CW01523899

ISBN 978-0-483-60931-0
PIBN 10791490

THE

COMPREHENSIVE CONCORDANCE

TO THE

HOLY SCRIPTURES

BY

REV. J. B. R. WALKER

A PRACTICAL, CONVENIENT, ACCURATE TEXT-FINDER. UNESSENTIAL WORDS OMITTED; ALL SERVICEABLE WORDS RETAINED. ONLY ONE ALPHABET FOR ALL WORDS, INCLUDING PROPER NAMES. PROPER NAMES ACCENTED. FIFTY THOUSAND MORE REFERENCES THAN IN CRUDEN

BASED ON THE AUTHORIZED VERSION

WITH AN INTRODUCTION

BY M. C. HAZARD, PH.D.

BOSTON AND CHICAGO, U.S.A.

Congregational Sunday-School and Publishing Society

INTRODUCTION.

BY M. C. HAZARD.

THE REASON AND PLAN FOR THIS WORK.

THAT there should be a new concordance is evident. "Cruden's Complete Concordance" has held the first place nearly ever since it was first issued in 1737. It certainly is a great testimony to its value that it has remained undisturbed in its supremacy for over a hundred and fifty years. Its defects have been apparent enough, but its great usefulness has caused scholars to be patient with them. There is no need, however, of perpetuating its faults in order to secure its excellences. The well-worn plates from which most of the editions are printed, together with the poor bindings into which they are put, would suggest the necessity of a fresh resetting, if nothing more; and if that much, then much more.

"Cruden's Complete" does not at all justify its name. It is very incomplete. It lacks tens of thousands of most important references, so that the diligent user of the concordance is continually annoyed by being unable to find the text for which he is searching under the principal word which should locate it without trouble. Failing to get it from one word he turns to another, and may have to look at one or two or three more before he finally discovers the object of his quest, or he may not succeed at all. It is difficult to conjecture why Cruden failed to incorporate so large a portion of Scripture into his concordance. Not only has he omitted thousands of essential texts, but he has given place to many words which are unimportant in the finding of passages, such as Not, So, Yet, Be, etc. His alphabetical arrangement is often faulty, and is annoying in the extreme under the letter I, under which he places all words beginning with J, so that one is perplexed just where to find words commencing with either of those letters. His introductory explanatory paragraphs are now looked upon as obsolete and as being of little value. Some of them, like the fifth paragraph under Wolf, are simply amusing. Why a concordance so incomplete, so defective in arrangement, and so unsatisfactory in many ways should have been allowed to stand unchallenged for so long a time seems a mystery.

In the Concordance herewith presented the design has been to issue one that should be comprehensive, correct, compact, and convenient. It is not "complete," for in order to be so it would have to contain every *a*, *an*, *in*, *the*, *this*, *that*, *not*, *so*, *he*, *her*, etc., occurring in the Bible. To put them all in would expand the volume into a cumbersome quarto of the size of

Webster's unabridged, instead of the present easily handled octavo. To insert them would be to encumber the work with words which are never sought in the effort to find a text. They would be a hindrance rather than a help, and might justly be characterized in a work of this sort as "wood, hay, and stubble."

The peculiarities and excellences of this Concordance may be thus summarized: —

1. *It is a concordance simply.* It is not a commentary nor a dictionary nor a compendium of Biblical information. It is a text-finder and nothing else. To attempt to combine in a concordance other features which demand extensive treatment in order to give reliable information is to attempt to impose upon the public and to secure patronage under false pretenses.

2. *It is rigidly alphabetical in its arrangement.* Cruden has numerous and gross errors in this respect. Young's Analytical Concordance, by force of its plan, is even more defective.

3. *Its passages and references under the alphabetical heads or divisions are in their strict Biblical order.* Young's Concordance disregards this essential rule. In that the texts are classified upon the basis of the Hebrew and Greek words which are translated into the same English word. Accordingly they are introduced heterogeneously, without Biblical sequence, and hence are confusing. A still more objectionable arrangement is the mingling of derivative words with their primaries instead of giving them a separate and alphabetical division. Thus under Forgive he places passages which contain the words *forgave, forgavest, forgiven, forgiveth, forgiving.* One searching for the passage, "Thy sins be forgiven thee," naturally would look for it under Forgiven, but in Young he would not find that as a caption word, and would discover his text under Forgive, in No. 6 of its Hebrew and Greek classifications.

4. *Proper names and appellatives will be found in their alphabetical order,* instead of being placed by themselves. The double arrangement in Cruden is inconvenient and confusing.

5. *Proper names are in every instance accented in order to help the student to the right pronunciation.*

6. *No irrelevant or needless matter is introduced.* The large size of Cruden's quarto or imperial octavo is owing to the insertion of long quotations not in the least degree essential or helpful. Young's Analytical Concordance is swollen into undue proportions by the incorporation of much which is not of the least practical utility to nine tenths of those who use a concordance. A large number of pages are given to *as, at, and, in, so, to, yet, of, for,* and many others of like unimportance to those who are simply seeking the whereabouts of a text.

7. *The page, though printed in small type, is very legible.* The caption words are in full-faced letters, so that they stand out clearly upon the page.

In the references the chapters are given in full-faced type and the verses in light-face. This avoids all confusion in determining whether the figures refer to chapters or to verses. After the first reference from a book it is not customary to repeat its abbreviated title, and then this arrangement of light and full face figures becomes necessary to perspicuity.

8. ***About fifty thousand more references are given than appear in Cruden's unabridged.*** If the unessential references were eliminated from that work, the preponderance over it in this would be still more remarkable. The fact will soon be discovered by the Bible student that this Concordance gives ready access to a great multitude of passages not incorporated in Cruden, and which are as prominent and important as any in the Scriptures.

9. *This Concordance is a compact and handy octavo* (5½x9¼ inches), instead of an inconvenient and cumbrous quarto. To secure this more desirable form narrower columns have been used, the references being condensed accordingly, though not beyond the point of ready recognition; and all unserviceable words have been omitted. By the use of thin but highly calendered paper the volume, though containing nearly a thousand pages, is but little thicker than the ordinary unabridged Cruden, which has but about seven hundred pages. The result is a thoroughly practical and usable concordance, inviting to the hand, pleasing to the eye, and satisfactory in every respect. One will consult this many times, where if it were a heavy quarto, he would not lift it from its place.

10. *This Concordance is cheap.* It is placed upon the market at the very low price of $2.00. Considering the great outlay this is very low indeed. Such a work is necessarily very expensive, and the disbursement in this case was increased by a change of plan when about half the pages were set up. The expenditures amount to thousands of dollars. Upon the supposition of a small demand, the price named is too low, but will be sufficient if the Concordance obtains the circulation which it deserves, and which, we believe, it will secure.

BIOGRAPHICAL.

The author of this work, Rev. James Bradford Richmond Walker, was born in Taunton, Mass., April 15, 1821. He graduated at Brown University in 1841, and at Andover Theological Seminary in 1846. As a pastor he served the Bucksport Church, Maine, Second Church, Holyoke, Mass., and Winsted Church, Connecticut. In 1861 he brought out "The Walkers of the Old Colony and Their Descendants," an octavo of 450 pages. He died of apoplexy, January 24, 1885, induced, it is believed, by his unremitting labors upon this Concordance.

Any one can see at a glance that the compilation of a concordance of the whole Bible is a task of no small magnitude. And yet no one can realize how great the labor is unless he undertakes it for himself, or carefully goes over the manuscript and the proofs of one who has done so. The collating of the words, the vigilant judgment required as to what shall be included or omitted, the selection of the identifying phrases, the verification of the references, the care needed in order to get all into correct alphabetical order, the patient scrutiny of proofs, all constitute an undertaking which is appalling to any but the most resolute will. It is not surprising to learn that the author devoted about twelve years to this work, the last two years and a half being almost uninterruptedly given to it, night hours as well as daytime often being occupied with it. That such a strain was more than even a vigorous constitution could stand, especially at his age, was in the nature of things. Mr. Walker lived to complete his task, but did not long survive its accomplishment. The intense application, prolonged often into unseasonable and unreasonable hours, proved too great a strain upon his vitality. It produced that condition which resulted in the stroke of which he died.

Mr. Walker began his Concordance upon one plan, and finished it upon another involving still more work. He decided upon this enlargement when his task was about half completed. His new purpose was to make the references still more complete and to add to the number of helpful divisions under the caption words. The plan was carried out in the latter half of the work, and then it became necessary to go all over the first half in order to make it correspond. This was indeed wearisome labor. The first half was already electrotyped. The rearrangement and additions necessitated the cutting up of plates, the "running over" of matter, and the making of new pages. The new pages thus introduced are indicated by enumerating them with superior figures. Thus at page 50 ten new pages are introduced which are foliod thus: 50^1, 50^2, 50^3, 50^4, etc. See also pages 52, 54, 342. It will be seen by an estimate of these pages that in carrying out his new plan he added about eight thousand new references to the first half of the book.

With these statements concerning the magnitude of the work, the changes made in it, and the time spent upon it, the reader is better qualified to appreciate the following memorandum made by the author upon the morning when he felt that it was concluded:—

BOSTON, 4.20 A.M., September 1, 1883.

At this morning hour, after an all night's work, preceded by work all day, I have revised the last page of my Concordance, and have laid it aside for the printer. After two years and five months of the most continuous and uninterrupted labor, day and night, I have at last reached the consummation for which I have struggled so long and so hard; for which I have prayed to be spared, and for which I now most gratefully render thanks to Him who has preserved and sustained me so remarkably under the burden of such intense application. That I have been able to do this work demands of me the most devout and grateful recognition of a Divine

Providence: and I cannot now, as I stand on the Mount Zion of my long and many years of labor, but have my heart deeply affected by my having been permitted to go through all this strenuous endeavor with such health and comfort. May the auspicious circumstances of this closing labor be prophetic of the success of this, the most comprehensive concordance of the Bible, adapted to the laity of the Church of Christ — a success which shall repair and counterbalance the disasters which were experienced years ago in the early history of the work!

May my heavenly Father set his seal of approval and usefulness upon this work, and may my humble plan and labor contribute to his glory in the help it shall furnish to the multitudes of the students of his Holy Word! May his name have all the glory, if any; his goodness have all the praise; his fatherly care and preservation have my grateful remembrance during all the years of my life! With this prayer, these acknowledgments, I lay down the pen, but with the never-to-be-forgotten record and memory of God's goodness and love cherished in my heart.

J. B. R. WALKER.

Not only had Mr. Walker put years of labor into the work, but thousands of dollars besides. Apparently his resources failed him before the beginning of the end, and probably it is this to which he refers as the disasters experienced in the early history of the undertaking. A firm was induced to advance the necessary funds to carry on the publication, and, with the exception of quite a number of insets incorporating changes, the plates were all made. Everything then bade fair for immediate issue, and hence the hopefulness of the memorandum. But owing to business complications and the death of the author, the matter was dropped, and for ten years the plates have been lying in the vaults where they were stored. It is to be hoped, now that the book is finally launched, that it may realize all the desires which he cherished concerning it.

Probably no one could have been found better fitted for this service than was Mr. Walker. It seems safe to say that his familiarity with the bibliography of this department is not excelled by any American scholar. He thoroughly knew what had been done in this line by others, and therefore was able intelligently to choose between methods. The writer hereof, as the Editor of the Society issuing the Concordance, has been obliged to test its accuracy and to pronounce upon the changes still to be made, and while doing so he has been struck with the patient collating, the extreme care, and the good judgment of the author. The proof corrections are enormous, and must have been very expensive, but he has never hesitated at any changes which would improve the book. In almost every case the alterations are distinct improvements. The boxes of memorandum papers and proof sheets, which came with the plates, are witnesses to his monumental labors.

But the Concordance itself must speak for him. Doubtless it has some faults and some inaccuracies. It would be strange if in a work involving hundreds of thousands of references some mistakes were not made. But if it is as perfect a help in its line as it is deemed to be, the years of labor bestowed upon it by the author will not have been in vain. Unless a wrong estimate is put upon it, his work will be more and more appreciated as years go by. It will, it is believed, take the place of Cruden, and be in the hands of almost every devout student of God's Word. And so it will come to pass, when many are having the benefit of the author's labors, that he, being dead, shall yet speak to multitudes.

BIBLIOGRAPHY.

THE history of concordance-making is of peculiar interest. Prior to the first published aid to the finding of texts doubtless there were those who had memorandums more or less full by which they could readily turn to passages when memory failed to give their location. The Vulgate being the clerical Bible at the time when the desire for such a convenience first found public expression, it was inevitable that the earliest concordances should be in

LATIN.

Antonius of Padua (1195–1231) is credited with having produced the first work of the kind, under the title *Concordantiæ Morales*. The concordance by Hugo de S. Caro, better known as Cardinal Hugo, however, is usually mentioned as being first, and probably deserves to stand first as being a concordance upon the whole Bible. He was born at Vienne in Dauphine, and studied in Paris, where he became a Dominican friar in 1225. In the year 1244, when preparing his Commentary on the Bible, as an aid in his work, he conceived the idea of making a concordance to the Latin Vulgate. With the aid of the five hundred Dominican monks in the convent, it is said, he carried out his plan. It was called *Concordantiæ S. Jacobi* because of its being prepared in the convent of St. Jacob in Paris. Invaluable as it was to its learned author, and helpful to the monks in the preparation of their sermons, it had the serious defect of indicating the location of references only in a general way. The chapters of the Bible had not then been divided into verses. Hugo adopted the expedient of supposing each chapter to have seven parts, which he indicated by the first seven letters of the alphabet. The fact that the word *terra* occurs in the first part of Genesis i was thus denoted: *terra*, Gen. i, *a*. The difficulty of finding the references was increased by the specification, as in the example given, of single words only. The first to remedy the deficiencies of this work were John of Derlington, Richard of Stavensby, and Hugo of Croyndon, who in about 1250 associated themselves together to revise it by adding the words in immediate connection with the key word. They being of English origin their production was called *The English Concordance*. The next to improve it was Conrad the Elder, of Halberstadt (1290), who, retaining the method of dividing the longer chapters into seven parts, assigned only four parts to the shorter chapters, indicating them by the letters *a* to *d*. He also shortened the citations made by the previous revisers, thus materially reducing the size of the volume. Conrad's edition supplanted the others, and its influence is seen as late as 1826 in an edition of the Vulgate printed at Frankfurt as shown by the letters on the margin indicating the chapter divisions as designated by him. It was again amended, as told in the Schaff–Herzog Encyclopædia, in the following way: —

"During the Council of Trent (1431–49)[1] a grave defect in the Concordance was discovered. John of Ragusa, a very learned man (d. 1444), held an animated discussion with Bohemians at the council upon the true meaning in the Bible of the particle *nisi*, and later with Greeks at Constantinople, whither the council had sent him, over the true meaning of *per* and *ex*. But the concordance failed him just here; for it did not contain particles. He determined to remedy this defect, and unable himself to command the time, entrusted the task to the Spanish doctor of theology, John of Suabia, who alphabetically arranged the particles, and then, in 1437, published the work, with an historical introduction. Sebastian Brant carried the first edition of it through the press of John Peter and John Froben, in Basel, 1496, under the title *Concordantiæ partium sive dictionum indeclinabilium totius Bibliæ* ('Concordance to the particles or indeclinable words in the entire Scriptures'), as the second part of Conrad's Concordance."

The first printed concordance bore the title *Fratris Conradi de Alemannia Ord. Predic. Concordantiæ Bibliorum*, etc. Argentorati (Strasburg), 1470. 2d ed., 1475. Bindzeil, in his *Ueber die Concordanzen*, 1870, gives a list of sixty-four concordances to the Vulgate, which were substantially reprints of this first edition. The last is the *Bibliorum Sacrorum Concordantiæ*, by F. P. Dutripon. This is the concordance used by the Catholic clergy, there being no concordance to the Douay translation of the Vulgate.

As directed by the Council of Trent, Sixtus V had published on the press of the Vatican an edition of the Septuagint in 1587, and soon after of the Vulgate. The latter especially was found to be so full of errors that a corrected edition had to be prepared under the auspices of his successor, Urban VII, 1590. After this revision a concordance appeared entitled *Concordantiæ Bibliorum Sacrorum Vulgatæ editionis ad recognitionem Jussu Sixti V, Pont. Max. Bibliis adhibitam, recensitæ atque amenditæ, opera et studio Francisi Lucae Brugensis*. Antwerp, 1617; Geneva, 1625; Paris, 1683. The greater number of the concordances to the Latin Vulgate are reprints of this edition. The best is that printed at Avignon in 1786, two vols. folio.

In 1600, published at Frankfurt for the heirs of "Andreæ VVecheli,"

[1] Council of Basel rather; the Council of Trent was a century later.

appeared the *Concordantiæ Bibliorum: id est Dictiones omnes qvæ in VVulgata editione Latina Librorum Veteris et Novi Testamenti leguntur*, etc. The name of the author does not appear. In the preface reference is made to a work by G. Bullock published at Antwerp in 1572, denominated *In Œconomiam Methodicam Concordantiæ S. Scripturæ* in which the author, by an arrangement which he calls analytical, divides his subjects into those referring to "Good Morals, Natural Matters, and Artificial Matters." This method the author of the Wecheli Concordance refused for "weighty reasons" to follow "lest we seem to turn concordances into controversies, misunderstandings and discordances." It is further shown in the preface that in preparing the work a little slip was devoted to each word, for it is said: "Certain things overlooked in the almost innumerable number of our little slips (*chartularum*) we have set off to the end of the work." "Finally," the author deprecatingly says, "if anything in all this index has been distinguished or described by us which in the smallest degree offends theological truth, or the holy Church of Christ, or is rightly displeasing, let it be unspoken and obliterated."

HEBREW.

To Rabbi Mordecai (or Isaac) Nathan is to be awarded the honor of having prepared the first Hebrew concordance. Beginning his task in 1438 he did not finish it even with the aid of many helpers until 1448. The reason for his undertaking it he states in his preface. Subjected to repeated challenges by some of his companions, in his search for materials with which to answer them he lighted upon a Latin concordance. This furnished him with an armory which his assailants could not resist. The thought came to him that a concordance of the Hebrew Bible would be of even greater value to the student of the Scriptures, and hence he set about its preparation. His work, a folio, was published in 1523 or 1524 at Venice by Daniel Bomberg. Its title, *The Light to the Way*, seems to have been suggested by the sudden light which was thrown upon his path by the discovery of the Latin concordance. A very defective Latin translation by Reuchlin appeared at Basel in 1556. Editions in Hebrew followed at Venice in 1564 and at Basel in 1581.

The errors in Nathan's concordance were so many that Marius de Calasio set out to correct them and to introduce some important improvements. He was a Franciscan friar, author of a Hebrew grammar and dictionary, and teacher of Hebrew at Rome by appointment of Pope Paul V. He was over seventy when he began his laborious work, but at the time of his death in 1620 left it almost ready for the printer. His mantle, by papal direction, fell upon Michael Angelus of St. Romulus, a professor of Hebrew and theology. By him the work was completed, and was published in 1621 at Rome in four folio volumes, under the title *Concordantiæ Sacrorum Bibliorum Hebraicorum*. The meaning of each word is given in both Hebrew and Latin, followed by the corresponding words in the other Shemitic languages, with Latin interpretations, and lastly the passages are given in which the word is found. Editions were published at Cologne in 1646, Rome 1657, and London in 1747–49. The London edition, under the direction of William Romaine, has the distinction of having had for its patrons his holiness the pope and all the monarchs of Europe.

Another effort which had the work of Nathan for its basis was that begun by Johann Buxtorf the elder and finished by his son. It was published in folio in 1632 at Basel with the title *Concordantiæ Bibliorum Hebraicæ, nova et artificiosa methodo dispositæ*, etc. Though better arranged and supplying many missing references, and especially valuable in furnishing a concordance at the end of the Chaldee words in the Old Testament, yet it was seriously defective in the omission of certain particles and all of the proper names. A fine copy of this is in the library of the American Congregational Association, Boston. Two abridgments were published, one at Wittemberg in 1653 and the other at Frankfurt in 1677, edited by Christian Raw, with the title *Fount of Sion.*

Supplying many deficiencies of Buxtorf's concordance, and far excelling it in other respects, is the work of Christian Nolde or Noldius, a professor at Copenhagen, entitled *Concordantiæ Particularum Ebraeo-Chaldaicarum*, etc. It was a quarto and published in 1679. A very important service was rendered by this Danish scholar to those engaged in the critical study of the Scriptures. Horne commends this work as of the highest importance to every Biblical critic. A new edition, containing in an appendix a lexicon to the Hebrew particles, by John Henry Michaelis and Christian Körber, was published at Jena in 1734.

William Robertson, A.M., was the author of *Thesaurus Linguæ Sanctæ sive Concordantiale Lexicon Hebraeo-Latino-Biblicum*, etc. London: 1680. Quarto. Mr. Robertson was distinguished for his knowledge of the Hebrew language, which he long taught in London. He was the author of several Hebrew grammatical works, and seems to have been a very zealous rabbinical scholar. His *Novum Testamentum Hebraicæ* was published in London in 1661. The nature of his Thesaurus is sufficiently indicated by the title. It is designed to answer both for a lexicon and a concordance to the Hebrew Scriptures. It is not complete enough for a concordance and is too cumbrous for a convenient lexicon.

While high honor is accorded to Noldius for his labor and scholarship, yet his valuable work was surpassed seventy-five years later by *Dr. John Taylor's Hebrew Concordance, adapted to the English Bible*, "disposed after the manner of Buxtorf." London: 1754. 2 vols. folio. The learned author devoted a vast amount of labor to this work, and had the encouragement and patronage of all the English and Irish bishops. It is still regarded as having value.

All previous concordances were eclipsed by the one prepared by Dr. Julius Fürst, assisted by Dr. Franz Delitzsch, called *Librorum Sacrorum Veteris Testamenti Concordantiæ Hebraicæ atque Chaldaicæ*, published at Leipzig, 1840, folio. Its groundwork and method are those of Buxtorf, but it includes much which makes it greatly superior to its pattern. It contains no less than eight appendixes, some of them quite valuable. Its usefulness unfortunately is restricted to those who are familiar with Latin.

While the two distinguished scholars just mentioned were preparing their concordance, a work requiring years of arduous labor and large pecuniary outlay was being carried on in the preparation of *The Englishman's Hebrew and Chaldee Concordance.* The editor was George V. Wigram, with S. B. Tregelles and B. Davidson as collaborators. Over ten years of work were expended upon it. It was begun in 1830, and was published in London in 1843 in two large quarto volumes. The account given in the preface by the editor of the labor and pains taken to secure fullness and accuracy is a graphic narration of a task so exacting and prolonged that few men would dare undertake it.

To the same indefatigable laborer Biblical scholars are indebted for the *Hebraist's Vade Mecum,* published in London in 1867. It is a valuable verbal index to the Hebrew and Chaldee Scriptures, the words being grammatically arranged, and the passages given under each form where they occur.

A revised and corrected edition of B. Davidson's excellent *Concordance of the Hebrew and Chaldee Scriptures* appeared in London in 1876, edited by Rev. Joseph Hughes, and issued by Bagster & Sons.

GREEK.

The statement that a concordance to the entire Bible in Greek was prepared by a monk, Euthalius Rhodius, about the year 1300 has come to be seriously doubted. It was never printed, and no handmade copy of it is in existence, so that the assertion of its having been written is traditionary only. To Conrad Kircher, a Lutheran minister at Augsburg, is given the credit of being the pioneer in this department of Biblical aids. His *Concordantiae Veteris Testamenti Græci Ebræis vocibvs respondentes* was published at Frankfort in two volumes, quarto, in 1607. He follows the order of the Hebrew words, putting after them the corresponding Greek words, so that it is really a Hebrew-Greek concordance.

The first Greek concordance, pure and simple, was the work of Abraham Tromm, issued in 1718 (2 vols. fol.) under the title *Concordantiae Græcæ Versionis vulgo dicta LXX Interpretum, cujus voces secundum ordinem elementorum sermonis Græci digestæ recensentur, contra atque in opere Kircheriano factum fuerat,* etc. This gives the Greek words in their order, with a Latin translation of each, followed by the corresponding Hebrew word or words. Then the passages in the Scripture are cited in which they occur, given in the order of the books and chapters, with quotations from the context as in English concordances. The passages from the Apocrypha follow those of the canonical books under their common title word. Annexed is a lexicon of all the words contained in the fragments of *Origen's Hexapla*, as published by Father Montfaucon, in 1713. The author was an eminent minister of Groningen. Only after sixteen years of prodigious labor, completed in his eighty-fifth year, did he give to Biblical literature this splendid contribution. So thorough and accurate was his work that it never has been superseded, but remains a monument to his labor and learning. After nearly two centuries it still retains its preëminence. Michaelis said of it: "I wish as earnestly that this concordance were in the hands of every theologian as that Pasor and other works of that nature were vanished from the schools." The author died in 1719, the year after the publication of his work.

The first Greek concordance to the New Testament was the work of a Lutheran divine at Augsburg (1500–1554), Xystus Buteleius, librarian of the city library. Its title, *Συμφώνια: ἡ συλλέξις τῆς διαθήκης καινῆς*, literally translated is: "Symphony: the gathering together of the New Testament." It cost him the labor of eight years, and was published at Basel in 1546.

The next similar work is that of Robert Stephens, who was the first to suggest and to adopt the division by verses. It was published at Geneva, in 1594, folio, by his son, Henry Stephens, the celebrated printer, who contributed a preface to the work. It appeared again with a supplement in 1600. An edition published in 1624 contains so many inaccuracies and is marked by so many deficiencies that it has been deemed to be spurious.

Erasmus Schmid, a Lutheran minister and professor of Greek in the University of Wittemberg, prepared a much more valuable work than either of the two foregoing, which was published in folio in 1638, at Wittemberg, a year after the death of its author. A revised edition followed at Gotha in 1717, and this was reprinted in Glasgow in two volumes octavo in 1819. The Bagsters have given it a place in a 32mo. edition on their list of invaluable helps to Christian scholars and students of the Bible. Its title was *Novum Testamentum, Tameion Jesv Christi; Græci; hoc est originalis Linguæ* (*aliis Concordantiæ*), etc. The title-page is symbolically illustrated, and has a picture of the author.

Next succeeding Schmid is the *Lexicon Anglo-Græco-Latinum Novi Testamenti*, etc., by Andrew Symson, London, 1658, folio. This, as indicated by the title, is partly a lexicon as well as a concordance. "By it," says the author, "any word may be rendered into Greek and Latin, English and Latin, and Greek and English." Its arrangement is singularly defective. Parkhurst says: "It is a performance which, while it exhibits the prodigious labor of its author, can give one no very high opinion of his genius or skill in the art of instruction. If indeed the method and ingenuity of this writer had been proportionable to his industry, he would have rendered all future Greek lexicons to the New Testament superfluous; but he has rendered his book in a manner useless to the young scholar, and in truth hardly manageable by any but a person of uncommon application."

A more portable work than these large concordances was published at London in 1767, entitled *A Concordance to the Greek Testament, with the English version to each word*, etc. By John Williams, LL.D. It is useful to the English reader, and is quite accurate.

Distancing all its predecessors, however, is *The Englishman's Greek Concordance of the New Testament*, published at London in 1840, reaching a fifth edition in 1868. It was republished in New York in 1848. This is a large octavo of more than a thousand pages, and was prepared by George V. Wigram, who had done such excellent work upon *The Englishman's Hebrew Concordance*, already mentioned. The same merits are apparent in this which distinguished that work. In fullness, accuracy, and copious indexes it leaves little to be desired by the student.

In 1842 the eminent publisher, Baron Karl Christian Tauchnitz, issued Karl Hermann Bruder's *Treasury of the Words of the New Testament* (*Ταμεῖον τῶν καινῆς διαθήκης λέξεων*), which the Schaff–Herzog Encyclopædia commends as the latest and best of the Greek concordances. Leipzig, 1842.

In 1870 appeared *A Critical Greek and English Concordance of the New Testament*, prepared by Charles F. Hudson, under the direction of Horace L. Hastings, editor of *The Christian*. The plan of the work was the conception of Mr. Hastings, but its execution was committed to Mr. Hudson. He labored upon it for nearly three years. The body of the work was completed, the index finished, and the supplement begun, when his health failed him, and upon his death the revision and completion of the work were entrusted to Dr. Ezra Abbot. Bagster's edition of Cruden containing the references only suggested that by omitting the quotations the work could be greatly condensed, and the result is a handy, convenient volume in which is packed a mine of information; for the references to the variant readings, obtained by a careful comparison of various MSS., make the book a repository of the best critical scholarship of the age up to the time of its issue. The preface contains an interesting account of the genesis and scope of the work.

A Critical Lexicon and Concordance to the English and Greek New Testament, by Rev. Ethelbert W. Bullinger, was published in London in 1877 by Longmans, Green & Co. It is a bulky octavo of about a thousand pages, and contains an index of Greek words with their various renderings besides several appendixes. Where there are variations in readings the different sources and authorities are cited. It is intended as a help to those unacquainted with Greek, and is really a valuable work.

Very much less commendable is *An Interpreting Concordance of the New Testament*, by Rev. James Gall. It shows with English letters the Greek original of every word. Thus abhor: *apostugeo, bdelussomai* puts the English reader in possession of the fact that abhor is the rendering of two Greek words, and the glossary at the end of the book gives the true meaning of each of those words; but the information at the best is of a superficial order. In works of this kind a thorough critical lexicon is needed.

In 1892 on the Clarendon Press, Oxford, was brought out *A Concordance to the Septuagint and the other Greek Versions*, including the apocryphal books, with which the scholars of this country should become familiar. It was begun by the late Dr. Edwin Hatch, and at his death was about half completed. The work was then taken up by Henry Redpath, M.A., assisted by other scholars. It has for its basis the texts of the Septuagint, Codex Alexandrinus A, Codex Vaticanus B, Codex Sinaiticus S, and the Sixtine edition of 1587 R, the comparisons being made from autotype and facsimile editions until the issue of Nestle's Supplement to Tischendorf's edition made this labor unnecessary. Painstaking and critical scholarship is evident throughout, while the large quarto page, clearly printed, makes it a luxury to examine.

SYRIAC.

The *Lexicon Syriacum Concordantiale, omnes Novi Testamenti Syraci voces — complectens*, by Charles Schaaf, a learned German, was published in Leyden in 1709. While it is more of a lexicon than a concordance, yet it is possible to use it as such. It was published at the same time with the very accurate edition of the Syriac New Testament edited by Leusden and Schaaf, which Michaelis characterizes as the very best edition that has been published. "The very excellent Lexicon," he adds, "which is annexed to it will ever retain its value, being, as far as regards the New Testament, extremely accurate and complete, and supplying in a measure the place of a concordance."

GERMAN.

To Germany belongs the distinction of bringing out the earliest concordance to any modern version of the Scriptures. Taking Luther's translation Johannes Schrötter as early as 1524 prepared his *Concordanz des Newen Testamentz zu teutsch*. This was a folio and was published at Strasburg.

It was nearly a century later (1610) before Schrötter had a successor. Then Conrad Agricola (Bauer) brought out his *Concordantia Bibliorum, Das ist Biblische Concordantz und Verzeichniss der Fürnembsten Wörter, Frankfurt-a-M.* Two years later he issued an appendix supplying its deficiencies, which appears in the editions published in 1621, 1632, and 1640. Christian Zeizius greatly improved upon it in his concordance published in Leipzig in 1658.

The most important service to readers and students of the German Bible was reserved for Friedrich Lanckisch. His *Concordantiæ Bibliorum Germanico-Hebraico-Græcæ, Deutsche, Hebraische und Griechische Bibel* was published at Leipzig and Frankfurt-a-M. in 1677. This was received with great favor. New editions, each carefully revised and improved, followed in 1688, 1696, 1705, and 1718, the latter under the supervision of Christian Reineck. The learned author died in 1669, eight years before the issue of his work. His purpose, as stated by Jackson in the Schaff–Herzog, was: "To revise, correct, and enlarge the Zeise edition of Agricola; to arrange under each German word the Greek or Hebrew words of which it was the translation; to place next to every Hebrew word a Greek letter, and to every Greek word a Latin letter, and then to use these letters to represent the word in the passages quoted from Luther's Bible, so that the reader seeing the letter would know of what Hebrew or Greek word the German was a translation."

But the work which has been the popular concordance of the Germans is that of Gottfried Büchner, who has been styled the Cruden of Germany. It appeared in two forms, a large and a *Hand Concordanz*. The larger work, consisting of two volumes, was published at Jena in 1750, new editions appearing in 1757 and 1765. The hand concordance was issued in 1740, and so great was the demand for it that fresh editions were put out in 1746, 1756, 1765, and 1776. In the latter year the publisher failed, and its great popularity and extensive sale were supplanted by Wichmann's Concordance issued at Leipzig and Dessau in 1782. That held the ground until 1840, when Büchner again came to the front through a revision by Dr. H. L. Heubner, and it now is the standard concordance of Germany. Its popularity is shown by the editions which have rapidly followed its reissue in 1844, 1850, 1859, 1877. In 1871 an American edition for the Germans of the United States was published in Philadelphia, edited by Dr. Schaff, by whom an appendix was added, contributed by Professor A. Spath, containing 8,060 omitted passages.

FRENCH.

The most noteworthy of the French concordances is that of Mark Wilks, entitled *Concordance des Saintes Escritures*, issued in Paris in 1840.

ENGLISH.

The earliest attempt to supply the English-speaking people with a concordance is thus entitled: "The Concordance of the New Teſtament, moſt neceſſary to be had in the hands of all ſoche as deſire the communication of any place contained in the New Teſtament. Imprinted by

Mr. Thomas Gybſon. *Cum privilegio regali.*" Though without date it must have been published before 1540, and from the preface to the reader it is inferred that it was the work of "John Day," aided by Gybson the printer.

This was the small beginning of larger efforts, the first of which appeared about ten years later with the following on its title-page: "A Concordance, that is to ſaie, a Worke wherein, by the ordre of the letters A, B, C, ye maie redely find any word conteigned in the whole Bible, ſo often as it is there expreſſed or mentioned." This was by John Marbeck, nearly a martyr, and was printed in London, folio, in 1550. In the detailed and graphic report given in Fox's Book of Martyrs of Marbeck's examination by the bishops, the author gives an interesting account of the way in which he was led to undertake the work. The story, as told to his judges, was as follows: —

When Thomas Matthews' Bible came first out in print (1537) I was much desirous to have one of them; and being a poor man, not able to buy one of them, determined with myself to borrow one amongst my friends, and to write it forth. And when I had written out the five books of Moses in fair great paper, and was entered into the book of Joshua, my friend, Master Turner, chanced to steal upon me unawares, and seeing me writing out the Bible, asked me what I meant thereby. And when I told him the cause: "Tush!" quoth he, "thou goest about a vain and tedious labour. But this were a profitable work for thee, to set out a concordance in English."

"A concordance," said I; "what is that?"

Then he told me it was a book to find out any word in the whole Bible by the letter, and that there was such a one in Latin already.

Then I told him I had no learning to go about such a thing.

"Enough," quoth he, "for that matter, for it requireth not so much learning as diligence. And seeing thou art so painful a man, and one that can not be unoccupied, it were a good exercise for thee."

And this, my lord, is all the instruction that I ever had, before or after, of any man.

Marbeck accordingly borrowed a Latin concordance, and had gone through with the letter L, when his papers were seized. When he was set at liberty they were not restored to him, and so he had to begin again. When he had completed his work he showed it to a friend, who promised to assist him in having it presented to the king, that it might have the sanction of his authority; but Henry VIII died before that could be brought about. This friend requested a copy of it, and as he could not deny him he laboriously transcribed one for him. When Edward VI was settled on the throne Marbeck renewed his thought of publishing his work. He consulted Grafton, the printer, concerning it, "who," he says in his introduction, "seeying the volume so houge and greate, saied the charges of imprinting thereof would not onely be importunate, but the bokes when finished would beare so excessive price as few would be able to attain vnto theim; wherefore by his aduice I yet once again a newe writte out, the same in such sorte as the worke now appereth."[1]

Marbeck's work, though defective and imperfect, and referring to chapters only, was an important contribution in its time to Biblical helps, and has the distinction of being the first concordance to the whole English Bible.

In the same year was published in London a translation of Conrad Pellicane's *Index Bibliorum*, a German work issued at Zurich probably in 1537. Its English title is as follows: "A Briefe and a Compendious Table, in maner of a Concordance, openying the waye to the principall Hiftories of the whole Bible, and the moft comon articles grounded and comprehended in the Newe Testament and Olde, in maner as amply as doeth the great Concordance of the Bible. Gathered and fet forth by Henry Bullinger, Leo Jude, Conrade Pellicane, and by the other minifters of the Church of Liguriæ (Zurich). Translated from the Hygh Almayne into Englifh by Walter Lynne. To which is added, a Tranflation of the Third Boke of Machabees." Lynne was an English printer, scholar, author, and translator.

The next to be mentioned appeared in 1578 at London, "imprinted" by the "Deputies" of Christopher Barker, and was thus entitled: "Tvvo right profitable and fruitfull Concordances, or large and ample Tables Alphabeticall. The first conteyning the interpretation of the Hebrue, Caldean, Greeke, and Latine wordes and names fcatteringly disperfed throughout the whole Bible, with their comon places following euery of them: and the feconde comprehending all such other principall wordes and matters, as concerne the fenfe and meaning of the Scriptures, or direct unto any neceffary and good inftruction. The further vfe of both the which Tables, (for breuitie fake) is expreffed more at large in the Preface to the Reader: and will ferue as well for the tranflation called Geneua, as for the other authorized to be read in the Churches. Collected by R. F. H." The signature to the Preface to the Christian Reader shows that the initials stand for Robert F. Herrey. The first "Table" is a dictionary of proper names, with scanty references to Scripture passages, and the second is more in the nature of a topical index than a concordance, "conducting unto moft of the neceffarieft and profitableft doctrines, fentences and inftructions, which are to be found in the old and Newe Teftament." It is a pamphlet, small quarto (8½x6¼), 162 pp., and was printed *cum privilegio Regiæ Maiestatis.*

In 1579 Christopher Barker published "A Concordance or Table, containing the principal wordes and matters which are comprehended in the New Teftament." The author was "J. W." and the book was an octavo.

Young, in his admirable Analytical Concordance, was in a measure anticipated by Richard Bernard, Rector of Batcombe, who in 1644 published

[1] Tounley's Bib. Lit. vol. iii, p. 118.

his *Thesaurus Biblicus seu Promptuarium Sacrum*, which he thus explains upon the caption page: (*That is,*) *The Bibles Treasury, or Holy Storehouse*. He however gives in Latin the various translations of the original word, and that which follows is more in the nature of a topical index. It has a supplement which is thus high-soundingly entitled: "The Bibles Abſtract and Epitomie, the Capital Heads, Examples, Sentences and Precepts of all the Principall Matters in Theologie, Collected together for the moſt part Alphabetically, with the Doctrines and Vſes compendiouſly explained, of all the chief Points therein conteyned. Taken out of the beſt Moderne Divines, both Reverend and Learned." The problems relating to God's decrees, predestination, election, affliction, etc., receive here treatment emphasized to the eye by brackets and other ingenious arrangements of rules and divisions, side heads and references. Large quarto.

In 1655 Rev. Robert Wickens brought out "A Compleat & Perfect Concordance of the Engliſh Bible, Compoſed after a new, and Compendious method, whereby may be readily found any place of Canonicall Scriptures: Very uſefull for all Students in Divinity, and all private Chriſtians, whoſe hearts God ſhall move to be ſearchers of His Word." It was published at Oxford by H. Hull, printer to the University, and is a small 12mo., containing the references only, and is far from being "complete and perfect."

The first to make a concordance approaching completeness was Clement Cotton, "a layman, of great understanding and of unwearied industry," who has furnished the model for all others succeeding him. He contented himself with making a concordance pure and simple. His first essay was made in 1622 on the New Testament according to the Genevan translation. In the year 1627 he published a concordance to the Old Testament under the title, "A Concordance to all the Bookes of the Old Teſtament, according to the Tranſlation allowed by His late Matie of Great Brittain, in which the moſt materiall words thereof are exactly gathered into their proper places, according to the order of the Alphabet. Whereby it will be eaſie (even for thoſe of meane capacitie) readily to turne unto any paſſage they deſire in ſaid Bookes; prouided that they rightly informe themſelves of ſome one principall word or mo, contained therein." It is a three-columned quarto, the text quotations usually being short and very judiciously made. The descriptive title of each psalm is included as though it were the first verse of the text. The dedication reads: "To his Deareſt and moſt Fertile and Frvitfvll Mother, the Church of England, a Carefvll Preſerver of both Teſtaments in their Prime and Native Pvritie." The author shows his humility in consecrating to her "theſe vntimely fruits of his weake and worthleſſe endeuours," and his patriotism by praying that she "may long continue to looke forth as the Morning, faire as the Moone, cleere as the Sunne, terrible as an Army with Banners; that ſhe may euen to old age grow into thouſands of millions, and that her ſeed may receive ſtrength from on high to poſſeſſe the gate of their enemies." On account of the infelicity of having one concordance following one translation and the other another, "like the Beare," says Gouge, "he still continued to lick over his works"; and in the year 1631 published "A Compleat Concordance of the Whole Bible, according to the aforeſaid laſt Tranſlation," afterwards adding a concordance to the Apocrypha. Its title-page was an attempt at fine ornamentation.

At the request of Clement Cotton, as appears by the preface, John Downame made a small pocket concordance, entitled *A Concordance to the whole Bible*, which is without date, but which must have been issued about 1635, inasmuch as it refers to the revised and enlarged concordance of Cotton. The effort was to cite only "the moſt principal and uſeful places," but even that was hardly possible in so small a book. A revised edition bearing date 1689 shows that it had some life.

The next to build upon Cotton was Rev. Samuel Newman, who began his ministry in England, but came to New England in 1636 or 1638, spending some time in Dorchester, settling in Weymouth in 1639, where he spent four and a half years, and finally locating at Rehoboth. His first edition was published in London in 1643, from which fact it is to be inferred that at least a portion of his labors was wrought in this country. The title-page frankly acknowledges his indebtedness to Cotton, and is as follows: "A Large and Complete Concordance to the Bible in Engliſh, According to the Laſt Tranſlation. Firſt collected by Clement Cotton, and now much enlarged and amended for the good both of Schollers and others: far exceeding the moſt perfect that ever was extant in our Language, both in ground-work and building. By Samuel Nevvman, a poor laborer in the Lord's vineyard. The manifold uſe and benefit of this work is ſufficiently declared in the Prefaces to the Reader." It is a heavy, bulky quarto, and amply justifies the claim of exceeding all others in its completeness. A second edition, revised by the aid of pine knots instead of candles, was published in 1650. A third was issued in 1658, still further corrected and amended, and including the Apocrypha. Newman's name on the title-page of this appears with the statement, "now Teacher of the Church at Rehoboth in New-England." In 1662, "A Concordance to the Holy Scriptures; with the various Readings both in Text and Margine, in a more exact Method then hath hitherto been extant. By S. N." was published at Cambridge, the initials presumptively standing for Samuel Newman. Apparently some redactor has shortened the text quotations made by Newman, has added references to the marginal readings, and has made the misimprovement of putting the proper names by themselves. This eventuated in the well-known *Cambridge Concordance*, printed in 1720, in which no credit of original authorship is given to Newman.

It may be worth while right here to dispose of a story which has gained some currency even among scholarly men, that Cruden really pirated Newman's work, publishing it under his own name. This fiction was started by a Rev. Samuel Peters, LL.D., who in a biography of Rev. Hugh Peters makes the statement that a Mr. Cruden, an eminent scholar of the University of Cambridge, was settled at Rehoboth by the direction of Drs. Mather and Cotton, who had a way of placing ministers wherever they chose, and that there he formed the first concordance of the Old and New Testaments which was ever made in the English tongue; that it was adopted and printed by the University of Cambridge in England, and with additions and improvements has passed through many editions still under the name of Cruden's Concordance. It would seem as if a greater number of errors could hardly be crowded into the same space. It is needless to point them all out, and is sufficient to say that Alexander Cruden did not publish his concordance until nearly a century afterward, at which time Newman's was so well known that he could not have filched it if he would, though unquestionably it was an aid to him in his work. Evidently Rev. Samuel Peters, LL.D., had learned of the fact that a superior concordance had been prepared at Rehoboth and jumped to the conclusion that Cruden was the author. Dr. Peters, by the way, was the Tory who invented the "Blue Laws" of Connecticut, and who was forced to leave that state on account of his misrepresentation of facts.

A brief concordance, which really was a topical text-book, appeared somewhere about 1653–54, the third edition being issued in 1656, entitled "The Fort-Royal of Holy Scriptures, or a new Concordance of the chief Heads of Scripture Common-placed, for ſuch as would ſuddenly command all the Rarities in the Book of God." One hundred and fourteen topics are concordanced. The first relating to God, after some "generals" shows by illustrative texts "What God is in himself, What God is not, What God will not do, What God cannot do, Where God is, What is with God," etc.

A curious work, "begun by that famous and worthy Man of God, Mr. Thomas Wilson, Miniſter of the Word of God at St. Georges in Canterbury, and one of the Six Preachers there," and continued by Mr. John Bagwell, was issued apparently about 1655, judging from the preface by Rev. Andrew Symson, though possibly it may have been earlier, for the seventh edition appeared in 1661. The title-page of that edition thus characterizes it: "A Complete Chriſtian Dictionary: wherein the Significations and ſeveral Acceptations of All the Words mentioned in the Holy Scriptures of the Old and New Teſtament, are fully Opened, Expreſſed, Explained. Alſo, Very many Ambiguous Speeches, Hard and difficult Phraſes therein contained, are plainly Interpreted, Cleered and Expounded. Tending to the increaſe of Chriſtian knowledge, and ſerving for the uſe of All; eſpecially the Unlearned, who have no ſkill in the Original Languages, Hebrew and Greek, wherein the Scriptures were firſt written; and may be unto

Miniſters of the Goſpel Maſters of Families Private Chriſtians	in ſtead of a	Concordance, Commentary on all the Scriptures.

It is a dictionary of phrases as well as of names and appellatives, and is a singular mixture of learning and of simplicity. The author exhibits his strong anti-Catholicism in his definition of *the cup of gold,* which he declares to be "the Title of the Catholick Church, of Peters chair, of Chriſts Vicar, and the whole external profeſſion of Chriſtian Religion; whereby, as by a fine goodly Cup, both people and Princes of the world have been enticed to drink up, and draw in, moſt abominable and filthy Superſtitions, Idolatry and Hereſies, which the Romiſh Church offered unto them," etc. Affliction he defines to be the evil of punishment, and with respect to the life to come is put for external torments, adding, "With relation unto this life, it 's taken either more or leſſe properly." Then follow in order illustrative citations in which it is taken "more properly" and "leſſe properly." Facing the title-page is a picture of the author, which is declared to be *vera effigies Thomæ Wilson,* and underneath which is this stanza:—

This Picture here preſented to thine eye,
Doth repreſent the comely Gravity
Of Wilſons Countenance: but oh! his Worth!
What Pen, beſides his Owne, can ſet it forth
I 'le ceaſe, Heres' but the Shadow of his Face
His Workes doe ſhew his Learning Vertue, Grace.

This work is a large quarto, and of the works previously mentioned is the first to be paged. pp. 754.

A very much condensed concordance (8¾x6½) with five narrow columus on the page was the work of Rev. John Jackson, published in 1668. Its title-page reads thus: "Index Biblicus: or an exact Concordance to the Holy Bible, According to the laſt Tranſlation. Whereunto are added the Marginal Readings, with the Acceptations and various Significations of the Principal Words contained in the Holy Scriptures of the Old and New Testaments. Compoſed in a New and moſt Comprehenſive Method, and Adorned with divers Significant and Pregnant Scripture-Phraſes." The condensation is carried too far, and proper names are omitted altogether. Printed by John Field, printer to the University of Cambridge.

A new conception was embodied in the "New and Useful Concordance to the Holy Bible," "begun by the induſtrious Labours of Mr. Vavaſor Powel, late deceaſed: and finiſhed by N. P. and J. F." Its specialty was the addition of "Marks to diſtinguiſh The { Commands / Promiſes and / Threatenings."

Each of these was severally indicated in the margin by the letters C,

P, T. In the concluding two pages was given a collection of prophecies relating to the calling of the Jews and the glory that shall be in the latter days. By Scripture references it was sought to be shown that the Jews shall be carried by the Gentiles to their own land; that the Gentiles shall join with them to become the Lord's people; that the River Euphrates shall be dried up; that rivers shall be made to flow in desert places; that prophets again shall be given to Israel; that the Lord Christ shall appear as the head and ruler of his people, etc. The book is a small one, and was published in 1671.

In 1696 Samuel Clark brought out "A Brief Concordance to the Holy Bible, of the Moſt Uſual and Uſeful Place, which one may have occaſion to ſeek for." It is more satisfactory than some of the brief concordances which preceded it.

The first edition of Cruden appeared in 1737 and soon supplanted all the concordances then in use. It has passed through numberless editions; has been abridged, enlarged, condensed, revised, changed in minor particulars by various hands, but to-day is essentially what he made it at the beginning. The concordances of Butterworth, Brown, Eadie, Cole, Hawker, Smith, Youngman, Taylor, are all merely modifications, and, generally, abridgments of Cruden. The defects of Cruden have been elsewhere referred to.

A work of almost incomparable labor was that of Rev. C. Cruttwell, which appeared in 1790: "A Concordance of Parallels, collected from Bibles and Commentaries which have been published in Hebrew, Latin, French, Italian, Spaniſh, Engliſh, and other Languages, with the authorities of each." The author, acting upon the motto that "Scripture is best interpreted by Scripture," noted from the sources referred to the passages which were deemed to throw light upon any text, and upon each verse has given an overwhelming number of "parallel" citations, ranging from good to indifferent and bad. The references being only to chapters and verses, the array of figures without a hint as to their value is discouraging, and hence it is no wonder that the work never obtained a very extensive circulation.

The work which has most commended itself in comparing the English with their Hebrew and Greek originals is that of Robert Young, LL.D., of Edinburgh, whose *Analytical Concordance* was published in 1879. It is the product of forty years of most exacting labor, nearly three years being occupied from 6 A.M. to 10 P.M. in carrying it through the press. Singularly enough with all the pains taken all reference to the Holy Spirit or Holy Ghost under the word Holy was missing in the first edition. The English words are in alphabetical order, and with each word is given the Hebrew or Greek word or words, with their meanings, of which it is a translation. When the English word is the representation of several words in the original the texts are classified in which those words occur, so that one can readily see where and how they are used, and so estimate their force and value. As a text-finder, as previously has been noted, it is inconvenient, but as a help to getting at those delicate shades of meaning which are hidden from the English reader it is invaluable. Quarto, pp. 1090. New York: Funk & Wagnalls.

In the foregoing the effort has not been to give an exhaustive list of the concordances which have been published, but rather to specify those which will best exhibit the progress of concordance-making through the centuries. It would be impossible as well as inadvisable to cite all.

The following named concordances had been gathered by Mr. Walker, and formed a part of his working library. It will be seen that some of the volumes are quite rare and of great interest. Nearly all the noteworthy English concordances are included in the list. Believing that such a collection should be kept together, the books have been presented, with the consent of Mr. Walker's daughter, to the library of the American Congregational Association, located in the Congregational House, Boston. There they will remain as a memorial to the author of this Concordance. The full titles are not cited, inasmuch as they have already been given.

Tvvo right profitable and fruitfull Concordances, or large and ample Tables Alphabeticall. Collected by R. F. F. 1578. 8½x6¼. pp. 162.

A Concordance to all the Bookes of the Old Testament, according to the Translation allowed by His late Matie of Great Brittain, etc. By Clement Cotton. 1627. 10½x7. pp. 787.

A Complete Concordance to the Bible of the Last Translation. By Clement Cotton. 1631. Two copies. 10½x7. pp. 1010.

A Concordance to the whole Bible. By John Downame. 1635 (?). Also edition of 1689. 5½x3. pp. 116.

A Large and Complete Concordance to the Bible in English, According to the Last Translation. By Samuel Newman. 1643. 13½x9. pp. 1373.

Thesaurus Biblicus seu Promptarium Sacrum. By Richard Bernard. 1644. 11x7. pp. 808.

The Fort-Royal of Holy Scriptures. By J. H. 5½x3½. pp. 414. 3d edition. 1656.

A large and Compleat Concordance to the Bible in English, According to the Last Translation. By Samuel Newman, Now Teacher of the Church at Rehoboth in New-England. 13x8. pp. 1380. 1658.

A Complete Christian Dictionary. By Mr. Thomas Wilson. 12½x8. pp. 754. 7th edition. 1661.

A Concordance to the Holy Scriptures. In a more exact Method then hath hitherto been extant. By S. N. Cambridge. 1662. 11½x7½.

The Proper Names of the Old Testament arranged Alphabetically from the Original Text with Historical and Geographical Illustrations. For the use of Hebrew students, schoolmasters and teachers. With an Appendix of the Hebrew and Aramaic names in the New Testament. London: Williams & Norgate. 1859. 9x5⅞. pp. 227.

The following are classified by themselves, inasmuch as they are all essentially different editions of Cruden:—

A Concordance to the Holy Scriptures of the Old and New Testament. By Thomas Taylor. Brooklyn. 1809. 7¼x4¼. pp. 360.

A Concordance to the Holy Scriptures of the Old and New Testament. By Rev. John Brown, of Haddington. London: Gale & Fenner. 1816. Miniature edition 4½x3. pp. 190.

Cruden's Concordance to the Bible. The three alphabets arranged in one. 8⅝x5½. Four cols. pp. 120. Pearl type. References only. London. Printed for Samuel Bagster & Son. 1833.

A Complete Concordance to the Holy Scriptures. By Alexander Cruden. Condensed edition. Introduction by David King, LL.D. Boston: Gould, Kendall & Lincoln. 1845.

A Concordance to the Canonical Books of the Old and New Testaments; to which are added a Concordance to the Books called Apocrypha; and a Concordance to the Psalter, contained in the Book of Common Prayer. London: Society for the Promotion of Christian Knowledge. 1859. 10⅛x6½. pp. 1523. Preface states that it is based upon Cruden.

A New and Complete Concordance to the Holy Scriptures, on the basis of Cruden. Edited by John Eadie, D.D., LL.D., Professor of Biblical Literature to the United Presbyterian Church, Scotland. With an introduction by David King, LL.D. 1850. Octavo, pp. 561. 14th edition. American Tract Society: New York.

A new edition of the preceding, with an introduction by Joel Hawes, D.D. 1867. Hartford: O. D. Case & Co.

A Concordance to the Old and New Testament, or a Dictionary and Alphabetical Index to the Bible. By Alexander Cruden, M.A. Edited by Rev. C. S. Carey. London: Routledge & Sons. 1867. 7x4¾. pp. 572. 3 cols.

A Complete Concordance to the Holy Scriptures of the Old and New Testament; or Dictionary and Alphabetical Index to the Bible, etc. Contains a concordance to the Apocrypha, and life of Cruden. 1867. Octavo, pp. 856. New York: M. W. Dodd.

A New Concordance to the Holy Scriptures, in a single Alphabet, etc. By Rev. John Butterworth. Revised by Adam Clarke, LL.D. Illustrated. 1867. Philadelphia: J. B. Lippincott & Co. 10x6½. pp. 280.

Cruden's Complete Concordance to the Old and New Testaments. Meanings of the proper names revised by Rev. Alfred Jones, M.A. About 1885. Octavo, pp. 757. Portrait of Cruden. London: Morgan & Scott.

A

COMPREHENSIVE

CONCORDANCE

TO THE

HOLY SCRIPTURES.

AA'RON.

Ex. 4 : 14. Is not A. thy brother ?
27. L. said unto A., Le. 10 : 8. Nu. 18 : 1, 8, 20. [spoken, 16 : 10.
30. A. spake all the words Lord
6 : 23. A. took Elisheba to wife
7 : 1. A. thy brother be thy prophet
9. shalt say unto A., 19.-8 : 5, 16.
12. A.'s rod swal-d up th. rods[17.
8 : 6. A. stretched hand ov. waters,
15 : 20. Miriam, prophetess, sis. of A.
16 : 34. A. laid up pot of manna
17 : 12. A. and Hur stayed up hands
18 : 12. A. came to eat bread with
19 : 24. sh. come up, they and A.[Jet.
24 : 14. A. and Hur are with you
28 : 2. shalt make holy garments for A., 3, 4.-29 : 29.-31 : 10.-35 : 19. -39 : 1, 41.-40 : 13. [29, 30.
12. A. sh. bear names before Lord,
30. sh. be upon A.'s heart, 35, 38.
29 : 5. put upon A. coat and robe
26. the ram of A.'s consecra-n, 27.
30 : 7. A. sh. burn sweet incense[3.
8. when A. lighteth lamps, Nu. 8 :
10. A. sh. make atonement [7:40.
32 : 1. peo. unto A., make us gods, Ac.
2. A. said, Break off earrings, 3.
5. A. saw it, A. made proclamation
22. A. said, Let not anger wax hot
25. A. had made people naked am.
35. they made calf which A. made
Le. 7 : 35. portion of anointing of A.
8 : 12. he poured oil upon A.'s h-d
9 : 8. A. slew calf of sin offering, 21.
22. A. lifted hand, blessed people
10 : 3. And A. held his peace | 4.
16 : 2. speak unto A., 21 : 17. Nu. 8 : 2.
3. A. shall come into holy place
6. A. shall offer his bullock of, 11.
8. A. shall cast lots upon two goats
21. A. sh. lay hands upon goat, 9.
23. A. shall come into tabernacle
22 : 4. what man of seed of A. is leper
24 : 3. shall A. order it from evening
Nu. 1 : 3. A. sh. number th. by armies
3 : 4. Ithamar ministered in sight
6. br. tribe of Levi before A. [of A.
32. Eleazar, son of A., be chief, Jos. 24 : 33. Ju. 20 : 28. Ezr. 7 : 5.
8 : 11. A. shall offer the Levites bef.
21. A. made atonement for them
12 : 5. Lord called A. and Miriam
10. A. looked upon Miriam, lepr-s
16 : 11. what is A. that ye murmur ?
16. Be thou and A. bef. the L. | 17.
40. no stranger not of seed of A.
46. Mos. said unto A., Take censer
17 : 3. write A.'s name on Levi's rod
6. rod of A. among their rods
8. rod of A. for Levi was budded
10. Bring A.'s rod bef. testimony
20 : 8. thou and A. speak unto rock
Nu. 20 : 24. A. be gath-d unto his, 26.
26. And strip A. of his garments
28. A. died there in top of mount, 27 : 13.-33 : 38. De. 10 : 6.-32 : 50.
29. cong-n mourned for A. 30 days
33 : 39. A. 123 years old wh. he died
De. 9 : 20. Lord very angry with A., I prayed for A. also same time
1 Ch. 24 : 19. acc-g to manner under A.
Ne. 10 : 38. priest, son of A. wi. Levites
Ps. 106 : 16. envied A., saint of the L.
115 : 10. O ho. of A., trust in the L.
12. Lord will bless the house of A.
118 : 3. Let house of A. now say th.
133 : 2. ointment upon A.'s beard
135 : 19. Bless Lord, O house of A.
Lu. 1 : 5. His wife of daughters of A.
He. 5 : 4. called of God as was A.
7 : 11. not called after order of A.
9 : 4. manna and A.'s rod th. budded

Children of AA'RON.

Le. 6 : 18. males among c.o. A. eat it
Jos. 21 : 4. lot came out for c.o. A.
10. cities which c.o. A. had, 13, 19.
1 Ch. 15 : 4. Da. assembled c.o. A. [A.
Ne. 12 : 47. sanctified them unto c.o.
See ELEAZAR, ITHAMAR, PRIEST

AA'RON, with Moses.

Ex. 4 : 28. M. told A. words of Lord
29. M. and A. gathered the elders
5 : 1. M and A. told Pharaoh, 7 : 10.-10 : 3, 8. [works, 20.
4. Whf. M. and A. let people from
6 : 13. Lord spake unto M. and A., 7 : 8.-9 : 8.-12 : 1, 43. Le. 11 : 1. -13 : 1.-14 : 33.-15 : 1. Nu. 2 : 1. -4 : 1, 17.-12 : 4.-14 : 26.-16 : 20. -19 : 1.-20 : 12, 23.
20. Jochebed bare A. and M., Nu. 26 : 59. 1 Ch. 6 : 3.-23 : 13.
7 : 6. M. and A. did as Lord commanded, 10, 20 -12 : 28, 50.
8 : 8. Pharaoh called for M. and A., 25.-9 : 27.-10 : 16.-12 : 31.
12. M. and A. went out from Pha.
11 : 10. M. and A. did wonders bef.
16 : 2. congregation murmured ag. M. and A., Nu. 14 : 2. -16 : 41.
6. M. and A. said unto chil. of Isr.
9. M. spake unto A., 33. Le. 8 : 31. -9 : 2, 7. -10 : 12. Nu. 16 : 46.
17 : 10. M. and A. went to top of hill
24 : 1. unto M. come thou and A., 9.
32 : 21. M. said unto A. What did peo.
34 : 30. when A. saw M. his face shone
31. M called unto them ; A. and
40 : 31. M. and A. washed thereat
Le. 8 : 10. M. took anointing oil, 30.
9 : 23. M. and A. went into tabern.
10 : 19. A. said unto M., this day
Nu. 1 : 17. M. and A. took men exp-d
44. that M. and A. numbered, 3 : 39.-4 : 34, 37, 41, 45, 46.-26 : 59, 64.
Nu. 3 : 1. are genera-s of A. and M
38. M. and A. keeping charge of
8 : 20. M. and A. did to Levites acc-g
9 : 6. men defiled came bef. M and A.
12 : 1. Miriam and A. spake ag. M.
11. A. said unto M., Alas, my lord
13 : 26. th. came to M. and A. [20 : 6.
14 : 5. M. and A. fell on their faces,
15 : 33. him gathering sticks unto M. and A. [42.-20 : 2.-26 : 9.
16 : 3. they gath-d ag. M. and A.,
18. stood in door with M. and A.
43. M. and A. came before tabern.
47. A took as M. com-ded and ran
50. A. returned unto M., and
20 : 10. M. and A. gathered the cong.
28. M. stripped A. of his garments
33 : 1. out of Egypt under M. and A.
Jos. 24 : 5. I sent M. and A., plagued Eg., 1 S. 12 : 8. Mi. 6 : 4.
1 S. 12 : 6. L. th. advanced M. and A.
1 Ch. 6 : 3. chil. of Amr., A., M., 23 : 13.
Ps. 77 : 20. leddest peo. by M. and A.
99 : 6. M. and A. among his priests
105 : 26. He sent M. his serv-t and A.
See SIN offering.

AA'RON, with sons.

Ex. 27 : 21. A. and s. shall order it
28 : 1. take unto thee A. and s., Nadab, Abihu, Eleazar, Ithamar A.'s s. Le. 10 : 1, 6, 12, 16. Nu. 3 : 2, 3, 4.-26 : 60. 1 Ch. 6 : 3, 50.-24 : 1.
40. for A.'s s. thou shalt make coats, girdles, 41, 43.-31 : 10.-39 : 27. Le. 8 : 13.
29 : 4. A. and s. thou shalt wash, 9.-30 : 19.-40 : 12, 31, 32. Le. 8 : 6.
9. consecrate A. and s., (2)30 : 30.
10. A, and his s. shall put hands upon head, 15, 19. Le. 8 : 14, 18, 22.
20. put blood upon top of right ear of A. and s., Le 8 : 23, 24.
21. oil, sprinkle it upon A. and s., Le. 8 : 30. [Le. 8 : 27.
24. put all in hands of A. and s.,
27. is for A. and s., 28. |29, 32, 35.
44. I will sanctify A. and his s.
31 : 10. holy garments for A. and s., 35 : 19.-39 : 41. [thereat
40 : 31. A. and his s. washed hands
Le. 1 : 5. A.'s s. shall sprinkle the blood, 11.-3 : 2.-8 : 13.-9 : 9, 12.
7. s. of A. shall put fire upon altar
8. A.'s s. shall lay parts in order
2 : 2. sh. bring meat off-g to A.'s s.
3. remnant shall be A.'s and s.(2)
3 : 5. A.'s s. shall burn it on altar
6 : 9. Command A. and s., This is the law | 14, 16, 20.-8 : 31.
25. Speak unto A. and to his s., saying, 10 : 12.-17 : 2.-21 : 1, 24. -22 : 2, 18. Nu. 6 : 23.

Le. 7 : 10. sh. s. of A. have one as another | 31, 33, 34, 35.
8 : 2. Take A. and s. and garments
30. Moses sanctified A. and his s.
36. A. and s., 9 : 1, 9, 12, 18.-10 : 1, 12.
10 : 16. Mos. was angry with s. of A.
13 : 2. leprosy; bro-t unto A. or one
16 : 1. after death of 2 s. of A ⌊of s.
21 : 1. Speak unto priests, s. of A.
24. Mos. told it unto A. and s. and
24 : 9. bread shall be A.'s and his s.
Nu. 3 : 9. give the Levites unto A. and s., 4 : 19, 27.-8 : 13, 19, 22.
10. thou shalt appoint A. and s.
38. Mos., A., and s. keep-g charge
48. give money unto A. and s., 51.
4 : 5. A. and s. shall take down rail
15. A. and s. made end of cover-g
10 : 8. s. of A. sh. blow wi trumpets
1 Ch. 6 : 49. A. and s. were appointed
50. And these are the s. of A. ⌈54.
57. to s. of A. gave cities of Judah,
23 : 13. A. separated, he and s. for ev.
28. Levites to wait on s. of A. | 32.
24 : 1. the divisions of the s. of A.
31. cast lots over ag. s. of A. ⌈of A.
2 Ch. 13 : 9. Have ye not cast out s.
10. minister unto L. are s. of A.
26 : 18. s. of A. are consecrated to
29 : 21. Hez-h com-ded s. of A. to of.
31 : 19. Also s. of A. in the fields ⌊fer
35 : 14. s. of A. busied in offering

AA'RONITES. ⌈of A.
1 Ch. 12 : 27. Jehoiada, the leader
27 : 17. Zadok was ruler of the A.

ABAD'DON. ⌈A.
Re. 9 : 11. angel of bottomless pit is

ABAG'THA.
Es. 1 : 10. A., Zethar, chamberlains

AB'ANA. ⌈Damas.
2 K. 5 : 12. A., Pharpar, rivers of

AB'ARIM.
Nu. 27 : 12. Moses, Get thee into mt. A., De. 32 : 49. ⌈Nebo, 48.
33 : 47. they pitched in A., before

ABASE, ED, ING. ⌈him
Jb. 40 : 11. Behold proud and a.
Is 31 : 4. as lion will not a. himself
32 : † 19. city shall be utterly a-d
Eze. 21 : 26. and a. him that is high
Da. 4 : 37. walk in pride he is able to a.
Mat. 23 : 12. whoso. exalt hims. sh. be a-d, Lu. 14 : 11.-18 : 14.
2 Co. 11 : 7. an offence in a-g myself
Ph. 4 : 12. I know how to be a-d

ABATED.
Ge. 8 : 3. the waters were a., 8, 11.
Le. 27 : 18. be a. from thy estimation
De. 34 : 7. nor was natural force a.
Ju. 8 : 3. their anger was a. tow. him

ABBA. ⌈possible
Mk. 14 : 36. A., Father, all things
Ro. 8 : 15. wh-by we cry, A., Father
Ga. 4 : 6. your hearts, crying, A., Fa.

AB'DA.
1 K. 4 : 6. Adoniram son of A., over
Ne. 11 : 17. A. was for thanksgiving

AB'DEEL. ⌈A.
Je. 36 : 26. king commanded son of

AB'DI. ⌈of A.
1 Ch. 6 : 44. Ethan son of Kishi son
2 Ch. 29 : 12. Levites; Kish, son of A.
Ezr. 10 : 26. had taken strange wives;

AB'DIEL. ⌊A.
1 Ch. 5 : 15. A., chief of the house

AB'DON. [Person.]
Ju. 12 : 13. A. judged Isr. | 15. A. died
1 Ch. 8 : 30. firstb. son, A., 23.-9 : 36.
2 Ch 34 : 20. A. to inquire of L. 2 K. 22 :

AB'DON. [Place.] ⌊† 12.
Jos. 21 : 30. A. with suburbs, 1 Ch.

ABED'NEGO. ⌊6 : 74.
See SHADRACH.

A'BEL. [Person.]
Ge. 4 : 2. A. was a keeper of sheep (2)
4. L. had respect unto A., and (2)
8. Cain rose up ag. A. his brother
Ge. 4 : 9. Where is A. thy brother?
25. me another seed instead of A.
Mat. 23 : 35. blood of A., Lu. 11 : 51.
He. 11 : 4. by faith A. offered sacrif.
12 : 24. better things than blood of

A'BEL. [Place.] ⌊A.
1 S. 6 : 18. gr. stone of A. th. set ark
2 S 20 : 15. besieged him in A. | 14.
18. they shall ask counsel at A.

A'BEL-BETH-MA'A-CHAH.
1 K. 15 : 20. captains smote Ijon, A.
2 K. 15 : 29. Tiglath-pileser took Ijon,

A'BEL-MA'IM. ⌊A.
2 Ch. 16 : 4. captains smote Ijon and

A'-BEL-MEHO'LAH. ⌊A.
Ju 7 : 22. host fled to A. | 1 K. 4 : 12.
1 K. 19 : 16. Elisha son of Shaphat

A'BEL-MIZ'RAIM. ⌊of A.
Ge. 50 : 11. name of it was called A.

A'BEL-SHIT'TIM.
Nu 33 : 49. A. in plains of Moab

A'BEZ. ⌈ward A.
Jos. 19 : 20. border of Issachar to-

ABHOR.
Le 26 : 11. my soul shall not a. you
15. if your soul a. my judgments
30. and my soul shall a. you
44. nor will I a. them to destroy
De. 7 : 26. thou shalt utterly a. it
23 : 7. not a. Edomite, Egyptian
1 S. 27 : 12. made his people a. him
Jb. 9 : 31 my clothes shall a. me
30 : 10. they a., they flee from me
42 : 6. I a. myself and repent in
Ps. 5 : 6. Lord will a. bloody man
119 : 163. I hate and a. lying: but
Pr. 24 : 24. nations shall a. him
Je 14 : 21. do not a. us for name's
Am. 5 : 10. they a. him th. speaketh
6 : 8. I a. the excellency of Jacob
Mi. 3 : 9. Hear, ye that a. judgment
Ro. 12 : 9. a. that which is evil

ABHORRED. ⌈a.
Ex. 5 : 21. ye made our savour to be
Le. 20 : 23. commit, thf. I a. them
26 : 43. their soul a. my statutes
De 32 : 19. Lord saw it, he a. them
1 S. 2 : 17. men a. the offering of L.
2 S. 16 : 21. thou art a. of thy father
1 K 11 : 25. Hadad a. Israel ⌈be a.
Jb. 9 : † 31. my clothes make me to
19 : 19. my inward friends a. me
Ps. 22 : 24. nor a. affliction of afflict-
78 : 59. God greatly a. Israel ⌊ed
89 : 38. thou hast cast off and a.
106 : 40. he a. his own inheritance
Pr. 22 : 14. he that is a. of L. sh. fall
La. 2 : 7. L. hath a. his sanctuary
Eze. 16 : 25. made thy beauty to be a.
Zch. 11 : 8. their soul a. me

ABHORREST.
Is. 7 : 16. land thou a. be forsaken
Ro. 2 : 22. thou that a. idols dost

ABHORRETH, ING.
Jb. 33 : 20. so th. his life a-h bread
Ps. 10 : 3. covetous, whom Lord a-h
36 : 4. on his bed, he a-h not evil
107 : 18. their soul a-h all meat ⌈a-h
Is. 49 : 7. to him whom the nation
66 : 24. they be an a-g unto all flesh

A'BI. ⌈name A.
2 K. 18 : 2. Hezekiah's mother's

ABI'A.
1 K. 14 : † 31. A., Rohoboam's son, reigned, 1 Ch. 3 : 10. Mat. 1 : 7.
Lu. 1 : 5. Zachar-s, of the course of A.

ABI'AH. ⌈Ashur
1 Ch. 2 : 24. A., Hezron's wife, bare
6 : 28. sons of Sam.; Vashni, A.,
7 : 8. sons of Becher; A. ⌊1 S. 8 : 2.

A'BI-AL'BON.
2 S. 23 : 31. of thirty; A 1 Ch. 11 : † 32.

ABI'ASAPH.
Ex. 6 : 24. sons of Korah, Assir, A.

ABI'ATHAR. ⌈6.
1 S. 22 : 20. A. fled after David, 23 :
1 S 22 : 21. A. shewed Da. S. had slain,
30 : 7. A. bro-t ephod to Da., 23 : 9. ⌊22.
2 S. 8 : 17. son of A. priest, 15 : 27, 36. 1 K. 1 : 42. 1 Ch. 18 : 16.-24 : 6.
15 : 24. A. went up until all the peo.
29. Zadok and A. carried the ark
35. Tell it to Zadok and A. priests, 17 : 15.-19 : 11.-20 : 25. 1 K. 4 : 4.
1 K. 1 : 7. Adonijah conferred wi. A., 19, 25.-2 : 22. ⌈thy of death
2 : 26. unto A. k. said, Thou wor-
27. Sol. thrust A. fr. being priest
35. Zadok did k. put in room of A.
1 Ch. 15 : 11. Da. called for Zadok, A.
27 : 34. aft. Ahithophel was A. ⌈A.
Mk. 2 : 26. into hou. of G. in days of
See PRIEST.

ABIB. ⌈34 : 18.
Ex. 13 : 4. ye came out in month A.,
23 : 15. feast of unleav-d bread keep in month A., 34 : 18. De. 16 : 1.

ABI'DA, ABI'DAH. ⌈33.
Ge. 25 : 4. sons of Midian, A., 1 Ch. 1 :

AB'IDAN. ⌈oni
Nu. 1 : 11. Of Benj.; A., son of Gide-
2 : 22. capt. of sons of Benj. sh. be A.
7 : 60. A. of Benjamin offered, 65.
10 : 24. over host of Benj. was A.

ABIDE.
Ge. 19 : 2. we a. in street all night
22 : 5. a. ye here with the ass, and I
24 : 55. Let the damsel a. with us
29 : 19. I give her to thee: a. wi. me
44 : 33. let servant a. instead of lad
Ex. 16 : 29. a. ye every man in place
Le. 8 : 35. a. at door of tabernacle
19 : 13. wages of him hired not a. wi.
Nu. 22 : 5. peo. of Eg. a. over ag. me
31 : 19. do ye a. without the camp
23. Every thing that may a. fire
35 : 25. a. unto death of high priest
De. 3 : 19. wives sh. a. in your cities
Jos. 18 : 5. Judah sh. a. in their coast
Ru. 2 : 8. a. here fast by my maidens
1 S. 1 : 22. bef. Lord and a. for ever
5 : 7. ark of God sh. not a. with us
19 : 2. a. in a secret place ⌈hold
22 : 5. Gad unto Dav., a. not in the
23. a. thou wi. me, fear not; for he
30 : 21. made to a. at brook Besor
2 S. 11 : 11. ark and Israel a. in tents
15 : 19. return and a. with the king
16 : 18. his will I be, and wi. him a.
1 K. 8 : 13. a settled place to a. in
2 Ch. 25 : 19. a. now at home; why
32 : 10. that ye a. in siege in Jerus.
Jb. 24 : 13. ag-t light, nor a. in paths
38 : 40. a. in covert to lie in wait
39 : 9. unicorn a. by thy crib?
Ps. 15 : 1. L., who shall a. in thy tab.
61 : 4. I will a. in thy tabernacle
7. he shall a. before God for ever
91 : 1. He shall a. under shadow of
Pr. 7 : 11. She is loud, feet a. not in
19 : 23. that hath it sh. a. satisfied
Ec. 8 : 15. that shall a. of his labour
Je. 10 : 10. not able to a. his indign.
42 : 10. if ye a. in this land ⌈-50 : 40.
49 : 18. no man sh. a. in Sodom, 33.
Ho. 3 : 3. Thou shalt a. for me many
4. Isr. shall a. without king ⌊days
11 : 6. sword shall a. on his cities
Jo. 2 : 11. day of L. who can a. it?
Mi. 5 : 4. they shall a., for now he
Na. 1 : 6. who can a. in his anger?
Mal. 3 : 2. who may a. his coming?
Mat. 10 : 11. whatso. town ye enter, there a. till, Mk 6 : 10. Lu. 9 : 4.
Lu. 19 : 5. I must a. at thy house
24 : 29. a. with us, it is toward even.
Jn. 12 : 46. should not a. in darkness
14 : 16. Comforter, that he may a.
15 : 4. a. in me; branch cannot bear except it a. in vine; no more can ye, except ye a. in me ⌈forth
6 if man a. not in me, he is cast
7. if a. in me, and my words a. in

Jn.15 .10.a. in my love as I a. in his
Ac. 15 : 34.it pleased Silas to a. there
16 : 15. come into my house and a.
20 : 23. bonds and afflictions a. me
27 : 31. except these a. in ship, ye
Ro. 11 : 23. if they a. not in unbelief
1 Co. 3 : 14. If any man's work a. he
7 : 8. is good if they a. even as I
20. let ev. man a. in same calling
24. wherein called, th-n a. wi. God
40. But she is happier if she so a.
16 : 6. I will a. and winter with you
Ph. 1 : 24. to a. in flesh more needful
25. I know th. I shall a. with you
1 Ti. 1 : 3. I besought thee to a. at
1 Jn. 2 : 24. Let that a. in you⌊Eph.
27. as taught you ye sh. a. in him
28. And now, little chil. a. in him

ABIDETH.

Nu. 31 : 23. all that a. not the fire
2 S. 16 : 3. Ziba said, he a. at Jerus.
Jb. 39 : 28. eagle a. upon the crag of
Ps. 49:12. man, be-g in honour a. not
55 : 19. God, even he that a. of old
119 : 90. established earth, and it a.
125 : 1. mount Zion, wh. a. for ever
Pr. 15 : 31. reproof of life a. am. wise
Ec. 1 : 4. but the earth a. for ever
Je. 21 : 9. that a. in city shall die
Jn. 3 : 36. the wrath of G. a. on him
8 : 35. servant a. not, son a. ever
12 : 24. Except corn die it a. alone
34. we heard Christ a. for ever
15 : 5. he th. a. in me bringeth forth
1 Co. 13 : 13. now a. faith, hope, charity
2 Ti. 2 : 13. yet he a. faithf.; he can-t
He. 7 : 3. Melchisedec a. a priest cont.
1 Pe. 1 : 23. by word of God which a.
1 Jn. 2 : 6. a. in him ought so to walk
10. loveth his brother a. in light
14. yo-g men, word of G. a. in you
17. doeth will of God a. for ever
27. the anointing of him a. in you
3 : 6. Whoso. a. in him sinneth not
14. loveth not brother a. in death
24. hereby know that he a. in us
2 Jn. 9. Whoso. a. not in doctr-e(2)

ABIDING. ⌈tents

Nu. 24 : 2. Balaam saw Israel a. in
Ju. 16 : 12. liers in wait a. in chamb.
1 S. 26 : 19. from a. in inheritance⌊9.
1 Ch. 29 : 15. shadow, there is none
Lu. 2 : 8. shepherds a. in field ⌊a.
Jn. 5 : 38. ye have not his word a.
Ac. 16 : 12. we were in that city a.
1 Jn. 3 : 15. no murderer hath etern.

ABI'EL. ⌊life a.

1 S. 9 : 1. a man of Benj. son of A.
14 : 51. Ner, fa. of Ab., was son of A.
1 Ch. 11 : 32. Hurai, A. the Arbath-e

ABIE'ZER. ⌈26 : † 30.

Jos. 17 : 2. lot for children of A., Nu.
Ju. 6 : 34. A. was gathered aft. Gid-n
8 : 2. better than the vintage of A.
2 S. 23 , 27. one of the thirty, A.
1 Ch. 7 : 18. Hammoleketh bare A.
11 : 28. val-t men of armies were A.
27 : 12. captain for 9th mo. was A.

ABIEZ'RITE, S. ⌈ash, A.

Ju. 6 : 11. Ophrah pertained unto Jo-
24. altar, yet in Ophrah of the A-s
8 : 32. seppl. in Ophrah of the A-s

AB'IGAIL. ⌈A., 14.

1 S. 25 : 3. Nabal's wife's name was
18. A., 23, 32, 36, 40, 42. ⌈take
39. David communed with A. to
27 : 3. David dwelt at Gath with A.
30 : 5. David's two wives, Ahinoam
and A., 2 S. 2 : 2-3 : 3. 1 Ch. 3 : 1.
2 S. 17 : 25. went in to A., dau. of N.
1 Ch. 2 : 16 whose sisters were Ze-
17. And A. bare Amasa⌊ruiah, A.

ABIHA'IL.

Nu. 3 : 35. chief was Zuriel son of A.
1 Ch. 2 : 29. name of wife of Abishur
5 : 14. children of Huri son of A.⌊A.
2 Ch. 11 : 18. Rehob. took A. dau. of
Es. 2 : 15. Esther dau. of A., 9 : 29.

ABI'HU. See NADAB.

See AARON with sons.

ABI'HUD. ⌈A.

1 Ch. 8 : 3. sons of Bela were Addar,

ABI'JAH, or ABI'JAM.

1 K. 14 : 1. A-h, son of Jerob., sick
31. A-m, Rehob.'s son, reigned in
his stead, 2 Ch. 12 : 16, A-h, †A-m
15 : 1. in 18th year of Jeroboam
reigned A-m, 2 Ch. 13 : 1, A-h
7. there was war between A-m and
Jeroboam (2), 2 Ch. 13 : 2, A-h
8. And A-m slept with his fathers,
2 Ch. 14 : 1, A-h ⌈son
1 Ch. 3 . † 10. Rehoboam, A-m his
24 : 10. lot to Hakkoz, 8th to A-h
2 Ch. 11 : 20. Maachah bare A-h
22. Rehob. made A-h the chief
13 : 3. A-h, 4, 15, 19, 20, 21, 22.
17. A-h slew th. with gr. slaughter
29 : 1. Hez-h's mo-'s name was A-h
Ne. 10 : 7. that sealed, Mesh-m, A-h
12 : 4. went up with Zeruh-l, Iddo,
17. Of A-h, Zichri ⌊A-h

ABILE'NE.

Lu. 3 : 1. Lysanias tetrarch of A.

ABILITY.

Le. 27 : 8. value him acc-g to his a.
Ezr. 2 : 69. they gave after their a.
Ne. 5 : 8. aft. our a. redeemed breth.
Da. 1 : 4. as had a. to stand in palace
Mat. 25 : 15. gave to each acc-g to a.
Ac. 11 : 29. ev. man acc. to a. to send
1 Pe. 4 : 11. do it as of a. God giveth

ABIM'AEL. ⌈1 : 22.

Ge. 10 : 28. Joktan begat A., 1 Ch.

ABIM'ELECH.

Ge. 20 : 2. A. sent and took Sarah
3. God came to A. in a dream | 8.
4. But A. had not come near her
9. A. called Abr. and said, What
hast th. done? 10.-21 : 22.-26 : 10.
14. A. gave sheep, oxen unto Abr.
15. A. said, My land is before thee
17. Abr. prayed; God healed A.
18. closed wombs of ho. of A., bec.
21 : 25. Abr. reproved A. bec. of well
26. A. said, I wot not who hath
27. Abr. gave sheep, oxen unto A.
29. A. said, What mean 7 lambs?
32. A. returned into land of Phil.
26 : 1. Isaac went unto A. k. of Phil.
8. A. saw Isaac sporting wi. Reb-h
9. A. said, She is thy wife ⌈eth
11. A. charged peo., He that touch-
16. A. said to Isaac, Go fr. us | 26.
Ju. 8 : 31. Gid-'s concubine bare son A.
9 : 1 A. son of Jerub-l went to Sh.
3. A., 16, 18, 19, 20, 21, 24, 25, 27,
28, 29, 31, 34, 35, 38, 39, 40, 41,
44, 45, 48, 49, 50, 52, 53, 55.
4. A. hired vain and light persons
6. men of She-m made A. k., 16, 18.
22. A. had reigned 3 years ov. Isr.
23. G. sent evil spirit betw. A. and
56. Thus G. rend-d wickedn. of A.
1 S. 21 : † 10. David fled to A., Ps. 34.
2 S. 11 : 21. Who smote A.? a woman
1 Ch. 18 : 16. Zadok and A. priests

ABIN'ADAB.

1 S. 7 : 1. bro-t ark into house of A.
16 : 8. Jesse called A., made him
17 : 13. A. followed S. to bat. ⌊pass
31 : 2. Philistines slew A., 1 Ch. 10 : 2.
2 S. 6 : 3 ark, and brought out of
house of A., 4.-1 Ch. 13 : 7.
1 K. 4 : 11. son of A. had Sol.'s dau-s
1 Ch. 2 : 13 Jesse begat Eliab, A. 2d
8 : 33. Saul begat Jona-n, A. 9 : 39.

Son of ABIN'OAM.

Ju. 4 : 6. Deborah called Barak – A.
12. Barak the – A. was gone to Tab.
5 : 1. Sang Deborah and Barak – A.
12. Barak lead captivity captive,

ABI'RAM. ⌊thou – A.

1 K. 16 : 34. Hiel laid founda-n in A.

ABI'RAM with Dathan.

Nu. 16 : 1. D. and A. sons of Eliab, 26 :
12. Moses sent to call D. and A.⌊9.
24. Get you up from tabernacle
of D. and A.
25. Moses went unto D. A., 27.
27. D. and A. stood in doors of tents
26 : 9. This is D. A famous in
congregation
De. 11 : 6. what he did unto D. and A.
Ps. 106 : 17. earth swallowed up D.
and covered the company of A.

AB'ISHAG.

See SHUNAMMITE.

ABISH'AI. ⌈thee

1 S. 26 : 6. A. said, I will go with
7. Da. and A. came by night⌈eneu.
8. said A. to Da., God hath deliv-d
9. Da. said to A., Destroy him not
2 S. 2 : 18. sons of Zeruiah, Joab, A., 1
24. Joab, A., pursued Abn.⌊Ch. 2 : 16
3 : 30. Joab, A., slew Abner bec. he
10 : 10. rest of people he delivered
into hand of A., 1 Ch. 19 : 11.
14. Ammonites fled before A., 1
Ch. 19 : 15. ⌈king? | 11.
16 : 9. said A., Why this dog curse
18 : 2. Da. sent 3d part of peo. und A.
5. k. com-ded A., Deal gently, 12.
19 : 21. A. said, Shall not Shimei be
put to death ⌈ba, 10.
20 : 6. David said to A., pursue She-
21 : 17. A. succoured David⌈11 : 20.
23 : 18. A. was chief am. three, 1 Ch.
1 Ch. 18 : 12. A. slew Edomites 18,000

ABISH'ALOM. ⌈10.

1 K. 15 : 2. Maachah, daughter of A.,

ABISH'UA. ⌈Ezr. 7 : 5.

1 Ch. 6 : 4. Phinehas begat A., 50.
5. And A. begat Bukki, and
8 : 4. sons of Bela, Gera, A., and Hu-m

AB'ISHUR. ⌈dab, A.

1 Ch. 2 : 28. sons of Shammai; Na-
29. the wife of A. was Abihail

AB'ITAL. ⌈Ch. 3 : 3.

2 S. 3 : 4. Shephatiah, son of A., 1

AB'ITUB.

1 Ch. 8 : 11. he begat A. and Elpaal

ABI'UD. ⌈Eliakim

Mat. 1 : 13. begat A., and A. begat

ABJECTS.

Ps. 35 : 15. the a. gathered ag. me

ABLE. ⌈men

Ex. 18 : 21. provide out of people a.
25. Moses chose a. men out of Isr.
Le. 14 : 22. such as he is a. to get, 31.
Nu. 1 : 3. all that are a. to go to war,
20, 22, 24, 26, 28, 30, 32, 34, 36,
38, 40, 42, 45.-26 : 2. 2 Ch. 25 : 5
13 : 30. we are well a. to overcome it
De 16 : 17. ev. man sh. give as he is a.
Jos. 23 : 9. no man a. to stand bef.
Ju. 8 : 3. what I a. to do in compar.
1 S. 6 : 20. who a. to stand bef. God?
1 K. 3 : 9. who is a. to judge gr. peo.?
2 K. 3 : 21. all a. to put on armour
1 Ch. 5 : 18. men a. to bear sword
9 : 13. very a. men for service, 26 : 8.
2 Ch. 2 : 6. who is a. to build house
20 : 6. none is able to withst-d thee
25 : 9. Lord is a. to give much more
32 : 13. were gods a. to deliv. lands
15. no god a. to deliver his people
Jb. 41 : 10. who a. to stand bef. me?
Pr. 27 : 4. who a. to stand bef. envy?
Eze. 46 : 11. lambs as he is a. to give
Da. 2 : 26. a. to make known dream?
3 : 17. our God is a. to deliver us
4 : 18. thou art a.; spirit is in thee
37. walk in pride, he is a. to abase
6 : 20. is G. a. to deliver from lions?
Mat. 3 : 9. God is a. of these stones
to raise up children, Lu. 3 : 8.
9 : 28. believe ye I am a. to do this?
10 : 28. a. to destroy soul in hell
19 : 12. he that is a. to receive it
20 : 22. are ye a. to drink of cup

Mat. 22 : 46. no man was a. to ans.
26 : 61. I am a. to destroy tem.⌊him
Mk. 4 : 33. as they were a. to hear
Jn. 10 : 29. no man is a. to pluck th.
Ac. 15 : 10. yoke fathers nor we a. to
20 : 32. word of grace, a. to build
25 : 5. wh. am. you are a.,go wi.me
Ro. 4 : 21. he was a. also to perform
11 : 23. God is a. to graff them in
14 : 4. God is a. to make him stand
15 : 14. ye a. to admonish one ano.
1 Co. 3 : 2. ye were not a., nei.now a.
10 : 13. tempted above that ye are a.
2 Co. 3 : 6. made us a. ministers of
9 : 8. G. is a. to make grace abound
Ep. 3 : 20. th. is a. to do abundantly
Ph. 3 : 21. he is a. to subdue all things
2 Ti. 1 : 12. he is a. to keep that wh. I
3 : 7. nev. a. to come to knowledge
15. Scriptures a. to make thee wise
He. 2 : 18. he is a. to succour them
5 : 7. unto him that was a. to save
7 : 25. he is a. to save to uttermost
11 : 19. that G. was a. to raise him
Ja. 1 : 21. word wh. is a. to save souls
3 : 2. a. to bridle the whole body
4 : 12. is one lawgiver a. to save and
Jude 24. a. to keep you from falling
Re. 5 : 3. no man a. to open the book
13 : 4. who a. to make war wi. him?
15 : 8. no man was a. to enter temp.

Be ABLE. ⌈ber

Ge. 15 : 5. stars, if thou b.a. to num-
33 : 14. children b.a. to endure
Ex. 18 : 23. thou sh. b.a. to endure
Le. 25 : 26. hims. b.a. to redeem it
49. if he b.a. may redeem hims.
Nu. 22 : 11. I shall b.a. to overc. th.
De. 7 : 24. no man b.a. to stand be-
fore thee, 11:25. Jos. 1:5. ⌈drive
Jos. 14 : 12. L. wi. me I sh. be a. to
1 S. 17 : 9. If he b.a. to fight me ⌈8.
2 K. 18 : 23. b.a. to set riders, Is. 36:
1 Ch. 29 : 14. b.a. to offer willingly
2 Ch. 32 : 14. y-r God b.a. to deliver
Is. 47 : 12. if so thou b.a. to profit
Eze. 33 : 12. nei. righte. b.a. to live
46 : 5. lambs as he b.a. to give, 11.
Zph. 1 : 18. nor gold b.a. to deliver
Lu. 14 : 31. whe. he b. a. with 10,000
Ro. 8 : 39. nei. death b.a. to separate
1 Co. 6 : 5. not one b.a. to judge betw.
10 : 13. ye b.a. to bear it ⌊breth.?
2 Co. 1 : 4. ye may b.a. to comfort
Ep. 3 : 18. May b.a. to comprehend
6 : 11. ye b.a. to stand ag. devil, 13.
16. ye shall b.a. to quench fiery
2 Ti. 2 : 2. who shall b.a. to teach
Tit. 1 : 9. may b.a. by sound doctr.
2 Pe. 1 : 15. ye b.a. after my decease
Re. 6 : 17. who shall b.a. to stand?

ABLE, with not or cannot.

Ge. 13 : 6. land was n.a. to bear th.
Ex. 10 : 5. one c. be a. to see the earth
18 : 18. thou art n.a. to perform it
40 : 35. Moses was n.a. to ent. tent
Le. 5 : 7. if n.a. to bring lamb, 11.-
14 : 32. hand is n.a. to get ⌊12 : 8.
25 : 28. if he be n.a. to restore it
Nu. 11 : 14. I am n.a. to bear th. peo.
13 : 31. We be n.a. to go ag. people
14 : 16. n.a. to bring peo., De. 9: 28.
22 : 37. am I n.a. to promote thee?
De. 1 : 9. I n.a. to bear you alone
14 : 24. thou art n.a. to carry it
1 S. 17 : 33. thou n.a. to go ag. Phil.
1 K. 9 : 21. Israel n.a. to destroy
2 K. 18 : 29. n.a. to deliver, Is. 36: 14.
2 Ch. 7 : 7. n.a. to receive offerings
20 : 37. ships n.a. to go to Tarshish
Ezr. 10 : 13. rain, we are n.a. to stand
Ne. 4 : 10. we are n.a. to build wall
Ps. 18:38. wounded them n.a. to rise
21 : 11. wh. they are n.a. to perform
36 : 12. down, shall n. be a. to rise
40 : 12. that I am n.a. to look up
Ec. 8 : 17. know yet n. be a. to find it
Is. 47 : 11. shalt n. be a. to put it off
Je. 10 : 10. sh. n. be a. to abide indign.
11 : 11. evil, they n. be a. to escape
49 : 10. sh. n. be a. to hide himself
La. 1 : 14. fr. whom I am n.a. to rise
Eze. 7 : 19. gold n. be a. to deliver th.
Da. 4 : 18. are n.a. to make known
Am. 7 : 10. land n.a. to bear words
Mat. 10 : 28. are n.a. to kill the soul
Lu. 1 : 20. sh. be dumb, n.a. to speak
12 : 26. If ye be n.a. to do least
13 : 24. seek to enter shall n. be a.
14 : 29. founda-n, is n.a. to finish, 30.
21 : 15. advers-s n. be a. to gainsay
Jn. 21 : 6. n.a. to draw net for the
Ac. 6 : 10. n.a. to resist the wisdom
1 Co. 3 : 2. ye were n.a. to bear it

AB'NER. ⌈20 : 25.

1 S. 14 : 51. Ner, father of A. | 57.-
17 : 55. Saul, said A., Whose son thou
26 : 7. A. and people lay round Saul
14. Da. cried, Answerest not A.? 15.
2 S. 2 : 14. A. said, Let yo. men play
17. sore battle, A. was beaten
19. A., 20, 21, 22, 24, 25, 26, 29, 30,
31.-3:9, 11, 12, 16, 17, 19, 20, 21,
22, 24, 25, 26, 31, 32.
23. A. smote Asahel under 5th rib
26. A. said, Sh. sword devour for ev.
3:6. A. made hims. strong for Saul
8. A. wroth for words of Ish-bo-h, 7.
27. Joab smote A. under 5th rib
30. Joab and Abishai slew A. bec.
32. David wept at grave of A.
33. Died A. as a fool dieth?
4:1. Saul's son heard A. was dead
12. head of Ish-bo. in sepulchre of
1 Ch. 27 : 21. Jaasiel son of A. ⌊A.
See **Abner son of NER.**

ABOARD.

Ac. 21 : 2. ship sailing, we went a.

ABODE. [Noun.]

2 K. 19 : 27. I know thy a., Is. 37:28.
Ezr. 9 : † 8. give us sure a. in holy
Jn. 14 : 23. will make our a. with him

ABODE. [Verb.]

Ge. 29 : 14. Jacob a. wi. him a month
49 : 24. But his bow a. in strength
Ex. 24 : 16. glory of L. a. upon Sinai
40 : 35. not enter tent bec. cloud a.
Nu. 9 : 17. where the cloud a., 18, 21.
20. chil. of Isr. a. in th. tents, 22.
11 : 35. peo. a. at Hazer-h⌈Ju. 11 : 17.
20 : 1. peo. a. in Kadesh, De. 1 : 46.
22 : 8. princes of Moab a. with Bal-m
25 : 1. Isr. a. in Shittim, and began
De. 3 : 29. we a. in valley ag. Beth-peor
9 : 9. I a. in the mount 40 days and
Jos. 5 : 8. a. in their places in camp
8 : 9. a. betw. Bethel, Ai ⌈Asher a.
Ju. 5 : 17. Gilead a. bey. Jordan,
19 : 4. Levite a. with him three days
20 : 47. 600 men a. in rock Rimmon
1 S. 1 : 23. wom. a. and gave her son
7 : 2. ark a. in Kirjath-jearim
13 : 16. Saul and Jonathan a. in
Gibeah, 22 : 6. ⌈25.-26 : 3.
23 : 14. Da. a. in wilderness, 18,
30 : 10. 2 hund. a. behind, so faint
2 S. 1 : 1. David a. 2 days in Ziklag
11 : 12 Uriah a. in Jerus. that day
15 : 8. vowed while I a. at Geshur
1 K. 17 : 19. into a loft where he a.
Je. 38 : 28. Jere. a. in court of prison
Mat. 17 : 22. while they a. in Galilee
Lu. 1 : 56. Mary a. wi. Elis-h 3 mos.
8 : 27. nei. a. in any hou. but tombs
21 : 37. Jesus a. in mount of Olives
Jn. 1 : 32. Spirit, and it a. upon him
39. came and a. with him that day
7 : 9. these words, he a. in Galilee
8 : 44. murderer, and a. not in truth
11 : 6. he a. two days in same place
Ac. 1 : 13. room where a. Peter, James
14 : 3. Long time a. they speaking
18 : 3. Paul a. wi. them and wrought
20 : 6. to Troas, where we a. 7 days
Ac. 21 : 7. we a. with breth. one day
8. house of Philip and a. with him
Ga. 1 : 18. I a. with Peter 15 days
2 Ti. 4 : 20. Erastus a. at Corinth

ABODE with there.

De. 1 : 46. acc-g unto days ye a.t.
Jos. 2 : 22. unto mt., and a.t. 3 days
Ju. 21 : 2. peo. a.t. till even bef. God
Ezr. 8 : 15. t.a. we in tents 3 days
32. we came to Jerus., a.t. 3 days
Jn. 4 : 40. Sychar, Jes. a.t. two days
10 : 40. where Jn. baptized and t.be
Ac. 12 : 19. to Cesarea, and t.a. ⌊a.
14 : 28. t.a. long time with discip.
17 : 14. Silas and Timotheus a.t.
20 : 3. Paul t.a. three months

ABODEST.

Ju. 5 : 16. why a. among sheepfolds?

ABOLISH, ED.

Is. 2 : 18. the idols he shall utterly a.
51 : 6. my righteousness not be a-d
Eze. 6 : 6. your works may be a-d
2 Co. 3 : 13. end of that which is a-d
Ep. 2 : 15. Having a-d in his flesh
2 Ti. 1 : 10. Ch. who hath a-d death

ABOMINABLE, BLY.

Le. 7 : 21. that touch any a. thing
11 : 43. not make yourselves a. wi.
18 : 30. commit not any a. customs
19 : 7. eaten on third day, it is a.
20 : 25. not make souls a. by beast
De. 14 : 3. shalt not eat any a. thing
1 K. 21 : 26. Ahab did very a-y in fol.
1 Ch. 21 : 6. king's word a. to Joab
2 Ch. 15 : 8. Asa put away a. idols
Jb. 15 : 16. How much more a. is man
Ps. 14 : 1. they have done a. works
53 : 1. they have done a. iniquity
Is. 14 : 19. cast out like an a. branch
65 : 4. broth of a. things in vessels
Je. 16 : 18. carcasses of their a. things
44 : 4. Oh, do not this a. thi. I hate
Eze. 4 : 14. nei. a. flesh in my mouth
8 : 10. behold ev. form of a. beasts
16 : 52. thy sins committed more a.
Mi. 6 : 10. scant measure that is a.
Na. 3 : 6. I will cast a. filth upon thee
Tit. 1 : 16. in works deny him be-g a.
1 Pe. 4 : 3. we walked in a. idolatries
Re. 21 : 8. the unbeliev-g and the a.

ABOMINATION. ⌈tians

Ge. 43 : 32. that is an a. unto Egyp-
46 : 34. ev. shepherd is a. unto Eg-s
Ex. 8 : 26. sacrifice the a. of Egyp-ns
Le. 7 : 18. it shall be an a., 11:41, 42.
11 : 10. an a. to you, 11, 12, 20, 23.
11. ye sh. have their carcasses in a.
13. wh. ye sh. have in a. am. fowls
18 : 22. wi. mankind; it is a., 20 : 13.
De. 7 : 25. it is a. to Lord, 17:1.-22:5.
26. Nei. sh. bring a. into thy hou.
12 : 31. every a. have they done
13 : 14. th. such a. is wrought, 17:4.
18 : 12. all th. do these are a., 22:5.
23 : 18. both these are an a. to God
24 : 4. that is an a. before the Lord
25 : 16. th. do unrighteously are a.
27 : 15. cursed th. maketh image, an
1 S. 13 : 4. Isr. was had in a. with⌊a.
1 K. 11 : 5. Milcom a. of Amorites
7. Chemosh the a. of Moab ⌈ans
2 K. 23 : 13. Ashtoreth, a. of Zidoni-
Ps. 88 : 8. thou hast made me an a.
Pr. 3 : 32. froward is an a. to Lord
6 : 16. seven things are a. unto him
8 : 7. wickedness is an a. to my lips
11 : 1. false balance is a. to the Lord
20. They of froward heart are a. to
12 : 22. Lying lips are a. to the Lord
13 : 19. a. to fools to depart fr. evil
15 : 8. sacri. of wicked is a., 21 : 27.
9. way of wicked is an a. unto L.
26. thoughts of wicked a. to Lord
16 : 5. Ev. one proud in heart is a.
12. a. to kings to commit wickedn.
17 : 15. both are a. to Lord, 20 : 10.
20 : 23. divers weights are a. to L.

Pr. 24 : 9. scorner is an a. to men
28 : 9. even his prayer shall be a.
29 : 27. An unjust man is a. to the just; upright is a. to wicked
Is. 1 : 13. incense is an a. unto me
41 : 24. a. is he that chooseth you
44 : 19. sh. I make the residue an a.
66 : 17. eating swine's flesh and a.
Je. 2 : 7. ye made mine heritage a.
32 : 35. that they should do this a.
Eze. 33 : 26. ye work a. and [12 : 11.
Da. 11 : 31. a. that maketh desolate,
Mat. 24 : 15. the a. of desolation, Mk.
Lu. 16 : 15. is a. with God [13 : 14.
Re. 21 : 27. nei. whatsoever worketh

ABOMINATIONS. [a.

De. 18 : 9. not learn to do after a. of
32 : 16. with a. provoked they him
1 K. 14 : 24. did acc. to a. of nations
2 K. 16 : 3. son thro. fire acc-g to a. of heathen, 2 Ch. 28 : 3. [Ch. 33 : 2.
21 : 2. Manasseh, aft. a. of heath., 2
23 : 24. a. Josiah put aw., 2 Ch. 34 :
2 Ch. 15 : †8. Asa put away a. of [33.
36 : 8. Jehoiakim and his a. [en
14. transgressed after a. of heath-
Pr. 26 : 25. are seven a. in his heart
Eze. 6 : 11. Alas for the evil a. of Isr.
8 : 6. thou sh. see greater a., 13, 15.
9. behold wicked a. that they do
9 : 4. men that sigh and cry for a.
11 : 18. sh. take away all a. thereof
14 : 6. turn your faces from your a.
16 : 2. cause Jerus. to know her a.
18 : 24. when the righteous doeth a.
20 : 4. to know a. of their fathers
7. Cast away every man a. of eyes
8. did not cast away a. of eyes
22 : 2. thou sh. shew her all her a.
36 : 31. sh. loathe yourselves for a.
44 : 6. O Israel, let it suffice of a.
7. broken covenant bec. of your a.
Da. 9 : 27. for the overspreading of a.
Zch. 9 : 7. take a. fr. betw. his teeth
Re. 17 : 4. hav-g golden cup full of a.
5. MOTHER OF HARLOTS AND A.

Commit, ted, teth
ABOMINATION, S. [a-s

Le. 18 : 26. Ye sh. not c. any of these
29. Whoso. c. these a-s be cut off
Je. 6 : 15. Were they ashamed when they had c-d a.? 8 : 12. [c-d
44 : 22. Lord no longer bec. of a-s
Eze. 8 : 6. seest thou a-s Israel c-h
17. Is it a light thing they c. a-s
16 : 50. haughty and c-d a-s bef. me
18 : 12. If he beget a son that c-d a.
22 : 11. c-d a. with neighbour's wife
33 : 29. land desolate bec. of a-s c-d
43 : 8. defiled my name by a-s c-d
44 : 13. sh. bear their shame, a-s c-d
Mal. 2 : 11. an a. is c-d in Judah

Their ABOMINATIONS.

De. 20 : 18. teach you not to do t.a.
29 : 17. ye have seen t.a., idols
Ezr. 9 : 1. people doing acc-g to t.a.
11. it is an unclean land with t.a.
Is. 66 : 3. soul delighteth in t.a. [34.
Je. 7 : 30. have set t.a. in house, 32 :
Eze. 6 : 9. evils committed in t.a.
7 : 20. they made the images of t.a.
11 : 21. heart walketh after t.a. [a.
12 : 16. that they may declare all t.
16 : 47. hast not done after t.a. [a.
20 : 30. commit whoredom after t.
23 : 36. yea, declare unto them t.a.
Ho. 9 : 10. t.a. were as they loved

These ABOMINATIONS.

Le. 18 : 27. all t.a. have men done
De. 18 : 12. bec. of t.a. Lord drive
2 K. 21 : 11. Manasseh hath done t.a.
Ezr. 9 : 14. affinity with peo. of t.a.?
Je. 7 : 10. are delivered to do all t.a.
Eze. 18 : 13. done t.a.; sh. surely die

Thine or Thy
ABOMINATIONS.

Je. 4 : 1. If thou wilt put away t.a.
Je. 13 : 27. I have seen t.a. on hills
Eze. 5 : 9. I do in thee, because of t.
11. defiled sanctuary with t.a. [a.
7 : 3. will recompense t.a., 4, 8, 9.
16 : 22. in t.a. not rememb-d youth
36. whoredoms with idols of t.a.
43. this lewdness above all t.a.
51. justified thy sisters in t.a. (2)
58. Thou hast borne t. a., saith L.

ABORTIVE. [an a.

1 Co. 15 : † 8. last was seen of me as

ABOUND, ED.

Pr. 28 : 20. faithful man shall a. wi.
Is. 2 : † 6. they a. with children of
Am. 6 : † 4. a. with superfluities [a.
Mat. 24 : 12. because iniquity shall
Ro. 3 : 7. if truth of God more a-d
5 : 15. grace by Jesus Ch. hath a-d
20. law, that the offence might a.; where sin a-d grace did more a.
6 : 1. in sin, that grace may a.?
15 : 13. that ye may a. in hope [us
2 Co. 1 : 5. as sufferings of Chr. a. in
8 : 2. deep poverty a-d unto riches
7. as ye a. in faith and love to us, see that ye a. in this grace also
9 : 8. God able to make all grace a.; that ye may a. in ev. good work
Ep. 1 : 8. a-d toward us in wisdom
Ph. 1 : 9. that your love may a. more
4 : 12. I know how to a.; am instructed how to a. and suffer
17. I desire fruit that may a. to
18. I have all and a.; I am full
1 Th. 3 : 12. Lord make you to a. in
4 : 1. so ye would a. more and [love
2 Pe. 1 : 8. if these be in you and a.

ABOUNDETH, ING.

Pr. 8 : 24. when were no fount-s a-g
29 : 22. furious man a-h in transg-n
1 Co. 15 : 58. always a-g in the work
2 Co. 1 : 5. so consolation a-h by Ch.
Col. 2 : 7. a-g with thanksgiving
2 Th. 1 : 3. charity of you all toward

ABOUT. [each a-h

Ge. 38 : 24. a. 3 months aft. was told
41 : 25. shewed Pha. what he a. to
42 : 24. Joseph turned a. [do, 28.
46 : 34. Thy servants trade a. cattle
Ex. 12 : 37. a. 600,000 on foot [wild-s
13 : 18. God led people a. through
19 : 23. Set bounds a. the mount
32 : 28. fell that day a. 3,000 men
Le. 6 : 5. a. which hath sworn falsely
Nu. 2 : 2. a. tabernacle shall ye pitch
4 : 4. sons of Kohath a. holy things
16 : 24. Get from a. tabern. of Kor.
De. 32 : 10. he led him a., kept him
Jos. 6 : 11. ark of Lord going a. city
10 : 13. sun hasted not a. a day [edst
Ju. 17 : shekels a. wh. thou curs-
Ru. 2 : 17. was a. an ephah of barley
1 S. 1 : 20. time come a. that Hannah
5 : 8. ark be carried a. unto Gath
9 : 26. a. spring of day S. called Saul
17 : 41. Philist-s looked a. and saw
21 : 5. women kept fr. us a. 3 days
25 : 38. a. ten days after Lord smote
2 S. 20 : 26. Ira, chief ruler a. Da. [Na.
24 : 6. came to Dan-jaan a. to Zidon
1 K. 2 : 15. the kingdom is turned a.
7 : 23. sea was round all a.; thirty cubits did compass it round a.
8 : 14. king turned his face a. and
18 : 32. Elijah made trench a. altar
22 : 36. a. going down of sun, 2 Ch.
2 K. 4 : 16. a. this season [18 : 34.
11 : 7. keep watch a. king [a. song
1 Ch. 15 : 22. Chenaniah instructed
2 Ch. 2 : 9. house I am a. to build
26 : 6. Uzziah built cities a. Ashdod
Ezr. 10 : 15. Jonath. employed a. this
Ne. 13 : 21. Why lodge ye a. wall?
Jb. 1 : 10. Hast thou made hedge a. him, a. his house, a. all he hath
Jb. 20 : 23. When a. to fill his belly
Can. 3 : 7. threesc. valiant men a. it
Can. 7 : 2. of wheat set a. with lilies
Is. 5 : † 2. beloved made wall a. it
50 : 11. compass yours. a. wi. sparks
Je. 32 : 44. witnesses in places a. Je
41 : 14. all the people cast a. and
Eze. 1 : 4. and a brightness was a. it
5 : 2. smite a. it with a knife
43 : 17. border a. it half a cubit (2)
Da. 5 : 31. Darius being a. 62 yrs. old
Ho. 7 : 2. doings have beset them a.
Mat. 14 : 21. eaten, a. 5,000 men, Mk. 6 : 44. Lu. 9 : 14. Jn. 6 : 10.
Mk. 2 : 2. was no room a. the door
3 : 8. a. Tyre, Sidon great multit-e
4 : 10. they a. him wi. twelve asked
5 : 13. the herd (they were a. 2,000)
6 : 48. a. the fourth watch of night
8 : 9. they that had eaten, a. 4,000
12 : 1. a vineyard, set hedge a. it
14 : 51. cloth a. his naked body
Lu. 1 : 56. Mary abode wi. her a. 3 mos.
2 : 37. she was a widow of a. 84 yrs.
49. must be a. Father's business
3 : 23. Jesus a. 30 years of age [ing
8 : 42. only dau., a. 12 years, a dy-
9 : 28. a. 8 days after, he took Peter
10 : 40. cumbered a. serving, 41.
12 : 35. Let your loins be girded a.
13 : 8. let it alone till I sh. dig a. it
22 : 41. withdrawn a. a stone's east
49. they a. him saw what would
Jn. 3 : 25. arose question a. purify-g
6 : 19. rowed a. 25 or 30 furlongs
11 : 18. Bethany a. 15 furlongs off
19 : 39. myrrh, aloes, a. 100 pound
20 : 7. napkin that was a. his head
Ac. 1 : 15. number of names a. 120
2 : 10. parts of Libya a. Cyrene
41. same day were added a. 3,000
3 : 3. Pet., John a. to go into temple
4 : 4. number of men was a. 5,000
5 : 36. to whom, a. 400 joined [phen
11 : 19. persecution was a. Ste-
13 : 20. judges a. space of 450 years
18 : 14. Paul a. to open his mouth
19 : 23. no small stir a. that way
20 : 3. he was a. to sail into Syria
27 : 30. shipmen a. to flee out of sh.
Ro. 4 : 19. when a. an 100 years old
10 : 3. going a. to establish their own righteousness
1 Co. 9 : 5. we not power to lead a. a sister?
2 Co. 4 : 10. always bearing a. in body
Ep. 6 : 14. Stand girt a. with truth
1 Ti. 5 : 13. wandering a. from house
2 Ti. 2 : 14. strive not a. words
Tit. 3 : 9. avoid strivings a. the law
He. 8 : 5. when a. to make tabern-e
Jude 9. disputed a. body of Moses
Re. 10 : 4. I was a. to write, and
16 : 21. ev. stone a. weight of talent

See CITY, COMPASSED, FETCH, GADDEST, GIRT, GO, GOETH, GONE, HIM, HOUR, S, JERUSALEM, LOINS, ME, MIDNIGHT, NECK, NOON, QUESTION, S, ROUND, SPACE, STOOD, THEE, THEM, THIS, WALKETH, WANDERED, WENT, WHOM, YOU. WHOM, YOU.

See **TIME** with **about**,
To morrow about this TIME

ABOVE. [earth

Ge. 1 : 20. fowl that may fly a. the
6 : 16. in a cubit finish window a.
27 : 39. of the dew of heaven from a.
48 : 22. thee one portion a. breth-n
49 : 26. a. blessings of progenitors
Ex. 25 : 21. mercy seat a., 40 : 20.
22. commune from a. mercy seat
26 : 14. covering a. of badgers' skins, 36 : 19. Nu. 4 : 25. [of it
24. boards sh. be coupled a. head
28 : 27. a. curious girdle, 28.-39 : 20.
30 : 14. numbered from 20 yrs. old and a., 1 Ch. 23 : 27. 2 Ch. 25 : 5.
40 : 19. Mos. put covering of tent a.

Le. 11 : 21. have legs **a.** their feet
27 : 7. if it be sixty years old and **a.**
Nu 16 : 3. lift yours. **a.** congregat-n
De. 17 : 20. be not lifted up **a.** breth.
25 : 3. if he sho. beat him **a.** these
28 : 13. thou sh. be **a.**, not beneath
30 : 5. multiply thee **a.** thy fathers
Jos 3 : 13. Jordan be cut off fr. **a.**, 16.
Ju. 5 : 24. blessed **a.** women Jael (2)
2 S. 22 : 17. He sent fr. **a.**, Ps. 18:16.
1 K. 7 : 3. house covered wi. cedar **a.**
11. **a.** were costly stones aft. meas.
20. chapiters had pomegranates **a.**
25. sea was **a.**, upon oxen, 2 Ch.
29. upon ledges was a base **a.** [4 : 4.
31. mouth of it **a.** was a cubit
8 : 7. the cherubim covered the ark
a., 2 Ch. 5 : 8. [52 : 32.
2 K. 25 : 28. **a.** throne of kings, Je.
1 Ch. 5 : 2. prevailed **a.** brethren
27 : 6. Benaiah was **a.** the thirty
Ne. 3 : 28. Fr. **a.** horse gate repaired
7 : 2. he feared G. **a.** many [priests
12 : 37. the wall **a.** house of David
39. fr. **a.** gate of Ephr. **a.** old gate (3)
Es. 5 : 11. advanced him **a.** princes
Jb. 3 : 4. let not God regard it fr. **a.**
18 : 16. **a.** sh. his branch be cut off
31 : 2. what portion of God from **a.**
28. I sho. have denied God th. is **a.**
Ps. 10 : 5. thy judgments are far **a.**
18 : 48. liftest me **a.** those ag-t me
27 : 6. be lifted up **a.** mine enemies
45 : 7. hath anointed thee **a.** thy
fellows, He. 1 : 9. [from **a.**
78 : 23. Tho. he commanded clouds
103 : 11. as heaven is high **a.** earth
119 : 127. I love thy com-ts **a.** gold
136 : 6. stretched earth **a.** the wat-s
137 : 6. Jerusalem **a.** my chief joy
144 : 7. Send thine hand from **a.**
Pr. 4 : † 23. keep heart **a.** all keeping
8 : 28. established the clouds **a.**
15 : 24. way of life is **a.** to the wise
Ec. 3 : 19. no preeminence **a.** a beast
Is. 2 : 2. L.'s house shall be exalted **a.**
6 : 2. **a.** it stood the seraphim [hills
7 : 11. Ask a sign in the height **a.**
14 : 13. exalt my throne **a.** the stars
14. will ascend **a.** heights of clouds
45 : 8. Drop down ye heavens fr. **a.**
Je. 15: 8. widows **a.** sand of the seas
35 : 4. **a.** the chamber of Maaseiah
La. 1 : 13. From **a.** he sent fire into
Eze. 1 : 22. stretched over heads **a.**
26. upon throne liken-s of man **a.**
10 : 1. **a.** the head of the cherubim
19. glory over cherubim **a.**, 11:22.
29 : 15. nei. exalt itself **a.** nations
37 : 8. lo, the skin covered them **a.**
41 : 20. **a.** door were cherubim, 17.
Da. 6 : 3. Daniel preferred **a.** princes
11 : 36. magnify hims. **a.** ev. god, 37.
Am. 2 : 9. I destroyed fruit from **a.**
Na. 3 : 16. merchants **a.** stars [6:40.
Mat. 10 : 24. not **a.** his mast. (2), Lu.
Jn. 3 : † 3. exc. man be born fr. **a.**, 7.
6 : 13. fragment-s of loaves ov. and **a.**
8 : 23. I am from **a.**; ye are of [**a.**
19 : 11. except it were given thee fr.
Ac. 4 : 22. man was **a.** 40 years old
26 : 13. light **a.** brightness of sun
Ro 10 : 6. to bring Christ from **a.**
14 : 5. esteemeth one day **a.** anoth.
1 Co. 15 : 6. seen of **a.** 500 brethren
2 Co. 1 : 8. were pressed **a.** strength
12 : 2. I knew man **a.** 14 years ago
Ga. 1 : 14. **a.** my equals in nation
4 : 26. Jerusalem which is **a.** is free
Ph. 2 : 9. him a name **a.** every name
Col. 3 : 1. seek things which are **a.**
2. set your affection on things **a.**
Phm. 16. not as servant but **a.** serv.
He. 10 : 8. **a.** when he said, Sacrifice
Ja. 1 : 17. every good gift is from **a.**
3 : 15. This wisdom not from **a.**
17. wisdom from **a.** is first pure

See **Above ALL, All the EARTH, Above THAT, Above all THAT, All PEOPLE, STOOD above,** CAUL, EARTH, HIM, ME, THEM.

Heaven, s ABOVE. [**a.**
Ge. 49 : 25. thee with blessings of **h.**
Ex. 20 : 4. not make likeness of thing
in **h. a.**, De. 5 : 8. [**a.**, Jos. 2 : 11.
De. 4 : 39. know that L. is God in **h.**
1 K. 8 : 23. no God like thee in **h. a.**
Ps. 50 : 4. He shall call to **h**-s fr. **a.**
Is. 45 : 8. Drop down ye **h**-s from **a.**
Je. 4 : 28. For this **h**-s **a.** be black
31 : 37. If **h. a.** can be measured [**a.**
Ac. 2 : 19. I will shew wonders in **h.**

A'BRAHAM = A'BRAM.
Ge. 17 : 5. Neither shall thy name be
called Abram, but A., 1 Ch. 1:27.
9. G. said unto A., 15.-18 : 13.-21 :
17. A. fell upon his face, and [12.
18. A. said, O that Ishmael might
22. God went up from A. [live
23. A. took Ishmael, every male
of A.'s house [cised, 26.
24. A. 99 years old when circum-
18 : 6. A. hastened unto Sarah
7. A. ran unto herd, fetched a calf
11. Now A. and Sarah were old
13. L. said to A., Wbf. did S. laugh
16. A. went to bring them on way
17. Shall I hide from A. thing I do
18. Seeing A. sh. become gr. nation
19. Lord may bring upon A. that
22. tow. Sodom; but A. stood bef.
23. A. said, Wilt destroy righteous
27. A. said, I have taken to speak
33. Lord left communing wi. A. (2)
19 : 27. A. gat up early to place [ont
29. God remembered A., sent Lot
20 : 1. A. journeyed toward south
2. A. said of his wife, She my sister
9. Abimelech called A., said, 10.
11. A. said, I thought they slay me
14. Abimelech gave oxen unto A.
17. A prayed unto God; G. healed
18. Lord closed wombs bec. of A.'s
21 : 2. Sarah bare A. son in old age
3. A. called name of his son Isaac
4. A. circumcised his son Isaac
5. A. 100 years old when Isaac was
7. A., 12, 14, 22, 24, 27. [born
8. A. made great feast same day
9. saw son of Hagar, borne unto A.
10. said unto A., Cast out bondw.
11. thing grievous in A.'s sight
25. A. reproved Abim. bec. of well
28. A. set seven ewe lambs by, 29.
33. A. planted grove in Beer-sheba
34. A. sojourned in Philis-s' land
22 : 1. God did tempt A. and said A.
3. A. rose up early in the morning
4. third day A. saw place afar off
5. A. said unto young men, Abide
6. A. took wood of burnt offering
8. A. said, My son, G. will provide
9. A. built an altar, bound Isaac
10. A. took knife to slay his son
11. Angel of the Lord called, A., A.
13. A. looked, behold, ram caught,
14. A. called place Jehovah-j-h (2)
15. Angel called unto A. out of h.
19. A. dwelt at Beer-sheba (2) | 20.
23. to Nahor, A.'s brother, 24 : 15.
23 : 2. A. came to mourn for Sarah
3. A. stood up from bef. his dead
5. children of Heth answered A.
7. A. bowed hims. to peo. of land, 12.
10. Ephron ans-d A. in audience,
16. A. weighed to Ephron (2) [14, 16.
19. A. buried Sarah in cave of Ma
20. cave unto A. for burying place,
18.-49 : 30.-50 : 13. [A. in all
24 : 1. A. was old; Lord had blessed
2. A. said unto his eldest servant
6. A. said, Beware, bring not my
9. put hand under thigh of A. [son

Ge. 24 : 12. O God of my master A. 42
27. Blessed be God of master A.,
34. he said, I am A.'s serv-t [48, 52.
59. sent aw Rebekah and A.'s serv.
25 : 1. A. took a wife, name Keturah
5. A. gave all he had unto Isaac
6. unto sons of concub-s A. gave (2)
7. these are years of A.'s life, 175
8. Then A. died in a good old age
10. field A. purchased of sons of
Heth; there was A. buried and
Sarah, 49 : 31. [Isaac
11. after death of A. God blessed
12. genera-s of Ishm-l, A.'s son (2)
19. genera-ns of Isaac, A.'s son (2)
26 : 1. besides famine in days of A.
5. Because A. obeyed my voice
18. stopped wells after death of A.
24. I will bless thee for A.'s sake
28 : 4. G. give thee blessing of A. (2)
9. Esau took dau. of Ishmael, A.'s
31 : 53 God of A. judge betw. us [son
35 : 12. land I gave A., to thee I will
27. Hebron, where A. sojourned
48 : 15 God bef. whom A. did walk
16. lads, on them name of A., Isaac
1 Ch. 1 : 27. Abram; the same as A.
28. The sons of A., Isaac, Ishmael
32. sons of Keturah, A.'s concub.
34. A. begat Isaac. The sons of
Isaac, Mat. 1 : 2. Ac. 7 : 8.
16 : 16. covenant he made with A.,
and oath unto Isaac, Ps. 105 : 9.
Ps. 47 : 9. even people of God of A.
105 : 42. he rememb-d A. his serv-t
Is. 29 : 22. saith L. who redeemed A.
63 : 16. though A. be ignorant of us
Eze. 33 : 24. A. was one, he inherited
Mi. 7 : 20. wilt perform mercy to A.
Mat. 1 : 1. Jes., son of Dav., son of A.
17. generations from A. to David
3 : 9. raise up chil. unto A., Lu. 3:8.
Lu. 3 : 34. Isaac, son of A. [A.
13 : 16. this woman being a dau. of
16 : 22. by angels into A.'s bosom
23. in hell he seeth A. afar off
25. A. said, Son, remember thou
29. A. saith, They have Moses and
19 : 9. forasmuch as he is son of A.
Jn. 8 : 39. If A.'s children ye would
do the works of A. [A.
40. ye seek to kill me; this did not
52. A is dead and the prophets
57. not 50 yrs. old; hast seen A.?
58. Jesus said, Before A. was, I am
Ac. 7 : 16. sepulchre A. bought of sons
17. which God had sworn unto A.
13 : 26. children of the stock of A.
Ro. 4 : 2. If A. justified by works
3. A. believed God, it was counted unto him, Ga. 3 : 6. Ja. 2 : 23.
9. faith was reckoned to A. for
Ga. 3 : 7. they of faith are chil. of A.
8. Scrip. preached gospel unto A.
9. they of faith are blessed with A.
14. That blessing of A. on Gentiles
18. God gave it to A. by promise
4 : 22. A. had 2 sons, one by bondm.
He. 6 : 13. God made promise to A.
7 : 1. Melchisedec met A., blessed
2. To whom A. gave a 10th of all, 4.
5. tho. they come out of loins of A.
6. he received tithes of A., blessed
9. Levi also paid tithes in A. [him
11 : 8. By faith, A. when he was called
17. By faith, A. when tried, offered
1 Pe. 3 : 6. as Sarah obeyed A., calling

A'BRAHAM with father.
Ge. 22 : 7. Isaac spake to A. his **f.**
26 : 3. perform oath unto A. thy **f.**
15. wells in days of A. his **f.**, 18.
24. am God of A. thy **f.** (2), 28 : 13.
31 : 42. Exc. God of my **f.** A. wi. me
32 : 9. Jac. said, O God of my **f.** A.
Jos. 24 : 2. Terah, **f.** of A., **f.** of Na-r
3. I took your **f.** A. from oth. side
Is. 51 : 2 Look unto A. your **f.**

Mat. 3 : 9. have A. to our f., Lu. 3 : 8.
Lu. 1 : 73. oath he sware to our f. A.
16 : 24. he said f. A. have mercy on
30. Nay, f. A., but if one went[me
Jn. 8 : 39. They said, A. is our f.
53. Art thou greater than our f. A.
56. f. A. rejoiced to see my day[A.
Ac. 7 : 2. God appeared unto our f.
Ro. 4 : 1. that A. our f. hath found?
12. steps of that faith of our f. A.
16. faith of A. who is f. of us all
Ja. 2 : 21. was not A. our f. justified

A'BRAHAM,
Isaac, and Jacob or Israel.

Ge. 50 : 24. bring you unto land wh.
he sware to A. -, Ex 6 : 8. - 32 :
13. -33 : 1. Nu. 32 : 11. De. 1 : 8. -
6 : 10. -30 : 20. -34 : 4. [with A. -
Ex. 2 : 24. God remembered covenant
3 : 6. I am the God of A., the God
of I., and the God of J., Mat.
22 : 32. Mk. 12 : 26. Ac. 7 : 32.
15. say, The God of A., God of I.,
God of J. hath sent me [4 : 5.
16. God of A, - appeared unto me,
6 : 3. And I appeared unto A. - by
32 : 13. Remember A., I., and Isr.
De. 9 : 5. Lord sware unto A. -, 29 : 13.
27. Remember thy servants A. -
1 K. 18 : 36. Elijah said, Lord God
of A., I., and Israel [with A. -
2 K. 13 : 23. because of his covenant
1 Ch. 29 : 18. O God of A., I., and Isr.
2 Ch. 30 : 6. turn again unto Lord
God of A., I., and Israel [A. -
Mat. 8 : 11. Many shall sit down wi.
Lu. 13 : 28. when ye see A. - in kingd.
20 : 37. calleth Lord the God of A. -
Ac. 3 : 13. God of A. - hath glorified

A'BRAHAM with seed.[(2)

Ge. 12 : 7. L. unto A., said, Unto thy s.
15 : 3. A. said, thou given me no s.
13. A., know thy s. sh. be stranger
2 Ch. 20 : 7. gavest it to s. of A. thy
Ps. 105 : 6. O ye s. of A. his servant
Is. 41 : 8. Israel, s. of A. my friend
Je. 33 : 26. to be rulers over s. of A.
Lu. 1 : 55. he spake to A. and his s.
Jn. 8 : 33. We be A.'s s. and never
37. A.'s s., but ye seek to kill me
Ac. 3 : 25. G. saying unto A., In thy s.
Ro. 4 : 13. promise not to A. or his s.
9 : 7. Nei. bec. they are the s. of A.
11 : 1. I also am of s. of A. [am I
2 Co. 11 : 22. they the s. of A.? So
Ga. 3 : 16. to A. and s. the promises
29. If Christ's, then are ye A.'s s.
He. 2 : 16. he took on him s. of A.

A'BRAM. [gat A., 27.

Ge. 11 : 26. Terah lived 70 years, be-
29. name of A.'s wife Sarai (2), 31.
31. Terah took A. into Canaan (2)
12 : 1. Lord had said unto A., Get
4. A. departed as L. had spok. (2)
5. A., Sarah his wife went into Ca.
6. A. passed thro. land unto Sichem
9. A. journeyed still toward south
10. A. went into Eg. to sojourn, 14.
16. entreated A. well for her sake
17. L. plagued Pha. bec. of A.'s wife
18. Pha. called A., said, What is
13 : 1. A. went out of Eg., he, wife
2. A. was very rich in cattle, gold
4. there A. called on name of Lord
5. Lot, went with A., had flocks
7. strife betw. herdsm. of A.'s catt.
8. A. said unto Lot, Let no strife
12. A. dwelt in Canaan, Lot in cit.
14. L. said unto A., Lift thine eyes
18. Then A. dwelt in plain Mamre
14 : 13. one that escaped told A.;
these were confederate with A.
14. A. heard his bro. was taken, 12.
19. Blessed be A. of most high God
21. k. of Sodom send unto A. | 22.
23. lest thou say I made A. rich
15 : 1. word of L. unto A., Fear not

Ge. 15 : 2. A. said, Lord, what give me
12. a deep sleep fell upon A. | 11.
18. Lord made covenant with A.
16 : 1. Sarai, A.'s wife, bare no chil.
2. A. heark-d to voice of Sarai (2)
3. A.'s wife gave Hagar to A. (3)
5. Sarai unto A., My wrong be | 6.
15. Hagar bare A. a son (')
17 : 1. when A. ninety years old (2)
3. A. fell on his face; God talked
5. Nei. any more thy name be A.
1 Ch. 1 : 27. A.; the same is Abraham
Ne. 9 : 7. Lord who didst choose A.

ABROAD. [Look

Ge. 15 : 5. bro-t Abraham a., said,
19 : 17. bro-t them a., said, Escape
Ex. 12 : 46. shalt not carry flesh a.
Le. 13 : 12. if a leprosy break out a.
14 : 8. leper sh. tarry a. out of tent
18 : 9. she be born at home or a.
De. 23 : 10. sh. go a. out of camp, 12.
13. when ease thyself a. shalt dig
24 : 11. bring pledge a. unto thee
32 : 11. as eagle spreadeth a. wings
Ju. 12 : 9. 30 sons, 30 dau-s he sent
a., 30 daugh-s from a. for sons
2 K. 4 : 3 Go, borrow thee vessels a.
2 Ch. 29 : 16. to carry uncleanness a.
31 : 5. soon as commandm-t came a.
Ps. 41 : 6. when he goeth a. telleth it
Pr. 5 : 16. fountains be dispersed a.
Is. 44 : 24. th. spreadeth a. the earth
Je. 6 : 11. pour fury upon children a.
La. 1 : 20. a. the sword bereaveth
Lu. 1 : 65. all sayings were noised a.
2 : 17. made known a. the saying
Ac. 2 : 6. when this was noised a.
Ro. 5 : 5. love of God is shed a. in our
16 : 19. your obedience is come a.
2 Co. 9 : 9. He hath dispersed a.; he
See BLAZE, CAST, COME, SCAT-
TER, ED, ETH, SEND, SPREAD,
STAND, WALK, WALKEST,
WANDERETH, WENT.

AB'SALOM.

2 S. 3 : 3. unto David sons, third, A.
of Maacah, 1 Ch. 3 : 2.
13 : 1. A. had a fair sister, Tamar
4. A. 20(2), 24, 25, 26, 27, 28, 29, 32.
22. A. hated Amnon bec. he forced
23. A. had sheepshearers in Baal-
ha-or; A. invited all king's sons
30. A. hath slain all the k.'s sons
37. But A. fled to Talmai, 34, 38.
39. soul of David longed to go to A.
14 : 1. king's heart was toward A.
21. Go thf. bring young man A., 23.
24. A., 28, 29, 30, 31, 32, 33 (2)[A.
25. none to be so much praised as
27. unto A. were born three sons
33. bowed to ground, k. kissed A.
15 : 1. A. prepared chariots, horses
2. A. (2), 3, 6. 7, 12, 37. [judge
4. A. said, Oh that I were made
6. So A. stole the hearts of Israel
10. A. sent spies thro-t all tribes;
ye sh. say, A. reigneth in Heb-n
11. with A. went 200 men out of J.
13. hearts of Israel are after A. | 12.
14. we sh. not else escape A.[wi. A.
31. Ahithophel, am-g conspirators
34. If say to A., I will be thy serv-t
16 : 8. kingdom into hand of A.
15. A. and all peo. came to Jerus.
16. Hushai said unto A., God save
17. A., 18, 20, 21, 22 (2) [king (2)
22. A. went in unto fa-'s concub-s
23. counsel of Ahithophel with A.
17 : 1. Ahith-l said unto A., Let me,
4. saying pleased A. well, and [15.
5. said A., Call Hushai, Archite, 6.
7. Hushai unto A., The counsel
9. slaughter among peo. th. follow
14. Lord bring evil upon A. (2)[A.
18. a lad saw them, and told A. | 20.
24. A. passed over Jordan, he and
25. A. made Amasa captain of host

2 S. 17 : 26. Isr., A. pitched in Gilead
18 : 5. Deal gently with A.; k. gave
all captains charge concerning
9. A. rode upon a mule (2) [A.
10. I saw A. hanged in an oak [A.
12. Beware none touch young man
14. thrust 3 darts thro. heart of A.
15. ten young men smote A., slew
17. they cast A. into great pit in
18. called unto this day A.'s place
29. Is young man A. safe? 32. [(2)
33. O my son A., my son A.! wou.
G. I had died for thee, O A.! 19:
19 : 1. weepeth, mourneth for A. [4.
6. if A. had lived and we had died
9. he is fled out of land for A.
10. A. whom we anointed is dead
20 : 6. Sheba do more harm than A.
1 K. 1 : 6. mother bare Adonij. after
2 : 7. when I fled because of A. [A.
28. Joab turned tho. not after A.
15 : †2. his moth. Maachah dau. of A.
2 Ch. 11 : 20. took Maachah dau. of A.
21. Rehoboam loved daugh-r of A.
Ps. 3.* Psalm of David when he fled

ABSENCE. [fr. A.

Lu. 22 : 6. betray him in a. of multi.
Ph. 2 : 12. now much more in my a.

ABSENT. [anoth.

Ge. 31 : 49. when we are a. one from
1 Co. 5 : 3. I verily as a. in body
2 Co. 5 : 6. in body we are a. fr. Lord
8. willing to be a. from the body
9. present or a. we be accepted
10 : 1. being a. am bold toward you
11. such as we are by letters when
13 : 2. being a. now I write, 10. [a.
Ph. 1 : 27. whe. I come, or else be a.
Col. 2 : 5. tho. I be a. in flesh, yet

ABSTAIN. [with you

Ac. 15 : 20. a. fr. pollutions of idols
29. a. from meats offered to idols
1 Th. 4 : 3. that ye a. from fornicat.
5 : 22. a. from all appearance of evil
1 Ti. 4 : 3. to a. from meats [war
1 Pe. 2 : 11. a. from fleshly lusts wh.

ABSTINENCE.

Ac. 27 : 21. after long a. Paul stood

ABSURD. [ets

Je. 23 : † 13. seen a. thing in proph-
2 Th. 3 : † 2. may be delivered fr. a.

ABUNDANCE. [men

De. 28 : 47. servedst not God for a.
33 : 19. shall suck of a. of the seas
1 S. 1 : 16. out of a. of my complaint
1 K. 10 : 10. no more such a. of spices
27. cedars made he as sycamore
trees for a., 2 Ch. 1 : 15. -9 : 27.
18 : 41. there is sound of a. of rain
2 Ch. 9 : 9. of spices great a.[38 : 34.
Jb. 22 : 11. a. of waters cover thee,
Ps. 72 : 7. In his days a. of peace
Ec. 5 : 10. not satisfied that loveth a.
12. a. of rich not suffer to sleep
Is. 7 : 22. for a. of milk, eat butter
15 : 7. a. gotten they carry away
47 : 9. a. of thine enchantments
60 : 5. a. of the sea sh. be converted
66 : 11. delighted wi. a. of her glory
Je. 33 : 6. reveal unto th. a. of peace
Eze. 16 : 49. a. of idleness was in her,
26 : 10. By a. of his horses dust sh.
Mat. 12 : 34. out of a. of heart mouth
speaketh, Lu. 6 : 45. [25 : 29.
13 : 12. and he shall have more a.,
Mk. 12 : 44. they did cast in of their
a., Lu. 21 : 4. [shall reign
Ro. 5 : 17. which receive a. of grace
2 Co. 8 : 2. a. of their joy abounded
14. your a. for their want, their a.
12 : 7. through a. of the revelations
Re. 18 : 3. rich thro. a. of her delica-

In ABUNDANCE. [cies

2 S. 12 : 30. spoil of city i. great a.
1 K. 1 : 19. slain oxen i. a., 25. [14.
1 Ch. 22 : 3. prepared iron, brass i. a.,
4. cedar trees i. a., 2 Ch. 9 : 27.

1 Ch. 22 : 15. workmen wi. thee i.a.
29 : 2. precious stones, marble i.a.
21. they offered sacrifices i. a. for
2 Ch. 2 : 9. to prepare me timber i.a.
4 : 18. Sol. made vessels i. great a.
9 : 1. queen of Sheba with gold i. a.
11 : 23. he gave chil. victuals i. a.
14 : 15. carried away sheep, camels,
15 : 9. they fell to Asa i. a. ⌊i. a.
16 : † 8. Were not the Lubim i. a.
17 : 5. Jehosh-t had riches i. a., 18 :
18 : 2. Ahab killed sheep i. a. ⌊1.
20 : 25. spoil, they found riches i. a.
24 : 11. they gathered money i. a.
29 : 35. burnt offerings were i. a.
31 : 5. Isr. brought i. a. firstfruits
32 : 5. Hez. made darts, shields i. a.
29. Hez-h provided him cities i.a.
Ne. 9 : 25. possessed fruit trees i. a.
Es. 1 : 7. gave them royal wine i. a.
Jb. 36 : 31. God giveth meat i. a.
Ps. 37 : 11. sh. delight i. a. of peace
52 : 7. trusted i. the a. of his riches
105 : 30. brought forth frogs i. a.
Zch. 14 : 14. gold, apparel i. great a.
Lu. 12 : 15. life consisteth not i.a.
2 Co. 8 : 20. that no man blame us i.

ABUNDANT. ⌊this a.

Ex. 34 : 6. Lord God a. in goodness
Pr. 12 : † 26. righteous more a. than
Is. 56 : 12. as this day, and more a.
Je. 51 : 13. Babylon a. in treasures
1 Co. 12 : 23. a. honour; uncomely
parts have more a. comeliness, 24.
2 Co. 4 : 15. a. grace might redound
7 : 15. his affection more a. tow. you
9 : 12. the administration is a. ⌈ons
11 : 23. in labours more a., in pris-
Ph. 1 : 26. your rejoicing be more a.
1 Ti. 1 : 14. grace of our Lord was a.
1 Pe. 1 : 3. Chr. acc. to his a. mercy

ABUNDANTLY. ⌈21.

Ge. 1 : 20. Let waters bring forth a.,
8 : 17. they may breed a. in earth
9 : 7. you bring forth a. in earth
Ex. 1 : 7. chil. of Israel increased a.
8 : 3. river shall bring forth frogs a.
Nu. 20 : 11. rock, water came out a.
1 Ch. 12 : 40. brought oxen, sheep a.
22 : 5. David prepared a. before his
8. Thou hast shed blood a. ⌊death
2 Ch. 31. 5. tithe brought they in a.
Jb. 12 : 6. into hand G. bringeth a.
36 : 28. clouds distil upon man a.
Ps. 36 : 8. They shall be a. satisfied
65 : 10. Thou waterest ridges th-f a.
132 : 15. I will a. bless her provis-n
145 : 7. a. utter the memory of thy
Can. 5 : 1. yea, drink a., O beloved
Is. 15 : 3. shall howl, weeping a.
35 : 2. it sh. blossom a. and rejoice
43 : †24. nei. a. moistened me with
55 : 7. G., for he will a. pardon ⌊fat
Mk. 14 : †72. wept a. when he thought
Jn. 10 : 10. might have life more a.
1 Co. 15 : 10. I laboured more a. than
2 Co. 1 : 12. and more a. to you-ward
10 : 15. be enlarged by you a. ⌈4.
12 : 15. the more a. I love you, 2 :
Ep. 3 : 20. is able to do exceeding a.
1 Th. 2 : 17. we endeavoured more a.
Tit. 3 : 6. Holy Gh. he shed on us a.
He. 6 : 17. G. willing more a. to shew
2 Pe. 1 : 11. entrance be ministered a.

ABUSE, ED. ⌈a-d

Le. 19 : † 20. lieth with a bondmaid,
Ju. 19 : 25. a-d her all night ⌈10 : 4.
1 S. 31 : 4. lest uncirc-d a. me, 1 Ch.
1 Co. 9 : 18. that I a. not my power

ABUSERS. ⌊in gosp.

1 Co. 6 : 9. nor a. of thems. with man-

ABUSING. ⌊kind

1 Co. 7 : 31. use this world as not a.

AC'CAD. ⌊it

Ge. 10 : 10. Nimrod, his kingdom A.

ACCEPT.

Ge. 32 : 20. peradv. he will a. of me
Ex. 22 : 11. owner of it shall a. th-of
Le. 26 : 41. th. a. of punishment, 43.
De. 33 : 11. Bless, Lord, and a. work
1 S. 26 : 19. let him a. an offering
2 S. 24 : 23. The L. thy God a. thee
Jb. 13 : 8. Will ye a. his person?
10. if ye do secretly a. persons
32 : 21. not a. any man's person
42 : 8. Job pray for you; him will I
Ps. 20 : 3. a. thy burnt sacrifice ⌊a.
82 : 2. a. the persons of wicked?
119 : 108. a. the freewill offerings
Pr. 6 : † 35. will not a. ransom ⌈ed
18 : 5. not good to a. person of wick-
Je. 14 : 10. Lord doth not a. them
12. I will not a. them, Am. 5 : 22.
Eze. 20 : 40. there will I a. them
41. I will a. you with sweet savour
43 : 27. I will a. you, saith the Lord
Mal. 1 : 8. pleased, or a. thy person?
10. neither will I a. an offering at
13. should I a. this of your hand?
Ac. 24 : 3. We a. it always and in all

ACCEPTABLE.

Le. 22 : 20. it shall not be a. for you
De. 33 : 24. be a. to his brethren ⌈a.
Ps. 19 : 14. meditation of my heart be
69 : 13. my prayer is in an a. time
Pr. 10 : 32. righteous know what is
21 : 3. To do justice is more a. ⌊a.
Ec. 12 : 10. Preacher sought a. words
Is. 49 : 8. In an a. time have I heard
58 : 5. wilt thou call this an a. day
61 : 2. To proclaim a. year of Lord
Je. 6 : 20. burnt offerings are not a.
Da. 4 : 27. O king, let my counsel be a.
Lu. 4 : 19. to preach the a. year of L.
Ro. 12 : 1. sacrifice, holy, a. unto God
2. is that good and a. will of God
14 : 18. is a. to God and approved
15 : 16. offering up of Gentiles might
Ep. 5 : 10. Proving what is a. ⌊be a.
Ph. 4 : 18. sacrifice a., well pleasing
1 Ti. 2 : 3. is a. in sight of God, 5 : 4.
1 Pe. 2 : 5. sacrifices a. to God by Ch.
20. if patiently, this is a. with God

ACCEPTABLY. ⌈a.

He. 12 : 28. whereby we may serve G.

ACCEPTANCE. ⌈altar

Is. 60 : 7. come up with a. on mine

ACCEPTATION. ⌈4 : 9.

1 Ti. 1 : 15. saying worthy of all a.,

ACCEPTED. ⌈a.?

Ge. 4 : 7. doest well sh. thou not be
19 : 21. I have a. thee concerning
Ex. 28 : 38. that they may be a. ⌊this
Le. 1 : 4. offering shall be a., 22 : 27.
7 : 18. not be a., 19 : 7.-22 : 23, 25.
10 : 19. should it have been a. in
22 : 21. offering perfect, to be a.
23 : 11. wave sheaf bef. Lord to be a.
1 S. 18 : 5. he was a. in sight of people
25 : 35. see, I have a. thy person
2 K. 5 : †1. Naaman, was a. in counten.
Es. 10 : 3. Mord-i, a. of his brethren
Jb 22 : †8. the man, a. for counten-
42 : 9. the Lord also a. Job ⌊ance
Is. 56 : 7. their sacrifices shall be a.
Je. 37 : 20. let my supplication be a.
Lu. 1 : † 28. art graciously a. ⌈try
4 : 24. No prophet a. in own coun-
Ac. 10 : 35. worketh righteousn. is a.
Ro. 15 : 31. my service may be a. of
2 Co. 5 : 9 or absent, we may be a.
6 : 2. in a time a.; now is the a. time
8 : 12. a. acc-g to that a man hath
17. indeed he a. the exhortation
11 : 4. anoth. gospel ye have not a.
Ep. 1 : 6. made us a. in the beloved

ACCEPTEST, ETH.

Jb. 34 : a-h not persons of princes
Ec. 9 : 7. God now a-h thy works
Ho. 8 : 13. the Lord a-h them not
Lu. 20 : 21. nei. a-t thou person of any
Ga. 2 : 6. God a-h no man's person

ACCEPTING. ⌈ance

He. 11 : 35. tortured, not a. deliver-

ACCESS. ⌈faith

Ro. 5 : 2. By whom we have a. by
Ep. 2 : 18. we have a. unto Father
3 : 12. In whom we have boldness,

AC'CHO. See AHLAB. ⌊a.

ACCOMPANY, IED, ING.

2 S. 6 : 4. they a-g the ark of God
Ac. 10 : 23. brethren from Joppa a-d
11 : 12. these six brethren a-d me
20 : 4. a-d Paul into Asia, Sopater
38. they a-d him unto the ship
He. 6 : 9. things that a. salvation

ACCOMPLISH.

Le. 22 : 21. offerings to a. his vow
1 K. 5 : 9. thou shalt a. my desire
Jb. 14 : 6. till he a. as a hireling his
Ps. 64 : 6. they a. a diligent search
Is. 55 : 11 it shall a. that wh. I please
Je. 44 : 25. will surely a. your vows
Eze. 6 : 12. will I a. my fury, 20 : 8, 21.
7 : 8. will I a. mine anger upon thee
13 : 15. will I a. my wrath upon wall
Da. 9 : 2. that he would a. 70 years
Lu. 9 : 31. decease he should a. at J.

ACCOMPLISHED. ⌈a.

2 Ch. 36 : 22. word by Jeremiah be
Es. 2 : 12. days of purifications a.
Jb. 15 : 32. It be a. before his time
Pr. 13 : 19. The desire a. is sweet to
Is. 40 : 2. cry that her warfare is a.
Je. 25 : 12. when 70 years are a., 29 :
34. days of dispersions are a. ⌊10.
39 : 16. my words shall be a. in
La. 4 : 11. The Lord hath a. his fury
22. punishment of thine iniquity
Eze. 4 : 6. When hast a. them ⌊a.
5 : 13. Thus shall mine anger be a.
Da. 8 : † 23. when transgressors are
11 : 36. till the indignation be a. ⌊a.
12 : 7. have a. to scatter the power
Lu. 1 : 23. days of his ministry a.
2 : 6. days a. that she be delivered
21. days were a. for circumcising
22. days of her purification were a.
12 : 50. I am straitened till it be a.
18 : 31. things conc. Son shall be a.
22 : 37. this must yet be a. in me
Jn. 19 : 28. all things were now a.
Ac. 21 : 5. wh. we had a. those days
1 Pe. 5 : 9. same afflictions are a. in

ACCOMPLISHING.

He. 9 : 6. priests a. the service of G.

ACCOMPLISHMENT.

Ac. 21 : 26. a. of days of purification

ACCORD. ⌈a.

Le. 25 : 5. That groweth of its own
Jos. 9 : 2. to fight Israel with one a.
Ac. 1 : 14. all with one a. in prayer
2 : 1. all with one a. in one place
46. daily with one a. in the temple
4 : 24. voice to God with one a.
5 : 12. with one a. in Sol-'s porch
7 : 57. ran upon Stephen wi. one a.
8 : 6. people with one a. gave heed
12 : 10. gate opened of his own a.
20. they came with one a. to him
15 : 25. assembled with one a. ⌈Paul
18 : 12. Jews with one a. made ag.
19 : 29. with one a. into theatre
2 Co. 8 : 17. forward of his own a.
Ph. 2 : 2. being of one a., of one

ACCORDING. ⌊mind

Ge. 18 : 21. who have done a. to cry
27 : 19. I have done a. as thou badest
41 : 54. dearth, a. as Joseph had said
43 : 7. told him a. to tenor of these
33. sat bef. him, firstb. a. to birthright, youngest a. to his youth
44 : 7. forbid servants do a. to this
47 : 12. and brethren a. to families
49 : 28. every one a. to his blessing
50 : 6. bury thy fath. a. as he made
Ex. 12 : 3. take a lamb a. to house, 4.
25. L. give you a. as he promised
39 : 14. stones a. to names of Isr. (2)
Le. 4 : 3. if priest sin a. to sin of peo.
26 : 21. more plagues a. to y-r sins

Le. 27 : 16. estimation of field a. to
25. estimations a. to shekel ⌊seed
Nu. 1 : 18. a. to number of their names
14 : 17. power of L. be great a. as
35 : 8. ev. one give a. to inheritance
De. 10 : 9. a. as Lord promised Levi
16 : 10. offering a. as L. blessed thee
25 : 2. man be beaten a. to his fault
Jos. 18 : 4. describe land a. to inheri.
1 S. 14 : 7. am wi. thee a. to thy heart
1 K. 3 : 6. a. as David walked in truth
2 K. 16 : 3. Ahaz walked a. to abom-s
2 Ch. 32 : 25. rendered not a. to ben-
34 : 32. did a. to cov-t of God ⌊efit
Ezr. 3 : 7. trees a. to grant of Cyrus
6 : 9. a. to appointment of priests
7 : 9. a. to good hand of his God
upon him, 6. Ne. 2 : 8. ⌈of lord
10 : 3. put away wives a. to counsel
Es. 8 : 9. to Jews a. to language⌈tion
Jb. 20 : 18. a. to his substance restitu-
33 : 6. I a. to thy wish in G.'s stead
42 : 9. Eliphaz did a. as L. com-ded
Ps. 33 : 22. mercy, O L , a. as we hope
48 : 10. a. to thy name so thy praise
55 : †18. thou a man a. to my rank
90 : 11. a. to thy fear so thy wrath
103 : 10. nor rewarded us a. to our
Pr. 26 : 4. answ. not fool a. to folly
Is. 9 : 3. joy a. to joy in harvest
44 : 13. a. to beauty of a man ⌈13.
Je. 2 : 28. a. to thy cities thy gods, 11:
40 : 3. Lord hath done a. as he said
Eze. 14 : 4. answer him a. to his idols
35 : 11. a. to thine anger a. to envy
39 : 24. a. to uncleann., a. to transg.
45 : 25. in feast a. to the offer-g (4)
47 : 12. new fruit a. to his months
Ho. 3 : 1. a. to love of L. tow. Israel
9 : 10. abominat-s a. as they loved
13 : 2. idols a. to own understand-g
6. a. to pasture so were they filled
Zch. 5 : 3. stealeth, be cut off a. to
it, sweareth, he cut off a. to it
Mal. 2 : 9. base a. as ye have not kept
Mk. 7 : 5. a. to the tradition of elders
Lu. 1 : 9. a. to custom of priest's office
5 : 14. offer a. as Moses commanded
Jn. 7 : 24. Judge not a. to appearance
Ac. 4 : 35. ev. man a. as he had need
7 : 44. make it a. to the fashion seen
Ro. 1 : 4. power a. to Spirit of holin-s
12 : 3. a. as G. hath dealt to ev. man
14 : †15. walkest not a. to charity
15 : 5. like minded a. to Christ Jes.
16 : 25. a. to revelation of mystery
1 Co. 3 : †3. carnal and walk a. to
8. ev. man receive a. to his labour
2 Co. 7 : †9. ye were made sorry a. to
9 : 7. a. as he purposeth so give⌊God
Ep. 1 : 4. a. as he hath chosen us
5. a. to good pleasure of his will, 9.
2 : 2. a. to the course of world (2)
3 : 7. a minister a. to gift of grace
4 : 22. old man corrupt a. to lusts
Ph. 1 : 20. a. to my earnest expecta-n
Col. 1 : 25. a minister a. to dispensat.
1 Ti. 1 : 18. Timothy a. prophecies
6 : 3. doctrine a. to godlin.⌊on thee
Tit. 3 : 7. heirs a. to hope of eter-l life
He. 8 : 9. Not a. to covenant I made
1 Pe 1 : 2. elect a. to foreknowledge
14. not fashion-g a. to former lusts
4 : 6. be judged a. to men in flesh,
but live a. to God in the spirit
2 Pe. 1 : 3. a. as his power hath given
2 : 22. it happened a. to true proverb
See **According to** or **unto ALL,**
According to THAT,
According to all THAT.
See **All THINGS.**
See ABILITY, ARMIES, CIRCUITS,
COMMANDMENT, DAYS, DEEDS,
DESERTS, DIVISION, S, DOING,
S, EATING, ELECTION, FAITH,
FLESH, GENERATIONS, GOSPEL,
GRACE, GREATNESS,
JUDGMENT, JUDGMENTS, KINDNESS,
KNOWLEDGE, LAW, LOT,
LOVINGKINDNESS, MEASURE,
MERCIES, MERCY, NUMBER
[Noun], NUMBERED, ORDER,
ORDINANCE, S, PATTERN,
PLEASURE, POWER, PROMISE,
RICHES, RIGHTEOUSNESS,
RULE, SAYING, SCRIPTURE, S,
SENTENCE, SERVICE, STATE,
TIME, TRIBES, TRUTH, VISION,
VOW, WAY, S, WICKEDNESS,
WILL, WISDOM, WISH, WORD, S,
WORK, S, WORKING, WRITING,
WRITTEN, YEARS.

ACCORDINGLY.

Is. 59 : 18. a. he will repay fury to

ACCOUNT. [Noun.] ⌈a.

2 K. 12 : 4. every one th. passeth the
1 Ch. 27 : 24. nei. was numb. put in a.
2 Ch. 26 : 11. numb. of their a. ⌈ters
Jb. 33 : 13. giveth not a. of his mat-
Ps. 144 : 3. man th. thou makest a.
Ec. 7 : 27 one by one to find a.⌊of him
Da. 6 : 2. that princes might give a.
Mat. 12 : 36. ev. idle word sh. give a.
18 : 23. king take a. of his servants
Lu. 16 : 2. give an a. of stewardship
Ac. 19 : 40. give an a. of this con-
Ro. 9 : †28. he will finish a. ⌊course
14 : 12. every one sh. give a. to God
Ph. 4 : 17. desire fruit to your a.⌈a.
Phm. 18. If oweth thee put on mine
He. 13 : 17. as they that must give a.
1 Pe. 4 : 5. who sh. give a. to him th.

ACCOUNT, ED, ING.

De. 2 : 11. which also were a-d giants
20. that also was a-d land of giants
1 K. 10 : 21. silver nothing a-d of
in days of Solomon, 2 Ch. 9 : 20.
Ps. 22 : 30. seed be a-d for generation
Is. 2 : 22. wherein is he to be a-d of?
59 : †15. departeth fr. evil a-d mad
Mk. 10 : 42. a-d to rule over Gentiles
Lu. 20 : 35. a-d worthy to obtain that
21 : 36. a-d worthy to escape⌊world
22 : 24. which sho. be a-d greatest
Ro. 8 : 36. we are a-d as sheep for sla.
1 Co. 4 : 1. Let a man so a. of us as
Ga. 3 : 6. a-d to him for righteousness
He. 11 : 19. a-g that God was able to
2 Pe. 3 : 15. a. that the longsuffering

ACCURSED.

De. 21 : 23. that is hanged is a. of God
Jos. 6 : 17. And the city shall be a.
18. lest ye make yourselves a. (3)
7 : 12. turned because a. : nei. will I
be with you except ye destroy a.
1 S. 3 : †13. sons made themselves a.
Is. 65 : 20 sinner 100 years old shall
Ro. 9 : 3. could wish myself a.⌊be a.
1 Co. 12 : 3. no man calleth Jesus a.
Ga. 1 : 8. preach other gospel be a.,
See **Accursed THING.** ⌊9.

ACCUSATION.

Ezr. 4 : 6. wrote an a. ag. Jud.⌈15 : 26.
Mat. 27 : 37. over head his a., Mk.
Lu. 6 : 7. might find an a. ag. him
19 : 8. if I taken thing by false a.
Jn. 18 : 29. What a. bring ye ag this
Ac. 25 : 18. Ag. whom bro-t none a.
1 Ti. 5 : 19. ag. an elder receive not a.
2 Pe. 2 : 11. angels bri. not railing a.
Jude 9. Michael durst not bring rail-

ACCUSE. ⌊ing a.

Pr. 30 : 10. a. not a serv. unto mast.
Mat. 12 : 10. that they might a. him,
Mk. 3 : 2. Lu. 11 : 54. Jn. 8 : 6.
Lu. 3 : 14. neither a. any falsely
23 : 2. they began to a. him, saying
14. touching things wh-f ye a. him
Jn. 5 : 45. th. I will a. you to Father
Ac. 24 : 2. Tertullus began to a. Paul
8. take knowl. of things wh-f we a.
13. nei. prove th-s wh-f they a. me
25 : 5. Let them go and a. this man
Ac. 25 : 11. none of things these a.
28 : 19. not aught to a. my nation
1 Pe. 3 : 16. falsely a. your good con-

ACCUSED. ⌊versation

Da. 3 : 8. certain Chaldeans a. Jews
6 : 24. bro-t men wh. had a. Daniel
Mat. 27 : 12. when a. he ans-d nothing
Mk. 15 : 3. chief priests a. him of
many things, Lu. 23 : 10. ⌈ed
Lu. 16 : 1. steward was a. th. he wast-
Ac. 22 : 30. certainty wh-f he was a.
23 : 28. known cause wheref. they
29. to be a. of questions of law⌊a.
25 : 16. before he wh. is a. have ac-
26 : 2. touch-g things I am a.⌊cusers
7. for which hope's sake I am a.
Tit. 1 : 6. not a. of riot or unruly
Re. 12 : 10. wh. a. them bef. our God

ACCUSER, S. ⌈a-s?

Jn. 8 : 10. Woman, where are thine
Ac. 23 : 30. I gave com-t to his a-s
35. hear when thine a-s are come
24 : 8. commanding his a-s to come
25 : 16. he have the a-s face to face
18. a-s bro-t none accusation of
2 Ti. 3 : 3. without affection, false a-s
Tit. 2 : 3. not false a-s, not given to
Re. 12 : 10. the a. of brethren is cast

ACCUSETH, ING. ⌊down

Jn. 5 : 45. is one th. a-h you, Moses
Ro. 2 : 15. thoughts a-g or excusing

ACCUSTOMED. ⌈evil

Je. 13 : 23. do good that are a. to do

ACEL'DAMA.

Ac. 1 : 19. called A. The field of blood

ACHA'IA. ⌈A.

Ac. 18 : 12. Gallio was the deputy of
27. Apollos disposed to pass into A.
19 : 21 purposed wh. passed thro. A.
Ro. 15 : 26. it hath pleased th. of A
16 : 5. Epenetus, firstfruits of A.
1 Co. 16 : 15. Stephanas, firstfruits
2 Co. 1 : 1. P. unto saints in A.⌊of A.
9 : 2. that A. was ready a year ago
11 : 10. no man shall stop me in A.
1 Th. 1 : 7. ye ensamples to all in A.
8. word sounded out not only in A.

ACHA'ICUS. ⌈A.

1 Co. 16 : 17. I am glad of coming of

A'CHAN = A'CHAR.

Jos. 7 : 1. A. took of accursed thing
18. A-n of Judah was taken, 19, 24.
20. A. ans-d I have sinned ag. L-
22 : 20. Did not A-n commit trespass
1 Ch. 2 : 7. A-r, troubler of Isr., † A-n

A'CHAZ = A'HAZ. ⌈begat

Mat. 1 : 9. Joatham begat A.; A.

ACH'BOR.

Ge. 36 : 38, 39, 2 K. 22 : 12, 14. 1 Ch.
1 : 49. 2 Ch. 34 : †20. Je. 26 : 22.

A'CHIM. ⌊-36 : 12.

Mat. 1 : 14. Sadoc begat A. ; A. begat

A'CHISH. ⌊Eliud

1 S. 21 : 10. David fled to A., king,
12. Dav. sore afraid of A. | 11.⌊27 : 2.
27 : 3. David dwelt with A. | 5, 9.
6. A. gave David Ziklag | 10, 12.
28 : 1. A. said, to battle with me, 2.
29 : 2. David passed on wi. A., 3, 6, 8.
9. A. said to David, Thou art good
1 K. 2 : 40. Shimei went to A. 39.
Ps. 34 : *†. David changed before A.

ACH'METHA.

Ezr. 6 : 2. found at A. in palace a roll

The valley of A'CHOR.

Jos. 7 : 24. Jos. bro-t Achan unto -A.
26. name of place was called - A.
15 : 7. the border went up from -A.
Is. 65 : 10. - A. place for herds to lie
Ho. 2 : 15. give - A. for door of hope

ACH'SA or ACH'SAH.

Jos. 15 : 16. will I give A-h my daughter to wife, 17. Ju. 1 : 12, 13.
1 Ch. 2 : 49. the dau. of Caleb was A-a

ACH'SHAPH. ⌈12 : 20.

Jos. 11 : 1. Jabin sent to king of A.,
19 : 25. their border was Hall, A.

ACH'ZIB. [Ju. 1 : 31.
Jos. 19 : 29. from coast to A.| 15 : 44.
Mi. 1 : 14. houses of A., shall be a lie
ACKNOWLEDGE, ED.
Ge. 38 : 26. Judah a-d them and said
De. 1 : † 17. sh. not a. faces in judg-t
21 : 17. he shall a. son of the hated
33 : 9. nei. did he a. his brethren
Ps. 32 : 5. I a-d my sin | 51 : 3. I a. my
Pr. 3 : 6. In thy ways a. him⌊transg.
Is. 33 : 13. ye th. are near a. my might
61 : 9. all that see shall a. them
63 : 16. though Israel a. us not
Je. 3 : 13. Only a. thine iniquity th.
14 : † 18. ag. a land and men a. it not
20. we a., O Lord, our wickedness
24 : 5. will I a. them th. are captive
Da. 11 : 39. strange god wh. he sh. a.
Ho. 5 : 15. will go till they a. offence
Ro. 1 : † 28. did not like to a. God
1 Co. 14 : 37. let him a. things I write
16 : 18. a. ye them that are such
2 Co. 1 : 13. what ye a. and shall a.
14. As ye have a-d us in part
ACKNOWLEDGETH, ING.
2 Ti. 2 : 25. repentance to a-g truth
Tit. 1 : 1. to the a-g the truth which
Phm. 6. by a-g of every good thing
1 Jn. 2 : 23. he that a-h the Son hath
ACKNOWLEDGMENT.
Ep. 1 : † 17. spirit of wisd. for a. of Ch.
Col. 2 : 2. to a. of the mystery of God
ACQUAINT.
Jb. 22 : 21. a. now thyself with him
ACQUAINTANCE.
2 K. 10 : † 11. Jehu slew all Ahab's a.
12 : 5. to every man of his a. [a.
7. receive no more money of your
Jb. 19 : 13. mine a. are estranged fr.
42 : 11. came all th. had been his a.
Ps. 31 : 11. I was a fear to mine a. [a.
55 : 13. it was thou mine equal, mine
88 : 8. hast put mine a. far from me
18. hast put mine a. into darkness
Lu. 2 : 44. they sought him among
23 : 49. all his a. stood afar off ⌊a.
Ac. 24 : 23. forbid none of his a. to
ACQUAINTED, ING. ⌊come
Ps. 139 : 3. art a-d with all my ways
Ec. 2 : 3. a-g mine heart with wisdom
Is. 53 : 3. He is a man a-d with grief
ACRAB'BIM = AKRAB'-BIM. [1 : † 36.
Jos. 15 : † 3. The going up to A., Ju.
ACQUIT.
Jb. 10 : 14. will not a. me fr. iniquity
Na. 1 : 3. L. will not at all a. wicked
ACRE, S.
1 S. 14 : 14. slaughter within half a.
Is. 5 : 10. ten a-s of vineyard yield
ACT. [a.
Is. 28 : 21. to pass his a., his strange
59 : 6. a. of violence in their hands
Jn. 8 : 4. taken in adultery, in very
ACTS. ⌊a.
De. 11 : 3. his a. wh. he did in Egypt
De. 11 : 7. eyes have seen great a. of
Ju. 5 : 11. rehearse righteous a. of L.
1 S. 12 : 7. reason of righteous a. of L.
2 S. 23 : 20. done many a. 1 Ch. 11 : 22.
1 K. 10 : 6. report I heard of thy a.,
11 : 41. book of a. of Sol.⌊2 Ch. 9 : 5.
2 K. 23 : 19. a. Josiah had done in B.
1 Ch. 29 : 29. a. of David [of Asa
2 Ch. 12 : 15. a. of Rehob.| 16 : 11. a.
Es. 10 : 2. And all the a. of his power
Ps. 103 : 7. his a. unto chil. of Israel
106 : 2. Who can utter mighty a. of
145 : 4. thy mighty a., 6, 12. ⌊L.?
150 : 2. Praise him for mighty a.
The rest of the ACTS.
1 K. 11 : 41. — a. of Sol-n, 2 Ch. 9 : 29.
14 : 19. — a. of Jerob. 2 K. 14 : 28.
29. — a. of Rehob in book of Chron.
15 : 7. — a. of Abijam, 2 Ch. 13 : 22.
23. — a. of Asa | 31. — a. of Nadab
16 : 5. — a. of Baasha | 14. — a. of Elah
1 K. 16 : 20. — a. of Zimri | 27. — a. of
22 : 39. — a. of Ahab, written⌊Omri
45. — a. of Jehoshaphat, 2 Ch. 20 : 34.
2 K. 1 : 18. — a. of Ahaziah [Jehu
8 : 23. — a. of Joram | 10 : 34. — a. of
12 : 19. — a. of Joash, 13 : 12. [ash
13 : 8. — a. of Jehoahaz | 14 : 15. Jeho-
14 : 18. — a. of Amaziah, 2 Ch. 25 : 26.
15 : 6. — a. of Azariah | 11. Zachariah
15. — a. of Shallum | 21. Menahem
26. — a. of Pekahiah | 31. Pekah
36. — a. of Jotham, 2 Ch. 27 : 7.
16 : 19. — a. of Ahaz, 2 Ch. 28 : 26.
20 : 20. — a. of Hezekiah, 2 Ch. 32 : 32.
21 : 17. — a. of Manasseh, 2 Ch. 33 : 18.
25. — a. of Amon in book of Chron.
23 : 28. — a. of Josiah, 2 Ch. 35 : 26.
24 : 5. — a. of Jehoiakim, 2 Ch. 36 : 8.
2 Ch. 26 : 22. — a. of Uzziah did Isai-
ACTIONS. ⌊ah write
1 S. 2 : 3. by Lord a. are weighed
ACTIVITY.
Ge. 47 : 6. if knowest any men of a.
AD'ADAH.
Jos. 15 : 22. cities of Judah were A.
A'DAH.
Ge. 4 : 19, 20, 23.—36 : 2, 4, 10, 12, 16.
ADAI'AH.
2 K. 22 : 1. daughter of A. of Boscath
1 Ch. 6 : † 21, 41.—8 : 21.—9 : 12. 2 Ch.
23 : 1. Ezr. 10 : 29, 39. Ne. 11 :
ADALI'A. ⌊5, 12.
Es. 9 : 8. in the palace Jews slew A.
AD'AM. [Person.]
Ge. 2 : † 15. God put A. into garden
20. A. gave names to all cattle, but
for A. was not a help meet, 19.
21. deep sleep to fall upon A.
23. A. said, This is bone of my bones
3 : 8. A. and his wife hid from Lord
9. God called unto A., 17. | 20, 21.—4 :
5 : 1. book of generations of A.⌊1, 25.
2. he called their name A. | 3, 4.
5. days A. lived were 930 years
De. 32 : 8. he separated sons of A.
1 Ch. 1 : 1. A., Sheth, Enosh [as A.
Jb. 31 : 33. If I covered my transg-ns
Ho. 6 : † 8. work iniquity and is like A.
Lu. 3 : 38. Seth, son of A., son of God
Ro. 5 : 14. death reigned from A.,
after similitude of A.'s transg-n
1 Co. 15 : 22. For as in A. all die
45. first A. a living soul, last A. a
1 Ti. 2 : 13. A. was first formed, then
14. A. was not deceived, but woman
Jude 14. Enoch the seventh from A.
AD'AM. [Place.]
Jos. 3 : 16. waters rose fr. the city A.
AD'AMAH. Jos. 19 : 36.
ADAMANT.
Eze. 3 : 9. As an a. thy forehead [a.
Zch. 7 : 12. made their hearts as an
AD'AMI. See ZAANANNIM.
A'DAR. [Month.] [A.
Ezr. 6 : 15. finished on third day of
Es. 3 : 7. they cast lot to 12th mo., A.
13. kill Jews on A., 8 : 12.—9 : 1, 17.
9 : 15. gathered on 14th day of A.
19. 14th day of A. day of gladness
21. keep 14th day and 15th of A.
A'DAR. [Place.]
Jos. 15 : 3. border went up to A. and
AD'BEEL. [1 : 29
Ge. 25 : 13. sons of Ishmael, A., 1 Ch.
ADD.
Ge. 30 : 24. Lord shall a. another son
Le. 5 : 16. a. fifth part, 6 : 5.—27 : 13,
15, 19, 27, 31. Nu. 5 : 7.
Nu. 35 : 6. ye sh. a. forty two cities
De. 4 : 2. Ye sh. not a. unto word, 12 :
19 : 9. thou shalt a. three cities⌊32.
29 : 19. to a. drunkenness to thirst
2 S. 24 : 3. L. thy God a. unto people
1 K. 12 : 11. Rehoboam said, I will a.
to your yoke, 14. 2 Ch. 10 : 14.
2 K. 20 : 6. I will a. 15 years, Is. 38 : 5.
1 Ch. 22 : 14. stones thou mayest a.
2 Ch. 28 : 13. intend to a. to our sins
Ps. 69 : 27. a. iniquity unto iniquity
Pr. 3 : 2. long life sh. they a. to thee
30 : 6. a. thou not unto his words
Is. 29 : 1. Woe! a. ye year to year
30 : 1. that they may a. sin to sin
13 : † 2. now they a. sin to sin [25.
Ma. 6 : 27. can a. one cubit, Lu. 12 :
Phi. 1 : 16. a. affliction to my bonds
2 Pe. 1 : 5. a. to faith virtue [saints
Re. 8 : † 3. that he a. it to prayers of
22 : 18. If any a., God sh. a. plagues
AD'DAN or AD'DON.
Ezr. 2 : 59. † went fr. Cherub, A., Ne.
AD'DAR. See ABIHUD.⌊7 : 61. †
ADDED.
De. 5 : 22. and the Lord a. no more
1 S. 12 : 19. we a. to our sins this evil
1 K. 10 : † 7. hast a. wisdom to fame
Je. 36 : 32. were a. many like words
45 : 3. L. hath a. grief to my sorrow
Da. 4 : 36. majesty was a. unto me
Mat. 6 : 33. be a. unto you, Lu. 12 : 31.
Lu. 3 : 20. Herod a. this above all
19 : 11. he a. and spake a parable
Ac. 2 : 41. there were a. 3,000 souls
47. Lord a. to the church daily
5 : 14. believers were a. to the Lord
11 : 24. much peo. was a. unto Lord
Ga. 2 : 6. in conference a. noth. to me
3 : 19. law was a. bec. of transgres-
ADDER, S. ⌊sions
Ge. 49 : 17. Dan. sh. be an a. in path
Ps. 58 : 4. they are like the deaf a.
91 : 13. shalt tread upon lion and a.
140 : 3. a-s' poison is und. their lips
Pr. 23 : 32. At last stingeth like an a.
Is. 11 : † 8. a-'s den | 14 : † 29. shall come
59 : † 5. They hatch a-'s eggs ⌊an a.
ADDETH.
Jb. 34 : 37. he a. rebellion unto sin
Pr. 10 : 22. he a. no sorrow with it
16 : 23. heart of the wise a. learning
Ga. 3 : 15. coven-t, no man a. there-
AD'DI. See COSAM. ⌊to
ADDICTED. [try
1 Co. 16 : 15. a. thems. to the minis-
ADDING. [head
Pr. 1 : † 9. be an a. of grace to thy
ADDITION, S.
1 K. 7 : 29. certain a-s made of thin
30. molten, at the side of every a.
36. he graved cherubim, and a-s
Is. 15 : † 9. I will bri. a-s upon Dimon
AD'DON. See ADDAN.
A'DER.
1 Ch. 8 : 15. Arad and A., sons of Be-
A'DIEL. ⌊riah
1 Ch. 4 : 36. Joel, A., princes, 9 : 12.
A'DIN. ⌊—27 : 25.
Ezr. 2 : 15.—8 : 6. Ne. 7 : 20.—10 : 16.
AD'INA. See SHIZA.
AD'INO. See EZNITE.
ADITHA'IM. [A.
Jos. 15 : 36. in the valley Enam and
ADJURE, ED. [time
Jos. 6 : 26. Joshua a-d them at that
1 S. 14 : 24. Saul had a-d the people
1 K. 22 : 16. How many times shall I
a. thee, th. thou tell, 2 Ch. 18 : 15.
Can. 2 : † 7. I a. you, O dau-s of Jerus.
Mat. 26 : 63. I a. thee by the liv. God
Mk. 5 : 7. I a. thee, torment me not
Ac. 19 : 13. We a. you by Jesus wh.
1 Th. 4 : † 27. I a. you this epis. be read
AD'LAI. See SHAPHAT.
AD'MAH. See ZEBOIM.
AD'MATHA. See CARSHENA.
ADMINISTERED.
2 Co. 8 : 19. a. by us to glory of Lord
20 abundance which is a. by us
ADMINISTRATION, S.
1 Co. 12 : 5. are differences of a-s, but
2 Co. 9 : 12. the a. of this service is
ADMIRATION.
Jude 16. Having men's persons in a.
Re. 17 : 6. I wondered with great a.

ADMIRED. [lieve
2 Th. 1 : 10. to be a. in all that be-
ADMONISH, ED, ING.
Ec 4 : 13. foolish king no more be a-d
12 : 12. And by these my son be a-d
Je. 42 : 19. know that I have a-d you
Ac. 27 : 9. fast now past, Paul a-d
Ro. 15 : 14. ye able to a. one another
Col. 3 : 16. a-g one another in psalms
1 Th. 5 : 12. over you in Lord and a.
2 Th. 3 : 15. but a. him as a brother
He. 8 : 5. as Moses was a-d of God
ADMONITION.
1 Co. 10 : 11. are written for our a.
Ep. 6 : 4. bring them up in a. of Lord
Tit. 3 : 10. heretic aft. second a. reject
AD'NA. [Ne. 12 : 15.
Ezr. 10 : 30. sons of Pahath-moab, A.,
AD'NAH.
1 Ch. 12 : 20. fell to David, A., and
2 Ch. 17 : 14. A. the chief, with him
ADO. ⌊300,000
Mk. 5 : 39. Why make ye this a.
ADON'I-BE'ZEK. [7.
Ju. 1 : 5. they found A. in Bezek, 6,
ADONI'JAH. [3 : 2.
2 S. 3 : 4. sons of David, 4th A., 1 Ch.
1 K. 1 : 5. Then A. exalted himself
7. Joab following A., helped him
8. A., 9, 41, 42, 43, 49. - 2 : 13, 19.
11. not heard A. doth reign? 13, 18,
25. they say, God save king A. ⌊24.
50. A. feared bec. of Solomon, 51.
2 : 21. Let Abishag be given A., 22.
24. A. sh. be put to death, 23. ⌊28.
2 Ch. 17 : 8. A., Tobijah taught in Jud.
Ne. 10 : 16. chief of the people, A.
ADONI'KAM.
Ezr. 2 : 13. children of A., Ne. 7 : 18.
8 : 13. last sons of A., whose names
ADONI'RAM = ADO'RAM.
1 K. 4 : 6. A. over tribute, 5 : 14.
ADON'I-ZE'DEK.
Jos. 10 : 1. A., king of Jerusalem, 3.
ADOPTION. [a.
Ro. 8 : 15. ye have received spirit of
23. waiting for the a., redemption
9 : 4. to whom pertaineth the a.
Ga. 4 : 5. might rec. the a. of sons
Ep. 1 : 5. predestinated us unto a. of
ADORA'IM. ⌊chil.
2 Ch. 11 : 9. built for defence A., and
ADO'RAM = ADONI'RAM.
2 S. 20 : 24. A. over tribute, 1 K. 12 : 18.
ADORN, ED, ETH.
Is. 61 : 10. as bride a-h with jewels
Je. 31 : 4. shalt be a-d with tabrets
Lu. 21 : 5. temple was a-d wi. stones
1 Ti. 2 : 9. that women a. in modest
Tit. 2 : 10. may a. the doctrine of G.
1 Pe. 3 : 5. holy women a-d themselves
Re. 21 : 2. bride a-d for her husband
ADORNING.
1 Pe. 3 : 3. a. not be that outward a.
ADRAM'MELECH.
2 K. 17 : 31. burnt children to A.
19 : 37. A. smote Sennach-b, Is. 37 :
ADRAMYT'TIUM. ⌊38.
Ac. 27 : 2. entering into a ship of A.
A'DRIA.
Ac. 27 : 27. as we were driven in A.
A'DRIEL. [21 : 8.
1 S. 18 : 19. Saul's dau-r to A., 2 S.
ADUL'LAM. [of A.
Jos. 12 : 15. kings Josh. smote, king
15 : 35. cities A., Socoh, 2 Ch. 11 : 7.
1 S. 22 : 1. David escaped to cave A.
2 S. 23 : 13. unto cave of A., 1 Ch. 11 : 15.
Ne. 11 : 30. chil. of Judah dwelt at A.
Mi. 1 : 15. unto A. the glory of Israel
ADUL'LAMITE. [12, 20.
Ge. 38 : 1. A., whose name Hirah,
ADULTERER, S.
Le. 20 : 10. a. be put to death [light
Jb. 24 : 15. eye of a. waiteth for twi-
Ps. 50 : 18. thou partaker with a-s
Is. 57 : 3. draw near ye seed of the a.
Je. 9 : 2. they be all a-s, assembly of
23 : 10. For the land is full of a-s
Ho. 7 : 4. all a-s, as an oven heated
Mal. 3 : 5. I will be witness ag-t a-s
Lu. 18 : 11. I not as other men, a-s
1 Co. 6 : 9. nor a-s shall inherit kingd.
He. 13 : 4. But a-s God will judge
Ja. 4 : 4. Ye a-s know ye not that
ADULTERESS, ES.
Le. 20 : 10. a. shall be put to death
Pr. 6 : 26. a. will hunt for pree. life
Eze. 23 : 45. judge them after manner
of a-s, because they are a-s [a.
Ho. 3 : 1. Go, love a woman, yet an
Ro. 7 : 3. if while husband liveth
she be married, she an a. (2)
Ja. 4 : 4. Ye a-s, know ye not that
2 Pe. 2 : † 14. Having eyes of an a.
ADULTERIES.
Je. 13 : 27. I have seen thine a.
Eze. 23 : 43. said I unto her old in a.
Ho. 2 : 2. let her put away her a. [21.
Mat. 15 : 19. out of heart, a., Mk. 7 :
ADULTEROUS.
Pr. 30 : 20. Such is way of a. woman
Mat. 12 : 39. An a. generation, 16 : 4.
Mk. 8 : 38. ashamed in this a. gen-
ADULTERY. ⌊eration
Jn. 8 : 3. bro-t woman taken in a., 4.
Ga. 5 : 19. works of the flesh are a.
2 Pe. 2 : 14. Having eyes full of a.
Commit, ted, teth, or **ting**
ADULTERY.
Ex. 20 : 14. Thou shalt not c. a., De. 5 :
18. Mat. 5 : 27.-19 : 18. Mk. 10 : 19.
Lu. 18 : 20. Ro. 13 : 9. Ja. 2 : 11.
Le. 20 : 10. man c-h a. put to death
Pr. 6 : 32. whoso c-h a. lacketh
Je. 3 : 8. backsliding Israel c-d a.
9. c-h a. with stones and stocks
5 : 7. fed to the full, they c-d a.
7 : 9. Will ye steal, murder, c. a.
23 : 14. prophets c. a., walk in lies
29 : 23. Because they have c-d a.
Eze. 16 : 32. But as a wife that c-h a.
23 : 37. with idols have they c-d a.
Ho. 4 : 2. by c-g a. they break out
13. your spouses shall c. a. [a.
14. I will not punish when they c.
Mat. 5 : 28. hath c-d a. in his heart
32. whoso-r shall put away wife,
causeth her to c. a.; whoso. sh.
marry her c-h a., 19 : 9. Lu. 16 : 18.
Mk. 10 : 11. Whoso. sh. put away wife,
marry ano., c-h a., Lu. 16 : 18.
12. if woman put away her husband and be married, she c-h a.
Ro. 2 : 22. sayest a man should not
c. a., dost thou c. a.?
Ja. 2 : 11. if thou c. no a., yet kill
Re. 2 : them that c. a. with her
ADUM'MIM. [17.
Jos. 15 : 7. bef. the going to A., 18 :
ADVANCED.
1 S. 12 : 6. It is that Lord that a. Mos.
Es. 3 : 1. Ahasuerus a. Haman [him
5 : 11. Haman told how king had a.
10 : 2. whereunto king a. Mordecai
ADVANTAGE. [me
Jb. 35 : 3. What a. will it be unto
Ro. 3 : 1. What a. hath the Jew?
2 Co. 2 : 11. Lest Satan get a. of us
Jude 16. in admiration because of a.
ADVANTAGED, ETH.
Lu. 9 : 25. what a-d if he gain world
1 Co. 15 : 32. what a-h me if dead rise
ADVENTURE, ED. ⌊not
De. 28 : 56. woman not a. to set foot
Ju. 9 : 17. my father for you a-d life
Ac. 19 : 31. th. he not a. into theatre
ADVENTURES. [me, 24.
Le. 26 : † 21. if ye walk at all a. with
ADVERSARIES. [a.
Ex. 23 : 22. an adversary unto thine
De. 32 : 27. lest a. behave strangely
43. he will render vengeance to
Jos. 5 : 13. Art for us or our a.? ⌊his a.
1 S. 2 : 10. a. of Lord shall be broken
2 S. 19 : 22. that ye be a. unto me?
Ezr. 4 : 1. when a. of Judah heard
Ne. 4 : 11. our a. said, They shall not
Ps. 38 : 20. evil for good, are my a.
69 : 19. mine a. are all before thee
71 : 13. that are a. to my soul [a.
81 : 14. turned my hand ag-t their
89 : 42. set up right hand of his a.
109 : 4. For my love they are my a.
20. Let this be reward of mine a.
29. mine a. be clothed with shame
Is. 1 : 24. I will ease me of mine a.
9 : 11. Lord shall set up a. of Rezin
11 : 13. a. of Judah shall be cut off
59 : 18. he will repay fury to his a.
63 : 18. a. trodden down sanctuary
64 : 2. make thy name known to a.
Je. 30 : 16. a. shall go into captivity
46 : 10. may avenge him of his a.
50 : 7. their a. said, We offend not
La. 1 : 5. Her a. are the chief [baths
7. a. saw her, did mock at her sab-
17. a. should be round about him
2 : 17. set up the horn of thine a.
Mi. 5 : 9. hand be lifted upon thine a.
Na. 1 : 2. L. take vengeance on his a.
Lu. 13 : 17. all his a. ashamed [say
21 : 15. your a. not able to gain-
1 Co. 16 : 9. and there are many a.
Ph. 1 : 28. noth-g terrified by your a.
He. 10 : 27. which shall devour the a.
ADVERSARY. [ries
Ex. 23 : 22. I a. unto thine adversa-
Nu. 22 : 22. angel an a. ag-t Balaam
† 32. I went to be an a. unto thee
1 S. 1 : 6. her a. provoked her sore
29 : 4. lest in battle he be a. to us
1 K. 5 : 4. is nei. a. nor evil occurrent
11 : 14. an a. unto Solomon, 23.
25. Rezon a. to Isr. all days of Sol.
Es. 7 : 6. The a. is wicked Haman
Jb. 1 : †6. a. came amo. them. The A.
31 : 35. that mine a. written a book
Ps. 74 : 10. how long sh. a. reproach?
109 : † 6. let an a. stand at his right
Is. 50 : 8. who is mine a.? let him
La. 1 : 10. a. hath spread out hand
2 : 4. stood with right hand as an a.
4 : 12. that a. into gates of Jerus.
Am. 3 : 11. An a. sh. be round about
Zch. 3 : † 1. an a. to be his a. [deliv.
Mat. 5 : 25. Agree with a., lest a.
Lu. 12 : 58. goest with a. to magis-
18 : 3. Avenge me of mine a. ⌊trate
1 Ti. 5 : 14. give none occasion to a.
1 Pe. 5 : 8. your a. the devil, as lion
ADVERSITY, IES.
1 S. 10 : 19. saved you out of all a-s
2 S. 4 : 9. my soul out of all a.
2 Ch. 15 : 6. G. did vex them with a.
Ps. 10 : 6. I shall never be in a.
31 : 7. hast known my soul in a-s
35 : 15. in mine a. they rejoiced
94 : 13. give him rest from days of a.
Pr. 17 : 17. a brother is born for a.
24 : 10. If thou faint in day of a.
Ec. 7 : 14. in the day of a. consider
Is. 30 : 20. tho. Lord give bread of a.
He. 13 : 3. remember them wh. suffer
ADVERTISE. ⌊a.
Nu. 24 : 14. I will a. thee what peo-
Ru. 4 : 4. I thought to a. thee ⌊ple
ADVICE.
Ju. 19 : 30. take a., speak your minds
20 : 7. give your a. and counsel
1 S. 25 : 33. blessed be thy a. and
2 S. 19 : 43. why our a. not be first
2 Ch. 10 : 9. What a. give ye ⌊had
14. answ-ed after a. of young men
25 : 17. Amaziah, k. of Jud. took a.
Pr. 20 : 18. with good a. make war
2 Co. 8 : 10. And herein I give my a.
ADVISE, ED.
2 S. 24 : 13. a. and see what answer
I shall return, 1 Ch. 21 : 12.
1 K. 12 : 6. How do ye a. that I ans.

Pr. 13 : 10. with well a-d is wisdom
Ac. 27 : 12. most part a-d to depart

ADVISEMENT.

1 Ch. 12 : 19. lords upon a. sent him
Pr. 1 : †4. to yo. man knowledge, a.

ADVOCATE. ⌈Father
1 Jn. 2 : 1. we have an a. with the

AENE'AS. See ÆNEAS.

AE'NON. See ENON.

AFAR off, AFAR. ⌈a.o.
Ge. 22 : 4. Abraham saw the place
37 : 18. brethren saw Joseph a. o.
Ex. 24 : 1. Come up, worship ye a. o.
33 : 7. pitched the tabernacle a. o.
Nu. 9 : 10. If any be in journey a. o.
2 K. 4 : 25. man of God saw her a.o.
Ezr. 3 : 13. the noise was heard a.o.
Ne. 12 : 43. joy of Jerus. heard a.o.
Jb 2 : 12. lifted up their eyes a. o.
36 : 3. fetch my knowledge from
25. man may behold it a. o. ⌊a.
39 : 29. prey, her eyes behold a. o.
Ps. 65 : 5. of them a.o. upon the sea
138 : 6. proud he knoweth a. o.⌈o.
139 : 2. understand-t my thought a.
Pr. 31 : 14. bringeth her food fr. a.
Is. 23 : 7. her feet sh. carry her a.o.
66 : 19. the isles a.o. Je. 31 : 10.
Je. 23 : 23. I a God at hand, not a.o.?
31 : † 3. L. appeared fr. a. unto me
46 : 27. I will save from a.o., 30 : 10.
51 : 50. Ye remember the Lord a.o.
Mi 4 : 3. he sh. rebuke nations a.o.
Mat. 26 : 58. Peter followed him a.
o., Mk. 14:54. Lu. 22:54. ⌈15:40.
27 : 55. women behold-g a.o., Mk.
Mk 5 : 6. saw Jesus a.o., he ran and
11 : 13. seeing fig tree a.o. he came
Lu. 16 : 23. he seeth Abraham a.o.
Ac. 2 : 39. the promise is to all a.o.
Ep 2 : 17. preached peace to you a.o.
He. 11 : 13. having seen promises a.o.
2 Pe. 1 : 9. blind and cannot see a.o.
See FAR, SMELLETH, STAND, STANDEST, ETH, ING. [Part.]
See **STOOD afar.**

AFFAIRS. ⌈of king
1 Ch. 26 : 32. pertaining to G. and a.
Ps. 112 : 5. guide his a. wi. discretion
Da. 2 : 49. Neb-r set Shadrach, M., and A. over a. of Bab-n, 3 : 12.
Ep. 6 : 21. th. ye may know my a., 22.
Ph. 1 : 27. I may hear of your a. ⌈life
2 Ti. 2 : 4. entangleth hims. wi. a. of

AFFECT, ED, ETH.

La 3 : 51. Mine eye a-h mine heart
Ac. 14 : 2. minds evil a-d ag. breth
Ga. 4 : 17. They zealously a. you not
well; that ye might a. them
18. good to be zealously a. in good

AFFECTION, S. ⌈of G.
1 Ch. 29 : 3. have set my a. to house
Ro. 1 : 26. G. gave them unto vile a-s
31. without natural a., 2 Ti 3 : 3
2 Co. 7 : 15. his inward a. toward you
Ga. 5 : 24. crucified the flesh wi. a-s
Col. 3 : 2. Set your a. on things above
5. mortify unclean-s, inordinate

AFFECTIONATELY. ⌊a.
1 Th. 2 : 8. being a. desirous of you

AFFECTIONED.

Ro. 12 : 10. Be kindly a. one to ano.

AFFINITY.

1 K. 3 : 1. Sol-n made a. with Pha-h
2 Ch. 18 : 1. Jehosh-t joined a. with
Ezr. 9 : 14. Should we join in a. with

AFFIRM, ED. ⌊peo.
Lu. 22 : 59. Another confidently a-d
Ac. 12 : 15. Rhoda a-d it was even so
25 : 19. Jesus Paul a. to be alive
Ro. 3 : 8. (as some a. that we say)
1 Ti. 1 : 7. what they say, nor wh-f a.
Tit. 3 : 8. these things a. constantly

AFFLICT.

Ge. 15 : 13. shall a. them 400 years
31 : 50. If thou shalt a. my daugh-s
Ex. 1 : 11. set taskmasters to a. them
Ex. 22 : 22. Ye sh. not a. any widow
23. If thou a. them in any wise
23 : † 22. I will a. them that a. thee
Le. 16 : 29. ye shall a. your souls,
31.-23 : 27, 32. Nu. 29 : 7.
Nu. 24 : 24. ships shall a. Asshur (2)
30 : 13. ev. binding oath to a. soul
Ju. 16 : 5. we may bind him to a. him
6. mightest be bound to a. thee
19. she began to a. him ⌈them
2 S. 7 : 10. nei. sh. chil. of wickedn-s a.
1 K. 11 : 39. I for this a. seed of Dav.
2 Ch. 6 : 26. if turn when thou dost a.
Ezr. 8 : 21. might a. ours. before God
Jb. 37 : 23. Almighty; he will not a.
Ps. 44 : . how thou didst a. people
55 : 19. God shall hear and a. them
89 : 22. nor son of wickedn-s a. him
94 : 5. they a. thine heritage
143 : 12. destroy all that a. my soul
Ec. 1 : †13. sore travail to men to a.
Is. 9 : 1. did more grievously a. her
51 : 23. hand of them that a. thee
58 : 5. day for a man to a. his soul?
64 : 12. wilt thou a. very sore? ⌈a.
Je. 31 : 28. as I watched ov. them to
La. 3 : 33. Lord doth not a. willingly
Am. 5 : 12. they a. the just ⌈math
6 : 14. they shall a. you from Ha-
Na. 1 : 12. I will a. thee no more
Zph. 3 : 19. I will undo all th. a. thee

AFFLICTED. ⌈fled
Ge. 16 : † 6. when Sarai a. her, she
Ex. 1 : 12. more a., more they grew
Le. 23 : 29. whatso. soul sh. not be a.
Nu. 11 : 11. Wheref. hast a. servant?
De. 26 : 6. Eg-ns a. us, laid bondage
Ru. 1 : 21. Almighty hath a. me
2 S. 22 : 28. a. people thou wilt save
1 K. 2 : 26. a. in all my father was a.
2 K. 17 : 20. L. rejected Israel and a.
Jb. 6 : 14. To him a., pity be shewed
30 : 11. hath loosed my cord, a. me
34 : 28. he heareth the cry of the a.
36 : † 6. He giveth right to the a.
† 15. He delivereth a. in affliction
Ps. 9 : † 12. he forgetteth not the a.
10 : † 12. Arise, O Lord, forget not a.
18 : 27. thou wilt save the a. people
22 : 24. nor abhorred afflict-n of a.
25 : 16. Turn thee; I am desolate, a.
35 : † 13. I a. my soul with fasting
82 : 3. do justice to a. and needy
88 : 7. hast a. me wi. all thy waves
15. I am a. and ready to die⌈a. us
90 : 15. glad acc. to days thou hast
102 : †23. He a. my strength in way
107 : 17. Fools, because of iniquities
116 : 10. I was greatly a. ⌊are a.
119 : 67. Bef. I was a. I went astray
71. it is good that I have been a.
75. Thou in faithfulness hast a.
107. I am a. very much ⌊me
129 : 1. Many a time have a. me, 2.
140 : 12. L. will maintain cause of a.
Pr. 15 : 15. all the days of a. are evil
22 : 22. nei. oppress the a. in gate
26 : 28. lying tongue hateth those a.
31 : 5. pervert judgment of a.⌊by it
Is. 9 : 1. he lightly a. land of Zeb-n
49 : 13. L. will have mercy upon a.
51 : 21. Thf. hear now this, thou a.
53 : 4. him smitten of God, and a.
7. was a., yet opened not mouth
54 : 11. O a., I will lay thy stones
58 : 3. wheref. have we a. our soul?
† 7. poor that are a. to thy house
10. and if thou satisfy the a. soul
60 : 14. sons of them that a. thee
63 : 9. In their affliction he was a.
La. 1 : 4. priests sigh, her virgins a.
5. Lord hath a. her for transg-ns
12. sorrow, wherew. L. hath a. me
Mi 4 : 6. I will gather her I have a.
Na. 1 : 12. Tho. I have a. thee, I will
Zph. 3 : 12. leave in thee an a. people
Mat. 24 : 9. shall deliver you to be a.
2 Co. 1 : 6. whether we be a., it is for
1 Ti. 5 : 10. if she have relieved the a.
He. 11 : 37. destitute, a., tormented
Ja. 4 : 9. Be a. and mourn, and weep
5 : 13. Is any among you a.? pray

AFFLICTEST. ⌈a.
1 K. 8 : 35. if turn fr. sin when thou

AFFLICTION.

Ge. 16 : 11. Lord hath heard thy a.
29 : 32. Lord hath looked upon my
31 : 42. God hath seen mine a. ⌊a.
41 : 52. me fruitful in land of my a.
Ex. 3 : 7. I have seen a. of my people in Egypt, Ac. 7 : 34. ⌈Egypt
17. I will bring you out of a. of
4 : 31. he had looked upon their a.
De. 16 : 3. seven days eat bread of a.
26 : 7. Lord looked on our a. ⌈maid
1 S. 1 : 11. if thou look on a. of hand-
2 : † 32. shalt see a. of tabernacle
2 S. 16 : 12. Lord will look on mine a.
1 K. 22 : 27. this fellow feed with
bread and water of a. (2) 2 Ch.
2 K. 14 : 26. L. saw a. of Israel⌊18 : 26.
2 Ch. 20 : 9. cry in our a., thou wilt
33 : 12. Manasseh was in a. ⌊hear
Ezr. 9 : † 5. I arose from my a. ⌈a.
Ne. 1 : 3. The remnant are in great
9 : 9. didst see a. of our fathers in
Jb. 5 : 6. Although a. cometh not of
10 : 15. thf. see thou mine a. ⌊dust
30 : 16. days of a. taken hold of me
27. the days of a. prevented me
36 : 8. if be holden in cords of a.
15. He delivereth poor in his a.
21. this thou chosen rather than a.
Ps. 22 : 24. he hath not abhorred a.
of the afflicted ⌈pain
25 : 18. Look upon mine a. and my
44 : 24. Wheref. forgettest our a.?
66 : 11. laidst a. upon our loins⌈a.
78 : †42. day he delivered them from
88 : 9. eye mourneth by reason of
106 : 44. he regarded their a. ⌊a.
107 : 10. being bound in a. and iron
39. they are brought low thro. a.
41. setteth the poor on high fr. a.
119 : 50. This my comfort in my a.
92. I should have perished in a.
153. Consider mine a., deliver me
Pr. 31 : † 5. Lest they pervert the
judgment of sons of a. ⌈of a.
Is. 30 : 20. tho. Lord give you water
48 : 10. chosen thee in furnace of a.
63 : 9. In their a. he was afflicted
Je. 4 : 15. publisheth a. fr. Ephraim
15 : 11. to entreat thee well in a.
16 : 19. Lord my refuge in day of a.
30 : 15. Why criest for thine a.?
48 : 16. Moab, his a. hasteth fast
La. 1 : 3. Jud. into captivity bec. of a.
7. Jerus. remembered in days of
9. O Lord, behold my a. ⌊a.
3 : 1. I am man that hath seen a.
19. Remembering mine a. ⌈early
Ho. 5 : 15. in their a. will seek me
Am. 6 : 6. not grieved for a. of Jos-h
Ob. 13. not have looked on their a.
Jon. 2 : 2. I cried by reason of a.
Na. 1 : 9. a. sh. not rise up sec. time
Ha. 3 : 7. saw tents of Cushan in a.
Zch. 1 : 15. they helped forward a.
8 : 10. nei. any peace because of a.
10 : 11. shall pass thro. sea with a.
Mk. 4 : 17. when a. ariseth, offended
13 : 19. in those days shall be a.
Ac. 7 : 11. came dearth and great a.
2 Co. 2 : 4. out of much a. I wrote
4 : 17. light a. wh. is but a moment
8 : 2. How that in great trial of a.
Ph. 1 : 16. to add a. to my bonds ⌈a.
4 : 14. did communicate with my
1 Th. 1 : 6. received word in much a.
3 : 7. comforted over you in our a.
He. 11 : 25. choosing to suffer a.
Ja. 1 : 27. to visit the fatherless in a.
5 : 10. for example of suffering a.

AFFLICTIONS.

Ps. 34 : 19. Many are a. of righteous
132 : 1. remember David and his a.
Ac. 7 : 10. delivered him out of all a.
20 : 23. bonds and a. abide me
2 Co. 6 : 4. in much patience, in a.
Col. 1 : 24. a. of Christ in my flesh
1 Th. 3 : 3. no man be moved by a.
2 Ti. 1 : 8. partakers of a. of gospel
3 : 11. a. wh. came unto me at Anti-
4 : 5. watch thou, endure a. ⌊och
He. 10 : 32. endured great fight of a.
33. ye were made gazingst-k by a.
1 Pe. 5 : 9. same a. in your brethren

AFFORDING. ⌈of store

Ps. 144 : 13. garners a. all manner

AFFRIGHT, ED. ⌈th.

De. 7 : 21. Thou shalt not be a-d at
2 Ch. 32 : 18. a loud voice to a. them
Jb. 18 : 20. that went before were a-d
39 : 22. He mocketh at fear, is not
Is. 21 : 4. fearfulness a-d me ⌊a-d
Je. 51 : 32. and men of war are a-d
Mk. 16 : 5. they were a-d, Lu. 24 : 37.
6. Be not a-d : Ye seek J. crucified
Re. 11 : 13. remnant a-d gave glory

AFOOT. ⌊to God

Mk. 6 : 33. and many ran a. thither
Ac. 20 : 13. Paul minding to go a.

AFORE. ⌈court

2 K. 20 : 4. a. Isaiah was gone into
Ps. 129 : 6. withereth a. it groweth
Is. 18 : 5. a. harvest, when bud ⌊up
Eze. 33 : 22. a. he that escaped came
Ro. 1 : 2. promised a. by prophets
9 : 23. had a. prepared unto glory
Ep. 3 : 3. mystery (as I wrote a. in)

AFOREHAND. ⌈my body

Mk. 14 . 8. she is come a. to anoint

AFORETIME. ⌈ings

Ne. 13 : 5. where a. they laid offer-
Jb. 17 : 6. and a. I was as a tabret
Is. 52 : 4. My people went a. into Eg.
Je. 30 : 20. children shall be as a.
Da. 6 : 10. he prayed before God as
Jn. 9 : 13. him that a. was blind⌊a.
Ro. 15 : 4. whatsoever things written

AFRAID. ⌊a.

Ge. 3 : 10. I was a. because naked
18 : 15. Sarah saying, I laughed
not; for she was a. ⌈this place
28 : 17. was a., said, How dreadful
31 : 31. Jacob said, Because I was a.
32 : 7. Jac. was greatly a., distres-d
42 : 35. saw the money they were a.,
43 : 18. men a. bec. brought ⌊28.
Ex. 3 : 6. Moses a. to look upon God
34 : 30. they a. to come nigh him
Le. 26 : 6. none make you a., Jb. 11:
De. 5 : 5. ye a. by reason of fire ⌊19.
7 : 19. people of whom thou art a.
9 : 19. I was a. of the anger and
28 : 60. diseases thou wast a. of
Ju. 7 : 3. proclaim, Whosoever is a.
Ru. 3 : 8. at midnight, the man was
1 S. 4 : 7. the Philistines were a.⌊a.
7 : 7. they were a. of Philistines⌈a.
17 : 11. Israel dismayed and greatly
18 : 12. Saul was a. of David ⌈a.
15. S. saw he behaved wisely, was
29. Saul was yet more a. of David
21 : 1. Abimelech was a. of David
28 : 5. Saul saw the host he was a.
2 S. 6 : 9. David was a. of the Lord
that day, 1 Ch. 13 . 12. ⌈me a.
14 : 15. because people have made
17 : 2. I will come and make him a.
22 : 5. floods of ungodly men made
me a., Ps. 18 : 4. ⌈were a.
1 K. 1 : 49. all guests with Adonijah
2 K. 10 : 4. they were exceedingly a.
25 : 26. a. of the Chaldees, Je. 41 : 18.
1 Ch. 21 : 30. David was a. because of
Ne. 6 : 9. they all made us a. ⌊sword
Es. 7 : 6. Haman was a. before king
Jb. 3 : 25. that I was a. of is come⌈a.
6 : 21. ye see my casting down ; are
Jb. 9 : 28. I am a. of my sorrows
13 : 11. his excellency make you a.
21. let not thy dread make me a.
15 : 24. anguish shall make him a.
18 : 11. Terrors shall make him a.
21 : 6. when I remember I am a.
23 : 15. I consider, I am a. of him
32 : 6. I was a., durst not shew you
33 : 7. my terror not make thee a.
39 : 20. Canst thou make him a.
41 : 25. raiseth hims. mighty are a.
Ps. 56 : 3. time I am a. I will trust
65 : 8. They are a. at thy tokens
77 : 16. waters saw thee ; they were
83 : 15. make a. with thy storm⌊a.
119 : 120. I am a. of thy judgments
Is. 10 : 29. Ramah is a. ; Gibeah is
17 : 2. none shall make them a.,
Eze. 34 : 28. Mi. 4 : 4. Zph. 3 : 13.
33 : 14. The sinners in Zion are a.
41 : 5. the ends of the earth were a.
57 : 11. of whom hast thou been a.
Je. 26 : 21. Urijah heard it, was a.
30 : 10. none shall make him a.,
36 : 16. a. both one and oth.⌊46 : 27.
38 : 19. Zed-h said, I am a. of Jews
39 : 17. men of whom thou art a.
42 : 11. King of Bab-n of whom ye
16. famine whereof ye a. ⌊are a.
Eze. 30 : 9. to make the careless
Ethiopians a. ⌈Na. 2 : 11.
39 : 26. dwelt, none made them a.,
Da. 4 : 5. dream, which made me a.
8 : 17. when he came, I was a. and
Jon. 1 : 5. the mariners were a., 10.
Ha. 2 : 17. a. because of men's blood
3 : 2. I heard thy speech and was a.
Mal. 2 : 5. he was a. before my name
Mat. 2 : 22. Joseph was a. to go ⌈a.
14 : 30. saw wind boisterous, was
25 : 25. I was a., and hid thy talent
Mk. 5 : 15. and they were a., Lu. 8 : 35.
9 : 32. But they were a. to ask him
10 : 32. as they followed, were a.
16 : 8. nei. said any thing, they a.
Lu. 8 : 25. they being a., wondered
24 : 5. they were a., bowed faces
Jn. 6 : 19. Jes. walking on sea, they a.
19 : 8. Pilate was the more a.
Ac. 9 : 26. they were all a. of Saul
10 : 4. Cornelius was a., said, What
22 : 9. they saw light and were a.
29. a. aft. he knew P. was a Roman
Ga. 4 : 11. I am a. of you, lest in vain

Be AFRAID.

Ex. 15 : 14. The people shall b. a.
De. 2 : 4. they sh. b. a. of you, 28 : 10.
1 S. 23 : 3. we b. a. here in Judah
2 S. 22 : 46. Strangers shall b. a.
out of close places, Ps. 18 : 45.
Ne. 6 : 13. was hired that I should b.
Jb. 19 : 29. b. ye a. of the sword⌊a.
Ps. 27 : 1. of whom shall I b. a.?
Ec. 12 : 5. b. a. of that which is high
Is. 13 : 8. they shall b. a. : pangs
19 : 16. Egypt b. a. bec. of shaking
17. every one sh. b. a. in himself
20 : 5. they shall b. a. of Ethiopia
31 : 9. princes shall b. a. of ensign
51 : 12. who, that thou b. a. of man
Je. 2 : 12. ye heavens, b. horribly a.
Eze. 32 : 10. kings sh. b. horribly a.
Mi. 7 : 17. they shall b. a. of our God
Ro. 13 : 4. But if thou do evil, b. a.

Be not AFRAID.

De. 20 : 1. - a. of them, Jos. 11 : 6.
Ne. 4 : 14. Je. 10 : 5. Eze. 2 : 6(3).
Jos 1 : 9. Be strong, - a. ; G. is with
1 S. 28 : 13. k. said unto her, - a.⌊thee
2 K. 1 : 15. said unto Elijah, - a. of
19 : 6. - a. of the words which
thou hast heard, Is. 37 : 6.
2 Ch. 20 : 15. - a. of this great mul-
titude, 32 : 7. ⌈rich
Ps. 49 : 16. - a. when one is made
Pr. 3 : 25. - a. of sudden fear, neither
Is. 10 : 24. - a. of the Assyrian ; he
Is. 40 : 9. Jerusa., lift thy voice, - a.
Je. 1 : 8. - a. of their faces, for I am
42 : 11. - a. of king of Babylon (2)
Eze. 2 : 6. - a. of their words nor (3)
Jo. 2 : 22. - a. ye beasts of the field
Mat. 14 : 27. good cheer ; it is I ; -
a., Mk. 6 : 50. Jn. 6 : 20.
17 : 7. Jesus said, Arise, and - a.
28 : 10. - a. ; go tell my brethren
Mk. 5 : 36. unto ruler, - a., believe
Lu. 12 : 4. - a. of them that kill body
Ac. 18 : 9. to Paul, - a., but speak
1 Pe. 3 : 14. - a. of their terror, nei.

Neither, Nor, or Not be AFRAID.

De. 1 : 17. ye sh. - a. of face of man
29. Dread not, n-r b. a., 31 . 6.
7 : 18. Thou sh - a. of them, 18 : 22.
Jb. 5 : 21. n-r shalt thou b. a. of
destruction when ⌈of earth
22. n-r shalt thou b. a. of beasts
Ps. 3 : 6. I will - a. of ten thousand
56 : 11. I will - a. what man can do
91 : 5. Thou - a. for terror by night
112 : 7. He shall - a. of evil tidings
8. heart established, he shall - a.
Pr. 3 : 24. liest down, thou shalt - a.
Is. 8 : 12. neither fear ye, n-r b. a.,
12 : 2. I will trust and - a. ⌊44 : 8.
31 : 4. he will - a. of their voice
51 : 7. n-r b. ye a. of their revilings
Eze. 2 : 6. n-r b. a. of their words
Am. 3 : 6. Shall a trumpet be blown
and the people - a.? ⌈b. a.
Jn. 14 : 27. not troubled, n-r let it
Ro. 13 : 3. Wilt thou - a. of power?

Not AFRAID. ⌈es?

Nu. 12 : 8. n. a. to speak ag-t Mos-
2 S. 1 : 14. thou n. a. to destroy L.'s
Pr. 31 : 21. is n. a. of snow⌊anointed?
Je. 36 : 24. n. a. nor rent garments
He. 11 : 23. n. a. of king's com-t⌈a.
1 Pe. 3 : 6. long as ye do well, and n.
2 Pe. 2 : 10. n. a. to speak evil of dig-

Sore AFRAID. ⌊nities

Ge. 20 : 8. Abimelech told, men s. a.
Ex. 14 : 10. chil. of Israel were s. a.
Nu. 22 : 3. Moab was s. a. of people
Jos. 9 : 24. we were s. a. of our lives
1 S. 17 : 24. men fled fr. Goliath, s. a.
21 : 12. David was s. a. of Achish
28 : 20. Saul fell on the earth s. a.
31 : 4. his armourbearer s. a., 1
Ne. 2 : 2. Then I was s. a.⌊Ch. 10 : 4.
Eze. 27 : 35. their kings shall be s. a.
Mat. 17 : 6. disciples fell, were s. a.
Mk. 9 : 6. Peter wist not : they s. a.
Lu. 2 : 9. glory of L. shone, they s. a.

AFRESH.

He. 6 : 6. they crucify Son of God a.

AFTER. ⌈I have

Ge. 18 : 12. a. I am waxed old shall
26 : 18. stopped wells a. death of A.
33 : 2. Jacob put Leah and chil. a.
7. a. came Joseph near and Rach.
38 : 24. 3 months a. it was told Jud.
39 : 7. a. these things, master's wife
50 : 14. a. had buried his father⌈48.
Le. 14 : 43. a. hath taken stones (2),
20 : 6. soul that turneth a. such
27 : 18. if sanctify field a. Jubilee
Nu. 15 : 39. seek not a. own heart (2)
32 : 42. called it Nobah, a. own na.
35 : 28. a. the death of high priest
De. 6 : 14. shall not go a. other gods
12 : 15. whatso. thy soul lusteth a.
20 : 18. to do a. all their abomina-s
Jos. 7 : 25. a. they had stoned them
10 : 14. no day like that bef. or a. it
Ju. 16 : 22. hair to grow a. he was
Ru. 2 : 18. a. she was sufficed⌊shaven
1 S. 1 : 9. rose up a. they had eaten
5 : 9. a. they had carried ark about
11 : 7. Whoso. cometh not a. S. (2)
15 : 31. So Samuel turned a. Saul
18 : 30. a. they went, Dav. behaved
24 : 8. David cried a. Saul, My lord

1 S. 24 : 14. a. whom is king of Israel come? a. a dead dog, a. a flea (4)
2 S. 11 : 1. a. year was expired D. sent
13 : 23. a. two years Abs. invited
18 : 22. let me also run a. Cushi [ass
1 K. 13 : 23. a. had eaten, saddled
17 : 13. a. make for thee and son
19 : 11. a. the wind an earthquake
1 Ch. 8 : 8. a. he had sent them away
Ezr. 7 : 18. do a. will of your God
Ne. 9 : 28. a. they had rest, did evil
13 : 19 not be opened till a. sabb-h
Es. 2 : 12. a. she had been 12 months
Jb. 10 : 6. inquirest a. mine iniquity
30 : 5. cried a. them as a. a thief
42 : 7. a. L. had spoken these words
Ps. 28 : 4. give th. a. work of hands
68 : 25. singers went bef., players a.
Ec. 1 : 11. those that shall come a.
4 : 16. that come a. not rejoice in
11 : 1. shalt find it a. many days
Is. 11 : 3. not judge a. sight of eyes: neither reprove a. the hearing
44 : 13. maketh it a. figure of man
Je. 16 : 16. a. will I send for hunters
Eze. 46 : 12. a. his going one shall
17. a. it sh. return to prince [shut
19. a. he brought me thro. entry
Ho. 11 : 10. They shall walk a. Lord
Mat. 1 : 12. a. they were bro-t to Bab.
6 : 32. a. all these do Gentiles seek
17 : 1. a. six days Jesus taketh Peter
23 : 3. but do not ye a. their works
24 : 29. a. tribulation of those days
25 : 19. a. long time the lord cometh
26 : 2. Ye know a. 2 days is passover
32. a. I am risen will go bef. you
73. a. a while they said to Peter, Thou art one, Mk. 14 : 70. [rec-n
27 : 53. out of graves a. his resur-
Mk. 2 : 1. into Capernaum a. some
16 : 14. seen him a. was risen [days
19 a. Lord had spoken, received
Lu. 1 : 59. Zacharias, a. name of fath.
6 : 1. sec. sabbath a. first he went
7 : 11. day a. he went into Nain
12 : 5. Fear him, wh. a. hath killed
14 : 29 Lest a. he hath laid founda.
15 : 13. not many days a. younger
22 : 59. hour a. anoth. affirmed [son
23 : 26. cross, that he bear it a. Jes.
Jn. 1 : 35. next day a. John stood
13 : 12. a. he had washed their feet
27. a. the sop Satan entered into
Ac. 3 : 24. from Samuel and those a.
5 : 4. a. it was sold, was it not in
7. three hours a. his wife came in
7 : 45. fathers that came a. brought
10 : 37. a. baptism, wh. Jn. preached
41. who did eat with him a. he rose
13 : 22. a man a. mine own heart
36 Dav. a. he had served generat.
15 : 13. a. they had held peace, Ja.
16 : 10. a. he had seen the vision
19 : 21. a. these things were ended
20 : 29. a. my departing sh. wolves
24 : 14. a. the way they call heresy
25 : 13. a. certain days, Agrippa
26 : 5. a. most straitest sect I lived
27 : 14. not long a. arose tempestu-s
21. a. long abstinence Paul stood
Ro. 2 : 5. a. thy impenitent heart
7 : 22. delight in law a. inward man
8 : 5. they that are a. the Spirit
1 Co. 7 : 40. happier, if she so abide, a. my judgment [sort
2 Co. 7 : 11. ye sorrowed a. a godly
10 : 7. ye look a. outward appear-
11 : 17. I speak it not a. Lord [ance?
Ga. 1 : 11. gospel preached is not a.
2 : 1. 14 years a. I went again [man
3 : 17. law which was 430 years a.
Ep. 1 : 11. a. counsel of his own will
4 : 24. new man, which a. God is
Col. 2 : 8. a. the rudiments of world
22. a. com-ts and doctrines of men
3 : 10. a. image of him that created

2 Th. 2 : 9. whose coming is a. the working of Satan [Satan
1 Ti. 5 : 15. some are turned aside a.
6 : 10. which, while some coveted a.
Tit. 1 : 1. truth which is a. godliness
4. mine own son a. common faith
3 : 10. a. second admonition reject
He. 3 : 5. of things to be spoken a.
4 : 11. lest any fall a. same example
6 : 15. a. he had patiently endured
7 : 16. not a. law of carnal com-t, but a. power of an endless life
10 : 26. if we sin a. we have received
36. patience a. have done will of G.
11 : 8. place he should a. receive
12 : 10. chastened us a. own pleas.
2 Pe. 2 : 6. that a. sho. live ungodly
20. if a. have escaped pollutions
Re. 11 : 11. a. 3 days and half, Spirit
12 : 15. serpent cast water a. wom.
13 : 3. all world wondered a. beast

AFTER him. [seeth me
Ge. 16 : 13. Have I looked a. h. that
19 : 6. Lot went out, shut door a. h.
31 : 23. Laban pursued a. h. 7 days
Nu. 25 : 13. have it, and seed a. h.
Ju. 3 : 31. a. h. was Shamgar which
4 : 14. Barak went and 10,000 a. h.
10 : 3. a. h. arose Jair, Judged Isr.
12 : 8. a. h. Ibzan Judged Israel
11. And a. h. Elon Judged Israel
13. And a. h. Abdon judged Israel
Ru. 2 : 2. Let me glean corn a. h.
2 S. 15 : 16. k. went and househ. a. h.
18. Pelethites, Gittites, 600, a. h.
20 : 6. take servants pursue a. h.
7. went out a. h. Joab's men, 14.
23 : 9. a. h. was Eleazar one of the three mighty, 1 Ch. 11 : 12.
11. a. h. was Shammah, Hararite
1 K 1 : 35. Ye shall come a. h., 40.
2 K 5 : 21. Naaman saw running a.
Mk. 1 : 20. left father, went a. h. [h.
36. Simon and they followed a. h.
Ac. 19 : 4. which should come a. h.

See **After the FLESH, After HIM, After the MANNER, After this MANNER, WENT after, YEAR after YEAR.**

See COME, CUSTOM, DEATH, GO, HER, LAW, LUSTS, ME, ORDER, SIMILITUDE, THAT, THEE, THEM, THIS, TRADITION, US, YOU.

AFTERBIRTH. [a.
De. 28 : †57. her eye be evil tow. her

AFTERNOON. [eat
Ju. 19 : 8. they tarried until a., did

AFTERWARD, S.
Ge. 10 : 18. a. were families of Can-s
15 : 14. a. sh. come with great sub-
30 : 21. a-s Leah bear a dau. [stance
32 : 20. and a. I will see his face
38 : 30. a. came out his brother
Ex. 5 : 1. a. Moses, Aaron told Pha.
11 : 1. a-s he will let you go hence
34 : 32. a. all chil. of Israel came
Le. 14 : 19. a. he sh. kill burnt off-g
36. a. priest shall go in to see hou.
16 : 26. sh. wash his clothes, bathe, and a. come into the camp, 28. Nu. 19 : 7.–31 : 24.
22 : 7. he shall a. eat of holy things
Nu. 5 : 26. a. woman to drink water
12 : 16. a. people removed fr. Haz.
31 : 2. a. sh. be gathered to people
32 : 22. a. ye shall return, guiltless
De. 13 : 9. thine hand first upon him, a-s hand of the people, 17 : 7.
24 : 21. vineyard, not glean it a.
Jos. 2 : 16. hide, a. may ye go y-r way
8 : 34. a. he read all words of law
10 : 26. a. Joshua hanged them on
24 : 5. and a. I brought you out
Ju. 1 : 9. a. Judah went to fight [ed
7 : 11. a. thy hands be strengthen-

Ju. 16 : 4. a. he loved wom. in Sorek
19 : 5. with bread, a. go your way
1 S. 9 : 13. blesseth sacrifice, a-s eat
24 : 5. a. David's heart smote him
8. David arose a., cried aft. Saul
2 S. 3 : 28. a. David said, I guiltless
1 Ch. 2 : 21. a. Hezron went in to Ma.
2 Ch. 35 : 14. a. they made ready
Ezr. 3 : 5. a. continual burnt offering
Ne. 6 : 10. a. I came unto house of
Jb. 18 : 2. mark, a-s we will speak
Ps. 73 : 24. a. receive me to glory
Pr. 20 : 17. deceit is sweet, but a-s
24 : 27. Prepare thy work, a-s build
28 : 23. a-s shall find more favour
29 : 11. wise keepeth it in till a-s
Is. 9 : 1. a. did grievously afflict her
Je. 21 : 7. a. I will deliver Zedekiah
34 : 11. a-s caused servants to retu.
46 : 26. a. sh. be inhabited as of old
49 : 6. a. I will bring captivity of
Ez. 11 : 24. a-s Spirit took me in vis.
41 : 1. a. he brought me to temple
43 : 1. a. he brought me to the gate
47 : 1. a. he brought me to door of
5. a. he measured a thousand
Da. 8 : 27. a. I rose, did k.'s business
Ho. 3 : 5. a. shall Israel seek Lord
Jo. 2 : 28. a. I will pour my Spirit
Mat. 4 : 2. he was a. a hungered,
21 : 29. a. he repented [Lu. 4 : 2.
32. ye had seen it, repented not a.
25 : 11. a. came the other virgins
Mk. 4 : 17. a. when affliction ariseth
16 : 14. a. he appeared unto eleven
Lu. 8 : 1. a. went thro-t every city
17 : 8. a. thou shalt eat and drink
18 : 4. a. he said, Tho. I fear not G.
Jn. 5 : 14. a. Jes. findeth him in tem.
13 : 36. thou shalt follow me a-s
Ac. 13 : 21. a. they desired a king
1 Co. 15 : 23. a. they th. are Christ's
46. and a. that which is spiritual
Ga. 1 : 21. a-s I came into Syria [ed
3 : 23. faith wh. should a-s be reveal-
He. 4 : 8. not a. spoken of anoth. day
12 : 11. a. yieldeth peaceable fruit
17. ye know a. Esau was rejected
Jude 5. a. destroyed them believed [not

A'GABUS.
Ac. 11 : 28. stood up one named A.
21 : 10. from Judea, a prophet A.

A'GAG. [than A.
Nu. 24 : 7. his king shall be higher
1 S. 15 : 8. Saul took A. k. of Amalek
9. Saul spared A. and the best of
20. I have bro-t A. king of Amalek
32. A. said, Surely the bitterness
33. Samuel hewed A. in pieces [(3)

A'GAGITE.
Es. 3 : 1. Haman the A., 10.–8 : 3, 5. See HAMAN.

AGAIN. [Abel
Ge. 4 : 2. she a. bare his brother
4 : 25. And Adam knew his wife a.
8 : 10. a. he sent, Nu. 22 : 15. Ju. 12 : 14. 1 S. 19 : 21. 2 K. 1 : 11, 13.–19 : 9. Mat. 21 : 36.–22 : 4. Mk. 12 : 4, 5. Lu. 20 : 11, 12. Ph. 4 : 16. Phm. 12.
21. I will not a. curse nor a. smite
15 : 16. they shall come hither a.
18 : 29. spake yet a., Ju. 9 : 37. Es. 8 : 3. Jb. 29 : 22. Is. 7 : 10.–8 : 5. Lu. 23 : 20. Jn 8 : 12. Ac. 10 : 15. Re. 10 : 8.
24 : 20. she ran a. unto the well [to draw
26 : 18. Isaac digged a. wells of wat.
29 : 3. put stone on well's mouth a.
33. conceived a., 34, 35.–30 : 19.
30 : 31. I will a. feed flock [–38 : 5.
35 : 9. God appeared unto Jacob a.
37 : 22. deliver him to his father a.
38 : 26. Judah knew her a. no more
43 : 2. Go a., 13. Ju. 20 : 23, 28. 1 K. 19 : 20. 2 Ch. 25 : 10. Jn. 11 : 7. Ac. 15 : 36.

Ge. 43 : 12. money, carry it a. in hand
Ex. 4 : 7. Put hand into bosom a. (3)
10 : 29. will see thy face a. no more
14 : 13. ye sh. see them a. no more
Le. 13 : 6. priest look on him a., 7.
20 : 2. a. say to Israel, Whosoever
24 : 20. so shall it be done to him a.
25 : 48. sold, he may be redeemed a.
52. sh. give a. price of his redemp.
26 : 26. deliver bread a. by weight
Nu. 11 : 4. children of Israel wept a.
12 : 14. aft. that let her be received
22 : 25. Balaam smote her a.⌊a., 15.
34. if displease, I will get back a.
32 : 15. yet a. leave them in wildern.
De. 5 : 30. Get you into your tents a.
13 : 16. it shall not be built a.
15 : 3. Of a foreigner exact it a. ⌈L.
18 : 16. Let me not hear a. voice of
22 : 2. thou sh. restore it to him a.
4. help him to lift them up a. ⌈a.
24 : 4. former husb-d not take her
13. deliver pledge a. when sun do.
20. sh. not go over the boughs a.
30 : 9. Lord a. rejoice over thee
33 : 11. smite, that they rise not a.
Jos. 5 : 2. circumcise a. chil. of Isr.
Ju. 3 : 12. did evil a., 4 : 1.- 10 : 6. -
13 : 1. Ne. 9 : 28. ⌈peaceably
11 : 13. now restore these lands a.
16 : 22. the hair began to grow a.
19 : 7. theref. Levite lodged there a.
20 : 22. men of Isr. set their battle a.
1 S. 3 : 6. L. called yet a., Samuel
21. the Lord appeared a. in Shiloh
4 : 5. the earth rang a., 1 K. 1 : 45.
5 : 3. they set Dagon in his place a.
9 : 8. answered a., 17 : 30. Da. 2 : 7.
Zch. 4 : 12. Mat. 22 : 1. Mk 15 :
12. Ac. 11 : 9. ⌈Philistines
19 : 8. there was war a. with the
20 : 17. caused David to swear a.
23 : 4. David inquired of Lord yet a.
27 : 4. sought no more a. for David
2 S. 2 : 22. said a., 18 : 22. Mk. 14 :
70.- 15 : 12. Lu. 13 : 20. Jn. 8 :
21.- 9 : 26.- 10 : 7.- 12 : 39.- 20 :
21. Re. 19 : 3. ⌈a.
3 : 11. he could not answer Abner
34. the people wept a. over Abner
14 : 13. k. not fetch home a. ban-
16 : 19. a., whom sho. I serve?⌊ished
20 : 10. Amasa, struck him not a.
21 : 15. Philistines had war a. with
Israel, 18, 19. ⌈against Israel
24 : 1. a. the anger of the Lord was
1 K. 13 : 4. hand dried so he could
not pull it in a. ⌈priests
33. he made a. of lowest of people
19 : 6. did eat, laid him down a. ⌈a.
2 K. 4 : 29. if any salute, answer not
9 : 20. He came, cometh not a., 18.
19 : 30. remnant of Judah shall yet
a. take root, Is. 37 : 31. ⌈thems.
1 Ch. 14 : 13. Philist-s yet a. spread
2 Ch. 13 : 20. Nei. did Jerob. recover
24 : 11. carried it to his place a.⌊a.
32 : 25. Hez-h rendered not a. acc.
Ezr. 4 : 16. if city be builded a., 13.
9 : 14. Should we a. break com-ts
Ne. 13 : 21. do so a. I will lay hands
Jb. 10 : 16. a. shewest thys. marvel-
12 : 23. nations, straiteneth a.⌊lous
14 : 14. If a man die, sh. he live a.?
20 : 15. riches, he shall vomit up a.
Ps. 37 : 21. borroweth, payeth not a.
71 : 20. Thou sh. quicken me a. (2)
85 : 6. Wilt thou not revive us a.?
107 : 39. a. they are minished and
140 : 10. into deep pits, rise not a.
Pr. 2 : 19. none th. go to her return
19 : 17. that given will L. pay a.⌊a.
19. if deliver, thou must do it a.
23 : 35. I will seek it yet a. ⌈a.
24 : 16. just man falleth, riseth up
Ec. 4 : 11. a., if two lie together
8 : 14. a., there be wicked men, to

Is. 10 : 20. no more a. stay upon th.
11 : 11. Lord shall set his hand a.
49 : 20. chil. sh. say a. in thine ears
51 : 22. thou shalt no more drink a.
Je. 18 : 4. he made it a. anoth. vessel
19 : 11. th. cannot be made whole a.
31 : 4. a. I will build thee, O virgin : thou shalt a. be adorned
32 : 15. Houses, fields a. possessed
33 : 10. a. be heard in this place, 12.
13. flocks pass a. under hands of
Eze. 4 : 6. lie a. on thy right side
7 : 7. not the sounding a. of mts.
26 : 21. yet thou never be found a.
33 : 15. if wicked give a. th. robbed
47 : 4. a. he measured a thous-d (2)
Am. 7 : 8. I not a. pass by them, 8 :
13. prophesy not a. at Beth-el ⌊2.
8 : 14. shall fall and never rise a.
Jon. 2 : 4. I will look a. tow. temple
Zch. 2 : 12. Lord sh. choose Jerus. a.
8 : 15. So a. have I thought to do
Mal. 2 : 13. have ye done a., wi. tears
Mat. 4 : 7. Jes. said, It is written, a.
8. a., 5 : 33.- 13 : 44, 45, 47.- 18 :
19.- 19 : 24. Jn. 16 : 28. Ro. 15 :
11. 1 Co. 3 : 20. 2 Co. 12 : 19.
He. 1 : 5, 6.- 2 : 13 (2).- 4 : 7.- 10 :
30. Re. 19 : 3. ⌈things
11 : 4. Go and shew John a. those
13 : 44. a. kingd. of heaven, 45, 47.
18 : 19. a. I say, That if two agree
19 : 24. a. I say, It is easier for a
26 : 43. he found them asleep a.,
52. Put up a. thy sword⌊Mk. 14 : 40
72. a. he denied, Mk. 14 : 70. Jn.
27 : 50. when Jes. had cried a.⌊18 : 27
Mk. 2 : 1. a. he entered into Capern.
3 : 1. he entered a. into synagogue
4 : 1. began a. to teach by sea side
5 : 21. when Jes. was passed over a.
7 : 31. a., departing from Tyre, he
8 : 13. entering ship, a. departed
25. put his hand a. upon his eyes
10 : 1. peo. resort unto him a. (2)
24. Jesus answered a., Children
15 : 13. they cried out a., Crucify
him, Jn. 18 : 40. ⌈many
Lu. 2 : 34. for fall and rising a. of
4 : 20. took, he gave a. to minister
6 : 30. taketh thy goods ask not a.
34. sinners lend to receive as much
35. lend, hoping for noth-g a.⌊a.
9 : 39. it teareth him, he foameth a.
14 : 6. they cou. not answer him a.
15 : 24. my son was dead, is alive a.,
Jn. 1 : 35. a., next day, John stood⌊32.
4 : 3. He departed a. into Galilee
13. Whoso. drinketh .. sh. thirst a.
54. This is a. the second miracle
6 : 15. he departed a. into a mount
8 : 8. a. he stooped down and wrote
9 : 24. a. called they the man that
27. Wheref. would ye hear it a.?
10 : 19. There was a division thf. a.
11 : 8. disciples say, goest thither a.
38. Jesus, thf., a. groaning in hims.
12 : 22. a. Andrew and Phil. tell Jes.
28. glorified, and will glorify it a.
13 : 12. after was set down a., said
16 : 16. a., a little while, ye sh. see
22. I will see you a. ⌊me, 17, 19.
19 : 37. a. another Scripture saith
20 : 26. After eight days a. disciples
21 : 1. Jesus shewed himself a. to
Ac. 1 : 6. wilt thou restore a. kingd
7 : 26. would have set them at one a.
10 : 16. vessel up a. into heaven,
11 : 9. answered a. fr. heaven⌊11 : 10.
13 : 37. raised a., saw no corrupt-n
15 : 16. build a. tabern-e of David
17 : 32. We will hear thee a. of ⌊(2)
27 : 28. sounded a., found it fifteen
Ro. 4 : 25. raised a. for our justifica-n
8 : 15. not spirit of bondage a. to
9 : †20. who thou that answerest a.
11 : 23. God able to graff them in a.

Ro. 15 : 10. And a., Praise Lord all
1 Co. 12 : 21. nor a. head to the feet
2 Co. 3 : 1. we begin a. to commend?
5 : 12. we commend not oursel-s a.
Ga. 1 : 9. as before, so say I now a.
2 : 18. For if I build a. the things I
4 : 9. desire a. to be in bondage? (2)
19. I travail in birth a. until Ch.
5 : 1. be not entangled a. with yoke
3. I testify a. to every man⌈you a.
Ph. 1 : 26. rejoicing by my coming to
2 : 28. when ye see him a. rejoice
4 : 4. Rejoice in Lord, and a. I say
10. your care of me flourished a.
16. once and a. unto my necessity
1 Th. 2 : 18. we would have come a.
4 : 14. if we believe Jesus rose a.
Tit. 2 : 9. servants not answering a.
He. 1 : 5. a., I will be to him a Fath.
2 : 13. a., I will put my trust in him
4 : 7. a., he limiteth a certain day
5 : 12. need that one teach you a.
6 : 1. not laying a. foundation of
6. impossible to renew them a.
10 : 3. remembrance a. of sins every
30. a., Lord shall judge his people
Ja. 5 : 18. prayed a., heaven gave rain
1 Pe. 1 : 3. God hath begotten us a.
2 : 23. when reviled reviled not a.
2 Pe. 2 : 20. they are a. entangled
22. dog is turned to his vomit a.
Re. 10 : 11. must prophesy a. bef many
20 : 5. rest of dead lived not a. till
See **BORN again, BRING again, BROUGHT again, CAME again, COME again, LIE down, TURN again, TURNED again, WENT again.**
See BID, BUILT, DELIVER, MEASURED, RAISED, RISE, RISEN, TOOK, WORD.

AGAINST.

Ge. 4 : 8. Cain rose a. Abel his broth.
16 : 12. his hand be a. every man (2)
30 : 2. a. Rachel, Jacob's anger
40 : 2. wroth a. chief of butlers (3)
43 : 25. the present a. Joseph came
44 : 18. let not anger burn a. serv-t
Ex. 7 : 15. by river's brink a. he come
11 : 7. a. any of Isr. not a dog move
12 : 12. a. gods of Eg. will I execute
14 : 27. sea, Egyptians fled a. it
Le. 4 : 2. If sin through ignorance a.
com-ts of Lord (2), 22, 27. ⌈peo.
19 : 18. not bear grudge a. chil. of
20 : 3. I will set my face a. that
man, De. 29 : 20. ⌈they came
Nu. 10 : 21. that set up tabernacle a.
11 : 18. sanctify yours a. to morrow
16 : 3. gath-d a. Moses, a. Aa., 20 : 2.
38. these sinners a. their own souls
17 : 10. to be a token a. the rebels
25 : 4. heads of people hang a. sun
De. 22 : 26. riseth a. his neighbour
Jos. 11 . 20. that they come a. Israel
Ju. 20 : 34. a. Gibeah, 10,000 chosen
1 S. 14 : 20. man's sword a. his fellow
47. Saul fought a. Moab, a. Z (6)
27 : 10. David said, a. south of J. (3)
1 K. 16 : 15. encamped a. Gibbethon
22 : 35. king was stayed up in chariot a. Syrians, 2 Ch. 18 : 34.
2 K. 16 : 11. Urijah made it a. Ahaz
18 : 25. Go up a. this land (2)⌊came
19 : 22. a. whom hast exalted thy
voice? even Holy One of Israel
25 : 4. Chaldees were a. city round
2 Ch. 20 : 12. we have no might a.
this great company (2) ⌈Hez-h
32 : 16. spake more a. God and a.
19. Spake a. the God of Jerus. as
a. the gods, work of men's hands
34 : 27. heardest his words a. this
place (2) ⌈have war
35 : 21. a. the house wherewith I
Ezr. 4 : 19. made insurrection a. k-s

Ezr. 7 : 23. why wrath a. realm of k.
8 : 22. to help us a. enemy in way
Ne. 2 : 19. will ye rebel a. king?
Es. 5 : 9. full of indignat-n a. Mord.
Jb. 38 : 23. reserved a. the time of
trouble, a. day of battle and war
Ps. 62 : 3. How long imagine mischief a. a man? [king a. it (2)
Ec. 9 : 14. little city, came a great
Is. 7 : 1. tow. Jerus. to war a. it (2)
19 : 2. I will set Eg-ns a. Eg-ns;
sh. fight ev. one a. brother (5)
17. counsel of L. determined a. it
40 : † 10. God will come a. strong
Je. 1 : 18. brazen walls a. land (5)
23 : 30. am a. prophets th. steal, 31.
25 : 9. bring Neb-r a. this land (3)
13. Jere-h prophesied a. nations
26 : 9. all the peo. a. Jeremiah [(4)
34 : 7. army fought a. cities of J.,
37 : 18. What have I offended a.
thee or a. people (3) [tiles, 2 (2)
46 : 1. word of L. to Jere-h a. Gen-
2. a. Eg., a. army of Pha-h-necho
Eze. 3 : 8. face strong a. their faces
4 : 2. lay siege a. it, build fort a.
it, set battering rams a. it, (5)
13 : 20. I am a. your pillows [drach
Da. 3 : 19. visage was changed a. Sha-
6 : 5. not find occasion a. Daniel, 4.
7 : 25. speak gr. words a. Most High
Mi. 2 : 3. a. this family do I devise
Ha. 3 : 8. was thine anger a. rivers (3)
Zch. 9 : 13. thy sons, O Zion, a. thy
sons, O Greece [Lu. 4 : 11.
Mat. 4 : 6. lest dash foot a. stone,
10 : 35. I am come to set a man a.
his father, the daughter a. her
mother (3). Lu. 12 : 53 (6).
12 : 25. kingdom divided a. itself
(2). Mk. 3 : 24, 25. Lu. 11 : 17 (2)
32. Whosoever speaketh a. Son
of man; whosoever speaketh
a. Holy Ghost, Lu. 12 : 10. [it
16 : 18. gates of hell not prevail a.
20 : 11. murmured a. the goodman
23 : 13. ye shut up kingdom a. men
24 : 7. nation shall rise a. nation
(2). Mk. 13 : 8 (2). Lu. 21 : 10 (2).
26 : 59. sought false witness a. Jes.,
Mk. 14 : 55. [a. Jesus
27 : 1. priests, elders took counsel
Mk. 3 : 26. if Satan rise up a. himself he cannot stand, Lu. 11 : 18.
29. he that shall blaspheme a.
Holy Ghost [any
11 : 25. forgive if ye have aught a.
13 : 12. chil. shall rise up a. parents
Lu. 2 : 34. sign which sh. be spok. a.
7 : 30. reject counsel of G. a. thems.
12 : 52. three a. two, two a. three
53. ye stretched no hands a. me
15 : 18. I have sinned a. heaven, 21.
Jn 13 : 29. we have need of a. feast
18 : 29. what accusation a. this man
19 : 12. hims. a king speaketh a. Ch.
Ac. 4 : 14. could say nothing a. it
26. a. the Lord, and a. his Christ
6 : 1. murmuring of Grecians a. H.
11. blasphemous words a. Moses,
and a. God [place
13. ceaseth not to speak a. holy
8 : 1. great persecution a. church
9 : 5. hard to kick a. pricks, 26 : 14.
29. Saul disputed a. the Grecians
19 : 36. these cannot be spoken a.
38. if craftsmen have matter a.
25 : 8 Nei. a. the law of Jews, nor
yet a. Cesar have I offended (8),
18. a. whom when accusers [28 : 17.
27 : 14. arose a. it tempestu-s wind
28 : 22. sect, every where spoken a.
Ro. 1 : 18. wrath of God a. ungodlin.
26. natural use into that a. nature
4 : 18. who a. hope believed in hope
1 Co. 6 : 18. sinneth a. his own body
8 : 12. sin a. breth. ye sin a. Christ
2 Co. 10 : 2. I think to bold a. some
5. exalteth itself a. knowl. of God
Ga. 3 : 21. Is the law a. promises? [a.
5 : 17. flesh lusteth a. spirit, spirit
23. a. such there is no law [devil
Ep. 6 : 11. able to stand a. wiles of
12. we wrestle not a. flesh and
blood, but a. principalities, a.
powers (5) [a. any
Col. 3 : 13. forgiving, if have quarrel
1 Ti. 5 : 19. a. elder rec. not accusa-n
6 : 19. foundation a. time to come
He. 12 : 3. endured contradiction of
sinners a. himself [a. sin
4. not resisted to blood, striving
Ja. 2 : 13. mercy rejoiceth a. judgm.
1 Pe. 2 : 11. lusts which war a. soul
Re. 12 : 7. Michael fought a. dragon
19 : 19. to make war a. his army
See ANOTHER, BRETHREN,
CHILD, DAY, DISCIPLES, EN-
CAMP, ED, ETH, FOUGHT, HER.
See **CRY against, FIGHT
against, Against GOD.**

AGAINST him.

[h.
Nu. 5 : 12. if wife commit trespass a.
Jos. 8 : 14. liers in ambush a. h.
Ju. 1 : 5. they fought a. h. and slew
6 : 31. Joab said unto all that stood
32. Let Baal plead a. h. [a. h.
16 : 5. by what means prevail a. h.
19 : 2. concub-e played whore a. h.
1 S. 17 : 9. if I prevail a. h., and kill
28 : 9. Saul practised mischief a. h.
24 : 6. to stretch mine hand a. h.
1 K. 22 : 32. capt-s turned to fight a.
2 K. 17 : 3. a. h. Shalmaneser [h.
24 : 1. Jehoiakim rebelled a. h. [h.
1 Ch. 19 : 10. Joab saw battle set a.
2 Ch. 13 : 3. Jerob-m set battle a. h.
14 : 10. Then Asa went out a. h.
24 : 21. conspired a. h., stoned him
23. host of Syria came up a. h.
25. his own servants conspired a.
h., 33 : 24. [Jehozabad
26. these conspired a. h., Zabad,
25 : 27. conspiring a. h. in Jerus-m
35 : 20. and Josiah went out a. h.
36 : 6. a. h. came Neb., bound him
Es. 7 : 7. Haman saw was evil determined a. h. [prevail a. h.
Jb. 15 : 24. Trouble, anguish shall
18 : 9. the robber sh. prevail a. h.
20 : 27. the earth shall rise up a. h.
39 : 23. The quiver rattleth a. h.
Ps. 13 : 4. Lest mine enemy say, I
prevailed a. h. [causeth shame
Pr. 14 : 35. but king's wrath a. h.
Is. 9 : 11. adversaries of Rezin a. h.
Eze. 17 : 15. But he rebelled a. h. in
19 : 8. nations a. h. on every side
Da. 6 : 5. except we find it a. h. concerning the law of his God [h.
8 : 7. he was moved with choler a.
9 : 9. mercies tho. we rebelled a. h.
11 : 25. shall forecast devices a. h.
30. ships of Chittim sh. come a. h.
40. king of north shall come a. h.
Mi. 5 : 5. raise a. h. seven shepherds
Mk. 6 : 19. Herodias a quarrel a. h.
14 : 56. bare false witness a. h., 57.
Lu. 6 : 7. might find accusation a. h.
22 : 65. blasphemously spake a. h.
Ac. 25 : 16. concerning crime laid a. h.
19. questions a. h. of superstit-n
27. not to signify crimes laid a. h.
Re. 19 : 19. was a. h. th. sat on horse
See **Against HIM.**
See **Against ISRAEL.**
See **Against JERUSALEM.**
See **Against GOD, LORD.**
See JESUS, JUDAH, ME.

Over AGAINST.

Ge. 21 : 16. Hagar sat o. a. him, wept
Ex. 14 : 2. encamp o. a. Baal-zephon
25 : 27. o. a. border sh. kings, 37 : 14.
26 : 35. candlest o. a. table, 40 : 24.
Ex. 28 : 27. o. a. coupling th-f, 39 : 20.
Nu. 8 : 2. seven lamps sh. give light
o. a. candlestick, 3. Ex. 25 : 37.
22 : 5. from Egypt, they abide o. a.
De. 1 : 1. in plain o. a. Red sea [me
2 : 19. when o. a. chil. of Ammon
3 : 29. in the valley o. a. Beth-peor,
4 : 46.-34 : 6. [o. a. Gilgal
11 : 30. Canaan-s in the champaign
32 : 49. m-t Nebo o. a. Jeri., 34 : 1.
Jos. 8 : 33. half o. a. Gerizim, and
half o. a. Ebal [Lebanon
9 : 1. in coasts of great sea o. a.
18 : 17. o. a. going up of Adum-m
18. passed tow. side o. a. Arabah
22 : 11. built altar o. a. land of Cana.
Ju. 19 : 10. Levite came o. a. Jebus
20 : 43. trode them down o. a. Gib-h
1 S. 14 : 5. one o. a. Mickmash; the
other o. a. Gibeah [a. Eg.
15 : 7. Havilah to Shur that is o.
2 S. 5 : 23. come upon them o. a.
mulberry trees, 1 Ch. 14 : 14.
16 : 13. Shimei on hill's side o. a. Da.
1 K. 7 : 20. o. a. belly by network
39. he set the sea eastward o. a.
the south, 2 Ch. 4 : 10. [7 days
20 : 29. pitched one o. a. the other
1 Ch. 5 : 11. chil. of Gad dwelt o. a.
8 : 32. also dwelt with brethren in
Jerusalem o. a. them, 9 : 38.
24 : 31. cast lots o. a. brethren (2)
Ne. 3 : 10. repaired o. a. his hou., 23,
25. o. a. turning of the wall [28.
7 : 3. watch ev. one o. a. his house
12 : 9. brethren o. a., 24, 38. | 37.
Es. 5 : 1. Esther stood in court o. a.
king's house; king sat o. a. gate
Ec. 7 : 14. God hath set one o. a. oth.
Je. 31 : 39. line shall go o. a. it [21.
Eze. 1 : 20. wheels lifted o. a. them,
3 : 13. noise of wheels o. a. them
40 : 18. o. a. the length of gates
23. gate o. a. gate toward north
41 : 15. building o. a. separate pla.
16. galleries o. a. the door [10 (2).
42 : 1. chamber o. a. separate pla.,
3. o. a. pavement for outer court
7. wall that was o. a. chambers
45 : 6. o a. oblation of holy portion, 7 (2). 48 : 18 (2). [a. it
46 : 9. not by gate he came, but o.
47 : 20. till man come o. a. Hamath
48 : 13. o. a. border of priests
15. 5,000 left in breadth o. a. 25,000
21. o. a. the 25,000 of oblation,
o. a. the portions for prince (8)
Da. 5 : 5. wrote o. a. candlestick
Mat. 21 : 2. Go into the village o.
a. you, Mk. 11 : 2. Lu. 19 : 30.
27 : 61. other Mary o. a. sepulchre
Mk. 12 : 41. Jesus sat o. a. treasury
13 : 3. as he sat o. a. the temple
15 : 39. centurion wh. stood o. a. him
Lu. 8 : 26. Gadarenes o. a. Galilee
Ac. 20 : 15. came next day o. a. Chios
27 : 7. scarce were come o. a. Cnidus, we sailed o. a. Salmone
See PARENTS, PAUL, PROPH-
ESIED, PROPHESY, THEE,
THEM, THIEF, TRUTH, US,
WALL, WARD, YOU.
See **The PEOPLE, STAND
against, WENT against.**

A'GAR.

[A.
Ga. 4 : 24. one from Sinai, which is
25. For this A. is mount Sinai in

AGATE, S.

[Arabia
Ex. 28 : 19. an a., an amethyst, 39 : 12.
Is. 54 : 12. make thy windows of a-s
Eze. 27 : 16. Syria in thy fairs with a.

AGE.

Ge. 18 : 11. Abr-m and Sarah were
well stricken in a., 24 : 1. [years
47 : 28. whole a. of Jacob was 147
48 : 10. eyes of Israel dim for a.
Nu. 8 : 25. from a. of 50 cease waiting

Jos. 23 : 1. Joshua stricken in a., 2.
1 S. 2 :33. sh. die in flower of their a.
1 K. 14 : 4. eyes set by reason of a.
1 Ch. 23 : 3. Levites were numbered
from a. of thirty [years
24. service from the a. of twenty
2 Ch. 36 :17. him that stooped for a.
Jb. 5 : 26. to thy grave in a full a.
8 : 8. For inquire of the former a.
11 :17. thine a. clearer than noond.
Ps. 39 : 5. mine a. is as nothing bef.
71 : † 18. unto old a. and gray hairs
Is. 38 : 12. Mine a. is departed and
Zch. 8 :4. every man with staff for a.
Mk. 5 : 42. she of a. of twelve years
Lu. 2 : 36. Anna was of great a.
† 52. Jes. increased in wisd.and a.
3 : 23. Jesus about 30 years of a.
8 : 42. one dau-r twelve years of a.
Jn. 9 : 21. he is of a. ; ask him, 23.
Ac. 13 : † 36. Da. in own a.served G.
1 Co. 7 : 36. if she pass flower of a.
14 : † 20. in underst-g be of ripe a.
Ep. 4 : † 13. unto a. of fulness of Ch.
He. 5 : 14. meat to them of full a.
11 : 11. Sarah delivered when past
See OLD age. [a.

AGES. [a.

Ps. 145 † 13. Thy kingdom is of all
Is. 26 : † 4. in Lord is the rock of a.
Ep. 2 : 7. in a. to come might shew
3 : 5. in other a. not made known
21. glory in church through all a.
Col. 1 : 26. mystery been hid from a.
Re. 15 : † 3. just, true, thou King of

AGED. [a.

2 S. 19 : 32. Barzillai a very a. man
Jb. 12 : 20. taketh understand-g of a.
15 :10. grayheaded and very a. men
29 : 8. the a. arose and stood up
32 : 9. neither do the a. understand
judgment [is full of days
Je. 6 : 11. taken, a. with him that
Tit. 2 : 2. That the a. men be sober
3. The a. women be as becometh
Phm. 9. being such as Paul the a.

AG'EE.

2 S. 23 : 11. Shammuah son of A.

AGO.

1 S. 9 : 20. asses lost three days a.
2 K. 19 : 25. Hast not heard long a.
how I have done it, Is. 37 : 26.
Ezr. 5 : 11. house builded years a.
Is. 22 : 11. that fashioned it long a.
Mat. 11 : 21. they would have repented long a., Lu. 10 : 13.
Mk. 9:21. how long a. since this came
Ac 10 : 30. four days a. I was fasting
15 : 7. ye know that a good while a.
2 Co. 8 : 10. to be forward a year a.
9 : 2. Achaia was ready a year a.
12 :2. I knew a man above 14 yrs. a.

AGONE.

1 S. 30 : 13. three days a. I fell sick

AGONY. [prayed

Lu. 22 : 44. and being in an a., he

AGREE, ED.

Am. 3 : 3. Can two walk together
except they be a-d [quickly
Mat. 5 : 25. a. with thine adversary
18 : 19. if two of you sh. a. on earth
20 : 2. he had a-d with labourers
13. didst not thou a. for a penny ?
Mk. 14 :56. their witness a-d not, 59.
Jn. 9 : 22. Jews had a-d if any man
Ac. 5 : 9. How is it ye a-d to tempt
40. And to him they a-d [Spirit
15 : 15. to this a. words of prophets
23 : 20. Jews have a-d to desire thee
28 :25. when a-d not among thems.
1 Jn. 5 : 8. these three a. in one
Re. 17 : 17. to a. and give their king-

AGREEMENT. [dom

2 K. 18 : 31. Make an a. with me by
a present, Is. 36 : 16. [we at a.
Is. 28 : 15. with death and hell are
18. your a. with hell sh. not stand

Da. 11 : 6. King of north to make a.
2 Co. 6 :16. what a. hath temple of G.

AGREETH. [a.

Mk. 14 : 70. art Galilean, thy speech
Lu. 5 : 36. new a. not with the old

AGRIP'PA. [to C.

Ac. 25 : 13. A. and Bernice came un-
22. A. said, I would hear the man
23. when A. was come, Paul [men
24. Festus said, King A. and all
26. specially before thee, O king A.
26 : 1. A. said unto Paul, Thou art
2. I think myself happy, king A.
7. For which hope's sake, king A.
19. O king A., I was not disobed-t
27. King A., believest prophets ?
28. A. said, Almost thou persuadest
32. said A. unto Festus, This man

AGROUND.

Ac. 27 : 41. they ran the ship a.

AGUE. [ing a.

Le. 26 : 16. I will appoint the burn-

A'GUR. [Jakeh

Pr. 30 : 1. The words of A. son of

AH.

Ps. 35 : 25. a., so would we have it
Is. 1 : 4. a., sinful nation, laden wi.
24. a., I will ease me of adversar-s
Je. 1 : 6. a., L. God ! I cannot speak
4 :10. a., L. God ! thou hast deceived
14 : 13. a., L. God ! prophets say
22 : 18. shall not lament for him,
saying, a., brother ! or a., sister ! a., lord ! or a., his glory !
32 : 17. a., Lord God ! thou hast
made heaven [lord !
34 : 5. will lament thee, saying, a.,
Eze. 4 : 14. a., Lord God ! my soul
hath not been polluted [stroy Isr.
9 : 8. a., Lord God ! wilt thou de-
11 :13. a., L. G. ! wilt make full end
20 : 49. a., L. God ! they say of me
21 :15. a. ! the sword is made bright
Mk. 15 : 29. a., thou that destroyest

AHA. [temple

Ps. 35 : 21. against me said, a., a.,
our eye hath seen it
40 : 15. be desolate that say unto
me a., a., 70 : 3.
Is. 44 : 16. he saith, a., I am warm
Eze. 25 :3. saidst, a., ag-t my sanct-y
26 : 2. bec. Tyrus said, ag-t Jerus.
36 : 2. a., ancient places are ours [a.

A'HAB. [28.

1 K. 16 : 29. A. reigned 22 years (2),
30. A. did evil above all before him
33. A. did more to provoke L. (2)
17 : 1. Elijah said unto A., As Lord
18 : 1. Go, shew thyself unto A., 2.
3. A. called Obadiah gover-r of, 5.
6. A. went one way, Obadiah went
9. deliver servant into hand of A.?
12. when I tell A. he shall slay me
16. Obadiah went to meet A. and
told him : A. went to meet Elij.
17. A. said, Art thou he th. troub-
20. A. sent unto all Israel [leth (2)
41. Elijah said unto A., Get thee
42. A went up to eat and drink
44. say unto A., Prepare chariot
45. A. rode and went to Jezreel
46. Elijah ran bef. A. to entrance
19 :1. A. told Jezebel all Elijah had
20 : 2. he sent messengers to A. [34.
13. there came a prophet unto A.
14. A. said, By whom ? by yo. meu
21 :1. vineyard hard by palace of A.
2. A. spake unto Naboth, Give me
3. Naboth said to A., Lord forbid
4. A. came into his house heavy
8. she wrote letters in A.'s name
15. Jezebel said to A., Take viney.
16. A. heard Naboth was dead, A
18. Arise, go down to meet A [rose
20. A. said, Hast found me, O ene.
21. cut off from A. him, 2 K. 9 : 8.
24. that dieth of A. dogs shall eat

1 K. 21: 25. none like A. wh. did sell
27. when A. heard, rent clothes
29. Seest how A. humbleth hims.
22 : 20. Lord said, Who shall persuade A. that he go and fall, 2
Ch. 18 : 19. [written in
39. rest of acts of A. are they not
41. Jehosh-t began in 4th y-r of A.
2 K. 1 : 1. Moab rebelled after the
death of A., 3 : 5. [reign
3 : 1. Jehoram, son of A. began to
8 : 16. fifth year of Joram son of A.
25. In 12th year of Joram son of A.
28. Ahaziah with Joram son of A.
against Hazael, 2 Ch. 22 : 5.
29. to see Joram son of A., bec. he
was sick, 2 Ch. 22 : 6. [A.
9 : 25. when I and thou rode after
29. 11th year of Joram son of A.
10 : 1. A. had 70 sons in Samaria(2)
18. A. served Baal a little [did A.
21 : 3. Manasseh made a grove as
2 Ch. 18 : 1. joined affinity with A.
2. Jehosh-t went down to A. (2)
3. A. said unto Jehosh-t, Wilt go
Je. 29 : 21. saith the Lord, of A. son
22. make thee like A. whom king
of Babylon roasted
See AHAZIAH.

House of A'HAB.

2 K. 8 : 18. he walked as did - A.,
for daughter of A. was his wife,
27 (8). 2 Ch. 21 : 6.-22 : 3, 4.
9 : 7. thou shalt smite - A., thy
8. the whole - A. shall perish
9. will make - A. like hou. of Jerob.
10 : 10. which Lord spake conc. - A.
11. Jehu slew all - A. in Jez-i, 17.
30. hast done unto - A. acc-g to
21 : 13. over Jerus. plummet of -A.
2 Ch. 21 : 13. like whoredoms of -A.
22 : 7. Lord anointed to cut off - A.
8. Jehu, executing judgment upon - A. [- A.
Mi. 6 : 16. are kept, all the works of

AHAR'AH.

1 Ch. 8 : 1. Benj-n begat A. the third

AHAR'HEL.

1 Ch. 4 : 8. Coz begat families of A.

AHAS'AI.

Ne. 11 : 13. Azareel son of A., son of

AHAS'BAI = UR.

2 S. 23 : 34. one of the thirty ; Eliphelet son of A., 1 Ch. 11 : † 35.

AHASUE'RUS.

Ezr. 4 : 6. in reign of A. wrote they
Es. 1 : 1. in days of A. (this is A.
which reigned unto Ethiopia)
2. days when A. sat on the throne
9. royal house wh. belonged to A.
10. chamberlains in presence of A.
15. Vashti not performed com-t of
16. to people in provinces of A. [A.
17. A. commanded Vashti be bro-t
19. Vashti come no more before A.
2 : 1. wh. wrath of A. was appeased
12. every maid's turn to go in to A.
16. So Esther was taken unto A.
21. sought to lay hand on A., 6 :2.
3 : 1. did A. promote Haman [A.
6. destroy Jews thro-t kingdom of
7. 12th year of A., they cast Pur
8. Haman said unto A., a people
12. in name of A. was it written
7 : 5. A. said unto Esth., Who is he
8 : 1. A. give house of Ha. unto Es.
7. A. said unto Esther, I have given
10. Mordecai wrote in A.'s name
12. Jews to slay upon one day in
all provinces of A., 9 : 2, 20, 30.
10 : 1. A laid tribute upon the land
3. Mordecai, Jew, was next unto A.
Da. 9 : 1. In first year of Darius, son

AHA'VA. [of A.

Ezr. 8 : 15. river that runneth to A.
21. proclaimed fast at river of A.
31. we departed from river of A.

A'HAZ = A'CHAZ.

2 K. 15 : 38. And Jotham slept, A. reigned, 16 : 1. 2 Ch. 27 : 9.
16 : 2. A. did not that which was right, 2 Ch. 28 : 1. [him
5. besieged A., could not overcome
7. A. sent messeng-s to Tiglath-p.
8. A. took gold in house of Lord
10. A. went to Damascus, saw altar; A. sent to Urijah patt. of it
11. U-h made it ag-t A. came
15. A. comm-ded Urijah, burn, 16.
17. A. cut off borders of the bases
19. rest of acts of A. are they not
20. And A. slept with his fathers, 2 Ch. 28 : 27. [Hoshea
17 : 1. In twelfth year of A. began
18 : 1. Hezekiah son of A. began to
20 : 11 down in dial of A., Is. 38:8.
23 : 12. altars on the chamber of A.
1 Ch. 3 : 13. A. his son, Hez-h, son
8 : 35. sons of Micah were, A 9:41.
36. And A begat Jehoadah ; and
9 : 42. And A. begat Jarah [As-a
2 Ch. 28 : 16. A. send unto kings of
19. Lord bro-t Judah low bec. of A.
21. A. took away portion out of
22. this is that king A. [hou. of L.
24. A. cut in pieces vessels of hou.
29 : 19. vessels which A. cast away
Is. 1 : 1. vision of Isaiah in days of A.
7 : 1. in days of A. Rezin ag-t Jerus.
3. Isaiah, Go forth to meet A.
10. the Lord spake again unto A.
12. A said, I will not tempt Lord
14 : 28. In year A. died, this burden
Ho. 1 : 1. The word of the Lord in the days of A., Mi. 1 : 1.

AHAZI'AH. [51.

1 K. 22 : 40 Ahab slept, A. reigned,
49. said A son of Ahab unto Je-
2 K. 1 : 2. A. fell thro. lattice[hosh.
18 rest of acts of A. are they not
8 : 24. Joram slept and A. reigned
25 12th yr. of Joram did A. begin
26. 22 yrs. old A began, 2 Ch. 22: 2.
29. A. went to see Joram because sick, 9 : 16. 2 Ch. 22 : † 6. [Jehu
9 : 21. Joram and A. went out ag-t
23. Joram said to A., treachery,
27. when A. saw this he fled[O A.
29. 11th year of Joram began A.
10 : 13. Jehu met brethren of A. (2)
11 : 1. when mother of A. saw her son was dead, 2 Ch. 22 : 10.
2. sister of A. took Joash, son of A. (2). 2 Ch. 22 : 11. [ed
12 : 18. took things A. had dedicat-
13 : 1. In three and twentieth year of Joash son of A. [son of A.
14 : 13. took Amaziah son of Jeh-h,
1 Ch. 3 : 11. Joram, A. his son [A.
2 Ch. 20 : 35. Jehosh-t did join with
37. Bec. hast joined with A. L. hath
21 : † 17 never a son left save A.
22 : 1. inhabitants made A. king
7. destruction of A. was of God[(2)
8. sons of brethren of A. Jehu slew
9. he sought A.; they caught him. So the hou. of A. had no power

AH'BAN. [A.

1 Ch. 2 : 29. Abihail bare Abishur,

A'HER = AHI'RAM. [A.

1 Ch. 7 : 12. and Hushim, the sons of

A'HI.

1 Ch. 5 : 15. A. the son of Abdiel
7 : 34. sons of Shamah ; A., Rohgah

AHI'AH = AHIM'ELECH.

1 S. 14 : 3. A. son of Ahitub, priest
18 Saul said unto A., Bring ark

AHI'AH.

1 K 4 : 3. Elihoreph and A. scribes
1 Ch. 8 : 7. A and Gera he removed

AHI'AM. [Ch. 11:35.

2 S. 23 : 33. one of the thirty ; A., 1

AHI'AN. [Amam

1 Ch. 7 : 19. sons of Shemidah, A.,

AHIE'ZER.

Nu. 1 : 12. Of Dan., A. ; son of Ammishaddai, 2 : 25.-7 : 66.-10:25.
7 : 66. On tenth day A. offered, 71.
10 : 25. and over his host was A.
1 Ch. 12 : 3. came to David ; chief [was A.

AHI'HUD.

Nu. 34 : 27. prince of Asher, A. son of
1 Ch. 8 : 7. Ehud begat Uzza and A.

AHI'JAH. [boam

1 K. 11 : 29. prophet A. found Jero-
30. A. caught new garment on him
12 : 15. Lord spake by A. the Shilonite, 14 : 18.-15 : 29. 2 Ch. 10:
14 : 2. there is A. the prophet [15.
4. Jerob.'s wife went to hou. of A.
A. could not see by reason of age
5. L. said unto A., wife of Jerob-m
6. when A. heard sound of her feet
1 Ch. 2 : 25. sons of Jerahmeel, Ram,
11 : 36. valiant men ; A. Pelonite[A.
26 : 20. of Levites, A. over treasures
2 Ch. 9 : 29. acts in prophecy of A.
Ne. 10 : 26. those th. sealed, A., Anan
See BAASHA.

AHI'KAM.

2 K. 22 : 12. Josiah commanded A., Go, inquire of Lord, 2 Ch. 34: 20.
14. A went unto Huldah, proph-ss
Je. 26 : 24. hand of A. was with Jer.

Gedaliah son of AHI'KAM.

2 K. 25 : 22. made G. - A. ruler, Je. 40 : 7, 11. [- A.
Je. 39 : 14. committed Jer-h unto G.
40 : 5. Go back to G. - A., dwell
6. Then went Jer-h unto G. - A.
9. G. - A. sware unto them, Fear
14. G. - A. believed them not[not
16. G. - A. said, Thou not do this
41 : 1. princes of k. came unto G. - A.
2. the ten men smote G. - A.
6. Ishmael said, Come to G. - A.
10. had committed to G. - A., 43:6.
16. after he had slain G. - A., 4, 18.

AHI'LUD.

2 S. 8 : 16. Jehoshaphat son of A., 20 : 24. 1 K. 4 : 3. 1 Ch. 18 : 15.
1 K. 4 : 12. Baana son of A. ; to him

AHIM'AAZ. [A

1 S. 14 : 50. Saul's wife, daughter of
2 S. 15 : 27. return with A. thy son
36. A., Zadok's son, Jonathan
17 : 17. Jona., A. stayed by En-rogel
20. Where is A. and Jonathan ?
18 : 19. said A., Let me bear tidings
22. said A., let me run aft. Cushi
23. Then A. ran by way of plain
27. foremost is like running of A.
28. A. said unto king, All is well
29. Is Absalom safe ? A. answered
1 K. 4 : 15. A. was in Naphtali[9, 53.
1 Ch. 6 : 8. Zadok begat A., A. begat,

AHI'MAN. [Anak

Nu. 13 : 22. A., Talmai, children of
Jos. 15 : 14. Caleb drove A., Talmai
Ju. 1 : 10. slew A., Sheshai, Talmai
1 Ch. 9 : 17. porters were Talmon, A.

AHIM'ELECH.

1 S. 14 : † 3. And A. son of Ahitub
21 : 1. came David to A., priest : A. was afraid of David [8.
2. David said unto A., The king,
22 : 9. saw son of Jesse coming to A.
11. king sent to call A. and priests
14. A. answ-d, who faithf. as Dav.
16. Thou shalt surely die, A., and
20. one of sons of A. escaped [thy
23 : 6. when son of A. fled to David
26 : 6. Dav said to A., Who will[son
30 : 7. David said to Abiathar, A.'s
2 S. 8 : 17. Zadok and A. were priests, 1 Ch. 18 : † 16. [Itamar
1 Ch. 24 : 3. A. of the sons of Ith-
6. wrote them bef. Zadok, A. [A.
31. cast lots, in presence of Zadok,
Ps. 52.* David is come to house of [A.
See AHITUB.

AHI'MOTH.

1 Ch. 6 : 25. sons of Elkanah ; A. and

AHIN'ADAB.

1 K. 4 : 14. A., son of Iddo, had Ma.

AHIN'OAM.

1 S. 14 : 50. Saul's wife was A., dau-r
25 : 43. David took A. of Jezreel
27 : 3. David, his two wives, A. and
2 S. 3 : 2. firstborn, Amnon of A., See ABIGAIL. [1 Ch. 3: 1.

AHI'O. [18 : 7.

2 S. 6 : 3. A. drave new cart, 1 Ch.
4. A. went before the ark [fathers
1 Ch. 8 : 14. A., Shashak, heads of
31. his firstborn, Abdon, A., 9:37.

AHI'RA son of Enan.

Nu. 1 : 15. Of Naphtali ; A. -, renowned of, 2 : 29.-10 : 27.
7 : 78 On 12th day, A. - offered, 83.

AHI'RAM, ITES.

Ge. 46 : † 21. sons of Benj., A., Rosh
Nu. 26 : 38. of A. the family of A-s
1 Ch. 7 : † 12. the Hushim, sons of A.

AHIS'AMACH.

Ex. 38 : 23. Aholiab, son of A., an engraver, 31 : 6.-35 : 34.

AHISH'AHAR. [A.

1 Ch. 7 : 10. sons of Bilhan ; Zethan,

AHI'SHAR.

1 K. 4 : 6. A. was over the household

AHITH'OPHEL.

2 S. 15 : 12. Absalom sent for A.
31 A. is among the conspirators. O Lord, turn counsel of A.[of A.
34. mayest for me defeat counsel
16 : 15. Absalom to Jerus-m and A.
20. said Absalom to A., Give counsel, what we shall do [cubines
21. A. said, Go in unto fath.'s con-
23. counsel of A. was as if a man(2)
17 : 1. A. said, Let me choose 12,000
6. A. hath spoken aft. this man-r
7. counsel A hath given not good
14. better than the counsel of A.(2)
15. Thus did A. counsel Absalom
21. thus hath A. counselled ag-t
23. A. saw his counsel not followed
23 : 34. Eliam son of A. ; Gilonite
1 Ch. 27 : 33. A. was king's counsel-r
34. after A. was Jehoiada son of

AHI'TUB.

1 S. 14 : 3. Ahiah son of A., priest
22 : 9. Ahimelech son of A., 11, 20.
12. Saul said, Hear, thou son of A.
2 S. 8 : 17. Zadok son of A., 1 Ch. 6 : 8, 12.-18 : 16. Ezr. 7 : 2.
1 Ch. 6 : 7 Amariah begat A., 11, 52.
9 : 11. A. ruler of house of God, Ne. See AHIMELECH. [11 : 11.

AH'LAB.

Ju. 1 : 31. Neither the inhabitants of Accho, nor A., Helbah, nor of

AH'LAI. [Aphik

1 Ch. 2 : 31. children of Shishan ; A.
11 : 41. valiant men, Zabad, son of

AHO'AH. [A.

1 Ch. 8 : 4. sons of Bela, Naaman, A

AHO'HITE.

2 S. 23 : 9. Eleazar, son of Dodo, the A., 1 Ch. 11 : 12. [the A.
23 : 28. one of the thirty ; Zalmon,
1 Ch. 11 : 29. valiant men, Hai, the A.
27 : 4. over the course, Dodai, an A.

AHO'LAH, AHO'LIBAH.

Eze. 23 : 4 A., the elder, A-bah her sister. Samaria is A.. Jerusalem is A-bah [was mine
5. A. played the harlot when she
11. When her sister A-bah saw this
22. O A-bah I will raise thy lovers against thee [and A-bah ?
36. Son of man, wilt thou judge A.
44. went in unto A and A-bah.

AHO'LIAB.

Ex. 31 : 6. I have given with him A.
35 : 34. may teach, both he and A.
36 : 1. Then wrought Bezaleel and A.

Ex.36 :2. Moses called A. and ev. wise
38 : 23. with him was A., engraver
AHO'LIBAH. See AHOLAH.
AHOLIBA'MAH. [Man.]
Ge. 36 : 41. dukes of Esau ; duke A.,
du. Elah, du. Pinon, 1 Ch. 1:52.
AHOLIBA'MAH.
[Woman.]
Ge. 36 :2. Esau took wives ; A., dau.
of Anah, 18, 25. [36 : 14, 18 (2).
5. A. bare Jeush, Jaalam, Korah,
AHU'MAI. [begat A.
1 Ch. 4 : 2. begat Jahath, Jahath
AHU'ZAM. [pher
1 Ch. 4 :6. Naarah bare him A., He-
AHUZ'ZATH. [friends
Ge. 26 : 26. Abim-h, A., one of his
A'I or HA'I. [13 : 3.
Ge. 12 : 8. pitched tent, H. on east,
Jos. 7 : 2. Joshua sent men to A. (2)
3. let 3,000 men go and smite A.
4. they fled before the men of A.
5. men of A. smote about 36 men
8 : 1. Joshua, arise, go up to A. ;
given into thy hand king of A.
2. do to A. and her king as thou
didst unto Jericho, 9 : 3.-10 : 1.
3. Joshua arose to go ag-t A., 10.
9. abode betw. Beth-el and A. (2)
11. people pitched on north side
of A. ; valley betw. them and A.
12. 5,000 in ambush betw. Beth-el
14. k. of A. saw it, hasted [and A.
16. all in A. were called to pursue
17. was not a man left in A. or [A.
18. Stretch out the spear toward
20. men of A. looked behind, saw
21 they turned, slew men of A.
23. king of A. they took alive [26.
24. slaying all inhabitants of A. (2)
25. fell that day all the men of A.
28. Joshua burnt A., made it heap
29. king of A. he hanged [than A.
10 : 2. feared bec. Gibeon greater
12 : 9. Joshua smote king of A. one
Ezr. 2 : 28. out of captivity men of
Beth-el and A., 223, Ne. 7 : 32.
Je. 49 : 3. Howl, O Heshbon, A. is
AI'AH. [spoiled
2 S. 3 : 7. Rizpah, daughter of A.,
21 : 8, 10, 11.
See AJAH, RIZPAH.
AI'ATH.
Is. 10 : 28. He is come to A., is passed
AIDED. [brethren
Ju. 9 : 24. a. Abim-h in killing his
AI'JA.
Ne. 11 : 31. chil. of Benj. dwelt at A.
AIJ'ALON, AJ'ALON.
Jos. 10 : 12. stand, moon, in valley
19 : 42. lot for Dan, Aj. [of Aj.
21 : 24. Ai. for families of children
of Kohath, 1 Ch. 6 : 69. Aj. [Ai.
Ju. 1 : 35. Amorites would dwell in
12 : 12. Elon was buried in Ai.
1 S. 14 : 31. smote Philistines to Ai.
1 Ch. 8 : 13. fathers of inhab-s of Aj.
2 Ch. 11 : 10. Rehob-m built Zorah,
28 : 18. Philist-s had taken Aj [Aj.
AIJ'ELETH SHA'HAR.
Ps. 22.* To chief musician upon A.
AILED, ETH. [S.
Ge. 21 : 17. What a-h thee, Hagar?
Ju. 18 : 23. Micah, What a-h thee
1 S. 11 : 5. What a-h the people that
2 S. 14 : 5. What a-h thee? I am widow
2 K. 6 : 28. What a-h thee? she ans-d
Ps. 114 : 5. What a-d thee, O thou sea
Is. 22 : 1. What a-h thee, thou city
AIMING. [turned
1 Ti. 1 : † 6. wh. some not a. at have
A'IN. [A.
Nu. 34 : 11. Riblah, on east side of
Jos. 15 : 32. of Judah, Lebaoth, A.
19 : 7. second lot to Simeon, A. ;
Ashan, 1 Ch. 4 : 32. [1 Ch. 6 : † 59.
21 ; 16. chil. of Aaron, A., Juttah,

AIR.
De. 4 : 17. fowl that flieth in the a.
2 S. 21 : 10. nei. birds of the a. to rest
Jb. 41 : 16. no a. can come between
Pr. 30 : 19. The way of an eagle in a.
Ec. 10 : 20. bird of a. sh. carry voice
Mat. 8 : 20. birds of a. have nests ;
but Son, Lu. 9 : 58. [32. Lu. 13 : 19.
13 : 32. birds of the a. lodge, Mk. 4:
Ac. 22 : 23. threw dust into the a.
1 Co. 9 : 26. as one that beateth a.
14 : 9. for ye shall speak into the a.
Ep. 2 : 2. to prince of powers of a.
1 Th. 4 : 17. to meet Lord in the a.
Re. 9 : 2. sun and a. were darkened
16 : 17. poured his vial into the a.
See **FOWL, S, of the air.**
AIRED.
Je. 22 : † 14. I will build a. chambers
A'JAH or AI'AH.
Ge. 36 : 24. children of Zibeon ; Aj.
and Anah, 1 Ch. 1 : 40. Ai.
AJ'ALON. See AIJALON.
A'KAN or JA'KAN.
Ge. 36 : 27. chil. of Ezer are Bilhan,
Zaavan, A. ; † J. 1 Ch. 1 : 42.,
AK'KUB. [J. ; † A.
1 Ch. 3 : 24. sons of Elioenai. A. and
9 : 17. porters were A., Talmon,
Ahiman, Ne. 11 : 19.-12 : 25.
Ezr. 2 : 42. out of captivity ; chil-
dren of A., Ne. 7 : 45.
45. The Nethinim ; the chil. of A.
Ne. 8 : 7. A. caused people to under-
AKRAB'BIM. [stand
Nu. 34 : 4. your border shall turn to
ascent of A., Jos. 15 : † 3. [to A.
Ju. 1 : 36. coast was from going up
See MAALEH-ACRABBIM.
ALABASTER.
Es. 1 : † 6. beds upon pavement of a.
Mat. 26 : 7. a woman having an a.
box of, Mk. 14 : 3. Lu. 7 : 37.
AL'AMETH. [A.
1 Ch. 7 : 8. sons of Becher, Abiah,
ALAM'MELECH.
Jos 19 : 26. Asher, their border A.
AL'AMOTH.
1 Ch. 15 : 20. with psalteries on A.
Ps. 46.* To musician, A song upon
ALARM. [A.
Nu. 10 :5. When ye blow an a., 6. (2)
6. shall blow a. for their journeys
7. ye shall blow, but not sound a.
9. if ye go to war, blow an a. [you
2 Ch. 13 : 12. priests to cry a. against
Is. 16 : † 9. a. is fal-n upon thy fruits
Je. 4 : 19. heard, O my soul, a. of war
49 : 2. I will cause an a. of war to
Jo. 2 : 1. sound an a. in my holy m-t
Zph. 1 : 16. of a. ag-t fenced cities
ALAS. [my lord
Nu. 12 : 11. Aaron unto Moses, a.,
24 : 23. a., who shall live when God
Jos. 7 : 7. Joshua said, a., O Lord
Ju. 6 : 22. Gideon said, a., O Lord!
I have seen an angel [me low
11 : 35. a., dau-r! thou hast bro-t
1 K 13 : 30. mourned, a., my bro.!
2 K. 3 : 10. a.! L. hath called these
6 : 5. a., master! it was borrowed
15. a., master! how shall we do?
Je. 30 : 7. a.! for that day is great
Eze. 6 : 11. Smite and say, a.! for
all abominations of Isr [hand
Jo 1 : 15 a., for day of Lord is at
Am. 5 : 16. say in highways, a.! a.!
Re. 18 : 10. a.! a.! Babylon, 16, 19.
ALBEIT.
Eze. 13 : 7. a. I have not spoken
Phm. 19. a. I do not say thou owest
ALE'METH. [Person.]
1 Ch. 8 : 36. Jehoadah begat A. and
9 : 42. Jarah begat A. and Azma-h
ALE'METH or AL'MON.
Jos. 21 : 18. † to sons of Aaron, Ge-
ba, A. with suburbs, 1 Ch. 6 : 60. †

ALEXAN'DER. [of A.
Mk. 15 : 21. compel Simon, father
Ac. 4 : 6. Annas, A. were gathered
19 : 33. drew A. out of multitude
1 Ti. 1 : 20. Of whom Hymeneus and
2 Ti. 4 : 14. A. the coppersmith [A.
ALEXAN'DRIA, ANS.
Ac. 6 : 9. the synagogue of the A-s
18 : 24. Apollos, born at A. [28 : 11
27 : 6. centurion found ship of A.,
ALGUM trees. See ALMUG.
ALI'AH. See ALVAH
ALI'AN. See ALVAN
ALIEN, S.
Ex. 18 : 3. I an a. in a strange land
De. 14 : 21. mayest sell it unto an a.
Jb. 19 : 15. I am an a. in their sight
Ps. 69 :8. I am a. unto my mother's
Is. 61 :5. sons of a. your ploughmen
La. 5 : 2. turned our houses to a-s
Ep. 2 : 12. a-s from commonwealth
He. 11 : 34. turned armies of the a-s
ALIENATE, ED. [a-d
Is. 1 : † 4. have forsaken Lord, are
Eze. 23 : 17. her mind was a-d from
18. my mind was a-d from her
22. fr. whom thy mind is a-d, 28.
48 : 14. sh. not a. firstfruits of land
Ep. 4 : 18. a-d from the life of God
Col. 1 : 21. you that were sometime
ALIKE. [a-d
De. 12 : 22. unclean and clean shall
eat of them a., 15 : 22. [a.
1 S. 30 : 24. the spoil they shall part
Jb. 21 : 26. shall lie down a. in dust
Ps. 33 : 15. He fashioneth hearts a.
62 : † 9. they a. lighter than vanity
139 : 12. darku. and light a. to thee
Pr. 20 : 10. Divers weights and measures a. abomination to L. [a.
27 :15. rainy day, contenti-s woman
Ec. 9 : 2. All things come a. to all
11 : 6. whether both sh. be a. good
Ro. 14 : 5. another esteemeth every
ALIVE. [day a.
Ge. 7 : 23. Noah only remained a.
12 :12. will kill me, but save thee a.
50 : 20. to save much people a.
Ex. 1 :17. saved the men chil. a., 18.
22. ev. daughter ye shall save a.
22 : 4. If theft be found in hand a.
Le. 10 : 16. the sons of Aaron left a.
14 : 4. to take two birds a., clean
16 :10. scapegoat shall be presented
26 :36. upon them left a. of you [a.
Nu. 16 : 33. went down a. into pit
21 : 35. smote Og until none left a.
22 :33. had slain thee, saved her a.
31 : 15. Have ye saved women a.?
De. 4 : 4. are a. every one of you
5 : 3. are all of us here a. this day
6 :24. that he might preserve us a.
20 : 16. shalt save a. nothing that
32 : 39. I kill, I make a., 1 S. 2 : 6.
Jos. 2 : 13. ye will save a. my father
6 : 25. Joshua saved Rahab a.
8 : 23. king of Ai they took a. and
14 : 10. the Lord hath kept me a.
Ju. 8 : 19. if ye had saved them a.
21 :14. gave wives they had saved a.
1 S. 15 : 8. he took Agag the king a.
27 : 9. D. left nei. man nor woman
1 K. 18 :5. grass to save horses a. [a.
20 : 18. for peace or war, take a. (2)
21 : 15. Naboth is not a., but dead
2 K. 5 : 7. Am I G. to kill, to make a.
7 : 4. if they save us a. we live [city
12. we sh. catch them a., get into
10 : 14. said, Take them a. And
they took them a., slew them
2 Ch. 25 : 12. 10,000 left a. Judah
cast from a rock [a.
Ps 30 : 3. Lord, thou hast kept me
Pr. 1 :12. Let us swallow them up a.
Je. 49 : 11. thy fatherless children I
will preserve a. [that come
Eze. 13 : 18. will ye save the souls a.

Eze. 13 : 19. souls a. that sho. not live
18 : 27. doeth right, save his soul a.
Da. 5 : 19. whom he would, he kept a.
Ha. 3 : † 2. L., preserve a. thy work
Mk. 16 : 11. when they heard he was
a., believed not ⌈again, 32.
Lu. 15 : 24. my son was dead, is a.
24 : 23. angels which said he was a.
Ac 1 : 3. To wh. he shewed hims. a.
9 : 41. called widows, presented her
20 : 12. brought young man a. ⌊a.
25 : 19. Jesus, Paul affirmed to be a.
Ro. 6 : 11. a. unto God thro. Christ
13. as those a. from the dead and
7 : 9. I was a. without the law once
1 Co. 15 : 22. in Christ all be made a.
1 Th. 4 : 17. we a. be caught up, 15.
2 Ti. 2 : †26. who are taken a. by him
Re. 1 : 18. I am a. forevermore
2 : 8. which was dead, and is a.
19 : 20. both were cast a. into lake
See **KEEP alive.** ⌊of fire

Yet ALIVE.

Ge. 43 : 7. Is your father y. a.? 27.
28. our father in good health is
45 : 26. Joseph is y. a., 28. ⌊y. a.
46 : 30. let me die bec. thou y. a.
Ex. 4 : 18. see whether they be y. a.
De. 31 : 27. while I am y. a. ⌈21, 22,
2 S. 12 : 18. while child was y. a. (2)
18 : 14. while y. a. in midst of oak
1 K. 20 : 32. Is he y. a.? he my bro.
Ec. 4 : 2. more than the living y. a.
Eze. 7 : 13. is sold, altho. they y. a.
Mat. 27 : 63. deceiver said, while y. a.

ALL. [Adj.] ⌈host

Ge. 2 : 1. heavens finished and a. the
3 : 20. Eve, bec. mother of a. living
7 : 11. a. fountains of deep broken
19. a. the high hills were covered
11 : 6. they have a. one language
12 : 5. Abr. took a. their substance
14 : 11. they took a. the goods of
Sodom and a. their victuals
18 : 26. I will spare a. the place
20 : 18. Lord had closed a. wombs
24 : 10. a. the goods, 31 : 18. Nu. 31 : 9.
20. she ran, drew for a. his camels
26 : 15 a. wells Philistines stopped
30 : 32. I will pass thro. a. thy flock,
removing a. speckled, a. brown
35. a. she goats that were speckled
and a. brown among the sheep
31 : 12. see, a. the rams are speckled
16. a. the riches taken fr. our fath.
34. Laban searched a. the tent ⌈(2)
37. what hast found of a. thy stuff
32 : 10. not worthy of least of a. thy
mercies, of a. the truth ⌈drove
33 : 8. What meanest by a. this
13. if overdrive, a. flock will die
34 : 25. brethren slew a. the males
29. a. wealth, a. little ones took
35 : 4. a. strange gods, a. earrings
36 : 6. Esau took a. persons of his
house, a. his beasts, a. subst-e
37 : 35. a. his sons, a. dau-s rose
up to comfort him ⌈a. wise men
41 : 8. Pha. sent for a. magicians,
30. a. the plenty shall be forgot-n
35. gather a. food of good yrs., 48.
51. forget a. toil, a. father's hou.
55. Pha-h said unto a. Egyptians
56. famine over a. face of earth:
Joseph opened a. storehouses
57. a. countries to Jos. to buy corn
47 : 12. nourished a. fa-'s househ-d
14. gathered a. the money in Eg.
15. a. Egyptians came unto Jos-h
48 : 15. G. wh. fed me a. my life.
50 : 7. with Joseph a. elders of Eg.
Ex. 27 : 17. a. pillars sh. be filleted
19. a. vessels in a. the service, a.
pins shall be of brass, 38 : 31.
29 : 12. pour a. the blood, Le. 4 :
13. take a. the fat, Le. 3 : 9. ⌊7, 18.
33 : 19. a. my goodn. pass bef. thee
Ex. 36 : 9. curtains were a. one size
Le. 3 : 16. a. the fat is the Lord's
4 : 26. burn a. his fat upon altar, 19.
7 : 9. a. meat offering sh. be priest's
10 : 11. teach a. statutes L. spoken
14 : 8. sh. shave off a. his hair, 9. (2)
15 : 16. he shall wash a. his flesh
16 : 30. may be clean fr. a. your sins
19 : 24. 4th year a. fruit sh. be holy
37. sh. ye observe a. my statutes,
a. my judgments, 20 : 22.
23 : 14. statute forever in a. dwellings, 21, 31. ⌈meat
25 : 7. shall a. increase thereof be
27 : 25. a. estimations acc. to shekel
Nu. 3 : 41. instead of a. firstborn ;
4 : 16. oversight of a. tabernacle ⌊a.
27. a. service of sons of Gershonites in a. their burdens (4)
5 : 30. execute upon her a. this law
11 : 22. sh. a. fish of sea be gathered
13 : 3. a. those men heads of Israel
16 : 16. Be a. thy company before
18 : 21. chil. of Levi a. tenth ⌊Lord
28. offer unto L. of a. your tithes
25 : 4. Take a. heads of people, hang
31 : 9. took a. women of Midian
captives, took spoil of a. (4)
10. burnt a. their cities, a. castles
11. they took a. the spoil, a. prey
of men and beasts ⌈De. 2 : 14.
32 : 13. a. generat-n was consumed
33 : 52. shall drive out a. inhabitants, destroy a. pictures (4)
De. 7 : 15. L. will take away a. sickn.
13 : 16. gather a. spoil into street (2)
14 : 22. tithe a. increase of thy seed
16 : 15. bless thee in a. increase, a.
20 : 14. a. in city a. the spoil ⌊works
22 : 3. so do with a. lost things of
26 : 12. an end of tithing a. tithes
28 : 60. upon thee a. diseases of Eg.
29 : 20. a. curses sh. lie upon him, 27.
21. separate him out of a. tribes,
according to a. curses written
31 : 18. hide my face for a. the evils
34 : 11. in a. signs which the Lord
12. in a. that mighty hand, in a.
the great terror ⌈kings (3)
Jos. 10 : 40. Joshua smote a. their
11 : 19. a. other took they in battle
12 : 24. a. the kings thirty and one
13 : 2. a. the borders of the Philistines and a. Geshuri
21 : 44. a. enemies (2), Ne. 6 : 16.
Ps. 6 : 7. La. 1 : 21.-3 : 46.
23 : 14. Ye know in a. your hearts
not one hath failed of a. things
Ju. 8 : 29. slew 10,000 men, a. lusty,
a. men of valour ⌈his miracles
6 : 13. Gideon said, Where be a.
18 : 31. Micah's image a. the time
Ru. 2 : 21. until ended a. my harvest
3 : 11. a. city doth know thou art
1 S. 9 : 20. a. the desire of Isr.? Is it
not on a. thy father's house?
10 : 9. a. those signs came to pass
12 : 7. of a. righteous acts of Lord
13 : 20. a. Isr-s went down to Phil-
17 : 47. a. assembly sh. know ⌊ist-s
22 : 22. death of a. persons of thy
23 : 23. a. places where he hideth
31 : 12. a. the valiant went a. night
2 S. 15 : 18. a. Cherethites, a. Git-s
16 : 6. a. mighty men on his right
8. upon thee a. blood of hou. of S.
23. so was a. the counsel of Ahith.
22 : 23. a. his judgments before me
23 : 5. this is a. my salvation, a.
1 K. 1 : 49. a. the guests were afraid
8 : 66. glad for a. the goodness for
10 : 3. Sol-n told a. her questions
11 : 8. did for a. his strange wives
28. made him ruler over a. charge
14 : 26. Shishak took a. shields of
15 : 12. Asa removed a. idols ⌊gold
19 : 18. a. knees wh. have not bowed
1 K. 22 : 22. lying spirit in a. proph-s
2 K. 4 : 13. for us with a. this care
5 : 12. better than a. waters of Isr.?
8 : 4. tell a. things Elisha hath done
10 : 19. call unto me a. the priests of
11 : 1. destroyed a. seed royal ⌊Baal
19 : 19. that a. kingdoms may know
24. I have dried up a. rivers of
23 : 26. a. provocations Manasseh
1 Ch. 6 : 49. a. work of place most
12 : 15. overflown a. his banks ⌊holy
29 : 16. a. this store is a. thine
2 Ch. 32 : 7. Be not afraid for a. mul-
33 : 7. Jerus. bef. a. tribes ⌊titude
14. put captains in a. fenced cities
15. a. the altars in Jerus. cast out
Ezr. 5 : 7. Unto Darius, k., a. peace
7 : 16. a. the gold in a. province of
21. a decree to a. the treasurers
25. judges which may judge a.
peo., a. such as know laws of G.
Ne. 7 : 60. a. the Nethinim were 392
73. a. Israel dwelt in their cities
10 : 33. charge ourselves for a. the
11 : 18. a. Levites in city 284 ⌊work
13 : 6. a. this time I not at Jerus.
30. cleansed I them fr. a. strang-s
Es. 2 : 17. favour more than a. virg.
Jb 19 : 19. a. my friends abhorred
31 : 4. he count a. my steps? ⌊me
12. wou. root out a. mine increase
33 : 11. he marketh a. my paths
34 : 21. and he seeth a. his goings
36 : 19. nor a. the forces of strength
Ps. 9 : 14. shew forth a. thy praise
10 : 4. God not in a. his thoughts
5. a. enemies, he puffeth at them
16 : 3. saints in wh. a. my delight
20 : 4. Lord, fulfil a. thy counsel, 5.
25 : 22. Redeem Isr. out of a. troub-s
34 : 4. delivered from a. my fears
39 : 12. sojourner as a. my fathers
41 : 3. make a. his bed in sickness
45 : 8. a. thy garments smell of m-h
56 : 5. a. their thoughts are ag. me
64 : 10. a. the upright shall glory
69 : 19. mine adversaries a. bef. thee
74 : 8. burned up a. the synagog-s
76 : 9. G. arose to save a. the meek
87 : 7. a. my springs are in thee
94 : 15. a. the upright sh. follow it
105 : 36. He smote chief of a. their
116 : 12. What for a. his benefits
119 : 14. as much as in a. riches
99. more than a. my teachers
132 : 1. David and a. his afflictions
Pr. 1 : 25. set at naught a. my coun-
3 : 9. firstfruits of a. increase ⌊sel
17. a. her paths are peace ⌈st-g
4 : 7. with a. thy getting get under-
31 : 8. a. such as are appointed to
21. a. her household with scarlet
Ec. 2 : 23. a. his days are sorrows ⌈go
5 : 16. in a. points as he came, sh.
7 : 28. woman among a. those not
Can. 4 : 4. bucklers, a. of mighty men
14. with a. trees, a. chief spices
8 : 7. if give a. substance for love
Is 2 : 13. day of L. upon a. cedars, a.
24 : 7. a. the merryhearted do sigh
39 : 2. shewed a. hou. of armour (3)
40 : 2. rec-d double for a. her sins
44 : 11. a. his fellows be ashamed
49 : 11. will make a. my mts. a way
60 : 21. people shall be a. righteous
63 : 9. in a. their affliction he was
Je. 8 : 2. bones of kings bef. a. host
3. death be chosen by a. residue
6 : 28. they are a. corrupters (2)
10 : 20. a. my cords are broken
12 : 14. L. ag. a. mine evil neighb-s
17 : 3. a. thy treasures to the spoil
18 : 23. knowest a. their counsel.
20 : 4. a terror to a. thy friends
5. I will deliver a. strength of city,
a. treasures (4) ⌈friends
6. there shalt die, thou and a. thy

Je. 20 : 10. a. my familiars watched
22 : 20. a. thy lovers are destroyed
22. wind sh. eat up a. thy pastors
28 : 4. bring king with a. captives
30 : 14. a. thy lovers forgotten thee
31 : 37. cast off a. seed of Israel [(2)
32 : 42. bring a. the good promised
33 : 9. shall hear a. the good I do, fear for a. the goodness (3)
38 : 23. shall bring out a. thy wives
41 : 11. when a. the captains heard
42 : 2. pray for us, a. this remnant
48 : 37. upon a. the hands cuttings
49 : 17. shall hiss at a. the plagues
32. I will scatter into a. winds, I will bring calamity from a. sides
50 : 27. Slay a. her bullocks [midst
51 : 47. a. her slain shall fall in the
52 : 14. a. the army break a. walls
30. captive were 4,600 ; a. persons
La. 1 : 2. among a. her lovers none
4. Zion ; a. her gates are desolate
15. trodden under foot a. mighty
3 : 51. of a. daughters of my city
60. Thou hast seen a. their vengeance against me (2) [mts.
Eze. 6 : 13. slain be in a. the tops of
7 : 17. a. hands shall be feeble, a. knees shall be weak [ness upon a.
18. shame be upon a. faces, bald-
13 : 18. sew pillows to a. armholes
17 : 21. a. his fugitives, a. bands
18 : 14. seeth a. his father's sins
21. If wicked turn from a. his sins and keep a. my statutes
20 : 43. remember a. your doings
21 : 15. sword against a. their gates
23 : 7. with a. idols defiled herself
30 : 8. a. her helpers be destroyed
31 : 12. in a. valleys branches fallen
32 : 16. lament for a. her multitude
36 : 25. fr. a. your idols cleanse you
43 : 11. shew them a. the forms, a. ordinances, a. laws (6), 44 : 5.
48 : 20. a. the oblation be 25,000
Da. 1 : 17. these four skill in a. learning ; Daniel had understanding in a. visions and
20. in a. matters better than a. magicians in a. his realm [8.
2 : 12. a. wise men, 48.-4 : 6, 18.-5:
3 : 5. what time ye hear a. kinds of music fall down, 7, 10, 15. [3.
2. gather judges, a. the rulers,
6 : 7. a. presidents have consulted
7 : 19. beast diverse fr. a. others, 7.
23. fourth diverse fr. a. kingdoms
27. a. dominions shall obey him
11 : 2. fourth be richer than they a.
Ho. 2 : 11. cause a. her mirth to cease, a. her solemn feasts
9 : 15. a. their princes are revolters
12 : 8. in a. my labours none iniquity
Am. 1 : 11. he did cast off a. pity
5 : 16. Wailing sh. be in a. streets ; shall say in a. highways, Alas !
8 : 10. a. your songs into lament-n
9 : 10. a. sinners shall die by sword
Ob. 15. day of L. near upon a. heath.
Na. 2 : 9. glory out of a. furniture
10. and much pain is in a. loins
3 : 10. children dashed at top of a. streets : a. her gr. men bound
12. a. thy strongholds like fig trees
Zph. 3 : 11. not be ashamed for a. thy
Zch. 10 : 11. a. the deeps dry [doings
12 : 14. a. the families that remain
Mal. 3 : 10. Bring ye a. tithes into
4 : 1. a. the proud shall be stubble
Mat. 2 : 4. gathered a. chief priests
3 : 15. to fulfil a. righteousness
4 : 23. about a. Galilee, Mk. 1 : 39.
6 : 29. Sol. in a. his glory, Lu. 12 : 27.
10 : 30. hairs a. numb-d, Lu. 12 : 7.
18 : 32. I forgave thee a. that debt
22 : 40. On two com-ts hang a. law
23 : 35. upon you a. righteous blo.

Mat. 24 : 47. ruler over a. his goods
25 : 7. Then a. those virgins arose
31. a. the holy angels with him
26 : 1. finished a. sayings, Lu. 7 : 1.
35. Likewise said a. the disciples
59. a. the counsel sought false witness, Mk. 14 : 55. [counsel
27 : 1. a. the chief priests took
Mk. 4 : 13. how know a. parables ?
32. becom-h greater than a. herbs
5 : 12. a. the devils besought him
33. the woman told him a. truth
7 : 19. into draught, purging a.
23. a. these evil things [meats ?
12 : 33. to love him with a. the heart is more than a. burnt offerings and sacrifices (5) [ing
44. but she did cast in a. her liv-
Lu. 1 : 6. both walking in a. com-ts
4 : 5. devil shewed him a. kingdoms
13. devil had ended a. temptation
14. fame of him thro. a. region
8 : 43. a. her living on physicians
9 : 1. gave them power ov. a. devils
10 : 19. power over a. power of ene.
11 : 22. stronger taketh a. armour
12 : 18. will bestow a. my fruits
13 : 17. a. adversaries ashamed (3)
15 : 1. drew near a. publicans to
21 : 15. a. your adversaries not able
29. Behold fig tree and a. trees [off
23 : 49. a. his acquaintance stood
24 : 27. expounded in a. Scriptures
Jn. 5 : 22. a. judgment unto the Son
16 : 13. will guide you into a. truth
17 : 10. a. mine are thine, and thine
Ac. 1 : 18. a. his bowels gushed out
19. known unto a. dwellers at Jer.
21. companied with us a. the time
3 : 18. shewed by a. his proph-s, 21.
25. in thy seed a. kindreds blessed
4 : 29. with a. boldness may speak
5 : 11. great fear upon a. church
21. called a. the senate of Israel
23. the prison shut with a. safety
7 : 10. out of a. afflictions ; Pha. made him governor over a. his
14. Joseph called a. his kindred
9 : 39. a. the widows stood weeping
10 : 2. feared God with a. his house
22. of good report among a. nation
12 : 11. from a. expectation of Jews
13 : 10. O full of a. subtlety and a. mischief, thou enemy of a.
22. which shall fulfil a. my will
15 : 17. a. Gentiles upon whom my
16 : 26. a. doors were opened [name
33. was baptized, he and a. his [8.
34. believing with a. his hou., 18 :
17 : 11. rec-d word with a. readiness
15. to come to him with a. speed
21. a. Athenians spent their time
22. in a. things too superstitious
26. dwell on a. the face of earth (2)
18 : 17. a. Greeks took Sosthenes
19 : 27. whom a. Asia worshippeth
20 : 18. what manner at a. seasons
19. serving Lord with a. humility
27. not shunned to declare a. coun.
28. Take heed theref. unto a. flock
21 : 18. a. the elders were present
22 : 5. a. the estate of elders [pear
30. com-ded a. their council ap-
23 : 1. I lived in a. good conscience
26 : 3. thee expert in a. customs
27 : 20. a. hope was then taken aw
28 : 31. teaching with a. confidence
Ro. 15 : 13. God fill you with a. joy
16 : 4. not only I, but a. churches
1 Co. 1 : 5. ye are enriched in a. utterance, a. knowledge [a.
9 : 24. they which run in a race run
10 : 1. a. our fathers were under the cloud, a. passed through the sea
2. And were a. baptized unto Mos.
3. did a. eat same spiritual meat
4. did a. drink same spirit-l drink

1 Co. 13 : 2. tho. I underst-d a. mysteries, tho. I have a. faith (3)
15 : 7. seen of James : then of a. apostles [a. rule (2)
24. when he shall have put down
25. reign till he hath put a. ene-s
2 Co. 1 : 3. the God of a. comfort
4. comforted us in a. tribulation
20. a. the promises of God are yea
7 : 4. I am joyful in a. tribulations
9 : 8. God able to make a. grace abound, that ye having a. (3)
11. enriched to a. bountifulness
10 : 6. in a readiness to revenge a. disobedience [patience
12 : 12. wrought among you in a.
Ga. 5 : 14. a. the law is fulfilled in
6 : 6. communicate in a. good thi-s
Ep. 1 : 3. with a. spiritual blessings
15. heard of y-r love unto a. saints
2 : 21. In whom a. the building
3 : 18. to comprehend with a. saints
4 : 31. Let a. bitterness be put away with a. malice [goodness
5 : 9. the fruit of the Spirit is in a.
6 : 16. to quench a. the fiery darts
18. Praying with a. prayer, watching with a. perseverance for a.
Ph. 1 : 9. love abound in a. judgm-t
13. my bonds are manifest in a. the palace (2) [magnified
20. that wi. a. boldness, Christ be
2 : 29. Receive him with a. gladn-s
4 : 7. peace wh. passeth a. underst-g
19. my God sh. supply a. your need
Col. 1 : 10. walk worthy, unto a. ple.
11. Strengthened with a. might, unto a. patience and [ance
2 : 2. unto a. riches of full assur-
10. which is head of a. principality
13. forgiven you a. trespasses
19. Head, from which a. the body
22. (Which a. are to perish with)
4 : 7. a. my state Tychicus declar-
12. complete in a. the will of God
1 Th. 3 : 7. comforted in a. our afflic.
13. coming of Lord with a. saints
4 : 10. a. brethren in a. Macedonia
5 : 22. Abstain fr. a. appearance of
2 Th. 1 : 4. patience in a. persec-nt-s
11. God fulfil a. the good pleasure
3 : 16. L give you peace by a. means
1 Ti. 1 : 15. faithful saying, worthy of a. acceptation, 4 : 9. [fering
16. might shew forth a. longsuf-
3 : 4. in subjection with a. gravity
5 : 2. the younger, with a. purity
6 : 1. masters worthy of a. honour
2 Ti. 4 : 17. a. Gentiles might hear
Tit. 2 : 10. shewing a. good fidelity
14. might redeem us fr. a. iniquity
He. 1 : 6. let a. angels worship him
2 : 11. he and they are a. of one
15. fear of death, a. their lifetime
3 : 2. Moses faithful in a. his hou., 5.
4 : 4. rest 7th day from a. his works
15. in a. points tempted as we are
6 : 16. an oath, end of a. strife [less
7 : 7. without a. contradiction the
9 : 21. he sprinkled a. the vessels
Ja. 1 : 2. count it a. joy when ye fall
1 Pe. 2 : 1. Wheref., laying aside a. malice, a. guile, a. evil speak-gs
18. servants be subject wi. a. fear
5 : 7. Casting a. your care upon him
10. God of a. grace make you perf.
2 Pe. 3 : 16. in a. his epistles speak-g
Jude 15. to convince of a. their ungodly deeds, and of a. hard [he
Re. 2 : 23. a. churches sh. know I am
7 : 4. 144,000 of a. tribes of Israel
11. a. angels stood about throne
17. shall wipe away a. tears, 21 : 4
8 : 3. incense wi. prayers of a. saints
7. trees and a. green grass burnt
11 : 6. smite earth with a. plagues
13 : 12. exercise a. power of 1st beast

Re. 18 : 12. gold and a. thyine wood
14. a. things goodly are departed
17. a. company in ships stood afar
21 : 8. a. liars sh. have their part in

Above ALL. [tle

Ge. 3 : 14. thou art cursed a. a. cat-
Nu. 12 : 3. Moses meek a. a. men
2 Ch. 11 : 21. loved Maachah a. a.
Ne. 9 : 5. exalted a. a. blessing[his
Es. 2 : 17. loved Esther a. a. women
Ps. 97 : 9. Lord high a. a. earth (2)
138 : 2. thy word a. a. thy name
Pr. 4 : † 23. keep heart a. a. keeping
Eze. 16 : 43. not commit lewdness a.
a. thine abominations [trees
31 : 5. his height was exalted a. a.
Lu. 13 : 2. sinners a. a. Galileans
4. those 18, sinners a. a. men?
Ep. 1 : 21. Ch. far a. a. principality
4 : 10. ascended far a. a. heavens
See **Above all THAT. All THINGS. According to** or **unto ALL.**

Nu. 9 : 3. keep 14th day - a. rites(2) 12.
De. 26 : 13. to widow - a. thy com-ts,
31 : 5. do unto them - a. com-ts[14.
Ju. 8 : 35. - a. the goodness shewed
1 S. 8 : 8. - a. works they have done
23 : 20. O king, come - a. desire of
25 : 30. done - a. the good spoken
1 K. 6 : 38. hou. finished - a. fashion
21 : 26 idols - a. things as Amorites
2 K. 16 : 10. pattern of altar - a. [ed
17 : 13. Turn ye - a. law I command-
21 : 8. do - a. law Mos. commanded
23 : 19. to them - a. acts done in B.
2 Ch. 2 : † 16. cut wood - a. thy need
6 : 33. do - a. that stranger calleth
Je. 21 : 2. if Lord deal with us - a. his
Eze. 18 : 24. when righteous doeth -
a. the abominations [beseech
Da. 9 : 16. - a. thy righteousness, I
See **According to all THAT.**
See LAW, VISION, WORDS.

Them ALL or **ALL them.**

Ezr. 1 : 5. a. t. whose spirit G. raised
8 : 22. wrath ag. a. t. that forsake
Ec. 2 : 14. I perceived one event hap-
peneth to t. a., 9 : 11. [t. a.
11 : 8. if many years, and rejoice in
Is. 8 : 12. A confederacy to a. t. [ered
44 : 11. workmen, let t. a. be gath-
Zph. 1 : 18. speedy riddance of a. t.
2 Ti. 4 : 8. a. t. that love his appear-g
He. 13 : 24. Salute a. t. that have
See **All them THAT.** [rule
See **THEM all, All of THEM.**

These ALL or **ALL these.**

Ge. 49 : 28. a. t. are twelve tribes of
Le. 6 : 3. in any of a. t. sinning[Isr.
1 Ch. 2 : 23. a. t. belonged to sons of
5 : 17. a. t. by genealogies[Machir
7 : 8. a. t. are the sons of Becher
2 Ch. 21 : 2. a. t. sons of Jehosh-h
Ezr. 1 : 11. a. t. Sheshbazzar bring
Jb. 12 : 9. Who knoweth not in a. t.
Is. 49 : 18. a. t. gather themselves
Ha. 2 : 6. Sh. not a. t. take parable
Zch. 8 : 17. a. t. are things I hate
Mat. 24 : 8. a. t. begin-g of sorrows
Ac. 2 : 7. Are not a. t. Galileans?
He. 11 : 13. t. a. died in faith, not
39. t. a. having obtained a good
See THESE. [report

Us ALL or **We ALL.**

Ge. 42 : 11. w. are a. one man's sons
Ex. 12 : 33. w. be a. dead men [fish
Nu. 17 : 12. saying, we die, w. a. per-
De. 5 : 3. who are a. of u. alive this
2 S. 18 : 25 son, let u. not a. go[day
19 : 6. if a. w. had died this day
2 K. 9 : 5. Which of a. u.? To thee
Pr. 1 : 14. let u. a. have one purse
Is. 53 : 6. a. w. have gone astray;
laid on him iniquity of u. a.
59 : 11. w. roar a. like bears, and
64 : 9. behold, w. are a. thy people
Mal. 2 : 10. Have w. not a. one fath.?
Jn. 1 : 16. of his fulness have a. w.
Ac. 2 : 32. wh-of w. a. are witnesses
10 : 33. Now are w. a. here bef. God
16 : 28. no harm; w. are a. here
26 : 14. w. were a. fallen to earth
Ro. 4 : 16. Abr.; who is fath. of u. a.
8 : 32. Son, delivered up for u. a.
14 : 10. w. shall a. stand before
judgment seat, 2 Co. 5 : 10.
1 Co. 8 : 1. we know that w. a. have
knowledge [bread
10 : 17. w. a. partakers of that one
12 : 13. w. are a. baptized into one
body, a. made to drink into one
15 : 51. w. shall not a. sleep, but
w. shall a. be changed[holding
2 Co. 3 : 18. w. a. with open face be-
Ga. 4 : 26. Jerus-m mother of u. a.
Ep. 2 : 3. w. a. had our conversation
4 : 13. Till w. a. come in the unity
Ja. 3 : 2. in many things w. offend a.
See **All CITIES, All the CONGREGATION, All the DAY, All the DAY long, All the DAYS, All the EARTH, From EVIL, All FLESH, All GODS, HEART with all, All ISRAEL, All the JEWS, All JUDAH, All LIVING, All MANNER, All MEN, All NATIONS, All the NATIONS, All PEOPLE, All the PEOPLE, All PRINCES, All the PROPHETS, All THAT, All they THAT, All those THAT, All THINGS, All these THINGS, All THEY, Than THEY, All THIS, THROUGHOUT all, All TIMES, All the WHILE, All the WORDS, All these WORDS, All WORDS of this law, WORKERS of iniquity, All Ye, All YOU.**
See ABOMINATIONS, AMAZED, AUTHORITY, BONES BRETHREN, CATTLE CHILDREN, CHURCHES, CITY, COASTS, COMMANDMENTS, COUNTRY, IES, DESIRE, DILIGENCE, DISCIPLES, DOINGS, ENEMIES, EVIL, EVILS, FAMILY, IES, FILTHINESS, FIRSTBORN, FLOCKS, FOWLS, FULNESS, GENERATIONS, HOUSE, IDOLS INCREASE, INHABITANTS, INIQUITY, INIQUITIES, JERUSALEM, JUDGMENTS, KINDREDS, KINGDOMS, KINGS, KNOWLEDGE, LABOUR, LABOURS, LAND, LANDS, MALES, MALICE, MEEKNESS, MEMBERS, MULTITUDE, MULTITUDES, NIGHT, OTHER, OTHERS, PLACES, PLAIN, PLEASURE, POWER, REGION, SAINTS, SAYINGS, SEED, SERVANTS, SERVICE, SINS, SONS, SORTS, SOULS, STREETS, SUCH, THEREIN, TREASURES, TRIBES, UNCLEANNESS, UNRIGHTEOUSNESS, VESSELS, WAYS, WICKEDNESS, WISDOM, WORK, WORKS, WORLD.

ALL. [Adv.]

Ge. 25 : 25. And the first came out
red a. over
Ex. 28 : 31. make robe of ephod a.
of blue, 39 : 22.
Nu. 11 : 32. quails a. abroad about
camp
Ju. 9 : 53. woman cast millstone a.
to brake Abimelech's skull
1 S. 28 : 20. Saul fell a. along on
the earth
2 S 17 : 3. the man as if a. returned
1 K. 14 : 10. taketh dung till a. gone
Ps. 45 : 13. King's dau-r a. glorious
Pr. 24 : 31. a. grown over wi. thorns
Can. 4 : 7. Thou art a. fair, my love
Je. 41 : 6. Ishmael wee ing a. along
Na. 3 : 1. the city! it is a. full of lies
Ha. 1 : 9. They shall come a. for vio-
Zch. 4 : 2. candlest. a. of gold[lence
Jn. 21 : 11. for a. there were so many

ALL. [Noun.] [chose

Ge. 6 : 2. took wives, of a. wh. they
7 : 22. a. in whose nostrils breath
14 : 20. Abram gave him tithes of a.
27 : 33. I eaten of a. bef. thou camest
Ex. 5 : 23. Nei. delivered people at
12 : 9. Eat not of it sodden at a.[a.
22 : 23. If they cry at a. unto me
26. If thou at a. take neighbour's
29 : 24. a. in hands of Aa.[raiment
37 : 22. a. of it work of pure gold[7.
Le. 7 : 18. if eaten at a., on 3d day, 19 :
15 : 24. if man lie with her at a. [a.
16 : 29. on tenth day do no work at
19 : 20. bondm. not at a. redeemed
27 : 10. if he sh. at a. change beast
13. if he will at a. redeem beast
31. if man at a. redeem his tithes
Nu. 11 : 6. is nothing at a. besides
22 : 38. I any power at a. [manna
23 : 25. Nei. curse at a. nor bless at
31 : 35. 32,000 in a. of women [a.
De. 2 : 36. Lord delivered a. unto us
8 : 19. if thou at a. forget thy God
21 : 14. not sell her at a. for money
Jos. 7 : 7. whf. hast at a. bro-t peo.
21 : 39. with suburbs; 4 cities in a.
45. a. came to pass, 23 : 14.[and a.
Ju. 16 : 3. Samson with them, bar
1 S. 20 : 6. If thy fath. at a. miss me
30 : 8. thou shalt overtake, recover
19. David recovered a., 18. [a.
2 S. 18 : 28. Ahimaaz said, a. is well
19 : 28. a. but dead men bef. king
30. let him take a. as king is come
42. we eaten at a. of king's cost?
23 : 39. the mighty men, 37 in a.
1 K. 2 : 26. thou been afflicted in a.
wherein my father was [ing me
9 : 6. if ye at a. turn from follow-
14 : 26. Shishak took treas-s, took a.
22 : 28. If thou return at a. in peace
2 K. 5 : 21. Naaman said, Is a. well?
9 : 11. unto Jehu, Is a. well? [22.
18 : 33. any of gods delivered at a.?
1 Ch. 2 : 6. sons of Zerah; five in a.
7 : 5. valiant men, in a. 87,000 [a.
21 : 23. Ornan said, Take, I give it
29 : 12. reignest over a.: in thine
hand to give strength unto a.
2 Ch. 35 : 7. Josiah gave a. for passover offerings, for a. present
Ne. 4 : 15. returned a. of us to wall
Jb. 34 : † 13. who hath disposed a.
38 : 18. earth? declare if knowest a.
Ps. 103 : 19. kingdom ruleth over a.
119 : 91. They continue, for a. are
145 : 9. Lord good to a. [thy serv-s.
15. The eyes of a. wait upon thee
Ec. 1 : 2. Vanity of vanities; a. is
vanity, 14.-2 : 11, 17.-3 : 19.-12 : 8.
3 : 20. a. go unto one place; a. are
of dust, a. turn to dust, 6 : 6.
5 : 9. profit of the earth is for a.
9 : 2. All things come alike to a.
3. that there is one event unto a.
11 : 5. works of God who maketh a.
8. a. th. cometh is vanity[defence
Is. 4 : 5. upon a., the glory shall be
29 : 11. vision of a. as a book sealed
50 : 2. Is my hand shortened at a.?
Je. 6 : 15. not at a. ashamed, 8 : 12.
11 : 12. not save at a. in trouble
13 : 19. Jud. be carried captive a.
23 : 32. not profit people at a. [of it
31 : 12. not sorrow any more at a.
50 : 32. it shall devour a. about him
Eze. 14 : 3. sho. I be inquired of at a.
16 : 4. thou wast not salted at a.,
nor swaddled at a.

Eze. 18 : 23. Have I any pleasure at
a. that the wicked should die?
20 : 32. into your mind not be at a.
that ye say [she doted (3)
23 : 7. whoredoms wi. a. on whom
37 : 22. two kingd-s any more at a.
Da. 4 : 12. in it was meat for a., 21.
10 : 3. neither did I anoint at a.
11 : 2. stir up at a. against Grecia
Ho. 11 : 7. none at a. wou. exalt him
13 : 2. a. of it work of craftsmen
Am. 3 : 5. snare taken nothing at a.
Mi. 1 : 10. weep ye not at a. [of thee
2 : 12. I will assemble, O Jacob, a.
Na. 1 : 3. L. not at a. acquit wicked
Ha. 2 : 19. stone; is no breath at a.
Zch. 7 : 5. did ye at a. fast to me?
Mat. 5 : 18. till a. be fulfilled, Lu.
34. I say, Swear not at a. [21 : 32.
18 : 26. patience, I will pay a., 29.
19 : 27. Peter said, Behold, we have
forsaken a., Mk. 10 : 28. Lu. 18 : 28.
21 : 26. a. hold John as a prophet
22 : 10. So servants gathered a. as
27. And last of a. the woman died,
Mk. 12 : 22. Lu. 20 : 32. [serve
23 : 3. a. whatso. they bid you ob-
28 : 9. Jes. met them, saying, a. hail
Mk. 6 : 39. make a. sit by companies
9 : 35. same shall be last of a., and
servant of a., 10 : 44. [of a.?
12 : 28. Which is first commandm-t
13 : 37. I say unto a., Watch[not I
14 : 29. Altho. a. be offended, yet
Lu. 2 : 3. a. went to be taxed, ev. one
4 : 7. if worship me, a. sh. be thine
15. he taught, being glorified of a.
22. a. bare him witness, wondered
5 : 11. they forsook a., followed him
28. Levi left a. and followed him
7 : 16. And there came a fear on a.
8 : 45. When a. denied, Peter said
52. And a. wept and bewailed her
12 : 1. unto disciples first of a. [a.
41. speakest parable unto us or to
15 : 13. younger son gathered a. [ine
14. when had spent a. arose fam-
20 : 38. G. of living; a. live unto h.
40. durst not ask him question at
Jn. 6 : 39. of a. given me lose noth. [a.
10 : 29. My Father greater than a.
11 : 49. ye know nothing at a.
18 : 38. I find in him no fault at a.
19 : 11. no power at a. ag. me, exc-t
Ac. 4 : 18. not speak at a. in name
5 : 36. a. as many as obeyed him, 37.
10 : 36. Jesus Ch. (he is Lord of a.)
11 : 10. a. were drawn up into heav.
17 : 25. giveth to a. life and breath
19 : 34. a. cried out, Great is Diana
20 : 38. sorrowing most of a. for
21 : 24. a. may know those things
conc-g thee are nothing [at a.
25 : 8. nor ag. Cesar have I offended
27 : 37. we were in a. 276 souls
Ro. 3 : 23. a. ha. sinned, come short
5 : 12. so death, for a. have sinned
9 : 5. Ch. came, who is over a., God
10 : 12. same L. over a., is rich unto
13 : 7. Render to a. their dues [a.
1 Co. 3 : 22. life or death; a. yours
9 : 19. made myself servant unto a.
10 : 31. do a. to the glory of God
11 : 18. first of a. there be divisions
12 : 6. God wh. worketh a. in a. [(4)
29. Are a. apostles? a. prophets?
30. Have a. gifts of healing? do a.
speak wi. tongues? do a. inter.
14 : 23. If a. speak with tongues
24. if a. prophesy, one unlearned
is convinced of a., judged of a.
31. may a. prophesy one by one
that a. may learn, and a. bo[a.
15 : 3. I delivered unto you first of
8. last of a. he was seen of me
22. as in Adam a. die, so in Christ
shall a. be made alive
1 Co. 15 : 28. that G. may be a. in a.
29. what do if dead rise not at a.
16 : 12. his will not at a. to come
2 Co. 5 : 14. that if one died for a.,
then were a. dead [unto him
15. he died for a. th. they sho. live
Ga. 3 : 22. concluded a. under sin
4 : 1. servant, tho. he be lord of a.
12. ye have not injured me at a.
Ep. 1 : 23. him that filleth a. in a.
4 : 6. One God and Father of a.,
who is above a., through a., in
6 : 13. having done a. stand [you a.
Ph. 2 : 21. a. seek their own, not
4 : 18. But I have a., and abound
Col. 1 : † 18. among a. have pre-em-
3 : 11. Christ is a. and in a. [inence
17. whatso. ye do, do a. in name
2 Th. 3 : 11. working not at a., busy-
1 Ti. 2 : 1. I exhort first of a. [bodies
6. Who gave hims. a ransom for a.
4 : 15. thy profiting may appear to a.
5 : 20. Them th. sin rebuke bef. a.
He. 7 . 2. Abraham gave tenth of a.
8 : 11. a. shall know me fr. least to
9 : 3. tabernacle called holiest of a.
8. way into holiest of a. not manif.
17. no strength at a. while testator
10 : 10. offering of Ch. once for a.
12 : 8. chastisement wh-f a. partak-
23. to God the Judge of a. [ers
13 : 4. marriage is honourable in a.
Ja. 2 : 10. offend in one point he is
guilty of a. [repentance
2 Pe. 3 : 9. that a. should come to
1 Jn. 1 : 5. in him no darkness at a.
Jude 15. execute judgm. upon a. (2)
Re. 13 : 16. causeth a. to rec. mark
18 : 14. sh. find them no more at a.
21. Bab-n be found no more at a.
22. voice of harpers no more at a.
23. candle shine no more at a.;
voice of bride no more at a. in
21 : 25. gates shall not be shut at a.

Above ALL. [a. a.

1 Ch. 29 : 11. Lord, exalted as head
Ec. 2 : 7. possessions a. a. in Jerus.
Da. 11 : 37. king shall magnify hims.
Lu. 3 : 20. Herod added this a. a. [a. a.
Jn. 3 : 31. He fr. heaven is a. a. (2)
Ep. 4 : 6. Father of a. who is a. a.
6 : 16. a. a. taking shield of faith

See Above all THAT.

ALL that.

Ge. 45 : 11. lest thou and a. t. thou
hast come to poverty [seen
13. tell my father of a. t. ye have
47 : 1. a. t. they have are come out
Ex. 31 : 6. a. t. are wise hearted [do.
Nu. 16 : 33. a. t. appertained went
19 : 14. the law: a. t. come into
tent, a. t. is in tent be unclean
De. 12 : 7. rejoice in a. t. ye put
hand to, 18.-15 : 10.-28 : 8, 20.
25 : 18. Amalek smote a. t. were fe.
Jos. 8 : 35. not a word of a. t. Moses
11 : 15. nothing undone of a. t. L.
22 : 2. Ye have kept a. t. Moses,
and obeyed in a. t. I com-ded
Ju. 6 : 9. of hand of a. t. oppressed
1 S. 25 : 21. in vain have I kept a. t.
this fellow hath (2) [ibosheth
2 S. 16 : 4. a. t. pertained unto Meph-
1 K. 16 : 25. Omri did worse than a. t.
1 Ch. 13 : 14. L. blessed a. t. he had
2 Ch. 35 : 7. gave for a. t. were pres.
Es. 2 : 15. favour in sight of a. t.
4 : 7. Mord. told of a. t. happened
Ps. 103 : 6. for a. t. are oppressed
Ec. 11 : 8. a. t. cometh is vanity
12 : † 13. a. t. hath been heard
Da. 9 : 16. reproach to a. t. are ab-t
Jude 15. convince a. t. are ungodly
Re. 18 : 19. made rich a. t. had ships
24. in her blood of a. t. were slain

See All THAT, All of THEM, All THAT he had.

ALLEGING. [fered

Ac. 17 : 3. a. Christ must have suf-

ALLEGORY.

Ga. 4 : 24. Which things are an a.

ALLELUIA. [3, 6.

Re. 19 : 1. much people, saying, A.,
4. elders worshipped, say-g, Amen;

ALLIED. [A.

Ne. 13 : 4. Eliashib was a. unto To-

AL'LON. [Person.] [biah

1 Ch. 4 : 37. son of Shiphi, son of A.

AL'LON. [Place.] [to Z.

Jos. 19 : 33. their coast was from A.

AL'LON-BA'CHUTH.

Ge. 35 : 8. under an oak called A.

ALLOW.

Lu. 11 : 48. ye a. deeds of y-r father
Ac. 24 : 15. hope which they also a.
Ro. 7 : 15. that which I do I a. not

ALLOWANCE.

2 K. 25 : 30. his a. was continual a.
Pr. 30 : † 8. feed with food of my a.
Lu. 3 : † 14. be content with your a.

ALLOWED, ETH.

Ro. 14 : 22. that thing which he a-h
1 Th. 2 : 4. as we were a-d of God

ALLURE. [ness

Ho. 2 : 14. I will a. her into wilder-
2 Pe. 2 : 18. they a. thro. lusts of

ALMIGHTY. [flesh

Ge. 17 : 1. I am the A. God; walk
28 : 3. G. A. bless thee, and make
35 : 11. I am G. A.: be fruitful and
43 : 14. G. A. give you mercy [Lus
48 : 3. G. A. appeared unto me at
49 : 25. by the A. who sh. bless thee
Ex. 6 : 3. I appeared unto Abraham,
Isaac, and Jacob by name G. A.
Nu. 24 : 4. which saw vision of A., 16.
Ru. 1 : 20. A. dealt bitterly with me
21. seeing A. hath afflicted me
Jb. 5 : 17. despise not chasten-g of A.
6 : 4. arrows of A. are within me
14. he forsaketh the fear of the A.
8 : 3. doth the A. pervert justice?
5. make thy supplication to the A.
11 : 7. Canst thou find out the A.
13 : 3. Surely I would speak to A.
15 : 25. he strengtheneth himself
against the A. [serve him?
21 : 15. What is the A. th. we should
20. shall drink of wrath of the A.
22 : 3. Is it any pleasure to the A.
that thou art righteous? [them?
17. said, what can the A. do for
23. If return to A. thou be built
25. the A. shall be thy defence
26. shalt have thy delight in the A.
23 : 16. heart soft, A. troubleth me
24 : 1. times are not hidden from A.
27 : 2. A. who hath vexed my soul
10. will he delight himself in A.?
11. what wi. A. I will not conceal
13. which they shall receive of A.
29 : 5. When the A. was with me
31 : 2. what inheritance of the A.
from on high? [answer me
35. my desire is that the A. would
32 : 8. inspiration of the A. giveth
understanding [me life
33 : 4. breath of the A. hath given
34 : 10. far from the A. that he commit iniquity [judgment
12. neither will the A. pervert
35 : 13. vanity, nei. will A. regard it
37 : 23. A., we cannot find him out
40 : 2. shall he that contendeth wi.
the A. instruct him? [it
Ps. 68 : 14. the A. scattered kings in
91 : 1. abide under shadow of the A.
Is. 13 : 6. come as a destruction from
the A., Jo. 1 : 15. [A., 10 : 5.
Eze. 1 : 24. their wings, as voice of
Da. 11 : † 38. A. God he shall honour
2 Co. 6 : 18. be my sons, saith Lord A.
Re. 1 : 8. Lord was, is to come, the A.
4 : 8. Holy, holy, holy Lord God A.

Re. 11 : 17. O Lord God A. which wast and art to come ⌈God A.
15 : 3. marvellous thy works, Lord
16 : 7. Even so, Lord G. A., true thy
14. to battle of great day of G. A.
19 : 15 : winepress of wrath of A. G.
21 : 22. God A. and Lamb are temple

ALMO'DAD. ⌈1 : 20.
Ge. 10 : 26. Joktan begat A., 1 Ch.

AL'MON. See ALEMETH.

AL'MON-DIBLATHA'IM.
Nu. 33 : 46. they encamped in A., 47.

ALMOND, S.
Ge. 43 : 11. carry the man myrrh, nuts, and a-s ⌈19 (2), 20.
Ex. 25 : 33. bowls like a-s (2), 34.-37 :
Nu. 17 : 8. rod of Aaron yielded a-s
Ec. 12 : 5. the a. tree shall flourish
Je. 1 : 11. I see a rod of an a. tree

ALMOST. ⌈me
Ex. 17 : 4. they be a. ready to stone
Ps. 73 : 2. But my feet were a. gone
94 : 17. my soul a. dwelt in silence
119 : 87. They had a. consumed me
Pr. 5 : 14. I was a. in all evil in the
Ac. 13 : 44. came a. the whole city
19 : 26. a. thro-t all Asia this Paul
21 : 27. seven days were a. ended
26 : 28. a. persuadest me to be C-n
29. both a. and altogether as I am
He. 9 : 22. a. all things purged with

ALMS. ⌊blood
Mat. 6 : 1. do not your a. before men
2. when doest thine a. do not, 3.
4. That thine a. may be in secret
Lu. 11 : 41. give a. of such things
12 : 33. Sell that ye have, give a.
Ac. 3 : 2. to ask a. of them that ent.
3. seeing Peter and John asked a.
10. knew it was he which sat for a.
10 : 2. Cornel. gave much a. to peo.
4. thine a. are come up for a, 31.
24 : 17. came to bring a. to my na-

ALMSDEEDS. ⌊tion
Ac. 9 : 36. Dorcas : woman full of a.

ALMUG or ALGUM trees.
1 K. 10 : 11.† from Ophir great plenty of a. t., 2 Ch. 9 : 10.†
12. king made of a-g t. pillars for hou. of L. (2), 2 Ch. 9 : 11 a-m t.
2 Ch. 2 : 8.† Send me a. t. out of Leb-

ALOES. ⌊anon
Ps. 45 : 8. thy garments smell of a.
Pr. 7 : 17. perfumed my bed with a.
Can. 4 : 14. myrrh and a. wi. spices
Jn. 19 : 39. mixture of myrrh and a.
See LIGNALOES.

ALOFT.
Pr. 18 : † 10. the righteous is set a.

ALONE. ⌈be a.
Ge. 2 : 18. not good that man should
Ex. 24 : 2. Moses a. come near Lord
Le. 13 : 46. the leper shall dwell a.
Nu. 11 : 14. I am not able to bear all this people a., De 1 : 9.
23 : 9. lo, the people shall dwell a.
De. 1 : 12. How can I a. bear your
32 : 12. Lord a. did lead him ⌊strife ?
33 : 28. Israel sh. dwell in safety a.
Jos. 22 : 20. Achan perished not a.
Ju. 3 : 20. parlour wh. Eglon had a.
2 S. 18 : 24. a man running a., 26.
25. If he be a. there is tidings in
1 K. 11 : 29. they two a. in the field
1 Ch. 29 : 1. Solomon whom a. God hath chosen ⌈decai a.
Es. 3 : 6. scorn to lay hands on Mor-
Jb. 1 : 15. I only am escaped a. to tell thee, 16, 17, 19. ⌈heavens
9 : 8. God which a. spreadeth the
15 : 19. to whom a. earth was given
31 : 17. If I have eaten my morsel a.
Ps. 83 : 18. name a. is JEHOVAH ⌈a.
102 : 7. I watch, and am as sparrow
136 : 4. who a. doeth great wonders
148 : 13. his name a. is excellent
Ec. 4 : 8. is one a. and not a second
Ec. 4 : 10. woe to him a. when he fall-
11. how can one be warm a. ? ⌊eth
Is. 2 : 11. Lord a. sh. be exalted, 17.
5 : 8. be placed a. in midst of earth
14 : 31. none a. in appointed times
44 : 24. stretched forth heavens a.
51 : 2. I called him a. and blessed
63 : 3. I have trodden winepress a.
Je. 15 : 17. I sat a. b. c. of thy hand
49 : 31. wealthy nation wh. dwell a.
La. 3 : 28. He sitteth a., keepeth si-
Da. 10 : 7. I Dan. a. saw vision ⌊lence
Ho. 8 : 9. Isr., a wild ass a. by hims.
Mat. 4 : 4. is written, Man shall not live by bread a., Lu. 4 : 4.
14 : 23. when the evening was come, he was there a., Lu. 9 : 18. ⌈a.
18 : 15. tell fault betw. thee and him
Mk. 4 : 10. when he was a. they asked
34. when they a. he expounded
6 : 47. ship in the sea, he a. on land
Lu. 5 : 21. forgive sins but God a. ?
6 : 4. not lawful but for priests a.
9 : 18. as Jesus was a. praying, his
36. voice past, Jesus was found a.
10 : 40. hath sister left me to serve a.
Jn. 6 : 15. he departed into a mt. a.
22. disciples were gone away a.
8 : 16. I am not a., but Fath., 16 : 32.
12 : 24. Except it die, it abideth a.
16 : 32. hour cometh ye leave me a.
17 : 20. Neither pray I for these a.
Ac. 19 : 26. ye see that not a. at Eph.
Ro. 4 : 23. not written for his sake a.
Ga. 6 : 4. have rejoicing in himself a.
1 Th. 3 : 1. we to be left at Athens a.
He. 9 : 7. went high priest a. once
Ja. 2 : 17. so faith is dead, being a.

Left ALONE. ⌈led
Ge. 32 : 24. Jacob was l. a. : wrest-
42 : 38. bro. dead, he is l. a.. 44 : 20.
Is. 49 : 21. I was l. a. ; these, where
Da 10 : 8. I was l. a. and saw vision
Jn. 8 : 9. Jesus was l. a. and woman
29. the Father hath not l. me a.
Ro. 11 : 3. am l. a., they seek my life

Let ALONE. ⌈Eg-ns
Ex. 14 : 12. l. us a. that we serve
32 : 10. l. me a. that my wrath wax
De. 9 : 14. l. me a. that I destroy
Ju. 11 : 37. l. me a. two months
2 S. 16 : 11. l. him a., let him curse
2 K. 4 : 27. l. her a. ; soul is vexed
23 : 18. l. him a., let no man move
Ezr. 6 : 7. l. work of house of God a.
Jb. 7 : 16. l. me a. ; my days vanity
10. nor l. me a. till I swallow my
10 : 20. l. me a. that I take comfort
13 : 13. l. me a. that I may speak
Ho. 4 : 17. joined to idols ; l. him a.
Mat. 15 : 14. l. th. a. : blind leaders
Mk. 1 : 24. l. us a., thou Jesus of Naz-h, Lu. 4 : 34. ⌈her, Jn. 12 : 7.
14 : 6. J. said, l. her a. ; why trouble
15 : 36. l. a. ; let us see wheth. Elias
Lu. 13 : 8. Lord, l. it a. this yr. also
Jn. 11 : 48. if we l. him a. all will
Ac. 5 : 38. Refrain fr. these men, l.
See THOU alone. ⌊th. a.

ALONG.
Ex. 2 : 5. her maidens walked a. by
9 : 23. fire ran a. upon the ground
Nu. 21 : 22. we will go a. by the king's highway, De. 2 : 27. ⌈Ed.
34 : 3. south quarter, a. by coast of
Jos. 10 : 10. L. chased them a. way
15 : 3. the border passed a. to (2), 6, 10, 11.-18 : 18, 19. ⌈to Ataroth
16 : 2. lot of Joseph passeth a. un-
19 : 13. passeth a. to Gittah-hepher
Ju. 7 : 12. chil. of east lay a. in vall.
13. overturned it, that tent lay a.
9 : 25, they robbed all that came a.
37. anoth. company come a. plain
11 : 26. cities a. by coasts of Arnon
20 : 37. liers in wait drew thems. a.
1 S. 28 : 20. Saul fell all a. on earth
2 K. 11 : 11. guard stood a. by the altar and temple, 2 Ch. 23 : 10.
See WENT along.

ALOOF. ⌈stand a.
Ps. 38 : 11. My lovers and friends

A'LOTH. ⌈A
1 K. 4 : 16. Baanoh was in Asher and

ALOUD. ⌈heard
Ge. 45 : 2. Joseph wept a. ; Egypt-s
Ezr. 3 : 12. many shouted a. for joy
Ps. 132 : 16. saints sh. shout a. for joy
Mk. 15 : 8. Multitude crying a. began

Cried ALOUD.
1 K. 18 : 28. c. a. and cut themselves
Da. 3 : 4 herald c. a., To you, O peo.
4 : 14. He c. a., Hew down the tree
5 : 7. king c. a. to bring astrologers
See CRY aloud, SING.

ALPHA. ⌈6.-22 : 13.
Re. 1 : 8. I am A. and Omega, 11.-21 :

ALPHE'US.
Mat. 10 : 3. James the son of A., Mk. 3 : 18. Lu. 6 : 15. Ac. 1 : 13.
Mk. 2 : 14. he saw Levi son of A. sit-

ALREADY. ⌊ting
Ex. 1 : 5. for Joseph was in Egypt a.
2 Ch. 28 : 13. have offended against Lord a. ⌈bondage a.
Ne. 5 : 5. some of our daughters into
Ec. 1 : 10. it hath been a. of old time
2 : 12. that wh. hath been a. done
3 : 15. that wh. is to be hath a. been
4 : 2. praised dead wh. are a. dead
6 : 10. That which been is named a.
Mal. 2 : 2. your blessings ; yea I have cursed them a. ⌈her a.
Mat. 5 : 28. committed adultery wi.
17 : 12. I say Elias is come a. ⌈dead
15 : 44. marvelled if he were a.
Lu. 12 : 49. what if it be a. kindled ?
Jn. 3 : 18. believeth not, condemned
4 : 35. are white a. to harvest ⌊a.
9 : 22. Jews had agreed a., if any
27. I have told you a., ye did not
11 : 17. lain in the grave 4 days a.
19 : 33. they saw he was dead a. ⌈I
Ac. 11 : 11. three men a. come where
27 : 9. bec. fast was a. past, Paul
1 Co. 5 : 3. I present in spirit have judged a. as though present
2 Co. 12 : 21. lest I shall bewail many which have sinned a.
Ph. 3 : 12. Not as though I had a. attained, either were a. perfect
16. whereto we have a. attained
2 Th. 2 : 7. iniquity doth a. work
1 Ti. 5 : 15. are a. turned aft. Satan
2 Ti. 2 : 18. resurrection is past a.
1 Jn. 4 : 3. antichrist a. in the world
Re. 2 : 25. that ye have a., hold fast

ALSO.
Ge. 1 : 16. he made the stars a.
2 : 9. tree of life a. in the garden
3 : 6. woman gave a. unto husband
4 : 4. Abel a. brought of firstlings
6 : 3. with man, for he a. is flesh
11. earth a. was corrupt bef. God
13 : 16. if number dust, thy seed a.
16 : 13. Have I a. looked after him
18 : 12. pleasure, my lord old a. ?
19 : 34. him drink wine this night a.
20 : 6. I a. withheld thee fr. sinning
24 : 14. give thy camels drink a., 46.
26 : 21. ano. well, strove for that a.
27 : 34. Bless me a., my father, 38.
30 : 30. provide for mine house a. ?
35 : 17. thou shalt have this son a.
38 : 10. wherefore Lord slew him a.
11. Lest Shelah die a. as his breth.
22. a. men said, no harlot in pla.
40 : 15. here a. have I done noth-g
16. baker said, I a. was in dream
42 : 22. thf. a. his blood is required
43 : 8. live, we, a. our little ones
44 : 16. we, he a. with whom cup is
45 : 20. a. regard not your stuff
48 : 19. he a. shall become a peo. (2)

Le. 23 : 27. a. on tenth of 7th month
Nu. 16 : 10. seek ye priesthood a. ?
De. 9 : 19. Lord hearkened unto me
at that time a., 10 : 10. [to thee
1 S. 8 : 8. forsaken me, so do a. un-
10 : 11. Is Saul a. among the prophets ? 12.-19 : 24. [Gibeah
26. And Saul a. went home to
14 : 44. God do so to me, and more
a., 2 S. 3 : 35.-19 : 13. [esied
19 : 21. messengers of Saul a. proph-
22. Then went Saul a. to Ramah
23. Spirit of God was upon him a.
24. he stripped off his clothes a.
25 : 22. more a. do God unto ene-s
26 : 25. do great things, a. prevail
2 S. 1 : 18. a. bade teach use of bow
11 : 17. Uriah, the Hittite, died a.
12 : 14. child a. born unto thee die
15 : 19. Whf. goest thou a. with us ?
thou art a stranger, a. an exile
18 : 2. I will surely go with you a.
1 K. 2 : 22. ask for him kingdom a.
13 : 18. I am a prophet a. as thou
22 : 22. shalt persuade him, prevail
2 K. 7 : 4. if we sit here we die a. [a.
9 : 27. Smite him a. in the chariot
16 : 14. Ahaz brought a. braz. altar
1 Ch. 8 : 32. these a. dwelt wi. breth.
2 Ch. 4 : 19. Sol-n made golden altar
5 : 12. a. singers arrayed in white[a.
34 : 27. I have even heard thee a.
Ezr. 5 : 10. We asked their names a.
14. vessels a. of gold, silver, 6 : 5.
Es. 4 : 16. I a. and maidens will fast
7 : 8. Will he force the queen a.
Jb. 11 : 11. he seeth wickedness a.
13 : 2. What ye know, I know a.
32 : 10. I a. will shew mine opinion,
17. I will answer a. my part [17.
Ps. 38 : 10. light of mine eyes a. gone
62 : 12. a. unto thee belongeth mer-
68 : 18. gifts for rebellious a. [cy
72 : 15. prayer a. for him contin-y
95 : 4. strength of the hills is his a.
Pr. 11 : 25. watereth, be watered a.
28 : 16. prince . . a. great oppressor
30 : 31. A greyhound ; a he goat a.
31 : 28. her husband a. praiseth her
Ec. 1 : 17. this a. is vexation of spirit
2 : 15. Then I said, this a. is vanity, 5 : 10.-6 : 9.-8 : 10, 14. [a. ?
Is. 7 : 13. but will ye weary my God
46 : 11. purposed, I will a. do it (2)
48 : 12. I am the first, I a. am last
56 : 6. a. the sons of the strangers
Je 3 : 8. Judah played the harlot a.
25 : 14. great kings serve thems. a.
28 : 14. I have given him beasts a.
38 : 25. a. what king said unto thee
Da. 6 : 22. a. have I done no hurt
Ha. 2 : 16. drink thou a., be uncov-d
Zeh. 8 : 21. to seek Lord ; I will go a.
Mat. 2 : 8. th. I may worship him a.
5 : 39. turn to him oth. a., Lu. 6 : 29.
6 : 21. there heart be a., Lu. 12 : 34.
13 : 26. then appeared the tares a.
23. a. beareth fruit, and bringeth
15 : 16. Are ye a. yet without understanding ? Mk. 7 : 18. [yard
20 : 7. He saith, Go ye a. into vine-
21 : 21. a. if ye say unto this mt.
24. I a. will ask you one thing,
Mk. 11 : 29. Lu. 20 : 3. [to 7th
22 : 26. Likewise the second a., un-
27. And last of all the woman died
a., Mk. 12 : 22. [clean a.
23 : 26. that the outside may be
24 : 27. so shall a. coming of Son of
man be, 37, 39. [12 : 40.
44. Therefore be ye a. ready, Lu.
25 : 17. he a. gained other two
26 : 13. there shall this a. be told
of her, Mk. 14 : 9. [ciples
35. Likewise a. said all the dis-
69. saying, Thou a. wast with Jesus of Galilee, 71. Mk. 14 : 67.

Mat. 26 : 73. thou a. art one of them,
Lu. 22 : 56, 59. Jn. 18 : 17, 25.
27 : 57. Joseph, who a. was disciple
Mk. 1 : 38. that I may preach there
a., Lu. 4 : 43. [Lu. 6 : 4.
2 : 26. gave a. to them with him,
28. Son of man is Lord a. of the
Sabbath, Lu. 6 : 5. [bef. them
8 : 7. commanded to set fishes a.
38. of him a. sh. Son be ashamed
12 : 6. beloved, he sent him a. last
Lu. 3 : 21. Jesus a. being baptized
6 : 31. do ye a. to them likewise
32. sinners a. love those th. love
33. sinners a. do the same [them
34. for sinners a. lend to sinners
36. Be merciful as your Fath. a. is
7 : 8. I a. am man under authority
49. Who is this forgiveth sins a. ?
10 : 1. Lord appointed other 70 a.
39. Mary wh. a. sat at Jesus' feet
11 : 40. did not he make that with-
45. thou reproachest us a. [in a. ?
49. Thf. a. said the wisdom of God
13 : 8. Lord, let it alone this year a.
14 : 26. if hate not his own life a.
16 : 10. is faithful a. in much (2)
17 : 24. so shall a. Son of man be
23 : 27. women, which a. lamented
Jn. 5 : 18. said a. ; God his fath. [him
19. what he doeth, a. doeth Son
27. authority to execute judgm. a.
6 : 36. ye a. have seen me, believe
67. said, Will ye a. go away ? [not
7 : 47. answered, Are ye a. deceived
52. said, Art thou a. of Galilee ?
8 : 19. known my Father a., 14 : 7.
9 : 27. will ye a. be his disciples [a. ?
40. Pharisees said, Are we blind
12 : 9. they might see Lazarus a.
26. where I am there a. my serv-t
42. among rulers a. many believed
13 : 9. not my feet only, a. my hands
14. ought a. to wash one anoth-'s
34. that ye a. love one another
14 : 1. believe in God, believe a. in
3. where I am ye may be a. [me
12. works that I do shall he do a.
19. because I live, ye shall live a.
15 : 20. they will a. persecute you (2)
23. hateth me, hateth my Fath. a.
27. ye a. shall bear witness, bec.
17 : 1. thy Son a. may glorify thee
19. they a. might be sanctified
20. for them a. wh. believe on me
24. I will that they a. be with me
21 : 3. They say, We a. go wi. thee
20. which a. leaned on his breast
25. are a. many other things Jes.
Ac. 2 : 22. wh. God did, as ye a. know
3 : 17. did it, as did a. your rulers
5 : 32. so is a. the Holy Ghost
37. rose up Judas ; he a. perished
8 : 13. Then Simon himself believed
9 : 32. Peter came a. to saints at [a.
10 : 26. Stand up ; I a. am a man
45. on Gentiles a. the Holy Ghost
11 : 18. a. to Gentiles repentance
30. relief : a. they sent by Saul
12 : 3. proceeded to take Peter a.
13 : 9. Saul (who a. is called Paul)
17 : 6. These are come hither a.
13. Jews came a., stirred up peo.
28. as certain a. of your own poets
19 : 27. but a. the temple of Diana
20 : 30. a. of your selves shall arise
23 : 11. so bear witness at Rome a.
24 : 26. He hoped a. that money be
Ro. 6 : 5. we shall be a. in likeness
of his resurrection [thee
11 : 21. heed lest he a. spare not
22. otherwise thou a. sh. be cut off
16 : 2. she a succourer of myself a.
1 Co. 4 : 8. we a. might reign wi. you
7 : 34. difference a. betw. wife and v.
9 : 8. saith not the law the same a.
10 : 6. not lust as they a. lusted

1 Co. 10 : 9. Nei. as some a. tempted
11 : 1. of me, as I am a. of Christ
12. so a. is the man by the woman
19. must be a. heresies amo. you
23. that which I a. delivered you
25. same manner a. he took cup
12 : 12. are one body ; so a. is Ch.
13 : 12. sh. know as a. I am known
14 : 15. pray with underst-g a. (2)
19. that I might teach others a.
34. obedience, as a. saith the law
15 : 8. last he was seen of me a. as
14. then your faith is a. vain
18. they a. which are fallen asleep
40. There are a. celestial bodies
42. So a. is the resurrection of
48. such they a. that are earthy
49. we shall a. bear image of [(2)
16 : 4. if meet that I go a., they sh.
2 Co. 1 : 7. sh. ye be a. of consolution
14. As a. ye have acknowledged us
4 : 11. shall raise us up a. by Jesus
8 : 6. a. finish in you same grace a.
10. but a. to be forward a year ago
10 : 11. word, will we be a. in deed
Ga. 2 : 17. if we a. are found sinners
6 : 1. lest thou a. be tempted
7. soweth, that shall he a. reap
Ep. 1 : 13. In whom ye a. trusted (2)
21. in this world, a. that to come
4 : 10. is the same a. that ascended
6 : 21. ye a. may know my affairs
Ph. 2 : 5. mind in you wh. was a. in
4 : 3. I entreat thee a. (2) [Christ
Col. 4 : 1. knowing ye a. ha. a Master
3. praying a. for us . . . mystery
of Christ for which I a. in bonds
1 Th. 1 : 5. not in word only, a. in p.
8. not only in Achaia, a. in ev. pla.
2 : 8. unto you a. our own souls
5 : 11. edify one another as a. ye do
24. Faithful he who a. will do it
1 Ti. 6 : 12. wh-unto thou art a. called
2 Ti. 1 : 5. persuaded that in thee a.
3 : 9. folly manifest as theirs a. was
4 : 15. Of whom be thou ware a.
Phm. 21. wilt a. do more than I say
He. 11 : 32. fail to tell of David a.
12 : 26. I shake the earth, a. heaven
13 : 3. as being yours. a. in the body
Ja. 2 : 2. if come in a. a poor man
26. faith without works is dead a.
1 Pe. 2 : 18. to the gentle, a. froward
2 Pe. 3 : 15. as brother Paul a. hath
16. As a. in all his epistles [written
1 Jn. 2 : 6. ought a. so to walk, as he
4 : 11. we ought a. to love one ano.
21. who loveth God, love broth. a.
5 : 1. loveth him a. that is begotten
Jude 8. a. filthy dreamers defile
Re. 1 : 7. they a. which pierced him
11 : 8. where a. our L. was crucified

ALTAR.

Ge. 8 : 20. Noah offered on the a.
12 : 7. a. unto the Lord, 8.-13 : 18.
Jos. 8 : 30. Ju. 6 : 26. 1 S. 7 : 17.
-14 : 35 (2). 2 S. 24 : 18, 21, 25.
13 : 4. Abr. went unto pla. of the a.
22 : 9. bound Isaac, laid him on a.
33 : 20. erected an a., called it El-
Elohe-Israel [unto God, 3.
35 : 1. go to Beth-el, make an a.
Ex. 20 : 24. a. of earth make unto me
25. if thou wilt make a. of stone
26. Nei. go up by steps unto mine a.
21 : 14. take him fr. a. that he die
24 : 6. blood he sprinkled on the a.
27 : 1. make an a. of shittim wood ;
a. shall be foursquare, 37 : 25
5. put grate under compass of a.
6. shalt make staves for a. [(2)
7. staves sh. be upon 2 sides of a.
28 : 43. when they come near the a.
29 : 12. pour all blood beside bottom
of a. (2), Le. 4 : 7 (2), 18 (2), 25
(2), 30 (2), 34 (2).-5 : 9 (2).-8 : 15
(2).-9 : 9 (2).

Ex. 29 : 13. fat, the caul, burn upon
a.,25. Le. 8 :16.-9:10,20.-16:25.
18. shalt burn the whole ram upon a., 25. Le. 8 : 21, 28. ⌈Aaron
21. blood upon a. sprinkle upon
36. cleanse the a. when atonem-t
37. Seven days make atonement
for a.; it shall be an a. most
holy; whatso. toucheth a. holy
38. offer upon a. two lambs day
44. I will sanctify tabernacle, a.
30 : 1. make an a. to burn incense
18. laver, put between tabernacle
and a., 40 : 7, 30. ⌈a., 40 : 32.
20. shall wash when come near to
38 : 3. he made all vessels of a., 30.
4. he made for a. a brazen grate
7. the staves into rings of the a.
40 : 5. set a. of gold before the ark
10. anoint the a.; sanctify the
a.; it shall be an a. most holy
33. he reared up court about a.
Le. 1 : 7. shall put fire upon a.,8,12.
9. priest shalt burn all on the a.,
13, 15, 17. - 3 : 5, 11, 16. - 4 : 10,
19, 26, 31, 35.-7 : 5, 31.-9 : 13,
14, 17. ⌈ward
11. kill it on side of the a. north-
15. pigeons priest shall bring unto a.; blood shall be wrung out
on the side of the a. (3) ⌈a.
16. crop, feathers cast beside the
2 : 2. burn memorial of it upon a.,
9.-5 : 12.-6 : 15. Nu. 5 : 26.
8. meat offering priest shall bring
unto the a., 6 : 14. ⌈on a.
12. firstfruits shall not be burnt
6 : 9. burning upon a. all night (2)
10. ashes upon the a. he shall put
beside a., Nu. 4 : 13. ⌈on a., 12.
13. fire shall ever be burning up-
8 : 11. Mos. anointed a. and vessels
15. Mos. took blood, purified a.(3)
30. blood upon a., sprinkled upon
9 : 7. Aaron, Go unto a., 8. ⌈a., 18.
12. blood Aaron sprinkled upon
24. fire consumed upon a. burnt o.
10 : 12. meat offering eat beside a.
14 : 20. offer burnt offer-g upon a.
16 : 12. censer full of coals off the a.
18. unto the a., make atonem., 33.
20. reconciling tabernacle and a.
17 : 11. blood; given you upon a.
21 : 23. not come nigh a., Nu. 18:3.
22 : 22. nor offer-g of them upon a.
Nu. 3 : 26. court wh. is by a., 4 : 26.
4 : 14. upon it censers, vessels of a.
5 . 25. jealousy offer-g upon the a.
26. memorial th-of burn upon a.
7 : 1. sanctified both a. and vessels
10. for dedicating of a. princes offered offering before the a., 11.
84. This was dedication of a., 88.
16 : 38. plates for covering of a., 39.
46. Take censer, put fire fr. off a.
18 : 5. ye sh. keep charge of the a.
7. your office for every thing of a.
23 : 2. Balak offered on every a. a
bullock, 4, 14, 30. ⌈thine a.
De. 33 : 10. burnt sacrifices upon
Jos. 8 : 31. an a. of whole stones
22 : 34. children of Gad called a. Ed
Ju. 6 : 25. throw down a. of Baal⌈(2)
28. the a. of Baal was cast down
30. may die, because he hath cast
down the a. of Baal, 31, 32.
13 : 20. when flame went up from
a., angel ascended in flame of a.
1 S. 2 : 28. him to offer upon mine a.
33. whom not cut off from mine a.
2 S. 24 : 18. to David, Go, rear an a.
in threshingfloor, 1 Ch. 21: 18.
1 K. 1 : 53. brought Adonijah fr. a.
2 : 29. was told Sol., he is by the a.
3 : 4. 1,000 did Sol-n offer upon a.
6 : 20. covered a., wh. was of cedar
22. whole a. he overlaid with gold

1 K. 7 : 48. Solomon made a. of gold
8 : 31. the oath come before thine
a., 2 Ch. 6 : 22. ⌈bef. Lord (2)
9 : 25. Sol-n burnt incense upon a.
12 : 32. Jerob. offered upon a., 33(2)
13 : 1. Jerob. by a. to burn incense
2. cried ag. the a., O a.. a., 4, 32.
3. Behold a. shall be rent, 5 (2)
4. Jerob. put forth his hand fr. a.
16 : 32. Ahab reared an a. for Baal
18 : 26. no voice; leaped upon a.
32. he made a trench about the a.
35. water ran round about the a.
2 K. 11 : 11. guard stood along by
the a. and temple, 2 Ch. 23 : 10.
12 : 9. Jehoiada set chest beside a.
16 : 10. Ahaz saw an a. at Damascus; sent fashion of a.
12 was come from Damascus, king
saw a., approached a. ⌈on a.
13. blood of his peace offering up-
14. Ahaz brought brazen a. from
between a. and house of L. (3)
15. Upon great a. burn the offer-g
18 : 22. Ye shall worship bef. this a.
in Jerus., 2 Ch. 32 : 12. Is. 36 : 7.
23 : 15. a. at Beth-el Josiah brake(2)
16. bones of sepulchres, burned
them upon a. ⌈el
17. hast done against a. of Beth-
2 Ch. 4 : 1. he made an a. of brass
5 : 12. singers stood at end of the a.
7 : 9. dedication of a. seven days
29 : 24. reconciliation with blood
upon a. ⌈upon a.
27. Hezekiah commanded to offer
Ezr. 3 : 3. they set a. upon his bases
7 : 17. offer them upon a. of God
Ps. 26 : 6. will compass thine a., O L.
43 : 4. will I go unto a. of God ⌈a.
51 : 19. offer bullocks upon thine
Is. 6 : 6. coal taken from off the a.
19 : 19. In that day shall be an a.
27 : 9. stones of a. as chalkstones
56 : 7. sh. be accepted upon mine a.
60 : 7. they shall come up on mine a.
La. 2 : 7. Lord hath cast off his a.
Eze. 8 : 5. at gate of a. this image
16. between porch and a. 25 men
40 : 46. keepers of the charge of a.
47. measured the a. before house
41 : 22. The a. of wood 3 cubits high
43 : 13. these are measures of the
a.; this sh. be higher place of a.
15. so the a. shall be four cubits;
from the a. and upward 4 horns
16. a. shall be twelve cubits long
18. These are ordinances of the a.
22. and they shall cleanse the a.
26. Seven days sh. they purge a.
27. make y-r burnt off-gs upon a.
45 : 19. put blood upon settle of a.
47 : 1. waters at south side of the a.
Jo. 1 : 13. howl, ye ministers of a.⌈a.
2 : 17. weep between the porch and
Am. 2 : 8. clothes, to pledge at ev. a.
9 : 1. I saw Lord standing upon a.
Zch. 9 : 15. be filled at corners of a.
14 : 20. pots be like bowls bef. the a.
Mal. 1 : 7. Ye offer polluted bread
upon mine a. ⌈for nought
10. neither kindle fire on mine a.
Mat. 5 : 23. if bring thy gift to a.⌈a.
24. Leave there thy gift before the
23 : 18. Whoso. sh. swear by a., 20.
19. whether greater the gift or a.
35. whom ye slew between temple
and a., Lu. 11 : 51. ⌈scription
Ac. 17 : 23. found an a. with this in-
1 Co. 9 : 13. which wait at a. are partakers with the a. ⌈a.?
10 : 18. eat of sacrifices partakers of
He. 7 : 13. tribe, of wh. no man at a.
13 : 10. an a. wh-f they have no ri.
Ja. 2 : 21. offered Isaac upon the a.
Re. 6 : 9. I saw under a. souls of th.
8 : 3. another angel stood at a. (2)

Re. 8 : 5. filled censer with fire of a.
11 : 1. measure temple of G. and a.
14 : 18. another angel came from a.
16 : 7. I heard another out of a. say

Brazen ALTAR.

Ex. 38 : 30. therewith made he b. a.
39 : 39. they bro-t unto Mos. b. a.
1 K. 8 : 64. because the b. a. too little, 2 Ch. 7 : 7. ⌈was bef. Lord
2 K. 16 : 14. Ahaz bro-t b. a. which
15. b. a. shall be for me to inquire
2 Ch. 1 : 5. b. a. that Bezaleel made
6. Sol-n went to b. a. and offered
Eze. 9 : 2. six men stood by the b. a.

ALTAR, S,
with build, ed, ing, or built.

Ge. 8 : 20. Noah b-d an a. unto Lord
12 : 7. there b-ed Abram an a., 8.
13 : 18. Abram, in Mamre, b-t an a.
22 : 9. Abr. b-t an a., bound Isaac
26 : 25. Isaac b-ed an a. there, and
35 : 7. Jacob b-t an a., El-b th-el
Ex. 17 : 15. Moses b-t a., called it
24 : 4. Moses b-ed an a. under hill
32 : 5. Aaron saw it, he b-t an a.
Nu. 23 : 1. b-d me here seven a-s, 29.
14. Balak b-t seven a-s and off-d
De. 27 : 5. there b-d a. of stones(2), 6.
Jos. 8 : 30. Joshua b-t an a. in Ebal
22 : 10. b-t an a. by Jordan, a great
a. to see to ⌈an a.
11. children of Reuben have b-t
16. trespass in th. ye have b-ed a.
19. nor rebel in b-g an a. besides
a. of Lord ⌈Lord
23. b-t us an a. to turn from the
26. Let us prepare to b-d an a.
29. God forbid, we b-d an a. besides a. of the Lord ⌈Lord
Ju. 6 : 24. Gideon b-t an a. unto the
26. b-d a. upon top of rock ⌈b-t
28. offered upon the a. that was
21 : 4. people rose early, b-t an a.
1 S. 7 : 17. Ramah; Samuel b-t an a.
14 : 35. Saul b-t an a.: same was
first a. that he b-t unto Lord
2 S. 24 : 21. David said, To b-d an a.
th. plague be stayed, 1 Ch. 21:22.
25. Da. b-t there an a., 1 Ch. 21:26.
1 K. 9 : 25. did Sol. offer upon a. wh.
he b-t (2), 2 Ch. 8 : 12. ⌈an a.
18 : 32. with the stones Elijah b-t
2 K. 16 : 11. Urijah b-t an a. acc. to
21 : 4. Manasseh b-t a-s in house
of Lord, 2 Ch. 33 : 4.⌈2 Ch. 33 : 5.
5. he b-t a-s for host of heaven,
2 Ch. 33 : 15. took away a-s he b-t
Ezr. 3 : 2. Then Joshua b-ed a. of G.

ALTAR of burnt offering.

Ex. 30 : 28. thou shalt anoint a. -
with vessels, 40 : 10.⌈a. -, 35:16.
31 : 9. wisdom that they may make
38 : 1. he made a. - of shittim wood
40 : 6. set a. - before the door of
the tabernacle, 29.
Le. 4 : 7. pour blood of bullock at
bottom of a. -, 18, 25, 30. ⌈a. -
10. priests shall burn them upon
34. blood of sin offering upon a. -
1 Ch. 6 : 49. Aaron offered upon a. -
16 : 40. to offer upon a. - continu-y
21 : 26. L. answ-d by fire upon a. -
29. tabern-e and a. - were at Gib-
22 : 1. this is the a. - for Israel⌊eon
2 Ch. 29 : 18. We have cleansed a. -

Golden ALTAR.

Ex. 39 : 38. brought to Moses g. a.
40 : 26. Moses put g. a. in tent of
Nu. 4 : 11. upon g. a. cloth of blue
2 Ch. 4 : 19. Sol-n made g. a. also
Re. 8 : 3. prayers of saints upon g. a.
9 : 13. a voice from g. a. before God

Horns of the ALTAR.

Ex. 29 : 12. shalt take blood, put it
upon the - a., Le. 4 : 7, 18, 25, 30,
34.-8 : 15.-9 : 9.-16 : 18.⌈- a., 51.
1 K. 1 : 50. Adonijah caught hold on

1 K. 2 : 28. Joab caught hold on - a.
Ps. 118 : 27. bind sacrifice unto - a.
Am. 3 : 14. - a. shall be cut off
Re. 9 : 13. a voice from the - a.

ALTAR, S, with incense.

Ex. 30 : 27. thou sh. anoint a. of i.
31 : 8. wisd. to make a. of i., 35: 15.
37 : 25. made i. a. of shittim wood
Le. 4 : 7. blood upon a. of sweet i.
1 Ch. 6 : 49. Aaron offered on a. of i.
28 : 18. for a. of i. refined gold
2 Ch. 26 : 16. Uzziah to burn incense
upon the a. of i. [a.
19. the leprosy rose from beside i.
30 : 14. a-s for i. cast into Kidron
Lu. 1 : 11. angel on right of a. of i.

ALTAR of the Lord.

Le. 17 : 6. sprinkle blood upon a. -
De. 12 : 27. burnt off-g upon a. - (2)
16 : 21. sh. not plant trees near a. -
26 : 4. take basket, set it before a. -
27 : 6. build a. - of whole stones
Jos. 9 : 27. And Joshua made them
hewers of wood for the a. -
22 : 19. nor rebel in building a. besides the a. -, 29. [of the a. -
28. we may say, Behold pattern
1 K. 8 : 22. Solomon stood before
the a. -, 2 Ch. 6 : 12. [a. -
54. Solomon arose from before the
18 : 30. Elijah repaired a. - broken
2 K. 23 : 9. priests came not to a. -
2 Ch. 8 : 12. Sol. offered burnt off-gs
15 : 8. Asa renewed a. - [on a. -
29 : 19. all the vessels are bef. a. -
21. priests to offer them on a. -
33 : 16. Manasseh repaired the a. -
35 : 16. offer upon a. - acc. to com-t
Ne. 10 : 34. wood off-g to burn upon
Mal. 2 : 13. cover-g a. - wi. tears [a. -
See SPRINKLE, SPRINKLED.

ALTARS.

Ex. 34 : 13. ye shall destroy their a.,
De. 7 : 5.-12 : 3. Ju. 2 : 2.
Nu. 3 : 31. their charge sh. be the a.
23 : 4. I have prepared seven a.
1 K. 19 : 10. Isr. thrown down a., 14.
2 K. 11 : 18. his a. brake they, and
slew Mattan bef. a., 2 Ch. 23: 17.
18 : 22. whose a. Hezekiah hath
taken, 2 Ch. 32 : 12. Is. 36 : 7.
21 : 3. Manasseh reared a. for Baal,
as did Ahab, 2 Ch. 33 : 3.
23 : 12. a. on top of chamber of Ahaz,
a. Manasseh made Josiah brake
20. slew all the priests upon the a.
2 Ch. 14 : 3. Asa took away a. of
strange gods, 30 : 14. [of Jerus.
28 : 24. Ahaz made a. in ev. corner
30 : 14. they took away a. in Jerus.
31 : 1. threw down a. out of Judah
34 : 4. brake down a. of Baalim, 7.
5. burnt bones of priests upon a.
Ps. 84 : 3. thine a., O Lord of hosts
Is. 17 : 8. he shall not look to the a.
65 : 3. incense upon a. of brick
Je. 11 : 13. a. to that shameful thing,
even a. to Baal [of your a.
17 : 1. sin graven upon the horns
2. their children rememb. their a.
Eze. 6 : 4. your a. sh. be desolate, 6.
5. scatter your bones about y-r a.
13. their slain men about their a.
Ho. 8 : 11. bec. many a. to sin, a.
shall be unto him to sin [a.
10 : 1. acc-g to his fruit, increased
2. he shall break down their a.
8. thistle sh. come up on their a.
12 : 11. their a. as heaps in furrows
Am. 3 : 14. I will visit a. of Beth-el
Ro. 11 : 3. they digged down thine a.

AL-TASCHITH.

Ps. 57.* To the chief Musician, A.,
58,* 59,* 75.*

ALTER. [change

Le. 27 : 10. He shall not a., it nor
Ezr. 6 : 11. Whoso. shall a. this word
Ezr. 6 : 12. destroy all that shall put
hand to a. this house [my lips
Ps. 89 : 34. nor a. thing gone out of
Pr. 31 : † 5. lest they a. the judgm-t

ALTERED, ETH. [a-d.

Es. 1 : 19. com-t written that it be not
Da. 6 : 8. law of Medes wh. a-h not, 12.
Lu. 9 : 29. his countenance was a-d

ALTERING. [pose

Nu. 14 : † 34. sh. know my a. of pur-

ALTHOUGH. [a. near

Ex. 13 : 17. not thro. land of Philis.,
Jos. 22 : 17. a. a plague in the cong.
2 S. 23 : 5. a. my house be not so (2)
1 K. 20 : 5. a. I have sent unto thee
Es. 7 : 4. a. enemy not countervail
Jb. 2 : 3. a. movedst me against him
5 : 6. a. affliction cometh not of dust
35 : 14. a. sayest thou sh. not see
Je. 31 : 32. a. I was a husband [him
Eze. 7 : 13. a. they were yet alive
11 : 16. a. I have cast them off (2)
Ha. 3 : 17. a. fig tree shall not blos.
Mk. 14 : 29. a. all shall be offended
Ga. 6 : † 1. a. man be overtak. in fault
He. 4 : 3. a. the works were finished

ALTOGETHER. [acc. to

Ge. 18 : 21. whe. they have done a.
Ex. 11 : 1. shall thrust you out a.
19 : 18. Sinai was a. on a smoke
Nu. 16 : 13. make thyself a. prince
23 : 11. hast blessed them a., 24: 10.
30 : 14. if husband a. hold his peace
De. 16 : 20. That wh. is a. just follow
2 Ch. 12 : 12. wou. not destroy him a.
Es. 4 : 14. if a. holdest thy peace
Jb. 13 : 5. Oh a. hold your peace!
27 : 12. Why are ye a. vain? [a.
Ps. 19 : 9. judgments of L. righteous
39 : 5. every man is a. vanity [self
50 : 21. that I was a. such as thy-
53 : 3. they are a. become filthy
62 : 9. they a. lighter than vanity
139 : 4. O Lord, thou knowest it a.
Can. 5 : 16. yea, he is a. lovely
Is. 10 : 8. Are not my princes a. k-s
Je. 5 : 5. these have a. broken yoke
10 : 8. they are a. brutish, foolish
15 : 18. thou be a. unto me as liar?
30 : 11. not leave thee a. unpunish.
49 : 12. thou a. go unpunished?
Jn. 9 : 34. Thou wast a. born in sins
Ac. 26 : 29. almost and a. such as I
1 Co. 5 : 10. not a. with fornicators
9 : 10. saith he it a. for our sakes?
2 Co. 4 : † 8. We not a. without help

A'LUSH.

Nu. 33 : 13. they encamped in A., 14.

AL'VAH or ALI'AH.

Ge. 36 : 40.† duke A., 1 Ch. 1 : 51.†

AL'VAN or ALI'AN.

Ge. 36 : 23.† children of Shobal were
these, A., Ebal, 1 Ch. 1 : 40.†

ALWAY.

Ex. 25: 30. set shewbread bef. me a.
Nu. 9 : 16. So it was a.; cloud by
De. 11 : 1. shalt keep his com-nts a.
28 : 33. be oppressed, crushed a.
2 S. 9 : 10. eat bread a. at my table
1 K. 11: 36. Dav. may have a light a.
2 K. 8 : 19. promised Dav. a. a light
Jb. 7 : 16. I would not live a.
Ps. 9 : 18. needy not a. be forgotten
119 : 112. to perform thy statutes a.
Pr. 28 : 14. Happy the man feareth a.
Mat. 28 : 20. and, lo, I am with you
Jn. 7 : 6. your time is a. ready [a.
Ac. 10 : 2. Cornelius prayed to G. a.
Ro. 11 : 10. bow down their back a.
2 Co. 4 : 11. are a. delivered unto d.
6 : 10. As sorrowful, yet a. rejoicing
Ph. 4 : 4. Rejoice in the Lord a.
Col. 4 : 6. Let your speech be a.
1 Th. 2 : 16. to fill up their sins a.
2 Th. 2 : 13. to give thanks a. to God
Tit. 1 : 12. The Cretians are a. liars
He. 3 : 10. They do a. err in heart

ALWAYS.

Ge. 6 : 3. My spirit sh. not a. strive
Ex. 27 : 20. cause the lamp to burn a.
28 : 38. plate a. be upon her foreh.
De. 5 : 29. would keep my com-ts a.
6 : 24. to fear Lord for our good a.
11 : 12. eyes of thy God a. upon it
14 : 23. mayest learn to fear Lord a.
1 Ch. 16 : 15. Be ye mindful a. of his
2 Ch. 18 : 7. for he never prophesied
good unto me, but a. evil
Jb. 27 : 10. will he a. call upon God?
32 : 9. Great men are not a. wise
Ps. 10 : 5. His ways are a. grievous
16 : 8. I have set Lord a. before me
103 : 9. He will not a. chide; neith.
Pr. 5 : 19. be ravished a. wi. her love
8 : 30. I his delight, rejoicing a.
Ec. 9 : 8. thy garment be a. white
Is. 57 : 16. neith. will I be a. wroth
Je. 20 : 17. her womb to be a. great
Eze. 38 : 8. mts. of Isr. been a. waste
Mat. 18 : 10. their angels do a. behold
26 : 11. have the poor a.; me ye
have not a., Mk. 14 : 7. Jn. 12 : 8.
Mk. 5 : 5. a., night and day, in mts.
Lu. 18 : 1. men ought a. to pray and
21 : 36. Watch, pray a. that ye be
Jn. 8 : 29. for I do a. things th. please
11 : 42. I knew thou hearest me a.
18 : 20. temple whi. Jews a. resort
Ac. 2 : 25. Lord a. before my face
7 : 51. ye do a. resist Holy Ghost
24 : 3. We accept it a. and in all
16. a. a conscience void of offence
Ro. 1 : 9. I make mention of you a.
in my prayers, Phm. 4. [behalf
1 Co. 1 : 4. I thank God a. on your
15 : 58. a. abounding in the work
2 Co. 2 : 14. God, which a. causeth
4 : 10. a. bearing about in body the
5 : 6. Therefore we are a. confident
9 : 8. a. having all sufficiency in all
Ga. 4 : 18. zealously affected a. in a
Ep. 5 : 20. Giving thanks a. for all
6 : 18. Praying a. with all prayer
Ph. 1 : 4. a. in every prayer for you
20. with all boldness, as a., so now
2 : 12. beloved, as ye have a. obeyed
Col. 1 : 3. praying a. for you
4 : 12. a. labouring fervently for you
1 Th. 1 : 2. We give thanks to God a.
3 : 6. good remembrance of us a.
2 Th. 1 : 3. We are bound to thank
God a. for you [our God
11. Wheref. we pray a. for you th.
3 : 16. The Lord give you peace a.
He. 9 : 6. priests went a. into tab.
1 Pe. 3 : 15. be ready a. to give ans-r
2 Pe. 1 : 12. put you a. in remembr-e
15. to have these a. in remembr-e

I AM or AM I.

[Relating to God or Christ.]

Ge. 15 : 1. I a. thy shield and [11.
17 : 1. I a. the Almighty God, 35 :
26 : 24. I a. the God of Abraham,
fear not, I a. with thee, 28 : 13.
-46 : 3. Mat. 22 : 32. Ac 7 : 32.
28 : 15. I a. with thee and will keep
46 : 3. I a. God, fear not to go down
Ex. 3 : 14. I AM THAT I AM; say
unto Israel, I AM hath sent me
22 : 27. I will hear; for I a. gracious
Nu. 18 : 20. I a. thy part and thine
De. 1 : 42. I a. not among you
Ps. 35 : 3. soul, I a. thy salvation
50 : 7. I a. God, even thy God [he
Is. 41 : 4. Who hath wro-t it? I a.
10. Fear not; I a. with thee; be
not dismayed; I a. thy G., 43 : 5.
44 : 6. I a. the first, I a. the last, 48 :
48 : 12. Hearken, O Isr., I a. he, 12.
58 : 9. cry, Lord shall say, Here I a.
Je. 1 : 8. Be not afraid, I a. wi. thee
6 : 11. I a. full of fury of the Lord;
I a. weary with holding in [off
23 : 23. a. I a God at hand, not afar

Je. 23 : 30. I a. ag-t prophets that steal my words, 31. ⌈false
32. I a. ag-t them that prophesy
Hag. 2 : 4. work ; for I a. with you
Mat. 16 : 13. Whom do men say that I a.? Mk. 8 : 27. Lu. 9 : 18.
15. But whom say ye that I a.? Mk. 8 : 29. Lu. 9 : 20.
18 : 20. where two or three in my name, there a. I in the midst
27 : 43. he said, I a. the Son of God
28 : 20. lo, I a. with you alway ⌈a.
Mk. 14 : 62. Art thou the Christ? I
Lu. 22 : 70. Son of God? Ye say I a.
Jn. 4 : 26. I that speak unto thee a.
6 : 35. I a. the bread of life ⌊he
7 : 28. ye know me, whence I a.
29. I a. fr. him ; he hath sent me
33. Yet a little while a. I with you
34. where I a. ye cannot come ⌈5.
8 : 12. I a. the light of the world, 9:
16. I a. not alone, I and Fa., 16, 23.
23. I a. fr above ; I a. not ⌈ this
58. Bef. Abraham was I a. ⌊world
9 : 5. As long as I a. in the world
9. is like him ; but he said, I a. he
10 : 9. I a. the door : by me if any
36. because I said, I a. Son of G.
11 : 25. Jes. said, I a. resurrection
12 : 26. where I a. shall servant be
13 : 13. Ye call me Lord ; so I a.
14 : 3. that where I a., ye may be
17 : 24. they be with me where I a.
18 : 5. Whom seek ye? I a. he, 8.
6. he had said, I a. he, they fell
19 : 21. write that he said, I a. King of the Jews ⌈-22 : 13.
Re. 1 : 8. I a. Alpha and Omega, 11.
17. I a. first and last, 11.-22 : 13.
18. I a. he that liveth ; I a. alive
2 : 23. I a. he wh. searcheth reins
See **I am the LORD,**
I am the LORD your God,
KNOW I am the Lord.
See **Against THEE.**

I AM or AM I.

Ge. 4 : 9. a. I my brother's keeper?
18 : 27. I wh. a. but dust and ashes
22 : 1. Here I a., 1 S. 12 : 3.-22 : 12.
7. Here a. I, 11.-27 : 1, 18.-31 : 11.
-37 : 13.-46 : 2. Ex. 3 : 4. 1 S. 3 : 4, 5, 6, 8, 16. 2 S. 1 : 7.-15 : 26.
25 : 22. If it be so, why a. I thus⌈a.
27 : 24. Art thou Esau? he said, I
46. Rebekah said, I a. weary of life
30 : 2 Jacob said, a. I in God's stead
13. Leah said, Happy a. I ⌈child
38 : 25. By the man . . . a. I with
Ex. 3 : 11. Who a. I that I go unto
4 : 10. I a. not eloquent ; I a.⌊Pha.
6 : 30. I a. of uncircumcised lips
Nu. 11 : 14. I a. not able to bear peo.
21. peo. among whom I a. 600,000
22 : 30. a. I not thine ass upon wh.
Jos. 14 : 10. I a. fourscore and five y.
11. yet I a. as strong as in the day
23 : 2. Josh. said, I a. old, stricken
Ju. 13 : 11. thou that spakest unto the woman? And he said, I a.
Ru. 3 : 9. who thou? I a. Ruth⌈sons?
1 S. 1 : 8. a. I not better than ten
26. I a. woman th. stood praying
9 : 19. Samuel said, I a. the seer
21. a. not I a Benjamite
12 : 2. I a. old and greyheaded
17 : 8. a. not I a Philistine, and ye
43. a. I a dog that thou comest
58. I a. son of Jesse, Beth-lehemite
30 : 13. I a. a young man of Egypt
2 S. 1 : 8. I a. an Amalekite, 13.
2 : 20. Art thou Asahel? I a. ⌈king
3 : 39. I a. weak, though anointed
9 : 8. look upon a dead dog as I a.
14 : 5. I a. indeed a widow woman
19 : 22. do not I know that I a. k-g
20 : 19. I a. one of them, faithful in
24 : 14. D. said, I a. in a great strait

1 K. 3 : 7. I a. but a little child : I
13 : 18. I a. a prophet as thou art
18 : 8. Art thou Elijah? I a. : go, tell
20 : 4. O king, I a. thine and all I
22 : 4. I a. as thou art, my people thy, 2 K. 3 : 7. 2 Ch. 18 : 3.
2 K. 5 : 7. a. I God to kill, make alive
16 : 7. Ahaz, saying, I a. thy serv-t
Ne. 6 : 11. who as I a. go into temple
Jb. 7 : 8. thine eyes upon me, and I
12. a. I a sea or a whale ⌊a. not
9 : 32. For he is not a man as I a.
10 : 15. I a. full of confusion, thf.
12 : 4. I a. as one mocked of neighb.
19 : 15. I a. an alien in their sight
32 : 6. Elihu said, I a. young, ye old
Ps. 39 : 4. may know how frail I a.
88 : 4. I a. as a man hath no stren
102 : 6. I a. like a pelican, I a. like
7. I a. as a sparrow alone ⌊an owl
120 : 7. I a. for peace, they for war
143 : 12. destroy them : for I a. thy
Pr. 26 : 19. a. not I in sport⌊servant
Is. 6 : 5. I a. undone because I a. of
8. Then said I, Here a. I, send me
19 : 11. how say, I a. son of the wise
47 : 8. sayest I a., and none else besides me, Zph. 2 : 15. ⌈child
Je. 1 : . I cannot speak : for I a. a
7. Lord said, Say not I a. a child
La. 3 : 1. I a. a man hath seen afflic-n
Mi. 3 : 8. I a. full of power by Spirit
7 : 1. I a. as when they gathered grape gleanings ⌈and Zion
Zch. 1 : 14. I a. jealous for Jerus-m
13 : 5. I a. no prophet, I a. husb-n
Lu. 1 : 19. angel said, I a. Gabriel
7 : 8. I a. a man under authority
15 : 19. I a. no more worthy to, 21.
18 : 11. thank thee I a. not as other
21 : 8. many shall come in my name, saying, I a. Christ ⌈Jn. 18 : 17.
22 : 58. Peter said, Man, I a. not,
Jn. 1 : 20. I a. not the Christ, 3 : 28.
21. Art thou Elias? he said, I a.
18 : 35. Pilate answ-d, a. I a Jew⌊not
Ac. 9 : 10. Ananias said, I a. here,
10 : 21. I a. he whom ye seek ⌊Lord
26. Stand up ; I also a. a man
13 : 25. John said, Whom think ye I a.? I a. not he ; whose shoes I a. not worthy to loose
21 : 39. Paul said, I a. a man wh. a. a Jew of Tarsus, 22 : 3.⌈bonds
26 : 29. such as I a., except these
27 : 23. God, whose I a., wh. I serve
1 Co. 3 : 4. I a. of Paul ; I a. of Apol.
9 : 1. a. I not apostle? a. I not free
2. If not unto oth-s, I a. unto you
11 : 1. followers of me as I a. of Ch.
12 : 15. Bec. I a. not the hand, I a.
16. Bec. I a. not the eye, I a. not
15 : 10. by grace of G. I a. what I a.
2 Co. 7 : 4. I a. joyful in tribulation
10 : 1. I Paul, who in presence a. base, but absent a. bold toward
11 : 2. I a. jealous over you ⌊you
21. any is bold, I a. bold also
22. Are they Hebrews? so a. I. Are they of Abr-m? so a. I (3)
23. ministers of Christ? I a. more
29. Who is weak and I a. not weak
12 : 10. when I a. weak a. I strong
Ga. 4 : 12. be as I a., for I a. as ye
Ep. 6 : 20. I a. an ambassador in
Ph. 4 : 11. in whatsoever state I a.
Col. 4 : 3. for which I a. in bonds
Re. 18 : 7. I sit a queen, a. no widow
19 : 10. I a. thy fellow servant
See Afraid, Come, Grieved.

A'MAD. See Alammelech.

A'MAL.

1 Ch. 7 : 35. sons of Helem ; Imna, ⌈A.

AM'ALEK.

Ge. 36 : 12. Timna bare to Eliphaz, ⌈A.
16. Duke Korah, duke Gatam,
Ex. 17 : 8. A. fought with Isr.⌊duke A.

Ex 17 : 9. Moses said, Go, fight wi. A.
10. So Joshua fought with A. ⌈ed
11. let down his hand, A. prevail-
13. Joshua discomfited A. and peo.
14. I will put out remembr-e of A.
16. Lord will have war with A.
Nu. 24 : 20. looked on A., he said, A. was first of nations ⌈1 S. 15 : 2.
De. 25 : 17. Remember what A. did,
19. blot out remembrance of A.
Ju. 3 : 13. Eglon gathered A., smote
5 : 14. Out of Ephr. root against A.
1 S. 15 : 3. Now go and smite A.
5. Saul came to a city of A. and
20. I brought Agag king of A. ⌈A.
28 : 18. nor executedst wrath upon
2 S. 8 : 12. gold David dedicated of Moab, of A., 1 Ch. 18 : 11. ⌈na, A.
1 Ch. 1 : 36. sons of Eliphaz : Tim-
Ps. 83 : 7. ag-t thee Am and A.

AM'ALEKITE. ⌈an A.

1 S. 30 : 13. I am of Eg., servant to
2 S. 1 : 8. Who art thou? I am an A.,

AM'ALEKITES. ⌊13.

Ge. 14 : 7. smote all country of A.
Nu. 13 : 29. A. dwell in land of south
14 : 25. (the A. dwelt in the valley)
43. the A. are there before you
45. Then A. came down, smote th.
Ju. 6 : 3. when Isr. had sown, A. ca.
33. A. were gathered, and pitched
7 : 12. A. lay along in the valley
10 : 12. A., Maonites did oppress you
12 : 15. Abdon buried in m-t of A.
1 S. 14 : 48. Saul gathered an host, smote A., delivered Israel ⌈(2)
15 : 6. Kenites, get from among A.
7. Saul smote A. fr. Havilah until
8. he took Agag king of A. alive
15. They have bro-t them from A.
18. L. said, Go, destroy sinners, A.
20. Saul said, I have destroyed A.
32. Bring me Agag king of the A.
27 : 8. David invaded Gezrites, A.
30 : 1. A. had smitten Ziklag
18. David recovered all that A. had
2 S. 1 : 1. David from slaughter of A.
1 Ch. 4 : 43. they smote the rest of A.

A'MAM. ⌈ma

Jos. 15 : 26. cities of Judah, A., She-

AM'ANA.

2 K. 5 : †12. Are not A., Pharpar⌈A.
Can. 4 : 8. spouse, look from top of

AMARI'AH.

1 Ch. 6 : 7. Meraioth begat A., A. begat Ahitub, 52 ⌈A-h, Ezr. 7 : 3.
11. Azariah begat A., A. begat
23 : 19. sons of Hebron, A. second,
2 Ch. 19 : 11. A. chief priest ⌊24 : 23.
31 : 15. next him Eden, A. in office
Ezr. 10 : 42. taken strange wives ; A.
Ne. 10 : 3. that sealed ; Pashur, A.
11 : 4. of chil. of Judah, A., son of
12 : 2. went up with Zerubbabel, A.
13. were priests of A., Jehohanan
Zph. 1 : 1. A. son of Hezekiah in days

AM'ASA.

2 S. 17 : 25. Absalom made A. capt. A. a man's son, name Ithra
19 : 13. A., Art not thou of my bone
20 : 4. king to A., Assemble Judah,
8. A. went before them ⌊5.
9. Joab said to A., Art in health?
Joab took A. by beard ⌈Joab's
10. A. took no heed to sword in
12. A. wallowed in blood in high-way ; peo. removed A. into field
1 K. 2 : 5. what Joab did unto A. 32.
2 Ch. 28 : 12. A. stood against them
See Ithra. ⌊from war

AMASA'I.

1 Ch. 6 : 25. sons of Elkanah ; A. and
35. Mahath, son of A. 2 Ch. 29 : 12.
12 : 18. spirit upon A., chief of capt-s
15 : 24. A., Zech. did blow trump-ts

AMASHA'I. ⌈A

Ne. 11 : 13. at Jerus., of the priests

AMASI'AH. [unto L.
2 Ch. 17 : 16. A., who offered himself

AMAZED. [a.
Ex. 15 : 15. dukes of Edom shall be
Ju. 20 : 41. men of Benjamin were a.
Jb. 32 : 15. were a., answ-d no more
Is. 13 : 8. shall be a. one at another
Eze. 32 : 10. many people a. at thee
Mat. 12 : 23. all the people were a.
19 : 25. disciples were exceedingly a.
Mk. 1 : 27. they were all a., saying
2 : 12. they were all a., and glorified God, Lu. 5 : 26. [dered
6 : 51. they were sore a., and won-
9 : 15. the people were greatly a.
10 : 32. they were a. and were afraid
14 : 33. he began to be sore a. and
16 : 8. they trembled and were a.
Lu. 2 : 48. saw him, they were a.
4 : 36. were all a. and spake among
9 : 43. were all a. at power of God
Ac. 2 : 7. were all a., marvelled, 12.
9 : 21. all that heard Saul were a.

AMAZEMENT.
Ac. 3 : 10. filled with wonder and a.
1 Pe. 3 : 6. not afraid with any a.

AMAZI'AH.
2 K. 12 : 21. Joash died; A. his son reigned, 2 Ch. 24 : 27. [Judah
13 : 12. Joash fought ag. A. king of
14 : 1. reigned A. the son of Joash king of Judah, 2 Ch. 25 : 1.
8. A. sent messengers to Jehoash, 2 Ch. 25 : 17. [ah, 2 Ch. 25 : 18.
9. Jehoash sent to A. king of Jud-
11. A. would not hear; he and A. looked in face at Beth-shemesh, 2 Ch. 25 : 20, 21. [2 Ch. 25 : 23.
13. Jehoash took A. k. of Judah,
15. Jehoash how he fought wi. A.
17. A. lived after death of Jehoash 15 years, 2 Ch. 25 : 25.
18. rest of acts of A. are they not in book of Chron., 2 Ch. 25 : 26.
21. made Azariah king instead of A., 15 : 1. 2 Ch. 26 : † 1.
23. In 15th year of A. Jeroboam began to reign [A., 2 Ch. 26 : 4.
15 : 3. Azariah did right acc. to all
1 Ch. 3 : 12. Joash his son, A. his son
4 : 34. and Joshah the son of A.
6 : 45. son of A. the son of Hilkiah
2 Ch. 25 : 5. A. gathered Judah and
9. A. said to the man of God [come
10. A. separated army that was
11. A. smote of chil. of Seir 10,000
13. army A. sent back fell upon Ju.
14. after A. was come fr. slaughter
15. Anger of L. was kindled ag. A.
27. after time A. did turn fr. Lord
Am. 7 : 10. A. priest of Beth-el sent
12. A. said unto Amos, O seer, flee
14. and Amos said to A., I was no

AMBASSADOR. [prophet
Pr. 13 : 17. a faithful a. is health
Je. 49 : 14. a. sent unto heath., Ob. 1.
Ep. 6 : 20. for wh. I am a. in bonds

AMBASSADORS. [a.
Jos. 9 : 4. made as if they had been
2 Ch. 32 : 31. business of a. of Bab-n
35 : 21. Necho sent a. to Josiah
Is. 18 : 2. That sendeth a. by sea
30 : 4. and his a. came to Hanes
33 : 7. a. of peace sh. weep bitterly
Eze. 17 : 15. he rebelled in sending a.
2 Co. 5 : 20. we are a. for Christ

AMBASSAGE. [eth
Lu. 14 : 32. sendeth an a. and desir-

AMBER.
Eze. 1 : 4. as colour of a., 27.-8 : 2.

AMBUSH, ES.
Jos. 8 : 2. lay thee an a. for the city
7. Then rise from a. and seize the
9. they went to lie in a. and [city
12. 5,000 : he set them to lie in a.
14. he wist not were liers in a. ag.
19. the a. rose quickly, ran [him
21. Joshua saw a. taken city
Je. 51 : 12. prepare the a-s; for Lord

AMBUSHMENT, S.
2 Ch. 13 : 13. Jeroboam caused an a.; the a. was behind them
20 : 22. the Lord set a-s ag. Ammon

A'MEN.
Re. 3 : 14. These things saith the A.

AMEN. [a.
Nu. 5 : 22. the woman shall say, A.,
De. 27 : 15. all the people sh. say, A., 16, 17, 18, 19, 20, 21, 22, 23, 24, 25, 26. [king, A.
1 K. 1 : 36. Benaiah answered the
1 Ch. 16 : 36. people said, A., praised the Lord, Ne. 5 : 13.-8 : 6. (2)
Ps. 41 : 13. Blessed be the Lord God. A. and A., 89 : 52. [glory; A. and A.
72 : 19. let earth be filled with his
106 : 48. let all the people say, A.
Je. 11 : † 5. answered I, A., O Lord
28 : 6. Even Jeremiah said, A. [A.
Mat. 6 : 13. thine the glory for ever.
28 : 20. unto the end of world. A.
Mk. 16 : 20. with signs following. A.
Lu. 24 : 53. praising, blessing G. A.
Jn. 21 : 25. not contain books. A.
Ro. 1 : 25. Creator, who is blessed for ever. A. [for ever. A.
9 : 5. Christ over all, God blessed
11 : 36. to whom be glory for ever. A. Ga. 1 : 5. Ep. 3 : 21. Ph. 4 : 20. 1 Ti. 1 : 17. 2 Ti. 4 : 18. He. 13 : 21. 2 Pe. 3 : 18. [all. A.
15 : 33. God of peace be with you
16 : 20. The grace of our Lord be with you. A. 24. 2 Co. 13 : 14. Ga. 6 : 18. Ph. 4 : 23. Col. 4 : 18. 1 Th. 5 : 28. 2 Th. 3 : 18. 1 Ti. 6 : 21. 2 Ti. 4 : 22. Tit. 3 : 15. Phm. 25. He. 13 : 25. Re. 22 : 21.
27. glory through Jesus Christ for ever. A. [thanks
1 Co. 14 : 16. say A., at thy giving of
16 : 24. My love be with you all in Christ Jesus. A.
2 Co. 1 : 20. all the promises of God in him are yea, and in him A.
Ep. 6 : 24. Grace be with all that love our Lord. A. [lasting. A.
1 Ti. 6 : 16. to whom be honour ever-
1 Pe. 4 : 11. To him be praise and dominion for ever. A. 5 : 11. Re. 1 : 6.
14. Peace be with you all. A. [A.
1 Jn. 5 : 21. keep yourselves fr. idols.
2 Jn. 13. chil. of . . greet thee. A.
Jude 25. To the only wise God our Saviour, glory now and ever. A.
Re. 1 : 7. he cometh with clouds; ev. eye shall see him. Even so, A.
18. I am alive for evermore, A.
5 : 14. And the four beasts said, A.
7 : 12. Saying, A. : Blessing unto our G. for ever and ev. A. [luia
19 : 4. four beasts, saying, A.; Alle-
22 : 20. Surely I come quickly. A.

AMEND.
2 Ch. 34 : 10. gave it to a. the house
Je. 7 : 3. saith Lord, a. your ways and your doings, 26 : 13.-35 : 15.
5. if ye thoroughly a. your ways
Jn. 4 : 52. inquired when he began

AMENDMENT. [to a.
Mat. 3 : † 8. fruits answerable to a.

AMENDS. [of life
Le. 5 : 16. he shall make a. for harm

AMERCE. [shekels
De. 22 : 19. they shall a. him in 100

AMETHYST.
See AGATE, JACINTH.

A'MI or A'MON.
Ezr. 2 : 57. † children of A., Ne. 7 : 59. †

AMIABLE.
Ps. 84 : 1. How a. thy tabernacles

AMIN'ADAB.
Mat. 1 : 4. Aram begat A.; A. begat Naasson, Lu. 3 : 33.

AMISS. [a.
2 Ch. 6 : 37. We have sinned, done
Da. 3 : 29. speak any thing a. ag. G.
Lu. 23 : 41. this man . . nothing a.
Ja. 4 : 3. receive not bec. ye ask a.

AMIT'TAI. [1 : 1.
2 K. 14 : 25. Jonah son of A., Jon.

AM'MAH.
2 S. 2 : 24. were come to hill of A.
8 : † 1. David took the bridle of A. See METHEG-AMMAH.

AM'MI.
Ho. 2 : 1. Say ye unto brethren, A.

AM'MIEL. [alli
Nu. 13 : 12. Of Dan, A. son of Gem-
2 S. 9 : 4. in house of Machir, the son of A., in Lo-debar, 5.-17 : 27.
1 Ch. 3 : 5. Bathshua daughter of A., 2 S. 11 : † 3. [sixth
26 : 5. sons of Obed-edom, Joab, A.

AM'MIHUD.
Nu. 1 : 10. Elishama son of A., 2 : 18.-7 : 48, 53.-10 : 22. 1 Ch. 7 : 26.
34 : 20. of Simeon; Shemuel son of
28. prince Pedahel son of A. [A.
2 S. 13 : 37. Talmai son of A., king
1 Ch. 9 : 4. Uthai son of A., son of

AM'MIHUR.
2 S. 13 : † 37. Talmai son of A. king

AMMIN'ADAB. [of A.
Ex. 6 : 23. Aaron took Elisheba dau.
Nu. 1 : 7. of Judah; Nahshon son of A., 2 : 3.-7 : 12, 17.-10 : 14.
1 Ch. 2 : 10. Ram begat A. and A. begat Nahshon, Ru. 4 : 19, 20.
6 : 22. The sons of Kohath; A.
15 : 10. Of sons of Uzziel; A. chief
11. Da. called for Levites, Uriel, A.

AMMI-NA'DIB. [A.
Can. 6 : 12. made me like chariots of

AMMISHAD'DAI.
See AHIEZER.

AMMIZ'ABAD.
1 Ch. 27 : 6. in his course was A.

AM'MON. [Moab
Ne. 13 : 23. married wives of A. and
Ps. 83 : 7. ag. thee; Gebal, A., Amalek

Children of AM'MON.
Ge. 19 : 38. Ben-ammi, father of - A.
Nu. 21 : 24. border of - A. strong (2)
De. 2 : 19. - A., distress them not; I not give thee land of - A. [not
37. Only unto land of - A. camest
3 : 11. is it not in Rabbah of - A.?
16. river Jabbok, which is border of - A., Jos. 12 : 2. [of - A.
Jos. 13 : 10. divide land unto border
25. Gad, their coast half la. of - A.
Ju. 3 : 13. Eglon gathered the - A.
10 : 6. Israel served gods of the - A.
7. L. sold them into hands of - A.
9. - A. passed over Jordan to fight
11. Did not I deliver you fr. - A.?
17. Then - A. encamped in Gilead
18. What man to fight against - A.
11 : 4. - A. made war ag-t Israel, 5.
6. Jephthah be captain that we may fight with - A., 8. [head?
9. If to fight - A. shall I be your
12. messengers unto k. of - A., 14.
13. king of - A. ans-d messengers
15. Israel took not land of - A. [A.
27. judge betw. chil. of Isr. and -
28. king of the - A. hearkened not
29. I passed over unto the - A., 32.
30. If deliver - A. into mine hands
31. when I return in peace fr. - A.
33. - A. were subdued before Israel
36. Lord taken vengeance of - A.
12 : 1. Wheref. passedst to fight - A.
2. I and people at strife with - A.
3. I passed over against - A. and
1 S. 12 : 12. king of - A. came ag. you
14 : 47. Saul fought ag. Moab, - A.
2 S. 8 : 12. David did dedicate gold of - A., 1 Ch. 18 : 11. [Ch. 19 : 1.
10 : 1. Nahash king of - A. died, 1

2 S. 10 : 2. David's servants into land of - A., 1 Ch. 19 : 2. [1 Ch. 19 : 3.
3. princes of - A. said unto Han.,
6. when - A. saw they stank before David, - A. hired 20,000 footmen, 1 Ch. 19 : 6. [1 Ch. 19 : 7, 9,
8. - A. put the battle in array at,
10. put them in array against - A., 1 Ch. 19 : 11. [1 Ch. 19 : 12.
11. if - A. too strong for thee, I,
14. when - A. saw Syrians were fled, fled they (2), 1 Ch. 19 : 15.
19. Syrians feared to help - A. any more, 1 Ch. 19 : 19.
11 : 1. Joab and Israel destroyed - A., 1 Ch. 20 : 1. [of - A.
12 : 9. hast slain Uriah with sword
26. Joab fought ag. Rab-h of - A.
12 : 31. thus did he unto cities of - A., 1 Ch. 20 : 3. [for David
17 : 27. Shobi of - A. brought beds
1 K. 11 : 7. Molech, the abomination of the - A., 2 K. 23 : 13. [the - A.
33. worshipped Milcom, god of
2 K. 24 : 2. ag. Jehoi-m bands of - A.
2 Ch. 20 : 1. - A. came ag. Jehosh-t
10. - A., behold how they rew. us
22. Lord set ambushments ag. - A.
23. - A. stood ag. inhabitants of S.
27 : 5. - A. gave Jotham 100 talents.
So much did - A. pay sec. year
Is 11 : 14. - A. shall obey them [A.
Je. 9 : 26. I will punish Edom and -
25. 21. To wit, Jerus., Moab, - A.
49 : 6. bring again captivity of - A.
Eze. 25 : † 10. men of the east ag. - A.
Da. 11 : 41. shall escape chief of - A.
Am. 1 : 13. For 3 trangres-ns of - A.
Zph. 2 : 8. revilings of - A. [rah
9. Moab as Sodom, - A. as Gomor-

AM'MONITE.

De. 23 : 3. An A. shall not enter congregation of the Lord [Ne. 13 : 1.
1 S. 11 : 1. Nahash the A. encamped,
2. Nahash the A. answered them
2 S. 23 : 37. one of the thirty, Zelek the A., 1 Ch. 11 : 39. [of it, 19
Ne. 2 : 10. When Tobiah, A., heard
4 : 3. Tobiah the A. said, if a fox go

AM'MONITES. [up

De. 2 : 20. A. call them Zamzummim
1 S. 11 : 11. slew A. until heat of day
1 K. 11 : 1. Solomon loved strange women of A. [tion of A.
5. Solomon went after abomina-
2 Ch. 20 : 1. besides A. ag. Jehosh-t
26 : 8. A. gave gifts to Uzziah [A.
27 : 5. Jotham fought with king of
Ezr. 9 : 1. abominations of A. [of J
Ne. 4 : 7. when A. heard that walls
Je. 27 : 3. yokes, send to king of A.
40 : 11. when Jews among A. heard
14. Baalis k. of A. hath sent Ishm.
41 : 10. Ishmael to go over to the A.
15. Ishmael escaped to A. [28.
49 : 1. Concerning the A., Eze. 21 :
2. an alarm of war in Rabbah of A.
Eze. 21 : 20. sword to Rabbah of A.
25 : 2. son of man, set face ag-t A.
3. say unto A., Hear word of Lord
5. A. a couching place for flocks
10. that A. not be remembered (2)

AMMONI'TESS.

1 K. 14 : 21. mother's name Naamah, an A., 31. 2 Ch. 12 : 13.
2 Ch. 24 : 26. Zabad, son of Shime-

AM'NON. [ath, an A.

2 S. 3 : 2. his firstborn was A. of Ahinoam, 1 Ch. 3 : 1. [her
13 : 1. Tamar; A. son of Dav. loved
2. A. fell sick for his sister Tamar. A. thought it hard [subtile man
3. A. had a friend, Jonadab, very
4. A. said unto him, I love Tamar
6. A. lay down, made hims. sick; A. said unto k., let Tamar come
7. Go to thy brother A.'s house, 8.

2 S. 13 : 9. A. said, Have out all men
10. A. said unto T., Bring meat (2)
15. Then A. hated her exceedingly. A. said unto her, Arise
20. A. thy brother been with thee?
22. Absalom spake unto A. neither good nor bad; for Abs. hated A.
26. said Abs., Let A. go with us
27. he let A. and king's sons go
28. Mark when A.'s heart is merry, and I say, Smite A., then kill
29. did unto A. as Abs. commanded
32. for A. only is dead, 33. [A
39. David was comforted concern-g
1 Ch. 4 : 20. sons of Shimon were A.

A'MOK. [Sallu, A.

Ne 12 : 7. priests with Zerubbabel,
20. chief of fathers; of A., Eber

A'MON.

1 K. 22 : 26. Take Micaiah back unto A., governor, 2 Ch. 18 : 25.
2 K. 21 : 18. A. his son reigned in his stead, 2 Ch. 33 : 20. [33 : 21.
19. A 22 years old began, 2 Ch.
23. servants of A. slew him
24. people slew all that conspired against A., 2 Ch. 33 : 25. [in bk.
25. rest of acts of A. are they not
1 Ch. 3 : 14. A. his son, Josiah his s.
2 Ch. 33 : 22. A. sacrificed unto im-
23. A. trespassed more and [ages
Je. 1 : 2. word of Lord in days of Josiah son of A., 25 : 3. Zph. 1 : 1.
Mat. 1 : 10. Manasses begat A.; A.
See AMI.

AMONG, AMONGST. [H.

Ge. 23 : 10. Ephron dwelt a. chil. of
24 : 3. Canaanites a. whom I dwell
30 : 33. ev. one not speckled a. goats
34 : 30. stink a. Canaanites (2) [(2)
40 : 20. lifted head of baker a. serv-s
42 : 5. came to buy corn a. those
Ex 2 : 5. when she saw ark a. flags
9 : 20. feared L. a. servants of Pha.
12 : 31. get you from a. my people
13 : 13 firstborn a. thy chil redeem
34 : 10. people a. wh. thou art shalt
Le. 7 : 33 He a. sons of Aaron that
11 : 13. in abomination a. the fowls
21 : 15. Nei. profane his seed a. peo
Nu. 4 : 2. Take sum of sons of Kohath a. sons of Levi [Levites
18. Cut not off Kohathites fr. a.
8 : 14. a. chil. of Israel, 16 -18 : 6.
11 : 21 peo. a. whom I am, 600,000
16 : 21 Separate from a. this cong-n
33. they perished fr a. congreg-n
45. Get you up from a. congreg-n
17 : 6. rod of Aaron a. their rods
19 : 20. soul be cut off fr. a. cong-n
25 : 7. Phinehas rose fr. a. cong-n
27 : 4. name done away a. his fam.
De. 2 : 14 wasted from a. the host
15. L. to destroy them fr. a. host
Jos. 13 : 13. Geshurites dwell a. Isr-s
15 : 13. unto Caleb a part a. chil. of
16 : 10. Canaanites dwell a. Ephr-s
17 : 6. dau-s of Manasseh inheritance a. his sons [asseh, 16 : 9.
9. cities of Ephr. a. cities of Man-
Ju. 1 : 32. Asherites dwelt a. Can-s
33. Naphtali dwelt a. Canaanites
3 : 5 chil. of Israel dwelt a. Can-s
5 : 16. Why abodest a. sheepfolds
12 : 4. ye fugitives a. Ephraim-s (2)
18 : 1. inheritance not a. tribes of
1 S. 10 : 11. Is Saul a. the prophets? [illegible] -19 : 24. [kites (2)
15 : 6 Kenites, Get you fr. a. Amale-
2 S. 15 : 31. Ahith-l a. conspirators
23 : 18. Abishai was chief a. three (2), 1 Ch. 11 : 20. [of Pha-h
1 K. 11 : 20. Genubath was a. sons
2 K. 11 : 2. stole Joash fr. a. k.'s sons
18 : 5. none like Hezekiah a. kings
1 Ch. 4 : 23. those dwelt a. hedges
11 : 24. Benaiah, a name a. three

2 Ch. 24 : 16. buried Jehoiada a. k-s
35 : 13. offerings they divided a. peo.
Ezr. 10 : 18. a. sons of priests that had taken strange wives [like S.
Ne. 13 : 26. a. many nations not k.
Jb. 2 : 8. he sat down a. the ashes
28 : 10. cutteth out rivers a. rocks
30 : 5. They were driven fr. a. men
33 : 23. If one a. thousand to shew
36 : 14. their life is a. the unclean
39 : 25. He saith a. trumpets, Ha!
Ps. 12 : 1 faithf. fail fr. a. men [ha!
21 : 10. destroy their seed fr. a. men
45 : 9. King's dau-s a. honourable
57 : 4. My soul is a. lions [women
82 : 1. God judgeth a. the gods
89 : 6. who a. sons of the mighty be likened unto Lord? [Sam. a.
99 : 6. Moses, Aaron a. his priests;
104 : 12. fowls wh. sing a. branches
109 : 30. I will praise him a. multi.
Pr. 15 : 31. heareth reproof abideth a. the wise [riotous
23 : 20. Be not a. winebibbers; a.
27 : 22. Tho. thou bray fool a. wheat
Ec. 6 : 1. an evil, common a. men
7 : 28. one man a. a thousand: but a woman a. all those not found
Can. 2 : 2. As the lily a. thorns so my love a. the daughters
3. As the apple tree a. trees, so is my beloved a. the sons
5 : 10. My beloved chiefest a. 10,000
Is. 10 : †22. remnant a. them return
44 : 4. they shall spring up a. grass
Je. 5 : 26. a. my people wicked men
10 : 7. a. wise men none like thee
11 : 9. conspiracy a. men of Jud. (2)
14 : 22. any a. vanities of Gentiles
29 : 32. not a man to dwell a. peo.
40 : 1. bound in chains a. captive
Eze. 1 : 1. as I a. captives by Chebar
6 : 13. slain men be a. their idols
7 : † 13. their life yet a. the living
11 : 1. a. whom I saw Jaazaniah
19 : 2 thy mother? she lay a. lions
6 went up and down a. lions [(2)
20 : 9. bef. heathen, a. whom they
29 : 12. her cities a. the cities waste
34 : 12. in day he is a. his sheep
Mi 7 : 2. is none upright a. men [of
Mat. 2 : 6. not Jud. least a. princes
27 : 56. a. which was Mary Magdalene and, Mk. 15 : 40. [tombs
Mk. 5 : 3 Who had his dwelling a.
6 : 4. not honour but a. his own kin
8 : 19 I brake five loaves a. 5,000
20. And when the seven a. 4,000
13 : 10 must be published a. nations, Lu. 24 : 47. [women, 42.
Lu. 1 : 28. Hail; blessed art thou a.
2 : 44. they sought him a. kinsfolk
7 : 28. a. those born of women
10 : 3. I send you as lambs a. wolves
30. certain man fell a. thieves, 36
16 : 15. esteemed a. men is abom-n
17 : † 21. kingdom of God is a. you
22 : 37 was reckoned a. transgr-rs
24 : 5. Why seek ye living a. dead?
Jn. 6 : 9. what are they a. so many?
11 : 54. no more openly a. Jews
12 : 42. a. chief rulers many believ.
Ac. 4 : 12. none other name given a.
10 : 22. of good report a. nat-n [men
12 : 18. no small stir a. the soldiers
17 : 34. believed; a. which Dionysius
20 : 25. a. whom I have gone prea.
26 : 3. expert in questions a. Jews
4. my life a. mine own nation at
Ro. 1 : 6. a. whom are ye the called
16 : 7. who are of note a. apostles
1 Co. 5 : 1. is fornication a. you (2)
Ep. 2 : 3. a. whom our conversation
Ph. 2 : 15. a. whom ye shine as lights
Col. 1 : † 18. a. all have pre-emin-e
2 Ti. 2 : 2. heard of me a. many wit.
He. 5 : 1. every high priest fr. a. men

Ja. 3 : 6. so is tongue a. members
See **Among the GODS, Among the HEATHEN, All NATIONS, Among the PEOPLE, All THEM, Among THEM, Among US, Among YOU.**
See BRETHREN, GENTILES, JEWS, MEN, MULTITUDE, NATIONS, THEMSELVES, THORNS, YOURSELVES.

AM'ORITE.

Ge. 10 : 16. Canaan begat Jebusite
and A., 1 Ch. 1 : 14. [re the A.
14 13 Abr. dwelt in plain of Mam-
48 22. wh. I took out of hand of A.
Ex. 33 : 2. I will drive out A., 34 : 11.
Nu. 32 : 39. dispossessed A. in Gilead
De. 2 . 24. into thine hand Sihon, A.
Jos. 9 : 1. when Hittite and A. heard
11 : 3. Jabin sent to A. in the mts.
Eze. 16 : 3. thy father was an A., 45.
Am. 2 : 9. I destroyed A. bef. them
10. I led you to possess land of A.

AM'ORITES. [A.

Ge. 14 : 7. smote all the country of
15 : 16. iniquity of A. not yet full
21. Unto thy seed given the A
Ex. 3 : 17. I will bring you into the
land of the A., 8. [service
13 : 5. when into land of A. keep
23 : 23. Angel sh. bring thee unto A.
Nu. 13 : 29. A. dwell in mountains
21 : 13. that comest out of coasts
of A. ; Arnon is betw. Moab, A.
25. Isr. dwelt in all cities of A., 31.
32. took villages, drove out the A.
22 : 2. saw all Israel had done to A.
De. 1 : 7. Turn, go to mount of the A.
19. ye saw by way of mount of A.
20. Ye are come unto mount of A.
27. brought us out to deliver us
into the hand of the A., Jos. 7 : 7.
44. A. chased you as bees do
3 : 9. Hermon : A. call it Shenir
7 : 1. When Lord hath cast out A.
20 : 17. utterly destroy Hittites, A.
Jos. 3 : 10. he will drive out the A.
10 : 12. day wh. L. delivered up A
12 : 8. Hittites, A., Hivites, Jebu-s
13 : 4. unto Aphek to borders of A.
24 : 8. I brought you into land of A.
11. fought ag-t you A. Perizzites
15. choose you gods your fathers
served or gods of A. [even A.
18. Lord drave out all the people,
Ju. 1 : 34. A. forced children of Dan
35. A. would dwell in m-t Heres
36. coast of A. was from going up
3 : 5. Israel dwelt among the A.
6 : 10. fear not the gods of the A.
10 : 8. oppressed Israel in land of A.
11. Did not I deliver you from A. ?
11 : 21. Isr. possessed land of A., 22.
23. Lord hath dispossessed the A.
1 S. 7 : 14. peace betw. Israel and A.
2 S. 21 : 2. Gibeonites, remnant of A.
1 K. 9 : 20. all the people left of the
A., 2 Ch. 8 : 7. [did A.
21 : 26. Ahab did abominably, as
2 K. 21 : 11. Manasseh done wickedly above all that A. did [of A.
Ezr. 9 : 1. according to abominations
Ne. 9 : 8. covenant to give land of A.
See **KINGS of Amorites, SIHON, king of Amorites.**

A'MOS. [herdmen

Am. 1 : 1. words of A. who was amo.
7 : 8. Lord said, A., what seest ? 8 :
10. A. hath conspired ag. thee [2.
11. A. saith, Jeroboam sh. die by
12. Amaziah said unto A., O seer,
14. ans-d A, I am no prophet [flee
Lu. 3 : 25. A. which was son of Naum

A'MOZ.

2 K. 19 : 2. Isaiah the prophet, the
son of A., 20.-20 : 1. 2 Ch. 26 :
22.-32 : 20, 32. Is. 1 : 1.-2 : 1.-
13 : 1.-20 : 2.-37 : 2, 21.-38 : 1.

AMPHIP'OLIS. [thro. A.

Ac. 17 : 1. when they had passed

AMPLI'AS. [the Lord

Ro. 16 : 8. Greet A., my beloved in

AM'RAM, ITES.

Ge. 36 : † 26. children of Dishon, A.,
Eshban, and Cheran, 1 Ch. 1 : 41.
Ex. 6 : 18. sons of Kohath ; A., Izhar, Nu. 3 : 19.-26 : 58. 1 Ch. 6 :
2, 18.-23 : 12. [26 : 59.
20. A. took Jochebed to wife, Nu.
20. years of life of A. 137 years
Nu. 3 . 27. of Kohath, family of A-s
26 : 59. and Jochebed bare unto A.
Aaron, Moses, 1 Ch. 6 : 3.-23 : 13.
1 Ch. 24 : 20. Of the sons of A. ; Shu-
26 . 23. of the A-s, Izharites [bael
Ezr. 10 : 34. sons of Bani ; A. ; Uel

AM'RAPHEL. [9.

Ge. 14 : 1. days of A. king of Shinar,

AM'ZI.

1 Ch. 6 : 46. son of A. son of Bani
Ne. 11 : 12. son of A. son of Zechar-h

A'NAB. [from A.

Jos. 11 : 21. Joshua cut off Anakim
15 : 50. in the mountains ; A., Anim

A'NAH. [Man.]

Ge. 36 : 20. sons of Seir the Horite,
Zibeon, A., 1 Ch. 1 : 38.
24. chil. of Zibeon ; Ajah and A. ;
A. that found mules, 1 Ch. 1 : 40.
29. dukes ; duke Zibeon, duke A.
1 Ch. 1 : 41. The sons of A. ; Dishon

A'NAH. [Woman. (?)]

Ge. 36 : 2. A. dau. of Zibeon, 14, 18.
25. children of A. ; Dishon and
Aholibamah the dau. of A., 2.

ANAH'ARATH. [A.

Jos. 19 : 19. border was tow. Shihon,

ANAI'AH. [stood A.

Ne. 8 : 4. Ezra stood : beside him
10 : 22. chief of the people ; A. and

A'NAK. [of A.

Nu. 13 : 22. Hebron, where children
33. we saw giants, sons of A., 28.
De. 9 : 2. Who stand bef. chil. of A.?
Jos. 15 : 13. city of Arba, father of
A., which is Hebron, 21 : 11.
14. Caleb drove thence three sons
of A. (2). Ju. 1 : 20.

AN'AKIM.

De. 1 : 28. we have seen sons of A.
2 : 10. Emim many and tall as A.
11. were accounted giants as A.
2 : 21. Zamzummim tall, as the A.
9 : 2. people tall, children of A.
Jos. 11 : 21. Joshua cut off the A. fr
22. none of A. left : only in Gaza
14 : 12. heardest how A. were there
15. Arba a gr. man among the A

AN'AMIM. [1 : 11.

Ge. 10 : 13. Mizraim begat A., 1 Ch.

ANAM'MELECH. [to A.

2 K. 17 : 31. Sepharvites burnt chil.

A'NAN. [A.

Ne. 10 : 26. chief of people ; Hanan,

ANA'NI. [A.

1 Ch. 3 : 24. sons of Elioenai ; Akkub,

ANANI'AH. [Person.]

Ne. 3 : 23. Maaseiah son of A.

ANANI'AH. [Place]

Ne. 11 : 32. chil. of Benj. dwelt at A.

ANANI'AS. [phira

Ac. 5 : 1. certain man, A., with Sap-
3. A., why hath Satan filled thine
5. A., hearing these words, fell do.
9 : 10. certain disciple, named A (2)
12. Saul, seen in vision a man, A.
13. A. ans-d, I have heard of this
17. A., putting hands on him, said
22 : 12. one A., a devout man, acc.
23 : 2. A. commanded to smite Paul
24 : 1. after five days, A. descended

A'NATH.

Ju. 3 : 31. Shamgar son of A., 5 : 6.

ANATHEMA.

1 Co. 12 : † 3. no man by Spirit calleth Jesus a. [him be A.
16 : 22. if love not Lord Jesus, let

AN'ATHOTH. [Person.]

1 Ch. 7 : 8. sons of Becher, A.
Ne. 10 19. chief of people A., Nebai

AN'ATHOTH. [Place.]

Jos. 21 : 18 to chil. of Aaron cities,
A. and, 1 Ch. 6 : 60. [fields
1 K. 2 : 26. Get thee to A., thine own
Ezr. 2 : 23. men of A. 128, Ne. 7 : 27.
Ne. 11 : 32. chil. of Benj. dwelt at A.
Is. 10 : 30. unto Laish, O poor A.
Je. 1 : 1. Hilkiah, of priests in A.
11 : 21. men of A. that seek thy life
23. bring evil on men of A. [of A.
29 : 27. why not reproved Jeremiah
32 : 7. say-g, Buy my field in A., 8.
9. I bought field of Hanameel in

ANCESTORS. [A.

Le. 26 : 45. remember covenant of

ANCHOR, S. [A.

Ac. 27 : 29. cast four a-s out of stern
30. as tho. would have cast a-s out
40. when they had taken up a-s
He. 6 : 19. hope as an a. of the soul

ANCIENT. [talus

De. 33 : 15. chief things of a. moun-
Ju. 5 : 21. that a. river, Kishon
1 Ch. 4 : 22. And these are a. things
Ezr. 3 : 12. a. men that had seen first
Jb. 12 : 12. With the a. is wisdom
Pr. 22 : 28. Remove not a. landmark
Can. 7 : † 9. lips of the a. to speak
Is. 3 : 2. a. the Lord doth take away
5. child shall behave proudly ag-t
9 : 15. The a. and honourable [a.
19 : 11. say, I am son of a. kings ?
23 : 7. whose antiquity is of a. days
44 : 7. I appointed a. people [time?
45 : 21. who declared this from a.
47 : 6. upon the a. hast laid yoke
51 : 9. Awake, O arm, as in a. days
Je. 5 : 15. it is an a. nation, whose
18 : 15. to stumble from a. paths
Eze. 9 : 6. they began at the a. men
36 2. the a. high places are ours
Da. 7 : 9. and the A. of days did sit
13. one like Son came to A of days
22. Until the A. of days came
Mal. 3 : † 4. pleasant unto L. as in a.
See TIMES. [years

ANCIENTS. [a.

1 S. 24 : 13. As saith proverb of the
Ps 119 : 100. I underst more than a.
Is. 3 : 14. enter into judgm-t with a.
24 : 23. Lord shall reign bef. his a.
Je. 19 : 1. take of the a. of people,
and of the a. of priests [the a.
Eze. 7 . 26. shall perish counsel from
8 : 11. stood 70 men of a. of Israel
12. hast seen what a. do in dark
27 : 9. The a. of Gebal were in thee

ANCLE bones.

See **ANKLE bones.**

ANCLES. See ANKLES.

ANDIRONS. [broad

Eze. 40 : † 43. within were a. a hand

AN'DREW.

Mat. 4 : 18. Simon called Peter and
A. his brother, 10 . 2. Mk 1 : 16.
Mk. 1 : 29. they entered house of A.
3 : 18. A., Philip, and Bartholomew
13 : 3. John, A. asked him privately
Lu. 6 : 14. chose 12, Simon, A and
Jn. 1 : 40. One which heard was A.
44. Philip of Bethsaida, city of A.
6 : 8. One of disciples, A., saith
12 : 22. Philip telleth A. : A . Phil.
Ac. 1 : 13. upper room, abode Peter,
James, A., and

ANDRONI'CUS. [men

Ro. 16 : 7. Salute A., Junia, my kins-

A'NEM.

1 Ch. 6 : 73. Unto sons of Gershom
Ramoth, A., with her suburbs

A'NER. [of A.
Ge. 14 : 13. plain of Mamre, brother
24. men with me, A., Eshcol, Ma.
1 Ch. 6 : 70. of tribe of Manasseh, A.

ANETH'OTHITE.
2 S. 23 : 27. one of 30, Abiezer the A.
See ANTOTHITE and

ANET'OTHITE. [the A.
1 Ch. 27 : 12. 9th captain was Abiezer

ANGEL. [thee, 40.
Ge. 24 : 7. shall send his a. before
48 : 16. The A. which redeemed me
Ex. 23 : 20. Behold, I send an A. before thee, 23.-32 : 34.-33 : 2. [a.
Nu. 20 : 16. we cried, Lord sent an
Ju. 13 : 19. the a. did wondrously
2 S. 24 : 16. when a. stretched out
hand, L. said to a., 1 Ch. 21 : 15.
17. when David saw a. that smote
1 K. 13 : 18. an a. spake unto me by
19 : 5. an a. touched Elijah, 7. [a.
1 Ch. 21 : 20. Ornan turned and saw
27. L. com-ded a. he put up sword
2 Ch. 32 : 21. Lord sent a. wh. cut off
Ec. 5 : 6. nei. say bef. a., it was error
Is. 63 : 9. A. of his presence saved th.
Da. 3 : 28. God, who hath sent his a.
6 : 22. sent a., shut lions' mouths
Ho. 12 : 4. he had power over the a.
Zch. 1 : 9. a. that talked with me
said, 13, 14, 19.-2 : 3.-4 : 1, 4, 5.
-5 : 5, 10.-6 : 4. [said, Cry
14. a. that communed with me
2 : 3. another a. went to meet him
3 : 3. Joshua stood before the a., 1.
6 : 5. a. answ-d, These are 4 spirits
Mat. 28 : 5. a. said unto the women,
Fear not ye [rias
Lu. 1 : 13. a. said, Fear not, Zacha-
18. Zacharias said unto a., Wh-by
19 a. said, I am Gabriel ⌊sh. I know
26. a. Gabriel was sent unto Naz-h
28. a. said, Hail, blessed among
30. a. said, Fear not, Mary ⌊women
34. said Mary unto a., How this
35. a. said, the Holy Ghost shall
38. the a. departed from her ⌊come
2 : 10. a. said unto shepherds, Fear
13. was with a. a multitude ⌊not
21. JESUS, so named of a. before
he was conceived [oning him
22 : 43. appeared an a., strength-
Jn. 5 : 4. an a. went down into pool
12 : 29. said, An a. spake to him
Ac. 6 : 15. his face as face of an a.
7 : 35. a. which appeared in bush
38. a. which spake to him in Sina
10 : 7. a. wh. spake unto Cornelius
22. Cornelius warned by a. to send
11 : 13. he had seen a. in his house
12 : 8 a. said unto Pet., Gird thys.
9. true which was done by the a.
10. the a. departed from him
11. Lord hath sent a. and deliv-
15. said they, It is his a. ⌊ered me
23 : 8. Sadducees say, nei. a. nor spi.
9. if an a. hath spoken to him
2 Co. 11 : 14. Satan into an a. of light
Ga. 1 : 8. tho. we or a. preach other
Re. 1 : 1. signified it by a. unto John
2 : 1. Unto the a. of the church, 8,
12, 18.-3 : 1, 7, 14. [ing
5 : 2. I saw a strong a. proclaim-
7 : 2. I saw another a. ascending
8 : 3. another a. stood at altar [hand
4. smoke ascended out of the a.'s
5. the a. took censer and filled it
7. first a. sounded | 8. second a.
10. third a. | 12. fourth a. [heaven
13. I heard an a. flying through
9 : 1. fifth a. sounded | 13. sixth a.
11. a king, a. of the bottomless pit
14. Saying to sixth a., Loose 4 a-s
10 : 1. I saw another mighty a.
come down fr. heaven, 18 : 1.-20 : 1.
5. a. which I saw stand upon sea
7. in days of voice of seventh a.
Re. 10 : 8. take book in hand of a.
9. I went unto a., said, Give me
10. book out of a.'s hand ⌊book
11 : 1. a. stood, saying, Rise, meas-
15. seventh a. sounded ⌊ure temp.
14 : 6. I saw another a. fly in heav-
en, having gospel [is fallen
8. another a. followed, say-g, Bab.
9. third a., saying, If any man
15. ano. a. crying, Thrust in sickle
17. ano. a. having sharp sickle, 18.
19. and the a. thrust in his sickle
16 : 3. sec. a. poured vial upon sea
4. third a. poured vial upon rivers
5. I heard the a. of the waters say
8. fourth a. poured vial upon sun
10. fifth a. vial upon seat of beast
12. sixth a. vial upon Euphrates
17. seventh a. poured vial into air
17 : 7. a. said, Wherefore marvel?
18 : 1. I saw anoth. a. from heaven
21. mighty a. took a stone, cast it
19 : 17. I saw an a. standing in sun
20 : 1. I saw an a. having key of pit
21 : 17. of a man, that is of the a.
22 : 6. God sent his a. to shew his
8. to worship before feet of the a.
16. I Jesus have sent mine a. to

ANGEL of God. [of h.
Ge. 21 : 17. a. - called to Hagar out
31 : 11. a. - spake unto me in dream
Ex. 14 : 19. a. - wh. went bef. camp
Ju. 6 : 20. a. - said, Take the flesh
13 : 6. his like countenance of a. -
9. a. - came again unto woman
1 S. 29 : 9. thou art good as an a. -
2 S. 14 : 17. as an a. -, so is my lord
the king, 19 : 27. [a. -
20. according to the wisdom of an
Ac. 10 : 3. an a. - coming in to him
27 : 23. stood by me this night a. -
Ga. 4 : 14. received me as an a. -

ANGEL of the Lord.
Ge. 16 : 7. the a. - found Hagar by
9. a. - said unto her, Return to
10. a. - said, I will multiply thy
11. a. - said, thou art with child
22 : 11. And the a. - called out of
heaven, Abr., 15. [Ac. 7 : 30.
Ex. 3 : 2. A. - unto him in a flame,
Nu. 22 : 22. a. - stood in way ag-t
Balaam, 24, 26. [way, 25, 27.
23. ass saw a. - standing in the
31. Balaam saw a. - stand-g in way
32. a. - said, Wheref. smitten ass
34. said unto a. -, I have sinned
35. a. - said unto B., Go with men
Ju. 2 : 1. An a. - came to Bochim
4. a. - spake unto Israel, they wept
5 : 23. Curse ye Meroz, said the a.
6 : 11. a. - sat under an oak [thee
12. a. - said unto Gideon, L. with
21. a. - put forth staff, touched
the cakes Then a. - departed
22. Gideon perceived he was a. -,
he said, Alas, I have seen an a. -
13 : 3. a. - appeared unto the wom.
13. a. - said unto Manoah, Of all
15. M. said unto a. -, let us detain
16. a. - said, I not eat thy bread.
M. knew not he was an a. -
17. Manoah said unto a. -, What
is thy name [est thou
18. a. - said unto him, Why ask-
20. a. - ascended in flame of altar
21. a. - did no more appear to M.
Then Manoah knew he was a. -
2 S. 24 : 16. a. - was by the thresh-
ingpl. of Araunah, 1 Ch. 21 : 15.
1 K. 19 : 7. a. - touched Elijah and
said, Arise and eat, 2 K. 1 : 3.
2 K. 1 : 15. a. - said unto Elijah, Go
19 : 35. a. - smote of Assyrians
185,000, Is. 37 : 36. [thro-t Isr.
1 Ch. 21 : 12. or the a. - destroying
16. David saw a. - having a sword
18. a. - com-ded Gad to say to Da.
1 Ch. 21 : 30. afraid of sword of a. -
Ps. 34 : 7. a. - encampeth about th.
35 : 5. and let the a. - chase them
6. and let the a. - persecute them
Zch. 1 : 11. a. - that stood among
the myrtle trees [hav mercy
12. a. - said, O L., how long not
3 : 1. Joshua, priest, standing be-
5. and the a. - stood by ⌊fore a. -
6. the a. - protested unto Joshua
12 : 8. house of David sh. be as a. -
Mat. 1 : 20. a. - in a dream, saying,
Joseph, 2 : 13, 19. [bidden
24. Then Joseph did as a. - had
28 : 2. a. - rolled back the stone
Lu. 1 : 11. appeared unto Zach-s a. -
2 : 9. shepherds, a. - came upon th.
Ac. 5 : 19. a. - opened prison doors
8 : 26. the a. - spake unto Philip
12 : 7. behold, a. - came upon Peter
23. the a. - smote Herod because

ANGELS. [even
Ge. 19 : 1. came two a. to Sodom at
15. morning arose a. hastened Lot
Ps. 8 : 5. made him a little lower th.
the a., He. 2 : 7, 9. [sands of a.
68 : 17. chariots of God are thou-
78 : 25. Man did eat a.' food [them
49. trouble, by sending evil a. am.
Mat. 4 : 11. a. came and ministered
unto him, Mk. 1 : 13. [the a.
13 : 39. end of world, reapers are
49. a. shall come and sever wicked
18 : 10. their a. do always behold
the face of my Father in heaven
24 : 36. that hour knoweth not the
a. of heaven, Mk. 13 : 32.
25 : 31. Son of man shall come and
all holy a. with him, Mk. 8 : 38.
Lu. 9 : 26. [of a.
26 : 53. more than twelve legions
Mk. 12 : 25. but are as a. in heaven
Lu. 2 : 15. as the a. were gone away
16 : 22. beggar was carried by a.
20 : 36. they are equal unto the a.
24 : 23. they had seen a vision of a.
Jn. 20 : 12. two a. in white, sitting
Ac. 7 : 53. the law by disposition of a.
Ro. 8 : 38 nor a. able to separate us
1 Co. 4 : 9. spectacle to a. and men
6 : 3. Know ye we shall judge a.?
11 : 10. power on her head bec. of a.
13 : 1. Tho. with tongues of men
Ga. 3 : 19. ordained by a. ⌊and a.
Col. 2 : 18. in worshipping of a. [a.
2 Th. 1 : 7. revealed with his mighty
1 Ti. 3 : 16. seen of a., preached unto
5 : 21. before God and the elect a.
He. 1 : 4. made much better than a.
5. unto which of a., said he, 13.
7. And of the a. he saith, Who
maketh his a. spirits [steadfast
2 : 2. if the word spoken by a. was
5. unto a. not put in subjection
16. took not on him nature of a.
12 : 22. innumerable company of a.
13 : 2. entertained a. unawares
1 Pe. 1 : 12. wh. a. desire to look into
3 : 22. a. powers being made subj-t
2 Pe. 2 : 4. if God spared not the a.
11. a. which are greater in power
Jude 6. a. which kept not first estate
Re. 1 : 20. a. of the seven churches
5 : 11. voice of many a. about throne
7 : 1. I saw four a. standing on four
2. cried with loud voice to four a.
11. all the a. stood about throne
8 : 13. trumpet of 3 a. yet to sound
9 : 14. Loose the four a. bound in
15. the four a. were loosed, which
14 : 10. tormented in presence of a.
21 : 12. twelve gates, at gates 12 a.

ANGELS of God.
Ge. 28 : 12. a. - ascending and descending, Jn. 1 : 51. [him
32 : 1. Jacob on his way, a. - met
Mat. 22 : 30. are as a. - in heaven

Lu. 12 :8. him Son confess before a.-
9. denieth me be denied before a.-
15 : 10. joy in presence of the a. -
He. 1 : 6. let all the a. - worship him
His ANGELS. [folly
Jb. 4 : 18. h. a. he charged with
Ps. 91 : 11. shall give h. a. charge
over thee, Mat. 4 : 6. Lu. 4 : 10.
103 : 20. Bless the Lord, ye h. a.
104 : 4. maketh h. a. spirits, He. 1 :
148 : 2. Praise ye him, all h. a. [7.
Mat. 13 : 41. Son shall send h. a.
16 : 27. glory of Father with h. a.
24 : 31. he shall send h. a., they
sh. gather the elect, Mk. 13 : 27.
25 : 41. fire prepared for the devil
and h. a. [and h. a.
Re. 3 : 5. his name before the Father
12 : 7. Michael and h. a. fought;
and the dragon fought and h. a.
9. Satan was cast out and h. a.
The seven ANGELS.
Re. 8 : 2. And I saw - a. which
stood before God [prepared
6. - a. which had 7 trumpets
15 : 1. I saw - a. having 7 plagues,
7. one of beasts gave - a. 7 vials [6.
8. till 7 plagues of - a. were fulfil-d
16 : 1. voice to - a., pour out vials
17 : 1. one of - a. talked with me,
ANGER, S. [Noun.] [21 : 9.
Ge. 27 : 45. Until brother's a. turn
44 : 18. let not thine a. burn ag-t
45 : † 5. neither be a. in your eyes
49 : 6. in their a. they slew a man
7. Cursed be their a. : it was fierce
Ex. 11 : 8. he went from Pha-h in a.
32 : 19. Moses' a. waxed hot, he
22. Let not a. of my lord wax [cast
De. 9 : 19. I was afraid of the a. [a.
13 : 17. L. turn fr. fierceness of his
29 : 23. Zeboim L. overthrew in a.
24. what meaneth this great a. ?
28. the Lord rooted them out in a.
32 : 22. For a fire is kindled in mine
a., Je. 15 : 14. [of his a.
Jos. 7 : 26 Lord turned fr. fierceness
Ju. 6 : 39. Let not a. be hot ag-t me
8 : 3. their a. was abated tow. him
1 S. 20 : 34. Jonathan arose from the
table in fierce a. [his a.
2 S. 22 : † 16. at blast of breath of
2 K. 23 : † 26. a-s Manasseh provok.
2 Ch. 25 : 10. returned home in gr. a.
Es. 1 : 12. king wroth, his a. burned
Jb. 4 : † 9. by his a. are consumed
9 : 5. overturneth them in his a.
13. If God will not withdraw his a.
18 : 4. He teareth himself in his a.
21 : 17. God distributeth sorrows in
35 : 15. hath visited in his a. [his a.
Ps. 6 : 1. rebuke me not in thine a.
7 : 6. O Lord, in thine a. lift thyself
21 : 9. as oven in time of thine a.
27 : 9. put not servant away in a.
30 : 5. his a. endureth but moment
37 : 8. Cease from a., forsake wrath
38 : 3. no soundness bec. of thine a.
56 : 7. in a. cast down peo. O Lord
69 : 24. let thy a. take hold of them
74 : 1. why thine a. smoke ag. sheep
77 : 9. in a. shut up his mercies?
78 : 21. a. came up against Israel
38. many a time turned he his a.
49. cast upon them fierceness of
50. He made a way to his a. [his a.
85 : 3. turned from fierceness of a.
4. cause thine a. tow. us to cease
5. draw out a. to all generations?
90 : 7. we are consumed by thine a.
11. Who know-h power of thine a.
103 : 9. neither keep his a. for ever
Pr. 15 : 1. grievous words stir up a.
19 : 11. discretion deferreth his a.
21 : 14. A gift in secret pacifieth a.
22 : 8. the rod of his a. shall fail
27 : 4. a. is outrageous; but who

Ec. 7 : † 3. a. is better than laughter
9. a. resteth in the bosom of fools
11 : † 10. remove a. from thy heart
Is. 5 : 25. for this his a. is not turned,
9 : 12, 17, 21.-10 : 4.
7 : 4. fear not for fierce a. of Rezin
10 : 5. O Assyrian, rod of mine a.
25. a little while sh. cease mine a.
12 : 1. tho. angry, thine a. is turned
13 : 3. my mighty ones for mine a.
9. day of the Lord with fierce a.
13. day of his fierce a., La. 1 : 12.
14 : 6. he that ruled nations in a.
30 : 27. name of the Lord cometh
burning with his a. [of his a.
30. L. shall shew the indignation
42 : 25. poured upon him fury of a.
48 : 9. name's sake defer mine a.
63 : 3. will tread them in mine a., 6.
65 : † 5. These are smoke in mine a.
66 : 15. L. to render his a. wi. fury
Je. 2 : 35. his a. shall turn from me
3 : 5. will he reserve his a. for ever?
3 : 12. not cause mine a. to fall upon you : I will not keep mine a.
4 : 26. cities broken by his fierce a.
7 : 20. a. be poured upon this place
10 : 24. Lord correct me ; not in a.
17 : 4. ye kindled a fire in mine a.
18 : 23. deal with them in thine a.
21 : 5. I will fight ag. you even in a.
25 : 38. desolate bec. of his fierce a.
32 : 31. as a provocation of mine a
37. have driven them in mine a.
33 : 5. whom I have slain in mine a.
36 : 7. great is the a. the Lord hath
42 : 18. mine a. hath been poured
upon Jerus-m, 44 : 6. [fierce a.
49 : 37. bring upon them, even my
La. 2 : 1. covered Zion in his a., remembered not footstool in his a.
3. cut off in fierce a. horn of Israel
6. despised in his a. king, priest
21. slain them in day of thine a.
3 : 43. Thou hast covered with a.
66. Persecute, destroy them in a.
4 : 11. L. hath poured his fierce a.
Eze. 3 : † 14. I went in hot a. of spi-t
5 : 13. Thus mine a. be accompl-d
15. execute judgm-ts in thee in a.
7 : 3. I will send mine a. upon thee
8. accomplish mine a. upon thee
13 : 13. overflowing shower in a.
20 : 8. accomp-h my a. ag. them, 21.
22 : 20. will gather you in mine a.
25 : 14. do in Edom acc. to mine a.
35 : 11. I will do acc-g to thine a.
43 : 8. I consumed them in mine a.
Da. 9 : 16. let thine a. be turned
11 : 20. be destroyed neither in a.
nor in battle, † a-s [mine a.
Ho. 11 : 9. nor execute fierceness of
13 : 11. I gave thee king in mine a.
14 : 4. mine a. is turned from him
Am. 1 : 11. his a. did tear perpetu-y
Jon. 3 : 9. Who can tell if God turn
from his fierce a. ? [in a.
Mi. 5 : 15. I will execute vengeance
7 : 18. retaineth not his a. for ever
Na. 1 : 6. who can abide in the fierceness of his a. ? [rivers?
Ha. 3 : 8. was thine a. against the
12. didst thresh the heathen in a.
Zph. 3 : 8. upon them all my fierce a.
Mk. 3 : 5. looked on them with a.
Ep. 4 : 31. Let all a., clamour be put
away, with all malice, Col. 3 : 8.
ANGER with kindled.
Ge. 30 : 2. Jacob's a. was k. ag. Ra-
Nu. 22 : 27. Balaam's a. was k. [chel
24 : 10. Balak's a. was k. ag. Ba-m
Ju. 9 : 30. Zebul heard, his a. was k.
14 : 19. Samson ; his a. was k. and
1 S. 11 : 6. Saul heard, his a. was k.
17 : 28. Eliab's a. was k. ag. David
20 : 30. Saul's a. was k. ag. Jonath.
2 S. 12 : 5. David's a. was k. ag. man

2 Ch. 25 : 10. their a. was k. ag Jud.
ANGER with kindled.
[Relating to God or Lord.]
Ex. 4 : 14. a. of L. was k. ag Moses
Nu. 11 : 1. Lord heard it ; a. was k.
10. a. of L. was k. greatly, 12 : 9.
22 : 22. G.'s a. was k. bec. Balaam
25 : 3. and the a. of the L. was k.
against Israel, 32 : 13. Jos. 7 : 1.
2 S. 24 : 1. 2 K. 13 : 3. [time
32 : 10. the L.'s a. was k. the same
De. 6 : 15 lest a. of L. be k. ag. thee
7 : 4. so will a. of the L. be k. ag-t
you, Jos. 23 : 16. [this land
29 : 27. a. of the L. was k. against
31 : 17. my a. shall be k. ag. them
2 S. 6 : 7. a. of the Lord was k. ag-t
Uzzah, 1 Ch. 13 : 10. [ag. Judah
2 K. 23 : 26. wherewith his a. was k.
2 Ch. 25 : 15. Wheref. a. of L. was
k. ag-t Amaziah [his people
Is. 5 : 25. Thf. is a. of Lord k. ag-t
Ho. 8 : 5. mine a. is k. against them
Zch. 10 : 3. Mine a. was k. ag. shep-
Lord's ANGER, or [h-ds
ANGER of the Lord.
Nu. 25 : 4. that fierce a. - be turned
32 : 14. to augment the fierce a. -
De. 29 : 20. a. - shall smoke against
Ju. 2 : 14. And the a. - was hot ag-t
Israel, 20.-3 : 8.-10 : 7.
2 K. 24 : 20. thro. the a.- it came to
pass in Jerusalem, Je. 52 : 3.
Je. 4 : 8. fierce a. - is not turned ba.
12 : 13. ashamed bec. of fierce a. -
25 : 37. cut down bec. of fierce a. -
30 : 24. fierce a. - not return, 23 : 20.
51 : 45. deliver every man his soul
from fierce a. - [caped
La. 2 : 22. in day of L.'s a. none es-
4 : 16. The a. - hath divided them
Zph. 2 : 2. bef. a. - come upon you,
bef. the day of the L.'s a. come
3. ye shall be hid in day of L.'s a.
See **ANGER with kindled.**
Provoke, ed, eth, ing to ANGER.
De. 4 : 25. When do evil to p. him t.
a., 9 : 18.-31 : 29. 2 K. 17 : 17.
2 Ch. 33 : 6. [to a.
32 : 16. with abominations p-d him
21. p-d me t. a. with vanities, I
will p. them t. a. with foolish
Ju. 2 : 12. they p-d the L. t. a. [na.
1 K. 14 : 9. made images to p. me t. a.
15. made groves, p-g the L. t. a.
15 : 30. wherew. Jerob-m p-d L. t. a.
16 : 2. Israel to p. me t. a. with
their sins, 2 K. 17 : 11 Je. 11 :
17.-32 : 29, 32. Eze. 8 : 17.-16 : 26.
7. Baasha p-g Lord t. a. with, 13.
26. Omri to p. L. God of Isr. t. a.
33. Ahab did more to p. L. t. a.
21 : 22. wherew. hast p-d me t. a.
22 : 53. Ahaziah p-d t. a. the Lord
2 K. 21 : 6 Manasseh, to p. Lord t.
15. they have p-d me t. a. [a.
22 : 17. that they might p. me t.
a. with, 2 Ch. 34 : 25. Je. 25 : 7.
23 : 19. houses of high places to p.
the Lord t. a. [his fathers
2 Ch. 28 : 25. Ahaz p-d t. a. God of
Ne. 4 : 5 p-d thee t. a. bef. builders
Ps. 78 : 58. they p-d him t. a. with
high places, 106 : 29. [own soul
Pr. 20 : 2. p-h him t. a. sinneth ag
Is. 1 : 4. have p-d Holy One u. a.
65 : 3. A people that p-h me t. a.
Je. 7 : 18. that they may p. me t. a.
19 Do they p. me t. a. ? saith L.
8 : 19. Why have they p-d me t. a.
25 : 6. p. me not t. a. with work of
32 : 30. Israel have p-d me t. a.
44 : 3. Because of their wickedness
to p. me t. a., Eze. 8 : 17. [peo.
Eze. 32 : † 9. I will p. t. a. hearts of
Ho. 12 : 14. Ephraim p-d him t. a.

Col. 3 : 21. Fathers, p. not chil. t.
See SLOW to anger. [a.

ANGER, ED. [sore

1 S. 1 : † 6. her adversary a-d her
Ps. 106 : 32. They a-d him at waters
Ro. 10 : 19. by foolish nation I will

ANGLE. [a. you

Is. 19 : 8. that cast a. shall lament
Ha. 1 : 15. They take up with the a.

ANGRY. [32.

Ge. 18 : 30. let not the Lord be a.,
45 : 5. be not a. that ye sold me
Le. 10 : 16. Moses a. with Eleazar
De. 1 : 37. Lord was a. with me, 4 :
9 : 8. Lord was a. with you [21.
20. Lord was very a. with Aaron
Ju. 18 : 25. lest a. fellows run upon
2 S. 19 : 42. wherefore be ye a. [thee
1 K. 8 : 46. If they sin ag. thee and
thou be a. with th., 2 Ch. 6 : 36.
11 : 9. Lord was a. with Solomon
2 K. 17 : 18. Lord was very a. with
Ezr. 9 : 14. not be a. with us [Israel
Ne. 5 : 6. I was very a. when I heard
Ps. 2 : 12. Kiss the Son, lest he be a.
7 : 11. God a. with wicked every day
76 : 7. who stand when thou art a.?
79 : 5. wilt be a. for ever? 85 : 5.
80 : 4. wilt thou be a. ag. prayer of
Pr. 14 : 17. He that is soon a. deal-
21 : 19. than with an a. woman [eth
22 : 24. no friendship with a. man
25 : 23. so doth an a. countenance
29 : 22. a. man stirreth up strife
Ec. 5 : 6. Whf. God a. at thy voice?
7 : 9. Be not hasty in spirit to be a.
Can. 1 : 6. my mother's children
were a. with me [me
Is. 12 : 1. though thou wast a. with
Eze. 16 : 42. I will be no more a.
Da. 2 : 12. for this the king was very
Jon. 4 : 1. Jonah was very a. [a.
4. Doest well to be a.? 9. [death
9. I do well to be a. even unto
Mat. 5 : 22. whoso. is a. with broth.
Lu. 14 : 21. master of house being a.
15 : 28. he was a., would not go in
Jn. 7 : 23. are ye a. at me because I
Ep. 4 : 26. Be ye a. and sin not
Tit. 1 : 7. be blameless, not soon a.
Re. 11 : 18. And the nations were a.

ANGUISH.

Ge. 42 : 21. we saw the a. of his soul
Ex. 6 : 9. hearkened not unto M. for
De. 2 : 25. tremble and be in a. [a.
2 S. 1 : 9. and slay me : for a. is come
Jb. 7 : 11. I will speak in a. of spirit
15 : 24. a. shall make him afraid
Ps. 119 : 143. Trouble and a. have
taken hold on me [eth
Pr. 1 : 27. when distress and a. com-
Is. 8 : 22. shall behold dimness of a.
30 : 6. into land of trouble and a.
Je. 4 : 31. a. as of her that bringeth
6 : 24. a. taken hold of us, 50 : 43.
49 : 24. a., sorrows have taken her
Jn. 16 : 21. rememb-th no more the a.
Ro. 2 : 9. Tribulation and a. upon
2 Co. 2 : 4. out of much a. of heart

A'NIAM. [hi, A.

1 Ch. 7 : 19. sons of Shemidah, Lik-

A'NIM. [A.

Jos. 15 : 50. in the mountains, Anab,

ANISE.

Mat. 23 : 23. ye pay tithe of mint, a.

ANKLE bones.

Ac. 3 : 7. his a. b. received strength

ANKLES. [36.

2 S. 22 : † 37. a. did not slip, Ps. 18 : †
Eze. 47 : 3. the waters were to the a.

AN'NA. [prophetess

Lu. 2 : 36. was daughter of one A., a

AN'NAS. [priests

Lu. 3 : 2. A. and Caiaphas being high
Jn. 18 : 13. led him away to A. first
24. A. had sent Jesus bound unto
Ac. 4 : 6. A. the high priest [Cai.

ANOINT. [a.

Ex. 28 : 41. coats, girdles, thou shalt
29 : 7. take oil and a. him, 40 : 13.
36. altar thou shalt a., 40 : 10. [9.
30 : 26. shalt a. the tabernacle, 40 :
30. thou shalt a. Aaron and his
sons, 40 : 13, 15 (2). [tify it
40 : 11. shalt a. the laver and sanc-
Le. 16 : 32. priest, whom he shall a.
De. 28 : 40. not a. thyself with oil
Ju. 9 : 8. The trees went to a. a king
15. If in truth ye a. me king over
Ru. 3 : 3. Wash thyself and a. thee
1 S. 9 : 16. shalt a. him to be captain
15 : 1. Lord sent me to a. thee king
16 : 3. shalt a. him whom I name
12. the Lord said, Arise, a. him
2 S. 14 : 2. a. not thyself with oil
1 K. 1 : 34. let Zadok a. him king
19 : 15. a. Hazael king over Syria
16. Jehu shalt thou a. to be king :
Elisha a. to be prophet [shield
Is. 21 : 5. arise, ye princes, a. the
Da. 9 : 24. to seal up the vision and
a. the Most Holy [weeks
10 : 3. nei. did I a. myself till three
Am. 6 : 6. That a. themselves with
chief ointments [not a. thee
Mi 6 : 15. shall tread olives, but
Mat. 6 : 17. when thou fastest, a. head
Mk. 14 : 8. she is come to a. my body
16 : 1. spices, th. they might a. him
Lu. 7 : 46. My head thou didst not a.
Re. 3 : 18. a. thine eyes with eyesalve

ANOINTED.

Ex. 29 : 29. garments, to be a. th-in
Le. 4 : 3. If priest that is a. do sin
5. priest a. shall take blood, 16.
6 : 20. they shall offer when he is a.
22. priest of his sons that is a. sh.
7 : 36. in the day that he a. them
8 : 10. M. a. the tabernacle, Nu. 7 : 1.
11. he a. altar and all, Nu. 7 : 1 (2)
12. oil on Aaron's head, a. him
Nu. 3 : 3. sons of Aaron wh. were a.
7 : 10. altar in day it was a., 84, 88.
1 S. 10 : 1. Is it not because Lord a.
thee to be captain? [rael?
15 : 17. Lord a. thee king over Is-
16 : 13. Samuel a. David in midst
2 S. 2 : 4. men of Jud. a. David king
7. house of Judah have a. me king
3 : 39. I am weak though a. king
5 : 3. elders of Israel a. David king,
17. 1 Ch. 11 : 3. [king, 1 Ch. 14 : 8.
17. Philistines heard David was a.
12 : 7. I a. thee king over Israel, 2
K. 9 : 3, 6, 12. [a. himself
12 : 20. David arose, washed, and
19 : 10. Absalom whom we a. is dead
23 : 1. David the a. of the God of
1 K. 1 : 39. Zadok took oil, a. Sol-n
45. a. Sol-n king in Gibeon, 5 : 1.
2 K. 11 : 12. made him king, a. him,
23 : 30. 1 Ch. 29 : 22. 2 Ch. 23 : 11.
2 Ch. 22 : 7. Lord a. to cut off Ahab
28 : 15. a. them and carried feeble
Ps. 2 : † 6. I a. my King upon Zion
Is. 61 : 1. a. me to preach, Lu. 4 : 18.
Eze. 28 : 14. Thou art the a. cherub
Lu. 7 : 38. kissed his feet, a. them
46. this woman hath a. my feet
Jn. 1 : † 41. Messiah which is the A.
9 : 6. he a. eyes of the blind man
11. Jesus made clay and a. eyes
11 : 2. that Mary wh. a. the Lord
12 : 3. took Mary oint. a. feet of Je.
Ac. 4 : 27. Jesus whom thou hast a.
10 : 38. how God a. Jesus of Naz-h
2 Co. 1 : 21. he wh. hath a. us is God

His ANOINTED. [a.

1 S. 2 : 10. he shall exalt horn of h.
12 : 3. witness against me before the
Lord and h. a. [day
5. The L. and h. a. is witness this
2 S. 22 : 51. mercy to h. a., Ps. 18 :
Ps. 2 : 2. ag-t Lord, ag-t h. a. [50.

Ps. 20 : 6. Now know I L. saveth h. a.
28 : 8. he is saving strength of h. a.
Is. 45 : 1. saith Lord to h. a., Cyrus

Lord's ANOINTED, or ANOINTED of the Lord.

1 S. 16 : 6. Surely L.'s a. is bef. him
24 : 6. God forbid I should do this
unto the L.'s a., seeing he is the
a. of the L., 10-26. 11. [L.'s a.
10. not against my lord, for he is
26 : 9. who can stretch his hand
against the L.'s a. g iltless
16. to die; because ye have not
kept the L.'s a. [against L.'s a.
23. I would not stretch mine hand
2 S. 1 : 14. not afraid to destroy L.'s
16. I have slain the L.'s a. [a.
19 : 21. death, bec. he cursed L.'s a.
La. 4 : 20. a. of L. taken in their

Mine ANOINTED. [pits

1 S. 2 : 35. walk before m. a. for ever
1 Ch. 16 : 22. Saying, Touch not m.
a., Ps. 105 : 15. [for m. a.
Ps. 132 : 17. I have ordained a lamp

ANOINTED with oil.

Ex. 29 : 2. Take wafers a. w. o.,
Le. 2 : 4.-7 : 12. Nu. 6 : 15.
Nu. 35 : 25. unto death of priest a.
w. holy o. [a. w. o.
2 S. 1 : 21. as though he had not been
Ps. 45 : 7. God hath a. thee w. o.
of gladness, He. 1 : 9. [him
89 : 20. w. my holy o. have I a.
92 : 10. I shall be a. w. fresh o. [o.
Eze. 16 : 9. I washed and a. thee w.
Mk. 6 : 13. they a. w. o. many sick

ANOINTED ones.

Zch. 4 : 14. These are the two a. o.

Thine ANOINTED.

2 Ch. 6 : 42. O Lord, turn not away
the face of t. a., Ps. 132 : 10. [a.
Ps. 84 : 9. O God, look upon face of t.
89 : 38. hast been wroth with t. a.
51. reproached footsteps of t. a.
Ha. 3 : 13. even for salvation with t.

ANOINTEDST, EST. [a.

Ge. 31 : 13. God of Beth-el, where
thou a-dst the pillar [oil
Ps. 23 : 5. thou a-est my head with

ANOINTING.

Ex. 40 : 15. a. shall be an everlasting priesthood [Aaron (2)
Le. 7 : 35. is the portion of the a. of
Nu. 18 : 8. given by reason of the a.
Is. 10 : 27. yoke destroyed bec. of a.
1 Jn. 2 : 27. a. ye have received of
him, same a. teacheth you of all

ANOINTING, with oil.

Ex. 25 : 6. Oil for the light, spices
for a. o., 35 : 8, 28. [Le. 8 : 2.
29 : 7. take the a. o., 21.-40 : 9.
30 : 25. be a holy a. o., 31.-37 : 29.
31 : 11. the a. o. and sweet incense,
35 : 15.-39 : 38. Nu. 4 : 16.
Le. 8 : 10. Moses took the a. o., 30.
12. poured a. o. upon Aaron's h.
10 : 7. a. o. of the Lord is upon you
21 : 10. upon priest's head a. o. was
12. a. o. of his God is upon him
Nu. 4 : 16. to Eleazar pertaineth a. o.
Ja. 5 : 14. a. him with o. in name of

ANON. [Lord

Mat. 13 : 20. heareth, and a. wi. joy
Mk. 1 : 30. a. they tell him of her

ANOTHER.

Ge. 4 : 25. me a. seed instead of Abel
26 : 21. digged a. well and strove,
30 : 24. L. sh. add to me a. son [22.
37 : 9. he dreamed a. dream, told it
43 : 7. asked us, have ye a. broth.?
Ex. 21 : 10. If he take a. wife [oth
22 : 9. any lost thing, a. challeng.
Nu. 5 : 19. if not to uncleann. with a-
20. gone to a. instead of husb., 29.
8 : 8. a. bullock take for offering
14 : 24. Caleb, bec. he had a. spirit
De. 4 : 34. a nation from midst of a.

De. 28 : 32. Thy sons unto a. people
29 : 28. Lord cast them into a. land
Ju. 2 : 10. a. genera-n that knew not
9 : 37. come a. company by plain
Ru. 2 : 8. Go not to glean in a. field
1 S. 10 : 9. God gave him a. heart⌈(2)
18 : 18. a. company turned to way
17 : 30. he turned from him tow. a.
1 K. 7 : 8. his house had a. court
11 : 23. God stirred up a. adversary
14 : 5. feign herself to be a. woman
6. why feignest thyself to be a.?
21 : 6. I will give thee a. vineyard
2 K. 1 : 11. king sent a. captain of 50
7 : 8. lepers entered into a. tent
1 Ch. 2 : 26. Jerahmeel had a. wife
2 Ch. 32 : 5. Hezekiah built a. wall
Ezr. 4 : 21. not builded until a. com-t
Ne. 9 : 3. a. 4th part, they confessed
Es. 1 : 19. royal estate unto a.⌈17, 18.
Jb. 1 : 16. while speaking came a.,
19 : 27. eyes sh. behold and not a.
31 : 8. let me sow, let a. eat ⌈a.
10. Then let my wife grind unto
Ps. 16 : 4. that hasten after a. god
109 : 8. and let a. take his office
Pr. 25 : 9. discover not secret to a.
Ec. 4 : 10. hath not a. to help him
Can. 5 : 9. What is thy beloved than
a. beloved (2) ⌈speak
Is. 28 : 11. with a. tongue will he
42 : 8. my glory not give to a., 48 :
44 : 5. a. shall call hims. Jac. (2)⌊11.
57 : 8. discovered thyself to a. than
65 : 15. servants by a. name ⌊me
22. They shall not build and a. inhabit; sh. not plant and a. eat
Je. 18 : 4. he made it a. vessel, as
22 : 26. will cast thee into a. country
36 : 28. Take a. roll and write, 32.
Eze. 12 : 3. remove fr. thy place to a.
15 : 7. a. fire shall devour them
17 : 7. there was a. great eagle with
19 : 5. she took a. of her whelps⌈(2)
22 : 11. a. hath defiled dau. in law
37 : 16. take a. stick, write upon it
Da. 2 : 39. after thee a. kingdom (2)
5 : 17. Dan. said, give rewards to a.
7 : 5. behold a. beast like to a bear
6. After this, lo, a., like a leopard
8. there came up a. little horn
24. a. shall rise after them ⌈a.
Ho. 4 : 4. Yet let no man reprove
Jo. 1 : 3. their children a. generat-n
Mat. 8 : 9. I say to a., Come, Lu. 7 : 8.
21. a. of disciples said, Lu. 9 : 61.
10 : 23. persecute you, flee into a.
11 : 3. do we look for a., Lu. 7 : 19.
19 : 9. Whosoever shall marry a. committeth adultery, Mk. 10 : 11, 12. Lu. 16 : 18. ⌈fellow
26 : 71. a. maid saw him, said, This
Mk. 12 : 4. he sent a. serv., Lu. 20 : 11.
5. he sent a.; and him they killed
14 : 19. and a. said, Is it I? ⌈a.
58. within three days I will build
16 : 12. he appeared in a. form unto
Lu. 6 : 6. on a. sabbath he entered
9 : 56. And they went to a. village
59. he said unto a., Follow me
61. a. said, I will follow thee⌈yoke
14 : 19. a. said, I have bought five
20. a. said, I have married a wife
31. what king, going to warag-t a.
16 : 7. said to a., How much owest
19 : 20. a. say-g, L., here is thy pound
22 : 58. after little while a. saw him
59. hour aft. a. affirmed, this fellow
Jn. 5 : 7. a. steppeth down before me
32. is a. that beareth witness of me
43. if a. come in his own name
14 : 16. he shall give a. Comforter
18 : 15. followed, so did a. disciple
19 : 37. a. Scrip. saith, They sh. look
21 : 18. when old a. shall gird thee
Ac. 1 : 20. his bishoprick let a. take
7 : 18. a. king wh. knew not Joseph
Ac. 10 : 28. to come unto one of a. na.
13 : 35. Whf. he saith in a. psalm
17 : 7. there is a. king, one Jesus
Ro. 2 : 1. wherein thou judgest a.
21. teachest a., teachest not thys.?
7 : 4. ye should be married to a.
23. I see a. law in my members
13 : 8. he that loveth a. hath ⌈eth
1 Co. 3 : 10. laid foundation, a. build-
4 : 7. who maketh thee differ fr. a.?
6 : 1. Dare any, hav-g matter ag. a.
10 : 24. seeketh ev. man a.-'s wealth
12 : 8. to a. the word of knowledge
9. To a. faith; to a. gifts of healing
10. To a. working of miracles; to a. prophecy; to a. tongues (5)
14 : 30. any thing be revealed to a.
2 Co. 11 : 4. If he preacheth a. Jesus, if ye rec. a. spirit, a. gospel
Ga. 1 : 6. soon removed unto a. gos-
7. gospel: (which is not a.) ⌊pel
6 : 4. have rejoicing in hims., not a.
He. 4 : 8. not have spoken of a. day
7 : 11. what need a. priest should
13. he pertaineth to a. tribe ⌊rise
15. ariseth a. priest who is made
Ja. 4 : 12. who thou that judgest a.?
Re. 6 : 4. went out a. horse, was red
12 : 3. appeared a. wonder in heaven
13 : 11. a. beast coming out of the
15 : 1. I saw a. sign in heav. ⌊earth
16 : 7. I heard a. out of altar say
18 : 4. I heard a. voice from heaven
20 : 12. a. book was opened, book
See ANGEL, DAY, WAY. ⌊of l.

ANOTHER man. ⌈m.

Ge. 29 : 19. her to thee than to a.
Ex. 22 : 5. if feed in a. m.-'s field
Le. 20 : 10. adultery wi. a. m.-'s wife
27 : 20. if he have sold field to a. m.
De. 20 : 5. a new house, lest he die, a. m. dedicate it ⌈of it
6. vineyard, lest he die, a. m. eat
7. lest die in battle, a. m. take her
24 : 2. may go and be a. m.-'s wife
28 : 30. wife, a. m. shall lie wi. her
Ju. 16 : 7. sh. be weak and as a. m., 11.
1 S. 10 : 6. shalt be turned into a. m.
2 S. 18 : 26. saw a. m. running and said, Behold a. m. run-g⌈Smite
1 K. 20 : 37. he found a. m., said,
Pr. 27 : 2. Let a. m. praise thee, not
Je. 3 : 1. If wife go, become a. m.-'s
Ho. 3 : 3. thou not be for a. m.⌈m.-'s
Lu. 16 : 12. not faithful in that is a.
Ro. 7 : 3. if be married to a. m. (2)
14 : 4. Who thou judgest a. m.-'s s.
15 : 20. lest I build upon a. m.-'s fo.
2 Co. 10 : 16. not boast in a. m.-'s line

ANOTHER, with one.

Ge. 11 : 7. not underst. o. a.-'s speech
Ex. 26 : 19. two sockets under o. board, two under a., 21, 25.-
36 : 24, 26. ⌈cherub on that
37 : 8. o. cherub on this side, a.
19. Three bowls in o., three in a.
Ju. 10 : 18. princes of G. said o. to a.
Ps. 105 : 13. they went from o. nation to a., from o. kingdom to a. people, 1 Ch. 16 : 20. ⌈a.
145 : 4. o. generation sh. praise to
Is. 66 : 23. from o. new moon to a., from o. sabbath to a. ⌈(2)
Je. 51 : 31. o. messenger to meet a.
Eze. 10 : 9. o. wheel by o. cherub, a. wheel by a. cherub ⌈a. on that
40 : 26. palm trees, o. on this side,
49. pillars, o. on this side, a. on
Da. 8 : 13. o. saint speaking, a. said
Am. 4 : 7. I caused to rain upon o. city, not upon a. city⌈stoned a.
Mat. 21 : 35. took servants, beat o.,
24 : 10. then many sh. hate o. a. (2)
1 Co. 15 : 39. o. kind of flesh of men, a. of beasts, a. of fishes, a. of
40. the glory of the celestial is o., glory of the terrestrial is a.
1 Co. 15 : 41. is o. glory of sun, a. glory of moon, and a. glory of stars: o. star differeth fr. a. star
Re. 11 : 10. shall send gifts o. to a.
. See ONE another.
See ONE, joined with another.
See PARABLE, PIECE, PLACE, WAY, WENT with way.

ANSWER, S.

Ge. 41 : 16. God gave Pha. a. of peace
De. 20 : 11. if city make a. of peace
Ju. 5 : 29. she returned a. to herself
2 S. 24 : 13. see what a. I sh. return
2 Ch. 10 : 6. What counsel give ye me to return a., 9. ⌈hum
Ezr. 4 : 17. sent king an a. unto Re-
5 : 5. they returned a. by letter
Es. 4 : 15. Esther bade them return Mordecai this a. ⌈no a.
Jb. 19 : 16. my servant, he gave me
21 : 34. in your a-s falsehood ⌈Job
32 : 3. no a., and yet condemned
5. no a. in mouth of these 3 men
34 : 36. bec. of Job's a-s for wicked
35 : 12. they cry, but none giveth a.
Pr. 15 : 1. A soft a. turneth wrath
23. hath joy by a. of his mouth
16 : 1. a. of tongue is from the Lord
24 : 26. kiss lips that giveth right a.
Can. 5 : 6. I called, he gave me no a.
Je. 44 : 20. wh. had given him that
Mi. 3 : 7. for there is no a. of God⌊a.
Lu. 2 : 47. all astonished at his a-s
20 : 26. they marvelled at his a. and
Jn. 1 : 22. that we may give a. to
19 : 9. Jesus gave him no a. ⌊them
Ro. 11 : 4. what saith the a. of God
1 Co. 9 : 3. Mine a. to them is this
2 Co. 1 : † 9. we had a. of death in
2 Ti. 4 : 16. At my first a. no man
1 Pe. 3 : 15. be ready to give an a.
21. a. of a good conscience toward

ANSWER. [Verb.] ⌊God

Ge. 30 : 33. my righteousn. a. for me
Nu. 21 : † 17. O well; a. ye unto it
De. 21 : 7. sh. a., Our hands not shed
25 : 9. wife shall a., So shall it be
27 : 15. the people shall a., Amen
Jos. 4 : 7. ye sh. a., waters of Jordan
1 S. 2 : 16. he would a., Nay, give
20 : 10. if thy father a. roughly?
1 K. 9 : 9. a., Bec. they forsook Lord
12 : 6. How advise that I may a., 9.
7. If wilt a. them, and speak good
18 : † 26. saying, O Baal, a. us
29. was nei. voice, nor any to a.
2 Ch. 10 : 10. a. people, Thy father
Ne. 5 : 8. they found nothing to a.
Es. 4 : 13. Mord. com-ded to a. Esth.
Jb. 5 : 1. Call, if any that will a. thee
9 : 14. How much less sh. I a. him
32. he not a man that I should a.
13 : 22. let me speak, and a. thou me
20 : 2. my thoughts cause me to a.
23 : 5. know words wh. he would a.
31 : 14. visiteth, what sh. I a. him
35. my desire, th. Almighty a. me
32 : 1. these three ceased to a. Job
33 : 5. If canst a. me set thy words
32. If hast any thing to say, a. me
38 : 3. I will demand of thee, a. me
40 : 2. reproveth God, let him a. it
4. I am vile; what shall I a. thee
Ps. 27 : 7. L., have mercy and a. me
65 : 5. By terrible things wilt a. us
86 : 7. thou wilt a. me, 38 : † 15.
102 : 2. when I call a. me speedily
108 : 6. save with right hand, a. me
119 : 42. wherewith to a. him that reproacheth me, Pr. 27 : 11.⌈me
143 : 1. O L., in thy faithfulness a.
Pr. 15 : 28. The heart studieth to a.
22 : 21. mightest a. words of truth
26 : 5. a. a fool accord-g to his folly
Is. 14 : 32. What sh. one a. messeng.
30 : 19. when hear it, he will a. thee
41 : 28. no counsellor that could a.

Is.50 :2. I called, was none to a.? 66 :
58 : 9. Thou sh. call, Lord sh. a.⌊4.
Je. 5 : 19. shalt a., Like as ye have
forsaken me, so ⌈forsaken cov-t
22 : 9. shall a., Because they have
42 : 4. whatso. Lord shall a. you, I
Eze. 21 : 7. Whf. sighest? thou sh.a.
Da. 3 : 16. we not careful to a. thee
Jo. 2 : 19. Lord will a. his people
Zch. 13 : 6. What are these wounds?
Then he shall a. ⌈proved
Ha. 2 : 1. what I shall a. when re-
11. beam out of timber shall a. it
Mat. 22 : 46. no man able to a. him
25 : 37. sh. a., Lord, when saw, 44.
40. King shall a. unto them, 45.
Mk. 11 : 29. I will ask of you one
question, and a. me, Lu. 20 : 3.
30. baptism of John, of men? a.
14 : 40. neith. wist they what to a.
Lu. 11 : 7. he from within sh. a. ⌈a.
12 : 11. take no thought what ye sh.
13 : 25. he shall a., I know you not
21 : 14. not meditate what ye sh. a.
Ac. 24 : 10. I the more cheerfully a.
25 : 16. have license to a. for hims.
26 : 2. happy bec. I sh. a. bef. thee
2 Co. 5 : 12. somewhat to a. them
Col. 4 : 6. how ye ought to a. every

I will ANSWER. ⌊man

Jb. 13 : 22. Then call thou, I w. a.,
14 : 15. Ps. 91 : 15. Je. 33 : 3.
32 : 14. neither w. I a. him with
your speeches ⌈will shew
17. I said, I w. a. also my part; I
20. I w. open my lips and a.
33 : 12. I w. a. that God is greater
35 : 4. I w. a. thee and companions
Ps. 91 : 15. He sh. call, and I w. a.
Is. 65 : 24. before they call, I w. a.
Eze 14 : 4. I the Lord w. a. him, 7.

ANSWER with
cannot, neither, or not.

Ge. 45 : 3. his brethren could n. a.
Ex. 23 : † 2. n. a. in a cause to de-
2 S. 3 : 11. Saul could n. a. Abner
2 K. 4 : 29. if any salute thee, a. n.
18 : 36. king's commandment was,
a. him n., Is. 36 : 21. ⌈sand, 15.
Jb. 9 : 3. he c. a. him one of a thou-
40 : 5. Once spoken; but I will n. a.
Pr. 1 : 28. they shall call, I will n. a.
26 : 4. a. n. a fool acc-g to his folly
29 : 19. tho. he understand, will n.
Is. 46 : 7. one cry, yet can he n. a.⌊a.
65 : 12. when I called, ye did n. a.
Je. 7 : 27. call; but they will n. a.
Lu. 14 : 6. they could n. a. him to
22 : 68. if I ask you, ye will n. a.

ANSWERABLE.

Ex. 38 : 18. a. to hangings of court
Mat. 3 : † 8. things a. to amendm-t

ANSWERED. ⌊of life

Ge. 23 : 10. Ephron a. Abraham in
34 : 13. sons of Jacob a. Shechem
43 : 28. a., our father is in health
Ex. 15 : 21. Miriam a., Sing ye to L.
De. 1 : 14. ye a. me. The thing is good
41. ye a., We have sinned ag. Lord
Jos. 1 : 16. They a. Josh., All we will
2 : 14. a. her, Our life for yours ⌊do
15 : 19. Who a., Give me a blessing
17 : 15. Josh. a., If thou be gr. peo-
Ju. 5 : 29. Her wise ladies a. her⌊ple
8 : 8. men of Penuel a. him as men
of Succoth had a. him ⌈they
18. they a., As thou art, so were
25. they a., We will willingly give
11 : 13. k. of Ammon a. messengers
15 : 6. hath done this? they a. Sam-
10. they a., To bind Samson ⌊son
18 : 14. a. the men that went to spy
19 : 28. let us be going. But none a.
Ru. 2 : 4. a. him, The L. bless thee
3 : 9. And she a., I am Ruth, thine
1 S. 3 : 4. Samuel a., Here am I, 16.
6. Eli a., I called not, my son
1 S. 3 : 10. Sam-l a., Speak; thy serv.
5 : 8. they a., Let ark be carried
6 : 4. They a., Five golden emerods
11 : 2. Nahash a., On this condition
12 : 5. And they a., He is witness
14 : 12. men of garrison a. Jonath.
39. not a man amo. people a. him
44. Saul a., God do so and more
17 : 30. people a. him after former
58. David a., I am son of Jesse
19 : 17. Michal a. Saul, David said
20 : 28. Jonathan a. Saul, David
22 : 12. Ahitub a., Here I am, lord
30 : 22. a. all the wicked men and
2 S. 1 : 4. he a., the people are fled
7. he called. And I a., Here am I
8. I a., I am an Amalekite, 13.
2 : 20. thou Asahel? he a., I am
4 : 9. David a. Rechab, As L. liveth
9 : 6. Mephib-h a., Behold thy serv.
13 : 12. she a., Nay, do not force me
14 : 5. she a., I am a widow woman
32. Abs. a. Joab, I sent unto thee
18 : 3. people a., Thou shalt not go
29. Is young man safe? Ahim-z a.
32. Is young man safe? Cushi a.
19 : 26. Mephib-h a., serv. deceived
38. king a., Chimham sh. go with
42. men of Judah a. men of Israel
20 : 17. he a., I am he. And he a., I
21 : 5. Gibeonites a. the king ⌊hear
1 K. 2 : 30. said Joab, thus he a. me
11 : 22. Hadad a., Nothing, let me
12 : 13. And the king a. the people
roughly, 2 Ch. 10 : 13. ⌈here
18 : 8. he a., tell thy lord, Elijah is
18. he a., I have not troubled Isr.
26. was no voice nor any that a.
20 : 14. order battle? he a., Thou
21 : 6. a., I will not give my viney.
20. Elijah a., I have found thee
22 : 15. Micaiah a., Go and prosper
2 K. 1 : 8. they a., He was hairy man
2 : 5. Elisha a., Yea, I know it ⌈ness
3 : 8. he a., The way thro. wilder-
4 : 13. she a., I dwell amo. mine own
14. Gehazi a., She hath no child
26. Is it well? she a., It is well
6 : 2. Let us go. Elisha a., Go ye
3. go with thy servants. He a., I
16. Elisha a., Fear not; for ⌊will
22. he a., Thou shalt not smite
28. aileth? She a., This woman
7 : 2. a lord a. the man of God, 19.
8 : 12. he a., Bec. I know the evil
13. Elisha a., Lord hath shewed
14. What said Elisha? Hazael a.
9 : 19. Jehu a., What thou wi. peace
22. he a., What peace so long as
10 : 13. Who are ye? They a., breth.
15. Is heart right? Jehonadab a.
20 : 10. Hez-h a., It is a light thing
15. What seen in thine house?
Hezekiah a., Is. 39 : 4. ⌈peo. more
1 Ch. 21 : 3. Joab a., Lord make his
2 Ch. 2 : 11. Huram, a. in writing
7 : 22. be a., Bec. they forsook L.
10 : 14. a. aft. advice of young men
16. people a., What portion we in
18 : 3. Jehosh. a., I am as Thou art
25 : 9. man of God a., Lord is able
34 : 23. Huldah a., Tell the man
Ne. 6 : 4. I a. them aft. same man-r
8 : 6. all the peo. a., Amen, Amen
Es. 1 : 16. Memucan a. before king
5 : 4. Esther a., let Haman come
6 : 7. Haman a. king, For the man
Jb. 9 : 16. If I had called and he a.
11 : 2. Sho. multitude of words be a.
32 : 12. none of you a. Job's words
15. were amazed, a. no more, 16.
Je. 36 : 18. How write all? Baruch a.
44 : 15. all people in Eg. a. Jere-h
Eze. 24 : 20. tell what these are? I a.
37 : 3. can these bones live? I a.
Da. 2 : 14. Daniel a. with wisdom
Mi. 6 : 5. what Balaam a. Balak⌊Ar.
Zch. 1 : 11. a. angel amo. myrtle trees
19. angel a., These are the horns
3 : 4. Joshua a., Take aw. garments
4 : 4. I a. angel that talked wi. me
6. he a., This is word unto Zerub-l
5 : 2. I a., I see a flying roll ⌈herd
10 : † 2. they a., there was no shep-
Mat. 12 : 38. a., we would see a sign
27 : 12. when he was accused, he a.
nothing, 14. Mk. 14 : 61.–15 : 3,
5. Lu. 23 : 9. ⌈man
Mk. 8 : 4. disciples a., Whence can
28. And they a., John the Baptist
9 : 12. he a., Elias cometh first ⌈well
12 : 28. one perceiving th. he had a.
34. Jesus saw that he a. discreetly
15 : 9. Pilate a., will ye th. I release
Lu. 10 : 28. thou hast a. right; this
11 : 45. Then a. one of the lawyers
13 : 14. ruler a. with indignation
20 : 7. a. they could not tell ⌈No
Jn. 1 : 21. thou that Prophet? he a.,
49. Nathanael a. and saith, Rabbi, thou art Son of God ⌈no man
5 : 7. impotent man a., Sir, I have
11. he a., He that made me whole
6 : 7. Philip a., 200 pennyworth of
68. Peter a., L., to whom sh. we go
7 : 46. officers a., Never man spake
47. a. Pharisees, Are ye deceived?
8 : 33. They a., We be Abr.'s seed
10 : 33. Jews a., For good work we
stone thee not ⌈out of the law
12 : 34. people a., We have heard
18 : 5. Whom seek ye? They a.,
35. Pilate a., Am I a Jew? ⌊Jesus
19 : 7. Jews a., We have a law ⌈Ce.
15. priests a., We have no k. but
22. Pilate a., What I have written
21 : 5. any meat? They a. him, No
Ac. 5 : 8. Peter a., Tell whe. ye sold
9 : 13. Ananias a., Lord I have
heard of this man ⌈bid water
10 : 46. a. Peter, Can any man for-
11 : 9. voice a. me again fr. heaven
15 : 13. James a., Men and breth-n
21 : 13. Paul a., What mean ye to
22 : 8. I a., Who art thou, L.? ⌊weep
28. chief capt. a., With a great
24 : 10. Paul a., Forasmuch ⌊sum
25. Felix a., Go thy way for ⌈12.
25 : 4. Festus a. that Paul be kept,
8. While he a. for himself, 26 : 1.
16. I a.; It is not manner of Ro-

ANSWERED. ⌊mans
[Relating to God.] ⌈tress

Ge. 35 : 3. God, who a. me in dis-
Ex. 19 : 19. Moses spake, God a. by v.
1 S. 7 : † 9. Samuel cried, the L. a.
10 : 22. L. a., he hath hid himself
14 : 37. he a. not Saul th. day, 28 : 6.
23 : 4. L. a. David, said, go to Kei-
30 : 8. he a. David, Pursue ⌊lah
2 S. 21 : 1. Lord a., It is for Saul
1 Ch. 21 : 26. L. a. Dav. by fire upon
28. a. him in threshingfl. of Ornan
Jb. 38 : 1. Then Lord a. Job out of
whirlwind, 40 : 1, 6. ⌈thunder
Ps. 81 : 7. I a. thee in the place of
99 : 6. they called upon Lord, he a.
118 : 5. L. a. set me in large place
Is. 6 : 11. he a., Until cities wasted
Je. 23 : 35. What hath Lord a., 37.
Ha. 2 : 2. Lord a. me, Write vision
Zch. 1 : 13. Lord a. angel that talked

ANSWERED.
[Relating to Jesus.]

Mk. 8 : 33. he a., Who is my mother
12 : 29. J. a., The first of all com-ts
Lu. 8 : 50. he a., Fear not · believe
14 : 5. he a., Which of you shall
have an ass fallen ⌈born of wat.
Jn. 3 : 5. Jesus a., Except a man be
5 : 17. J. a., My Father worketh, I
6 : 70. J. a., Have not I chosen you
8 : 19. J. a., Ye nei. know me nor
34. J. a., Whoso. committeth sin

Jn. 8 : 49. Jes. a., I have not a devil
54. J. a., If I honour myself, my
9 : 3. J. a., Neither this man sinned
27. he a., I have told you already
10 : 25. J. a., I told you, and ye believed not [I shewed
32. J. a., Many good works have
34. J. a., Is it not written in law
11 : 9. J. a., Are there not 12 hours
12 : 23. J. a., The hour is come th.
13 : 8. J. a., If I wash thee not [sop
26. J. a., He it is to whom I give a
36. J. a., Whither I go thou canst
38. J. a., Wilt lay down life [not
16 : 31. J. a., Do ye now believe?
18 : 8. J. a., I have told you, I am
20. J. a., I spake openly to w. [he
23. J. a., If I have spoken evil
34. J. a., Sayest this of thyself
36. J. a., My kingdom is not of
37. J. a., Thou sayest, I am a k-g
19 : 11. J. a., Thou no power ag-t

ANSWERED not. [it

1 S. 4 : 20. she a. n. nei. did regard
14 : 37. he a. Saul n. th. day, 28 : 6.
2 S. 22 : 42. L. a. them n., Ps. 18 : 41.
1 K. 18 : 21. people a. him n. a word, 2 K. 18 : 36. Is. 36 : 21. [35 : 17.
Je. 7 : 13. I called you, but ye a. n.,
Mat. 15 : 23. Jesus a. her n. a word

ANSWERED and said.

[Relating to Jesus.]

Mat. 4 : 4. he a. -, It is written, Man shall not live by, Lu. 4 : 4.
11 : 4. J. a. -, Go shew John things
25. J. a. -, I thank thee, O Fath.
12 : 39. he a. -, An evil and adult-s
48. he a. -, Who is my mother? and who my, Lu. 8 : 21. [to know
13 : 11. he a. -, Bec. it is given you
37. he a. -, He th. soweth good s.
15 : 3. he a. -, Why ye transgress
13. he a. -, Every plant which Fa.
24. he a. -, I am not sent but unto
26. he a. -, It is not meet to take
28. J. a. -, O woman, gr. thy faith
16 : 2. he a. -, When it is evening
17. J. a. -, Blessed art thou, Sim.
17 : 11. J. a. -, Elias sh. first come
17. J. a. -, O faithless generation
19 : 4. he a. -, Have ye not read th.
20 : 22. J. a. -, Ye know not what
21 : 21. J. a. -, If ye have faith ye
24. J. a. -, I will ask you one thing, Mk. 11 : 29. Lu. 20 : 3.
22 : 1. J. a. -, The kingd. of heaven
29. J. a. -, Ye do err, not knowing
24 : 4. J. a. -, Take heed th. no man
26 : 23. J. a. -, He that dippeth his hand with me, Mk. 14 : 20. [eat
Mk. 6 : 37. he a. -, Give ye them to
7 : 6. J. a. -, Well Esaias prophesied
10 : 3. J. a. -, What did M. command
5. J. a. -, For hardness of heart
29. J. a. -, is no man hath left ho.
51. J. a. -, What wilt thou I do
11 : 14. J. a. -, No man eat fruit of
12 : 35. J. a. -, How say scribes
14 : 48. J. a. -, Are ye come as ag-t
Lu. 4 : 8. J. a. -, Get behind me, Sa.
10 : 41. J. a. -, Martha, thou art
13 : 15. L. a. -, Thou hypocrite
17 : 20. he a. -, The kingdom of G.
19 : 40. he a. -, I tell you if these
22 : 51. J. a. -, Suffer ye thus far
23 : 3. he a. -, Thou sayest it
Jn. 1 : 48. J. a. -, when wast under fig tree I saw thee [believest
50. J. a. -, Bec. I said, I saw thee,
2 : 19. J. a. -, Destroy temple, and
3 : 3. J. a. -, Except a man be born
3 : 10. J. a. -, Art thou a master of
4 : 10. J. a. -, If knewest gift of God
13. J. a. -, Whoso. drinketh this
5 : 19. a. J. and s., The Son can do nothing of himself [ye did eat
6 : 26. J. a. -, Ye seek me because

Jn. 6 : 29. J. a. -, This is work of God
43. J. a. -, Murmur not among
7 : 16. J. a. -, My doctrine is not m.
21. J. a. -, I have done one work
8 : 14. J. a. -, Though I bear record
12 : 30. J. a. -, This voice came not bec. of me, but for your [est not
13 : 7. J. a. -, What I do thou know-
14 : 23. J. a. -, If any man love me

See **JESUS said.**

ANSWERED and said.

Ge. 18 : 27. Abr. a. -, I have taken
24 : 50. Laban a. -, The thing from
27 : 37. Isaac a. - unto Esau, 39. [L.
31 : 14. Leah a. -, Is any portion
31. Jacob a. -, Bec. I was afraid
36. Jacob a. -, What is my tresp.?
43. Laban a. -, These are my dau-s
40 : 18. Joseph a. -, This is interp-n
Ex. 4 : 1. Moses a. -, But they will not believe me [24 : 3.
19 : 8. people a. -, All we will do,
Nu. 11 : 28. Joshua a. -, My lord Mo.
22 : 18. Balaam a. -, unto servants
23 : 12. B. a. -, Must I not take heed
26. B. a. - unto Balak, Told I not
De. 1 : 14. ye a. -, The thing spoken
41. ye a. -, We have sinned ag. L.
Jos. 7 : 20. Achan a. -, I have sinned
9 : 24. a. -, we were afraid of you
22 : 21. Gad a. -, unto heads of Isr.
26 : 16. peo. a. -, God forbid [else
Ju. 7 : 14. fellow a. -, This is noth.
20 : 4. Levite a. -, I came into Gib-h
Ru. 2 : 6. servant a. -, It is the Moabitish damsel [shewed me
11. Boaz a. -, It hath been fully
1 S. 1 : 15. Hannah a. -, No, my lord
17. Eli a. -, Go in peace; and God
4 : 17. messenger a. -, Israel is fled
9 : 8. serv. a. -, I have part of shek.
12. Is seer here? Maidens a. -, He
19. Sam-l a. -, I am the seer [ite
21. Saul a. -, Am not I a Benjam-
10 : 12. one a. -, who is their fath.?
14 : 28. a. -, Thy fath. charged peo.
16 : 18. a. -, I have seen son of Jes.
18 : 7. women a. -, Saul hath slain
20 : 32. Jonathan a. - unto Saul, Whf. he be slain? [mon bread
21 : 4. priest a. -, There is no com-
5. David a. -, women been kept fr.
22 : 9. Doeg a. -, I saw son of Jesse
14. Ahim-h a. -, who so faithful
25 : 10. Nabal a. -, Who is David?
26 : 6. David a. - to Ahimelech, Who will go with me [est to king
14. Abner a. -, Who thou that cri-
22. David a. -, Behold, k.'s spear!
29 : 9. Achish a. -, thou art good
30 : 22. a. all the wicked men and s.
2 S. 13 : 32. And Jonadab a. -, Amnon only is dead [not from me
14 : 18. k-g a. - unto woman, Hide
19. woman a. -, As thy soul liveth
15 : 21. Ittai a. -, As Lord liveth [ei
19 : 21. Abishai a. -, Sh. not Shim-
43. Isr. a. -, We have ten parts in
20 : 20. Joab a. -, Far be it from me
1 K. 1 : 28. David a. -, Call Bath-sh.
36. Benaiah a. -; Amen; L. say
43. Jonathan a. -, David hath made Solomon king [er, Why
2 : 22. Solomon a. - unto his moth-
3 : 27. k. a. -, Give her living child
13 : 6. Jerob. a. -, Entreat L. for me
18 : 24. people a. -, It is well spok.
20 : 4. king of Isr. a. -, I am thine
11. a. -, Let not him that girdeth
2 K. 1 : 10. Elijah a. - to captain, 12.
11. capt. a. -, O man of God, Come
8 : 11. one of the servants a. -, Here is Elisha [of horses
7 : 13. one a. -, Let some take five
19. lord a. -, If L. make windows, 2.
1 Ch. 12 : 17. David a. -, If ye be come peaceably

2 Ch. 29 : 31. Hezekiah a. -, ye have
31 : 10. Azariah a. -, Since the peo.
34 : 15. Hilkiah a. - to Shaphan
Ezr. 10 : 2. Shecaniah a. - unto Ezra, We have trespassed ag. God
12. all congregation a. -, so must
Ne. 2 : 20. I a. -, God will prosper us
Es. 5 : 7. Esther a. -, My petition is
7 : 3. Esther a. -, If favour in thy
5. k. a. - unto Esther, Who is he
Jb. 1 : 7. Whence comest thou? Satan a. -, From going, 2 : 2.
9. Satan a. -, Doth Job fear God for nought? [for his life
2 : 4. Satan a. -, Skin for skin, all
3 : † 2. Job a. -, 6 : 1.-9 : 1.-12 : 1. -16 : 1.-19 : 1.-21 : 1.-23 : 1.-26 : 1.-40 : 3.-42 : 1. [15 : 1.-22 : 1.
4 : 1. Eliphaz the Temanite a. -,
8 : 1. Then a. Bildad the Shuhite and s., 18 : 1.-25 : 1. [s., 20 : 1.
11 : 1. a. Zophar, Naamathite and
32 : 6. Elihu, Buzite, a. -, 34 : 1.
40 : 1. Moreover L. a. Job and s., 6.
Is. 21 : 9. he a. -, Babylon is fallen
Je. 11 : 5. a. I and s., So be it, O L.
Da. 2 : 5. king a. - to the Chaldeans
7. They a. -, Let king tell dream
8. king a. -, ye would gain time
10. Chaldeans a. -, not a man can
15. Daniel a. -, Why is decree so
20. Dan. a. -, Blessed be name of G.
26. king a. - to Daniel, thou able
27. Dan. a. - in presence of king
47. king a. - unto Dan. your God
3 : 16. Shadrach, Meshach a. - to k.
24. counsellors a. -, True, O king
25. king a. -, Lo, I see 4 men loose
4 : 19. Belteshazzar a. -, My lord
5 : 17. Daniel a. -, Let gifts be to
6 : 12. king a. -, The thing is true
13. a. -, Dan. regardeth not thee
Am. 7 : 14. Amos a. -, I no prophet
Hag. 2 : 12. holy? priests a. -, No, 13.
14. Haggai a. -, So is this people
Zch. 1 : 10. man am myrtle trees a. -
12. angel a. -, O Lord, how long not have mercy [these be? 13.
4 : 5. angel a. -, knowest what
11. I a. -, What these two olive trees, 12.-6 : 4. [spirits
6 : 5. angel a. -, These are the four
Mat. 8 : 8. centurion a. -, I am not
14 : 28. Peter a. -, 15 : 15.-16 : 16.-17 : 4.-19 : 27.-26 : 33. Mk. 9 : 5. Lu. 7 : 43. [no wrong
20 : 13. he a. -, Friend, I do thee
21 : 27. priests and elders a. -, We cannot tell, Mk. 11 : 33. [went
29. He a. -, I will not; but afterw.
30. second a. -, I go, sir; went not
25 : 12. he a. -, Verily I kno. you not
26. lord a. -, Thou wicked servant
26 : 25. Judas a. -, Master, is it I?
63. high priest a. -, I adjure thee by living God [death
66. They a. -, He is guilty of
27 : 21. governor a. -, Whether of the twain will ye that I release
25. people a. -, His blood be on us
28 : 5. angel a. - unto wom[n [dogs
Mk. 7 : 28. she a. -, Yes, Lord; yet
9 : 17. one a. -, I have brought son
10 : 20. he a. -, these have I ob-
15 : 12. Pilate a. -, What [served
Lu. 1 : 35. angel a. -, Holy Gh. shall
60. his mother a. -. Not so [come
9 : 49. John a. -, Master, we saw one casting out devils [said
17 : 37. they a. -, Where, Lord? he
20 : 24. what image, They a. -, Ce-
Jn. 2 : 18. Jews a. -, What sign [sar's
3 : 9. Nicodemus a. -, How can th.
27. John a. -, A man can receive nothing exc. from heaven [band
4 : 17. woman a. -, I have no hus-
7 : 20. peo. a. -, Thou hast a devil

Jn. 7 : 52. a. -, Art thou of Galilee?
8 : 39. They a. -, Abr. is our father
48. Jews a. -, Say we not well, th.
9 : 11. He a. -, A man Jes. made clay
20. His parents a. -, this our son
25. He a. -, Whe. he a sinner or no
30. man a. -, herein is marvellous
34. They a. -, Thou wast b. in sins
36. He a. -, Who is he, Lord, that
18 : 30. a. -, If he not a malefactor
20 : 28. Thomas a. -, My L. and my
Ac. 4 : 19. But Peter and John a. -,
Whether it be right, 5 : 29.
8 : 24. Simon a. -, Pray ye for me
34 eunuch a. -, of whom speaketh
37. he a. -, I believe Jes. [prophet
19 : 15. evil spirit a. -, Jes. I know
25 : 9. Festus a. -, Wilt go to Jerus.

ANSWERED, saying. [s.
Ge. 23 : 5. children of Heth a. Abr.,
14. Ephron a. Abr., s., land worth
41 : 16. Joseph a., s., It not in me
42 : 22. Reuben a., s., Do not sin
Nu. 32 : 31. children of Gad a., s.,
As the Lord said, Jos. 22 : 21.
Jos. 1 : 16. they a. Joshua, s., All
that . . . we will do [be
1 S. 17 : 27. people a., s., So shall it
1 K. 12 : 16. people a. king, s., What
portion in David? [Jeremiah, s.
Je. 44 : 15. the people in Pathros a.
Mat. 25 : 9. the wise a., s., Not so
Mk. 3 : 33. a., s., Lu. 8 : 50.-14 : 5.
5 : 9. he a., s., My name is Legion
9 : 38. John a., s., Master, we saw
Lu. 3 : 16. John a., s., I baptize you
with water, Jn. 1 : 26. [these
Re. 7 : 13. one of elders a., s., What

ANSWEREDST.
Ps. 99 : 8. Thou a. them, O Lord
138 : 3. when I cried thou a. me

ANSWEREST. [Abner?
1 S. 26 : 14. Dav. cried, a. thou not,
Jb. 16 : 3. emboldeneth that thou a.
Mat. 26 : 62. the high priest said, a.
thou nothing? Mk. 14 : 60.-15 : 4.
Jn. 18 : 22. a. thou high priest so?
Ro. 9 : † 20. who art thou that a. G.

ANSWERETH.
1 S. 28 : 15. God a. me no more [God
1 K. 18 : 24. th. a. by fire let him be
Jb. 12 : 4. calleth upon God, he a.
33 : † 13. he a. not of his matters
Pr. 18 : 13. a. a matter bef. he hear-
23. but the rich a. roughly [eth it
24 : †26. sh. kiss his lips th. a. right
27 : 19. As face a. to face so heart
Ec. 5 : 20. God a. him in the joy of
10 : 19. but money a. all things [a.
Mal. 2 : † 12. L. will cut off him that
Mk. 8 : 29. Pet. a., Thou art the Ch.
9 : 19. He a., O faithless generation
10 : 24. Jes. a., Chil., how hard is it
Lu. 3 : 11. He a., He th. hath 2 coats
Ga. 4 : 25. Agar a. to Jerus-m which

ANSWERING. [now is
Jb. 32 : † 1. men ceased from a. Job
Lu. 23 : 40. other a., rebuked him
Tit. 2 : 9. servants obedient, not a.

ANSWERING, said.
Lu. 1 : 19. angel a. s., I am Gabriel
5 : 5. Simon a. s., We have toiled
9 : 19. They a. s., John the Baptist
20. Peter a. s., The Christ of God
13 : 8. he a. s., let it alone this yr.
15 : 29. he a. s. to his father, Lo
20 : 39. scr. bes a. s., Thou well said
24 : 18. Cleopas a. s., thou stranger

Jesus ANSWERING, with
said, saith, say, or spake.
Mat. 3 : 15. J. a. s-d, Suffer it to be
Mk. 11 : 22. J. a. s-h, Have faith in G.
33. J. a. s-h, Neither do I tell you
12 : 17. J. a. s-d, Render to Cesar
24. J. a. s-d, Do ye theref. not err
13 : 2. J. a. s-d, Seest buildings?
5. Jes. a. began to s-y, Take heed

Mk. 15 : 2. J. a. s-d, Thou sayest it
Lu. 4 : 12. J. a. s-d, Thou not tempt
5 : 22. J. a. s-d, What reason ye in
31. J. a. s-d, They that are whole
6 : 3. J. a. s-d, Have ye not read so
7 : 22. J. a. s-d, Go your way, tell
40. J. a. s-d, Simon, I have somew.
9 : 41. J. a. s-d, O faithless genera.
10 : 27. J. a. s-d, Thou sh. love L.
30. J. a. s-d, A certain man went
13 : 2. J a. s-d, Suppose ye these
14 : 3. J. a. s-e unto lawyers, Is it
lawful to heal [cleansed?
17 : 17. And J. a. s-d, Were not ten
20 : 34. J. a. s-d, chil. of this world

ANT, S. [marry
Pr. 6 : 6. Go to the a., thou sluggard
30 : 25. a-s are a people not strong

ANTICHRIST, S.
1 Jn. 2 : 18. A. shall come, even now
there are many a-s
22. He is a. that denieth the Fath.
4 : 3. and this is that spirit of a.
2 Jn. 7. This is a deceiver and an a.

AN'TIOCH.
Ac. 6 : 5. Nicolas, a proselyte of A.
11 : 19. they travelled as far as A.
20. when were come to A., spake
22. Barnabas th. he go as far as A.
26. B. found Saul bro-t him unto
A.; called Christians first in A.
27. prophets from Jerus. unto A.
13 : 1. in church at A. cert. prophet
14. they came to A. in Pisidia [P-l
14 : 19. Jews from A. having stoned
21. had preached, returned to A.
26. into Attalia; thence sailed to
15 : 22. send chosen men to A. [A.
23. greeting unto brethren in A.
30. when dismissed, came to A. [A.
35. Paul, Barnabas continued in
18 : 22 saluted church, went to A.
Ga. 2 : 11. When Pet. was come to A.
2 Ti. 3 : 11. my persecutions at A.

AN'TIPAS. See MARTYR.

ANTIPA'TRIS. [A.
Ac. 23 : 31. bro-t Paul by night to

ANTIQUITY. [days
Is. 23 : 7. city, whose a. is of ancient

ANTOTHI'JAH.
1 Ch. 8 : 24. heads of the fathers, A.

AN'TOTHITE. [the A.
1 Ch. 11 : 28. valiant men, Abiezer
12 : 3. came to David Jehu the A.

AN'UB. [bah
1 Ch. 4 : 8. Coz begat A. and Zobe-

ANVIL.
Is. 41 : 7. him that smote the a.

ANY. [Adj.] [stranger
Ge 17 : 12. bought with money of a.
31 : 14. a. portion for us in father's
36 : 31. kings in the land before a.
king of Israel, 1 Ch. 1 : 43. [you
42 : 16. proved, whether a. truth in
Ex. 1 : 10. when falleth out a. war
12 : 39. neither prepared a. victuals
16 : 24. neither was a. worm therein
20 : 4. Thou shalt not make a.
graven image, or a. likeness,
Le. 26 : 1. De. 4 : 16, 17 (2), 18
(2).-16 : 22. [give life for life
21 : 23. if a. mischief follow, then
22 : 22. Ye shall not afflict a. widow
31. nei. eat a. flesh torn of beasts
32 : 24. Whoso. hath a. gold, break
34 : 10. not been done in a. nat. [ey
Le. 2 : 11. burn no leaven nor a. hon-
6 : 27. is sprinkled upon a. garm-t
11 : 38. if a. water upon the seed,
and a. part of carcass fall
13 : 24. if a. flesh, in skin whereof
18 : 30. commit not a. one of these
19 : 18. Thou sha. not bear a. grudge
28. not make a. cuttings in your
flesh, nor print a. marks, 21 : 5.
21 : 9. dau. of a. priest, if profane
17. Whosoever hath a. blemish

Nu. 5 : 6. man or wom. commit a. sin
6 : 3. nei. drink a. liquor of grapes
9 : 12. nor break a. bone of it
15 : 27. if a. soul sin thro. ignorance
21 : 5. no bread, nei. a. water, 20 : 5.
23 : 23. nei. a. divination ag. Israel
De. 2 : 19. not of land a. possession
4 : 16. Lest similitude of a. figure
17. likeness of a. [wl | 18. a. fish
7 : 7. ye were not more than a. people
14 : 1. nor a. baldness for the dead
15 : 21. if a. blemish, not sacrifice it
16 : 21. not plant a. trees near altar
17 : 1. shalt not sacrifice a. bullock
wh-in is a. evilfavouredness [son
18 : 10. not be a. one that maketh
19 : 15. One witness shall not rise
against a man for a. iniquity or
a. sin, in a. sin that he sinneth
20. commit no more a. such evil
24 : 5. nei. be charged with a. busi.
29 : 23. nor a. grass groweth [them
32 : 28. nei. a. understanding in
Jos. 6 : 10. not shout, nor make a.
noise, nei. a. word out of mouth
13 : 33. unto Levi not a. inherit-e
Ru. 2 : 22. that they meet thee not
in a. other field [to blind
1 S. 12 : 3. have I received a. bribe
14 : 24. Cursed th. eateth a. food, 28.
2 S. 7 : 6. I not dwelt in a. house
14 : 32. if a. iniquity in me, kill me
19 : 42. hath he given us a. gift?
1 K. 10 : 20. not the like in a. kingd.
2 K. 10 : 5. we will not make a. king
1 Ch. 29 : 25. as not on a. king bef.
2 Ch. 9 : 9. neither a. spice as queen
Jb. 6 : 6. a. taste in white of an egg?
8 : 12. flag withereth bef. a. herb
9 : 33. Nei. a. daysman betwixt us
10 : 22. of darkn., without a. order
16 : 17. Not for a. injustice in mine
25 : 3. Is a. number of his armies?
Ps. 4 : 6. Who will shew us a. good?
38 : 3. neith. a. rest bec. of my sin
59 : 5. be not merciful to a. trans-
74 : 9. no more a. prophet [gressors
86 : 8. nei. a. works like thy works
91 : 10. neith. a. plague come nigh
119 : 133. let not a. iniquity have
dominion over me [mouths
135 : 17. neither a. breath in their
139 : 24. see if a. wicked way in me
141 : 4. Incline not my heart to a.
evil thing [a. being
146 : 2. sing praises, while I have
147 : 20. not dealt so with a. nation
Pr. 6 : 35. will not regard a. ransom
14 : 34. sin a reproach to a. people
Ec. 1 : 11. neith. a. remembrance of
2 : 10. not my heart from a. joy
Is. 2 : 7. nei. a. end of treasures (2)
26 : 18. not wrought a. deliverance
53 : 9. neith. a. deceit in his mouth
56 : 2. keepeth hand fr. doing a. evil
Je. 9 : 4. trust ye not in a. brother
37 : 17. Is there a. word from Lord?
50 : 40. nei. a. son of man dwell th-n
51 : 43. nei. doth a. son of man pass
La. 1 : 12. see if a. sorrow like my
3 : 49. mine eye trickleth without
a. intermission [pity
Eze. 5 : 11. neither will I have a.
8 : † 17. Is a. thing lighter than to
12 : 24. be no more a. vain vision
18 : 8. nei. hath taken a. increase
23. I a. pleasure that wicked die?
31 : 8. not a. tree like him [wine
44 : 21. Neith. shall a. priest drink
Da. 2 : 10. no king asked at a. magi-
30. not for a. wisdom I have [cian
6 : 4. nei. a. error or fault in him
5. not find a. occasion ag. Daniel
8 : 4. nei. a. that could deliver out
11 : 15. neith. there be a. strength
to withstand [tans enter not
Mat. 10 : 5. into a. city of Samari-

Mat. 13 : 19. When a. one heareth w
Mk. 12 : 34. no man after that durst
ask him a. question, Lu. 20:40.
14 : 63. What need we a. further
witnesses, Lu. 22 : 71. [rection
Lu. 20 : 27. deny there is a. resur-
24 : 41. Have ye here a. meat? Jn.
Ac. 13 : 15. a. word of exhort-n [21:5.
19 : 2. whether be a. Holy Ghost
24 : 20. if found a. evil doing in me
25 : 5. if be a. wickedness in him
17. with-t a. delay I sat on judgm.
Ro. 9 : 11. not having done a. good
1 Co. 7 : 12. if a. brother have a wife
2 Co. 1 : 4. which are in a. trouble
Ga. 1 : 8. preach a. other gospel, 9.
Ep. 5 : 5. nor hath a. inheritance in
Ph. 2 : 1. If be a. consolation in Ch.,
a. comfort, a. fellowship (4)
4 : 8. if a. virtue, a. praise, think
Col. 2 : 23. not in a. honour to satisfying of the flesh [matter
1 Th. 4 : 6. no man defraud in a.
He. 4 : 12. than a. twoedged sword
13. Nei. is a. creature not manif-t
12 : 15. lest a. root of bitterness
16. Lest be a. fornicat-r or profane
1 Pe. 3 : 6. not with a. amazement
2 Pe. 1 : 20. no Scripture is of a. private interpretation [tree
Re. 7 : 1. not blow on sea nor on a.
16. nei. sun on them nor a. heat
9 : 4. they should not hurt a. green
thing, neither a. tree, but those
See BEAST, CASE, MANNER, MEANS, OTHER, PERSON, WORK.

See **Any GOD, Any MAN, Any MORE, Any THING, Any TIME, Any WAYS, Any WHILE, Any WISE, Of YOU.**

ANY. [Adv.] [further
Mk. 5 : 35. why troublest Master a.
See LONGER, WHITHER.

ANY more. [a. m.
2 S. 2 : 28. people stood, nei. fought
14 : 10. he sh. not touch thee a. m.
11. not revengers to destroy a. m.
1 Ch. 17 : 9. nei. waste Israel a. m.
Eze. 28 : 19. never sh. thou be a. m.
Jo. 2 : 2. not been the like, nei. be
Re. 7 : 16. nei. thirst a. m. [a. m.
12 : 8. nei. their pla. be found a. m.
18 : 11. no man buyeth their merchandise a. m. [in thee
22. no craftsmen be found a. m.
See **Any MORE.**

ANY. [Pronoun.] [him
Ge. 4 : 15. lest a. finding sho kill
19 : 12. Hast thou here a. besides?
43 : 34. five times as much as a. of
Ex. 10 : 23. nei. rose a. from his pla.
11 : 7. ag-t a. of Isr. not a dog move
22 : 25. If lend money to a. of peo.
30 : 33. compoundeth a. like it, or
Le. 2 : 1. when a. will offer meat off.
4 : 2. If a soul sin against a. of the
commandments, 13, 22, 27 (2).
-5 : 17. Nu. 15 : 27. [ple sin
27. if a. one of the common peo-
5 : 17. if a soul commit a. of these
6 : 3. in a. of all these sinning th-in
30. no offering wh-of a. of blood
7 : 15. not leave a. of it until morn-g
18. if a. of the flesh be eaten on
26. eat no blood in a. of dwell-gs
11 : 32. upon whatso-r a. doth fall
33. whereinto a. of them falleth
18 : 6. None approach to a. of kin
21. not let a. of thy seed pass
thro. fire to Molech, De. 18 : 10.
24. Defile not yours. in a. of these
26. not commit a. of these abominations; neither a. of your
nation, nor a. stranger. 30. [a.
9 : † 20. with bondmaid abused by

Le. 20 : 2. a. of his seed unto Molech
22 : 25. Nei. ye offer a. of these, 24.
25 : 25. if a. of kin redeem it, 49.
Nu. 14 : 23. land, nei. shall a. see it
30 : 5. not a. of her vows sh. stand
36 : 3. if married to a. of the other
tribes of Israel [vows which
De. 12 : 17. mayest not eat a. of thy
15 : 7. if poor within a. of thy gates
16 : 5. not sacrifice passover within
a. of thy gates [or woman
17 : 2. if within a. of thy gates, man
18 : 6. if Levite from a. of thy gates
23 : 24. grapes, not put a. in vessel
24 : 7. If a man, stealing a. of breth.
28 : 14. not go aside fr. a. of words
55. not give to a. of flesh of chil.
32 : 39. neither is a. that can deliver out of my hand [a. of Israel
Jos. 10 : 21. none moved tongue ag-t
11 : 11. not a. left to breathe, 14.
23 : 13. God will no more drive out
a. of the nations, Ju. 2 : 21.
Ju. 20 : 8. not a. of us go to his tent,
nei. a. of us turn into his house
21 : 1. not a. give dau-r unto Benj.
1 S. 5 : 5. neither a. that come into
Dagon's house [10 : 23.
9 : 2. Saul higher than a. of people,
13 : 22. nor spear in hand of a. of
25 : 22. a. that pisseth ag-t the wall
30 : 2. they slew not a., great or
2 S. 2 : 1. shall I go into a. of cities
7 : 7. spake I with a. of tribes of
Israel, 1 Ch. 17 : 6. [3.
9 : 1. Is yet a. left of house of Saul,
21 : 5. fr. remaining in a. of coasts
1 K. 3 : 12. nei. a. arise like thee, 13.
5 : 6. not a. that can skill to hew
15 : 17. not suffer a. to go out or
29. smote all; left not to Jerob. a.
18 : 26. no voice nor a. that answ-d
2 K. 10 : 14. neith. left he a. of them
24. If a. of the men escape, he th.
14 : 26. was not a. shut up, nor a.
left, nor a. helper for Israel
18 : 33. Hath a. of the gods delivered at all his land, Is. 36 : 18.
23 : 25. Josiah, neith. arose a. like
Ezr. 7 : 24. touching a. of priests
Jb. 4 : 20. perish with-t a. regarding
5 : 1. Call, if be a. that will answer
4. nei. is there a. to deliver them
18 : 19. nor a. remaining in dwel-gs
21 : 22. Shall a. teach God knowl.?
31 : 19. If I have seen a. perish for
want, or a. poor without cov-g
33 : 13. giveth not acc-t of a. of his
27. and if a. say, I have sinned
34 : 27. not consider a. of his ways
36 : 5. God mighty, despis-h not a.
37 : 24. he respecteth not a. that is
Ps. 5 : † 9. no faithfulness in a. [wise
14 : 2. L. looked to see if a. that did
seek God, 53 : 2. [strength
33 : 17. horse, nei. deliver a. by his
74 : 9. nei. a. th. knoweth how long
109 : 12. nei. a. to favour his chil.
115 : 17. nei. a. that go into silence
Pr. 30 : 30. lion turneth not for a.
31 : 5. Lest pervert judgment of a.
Is. 27 : 3. lest a. hurt it, I will keep
33 : 20. neith. a. of cords be broken
44 : 8. G. besides me? I know not a.
51 : 18. nei. a. taketh her by hand
59 : 4. nor a. pleadeth for truth
Je. 5 : 1. if a. that seeketh truth
14 : 22. Are a. among vanities that
18 : 18. not give heed to a. of words
23 : 24. Can a. hide in secret places
33 : 26. not a. of his seed be rulers
36 : 24. afraid, neith. king nor a. of
48 : 9. Moab without a. to dwell
Eze. 7 : 11. none shall remain nor a.
of theirs [self in iniquity
13. neith. shall a. strengthen him-
16 : 5. None eye pitied thee, to do a.

Eze. 18 : 7. not oppressed a., 16.
39 : 15. when a. seeth a man's bone
44 : 13. nor near to a. of my holy
46 : 16. if prince give unto a. of his
Da. 8 : 4. nei. a. could deliver [sons
Am. 6 : 10. Is yet a. with thee?
8 : 7. never forget a. of their works
Ob. 18. not be a. of house of Esau
Zch. 13 : 3. when a. shall prophesy
Mk. 8 : 26. nor tell it to a. in town
11 : 25. forgiving if aught against a.
Lu. 3 : 14. neither accuse a. falsely
8 : 43. neither could be healed of a.
9 : 36. told no man a. of those thi-s
11 : 11. If son ask bread of a. of you
20 : 21. neith. acceptest person of a.
Jn. 2 : 25. needed not a. sho. testify
7 : 48. Have a. of rulers believed
Ac. 4 : 32. nei. said a. that aught of
34. Nei. a. among them th. lacked
9 : 2. that if he found a. of this way
27 : 42. lest a. swim out, and escape
28 : 21. nei. a. spake a. harm of thee
Ro. 15 : 18. I not dare to speak of a.
1 Co. 1 : 15. lest a. say I had baptized
6 : 12. not bro-t under power of a.
10 : 27. If a. that believe not bid
2 Co. 2 : 5. if a. have caused grief
8 : 23. whether a. do inquire of Tit.
11 : 21. Whereinsoever a. is bold, I
12 : 17. Did I make a gain of you
by a. of them [against a.
Col. 3 : 13. if a. man have a quarrel
2 Th. 3 : 10. if a. would not work
1 Ti. 5 : 8. if a. provide not for own
Tit. 1 : 6. If a. be blameless, husb.
Ja. 1 : 23. if a. be a hearer of word
5 : 13. Is a. afflicted? Is a. merry
14. Is a. sick among you? let him
1 Pe. 3 : 1. if a. obey not the word
2 Pe. 3 : 9. not willing a. sho. perish
2 Jn. 10. if a. bring not this doctrine

APACE. [near
2 S. 18 : 25. he came a. and drew
Je. 46 : 5. their mighty ones are fled
See FLEE. [a.

APART. [trix
Ex. 13 : 12. set a. all that open ma-
Le. 15 : 19. she shall be put a. 7 days
18 : 19. not approach as long as she
Ne. 12 : † 47. set a. holy things [is a.
Ps. 4 : 3. Lord hath set a. godly for
Eze. 22 : 10. humbled her, set a. for
Zch. 12 : 12. mourn, every family
a.; family of house of David
a., wives a. (5), 13(4), 14(2). [a.
Mat. 14 : 13. Jes. into a desert place
23. he went into a mt. a. to pray
17 : 1. Jesus taketh Peter, John,
into a high mt. a., Mk. 9 : 2.
19. came the disciples to Jesus a.
20 : 17. Jesus took 12 disciples a.
Mk. 6 : 31. Come ye a., rest awhile
Ja. 1 : 21. lay a. all filthiness and

APEL'LES.
Ro. 16 : 10. Salute A. approved in

APES. [Christ
1 K. 10 : 22. navy bringing silver,
ivory, a., peacocks, 2 Ch. 9 : 21.

APHAR'SACHITES. [6.
Ezr. 5 : 6. his companions the A., 6 :

APHAR'SATHCHITES, APHAR'SITES.
Ezr. 4 : 9. wrote Rehum, Shimshai,
and companions; the A., the A.

A'PHEK. [A. one
Jos. 12 : 18. kings Josh. smote, k. of
13 : 4. all the land of Can-s unto A.
19 : 30. lot for Asher; A., Rehob
1 S. 4 : 1. Philist-s pitched in A., 29 : 1.
1 K. 20 : 26. Ben-hadad to A. to fight
30. rest fled to A. into city [Israel
2 K. 13 : 17. thou shalt smite Syrians

APHE'KAH. [in A.
Jos. 15 : 53. cities in mts.; Janum,

APHI'AH. [A.
1 S. 9 : 1. son of Bechorath, son of A.

A'PHIK. See AHLAB.
APH'RAH. [in dust
Mi. 1 : 10. in house of A. roll thyself
APH'SES.
1 Ch. 24 : 15. lot came forth, 17th to
APIECE. [A.
Nu. 3 : 47. take 5 shekels a. by poll
7 : 86. spoons weighing ten shekels
17 : 6. princes gave him a rod a. [a.
1 K. 7 : 15. pillars 18 cubits high a.
Eze. 10 : 21. Every one had 4 faces a.
41 : 24. the doors had two leaves a.
Lu. 9 : 3. neither have two coats a.
Jn. 2 : 6. two or three firkins a.
APOLLO'NIA. [A.
Ac. 17 : 1. they had passed through
APOL'LOS.
Ac. 18 : 24. a certain Jew named A.
19 : 1. while A. at Corinth, Paul
1 Co. 1 : 12. I am of P. ; I of A., 3 : 4.
3 : 5. Who then is Paul, and who A.
6. I have planted, A. watered [phas
22. Whether Paul, or A., or Ce-
4 : 6. I in figure transferred to A.
16 : 12. As touching our brother A.
Tit. 3 : 13. Bring Zenas, A. on the way
APOL'LYON. [A.
Re. 9 : 11. in Greek hath his name
APOSTLE. [Co. 1 : 1.
Ro. 1 : 1. Paul called to be an a., 1
11 : 13. as I am the a. of Gentiles
1 Co. 9 : 1. Am I not an a. ? free?
2. If I be not an a. unto others
15 : 9. not meet to be called an a.
2 Co. 1 : 1. Paul an a. by the will of
God, Ep. 1 : 1. Col. 1 : 1. 1 Ti.
1 : 1. 2 Ti. 1 : 1. [among you
12 : 12. signs of an a. were wrought
Ga. 1 : 1. Paul an a. (not of men)
1 Ti. 2 : 7. whereunto I am ordained
an a., 2 Ti. 1 : 11. [of Jes. Chr.
Tit. 1 : 1. Paul, serv-t of God, an a.
He. 3 : 1. consider the A. and High
Priest, Christ Jesus [Pe. 1 : 1.
1 Pe. 1 : 1. Peter an a. of Jesus, 2
APOSTLES. [are
Mat. 10 : 2. names of the twelve a.
Mk. 6 : 30. a. gathered unto Jesus
Lu. 6 : 13. twelve whom he named a.
9 : 10. a. when they were returned
11 : 49. I will send prophets and a.
17 : 5. a. said, Increase our faith
22 : 14. he sat, twelve a. with him
24 : 10. women told things unto a.
Ac. 1 : 2. had given comm-t unto a.
26. was numbered with eleven a.
2 : 37. said unto Peter and rest of a.
42. steadfastly in the a.' doctrine
43. many signs done by a., 5 : 12.
4 : 33. gave a. witness of resurrect.
36. Joses by a. surnamed Barna-
37. laid it at a.' feet, 35.-5 : 2. [bas
5 : 18. laid their hands on the a.
29. Peter and a. said, We ought to
34. commanded to put a. forth
40. had called a. and beaten them
6 : 6. Whom they set before the a.
8 : 1. all scattered abroad except a.
14. when a. heard that Samaria
18. thro. laying on of a.' hands
9 : 27. Barnabas brought Paul to a.
11 : 1. a. heard Gentiles had rec-d
14 : 4. part with Jews, part with a.
14. a., Barnabas and Paul ran in
15 : 2. Paul and B. to Jerus. unto
a. and elders about this, 4. [ter
6. a., elders came to consider mat-
22. pleased a., elders to send chos-
23. a., elders send greeting [en m.
33. were let go in peace unto a.
16 : 4. decrees ordained of a., elders
Ro. 16 : 7. who are of note among a.
1 Co. 4 : 9. God set forth us a. last
9 : 5. to lead about wife as other a.?
12 : 28 God hath set in church first
29. Are all a.? all prophets? [a.
15 : 7. seen of James; then of all a.
1 Co. 15 : 9. I am least of a. [12 : 11.
2 Co. 11 : 5. I not behind chiefest a.,
13. such are false a., deceitful,
transform-g thems. into a. of C.
Ga. 1 : 17. which were a. before me
19. of a. saw I none save James
Ep. 2 : 20. upon foundation of a.
3 : 5. as it is now revealed unto a.
4 : 11. he gave some a. ; and some
1 Th. 2 : 6. burdensome, as a. of Ch.
2 Pe. 3 : 2. comm-t of us a. of Lord
Jude 17. rememb. words spoken of a.
Re. 2 : 2. say they are a., and are not
18 : 20. Rejoice over her, ye a. [a.
21 : 14. in them names of the twelve
APOSTLESHIP. [a.
Ac. 1 : 25. he may take part of this
Ro. 1 : 5. By whom we have rec-d a.
1 Co. 9 : 2. seal of mine a. are ye
Ga. 2 : 8. Peter to a. of circumcision
APOTHECARY, IES.
Ex. 30 : 25. ointment after art of a.
35. confection aft. art of a., 37 : 29.
2 Ch. 16 : 14. of spices by the a-s' art
Ne. 3 : 8. Hananiah, son of one of a-s
Ec. 10 : 1. flies cause ointment of a.
AP'PAIM.
1 Ch. 2 : 30. sons of Nadab ; A., 31.
APPAREL. [a.
Ju. 14 : † 19. Samson slew 30, took
17 : 10. I will give thee suit of a.
1 S. 27 : 9. David took oxen, asses, a.
2 S. 1 : 24. ornaments upon your a.
12 : 20. David arose, changed his a.
14 : 2. put on now mourning a.
1 K. 10 : 5. queen of Sheba had seen
ministers, their a., 2 Ch. 9 : 4. (2)
Ezr. 3 : 10. set the priests in their a.
Es. 6 : 9. let a. and horse be delivered
11. took Haman the a., arrayed
Is. 3 : 22. changeable suits a. [M., 10.
4 : 1. We will wear our own a. [a.?
63 : 1. Who is this glorious in his
2. Wheref. art thou red in thine a.
Eze. 27 : 24. and in chests of rich a.
Zph. 1 : 8. all clothed wi. strange a.
Zch. 14 : 14. wealth of heath., gold, a.
Ac. 1 : 10. two men stood in white a.
20 : 33. I have coveted no man's a.
1 Ti. 2 : 9. that women in modest a.
Ja. 2 : 2. if come a man in goodly a.
1 Pe. 3 : 3. of gold, or putting on of
See ROYAL. [a.
APPARELLED. [a.
2 S. 13 : 18. king's dau-s were virgins
Lu. 7 : 25. which are gorgeously a.
APPARENTLY.
Nu. 12 : 8. With him will I speak a.
APPEAL, ED.
Ac. 25 : 11. I a. unto Cesar
12. Hast thou a-d unto Cesar?
21. P. had a-d unto Augustus, 25
26 : 32. at liberty, if he had not a-d
28 : 19. I was constrained to a. un-
APPEAR. [to Cesar
[Relating to God or Jesus.] [6.
Le. 9 : 4. to day L. will a. unto you,
16 : 2. I will a. in the cloud upon
1 S. 2 : 27. Did I plainly a. unto hou.
of thy father [unto Sol.
2 Ch. 1 : 7. that night did God a.
Ps. 102 : 16. he shall a. in his glory
Is. 66 : 5. but he shall a. to your joy
Ac. 26 : 16. things in which I will a.
APPEAR.
Ge. 1 : 9. God said, let dry land a.
30 : 37. Jac. made white a. in rods
Ex. 23 : 15. none shall a. before me
empty, 34 : 20. De. 16 : 16.
17. Three times in the year all thy
males shall a. before the Lord,
34 : 23, 24. De. 16 : 16 (2).
Le. 13 : 57. if it a. still in garment
De. 31 : 11. when all Israel is come
to a. before the Lord [Manoah
Ju. 13 : 21. angel did no more a. to
1 S. 1 : 22. child, that he a. before L.
Ps. 42 : 2. when shall I a. before God
90 : 16. Let thy work a. unto serv-ts
Can. 2 : 12. The flowers a. on earth
4 : 1. goats that a. from Gilead, 6 :
7 : 12. whether tender grape a. [5.
Is. 1 : 12. When ye come to a. before
Je. 13 : 26. that thy shame a. [me
Eze. 21 : 24. in your doings sins do a.
Mat. 6 : 16. may a. unto men to fast
18. thou a. not unto men to fast
23 : 27. sepulchres wh. a. beautiful
28. so ye outwardly a. righteous
24 : 30. shall a. sign of Son of man
Lu. 11 : 44. ye as graves wh. a. not
19 : 11. thought kingdom of God
should immediately a. [to a.
Ac. 22 : 30. commanded all council
Ro. 7 : 13. sin, that it might a. sin
2 Co. 5 : 10. must all a. bef. judgm-t
7 : 12. our care for you might a.
13 : 7. not that we sho. a. approved
Col. 3 : 4. When Chr. our life shall a.
1 Ti. 4 : 15. that thy profiting may a.
He. 9 : 24. a. in presence of G. for us
28. to them sh. he a. second time
11 : 3. not made of things wh. do a.
1 Pe. 4 : 18. where shall ungodly a.?
5 : 4. when chief Shepherd shall a.
1 Jn. 2 : 28. when he shall a. we may
3 : 2. not yet a. what we shall be :
we know that when he shall a.
Re. 3 : 18. shame of nakedn-s not a.
APPEARANCE, S. [16.
Nu. 9 : 15. upon tabern. as a. of fire,
1 S. 16 : 7. man looketh on outw. a.
Eze. 1 : 5. creatures, this was their a.
13. their a. was like burning coals,
and like a. of lamps [ning
14. ran as the a. of a flash of light-
16. a. of wheels was like a beryl :
a. as a wheel in a wheel, 10 : 9.
26. throne as the a. of a sapphire
stone : and a. of a man upon it
27. as the a. of fire round about,
from the a. of his loins upward,
and from the a. of his loins
downward, as a. of fire, 8 : 2.
28. As the a. of the bow in cloud,
so was the a. of the brightness.
This was the a. of the glory of L.
10 : 1. abo. cherubim as a. of throne
10. as for a-s, they had one liken.
22. the same faces I saw, their a-s
40 : 3. man whose a. like a. of brass
41 : 21. posts, a. of one as a. of other
42 : 11. the way like a. of chambers
43 : 3. was according to a. of vision
Da. 8 : 15. there stood before me as
the a. of a man, 10 : 18 [ning
10 : 6. and his face as the a. of light-
Jo. 2 : 4. The a. is as the a. of horses
Jn. 7 : 24. Judge not acc-g to the a.
2 Co. 5 : 12. glory in a., not in heart
10 : † 1. who in outward a. am base
7. Look on things aft. outward a.?
1 Th. 5 : 22. Abstain fr. all a. of evil
APPEARED.
[Relating to God or Christ.]
Ge. 12 : 7. the Lord a. unto Abram
(2), 17 : 1.-18 : 1. [not into Eg., 24.
26 : 2. Lord a. unto Isaac, said, Go
35 : 1. G that a. when thou fleddest
7. El-beth-el, because there G. a.
9. God a. unto Jacob again [Lus
48 : 3. God Almighty a. unto me at
Ex. 3 : 16. God of fathers a. unto me
4 : 1. will say, Lord not a. unto me
5. may believe L. G. a. unto thee
6 : 3. I a. unto Abr. by name of G.
De. 31 : 15. Lord a. in the tabernacle
1 S. 3 : 21. the L. a. again in Shiloh
1 K. 3 : 5. In Gibeon Lord a. to Sol-n
by night, 2 Ch. 1 : 7.-7 : 12. [9.
9 : 2. L. a. to Sol-n second time, 11 :
2 Ch. 3 : 1. where Lord a. unto David
Je. 31 : 3. The L. a. of old unto me
Mk. 16 : 9. he a. first to Mary Magd.

Mk.16 : 12. After that he a. unto two
14. Afterw. he a. unto the eleven
Lu. 24 :34. L.risen, hath a. to Simon
Ac. 7 : 2 God of glory a. unto Abr.
9 : 17. Jesus that a. unto thee in
26 : 16. I have a. unto thee for this
He. 9 : 26. hath he a. to put away

APPEARED. [sin

Ex. 3 : 2. Angel of the Lord a. in a flame out of a bush, Ac. 7:30,35.
14 : 27. sea returned when morning
16 : 10. glory of Lord a. in cloud[a.
Le. 9 : 23. glory of Lord a. to peo., Nu. 14 : 10.-16 : 19, 42. [Aaron
Nu. 20 : 6.glory of L. a. unto Moses,
Ju. 6 : 12.angel of L. a. unto Gideon
13 : 3. angel of L. a. unto woman
10. Behold, man hath a. unto me
2 S. 22 : 16.the channels of the sea a.
2 K. 2 : 11. a. chariot of fire, horses
Ne. 4 : 21. we laboured till stars a.
Eze. 10 : 1. in firmament, a. as it were a sapphire stone [hand
8. a. in cherubim, form of a man's
19 : 11. a. in her height wi. branches
Da. 1 : 15. countenances a. fairer
8 : 1. a vision a. unto me, Daniel, after that which a. at the first
Mat. 1 : 20. angel of the Lord a. in a dream, saying, Joseph [a.
2 : 7. inquired what time the star
13 : 26. fruit, then a. the tares
17 : 3. a. unto them, Moses and Elias talking with him, Mk. 9:4.
27 : 53.out of graves, a. unto many
Lu. 1 : 11. a. unto Zacha-s angel of
9 : 8. said of some, Elias had a. [L.
31. Who a. in glory and spake
22 : 43.a. angel strengthening him
Ac. 2 : 3. a. unto th. cloven tongues
16 : 9. a vision a. to Paul in night
27 : 20. when nei. sun nor stars a.
Tit. 2 : 11.grace of God hath a. to all
3 : 4. aft.love of God toward man a.
Re.12 : 1.a. a great wonder in heav., [3.

APPEARETH.

Le. 13 : 14. raw flesh a., he unclean
43. as leprosy a. in skin of flesh
De. 2 : 30. deliver him as a. this day
Ps. 46 : †5.help her,when morn-g a.
84 : 7. every one in Zion a. bef. God
Pr. 27 : 25. The hay a. and the grass
Je. 6 : 1. for evil a. out of the north
Mal. 3 : 2.who sh. stand when he a.?
Mat. 2 : 13. angel of the Lord a. to Joseph, saying, 19. [little time
Ja. 4 : 14. life is a vapour, that a. a

APPEARING. [Lord

1 Ti. 6 : 14. keep comm-t until a. of
2 Ti. 1 : 10.manifest by a. of Saviour
4 : 1.judge quick and dead at his a.
8. unto all them that love his a.
Tit. 2 :13.look-g for glorious a. of G.
1 Pe. 1 : 7. unto praise at a. of Jesus

APPEASE, ED, ETH.

Ge.32 : 20.I will a. him with present
Es. 2 : 1. Ahasuerus was a-d, he remembered Vashti [a-h strife
Pr. 15 : 18. he that is slow to anger
Ac.19 : 35. townclerk had a-d people

APPERTAIN, ED, ETH.

Le. 6 : 5. unto him to whom it a-h
Nu. 16 :30. swallow up with all th.a.
32. men that a-d unto Korah, 33.
Ne. 2 : 8. beams for gates of palace which a. to house [Uzziah
2 Ch. 26 : 18. It a-h not unto thee,
Je.10 :7. fear thee, to thee doth it a.
See PERTAIN, ED, ETH, ING.

APPETITE.

Jb. 38 : 39. Wilt thou fill a. of lions
Pr. 23 : 2. if thou be a man given to
Ec. 6 : 7. is a. yet not filled [a.
Is. 29 : 8. he awaketh, soul hath a.
56 : † 11. Yea, they are strong of a.

APPHI'A.

Phm. 2. And to our beloved A., and

AP'PII FO'RUM.

Ac. 28 : 15. they came as far as A. F.

APPLE with eye. [e.

De. 32 : 10. he kept him as a. of his
Ps. 17 : 8. Keep me as a. of thine e.
Pr. 7 : 2. Keep law as a. of thine e.
La. 2 : 18. not a. of thine e. cease
Zch. 2 : 8. toucheth the a. of his e.

APPLE tree.

Can. 2 : 3. As the a. t. among trees
8 : 5. I raised thee up under a. t.
Jo. 1 : 12. a. t., all trees are with-d

APPLES. [silver

Pr. 25 : 11. a. of gold in pictures of
Can. 2 : 5. comfort me with a. : for I
7 : 8. the smell of thy nose like a.

APPLY, IED. [dom

Ps. 90 : 12. a. our hearts unto wis-
Pr. 2 : 2. a. thine heart to underst-g
22 :17.a. heart unto my knowledge
23 : 12.a. thine heart unto instruc.
Ec. 7 : 25. I a-d my heart to know
8 : 9. I a-d my heart unto ev. work
16. When I a-d heart to wisdom
Ho. 7 : † 6. a-d their heart like an

APPOINT. [oven

Ge. 30 : 28. a. thy wages, I will give
41 : 34. let Pharaoh a. officers [it
Ex. 21 : 13. I will a. thee a place
30 : 16. atonement money, a. it for
Le. 26 : 16. I will a. over you terror
Nu. 1 : 50.a. Levites over tabernacle
3 : 10. shalt a. Aaron and his sons
4 : 19. Aaron and his sons shall a. every one to service [burdens
27. ye shall in charge a. all their
35 : 6. six cities for refuge which ye shall a., 11. Jos. 20 : 2.[himself
1 S. 8 : 11. He will a. your sons for
12.will a.captains over thousands
2 S. 6 : 21. to a. me ruler over people
7 : 10. I will a. place for my people
15 : 15. ready to do whatso. king a.
1 K. 5 : 6. will I give hire according to all thou shalt a. [thou a.
9. I will convey them unto place
1 Ch. 15 : 16. a. breth. to be singers
Ne. 7 : 3. a. watches of the inhabit-s
Es. 2 : 3. let the king a. officers in all
Jb. 14 :13.wouldest a. me a set time
Is. 26 : 1. salvation will God a. for
61 : 3. a. unto them that mourn in
Je. 15 : 3. I will a. four kinds [Zion
49 : 19. who is chosen man I may a.? who a. me time? 50 : 44.
51 :27. a. a captain ag-t her: cause
Eze. 21 : 19. a. two ways, that sword
20. a. a way that sword may come
22. divination for Jerusalem to a. captains, to a. battering rams
45 : 6. ye shall a. possession of city
Ho. 1 : 11. shall a. thems. one head
Mat. 24 : 51. a. him with hypocrites
Lu. 12 : 46. a. him with unbelievers
22 : 29. I a. unto you a kingdom as
Ac. 6 :3.seven men whom we may a.

APPOINTED. [seed

Ge. 4 : 25. God hath a. me another
24 :14.same be she a. for Isaac, 44.
Nu.9 :2.keep passover at a.season,3.
7. may not offer in his a. season
13. bro-t not offering in a. season
Jos. 20 : 7. they a. Kedesh in Galilee
9. the cities a. that whoso. killeth
Ju. 18 : 11. 600 men a. with weapons of war, 16, 17. [rael and
20 : 38. was an a. sign between Is-
1 S.13 : 11. camest not within days a.
19 : 20. Samuel, as a. over them
21 : 2. I have a. servants to such
25 : 30. L. shall have a. thee ruler
29 : 4.make fellow return to pla. a.
2 S. 17 : 14. Lord a. to defeat counsel
1 K. 1 : 35. I have a. him to be ruler
11 : 18. Pharaoh a. Hadad victuals
12 : 12. Jerob. came as king had a.
20 : 42. a man I a. to destruction

2 K. 7 : 17. king a. the lord to have
8 : 6. king a. unto her cert. officer
10 : 24. Jehu a. fourscore men
11 : 18. priest a. officers over house
18 : 14. k. a. unto Hez. 300 talents
1 Ch. 6 : 48. Levites were a. unto ser.
49. Aaron and sons a. for work
9 : 29. were a. to oversee vessels
15 : 17. Levites a. Heman [Ne. 7 : 1.
19. singers were a., 2 Ch. 20 : 21.
16 : 4. a. of Levites to minister [2.
2 Ch. 8 : 14. a. courses of priests, 31 :
23 : 18. Jehoiada a. the offices
33 : 8. land I a. for your fathers
34 : 22. that king a. went to Huldah
Ezr. 3 : 8. a. Levites from 20 yrs. old
8 : 20. Nethinim whom David a.
Ne. 5 : 14. time I was a. governor
6 : 7. a. prophets to preach of thee
9 : 17. in rebellion a. a captain to
12 : 31. I a. two great companies
44.† were some a. over chambers to gather portions a. by law for
13 : 30. I a. the wards of the priests
Es. 1 : 8. so king had a. to officers
2 : 15.what the keeper of women a.
4 : 5. Hatach, he a. to attend Esth.
Jb. 7 : 3 wearisome nights are a. me
14 : 5.thou hast a. his bounds that
20 : 29. heritage a. unto him by G.
23 : 14. performeth thing a. for me
30 :23. to the house a. for all living
Ps. 44 : 11. us like sheep a. for meat
78 : 5. For he a. a law in Israel[die
79 : 11. preserve thou those a. to
102 : 20. to loose those a. to death
104 : 19.He a. the moon for seasons
Pr. 7 : 20. will come home at day a.
8 : 29. he a. foundations of earth
31 : 8. such as are a. to destruction
Is. 1 : 14. your a. feasts my soul hat-
28 : 25. cast in the a. barley [eth
44 : 7. since I a. the ancient people
Je. 5 : 24. the a. weeks of harvest
33 : 25. a. ordinances of heaven
47 : 7. ag. sea shore? hath he a. it
Eze. 4 : 6. I have a. thee each day
36 : 5.a. my land (into possession)
43 : 21. burn bullock in a. place
Da. 1 : 5. king a. them daily provi-
10. king who a. your meat [sion
Mi 6 : 9. hear ye rod, and who a. it
Mat. 26 : 19.disciples did as Jesus a.
27 : 10. potter's field, as Lord a. me
28 : 16. into mt. where Jes. had a.
Lu. 3 : 13. Exact no more than is a.
10 : 1. After these Lord a. other 70
22 : 29. to you a kingd. as Father a.
Ac. 1 : 23. they a. two, Joseph [me
7 : 44. had tabernacle as he had a.
17 : 31. a. a day he will judge world
20 : 13. for so he had a., minding to
22 : 10. which are a. for thee to do
28 : 23.when they had a. him a day
1 Co. 4 :9.apostles last,as a. to death
1 Th. 3 :3.know we are a. thereunto
5 : 9. God hath not a. us to wrath
2 Ti. 1 : 11. I am a. a preacher and
Tit. 1 : 5. elders in every city as I a.
He. 1 : 2.whom he hath a. heir of all
3 : 2. faithful to him that a. him
9 : 27. it is a. unto men once to die
1 Pe. 2 : 8. whereunto they were a.
See TIME, S, with appointed.

APPOINTETH. [will

Da. 5 : 21. a. over it whomsoever he

APPOINTMENT. [sons

Nu. 4 : 27. At the a. of Aaron and
Jos. 11 : † 5. kings assembled by a.
2 S. 13 :32. by a. of Abs-m this hath
Ezr. 6 : 9. acc-g to a. of the priests
Jb. 2 : 11. had made an a. to mourn

APPREHEND.

1 K. 18:†40. a. the prophets of Baal
2 Co. 11 : 32. gov-r desirous to a. me
Ph. 3 : 12. may a. that for which I am apprehended of Christ Jesus

APPREHENDED.
Ac. 12 : 4. a. Peter, put him in prison
Ph. 3 : 12. for wh. I am a. of Christ
13. I count not myself to have a.
APPROACH. [kin
Le. 18 : 6. None shall a. to near of
14. thou shalt not a. to his wife
19. shalt not a. woman put apart
20 : 16. if a wom. a. unto any beast
21 : 17. not a. to offer bread, 18.
Nu. 4 : 19. when a. most holy things
De. 20 : 2. priest a., speak unto peo.
3. ye a. this day to battle against
31 : 14 thy days a. thou must die
Jos 8 : 5. with me will a. city [him
Jb 40 : 19. make sword to a. unto
Ps. 65 : 4. whom thou causest to a.
Je. 30 : 21. he shall a. unto me : who
engaged heart to a. unto me?
Eze. 42 : 13 priests that a. unto L.
14. a. to things wh. are for people
43 : 19. a. unto me to minister [a.
1 Ti 6 : 16. in light wh. no man can
APPROACHED, ETH.
2 S. 11 : 20. Whf. a-d ye so nigh city
1 K. 20 : † 13 a-d a prophet unto Ahab
2 K. 16 : 12. king a-d to altar, offered
Ps. 27 : † 2. when mine enemies a-d
Is 8 : † 3. I a-d unto the prophetess
Lu. 12 : 33 where no thief a-h, nei.
APPROACHING. [God
Is. 58 : 2. they take delight in a. to
He. 10 : 25. the more, as ye see the day
APPROVE. [a.
Ps. 49 : 13. posterity a. their sayings
1 Co 16 : 3 whomso. ye a. by letters
Ph 1 : 10. That ye a. things excellent
APPROVED.
Ac. 2 : 22. Jesus, a man a. of God by
Ro 14 : 18. acceptable to God, a. of
16 : 10 Salute Apelles, a. in Christ
1 Co. 11 : 19. wh. are a. be manifest
2 Co. 7 : 11. In all ye a. yourselves
10 : 18. For not he that commend-
eth himself is a., but [a.
13 : 7. not that we should appear
2 Ti. 2 : 15. Study to shew thyself a.
APPROVEST, ETH, ING.
La 3 : 36. To subvert, Lord a-h not
Ro. 2 : 18. a-t things more excellent
2 Co. 6 : 4. in all things a-g ourselves
APPURTENANCES. [a.
1 K. 6 : † 38. house finished with all
APRON, S.
Ge 3 : 7 sewed fig leaves, made a-s
Ru. 3 : † 15. Bring the a. upon thee
Ac. 19 : 12. brought unto the sick
APT. [a s
2 K. 24 : 16. all strong and a. for
war, 1 Ch. 7 : 40 [Ti. 2 : 24.
1 Ti. 3 : 2 bishop be a. to teach, 2
AQ'UILA with PRISCIL'LA.
Ac. 18 : 2. Paul found a Jew named
A. with P. his wife [him P., A.
18. Paul sailed into Syria, with
26. when A. and P. heard Apollos
Ro. 16 : 3. Greet A. and P., 2 Ti. 4 : 19.
1 Co. 16 : 19. A. and P. salute you in
AR. [Lord
Nu. 21 : 15 stream that goeth to A.
28. fire hath consumed A. of Moab
De. 2 : 9. given A. unto chil. of Lot
18. Thou to pass thro. A. this day
29. As the Moabites in A. did
Is. 15 : 1. A. of Moab is laid waste
A'RA. [A.
1 Ch. 7 : 38. sons of Jether ; Pispah,
A'RAB. [Eshean
Jos. 15 : 52. cities in the mts. ; A.
AR'ABAH. [to A. (2)
Jos. 18 : 18. of Benj. ; border went
ARA'BIA.
1 K 10 : 15 Besides that Sol-n had
of all kings of A., 2 Ch. 9 : 14
Is. 21 : 13. The burden upon A. In
the forest of A shall ye lodge
Je. 25 : 24. kings of A., if refuse cup
Eze. 27 : 21. A. occupied with thee
Ga. 1 : 17. I went into A., returned
4 : 25. this Agar is mount Sinai in
ARA'BIAN, S. [A.
2 Ch. 17 : 11. A-s brought him flocks
21 : 16. Lord stirred up spirit of A-s
22 : 1. band with A-s had slain all
26 : 7. God helped Uzziah ag-t A-s
Ne. 2 : 19. Geshem, A., laughed us to
4 : 7. when A-s heard that walls of
Jerus-m were made up [builded
6 : 1. when G-shem, A., heard I
Is. 13 : 20. neith. shall A. pitch tent
15 : † 7. carry away to valley of A-s
Je. 3 : 2. In the ways hast sat as A.
Ac. 2 : 11 Cretes, A-s, we do hear in
A'RAD. [Person.]
Nu. 21 : 1. when king A. the Canaanite heard tell that Israel, 33 : 40.
1 Ch. 8 : 15. sons of Elpaal ; A. and
A'RAD. [Place.] [A. one
Jos. 12 : 14. kings Isr. smote, k. of
Ju. 1 : 16. wilderness in south of A.
A'RAH. [niel
1 Ch. 7 : 39. sons of Ulla ; A., Ha-
Ezr. 2 : 5. chil. of A. 775 | Ne. 7 : 10. 652
Ne. 6 : 18. of Shechaniah son of A.
A'RAM. [Person.]
Ge 10 : 22. chil. of Shem ; Lud, A.
23 chil. of A. ; Hul, Gether, Mash
22 : 21. Kemuel, father of A. [Gether
1 Ch. 1 : 17. sons of Shem ; A., Hul,
7 : 34. sons of Shamer ; Ahi, A.
Mat. 1 : 3. begat A. | 4. A. begat
Lu. 3 : 33 Aminadab was son of A.
A'RAM. [Place.] [A.
Nu. 23 : 7. Balak brought me from
1 Ch. 2 : 23. Segub took Geshur, A.
See PADAN-ARAM.
ARAMI'TESS.
1 Ch. 7 : 14. his concubine the A.
A'RAM-NAHARA'IM.
Ju 3 : † 8. Chushan-rishathaim k-g
Ps. 60.* when Da. strove wi A. [of A.
A'RAM-ZO'BAH.
Ps. 60.* when David strove with A.
A'RAN.
Ge. 36 : 28. chil. of Dishan ; Uz and
A., 1 Ch. 1 : 42.
AR'ARAT.
Ge. 8 : 4. ark rested upon mts. of A.
2 K 19 : † 37 his sons escaped into
land of A., Is. 37 : † 38. [A.
Je. 51 : 27. call ag. her kingdoms of
ARAU'NAH = ORNAN.
2 S. 24 : 16. angel by threshingplace
of A., 18 1 Ch. 21 : † 15. 2 Ch.
3 : † 1 [22, 24.
20. A. bowed before king (2), 21,
23. these did A. give unto Da. (2)
AR'BA. [A.
Ge. 35 : 27. Jacob came unto city of
Jos. 14 : 15. A. a great man among
15 : 13. unto Caleb gave city of A.
21 : 11 gave city of A. wh. is Heb-n
See ANAK, KIRJATH-ARBA.
AR'BAH = ARBA. See ARBA.
AR'BATHITE.
2 S. 23 : 31. one of the thirty, Abi-
albon the A., 1 Ch 11 : 32
AR'BITE. [the A.
2 S. 23 : 35. one of the 30 ; Paarai
ARCHANGEL. [of a.
1 Th. 4 : 16. L. sh. descend with voice
Jude 9. Michael the a. contending
ARCHELA'US. [in Ju.
Mat. 2 : 22. heard that A. did reign
ARCHER, S.
Ge. 21 : 20. Ishmael became an a.
49 : 23. Jos-h, a-s sorely grieved him
Ju. 5 : 11. delivered from noise of a-s
1 S. 31 : 3. a-s hit Saul, 1 Ch. 10 : 3.
1 Ch. 8 : 40. mighty men of valour, a-s
2 Ch. 35 : 23. a-s shot at king Josiah
Jb 16 : 13. His a-s compass me [men
Is. 21 : 17. residue of a-s ; mighty
22 : 3. thy rulers are bound by a-s
Je. 50 : 29. Call the a-s ag. Babylon
51 : 3. Against him that bendeth let-
ARCHES. [a. bend
Eze. 40 : 16. narrow windows to a.
21. the a. thereof 22 (2), 24, 25,
26, 29 (2), 30, 31, 33 (2), 34, 36.
30. a. were 5 and 20 cubits long
AR'CHEVITES. [ria
Ezr. 4 : 9. A. Asnapper set in Sama-
AR'CHI. [of A.
Jos. 16 : 2. lot of Joseph unto borders
ARCHIP'PUS. [try
Col. 4 : 17. A., Take heed to minis-
Phm. 2. Paul to A. our fellow soldier
Hushai the AR'CHITE.
2 S. 15 : 32. H. A. came to meet Dav.
16 : 16. when H. A., David's friend
17 : 5. said Abs-m, Call now H. A.
14 Counsel of H. A. better than
1 Ch. 27 : 33. H. A., king's compan-
ARCTU'RUS. [ion
Jb. 9 : 9. Which maketh A., Orion
38 : 32. canst thou guide A., sons
ARD, ARD'ITES. [A.
Ge. 46 : 21. sons of Benjamin, Belah,
Nu. 26 : 40. sons of Bela were A. ;
of A. the family of A-s, 1 Ch. 8 : † 3.
AR'DON. [A.
1 Ch. 2 : 18. chil. of Azubah, Jesher,
ARE. [therein
Ge. 18 : 24. for 50 righteous that a.
19 : 5. Where a. the men that came
15. take thy 2 dau-s which a. here
20 : 7. sh. die and all that a. thine
16. covering unto all a. with thee
25 : 23. Two nations a. in thy womb
27 : 22. the hands a. hands of Esau
41. days of mourning a. at hand
46. these, which a. dau-s of land
29 : 4. they said, Of Haran a. we
31 : 15. a. we not counted strangers
43. said, These a. my daugh-s (3)
33 : 13. knoweth chil. a. tender (2)
35 : 2. strange gods that a. amo. you
40 : 12. The 3 branches a. 3 days | 18.
41 : 26. seven good kine a. 7 yrs. (2)
42 : 9. Jos. said, Ye a. spies, 14, 16.
11. We a. all one man's sons (2)
21. We a. guilty conc. our brother
36. all these things a. against me
44 : 16. we a. my lord's servants
45 : 6. a. five years, nei. earing nor
47 : 3. Thy servants a. shepherds
48 : 9 Jos-h said, They a. my sons
Ex 5 : 17. said, Ye a. idle, ye a. idle
8 : 21 flies, ground whereon they a.
Le. 23 : 17. they a. firstfruits unto L.
Nu 15 : 15. as ye a., so sh. stranger
20 : 16. behold, we a. in Kadesh [be
35 : 33. not pollute land wh-in ye a.
De. 1 : 2. a., 7 : 6.-13 : 7.-14 : 9 -16 :
11, 14 -17 : 14.-21 : 6.-24 : 14.
11. one thousand times so many
more as ye a. [heaven
28. cities a. great, walled up to
4 : 4. that did cleave unto L. a. alive
7 : 17. These nations a. more than I
9 : 29. Yet they a. thy peo. [Jordan
11 : 30. a. they not on other side
12 : 1. These a. statutes ye shall do
14 : 1. Ye a. children of the Lord
20 : 15. unto cities wh. a. far off (2)
29 : 1. These a. words of covenant
32 : 4. all his ways a. judgment
5. they a. a crooked generation
21. to jealousy with those which
a. not a people, Ro. 10 : 19.
28. they a. nation void of counsel
37. he sh. say, Where a. their gods
33 : 3. all his saints a. in thy hand
17. his a. like horns of unicorns ;
a. the ten thousands of Ephr. (3)
27. underneath a. overlast-g arms
Jos. 4 : 9. they a. there unto this day
9 : 8 We a. thy servants. Joshua
said, Who a. ye? 11. [you
22 Wheref. saying, We a. far from

Ju. 7 : 18. I and all that **a.** with me
8 : 6. **a.** the hands of Zeba in thine
20 : 7. Ye **a.** all children of Israel
Ru. 4 : 9. Ye **a.** witnesses this day
1 S. 12 : 21 can-t profit, they **a.** vain
2 S. 19 : †6. th. princes **a.** not to thee
1 K. 8 : 8. there they **a.** unto this day
2 K. 5 : 12. **a.** not Abana, Pharpar
1 Ch. 6 : 33. these **a.** they Da set over
50. And these **a.** the sons of Aaron
54. these **a.** their dwellingplaces
7 : 33. These **a.** the chil. of Japhlet
15 : 12. Ye **a.** chief of fathers of Lev.
Ne. 2 : 17. Ye see distress we **a.** in
12 : 1. These **a.** priests that went up
Jb. 3 : 19. small and great **a.** there
5 : 4. His chil. **a.** far from safety [me
6 : 4. arrows of Almighty **a.** within
7. **a.** as my sorrowful meat [ling?
7 : 1. **a.** not his like days of hire-
6. My days **a.** swifter than shuttle
8. thine eyes **a.** upon me, I am not
8 : 13. So **a.** paths of all forget God
10 : 5. **a.** thy years as man's days?
20. **a.** not my days few? cease [(2)
12 : 16. deceived and deceiver **a.** his
13 : 12. remembrances **a.** like ashes
23. How many **a.** my sins [thee
14 : 5. number of his months **a.** wi.
15 : 10. With us **a.** very aged men
11. **a.** consolations of God small
15. heavens **a.** not clean in his si-t
17 : 1. my days **a.** extinct, the
graves **a.** ready for me
2. **a.** there not mockers with me?
7. all my members **a.** as a shadow
11. My days **a.** past, my purposes
20 : 11. His bones **a.** full of sin [a.
21 : 9. Their houses **a.** safe fr. fear
18. They **a.** as stubble before wind
24. His breasts **a.** full of milk [thee
22 : 10. Therefore snares **a.** round
12. behold stars, how high they **a.**!
14. Thick clouds **a.** a covering to
19. The righteous see it, **a.** glad
23 : 14. many such things **a.** with
24 : 8. They **a.** wet with the showers
13. They **a.** those rebel ag-t light
23. his eyes **a.** upon their ways
24 : † 24. a little while, but **a.** not
25 : 5. stars **a.** not pure in his sight
26 : 14. Lo, these **a.** parts of his ways
27 : 12. why **a.** ye altogether vain?
28 : 6. stones **a.** place of sapphires
30 : 1. they that **a.** younger than I
32 : 9. Great men **a.** not alw. wise
34 : 18. to princes Ye **a.** ungodly?
21. his eyes **a.** upon ways of man
36 : 7. with kings **a.** they on throne
37 : 17. How thy garments **a.** warm
38 : 35. Canst send lightnings, that
they say unto thee, Here we **a.**?
39 : 4. young ones **a.** in good liking
30. where the slain **a.**, there is she
40 : 18. his bones **a.** like bars of iron
41 : 15. His scales **a.** his pride [(2)
23. The flakes of his flesh **a.** firm
30. sharp stones **a.** under him: he
Ps. 1 : 4. The ungodly **a.** not so (2)
3 : 1. many **a.** they that rise ag. me
10 : 5. his ways **a.** always grievous; thy judgm-ts **a.** out of sight
12 : 4. have said, our lips **a.** our own
6. words of the L. **a.** pure words
17 : 14. From men which **a.** thy
hand, they **a.** full of children
19 : 8. statutes of the Lord **a.** right
9. judgments of Lord **a.** true [gold
10. More to be desired **a.** they than
25 : 10. All paths of Lord **a.** mercy
15. Mine eyes **a.** ever toward Lord
19. mine enemies; they **a.** many
34 : 19. Many **a.** afflictions of right-s
36 : 3. words of his mouth **a.** deceit
6. thy judgments **a.** a great deep
38 : 5. My wounds **a.** corrupt bec.
19. mine enemies **a.** lively, **a.** str.

Ps. 38 : 20 that render evil for good
a. mine adversaries [enemies
45 : 5. Thine arrows **a.** sharp in K-'s
50 : 11. wild beasts of field **a.** mine
51 : 17. sacrifices of G. **a.** broken spi.
55 : 10. mischief, sorrow **a.** in midst
56 : 5. all their thoughts **a.** ag. me
8. my tears; **a.** they not in thy b.
12. Thy vows **a.** upon me, O God
57 : 4. I lie among them that **a.** set
on fire, whose teeth **a.** spears
58 : 4. they **a.** like the deaf adder
59 : 7. belch; swords **a.** in their lips
62 : 9. men of high degree **a.** lie (3)
65 : 5 that **a.** afar off upon the sea
8. They **a.** afraid at thy tokens
68 : †26. ye th. **a.** of fountain of Isr.
69 : 4. hate me **a.** more than hairs
73 : 4. **a.** no bands in their death
5. They **a.** not in trouble as other
8. They **a.** corrupt, speak wickedly
27. that **a.** far from thee sh. perish
74 : 20. dark places of earth **a.** full
82 : 5. foundations **a.** out of course
6. all of you **a.** chil. of Most High
84 : 5. in whose heart **a.** ways of [(2)
89 : 11. The heavens **a.** thine [ses
49. L. where **a.** thy lovingkindnes-
90 : 4. 1,000 years **a.** but as yesterd.
5. they **a.** as a sleep [and ten
10. days of our years **a.** threescore
92 : 5. O Lord, how great **a.** thy
works! thy thoughts **a.** deep
93 : 5. Thy testimonies **a.** very sure
94 : 11. thoughts of man **a.** vanity
95 : 4. In his hand **a.** deep places
96 : 5. all gods of nations **a.** idols
6. Honour, majesty **a.** before him
97 : 2. Clouds, darkn **a.** about him,
102 : 8. they that **a.** mad ag. me [(2)
24. thy yrs. **a.** thro-t generations
25. heavens **a.** work of thy hands
103 : 14. he remember-h we **a.** dust
15. As for man, his days **a.** as grass
104 : 16. trees of Lord **a.** full of sap
17. stork, the fir trees **a.** her hou.
18. high hills **a.** a refuge for goats
24. Lord, how manifold **a.** works!
25. sea, wh-in **a.** things innumer.
107 : 27. reel, **a.** at their wit's end
30. Then **a.** they glad bec. quiet
109 : 4. For my love **a.** my adversa-s
115 : 4. Their idols **a.** silver and
15. Ye **a.** blessed of the Lord, wh.
16. heavens **a.** the L.'s; but earth
119 : 75. thy judgments **a.** right
84. How many **a.** days of servant?
85. digged pits which **a.** not after
86. all thy com-ts **a.** faithful [law
91. continue, for all **a.** thy serv-ts
98. com-ts; they **a.** ever with me
99. testimonies **a.** my meditation
103. How sweet **a.** thy words unto
111. They **a.** rejoicing of my heart
137. L., upright **a.** thy judgments
138. Thy testimonies **a.** faithful
143. Trouble, yet com-ts **a.** delight
150. mischief; they **a.** far fr. thy
151. all thy com-ts **a.** truth [law
156. Great **a.** thy tender mercies
157. Many **a.** my persecutors, yet
172. thy com-ts **a.** righteousness
125 : 4. good to them th. **a.** upright
127 : 3. chil. **a.** a heritage of Lord
4. As arrows **a.** in hand of mighty;
so **a.** children of the youth
139 : 12. darkness, light **a.** alike to
14. marvellous **a.** th. works [thee
17. How precious **a.** thy thoughts
141 : 6. hear words; they **a.** sweet
8. mine eyes **a.** unto thee, O God
142 : 6. persecutors; **a.** stronger
144 : 4. his days **a.** as a shadow [all
145 : 9. his tender mercies **a.** over
Pr. 1 : 19. So **a.** the ways of every
one greedy of gain [righteousn.
8 : 9. words of my mouth **a.** in

Pr. 8 : 18. Riches, honour **a.** with me
10 : 6. Blessings **a.** upon head of just
11 : 20. They that **a.** of froward
heart **a.** abomination; but upright **a.** his delight (4), 15 : 26.
12 : 5. thoughts of the righteous **a.**
right; but counsels of wicked **a.**
7. wicked **a.** overthrown, **a.** not
22 Lying lips **a.** abomination (2)
14 : 4. Where no oxen **a.**, crib clean
12. end **a.** ways of death, 16 : 25.
15 : 3. eyes of L. **a.** in every place
11. Hell, destruction **a.** bef. Lord
26. words of pure **a.** pleasant (2)
16 : 2. ways of man **a.** clean in own
11. just weight, balance **a.** L.'s (2)
13. Righteous lips **a.** delight of K-s
24. Pleasant words **a.** as honeyco.
17 : 6. glory of chil. **a.** their fa-s (2)
24. eyes of fool **a.** in ends of earth
18 : 7. fool's lips **a.** snare of his soul
8. The words of a talebearer **a.** as
wounds, 26 : 22. [of a castle
19. their contentions **a.** like bars
21. Death and life **a.** in the tongue
20 : 10. Divers weights **a.** abomin-n,
24. Man's goings **a.** of Lord [23.
22 : 5. snares **a.** in way of froward
26. Be not of them that **a.** sureties
26 : 7. legs of the lame **a.** not equal
21. As coals **a.** to burning coals
23. Burning lips **a.** like a potsherd
25. **a.** 7 abominations in his heart
27 : 6. Faithful **a.** the wounds of a
friend; kisses of an enemy **a.** de.
20. Hell and destruction **a.** never
24. For riches **a.** not for ever [full
26. the goats **a.** price of field (2)
28 : 1. righteous **a.** bold as lion [ity
29 : 2. When righteous **a.** in author-
30 : 12. generation that **a.** pure in
13. O how lofty **a.** their eyes [own
18. three things **a.** too wonderful
24. four thi-s **a.** little, but **a.** wise
25. The ants **a.** a people not strong
26. The conies **a.** but a feeble folk
29 yea, four **a.** comely in going
Ec. 2 : 14. wise man's eyes **a.** in his
23. all his days **a.** sorrows [head
4 : 2. I praised dead which **a.** dead
more than living which **a.** alive
5 : 7. in many words **a.** vanities [ow
8 : 13. wicked, his days **a.** as shad-
9 : 1. the wise and their works **a.** in
hand of God [a. gracious
10 : 12. words of wise man's mouth
12 : 11. words of wise **a.** as goads
Can. 1 : 10. Thy cheeks **a.** comely wi.
17. The beams of our hou **a.** cedar
4 : 2. Thy teeth **a.** like a flock, 6 : 6.
3. Thy lips **a.** like thread of scarlet
5. Thy breasts **a.** like 2 roes, 7 : 3 (2)
5 : 11. His locks **a.** black as raven
12. His cheeks **a.** as bed of spices
14. His hands **a.** as gold rings set
15. His legs **a.** as pillars of marble
6 : 7. As pomegranate **a.** thy tem-
8. There **a.** threescore queens [ples
7 : 1. How beautiful **a.** thy feet
Is. 1 : 14. they **a.** a trouble unto me
15. your hands **a.** full of blood
23. princes **a.** compan-s of thieves
3 : 8. tongue and doings **a.** ag Lord
5 : 21. Woe unto them th. **a.** wise in
22. Woe unto them **a.** mighty to
28. Whose arrows **a.** sharp [drink
8 : 18. I and chil. **a.** for signs and
10 : 8 **a.** not my princes kings?
19 : 11. Surely princes of Zoan **a.**
fools, 13 (3) [wise men?
12. Where **a.** they? where **a.** thy
23 : 8. merchants **a.** princes (2)
24 : 17. Fear, pit, snare **a.** upon thee
18. windows from on high **a.** open
21. Lord punish ones **a.** on high
25 : 1. thy counsels **a.** faithfulness
26 : 14. They **a.** dead, sh not rise (2)

Is. 28 : 1. a. on head of fat valleys
7.Thro. strong drink a. out of way
8. all tables a. full of filthiness
15. with hell a. we at agreement
30 : 27.his lips a. full of indignat-n
31 : 1. trust in chariots bec. they
a. many ; in horsemen because
they a. strong [not God
3.Now the Egyptians a. men, and
32 : 7. instruments of churl a. evil
9.Rise, ye women th. a. at ease, 11.
33 : 13. Hear, ye that a. far off (2)
35 : 4.them that a. of fearful heart
36 : 5. (but they a. but vain words)
11. ears of peo. th. a. on the wall
19. Where a. gods of Hamath ? (2)
40 : 15.nations a. as drop of bucket
41 : 23.Shew things that a. to come
29. Behold, they a. all vanity ;
their molten images a. wind (3)
42 : 17. to images, Ye a. our gods
22. a people, they a. for a prey (3)
43 : 10. Ye a. my witn-s, 12.-44 : 8.
44 : 9. that make a graven image a.
all vanity (2) | 11. they a. of men
46 : 1. th. a. burden to weary beast
12. that a. far from righteousness
52 : 7. How beautiful a. feet of him
th. publisheth peace, Ro. 10:15.
54 : 1. more a. chil. of desolate than
55 : 8. my thoughts a. not your (2)
9 as heavens a. higher than (2)
56 : 10. His watchmen a. blind ;
they a. all dumb dogs (3)
11. Yea, they a. greedy dogs, a.
57 : 20. wicked a. like troubled sea
59 : 6. their works a. works of iniq.
7. thoughts a. tho-ts of iniq-y (2)
12. our transgressions a. with us
61 : 9. they a. seed L. hath blessed
63 : 8. Surely they a. my people
65 : 22. as days of tree a. days of
23. they a. the seed of blessed[peo.
Je. 2 : 11. gods which a. yet no gods
28. where a. gods thou hast made?
acc-g to thy cities a. thy gods
31. wheref. say people, We a. lords
4 : 17. As keepers of field a. ag-t her
5 : 6. their transgressions a. many
10. her battlements ; a. not Lord's
6 : 20. offerings a. not acceptable
23. they a. cruel, have no mercy
28. they a. brass and iron ; they
a. all corrupters (3)
8 : 8. How do ye say, We a. wise?
9 : 3. they a. not valiant for truth
25. punish all wh. a. circumc-d[(3)
26. all these nations a. uncircum.
10 : 5. They a. upright as palm tr.
8. they a. altogether brutish [18.
15. a. vanity, work of errors, 51 :
20. my chil. a. gone forth, a. not
14 : 22. a. any among the vanities
15 : 2.Such as a. for death to de.(4)
16 : 17. mine eyes a. upon th. ways
20.make gods, and they a. no gods
22 : 17.thine eyes a. not for covet-s
23 : 11. prophet, priest a. profane
26. they a. prophets of deceit of
24 : 2. good like figs that a. first ripe
30 : 4. these a. words Lord spake
32 : 35. places of Baal which a. in
valley of Hinnom [ets
37 : 19. Where a. now your proph-
44 : 2. this day they a. a desolation
24. all Judah that a. in Egypt, 27.
46 : 23. a. more than grasshop-s(2)
48 : 14. How say ye, We a. mighty
17. ye that a. about him bemoan
50 : 38. and they a. mad upon idols
42. they a. cruel, not shew mercy
51 : 7.drunken, thf. nations a. mad
43. Her cities a. a desolation and
64. Thus far a. words of Jeremiah
La. 1 : 22. my sighs a. many ; heart
3 : 23. They a. new every morning
4 : 9. slain with sword a. better th.

La. 4 : 19. Our persecutors a. swifter
5 : 3. We a. orphans and fatherless,
our mothers a. as widows
5.Our necks a. under persecution
7. Our fathers sinned and a. not
Eze. 2 : 4.they a. impudent chil., 3:7.
5.(for they a. a rebellious house),
yet, 7.-3 : 26, 27.-12 : 2.
5 : 5. of the nations that a. round
about her, 6, 7, 14, 15.-16 : 57.
7 : 9.abominations that a. in midst
11 : 7. Your slain, they a. the flesh
12 : 23. The days a. at hand[far off
27. prophesieth of times that a.
13 : 4. thy prophets a. like foxes
16 : 52. a. more righteous than th.
18 : 4. Behold, all souls a. mine
25. a. not your ways unequal, 29.
29. Israel, a. not my ways equal ?
22 : 9. In thee a. men th. carry tales
18. they a. the dross of silver
23 : 45. they a. adulteresses [us
24 : 19. tell what these things a. to
32 : 22. Asshur, his graves a. about
33 : 24. Abr. one, but we a. many
27. they that a. in the wastes fall
34 : 31. ye a. men, and I am God
36 : 2. ancient high places a. ours
3. ye a. an infamy of the people
8. Israel ; they a. at hand to come
38 : 11. I will go to them a. at rest
45 : 14. for ten baths a. a homer
48 : 1. these a. his sides, east [Bab.
Da. 3 : 12. a. certain Jews set over
4 : 3. How great a. his signs ! (2)
18. all the wise men a. not able to
5 : 23. God, whose a. all thy ways
7 : 17. beasts, which a. four, a. four
24. ten horns a. ten kings [kings
8 : 20. ram having 2 horns a. kings
9 : 7. Isr. that a. near, that a. far
Ho. 1 : 9. ye a. not my people, 10.
10. Ye a. sons of the living God
2 : 12. These a. rewards my lovers
4 : 4. people a. as they that strive
7 : 2. their doings, a. bef. my face
16. they a. like a deceitful bow
9 : 15. all their princes a. revolters
12 : 7.balances of deceit a. in his h.
11. prophets : they a. vanity, their
altars a. as heaps in furrows
14 : 3. nei will we say, Ye a. gods
Am. 9 : 7.a. ye not as chil. of Ethiop.
Jon. 4 : 11.wh-in a. more th.120,000
Mi. 1 : 5. what a. high places of Jud.
6 : 10. a. treasures of wickedn. [(2)
12. rich men a. full of violence
7 : 6. man's enemies a. of own hou.
Na. 3 : 17. Thy crowned a. as locusts : not know where they a.
Ha. 1 : 3.there a. that raise strife (2)
6. dwellingplaces th. a. not theirs
7. They a. terrible and dreadful
8. Their horses a. more fierce th.
3 : 6. ways a. everlasting[wolves(2)
Zph. 3 : 3. princes a. roaring lions ;
Judges a. evening wolves [ous
4.Her prophets a. light, treacher-
18. them that a. sorrowful for
solemn assembly, who a. of thee
Zch. 4 : 11. What a. these two olive
6 : 5.These a. four spirits of heavens
6. The black horses wh. a. th-in
15. they that a. far off shall come
Mat. 2 : 18. Rachel weeping for children bec. they a. not [Lu.12:24.
6 : 26. fowls. a. ye not much better,
9 : 37.harvest, but labourers a. few
10 : 29.a. not two sparrows sold for
12 : 48. he said, who a. my breth. ?
13 : 38.good seed a. chil. of kingd.(2)
15 : 20.These a. things which defile
17 : 26.Jes. saith, Then a. chil. free
19 : 26. but with God all things a.
possible, Mk. 14:36. Lu. 18 : 27.
30. But many that a. first shall be
last, Mk. 10 : 31. Lu. 13 : 30(2).

Mat. 20 : 22. a. ye able to drink of
cup that I. sh. drink ? We a. able
22 : 21. Render Cesar things which
a. Cesar's (2), Mk. 12 : 17(2).
30. a. as angels of God, Mk. 12:25.
23 : 31. ye a. chil. of them th. killed
Mk. 5 : 9. name Legion ; we a. many
6 : 3. a. not his sisters with us ?
13 : 1. see what buildings a. here !
14 : 48. a. ye come out as ag. thief
Lu. 6 : 25. Woe unto you th. a. full
7 : 31. what a. they like? [market
32.They a. like chil. sitting in the
9 : 55. ye know not spirit ye a. of
11 : 7. my chil. a. with me in bed
21. man armed, goods a. in peace
41. all things a. clean unto you
44. ye a. as graves which appear
not, men a. not aware of them
12 : 6. a. not five sparrows sold for
7. ye a. of more value than many
13 : 14.a. six days in which to work
23.a. there few that be saved ? [27.
25. I know you not whence ye a.,
16 : 8. chil. of this world a. wiser
17 : 17. cleansed ? where a. the 9 ?
18 : 11. I am not as other men a.
20 : 36. they a. equal unto angels
22 : 38. Lord, here a. 2 swords [(2)
24 : 17. as ye walk and a. sad (2)
48. ye a. witnesses of these things
Jn. 4 : 35. say not, There a. 4 mos.
5 : 28. all that a. in graves sh. hear
7 : 47. answ-d, a. ye also deceived ?
8 : 37. I know ye a. Abr-'s seed
44. Ye a. of your father the devil
47. hear not bec. ye a. not of God
10 : 26.believe not, bec. ye a. not of
30. I and my Father a. one [gods?
34. Is it not written I said, Ye a.
11 : 9. a. not 12 hours in the day ?
13 : 10. ye a. clean, but not all, 11.
14 : 2.In Fa.'s house a. many man-
15 : 3. Ye a. clean thro. word[sions
5. I am the vine, ye a. branches
14. Ye a. my friends if do whatso.
19. ye a. not of the world, theref.
17 : 7.all things given me a. of thee
9. I pray for them ; they a. thine
10. mine a. thine, thine a. mine
11. they may be one as we a., 22.
14. They a. not of world as I, 16.
21 : 25. a. other things Jesus did
Ac. 2 : 13. These a. full of new wine
32. wh-of we all a. witnesses, 3:15.
5 : 9.buried thy husband a. at door
7 : 1.said priest, a. these things so ?
26. Sirs, ye a. brethren ; why do
15 : 23. brethren wh. a. of Gentiles
16 : 28. Do no harm ; we a. all here
17 : 28.we a. his offsp-g, 29.-21 :20.
25 : 5.let them wh. a. able go down
28 : 27. their ears a. dull of hearing
Ro. 1 : 6. a. ye the called of Jes. Ch.
15. preach to you that a. at Rome
20.so that they a. without excuse
28. things wh. a. not convenient
32. such things a. worthy of death
2 : 2. we a. sure judgment of God is
8. unto them that a. contentious
14. these a. law unto themselves
19. light of them which a. in dark-
3 : 9. a. we better than they ? [ness
15. Their feet a. swift to shed blo.
16. Destruction, misery, a. in th.
4 : 12. which a. not of circumcision
6 : 13. those that a. alive from dead
14. ye a. not under law, but grace
8 : 1. to them which a. in Christ
9. ye a. not in the flesh [the flesh
12.brethren, we a. debtors, not to
16. beareth witn-s we a. chil. of G.
18. a. not worthy to be compared
37. we a. more than conquerors
9 : 4. Who a. Israelites ; to whom
5. Whose a. the fathers, of whom
8. They which a. chil. of flesh(2)

Ro. 9 : 26. said, Ye a. not my people
11 : 14. provoke them which a. my
16. if root be holy so a. branches
28. they a. enemies for y-r sakes ;
they a. beloved for fath-s' sakes
33. unsearchable a. his judgm-ts
36. of him, to him a. all things
13 : 6. for they a. God's ministers
14 : 20. All things indeed a. pure
15 : 26. for poor saints which a. at
27. and their debtors they a. ⌊Jer.
16 : 15. Salute saints which a. with
1 Co. 1 : 27. weak to confound things
which a. mighty ⌈things th. a.
28. wh. a. not, to bring to nought
3 : 17. temple of God holy, wh. ye a.
6 : 19. and ye a. not your own ⌈G.'s
20. your body and spirit wh. a.
8 : 6. one God of wh. a. all things ;
one Jes. by whom a. all things
9 : 2. seal of mine apostleship a. ye
12. If others partakers, a. not we
20. gain them that a. und. law (2)
21. them that a. without law (2)
12 : 12. memb-s many, a. one body,
22. more feeble a. necessary ⌊20.
27. Now ye a. the body of Christ
29. a. all apostles? a. all proph. (4)
14 : 10. a. so many voices in world
22. Wheref. tongues a. for a sign
23. will they not say ye a. mad ? (2)
15 : 40. There a. celestial bodies
16 : 9. there a. many adversaries
2 Co. 2 : 16. we a. savour unto death
3 : 5. Not that we a. sufficient to
5 : 4. we that a. in this tabernacle
6. whilst we a. at home in body (3)
18. all things a. of God, who hath
20. Now then we a. ambassadors
10 : 4. weapons of warfare a. not c.
7. as he is Christ's, even so a. we
12. measuring thems. a. not wise
11 : 22. a. they Hebrews ? so am I (3)
23. a. they ministers of Christ ⌈(2)
Ga. 5 : 19. works of flesh a. manifest
Ep. 2 : 19. ye a. no more strangers
Ph. 1 : 13. my bonds a. manifest in
3 : 3. we a. the circumcision ⌊palace
4 : 8. whatsoever things a. true (6)
22. saints salute you that a. of Ce.
Col. 2 : 10. ye a. complete in him
17. a. a shadow of things to come
20. why a. ye subject to ordinan-s
22. Which a. to perish with using
3 : 1. seek those things wh. a. above
3. For ye a. dead, your life is hid
5. mortify members wh. a. upon
1 Th. 2 : 10. ye a. witnesses ⌊earth
14. churches which in Judea a. in
15. please not God, a. contrary to
5 : 5. Ye a. children of the light (2)
7. they drunken a. drunken in ni.
8. let us who a. of day be sober
12. to know them wh. a. over you
14. warn them that a. unruly ⌈ies
2 Th. 3 : 11. working not a. busybod-
12. them that a. such we comm-d
1 Ti. 5 : 3. Honour widows that a.
16. relieve them that a. widows
25. good works of some a. manifest ; they that a. otherwise
Tit. 1 : 10. a. many unruly talkers
12. The Cretians a. always liars
15. Unto pure all things a. pure (2)
3 : 9. they a. unprofitable, vain
15. All that a. with me salute thee
He. 1 : 10. heavens a. works of thine
4 : 13. all things a. naked unto him
15. was tempted like as we a. ⌈age
5 : 14. meat to them that a. of full
12 : 8. without chastisement wh-of
all a. partakers, a. ye bastards
Ja. 5 : 2. your garm-ts a. motheaten
17. to like passions as we a. ⌈tion
2 Pe. 2 : 19. a. servants of corrup-
1 Jn. 2 : 18. now a. many antichrists
3 : 22. we do things that a. pleasing

1 Jn. 4 : 1. spirits whe. they a. of God
5 : 7. a. three th. bear record (2), 8.
Jude 4. a. certain men crept in
12. clouds they a. without water
Re. 1 : 4. Spirits wh. a. bef. throne
19. Write things wh. a. and sh. be
2 : 2. not bear them which a. evil,
say they a. apostles, a. not, 9.
18. his feet a. like fine brass ⌈God
4 : 5. seven lamps a. seven Spirits of
11. all, for thy pleasure they a.
5 : 8. odours wh. a. prayers of saints
13. and such as a. in the sea (2)
8 : 13. three angels wh. a. to sound!
10 : 6. heaven and things th-in a. (3)
20 : 10. where beast, false prophet a.
See ALL, AS, BLESSED, FULL,
THEY, WE, WHICH, YE.
See **BLESSED are ye,**
All THAT, THEM that,
THESE are, THEY all,
Blessed are THEY,
THEY that, YE all.

ARE'LI, ITES. ⌈A.
Ge. 46 : 16. sons of Gad ; Ziphion,
Nu. 26 : 17. of A., family of the A-s

AREOP'AGITE. ⌈A.
Ac. 17 : 34. believed ; Dionysius the

AREOP'AGUS. ⌈A.
Ac. 17 : 19. they brought Paul unto

ARE'TAS. ⌈king
2 Co. 11 : 32. governor under A. the

AR'GOB. [Person.]
2 K. 15 : 25. Pekah smote A., Arieh

AR'GOB. [Place.]
De. 3 : 4. we took all region of A., 13.
14. Jair took all the country of A.
1 K. 4 : 13. pertained the region of A.

ARGUE, ED.
Jb. 9 : †33. Neith. is one that should
a. betwixt us ⌈before him
13 : † 15. I will a. mine own ways
Is. 11 : †4. sh. a. with equity for meek
Ha. 2 : †1. answer when I am a-d wi.

ARGUING. ⌈prove
Jb. 6 : 25. what doth your a. re-
Ha. 2 : † 1. what answer upon my a.

ARGUMENTS. ⌈a.
Jb. 23 : 4. would fill my mouth with

ARID'AI.
Es. 9 : 9. Jews slew Arisai and A.

ARID'ATHA.
Es. 9 : 8. Jews slew A., the sons of

ARI'EH. ⌊Haman
See ARGOB. [Person.]

A'RIEL. [Person.]
Ezr. 8 : 16. sent for Eliezer, A., chief

A'RIEL. [Place.]
Is. 29 : 1. Woe to A., to A., the city
2. Yet I will distress A. : it shall be
unto me as A. ⌈A. shall be
7. all nations that fight against

ARIGHT. ⌈a.
Ps. 50 : 23. ordereth his conversat-n
78 : 8. that set not their heart a.
Pr. 4 : † 26. thy ways be ordered a.
15 : 2. the wise useth knowledge a.
23 : 31. wine when it moveth itself
Je. 8 : 6. but they spake not a. ⌊a.

ARIMATHE'A.
Mat. 27 : 57. came a rich man of A. ;
Joseph, Mk. 15 : 43. Jn. 19 : 38.
Lu. 23 : 51. Jos-h, a good man of A.

A'RIOCH. ⌈9.
Ge. 14 : 1. days of A. king of Ellasar,
Da. 2 : 14. Daniel answered A., captain of king's guard, 15. ⌈iel
15. A. made thing known to Dan-
24. Therefore Daniel went unto A.
25. A. brought in Daniel bef. king

ARIS'AI. See ARIDAI.

ARISE. ⌈land
Ge. 13 : 17. a., walk through the
19 : 15. hastened Lot, saying, a.
21 : 18. a., lift up the lad, hold him
27 : 19. a. and eat of my venison
31. Let my father a. and eat of

Ge. 27 : 43. son, a., flee to Laban my
28 : 2. a., go to Bethuel, thy mo.'s
31 : 13. a., get thee out from land
35 : 1. a., go up to Beth-el and, 3.
41 : 30. shall a. seven yrs. of famine
43 : 8. Send lad, we will a. and go
13. and a., go again unto the man
De. 9 : 12. a., get thee quickly hence
10 : 11. a., take journey bef. people
13 : 1. If a. a prophet or a dreamer
17 : 8. then shalt a. and get thee
Jos. 1 : 2. a., go over this Jordan
8 : 1. take the people, a., go to Ai
Ju. 5 : 12. a., Barak, lead captivity
7 : 9. a., get thee unto the host
15. Gid-n said, a. ; Lord delivered
18 : 9. a., that we may go ag. them
20 : 40. flame began to a. out of city
1 S. 9 : 3. said to Saul, a., seek asses
16 : 12. a., anoint him, this is he
23 : 4. answ-d Dav., a., go to Keilah
2 S. 2 : 14. Let young men a., play (2)
3 : 21. I will a. and gather Israel
11 : 20. if so be that king's wrath a.
13 : 15. Amnon said unto her, a.,
15 : 14. a. and let us flee ⌊be gone
17 : 1. I will a., pursue after David
21. said unto David, a., pass over
19 : 7. a., speak comfortably unto
22 : 39. wounded, they could not a.
1 K. 3 : 12. nor shall any a. like thee
14 : 2. Jerob-m to wife, a., disguise
12. a., get thee to thine house
17 : 9. Elijah, a., get to Zarephath
19 : 5. angel touched him, said, a.,
21 : 7. a., eat bread, be merry ⌊7.
15. Ahab, a., take vineyard of Na.
18. a., go down to meet Ahab, k-g
2 K. 1 : 3. Elijah, a., meet messen-
8 : 1. Elisha unto woman, a. ⌊gers
9 : 2. make Jehu a. amo. brethren
1 Ch. 22 : 16. a., be doing, the Lord
19. a., build ye sanctuary of Lord
2 Ch. 6 : 41. a., O Lord, into resting
Ne. 2 : 20. we will a. and build ⌊pla.
Ezr. 10 : 4. a. ; this matter belongeth
Es. 1 : 18. sh. a. too much contempt
4 : 14. shall deliverance a. to Jews
Jb. 7 : 4. When sh. I a., night be gone?
11 : †17. age shall a. above noonday
25 : 3. upon wh. doth not his light a.
Ps. 3 : 7. a., O Lord ; save me, my G.
7 : 6. a., O Lord, in thine anger
9 : 19. a., O Lord ; let not man
10 : 12. a., O Lord ; lift thine hand
12 : 5. now will I a., saith the Lord
17 : 13. a., O Lord ; disappoint him
44 : 23. a., cast us not off forever
26. a. for our help, redeem us for
68 : 1. Let G. a., let his enemies be
74 : 22. a., O God ; plead own cause
78 : 6. chil. a., declare to their chil.
82 : 8. a., O God ; judge the earth
88 : 10. shall dead a. and praise ?
89 : 9. when waves a. thou stillest
102 : 13. Thou shalt a. and have
mercy upon Zion ⌈ashamed
109 : 28. when they a. let them be
132 : 8. a., O Lord, into thy rest
Pr. 6 : 9. when a. out of thy sleep?
31 : 28. Her chil. a., call her blessed
Can. 2 : 13. a. my love, my fair one
Is. 21 : 5. a. ye princes, anoint shield
23 : 12. daughter of Zidon ; a. pass
over to Chittim ⌈they a.
26 : 19. with my dead body shall
31 : 2. he will a. against evil doers
49 : 7. k-s shall a., princes worship
52 : 2. a., O Jerusalem ; loose thys.
60 : 1. a., shine ; thy light is come
2. the Lord shall a. upon thee
Je. 1 : 17. a., speak all I command
2 : 27. in trouble will say, a., save
28. gods, let th. a. if can save ⌊us
6 : 4. a., and let us go up at noon
5. a. and let us go by night and
8 : 4. Shall they fall and not a. ?

Je. 13 : 4. Take girdle, a., go hide it
6. a., go to Euphrates, take girdle
18 : 2. a., go to the potter's house
31 : 6. a. ye, let us go up to Zion
46 : 16. a., let us go to our own peo.
49 : 28. a., go to Kedar, spoil men
31 a., get you unto wealthy nat-n
La. 2 : 19. a., cry out in the night
Eze. 3 :22. a., go forth into the plain
Da. 2 : 39. shall a. another kingdom
7 : 5. beast, a., devour much flesh
17. beasts are 4 kings which sh. a.
24. horses are 10 kings that sh. a.
Ho. 10 : 14. tumult a. among people
Am. 7 : 2. by whom sh. Jacob a.? 5.
Ob. 1. a. and let us rise against her
Jon. 1 : 2. a., go to Nineveh, 3 : 2.
6 O sleeper, a., call upon thy God
4 : 8. when sun did a. G. prepared
Mi. 2 : 10. a.; this is not your rest
4 :13. a., thresh, O daugh-r of Zien
6 : 1. a., contend before the mts.
7 : 8. O enemy; when I fall I sh. a.
Ha. 2 : 19. saith to dumb stone, a.
Mal. 4 :2. sh. sun of righteousn-s a.
Mat. 2 : 13. a., take young child, 20.
9 : 5. is it easier to say, a.? Mk. 2:9.
6. a., take up thy bed, and go unto, Mk. 2 : 11. Lu. 5 : 24.
17 : 7. Jesus said, a., be not afraid
24 : 24. there shall a. false Christs
Mk. 3 : †3. he saith unto the man, a.
5 : 41. Damsel (I say), a., Lu. 8 :54.
Lu. 7 : 14. Lord said, Young man, a.
15 : 18. I will a., go to my father
17 : 19. a., go thy way: thy faith
24 : 38. why do thoughts a. in your [hearts
Jn. 14 :31. a., let us go hence
Ac. 8 : 26. a., go toward the south
9 : 6. L. said unto Saul, a., go into
11. a., go into street called Straight
34. Eucas, a. and make thy bed [a.
40. Peter, turning, said, Tabitha,
10 : 20. the Spirit said, a., go with [them
11 : 7. a., Peter, slay and eat
12 : 7. a. quickly. And his chains
20 : 30. men a., speaking perverse
22 : 10. L. said, a., go into Damasc.
16. why tarriest? a., be baptized
Ep. 5 : 14. a. from the dead, and Chr.
2 Pe. 1 : 19. until daystar a. in your [hearts
See RISE.

ARISETH.

1 K 18 : 44. a. little cloud out of sea
Ps. 104 : 22. The sun a., they gather
112 : 4. Unto the upright a. light
Ec. 1 : 5. The sun a. and goeth down
Is. 2 : 19. a. to shake the earth, 21.
Na. 3 : 17. when sun a. they flee [17.
Mat. 13 : 21. persecution a., Mk. 4 :
Jn. 7 :52. out of Gali. a. no prophet
He. 7 :15. of Melchizedec a. another [priest

ARISING.

Es. 7 : 7. k-g a. fr. banquet in wrath

ARISTAR'CHUS.

Ac. 19 : 29. having caught Gaius, A.
20 : 4. accompanied Paul, A., and
27 : 2. A., a Macedonian, with us
Col. 4 : 10. A., fellow prisoner, Phm. [24.

ARISTOBU'LUS.

Ro. 16 : 10. Salute them of A.' house- [hold

ARK.

Ge. 6 :14. Make a. of gopher wood (2)
15. length of a. shall be 300 cubits
16. windows sh. thou make to a. (2)
18. thou shalt come into a. and
19. two of every sort bring into a.
7 : 1. Come thou and all into a. [13.
7. Noah went into a. bec. of flood,
9. went two and two into a., 15.
17. waters increased, bare up a.
18. a. went on face of the waters
23. Noah only alive, and they in a.
8 : 1. G. remembered Noah and all [in a.
4. a. rested in 7th month
6. Noah opened window of the a.
9. dove returned into the a. (2)
Ge. 8. 10. again sent dove out of a.
13. Noah removed covering of a.
16. Go forth of a. thou, wife, and
19. Every beast went out of the a.
9 : 10. covenant with all go out of [a.
18. sons that went forth of a.
Ex. 2 : 3. she took a. of bulrushes
5. when she saw a. among flags
25 : 10. make an a. of shittim wood
14. put staves by sides of a. that a. be borne, 15.–35 : 12.–37 : 5.
21. put mercy seat above upon a., 26 : 34.–40 : 20. Le. 16 : 2.
35 : 12. wise hearted shall make a.
37 : 1. Bezaleel made a. of shittim w.
40 : 3. shalt cover the a. with vail
20. he put the testimony into a.
21. he brought the a. into taberu.
Nu. 3 : 31. their charge sh. be the a.
10 : 35. when a. set forward, Moses
De. 10 : 1. come into mt., make an a.
2. tables thou shalt put in the a.,
5. 2 Ch. 5 : 10. [and hewed
3. I made an a. of shittim wood,
Jos. 3 : 15. bare a. unto Jordan (2)
4 : 10. which bare a. stood in Jord.
6 : 4. bear before a. seven trumpets
9. rearward came after the a. [a.
8 : 33. Israel stood on this side the
1 S. 6 : 13. they saw a. and rejoiced
7:2. while the a. abode in Kirjath-j.
2 S. 6 : 4. Ahio went before the a.
11 : 11. a. and Israel abide in tents
1 K. 8 : 3. elders came, priests took up the a., 2 Ch. 5 : 4, 5. [5 : 6.
5. all Isr. bef. a. sacrificing, 2 Ch.
7 cherubim spread wings over the a. and covered a., 2 Ch 5 : 8. (2)
9. nothing in the a. save the two tables, 2 Ch. 5 : 10. [the a.
21. I have set there a place for
1 Ch. 6 : 31. after that a. had rest
13 : 9. Uzza put hand to hold a., 10.
13. Dav. brought not the a. home
15 : 23. doorkeepers for the a., 24.
27. fine linen, Levites that bare a.
16 :37. Asaph to minister bef. a., (2)
2 Ch. 5 : 9. staves were seen from a. before oracle (2), 1 K. 8 : † 8.
6 : 11. in it have put a., wh-in is
41. arise, O Lord, and a. of thy strength, Ps. 132 : 8. [did build
35 : 3. Put a. in house that Solo-n
Mat. 24 : 38. until day Noe entered into a., Lu. 17 : 27. [an a.
He. 11 : 7. By faith Noah prepared
1 Pe. 3 : 20. while the a. was prep-g
Re. 11 :19. in temple a. of his testam.

ARK of the covenant.

Jos. 3 : 6. Take up a. –, pass over (2)
8. command priests that bear a. –
14. priests bearing a. – before peo.
4 : 9. stones where priests bare a. –
6 : 6. Joshua said, Take up a. –
He. 9 : 4. holiest of all had the a. –

ARK of covenant of God or Lord.

Nu. 10 : 33. a. – went bef. to search
14 : 44. a. – departed not out of ca.
De. 10 : 8. tribe of Levi to bear a. –
31 : 9. the sons of Levi which bare a. –, 25. 1 Ch. 15 : 26. [of a. –
26. book of law put it in the side
Jos. 3 : 3. When ye see a. –, go after
11. a. – passeth over into Jordan
17. priests th. bare a. – stood firm
4 : 7. waters were cut off before a. –
18. when priests that bare a. – out
6 : 8. seven priests; a. – followed
8 : 33. stood bef. priests wh. bare a. –
Ju. 20 : 27. a. – there in those days
1 S. 4 : 3. Let us fetch the a. –, 4.
4. two sons of Eli were with a. –
5. a. – came into camp Isr. shouted
2 S. 15 :24. Zadok, Levites bear-g a. –
1 K. 3 : 15. Sol-n before a. – offered
6 : 19. oracle, to set there the a. –
1 K. 8 : 1. bring the a. – out of city of David, 1 Ch. 15:25. 2 Ch. 5:2.
6. priests brought a. – unto his place, 2 Ch. 5 : 7. [shouting
1 Ch. 15 : 28. brought the a. – with
29. as a. – came, Michal saw Dav.
16 :6. priests with trumpets bef. a. –
37. So he left bef. a. – Asaph and
17:1. a. – remaineth under curtains
28 : 2. to build house for a. –, 22 :19.
18. cherubim th. covered the a. –
Je. 3 : 16. s. say no more, The a. –

ARK of God.

1 S. 3 : 3. in temple where a. – was
4 : 11. the a. – was taken, 17, 19.
13. Eli, his heart trembled for a. –
18. made mention of a. –, Eli fell
21. named I-chabod, because a. –
22. glory departed, for a. – taken
5 : 2. Philistines took a. – and set it by Dagon, 1. [with us
7. The a. – of Isr. shall not abide
8. What shall we do with the a. –. Let a. – be carried unto Gath (3)
10. Thf. they sent a. – to Ekron (3)
11. Send aw. a. – th. it slay us not
6 : 3. If send a. – send it not empty
14 : 18. Saul said, Bring a. – (2)
2 S. 6 : 2. David went from Baale to bring up a. –, 1 Ch. 13 :6. [13:7.
3. set a. – upon a new cart, 4. 1 Ch.
6. Uzzah put forth hand to a. –
7. God smote him; he died by a. –
12. L. blessed Obed-edom because of a. –; David brought up a. –
7 : 2. a. – dwelleth within curtains
15 : 24. priests set down a. – [city
25. Zadok, Carry back a. – into
29. Zadok carried a. – again to Je.
1 Ch. 13 : 3. let us bring again a. –
5. gathered all Isr. to bring a. – fr. Kirjath-j, 6. 2 Ch. 1 : 4.
12. How shall I bring a. – home?
14. a. – remained with Obed-edom
15 : 1. David prepared place for a. –
2. None ought to carry a. – but (2)
12. sanctify, that ye may bring a. –
15. Levites bare a. – upon should-s
24. did blow with trumpets before [a. –
16 :1. So they brought the a. –

ARK of the Lord.

Jos. 3 : 13. soon as priests that bear a. – rest in Jordan, 17. – 4 : 10,
4 : 5. Pass over before a. – [16.
11. people were passed, a. – passed
6 : 6. bear 7 trumpets bef. a. –, 13.
7. let him, armed, pass bef. a. –
11. So the a. – compassed the city
12. Josh. rose early, priests took
13. the rearward came aft. a. – [a. –
7. 6. Joshua fell upon face bef. a. –
1 S. 4 : 6. understood a. – was come
5 : 3. Dagon was fallen bef. a. –, 4.
6 : 1. a. – in country of Phil. seven [mos.
2. What shall we do to a. –?
8. take a. –, lay it upon cart, 11.
15. Levites took down a. – and cof.
18. stone wh-on they set a. – [a. –
19. he smote bec. they looked into
21. Philis. have brought the a. –
7 :1. men of Kirjath-j. fetched a. –, sanctified Eleazar to keep a. –
2 S. 6 : 9. How shall a. – come to me
10. David would not remove a. –
11. a. – in house of Obed-edom 3 [mos.
13. they that bare a. – gone
15. Isr. brought a. – with shouting
16. as a. – came into city, Michal
17. brought in a. –, set it in place
1 K. 2 : 26. not to death, bec. bar. [est a. –
8 : 4. priests brought a. –
1 Ch. 15 : 3. bring a. –, 12, 14.
16 : 4. Levites to minister bef. a. –
2 Ch 8:11. places are holy wh-to a. –
See **Ark of TESTIMONY.**

ARK'ITE.

Ge. 10 : 17. Canaan begat A., 1 Ch. [1 : 15.

ARM. [Noun.]
Ex. 15 : 16. by greatness of thine a.
De. 33 : 20. he teareth a. wi. crown
1 S. 2 : 31. I will cut off thine a. and a. of thy father's house [a.
2 S. 1 : 10 I took the bracelet on his
2 Ch. 32 :8. With him is an a. of flesh
Ezr. 4 : † 23. made Jews cease by a.
Jb. 22 : † 8. man of a. had the earth
26 : 2. how savest thou the a. that
31 : 22. let mine a. fall fr. shoulder
35 : 9. cry out by a. of the mighty
38 : 15. high a. shall be broken
40 : 9. Hast thou an a. like God?
Ps. 10 :15. Break thou a. of wicked
44 : 3. neither did their own a. save, but thine a. [generation
71 : † 18. shewed thine a. unto this
77 . 15. with thine a. redeemed peo.
79 : † 11. acc. to thine a. preserve
83 : † 8. been an a. to child-n of Lot
89 : 10. scattered enemies with thy
13. Thou hast a mighty a. [a.
21. mine a. shall strengthen him
98 : 1. his holy a. gotten victory [a.
Can. 8 : 6. set me as seal upon thine
Is. 9 : 20. eat ev. man flesh of his a.
17 : 5. reapeth ears with his a. [a.
30 : 30. shew lighting down of his
33 : 2. be their a. every morning
40 : 10. his a. shall rule for him
11. shall gather lambs with his a.
48 :14. his a. shall be on Chaldeans
51 :5. isles on mine a. sh. they trust
9. put on strength, O a. of Lord
52 : 10. Lord hath made bare his a.
53 : 1. to whom is the a. of Lord revealed? Jn. 12 : 38. [63 : 5.
59 : 16. his a. brought salvation.
62 : 8. Lord hath sworn by a. of his
63 :12. led them with his glorious a.
Je 17 : 5. he that maketh flesh his a.
21 : 5. fight ag. you with strong a.
48 : 25. of Moab, his a. is broken
Eze. 4 : 7. thine a. sh. be uncovered
22 : † 6. to their a. to shed blood
30 : 21. I have broken a. of Pha-h
31 : 17. into hell that were his a.
Da. 11 : 6. she not retain power of a.
Zch. 11 : 17. sword shall be upon his a. ; his a. sh. be clean dried up
Lu. 1 : 51. shewed strength with a.
Ac. 13 : 17. with high a. bro-t them
See **STRETCHED out arm.**
See OUTSTRETCHED.

ARMS.
Ge. 49 :24. the a. of his hands strong
De. 33 : 27. underneath are everl-g a.
Ju. 15 : 14. cords upon his a. as flax
16 : 12. he brake them fr. off his a.
2 S. 22 : 35. a bow of steel is broken by mine a., Ps. 18 : 34. [his a.
2 K. 9 : 24. smote Jehoram between
Jb. 22 : 9. a. of the fatherless brok.
Ps. 37 : 17. a. of wicked be broken
Pr. 31 : 17. she strength-h her a. [a.
Is. 44 : 12. worketh it wi. strength of
49 : 22. bring thy sons in their a.
51 : 5. mine a. shall judge people
Eze. 13 :20. I tear them from your a.
30 : 22. I will break Pha-'s a., 24.
25. I will strengthen a. of king of Bab-n, a. of Pha. shall fall, 24.
Da. 2 : 32. his breast and a. of silver
10 : 6. his a. like to polished brass
11 : 15. a. of south not withstand
22. with a. of flood be overflown
31. a. shall stand on his part [a.
Ho. 7 : 15. I have strengthened their
11 : 3. taking Ephraim by their a.
Mk. 9 : 36. had taken him in his a.
10 : 16. Jes. took them up in his a.
Lu. 2 : 28. Simeon took Jes. in his a.
Ro: 6 : † 13. nei. yield your members as a. of unrighteousness

ARM. [Verb.] [war
Nu. 31 : 3. a. some of yours. unto
1 Pe. 4 : 1. a. yours. with same mind

ARMAGED'DON.
Re. 16 : 16. he gathered them into A.

ARMED.
Ge. 14 : 14. Abram a. his servants
41 : † 40. thy word, my people be a.
Nu. 31 : 5. ev. tribe, 12,000 a. for war
32 : 17. will go ready a. bef. Israel
20. if ye will go a. before Lord, 21.
27. will pass over, ev. man a., 29.
30. if not pass over with you a.
32. We will pass a. into Canaan
De. 3 : 18. ye shall pass over a. bef. your brethren, Jos. 1 : 14. [rael
Jos. 4 : 12. passed over a. before Is-
† 13. 40,000 a. for war passed over
6 : 7. let him that is a. pass on
9. a. men went before priests, 13.
Ju. 7 : 11. Gid. unto outside of a. m.
1 S. 17 : 5. was a. with coat of mail
38. Saul a. Dav. with his armour; also he a. him with coat of mail
1 Ch. 12 : 2. They were a. with bows
23. bands ready a. came to David
24. children of Jud. 6,000 ready a.
2 Ch. 17 : 17. with Eliada, a. 200,000
28 : 14. So a. men left the captives
Jb. 39 : 21. goeth on to meet a. men
Ps. 78 : 9. chil. of Ephraim being a.
Pr. 6 : 11. want as an a. man, 24 :34.
Is. 15 : 4. a. soldiers of Moab sh. cry
Lu. 11 : 21. man a. keepeth palace

ARME'NIA.
2 K. 19 : 37. his sons smote him and escaped into A., Is. 37 : 38.

ARMHOLES. [a.
Je. 38 :12. Put rotten rags und. thine
Eze. 13 : 18. women that sew pillows

ARMIES. [to a.
Ex. 6 : 26. Bring out Israel acc. to
7 : 4. bring mine a. out of Egypt [a.
12 : 17. this day I brought your a. out of Egypt, 51. [them by a.
Nu. 1 : 3. thou and Aaron number
2 : 3. east shall Jud. pitch thro-t a.
9. camp of Jud. 186,400 thro-t a.
10. On south Reuben, acc-g to a.
16. in camp of R., 151,450 thro-t a.
18. On west Ephraim acc-g to a.
24. of camp of E 108,100 thro-t a.
25. standard of Dan on north by a.
10 : 14. first went Judah acc. to a.
18. Reuben set forward acc. to a.
22. Ephraim set forward acc. to a.
28 journeyings of Israel acc. to a.
33 : 1. out of Eg. with a. under Mo.
De. 20 : 9. make capt-s of a. to lead
1 S. 17 : 1. Philis. gathered their a. to battle, 28 : 1.-29 : 1. [rael
8. Goliath cried unto the a. of Is-
10. I defy the a. of Israel this day
23. champion out of a. of Philist.
26. who this that he defy a. of God
36. Philist-e hath defied a. of God
45. I in name of God of a. of Israel
23 : 3. if we come ag. a. of Philist-s
2 K. 25 : 23. when capt-s of a. heard
26. people, capt-s of a. came to Eg.
1 Ch. 11 : 26. valiant men of a. were
2 Ch. 16 : 4. sent capt-s of a. ag. Isr.
Jb. 25 : 3. Is any number of his a. ?
Ps. 44 : 9. But thou goest not forth with our a., 60 : 10.
68 : 12. Kings of a. did flee apace
Can. 6 . 13. As company of two a.
Is 34 : 2. his fury upon all their a.
Mat. 22 : 7. sent his a., burned city
Lu. 21 : 20. Jerus. compassed wi. a.
He. 11 : 34. to flight a. of the aliens
Re. 19 : 14. a. in heaven followed
19. I saw kings, their a. gathered

ARMO'NI. [A. and
2 S. 21 : 8. took two sons of Rizpah,

ARMOUR. [a., 6.
1 S. 14 : 1. young man that bare his
17 : 38 Saul armed David with a.
39. Dav. girded sword upon his a.
1 S. 17 :54. David put Goliath's a. in
31 : 9. found Saul, stripped off his a., 1 Ch. 10 : 9. [1 Ch. 10 : 10.
10. put his a. in house of Ash-t-h,
2 S. 2 : 21. Turn aside, take his a.
18 : 15. ten y-g men bare Joab's a.
1 K. 10 : 25. Brought every man a.
22 : 38. blood ; they washed his a.
2 K. 3 : 21. all able to put on a. [a.
10 : 2. with you a fenced city and
20 : 13. Hezekiah shewed all the house of his a., Is. 39 : 2. [a.
Jb. 39 : † 21. he go on to meet the
Is 22 : 8. didst look to a. of house
Eze. 38 :4. all of them clothed wi. a.
Lu. 11 : 22. taketh a. wh-in he trust.
Ro. 13 : 12. let us put on a. of light
2 Co. 6 : 7. by the a. of righteousn-s
Ep. 6 : 11. Put on whole a. of God
13. whf. take the whole a. of God

ARMOURBEARER.
Ju. 9 : 54. Abimelech called his a.
1 S. 14 : 7. his a. said, Do all th. [17.
12. Jonathan and a. (2), 13 (2), 14,
16 : 21. Saul loved David greatly ; he became his a., 1 Ch. 10 : 4.
31 : 4. said Saul unto a., thrust me through ; his a. would not [5.
5. when a. saw Saul dead, 1 Ch. 10:
6. Saul died and a., 1 Ch. 10 : 5.
2 S. 23 : 37. Nahari, the Beerothite, a. to Joab, 1 Ch. 11 : 39.

ARMOURY. [a.
Ne. 3 : 19. over ag-t the going up to
Can. 4 : 4. tower builded for an a.
Je. 50 : 25. Lord hath opened his a.

ARMY. [his a.
Ge. 26 : 26. Phichol chief captain of
Ex. 14 : 9. his a. overtook them
De. 11 : 4. what he did to a. of Egypt
Ju. 4 : 7. Sisera, capt. of Jabin's a.
8 : 6. we give bread unto thine a. ?
9 : 29. Increase thine a., come out
1 S. 4 : 2. Philistines slew of a. 4,000
12. ran a man of Benj-n out of a.
16. I fled to day out of the a. (2)
17 :21. Philistines had put a. ag. a.
22. David left carriage, ran into a.
48. D. toward a. to meet Philist-e
1 K. 20 : 19. young men came out a.
25. number thee an a. like a. lost
2 K. 25 : 5. a. of Chaldees pursued Z-h ; all his a. scattered, Je 52:8.
10. a. of Chaldees brake walls of Jerusalem, Je. 52 : 14. [the a.
1 Ch. 20 : 1. Joab led the power of
27 : 34. general of k-'s a. was Joab
2 Ch. 13 :3. Abijah with a. of 400,000
14 : 8. Asa an a. 580,000, all mighty
20 : 21. praise as they went bef. a.
24 : 24. a. of Syrians came wi small
25 : 7. not a. of Israel go with thee
9. what for 100 talents given to a.
10 a. that was come out of Ephr.
13. soldiers of a. wh. Amaz-h sent
26 : 13. under their hand a., 307,500
Ne. 2 : 9. sent captains of a. with me
4 : 2 he spake before a. of Samaria
Jb. 29 : 25. I dwelt as king in the a.
Ps. 68 : † 11. great a. that published
Can. 6 : 4. as an a. with banners, 10.
Is. 36 : 2. sent Rabshakeh with gr. a.
43 : 17. bring-h forth a. and power
Je. 32 : 2. Babylon's a. besieged Jerusalem, 34 : 1, 7.-39 : 1.-52:4.
35 : 11. let us go to Jerus. for fear of a. of Chaldeans and a. of Syr-ns
37 : 5. Pha-'s a. was come out of E.
7. Pha-'s a. shall return to Egypt
10. smitten whole a. of Chalde-ns
11. a. of Chaldeans broken from Jerusalem, for fear of Pha-'s a.
38 : 3. city into the hand of Babylon's a., 34 : 21. [ekiah
39 : 5. Chaldeans' a. overtook Zed-
46 : 2. word of Lord ag. a. of Pha
22. they shall march with an a.

Eze. 17 : 17. Neith. Pha-h with his a.
27 : 10. They of Phut in thine a.
11. The men of Arvad wi. thine a.
29 : 18. Neb-r caused his a. to serve
service, yet no wages, nor his a.
19. Egypt shall be wages for her a.
32 : 31. Pharaoh and all his a. slain
37 : 10. stood an exceeding great a.
38 : 4. bring thee forth and thine a.
15. rid-g upon horses, a mighty a.
Da. 3 : 20. men in a. to bind Shad-h
4 : 35. acc. to his will in a. of heav.
11 : 7. one which sh. come wi. an a.
13. king of north with great a., 25.
25. king of south with very great a.
26. his a. sh. overflow; many slain
Jo. 2 : 11. Lord utter voice bef. his a.
20. I will remove the northern a.
25. locust, palmerworm, my gr. a.
Zch. 4 : † 6. Not by a. nor by power
9 : 8. I will encamp bec. of the a.
Ac. 23 : 27. I with an a. rescued him
Re. 9 : 16. number of a. of horsemen
19 : 19. ag. him on the horse, against ⌊his a.

AR'NAN.

1 Ch. 3 : 21. the sons of A.; the sons

ARNON.

Nu. 21 : 13. pitched on other side of
A.; for A. is the border of Moab
14. What he did in the brook of A.
24. Israel possessed Sihon's land
from A., Jos. 12 : 1. Ju. 11 : 22.
26. Sihon had taken land unto A.
28. lords of the high places of A.
22 : 36. met Balaam in border of A.
De. 2 : 24. Rise, pass over river A.
36. Aroer, which is by the river of
A., 3 : 12.-4 : 48. Jos. 12 : 2.-13:
9, 16. 2 K. 10 : 33.
3 : 8. we took the land from river A.
unto mount Hermon, Jos. 12: 1.
16. I gave fr. Gilead unto river A.
Ju. 11 : 13. took my land fr. A. unto
26. Isr. dwelt by coasts of A. ⌊Jab.
Is. 16 : 2. daughters be at fords of A.
Je. 48 : 20. tell in A., Moab is spoiled

A'ROD or AR'ODI, ITES.

Ge. 46 : 16. † sons of Gad; Eri, A-i
Nu. 26 : 17. † Of A-d, family of A-s

ARO'ER. ⌈A.

Nu. 32 : 34. chil. of Gad built Dibon,
Jos. 13 : 25. coast unto A. bef. Rab-h
Ju. 11 : 26. While Israel dwelt in A.
33. smote them from A. to Minnith
1 S. 30 : 28. a present to them in A.
2 S. 24 : 5. over Jordan, pitched in A.
1 Ch. 5 : 8. of Joel, who dwelt in A.
Is. 17 : 2. The cities of A. forsaken
Je. 48 : 19. O inhabitant of A., stand
See ARNON.

ARO'ERITE.

1 Ch. 11 : 44. sons of Hothan the A.

AROSE. ⌈tened Lot

Ge. 19 : 15. morning a., angels has-
33. Lot perceived not when she a.
24 : 61. Rebekah a. and damsels
37 : 7. my sheaf a., stood upright
Ex. 1 : 8. a. new king over Egypt,
wh. knew not Joseph, Ac. 7 : 18.
De. 34 : 10. a. not a prophet like Mo.
Jos. 8 : 3. Joshua a. and peo. of war
19. ambush a. quickly out of their
24 : 9. Balak a., warred ag-t Israel
Ju. 2 : 10. a. generation wh. knew
3 : 20. Eglon a. out of his seat ⌊not L.
5 : 7. until I Deborah a. a mother
6 : 28. when men of city a. early ⌊(2)
8 : 21. Gideon a., slew Zeba, Zal.
10 : 1. a. to defend Israel Tola; he
3. after him a. Jair, a Gideonite
16 : 3. Samson a. at midnight ⌈ly
19 : 5. fourth day, when they a. ear-
8. he a. early on 5th day to depart
20 : 8. all the people a. as one man
Ru. 1 : 6. she a. with daugh-s in law
1 S. 5 : 3. when they of Ashdod a.
early, Dagon fallen before ark, 4.
1 S. 9 : 26. Samuel with Saul; they
a. early; Saul a., went out
13 : 15. Sam-l a. got him from Gilgal
17 : 35. when he a. ag-t me I slew
48. Philistine a., came to meet Da.
52. men of Israel a. and shouted
20 : 25. Jonathan a., Abner sat by
34. Jonathan a. fr. table in anger
41. David a., bowed hims. 3 times
42. David a., departed; Jonathan
21 : 10. Dav. a., fled for fear of Saul
23 : 13. David and men a., departed
24 : 4. Dav. a., cut off skirt of Saul
25 : 41. Abigail a., bowed to earth
42. Abigail a., rode upon an ass⌈ed
26 : 5. Dav. a., came where S. pitch-
27 : 2. Dav. a., passed over with 600
28 : 23. Saul a. from earth, sat ⌈roof
2 S. 11 : 2. Dav. a. and walked upon
12 : 17. And elders of his house a.
12 : 20. David a. fr. earth, washed
13 : 29. all king's sons a. and fled
31. king a., and tare his garments
14 : 31. Joab a., and came to Abs.
17 : 22. David a., passed over Jor.
23. Ahithophel a., gat him home
19 : 8. Then king a., sat in the gate
23 : 10. He a., smote the Philistines
1 K. 2 : 40. Shimei a., saddled his ass
8 : 20. she a. at midnight, took my
8 : 54. Sol. a. from before altar ⌊son
11 : 18. they a. out of Midian, came
40. Jeroboam a., fled into Egypt
14 : 17. Jerob-'s wife a., departed
19 : 8. Elijah a., did eat and drink
2 K. 4 : 30. Elijah a., followed her
7 : 7. Syrians a., fled in twilight
12. king a. in the night and said
8 : 2. woman a., did after saying of
10 : 12. Jehu a., came to Samaria
11 : 1. Athaliah a., destroyed all
the seed royal, 2 Ch. 22 : 10.
12 : 20. his servants a., slew Joash
19 : 35. when they a. early, they
were all dead corpses, Is. 37 : 36.
23 : 25. nei. after him a. any like
25 : 26. people, captains a., came to
1 Ch. 10 : 12. They a., took body of S.
2 Ch. 29 : 12. Levites a., sanctified
30 : 14. a., took away altars in Jer.
27. Levites a. and blessed people
36 : 16. mocked until wrath of L. a.
Ezr. 9 : 5. I a. from my heaviness
10 : 5. a. Ezra, made Israel swear
Ne. 2 : 12. I a. in night, few with me
Es. 8 : 4. Esther a. stood before king
Jb. 1 : 20. Job a., rent his mantle
19 : 18. I a. and they spake ag. me
29 : 8. saw me, aged a. and stood
Ps. 76 : 9. When God a. to judgm-t
Ec. 1 : 5. sun hasteth to where he a.
Je. 41 : 2. a. Ishmael, smote Gedal.
Da. 6 : 19. king a. early, went unto
Jon. 3 : 6. the king a., sat in ashes ⌊den
Mat. 2 : 21. he a. and took the young
child into Egypt, 14. ⌈4 : 39.
8 : 15. she a. and ministered, Lu.
24. a. a great tempest, Mk. 4 : 37.
26. he a. and rebuked the winds,
Mk. 4 : 39. Lu. 8 : 24. ⌈2 : 14.
9 : 9. he a. and followed him, Mk.
19. ruler, Jesus a. and followed
25. took her by hand, the maid a.
25 : 7. virgins a., trimmed lamps
26 : 62. the high priest a. and said
27 : 52. bodies of saints wh. slept a.
Mk. 2 : 12 a., took up bed, Mat. 9 : 7.
5 : 42. the damsel a. and, Lu. 8 : 55.
9 : 27. Jesus lifted him, and he a.
10 : 1. he a. and cometh into Judea
14 : 57. a. certain, bare false witn.
Lu. 1 : 39. Mary a. in those days
4 : 38. he a. out of synagogue ⌈a.
6 : 8. man which had withered hand
48. when flood a. the stream beat
9 : 46. a. a reasoning among them
15 : 14. a. mighty famine in land
Lu. 15 : 20. a., came to his fath. ⌈late
23 : 1. multitude a., led him to Pi-
24 : 12. a. Peter, ran unto sepule.
Jn. 3 : 25. a. question betw. some
6 : 18. the sea a. by a great wind
11 : 29. heard that, she a. quickly
Ac. 5 : 6. young men a. and buried
6 : 1. There a. a murmuring ⌊him
9. there a. certain of synagogue
9 : 8. Saul a. from the earth ⌈tized
18. received sight, a., and was bap-
34. Arise, make thy bed. And he a.
11 : 19. persecution that a. about
19 : 23. a. no small stir ⌊Stephen
23 : 7. a. a dissension between, 10.
9. a. a great cry; and scribes a.
27 : 14. a. against it a tempestuous
Re. 9 : 2. a. smoke out of pit ⌊wind
See ROSE,

Arose and WENT.

AR'PAD or AR'PHAD.

2 K. 18 : 34. Where are the gods of
Hamath, of A.? Is. 36 : 19. ⌈13.
19 : 13. Where is king of A.? Is. 37:
Is. 10 : 9. is not Hamath as A.? is not
Je. 49 : 23. Hamath is confounded,

ARPHAX'AD. ⌊and A.

Ge. 10 : 22. the children of Shem;
Elam, A., 1 Ch. 1 : 17. ⌈1 : 18.
24. A. begat Salah, 11 : 12. 1 Ch.
11 : 10. Shem begat A. aft. flood, 11.
13. A. lived after begat Salah 430
1 Ch. 1 : 24. Shem, A., Shelah ⌊yrs.
Lu. 3 : 36. A. which was son of Sem

ARRAY. [Noun]

Ju. 20 : 20. Israel put themselves in
a., 22 (2), 30, 33. ⌈ag. Israel
1 S. 4 : 2. Philst-s put thems. in a.
† 2. they slew of the a. ab-t 4,000
2 S. 10 : 9. Joab put choice men in
a. against Syrians, 1 Ch. 19 : 10.
10. put rest in a. against children
of Ammon, 1 Ch. 19 : 11. ⌈Dav.
17. Syrians set thems. in a. ag-t
1 K. 20 : 12. Set yourselves in a.
And they set themselves in a.
Jb. 6 : 4. terrors of G. set thems. in a.
Is. 22 : 7. horsemen set thems. in a.
Je. 6 : 23. set in a. for war ag-t thee
50 : 9. set themselves in a. ag-t her
14. Put yours. in a. ag-t Babylon
42. upon horses every one in a.
Jo. 2 : 5. as a people set in battle a.
1 Ti. 2 : 9. not with pearls or costly a.
See **BATTLE in array.**

ARRAY. [Verb.]

Es. 6 : 9. may a. the man whom king
Jb. 40 : 10. a. thyself with glory ⌈Eg.
Je. 43 : 12. a. himself with land of

ARRAYED. ⌈of linen

Ge. 41 : 42. Pha. a. him in vestures
2 Ch. 5 : 12. being a. in white linen
28 : 15. clothed naked, and a. them
Es. 6 : 11. Haman a. Mordecai and
Mat. 6 : 29. Solomon was not a. like
one of these, Lu. 12 : 27. ⌈geous
Lu. 23 : 11. Jesus, Herod a. in gor-
Ac. 12 : 21. Herod a. in royal apparel
Re. 7 : 13. What are these a. in white
17 : 4. the woman was a. in purple
19 : 8. that she be a. in fine linen

ARRIVED. ⌈cues

Lu. 8 : 26. a. at country of Gadar-
Ac. 20 : 15. next day we a. at Samos

ARROGANCY. ⌈mouth

1 S. 2 : 3. let not a. come out of your
Pr. 8 : 13. pride and a. do I hate
Is. 13 : 11. cause a. of proud to cease
Je. 48 : 29. pride of Moab and his a.

ARROW. ⌈an a.

1 S. 20 : 36. Jonath., as lad ran, shot
37. when lad was come to place of
a., Jonath. said, Is not a. bey.
2 K. 9 : 24. a. went out at his heart
13 : 17. The a. of L.'s deliverance,
and a. of deliverance from Syria
19 : 32 nor shoot a. there, Is. 37 : 33.

Jb. 34 : † 6. mine a. is incurable
41 : 28. a. cannot make him flee
Ps. 11 : 2. wicked make ready a. [a.
64 : 7. God shall shoot at them wi.
91 : 5. not be afraid for a. by day
Pr. 25 : 18. false witness is sharp a.
Je. 9 : 8. tongue is as an a. shot out
La. 3 : 12. set me as mark for the a.
Zch. 9 : 14. his a. shall go as light-
ARROWS. [ning
Nu. 24 : 8. pierce them with his a.
De. 32 : 23. spend mine a. upon them
42. make mine a. drunk with blo.
1 S. 20 : 20. I will shoot three a. on
21. I will send lad, saying, find a.
If I say the a. are on this side
22. If I say the a. are beyond thee
36. lad, Run now, find a. I shoot
38. Jonathan's lad gathered up a.
2 S. 22 : 15. the Lord sent out a. and
scattered them, Ps. 18 : 14.
2 K. 13 : 15. Elisha said, Take bow
and a. And he took bow and a.
18. Take a. and smite the ground
1 Ch. 12 : 2. stones and shooting a.
2 Ch. 26 : 15. to shoot a. and stones
Jb. 6 : 4. a. of Almighty within me
Ps. 7 : 13. ordaineth a. ag. persecu-
21 : 12. make ready thine a. [tors
38 : 2. thine a. stick fast in me
45 : 5. Thine a. are sharp in heart
of the King's enemies [a.
57 : 4. whose teeth are spears and
58 : 7. he bendeth bow to shoot a.
64 : 3. shoot a., even bitter words
76 : 3. There brake he a. of the bow
77 : 17. thine a. also went abroad
120 : 4. Sharp a. of the mighty
127 : 4. As a. in hand of a mighty
144 : 6. shoot thine a. destroy them
Pr. 26 : 18. who casteth firebrands, a.
Is. 5 : 28. Whose a. are sharp, and
7 : 24. With a., bows sh. men come
Je. 50 : 9. their a. as of expert man
14. shoot at Babylon, spare no a.
51 : 11. Make bright the a.; gather
La. 3 : 13. caused a. of his quiver to
enter my reins [famine
Eze. 5 : 16. upon them the evil a. of
21 : 21. he made his a. bright, he
39 : 3. cause a. to fall out of hand
9. Israel shall burn bows and a.
Ha. 3 : 11. at light of thine a. that
ARROWSNAKE. [path
Ge. 49 : † 17. Dan shall be an a. in
ART. [Verb.]
Ps. 65 : 5. who a. the confidence of
all the earth [stroyed
137 : 8. Babylon, who a. to be de-
Can. 2 : 14 my dove that a. in clefts
Eze. 22 : 5. mock thee, which a. infa-
27 : 3. wh. a. merchant fr. isles [mous
Re. 11 : 17. Lord Almighty, which a.,
and wast, and a. to come, 16 : 5
Thou ART or **ART thou.**
De. 4 : 30. When t. a. in tribulation
7 : 6. t. a. a holy people, 14 : 2.
8 : 10. When t. a. full, thou shalt
bless Lord for land, 12. [to be
Jos. 13 : 1. t. a. old, yet much land
Ru. 3 : 9. Who a. t.? she answered,
I am Ruth; t. a. a near kinsm.
11. city doth know t. a. virtuous
16. she said, Who a. t., my dau.?
1 S. 26 : 14. Who a. t. criest to king?
15. Abner, a. t. not valiant man?
2 S. 18 : 3. t. a. worth 10,000 of us
2 Ch. 14 : 11. O Lord, t. a. our God
Jb. 15 : 7. a. t. first man was born?
17 : 14. I said to corruption, t. a.
my fath.; to worm, t. a. my mo.
22 : 3. pleasure that t. a. righteous
31 : 24. gold, t. a. my confidence
34 : 18. fit to say to k., t. a. wicked?
Ps. 3 : 3. t., Lord, a. shield for me
5 : 4. For t. a. not a God that hath
pleasure in wickedness

Ps. 16 : 2. said unto Lord, t. a. my L.
22 : 1. why a. t. so far from helping
3. t. a. holy that inhabitest [me
10. t. a. my God, fr. my mother's,
25 : 5. t. a. God of my salvation [9.
31 : 3. t. a. my rock, my fortress
14. O Lord : I said, t. a. my God
32 : 7. t. a. my hiding place; thou
40 : 17. t. a. my deliverer, 70 : 5.
42 : 5. Why a. t. cast down, O my
soul? (2) 11 (2), 43 : 5 (2).
43 : 2. For t. a. God of my strength
44 : 4. t. a. my King, O God [men
45 : 2. t. a. fairer than the chil. of
63 : 1. O God, t. a. my God; my
66 : 3. Say unto God, How terrible
a. t. in thy works! 68 : 35. [ress
71 : 3. t. a. my rock and my fort-
5. For t. a. my hope, O Lord God:
t. a. my trust from my youth
7. but t. a. my strong refuge
76 : 4. t. a. more glorious than mts.
7. t., even t., a. to be feared : and
77 : 14. t. a. the God doest wonders
86 : 5. t., Lord, a. ready to forgive
10. For t. a. great; t. a. G. alone
15. t. a. a God full of compassion
89 : 17. t. a. glory of their strength
26. sh. cry, t. a. my Fa., my God
90 : 2. from everlasting t. a. God
92 : 8. t., L., a. most high evermore
110 : 4. t. a. a priest for ever, after
118 : 28. t. a. my G., I will exalt (2)
119 : 57. t. a. my portion, O Lord
68. t. a. good and doest good
137. Righteous a. t., O Lord, and
151. t. a. near, O Lord; thy com-ts
142 : 5. t. a. my refuge, my portion
143 : 10. Teach me, for t. a. my G.
Pr. 7 : 4. unto wisdom, t. a. my sis-
Ec. 10 : 17. Blessed a. t., O land [ter
Can. 1 : 15. Behold, t. a. fair, my
love (2), 16.-4 : 1 (2), 7.-6 . 4.
7 : 6. fair a. t., O love, for delights
Is. 41 : 9. t. a. my servant; chosen
43 : 1. by thy name; t. a. mine (2)
44 : 21. O Israel, t. a. my servant,
48 : 4. I knew that t. a. obstinate
51 : 16. unto Zion, t. a. my people
63 : 2. Wheref. a. t. red in apparel
Je. 2 : 23. t. a. a swift dromedary
27. Saying to stock, t. a. my fath.
3 : 4. father, t. a. guide of my youth
22. we come unto thee; t. a. our
10 : 6. t. a. great, thy name gr. [G.
12 : 1. Righteous a. t., O Lord [far
2. t. a. near in their mouth, and
14 : 9. t., O Lord, a. in midst of us
17 : 14. save, O Lord, t. a. my praise
17. t. a. my hope in day of evil
20 : 7. Lord, t. a. stronger than I
49 : 12. a. t. he shall go unpunish-
51 : 20. t. a. my battle axe, and [ed?
Eze. 16 : 34. therefore t. a. contrary
45. t. a. thy mother's daughter.
t. a. sister of thy sisters [them
54. in that t. a. a comfort unto
22 : 24. t. a. land th. is not cleansed
27 : 3. O t. that a. situate at entry
28 : 2. yet t. a. a man and not God
3. Behold t. a. wiser than Daniel
31 : 2. Whom a. t. like in greatness
32 : 2. t. a. like a young lion of the
nations, t. a. as a whale [song
33 : 32. t. a. unto them as a lovely
38 : 17. a. t. he of whom I spoken
Da. 2 : 26. Daniel, a. t. able to make
known the dream [but t. a.
4 : 18. all the wise men not able;
Ho. 2 : 23. I will say, t. a. my people;
they shall say, t. a. my God
Jon. 4 : 2. I knew t. a. merciful [No
Na. 3 : 8. a. t. better than populous
Ha. 1 : 13. t. a. of purer eyes than to
Mat. 16 : 14. Some say th. t. a. John
17. Blessed a. t. Simon Bar-jona
23. Satan : t. a. an offence unto

Mat. 22 : 16. Master, we know that t.
a. true, Mk. 12 : 14. [Lu. 19 : 21.
25 : 24. I knew t. a. a hard man,
Mk. 14 : 70. Surely t. a. one of them;
for t. a. a Galilean, Lu. 22 : 58.
Lu. 1 : 28. Blessed a. t. am. women
Jn. 17 : 21. as t. Father, a. in me
Ac. 12 : 15. said unto her, t. a. mad
26 : 24. Paul, t. a. beside thyself
Ro. 2 : 1. Therefore t. a. inexcus-
able, O man, whosoever t. a.
1 Co. 7 : 27. a. t. bound unto a wife?
a. t. loosed from a wife?
Ga. 4 : 7. t. a. no more serv. but son
He. 5 : 6. t. a. a priest for ever [16.
Re. 3 : 15. t. a. neither cold nor hot,
17. knowest not t. a. blind and
16 : 5. t. a. righteous, O L. [naked
See **Art THOU**, or **THOU art.**
ART, S. [device
Ac. 17 : 29. graven by a. or man's
19 : 19. Many which used curious
See APOTHECARY. [a-s
ARTAXER'XES. [(2)
Ezr. 4 : 7. In days of A. wrote Bishlam
8. Rehum wrote ag-t Jerus. to A.
11. copy of the letter sent unto A.
23. when copy of k. A-s' letter was
6 : 14. acc. to commandment of A.
7 : 1. in the reign of A., Ezra, 8 : 1.
7. went up in seventh year of A.
11. copy of letter A. gave to Ezra
12. A., king of kings, unto Ezra
21. I, A., king, do make a decree
Ne. 2 : 1. to pass in 20th year of A.
5 : 14. unto two and 30th year of A.,
AR'TEMAS. [13 : 6.
Tit. 3 : 12. When I send A. unto thee
ARTIFICER. [of ev. a.
Ge. 4 : 22. Tubal-cain an instructor
1 Ch. 29 : 5. work to be made by a-s
2 Ch. 34 : 11. to a-s gave they money
Is. 3 : 3. L. doth take away cunning
ARTILLERY. [a.
1 S. 20 : 40. Jonath. gave a. unto
AR'UBOTH. [lad
1 K. 4 : 10. The son of Hesed, in A.
ARU'MAH.
Ju. 9 : 41. Abimelech dwelt at A
AR'VAD. [ners
Eze. 27 : 8. inhabitants of A. mari-
11. men of A. with thine army
AR'VADITE. [1 : 16.
Ge. 10 : 18. Canaan begat A., 1 Ch.
AR'ZA.
1 K. 16 : 9. in house of A., steward
AS. [fore him
Ge. 2 : † 18. make him a help a. be-
3 : 5. ye shall be a. gods, knowing
22. the man is become a. one of us
22 : 14. a. it is said, He. 4 . 7. [48.8.
24 : 51. a. Lord hath spoken, Je.
31 : 2. Laban not toward him a. bef.,
26. away my dau-s a. captives [5.
32 : 25. a. he wrestled with him
28. a. prince hast power with G.
Ex. 15 : 5. they sank a. a stone
Nu. 13 : 33. we in own sight a. grass-
15 : 14. a. ye do, so he shall do [hop.
15. a. ye are, so shall stranger be
32 : 31. a. Lord said, so will we do
De. 1 : 11. a. God hath promised you
6 : 8. be a. frontlets bet. thine eyes
16. a. ye tempted him in Massah
12 : 9. not a. yet come to the rest
Jos. 3 : 5. a.. Ps. 104 : 17.-147 : 20.
Pr. 12 : 4. Can. 4 : 11 Is. 10 : 10,
18, 32.-13 : 6.-14 : 17.-16 : 14.-
22 : 16.-24 : 22.-30 : 14.-31 : 4.-
33 : 11, 12.-37 : 27 (4).-38 : 13.-
44 : 4 (2).-47 : 8, 14.-48 : 19 -49 :
18 (2).-58 : 5.-61 : 10 (2), 11.-62 :
1. Je. 4 : 13 (2).-14 : 8 -23 : 34.-
50 : 8, 26. La. 1 : 17 -2 : 4, 5, 12.
-4 : 2.-5 : 3. Eze. 1 : 10, 13, 15.-
3 : 9.-10 : 10.-12 : 4.-15 : 6 -16 :
4, 32.-17 : 5.-20 : 32 (2).-22 : 20,

22.-23 : 18, 44.-26 : 3. -28 : 16.-
33 : 32. -34 : 12, 17, 19.-35 : 15.
-37 : 10. 41 : 21,25. Da. 2 : 42.-
4 : 25.-5 : 12.-7 : 9. Ho. 2 : 3.-5:
12. -7:12 (2). -9:1,11,13.-10 : 4,
7, 11.-12 : 11.-13 : 7. Jo. 2:2, 3,
5. Am. 2:9,13. -4:11. -5:24 (2).
8:8, 10. -9:5, 7, 11. Mi. 1: 4, 6.
-3 : 12.-4 : 12.-5 : 7.-7: 10. Ha.
1 :8, 14.-2 : 14.-3 : 14. Zch.4:1.
-7 : 12, 13.-9 : 13.-10 : 5.-14: 10.
Mat. 1 : 18. 2 Co. 8 : 13. He.
5 : 4. -10 : 25.
Jos. 10 : 1. a. had done to Jericho
14 : 11. I am a. strong a. I was (4)
23 : 8. cleave unto Lord a. ye have
15. a. all good things upon you
Ju. 6 : 5. came up a. grasshoppers
8 : 8. answered a. men of Succoth
20 : 30. in array a. at other times
32. They are smitten a. at first
1 S. 9 : 11. a. they went up to city
12 : 23. a. for me, God forbid I sin
15 : 22. Hath Lord a. great delight
33. a. sword made women childl-s
16 : 7. Lord seeth not a. man seeth
18 : 1. Jonath. loved him a. own soul
26 : 24. a. thy life was much set by
28 : 17. Lord hath done a. he spake
30 : 24. a. his part that goeth to bat.
2 S. 3 : 9. a. Lord hath sworn, so I do
6 : 16. a. ark came into city of Dav.
9 : 11. a. for Mephib-h, he sh. eat at
16 : 19. a. I have served in thy fa-'s
18 : † 3. thou art a. 10,000 of us
22 : 31. a. for God, his way is perf-t
1 K. 8 : 6. a. it is this day (2) ⌈8 : 25.
14. a. thy father David did walk,
2 K. 8 : 19. a. he promised to give
27. did evil, a. did house of Ahab
17 : 2. did evil, but not a. k-s of Isr.
4. a. he had done year by year
24 : 13. a. Lord had said, 17 : 23.
2 Ch. 33 : 23. humbled not a. Man-h
34 : 26. a. for king, say unto him
Ne. 9 : 24. might do a. they would
Es. 5 : 8. do to morrow a. king said
7 : 8. a. went out of king's mouth
9 : 23. Jews to do a. they had begun
Jb. 8 : 16. a. infants wh. never saw
7 : 2. a. servant desireth shadow(2)
9. a. cloud vanisheth, so he shall
20. passed away a. the swift ships
10 : 4. or seest thou a. man seeth ?
5. are thy days a. days of man ? (2)
9. thou hast made me a. the clay
10. Hast not poured me a. milk ?
14 : 11. a. waters fail, so man lieth
16 : 4. I could speak a. ye do⌊down
17 : 10. a. for you, I can-t find one
19 : 22. why persecute me a. G.⌊wise
22 : 2. profitable unto G. a. himself
8. a. for mighty, he had the earth
24. shalt thou lay up gold a. dust
27 : 21. a. a storm hurleth him out
31 : 36. I would bind it a. a crown
34 : 26. striketh them a. wicked m.
41 : 24. a. hard a. nether millstone
Ps. 32 : 9. be not a. horse, a. mule
41 : 12. a. for me, thou upholdest
42 : 1. a. hart panteth after brooks
48 : 8. a. we have heard, so seen
55 : 16. a. for me, I will call upon G.
58 : 9. take them a. with whirlwind
† 9. whirlwind a. living a. wrath
73 : 2. a. for me, feet almost gone
20. a. a dream when one awaketh
78 : 8. might not be a. their fathers
83 : 11. make princes a. Zebah, a.
89 : 11. a. for world, thou founded
37. be established a. the moon (2)
90 : 5. carriest them away a. with
flood ; they are a. a sleep ⌈told
9. we spend our years a. a tale
103 : 15. a. a flower, he flourisheth
125 : 2. a. mountains about Jerus.
5. a. for such a. turn aside unto
Ps. 137 : 8. rewardeth thee a. thou
141 : 7. a. when one cutteth⌊served
144 : 12. our sons be a. plants (2)
Pr. 5 : 4. her end bitter a. wormw. (2)
19. Let her be a. loving hind
6 : 5. Deliver thyself a. roe from
11. come thy want a. armed man
7 : 2. my law a. apple of thine eye
22. after her a. ox to slaughter (2)
23. a. a bird hasteth to the snare
9 : 16. a. for him, she saith, Stolen
10 : 20. tongue of just is a. silver
23. a. sport to fool to do mischief
25. a. whirlwind, wicked no more
26. a. smoke to eyes, so sluggard
11 : 22. a. jewel in swine's snout⌊(2)
15 : 19. slothful a. hedge of thorns
16 : 14. wrath of k. a. death, 19 : 12.
15. k-'s favour a. cloud of r., 19 : 12.
17 : 14. beginning of strife is a. wh.
18 : 4. words are a. deep waters (2)
24 : 29. Say not, I will do a. he to me
25 : 12. a. earring of gold, so is wise
20. a. vinegar upon nitre, so is he
25. a. cold waters to thirsty ⌊(2)
26 : 2. a. swallow by flying, so curse
8. a. he that bindeth stone, so⌊(2)
9. a. thorn into hand of drunkard
11. a. dog returneth to his vomit
14. a. door turneth, so doth slothf.
18. a. mad man who casteth firebr.
27 : 8. a. bird wandereth from nest
19. a. in water face answereth, so
21. a. the fining pot for silver, so
28 : 15. a. ranging bear, so wicked
Ec. 2 : 15. a. happeneth to fool
5 : 16. a. he came, so shall he go, 15.
7 : 6. a. the crackling of thorns, so
9 : 12. a. fishes taken in net, so (2)
11 : 5. a. knowest not way of spirit
Can. 5 : 11. His head a. fine gold (2)
12. His eyes are a. eyes of doves
15. his countenance is a. Leb-n (2)
6 : 4. Thou art beautiful a. Tirzah,
terrible a. an army (3), 10. ⌈Gil.
5. thy hair is a. flock of goats from
6. Thy teeth are a. a flock of sheep
10. fair a. moon, clear a. sun (4)
7 : 4. Thy neck a. tower of ivory (2)
8. thy breasts shall be a. clusters
8 : 6. Set me a. a seal upon thine
heart ; love is strong a. dea. (4)
Is. 1 : 30. ye shall be a. an oak, leaf
31. strong sh. be a. tow(2) ⌊fadeth
3 : 9. Declare their sin a. Sodom
12. a. for people, chil. oppressors
10 : 9. Is not Hamath a. Arpad ? (3)
11. a. unto Samaria, so do to Jer.
15. a. if rod should shake itself (3)
26. a. his rod upon sea, so shall he
13 : 14. it shall be a. chased roe⌈we
14 : 10. Art thou become weak a.
16 : 2. a. a bird cast out, so daugh-s
17 : 5. a. he that gathereth ears (2)
13. be chased a. chaff of mount-s
23 : 5. a. at report conc. Egypt, so
24 : 2. a. with buyer, so seller (6)
13. be a. shaking of olive tree (2)
26 : 17. Like a. woman in pain, so
28 : 2. one a. a tempest sh. cast (2)
29 : 8. a. when hungry dream-h(2)
30 : 13. iniquity a. a breach ready
31 : 5. a. birds flying, so L. defend
32 : 2. a. shadow of a great rock (3)
34 : 4. a. leaf falleth from vine (3)
38 : 12. mine age is removed a. tent
47 : 4. a. for our Redeemer, Lord is
48 : 18. thy peace been a. a river(2)
49 : 18. bind them a. bride doeth(2)
51 : 13. a. if he were ready to destr.
23. laid thy body a. ground (2)
54 : 6. called thee a. woman grieved
9. this a. waters of Noah unto (2)
55 : 9. a. heavens are higher than
58 : 4. sh. not fast a. ye do this day
10. sh. thy darkness be a. noonday
59 : 10. grope a. if we had no eyes (3)
Is. 59 : 12. a. for our iniquities, we
17. clad with zeal a. with cloak(2)
60 : 8. that fly a. a cloud a. doves
62 : 5. a. man marrieth virgin (2)
64 : 6. But we are all a. an unclean
thing ; we all fade a. a leaf (3)
66 : 3. a. if he slew a man, a. if he
cut off a dog's neck (4)⌈your seed
22. a. new earth shall remain, so
Je. 4 : 31. a. of her that bringeth
forth first child (2) ⌈ulchre
5 : 16. Their quiver a. an open sep-
27. a. a cage is full of birds, so
6 : 7. a. fountain casteth out waters
13 : 10. people shall be a. girdle
14 : 8. why be a. stranger in land(2)
9. why be a. man cannot save ? (2)
15 : 18. wilt be unto me a. a liar ?(2)
17 : 8. he sh. be a. a tree by waters
11. a. partridge sitting on eggs
16. a. for me, I have not hastened
18 : 6. a. clay in potter's hand, so
24 : 8. a. the evil figs are so evil⌊ye
44 : 6. they are wasted a. at this
50 : 9. their a. of expert man ⌊day
11. ye fat a. heifer, bellow a. bulls
51 : 49. a. Babylon caused slain, so
La. 1 : 20. at home there is a. death
4 : 6. S. overthrown a. in a moment
17. a. for us, our eyes a. yet failed
5 : 21. L., renew our days a. of old
Eze. 1 : 18. a. for their rings dread-
24. wings a. noise of host (2) ⌊ful
27. I saw a. colour of amber, a.
9 : 10. a. for me, mine eye not spare
10 : 13. a. for the wheels : O wheel
11 : 21. a. for them whose heart w.
16 : 47. a. if that were little thing
50. I took them away a. I saw good
18 : 4. a. soul of father, so of son
18. a. for his father, die in iniquity
20 : 39. a. for you, O Isr., serve idols
24 : 22. ye shall do a. I have done
33 : 17. a. for them, ways not equal
34 : 17. a. for you, O flock, I judge
42 : 11. the way a. broad a. they (3)
48 : 23. a. for rest of tribes, Benj-n
Da. 2 : 29 a. for thee, thy thoughts
30. a. for me, this secret not for
8 : 5. a. I was considering, a goat
10 : 4 a. I was by side of great river
Ho. 4 : 7. a. were increased, so sinned
6 : 3. L. .. going forth a. morning(3)
4. your goodn. a. morning cloud,
a. early dew it goeth, 13 : 3 (4).
9. a. robbers wait, priests murder
8 : 12. were counted a. strange thi.
11 : 2. a. they called them, so went
14 : 5 I will be a. dew unto Isr. (3)
6. his beauty sh. be a. olive tree (2)
7. they shall grow a. the vine (3)
Jo. 2 : 4. a. horsemen so sh. they run
Ob. 16. a. ye have drunk, so heath.
Mi. 3 : 3. bones a. for pot, a. flesh
7 : 1. I am a. when they gathered
4. best of them is a. a brier⌊fruits
Zch. 1 : 4. Be not a. your fathers
8 : 13. a. ye were a curse, O Jud., so
14. a. I thought to punish you, so
9 : 3. heaped up gold a. the mire (2)
15. sh. make noise a. thro. wine(2)
16. shall be a. stones of crown (3)
12 : 8. house of David sh. be a. G.,
a. the angel of Lord (3) ⌈in bat.
14 : 3. Lord ag-t nations, a. when
14 : 15. so plague of horse be a. this
Mal. 3 : 3. he shall sit a. a refiner(2)
Mat. 6 : 2. do not a. hypocrites, 5, 16.
7. not vain repetitions a. heathen
10. Thy will be done in earth a.
it is in heaven, Lu. 11 : 2. ⌈give
12. forgive us our debts, a. we for-
7 : 29. taught not a. scribes, Mk. 1:
8 : 13. a. thou hast believed, so⌊22.
10 : 16. wise a. serpents .. a. doves(3)
25. disciple that he be a. mast. (2)
12 : 40. a. Jonas was 3 days in wha.

Mat 13 : 40. a. tares are burned, so
14 : 5. they counted him a. prophet
15 : 33. a. to fill so great multitude
17 : 20. If ye have faith a. grain of
mustard, Lu. 17 : 6. [children
18 : 3. Except ye become a. little
4. Whosoever humble himself a.
this child, Mk. 10 : 15. Lu. 18 : 17.
17. let him be unto thee a. heath.
19 : 19. shalt love thy neighbour a.
thyself, 22 : 39. Mk. 12 : 31, 33.
Lu. 10 : 27. Ro. 13 : 9. Ga. 5 : 14.
Ja. 2 : 8. [a prophet
21 : 26. peo. ; for all hold John a.
24 : 27. a. the lightning out of east,
so coming of, Lu. 17 : 24. [Son, 38.
37. a. days of Noe, so coming of
25 : 14. kingdom is a. man travelling into, Mk. 13 : 34. [divideth
32. sh. separate them a. shepherd
26 : 21. a. they did eat, Mk. 14 : 18.
39. Father, not a. I will, but a.
27 : 65. make it a. sure a. ye can
28 : 6. a. . . . . said, Mk. 14 : 16.-
16 : 7. Lu. 22 : 13. Jn. 1 : 23.-7 :
38.-10 : 26. Ro. 9 : 29. 2 Co. 6 :
16.-9 : 3. He. 4 : 3. 7.
9. a. they went to tell disciples
Mk. 3 : 5. his hand . . restored whole
a. the other, Lu. 6 : 10. [ground
4 : 26. a. if a man sho. cast seed into
33. spake, a. they were able to he.
8 : 24. I see men a. trees walking
9 : 3. white a. snow, so a. no fuller
10 : 1. a. he was wont, he taught
14 : 3. a. he sat at meat, a woman
15 : 8. to do a. he had ever done
16 : 7. shall ye see him, a. he said
Lu. 1 : 55. a. he spake, 70.-11 : 27.
2 : 15. a. the angels were gone away
20. a. it was told unto them
3 : 23. Jesus (a. was supposed), son
4 : 16. a. his custom was [of Joseph
6 : 22. cast out your name a. evil
31. a. ye would that men do to you
36. Be ye merciful a. your Father
40. one perfect sh. be a. his master
8 : 5. a. he sowed, some fell by way
10 : 3. I send you a. lambs among
18. I beheld Satan a. lightning fall
11 : 1. L. teach us to pray a. John
36. a. when a candle give light [(2)
13 : 34. a. a hen doth gather brood
14 : 22. is done a. thou commanded
15 : 25. a. he drew nigh to house
21 : 35. a. snare shall it come on all
22 : 26. greatest be a. the younger ;
chief a. he that doth serve [eth
27. I among you a. he that serv-
31. that he may sift you a. wheat
39. a. he was wont, to m-t of Olives
23 : 26. a. they led him away, laid
24 : 11. words seemed a. idle tales
39. not flesh, a. ye see me have
Jn. 1 : 14. glory a. of only begotten
3 : 14. a. Moses lifted serpent, so
5 : 21. a. Father raiseth dead, so
26. a. Father hath life in himself
30. a. I hear I judge ; and my
6 : 57. a. Father hath sent me ; so
58. not a. fathers did eat manna
8 : 28. a. my Father taught I speak
10 : 15. a. Father knoweth me ; so
13 : 15. ye should do a. I have done
33. a. I said unto Jews, so I say
34. love one another, a. I loved
you, 15 : 12. [unto you
14 : 27. not a. world giveth, give I
31. a. Father gave com-t, so I do
15 : 4. a. branch can-t bear of itself
6. If not in me is cast a. a branch
9. a. Father loved me, so I you
17 : 2. a. thou hast given him power
11. th. they may be one, a. we, 21.
21. a. thou art in me, I in thee
23. loved them a. thou loved me
19 : 40. a. manner of Jews to bury
Jn. 20 : 11. a. she wept, she stooped
21. a. my Father sent me, 17 : 18.
Ac. 2 : 2. a sound a. of mighty wind
4. speak a. Spirit gave utterance
15. are not drunken, a. ye suppose
22. by miracles, signs a. ye know
45. to all, a. ev. man had need, 4 : 35.
7 : 28. Wilt kill me, a. didst Eg-n ?
†37. Prophet L. raise up a. myself
40. a. for this Moses, we wot not
48. a. saith . . . . 1 Co. 14 : 34. He.
3 : 7.-5 : 6. [unto water
8 : 36. And a. they went, came
10 : 25. a. Peter was coming in, Cor.
11 : 15 Holy Gh. on them, a. on us
13 : 25. a. John fulfilled his course
16 : 4. a. they went thro. the cities
17 : 2. Paul, a. manner was, went
28. a. certain of your poets said
22 : 3. I was zealous tow. God a. ye
5. a. high priest doth bear witness
25. a. they bound him, Paul said
23 : 11. a. thou hast testified of me
31. a. it was commanded, took P-l
25 : 10. no wrong, a. thou knowest
27 : 30. a. shipm. were about to flee
Ro. 1 : 21. glorified him not a. God
3 : 5. (I speak a. a man) God forbid
7. why am I judged a. a sinner ?
8. a. we be slanderously reported
5 : 12. a. by one man sin ent-d [(2)
16. not a. by one that sinned, so
18. a. by offence of one, judgment
19. a. by one man's disobedi-e, so
21. a. sin hath reigned unto death
6 : 4. like a. Christ was raised, so
13. a. those th are alive fr. dead (3)
19 a. ye have yielded to iniquity
8 : 26. what pray for a. we ought
9 : 27. Tho. Israel be a. sand of sea
29. we had been a. Sodoma [ed
11 : 30. a. ye in times past not believ-
12 : 4. a. we have many members
13 : 13. walk honestly a. in the day
15 : 7. receive one anoth. a. Christ
15. a. putting you in mind [rec. us
1 Co. 3 : 1. I could not speak a. unto
spiritual, but a. unto carnal (3)
3. are ye not carnal, walk a. men ?
10. unto me, a. wise masterbuild.
15. shall be saved yet so a. by fire
4 : 1. account of us a. ministers of C.
7. why glory, a. if not received it ?
13. we are made a. filth of world
17. ways, a. I teach in ev. church
14. a. my beloved sons I warn you
5 : 3. I, a. absent in body, have
judged already (2) [leavened
7. be a new lump, a. ye are un-
7 : 17. a. L. hath called ev. one (2)
31. use this world a. not abusing
8 : 2. knoweth nothing a. he ought
5 a. there be gods many and lords
7. some eat it a. offered unto idol
9 : 8. Say I these things a. a man ?
20. I, to them under law, a. und.
21. To them without law, a. wi-t
22. To the weak, I a. weak [law
10 : 6. not after evil things, a. they
15. I speak a. to wise men ; judge
11 : 2. keep ordinances a. I deliv-d
12. a. the woman is of the man, so
12 : 11. dividing to every man a. he
12. a. the body is one, so is Christ
18. God set members a. it pleased
13 : 1. am become a. sounding brass
11. a child, I spake a. a child (3)
14 : 33. of peace, a. in all churches
15 : 8. a. of one born out of time
22 a. in Adam all die, so in Christ
38. G. giveth it a body a. it pleased
48. a. the earthy ; a. is heavenly
49. a. we have borne image of eart.
16 : 1. a. I have given order, so do
2. lay by him, a. G. hath prosp-d
10. worketh work of Lord, a. I do
2 Co. 1 : 5. a. sufferings of Ch. in us
2 Co. 1 : 7. a. partakers of sufferings
14. a. ye have acknowledged us
18. a. G. is true, our word not yea
2 : 17. not a. many ; but a. of sincerity, a. of God, speak we
3 : 5. Not sufficient to think a. of
13. Not a. Moses wh. put vail over
4 : 1. a. we have received mercy, we
6 : 4. approving ourselves a. minis-
8. a. deceivers, and yet true [ters
9. a. unknown ; a. dying ; a. [(8)
10. a. sorrowful, a. having noth.
13. I speak a. unto children ; be ye
7 : 14. a. we spake to you in truth
8 : 5. they did not a. we hoped
6. a. he had begun, so finish in you
7. Thf. a. ye abound in faith, love
11. a. was a readiness to will, so
9 : 5. a. matter of bounty, not cov.
10 : 2. a. if we walked acc. to flesh
11 : 3. a. serpent beguiled Eve, so
10. a. the truth of Christ is in me
15. transformed a. ministers of
13 : 2. I foretell you a. if present
7. ye honest, tho. we a. reprobates
Ga. 1 : 9. a. we said before, so I now
2 : 7. a. gospel of uncirc-n unto Pet.
14. If th. livest not a. do Jews (2)
3 : 16. not to seeds, a. of many ; but
4 : 12. be a. I am ; I am a. ye [a.
28. we, a. Isaac was, chil. of promise
29. a. he born aft. flesh persecuted
5 : 21. I tell you a. I have told you
6 : 10. a. opportunity, let us do good
Ep. 3 : 3. a. I wrote afore in few w-s
5. a. now revealed unto apostles
4 : 17. walk not a. other Gentiles
21. taught, a. the truth is in Jes.
5 : 1. Be followers of G. a. dear chil.
2. walk in love, a. Christ loved us
3. not named, a. becometh saints
8. walk a. children of light [wise
15. ye walk not a. fools, but a.
22. Wives, submit unto husbands,
a. unto the Lord, Col. 3 : 18.
24. a. church is subject unto Chr.
28. So to love wives a. our bodies
6 : 5. obed-t to masters a. unto Chr.
6. not a. menpleasers, but a.
servants of Christ, Col. 3 : 22.
7. doing service, a. to the Lord,
not to men, Col 3 : 23. [4 : 4.
20. speak boldly, a. I ought, Col.
Ph. 1 : 20. with boldness, a. always
2 : 8. found in fashion a. a man
12. a. ye have always obeyed, not
a. in my presence only, but in
15. among wh. ye shine a. lights
22. a. a son he hath served wi. me
3 : 17. so a. ye have us for ensample
Col. 1 : 6. a. it is in all the world (2)
7. a. ye learned of Epaphras, our
2 : 6. a. ye have received Christ, so
7. stablished in the faith a. taught
3 : 12. Put on a. the elect of God
1 Th. 1 : 5. a. ye know what men we
2 : 2. shamefully, a. ye know, at P.
4. not a. pleasing men, but God (2)
5. neither flattering words, a. ye
11. we charged you a. a father (2)
13. ye received it not a. word of
men, but a. it is in truth, of G.
4 : 1. a. ye have received of us
6. avenger, a. we forewarned you
11. that ye work a. we comm-ded
5 : 6. let us not sleep a. do others
2 Th. 1 : 3. thank God, a. it is meet
2 : 2. nor by letter, a. from us, a.
4. he, a. God, sitteth in temp. of G.
3 : 15. count him not a. an enemy,
admonish him a. a brother
1 Ti. 1 : 3. a. I besought thee to
abide at Ephesus [young men a.
5 : 1. an elder, entreat a. a father ;
2. elder women a. mothers : the
younger a. sisters [soldier
2 Ti. 2 : 3. endure hardness, a. good

2 Ti. 2:9. I suffer trouble a. evil doer
17. their word will eat a. a canker
3. 8. a. Jannes withstood Moses
9. folly be manifest, a. theirs was
Tit. 1 : 7. blameless, a. steward of
9 Holding the word a. taught⌊G.
2 : 3. aged women, a. becometh ho.
Phm 9. such a. Paul the aged, and
16 Not now a. servant, but broth.
17. If count me a partner, receive
him a. myself ⌈lent name
He. 1 : 4 a. he obtained more excel-
11. shall wax old a. doth garment
12 a. vesture sh thou fold them
3 : 2. a. Moses was faithful in all, 5.
6 Christ, a. son, over own house
8. Harden not a. in provocat-n, 15.
4 : 3. a. I have sworn in my wrath
5 : 3. a. for people, so for hims. to
6 : 19 hope we have a. an anchor
7 : 9. a. I may so say, Levi paid
27. not daily, a. those priests, to
8 : 5. a. Moses was admonished of
9 : 25. a. high priest entereth holy
10 : 25 a. manner of some is : the
more a. ye see day approaching
11 : 9. sojourned a. in strange cou.
12. sprang of one a. good a. dead,
so many a. the stars and a. sand
27 a. seeing him who is invisible
29. through Red sea a. by dry la.
12. 5. speaketh unto you a. chil-n
7. God dealeth with you a. sons
16 a. Esau, who sold his birthri.
27. shaken, a. of things are made
13 : 3. bonds, a. bound wi. them (2)
17. a. they that must give account
Ja 1 : 10. a. the flower he pass away
2 : 12. So speak, so do, a., they th.
shall be judged ⌈so faith
26. a. body without spirit is dead,
5 : 5. hearts, a. in day of slaugh-
1 Pe. 1 : 14. a. obedient children⌊ter
15. a. he which called you is holy
19. blood of Christ a. of a lamb
2 : 2. a. newborn babes, desire the
5. Ye, a. lively stones, are built
11. I beseech you a. strangers
12. they speak against you a. evil
doers, 3 : 16 ⌈are sent
14. governors, a. unto them that
16 a. free, but a. servants of God
3 : 7. unto wife, a. unto the weaker
vessel, and a. being heirs togeth.
8. Finally, live a. brethren ⌈God
4 : 10. a. good stewards of grace of
11. Let him speak a. oracles of
God ; a. of ability God giveth
15 let none suffer a. a murderer (4)
16. if any man suffer a. Christian
19. souls to him, a. unto faithful
5 : 3. Nei. a. being lords over God's
8 devil, a. roaring lion ⌊heritage
12. a faithful brother, a. I suppose
2 Pe 1 : 21 holy men spake a. moved
2 12. these a. natural brute beasts
3 : 4. all continue a. they were ⌈(2)
8. one day with L. a.. thous. years
16 a. in all his epistles speaking :
wrest a. they do other script-s
1 Jn 1 : 7. if we walk in light, a. he
2 : 18. a. ye have heard that antichrist shall come ⌈you all
27. a. same anointing teacheth
3 : 2. for we shall see him a. he is
12. Not a. Cain, who was of wicked
23. love one another, a. he gave
4 : 17. a. he is, so are we in world
2 Jn. 4. a. we com-t from the Father
6. a. ye have heard from beginn-g
Jude 10. naturally a. brute beasts
Re. 1 : 10. great voice, a. of trumpet
14. his eyes were a. flame of fire (3)
15. feet a. if they burned in fur-
17. I fell at his feet a. dead⌊nace (2)
2. 24. not known Satan, a. they
27. a. vessels of a potter be broken

Re. 4 : 7. third beast face a. a man
6 : 11. brethren be killed a. they
14. the heaven departed a. a scroll
8 : 12. so a. third part was darkened
9 : 2. out of pit a. smoke of furnace
3. unto locusts power, a. scorpi-s
5. torment a. torment of scorpion
7. their faces were a. faces of men
8. they had hair a. hair of women,
their teeth a. teeth of lions
9. sound of wings a. of chariots (2)
17. heads of horses a. heads of li-
10 : 1. angel, feet a. pillars of fire⌊ons
3. loud voice, a. when lion roareth
7 a. he hath declared to prophets
12 : 15. cast water a. flood aft. wom-
13 : 2. beast, feet a. feet of bear⌊an
11. another beast, spake a. dragon
17 : 12. a. king's one hour wi. beast
19 : 12. His eyes a. a flame of fire
21 : 2. saw new Jerusalem a. bride
16. city, length a. large a. breadth
22 : 1. water of life clear a. crystal

AS it had been. ⌈angel

Ac. 6 : 15. saw his face a. - face of
9 : 18. fell from his eyes a. - scales
10 : 11. saw a vessel descending, a.
- a great sheet let down, 11 : 5.
Re. 5 : 6. stood a Lamb a. - slain

Even AS. ⌈hunter

Ge. 10 : 9. e. a. Nimrod, mighty
44 : 18. for thou art e. a. Pharaoh
Jos. 13 : 8. e. a. Moses gave them
Mat. 5 : 48. Be ye perfect e. a. Fath.
15 : 28. be it unto thee e. a. thou
18 : 33. e. a. I had pity on thee
20 : 14 give unto last e. a. unto 1st
28. e. a. Son came not to be minis.
23 : 37. e. a. hen gathereth chick-s
Mk. 4 : 36. e. a. he was in the ship
11 : 6. e. a. Jesus had commanded
Lu. 1 : 2. e. a. they delivered unto
9 : 54. consume e. a. Elias did ⌊us
18 : 11. I am not a. other men, or
e. a. this publican ⌈said
19 : 32. they found, e. a. he had
24 : 24. found it e. so a. wom. said
Jn. 5 : 23. honor Son e. a. Father
12 : 50. e. a. Father said, so I speak
15 : 10. e. a. I have kept Father's
17 : 14. e. a. I am not of world, 16.
22. they may be one e. a. we are
Ac. 15 : 8. Holy Ghost, unto us, e. a.
11. believe we be saved e. a. they
27 : 25. sh. be e. a. it was told me
Ro. 1 : 13. fruit, e. a. am. Gentiles
28. e. a. they did not like to retain God in knowledge ⌈edness
4 : 6. e. a. David describeth bless-
1 Co. 1 : 6. e. a. testimony of Chr. was
3 : 1. speak, e. a. unto babes in C.
5. e. a. the Lord gave to ev. man
7 : 7. I would all men were e. a. I
8. It is good if they abide e. a. I
10 : 33. e. a. I please all men in all
11 : 1. of me, e. a. I am of Christ
12 : 2. unto idols, e. a. ye were led
13 : 12 sh. know, e. a. I am known
2 Co. 1 : 14. we your rejoicing, e. a.
3 : 18. changed e. a. by Spirit of L.
11 : 12. they may be found e. a. we
Ga. 3 : 6. e. a. Abrah. believed God
4 : 14. me a. an angel, e. a. Christ
Ep. 2 : 3. chil. of wrath, e. a. others
4 : 4. e. a. ye are called in one hope
32. forgiving, e. a. G. forgiven you
5 : 23. husb. head of wife e. a. Chr.
25. love your wives e. a. Chr. loved
29. cherisheth it e. a. Lord the ch.
33. so love his wife e. a. himself
Phil. 1 : 7. e. a. it is meet for me to
Col. 3 : 13. e. a. Christ forgave you
1 Th. 2 : 7. e. a. a nurse cherisheth
14. ye suffered of your own, e. a.
3 : 4. we told you, e. a. it came⌈you
12. in love tow-d all, e. a. we tow.
4 : 5. Not in lust, e. a. the Gentiles

1 Th. 4 : 13. sorrow not, e. a. oth-s
5 : 4. edify one another e. a. ye do
2 Th. 3 : 1. glorified e. a. with you
1 Pe. 3 : 6. e. a. Sarah obeyed Abr.
2 Pe. 1 : 14. e. a. Christ shewed me
2 : 1. e. a. shall be false teachers
3 : 15. e. a. bro. Paul hath written
1 Jn. 2 : 6. to walk e. a. he walked
27. e. a. it taught, ye shall abide
3 : 3. purifieth himself e. a. he is
7. is righteous, e. a. he is ⌊pure
3 Jn. 2. e. a. thy soul prospereth
3. e. a. thou walkest in the truth
Jude 7. e. a. Sodom and Gomorrah
Re. 2 : 27. e. a. I received of my Fa.
3 : 21. e. a. I also overcame ⌈figs
6 : 13. e. a. a fig tree casteth her
18 : 6. Reward her, e. a. she rew-d

See **DID** with as, **As I LIVE, As the Lord LIVETH, As thy soul LIVETH, As LONG as, As MANY as, As MUCH, So MUCH, As ONE, As SHEEP, As SOON as, As it WAS, As WELL, As it WERE, As if it WERE, As it is WRITTEN.**

See ACCORDING, APPEARANCE, APPOINTED, ARE, BECAME, CONCERNING, DAY, DAYS, DREAM, FAR, FIRE, FORASMUCH, GRASS, HONEY, HYPOCRITES, INASMUCH, LIGHT, LIKE, LION, NOISE, OFT, OFTEN, PERTAINING, PROPHET, RAIN, SAND, SNOW, SO, SOME, STARS, SUCH, SUN, THIEF, THOUGH, TOUCHING, TRAVAIL, VOICE, WOMAN, YET.

A'SA. ⌈1

1 K. 15 : 8. A. reigned, 9. 2 Ch. 14 :
11. A. did that was right, 2 Ch 14 : 2.
13. mother ; A. destroyed her idol,
burnt it, 2 Ch. 15 : 16 (2) ⌈15 : 17.
14. A.'s heart was perfect, 2 Ch.
16. war between A. and Baasha, 32.
17. Baasha not suffer any to go out
or come in to A., 2 Ch. 16 : 1 (2).
18. A. took all the silver and gold
in treasures (2), 2 Ch. 16 : 2.
20. So Ben-hadad hearkened unto
king A., 2 Ch. 16 : 4.
22. A. made proclamation thro-t
Judah ; A. built Geba, 2 Ch 16 :
23. rest of acts of A., 2 Ch. 16 : 11. ⌊6.
24. A. was buried, 2 Ch. 16 : 13.
25. Nadab began in second yr. of A.
28. 3d yr. of A. did Baasha slay, 33
16 : 8. In 26th yr. of A. began Elah
10. smote Elah in 27th yr. of A. ⌊15.
23. In 31st year of A. began Omri
29. In 38th year of A. began Ahab
22 : 41. Jehosh-t son of A. began to
43. walked in ways of A., 2 Ch. 20 :
46. sodomites in days of A. he⌊32.
1 Ch. 3 : 10. Abia, A. his son, Jehosh.
9 : 16. Berechiah son of A. ⌈targets
2 Ch. 14 : 8. A. had army that bare
10. A. went ag-t Zerah, set battle
11. A. cried unto the Lord, help
12. Lord smote Ethiopians bef. A.
13 A., people pursued unto Gerar
15 : 2. Azariah went to meet A. (2)
8. when A. heard, he took courage
10. gath-d at Jerus., 15th yr. of A.
19. no more war unto 35th yr. of A.
16 : 7. Hanani, seer, came to A., said
10. Then A. was wroth with the
seer : A. oppressed some of peo.
12. A. was diseased in his feet until
17 : 2. in cities of Ephr. A. had tak-
21 : 12. not walked in ways of A.⌊en
Je. 41 : 9. pit A. had made for fear
Mat. 1 : 7. begat Abia ; Abia begat A.
8. A. begat Josaphat ; Josaphat

AS'AHEL.

2 S. 2 : 18. sons of Zeruiah, Joab
and A., 1 Ch. 2 : 16. ⌈roe
18. A. was as light of foot as a wild
19. A. pursued after Abner; and
20. Art thou A.? he answ-d, I am
21. A. would not turn fr. following
22. Abner said to A., Turn aside
23. place where A. fell and died⌈A.
30. lacked of David's serv-s 19 and
32. took A., buried him in Beth-le.
3 : 27. Abner died for blood of A.,
30. slew Abner, he had slain A.⌊30.
23 : 24. A. one of the 30, 1 Ch. 11 : 26.
1 Ch. 27 : 7. captain, A., bro. of Joab
2 Ch. 17 : 8. sent A. and . . to teach
31 : 13. Nahath, A. were overseers
Ezr. 10 : 15. Jonathan, son of A.

ASAHI'AH[1] or ASAI'AH.[2]

2 K. 22 : 12. king commanded A.[1], a
servant of king, 2 Ch. 34 : 20.[2]
14. A.[1] went unto Huldah, proph-
⌊etess

ASAI'AH.

1 Ch. 4 : 36. A., Adiel were princes
6 : 30. Haggiah, A., whom David set
over service of song
9 : 5. of Shilonites; A. firstborn
15 : 6. Of the sons of Merari; A.
11. David called for Uriel, A.⌊chief

A'SAPH.

2 K. 18 : 18. Joah the son of A. the
recorder, 37. Is. 36 : 3, 22. ⌈(2)
1 Ch. 6 : 39. his broth. A., who stood
9 : 15. of Levites; Zichri son of A.
15 : 19. singers, Heman, A. to sound
with cymbals of brass, 17.-16 : 5.
16 : 5. to praise the Lord, A. chief
7. David, this psalm into ha. of A.
37. he left bef. ark A. and brethren
25 : 1. to the service of sons of A
2. sons of A. under hands of A. (3)
6. these, acc. to king's order to A.
9. first lot came for A. to Joseph
26 : 1. Cone-g porters of sons of A.
2 Ch. 5 : 12. singers, all of them of A
20 : 14. upon a Levite of the sons of
A. came the Spirit ⌈thems.
29 : 13. of sons of A.; they sanctified
30. praise with words of Da. and A.
35 : 15. singers, sons of A., in pla.,
according to commandm-t of A.
Ezr. 2 : 41. singers, children of A.,
128, Ne. 7 : 44. 148 ⌈cymbals
3 : 10. they set the sons of A. with
Ne. 2 : 8. unto A., keeper of forest
11 : 17. son of A. principal in prayer
22. Of sons of A., singers over the
12 : 35. trumpets; son of A.⌊busin.
46. in days of David and A. of old
Ps. 50.* Psalm of A., 73,* 79,* 82.*
74.* Maschil of A., 78.* ⌈of A.
75.* Al-taschith. A Psalm or Song
76.* on Neginoth, A Psalm or Song
77.* to Jeduthun, Psalm of A.⌊of A.
80.* To Musician upon Shoshan-
nim-Eduth, A Psalm of A.
81.* upon Gittith, A Psalm of A.
83.* A Song or Psalm of A.

ASARE'EL.

1 Ch. 4 : 16. And the sons of Jehaleleel; Ziph, A.

ASARE'LAH.

1 Ch. 25 : 2. Of the sons of Asaph;
Zaccur, and Joseph, and A.

ASCEND. ⌈to a.

Ex. 25 : † 37. they shall cause lamps
27 : † 20. pure oil to cause lamp to
a. always, Le. 24 : † 2. ⌈to a.
30 : † 8 when Aaron causeth lamps
Le. 2 : † 12. firstfruits not a. on altar
Nu. 21 : † 17. Israel sang, a., O well
De. 28 : † 61. plague to a. upon thee
Jos. 6 : 5. city sh. fall, a., every man
2 Ch. 3 : † 14. vail, cherubim, to a.
20 : † 34. made to a. in book of k-s
Ps. 24 : 3. Who sh. a. into hill of L.
104 : † 8. The mts. a.; valleys desc.
Ps. 135 : 7. He causeth vapours to a.
from earth, Je. 10 : 13.-51 : 16.
139 : 8. If I a. up into heaven, thou
Is. 14 : 13. I will a. into heaven, 14.
Je. 37 : † 11. army of Chal. made to a.
Eze. 38 : 9. shalt a., come like storm
Jn. 6 : 62. if ye see Son of man a. up
20 : 17. I a. to my Father and your
Ro. 10 : 6. Say not, Who a. into h.?
Re. 17 : 8. beast shall a. out of pit

ASCENDED.

Ex. 19 : 18. smoke th-of a. as smoke
Nu. 13 : 22. a. by south unto Heb-n
Jos. 8 : 20. smoke of city a. to, 21.
10 : 7. Joshua a. from Gilgal and
15 : 3. border a. up on south side
Ju. 13 : 20. angel a. in flame of alt.
20 : 40. flame of city a. to heaven
1 K. 22 : † 35. the battle a. that day
1 Ch. 27 : † 24. neither a. the number in the Chronicles ⌈alem a.
Ne. 4 : † 7. heard that walls of Jerus-
Ps. 68 : 18. Thou hast a. on high
Pr. 30 : 4. Who hath a. into heaven
Jn. 3 : 13. no man hath a. to heaven
20 : 17. I am not yet a. to my Fath.
Ac. 2 : 34. David is not a. into heav.
25 : 1. Festus a. from Cesarea to Je.
Ep. 4 : 8. When he a. up on high, he
9. Now that he a., what is it ⌈a.
10. that descended is same that
Re. 8 : 4. smoke of incense a. bef. G.
11 : 12. they a. to heaven in cloud

ASCENDETH, ING.

Ge. 28 : 12. angels a-g, descending
32 : † 24. wrestled until a-g of mor.
1 S. 28 : 13. saw gods a-g out of earth
1 K. 18 : † 29. a-g of evening sacrifice
2 K. 12 : † 4. money th. a-h on heart
Jb. 5 : † 26. as shock of corn a-h in
Ps. 74 : † 23. tumult of those ag-t
thee a-h continually ⌈a-g
Ec. 3 : † 21. the spirit of man that is
Lu 19 : 28. he went bef.. a-g to Jerus.
Jn. 1 : 51. angels of God a-g and des.
Re. 7 : 2. I saw angel a-g from east
11 : 7. beast that a-h out of the pit
14 : 11. smoke of torment a-h for-
⌊ever

ASCENSIONS.

Am. 9 : † 6. buildeth his a. in heav-
⌊en

ASCENT.

Nu. 34 : 4. turn to a. of Akrabbim
1 S. 9 : † 11. in a. they found maidens
2 S. 15 : 30. David went by a. of Oliv.
1 K. 10 : 5. a. by which he went unto house of Lord, 2 Ch. 9 : 4.
2 Ch. 20 : † 16. they come by a. of
⌊Ziz

ASCRIBE, ED.

De. 32 : 3. a. ye greatness unto God
1 S. 18 : 8. a-d unto David ten thousands; and to me a-d but thou-s
Jb. 36 : 3. I will a. righteousness to
my Maker . . my words not false
Ps. 68 : 34. a. ye strength unto God

AS'ENATH. ⌈A.

Ge. 41 : 45. Pha. gave Joseph to wife
50. A. daugh. of priest of On, 45.-
⌊46 : 20.

A'SER.

See Tribe of ASHER.

ASH.

Is. 44 : 14. he planteth an a., and rain

ASHAMED.

Ju. 3 : 25. tarried till they were a.
2 S. 10 : 5. because the men were
greatly a., 1 Ch. 19 : 5. ⌈when
19 : 3. as people being a. steal away
2 K. 2 : 17. they urged till he was a.
8 : 11. settled countenance until a.
2 Ch. 30 : 15. priests and Lev. were a.
Ezr. 8 : 22. I was a. to require of k.
9 : 6. am a. to lift my face to thee
Jb. 6 : 20. they came and were a.
11 : 3. when thou mockest shall no
man make thee a.? ⌈a. (2)
Ps. 6 : 10. Let all mine enemies be
25 : 3. let none that wait on thee be
a.; let them be a. who transg-s
Ps. 31 : 17. let the wicked be a.⌈mine
35 : 26. Let them be a. th. rejoice at
69 : 6. Let not them be a. for my sa.
74 : 21. let not oppressed return a.
86 : 17. that they wh. hate me be a.
109 : 28. when arise, let them be a.
119 : 78. Let proud be a.; for they
dealt perversely ⌈rottenness
Pr. 12 : 4. she that maketh a. is as
Is. 1 : 29. they sh. be a. of the oaks
20 : 5. they shall be a. of Ethiopia
23 : 4. Be thou a., O Zidon, the sea
26 : 11. shall be a. for their envy
30 : 5. all a. of people that could
not profit them ⌈anon is a.
33 : 9. The earth mourneth; Leb.
42 : 17. be a. that trust in images
44 : 9. see not; that they may be a.
11. all his fellows shall be a.; let
them all be a. together (2) ⌈a.
45 : 24 all incensed against him be
65 : 13. my servants shall rejoice,
ye shall be a. ⌈shall be a.
66 : 5. he appear to your joy, they
Je. 2 : 26. As thief is a. when found,
so is the house of Israel a.
36. shalt be a. of Egypt as thou
wast a. of Assyria ⌈to be a.
3 : 3. whore's forehead, refusedst
6 : 15. Were they a.? nay, they
were not at all a., 8 : 12. ⌈ed
8 : 9. wise men are a., are dismay-
12 : 13. shall be a. of your revenues
14 : 4. no rain; ploughmen were a.
17 : 13. that forsake thee shall be a.
20 : 11. my persecutors shall be a.
48 : 13. Moab shall be a. of Chemosh, as Isr. was a. of Beth-el
50 : 12. she that bare you sh. be a.
Eze. 16 : 27. daughters a. of lewdn-s
61. shalt remember thy ways and
32 : 30. with terror are a. ⌊be a.
43 : 10. they may be a. of iniquities
11. if be a. of all they have done
Ho. 4 : 19. they shall be a. because
of their sacrifices ⌈counsel
10 : 6. Israel shall be a. of his own
Jo. 1 : † 10. corn wasted, new wine is
11. Be ye a., O ye husbandmen⌊a.
Zch. 9 : 5. her expectation shall be a.
10 : † 5. make riders on horses a.
13 : 4. prophets shall be a. every
one of his vision ⌈Lu. 9 : 26.
Mk. 8 : 38. Whoso. shall be a. of me,
Lu. 13 : 17. his adversaries were a.
16 : 3. I cannot dig, to beg I am a.
Ro. 6 : 21. things wh-of ye are now a.
2 Co. 9 : 4. Lest we be a. in boasting
Ph. 1 : 20. in nothing I shall be a.
2 Th. 3 : 14. have no company with
him, that he may be a. ⌈a.
Tit. 2 : 8. he of contrary part may be
1 Pe. 3 : 16 be a. that falsely accuse

ASHAMED, confounded.

Ps. 40 : 14. Let them be a. and c. that
seek my soul, 70 : 2. ⌈when Lord
Is. 24 : 23. moon be c. and sun a.
41 : 11. all ag-t thee shall be a., c.
45 : 16. be a. and c. makers of idols
17. ye shall not be a. nor c. ⌈c.
54 : 4. thou shalt not be a.; neither
Je. 14 : 3. found no water; were a., c.
15 : 9. She th. hath borne seven, a.,
22 : 22. a., c. for thy wickedn-s⌊c.
31 : 19. I was a., c., bec. I did bear
reproach of my youth ⌈O Israel
Eze. 36 : 32 be a., c. for your ways,
Mi. 3 : 7. sh. seers be a., diviners c.

ASHAMED, with not or never. ⌈n. a.

Ge. 2 : 25. naked, man and wife, and
Nu. 12 : 14. sho. she n. be a. 7 days?
Jb. 19 : 3. n. a. that ye make yourselves strange to me ⌈a., 20.
Ps. 25 : 2. O my God, let me n. be
31 : 1. my trust; let me n-r be a.
17. Let me n. be a., 119 : 116.

Ps. 34 : 5. They looked; faces were n.
37 : 19. sh. n. be a. in evil time [a.
119 : 6. Then shall I n. be a. when
46. speak of testimonies, n. be a.
80. heart be sound, th. I be n. a.
127 : 5. they sh. n. be a., but speak
Is. 29 : 22. Jacob shall n. now be a.
45 : 17. n. be a., world without end
49 : 23. n. be a. that wait for me
50 : 7. face like flint, I sh. n. be a.
54 : 4. Fear not, thou shalt n. be a.
Jo. 2 : 26. my people n-r be a., 27.
Zph 3 : 11. In that day thou n. be a.
Ro. 1 : 16. I am n. a. of gospel of C.
5 : 5. hope maketh n. a.; bec. love
9 : 33. whosoever believeth on him
shall n. be a., 10 : 11. [n. a.
2 Co. 7 : 14. If I have boasted I am
10 : 8. tho. boast, I should n. be a.
2 Ti. 1 : 8. Be thou n. a. of testimony
12. I am n. a.; for I know whom
16. Onesiph-s; n. a. of my chain
2 : 15. to shew thyself a workman
that needeth n. to be a. [ren
He. 2 : 11. he n. a. to call them breth-
11 : 16. God n. a. to be called their
1 Pe. 4 : 16. if suffer as a Christian,
let him n. be a. [coming
1 Jn. 2 : 28. we may n. be a. at his
See SHAMED.

A'SHAN.

Jos. 15 : 42. cities of Judah, Ether,
A., 19 : 7. 1 Ch. 4 : 32.-6 : 59.
21 : † 16. to chil. of Aaron, A. Jut-

ASH'BEA. [tah

1 Ch. 4 : 21. families of house of A.

ASH'BEL, ITES.

Ge. 46 : 21. sons of Benjamin, Belah,
A., Ehi, 1 Ch. 8 : 1.
Nu. 26 : 38. of A. the family of A-s

ASH'CHENAZ.

See ASHKENAZ.

ASH'DOD. [A.

Jos. 11 : 22. Anakim, only in Gaza,
15 : 46. all that lay near A., 47. [A.
1 S. 5 : 1. Philistines brought ark to
3. when they of A. arose on [in A.
5. nor tread threshold of Dagon
6. hand of Lord heavy upon A. (2)
7. when men of A. saw it was so
6 : 17. golden emerods; for A. one
2 Ch. 26 : 6. Uzziah brake down wall
of A., built cities about A.
Ne. 13 : 23. Jews that had married
wives of A. [of A.
24. children spake half in speech
Is. 20 : 1. Tartan fought ag-t A. (2)
Je. 25 : 20. I made nations drink; A.
Am. 1 : 8. I will cut off inhabitant fr.
3 : 9. Publish in the palaces at A [A
Zph. 2 : 4. sh. drive out A. at noonday
Zch. 9 : 6. a bastard shall dwell in A.

ASH'DODITES[1]
or ASH'DOTHITES.[2]

Jos. 13 : 3. the A.[2], Gittites, Avites
Ne. 4 : 7. when A.[1] heard that walls

ASH'DOTH-PIS'GAH.

De. 3 : 17. unto salt sea, under A.,
eastward, Jos. 12 : 3.-13 : 20.

ASH'ER. [Person.]

Ge. 30 : 13. Leah called his name A.
35 : 26. sons of Zilpah, Gad and A.
46 : 17. the sons of A.; Jimnah,
Ishuah, and, 1 Ch. 7 : 30. [fat
49 : 20. Out of A. his bread shall be
Ex. 1 : 4. into Egypt with Jacob, A.
Nu. 26 : 46. daughter of A. was Sarah
1 Ch. 2 : 2. the sons of Israel; Gad, A.

ASH'ER.
[Tribe or territory.]

Nu. 1 : 13. Of A.; Pagiel son of Ocran
40. Of chil. of A. able to go to war
2 : 27. captain of children of A.,
Pagiel, 7 : 72.-10 : 26. [of A., 44.
26 : 47. These are families of sons
De. 27 : 13. stand to curse: Gad, A.
33 : 24. Let A. be blessed with chil.
Jos. 17 : 10. they met in A. on nor. [(2)
11. Manasseh had in A. Beth-shean
19 : 34. coast reacheth to A. on west
Ju. 1 : 31. Nei. did A. drive inhab-ts
5 : 17. A. continued on the sea shore
6 : 35. Gid. sent messengers unto A.
7 : 23. men out of A. pursued Midi-
1 K. 4 : 16. Baanah was in A. [anites
1 Ch. 7 : 40. chil. of A.; choice men
12 : 36. of A., expert in war, 40,000
2 Ch. 30 : 11. divers of A humbled
Eze. 48 : 2. by Dan, a portion for A.
34. one gate of Gad, one of A., one

Tribe of
ASH'ER or A'SER.[2]

Nu. 1 : 41. numbered, of - A., 41,500
2 : 27. encamp by Dan shall be - A.
10 : 26. over host of - A. Pagiel [la.
13 : 13. Of - A., Sethur to spy out
34 : 27. prince of - A., Ahihud; to
Jos. 19 : 24. fifth lot came for - A.
31. this is the inheritance of - A.
21 : 6. children of Gershom had out
of - A., 30. 1 Ch. 6 : 62, 74.
Lu. 2 : 36. dau-r of Phanuel of - A.[2]
Re. 7 : 6. Of - A.[2] were sealed 12,000

ASH'ER. [Place.] [to M.

Jos. 17 : 7. coast of Manasseh fr. A.

ASH'ERITES.

Ju. 1 : 32. A. dwelt amo. Canaanites

ASHES. [a.

Ge. 18 : 27. I which am but dust and
Ex. 9 : 8. Take handfuls of a. of fur.
10. took a. and stood before Pha-h
27 : 3. make pans to receive his a.
Le. 1 : 16. beside altar, by place of a.
4 : 12. where a. are poured, burn
6 : 10. priest shall take up the a. [2)
11. sh. carry a. without the camp
Nu. 4 : 13. they shall take a. fr. altar
19 : 9. a man clean shall gather a.
10. that gathereth a. shall wash
17. unclean person take a. of heif.
2 S. 13 : 19. Tamar put a. on head
1 K. 13 : 3. altar be rent, a. poured, 5.
20 : 38. prophet disguised with a.
41. he took away a. from his face
2 K. 23 : 4. carried a. unto Beth-el
Jb. 2 : 8. Job sat down among the a.
13 : 12. Your remembr-s are like a.
30 : 19. I am become like dust and
42 : 6. I repent in dust and a. [a.
Ps. 20 : † 3. turn to a. thy sacrifices
102 : 9. I have eaten a. like bread
147 : 16. scatter-h hoar frost like a.
Is. 44 : 20. He feedeth on a. [for a.
61 : 3. to give unto them beauty
Je. 25 : 34. ye shepherds wallow in a.
31 : 40. valley of a. be holy unto L.
52 : † 18. instruments to remove a.
La. 3 : 16. hath covered me with a.
Eze. 27 : 30. pilots shall wallow in a.
28 : 18. I will bring thee to a. [feet
Mal. 4 : 3. wicked be a. under your
He. 9 : 13. if a. of heifer sanctifieth
2 Pe. 2 : 6. Sodom, Gomorrah into a.

ASHES with sackcloth.

Es. 4 : 1. Mordecai put on s. with a.
3. mourning, many lay in s. and
Is. 58 : 5. is it to spread s. and a. [a.
Je. 6 : 26. O daughter, gird thee with
s., wallow in a. [s. and a.
Da. 9 : 3. I set my face to seek with
Jon. 3 : 6. king of N. with s. sat in a.
Mat. 11 : 21. Tyre, Sidon wou. have
repented in s. and a., Lu 10 : 13.

ASH'IMA. [A.

2 K. 17 : 30. men of Hamath made

ASH'KELON,[1]
AS'KELON.[2]

Ju. 1 : 18. Judah took A.[2] wi. coast
14 : 19. Samson went to A.[1], slew 30
1 S. 6 : 17. emerods for A.[2], one for
2 S. 1 : 20. publish it not in A.[2] [zah
Je. 25 : 20. fury, they sh. drink, A.[1], Az-
47 : 5. A.[1] is cut off with remnant
7. Lord given it a charge ag-t A.[1]
Am. 1 : 8. that holdeth sceptre fr. A.[1]
Zph. 2 : 4. forsaken, A.[1] a desolation
7. in houses of A.[1] shall lie down
Zch. 9 : 5. A.[1] shall see it and fear.
and A.[1] shall not be inhabited

ASH'KENAZ,[1]
or ASH'CHENAZ.[2]

Ge. 10 : 3. sons of Gomer; A.[1], and
Riphath, and, 1 Ch. 1 : 6.[2]
Je. 51 : 27. call ag-t her kingdoms of

ASH'NAH. [A.[2]

Jos. 15 : 33. in the valley, Eshtaol, A.
43. Jiphtah, A., Nezib, wi. villages

ASHPANS. [gold

1 K. 7 : † 50. spoons and a. of pure

ASH'PENAZ.

Da. 1 : 3. A., master of his eunuchs

ASH'RIEL. See ASRIEL.

ASH'TAROTH,[1]
ASH'TORETH,[2]
or AS'TAROTH.[3] [Idol.]

Ju. 2 : 13. Israel served Baal a
A.[1], 10 : 6.[1] 1 S. 12 : 10.[1] [A.[1], and 3.
1 S. 7 : 4. Isr. did put away Baalim,
31 : 10. his armour in house of A.[1]
1 K. 11 : 5. Solomon went after A.[2],
goddess of the Zidonians, 33.
2 K. 23 : 13. places Sol. builded for A.[2]
[Place.]
De. 1 : 4. Og, which dwelt in A.[3],
Jos. 9 : 10.[1]-12 : 4.[1]-13 : 12.[1] [shan
Jos. 13 : 31. A.[1], Edrei, cities in Ba-
1 Ch. 6 : 71. Unto sons of Gershom,

ASHTE'RATHITE. [A.[1]

1 Ch. 11 : 44. valiant men, Uzzia, A.

ASH'TEROTH
KAR'NAIM. [A. K.

Ge. 14 : 5. kings smote Rephaim in

ASH'TORETH.

See ASHTAROTH.

ASH'UR. [bare A.

1 Ch. 2 : 24. Abiah, Hezron's wife,
4 : 5. A., father of Tekoa had two

ASH'URITES. [wives

2 S. 2 : 9. Ish-bosheth king over A.
Eze. 27 : 6. A. made benches of ivory

ASH'VATH. [A.

1 Ch. 7 : 33. sons of Japhlet, Bimhal,

A'SIA.

Ac. 2 : 9. dwellers in Pontus and A.
6 : 9. them of A. disputing wi. Steph.
16 : 6. were forbid. to preach in A.
19 : 10. all in A. heard the word
22. Paul stayed in A. for a season
26. thro-t A. Paul hath turned peo.
27. Diana, whom A. worshippeth
31. certain of chief of A., friends
20 : 4. accompanied him into A.
Sopater; and of A. Tychicus [A.
16. Paul would not spend time in
18. from first day I came into A
21 : 27. Jews of A. stirred up people
24 : 18. Jews of A. found me purified
27 : 2. meaning to sail by coasts of A.
1 Co. 16 : 19. churches of A. salute
2 Co. 1 : 8. of our trouble in A. [you
2 Ti. 1 : 15. all in A. be turned from me
1 Pe. 1 : 1. strangers scattered thro-t
Re. 1 : 4. John to churches in A. [A.
11. write in book unto churches

ASIDE. [in A.

2 S. 3 : 27. Joab took him a., smote
6 : 10. carried ark a. into house of
Obed-edom, 1 Ch. 13 : 13 [full
2 K. 4 : 4. shalt set a. that which is
Jb. 1 : † 19. came great wind from a.
Mk. 7 : 33. took him a. fr. multitude
Jn. 13 : 4. He laid a. his garment
He. 12 : 1. let us lay a. every weight
See GO aside, GONE aside,
TURN aside, TURNED
aside, WENT aside.

A'SIEL.

1 Ch. 4 : 35. Seraiah the son of A.

ASK. [name

Ge. 32 : 29. Wherefore a. after my
34 : 12. a. me never so much dower

De. 4 : 32. a. now of days th. are past
13 : 14. a. diligently ; if it be truth
32 : 7. a. thy fa., he will shew thee
Jos. 4 : 6. when chil. a. fathers, 21.
15 : 18. moved him to a. of her father a field, Ju. 1 : 14. [peace
1 S. 10 : † 4. they will a. thee of
12 : 19. added this evil to a. a king
25 : † 5. go and a. him of peace, 2
8. a. thy young men [S. 8 : † 10,
28 : 16. Wheref. dost thou a. of me
2 S. 14 : 18. hide not thing I shall a.
1 K. 2 : 16. I a. one petition of thee
20. king said, a. on, my mother
22. why dost a. Abishag for Adonijah ? a. for him kingdom also
3 : 5. God said, a. what I shall give
thee, 2 Ch. 1 : 7. [a. of thee
14 : 5. wife of Jeroboam cometh to
2 K. 2 : 9. Elijah said, a. what I shall
do for thee [help of L.
2 Ch. 20 : 4. Judah gathered to a.
Jb. 12 : 7. a. beasts, they shall teach
Ps. 2 : 8. a. of me, I shall give thee
Is. 7 : 11. a. thee a sign of L. ; a. it
12. I will not a. neither tempt L.
45 : 11. saith Lord, a. me of things
concerning my sons [justice
58 : 2. they a. of me ordinances of
Je. 6 : 16. a. for the old paths [doest?
15 : 5. who go aside to a. how thou
18 : 13. a. ye among heathen [of L.?
23 : 33. people a., What is burden
30 : 6. a. whether man doth travail
38 : 14. king said, I will a. a thing
48 : 19. a. him that fleeth and her
50 : 5. They shall a. way to Zion
La. 4 : 4. young children a. bread
Da. 6 : 7. whoso. shall a. of any God
or man for 30 days, 12. [the law
Hag. 2 : 11. a. now the priests conc.
Zch. 10 : 1. a. rain in time of latter
Mat. 6 : 8. what need of, before ye a.
7 : 7. a. and it shall be given you,
seek, and, Lu. 11 : 9. [11 : 11.
9. if son a. bread, give stone? Lu.
10. Or if he a. a fish, Lu. 11 : 11.
11. good things to them th. a. him
14 : 7. give her whatso. she wou a.
18 : 19. touching any thing they a.
20 : 22 Jesus said, Ye know not
what ye a., Mk. 10 : 38.
21 : 22. whatsoever ye a. in prayer
24. I also will a. you one question,
Lu. 6 : 9.-20 : 3. Mk. 11 : 29.
22 : 46. nei. durst a. him any more
questions, Mk. 12 : 34. Lu. 20 : 40.
27 : 20. that they sho. a. Barabbas
Mk. 6 : 22. a. whatso-r thou wilt, 23.
24. unto mother, What shall I a.
9 : 32. afraid to a. him, Lu. 9 : 45.
Lu. 6 : 30. taketh goods, a. not again
11 : 12. Or, if he shall a. an egg [a.
13. give Holy Spirit to them that
12 : 48. to wh. much, of him a. more
19 : 31. if man a., Why loose him
22 : 68. if I a. you, ye will not answ.
Jn. 1 : 19. Jews sent priests to a. him
9 : 21. he is of age ; a. him, 23.
11 : 22. wilt a. of God, G. will give it
13 : 24. Peter beckoned that he a.
14 : 13. whatsoever ye shall a. in
my name, 15 : 16.-16 : 23.
14. if ye a. in my name I will do it
15 : 7. if abide in me, a. what ye will
16 : 19. they were desirous to a. him
23. that day ye shall a. me nothing
24. a., ye shall receive, that joy
26. that day ye sh. a. in my name
30. needest not any man a. thee
18 : 21. a. them wh. heard me [him
21 : 12. none of disciples durst a.
Ac. 3 : 2. to a. alms of them that ent.
10 : 29. I a. for what intent ye sent
12 : † 13. damsel to a. who was th-e
1 Co. 14 : 35. a. husbands at home
Ep. 3 : 20. to do above all we a. or
Ja. 1 : 5. If lack wisdom, let him a.
6. But let him a. in faith [of God
4 : 2. ye have not because ye a. not
3. Ye a., and receive not, because
ye a. amiss [receive
1 Jn. 3 : 22. whatsoever we a. we
5 : 14. if we a. acc-g to his will, he
15. if he hear us whatsoever we a.
16. If sin not unto death, he shall
See COUNSEL [a. and

ASKED. [thou?

Ge. 24 : 47. I a., Whose daughter
26 : 7. the men a. him of his wife
32 : 29. Jacob a., Tell me thy name
37 : 15. man a., What seekest thou?
38 : 21. Judah, he a., Where harlot
40 : 7. he a. Pha-'s officers wi. him
43 : 7. the man a. us of our kindred
27. Jos-h a. them of their welfare
44 : 19. My lord a., Have ye a fath.
Ex. 18 : 7. a. each other of welfare
Jos. 19 : 50. gave him city wh. he a.
Ju. 5 : 25. He a. water, she gave milk
6 : 29. when they a., they said, Gid.
13 : 6. I a. him not whence he was
18 : † 15. they a. him of peace [a.
1 S. 1 : 17. God grant petition thou
20. name Sam-l, Bec I a. him of L.
† 20. H. called his name, A. of God
27. Lord given petition I a., 2 : † 20.
8 : 10. L. unto people that a. king
17 : † 22. David a. his brethren of
peace, 30 : † 21. [and David?
19 : 22. Saul a., Where are Samuel
20 : 6. say, David a. that he might
run to Beth-lehem, 28. [did
30 : † 21. David a. them how they
1 K. 3 : 10. pleased L. Sol-n a. this
11. Bec. thou hast a. this, and not
a. long life, nei. a.(5), 2 Ch. 1 : 11.
13. I given that thou hast not a.
10 : 13. Solomon gave queen of Sheba whatsoever she a., 2 Ch. 9 : 12.
2 K. 2 : 10. Thou hast a. hard thing
8 : 6. when king a. woman, she told
Ezr. 5 : 9. a. we, Who commanded
10. We a. their names [you to build
Ne. 1 : 2. I a. conc-g Jews escaped
Jb. 21 : 29. Have ye a. them that go
Ps. 21 : 4. He a. life of thee, thou
35 : † 11. they a. things I knew not
105 : 40. people a., he bro-t quails
Is. 30 : 2. have not a. at my mouth
41 : 28. was no counsellor, th. when
I a., could answer [not after
65 : 1. I am sought of them that a.
Je. 36 : 17. a. Baruch, How write
37 : 17. king a. him secretly, Is any
word from the Lord? [and a.
38 : 27. came princes unto Jerem-h
Da. 2 : 10. no k. that a. such things
7 : 16. I a. him the truth of all this
Mat. 12 : 10. a., Is it lawful to heal
16 : 13. he a. his disciples, Mk. 8 : 27.
Lu. 9 : 18. [Lu. 8 : 9.
17 : 10. disciples a. him, Mk 7 : 17.
22 : 23. Sadducees a. him, If a man
die, Mk. 12 : 18. Lu. 20 : 27. [him
35. a lawyer a. question, tempt-g
41. Jes. a., What think ye of Chr.
Mk. 4 : 10. they a. of him the parable
5 : 9. Jesus a. him, What is thy
name? Lu. 8 : 30. [head of John
6 : 25. she a., I will thou give me
7 : 5. scribes a., Why walk not disci.
8 : 5. he a., How many loaves have
23. he a. him if he saw aught [ye
9 : 11. they a. him, Why say scribes
16. he a. scribes, What question
21. a. his father, How long since
28. disciples a., Why could not we
33. a., What was it ye disputed
10 : 2. Pharisees a., Is it lawful for
10. his disciples a. him again of
17. one a. him, What shall I do
that I may inherit, Lu. 18 : 18.
12 : 28. one a., Which is first com-t?
Mk. 13 : 3. James, John a., When sh
these things be? Lu. 21 : 7.
14 : 60. high priest a. Jesus, Answerest thou nothing?
61. a. him, Art thou the Christ?
15 : 2. Pilate a., Art thou King of
the Jews, Mat. 27 : 11. Lu. 23 : 3.
4. Pilate a., Answerest nothing
44. a. wheth. been any while dead
Lu. 1 : 63. he a. for a writing table
3 : 10. people a., What we do then?
9 : 18. he a., Whom say peo. I am
15 : 26. son a. what these meant
18 : 36. blind man a. what it meant
40. a., What wilt that I do unto
20 : 21. a., Is it lawful to give tribute
22 : 64. they a., who is it smote thee
23 : 6. Pilate a. whe. man Galilean
Jn. 1 : 21. they a., Art thou Elias?
25. they a., Why baptizest thou
4 : 10. thou wouldest have a. of him
5 : 12. a., What man said, Take thy
9 : 2. disciples a. who did sin [bed
15. Phari. a. how he received sight
19. Jews a. them, Is this your son
16 : 24. have ye a. nothing in my
18 : 7. a. he, Whom seek ye [name
19. a. Jes. of disciples and doctrine
Ac. 1 : 6. a., Lord, wilt thou restore
3 : 3. seeing Peter, John, a. an alms
4 : 7. a., By what power done this?
5 : 27. priest a., Did not we com-d
10 : 18. a. whe. Simon lodged there
23 : 19. a., What hast to tell me?
34. he a. of what province he was
25 : 20. I a. whe. he would go to Je.
Ro. 10 : 20. I was made manifest unto them that a. not after me

AS'KELON. See ASHKELON.

ASKEST.

Ju. 13 : 18. Why a. after my name?
Jn. 4 : 9. a. drink of me, a woman of
18 : 21. Why a. thou me? ask them

ASKETH. [a.

Ge. 32 : 17. When Esau my brother
Ex. 13 : 14. when thy son a., in time
to come, De. 6 : 20. [of thee
De. 14 : † 26. whatsoever thy soul a.
Mi. 7 : 3. the prince a. and the judge
a. for reward [Lu. 6 : 30.
Mat. 5 : 42. Give to him that a. thee,
7 : 8. For every one that a. receiveth, Lu. 11 : 10. [est thou?
Jn. 16 : 5. none a. me, Whither go-
1 Pe. 3 : 15. a. you a reason of hope

ASKING. [state

Ge. 43 : † 7. man a. asked us of our
1 S. 12 : 17. wickedness in a. a king
2 K. 2 : † 10. hast done hard in a.
1 Ch. 10 : 13. Saul died for a. counsel
Ps. 78 : 18. tempted God by a. meat
Lu. 2 : 46. in temple a. questions
Jn. 8 : 7. when they continued a. he
1 Co. 10 : 25. eat, a. no question for,

ASLEEP. [27.

Ju. 4 : 21. Sisera was fast a., weary
1 S. 26 : 12. no man saw it; all a.
Can. 7 : 9. lips of those a. to speak
Jon. 1 : 5. Jonah lay, and was fast a.
Mat. 8 : 24. arose a tempest, but he
was a., Mk. 4 : 38. Lu. 8 : 23.
26 : 40. unto disciples, and findeth
them a., 43. Mk. 14 : 40. [fell a.
Ac. 7 : 60. Stephen had said this, he
1 Co. 15 : 6. but some are fallen a.
18. they which are fallen a. in Ch.
1 Th. 4 : 13. ignorant conc-g them a.
15. not prevent them which are a.
2 Pe. 3 : 4. since fathers fell a. all

AS'NAH. [things

Ezr. 2 : 50. The Nethinim : chil. of A.

AS'NAPPER. [over

Ezr. 4 : 10. nations noble A. brought

ASP, S. [a-s

De. 32 : 33. their wine is venom of
Jb. 20 : 14. his meat is the gall of a-s
16. he shall suck the poison of a-s

Ps. 58 : † 4. like **a.** that stoppeth ear
91 : †13. sh. tread upon lion and **a.**
Is. 11 :8. child sh. play on hole of **a.**
Ro. 3 : 13. poison of a-s under their [lips

AS'PATHA.

Es. 9 : 7. slew A. and sons of Haman

AS'RIEL,[1] ITES, ASH'RIEL.[2]

Nu. 26 : 31. of A.[1], the family of A-s
Jos. 17 : 2. lot for children of A.[1]
1 Ch. 7 : 14. sons of Manasseh ; A.[2]

ASS.

Ge. 22 : 5. Abide ye here with the **a.**
42 : 27. to give his **a.** provender in
44 : 13. laded every man his **a.** [ing
49 : 14. Issachar is strong **a.** couch-
Ex. 4 : 20. Moses set them upon **a.**
13 : 13. every firstling of an **a.** shalt
redeem. 34 : 20. [a., De. 5 :21.
20 : 17. not covet neighb-'s ox nor
21 : 33. if a man dig pit, and **a.** fall
22 : 4. theft, whe. ox or a., restore
9. For trespass for **a.**, cause come
10. if man deliver **a.** to keep [5.
23 : 4. If meet enemy's **a.** astray,
12. 7th day rest: that thine **a.** may
Nu. 16 : 15. I have not taken one **a.**
22 : 22. Balaam riding upon his **a.**
23. **a.** saw angel in the way ; **a.**
turned ; Balaam smote **a.**, 27 (2).
25. the **a.** crushed Balaam's foot
28. L. opened mouth of **a.** [ed me
29. said unto **a.**, thou hast mock-
30. **a.** said, Am not I thine **a.**
32. Wherefore smitten thine **a.**
33. **a.** saw me, turned 3 times [a.
De. 5 : 14. sab. ; not do any work, nor
22 : 3. in like manner do with his **a.**
4. not see broth-'s **a.** fall, and hide
10. sh. not plough with ox and **a.**
28 : 31. thine **a.** shall be taken away
Jos. 6 : 21. destroyed all, man, ox, **a.**
15 : 18. Achsah lighted off her **a.** ;
Caleb said, Ju. 1 : 14. [ox nor **a.**
Ju. 6 : 4. left no sustenance, neither
15 : 15. found new Jawbone of an **a.**
16. with jaw of an **a.** slain 1,000 (2)
19 : 28. man took her up upon an **a.**
1 S. 12 : 3. whose **a.** have I taken?
15 : 3. slay man, woman, camel, **a.**
16 : 20. Jesse took **a.** laden with b.
25 : 20. as Abigail rode on the **a.**
23. Abigail hasted, lighted off **a.**
42. rode upon an **a.** with damsels
1 K. 2 : 40. Shimei saddled his **a.**
13 : 24. **a.**, lion stood by carcass,
28. lion had not torn the **a.** [28.
29. prophet laid carcass upon **a.**
2 K. 6 : 25. a-'s head sold for 80 pieces
Jb. 24 : 3. drive away **a.** of fatherless
Pr. 26 : 3. bridle for **a.** and rod for f.
Is. 1 : 3. knoweth **a.** his master's crib
32 : 20. that send forth feet of ox, **a.**
Je. 22 : 19. buried with burial of **a.**
Zch. 9 : 9. thy King cometh, riding
upon an **a.**, and colt, the foal of
an **a.**, Mat. 21 : 5. Jn. 12 : 15.
14 : 15. so be plague of horse, of **a.**
Mat. 21 : 2. ye shall find an **a.** tied
7. disciples brought **a.** and colt
Lu. 13 : 15. each loose his **a.** on sab.
14 : 5. sh. have an **a.** fallen into pit
2 Pe. 2 : 16. dumb **a.** forbade proph.

ASS colts. [a. c.

Ju. 10 : 4. thirty sons rode on thirty
12 : 14. 40 sons, 30 nephews, on 70

ASS'S colt. [a. c.

Ge. 49 : 11. binding **a. c.** unto vine
Jb. 11 : 12. man born like wild **a. c.**
Jn. 12 : 15. thy King sitting on **a. c.**
See SADDLE, SADDLED.
See **WILD** ass, es.
See **YOUNG** ass, es.

ASSES. [a.

Ge. 12 : 16. Abr. had he **a.** and she
24 : 35. L. hath given him camels, **a.**
30 : 43. Jacob had much cattle, **a.**
32 : 5. have oxen, and **a.** ; flocks
15. present for Esau ; 200 ewes, 20
34 : 28. sons of Jacob took **a.** [she **a.**
36 : 24. as he fed the **a.** of Zibeon
42 : 26. laded their **a.** with corn [a.
43 : 18. take us for bondmen, our
24. he gave their **a.** provender
44 : 3. men sent away and **a.** [a.
45 : 23. to father ; ten **a.**, ten she
47 : 17. bread in exchange for the **a.**
Ex. 9 : 3. hand of L. is upon **a.**, oxen
Nu. 31 : 28. levy tribute of **a.**, sheep
30. take one portion of fifty of **a.**
34. booty 72,000 beeves, 61,000 **a.**
39. portion of them was **a.** 30,500
45. half unto cong-n was 30,500 **a.**
Jos. 7 : 24. took Achan, his sons, **a.**
9 : 4. took old sacks upon their **a.**
Ju. 5 : 10. ye that ride on white **a.**
Ju. 19 : 3. after her, having couple **a.**
19. provender for our **a.**, 21 [and **a.**
1 S. 8 : 16. he take your young men
9 : 3. **a.** of Kish were lost. Kish
said to Saul, Go, seek the **a.** [a.
5. lest my father leave caring for
10 : 2. The **a.** are found ; thy father
hath left care of **a.**, 9 : 20 [a.
14. Whither went ye? To seek the
16. told us plainly **a.** were found
22 : 19. Doeg smote men, women, **a.**
25 : 18. Abigail took wine, corn on **a.**
27 : 9 David took away oxen, **a.**
2 S. 16 : 2. The **a.** for king's househ.
2 K. 4 : 22. Send me one of the **a.**
7 : 7. left tents, horses, **a.** and fled
10. no man there, but horses, **a.**
1 Ch 5 : 21. they took of **a.** 2,000
12 : 40. they nigh brought bread on
27 : 30. over the **a.** was Jehdeiah [a.
2 Ch. 28 : 15. carried feeble upon **a.**
Ezr. 2 : 67. Their camels, 435 ; **a.**,
6,720, Ne. 7 : 69. [lading **a.**
Ne. 13 : 15. on sab., bringing sheaves,
Jb. 1 : 3. Job. His substance 500 she **a.**
14. oxen, **a.** ; Sabeans took [a.
42 : 12. Job, 6,000 camels, 1,000 she
Is. 21 : 7. watchman saw chariot of **a.**
Eze. 23 : 20. whose flesh as flesh of **a.**

ASSAULT. [Noun.]

Ac. 14 : 5. an **a.** made of Jews with

ASSAULT, ED. [them

Es. 8 : 11. to slay all that would **a.**
Ac. 17 : 5. Jews a-d house of Jason

ASSAY, ED, ING. [tion

De. 4 : 34. hath God a-d to take na-
1 S. 17 : 39. David a-d to go [thee
Jb. 4 : 2. If we **a.** to commune with
Ac. 9 : 26. Saul a-d to join disciples
16 : 7. they a-d to go into Bithynia
He. 11 : 29. Egypt-s a-g, were drowned

ASSEMBLE. [5.

2 S. 20 : 4. **a.** me the men of Judah,
Ps. 2 : † 1. Why do the heathen **a.**
Is. 11 : 12. he shall **a.** outcasts of Is-
Je. 12 : 9. **a.** beasts to devour [rael
21 : 4. I will **a.** them into this city
Eze. 11 : 17. **a.** you out of countries
Da. 11 : 10. **a.** a multitude of forces
Jo. 2 : 16. **a.** elders, gather children
Mi. 2 : 12. I will **a.**, O Jacob, all of
4 : 6. will I **a.** her that halteth, and
Zph. 3 : 8. that I may **a.** kingdoms

ASSEMBLE themselves or yourselves.

Nu. 10 : 3. when blow, assembly **a. t.**
Is. 45 : 20. **a. y.** ye that are escaped
48 : 14 All ye, **a. y.**, and hear
Je. 4 : 5. **a. y.**, let us go into the de-
fenced cities, 8 : 14. [**a. y.** to my
Eze. 39 : 17. Speak to every beast,
Ho. 7 : 14. they **a. t.** for corn, wine
Jo. 3 : 11. **a. y.**, come, all ye heathen
Am. 3 : 9. **a. y.** upon mts. of Samaria

ASSEMBLED. [tabern.

Ex. 38 : 8. women which **a.** at door of
Nu. 1 : 18. **a.** all congreg-n together
Jos. 11 : † 5. when all these kings **a.**
18 : 1. Isr **a.** together at Shiloh
1 S. 2 : 22. lay with women that **a.**
1 K. 8 : 1. Solomon **a.** elders of Israel, 2. 2 Ch. 5 : 2, 3.
5. congregation that were **a.** were
before ark, 2 Ch. 5 : 6. [Judah
12 : 21. Rehoboam **a.** all house of
1 Ch 15 : 4. David **a.** child-n of Aaron
28 : 1 David **a.** all princes of Israel
2 Ch. 30 : 13. **a.** people to keep feast
Ezr. 9 : 4. **a.** every one that trembled
10 : 1. Ezra had prayed, **a.** a cong-n
Ne. 9 : 1. Israel were **a.** with fasting
Es. 9 : 18. Jews at Shushan **a.** to-
Ps. 48 : 4. For, lo, kings were **a.** [gether
Is. 43 : 9. let the people be **a.** [a.
Eze. 38 : 7. all thy company that are
Da. 6 : 6. princes **a.** together, 15.
11. men **a.**, found Daniel praying
Mat. 26 : 3. **a.** together chief priests
57. the elders were **a.**, Mk. 14 : 53.
28 : 12. when **a.**, gave large money
Jn 20 : 19. disciples were **a.** for fear
Ac. 1 : 4. Jes. being **a.** together with
4 : 31. the place shaken where they
were **a.** together [a. together
15 : 25. seemed good unto us, being
See **Assemble, Assembled THEMSELVES.**

ASSEMBLIES. [a.

Ne. 12 : † 25. porters keeping ward at
Ps. 86 : 14. **a.** of violent men sought
Ec. 12 : 11. as nails by masters of **a.**
Is. 1 : 13. calling of **a.** I can-t away
4 : 5. upon her **a.** a cloud by day
14 : †31. shall not be alone in his **a.**
Eze. 44 : 24. keep my laws in mine **a.**
Am. 5 : 21. not smell in y-r solemn **a.**

ASSEMBLING. [a.

Ex. 38 : 8. looking glasses of women
He. 10 : 25. Not forsaking **a.** of our-

ASSEMBLY. [selves

Ge. 28 : † 3. thou be an **a.** of people
49 : 6. unto their **a.** be not united
Ex. 12 : 6. whole **a.**, kill it in even-g
16 : 3. to kill whole **a.** with hunger
Le. 4 : 13. if the thing be hid from **a.**
8 : 4 **a.** was gathered unto the door
Nu. 8 : 9. gather the whole **a.** of Isr.
10 : 2. trumpets for calling of whole
14 : 5. fell on faces before all **a.** [a.
16 : 2. 250 princes of the **a.** [the **a.**
20 : 6. Moses and Aaron went from
8. Take the rod and gather the **a.**
De. 5 : 22. words Lord spake unto **a.**
9 : 10. spake in mount, out of fire,
in day of the **a.**, 10 : 4.-18 : 16.
Ju. 20 : 2. presented thems. in the **a.**
21 : 8. none from Jabesh-gil-d to **a.**
1 S. 17 : 47. **a.** sh. know L. saveth not
2 Ch. 30 : 23. whole **a.** took counsel
Ne. 5 : 7. I set a great **a.** ag-t them
Ps. 22 : 16. **a.** of wicked inclosed me
89 : 7 G. to be feared in **a.** of saints
107 : 32. praise him in **a.** of elders
111 : 1. praise in **a.** of upright [a.
Pr. 5 : 14. I was almost in all evil in
Je. 6 : 11. pour upon **a.** of young men
9 : 2. be an **a.** of treacherous men
15 : 17. I sat not in **a.** of mockers
26 : 17. elders spake to all the **a.**
50 : 9. ag. Bab-n **a.** of great nations
La. 1 : 15. **a.** to crush my young men
2 : 6. he hath destroyed places of **a.**
Eze. 13 : 9. they shall not be in the **a.**
23 : 24. ag-t Aholibah with an **a.**
Ac. 19 : 32. **a.** was confused ; part
39. it be determined in a lawful **a.**
41. had spoken, he dismissed **a.**
He. 12 : 23. general **a.** of firstborn
Ja. 2 : 2. unto your **a.** man with gold
See **SOLEMN** assembly, ies.

ASSENT. [one a

2 Ch. 18 : 12. declare to king with

ASSENTED. [quired

Lu. 23 : † 24. Pilate **a.** as they re-
Ac. 24 : 9. Jews **a.** that these were so

AS'SHUR.
Ge. 10 : 11. went A. builded Nineveh
22. The children of Shem ; Elam, A., 1 Ch. 1 : 17.

AS'SHUR,[1] AS'SUR.[2]
[Assyria or Assyrians.]
Nu. 24 : 22. until A.[1] carry thee cap.
24. ships fr. Chittim sh. afflict A.[1]
Ezr. 4 : 2. Esar-haddon, king of A.[2]
Ps. 83 : 8. A.[2] also is joined with them
Is. 10 : † 5. O A., rod of mine anger
Eze. 23 : † 7. whoredoms with the choice of chil. of A.[1] [thy merc.
27 : 23. merchants of Sheba, A.[1],
32 : 22. A.[1] is there and company
Ho. 14 : 3. A.[1] shall not save us ; we

ASSHU'RIM. [shim
Ge. 25 : 3. sons of Dedan, A., Letu-

ASSIGNED. [Pha.
Ge. 47 : 22. priests had portion a. of
Jos. 20 : 8. a. Bezer in wilderness
2 S. 11 : 16. Joab a. Uriah unto pla.

AS'SIR.
Ex. 6 : 24. the sons of Korah ; A. and Elkanah, 1 Ch. 6 : 22.
1 Ch. 3 : 17. sons of Jeconiah ; A.
6 : 23. Ebiasaph, A. his son, 37.

ASSIST.
Ro. 16 : 2. a. her in whatso. business

ASSOCIATE.
Is. 8 : 9. a. yourselves, ye people [a.
Da. 11 : † 6. in end of years they sh.

AS'SOS. [tending
Ac. 20 : 13. we sailed unto A., in-
14. Paul met with us at A., we

ASSUAGE, ED.
Ge. 8 : 1. a wind, and waters were a-d
Jb. 16 : 5. moving of my lips a. grief
6. Tho. I speak, my grief not a-d

AS'SUR. See ASSHUR.

ASSURANCE. [life
De. 28 : 66. shalt have none a. of thy
Is. 32 : 17. effect of righteousn-s, a.
Ac. 17 : 31. hath given a. unto all
Col. 2 : 2. riches of full a. of under-g
1 Th. 1 : 5. gospel came in much a.
He. 6 : 11. to full a. of hope unto end
10 : 22. draw near in full a. of faith

ASSURE.
1 Jn. 3 : 19. we shall a. our hearts

ASSURED.
Le. 27 : 19. and it shall be a. to him
Je. 14 : 13. I will give you a. peace
Ro. 14 : † 5. Let every man be fully a.
2 Ti. 3 : 14. things thou hast been a.

ASSUREDLY. [me
1 S. 28 : 1. Know a. thou sh. go with
1 K. 1 : 13. a. Solomon thy son shall reign, 17. 30. [land a.
Je. 32 : 41. I will plant them in this
38 : 17 If thou a. go unto king of B.
49 : 12. they have a. drunken and
Ac. 2 : 36. let house of Israel know a.
16 : 10. a. gathering that L. called

ASSWAGE. See ASSUAGE.

ASSYR'IA. [A.
Ge. 2 : 14. Hiddekel goeth toward
25 : 18. dwelt as thou goest tow. A.
2 K. 15 : 29. carried them captive to A., 17 : 6, 23.-18 : 11. [of A.
Is. 7 : 18. hiss for the bee in the land
11 : 11. remnant of peo. from A., 16.
19 : 23. highway out of Eg. to A. (2)
24. Israel be third with Eg. and A.
25. Blessed be A., the work of my
27 : 13. ready to perish in A. [hands
Je. 2 : 18. what thou to do in way of
36. ashamed of Egypt as of A. [A.
Eze. 23 : 7. whoredoms wi. men of A.
Ho. 7 : 11. they call to Eg., go to A.
8 : 9. they are gone to A., a wild ass
9 : 3. shall eat unclean things in A.
10 : 6. It shall be carried unto A.
11 : 11. sh. tremble as dove out of A.
Mi. 5 : 6. shall waste the land of A.
7 : 12. that day he shall come fr. A.
Zph. 2 : 13. And he will destroy A.
Zch. 10 : 10. I will gather out of A.
11. pride of A. shall be bro-t down

King, s[2] of ASSYR'IA.
2 K. 15 : 20, So the - A. turned back
29. Tiglath-p-r - A. took Gilead, Galilee, 2 Ch. 28 : 20. [28 : 16.[2]
16 : 7. So Ahaz sent to - A., 2 Ch.
9. - A. went ag-t Damascus (2) [A.
10. Ahaz went to meet Tiglath.-
17 : 3. Ag-t Hoshea came the - A.
4. Hoshea, - A. shut in prison (3)
5. - A. to Samaria, besieged it, 18 : 9.
24. - A. bro-t men, placed in Sam.
26. spake to - A. The nations in Sa.
27. - A. commanded, Carry one of
18 : 7. Hez-h rebelled ag. - A [priests
13. Sennach-b - A. come against Judah, 2 Ch. 32 : 1. Is. 36 : 1.
14. the - A. appointed unto Hezekiah 300 talents (2) [- A.
16. cut gold from temple, gave to
17. the - A. sent Tartan to Hezekiah, 2 Ch. 32 : 9. Is. 36 : 2.
28. saying, Hear the word of the great king, the - A., Is. 36 : 13.
30. not be delivered into hand of - A., 19 : 10. 2 Ch. 32 : 11. Is 37 : 10.
31. saith - A., Make agreement with me, Is. 36 : 16. [Is. 37 : 4.
19 : 4. - A. sent to reproach God,
6. the servants of - A. have blasphemed me, Is. 37 : 6. [Is. 37 : 8
8. found - A, warring ag. Libnah,
11. heard - A.[2] have done to all lands, Is. 37 : 11. [Is. 37 : 18.
17. - A.[2] have destroyed nations,
20. thou hast prayed ag-t - A., I have heard, Is. 37 : 21. [Is. 37 : 37.
36. So Sennach-b - A. departed,
20 : 6. I will deliver thee out of hand of - A., Is. 38 : 6. [- A.
23 : 29. king of Eg. went up against
1 Ch. 5 : 6. Beerah - A. carried capt.
26. God stirred up Pul - A. (2)
2 Ch. 28 : 21. out of house of Lord, gave it unto - A. [A.[2]
30 : 6. are escaped out of hand of -
32 : 4. saying, Why sho - A.[2] come
10. saith - A., Wh-on do ye trust, 2 K. 18 : 19. Is. 36 : 4. [- A.
21. angel cut off mighty men of
22. Lord saved Hezekiah from - A.
Ne. 9 : 32. trouble since time of - A.[2]
Is. 8 : 4. spoil of Samaria before - A.
7. Lord bringeth upon them - A.
20 : 1. when Sargon - A. sent Tart.
36 : 18. Hath any gods delivered out of the hand of - A.? [O - A.
Na. 3 : 18. thy shepherds slumber,
See **KING of Assyria.**

ASSYRIAN, S.
2 K. 19 : 35. smote in the camp of A-s 185,000 men, Is. 37 : 36.
Is. 10 : 5. O A., the rod of mine anger
24. O my peo., be not afraid of A.
14 : 25. I will break A. in my land
19 : 23. A. shall come into Egypt, Eg-ns shall serve with A-s [it
23 : 13. people not, till A. founded
30 : 31. shall the A. be beaten down
31 : 8. Then shall A. fall with sword
52 : 4. A. oppressed without cause
La. 5 : 6. We have given hand to A-s
Eze. 16 : 28. hast played whore with
23 : 5. She doted on A-s, 9, 12. [A-s
9. I delivered her into hand of A-s
23. I will bring against thee all A-s
31 : 3. A. was a cedar in Lebanon
Ho. 5 : 13. went Ephraim to the A.
11 : 5. but the A. shall be his king
12 : 1. I do make covenant with A-s
Mi. 5 : 5. be peace when A. sh. come
6. shall he deliver us from the A.

AS'TAROTH.
See ASHTAROTH.

ASTONIED. [a., 4.
Ezr. 9 : 3. I plucked off my hair, sat
Jb. 17 : 8. Upright men be a. at this
18 : 20. that come after shall be a.
Is. 52 : 14. As many were a. at thee
Je 14 : 9. why thou be as a man a.
Eze. 4 : 17. may be a. one with ano.
Da. 3 : 24. Neb-r was a., rose in haste
4 : 19. Daniel was a. for one hour
5 : 9. countenance changed, lords

ASTONISHED. [a.
Le. 26 : 32. your enemies shall be a.
1 K. 9 : 8. that passeth by shall be a., Je. 18 : 16 -19 : 8. -49 : 17. -50:
Jb 21 : 5. Mark me, and be a. [13.
26 : 11. pillars of heaven are a. at
Je. 2 : 12. Be a., O ye heavens, at this
4 : 9. priests be a., and prophets
Eze. 3 : 15. I remained a. seven days
26 : 16. princes shall be a. at thee
27 : 35. inhabitants of isles sh. be a.
28 : 19. that know thee shall be a.
Da. 8 : 27. I Daniel was a. at vision
Mat. 7 : 28. people were a. at his doctrine, 13 : 54. - 22 : 33. Mk. 1 : 22.-6 : 2.-11 : 18. Lu. 4 : 32.
Mk. 5 : 42. a. with great astonishm-t
7 : 37. beyond measure a., 10 : 26.
10 : 24. discip. were a. at his words
Lu. 2 : 47. a. at his understanding
5 : 9. he was a. at draught of fishes
8 : 56. her parents were a. ; but he
24 : 22. certain women made us a.
Ac. 9 : 6. Saul, trembling and a.. said
10 : 45. they of the circumcision which believed were a. [were a.
12 : 16. when they saw Peter they
13 : 12. deputy believed, being a.

ASTONISHETH.
Da. 11 : † 31. they shall place the abomination that a., 12 : † 11.

ASTONISHMENT.
De. 28 : 28. Lord sh. smite thee with
37. thou shalt become an a. [a.
2 Ch. 7 : 21. this house sh. be an a.
29 : 8. he hath delivered them to a.
Ps. 60 : 3. made us drink wine of a.
Je. 5 : † 30. a. is committed in land
8 : 21. a. hath taken hold on me
25 : 9. I will make them an a., 18.
11. land shall be desolation and a.
29 : 18. I will deliv. them to be an a.
42 : 18. ye shall be an a., 44 : 12
44 : 22. therefore is your land an a.
51 : 37. Babylon shall become an a.
41. how is Babylon become an a.
Eze. 4 : 16. they shall drink water by measure, and with a., 12 : 19.
5 : 15. be an a. unto nations about
23 : 33. be filled with cup of a. and
Mi. 6 : † 16. that I make thee an a.
Zch. 12 : 4. smite every horse with a.
Mk. 5 : 42. astonished with great a.

ASTRAY. [a.
Ex. 23 : 4. if meet enemy's ass going
1 Pe. 2 : 25. were as sheep going a.
See **GO astray, GONE astray, WENT astray.**

ASTROLOGER, S.
Is. 47 : 13. Let now the a-s save thee
Da. 1 : 20. ten times better than a-s
2 : 2. commanded to call a-s, 5 : 7.
10. no king asked such at any a.
27. secrets cannot a-s shew unto
4 : 7. came in magicians, a-s [king
5 : 11. master of the magicians, a-s
15. wise men, a-s could not shew

ASUNDER. [5 : 8.
Le. 1 : 17. he shall not divide it a.,
Nu. 16 : 31. ground clave a. und. them
2 K. 2 : 11. and parted them both a.
Jb. 16 : 12. but he hath broken me
13. he cleaveth my reins a. [a.
Ps. 2 : 3. Let us break their bands a.
Eze. 30 : 16. and No shall be rent a.
Ha. 3 : 6. he drove a. the nations
Mat. 19 : 6. God hath joined, let not man put a., Mk 10 : 9. [a.
Mk. 5 : 4. chains had been plucked

Ac. 1 : 18. falling headlong burst a.
Ac. 15 : 39. departed a., one fr other
He. 4 : 12. dividing a. of soul and [spirit
11 : 37. they were sawn a.
See **CUT asunder.**

ASUP'PIM.
1 Ch. 26 : 15. to her sons, house of [A.
17. Levites toward A., two and two

ASYN'CRITUS.
Ro. 16 : 14. Salute A., Phlegon

AT.
See ALL, DAY, DOCTRINE, DOOR, DOORS, FEAST, 8, FEET, GATE, GATES, HOME, LAST, ME, ONCE, RECEIPT, SEASON, TIME.
See **At FIRST, At HIM, At LEAST, STOOD at, At THEE, At THEM, At US.**

A'TAD.
Ge. 50 : 10. came to threshingfloor [of A.
11. saw mourning in the floor of A.

AT'ARAH.
1 Ch. 2 : 26. wife A.; she mother of [Onam

AT'ARITES,
or **AT'AROTH.**
1 Ch. 2 : 54. † of Salma; A., house of [Joab

AT'AROTH.
Nu. 32 : 3. A. is land for cattle
34. children of Gad built Dibon, [A.
Jos. 16 : 2. lot of Joseph along to A.
7. border of Ephraim went to A.

AT'AROTH-A'DAR,[1]
or **AT'AROTH-AD'DAR.**[2]
Jos. 16 : 5. border of Ephr. on east
18 : 13. border descended to A.[1] [A.[2]

ATE.
Ps. 106 : 28. They a. sacrifices of the [dead
Da 10 : 3. I a. no pleasant bread
Re. 10 : 10. I took the book and a. it

A'TER.
Ezr. 2 : 16. chil. of A. of Hezekiah, ninety eight, Ne. 7 : 21. [45.
42. the porters; chil. of A., Ne. 7 :
Ne. 10 : 17. that sealed were A., Az- [zur

A'THACH.
1 S. 30 : 30. of spoil to them in A.

ATHAI'AH.
Ne. 11 : 4. at Jerus. dwelt A., son of

ATHALI'AH. [Man.]
1 Ch 8 : 26. A., sons of Jeroham
Ezr. 8 : 7. Jeshaiah, son of A., and

ATHALI'AH. [Woman.]
2 K. 8 : 26. Ahaziah, his mother's name A., 2 Ch. 22 : 2. [Ch. 22 : 10.
11 : 1. A. destroyed seed royal, 2
2. hid Joash from A., 2 Ch. 22 : 11.
3. A. did reign over the land, 2 Ch. 22 : 12. [2 Ch. 23 : 12.
13. when A. heard noise of guard,
14. A. rent her clothes, and cried, Treason, 2 Ch. 23 : 13. [23 : 21.
20. slew A. beside k.'s house, 2 Ch.
2 Ch. 24 : 7. sons of A., that wicked [wom.

ATHE'NIANS.
Ac. 17 : 21. A. spent their time to tell [or hear

ATH'ENS.
Ac. 17 : 15. conducted Paul unto A.
16. Now while Paul waited at A.
22. men of A., ye are superstitious
18 : 1. Paul departed from A. and
1 Th. 3 : 1. thought good to be left [at A.

ATHIRST.
Ju. 15 : 18. Samson was sore a. and
Ru. 2 : 9. when a. go unto the vessels
Mat. 25 : 44. L., when saw we thee a.
Re. 21 : 6. I will give unto him that
22 : 17. let him that is a. come [is a.

ATH'LAI.
Ezr. 10 : 28. Of the sons of Bebai, A.

ATONEMENT.
Ex. 29 : 33. eat things wherewith a.
36. offer every day bullock for a.; cleanse altar when a. made
37. Seven days make a. for altar
30 : 15. half a shekel to make a. for your souls, 16. [tabernacle
16. take a. money for service of
Ex. 32 : 30. peradv. I make a. for y-r
Le. 1 : 4. sh. be accepted to make a.
4 : 20. the priest shall make an a. for them, 26, 31, 35.-5 : 6, 10, 13, 16, 18.-6 : 7.-14 : 18, 19, 20, 31. -15 : 15.-19 : 22. Nu. 15 : 25.
7 : 7. priest that maketh a. shall
8 : 34. Lord commanded to make a.
9 : 7. make a. for thyself and a. for them, 16 : 24. [make a.
10 : 17. holy, God hath given it to
12 : 7. make a. for her, 8.-15 : 30.
14 : 21. one lamb to make a. for him
29. oil upon head to make a. for
53. shall make an a. for the house
16 : 6. Aaron shall make an a. for himself and house, 11, 17.
10. the scapegoat alive to make an a. with him [place
16. he shall make a. for the holy
17. when he goeth in to make an a.
18. he shall go unto the altar and make a. for it [make a.
27. whose blood was brought in to
30. priest sh. make a. for you, 32.
33. he sh. make a. for sanctuary, a. for tabernacle, a. for priests
34. statute to make a. once a year
17 : 11. it is blood that maketh an a. for the soul (2) [day of a.
23 : 27. tenth day of 7th month be
28. do no work; is a day of a. to make a. for you [sound
25 : 9. day of a. make the trumpet
Nu. 5 : 8. ram of a. whereby an a.
6 : 11. a. for him, he sinned by the [dead
8 : 12. to make a. for Levites
19. Levites to make a. for Israel
21. Levites, Aaron made a. for th.
15 : 28. priest make a. for soul that sinneth ignorantly (2) [for them
16 : 46. go quickly, and make an a.
47. Aaron made a. for the people
25 : 13. Phinehas, bec. he made a.
28 : 22. one goat to make a. for you,
29 : 5. kid to make an a. for you [30.
11. beside the sin offering of a.
31 : 50. chains, earrings, to make a.
2 S. 21 : 3. wherew. shall I make a.?
1 Ch. 6 : 49. Aa. and sons to make a.
2 Ch 29 : 24. killed goats to make a.
Ne. 10 : 33. offerings to make a. for [Isr.
Jb. 33 : †24. I have found an a.
Ro. 5 : 11. by whom we received a.

ATONEMENT, S.
Ex. 30 : 10. Aaron make a. once a year with blood of sin offerings [of a-s (3)

AT'ROTH.
Nu. 32 : 35. the chil. of Gad built A.,

AT'TAI.
1 Ch. 2 : 35. to Jarha to wife; she [Shophan
36. A. begat Nathan [bare A.
12 : 11. unto David men of might, A. the sixth [bare him A.
2 Ch. 11 : 20. took Maachah; which

ATTAIN.
Ps. 139 : 6. high, I cannot a. unto it
Pr. 1 : 5. and man of understanding shall a. unto wise counsels
Eze. 46 : 7. acc-g as his hand shall a.
Ho. 8 : 5. ere they a. to innocency?
Ac. 27 : 12. if might a. to Phenice
Ph. 3 : 11. I might a. unto resurrec- [tion of

ATTAINED.
Ge. 47 : 9. years of my life not a. unto years of my fathers [ficiency
Le. 25 : † 26. if his hand hath a. suf-
2 S. 23 : 19. he a. not unto the first three, 23. 1 Ch. 11 : 21, 25.
Ro. 9 : 30. That the Gentiles have a. to righteousness [righteousness
31. Israel hath not a. to the law of
Ph. 3 : 12. Not as though I had a.
16. whereto we have a. let us walk
1 Ti. 4 : 6. doctrine whereunto hast [a.

ATTA'LIA.
Ac. 14 : 25. they went down into A.

ATTEND.
Es. 4 : 5. he appointed to a. upon [her
Ps. 17 : 1. O Lord, a. unto my cry
61 : 1.-142 : 6. [complaint
55 : 2. a. unto me: I mourn in my
86 : 6. a. to voice of my supplications
Pr. 4 : 1. a. to know understanding
20. My son a. to my words; incline
5 : 1. My son, a. unto my wisdom
7 : 24. O ye chil. a. to words of my
1 Co. 7 : 35. a. upon L. with-t distrac- [tion

ATTENDANCE.
1 K. 10 : 5. a. of his ministers, 2 Ch. [9 : 4.
1 Ti. 4 : 13. give a. to reading
He. 7 : 13. no man gave a. at altar

ATTENDED, ING.
Jb. 32 : 12. I a-d, none convinced [Job
Ps. 66 : 19. he hath a-d to my prayer
Ac. 16 : 14. she a-d unto things spok.
Ro. 13 : 6. ministers a-g continually

ATTENT.
2 Ch. 6 : 40. let ears be a. unto prayer
7 : 15. mine ears a. unto the prayer

ATTENTIVE, LY.
Ne. 1 : 11. O Lord, let thine ear be a. to prayer, 6. Ps. 130 : 2. [48.
8 : 3. all the people were a., Lu. 19 :
Jb. 37 : 2. Hear a-y noise of his voice

ATTENTION.
1 K. 18 : † 29. there was nei. voice [nor a.
2 K. 4 : † 31. staff upon child; neither voice nor a.

ATTIRE. [Noun.]
Pr. 7 : 10. a woman with a. of harlot
Je. 2 : 32. Can a bride forget her a.
Eze. 23 : 15. exceeding in dyed a. up- [on heads

ATTIRED.
Le. 16 : 4. Aaron with mitre shall be [a.

ATTRIBUTED.
Jb. 1 : † 22. Job not a. folly to God

AUDIENCE.
Ge. 23 : 10. Abr. in the a. of chil. of [Heth
13. Abr. unto Ephron in a. of peo.,
Ex. 24 : 7. Mos. read in a. of peo. [16.
1 S. 25 : 24. let thine handmaid speak in thine a. [command-ts
1 Ch. 28 : 8. in a. of our God seek for
Ne. 13 : 1. read in book of Moses in a. of the people [people
Lu. 7 : 1. ended his sayings in a. of
20 : 45. in a. of peo. said to disciples
Ac. 13 : 16. ye that fear God, give a.
15 : 12. gave a. to Barnabas, Paul
22 : 22. gave him a. unto this word

AUGHT. [Noun.]
Ge. 39 : 6. knew not a. he had, save
47 : 18. not a. left, but our bodies
Ex. 5 : 8. sh. not diminish a., 11, 19.
12 : 46. not carry forth a. of flesh
22 : 14. if man borrow a. of neighb.
29 : 34. if a. of flesh of consecrations remain, then burn [cass
Le. 11 : 25 whoso beareth a. of car-
19 : 6. if a. remain until third day
25 : 14. if thou sell a. or buyest a.
27 : 31. if a man will redeem a. of
Nu. 15 : 24 if a. be committed by ignorance, the congr-n [tuously
30. soul that doeth a. presump-
30 : 6. or uttered a. out of her lips
De. 4 : 2. sh. not add, nei. diminish a.
15 : 2. that lendeth a. unto neighb.
26 : 14. neith. taken a. for unclean use, nor given a. for the dead
Jos. 21 : 45. failed not a. of any good
Ru. 1 : 17. if a. but death part thee
1 S. 12 : 4. nei. taken a. of any man's
5. ye not found a. in my hand
25 : 7. nei. was a. missing [of spoil
30 : 22. we will not give them a.
2 S. 3 : 35. If I taste bread or a. else
14 : 10. Whoso-r saith a. unto thee
19. none can turn from a. my lord hath spoken [thee
Mat. 5 : 23. that brother hath [a. ag.
21 : 3. if any man say a. unto you
Mk. 7 : 12. suf. him no more to do a.

Mk. 8 : 23. asked him if he saw **a.**
11 : 25.forgive, if ye have **a.** against
Ju. 4 : 33. any bro-t him **a.** to eat?
Ac. 4 : 32. neith. said any **a.** was his
24 : 19. if they had **a.** against me
28 : 19. not **a.** to accuse my nation
Phm. 18. if he oweth thee **a.**, put on

AUGMENT. [the L.
Nu. 32: 14. to **a.** the fierce anger of

AUGUS'TUS. [A.
Lu. 2 : 1. went a decree from Cesar
Ac. 25 : 21. Paul appealed unto A., 25.
27 : 1. Julius, a centurion of A-'s

AUL. See AWL. [band

AUNT. [thy **a.**
Le. 18 : 14. not to his wife; she is

AUSTERE. [22.
Lu. 19 : 21. bec. thou art an **a.** man,

AUTHOR.
Ac. 3 . † 15. ye killed the A. of life
1 Co. 14 : 33. God not **a.** of confusion
He. 5 : 9. became the **a.** of salvation
12 : 2. Jes., **a.** and finisher of faith

AUTHORITY, IES.
Es. 9 : 29. Esther wrote with all **a.**
Pr. 29 : 2. when righteous are in **a.**
Mat. 7 : 29. as one having **a.**, Mk. 1:
8 : 9. am man under **a.**, Lu. 7:8.[22.
20 : 25. great exercise **a.**, Mk. 10:42.
21 : 23. By what **a.** doest thou these
things? and who gave thee this
a.? Mk. 11 : 28 (2). Lu. 20 : 2(2).
24. I will tell you by what **a.** I do
these things, Mk. 11 : 29.
27. Neither tell I by what **a.** I do
these, Mk. 11 : 33. Lu. 20 : 8.
Mk. 1 : 27. with **a.** commandeth he
unclean spirits, Lu. 4 : 36.
13 : 34. who gave **a.** to his servants
Lu. 9 : 1. he gave **a.** over all devils
19 : 17. have thou **a.** over ten cities
20 : 20. deliver him unto **a.** of gov-r
22 : 25. exercise **a.** called benefac-rs
Jn. 5 : 27. **a.** to execute judgment
Ac. 8 : 27. eunuch of great **a.** under
9 : 14. he hath **a.** to bind. 26: 10, 12.
1 Co. 15 : 24. sh. have put down all **a.**
2 Co. 10 : 8. I should boast more of **a.**
1 Th. 2 : † 6 we might have used **a.**
1 Ti. 2 : 2. supplication for all in **a.**
12. I suffer not woman to usurp **a.**
Tit. 2 : 15. exhort, rebuke with all **a.**
1 Pe. 3 : 22. **a**-s made subject unto
Re. 13 : 2. dragon gave him great **a.**

A'VA = I'VAH.
2 K. 17 : 24. king bring men from A.
18 : † 34. where are the gods of A.?

AVAILETH.
Es. 5 : 13. this **a.** me nothing, so long
Ga. 5 : 6. in Christ nei. circumcision
a. any thing, 6 : 15. [much
Ja. 5 : 16. prayer of a righteous **a.**

A'VEN. [fall
Eze. 30 : 17. young men of A. shall
Ho. 10 : 8. The high places of A. sh.
be destroyed [from A.
Am. 1 : 5. I will cut off inhabitant
See BETH-AVEN, BIKATH-AVEN.

AVENGE.
Le. 19 : 18. Thou shalt not **a.** nor
26 : 25. shall **a.** quarrel of my cov-t
Nu. 31 : 2. **a.** Israel of Midianites, 3.
De. 32 : 43. will **a.** blood of his serv-s
1 S. 24 : 12. the Lord **a.** me of thee
2 K. 9 : 7. smite Ahab that I may **a.**
Es. 8 : 13. Jews to **a.** themselves on
Is. 1 : 24. I will **a.** me of enemies
Je. 46 : 10. day of L., that he may **a.**
Ho. 1 : 4. I will **a.** blood of Jezreel
Lu. 18 : 3. **a.** me of mine adversary
5. bec. widow troubleth I **a.** her
7. shall not God **a.** his own elect
8. that he will **a.** them speedily
Ro. 12 : 19. beloved, **a.** not yoursel-s
Re. 6 : 10. how long dost not **a.** our

AVENGED. [blood
Ge. 4 : 24. If Cain sh. be **a.** sevenfold

Ex. 21 : † 20. he shall be surely **a.**
Jos. 10 : 13. sun stood until people **a.**
Ju. 15 : 7. done this, yet I will be **a.**
16 : 28. be **a.** of Philist. for my eyes
1 S. 14 : 24. that I may be **a.** on mine
18 : 25. 100 foreskins, to be **a.** [self
25 : 31. that my lord hath **a.** him-
2 S. 4 : 8. the Lord hath **a.** my lord
18 : 19. L. hath **a.** him of enemies
31. L. hath **a.** thee this day of all
Je. 5 : 9. shall not my soul be **a.** on
such a nation as this? 29.-9 : 9.
Ac. 7 : 24. Moses **a.** him oppressed
Re. 18 : 20. God hath **a.** you on her
19 : 2. hath **a.** blood of his servants

AVENGEMENT. [me
2 S. 22 : † 48. God that giveth **a.** for

AVENGER.
Nu. 35 : 12. cities for refuge from
the **a.**, Jos. 20 : 3.
Ps. 8 : 2. mightest still the enemy
44 : 16. by reason of the **a.** [and **a.**
1 Th. 4 : 6. Lord is the **a.** of all such

AVENGER of blood.
De. 19 : 6. Lest the **a.** - pursue slayer
12. deliver him into hand of **a.** -
Jos. 20 : 3. sh. be your refuge fr. **a.** -
5. if the **a.** - pursue after him
9. not die by the hand of the **a.** -

AVENGETH, ING. [Isr.
Ju. 5 : 2. Praise Lord for the **a**-g of
1 S. 25 : 26. L. withholden thee fr. **a**-g
33. blessed wh. kept me from **a**-g
2 S. 22 : 48. God that **a**-h me, Ps. 18 : 47.

AVERSE.
Mi. 2 : 8. pass as men **a.** from war

A'VIM. [Place.]
Jos. 18 : 23. cities of Benj-n, A., Parah

A'VIM, A'VITES.
De. 2 : 23. A., wh. dwelt in Hazerim
Jos. 13 : 3. the Ekronites; also A-s
2 K. 17 : 31. A-s made Nibhaz and

A'VITH. [46.
Ge. 36 : 35. his city was A., 1 Ch. 1 :

AVOID, ED, ING. [ence
1 S. 18 : 11. David **a**-d out of his pres-
Pr. 4 : 15. **a.** it, pass not by it [**a.**
Ro. 16 : 17. which cause divisions,
1 Co. 7 : 2. **a.** fornication [blame
2 Co. 8 : 20. **a**-g this, that no man
1 Ti. 6 : 20. **a**-g profane babblings
2 Ti. 2 : 23. unlearned questions **a.**
Tit. 3 : 9. **a.** foolish questions and

AVOUCHED. [God
De. 26 : 17. hast **a.** Lord to be thy
18. Lord **a.** thee to be his people

AWAIT = WAIT. [Saul
Ac. 9 : 24. laying **a.** was known of

AWAKE.
Ju. 5 : 12. **a.**, **a.**, Deborah; **a.**, **a.**
Jb. 8 : 6. he would **a.** for thee[not **a.**
14 : 12. till heavens be no more.
19 : † 26. **a.**, tho. body be destroyed
Ps. 7 : 6. **a.** for me to judgment, 35 :
17 : 15. I **a.** with thy likeness [23
44 : 23. **a.**, why sleepest thou, O L.?
57 : 8. **a.** up, my glory; **a.**, psaltery
and harp; I will **a.** early, 108 : 2.
59 : 4. They prepare : **a.** to help me
5. O Lord, **a.** to visit the heathen
139 : 18. when I **a.** I am with thee
Pr. 23 : 35. when shall I **a.**? [8 : 4.
Can. 2 : 7. nor **a.** my love, till, 3 : 5.-
4 : 16. **a.**, O north wind : and come
Is. 26 : 19. **a.** ye that dwell in dust
51 : 9. **a.**, **a.**, put on strength, O
arm of the Lord; **a.**, as in the
ancient days, 52 : 1.
17. **a.**, **a.**, stand up, O Jerusalem
Da. 12 : 2. that sleep in dust shall **a.**
Jo. 1 : 5. **a.**, ye drunkards, and weep
Ha. 2 : 7. not **a.** that shall vex thee?
19. woe, that saith to the wood, **a.**
Zch. 13 : 7. **a.**, O sword, ag. shepherd
Mk. 4 : 38. was asleep, they **a.** him
Lu. 9 : 32. when **a.**, they saw his glo.
Jn. 11 : 11. I go that I may **a.** him

Ro. 13 : 11. now it is high time to **a.**
1 Co. 15 : 34. **a.** to righteousness
Ep. 5 : 14. **a.**, thou that sleepest, rise
2 Ti. 2 : † 26. may **a.** thems. out of

AWAKED. [snare
Ge. 28 : 16. Jacob **a.** out of his sleep
Ju. 16 : 14. Samson **a.**, went with pin
1 S. 26 : 12. no man knew it, nei. **a.**
1 K. 18 : 27. sleepeth and must be **a.**
2 K. 4 : 31. the child is not **a.** [me
Ps. 3 : 5. slept; **a.**; for L. sustained
78 : 65. Lord **a.** as one out of sleep
Je. 31 : 26. Upon this I **a.**, beheld

AWAKEST, ETH, ING.
Ps. 73 : 20. As a dream when one **a**-h;
so, O Lord, when thou **a**-t[thee
Pr. 6 : 22. when thou **a**-t, talk with
Is. 29 : 8. he **a**-h his soul is empty;
he **a**-h, and behold he is faint
Eze. 7 : † 6. the end; it **a**-h ag. thee
Ac. 16 : 27. keeper of the prison **a**-g

AWARE.
Can. 6 : 12. Or ever I was **a.**, my soul
Je. 50 : 24. O Bab., thou wast not **a.**
Mat. 24 : 50. in an hour that he is
not **a.** of, Lu. 12 : 46.[are not **a.**
Lu. 11 : 44. men that walk over them
See WARE.

AWAY. [**a.**
Ge. 15 : 11. fowls, Abr. drove them
31 : 20. Jacob stole **a.** unawares to
26. hast stolen **a.** unawares to me
40 : 15. I was stolen **a.** out of land
44 : 3. soon as light, men were sent
Ex. 2 : 17. shepherds drove th. **a.**[**a.**
19 : 24. L. said unto Moses, **a.**, get
Le. 1 : 16. pluck **a.** crop wi. feathers
25 : 25. If brother sold **a.** possess-n
Nu. 11 : 6. now our soul is dried **a.**
De. 26 : 13. thou shalt say, I have
brought **a.** hallowed things [**a.**
Ju. 5 : 21. river of Kishon swept th.
1 S. 14 : 16. the multitude melted **a.**
19 : 10. slipped **a.** out of S-'s pres.
25 : 10. be many servants nowadays
that break **a.** [en thee **a.**
2 S. 19 : 41. Why men of Judah stol-
1 K. 2 : 39. servants of Shimei ran **a.**
11 : 13. I will not rend **a.** all kingd.
14 : 8. rent kingdom **a.** fr. house of
2 K. 5 : 2. brought **a.** little maid[Da.
1 Ch. 21 : 8. do **a.** iniquity of serv-t
2 Ch. 28 : 21. Ahaz took **a.** portion
35 : 23. Have me **a.**, I am wounded
Es. 8 : 3. besought to put **a.** mischief
Jb. 9 : 26. passed **a.** as swift ships
14 : 10. But man dieth, wasteth **a.**
19. washest **a.** things which grow
20 : 8. he shall be chased **a.** as vision
28. his goods flow **a.** in day of wra.
30 : 12. youth; they push **a.** my feet
Ps. 1 : 4. The ungodly, like chaff
which the wind driveth **a.** [**a.**
34.* Abimelech; who drove David
48 : 5. were troubled, and hasted **a.**
58 : 8. As snail, let every one pass **a.**
90 : 5. carriest them **a.** as wi. flood
104 : 7. at thy thunder hasted **a.**
119 : 119. Thou puttest **a.** wicked
Pr. 10 : 3. L. casteth **a.** substance of.
19 : 26. that chaseth **a.** his mother
20 : 8. A king scattereth **a.** all evil
25 : 23. north wind driveth **a.** rain
Is. 1 : 13. assemblies I cannot **a.** wi.
25. I will purely purge **a.** thy dross
22 : 4. Th. said I, Look **a.** from me
24 : 4. earth mourneth, fadeth **a.**(2)
28 : 17. hail shall sweep **a.** refuge of
59 : 13. departing **a.** from our God
Je. 1 : 3. unto the carrying **a.** of Jerusalem captive, Mat. 1 : 17.
6 : 29. the wicked are not plucked **a.**
37 : 13. Thou fallest **a.** to Chaldeans
14. said Je., It is false; I fall not **a.**
46 : 15. Why valiant men swept **a.**?
La. 4 : 15. when they fled **a.** they
Eze. 16 : 9. I washed **a.** thy blood

Eze. 26 : 16. princes of sea lay a. robes
Ho. 6 : 4. as the early dew it goeth a.
Na. 3 : 16. the cankerworm fleeth a.
Zch. 7 : 11. they pulled a. shoulder
Mat. 13 : 19. wicked one catcheth a.
27 : 2. they led him a. to Pilate
31. they led him a. to crucify him
28 : 13. Say, disciples stole him a.
Mk. 15 : 16. led him a. unto hall ⌈a.
Lu. 4 : † 34. man wh. had devil cried,
16 : 18. Whosoever putteth a. wife
23 : 18. a. with this man, release B.
Jn. 5 : 13. Jesus conveyed himself a.
19 : 15. a. with him, a. ; crucify h.
Ac. 5 : 37. Judas drew a. much peo.
20 : 6. we sailed a. from Philippi
30. men arise to draw a. disciples
21 : 36. multitude crying, a. with
22 : 16. arise, wash a. thy sins ⌊him
22. a. with such a fellow fr. earth
Ro. 11 : 15. if casting a. be reconcil-g
2 Co. 3 : 14. same vail untaken a.
Col. 1 : 23. If in faith not moved a.
1 Pe. 1 : 24. flower thereof falleth a.
Re. 16 : 20. every island fled a., mts.
20 : 11. fr. whose face heaven fled a.

See **CARRIED away, CARRY away, CAST away, FALL away, FLEE away, GO away, GONE away, PUT away, Put away EVIL, SENT away, TAKE away, TAKEN away, TOOK away, TURN away, TURNED away, WENT away.**

See CARRIETH, CASTAWAY, CONSUME, DONE, DRAWN, DRIVE, DRIVEN, FADE, FADETH, FAR, FELL, FLED, FLY, GAT, GET, GOETH, LEAD, LED, MELT, PASSETH, PINE, ETH, PUTTING, ROLL, ED, SEND, STEAL, STEALETH, TAKETH, TURNETH, TURNING, VANISH, VANISHETH, WEAR, WIPE, WITHERED.

AWE. [Noun.]

Ps. 4 : 4. Stand in a. and sin not
33 : 8. inhab-ts of world stand in a.
119 : 161. my heart standeth in a.

AWETH.

⌈man
Pr. 17 : † 10. reproof a. more a wise

AWL = AUL.

Ex. 21 : 6. master shall bore his ear through with an a., De. 15 : 17.

AWOKE.

⌈knew
Ge. 9 : 24. Noah a. from his wine and
41 : 4. So Pharaoh a., 7, 21. ⌈son a.
Ju. 16 : 20. she said, Philist. ; Sam-
1 K. 3 : 15. Solomon a. ; was dream
Mat. 8 : 25. disciples a. him, Lu. 8 :

AWORK.

⌊24.
2 Ch. 2 : 18. overseers to set people

AXE.

⌊a.
De. 19 : 5. fetcheth stroke with an a.
20 : 19. shall not destroy trees by a.
Ju. 9 : 48. Abimelech took an a.
1 S. 13 : 20. to sharpen ev. man his a.
1 K. 6 : 7. hammer nor a. heard in
Is. 10 : 15. Sh. a. boast itself ag. him
44 : † 12. The smith wi. a. worketh
Je. 10 : 3. one cutteth a tree with a.
Mat. 3 : 10. a. is laid unto root, Lu.
See **BATTLE axe.** ⌊3 : 9.

AXE head.

2 K. 6 : 5. a. h. fell into the water

AXES.

1 S. 13 : 21. Yet they had a file for a.
2 S. 12 : 31. he put them under saws and a. of iron, 1 Ch. 20 : 3. ⌈a.
Ps. 74 : 5. famous as he had lifted up
6. break the carved work with a.
Je. 46 : 22. come ag-t her with a. as
Eze. 26 : 9. with his a. break towers

AXLETREES.

1 K. 7 : 32. a. of wheels were joined
33. a. and their naves all molten

A'ZAL.

⌈A.
Zch. 14 : 5. valley of mts. sh. reach

AZALI'AH.

⌊34 : 8.
2 K. 22 : 3. king sent son of A., 2 Ch.

AZANI'AH.

Ne. 10 : 9. Levites ; Jeshua son of A.

AZA'RAEL[1] or AZA'REEL[2]

Ne. 11 : 13. at Jerus. A.[2] son of A-h.
12 : 36. A.[1] with musical instrum-ts

AZA'REEL.

1 Ch. 12 : 6. among mighty men ; A.
25 : † 4. sons of Heman ; A. ⌈to A.
18. they cast lots. The eleventh
27 : 22. Of Dan, A. son of Jeroham
Ezr. 10 : 41. Of sons of Bani ; A.

AZARI'AH.

1 K. 4 : 2. princes Solomon had ; A.
5. A. son of Nathan, over officers
2 K. 14 : 21. people of Judah took A., made him king, 2 Ch. 26 : † 1.
15 : 1. began A. son of Amaziah to
6. rest of acts of A. written in book
7. So A. slept with his fathers ⌈ah
8. In 38th year of A. did Zachari-
17. 39th year of A. began Mena-m
23. 50th year of A. Pekahiah began
27. two and 50th year of A. Pekah
1 Ch. 2 : 8. the sons of Ethan ; A.
38. Obed begat A. ⌊ 39. A. begat H.
3 : † 11. Joram, A. his son, Joash
12. Amaziah, A. his son, Jotham
6 : 9. Ahimaaz begat A., A. begat
10. A. (he executed priest's office
11. A. begat Amaziah ⌊in Jerus.)
13. Hilkiah begat A., 9 : 11. ⌈† 24
14. A. begat | 36. A. son of Zeph.,
2 Ch. 15 : 1. Spirit of G. came upon A.
21 : 2. sons of Jehosh-t, A. (2) ⌈† 24.
22 : 6. A., son of Jehoram, 2 K. 8 :
23 : 1. took captains of hundreds, A., son of Jeroham, A. son of O.
26 : 17. A., priest, went in aft him
20. A. looked, Uzziah was leprous
28 : 12. heads of Ephr., A. son of J.
29 : 12. Levites arose ; Joel son of A.
31 : 10. A., priest of hou. of Zadok
13. A., the ruler of house of God
Ezr. 7 : 1. A. the son of Hilkiah, son
3. A. son of Meraioth, son of Zer-h
Ne. 3 : 23. After him repaired A.
24. from house of A. unto turning
7 : 7. with Zerubbabel, A., Ezr. 2 : † 2.
8 : 7. A. caused people to understand
10 : 2. those that sealed were A., Jer.
12 : 33. princes of Judah, A., Ezra
Je. 43 : 2. spake A. and proud men
Da. 1 : 6. of chil. of Judah, Daniel, A
7. gave names ; to A., of Abed-nego
11. Melzar, prince had set over A
19. among all, none like Dan-l, A.
2 : 17. Daniel make thing known to

A'ZAZ.

⌊A.
1 Ch. 5 : 8. Bela son of A., son of

AZAZI'AH.

1 Ch. 15 : 21. Jeiel, A., with harps on
27 : 20. of Ephr., Hoshea son of A.
2 Ch. 31 : 13. Jehiel, A., were over- ⌊seers

AZ'BUK.

Ne. 3 : 16. repaired Nehemiah son of

AZE'KAH.

⌊A.
Jos. 10 : 10. Lord smote them to A.
11. cast stones upon them unto A.
15 : 35. in valley, Socoh, A. ⌈and A.
1 S. 17 : 1. pitched between Shochoh
2 Ch. 11 : 9. Rehoboam built Gath, A.
Ne. 11 : 30. dwelt at A. and in villages
Je. 34 : 7. Bab-n's army fought ag.

A'ZEL.

⌊A.
1 Ch. 8 : 37. Eleasah, A. his son, 9 : 43.
38. A. had six sons (2), 9 : 44 (2).

A'ZEM or E'ZEM.

Jos. 15 : 29. cities of Judah, Iim, A.
19 : 3. chil. of Simeon had Balah, A.
1 Ch. 4 : 29. They dwelt at Bilhah, E

AZ'GAD.

⌈2,322
Ezr. 2 : 12. chil. of A. 1,222, Ne. 7 : 17.
8 : 12. of sons of A. ; Johanan, son
Ne. 10 : 15. chief of people, Bunni, A.

A'ZIEL.

⌈teries
1 Ch. 15 : 20. Zech-h, A., with psal-

AZI'ZA.

Ezr. 10 : 27. of sons of Zattu ; A.

AZ'MAVETH. [Person.]

2 S. 23 : 31. one of the thirty ; A. the Barhumite, 1 Ch. 11 : 33. ⌈Ch. 9 : 42.
1 Ch. 8 : 36. Jehoadah begat A., 1
12 : 3. came to David, the sons of A.
27 : 25. over king's treasures ; A.

AZ'MAVETH or BETH-AZ'MAVETH. [Place.]

Ezr. 2 : 24. † The children of A. forty and two, Ne. 7 : 28. B. † A. ⌈Geba, A.
Ne. 12 : 29. singers out of fields of

AZ'MON.

Nu. 34 : 4. Your border pass on to A.
5. border fetch a compass from A.
Jos. 15 : 4. border passed toward A.

AZ'NOTH-TA'BOR.

Jos. 19 : 34. coast turneth to A : and

A'ZOR.

⌈Sadoc
Mat. 1 : 13. begat A. | 14. A. begat

AZO'TUS.

Ac. 8 : 40. Philip was found at A.

AZ'RIEL.

1 Ch. 5 : 24. heads of house, Ishi, A.
27 : 19. ruler, Jerimoth son of A.
Je. 36 : 26. commanded Seraiah son ⌊of A.

AZ'RIKAM.

1 Ch. 3 : 23 sons of Neariah ; A.
8 : 38. Azel had 6 sons, A. and, 9 : 44.
9 : 14. of Levites ; A. son of Hashabiah, Ne. 11 : 15. ⌈of house
2 Ch. 28 : 7. Zichri slew A., governor

AZU'BAH.

1 K. 22 : 42. his mother's name A., daughter of Shilhi, 2 Ch. 20 : 31.
1 Ch. 2 : 18. Caleb begat of A. his wife
19. when A. dead, Caleb took Eph- ⌊rath

A'ZUR.

Je. 28 : 1. Hananiah son of A., proph.
Eze. 11 : 1. I saw Jaazaniah son of A.

AZ'ZAH = GA'ZA.

⌈to A.
Ge. 10 : † 19. border of Canaanites un-
De. 2 : 23. Avim wh. dwelt unto A.
1 K. 4 : 24. Sol-n dominion even to A.
2 K. 18 : † 8. He smote Philist-s unto A.
Je. 25 : 20. fury they shall drink, A.
14 : † 1. before Pharaoh smote A.

AZ'ZAN.

Nu. 34 : 26. prince, Paltiel son of A.

AZ'ZUR.

Ne. 10 : 17. chief of people, Ater, A.

B.

BA'AL or BA'ALIM.[2]

[Idol, god.] ⌈of B.
Nu. 22 : 41. Balaam into high places
Jos. 13 : † 17. the high places of B.
Ju. 2 : 11. Israel served B.[2], 3 : 7.
10 : 6, 10. 1 S. 12 : 10. ⌈K. 17 : 16.
13. they served B., Ashtaroth, 2
6 : 25. throw down altar of B., 28.
30. bec. he cast down altar of B.
31. Joash said, Will ye plead for B.
32. Let B. plead ag-t him, bec. he
8 : 33. Isr. went a whoring after B.[2]
1 S. 7 : 4. Then Israel put away B.[2]
1 K. 16 : 31. Ahab went, served B.
32. he reared an altar for B. in the house of B. ⌈B.[2]
18 : 18. in that thou hast followed
19. gather to me prophets of B.
21. But if B., then follow him | 450
22. I only prophet of L., B.'s 450
25. Elijah said unto prophets of B.
26. called on B. from morning until noon, O B., hear us ⌈escape
40. Take prophets of B., let not one
19 : 18. 7,000 in Israel which have not bowed unto B., Ro. 11 : 4.
22 : 53. Ahaziah served B.

2 K. 3 : 2. Jehoram put away image
10 : 18. Ahab served B. a little⌊of B.
19. call unto me prophets of B. ;
I have great sacrifice to do to B. ;
. . . destroy worshippers of B.
20. And Jehu said, Proclaim a
solemn assembly for B.
21. all worshippers of B. came ;
house of B. was full(3)⌈pers of B.
22. Bring vestments for worship-
23. Jehu went into house of B.,
said, Search, that none but worshippers of B. only (3) ⌈of B.
25. captains went to city of house
26. images out of house of B. ⌈B.
27. brake down image, house of
28. Jehu destroyed B. out of Isr-l
11 : 18. house of B. and brake it
down ; slew Mattan, priest of
B., 2 Ch. 23:17.⌈B., 2 Ch. 33 :3.[2]
21 : 3. Manasseh reared altars for
23 : 4. out all vessels made for B.
5. burned incense unto B. ⌈to B.[2]
2 Ch. 17 : 3. Jehosh-t sought not un-
24 : 7. dedicated things of L. upon
28 :2. Ahaz made images for B.[2]⌊B.[2]
34 :4. they brake down altars of B.[2]
Je. 2 : 8. prophets prophesied by B.
23. say, I have not gone after B.[2]?
7 : 9. Will ye burn incense unto B.,
11 : 13, 17.-32 : 29.⌈thers taught
9 : 14. walked after B.[2], which fa-
12 : 16 taught people to swear by B.
19 : 5 They built places of B. to
burn sons unto B , 32 : 35.
23 : 13. they prophesied in B. ⌈B.
27. fathers forgotten my name for
Ho. 2 :8. silver, gold, prepared for B
13. will visit upon her days of B.[2]
17. I will take away names of B.[2]
11 : 2. they sacrificed unto B.[2]⌈in B.
13 : 1. Ephraim when he offended
Zph. 1 : 4. will cut off remnant of B.

BA'AL. [Person.]

1 Ch. 5 : 5. sons of Joel ; Reaia, B.
8 : 30. firstb son Abdon, B., 9 : 36.

BA'AL. [Place.] ⌈B.

1 Ch. 4 : 33. all their villages unto
See BAALATH-BEER.

BA'ALAH. ⌈B.

Jos. 15 : 9 the border was drawn to
10. the border from B. unto Seir
11. border passed along to mt B
29. cities of Judah, B.. Iim, Azem
See BAALE, BALAH.

BA'ALATH. ⌈keh, B.

Jos. 19 : 44. Dan . . . coast was Elte-
1 K. 9 : 18. Solomon built B., Tadmor, and store cities, 2 Ch. 8 :6.

BA'ALATH-BE'ER.

Jos. 19 : 8. for Simeon ; Ain, Ashan,
and all villages to B , 1 Ch 4:†33.

BA'AL-BE'RITH.

Ju 8 : 33 Israel made B. their god
9 : 4. gave silver out of house of B.

BA'ALE or BA'ALAH.

2 S 6 : 2.† David went with people
from B. to bring ark. 1 Ch. 13:6 †

BA'AL-GAD.

Jos. 11 : 17. Joshua took land unto
B. in valley of Lebanon, 12 : 7.
13 : 5. land from B. unto Hamath

BA'AL-HA'MON. ⌈B.

Can. 8 : 11. Solo-n had vineyard at

BA'AL-HA'NAN.

Ge. 36 : 38 Saul died, B son of Achbor reigned, 1 Ch. 1 : 49 ⌈49 :50.
39. B. died, Hadar reigned, 1 Ch.
1 Ch. 27 : 28. over olive trees was B.

BA'AL-HA'ZOR. ⌈in B.

2 S. 13 : 23. Abs had sheepshearers

BA'AL-HER'MON. ⌈B.

Ju. 3 : 3 Hivites dwelt from mount
1 Ch. 5 :23. Manasseh fr Bashan unto

BA'ALI. ⌊B.

Ho 2 : 16. call me Ishi ; no more B.

BA'ALIM. See BAAL.

BA'ALIS. ⌈slay thee?

Je. 40 : 14. know B. hath sent to

BA'AL-ME'ON. ⌈cattle

Nu. 32 : †3. Nebo, B., a land for
38. children of Reuben built B.
Jos. 13 : † 17. Dibon and house of B.
1 Ch. 5:8. Joel dwelt in Aroer unto B.
Eze. 25 : 9. glory of the country B.
See BETH-BAAL-MEON.

BA'AL-PE'OR.

Nu. 25 : 3. Israel joined himself un-
to B., Ps. 106 : 28. ⌈unto B.
5. Slay ye every one, men joined
De. 4 : 3. what Lord did because of
B., all that followed B. God de-
Ho. 9 : 10. fathers went to B.⌊stroyed

BA'AL-PER'AZIM.

2 S. 5 : 20 David to B., smote them
Theref. called place B., 1 Ch. 14 :
See PERAZIM. ⌊11 (2).

BA'AL-SHAL'ISHA.

2 K. 4 : 42. man from B. bro-t bread

BA'AL-TA'MAR. ⌈at B.

Ju. 20 : 33. Isr. put thems. in array

BA'AL-ZE'BUB. ⌈ron

2 K. 1 : 2. inquire of B., God of Ek-
3. because not a God in Israel that
ye inquire of B.. god of ? 6, 16.

BA'AL-ZE'PHON. ⌈9.

Ex. 14 : 2. encamp over against B.,
Nu. 33 : 7. unto Pi-hahiroth, bef. B.

BA'ANA.

1 K. 4 : 12. B. son of Ahilud ; to him
Ne. 3 : 4. repaired Zadok son of B.

BA'ANAH. ⌈Rechab

2 S. 4 : 2. captains ; one B., other
5. sons of Rimmon, Rechab and B.
6. Rechab and B. his bro. escaped
9. David answered Rechab and B.
23 : 29. Heleb son of B. 1 Ch. 11:30.
1 K. 4 : 16. B. son of Hushai in Asher
Ezr. 2 : 2. Which came with Zerubbabel : B., Ne. 7 : 7. ⌈rim, B.
Ne. 10 : 27. those that sealed ; Ha-

BA'ARA.

1 Ch. 8 : 8. Hushim, B. were his wives

BAASEI'AH. ⌈ah

1 Ch. 6 : 40 son of B. son of Malchi-

BA'ASHA. ⌈32.

1 K. 15 : 16. war betw. Asa and B.,
17. B. went ag-t Judah, 2 Ch. 16:1.
19. break league wi. B., 2 Ch. 16:3.
21 And when B. heard, he left off
building, 2 Ch. 16 : 5.⌈2 Ch. 16:6.
22. timber wh-h B. had builded,
27 B. son of Ahijah conspired (2)
28. Nadab did B. slay, and reigned
33. began B. son of Ahijah to reign
16 : 1. word of L. to Jehu ag. B., 7, 12.
3. I will take away posterity of B.
4. that dieth of B. shall dogs eat
5. rest of acts of B., are they not
6 B. slept with his fathers, and
8. began Elah son of B. to reign
11. Zimri slew all house of B., 12.
13. For all the sins of B. and son
21 : 22. make thine like house of
B. son of Ahijah, 2 K. 9 : 9.
Je. 41 : 9. pit Asa made for fear of B.

BABBLER. ⌈ter

Ec. 10 : 11. serpent ; a **b.** is no bet-
Ac. 17 : 18. What will this **b.** say ?

BABBLING, S. ⌈**b.**?

Pr. 23 :29. Who hath woe ? who hath
1 Ti. 6 : 20. avoiding vain **b**-s and
2 Ti. 2:16. shun profane and vain **b**-s

BABE.

Ex. 2 : 6. and behold the **b.** wept
Lu. 1 :41. the **b.** leaped in her womb
44. **b.** leaped in my womb for joy
2 : 12. find **b.** wrapped in swaddling
16. found Mary and **b.** in manger
He. 5 : 13. unskilful, for he is a **b.**

BABES.

Ps. 8 : 2. Out of mouth of **b.** and
sucklings, Mat. 21 : 16. ⌈**b.**
17 :14. they leave substance to their
Is. 3 : 4. **b.** shall rule over them
Mat. 11 : 25. hast revealed them unto **b.**, Lu. 10 : 21. ⌈teacher of **b.**
Ro. 2 : 20. instructor of the foolish,
1 Co. 3 : 1. even as unto **b.** in Christ
1 Pe. 2 :2. as new born **b.** desire milk

BABEL. ⌈was B.

Ge. 10 : 10. beginning of kingdom
11 : 9. therefore is the name of it B.
Eze. 23 : † 17. chil. of B. to her into

BAB'YLON. ⌊bed

Ge. 10 : † 10. Nimrod, beginning of
his kingdom was B. ⌈coth, 24.
2 K. 17 : 30. men of B. made Suc-
20 : 14. far country fr. B., Is. 39 :3.
17. be carried unto B., 1 Ch. 9 : 1.
24 : 15. carried away Jehoiachin to
B. (2) 2 Ch. 36 : 10. Je. 24 : 1.
16. smiths captive to B. ⌊-27 : 20.
25 : 7. they carried Zedekiah to B.,
Je. 39 : 7.-52 : 11.
13. the brass in house of L. Chaldees carried to B., Je 52 : 17.
28 above kings in B., Je. 52 : 32.
2 Ch. 32 : 31. the ambassadors of B.
33 : 11. Manasseh, with fetters to B.
36 : 6. Jehoiakim in fetters to B.
7. Neb-r carried vessels of house
of L. to B. (2), 18. Ezr. 5 : 14.-
6 : 5. Je. 28 : 3. ⌈from B.
Ezr. 1 : 11. vessels Sheshbazzar bring
2 : 1. whom Neb-r had carried away
to B., Je. 29 : 1, 4.-39 : 9.-40 : 1.
5 :14. Cyrus take out of temple of B.
17. king's treasure house at B.
6 : 1. treasures were laid up in B.
7 : 6. This Ezra went up from B.
9. day began he to go up from B.
16. all gold thou canst find in B.
8 : 1. that went up with me from B.
Ps. 87 : 4. mention of Rahab and B.
137 : 1. By the rivers of B. we sat
Is. 13 : 1. burden of B. which Isaiah
19. B. as when God overthrew Sod.
14 : 22. I will cut off from B. name
21 : 9. B. is fallen, is fallen, Je. 51 :
8. Re. 14 : 8. - 18 : 2. ⌈to B.
43 : 14. For your sake I have sent
48 : 14. Lord will do pleasure on B.
20. Go ye forth of B , flee fr. Chal.
Je. 20 : 4. carry captive into B., 5.
6. Pashur, shalt come to B. and die
27 : 16. vessels sh. be brought from
18. that vessels left go not to B.⌊B.
22. vessels left sh. be carried to B.
28 :4. captives that went into B.⌈B.
6. Lord do so ; bring vessels from
29 : 3. whom Zedekiah sent unto B.
10. aft. 70 yrs. at B. I will visit you
15. Lord raised us prophets in B.
20. Hear all ye whom I sent to B.
22. curse by all of Judah in B. ⌈B.
28. For therefore he sent us unto
32 : 5. he shall lead Zedekiah to B.
34 : 3. Zedekiah, thou shalt go to B.
40 : 4. If it seem good to come with
me into B. (2) ⌈to B.
7. them not carried away captive
43 : 3. carry us away captives into
50 : 1. The word L. spake ag. B. ⌊B.
2. B. is taken, Bel is confounded
8. Remove out of B., go forth
9. cause to come ag. B. great nat-s
13. that goeth by B sh. hiss at her
14. Put yourselves in array ag. B.
16. Cut off the sower from B. and
23. how is B. become a desolation
24. thou art also taken, O B.⌈of B.
28. The voice of them that flee out
29. Call together archers ag-t B.
34. may disquiet inhabitants of B.
35. A sword is upon inhab-s of B
45. hear ye counsel of Lord ag-t B.
46 At the noise of the taking of B.
51 : 1. I will raise ag. B. destroying
2. will send unto B. fanners⌊wind
6. Flee out of B. ; be not cut off

Je. 51 : 7. B. golden cup in L-'s hand
8. B. is suddenly fallen ; howl for
9. We would have healed B., but
11. his device is ag-t B. to destroy
12. Set standard upon walls of B.:
for L. hath done that he spake
24. render unto B. their evil⌊ag.B.
29. purpose of Lord shall be performed ag. B. to make B. desol-n
30. mighty men of B. forborne to
35. violence to me be upon B.⌊fight
37. B. sh. become heaps, a hissing
41. how is B. become astonishm-t
42. The sea is come up upon B.
44. will punish Bel in B. (2) ⌈of B.
47. I will do judgment ag. images
48. heaven, earth shall sing for B.
49. at B. shall fall slain of earth(2)
53. Tho. B. mount up to heaven
54. sound of a cry cometh from B
55. Bec. Lord hath spoiled B., 56.
58. walls of B. shall be broken
59. Seraiah with Zedekiah into B.
60 evil that shall come upon B. (2)
61. When thou comest to B., say
64. shall B. sink and not rise ⌈20.
Eze. 12 : 13. I will bring him to B., 17:
17 : 12. king, princes, led them to B.
16. with him in B. he shall die
Da. 2 : 48. Daniel over province of B.
4 : 29. Neb-r walked in palace of B.
30. Is not this great B. I built ⌈B.
Mi. 4 : 10. daugh-r of Zion shall go to
Zch. 6 : 10. Take of them come fr. B.
Mat. 1 : 11. time they were carried
away to B., 12. ⌈into B. (2)
17. fr. David, until carrying away
Ac. 7 : 43. I will carry you beyond B.
1 Pe. 5 : 13. church at B. saluteth
Re. 14 : 8. B. is fallen, great city ⌊you
16 : 19. B. in remembrance bef. God
17 : 5. B., GREAT, MOTHER OF HAR-
18 : 10. Alas, alas, great city B.⌊LOTS
21. great city, B. be thrown down

See **DAUGHTER of Babylon.**

King of BABYLON.

2 K. 20 : 12. son of Baladan - B. sent
letters unto Hezekiah, Is. 39 : 1.
18. they shall be eunuchs in palace of - B., Is. 39 : 7. ⌈tained to k.
24 : 7. - B. had taken all that per-
11. Nebuchadnezzar - B. came
against the city, 10. - 25 : 8 (2).
Je. 39 : 1. - 52 : 4, 12.
12. Jehoiachin went out to - B.;
- B. took him, Je. 24 : 1. ⌈B.
16. men of might - B. brought to
17. - B. made Matt-h k., Je. 37 : 1.
20. Zed-h rebelled ag. - B., Je. 52 : 3.
25 : 6. took Zed-h, brought him to
- B., Je. 39 : 5. - 44 : 30. - 52 : 9, 11.
11. people and fugitives that fell
away to - B., Je. 52 : 15.
20. Nebuzar-adan took these, and
brought them to - B., Je. 52 : 26.
21. And - B. slew them at Riblah,
Je. 52 : 27. ⌈Je. 40 : 11.
22. people whom the - B. had left,
23. - B. had made Gedaliah governor, Je. 40 : 5, 7. - 41 : 2, 18.
24. Gedaliah said, serve the - B.,
Je. 27 : 17. - 40 : 9. ⌈Je. 52 : 31.
27. - B. did lift head of Jehoia-n,
2 Ch. 36 : 6. came - B., bound him
in fetters, 2 K. 24 : 1. ⌈Ne. 7 : 6.
Ezr. 2 : 1. whom - B. had carried aw.,
5 : 12. gave them into hand of - B.
13. 1st year of Cyrus - B., a decree
Ne. 13 : 6. two and 30th year of - B.
Es. 2 : 6. whom - B. had carried aw.
Is. 14 : 4. take this proverb ag-t - B.
Je. 20 : 4. Judah into hand of - B.,
21 : 2. - B. maketh war ag. us⌊21 : 10.
4. weapons wherew. ye fight ag. - B.
7. I will deliver Zedekiah into the
hand of - B., 32 : 4. - 34 : 21. - 37 : 17.

Je. 22 : 25. give thee into hand of - B.
25 : 1. word to Jeremiah in ⌈first
year of - B. ⌈and
9. I will send the - B. against this
11. nations shall serve - B. 70 yrs.
12. I will punish the - B. and nation for iniquity, 50 : 18. ⌈of - B.
27 : 6. given these lands into hand
8. nation which will not serve - B.
will I punish (2), 13. ⌈14.
9. saying, Ye shall not serve - B.,
11. bring neck under yoke of - B.
12. Bring necks under yoke of - B.
17. Hearken not ; serve - B., live
20 vessels which - B. took not
28 : 2. I have broken yoke of - B.
3. will I bring all vessels - B. took
4. I will break yoke of - B., 11.
14. nations th. they may serve - B.
29 : 3. (whom Zedekiah sent to - B.)
21. into hand of - B.; he shall slay
22. thee like Ahab, wh. - B. roasted
32 : 2. - B.'s army besieged Jerus.
3. I will give this city into hand of
- B., 28, 36. - 34 : 2. - 38 : 3. ⌈Jerus. , 7.
34 : 1. when Neb-r - B. fought ag-t
3. thine eyes sh. behold eyes of - B.
35 : 11. when - B. came up into land
36 : 29. The - B. shall destroy land
37 : 19. prophesied, - B. sh. not come
38 : 17. If wilt go unto - B.'s princes
18. if wilt not go unto - B.'s princes
22. women be bro-t to - B.'s princes
23. Thou shalt be taken by - B.
39 : 3. all princes of - B. came in (2)
6. - B. slew sons of Zedekiah and
nobles (2), 52 : 10. ⌈ing Jeremiah
11. Now - B. gave charge concern-
13. - B.'s princes sent, took J. out
42 : 11. Be not afraid of - B. ⌈throne
43 : 10. I will take - B. and set his
46 : 2. army of Eg. which - B. smote
13. how - B. should smite Egypt
26. deliver them into hand of - B.
49 : 28. kingdoms wh. - B. sh. smite
30. - B. hath taken counsel ag. you
50 : 17. - B. hath broken his bones
43. - B. hath heard the report of
51 : 31. to shew - B. city is taken
34. Neb-r - B. hath devoured me
52 : 12. 19th year of - B. came captain which served - B ⌈day
34. diet given him of - B. every
Eze. 17 : 12. - B. is come to Jerusa-m
19 : 9. they brought him to the - B.
21 : 19. that the sword of - B. may
come, 32 : 11. ⌈way
21. - B. stood at the parting of the
24 : 2. - B. set himself ag. Jerus-m
26 : 7. I will bring upon Tyrus, - B.
29 : 18. - B. caused his army to serve
19. I will give Egypt unto the - B.
30 : 10. I will make multitude of
Egypt to cease by - B. ⌈25.
24. I will strengthen arms of - B.,
25. shall put sword into hand of - B.
Da. 1 : 1. - B. unto Jerus., besieged
7 : 1. first year of - B., Daniel had
See PROVINCE. ⌊dream

Wise men of BABYLON.

Da. 2 : 12. to destroy all the - B., 24.
14. king's guard gone to slay - B.
18. th. Daniel not perish with - B.
24. Daniel said, Destroy not - B.
48. Dan. chief of governors over -
4 : 6. a decree to bring in all - B.⌊B.
5 : 7. king said to - B., Whoso, shew

BABYLO'NIANS. ⌈B.

Ezr. 4 : 9. Then wrote Rehum and
Eze. 23 : 15. attire after manner of B.
17. B. came to her into bed of love
23. raise ag-t thee thy lovers, B.

BABYLO'NISH. ⌈ment

Jos. 7 : 21. I saw among spoils B. gar-

BA'CA.

Ps. 84 : 6. Who passing thro. valley
of B. make it a well

BACH'RITES.

Nu. 26 : 35. of Becher, family of B.

BACK. [Adv.] ⌈b.

Ex. 18 : 2. after Moses had sent her
Nu. 22 : 34. if it displease, I will get b.
Jos. 8 : 26. Joshua drew not hand b.
Ru. 2 : 6. damsel that came b. with
2 S. 12 : 23. can I bring him b. again ?
15 : 20. return, take b. thy broth-n
18 : 16. Joab held b. the people
19 : 10. why speak ye not of bringing the king b. ? 43. ⌈b., 12.
11. Why ye last to bring the king
1 K. 13 : 22. as thou camest b., thy
19 : 21. returned b., took yoke of
2 Ch. 13 : 14. Judah looked b. ⌊oxen
25 : 13. soldiers Amaziah sent b.
Jb. 26 : 9. holdeth b. face of throne
33 : 18. He keepeth b. soul from pit
39 : 22. nei. turneth he b. fr. sword
Ps. 14 : 7. when Lord bringeth b.
captivity of people, 53 : 6. ⌈5.
114 : 3. sea fled : Jordan driven b.,
Je. 8 : 5. Why this people slidden b.
48 : 10. cursed th. keepeth b. sword
La. 2 : 3. L. drawn b. his right hand
Ho. 4 : 16. Israel slideth b. as heifer
Mat. 24 : 18. neither return b. to
take his clothes, Lu. 17 : 31.
28 : 2. angel rolled b. the stone,
sat upon it ⌈returned b.
Lu. 8 : 37. he went into ship, and
9 : 62. hand to plough, and looking
Ga. 5 : † 7. who did drive you b. ?⌊b.

See **BROUGHT back, CARRY back, DRAW back, GO back, GONE back, TURN back, TURNED back, WENT back.**

See BRING, KEEP, KEPT, LOOK.

BACK. [Adj.]

Ex. 33 : 23. shalt see my b. parts

BACK side.

Ex. 3 : 1. led flock to b. s. of desert
26 : 12. curtain hang over b. s. of
Re. 5 : 1. book written within on b. s.

BACK. [Noun.] ⌈Sam-l

1 S. 10 : 9. turned his b. to go from
1 K. 14 : 9. thou hast cast me behind
thy b., Eze. 23 : 35.
Ps. 21 : 12. shalt thou make them
turn their b. ⌈upon my b.
129 : 3. The ploughers ploughed
Pr. 10 : 13. a rod is for b. of him th.
is void of understanding, 26 : 3.
19 : 29 stripes for the b. of fools
Is. 38 : 17. cast my sins behind thy b.
50 : 6. I gave my b. to the smiters
Je 2 : 27. turned their b. unto me
18 : 17. I will shew them the b., not
32 : 33. have turned unto me the b.
48 : 39. Moab turned b. with shame
Da. 7 : 6. had upon b. of it four wings
Ro. 11 : 10. bow down their b. alway

BACKS. ⌈b.

Ex. 23 : 27. thine enemies turn their
Jos. 7 : 8. Israel turneth their b., 12.
Ju. 20 : 42. men of Benj-n turned b.
2 Ch 29 : 6. our fath-s turned their b.
Ne. 9 : 26. cast law behind their b.
Eze. 8 : 16. men with b. tow. temple
10 : 12. body, b., and hands full of

BACKBITERS. ⌊eyes

Ro. 1 : 30. b., haters of God, despite-

BACKBITETH, ING. ⌊ful

Ps. 15 : 3. who dwell in holy hill ?
He that b-h not with tongue
Pr. 25 : 23. so doth an angry countenance b. g tongue

BACKBITINGS. ⌈b.

2 Co. 12 : 20. lest be debates, wrath,

BACKBONE. ⌈b.

Le. 3 : 9. rump, take off hard by the

BACKSIDE.

See **BACK side.**

BACKSLIDER. ⌈ways

Pr. 14 : 14. b. sh. be filled with own

BACKSLIDING. [Adj.]
Je. 3 : 6. seen that b. Isr. hath done?
8. b. Israel committed adultery
11. b. Israel hath Justified herself
12. Return, thou b. Isr., saith L.
14. Turn, O b. chil., saith L., 22.
31 : 22. how long, O b. dau-r, 49 : 4.
Ho. 4 : 16. For Israel as a b. heifer
Zch. 7 : † 11. they gave b. shoulder

BACKSLIDING, S.
Je. 2 : 19. thy b-s shall reprove thee
3 : 22. I will heal b-s, Ho. 14 : 4.
5 : 6. bec. their b-s are increased
8 : 5. Jerus. slidden back by perpet-
14 : 7 our b-s are many ⌊ual b.?
Ho. 11 : 7. my people are bent to b.

BACKWARD.
Ge. 9 : 23. went b., covered father;
their faces were b., they saw not
49 : 17. so that his rider shall fall b.
1 S. 4 : 18. Eli fell from off the seat b.
2 K. 20 : 10. let the shadow return
b. ten degrees, Is. 38 : 8. ⌈b.
11. Lord brought shadow 10 deg-s
Jb. 23 : 8. b., I cannot perceive him
Ps. 40 : 14. let them be driven b. th.
wish me evil, 70 : 2. ⌈gone b.
Is. 1 : 4. Ah, sinful nation. they are
28 : 13. might fall b. and be broken
44 : 25. I Lord turneth wise men b.
59 : 14. judgment is turned away b.
Je. 7 : 24. they went b., not forward
15 : 6. thou art gone b., thf. will I
La. 1 : 8. Jerus. sigheth, turneth b.
Jn. 18 : 6. went b. and fell to ground

BAD. [Adj.] ⌈b. city
Ezr. 4 : 12. building the rebellious,
Je. 24 : 2. figs not eaten, they so b.

BAD with good.
Ge. 24 : 50. we cannot speak b. or g.
31 : 24. speak not to Jacob g. or b.,
Le. 27 : 10. g. for b., or b. for g. ⌊29.
12. priest value it, wheth. g. or b.
14. estimate house, whe. g. or b.
33. not search whe. it be g. or b.
Nu. 13 : 19. what the land is, g. or b.
24 : 13. I cannot go beyond commandment to do g. or b. ⌈b.
2 S. 13 : 22. Absalom spake nei. g. or
14 : 17. so king to discern g. and b.
1 K. 3 : 9. I may discern g. and b.
Mat. 13 : 48. gathered the g. and
cast the b. away ⌈wedding was
22 : 10. gath-d both b. and g., and
2 Co. 5 : 10. acc-g to that done, whe.

BADE, EST. ⌊g. or b.
Ge. 27 : 19. I have done as thou b-t
43 : 17. the man did as Joseph b.
Ex. 16 : 24. they laid it up as Mos. b.
Nu. 14 : 10. cong-n b. stone them ⌈b.
Jos. 11 : 9 Josh. did unto them as L.
Ru. 3 : 6. to all her mother in law b.
1 S. 24 : 10. some b. me kill thee
2 S. 1 : 18. David b. them teach Jud.
14 : 19. thy servant Joab, he b. me
2 Ch. 10 : 12. on third day, as king b.
Es 4 : 15. Es. b. return answer ⌈en
Mat. 16 : 12. he b. not beware of leav-
Lu. 14 : 9. that b. thee and him, 10.
12. said he to him that b. him
16. made a supper, b. many, 12.
Ac. 11 : 12. the Spirit b. me go with
18 : 21. Paul b. them farew-l ⌊them
22 : 24. b. that he be examined by

BADGERS' skin, s.
Ex. 25 : 5. this is the offering, rams'
skins dyed red, b. s-s, 35 : 7, 23.
26 : 14. covering of b. s-s, 36 : 19. -
39 : 34. Nu. 4 : 6, 8, 10, 11, 12, 14, 25.
35 : 23. every man with whom b. s-s
Eze. 16 : 10. I shod thee with b. s.

BADNESS. ⌈for b.
Ge. 41 : 19. such I never saw in Eg-t
Je. 24 : † 2. figs not to be eaten for b.

BAG, S. ⌈weights
De. 25 : 13. not have in thy b. divers
1 S. 17 : 40. five smooth stones in a b.
1 S. 17 : 49. hand in b., took a stone
2 K. 5 : 23. bound two talents in two
12 : 10. money they put in b-s ⌊b-s
Jb. 14 : 17. My transgr-n sealed in b.
Pr. 7 : 20. hath taken b. of money
16 : 11. weights of b. are his work
Is. 46 : 6. They lavish gold out of b.
Mi. 6 : 11. wi. b. of deceitful weights
Hag. 1 : 6. wages into a b. with holes
Lu. 12 : 33. provide b-s wh. wax not
Jn. 12 : 6. he was a thief, had b. ⌊old
13 : 29. because Judas had the b.

BAHA'RUMITE[1]
or BAR'HUMITE.[2]
2 S. 23 : 31. one of the thirty; Azmaveth the B.[2], 1 Ch. 11 : 33.[1]

BAHU'RIM.
2 S. 3 : 16. husband behind her to B.
16 : 5. David came to B.; Shimei
cursed, cast stones at D., 1 K 2 : 8.
17 : 18. came to a man's house in B.
19 : 16. Shimei of B hasted to meet

BA'JITH. ⌊David
Is. 15 : 2. He is gone up to B. to weep

BAKBAK'KAR.
1 Ch. 9 : 15. of Levites; B., Heresh

BAK'BUK. ⌈Ne. 7 : 53.
Ezr. 2 : 51. Nethinim; chil. of B.,

BAKBUKI'AH.
Ne. 11 : 17. B. second am-g brethren
12 : 9. B and Unni in the watches
25. B., Akkub, porters at thresh-

BAKE. ⌊old
Ge. 19 : 3 Lot did b. unleav-d bread
Ex. 16 : 23. b. that ye will b. to day
Le. 24 : 5. take flour, b. twelve cakes
26 : 26. ten women sh b. y-r bread
1 S. 28 : 24. woman at En-dor did b.
2 S. 13 : 8. Tamar did b. the cakes
Eze. 4 : 12. b. it with dung of a man
46 : 20. where they sh. b. meat off-g

BAKED, ETH.
Ex. 12 : 39. they b-d unleav-d cakes
Nu. 11 : 8. manna people b-d in pans
1 Ch. 23 : 29. that which is b-d in pan
Is. 44 . 15. b-h bread; maketh a ged
19. I have b-d bread upon coals

BAKEMEATS.
Ge. 40 : 17. in basket b. for Pharaoh

BAKEN. ⌈9.
Le. 2 : 4. a meat offering b., 5, 7.-7 :
6 : 17. It sh. not be b. with leaven
21. when it is b., b. pieces offer
23 : 17. wave loaves be b. wi. leaven
1 K. 19 : 6. was a cake b. on the coals

BAKER, S. ⌈Eg.
Ge. 40 : 1 b. had offended king of
2. Pharaoh wroth ag-t chief of b-s
5. butler and b. in prison ⌈good
16. chief b. saw interpreta-n was
20. Pha. lifted up head of chief b.
22. hanged chief b., as Joseph had
41 : 10. Pha-h put in ward chief b.
1 S 8 : 13. your daughters to be b-s
Je. 37 : 21. Jere-h bread out of b-s'
Ho. 7 : 4. as oven heated by b. ⌊street
6. their b. sleepeth all the night

BA'LAAM. ⌈unto B.
Nu. 22 : 5. Balak sent messengers
7. elders of Moab came unto B.,
and spake the words of Balak ⌈B.
8. the princes of Moab abode with
9. God came unto B., said, What
10. B. said unto God, Balak sent
12. G. said unto B., Thou sh. not go
13. B. said unto princes of Balak
14. princes went unto Balak and
said, B. refuseth to come ⌈Let
16. came to B., said, saith Balak.
18. B. answered servants of Balak
20. God came unto B. at night
21. B. went with princes of Moab
23. and B. smote the ass, to turn
25. ass crushed B-'s foot ag. wall
27. ass fell under B.; B-'s anger
28. said unto B, What have I done
29. B. said unto ass, thou mocked
Nu. 22 : 30. ass said unto B., Am not I
31 Lord opened eyes of B. ⌊thine
34. B. said unto angel, I sinned
35. angel of Lord said unto B, Go.
So B. went with princes of Balak
36. when Balak heard B. was come
37. Balak said unto B., Did I not
38. B. said unto Balak, I am come
39. B. went with Balak, they came
40. Balak offered oxen, sent to B.
41. Balak took B. into high places
23 : 1. B. said to Balak, Build me
seven altars, 29. ⌈altar (2), 30.
2. Balak and B. offered on every
3. B. said to Balak, Stand by off-g
4. God met B.: he said unto him
5. L. put word in B-'s mouth, said,
Return unto Balak, 16. ⌈done?
11. Balak said unto B., What hast
25. Balak said unto B., Nei. curse
26. B. said unto Balak, Told not I
27. Balak said unto B., Come, I
28. Balak bro-t B. unto top of Peor
24 : 1. when B saw it pleased L. to
2. B. lifted his eyes and saw Israel
3. B. son of Beor hath said, 15. ⌈(2)
10. Balak's anger was kindled ag. B.
12. B. said unto Balak, Spake I not
25. B. returned to his place: Balak went his way ⌈Jos. 13 : 22.
31 : 8. B. son of Beor they slew,
16. counsel of B. to commit tresp.
De. 23 : 4. bec. they hired B., Ne. 13 :
5. Lord not hearken unto B. ⌊2.
Jos. 24 : 9. Balak warred ag. Israel,
and called B. to curse ⌈B.
10. but I would not hearken unto
Mi. 6 : 5. remember what Balak consulted, and what B. answered
2 Pe. 2 : 15. following the way of B.
Jude 11. greedily aft. the error of B.
Re. 2 : 14. that hold doctrine of B.
See BEOR.

BA'LAC. See BALAK.

BAL'ADAN.
2 K. 20 : 12. Berodach-baladan the
son of B. sent, Is. 39 : 1.

BA'LAH[1] or BIL'HAH.[2]
[Place.]
Jos. 19 : 3. the tribe of Simeon had
B.[1] and Azem, 1 Ch. 4 : 29. *B.*[2] † [1]

BA'LAK or BA'LAC.
Nu. 22 : 2 B. saw all Isr. had done to
4. B., king of Moabites at that time
15. B. sent princes more honourab.
23 : 7. B. hath bro-t me from Aram
13 B. said, Come with me, 27.
15. said unto B., Stand by offer-g
17. B. said, What hath L. spoken?
18. he said, Rise up B. and hear
24 : 13 If B. give me house full of
Ju. 11 : 25. thou better than B.? ⌊gold
Re. 2 : 14. taught B-c to cast stum-
See BALAAM. ⌊blingbl.
See **Balak son of ZIP'POR.**

BALANCE. ⌈b.
Jb. 31 : 6. Let me be weighed in even
Ps. 62 : 9. laid in b., they are vanity
Pr. 11 : 1. false b. is an abom-n, 20 : 23.
16 : 11. just weight and b. are L.'s
Is. 40 : 12. Who weighed hills in b.?
15. nations as small dust of the b.
46 : 6. They weigh silver in the b.

BALANCES.
Le. 19 : 36. Just b., just, Eze. 45 : 10.
Jb. 6 : 2. my calamity laid in the b.
Je 32 : 10. weighed him money in b.
Eze. 5 : 1. take b. to weigh the hair
Da. 5 : 27. thou art weighed in the b.
Ho. 12 : 7. b. of deceit in his hand
Am. 8 : 5, falsifying the b. by deceit
Mi. 6 : 11. them pure, wi. wicked b.?
Re. 6 : 5. he that sat on him had b.

BALANCINGS.
Jb. 37 : 16. Dost know the b. of the

BALD. ⌊clouds?
Le 13 : 40. he is b.; yet is clean, 41.

Le. 13 : 42. if in **b.** head or **b.** forehead
a white sore; it is leprosy(4), 43.
† 55. it is fret, whether **b.** in head
2 K. 2 : 23. Go up thou **b.** head (2)
Je. 16 : 6. nor make themselves **b.**
48 : 37. every head shall be **b.** and
Eze. 27 : 31. make thems. **b.** for thee
29 : 18. every head was made **b.**
Mi. 1 : 16. Make thee **b.** and poll thee

BALD locust.

Le. 11 : 22. and ye may eat the **b. l.**

BALDNESS. ⌈head

Le. 21 : 5. not make **b.** upon their
De. 14 : 1. nor make **b.** between eyes
Is. 3 : 24. instead of well set hair, **b.**
15 : 2. on heads **b.** and beard cut
22 : 12. that day did Lord call to **b.**
Je. 47 : 5. **b.** is come upon Gaza ⌈10.
Eze. 7 : 18. **b.** upon heads, Am. 8:
Mi. 1 : 16. enlarge thy **b.** as the eagle

BALL, S. ⌈b-s

Is. 3 : † 19. L. will take their sweet
22 : 18. he will toss thee like a **b.**

BALM.

Ge. 37 : 25. Ishmaelites with **b.** and
43 : 11. take a little **b.** and honey
Je. 8 : 22. Is there no **b.** in Gilead?
46 : 11. into Gilead, take **b.**, O virgin
51 : 8. howl; take **b.** for her pain
Eze. 27 : 17. Judah traded in wheat,

BA'MAH. ⌊b.

Eze. 20 : 29. name is B. unto this day

BA'MOTH. ⌈to B.

Nu. 21 : 19. they went up fr. Nahaliel
20. and from B. in Moab to Pisgah

BA'MOTH-BA'AL.

Jos. 13 : 17. gave Reuben, Dibon, B.

BAND, S. ⌈rend

Ex. 39 : 23. a **b.** that it should not
Le. 26 : 13. I broken **b-s** of your yoke
Ju. 15 : 14. **b-s** loosed off his hands
2 K. 23 : 33. Jehoahaz Pha. put in **b-s**
Jb. 38 : 9. darkness a swaddling **b.**
31. Canst thou loose **b-s** of Orion?
39 : 5. who loosed **b-s** of wild ass?
10. Canst bind unicorn wi. his **b.**?
Ps. 2 : 3. Let us b-k their **b-s** asunder
73 : 4. are no **b-s** in their death
107 : 14. he brake **b-s** in sunder ⌈b-s
Ec 7 : 26. the woman whose hands as
Is. 28 : 22. lest **b-s** be made strong
52 : 2. loose thyself from **b-s** of neck
58 : 6. to loose **b-s** of wickedness
Je. 2 : 20. For I have burst thy **b-s**
Eze. 3 : 25. they shall put **b-s** upon
4 : 8. I will lay **b-s** upon thee ⌊thee
34 : 27. I broken **b-s** of their yoke
Da. 4 : 15. with a **b.** of iron, 23. ⌈love
Ho. 11 : 4. I drew them with **b-s** of
Zch. 11 : 7. two staves, one I called
Beauty, the other B-s ⌈B-s
14. I cut mine other staff, even
Lu. 8 : 29. he brake **b-s** was driven
Ac. 16 : 26. every one's **b-s** loosed
22 : 30. capt. loosed Paul from **b-s**
27 : 40. loosed rudder **b.**, hoised sail
Col. 2 : 19. from which all body by
See BONDS. ⌊b-s

BAND, S.

[Company, ies.]

Ge. 32 : 7. divided flocks into two
10. now I am become two **b-s** ⌊b-s
33 : † 8. What is all this **b.** to thee?
1 S. 10 : 26. **b.** whose hearts G. touched
2 S. 4 : 2. two men, captains of **b-s**
1 K. 11 : 24. became captain over a **b.**
2 K. 6 : 23. **b-s** of Syria came no more
11 : † 7. two **b-s** that go on sabbath
13 : 20. **b-s** of Moabites invaded la.
21. burying a man they spied a **b.**
24 : 2. Lord sent against him **b-s** of
Chaldees, **b-s** of Moabites (4)
1 Ch. 7 : 4. with them **b-s** of soldiers
12 : 18. David made captains of **b.**
21. helped David ag-t **b.** of rovers
23. numbers of **b-s** armed ⌈bians
2 Ch. 22 : 1. **b.** that came with Ara-
2 Ch. 25 : † 9. 100 talents given to **b.** of
† 13. sons of **b.** which Ama-h ⌊Isr.
26 : 11. men that went to war by **b-s**
Ezr. 8 : 22. ashamed to require of
the king **b.** of soldiers ⌈three **b-s**
Jb. 1 : 17. The Chaldeans made out
Ps. 119 : 61. **b-s** of wicked robbed me
Pr. 30 : 27. locusts go forth by **b-s**
Eze. 12 : 14. I will scatter all his **b-s**
17 : 21. all his **b-s** sh. fall by sword
38 : 6. Gomer, and all his **b-s**; Togarmah, his **b-s** ⌈and thy **b-s**
9. like cloud to cover land, thou
22. I will rain upon his **b-s** ⌈b-s
39 : 4. fall upon mts. thou and thy
Mat. 27 : 27. gathered unto him the
whole **b.**, Mk. 15 : 16. ⌈of men
Jn. 18 : 3. Judas having received a **b.**
12. **b.** and captain took Jesus ⌈b.
Ac. 10 : 1. the **b.** called the Italian
21 : 31. tidings came unto chief
captain of **b.** ⌈gustus' **b.**
27 : 1. to Julius, centurion of Au-

BANDED. ⌈gether

Ac. 23 : 12. certain of Jews, **b.** to-

BA'NI. ⌈Gadite

2 S. 23 : 36. one of the thirty; B.,
1 Ch. 6 : 46. Of Kohathites; son of B.
Ezr. 2 : 10. The chil. of B., Ne. 7 : † 15.
10 : 29. taken strange wives; sons
34. Of sons of B.; Maadai ⌊of B.
38. and B., Binnui, Shimei, and
Ne. 3 : 17. repaired Rehum son of B.
8 : 7. B. caused people to underst-d
9 : 4. stood upon stairs, B., Bunni, B.
5. B. said, Stand up, bless Lord
10 : 13. those that sealed; B., Ben-
14. chief of people; Elam, B. ⌊inu
11 : 22. The overseer, Uzzi son of B.

BANISHED. ⌈b.

2 S. 14 : 13. doth not fetch home his
14. that his **b.** be not expelled fr.

BANISHMENT. ⌊him

Ezr. 7 : 26. whether unto death or **b.**
La. 2 : 14. have seen for thee causes

BANK. ⌊of b.

Ge. 41 : 17. I stood upon **b.** of river
De. 4 : 48. Aroer by **b.** of river Arnon, Jos. 12 : 2.-13 : 9, 16. ⌈city
2 S. 20 : 15. they cast up **b.** ag-t the
2 K. 2 : 13. Elisha by **b.** of Jordan
19 : 32. He sh. not cast a **b.** against
it, Is. 37 : 33. ⌈many trees
Eze. 47 : 7. at the **b.** of the river
12. by the river upon **b.** all trees
Da. 12 : 5. one on this side of the **b.**
other on that side of **b.** ⌈to b.?
Lu. 19 : 23. Whf. not my money in-

BANKS. ⌈4 : 18.

Jos. 3 : 15. Jordan overflow-h his **b.**,
1 Ch. 12 : 15. Jordan had overfl-n **b.**
Is. 8 : 7. k. of Assyria go over his **b.**
Da. 8 : 16. I heard voice between **b.**

BANNER, S. ⌈my b.

Ex. 17 : † 15. altar, called it, The L.,
Ps. 20 : 5. in name of God set up **b-s**
60 : 4. a **b.** to them that fear thee
Can. 2 : 4. his **b.** over me was love
6 : 4. terrible as army with **b-s**, 10.
Is. 13 : 2. Lift up a **b.** upon moun-

BANQUET. [Verb.] ⌊tain

Es. 7 : 1. king, Haman came to **b.** wi.

BANQUET. ⌊Esther

Es. 5 : 4. let king and Haman come
unto the **b.**, 5 8. ⌈wine, 7 : 2.
6. king said unto Esther at **b.** of
12. did let no man come unto **b.**
14. go in with king unto **b.** ⌈to b.
6 : 14. hasted to bring Haman un-
7 : 7. king arising from **b.** in wrath
8. k. into place of **b.**; Haman was
Jb. 41 : 6. companions make **b.** of him
Am. 6 : 7. **b.** of them that stretched

BANQUET house. ⌈h.

Da. 5 : 10. now queen came into **b.**

BANQUETING house.

Can. 2 : 4. He brought me to **b. h.**

BANQUETINGS. ⌈b.

1 Pe. 4 : 3. when we walked in lusts,

BAPTISM, S. ⌈b.

Mat. 3 : 7. saw Pharisees come to his
21 : 25. The **b.** of John, whence
was it? Mk. 11 : 30. Lu. 20 : 4.
Mk. 1 : 4. John did baptize and
preach **b.** of repentance, Lu. 3 : 3.
Ac. 1 : 22. Beginning from **b.** of John
10 : 37. after **b.** wh. John preached
13 : 24. John preached **b.** of repent.
18 : 25. Apollos knowing **b.** of John
Ro. 6 : 4. are buried with him by **b.**
Eph. 4 : 5. one Lord, one faith, one **b.**
Col. 2 : 12. Buried with him in **b.**
He. 6 : 2. Of the doctrine of **b-s** ⌈us
1 Pe. 3 : 21. even **b.** doth now save
See BAPTIZED.

BAP'TIST. ⌈ing

Mat. 3 : 1. came John the B. preach-
11 : 11. hath not risen a greater
than John the B., Lu. 7 : 28.
11 : 12. from the days of John the B.
14 : 2. This is John the B.; is risen
8. Give me here John B-'s head in
a charger, Mk. 6 : 25.
16 : 14. Some say thou art John the
B.; some Elias, Mk. 8 : 28. Lu.
17 : 13. spake of John the B. ⌊9 : 19.
Mk. 6 : 14. Herod said, That John
the B. was risen ⌈John the B.
24. What sh. I ask? The head of
Lu. 7 : 20. John B. hath sent us
33. John the B. came nei. eating

BAPTIZE.

Mat. 3 : 11. I **b.** you with water, he
shall **b.** with Holy Ghost, Mk.
1 : 8. Lu. 3 : 16. Jn. 1 : 26, 33.
Mk. 1 : 4. John did **b.** in wilderness
Jn. 1 : 33. sent me to **b.** with water
1 Co. 1 : 17. Christ sent me not to **b.**

BAPTIZED. ⌈1 : 5.

Mat. 3 : 6. were **b.** in Jordan, Mk.
13. cometh Jesus unto John to be
14. I have need to be **b.** of thee ⌊b.
16. Jesus, when he was **b.** went
20 : 22. ye able to be **b.** with baptism that I am **b.** with? 23.
Mk. 10 : 38, 39. ⌈water
Mk. 1 : 8. I indeed have **b.** you with
9. Jesus was **b.** of John in Jordan
16 : 16. believeth and is **b.** be saved
Lu. 3 : 7. multitude th. came to be **b.**
12. Then came publicans to be **b.**
21. when people were **b.**, Jesus
being **b.**, heaven was opened
7 : 29. publicans being **b.** with the
baptism of John ⌈b. of him
30. Pharisees, lawyers, being not
12 : 50. I have baptism to be **b.** with
Jn. 3 : 22. tarried with them and **b.**
23. much water, and they were **b.**
4 : 1. Jesus **b.** more disciples than
2. Tho. Jesus himself **b.** not ⌊John
10 : 40. place where John first **b.**
Ac. 1 : 5. John **b.** with water, ye sh.
be **b.** with Holy Ghost, 11 : 16.
2 : 38. Repent, be **b.** every one ⌈b.
41. that gladly received word were
8 : 12. were **b.** both men and wom.
13. Simon believed; when **b.** he
16. they were **b.** in name of L. Jes.
36. what doth hinder me to be **b.**?
38. into the water, Philip and the
eunuch; and he **b.** him
9 : 18. Saul arose and was **b.**
10 : 47. any forbid water that these
should not be **b.**? ⌈b. in name
48. Peter commanded them to be
16 : 15. Lydia, and when she was **b.**
33. jailer was **b.** and all his ⌈b.
18 : 8. many of Corinthians were
19 : 3. Unto what then were ye **b.**?
they said, Unto John's baptism
4. John **b.** with baptism of repen.
5. when heard this they were **b.**
22 : 16. be **b.**, wash away thy sins

Ro. 6 : 3. so many as were b. into
Christ were b. into his death?
1Co.1:13.were ye b. in name of P-l?
14. I thank God I b. none of you
15.lest any say, I b. in own name
16. I b. household of Stephanas;
know not wh-r I b. any other
10 : 2.were all b. unto Moses⌈body
12 : 13. by one Spirit b. into one
15:29.what do wh.are b. for dead?
why are they b. for the dead?
Ga. 3 :27. many as have been b. in-
See Baptism ⌊to Christ

BAPTIZEST, ETH.

Jn. 1 : 25. why b-t thou if not Chr.
33. he which b-h with Holy Gh-t
8:26. b-h and all men come to him

BAPTIZING. ⌈them

Mat. 28 : 19. teach all nations, b.
Jn.1:28. Jordan,where John was b.
31. thf. am I come b. with water
3 : 23. John was also b. in Enon

BAR. [Verb.]

Ne.7:3. shut the doors and b. them

BAR. [Noun.] ⌈boards

Ex. 26 : 28. middle b. in midst of
36:33. made middle b. shoot thro.
Nu. 4:10. shall put it upon a b., 12.
Ju. 16 : 3. S-n took doors of city, b.
Is. 27 : † 1. Lord shall punish levia-
than, crossing like a b. ⌈cus
Am. 1 : 5. I will break b. of Damas-

BARS. ⌈31.

Ex. 26 : 26. b. of Shittim wood, 36:
27.and five b. for boards of other
side (2), 36 : 32 (2). ⌈36 : 34 (2).
29. shalt overlay b.with gold (2),
35:11. make tabernacle, b., 39:33.
40:18. reared tabernacle, put in b.
Nu. 3 : 36. charge of Merari boards
of tabernacle and b., 4 : 31.
De. 3:5.All cities fenced with walls,
b., 1 K. 4 : 13. 2 Ch. 8 : 5.
1 S. 23 :7. into a town that hath b.
2 Ch.14:7. build cities, make gates,
Ne. 3:3. set up b., 6, 13, 14, 15. ⌊b.
Jb. 17:16. shall go down to b. of pit
18 : † 13. devour the b. of his skin
38 : 10. who shut up sea and set b.
40:18. his bones are like b. of iron
Ps. 107 : 16. cut b. of iron, Is. 45:2.
147 : 13. strengthened b. of gates
Pr. 18 : 19. contentions are like the
b. of a castle ⌈their b.
Is. 43:†14. I have brought down all
Je. 48:†30. on whom stayeth his b.
50 : † 36. A sword is upon the b.
51:30. Babylon; her b. are broken
La. 2 : 9. Lord hath broken her b.
Eze. 38 : 11. dwelling without walls
hav-g nei. b.nor gates, Je.49:31.
Jon. 2 : 6. earth with her b. about
Na.3:13. fire sh. devour thy b.⌊me

BARAB'BAS.

Mat. 27:16. they had a notable prisoner, B., Mk. 15:7. ⌈Jesus, 21.
17. Whom will ye I release? B. or
20.persuaded multitude that they
ask B., Mk. 15 : 11. ⌈said B.
21. Whether of the twain. They
26. released he B., Mk. 15:15. ⌈B.
Lu. 23 : 18. Away with this, release
Jn. 18:40.cried they, Not this man,
but B. Now B. was a robber

BAR'ACHEL. ⌈6.

Jb. 32:2. wrath of Elihu son of B.,

BARACHI'AS. ⌈of B.

Mat. 23 : 35. blood of Zacharias son

BA'RAK. ⌈desh

Ju. 4:6. Deborah called B. out of Ke-
8. B. said, If thou wilt go, I will
9. Deborah went wi. B. to Kedesh
10. B. called Zebulun to Kedesh
12.shewed Sisera that B. was gone
14. Deb-h said unto B., Up: So B.
15. L. discomfited Sisera before
16. B. pursued after host unto⌊B.

Ju. 4:22. as B. pursued Sisera, Jael
5 : 1. Then sang Deborah and B.
12. arise, B., lead thy captivity c.
15. Issachar, and also B.
He. 11: 32. time would fail to tell of
See Son of ABINOAM. ⌊B.

BARBARIAN, S.

Ac. 28 : 4. when b-s saw the beast
Ro. 1:14. I am debtor to Gr.and B-s
1 Co. 14 :11. unto him a b.; he a b.
Col. 3:11.neither Greek nor Jew, B.

BARBAROUS. ⌈ness

Ac. 28 : 2. b. people shewed kind-

BARBED.

Jb. 41:7. fill his skin with b. irons?

BARBER.

Eze. 5 : 1. take thee a b-s razor and

BARE. [Adj.] ⌈head b.

Le. 13: 45. his clothes shall be rent,
55. it is fret, whether b. within or
Ps. 137 : † 7. make b. to foundation
141:†8.O God, make not my soul b.
Is. 32 : 11. strip you, make you b.
47 : 2. make b. leg, uncover thigh
52: 10. Lord made b. his holy arm
Je. 13:22.for iniquity thy heels made
49 : 10. I have made Esau b. ⌊b.
Eze. 16 : 7. wast naked and b., 22.
39.sh. leave thee naked, b., 23:29.
Jo. 1 : 7. my fig tree; made it b.

BARE grain. ⌈but b.g.

1 Co. 15 :37. not body that shall be,

BARE. [Brought forth.]

Ge. 4: 1. she conceived and b. Cain
2. she again b. his brother. Abel
17. and she conceived, b. Enoch
20. Adah b. Jabal; he fa. of such
22. Zillah, she b. Tubal-cain, an
25. she b. a son, his name Seth
6 : 4. they b. to them mighty men
16:1. Sarai, Abr-'s wife, b. no chil.
15. Hagar b. Abram a son; name
Ishmael (2), 16.-25:12. ⌈Moab
19:37. the firstborn b. a son, name
38. younger b. a son, Ben-ammi
20: 17. healed maidserv-ts; they b.
21:2. Sarah b.A son in his old age
3. A. called son Sarah b. Isaac
22 : 24. his concubine b. Tebah
24 : 24. Bethuel the son of Milcah,
which Milcah b., 47. ⌈old
36. Sarah b. a son when she was
25 : 2. Abr. took Keturah, she b.
Zimran, Jokshan, 1 Ch. 1 : 32.
26. Isaac 60 years old when she b.
29:32.Leah b.a son; name Reuben
33.conceived again, b.son, 34, 35.
30 : 1. Rachel saw she b. no chil-n
5. Bilhah conceived, b. J.a son, 7.
10. Zilpah, Leah's maid, b. a son
12. Zilpah b. Jacob a second son
17. Leah conceived, b. J. son, 19.
21.Leah afterw-ds b. Dinah, 34:1.
23. Rachel conceived and b.a son
31 : 8. all the cattle b. speckled;
then b. all cattle ringstreaked
36 : 4. Adah b. to Esau Eliphaz;
and Bashemath b. Reuel ⌈14.
5. Aholibamah b. Jeush, Korah,
12. Timna b. to Eliphaz Amalek
38:3. Shuah conceived, b. son; Er
4. conceived again, b. son; Onan
5. conceived again, b. Shelah: he
was at Chezib when she b. him
41:50. born unto Joseph two sons:
which Asenath b., 46:20. ⌈sons
44:27. Ye know my wife b. me two
46:15. sons of Leah, which she b.
18.sons of Zilpah; she b. 16 souls
25. Bilhah; she b. unto Jacob
Ex. 2 : 2. woman conceived, b. son
22. Zipporah b. a son, Gershom
6 : 23. Elisheba; she b. Nadab, A.
25. Eleazar she b. him Phinehas
Nu. 26 : 59. Jochebed, whom her
mother b. to Levi in Egypt; she
b. Aaron and Moses, Ex. 6:20.

Ju. 8:31. his concubine b. Abimel.
11:2. Gilead's wife b.him sons⌊ech
13:2. Manoah; wife barren, b. not
24. the woman b. a son, Samson
Ru. 4: 12. Pharez, whom Tamar b.
unto Judah, 1 Ch. 2 : 4. ⌈son
13. So Boaz took Ruth; she b. a
1 S. 1 : 20. Hannah b. son, Samuel
2:21. Lord visited Hannah, she b.
2 S. 11: 27. David fetched her to his
house; she b. a son ⌈wife b.
12 : 15. Lord struck child Uriah's
24.Bath-sheba b. a son, Solomon
21 : 8. sons Rizpah b. unto Saul
† 8. sons of Michal, she b. to Adriel
1 K. 1 : 6. b. him after Absalom
11:20. sister of Tahpenes b. Genu.
2 K. 4 :17. woman b. son th. season
1 Ch. 2:17. Abigail b. Amasa ⌈Hur
19. Caleb took Ephrath which b.
21. daughter of Machir b. Segub
24.Abiah Hezron's wife b. Ashur
29. Abihail b. him Ahban, Molid
35. to Jarha to wife; she b.Attai
46. Ephah Caleb's concubine b.
48.Maachah Caleb's concubine b.,
4 : 6. Naarah b. him Ahuzam ⌊49.
9.Jabez,Because I b. him wi.sor-
17. she b. Miriam, Ishbah ⌊row
18. Jehudijah b. Jered father of
7 : 14. sons of Manasseh; Ashriel,
wh. she b.; (his concu. b. Machir
16.wife of Machir b.a son, Peresh
18. sister Hammoleketh b. Ishod
23.Ephraim in to wife; she b.son
2 Ch. 11 : 19. Rehoboam took Abihail . . . which b. him children
20. Maachah which b. him Attai
Pr.17:25.bitterness to her th.b.him
23 : 25. she th. b. thee sh. rejoice
Can. 6 : 9. choice one of her that b.
8:5. there bro-t forth that b. thee
Is. 8 : 3. prophetess; she b. a son
51:2. Look unto Sarah that b.you
Je. 16:3.conc. mothers th. b. them
20 : 14. day wherein mother b. me
22:26.cast out mother that b. thee
50:12. that b. you sh. be ashamed
Eze. 23:4. mine, they b.sons, dau-s
37. caused sons they b.to pass⌈8.
Ho. 1:3. took Gomer, who b. a son,
6.conceived again, b. a daughter
Lu. 23:29. Blessed, wombs never b.

BARE fruit, s. ⌈dredf.

Lu.8:8. on good ground b.f. a hun-
Re. 22:2.tree of life b. 12 manner of

BARE. [Carried.] ⌊f-s

Ge. 7 : 17. the waters b. up the ark
31:39. torn of beasts; I b.the loss
Ex. 19 : 4. I b. you on eagle's wings
Nu. 13:23. cluster they b.upon staff
De. 1:31. God b. thee as a man doth
31 : 9. priests which b. the ark of
the covenant, 25. Jos. 3:15 (2),
17.-4:9, 10, 18 -8:33. ⌈pres-ts
Ju. 3:18. sent away people that b.
1S.14:1. man that b. his armour, 6.
17:41.man that b. shield went bef.
2 S. 6:13. when they that b. ark of
Lord, 1 Ch. 15:15. 26, 27. ⌈ab's
18 :15. ten young men that b. Jo-
1 K. 5 : 15. 70,000 that b. burdens
10 : 2. queen of Sheba, with camels
that b. spices, 2 Ch. 9:1.⌈them
14:28. brazen shields, the guard b.
2 K.5:23. talents they b. before him
1 Ch. 12:24. of Judah that b. shield
and spear, 2 Ch. 14 : 8 (2).
Ne. 4 : 17. they that b. burdens
Is.22:6. Elam b. quiver wi.chariots
53 : 12. he b. the sin of many and
63:9. he b. them all days of old
Eze. 12:7. stuff I b. upon my shoul.
Mat. 8 : 17. Hims. b. our sicknesses
Lu. 7:14. they th. b. him stood still
11:27. Blessed is womb th. b. thee
Jn. 2:8. they b. it water made wine

Jn. 12 : 6. had the bag and **b.** what
Ac. 12:†20. Herod **b.** a hostile mind
1 Pe. 2:24. Who **b.** our sins on tree
BARE record. ⌈Spirit
Jn. 1: 32. John **b. r.**, saying, I saw
34. I **b. r.** that this is Son of God
12 : 17. the people with him **b. r.**
19:35. he that saw it, **b. r.** and his
Re. 1:2. Who **b. r.** of word of G. ⌊r.
BARE rule.
1 K. 9:23. 550 which **b. r.** over people that wrought, 2 Ch. 8 : 10.
Ne. 5:15. servants **b. r.** over people
Eze. 19:11. rods for them that **b. r.**
See Bare WITNESS.
BAREFOOT.
2 S. 15 : 30. David went up **b.** ⌈3.
Is. 20: 2. Isaiah walking naked, **b.**,
4. lead Egyptians naked and **b.**
BAREST. ⌈Lord
1 K. 2 : 26. because thou **b.** ark of
Is. 63: 19. thou never **b.** rule over th.
Jn. 3 : 26. to whom thou **b.** witness
BARHU'MITE.
See BAHARUMITE.
BARI'AH. ⌈B.
1 Ch 3:22. sons of Shemaiah: Igeal,
BAR-JESUS. ⌈B.
Ac. 13 : 6. found a sorcerer, a Jew,
BAR-JO'NA. ⌈B
Mat. 16:17. Blessed art thou Simon
BARK. ⌈b.
Is. 56 : 10. dumb dogs, they cannot
BARKED.
Jo. 1 : 7. He hath **b.** my fig tree
BARKING. ⌈b.
Jo. 1 : † 7. He laid my fig tree for a
BAR'KOS.
Ezr. 2:53. children of B , Ne. 7 : 55
BARLEY.
Ex. 9:31. **b.** was smitten : for **b.** was
Le. 27:16. a homer of **b.** seed at fifty
Nu. 5 : 15. of an ephah of **b.** meal
Ju. 7:13. a cake of **b.** tumbled into
Ru. 1 : 22. beginning of **b.** harvest
2 : 17. she gleaned an ephah of **b.**
23. to glean unto end of **b.** harvest
3 : 2. Boaz winnoweth **b.** to-night
15. measured six measures of **b.**
17. six measures of **b.** gave he me
2 S. 14: 30. Joab's field, he hath **b.**
21 : 9. were hanged in **b.** harvest
1 K. 4 : 28. **b.** and straw for horses
2 K. 4 : 42. brought 20 loaves of **b.**
7:1. two measures of **b.** for, 16, 18.
1 Ch. 11:13. was a ground full of **b.**
Eze. 4 : 12. shalt eat it as **b.** cakes
13 : 19. will ye pollute me for **b.**
45:13. give part of homer of **b.** ⌈(2)
Ho. 3:2. bought her for homer of **b.**
Jn. 6 : 9. a lad hath five **b.** loaves
13. fragments of five **b.** loaves
Re. 6: 6. Three measures of **b.** for a
See **WHEAT** with **barley.**
BARN.
Jb. 39 : 12. thy seed gather into **b.**
Hag. 2 : 19. Is the seed yet in **b.** ?
Mat. 13:30. gather wheat into my **b.**
Lu. 12:24. nei. have storehouse nor
See BARNFLOOR. ⌊b.
BARNS. ⌈thy **b.**
De. 28 : †8. L. command blessing in
Pr. 3 : 10. So shall thy **b.** be filled
Jo. 1 : 17. the **b.** are broken down
Mat. 6 : 26 reap nor gather into **b.**
Lu. 12 : 18. I will pull down my **b.**
BAR'NABAS.
Ac. 4 : 36. Joses was surnamed B.
9 : 27. B. brought him to apostles
11:22. that B. go as far as Antioch
25. Then departed B. to seek Saul
30. They sent it by the hands of B.
12:25. B., Saul returned fr. Jerus.
13 : 1. Antioch; teachers, B., Saul
2. said, Separate me B. and Saul
7. Paulus called for B. and Saul
43. many of Jews followed Paul, B.

Ac. 13 : 46. Paul and B. waxed bold
50. persecution ag-t Paul and B
14:12. they called B. Jupiter ⌈ran
14. when B. and Paul heard, they
20. he departed with B. to Derbe
15 : 2. Paul, B. had dissension (2)
12. all gave audience to B., Paul
22. chosen men with Paul, B., 25.
25. our beloved B. and Paul
35 Paul, B continued in Antioch
36. some days af. Paul said unto B.
37. B. determined to take John Mk
39. B. took Mark, sailed unto Cy-
1 Co. 9:6 Or I only and B. ⌊prus
Ga. 2: 1. I went to Jerusalem with B.
9. gave to me and B. right hands
13. B. was carried away with their dissimulation ⌈receive
Col. 4:10. Marcus, sister's son to B.
See PAUL, SAUL = PAUL.
BARNFLOOR. ⌈or
2 K. 6:27. sh I help thee ? out of **b.**,
BARRED. ⌈ter
Can. 4 : † 12. a garden **b.** is my sis-
BARREL, S.
1 K. 17: 12. handful of meal in a **b.**
14. **b.** of meal shall not waste
16. **b.** of meal wasted not
18 : 33. Fill four **b-s** with water
BARREN.
Ge. 11 : 30. But Sarai was **b.**
25:21. Isaac entreated the Lord for his wife, because she was **b.** ⌈**b.**
29:31. Leah was hated ; but Rachel
Ex. 23 : 26. cast young, nor be **b.**
De. 7 : 14. not be male or female **b.**
Ju. 13 : 2. Manoah ; his wife was **b.**
3. thou art **b.**, but shalt bear son
1 S. 2 : 5. the **b.** hath borne seven
2 K. 2: 19. water naught, ground **b.**
21. not be any death or **b.** land
Jb. 24:21. He evil entreateth the **b.**
39 : 6. made **b.** land his dwellings
Ps. 113:9. **b.** woman to keep house
Pr. 30:16. never satisfied; **b.** womb
Can. 4:2. none is **b.** amo. them, 6:6.
Isa. 54: 1. Sing, O **b.**, that didst not
Jo. 2 : 20. drive him into a land **b.**
Lu. 1 : 7. because Elisabeth was **b.**
36. 6th month with her who was
23:29. Blessed are the **b.** ⌊called **b.**
Ga 4 : 27. written, Rejoice, thou **b.**
2 Pe. 1:8. ye nei be **b.** nor unfruit-
BARRENNESS. ⌊ful
Ps. 107 : 34. A fruitful land into **b.**
BAR'SABAS. ⌈B.
Ac. 1 : 23. appointed Joseph called
15 : 22. Judas surnamed B. and
BARTHOL'OMEW.
Mat. 10 : 3. the apostles are these ;
Philip, B . Mk 3:18. Lu. 6:14.
Ac. 1 : 13. where abode Philip, B.
BARTIME'US.
Mk. 10:46. blind B. sat by highway
BA'RUCH.
Ne. 3: 20. B. son of Zabbai repaired
10: 6. those that sealed, Daniel, B
11: 5. at Jerus. Maaseiah son of B.
Je. 32: 12. I gave evidence unto B.,
13. I charged B. before them ⌊16.
36: 4. Jeremiah called B ; B wrote
5. Jer-h commanded B., saying
8. B. did acc-g to all th. Jer-h ⌈13.
10. read B. in book words of Jer-h,
14. princes sent Jehudi unto B
So B. took roll in his hand ⌈it
15. Sit down, read it. So B. read
16. they were afraid, said unto B.
17. asked B., How didst write these
18. B. answered, He pronounced all
19. said princes unto B., Go hide
26. k. commanded to take B., Jer.
27. king burned the roll B. wrote
32. took J. another roll, gave to B.
43: 3. B. setteth thee on against us
6. Johanan took B. into Egypt
45: 1. word Jeremiah spake unto B.

Je. 45 : 2. Thus saith the Lord, the God of Israel, unto thee, O B.
See NERIAH.
BARZIL'LAI.
2 S. 17 : 27. B., Gileadite, brought wheat, sheep for David ⌈king
19 : 31. B. the Gileadite went with
32. Now B. was a very aged man
33. king said unto B., Come wi me
34. B said, How long have I to live
39. king kissed B., blessed him
21 : 8. brought up for Adriel son of B. the Meholathite ⌈Gileadite
1 K. 2:7. kindness unto sons of B.,
Ezr. 2:61. the children of B. ; which took a wife of the daughters of B. the Gileadite, Ne. 7 : 63.
BASE, S.
1 K. 7 : 27. ten **b-s** of brass; four cubits length of one **b.** ⌈ner, 37.
28. work of **b-s** was on this man-
29. upon the ledges was a **b.** above
30. every **b.** had 4 brazen wheels
31. mou. was round aft. work of **b.**
32. axletrees were joined to the **b.**
34. four undersetters to one **b.** (2)
35. in top of **b.** round compass (2)
37. made the ten **b-s**
38. upon ev. one of ten **b-s** 1 laver
39. he put five **b-s** on right side of house, five on ⌈**b-s**, 2 Ch. 4: 14.
43. ten **b-s**, and ten lavers on the
2 K. 16 : 17. cut off borders of **b-s**
25:13. **b-s** and brazen sea of hou.,
Ezr. 3:3. they set altar upon **b-s** ⌊16.
Ps. 104 : † 5. He hath founded the earth upon her **b-s** ⌈sea and **b-s**
Je. 27 : 19. saith Lord, concerning
52:17. **b-s** and sea Chaldeans brake
20. twelve brazen bulls under **b-s**
Zch. 5 : 11. be set upon her own **b.**
BASE. [Adj.]
2 S. 6:22. be **b.** in mine own sight
Jb. 30 : 8. were children of **b.** men
Is. 3 : 5. **b.** ag-t the honourable ⌈**b.**
Eze. 17 : 14. that kingdom might be
29 : 14. they shall be a **b.** kingdom
Mal. 2 : 9. I also made you **b.** ⌈say
Ac. 17:†18. What will this **b.** fellow
1 Co. 1 : 28. **b.** things of the world
2 Co. 10 : 1. I, Paul, in presence am
BASER, EST. ⌊**b.**
Eze 29 : 15. Pathros, **b-t** of kingd-s
Da. 4 : 17. setteth over it **b-t** of men
Ac. 17 : 5. lewd fellows of **b-r** sort
BA'SHAN. ⌈3 : 1.
Nu. 21 : 23. went by way of B., De.
33. Og king of B. went out ag-t them, De. 3 : 1. -29 : 7.
32 : 33. Moses gave kingdom of Og king of B., Jos. 13: 12, 30(3), 31.
De. 1:4. After he had slain Og king of B., 3 : 3. Jos. 12 : 4.
3 : 10. we took Gilead, all B. unto
. . cities of Og in B., 4. ⌈ants
11. only Og of B. remained of gi-
13. Gilead, all B. gave I unto Manasseh, Jos. 13 : 11, 30. ⌈giants
13. B., which was called land of
4:43. Golan in B., Jos. 20:8.-21:27.
47. and they possessed land of Og king of B., Ne. 9 : 22.
32:14. rams of the breed of B ⌈B
33 : 22. of Dan ; he shall leap from
Jos. 9:10 all that he did to Og king
12:5. Og reigned in Salcah, B. ⌊of B.
17: 1. theref. he had Gilead and B.
5. to Manasseh, besides Gilead, B.
21 : 6. Gershon had in B. thirteen cities, 1 Ch. 6 : 62. ⌈B.
22:7. to Manasseh, Moses given in
1 K. 4: 13. to him Argob wh. is in B.
19. Geber was in the country of Gilead and Og king of B.
2 K. 10:33. Hazael smote Gilead, B.
1 Ch. 5 : 11. Gad dwelt in B. unto S.
12. Joel. chief, and Shaphat in B.

1 Ch.5:16. they dwelt in Gilead in B.
23. Manasseh increased fr.B. unto
6 : 71. Unto Gershom Golan in B.
Ps. 22 : 12. strong bulls of B. beset
68 : 15. hill of G. as hill of B.(2)⌊une
22. said, I will bring again from B.
135 : 11. Who slew mighty kings;
Og king of B., 136 : 20. ⌈fruits
Is. 33 : 9. B., Carmel, shake off their
Je. 22 : 20. lift up thy voice in B.⌈B.
50 : 19. Israel shall feed on Carmel,
Eze. 39 : 18. all of them fatlings of B.
Am. 4 : 1. Hear this, ye kine of B.
Mi. 7 : 14. let them feed in B. as in
Na. 1 : 4. B. languisheth, and Carmel
See OAKS.

BA'SHAN-HA'VOTH-JA'IR.

De. 3 : 14. Jair called them B.

BASH'EMATH.

Ge. 26 : 34. Esau took to wife B.
36 : 3. Esau took B., Ishmael's dau.
4. to Esau B. bare Reuel, 10. ⌈17
13. the sons of B. Esau's wife,

BASIN. ⌈(2)

Ex. 12 : 22. dip it in blood in the **b.**
1 Ch. 28 : 17. gave gold for every **b.**
Jn. 13 : 5. he poureth water into **b.**

BASINS. ⌈in **b.**

Ex. 24 : 6. Moses took blood, put it
27 : 3. shalt make his pans, **b.**, 38:3.
Nu. 4 : 14. they shall put upon it **b.**
2 S. 17 : 28. Barzillai brought beds, **b.**
1 K. 7 : 40. Hiram made lavers, **b.**,
45. 2 Ch. 4 : 8, 11. ⌈4 : 22.
50. snuffers, **b.** of pure gold, 2 Ch.
2 K. 12 : 13. not made **b.** of money
1 Ch. 28 : 17. for **b.** gold by weight
Ezr. 1 : 10. 30 **b.** of gold, silver **b.**
8 : 27. 20 **b.** of gold of 1,000 drams
Ne. 7 : 70. Tirshatha gave fifty **b.**
Je. 52 : † 18. shovels, **b.** took they
19. **b.**, spoons took captain away

BASKET.

Ge. 40 : 17. in **b.** all bakemeats, the
birds did eat them out of **b.**
Ex. 29 : 3. cakes, wafers, put them in
one **b.**, and bring them in **b.**
23. **b.** of the unleavened bread.
Le. 8 : 2, 26. Nu. 6 : 15, 17. ⌈**b.**
32. Aaron sh. eat bread that is in
Le. 8 : 31. in the **b.** of consecrations
Nu. 6 : 19. take one cake out of the **b.**
De. 26 : 2. first of fruit put in the **b.**
4. priest take **b.**, set it before altar
28 : 5. Blessed shall be thy **b.** and
17. Cursed sh. be thy **b.** and store
Ju. 6 : 19. flesh Gideon put in a **b.**
Ps. 126 : † 6. goeth, bearing seed **b.**
Je. 24 : 2. One **b.** good figs, other **b.**
Am. 8 : 2. A **b.** of summer fruit, 1.
Ac. 9 : 25. disciples let him down by
the wall in a **b.**, 2 Co. 11 : 33.

BASKETS. ⌈head

Ge. 40 : 16. I had three white **b.** on
18. Joseph said, three **b.** are 3 days
2 K. 10 : 7. slew 70, put heads in **b.**
Je. 6 : 9. as a grapegatherer into **b.**
24 : 1 two **b.** of figs before temple
Mat. 14 : 20. took up twelve **b.** full,
Mk. 6 : 43. Lu. 9 : 17. Jn. 6 : 13.
15 : 37. did all eat, and took up of
broken meat left 7 **b.**, Mk. 8 : 8.
16 : 9. nei. remember how many **b.**
ye took up? 10. Mk. 8 : 19, 20.

BAS'MATH. ⌈mon

1 K. 4 : 15. he took B. dau-r of Solo-

BASON, BASONS.

See BASIN, BASINS

BASTARD, S. ⌈cong-n

De. 23 : 2. A **b.** shall not enter into
Zch. 9 : 6. **b.** shall dwell in Ashdod
He. 12 : 8. if without chastisement.

BAT, S. ⌊**b**-s

Le. 11 : 19. lapwing and **b.** shall be
an abomination, De 14 : 18.⌈**b**-s
Is. 2 : 20. sh. cast his idols to moles

BATH, S. ⌈**b**-s

1 K. 7 : 26. the sea contained 2,000
38. one laver containing forty **b**-s
2 Ch. 2 : 10. give 20,000 **b**-s of wine
4 : 5. the sea received 3,000 **b**-s ⌊(2)
Ezr. 7 : 22. 100 **b**-s of wine, 100 **b**-s
Is. 5 : 10. ten acres shall yield one **b.**
Eze. 45 : 10. a just ephah, a just **b.**
11. ephah and **b.** be of one measure, **b.** contain tenth part homer
14. shall offer tenth part of a **b.**;
for ten **b**-s are a homer (3)

BATHE, ED.

Le. 17 : 16. if wash not nor **b.** flesh
Is. 34 : 5. my sword be **b**-d in heaven
See Bathe in WATER.

BATH-RAB'BIM.

Can. 7 : 4. fishpools by the gate of B.

BATH'-SHEBA or BATH'-SHUA.[2] ⌈am

2 S. 11 : 3. † Is not this B.[2] dau. of Eli-
12 : 24. David comforted B. his wife
1 K. 1 : 11. Nathan spake unto B.
15. B. went unto k. into chamber
16. B did obeisance unto king, 31.
28. Then David said, Call me B.
2 : 13. Adonijah came to B. ⌈thee
18. B. said, Well; I will speak for
19. B. went unto Sol-n for Adon-h
Ps. 51.* aft. David had gone in to B.
1 Ch. 3 : 5. † these born unto him of
B.[2] daughter of Ammiel, † B.

BATTERED, ING.

2 S. 20 : 15. peo. with Joab **b**-d wall
Eze. 4 : 2. and set **b**-g rams against it
21 : 22 † appoint **b**-g rams ag. gates

BATTLE.

Ge. 14 : 8. they joined **b.** in Siddim
Nu. 21 : 33. Og to **b.** at Edrei, De. 3 : 1.
31 : 14. wroth with captains from **b.**
21. which went to the **b.**, 27, 28.
32 : 27. pass over before Lord to **b.**,
De. 2 : 9. neither contend in **b.** ⌊29.
24. Sihon, contend with him in **b.**
20 : 1. thou goest to **b.** ag-t thine
2. when ye are come nigh unto **b.**
3. O Israel, ye approach unto **b.**
5. return, lest he die in **b.**, 6, 7.
29 : 7. came unto **b.** we smote them
Jos. 4 : 13. 40,000 passed over unto **b.**
8 : 14. city went against Israel to
11 : 19. all other they took in **b.**⌊**b.**
20. of the Lord, that they come
against Israel in **b.** ⌈them in **b.**
22 : 33. not intend to go against
Ju. 8 : 13. Gideon from **b.** before sun
20 : 14. to **b.** ag-t chil. of Israel⌊up
18. Which of us go up first to **b.**
20. Israel went to **b.** ag. Benjamin
23. Shall I go again to **b.** ag. Benj.,
34. ag. Gibeah the **b.** was sore⌊28.
39. when Israel retired in **b.**, B-n
said, they are smitten as in first
42. but the **b.** overtook them ⌊**b.**
1 S. 4 : 1. Israel ag-t Philistines to **b.**
2. joined **b.**, Israel was smitten
7 : 10. Philistines drew near to **b.**
14 : 20. Saul and people came to **b.**
22. Israel followed hard after in **b.**
23. **b.** passed over unto Beth-aven
17 : 1. Philist. gathered armies to **b.**
13. sons of Jesse followed S to **b.**
20. as the host shouted for **b.** ⌊(2)
28. art come thou mightest see **b.**
47. the **b.** is the Lord's, 2 Ch. 20 : 15.
26 : 10. sh. descend into **b.**, perish
28 : 1. thou shalt go with me to **b.**
29 : 4. let him not go with us to **b.**,
. . lest in **b.** he be an adversary
9. He shall not go with us to the **b.**
30 : 24. his part th. goeth down to **b.**
31 : 3. And the **b.** went sore against
Saul, 1 Ch. 10 : 3. ⌈dead
2 S. 1 : 4. people are fled fr. **b.**, many
25. How are mighty fallen in **b.**!
2 : 17. very sore **b.**; Abner beaten
3 : 30. bec. he had slain Asahel in **b.**

2 S. 10 : 9. When Joab saw front of
b. was against him, 1 Ch. 19 : 10.
13. Joab drew nigh the **b.** against
Syrians, 1 Ch. 19 : 14 ⌈Ch. 20 : 1.
11 : 1. when kings go forth to **b.**, 1
15. Set ye Uriah in forefront of **b.**
25. make **b.** more strong ag-t city
17 : 11. go to **b.** in thine own person
18 : 6. **b.** was in wood of Ephraim
8. **b.** was scattered over country
19 : 3. as people when they flee in
10. And Absalom is dead in **b.**⌊**b.**
21 : 17. Thou shalt go no more to **b.**
18. again **b.** with Philist-s at Gob,
20. And there was a **b.** in Gath⌊19.
22 : 40. For thou hast girded me
to **b.**, Ps. 18 : 39. ⌈to **b.**
23 : 9. defied Philistines gathered
1 K. 8 : 44. If thy people go to **b.**
20 : 14. Who shall order the **b.**?
29. in seventh day **b.** was joined
39. Thy servant went out into **b.**
22 : 4. Wilt thou go with me to **b.**?
6. Shall I go against Ramoth-gilead to **b.**, 15. 2 Ch. 18 : 5, 14.
30. I will disguise myself, enter
into **b.** (2), 2 Ch. 18 : 29 (2).
35. And the **b.** increased that day,
2 Ch. 18 : 34. ⌈to **b.**?
2 K. 3 : 7. wilt thou go against Moab
26. Moab saw the **b.** was too sore
1 Ch. 5 : 20. they cried to God in **b.**
7 : 11. 17,200 fit to go out for **b.**
40. of Asher, apt to **b.**, 26,000 ⌈**b.**
11 : 13. Philistines were gathered to
12 : 8. unto David men fit for **b.**⌈**b.**
19. Da. with Philistines ag. Saul to
33. Of Zebulun, went to **b.** 50,000
36. of Asher, to **b.**, expert, 40,000
37. all instruments of war for **b.**
14 : 15. a sound, then go out to **b.**
19 : 7. chil. of Ammon came to **b.**
2 Ch. 13 : 14. **b.** was before, behind
20 : 1. Moab ag-t Jehoshaphat to **b.**
15. the **b.** is not yours, but God's
17. Ye not need to fight in this **b.**
25 : 8. do it, be strong for the **b.**
13. that they not go with him to **b.**
Jb. 15 : 24. as a king ready to the **b.**
39 : 25. he smelleth the **b.** afar off
41 : 8. remember the **b.**, do no more
Ps. 24 : 8. The Lord mighty in **b.**⌈**b.**
55 : 18. He delivered my soul from
76 : 3. There brake the sword and **b.**
89 : 43. not made him to stand in **b.**
Ec. 9 : 11. swift, nor **b.** to the strong
Is. 9 : 5 **b.** of warrior is with noise
13 : 4. Lord mustereth host of **b.**
22 : 2. thy slain are not dead in **b.**
27 : 4. who set briers ag-t me in **b.**?
28 : 6. strength to them th. turn **b.**
42 : 25. upon him strength of the **b.**
Je. 8 : 6. as horse rusheth into **b.**
18 : 21. let young men be slain in **b.**
46 : 3. Order shield, draw near to **b.**
49 : 14. come ag-t her, rise up to **b.**
50 : 22. A sound of **b.** is in the land
42. put in array, like a man to **b.**
Eze. 7 : 14. none goeth to the **b.**: for
13 : 5. to stand in **b.** in day of Lord
Da. 11 : 20. neith. in anger nor in **b.**
25. king shall be stirred up to **b.**
Ho. 1 : 7. will not save by bow nor **b.**
2 : 18. I will break **b.** out of earth
10 : 9. **b.** in Gibeah ag-t iniquity
Jo. 2 : 5. strong people set in **b.** ar-
Ob. 1. rise up ag-t Edom in **b.** ⌊ray
Zch. 10 : 3. as his goodly horse in **b.**
5. which tread down enemies in **b.**
14 : 2. all nations ag-t Jerus. to **b.**
1 Co. 14 : 8. who shall prepare to **b.**?
Re. 9 : 7. locusts were like horses
prepared unto **b.** ⌈ning to **b.**
9. chariots of many horses run-
16 : 14. to **b.** of that great day, 20 : 8.

BATTLE in array. ⌈**b.**-

Ju. 20 : 22. men of Israel set their

1 S. 17 : 2. Israel set **b.** - ag. Philist.
8. Why come out to set **b.** -? [-
21. Israel, Philistines, had put **b.**
2 S. 10 : 8 Am-n put **b.** -, 1 Ch. 19 : 9.
1 Ch. 12 : † 33. which could set **b.** -
19 : 17. Dav. set **b.** - ag. Syrians (2)
2 Ch. 13 : 3. Abija set the **b.** -;
Jeroboam set **b.** - against him
14 : 10. Asa set **b.** - in valley of Zeph-

BATTLE axe. [athah

Je. 51 : 20. Thou art my **b. a.** and

BATTLE bow.

Zch. 9 : 10. the **b. b.** shall be cut off
10 : 4. came forth out of him **b. b.**

Day of BATTLE.

1 S. 13 : 22. in - **b.** neith. sword nor
Jb 38 : 23. which I reserved ag-t - **b.**
Ps. 78 : 9 Ephraim turned in - **b.**
140 : 7. God covered my head in - **b.**
Pr 21 : 31. horse prepared ag-t - **b.**
Ho. 10 : 14. spoiled Beth-arbel in - **b.**
Am. 1 : 14. sh. devour palaces in - **b.**
Zch. 14 : 3 as when L fought in - **b.**

BATTLES.

1 S. 8 : 20. our king may fight our **b.**
18 : 17. be valiant, fight Lord's **b.**
25 : 28. my lord fighteth **b.** of Lord
1 Ch. 26 : 27. spoils won in **b.** dedica.
2 Ch. 32 : 8. is God, to fight our **b.**
Is. 30 : 32. in **b.** of shakings he fight

BATTLEMENT, S.

De. 22 : 8. make a **b.** for thy roof
Je. 5 : 10. take away her **b-s**; they
Da. 9 : † 27. upon **b-s** shall be idols

BA'VAI. [dad

Ne. 3 : 18. repaired B. son of Hena-

BAY. [Noun.]

Jos. 15 : 2. sea from **b.** southward
5. **b.** at uttermost part of Jordan
18 : 19. at north **b.** of the salt sea

BAY. [Adj.] [**b.**

Zch. 1 : † 8. behind him red horses,
6 : 3 in fourth chariot **b.** horses
7. the **b.** sought to go thro. earth

BAY tree.

Ps. 37 : 35. wicked like a green **b. t.**

BAZ'LITH, or BAZ'LUTH.

Ezr. 2 : 52. † the chil. of B., Ne. 7 : 54. †

BDELLIUM.

Ge. 2 : 12. Havilah . . and there is **b.**
Nu. 11 : 7. manna, colour was as of **b.**

BE.

Ge. 1 : 14. let them **b.** for signs and
15. let them **b.** for lights in firma.
22. **b.** fruitful and multiply, 28.-
8 : 17.-9 : 7.-35 : 11. [alone
2 : 18. It is not good that man **b.**
13 : 8. no strife, for we **b.** brethren
16 : 5. said, My wrong **b.** upon thee
17 : 1. walk before me, **b.** thou per.
18 : 24. Peradvent. **b.** 50 righteous
24 : 14. let the same **b.** she that
51. let her **b.** master's son's wife
60. **b.** thou mother of millions
27 : 13. Upon me **b.** curse, my son
21. whether thou **b.** my very son
29. **b.** lord over thy brethren:
cursed **b.** ev. one curseth thee (3)
31 : 44. let it **b.** for a witness, 52 (2)
32 : 18. they **b.** thy servant Jacob's
33 : † 9. **b.** that to thee that is thine
34 : 23. ev. beast of their's **b.** ours?
35 : 2. **b.** clean, change garments
37 : 27. let not our hand **b.** upon h.
32. whether it **b.** thy son's coat or
38 : 29. this breach **b.** upon thee
42 : 16. whether **b.** any truth in you
32. We **b.** twelve brethren, sons
44 : 10. let it **b.** acc. unto your words
26. if youngest brother **b.** with us
50 : 18. Behold, we **b.** thy servants
Ex. 8 : 10. **b.** it acc-g to thy word
10 : 10. Let the Lord **b.** so with you
12 : 33. they said, We **b.** all dead m.
18 : 19. **b.** thou for peo. to God-ward
Le. 8 : 33. consecration **b.** at an end
13 : 26. **b.** no white hair in spot (3)
Le. 15 : 24. if her flowers **b.** upon h.
23 : 29. whatso. soul it **b.** not afflicted
25 : 51. If **b.** yet many years behind
Nu. 1 : 53. **b.** no wrath upon cong-n
5 : 13. If **b.** no witness against her
13 : 20. land, whether **b.** wood th-in
or not And **b.** ye of good cour.
14 : 3. wives and chil. **b.** prey? [Lord
16 : 16. **b.** thou and company before
De. 10 : 5. they **b.** as Lord com-ded
15 : 6. If **b.** among you a poor man
21. if **b.** any blemish therein as if
29 : 18. Lest **b.** man . . whose heart
turneth; **b.** root that beareth
Jos. 9 : 21. let them **b.** hewers of w.
14 : 12. if so **b.** Lord **b.** with me (3)
Ju. 6 : 13. if Lord **b.** with us, why
this? where **b.** all his miracles
31. if he **b.** a god, let him plead
15 : † 2. her sister, let her **b.** thine
17 : 10. **b.** unto me a father, priest
1 S. 10 : 7. let it **b.** when signs [sh. die
14 : 39 tho. it **b.** in Jonathan he
18 : 22. now **b.** king's son in law
20 : 7. if he **b.** very wroth, **b.** sure
8. if **b.** in me iniquity slay me thyself, 2 S. 14 : 32. [Father
13. Lord **b.** with thee as with my
42. Lord **b.** between me and thee
23 : 23. if he **b.** in land I will search
25 : 11. I know not whence they **b.**
2 S. 1 : 21. Ye mts., **b.** dew upon you
18 : 32. enemies **b.** as that young m.
24 : 17. let thine hand **b.** against me
1 K. 1 : 37. even so **b.** he with Sol-n
8 : 37. if **b.** in the land famine (4)
57. Lord **b.** with us as with fath-s
12 : 7. If **b.** servant unto people (2)
18 : 21. if Lord **b.** God, follow him
2 K. 2 : 16. **b.** with thy servants 50
6 : 16. that **b.** with us more than (2)
10 : 23. look that **b.** none of serv-ts
19 : 25. thou **b.** to lay waste [of L.
20 : 19. good; if peace **b.** in my days
1 Ch. 21 : 3. 100 times more as they **b.**
2 Ch. 36 : 23. The Lord his God **b.**
with him, Ezr. 1 : 3. [**b.** so
Ezr. 5 : 17. let **b.** search whether it
9 : 14. wouldst not thou **b.** angry
so there **b.** no escaping?
Ne. 1 : 6. Let thine ear **b.** attentive
Jb. 5 : 1. Call if **b.** any that will ans.
10 : 15. If I **b.** wicked, woe unto
me; and if I **b.** righteous, 9 : 29.
15 : 14. What is man th. he **b.** clean
19 : 4. **b.** it indeed th. I have erred
33 : 23. If **b.** a messenger with him
Ps. 3 : 2. **b.** wise now, O ye kings
7 : 3. if **b.** iniquity in my hands
19 : 14. Let words of . . **b.** accept-
28 : 1. if thou **b.** silent to me [able
31 : 17. let them **b.** silent in grave
24. **b.** of good courage, Is. 41 : 6.
33 : 22. Let thy mercy, L. be upon
35 : 5. Let them **b.** as chaff [pery
6. Let their way **b.** dark, slip-
39 : 13. bef. I go hence, **b.** no more
58 : 7. let them **b.** as cut in pieces
67 : 1 God **b.** merciful unto us
71 : 3. **b.** my strong habitation
80 : 17. Let thy hand **b.** upon man
90 : 17. let beauty of Lord **b.** upon
109 : 8. Let his days **b.** few [us
10. Let his chil. **b.** vagabonds, 9.
15. Let them **b.** bef. L. continu-y
17. blessing, let it **b.** far from him
19. cursing. Let it **b.** for a girdle
20. Let this **b.** reward of adversar.
129 : 6. Let them **b.** as the grass
8. The blessing of Lord **b.** upon y.
139 : 24. if **b.** any wicked way in me
149 : 6. Let high praises of God **b.**
Pr. 23 : 17. **b.** in fear of Lord all day
Ec. 6 : 11. **b.** many things that incr.
8 : 14. **b.** just men; **b.** wicked men
Can. 1 : 7. why I **b.** as one that turn-
2 : 17. **b.** thou like a roe, 8 : 14. [eth
Can. 8 : 9. If she **b.** wall, if **b.** door
Is. 1 : 18. tho. sins **b.** as scarlet (4)
19. If ye **b.** obedient, sh. eat good
3 : 6. hast clothing, **b.** our ruler (2)
8 : 13. Lord, let him **b.** your fear,
let him **b.** your dread [cept
28 : 10. precept must **b.** upon pre-
41 : 22. former things, what they **b.**
47 : 12. if so **b.** thou **b.** able to profit, if so **b.** thou mayest prevail
Je. 5 : 1. if **b.** any that executeth
7 : 32. bury in Tophet till **b.** no pl.
14 : 8 why thou **b.** as a stranger
9. Why thou **b.** as man astonished
15 : 18. wilt thou **b.** unto me as liar
21 : 2. if so **b.** L. will deal with us
26 : 3. If so **b.** they turn from me
27 : 18. if word of L. **b.** wi. them (2)
42 : 6. whe. it **b.** good or it **b.** evil
Eze. 22 : 5. Those that **b.** near **b.** far
La. 1 : 12. see if **b.** sorrow like my
3 : 29. if so **b.** there may **b.** hope
Da. 3 : 15. **b.** at what time hear cornet
4 : 19. dream **b.** to them hate thee
5 : 7. that he **b.** 3d ruler in kingd.
12 : 13. go thy way till the end **b.**
Ho. 3 : 3. so will I also **b.** for thee
8 : 7. if so **b.** it yield, strangers sh.
13 : 15. Tho. he **b.** fruitful among
Jon. 1 : 6. if so **b.** G. think upon us
Na. 1 : 12. Tho. they **b.** many [eyes?
Zch. 8 : 6. it **b.** marvellous in mine
Mat. 2 : 13. **b.** there till I bring word
4 : 3. If thou **b.** the Son of God, 6.
-27 : 40. Lu. 4 : 3. [thereat
7 : 13. many there **b.** which go in
14. few there **b.** that find it [you
9 : 29. Acc-g to your faith **b.** it unto
10 : 25. disciple, he **b.** as his master
15 : 28. **b.** it unto thee as thou wilt
16 : 22. **b.** it far from thee, Lord
23. savourest not things that **b.**
of God, but **b.** of men, Mk. 8 : 33.
18 : 13. if so **b.** he find it, rejoiceth
17. let him **b.** as a heathen man
19 : 9. except it **b.** for fornication
10. If case of the man **b.** so [(2)
20 : 26. let him **b.** your minister
26 : 5. lest there **b.** an uproar
27 : 49. Let **b.**, Let us see whe. Elias
Mk. 3 : 14. twelve, that they **b.** with
7 : 4. many other things **b.** [him
13 : 7. such things must needs **b.**
14. let them that **b.** in Judea flee
Lu. 1 : 29. what salutat-n this sho. **b.**
38. **b.** it unto me acc-g to thy word
10 : 6. if the son of peace **b.** there
14 : 33. whoso-r he **b.** forsaketh not
19 : 19. **b.** thou also over five cities
22 : 26. greatest, let **b.** as younger
23 : 24. it sho. **b.** as they required
37. If thou **b.** king of the Jews [35.
39. If thou **b.** Christ, save thyself,
Jn. 3 : 2. miracles, exc. God **b.** with
9. How can these things **b.**? [him
7 : 17. doctrine, whe. it **b.** of God
8 : 33. answ-d, We **b.** Abr-'s seed
9 : 25. Wheth. he **b.** a sinner or no
31. if any man **b.** worshipper of G.
10 : 24. If thou **b.** the Christ, tell
13 : 24. that he ask who it should **b.**
16 : 33 tribulation; **b.** of good ch.
Ac. 13 : 47. **b.** for salvat-n unto ends
19 : 2. whe. there **b.** any Holy Gho.
26. they **b.** no gods wh. are made
24 : 21. exc. it **b.** for this one voice
27 : 25. Wheref., sirs, **b.** of good c.
Ro. 3 : 4. let G. **b.** true, but ev. man
8 : 9. if so **b.** Spirit of God dwell in
17. if so **b.** we suffer with him [you
31. If God **b.** for us, who can **b.**
11 : 15. if casting away **b.** reconcil-g
12 : 16. **b.** of same mind one toward
13 : 1. Let every soul **b.** subject unto . . powers that **b.** are orda-d
15 : 16. **b.** minister to Gentiles,
that offering of G-s **b.** acceptab

Ro. 15:33. God of peace **b.** with you
1 Co. 8 : 5. though there **b.** that are
called gods,(there **b.** gods many)
9 : 19. tho. I **b.** free from all men
23. that I might **b.** partaker with
27. lest I should **b.** a castaw.⌊you
10 : 1. I would not that ye **b.** igno-
30. if I by grace **b.** partaker ⌊rant
11 : 18. I hear there **b.** divisions
12 : 25. there **b.** no schism in body
14 : 20. Brethren, in understan-g **b.**
27. let it **b.** by two or three ⌊men
28. if **b.** no interpreter, let him
15 : 13. if **b.** no resurrection, then
15. if so **b.** that the dead rise not
57. But thanks **b.** to God ⌈come
16 : 2. **b.** no gatherings when I
22. if love not Ch., **b.** Anathema
24. My love **b.** with you in Christ
2 Co. 1 : 17. with me sho. **b.** yea and
5 : 3. If so **b.** that being clothed we
10. done, whether it **b.** good or b.
17. Thf. if any man **b.** in Christ
† 17. let him **b.** a new creature
8 : 12. if **b.** first a willing mind, it
12 : 11. chiefest. tho. I **b.** nothing
16. **b.** it so, I did not burden you
13 : 7. though we **b.** as reprobates
11. **b.** perfect, **b.** of good comfort,
Ga. 3 : 9. wh. **b.** of faith, blessed⌊**b.**
4 : 12. I beseech you, **b.** as I am ⌈**b.**
5 : 10. bear his judgment whoso. he
Ep. 1 : 12. That we **b.** to praise of
4 : 21. If so **b.** ye have heard him
Ph. 2 : 5. Let this mind **b.** in you
4 : 6. **b.** careful for nothing ; but
8. if **b.** any virtue, if **b.** any praise
1 Th. 3 : 5. lest our labour **b.** in vain
1 Ti. 4 : 12. **b.** thou an example of
He. 2 : 17. might **b.** merciful priest
Ja. 2 : 15. If a brother **b.** naked, and
1 Pe. 1 : 6. if need **b.**, ye in heavin-s
15. as he is holy, so **b.** ye holy, 16.
2 : 3. If so **b.** ye have tasted that
13. Submit, whether it **b.** to king
18. servants **b.** subject to masters
3 : 1. wives **b.** in subject-n to husb-s
4. adorning, let it **b.** the hidden m.
15. **b.** ready always to give answer
17. better if the will of God **b.** so
5 : 5. all **b.** subject one to another
8. **b.** sober, **b.** vigilant ; bec. devil
2 Pe. 1 : 4. that ye might **b.** partak-
8. if these things **b.** in you ⌊ers
3 Jn. 8. we might **b.** fellow helpers
Re. 2 : 10. **b.** thou faithful unto d-h
3 : 2. **b.** watchful, strengthen thi-s
18 : 22. of whatsoever craft he **b.**
22 : 11. unjust, let him **b.** unjust
still ; he holy, let him **b.** holy(4)

See **Be ABLE, Be AFRAID.**
See **BLOOD be on or upon,**
BEGAN, BLESSED, CHILDREN,
CLEAN, DESOLATE, FAR,
FOLLOWERS, GLAD, IF, IT,
JOYFUL, LET.

If it BE.

Ge. 23 : 8. - **b.** your mind that I bury
25 : 22. - **b.** so, why am I thus?
Ex. 1 : 16. - **b.** a son, kill, - **b.** dau.
Le. 15 : 23. - **b.** on her bed, unclean
De. 15 : 21. - **b.** lame, not sacrifice it
2 K. 9 : 15. - **b.** your minds, let none
10 : 15. - **b.**, give me thine hand
Da. 3 : 17. - **b.** so, our God is able to
Zch. 8 : 6. - **b.** marvellous in eyes
Mat. 14 : 28. - **b.** thou, bid me come
Ac. 5 : 39. - **b.** of God, cannot overth.
18 : 15. - **b.** question of words⌈ably
Ro. 12 : 18. - **b.** possible, live peace-
Ga. 3 : 4. suffered in vain? - **b.** in

Let there BE. ⌊vain

Ge. 1 : 3. God said, - **b.** light ⌈ment
6. And God said, - **b.** a firma-
13 : 8. - **b.** no strife betw. me and
26 : 28. - **b.** an oath betwixt us and
Ex. 5 : 9. - more work **b.** upon men
Ezr. 5 : 17. - **b.** search in treasure ho.
Ps. 109 : 12. - **b.** none to extend mercy ; nei. - **b.** any to favour chil.

May BE.

Ex. 7 : 19. **m. b.** blood thro-t Egypt
9 : 22. **m. b.** hail in all Egypt⌈felt
10 : 21. **m. b.** darkness which **m. b.**
27 : 5. net **m. b.** to midst of altar
28 : 28. that it **m. b.** above girdle
37 plate, that it **m. b.** upon mitre
30 : 16. that it **m. b.** a memorial
29. sanctify, that they **m. b.** holy
Le. 14 : 8. wash that he **m. b.** clean
24 : 7. **m. b.** on bread for a memor-l
Nu. 7 : 5. they **m. b.** to do service
De. 6 : 3. that it **m. b.** well wi. thee,
18.-22 : 7. Ru. 3 : 1. Ep. 6 : 3.
11 : 18. that they **m. b.** as frontlets
31 : 19. this song **m. b.** a witness
Jos. 4 : 6. this **m. b.** a sign amo you
Ju. 19 : 9. thine heart **m. b.** merry
Ru. 1 : 11. they **m. b.** your husb-ds?
4 : 14. name **m. b.** famous in Israel
1 S. 8 : 20. we **m. b.** like all nations
2 S. 18 : † 22. **b.** what **m.**, let me run
2 Ch. 7 : 16. my name **m. b.** there
13 : 9. same **m. b.** a priest ⌊forever
Ne. 4 : 22. in night **m. b.** a guard
Jb. 22 : 2. **m. b.** profitable to hims.
Is. 10 : 2. widows **m. b.** their prey
Eze. 24 : 11. that brass **m. b.** hot (2)
Jon. 1 : 11. do that sea **m. b.** calm
Mat. 23 : 26. that outside **m. b.** clean
Jn. 12 : 36. ye **m. b.** child-n of light
16 : 24. shall receive, that your joy
m. b. full, 1 Jn. 1 : 4. ⌈ity (3)
2 Co. 8 : 14. that there **m. b.** equal-
2 Pe. 3 : 2. ye **m. b.** mindf. of words

See **Be ABLE, MAY be,**
Might BE, Mightest BE.
See MAYEST, MUST.

BE.

with cannot, neither, or **not.**

Ge. 21 : 12. Let it **n. b.** grievous bec.
38 : 9. Onan knew seed **n. b.** his
44 : 30. and the lad **n. b.** with us
45 : 6. five years, n-r **b.** earing nor
Ex. 9 : 29. n-r shall **b.** any more hail
Le. 26 : 13. ye **b. n.** their bondmen
Nu. 12 : 12. Let her **n. b.** as one dead
16 : 40. that he **n. b.** as Korah
De. 15 : 9. Beware, **b. n.** a thought
in thy wicked heart ⌈except
Jos. 7 : 12. n-r will I **b.** wi. you more
2 Ch. 30 : 7. **b. n.** like your fathers,
which trespassed, 8. Zch 1 : 4.
Ps. 22 : 19. **b. n.** thou far from me,
O Lord, 35 : 22.-38 : 21.-71 : 12.
28 : 1. O Lord, **b. n.** silent to me
32 : 9. **b.** ye **n.** as the horse or as
69 : † 25. let **n. b.** a dweller in tents
Ec. 5 : 2. **b. n.** rash with mouth (2)
Is. 3 : 7. swear, I will **n. b.** a healer
7 : 8. Ephr., that it **b. n.** a people
28 : 22. **b.** ye **n.** mockers ⌈**b.** aft.
43 : 10. before me no God, **n-r** shall
Je. 49 : 23. the sea : it **c. b.** quiet
Eze. 16 : 16. **n-r** shall it **b.**, 20. ⌈th.
34 : 10. they may **n. b.** meat for
Mat. 6 : 16. when fast, **b. n.** as hypo.
24 : 20. pray that your flight **b. n.**
in winter, Mk. 13 : 18. ⌈troub.
Mk. 13 : 7. hear of wars, **b.** ye **n.**
Lu. 12 : 29. **n-r b.** ye of doubtful
13 : 33. **c. b.** that prophet perish
14 : 26. he **c. b.** my disciple, 33.
Jn. 1 : 25. if thou **b. n.** that Christ
20 : 27. **b. n.** faithless, but believ-g
Ac. 17 : 27. tho. he **b. n.** far from us
Ro. 4 : 17. calleth things which **b. n.**
12 : 16. **b. n.** wise in own conceits
1 Co. 2 : † 5. faith **n. b.** in wisdom of
7 : 23. **b. n.** ye the servants of men
9 : 2. If I **b. n.** apostle unto others
10 : 7. n-r **b.** ye idolators as some
14 : 20 **b. n.** children in underst-g
2 Co. 6 : 14. **b.** ye **n.** unequally yoked
Ga. 1 : 10. if I pleased men, should
n. b. servant of Christ ⌈glory
5 : 26. Let us **n. b.** desirous of vain-
Ep. 5 : 7. **b. n.** partakers with them
17. **b.** ye **n.** unwise, but underst-g
Tit. 3 : 14. that they **b. n.** unfruitf.
Phm 14. thy benefit **n. b.** of necessi-
He. 6 : 12. That ye **b. n.** slothful⌊ty
8 : 4. if on earth he **n. b.** priest⌈ters
Ja. 3 : 1. brethren **b. n.** many mas-
1 Pe. 3 : 3. let it **n. b.** outw. adorning
2 Pe. 1 : 8. ye shall n-r **b.** barren

See **Neither be AFRAID,**
Be not AFRAID,
WILL not be.
See **PEACE be,** QUIET.

Shall BE or **Shalt BE.**

Ge. 1 : 29. to you it **s. b.** for meat
2 : 24. his wife ; they **s. b.** one flesh
3 : 16. desire **s. b.** to thy husband
4 : 7. unto thee **s. b.** his desire and
12. vagabond s-t thou **b.** in earth,
6 : 3. his days **s. b.** 120 years ⌊14.
15. length of ark **s. b.** 300 cubits
19. two ; they **s. b.** male and fe.
21. it **s. b.** food for thee and them
9 : 2. fear of you **s. b.** upon beast
3. Ev. thing that liveth **s. b.** meat
11. neither **s.** any more **b.** a flood
13. bow in cloud **s. b.** a token, 16.
25. Cursed **b.** Canaan ; a serv-t **s.**
he **b.** unto his brethren, 26, 27.
12 : 2. thou **s-t b.** a blessing ⌈heir
15 : 4. out of own bowels **s. b.** thine
5. So **s.** thy seed **b.**, Ro. 4 : 18.
13. Abram, thy seed **s. b.** stranger
17 : 4. thou **s-t b.** father of nations
5. but thy name **s. b.** Abraham
11. it **s. b.** a token of a covenant
13. my coven-t **s. b.** in your flesh
15. but Sarah **s.** her name **b.**
16. she **s. b.** mother of nations ;
kings of people **s. b.** of her
24 : 8. thou s-t **b.** clear fr. my oath,
25 : 23. one peo. **s. b.** stronger ⌊41.
26 : 22. room for us, we **s. b.** fruitf.
27 : 39 thy dwelling **s. b.** fatness
28 : 14. thy seed **s. b.** as dust of e-h
21. then **s.** the Lord **b.** my God
22. this stone **s. b.** God's house
29 : 15. tell me what **s.** thy wages **b.**
30 : 32. speckled **s. b.** my hire,
31 : 8. ringstreaked **s. b.** thy hire(2)
34 : 10. land **s. b.** bef. you ⌈18 : 31.
35 : 10. Israel **s. b.** thy name, 1 K.
11. of nations **s. b.** of thee ⌈well
40 : 14. think on me when it **s. b.**
41 : 27. **s. b.** seven years of famine
36. that food **s. b.** for store ag-t
the famine which **s. b.** ⌈blamel.
44 : 10. he **s. b.** my serv-t ; ye **s. b.**
45 : 10. thou **s-t b.** near unto me
47 : 24. four parts **s. b.** your own
48 : 5. Reuben, Simeon **s. b.** mine
19. he **s. b.** great ; his bro. **s. b.**
21. God **s. b.** with you ⌊greater
49 : 10. unto him **s.** gathering **b.**
13. Zebulun **s. b.** for a haven (2)
26. they **s. b.** on the head of Jos-h
Ex. 4 : † 9. river **s. b.** and **s. b.** blood
16. he **s. b.** thy spokesman : thou
s-t b. to him instead of God (3)
7 : 1. Aaron's **b.** thy prophet ⌈(2)
11 : 6. **s. b.** great cry thro-t Egypt
13 : 5. it **s. b.** when Lord bring thee.
9. it **s. b.** for a sign unto thee ⌊10
14. it **s. b.** when thy son asketh
16 : 5. it **s. b.** twice as much as⌈(2)
18 : 22. so **s.** it **b.** easier for thys.,
19 : 5. ye **s. b.** a peculiar treasure
6. ye **s. b.** a kingdom of priests
21 : 36. pay ox for ox, dead **s. b.** his
25 : 20. toward mercy seat **s.** faces **b.**
26 : 24. they **s. b.** for 2 corners (2)
28 : 37. forefront of mitre it **s. b.**
29 : 28. it **s. b.** Aaron's by statute
30 : 2. altar foursquare **s.** it **b.** (4)

Ex. 30 . 4. s. b. for places for staves
13. half shekel s. b. offering of L.
25. it s. b. a holy anointing oil,
31, 32, 36, 37. [b. holy
29. whatsoever toucheth them s.
34. of each s. there b. like weight
40 : 10. it s. b. an altar most holy
Le 2 : 1. offering s. b. of fine flour
13 : 46. days, plague s. b. in him ;
with-t camp s. his habitation b.
15 : 3. this s. b. his uncleanness
19 : 23. yrs. s. it b. as uncircumc-d
20 : 21. they s. b. childless [(2.
23 : 27. it s. b. a holy convocation
25 : 45. they s. b. your possession
53. as hired serv-t s. he b. [-30 : 22.
26 : 12. ye s. b. my people, Je. 7 : 23.
Nu. 3 : 12. the Levites s. b. mine
10 : 8. they s. b. for an ordinance
15 : 15. as ye are, so s. stranger b.
33 : 55. s. b. pricks in your eyes [b.
36 : † 3. tribe, unto whom they s.
De. 2 : 25. s. b. in anguish bec. of
6 : 25. it s. b. our righteousness if
15 : 16. it s. b. if he say unto thee
17 : 19. book s. b. wi. him all his life
18 : 3. this s. b. priest's due [21.
24 : 19. it s. b. for the stranger, 20,
28 : 13. not the tail, thou s-t b. above
44. he s. b. head, thou s-t b. tail
32 : 20. will see what their end s. b.
Jos. 4 : 7. stones s. b. for memorial
7 : 15. s. b., that be with accursed
22 : 28. it s. b. when they say to us
Ju. 7 : 4. it s. b. of whom I sh. say
11 : 9 Jephthah said, s. I b. head ?
31. it s. b. that whoso. cometh to
meet me s. b. the Lord's [less
1 S. 15 : 33. so s. thy moth. b. child-
17 : 36. Philist-s s. b. as one of th.
22 : 23. with me s-t thou b. in safeg.
2 S. 2 : 26. how long s. it b. ere thou
5 : 8. he s. b. chief and captain
15 : 20. mercy, truth s. b. with thee
21. place king s. b. servant b.
1 K. 18 : 31. Israel s. b. thy name
20 : 40. So s. thy judgment b.
2 K. 2 : 10. if see me taken it s. b. so
2 Ch. 19 : 11. Lord s. b. with the good
33 : 4. In Jerus. s. my name b. forev.
Ne. 2 : 6. how long s. thy journey b. ?
Jb. 11 : 15. yea, thou s-t b. steadfast
17. thine age s. b. clearer than
noonday ; thou s-t b. as morn-g
18. thou s-t b. secure bec. is hope
20 : 18. according to his substance
s. restitution b. [straits
22. In his sufficiency he s. b. in
22 : 25. Almighty s. b. thy defence
Ps. 62 : 3. as a bowing wall s. ye b.
104 : † 31 glory of Lord s. b. for ev.
34. My meditation s. b. sweet [day
110 : 3. Thy people s. b. willing in
125 : 5. but peace s. b. upon Israel
128 : 2. happy s-t thou b., it s. b.
3. Thy wife s. b. as fruitful vine
137 : 8. happy s. b. that rewardeth
9. happy s. b. that dasheth little
141 : 5. smite me ; it s. b. a kindn-s,
my prayer s. b. in their calamity (3) [thy soul (2)
Pr. 24 : 14. So s. wisdom b. unto
Ec. 1 : 9. hath been, is that wh. s. b.
10 : 14. man cannot tell wh. s. b. (2)
11 : 3. where tree falleth th. it s. b.
Is. 1 : 18. sins s. b. white as snow (2)
30. ye s. b. as oak whose leaf fad-h
31. strong s. b. as tow and burn
2 : 12. day of L. s. b. upon proud
3 : 11. wicked ! it s. b. ill with him
4 : 2. s. branch of Lord b. glorious
5. upon all the glory s. b. defence
6. s. b. a tabernacle from the heat
6 : 13. in it s. b. a tenth ; holy seed
s. b. substance thereof [s. b. for
7 : 23. place where 1,000 vines, it
25. it s. b. for the sending of oxen

Is. 8 : 14. he s. b. for sanctuary [God
21. they s. b. hungry, sh curse
9 : 19. people s. b. as fuel of fire
10 : 17. light of Israel s. b. for fire
11 : 5. righteousness s. b. the girdle
10. that day s. b. a root of Jesse
17 : 5. it s. b. as he that gathereth
19 : 16 s. Egypt b. like unto wom.
19. that day s. b. an altar in Eg.
20. s. b. for sign unto L. of hosts
22 : 23. he s. b. for glorious throne
23 : 18. her hire s. b. holiness to L.
24 : 2. it s. b. as wi. people, so priest
29 : 7. all s. b. as dream of a night
8. It s. b. as when a hungry man
35 : 8. and a highway s. b. there (2)
9. No lion s. b. there, nor raven-s
47 : 14. Behold, they s. b. as stubble
15. Thus s. they b. unto thee
58 : 8. Glory of Lord s. b. rearward
Je. 7 : 33. people s. b. meat for fowls
13 : 27. O Jerus. ! when s. it once b.
15 : 19. thou s-t b. as my mouth
23 : 26. How long s. this b. in the
heart of prophets [sword
25 : 16. they s. b. mad because of
31 : 6. s. b. day, watchmen sh. cry
32 : 5. Babylon, there s. he b. until
33 : 9. it s. b. to me a name of joy
42 : 17. So s. it b. with all men th.
18. ye s. b. an execration, a curse
49 : 22. s. b. as heart of a woman in
32. their camels s. b. booty [pangs
36. s. b. no nation, whi. outcasts
51 : 58. folk in the fire s. b. weary
63. it s. b. when an end of read-g
Eze. 13 : 9. hand s. b. upon proph-s
18 : 20. righteousness of righteous
s. b. upon him (2) [of nets
26 : 5. It s. b. place for spreading
27 : 36. thou s-t b. a terror, and
never s-t b. any more [8 : 19.
Da. 2 : 28. what s. b. in latter days,
8 : 17. at time of end s. b. vision
19. at the time the end s. b. [chief
11 : 27. kings' hearts s. b. to do mis-
Ho. 1 : 11. great s. b. day of Jezreel
4 : 6. thou s-t b. no priest to me
9. s. b. like people, like priest
5 : 9. made known that which s. b.
8 : 8. s. b. as vessel wh-in no pleas.
11. altars s. b. unto him to sin
13 : 3. they s. b. as morning cloud
14 : 7. scent s. b. as wine of Leb-n
Am 5 : 14. God of hosts s. b. wi. you
Ob. 16. s. b. as tho. they had not b.
Mi. 2 : 11. he s. b. prophet of people
5 : 5. this man s. b. the peace when
7 : 4. now s. b. their perplexity
8. the Lord s. b. a light unto me
Ha. 2 : 7. thou s-t b. for booties [gl-y
16. shameful spewing s. b. on thy
3 : 17. s. b. no herd in the stalls (2)
Hag. 2 : 12. s. it b. holy ? priests said,
13. s. it b. unclean ? It s. b. [No
Zch. 2 : 11. nations s. b. my people
6 : 13. he s. b. a priest upon his
throne ; counsel of peace s. b.
14. the crowns s. b. to Helem and
8 : 5. streets s. b. full of boys, girls
13. were a curse ; ye s. b. a bless-
9 : 7. he s. b. for our God (2) [ing
12 : 8. feeble s. b. as David ; and
house of David s. b. as God
14 : 8. it s. b. that living waters (2)
17. And it s. b. that s. b. no rain
18. s. b. plague wherew. L. smite
19. This s. b. punishment of Eg.
20. s. b. upon bells HOLINESS (2)
21. every pot s. b. holiness unto
Lord ; s. b. no more the C., 20.
Mal. 3 : 12. ye s. b. delightsome la.
Mat. 5 : 22. s. b. in danger of hell f.
10 : 36. man's foes s. b. they of his
12 : 27. therefore they s. b. your
judges, Lu. 11 : 19. [generation
45. so s. it b. unto this wicked

Mat. 22 : 28. whose wife s. she b. of
seven, Mk. 12 : 23. [Mk. 13 : 19 (2).
24 : 21. s. b. great tribulation (2).
27. so s. coming of Son of man b.,
37, 39. Lu. 17 : 24, 26, 30. [36.
40. Then s. two b. in field, Lu. 17 :
Mk. 9 : 19. O, how long s. I b. with
you ? Lu. 9 : 41. [day that
Lu. 1 : 20. so thou s-t b. dumb until
34. Mary unto angel, How s. th. b.
66. Wh. manner of child s. this b. ?
6 : 35. ye s. b. children of Highest
40. one perfect, s. b. as his master
11 : 30. a sign, so s. Son of man b.
12 : 20. whose s. those things b.
17 : 31. he wh. s. b. upon housetop
34. that night s. b. 2 men in bed
35. two women s. b. grinding
23 : 43. To day s-t b. in paradise
Jn. 4 : 14. s. b. in him a well of water
8 : 55. If I say . . I s. b. liar like you
10 : 16. s. b. one fold, one shepherd
12 : 26. where I am s. my serv-t b.
14 : 17. he wi. you, and s. b. in you
15 : 8. so s. ye b. my disciples [b.
19 : 24. Let us cast lots whose it s.
Ac. 1 : 8. ye s. b. witnesses in all Je.
22 : 15. thou s-t b. his witness unto
24 : 15. hope that s. b. a resurrect-n
27 : 25. it s. b. even as was told me
1 Co. 14 : 11. I s. b. unto him a barbarian ; he s. b. a barbarian
15 : 28. then s. Son b. subject unto
37. sowest not that body that s. b.
2 Co. 6 : 16. and they s. b. my people, He. 8 : 10. Re. 21 : 3. [ters
18. ye s. b. my sons and daugh-
11 : 15. whose end s. b. acc. to works
13 : 11. God of love and peace s. b.
with you, Ph. 4 : 9. [Lord
1 Th. 4 : 17. so s. we ever b. with the
1 Ti 4 : 6. thou s-t b. a good minister
He. 1 : 5. I a Father, he s. b. a Son
14. who s. b. heirs of salvation ?
1 Jn. 3 : 2. but we s. b. like him (2)
Re. 1 : 19. Write things which s. b.
16 : 5. Thou, O Lord, wast and s-t b.
21 : 3. God s. b. with them, their G.
22 : 12. To give ev. man as work s. b.

See Shall be DESOLATE.
See Statute for EVER,
BLESSED, SO, UNCLEAN.

Shall not or Shalt not BE.

Ge. 15 : 4. This - b. thine heir [for
16 : 10. thy seed, it - b. numbered
21 : 10. - b. heir with my son Isaac
Ex. 12 : 13 the plague - b. upon you
22 : 25. thou - b. to him as a usurer
De. 28 : 13. head ; thou - b. beneath
1 S. 24 : 12. hand - b. upon thee, 13.
2 S. 18 : † 20. Thou - b. man of tid-
1 K. 3 : 13. - b. any like thee [ings
2 K. 2 : 10. but if not, it - b. so [land
21. - b. any more death or barren
20 : † 19. - b. peace in my days ?
Ezr. 7 : 24. - b. lawful to impose toll
Jb. 7 : 21. seek me in morning, I - b.
8 : † 22. dwellingplace of wicked - b.
Ps. 37 : 10. little while wicked - b. (2)
Ec. 8 : 13. it - b. well with wicked
Is. 9 : 1. dimness - b. such as was in
16 : 6. but his lies - b. so, Je. 48 : 30.
47 : 14. there - b. a fire to warm at
Je. 14 : 15. Sword and famine - b.
30 : 19. they - b. few, they - b. small
Eze. 13 : 9. they - b. in assembly of
18 : 30. so iniquity - b. your ruin
20 : 32. cometh into your mind - b.
Da. 11 : 29. it - b. as former or [at all
Ho. 3 : 3. thou - b. for another
Am. 7 : 3. This - b. saith the L., 6.
Mat. 6 : 5. thou - b. as hypocrites
16 : 22. Lord ; this - b. unto thee
20 : 26. But it - b. so among you,
Mk. 10 : 43. Lu. 22 : 26. [b. yet
Mk. 13 : 7. hear of wars, but end -

2 Co 12 : 6. I • b. a fool ; I forbear
See Not be ABLE,
BE with neither,
So, SO be it, Be STRONG.

To BE. ⌈with me
Ge. 3 : 12. woman thou gavest **t. b.**
16 : 3. Hagar to Abr. **t. b.** his wife
17 : 7. **t. b.** a G. unto thee and thy
18 : 11. it ceased **t. b.** with Sarah
28 : 9. sister of Nebajoth **t. b.** wife
29 : 29. gave Bilhah **t. b.** her maid
34 : 22. dwell with us, **t. b.** one peo.
38 : 15. he thought her **t. b.** harlot
39 : 10. not lie by nor **t. b.** with her
41 : 52. G. caused me **t. b.** fruitful
Ex. 21 : 16. endow her **t. b.** his wife
Le. 22 : 33. brought you out of Egypt
t. b. your God, 25 : 38. ⌊ance
De. 4 : 20. **t. b.** a people of inherit-
26 : 17. avouched Lord **t. b.** thy G.
18. L. avouched thee **t. b.** his peo.
Ju. 14 : 11. thirty **t. b.** with him
1 S. 3 : 20. knew Sam-l **t. b.** prophet
2 S. 12 : 10. wife of Uriah **t. b.** thy w.
1 K. 14 : 5. feign herself **t. b.** anoth.
1 Ch. 28 : 6. chosen him **t. b.** my son
Ps. 9 : 20. know thems. **t. b.** but m.
36 : 2. his iniquity found **t. b.** hate-
3. he hath left off **t. b.** wise ⌊ful
79 : 2. thy servants **t. b.** meat for
113 : 9. barren **t. b.** joyful mother
Pr. 16 : 7. his enemies **t. b.** at peace
24 : 1. neith. desire **t. b.** with them
Ec. 3 : 15. which is **t. b.** hath been
Is. 3 : 4. children **t. b.** their princes
Mat. 3 : 15. Suffer it **t. b.** so now
Ac. 1 : 22. one **t. b.** witness with us
5 : 31. Him G. exalted **t. b.** a Prince
7 : 35. same did G. send **t. b.** a ruler
13 : 47. thee **t. b.** light of Gentiles
20 : 16. **t. b.** at Jerus. day of Pent.
26 : 28. almost . . **t. b.** a Christian
1 Co. 7 : 26. is good for man so **t. b.**
12 : 22. wh. seem **t. b.** more feeble
2 Co. 12 : 6. that he seeth me **t. b.**
Ga. 6 : 3. think hims. **t. b.** somethi.
Ph. 1 : 23. a desire **t. b.** with Christ
Ja. 3 : 10. things ought not so **t. b.**
2 Pe. 3 : 11. wh. persons ought ye **t. b.**
See WILL be, WILL not be.
See WE, WELL [Adj.], YE.

BEACON. ⌈mt.
Is. 30 : 17. be left as **b.** upon top of

BEALI'AH.
1 Ch. 12 : 5. among mighty men, B.

BE'ALOTH. ⌈B.
Jos. 15 : 24. cities of Judah, Ziph,

BEAM, S. ⌈b.
Ju. 16 : 14. Samson went away with
1 S. 17 : 7. his spear was like weaver's
b., 2 S. 21 : 19. 1 Ch. 11 : 23.-20 : 5.
1 K. 6 : 6. that **b-s** not be fastened
9. covered the house with **b-s** of
cedar, 7 : 2, 3. ⌈7 : 12.
36. court with row of cedar **b-s**,
7 : 6. other pillars and the thick **b.**
2 K. 6 : 2. go to Jordan and take a **b.**
5. one felling a **b.**, axe head fell
2 Ch. 3 : 7. he overlaid the **b-s**, posts
Ne. 2 : 8. he gave timber to make **b-s**
3 : 3. who laid **b-s** thereof, set, 6.
Ps. 104 : 3. Who layeth **b-s** in waters
Can. 1 : 17. **b-s** of our house cedar
Ha. 2 : 11. **b.** out of timber sh. ans-r
3 : †4. God ; bright **b-s** out of his h.
Mat. 7 : 3. why considerest not **b.** in
own eye? Lu. 6 : 41, 42. ⌈own eye
4. and, behold, a **b.** is in thine
5. cast **b.** out of own eye, Lu. 6 : 42.

BEANS. ⌈David
2 S. 17 : 28. Barzillai brought **b.** to
Eze. 4 : 9. Take unto thee wheat, **b.**

BEAR, S. ⌈took
1 S. 17 : 34. came a lion and **b.** and
36. Thy servant slew lion and **b.**
37. delivered me out of paw of **b.**
2 S. 17 : 8. be chafed as a **b.** robbed
2 K. 2 : 24. came two she **b-s** ⌈man
Pr. 17 : 12. Let a **b.** robbed meet a
28 : 15. As roaring lion, a ranging **b.**
Is. 11 : 7. the cow and **b.** shall feed
59 : 11. We roar all like **b-s**, mourn
La. 3 : 10. He was unto me as a **b.**
Da. 7 : 5. another beast like a **b.** ⌈ed
Ho. 13 : 8. meet them as a **b.** bereav-
Am. 5 : 19. did flee fr. lion, **b.** met
Re. 13 : 2. his as the feet of a **b.** ⌊him

BEAR. [To bring forth.]
Ge 16 : 11. angel said, thou sh. **b.** son
17 : 17. sh. Sarah 90 years old **b.**?
19. Sarah shall **b.** thee a son, 21.
18 : 13. Sh. I **b.** a child wh. am old?
22 : 23. eight did Milcah **b.** Nahor
30 : 3. Bilhah sh. **b.** upon my knees
Le. 12 : 5. if she **b.** a maid child ⌈b.
De 28 : 57. evil toward chil. she sh.
Ju. 13 : 3. said, thou sh. **b.** son, 5, 7.
Ru. 1 : 12. if I **b.** sons ; wou. ye tarry
1 K. 3 : 21. it was not son which I **b.**
Ec. 3 : †2. A time to **b.**, a time to die
Can. 4 : 2. sheep, every one **b.** twins
Is. 7 : 14. a virgin shall **b.** a son, and
54 : 1. Sing, thou that didst not **b.**
Je. 29 : 6. give dau-s th. they may **b.**
Lu. 1 : 13. Elisabeth shall **b.** a son
1 Ti. 5 : 14. younger marry, **b.** child-n

BEAR.
[To carry or endure.]
Ge. 4 : 13. My punishment is greater
than I can **b.** ⌈36 : 7.
13 : 6. the land not able to **b.** them,
43 : 9. let me **b.** blame, 44 : 32. ⌈to **b.**
49 : 15. Issachar, bowed shoulder
Ex. 18 : 22. they shall **b.** the burden
with thee, Nu. 11 : 17. ⌈37 : 14, 15.
25 : 27. places of staves to **b.** table.
27 : 7. staves upon altar to **b.** it,
30 : 4.-37 : 27.-38 : 7. ⌈bef. L., 29.
28 : 12. Aaron shall **b.** their names
37 : 5. staves into rings to **b.** ark
Le. 19 : † 17. neighbour, **b.** not sin
18. shalt not **b.** any grudge ⌊for h.
Nu. 1 : 50. Levites shall **b.** tabernacle and vessels, 4 : 15, 25.-7 : 9.
11 : 14. I am not able to **b.** this people alone, 17. De. 1 : 9 ⌈cong-n?
14 : 27. How long shall I **b.** wi. this
33. chil. shall **b.** your whoredoms
De. 1 : 12. How can I **b.** your strife?
31. God bare thee as man doth **b.**
10 : 8. tribe of Levi to **b.** ark ⌊son
Jos. 3 : 8. command the priests that
b. the ark, 13.-4 : 16. ⌈pets, 6.
6 : 4. priests sh. **b.** bef. ark 7 trum-
2 S. 18 : 19. Let me **b.** king tidings
20. shalt not **b.** tidings this day (3)
2 K. 18 : 14. puttest on me will I **b.**
1 Ch. 5 : 18. men able to **b.** sword
2 Ch. 2 : 2. 70,000 men to **b.** burdens
Ps. 75 : 3. earth, I **b.** up pillars of it
89 : 50. how I do **b.** reproach of peo.
91 : 12. They shall **b.** thee up in
hands, Mat. 4 : 6. Lu 4 : 11.
144 † 14. oxen be able to **b.** burdens
Pr. 9 : 12. scornest, thou shalt **b.** it
18 : 14. wounded spirit, who can **b.**?
30 : 21. for four which it cannot **b.**
Is. 1 : 14. feasts ; I am weary to **b.**
46 : 4. I made and I will **b.** you
7. they **b.** him upon the shoulder
52 : 11. be clean that **b.** vessels of
Je. 10 : 19. a grief, and I must **b.** it
17 : 21. **b.** no burden on sab-h, 27.
31 : 19. did **b.** reproach of my youth
44 : 22. Lord could no longer **b.**
La. 3 : 27. that he **b.** yoke in youth
Eze. 12 : 6. In their sight shalt **b.** it
12. prince shalt **b.** upon shoulder
14 : 10. they shall **b.** punishment
16 : 52. also **b.** thine own shame (2)
23 : 35. **b.** thou thy lewdness and
32 : 30. **b.** their shame, 36 : 7.-44 : 13.
34 : 29. nei. **b.** shame of heathen
36 : 15. nei. **b.** reproach of people
Eze. 46 : 20. **b.** th. not into outer court
Am. 7 : 10. land not able to **b.** words
Mi. 6 : 16. ye sh. **b.** reproach of peo.
7 : 9. I will **b.** indignation of Lord
Zph. 1 : 11. that **b.** silver are cut off
Hag. 2 : 12. If one **b.** holy flesh in
Zch. 5 : 10. Whither **b.** the ephah,
6 : 13. he shall **b.** the glory and rule
11 : † 16. nor **b.** that that standeth
Mat. 3 : 11. shoes I not worthy to **b.**
27 : 32. Simon : they compelled to
b. cross, Mk. 15 : 21. Lu. 23 : 26.
Lu. 14 : 27. whoso doth not **b.** cross
18 : 7. avenge elect, tho. he **b.** long?
Jn. 2 : 8. **b.** unto governor of feast
16 : 12. ye cannot **b.** them now
Ac. 9 : 15. chosen vessel to **b.** name
15 : 10. yoke, fa-s nor we able to **b.**?
18 : 14. reason I should **b.** wi. you
27 : 15. could not **b.** up into wind
Ro. 15 : 1. to **b.** infirmities of weak
1 Co 3 : 2. ye were not able to **b.** it
10 : 13. that ye may be able to **b.** it
15 : 49. we sh. **b.** image of heavenly
2 Co. 11 : 1. Would ye could **b.** wi. me
4. ye might well **b.** with him ⌊(2)
Ga. 6 : 2. **b.** one another's burdens
5. man shall **b.** his own burden
17. I **b.** in my body the marks of
He. 5 : † 2. Who can **b.** wi. ignorant
Ja. 3 : 12. fig tree **b.** olive berries?
Re. 2 : 2. canst not **b.** them wh. are
See Bear FRUIT. ⌊evil

BEAR iniquity, ies.
Ex. 28 : 38. Aaron **b. i.** of holy thi-s
43. linen breeches, th. they **b.** not **i.**
Le. 5 : 1. he shall **b.** his **i.**, 17.-7 :
18.-17 : 16.-19 : 8.-20 : 17.
10 : 17. to you to **b. i.** of congrega-n
16 : 22. goat shall **b.** all their **i-s**
20 : 19. they shall **b.** their **i.**, Nu.
18 : 23. Eze. 44 : 10, 12. ⌈tresp.
22 : 16. Or suffer them to **b. i.** of
Nu. 5 : 31. this woman sh. **b.** her **i.**
14 : 34. sh. **b.** your **i-s** forty years
18 : 1. Thou and sons **b. i.** of (2)
30 : 15. he shall **b.** her **i.** ⌈their **i-s**
Is. 53 : 11. my righteous servant **b.**
Eze. 4 : 5. **b. i.** of house of Isr., 4, 6.
18 : 19. doth not son **b. i.** of fa.?
20. son shall not **b. i.** of father,
neither shall father **b. i.** of son

BEAR judgment.
Ex. 28 : 30. Aaron shall **b. j.** of Isr.
Ga. 5 : 10. that troubleth you shall
See RECORD. ⌊**b.** his **j.**

BEAR rule.
Es. 1 : 22. man should **b. r.** in house
Pr. 12 : 24. hand of diligent sh. **b. r.**
Je. 5 : 31. priests **b. r.** by their means
Da. 2 : 39. kingdom of brass sh. **b. r.**

BEAR sin, s.
Le. 19 : †17. neighbour, **b.** not **s.** for
20 : 20. they shall **b.** their **s.** ⌊him
22 : 9. lest they **b. s.** for it and die
24 : 15. curseth God shall **b.** his **s.**
Nu. 9 : 13. that man shall **b.** his **s.**
18 : 22. lest they **b. s.** and die ⌈best
32. **b.** no **s.** when ye heaved the
Eze. 23 : 49. shall **b. s-s** of your idols
He. 9 : 28. Christ was offered to **b.**
See Bear WITNESS. ⌊s-s

BEARD, S. ⌈30.
Le. 13 : 29. a plague upon head or **b.**,
14 : 9. shall shave all hair off his **b.**
19 : 27. sh. mar corners of **b.**, 21 : 5.
1 S. 17 : 35. I caught him by **b.** ⌈b.
21 : 13. David let spittle fall upon
2 S. 10 : 4. shaved off half of **b-s** ⌈5.
5. until y-r **b-s** be grown, 1 Ch. 19 :
19 : 24. Mephib. nei. trimmed his **b.**
20 : 9. Joab took Amasa by **b.** to k.
Ezr. 9 : 3. plucked off hair of my **b.**
Ps. 133 : 2. ran down upon A-'s **b.** (2)
Is. 7 : 20. and it sh. consume the **b.**
15 : 2. baldn-s, and every **b.** cut off
Je. 41 : 5. men, having **b-s** shaven

1 Co.15 : 32. I have fought with b. at
39. another flesh of b. [Ephe.
Tit. 1 : 12. Cretians are evil b.
He. 13 : 11. bodies of b. whose blood
Ja. 3 : 7. b. is tamed, but tongue
2 Pe. 2 : 12. as natural brute b.
Jude 10. naturally as brute b.
Re. 4 : 6. four b. full of eyes before
8. four b. had each six wings
4 : 9. when those b. give glory
5 : 6. midst of four b. a Lamb
8. had taken book the four b.
11. about the throne and the b.
14. the four b. said Amen [7.
6 : 1. b. saying, Come and see, 15:
7 : 11. angels stood about four b.
14 : 3. a new song before four b.
15 : 7. one of four b. gave angels
18 : 13. fine flour, wheat, b.
19 : 4. four b. fell down to worship

BEASTS of the Earth.

De. 28 : 26. carcass be meat to b.-
1 S. 17 : 46. carcasses of Phil. to b.-
Jb. 5 : 22. nor shalt be afraid of b.-
35 : 11. who teacheth more than b.-
Ps. 79 : 2. flesh of thy saints to b.-
Is. 18 : 6. they shall be left to b.-
Je. 7 : 33. carcasses of peo. meat for
b.-, 16 : 4.-19 : 7.-34 : 20. [vour
15 : 3. appoint over them b.- to de-
Ac. 10 : 12. of four-footed b.-, 11 : 6.
Re. 6 : 8. kill with hunger and b.-

BEASTS of the Field.

Ex. 23 : 11. what poor leave b.- eat
De. 7 : 22. lest the b.- increase
1 S. 17 : 44. I will give thy flesh to b.-
2 S. 21 : 10. birds nor b.- by night
Jb. 5 : 23. b.- at peace with thee
40 : 20. mountains, where b.- play
Ps. 8 : 7. put b.- under his feet
Is. 56 : 9. ye b.- come to devour
Je. 12 : 9. assemble all b.-, come
27 : 6. b.- given him, 28 : 14. Da.
2 : 38. [b.-, 34 : 5.-39 : 4.
Eze. 29 : 5. given thee for meat to
31 : 6. under br-s b.- bring forth
13. b.- shall be on his branches
38 : 20 b.- shall shake at my pres.
Da. 4 : 12. b.- had shadow under, 21.
25. dwelling be with b.-, 23, 32.
Ho. 2 : 18. make covenant with b.-
4 : 3. the land mourn with b.-
Jo. 1 : 20. b.- cry also to thee
2 : 22. Be not afraid ye b.-

Wild BEASTS.

Le. 26 : 22. I will send w. b. [b.
1 S. 17 : 46. carcasses of Philis. to w.
Ps. 50 : 11. w. b. of field are mine
Is 13 : 21. w. b. shall lie there
22. w. b. of islands shall cry
34 : 14. w. b. of desert meet w.
b. of island, Je. 50 : 39.
Mk. 1 : 13. Christ was with w. b.
Ac. 10 : 12. sheet, were all w. b.,

BEAT. [11 : 6.

Ex. 30 : 36. spices shall b. small
39 : 3. did b. gold into thin plates
Nu. 11 : 8. people b. manna in
De. 25 : 3. if he b. him above these
Ju. 8 : 17. he b. down tower of Pen.
9 : 45. Abimelech b. down city
19 : 22. sons of Belial b. at door
Ru. 2 : 17. she b. that she gleaned
2 S. 22 : 43. I b. them small, Ps. 18 :
2 K. 3 : 25. Israeli. b. down cities [42.
13 : 25. Joash b. Ben-hadad
23 : 12. altars did king b. down
Ps. 52 : † 5. God shall b. thee down
89 : 23. I will b. down his foes
Pr. 23 : 14. thou shalt b. him
Is. 2 : 4. b. swords into, Mi. 4 : 3.
3 : 15. mean ye that ye b. my peo.
27 : 12. L. sh. b. off from channel
41 : 15. thresh mountains, b. small
Jo. 3 : 10. b. plough-sha. into swo.
Jon. 4 : 8. sun b. on head of Jonah
Mi. 4 : 13. b. in pieces many peo.

Mat. 7 : 25. winds blew and b. upon
that house, 27. Lu. 6 : 48, 49.
21 : 35. husbandmen took serv-ts,
b. one, Mk. 12 : 3. Lu. 20 : 10, 11.
Mk. 4 : 37. waves b. into ship,
Lu. 12 : 45. begin to b. menservants
Ac. 16 : 22. magistrates com-ded to b.
18 : 17. took Sosthenes, b. him [them
22 : 19. I b. in every synagogue th.
27 : † 14. b. a wind, called Euroc-

BEATEN. [lydon

Ex. 5 : 14. officers of Isr. were b., 16.
37 : 7. cherubim of gold b. out of
Le. 2 : 14. corn b. out of full ears, 16.
16 : 12. of sweet incense b. small
De. 25 : 2. if man be worthy to be b.
Jos. 8 : 15. Joshua, Isr. made as if b.
2 S. 2 : 17. Abner was b. and Israel
2 Ch. 2 : 10. 20,000 meas. b. wheat
15 : † 6. nation b. in pieces of nat-n
34 : 7. he had b. images to powder
Jb. 4 : † 20. They are b. in pieces
Pr. 10 : † 8. a prating fool be b., † 10.
23 : 35. have b. me, I felt it not
Is. 27 : 9. of altar, as chalkstones b.
28 : 27. fitches are b. out with staff
30 : 31. shall Assyrian be b. down
Je. 46 : 5. mighty ones are b. down
Mi. 1 : 7. images sh. be b. to pieces
Mk. 13 : 9. in synagogues ye sh. be b.
Lu. 12 : 47. be b. with many stripes
48 knew not, be b. with few stripes
Ac. 5 : 40. called apostles and b. th.
16 : 37. They have b. us openly
2 Co. 11 : 25. Thrice was I b. wi. rods

BEATEN gold.

Nu. 8 : 4. candlestick was of b. g.
1 K. 10 : 16. Sol-n made 200 targets
of b. g.. 2 Ch. 9 : 15 (2). [16.
17. 300 shields of b. g., 2 Ch. 9 :

BEATEN oil. [2.

Ex. 27 : 20. pure o. olive b., Le. 24 :
29 : 40. part of hin of b. o., Nu. 28 :
See **Beaten WORK.** [5.

BEATEST, ETH.

De. 24 : 20 When thou b-t olive tree
Pr. 23 : 13. if b-t with rod he not die
1 Co. 9 : 26. not as one that b-h the

BEATING. [air

1 S. 14 : 16. went b. down one anoth.
Mk. 12 : 5. b. some, killing some [P.
Ac. 21 : 32. saw soldiers, they left b.

BEAUTIES. See Beauty.

BEAUTIFUL.

Ge. 29 : 17. Rachel was b. and well
De. 21 : 11. amo. captives b. woman
1 S. 16 : 12. David of b. countenance
25 : 3. Abigail of b. countenance
2 S. 11 : 2. Bath-sheba was very b.
14 : † 25. in Israel not a man b. as
Es. 2 : 7. Esther was fair and b. [Abs
Ps. 48 : 2. b. for situation is m-t Zion
Ec. 3 : 11. hath made every thing b.
Can. 6 : 4. Thou art b., O my love
7 : 1. How b. are thy feet wi shoes
Is. 4 : 2. shall branch of the L be b.
52 : 1. put on thy b. garments, Je.
7. How b. are the feet of, Ro. 10 : 15.
64 : 11. Our b. house is burned
Je. 13 : 20. where is thy b. flock?
48 : 17. the staff broken and b. rod!
Eze. 16 : 12. a b. crown upon thine
13. thou wast exceeding b. [head
23 : 42. Sabeans put b. crowns upon
Mat. 23 : 27. sepulchres wh. appear
Ac. 3 : 2. at the gate called B., 10. [b.

BEAUTIFY. [of L.

Ezr. 7 : 27. king's heart to b. house
Ps. 149 : 4. will b. meek with salvat.
Is. 60 : 13. Leb-n to b. my sanctuary

BEAUTY, IES. [40.

Ex. 28 : 2. garments for glory and b.,
2 S. 1 : 19. The b. of Israel is slain
14 : 25. none praised as Absal. for b.
2 Ch. 3 : 6. with precious stones for b.
Es. 1 : 11. to shew the people her b.
Jb. 40 : 10. array thyself with b.

Ps. 27 : 4. to behold b. of the Lord
39 : 11. makest his b. to consume
45 : 11. king greatly desire thy b.
49 : 14. b. shall consume in grave
50 : 2. Out of Zion perfection of b.
90 : 17. let b. of our G. b. upon us
96 : 6. strength and b. in sanctuary
110 : 3. in b-s of holiness fr. morn.
Pr. 6 : 25. Lust not after her b. [ing
20 : 29. b. of old men is the gray h.
31 : 30. Favour deceitful, b. is vain
Is. 3 : 24. and burning instead of b.
4 : † 2. branch of L. sh. be b., glory
13 : 19. b. of Chaldees' excellency
28 : 1. whose b. is fading flower, 4.
5. shall Lord be for a diadem of b.
33 : 17. shall see the King in his b.
44 : 13. according to the b. of a man
53 : 2. no b. we should desire him
61 : 3. give unto them b. for ashes
Je. 3 : † 19. How shall I give thee a
heritage of b.? [parted
La. 1 : 6. from Zion all her b. is de-
2 : 1. Lord hath cast down b. of Isr.
15. city men call perfection of b.?
Eze. 7 : 20. As for b. of his ornament
16 : 14. renown among heathen for
15. didst trust in thine own b. [b.
25. made thy b. to be abhorred
27 : 3. hast said, I am of perfect b.
4. builders perfected thy b., 11.
28 : 7. swords ag. b. of thy wisdom
12. full of wisdom, perfect in b.
17. heart was lifted bec. of thy b.
31 : 8. not any tree like him in b.
32 : 19. Whom dost thou pass in b.?
Ho. 10 : † 11. upon b. of her neck
14 : 6. Israel his b. be as olive tree
Zch. 9 : 17. For how great is his b.!
11 : 7. two staves; one I called B.
10. I took my staff B., cut it asun-
See Holiness. [der

BE'BAI.

Ezr. 2 : 11. The chil. of B., Ne. 7 : 16.
8 : 11. up from Bab-n; of sons of B.,
Zech-h son of B., and 28 males
10 : 28. taken strange wives; of sons
Ne. 10 : 15. th. sealed; Bunni, B. [of B.

BECAME.

Ge. 2 : 7. and man b. a living soul
10. river was parted, b. four heads
6 : 4. the same b. mighty men
19 : 26. his wife b. pillar of salt [wife
20 : 12. dau. of my fath., she b. my
24 : 67. Rebekah, she b. his wife
26 : 13. Isaac grew until he b. great
44 : 32. thy servants b. surety for
47 : 20. so the land b. Phar-'s [lad
26. land of priests b. not Phar-'s
49 : 15. Issachar b. servant unto
Ex. 2 : 10. child b. her son [tribute
4 : 3. A rod, it b. a serpent [hand
4. Moses caught it, it b. rod in his
7 : 10. rod bef. Pha-h, it b. serpent
12. every man his rod, b. serpents
8 : 17. all dust of the land b. lice (2)
9 : 10. ashes, it b. a boil breaking
24. none like it in Eg. since b. nat-n
36 : 13. coupled so it b. one tabern.
Nu. 12 : 10. behold, Miriam b. leprous
26 : 10. devoured 250; they b. sign
De. 26 : 5. father into Eg., b. nation
Jos. 7 : 5. hearts of peo. b. as water
14 : 14. Hebron b. inherit. of Caleb
24 : 32. b. inherit. of chil of Joseph
Ju. 1 : 30. Canaanites b. tributaries
15 : 14. cords of his arms b. as flax
17 : 5. one of his sons b. his priest
12. young man b. priest in hou. of
Ru. 4 : 16. Naomi b. nurse [Micah
1 S. 10 : 12. it b. a proverb. Is Saul
16 : 21. loved David, b. armourb-r
18 : 29. and Saul b. David's enemy
25 : 37. heart died within, he b. as a
42. And Abigail b. his wife [stone
2 S. 2 : 25. chil. of Benj. b. one troop
4 : 4. fell, b. lame: name Mephib-h

2 S. 8 : 2. **b.** David's servants, bro-t
gifts, 6, 14. 1 Ch. 18 : 6, 13.-19 :
11 : 27. Da. sent, she **b.** his wife⌊19
1 K. 12 : 30. this thing **b.** sin, 13:34.
13 . 6. king's hand **b.** as it was
33. whoso would **b.** one of priests
2 K 17 : 3. Hoshea **b.** his servant
15 they **b.** vain, went aft. heath-
24 : 1. Jehoiakim **b.** his servant⌊en
2 Ch. 27 . 6. Jotham **b.** mighty bec.
Ne. 9 : 25. so they did eat, **b.** fat and
Es. 8 : 17. many of people **b.** Jews
Ps. 69 : 11. I **b.** a proverb to them
83 : 10 they **b.** as dung for earth
Eze. 17 : 6. **b.** a vine, brought forth
19 : 3. it **b.** a young lion, and, 6.
23 : 10. she **b.** famous amo. women
31 : 5. his branches **b.** long because
34 : 5. they **b.** meat to all beasts
8 because my flock **b.** a prey ; **b.**
36 : 4. cities which **b.** a prey ⌊meat
Da 2 : 35. iron, gold **b.** like chaff ;
stone that smote **b.** a great mt
8 : 4 ram did acc-g to . . **b.** great
10 : 15. face tow. ground, I **b.** dumb
Ob. 12. in day that he **b.** a brother
Zch 8 : † 10. hire of man **b.** nothing
Mat. 28 : 4. Keepers **b.** as dead men
Mk 9 : 3. And his raiment **b.** shining
Ac. 10 : 10. Peter **b.** very hungry
Ro. 1 : 21. but **b.** vain in imaginat-s
22. Professing to be wise **b.** fools
6 : 18. ye **b.** servants of righteousn.
1 Co. 9 : 20. unto Jews I **b.** as a Jew
22. To the weak **b.** I as weak, that
13 : 11. when I **b.** a man I put away
2 Co. 8 : 9. for your sakes he **b.** poor
Ph. 2 : 8. he **b.** obedient unto death
1 Th. 1 : 6. ye **b.** followers of us and
2 : 14. ye **b.** followers of churches
He. 2 10. it **b.** him for whom are all
5 9. **b.** author of eternal salvat-n
7 . 26. For such a high priest **b.** us
10 : 33. whilst ye **b.** companions of
11 . 7 **b.** heir of the righteousness
Re. 6 . 12. sun **b.** black, moon **b.** as
8 : 8. third part of sea **b.** blood
11. third part of waters **b.** wormw.
16 : 3. sea **b.** as blood of dead men
4. rivers and fountains **b.** blood

BECAMEST. ⌈God
1 Ch. 17 : 22. thou, Lord, **b.** their
Eze 16 : 8. a covenant, and thou **b.**

BECAUSE. ⌊mine
Ge 2 : 3. **b.** in it he had rested⌈man
23. called Woman, **b.** taken out of
3 . † 1. Yea, **b.** God said, ye sh. not
14. **b.** thou hast done this ⌈wife
17. **b.** hast hearkened unto thy
5 : 29. **b.** of ground which G. cursed
7 : 7. went into ark **b.** of the flood
12 : 13. my soul shall live **b.** of thee
17. Lord plagued Pha **b.** of Sarai
20 : 11. **b.** I tho-t, fear of G is not
18. Lord closed wombs **b.** of Sarah
21 : 11. thing grievous in Abr-'s
sight **b.** of his son, 12. ⌈of well
25 Abr. reproved Abimelech **b.**
22 : 16. **b.** thou hast done this thi.
18. blessed : **b.** thou hast obeyed
25 : 21. entreated for wife **b.** bar-n
26 : 5. be blessed ; **b.** Abr obeyed
27 : 41. Esau hated Jac. **b.** of bles-g
46. am weary **b.** of dau-s of Heth
29 : 15. **b.** my bro ,serve for nought?
30 : 18. **b.** I have given my maiden
36 : 7. land not bear them **b.** of catt.
38 : 15. harlot; **b.** she covered face
26. **b.** I gave her not to Shelah
39 : 9. kept fr. me, **b.** thou his wife
41 : 32. **b.** thing is established by G.
43 : 18. afraid **b.** bro-t into Joseph's
46 : 30. let me die, **b.** thou yet alive
49 : 4. **b.** thou wentest to fath-'s bed
Ex. 1 : 12. grieved **b.** of chil. of Isr.
8 : 12. cried unto Lord **b.** of frogs
9 : 11. could not stand **b.** of boils

Ex 13 : 8. This **b.** of that wh Lord
19 : 18. Sinai on a smoke **b.** Lord
32 : 35. plagued peo. **b.** made calf
Le. 19 : 8. **b.** be profaned hallowed
20. not to death, **b.** she not free
20 : 3. **b.** hath given seed unto Mol.
21 : 23. not in vail, **b.** hath blemish
26 : 43. **b.**, even **b.** they despised my
judgments, and **b.** their soul
Nu 7 : 9. **b.** service of sanctuary was
11 . 14. **b.** it is too heavy for me
20 **b.** ye have despised the Lord
12 : 1. ag-t Moses **b.** of Ethiopian
13 : 24. called Eshcol **b.** of grapes
14 : 16. **b.** L. not able to bring peo.
24 Caleb, **b.** he had another spirit
21 : 4. people discouraged b. of way
25 : 13. **b.** he was zealous for his G.
30 : 5. **b.** her father disallowed her
32 : 17. in fenced cities **b.** of inhab-s
De. 1 : 36. Caleb, **b.** he followed Lord
2 : 25. shall be in anguish **b.** of thee
7 : †12. **b.** ye hearken to judgments
8 : 20. perish ; **b.** ye not obedient
9 : 25. **b.** L. said he would destroy
15 : 10. **b.** for this G. sh. bless thee
16. **b.** he loveth thee and thine (2)
18 : 12. **b.** of abominations L. doth
20 : 3. neith. be terrified **b.** of them
21 : 14. not sell her **b.** humbled her
22 : 24 shall stone the damsel **b.**
she cried not ; and man **b.** he
23 : 4. **b.** they met you not wi. bread
24 : 1. **b.** found uncleanness in her
28 : 47. **b.** thou servedst not thy G.
Jos 2 : 9. all faint **b.** of you, 11, 24.
5 : 1. nei. spirit in them **b.** of Israel
6 : 1. Jericho was shut **b.** of Israel
17. **b.** she hid the messengers, 25
7 : 12. th. turned backs **b.** accursed
9 : 24. we were sore afraid **b.** of you
11 : 6. Be not afraid **b.** of them
23 : 3. done unto nations **b.** of you
Ju. 2 : 18. repented L. **b.** of groan-gs
6 : 2. **b.** of Midianites Isr. made dens
6. Isr. impoverished **b.** of Mid-ites
7. Isr. cried unto L. **b.** of Mid-ites
22. Alas ! O God ! **b.** I seen angel
14 : 17. told, **b.** she lay sore upon
1 S. 4 : 21. I-chabod ; **b.** ark of God
taken, and **b.** of her husband
8 : 18. ye shall cry out **b.** of your k.
19 : 4. **b.** hath not sinned ag. thee
24 : 5 **b.** he had cut off Saul's skirt
26 . 12. **b.** deep sleep was upon th.
21. **b.** my soul precious in thine
28 : 18. **b.** thou obeyedst not the L
20 Saul sore afraid **b.** of words of
30 : 13 **b.** 3 days agone I fell sick
2 S. 2 : 6. I will requite **b.** ye have
12 : 6 lamb fourfold, **b.** he did this
thing, and **b.** he had no pity
10. **b.** thou hast taken wife of U
13 : 22. Amnon, **b.** he forced sister
18 : 20. **b.** the king's son is dead
1 K. 1 : 50. Adonijah feared b. of Sol
2 : 7. I fled **b.** of Absalom, thy bro.
3 : 19. child died ; **b.** she overlaid it
8 : 11. not to minister **b.** of cloud
64. **b.** brazen altar was too little
9 : 9. **b.** they forsook the Lord God
11 : 34. **b.** he kept my command-ts
14 : 16. give Isr. up **b.** of sins of J.
20 : 42. **b.** thou hast let go a man
21 : 29. **b.** he humbleth hims. I will
2 K. 9 : 14. Joram kept Ramoth-gilead **b.** of Hazael of Syria ⌈ing
10 : 30. **b.** hast done well in execut-
13 : 23. L. was gracious **b.** of cov-t
18 : 12. **b.** they obeyed not voice of L.
19 : 28. **b.** thy rage against me is
21 : 15 **b.** they have done evil in
22 : 17. **b.** they have forsaken me
19. **b.** thine heart was tender and
hast wept bef. me, 2 Ch. 34 : 27.
1 Ch. 4 : 41. **b.** was pasture for flocks
15 : 13. **b.** ye did it not at the first

1 Ch. 21 : 8. sinned **b.** I have done
2 Ch. 2 : 11. **b.** Lord loved his people
12 : 5. princes to Jer. **b.** of Shishak
27 : 6 **b.** prepared his ways before L.
28 : 6. **b.** had forsaken G. of fath-s
9. **b.** Lord was wroth with Judah
Ezr 4 : 14. **b.** we have maintenance
9 : 15. we cannot stand **b.** of this
Ne. 4 : 9. we set a watch **b.** of them
5 : 15. so did not I **b.** of fear of God
9 : 38. **b.** of this we make covenant
Jb 3 : 10. **b.** shut not moth-'s womb
11 : 16 **b.** thou shalt forget misery
18. sh. be secure **b.** there is hope
15 . 27. **b.** he maketh collops of fat
17 : 12. light is short **b.** of darkn-s
20 : 19 **b.** hath oppressed poor (2)
23 : 17. **b.** I was not cut off before
29 : 12. **b.** I delivered poor ⌊darkn
30 : 11 **b.** he hath loosed my cord
32 : 1. Job ; **b.** he was righteous in
his own eyes ' ⌈hims
2. against Job wrath **b.** justified
3. ag. his three friends, **b.** no ans.
4. waited **b.** they elder than he
34 . 27. **b.** they turned back fr. him
35 : 12. **b.** of the pride of evil men
15. But **b.** it is not so ; he in anger
36 : 18. **b.** there is wrath, beware
38 : 21. Knowest it **b.** then born?(2)
39 : 11. trust him, **b.** strength gr-t
17 **b.** God deprived her of wisdom
Ps. 37 : 7 fret not **b.** of him who
prospereth, **b.** of man who ⌈(2)
38 : 3. neither any rest **b.** of my sin,
5. My wounds stink **b.** of foolishn.
45 : 4. ride prosperously **b.** of truth
55 : 3. I mourn **b.** of the enemy (2)
59 : 9. **b.** of his strength will I wait
60 : 4. given a banner **b.** of truth
8. Philistia, triumph **b.** of me
63 : 3. **b.** thy lovingkindness is bet-
7. **b.** thou hast been my help ⌊ter
68 : 29 **b.** of thy temple at Jerus.
69 : 7. **b.** for thy sake borne repro-h
78 : 22. **b.** they believed not in God
91 : 14. **b.** hath set his love upon me
102 : 10. eaten ashes **b.** of thy wrath
106 : 33. **b.** they provoked his spir.
107 : 17. Fools **b.** of their iniquities are afflicted (2) ⌈quiet
30 Then are they glad **b.** they be
109 : 16. **b.** he remembered not
122 : 9. **b.** of house of our God I will
Pr. 1 24. **b.** I called and ye refused
Ec. 8 : 6. **b.** to every purpose is time
11. **b.** sentence against evil work
15. mirth, **b.** man hath no better
thing than to eat and ⌈not find
17. **b.** tho. man labour to seek it,
Is. 3 . 8. **b.** their doings are ag-t L.
16. **b.** dau-s of Zion are haughty
5 : 13. captivity, **b.** no knowledge
24. **b.** they cast away law of Lord
6 : 5. **b.** I am man of unclean lips
7 : 5. **b.** Syria taken evil counsel
† 9. not believe ? **b.** ye not stable
24. **b.** all land shall become briers
10 : 27. yoke destroyed **b.** of anoint
17 : 9 left **b.** of children of Israel
10. **b.** thou hast forgotten God of
19 : 16 Eg. shall fear **b.** of shaking
17. be afraid b. of counsel of Lord
20. cry unto Lord **b.** of oppressors
22 : 4. weep, **b.** of spoiling of people
30 : 12. **b.** ye trust in oppression
31 : 1. trust in chariots **b.** many
32 : 14. **b.** palaces shall be forsaken
37 : 29. **b.** thy rage ag-t me is come
48 : 4. **b.** I knew thou art obstinate
50 : 2. their fish stinketh **b.** no wa.
51 : 13. hast feared **b.** of oppressor
53 : 9. **b.** he had done no violence
12. **b.** he poured out soul unto d.
55 : 5. nations unto thee **b.** of thy G.
60 : 9. G., **b.** he hath glorified thee
65 : 12. **b.** when I called ye did not

Is. 65 : 16. **b.** troubles forgotten (2)
Je. 2 : 35. **b.** I am innocent (2)
4 : 4. lest my fury, **b.** of evil of
your doings, 21 : 12. ⌈bitter (2)
18. this is thy wickedness, **b.** it is
28. heavens be black : **b.** I have
5 : 14. **b.** ye speak this word I will
6 : 30. Reprobate silver shall men
call them, **b.** Lord rejected
7 : 13. **b.** have done all these works
8 : 19. **b.** of them that dwell in far
9 : 13. **b.** they have forsaken my law,
I will, 17 : 13.-18 : 15.
19. confounded, **b.** forsaken land,
b. our dwellings cast us out
10 : 5. be borne **b.** they cannot go
12 : 4. **b.** they said, He shall not see
13 : 17. tears, **b.** L.'s flock is carried
14 : 4. ashamed, **b.** ground chap-
6. eyes did fail **b.** was no grass⌊ped
16. people be cast out **b.** of famine
15 : 4. be removed **b.** of Manasseh
17. I sat alone **b.** of thy hand
16 : 11. **b.** your fathers forsaken me
18. double ; **b.** they defiled my la.
19 : 4. **b.** they have forsaken me
8. shall hiss **b.** of all the plagues
13. **b.** of houses upon whose roofs
20 : 17 **b.** he slew me not fr. womb
22 : 15. **b.** closest thyself in cedar
23 : 9. Mine heart is broken **b.** of
the prophets ; **b.** of Lord, and **b.**
10. **b.** of swearing land mourneth
38. **b.** ye say this, The burden of
25 . 8. **b.** ye have not heard words
16. they shall drink, be mad **b.**
of the sword, 27. ⌈Lord
37. are cut down **b.** of anger of
38. land desolate **b.** of oppressor
26 : 3. evil I purpose **b.** of their⌊(2)
29 : 15. **b.** ye said, Lord hath raised
19. **b.** they have not hearkened
23. **b.** they have committed villany
25. **b.** has sent letters unto Jerus.
31. **b.** Shemaiah hath prophesied
32. **b.** he taught rebellion ag-t L.
31 : 15. Rachel weeping for her chil.
b. they were not, Mat. 2 : 18.
19. **b.** I did bear reproach of my y.
32 : 24. hand of Chald-s **b.** of sword
32. **b.** of all the evil of Israel, and
35 : 16. **b.** sons of Jonadab perform
17. **b.** I have spoken, but they
18. Israel ; **b.** ye have obeyed the
40 : 3. **b.** ye have sinned, this is c.
41 : 9. he had slain **b.** of Gedaliah
18. dwelt in Chimham **b.** of Chal.
44 : 3. desolation **b.** of wickedness
22. no longer bear **b.** of doings (2)
23. **b.** ye have sinned, thf. evil (2)
46 : 15. stood not, **b.** Lord did drive
23. **b.** they are innumerable⌊them
47 : 4. **b.** of the day to spoil Philis.
48 : 7. **b.** hast trusted in thy works
36. **b.** riches gotten are perished
42. **b.** he magnified hims. ag-t L.
45. stood under shadow **b.** of force
50 : 7. we offend not **b.** they sinned
11. **b.** ye were glad, O destroyers,
b. ye are grown fat (3) ⌈lited
13. **b.** of wrath of L. not be inhab-
24. caught, **b.** hast striven ag. L
51 : 11. **b.** it is vengeance of the L.
55. **b.** the Lord spoiled Babylon
56. **b.** spoiler is come upon her
La. 1 : 3. Judah into captivity **b.** of
affliction, **b.** of great servitude
16. I weep ; **b.** comforter is far fr.
me ; **b.** the enemy prevailed
3 : 28. alone, **b.** he hath borne it
51. affecteth mine heart **b.** of
5 : 9. gat bread with peril **b.** of sw.
10. our skin black **b.** of famine
18. **b.** of Zion, foxes walk upon it
Eze. 5 : 7. **b.** ye multiplied more than
9. I will do **b.** of thine abomina-s
11. **b.** thou has defiled my sanct-y

Eze. 7 : 19. **b.** it is stumblingblock
13 : 8. **b.** ye have spoken vanity
10. **b.**, even **b.** they have seduced
my people, saying, Peace ⌈sad
22. **b.** with lies ye made righteous
14 : 15. that no man pass **b.** of beasts
16 : 15. But thou playedst harlot
b. of thy renown ⌈unsatiable
28. hast played the whore also **b.**
43. **b.** not remembered thy youth
63. never open mouth **b.** of shame
18 : 18 **b.** he spoiled broth., sh. die
28. **b.** he turneth from transgres.
20 : 16. **b.** despised my judgm-ts, 24.
21 : 7. For the tidings **b.** it cometh
13. **b.** it is a trial, what if sword
24. **b.** ye made iniq rememb-d (2)
28. to consume **b.** of the glittering
22 : 19. **b.** ye are all become dross
23 : 30. **b.** art polluted with idols (2)
35. **b.** thou hast forgotten me ⌈is
45. **b.** they are adulteresses, blood
25 : 3. **b.** saidst, Aha ag-t my sanct
6. **b.** hast clapped thine hands
8. **b.** Moab and Seir do say, Judah
12. **b.** Edom hath dealt ag-t Judah
15. **b.** Philistines dealt by revenge
26 : 2. **b.** Tyrus said ag. Jerus., Aha
28 : 2. **b.** thou hast said, I am a god,
17. heart lifted **b.** of thy beauty⌊6.
29 : 9. **b.** he said, river is mine ⌈me
20. given Eg. **b.** they wrought for
31 : 5. branches long **b.** of waters
10. **b.** thou lifted thys. in height
34 : 8. **b.** my flock became a prey,
b. there was no shepherd
21. **b.** ye have thrust with side
35 : 5. **b.** hast shed blood of Israel
10. **b.** said, These nations mine
15. didst rejoice at Isr. **b.** desolate
36 : 2. **b.** the enemy hath said, Aha
3. †**b.** they have made you desolate
6 **b.** have borne shame of heathen
13. **b.** they say, Thou devourest
Da. 2 : 8. **b.** thing is gone fr. me⌊men
3 : 22. Theref. **b.** king's com-t urgent
29. **b.** is no other God can deliver
6 : 3. **b.** an excellent spirit in him
7 : 11. **b.** of great words horn spake
9 : 8. confusion, **b.** we have sinned
16 **b.** for sins people a reproach
Ho. 4 : 6. **b.** hast rejected knowledge
19. ashamed **b.** of their sacrifices
5 : 11. **b.** he walked after the com-t
8 : 11. **b.** Ephraim hath made many
altars to sin ⌈wickedness
10 : 15. So sh. Beth-el do **b.** of your
Jo. 3 : 5. **b.** ye have taken my silver
Am. 4 : 12. **b.** I will do this, prepare
Mi. 2 : 10. **b.** polluted, sh. destroy you
7 : 9. indignation of L. **b.** I sinned
13. land sh. be desolate **b.** of them
17. and they shall fear **b.** of thee
18. **b.** he delighteth in mercy
Na. 3 : 4. corpses ; **b.** of whoredoms
11. seek strength **b.** of ene. ⌈lence
Ha 2 : 17. **b.** of men's blood, vio-
Zch. 8 : 10. nei. peace **b.** of affliction
9 : 8. I will encamp about mine
house **b.** of army and **b.** (3)
10 : 5. shall fight **b.** Lord is wi. them
Mal. 2 : 14. **b.** Lord hath been witn.
Mat. 5 : 36. **b.** canst not make hair
7 : 14. **b.** strait is the gate ⌊white
9 : 36. with compassion on them **b.**
they fainted, Mk. 6 : 34 ⌈not
11 : 20. upbraid cities **b.** repented
25. **b.** hast hid these things from
12 : 41. **b.** repented at preaching of
13 : 5. they sprung up **b.** they had
no deepness of earth, Mk. 4 : 5.
6. **b.** they had no root withered,
Mk. 4 : 6. Lu. 8 : 6. ⌈mysteries
11. **b.** it is given unto you to know
13. parables ; **b.** they see-g see not
21. when persecution **b.** of word
58. did not mighty works **b.** of un.

Mat. 14 : 5. multitude, **b.** counted
him a prophet, 21 : 46. ⌈Mk. 8 : 2.
15 : 32. **b.** they have nothing to eat,
16 : 7. It is **b.** we have no bread, 8.
Mk. 8 : 16, 17. ⌈unbelief
17 : 20. Why not we? **b.** of your
18 : 7. Woe unto world **b.** of offen-
32. I forgave **b.** thou desiredst⌊ces
19 : 8. **b.** of hardness of your hearts
20 : 7. say, **b.** no man hath hired us
15. Is thine eye evil **b.** I am good?
31. rebuked, **b.** should hold peace
23 : 29. **b.** ye build tombs of proph-s
24 : 12. **b.** iniquity sh. abound, love
26 : 31. All ye shall be offended **b.**
of me this night, Mk. 14 : 27.
33. Tho. all be offended **b.** of thee
27 : 6. **b.** it is the price of blood
19. suffered in a dream, **b.** of him
Mk. 1 : 34. and suffered not devils to
speak **b.** they knew him ⌈tude
3 : 9. ship wait on him **b.** of multi-
30. **b.** said, He hath unclean spirit
4 : 29. putteth in sickle **b.** harvest
5 : 4. **b.** he had been often bound
6 : 6. marvelled **b.** of their unbelief
7 : 19. **b.** it entereth not his heart
9 : 38. we forbade him, **b.** he followeth not us, Lu. 9 : 49. ⌈to Ch.
41. give cup of water **b.** ye belong
12 : 24. err, **b.** ye know not Script.?
15 : 42. **b.** it was the preparation
16 : 14. **b.** they believed not them
Lu. 1 : 7. no child, **b.** Elis-h barren
20. be dumb, **b.** thou believ-t not
2 : 4. **b.** he was of lineage of David
7. manger ; **b.** no room in the inn
4 : 18. **b.** he anointed me to preach
5 : 19. not find by what way **b.** of
8 : 30. Legion : **b.** many devils
9 : 7. **b.** it was said, John was risen
53. **b.** his face as tho. he would go
10 : 20. rejoice **b.** your names in h.
11 : 8. not rise **b.** he is his friend,
yet **b.** of importunity will rise
18. **b.** ye say I cast out devils thro.
12 : 17. **b.** I have no room where to
13 : 2. sinners above all **b.** they suf-
14. **b.** Jesus healed on sab.⌊fered?
15 : 27. **b.** he hath received him safe
16 : 8. commended steward, **b.** he
had done wisely ⌈comm-ded?
17 : 9 thank servant **b.** he did things
18 : 5. **b.** this widow troubleth me
19 : 3. could not, **b.** little of stature
11. parable, **b.** they thought kingdom immediately appear (2)
17. **b.** thou hast been faithful in
21. **b.** thou art an austere man
31. say, **b.** Lord hath need of him
44. **b.** thou knowest not the time
23 : 8. **b.** he heard many things of
Jn. 1 : 50. **b.** I said, I saw thee und.
2 : 24. **b.** he knew all men ⌊tree
3 : 18. condemned **b.** he not believed
19. loved darkness **b.** deeds evil
23. baptiz-g in Enon **b.** much wa.
29. rejoiceth **b.** of bridegr-'s voice
4 : 41. more believed **b.** of his word
42. we believe not **b.** of thy say-g
5 : 16 **b.** he had done these on sabb.
18. **b.** he had not only broken sabb.
27. **b.** he is the Son of man ⌈will
30. just : **b.** I seek not mine own
6 : 2. followed **b.** they saw miracles
26. not **b.** ye saw miracles, but
b. ye did eat of loaves ⌈bread
41. murmured **b.** he said, I am the
7 : 1. **b.** Jews sought to kill him
7. me it hateth, **b.** I testify of it
22. (not **b.** it is of Moses, but fath-s)
23. angry, **b.** I made a man whole
30. **b.** his hour was not yet come
39. **b.** Jesus was not yet glorified
43. division amo. people **b.** of him
8 : 22. **b.** he saith, Whither I go, ye
37. to kill me, **b.** my word no pla.

Jn.8 :43. b. ye cannot hear my word
44. not in truth, b. no truth in h.
45. b. I tell you the truth, ye ⌈G.
47. thf. hear not b. ye are not of
9 :16. not of God, b. he keepeth not
22. b. they feared the Jews ⌊sabb.
10 : 13. fleeth, b. he is a hireling
17. love me, b. I lay down my life
26. believe not, b. not of my sheep
33. but b. thou makest thyself G.
36. b. I said I am the Son of God
11: 9. stumbleth not, b. seeth light
10. in night stumbleth b. no light
42. but b. of the people I said it
12 : 6. b. he was a thief, had bag
11. b. by him many believed on J.
30. This voice came not b. of me
39. not believe, b. Esaias said⌈fess
42. b. of Pharisees, did not con-
13 : 29. tho-t, b. Judas had the bag
14 : 12. b. I go unto my Father,
28.-16 : 10, 17. ⌈seeth him not
17. the world cannot receive, b. it
19. me; b. I live, ye shall live also
15 : 19. b. ye are not of world ⌈me
21. b. they know not him th. sent
27. b. ye with me from beginning
16 : 3. b. they have not known Fa.
4. not at beginning, b. I with you
6. b. I said these things, sorrow
9. sin, b. they believe not on me
10. Of righteousn. b. I go to Fath.
11. b. prince of world is judged
16. sh. see me b. I go to Father, 17.
21. sorrow, b. her hour is come
27. Fa. loveth you b. ye loved me
32. Not alone, b. Father with me
17 : 14. b. they are not of the world
19 : 7. b. made himself Son of God
42. b. of Jews' preparat-n day, 31.
20 : 13. b. they have taken my L.
29. b. hast seen me hast believed
21 : 17. Peter was grieved b. he said
Ac. 2 : 6. b. every man heard them
24. b. not possible that he be hold-
27. b. thou not leave my soul ⌊en
4 : 21. they let them go b. of people
6 : 1. b. widows were neglected in
8 : 11. b. he had bewitched them
20. Thy money perish wi. thee b.
10 : 45 b. on Gentiles the Holy Gh.
12: 3. b. he saw it pleased Jews
20. b. nourished by king's money
23. b. gave not God glory⌈speaker
14 : 12. Paul, Mercurius, b. chief
16 : 3. circumcised him b. of Jews
17 : 18. b. he preached Jesus and
31. b. he hath appointed a day in
18 : 2. (b. Claudius com-ded Jews)
3. b. of same craft, he wrought
20 : 16. b. he not spend time in Asia
22 : 29. afraid b. he had bound him
27 : 4. Cyprus, b. winds contrary
9. b. fast was already past, Paul
28 : 2. received us b. of the rain, b.
18. b. was no cause of death in me
20. b. for hope of Isr. I am bound
Ro. 1 : 19. b. that wh. may be known
21. b. when they knew God ⌊of G.
4 : 15. b. the law worketh wrath
5 : 5. b. love of God is shed in our
6 : 15. shall we sin b. not under law
19. b. of infirmity of your flesh
8 : 7. b. carnal mind enmity ag. G.
10. body is dead, b. of sin ; Spirit
is life b. of righteousness⌈Spirit
† 11. sh. quicken your bodies b. of
21. b. creature shall be delivered
27. b. he maketh intercession for
9 : 7. b. they are seed of Abraham
28. b. a short work will L. make
32. b. they sought it not by faith
14 : 23. b. he eateth not of faith⌈me
15 : 15. boldly, b. of grace given to
1 Co. 1 : 25. b. foolishness of G. wiser
2 : 14. b. are spiritually discerned
3 : 13. b. it shall be revealed by fire

1 Co. 6 : 7. fault b. ye go to law ⌈gels
11 : 10. power on her head b. of an-
12 : 15. b. I am not the hand, is it
16. if ear say, b. I am not the eye
15 : 9. b. I persecuted the church
15. b. we have testified of God
2 Co. 5 : 14. b. we judge, if one died
7 : 13. b. his spirit was refreshed
11 : 7. b. I preached to you gospel
11. b. I love you not? G knoweth
Ga. 2 : 4. b. of false brethren who . .
11. b. he was to be blamed⌊to spy
3 : 19. Whf. law ? b. of transgr-ns
4 : 6. b. ye are sons, God sent Spirit
16. I your enemy b. I tell truth
Ep. 4 : 18. b. of blindness of heart
5 : 6. b. of these things wrath of G.
16. Redeeming time b. days evil
Ph. 1 : 7. b. I love you in my heart
2 : 26. b. ye heard he had been sick
30. b. for work of Christ nigh un-
4 : 17. Not b. I desire a gift⌊to dea.
1 Th. 2 : 8. b. ye were dear unto us
9. b. we would not be chargeable
13. b. ye received it not as word of
4 : 6. b. Lord is avenger of all such
2 Th. 1 : 3. b. your faith groweth
10. b. our testimony was believed
2 : 10. b. received not love of truth
13. b. God chosen you to salvat-n
3 : 9. Not b. we have not power
1 Ti. 1 : 13. b. I did it ignorantly in
4 : 10. b. we trust in the living God
5 : 12. b. they have cast off faith
6 : 2. not despise, b. they are brethren, do them service, b. beloved
Phm. 7. b. saints refreshed by thee
He. 3 : 19. not enter b. of unbelief
4 : † 2. b. they not united by faith
6. they entered not in b. of unbel.
6 : 13. b. could swear by no greater
7 : 23. b. not suffered to continue
24. this man b. he continueth ev.
8 : 9. b. they continued not in cov.
10 : 2. b. worshippers once purged
11 : 5. b. God had translated him
11. Sarah, b. she judged him faithf
23. b. they saw he was proper chi.
Ja. 1 : 10. b. as flower he pass away
4 : 2. ye have not, b. ye ask not
3. Ye receive not, b. ye ask amiss
1 Pe. 1 : 16. b. it is written, Be holy
2 : 21. b. Christ also suffered for us
5 : 8. b. your adversary the devil
1 Jn. 2 : 8. b. the darkness is past
11. b. darkness hath blinded his
12. b. your sins are forgiven⌊eyes
13. I write b. ye have overcome,
. . . b. ye have known Fa.(3), 14(2)
21. not written b. ye know not
truth, but b. ye know it⌈him n.
3 : 1. knoweth us not, b. it knew
9. cannot sin, b. he is born of G.
12. b. his own works were evil
14. unto life b. we love brethren
16. love, b. he laid down his life
22. we receive, b. we keep com-ts
4 : 1. b. many false prophets are
4. B. greater is he that is in you
9. b. God sent his only Son into
13. b. he hath given us of Spirit
17. b. as he is so we in this world
18. b. fear hath torment ⌈us
19. We love him, b. he first loved
5 : 6. witness, b. the Spirit is truth
10. b. he believeth not record, G.
3 Jn. 7. b. for his name's sake they
Jude 16. admiration b. of advantage
Re. 1 : 7. kindreds sh. wail b. of him
2 : 4. b. thou hast left thy 1st love
14. b. hast them th. hold doctrine
20. b. sufferest that woman Jezebel
3 : 10. b. hast kept word of patience
16. So then b. thou art lukewarm
17. b. thou sayest I am rich, and
5 : 4. b. no man was found worthy
8 : 11. many died of waters b. bitter

Re. 11 : 10. b. th. prophets tormented
17. b. thou hast taken thy power
14 : 8. b. she made nations drink
16 : 5. righteous b. hast judged thus
11. blasphemed God b. of pains, ⌊21.

BE'CHER.

Ge. 46 : 21. sons of Benjamin were
Belah, B., and 1 Ch. 7 : 6.
Nu. 26 : 35. of B., family of Bachrites
1 Ch. 7 : 8. sons of B., Zemira and(2)

BECHO'RATH.

1 S. 9 : 1. son of Zeror, the son of B.

BECKONED, ING.

Lu. 1 : 22. Zacharias b-d, speechless
5 : 7. they b-d unto partners in ship
Jn. 13 : 24. Peter b-d he should ask
Ac. 12 : 17. Peter b-g unto them wi.
13 : 16. Paul, b-g with hand, said
19 : 33. Alexander b-d with hand
21 : 40. Paul stood on stairs and b-d
24 : 10. Paul, aft. governor had b-d,

BECOME. ⌊anew-d

Ge. 3 : 22. the man is b. as one of us
9 : 15. waters sh. no more b. a flood
17 : † 16. and she shall b. nations
18 : 18. Abr. sh. b. a mighty nation
24 : 35. my master, he is b. great
32 : 10. and now am I b. two bands
34 : 16. with you we will b. one peo.
37 : 20. what will b. of his dreams
38 : † 23. lest we b. a contempt
48 : 19. he shall b. a people ; his
brother b. multitude of nations
Ex. 4 : 9. water shall b. blood upon l.
7 : 9. Take thy rod, it sh. b. serpent
19. rivers, that they may b. blood
8 : 16 smite dust, that it b. lice
9 : 9. ashes, it shall b. small dust
15 : 2. The Lord, he is b. my salvation, Ps. 118 : 14, 21. Is. 12 : 2.
6. right hand, O L., is b. glorious
23 : 29. lest the land b. desolate
32 : 1. Moses, we wot not what is
b. of him, 23. Ac. 7 : 40. ⌈ness
Le. 19 : 29. lest land b. full of wicked-
Nu. 5 : 24. water into her b. bitter, 27.
De. 27 : 9. thou art b. people of God
28 : 37. thou sh. b. an astonishm-t
Jos. 9 : 13. our shoes are b. old by
Ju. 16 : 17. if shaven I shall b. weak
1 S. 28 : 16. Lord is b. thine enemy
2 S. 7 : 24. thou, Lord, art b. their G.
1 K. 2 : 15. kingdom is b. my bro-'s
14 : 3. tell thee what sh. b. of child
2 K. 21 : 14. sh. b. a prey to enemies
22 : 19. that they should b. a curse
Es. 2 : 11. Esther, what sho. b. of her
Jb. 7 : 5. my skin is b. loathsome
15 : 28. in houses ready to b. heaps
21 : 7. Wherefore do wicked b. old
30 : 19. I am b. like dust and ashes
21. Thou art b. cruel to me
Ps. 14 : 3. they are all together b.
filthy, 53 : 3. Ro. 3 : 12. ⌈down
28 : 1. lest I b. like them that go
62 : 10. and b. not vain in robbery
69 : 8. I am b. stranger unto breth.
22. Let their table b. a snare ; th.
welfare, let it b. a trap⌈neighb-s
79 : 4. We are b. a reproach to our
109 : 7. let his prayer b. sin⌈corner
118 : 22. stone is b. headstone of
119 : 83. I am b. like bottle in smo.
148 : † 7. I am b. like them that go
Pr. 29 : 21. shall have him b. his son
Is. 1 : 21. How is city b. a harlot !
22. Thy silver is b. dross ; thy
7 : 24. bec. the land shall b. briers
14 : 10. Art thou b. weak as we ?(2)
19 : 11. counsel of . . . is b. brutish
13. The princes of Zoan are b. fools
29 : 11. vision has b. unto you as a
34 : 9. land shall b. burning pitch
35 : 7. parched ground shall b. pool
59 : 6. Their webs not b. garments
60 : 22. little one sh. b. a thousand
Je. 2 : 5. your fathers are b. vain

Je 2 :† 14. Israel, why is he b. spoil
3 : 1. If his wife b. another man's
5 : 13. prophets shall b. wind [rich
27. theref. they are b. great and
7 : 11. Is this house b. den of rob-
10 : 21. pastors are b. brutish[bers
22 : 5. this house shall b. desolation
26 : 18. Jerusalem sh. b. heaps, and
49 : 13. Bozrah shall b. a desolation
50 : 23. how is Babylon b. a desola-
37. they shall b. as women [tion
51 : 37. Babylon shall b. heaps
La. 1 : 1. how is she b. as a widow!
how is she b. tributary!
2. all her friends are b. her enemies
6. her princes are b. like harts
11. see, O Lord, for I am b. vile
4 : 1. How is the gold b. dim!
3. daughter of my peo. is b. cruel
8. withered, it is b. like a stick!
Eze. 22 : 4. art b. guilty in thy blood
18. house of Isr. is to me b. dross
19. Because ye are all b. dross
26 : 5. Tyrus sh. b. spoil to nations
36 : 35. and desolate is b. like Eden;
ruined cities are b. fenced [ha.
37 : 17. they shall b. one in thine
Da. 4 : 22. thou, O king, art b. strong
9 : 16. thy people are b. a reproach
11 : 23. b. strong with a small peo.
Ho. 12 : 8. Ephr. said, I am b. rich
13 : 15. Ephr.; his spring shall b.
16. Samaria shall b. desolate [dry
Jon. 4 : 5. see what would b. of city
Mi. 3 : 12. Jerusalem shall b. heaps
Zph. 1 : 13. their goods sh. b. booty
2 : 15. how is she b. a desolation
Zch. 4 : 7. O mountain? before Zerubbabel b. a plain [children
Mat. 18 : 3. Except ye b. as little
21 : 42. same is b. head of corner,
Mk. 12 : 10. Lu. 20 : 17. Ac. 4 : 11
Mk. 1 : 17. you to b. fishers of men
Jn. 1 : 12. power to b. sons of God
Ac. 12 : 18. stir, what was b. of Peter
Ro. 3 : 12. they are b. unprofitable
19. that all world may b. guilty
4 : 18. he might b. father of nations
6 : 22. being now free and b. servants to God [of Christ
7 : 4. ye are b. dead to law by body
13. sin by com-t might b. sinful
1 Co. 3 : 18. let him b. a fool, that
7 : 18. let him not b. uncircumc-d
8 : 9. lest liberty b. stumblingbl-k
13 : 1. I am b. as sounding brass
15 : 20. now is Christ b. firstfruits
2 Co. 5 : 17. in Ch. all things are b.
12 : 11. I am b. fool in glorying[new
Ga. 4 : 16. am I tht. b. your enemy
5 : 4. Christ is b. of no effect unto y.
Tit. 2 : 1. which b. sound doctrine
Phm. 6. communication of thy faith
may b. effectual [of milk
He. 5 : 12. are b. such as have need
Ja. 2 : 4. b. judges of evil thoughts?
11. if kill, art b. a transgressor
Re. 11 : 15. are b. kingdoms of our L.
18 : 2. Bab. is b. habitation of devils

BECOMETH.

Ps. 93 : 5. holiness b. thine house
Pr. 10 : 4. He b. poor that dealeth
17 : 7. Excellent speech b. not a fool
18. void of understand-g b. surety
Ec. 4 : 14. born in his kingd. b. poor
Mat. 3 : 15. b. us to fulfil righteousn.
13 : 22. riches choke the word, he
b. unfruitful, Mk. 4 : 19. [4 : 32.
32. is least of seeds, b. a tree, Mk.
Ro. 16 : 2. Phebe receive as b. saints
Ep. 5 : 3. not once named as b. saints
Ph. 1 : 27. conversat-n be as b. gospel
1 Ti. 2 : 10. (b. women professing god.)
Tit. 2 : 3. aged women, as b. holiness

BED.

Ge. 47 : 31. bowed upon b.-'s head, 1
48 : 2. Israel sat upon b. [K. 1 : 47.
49 : 4. Reuben, wentest up to thy
fath-'s b., defiledst it, 1 Ch. 5 : 1.
33. Jacob gathered his feet into b.
Ex. 8 : 3. frogs sh. come upon thy b.
21 : 18. if die not, but keepeth his
Le. 15 : 4. b. whereon he lieth, 24. [b.
5. toucheth his b. shall wash,
21. toucheth her b. sh. wash, 23.
26. Every b. whereon she lieth
shall be as b. of her separation
1 S. 19 : 13. Michal took an image
and laid it in b., 16. [slay him
15. Bring him up in b. that I may
28 : 23. he arose and sat upon b.
2 S. 3 : † 31. David followed the b.
4 : 5. Ish-bosheth, who lay on a b.
7. lay on his b. and they slew him
11. slain righteous upon his b.?
11 : 2. David arose from off his b.
13. Uriah went out to lie on his b.
13 : 5. lay on thy b., make thys. sick
1 K. 17 : 19. laid him upon his own b.
21 : 4. Ahab upon his b. and turned
2 K. 1 : 4. shalt not come down from
that b., but surely die, 6, 16.
4 : 10. let us set there for him a b.
21. laid him on b. of man of God
32. child dead and laid upon b.
2 Ch. 16 : 14. in b. with sweet odours
24 : 25. slew him on his b. [Esther
Es. 7 : 8. Haman fallen upon b. wh-on
Jb. 7 : 13. My b. shall comfort me
17 : 13. I made my b. in darkness
33 : 15. in slumberings upon the b.
19. He is chastened upon his b.
Ps. 4 : 4. commune with heart upon
6 : 6. all night make my b. swim [b.
36 : 4. deviseth mischief upon his b.
41 : 3. Lord will strengthen him upon b. of languishing; thou wilt
make all his b. in his sickness
63 : 6. When I remember thee upon
132 : 3. I will go up into my b. [b.
139 : 8. If I make my b. in hell [17.
Pr. 7 : 16. decked my b. with tapestry,
17. I perfumed my b. with myrrh
22 : 27. why should he take thy b.
26 : 14. so doth slothful upon his b.
Can. 1 : 16. thou fair; our b. is green
3 : 1. by night on b. I sought him
7. Behold his b., which is Solo-n's
† 9. Sol. made b. of wood of Leb-n
Is. 28 : 20. b. shorter than that a m.
57 : 7. upon high mt. hast set thy b.
8. enlarged thy b., lovedst their b.
Eze. 23 : 41. satest upon a stately b.
32 : 25. her a b. in midst of slain
Da. 2 : 28. visions upon thy b., 29.
4 : 5. thoughts upon my b., 10, 13.
7 : 1. a dream and visions upon b.
Am. 3 : 12. dwell in Samaria in cor-
ner of a b. | † and on b-'s feet
Mat. 9 : 2. brought a man sick of
palsy, lying on a b., Lu. 5 : 18.
6. Take up thy b. and walk, Mk.
2 : 9, 11. Jn. 5 : 8, 11, 12. [lay
Mk. 2 : 4. let down b. wherein sick
12. he took up b. and went forth
4 : 21. Is a candle to be put under a
b.? Lu. 8 : 16. [upon the b.
7 : 30. she found her daughter laid
Lu. 11 : 7. my chil. are with me in b.
17 : 34. two men in one b.; one taken
Jn. 5 : 9. took up his b. and walked
10. sab.; not lawful to carry thy b.
Ac. 9 : 33. had kept his b. 8 years
34. Peter said, Eneas, make thy b.
Re. 2 : 22. I will cast her into a b.

BED of love. [to b.-

Eze. 23 : 17. Babyl-s came to her in-

BED, S, of spices.

Can. 5 : 13. His cheeks are as a b.-
6 : 2. My beloved is gone down to

BED undefiled. [b-s-

He. 13 : 4. marriage honourable and

BEDS. [b. u.

2 S. 17 : 28. Barzillai brought b. and
Es. 1 : 6. b. were of gold and silver
Ps. 149 : 5. Let saints sing upon b.
Is. 57 : 2. they shall rest in their b.
Ho. 7 : 14. when they howled upon b.
Am. 6 : 4. lie upon b. of ivory, and
Mi. 2 : 1. them that work evil upon
Mk. 6 : 55. carry in b. those sick [b.
7 : † 4. the washing of cups and b.
Ac. 5 : 15. sick into streets, on b. and

BE'DAD. [couches

Ge. 36 : 35. Hadad son of B., 1 Ch. 1:

BE'DAN. [46.

1 S. 12 : 11. Lord sent B., delivered
1 Ch. 7 : 17. sons of Ulam; B. [you

BEDCHAMBER.

Ex. 8 : 3. frogs shall come into thy b.
2 S. 4 : 7. Ish-bosheth lay in his b.
2 K. 6 : 12. words thou speakest in b.
11 : 2. hid him in b., 2 Ch. 22 : 11.
Ec. 10 : 20. curse not rich in thy b.
Ac. 12 : † 20. Blastus over king's b.

BEDEI'AH.

Ezr. 10 : 35. of the sons of Bani; B.

BEDSTEAD.

De. 3 : 11. his b. was a b. of iron

BEE, BEES. [b-s

De. 1 : 44. Amorites chased you as
Ju. 14 : 8. a swarm of b-s in the lion
Ps. 118 : 12. compassed me like b-s
Is. 7 : 18. shall hiss for b. in Assyria

BEELI'ADA or ELI'ADA.

2 S. 5 : 16. † sons born to David in
Jerusalem, Ibhar, E. † B., 1 Ch.
3 : 8. †-14 : 7. †

BEEL'ZEBUB. [B.

Mat. 10 : 25. called master of house
12 : 24. doth not cast out devils,
but by B., Mk. 3 : 22. Lu. 11 : 15.
27. if I by B. cast out devils, by
whom do your, Lu. 11 : 18, 19.

BEEL'ZEBUL.

Mat. 10 : † 25.-12 : † 24, † 27. Mk. 3 :
† 22. Lu. 11 : † 15, † 18, † 19.

BEEN. [b.

Ge. 13 : 3. Abr. where his tent had
26 : 8. when had b. there long time
31 : 5. God of my father b. with me
38. 20 years have I b. with thee, 41.
42. Exc. God of Abr. b. with me
38 : 26. She b. more righteous than
45 : 6. two years hath famine b. [I
46 : 32. their trade b. to feed cattle,
47 : 9. few ha. days of my life b. [34.
Ex. 2 : 22. I have b. a stranger, 18 : 3.
De. 2 : 7. thy God hath b. with thee
4 : 32. whe. hath b. any such thing
9 : 7. ye have b. rebellious against
the Lord, 24.-31 : 27. [servant
15 : 18. he b. worth a double hired
Jos. 7 : 7. would God we b. content
9 : 4. as if they had b. embassadors
10 : 27. cave wherein they had b.
Ju. 16 : 17. I have b. a Nazarite [hid
1 S. 1 : 13. Eli tho-t she b. drunken
4 : 9. not servants as they have b.
17. b. great slaughter amo. people
9 : 24. hath it b. kept for thee [deaf
10 : † 27. Saul as though he had b.
14 : 38. see wherein this sin hath b.
19 : 4. his works b. to thee-ward g.
20 : 13. as he hath b. with my fath.
29 : 3. David which hath b. wi. me
6. as Lord liveth thou hast b. upr.
8. so long as I have b. with thee
2 S. 1 : 26. pleasant hast b. unto me
12 : 8. if that had b. too little I
13 : 20. Hath Amnon b. with thee?
14 : 32. it had b. good for me to
have b. there still [king
1 K. 1 : 37. As the Lord hath b. with
16 : 31. as if it had b. a light thing
17 : 7. had b. no rain in the land
19 : 10. I have b. zealous for L., 14.
2 K. 4 : 13. thou hast b. careful for
20 : 12. Hez. had b. sick, Is. 39 : 1.
1 Ch. 17 : † 5. I have b. fr. tent to tent
8. I have b. with thee whitherso

2 Ch. 1 : 12. as none th. have b. before
15 : 3. Isr. hath b. without true G
23 . 9. shields that had b. k David's
Ezr. 4 : 20. have b. mighty k-s over
5 : 16. hath it b. in building⌊Jeru.
9 : 2. rulers b. chief in trespass
7. have we b. in a great trespass
Ne. 5 : 15. you that had b. bef. me
Es. 2 : 12. after she had b. 12 mos.
Jb. 3 : 13. now should I have b.
quiet; then had I b. at rest ⌈b.
10 : 19. I should have b. as tho. not
42 : 11. had b. of his acquaintance
Ps. 25 : 6. mercies have b. ever of old
27 : 9. thou hast b. my help, 63 : 7.
35 : 14. as tho. he had b. my friend
37 : 25. have b. young, now am old
42 : 3. tears have b. my meat day
50 : 8. have b. continually bef. me
18. thou b. partaker with adulter-
59 : 16. thou hast b. my defence⌊ers
61 : 3. thou hast b. a shelter for me
69 : 22. sho. have b. for their welfa.
83 : † 8. b. an arm to child-n of Lot
85 : 1. hast b. favourable unto land
89 : 38. b. wroth wi. thine anointed
90 : 1. hast b. our dwellingplace in
94 : 17. Unless Lord had b. my help
115 : 12. Lord hath b. mindful of us
119 : 54. statutes have b. my songs
92. Unless law had b. my delights
143 : 3. those that have b. long dead
Ec. 1 : 9. thing that hath b. shall be
10. it hath b. already of old time
16. more wisdom than all have b.
3 : 15. That which hath b. is now;
that wh. is to be hath b., 6 : 10.
4 : 16. no end of all that have b.⌈(2)
Is. 1 : 9. we sho. have b. as Sodom,
25 : 4. hast b. a strength to poor
26 : 17. so have we b. in thy sight
18. We have b. with child, we
have b. in pain ⌈precept
28 : † 10. For precept hath b. upon
42 : 14. I have b. still and refrained
43 : 4. thou hast b. honourable
22. thou hast b. weary of me, O Isr.
48 : 18. had thy peace b. as a river
19. thy seed had b. as the sand
49 : 21. these, where had they b.?
57 : 11. of whom hast thou b. afraid
66 : 2. all those things have b.⌈Isr.
Je. 2 : 31 Have I b. a wildern-s unto
4 : 17. she hath b. rebellious ag. me
20 : 17. mother might have b. my
22 : 21. This b. thy manner⌊grave
28 : 8. prophets that have b. bef. me
32 : 31. city had b. a provocation
48 : 11. Moab hath b. at ease from
50 : 6. My people hath b. lost sheep
29. she hath b. proud ag-t Lord
51 : 7. Babylon hath b. a golden cup
Eze. 2 : 5. yet shall know hath b. a
prophet among them, 33 : 33.
10 : 10. as if wheel had b. in midst
21 : † 13. trial hath b., what then?
22 : 13. at blood wh. hath b. in thee
28 : 13. thou hast b. in garden of G.
29 : 6. bec. they have b. staff of reed
38 : 8 mts. of Isr. b. always waste
Ho. 5 : 1. ye have b. a snare on Miz-
2. tho. I have b. a rebuker ⌊pah
Jo 1 : 2. Hath this b. in your days
Mi. 5 : 2. whose goings b. from of old
7 : † 13. After land hath b. desolate
Na. 1 : † 12. If they would have b.
at peace, sho. have b. many(3)
Mal. 2 : 9. have b. partial in the law
14. L. hath b. witness betw. thee
3 : 13. Your words have b. stout ag.
Mat. 1 : 6. had b. wife of Urias ⌊me
23 : 30. If we had b. in days of fa-s
we would not have b. partakers
26 : 24. it had b. good for that man
if not b. born, Mk. 14 : 21.
28 : † 2. there had b. a great earthq.
Mk. 6 : 49. supposed it had b. spirit
Mk. 8 : 2 have b. with me three days
15 : 44. whe. he b. any while dead
16 : 10. told them th. had b. wi. him
Lu. 1 : 70. prophets have b. since w.
2 : 44. him to have b. in company
7 : 10. servant whole that had b. s.
19 : 17. bec. hast b. faithful in little
24 : 21. we trusted it had b. he
Jn. 5 : 6. b. long time in that case
9 : 18. not believe he had b. blind
11 : 21. L., if thou hadst b. here, 32.
39. he hath b. dead four days
12 : 1. Lazarus which had b. dead
14 : 9. Have I b. so long with you
15 : 27. ye have b. with me fr. begin-g
Ac. 4 : 13. that they had b. with Jes.
6 : 15. his face as it had b. face of
7 : 52. of whom ye have b. betrayers
9 : 18. from eyes as it had b. scales
10 : 11. as it had b. gr. sheet, 11 : 5.
14 : 19. supposing he had b. dead
15 : 7. when had b. much disputing
19 : 21. After I have b. there see R.
20 : 18. manner I have b. with you
24 : 10. hast b. of many years judge
19. Who ought to have b. here
25 : 14. had b. there many days
Ro. 9 : 29. we had b. as Sodoma
11 : 34. who hath b. his counsellor?
16 : 2. she b. a succourer of many
2 Co. 11 : 21. as tho. we had b. weak
25. a night and day I ha b. in deep
Ga. 3 : 21. if a law . . . righteousness
sho. have b. by the law ⌈have
4 : 15. if it had b. possible, ye would
Col. 4 : 11. have b. a comfort unto me
1 Th. 2 : 6. might have b. burdenso.
1 Ti. 5 : 9. having b. wife of one man
2 Ti. 3 : † 10. thou hast b. a diligent
follower of my doctrine
He. 8 : 7. if 1st covenant had b. fault-
Ja 5 : 5. Ye have b. wanton ⌊less
2 Pe. 2 : 21. b. better not have kno.
1 Jn. 2 : 19. for if they had b. of us

Not BEEN. ⌈in Eg.

Ex. 9 : 18. hail, such as hath n. b.
1 S. 4 : 7. hath n. b. such a thing
14 : 30. had n. b. greater slaughter
1 K. 3 : † 13. hath n. b. any among
kings like thee, 1 Ch. 29 : 25.⌈Da.
14 : 8. thou hast n. b. as my serv-t
Ne. 2 : 1. I had n. b. sad in his pr.
Jb. 3 : 16. Or as a hidden untimely
birth I had n. b. ⌈had n. b.
10 : 19. I should have been as tho. I
Ps. 124 : 1. If it had n. b. the Lord, 2.
Ec. 4 : 3. better is he wh. hath n. b.
Is. 17 : 10. n. b. mindful of the Rock
Eze. 16 : 31. hast n. b. as a harlot
Jo. 2 : 2. hath n. b. ever the like
Ob. 16. be as though they had n. b.
Mat. 26 : 24. good if he had n. b. born
Lu. 16 : 11. If ye have n. b. faithf., 12.

BE'ER. ⌈spake

Nu. 21 : 16. to B.; well wherew. Lord
Ju. 9 : 21. Jotham ran away, fled to

BEE'RA. ⌊B.

1 Ch. 7 : 37. sons of Zophah; Ithran,

BEE'RAH. ⌊B.

1 Ch. 5 : 6. B., prince of Reubenites

BE'ER-E'LIM.

Is. 15 : 8. howling thereof unto B.

BEE'RI.

Ge. 26 : 34. to wife Judith dau. of B.
Ho. 1 : 1. word unto Hosea son of B.

BE'ER-LAHA'I-ROI.

Ge. 16 : 14. Wh' the well was called B.
See LAHAI-ROI.

BEE'ROTH.

De. 10 : 6. Israel took journey fr. B.
Jos. 9 : 17. their cities Gibeon, B.
18 : 25. cities of Benjamin. Gibeon,
B., 2 S 4 : 2. ⌈Ne. 7 : 29.
Ezr. 2 : 25. children of Chephirah, B.,

BEER'OTHITE, S, or **BE'ROTHITE.**[2]

2 S. 4 : 2. sons of Rimmon a B., 5, 9.
2 S. 4 : 3. (the B-s fled to Gittaim)
23 : 37. Nahari the B., armourbearer to Joab, 1 Ch. 11 : 39. B.[2]

BEER'-SHEBA. ⌈B.

Ge. 21 : 14. Hagar in wilderness of
31. Wherf. he called that place B.
32. Thus they made coven-t at B.
33. Abraham planted a grove in B.
22 : 19. his young men went to B.;
Abraham dwelt at B. ⌈B.
26 : 23. Isaac went from thence to
33. name of city is B. unto this day
28 : 10. Jacob from B. toward Har-
46 : 1. Israel with all came to B⌊an
5. Jacob rose up from B.: sons
Jos. 15 : 28. cities of Judah, B., and
19 . 2. tribe of Simeon had B. and
Moladah, 1 Ch. 4 : 28. ⌈in B.
1 S. 8 : 2. Joel, Abiah; were Judges
2 S. 24 : 7. they went out even to B.
1 K. 19 : 3. Elijah went for his life to B.
2 K. 12 : 1. his mother's name Zibi-
ah of B., 2 Ch. 24 : 1. ⌈to B.
23 : 8. defiled high places fr. Geba
2 Ch. 19 : 4. Jehosh-t went from B.
Ne. 11 : 27. some of Judah dwelt at B.
30. they dwelt from B. unto Hin.
Am. 5 : 5. not Beth-el; pass not to B.
7 : † 9. B. of Isaac shall be desolate
8 : 14. The manner of B. liveth

BEER'-SHEBA with Dan.

Ju. 20 : 1. gathered fr. D. even to B.
1 S. 3 : 20. Israel from D. to B. knew
Samuel to be prophet ⌈to B.
2 S. 3 : 10. throne of David from D.
17 : 11. Isr. be gathered fr. D. to B.
24 : 2. Go from D. to B., number ye
the people, 1 Ch. 21 : 2.
15. died from D. to B. 70,000 men
1 K. 4 : 25. Isr. dwelt safely fr. D. to B.
2 Ch. 30 : 5. proclamation fr. B. to D.

BEESH'-TERAH.

Jos 21 : 27. unto child-n of Gershon

BEETLE. ⌊gave B.

Le. 11 : 22. these ye may eat, the b.

BEEVES. ⌈b.

Le. 22 : 19. offer without blemish of
21. offering in b., it sh. be perfect
Nu. 31 : 28. levy a tribute of b., 30.
33. booty was 72,000 b.⌈36,000 b.
38. portion of them th. went to war
44. half unto congreg-n, 36,000 b.

BEFALL. ⌈him

Ge. 42 : 4. Lest peradv. mischief b.
38. if mischief b. him, 44 : 29.
49 : 1. which shall b. you in the last
days, De. 31 : 29. Da. 10 : 14.
De. 31 : 17. many evils shall b. them
Ps. 91 : 10. There sh. no evil b. thee
Ac. 20 : 22. things that shall b. me

BEFALLEN, ETH.

Le. 10 : 19. such things have b-n me
Nu. 20 : 14. all travail th. hath b-n us
De. 31 : 21. what troubles are b-n th.
Ju. 6 : 13. why is all this b-n us?
1 S. 20 : 26. Something b-n him⌈him
Es. 6 : 13. told everything had b-n
Ec. 3 : 19. that which b-h men b-h
beasts, even one thing b-h them
Mat 8 : 33. was b-n to the possessed

BEFELL. ⌊of devils

Ge. 42 : 29. told Jacob all that b. th.
Jos. 2 : 23. to Joshua told all that b.
2 S. 19 : 7 worse than all that b. thee
Mk. 5 : 16. they told how it b. him
Ac. 20 : 19. b. me lying in wait of

BEFORE. [Adv.] ⌊Jews

Ge. 31 : 5. your father's countenance
not toward me as b. ⌈lost
Nu. 6 : 12. days that were b. shall be
Jos. 4 : 18. Jordan ov. his banks as b.
8 : 33. as Moses commanded b.
14 : 15. name of Hebron b. was Kirjath-arba, Ju. 1 : 10. ⌈jath-sepher
Ju. 1 : 11. name of Debir b. was Kir-
23. the name of Beth-el b. was Luz
3 : 2. such as b. knew nothing th-f

Ju. 16 : 20. I will go as b. and shake
1 K. 13 : 6. king's hand as it was b.
Jb. 42 : 10. Job twice as much as b.
11. came all of his acquaintance b.
Eze. 44 : 22. widow that had priest b.
Jon. 4 : 2. I fled b. unto Tarshish
Mat. 14 : 8. she being b. instructed
24 : 25. Behold, I have told you b.
Mk. 6 . 45. to go to the other side b.
Lu. 19 : 4. he ran b., climbed into
21 : 14. not to meditate b. what ye
23 : 12. b. they were at enmity⌊ans.
53. wherein never man b. was laid
Jn. 6 : 62. Son ascend where he was
9 : 8. they wh. b. had seen him ⌊b.
Ac. 1 : 16. Dav. spake b. conc. Judas
2 : 31. He, seeing this b., spake of
3 : 18 God shewed b. by prophets
20. send Jes., wh. was b. preached
4 : 28. counsel determined b. to be
7 : 52. slain them wh. shewed b. of
10 : 41. witnesses chosen b. of God
17 : 26. be determined the times b.
20 : 5. These going b. tarried for us
21 : 29. (seen b. wi. him Trophimus)
Ro. 3 : 9. we have b. proved Jews
9 : 29. as Esaias said b., Exc Lord
2 Co. 1 : 15. I was minded to come
unto you b., that ⌈to die
7 : 3. I said b.; ye are in our hearts
8 : 10. who have begun b. to do and
9 : 5. that they go b. unto you, and
make up bounty whereof ye had
13 : 2. I told you b., and ⌊notice b.
Ga. 1 : 9. As we said b. so say I now
3 : 8. preached b. gospel unto Abr.
17. covenant confirmed b. in Ch-t
5 : 21. of the which I tell you b.
Ep. 2 : 10. good works which God
b. ordained we should walk in
3 : †3. (wrote a little b. in few)⌈are b.
Ph. 3 : 13. reaching unto things wh.
Col. 1 : 5. hope whereof ye heard b.
1 Th. 2 : 2. after we had suffered b.
3 : 4. we told you b. we sho. suffer
1 Ti. 1 : 13. Who was b. blasphemer
5 : 24. men's sins going b. to judgm.
He. 7 : 18. of commandment going b.
10 : 15. after th. he had said b. ⌈b.
2 Pe 3 : 2. mindful of words spoken
17. seeing ye know these things b.
Jude 4. b. ordained to condemnat-n
17. remember ye words spoken b.

BEFORE with behind.

2 S. 10 : 9. Joab saw battle against
him b-e and b-d, 1 Ch. 19 : 10.
2 Ch. 13 : 14. Judah looked back,
battle was b-e and b-d ⌈b-e
Ps. 139 : 5. hast beset me b-d and
Is. 9 : 12. Syrians b-e, Philistines b-d
Re. 4 : 6. beasts full of eyes b-e, b-d

BEFORE. [Prep.] ⌈(2)

Ge. 2 : 5 God made herb b. it grew
11 : 28. Haran died b. his fa. Terah
12 : 15. commended Sarai b. Pha-h
19 : 4. b. they lay down, men of city
24 : 15. b. he had done speaking,
45. b. I had done speaking⌊Rebek.
25 : 18. unto Shur, that is b. Egypt
27 : 4. soul may bless thee b. I die
33. I have eaten b. thou camest
29 : 26. not give younger b. firstb.
30 : 30. little thou hadst b. I came
38. set the rods b. the flocks, 41.
39 flocks conceived b. the rods
31 : 32. b. brethren discern thine
33 : 14. lord pass over b. his servant
36 : 31. b. there reigned any king
over Israel, 1 Ch. 1 : 43. ⌈spired
37 : 18. b. he came near, they con-
41 : 46. Joseph when stood b. Pha-h
50. unto Joseph 2 sons b. famine
43 : 14. God give you mercy b. man
45 : 28. I will go and see him b. I die
48 : 5. sons born in Eg-t b. I came
20. Jac. set Ephraim b. Manasseh
50 : 16. father command b. he died

Ex. 12 : 34. dough b. it was leavened
16 : 34. Aa. laid it up b. Testimony
34 : 3. nor herds feed b. that mount
Le. 10 : 4. brethren fr. b. sanctuary
14 : 36. empty house, b. priest go
19 : 14. nor stumblingblock b. blind
26 : 37. they shall fall b. a sword
Nu. 13 : 22. Hebron 7 years b. Zoan
14 : 5. fell on faces b. the assembly
20 : 10. Moses gath-d cong-n b. rock
21 : 11. Ije-Ab., in wildern. b. Moab
33 : 47. pitched in mts. b. Nebo
36 : 1. chief of families spake b. M.
De. 1 : 42. lest be smitten b. enemies
21 : 16. not make son of beloved
firstborn b. son of hated ⌈b. I
31 : 21. I know their imagination,
Jos. 2 : 8. b. they were laid down she
8 : 33. all Israel stood b. the priests
13 : 3. from Sihor, wh. is b. Egypt
15 : 7. b. the going to Adummim
19 : 11. border to river b. Jokneam
46 Rakkon, with border b. Japho
Ju. 4 : 15. discomfited Sisera, b. Ba.
8 : 13. Gideon fr. battle b. sun up
11 : 33. Ammon subdued b. Israel
12 : 5. passages of Jordan b. Eph-s
16 : 3. to top of a hill b. Hebron
18 : 6. Go : b. the Lord is your way
Ru. 3 : 14. she rose b. one could kn.
4 : 4. Buy it b. the inhabitants,
and b. the elders ⌈Eli, 3 : 1.
1 S. 2 : 11. the child did minister b.
35. he sh. walk b. mine anointed
8 : 11. some sh. run b. his chariots
9 : 13. ye shall find him b. he go to
15. Lord told Samuel b. Saul came
24. took shoulder, set it b. Saul
14 : 21. Hebrews with Philis. b. that
15 : 30. honour me b. elders, b. Isr.
16 : 8. Abinadab pass b. Samuel
17 : 57. Abner brought Dav. b. Saul
20 : 1. what is my sin b. thy father
26 : 1. Dav. hide in hill b. Jeshi-n?
30 : 20. they drave b. other cattle
31 : 1. men of Israel fled from b.
the Philistines, 1 Ch. 10 : 1. ⌈Da.
2 S. 2 : 17. Abner beaten b. serv-ts of
3 : 31. David said, mourn b. Abner
34. as man falleth b. wicked men
6 : 21. David said, It was b. the L.,
which chose me b. thy father;
b. all his house ⌈the sun
12 : 12. I will do this b. Israel, b.
1 K. 6 : 7. ready b. it was brought
7 : 49. candlesticks of gold b. oracle
8 : 8. staves were seen b. the oracle
12 : 30. went to worship b. the one
18 : 46. Elij. ran b. Ahab to entrance
2 K. 1 : 13. captain on knees b. Elij.
4 : 43. I set this b. a hundred men?
5 : † 1. a great man b. his master
1 Ch. 6 : 32. ministered b. dwellingplace of tabernacle ⌈Asa (2)
2 Ch. 14 : 12. L. smote Ethiopians b.
28 : 9. a prophet went out b. host
33 : 19. his sins b. be was humbled
Ezr. 4 : 23. letter was read b. Rehum
7 : † 14. art sent from b. king ⌈well
Ne. 2 : 13. I went out b. the dragon
4 : 5. provoked thee b. the builders
8 : 1. people gathered b. water gate
3. Ezra read b. street that was b.
the water gate, b. men ⌈Tobiah
13 : 4. b. this, Eliashib allied unto
19. gates began to be dark b. sab.
Es. 3 : 7. they cast the lot b. Haman
Jb. 3 : 24. sighing cometh b. I eat
8 : 12. withereth b. any other herb
16. He is green b. the sun ⌈turn
10 : 21. b. I go whence I sh. not re.
15 : 7. wast thou made b. the hills?
32. be accomplished b. his time
21 : 18. They are as stubble b. wind
23 : 17. I was not cut off b. darkn-s
Ps. 31 : 19. trust in thee b. sons of
39 : 13. O spare me b. I go hence

Ps. 52 : 9. thy name; good b. saints
58 : 9. b. your pots can feel thorns
68 : 2. as wax melteth b. the fire
80 : 2. b. Ephraim, Benj-n stir thy
83 : 13. them as stubble b. the wind
90 : 2. b. mts. were brought forth
119 : 46. of thy testimonies b. kings
67. b. I was afflicted I went astray
138 : 1. b. gods will I sing unto thee
141 : 3. Set a watch, O Lord, b. my
Pr. 8 : 22. me b. his works of old⌊mou.
25. b. mts. were settled, b. hills
14 : 19. The evil bow b. the good
15 : 33. b. honour is humility, 18 : 12.
16 : 18. Pride goeth b. destruction
17 : 14. leave off contention, b.⌊(2)
18 : 12. b. destruction man haughty
13. answereth matter b. heareth
16. bringeth him b. great men
25 : 26. A righteous man falling
down b. the wicked ⌈cong-n
26 : 26. his wickedness be shewed b.
30 : 7. deny me them not b. I die
Ec. 6 : 8. knoweth to walk b. living
7 : 17. why should-t die b. thy time?
10 : † 5. as an error from b. ruler
Is. 7 : 16. b. child sh. know to refuse
8 : 4. b. child have knowledge to cry,
17 : 14. b. morning he is not⌊My, (2)
24 : 23. when L. reign b. his ancients
42 : 9. b. they spring forth I tell you
43 : 13. b. the day was, I am he
48 : 5. b. it came to pass I shewed
7. b. day when thou heardest not
53 : 7. as sheep b. shearers is dumb
65 : 24. b. they call, I will answer
66 : 7. b. she travailed, she brought
forth; b. her pain came, she
Je. 1 : 5. b. I formed I knew thee;
b. camest forth I sanctified thee
13 : 16. b. he cause darkness, and
b. your feet stumble⌈b. temple
24 : 1. two baskets of figs were set
35 : 5. I set b. sons of Rechabites
38 : 10. Jer-h out of dungeon b. he
Eze. 6 : 4. cast slain b. y-r idols ⌊die
9 : 6. ancient men wh. were b. house
16 : 57. b. wickedn was discovered
20 : 9. not be polluted b. heath., 14.
40 : 47. measured altar b. the house
41 : 12. building b. separate place
42 : 2. b. length of 100 cubits door
4. b. chambers walk of ten cubits
13. south chambers b. sep. place
44 : 4. way of north gate b. house
12. bec ministered b. their idols
Da. 5 : 1. drank wine b. the thous-d
8 : 6. to ram, seen standing b. river
Jo. 2 : 11. L. utter his voice b. army
Am. 1 : 1. two years b. earthquake
4 : 3. every cow at that wh. is b. her
Mi. 1 : 4. valleys cleft as wax b. fire
6 : 1. contend thou b. the mount-s
Zph. 2 : 2. b. the decree bring forth,
b. anger of Lord come (4) ⌈a st.
Hag. 2 : 15. b. a stone was laid upon
Zch. 3 : 1. Joshua b. angel of Lord
9. stone that I have laid b. Joshua
4 : 7. O mountain? b. Zerubbabel
thou become a plain ⌈for man
8 : 10. b. these days was no hire
14 : 4. mount of Olives, b. Jerusal.
5. flee, as ye fled b. earthquake
Mal. 2 : 5. he was afraid b. my name
3 : 11. your vine cast fruit b. time
4 : 5. I will send Elijah b. coming
Mat. 1 : 18. b. they came together
6 : 8. what ye have need of b. ye ask
7 : 6. neither cast pearls b. swine
8 : 29 come to torment us b. time?
10 : 18. ye shall be brought b. kings
for my sake, Mk. 13 : 9. Lu. 21 : 12
32. Whoso. sh. confess me b. men,
him (2), Lu. 12 : 8. ⌈Lu. 12 : 9 (2).
33. whosoev. shall deny me b. men,
24 : 38. as in days b. flood, eating
27 : 11. Jesus stood b. the governor

Mat.27:24.P.washed hands **b.** mult.
Mk. 1 : 35.rising **b.** day, he went out
15 : 42. bec. it was the day **b.** sabb.
Lu. 2 : 21. so named **b.** conceived
26. not see death, b. had seen Ch.
5 : 19. let him down **b.** Jesus ⌈tude
9 : 16. to disciples to set **b.** multi-
11 : 38. had not washed **b.** dinner
21 : 12.**b.** these sh.lay hands on you
36. worthy to stand **b.** Son of man
22 : 15. to eat passover **b.** I suffer
Jn. 1 : 48. **b.** Philip called thee, I
7 :51. Doth our law judge **b.** it hear
8 : 58. **b.** Abraham was, I am⌈over
11 : 55. many to Jerusalem **b.** pass-
12 :1.Jes.,6 days **b.** passover, came
13 : 1. **b.** feast of passover, when J.
19. I tell you **b.** it come, 14 : 29.
15 : 18. it hated me **b.** it hated you
Ac. 2 :20.moon into blood **b.** gr.day
5:23.found keepers stand-g **b.** doors
27. they set them **b.** the council
36. **b.** these days rose up Theudas
6 : 6. Whom they set **b.** apostles
7 : 2. Abr. **b.** he dwelt in Charran
8 : 32. like a lamb dumb **b.** shearer
9 : 15. to bear my name **b.** Gentiles
10 :17.behold,the men stood **b.** gate
12 : 6. keepers **b.** door kept prison
14. told how Peter stood **b.** gate
13 : 24.John preached **b.** his com-g
14 : 13. the priest of Jupiter **b.** city
16 : 29. fell down **b.** Paul and Silas
18 : 17. beat Sosthenes **b.** judgm-t
19 : 9.evil of that way **b.** mult.⌊seat
21 :38.Egyptian, wh. **b.** these days
24 : 20.while I stood **b.** the council
25:16.**b.** he have accusers face to fa.
27 : 24. thou must be bro-t **b.** Cesar
1 Co. 4 :5. judge nothing **b.** the time
6 :1.Dare any,go to law **b.** unjust(2)
6. brother to law **b.** unbelievers
11 : 21. taketh **b.** other his supper
2 Co.5 : 10.all appear **b.** judgment s.
7 : 14. boasting,wh.I made **b.** Titus
8 : 24. shew **b.** churches your love
Ga. 2 : 12. **b.** certain came fr. James
3 :23. **b.** faith came, we under law
Col. 1 :17.he is **b.** all things, by him
1 Ti. 5 : 19. but **b.** two or 3 witnesses
20. Them that sin rebuke **b.** all
21.with-t preferring one **b.** anoth.
6 : 12. good profession **b.** witnesses
13. I give thee charge, **b.** Christ
Jesus, who **b.** Pilate witnessed
2 Ti.4:21.diligence to come **b.** winter
He. 11 : 5. **b.** his translation he had
Ja. 2 : 6.draw you **b.** judgm-t seats?
3 Jn 6.witness of thy charity **b.** ch
Jude 24 present you faultless **b.** the
presence of his glory⌈my Fa. (2)
Re. 3 : 5 I will confess his name **b.**
9. make them worship **b.** thy feet
5 : 8. elders fell down **b.** the Lamb
10 : 11.Th.must prophesy **b.** many
22:8.I fell down to worship **b.** angel

Come BEFORE.

Ex 22 . 9.cause of both **c. b.** judges
Ps. 42 . 2 when shall I **c. b.** God?
79 :11. sighing of prisoner **c. b.** thee
86 : 9. All nations shall **c.** and worship **b.** thee, O L.,Re.15:4.⌈170.
88:2. Let my prayer **c. b.** thee, 119:
95 : 2.Let us **c. b.** his presence with
thanksgiving, 100 : 2. ⌈**b.** thee
La. 1 : 22. Let their wickedness **c.**
2 Ti. 4 : 21.Do diligence to **c. b.** win-
See **Before the LORD.** ⌊ter

BEFORE God. ⌈G.

Lu. 1 : 8. executed priest's office **b.**
1 Th. 3 : 9. joy for your sakes **b.** G.
Re. 8 : 2. I saw angels wh. stood **b.**
4. incense ascended up **b.** G. ⌊G.
11 : 4. candlestick standing **b.** G.
16. elders wh. sat **b.** G. fell upon
20 :12.I saw dead stand **b.** G ⌊faces
See **Before GOD.**

BEFORE him. ⌈b. h.

Ge. 2 : † 18. will make him a help as
42 : 6. brethren bowed down **b. h.**
43 : 34. messes unto them fr. **b. h.**
46 :28. sent Jud. **b. h.** unto Joseph
Ex. 10 : 1.shew these my signs **b. h.**
Nu. 32 : 21.driven out enemies **b. h.**
Jos. 6 : 20. every man straight **b. h.**
1 S. 17 : 41.th.bare shield went **b. h.**
2 S. 13 :9.she poured them out **b. h.**
22 : 13. Through brightness **b. h.**
1 K. 1 : 25. they eat and drink **b. h.**
15 : 3. sins father had done **b. h.**
19 : 19. with 12 yoke of oxen **b. h.**
21 : 13. two men of Belial sat **b. h.**
2 K. 5 : 23. two talents; bare **b. h.**
2 Ch. 2 : 6. only burn sacrifice **b. h.**
Es. 1 : 3. nobles, princes being **b. h.**
17. Vashti to be brought in **b. h.**
Ps. 142 : 2.I poured complaint **b. h.**
Ec. 2 : †26. God giveth to man **b. h.**
Is. 45 :1. open **b. h.** twoleaved gates
Eze.8 :20.I lay stumblingblock **b. h.**
Da. 4 : 8. **b. h.** I told the dream
5 : 19. people trembled **b. h.**⌈**b. h.**
6 : 18. neith. instruments of music
22.as **b. h.** innocency found in me
7 : 10. A fiery stream issued **b. h.**
13. they brought him near **b. h.**
Mat. 14 :22. to go **b. h.** unto oth.side
Lu. 8 : 28. cried out, fell down **b. h.**
47. woman trembling, fall-g **b. h.**
14 : 2. a man **b. h.** wh. had dropsy
Re. 4 : 10. elders fall **b. h.** that sat
19 : 20. that wrought miracles **b. h.**
See **Before HIM.**

BEFORE it. ⌈i.

Ex. 4 : 3. serpent; Moses fled fr. **b.**
14 : 2. **b. i.** shall ye encamp by sea
32 : 5. Aaron built an altar **b. i.**
39:18.shoulderpieces of ephod **b. i.**
Jos. 10 :14. no day like that **b. i.**, or
Ps. 80:9. Thou preparedst room **b. i.**
Is. 47 : 14. not be fire, to sit **b. i.** ⌈i.
Eze. 23 :41. satest upon bed, table **b.**
Da. 7 : 7. diverse from all beasts **b. i.**

BEFORE the Lord.

Le. 4 : 15. bullock be killed **b.** – (2)
18. blood upon altar which is **b.** –
24.wh.they kill offering **b.** –,6:25.
6 : 7. make atonement **b.** –, 10:17.-
14:18,29,31.-15:15.-19:22.-23:28.
14. sons of Aaron sh. offer it **b.** –
8 : 26. of unleavened bread **b.** –
27. he waved them for a wave offering **b.** –, 29.-9 : 21.-10 : 15.-
14 : 12, 24.-23 : 11, 20. Nu. 6:20
9 : 2. calf for sin offering, ram, offer
them **b.** –, 4. Eze. 43 : 24. ⌈**b.** –
10 : 19. this day have they offered
12 : 7. Who shall offer it **b.** – for her
14 : 11. priest sh. present man **b.** –
23.bring them on 8th day **b.** –,15:
31. make atonem-t for her **b.** –⌊14.
16 : 12 censer of coals fr. altar **b.** –
13. shall put incense on fire **b.** –
18 he shall go out unto altar **b.** –
30. be clean from all your sins **b.** –
24 : 3. order it **b.** – continually,4,8.
6. cakes upon table **b.** –, Nu. 6:16.
Nu. 5 : 25 shall wave offering **b.** –
7 : 3. princes brought offering **b.** –
8 : 11. shall offer Levites **b.** –,10,21.
14 : 37. men died by the plague **b.** –
15 : 15. as ye, so stranger be **b.** –
25. sin offering **b.** – for ignorance,
16 : 38. censers, th.offered **b.** – ⌊28.
40.no stranger to offer incense **b.** –
17 : 7. Moses laid up rods **b.** – ⌊ 9.
9. Moses bro-t out the rods fr. **b.** –
20 : 3. when our brethren died **b.** –
9. Moses took the rod from **b.** –
27 : 21. sh. ask counsel for him **b.** –
31 : 50. atonem-t for our souls **b.** –
32 : 20. Moses said, If ye will go
armed **b.** – to war, 21, 27, 29.
22. until land be subdued **b.** – (3)
De. 1 : 45. ye returned and wept **b.** –
4 : 10. day thou stoodest **b.** – in H.
9 : 25. I fell down **b.** – forty days
12 : 7. and there shall ye eat **b.** –
24 : 4. that is an abomination **b.** –
13.if be righteousn. unto thee **b.** –
26 : 10. firstfruits of land set **b.** –(2)
Jos. 4 : 13.40,000 over **b.** – unto bat.
6 : 8. seven priests passed on **b.** –
7 : 23. and they laid them out **b.** –
18 :8. may cast lots for you **b.** –,10.
19 : 51. divided by lot in Shiloh **b.** –
Ju. 5 : 5.mountains melted **b.** – (2)
20 : 23. Israel wept **b.** – until even,
1 S. 1 : 12. as she praying **b.** –⌊26(2).
19. they rose up, worshipped **b.** –
2 : 18. Samuel ministered **b.** –, a
21. child Samuel grew **b.** – ⌊child
7 : 6. drew water, poured it out **b.** –
10 : 25. wrote in book, laid it up **b.** –
11 :15.made Saul king **b.** – in G. (2)
15 : 33. Samuel hewed Agag **b.** –
21 : 6. but shewbread taken fr. **b.** –
23 :18. they two made covenant **b.** –
2 S. 3 : 28.I guiltless **b.** – from blood
of Abner ⌈1 Ch. 11 : 3.
5 : 3.David a league with them **b.** –,
6 :5.David and all Israel played **b.** –
16.M. saw Dav. dancing **b.** –,6:14.
17. David offered burnt off-gs **b.** –
21. said unto Michal,It was **b.** –(2)
7 : 18. David sat **b.** –, said, Who
am I, 1 Ch 17 : 16. ⌈**b.** –
1 K. 2 : 45. throne of Da.established
8 : 59. words wh w.supplication **b.** –
62. king and Israel offered sacrifice **b.** –, 2 Ch. 7 : 4. ⌈little
64. because the altar **b.** – was too
9 : 25.burnt incense upon altar **b.** –
19 : 11.Go, stand upon mount **b.** –;
wind brake the rocks **b.** – ⌈**b.** –
2 K. 16 :14.he brought altar wh.was
19 : 15. Hezekiah prayed **b.** – and
22 :19.Bec. hast humbled thys.**b.** –
23 : 3. Josiah made a covenant **b.**
–, 2 Ch. 34 : 31. ⌈incense **b.** –
1 Ch. 23 : 13. sons for ever to burn
31. And to offer continually **b.** –
2 Ch. 1 : 6. Sol. went up to altar **b.** –
14 : 13. Ethiopians destroyed **b.** –
20 : 18.all Judah fell **b.** – worship-g
31 : 20. Heze-h wrought right **b.** –
33 : 23. Manasseh humbled not **b.** –
Ps. 98 : 6. made a joyful noise **b.** –
Je. 36 : 9. they proclaimed fast **b.** –
Eze. 41 : 22. This is the table **b.** –
Hag. 1 : 12. the people did fear **b.** –
See **Before the LORD,**
APPEAR, PRESENT, PRESENTED.

BEFORE me.

Ge. 32 : 16. servants pass over **b. m.**
20. with present that goeth **b. m.**
33 : 14. as cattle that goeth **b. m.**
Ex. 10 : 3. to humble thyself **b. m.**
25 : 30.upon table of shewbr. **b. m.**
Ju. 11 :9.If Lord deliver them **b. m.**
1 S. 2 : 28. to wear an ephod **b. m.**?
2 S.5:20.broken forth on ene-s **b. m.**
19 : 13. if not captain of host **b. m.**
1 K. 9 : 3. supplication made **b. m.**
Ne. 6 : 19.reported good deeds **b. m.**
Jb. 30 : 11. ha.let loose bridle **b. m.**
33 : 5. set thy words in order **b. m.**
Ps. 57 : 6. they digged a pit **b. m.**
Is. 48 : 19. name not cut off fr. **b. m.**
66 : 23. to worship **b. m.**, saith L.
Je 30:20. cong. be established **b. m.**
31:36.If ordinances depart fr. **b. m.**,
Isr.cease fr. being a nation **b. m.**
34 : 18. covenant they made **b. m.**
Eze. 2 : 10. roll; he spread it **b. m.**
16:50.committed abominat-s **b. m.**
36 : 17.their way **b. m.** as unclean-s
Da. 2 : 9.lying words to speak **b. m.**
4 :6.wise men of Bab-n **b. m.**, 6:15.
8. at last Daniel came in **b. m.**
Jn. 10 :8. All **b. m.** are thieves and

Ga. 1 : 17. which were apostles **b.** m.
See **Before ME.**
BEFORE thee.
Ge. 17 : 18. that Ishmael live **b. t.**
20 : 15. my land is **b. t.**, dwell, 47 :
31 : 35. I cannot rise up **b. t.** [6.
Ex. 23 : 27. I will send my fear **b. t.**
De. 20 : † 19. the tree is to go **b. t.** [t.
32 : 52. thou shalt see the land **b.**
33 : 10. they shall put incense **b. t.**
Ezr. 9 : 15. we are **b. t.** in trespasses
Ne. 4 : 5. let not sin be blotted out
9 : 8. his heart faithful **b. t.** [**b. t.**
32. let not trouble seem little **b. t.**
Ps. 39 : 5. mine age as nothing **b. t.**
69 : 19. mine adversaries are all **b.**
73 : 22. I was as a beast **b. t.** [t.
Is. 9 : 3. they joy **b. t.** as men [**b. t.**
Je. 17 : 16. that out of my lips right
Da. 6 : 22. **b. t.** have I done no hurt
Mat. 6 : 2. do not sound trumpet **b. t.**
11 : 10. my messenger to prepare
way **b. t.**, Mk. 1 : 2. Lu. 7 . 27.
Re. 3 : 8. I have set **b. t.** open door
See **Before THEE.**
See **Come BEFORE.**
See **CHILDREN of Israel, Fell before FACE, FACE of the Lord, Before the PEOPLE, His PEOPLE, STAND before, STOOD before, Before THEM, Before US, WENT before, Before WHOM, Before YOU.**
See AARON, ALL, ALTAR, S, ARK, BRETHREN, COCK, DAY, DEATH, DOOR, S, ENEMIES, ENEMY, EYES, FACE, S, FOUNDATION, GO, HEATHEN, KING, MAMRE, MEN, MOUNT, MULTITUDE, PRIEST, SET, TABERNACLE, TIME, THRONE, VAIL, WEEPING, WIND, WORLD.
BEFOREHAND.
Mk. 13 : 11. take no thought **b.** what
2 Co. 9 : 5. make up **b.** your bounty
1 Ti. 5 : 24. Some men's sins open **b.**
25. good works of some manif. **b.**
1 Pe. 1 : 11. testified **b.** sufferings of
BEFORETIME. [Chr.
De. 2 : 12. Horim dwelt in Seir **b.**
Jos. 20 : 5. bec. he hated him not **b.**
1 S. 9 : 9. (**b.** in Israel a man spake ;
a Prophet was **b.** called a Seer)
10 : 11. all that knew him **b.** saw
2 S. 7 : 10. nei. sh. afflict them as **b.**
2 K. 13 : 5 Israel dwelt in tents as **b.**
Ne. 2 : 1. I had not been **b.** sad in
Is. 41 : 26. Who hath declared **b.**
Ac. 8 : 9. Simon wh. **b.** used sorcery
BEG. [bonds, **b.**
Ps. 109 : 10. let his children be vag-
Pr. 20 : 4. sluggard sh. **b.** in harvest
Lu. 16 : 3 What shall I do? I cannot dig : to **b.** I am ashamed
BEGAN.
Ge. 4 : 26. then **b.** men to call upon
6 : 1. when men **b.** to multiply [L.
9 : 20. Noah **b.** to be husbandman
10 : 8. begat Nimrod : he **b.** to be a
mighty one, 1 Ch. 1 : 10. [Jos. said
41 : 54. seven years of dearth **b.** as
44 : 12. he searched, **b.** at eldest
Nu. 25 : 1. the people **b.** to commit
whoredom with dau-s [clare law
De. 1 : 5. in Moab, **b.** Moses to de-
Ju. 13 : 25. Spirit of Lord **b.** to move
16 : 19. she **b.** to afflict him [him
22. hair of his head **b.** to grow
19 : 25. when day **b.** they let her go
20 : 31. Benj. **b.** to smite Israel, 39.
40. flame **b.** to arise out of city
1 S. 3 : 2. his eyes **b.** to wax dim [L.
14 : †35. altar Saul **b.** to build unto
1 K. 6 : 1. in Zif he **b.** to build the
house of the Lord, 2 Ch. 3 : 1, 2.

2 K. 10 : 32. Lord **b.** to cut Isr. short
15 : 37. Lord **b.** to send ag-t Judah
1 Ch. 27 : 24. Joab **b.** to number, but
2 Ch. 20 : 22. when they **b.** to sing,
Lord set ambushments ag. Am.
29 : 17. **b.** on first day to sanctify
27. when burnt offering **b.** song of
the Lord **b.** [heaps
31 : 7. they **b.** to lay foundation of
10. Since people **b.** to bring off-gs
21. Hez-h in every work that he **b.**
34 : 3. Josiah, while young, **b.** to
seek God : he **b.** to purge Jerus.
Ezr. 3 : 6. **b.** to offer burnt offerings
8. in second year **b.** Zerubbabel
5 : 2. Zerubb-l **b.** to build house of
7 : 9. Ezra **b.** to go up fr. Babylon
Ne. 4 : 7. breaches **b.** to be stopped
13 : 19. gates of Jerus. **b.** to be dark
Eze. 9 : 6. they **b.** at the ancient men
Jon 3 : 4. Jonah **b.** to enter into city
Mat. 4 : 17. time Jesus **b.** to preach
11 : 20. **b.** he to upbraid the cities
12 : 1. his disciples **b.** to pluck ears
of corn, Mk. 2 : 23. [Mk. 10 : 32.
16 : 21. **b.** Jes. to shew how he must,
22. Then Peter took him, **b.** to
rebuke him, Mk. 8 : 32. [14 : 33.
26 : 37. he **b.** to be sorrowful, Mk.
74. Then **b.** he to curse and to
swear, Mk. 14 : 71. [first day
28 : 1. as it **b.** to dawn toward the
Mk. 1 : 45. he **b.** to publish it, 5 : 20.
5 : 17. **b.** to pray him to depart
6 : 7. **b.** to send them by 2 and two
55. **b.** to carry those sick, where
8 : 11. Pharisees **b.** to question him
10 : 32. he **b.** to tell what things
41. **b.** to be displeased with James
47. **b.** to cry out, Jesus have mercy
11 : 15. Jesus **b.** to cast out them
that sold, Lu. 19 : 45. [Lu. 20 : 9
12 : 1. he **b.** to speak by parables,
14 : 65 some **b.** to spit on him and
†72. he **b.** to weep when he thought
15 : 8. multitude **b.** to desire him to
18. they **b.** to salute him, Hail [do
Lu. 3 : 23. Jesus **b.** to be about 30 y.
5 : 7. filled ships, they **b.** to sink
21. Pharisees **b.** to reason, Who
7 : 15. he that was dead **b.** to speak
24. he **b.** to speak concern-g John
38. **b.** to wash his feet with tears
9 : 12. when the day **b.** to wear aw.
11 : 53. Pharisees **b.** to provoke him
14 : 18. they all **b.** to make excuse
30. This man **b.** to build, not able
15 : 14. famine; he **b.** to be in want
24. son alive; they **b.** to be merry
19 : 37. disciples **b.** to praise God
22 . 23. they **b.** to inquire wh it was
23 : 2. they **b.** to accuse him, say-g
Jn. 4 . 52. hour when he **b.** to amend
13 . 5 he **b.** to wash disciples' feet
Ac. 1 : 1. of all Jesus **b.** to do and
2 : 4. **b.** to speak wi. other tongues
8 : 35. Philip **b.** at same Scripture
10 : 37. word which **b.** from Galilee
11 : 15. as I **b.** to speak, Holy Ghost
12 : † 1. Herod **b.** to vex the church
18 : 26. Apollos **b.** to speak boldly
24 : 2. Tertullus **b.** to accuse him
27 : 35. had broken it, he **b.** to eat
He. 2 . 3 salvation which **b.** to be
See ASA, COCK, WORLD.
See **Began to REIGN.**
BEGAN to say.
Mat. 11 : 7. Jesus **b.** - unto multitude cone-g John [Mk. 14 : 19.
26 : 22 **b.** every one **t. s.**, Is it I?
Mk. 10 : 28. Peter **b.** -, Lo, we left all
13 : 5. Jesus **b.** -, Take heed lest
14 : 69. maid **b.** -, This is one of th.
Lu. 4 : 21. **b.** -, This day this Scrip.
7 : 49. they **b.** -, Who is this that
forgiveth sins also? [eration
11 : 29. he **b.** -, This is an evil gen-

Lu. 12 : 1. **b.** - to his disciples, Beware
See **Began to TEACH.**
BEGAT.
Ge. 4 : 18. and Irad **b.** Mehujael (3)
5 : 3. Adam lived 130 years, **b.** Seth
4. **b.** sons and daughters, 7, 10, 13,
16, 19, 22, 26, 30.-11 : 11, 13, 15,
17, 19, 21, 23, 25. [Enos, 7.
6. Seth lived 105 years, and **b.**
7. lived after he **b.** . . . years, 10,
13, 16, 19, 22, 26, 30.-11 : 11, 13,
15, 17, 19, 21, 23, 25. [nan
9. Enos lived 90 years, and **b.** Cai-
12. Cainan lived 70 y-s, **b.** Mahal-l
15. M. lived 65 years, and **b.** Jared
18. Jared lived 162 years, **b.** Enoch
21. E. lived 65 y-rs, **b.** Methuselah
25. M-h lived 187 years, **b.** Lamech
28. Lamech lived 182 years, **b.** a son
32. Noah **b.** Shem, Ham, J., 6 : 10.
10 : 8. And Cush **b.** Nimrod : he a
mighty one in earth, 1 Ch. 1 : 10.
13. Mizraim **b.** Ludim, 1 Ch. 1 : 11.
15. Canaan **b.** Sidon, Heth, Jebusite, 1 Ch. 1 : 13. [1 Ch. 1 : 18.
24. Arphaxad **b.** Salah ; Salah **b.**,
26. Joktan **b.** Almodad, 1 Ch. 1 : 20.
11 : 10. Shem 100 years old, and **b.**
Arphaxad two years after flood
12. Arphaxad lived 35 yrs. **b.** Salah
14. Salah lived 30 years, **b.** Eber
16. Eber lived 430 years, **b.** Peleg
18. Peleg lived 30 years, **b.** Reu
20. Reu lived 32 years and **b.** Serug
22. Serug lived 30 years, **b.** Nahor
24. Nahor lived 29 years, **b.** Terah
26. Terah lived 70 yrs., **b.** Abram,
27. Haran **b.** Lot [Haran, 27.
22 : 23. And Bethuel **b.** Rebekah
25 : 3. Jokshan **b.** Sheba and Dedan
19. Abraham **b.** Isaac, 1 Ch. 1 :
34. Mat. 1 : 2. Ac. 7 : 8. [land
Le. 25 : 45. buy of families they **b.** in
Nu. 26 : 29. and Machir **b.** Gilead
58. And Kohath **b.** Amram [thou
De. 32 : 18. Of the Rock that **b.** thee
Ju. 11 : 1. Gilead **b.** Jephthah [1 : 3.
Ru. 4 : 18. Pharez **b.** Hezron, Mat.
19. Hezron **b.** Ram, Ram **b.** Amminadab, 1 Ch. 2 : 10. Mat. 1 : 3, 4.
20. And Amminadab **b.** Nahshon,
and Nahshon **b.** Salmon, 1 Ch.
2 : 10, 11. Mat. 1 : 4.
21. Salmon **b.** Boaz, Boaz **b.** Obed,
1 Ch. 2 : 11, 12. Mat. 1 : 5.
22. Obed **b.** Jesse, and Jesse **b.**
David, Mat. 1 : 6. [Eliab
1 Ch. 2 13. Jesse **b.** his firstborn
18. Caleb **b.** children of Azubah
20. Hur **b.** Uri, Uri **b.** Bezaleel
22. Segub **b.** Jair. who had 23 cities
36. Attai **b.** Nathan, N. **b.** Zabad
37. Zabad **b.** Ephlal, E. **b.** Obed
38 Obed **b.** Jehu, J. **b.** Azariah
39. Azariah **b.** Helez, H. **b.** Eleasah
40. Eleasah **b.** Sisamai, S. Shal-m
41. Shallum **b.** Jekamiah, J. **b.**
44. Shema **b.** Raham, Rekem **b.**
46. Haran **b.** Gazez [Shammai
4 : 2. Reaiah **b.** Jahath, J. **b.** Ahumai
8. Coz **b.** Anub, Zobebah [mai
11. Chelub **b.** Mehir, fa. of Eshton
12 Eshton **b.** Beth-rapha, Paseah
14. Meonothai **b.** Ophrah : Seraiah **b.** Joab father of [Abishua
6 : 4. Eleazar **b.** Phinehas, P. **b.**
5. A. **b.** Bukki, and B. **b.** Uzzi
6. U. **b.** Zerahiah, Z. **b.** Meraioth
7. M. **b.** Amariah, A. **b.** Ahitub
8. A. **b.** Zadok, Z. **b.** Ahimaaz
9. A. **b.** Azariah, A. **b.** Johanan
10. J. **b.** Azariah (he it is that)
11. A. **b.** Amariah, A. **b.** Ahitub
12. A. **b.** Zadok, Z. **b.** Shallum
13. S. **b.** Hilkiah, H. **b.** Azariah
14 A. **b.** Seraiah, S. **b.** Jehozadak
7 : 32. Heber **b.** Japhlet, Shomer

1 Ch. 8 : 1. Benjamin b. Bela, Ashbel
7. Ehud : he b. Uzza and Ahihud
8. Shaharaim b. children in Moab
9. he b. of Hodesh Jobab, Zibia
11. of Hushim he b. Ahitub, Elpa-
32 Mikloth b. Shimeah, 9 : 38. [al
33. Ner b. Kish, Kish b. Saul,
Saul b. Jonathan, and, 9 : 39.
34. son of Jonathan, Merib-baal,
Merib-baal b. Micah, 9 : 40.
36. Ahaz b. Jehoadah ; J. b. Zimri ; Zimri b. Moza, 9 : 42.
37. And Moza b. Binea, 9 : 43.
14 : 3. David b. more sons and dau-s
2 Ch. 11 : 21. Reho. b. 28 sons, 60 d-s
13 : 21. Abijah b. 22 sons, 16 dau-s
24 : 3. Joash b. sons and daughters
Ne. 12 : 10. Jeshua b. Joiakim, J. b.
Eliashib, and E. b. Joiada [Jad-a
11. Jolada b. Jonathan, J. b.
Pr. 23 : 22. Hearken unto fath. th. b.
Je. 16 : 3. fathers that b. them [thee
Da. 11 : 6. given up, and he th. b. her
Zch. 13 : 3. father and mother that
b. him shall thrust him thro (2)
Mat. 1 : 2. Isaac b. Jacob ; Jacob b.
Judas and brethren, Ac. 7 : 8.
3. Judas b. Pharez and Zara of T.
6. David b. Sol-n of wife of Urias
7. And . . b. . . (3), 8 (3), 9(3), 10
(3), 11, 12(2), 13 (3), 14(3), 15 (3).
16. Jacob b. Joseph husband of
Mary, of whom Jesus [sons
Ac. 7 : 29. Moses in Madian, b. two
Ja. 1 : 18. Of his own will b. he us
1 Jn. 5 : 1. one that loveth him th. b.

BEGET. [he b.
Ge. 17 : 20. Ishmael, 12 princes sh.
De 4 : 25. When thou shalt b. chil.
28 : 41. shalt b. sons, but not enjoy
2 K. 20 : 18. sons thou shalt b. shall
they make eunnchs, Is. 39 : 7.
Ec. 6 : 3. If a man b. 100 child-n [b.
Is. 66 : † 9. Sh. I bring to birth, not
Je. 29 : 6. Take wives, and b. sons
Eze. 18 : 10. if he b. son th. is robber
14. if b. son that seeth fath-'s sins
47 : 22. strangers wh. b. chil. among

BEGETTEST. [yon
Ge. 48 : 6. issue thou b. sh. be thine
Is. 45 : 10. unto fath., What b. thou?

BEGETTETH. [sorrow
Pr. 17 : 21. b. a fool doeth it to his
23 : 24. b. wise child shall have joy
Ec. 5 : 14. he b. a son and is noth-g

BEGGAR, LY. [hill
1 S. 2 : 8. he lifteth b. from dung-
Lu. 16 : 20. was a b. named Lazarus
22. b. died, was carried by angels
Ga. 4 : 9. turn again to b-y elements

BEGGED.
Mat. 27 : 58. Joseph to Pilate, b.
body of Jesus, Lu. 23 : 52. [b.?
Jn. 9 : 8. Is not this he that sat and

BEGGING. [bread
Ps. 37 : 25. I ha. not seen his seed b.
Mk 10 : 46. Bartimeus sat b., Lu.

BEGIN. [18 : 35.
Ge. 11 : 6. L. said, this they b. to do
De. 2 : 24. b. to possess it, contend
25. will I b. to put dread of thee
16 : 9. b. to number 7 weeks fr. time
Jos. 3 : 7. will I b. to magnify thee
Ju. 10 : 18. What man b. to fight A.
13 : 5. he shall b. to deliver Israel
1 S. 3 : 12. when I b. will make end
22 : 15. Did I b. to inquire of God
2 K. 8 : 25. did Ahaziah b. to reign
Ne. 11 : 17. Mattaniah to b. thanksg.
Je. 25 : 29. I b. to bring evil on city
Eze. 9 : 6. slay, b. at my sanctuary
Ho. 8 : † 10. sh. b. a little for burden
Mat. 24 : 49. if servant b. to smite
his fellow, Lu. 12 : 45. [selves
Lu. 3 : 8. b. not to say within your-
13 : 25. ye b. to stand without and
26. sh. ye b. to say, We have eaten
Lu. 14 : 9 b. wi. shame to take lowest
29. that behold it b. to mock him
21 : 28. when these things b. to co.
23 : 30. b. to say to mts., Fall on us
2 Co. 3 : 1. we b. to commend ours.?
1 Pe. 4 : 17. judgment b. at house
of God, if it b. at us [to sound
Re. 10 : 7. angel, when he shall b.

BEGINNER.
Ho. 12 : † 2. Jes., the b. of our faith

BEGINNEST. [to corn
De. 16 : 9. time thou b. to put sickle

BEGINNING. [Part.]
Mat. 14 : 30. b. to sink, he cried, L.
20 : 8. hire, b. from last unto first
Lu. 23 : 5. b. fr. Galilee to this place
24 : 27. b. at Moses and prophets
47. all nations, b. at Jerusalem
Jn. 8 : 9. went out, b. at the eldest
Ac. 1 : 22. b. from baptism of John

BEGINNING. [Noun.]
Ge. 10 : 10. b. of kingdom was Babel
49 : 3. Reuben, b. of my strength
Ex. 12 : 2. This he the b. of months
De. 21 : 17. he is b. of his strength
1 S. 3 : † 12. perform ag. Eli b. and
Jb. 8 : 7. Tho. thy b. was small, yet
42 : 12. end of Job more than his b.
Ps. 111 : 10. The fear of the Lord is
the b. of wisdom, Pr. 9 : 10.
Pr. 1 : 7. fear of L. b. of knowledge
17 : 14. b. of strife is as when one
Ec. 7 : 8. Better is the end than b.
10 : 13. b. of words . . is foolishness
Is. 18 : 2. peo. terrible fr. their b., 7.
64 : 4. since the b. men not heard
Ho. 1 : 2. b. of word of Lord by Hosea
Mi. 1 : 13. she is the b. of sin to Zion
Mat. 24 : 8. all these are b. of sorrows
21. be tribulation as not since b.
Mk. 1 : 1. The b. of gospel of Christ
Jn. 2 : 11. This b. of miracles did Jes.
Col. 1 : 18. who is the b. fr. firstborn
He. 3 : 14. if we hold b. of confidence
6 : † 1. leaving word of b. of Christ
7 : 3. having neither b. of days, nor
2 Pe. 2 : 20. end is worse than the b.
Re. 1 : 8. I am the b., 21 : 6.-22 : 13.
3 : 14. saith the Amen, b. of creation

At the BEGINNING.
Ge. 13 : 3. where tent had been - b.
41 : 21. were ill favoured as - b.
Ru 3 10. more kindness than - b.
2 K. 17 : 25. so - b. of their dwelling
1 Ch. 17 : 9. nei. sh. waste them as - b.
Pr. 20 : 21. An inheritance may be
gotten hastily - b. [- b.
Is. 1 : 26. I will restore counsellors
Da. 9 : 21. I had seen in vision - b.
23. - b. of thy supplications [and
Mat. 19 : 4. he - b. made them mal-
Jn. 2 : 10. - b. doth set good wine
16 : 4. these, I said not unto you - b.
Ac. 11 : 15. Holy Ghost, as on us - b.

From the BEGINNING.
De. 11 : 12. eyes of L. upon it - b. of
year unto end [enemy
32 : 42. - b. of revenges upon the
2 S. 21 : 10. - b. of harvest until wat.
Ps. 119 : 160. Thy word is true - b.
Pr. 8 : 23. I was set up - b., or ever
Ec. 3 : 11. no man find out work that
God maketh - b. to the end
Is. 40 : 21. not been told you - b.?
41 : 4. Who calling generations - b.?
26. Who hath declared - b.?
46 : 10. Declaring the end - b. [- b.
48 : 3. I ha. declared former things
5. I have - b. declared it to thee
7. They are created now, not - b.
16. I not spoken in secret - b. [- b.
Je. 17 : 12. A glorious high throne
Mat. 19 : 8. - b. it was not so [fem.
Mk. 10 : 6. - b. of creation, male and
13 : 19. affliction such as was not
- b. of creation [nesses
Lu. 1 : 2. which - b. were eyewit-
Jn. 6 : 64. Jesus knew - b. who they
8 : 25. same I said unto you - b.
44. He a murderer - b., abode not
15 : 27. ye have been with me - b.
Ac. 11 : 4. Peter rehearsed matter - b.
15 : 18. Known unto God his works
26 : 5. Which knew me - b. [- b.
Ep. 3 : 9. which hath - b. been hid
2 Th. 2 : 13. God hath - b. chosen
2 Pe. 3 : 4. all continue as - b. [you
1 Jn. 1 : 1. which was - b., we heard
2 : 7. The old commandment is the
word ye heard - b. (2) [is - b.
13. fath-s, ye have known him th.
24. abide in you ye heard - b. (2)
3 : 8. of devil ; for devil sinneth - b.
11. ye heard - b., love one anoth.
2 Jn. 5. we heard - b. that we love
6. as ye heard - b. ye should walk

In the BEGINNING.
Ge. 1 : 1. - b. God created heaven
Ju. 7 : 19. Gideon came - b. of watch
Ru. 1 : 22. to Beth-le. - b. of harvest
2 S. 20 : † 18. spake - b., Surely they
will ask of Abel [harvest
21 : 9. were put to death - b. of
Pr. 8 : 22. The Lord possessed me - b.
La. 2 : 19. - b. of watches pour out
Eze. 40 : 1. - b. of year Lord bro-t me
Am. 7 : 1. grasshoppers - b. of latter
Jn. 1 : 1. - b. was the Word, and W.
2. The same was - b. with God
Ph. 4 : 15. know that - b. of the gos.
He. 1 : 10. Thou, Lord, - b. laid
See Reign. [founda-n

BEGINNINGS. [blow
Nu. 10 : 10. in the b. of y-r months
28 : 11. in b. of your months offer
Eze. 36 : 11. will do better unto you
than at your b. [rows
Mk. 13 : 8. these are the b. of sor-

BEGOTTEN.
Le. 18 : 11. b. of thy father, she is
Nu. 11 : 12. people, have b. them?
De. 23 : 8. chil. b. of them sh. enter
Ju. 8 : 30. Gideon had 70 sons b.
Jb. 38 : 28. or who b. drops of dew?
Ps. 2 : 7. my Son; this day have I b.
thee, Ac. 13 : 33. He. 1 : 5.-5 : 5.
Is. 49 : 21. Who hath b. me these
Je. 2 : † 27. stone, Thou hast b. me
Ho 5 : 7. they have b. strange chil.
Mat. 1 : † 20. b. in her is of Holy Gh.
1 Co. 4 : 15. I have b. you thro. gospel
Phm. 10. Onesimus, whom I have b.
1 Pe. 1 : 3. hath b. us unto lively
1 Jn. 5 : 1. loveth him th. is b. [hope
18. that is b. of God keepeth him-
See Firstbegotten. [self

Only BEGOTTEN.
Jn 1 : 14. glory as of o. b. of Father
18. o. b. Son, he hath declared
3 : 16. so loved, gave his o. b. Son
18. hath not believed in o. b. Son
He. 11 : 17. Abr. offered up o. b. son
1 Jn. 4 : 9. God sent his o. b. Son

BEGUILE. [you
Col. 2 : 4. lest any man should b.
18. Let no man b. you of reward

BEGUILED. [b. me
Ge. 3 : 13. woman said, The serpent
29 : 25. wherefore hast thou b. me!
Nu. 25 : 18. b. you in matter of Peor
Jos. 9 : 22. Wherefore have ye b. us?
2 Co. 11 : 3. fear lest as serpent b. Eve

BEGUILING.
2 Pe. 2 : 14. b. unstable souls : curs-

BEGUN. [ed chil.
Nu. 16 : 46. is wrath; the plague is b.
De. 2 : 31. I have b. to give Sihon
3 : 24. hast b. to shew thy greatn-s
Es. 6 : 13. bef. whom hast b. to fall
9 : 23. Jews to do as they had b.
Mat. 18 : 24. wh. he had b. to reckon
2 Co. 8 : 6. as he had b., so finish in
10. expedient for you who have b.
Ga. 3 : 3. foolish, having b. in Spirit

Ph. 1 : 6. hath **b.** a good work in you
1 Ti. 5 : 11. have **b.** to wax wanton

BEHALF.

Ex. 27 : 21. a statute on **b.** of Israel
2 S. 3 : 12. Abner to David on his **b.**
2 Ch. 16 : 9. strong in **b.** of them
Jb. 36 : 2. I yet to speak on God's **b.**
Je. 51 : † 59. went on **b.** of Zedekiah
Da. 11 : 18. prince for own **b.** sh. cause
Ro. 16 : 19. I am glad on your **b.** [b.
1 Co. 1 : 4. I thank my God on your
2 Co. 1 : 11. thanks given on our **b.**
5 : 12. occasion to glory on our **b.**
8 : 24. our boasting on your **b.** [b.
9 : 3. boasting of you vain in this
Ph. 1 . 29. unto you given in **b.** of C.
1 Pe. 4 : 16. glorify God on this **b.**

BEHAVE.

De. 32 : 27. adversaries **b.** strangely
1 Ch. 19 : 13. let us b. ours. valiantly
Jb. 41 : † 33. who b. without fear [in
Ps. 101 : 2. I will **b.** myself wisely
Is. 3 : 5. child shall **b.** proudly ag-t
42 : † 13. Lord will b. mightily ag-t
1 Co. 13 : 5. charity not b. unseemly
1 Ti. 3 : 15. oughtest to **b.** in house

BEHAVED. [of G.

1 S. 18 : 14. David b. wisely in all, 5.
15. Saul saw he b. wisely, afraid
30. David b. more wisely than all
Ps. 35 : 14. I **b.** as tho. he my friend
131 : 2. I have **b.** as a child weaned
Ho. 12 : † 3. Jacob **b.** hims. princely
Mi. 3 : 4. have **b.** ill in their doings
1 Th. 2 : 10. how holily we **b.** among
2 Th. 3 : 7. we **b.** not disorderly [you

BEHAVETH. [gin

1 Co. 7 : 36. if **b.** uncomely tow. vir-

BEHAVIOUR. [Ps. 34.*

1 S. 21 : 13. David changed his **b.**,
1 Ti. 3 : 2. bishop must be of good **b.**
Tit. 2 : 3. aged women be in **b.** as be-

BEHEAD. [cometh

Ho. 10 : † 2. he shall **b.** their altar

BEHEADED. [b.

De. 21 : 6. sh. wash hands over heifer
2 S. 4 : 7. smote Ish-bosheth, **b.** him
Mat. 14 : 10. and Herod sent, and **b.**
John in prison, Mk. 6 : 27.
Mk. 6 : 16. Herod said, It is John
whom I **b.**, Lu. 9 : 9. [b. for
Re. 20 : 4. I saw the souls of them

BEHELD. [fair

Ge. 12 : 14. Egyptians **b.** woman was
13 : 10. Lot **b.** all plain of Jordan
19 : 28. Abraham **b.**, and lo, smoke
31 : 2. Jacob **b.** countenance of La-
48 : 8. Israel **b.** Joseph's sons [ban
Nu. 21 : 9. when **b.** serpent of brass
23 : 21. hath not **b.** iniquity in Jac.
Ju. 16 : 27. **b.** while Sams. made sport
1 S. 26 : 5. David **b.** place Saul lay
1 Ch. 21 : 15. angel destroying, L. **b.**
Jb. 31 : 26. If I **b.** sun when it shined
Ps. 119 : 158. I **b.** transgressors [me
142 : 4. I **b.**, no man would know
Pr. 7 : 7. I **b.** among the simple ones
Ec. 8 : 17. then I **b.** all work of God
Is. 41 : 28. For I **b.**, and there was
no man, Je. 4 : 25. [with-t form
Je. 4 : 23. I **b.** the earth, lo, it was
24. I **b.** mountains, they trembled
26. I **b.**, fruitful place was wilder-
31 : 26. Upon this I awaked, **b.** [ness
Eze. 1 : 15. as I **b.** living creatures
8 : 2. I **b.**, lo, a likeness as of fire
37 : 8. I **b.**, lo, sinews, flesh came
Da. 7 : 4. I **b.** till wings were plucked
6. I **b.**, lo, another, like a leopard
9. I **b.** till thrones were cast down
11. I **b.**, bec. of the words the horn
spake : I **b.** till beast was slain
21. I **b.**, and same horn made war
Ha. 3 : 6. he **b.**, and drove nations
Mat. 19 : 26. Jesus **b.**, said, With men
Mk. 9 : 15. all people **b.** him, amazed
12 : 41. **b.**, how people cast money
15 : 47. Mary M. and Mary **b.** wh.
he was laid, Lu. 23 : 55. [fall
Lu. 10 : 18. I **b.** Satan as lightning
19 : 41. he **b.** city, and wept over it
20 : 17. he **b.** them, said, The stone
22 : 56. a maid **b.** him by the fire
24 : 12. he **b.** the linen clothes laid
Jn. 1 : 14. we **b.** his glory as of the
42. Jes. **b.** him, said, Thou art S.
Ac. 1 : 9. while they **b.**, he was taken
17 . 23. For as I **b.** your devotions
Re. 5 : 6. I **b.**, and lo, a Lamb as slain
11. I **b.**, heard the voice of angels
6 : 5. I **b.**, lo, a black horse [seal
12. I **b.**, when he had opened 6th
7 : 9. I **b.**, and lo, great multitude
8 : 13. I **b.**, heard an angel flying
11 : 12. ascended, their enemies **b.**
13 : 11. I **b.** another beast [them

BEHEMOTH. [made

Jb. 40 : 15. Behold now **b.** which I

BEHIND. [b.

Ex. 10 : 26. shall not a hoof be left
11 : 5. firstborn of maidservant **b.**
Le. 25 : 51. If be many yrs **b.** [mine
Nu. 3 : 23. Gershonites pitch **b.** tab.
Jos. 8 : 2. lay ambush for city **b.** it
4. ye shall lie in wait **b.** city, 14.
Ju. 18 : 12. behold, it is **b.** Kirjath-j.
1 S. 21 : 9. wrapped in cloth **b.** ephod
30 : 9. Besor, where those left **b.**
10. men abode **b.**, faint [stayed
2 S. 3 : 16. husband weeping **b.** her
1 K. 10 : 19. top of throne round **b.**
14 : 9. thou hast cast me **b.** thy back,
Eze. 23 : 35. [the guard
2 K. 11 : 6. a third part at gate **b.**
Ne. 4 : 13. I set **b.** wall the people
16. rulers were **b.** house of Judah
9 : 26. cast thy law **b.** their backs
Can. 2 : 9. he standeth **b.** our wall
Is. 38 : 17. hast cast all my sins **b.**
57 : 8. **b.** doors hast set remembr-e
66 : 17. **b.** tree eating swine's flesh
Eze. 41 : 15. building the place **b.** it
Am. 7 : † 15. L. took me from **b.** flock
Mk. 5 : 27. she came in the press **b.**
Lu. 2 : 43. child Jes. tarried **b.** in J.
1 Co. 1 : 7. So ye come **b.** in no gift
2 Co. 11 : 5. I was not a whit **b.** the
chiefest apostles, 12 : 11. [b.
Ph. 3 : 13. forgetting things wh. are
Col. 1 : 24. fill up that **b.** of afflict-n
See **BEFORE** with **behind.**

BEHIND him.

Ge. 22 : 13. **b. h.** a ram caught in
1 S. 24 : 8. when Saul looked **b. h.**
2 S. 1 : 7. when he looked **b. h.**, saw
2 : 20. Abner looked **b. h.**, said [me
13 : 34. came much people **b. h.**
Lu. 7 : 38. woman stood **b. h.** weep-g
See **Behind HIM, Behind ME, Behind THEE, Behind THEM, Behind US.**

BEHOLD. [herb

Ge. 1 : 29. **b.**, I have given you every
31. made, and, **b.** it was very good
3 : 22. **b.**, man is become as one of
4 : 14. **b.**, thou hast driven me out
6 : 13. **b.**, I will destroy them with
17. **b.**, I do bring a flood of waters
8 : 13. **b.**, face of ground was dry
9 : 9. I, **b.**, I establish my covenant
11 : 6. L. said, **b.**, the people is one
15 : 3. **b.**, to me hast given no seed
4. **b.**, word of Lord came unto him
17. **b.** smoking furnace, burning
16 : 6. **b.**, thy maid is in thy hand
11. **b.**, thou art with child, shalt
17 : 4. **b.**, my covenant is with thee
20. Ishmael, **b.**, I have blessed h.
18 : 9. Where is Sarah ? **b.**, in tent
19 : 34. **b.**, I lay yesternight wi. fath.
20 : 3. **b.**, thou art but a dead man
15. **b.**, my land is bef. thee ; dwell
16. **b.**, I have given thy brother
1,000 pieces : **b.**, he is to thee a
Ge. 22 : 1. he said, **b.**, here I am, 27 :
1.—1 S. 12 : 3. Ac. 9 : 10. [is lamb
7. **b.**, the fire and wood : but where
13. **b.**, behind him a ram caught
20. **b.**, Milcah, she hath borne chil.
24 : 13. **b.**, I stand here by the well
15. done speaking, **b.**, Rebekah
30. **b.**, he stood by camels at well
51. **b.**, Rebekah is bef. thee ; take
63. **b.**, camels were coming [38 : 27.
25 : 24. **b.**, were twins in her womb,
32. **b.**, I am at the point to die [ah
26 : 8. **b.**, Isaac sporting wi. Rebek-
9. **b.**, of a surety she is thy wife
27 : 6. **b.**, I heard thy father speak
11. **b.**, Esau my brother is hairy
37. **b.**, I have made him thy lord
39. **b.**, thy dwelling sh. be fatness
42. **b.**, Esau purposing to kill thee
28 : 12. **b.** a ladder set up on earth ;
b. angels of G. ascending, desc.
13. **b.**, the Lord stood above it
15. **b.**, I am with thee, will keep
29 : 2. Jacob looked, and **b.**, a well
30 : 3. **b.**, my maid Bilhah, go in un-
34. **b.**, I would it might be acc. [to
31 : 10. **b.**, rams which leaped upon
51. **b.** this heap, **b.** pillar [cattle
32 : 18. **b.**, he is behind us, 20. [400
33 : 1. **b.**, Esau came, with him
37 : 7. **b.**, sheaves made obeisance (2)
9. **b.**, I have dreamed more (2)
15. **b.**, he was wandering in field
19. said, **b.**, this dreamer cometh
25. **b.**, a company of Ishmaelites
29. **b.**, Joseph was not in the pit
38 : 13. **b.**, thy father in law goeth
23. **b.**, I sent this kid, thou hast
24. **b.**, she with child by whored.
29. back his hand, **b.**, bro. came
39 : 8. **b.**, my master wotteth not
40 : 6. Joseph came in, **b.**, they sad
9. in dream, **b.** a vine was bef. me
16. **b.**, I had baskets on my head
41 : 1. **b.**, he stood by the river, 17.
2. And **b.**, 7 well favoured kine
3. **b.**, seven other kine came up, 19.
5. **b.**, seven ears of corn came up
6. **b.**, seven thin ears, blasted, 23.
29. **b.**, come seven years of plenty
42 : 2. **b.**, I have heard is corn in Eg.
13. **b.**, youngest is with our fath.
22. thf., **b.**, his blood is required
35. **b.**, every man's money, 43 : 21.
44 : 8. **b.**, the money wh. we found
16. **b.**, we are my lord's servants,
45 : 12. **b.**, your eyes see [50 : 18.
47 : 1. **b.**, they are in land of Gosh.
23. **b.**, I have bought you this day
48 : 1. Joseph, **b.**, thy father is sick
2. told Jacob, **b.**, Joseph cometh
4. **b.**, I will make thee fruitful
21. **b.**, I die ; God shall be wi. you
Ex. 1 : 9. **b.**, Israel are more than we
2 . 6. she saw child ; **b.**, babe wept
13. **b.**, two men of Hebrews strove
3 : 2. **b.**, the bush burned with fire
9. **b.**, the cry of Israel is come up
13. **b.**, when I come unto chil. of
4 : 1. **b.**, they will not believe me
6. **b.**, his hand leprous as snow
14. **b.**, Aaron cometh to meet thee
23. **b.**, I will slay thy son, firstb.
5 : 5. **b.**, people of land are many
16. **b.**, thy servants are beaten
6 : 12. **b.**, Isr. have not hearkened
30. **b.**, I am of uncircumcised lips
7 : 16. **b.**, thou wouldest not hear
17. **b.**, I will smite with rod in m.
8 : 2. **b.**, I will smite with frogs
21. **b.**, I will send swarms of flies
29. **b.**, I go fr. thee, I will entreat
9 : 3. **b.**, hand of L. is upon cattle
18. **b.**, to morrow a grievous hail
10 : 4. **b.**, to morrow will I bring loc.
14 : 10. **b.**, Egyptians marched aft.
16 : 4. **b.**, I will rain bread from h.

Ex. 16 : 10. **b.**, glory of L. appeared
17 : 6. **b.**, I will stand before thee
23 : 20. **b.**, I send an Angel bef. thee
24 : 8. **b.** the blood of the covenant
32 : 34. **b.**, mine Angel sh. go before
33 : 21. **b.**, there is a place by me
34 : 10. **b.**, I make a covenant ⌈ite
11. **b.**, I drive out bef. thee Amor-
30. **b.**, the skin of his face shone
39 : 43. **b.**, they had done it as Lord
Le. 10 : 18. **b.**, blood of it not bro-t
19. **b.**, this day have they offered
13 : 5. **b.**, if the plague be at a stay
8. **b.**, scab spreadeth in the skin
25. and **b.**, if, 26, 30, 31, 32, 34,
36, 39, 43, 53, 55, 56.
14 : 3. **b.**, if leprosy be healed ⌈44.
37. **b.**, if plague in walls of ho., 39,
48. **b.**, plague not spread in house
25 : 20. **b.**, we shall not sow nor ⌈**b.**
Nu. 12 : 8. similitude of Lord sh. he
10. **b.**, Miriam became leprous⌈p.
16 : 47. **b.**, plague was begun among
17 : 8. **b.**, rod of Aaron was budded
12. **b.**, we die, we perish, we all
20 : 16. **b.**, we are in Kadesh ⌈of Eg.
22 : 11. **b.**, there is a peo. come out
23 : 9. from the hills I **b.** him : lo
24 : 17. I shall **b.** him, but not nigh
25 : 6. **b.**, 12.-31 : 16. Ju. 20 : 7.
32 : 23. **b.**, ye have sinned, De. 9 : 16.
De. 1 : 8. **b.**, I have set land bef. you, 21
2 : 24. **b.**, into thine hand Sihon, 31.
3 : 11. **b.**, his was a bedstead of iron
27. Get thee into top of Pisgah, **b.**
4 : 5. **b.**, I have taught you statutes
11 : 26. **b.**, I set bef. you blessings
: 49. Get thee up and **b.** Canaan
Jos. 2 : 2. **b.**, came men in to search
7 : 21. **b.**, they are hid in my tent, 22.
8 : 4. **b.**, ye shall lie in wait ag. city
22 : 11. **b.**, Reub. . . have built altar
28. **b.** pattern of the altar of Lord
23 : 4. **b.**, I have divided the nations
14. **b.**, I am going way of all earth
Ju. 1 : 2. **b.**, I have delivered land
3. 24. **b.**, the doors of parlour were
25. **b.**, their lord fallen dead⌊locked
4 : 22. **b.**, as Barak pursued Sisera
6 : 15. **b.**, my family is poor in Ma.
28. **b.**, altar of Baal was cast do.
37. **b.**, I will put a fleece of wool
8 : 15. **b.** Zebah and Zalmunna
9 : 31. **b.**, Gaal be come to Shechem
11 : 34. **b.**, dau. came to meet him
13 10. **b.**, the man hath appeared
14 . 5. **b.**, a young lion roared ag.
16. **b.**, I have not told my fa.⌊him
16 : 10. **b.**, thou hast mocked me
19 : 9. **b.**, day draweth tow. evening
16. **b.**, there came an old man⌊(2)
24. **b.**, here is my dau-r, a maiden
20 : 40. **b.**, flame of city ascended
Ru. 2 : 4. **b.**, Boaz came from Beth-le.
1 S. 2 : 31. **b.**, 14 : 11.-21 : 9. - 24 :
20 -30 : 3. 2 S. 18 : † 31. 2 Ch.
16 : 11.-23 : 13. Je. 7 : 32.-19 :
6.-24 : 1. Eze. 21 : 7. Jo. 3 : 1, 7.
Am. 6 : 14.-7 : 4, 7. Mi. 1 : 3. Re.
19 : 11.-21 : 3, 5.-22 : 7.
1 S. 5 : 3. **b.**, Dagon was fallen, 4.
8 : 5. **b.**, thou art old, sons walk not
9 : 7. **b.**, if we go, what sh. we bring
8 **b.** I have fourth part of shekel
12. **b.**, he is bef. you : make haste
17 **b.** the man whom I spake of
24. Samuel said, **b.** that wh. is left
10 : 10. **b.**, company of prophets met
11. **b.**, he prophesied am. prophets
22. **b.**, he hath hid among the stuff
11 : 5. **b.**, Saul came after the herd
12 : 1. **b.**, I hearkened unto voice
13. **b.**, Lord hath set king ov. you
14 : 7. **b.**, I am with thee acc. to thy
8. **b.**, we will pass over unto these
16. **b.**, the multitude melted away
17. **b.**, Jonathan and armourb-r

1 S. 14 : 20. **b.**, ev. man's sword ag. fel-
33. **b.**, people sin ag. the Lord⌊low
15 : 12. **b.**, he set him up a place
22. **b.**, to obey better than sacrifice
16 : 11. youngest, **b.**, keepeth sheep
18 : 17. **b.**, daugh-r Merab will I give
22. **b.**, king hath delight in thee
19 : 19. **b.**, David is at Naioth, 22.
20 : 2. **b.**, my father will do nothing
5. **b.**, to morrow is the new moon
12. **b.**, if there be good tow. David
21. **b.**, the arrows are on this side
22 : †12 **b.** me, my lord, 2 S. 1 : †7.⌊(2)
23 : 1. **b.**, Philistines fight ag. Kei-
3. **b.** we be afraid in Judah ⌊lah
24 : 1. **b.**, David is in wilderness of
4. **b.**, I will deliv. thine enemy into
9. **b.**, David seeketh thy hurt?
10. **b.**, this day thine eyes seen
25 : 14. **b.**, David sent messengers
36. **b.**, he held a feast in his house
26 : 24. **b.**, thy life was much set by
28 : 7. **b.**, is woman hath a familiar
21. **b.**, handmaid hath obeyed th.
2 S. 9 : 6. he answered, **b.**, thy serv '
12 : 18. **b.**, while child was yet alive
17 : 9. **b.**, he is hid now in some pit
18 : 10. **b.**, I saw Absalom hanged
24 : 22. **b.**, here be oxen for sacrif.
1 K. 8 : 27. **b.**, the heaven of heavens
cannot contain thee, 2 Ch. 6 : 18.
13 : 2. **b.**, a child shall be born unto the house of David ⌈et
14 : 2. **b.**, there is Ahijah the proph-
10. **b.**, I will bring evil upon Jero.
16 : 3. **b.**, I will take away posterity
17 : 9. **b.**, I commanded a widow
18 : 7. Obadiah, **b.**, Elijah met him
8. tell thy lord, **b.**, Elijah is here,
44. **b.**, ariseth little cloud⌊11, 14.
19 : 5. **b.**, an angel touched him
11. **b.**, strong wind rent mountain
13. **b.**, a voice, What doest, Elijah?
20 : 13. **b.**, prophet unto Ahab (2)
22 : 25. Micaiah said, **b.**, thou shalt
see in that day, 2 Ch. 18 : 24.
2 K. 1 : 9. **b.**, he sat on top of a hill
2 : 11. **b.**, appeared chariot of fire
19. **b.**, situation of city is pleasant
3 : 20. **b.**, came water by way of E.
4 : 13. **b.**, thou hast been careful for
25. **b.**, yonder is Shunammite⌊us
5 : 11. **b.**, I thought, He will come
20. **b.**, my master spared Naaman
6 : 13. **b.**, he is in Dothan ⌈head
25. **b.**, they besieged it until ass's
33. **b.**, this evil is of the Lord (2)
7 : 2. **b.**, if L make windows(2), 19.
13 : 21. **b.**, they spied band of men
15 : 26. **b.**, they are in book of Chr., 31
19 : 7. **b.**, I will send a blast upon
him, and he, Is. 37 : 7. ⌈thee
9. **b.**, he is come to fight against
11. **b.**, thou heard what kings of A.
35. **b.**, they were all dead corpses
20 : 5. Hez-h ; **b.**, I will heal thee
17. **b.**, all in thine house sh. be
carried to Babylon, Is. 39 : 6.
22 : 16. **b.**, I will bring evil upon
this place, 2 Ch. 34 : 24.
20. **b.**, I will gather thee unto thy
fathers, 2 Ch. 34 : 28. ⌈amo. 30
1 Ch. 11 : 25. **b.**, he was honourable
2 Ch. 19 : 11. **b.**, Amariah is ov. you
20 : 11. **b.**, how they reward us
26 : 20. **b.**, he was leprous in forch.
28 : 9. **b.**, because Lord was wroth
29 : 19. **b.**, they are bef. altar of L.
33 : 19. **b.**, they are written among
35 : 25. **b.**, are written in lamenta-s
Ne. 9 : 36. **b.**, we are servants this d.
Es. 6 : 5. **b.**, Haman standeth in court
7 : 9. **b.** gallows fifty cubits high
Jb. 1 : 12. **b.**, all he hath, in thy pos.
2 . 6. **b.**, he is thine hand; but save
4 : 3. **b.**, thou hast instructed many
18. **b.**, he put no trust in servants

Jb. 5 : 17. **b.**, happy the man whom G.
8 : 19. **b.**, this is the joy of his way
20. **b.**, G. not cast aw. perfect man
9 : 12. **b.**, he taketh aw., who hinder
12 : 14. **b.**, he shutteth up a man
15. **b.**, he withholdeth the waters
15 : 15. **b.**, he putteth no trust in
19 : 7. **b.**, I cry out of wrong⌊saints
27. Whom mine eyes shall **b.**⌈him
20 : 9 neith. his place any more **b.**
21 : 27. **b.**, I know your thoughts
22 : 12. **b.** height of the stars ⌈there
23 : 8. **b.**, I go forward, but he is not
9. doth work, but I cannot **b.** him
24 : 5. **b.**, as wild asses go they to
25 : 5. **b.** to moon, shineth not⌊work
27 : 12. **b.**, all ye have seen it; why
28 : 28. **b.**, fear of Lord is wisdom
31 : 35. **b.**, my desire is th. Almighty
32 : 11. **b.**, I waited for your words
12. **b.**, none of you that convinced
19. **b.**, my belly as wine, no vent
33 : 6. **b.**, I am in God's stead : I am
7. **b.**, my terror not make thee af.
10. **b.**, he findeth occasions ag. me
12 **b.**, in this thou art not just
34 : 29 when hideth who can **b.** him?
35 : 5. **b.** the clouds wh. are higher
36 : 5. **b.**, God is mighty, despiseth
22. **b.**, God exalteth by power⌊not
24. magnify his work wh. men **b.**
25. man may **b.** it afar off ⌈not
26. **b.**, God is great, we know him
30. **b.**, he spreadeth light upon it
38 : † 35. lightnings th. may say, **b.**
39 : 29. eagle, her eyes **b.** afar ⌊us
40 : 4. **b.**, I am vile; what I answer
11. **b.** every one proud, abase him
23. **b.**, he drinketh up a river and
Ps. 11 : 4. his eyes **b.** ; his eyelids
7. countenance doth **b.** upright
17 : 2. let eyes **b.** the things equal
15. I will **b.** thy face in righteousn.
27 : 4. to **b.** the beauty of the Lord
33 : 18. **b.**, eye of Lord is upon them
37 : 37. Mark perfect man, **b.** upri-t
39 : 5. **b.**, thou made my days as a
46 : 8. Come, **b.** works of the Lord
51 : 5. **b.**, I was shapen in iniquity
54 : 4. **b.**, God is mine helper, the
59 : 4. awake to help me, and **b.** ⌊L.
7. **b.**, they belch out with mouth
66 : 7. his eyes **b.** the nations ; let
73 : 12. **b.**, these are the ungodly
78 : 20. **b.**, he smote the rock ⌈vine
80 : 14. look down, **b.**, and visit
84 : 9. **b.**, O God, thine anointed
91 : 8. sh. thou **b.** reward of wicked
102 : 19. fr. heaven did L. **b.** earth
113 : 6. Who humbleth to **b.** things
119 : 18. Open mine eyes th. I may **b.**
40. **b.**, I have longed aft. precepts
121 : 4. **b.**, he that keepeth Israel
128 : 4. **b.**, that thus man be blessed
133 : 1. **b.**, how good, how pleasant
134 : 1. **b.**, bless Lord, all ye serv-ts
139 : 8. if my bed in hell, **b.**, thou
Pr. 23 : 33. eyes sh. **b.** strange wom-
Ec. 1 : 14. **b.**, all is vanity, 2 : 11. ⌊en
2 : 12. I turned to **b.** wisdom, folly
4 : 1. **b.**, tears of such as were op-
5 : 18. **b.**, that I have seen⌊pressed
7 : 27. **b.**, this have I found, saith
11 : 7. pleasant it is to **b.** the sun
Can. 1 : 15. **b.**, thou art fair, my love;
b., thou art fair, 16.-4 : 1(2). ⌈wall
2 : 9. **b.**, he standeth behind our
3 : 7. **b.** his bed, wh. is Solomon's
11. **b.**, O dau-s, Sol-n with crown
Is. 3 : 1. **b.**, Lord doth take aw. stay
5 : 7. for judgment, **b.** oppression,
for righteousness, but **b.** a cry
26. **b.**, they shall come with speed
30. if one look, **b.** darkness, sor-w
6 : †8. Then said I, **b.** me ; send me
7 : 14. **b.**, a virgin shall conceive,
bear a son, Mat. 1 : 23.

Is. 8 : 18. **b.**, I and children which
the Lord hath given, He. 2 : 13.
22. look unto the earth, **b.** trouble
10 · 33. **b.**. L. shall lop the bough
12 : 2. **b.**, God is my salvation I
13 : 9. **b.**, day of the Lord cometh
17. **b.**. I will stir up the Medes ag.
17 : 1. **b.**, Damascus shall be a heap
14. And **b.** at eveningtide trouble
19 · 1 **b.**, Lord rideth upon a swift
20 : 6. **b.**, such is our expectation
21 · 9. **b.**, cometh a chariot of men
22 : 13. **b.** joy, gladn. slaying oxen
17. **b.**, the L. will carry thee away
23 : 13. **b.** the land of the Chaldeans
24 : 1. **b.**, Lord maketh earth empty
26 : 10. will not **b.** majesty of Lord
21. **b.**, the Lord cometh to punish
28 2. **b.**, Lord hath a mighty one
16. **b.**, I lay in Zion for a foundation, a stone, 1 Pe. 2:6. [he eat-h
29 : 8. a hungry man dreameth, **b.**
14. **b.**, I will do a marvellous work
30 · 27. **b.**, name of Lord cometh
32 : 1. **b.**, King sh reign in right-s
33 : 7. **b.**, their valiant ones sh. cry
17. they shall **b.** land very far off
34 : 5. **b.**, it shall come upon Idumea
35 : 4. **b.**, G. will come with venge-e
37 : 11. **b.**, thou hast heard what k-s
38 : 5. **b.**, I will add unto thy days
8. **b.**, I will bring again shadow
11. I shall **b.** man no more [ness
17. **b.**, for peace I had great bitter-
40 : 9. cities of Judah, **b.** your God!
10 **b.**, Lord will come. **b.**, his
15. **b.**, nations are as a drop of a
bucket; **b.**, he taketh up isles
26 **b.**, who hath created these thi-s
41 : 11. **b.**, they shall be confounded
15. **b.**, I will make thee a thresh-g
23. do good or evil that we may **b.**
24. **b.**, ye are of nothing; your
27. first sh. say to Zion, **b.**, **b.** th.
29. **b.**, they are all vanity : works
42 : 1. **b.** my servant, wh. I uphold
43 : 19. **b.**, I will do a new thing
44 : 11. **b.**, his fellows sh. be asham.
47 : 14. **b.**, they shall be as stubble
48 : 7. lest thou say, **b.**, I knew th.
10. **b.**, I have refined thee, but
49 : 12. **b.**, these shall come fr. far
16. **b.**, I have graven thee upon
18. Lift thine eyes, and **b.** [palms
21. **b.**, I was left alone; these
22. **b.**, I will lift hand to Gentiles
50 : 1. **b.**, for iniquities sold yours.
2. **b.**, at my rebuke I dry up sea
9. **b.**, the Lord God will help me
11. **b.**, all ye that kindle a fire
51 : 22. **b.**, I have taken out of thine
hand cup of tremb-g [prudently
52 : 13. **b.**, my servant shall deal
54 : 11. **b.**, I will lay thy stones wi
15. **b.**, they shall gather, but not
16. **b.**, I have created the smith
55 : 4. **b.**, I have given for a witness
5 **b.**, thou shalt call a nation, and
56 : 3. nei. say, **b.**, I am a dry tree
58 : 3. **b.**, in your fast ye find pleas-
4. **b.**, ye fast for strife, debate[ure
59 : 1. **b.**, Lord's hand not shortened
60 : 2. **b.**, darkness sh. cover earth
62 : 11. to Zion, **b.**, thy salvation
cometh : **b.**, his rew-d is (3) [ry
63 : 15. **b.**, fr. habitation of thy glo-
64 : 9. Lord, **b.**, we are all thy peo.
65 : 1. I said, **b.** me, **b.** me, unto a
6. **b.**, it is written bef. me[nation
13. **b.**, my servants shall eat (3)
14. **b.**, my servants shall sing for
17. **b.**, I create new heavens and
18. **b.**, I create Jerusa. a rejoicing
66 : 12. **b.**, I will extend peace to h.
15 **b.**, the Lord will come with fire
Je. 1 : 6. Ah, L.! **b.**, I cannot speak
18. **b.**, I have made thee a defenced

Je 2 : 35. **b.**, I will plead with thee
3 . 5. **b.**, done evil as thou couldest
22. **b.**, we come unto thee : thou
4 : 13. **b.**, he sh come up as clouds
16 **b.**, watchers from far country
5 : 14. **b.**, I will make my words fire
6 : 10. **b.**, their ear is uncircumc-d
19. **b.**, I will bri. evil upon peo.[(2)
21. **b.**, I will lay stumblingblocks
22. **b.**, a people cometh from north
7 · 8. **b.**, ye trust in lying words
11. **b.**, I have seen it, saith Lord
20. **b.**, my fury shall be poured
upon this place, 11 : 11.-19 3.
8 : 15. We looked for a time of health,
b., trouble, 14 : 19. [amo. you
17. For **b.**, I will send serpents
19. **b.** cry of my people because of
9 : 7. **b.**, I will meet them, try them
15. **b.**, I will feed this people with
wormwood, and give, 23 : 15.
25. **b.**, I will punish circumcised
10 · 22. **b.**, noise of bruit is come
11 . 22. **b.**, young men sh. die by s.
13 : 7. **b.**, the girdle was marred
20. **b.** them that come fr. the north
16 : 12. **b.**, ye walk aft. imagination
14. **b.**, it shall no more be said,
The Lord liveth, 23 · 7. [ers
16. **b.**, I will send for many fish-
18 : 3. **b.**, he wro-t work in wheels
6. **b.**, as clay is in potter's hand
11. **b.**, I frame evil ag. you; return
20 : 4. terror, thine eyes shall **b.** it
21 : 4. **b.**, I will turn back weapons
8. **b.**, I set before you way of life
13. **b.**, I am ag. thee, O inhabitant
23 : 2. **b.**, I will visit upon you evil
5. **b.**, I will raise righteous Branch
19. **b.**, whirlwind of L. gone forth
30. **b.**, I am ag. prophets th. steal
32. **b.**, I am ag. them th. prophesy
25 : 9. **b.**, I will take all families of
32. **b.**, evil shall go fr. nation to na.
26 : 14. **b.** I am in your hand; do
27 : 16. saying, **b.**, vessels of L.'s ho.
28 : 16. **b.**, I will cast thee fr. earth
29 : 17. **b.**, I will send sword, fam.
21. **b.**, I will deliver them into ha.
32. **b.**, I will punish Shemaiah :
neith. shall he **b.** good I will do
30 : 18. **b.**, I will bring again capt-y
23. **b.**, whirlwind of Lord goeth
31 : 8. **b.**, I will bring from north
27. **b.**, I will sow the house of Isr.
31. **b.**, I will make new cov-t with
38. **b.**, city be built to Lord [Isr.
32 : 3. **b.**, I will give this city into
4. his eyes shall **b.** his eyes, 34 : 3.
7 **b.**, Hanameel shall come, say-g
17. **b.**, thou hast made heaven
24. **b.** the mounts, they are come to
27. **b.**, I am God of all flesh [take
28. **b.**, I will give this city into ha.
37. **b.**, I will gather them out of all
33 · 6. **b.**, I will bring it health, and
14. **b.**, I will perform good thing
34 : 17. **b.**, I proclaim a liberty for
22 **b.**, I will make cities desolat-n
35 : 17. **b.** I will bring upon Jud. evil
37 : 7. **b.**, Pharaoh's army sh return
38 : 5. **b.**, he is in your hand [city
39 : 16. **b.** I will bring words upon
40 : 4. **b.**, all the land is before thee
10. **b.**, I will dwell at Mizpah, to
42 : 2. (we but few, as thine eyes **b.**)
43 : 10. **b.**, I will take Nebu-r, set
44 : 2. **b.**, they are a desolation
11. **b.**, I will set my face ag-t you
27. **b.**, I will watch over th. for evil
30. **b.**, I will give Pharaoh-hophra
45 : 4. **b.**, that I built I will break
46 : 25. **b.**, I will punish mult-e of
27. **b.**, I will save thee from afar
47 : 2. **b.**, waters sh. overflow land
48 : 12. **b.**, I will send wanderers
40. **b.**, he sh. fly as eagle ov. Moab

Je. 49 : 2. **b.**, will cause alarm in Rab
5. **b.**, I will bring fear upon thee
12. **b.**, they assuredly drunken
19. **b.**, he sh. come like lion, 50 : 44.
22. **b.**, he shall spread wings over
35. **b.**, I will break bow of Elam
50 . 12. **b.**, hindermost of nations a
18. **b.**, I will punish king of Bab-n
31. **b.**, I am against thee, O proud
41. **b.**, a people shall come fr. north
44. **b.**, he shall come like a lion
51 : 1. **b.**, I will raise ag-t Babylon
25. **b.**, I am ag. thee, O mountain
36. **b.**, I will plead thy cause [52.
47. **b.** I do judgment upon images.
La. 1 : 9. O Lord, **b.** my affliction
12. **b.**, see if any sorrow like my s
18 hear all people, **b.** my sorrow
20. **b.**, O Lord; I am in distress
2 : 20. **b.**, O Lord; to whom done
3 · 50. Till Lord **b.** from heaven
63. **b.** their sitting down and ris-
5 : 1. O L., **b.** our reproach [ing up
Eze. 1 : 4. **b.**, a whirlwind came out
15. **b.** one wheel upon the earth
2 : 9. **b.**, a hand was sent unto me
3 : 8. **b.**, I have made thy face str.
23 **b.**, the glory of L. stood there,
4 : 8. **b.**, I lay hands upon thee[8:4.
5 : 8. **b.**, I, even I, am ag. thee, 13.8.
6 . 3. **b.**, I, even I, will bring sword
7 : 5. An evil, only evil, **b.**, is come
6. watcheth for thee; **b.**, it is come
10. **b.** the day, **b.**, it is come; the
8 : 7. I looked, **b.**, a hole in the wall
8. I had digged in wall, **b.** a door
9. Go in, **b.** abominations they do
10. **b.** abominable beasts, idols
14. **b.**, women weep-g for Tammuz
16. **b.**, at door of temple 25 men,
9 : 2. **b.**, six men came fr. way[11:1.
11. **b.**, man clothed with linen
10 : 1. **b.**, above cherubim, as saph.
9. **b.** the four wheels by cherubim
12 : 27. Son of man, **b.**, Israel say
14 : 22 **b.**, shall be left a remnant
15 : 4. **b.**, it is cast into the fire [(2)
5. **b.**, it was meet for no work[love
16 : 8. **b.**, thy time was the time of
27. **b.**, I stretched hand over thee
37. **b.**, I will gather all thy lovers
43. **b.**, I will recompense thy way
44. **b.**, ev. one shall use this prov.
49. **b.**, this was iniquity of sister
17 : 7. **b.**, vine did bend tow. him
10. **b.**, being planted, sh. it prosper
12. **b.**, k. of Bab. is come to Jerus
18 : 4. **b.**, all souls are mine; as
20 : 47. **b.**, I will kindle a fire in thee
21 : 3. **b.**, I am ag. thee. saith Lord,
28 : 22.-29 : 10.-38 : 3. Na. 2 · 13 -3 5.
22 : 6. **b.**, princes of Isr. to shed bl
13. **b.**, I have smitten mine hand
19. **b.**, I will gather you into Jeru.
23 : 22. **b.**, I will raise thy lovers
28. **b.**, I will deliver thee into hand
of them thou hatest, 25 : 4, 7.
24 : 16. **b.**, I take from thee desire
21. **b.**, I will profane my sanctu-y
25 : 8. **b.**, Judah is like all heathen
9. **b.**, I will open the side of Moab
16. **b.**, I will cut off the Cherethim
26 : 3. **b.**, I am ag. thee, O Tyrus, 7.
28 : 3. **b.**, thou art wiser than Dan-l
7. **b.**, I will bring strangers upon
17. bef. kings th. they may **b.** thee
18. to ashes in sight of all that **b.**
29 : 8. **b.**, I will bring sword upon
30 : 22. **b.**, I am against Pharaoh
31 : 3. **b.**, Assyrian was a cedar in
34 : 10. **b.**, I am ag. shepherds[Leb.
11. **b.**, I will search my sheep [20.
17. **b.**, I judge between cattle and,
36 : 6. **b.**, I have spoken in my fury
9. **b.**, I am for you, I will turn
37 . 11. **b.**, they say, our hope is lost
12. **b.**, O people, I will open graves

Eze. 37 : 19. b., I will take stick of J
21. b., I will take Israel fr. heath.
39 : 1. b., I am against thee, O Gog
8. b., it is come, saith the Lord
40 : 4. Son of man b. and hear, 44 : 5.
43 . 2. b., glory of God came fr. east
5. b., glory of Lord filled house
12. b., this is the law of the house
44 : 4. b., glory filled hou. of Lord
47 : 1. b., waters issued und. thresh-
2. b., ran waters on right side⌊old
7. b., many trees on one side and
Da. 2 : 31. sawest, and b. gr-t image
4 : 10. I saw, and b. a tree in midst
13. b., a watcher, and a holy one
7 : 2. b., four winds strove upon sea
5. b. another beast, like to a bear
7. b. a fourth beast, dreadful, ter.
8. b., in this hour were eyes (2)
13. b., one like Son of man came
8 : 19. b., I will make thee know
9 : 18. O God, b. our desolations
11 : 2. b., sh. stand 3 kings in Per.
Ho 2 : 14. b., I will allure her and
Jo. 2 : 19. b., I will send you corn
Am. 2 : 13. b., I am pressed und. you
3 : 9. Assemble, b. great tumults
7 : 1. b., he formed grasshoppers
8. b., I will set plumbline in Israel
8 : 11. b., I will send a famine of
9 : 8. b., eyes of Lord upon sinful
13. b., ploughman overtake reap-
Ob. 2. b., I have made thee small⌊er
† 12. do not b. day of thy brother
Mi. 2 : 3. b., ag-t this family I devise
7 : 9. I shall b. his righteousness
10. enemy, mine eyes shall b. her
Na. 1 : 15. b. upon mts. feet of him
3 : 13. b., thy people are women
Ha. 1 : 3. Why cause me to b. griev-
5. b. ye among heathen ⌊ance?
13. of purer eyes than to b. evil
2 : 4. b., his soul is not upright
13. b., is it not of Lord of hosts
Zph. 3 : 19. b., I will undo all that
Zch. 1 : 8. b. a man upon red horse
11. b.. all the earth sitteth still
18. lifted mine eyes, b. four horns
2 : 1. b. a man with measuring line
3. b., angel went, anoth. angel met
9. b. I will shake my hand ⌈pass
3 : 4. b., I caused thine iniquity to
8. b., I will bring forth BRANCH
9. b. the stone I laid bef. Josh. (2)
4 : 2. b. a candlestick all of gold
5 : 1. I looked, and b. a flying roll
9. b., two women, wind in wings
6 : 1. b., came four chariots fr. mts.
8. b., these have quieted my spirit
in the north country ⌈BRANCH
12. b. man whose name is The
8 : 7. b., I will save my people from
9 : 4. b., the Lord will cast her out
9. b., thy King cometh, Mat. 21 :
5. Jn. 12 : 15. ⌈of trembling
12 : 2. b., I will make Jerus. a cup
14 : 1. b., day of L. cometh, Mal. 4 : 1.
Mal. 1 : 13. ye said, b., what wearin.
2 : 3. b., I will corrupt your seed
3 : 1. b., I will send my messenger,
he shall prepare, 4 : 5. Mat. 11 :
10. Mk. 1 : 2. Lu. 7 : 27. ⌈2 : 13, 19.
Mat. 1 : 20. b., angel of L. appeared,
23. b., a virgin shall be wi. child
2 : 1. b., came wise men fr. the east
4 : 11. b., angels ministered unto
6 : 26. b., fowls of the air sow not
7 : 4. b., a beam is in thine own eye
8 : 2. b., came a leper, saying. Lord
24. b., there arose a great tempest
29. And b., they cried out, saying
32. b., whole herd ran violently
34. b., city came out to meet Jes.
9 : 2. b., they brought him a man
sick of palsy, Lu. 5 : 18. ⌈phem-h
3. b., scribes said, This man blas-
10 b., publicans and sinn-s came
Mat. 9 : 18. b., came a ruler, say-g, My
dau. is dead, Mk. 5 : 22. Lu. 8 : 41.
20. b., a woman, diseased wi. issue
32. b., they brought a dumb man
10 : 16. b., I send you forth as sheep
in midst of wolves, Lu. 10 : 3. ⌈ing
11 : 8. b., they that wear soft cloth-
19. b. a man gluttonous, Lu. 7 : 34.
12 . 2. b., disciples do that not lawf.
10. b., man wh. had hand wither.
18. b., servant wh. I have chosen
41. b., greater than Jonas is here,
Lu. 11 : 32. ⌈Lu. 11 : 31.
42. b., a greater than Sol. is here,
47. b., thy mother and brethren
stand without. 46. Mk. 3 : 32.
49. b. my mother and my brethren! Mk. 3 : 34. ⌈Mk. 4 : 3.
13 : 3. b., a sower went forth to sow,
15 : 22. b., woman of Canaan came
17 : 3. b., appeared Moses and Elias
5. b., a bright cloud, b., a voice
18 : 10. their angels always b. face
19 : 16. b., one said, Good Master
27. b., we have forsaken all; what
20 : 18. b., we go up to Jerusalem,
Mk. 10 : 33. Lu. 18 : 31. ⌈cried out
30. b., two blind men by way side
22 : 4. b., I have prepared my din.
23 : 34. b., I send unto you proph-s
38. b., your house is left unto you
desolate, Lu. 13 : 35. ⌈13 : 23.
24 : 25. b., I told you before, Mk.
26. if they say, b., he is in the desert; b., he is in secret chamb-s
25 : 6. b., the bridegroom cometh
20. b., I have gained five talents
22. b., I have gained 2 other tal-s
26 : 45. b., the hour is at hand, let
us be going, Jn. 16 : 32. ⌈tray me
46. b., he is at hand that doth be-
51. b., one of them drew his sword
27 : 51. b., vail of temple was rent
28 : 7. b., he goeth bef. you into Ga.
9. b., Jesus met them, saying, All
11. b., some of watch ca. into city
Mk. 2 : 24. b., why do they on sabb
11 : 21. b., the fig tree thou cursedst
14 : 41. b., Son of man is betrayed
15 : 4. b., how many things they
35. b., he calleth Elias ⌊witness
16 : 6. b. place where they laid him
Lu. 1 : 20. b., thou shalt be dumb
31. b., thou sh. conceive in womb
36. b., thy cousin hath conceived
38. b., the handmaid of the Lord
48. b., all generations sh. call me
2 : 10. b., I bring you tidings of gr.
34. b., this child is set for the fall
48. b., thy fath. and I have sought
5 : 12. b., a man full of leprosy
6 : 23. b., your reward is great in h.
7 : 25. b., they which are gorgeously
37. b., a woman, wh. was a sinner
9 : 30. b., talked with him two men
38. b., man of company cried out
10 : 19. b., I give you power to tread
25. b., a certain lawyer stood ⌈you
11 : 41. b., all things are clean unto
13 : 7. b., these three years I come
30. b., are last, which sh. be first
32. b., I cast out devils, and I do
14 : 29. all that b. it begin to mock
17 : 21. b., kingdom of G. is within
19 : 8. b. Lord, half of my goods I
20. Lord, b., here is thy pound ⌈b.
21 : 6. As for these things which ye
29. b. the fig tree and all trees
22 : 10. b., when entered into city
21. b., hand of him th. betrayeth
31. b., Satan desired to have you
38. Lord, b., here are two swords
47. b. a multit-e, Judas went bef.
23 : 14. b., I have found no fault
29. b., the days are coming in wh.
24 : 4. b., two men stood by them
13. b., two went th. day to Emm.
Lu. 24 . 39. b. my hands and my feet,
that it is I, Jn. 20 : 27. ⌈Father
49. b., I send the promise of my
Jn. 1 : 29. b. the Lamb of God, 36.
47. b. an Israelite, in wh. no guile!
3 . 26. b., the same baptizeth, and
4 : 35. b., I say, Lift up your eyes
5 : 14. b., thou art made whole
11 : 3. b., he wh. thou lovest is sick
36. said Jews, b., how he loved him
12 : 19. b., world is gone after him
17 : 24. that they may b. my glory
18 : 21. b., they know what I said
19 : 4. b., I bring him forth to you
5. P. saith unto them, b. the man!
14. saith unto Jews, b. y-r King!
26. Jesus saith, Woman, b. thy son
27. saith to disciple, b. thy moth.
Ac. 1 : 10. b., two stood by in white
2 . 7. b., are not these Galileans?
5 : 9. b., feet of them wh. buried thy
25. b., men ye put in prison are
28. b., ye have filled Jerusalem
7 : 31. as he drew near to b. it ⌈b.
32. Moses trembled, and durst not
56. b., I see the heavens opened
8 : 27. b., a man of Ethiopia, a eu.
9 : 10. Ananias said, b., I am here
11. inquire for Saul; b., he pray-h
10 : 17. b., men sent fr. Cornelius
19. Spirit said, b., 3 men seek thee
21. Peter said, b., I am he ye seek
30. b., man stood bef. me in bright
11 : 11. b., were three men come
12 : 7. b., angel of L. came upon him
13 : 11. b., hand of L. is upon thee
25. b., cometh one after me, whose
41. b., ye despisers wonder, perish
16 : 1. b., a certain disciple there
20 : 22. b., I go bound in the spirit
25. b., ye sh. see my face no more
Ro. 2 : 17. b., thou art called a Jew
9 : 33. b., I lay in Sion stumblingst.
11 : 22. b. goodn. and severity of G.
1 Co. 10 : 18. b. Israel after the flesh
15 : 51. b., I shew you a mystery
2 Co. 3 : 7. could not b. face of Mos.
5 : 17. b., all things are become new
6 : 9. as dying, and, b., we live; as
7 : 11. b. this selfsame thing, that
12 : 14. b., I am ready to come to y.
Ga. 1 : 20. b., before God, I lie not
5 : 2. b., I Paul say, if ye be circum.
He. 8 : 8. b., the days come when I
Ja. 3 : 3. b., we put bits in horses' m.
4. b. ships, which though so great
5. b., how gr. a matter a little fire
5 : 4. b., hire of the labourers crieth
7. b., husbandm. waiteth for fruit
9. b., the judge standeth bef. door
11. b., we count them happy wh.
1 Pe. 2 : 12. good works, wh. they b.
3 : 2. b. your chaste conversation
1 Jn. 3 : 1. b., manner of love the Fa.
Jude 14. b., Lord cometh wi. 10,000
Re. 1 : 7. b., he cometh with clouds
18. b., I am alive for evermore
2 : 10. b., devil shall cast some into
22. b., I will cast her into a bed
3 : 8. b., I have set an open door
9. b., I will make them worship (2)
11. b., I come quickly : hold fast
20. b., I stand at door and knock
4 : 1. b., a door was opened in heav.
2. b., a throne was set in heaven
5 : 5. b., the Lion of the tribe of Ju.
6 : 2. b., a white horse : he that sat
8. b. pale horse: th. sat was Death
9 : 12. b., there come two woes more
11 : 14. b.. 3d woe cometh quickly
12 : 3. b. a great red dragon ⌈sat
14 : 14. b. a white cloud, and one
15 : 5. b., the temple in heaven was
16 : 15. b., I come as a thief ⌊opened
17 : 8. when they b. the beast that

BEHOLD, it is.

Ge. 16 : 14. well: b. - betw. Kadesh

Ge.34 . 21. land, b. - large enough
Ex. 32 : 9. this people, b. - a stiff-necked people, De.9:13. [mouldy
Jos. 9 : 12. our bread; now, b. - dry,
Ju. 18 : 9. the land, b. - very good
12. Mahaneh-dan; b. - behind K.
Is. 52 : 6. I am he doth speak: b. - I

BEHOLD with now.

Ge. 12 : 11. b. n., I know thou art
19. n. b. thy wife, take her[fair w.
16 : 2. b. n., L. hath restrained me
18 : 27. b. n., I have taken it upon me to speak unto Lord, 31.
19 : 2. b. n., my lords, tarry all ni.
8. b. n., I have two dau-s [grace
19. b. n., thy servant hath found
20. b. n., city is near to flee unto
27 : 2. b. n., I am old, I know not
36. b., n. he hath taken my bles-g
De.26:10. n., b., I brought firstfruits
Ju. 13 : 3. b., n., thou art barren
19 : 9. b., n. day draweth tow. ev-g
1 S. 9 : 6. b. n., is in this city a man
12 : 2. n., b., king walketh bef. you
13. n., b. k. whom ye have chosen
16 : 15. b. n., an evil spirit from God
24 : 20. n., b., I know thou sh. be k.
2 S. 14 : 21. b. n., I have done this
1 K. 1 : 18. n., b., Adonijah reigneth
20 : 31. b. n., k-s of Isr. are merciful
22 : 23. n., b., L. hath put lying spi.
2 K. 2 : 16. b. n., with thy serv-ts
4 : 9. b. n., this a holy man[50 men
5 : 15. b., n. I know is no G. in earth
22. b., n. there be two young men
6 : 1. b. n., place is too strait for us
18 : 21. n., b., thou trustest upon bruised reed, even Egypt[cause
Jb. 13 : 18. b. n., I have ordered my
16 : 19. n., b., my witness in heav.
33 : 2. b., n. I have opened my mou.
40 : 15. b. n. behemoth, wh. I made
Is. 8 : 7. n., b., L. bringeth up wat-s
Je. 40 : 4. n., b., I loose thee this d.
Mat. 26 : 65. b., n., ye have heard his blasphemy [threatenings
Ac. 4 : 29. And, n., Lord, b. their
13 : 11. n. b., hand of L. upon thee
20 : 22. n. b., I go bound in spirit
2 Co. 6 : 2. b., n. is the accepted time, b., n. is the day of salvat.
See **Behold, it WAS.**
See **Behold, there WAS.**

BEHOLDERS. [of b.
Jb. 34 : † 26. striketh them in place

BEHOLDEST.
Ps. 10 : 14. thou b. mischief, spite
Mat. 7 : 3. why b. mote in, Lu. 6:41.
Lu. 6 : 42. b. not beam in own eye

BEHOLDETH.
Jb. 24 : 18. he b. not way of vine-
41 : 34. He b. all high things[yards
Ps. 33 : 13. L. b. all the sons of men
Ja. 1 : 24. b. himself, goeth his way

BEHOLDING. [ity
Ps. 119 : 37. mine eyes from b. van-
Pr. 15 : 3. Lord b. the evil and good
Ec. 5 : 11. what good, saving the b. of
Mat. 27: 55. many women were there b. afar off, Lu. 23:49. [said, One
Mk. 10 : 21. Jesus b. him, loved him,
Lu. 23 : 35. And the people stood b.
48. b. things done, smote breasts
Ac. 4 : 14. b. man which was healed
8 : 13. Simon b. miracles and signs
14 : 9. Paul, steadfastly b. him [sel
23 : 1. Paul earnestly b. the coun-
2 Co. 3 : 18. b. as in glass, glory of L.
Col. 2 : 5. joying and b. your order
Ja. 1 : 23. like man b. face in a glass

BEHOOVED. [rise
Lu. 24 : 46. it b. Christ to suffer and
He. 2 : 17. it b. him to be made like

BEING. [Noun.] [breth.
Ps. 104:33. praise my God while I have my b., 146 : 2. [have our b.
Ac. 17 : 28. in him we live and move,

BEING. [Part.] [b. old?
Ge. 18 : 12. I have pleasure, my lord
21 : 4. circumcised son, b. 8 days
24 : 27. I b. in way, L. led me [old
34 : 30. I b. few, they shall slay me
35 : 29. Isaac died, b. old, full of d-s
37 : 2. Joseph, b. seventeen years
50 : 26. So Joseph died, b. 110 yrs.
Ex. 13 : 15. I sacrifice all, b. males
22 : 14. it die, owner b. not with it
Le. 21 : 4. not defile, b. a chief man
Nu. 22 : 24. a wall b. on this side
30 : 3. b. in her father's house, 16.
De. 17 : 8. b. matters of controversy
22 : 24. she cried not, b. in the city
32 : 31. our enemies b. judges[men
Jos. 9 : 23. none freed from b. bond-
21 : 10. b. of families of Kohathites
24 : 29. Joshua died, b. 110 years old, Ju. 2 : 8. [child
1 S. 2 : 18. Samuel ministered, b. a
15 : 23. rejected thee fr. b. king, 26.
26 : 13. great space b. betw. them
2 S. 13 : 4. Why, b. king's son, lean
1 K. 1 : 41. the city b. in an uproar
11 : 17. Hadad b. yet a little child
15 : 13. Maachah he removed from b. queen, 2 Ch. 15 : 16. [boam
16 : 7. in b. like the house of Jero-
2 Ch. 26 : 21. in a several hou., b. leper
Ezr. 10 : 19. b. guilty, offered a ram
Ne. 6 : 11. who, b. as I am, would go
Es. 1 : 3. nobles, princes, b. bef. him
Jb. 27 : † 11. I will teach you, b. in
Ps. 49 : 12. man b. in honour abideth
83 : 4. cut them off fr. b. nation[not
Je. 34 : 9. b. a Hebrew, or Hebrewess
Eze. 48 : 22. b. in the midst of that
Da. 5 : 31. Darius took kingdom, b. 62
Mat. 1 : 19. Joseph, b. a just man
7 : 11. If ye b. evil know how to give gifts, Lu. 11 : 13. [things?
12 : 34. how ye, b. evil, speak good
Mk. 8 : 1. multitude b. great, Jesus
9 : 33. b. in the house, he asked
14 : 3. b. in Bethany, in house of
Lu. 2 : 5. Mary, b. great with child
3 : 23. b. (as supposed) son of Jos-h
13 : 16. this woman, b. dau. of Abr.
16 : 23. lifted his eyes, b. in torm-ts
18 : † 9. which trusted in themselves as b. righteous [rection
20 : 36. b. the children of resur-
22 : 3. Satan into Judas, b. of twelve
44. And b. in an agony, he prayed
Jn. 4 : 9. How, b. a Jew, askest drink
5 : 13. multitude b. in that place
6 : 71. spake of Judas; b. one of 12
7 : 50. he th. came by night, b. one
10 : 33. b. a man, makest thys. God
11 : 49. b. high priest that year, 51.
*18 : 26. (b. his kinsm. whose ear Pe.)
19 : 38. Joseph, b. a disciple of Jes.
Ac. 2 : 30. David, b. a prophet, spake
3 : 1. hour of prayer, b. ninth hour
7 : 55. Stephen, b. full of Holy Gh.
14 : 8. b. cripple fr. moth-'s womb
15 : 32. Judas, Silas, b. prophets
16 : 20. These, b. Jews, trouble city
21. not lawf. to observe, b. Rom-s
37. beaten us uncondemned, b. R-s
19 : 40. b. no cause wh-by we may
27 : 2. one Aristarchus b. with us
Ro. 11 : 17. if thou, b. a wild olive tr.
1 Co. 7 : 21. Art called, b. a servant?
22. in the Lord, b. servant, is freeman; he b. free is Christ's ser.
8 : 7. conscience, b. weak is defiled
9 : 21. b. not without law to God
10 : 17. we b. many are one bread
12 : 12. members b. many, are one
2 Co. 8 : 17. b. more forward, Titus
12 : 16. b. crafty, I caught you
Ga. 1 : 14. b. zealous of traditions
2 : 3. neither Titus, b. Greek, was circumcised [ner of Gentiles
14. if thou, b. Jew, livest aft. man-
Ep. 2 : 20. Christ b. chief corner sto-
4 : † 15. b. sincere in love may grow
18. b. alienated from life of God
Ph. 2 : 2. b. of one accord, one mind
6. Who, b. in form of G., thoug it
Col. 2 : 13. And you, b. dead in sins
Tit. 1 : 16. deny him, b. abominable
Phm. 9. I b. such an one as Paul[ry
He. 1 : 3. Who b. brightn-s of his glo-
13 : 3. as b. yourselves in the body
Ja. 1 : 25. he b. not forgetful hearer
1 Pe. 5 : 3. Neither as b. lords over God's heritage, but b. ensamp.
Re. 12 : 2. she, b. with child, cried

BEKAH. [bered
Ex. 38 : 26. A b. for every man num-

BEL. [stoopeth
Is. 46 : 1. B. boweth down, Nebo
Je. 50 : 2. B. is confounded [lon
51 : 44. I will punish B. in Baby-

BE'LA. [Place.]
Ge. 14 : 2. war with king of B., 8.

BE'LA or BE'LAH.
Ge. 36 : 32. B. son of Beor reigned in Edom, 1 Ch. 1 : 43. [Ch. 1:44.
33. B. died, Jobab reigned in st-d, 1
46 : 21. sons of Benj. were B-h, Becher, Ashbel, 1 Ch. 7:6. B-a
Nu. 26 : 38. of B. family of Belaites
40. sons of B. were Ard, Naaman
1 Ch. 5 : 8. chief, B. the son of Azaz
7 : 7. sons of B.; Ezbon, Uzzi, Iri
8 : 1. Benj-n begat B. his firstborn
3. sons of B., Addar, Gera, Abihud

BE'LAITES. See BELA.

BELCH, ETH. [mouth
Ps. 59 : 7. Behold, they b. out with
Pr. 15 : † 2. mouth of fools b-h out

BE'LIAL. [out
De. 13 : 13. men, children of B., gone
15 : † 9. not a tho-t in thy B. heart
Ju. 19. 22. sons of B. beset the hou.
20 : 13. deliver us chil. of B. [of B.
1 S. 1 : 16. count not handmaid dau.
2 : 12. sons of Eli were sons of B.
10 . 27. chil. of B. said, How sh. this
25 : 17. he is such a son of B. that
25. not Lord regard this man of B.
30 : 22. Then answered men of B.
2 S. 16 : 7. Come out, thou man of B.
20 : 1. happened there a man of B.
22 : † 5. the floods of B. made me afraid, Ps. 18 : † 4. [thrust aw.
23 : 6. sons of B. shall be as thorns
1 K. 21 : 10 set two sons of B. to bear witness against Naboth, 13 (2).
2 Ch. 13 . 7. gathered unto Jerob-m vain children of B. [unto him
Ps. 41 : † 8. A thing of B. cleaveth
101 : † 3 no thing of B. bef. m. eyes
Pr. 16 : † 27. man of B. diggeth up evil
19 : † 28. A witness of B. scorneth
Na. 1 : † 11. is one, a counsellor of B.
† 15. B. shall no more pass through
2 Co. 6 : 15 what concord Christ wi.

BELIE, BELIED. [B.
Pr. 30 : † 9. lest I be full and b. thee
Je. 5 : 12. They have b-d the Lord

BELIEF.
2 Th. 2 : 13. of Spirit and b. of truth

BELIEVE. [peared,
Ex. 4 : 5. may b. the Lord hath ap-
8. they will b. voice of latter sign
19 : 9. people may b. thee for ever
Nu. 14 : 11. how long ere they b. me?
2 Ch. 20 : 20. b. in Lord; b. proph-
32 : 15. Hezekiah, neith. b. him Lets
Jb. 39 : 12. Wilt thou b. him, that
Is. 43 : 10. that ye may b. me, and
Mat. 9 : 28. b. I am able to do this?
18 : 6. whoso offend one of little ones wh. b. in me. Mk. 9:42. [b.
21 : 32. repented not that ye might
27 : 42. come from cross we will b.
Mk. 1 : 15. repent ye and b. gospel
5 : 36. not afraid, only b., Lu. 8:50.
9 : 23. If canst b., all things possibl

Mk. 9 : 24. Lord, I b. help, Jn. 9 : 38.
11 : 23. sh. b. things he saith sh. come
24. b. ye receive them, and ye
15 : 32. descend, that we may b.
16 : 17. signs sh. follow them wh. b.
Lu. 8 : 12. tak. word, lest they b.
13. no root, wh. for a while b.
24 : 25. and slow of heart to b.
Jn. 1 : 7. that all through him b.
12. to them that b. on his name
3 : 12. how b. if I tell you of heav.?
4 : 21. Woman, b. me, hour cometh
42. we b. not bec. of thy saying
5 : 44. How b. which rec. honour
47. how shall ye b. my words?
6 : 29. that ye b. on him he sent
30. what sign, that we may b.
69. we b. thou art Christ
7 : 5. neither did breth. b. in him
39. Spirit, wh. they that b. receive
9 : 35. Dost thou b. on Son of G ?
36. Who is he, L., th. I might b.
38. And he said, Lord, I b.
10 : 38. b. works, that ye may b.
11 : 15. to the intent ye may b.
27. I b. that thou art the Christ
40. Said I not, if thou wouldst b.
42. may b. thou sent me [thou
48. let him alone, all men will b.
12 : 36. while light, b. in light
13 : 19. to pass, ye may b. I am he
14 : 1. ye b. in G., b. also in me
11. b. I am in Fa., or b. for works'
29. come to pass ye might b.
16 : 30 : we b. thou camest fr. God
31. Jes. ans. them, do ye now b.?
17 : 20. I pray for them wh. sh. b.
21. world may b. thou sent me
19 : 35. saith true, th. ye might b.
20 : 31. written that ye might b.
Ac. 8 : 37. I b. J. C. is Son of God
13 : 39. by him all th. b. are justifi.
41. work you shall in no wise b.
15 : 7. that Gent. by me should b.
11. b. thro' grace we sh. be saved
16 : 31. b. on L. J., thou sh. be sav.
19 : 4. b. on him th. should come
21 : 20. seest how many Jews b.
25. touching Gentiles which b.
27 : 25. I b. G. that it shall be as
Ro. 3 : 22. righte. of G. on all th. b.
4 : 11. might be fa. of all that b.
24. shall be imputed, if we b.
6 : 8. if dead, we b. we shall live
10 : 9. and shalt b. G. raised him
14. how b. in him not heard?
1 Co. 1 : 21. preach. to save that b.
11 : 18. divisions, and I partly b. it
14 : 22. tongues a sign, not to th. b.
prophesying for them which b.
2 Co. 4 : 13. we b. and theref. speak
Ga. 3 : 22. promise to them that b.
Ep. 1 : 19. of his power to us who b.
Ph. 1 : 29. to us given not only to b.
1 Th. 1 : 7. ensamples to all that b.
2 : 10. we behaved am. you that b.
13. word worketh in you that b.
4 : 14. if we b. Jesus died and rose
2 Th. 1 : 10. admired in all that b.
2 : 11. that they should b. a lie
1 Ti. 1 : 16. pattern to them that b.
4 : 3. with thanksg. of them th. b.
10. Saviour, espec. of those th. b.
He. 10 : 39. that b. to saving of soul
11 : 6. cometh to G. must b. he is
Ja. 2 : 19. devils b. and tremble
1 Pe. 1 : 21. Who by him do b. in G.
2 : 7. to you wh. b. he is precious
1 Jn. 3 : 23. his com-t. that we sho. b.
5 : 13. to you that b. th. ye may b.

BELIEVE not, or not BELIEVE.

Ex. 4 : 1. behold they will n. b. me
8. if they will n. b. thee, 9.
De. 1 : 32. in this ye did n. b. L.
2 K. 17 : 14. like fa. did n. b. in L.
Jb. 9 : 16. I n. b. he had hearkened
Pr. 26 : 25. speaketh fair, b. him n.
Is. 7 : 9. if will n. b. not be estab.
Je. 12 : 6. b. n. tho. they speak fair
Ha. 1 : 5. ye will n. b. tho. told you
Mat. 21 : 25. Why n. b. him? Mk.
11 : 31. [26. Mk. 13 : 21.
24 : 23. Lo here is Christ, b. it n.,
Lu. 22 : 67. If I tell you, you will n.
b. [things and ye b. n.
Jn. 3 : 12. If I have told earthly
4 : 48. Except ye see signs will n. b.
5 : 38. whom sent, him ye b. n.
47. if b. n. writ. how b. my words
6 : 36. ye have seen me and b. n.
64. are some of you which b. n.
8 : 24. if ye b. n. I am he, ye die
45. I tell you truth, ye b. me n.
46. if I say truth, why n. b. me?
9 : 18. concern. the Jews did n. b.
10 : 26. ye b. n. bec. not of my sheep
37. if I do not works of Fa. b. n.
38. tho. ye b. n. me, bel. works
12 : 39. could n. b. bec. Isa. said
47. If any hear words and b. n.
16 : 9. reprove of sin. bec. th. b. n.
20 : 25. hand into his side I n. b.
Ro. 3 : 3. what if some did n. b.
15 : 31. be deliv. fr. them do n. b.
1 Co. 10 : 27. b. n. bid you to feast
14 : 22. tongues a sign to th. b. n.
2 Co. 4 : 4. blinded them that b. n.
2 Ti. 2 : 13. if we b. n. he faithful
1 Jn. 4 : 1. b. n. every spirit, but

BELIEVED.

Ge. 15 : 6. he b. counted for righte.,
Ro. 4 : 3. Ga. 3 : 6. Ja. 2 : 23.
Ex. 4 : 31. Aaron spake, people b.
14 : 31. they b. the L. and Moses
1 S. 27 : 12. and Achish b. David
Ps. 27 : 13. fainted unless I had b.
106 : 12. Then b. they his words
116 : 10. I b. thf. spok., 2 Co. 4 : 13.
119 : 66. for I have b. thy com-t
Is. 53 : 1. Who hath b. our report?
Jn. 12 : 38. Ro. 10 : 16.
Da. 6 : 23. no hurt bec. he b. in G.
Jon. 3 : 5. so peo. of Nineveh b. G.
Mat. 8 : 13. b. so be it done to thee
21 : 32. publicans and harlots b.
Mk. 16 : 13. neither b. they them
Lu. 1 : 1. things most surely b.
45. blessed is she that b. for there
Jn. 2 : 11. his disciples b. on him
22. they b. scripture and word
4 : 39. the Samaritans of city b.
50. man b. word Jes. had spoken
53. the father b. and whole house
5 : 46. b. Moses, ye would ha. b. me
7 : 48. have any Phari. b. on him?
8 : 31. said Jesus to Jews that b.
11 : 45. seen things Jesus did, b.
12 : 11. many of Jews b. on Jesus
16 : 27. Fa. loveth you bec. you b.
17 : 8. have b. thou didst send me
20 : 8. went other disci. saw and b.
29. thou hast b. blessed they th.
have not seen and yet b.
Ac. 2 : 44. all that b. had things
4 : 4. many wh. heard word b.
32. that b. were of one heart
5 : † 36. as many as b. Theudas
8 : 12. But when they b. Philip
13. Simon b. and was baptized
10 : 45. circum. who b. were aston.
11 : 17. like gift as to us who b.
21. great number b. turned to L.
13 : 12. then deputy b. astonished
48. as were ord. to eter. life b.
14 : 1. mult. of Jews and Gr. b.
23. to Lord on whom they b.
15 : 5. certain of Pharisees b.
16 : 1. certain woman, Jewess, b.
17 : 4. b. and consorted with Paul
34. certain clave to him and b.
18 : 8. Crispus chief ruler, b.
27. helped them which had b.
19 : 2. receiv. ye H. G. since ye b.?
Ac. 22 : 19. I beat them that b.
27 : 11. centurion b. master of ship
28 : 24. some b. and some b. not
Ro. 4 : 3. Ab. b. God, Ga. 3 : 6. Ja.
17. bef. him whom he b. [2 : 23.
18. who against hope b. in hope
13 : 11. nearer than when we b.
1 Co. 3 : 5. ministers by whom ye b.
15 : 2. unless ye have b. in vain
11. so we preach and so ye b.
Ga. 2 : 16. even we have b. in J. C.
Ep. 1 : 13. aft. ye b. ye were sealed
2 Th. 1 : 10. our testimony was b.
1 Ti. 3 : 16. b. on in world, receiv.
2 Ti. 1 : 12. I know whom I have b.
Tit. 3 : 8. wh. have b. be careful to
He. 4 : 3. we wh. have b. do enter
1 Jn. 4 : 16. we have b. love of G.

Many BELIEVED.

Jn. 2 : 23. at the passover m. b.
4 : 39. m. of the Samaritans b.
41. m. b. because of his word
7 : 31. m. of people b.
8 : 30. as he spake m. b.
10 : 42. m. b. on him there [b.
11 : 45. m. Jews wh. came to Mary
12 : 42. among chief rulers also m.
Ac. 9 : 42. Joppa, and m. b. [b.
17 : 12. m. of them b.
18 : 8. m. of the Corinthians b.
19 : 18. m. that b. confessed deeds

BELIEVED not, or not BELIEVED.

Ge. 45 : 26. heart fainted he b. n.
Nu. 20 : 12. Because ye b. me n.
De. 9 : 23. rebelled and b. him n.
1 K. 10 : 7. I b. n. words, 2 Ch 9 : 6.
Jb. 29 : 24. if I laughed, they b. it n.
Ps. 78 : 22. Because they b. n. in G.
32. b. n. for his wondrous works
106 : 24. despised land b. n. word
Je. 40 : 14. Gedaliah b. them n.
La. 4 : 12. of world would n. have b.
Mat. 21 : 32. John came ye b. n.
Mk. 16 : 11. heard he was alive b. n.
14. upbraided bec. they b. n.
Lu. 20 : 5. will say, Why b. ye n.?
24 : 11. as idle tales they b. n.
41. while they b. n. for joy
Jn. 3 : 18. condemned bec. he n. b.
6 : 64. Jesus knew who b. n. [n.
10 : 25. ans. I told you and ye b.
12 : 37. many miracles yet b. n.
Ac. 9 : 26. b. n. that he was a disci.
17 : 5. Jews wh. b. n. moved with
19 : 9. divers hardened and b. n.
28 : 24. spoken, and some b. n.
Ro. 10 : 14. how call on wh. ha. n. b.
11 : 30. in times past n. b. God
31. so have these now n. b.
2 Th. 2 : 12. be damned who b. n.
He. 3 : 18. not enter rest that b. n.
11 : 31. Rahab per. not wi. th. b. n.
Jude 5. L. destroyed them b. n.

BELIEVERS.

Ac. 5 : 14. b. were the more added
1 Ti. 4 : 12. be example of the b.

BELIEVEST.

Lu. 1 : 20. be dumb bec. thou b. not
Jn. 1 : 50. under fig-tree, b. thou?
11 : 26. never die, b. thou this?
14 : 10. b. thou not I am in Fa.
Ac. 8 : 37. if thou b. with all heart
26 : 27. b. prophets? I kn. thou b.
Ja. 2 : 19. Thou b. there is one G.

BELIEVETH.

Jb. 15 : 22. he b. not he sh. return
39 : 24. neither b. it is trumpet
Pr. 14 : 15. simple b. every word
Is. 28 : 16. that b. not make haste
Mk. 9 : 23. all possible to him b.
16 : 16. He that b. shall be saved,
he that b. not sh. be damned
Jn. 3 : 15. whoso b. not perish, 16
18. he that b. is not condemned,
he that b. not is condemned
36. that b. hath everl. life, 6 : 47.

Jn. 5 : 24. b. on him hath everl. life
6 : 35. he that b. on me never thirst
40. seeth Son and b. hath life
7 : 38. that b. on me, out of belly
11 : 25. that b. tho. dead yet sh. live
26. whoso. b. in me sh. never die
12 : 44. that b. b. not on me, but
46. whoso. b. not abide in darkn.
14 : 12. that b. on me, works I do
Ac. 10 : 43. whosoever b. in him
shall receive remission of sins
Ro. 1 : 16. power of G. to ev. one th. b.
3 : 26. justifier of him th. b. in Jes.
4 : 5. that worketh not but b. on
9 : 33. b. sh. not be asha., 10 : 11.
10 : 4. C. is end of law to ev. one b.
10. with heart man b. to righte.
14 : 2. one b. he may eat all things
1 Co. 7 : 12. hath a wife that b. not
13. husband that b. not
13 : 7. love b. all things, hopeth
14 : 24. come in one that b. not
2 Co. 6 : 15. hath he th. b. with infi.
1 Ti. 5 : 16. if any that b. have wid.
1 Pe. 2 : 6. he b. not be confounded
1 Jn. 5 : 1. Whoso. b. Jes. is Christ
5. overcometh, but he that b.
10. that b. on Son of G., b. not
God because he b. not record

BELIEVING.

Mat. 21 : 22. ask b. ye shall receive
Jn. 20 : 27. said to Thomas, be not
faithless but b.
31. that b. ye might have life
Ac. 16 : 34. b. in G. with his house
24 : 14. b. all things written in law
Ro. 15 : 13. all joy and peace in b.
1 Ti. 6 : 2. that have b. masters †
service because they are b.
1 Pe. 1 : 8. yet b. ye rejoice with joy

BELL, S.

Ex. 28 : 33. b. of gold betw., 39 : 25.
34. a golden b. and pomegr., 39 : 26.
Zch. 14 : 20. upon the b-s of horses

BELLOW. See BULLS.

BELLOWS.

Je. 6 : 29. the b. are burnt, lead is

BELLY, BELLIES.

Ge. 3 : 14. on thy b. shalt thou go
Le. 11 : 42. goeth on b. be abom.
Nu. 5 : 21. thy b. to swell, 22, 27.
25 : 8. thrust man and wom. thro. b.
De. 28 : † 11. fruit of thy b., † 53.
Ju. 3 : 21. the dagger in his b. | 22.
1 K. 7 : 20. pomegra. over ag. the b.
Jb. 3 : 11. when I came out of b.
15 : 2. fill b. with east wind
35. their b. prepareth deceit
19 : † 17. for chil.'s sake of my b.
20 : 15. G. shall cast out of his b.
20. not feel quietness in his b.
23. When about to fill his b.
32 : † 18. spirit of my b. constrain-
19. my b. is as wine which [eth
Ps. 17 : 14. b. fillest with thy treas.
22 : 10. my God from mother's b.
31 : 9. consumed with grief, my b.
44 : 25. our b. cleaveth to earth
58 : † 3. they go astray from b.
132 : † 11. of the fruit of thy b.
Pr. 13 : 25. b. of wicked shall want
18 : 8. innerm. parts of b., 26 : 22.
20. man's b. be satisfied
20 : 27. searching inw. parts of b.
30. so stripes inward parts of b.
22 : † 18. if keep them in thy b.
Can. 5 : 14. b. is as bright ivory
7 : 2. b. is like heap of wheat
Is. 46 : 3. borne by me from b.
Je. 1 : 5. formed thee in the b.
51 : 34. filled b. with delicates
Eze. 3 : 3. cause thy b. to eat
Da. 2 : 32. image's b. of brass
Jon. 1 : 17. b. of fish, Mat. 12 : 40.
2 : 1. unto Lord out of fish's b.
2. out of b. of hell cried I
Mi. 6 : † 7. fruit of my b. for sin
Ha. 3 : 16. heard, my b. trembled
Mat. 15 : 17. whatso. goeth into b.
is cast out into dr., Mk. 7 : 19.
Lu. 15 : 16. filled his b. with husks
Jn. 7 : 38. out of b. sh. flow rivers
Ro. 16 : 18. they serve their own b.
1 Co. 6 : 13. Meats for b. and b.
Ph. 3 : 19. whose God is their b.
Tit. 1 : 12. Cretians are slow b-s
Re. 10 : 9. it make thy b. bitter
10. eaten it, my b. was bitter

BELONG.

Ge. 40 : 8. interpreta. b. to God?
Le. 27 : 24. return to wh. it did b.
De. 29 : 29. secret things b. to God
Nu. 1 : 50. over all that b. to it
Ps. 47 : 9. shields b. to God
68 : 20. to our God b. the issues
Pr. 24 : 23. These b. to the wise
Eze. 21 : † 13. b. to despising rod
Da. 9 : 9. To the Lord b. mercies
Mk. 9 : 41. because ye b. to Christ
Lu. 19 : 42. which b. to thy peace
1 Co. 7 : 32. things that b. to Lord

BELONGED, EST.

Jos. 17 : 8. Tappuah b. to
1 S. 21 : 7. herdmen that b. to Saul
30 : 13. to whom b. thou?
1 K. 1 : 8. men which b. to David
2 K. 7 : † 2. lord which b. to king
1 Ch. 2 : 23. b. to sons of Machir
13 : 6. Kirjath-jearim b. to Judah
2 Ch. 26 : 23. field of burial wh. b.
Lu. 23 : 7. knew he b. to Herod's

BELONGETH.

Nu. 8 : 24. that b. unto Levites
De. 32 : 35. To me b. vengeance,
Ps. 94 : 1. He. 10 : 30.
Ju. 19 : 14. b. to Benjamin, 20 : 4.
1 S. 17 : 1. wh. b. to Judah. 30 : 14.
1 K. 19 : 3. 2 K. 14 : 11. 2 Ch.
25 : 21.
Ezr. 10 : 4. this matter b. to thee
Ps. 3 : 8. Salvation b. unto Lord
62 : 11. power b. unto God
12. unto thee, O Lord, b. mercy
94 : 1. to whom vengeance b.
Da. 9 : 7. O Lord, righte b. to thee
8. to us b. confusion of face
He. 5 : 14. strong meat b. to them

BELONGING.

Nu. 7 : 9. the service b. to them
Ru. 2 : 3. part of a field b. to Boaz
1 S. 6 : 18. cities b. to five lords
Pr. 26 : 17. strife b. not to him
Lu. 9 : 10. desert b. to Bethsaida

BELOVED.

De. 21 : 15. wives, one b. the other
16. make son of b. firstborn
33 : 12. b. of L. dwell in safety
2 S. 12 : † 25. that is b. of the L.
Ne. 13 : 26. Sol. was b. of his God
Ps. 60 : 5. b. be delivered, 108 : 6.
127 : 2. so he giveth his b. sleep
Pr. 4 : 3. b. in sight of my mother
Can. 5 : 1. drink abundantly, O b.
9. thy b. more than another b.
6 : 1. Whither is thy b. gone?
8 : 5. leaning on her b.?
Da. 9 : 23. greatly b., 10 : 11, 19.
Ho. 3 : 1. love a woman b. of her
9 : 16. I will slay b. fruit of womb
Ac. 15 : 25. men with b. Barnabas
Ro. 1 : 7. To all in Rome, b. of God
9 : 25. call her b. which was not b.
11 : 28. are b. for Father's sake
16 : 12. Salute b. Persis who labour-
Ep. 1 : 6. made us accepted in b. [ed
6 : 21. Tychicus b. bro., Col. 4 : 7.
Col. 3 : 12. elect of God holy and b.
4 : 9. Onesimus, a b. brother
14. Luke the b. physician
1 Th. 1 : 4. b. your election of God
2 Th. 2 : 13. you breth. b. of Lord
1 Ti. 6 : 2. do them service bec. b.
Phm. 2. And to our b. Apphia
16. above a servant a brother b.
He. 6 : 9. b. we are persuaded of
1 Pe. 4 : 12. b. think it not str
2 Pe. 3 : 1. This sec. epistle b. I
8. b. be not ignorant of
14. b. seeing that ye look
15. b. brother Paul hath wri
17. b. seeing ye know these
1 Jn. 3 : 2. b. now we are sons
21. b. if heart condemn us n
4 : 1. b. believe not every spir
7. b. let us love one another
11. b. if God so loved us we
3 Jn. 2. b. I wish above all
5. b. thou doest faithfully
11. b. follow not evil, but go
Jude 3. b. I gave all diligence
17. b. remember words spoke
20. ye b. building yourselves
Re. 20 : 9. compassed b. city

Dearly BELOVED.

See DEARLY.

My BELOVED.

Can. 1 : 14. m. b. is to me a clu
16. art fair, m. b. yea pleasa
2 : 3. as the apple-tree, so is m
8. The voice of m. b.! behold
9. m. b. is like a roe or hart
10. m. b. said unto me, Rise
16. m. b. is mine, I am his, 6
17. turn m. b. and be like a
4 : 16. Let m. b. come into gar
5 : 2. it is voice of m. b., 2 : 8.
4. m. b. put in his hand
5. to open to m. b. | 6. I ope
10. m. b. is white | 16. This is
6 : 2. m. b. is gone
3. I am m. b. m. b. mine, 7 :
7 : 9. like best wine for m. b.
11. Come m. b. let us go into
13. laid up for thee, O m. b.
8 : 14. Make haste m. b.
Is. 5 : 1. a song of m. b. touch
Je. 11 : 15. m. b. to do in my ho
Mat. 3 : 17. This is m. b. Son,
5. Mk. 1 : 11. -9 : 7. Lu. 3 : 2
9 : 35. 2 Pe. 1 : 17.
12 : 18. m. b. in whom my sou
Lu. 20 : 13. I will send m. b. &
Ro. 16 : 8. Greet Amplias m. b. in
9. salute Stachys m. b.
1 Co. 4 : 14. as m. b. sons I wa
17. Tim m. b. son, 2 Ti. 1 : 2
15 : 58. m. b. brethren be ye ste
Ph. 2 : 12. m. b. as ye have obe
Ja. 1 : 16. Do not err, m. b. bre
19. m. b. brethren swift to h
2 : 5. Hearken m. b. hath not

BELSHAZ'ZAR.

Da. 5 : 1. B. the king | 2, 9, 29,
22. O B. hast not humbl. thy he
7 : 1. 1st yr. of B. | 8 : 1. 3d yr. of

BELTESHAZ'ZAR.

Da. 1 : 7. gave to Dan. name of
2 : 26. name was B., 4 : 8, 9,
5 : 12. -10 : 1. O B. 4 : 18.

BEMOAN, ED. ING.

Jb. 42 : 11. they b-d Job, and com
Je. 15 : 5. who b. thee, O Jerus.
16 : 5. lament nor b. them
22 : 10. Weep not for dead, nor
31 : 18. I have heard Ephr. b-g him
48 : 17. All ye about him b. him
Na. 3 : 7. Nineveh, who will b. h

BEN.

1 Ch. 15 : 18. breth. of sec. degree.

BENA'IAH.

2 S. 8 : 18. B. son of Jehoi., 20 : 2
-23 : 20. 1 K. 1 : 8. -2 : 25. 1 C
18 : 17. -27 : 5, 34.
2 S. 23 : 22. thing did B., 1 Ch. 11 : 2
1 K. 1 : 32. king said, Call B.
2 : 35. put B. in Joab's room
4 : 4. B. was over the host
1 Ch. 4 : 36. and B. sons of Sime
| 15 : 24. 2 Ch. 20 : 14.
11 : 31. B. a mighty man
15 : 18. of sec. degree, B., 20. -1

1 Ch 27 : 5. the third captain, B.
14. captain for 11th month, B.
2 Ch. 31 : 13. and B. overseers
Ezr. 10 : 25. B. son of Parosh
30. B. son of Pahath-moab
35. B. son of Bani | 43. B. son of
Eze. 11 : 1. I saw Pelatiah son of B.
13. the son of B. died

BEN-AM'MI.

Ge. 19 : 38. called his name B.

BENCHES.

Eze. 27 : 6. made thy b. of ivory

BEND.

Ps. 11 : 2. wicked b. their bow
64 : 3. who b. bows to shoot
Je. 9 : 3. b. their tongue for lies
46 : 9. Lydians, that b. the bow
50 : 14 th. b. bow shoot at her, 29.
51 : 3. Ag. him let the archer b.
Eze. 17 : 7. vine did b. her roots

BENDETH, ING.

Ps. 58 : 7. when he b. his bow to
Is. 60 : 14. sons of them that afflict-
ed thee shall come b. [archer
Je. 51 : 3. Against him that b. let

BENEATH.

Ex. 20 : 4. in earth b., De. 5 : 8.
32 : 19. he brake tables b. mount
De. 4 : 39. on earth b. is none else
28 : 13. shalt be above and not b.
33 : 13. the deep that coucheth b.
Ezr. 9 : † 13. withheld b. our iniq.
Jb. 18 : 16. roots sh. be dried up b.
Pr. 15 : 24. may depart from hell b.
Is. 14 : 9. hell from b. is moved
51 : 6. lift eyes, look on earth b.
Je. 31 : 37. if founda. searched b.
Mk. 14 : 66. Peter was b. in palace
Jn. 8 : 23. ye are fr. b. I fr. above

BEN'E-BE'RAK.

Jos. 19 : 45. their inheritance B.

BENEFACTORS.

Lu. 22 : 25. exercise authori. are b.

BENEFIT. [Verb.]

Je. 18 : 10. good wherew. I b. them

BENEFIT, S.

1 S. 12 : † 7. reason of all b. of L.
2 Ch. 32 : 25. Hezekiah rendered not
according to b.
Ps. 68 : 19. L. daily loadeth with b.
103 : 2. and forget not all his b.
116 : 12. what render to L. for b.?
2 Co. 1 : 15. to come before that
ye might have a 2d b.
1 Ti. 6 : 2. partakers of the b.
Phm. 14 thy b. not be of necessity

BEN'E-JA'AKAN.

Nu. 33 : 31. pitched in B. | 32.

BENEVOLENCE. [b.

1 Co. 7 : 3. husb. render to wife due

BEN-HA'DAD. [16 : 2.

1 K. 15 : 18. Asa sent to B., 2 Ch.
20 : 2. saith B. Thy silver is mine
16. B. was drinking hims. drunk
20. B. escaped on a horse
32. B. saith, Let me live
2 K. 6 : 24. B. besieged Samaria
8 : 7. B. was sick | 9. thy son B.
13 : 3. deliv. Isr. into hand of B.
25. took out of hand of B.
Je. 49 : 27. palaces of B., Am. 1 : 4.

BEN-HA'IL.

2 Ch. 17 : 7. sent to his princes B.

BEN-HA'NAN.

1 Ch. 4 : 20. sons of Shimon, B.

BEN'INU.

Ne. 10 : 13. their brethren, B.

BEN'JAMIN.

Ge. 35 : 18. father called him B.
24. sons of Rachel, Jo. B., 46 : 19.
42 : 36. and ye will take B. also
43 : 14. send away your bro. and B.
16. when Joseph saw B., 29.
34. B. mess was five times
44 : 12. cup was found in B. sack
45 : 14. fell on his bro. B. neck, 22.
46 : 21. the sons of B., Nu. 26 : 38,
41. 1 Ch. 7 : 6.-8 : 1, 40.-9 : 7.
Ne. 11 : 7.
49 : 27. B. shall ravin as a wolf
Nu. 1 : 11. prince of B. Abidan
De. 27 : 12. stand to bless, Jo. B.
33 : 12. of B. the beloved of Lord
Ju. 5 : 14. B. among thy people
19 : 14. Gibeah wh. belongs to B.
20 : 20. Isr. went to battle ag. B.
35. Lord smote B. before Israel
46. all that fell of B. 25,000
21 : 1. not any give dau. to B., 18.
16. women are destr. out of B.
1 S. 4 : 12. ran a man of B. out
9 : 1. was a man of B. Kish [B.
10 : 2. Rachel's sepul. in border of
13 : 2. in Gibeah of B., 15, 16.-14 :
2 S. 2 : 15. there arose 12 of B. [16.
3 : 19. Abner spake in ears of B.
19 : 17. thous. men of B. with him
21 : 14. bones of Saul buried in B.
1 K. 4 : 18. Shimei officer in B.
1 Ch. 7 : 10. the sons of Bilhan, B.
21 : 6. B. counted not amo. them
27 : 21. over B. was Jaasiel
2 Ch. 17 : 17. of B. Eliada mighty
34 : 32. caused all in B. to stand
Ne. 3 : 23. After him repaired B.
Ps. 68 : 27. is little B. with ruler
80 : 2. Bef. B. and Manas. stir up
Je. 37 : 13. in gate of B., 20 : 2.-38 : 7.
38 : 7. king sitting in gate of B.
Eze. 48 : 23. B. portion | 32. gate of B.
Ho. 5 : 8. cry after thee, O B.
Ob. 19. B. shall possess Gilead
Zch. 14 : 10. inhabited from B. gate

See CHILDREN.

BEN'JAMIN with Judah.

Ju. 10 : 9. passed to fight J. and B
1 K. 12 : 23. Speak to J. and B., 2
Ch. 11 : 3.
1 Ch. 12 : 16. of B. and J. to David
2 Ch. 11 : 12. Rehob. hav. J. and B.
15 : 2. Hear ye me, all J. and B.
8. put idols out of J. and B.
25 : 5. captain's thro. J. and B.
31 : 1. down the altars of J. and B.
34 : 9. money gathered of J. and B.
Ezr. 1 : 5. chief fathers of J. and B.
4 : 1. adversaries of J. and B.
Ne. 11 : 4. dwelt of J. and B.
12 : 34. after them went J. B. and
Eze. 48 : 22. the border of J. and B.

Land of BEN'JAMIN.

Ju. 21 : 21. take wife into l. o. B.
1 S. 9 : 16. man out of l. o. B.
2 Ch. 15 : 8. idols out of l. o. B.
Je. 17 : 26. come fr. l. o. B. bring.
32 : 44. take witnesses in l. o. B.
33 : 13. in the l. o. B. flocks pass
37 : 12. Jere. to go into l. o. B.

Tribe of BEN'JAMIN.

Nu. 1 : 37. of the t. o. B. 35,400
2 : 22. captain of t. o. B., 10 : 24.
13 : 9. Of t. o. B. to spy the land
34 : 21. Of t. o. B. to divide
Jos. 18 : 11. lot of t. o. B. came
21. cities of t. o. B. Jericho
21 : 4. cities to Levites out of t. o.
B., 17. 1 Ch. 6 : 60, 65.
Ju. 20 : 12. sent men thro. t. o. B.
1 S. 9 : 21. least of families of t. o. B.
10 : 20. tribes near t. o. B. taken
Ac. 13 : 21. Saul a man of t. o. B.
Ro. 11 : 1. I am of the t. o. B. Ph. 3 : 5.
Re. 7 : 8. of t. o. B. were sealed

BEN'JAMITE.

Ju. 3 : 15. Ehud a B.
1 S. 9 : 1. Kish a B man of power
21. Saul said, Am not I a B.
2 S. 16 : 11. Shimei a B., 19 : 16. 1
K. 2 : 8. [decai a B.
20 : 1. Sheba a B. | Es. 2 : 5. Mor-

BEN'JAMITES.

Ju. 19 : 16. the men were B.
20 : 35. Israel destr. of B. 25,100
43. Thus they inclosed the B.
1 S. 22 : 7. said Saul, Hear ye B.
1 Ch. 27 : 12. was Abiezer of B.

BE'NO.

1 Ch. 24 : 26, 27. sons of Jaaziah, B.

BENO'NI.

Ge. 35 : 18. called his name B.

BENT. [12.

Ps. 7 : 12. b. his bow, La. 2 : 4.-3 :
37 : 14. b. bow to cast down poor
Is. 5 : 28. arrows sharp, bows b.
21 : 15. they fled from b. bow
Ho. 11 : 7. my peo. are b. to backsli.
Zch. 9 : 13. When I have b. Judah

BEN-ZO'HETH.

1 Ch. 4 : 20. sons of Ishi, B.

BE'ON.

Nu. 32 : 3. B. a land for cattle

BE'OR.

Ge. 36 : 32. Bela son of B., 1 Ch. 1 : 43.
Nu. 22 : 5. Balaam the son of B.,
24 : 3, 15.-31 : 8. De. 23 : 4.
Jos. 13 : 22.-24 : 9. Mi. 6 : 5.

BE'RA.

Ge. 14 : 2. made war with B.

BER'ACHAH.

1 Ch. 12 : 3. B. came to David
2 Ch. 20 : 26. called the valley of B.

BERACHI'AH.

1 Ch. 6 : 39. Asaph son of B.

BERAI'AH.

1 Ch. 8 : 21. B. the sons of Shimhi

BERE'A.

Ac. 17 : 10. sent Paul by night to B.
13. heard Paul preached at B.
20 : 4. Sopater of B. accompanied

BEREAVE.

De. 32 : † 25. sword sh. b. young men
Ec. 4 : 8. for who. b. my soul of good
Je. 15 : 7. will b. th. of chil., 18 : 21.
Eze. 5 : 17. evil beasts shall b. thee
14 : † 15. noisome beasts to b. land
36 : 12. no more b. of men, 14.
Ho. 9 : 12. children, will I b. them

BEREAVED, ETH.

Ge. 42 : 36. Jac. said, Me ye have b.
43 : 14. b. of my chil. I am b.
La. 1 : 20. abroad the sword b-h
Eze. 36 : 13. hast b. thy nations
Ho. 13 : 8. will meet them as bear b.

BERECHI'AH.

1 Ch. 3 : 20.-9 : 16.-15 : 17, 23. 2
Ch. 28 : 12. Ne. 3 : 4, 30.-6 : 18.
Zch. 1 : 1, 7.

BE'RED. [Place, person.]

Ge. 16 : 14. betw. Kadesh and B., 1

BE'RI. [Ch. 7 : 20.

1 Ch. 7 : 36. sons of Zophah, B.

BERI'AH.

Ge. 46 : 17. Nu. 26 : 44, 45. 1 Ch. 7 : 23,
30, 31. -8 : 13, 16. -23 : 10, 11.

BERI'ITES, BE'RITES.

Nu. 26 : 44. family of B. | 2 S. 20 : 14.

BE'RITH.

Ju. 9 : 46. house of their god B.

BERNI'CE.

Ac. 25 : 13. Agrippa and B. came, 23.
26 : 30. the governor and B.

BERO'DACH-BAL'ADAN.

2 K. 20 : 12. B. king of Babylon

BERO'THAH.

Eze. 47 : 16. B. betw. Damascus and

BERO'THAI.

2 S. 8 : 8. B., cities of Hadadezer

BERO'THITE.

1 Ch. 11 : 39. Naharai, B. armour-b.

BERRIES.

Is. 17 : 6. two or three b. in the top
Ja. 3 : 12. can fig-tree bear olive b.

BERYL.

Ex. 28 : 20. fourth row a b., 39 : 13.
Can. 5 : 14. hands as rings with b.
Eze. 1 : 16. work like colour of b.,
28 : 13. diamond, b. onyx [10 : 9.
Da. 10 : 6. His body was like b.
Re. 21 : 20. eighth founda. was b.

BESAI.

Eze. 2 : 49. chil. of B. | Ne. 7 : 52.

BESEECH.
Ex. 33 : 18. I **b.** shew thy glory
Nu. 12 : 11. I **b.** lay not her sin
13. Heal her now, O Lord, I **b.**
14 : 17. I **b.** let power of my L.
Jb. 42 : 4. Hear, I **b.** and I will
Ps. 80 : 14. Return, we **b.** O God
116 : 4. I **b.** thee deliver my soul
118 : 25. Save I **b.** O L. send pros.
119 : 108. Accept I **b.** free-will off.
Is. 64 : 9. see, we **b.**, we thy people
Je. 38 : 20. Obey, I **b.** voice of L.
Am. 7 : 2. O L. forgive, I **b.** thee
Jon. 1 : 14. said, We **b.** thee, O L.
4 : 3. O L. take, I **b.** my life
Mal. 1 : 9. **b.** God he be gracious
Mk. 7 : 32. they **b.** him to put hand
Lu. 8 : 28. Jesus I **b.** torment not
9 : 38. I **b.** thee look on my son
Ac. 21 : 39. I **b.** thee suffer me to
26 : 3. I **b.** thee to hear me patient.
Ro. 12 : 1. I **b.** by mercies of God
15 : 30. I **b.** you brethren, 16 : 17.
1 Co. 1 : 10.-16 : 15. He. 13 : 22.
1 Co. 4 : 16. I **b.** be ye followers
2 Co. 2 : 8. I **b.** confirm your love
5 : 20. as tho. G. did **b.** you by us
6 : 1. we **b.** rece. not grace in vain
10 : 1. I Paul **b.** you by meekness
Ga. 4 : 12. I **b.** you be as I am
Ep. 4 : 1. I **b.** you to walk
Ph. 4 : 2. I **b.** Euodias and **b.** Syn.
1 Th. 4 : 1. we **b.** you brethren, 10.
-5 : 12. 2 Th. 2 : 1.
Phm. 9. for love's sake I **b.** thee
10. I **b.** thee for my son Onesim.
He. 13 : 19. I **b.** you to do this
1 Pe. 2 : 11. I **b.** you as strangers
2 Jn. 5. now I **b.** thee, lady, not
See BRETHREN.

BESEECHING.
Mat. 8 : 5. centurion **b.** him, Lu. 7 : 3.
Mk. 1 : 40. leper to him **b.** him

BESET.
Ju. 19 : 22. sons of Belial **b.**, 20 : 5.
Ps. 22 : 12. bulls of Bashan **b.** me
139 : 5. **b.** me behind and before
Ho. 7 : 2. their doings have **b.** them
He. 12 : 1. sin doth so easily **b.** us

BESIDE.
Ge. 26 : 1. a famine **b.** first famine
Le. 18 : 18. **b.** other in her life
23 : 38. **b.** sabbaths, **b.** gifts, **b.** vows, **b.** free-will offerings
Nu. 5 : 20. lain with thee **b.** hush.
6 : 21. **b.** that his hand shall get
11 : 6. nothing **b.** this manna
28 : 23. **b.** burnt-offering, 29 : 6.
De. 29 : 1. **b.** cov. made in Horeb
Jos. 7 : 2. Ai wh. is **b.** Beth-aven
22 : 19. an altar **b.** altar of L., 29.
Ju. 6 : 37. dry on all the earth **b.**
11 : 34. **b.** her Jeph. nei. son nor
1 S. 19 : 3. I will stand **b.** my fa.
1 K. 10 : 13. **b.** that Sol. gave her
2 K. 21 : 16. **b.** his sin he made Jud.
Ps. 23 : 2. leadeth **b.** still waters
Can. 1 : 8. feed thy kids **b.** tents
Is. 32 : 20. sow **b.** all waters
56 : 8. I will gather oth. **b.** those
Mat. 14 : 21. five thousand **b.** women and children, 15 : 38.
25 : 20. I have gained **b.** them five
22. two other talents **b.** them
Lu. 16 : 26. **b.** all this, betw. us and
24 : 21. **b.** all this, to-day is third
2 Co. 11 : 28. **b.** those things th. are

BESIDE,
With **self** or **selves.**
Mk. 3 : 21. said, he is **b.** himself
Ac. 26 : 24. Paul, thou art **b.** thys.
2 Co. 5 : 13. whether we be **b.** ours.

BESIDES.
Ge. 19 : 12. Hast thou here any **b.**
1 K. 22 : 7. proph. of L. **b.**, 2 Ch. 18 : 6.
1 Co. 1 : 16. **b.** I know not whether
Phm. 19. owest me thine own self **b.**

BESIEGE.
De. 20 : 12. war ag. thee, then **b.**
19. When **b.** city long time
28 : 52. he shall **b.** thee in gates
1 S. 23 : 8. to Keilah to **b.** David
1 K. 8 : 37. if enemies **b.**, 2 Ch. 6 : 28.
2 K. 24 : 11. his servant did **b.** it
Is. 21 : 2. O Elam, **b.** O Media
Je. 21 : 4. Chaldeans wh. **b.** you, 9

BESIEGED.
2 K. 6 : 25. **b.** it until ass's head
19 : 24. with feet I have dried up all rivers of **b.** pl. Is. 37 : 25.
25 : 2. city was **b.**, Je. 52 : 5.
Ec. 9 : 14. a great king **b.** it
Is. 1 : 8. Zion is left as a **b.** city
Eze. 4 : 3. it shall be **b.**
6 : 12. he **b.** shall die by famine

BESODEI'AH.
Ne. 3 : 6. Meshullam son of B.

BESOM.
Is. 14 : 23. sweep it with **b.** of destr.

BE'SOR.
1 S. 30 : 9. men to brook B. | 10, 21.

BESOUGHT.
Ge. 42 : 21. he **b.** us we not hear
Ex. 32 : 11. Moses **b.** L., De. 3 : 23.
2 S. 12 : 16. Da. **b.** G. for the child
1 K. 13 : 6. man of God **b.** the L.
2 K. 1 : 13. cap. fell on his knees **b.**
13 : 4. Jehoahaz **b.** L., L. heark.
2 Ch. 33 : 12. Manas. in afflic. **b.** L.
Ezr. 8 : 23. we fasted and **b.** our G.
Es. 8 : 3. **b.** him with tears to put
Je. 26 : 19. did not Hez. fear, **b.** L.
Mat. 8 : 31. so the devils **b.** him, Mk. 5 : 10, 12. Lu. 8 : 31, 32.
34. **b.** him to depart, Lu. 8 : 37.
14 : 36. **b.** that th. touch, Mk. 6 : 56.
15 : 23. **b.** saying, Send her
18 : 29. **b.** saying, Have patience
18 : † 26. serv. **b.** L. have patience
Mk. 5 : 23. Jairus **b.** him, Lu. 8 : 41.
7 : 26. **b.** that he cast devil out of
8 : 22. blind, **b.** him to touch
Lu. 4 : 38. they **b.** him for her
5 : 12. **b.** saying, Lord if thou
7 : 4. **b.** saying, he was worthy
8 : 38. **b.** that he be with him
9 : 40. **b.** disciples to cast out
11 : 37. Pharisee **b.** him to dine
Jn. 4 : 40. Samari. **b.** that he tarry
47. nobleman of Capern. **b.** him
19 : 31. **b.** that legs be broken
38. **b.** Pilate he might take body
Ac. 13 : 42. Gent. **b.** these words be
16 : 15. Lydia **b.** us, saying, If ye
39. magistrates **b.** and bro. th. out
21 : 12. we **b.** him not to go to Jerus
27 : 33. Paul **b.** th. to take meat
2 Co. 12 : 8. For this I **b.** L. thrice
1 Ti. 1 : 3. **b.** thee to abide at

BEST.
Ge. 43 : 11. take of **b.** fruits in land
47 : 6. in **b.** of land make fa. dwell,
Ex. 22 : 5. of **b.** make restitut.
Nu. 18 : 12. all the **b.** of oil, **b.** of
29. heave-offering be of **b.**
36 : 6. marry whom they think **b.**
De. 23 : 16. he dwell it likes him **b.**
1 S. 8 : 14. take **b.** of your viney
15 : 9. Saul spared **b.** of sheep, 15.
2 S. 18 : 4. what seemeth you **b.** I will do
1 K. 10 : 18. overlaid with **b.** gold
2 K. 10 : 3. look out **b.** of master's sons
Es. 2 : 9. her unto **b.** place
Ps. 39 : 5. man at **b.** state vanity
Can. 7 : 9. roof of mouth like **b.** wine
Eze. 31 : 16. choice and **b.** of Leb.
Mi. 7 : 4. **b.** of them is as a brier
Lu. 15 : 22. Bring forth the **b.** robe
1 Co. 12 : 31. covet earnest. **b.** gifts

BESTEAD.
Is. 8 : 21. pass thro. it hardly **b.**

BESTIR.
2 S. 5 : 24. hearest sound then **b.** thyself

BESTOW.
Ex. 32 : 29. may **b.** on you a bless.
De. 14 : 26. **b.** money for what thy soul
2 Ch. 24 : 7. they did **b.** on Baalim
Ezr. 7 : 20. shalt have occasion to **b.** **b.** it of king's treasure-ho.
Lu. 12 : 17. I no room to **b.** my fruits
18. there will I **b.** all my fruits
1 Co. 12 : 23. we **b.** more honour
13 : 3. tho. I **b.** all my goods to feed

BESTOWED.
1 K. 10 : 26. **b.** in cities, 2 Ch. 9 : 25.
2 K. 5 : 24. Gehazi **b.** them in house
1 Ch. 29 : 25. L. **b.** upon Sol. royal maj.
Is. 63 : 7. acc. to all Lord **b.** on us
Jn. 4 : 38. reap that ye **b.** no lab.
Ro. 16 : 6. Greet Mary who **b.** much
1 Co. 15 : 10. grace **b.** upon me not in vain
2 Co. 1 : 11. gift **b.** upon us by many persons
8 : 1. grace **b.** on the churches
Ga. 4 : 11. lest I **b.** labour in vain
1 Jn. 3 : 1. manner of love Fa. **b.**

BE'TAH.
2 S. 8 : 8. B. cities of Hadadezer

BETAKE.
Is. 14 : † 32. poor of peo. **b.** thems.

BE'TEN.
Jos. 19 : 25. their border was B.

BETHAB'ARA.
Jn. 1 : 28. in B. beyond Jordan

BETH'ANATH.
Jos. 19 : 38. fenced cities, B. Ju. 1 : 33.

BETH'ANOTH.
Jos. 15 : 59. in the mountains, B.

BETH'ANY.
Mat. 21 : 17. Jes. went into B., 26 : 6. Mk. 11 : 1, 11.-14 : 3. Lu. 19 : 29. Jn. 12 : 1.
Mk. 11 : 12. when come from B.
Lu. 24 : 50. led them out far as B.
Jn. 11 : 1. named Lazarus of B.
18. B. was nigh unto Jerusalem

BETH-AR'ABAH.
Jos. 15 : 61. in wilderness B., 6.-18 : 22.

BETH'ARAM.
Jos. 13 : 27. in the valley B.

BETHAR'BEL.
Ho. 10 : 14. B. in the day of battle

BETH-A'VEN.
Jos. 7 : 2. Ai, which is beside B.
1 S. 14 : 23. battle passed over to B.
Ho. 4 : 15. nor go ye up to B.
5 : 8. cry aloud at B. after thee
10 : 5. fear, because of calves of B.

BETH-AZ'MAVETH.
Ne. 7 : 28. the men of B., 42.

BETH-BAAL-ME'ON.
Jos. 13 : 17. cities in the plain B.

BETH-BA'RAH.
Ju. 7 : 24. take waters unto B.

BETH-BIR'EI.
1 Ch. 4 : 31. they dwelt at B.

BETH'-CAR.
1 S. 7 : 11. smote them under B.

BETH-DA'GON.
Jos. 15 : 41. cities B., 19 : 27.

BETH-DIBLATHA'IM.
Je. 48 : 22. judgm. is come upon B

BETH'-EL.
Ge. 12 : 8. tent having B. on west
28 : 19. called the place B., 35 : 15
31 : 13. I am God of B. where thou
35 : 1. go to B., 3. | 6. Jacob to B
Jos. 16 : 2. lot of Jo. goeth from B
Ju. 1 : 22. house of Jo. went ag. B.
4 : 5. dwelt betw. Ramah and B.
21 : 19. in a place on north of B.
1 S. 7 : 16. went fr. year to yr. to B.
10 : 3. three men going up to B.
13 : 2. two thousand with Saul in B
30 : 27. a present to them in B.
1 K. 12 : 29. set one calf in B., 33.
32. he placed in B. the priests
13 : 1. there came a man of G. to B
4. had cried ag. altar in B., 32.

1 K. 13 : 11. dwelt an old proph. in B.
2 K. 2 : 2. the L. hath sent me to B.
23. and he went up unto B.
10 : 29. Jehu dep. not fr. calves in B.
17 : 28. one of priests dwelt in B.
23 : 4. he burnt carried ashes to B.
15. the altar at B. Josiah brake
17. who proclaim. ag. altar of B.
19. acc. to all he had done in B.
Ezr. 2 : 28. the men of B., Ne. 7 : 32
Je. 48 : 13. Isr. was ashamed of B.
Ho. 10 : 15. So shall B. do to you
12 : 4. he found him in B. there he
Am. 3 : 14. I will visit altars of B.
4 : 4. Come to B. and transgress
5 : 5. seek not B. for B. sh. come
6. lest be none to quench it in B.
7 : 13. but prophesy not more at B.

BETH'-ELITE.

1 K. 16 : 34. Hiel B. did build Jeri.

BETH-E'MEK.

Jos. 19 : 27. north side of B.

BE'THER.

Can. 2 : 17. hart on mountains of B.

BETHES'DA.

Jn. 5 : 2. there is a pool B.

BETH-E'ZEL.

Mi. 1 : 11. not in mourning of B.

BETH-GA'DER.

1 Ch. 2 : 51. Hareph father of B.

BETH-GA'MUL.

Je. 48 : 23. judgm. is come upon B.

BETH-HAC'CEREM.

Ne. 3 : 14. ruler of part of B.
Je. 6 : 1. set sign of fire in B.

BETH-HA'RAN.

Nu. 32 : 36. built B. fenced cities

BETH-HOG'LA, H.

Jos. 15 : 6. border to B. | 18 : 19, 21.

BETH-HO'RON.

Jos. 10 : 11. going down to B. the L.
16 : 3. unto coast of B. | 5.
18 : 13. near hill on south of B. [68.
21 : 22. gave Levites B., 1 Ch. 6 :
1 S. 13 : 18. company turned to B.
1 K. 9 : 17. Sol. built B., 2 Ch. 8 : 5.
1 Ch. 7 : 24. dau. Sherah built B.
2 Ch. 25 : 13. Samaria even unto B.

BETHINK.

1 K. 8 : 47. if b. thems., 2 Ch. 6 : 37.

BETH-JES'HIMOTH, and BETH-JES'IMOTH.

Nu. 33 : 49. Jos. 12 : 3.-13 : 20. Eze 25 : 9.

BETH-LEB'AOTH.

Jos. 19 : 6. in their inheritance B.

BETH'LEHEM.

Ge. 35 : 19. died in way to B., 48 : 7.
Jos. 19 : 15. B. cities of Zebulun
Ju. 12 : 8. Ibzan of B. judged Isr.
Ru. 1 : 19. two went till came to B.
2 : 4. Boaz came from B.
4 : 11. be famous in B.
1 S. 16 : 4. Samuel came to B.
20 : 6. leave to run to B., 28.
2 S. 23 : 15. give me water of well of B., 1 Ch. 11 : 17.
1 Ch. 2 : 51. Salma father of B., 54.
4 : 4. of Ephratah, father of B.
2 Ch. 11 : 6. Rehob. built B. and
Ezr. 2 : 21. chil. of B., Ne. 7 : 26.
Je. 41 : 17. of Chimham by B.
Mat. 2 : 1. Jesus was born in B., 5.
6. thou B. in land of Juda
16. Herod slew all children in B.
Lu. 2 : 4. Joseph went up to B.
15. Let us go to B. and see
Jn. 7 : 42. Christ cometh out of B.

BETH'-LEHEM-EPH'RA-TAH.

Mi. 5 : 2. B. though thou be little

BETH'-LEHEMITE.

1 S. 16 : 1. Jesse B., 18. -17 : 58.
2 S. 21 : 19. B. slew Goliath's bro.

BETH'-LEHEM-JU'DAH.

Ju. 17 : 7. a Levite of B., 8, 9.
19 : 1. a concubine out of B.
Ju. 19 : 18. passing fr. B. and I to B.
Ru. 1 : 1. Elimelech of B. went to
1 S. 17 : 12. an Ephrathite of B.

BETH-MA'ACHAH.

2 S. 20 : 14. went through to B., 15.

BETH-MAR'CABOTH.

Jos. 19 : 5. cities B. | 1 Ch. 4 : 31.

BETH-ME'ON.

Je. 48 : 23. judgment come upon B.

BETH-NIM'RAH.

Nu. 32 : 36. cities B. | Jos. 13 : 27.

BETH-PA'LET, or PHE'-LET. [11 : 26.

Jos. 15 : 27. utterm. cities, B., Ne.

BETH'-PAZ'ZEZ.

Jos. 19 : 21. border was toward B.

BETH-PE'OR.

De. 3 : 29. in the valley over ag. B.
4 : 46. Moses spake over ag. B.
34 : 6. buried Moses over ag. B.
Jos. 13 : 20. B. and all cities of plain

BETH'-PHAGE.

Mat. 21 : 1. when come to B., Mk. 11 : 1. Lu. 19 : 29.

BETH'-RAPHA.

1 Ch. 4 : 12. Eshton begat B.

BETH'-REHOB.

Ju. 18 : 28. in valley of B. | 2 S. 10 : [6.

BETHSAI'DA.

Mat. 11 : 21. woe B., Lu. 10 : 13
Mk. 6 : 45. disciples to go to B.
8 : 22. cometh to B. they bring
Lu. 9 : 10. a desert belonging to B.
Jn. 1 : 44. Philip was of B., 12 : 21.

BETH'-SHAN.

1 S. 31 : 10. Saul's body to wall of B. | 12. 2 S. 21 : 12.

BETH-SHE'AN.

Jos. 17 : 11. Manasseh had B. and towns, 16.
Ju. 1 : 27. 1 K. 4 : 12. 1 Ch. 7 : 29.

BETH'-SHEMESH.

Jos. 15 : 10. the border of Jud. to B.
19 : 22. Issa.'s coast reacheth to B.
38. and B. cities of Naphtali
21 : 16. Judah gave to Levites B.
Ju. 1 : 33. not drive inhab. of B.
1 S. 6 : 9. goeth by way of B.
12. the kine took way to B.
19. he smote the men of B.
1 K. 4 : 9. son of Dekar was in B.
2 K. 14 : 11. kings looked in the face at B., 2 Ch. 25 : 21.
2 Ch. 28 : 18. the Philis. had tak. B.
Je. 43 : 13. shall break images of B.

BETH'-SHEMITE.

1 S. 6 : 14. field of Joshua the B., 18.

BETH-SHIT'TAH.

Ju. 7 : 22. the host fled to B.

BETH-TAP'PUAH.

Jos. 15 : 53. in mountains, B.

BETHU'EL.

Ge. 22 : 22. bare to Nahor, B. [20.
23. B. begat Rebek., 24 : 15.-25 :
24 : 24. I am the dau. of B., 47
50. Laban and B. answered
28 : 2. go to the house of B. | 5.

BETHU'EL, or BE'THUL.

Jos. 19 : 4. chil. of Sim. had B. | 1 Ch. [4 : 30.

BETH'ZUR.

Jos. 15 : 58. cities in mountains, B.
1 Ch. 2 : 45. 2 Ch. 11 : 7. Ne. 3 : 16.

BETIMES.

Ge. 26 : 31. rose up b. and sware
2 Ch. 36 : 15. messengers rising b.
Jb. 8 : 5. wouldest seek unto G. b.
24 : 5. as asses rising b. for prey
Pr. 13 : 24. chasteneth him b.

BET'ONIM.

Jos. 13 : 26. fr. Heshbon under B.

BETRAY.

1 Ch. 12 : 17. if come to b. me
Mat. 24 : 10. shall b. one another
26 : 16. sought opportunity to b. him, Mk. 14 : 11. Lu. 22 : 6.
21. I say one of you shall b. me,
23. Mk. 14 : 18. Jn. 13 : 21.
Mat. 26 : 46. he is at hand doth b. me
Mk. 13 : 12. brother shall b. brother
14 : 10. prs. to b. him unto them
Lu. 22 : 4. how he might b. him
Jn. 6 : 64. Jesus knew who should b. him, 71.-12 : 4.-13 : 11.
71. he it was that should b. him
12 : 4. Simon's son wh. sho. b. him
13 : 2. into heart of Judas to b. him

BETRAYED. [8 : 19.

Mat. 10 : 4. Judas who b. him, Mk.
17 : 22. Son of man shall be b.,
20 : 18.-26 : 2, 45. Mk. 14 : 41.
26 : 24. woe by wh. Son of man is b., Mk. 14 : 21. Lu. 22 : 22.
25. which b. him ans., 27 : 3.
48. that b. gave sign, Mk. 14 : 44.
27 : 4. in that I b. innocent blood
Lu. 21 : 16. be b. both by parents
Jn. 18 : 2. Judas wh. b. him knew
5. which b. him stood with them
1 Co. 11 : 23. night he was b. took

BETRAYERS.

Ac. 7 : 52. One, of whom ye the b.

BETRAYEST, ETH.

Mk. 14 : 42. he that b. me is at hand
Lu. 22 : 21. hand of him that b. me
48. Judas, b. thou with a kiss?
Jn. 21 : 20. which is he th. b. thee

BETROTH.

De. 28 : 30. b. a wife another sh. lie
Ho. 2 : 19. b. thee in righteousn.
20. I will b. thee to me in faithful.

BETROTHED.

Ex. 21 : 8. master who b. her
9. if he b. her unto his son [28.
22 : 16. entice maid not b., De. 22 :
Le. 19 : 20. lieth with woman b.
De. 20 : 7. who hath b. a wife
22 : 23. if find virgin b. and lie
25. find b. damsel in field
27. b. damsel cried, was none

BETTER.

Ge. 29 : 19. b. I give her to thee
Ex. 14 : 12. b. to have served Egyp.
Nu. 14 : 3. not b. to return to Egypt
Ju. 8 : 2. gleanings b. than vintage
11 : 25 nor thou b. than Balak
18 : 19. b. be priest unto one man
1 S. 1 : 8. am I b. than ten sons?
27 : 1. nothing b. than to Philis.
1 K. 1 : 47. G. make name of k. Sol. b.
2 : 32. fell upon two men b. than he
19 : 4. I am not b. than my fathers
21 : 2. give thee a b. vineyard
2 K. 5 : 12. rivers of Damascus b.
2 Ch. 21 : 13. slain breth. b. th. thys.
Ps. 69 : 31. please L. b. than an ox
Ec. 2 : 24. nothing b. than to eat
3 : 22. nothing b. than to rejoice in
4 : 3. b. is he than both they
9. two are b. | 6 : 11. is man b.? 8 :
7 : 10. that former days were b. [15.
11. wisd. good as inheri. yea b. too
10 : 11. serp. bite, babbler is no b.
Is. 56 : 5. give a name b. than of sons
La. 4 : 9. they that be slain are b.
Ez. 36 : 11. settle you, and do b. [b.
Da. 1 : 20. he found them ten times
Ho. 2 : 7. then was it b. with me
Am. 6 : 2. b. than these kingdoms?
Na. 3 : 8. Art thou b. than No?
Mat. 6 : 26. fowls of the air, Are ye not b. than they? Lu. 12 : 24.
12 : 12. is a man b. than a sheep?
18 : 6. it were b. for him that a millstone, Mk. 9 : 42. Lu. 17 : 2.
Ro. 3 : 9. are we b. than they?
1 Co. 7 : 38. not in marriage doth b.
8 : 8. neither if we eat are we b.
9 : 15. b. for me to die than make
11 : 17. come together not for b.
Ph. 2 : 3. esteem other b. than hims.
He. 1 : 4. made b. than the angels
6 : 9. persuaded b. things of you
7 : 7. the less is blessed of the b.
19. but bringing in of a b. hope

He. 7 : 22. surety of a b. testament
8 : 6. mediator of a b. covenant
established on b. promises
9 : 23. heav. things with b. sacri.
10 : 34. in heaven a b. substance
11 : 16. they desire a b. country
35. might obtain a b. resurrection
40. God provided some b. thing
12 : 24. b. things than that of Abel
2 Pe. 2 : 21. b. not to have kn. way

BETTER is.

Pr. 15 : 16. b. i. little with fear
17. b. i. dinner of herbs where
16 : 8. b. i. a little with righte.
16. much b. i. it to get wisdom
17 : 1. b. i. a dry morsel [28 : 6.
19 : 1. b.i. poor walks in integrity,
27 : 10. b. i. a neighbour near
Ec. 4 : 6. b. i. a handful with
13. b. i. a poor wise child than
6 : 9. b. i. the sight of the eyes
7 : 8. b. i. end than beginning
Can. 4 : 10. b. i. thy love than

Is BETTER, or is it BETTER.

Ju. 9 : 2. Whether i. b. all reign
18 : 19. i. i. b. to be priest to one
Ru. 4 : 15. thy daughter i.b. to thee
1 S. 15 : 22. to obey i. b. than sac
28. neighb. that i. b. than thou
2 S. 17 : 14. counsel of Hushai i. b.
Es. 1 : 19. ano. that i. b. than she
Ps. 37 : 16. little righte. hath i. b.
63 : 3. loving-k. i. b. than life
84 : 10. a day in thy courts i. b.
than a thousand
119 : 72. law i. b. to me than gold
Pr. 3 : 14. merch. of wisdom i. b.
8 : 11. wisdom i. b. than rubies
19. My fruit i. b. than gold
12 : 9. i. b. than he that honour.
16 : 32. that is slow to anger i. b.
19 : 22. poor man i. b. than liar
22 : † 1. favour i. b. than silver
27 : 5. rebuke i. b. than love
Ec. 6 : 3. an untimely birth i. b.
7 : 1. good name i. b. than oint.
3. Sorrow i. b. than laughter, by
sadness heart i. made b.
8. the patient in spirit i. b.
9 : 4. a living dog i. b. than a
16. Wisdom i. b. than strength
18. Wisdom i. b. than weapons
Can. 1 : 2. thy love i. b. than wine
Lu. 5 : 39. the old i. b.
Ph. 1 : 23. with Christ wh. i. far b.

It is BETTER, or BETTER it is.

Ge. 29 : 19. i. i. b. I give her to thee
2 S. 18 : 3. i. i. b. thou succour us
Ps. 118 : 8. i.i.b. to trust in L., 9.
Pr. 16 : 19. b. i. i. to be humble
21 : 9. i. i. b. to dwell in, 25 : 24.
19. i. i. b. to dwell in wilderness
25 : 7. b. i. i. it be said, Come
Ec. 5 : 5. b. i. i. thou sho. not vow
7 : 2. i. i. b. to go to house of
5. i. i. b. to hear rebuke of
Jon. 4 : 3. i. i. b. for me to die, 8.
Mat. 18 : 8. i. i. b. to enter into
life halt, 9. Mk. 9 : 43, 45, 47.
1 Co. 7 : 9. i. i. b. to marry than
1 Pe. 3 : 17.i.i.b. ye suffer for well-d

BETTERED.

Mk. 5 : 26. she was nothing b. but

BETWEEN.

Ge. 1 : † 4. God divided b. light and
† 14. to divide b. light and darkn.
3 : 15. will put enmity b. thy seed
9 : 16. covenant b. God and every
15 : 17. lamp passed b. pieces
49 : 10. nor lawgiver from b. feet
Ex. 8 : 23. division b. my people
12 : † 6. kill it b. ev-g Nu. : 9 † 3.
13 : 9. a memorial b. thine eyes,
16. De. 6 : 8.–11 : 18.
18 : 16. I judge b. one and another
Ex. 26 : 33. vail sh. divide b. holy and
Nu. 11 : 33. flesh was b. their teeth
28 : † 4. other lamb offer b. 2 eve.
De. 17 : 8. b. bl., b. plea, b. stroke
33 : 12. dwell b. his shoulders
Ju. 4 : 5. Deb. dwelt b. Ramah
1 S. 7 : 14. peace b. Isr. and Amor.
2 S. 19 : 35. b. good and evil, 1 K.
3 : 9.
1 K. 18 : 21. halt ye b. two opinions
Pr. 18 : 18. parteth b. the mighty
Je. 34 : 18. pass. b. parts of calf, 19.
Eze. 34 : 17. I judge b. cattle b.
Ho. 2 : 2. adulteries fr. b. breasts
Jo. 2 : 17. priests weep b. porch
Zch. 11 : 14. break brotherh. b. Jud.
Mat. 18 : 15. tell him his fault b. thee
23 : 35. ye slew b. temple and
Lu. 11 : 51. b. the altar and temple
16 : 26. b. us and you great gulf
23 : 12. at enmity b. themselves
Jn. 3 : 25. b. John's disci. and Jews
Ac. 12 : 6. sleeping b. two soldiers
13 : † 42. be preached sabbath b.
15 : 9. no diff. b. us and them
26 : 31. they talked b. themselves
Ro. 1 : 24. their own bodies b. thems.
10 : 12. no differ. b. Jew and Gr.
1 Co. 6 : 5. able to judge b. breth.
7 : 34. differ. b. wife and a virgin
1 Ti. 2 : 5. one mediator b. G. and

BETWIXT.

Jb. 36 : 32. cloud that cometh b.
Can. 1 : 13. all night b. my breasts
Ph. 1 : 23. I am in a strait b. two

BEU'LAH.

Is. 62 : 4. call thy land B., for Lord

BEWAIL.

Le. 10 : 6. b. burning L. hath kind.
De. 21 : 13. b. her fa. and mother
Ju. 11 : 37. and b. my virginity, 38.
Is. 16 : 9. b. with weeping of Jazer
2 Co. 12 : 21. b. many who have sin.
Re. 18 : 9. shall b. her when they

BEWAILED, ETH.

Ju. 11 : 38. b. her virgin. upon mts.
Je. 4 : 31. dau. of Zion that b-h hers.
Lu. 8 : 52. all wept and b. her
23 : 27. of women which b. him

BEWARE.

Ge. 24 : 6. b. bring not my son
Ex. 23 : 21. b. of him, obey his
De. 6 : 12. b. lest forget L., 8 : 11.
15 : 9. b. be not wicked thought
Ju. 13 : 4. b. drink no wine, 13.
2 S. 18 : 12. b. none touch young
2 K. 6 : 9. b. thou pass not such pl.
Jb. 36 : 18. b. lest he take thee away
Pr. 19 : 25. and the simple will b.
Is. 36 : 18. b. lest Hez. persuade you
Mat. 7 : 15. b. of false prophets
10 : 17. But b. of men
16 : 6. b. of leaven of Pharisees, 11.
Mk. 8 : 15. Lu. 12 : 1.
Mk. 12 : 38. b. of scribes, Lu. 20 : 46.
Lu. 12 : 15. b. of covetousness
Ac. 13 : 40. b. lest that come which
Ph. 3 : 2. b. of dogs, b. of evil workers, b. of concision
Col. 2 : 8. b. lest any man spoil you
2 Pe. 3 : 17. b. lest being led away

BEWITCHED.

Ac. 8 : 9. Simon b. the people, 11.
Ga. 3 : 1. who hath b. you

BEWRAY.

Is. 16 : 3. b. not him that wander.

BEWRAYETH.

Pr. 27 : 16. oint. of his hand b. its.
29 : 24. heareth cursing, b. it not
Mat. 26 : 73. thy speech b. thee

BEYOND.

Nu. 22 : 18. Balaam said, I cannot
go b. word of Lord, 24 : 13.
De. 30 : 13. nor is it b. the sea
1 S. 20 : 22. arrows b. thee, 36, 37.
2 S. 10 : 16. b. the river, 1 K. 14 :
15. 1 Ch. 19 : 16. Ezr. 4 : 17,
20.–6 : 6, 8.–7 : 21, 25. Ne. 2 : 7,
9. Is. 7 : 20.–18 : 1. Zph. 3 : 10.
2 Ch. 20 : 2. mult. b. sea, Je. 25 : 22.
Mk. 6 : 51. amazed b. meas., 7 : 37.
2 Co. 8 : 3. b. their power willing
10 : 14. stretch not b. measure
16. preach gospel in regions b.
Ga. 1 : 13. b. measure I persecuted
1 Th. 4 : 6. man go b. and defraud

BEYOND Jordan.

See JORDAN.

BE'ZAI.

Ezr. 2 : 17. Ne. 7 : 23.–10 : 18.

BEZAL'EEL.

Ex. 31 : 2. have called by name B.
son of Uri, 35 : 30. 1 Ch. 2 : 20.
36 : 1. Then wrought B. and Aholiab
37 : 1. And B. made the ark
38 : 22. B. made all Lord com-d
2 Ch. 1 : 5. brazen altar that B.
Ezr. 10 : 30. sons of Pahath-m., B

BE'ZEK.

Ju. 1 : 4. they slew in B. 10.000, 5.
1 S. 11 : 8. numbered Israel in B.

BE'ZER. [Person, place.]

De. 4 : 43. Jos. 20 : 8.–21 : 36. 1 Ch.
6 : 78.
1 Ch. 7 : 37. sons of Zophah, B.

BIBBER. See WINE.

BICH'RI.

2 S. 20 : 1. Sheba son of B , 2, 6, 7,
10, 13, 21.
22. cut off head of son of B.

BID.

Nu. 15 : 38. b. them make fringes
Jos. 6 : 10. until day I b. you shout
1 S. 9 : 27. b. servant pass before
2 S. 2 : 26. how long ere b. peo. ret.
2 K. 4 : 24. slack not except I b.
5 : 13. if had b. thee do gr. thing
10 : 5. we will do all thou sh b. us
Jon. 3 : 2. preaching that I b. thee
Zph. 1 : 7. Lord hath b. his guests
Mat. 14 : 28. b. me come on water
22 : 9. as ye find b. to marriage
23 : 3. what they b. you observe,
that observe and do
Lu. 9 : 61. let me first b. farewell
10 : 40. b. her that she help me
14 : 12. lest they also b. thee again
1 Co. 10 : 27. that believe not b. you
2 Jn. 10. nor b. him God speed, 11.

BIDDEN.

1 S. 9 : 13. afterw. they eat th. be b.
22. among them that were b.
2 S. 16 : 11. let him curse, L. hath b.
Mat. 1 : 24. Jo. did as angel b. him
22 : 3. to call them b. to wedding
4. Tell them b. I have prepared
8. they who were b. not worthy
Lu. 7 : 39. when Pharisee who had
b. him
14 : 7. put parable to those b.
8. art b. lest a more hon. be b.
10. art b. sit in lowest room
17. say to them b. Come
24. none of men b. sh. taste of sup.

BIDDETH, BIDDING.

1 S. 22 : 14. goeth at thy b. and
2 Jn. 11. he that b. him God speed

BID'KAR.

2 K. 9 : 25. Jehu said to B. capt.

BIER.

2 S. 3 : 31. David followed the b.
Lu. 7 : 14. he came and touched b

BIG'THA.

Es. 1 : 10. B. of 7 chamberlains

BIG'THAN,

Es. 2 : 21. B. to lay hand on king

BIG'THANA.

Es. 6 : 2. Mordecai had told of B.

BIG'VAI.

Ezr. 2 : 2. went out of captiv. B. | 14
Ezr. 8 : 14. Ne. 7 : 7. 19.–10 : 16.

BIL'DAD.

Jb. 2 : 11. B. the Shuhite, 8 : 1
18 : 1.–25 : 1.–42 : 9.

BIL'EAM.
5: 70. B. with suburbs
BIL'GAH.
24: 14. Ne. 12: 5, 18.
BIL'GAI.
: 8. B. these were priests
BIL'HAH.
: 29. Laban gave Rachel B.
. Behold my maid B., 4.
. conceived, 7.
2. Reuben lay with B.
he sons of B. 37: 2.-46: 25.
Ch. 7: 13.
4: 29: his sons dwelt at B.
BIL'HAN.
: 27. 1 Ch. 1: 42.-7: 10.
BILL.
: 1. b. of divorcement, Is.
: 1. Je. 3: 8. Mk. 10: 4.
i: 6. Take thy b. and write,
See DIVORCE. [7.
BILLOWS.
7. b. gone over me, Jon. 2: 3.
BIL'SHAN.
: 2. B. came with Zeruh., Ne.
BIM'HAL. [7: 7.
7: 33. sons of Japhlet, B.
BIND. [39: 21.
: 28. shall b. breast-plate,
: 2. swear to b. his soul, 3.
8. thou shalt b. them for a
m, 11: 18.
5. shalt b. up the money
: 18. b. this line in window
: 10. To b. Samson are we
We are come to b. thee
10, we will b. thee fast
. b. Samson to afflict him
b. with 7 green withs
f b. me with new ropes
: 36. I will b. it as a crown
17. he that hateth right b.?
1. Canst b. infl. of Pleiades?
0. Canst thou b. unicorn?
3. b. their faces in secret
. wilt thou b. Leviathan
5: 22. To b. his princes
27. b. sacrifice with cords
8. To b. kings with chains
3. b. them about thy neck
. b. them upon thine heart
b. them upon thy fingers
16. b. up the testimony
8. b. them on as bride doth
. to b. up broken-hearted
: 63. book b. a stone to it
: 25. bands, and shall b. thee
ew b. them in thy skirts
7. b. tire of thine head
1. put a roller to b. it
5. I will b. up broken
20. com-d mighty men to b.
1. hath smit. will b. us up
0. b. thems. in two furrows
13. b. chariot to swift beast
: 29. b. strong man. Mk. 3: 27.
0. b. the tares in bundles
. whatso. b. on earth, 18: 18.
. b. him hand and foot
b. heavy burdens grievous
: 3. no man could b. him
14. authority to b. all that
angel said, b. on thy sandals
1. So shall Jews b. man
BINDETH.
18. he maketh sore and b.
He b. up waters in clouds
. He b. floods from overfl.
. it b. me as the collar
. they cry not when he b.
: 7. nor he that b. sheaves
. he healeth and b. up
8. that b. stone in sling
26. in day L. b. up breach
BINDING.
7. we were b. sheaves in field
. b. his foal to the vine

Ex. 28: 32. have b. of woven work
Nu. 30: 13. b. oath to afflict soul
Ac. 22: 4. b. and deliv. into prisons
BIN'EA.
1 Ch. 8: 37. Moza begat B., 9: 43.
BIN'NUI.
Ezr. 8: 33. Noadiah son of B. | 10:
30, 38. Ne. 3: 24.-7: 15.-10: 9.
-12: 8.
BIRD.
Ge. 7: 14. ev. b. of ev. sort into ark
Le. 14: 6. living b., 7, 51, 52, 53.
51. slain b. | 52. blood of b.
52. cleanse house with living b.
De. 22: 6. If b. nest chance
Jb. 41: 5. play with him as a b.
Ps. 11: 1. to my soul, flee as a b.
124: 7. our soul is escaped as a b.
Pr. 1: 17. in vain net in sight of b.
6: 5. and as a b. from the fowler
7: 23. as a b. hasteth to snare
26: 2. As b. by wandering so curse
27: 8. As b. that wander fr. nest
Ec. 10: 20. b. shall tell matter
12: 4. shall rise at voice of b.
Is. 16: 2. as wandering b. cast
46: 11. a ravenous b. from east
Je. 12: 9. heritage as speckled b.
La. 3: 52. chased me like a b.
Ho. 9: 11. their glory fly like b.
11: 11. shall tremble as a b.
Am. 3: 5. b. fall where no gin is
Re. 18: 2. cage of every unclean b.
BIRDS.
Ge. 15: 10. b. divided he not
40: 17. b. did eat them out
19. the b. shall eat thy flesh
Le. 14. 4. to take two b. alive
5. one of b. be killed in, 50.
49. to cleanse house two b.
De. 14: 11. clean b. ye shall eat
2 S. 21: 10. suff. not b. to rest
Ps. 104: 17. Where b. make nests
148: † 10. praise the Lord ye b.
Ec. 9: 12. b. caught in the snare
Can. 2: 12. time of singing of b.
Is. 31: 5. As. b. flying, so L. defend
Je. 4: 25. b. of the heavens fled
5: 27. As cage full of b. so are
12: 4. beasts are consumed and b.
9. b. round about are ag. her
Eze. 39: 4. I will give thee to rav. b.
Da. 4: 33. his nails like b. claws
Mat. 8: 20. b. have nests, Lu. 9: 58.
13: 32. b. lodge in the branches
Ro. 1: 23. into an image like to b.
1 Co. 15: 39. of fishes, ano. of b.
Ja. 3: 7. every kind of b. is tamed
BIR'SHA.
Ge. 14: 2. B. king of Gomorrah
BIRTH.
Ex. 28: 10. other stone acc. to b.
2 K. 19: 3. chil. to the b., Is. 37: 3.
Jb. 3: 16. as a hidden untimely b.
Ps. 58: 8. pass like untimely b.
Ec. 6: 3. an untimely b. is better
7: 1. day of death better than b.
Is. 66: 9. Shall I bring to the b.
Eze. 16: 3. Thy b. is of Canaan
Ho. 9: 11. glory of Ephr. fly fr. b.
Mat. 1: 18. b. of J. C. on this wise
Lu. 1: 14. many sh. rejoice at his b.
Jn. 9: 1. a man blind from his b.
Ga. 4: 19. of whom I travail in b.
Re. 12: 2. she cried, travailing in b.
BIRTH-DAY.
Ge. 40: 20. wh. was Phar-'s b.
Mat. 14: 16. Herod's b., Mk. 6: 21.
BIRTH-RIGHT.
Ge. 25: 31. Jac. said, Sell me thy b.
32. what profit this b. to me
33. sware and sold his b.
34. thus Esau despised his b.
27: 36. took away my b. and bless.
43: 33. first-born acc. to his b.
1 Ch. 5: 1. Reuben's b. to sons of Jo.
He. 12: 16. for morsel sold his b.

BIR'ZAVITH.
1 Ch. 7: 31. Malchiel father of B.
BISH'LAM.
Ezr. 4: 7. wrote B. unto Artaxerxes
BISHOP, S.
Ph. 1: 1. to saints at Philippi with
1 Ti. 3: 1. If des re office of b. [b-s
2. A b. be blameless, Tit. 1: 7.
1 Pe. 2: 25. to the b. of your souls
BISHOPRIC.
Ac. 1: 20. his b. let another take
BIT, S.
Ps. 32: 9. mouth be held in with b.
Ja. 3: 3. put b-s in horses' mouths
BIT.
Nu. 21: 6. fiery serpents b. people
Am. 5: 19. leaned on wall serp. b.
BITE, BITETH. [him
Ge. 49: 17. Dan an adder, that b-h
Pr. 23: 32. At last it b-h like a serp.
Ec. 10: 8. breaketh hedge, serp. b.
11. serp. b. without enchantment
Je. 8: 17. serpents, they sh. b. you
Am. 9: 3. command serp. he sh. b.
Mi. 3: 5. prophets that b. with
Ha. 2: 7. not rise that b. thee
Ga. 5: 15. if ye b. and devour one
BITHI'AH.
1 Ch. 4: 18. the sons of B.
BITH'RON.
2 S. 2: 29. Abner went through B.
BITHYN'IA.
Ac. 16: 7. assayed to go into B.
1 Pe. 1: 1. through Asia and B.
BITTEN.
Nu. 21: 8. that is b. when he looks
9. if a serpent had b. any man
BITTER.
Ge. 27: 34. Esau cried with b. cry
Ex. 1: 14. Egyp. made their lives b.
12: 8. with b. herbs eat, Nu. 9: 11.
15: 23. not of waters, they were b.
Nu. 5: 24. enter her, become b., 27.
De. 32: 24. devoured with b. destru.
32. of gall, their clusters are b.
Ju. 18: † 25. fellows b. of soul run
Ru. 1: † 20. not Naomi, but b.
1 S. 1: † 10. Hannah was b. of soul
22: † 2. ev. one b. of soul gath. to
30: † 6. the people's soul was b.
2 S. 17: † 8. mighty, and b. of soul
2 K. 4: † 27. her soul is b. in her
14: 26. afflic. of Isr. that it was b.
Es. 4: 1. Mord. cried with a b. cry
Jb. 3: † 5. those who have a b. day
20. why is life to b. in soul?
13: 26. writest b. things ag. me
23: 2. to-day is my complaint b.
27: † 2. Alm. made my soul b.
Ps. 64: 3. shoot arrows, b. words
Pr. 5: 4. her end is b. as wormw.
27: 7. to hungry b. thing is sweet
31: † 6. wine to those b. of soul
Ec. 7: 26. more b. than death the
Is. 5: 20. b. for sweet, sweet for b.
22: † 4. I will be b. in weeping
24: 9. strong drink shall be b. to
Je. 2: 19. it is an evil thing and b.
4: 18. thy wickedness, it is b.
6: 26. b. lamentation as for son
31: 15. in Ramah, b. weeping
Eze. 3: † 14. and I went b.
27: 31. shall weep with b. wailing
Am. 8: 10. end as a b. day
Ha. 1: 6. Chaldeans, that b. nation
Col. 3: 19. love wives, be not b. ag.
Ja. 3: 14. if ye have b. envying
Re. 8: 11. men died of wat-s bec. b.
10: 9. it shall make thy belly b.
10. as I had eaten it my belly was
BITTER water. [b.
Nu. 5: 18 b. w. causeth curse 19,
23. blot them out with b. w. [24.
Ja. 3: 11. send sweet w. and b.
BITTERLY.
Ju. 5: 23. curse ye b. the inhabi.
Ru. 1: 20. Alm. dealt b. with me

Is. 22 : 4. I will weep b.
33: 7. ambassadors shall weep b.
Eze. 27 : 30. pilots of Tyre sh. cry b.
Ho. 12 : 14. Ephr. provoked him b.
Zph. 1 : 14. mighty man sh. cry b.
Mat. 26 : 75. Peter wept b., Lu. 22 : 62.

BITTERN.

Is. 14 : 23. possession for b., 34 : 11.
Zph. 2 : 14. b. shall lodge in

BITTERNESS.

Ge. 26 : † 35. b. of spirit to Isaac
Ex. 15 : † 23. name of it was b.
Ru. 1 : † 13. I have b. for your
1 S. 1 : 10. Hannah was in b. of soul
15 : 32. the b. of death is past
2 S. 2 : 26. the sword will be b.
Jb. 7 : 11. I will complain in b.
9 : 18. but filleth me with b.
10 : 1. I will speak in b. of soul
21 : 25. another dieth in b. of soul
Pr. 14 : 10. the heart knoweth his b.
17 : 25. a foolish son is b. to her
Is. 38 : 15. go softly all my life in b.
17. behold, for peace I had gr. b.
La. 1 : 4. virgins afflicted, she in b.
3 : 15. he hath filled me with b.
Eze. 3 : 14. Spi. took me I went in b.
21 : 6. with b. sigh bef. their eyes
27 : 31. sh. weep for thee with b.
Ho. 12 : † 14. Ephr. provoked him with b. [in b. for first-born
Zch. 12 : 10. in b. for him as one
Ac. 8 : 23. I perceive thou art in the gall of b.
Ro. 3 : 14. mouth is full of b.
Ep. 4 : 31. Let all b. be put away
He. 12 : 15. lest any root of b.

BIZJOTH'JAH.

Jos. 15 : 28. uttermost cities were B.

BIZ'THA.

Es. 1 : 10. B. the 7 chamberlains

BLACK.

Le. 13 : 31. there is no b. hair in it
37. and there is b. hair grown
1 K. 18 : 45. the heaven was b. with clouds
Es. 1 : 6. white and b. marble
Jb. 30 : 30. my skin is b. upon me
Pr. 7 : 9. in the b. and dark night
Can. 1 : 5. I am b. but comely, O dau
6. Look not upon me, I am b.
5 : 11. his locks are b. as a raven
Je. 4 : 28. for this sh. heavens be b.
8 : 21. for peo. I am hurt, I am b.
14 : 2. gates languish, they are b.
La. 5 : 10. Our skin was b. like
Eze. 31 : † 15. caused Leb. to be b.
Zch. 6 : 2. in sec. chariot b. horses
6. b. horses go forth into north
Mal. 3 : † 14. what profit in b.?
Mat. 5 : 36. one hair white or b.
Re. 6 : 5. and lo a b. horse
12. sun became b. as sackcloth

BLACKER, ISH.

La. 4 : 8. visage b. than a coal
Jb. 6 : 16. Which are b-h by ice

BLACKNESS.

Jb. 3 : 5. let b. of day terrify
Is. 50 : 3. I clothe heavens with b.
La. 4 : † 8. visage darker than b.
Jo. 2 : 6. faces gather b., Na. 2 : 10.
He. 12 : 18. ye are not come to b.
Jude 13. to whom is reserved the b.

BLADE.

Ju. 3 : 22. the haft went in after b.
Jb. 31 : 22. fall from shoulder-b.
Mat. 13 : 26. b. was sprung
Mk. 4 : 28. first the b. then the ear

BLAINS.

Ex. 9 : 9. a boil with b., 10.

BLAME. [Noun.]

Ge. 43 : 9. me bear b. for ever, 44 : 32.
Ep. 1 : 4. holy and without b.

BLAME, ED.

2 Co. 6 : 3. that ministry be not b.
8 : 20. that no man should b. us
Ga. 2 : 11. because he was to be b.

BLAMELESS.

Ge. 44 : 10. he my serv. ye sh. be b.
Jos. 2 : 17. we will be b. of oath
Ju. 15 : 3. be more b. than Philis.
Mat. 12 : 5. profane sabbath, are b.
Lu. 1 : 6. in ordinances of L b.
1 Co. 1 : 8. ye be b. in day of Lord
Ph. 2 : 15. that ye may be b. and
3 : 6. touching righte. in law b.
1 Th. 5 : 23. body preserved b.
1 Ti. 3 : 2. bishop be b., Tit 1 : 7.
10. use office of deacon b.
5 : 7. charge, that they may be b.
Tit. 1 : 6. If any be b. the husband
2 Pe. 3 : 14. ye may be found b.

BLASPHEME.

2 S. 12 : 14. occasion to ene. to b.
1 K. 21 : 10. Thou didst b. God, 13.
Ps. 74 : 10. shall the enemy b. thy
Mk. 3 : 28. wherewith they shall b.
29. but he shall b. against H. G.
Ac. 26 : 11. I compelled them to b.
1 Ti. 1 : 20. may learn not to b.
Ja. 2 : 7. Do not they b. thy name
Re. 13 : 6. to b. his name and tab.

BLASPHEMED.

Le. 24 : 11. Israelitish wom.'s son b.
2 K. 19 : 6. serv. of king of Assyria b. me. 22. Is. 37 : 6, 23.
Ps. 74 : 18. foolish peo. b. thy name
Is. 52 : 5. my name every day is b.
65 : 7. have b. me on the hills
Eze. 20 : 27. your fathers b. me
Ac. 18 : 6. they opposed and b.
Ro. 2 : 24. name of G. is b. thro.
1 Ti. 6 : 1. name of G. be not b.
Tit. 2 : 5. that word of G. be not b.
Re. 16 : 9. men scorched and b.
11. b. because of their pains
21. men b. God because of hail

BLASPHEMEST, ETH, ING.

Le. 24 : 16. b. Lord be put to death
Ps. 44 : 16. voice of him that b.
Mat. 9 : 3. scribes said, This man b.
Lu. 12 : 10. b-h ag. H. G. not be forgiv
Jn. 10 : 36. Fa. sanctified Thou b-t
Ac. 18 : 45. Jews spake ag. Paul b-g

BLASPHEMER, S.

Ac. 19 : 37. are not b-s of goddess
1 Ti. 1 : 13. Who was before a b.
2 Ti. 3 : 2. last days men be b-s

BLASPHEMIES.

Eze. 35 : 12. th. I have heard thy b.
Mat. 15 : 19. out of the heart b.
Mk. 2 : 7. why this man speak b.?
3 : 28. b. they shall blaspheme
Lu. 5 : 21. Who this speaketh b.?
Re. 13 : 5. mouth giv. speaking b.

BLASPHEMOUS, LY.

Lu. 22 : 65. things b-y spake they
Ac. 6 : 11. heard him speak b. words
13. ceaseth not to speak b. words

BLASPHEMY.

2 K. 19 : 3. is a day of b., Is. 37 : 3.
Mat. 12 : 31. all manner of b. be forgiv. but b. against H. G.
26 : 65. He hath spok. b. ye heard his b., Mk. 14 : 64.
Mk. 7 : 22. out of the heart b.
Jn. 10 : 33. we stone for b.
Col. 3 : 8. now ye also put off b.
Re. 2 : 9. I know b. of th. that say
13 : 1. and upon his heads b.
6. he opened his mouth in b.
17 : 3. full of names of b.

BLAST.

Ex. 15 : 8. with b. of thy nostrils
Jos. 6 : 5. th. make long b. with horns
2 S. 22 : 16. rebuke of L. at b. of breath of his nostrils, Ps. 18 : 15.
2 K 19 : 7. b. on Sennach., Is. 37 : 7.
Jb. 4 : 9. By b. of God they perish
Is. 25 : 4. b. of terrible is as storm

BLASTED.

Ge. 41 : 6. thin ears b., 23, 27.
2 K. 19 : 26. as corn b., Is. 37 : 27.

BLASTING. [N and adj.]

De. 28 : 22. L. smite thee with b.
1 K. 8 : 37. be b. mildew. 2 Ch. 6 : 28
Am. 4 : 9. smitten you with b.
Hag. 2 : 17. I smote you with b.

BLAS'TUS.

Ac. 12 : 20. made B. their friend

BLAZE.

Mk. 1 : 45. b. abroad the matter

BLEATING, S.

Ju. 5 : 16. abodest to hear b-s of flocks
1 S. 15 : 14. meaneth b. of sheep

BLEMISH, ES.

Ex. 12 : 5. lamb shall be without b. a male of, Le. 9 : 3.-14 : 10.-23 : 12. Nu. 6 : 14.-Eze. 46 : 13.
29 : 1. two rams without b., Le. 5 : 15, 18.-6 : 6.-9 : 2. Eze. 46 : 4
Le. 1 : 3. offer a male without b., 10.-4 : 23.-22 : 19.
3 : 1. male or female without b., 6.
4 : 3. a bullock without b., De. 17 : 1. Eze. 45 : 18. [32.
28. he shall bring kid, without b.,
21 : 17. hath b. not approach, 18,
20. dwarf or b. in his eye [21, 23.
22 : 20. whatso. hath a b. that sh. ye not offer, De. 15 : 21.
21. in free-will offering no b.
25. b-s in them not be accepted
23 : 18. sh. offer 7 lambs without b. Nu. 28 : 19.-29 : 2, 8, 36.
24 : 19. if man cause b. in neighb.
20. as he hath caused b. in man
Nu. 19 : 2. a red heifer without b.
28 : 31. shall b. unto without b.
29 : 13. offer 14 lambs without b., 20, 23, 29, 32.
De. 17 : 1. any sheep wherein is b.
2 S. 14 : 25. was no b. in Absalom
Da. 1 : 4. Chil. in whom was no b.
Ep. 5 : 27. be holy and without b.
1 Pe. 1 : 19. as of a lamb without b.
2 Pe. 2 : 13. Spots they are and b-s

BLESS. [God being agent.]

Ge. 12 : 2. I will b. thee. 26 : 3, 24.
3. I will b. them that b. thee
17 : 16. I will b. her and give a son
22 : 17. I will b. thee, He. 6 : 14.
28 : 3. G. Al. b. thee, multiply thee
32 : 26. not let thee go, exc. thou b.
48 : 16. b. lads, and let my name
49 : 25. by Al. who shall b. thee
Ex. 20 : 24. I will come b. thee
23 : 25. sh. b. thy bread and water
Nu. 6 : 24. L. b. thee and keep thee
27. name on Isr., I will b. them
24 : 1. it pleased the L. to b. Israel
De. 1 : 11. b. you as he hath prom.
7 : 13. b. thee, b. fruit of womb
14 : 29. that the Lord may b. thee, 23 : 20.-24 : 19.
15 : 4. no poor, for L. shall b. thee
10. for this thing L. shall b. thee
18. L. shall b. thee in all, 30 : 16.
16 : 15. bec. L. shall b. thee in all
26 : 15. look down b. thy peo. Isr.
28 : 8. he shall b. thee in the land
12. to b. all work of thine hand
33 : 11. b. Lord, his substance
Ru. 2 : 4. The L. b. thee, Je. 31 : 23.
2 S. 7 : 29. theref. let it please thee to b. house of thy servant, 1 Ch. 17 : 27.
1 Ch. 4 : 10. O that wouldest b. me
Ps. 5 : 12. thou L. wilt b. righte.
28 : 9. save peo. b. thine inheri.
29 : 11. L. will b. his peo. with peace
67 : 1. G. our G. shall b. us, 6, 7.
115 : 12. L. will b. us, will b. house of Isr., will b. house of Aaron
13. He will b. them that fear L.
128 : 5. L. shall b. thee out of Zion
132 : 15. I will abun. b. her provis.
134 : 3. Lord b. thee out of Zion
Is. 19 : 25. whom L. of hosts sh. b.

Hag. 2 : 19. fr. this day will I **b.** you
Ac. 3 : 26. sent him to **b.** you
BLESS. [God being the object.]
De. 8 : 10. full, thou shalt **b.** the L.
Ju. 5 : 9. **b.** ye the Lord, Ps. 103 : 21.-134 : 1.
1 Ch. 29 : 20. David said, Now **b.** L.
Ne. 9 : 5. stand up and **b.** Lord for
Ps. 16 : 7. I will **b.** L. who given me
26 : 12. in cong. will I **b.** the Lord
34 : 1. I will **b.** the L. at all times
63 : 4. will I **b.** thee while I live
66 : 8. O **b.** our G. make his praise
68 : 26. **b.** ye God in congregations
96 : 2. sing to the L. **b.** his name
100 : 4. thankful, **b.** his name, 103 : 1.
103 : 1. **b.** the Lord, O my soul, 2, 22.-104 : 1, 35.
20. **b.** L. ye angels | 21. **b.** ye hosts
22. **b.** the Lord all his works in
115 : 18. we will **b.** L. fr. this time
134 : 2. lift hands, and **b.** the L.
135 : 19. **b.** L. O house of Isr., **b.** L. O house of Aaron
20. ye that fear L. **b.** the Lord
145 : 1. I will **b.** thy name for ever
2. Every day will I **b.** thee, and
10. O L. thy saints shall **b.** thee
21. let all flesh **b.** his holy name
Ja. 3 : 9. **b.** we God, even the Fa.
BLESS. [Man agent and object.]
Ge. 27 : 4. may **b.** thee bef. I die, 25.
10. may **b.** thee before his death
19. thy soul may **b.** me, 31.
34. **b.** me, even me, O my fa., 38.
48 : 9. Bring to me, I will **b.** them
20. In thee shall Israel **b.** saying
Ex. 12 : 32. take flocks **b.** me also
Nu. 6 : 23. this wise ye shall **b.** Isr.
23 : 20. I have received com-t to **b.**
25. Neither curse them nor **b.** th.
De. 10 : 8. L. separa. Levi to **b.**, 21 : 5.
24 : 13. sleep in his raim. **b.** thee
27 : 12. sh. stand on Gerizim to **b.**
29 : 19. heareth this curse, he **b.** himself [they should **b.**
Jos. 8 : 33. as Moses commanded
1 S. 9 : 13. bec. he doth **b.** sacrifice
13 : †10. went to meet Sam. to **b.** him
2 S. 6 : 20. to **b.** household, 1 Ch. 16 : 43.
8 : 10. Toi sent Joram to **b.** David
21 : 3. ye may **b.** inheritance of L.
1 K. 1 : 47. to **b.** our lord k. David
1 Ch. 23 : 13. to **b.** in his name
Ps. 62 : 4. **b.** with their mouths
109 : 28. them curse, but **b.** thou
129 : 8. we **b.** you in name of L.
Pr. 30 : 11. that not **b.** their moth.
Is. 65 : 16. shall **b.** himself in God
Je. 4 : 2. nations shall **b.** thems.
Mat. 5 : 44. **b.** that curse, Lu. 6 : 28.
Ro. 12 : 14. **b.** and curse not
1 Co. 4 : 12. being reviled we **b.**
10 : 16. cup of blessing we **b.**
14 : 16. thou **b.** with the spirit

BLESSED.
[Man agent and object.]
Ge. 14 : 19. **b.** Abram, and said, **b.** [be Ab.
24 : 60. they **b.** Rebekah
27 : 23. so Isaac **b.** Jacob, 27.
29. **b.** he that blesseth thee
33. I have **b.** and he shall be **b.**
41. blessing whw. his fa. **b.** him
28 : 1. Isaac called Jacob, **b.** him
6. **b.** him gave charge, He. 11 : 20.
30 : 13. daughters will call me **b.**
31 : 55. kissed sons dau-s and **b.** th.
47 : 7. **b.** Pha., 10 | 48 : 15. he **b.** Jo.
48 : 20. Jacob **b.** Manas., He. 11 : 21.
49 : 28. Jacob **b.** his sons
Ex. 39 : 43. Moses **b.** them, De. 33 : 1.
Le. 9 : 22. Aaron and **b.** them
23. Moses and Aaron **b.** people
Nu. 22 : 6. whom thou blessest is **b.**
23 : 11. thou hast **b.** them, 24 : 10.
De. 28 : 6. **b.** when comest in, **b.**
33 : 1. **b.** chil. of Isr. before death
De. 33 : 20. **b.** that enlargeth Gad
24. let Asher be **b.** with children
Jos. 14 : 13. Joshua **b.** Caleb
22 : 6. Josh. **b.** them and sent, 7.
24 : 10. Balaam **b.** you still
Ju. 5 : 24. **b.** above women, Jael
Ru. 2 : 19. **b.** he that took knowl.
1 S. 2 : 20. Eli **b.** Elkanah
25 : 33. **b.** be thy advice, **b.** thou
26 : 25. Saul said, **b.** be thou my
2 S. 6 : 18. Da. **b.** peo., 1 Ch. 16 : 2.
13 : 25. would not go, but **b.** him
19 : 39. kissed Barzillai, **b.** him
1 K. 2 : 45. king Sol. shall be **b.**
8 : 14. king Sol. **b.** all con., 55.
66. cong. **b.** Solomon, 2 Ch. 6 : 3.
2 Ch. 30 : 27. Levites **b.** people
Ne. 11 : 2. peo. **b.** all that offered
Jb. 29 : 11. ear heard it **b.** me
31 : 20. If loins have not **b.** me
Ps. 49 : 18. he lived he **b.** his soul
72 : 17. be **b.** in him, called him **b.**
118 : 26. **b.** he cometh in name of the Lord, we have **b.** you
Pr. 31 : 28. Her children call her **b.**
Ec. 10 : 17. **b.** art thou, O land
Can. 6 : 9. dau-s saw and **b.** her
Is. 66 : 3. as if he **b.** an idol
Je. 20 : 14. day my moth. bare be **b.**
Mal. 3 : 12. nations sh. call you **b.**
Mk. 11 : 10. **b.** be kingd. of our fa.
Lu. 1 : 48. all gen. shall call me **b.**
2 : 34. Simeon **b.** them, and
Ac. 20 : 35. It is more **b.** to give
Tit. 2 : 13. Looking for **b.** hope
He. 7 : 1. met Ab. and **b.** him, 6.
7. the less is **b.** of the better
11 : 20. By faith Isaac **b.** Jacob
21. dying, **b.** sons of Joseph
BLESSED. [God the agent.]
Ge. 1 : 22. God **b.** them, saying, be fruitful, 28.-5 : 2.
2 : 3. God **b.** 7th day, Ex. 20 : 11.
9 : 1. God **b.** Noah and his sons
12 : 3. in thee all families be **b.**, 18 : 18.-22 : 18.-26 : 4.-28 : 14. Ac. 3 : 25. Ga. 3 : 8.
17 : 20. **b.** Ishmael | 24 : 1. L. **b.** Ab.
24 : 31. come in thou **b.** of Lord
25 : 11. God **b.** Isaac, 26 : 12.
26 : 29. thou art now **b.** of Lord
27 : 27. field which Lord hath **b.**
30 : 27. L. hath **b.** me for thy sake
30. **b.** thee since my coming
32 : 29. he **b.** Jacob, 35 : 9. | 48 : 3.
39 : 5. L. **b.** Egyptian's house
Nu. 22 : 12. for the people are **b.**
23 : 20. he hath **b.** I cannot reverse
De. 2 : 7. thy God hath **b.** thee, 12 : 7.-15 : 14.-16 : 10.
7 : 14. shalt be **b.** above all people
14 : 24. if place when Lord hath **b.**
28 : 3. **b.** shalt thou be in city, **b.**
4. **b.** be fruit of body | 5. basket
33 : 13. of Jo. he said, **b.** of Lord
Jos. 17 : 14. as Lord hath **b.** me
Ju. 13 : 24. Samson, Lord **b.** him
17 : 2. **b.** be thou of Lord, Ru. 3 : 10. 1 S. 15 : 13.
Ru. 2 : 20. **b.** be he of L. who hath
3 : 10. **b.** be thou L. my daughter
1 S. 23 : 21. **b.** be ye of L., 2 S. 2 : 5.
2 S. 6 : 11. Lord **b.** Obed-edom, 12. 1 Ch. 13 : 14.-26 : 5.
7 : 29. house of thy servant be **b.**
1 Ch. 17 : 27. blessest, it shall be **b.**
2 Ch. 31 : 10. Lord hath **b.** his peo.
Jb. 1 : 10. hast **b.** work of hands
42 : 12. Lord **b.** latter end of Job
Ps. 21 : 6. hast made him most **b.**
33 : 12. **b.** is nation whose God
37 : 22. **b.** of him sh. inherit
26. lendeth, and his seed is **b.**
41 : 2. keep him, he shall be **b.**
45 : 2. God hath **b.** thee for ever
89 : 15. **b.** is people that know
112 : 2. gen. of upright shall be **b.**
Ps. 115 : 15. you are **b.** of the Lord
119 : 1. **b.** are undefiled in way
128 : 1. **b.** is every one that feareth
4. man be **b.** that feareth Lord
147 : 13. he hath **b.** thy children
Pr. 5 : 18. Let thy fountain be **b.**
10 : 7. memory of the just is **b.**
20 : 7. the just man's chil. are **b.**
21. end thereof shall not be **b.**
22 : 9. bountiful eye shall be **b.**
Is. 19 : 25. **b.** be Egypt my people
51 : 2. called him alone and **b.** him
61. 9 seed L. hath **b.**, 65 : 23.
Mat. 5 : 3. **b.** poor in spi. | 5. **b.** meek
7. **b.** merciful | 8. **b.** pure in heart
9. **b.** peacemakers | 10. persecut.
13 : 16. **b.** are your eyes, Lu. 10 : 23.
14 : 19. he **b.** and brake, 26 : 26. Mk. 6 : 41.-14 : 22. Lu. 9 : 16.-24 : 30. [mon
16 : 17. Jes. said, **b.** art thou Si-
24 : 46. **b.** is that serv., Lu. 12 : 43.
25 : 34. Come, ye **b.** of my Father
Mk. 8 : 7. he **b.** and commanded
10 : 16. in his arms and **b.** them
14 : 61. thou art C. Son of the **b.**
Lu. 1 : 28. **b.** among women, 42.
42 **b.** is the fruit of thy womb
45. **b.** is she that believed
6 : 20 : **b.** be ye poor
11 : 27. **b.** is womb that bare thee
12 : 37. **b.** are those servants, 38.
14 : 14. thou shalt be **b.** they
19 : 38. **b.** be King that cometh
23 : 29. **b.** are the barren
24 : 50. he **b.** them | 51. while **b.**
Ga. 3 : 9. **b.** with faithful Ab.
Ep. 1 : 3. **b.** us with spiritual bl-s
Ja. 1 : 25. shall be **b.** in his deed
Re. 14 : 13. **b.** are dead die in the L
BLESSED. [God the object.]
Ge. 14 : 20. **b.** be most high God
24 : 48. **b.** God of my master Ab.
Jos. 22 : 33. chil. of Israel **b.** God
2 S. 22 : 47. **b.** be my rock, Ps. 18 : 46.
1 Ch. 29 : 10. Da. **b.** L. **b.** thou, O L.
20. all the cong. **b.** the Lord
2 Ch. 20 : 26. there they **b.** Lord
31 : 8. saw the heaps, they **b.** L.
Ne. 8 : 6. and Ezra **b.** the Lord
9 : 5. **b.** be thy name, Ps. 72 : 19.
Jb. 1 : 21. **b.** be name, Ps. 113 : 2.
Ps. 66 : 20. **b.** be G., 68 : 35. 2 Co. 1 : 3
119 : 12. **b.** art thou, O L. teach
Eze. 3 : 12. **b.** be glory of the Lord
Da. 2 : 19. Dan. **b.** the God of, 20.
3 : 28. **b.** be God of Shadrach
4 : 34. Neb. **b.** the most High
Mk. 14 : 61. Art thou C. Son of the **b.**
Lu. 2 : 28. in his arms and **b.** God
Jn. 12 : 13. **b.** is the King of Israel
Ro. 1 : 25. Creator who is **b.** forever
9 : 5. C. who is over all, God **b.**
2 Co. 11 : 31. is **b.** for evermore
Ep. 1 : 3. **b.** be the Fa., 1 Pe. 1 : 3.
1 Ti. 1 : 11. glori. gospel of **b.** God
6 : 15. **b.** and only Potentate
BLESSED are they.
Ps. 2 : 12. **b. a. t.** that put trust
84 : 4. **b. a. t.** dwell in thy house
106 : 3. **b. a. t.** that keep judgm.
119 : 2. **b. a. t.** that keep testimo.
Pr. 8 : 32. **b. a. t.** keep my ways
Is. 30 : 18. **b. a. t.** th. wait for him
Mat. 5 : 4. **b. a. t.** that mourn
6. **b.** who hunger | 10. persecuted
Lu. 11 : 28. **b. a. t.** that hear word
Jn. 20 : 29. **b. a. t.** that have not seen [forgiven
Ro. 4 : 7. **b. a. t.** whose iniq. are
Re. 19 : 9. **b. a. t.** called to marri.
22 : 14. **b. a. t.** that do his com-ts
BLESSED are ye.
Is. 32 : 20. **b. a. y.** sow beside [vile
Mat. 5 : 11. **b. a. y.** when men re-
Lu. 6 : 21. **b. a. y.** that hunger now
b. a. y. that weep now

Lu. 6 : 22. **b. a. y.** when men hate [you
BLESSED is he.
Nu. 24 : 9. **b.i.h.** that blesseth thee
Ps. 32 : 1. **b. i. h.** whose transgr. is
41 : 1. **b.i. h.** th. considereth poor
Da. 12 : 12. **b. i. h.** that waiteth
Mat. 11 : 6. **b. i. h.** whoso. not offended in me, Lu. 7 : 23.
21 : 9. **b.i.h.** cometh in name, 23 : 39. Mk. 11 : 9. Lu. 13 : 35.
Lu. 14 : 15. b. i. **h.** shall eat bread
Re. 1 : 3. **b. i. h.** that readeth
16 : 15. b. i. **h.** that watcheth
20 : 6 **b.i.h.** hath part in first resur
22 : 7. **b.i.h.** that keepeth sayings
BLESSED is the man.
Ps. 1 : 1. **b.i.m.** walk. not in couns.
32 : 2. **b.i.m.** to whom L. imputeth not iniquity, Ro. 4 : 8.
34 : 8. **b. i. m.** that trusteth in him, 84 : 12. Je. 17 : 7.
40 : 4. **b.i.m.** maketh L. his trust
65 : 4. **b.i.m.** whom thou choosest
84 : 5. **b.i.m.** whose strength in
94 : 12. **b.i.m.** whom thou chast.
112 : 1. **b.i.m.** that feareth Lord
Pr. 8 : 34. **b.i.m.** that heareth me
Is. 56 : 2. **b.i.m.** that doeth this
Ja. 1 : 12. **b.i.m.** th. endur. tempt.
BLESSEDNESS.
Ro. 4 : 6. as David describeth the **b.**
9. Cometh this **b.** on circ. only?
Ga. 4 : 15. Where b. ye spake of?
BLESSEST, ETH.
Ge. 27 : 29. bl. that **b.** thee, Nu. 24 : 9.
Nu. 22 : 6. whom thou **b.** is blessed
De. 15 : 6. God **b.** thee as he prom.
1 Ch. 17 : 27. thou b. O Lord, and it be blessed [abhorreth
Ps. 10 : 3. **b-h** covetous whom Lord
65 : 10. thou b. springing thereof
107 : 38. He b. they are multiplied
Pr. 3 : 33. he b. habitation of just
27 : 14. **b-h** friend with loud voice
Is. 65 : 16. who b. himself in earth
BLESSING. [Part.]
Lu. 24 : 53. in the temple **b.** God
He. 6 : 14. Surely b. I will bless thee
BLESSING. [Noun.]
Ge. 12 : 2. thou shalt be a **b.**
22 : 17. in b. I will bless, He. 6 : 14.
27 : 12. a curse on me and not a **b.**
30. Isaac made end of **b.** Jacob
35. thy brother hath taken thy **b.**
36. Hast not reserved **b.** for me?
38. Hast but one **b.** my father?
41. Esau hated Jacob bec. of **b.**
28 : 4. God give thee the **b.** of Ab.
33 : 11. Take my **b.** that is bro't
39 : 5. **b.** of L. was on all he had
49 : 28. ev. one acc. to his **b.** he bl.
Ex. 32 : 29. may bestow on you a **b.**
Le. 25 : 21. will com. my **b.** upon you
De. 11 : 26. I set bef. you a **b.** 30 : 19.
27. a **b.** if ye obey com-ts of L.
29. thou shalt put **b.** on Gerizim
12 : 15. acc. to **b.** of L., 16 : 17.
23 : 5. L. turned curse into a b.
28 : 8. L. shall com. **b.** on store-h
30 : 1. upon thee **b.** and curse
19. set bef. you **b.** and cursing
33 : 1. this is **b.** Moses blessed, 7.
16. let the **b.** come upon Joseph
23. Naphtali full with **b.** of Lord
Jos. 15 : 19. Give me a **b.**, Ju. 1 : 15.
1 S. 25 : 27. this **b.** thy handmaid
30 : † 26. a **b.** for you from spoil
2 S. 7 : 29. with thy **b.** let house
2 K. 5 : 15. take **b.** of thy servant
18 : † 31 make with me a b., Is. 36 † 16.
Ne. 9 : 5. wh. is exalted above all **b.**
13 : 2. our G. turned curse into **b.**
Jb. 29 : 13. **b.** of him ready to perish
Ps. 3 : 8. thy **b.** is upon thy people
24 : 5. he shall receive **b.** from L.
109 : 17. as he delighted not in **b.**
Ps. 129 : 8. **b.** of L. be upon you
133 : 3. L. commanded **b.** even life
Pr. 10 : 22. **b.** of L. maketh rich
11 : 11. by **b.** of upright city is
† 25. soul of **b.** sh. be made fat
26. b. upon him that selleth it
24 : 25. **b.** come upon them that rebuke
Is. 19 : 24. **b.** in midst of the land
44 : 3. will pour my **b.** on thy offsp.
65 : 8. destroy it not, a **b.** is in it
Eze. 34 : 26. will make pla. about my hill a **b.** showers of b.
44 : 30. the b. to rest in thy house
Jo. 2 : 14. leave a **b.** behind him
Zch. 8 : 13. and ye shall be a **b.**
Mal. 3 : 10. and pour you out a **b.**
Ro. 15 : 29. fulness of **b.** of gospel
1 Co. 10 : 16. cup of **b.** we bless [b.
2 Co. 9 : † 5. make up beforeh. your
Ga. 3 : 14. that **b.** of Ab. might come
He. 6 : 7. earth receiveth **b.** fr. God
12 : 17. would have inherited **b.**
Ja. 3 : 10. same mouth **b.** cursing
1 Pe. 3 : 9. but contrariwise **b.** that ye should inherit a **b.**
Re. 5 : 12. worthy to receive **b.**
13. **b.** to him sitteth on throne
7 : 12. **b.** and glory to our G. for
BLESSINGS.
Ge. 49 : 25. shall bless thee with **b.** of heaven, **b.** of deep, **b.** of breasts
26. **b.** of thy father prevailed above the **b.** of my [thee
De. 28 : 2. all these **b.** sh. come on
Jos. 8 : 34. he read **b.** and cursings
Ps. 21 : 3. preventest him with **b.**
† 6. thou hast set him to be **b.**
Pr. 10 : 6. b. are upon the just
28 : 20. a faithful abound with **b.**
Mal. 2 : 2. and will curse your **b.**
Ep. 1 : 3. blessed us with spiritual [b.
BLEW.
Jos. 6 : 8. priests passed bef L. and **b.**, 9, 13, 16, 20. 2 K. 9 : 13.-11 : 14.
Ju. 3 : 27. Ehud **b.** a trumpet in
6 : 34. Spirit upon Gideon, he **b.** a
7 : 19. they **b.** the trumpets, 20, 22.
1 S. 13 : 3. Saul **b.** saying, Let
2 S. 2 : 28. Joab **b.**, 18 : 16.-20 : 22.
20 : 1. Sheba **b.** a trumpet and said
1 K. 1 : 39. **b.** trumpet, said, God save king Sol. | 2 K. 11 : 14.
2 K. 9 : 13. **b.** saying, Jehu is king
Mat. 7 : 25. winds **b.** and beat upon that house, 27.
Jn. 6 : 18. sea arose by wind that **b.**
Ac. 27 : 13. south-wind **b.**, 28 : 13.
BLIND. [Adjective.]
Ex. 4 : 11. who maketh the **b.**
Le. 19 : 14. not stumbling-bl. bef. **b.**
21 : 18. a **b.** man not approach
22 : 22. not offer **b.**, De. 15 : 21.
De. 27 : 18. that maketh **b.** wander
28 : 29. grope at noon as **b.** gropeth
2 S. 5 : 6. Except thou take away **b.**
8. **b.** hated of David, **b.** not come into house
Jb. 29 : 15. I was eyes to the **b.**
Ps. 146 : 8. L. openeth eyes of **b.**
Is. 29 : 18. eyes of **b.** sh. see, 35 : 5.
42 : 7. for a light to open **b.** eyes
16. bring **b.** by way they kn. not
18. look, ye **b.** that ye may see
19. who is **b.** but my serv.? who is **b.** as he th. is perf., and **b.**
43 : 8. bring **b.** peo. th. have eyes
56 : 10. His watchmen are **b.** they
59 : 10. we grope for wall like **b.**
Je. 31 : 8. will gath. with them **b.**
La. 4 : 14. they wandered as **b.** men
Zph. 1 : 17. shall walk like **b.** men
Mal. 1 : 8. **b.** for sacrifice is it not evil? [20 : 30.
Mat. 9 : 27. two **b.** men foll., 28.-
Mat. 11 : 5. the **b.** receive their sight, 12 : 22. Lu. 7 : 22.
15 : 14. be **b.** leaders of **b.**, if **b.** lead **b.** both shall, Lu. 6 : 39.
30. having with them lame, **b.**
31. lame to walk, **b.** to see
21 : 14. **b.** came to him in temple
23 : 16. Woe to you, ye b. guides
17. Ye b. whether is greater, 19.
24. Ye **b.** guides, strain at
26. thou b. Pharisee, cleanse first
Mk. 8 : 22. bring **b.** man unto him
23. took **b.** man by hand
10 : 46. b. Bartimeus sat begging
49. they call b. man, saying
51. **b.** man said, Lord, that I
Lu. 4 : 18. recovery of sight to **b.**
7 : 21. to many **b.** he gave sight
14 : 13. thou makest a feast, call **b.**
21. and the halt and the **b.**
18 : 35. **b.** man sat begging
Jn. 5 : 3. lay a great mult. of **b.**
9 : 1. man that was **b.** fr. birth | 2, 19, 20, 32.
6. anointed eyes of **b.** man
8. seen him that was **b.**
13. to Phari. him that was **b.**
17. unto **b.** What sayest thou
18. not believe he born **b.**
24. again called man was **b.**
25. I know, whereas I was **b.**
39. which see might be made **b.**
40. are we **b.** | 41. ye were **b.**
10 : 21. can devil open eyes of **b.**?
11 : 37. man wh. open. eyes of **b.**
Ac. 13 : 11. thou shalt be **b.** not
Ro. 2 : 19. thou art a guide to the **b.**
2 Pe. 1 : 9. lacketh these things is **b.**
Re. 3 : 17. knowest not thou art **b.**
BLIND. [Verb.]
De. 16 : 19. gift doth **b.** the eyes
1 S. 12 : 3. received I a bribe to **b.**
BLINDED, ETH.
Ex. 23 : 8. for a gift **b-h** the wise
Je. 52 : † 11. he **b-d** eyes of Zede.
Jn. 12 : 40. he hath **b.** their eyes
Ro. 11 : 7. obtained, the rest are **b.**
2 Co. 3 : 14. but their minds were **b.**
4 : 4. god of this world hath **b.** minds [eyes
1 Jn. 2 : 11. bec. darkn. hath **b.** his
BLINDFOLDED.
Lu. 22 : 64. when they had **b.** him
BLINDNESS.
Ge. 19 : 11. smote the men with **b.**
De. 28 : 28. L. sh. smite thee with **b.**
2 K. 6 : 18. Elisha prayed, Smite peo. with **b.** he smote with **b.**
Zch. 12 : 4. smite ev. horse with **b.**
Mk. 3 : † 5. grieved for **b.** of heart
Ro. 11 : 25. **b.** in part has happen.
Eph. 4 : 18. bec. of **b.** of their heart
BLOCK. See STUMBLING.
BLOOD, S.
[Where marked with † it is in the Hebrew BLOODS.] [11.
Ge. 4 : † 10. voice of bro's **b-s** crieth
9 : 4. the life which is **b.** shall you not eat, Le. 17 : 14.
5. **b.** of your lives will I require
37 : 31. they dipped the coat in **b.**
49 : 11. clothes in **b.** of grapes
Ex. 4 : 9. water shall become **b.**
7 : 17. waters be turned into **b.**, 20.
19. be **b.** through all Egypt, 21.
12 : 7. **b.** strike it on posts
13. **b.** for a token when I see **b.**
22. hyssop dip it in **b.**
23. **b.** be upon the lintel
23 : 18. not **b.** with leaven, 34 : 25.
29 : 20. his **b.** put upon tip of ear, Le. 8 : 23, 24.-14 : 14, 25.
21. shalt take of **b.** upon altar
30 : 10. once in a year with **b.**
Le. 1 : 15. **b.** shall be wrung out, 5 : 9.
4 : 6. dip finger in **b.**, 30, 34.-9 : 9.
10 : 18. **b.** of it was not bro't in

2: 4. in b. of her purifying, 5.
cleansed from issue of her b.
6. living bird in b. of bird
19. if issue in her flesh be b.
. if woman have issue of b.
4. b. be imput. unto th. man
. it is b. maketh atonement
16. not stand ag. b. of neighb.
11. b. upon them, 12, 13, 16,
. uncov. fountain of her b. ⌊27.
23: 24. drink b. of the slain
19. The revenger of b., 21, 24,
25, 27. De. 19: 6, 12. Jos. 20:
3, 5, 9.
. not cleansed but by b. of him
12: 27. b. of sacri. be poured
8. betw. b. and b., 2 Ch.19: 10.
10. and so b. be upon thee
8. b. shall be forgiven them
8. that thou bring not b.
43. avenge b. of his servants
9: 24. their b. be upon Abim.
26: 20. not my b. fall to earth
1: 16. thy b. be on thy head
. from the b. of the slain from
28. I guiltless from the b-s
11. suffer revengers of b.
† 7. come out, thou man of b-s
L. returned upon thee all b.
12. Amasa wallowed in b.
17. this b. of the men? 1 Ch.
11: 19.
2: 5. b. of war on girdle
. Their b. returned upon Joab
. b. on thy head, Eze. 33: 4.
28. till b. gushed out upon th.
: 19. dogs licked b. of Naboth
35. b. ran out of wound
3: 22. saw the waters red as b.
. This is b. kings are slain
7. avenge b. of my servant
26. b-s of Naboth, b-s of sons
16: 18. cover not thou my b.
: 30. eagles' young suck up b.
16: 4. drink-offerings of b.
: 9. What profit is in my b.?
: 13. will I drink b. of goats?
: 10. wash feet in b. of wicked
: 23. foot in b. of thine enemy
: 14. precious b. be in his sight
: 44. turned rivers into b., 105:
28: 17. violence to b. any ⌊29.
: 33. wringing of nose bringeth
: † 15. hands are full of b-s ⌊b.
4. L. shall purge b. of Jerus.
5. garments rolled in b. wash
: 9. waters of Dimon full of b.
: † 21. earth sh. disclose her b-s
: † 15. stopp. ear fr. hearing b-s
: 3. mountains melted with b.
: 3. as if he offered swine's b.
2: 34. b. of poor innocents
: 21. pour their b. by force of
: 10. cursed that keep. sw. fr. b.
: 35. my b. be upon inhab. of
4: 14. polluted thems. with b.
. 5: 17. pestilence and b. pass
9. land is full of b. and city
: 19. pour fury upon it in b.
: 6. I said when wast in thy b.
9. I washed away thy b-s
. wast polluted in thy b.
. by the b. of thy children
. I will give thee b. in fury
: 10. son that is a shedder of b.
13. his b-s shall be upon him
: 10. mother like vine in thy b.
: 32. thy b. in midst of land, 22:
: 3. the city sheddeth b. ⌊12.
. at thy b. in the midst of thee
: 37. b. is in their hands, 45.
: 7. her b. is in midst of her
I have set her b. on rock
: 23. will send b. into her streets
: 6. water with thy b. the land
: 6. prepare thee to b. thou hast
not hated b. b. shall pursue

Eze. 39: 17. eat fl., drink b., 18, 19.
44: 7. when ye offer my bread, b.,
Ho. 1: 4. avenge b. of Jezreel ⌊15.
4: † 2. and b-s toucheth b-s
Jo. 2: 30. b. fire, smoke, Ac. 2: 19.
31. moon turned into b., Ac.2: 20.
3: 21. I will cleanse their b.
Ha. 2: 8. because of men's b., 17.
Zph. 1: 17. b. be poured as dust
Mat. 9: 20. woman with an issue
of b., Mk. 5: 25. Lu. 8: 43.
16: 17. b. hath not revealed it
23: 30. not partakers in b. of proph
35. b. of Abel, Lu. 11: 51.
26: 28. my b. of new test., Mk. 14:
27: 6. because it is price of b. ⌊24.
8. called field of b., Ac. 1: 19.
24. am innocent of b. of this just
Mk. 5: 29. fountain of her b. dried
Lu. 8: 44. her issue of b. stanched
11: 50. b. of all the prophets
13: 1. whose b. Pilate mingled
22: 20. new testament in my b., 1
Co. 11: 25.
44. sweat as great drops of b.
Jn. 1: 13. were born not of b.
6: 54. who drinketh my b., 56.
55. my b. is drink indeed
19: 34. forthwith came out b. ⌈us
Ac. 5: 28. to bring this man's b. on
15: 20. abstain from b., 29.
17: 26. made of one b. all nations
18: 6. b. be on your own heads
20: 26. pure from b. of all men
21: 25. keep thems. fr. b. fornica.
1 Co. 11: 27. guilty of body and b.
15: 50. b. cannot inherit kingdom
Ep. 6: 12. we wrestle not ag. b.
Col. 1: 20. peace thro. b. of cross
He. 2: 14. chil. partakers of b.
9: 7. not without b. which he off.
12. b. of goats, but by his b.
13. if the b. of bulls sanctifieth
18. neither 1st testa. without b.
19. he took b. of calves with
20. this is b. of the testament
22. without shedding of b. there
10: 4. not possible b. of bulls
19. into holiest by b. of Jesus
11: 28. he kept sprinkling of b.
12: 4. not yet resisted unto b. ⌈eth
24. to b. of sprinkling that speak-
13: 11. whose b. is brought into
1 Pe. 1: 2. sprinkling of b. of Jes.
1 Jn. 1: 7. the b. of J. C. cleanseth
5: 6. that came by water and b.
8. the spirit, the water, and b.
Re. 5: 9. redeemed us by thy b.
6: 10. long dost not avenge our b.
12. the moon became as b.
7: 14. white in the b. of the Lamb
8: 8. part of sea became b., 16: 3.
11: 6. to turn the waters into b.
12: 11. overcame by b. of Lamb
14: 20. b. came out of wine-press
16: 4. waters, they became b.
6. hast giv. them b. to drink
18: 24. was found b. of prophets
19: 2. avenged the b. of his serv.
13. with a vesture dipped in b.
See AVENGER, REVENGER.

BLOOD be upon.

Le. 20: 9. curseth father, b.b.u. him
11. incest | 13. sodomy. b. b. u.
16. bestiality | 27. wizard, b.b.u.
De 19: 10. innoc. b. so b.b.u. thee
Eze. 18: 13. done abom. b.b.u. him
33: 5. not warning, b.b.u. him

BLOOD with bullock.

Ex. 29: 12. take b. of b., Le. 4: 5.
-16: 14, 18.
Le. 4: 7. pour b. of b. at altar, 18,
25, 30, 34. -8: 15. -9: 9. Eze.
43: 20 -45: 19. ⌈b.
16: 15 do with that as with b. of
15. shall bring of b. of b.
Is. 1: 11 I delight not in b. of b.

BLOOD of Christ.

1 Co. 10: 16. communion of b.o.C.
Ep. 2: 13. are made nigh by b.o.C.
He. 9: 14. much more shall b. o.
C. purge?
1 Pe. 1: 19. with precious b. o. C.
1 Jn. 1: 7. b. o. C. cleanseth us
from sin

BLOOD of the Covenant.

Ex. 24: 8. Moses said, Behold b.
o. c. ⌈c.
Zch. 9: 11. as for thee by b. o. thy
He. 10: 29. counted b.o.c. unholy
13: 20. thro. b. o. everlasting c.

BLOOD with eat.

Le. 3: 17. ye e. neither fat nor b.
7: 26. e. no manner of b., 27.-
17: 14. De. 12: 16, 23.-15: 23.
27. that e. b. be cut off, 17: 10.
1 S. 14: 32. peo. e. them with b.,
33, 34. ⌈your eyes
Eze. 33: 25. ye e. with b. and lift up

For BLOOD.

Nu. 35: 33. f. b. it defileth land
2 S. 3: 27. he died f. b. of Asahel
2 Ch. 24: 25. f. b. of sons of Jehoi.
Ps. 9: 12. maketh inquisition f. b.
Pr. 1: 11. let us lay wait f. b., 18.
12: 6. are to lie in wait f. b.
Mi. 7: 2. they all lie in wait f. b.

His BLOOD.

Ge. 37: 26. slay bro. and conceal h.
42: 22. behold h.b. is required ⌊b.
Ex. 29: 20. take h. b. put it upon
ear, Le. 8: 23, 24.-14: 14, 25.
Le. 20: 9. h. b. shall be upon him
Jos. 2: 19. h.b. sh. be upon his head
2 S. 4: 11. shall I not require h.b.
1 K. 2: 32. L. sh. return h.b. upon
1 K. 22: 38. dogs licked up h. b.
Eze. 3: 18. h. b. will I require at
thy hand, 20.-33: 4, 6, 8.
Ho. 12: 14. shall leave h.b. on him
Zch. 9: † 7. take h.b. out of mouth
Mat. 27: 25. h.b. be on us and ⌈b.
Jn. 6: 53. Son of man and drink h.
Ac. 20: 28. church purch. with h.b.
Ro. 3: 25. through faith in h. b.
5: 9. being justified by h.b. ⌈1: 14.
Ep. 1: 7. redemp. thro. h. b., Col.
He. 9: 12. by h. own b. he entered
13: 12. sanctify people with h. b.
Re. 1: 5. washed us in h. b.

Innocent BLOOD.

De. 19: 10. That i. b. be not shed
13. put away guilt of i. b., 21: 9.
21: 8. lay not i.b. to peo.'s charge
1 S. 19: 5. wilt thou sin against i.b.
1 K. 2: 31. i. b. that Joab shed
2 K. 21: 16. Manas. shed i.b., 24: 4.
Ps. 94: 21. they condemn i. b.
106: 38. shed i. b. even b. of sons
Pr. 6: 17. L. hateth hands shed i.b.
Is. 59: 7. make haste to shed i. b.
Je. 7: 6. shed not i. b., 22: 3.
22: 17. and heart are to shed i. b.
26: 15. surely bring i.b. on yours.
Jo. 3: 19. bec. they have shed i. b.
Jon. 1: 14. O L. lay not upon us i.b.
Mat. 27: 4. in that I betrayed i. b.

Shed BLOOD. ⌈s.

Ge. 9: 6. man's b. by man his b. be
37: 22. Reuben said to th. s. no b.
Ex. 22: 2. shall no b. be s. for him
3. if sun risen b. be s. ⌈off
Le. 17: 4. s. b. that man sh. be cut
Nu. 35: 33. cleansed of b. s. but by
De. 21: 7. hands not s. this b. ⌊b.
1 S. 25: 26. from coming to s. b.
31. hast s. b. causeless, or
33. kept me fr. coming to s. b.
1 K. 2: 5. s. b. of war in peace
1 Ch. 22: 8. hast s. b. much. 28: 3.
Ps. 79: 3. Their b. s. like water
10. revenging b. of thy serv. s.
Pr. 1: 16. haste to s. b., Ro. 3: 15
La. 4: 13. proph. s. b. of the just

Eze. 16 : 38. as women that s. b., 23 : 45.
22 : 4. guilty in b. thou hast s.
6. the princes power to s. b.
9. that carry tales to s. b.
12. taken gifts to s. b.
27. like wolves to s. b.
23 : 45. manner of wom. that s.b.
33 : 25. ye s. b. and shall ye poss.
35 : 5. hast s. b. of chil. of Israel
36 : 18. fury on th. for b. they s.
Mat. 23 : 35. on you righteous b.s.
Mk. 14 : 24. this is my b. which is s., Lu. 22 : 20.
Lu. 11 : 50. b. of all prophets s.
Ac. 22 : 20. when b. of Steph. was s.
Ro. 3 : 15. Their feet swift to s. b.
Re. 16 : 6. have s. b. of saints

Sprinkle, eth, BLOOD.

Ex. 29 : 16. take the ram's b. and s.
20. s. b. upon altar, Le. 1 : 5, 11.-3 : 2, 8, 13.-7 : 2.-17 : 6. Nu. 18 : 17.
Le. 4 : 6. priest s. b., 17. | 16 : 14, 19.
5 : 9. s. b. of sin-off. on side of altar
7 : 14. be the priests that s. the b.
Nu. 19 : 4. s. of the b. bef. tabern.
2 K. 16 : 15. s. on it b. of burnt-off.
Eze. 43 : 18. make an altar to s. b.

BLOOD Sprinkled. [24.

Ex. 24 : 6. of b. Moses s., Le. 8 : 19,
8. Moses took b. and s. on peo.
Le. 6 : 27. s. b. on any garment
8 : 30. Moses took b. s. on Aaron
9 : 12. Aaron's sons pres. b. he s., 18.
2 K. 9 : 33. Athaliah's b. s. on wall
16 : 13. Ahaz s. b. of his peace-off.
2 Ch. 29 : 22. s. b. of bullocks, 30 : 16.
35 : 11. priests s. b. fr. their hands
Is. 63 : 3. b. shall be s. on my garm.
He. 9 : 21. he s. with b. tabern.

With BLOOD.

Ex. 30 : 10. Aaron make atone. w. b.
Le. 14 : 52. cleanse house w. b.
19 : 26. sh. not eat anything w. b.
De. 32 : 42. drunk w. b. of slain
1 K. 2 : 9. hoar head br. down w. b.
2 Ch. 29 : 24. reconcilia. w. their b.
Ps. 106 : 38. land was pollut. w. b.
Is. 34 : 6. sword of L. filled w. b. (2)
7. their land sh. be soaked w. b.
49 : 26. be drunken w. own b.
59 : 3. your hands are defiled w. b.
Je. 19 : 4. filled place w. b. of
46 : 10. be made drunk w. their b.
La. 4 : 14. have pollut. thems. w. b.
Eze. 38 : 22. will plead ag. him w. b.
Ho. 6 : 8. Gilead is polluted w. b.
Mi. 3 : 10. they build up Zion w. b.
Ha. 2 : 12. that buildeth town w. b.
Ga. 1 : 16. I conferred not w. b.
He. 9 : 21. sprinkled w. b. the tab.
22. all things are purged w. b.
25. into holy place w. b.
Re. 8 : 7. fire, mingled w. b.
17 : 6. saw woman drunken w. b.

BLOOD-GUILTINESS.

Ps. 51 : 14. Deliver me from b. O God of my salvation

BLOOD-THIRSTY.

Pr. 29 : 10. b. hate upright

BLOODY. [26.

Ex. 4 : 25. a b. husband art thou,
2 S. 16 : 7. Come out, thou b. man
8. taken in mischief, a b. man
21 : 1. famine for Saul, his b. hou.
Ps. 5 : 6. L. will abhor b. man
26 : 9. gath. not my life with b. men
55 : 23. b. men not live half days
59 : 2. deliv. save me from b. men
139 : 19. depart fr. me ye b. men
Eze. 7 : 23. land is full of b. crimes
22 : 2. wilt thou judge the b. city
24 : 6. Woe to b. city, 9. Na. 3 : 1.
Ac. 28 : 8. lay sick of a b. flux

BLOOMED.

Nu. 17 : 8. Aaron's rod b. blossoms

BLOSSOM, S.

Ge. 40 : 10. her b-s shot forth
Is. 5 : 24. b. shall go up as dust

BLOSSOM, ED.

Nu. 17 : 5. the man's rod shall b.
Is. 27 : 6. Israel shall b. and bud
35 : 1. desert shall b. as the rose
2. it shall b. abundantly and
Eze. 7 : 10. rod hath b. pride
Ho. 14 : † 5. he shall b. as lily
Ha. 3 : 17. Although fig-tree not b.

BLOT. [Noun.]

De. 32 : † 5. their b. not of his chil.
Jb. 31 : 7. if b. hath cleaved to my hands [teth b.
Pr. 9 : 7. that rebukes wicked, get-

BLOT out.

Ge. 7 : † 4. living thing I b. o.
Ex. 32 : 32. b. me o. of thy book
33. hath sinned, him I b. o.
Nu. 5 : 23. shall b. them o.
De. 9 : 14. that I b. o. their name
25 : 19. sh. b. o. remem. of Amal.
29 : 20. L. shall b. o. his name
2 K. 14 : 27. said not, would b. o. Isr.
Ps. 51 : 1. O God, b. o. transgr.
9. hide sins, b. o. mine iniq.
Je. 18 : 23. nor b. o. their sin from
Re. 3 : 5. not b. o. of book of life

BLOTTED out.

Ne. 4 : 5. let not their sin be b. o.
Ps. 69 : 28. b. o. of book of living
109 : 13. let their name be b. o.
14. let not sin of mother be b. o.
Is. 44 : 22. b. o. as a thick cloud
Ac. 3 : 19. that your sins be b. o.

BLOTTETH, ING, out.

Is. 43 : 25. that b. o. thy transgr.
Col. 2 : 14. b-g o. hand-writing

BLOW. [Noun.]

Ps. 39 : 10. I am consumed by b.
Je. 14 : 17. broken with grievous b.

BLOW. [Verb.]

Ex. 15 : 10. didst b. with wind
Nu. 10 : 3. when they sh. b. with
5. When ye b. alarm, 6. [them
7. ye shall b. but not alarm
9. then ye shall b. an alarm
Ju. 7 : 18. When I b. then b. ye
1 K. 1 : 34. b. ye, say, God save
Ps. 78 : 26. caused east wind to b.
147 : 18. causeth his wind to b.
Can. 4 : 16. b. upon my garden
Is. 40 : 24. he shall b. upon them
Eze. 21 : 31. b. against thee, 22 : 21.
22 : 20. furnace to b. fire upon it
Ho. 5 : 8. b. cornet in Gibeah
Hag. 1 : 9. ye bro't I did b. upon it
Lu. 12 : 55. ye see south wind b.
Re. 7 : 1. that wind should not b.
See TRUMPET, S.

BLOWETH.

Is. 40 : 7. bec. Spirit of L. b. upon it
54 : 16. created smith that b. coals
Jn. 3 : 8. wind b. where it listeth

BLOWING.

Le. 23 : 24. memorial of b. trumpets
Nu. 29 : 1. is a day of b. trumpets
Jos. 6 : 9. going on and b. with

BLOWN.

Jb. 20 : 26. fire not b. consume
Is. 27 : 13. that trumpet be b.
Eze. 7 : 14. They have b. trumpet
Am. 3 : 6. sh. trumpet be b. in city
Mal. 1 : † 13. ye might have b. it

BLUE. [away

Ex. 25 : 4. b. purple, scarlet, 26 : 1, 31, 36.-27 : 16.-28 : 5, 6, 8, 15, 33.-35 : 6, 23, 25, 35.-36 : 8, 35, 37.-38 : 18, 23.-39 : 1, 2, 5, 8, 24, 29.
28 : 31. robe of ephod b., 39 : 22.
39 : 3. cut gold to work it in b.
Nu. 4 : 6. cloth of b., 7, 9, 11, 12.
15 : 38. upon fringes riband of b.
2 Ch. 2 : 7. cunning to work in b.,
3 : 14 vail of b. and purple [14.
Es. 1 : 6. b. hangings. b. marble
8 : 15. Mord. in apparel of b.
Eze. 23 : 6. Assyr. clothed with b.
27 : 7. b. and purple from isles
24. b. clothes and broidered
See PURPLE, CLOTH, LACE, LOOPS.

BLUENESS.

Pr. 20 : 30. b. of wound cleanseth

BLUNT.

Ec. 10 : 10. if iron be b. and he

BLUSH.

Ezr. 9 : 6. I b. to lift up my face
Je. 6 : 15. nor could they b., 8 : 12

BOANER'GES.

Mk. 3 : 17. surnamed them B.

BOAR.

Ps. 80 : 13. b. out of the wood

BOARD, S. [36 : 21.

Ex. 26 : 16. length, breadth of b.,
17. b. of tab., 18.-36 : 22, 23.
29. overlay b-s with gold, 36 : 34.
27 : 8. Hollow with b-s, -38 : 7.
36 : 20. he made b-s for tab.
30. under ev. b. two sockets
Nu. 3 : 36. of Merari shall be b.
1 K. 6 : 9. b-s of cedar, 15, 16.
Can. 8 : 9. inclose her with b-s of
Ac. 27 : 44. some on b-s came to land

BOAST. [Noun.]

Ps. 34 : 2. My soul sh. make her b.
Ro. 2 : 17. Jew, and makest b. of G.
23. makest thy b. of the law

BOAST, ED. [off

1 K. 20 : 11. not b. as he that put
2 Ch. 25 : 19. heart lifteth thee to b.
Ps. 44 : 8. In God we b. all the day
49 : 6. b. thems. in their riches
94 : 4. workers of iniq. b. thems.
97 : 7. confounded that b. of idols
Pr. 27 : 1. b. not of to-morrow
Is. 10 : 15. Shall axe b. itself ag.
61 : 6. in their glory shall you b.
Eze. 35 : 13. ye have b-d ag. me
Ro. 11 : 18. b. not ag. branches (2)
2 Co. 7 : 14. if I have b-d any th.
9 : 2. I b. to them of Macedonia
10 : 8. tho. I sho. b. somewhat
13. we will not b. of things
16. not to b. in ano. man's line
11 : 16. that I may b. a little
Ep. 2 : 9. Not works, lest any b.

BOASTERS.

Ro. 1 : 30. b. inventors of evil th.
2 Ti. 3 : 2. b. proud, blasphemers

BOASTEST, ETH.

Ps. 10 : 3. wicked b. of heart's
52 : 1. Why b-t thou in mischief?
Pr. 20 : 14. when gone then he b.
25 : 14. Whoso b. of false gift
Ja. 3 : 5. tongue little b. great th.

BOASTING. [Participle.]

Ac. 5 : 36. rose Theudas b. himself
2 Co. 10 : 15. Not b. without meas.

BOASTING, S. [Noun.]

Ro. 3 : 27. Where is b. then? it is excluded
2 Co. 7 : 14. so our b. is found truth
8 : 24. shew ye proof of our b.
9 : 3. lest our b. of you be in vain
4. ashamed in this confident b.
11 : 10. no man sh. stop me of th. b.
17. as it were foolishly in this b.
Ja. 4 : 16. now ye rejoice in your b.

BOAT, S.

Jn. 6 : 22. peo. saw was no other b.
that Jesus went not into b.
23. came other b-s from Tiberias
Ac. 27 : 16. work to come by the b.
30. when they had let down b.
32. soldiers cut off ropes of b.

BO'AZ. [3 : 17.

1 K. 7 : 21. pillar called B., 2 Ch.

BO'AZ, and BO'OZ.

Ru. 2 : 1. kinsman, his name was B.
19. with whom I wrought is B.
3 : 2. is not B. of our kindred

Ru. 3 : 7. when B. had eaten
4 : 1. Then went B. up to gate
13. So B. took Ruth and
21. B. begat Obed, 1 Ch. 2 : 11, 12. Mat. 1 : 5.
Lu. 3 : 32. Obed was son of B.

BOCH'ERU.

1 Ch. 8 : 38. Azel's sons, B., 9 : 44.

BO'CHIM.

Ju. 2 : 1. angel came up to B.
5. called that place B.

BODIES.

Ge. 47 : 18. not aught left, but **b.**
1 S. 31 : 12. took **b.** of Saul's sons, 1 Ch. 10 : 12.
Ne. 9 : 37. dominion over our **b.**
Jb. 13 : 12. your **b.** like **b.** of clay
Eze. 1 : 11. two wings cov. **b.**, 23.
Da. 3 : 27. whose **b.** fire no power
28. yielded **b.** th. might not serve
Mat. 27 : 52. **b.** of saints arose
Jn. 19 : 31. **b.** not remain on cross
Ro. 1 : 24. to dishonour their **b.**
8 : 11. sh. quicken your mortal **b.**
12 : 1. present your **b.** a living sacri.
1 Co. 6 : 15. your **b.** members of C.
15 : 40. are celestial **b.** and **b.**
Ep. 5 : 28. love wives as own **b.**
He. 10 : 22. **b.** washed with pure wa.
13 : 11. **b.** of beasts, whose blood
Re. 18 : † 13. merchandise of **b.** and

Dead BODIES.

2 Ch. 20 : 24. they were **d. b.** fallen
25. found with **d. b.** jewels
Ps. 79 : 2. **d. b.** given to be meat
110 : 6. fill places with the **d. b.**
Je. 31 : 40. valley of **d. b.** be holy
33 : 5. it is to fill them with **d. b.**
34 : 20. their **d. b.** shall be for meat
41 : 9. pit wherein Ish. cast **d. b.**
Am. 8 : 3. many **d. b.** in ev. place
Re. 11 : 8. **d. b.** shall lie in street
9. nations see their **d. b.** nor suffer **d. b.** to be put

BODILY.

Lu. 3 : 22. H. G. in a **b.** shape
2 Co. 10 : 10. **b.** presence is weak
Col. 2 : 9. fullness of Godhead **b.**
1 Ti. 4 : 8. **b.** exercise profit. little

BODY.

Ex. 24 : 10. as **b.** of heaven
1 S. 31 : 12. **b.** of Saul, 1 Ch. 10 : 12.
Jb. 19 : 17. chil.'s sake of my **b.**
26. tho. worms destroy this **b.**
20 : 25. It cometh out of the **b.**
Ps. 139 : † 15. my **b.** was not hid
Pr. 5 : 11. and **b.** are consumed
Is. 10 : 18. consume soul and **b.**
51 : 23. laid thy **b.** as ground
Eze. 10 : 12. **b.** was full of eyes
Da. 7 : 15. grieved in spirit in **b.**
Mat. 5 : 29. **b.** cast into hell, 30.
6 : 22. light of **b.** eye, Lu. 11 : 34. **b.** full of light, Lu. 11 : 34, 36.
23. **b.** shall be full of darkness
25. no thought for **b.**, Lu. 12 : 22. **b.** more than raim., Lu. 12 : 23.
10 : 28. that kill **b.**, Lu. 12 : 4.
14 : 12. John's disciples took **b.**
26 : 12. poured this oint. on my **b.**
26. Jes. said, Take, eat, this is my **b.**, Mk. 14 : 22. Lu. 22 : 19. 1 Co. 11 : 24.
27 : 58. Jo. begged **b.** of Jes., Mk. 15 : 43. Lu. 23 : 52. Jn. 19 : 38.
59. taken **b.** he wrapped it
Mk. 5 : 29. she felt in her **b.** that
14 : 8. she come to anoint my **b.**
51. linen cloth about his **b.**
15 : 45. Pilate gave **b.**, Mat. 27 : 58.
Lu. 17 : 37. **b.** is, thither eagles
24 : 3. they found not **b.** of L.
Jn. 19 : 40. took they **b.** of Jesus
20 : 12. **b.** of Jesus had lain
Ac. 9 : 40. to **b.** said Tabitha
Ro. 6 : 6. that **b.** of sin be destroyed
7 : 4. dead to law by **b.** of Christ
Ro. 7 : 24. deliv. from **b.** of this death?
8 : 10. **b.** is dead bec. of in
13. Spirit mortify deeds of **b.**
23. the redemption of our **b.**
1 Co. 6 : 13. **b.** is not for fornication, but for L. and L. for **b.**
18. Every sin is without **b.**
6 : 19. **b.** is temple of H. Ghost
7 : 4. wife no power of her **b.**
9 : 27. but I keep under my **b.**
10 : 16. communion of **b.** of C.
11 : 27. guilty of **b.** and blood
29. not discerning the Lord's **b.**
12 : 14. **b.** is not one member
15. is it theref. not of the **b.**? 16.
17. if whole **b.** were an eye
19. where were **b.** | 20. one **b.**
22. members of **b.** wh. seem, 23.
24. G. hath tempered **b.** together
27. Now ye are **b.** of Christ
13 : 3. tho. I give **b.** to be burned
15 : 35. what **b.** do dead come?
37. sowest not **b.** that shall be
38. G. giveth it a **b.** as it hath
44. natural **b.** raised a spirit. **b.**
2 Co. 5 : 8. willing to be absent fr. **b.**
Ep. 3 : 6. fellow-heirs of same **b.**
4 : 12. edifying of **b.** of Christ
16. whole **b.** fitly joined together
5 : 23. he is Saviour of the **b.**
Ph. 3 : 21. who shall change vile **b.**
Col. 1 : 18. head of the **b.** church
2 : 11. in putting off the **b.** of sins
17. shadow, but **b.** is of Christ
19. from which the **b.** by joints
23. a shew of wisdom in negl. **b.**
1 Th. 5 : 23. I pray your **b.** be pres.
He. 10 : 5. **b.** hast thou prepared
10. thro. offering of **b.** of Jesus
Ja. 2 : 16. not things needful to **b.**
26 as **b.** without spirit is dead
3 : 2. is able to bridle whole **b.**
3. we turn their whole **b.**
6. tongue defileth the whole **b.**, 3.
Jude 9. disputed about **b.** of Moses

Dead BODY.

Le. 21 : 11. nor go in to **d. b.**, Nu. 6 : 6.
Nu. 9 : 6. men defiled by **d. b.**, 7.
10. be uncl. by **d. b.**, Hag. 2 : 13.
19 : 11. toucheth **d. b.** unclean, 16.
2 K. 8 : 5. restored a **d. b.** to life
Is. 26 : 19. with my **d. b.** sh. arise
Je. 26 : 23. cast his **d. b.** into graves
36 : 30. his **d. b.** shall be cast out

Fruit of thy BODY.

De. 28 : 4. Blessed shall be **f. o. b.**
11. make thee plenteous in the **f. o. b.**, 30 : 9. [land
18. Cursed shall be **f. o. b.** and
53. shalt eat **f. o. b.** in siege
Ps. 132 : 11. **f. o. b.** will I set on thy throne [of soul
Mi. 6 : 7. give **f. o.** my **b.** for sin

His BODY.

Ex. 21 : † 3. if he came in with **h. b.**
De. 21 : 23. **h. b.** not remain all night
Ju. 8 : 30. Gid. had 70 sons of **h. b.**
1 S. 31 : 10. fastened **h. b.** to wall
Da. 4 : 33. **h. b.** wet with dew, 5 : 21.
7 : 11. beast slain and **h. b.** destr.
10 : 6. **h. b.** was like the beryl
Lu. 23 : 55. beheld how **h. b.** was laid
24 : 23. when they found not **h. b.**
Jn. 2 : 21. spake of tem. of **h. b.**
Ac. 19 : 12. from **h. b.** were bro't to the sick
Ro. 4 : 19. he considered not **h. b.**
1 Co. 6 : 18. commits fornication sinneth ag. **h. b.**
7 : 4. husband not power of **h. b.**
2 Co. 5 : 10. rec. things done in **h. b.**
Ep. 1 : 23. is **h. b.** fulness of him
5 : 30. For we are members of **h. b.**
Ph. 3 : 21. fashioned like **h.** glori. **b.**
Col. 1 : 24. for **h. b.** sake church
1 Pe. 2 : 24. bare our sins in **h. b.**

In BODY.

La. 4 : 7. more ruddy **i. b.** than
Ro. 6 : 12. Let not sin reign **i. b.**
1 Co. 5 : 3. I verily as absent **i. b.**
6 : 20. glorify G. **i.** your **b.** and spi
7 : 34. that she may be holy **i. b.**
12 : 18. set members ev. one **i. b.**
25. should be no schism **i. b.**
2 Co. 4 : 10. bearing **i. b.** dying of our L. that life be **i.** our **b.**
5 : 6. whilst we are at home **i. b.**
12 : 2. whether **i. b.** or out of, 3.
Ga. 6 : 17. I bear **i. b.** marks of L.
Ph. 1 : 20. C. be magnified **i.** my **b.**
Col. 1 : 22. reconciled **i. b.** of his flesh
He. 13 : 3. being yours. **i.** the **b.**

One BODY.

Ro. 12 : 4. many members in **o. b.**
5. we are **o. b.** in C., 1 Co. 10 : 17.
1 Co. 6 : 16. joined to harlot, is **o. b.**
12 : 12. as **b.** is **o.** and hath many
13. we are baptised into **o. b.**
20. many members, yet but **o. b.**
Ep. 2 : 16. reconcile both to G. in **o. b.**
4 : 4. There is **o. b.** and one Spirit
Col. 3 : 15. ye are called in **o. b.**

BO'HAN.

Jos. 15 : 6. stone of B. 18 : 17

BOIL, S. [Noun.]

Ex. 9 : 9. be a **b.** with blains
10. became a **b.** with blains
11. not stand, bec. of the **b.**
Le. 13 : 18. in which a **b.** | 19, 20, 23.
2 K. 20 : 7. figs on **b.**, Is. 38 : 21.
Jb. 2 : 7. Satan smote Job with **b-s**

BOIL. [Verb.]

Le. 8 : 31. **b.** flesh at door of tab.
Jb. 41 : 31. maketh deep to **b.** like
Is. 64 : 2. fire causeth waters to **b.**
Eze. 24 : 5. burn bones, make it **b.**
46 : 20. place where priests shall **b.**, 24.

BOILED.

1 K. 19 : 21. yoke of oxen and **b.** th.
2 K. 6 : 29. So we **b.** my son
Jb. 30 : 27. My bowels **b.** and

BOILETH, ING.

Ps. 45 : † 1. heart **b.** up a good
Eze. 46 : 23. made with **b.** places

BOISTEROUS.

Mat. 14 : 30. wind **b.** he was afraid

BOLD.

Pr. 28 : 1. righteous **b.** as a lion
Ac. 13 : 46. Paul and Bar. waxed **b.**
Ro. 10 : 20. Esaias is very **b.** and
2 Co. 10 : 1. being absent, am **b.**
2. not be **b.** wh. I think to be **b.**
11 : 21. any is **b.** I am **b.** also
Ph. 1 : 14. are much more **b.** to speak
1 Th. 2 : 2. we were **b.** in our God
Phm. 8. might be much **b.** in C.

BOLDLY.

Ge. 34 : 25. Levi came upon city **b.**
Mk. 15 : 43. Jo. went in **b.** to Pilate
Jn. 7 : 26. he speaketh **b.** and they
Ac. 9 : 27. preached **b.** at Damas.
29. he spake **b.** in name of L.
14 : 3. abode, speaking **b.** in L.
18 : 26. Apollos began to speak **b.**
19 : 8. spake **b.** for three months
Ro. 15 : 15. written more **b.** to you
Ep. 6 : 19. I may open my mouth **b.**
20. speak **b.** as I ought to speak
He. 4 : 16. let us come **b.** to throne
13 : 6. **b.** say, L. is my helper

BOLDNESS.

Ec. 8 : 1. **b.** of face be changed
Ac. 4 : 13. when they saw **b.** of P
29. with all **b.** they may speak
31. spake word of God with **b.**
2 Co. 3 : † 12. great **b.** of speech
7 : 4. Great is my **b.** of speech tow.
Ep. 3 : 12. in whom we have **b.**
Ph. 1 : 20. with all **b.** as always
1 Ti. 3 : 13. they purchase great **b.**
He. 10 : 19. **b.** to enter holiest
1 Jn. 4 : 17. may have **b.** in judgm.

BOLLED.
Ex. 9 : 31. and the flax b.
BOLSTER.
1 S.19 : 13.goats' hair for his b., 16.
26 : 7.spear at b.,11,12 | 16. water
BOLT, ED.
2 S.13 : 17. b. door | 18.he b-d door
BOND. [Adjective.]
1 Co. 12 : 13. into one body, b. or
See FREE. [free
BOND. [Noun.]
Nu. 30 : 2. bind his soul with b.
3. if woman bind herself by b.
4. her father hear her b.
12. conc. b. of her soul
Jb. 12 : 18. He looseth b. of kings
Eze. 20 : 37. I will bring you into b.
Lu. 13 : 16. loosed fr. his b. on sab.
Ac. 8 : 23. thou art in b. of iniquity
Ep. 4 : 3. of Spirit in b. of peace
Col. 3 : 14.charity, b. of perfectness
BONDS.
Nu. 30 : 5. not her b. shall stand
7. b. whw. she bound her soul
14. he established all her b. wh.
Ps. 116 : 16. thou hast loosed my b.
Je. 5 : 5. broken yoke, burst b.
27 : 2.make b. and yokes, Na.1 : 13.
30 : 8. I will burst thy b.
Na. 1 : 13. and I will burst thy b.
Ac. 20 : 23. b. and afflic. abide me
23 : 29.nothing worthy of b.,26:31.
25 : 14. man left in b. by Felix
26 : 29. such as I am exc. these b.
Ep. 6 : 20. am ambassador in b.
Ph. 1 : 7. in b. partakers of grace
13. my b. in C. are manifest
14. breth. confident by my b.
16. to add affliction to my b.
Col.4 : 3.I am in b. | 18.Rem. my b.
2 Ti. 2 : 9. suffer troub. even to b.
Phm. 10. whom begotten in my b.
13. ministered to me in b. of gos.
He. 10 : 34. compassion of me in b.
11 : 36. others had trial of b. and
13 : 3.Remem. them in b. as bound
BONDAGE.
Ex. 1 : 14. lives bitter with hard b.
2 : 23. Isr. sighed by reason of b.
cried to G. by reason of b.
6 : 6. I will rid you out of their b.
9. hearkened not for cruel b. [b.
13 : 3. day ye came out of house of
14. L. brought us out of house of
b., 20 : 2. De. 5 : 6.–6 : 12.–8 :
14.–13 : 5, 10. Jos. 24 : 17. Ju.
6 : 8. [b.
De. 26 : 6. Egyp. laid upon us hard
Ne. 5 : 5. we bring into b. our sons,
dau-s are brought into b.
18. bec. b. was heavy upon peo.
9 : 17.app.a captain to return to b.
Is. 14 : 3. L. give rest from hard b.
Ro. 8 : 15. not received spirit of b.
21. delivered fr. b. of corruption
Ga.4 : 24.Sinai, wh. gendereth to b.
5 : 1. not entangled with yoke of b.
He. 2 : 15. all lifetime subject to b.
In, into, or under BONDAGE.
Ex. 6 : 5. Isr. the Egyp. keep i. b.
Ezr. 9 : 8. a little reviving i. our b.
9.G. hath not forsak. us i. our b.
Jn. 8 : 33. never i. b. to any man
Ac. 7 : 6. they sho. bring them i.b.
7. nation to wh. shall be i. b.
1 Co. 7 : 15. bro. or sister not u. b.
2 Co.11 : 20.if a man bring you i.b.
Ga. 2 : 4. they might bring us i. b.
4 : 3. were i.b. under the elements
9. whereunto ye desire to be i. b.
25. ans. to Jerus. which is i. b.
2 Pe. 2 : 19. same is he brought i.b.
BONDMAID, S.
Le. 19 : 20. whoso. lieth with a b.
25 : 44.thy b-s be of heath.buy b-s
Ga. 4 : 22. one by a b. the other by

BONDMAN.
Ge. 44 : 33. let me inst. of lad a b.
De. 15 : 15. remember thou wast a
b. in E., 16 : 12.–24 : 18, 22.
Re. 6 : 15. every b. hid in the dens
BONDMEN.
Ge. 43 : 18. he may take us for b.
44 : 9. and we will be my lord's b.
Le. 25 : 42.they sh. not be sold as b.
44. b. sh. be of heath. buy b.
46. they sh. be your b. for ever
26 : 13. that ye sho. not be th ir b.
De. 6 : † 12. lest forget L. who bro't
thee out of b., 13 : † 10.
21. then say, We were Pha.'s b.
7 : 8. redeemed you out of b.
28 : 68. there ye shall be sold for b.
Jos. 9 : 23. none freed fr. being b.
1 K. 9 : 22. of Isr. Sol. made no b.
2 K. 4 : 1.to take my 2 sons to be b.
2 Ch. 28 : 10. to keep chil. of Judah
for b. [not forsak.
Ezr. 9 : 9. we were b. yet G. hath
Es. 7 : 4. if we had been sold for b.
Je. 34 : 13. I bro't them out of b.
BOND-SERVANT.
Le. 25 : 39. not compel to serve as b.
BOND-SERVICE.
1 K.9 : 21.Sol. did levy tribute of b.
BONDWOMAN.
Ge. 21 : 10. Cast out this b. son of
b. shall not be heir, Ga. 4 : 30.
12. let it not grieve thee bec. of b.
13. son of b. will I make nation
Ga. 4 : 23. son of b. born aft. flesh
31. we are not children of the b.
BONDWOMEN.
De. 28 : 68. sold for b., Es. 7 : 4.
BONE.
Ge. 2 : 23. This is b. of my bones
29 : 14. Surely thou art my b. and
Ex.12 : 46.neith. break b., Nu.9:12.
Nu. 19 : 16. toucheth a b. of a man,
be unclean [b. and flesh
Ju. 9 : 2. remember that I am your
2 S. 5 : 1. we are thy b., 1 Ch.11 : 1.
19 : 13. Art thou not of my b.
Jb. 2 : 5. touch his b. he will curse
19 : 20. My b. cleaveth to my skin
31 : 22. let my arm be broken fr. b.
Pr. 25 : 15. soft tongue breaketh b.
Eze. 37 : 7. bones came b. to his b.
39 : 15. when any seeth a man's b.
Jn. 19 : 36. b. of him sh. not be
BONES. [broken
Ex. 13 : 19. Moses took b. of Joseph
Jos. 24 : 32. b. of Joseph buried
Ju. 19 : 29. divided concu. with b.
2 S.21:12.b. of Saul, b. of Jona.,14.
1 K. 13 : 2. men's b. shall be burnt
2 K. 13 : 21. touched b. of Elisha
23 : 14. filled places with b. of men
16. took b. out of sepulchres
20.he burnt men's b.upon altars
2 Ch. 34 : 5. he burnt b. of priests
Jb. 10 : 11. hast fenced me with b.
Ps. 51 : 8. b. thou hast brok. may
53 : 5. G. scattereth b. of him that
141 : 7. Our b. are scatt. at grave's
Pr. 3 : 8. fear L. it be marrow to b.
14 : 30. envy the rottenness of b.
15 : 30. good report maketh b. fat
16 : 24.pleasant words health to b.
17 : 22. broken spirit drieth the b.
Ec. 11 : 5. how b. grow in womb
Is. 58 : 11. L. shall make fat thy b.
66 : 14. your b. shall flourish like
Je. 8 : 1. bring b. of kings, b. of
priests, b. of prophets, b. of
Eze. 6 : 5. scatt. your b. ab. altars
24:4.with choice b. | 5.burn b.,10.
37 : 1. valley full of b. | 3. b. live?
4. Prophesy upon b. O ye dry b.
5. saith God unto b. | 7. [b.
11. these b. are house of Isr. our
Am. 2 : 1. bec. he burnt b. of king
6 : 10.burneth him, to bring out b.

Zph. 3 : 3. they gnaw not b. til
Mat. 23 : 27. full of dead men's
Lu. 24 : 39. for a spirit hath no
His BONES. [h
1 K. 13 : 31. dead lay my b. be
2 K. 23 : 18. let no man move h
Jb. 20 : 11. h.b. are full of the
21 : 24. h.b. moistened with m
33 : 19. mult. of h.b. with str. p
21. h. b. not seen, stick out
40 : 18. h.b. as brass, h.b. as
Ps. 34 : 20. He keepeth all h.
not one is broken
109 : 18. let come like oil into h
Pr. 12 : 4. is as rottenness in h.
Je. 50 : 17. Neb. hath broken h.
Ep. 5 : 30. we are members of h.
He. 11 : 22. gave com. conc. h.
My BONES. [
Ge. 50 : 25. carry up m.b., Ex.
2 S. 19 : 12. Ye are m.b. and fle
1 K.13 : 31.dead m.b. beside his
Jb. 4 : 14. made all m. b. to sh
7 : † 15. chooseth death than m.
30 : 17. m. b. are pierced in m
30. my skin is black, m.b. bu
Ps. 6 : 2. heal me, m. b. are ve
22 : 14. all m.b. are out of join
17. I may tell all m. b.
31 : 10. m. b. are consumed [
32 : 3. kept silence m. b. wa
35 : 10. All m.b. shall say, L. w
38 : 3. neither is any rest in m.
42 : 10. As with a sword in m.
102 : 3. m. b. are burnt as hea
5. groaning m. b. cleave to s
Is. 38 : 13. so will he break all m.
Je. 20 : 9. as a fire shut up in m.
23 : 9. heart broken, m. b. sha
La. 1 : 13. hath sent fire into m.
3 : 4. he hath broken m. b.
Ha. 3 : 16. rottenness entered in
Their BONES. [m.
Nu. 24 : 8. Israel shall break t.
1 S. 31 : 13. t. b. and buried at
besh [c
1 Ch. 10 : 12. buried t. b. under
La. 4 : 8. their skin cleaveth to t.
Eze.32 : 27.their iniq. sh. be en t.
Da. 6 : 24. the lions brake all t.
Mi. 3 : 2. pluck off flesh from t.
3.they break t. b. and chop th
BONNETS.
Ex. 28 : 40. for Aaron's sons th
shalt make b. [them, Le. 8:
29 : 9. thou shalt put the b.
39 : 28. they make goodly b.
fine linen [the
Is. 3 : 20. the Lord will take aw
Eze. 44 : 18. they shall have lin
b. on their heads
BOOK.
Ex. 17 : 14. for a memorial in a
32 : 32. blot me out of thy b.
33.sinned, will I blot out of my
Nu. 5 : 23. write these curses in a
21 : 14. in b. of the wars of the
De. 17 : 18.a copy of this law in a
31 : 24. end of writing law in b
Jos. 10 : 13.in b. of Jasher,2S.1:
18 : 9. describ. it into 7 parts in
1 S. 10 : 25. Samuel wrote it in
1 K.11 : 41.writ. in b. of acts of
2 K. 22 : 8. Hilkiah gave b. to S
10. Hilkiah delivered me a b.
Ch. 34 : 15, 18.
16. I will bring all words of the
23 : 24. might perform words in
1 Ch. 9 : 1. written the b. of kin
29 : 29.are written in b. of Sam
2 Ch. 9 : 29. acts of Sol. in b. of
12 : 15. acts of Rehob. in b. of S
20 : 34.acts of Jehosh.in b. of J
34 : 16. Shaphan carried b. to
21.conc. words of b. that is fo
24. curses that are written in
Ezr. 4 : 15.search made in b. of

Ne. 8 : 5. Ezra open. b. in the sight
Es. 9 : 32. it was written in the b.
Jb.19 : 23.oh that they were in a b.
31 : 35. that adversary had writ. b.
Ps. 40 : 7. volume of b., He. 10 : 7.
56 : 8. tears, are they not in thy b.
69: 28.let them be blotted out of b.
139 : 16. in thy b. all my members
Is. 29 : 11. words of a b. sealed
12. b. is deliv. to him not learned
18. deaf sh. hear words of b.
30 : 8. Now go and note it in a b.
34: 16. seek ye out of b. of the L.
Je. 30 : 2. write words spoken in b.
32 : † 10. I wrote in b. evidence
12. witnesses that subscribed b.
36 : 2.take roll of b. | 10.read in b.
11. had heard out of b.
18. I wrote them in b.
32. words of b. which Jehoiada
45 : 1. writ. words in b. from Jere.
51 : 60. Jere.wrote in b. all the evil
Eze. 2 : 9. roll of a b. was therein
Da. 12 : 1. ev. one found writt. in b.
4. O Daniel, seal the b.
Na. 1 : 1. b. of vision of Nahum
Mal.3 : 16.b. of remem. was written
Mat. 1 : 1. b. of generation of Jes.
Lu. 3 : 4. as writt. in b. of Esaias
4 : 17. was delivered to Jes. b. of Esaias, when he had opened b.
20. he closed the b. and gave it
20 : 42. in the b. of Ps., Ac. 1 : 20.
Ac. 7 : 42. written in b. of prophets
He. 9 : 19. he sprinkled b. and peo.
Re. 1 : 11. what seest, write in a b.
5 : 1.a b.writt. within, on backside
2. Who is worthy to open the b.
3. no man was able to open b.
4. worthy to open b. | 5. 7, 8, 9.
10 : 2. had in his hand a little b.
8. Go and take little b. open
9. give me little b. | 10. I took b.
20 : 12. b. was opened, b. of life
22 : 19. if any take fr. words of b.
See COVENANT.

BOOK of the Law.

De.28 : 61.plague not writ. in b.o.l.
29 : 21. acc. to curses in b. o. l.
30 : 10. to keep statutes in b. o. l.
31 : 26. this b. o. l. put it in ark
Jos. 1 : 8. this b.o.l. sh. not depart
8 : 31. written in b. o. l. of Moses, 34. | 23 : 6. 2 K. 14 : 6.
24 : 26. Josh. wrote in b. o. l.
2 K. 22 : 8. I have found b. o. l. in house, 2 Ch. 34 : 14, 15.
11. k. heard words of b. o. l.
2 Ch 17 : 9. had b. o. l. of Lord
Ne. 8 : 1. Ezr. to bring b. o. l.
3. peo. attentive unto b. o. l.
8. read in b. o. l., 18.-9 : 3.
Ga.3: 10. writ. in b. o. l. to do them

BOOK of Life. [l.

Ph. 4 : 3. whose names are in b. o.
Re.3 : 5.not blot name out of b.o.l.
13 : 8. names not in b.o.l., 17 : 8.
20 : 12. another b. opened, b. o. l.
15. not found in b. o. l. was cast
21 : 27. are writ. in Lamb s b. o. l.
22 : 19. take his part out of b. o. l.

BOOK of Moses.

2 Ch. 25 : 4. did as writ. in b. M.
35 : 12. to offer as writ. in b. M.
Ezr.6 : 18.set priests,as writ.in b.M.
Ne. 13 : 1. that day read in b. M.
Mk. 12 : 26. have ye read in b. M.?

This BOOK.

Ge. 5 : 1. t. is b. of gen. of Adam
De.28 : 58. writ.in t. b., 2 Ch. 34 : 21.
29 : 20. curses written in t. b., 27.
2 K. 22 : 13.inq. conc. words of t. b. not heark. to words of t. b.
23 : 3. perform words writ. in t. b.
Je. 25 : 13. bring all writ. in t. b.
51 : 63. made end of reading t. b.
Jn. 20 : 30. signs not writ. in t. b.
Re. 22 : 7. sayings of proph. of t. b.
9. which keep sayings of t. b.
10. Seal not the sayings of t. b.
18. heareth words of t. b., add to him plagues in t. b.
19. his part from things in t. b.

BOOKS.

Ezr. 6 : † 1. search was made of b.
Ec. 12 : 12. of making many b.
Da. 7 : 10. b. were open., Re. 20 : 12.
9 : 2. I underst. by b. num. of yrs.
Jn. 21 : 25. world not contain b.
Ac.19: 19.brought b.and burned th.
2 Ti. 4 : 13. bring b. parchments
Re. 20 : 12. judged out of things in [b.

BOOTH.

Jb. 27 : 18. b. that keeper maketh
Jon. 4 : 5. Jonah made him a b.

BOOTHS.

Ge. 33 : 17. Jacob made b. for
† the name of the place is b.
Le. 23 : 42. dwell in b. seven days
43. I made Israel dwell in b.
Ne. 8 : 14. Isr. should dwell in b.
15. to make b. | 16. made b.

BOOTY, IES.

Nu. 31 : 32. b. the rest of the prey
Je. 49 : 32. their camels sh. be a b.
Ha. 2 : 7. thou shalt be for b-s
Zph. 1 : 13. goods sh. become a b.

BO'OZ. See BOAZ.

BORDER. [Verb]

Zch. 9 : 2. Hamath also shall b.

BORDER. [Noun.]

Ge. 49 : 13. Zebulun his b. sh. be
Ex. 19 : 12. touch b. of mount
25 : 25. make to it a b. (2)
Nu. 20 : 16. city in utterm. of b.
21. refused Isr. pass thro' b.
21 : 23. suffer Isr. thro' b.
34 : 8. From Hor point out b.
35 : 26. slayer come without b.
De. 12 : 20. When L. enlarge b.
Jos. 22 : 25. L. made Jordan a b.
24 : 30. buried Josh. in b. of his inheri. in mt. Ephr., Ju. 2 : 9.
2 S. 8 : 3. went to recover his b.
1 K. 4 : 21. Sol. reigned unto b. of E., 2 Ch. 9 : 26.
2 K. 3 : 21. all able stood in b.
Ps. 78 : 54. to b. of his sanctuary
Pr. 15 : 25. establish b. of widow
Is. 19 : 19. a pillar at the b.
28 : † 25. cast rye in their b.
37 : 24. enter into height of his b.
Je. 31 : 17. chil. come to their b.
50 : 26. ag. her from utmost b.
Eze. 11 : 10. judge in b. of Isr., 11.
47 : 13. This shall be the b.
48 : 12. b. of Lev. | 13. of priests
Jo. 3 : 6. remove them from b.
Am. 1 : 13. might enlarge their b.
6 : 2. b. greater than your b.
Ob. 7. brought thee even to b.
Zph. 2 : 8. magnified ag. their b.
Mal. 1 : 4. call them b. of wickedn.
5. will be magnifi. from b. of Isr.
Mk. 6 : 56. touch. if but b. of garm.
Lu. 8 : 44. touched b. of his garm.
See EAST, SOUTH.

BORDERS.

Ge. 23 : 17. trees in all b. sure
Ex. 8 : 2. smite thy b. with frogs
16 : 35. come to b. of Canaan
34 : 24. I will enlarge thy b.
Nu. 15 : 38. in b. on fringe of b.
20 : 17. have passed thy b., 21 : 22.
1 K. 7 : 28. had b. and b. were
2 K. 16 : 17. Ahaz cut off b.
19 : 23. enter lodgings of his b.
1 Ch. 5 : 16. Sharon, upon their b.
Ps. 74 : 17. hast set b. of earth
147 : 14. maketh peace in thy b.
Can. 1 : 11. make thee b. of gold
Is. 15 : † 5. heart cry to the b.
54 : 12. thy b. of pleasant stones
60 : 18. nor destruc. within b.
Jo. 15 : 13. thy sins, in all thy b.
17 : 3. places for sin thro' thy b.
Eze. 27 : 4. Thy b. in midst of seas
45 : 1. shall be holy in thy b.
Mi. 5 : 6. he treadeth within our b.
Mat. 4 : 13. in the b. of Zabulon
23 : 5. and enlarge the b. of their garments
Mk. 7 : 24. b. of Tyre and Sidon

BORE, ED.

Ex. 21 : 6. his master sh. b. his ear
Nu.16: † 14. b.out eyes of these men?
Ju.16 : † 21. Philis. b-d out his eyes
2 K. 12: 9. Jehoi. took chest and b-d
Jb. 40 : † 24. will any b. his nose?
41 : 2. canst thou b. his jaw thro'?

BORN.

Ge.17: 17. child b. 100 yrs. old, 21 : 5.
24 : 15. Rebekah was b. to Bethuel
Ex. 1 : 22. every son b. ye shall cast into the river
Le. 18 : 9. whether b. at home or b.
19 : 34. stranger b.as one b.am.you
23 : 42. Israelites b. shall dwell in booths
Nu. 15 : 13. all b. of the country
29. one law for him that is b.
Jos.5 : 5.b. in wilder. had not circ.
8 : 33. stranger, as he that was b.
Ju 13 : 8. do to child that sh. be b.
18 : 29. city after name of Dan. b. to Israel
2 S. 12 : 14. child b. sh. surely die
1 K. 13 : 2. a child sh. be b. to Da.
1 Ch. 7 : 21. men of Gath b. in land
20 : † 6. he was b. to the giant
22 : 9. a son shall be b. to thee
Jb. 3 : 3. day perish wherein I was b.
5 : 7. man is b. to trouble as sparks
11 : 12. tho' man be b. like colt
15 : 7. art thou first man th. was b.?
38 : 21. Knowest it, bec. then b.?
Ps. 22 : 31. declare to peo. sh. be b.
58 : 3. they go astray as soon as b.
78 : 6. even chil. that should be b.
87 : 4. this man b. there, 6. | 5.
Pr. 17 : 17. bro. is b. for adversity
Ec. 3 : 2. a time to be b. and to die
4 : 14. b. in kingd. becometh poor
Is. 9 : 6. unto us a child is b. to us
66 : 8. shall nation be b. at once?
16 : 3. conc. sons and daus. b. in
Je.20:14. Cursed be the day I was b.
22 : 26. where not b. shall ye die
Eze. 16 : 4. in day thou wast b. thy
5. to loathing in day thou wast b.
47 : 22. be as b. in the country
Ho. 2 : 3. set her as in day she was b.
Mat. 1 : 16. of whom was b. Jesus
2 : 1. when Jesus was b. in Bethle.
2. where be b. king of Jews?
4. demanded where C. sho. be b.
19 : 12. some eunuchs were so b.
26 : 24. good if he had not been b., Mk. 14 : 21.
Lu. 1 : 35. holy thing th. sh. be b.
2 : 11. to you is b. this day in city
Jn. 1 : 13. Which was b. not of blood
3 : 4. How be b. when he is old?
5. Except a man be b. of water
6. b. of flesh is flesh, that b. of Spi
8. so is every one b. of the Spirit
8 : 41. We be not b. of fornication
9 : 2. who sin, that he was b. blind?
19. son wh. ye say was b. blind
20. Our son, and was b. blind
32. eyes of one b. blind
34. wast b. in sins, and teach us?
16 : 21. for joy that a man is b.
18 : 37. To this end was I b.
Ac. 2 : 8. tongue wherein we were b.
7 : 20. in which time Moses was b.
18 : 2. a Jew Aquila b. in Pontus
24. Apollos b. at Alexandria
22 : 3. b. in Tarsus | 28. I free-b.
Ro. 9 : 11. chil. being not yet b.
1 Co. 15 : 8. one b. out of due time

Ga. 4 : 23. was b. after the flesh, 29.
He. 11 : 23. Moses when b. was hid
1 Pe. 2 : 2. as new-b. babes desire
1 Jn.2 : 29.doeth righte.is b. of him
Re. 12 : 4. devour child soon as b.

BORN again.

Jn. 3 : 3. except a man b. a., 5.
7. marvel not, ye must be b. a.
1 Pe. 1 : 23. b.a. not of corrup. seed
See FIRSTBORN, WITNESS.

BORN of God.

Jn. 1 : 13. b. not of blood, but o. G.
1 Jn. 3 : 9. b. o. G. doth not commit sin, because b. [G.
4 : 7. every one that loveth is b.o.
5 . 1. believ. J. is C. is b.o.G.
4. whatso. is b.o.G.' overcometh
18. whoso. is b. o. G. sinneth not

BORN in house.

Ge. 14 : 14. armed serv. b. i. his h.
15 : 3. one b. i. my h. is my heir
17 : 12.b.i.h.be circumc., 13,23,27.
Le. 22 : 11. b.i. priest's h. eat of his
Ec. 2 : 7. I had servants b.i. my h.

BORN in the land.

Ex. 12 : 19. stranger or b. i. l.
48. stranger be as one b. i. l.
Le. 24 : 16. b.i.l. that blasphemeth
Nu. 9 : 14. for stranger and b. i. l.
15 : 30. doeth aught whether b.i.l.

BORN of a woman, or women. [days

Jb. 14 : 1. Man b. o. w. is of few
15 : 14. b. o. w. that he should be righteous
25 : 4. how clean that is b. o. w.
Mat.11 : 11.that are b.o.w.,Lu. 7 : [28.

BORNE. [Brought forth.]

Ge. 21 : 7. b. him a son in old age
29 : 34. I have b. him three sons
30 : 20. I have b. him six sons
31 : 43. what to chil. they have b.
Le. 12 : 2. b. a man child
7. law of her b. a male [belov.
De. 21 : 15. b. him chil. both the
Ru. 4 : 15. dau.-in-l. hath b. him
1 S. 2 : 5. barren hath b. seven
4 : 20. fear not, hast b. a son
Je. 15 : 9. she that hath b. seven
10. hast b. me a man of strife
Eze.16 : 20.sons thou hast b.unto me

BORNE. [Carried.]

Ge 50 : †23.chil.b.on Joseph's knees
Ex.25 : 14.that ark be b. with them
28. that table be b. with them
Ju.16 : 29.pillars on wh. house b.up
Is. 46 : 3. b. by me from belly
66 : 12.ye shall be b. upon her sides
Je. 10 : 5. must be b. bec. cannot go
Am. 5 : 26. b. tab. of Moloch
Mk. 2 : 3. one sick of palsy was b. of
Jn. 20 : 15. if hast b. him hence
Ac. 21 : 35. he was b. of soldiers
1 Co. 15 : 49. b. image of earthly

BORNE. [Endured.]

Jb. 34 : 31. I have b. chastisement
Ps. 55 : 12. enemy, then I could have b.
69 : 7. thy sake I have b. reproach
Is. 53 : 4. Surely he hath b. griefs
La. 3 : 28. he hath b. it upon him
5 : 7.fathers we have b. their iniq.
Eze. 16 : 58. Thou hast b. thy lewd.
32 : 24.b.shame,25 -36 : 6.-39:26.
Mat. 20 : 12. b. burden and heat
23 : 4. grievous to be b.,Lu.11 : 46.
Re. 2 : 3. hast b. and hast patience

BORROW. [11 : 2.

Ex. 3 : 22. woman b. of neighbour,
22 : 14. if man b. aught, and it be
De. 15 : 6. lend, but not b., 28 : 12.
2 K. 4 : 3. Go b. vessels abroad, b. not few [not away
Mat. 5 : 42.from him would b. turn

BORROWED, ETH.

Ex. 12 : 35. b-d of Egyp. jewels
2 K. 6 : 5. Alas, master, it was b.
Ne. 5 : 4. b-d money for king's trib.
Ps. 37 : 21. wicked b-h payeth not

BORROWER.

Pr. 22 : 7. b. is servant to lender
Is. 24 : 2. as with lender so b.

BOS'CATH=BOZ'KATH.

2 K. 22 : 1. Adulah of B. | Jos. 15 : 39.

BOSOM. [b.

Ge. 16 : 5. given my maid into thy
Ex. 4 : 6. Put hand into thy b., 7.
Nu. 11 : 12. Carry them in thy b.
De. 13 : 6. if wife of thy b. entice
28 : 54. eye evil tow. wife of his b.
56. eye evil tow. husb. of her b.
Ru. 4 : 16. child and laid it in her b.
2 S. 12 : 3. and lay in his b.
8. thy master's wives into thy b.
1 K. 1 : 2. virgin, let lie in thy b.
3 : 20. took my son, laid it in her b. her dead child in my b.
17 : 19. Elij. took him out of her b.
22 : † 35. blood into b. of chariot
Jb.19 : †27.reins consumed in my b.
31 : 33. hiding mine iniq. in my b.
Ps. 35 : 13. prayer ret. into own b.
74 : 11. pluck hand out of thy b.
79 : 12. render seven-fold into b.
89 : 50. bear in my b. reproach
129 : 7. bindeth sheaves, his b.
Pr. 5 : 20. embrace b. of stranger?
6 : 27. can man take fire in his b.?
17 : 23. wicked taketh gift out of b.
19 : 24.hideth his hand in b.,26:15.
21 : 14. reward in b. pacifieth
Ec. 7 : 9. anger rest. in b. of fools
Is. 40 : 11. carry lambs in his b.
49 : † 22. bring thy sons in their b.
65 : 6. even recomp. into their b.
7. measure work into their b.
Je.32 : 18. iniq. of fa. into b. of chil.
La. 2 : 12. soul into mother's b.
Eze. 43 : † 13. b. of altar be a cubit
Mi. 7 : 5. her that lieth in thy b.
Lu.6 : 38.good measure into your b.
16:22.by angels into Abraham's b.
23.seeth Ab.and Lazarus in his b.
Jn. 1 : 18. in b. of the Father
13 : 23. was leaning on Jesus' b.

BO'SOR. See BA'LAAM.

BOSSES.

Jb. 15 : 26. thick b. of his bucklers

BOTCH.

De.28 : 27. L. smite thee with b., 35.

BOTH.

Ge. 2 : 25.b. naked | 3 : 7.eyes of b.
19 : 36. b. daus. of Lot with child
21 : 27. b. of them made a coven.
31. bec. there they sware b.
22 : 8. went b. of them together
27 : 45. why be deprived of you b.
31 : 37. may judge betwixt us b.
Ex. 22 : 9. cause of b. bef. judges
11. oath of Lord be between b.
32 : 15. tables written on b. sides
Le. 20 : 11. b. of them surely be put to death, 12. De. 22 : 22.
Nu. 12 : 5. Aaron, Miriam, b. came
25 : 8. Phinehas thrust b. through
De. 19 : 17. b. men sh. stand bef. L.
1 S. 2 : 34. in one day shall die b.
9 : 26.went b.of them,he and Sam.
20 : 42. as we have sworn b. of us
25 : 43. they were b. his wives
Jb. 9 : 33. days-man lay hand on b.
Pr. 17 : 15. b. are abom., 20 : 10.
20 : 12. L. hath made even b. of th.
24 : 22. knoweth ruin of them b.
Ec. 4 : 3. better than b. is he that
Is.1 : 31.they shall b.burn together
7 : 16. land be forsaken of b. kings
Je. 46 : 12. are fallen b. together
Eze. 21 : 19. b. sh. come of one land
23 : 13. saw they b. took one way
Mi. 7 : 3. do evil with b. hands
Zch. 6 : 13. couns. of peace betw. b.
9 : † 15. shall fill b. bowls
Mat.9 : 17. b.are preserved, Lu.5:38.
Mat. 13:30. Let b. grow until harv.
15 : 14. b. fall into ditch, Lu. 6:39.
Lu. 1 : 6. were b. righteous before
7. b. were now well stricken
5 : 7. came and filled b. ships
7 : 42. frankly forgave them b.
Ac. 8 : 38. down b. into the water
23 : 8. but Pharis. confess b.
Ep. 2 : 14. who hath made b. one
16. might reconcile b. unto God
2 Pe. 3 : 1. in b. I stir your minds
Re. 19 : 20. b. were cast into lake

BOTTLE.

Ge. 21 : 14. b. of wat. gave it Hagar
15. wat. spent in b. | 19. filled b.
Ju. 4 : 19. she opened a b. of milk
1 S. 1 : 24. Hannah took b. of wine
10 : 3. ano. carrying a b. of wine
16 : 20. Jesse took a b. of wine
2 S. 16 : 1. Ziba to Da. b. of wine
Ps. 56 : 8. put my tears into thy b.
119 : 83. I am like b. in the smoke
Is. 30 : † 14. break it as b. of potters
Je. 13 : 12. Ev. b. filled with wine
19 : 1. potter's b. | 10.break the b.
Ha. 2 : 15.puttest thy b. to him and

BOTTLES.

Jos. 9 : 4. Gibeonites took wine b.
13. these b. of wine were new
1 S.25 : 18. Abig.took two b.of wine
Jb. 32 : 19.belly to burst like new b.
38 : 37. who stay b. of heaven?
Je. 48 : 12. empty vessels, break b.
Ho. 7 : 5. made sick with b. of wine
Mat. 9 : 17. new wine into old b. b. break, Mk. 2 : 22. Lu. 5 : 37,38.

BOTTOM, S.

Ex. 15 : 5. sank into b. as stone
29 : 12. pour blood beside b. of altar, Le. 4 : 7, 18, 25, 30.-5 : 9.-8 : 15.-9 : 9.
Jb. 36 : 30. G. covereth b. of sea
Can. 3 : 10. he made b. of gold
Eze.36 : † 4. saith L. to hills and b-s
43 : 13. b. shall be a cubit, 17.
Da. 6 : 24. came at the b. of den
Am. 9 : 3. hid from my sight in b.
Jon. 2 : 6. I went to b-s of mount-s
Zch. 1 : 8. myrtle-trees in the b.
Mat. 27 : 51. vail rent from top to b., Mk. 15 : 38.

BOTTOMLESS.

Re. 9 : 1. to him key of b. pit
2. opened b. pit, arose smoke
11. a k. which is angel of b. pit
11 : 7. beast that asc. out of b. pit
17 : 8. beast sh. ascend out of b. pit
20 : 1. angel having key of b. pit
3. cast him into the b. pit, and

BOUGH.

Ge. 49 : 22. Joseph is a fruitful b. b. by a well, whose branches run over the wall
Ju. 9 : 48. Abimelech cut down a b.
49. cut down every man his b.
Is. 10 : 33.L. shall lop b. with terror
17 : 6. berries in top of utterm. b.
9. strong cities be as a forsak. b.

BOUGHS.

Le. 23 : 40. b. of goodly trees, b. of
De.24 : 20.shalt not go over b.again
2 S. 18 : 9. mule went under b. of
Jb. 14 : 9. brought b. like a plant
Ps. 80 : 10. b. like goodly cedar-tr.
11. She sent out her b. to the sea
Can. 7 : 8. I will take hold of the b.
Is. 27 : 11. When b. are withered.
30 : † 17. left as tree bereft of b.
Eze. 17 : 23. it shall bring forth b.
31 : 3. his top was am. thick b., 14.
5. his b. were multiplied
6. their nests in his b., Da. 4 : 12.
8. fir-trees not like his b.
10. shot up his top am. b.
12. his b. are broken

BOUGHT. [Noun.]

1 S. 25 : † 29. midst of b. of a sling

BOUGHT. [Verb.]
Ge. 17 : 12. circ. man-ch. **b.** with money, 13, 23, 27. Ex. 12 : 44.
33 : 19. Jacob **b.** a field, Jos. 24 : 32.
39 : 1. Potiphar **b.** Joseph of Ish.
47 : 14. gath. money for corn th. **b.**
20. Joseph **b.** all land of E., 23.
22. land of priests **b.** he not [16.
49 : 30. which Ab. **b.**, 50 : 13. Ac.7 :
Le.25 : 28.remain in hand that **b.** it
30. be estab. to him that **b.** it
50. reckon with him that **b.** him
25 : 51. of money he was **b.** for
27 : 22. sanctify to L. field he **b.**
24. return to him of wh. it was **b.**
De. 32 : 6. he thy fa. that **b.** thee?
Jos. 24 : 32. ground Jacob **b.** of
Ru. 4 : 9. have **b.** all was Elimel.'s
2 S. 12 : 3. ewe-lamb he had **b.**
24 : 24. David **b.** threshing-floor
1 K.16 : 24.Omri **b.** the hill Samaria
Ne. 5 : 16. nor **b.** we any land
Je. 32 : 9. I **b.** the field of Hanameel
43. fields sh. be **b.** in this land
Ho. 3 : 2. I **b.** her for 15 pieces
Mat. 13 : 46. he sold all **b.** that field
21 : 12. Jesus cast out them **b.**, Mk. 11 : 15. Lu. 19 : 45.
27 : 7. **b.** with them potters' field
† 9. they **b.** of chil. of Israel
Mk. 15 : 46. Joseph **b.** fine linen and
16 : 1. **b.** sweet spices to anoint
Lu.14:18.I have **b.**a piece of ground
19. I have **b.** five yoke of oxen
17 : 28. they drank, **b.** and sold
1 Co. 6 : 20. **b.** with a price, 7 : 23.
2 Pe. 2 : 1. denying L. that **b.** them
Re. 14 : † 4. were **b.** from am. men

BOUND. [Actively.]
Ge. 22 : 9. **b.** Isaac his son laid him
38 : 28. midwife **b.** on his hand a
42 : 24. took Simeon and **b.** him
Le. 8 : 7. **b.** ephod with girdle
† 13. he **b.** bonnets on A.'s sons
Nu. 30 : 4. she had **b.** her soul, 5, 6, 7, 8, 9, 10, 11.
Jos. 2 : 21. she **b.** a scarlet line in
Ju.15: 13.**b.**Samson with two cords
16 : 8. she **b.** him with 7 withs
12. **b.** him with ropes | 21.fetters
2 K. 5 : 23. he **b.** 2 talents in 2 bags
17 : 4. he **b.** Hoshea in prison
25 : 7. they **b.** Zed. with fetters
2 Ch. 33 : 11. king **b.** Manasseh
36 : 6. Neb. **b.** Jehoiakim
Pr. 30 : 4. hath **b.** waters in garm.
Ho.7 : 15.Tho. I have **b.** their arms
Mat.14 : 3.Herod **b.** John, Mk.6:17.
27 : 2. **b.** Jesus, Mk.15:1.Jn.18:12.
Lu. 13 : 16. this dau. Satan hath **b.**
Ac.21 : 11.Agabus **b.** his own hands
22 : 25. they **b.** Paul with thongs, 29. [14, 21.
23: 12.**b.** themselves under curse,
Re.20 : 2.he **b.** Sat. thousand years

BOUND. [Passively.]
Ge. 39 : 20. wh. k.'s prisoners are **b.**
40 : 3.prison where Joseph was **b.**
5. butler and baker **b.** in prison
42 : † 16.ye shall be **b.** in prison to
19. let one of breth. be **b.** in pris.
Nu. 19 : 15. vessel no cover **b.** upon
Ju. 16 : 6. mightest be **b.**, 10, 13. [it
1 S. 25:29. soul of my lord sh. be **b.**
2 S. 3 : 34. thy hands were not **b.**
Jb. 36 : 8. if they be **b.** in fetters
Ps. 107 : 10. being **b.** in affliction
Pr. 22 : 15. Foolishness is **b.**in child
Is.22 : 3.are **b.**by archers, all are **b.**
61 : 1.opening of prison to them **b.**
La. 1 : 14. yoke of my transgr. is **b.**
Da. 3 : 21. **b.** in coats | 23. fell **b.**
24.cast three men **b.** into furnace
Mat. 16 : 19. earth, be **b.** in heaven
18 : 18.
23 : † 18. sweareth by gift, he is **b.**
Mk. 15 : 7.**b.**with them made insur
Jn.11 : 44.**b.** hand and foot, face **b.**
18 : 24.Annas had sent him **b.**,† 13.
Ac. 9 : 2. might br. them **b.**, 21.- 22 : 5.
12 : 6. Peter **b.** | 24 : 27. Paul **b.**
20 : 22. behold I go **b.** in the Spirit
21 : 13. am ready not to be **b.** only
Ro. 7 : 2. is **b.** to her husb., 1 Co. 7 : 39.
1 Co. 7 : 27. Art thou **b.** unto a wife
2 Th. 1 : 3. we are **b.** to thank G.,
2 Ti.2 : 9.word of G. is not **b.** [2:13.
He.13 : 3.them in bonds, as **b.** with
Re. 9 : 14. loose angels **b.** in Euphrates

BOUND in or **with chain, s.**
2 Ch. 33: † 11. **b.** Manasseh, **w.c-s**
36 : † 6. Neb. **b.** Jehoiakim **i. c-s**
Ps. 68 : 6.G. bringeth out those **b.**-
Je. 39 : 7. **b.**- Zedekiah, 52 : 11.
40 : 1. Jeremiah, **b.i.c-s** [**i.c-s**
Na. 3 : 10. all her great men were **b.**
Mk. 5 : 4. bec.he had been often **b.**-
Lu. 8 : 29. he was kept **b. w. c-s**
Ac. 21 : 33. com-d Paul to be **b. w.** two **c.** [this **c.**
28 : 20. for hope of Isr. I am **b.w.**

BOUND up.
Ge. 44 : 30. his life is **b. u.** in lad's
2 S. 20 : † 3. **b. u.** living in widowhood
2 K. 12 : † 10. **b. u.** money in bags
Is. 1 : 6. they have not been **b. u.**
Je. 30 : 13. th. thou mayest be **b.u.**
Eze. 30 : 21. it shall not be **b. u.**
34 : 4. nor have ye **b.u.** that brok.
Ho. 4 : 19. the wind hath **b.** her **u.**
13 : 12. the iniq. of Ephraim is **b.**
Lu. 10 : 34. he **b.u.** his wounds [**u.**

BOUND. [Noun.]
Ge. 49 : 26. to utmost **b.** of hills [**b.**
Jb. 38 : 20. shouldest take it to the
Ps. 104 : 9. to waters set a **b.** not
Pr. 22 : † 28. remove not ancient **b.**, 23 : † 10.
Je. 5 : 22. placed sand for **b.** of sea
Eze. 40 : † 12.**b.** bef. little chambers
Ho. 5 : 10. like them that remove

BOUNDS. [the **b.**
Ex. 19 : 12. shalt set **b.** to people
23. Set **b.** about the mount, and
23 : 31. I will set thy **b.** fr. Red sea
De. 32 : 8. he set **b.** of the people
Jb.14 : 5.hast appointed his **b.** that
26 : 10. compassed the waters with
Is. 10 : 13.removed **b.** of people [**b.**
Ac. 17 : 26. hast determined **b.** of

BOUNTIFUL. [their
Ps.145 : † 17.L. is **b.**in all his works
Pr. 22 : 9. hath a **b.** eye shall be blessed
Is. 32 : 5. nor churl be said to be **b.**

BOUNTIFULLY. [me
Ps. 13 : 6. bec. hath dealt **b.** with
116 : 7. L. hath dealt **b.** with thee
119 : 17. Deal **b.** with thy servant
142 : 7. shalt deal **b.** with me
2 Co. 9 : 6. soweth **b.** shall reap **b.**

BOUNTIFULNESS.
2 Co. 9 : 11. Being enriched to all **b.**

BOUNTY. [**b.**
1 K.3 : † 6.hast shewed to Da. great
10 : 13.Sol.gave her of his royal **b.**
Pr. 20 : † 6. most proclaim own **b.**
2 Co. 9 : 5. make beforehand your **b.** th. same be ready as matter of **b.**

BOW. [Noun.]
Ge. 9 : 13. set my **b.** in cloud
14. that the **b.** shall be seen, 16.
27 : 3. take thy quiver and **b.**
48 : 22. I took of Amorite with **b.**
49 : 24. his **b.** abode in strength
Jos. 24 : 12. not with thy sw. nor **b.**
1 S. 18 : 4. gave David his sword, **b.**
2 S. 1 : 18. teach Judah use of **b.**
22. **b.** of Jonathan turned not
2 S. 22 : 35. **b.** of steel is broken by mine arms, Ps. 18 : 34. [18 : 33.
1 K. 22 : 34. **b.** at a venture, 2 Ch.
2 K. 6 : 22. smite taken with **b.**
9 : 24. Jehu drew a **b.** with full
13 : 15. take **b.** and arrows, took **b.**
16. Put thy hand upon the **b.** he
1 Ch. 5 : 18. able to shoot with **b.**
12 : 2. with **b.** shooting out of **b.**
Jb. 20 : 24. **b.** of steel sh. strike him
29 : 20. my **b.** was renewed
Ps. 44 : 6. I will not trust in my **b.**
46 : 9. he breaketh **b.** cutteth
76 : 3. brake he arrows of the **b.**
78 : 57. turned like deceitful **b.**
Is. 41 : 2. as stubble to his **b.**
66 : 19. to nations that draw **b.**
Je. 6 : 23. they sh. lay hold on **b.**
49 : 35. I will break **b.** of Elam
50 : 42. they shall hold the **b.**
La. 2 : 4. bent **b.** like an enemy
Eze. 1 : 28. as the **b.** in the cloud
39 : 3. smite thy **b.** out of hand
Ho. 1 : 5. I will break **b.** of Israel
7. I will not save them by **b.**
2 : 18. will break **b.** and sword
7 : 16. they like deceitful **b.**
Am. 2 : 15. he that handleth **b.**
Ha. 3 : 9. **b.** made quite naked
Zch. 9 : 13. filled **b.** with Ephr.
Re. 6 : 2. on white horse had **b.**
See Bend, bent, battle-bow.

BOWS.
1 S. 2 : 4. **b.** of mighty are broken
31:† 3. with **b.** hit him, 1 Ch.10:† 3.
1Ch.12:2. they were armed with **b.**
2 Ch. 14 : 8. army that drew **b.**
26 : 14. Uzziah prepared **b.**
Ne.4 : 13. I even set peo. with their
16.other half of them held **b.** [**b.**
Ps. 37 : 15. their **b.** sh. be broken
64 : 3. bend **b.** to shoot
78 : 9. carrying **b.** turned back
Is. 5 : 28. arrows sharp, **b.** bent
7 : 24. With **b.** shall men come
13 : 18. **b.** shall dash young men
21 : † 17. **b.** shall be diminished
Je. 51 : 56 ev. one of **b.** is broken
Eze. 39 : 9. they shall burn the **b.**

BOW. [Verb.] [arrows
Jos 23 : 7. nor serve, nor **b.** to their gods, 2 K. 17 : 35.
2 K. 5 : 18. I **b.** in hou. of Rimmon
Jb. 39 : 3. They **b.** bring forth
Ps. 22 : 29. to the dust, shall **b.**
72 : 9.in wildern. shall **b.** bef. him
78 : † 31. **b.** down chosen men
144 : 5. **b.** thy heavens, O Lord
Pr. 5 : 1. **b.** thine ear, to my
14 : 19. evil **b.** before the good
Ec. 12 : 3. the strong men shall **b.**
Mi. 6 : 6. **b.** myself bef. high G.
Ha. 3 : 6. the perpetual hills did **b.**

BOW down.
Ge. 27 : 29. nations **b.d.** sons **b. d.**
37 : 10.shall I, mother, breth. **b.d.**
49 : 8. father's chil. shall **b. d.**
Ex.11 : 8. thy serv. shall **b.d.** to me
20 : 5. not **b. d.** to them, De. 5 : 9.
23 : 24. shalt not **b. d.** to th. gods
Le. 26 : 1. neith. image to **b.d.**to it
Ju. 2 : 19. in foll. other gods to **b.d.**
2 K. 5 : 18. **b. d.** in h. of Rimmon
19 : 16. L. **b. d.** thine ear, Ps.86:1.
Jb. 31 : 10. let others **b.d.**upon her
Ps. 31 : 2. **b. d.** thine ear, Pr.22:17.
95 : 6. let us worship and **b. d.**
Is. 10 : 4. they **b.d.**under prisoners
46 : 2. They stoop, **b. d.** together
49 : 23. queens shall **b. d.** to thee
51 : 23. **b. d.** that we may go over
58 : 5. to **b. d.** head as a bulrush?
60 : 14. that despised thee sh.**b.d.**
65 : 12. sh. all **b. d.** to slaughter
Ro. 11 : 10. **b. d.** their back alway

BOW, ED knee, s.
Ge. 41 : 43. cried before him, **b. k.**

1 K. 19 : 18. k-s not b-d unto Baal
Is. 45 :23.every k.shall b.,Ro.14:11.
Mat. 27 : 29. b-d the k. before him
Ro. 11 : 4. have not b-d k. to Baal
Ep.3 : 14 I b.my k-s to Fa.of our L.
Ph. 2 : 10. name of J. every k. sh.b.

BOWED. [bear
Ge. 49 : 15. Issachar b. shoulder to
Jos. 23 : 16. other gods, b. yours. to
Ju. 5 : 27. At her feet he b., where
he b. he fell [men of Jud.
2 S. 19 : 14. David b. the hearts of
22 : 10.he b. the heavens, Ps. 18 :9.
1K.1:16.Bath-sheba b.obeisance,31.
2 K.1:†13. thirdcaptain b.bef.Elijah
Es. 3 : 2. b. and reverenced Haman
5. Haman saw Mordecai b. not, 2.
La. 3 : † 20. My soul is b. in me [er
Lu. 13:11.woman wh. was b., togeth-

BOWED down. [him
Ge. 42 : 6. Joseph's breth. b. d. bef.
Nu. 25 :2. people b. d. to their gods
Ju. 7 : 6. b. d. upon knees to drink
2 K. 9 : †24. Jehoram b. d. in chari-
Ps. 35 :14. I b. d. heavily as one [ot
38 : 6.troubled ; I am b. d. greatly
42 : † 5. Why art b. d., O my soul?
44 : 25. our soul is b.d. to the dust
57 : 6. my soul is b.d.; they digged
145 : 14. raiseth those b. d., 146:8.
Is.2:11.haughtiness of men be b. d.
17. loftiness of man shall be b. d
21 : 3. I was b. d. at hearing of it
Lu.24 :5. afraid and b. d. their faces

BOWED head, s. [sance
Ge. 43 : 28. they b. h-s, made obei-
Ex. 4 : 31. b. their h-s, worshipped,
12 : 27. 2 Ch. 29 : 30. Ne 8 : 6.
34 : 8. Moses made haste, b. his h.
2 Ch. 20 : 18. Jehoshaphat b. his h.
Jn. 19 : 30. Jes. b. h.,gave up ghost

BOWED down head, s.
Ge. 24 : 26. man b. -, worsh-d L.,48.
43 : 28. they b. -, made obeisance
Nu. 22 : 31. Balaam b. - and fell
1 Ch 29 : 20. they b. -, worshipped

BOWED herself.
Ru. 2 : 10. she fell on her face, b. h.
1 S. 4 : 19. Phinehas' wife b. h. and
25 : 23. Abigail before David, b. h.
2 K.4 :37.she b. h., took up her son

BOWED himself. [h.
Ge. 18 : 2.Abr. ran to meet them. b.
19 : 1. Lot b. h. toward the ground
23 : 7. Abr. b. h. to peo. of la., 12.
33 : 3. Jacob b. h. seven times
47 : 31. Israel b. h. upon bed's h-d
48 : 12. Joseph b. h. face to earth
Nu. 22 : † 31. Balaam b. h. on face
Ju. 16 : 30.Samson b. h.with might
1 S. 20 : 41. David b. h. three times
24 : 8. Saul looked, David b. h.
28 : 14. Saul perceived Sam-l, b. h.
2 S.9 :8.Mephibosheth b. h. to Dav.
14 : 22. Joab b. h., thanked king
33. Absalom b. h. before the king
18 : 21. Cushi b. h. unto Joab and
24:20. Araunah b. h., 1 Ch. 21:21.
1 K. 1 : 23.Nathan b. h. before king
47. the king b. h. upon the bed
53. Adonijah b. h. to king Sol-n
2 : 19.Solomon b. h. to his mother
2 Ch.25:14. set his gods, b. down h.
See Bow,ed THEMSELVES.

BOWELS.
Ge. 15 : 4. out of own b. thine heir
25 : 23. two people sh. be fr. thy b.
43 : 30. his b. did yearn upon bro.
Nu. 5 : 22. this water that causeth
curse sh.go into thy b.[of thy b.
2 S. 7 : 12.seed wh.shall proceed out
16:11. son wh. came forth of my b.
20 : 10. Joab shed out Amasa's b.
1 K.3 : 26. b. yearned upon her son
2 Ch. 21 : 15. shalt have sickness by
disease of b.until b. fall out,19.
2 Ch.21:18.Lord smote him in his b.
2 Ch. 32 : 21. they of his b. slew him
Jb. 20 : 14. meat in his b. is turned
30 : 27. My b. boiled and rested not
Ps. 22 : 14. heart is melted in my b.
25 : † 6 Remember, O Lord, thy b.
40 : †8. thy law is in midst of my b.
71 : 6. took me out of mother's b.
109 : 18. so let it come into his b.
Pr. 12 : † 10. b. of wicked are cruel
Can. 5 : 4.my b.were moved for him
Is. 16 : 11. my b. sound like an harp
48:19.offspring of thy b.like gravel
49 : 1. from b. of my mother hath
63 : 15. where is sounding of thy b.
Je.4 :19.My b., my b.! I am pained
31 : 20. my b. are troubled for him
La. 1 : 20. my b. are troubled, 2 : 11.
Eze. 3 : 3. fill thy b. with this roll
7 : 19. not satisfy souls, nei. fill b.
Jon. 1 : † 17. Jonah was in b. of fish
Lu 1 : †78.thro. b.of mercy of our G.
Ac.1:18.Judas burst, his b. gushed
2 Co. 6 : 12. are straitened in your b.
7 : †15.Titus, his b. abundant tow.
Ph. 1 : 8. I long aft. you in b. of Ch.
2 : 1. If there be any b. and mercies
Col. 3 : 12. Put on, thf. b. of mercies
Phm. 7 b. of saints are refreshed [b.
12. receive him, that is, mine own
20. broth.,refresh my b. in the L.
1 Jn. 3 : 17. shutteth b. of compas-n

BOWETH, BOWING.
Ge. 24 : 52. Eliezer b-g to the earth
Ju.7 : 5.b-h upon his knees to drink
Jb. 4 : † 4. strengthened b-g knees
Ps. 17 : 11. set their eyes, b-g down
62 : 3. as a b-g wall shall ye be
Pr. 16 : † 26. for his mouth b-h unto
Is. 2 : 9. mean man b-h down [him
46 : 1. Bel b-h down, Nebo stoopeth
Mk. 15 : 19. spit upon him, and b-g

BOWL. [knees
Nu. 7 : 19. He offered silver b. of 70
shekels, 13, 25, 31, 37, 43, 49,
55, 61, 67, 73, 79, 85. [of water
Ju 6 : 38. wringed the dew,a b. full
Ec. 12 : 6 or golden b. be broken [it
Zch. 4 : 2. candlestick with b. upon
3. trees, one upon right side of b.

BOWLS. [16.
Ex. 25 : 29. make the b. of gold, 37 :
31. candlestick of gold ; b., 37:17.
34. in candlestick 4 b. like, 37:20.
Nu. 4 : 7. table of shewbread put b.
† 14. censers, b. of the altar [b.
7 : 84. dedication of altar 12 silver
1 K. 7 :41. two b. of chapiters(2),42.
50. b., censers of gold, 1 Ch. 28:17.
2 K.12 :13.house of Lord b. of silver
25 : 15. b. and things of gold the
capt. took away, Je. 52 : 18, 19.
2 Ch. 4 : † 8. Sol.made 100 b.of gold
† 11. Huram made pots, shovels,
Am. 6 : 6. That drink wine in b. [b.
Zch. 9 :15.they shall be filled like b.
14 : 20. pots be like b. before altar
See BRANCH. [Noun.]

BOWMEN.
Je. 4 : 29. flee for the noise of the b.

BOWSHOT. [a b.
Ge. 21 : 16. Hagar sat over ag-t him

BOX. [3
2 K. 9 :1. take this b. of oil in hand,
Mat. 26 : 7. alabaster b., Mk. 14 : 3.
Mk. 14 : 3. she brake b., Lu. 7 : 37.

BOX or BOX tree.
Is. 41 : 19. I will set in desert b. t.
60 : 13. glory of Lebanon, the b.

BOY, S.
Ge. 25 : 27. the b-s grew ; Esau was
Jo. 3 : 3. have given a b. for a harlot
Zch. 8 : 5. streets shall be full of b-s

BO'ZEZ.
1 S. 14 : 4.rock, name of one was B.
BOZ'KATH. See BOSCATH.

BOZ'RAH. [Ch.1:44.
Ge. 36 : 33. Jobab of B. reigned, 1
Is. 34 : 6. Lord hath a sacrifice in B
63 : 1. with dyed garments from B.?
Je. 48 : 24. judgm-t is come upon B.
49 : 13.B. shall become a desolation
22. shall spread his wings over B.
Am. 1 :12. shall devour palaces of B.
Mi. 2 : 12. put them as the sheep of

BRACELET, S. [B.
Ge. 24 :22.two b-s for her hands, 47.
30.saw b-s upon his sister's hands
38 : 18.Thy signet,b-s,and staff, 25.
Ex. 35 : 22. brought b-s, Nu. 31 :50.
2 S. 1 : 10. I took the b. on his arm
Is. 3 : 19. L. will take away the b-s
Eze.16:11. I put b-s upon thy hands
23 : 42. put b-s upon their hands

BRAIDED = BROIDED.
1 Ti. 2 : 9. not with b. hair or gold

BRAKE. [field
Ex. 9 : 25. the hail b. every tree of
32 : 3. people b. off their earrings
19. cast tables and b.-, De. 9 : 17.
Ju. 7 : 19. they b. the pitchers, 20.
9 : 53. millstone all to b. his skull
16:9. b.the withs | 12. b.new ropes
1 S. 4 : 18. Eli fell and his neck b.
2 S.23:16.b. thro. host, 1 Ch. 11 : 18.
2 Ch. 21 :17.Arabians b. into Judah
31 : 1. Isr. b. images, threw down
† 5. soon as commandm-t b. forth
Jb. 29 : 17. I b. the Jaws of wicked
38:8.who shut sea when it b.forth?
10. b. up for it my decreed place
Ps. 76 : 3. There b. be the arrows
105 : 16. he b. whole staff of bread
33. He b. the trees of their coast
106 : 29. plague b. in upon them
107:14. he b. their bands in sunder
Is. 59 : † 5. as if there b. out a viper
Je. 28 : 10. yoke fr.Jeremiah's neck,
31: 32. my covenant they b. [b. it
52 : 17. pillars of brass Chaldeans b.
Eze. 17 : 16. king, whose cov-t he b.
Da. 2 : 1. troubled,sleep b.from him
34. smote his feet, and b.them, 45.
8 : 7. goat smote ram, b. his horns
Mat. 14 : 19. he blessed and b. and
gave loaves, 15 : 36.-26 :26. Mk.
6 : 41.-8 : 6.-14 : 22. Lu. 9 : 16.
-22 : 19.-24 : 30. 1 Co. 11 : 24.
Mk. 8 : 19.When I b. the five loaves
14 : 3. she b. the box and poured it
Lu. 5 : 6. their net b. | 8:29.b. bands
Jn. 19 :32.soldiers b.legs of the first
33. Jes. dead, they b. not his legs
See IMAGES.
BRAKE in pieces. See PIECES

BRAKE down.
2 K. 10 : 27. b. d. image of Baal, b.
d.house of B.,11:18. 2 Ch.23:17.
23 : 7. he b. d. houses of sodomites
8. b.d.high places | 12. b.d.altars,
2 Ch. 14 : 3. Asa, b. d. images [15.
26 : 6. Uzziah b. d. wall of Gath
34 : 4. they b. d. altars of Baalim ;
images Josiah b., 2 K. 23 : 14.
See WALL, S, with Jerusalem.

BRAKEST. [De.10:2.
Ex 34 : 1. first tables wh thou b.,
Ps. 74 : 13. b. heads of dragons, 14.
Is. 9 : † 4. b. the yoke of his burden
Eze. 29 : 7. leaned upon thee, thou

BRAMBLE, S. [b.
Ju. 9 : 14. said all trees unto the b.
15. b. said, let fire come out of b.
Is.34:13.sh.come up b-s in fortresses
Lu. 6 : 44. nor of b.bush gath.grapes

BRANCH. [Verb.] [him
Zch. 6 : †12. he shall b. up fr. under

BRANCH. [Noun.]
Ex. 25 : 33. Three bowls in one b. ;
three bowls in oth b., 37:19(2).
37:17.of gold ; his b., his bowls, his
Nu. 13 : 23. cut b. with one cluster
Jb. 8 : 16. his b. shooteth forth in
14 : 7. the tender b. will not cease
15 : 32. his b. shall not be green

Jb.18 : 16.above sh.his **b.** be cut off
29:19.dew lay all night upon my **b.**
Ps.80:15. **b.** thou madest strong for
Pr.11:28. righte. shall flourish as **b.**
Is. 4 : 2. shall **b.** of L. be beautiful
9 :14.Lord will cut off **b.** and rush
11: 1. **b.** shall grow out of his roots
14 : 19. art cast out like abomi. **b.**
17 : 9. cities as an uppermost **b.**
19:15. work wh. **b.** or rush may do
25:5.**b.** of terrible ones sh. be low
60: 21. **b.** of my planting, the work
Je.23: 5. raise to Da. a righteous **b.**
33 : 15. cause **b.** of righte. to grow
Eze. 8 : 17. they put **b.** to their nose
15:2.what vine tree more than **b.**?
17:3. an eagle took highest **b.**, 22.
Da. 11 : 7. out of a **b.** of her roots
Zch.3:8.bring forth my serv. the **b.**
6 : 12. man whose name is the **b.**
Ma. 4 : 1. shall leave root nor **b.**
Mat. 24 : 32 **b.** is tender,Mk.13:28.
Lu. 1 : † 78. **b.** fr.on high hath vis.
Jn. 15 : 2. Ev. **b.** that beareth not,
ev. **b.** that beareth
4.As the **b.**cannot bear fruit itself
6. he is cast forth as a **b.**

BRANCHES.

Ge.40: 10. in the vine were three **b.**
12. The three **b.** are three days
49 : 22. whose **b.** run over the wall
Ex. 25 : 32. six **b.** out of candlest.
b. out, 33, 35.-37 : 18, 19, 21.
Le.23 : 40.**b.** of palm trees, Ne.8:15.
Jb. 15 : 30.flame shall dry up his **b.**
Ps. 80 : 11. sent out her **b.** to river
104 : 12. fowls which sing amo. **b.**
Is. 16 : 8. Moab's **b.** are stretched
17 : 6. four or five in outmost **b.**
18 : 5. he shall cut down the **b.**
27 : 10. there shall he consume **b.**
30 : † 17. left as a tree bereft of **b.**
Je. 11 : 16. the **b.** of it are broken
Eze. 17 : 6. spreading vine whose **b.**
19 : 10. she fruitful and full of **b.**
11. thick **b.** mult. of her **b.**
14. fire out of a rod of her **b.**
31 : 3. Assyr. as cedar with **b.**
5. **b.** became long
6. under his **b.** did beasts
7. fair in length of his **b.**, 9.
8. not like the Assyrian's **b.**
12. in valleys his **b.** fallen
13. all beasts be upon his **b.**
36 : 8. O mts. ye sh. shoot **b.**
Da. 4 : 14. Hew tree, cut off **b.**
21. upon whose **b.** fowls of heav.
Ho.11 : 6.sword consume Ephr.'s **b.**
14 : 6. his **b.** shall spread, and his
Jo. 1 : 7. my vine waste, **b.** white
Na. 2 : 2. emptiers marred vine **b.**
Zch. 4 : 12. What be these 2 olive **b.**
Mat. 13 : 32. lodge in **b.**,Lu.13 : 19.
21: 8. others cut down **b.**, Mk.
11: 8. Jn. 12 : 13. [out **b.**
Mk. 4 : 32. than all herbs shooteth
Jn. 15 : 5. I am vine, ye are the **b.**
Ro. 11 : 16. if root be holy, so **b.**
17. if some of **b.** be broken, 19.
18. Boast not ag. **b.** but if boast
21. if God spared not natural **b.**
24. much more, natural **b.**

BRAND, S.

Ju. 15 : 5. he had set **b.** on fire
Zch. 3 : 2. is not this a **b.** plucked

BRANDISH. [sword

Eze. 32 : 10. when I shall **b.** my

BRASEN. See BRAZEN.

BRASS.

Ex. 25 : 3. take gold, silver, **b.**,35:5.
26 : 11. taches of **b.**, 36 : 18.
37. cast five sockets of **b.**, 27 : 10,
17, 18.-36 : 38.-38 : 11, 17, 19.
27 : 2.overlay altar with **b.**,6.-38:2.
3. all vessels make of **b.**, 38 : 3.
4. net work of **b.** | 19. pins of **b.**
30 : 18. make a laver of **b.**, 38 : 8.
Ex. 31 : 4. to work in **b.**, 35 : 32.
35 : 24. offering of silver and **b.**
38 : 5.rings of **b.** | 6.staves with **b.**
29. **b.** of offering was 70 talents
39 : 39. brazen alt. and grate of **b.**
Nu. 21 : 9. made a serpent of **b.**, beheld serp. of **b.** he lived
De. 8 : 9. out of hills mayest dig **b.**
28 : 23. the heaven shall be **b.**
Ju. 16 : 21. bound with fetters of **b.**
1 S. 17 : 5. Goliath helmet of **b.**,38.
6. had greaves of **b.** on his legs
2 S. 8 : 8. Da. took **b.**, 1 Ch. 18 : 8.
1 K. 7 : 14. Hiram a worker in **b.**
15. cast pillars of **b.**, 2 K. 25 : 13.
16. chapiters of **b.**, 2 K. 25 : 17.
Je. 52 : 22.
27. bases of **b.** | 30. plates
38. made lavers, 2 Ch. 4 : 16.
45. pots and shovels of bright **b.**
47. weight of the **b.**, 2 Ch. 4 : 18.
2 K. 25 : 7. Zede. with fetters of **b.**
13. carried **b.** to Bab., Je. 52 : 17.
1 Ch. 15 : 19. with cymbals of **b.**
22 : 3. David prepared **b.**, 29 : 7.
29 : 2. prepared **b.** for things of **b.**
2 Ch. 4 : 1. he made altar of **b.**
9. overlaid doors with **b.**
12 : 10. Rehob. made shields of **b.**
Jb. 6 : 12. stones, or is my flesh **b.**?
40 : 18. his bones as pieces of **b.**
41 : 27. Leviathan esteem. **b.** as rotten wood
Ps. 107 : 16. broken gates of **b.**
Is. 45 : 2. I will break gates of **b.**
60 : 17.for wood bring **b.** for **b.**gold
Eze. 1 : 7. sparkled like burnish. **b.**
24 : 11. that **b.** of it may be hot
40 : 3. like appearance of **b.**
Da. 2 : 32. his belly and thighs of **b.**
39. shall arise third kingd. of **b.**
7 : 19.beast, whose nails were of **b.**
10 : 6. his feet like polished **b.**
Mi. 4 : 13. will make thine hoofs **b.**
Zch. 6 : 1.mountains mount-s of **b.**
Mat. 10 : 9. Provide neith. gold nor
1 Co. 13 : 1. I am as sounding **b.** [**b.**
Re. 1 : 15. feet like to fine **b.**, 2 : 18.
9 : 20. sho. not worship idols of **b.**

Iron and BRASS.

Ge. 4 : 22. instructor in **b. a. i.**
Le. 26 : 19. your heaven **i.** earth **b.**
Nu. 31 : 22. **b. a. i.** wh. abide fire
De. 33 : 25.thy shoes shall be **i.a.b.**
Jos. 22 : 8. return with **b.a.i.** and
1 Ch. 22 : 14. prep. **b. a. i.**, 16.
2 Ch. 2 : 7. cunning to work in **b. a. i.**, 14.
24 : 12. such as wrought in **i.a.b.**
Jb.28 : 2.**i.**taken out of earth, **a.b.**
Is.48 : 4.neck an **i.**sinew,**a.**brow **b.**
60 : 17. for **b.** gold, for **i.** silver
Je. 6 : 28. are **b. a. i.**, Eze. 22 : 18.
Eze. 22 : 20. **i. a. b.** into furnaces
Da. 2 : 35. was **i.** clay, **b.** brok., 45.
4 : 15. with a band of **i. a. b.**, 23.
5 : 4. praised gods of silver, **b.a.i.**
Re. 18 : 12. of precious wood, **b.a.i.**

Vessels of BRASS.

Ex. 27 : 3. make all **v. o. b.**
38 : 3. all the **v.** made he **o. b.**
Jos. 6 : 19. all **v.o.b.** are consecrat.
24. **v.o.b.** they put into treasury
2 S. 8 : 10.brought **v.o.b.**,1 Ch.18:10.
2 K. 25 : 14. **v. o. b.** took they, Je. 52 : 18.
16. wh. Sol. made, **b. o.** all these
v. without weight, Je. 52 : 20.
1 Ch. 18 : 8. pillars and **v. o. b.**
Ezr. 8 : † 27. two **v. o.** yellow **b.**
Eze. 27 : 13. traded in **v. o. b.**, Re. 18 : 12.

BRAVERY.

Is. 3 : 18. L. will take away their **b.**

BRAWLER, S.

1 Ti. 3 : 3. a bishop must be no **b.**
Tit. 3 : 2. to be no **b**-s but gentle

BRAWLING, S. [Adj. and N.]

Pr. 25 : 24. with a **b.** woman, 21 : 19.
Ja. 4 : † 1. fr. whence come **b**-s ?

BRAY, ED, ETH.

Jb. 6 : 5. Doth the wild ass **b.** when
30 : 7. Among the bushes they **b**-d
Ps. 42 : † 1. hart **b**-d aft. water-br.
Pr. 27 : 22. tho. **b.** a fool in mortar

BRAZEN. [38:4.

Ex.27 : 4. **b.** rings | 35 : 16.**b.** grate,
38 : † 8. **b.** glasses | 10. **b.** sockets
30. the **b.** altar, 39 : 39. 1 K. 8 :
64. 2 K. 16 : 14, 15. 2 Ch. 1 : 5,
6.-7 : 7. Eze. 9 : 2.
Le. 6 : 28. sin-off. sodden in **b.** pot
Nu. 16 : 39. **b.** censers [bars
1 K. 4 : 13. cities with walls and **b.**
7 : 30. base had four **b.** wheels
14 : 27. made **b.** shields
2 K.16 : 17.**b.** oxen | 18:4.**b.**serpent
25 : 13. **b.** sea did Chald., Je.52:17.
2 Ch. 6 : 13. Sol. made **b.** scaffold
Jb. 6 : † 12. stones, or is my flesh **b.**
Je.1 : 18.made thee this day **b.** walls
15 : 20. I will make thee a **b.** wall
52 : 20.**b.** bulls | Mk.7 : 4.**b.**vessels
See ALTAR.

BREACH.

Ge. 38 : 29. midwife said, this **b.** be
† theref. his name was called a **b.**
Le. 24 : 20. **b.** for **b.** eye for eye
Nu. 14 : 34. know my **b.** of promise
Ju 21 : 15. L. hath made **b.** in tribes
2 S. 5 : 20. broken as **b.** of waters
6 : 8. a **b.** on Uzzah. 1 Ch. 13 : 11.
2 K. 12 : 5. whereso. **b.** be found
1 Ch. 15 : 13. L. made **b.** upon us
Ne. 6 : 1. builded wall, and no **b.**
Jb.16 : 14.break.me with **b.**upon **b.**
Ps. 106 : 23. had not Mo.stood in **b.**
Pr. 15 : 4. perverseness is a **b.** in
Is. 7 : 6. let us make a **b.** for us
30 : 13.this iniq.sh. be to you as **b.**
26. day L. bindeth up **b.**
58 : 12. be called repairer of **b.**
Je. 6 : † 14. healed the **b.** slightly
14 : 17. of my peo broken with **b.**
17 : † 18. break with a double **b.**
La. 2 : 13. thy **b.** is great like sea
Eze. 26 : 10. city wherein is made **b.**
Da. 9 : † 25. **b.** built in troublous
Am. 6 : † 6. not grieved for **b.** of Jo.

BREACHES.

Ju. 5 : 17. Asher abode in his **b.**
2 S. 5 : † 20. plain of **b.**, 1 Ch.14†11.
1 K. 11 : 27. rep. **b.** of city of Da.
2 K 12 : 5. repair **b.** of house
6. priests not repair. **b.** of house
12. repair **b.** of house of L.,22 : 5.
Ne. 4 : 7. **b.** began to be stopped
Ps. 60 : 2. heal **b.** for it shaketh
Is. 22 : 9. Ye have seen **b.** of city
Eze. 13 : † 5. ye not gone into **b.**
Am. 4 : 3. ye shall go out at **b.**
6 : 11. L. will smite house with **b.**
9 : 11. and I will close up the **b.**

BREAD.

Ge. 14 : 18. king of Salem bro. **b.**
18 : 5. will fetch a morsel of **b.**
21 : 14. Ab. took **b.** gave Hagar
25 : 34. then Jacob gave Esau **b.**
27 : 17.savoury meat and **b.** to Jac.
41 : 54. in Egypt there was **b.**
55. people cried to Pha. for **b.**
43 : 31. set on **b.** | 45 : 23. **b.** for fa.
47:12.nourished father's h.with **b.**
15. give us **b.** | 17. **b.** for horses
19. buy us and our land for **b.**
49 : 20 Out of Asher his **b.** be fat
Ex. 16 : 4. will rain **b.** from heav.
8. in morning **b.** to full, 12.
29. on sixth day **b.** of two days
32. they may see **b.** I fed you
23 : 25. he shall bless thy **b.** and
29 : 32. **b.** in basket by the door
34. if aught of the **b.** remain
40 : 23. set **b.** in order upon table

Le. 8 : 26. took a cake of oiled b.
32. what remaineth of b. burn
21 : 6. b. of their G., 8, 17, 21, 22.
22 : 25. nor fr. stranger offer b.
23 : 18. offer with b. 7 lambs
20. wave with b. of first-fruits
24 : 7. on the b. for memorial
26 : 26. ten women shall bake b.
Nu. 4 : 7. continual b. be thereon
14 : 9. people of land are b. for
21 : 5. no b. soul loatheth this b.
28 : 2. My b. for my sacrifices
De. 8 : 3. man doth not live by b.
only, Mat. 4 : 4. Lu. 4 : 4.
16 : 3. b. of affliction, 1 K. 22 : 27.
2 Ch. 18 : 26.
23 : 4. they met you not with b.
29 : 6. Ye have not eaten b. nor
Jos. 9 : 5. b. was dry and mouldy
12. This our b. we took hot for
Ju. 7 : 13. cake of barley b. tumbled
8 : 6. sho. give b. to thy army, 15.
19 : 5. Comfort thy heart with b.
19. is b. and wine also for me
Ru. 1 : 6. L. visited peo. in giving b.
1 S. 2 : 5. they hired out for b.
36. shall crouch for morsel of b.
9 : 7. the b. is spent in our vessels
16 : 20. Jesse took an ass with b.
21 : 4. no common but hallowed b.
5. the b. is in a manner common
6. gave hallowed b.; for no b.
but shew-b. to put hot b.
22 : 13. thou hast given him b.
25 : 11. shall I take my b. to give
28 : 22. let me set a morsel of b.
30 : 11. found an Egyp gave him b.
2 S. 3 : 29. not fail one that lacketh b.
35. if I taste b. till sun be down
6 : 19. he dealt to ev. one a cake of b.
1 K. 4 : † 22. Sol.'s b. for one day was
13 : 22. camest back hast eaten b.
23. after he had eaten b. and
17 : 6. ravens brought b. and flesh
11. Bring me a morsel of b.
18 : 4. fed them with b. and wat., 13.
2 K. 4 : 42. bro't man of G. b.
18 : 32. take to land of b., Is. 36 : 17.
1 Ch. 12 : 40. of Zebulun brought b.
Ne. 5 : 14. not eaten b. of gov., 18.
15. taken of their b. and wine
9 : 15. gavest them b. fr. heaven
13 : 2. bec. they met not Isr. with b.
Jb. 15 : 23. wandereth abroad for b.
22 : 7. withholden b. from hungry
27 : 14. offsp. not be satisf. with b.
28 : 5. earth, out of it cometh b.
33 : 20. his life abhorreth b. and
Ps. 37 : 25. nor seen seed begging b.
78 : 20. give b.? | 102 : 9 ashes like b.
80 : 5. feedest them with b. of tears
104 : 15. b. wh. strengt. man's heart
105 : 40. satisfied them with b. [es
109 : 10. seek b. out of desolate plac-
132 : 15. satisfy her poor with b.
Pr. 9 : 17. b. eat. secret is pleas. [b.
12 : 9. honoureth hims. and lack.
11. tilleth be satisfied with b., 28 :
20 : 13. shalt be satis. with b. [19.
17. b. of deceit is sweet to a man
22 : 9. giveth of his b. to the poor
31 : 27. she eateth not b. of idleness
Ec. 9 : 11. not to swift, nor b. to wise
11 : 1. cast thy b. upon the waters
Is. 3 : 1. L. take whole stay of b.
7. in my house is neither b. nor
21 : 14. they prevented with b. him
30 : 20. tho. L. give b. of adversity
33 : 16. his b. shall be given him
44 : 15. he baketh b. on coals, 19.
51 : 14. nor that his b. should fail
55 : 2. why spend for that not b.?
10. that it may give b. to eater
58 : 7. to deal thy b. to hungry?
Je. 11 : † 19. destroy stalk with b.
42 : 14. nor have hunger of b.
44 : † 17. then had we plenty of b.

La. 1 : 11. people sigh, they seek b.
4 : 4. young chil. ask b. no man
breaks [with b.
5 : 6. to Egyptians to be satisfied
9. We gat our b. with peril of
Eze. 4 : 15. thou sh. prepare thy b.
17. that they may want b. and wa
16 : 49. pride, fulness of b. and
18 : 7. given his b. to hungry, 16.
44 : 7. when ye offer my b.
Ho. 2 : 5. my lovers that give me b.
9 : 4. sacrifices be as b. of mourners
Am. 4 : 6. given you want of b. in
8 : 11. not famine of b. but hearing
Hag. 2 : 12. if one with skirt touch b.
Mal. 1 : 7. Ye offer polluted b. [4 : 3.
Mat. 4 : 3. stones be made b., Lu
6 : 11. give us daily b., Lu. 11 : 3.
7 : 9. if son ask b. will he give him
a stone? Lu. 11 : 11.
15 : 26. to take chil.'s b., Mk. 7 : 27.
33. whence so much b., Mk. 8 : 4.
16 : 5. forgot. to take b., Mk. 8 : 14.
11. I spake it not cone. b.
12. not beware of leaven of b.
26 : 26. Jesus took b. and blessed
it. Mk. 14 : 22.
Mk. 6 : 36. buy themselves b.
37. 200 pennyworth of b., Jn. 6 : 7.
Lu. 7 : 33. Baptist neith. eating b.
9 : 3. noth. for journey, neither b.
15 : 17. servants of my fa. have b.
22 : 19. took b. gave thanks, 24 : 30.
24 : 35. known in breaking b.
Jn. 6 : 32. Moses gave not that b.,
my Fa. giveth true b.
33. the b. of God is he wh. cometh
34. L., evermore give us this b.
35. Jes. said, I am b. of life, 48.
41. I am b. wh. came, 50 : 58.
51. I am living b., b. I give
58. that eateth of this b. sh. live
13 : 18. eateth b. with me lifted
21 : 9. saw fire, fish and b. [heel
13. Jesus then taketh b. and giv.
Ac. 2 : 42. contin. in breaking of b.
46. breaking b. fr. house to house
20 : 7. when disci. came to break b.
11. when he had broken b. and
27 : 35. he took b. and gave thanks
1 Co. 10 : 16. b. we break, is it not
17. we being many are one. b.
11 : 23. night he was betr. took b.
2 Co. 9 : 10. minister b. for food
See AFFLICTION.

BREAD-CORN.

Is. 28 : 28. b. is bruised, bec. he will

BREAD with eat.

Ge. 3 : 19. In sweat of face shalt e. b.
28 : 20. if L. will give me b. to e.
31 : 54. Jacob called breth. to e. b.
37 : 25. Joseph's breth. sat to e. b.
39 : 6. aught he had, save b. he e.
43 : 25. heard they sho. e. b. there
32. Egypt. not e. b. with Hebrews
Ex. 2 : 20. call him th. he may e. b.
16 : 3. we did e. b. to the full
15. b. Lord hath given you to e.
18 : 12. to e. b. with Moses' fa.-in-l.
34 : 28. not e. b. 40 days, De. 9 : 9, 18.
Le. 8 : 31. e. it, with b. in basket
21 : 22. He shall e. the b. of his G.
23 : 14. neither e. b. nor parched
26 : 5. shall e. your b. to the full
Nu. 15 : 19. when ye e. b. of land
De. 8 : 9. e. b. without scarceness
Ju. 13 : 16. I will not e. thy b.
Ru. 2 : 14. at meal-time e. b.
2 S. 9 : 7. shalt e. b. at my table, 10.
12 : 17. neith. did he e. b. with th.
20. set b. and he did e.
21. didst rise and e. b.
16 : 2. b. for young men to e.
1 K. 13 : 8. nor will I e. b. 16.
9. charged me, saying e. no b.
15. Come home with me and e. b.
21 : 7. e. b. let thy heart be merry

2 K. 4 : 8. constrained Elisha to e. b.
6 : 22. set b. and wat., they may e.
23 : 9. did e. of the unleav. b.
25 : 29. did e. b. bef. him, Je. 52 : 33.
Job 42 : 11. and did e. b. with Job
Ps. 14 : 4. eat my peo. as e. b. 53 : 4.
41 : 9. e. of my b. hath lifted heel
78 : † 25. did e. the b. of mighty
102 : 4. so that I forgot to e. my b.
127 : 2. sit late to e. b. of sorrows
Pr. 4 : 17. they e. b. of wickedness
9 : 5. Come e. of my b. [eye
23 : 6. e. not b. of him hath evil
25 : 21. if ene. hunger, give b. to e.
Ec. 9 : 7. Go e. thy b. with joy
Is. 4 : 1. We will e. our b. and wear
Je. 5 : 17. they shall e. up thy b.
41 : 1. did e. b. togeth. in Mizpah
Eze. 4 : 13. thus sh. Isr. e. defiled b.
16. they shall e. b. by weight
12 : 18. e. thy b. with quaking
19. shall e. b. with carefulness
24 : 17. and e. not b. of men, 22.
44 : 3. prince sit in it to e. b.
Am. 7 : 12. flee into Judah, there e. b.
Ob. 7. e. thy b. have laid wound
Mat. 15 : 2. wash not when th e. b.
Mk. 3 : 20. could not so much as e. b
6 : 36 buy b. they have noth. to e.
7 : 2. disci. e. b. with defiled hands, 5.
Lu. 14 : 1. to Pharisee's house to e. b.
15. Blessed that sh. e. b. in kingd.
Jn. 6 : 5. whence buy b. these may e.
23. nigh pla. where they did e. b.
31. he gave b. from heaven to e.
51. if any e. of this b. be sh. live
1 Co. 11 : 26. as often as ye e. this b.
27. whosoever shall e. this b.
28. so let him e. of that b.
2 Th. 3 : 8. did we e. b. for naught?
12. that with quietness they e. b.

Leavened BREAD. [off

Ex. 12 : 15. eateth l. b. soul be cut
13 : 3. there shall no l. b. be eaten
7. no l. b. be seen, De. 16 : 3, 4.
23 : 18. not offer blood with l. b.
Le. 7 : 13. he shall offer for off. l. b.

Loaf, or Loaves of BREAD.

Ex. 29 : 23. one l. o. b. with ram
of consecration [follow
Ju. 8 : 5. Give l-s o. b. to peo. that
1 S. 10 : 3. carrying three l. o. b.
4. salute, and give thee 2 l. o. b.
21 : 3. give me five l. o. b. in hand
2 S. 16 : 1. upon asses 200 l. o. b.
1 Ch. 16 : 3. dealt to ev. one a l. o. b.

No BREAD.

Ge. 47 : 13. was n. b. in all land
Nu. 21 : 5. n. b. and our soul loath.
1 S. 21 : 4. there is n. common b.
6. n. b. there, but shew-bread
28 : 20. Saul had eaten n. b. all
30 : 12. Egypt. had eaten n. b. 3 days
1 K. 13 : 9. Eat n. b. nor, 17, 22.
21 : 4. turned, and would eat n. b.
5. Why so sad, that eatest n. b.
2 K. 25 : 3. n. b. for people, Je. 52 : 6.
Ezr. 10 : 6. he came, he did eat n. b.
Je. 38 : 9. is n. more b. in city.
Da. 10 : 3. I ate n. pleasant b.
Mat. 16 : 7. reasoned, It is bec. we
have tak. n. b., 8. Mk. 8 : 16, 17.
Mk. 6 : 8. take no scrip, n. b. no

Piece, or Pieces of BREAD.

1 S. 2 : 36. that I may eat a p. o. b.
Pr. 6 : 26. a man is bro. to p. o. b.
28 : 21. for p. o. b. man will transgr.
Je. 37 : 21. to give Jere. daily p. o. b.
Eze. 13 : 19. ye pollute me for p-s o. b.

SHEW-BREAD. See SHEW.

Staff of BREAD.

Le. 26 : 26. have broken s. o. your b.
Ps. 105 : 16. he brake whole s. o. b.
Eze. 4 : 16. I will break s. o. b. 5 :
16. 14 : 13.

Unleavened BREAD.

Ge. 19 : 3. Lot did bake u. b. they eat

Ex. 12 : 8. passo. with u. b. Nu. 9: 11.
15. seven days eat u. b. 13 : 6, 7.–
23 : 15.–34 : 18. Le. 23 : 6. Nu. 28:
17. De. 16 : 3.
18. on 14th day of month eat u. b.
20. in all your habita. eat u. b.
29 : 2. take u. b. to hallow priests
Le. 6: 16. meat-off. ye sh. eat with u. b.
Nu. 6 : 15. wafers of u. b. with oil
De. 16 : 8. Six days shalt eat u. b.
1 S. 28 : 24. witch of E. bake u. b.
2 K. 23 : 9. did eat u. b. am. breth.
Eze. 45 : 21. on 14th day passo. of
Mk. 14 : 12. first day of u. b. ⌊u. b.
Lu. 22: 7. came days of u. b. Ac. 12: 3.
Ac. 20 : 6. after days of u. b., sailed
1 Co. 5 : 8. with u. b. of sincerity
See BASKET, FEAST.

BREADTH.

Ge. 6 : 15. ark ; the b. fifty cubits
13 : 17. walk thro. land in b. of it
Ex. 27 : 18. b. of the court 50 cubits
28 : 16. breast-pl., a span b., 39 : 9.
38 : 1. the altar, five cubits the b.
De. 2 : 5. not give of land, a foot b.
Ju. 20 : 16. sling stones at hair's b.
1 K. 6 : 2. b. of L's house, 2 Ch. 3 : 3.
7 : 6. b. of porch was 30 cubits
2 Ch. 4 : 1. b. of altar 20 cubits
Ezr. 6 : 3. b. of L's house 60 cubits
Jb. 37 : 10. b. of waters is straitened
38 : 18. Hast perceived b. of earth ?
Is. 8 : 8. his wings sh. fill b. of land
Eze. 40 : 5. b. of building | 11. entry
13. b. of gate, 20, 48. | 49. porch
41 : 1. b. of taber. | 2. b. of door, 3.
5. b. of side chamb. | 7. b. of house
11. b. of place left | 14. face of h.
45 : 1. b. of holy portion of land
Da. 3 : 1. b. of image six cubits
Ha. 1: 6. shall march thro' b. of land
Zch. 2 : 2. measure Jerus., to see b.
5 : 2. I see flying roll, b. 10 cubits
Ep. 3 : 18. what is b. and length
Re. 20 : 9. went up on b. of earth
21 : 16. length of city large as b.

BREAK. [Noun.]

2 S. 2 : 32. Joab came at b. of day
Ac. 20 : 11. he talked till b. of day

BREAK. [Verb.]

Ge. 19 : 9. they came near to b. door
27 : 40. b. his yoke off thy neck
Ex. 12 : 46. nor b. bone, Nu. 9 : 12.
13 : 13. shalt b. his neck, 34 : 20.
34 : 13. ye shall b. their images
Le. 11: 33. vessel unclean ye shall b.
26 : 19. I will b. pride of your power
Nu. 24 : 8. Isr. shall b. their bones
30 : 2. if vow, he sh. not b. his word
32 : † 7. wheref. b. ye heart of Isr. ?
De. 12 : 3. ye shall b. their pillars
1 S. 25 : 10. b. ev. man fr. master
1 K. 15 : 19. b. thy league, 2 Ch. 16: 3.
Ezr. 9 : 14. Sho. we again b. com-ts
Jb. 13 : 25. Wilt b. a leaf driven ?
39 : 15. forget. wild beast may b. th.
Ps. 2 : 3. Let us b. their bands
9. shalt b. them with rod of iron
10 : 15. b. thou the arm of wicked
58 : 6. b. their teeth, O God
74 : † 8. they said, Let us b. them
89 : 31. if they b. my statutes and
104 : † 11. wild asses b. their thirst
141: 5. an oil wh. sh. not b. my head
Can. 2 : 17. until day b. and, 4 : 6.
Is. 14 : 25. I will b. the Assyrians
28 : 24. b. clods | 28. nor b. it with
30 : 14. b. it as a potter's vessel
38 : 13. so will be b. all my bones
42 : 3. bruised reed not b. Mat. 12: 20.
58 : 6. fast, that ye b. every yoke ?
Je. 15: 12. sh. iron b. northern iron ?
16 : † 7. neither shall men b. bread
17 : † 18. b. with a double breach
19 : 10. b. bottle, so I b. peo. 11.
28 : 4. I will b. yoke of king, 11.–
30 : 8,
Je. 43 : 13. He shall b. images
48 : 12. I will b. Moab's bottles
49 : 35. I will b. the bow of Elam
Eze. 4 : 16. I will b. the staff of
bread, 5 : 16.–14 : 13.
16 : 38. as women that b. wedlock
23 : 34. thou shalt b. the sherds
29 : 7. they took hold thou didst b.
30 : 18. when I sh. b. yokes of E.
22. I will b. Pharaoh's arms, 24.
Ho. 1 : 5. I will b. bow of Isr. in
2 : 18. I will b. the bow, sword
10 : 11. Jud. plough, Jac. b. clods
Jo. 2 : 7. sh. march not b. ranks
Am. 1 : 5. I will b. bar of Damascus
Mi. 3 : 3. flay skin, and b. bones
Na. 1 : 13. now will I b. his yoke
Zch. 11 : 14. I might b. brotherh.
Mat. 5: 19. b. one of these least com.
9 : 17. else bottles b. and the wine
Ac. 20 : 7. disciples came to b. bread
21: 13. what mean ye to b. my heart?
1 Co. 10 : 16. bread we b. is it not

BREAK covenant.

Le. 26 : 15. but that ye b. my c.
44. I will not b. my c.
De. 31 : 16. this peo. will b. my c., 20.
Ju. 2 : 1. said, I will never b. my c.
Ps. 89 : 34. my c. will I not b.
Je. 14 : 21. b. not thy c. with us
33 : 20. if ye can b. my c. of day
Eze. 17 : 15. sh. he b. c. and be deliv. ?
Zch. 11 : 10. that I might b. my c.

BREAK down.

Ex. 23: 24. b. d. their images, De. 7: 5.
Le. 14 : 45. and he shall b. d. house
De. 12 : † 3. ye sh. b. d. their altars
Ju. 8 : 9. I come will b. d. tower
Ne. 4 : 3. fox, he sh. b. d. stone wall
Ps. 74 : 6. they b. d. carved work
Ec. 3 : 3. a time to b. d. and a time
Is. 5 : 5. I will b. d. wall of viney.
Je. 31 : 28. watched over them to b. d.
45 : 4. that I have built will I b. d.
Eze. 13 : 14. I b. d. wall ye daubed
16 : 39. sh. b. d. thy high places
26 : 4. they sh. b. d. towers of Tyrus
12. they shall b. d. thy walls
Ho. 10 : 2. he sh. b. d. their altars

BREAK forth.

Ex. 19: 22. lest L. b. f. upon them, 24.
Is. 14 : 7. they b. f. into singing,
44 : 23.–49 : 13.–54 : 1. ⌈ye
52 : 9. b. f. into joy, sing together,
54 : 3. shalt b. f. on right hand
55 : 12. hills sh. b. f. into singing
58 : 8. sh. thy light b. f. as morning
Je. 1 : 14. out of north evil sh. b. f.
Ga. 4 : 27. b. f. that travailest not

BREAK off.

Ge. 27 : 40. thou shalt b. his yoke o.
Ex. 32 : 2. b. o. golden ear-rings, 24.
Da. 4 : 27. O king, b. o. thy sins by

BREAK out.

Ex. 22 : 6. if fire b. o. so that corn
Le. 13 : 12. if leprosy b. o. in the skin
14 : 43. if the plague b. o.
Ps. 58 : 6. b. o. great teeth of lion
Is. 35 : 6. in wilder. sh. waters b. o.
Ho. 4 : 2. they b. o., and blood
Am. 5 : 6. he b. o. like fire in house

BREAK in pieces.

2 K. 25 : 13. Chaldeans b. i. p. pillars
Jb. 19: 2. how long will ye b. me i. p.
34 : 24. shall b. i. p. mighty men
Ps. 72 : 4. he shall b. i. p. oppressor
94 : 5. They b. i. p. thy people, O L.
Is. 45 : 2. I will b. i. p. gates of brass
Je. 1 : † 17. lest I b. thee i. p. bef.
51 : 20. with thee will I b. i. p.
nations. ⌈and rider
21. with thee will I b. i. p. horse
22. with thee b. i. p. man, woman,
old, young, young man, maid
23. b. i. p. shepherd and flock
Da. 2 : 40. sh. it b. i. p. kingd., 44.
7: 23. beast shall b. i. p. whole earth

BREAK through.

Ex. 19 : 21. lest they b. t. to the L.
24. let not priests and people b. t.
2 K. 3 : 26. to b. t. to king of Edom
Mat. 6 : 19. thieves b. t. | 20. b. not t.

BREAK up. ⌈u.

2 Ch. 32 : † 1. Sennach. to b. them
Je. 4 : 3. b. u. your fallow gr., Ho.

BREAKER, S. ⌊10: 12.

Eze. 18 : † 10. son, a b. up of a house
Mi. 2 : 13. b. is come up
Ro. 1 : 31. covenant b-s ⌈cum.
2 : 25. if thou b. of law thy cir-

BREAKEST, ETH.

Ge. 32 : 26. Let me go, for day b.
Jb 9 : 17. for he b. me with tempest
12 : 14. he b., it cannot be built
16 : 14. He b. me with breach
28 : 4. blood b. out fr. inhabitants
Ps. 10 : † 10. b. hims. that poor fall
29 : 5. b. cedars | 46 : 9. he b. bow
48 : 7 thou b. ships of Tarshish
119 : 20. My soul b. for the longing
Pr. 25 : 15. soft tongue b. the bone
Ec. 10 : 8. b. a hedge, serpent bite
Is. 59 : 5. is crushed b. into a viper
Je. 19 : 11. as one b. a potter's vessel
23 : 29. word like hammer b. rock
La. 4 : 4. chil. ask br. no man b. it
Da. 2 : 40. iron b. in pieces all these

BREAKING. [Participle.]

Ex. 9 : 9. sh. be a boil b. forth, 10.
22 : 2. if a thief be found b. up
Ac. 2 : 46. b. bread fr. house to house

BREAKING, S.

Ge. 32 : 24. wrestled until b. of day
Ju. 7 : † 15. Gideon heard dream,
and b. ⌈up
2 K. 11 : † 6. keep watch of h. fr. b.
1 Ch 14 : 11. upon enem. like b. of
waters ⌈wat.
Jb. 30 : 14. came as wide b. in of
41 : 25. by reason of b-s they purify
Ps. 144 : 14. that there be no b. in
Is. 22 : 5. a day of b. down walls
30 : 13. whose b. cometh suddenly
14. break it as b. of potter's ves.
Eze. 16 : 59. oath in b. cov., 17: 18.
21 : 6. sigh, with b. of thy loins
Ho. 13: 13. in place of b. forth of chil.
Lu. 24 : 35. known in b. of bread
Jn. 7 : † 23. without b. law of Moses
Ac. 2 : 42. continued in b. of bread
Ro. 2 : 23. thro. b. law, dishon. G.

BREAST.

Ex. 29 : 26. take b. of ram of cons.
27. sh. sanctify b. of wave-off.
Le. 7 : 30. b. waved, fat with b.
31. but the b. shall be Aaron's
34. wave-b. have I taken
8 : 29. Moses took b. and waved it
10 : 14. the wave-b. shall ye eat
Nu. 6 : 20. to priest, with wave-b.
18 : 18. wave-b. shoulder thine
Jb. 24 : 9. pluck fatherless fr. b.
Is. 60 : 16. shalt suck b. of kings
La. 4 : 3. sea monsters draw out b.
Da. 2 : 32. head of gold, his b. and
Lu. 18 : 13. publican smote his b.
Jn. 13 : 25. lying on Jesus' b., 21: 20.

BREASTS.

Ge. 49 : 25. bless with blessings of b.
Le. 9 : 20. fat on b. | 21. b. waved
Jb. 3 : 12. why b. that I sho. suck
21 : 24. His b. full of milk, his
Ps. 22 : 9. hope when on mother's b.
Pr. 5 : 19. let her b. satisfy thee
Can. 1 : 13. all night betwixt my b.
4 : 5. thy two b. like roes, 7 : 3.
7 : 7. b. like clusters of grapes
8. thy b. as clusters of the vine
8 : 1. bro. sucked b. of my moth.
8. little sister, and she hath no b.
10. am a wall my b. like towers
Is. 28: 9. weaned fr. milk drawn fr. b.
66 : 11. with b. of her consolation

Eze. 16 : 7. thy b. are fashioned
23 : 3. there were their b. pressed
8. bruised b. of her virginity
34. shalt pluck off thine own b.
Ho. 2 : 2. put aw. adulteries fr. her b.
9 : 14. miscarrying womb dry b.
Jo. 2 : 16. gather those th. suck b.
Na. 2 : 7. doves tabering on their b.
Lu. 23 : 48. people smote their b.
Re. 15 : 6. having their b. girded

BREAST-PLATE, S.

Ex. 25 : 7. stones set in b., 35 : 9.
28 : 4. shall make a b., 15.-39 : 8.
22. shalt make upon b. chains
23. put rings on b., 24, 26.-39 : 16, 17, 19.
28. bind b. by rings, 39 : 21.
29. the names of Israel in b.
30. put in b. the Urim, Le. 8 : 8.
39 : 9. they made b. double
15. made upon b. chains
Le. 8 : 8. put b. on him, Ex. 29 : 5.
1 K. 22 : † 34 Ahab bet. joints and b.
Is. 59 : 17. he put on righte. as b.
Ep. 6 : 14. having b. of righte.
1 Th. 5 : 8. putting on b. of faith
Re. 9 : 9. b-s as it were b-s of iron
17. having b-s of fire, of jacinth

BREATH.

Ge. 2 : 7. into nostrils b. of life
6 : 17. destr. flesh wherein is b.
7 : 15. ent. two and two wh. is b.
22. all in whose nostrils b. died
Jos. 11 : † 11. there was not any b.
2 S. 22 : 16. at the blast of the b. of his nostrils, Ps. 18 : 15.
1 K. 17 : 17. was no b. left in him
Jb. 4 : 9. by b. of nostrils consum.
9 : 18. not suffer me to take my b.
11 : † 20. their hope a puff of b.
12 : 10. in whose hand is b. of all
15 : 30. by b. of his mouth go
17 : 1. My b. is corrupt, my days
19 : 17. My b. is strange to my wife
27 : 3. All while my b. is in me
33 : 4. b. of Al. hath giv. me life
34 : 14. if he gath. his spirit and b.
37 : 10. By b. of G. frost is given
41 : 21. His b. kindleth coals
Ps. 33 : 6. all made by b. of his
104 : 29. takest their b. they die
135 : 17. nor any b. in mouths
146 : 4. His b. goeth forth, he ret.
150 : 6. that hath b. praise the L.
Ec. 3 : 19. yea, they have all one b.
Is. 2 : 22. Cease from man, whose b.
11 : 4. with b. will slay wicked
30 : 28. his b. as overfl. stream
33. b. of L. like stream of brimst.
33 : 11. your b. as fire sh. devour
42 : 5. he that giveth b. to people
Je. 10 : 14. no b. in them, 51 : 17.
La. 4 : 20. the b. of our nostrils
Eze. 37 : 5. b. to enter you sh. live
6. cover you and put b. in you
8. no b. in them | 9. Come, O b.
10. b. came and they lived
Da. 5 : 23. G. in whose hand thy b.
10 : 17. neither is b. left in me
Ha. 2 : 19. no b. at all in image
Ac. 17 : 25. giveth to all life and b.
Ja. 2 : † 26. body without b. dead
Re. 13 : † 15. to give b. to image

BREATHE.

Jos. 11 : 11. not any left to b., 14.
Jb. 31 : † 39. soul of owners to b. out
Ps. 27 : 12. such as b. out cruelty
Can. 4 : † 6. till the day b. and
Eze. 37 : 9. O breath, b. on slain

BREATHED.

Ge. 2 : 7. b. into nostrils b. of life
Jos. 10 : 40. destroyed all that b.
1 K. 15 : 29. not to Jerob. any that b.
Jn. 20 : 22. b. on them, Receive ye

BREATHETH, ING.

De. 20 : 16. save alive nothing th. b.
La. 3 : 56. hide not ear at my b-g
Ac. 9 : 1. Saul yet b-g threatenings

BRED.

Ex. 16 : 20. some left b. worms

BREECHES.

Ex. 28 : 42. make linen b., 39 : 28.
Le. 6 : 10. priest put on linen b.
16 : 4. he shall have linen b.
Eze. 44 : 18. they sh. have linen b.

BREED. [Verb.]

Ge. 8 : 17. they may b. abundantly

BREED, BREEDING.

De. 22 : 14. rams of b. of Bashan
Zph. 2 : 9. Moab be as b-g of nettles

BRETHREN.

Ge. 13 : 8. no strife, for we be b.
19 : 7. Lot said, b. do not so wick.
24 : 27. L. led me to master's b.
34 : 11. Shechem said to her b.
25. Dinah's b. took each his sw.
42 : 3. Jo.'s b. went to buy corn
6. b. bowed | 13. we 12 b., 32.
45 : 16. saying Jo.'s b. are come
49 : 5. Simeon and Levi are b.
50 : 15. Jo.'s b. saw fa. was dead
Nu. 27 : 4. give us possession among the b., 7. Jos. 17 : 4.
10. no b. give it to father's b.
11. if his father have no b. ye
De. 25 : 5. If b. dwell tog. one die
Jos. 6 : 23. brought Rahab and b.
17 : 4. he gave inherit. am. b.
Ju. 9 : 1. Abim. went to moth.'s b.
3. mother's b. spake of him to
2 K. 10 : 13. We are b. of Ahaziah
1 Ch. 12 : 2. to Da. of Saul's b.
26 : 7. whose b. were strong men, 9.
11. all the sons and b. of Hosah
27 : 18. Elihu, one of b. of David
2 Ch. 21 : 2. had b. sons of Jehosh.
22 : 8. Jehu found b. of Ahaziah
Ps. 133 : 1. for b. to dwell in unity
Pr. 6 : 19. soweth discord am. b.
17 : 2. part of inherit. among b.
19 : 7. all b. of poor hate him
Am. 1 : † 9. remem. not cov. of b.
Mat. 4 : 18. Jesus saw two b. | 21.
19 : 29. hath forsaken houses, b.
20 : 24. indignation against two b.
22 : 25. with us seven b., Mk. 12 : 20. Lu. 20 : 29.
23 : 8. one Master, all ye are b.
Mk. 10 : 29. no man hath left b. father, for my sake, Lu. 18 : 29.
30. hundred-fold, houses, b.
Lu. 14 : 26. if any hate not chil., b.
16 : 28. I have five b. that he may
21 : 16. ye shall be betrayed by b.
Jn. 21 : 23. this saying went am. b.
Ac. 3 : 17. b. I wot thro. ignorance
6 : 3. b. look out seven men [knew
7 : 26. Sirs, ye are b. | 9 : 30. b.
10 : 23. b. from Joppa accomp.
11 : 1. apostles and b. in Judea
12. these six b. accomp. me
29. determ. to send relief to b.
12 : 17. Go shew these things to b.
14 : 2. minds evil-affected ag. b.
15 : 1. men fr. Judea taught b.
3. caused great joy to all b.
22. and Silas chief among b.
23. b. send greeting to b. of Gentiles in Antioch
32. exhorted b. with many words
33. were let go in peace fr. b.
40. recom. by b. to grace of G.
16 : 2. Tim. well reported by b.
40. seen b. they comforted
17 : 6. drew certain b. to the rulers
10. b. sent away Paul, 14.
18 : 18. Paul took leave of b.
27. b. wrote to rec. Apollos
20 : 32. b. I commend you to G.
21 : 7. to Ptolemais, saluted b.
17. to Jerus. b. recei. us gladly
22 : 5. I received letters to b.
23 : 5. I wist not b. he was high pr.
28 : 14. where we found b. and were
Ac. 28 : 15. b. heard of us, c. to meet
21. nor any of b. spake harm
Ro. 1 : 13. not have you ignorant b., 11 : 25. 1 Co. 10 : 1.-12 : 1. 1 Th. 4 : 13.
7 : 1. Know ye not b. law hath
8 : 12. b. we are debtors, not to fl.
29. be first-born am. many b.
10 : 1. b. my prayer to G. for Isr. is
12 : 1. beseech b. by mercies of G., 15 : 30.-16 : 17. 1 Co. 1 : 10.-16 : 15. Ga. 4 : 12. He. 13 : 22.
† 10. kindly affec. in love of b.
Ro. 15 : 15. b. I have written boldly
16 : 14. salute the b., Col. 4 : 15.
1 Co. 1 : 26. ye see your calling b.
2 : 1. I b. when I came to you
3 : 1. I b. could not speak to you
4 : 6. these things b. I in a figure
7 : 24. b. let ev. man abide with G.
29. b. time is short, 15 : 50.
8 : 12. sin so ag. b. ye sin ag. C.
9 : 5. as b. of Lord and Cephas
11 : 2. Now I praise you b. that
14 : 20. b. be not chil. in underst.
26. How is it b. when ye come
39. b. covet to prophesy
15 : 6. he was seen of above 500 b.
50. I say b. flesh and blood
58. my beloved b. be steadfast
16 : 11. I look for him with b.
12. desired him to come with b.
20. All b. greet you, Ph. 4 : 21.
2 Co. 9 : 3. sent b. lest our boasting
5. I thought it nec. to exhort b.
11 : 9. b. wh. came fr. Maced. supplied
26. been in perils among false b.
13 : 11. Finally b. farewell, be perfect
Ga. 1 : 2. b. with me to churches
11. I certify you b.
2 : 4. because of false b. brought in
4 : 12. b. I beseech be as I
Ep. 6 : 23. Peace be to the b.
Ph. 1 : 14. many b. waxing confident
Col. 1 : 2. to saints and faithful b.
4 : 15. Salute b. in Laodicea
1 Th. 4 : 1. we beseech b., 10.-5 : 12.
10. ye do it tow. all b. [2 Th. 2 : 1.
5 : 14. we exhort you b. warn
5 : 25. b. pray for us, 2 Th. 3 : 1.
26. Greet all b. with a holy kiss
27. this epistle be read to holy b.
2 Th. 2 : 15. Therefore b. stand fast
1 Ti. 4 : 6. put b. in remem. of these
5 : 1. entreat younger men as b.
6 : 2. not despise bec. they are b.
He. 2 : 11. not asha. to call them b.
3 : 1. holy b. consider Apostle
12. Take heed b. lest
Ja. 2 : 5. belov. b. hath not G. chosen
1 Pe. 1 : 22. unfeigned love of the b.
3 : 8. one mind, love as b. be pitiful
1 Jn. 3 : 14. to life, bec. we love b.
16. lay down our lives for b.
3 Jn. 3. rejoiced when b. testified
5. whatso. thou doest to b.
10. neither doth he receive b.

His BRETHREN.

Ge. 9 : 22. Ham told h. two b.
25. Canaan, serv. of serv. to h. b.
16 : 12. dwell in pres. of h. b., 25 : 18.
27 : 37. h. b. to him for servants
31 : 54. called h. b. to eat bread
37 : 2. Jo. feeding flock with h. b.
4. loved him more than h. b.
5. Jo. dreamed told it h. b.
11. h. b. envied him, his father obs.
23. when Jo. was come unto h. b.
27. and h. b. were content
30. Reuben retur. to h. b. and said
38 : 11. Lest he die also as h. b.
42 : 7. Jo. saw h. b. and knew, 8.
44 : 33. let lad go up with h. b.
45 : 3. Joseph said unto h. b., 4.-46 : 31.-50 : 24.
47 : 12. Jo. nourished fa. and h. b.
49 : 26. separate fr. h. b., De. 33 : 16

Ex 1: 6. Joseph died, h. b. and all
2:11.Egyp. smiting one of h. b. (2)
Le. 21: 10. high-priest am. h. b.
25:48. one of h.b. may redeem him
Nu.25:6. to h. b. a Midian. woman
27: 9. give his inherit. to h. b.
De. 10: 9. Levi no part with h. b.
17: 20. heart be not lifted ab.h.b.
18: 7. he sh. minister as all h. b.
20: 8. lest h. b. heart faint as well
24: 7. found stealing any of h. b.
33: 9. nor did he acknowl. h. b.
24. let Asher be accept. to h. b.
Ju. 9: 5. Abim. slew h. b. being 70
26. Gaal with h. b. went to She.
56. to fa. in slaying h. 70 b.
11: 3. Jephthah fled from h. b.
Ru. 4: 10. name not cut off fr. h.b.
1 S. 16: 13. anointed him in midst of h. b.
17: 22. into army and salute h.b.
22: 1. h. b. and fa's. h. heard it
1 K.1:9. called all h. b. king's sons
2 K.9:2.him rise up from am. h. b.
1 Ch. 4: 9. Jabez more than h. b.
5:2. for Jud. prevailed above h. b.
7:22. Eph.,h.b.came to comf. him
25: 9. with h. b. and sons were 12
[So to the end of the chapter.]
2 Ch. 21: 4. Jehoram slew all h.b.
Ne. 4: 2. he spake bef. h. b.
Es.10:3.Mord. was accepted of h.b.
Jb.42: 11. came unto him all h. b.
Ho. 13: 15. tho. fruitful am. h. b.
Mi. 5: 3. remn. of h. b. return
Mat. 1: 2. begat Judas and h. b.
11. begat Jechonias and h. b.
12: 46. h. b. stood without, Mk.
3: 31. Lu. 8: 19. [Ac. 1: 14.
13: 55. mother Mary and h. b.
Jn. 7: 3. h. b. said to him, Depart
5 neither did h. b. believe
10. But when h. b. were gone up
Ac. 7: 13. Jo. was made kn. to h.b.
23. Moses' heart to visit h. b.
25. supposed h. b. understood
1 Co. 6:5. able to judge betw. h. b.
He. 2:17. it behoved to be like h. b.

Men and BRETHREN.

Ac. 1: 16. m. a. b. this scripture
2:29. m. a. b. let me freely speak
37. m. a. b. what shall we do
7:2. m., b., and fathers, hearken
13:15. m.a.b. if ye have any word
26. m. a. b. chil. of stock of Ab.
38. Be it known to you, m. a. b.
15: 7. m. a. b. G. made choice
13. James ans., m. a. b. hearken
22: 1. m. b., hear my defence
23: 1. m. a. b. I have lived in all
6. m. a. b. I am a Pharisee, son
28: 17. m. a. b. tho. I have com.

My BRETHREN. [noth.

Ge. 29: 4. Jac. said, m. b. whence?
31: 37. set it bef. m. b. and thy
37: 16. I seek m. b. tell me where
46: 31. m. b. are come to me, 47:1.
Ex. 4: 18. Let me return to m. b.
Jos. 2:13. they will save alive m.b.
14: 8. m. b. made heart melt
Ju.8:19. Gid. said, They were m.b.
19: 23. m. b. do not so wickedly
1 S. 20:29. let me, I pray, see m.b.
30: 23. ye shall not do so, m. b.
2 S. 19: 12. Ye are m. b. my bones
1 Ch.28:2. Da. said, Hear me.m.b.
Ne. 1: 2. Hanani, one of m. b.
4: 23. I nor m. b. put off clothes
5: 10. m. b. might exact money
14. I m. b. have not eaten bread
Jb. 6: 15. m. b. have dealt deceit.
19: 13. He hath put m. b. far
Ps.22:22.thy name to m.b.,He.2:12.
69: 8. I am a stranger to m. b.
122:8.For m. b. and compan.sake
Mat.12:48. who are m. b.?Mk.3:33.
49. mother and m. b., Mk. 3: 34.
Mat.25: 40.done it to least of m.b.
28: 10. tell m. b. they go into Gal.
Lu. 8: 21. m. b. are wh. hear word
Jn. 20: 17. m.b. and say, I ascend
Ro. 7: 4. m. b. ye are become dead
9: 3. accursed from C. for m. b.
15: 14. am persuaded of you m.b.
Ja. 1: 16. Do not err m. belov. b.
19. m. beloved b. let every man
Ja. 5: 10. Take m. b. the prophets
12. all things, m. b. swear not

Our BRETHREN.

Ge. 31: 32. bef. o.b. discern what is
Nu. 20: 3. when o. b. died bef. L.
De. 1: 28. o. b. discour. our hearts
Jos. 17: 4. to give inherit am.o.b.
2 S. 19: 41. why o. b. stolen thee
1Ch.13:2.let us send abroad to o.b.
Ne. 5: 5. our flesh as flesh of o. b.
8. have redeemed o. b. Jews
Ac. 15: 36. visit o. b. in every city
2 Co. 8: 23. or o. b. be inquired of
Re.12:10. accuser of o. b. is cast

Their BRETHREN.

Nu.8:26. minister with t. b. in tab.
De. 18: 2. Levites no inherit. am.
18.a prophet from am. t.b. [t.b.
Ju. 20: 13. not hearken to t. b.
21: 22. t. b. come to complain
2 S. 2:26. bid peo. from follow. t.b.
2 K 23: 9. unleav. bread am. t. b.
1Ch.8:32. with t. b. in Jerus.,9:38.
12: 32. all t. b. were at their com.
39. drinking, for t. b. had prep.
1 Ch. 15: 16. appoint t. b. singers
18 with them t. b. of sec. degree
2 Ch. 28: 15. brought them to t.b.
Ne. 5: 1. great cry ag. t. b. Jews
13: 13. office to distribute to t. b.
Jb. 42:15. fa. gave inherit. am. t.b.
Je. 41: 8. slew them not am. t. b.
He. 7: 5. take tithes of peo., of t.b.
Re. 6: 11. till t. b. should be killed

Thy BRETHREN.

Ge. 27: 29. be lord over t. b. let
31: 37. before t. b. that they judge
37: 10. I and t. b. come to bow
13. Do not t. b. feed the flock
14. whether it be well with t. b.
45: 17. Say unto t. b., This do
47: 5. Thy fa. and t. b. are come
48: 22. given one portion ab. t. b.
49: 8. he whom t. b. shall praise
De. 15: 7. if a poor man of t. b.
17: 15. from am. t.b. set king over
18: 15. raise up a prophet of t. b.
24: 14. not oppress poor of t. b.
Jos. 2: 18. bring t. b. home unto
Ju. 14: 3. no woman among t. b.
1 S.17: 17. take for t. b. run to t.b.
18. look how t. b. fare, and
2 S. 15: 20. take back t. b. with
2 Ch. 21: 13. hast slain t. b. better
Je. 12: 6. t. b. have dealt treach.
Eze. 11: 15. t. b. even t. b. men
Mat. 12: 47. mother and t. b. stand
without, Mk. 3: 32. Lu. 8: 20.
Lu. 14: 12. call not t. b. lest they
22: 32. art converted strengt. t. b.
Re. 19: 10. I am of t. b., 22: 9.

Your BRETHREN.

Ge. 42: 19. one of y. b. be bound
33. leave one of y. b. here
Le. 10: 4. carry y. b. from sanct.
6. let y. b. bewail the burning
25: 46. over y. b. ye sh. not rule
Nu. 18: 6. taken y. b. Levites
32: 6. y. b. go to war and ye sit
De. 1: 16. hear causes betw. y. b.
3: 18.pass over bef. y. b., Jos.1:14.
20. given rest to y. b., Jos. 1: 15.
Jos. 22: 3. Ye have not left y. b.
4. L. hath given rest to y. b.
8. divide spoil with y. b. [11: 4.
1 K. 12: 24. not fight ag. y.b. 2 Ch.
2 Ch. 19: 10. what cause of y. b. so
wrath upon y. b.
2 Ch. 28: 11. deliver captives of y. b.
30: 7. be ye not like y. b. wh. tresp.
9. if turn, y. b. sh. find compass.
Ne. 4: 14. fight for y. b. your wives
5: 8. will ye even sell y. b. or
Is. 66: 5. y. b. that hated you
20. y. b. for offering to Lord
Je. 7: 15. as I have cast out y. b.
Ho. 2: 1. Say to y. b. Ammi, to
Mat. 5: 47. if ye salute y. b. only
Ac. 3: 22. a prophet of y. b., 7: 37.
1 Co. 6: 8. defraud and that y. b.
1 Pe. 5: 9. same afflictions in y. b.

BRIBE, S.

1 S. 8: 3. Samuel's sons took b-s
12: 3. hand have I receiv. any b.?
Ps. 26: 10. right hand full of b-s
Is. 33: 15. hands from holding b-s
Am. 5: 12. they take a b. and

BRIBERY.

Jb. 15: 34. fire consume tab. of b.

BRICK, S.

Ge. 11: 3. make b. they had b.
Ex. 1: 14. their lives bitter in b.
5: 7. no more straw to make b., 16.
8. tale of b-s lay upon them
14. your task in making b-s
18. shall deliver tale of b-s, 19.
Is. 9: 10. The b-s are fallen down
65: 3. incense on altars of b.

BRICKKILN.

2 S. 12: 31. made them pass thro. b.
Je. 43: 9. hide stones in clay in b.
Na. 3: 14. make strong the b.

BRIDE.

Is. 49: 18. bind them, as b. doth
61: 10. b. adorneth with jewels
62: 5. bridegr. rejoiceth over b.
Je. 2: 32. can b. forget attire?
7: 34. voice of b. 16: 9.–25: 10.
33: 11. be heard voice of b.
Jo. 2: 16. b. go out of her closet
Jn. 3: 29. He that hath b. is
Re. 18: 23. voice of b. heard no more
21: 2. b. adorned for her husband
9. shew thee b. Lamb's wife
22: 17. Spirit and b. say, Come

BRIDECHAMBER.

Mat. 9: 15. chil. of b. mourn
Mk. 2: 19. chil. of b. fast? Lu. 5: 34.

BRIDEGROOM.

Ps. 19: 5. b. coming out of cham.
Is. 61: 10. as b. decketh himself
62: 5. as b. rejoiceth over bride
Mat. 9: 15. mourn while b. is with
them? Mk. 2: 19. Lu. 5: 34.
25: 1. ten virgins to meet b.
5. b. tarried | 6. b. cometh, 10.
Jn. 2: 9. governor called the b.
3: 29. hath bride is b.; friend of b.
rejoiceth bec. of b. voice

BRIDLE, S.

2 K.19:28.my b. in thy lips, Is.37:29.
Jb. 30: 11. they have let loose b.
41: 13. who with double b.?
Ps. 32: 9. must be held with b.?
39: 1. keep my mouth with b.
Pr. 26: 3. a b. for the ass, a rod
Is. 30: 28. b. in jaws of people
Zch. 14: † 20. on b-s holiness to L.
Re. 14: 20. blood came to horse b-s

BRIDLE, ETH.

Ja. 1: 26. and b-h not his tongue
3: 2. able to b. whole body

BRIEFLY.

Ro. 13: 9. it is b. comprehended
1 Pe. 5: 12. by Sylva. have writ. b.

BRIER.

Is. 55: 13. instead of b. myrtle-tree
Eze. 28: 24. no more a pricking b.
Mi. 7: 4. best of them is as a b.

BRIERS.

Ju. 8: 7. tear your flesh with b.
16. he took the elders and b.
Is. 5: 6. there shall come up b.
7: 23. it shall even be for b.
24. land sh. become b. and thorns

Is. 7 : 25. not come thither fear of b.
9 : 18. wickedn. shall devour b.
10 : 17. devour his b. in one day
27 : 4. set b. ag. me in battle
32 : 13. on land shall come up b.
Eze. 2: 6. son of man, tho' b. be with
He. 6 : 8. heareth b. is rejected

BRIGANDINE, S.

Je. 46 : 4. and put on the b-s
51 : 3. lifteth up himself in his b.

BRIGHT.

Le. 13 : 2. when man have a b. spot,
19, 24, 25, 26, 38, 39.
4. if b. spot be white in skin
23. if b. spot stay in place, 28.
14 : 56. this is law for b. spot
1 K. 7 : 45. vessels of b. brass, 2 Ch.
Jb. 37 : 11. scat. his b. cloud [4 : 16.
21. see not b. light in clouds
Can. 5 : 14. belly is as b. ivory
Je. 51 : 11. Make b. the arrows
Eze. 1 : 13. fire b. and out of fire
21 : 15. sword is made b. it is
21. k. of Bab. made arrows b.
27 : 19. b. iron in thy market
32 : 8. b. lights I will make dark
Na. 3 : 3. lifteth up b. sword
Zch. 10 : 1. L. shall make b. clouds
Mat. 17 : 5. b. cloud overshad. them
Lu. 11 : 36. b. shining of a candle
Ac. 10 : 30. stood in b. clothing
Re. 22 : 16. b. and morning star

BRIGHTNESS.

2 S. 22 : 13. Thro. b. bef. him were
coals kindled, Ps. 18 : 12.
Jb. 31 : 26. moon walking in b.
Ps. 89 : † 44. madest b. to cease
Is. 59 : 9. we wait for b. but walk
60 : 3. kings to b. of thy rising
19: nor for b. moon give light
62 : 1. till righte. go forth as b.
66 : † 11. with b. of her glory
Eze. 1 : 4. a b. was about it, 27.
28. so appearance of b., 8 : 2.
10 : 4. court full of b. of glory
28 : 7. strangers shall defile thy b.
17. hast corrupted by thy b.
Da. 2 : 31. image, whose b. excellent
4 : 36. my b. returned unto me
5 : † 6. k.'s b. was changed, † 9.
12 : 3. wise shall shine as the b.
Am. 5: 20. day of L. be dark and no b.
Ha. 3 : 4. his b. was as the light
Ac. 26 : 13. light above b. of sun
2 Th. 2 : 8. with b. of his coming
He. 1 : 3. being b. of his glory

BRIM.

Jos. 3 : 15. feet dipp. in b. of water
1 K. 7: 26. b. like b. of cup, 2 Ch. 4: 5.
2 Ch. 4 : 2. molten sea fr. b. to b.
Jn. 2 : 7. they filled them to b.

BRIMSTONE.

Ge. 19 : 24. upon Gom. b., Lu. 17 :
De. 29 : 23. whole land is b. [29.
Jb. 18 : 15. b. scatt. on his habi.
Ps. 11 : 6. upon wicked he shall
rain fire and b., Eze. 38 : 22.
Is. 30 : 33. breath like stream of b.
34 : 9. dust turned into b.
Re. 9 : 17. out of their mouths b.
18. part of men killed by b.
14 : 10. he be tormented with b.
19: 20. lake, burning with b., 20: 10.
21 : 8. lake burn. with fire and b.

BRING.

Ge. 6 : 17. b. flood on earth
19 : two of every sort b. into ark
9 : 14. wh. I b. cloud over earth
18: 16. Ab. did b. them on their way
19. b. upon Ab. he hath spoken
27 : 4. b. it to me I may eat, 25.
5. b. me venison
10. shalt b. it to thy father
12. I shall b. a curse upon me
42 : 20. b. youngest brother, 34.
37. if I b. him not, 43 : 9.—44 : 32.
43 : 16. b. these men home
45 : 19. take wagons b. your fa.
48 : 9. b. them, I will bless them
Ex. 10 : 4. I will b. the locusts
11 : 1. will I b. one plague more
13 : 5. when Lord shall b. thee, 11.
18 : 19. mayest b. causes to God
21 : 6. master sh. b. him to Judges
22 : 13. if torn, b. it for witness
23 : 4. shalt surely b. it back
19. first of first-fruits, b. 34 : 26.
20. send an angel to b. thee
25 : 2. that they b. me an offering
35 : 5. of willing heart, let him b.
29. heart made them willing to b.
36 : 5. peo. b. more than enough
Le. 5 : 7. if not able to b., 11.—12 : 8.
8. shall b. them to priest, 12.
16 : 12. shall b. fire within vail
17 : 5. that Isr. may b. sacrifices
Nu. 8 : 9. shalt b. Levites, 10.
14 : 8. if L. delight in us, will b.
16. L. not able to b., De. 9 : 28.
24. Caleb, will I b. into the land
15 : 18. into land whither I b. you
16 : 9. to b. you near to himself
16 : 17. b. every man his censer
20 : 12. ye shall not b. this cong.
23 : 27. b. thee unto another place
32 : 5. b. us not over Jordan
De. 1 : 17. cause too hard b. to me
7 : 1. when L. b. thee into land
21 : 12. shalt b. her to thy house
22 : 2. b. it unto thine house
8. thou b. not blood upon house
28 : 49. L. shall b. nation ag. hou.
30 : 12. b. it, that we may do, 13.
33: 7. Hear, L. and b. Jud. to his peo.
1 S. 1 : 22. weaned, I will b. him
9 : 7. said Saul, what we b. man?
23. b. the portion I gave thee
11: 12. b. men, we may put to death
20 : 8. why b. me to thy father?
27 : 11. man nor wom. alive to b.
2 S. 3 : 12. my hand, to b. Isr. to
13. except thou b. Michal when
14 : 10. saith aught b. him to me
17 : 3. will b. back peo. unto thee
19 : 11. Why last to b. k. back?
1 K. 3 : 24. king said, b. me a sword
8 : 32. to b. his way on his head
† 47. if b. to heart, 2 Ch. 6 : † 37.
13 : 18. b. him back to thine house
17 : 11. b. me a morsel of bread
20 : 33. he said, Go ye b. him
2 K. 2 : 20. b. me a new cruse
4 : 6. b. a vessel | 41. b. meal
6 : 19. I will b. you to man ye seek
1 Ch. 13 : † 3. let us b. about the
ark of our God
16 : 29. b. an offering and come
21 : 2. b. the number of them to
me, that I may [ings
2 Ch. 31 : 10. peo. began to b. offer-
Ezr. 8 : 17. should b. us ministers
Ne. 13 : 18. our God b. this on us?
Jb. 6 : 22. Did I say b. unto me
10 : 9. wilt thou b. me into dust?
14 : 4. Who can b. clean thing out
18 : 14. b. him to king of terrors
30 : 23. thou wilt b. me to death
33 : 30. b. back his soul from pit
Ps. 43 : 3. b. me to thy holy hill
60: 9. b. me into strong city? 108: 10.
72 : 3. mts. shall b. peace to peo.
94 : 23. b. on them own iniquity
Pr. 4 : 8. she sh. b. thee to honour
29 : 8. Scornful b. a city into
Ec. 3 : 22. who shall b. him to see?
11 : 9. G. will b. thee into judgm.
12: 14. G. b. every work into judgm.
Can. 8 : 2. b. thee into my mother's
Is. 7 : 17. L. shall b. on thee and
14 : 2. shall b. them to their pl.
15 : 9. I will b. more upon Dimon
16 : † 3. b. counsel, execute judg.
25 : 12. shall he b. to the ground
43 : 5. b. thy seed from east
Is. 43: 6. b. my sons fr. far, 49: 22.—60: 9.
45 : 21. Tell ye and b. them near
46 : 13. I b. near my righteousness
56 : 7. will I b. to my holy mt.
58 : 7. b. poor to thy house
60 : 17. For brass b. gold, for iron b.
66 : 4. I will b. their fears upon
Je. 3 : 14. I will b. you to Zion
10 : 24. lest thou b. me to nothing
11 : 8. I will b. on them this cov.
17 : 18. b. upon them day of evil
31 : 8. I will b. them fr. the north
32 : 42. b. on them all good prom.
33 : 6. I will b. it health and cure
11. that sh. b. sacrifice of praise
49 : 5. I will b. a fear upon thee
La. 1 : † 16. b. back my soul is far
Eze. 6 : 3. I, will b. sword upon you
11: 9. I will b. you out of the midst
20 : 15. not b. them into the land
21 : 29. I will b. on necks of slain
23 : 22. b. them aga. thee on every
28 : 8. I will b. thee to ashes [side
34 : 13. I will b. them to their land,
36 : 24.—37 : 21.
38 : 17. I would b. thee aga. them
Ho. 2 : 14. I will b. her to wilder.
Am. 4 : 1. b. and drink | 4. b. sacri.
Mi. 1 : 15. will I b. an heir to thee
Zch. 8 : 8. I will b. them, and they
Mal. 1 : † 7. ye b. polluted bread
3 : 10. b. all the tithes into store-h.
Mat. 2 : 13. there till I b. thee word
5 : 23. if thou b. gift to the altar
14 : 18. He said b. them to me
17 : 17. b. him hither to me, Mk. 9 :
19. Lu. 9 : 41.
21 : 2. an ass and a colt, b. them to
me, Mk. 11 : 2. Lu. 19 : 30.
Mk. 7: 32. they b. to him one deaf
8 : 22. they b. a blind man unto
9 : 19. how long suffer you b. him
12 : 15. b. me a penny that I may
15 : 22. they b. him unto place
Lu. 2 : 10. I b. you good tidings
8 : 14. and b. no fruit to perfection
12 : 11. b. you into synagogues
15 : 23. b. hither fatted calf
19 : 27. b. and slay them bef. me
Jn. 10 : 16. other sheep, I must b.
14 : 26. b. all things to your remem
18 : 29. What accusation b. you?
21 : 10. b. of fish ye have caught
Ac. 5: 28. to b. this man's bl. upon us
7 : 6. should b. them into bondage
9 : 2. he might b. them bound, 21.
22 : 5. to Damas. to b. them bound
23 : 10. com. to b. Paul into castle
17. b. young man to chief capt.
18. to b. this young man unto
24. b. him safe unto Felix
24 : 17. I came to b. alms to my
1 Co. 1 : 19. I will b. to uoth. under
28. b. to naught things that are
4 : 5. b. to light hidden things
17. b. you into remem. of my ways
9 : 27. body, I b. it into subjection
16 : 3. send to b. your liberality
6. that ye may b. me on journey
2 Co. 11 : 20. if a man b. you into
bondage [us to C.
Ga. 3 : 24. our school-master to b.
1 Th. 4: 14. them that sleep will G. b.
2 Ti. 4 : 11. Mark b. him with thee
13. b. cloak with thee and books
Tit. 3 : 13. b. Zenas and A. on jour.
1 Pe. 3 : 18. tha. he might b. us to G.
2 Pe. 2 : 11. b. not railing accu.,
2 Jn. 10. if b. not this doct. [Jude 9.
3 Jn. 6. whom if thou b. journey
Rev. 21 : 24. kings do b. their glory
26. b. the glory of nations into it
See HOME, HITHER.

BRING again.

Ge. 24 : 5. must I b. thy son a. to?
6. beware thou b. not my son a., 8.
28 : 15. b. thee a. iuto land, 48 : 21.

Ge. 37 : 14. well with breth. **b.** word **a.**
42 : 37. deliv. I'll **b.** him to thee **a.**
Ex. 23 : 4. shalt **b.** it back to him **a.**
Nu. 17 : 10. **b.** Aaron's rod **a.**
22 : 8. Lodge I'll **b.** you word **a.**
De. 1 : 22. **b.** us word **a.** what way
22 : 1. any case **b.** them **a.** to bro.
28 : 68. L. shall **b.** thee into Eg. **a.**
Ju. 11 : 9. If ye **b.** me home **a.**
19 : 3. her husb. went to **b.** her **a.**
2 S. 12 : 23. can I **b.** him **a.**, I sh. go
14 : 21. **b.** young man Absalom **a.**
15 : 8. If L. sh. **b.** me **a.** to Jerus.
25. he will **b.** me **a.** and shew it
1 K. 8 : 34. and **b.** them **a.**, 2 Ch. 6 : 25.
12 : 21. Jud. ag. Israel to **b.** kingd.
a. to Rehob., 2 Ch. 11 : 1.
1 Ch. 13 : 3. let us **b.** **a.** ark of G.
21 : 12. advise word I shall **b.** **a.**
2 Ch. 24 : 19. prophets to **b.** them **a.**
Ne. 9 : 29. mightest **b.** them **a.** to law
Ps. 68 : 22. I will **b.** **a.** from Bashan,
I will **b.** **a.** my peo. from sea
Pr. 19 : 24. not **b.** it to his mouth **a.**
26 : 15. grieveth to **b.** it **a.** to mouth
Is. 38 : 8. will **b.** **a.** shadow of degrees
46 : 8. **b.** it **a.** to mind, O transg.
49 : 5. saith L., to **b.** Jac. **a.** to him
52 : 8. sh. see when L. **b.** **a.** Zion
Je. 12 : 15. I will **b.** them **a.**, 50 : 19.
15 : 19. wilt return, then I **b.** thee **a.**
16 : 15. I will **b.** them **a.** to their
land, 24 : 6.–32 : 37.
23 : 3. I will **b.** them **a.** into folds
28 : 3. I will **b.** **a.** the vessels
4. I will **b.** **a.** Jeconiah, 6.
29 : 14. will **b.** you **a.** into place
30 : 3. I **b.** **a.** captiv. of peo. Isr.
and Jud., 18.–31 : 23. Eze. 39 :
25. Jo. 3 : 1. Am. 9 : 14.
32 : 37. **b.** them **a.** unto place
48 : 47. will **b.** **a.** captivity of Moab
49 : 6. **b.** **a.** captiv. of Ammon
39. **b.** **a.** captivity of Elam
50 : 19. **b.** Isr. **a.** to his habitation
Eze. 16 : 53. when I **b.** **a.** their
captiv. I will **b.** **a.**
29 : 14. I will **b.** **a.** captivity of E.
34 : 16. will **b.** **a.** which was driv.
Zph. 3 : 20. that time I **b.** you **a.**
Zch. 10 : 6. **b.** them **a.** to place them
10. I will **b.** them **a.** out of E.
Mat. 2 : 8. **b.** word **a.** that I may
See CAPTIVITY. ⌊worsh.

BRING down.

Ge. 42 : 38. **b.** **d.** grey hairs, 44 : 29, ⌈31.
43 : 7. say, **b.** your bro. **d.**, 44 : 21.
45 : 13. sh. haste and **b.** **d.** my fa.
De. 9 : 3. **b.** them **d.** before thy face
21 : 4. **b.** **d.** heifer unto valley
Ju. 7 : 4. **b.** them **d.** to the water
1 S. 30 : 15. Canst **b.** me **d.** I will
b. thee **d.**
2 S. 22 : 28. eyes on haughty to **b.** **d.**
1 K. 1 : 33. Sol. **b.** him **d.** to Gihon
2 : 9. hoary head **b.** **d.** with blood
5 : 9. **b.** them **d.** from Lebanon
Ps. 18 : 27. wilt **b.** **d.** high looks
55 : 23. shalt **b.** them **d.** to pit of
Is. 25 : 5. shalt **b.** **d.** noise of strang.
11. he sh. **b.** **d.** their pride together
12. the high fort shall he **b.** **d.**
63 : 6. I will **b.** **d.** their strength
Je. 49 : 16. I will **b.** thee **d.**, Ob. 4.
51 : 40. I will **b.** them **d.** like lambs
Eze. 13 : 14. **b.** it **d.** to the ground
26 : 20. when I shall **b.** thee **d.**
28 : 8. They shall **b.** thee **d.** to pit
Ho. 7 : 12. I will **b.** them **d.** as fowls
Jo. 3 : 2. **b.** them **d.** to valley of J.
† 11. L. sh. **b.** **d.** thy mighty ones
Am. 3 : 11. he shall **b.** **d.** thy strength
9 : 2. though they climb to heaven
thence will I **b.** them **d.**
Ob. 3. saith in heart, Who **b.** me **d.**
Ac. 23 : 15. he **b.** him **d.** to you
20. desire thou wouldst **b.** **d.** Paul

Ro. 10 : 6. that is to **b.** C. **d.** from
See EVIL. ⌊above

BRING forth.

Ge. 1 : 11. Let the earth **b.** **f.**, 24.
20. Let waters **b.** **f.** abundantly
3 : 16. in sorrow shalt **b.** **f.** chil.
18. Thorns and thistles sh. it **b.** **f.**
8 : 17. **b.** **f.** every living thing
9 : 7. **b.** **f.** abundantly in earth
38 : 24. **b.** her **f.** let her be burnt
Ex. 3 : 10. mayest **b.** **f.** my peo. Isr.
11. who I, that I **b.** **f.** Israel?
7 : 4. that I may **b.** **f.** my armies
8 : 3. river shall **b.** **f.** frogs abun.
18. magicians did so to **b.** **f.** lice
Le. 24 : 14. **b.** **f.** him hath cursed, 23.
25 : 21. shall **b.** **f.** fruit 3 years
26 : 10. eat and **b.** **f.** old, bec. of new
Nu. 19 : 3. **b.** her **f.** without camp
20 : 8. **b.** **f.** water out of rock
De. 14 : 28. thou shalt **b.** **f.** all tithe
17 : 5. shalt **b.** **f.** that man or wom.
22 : 15. **b.** **f.** tokens of damsel's virg.
Jos. 2 : 3. **b.** **f.** men that are come to
Ju. 6 : 18. until I **b.** **f.** my present
19 : 22. **b.** **f.** man came to thy house
2 K. 10 : 22. **b.** **f.** vestments for worsh.
19 : 3. no strength to **b.** **f.**, Is. 37 : 3.
23 : 4. to **b.** **f.** vessels made for Baal
Ezr. 1 : 8. those did Cyrus **b.** **f.** by
10 : † 3. a cov. to **b.** **f.** our wives
Jb. 14 : 9. **b.** **f.** boughs like a plant
15 : 35. mischief, and **b.** **f.** vanity
38 : 32. Canst thou **b.** **f.** Mazzaroth
39 : 1. kn. when wild goats **b.** **f.**? 2, 3.
40 : 20. mountains **b.** him **f.** food
Ps. 25 : † 15. **b.** **f.** my feet out of net
37 : 6. sh. **b.** **f.** thy righte. as light
92 : 14. shall **b.** **f.** fruit in old age
104 : 14. may **b.** **f.** food out of earth
144 : 13. sheep may **b.** **f.** thousands
Pr. 8 : † 35. findeth me sh. **b.** **f.** favour
27 : 1. kn. not what day may **b.** **f.**
Is. 5 : 2. that it should **b.** **f.** grapes. 4.
23 : 4. I travail not, nor **b.** **f.** chil.
33 : 11. conceive chaff, **b.** **f.** stubble
41 : 21. **b.** **f.** your strong reasons
22. **b.** **f.** and shew what sh. happen
42 : 1. he sh. **b.** **f.** judgm. to Gent.
3. he sh. **b.** **f.** judgm. unto truth
43 : 8. **b.** **f.** blind peo. that have eyes
9. let them **b.** **f.** their witnesses
45 : 8. open, let them **b.** **f.** salva.
55 : 10. water. earth. maketh it **b.** **f.**
59 : 4. conceive mischief, **b.** **f.** iniq.
65 : 9. will **b.** **f.** a seed out of Jac.
23. not in vain, nor **b.** **f.** for troub.
66 : 8. shall earth **b.** **f.** in one day?
9. to birth, and not cause to **b.** **f.**
Je. 12 : 2. grow, yea they **b.** **f.** fruit
51 : 44. I'll **b.** **f.** what he swallowed
Eze. 12 : 4. thou shalt **b.** **f.** thy stuff
17 : 8. it might **b.** **f.** branches
23. and it shall **b.** **f.** boughs
20 : 6. to **b.** them **f.** of land of E.
38. will **b.** them **f.** out of country
28 : 18. will I **b.** **f.** a fire in midst
38 : 4. I will **b.** thee **f.** thy army
47 : 12. **b.** **f.** new fruit acc. to month
Ho. 9 : 13. Ephr. shall **b.** **f.** his chil.
16. tho. they **b.** **f.** yet will I slay
Mi. 4 : 10. in labour to **b.** **f.** O Zion
7 : 9. he will **b.** me **f.** to the light
Zph. 2 : 2. Bef. decree **b.** **f.** day pass
Zch. 3 : 8. **b.** **f.** my serv. Branch
4 : 7. **b.** **f.** head-stone with shout.
5 : 4. **b.** **f.** a curse, it shall ent. h.
Mat. 1 : 23. a virgin sh. **b.** **f.** son, 21.
3 : 8. **b.** **f.** fruits for rep., Lu. 3 : 8.
7 : 18. can-t **b.** **f.** evil fr., Lu. 6 : 43.
Mk. 4 : 20 **b.** **f.** fruit, some 30 fold
Lu. 1 : 31 **b.** **f.** a son, call Jesus
8 : 15. heard word, **b.** **f.** fruit
15 : 22. **b.** **f.** best robe put it on him
Jn. 15 : 2. that it **b.** **f.** more fruit
16. I ord. you, sho. **b.** **f.** fruit
19 : 4. I **b.** him **f.** th. ye may know

Ac. 12 : 4. after Easter to **b.** him **f.**
Ro. 7 : 4 sho. **b.** **f.** fruit unto G
5. motions of sin to **b.** **f.** death

BRING in.

Ex. 6 : 8. I **b.** you **i.** land I swear
15 : 17. shall **b.** **i.** and plant them
16 : 5. prepare that they **b.** **i.**
23 : 23. my Angel shall **b.** thee **i.**
26 : 33. **b.** **i.** within the vail
40 : 4. thou shalt **b.** **i.** the table
Le. 6 : 21. baken, shalt **b.** it **i.**
Nu. 14 : 31. little ones, will I **b.** **i.**
20 : 5. to **b.** us **i.** unto this evil pl.
De. 4 : 38. **b.** thee **i.** to give land
6 : 23. **b.** us **i.** to give us land
2 S. 9 : 10. shalt **b.** **i.** the fruits
2 Ch. 24 : 9. to **b.** **i.** to L. collection
28 : 13. Ye shall not **b.** **i.** captives
Je. 17 : 24. **b.** **i.** no burden on sab.
Da. 2 : 24. **b.** me **i.** before the king
5 : 7. k. cried to **b.** **i.** astrologers
9 : 24. to **b.** **i.** everlasting righte.
Hag. 1 : 6. sown much **b.** **i.** little
Lu. 5 : 18. sought to **b.** him **i.**
19. they might **b.** him **i.** because
14 : 21. **b.** **i.** hither poor, maimed
2 Pe. 2 : 1. **b.** **i.** damnable heresies

BRING out.

Ge. 19 : 5. **b.** them **o.** to us, 8, 12.
40 : 14. **b.** me **o.** of this house
50 : 24. G. will **b.** you **o.** of this
Ex. 6 : 6. **b.** you **o.** from under burd.
13. **b.** chil. of Isr. **o.** of E., 26, 27.
–7 : 5.–12 : 51. Je. 31 : 32.
32 : 12. For mischief did **b.** them **o.**
De. 21 : 19. **b.** him **o.** to elders
22 : 21. **b.** **o.** damsel \| 24. **b.** both **o.**
24 : 11. **b.** **o.** pledge unto thee
Jos. 6 : 22. **b.** **o.** thence Rahab
10 : 22. **b.** **o.** those five kings
Ju. 6 : 30. **b.** **o.** son that he die
19 : 24. I will **b.** **o.** humble ye them
Ps. 25 : 17. O **b.** me **o.** of my distr.
142 : 7. **b.** my soul **o.** of prison
143 : 11. **b.** my soul **o.** of trouble
Is. 42 : 7. to **b.** **o.** prisoners from
Je. 8 : 1. **b.** **o.** bones of kings of Jud.
38 : 23. **b.** **o.** thy wives and chil.
Eze. 11 : 7. I will **b.** you **o.** of midst
20 : 34. **b.** you **o.** from peo., 34 : 13.
41. accept you, when I **b.** you **o.**
24 : 6. **b.** it **o.** piece by piece, let
Am. 6 : 10. burneth to **b.** **o.** bones
Ac. 17 : 5. sought to **b.** them **o.** to

BRING to pass.

Ge. 41 : 32. dream, G. will **b.** **t.** **p.**
50 : 20. to **b.** **t.** **p.** as at this day
Ps. 37 : 5. trust in him, sh. **b.** it **t.** **p.**
Is. 28 : 21. **b.** **t.** **p.** his strange act
46 : 11. spoken, I will **b.** it **t.** **p.**

BRING up.

Ge. 46 : 4. I will **b.** thee **u.** again
Ex. 3 : 8. **b.** them **u.** out of th. land
17. I will **b.** you **u.** out of afflic.
33 : 12. sayest **b.** **u.** this people
Nu. 14 : 37. that **b.** **u.** evil report
20 : 25. **b.** **u.** Aaron to mt. Hor
De. 22 : 14. **b.** **u.** an evil name on her
Ju. 6 : 13. Did not L. **b.** us **u.** from
1 S. 19 : 15. **b.** him **u.** in the bed
28 : 8. **b.** me him **u.** I name
11. Whom **b.** **u.**, **b.** **u.** Samuel
15. Why disquiet to **b.** me **u.**?
2 S. 2 : 3. his men did David **b.** **u.**
6 : 2. to **b.** **u.** ark of God, 1 K. 8 :
1, 4. 1 Ch. 13 : 6.–15 : 3, 12, 14,
25. 2 Ch. 5 : 2, 5. ⌈day
1 Ch. 17 : 5. since **b.** **u.** Isr. to this
Ezr. 1 : 11. did Sheshbazzar **b.** **u.**
Ne. 10 : 38. shall **b.** **u.** tithes to G.
Is. 23 : 4. nor **b.** **u.** virgins
Je. 27 : 22. then will I **b.** them **u.**
Eze. 16 : 40. **b.** **u.** company ag. thee
23 : 46. **b.** **u.** company upon them
26 : 19. when I shall **b.** **u.** the
deep upon thee
29 : 4. will **b.** thee **u.** out of rivers

Eze.32 : 3.shall b. thee u. in my net
37 : 6. I will b. u. flesh on you
Ho. 9 : 12. Though they b. u. chil.
Am. 8 : 10. I will b. u. sackcloth
Ro. 10 : 7. to b.u. C. again fr. dead
Ep. 6 : 4.b.them u.in nurture of L.

BRINGERS.

2 K.10 : 5.b.up of chil. sent to Jehu

BRINGEST.

1 K. 1 : 42. valiant b. good tidings
Jb. 14 : 3. b. me unto judgm. with
Is. 40 : 9.O Jerus.th.b.good tidings
Ac. 17 : 20.b. strange things to ears

BRINGETH.

Ex. 6 : 7. who b. you out fr. burden
Le. 11 : 45. L. that b. you out of E.
17 : 4.b. it not to door of taber., 9.
De. 8 : 7. L. b. thee into good land
1 S.2 : 6. he b. down to grave, b. up
7. L. maketh poor, he b. low
2 S.18 : 26.k.said,He b. good tidings
22 : 48. that b. peo. under me
49. that b. me forth fr. enemies
Jb. 12 : 6. into hand G. b. abund.
22. he b. to light shadow of dea.
19 : 29. wrath b. punishm. of sw.
28 : 11. thing hid b. he to light
Ps. 1 : 3. b. forth fruit in his season
14 : 7. L. b. back captivity, 53 : 6.
33 : 10. L. b. counsel of heathen to
37 : 7. who b. wick. devices to pass
68 : 6. he b. out them are bound
Ps. 107 : 28. b. them out of distress.
30. he b. them to desired haven
135 : 7. b. wind out of treasuries,
Je. 10 : 13.–51 : 16.
Pr. 10 : 31. mouth of just b. wisdom
16 : 30. moving his lips he b. evil
18 : 16. gift b. him bef. great men
19 : 26. a son that b. reproach
20 : 26. wise k. b. wheel over them
21 : 27. when he b. it with a wick.
29 : 15.child left, b.moth.to shame
21. that delicately b. up his serv.
25. The fear of man b. a snare
30 : 33.b. butter, b. blood, b.strife
31 : 14. she b. her food from afar
Ec. 2 : 6. wood that b. forth trees
Is. 8 : 7. L. b. on them the waters
26 : 5. b. down them on high, b.
40 : 23. b.princes to noth. [to dust
26. b. out their host by number
41:27. to Jerus. one b. good tidings
43 : 17. Which b. forth the chariot
52 : 7. How beautiful feet of him b.
good tidings, b. good, Na.1 : 15.
54 : 16. smith that b. forth instru.
61 : 11. as earth b. forth her bud
Je.4 : 31.that b. forth her first child
Eze.29 : 16.which b. iniq.to remem.
Ho. 10 : 1.Isr.b.forth fruit to hims.
Hag.1:11.drought upon that which
ground b. forth
Mat. 3 : 10. tree th. b. not forth
good fruit hewn down, 7 : 19.
Lu. 3 : 9.
7 : 17. good tree, b. forth good fru.
12 : 35.good man b. forth good thi.
evil man b. evil, Lu. 6 : 45.
13 : 23. b. forth some a 100 fold
52. who b. out of treasure new
17 : 1. Jesus b. them into high mt.
Mk. 4 : 28. earth b. forth of hers.
Lu. 6 : 43. good tree b. not corrupt
Jn. 12 : 24. if die, it b. forth, 15 : 5.
Col. 1 : 6. gospel b. forth fruit, as it
Tit.2 : 11. grace of G. that b. salva.
He. 1 : 6. b. first-begot. into world
6 : 7. earth b. forth herbs meet
Ja. 1 : 15. lust b. forth sin, sin b.
See TIDINGS. [death

BRINGING. [Part.]

Nu.5 : 15.offering b.iniq.to remem.
1 K. 10 : 22. navy b. gold,2 Ch.9:21.
2 K.21 : 12.am b.such evil on Jerus.
Ne. 13 : 15. on sab. b. in sheaves
Ps. 126 : 6. rejoicing, b. his sheaves
Je. 17 : 26. b. burnt-off. b.sacrifices
Mat. 21 : 43. nation b. forth fruit
Mk. 2 : 3. b. one sick of the palsy
Lu. 24 : 1. b. spices prepared
Ac. 5 : 16. multitude b. sick folks
Ro. 7 : 23. b. me into captiv. to sin
2 Co. 10 : 5. b. into captiv. thought
2 Pe. 2 : 5. b. in flood on the world

BRINGING. [Noun.]

Ex. 12 : 42.observed for b.them out
36 : 6. peo. were restrained from b.
Nu.14:36.b. up a slander upon land
2 S. 19 : 10. of b. king back, 43.
Eze.20 : 9.myself kn. in b.them out
Da. 9 : 12. by b. upon us gr. evil
He. 2 : 10. b. many sons unto glory
7 : 19. b. in of a better hope did

BRINK.

Ge. 41 : 3. stood on the b. of river
Ex. 2 : 3. laid ark by river's b.
7 : 15. shalt stand by the river's b.
De. 2 : 36. fr. Aroer by b. of river
Jos. 3 : 8. When come to b. of Jor.
Eze. 47 : 6. me return to b. of river

BROAD.

Nu. 16 : 38. make b. plates, 39.
Ne. 3 : 8. Uzziel Hananiah fortified
Jerusalem to b. wall, 12 : 38.
7 : † 4. the city was b. in spaces
Jb. 36 : 16. removed into a b. place
Ps. 119: 96.thy com. is exceeding b.
Can. 3:2. in b. ways I will seek him
Is.33 : 21.L. will be pla. of b. rivers
Je.5 : 1. know and seek in b. places
51 : 58. b. walls of Bab. be broken
Na. 2 : 4. chari. justle in b. ways
Mat. 7 : 13.b. is the way th. leadeth
23 : 5. make b. their phylacteries

BROADER.

Jb.11 : 9.measure is b. than the sea

BROIDERED.

Ex. 28 : 4. make a b. coat [work
Eze. 16 : 10. I clothed thee with b.
13. thy raiment was of b. work
18. tookest thy b. garments
26 : 16. princes put off b. garm.
27 : 7. linen with b. work thy sail
16. in thy fairs with b. work
24. thy merchants in b. work
1 Ti. 2 : 9. adorn not with b. hair

BROILED.

Lu. 24 : 42. gave him piece of b. fish

BROKEN.

Ge. 17 : 14. he hath b. my cov., Ps.
55 : 20.Is.24 : 5.–33 : 8.Je.11:10.
Le. 6 : 28. earthen vessel shall be b.
15 : 12. vessel he touched sh. be b.
21:19.man b.-footed, or b.-handed
20. his stones b. let him not offer
22 : 22.blind, b. ye sh. not offer,24.
26 : 13.have b. bands of your yoke
26. I have b. staff of your bread
Nu. 15 : 31.bec. he hath b.his com.
Ju.5:22.horse-hoofs b.by prancings
16 : 9. brake withs as tow is b.
1 S.2 : 4.bows of mighty men are b.
2 S.22 : 35.bow of steel b.,Ps.18:34.
1 K. 22 : 48. ships b. at Ezion-ge.
1 Ch.14:11.G.b.in upon mine enem.
2 Ch. 20 : 37. b. thy works,ships b.
32 : 5. he built wall that was b.
Jb. 4 : 10. teeth of young lions b.
7 : 5. my skin is b. and loathsome
16 : 12.at ease,he hath b.me asun.
22 : 9. arms of fatherless been b.
24 : 20.wickedness sh.be b. as tree
31 : 22. let arm be b. fr. bone
38 : 15. the high arm shall be b.
Ps. 3 : 7. hast b. teeth of ungodly
31 : 12. I am like a b. vessel
34:18.nigh them of b.heart,51:17.
20. keepeth bones, not one is b.
37 : 15.bows sh. be b. | 17.arms b.
38 : 8. I am feeble and sore b.
44 : 19.hast b. us in pla. of dragons
51 : 8. that hast b. may rejoice
17. sacrifices of G. are a b. spirit
Ps. 60 : † 1. cast us off, hast b. us
2.earth to tremble,thou hast b. it
69 : 20. Reproach hath b.my heart
107 : 16. he hath b. gates of brass
109 : 16. he might slay b. in heart
124 : 7. snare is b. we are escaped
147 : 3. He healeth the b. in heart
Pr. 6 : 15. suddenly shall he be b.
11 : † 15. is surety shall be sore b.
13 : † 20. companion of fools be b.
15 : 13. by sorrow the spirit is b.
17 : 22. b. spirit drieth the bones
25 : 19. is like b. tooth and a foot
Ec. 4 : 12. threefold cord is not b.
12 : 6. or the golden bowl be b. or
pitcher be b.
Is. 5 : 27.nor latchet of shoes be b.
7 : 8.within 65 years sh.Ephr.be b.
8 : 15. many among them sh.be b.
9 : 4. hast b. yoke of his burden
14 : 5. L. hath b. staff of wicked
29.rod of him th. smote thee is b.
19 : 10.they shall be b. in purposes
21 : 9.all graven images he hath b.
24 : 5. they have b. the everl. cov
28 : 13. might fall backw.and be b.
33 : 8. he hath b. covenant, he
20. nor shall any of cords be b.
36 : 6. trustest in staff of b. reed
42 : † 4. he shall not fail nor be b.
Je. 2 : 13. hewed out b. cisterns
16. chil. b. crown of thy head
20. of old I have b. thy yoke
5 : 5. these have b. thy yoke
10 : 20.all my cords are b.my chil.
11 : 16. the branches of it are b.
14:17.virgin dau.of my people is b.
22 :28. Is man Coniah b. idol?
23 : 9.my heart is b.bec. of proph.
28 : 2. I have b. yoke of k. of Bab.
12. b. yoke off neck of prophet
13. Thou hast b. yokes of wood
33 : 21.may my cov. be b.with Da.
48 : 17. How is the strong staff b.
25. arm of Moab is b. saith L.
38. I have b. Moab like a vessel
50:17.this Neb.hath b.Isr.'s bones
23.the hammer of whole earth b.
51 : 30. her bars are b.
56. Bab. ev. one of bows is b.
58. broad walls of Bab. sh. be b.
La. 2 : 9. he hath b. her bars
3 : 4. b. my bones | 16.b.my teeth
Eze.6 : 4.your images shall be b.,6.
9. I am b. with their whorish
17 : 19. my cov. he hath b. [heart
19 : 12. her strong rods were b.
26:2. Aha, she is b. that was gates
27 : 26. east wind b. thee in seas
34. thou shalt be b. by the seas
30 : 21. I have b. arm of Pharaoh
22.I will break strong and that b.
31 : 12.his boughs are b. by rivers
32 : 28. be b. in midst of uncirc.
34 : 4. nor have ye bound up b.
16. I will bind up that was b.
27. when I have b. bands of yoke
44 : 7. they have b. my covenant
Da. 2 : 42. so kingdom partly b. [b.
8 : 8. when he strong gr. horn was
22. that being b. whereas 4 stood
25. he shall be b. without hand
11 : 4.his kingdom shall be b. and
22.with the arms of a flood be b.
Ho. 5 : 11.Ephr.is oppressed and b.
Jo. 1 : 4. so ship was like to be b.
Zch. 11 : 11. it was b. in that day
16. a shep. shall not heal that b.
Mat. 15 : 37. of b. meat, Mk. 8 : 8.
21:44. on stone sh. be b.,Lu.20:18.
Lu. 12 : 39. not suff. house to be b.
Jn. 5 : 18. he had not only b. sab.
7 : 23. that law of Moses not be b.
10 : 35. and scripture cannot be b.
19 : 31. besought legs might be b.
36. A bone of him shall not be b.
21 : 11. many, yet was not net b.

Ac.20 : 11. had b. bread and talked
27:35.gave thanks,when he had b.
41.hinder part was b. with waves
44. some on pieces of b. ship
1 Co. 11 : 24. is my body b. for you
Re. 2 : 27.as vessels shall they be b.

BROKEN down.

Le. 11 : 35. oven or ranges b. d. for
1 K. 18 : 30. repaired altar of L. b.d.
2 K.11 : 6.watch, that it be not b.d.
2 Ch.33:3.built places Hez.had b.d.
34 : 7. Josiah had b. d. the altars
Ne. 1 : 3. wall of Jerusalem is b. d.
2 : 13. I viewed the walls b. d.
Ps 80 : 12.Why hast b.d.her hedges
89: 40. hast b. d. all his hedges
Pr. 24 : 31. stone-wall b. d. [b. d.
25 : 28. no rule over spirit like city
Is. 16 : 8.have b.d. principal plants
22: 10. houses ye b. d. to fortify
24 : 10. city of confusion is b. d.
19. the earth is utterly b. d.
Je.4:26.cities b.d. | 48:20.Moab,39.
Eze. 30 : 4. her founda. sh. be b. d.
Jo. 1 : 17. barns b.d.corn withered
Ep. 2 : 14. C. hath b.d. middle wall

BROKEN forth.

Ge. 30 : † 30. it is b. f. to a mult.
38: 29. How hast thou b. f.?
2 S. 5 : 20. L. hath b.f. on mine ene.

BROKEN in.

1 Ch. 14 : 11. G. hath b. i. on mine

BROKEN off. [enem.

Jb. 17 : 11. my purposes are b. o.
Is.27:11.boughswithered sh.be b.o.
Ro. 11 : 17. if branches be b. o.
20. bec. of unbelief were b.o.,19.

BROKEN out.

Le.13: 20. plague of leprosy b.o.,25.

BROKEN in, or to pieces.

1 S. 2 : 10. adversaries of L. be b.t.
2 Ch.25 : 12.cast fr. rock, b.i.p.[p.
Ps.89 : 10.thou hast b. Rahab i. p.
Is. 8 : 9. associate ye, sh. be b.i.p.
30:14.as potter's vessel th is b.i.p.
Je. 50 : 2. Merodach is b. i. p., her
images b. i. p.
Da. 2 : 35. brass, silver, gold b.t.p.
Ho. 8 : 6. calf of Samaria be b.i.p.
Mk. 5 : 4. and fetters been b. i. p.

BROKEN up.

Ge.7 : 11.fountains of gr. deep b.u.
2 K. 25 : 4. city Jerus. b.u., Je.39:
2.-52: 7. [house of G.
2 Ch. 24 : 7. sons of Athaliah b. u.
Pr. 3:20. By his knowl. depths b.u.
Je. 37:11. army of Chal. was b. u.
Mi. 2 : 13. they have b. u. the gate
Mat. 24 : 43. not suff. house b. u.
Mk. 2 : 4. when had b. roof u.
Ac. 13 : 43. when cong. was b. u.

BROKEN-FOOTED.

BROKEN-HANDED.

Le. 21 : 19. man that is b.f.or b.h.

BROKEN-HEARTED.

Is. 61 : 1. sent me to bind up b.
Lu. 4 : 18. to heal b., to preach

BROOD.

Lu. 13 : 34. hen doth gather her b.

BROOK.

Ge. 32 : 23. sent them over b.
Le. 23 : 40. take willows of b.
Nu. 13 . 23. came to b. Eschol
24. called b. Eschol because of
De. 2 : 13. b. Zered, over b., 14.
9 : 21. and I cast dust into the b.
1 S. 17 : 40. five stones out of b.
30 : 9. David came to b. Besor
2 S. 15 : 23. king passed b. Kidron
17 : 20. They be gone over b.
1 K. 2 : 37.day thou passest over b.
15:13.idol burnt by b.,2 Ch.15:16.
17 : 3. hide by b. Cherith, 5.
6. he drank of the b.
18 : 40. Elijah brought them to b.
2 K. 23 : 6. burnt grove at b. Kid.
12. cast dust into b., 2 Ch. 30: 14.
2 Ch. 20 : 16. find them at end of b.
29 : 16. carried it to b. Kidron
32 : 4. much people stopped the b.
Ne. 2 : 15. by b. viewed wall
Jb. 6 : 15. dealt deceitfully as b.
40 : 22. willows of b. compass
Ps. 83 : 9. as to Jabin at b. Kison
110 : 7. He shall drink of b. in way
Pr. 18 : 4. well-sp of wisd. as b.
30:†17.ravens of b.shall pick it out
Is. 15 : 7. carry to b. of willows
Je. 31 : 40. fields to b. Kidron holy
Jn. 18 : 1. went over b. Cedron

BROOKS.

Nu. 21 : 14. did in b. of Arnon
15. stream of b. that goeth to Ar
De. 8 : 7. a land of b. of water
2 S.23 : 30. b. of Gaash, 1 Ch.11:32.
1 K. 18 : 5. said, Go unto all b.
Jb. 6 : 15. as stream of b. th. pass
20 : 17. shall not see b. of honey
22 : 24. lay up gold as stones of b.
Ps. 42 : 1. panteth after water-b.
Is. 19 : 6. b. of defence be emptied
7. reeds by b. by mouth of b. ev.
thing by b.
8. cast angle into b. sh. lament

BROTH.

Ju. 6 : 19. Gideon put b. in pot
20. angel said, pour out the b.
Is. 65 : 4. b. of abominable things

BROTHER. [life

Ge. 9 : 5. of every man's b. require
24 : 29. Rebekah had b. Laban
53. gave to her b. and mother
28 : 2. Laban thy mother's b.
29 : 12. told Rachel he her fa.'s b.
43 : 6. as to tell ye had a b.
7. have ye another b., 44 : 19.
De. 25 : 5. husband's b. go to her
Ju. 9 : 24. blood on Abim. their b.
21:6 Isr.repented them for Benj.b.
2 S.13 : 20.desolate in b. Abs.house
21 : 19.slew b.of Goliath,1 Ch.20:5.
Jb. 1 : 13 in eldest b. house, 18.
30 : 29. I am a b. to dragons
Pr. 17 : 17. b. is born for adversity
18 : 9. slothful is b. to waster
19. b. offend. harder to be won
24. sticketh closer than a b.
27 : 10. a neighb. than b. far off
Ec. 4 : 8. he hath child nor b.
Je. 9 : 4. trust not in b. for ev. b.
Eze. 44 : 25. for b. they may defile
Mal. 1 : 2. Was Esau Jacob's b.?
Mat. 10 : 21. b. deliv. b.,Mk.13:12.
Mk.12 : 19.If man s b.die,Lu.20:28.
Jn. 11 : 2. b. Lazarus was sick
19. Jews came to comf. conc. b.
Ac. 9 : 17. b. Saul, rec. sight,22:13.
12 : 2. he killed Jas. b. of John
21 : 20. seest, b. how many believe
Ro. 16 : 23. Quartus a b.
1 Co. 5 : 11. if a b. be a fornicator
6 : 6. b. goeth to law with b. bef.
7 : 12. b. hath wife believ. not
15. b. or sister is not under bond.
8 : 11. thro. thy knowl. weak b.
2 Co. 8 : 18. ha. sent with him b.
Ga. 1 : 19. save James the L.'s b.
2 Th. 3 : 6. b. that walketh disor-
15. admonish him as b. [derly
Phm. 7. saints refreshed by thee, b.
16. above a serv. a b. beloved
20. b. let me have joy of thee
Ja. 1 : 9. b. of low degree rejoice
2 : 15. If a b. be naked

His BROTHER.

Ge. 25 : 26. after came h. b. out
33 : 3. until came near h. b.
35 : 7. fled from face of h. b.
38 : 9.le t he sho. give seed to h.b.
42 : 38. h. b. is dead, 44 : 20.
Ex. 32 : 27. slay every man h. b.
Le. 21 : 2. for h.b. he may be defil.
Nu.6:7.not make hims unc.for h.b.
De. 15 : 2. not exact it of h. b.
De. 19:19.thou-t to ha. done to h.b.
25 : 6. sh.succeed in name of h.b.
28 : 54. his eye be evil tow. h. b.
Ju. 9 : 21.Jotham fled for fear of h.
2 S. 3 : 27. smote for bl. of h.b. [b.
1 K. 1 : 10. Sol. h. b. he called not
Ne. 5 : 7. usury every one of h. b.
Ps. 49 : 7. None can redeem h. b.
Is. 3 : 6. when man take hold h. b.
9 : 19.peo. fuel, no man spare h.b.
19 : 2. shall fight ev. one ag. h. b.
41 : 6. to h.b. Be of good courage
Je. 13 : † 14. dash man ag. h. b.
31:34.teach no more h.b.,He.8:11.
34 : 9.that none serve hims.of h.b.
14. let go ev. man h. b. a Hebrew
17. liberty every one to h. b.
Eze.18 : 18. spoiled h.b. by violence
33 : 30.speak ev. one to h.b.,Come
Ho. 12 : 3.Jac.took h.b. by the heel
Am. 1 : 11. pursue h. b. with sword
Mi. 7 : 2.they hunt every man h.b.
Hag 2 : 22.ev. one by sword of h.b.
Zch. 7 : 9. mercy ev. man to h. b.
10. let none imagine evil ag. h.b.
Mal.2 : 10.why deal treach. ag.h.b.
Mat.4 : 18.Simon and Andrew h.b.
21. of Zeb. and John h. b.
5 : 22. whoso. sayeth Raca to h.b.
18 : 35. if forgive not ev. one h. b.
22 : 24. raise seed to h.b., Mk.12:
19. Lu. 20: 28.
25. no issue. left his wife to h.b.
Mk.6 : 17.Herodias' sake h.b. Philip's wife, Lu. 3 : 19.
Lu. 3 : 1. h. b. Philip tetrarch of
Jn. 1 : 41. He findeth h. b. Simon
Ro. 14 : 13. occa. to fall in h.b.way
1 Th.4 : 6.that no man defraud h.b.
Ja.4:11 sp.evil of h.b.judgeth h.b.
1 Jn. 2 : 9. and hateth h. b., 11.
10. loveth h. b. abideth in light
3 : 10. he that loveth not h. b.,14.
12. not as Cain, slew h. b. bec
h. b. works righteous
15.hateth h.b. is murderer, 4:20.
17. and seeth h. b. have need
1 Jn. 4 : 21.loveth G.,love h.b. also
5 : 16. if any see h. b. sin a sin

My BROTHER.

Ge. 4 : 9. said, Am I m. b. keeper?
20 : 5. He is m.b.,13. 1 K. 20 : 32.
27:41.Then will I slay m.b. Jacob
29 : 15. to Jac. bec. thou art m.b.
32 : 11. Deliver me from m. b.
33 : 9. I have enough, m. b.
Ju.20 : 23.battle ag. Benj.m.b.,28.
1 S. 20 : 29. m. b. hath com-d me
2 S.1 : 26. distressed for thee, m.b.
13 : 12. nay m. b. do not force me
1 K.13 : 30.they mourned, Alas, m.
20 : 32.Is he alive? he is m.b.[b.
Ps.35 : 14.as tho. he had been m.b.
Can.8 : 1.O that thou wert as m.b.
Je. 22 : 18. not lament, Ah m. b.
Mat. 12 : 50. same is m.b.,Mk.3:35.
18 : 21. L.how oft m.b.sin ag. me?
Lu.12 : 13.sp.to m.b.that he divide
Jn. 11 : 21. if here, m.b. not died
21 : 32. been here m. b. not died
1 Co.8 : 13.if meat make m.b.to off.
2 Co. 2 : 13.I found not Titus m.b.
Ph. 2 : 25. to you Epaphrod. m.b.

Our BROTHER.

Ge. 37 : 26. what profit if slay o. b.
27. for he is o. b., Ju. 9 : 3.
42 : 21. We are guilty conc. o. b.
43 : 4. if wilt send o. b. we will go
44:26.exc.o.youngest b.be with us
Ju. 9 : 3. they said, He is o. b.
2 Co. 1 : 1. Timothy o.b., Col. 1 : 1.
1 Th. 3 : 2. He 13 : 23.
8 : 22. have sent with them o. b.
2 Pe. 3:15.even as o.beloved b.Paul
Phm. 1. Tim. o. b. to Philemon

Thy BROTHER.

Ge. 4:9. Cain, Where is Abel t. b.?

Ge. 4: 10. voice of t. b. bl. crieth, 11.
20: 16. given t. b. a thous. pieces
27: 35. t. b. came with subtilty
40. live by sword, serve t. b.
44. until t. b. fury turn, 45.
38: 8. go in to t. b. wife and raise up seed to t. b.
Ex. 4: 14. Is not Aaron t. b.?
28: 1. take to thee Aaron t. b.
Le. 19: 17. thou shalt not hate t. b.
25: 25. If t. b. be waxen poor
36. fear G. that t. b. may live
Nu. 27: 13. as Aa. t. b., De. 32: 50.
De. 13: 6. If t. b. entice thee
15: 3. which is thine with t. b.
7. nor shut hand from t. poor b.
9. eye evil against t. poor b.
11. open hand wide to t. b.
12. if t. b. Hebr. be sold to thee
17: 15. stranger over thee not t. b.
22: 1. bring them again to t. b.
2. with thee until t. b. seek
3. with lost things of t. b.
23: 7. not abhor Edomite, he t. b.
19. not lend upon usury to t. b.
24: 10. when lend t. b. anything
25: 3. t. b. seem vile unto thee
2 S. 2: 22. how hold face to Joab t. b.
13: 20. hold thy peace, he is t. b.
1 K. 20: 33. said, t. b. Benhadad
Jb. 22: 6. pledge fr. t. b. for naught
Ps. 50: 20. Thou speakest ag. t. b.
Pr. 27: 10. t. b. house in calamity
Ob. 10. violence ag. t. b. Jacob
12. not have looked on day of t. b.
Mat. 5: 23. remem. t. b. hath aught
24. first be reconciled to t. b.
7: 3. mote in t. b. eye, 4, 5. Lu. 6: 41, 42. [b., Lu. 17: 3.
18: 15. t. b. trespass, hast gained t.
Mk. 6: 18. not lawf. to have t. b. wife
Lu. 15: 27. said t. b. is come
32. this t. b. was dead, and
Jn. 11: 23. t. b. shall rise again
Ro. 14: 10. why judge t. b.? why dost thou set at naught t. b.?
15. if t. b. grieved with thy
21. whereby t. b. stumbleth

Your BROTHER.

Ge. 42: 16. let him fetch y. b.
20. bring y. youngest b., 34.
34. will I deliv. you y. b. (2)
43: 3. except y. b. be with you
7. say, Bring y. b. down
13. Take y. b. and go again
14. send away y. other b.
29. Is this y. youngest b.
44: 23. Exc. y. youngest b. come
45: 4. I am Joseph, y. b. whom ye
Ju. 9: 18. Abim., because he is y. b.
Re. 1: 9. John, who also am y. b.

BROTHERHOOD.

Zch. 11: 14. break b. betw. Judah
1 Pe. 2: 17. Love the b. Fear God

BROTHERLY.

Am. 1: 9. they remember not b. cov.
Ro. 12: 10. affectioned, with b. love
1 Th. 4: 9. as touching b. love, ye
He. 13: 1. Let b. love continue
2 Pe. 1: 7. to godliness b. kindn. (2)

BROUGHT.

Ge. 20: 9. b. on me a great sin.
27: 20. Because Lord b. it to me
31: 39. torn I b. not to thee
43: 26. they b. him the present
Ex. 9: 19. beast not b. home sh. die
10: 13. b. east-wind, east-wind b.
15: 22. Moses b. Isr. from Red Sea
18: 26. hard causes they b. to M.
19: 4. how I b. you to myself
32: 1. man that b. us up, 23.
21. thou hast b. so great a sin
35: 21. they b. Lord's offering, 24.
23. ev. man with whom scarlet b.
Le. 13: 2. shall be b. to Aaron, 9.
23: 14. till he have b. an off. to
24: 11. b. blasphemer to Moses

Nu. 6: 13. he shall be b. to door of
9: 13. b. not offering in his season
11: 31. wind from L. b. quails
14: 3. wheref. b. us to this land?
16: 10. hath b. thee near to him
27: 5. Moses b. their cause before
31: 50. b. an oblation for L.
32: 17. till we have b. them to pl.
De. 5: 15. G. b. thee out thence
26: 10. I have b. the first-fruits
13. b. away hallowed things
Jos. 7: 7. hast b. peo. over Jordan?
14. in morning ye shall be b.
23. they b. them to Joshua
24. b. them to valley of Achor
24: 7. L. b. the sea upon them
Ju. 2: 1. I b. you unto the land
16: 18. the Philistines b. money
18: 3. Who b. thee hither? and
1 S. 1: 24. she b. Sam. to h. of L.
25. they b. the child to Eli
2: 19. little coat b. to him
10: 27. they b. him no presents
21: 14. wheref. ye b. him to me?
25: 35. Da. received what she b.
30: 11. they b. an Egypt. to Da.
2 S. 1: 10. and bracelet, b. them to
4: 10. to have b. good tidings
7: 18. who am I, that thou hast b. me hitherto? 1 Ch. 17: 16.
1 K. 9: 9. L. b. this evil, 2 Ch. 7: 22.
10: 25. b. each his, 2 Ch. 9: 24.
17: 20. hast b. evil upon widow?
20: 39. b. a man unto me
22: 37. king died, was b. to Sama.
2 K. 5: 20. not receiving what he b.
17: 4. Hoshea b. no presents to k.
27: carry priest ye b. thence
20: 11. b. shadow ten degrees
24: 16. craftsmen king b. captive
1 Ch. 11: 19. with jeop. of lives b. it
14: 17. b. fear of him on all natio.
2 Ch. 13: 18. child. of Isr. b. under
17: 5. Jud. b. to Jehosh. presents
22: 9. b. Ahaziah to Jehu
25: 12. b. unto top of rock
28: 5. k. of Syria b. Isr. to Damas.
15. b. captives to Jericho to
32: 23. many b. gifts to L. to Je.
Ezr. 8: 18. b. us man of underst.
10: † 10. ye have b. strange wives
Ne. 4: 15. b. their coun. to naught
5: 5. daughters b. into bondage
8: 16. people b. them and made
9: 33. art just in all b. upon us
13: 12. Judah b. tithe of corn
Es. 6: 8. Let royal apparel be b.
9: 11. number of slain b. to k.
Jb. 4: 12. thing secretly b. to me
21: 32. shall he be b. to grave
Ps. 35: 4. be b. to confusion, 26.
45: 15. With joy shall they be b.
71: 24. b. to shame seek my hurt
78: 71. b. him to feed Jacob
Pr. 6: 26. man b. to piece of bread
Can. 2: 4. b. me to banqueting-h.
Is. 15: 1. Ar b. Kir b. to silence
23: 13. b. land of Chald. to ruin
29: 20. terrible one b. to naught
43: 23. not b. small cattle, 24.
48: 15. called him, I have b. him
53: 7. b. as a lamb to slaughter
59: 16. his arm b. salvation, 63: 5.
60: 11. that their kings may be b.
62: 9. they that b. it shall drink
Je. 11: 19. as ox b. to slaughter
15: 8. I have b. on them a spoiler
32: 42. as I have b. all this evil
40: 3. Now Lord hath b. it and
Eze. 14: 22. comfort. conc. evil I b.
23: 8. nor left whoredoms b. fr. E.
29: 5. shalt not be b. together
40: 4. I might shew, art thou b.
47: 3. he b. me through waters, 4.
Da. 6: 18. nor instru. of music b.
7: 13. b. him bef. ancient of days
9: 14. L. watched evil, and b. it

Da. 11: 6. given up, and that b. her
Hag. 1: 9. ye b. it home I did blow
Mal. 1: 13. ye b. what was torn
Mat. 1: 12. after they were b. to Bab.
9: 2. they b. to him a man sick
32: they b. to him a dumb man
10: 18. ye shall be b. bef. kings for my sake, Mk. 13: 9. Lu. 21: 12.
12: 25. kingd. b. to deso., Lu. 11: 17.
14: 11. b. John Baptist's head to her mother, Mk. 6: 28.
16: 8. ye have b. no bread
17: 16. I b. him to thy disciples
18: 24. one was b. owed 10,000
19: 13. were b. to him little children, Mk. 10: 13. Lu. 18: 15.
21: 7. b. the ass, and the colt, Mk. 11: 7. Lu. 19: 35.
25: 20. came and b. other 5 talents
Mk. 4: 21. candle b. to be put under
6: 27. k. com-d his head to be b.
10: 13. disci. rebuked those b. them
12: 16. bring penny and they b. it
Lu. 2: 22. b. him to Jerus. to present
4: 9. he b. him to Jerusalem
5: 11. had b. ships to land
18. men b. in a bed a man
7: 37. woman b. alabaster-box
10: 34. b. him to an inn took care
18: 40. Jesus com-d him to be b.
23: 14. Ye have b. this man
Jn. 1: 42. he b. Simon to Jesus
4: 33. any b. him aught to eat?
7: 45. Why have ye not b. him
9: 13. They b. to Pharis. him blind
19: 39. b. a mixture of myrrh
Ac. 4: 34. b. prices of things, 37.—5: 2.
5: 21. to prison to have them b.
27. and when they had b. them
36. scattered and b. to naught
6: 12. caught Stephen and b. him
9: 27. Barnabas b. him to apostles
15: 3. b. on way by the church
16: 16. who b. her masters gain
20. b. them to the magistrates
18: 12. b. Paul to judgment seat
19: 12. were b. to sick, aprons
19. b. their books, and burned
24. Demetrius b. no small gain
37. ye b. these men, no robbers
20: 12. they b. young man alive
21: 5. they all b. us on our way
16. b. with them one Mnason
23: 31. b. Paul by night
25: 6. commanded Paul to be b.
18. they b. none accusation
27: 24. Paul, thou must b. bef. Ce.
Ro. 15: 24. to be b. thith. by you [any
1 Co. 6: 12. not be b. und. power of
2 Co. 1: 16. b. on way to Judea
1 Th. 3: 6. b. tidings of your faith
2 Ti. 1: 10. b. life and immortality
1 Pe. 1: 13. grace to be b. to you
2 Pe. 2: 19. of same is b. in bond.

BROUGHT again.

Ge. 14: 16. Abram b. a. bro. Lot
43: 12. money th. was b. a. in sacks
Ex. 10: 8. Moses b. a. to Pharaoh
15: 19. Lord b. a. waters of sea
De. 1: 25. b. us word a. a good land
Jos. 14: 7. I b. him word a. as it
Ru. 1: 21. b. me home a. empty
1 S. 6: 21. Philis. b. a. ark of L.
2 S. 3: 26. b. a. Abner from well
1 K. 2: 30. b. king word a.
2 K. 22: 9. Shaphan b. word a., 20. 1 K. 20: 9. 2 Ch. 34: 28.
2 Ch. 33: 13. L. b. Manas. a. to Jeru.
Ne. 13: 9. thither b. I a. vessels
Je. 27: 16. vessels shall be b. a.
Eze. 34: 4. ye not b. a. wh. was driven
39: 27. b. them a. from peo.
Mat. 27: 3. b. a. 30 pieces of silver
He. 13: 20. that b. a. from dead

BROUGHT back.

Ge. 14: 16. Ab. b. b. all goods
Nu. 13: 26. b. b. word to them and

1 K. 13: 23. for prophet whom he b. b.
2 Ch. 19: 4. Jehosh. b. them b. to L.
Ps. 85: 1. hast b. b. captivity
Eze. 38: 8. land b. b. from sword

BROUGHT down.

Ge. 39: 1. Jo. was b. d. into Egypt
Ju. 7: 5. he b. d. peo. to waters
16: 21. Philistines b. d. Samson
1 S. 30: 16. when he had b. him d.
1 K. 1: 53. b. Adonijah d. fr. altar
17: 23. Elijah b. child d. out
18: 40. b. them d. to brook Kishon
2 K. 11: 19. b. d. the king. 2 Ch. 23: 20.
Ps. 20: 8. They are b. d. and fallen
107: 12. he b. d. their heart with
Is. 5: 15. mean man shall be b. d.
14: 11. pomp is b. d. to grave
15. thou shalt be b. d. to hell
29: 4. shalt be b. d. and speak
43: 14. I have b. d. all nobles
La. 2: 2. b. them d. to ground
Eze. 17: 24. I L. have b. d. tree
31: 18. b. d. with trees of Eden
Zch. 10: 11. pride of Assy. be b. d.
Mat. 11: 23. Caper. b. d. to hell
Ac. 9: 30. breth. b. him d. to Cesa.
22: 30. he b. Paul d. and set him

BROUGHT forth.

Ge. 1: 12. earth b. f. grass and herbs
1: 21. waters b. f. abundantly
14: 18. king of Salem b. f. bread
15: 5. Lord b. f. Abram abroad
19: 16. angels b. Lot f. and set
24: 53. the servant b. f. jewels
38: 25. When b. f. she sent to fa.
41: 47. earth b. f. by handfuls
Ex. 3: 12. When hast b. f. people
16: 3. ye have b. us f. into wilder.
29: 46. shall kn. I L. b. them f., Le.
25: 38.–26: 13, 45. De. 16: 1.
32: 11. peo. thou hast b. f., De. 9: 26.
Le. 25: 42. I b. f. out of Egypt, 55.
Nu. 17: 8. Aaron's rod b. f. buds
20: 16. angel, and b. us f. out of E.
24: 8. God b. him f. out of Egypt.
De. 6: 12. forget L. b. thee f., 8: 14.
8: 15. b. f. water out of rock [ed
9: 12. peo. thou b. f. have corrupt-
26: 8. Lord b. us f. with a mighty
29: 25. cov. made wh. he b. them f.
33: 14. precious fruits b. f. by sun
Jos. 10: 23. b. f. those five kings
Ju. 5: 25. she b. f. butter in dish
6: 8. I b. you f. out of house of b.
1 S. 12: 8. who b. f. your fathers
2 S. 22: 20. b. me f. into large place,
Ps. 18: 19. [2 Ch. 6: 5.
1 K. 8: 16. since day I b. f. my peo.,
9: 9. they forsook L. who b. f. fathers, 2 Ch. 7: 22.
2 K. 10: 22. b. f. vestments for
11: 12. b. f. king's son, put the cr.
Ezr. 1: 7. Cyrus b. f. vessels
Jb. 10: 18. Wherefore hast b. me f.
21: 30. wick. be b. f. to d. of wrath
Ps. 7: 14. mischief, b. f. falsehood
90: 2. Before mountains were b. f.
105: 30. land b. f. frogs in abnnd.
37. b. them f. with silver
43. he b. f. his people with joy
Pr. 8: 24. When no depths, I was b. f.
25. before the hills was I b. f.
Can. 8: 5. mother b. thee f. she b. f.
Is. 5: 2. and it b. f. wild grapes
26: 18. b. f. wind | 45: 10. what b. f.
51: 18. to guide her she hath b. f.
66: 7. Bef. she travailed, she b. f.
8. as Zion travailed, she b. f.
Je. 2: 27. stone, Thou hast b. me f.
11: 4. in day I b. them f., 34: 13.
17: †11. gathereth young he not b. f.
20: 3. Pashur b. f. Jere. out of
32: 21. hast b. f. Israel with signs
50: 25. L. b. f. weapons of indig.
51: 10. L. hath b. f. our righte.
Eze. 12: 7. I b. f. my stuff by day
14: 22. remn. b. f. sons daughters
Eze. 17: 6. became vine and b. f.
20: 22. in whose sight I b. them f.
Mi. 5: 3. which travaileth hath b. f.
Hag. 2: 19. olive-tree hath not b. f.
Mat. 1: 25. till she b. f. first-born
13: 8. b. f. fruit 100 fold, Mk. 4: 8.
26. blade sprung up and b. f.
Mk. 4: 29. when fruit is b. f. [son
Lu. 1: 57. Elisabeth's time she b. f.
2: 7. she b. f. her first-born son
12: 16. ground of rich man b. f.
Jn. 19: 13. Pilate heard that, b. f.
Ac. 5: 15. b. f. sick into streets [Jes.
19. opened prison b. them f.
12: 6. Herod would have b. him f.
23: 28. I b. him f. into council
25: 17. I com-d man to be b. f.
23. at Festus com-d Paul was b. f.
26. I have b. him f. before you
Ja. 5: 18. prayed, and earth b. f. fr.
Re. 12: 5. she b. f. a man-child
13. dragon persecu. wom. which b.
[f.

BROUGHT in.

Ge. 39: 14. b. i. Hebrew to mock
47: 7. Joseph b. i. Jacob his father
Le. 10: 18. blood was not b. i.
16: 27. goat, wh. blood was b. i.
Nu. 12: 15. till Miriam was b. i.
De. 9: 4. for my righte. L. b. me i.
11: 29. when L. hath b. thee i.
2 S. 3: 22. Joab b. i. a great spoil
6: 17. they b. i. ark of L., 1 K. 8: 6.
Ne. 13: 19. no burden b. i. on sab.
Ps. 78: 26. he b. i. the south-wind
Da. 5: 13. was Daniel b. i. bef. king
Mat. 14: 11. John's head was b. i.
Lu. 2: 27. parents b. i. child Jesus
Jn. 18: 16. opened door b. i. Peter
Ac. 7: 45. b. i. with Jes. into poss.
Ga. 2: 4. false brethren b. i. to spy
He. 9: †16. must be b. i. death of
testator

BROUGHT into.

Le. 26: 41. b. them i. land of enem.
Nu. 16: 14. not b. us i. land that
23: 14. b. him i. field of Zophim
De. 6: 10. L. b. thee i., 31: 20.
1 S. 5: 2. b. ark i. Dagon's house
9: 22. b. them i. the parlour
20: 8. b. thy serv. i. a cov. with thee
2 K. 12: 16. sin-money not b. i. h.
Ps. 22: 15. b. me i. dust of death
73: 19. How are b. i. desolation
106: 42. b. i. subjec. Je. 34: 11, 16.
Can. 1: 4. k. b. me i. his chambers
Je. 2: 7. I b. i. plentiful country
La. 3: 2. hath b. me i. darkness
Eze. 20: 10. b. them i. wilderness
28. had b. them i. land
27: 26. rowers b. thee i. water
44: 7. b. i. my sanct. strangers
Lu. 22: 54. b. him i. high priest's
Ac. 9: 8. they b. him i. Damascus
39. they b. him i. upper chamber
16: 34. he had b. them i. house
21: 28. b. Greeks i. the temple, 29.
22: 24. to be b. i. castle
1 Ti. 6: 7. we b. noth. i. this world
He. 13: 11. whose bl. is b. i. sanct.

BROUGHT low.

Ju. 11: 35. dau. hast b. me very l.
2 Ch. 28: 19. L. b. Judah l. bec. of
Jb. 14: 21. they are b. l. [Ahas
24: 24. wicked are gone and b. l.
Ps. 79: 8. let mercies prev. us, b. l.
106: 43. were b. l. for their iniq.
107: 39. they are b. l. thro. oppres.
116: 6. I was b. l., he helped me
142: 6. attend, for I am b. very l.
Ec. 12: 4. dau-s of music be b. l.
Is. 2: 12. lifted up, he shall be b. l.
25: 5. branch of terri. ones be b. l.
Lu. 3: 5. every hill b. l., Is. 40: 4.

BROUGHT out.

Ge. 15: 7. that b. thee o. of Ur
41: 14. b. him o. of the dungeon
43: 23. he b. Simeon o. unto them
Ex. 13: 3. by strength L. b. you o.
9, 14, 16. De. 6: 21.–7: 8, 19.
20: 2. I am the L. which b. thee o.,
Le. 19: 36.–22: 33. Nu. 15: 41.
De. 5: 6.–13: 5, 10. Ps. 81: 10.
Le. 23: 43. I b. them o., 1 K. 8: 21.
De. 4: 37. b. thee o. in his sight
5: 15. remember L. b. thee o.
6: 23. he b. us o. from thence
9: 28. b. them o. to slay in wilder.
Jos. 6: 23. young men b. o. Rahab
24: 5. plagued E., and I b. you o.
2 S. 13: 18. serv. b. her o. and bolted
2 K. 23: 6. he b. out grove fr. h. of L.
1 Ch. 20: 3. he b. o. the peo. in it
2 Ch. 23: 11. th. they b. o. k's son
29: 16. priests b. o. all uncleann.
Ps. 78: 16. b. streams o. of rock
80: 8. thou hast b. a vine o. of E.
107: 14. He b. them o. of darkness
136: 11. b. o. Israel fr. am. them
Je. 7: 22. in day I b. them o. of E.
Eze. 20: 14. whose sight I b. th. o.
Da. 5: 13. whom king b. o. of Jewry
Ho. 12: 13. by prophet L. b. Isr. o.
Ac. 7: 36. b. them o. after he had
40. this Moses, which b. us o.
12: 17. declare how L. b. him o.
13: 17. with a high arm b. th. o.
16: 30. b. o., said, What do to be
39. besought, and b. them o. [sav.?

BROUGHT to pass.

2 K. 19: 25. have b. it t. p., Is. 37: 26.
Eze. 21: 7. it shall be b. t. p.
1 Co. 15: 54. sh. be b. t. p. saying

BROUGHT unto.

Mat. 4: 24. they b. u. him all sick
14: 35. Mk. 1: 32. Lu. 4: 40.
8: 16. b. u. him many possessed
12: 22. Th. was b. u. him one with
22: 19. they b. u. him a penny
Mk. 9: 17. b. u. thee my son, 20.
Lu. 18: 15. they b. u. him infants
23: 14. Ye have b. this man u. me
Ac. 11: 26. he b. him u. Antioch
14: 13. b. ox. and garlands u. gates
17: 15. they b. Paul u. Athens
19. b. him u. Areopagus

BROUGHT up.

Ge. 50: 23. b. u. upon Jo's knees
Ex. 17: 3. Wherefore hast b. us u.?
Nu. 21: 5. [23.
32: 1. as for Moses that b. us u.,
4. gods b. thee u., 8. 1 K. 12: 28.
33: 1. people wh. thou hast b. u.
Nu. 13: 32. b. u. evil report of land
16: 13. sm. thing th. hast b. us u.?
20: 4. why have ye b. u. cong.
De. 20: 1. L. with thee, wh. b. u.
22: 19. b. u. evil name upon virgin
Jos. 24: 17. he it is that b. us u.
32. bones of Jo. b. u., buried they
Ju. 6: 8. I b. you u. fr. Egypt, 1 S.
15: 13. b. Sams. u. fr. rock [10: 18.
16: 8. lords b. u. sev. green withs
31. b. Samson u. and buried
1 S. 2: 14. all the flesh-hook b. u.
8: 8. done since the day I b. them
u., 2 S. 7: 6. 1 Ch. 17: 5.
10: 18. I b. u. Isr. out of Egypt
12: 6. L. that b. your fathers u.
2 S. 6: 12. Dav. b. u. ark of God, 15.
1 K. 8: 4. 1 Ch. 15: 28. 2 Ch. 1: 4.
21: 8. sons she b. u. for Adriel
13. b. u. the bones of Saul
2 K. 10: 1. that b. u. Ahab's chil., 6.
17: 7. Isr. sinned ag. L. wh. b. th. u.
36. L. who b. you u., him fear
25: 6. b. u. Zed. to King, Jer. 39: 5.
2 Ch. 1: 4. ark had David b. u.
8: 11. Solo. b. u. daughter of Pha.
10: 8. young men b. u. w. him, 10.
Ezr. 1: 11. vessels b. u. from Bab.
4: 2. Ezar-haddon king b. us u.
Ne. 9: 18. This is thy G. b. thee u.
12: 31. I b. u. princes of Judah
Es. 2: 7. Mordecai b. u. Esther

Es. 2:20. like as when she was b. u.
Jb. 31: 18. fr. youth b. u. with me
Ps. 30:3. b. u. my soul from grave
40: 2. He b. me u. out of hor. pit
Pr. 8:30. was, as one b. u. with him
Is. 1: 2. I have nourished and b.
49: 21. who. b.u.these? [u. chil.
51: 18. none of all sons she b. u.
63: 11. that b. them u.? Je. 2: 6.
Je. 11: 7 protes. in day I b. them u.
16: 14. b. u. Isr. out of E., 23: 7.
15. L. that b.u.Isr. fr.north,23:8.
La. 2:22.those I b.u. enemy consu.
4: 5. were b. u. in scarlet embrace
Eze. 19: 3. b. u. one of her whelps
31: † 4. the deep b. him u. on high
37:13. b. you u. out of your graves
Am. 2: 10. I b. you u., 3: 1.-9: 7.
Mi. 6: 4. [tion
Jon. 2: 6. b. u. my life fr. corrup-
Na. 2: 7. she sh. be b.u. and maids
Lu. 4: 16. Naz. where he been b.u.
Ac. 13:1. had been b.u. with Herod
22: 3. b. u. at feet of Gamaliel
1 Ti. 5: 10. if she have b. u. chil.

BROUGHTEST. [ed
Ex. 32: 7. peo. b. out have corrupt-
Nu. 14: 13. b. up people in might
De. 9: 28. land whence thou b. us
29. thy inheri. thou b., 1 K.8:51.
2 S. 5: 2. that b. in Isr., 1 Ch.11:2.
1 K. 8: 53. when b. fathers out
Ne. 9: 7. b. him forth.out of Ur
15. thou b. water out of rock
23. b. them into land promised
Ps. 66: 11. Thou b. us into the net
12. b. us out into wealthy place

BROW.
Is. 48: 4. neck iron thy b. brass
Lu. 4: 29. led him to b. of hill

BROWN.
Ge. 30: 32. all b. cattle, 35, 40.
33. every one not b. be accounted

BRUISE, S. [stolen
Is. 1: 6. no soundness, but b-s and
53: † 5. with his b. we are healed
Je.6: † 14.healed b. of peo. slightly
30: 12. saith L. Thy b. is incura.
Eze.47: † 12. the leaf thereof for b-s
Na. 3: 19. there is no healing of thy

BRUISE. [Verb.] [b.
Ge. 3: 15. it shall b. thy head,
thou shalt b. his heel
Is. 28: 28. nor b. it with horsemen
53: 10. it pleased the L. to b. him
Da. 2: 40. as iron it break and b.
Ro. 16: 20. G. of peace sh. b. Sat-

BRUISED, ING. [an
Le. 22: 24. sh. not offer what is b.
2 K. 18: 21. trusteth this b. reed
Is. 28: 28. Bread corn is b.
42: 3. b. reed not break, Mat. 12:
53: 5. he was b. for our iniq. [20.
Eze. 23: 3. b. teats of their virgin.
8. b. the breasts of her virginity
21. in b-g thy teats by Egyptians
Lu. 4: 18. to set at liberty them b.
9: 39. spirit b-g him, hardly de-

BRUIT. [parteth
Je. 10: 22. noise of the b. is come
Na. 3: 19. all that hear b. of thee

BRUTE. See BEASTS.

BRUTISH.
Ps. 49: 10. fool and the b. perish
92: 6. a b. man knoweth not
94: 8. Underst. ye b. am. people
Pr. 12: 1. that hateth reproof is b.
30: 2. I am more b. than any man
Is.19: 11. counsel of wise become b.
Je. 10: 8. they are altogether b.
14. man b., 51: 17. | 21. pastors b.
Eze. 21: 31. deliv. into hand of b.

BUCKET, S. [men
Nu. 24: 7. pour water out of his b.
Is. 40: 15. nations as drop of a b.

BUCKLER. [18:30.
2 S. 22: 31. b. to all th. trust, Ps.
1 Ch. 5: 18. men able to bear b.
12:8. Gadites that could handle b.
Ps. 18: 2. Lord is my God, my b.
35: 2. Take hold of shield and b.
91: 4. his truth shall be thy b.
Pr. 2: 7. b. to them walk upright.
Je.46: 3. Order ye the b. and shield
Eze. 23: 24. shall set ag. thee b.
26: 8. he sh. lift up the b. ag. thee

BUCKLERS.
2 Ch.23: 9. Jehoiada deliv. spears, b.
Jb. 15: 26. runneth upon bosses of
Can. 4: 4. hanged 1000 b. [his b.
Eze. 38: 4. a great company with b.
39: 9. they sh. set on fire shields,

BUD, S. [b.
Nu. 17: 8. Aa.'s rod bro't forth b.
Jb. 38: 27. b. of tender herb to spr.
Is. 18: 5. when the b. is perfect
61: 11. earth bring. forth her b.
Eze. 16: 7. to multiply as b. of field
Ho. 8: 7. b. shall yield no meal

BUD. [Verb.]
Ge.3: † 18. thistles sh. it cause to b.
Jb.14:9. thro. scent of water it will b.
Ps. 132: 17. make horn of David b.
Can. 7: 12. see if pomegranates b.
Is. 27: 6. Israel shall bloom and b.
55: 10. earth to bring forth and b.
Eze. 29: 21. cause horn of Isr. to b.

BUDDED.
Ge. 40: 10. vine was as though it b.
Nu. 17: 8. Aa.'s rod for Levi b.
Can. 6: 11. to see whe. pomegran-
Eze. 7: 10. pride hath b. [ates b.
He. 9: 4. ark wherein rod b.

BUFFET, ED.
Mat. 26: 67. spit and b. him, Mk.
Mk. 14: 65. began to b. him [14:65.
1 Co. 4: 11. to pres. hour we are b.
2 Co.12: 7. messen. of Sat. to b. me
1 Pe. 2: 20. if be b. for your faults

BUILD. [Referred to God.]
1 S. 2: 35. and will b. him a sure
house, 2 S. 7: 27. 1 K. 11: 38.
1 Ch. 17: 10. L. will b. thee a house
25. told thou wilt b. him house
Ps.28: 5. destroy, and not b. them
51: 18. to Sion, b. walls of Jerus.
69: 35. G. will b. cities of Judah
89: 4. b. up thy throne to all gene.
102: 16. When L. shall b. up Zion
127: 1. except L. b. house, they lab.
147: 2. L. doth b. up Jerusalem
Je. 18: 9. conc. nation to b. it
24: 6. will b. not pull down, 31:28.
31: 4. I will b. thee, O virgin
28. will watch over them to b.
33: 7. I will b. Jud. and Isr. as at
42: 10. if abide in land will b. you
Eze. 36: 36. I L. b. ruined places
Am. 9: 11. I will b. it as of old
Mat.16: 18. on this rock b. my ch.
26: 61. to b. it in 3 days, Mk.14:58.
Ac. 15: 16. I will b. taberu. of Da.

BUILD. [Man the agent.]
Ge. 11: 4. go to, let us b. us a city
8. and they left off to b. the city
Nu. 32: 16. We will b. sheep-folds
24. b. cities for your little ones
De. 20: 20. b. bulwarks ag. city
1 K. 9: 19. all the cities of store,
and that which Solomon desired to b. in Jerusalem, 2 Ch.
24. then did b. Millo [8: 6.
11: 7. Sol. did b. pl. for Chemosh
16: 34. Hiel, Bethelite b. Jericho
1 Ch. 22: 19. b. ye sanctuary of L.
29: 19. to Sol. heart to b. palace
2 Ch. 14: 7. let us b. these cities
Ezr. 4: 2. Let us b. with you. we
5: † 4. men that b. this building
Ne. 2: 5. b. city of my fa. sepul.
17. b. the wall | 18. rise and b.
20. we his serv. will rise and b.
3: 3. fish-gate did the sons b.
4: 3. which they b. if a fox go up,
Ne.4: 10. we are not able to b. wall
Ec. 3: 3. and a time to b. up
Can. 8: 9. we will b. upon her
Is. 9. 10. fallen, but we will b.
45: 13. he shall b. my city
58: 12. b. old waste places, 61: 4
60: 10. sons of strangers b. walls
65: 22. not b. another inhabit
Je. 1: 10. have set thee to b.
Eze. 4: 2. b. a fort ag. it, 21: 22.
39: † 15. then shall ye b. up a sign
Da. 9: 25. to restore and b. Jerus.
Am. 9: 11. b. it as in days of old
14. Israel shall b. waste cities
Mi. 3: 10. They b. Zion with blood
Zch. 6: 12. he shall b. temple, 13.
15. that far off shall b. in tem.
9: 3. Tyrus did b. a strong hold
Mal. 1: 4. b. but I throw down
Mat. 23: 29. ye b. tombs of proph-
ets, Lu. 11: 47, 48.
Lu. 12: 18. my barns and b. greater
14: 28. intending to b. a tower?
30. to b. and not able to finish
Ac. 20: 32. grace, able to b. you up
Ro. 15: 20. lest I b. on ano. man's
1 Co. 3:12. if any b. on this founda.
Ga. 2: 18. b. again things I destroy-

BUILD altar, s. [ed
Ex. 20: 25. not b. a. of hewn stone
Nu. 23: 1. said, b. me here 7 a., 29.
De. 27: 5. there shalt b. an a. to L.
6. shalt b. a. of L. of whole stones
Jos. 22: 26. Let us prep. to b. an a.
29. G. forbid, we b. an a.
See BEGAN.

BUILD joined with house, s.
De. 25: 9. that will not b. bro.'s h.
28: 30. b. a h., not dw., Zph.1:13.
Ru. 4: 11. wh. two did b. h. of Isr.
1 S.2: 35. b. him sure h., 1 K.11:38.
2 S. 7: 5. thou b. me h. to dwell in
7. Why b. ye not me a h. of cedar
13. shall b. h. for my name, 1 K.
5: 5.-8: 19. 1 Ch. 17:12.-22:10.
27. saying, I will b. thee an h.
1 K. 2: 36. b. thee a h. in Jerus.
5: 3. David not b. a h. for wars
5. I purpose to b. h. to L., 2 Ch.2:1.
18. timber and stones to b. h.
8: 16. no city to b. a h., 2 Ch. 6:5.
17. in heart of David to b. a h.,
1 Ch. 28: 2. 2 Ch. 6: 7.
18. in heart to b. h., 2 Ch. 6: 8.
19. shalt not b. h., 1 Ch. 17: 4.
-22: 8.-28: 3. 2 Ch. 6: 9.
1 Ch. 17: 10. L. will b. thee an h.
12. b. me a h., 2 Ch. 6: 9.
25. told thou wilt b. him h.
22: 6. charged him to b. h.
7. in my mind to b. h., 28: 2.
8. not b. a h., thou shed blood
11. my son, b. the h. of Lord
28: 6. Sol. shall b. my h. and my
10. L. chosen thee to b. h.
29: 16. have prep. to b. thee h.
2 Ch. 2: 4. Behold I b. a h. to L.
5. h. I b. is great, for gr. is our G
6. who able to b. him a h.? (2)
36: 23. charged to b. h., Ezr. 1: 2.
Ezr. 1: 3. go to Jerus. b. h. of L.
5:3. Who com-d you to b. this h.? 9.
13. Cyrus decree to b. this h.
6: 7. let governor of Jews b. h.
Ps. 127: 1. labour in vain th. b. h.
Pr. 24: 27. prepare and b. thine h.
Is. 65: 21. shall b. h-s and inhabit
66: 1. wh. is h. ye b. unto me?
Je. 22: 14. I will b. me a wide h.
29: 5. b. h-s dwell in them, 28.
35: 7. Neither sh. ye b. h. nor sow
9. Nor to b. h-s to dwell in
Eze.11:3. It is not near, let us b. h-s
28: 26. dwell safely, and sh. b. h-s
Zph. 1: 13. shall b. h-s not inhab.
Hag. 1: 8. bring wood, b. h.
Zch. 5: 11. To b. it a h. in Shinar

Ac. 7 : 49. what h. will ye b. me

BUILDED.

Ge. 2 : † 22. of rib L. b. woman
4 : 17. Cain b. city called Enoch
8 : 20. Noah b. an altar to the L.
10 : 11. Asher b. Nineveh, Reho.
11 : 5. L. came to see tower men b.
12 : 7. Ab. b. altar to L., 13 : 18.
16 : † 2. I may be b. by her, 30 : † 3.
26 : 25. Isaac b. | Ex. 24 : 4. Moses b.
Jos. 22 : 16. in that ye b. an altar
1 K. 8 : 27. how much less this house
I have b., 43. [had b.
15 : 22. stones wherewith Baasha
2 K. 23 : 13. Sol. b. for Ashtoreth
1 Ch. 22 : 5. h. b. must be magnifical
Ezr. 3 : 2. b. altar of G. of Israel
4 : 1. heard that they b.
13. be it known if city be b., 16.
21. give com-t that city be not b.
5 : 8. we went to house of G. b.
11. we build house b. years ago
15. let house of G. be b., 6 : 3.
6 : 14. elders of Jews b. and prosp.
Ne. 4 : 18. sword girded, and so b.
6 : 1. enemies heard I had b.
Jb. 20 : 19. taken house he b. not
Ps. 122 : 3. Jerus. is b. a city comp.
Pr. 9 : 1. Wisd. hath b. her house
24 : 3. Thro. wisdom is a house b.
Ec. 2 : 4. I b. me houses, I planted
Can. 4 : 4. tower of D. b. for armoury
Je. 30 : 18. city be b. on own heap
La. 3 : 5. He hath b. against me
Eze. 36 : 10. wastes shall be b., 33.
Lu. 17 : 28. they plant, they b.
Ep. 2 : 22. In whom ye are b. toge.
He. 3 : 3. b. house more honour
4. ev. house is b. by some man

BUILDEDST, EST. [not
De. 6 : 10. goodly cities thou b-dst
22 : 8. When thou b. a new house
Ne. 6 : 6. for cause thou b. wall
Eze. 16 : 31. b. eminent place
Mat. 27 : 40. destroyest tem. and b.
it in three days, Mk. 15 : 29.

BUILDER.

1 Co. 3 : 10. as a wise master-b.
He. 11 : 10. for a city whose b. is G.

BUILDERS.

1 K. 5 : 18. and Hiram's b. did hew
2 K. 12 : 11. laid money out to b.
22 : 6. give it to b-s, 2 Ch. 34 : 11.
Ezr. 3 : 10. when b. laid foundation
Ne. 4 : 5. have provoked thee bef. b.
18. b., ev. one had sword girded
Ps. 118 : 22. stone b. refus. become
headstone, Mat. 21 : 42. Mk.
12 : 10. Lu. 20 : 17. Ac. 4 : 11.
127 : † 1. labour in vain that are b.
Eze. 27 : 4. b. have perfec. thy beauty
1 Pe. 2 : 7. stone wh. b. disallowed

BUILDETH.

Jos. 6 : 26. cursed that b. this city
Jb. 27 : 18. He b. house as a moth
Pr. 14 : 1. wise woman b. her house
Je. 22 : 13. woe to him that b. by
unrighteousness
Ho. 8 : 14. Israel b. temples
Am. 9 : 6. b. his stories in heavens
Ha. 2 : 12. b. a town with blood
1 Co. 3 : 10. I laid founda. ano. b.

BUILDING. [Participle.]

1 K. 6 : 7. no tool heard in h. while b.
7 : 1. Sol. was b. his h. 13 years
2 Ch. 16 : 6. wherew Baasha was b.
Ezr. 4 : 12. b. rebellious bad city
Jude 20. b. up on most holy faith

BUILDING, S.

Jos. 22 : 19. rebel not in b. altar
1 K. 3 : 1. made an end of b. his house
6 : 38. was Sol. 7 years in b. it
9 : 1. Sol. finished the b. of h. of L.
15 : 21. he left off b. of Ramah, 2
Ch. 16 : 5.
1 Ch. 28 : 2. made ready for the b.
2 Ch. 3 : 3. Sol. was instructed for b.
Ezr. 4 : 4. and troubled them in b.
5 : 4. names of men made b.
16. since that time it been in b.
6 : 8. what do for b. of house of G.
Ec. 10 : 18. By slothf. b. decayeth
Eze. 17 : 17. by b. forts to cut off
40 : 5. he measured the b., 41 : 15.
42 : 6. the b. was straitened
46 : 23. there was a row of b. round
Mat. 24 : 1. to shew him b-s of temple
Mk. 13 : 1. see what b-s are here, 2.
Jn. 2 : 20. temple was 46 yrs. in b.
1 Co. 3 : 9. ye are God's b.
2 Co. 5 : 1. we have a b. of God
Ep. 2 : 21. in wh. b. fitly framed
He. 9 : 11. by tabern. not of this b.
Re. 21 : 18. b. of wall of jasper

BUILT.

De. 13 : 16. it shall not be b. again
1 K. 22 : 39. cities that Ahab b. are
2 Ch. 14 : 7. So they b. and prospered
20 : 8. they have b. thee a sanctuary
26 : 9. Uzziah b. towers in, 10.
27 : 3. on wall of Ophel he b.
4. Jotham b. castles and
Jb. 3 : 14. who b. desolate places
12 : 14. breaketh it cannot be b.
22 : 23. if return shalt be b. up
Ps. 78 : 69. b. his sanctu. like high
89 : 2. Mercy sh. be b. up for ever
Ec. 9 : 14. b. great bulwarks
Is. 5 : 2. b. a tower in vineyard
44 : 26. to the cities, Ye shall be b.
28. to Jerus. Thou shalt be b.
Je. 12 : 16. shall they be b. in
31 : 4. thou shalt be b. O virgin
32 : 31. provoca. fr. day they b. it
45 : 4. which I b. will break down
Eze. 16 : 24. hast b. eminent place
25. hast b. thy high place at ev.
26 : 14. thou shalt be b. no more
Da. 4 : 30. great Bab. I have b.?
9 : 25. the street shall be b. again
Zch. 8 : 9. strong, that tem. be b.
Mat. 21 : 33. b. a tower, Mk. 12 : 1.
Lu. 7 : 5. hath b. us a synagogue
1 Co. 3 : 14. if work abide he hath b.
Ep. 2 : 20. b. on founda. of apostles
Col. 2 : 7. Rooted and b. up in him
He. 3 : 4. he that b. all things is G.

BUILT altar.

Ge. 22 : 9. Ab. b. a. there, 13 : 18.
33 : † 20. Jacob b. an a., El-elohe
Ex. 17 : 15. Mo. b. a., 24 : 4. | 32 : 5.
Jos. 8 : 30. Joshua b. a. [Aaron b. a.
22 : 10. half-tribe Manas. b. great a.
Ju. 6 : 24. Gid. b. a. | 21 : 4. peo. b. a.
1 S. 7 : 17. Sam. | 14 : 35. Saul b. a.
2 S. 24 : 25. David b. a. to the L.
1 K. 9 : 25. Sol. offered on a. he b.
18 : 32. with stones Elisha b. a.
2 K. 16 : 11. Urijah the priest b. an a.

BUILT altars.

Nu. 23 : 14. Balak b. seven a. and
2 K. 21 : 4. he b. a. in house of L.
5. b. a. for host of heav., 2 Ch. 33 : 5
2 Ch. 33 : 15. took away a. he had b.

BUILT city.

Nu. 21 : 27. let the c. of Sihon be b.
Jos. 19 : 50. Joshua b. c. and dwelt
Ju. 1 : 26. b. a c. called Luz
18 : 28. Danites b. c. and dwelt
1 K. 16 : 24. name of c. he b. Shemer
1 Ch. 11 : 8. David b. c. from Millo
Is. 25 : 2. to be no c. never be b.
Je. 31 : 38. days come c. be b. to L.
Lu. 4 : 29. hill whereon c. was b.

BUILT cities.

Ex. 1 : 11. b. for Pha. treasure c.
Jos. 24 : 13. given you c. ye b. not
1 K. 15 : 23. c. Asa b. are written
2 Ch. 8 : 2. c. Huram restored, Sol. b.
11 : 5. Rehob. b. c. for defence in Jud.
14 : 6. Asa b. fenced c. in Judah
17 : 12. Jehoshaphat b. c. of store
26 : 6. Uzziah b. c. about Ashdod
27 : 4. Jotham b. c. in the mount-s
Is. 44 : 26. to c. of Jud. Ye shall be b.

BUILT high places.

1 K. 14 : 23 Judah b. h. p. images, and
2 K. 17 : 9. chil. of Isr. b. h. p. in cities
21 : 3. Manasseh b. h. p., 2 Ch. 33 : 3.
2 Ch. 33 : 19. places wherein he b. h. p.
Je. 7 : 31. b. h. p. of Tophet
19 : 5. b. h. p. of Baal, 32 : 35.

BUILT house, s.

Ge. 33 : 17. to Succoth and b. h.
De. 8 : 12. when hast b. goodly h-s
20 : 5. what man hath b. a new h.
2 S. 5 : 11. Masons b. David a h.
1 K. 3 : 2. was no h. b. to name of L.
6 : 9. Sol. b. h., 14. | 8 : 13. I b. thee h.
7 : 2. b. h. of forest of Lebanon
8 : 20. have b. h. for name of L.
44. toward the h. I have b., 48.
2 Ch. 6 : 33, 34, 38.
9 : 3. hallowed h. thou hast b.
10. when Sol. had b. two h-s
24. h. Sol. b. for her, 2 Ch. 8 : 11.
10 : 4. seen h. Sol. b., 2 Ch. 9 : 3.
11 : 38. build sure h. as I b. for Da.
1 Ch. 6 : 32. until Sol. had b. h. of L.
17 : 6. Why have ye not b. me a h.
2 Ch. 6 : 2. b. h. of habita. for thee
18. how much less h. I b.?
Am. 5 : 11. ye b. h-s of hewn stone
Hag. 1 : 2. time L.'s h. should be b.
Zch. 1 : 16. my h. shall be b. in it
Mat. 7 : 24. b. h. on rock, Lu. 6 : 48.
26. foolish b. h. on sand, Lu. 6 : 49.
Ac. 7 : 47. but Solomon b. him a h.
1 Pe. 2 : 5. ye are b. up spiritual h.

BUILT wall, s.

1 K. 6 : 15. Sol. b. w-s of house
2 Ch. 27 : 3. on w-s of Ophel he b.
32 : 5. Hezekiah b. up w. broken
33 : 14. Manasseh b. w. without city
Ne. 4 : 6. So b. we w. | 7 : 1. w. was b.
Eze. 13 : 10. one b. up w., another
Da. 9 : 25. street be b. again and w.
Mi. 7 : 11. day thy w-s are to be b.

BUK'KI.

Nu. 34 : 22. 1 Ch. 6 : 5, 51. Ezr. 7 : 4.

BUKKI'AH.

1 Ch. 25 : 4. sons of Heman, B., 13.

BUL.

1 K. 6 : 38. in month B. the house

BULL.

Jb. 21 : 10. Their b. gendereth and
Is. 51 : 20. thy sons lie as a wild b.

BULLS.

Ge. 32 : 15. Jac. took ten b. as pres.
Ps. 22 : 12. b. have compassed me,
strong b. of Bashan
50 : 13. will I eat flesh of b.
68 : 30. rebuke the multitude of b.
Is. 34 : 7. with b. shall come down
Je. 50 : 11. ye bellow as b. O destroy.
52 : 20. twelve brasen b. under bases
He. 9 : 13. if blood of b. sanctifieth
10 : 4. not possible bl. of b. take

BULLOCK. [aw. sins
Ex. 29 : 3. in basket with the b.
10. on head of b., Le. 4 : 15.-8 : 14.
11. shalt kill b., Le. 1 : 5.-9 : 18.
Le. 4 : 4. bring b. to door of taberu.
12. whole b. shall he carry
9 : 18. He slew also the b.
19. fat of b. and ram
Nu. 15 : 9. with b. meat-off., 29 : 37.
23 : 2. offered on ev. altar a b., 4.
De. 15 : 19. no work with firstling of b.
17 : 1. not sacri. b. with blemish
33 : 17. glory like firstling of b.
Ju. 6 : 25. young b. sec. b., 26.
1 K. 18 : 23. let choose one b. 25.
33. Elijah cut b. in pieces, and
Ps. 50 : 9. I will take no b. out of house
69 : 31. better than b. that hath
Is. 65 : 25. lion eat straw like b.
Je. 31 : 18. b. unaccust. to yoke

BULLOCK
with sin-offering.

Ex. 29 : 36. offer ev. day a b. for a s.

Le. 16: 6. shall offer his b. of s.
Eze. 45: 22. shall prepare b. for a s.
See BLOOD.

Young BULLOCK.

Ex. 29: 1. one y. b., Le. 23: 18.
Le. 4: 3. sin. bring y. b., Eze. 43: 19.
14. cong. offer. y. b., Nu. 15: 24.
16: 3. into holy place with y. b.
Nu. 7: 15. One y. b. one ram, 21, 27,
33, 39, 45, 51, 57, 63, 69, 75, 81.
8: 8. take a y. b. another y. b.
Ju. 6: 25. Take thy father's y. b.
2 Ch. 13: 9. to consecrate with y. b.
Eze. 45: 18. y. b. and cleanse sanc.
46: 6. in day of new moon a y. b.

BULLOCKS.

Nu. 8: 12. hands upon heads of b.
29: 23. on fourth day ten b.
1 K. 18: 23. Let them give two b.
1 Ch. 29: 21. they offered a thous. b.
Ezr. 6: 17. at dedication 100 b.
Ps. 51: 19. offer b. upon thine altar
66: 15. I will offer unto thee b.
Is. 1: 11. I delight not in blood of b.
34: 7. the b. shall come down
Je. 46: 21. hired men like fatted b.
50: 27. Slay all her b.
Eze. 39: 18. ye sh. drink blood of b.
Ho. 12: 11. sacrifice b. in Gilgal
See SEVEN.

BULRUSH, ES.

Ex. 2: 3. she took for him an ark of b-s
Is. 18: 2. ambassa. in vessels of b-s
58: 5. to bow his head like a b.?

BULWARKS.

De. 20: 20. shalt build b. ag. city
2 Ch. 26: 15. made engines on b.
Ps. 48: 13. Mark well her b.
Ec. 9: 14. a great king built b. ag. it
Is. 26: 1. salvation appoint for b.

BU'NAH.

1 Ch. 2: 25. sons of Jerahmeel, B.

BUNCH, ES.

Ex 12: 22. take a b. of hyssop
2 S. 16: 1. with 100 b. of raisins
1 Ch. 12: 40. Zeb. brought b. of raisins
Is. 30: 6. treasures upon b. of camels

BUNDLE, S.

Ge. 42: 35. man's b. of money in
1 S. 25: 29. soul bound in b. of life
Can. 1: 13. b. of myrrh my well-bel.
Is. 58: † 6. to undo b. of the yoke
Am. 9: † 6. founded b. in the earth
Mat. 13: 30. bind the tares in b-s
Ac. 28: 3. Paul gath. b. of sticks

BUN'NI.

Ne. 9: 4.–10: 15.–11: 15.

BURDEN. [Noun.]

Ex. 18: 22. b. with thee, Nu. 11: 17.
23: 5. ass of him lying under b.
Nu. 4: 15. b. of sons of Kohath
19. appoint each to his b.
11: 11. b. of all this peo. on me
De. 1: 12. how alone bear your b.?
2 S. 15: 33. shalt be a b. to me
19: 35. why thy servant be b. to
my lord? [of Joseph
1 K. 11: † 28. Jerob. ruler over b.
2 K. 5: 17. two mules' b. of earth
8: 9. forty camels b. to Elisha
9: 25. L. laid this b. upon him
2 Ch. 35: 3. not be b. on yr. shoul.
Ne. 13: 19. no b. brought on sab.
Jb. 7: 20. so that I am b. to myself
Ps. 38: 4. iniquit. as a b. too heavy
55: 22. Cast thy b. on the Lord
81: 6. I remov. his shoulder fr. b.
Ec. 12: 5. grasshopper be a b.
Is. 9: 4. hast broken yoke of his b.
10: 27. b. be taken off thy shoul.
13: 1. b. of Bab. Isaiah did see
14: 25. b. depart off their shoulder
28. year Ahaz died, was this b.
15: 1. b. of Moab | 17: 1. b. of Dam.
19: 1. b. of E. | 23: 1. b. of Tyre
21: 1. b. of the desert of the sea
11. b. of Dumah | 13. upon Arabia

Is. 22: 1. b. of valley of vision
25. b. upon it shall be cut off
30: 6. b. of beasts of the south
27. name of Lord the b. is heavy
46: 1. carriages b. to weary beast
2. they could not deliver the b.
Je. 17: 21. no b. on sabbath, 22, 27.
23: 33. b. of the Lord? What b.
36. the b. of L. mention no more
38. since ye say, The b. of the L.
Eze. 12: 10. this b. concern. prince
Ho. 8: 10. sorrow for b. of king
Na. 1: 1. b. of Nineveh, the book
Ha. 1: 1. b. Habakkuk did see
Zph. 3: 18. reproach of it was a b.
Zch. 9: 1. b. of Lord in Hadrach
12: 1. b. of word of L. for Israel
Mal. 1: 1. b. of word of L. to Israel
Mat. 11: 30. easy, and my b. is light
20: 12. the b. and heat of the day
Ac. 15: 28. good to lay no greater b.
21: 3. their ship was to unlade b.
Ga. 6: 5. every man bear his own b.
Re. 2: 24. upon you none other b.

BURDENS.

Ge. 49: 14. Issa. couch. betw. two b.
Ex. 1: 11. to afflict them with th. b.
2: 11. Moses looked on their b.
5: 4. King said, Get you to your b.
5. make them rest from their b.
6: 6. bring you fr. b. of Egypt., 7.
Nu. 4: 27. appoint all their b. [18.
1 K. 5: 15. 70,000 bear b., 2 Ch. 2: 2,
2 Ch. 24: 27. greatness of the b.
34: 13. over the bearers of b.
Ne. 4: 10. str. of bearers of b-s decay-
17. that bare b. held a weap. [ed
13: 15. manner of b. bro. on sab.
Is. 58: 6. fast, to undo heavy b.
La. 2: 14. prophets seen false b.
Am. 5: 11. take fr. poor b. of wheat
Mat. 23: 4. bind heavy b., Lu. 11: 46.
Ga. 6: 2. Bear ye one another's b.

BURDEN, ED.

Zch. 12: 3. b. thems. be cut in pieces
2 Co. 5: 4. in tab. we groan being b.
8: 13. not others be eased, and you b.
12: 16. be it so, I did not b. you

BURDENSOME.

Zch. 12: 3. make Jeru. a b. stone
2 Co. 11: 9. I have kept fr. being b.
12: 13. except I was not b. to you
14. third time I come, not be b.
1 Th. 2: 6. might be b. as apostles

BURIAL. [longed

2 Ch. 26: 23. in field of b. wh. be-
Ec. 6: 3. also that he have no b.
Is. 14: 20. not joined with th. in b.
Je. 22: 19. buried with b. of an ass
Mat. 26: 12. she did it for my b.
Ac. 8: 2. carried Stephen to his b.

BURIED.

Ge. 25: 10. there was Abraham b.
35: 8. she was b. under oak
49: 31. There they b. Abr., Sarah,
Isaac, Rebekah, I b. Leah
Nu. 11: 34. b. people that lusted
20: 1. Miriam was b. there
33: 4. Egyp. b. all their first-born
De. 10: 6. Aaron, he was b.
Jos. 24: 32. bones of Joseph b. they
Ru. 1: 17. and there will be b.
1 S. 31: 13. b. them under tree
2 S. 2: 4. they that b. Saul
19: 37. b. by grave of my father
4: 12. head of Ish-b. and b. it
21: 14. bones of Saul b. in Zelah
1 K. 13: 31. wherein man of G. is b.
Ec. 8: 10. so I saw wicked b.
Je. 8: 2. not gather, nor b., 16: 6.–
20: 6.–25: 33.
16: 4. not be lamented nor b.
22: 19. b. with burial of an ass
Eze. 39: 15. till buriers have b. it
Mat. 14: 12. discip. took body b. it
Lu. 16: 22. rich man died was b.
Ac. 2: 29. David both dead and b.

Ac. 5: 9. feet of th. which b. hush
10. b. her by her husband
Ro. 6: 4. b. with him by baptism
1 Co. 15: 4. he was b. and rose
Col. 2: 12. b. with him in baptism

BURIED him.

Ge. 50: 13. b. h. in field of Machpe.
De. 34: 6. he b. h. in a valley
Jos. 24: 30. b. h. in border, Ju. 2: 9.
33. b. h. in a hill that
Ju. 16: 31. b. h. between Zorah
1 S. 25: 1. b. h. in his house, 28: 3.
2 S. 2: 5. kindn. unto Saul and b. h.
1 K. 14: 18. b. h., all Isr. mourned
2 K. 13: 20. Elisha, they b. h.
2 Ch. 24: 25. b. h. not in sepul. of kings
Ac. 5: 6. young men b. h.

BURIED in.

Ge. 15: 15. be b. i. good old age
23: 19. Ab. b. Sarah i. a cave
35: 19. Rachel was b. i., 48: 7.
2 S. 17: 23. b. i. sepulchre of fa.
1 K. 2: 34. Joab b. i. his own house
2 K. 21: 18. Manass. was b. i. gar-
26. Amon was b. i. sepulchre [den
Jb. 27: 15. remain be b. i. death

BURIED in city of David.

1 K. 2: 10. Dav. was b. i. c. o. D.
11: 43. Sol. b. i. c. o. D., 2 Ch. 9: 31.
15: 8. b. Abijam i. c. o. D., 2 Ch.
24. Asa b. i. c. o. David [14: 1.
22: 50. Jehosh. b. i. c. o. David,
2 Ch. 21: 1. [2 Ch. 21: 20.
2 K. 8: 24. Joram b. i. c. o. David,
9: 28. Ahaziah | 14: 20. Amaziah
12: 21. Jehoash b. i. c. o. David,
2 Ch. 24: 25.
15: 7. Azariah b. i. c. o. David
38. Jotham b. i. c. o. David, 2 Ch.
27: 9. [28: 27.
16: 20. Ahaz b. i. c. o. D., 2 Ch.
2 Ch. 12: 16. Rehoboam b. i. c. o. D.
21: 20. b. Jehoram in c. o. D.
24: 16. b. Jehoiada i. c. o. D.

BURIED with his fathers.

1 K. 14: 31. Rehob. | 15: 24. Asa b.–
22: 50. Jehos. | 2 K. 8: 24. Joram b.–
2 K. 12: 21. Joash | 14: 20. Amaz. b.–
15: 7. Azariah b.– | 38. Jotham b.–
16: 20. Ahaz b., 2 Ch. 21: 1.–26: 28.

BURIERS.

Eze. 39: 15. a sign till b. have buried

BURN.

Ge. 44: 18. let not thine anger b.
Ex. 27: 20. lamp to b. alw., Le. 24: 2.
29: 13. shalt take caul, and b., 18,
25. Le. 1: 9, 15.–2: 2, 9, 16.–
3: 5, 11, 16.–5: 12.–6: 15.–9: 17.–
Nu. 5: 26.
Le. 4: 19. priest take fat and b., 26,
31.–7: 31.–16: 25.–17. 6. Nu. 18: 17.
6: 12. priest b. wood on it
13: 52. shall b. that garment
Nu. 19: 5. one shall b. heifer
Jos. 11: 13. Hazor, did Joshua b.
1 S. 2: 16. not fail to b. the fat
2 Ch. 2: 6. save only to b. sacrifice
13: 11. they b. to L. every morn.
Is. 1: 31. they sh. both b. together
10: 17. b. and devour his thorns
27: 4. I would go thro., and b. th.
40: 16. Leb. is not sufficient to b.
44: 15. sh. it be for a man to b.
Je. 7: 20. my fury shall b. and
34: 5. sh. they b. odours for thee
36: 25. king would not b. roll
Eze. 24: 5. b. also bones under it
11. that brass of it may b.
39: 9. they shall b. the weapons
43: 21. he shall b. bullock in pl.
Na. 2: 13. I will b. her chariots
Mal. 4: 1. day that shall b. as oven
Mat. 13: 30. tares in bundles to b.
Lu. 3: 17. chaff he will b. with fire
24: 32. Did not our heart b. with.?
1 Co. 7: 9. better to marry than b.
2 Co. 11: 29. offended, I b. not?

BURN, joined with fire.
Ex. 12 : 10. that remaineth shall b. with f., 29 : 34. Le. 8 : 32.
Le. 13 : 57. b. wherein plague is with
16 : 27. b. with f. their skins [f.
De. 5 : 23. mountain did b. with f.
7 : 5. b. images, 25. | 12 : 3. b. groves
32 : 22. f. shall b. to the lowest hell, Je. 17 : 4.
Jos. 11 : 6. b. their chariots with f.
Ju. 9 : 52. tower to b. it with f.
12 : 1. b. house | 14 : 15. b. thee wi. f.
Ps. 79 : 5. long jealousy b. like f.?
89 : 46. L. shall thy wrath b. like f.?
Is. 47 : 14. as stubble, f. sh. b. them
Je. 4 : 4. fury like f. and b., 21 : 12.
7 : 31. b. sons and d. in f., 19 : 5.
21 : 10. Neb. shall b. city with f., 32 : 29.–34 : 2, 22.–37 : 8, 10.–38 : 18.
Eze. 5 : 2. b. with f. part of city.
16 : 41. b. houses with f., 23 : 47.
Mat. 3 : 12. he will b. chaff with unquenchable f., Lu. 3 : 17.
Re. 17 : 16. and b. her with f.

BURN incense.
Ex. 30 : 1. make an altar to b. i.
7. Aaron shall b. sweet i., 8.
1 K. 13 : 1. Jeroh. stood to b. i. [it.
2 K. 18 : 4. child. of Isr. did b. i. to
1 Ch. 23 : 13. sons for ever to b. i.
2 Ch. 2 : 4. house to b. sweet i.
13 : 11. b. every morning sweet i.
26 : 16. Uzziah went to b. i., 19.
28 : 25. Ahaz made high pl. to b. i.
29 : 11. L. hath chosen you to b. i.
32 : 12. wersh. bef. one altar, b. i.
Je. 7 : 9. will ye b. i. to Baal ? 11 : 13.
44 : 17. b. i. to queen of heaven
Ho. 4 : 13. b. i. on hills under oaks
Ha. 1 : 16. they b. i. to their drag
Lu. 1 : 9. Zacharias his lot to b. i.

BURNED.
Ex. 3 : 2. bush b. was not consumed
De. 9 : 15. mount b. with fire
32 : † 22. fire hath b. to lowest hell
Jos. 7 : 25. b. them with fire
2 S. 5 : 21. David b. their images
2 K. 23 : 6. he b. grove at brook
15. he b. the high place, and
16. bones out of sepul. and b.
2 Ch. 25 : 14. Amaziah b. incense
34 : 25. forsaken me, b. incense
Es. 1 : 12. king, anger b. in him
Jb. 30 : 30. and my bones are b.
Ps. 39 : 3. while musing fire b.
102 : 3. my skin black, bones b.
Pr. 6 : 27. take fire, clothes not b.?
28. go upon coals and feet not b.?
Is. 24 : 6. inhabit. of earth are b.
42 : 25. it b. him, laid it not to
Je. 2 : 15. cities b. | 6 : 29. bellows b.
36 : 28. in the roll Jehoiakim b.
La. 2 : 3. b. ag. Jacob like flaming
Eze. 20 : 47. all faces be b. therein
24 : 10. and let the bones be b.
Jo. 1 : 19. flame hath b. all trees
Am. 2 : 1. bec. he b. bones of king
Na. 1 : 5. earth is b. at his presence
Mat. 13 : 40. tares are gath. and b.
Jn. 15 : 6. branch withered, th. are b.
Ac. 19 : 19. their books and b. them
Ro. 1 : 27. b. in their lust one tow.
1 Co. 3 : 15. if any man's work be b.
13 : 3. though give body to be b.
He. 6 : 8. whose end is to be b.
12 : 18. not come to mount that b.
13 : 11. beasts b. without camp
Re. 1 : 15. feet like brass, as if b.
16 : † 9. men were b. with gr. heat

BURNED joined with fire.
De. 4 : 11. the mountain b. with f.
1 S. 30 : 1. Amal. b. Ziklag with f.
2 S. 23 : 7. they shall be b. with f.
2 K. 23 : 11. b. chari. of sun with f.
1 Ch. 14 : 12. gods were b. with f.
Ne. 1 : 3. gates are b. with f., 2 : 17.
Ps. 80 : 16. it is b. with f., it is
Is. 1 : 7. your cities are b. with f.
43 : 2. walkest through f. not be b.
64 : 11. our beaut. h. is b. with f.
Je. 38 : 17. city not be b. with f.
23. cause city to be b. with f.
49 : 2. her dau-s be b. with f.
51 : 32. reeds they have b. with f.
58. Bab.'s gates be b. with f.
Mi. 1 : 7. hires be b. with the f.
Re. 18 : 8. she shall be b. with f.

BURNED incense.
2 Ch. 29 : 7. lamps and not b. i.
Is. 65 : 7. have b. i. upon mountains
Je. 18 : 15. my peo. b. i. to vanity
44 : 15. knew their wives had b. i.
Ho. 2 : 13. days she b. i. to them
11 : 2. they b. i. to graven images

BURNED up.
Jb. 1 : 16. fire of G. b. u. sheep
Ps. 74 : 8. b. u. all synagogues
106 : 18. flame b. u. the wicked
Is. 64 : 11. and beau. house is b. u.
Je. 9 : 10. b. u. none can pass, 12.
Mat. 22 : 7. king b. u. their city
2 Pe. 3 : 10. earth, and works be b. u.

BURNETH.
Le. 16 : 28. that b. them, Nu. 19 : 8.
Ps. 46 : 9. he b. chariot
83 : 14. As the fire b. wood, and
97 : 3. a fire b. up his enemies
Is. 9 : 18. wickedness b. as fire
44 : 16. He b. part thereof in fire
62 : 1. salvation as a lamp that b.
64 : 2. when melting fire b.
65 : 5. these a fire that b. all day
66 : 3. b. inc. as if blessed idol
Je. 48 : 35. cease that b. incense
Jo. 2 : 3. behind them a flame b.
Re. 21 : 8. lake which b. with fire

BURNING. [Part. and Adj.]
Ge. 15 : 17. b. lamp passed between
Le. 6 : 9. fire of altar be b., 12, 13.
26 : 16. I will appoint b. ague
De. 32 : 24. devoured with b. heat
Jb. 5 : † 7. as sons of b. coal lift
41 : 19. Out of mouth go b. lamps
Ps. 11 : † 6. on wick. rain b. temp.
140 : 10. Let b. coals fall upon th.
Pr. 16 : 27. in his lips is as b. fire
26 : 21. as coals are to b. coals
23. b. lips and wicked heart
Is. 30 : 27. name of L. cometh far, b.
34 : 9. land shall become b. pitch
Je. 20 : 9. his word was as b. fire
Eze. 1 : 13. appearance like b. coals
21 : † 31. deliv. in. hand of b. men
Da. 3 : 6. be cast into b. furn., 11.
17. able to deliv. fr. b. furnace
20. to cast into b. furnace, 21, 23.
26. Neb. came near b. furnace [fire
7 : 9. throne like flame, wheels as b.
Ha. 3 : 5. b. coals forth at his feet
Lu. 12 : 35. loins be girded, lights b.
Jn. 5 : 35. John b. shining light
Ja. 1 : 11. no sooner risen w. b. heat
Re. 4 : 5. seven lamps b. bef. throne
8 : 8. as great mountain b. with
10. fell a great star b. as lamp
19 : 20. both cast alive into lake b.

BURNING, S.
Ge. 11 : † 3. burn the bricks to a b.
Ex. 21 : 25. b. for b-s, wound for
Le. 10 : 6. bewail b. wh. L. kindled
13 : 28. spot stay, it is rising of b.
Nu. 11 : † 3. he called place a b.
De. 28 : 22. smite with extreme b.
29 : 23. whole land brimstone, b.
Jos. 11 : † 8. chased to b-s of waters
2 Ch. 16 : 14. very great b. for him
21 : 19. made no b. like b. of fath.
Is. 3 : 24. be b. instead of beauty
4 : 4. purged Jerus. by spirit of b.
9 : 5. this shall be with b. and
10 : 16. kindle b. like b. of fire
32 : † 13. b. upon all hous. of joy
33 : 12. people be as b. of lime
14. who sh. dwell with everl. b-s?
Je. 34 : 5. with b-s of thy fathers
Am. 4 : 11. as a firebrand out of b.
Re. 18 : 9. shall see smoke of her b.

BURNISHED.
Eze. 1 : 7. sparkl. like col. of b. brass

BURNT.
Ge. 38 : 24. bring her, let her be b.
Ex. 3 : 3. why bush is not b.
Le. 2 : 12. shall not be b. on altar
6 : 22. meat-off. b., 23.–8 : 21.
10 : 16. sought goat, and it was b.
Nu. 16 : 39. they that were b. had off.
De. 32 : 24. shall be b. with hunger
1 S. 2 : 15. bef. they b. fat, priests ser.
1 K. 13 : 2. men's bones be b. upon th.
15 : 13. Asa b. her idol, 2 Ch. 15 : 16.
2 K. 25 : 9. b. the house of L., 2 Ch. 36 : 19. Je. 52 : 13.
Je. 51 : 25. make thee a b. mountain

BURNT, joined with fire.
Ex. 32 : 20. b. calf in f., De. 9 : 21.
Le. 6 : 30. sin-offer. be b. in f.
7 : 17. flesh of sacrifice on 3d day be b. with f., 19 : 6.
20 : 14. if man take wife and her mother, they be b. with f.
21 : 9. dau. of priest playing whore, she shall be b. with f.
Nu. 11 : 1. f. of L. b. among them, 3.
De. 12 : 31. sons and dau-s th. b. in f.
Jos. 6 : 24. they b. Jericho with f.
7 : 15. he taken with accursed thing shall be b. with f.
11 : 9. Joshua b. chariots with f.
11. took Hazor and b. it with f.
Ju. 15 : 6. b. her and fath. with f.
14. cords bec. as flax b. with f.
18 : 27. came to Laish b. it with f.
1 K. 9 : 16. Pha. had b. Gezer w. f.
16 : 18. Zimri b. king's hou. with f.
2 K. 1 : 14. f. from heav. b. 2 captains
17 : 31. Sepharvites b. chil. in f.
25 : 9. gr. man's house b. with f.
2 Ch. 28 : 3. Ahaz b. his chil. in f.

BURNT incense.
Ex. 40 : 27. b. sweet i. thereon
1 K. 3 : 3. Sol. b. i. in high places
9 : 25. Sol. b. i. upon altar bef. L.
12 : 33. Jerob. offered on altar b. i.
22 : 43. people b. i. in high places, 2 K. 12 : 3.–14 : 4.–15 : 4, 35.
2 K. 16 : 4. Ahaz b. i., 2 Ch. 28 : 3, 4.

BURNT-OFFERING.
Ge. 22 : 7. where is the lamb for b.?
8. G. will provide lamb for b.
13. for a b. instead of Isaac
Ex. 18 : 12. Jethro took b. for God
29 : 18. ram is a b. unto the Lord
Le. 1 : 4. sh. put hand on head of b.
4 : 29. slay sin-off. in place of b., 33.–6 : 25.–7 : 2.–14 : 13.
5 : 7. other pigeon for a b., 10 : 19.–12 : 8.–14 : 22, 31.
6 : 9. This is law of b., 7 : 37.
7 : 8. priest shall have skin of b.
9 : 2. ram for a b., 16 : 3, 5.–23 : 18.
3. and lamb for b., 12 : 6.–23 : 12.
Nu. 7 : 15. one lamb for a b., 21, 27, 33, 39, 51, 57, 63, 69, 75, 81. Eze. 45 : 15.
23 : 3. Stand by thy b. I will go, 15.
28 : 10. this is the b. of ev. sabbath
13. for a b. of a sweet savour
14. this is the b. of every month
29 : 6. beside meat-off. and daily b.
Jos. 22 : 26. to build altar not for a b.
Ju. 13 : 23. would not have rec. b.
1 S. 7 : 10. as Samuel was offering b.
13 : 12. forced myself and offered b.
2 K. 3 : 27. offered him for a b.
2 Ch. 7 : 1. fire came and consum. b.
29 : 24. b. be made for all Israel
Ps. 40 : 6. b. hast thou not required
51 : 16. thou delightest not in b.
19. be pleased with b. whole b.
Is. 40 : 16. nor the beasts for a b.
61 : 8. I the L. hate robbery for b.

Eze. 44 : 11. they shall slay the **b.**
45 : 17. princes shall prepare the **b.**
46 : 2. priest sh. prepare prince's **b.**
13. thou shalt daily prepare a **b.**

Continual BURNT-OFFERING.

Ex. 29 : 42. a c. o., Nu. 28 : 3, 6, 10, 15, 24, 31.-29 : 11, 16, 19, 22, 25, 28, 31, 34, 38. Ezr. 3 : 5. Ne. 10 : 33. Eze. 46 : 15.

Offer, or offered BURNT-OFFERING.

Ge. 22 : 2. take Isaac **o.** him for a **b.**
Le. 9 : 7. go to altar and **o.** thy **b.**
15 : 15, 30. Nu. 6 : 16.-15 : 24.
Nu. 28 : 11. in beginn. of months **o.**
23. shall **o.** these besides **b.** [**b.**
Ju. 11 : 31. I will **o.** it up for a **b.**
13 : 16. if thou **o.** a **b.** it unto L.
1 S. 6 : 14. and **o-d** the kine for a **b.**
7 : 9. Sam. **o-d** sucking lamb for **b.**
2 K. 5 : 17. will hencef. **o.** neither **b.**
2 Ch. 29 : 27. Hez. commanded to **o. b.**
Jb. 42 : 8. **o.** up for yourselves a **b.**
Je. 14 : 12. when **o. b.** I will not
Eze. 46 : 4. **b.** prince shall **o.** in sab.

BURNT-OFFERINGS.

Ge. 8 : 20. Noah offered **b.** on altar
Ex. 10 : 25. give us sacrifices and **b.**
20 : 24. shalt sacrifice thereon **b.**
Nu. 10 : 10. blow over your **b.**
De. 12 : 6. bring your **b.**, 11, 14, 27.
Jos. 22 : 27. do service of L. with **b.**
1 S. 15 : 22. Hath L. as great delight in **b.**
2 S. 6 : 17. David offered **b.**, 24 : 25.
1 K. 3 : 15. Sol. stood and offered **b.**
8 : 64. middle of court, he offered **b.**
1 Ch. 29 : 21. they offered **b.** to L.
2 Ch. 2 : 4. I build a house for **b.**
7 : 7. altar not able to receive **b.**
29 : 7. have not offered **b.** in
34. priest could not slay all **b.**
30 : 15. Levites, brought **b.**
35 : 14. sons busied in offering **b.**
Ezr. 3 : 4. offered the daily **b.**
6 : 9. they have need of for **b.**
8 : 35. offered **b.** unto G. of Israel
Jb. 1 : 5. offered **b.** acco. to number
Ps. 50 : 8. not reprove for **b.**
66 : 13. into thy house with **b.**
Is. 1 : 11. I am full of the **b.**
43 : 23. nor small cattle of **b.**
56 : 7. their **b.** shall be accepted
Je. 6 : 20. your **b.** are not acceptable
7 : 21. Put your **b.** to sacrifices
22. to your fathers concerning **b.**
17 : 26. from south, bringing **b.**
19 : 5. burn sons for **b.** to Baal
Eze. 45 : 17. princes to give **b.**
Ho. 6 : 6. knowledge of G. than **b.**
Mi. 6 : 6. come before him with **b.**?
Mk. 12 : 33. love neighb. than **b.**
He. 10 : 6. In **b.** for sin no pleasure
8. and **b.** and offering

Offer BURNT-OFFERINGS.

De. 12 : 13. **o.** not **b.** in every place
14. there **o.** thy **b.**, 27.
1 S. 10 : 8. down to thee to **o. b.**
2 S. 24 : 24. nor **o. b.** that cost me nothing, 1 Ch. 21 : 24.
1 K. 3 : 4. a 1,000 **b.** did Sol. **o.**
9 : 25. times a year did Sol. **o. b.**
Ezr. 3 : 2. builded altar to **o. b.**
Je. 33 : 18. not want man to **o. b.**
Eze. 43 : 18. they make it to **o. b.**
Am. 5 : 22. Tho. ye **o.** me **b.** I will

BURNT-SACRIFICE.

Ex. 30 : 9. offer no **b.** thereon
Le. 1 : 9. burn all to be a **b.**, 3 : 5.
Nu. 23 : 6. lo he stood by his **b.**
De. 33 : 10. shall put **b.** on altar
2 S. 24 : 22. here be oxen for **b.**
1 K. 18 : 38. fire consumed **b.**
2 K. 16 : 15. altar burn king's **b.**
Ps. 20 : 3. and accept thy **b.**

BURNT-SACRIFICES.

1 Ch. 23 : 31. to offer all **b.** in sab.
2 Ch. 13 : 11. morn. and even. **b.**
Ps. 66 : 15. offer **b.** of fatlings

BURNT up.

Ju. 15 : 5. foxes **b. u.** shocks
2 K. 1 : 14. fire **b. u.** to captains
Is. 3 : † 14. have **b. u.** vineyard
Re. 8 : 7. third part of trees **b. u.**, all green grass **b. u.**

BURST, BURSTING.

Jb. 32 : 19. it is ready to **b.** like
Pr. 3 : 10. presses **b.** with new
Is. 30 : 14. in **b-g** of it a sherd
Je. 2 : 20. I have **b.** thy bands, 5 : 5.-30 : 8. Na. 1 : 13.
Mk. 2 : 22. **b.** bottles, Lu. 5 : 37.
Ac. 1 : 18. he **b.** asunder in midst

BURY.

Ge. 23 : 4. that I may **b.** my dead
6. in our sepulchres **b.** dead, 11, 15.
13. I will **b.** my dead there
47 : 29. **b.** me not in E., 49 : 29.
30. out of E. and **b.** me in their
50 : 5. let me go and **b.** my father
6. Go up and **b.** thy father, as he
7. Jo. went to **b.** his father, 14.
De. 21 : 23. shalt **b.** him that day
1 K. 2 : 31. upon Joab and **b.** him
11 : 15. Joab was gone to **b.** slain
13 : 29. old proph. came to **b.** him
31. when dead, **b.** me in sepul.
14 : 13. Isr. shall mourn and **b.** him
2 K. 9 : 10. shall be none to **b.** Jezebel
34. Go see cursed woman, **b.** her
9 : 35. to **b.** her, found only skull
Ps. 79 : 3. was none to **b.** them
Je. 7 : 32. **b.** in Tophet, 19 : 11.
14 : 16. they sh. have none to **b.** them
Eze. 39 : 11. there shall they **b.** Gog
13. all the people shall **b.** them
14. passing thro. the land to **b.**
Ho. 9 : 6. Memphis shall **b.** them
Mat. 8 : 21. to go **b.** my fa., Lu. 9 : 59.
22. let dead **b.** dead, Lu. 9 : 60.
27 : 7. potter's field to **b.** strangers
Jn. 19 : 40. manner of Jews to **b.**

BURYING. [P. and N.]

2 K. 13 : 21. as they were **b.** a man
Eze. 39 : 12. seven months be **b.** of
Mk. 14 : 8. to anoint my body to **b.**
Jn. 12 : 7. ag. my **b.** hath she this

BURYINGPLACE.

Ge. 23 : 4. possession of a **b.**, 9.-49 : 30.-50 : 13. [their **b.**
47 : 30. out of E. and bury me in
Ju. 16 : 31. Samson in **b.** of Manoah

BUSH, ES.

Ex. 3 : 2. flame of fire in **b.** Ac. 7 : 30.
3. why **b.** is not burnt
4. God called to him out of **b.**
De. 33 : 16. good-will of him in **b.**
Jb. 30 : 4. cut mallows by the **b-s**
7. Among the **b-s** they brayed
Is. 7 : 19. they shall rest upon all **b-s**
Mk. 12 : 26. how in **b.** G. spake
Lu. 6 : 44. nor of bramble **b.** grapes
20 : 37. Moses shewed at the **b.**
Ac. 7 : 35. angel which appeared in [**b.**

BUSHEL.

Mat. 5 : 15. light candle put it under **b.**, Mk. 4 : 21. Lu. 11 : 33.

BUSHY.

Can. 5 : 11. his locks are **b.** and

BUSINESS.

Ge. 39 : 11. Jo. went to do his **b.**
De. 24 : 5. nor be charged with **b.**
Jos. 2 : 14. if ye utter not our **b.**
20. if thou utter this our **b.**, we
Ju. 18 : 7. had no **b.** with any, 28.
1 S. 10 : † 2. left the **b.** of the asses
20 : 19. didst hide thyself when **b.**
21 : 2. let no man know of **b.**
8. the king's **b.** required haste
25 : † 2. man whose **b.** was in Carmel
1 Ch. 26 : 29. outward **b.** over Isr.
30. in all the **b.** of the Lord
2 Ch. 13 : 10. Levites wait on their **b.**
17 : 13. he had much **b.** in cities
29 : † 15. gath. breth. in **b.** of Lord
32 : 31. in the **b.** of ambassadors
Ne. 11 : 16. oversight of outward **b.**
22. singers over **b.** of house
13 : 30. every man in his **b.**
Es. 3 : 9. that have charge of the **b.**
9 : † 3. did king's **b.** helped the Jews
Ps. 107 : 23. do **b.** in great waters
Pr. 18 : † 1. intermeddl. in every **b.**
22 : 29. a man diligent in his **b.**?
Ec. 5 : 3. a dream thro. mult. of **b.**
8 : 16. see the **b.** upon earth
Da. 8 : 27. I rose, did the king's **b.**
Lu. 2 : 49. must be about my Fa.'s **b.**
Ac. 6 : 3. may appoint over this **b.**
Ro. 12 : 11. Not slothful in **b.**
16 : 2. assist in **b.** she hath need
1 Th. 4 : 11. study to do your own **b.**

BUSY, IED.

1 K. 20 : 40. as thy servant was **b-d**
2 Ch. 35 : 14. sons of Aaron **b.** in off.

BUSY-BODY, IES.

2 Th. 3 : 11. some are **b.**, 1 Ti. 5 : 13.
1 Pe. 4 : 15. let none suffer as **b.**

BUT.

1 S. 20 : 3. **b.** a step between me and
2 K. 7 : 4. kill us, we shall **b.** die
Ps. 115 : 5. mouths **b.** speak not, (2)
6. ears **b.** hear not; noses **b.**
7. hands **b.** handle not; feet **b.**
Mat. 24 : 36. **b.** of that day and hour
37. **b.** as the days of Noe were, so
Mk. 5 : 28. if I touch **b.** his clothes
1 Co. 4 : 19. not speech, **b.** the power
6 : 11. **b.** ye are washed
7 : 10. yet not I, **b.** the Lord
12 : 4. diversities **b.** same Spirit
5. differences **b.** the same Lord
6. **b.** it is same G. which worketh
2 Co. 2 : 5. not grieved me **b.** in part
4 : 17. affliction, **b.** for a moment
Ga. 1 : 12. **b.** by revelation of Jesus

BUT the end. See END.

BUTLER, S.

Ge. 40 : 1. **b.** of king of Egypt, 5.
2. against the chief of **b-s** | 13.
9. chief **b.** told his dream to Jo.
20. lifted up head of chief **b.**
21. restored his chief **b.** to | 23.
41 : 9. **b.** said, I rememb. my faults

BUTTER.

Ge. 18 : 8. Ab. took **b.** and milk
De. 32 : 14. **b.** of kine, milk of sheep
Ju. 5 : 25. she brought **b.** in a dish
2 S. 17 : 29. Barzil. brought **b.** for Da.
Jb. 20 : 17. brooks of honey and **b.**
29 : 6. I washed my steps with **b.**
Ps. 55 : 21. words smoother than **b.**
Pr. 30 : 33. churning bringeth **b.**
Is. 7 : 15. **b.** shall he eat, 22.

BUTTOCKS.

2 S. 10 : 4. garm. to their **b.**, 1 Ch. 19 : 4.
Is. 20 : 4. **b.** uncovered to shame

BUY.

Ge. 42 : 2. get you to Egypt and **b.**
7. From Canaan to **b.** food, 43 : 20.
10. to **b.** food are thy servants
43 : 2. Go again, **b.** food, 44 : 25.
4. we will go and **b.** | 22.
47 : 19. **b.** us and our land for bread
Ex. 21 : 2. If thou **b.** a Heb. serv.
Le. 22 : 11. if priests **b.** any soul
25 : 15. after jubilee **b.** of neighb.
44. of them sh. ye **b.** bondmen, 45.
De. 2 : 6. shall **b.** meat for money
28 : 68. and no man shall **b.** you
Ru. 4 : 4. **b.** it before the inhabi.
5. thou must **b.** it also of Ruth
8. unto Boaz, **b.** it for thee
2 S. 24 : 21. David said, To **b.** thresh ing-floor, 24. 1 Ch. 21 : 24. [22 : 6
2 K. 12 : 12. masons to **b.** timber,
2 Ch. 34 : 11. to **b.** hewn stone
Ezr. 7 : 17. **b.** speedily with this
Ne. 10 : 31. not **b.** it on the sabbath

Is. 55 : 1. come, b. and eat, b. wine
Je. 32 : 7. b. field in Anathoth
25. b. thee the field for money
44. Men shall b. fields for money
Mat. 14 : 15. b. victuals, Mk. 6 : 36.
25 : 9. go to them that sell, and b.
10. went to b. bridegroom came
Mk. 6 : 37. Shall b. 200 pennyw.?
Lu. 9 : 13. exc. we b. meat for peo.
22 : 36. let him sell garm. b. one
Jn. 4 : 8. disciples gone to b. meat
6 : 5. Whence shall we b. bread?
13 : 29. b. things we have need of
1 Co. 7 : 30. b. as tho' possessed not
Ja. 4 : 13. b. and sell, and get gain
Ro. 3 : 18. b. of me gold tried in fire
13 : 17. no man b. or sell, save he

BUY corn.

Ge. 41 : 57. all came to Jo. to b. c.
42:3. Jo's breth. went down to b. c.
Ne. 5 : 3. mortgaged lands to b. c.

BUY poor.

Am. 8 : 6. may b. the p. for silver

BUY truth.

Pr. 23 : 23. b. the t. and sell it not

BUYER.

Pr. 20 : 14. it is naught, saith the b.
Is. 24 : 2. as with b. so with seller
Eze. 7 : 12. let not the b. rejoice, nor

BUYEST, ETH.

Le. 25 : 14. if sell aught, or b-t aught
Ru. 4 : 5. what day b-t field of Nao.
Pr. 31 : 16. she consid. field b-h it
Mat. 13 : 44. selleth all b-h field
Re. 18 : 11. no man b-h her merch.

BUZ.

Ge. 22 : 21. Milcah bare to Nahor B.
1 Ch. 5 : 14. son of Jahdo, son of B.
Je. 25 : 23. I made B. drink cup [of B.

BU'ZI.

Eze. 1 : 3. word came to Ezekiel son

BU'ZITE.

Jb. 32 : 2. son of Barachel B., 6.

BY and BY.

Mat. 13 : 21. b. a. b. is offended
Mk. 6 : 25. give me b.a.b. the head
Lu. 17 : 7. say b. a. b. sit to meat
21 : 9. but the end is not b. a. b.

BY-WAYS.

Ju. 5 : 6. travellers walked thro. b.

BY-WORD.

De. 28 : 37. a b. among all nations
1 K. 9 : 7. Isr. be a b. am. all peo.
2 Ch. 7 : 20. make this house a b.
Jb. 17 : 6. made me a b. of people
30 : 9. their song, yea, I am their b.
Ps. 44 : 14. Thou makest us a b.
Jo. 2 : † 17. why heathen use a b.

C.

CAB.

2 K. 6 : 25. of a c. of dove's dung

CAB'BON.

Jos. 15 : 40. cities in valley C.

CABINS.

Je. 37 : 16. when Jeremiah was ent. [into c.

CA'BUL.

1 K. 9 : 13. called them C., Jos. 19 : 27.

CÆ'SAR. See CE'SAR.

CÆS'AREA. See CES'AREA.

CAGE.

Je. 5 : 27. As a c. is full of birds, so
Re. 18 : 2. Bab., is a cage of ev. nuel. [bird

CA'IAPHAS.

Mat. 26 : 3. the high-priest C.
57. they led Jesus away to C.
Jn. 11 : 49. C. said, ye know noth.
18 : 14. C. was he th. gave counsel
28. led Jesus from C. to hall
See ANNAS.

CAIN. [Place.] [Jud.

Jos. 15 : 57. C. and Gibeah, cities of

CAIN. [Person.]

Ge. 4 : 2. C. was tiller of ground
5. to C. and off. he had not respect
15. L. set a mark on C. lest any
Ge. 4 : 25. instead of Abel wh. C. slew
He. 11 : 4. excellent sac. than C.
1 Jn. 3 : 12. not as C. who was of
Jude 11. have gone in way of C.

CAI'NAN.

Ge. 5 : 9. begat C. | 14. C. died
Lu. 3 : 36. was son of C., 37.

CAKE, S.

Ge. 18 : 6. make c-s upon the dough
Ex. 12 : 39. they baked unleav. c-s
Le. 7 : 12. with sacrifice, unleav. c-s
13. Beside c-s he shall offer [c-s
24 : 5. take flour, and bake twelve
Nu. 11 : 8. baked in pans made c-s
15 : 20. offer up a c. of the first
Ju. 7 : 13. a c. tumbled into host
1 S. 30 : 12. gave piece of c. of figs
2 S. 6 : 19. Da. dealt to ev. one a c.
13 : 6. make me a couple of c. [c.
1 K. 17 : 12. L. liveth, I have not a
13. make me a little c. first
19 : 6. there was a c. baken on coals
Je. 7 : 18. make c-s to queen, 44 : 19.
Ez. 4 : 12. shalt eat it as barley c-s
Ho. 7 : 8. Ephraim is a c. not turned
See FIGS, UNLEAVENED.

CA'LAH.

Ge. 10 : 11. Asshur builded C. | 12.

CAL'COL. See CHALCOL.

CALAMITY, IES.

De. 32 : 35. day of their c. at hand
2 S. 22 : 19. me in day of c., Ps. 18 : 18.
Jb. 6 : 2. my c. laid in balances
30 : 13. they set forward my c.
Ps. 57 : 1. until these c-s be overpast
141 : 5. my prayer sh. be in their c.
Pr. 1 : 26. I will laugh at your c.
6 : 15. his c. shall come suddenly
17 : 5. he that is glad at c. shall be
19 : 13. foolish son is c. of his fa.
24 : 22. their c. shall rise suddenly
27 : 10. nor into bro. house in c.
Je. 18 : 17. shew the back in c.
46 : 21. day of their c. was come
48 : 16. c. of Moab is near to come
49 : 8. bring c. of Esau upon him
32. will bring their c. fr. all sides
Eze. 35 : 5. blood of Isr. in day of c.
Ob. 13. their substance in their c.

CALAMUS.

Ex. 30 : 23. take of sweet c., 250
Can. 4 : 14. Spikenard, saffron, c.
Eze. 27 : 19. c. in market of Tyrus

CALDRON, S. [c-s

2 Ch. 35 : 13. offerings sold they in
1 S. 2 : 14. he struck into c.
Jb. 41 : 20. smoke, as out of a c.
Je. 52 : 18. c-s took they away, 19.
Eze. 11 : 3. this city is the c., 7.
11. This city shall not be your c.
Mi. 3 : 3. chop as flesh within c.

CA'LEB. [Person.]

Nu. 13 : 6. C. to spy the land
30. C. stilled the people bef. Mo.
14 : 24. C. having another spirit,
30.-32 : 12. De. 1 : 36.
38. C. lived still, 26 : 65.
34 : 19. C. to divide the land
Jos. 14 : 13. Jos. gave C. Hebron
15 : 14. C. drove sons of Anak
16. C. said, he that smiteth
Ju. 1 : 15. C. gave her springs
1 S. 25 : 3. Nabal of house of C.
1 Ch. 2 : 18. C. begat, 42, 50.-4 : 15.

CA'LEB. [Place.]

1 S. 30 : 14. on south of C.

CALEB-EPH'RATAH.

1 Ch. 2 : 24. Hezron dead in C.

CALF.

Ge. 18 : 7. Abraham fetched a c.
Ex. 32 : 4. had made it a molten c.,
19. saw c. and dancing [8.
20. Moses burnt c. and, De. 9 : 21.
24. cast into fire came out c.
35. plagued peo. because made c.
Le. 9 : 2. Take young c. for a sin-off.
3. take c. for a burnt-offering
De. 9 : 16. ye had made you molten
c., Ne. 9 : 18. Ps. 106 : 19.
1 S. 28 : 4. wom. had fat c. in house
Jb. 21 : 10. cow casteth not her c.
Ps. 29 : 6. He maketh to skip like c.
Is. 11 : 6. c. and young lion togeth.
27 : 10. there shall the c. feed and
Je. 34 : 18. when they cut c. in twain
Eze. 1 : 7. feet were like a c. foot
Ho. 8 : 5. Thy c. O Samaria hath cast
6. c. of Samaria shall be broken
Lu. 15 : 23. bring hither the fatted c.
27. father hath killed fatted c., 30
Ac. 7 : 41. made a c. in those days
Re. 4 : 7. second beast was like a c.

CALKERS.

Eze. 27 : 9. ancients of Gebal thy c.
27. c. shall fall into seas

CALL.

Ge. 2 : 19. what he would c. them
Ex. 2 : 7. c. to thee a nurse of Heb.
20. c. him that he eat bread
Nu. 16 : 12. Moses sent to c. Dathan
22 : 20. the men c. thee, go [for
De. 4 : 7. God is in all things we c.
26. I c. heaven and earth to witness against you, 30 : 19.-31 : 28.
Ju. 16 : 25. c. for Samson that he may make us sport
21 : 13. to c. peaceably unto them
Ru. 1 : 21. why c. ye me Naomi
1 S. 3 : 6. for thou didst c. me, 8.
16 : 3. c. Jesse to the sacrifice
22 : 11. king sent to c. Ahimelech
2 S. 17 : 5. c. now Hushai
1 K. 1 : 28. c. Bathsh. | 32. c. Zadok
8 : 52. hearken in all they c. for
17 : 18. come to c. my sin to rem
18 : 24. c. ye on your gods, 25.
2 K. 4 : 12. c. this Shunamite, 36.
10 : 19. c. all prophets of Baal
Jo. 5 : 1. c. now if any will answer
13 : 22. then c. I will ans., 14 : 15.
Ps. 4 : 1. Hear when I c., O God
3. Lord will hear when I c.
14 : 4. eat my peo. c. not upon L.
20 : 9. let k. hear when we c.
49 : 11. c. lands after own names
77 : 6. I c. to rem. my song in the
86 : 5. plenteous in mercy to all c.
99 : 6. Sam. am. them c. on name
102 : 2. when I c. ans. me speedily
145 : 18. L. is nigh all c. upon him
Pr. 7 : 4. c. understanding thy kins.
8 : 4. to you, O men, I c., my voice
9 : 15. c. passengers who go right
31 : 28. chil. arise, and c. her blessed
Is 3 : † 12. who c. thee blessed, 9 : † 16.
5 : 20. Woe to them c. evil good
22 : 12. did L. c. to weeping
45 : 3. I L. wh. c. thee by name
48 : 2. c. thems. of the holy city
13. when I c. they stand up
55 : 6. c. ye upon him while he near
58 : 5. wilt thou c. this a fast?
13. c. the sabbath a delight
65 : 15. c. his serv. by ano. name
24. bef. they c. I will answer
Je. 9 : 17. c. for mourning women
33 : 3. c. unto me, I will ans. thee
50 : 29. c. the archers against Bab.
51 : 27. c. against her the kingdoms
La. 2 : 15. city men c. perfection
Da. 2 : 2. com-d to c. magicians
Ho. 1 : 4. c. his name Jezreel
6. c. her name Lo-ruhamah
9. c. his name Lo-ammi, for ye
7 : 11. they c. to Egypt, go to Ass.
Jo. 1 : 14. c. solemn assemb., 2 : 15.
Jon. 1 : 6. O sleeper, c. upon G.
Zch. 3 : 10. c. ev. man his neighb.
Mal. 3 : 15. we c. proud happy
Mat. 9 : 13. not come to c. righteous but, Mk. 2 : 17. Lu. 5 : 32.
20 : 8. c. labourers and give them
22 : 3. servants to c. them bidden
43. David in spirit c. him Lord?

Mat. 23: 9. c. no man fa. upon earth
Mk. 15: 12. whom ye c. King of Jews
16. they c. the whole band
Lu. 6: 46. why c. ye me L. and do
14: 13. makest a feast c. poor
Jn. 4: 16. Go c. thy husband and
13: 13. Ye c. me Master and L.
Ac. 9: 14. bind all c. on thy name
10: 5. c. for Simon, 32.-11: 13.
19: 13. c. over th. had evil spirits
24: 14. way they c. heresy
Ro. 10: 12. rich to all c. upon him
2 Co. 1: 23. I c. God for a record
2 Ti. 1: 5. I c. to rem. the faith
2: 22. peace with them c. on Lord
He. 2: 11. not ash. to c. th. breth.
10: 32. c. to remem. former days
Ja. 5: 14. let him c. the elders
1 Pe. 1: 17. if ye c. on Father who

CALL on or upon the name of the Lord.

Ge. 4: 26. began men to c. u. n. o. L.
1 K. 18: 24. I will c. o. n. o. Lord, Ps. 116: 17.
2 K. 5: 11. he will come and c. o. n. o. Lord [Is. 12: 4.
1 Ch. 16: 8. c. u. n. o. L., Ps. 105: 1.
Jo. 2: 32. whoso. sh. c. o. n. o. L., Ac. 2: 21. Ro. 10: 13.
Zph. 3: 9. may all c. u. n. o. L.
1 Co. 1: 2. in ev. place c. u. n. o. L.

Not CALL.

Ge. 17: 15. shall n. c. her name Sarai but Sarah [with thee
Ju. 12: 1. and didst n. c. us to go
Ru. 1: 20. c. me n. Naomi, c. me
Ps. 14: 4. they c. n. upon L. [Mara
Is. 31: 2. will n. c. back his words
Je. 10: 25. families th. c. n. on name
Lu. 14: 12. c. n. thy friends
Jn. 15: 15. I c. you n. servants
Ac. 10: 15. c. n. common, 11: 9.
28. n. to c. any man common

Shall, or Shalt CALL.

Ge. 17: 19. s. c. his name Isaac
De. 25: 8. elders of his city s. c. him
30: 1. thou s. c. them to mind
33: 19. They s. c. peo. to mount.
Jb. 14: 15. s. c. I will answer
Ps. 50: 4. He s. c. to heavens
72: 17. nations s. c. him blessed
Is. 7: 14. s. c. Immanuel, Mat. 1: 23.
34: 12. s. c. nobles to
41: 25. from rising of sun s. he c.
44: 5. another s. c. hims. Jacob
7. who, s. c. and declare it?
55: 5. s. c. nation knowest not
58: 9. s. c. and the Lord answer
60: 14. s. c. thee city of Lord
18. s. c. thy walls salvation
61: 6. s. c. you ministers of God
62: 12. s. c. them holy people
Je. 3: 17. s. c. Jeru. throne of L.
19. s. c. me, my father [them
6: 30. Reprobate silver s. men c.
7: 27. s. c. to them, not answer
Ho. 2: 16. s. c. me no more Baali
Jo. 2: 32. in remnant Lord s. c.
Am. 5: 16. they s. c. the husbandm.
Zch. 13: 9. s. c. on my name
Mal. 1: 4. s. c. th. border of wick.
3: 12. nations s. c. you blessed
Mat. 1: 21. s. c. name Jes., Lu. 1: 31.
10: 25. s. c. them of household?
Lu. 1: 13. s. c. his name John
48. all gene. s. c. me blessed
Ac. 2: 39. as many as Lord s. c.
Ro. 10: 14. how s. they c. on him

CALL upon me.

Ps. 50: 15. c. u. m. in day of trou.
91: 15. shall c. u. m. I will answ.
Pr. 1: 28. shall c. u. m. not answ.
Je. 29: 12. shall ye c. u. m. and

Will CALL.

Ge. 24: 57. We w. c. damsel
30: 13. dau-s w. c. me blessed
1 S. 12: 17. I w. c. unto L., he send
2 S. 22: 4. I w. c. on L., Ps. 18: 3.
Jb. 27: 10. w. hyp. c. upon God?
Ps. 55: 16. I w. c. upon God, 86: 7.
80: 18. quicken us, we w. c. upon
116: 2. w. I c. upon him long as I
Is. 22: 20. I w. c. my serv. Eliakim
Je. 1: 15. I w. c. families of
25: 29. w. c. for sword, Eze. 38: 21.
Eze. 21: 23. he w. c. to remem. iniq.
36: 29. I w. c. for the corn, and
Ac. 24: 25. a conv. season I w. c. for
Ro. 9: 25. I w. c. them my people

CALLED.

Ge. 2: 19. whatso. Adam c. every
11: 9. name of it c. Babel
12: 8. c. upon name of L., 13: 4.-21: 33.-26: 25.
21: 17. angel c. to Hagar
22: 11. angel c. unto Abraham
35: 10. not be c. any more Jacob
18. c. him Ben-oni, fa. c. him Benj.
39: 14. she c. to the men
Ex. 1: 18. king c. midwives
8: 8. Pha. c. for Moses, 25.-9: 27.-10: 16, 24.-12: 31.
Nu. 13: 16. Moses c. Oshea
De. 5: 1. Moses c. all Israel, 29: 2.
15: 2. it is c. the Lord's release
28: 10. art c. by name of Lord
Jos. 21: † 9. cities here c. by name
Ju. 12: † 1. men of Ephr. were c.
14: 15. have ye c. us to take
15: 17. cast jaw-bone, c. place
18. Samson athirst, c. on Lord
16: 28. Samson c. unto the Lord
1 S. 3: 16. Then Eli c. Samuel
9: 9. now c. proph., was c. a seer
12: 18. So Samuel c. unto Lord
2 S. 6: 2. name is c. by name of L.
12: 28. lest city be c. aft. my name
18: 26. watchm. c. unto the porter
21: 2. the king c. the Gibeonites
1 K. 1: 9. Adonijah c. breth., 19: 25.
18: 3. Ahab c. Obadiah, the gov.
26. they c. on the name of Baal
2 K. 4: 22. she c. unto her husband
7: 10. they c. unto porter of city
1 Ch. 4: 10. Jabez c. on G. of Isr.
13: 6. ark of G., wh. name is c. on it
21: 26. David c. upon L., he ans. him
Es. 2: 14. exc. she were c. by name
4: 11. who is not c., law to put him to death, I have not been c.
Jb. 17: † 14. I have c. to corrupt.
Ps. 53: 4. have not c. upon G. [name
79: 6. kingd. th. not c. upon thy
Is. 31: 4. a mult. of shepherds is c.
43: 22. hast not c. upon me, O Jac.
48: 1. O Jacob, ye c. by name of Isr.
12. Hearken unto me, O Isr. my c.
61: 3. might be c. trees of righte.
Je. 7: 32. no more be c. Tophet
La. 1: 21. bring day thou hast c.
2: 22. thou hast c. my terrors
Eze. 20: 29. the name is c. Bamah
Da. 5: 12. now let Daniel be c.
Mat. 1: 16. horn Jes., who is c. Christ
2: 7. Herod privily c. wise men
23. dwelt in a city c. Nazareth
4: 18. Simon c. Peter and Andrew
10: 2. first Simon, who is c. Peter
13: 55. is not his mother c. Mary?
15: 32. Jes. c. his disciples, 20: 25. Mk. 6: 7. -8: 1. -10: 42. -12: 43. Lu. 6: 13. -9: 1. -18: 16.
18: 2. Jes. c. a little child unto him
20: 16. many be c. but few, 22: 14.
32. Jesus stood still, and c. them
23: 7. to be c. of men Rabbi
8. be ye not c. Rabbi, 10 [livered
25: 14. c. his own servants and de-
26: 14. one of the 12 c. Jud. Iscar.
36. unto a place c. Gethsemane
27: 16. notable prisoner c. Barab.
17. sh release Jesus, c. Christ? 22.
33. unto a place c. Golgotha
Mk. 10: 49. Jesus com. him to be c.
Mk. 14: 72. Peter c. to mind word Jes
15: 16. led into hall c. Pretorium
Lu. 1: 61. none of thy kindr. is c.
62. signs how he have him c.
2: 4. city of David c. Bethlehem
23. dwelt in city c. Nazareth
6: 15. and Simon c. Zelotes
7: 11. into a city c. Nain
8: 2. Mary c. Magdalene out of
9: 10. into desert place c. Bethsai.
10: 39. she had a sister c. Mary
15: 19. worthy to be c. thy son, 21.
19: 15. he com. the serv. to be c.
29. at the mount c. mount of Olives, Lu. 21: 37. Ac. 1: 12.
22: 25. upon them are c. benefac.
23: 33. to place that is c. Calvary
24: 13. went to village c. Emmaus
Jn. 1: 48. Bef. Philip c. thee I saw
2: 9. gov. of feast c. bridegroom
4: 5. to a city of Sa. c. Sychar
25. Messiah cometh, wh. is c. C.
5: 2. a pool c. Bethesda
9: 11. man c. Jesus made clay
11: 16. Thomas c. Didy., 20: 24. 21: 2.
28. she c. Mary, The Master is
54. into a city c. Ephraim
18: 33. Pilate c. Jesus, Art thou
19: 13. judgm. seat in pl. c. Pave.
17. into place c. place of a skull
Ac. 1: 19. field is c. Aceldama
23. Joseph c. Barsabas and
3: 2. at gate of temp. c. Beautiful
11. ran unto porch c. Solomon's
5: 21. high priest c. coun. togeth.
6: 2. twelve c. mult. of disc. unto
9. syn. c. syn. of Libertines
7: 14. Jo. c. his fa. Jacob to him
8: 9. man c. Simon used sorcery
9: 11. street c. Straight, for one c.
21. destroyed them wh. c. [Saul
36. by interpretation is c. Dorcas
10: 1. man in Cesarea c. Corne. (2)
18. men c. and asked wh. P. lodg.
24. Corne. c. kinsmen, near friends
11: 26. were c. Christ. first at An.
13: 7. who c. for Barna. and Saul
9. Saul, c. Paul, filled with H. G.
15: 17. Gent. upon wh. my n. is c.
19: 40. c. in ques. for this day's
20: 1. Paul c. unto him disciples
17. c. elders of church
23: 6. I am c. in question, 24: 21.
17. Paul c. centurion unto him
18. Paul prisoner c. me to
27: 8. came to pl. c. Fair Havens
14. tempest. wind c. Euroclydon
16. under an island c. Clauda
28: 17. Paul c. chief of Jews togeth.
Ro. 1: 1. Paul c. to be apos., 1 Co. 1: 1.
6. am. whom are ye the c. of Jes.
7. them c. to be saints, 1 Co. 1: 2.
2: 17. thou art c. a Jew, and restest
8: 28. who are the c. acc. to his pur.
1 Co. 1: 1. Paul c. to be an apostle
2. unto them c. to be saints
9. ye were c. to fellowship
24. to them c. both Jews and Gr.
26. not many noble are c. [nica.
5: 11. if any c. a broth. be a for-
7: 18. c. being circum.? is any c.
21. Art thou c. being a servant?
22. he that is c. is the Lord's
24. man wherein he is c. abide
8: 5. there be that are c. gods
15: 9. not meet to be c. an apostle
Ga. 1: 6. removed from him c. you
5: 13. ye have been c. to liberty
Ep. 2: 11. are c. uncirc. by that c.
4: 1. of vocation wherew. ye are c.
4. even as ye are c. in one hope
Col. 3: 15. to wh. ye are c. in one
4: 11. Jesus, which is c. Justus
2 Th. 2: 4. exalteth above all is c. G.
14. c. you by our gospel
1 Ti. 6: 12. eter. life, whereto art c.
20. opposit. of sci. falsely so c.

He. 3: 13. exhort while it is c. to-day
7: 11. not be c. after order of
9: 2. tab. which is c. sanctuary
3. which is c. Holiest of all
15. that are c. might rec. promise
11: 16. not ash. to be c. their God
24. ref. to be c. son of Pha.'s dau.
Ja. 2: 7. blasp. name by wh. ye are c.
1 Pe. 2: 9. hath c. you out of dark
21. hereunto were ye c. bec. Ch.
3: 9. knowing ye are thereunto c.
2 Pe. 1: 3. that hath c. us to glory
1 Jn. 3: 1. should be c. sons of God
Jude 1. preserved in J. Christ and c.
Re. 1: 9. I was in isle c. Patmos
8: 11. the star is c. Wormwood
11: 8. city wh. spiritually is c. Sod.
12: 9. that old serpent c. Devil
16: 16. unto place c. Armageddon
17: 14. that are with him, are c.
19: 9. blessed that are c. to mar.

CALLED,
joined with **God,** or **Lord.**

Ge. 1: 5 G. c. light day, dark. he c.
8. God c. firmament, Heaven
10. G. c. dry land Earth, wat. c.
3: 9. Lord c. unto Adam
5: 2. G. c. their name Adam
Ex. 3: 4. G. c. unto him out of bush
19: 3. Lord c. unto him out of mt.
20. Lord c. Moses to top of mt.
35: 30. L. hath c. name Bezaleel
Nu. 12: 5. L. c. Aaron and Miriam
1 S. 3: 4. L. c. Samuel, 6, 8, 10.
2 K. 3: 10. L. hath c. 3 kings, 13.
8: 1. L. hath c. for famine
Ps. 50: 1. L. c. earth from rising
Is. 41: 2. L. c. him to his foot
42: 6. I have c. thee in rights.
49: 1. L. hath c. me from womb
54: 6. L. c. thee as wom. forsaken
Je. 11: 16. c. name olive-tree
20: 3. not c. thy name Pashur
Am. 7: 4. G. c. to contend by fire
16: 10. gathering that L. c. us
1 Co. 7: 15. G. hath c. us to peace
17. as L. c. every one, so let
Ga. 1: 15. G. who c. me by grace
1 Th. 2: 12. c. you to his kingd.
4: 7. G. not c. us to uncleanness
2 Th. 2: 14. G. c. you by our gospel
2 Ti. 1: 9. c. us with holy calling
He. 5: 4. c. of G. as was Aaron
10. c. of G. a high-priest after
1 Pe. 5: 10. G. of all grace, c. us

He CALLED.

Ge. 21: 31. h. c. place Beer-sheba
26: 18. h. c. names as father
35: 10. h. c. his name Israel
Ex. 24: 16. c. to Moses out of cloud
Ju. 6: 32. h. c. him Jerubbaal
15: † 19. h. c. it well of him that c.
2 S. 1: 7. h. saw and c. unto me
13: 17. h. c. his serv. that minist.
1 K. 1: 10. Sol. h. c. not, 19, 26.
9: 13. h. c. them land of Cabul
2 K. 4: 36. h. c. to Gehazi, so h. c.
18: 4. serpent, h. c. it Nehushtan
Ps. 105: 16. h. c. for a famine
Je. 42: 8. c. h. Johanan and capts.
La. 1: 15. h. c. assembly ag. me
Eze. 9: 3. h. c. to man clothed
Mat. 4: 21. mending nets, h. c. them
10: 1. when h. had c. his twelve
15: 10. h. c. the multitude
18: 32. lord said aft. h. had c. him
Mk. 1: 20. h. c. and they left
3: 23. h. c. scribes unto him
6: 7. h. c. the twelve, 9: 35. Lu. 9: 1.
7: 14. h. had c. people, 8: 34.
Lu. 13: 12. Jes. saw h. c. her to him
15: 26. h. c. one of the servants
16: 2. h. c. him said, How is it
5. h. c. ev. one of Lord's debtors
19: 13. h. c. his ten serv-s and deliv.
Jn. 10: 35. If h. c. them Gods
12: 17. with him when h. c. Laz.

Ac. 9: 41. when h. had c. saints
10: 7. angel dep. h. c. two of serv-s
23. c. h. them in, and lodged
16: 29. Then h. c. for a light
19: 25. Whom h. c. with workm.
23: 23. h. c. two centurions
Ro. 8: 30. them h. c. whom h. c. he
9: 24. Even us whom h. hath c.
1 Pe. 1: 15. h. wh. hath c. you is holy
See CALLED **the name.**

I CALLED or, I have CALLED.

Nu. 24: 10. I c. thee to curse ene.
Ju. 12: 2. when I c. you, ye
1 S. 3: 5. Eli, said, I c. not, 6.
28: 15. I h. c. thee, mayest make
2 S. 22: 7. in my distress I c., Ps. 18: 6.-118: 5.
Ne. 5: 12. I c. priests, and took
Jb. 9: 16. if I had c. and he ans.
19: 16. I c. my serv. and no answer
Ps. 17: 6. I h. c. upon thee, for
31: 17. me not be asha. for I h. c.
88: 9. I h. c. daily upon thee
116: 4. c. I upon the name of L.
Pr. 1: 24. I h. c. and ye refused
Can. 5: 6. I c. him, gave no answer
Is. 13: 3. I h. c. my mighty ones
41: 9. I h. c. thee from chief men
43: 1. I c. thee by name, 45: 4.
48: 15. I h. c. him, I have bro't
50: 2. when I c. none to answer
51: 2. I c. him alone, and blessed
65: 12. I c. ye not ans., Je. 7: 13.
66: 4. when I c. none did answer
Je. 7: 13. I c. you, ye ans. not
35: 17. bec. I h. c. to them
La. 1: 19. I c. for my lovers, but
3: 55. I c. out of low dungeon
57. drewest near in day I c.
Ho. 11: 1. I c. my Son, Mat. 2: 15.
Hag. 1: 11. I c. for drought
Zch. 11: 7. I c. Beauty, other I c.
Jn. 15: 15. I h. c. you friends
Ac. 13: 2. work wh. I h. c. them
28: 20. this cause h. I c. you

CALLED by my name.

2 Ch. 7: 14. my peo. wh. are c. b. m. n.
Is. 43: 7. bring, ev. one c. b. m. n.
65: 1. behold, to na. not c. b. m. n.
Je. 7: 10. house c. b. m. n., 11, 14, 30.-32: 34.-34: 15.
25: 29. evil on city c. b. m. n.
Am. 9: 12. remna. of heath. c. b. m. n.

CALLED by thy name.

1 K. 8: 43. house c. b. t. n., 2 Ch. 6: 33.
Is 4: 1. let us be c. b. t. n. to
Is. 43: 1. I have c. thee b. t. n., 45: 4.
63: 19. they were not c. b. t. n.
Je. 14: 9. O Lord, we are c. b. t. n.
15: 16. for I am c. b. t. n. O L.
Da. 9: 18. beh. city wh. is c. b. t. n.
19. for city and peo. are c. b. t. n.

CALLED his name.

Ge. 35: 10. Jacob, he c. h. n. Israel
18. She c. h. n. Benoni, but
1 Ch. 4: 9. mother c. h. n. Jabez
7: 16. she c. h. n. Peresh
23. c. h. n. Beriah
Mat. 1: 25. son, he c. h. n. Jesus
Re. 19: 13. h. n. is c. Word of God

CALLED the name.

Ge. 28. 19. c. t. n. Beth-el, 35: 15.
Ex. 16: 31. Israel c. t. n. Manna
17: 7. he c. t. n. of place Massah
15. Moses c. t. n. JEHOVAH-nissi
Ju. 15: 19. Samson c. t. n. En-hakk.
2 S. 5: 20. c. t. n. Baal-perazim, 2 Ch. 14: 11.
1 K. 7: 21. c. t. n. Jachin, 2 Ch. 3: 17.
Jb. 42: 14. c. t. n. of first, Jemima

Sent and CALLED.

Ge 27: 42. she s. a. c. Jacob her
31: 4. Jac. s. a. c. Rach. and Leah
41: 14. then Pha s. a. c. Joseph
Jos. 24: 9. Balak s. a. c. Balaam
Ju. 4: 6. she s. a. c. Barak out

Ju. 16: 18. she s. a. c. lords of Philis
2 S. 12: 25. he s. a. c. Jedidiah
1 K. 2: 36. king s. a. c. Shimei, 42.
12: 3. they s. a. c. Jerob., 2 Ch. 10: 3.
Es. 5: 10. Haman s. a. c. his friends
Jb. 1: 4. Job's. a. c. three sisters
Ac. 20: 17. s. to Ephesus, a. c. eld.

Shall be CALLED.

Ge. 2: 23. s. b. c. Woman, bec. taken
17: 5. thy name s. b. c. Abraham
21: 12. for in Isaac s. thy seed b. c., Ro. 9: 7. He. 11: 18.
32: 28. name s. b. c. no more Jacob
48: 6. thy issue s. b. c. aft. breth.
De. 25: 10. his name s. b. c. in Isr.
Pr. 16: 21. wise in heart s. b. c. pru.
24: 8. devis. evil, s. b. c. a mischiev.
Is. 4: 3. remain. in Jeru. s. b. c. holy
9: 6. his name s. b. c. Wonderful
19: 18. s. b. c. The city of destruc.
32: 5. vile per. s. b. no more c. lib.
35: 8. and it s. b. c. way of holiness
54: 5. God of whole earth s. he b. c.
56: 7. house s. b. c. hou. of prayer, Mat. 21: 13. [19: 6.
Je. 7: 32. it s. no more b. c. Tophet,
23: 6. s. b. c. L. our Righte., 33: 16.
Zch. 8: 3. Jer. s. b. c. A city of truth
Mat. 1: † 23. name s. b. c. Emmanuel
2: 23. be fulfill. s. b. c. a Nazarene
5: 9. peace-makers s. b. c. children
19. he s. b. c. least in the kingdom
Mk. 11: 17. my house s. b. c. hou. of
Lu. 1: 32. he s. b. c. Son of Highest
35. holy thing s. b. c. Son of God
60. said, Not so; he s. b. c. John
2: 23. Ev. male s. b. c. holy to L.
Ro. 7: 3. s. b. c. an adulteress
9: 26. they s. b. c. chil. of God

Shalt be CALLED.

Is. 1: 26. thou s. b. c. city of righte.
47: 1. thou s. b. c. no more tender
5. s. no more b. c. The lady of
58: 12. thou s. b. c. The repairer
62: 2. s. b. c. by a new name
4. thou s. b. c. Hephzi-bah, thy
12. thou s. b. c. Sought out, A city
Lu. 1: 76. thou s. b. c. prophet of
Jn. 1: 42. thou s. b. c. Cephas

They CALLED. [men?

Ge. 19: 5. t. c. Lot, and said, Where
24: 58. t. c. Rebekah and said
Nu. 25: 2. t. c. peo. unto sacrifices
Ju. 16: 25. t. c. for Samson out of
18: 12. t. c. that place Mahaneh-
1 S. 23: 28. t. c. that pl. Sela-ham
1 Ch. 11: 7. t. c. it The city of Da.
Es. 9: 26. t. c. these days Purim
Ps. 99: 6. t. c. upon the Lord, and
Je. 12: 6. t. c. a multitude aft. thee
30: 17. bec. t. c. thee an outcast
Ho. 11: 2. as t. c. them, so they
7. tho. t. c. them to Most High
Mat. 10: 25. if t. c. mast. Beelzebub
Lu. 1: 59. t. c. him Zacharias, after
Jn. 9: 18. t. c. parents of him receiv
24. again c. t. man that was blind
Ac. 4: 18. t. c. and com. not to speak
5: 40. when t. had c. the apostles
14: 12. t. c. Barnabas, Jupiter.

Was or wast CALLED.

De. 3: 13. wh. w. c. land of giants
Ju. 6: † 34. Abiezer w. c. after him
2 Ch. 20: 26. place w. c. Berachah
Ezr. 2: 61. w. c. after their name, Ne. 7: 63. [the womb
Is. 48: 8. w-t c. a transgressor from
Da. 10: 1. name w. c. Belteshazzar
Mat. 26: 3. high pr. w. c. Caiaphas
27: 8. w. c. The field of blood
Lu. 1: 36. with her who w. c. barren
2: 21. his name w. c. JESUS
22: 47. he that w. c. Judas one of
Jn. 2: 2. Jesus w. c. to marriage
Ac. 13: 1. Simeon, that w. c. Niger
24: 2. when he w. c., Tertullus beg.
28: 1. they knew island w. c. Melita

1 Co. 7:20. abide in calling he w.c.
He. 11:8. Abr.wh. he w. c. obeyed
Ja. 2:23. he w. c. the Friend of G.
Re.19:11. sat on him w.c. Faithful

CALLEDST, CALLEST.

Ju. 8:1. c. us not when wentest
1 S. 3:5. Here am I, for thou c. me
Ps. 81:7. Thou c. in troub., I deliv.
Eze. 23:21. c. to remem. lewdness
Mat. 19:17. Why c. thou me good?
none good, Mk.10:18. Lu.18:19.

CALLETH.

1 K. 8:43. do accord. to all stranger
c. to thee for,2Ch.6:33. [answ.
Jb. 12:4. who c. upon God, and he
Ps. 42:7. Deep c. unto deep
147:4. c. th. by names, Is. 40:26.
Pr.18:6. fool's mouth c. for strokes
Is. 21:11. he c. to me out of Seir
59:4. None c. for justice, nor any
64:7. is none that c. upon thy n.
Ho. 7:7. none that c. unto me
Am. 5:8. c. for waters of sea, 9:6.
Mat. 27:47. c. for Elias, Mk. 15:35.
Mk. 3:13. c. unto him wh. he would
10:49. Be of good comf., he c. thee
12:37. if Dav. c. him L., Lu.20:44.
Lu. 15:6. he c. together his friends
9. she c. her friends and neighb.
20:37. when he c. the L. the God
Jn. 10:3. he c. his sheep by name
11:28. The Master is come and c.
Ro. 4:17. c. things which be not
9:11. elect. might stand, of him c.
1 Co. 12:3. no man by Spirit c.
Jesus accursed [him c. you
Ga. 5:8. persuasion cometh not of
1Th.5:24. Faithful is he that c. you
Re. 2:20. c. herself a prophetess

CALLING. [Noun.]

Nu.10:2. trumpets for c. assembly
Is. 1:13. c. of assemblies, I cannot
Eze. 23:19. in c. to rem. her youth
Ro. 11:29. c. of God witho. repent.
1 Co. 1:26. ye see your c. brethren
7:20. Let every man abide same c.
Ep. 1:18. kno. what is hope of h. c.
4:4. called in one hope of your c.
Ph. 3:14. prize of the high c. of G.
2 Th. 1:11. count you worthy of c.
2 Ti. 1:9. called us with a holy c.
He. 3:1. partakers of heavenly c.
2 Pe. 1:10. to make your c. sure

CALLING. [Participle.]

Is. 41:4. c. genera. from beginning
46:11. c. ravenous bird from east
Mat. 11:16. c. to fellows, Lu. 7:32.
Mk. 3:31. sent unto him c. him
11:21. Peter c. to remembrance
15:41. c. unto him centurion
Lu. 7:19. John c. two of his discip.
Ac. 7:59. stoned Ste. c. upon God
22:16. wash aw. thy sins, c. on L.
1 Pe. 3:6. Sarah obeyed Abra., c.
[him lord

CALM.

Ps. 107:29. He maketh storm a c.
Jon. 1:11. that sea be c. unto us
12. cast me forth, so sea be c.
Mat. 8:26. there was a great c., Mk.
4:39. Lu. 8:24.

CAL'NEH.

Ge. 10:10. Babel and C. in Shinar
Am. 6:2. pass ye unto C. thence to

CAL'NO.

Is. 10:9. Is not C. as Carchemish?

CAL'VARY.

Lu. 23:33. come to place called C.

CALVE, ED, ETH.

Jb. 21:10. their cow c-h casteth not
39:1. canst mark when hinds c.?
Ps.29:9. voice of L. maketh hinds c.
Je. 14:5. the hind c-d in the field

CALVES.

1 S. 6:7. bring their c. home | 10.
14:32. spoil, and took oxen c.
1 K. 12:28. k. made two c. of gold
32. sacrificing to c. he had made

2 K. 10:29. departed not fr. gold c.
17:16. made images even two c.
2 Ch. 11:15. ordained priests, for c.
13:8. there are with you gold c.
Ps. 68:30. rebuke bulls with the c.
Hos. 10:5. fear, bec. of c. of Beth-a
13:2. let men that sacri. kiss the c.
14:2. will render c. of our lips
Am. 6:4. eat c. out of the stall
Mi. 6:6. come with c. of year old?
Mal. 4:2. ye shall grow up as c.
He. 9:12. Neith. by blood of c. but
19. took bl. of c. sprinkled book

CAME.

Ge. 10:14. c. Philistim, 1 Ch. 1:12.
19:1. two angels c. to Sodom at
20:3. G. c. to Abim. in dream
27:35 brother c. with subtilty
29:1. Rachel c. with sheep
31:24. God c. to Laban in dream
32:6. c. to thy brother Esau, he
33:1. Esau c. and 400 men
34:25. c. upon city boldly
39:16. laid up garm. until lord c.
47:15. all Egypt c. unto Joseph
Ex. 8:6. and the frogs c. up and
36:4. c. every man from his work
Nu. 13:27. c. to land sentest us
19:2. heifer upon wh. never c. yoke
22:9. God c. unto Balaam at, 20.
24:2. Sp of G. c. upon him, Ju. 3:
10. 1 S. 10:10.
De. 1:19. we c. to Kadesh-barnea
33:2. Lord c. from Sinai
Jos. 15:18. she c. to him, Ju.1:14.
Ju. 5:19. kings c. and fought
7:13. cake of bread c. to a tent
9:25. they robbed all that c. along
57. upon th. c. curse of Jotham
11:18. c. not within bor. of Moab
13:6. A man of God c. unto me
10. man that c. unto me the
11. Manoah arose c. to man
19:22. Bring man c. into thy house
20:48. Isr smote Benj. all that c.
Ru. 2:6. Moab. damsel th. c. back
1 S. 2:13. priest's servant c. 15.
14. did to all Israelites that c.
27. c. a man of God to Eli
4:1. word of Samuel c. to all Israel
7:13. c. no more into coasts of
9:15. Lord told Sam. bef. Saul c.
10:14. asses no where, c. to Sam.
13:8. Samuel c. not to Gilgal
15:35. Sam. c. no more to Saul
17:34. there c. a lion and a bear
26:3. Da. saw that Saul c. after him
2 S. 2:4. men of Jud. c. anoin. Da.
3:25. Abner, that c. to deceive th.
13:30. in way tidings c. to David
36. king's sons c. and wept
15:2. when any c. to k. for judgm.
16:15. Absalom c. to Jerusalem
18:25. c. apace, drew near
20:12. every one that c. stood
1 K. 1:42. while he spake, Jonat. c.
4:34. c. of all people to hear Sol.
10:10. c. no more such spices
12. c. no such almug-trees
12:12. all people c., 2 Ch. 10:12.
13:10. returned not by way he c.
19:9. he c. to cave and lodged
20:43. k. of Isr. c. heavy to Sama.
2 K. 3:15. hand of L. c. upon him
4:11. on day he c. thither
27. when she c. to man of God
5:15. Naaman c. stood bef. Elisha
6:23. bands of Syria c. no more
32. ere messenger c. he said
8:14. Hazael c. to his master
9:11. wheref. c. this mad fellow
10:12. Jehu arose, c. to Samaria
21. all worshippers of Baal c.
17:28. one of the priests c. and
19:33. way he c. shall he return
24:3. at com. of L. c. this on Jud.
1Ch. 1:12. of wh. c. Philis., Ge.10:14.

1 Ch. 4:41 c. in days of Hez.
5:2. of him c. the chief ruler
7:22. Eph.'s breth. c. to comfort
12:1. these are that c. to David
16. c. of children of Benjamin
22. c. to Da. to help him gr. host
2 Ch. 11:14. Levites c. to Judah
12:11. guard c. fetched shields
14:14. fear of L. c. upon them
22:1. men that c. with Arabians
24:18. wrath c. on Jud. and Jerus.
25:20. Amaz. not hear it c. of G.
30:11. divers humbl. c. to Jerus.
31:5. soon as com-t c. abroad
Ezr. 2:2. Which c. with Zerub.
5:5. till matter c. to Darius
Ne. 7:73. when seventh month c.
Es. 1:17. Vashti, but she c. not
2:13. thus c. ev. maiden to k.
4:2. Mordecai c. bef. king's gate
8:17. k.'s decree c. Jews had joy
9:25. when Es. c. before king
Jb. 1:6. sons of God c., 2:1.
3:† 25. fear and it c. upon me
26. not in safety yet trouble c.
26:4. whose spirit c. fr. thee? [c.
29:13. bless. of him ready to perish
30:26. for good, evil c. darkn. c.
Ps. 18:6. my cry c. before me
27:2. when my foes c. upon me
78:31. wrath of G. c. upon them
105:19. Until time his word c.
31. there c. divers sorts of flies
34. he spake, and locusts c.
Ec. 5:15. to go as he c., 16.
Is. 20:1. year Tartan c. to Ashdod
30:4. ambassadors c. to Hanes
41:5. ends of earth afraid, c.
Je. 7:31. nor c. it into my mind,
19:5.-32:35.
8:15. for peace, but no good c.
44:21. c. it not into his mind
Eze. 4:14. nor c. abom. flesh into
17:3. c. to Leb. and took branch
33:22. afore he that escaped c.
37:7. bones c. together, bone to
10. breath c. into them, they lived
43:2. glory of God c. from east
Da. 2:† 29. thoughts c. into mind
4:28. All this c. on the king Neb
7:13. one like son of man c. with
22. Till the Ancient of days c. and
Am. 6:1. to whom house of Isr. c.
Jon. 3:6. word c. to king of Nine.
Ha. 3:3. God c. from Teman
Hag. 1:9. much, and lo it c. to little
2:16. when one c. to the press-fat
Zch. 7:12. c. a great wrath from L.
14:16. all nations that c. ag. Jerus.
Mat. 2:1. there c. wise men fr. east
9. Till it c. and stood over child
3:1. In those days c. John Baptist
7:25. rains descended floods c., 27.
9:1. he c. into his own city
20. a woman c. behind, touched
28. blind men c. to Jesus
20:28. Son of man c. not to be
ministered unto, Mk. 10:45.
21:28. c. to first and said, Son, go
30. he c. to the second, and said
32. Jn. c. to you in way of righte.
25:10. went to buy, bridegr. c.
36. I was in prison, ye c. to me
26:49. he c. to Jes. and kissed him
60. false witnesses c. yet found
28:1. c. Mary Mag. and other M.
13. disciples c. by night, stole
Mk. 3:8. heard gr. things he did, c.
6:33. peo. c. together unto him
7:25. c. and fell at his feet
8:3. divers c. from far
9:21. how long since this c. to him
12:28. one of scribes c. and ask.
42. c. a certain poor widow
Lu.1:57. now Elisabeth's full time c.
9:34. c. cloud and overshad. them
35. there c. voice out of cloud

Lu.15. 17. when he c. to hims. he said
20. he arose and c. to his father
Jn. 1: 7. same c. to bear witness
11. He c. to his own, his own rec.
17. grace and truth c. by J. C.
3: 2. same c. to Jesus by night, 7: 50.—19: 39.
23. they c. and were baptized
4: 27. upon this c. his disciples
10: 35. gods to whom word of G. c.
12: 21. The same c. to Philip
30. the voice c. not bec. of me
18: 39. there c. also Nicodemus
20: 8. wh. c. first to sepulchre
19. at even c. Jesus, and stood
Ac. 8: 40. cities, till he c. to Cesarea
9: 21. c. hither for that intent, to
10: 45. many as c. with Pet. were
11: 5. vessel descended, c. to me
23. he c. and had seen grace of G.
19: 18. that believ. c. and confessed
20: 7. when disciples c. together
28: 21. nor breth. th. c. spake harm
Ro. 5: 18. judgm. c. the free gift c.
7: 9. when com-t c. sin revived
9: 5. of whom, concern. flesh, C. c.
1 Co. 15: 21. by man c. death, by man c. also resurrection
2 Co. 1: 8. trouble wh. c. to us in A.
Ga. 2: 12. bef. that certain c. fr. Ja.
3: 23. bef. faith c. we were kept
Ep. 2: 17. c. and preached peace to
1 Th. 1: 5. our gospel c. not in word
1 Ti. 1: 15. that C. c. to save sin.
2 Ti. 3: 11. persecu. which c. to me
2 Pe. 1: 17. c. such a voice to him
18. this voice which c. from heav.
21. prophecy c. by will of man
1 Jn. 5: 6. that c. by wat. and bl.
3 Ju. 3. breth. c. and testi. of truth
Re 16: 19. great Bab. c. in remem.

See Spirit of the LORD.

CAME again.

Ju. 13: 9. angel c. a. to the woman
15: 19. his spirit c. a., 1 S. 30: 12.
21: 14. Benj. c. a. at that time
1 K. 17: 22. the soul of the child c. a.
19: 7. angel of L. c. a. sec. time
2 K. 5: 14. his flesh c. a. like flesh
7: 8. lepers c. a., and en. into tent
Ezr. 2: 1. these c. a. to Jud., Ne. 7: 6.
Es. 6: 12. Mordecai c. a. to king's
Da. 10: 18. c. a. and touched me
Zch. 4: 1. angel c. a. and waked me
Lu. 8: 55. her spir. c. a. and she aro.
Jn. 8: 2. early he c. a. into temple

CAME down.

Ge. 11: 5. Lord c. d. to see the city
15: 11. when fowls c. d. on carcass.
43: 20. O sir, we c. d. to buy food
Ex. 19: 20. L. c. d. upon mount Sinai
34: 29. when Moses c. d. fr. Sinai
Le. 9: 22. Aaron c. d. fr. offering
Nu. 11: 25. L. c. d. in cloud, 12: 5.
14: 45. Amalekites c. d. and smote
De. 9: 15. I c. d. from mount, 10: 5.
Jos. 3: 16. That water which c. d.
Ju. 5: 14. out of Machir c. d. gov.
1 S. 25: 20. she c. d. by the covert
2 S. 22: 10. bowed heavens c. d., Ps. 18: 9.
2 K. 1: 10. c. d. fire fr. heav., 12: 14.
1 Ch. 7: 21. c. d. to take their cattle
2 Ch. 7: 1. end of praying, fire c. d., 3.
La. 1: 9. she c. d. wonderfully
Da. 4: 13. holy one c. d. fr. heaven
Mi. 1: 12. evil c. d. from Lord to
Mat. 17: 9. c. d. fr. mt., Mk. 9: 9.
Lu. 10: 31. c. d. a certain priest
19: 6. he made haste and c. d. and
Jn. 3: 13. he that c. d. from heaven
6: 38. I c. d. from heaven, not to do
41. bread wh. c. d. fr. heav. 51, 58.
Ac. 9: 32. c. d. to saints at Lydda
15: 1. men which c. d. fr. Judea
21: 10. c. d. from Judea a prophet
Re. 20: 9. fire c. d. from God

CAME forth.

Ge. 24: 45. Rebek. c. f. with pitcher
Ex. 5: 20. as they c. f. from Pha.
13: 8. to me when I c. f. out of E.
Nu. 11: 20. Why c. f. out of Egypt
12: 5. Aaron and Miriam, c. f.
De. 23: 4. met not when ye c. f.
Jos. 9: 12. on day we c. f. to you
Ju. 14: 14. Out of eater c. f. meat, out of strong c. f. sweetness
20: 21. chil. of Benj. c. f. out of
33. liers in wait of Israel c. f.
2 S. 16: 5. Shimei c. f. and cursed
11. son which c. f. of my bowels
1 K. 22: 21. c. f. a spirit, and stood
2 K. 2: 23. c. f. chil. and mocked him
24. c. f. two she-bears and tare
21: 15. fathers c. f. of E., Je. 7: 25.
2 Ch. 32: 21. c. f. of his bowels
Pr. 7: 15. c. I f. to meet thee
Ec. 5: 15. As he c. f. naked, sh. ret.
Je. 20: 18. Whf. c. I f. out of womb?
Da. 3: 26. they c. f. of the fire
5: 5. c. f. fingers wrote upon wall
7: 10. fiery stream c. f. fr. bef. him
8: 9. out of one c. f. little horn
9: 23. command c. f. and I am come
Zch. 10: 4. out of him c. f. corner
Mk. 1: 38. that I may preach, c. I f.
Jn. 11: 44. he was dead c. f. bound
16: 28. I c. f. fr. Father into world
19: 5. Jesus c. f. wearing crown

I CAME.

Ge. 24: 42. I c. this day to well
30: 30. little thou hadst bef. I c.
48: 5. were born bef. I c. into Eg.
7 when I c. fr. Padan, Rachel died
Ex. 5: 23. since I c. to speak to Pha.
De. 22: 14. I c. to her not a maid
Ju. 20: 4. I c. into Gibeah of Benj.
1 K. 10: 7. I bel. not till I c., 2 Ch. 9: 6.
Ne. 6: 10. I c. to house of Shemaiah
13: 6. I c. to k. and obtained leave
7. I c. to Jerus. and underst. evil
Is. 50: 2. when I c. was there no man
Eze. 3: 15. I c. to th. of captivity
43: 3. when I c. to destroy city
Mat. 10: 34. I c. not to send peace
Mk. 2: 17. I c. not to call righteous, Lu. 5: 32.
Jn. 8: 14. I know whence I c.
42. I c. fr. G., nor c. I of myself
12: 27. this cause I c. to this hour
47. for I c. not to judge world
18: 37. this cause c. I into world
Ac. 10: 29. c. I soon as I was sent for
20: 18. fr. first day I c. into Asia
22: 11. being led, I c. into Dam.
23: 27. then c. I with an army
24: 17. I c. to bring alms to my nation [excellency
1 Co. 2: 1. when I c. I c. not with
2 Co. 1: 23. to spare you I c. not
2: 3. lest wh. I c. I sho. have sorrow
12. when I c. to Troas to preach
Ga. 1: 21. Afterwards I c. into Syria

CAME in.

Ge. 6: 4. sons of G. c. i. unto dau-s
19: 5. Where are men that c. i. to thee
38: 18. Judah c. i. unto her
39: 14. he c. i. to lie with me
40: 6. Joseph c. i. unto them
41: 14. c. i. unto Pharaoh
Ex. 10: 3. Moses c. i. unto Pharaoh
21: 3. If he c. i. by hims. sh. go out
Jos. 6: 1. and none c. i. to Jericho
1 S. 18: 13. went out and c. i., 16.
2 S. 11: 4. she c. i. unto him, he lay
1 K. 14: 6. as she c. i. at door, Ahijah
1 Ch. 27: 1. c. i. and went out by
2 Ch. 15: 5. no peace to him that c. i., Zch. 8: 10.
Es. 2: 14. she c. i. unto k. no more
Je. 32: 23. they c. i. and possess. it
37: 4. Jere. c. i. and out am. people
Eze. 46: 9. not return way he c. i.
Da. 4: 7. c. i. magicians, 5: 8.

Da. 4: 8. at last Daniel c. i. bef. me
Jon. 2: 7. my prayer c. i. unto tem.
Mat. 22: 11. king c. i. to see guests
Mk. 6: 25. she c. i. unto king
Lu. 1: 28. the angel c. i. unto Mary
7: 45. this wom. since I c. i. kissed
Ac. 5: 7. wife not knowing c. i.
10. young men c. i. and found her
28: 30. received all that c. i.
Ga. 2: 4. who c. i. privily to spy

CAME near.

Ge. 19: 9. they c. n. to break door
33: 3. until he c. n. his brother
Ex. 14: 20. one c. not n. other
40: 32. when they c. n. altar
Nu. 31: 48. and captains c. n. to Mo.
36: 1. chief of Joseph c. n. bef Mo.
De. 1: 22. ye c. n. to me ev. one, 5: 23.
Jos. 10: 24 c. n. and put your feet
17: 4. they c. n. bef. Eleazar, 21: 1.
1 K. 18: 36. Elijah c. n. and said
2 K. 4: 27. Gehazi c. n. to thrust
2 Ch. 18: 23. Zedekiah c. n. smote
Je. 42: 1. least to greatest c. n.
Da. 3: 8. Chald. c. n. and accused
26. Nebu. c. n. to the furnace
8: 17. So he c. n. where I stood
Ac. 9: 3. he c. n. to Damascus

CAME nigh.

Ex. 32: 19. he c. n. he saw calf
34: 32. afterw. all chil of Isr. c. n.
2 S. 15: 5. c. n. to do him obeis.
Mat. 15: 29. Jesus c. n. to sea of Gal.
Mk. 11: 1. they c. n. to Jerusalem
Lu. 7: 12. when he c. n. to gate of

CAME out.

Ge. 24: 15. behold Rebekah c. o.
25: 25. first c. o. red, all over like
38: 28. midwife said, This c. o. first
46: 26. souls wh. c. o. of his loins
Ex. 13: 3. Remember day ye c. o., 4.
34: 34. vail off until he c. o.
Le. 9: 24. fire c. o. fr. L., Nu. 16: 35.
Nu. 12: 4. L. spake, they three c. o.
16: 27. Dathan and Abiram c. o.
20: 11. he smote rock, and water
De. 11: 10. as whence ye c. o. [c. o.
Jos. 5: 4. c. o. were circumcised, 5.
6. till all th. c. o. of E. were consu.
Ju. 4: 22. Jael c. o. to meet him
11: 34. dau. c. o. to meet him
1 S. 4: 16. I am he that c. o. of army
21: 5. about 3 days since I c. o.
2 S. 2: 23. spear c. o. behind him
6: 20. Michal c. o. to meet David
11: 23. men prevailed aga. us c. o.
18: 4. all peo. c. o. by hundreds
1 K. 8: 9. cov. with Isr. when they c. o. of Egypt, 2 Ch. 5: 10.
20: 19. princes of provinces c. o.
2 Ch. 20: 10. invade, when they c. o.
Jb. 1: 21. Naked c. I o. of my mo.'s
3: 11. why died I not from womb? when I c. o. of the belly?
Je. 17: 16. wh. c. o. of lips right
Eze. 1: 4. whirlwind c. o. of north
Ha. 3: 14. they c. o. as a whirlwind
Hag. 2: 5. I covenanted with you when ye c. o. [wind
Zch. 5: 9. c. o. two women, and
Mat. 8: 34. city c. o. to meet Jesus
12: 44. house whence I c. o., Lu. 11: 24.
27: 32. as they c. o. found Simon
53. c. o. of graves after his resurr.
Mk. 1: 26. unclean spirit cried, he c. o., 9: 26.
6: 34. when he c. o. saw much peo.
9: 7. a voice c. o. of the cloud
Lu. 1: 22. when he c. o. he not speak
4: 35. he c. o. of him, and hurt
41. devils c. o. of many, Ac. 8: 7.
15: 28. c. o. his father and entreated
Jn. 16: 27. ye beli. I c. o. from G.
17: 8. have known I c. o. fr. thee
19: 34. forthw. c. o. blood and water
Ac. 7: 4. c. o. of land of Chaldea

Ac. 8 : 7. uncl. spirits c. o. of many
16 : 18. spirits c. o. the same hour
1 Co. 14 : 36. c. word of G. o. fr. you
He. 3 : 16. not all that c. o. of E.
Re. 7 : 14. c. o. of great tribulation
14 : 15. angel c. o. of temple, 17.
18. another angel c. o. from altar
15 : 6. seven angels c. o. of temple
19 : 5 a voice c. o. of the thröne

CAME over.

Jos. 4 : 22. Israel c. o. this Jordan
Ju. 19 : 10. Levite c. o. ag. Jebus
Mk. 5 : 1. c. o. to other side of sea

CAME to pass.

Ex. 12 : 41. it c. t. p. at end, selfsame day it c. t. p., 51.
De. 2 : 16. So it c. t. p., 1 S. 13 : 22.
2 K. 15 : 12. Es. 2 : 8. Ac. 27 : 44.
Jos. 17 : 13. it c. t. p. when Isr. grew
21 : 45. there failed not ; all c. t. p.
Ju. 13 : 20. For it c. t. p., 15 : 1.
1 K. 11 : 4, 15. 2 K. 8 : 5. Ne.
2 : 1.-4 : 1, 7.-6 : 1.-7 : 1. Je.
35 : 11.
1 S. 1 : 20. it c. t. p. when time was
10 : 9. those signs c. t. p. that day
16 : 23. c. t. p. when evil spirit
2 S. 2 : 1. it c. t. p. after this, 8 : 1.
-10 : 1. 2 K. 6 : 24. 2 Ch. 20 : 1.
2 K. 8 : 15. it c. t. p. on morrow, 1
Ch. 10 : 8. Je. 20 : 3. Ac. 4 : 5.
Is. 48 : 3. I did them suddenly, and
they c. t. p.
5. bef. it c. t. p. I shewed it thee
1 Th. 3 : 4. as it c. t. p. ye know

Then CAME.

Ex. 17 : 8. t. c. Amalek and fought
Nu. 27 : 1. t. c. dau-s of Zeloph.
1 S. 21 : 1. t. c. Da. to Ahimelech
2 S. 5 : 1. t. c. rall the tribes to Da.
24 : 6. they t. c. to Gilead, and
2 K. 18 : 37. t. c. Eliak. Is. 36 : 22.
2 Ch. 1 : 13. t. c. Sol. fr. his journey
12 : 5. t. c. Shemaiah to Rehob.
Ezr. 5 : 16. t. c. Sheshbazzar and
Ne. 1 : 2. t. Hanam of my breth. c.
2 : 9. t. I c. to governors
Jb. 30 : 26. looked for good, t. evil c.
42 : 11. t. c. all his brethren
Je. 19 : 14. t. c. Jere. from Tophet
38 : 27. t. c. all princes unto Jere.
Eze. 14 : 1. t. c. of the elders of Isr.
23 : 39. t. c. same day into
Mat. 9 : 14. t. c. disciples of John
15 : 1. t. c. to Jesus scribes and
12. t. c. his disciples, 17 : 19.
25. t. c. she, and worshipped him,
18 : 21. t. c. Pe. to him [Mk. 7 : 25.
20 : 20. t. c. mother of Zeb's chil.
26 : 50. t. c. and laid hands on Jesus
Lu. 3 : 12. t. c. publicans to be bapt.
22 : 7. t. c. day of unleav. bread
Jn. 7 : 45. t. c. officers to chief pr.
12 : 28. t. c. a voice from heaven
20 : 26. t. c. Jes. doors being shut
Ac. 16 : 1. t. c. he to Derbe

They CAME, or CAME they.

Ge. 11 : 31. t. c. to Haran and dwelt
12 : 5. into land of Canaan, t. c.
22 : 9. t. c. to place G. told him of
Ex. 16 : 35. until t. c. to land inhab.
19 : 1. c. t. into wildern. of Sinai
35 : 22. t. c. both men and women
Ju. 5 : 23. t. c. not to help of Lord
2 S. 4 : 7. when t. c. he lay on bed
1 K. 1 : 32. Zadok and Nathan, t. c.
2 : 7. so t. c. to me, when I fled
13 : 25. t. c. and told it in city
2 K. 2 : 4. t. c. to Jericho
6 : 4. t. c. to Jordan, cut wood
20 : 14. whence c. t. to thee, Is. 39 : 3.
2 Ch. 20 : 4. out of Ju. t. c. to seek L.
29 : 17. 8th day c. t. to porch of L.
Ezr. 2 : 68. when t. c. offered freely
Ne. 13 : 21. c. t. no more on sab.
Jb. 6 : 20. t. c. thith. were asham.
Jb. 30 : 14. t. c. as wide breaking
Ps. 88 : 17. t. c. round me like wat·
Je. 14 : 3. t. c. to pits found no wat·
43 : 7. thus c. t. to Tahpanhes
Eze. 23 : 40. messen. sent, lo t. c.
Da. 2 : 2. t. c. and stood bef. king
6 : 24. ever t. c. at bottom of den
Mat. 1 : 18. bef. t. c. togeth. she was
14 : 34. t. c. into land of Gennesa.
18 : 31. t. c. and told L., Lu. 14 : 21.
26 : 73. aft. while c. t. th. stood by
Mk. 1 : 45. t. c. from ev. quarter
3 : 13. called he would, and t. c.
Lu. 2 : 16. t. c. and found Mary
24 : 23. t. c. saying had seen vision
Jn. 12 : 9. t. c. not for Jesus' sake
Ac. 8 : 36. t. c. unto a certain water
12 : 10. t. c. to the iron gate
20. t. c. with one accord and
17 : 13. t. c. thither and stirred
23 : 14. t. c. to the chief priests
33. Who when t. c. to Cesarea
Re. 7 : 13. these, and whence c. t.

Word of the Lord CAME.

Ge. 15 : 1. w. o. l. c. to Abram, 4.
1 S. 15 : 10. w.- c. unto Samuel
2 S. 7 : 4. w.- c. unto Nathan, 1 Ch.
24 : 11. w.- c. unto Gad [17 : 3.
1 K. 6 : 11. w.- c. unto Solomon
16 : 1. w.- c. to Jehu, 7.
13 : 20. w.- c. unto prophet
17 : 2. w.- c. unto Elijah, 8.-18 : 1.
-19 : 9.-21 : 17, 28.
18 : 31. w.- c. saying, Isr. thy name
2 K. 20 : 4. w.- c. to Isaiah, Is. 38 : 4.
1 Ch. 22 : 8. w.- c. to David
2 Ch. 11 : 2. w.- c. to Shemaiah, 12 : 7.
1 K. 12 : 22.
Je. 1 : 11. w.- c. unto me saying, 18 :
3, 8.-16 : 1.-18 : 5-24 : 4-32 : 6.
Eze. 6 : 1.-7 : 1.-11 : 14.-12 : 1, 8,
17, 21, 26.-13 : 1.-14 : 2, 12.-15 :
1.-16 : 1.-17 : 1, 11.-18 : 1.-20 :
2, 45.-21 : 1, 8, 18.-22 : 1, 17, 23.
-23 : 1.-24 : 1, 15, 20.-25 : 1.-
26 : 1.-27 : 1.-28 : 1, 11, 20.-
29 : 1, 17.-30 : 1.-31 : 1.-32 : 1,
17.-33 : 1, 23.-34 : 1.- 35 : 1.-
36 : 16.-37 : 15.-38 : 1. Zch. 4 : 8.-
6 : 9.
14 : 1. w.- c. to Jeremiah, 1 : 2, 4.
-2 : 1.-28 : 12.-29 : 30.-32 : 26.-
33 : 1, 19, 23.-34 : 12.-35 : 12.-36 :
27.-37 : 6.-39 : 15.-42 : 7.-43 : 8.-
46 : 1.-47 : 1.-49 : 34. Da. 9 : 2.
Eze. 1 : 3. w.- c. unto Ezekiel, 3 : 16.
Ho. 1 : 1. w.- c. unto Hosea
Jo. 1 : 1. w.- c. to Joel
Jon. 1 : 1. w.- c. unto Jonah, 3 : 1.
Mi. 1 : 1. w.- c. to Micah
Zph. 1 : 1. w.- c. unto Zephaniah
Hag. 1 : 1. w.- c. by Hag., 3.-2 : 1,
10, 20. Zch. 7 : 1, 8.
Zch. 1 : 1. w.- c. unto Zechariah.
7 : 4. w.- c. unto me, 8 : 1, 18.

CAMEL.

Ge. 24 : 64. Rebekah lighted off c.
31 : 34. put them in c.'s furniture
Le. 11 : 4. shall not eat c., De. 14 : 7.
1 S. 15 : 3. slay infant, ox, and c.
Zch. 14 : 15. so shall be plague of c.
Mat. 19 : 24. It is easier for a c. to
go thro. Mk. 10 : 25. Lu. 18 : 25.
23 : 24. strain at gnat swallow c.

CAMELS.

Ge. 12 : 16. Abram had sh. and c.
24 : 10. serv. took 10 c. of the c. | 11.
14. will give c. drink | 30, 63.
19. will draw water for thy c., 44.
30 : 43. Jacob had much cattle and c.
32 : 15. Thirty milch c. and
37 : 25. Ishmaelites came with c.
Ex. 9 : 3. hand of the L. on the c.
Ju. 6 : 5. c. without number, 7 : 12.
8 : 21. took ornam. on c. necks, 26.
1 S. 27 : 9. David took away c. [c.
30 : 17. 400 y-g men who rode upon
1 K. 10 : 2. to Jeru. with c., 2 Ch. 9 : 1.
2 K. 8 : 9. present forty c. burden
1 Ch. 5 : 21. Reub. took of c. 50,000
12 : 40. of Zebulun bro-t br. on c.
27 : 30. Over c. was Obil the Ishm
Ezr. 2 : 67. their c. 435, Ne. 7 : 69.
Es. 8 : 10. letters by post on c., 14.
Jb. 1 : 3. his substance was 3,000 c.
17. Chaldeans fell upon the c.
42 : 12. he had 6,000 c.
Is. 21 : 7. he saw a chariot of c.
30 : 6. treasures on bunches of c.
60 : 6. mult. of c. shall cover thee
Je. 49 : 29. they shall take their c.
32. their c. shall be a booty
Eze. 25 : 5. Rabbah a stable for c.
Mat. 3 : 4. raiment of c. hair, Mk. 1 : 6.

CAMEST.

Ge. 16 : 8. Hagar, Whence c. thou?
24 : 5. bring again to land whence c.
27 : 33. I have eat. of all bef. thou c.
Ex. 23 : 15. in it c. out fr. E., 34 : 18.
Nu. 22 : 37. whf. c. th. not unto me?
De. 2 : 37. to land of Ammon c. not
16 : 3. rem. day thou c. in haste
6. season thou c. out of Egypt
1 S. 13 : 11. c. not within days ap.
17 : 28. Why c. thou down hither?
2 S. 11 : 10. c. thou not fr. journey?
15 : 20. thou c. but yesterday [17.
1 K. 13 : 9. not return way thou c.,
14. art man of God c. fr. Judah?
22. c. back and hast eaten
2 K. 19 : 28. I will turn thee back by
way thou c., Is. 37 : 29.
Ne. 9 : 13. c. down upon mount Sinai
Is. 64 : 3. c. down, mts. flowed
Je. 1 : 5. bef. c. forth, I sanct. thee
Eze. 32 : 2. c. forth with thy rivers
Mat. 22 : 12. Friend, how c. in hith.
Jn. 6 : 25. Rabbi, when c. hither?
16 : 30. we believe thou c. fr. God
Ac. 9 : 17. Jesus app. in way, as th. c.

CA'MON.

Ju. 10 : 5. Jair was buried in C.

CAMP. [Noun.]

Ex. 14 : 19. angel of L. went bef. c.
16 : 13. at even quails covered c.
32 : 17. there is noise of war in c.
19. as he came nigh the c.
27. go thro. c. slay every man bro.
36 : 6. caused it proclaimed thro. c.
Le. 17 : 3. man killeth goat in c.?
24 : 10. they strove together in c.
Nu. 1 : 52. sh. pitch ev. one by own c.
2 : 3. on east-side c. of Jud. pitch
4 : 5. when c. setteth forward
15. as c. is to set forward, after
11 : 1. consu. in utmost parts of c.
26. Eldad and Medad proph. in c.
De. 23 : 10. shall not come witho. c.
14. Lord walked in midst of thy c.
Jos. 6 : 18. make c. of Isr. a curse
Ju. 7 : 17. I come to outside of c.
13 : 25. Sp. of G. to move him in c.
21 : 8. came none to c. fr. Jabesh
12. virgins, th. brought to the c.
1 S. 4 : 6. meaneth gr. shout in c.
13 : † 23. c. of the Philis. went
17 : 17. run to the c. to thy breth.
1 K. 16 : 16. made Omri king in c.
2 K. 6 : 8. in such a place be my c.
7 : 7. they left c. as it was, fled
8. when these lepers came to c.
2 K. 19 : 35. smote in c. of Assyrians 185,000, 2 Ch. 32 : 21. Is. 37 : 36.
2 Ch. 22 : 1. came with Arabi. to c.
Ps. 78 : 28. let it fall in midst of c.
106 : 16. they envied Moses in c.
Eze. 4 : 2. lay siege, set c. against it
Jo. 2 : 11. for his c. is very great
Re. 20 : 9. compassed c. of saints

Into the CAMP.

Le. 14 : 8. sh. come i. c., 16 : 26, 28.
Nu. 11 : 30. Mos. gat him i. c. [i. c.
De. 23 : 11. sun down, he sh. come
1 S. 4 : 7. Philis. said, G. is come i. c.

Out of the CAMP.
Ex. 19 : 17. Moses bro-t peo. o.o.c.
Le. 10 : 4. carry your breth. o.o.c.
5. carried in coats o. o. c.
14 : 3. priest shall go forth o.o.c.
17 : 3. wh. man kill. goat o. o. c.
24:23. bring him had ours. o.o.c.
Nu. 5:2. com. put ev. leper o.o.c.
12 : 14. let Miriam be shut o.o.c.
14 : 44. Moses departed not o.o.c.
De. 23 : 10. uncl. person sh. go o.o.
1 S. 13 :17. spoilers came o.o.c. [c.
2 S. 1 : 2. man o. o. c. from Saul
3. o. o. c. of Israel am I escaped

Round about the CAMP.
Nu. 11 : 31. spread them r.a.c.,32.
Ju. 7 : 21. ev. man in pl. r. a. c.

Without the CAMP.
Ex. 29 : 14. bullock shalt burn w.
c., Le. 8 : 17.-9 : 11.-16 : 27.
33 : 7. sought Lord, went w. c.
Le. 4 : 21. carry bullock w. c., 12.
6 : 11. shall carry ashes w. c.
13 : 46. hath plague dwell w. c.
Nu. 5 : 3. ev. leper be put w. c.
15 : 35. gath. of sticks stoned w.c.
19 : 3. red heifer w. c. slay her
31 : 19. abide w. c. seven days
De. 23 : 12. shalt have place w. c.
Jos. 6 : 23. Rahab left kindr. w. c.
He. 13 : 11. beasts are burnt w. c.
13. Let us go forth to him w. c.

CAMPS.
Ge. 32 : † 2. he called place two c.
Nu. 5 : 3. that they defile not c.
10 : 2. for journeying of c.
Am. 4 : 10. stink of your c. come

CAMP, ED.
Ex. 19 : 2. Isr. c-d before mount
Is. 29 : 3. I will c. against thee
Je. 50 : 29. that bend bow c. ag. it
Na. 3 : 17. c. in hedges in cold

CAMPHIRE.
Can. 1 : 14. My beloved is as c.
4 : 13. thy plants an orchard of c.

CAN.
Ge. 41 : 38. c. we find such a one
De. 31 : 2. I c. no more go out
2 S. 12 : 23. c. I bring him back
19 : 35. c. I discern, c. I hear
Jb. 6 : 6. c. that unsav. be eaten?
8 : 11. c. rush grow? c. flag?
22 : 2. c. man be profita. to God?
13. c. he judge thro. dark cloud?
36 : 29. c. any underst. the clouds?
Ps. 78 : 19. c. God furnish a table?
20. c. he give bread? c. he flesh?
89 : 6. wh. c. be comp.? lik. to L.?
Pr. 6 : 27. c. a man take fire in
28. c. one go on hot coals and
Is. 46 : 7. cry, yet c. he not answ.
49:15. c. woman forget her suck.
Je. 2 : 32. c. maid forget her orna.
23 : 24. c. any hide in secret pla.
Am. 3 : 3. c. two walk togeth. exc.
5. c. a bird fall in snare where
8. who c. but prophesy?
Mat. 19 : 25. who c. be saved? Mk.
10 : 26. Lu. 18 : 26.
27 : 65. make it sure as you c.
Mk. 2 : 19. c. chil. of bride-cham.
9:29. kind c. come forth but [fast?
39. they said unto him, We c.
10 : 38. c. ye drink of cup that I
Lu. 6 : 39. c. the blind lead blind?
Jn. 1 : 46. c. good c. of Nazareth?
6 : 60. hard saying, who c. hear it?
10 : 21, c. a devil open eyes
15 : 4. no more c. ye, except ye
Ac. 10 : 47. c. any forbid water
Ro. 8 : 7. subject to law, nor c. be
He. 5 : 2. c. have compas. on igno.
Ja. 2 : 14. c. faith save him?
3 : 12. c. fig-tree bear oliv.-berries?

How CAN.
De. 1 : 12. h. c. I bear your cumbr.?
1 S. 16 : 2. h. c. I go, if Saul hear
Es. 8 : 6. h. c. I endure to see evil
Jb. 25 : 4. h. c. man be justified
Pr. 20 : 24. h. c. a man understand
his way?
Ec. 4 : 11. h. c. one be warm alone?
Je. 47 : 7. h. c. it be quiet
Mat. 12 : 34. h. c. ye being evil?
Mk. 3 : 23. h. c. Satan cast out Sat.
Jn. 3 : 4. h. c. man be born
9. Nico. said, h. c. th things be?
5 : 44. h. c. ye believe which rec.
6:52. h. c. this man give his flesh
14:5. Lord, h. c. we know the way?
Ac. 8 : 31. h. c. I exc. man guide
1 Jn. 4 : 20. h. c. he love G. wh. he
See BE, DO, COME, ENTER.

CA'NA.
Jn. 2 : 1. was a marriage in C.
11. beginning of miracles in C.
4 : 46. Jesus came again into C.
21 : 2. Thomas and Nath. of C.

CA'NAAN. [Person.]
Ge. 9 : 18. Ham is father of C., 22.
25. Cursed be C. | 26. C. be serv., 27.
10 : 15. C. begat Sidon, 1 Ch. 1:13.
Ge. 28 : 1. not wife of dau. of C., 6.

CA'NAAN. [Place.]
Ex. 15 : 15. inhab. of C. shall melt
Ju. 3 : 1. not known all wars of C.
4 : 2. L. sold them to Jabin of C.
23. G. subdued Jabin k. of C., 24.
5 : 19. fought kings of C. in Taan.
Ps. 106 : 38. they sacr. to idols of C.
135 : 11. smote all kingdoms of C.
Is. 19:18. cities in E. speak lang. of C.
Zph. 2 : 5. O C. I will destroy thee
Mat. 15 : 22. wom. of C. cried to J.

Land of CA'NAAN.
Ge. 12 : 5. forth to go into l. o. C.
16 : 3. Ab. dwelt ten y. in l. o. C.
17 : 8. I will give thee l. o. C., Le.
25 : 38. Nu. 34 : 2. De. 32 : 49.
1 Ch. 16 : 18. Ps. 105 : 11.
37 : 1. Jacob dwelt in l. o. C.
42 : 5. the famine was in l. o. C.
7. whence they said, From l.o.C.
13. We are s. of one man in l.o.C.
45 : 17. go, get ye up unto l. o. C.
50 : 13. carried him into l. o. C.
Le. 14 : 34. When ye be come into l.
o.C., Nu. 34 : 2. [C.
18 : 3. do not after doings of l. o.
Nu. 13:17. Moses sent to spy l.o.C.
32 : 32. pass over armed into l.o.C.
Jos. 5 : 12. did eat fruit of l. o. C.
22 : 11. built altar over ag. l. o. C.
24 : 3. I led him thro. all l.o. C.
Eze. 16 : 3. thy nativity of l. o. C.
Ac. 7 : 11. dearth over all l. o. Ch.
13 : 19. destr. 7 nations in l.o.Ch.

CA'NAANITE, S.
Ge. 10 : 18. families of C. spread
12 : 6. C. was in land, 13, 7.
15 : 21. Amorites, C. Girgashites,
Ex. 3 : 8, 17.-23 : 23. De. 7 : 1.-
20 : 17. Jos. 3 : 10.-12 : 8. Ju.
3 : 5. Ne. 9 : 8.
24 : 3. shall not take a wife of C.
34 : 30. make me stink amongst C.
38 : 2. Jud. saw dau. of certain C.
Ex. 23 : 28. I will drive out the C.,
33 : 2.-34 : 11.
Nu. 13 : 29. C. dwell by the sea
21 : 3. Lord deliv. up C., Ne. 9:24.
Jos. 17 : 12. C. would dwell in land,
Ju. 1 : 27. [chariots
18. drive out C. tho. have iron
Ju. 1:1. Who go up against C. first?
9. Jud. went to fight ag. C., 10.
29. Neither did Ephr. drive out C.
30. C. dwelt among them, 28, 29.
Jos. 16 : 10.
33. Naphtali dwelt among C.
1 K. 9 : 16. Phar. had slain C. in
Ezr. 9 : 1. doing acc. to abom. of C.
Ob. 20. shall possess that of C.
Zch. 14 : 21. no more C. in h. of L.
Mat. 10 : 4. Simon the C., Mk. 3:18.

CANAANI'TESS.
1 Ch. 2 : 3. born to Jud. of Shua C.

CANAANI'TISH.
Ge. 46:10. Shaul son of C., Ex.6:15.

CAN'DACE.
Ac. 8 : 27. a eunuch under C.

CANDLE, S.
Jb. 18 : 6. his c. shall be put out
21 : 17. is c. of wicked put out?
29 : 3. his c. shined upon my head
Ps. 18 : 28. for thou wilt light my c.
Pr. 20 : 27. spirit of man is c. of L.
24 : 20. c. of wicked be put out
31 : 18. her c. goeth not out by
Je. 25 : 10. fr. them light of the c.
Zph. 1:12. will search Jerus. with c-s
Mat. 5 : 15. Nor do men light a c.
Mk. 4 : 21. Lu. 8 : 16.-11 : 33.
Lu. 11 : 36. shining of c. giveth light
15 : 8. doth not she light a c. and
Re. 18 : 23. c. shine no more in thee
22 : 5. they need no c. nor sun

CANDLESTICK.
Ex. 25 : 31. make c., 37 : 17. Nu. 8:4.
32. branches of c. out of side, 37 : 18.
33. six branches out of c., 37 : 19.
34. in c. four bowls, 37 : 20.
26 : 35. shalt set c. over ag. table
31 : 8. pure c., 39:37 | 40:4. bring c.
40 : 24. put c. in tent of cong.
Le. 24 : 4. shall order lamps upon c.
Nu. 3 : 31. their charge shall be c.
4 : 9. shall take cloth and cover c.
8 : 2. lamps give light over ag. c., 3.
4. c. beaten gold, he made c.
1 K. 7 : 49. c-s of gold, 2 Ch. 4:7. [c.
2 K. 4:10. let us set for him a bed, a
1 Ch. 28 : 15. Even weight for c-s
of gold, by weight for every c.
2 Ch. 4 : 7. made ten c. of gold
20. the c-s with their lamps
13 : 11. set they in order c.
Je. 52 : 19. he took away c-s, spoons
Da. 5 : 5. wrote over ag. c. on plaster
Zch. 4 : 2. behold a c. all of gold
11. two olive-trees upon side of c.
Mat. 5 : 15. but on a c. and it giveth light. Lu. 8 : 16.-11 : 33.
Mk. 4 : 21. candle not to be set on c.
He. 9 : 2. first, wherein was c.
Re. 2 : 5. else I will remove thy c.
11 : 4. two c-s standing before G.
See SEVEN.

CANDY.
Ac. 27 : † 7. wind not suff-g we sailed

CANE. [under C.
Is. 43:24. hast bought me no sweet c.
Je. 6 : 20. sweet c. from far country

CANKER. [Noun.]
2 Ti. 2 : 17. their word will eat as c.

CANKERED.
Ja. 5 : 3. Your gold and silver is c.

CANKER-WORM.
Jo. 1 : 4. c. eaten, wh. c. left, 2 : 25.
Na. 3 : 15. eat thee like c. make as c.
16. c. spoileth, and flieth away

CAN'NEH.
Eze. 27 : 23. Haran and C. thy merch.

CANNOT.
Is. 1 : 13. assemblies I c. away
29 : 11. saith, I c. for it is sealed
Je. 5 : 22. waves c. prevail, c. pass
18 : 6. c. I do with you as potter?
Da. 2 : 27. c. astrologers
Mat. 16 : 3. c. ye discern the signs
21 : 27. We c. tell, Mk. 11 : 33. Lu.
20 : 7. Jn. 3 : 8.-16 : 18.
Lu. 18 : 33. c. be that proph. perish
16 : 26. pass from hence to you c.
1 Co. 11 : † 20. ye c. eat L.'s supper
2 Co. 12 : 2. in body I c. tell, 3.
He. 9 : 5. of wh. we c. now speak
See BE, CEASE, COME, STAND.

CANST.
Ex. 33 : 20. c. not see my face and
De. 28 : 27. itch, thou c. be healed

Jb. 33:5. if c.ans. me, set thy words
Je. 47 : † 7. how c. thou be quiet
Mat.8:2.L. if wilt, thou c. make me
clean, Mk. 1: 40. Lu. 5 : 12.
Mk. 9 : 22. if thou c. do any thing
Ac. 21:37. capt. said, c.speak Greek

CAPER'NAUM.

Mat. 4 : 13. Jesus dwelt in C.
8 : 5. when Jes. was entered into C.
11: 23. thou C. exalted, Lu. 10:15.
17 : 24. when they were come to C.
Mk. 1: 21. they went into C., 2 : 1.
9 : 33. be came to C., Lu. 4 : 31.
Lu. 4 : 23. we have heard done in C.
Jn. 2 : 12. they continued not in C.
4 : 46. nobleman wh. son sick at C.
6 : 17. disci. went over sea tow. C.
24. people came to C. seeking Jes.
59. these said as he taught in C.

CAPH'TOR.

Je. 47 : 4. spoil country of C.
Am. 9:7. Philis. from C. | De.2 : 23.

CAPPADO'CIA.

Ac. 2 : 9. dwellers in C. we hear
1 Pe. 1 : 1. scattered thro. C., Asia

CAPH'TORIM, S.

Ge. 10 : 14. De. 2 : 23. 1 Ch. 1: 12.

CAPH'THORIM. See above.

CAPTAIN.

Ge. 37:36. sold him to Potiphar,c.of
40 : 4. c.charged Joseph with them
Nu. 2 : 3. Nahshon, c. of Israel
5. Nethaneel, c. of chil. of Issa.
14 : 4. let us make a c., Ne. 9 : 17.
Jos. 5 : 14. as c. of host of the L.
15. c. of Lord's host said to Josh.
Ju. 4 : 2. c. was Sisera, 7. 1 S. 12: 9.
11 : 6. said to Jephthah, be our c.
11. peo. made him c. over them
1 S. 9 : 16. shalt anoint him c.,10: 1.
13 : 14.L.commanded him to be c.
17:18. carry these ten cheeses to c.
18 : 13. made c. over a thousand
22 : 2. Da. became a c. over them
2 S. 5:2. Thou shalt be a c.over Isr.
8. he shall be c., 1 Ch. 11 : 6.
10:18.smote Shobach c.,1Ch.19:18.
19 : 13. if thou be not c. of host
23 : 19. Abishai was theref. their c.
1 K. 16 : 16. Isr.made Omri, c. king
2 K. 1 : 9. king sent c. with 50
11. he sent to him another c., 13.
4 : 13. wouldest be spoken for to c.
5 : 1. Naaman, c. of host of Syria
9 : 5.I have an errand.to thee, O c.
15:25.Pekah, a c. of his, conspired
18 : 24. turn face of one c., Is.36:9.
20 : 5. tell Hezekiah c. of my peo.
25 : 8. Nebuzar-adan, c., Je.52:12.
12. c. of guard left, Je. 39 : 10.
15. c. of guard took, Je. 52 : 19.
† 19. took scribe of c., Je.52 : † 25.
1 Ch.11 : 21.honourable, he their c.
19:18.Shophach c.of host,2 S.10:18
27:5.third c. Benaiah | 7.fourth c.
8. fifth c. | 9. sixth c.
10. seventh c. | 11. eighth c.
12. ninth c. | 13. tenth c.
14. eleventh c. | 15. twelfth c.
2 Ch. 13 : 12. God himself is our c.
Ne. 9 : 17. appointed c. to return
Is. 3 : 3. L. doth take away c. of 50
Je. 37 : 13. a c., Irijah, took Jere.
40 : 2. c. of guard took Jeremiah
5. c. gave Jere. victuals and a
51 : 27. appoint a c. against her
Hag.1 : † 1.word to Zerub. c. of Jud.
Jn. 18 : 12. band and c. took Jesus
Ac. 4 : 1. c. of temple, 5 : 24.
5 : 26. then c. with officers bro-t
28 : 16. delivered prisoners to c.
He. 2 : 10. c. of their salva. perfect

Chief CAPTAIN, S.

2 S. 23 : 8.that sat c. among the c-s
1 Ch. 12 : 18. Amasai c. of c-s said
27:3.c.of c-s of host for first month
2 Ch. 8:9. c. of c-s and c.of chariots
Lu. 22 : 52. to c. priests and c-s of
Ac. 21 : 31. tidings came unto c. c.
32. saw c. c. and soldiers
33. c. c. came and took | 22 : 27.
37. said unto c. c. May I speak to
22 : 24. c. c. com-d him to be bro-t
26. centur. told c. c. Take heed
28. c.c. ans. With a great sum
29. c.c. afraid after he knew
23 : 10. c.c. lest Paul be torn
15. signify to c. c. that he br. him
17. Bring y-g man unto c.c. | 18.
19. c. c. took him by hand | 22.
24 : 7. c.c. Lysias came upon | 22.
25 : 23. with c.c. and princ. men
Re. 6 : 15. rich men and c. c-s hid

CAPTAINS.

Ex. 14 : 7. c. over ev. one of them
15 : 4. his chosen c. are drowned
Nu. 31 : 14.Moses was wroth with c.
De. 1 : 15. I made wise men c.
20 : 9. sh. make c. to lead people
29 : 10. your c. of tribes, your
Jos. 10 : 24. said to c. of men of war
1 S. 8 : 12. he will appoint him c.
22 : 7. son of Jesse make you all c.
2 S. 18 : 5. gave c. charge conc. Abs.
† 13. three c. came to cave of
1 K. 2 : 5. kno. what Joab did to c.
9 : 22. they were his princes, c.
15 : 20. sent c. of hosts which
20 : 24. take kings away, and put c.
22 : 33. when c. perceived he was
not the king, 2 Ch. 18 : 32.
2 K. 1 : 14. burnt two c. of fifties
9 : 5. c. of host were sitting
11 : 15. Jehoiada commanded c.
1 Ch. 4:42. c. Pelatiah and Neariah
11 : 15. three of 30 c.went to David
12 : 34. of Naphtali a thousand c.
2 Ch. 21 : 9. Jehoram smote the c.
33 : 11. L. brought upon them c.
Ne. 2 : 9. king had sent c. with me
Jb. 39 : 25. the thunder of the c.
Je.13 : 21.hast taught them to be c.
51 : 23. will I break in pieces c.
57. I will make drunk her c.
Eze. 21 : 22. c. to open the mouth
23 : 6. c. all desirable young men,
Da. 3 : 27. c.saw these men [12, 23.
6 : 7. c. consulted to estab. statute
Na. 3 : 17. thy c. as great grasshop.
Mk. 6 : 21. Herod made supper to c.
Lu. 22 : 4. Judas communed with c.
Re. 19 : 18. may eat the flesh of c.

CAPTIVE.

Ge. 14 : 14. heard his bro. was tak.c.
34 : 29. their wives took they c.
Ex. 12 : 29.unto the first-born of c.
De. 21 : 10. thou hast taken them c.
2 K. 5 : 2. brought c. little maid
6 : 22. smite those taken c.
Is. 49 : 21. I am desolate, a c.
24. shall lawful c. be delivered ?
51 : 14. c. exile hasten it that he
52 : 2. loose thyself, O c. dau. of Z.
Am. 6 : 7. go c. with first that go c.
2 Ti. 2 : 26.taken c. by him at will

Carry, led CAPTIVE.

Ge. 31 : 26. c. away my dau-s as c.
Nu. 24 : 22. until Ashur c. thee c.
1 K. 8 : 46. c. them c., 2 Ch. 6 : 36.
47. if they bethink thems. in land
whither c-d c., 2 Ch. 6 : 37.
50. before them wh. c-d them c.
2K.15:29.Tiglath-pileser c-d them c.
16 : 9. he c-d peo. of Damascus c.
1 Ch.5: 6.whom k.of Assyria c-d c.
2 Ch. 25 : 12. 10,000 Judah c-d c.
28 : 5 they c-d great multitude c.
8. Israel c-d c. of breth. 200,000
17. smitten Jud. and c-d away c.
Ps.106:46.pitied of those c-d them c.
137 : 3.that c-d us c. required song
Je. 13 : 17. bec. Lord's flock is c-d c.
19. Judah shall be wholly c-d c.
20 : 4. he sh.c. them c.to Babylon
Je.24:1.c-d away c. Jeconiah, 27:20.
5. I will acknowl. them c-d c.
29 : 1. elders wh. were c-d away c.
4. saith L. to all that are c-d c.
7. caused you to be c-d away c.
14. whence I caused you c-d c.
39 : 9. c-d away c. into Bab.
40 : 1.Judah wh.were c-d c.,52:27.
7. them that were not c-d c. to
41 : 10. Ishmael c-d c. all residue
43 : 3. c. us away c. into Bab.
12. shall c. the Egyptians c.
52 : 15. c-d away c. certain of
28. peo. whom Neb. c-d away c.
29. Neb. c-d c. 832 persons
30. c-d c. of Jews 745 persons
La. 4 : † 22. will c. thee c. for sins
Eze.6:9. whither they shall be c-d c.
Da. 11 : 8. and shall c. c. into E.
Am. 1 : 6.bec. they c-d c. captivity
Ob.11. day strangers c-d c.his forces

Carrying CAPTIVE.

Je. 1 : 3. to the c. away of Jerus.c.

Lead or led CAPTIVE.

Ju. 5 : 12. l. thy captivity c. thou
1 K. 8 : 48. in land of enemies who
l. them c. [l. c.
2 Ch. 30 : 9. compas. bef. them that
Ps. 68 : 18. l. captivity c., Ep. 4 : 8.
Je. 22 : 12. die whither l. him c.
Am. 7 : 11. Israel shall be l. c. out
Na. 2 : 7. Huzzab shall be l. c. her
maids shall l. her [tions
Lu. 21 : 24. shall be l. c. into all na-
2 Ti. 3 : 6. l. c. silly women laden

CAPTIVES.

Nu. 31 : 9. took wom. of Midian c.
12. brought the c. | 19.purify c.
De. 21:11. am.c. a beautiful woman
32:42. arrows dru. with blood of c.
1 S. 30 : 2. had taken women c.
5. David's two wives c.
2 K. 24 : 14. from Jerus. 10,000 c.
2 Ch. 28 : 11. and deliver c. again
13.Ye shall not bring in c. hither
14. armed men left c. and
Is. 14 : 2. sh. take them c. whose c.
20 : 4. lead away Ethiopians c.
45 : 13. let go my c. not for price
49 : 25. c. of mighty shall be taken
61 : 1. liberty to the c., Lu. 4 : 18.
Je.28:4.c. of Jud.th.went into Bab.
48:46.sons and dau-s c.
50 : 33.that took c. held them fast
Eze. 1 : 1. as I was am. c. by Chebar
16 : 53. bring again captiv. of c.
Da. 2 : 25. found a man of c. of Ju.

CAPTIVITY.

Nu. 21 : 29. given his dau-s into c.
De. 21 : 13. put raiment of c. fr. her
30 : 3. Lord will turn thy c.
Ju. 5 : 12. lead c. cap. son of Abin.
18 : 30. until day of c. of land
2 K. 24 : 15. carried into c. to Bab
25 : 27. in 37th year of c., Je.52:31
1 Ch. 5 : 22. their steads until c.
6 : 15. Jehozadak went into c.
2 Ch. 6 : 37. if they pray in c.
38. if they return to thee in c.
29 : 9. sons and our wives are in c.
Ezr.1 : 11.them of c. that were bro-t
9 : 7. have been delivered to c.
Ne. 1 : 2. Jews left of the c.
4 : 4. give them for a prey in c.
Es. 2 : 6. Mord. carried with c.
Jb. 42 : 10. Lord turned c. of Job
Ps. 14 : 7. L. bringeth back c., 85:1.
68 : 18. led c. captive, Ep. 4 : 8.
78 : 61. deliv. his strength into c.
85 : 1. hast brought back c. of Jac.
126 : 1. L. turned again c. of Z.
4. Turn again our c. O Lord, as
Is. 5 : 13. my peo. are gone into c.
20: † 4. Assyria sh. lead c. of Egypt
22 : 17. carry thee with mighty c.
46 : 2. themsel. are gone into c.
49 : † 25. c. of mighty be taken

Je. 15 : 2. for c. to the c., 43 : 11.
24 : † 5. so will I acknowl. the c.
29 : 14. I will turn your c., 30 : 3.
-32 : 44.-33 : 7, 11, 26. [c.
16. breth. not gone with you into
29 : 20. hear word of L., all ye of c.
22. a curse by all c. of Judah
28. saying, this c. is long
31. Send to all them of the c.
30 : 10. thy seed from c., 46 : 27.
32 : 44. c. to return, 33 : 7, 11, 26.
48 : 11. Moab at ease, nor into c.
† 46. O Moab, thy sons are into c.
La. 1 : 3. Judah is gone into c.
5. her children are gone into c.
18. and young men gone into c.
2 : 14. not discov., to turn thy c.
4 : 22. no more carry into c.
Eze. 1 : 2. of Jehoiachin's c.
3 : 11. get to them of c. speak
15. came to them of c., 11 : 24.
11 : 25. I spake to them of the c.
12 : 7. my stuff, as stuff for c.
16 : 53. bring their c., c. of Sodom, c. of Samaria, c. of thy captives
25 : 3. into c. thou saidst, Aha
33 : 21. year of c. one escaped
39 : 23. of Israel went into c.
28. led into c. among heathen
40 : 1. in 5 and 20th year of our c.
Da. 6 : 13. Daniel of c. of Judah
11 : 33. shall fall by c. and by spoil
Hos. 6 : 11. returned c. of my peo.
Am. 1 : 6. carried captive whole c.
9. they deliv. whole c. to Edom
4 : † 10. with c. of your horses
Ob. 20. c. of host, c. of Jerusalem
Mi. 1 : 16. gone into c. from thee
Na. 3 : 10. No went into c.
Ha. 1 : † 7. proceed c. of these
9. shall gather the c. as sand
Zph. 2 : 7. Lord sh. turn c., 3 : 20.
Zch. 6 : 10. Take of them of the c.
Ro. 7 : 23. into c. to law of sin
2 Co. 10 : 5. into c. every thought
See CAPTIVE

Bring CAPTIVITY.

Ezr. 1 : 11. b. up with them of c.
Ps. 53 : 6. when G. b. back c. of peo.
Je. 30 : 18. b. c. of Jacob's tents
3. I will b. again c. of people
31 : 23. shall b. again their c.
48 : 47. will b. again c. of Moab
49 : 6. b. again c. of Ammon
39. I will b. again c. of Elam
Eze. 16 : 53. b. again c. | c. of thy cap.
29 : 14. b. again c. of Egypt
39 : 25. will I b. again c. of Jacob
Jo. 3 : 1. when I b. c. of Judah
Am. 9 : 14. b. again c. of my peo.

Children of CAPTIVITY.

Ezr. 4 : 1. c. o. c. builded temple
6 : 16. rest of c. o. c. kept dedica.
19. c. o. c. kept passover on 14th
20. killed passover for c. o. c.
10 : 7. proclamation to c. o. c.
16. c. o. c. did so, and were separa.
Da. 5 : 13. Dan. of c. o. c. of Judah

Go into CAPTIVITY.

De. 28 : 41. sons and dau-s g. i. c.
Je. 20 : 6. thou and ho. shall g. i. c.
22 : 22. thy lovers shall g. i. c.
30 : 16. adversaries shall g. i. c.
46 : 19. O dau., furnish to g. i. c.
48 : 7. Chemosh g. i. c.
49 : 3. their king shall g. i. c.
Eze. 12 : 4. go, as they that g. i. c.
30 : 17. these cities shall g. i. c.
18. Egypt, her dau-s shall g. i. c.
Am. 1 : 5. people of Syria shall g. i. c.
15. their king shall g. i. c.
5 : 5. Gilgal shall surely g. i. c.
27. will I cause you to g. i. c.
7 : 17. Israel shall surely g. i. c.
9 : 4. tho. they g. i. c. bef. enem.
Zch. 14 : 2. half of city shall g. i. c.
Re. 13 : 10. leadeth into c. sh. g. i. c.

Out of CAPTIVITY.

Ezr. 2 : 1. went up o. o. c., Ne. 7 : 6.
3 : 8. come up o. o. c., Ne. 8 : 17.
6 : 21. Isr. o. o. c. kept feast with joy
8 : 35. come o. o. c. offered to God

CARBUNCLE, S.

Ex. 28 : 17. first row a c., 39 : 10.
Is. 54 : 12. make thy gates of c-s
Eze. 28 : 13. and c. thy covering

CAR'CAS.

Es. 1 : 10. of 7 chamberlains, C.

CARCASS.

Le. 5 : 2. touch c. of unclean thing
7 : † 24. fat of c. may be used
11 : 8. c. not touch, De. 14 : 8.
24. whoso. toucheth c., 27, 36, 39.
25. whoso. beareth aught of c., 28, 40. [37, 38.
35. whereupon any of c. falleth,
40. he that eateth of c.
17 : † 15. that eateth a c. sh. wash
De. 28 : 26. thy c. shall be meat
Jos. 8 : 29. take his c. down
Ju. 14 : 8. c. of lion, honey in c.
1 K. 13 : 22. c. not come to sepul.
24. c. in way, lion by c., 25, 28.
29. proph. took c. of man of G.
30. laid c. in his own grave
2 K. 9 : 37. c. of Jezebel as dung
Is. 14 : 19. cast out as c. trodden
Mat. 24 : 28. c. is, there eagles be

CARCASSES.

Ge. 15 : 11. fowls came on c.
Le. 11 : 11. their c. in abomina., 26.
26. c. of ev. beast divideth hoof
26 : 30. your c. upon c. of idols
Nu. 14 : 29. c. shall fall in wilder.
1 S. 17 : 46. give c. of the Philis.
Is. 5 : 25. c. were torn in streets
34 : 3. stink shall come out of c.
66 : 24. look upon c. of the men
Je. 7 : 33. c. of this peo. sh. be meat for fowls, 16 : 4.-19 : 7.
9 : 22. c. of men shall fall as dung
16 : 18. they filled mine inh. with c.
Eze. 6 : 5. lay c. of Israel bef. idols
43 : 7. defile by c. of their kings
9. put c. of th. kings far fr. me
Na. 3 : 3. is a great number of c.
He. 3 : 17. whose c. fell in wilder.

CAR'CHEMISH.

2 Ch. 35 : 20. came to fight ag-st C.
Is. 10 : 9. is not Calno as C.?
Je. 46 : 2. river Euphrates in C.

CARE, S.

1 S. 10 : 2. fath. hath left c. of asses
2 K. 4 : 13. careful with all this c.
Je. 49 : 31. nation without c.
Eze. 4 : 16. shall eat bread with c.
Mat. 13 : 22. c. of world chokes the
Mk. 4 : 19. c-s of world choke word
Lu. 8 : 14. they are choked with c-s
10 : 34. he took c. | 35. c. of him
21 : 34. be overcharged with c-s
1 Co. 9 : 9. Doth G. take c. for oxen?
12 : 25. same c. one for another
2 Co. 7 : 12. our c. for you might ap.
8 : 16. same earnest c. in Titus for
11 : 28. besides c. of all churches
1 Ti. 3 : 5. how take c. of ch. of G.
1 Pe. 5 : 7. Casting your c. upon [him

CARE, ED.

2 S. 18 : 3. if flee, not c. for us
Ps. 142 : 4. no man c-d for my soul
Lu. 10 : 40. not c. that sist. left me?
Jn. 12 : 6. not that he c-d for poor
Ac. 18 : 17. Gallio c-d for none of tho.
1 Co. 7 : 21. a servant, c. not for it
Ph. 2 : 20. who will c. for your state

CARE'AH. See KARE'AH.

CAREFUL.

2 K. 4 : 13. thou hast been c. for us
Je. 17 : 8. sh. not be c. in drought
Da. 3 : 16. O Nebu. not c. to ans. thee
Lu. 10 : 41. Martha, thou art c.
12 : † 29. live not in c. suspense
Ph. 4 : 6. c. for noth., but by prayer
Ph. 4 : 10. ye were c. but lacked
Ti. 3 : 8. be c. to maint. good works

CAREFULLY.

De. 15 : 5. if c. hearken unto Lord
2 Ch. 36 : † 15. sending messenger c.
Mi. 1 : 12. inhab. of Maroth waited c.
Ph. 2 : 28. I sent him the more c.
He. 12 : 17. sought it c. with tears

CAREFULNESS.

Eze. 12 : 18. drink thy water with c.
19. They shall eat bread with c.
1 Co. 7 : 32. have you without c.
2 Co. 7 : 11. what c. it wro-t in you

CARELESS.

Ju. 18 : 7. saw how they dwelt c.
Is. 32 : 9. hear my voice, ye c. dau.
10. ye c. women | 11. ye c. ones
Eze. 30 : 9. c. Ethiopians afraid

CARELESSLY.

Is. 47 : 8. hear that dwellest c.
Eze. 39 : 6. fire am. them that dwell c.
Zph. 2 : 15. rejoicing city dwelt c.

CAREST, ETH, ING.

De. 11 : 12. land L. thy God c-h for
1 S. 9 : 5. fa. leave c-g for the asses
Mat. 22 : 16. nor c-t thou for any
Mk. 4 : 38. c. thou not th. we perish?
12 : 14. true, and c-t for no man
Jn. 10 : 13. hireling c-h not for sheep
1 Co. 7 : 32. unmarried c-h for, 34.
33. married, c-h for world, 34.
1 Pe. 5 : 7. care upon him, for he c.

CAR'MEL. [Judah

Jos. 15 : 55. C. and Ziph inherit. of
1 S. 15 : 12. Saul came to C.
25 : 2. Nabal's possessions in C.
7. nothing missing while in C.
40. David's serv-ts to Abigail to C.
1 K. 18 : 19. gath. all Isr. to mt. C.
42. Elijah went up to top of C.
2 K. 2 : 25. Elisha went to mount C.
4 : 25. wom. of Shunem to mt. C.
19 : 23. forest of his C., Is. 37 : 24.
2 Ch. 26 : 10. had vine-dressers in C.
Can. 7 : 5. thine head is like C.
Is. 33 : 9. C. shake off fruits
35 : 2. excellency of C. and Sharon
Je. 46 : 18. as C. by sea, so shall he
Am. 1 : 2. the top of C. shall wither
9 : 3. though they hide in top of C.
Mi. 7 : 14. which dwell solitary in C.
See BASHAN.

CAR'MELITE.

1 S. 30 : 5. Abigail, wife of Nabal C.
2 S. 2 : 2.-3 : 3.
2 S. 23 : 35. Hezrai C., 1 Ch. 11 : 37.

CAR'MELITESS.

1 S. 27 : 3. Abigail the C., 1 Ch. 3 : 1.

CARMI.

Ge. 46 : 9. sons of Reuben, C.
Nu. 26 : 6. of C. family of Carmites
Jos. 7 : 1. son of C., 18. 1 Ch. 2 : 7.
1 Ch. 4 : 1. sons of Judah, C. | 5 : 3.

CAR'MITES. See CAR'MI.

CARNAL.

Ro. 7 : 14. but I am c. sold under
8 : 7. c. mind is enmity against God
15 : 27. minister in c. things
1 Co. 3 : 1. as unto c. even to babes
3. ye are yet c. | 4. ye not c.?
9 : 11. if we reap your c. things?
2 Co. 10 : 4. weapons of are not c.
He. 7 : 16. law of a c. command-t
9 : 10. which stood in c. ordinances

CARNALLY.

Le. 18 : 20. not lie c. with neighbor's wife.
19 : 20. lieth c. with a bond-maid
Nu. 5 : 13. a man lie with her c.
Ro. 8 : 6. to be c. minded is death

CARPENTER, S.

2 S. 5 : 11. sent c. to Dav., 1 Ch. 14 : 1
2 K. 12 : 11. th. laid it out to c., 22 : 6.
2 Ch. 24 : 12. they hired c., Ezr. 3 : 7.
Is. 41 : 7. c. encouraged goldsmith
44 : 13. c. stretcheth out his rule
Je. 24 : 1. c. he carried away, 29 : 2.

Zch. 1 : 20. Lord shewed me four c.
Mat. 13 : 55. is not this the c.'s son?
Mk. 6 : 3. Is not this the c., son of

CAR'PUS.

2 Ti. 4 : 13. cloak I left with C.

CARRIAGE, S.

Nu. 4 : † 24. c. of Gershonites
Ju. 18 : 21. Danites, and c. before
1 S. 17 : † 20. David came to pl. of c.
22. left c. with keeper of c.
Is. 10 : 28. hath laid up his c.
46 : 1. your c. were heavy laden
Ac. 21 : 15. took up c. went to Jer.

CARRIED.

Ge. 46 : 5. sons of Isr. c. Jac., 50 : 13.
Le. 10 : 5. c. them in their coasts
Jos. 4 : 8. they c. the stones over
Ju. 16 : 3. he c. them to top of
1 S. 5 : 8. let ark be c. unto Gath
9. that after they had c. it
2 S. 6 : 10. c. ark aside, 1 Ch. 13 : 13.
15 : 29. Abiathar c. ark of God to
1 K. 17 : 19. he c. him into a loft
21 : 13. c. Naboth forth and stoned
2 K. 7 : 8. c. thence silver and gold
9 : 28. c. him in a chariot, 23 : 30.
20 : 17. wh. fathers have laid up in store be c. to Bab., Is. 39 : 6.
23 : 4. c. the ashes to Beth-el
24 : 13. he c. out all the treasures
15. c. he into cap. from Jerus.
25 : 7. bound Zed. c. him to Bab.
13. c. brass to Bab., Je. 52 : 17.
1 Ch. 13 : 7. c. ark of G. in new cart
2 Ch. 24 : 11. c. chests to his place
28 : 15. c. the feeble upon asses
33 : 11. who c. Manasseh to Bab.
34 : 16. Shaphan c. book to king
36 : 4. Necho c. Jehoahaz to Egypt
Jb. 5 : 13. of froward is c. headlong
10 : 19. sho. have been c. fr. womb
Ps. 46 : 2. tho. mts. be c. into sea
Is. 46 : 3. remn. wh. are c. fr. womb
49 : 22. thy dau-s be c. on shoul.
53 : 4. he hath c. our sorrows
63 : 9. he c. them all days of old
Je. 27 : 22. be c. into Babylon, 28 : 3.-52 : 11, 17.
Eze. 17 : 4. he c. twigs into a land
37 : 1. c. me out in Spirit of Lord
Da. 1 : 2. which he c. into Shinar
Ho. 10 : 6. it shall be c. into Assyr.
12 : 1. make cov., oil is c. into E.
Jo. 3 : 5. ye have c. into your tem.
Mk. 15 : 1. bound Jesus and c. him
Lu. 7 : 12. was a dead man c. out
16 : 22. beggar was c. by angels
24 : 51. parted fr. them, and c. up
Ac. 3 : 2. one lame fr. womb was c.
5 : 6. young men c. Ananias out
7 : 16. our fa-s were c. into Sychem
8 : 2. c. Stephen to his burial
21 : 34. com. him to be c. into castle
Ep. 4 : 14. c. with ev. wind of doct
He. 13 : 19. be not c. with divers doctrines
2 Pe. 2 : 17. clouds c. with tempest
Jude 12. clouds c. of winds
See CAPTIVE.

CARRIED away.

Ge. 31 : 18. Jacob c.a. all his goods
26. hath c. a. my dau-s captives
1 S. 30 : 2. slew not, c. th. a., 18.
2 K. 17 : 6. c. Isr. a. into Assyr., 23.
11. heathen whom L. c. a. before
28. one of priests they had c. a.
33. nations they c. a. fr. thence
24 : 14. c. a. all Jerus. and princes
15. c. a. Jehoiachin to Babylon
25 : 21. Jud. was c. a. out of land
1 Ch. 5 : 26. Tilgath-pilneser c. a.
6 : 15. when L. c.a. Jud. and Jerus.
9 : 1. who were c. a. for transgr.
2 Ch. 12 : 9 Shishak c.a. shields of
14 : 13. peo. c.a. much spoil, 21 : 17.
15. they c. a. sheep and camels
16 : 6. c. a. stones of Ramah
2 Ch. 36 : 20. escaped fr. sword, c. he a.
Ezr. 2 : 1. these been c. a., Ne. 7 : 6.
5 : 12. c. people a. into Babylon
8 : 35. chil of those th. been c.a.
9 : 4. transgr. of those c.a., 10 : 6.
10 : 8. from cong. of those c. a.
Jb. 1 : 17. fell upon camels, c. th. a.
Je. 29 : 4. whom I caused to be c.a.
Da. 2 : 35. iron, gold, winds c. th. a.
Na. 3 : 10. No was c. a. into captiv.
Mat. 1 : 11. time were c. a. to Bab.
Mk. 15 : 1. c. Jesus a. to Pilate
1 Co. 12 : 2. Gent. c.a. to dumb idols
Ga. 2 : 13. Barnabas was c. a. with dissimulation [flood
Re. 12 : 15. cause her be c. a. of
17 : 3. he c. me a. in spirit, 21 : 10.

CARRIEST, ETH, YING.

Ge. 45 : † 23. ten asses c-g good thi.
1 S. 10 : 3. one c-g 3 kids, c. 3 loaves
Jb. 21 : 18. as chaff storm c-h away
27 : 21. east-wind c-h rich man aw.
Ps. 78 : 9. Ephr. c-g bows, turned
90 : 5. thou c-t them as with flood
Mat. 1 : 17. until c-g into Bab. (2)
Ac. 5 : 10. young men c-g bur. her
Re. 17 : 7. mystery of beast c-h her

CARRY.

Ge. 37 : 25. to c. spicery to Egypt
42 : 19. go ye, c. corn for the famine
43 : 11. c. the man a present
12. money, c. it again in your hand
44 : 1. fill sacks as they can c.
45 : 27. wagons sent to c. him, 46 : 5.
50 : 25. c. up my bones, Ex. 13 : 19.
Ex. 33 : 15. pres. go not. c. us not
Le. 10 : 4. c. brethren out of camp
Nu 11 : 12. c. them in thy bosom
De. 14 : 24. art not able to c. it
Jos. 4 : 3. c. twelve stones over
1 S. 17 : 18. c. these ten cheeses
20 : 40. said, Go, c. them to city
2 S. 19 : 18. ferry-boat to c. k.'s hou.
1 K. 18 : 12. Spirit of L. sh. c. thee
2 K. 4 : 19. c. him to his mother
9 : 2. c. Jehu to an inner chamber
17 : 27. c. thither one of priests
1 Ch. 10 : 9. to Philis. to c. tidings
15 : 2. none ought to c. ark but
23 : 26. Levites no more c. tabern.
2 Ch. 2 : 16. c. wood up to Jerus.
36 : 6. in fetters, to c. him to Bab.
Ezr 5 : 15. c. these vessels into temple
7 : 15. c. silver and gold freely off.
Ec. 10 : 20. a bird shall c. voice
Is. 23 : 7. own feet shall c. her afar
30 : 6. c. riches on young asses
40 : 11. c. the lambs in his bosom
46 : 4. even to hoar hairs will c. you
7. c. and set him in his place
Je. 20 : 5. will I c. them to Bab.
39 : 7. in chains to c. him to Bab.
14. Gedaliah c. Jere. home
Eze. 22 : 9. c. tales to shed blood
Mk. 6 : 55. to c. in beds the sick
11 : 16. to c. vessel through temple
Lu. 10 : 4. c. neither purse nor scrip
Jn. 5 : 10. not lawful to c. thy bed
21 : 18. c. thee whither thou wouldest [not

CARRY away.

2 K. 18 : 11. k. of Assyr. did c.a. Isr.
25 : 11. fugitives did Nebuzar. c.a.
2 Ch. 20 : 25. more than could c. a.
Jb. 15 : 12. Why heart c. thee a.
Ps. 49 : 17. dieth he sh. c. noth. a.
Ec. 5 : 15. nothing left he may c.a.
Is. 5 : 29. they sh. c. prey a. safe
15 : 7. have laid up, shall they c.a.
22 : 17. the Lord will c. thee a.
41 : 16. wind shall c. them a., 57 : 13.
La. 4 : 22. no more c. thee a. O Zion
Eze. 38 : 13. come to c. a. silver
Ac. 7 : 43. will c. you a. beyond Bab.
See CAPTIVE.

CARRY back.

2 S. 15 : 25. c.b. ark of G. into city
1 K. 22 : 26. c. Micaiah b., 2 Ch. 18 : 25.

CARRY forth.

Ex. 12 : 46. not c.f. aught of passo
14 : 11. dealt to c. us f. out of E.
Le. 4 : 21. he shall c.f. bullock, 12.
6 : 11. c. f. ashes, 14 : 45.-16 : 27.
2 Ch. 29 : 5. c.f. filthiness out of holy
Je. 17 : 22. Nor c.f. burden on sab.
Eze. 12 : 6. c. it f. in the twilight

CARRY out.

Ge. 47 : 30. thou shalt c. me o. of E.
De. 28 : 38. shall c. much seed o.
1 K. 21 : 10. then c. him o. and stone
22 : 34 c. me o. of host, 2 Ch. 18 : 33.
2 Ch. 29 : 16. c. it o. into Kidron
Eze. 12 : 5. dig thro. wall and c.o., 12.
Ac. 5 : 9. feet at door shall c. thee o.
1 Ti. 6 : 7. certain we can c. noth. o.

CARSHE'NA.

Es. 1 : 14. C. of 7 chamberlains

CART.

1 S. 6 : 7. make new c. tie kine to c.
8. ark of L. and lay upon c., 11.
10. kine and tied them to c.
14. c. came into field of Joshua
2 S. 6 : 3. they set ark upon new c.
1 Ch. 13 : 7. Uzza and Ahio drave c.
Is. 28 : 28. corn with wheel of c.
Am. 2 : 13. as c. is pressed th. is full

CART-ROPE.

Is. 5 : 18. that draw sin as with c.

CART-WHEEL. [min

Is. 28 : 27. nor is c. turned on cum-

CARVED, ING, INGS.

Ex. 31 : 5. Bezaleel in c., 35 : 33.
Ju. 18 : 18. man fetched the c. image
1 K. 6 : 18. cedar of house was c.
29. he c. all the walls of house
32. he c. c-s of cherubim
2 Ch. 33 : 7. set c. image in h. of God
22. Amon sacrifi. to c. images
34 : 3. Josi. purged Jud. fr. c. images
4. he cut down c. images
Ps. 74 : 6. they break the c. work
Pr. 7 : 16. decked my bed with c. [work

CASE, S.

Ex. 5 : 19. see they were in evil c.
De. 19 : 4. c. of slayer who shall flee
22 : 1. shalt in any c. bring them
24 : 13. in any c. shalt deliver pledge [such a c.
Ps. 144 : 15. Happy that people in
Je. 2 : † 25. saidst, Is the c. desperate
12 : † 1. let me reason the c. with thee [kingdom
Mat. 5 : 20. ye shall in no c. enter
19 : 10. if c. of man be so with wife
Jn. 5 : 6. been long time in that c.
1 Co. 7 : 15. under bondage in such [c-s

CASEMENT.

Pr. 7 : 6. I looked through my c.

CASIPH'IA.

Ezr. 8 : 17. at the place C.

CAS'LUHIM. [1 : 12.

Ge. 10 : 14. C. of whom Philis., 1 Ch.

CASSIA.

Ex. 30 : 24. take of c. 500 shekels
Ps. 45 : 8. all thy garments smell of c.
Eze. 27 : 19. c. in thy market

CAST. [Noun.]

Lu. 22 : 41. withdrawn about a stone's [c.

CAST. [Passive.]

Ex. 38 : 27. of the silver were c. sockets [rows
1 K. 7 : 24. Knobs were c. in two
13 : 24. carcass c. in way, 25, 28.
2 Ch. 4 : 3. Two rows oxen were c.
Jb. 18 : 8. c. into net by his own feet
Ps. 22 : 10. I was c. upon thee fr. womb
76 : 6. horse are c. into dead sleep
140 : 10. let them be c. into the fire
Pr. 16 : 33. the lot is c. into the lap
Is. 25 : 7. covering c. over all peo.
Je 22 : 28. c. into land they kn. not
38 : 11. took old c. clouts and rags
12. put old c. clouts under arm
Eze. 15 : 4. vine-tree is c. into fire
Da. 3 : 6. be c. into fiery furnace

Da. 3:21. these were c. into furnace
6:7. shall be c. into den of lions, 16.
Jon. 2: 4. I am c. out of thy sight
Mi. 4:7. her that was c.a strong na.
Mat. 3: 10. tree is hewn down, c. into fire, 7: 19. Lu. 3: 9.
4: 12. that John was c. into prison
5: 25. to judge, and be c. into pris.
13. good for noth. but to be c.
29. body be c. into hell, 30.
6: 30. is c. into the oven, Lu. 12:28.
13: 47. a net c. into the sea
21: 21. to mt. Be c. into sea
Mk. 9: 42. better he were c. into sea, Lu. 17: 2. [Mat. 18: 8, 9.
45. two eyes to be c. into hell, 47.
Lu. 23: 19. for murder c. in pris., 25.
Jn. 3: 24. John not yet c. into pris.
Ac. 16: 37. have c. us into prison
27: 26. must be c. on a certain isl-
Re. 8:7. fire were c. upon earth [and
8. mountain burning c. into sea
12: 13. dragon was c. unto the earth
19: 20. both c. alive into lake
20: 10. devil c. into lake of fire
14. death and hell c. into lake
15. not in book of life, c. into lake

CAST. [Active.]

Ge. 21: 15. Hagar c. child under
31: 38. she-goats not c. young
51. pillar c. betw. me and thee
37: 20. slay and c. him into pit
39: 7. wife c. her eyes upon Joseph
Ex. 1: 22. ev. son ye sh. c. into river
4: 3. said c. it he c. rod on ground
25. Zipporah c. foreskin at feet
7: 9. Take rod, c. it bef. Pharaoh
10: 19. locusts and c. into Red sea
15: 4. Pha. char he c. into sea
25. when he had c. tree into wat.
22: 31. flesh torn of beasts, c. to
23: 26. sh. noth. c. their young
25: 12. shall c. four rings of gold, 37: 3, 13.-38: 5.
32: 19. Moses c. tables out of hand
24. I c. into fire, came out calf
Le. 1: 16. c. it beside altar on east
14: 40. sh. c. them into uncl. place
Nu. 19: 6. priest c. cedar wood into
35: 22. if c. upon him anything
23. c. it upon him that he die
De. 9: 21. I c. dust into brook
28: 40. olive shall c. his fruit
29: 28. L. c. them into another land
Jos. 8: 29. c. king of Ai at gate
10: 27. c. them into cave wherein
Ju. 8: 25. c. ev. one ear-rings of
9: † 17. my father c. his life far
53. a woman c. a piece of millstone, 2 S. 11: 21.
1 S. 18: 11. Saul c. javelin, 20: 33.
2 S. 16: 6. Shimei c. stones at David
13. Shimei cursed, and c. dust
18: 17. they c. Abs. into a great pit
20: 12. man c. cloth upon Amasa
1 K. 7: 15. he c. two pillars of brass
7: 46. In plain c. them, 2 Ch. 4: 17.
14: 9. hast c. me behind thy back
19: 19. Elijah c. mantle upon Elisha
2 K. 2: 16. Spirit c. him upon mt.
21. went to spring and c. salt in
3: 25. on good land c. each his stone
4: 41. meal, and he c. it into the pot
6: 6. he c. in stick, iron swam
9: 25. c. in portion of Naboth, 26.
13: 21. c. man into sepul. of Elis.
23. neith. c. he them fr. his pres.
19: 18. c. gods into fire, Is. 37: 19.
32. nor c. bank against it, Is. 37: 33.
23: 6. c. powder thereof upon graves
12. c. dust into Kidron, 2 Ch. 30: 14.
2 Ch. 24: 10. bro-t and c. into chest
26: 14. bows and slings to c. stones
Ne. 9: 26. c. thy law behind backs
Es. 3: 7. they c. Pur, that is the lot
9: 24. Haman had c. Pur, the lot
Jb. 20: 23. G. sh. c. fury upon him
Jb. 27: 22. God shall c. upon him
29: † 17. I c. spoil out of his teeth
30: 19. he hath c. me into the mire
40: 11. c. abroad rage of thy wrath
Ps. 55: 3. they c. iniquity upon me
22. c. thy burden upon the Lord
74: 7. have c. fire into thy sanct.
78: 49. he c. upon them his wrath
Pr. 1: 14. c. in thy lot among us
Ec. 11: 1. c. thy bread upon the wat.
Is. 2: 20. man sh. c. his idols to bats
28: 25. c. abroad fitches, c. in wheat
38: 17. hast c. all my sins behind
Je. 6: 6. c. a mount ag., Eze. 4: 2.
22: 7. choice cedars c. into fire
26: 23. c. Urijah's body into graves
36: 23. c. it into fire on the hearth
38: 6. they c. Jere. into dungeon, 9.
41: 7. Ishm. slew, c. them into pit
14. c. about and went to Johan.
51: 63. c. it into Euphrates
La. 3: 53. life and c. stone upon me
Eze. 5: 4. c. them into midst of fire
7: 19. they shall c. their silver in the streets [off
11: 16. Altho. I have c. them far
23: 35. hast c. me behind thy back
26: 8. c. mount ag. thee and lift
28: 17. I will c. thee to the ground
43: 24. priests sh. c. salt upon them
Da. 3: 20. to c. them into furnace
24. Did not we c. 3 men into fire
6: 16. c. into den of lions, 24.
Am. 4: 3. sh. c. them into palace
Jon. 2: 3. hadst c. me into the deep
Mi. 2: 5. none that c. a cord by lot
4: 7. I will make her c. off
7: 19. wilt c. all their sins into sea
Na. 3: 6. I will c. filth upon thee
Zch. 5: 8. he c. it into ephah, c.
11: 13. c. it unto potter, c. them
Mal. 3: 11. nor vine c. her fruit
Mat. 5: 29. c. it from thee, 30.-18: 8, 9. [swine
7: 6. nor c. your pearls before
13: 42. c. into furnace, 50, Jn. 15: 6.
48. good into vessels, but c. the
15: 26. bread c. it to dogs, Mk. 7: 27.
17: 27. c. a hook and take up fish
18: 30. c. into prison till he pay
22: 13. c. into outer darkn., 25: 30.
27: 44. thieves c. same in his teeth
Mk. 4: 26. as if man sho. c. seed
9: 22. oft-times c. him into fire
11: 7. garm. on him, Lu. 19: 35.
12: 4. servant, at him they c. stones
41. c. money into treas., Lu. 21: 4.
43. widow hath c. more in, 44.
Lu. 1: 29. c. in her mind wh. manner
12: 5. hath power to c. into hell
58. officer c. thee into prison
13: 19. man c. into his garden
19: 43. enemies shall c. a trench
Jn. 8: 7. first c. a stone at her
59. took up stones to c. at him
21: 6. c. net | 7. c. hims. into sea
Ac. 12: 8. c. thy garment ab. thee
16: 23. c. Paul and Silas into pris.
27: 43. swim c. thems. into sea
1 Co. 7: 35. not that I may c. a
Re. 2: 10. devil c. some into prison
14. Balak to c. a stumbling-bl.
22. I will c. her into a bed, and
4: 10. elders c. crowns bef. throne
8: 5. c. it into the earth | 12: 4.
14: 19. c. it into wine press of wrath
18: 19. c. dust on heads, and cried
21. millstone and c. it into sea
20: 3. c. him into bottomless pit

CAST away.

Le. 26: 44. I will not c. them a. nor
Ju. 15: 17. c.a. jawbone out of ha.
2 S. 1: 21. shield of mighty is c. a.
2 K. 7: 15. vessels Syrians had c.a.
2 Ch. 29: 19. vessels Ahaz did c. a.
Jb. 8: 4. have c. them a. for transgr.
20. God will not c.a. a perf. man
Ps. 2: 3. let us c. a. their cords
51: 11. c. me not a. from thy pres.
Ec. 3: 5. time to c. a. stones, 6.
Is. 5: 24. bec. they have c. a. law
30: 22. c.a. as a menstruous cloth
31: 7. ev. man shall c.a. his idols
41: 9. I have chos. not c. thee a.
Je. 7: 29. cut hair, O Jeru., c. it a.
33: 26. then will I c.a. seed of Jac.
Eze. 18: 31. c.a. all your transgr.
20: 7. c. a. every man abominations of eyes [eyes
8. did not c. a. abominations of
Ho. 9: 17. My God will c. them a.
Jo. 1: 7. made bare and c. it a.
Mat. 13: 48. gathered good, c. bad a.
Lu. 9: 25. if a man be c. a.
Ro. 11: 1. Hath God c.a. his people
2. God hath not c. a. his people
He. 10: 35. c. not a. your confidence

CAST down.

Ex. 7: 10. Aaron c. d. his rod
12. they c. d. every man his rod
Jos. 10: 11. Lord c. d. great stones
Ju. 6: 28. altar of Baal was c. d.
1 K. 18: 42. Elijah c. himself d.
2 Ch. 25: 8. God hath power to c. d.
12. c. them d. from top of rock
Ne. 6: 16. were c. d. in own eyes
Jb. 18: 7. own counsel sh. c. him d.
22: 29. When men are c. d. then say
29: 24. of my counte. they c. not d.
41: 9. one be c. d. at sight of him
Ps. 17: 13. disappoint him, c. him d.
36: 12. they are c. d. and shall not
37: 14. bent bow to c. d. poor
24. fall, he sh. not be utterly c.d.
42: 5. Why art thou c. d. O my soul, 11.-43: 5.
6. O my God, my soul is c. d.
56: 7. in thine anger c. d. people
62: 4. consult to c. him d. from his
89: 44. thou hast c. his throne d.
102: 10. hast lifted me up, and c.d.
Pr. 7: 26. she c. d. many wounded
Is. 28: 2. L. shall c. d. with hand
Je. 6: 15. they shall be c.d., 8: 12.
La. 2: 1. c. d. the beauty of Israel
Eze. 6: 4. c. d. your slain bef. idols
19: 12. thy mother was c. d. to
31: 16. when I c. Assyr. d. to hell
32: 18. wail for Egypt and c. her d.
Da. 7: 9. till thrones were c. d.
8: 7. he-goat c. d. ram to ground
10. it c.d. some of host, and stars
11. sanct. was c.d. | 12. c.d. truth
11: 12. he sh. c. d. ten thousands
Mat. 4: 6. if Son, c. thys. d., Lu. 4: 9.
15: 30. c. them d. at Jesus' feet
27: 5. he c.d. pieces of silver in tem.
Lu. 4: 29. might c. Jes. d. headlong
2 Co. 4: 9. we are c.d. but not destr
7: 6. G. that comforteth those c.d.
2 Pe. 2: 4. but c. the angels d. to hell
Re. 12: 10. accuser of brethren is [c. d.

CAST forth.

Ne. 13: 8. I c. f. household stuff
Ps. 144: 6. c. f. lightning, and
Je. 22: 19. Jehoia. c. f. beyond gates
Eze. 32: 4. c. thee f. upon open field
Ho. 14: 5. c.f. his roots as Lebanon
Jon. 1: † 4. L. will c. f. great wind
5. mariners c. f. wares in ship
12. c. me f. into sea, so sea be
15. took Jonah and c. him f.
Mk. 7: 26. c. f. devil out of dau.
Jn. 15: 6. he is c. f. as a branch

CAST lots.

Le. 16: 8. c. l. on two goats
Jos. 18: 6. I may c. l. for you, 8.
10. Joshua c. l. in Shiloh
1 S. 14: 42. c. l. betw. me and Jona.
1 Ch. 25: 8. c. l. ward ag. ward
26: 13. they c. l. small as great
14. they c. l., his came out
Ne. 10: 34. we c. l. among priests
11: 1. rest of people also c. l.

Ps. 22 : 18. c. l. upon my vesture,
Mat 27: 35. Lu. 23: 34. Jn.19:24
Is. 34 : 17. he hath c. l. for them
Jo. 3 : 3. have c. l. for my people
Ob. 11. foreigners c. l. upon Jeru.
Jon. 1 : 7. c. l. that we may know
Na. 3 : 10. c. l. for her hon. men

CAST off.

2 K. 23 : 27. I will c. o. Jerusalem
1 Ch. 28 : 9. will c. thee o. for ever
2 Ch. 11 : 14. Jerob. had c. them o.
Jb 15 : 33. c. o. his flower as
Ps 43 : 2. why dost c. me o.?
44 : 9 thou hast c. o., 60 : 1, 10.-
89 : 38.-108 : 11.
23. O L. c. us not o. for ever
71 : 9. c. me not o. in old age
74: 1. why c. us o. for ever?
77 : 7. Will Lord c. o. for ever?
94 : 14. not c. o. his peo , La.3 : 31
Je. 28 : 16. I will c. Hananiah o.
31 : 37. I will c. o. seed, 33 : 24.
La. 2 : 7. L. hath c. o. his altar
Ho 8 : 3. Israel hath c. o. good
5. Thy calf, O Sama. c. thee o.
Am 1 : 11. Edom did c. o. pity
Zech. 10 : 6. as tho. I not c. them o.
Ac. 22 : 23. c. o. their clothes
Ro. 13 : 12. c. o. works of darkness
1 Ti. 5 : 12. have c. o. first faith

CAST out.

Ge 21 : 10. c. o. this bondwoman
Ex 34 : 24. I will c. o. nations
Le. 18: 24. nations are defiled which
I c. o., 20 : 23. De. 7 : 1.
De 6 : 19. c. o. all thine enemies
9 : 4 G. hath c. them o. fr. bef. thee
17. I c. two tables o. of my
Jos. 13 : 12. these did Moses c. o.
2 S. 20 : 22. c. o. Sheba's head [20
1 K. 9 : 7. house will I c. o., 2 Ch. 7:
21 : 26. Amorites, whom the L. c.
o. before Israel, 2 K. 16 : 3.
2 K. 10 : 25. captains c. them o.
17 : 20. c. them o. of sight, 24 : 20
2 Ch. 13 : 9. Have ye c. o. priests
20 : 11. to c. us o. of thy possess.
33 : 15. c. them o. of the city
Ne. 1 : 9. tho. there were of you c.o.
Jb 20 : 15. c. them o. of his belly
39 : 3. they c. o. their sorrows
Ps 5 : 10. c. them o. in transgr.
18 : 42. I did c. them o. as dirt
44 : 2. didst afflict peo and c. o.
60 : 8. will I c. o. my shoe, 108 : 9.
78 : 55. He c. o. heathen, 80 : 8.
Pr. 22 : 10. c. o. scorner and conten.
Is. 14 : 19. art c. o. of thy grave
16 : 2. as a bird c. o. of the nest
26 : 19. earth shall c. o. the dead
34 : 3 Their slain also shall be c.o.
58 : 7. that thou bring poor c. o.
66 : 5. c. you o. for my name's sa.
Je. 7 : 15. I will c. you o. of my
sight, as I have c. o.
9 : 19. dwellings have c. us o.
14 : 16. sh. be c.o. in streets of Jeru.
15 : 1. c. them o., 23 : 39.-52 : 3.
16 : 13. will I c. you o. of land
22 : 26. I will c. thee o. and moth.
28. wheref. are they c. o. he and
36 : 30. his dead body be c. o.
51 : 34 Neb hath c. me o.
Eze. 16 : 5 c. o. in the open field
28 : 16. c. thee o. of mount of G.
36 : 5. with despitef. minds to c. it o.
Am. 8 : 8. the land shall be c. o.
Mi 2 : 9 women have ye c. o.
Zep. 3 : 15. hath c. o. thine enemy
Zech. 1 : 21. to c. o. horns of Gent.
: 4 L. will c. her o. and smite
Mat. 5 : 13 salt to be c.o., Lu.14:35.
7 : 5. first c. o. beam, Lu. 6 : 42.
22. L , have we not c. o. devils?
8 : 12. chil. of kingd. be c. o.
16. he c. o. spirits with word
31. if thou c. us o. suffer us

Mat. 9 : 33. devil c. o. dumb spake
10 : 1. power ag. spirits to c. o.
8. raise the dead, c. o. devils
12 : 24. c. o. but by Beelz., Lu. 11:
26. if Satan c. o. Satan [18.
27. if I c. o. devils, Lu. 11 : 19.
28. if I c. o. devils by Spirit of G.
15 : 17. is c. o. into draught
17 : 19. not we c. him o.? Mk.9:28.
21 : 12. c. o. all that sold, Mk. 11:
15. Lu. 19 : 45. [8. Lu. 20 : 15.
39. c. him o. of vineyard, Mk.12:
Mk. 1 : 34. c.o. many dev.,39 -6:13.
3 : 15. power to c. o. devils
23. How can Satan c. o. Satan?
9 : 18. to disciples to c. him o.,
Lu. 9 : 40.
28. Why c'd not we c. him o.?
16 : 9. o. of whom c. seven devils
17. In my name shall c. o. devils
Lu. 6 : 22. c. o. your name as evil
11 : 18. I c. o. devils through Beelz.
20. if I with finger of G. c. o. dev.
13 : 32. I c. o. devils, and do cures
20 : 12. they wounded and c. him o.
Jn. 6 : 37. I will in no wise c. o.
9 : 34. thou teach us? they c. him o.
35. J. heard they had c. him o.
12 : 31. prince of this world be c.o.
Ac. 7 : 19. that they c.o. young chil.
21. when Mos. was c.o. Pha.'s dau.
58. they c. Stephen o. of the city
27 : 19. we c. o. tackling of ship
29 c. 4 anchors o. | 38. c.o. wheat
Ga 4 : 30. c. o. the bondwoman
Re. 12 : 9. great dragon was c. o.
15. the serpent c. o. water, 16.

Lord CAST out.

1 K. 14 : 24. wh. L. c.o. bef chil. of
Isr., 2 K.16:3. 2 Ch.28 : 3.-33 : 2
2 K. 17 : 8. L. c. o. bef. Israel, 21:2
Zch. 9 : 4. L. will c. her o. and

CAST up. [smite

2 S. 20 : 15. c. u. a bank ag. city
Is 57 : 14. c.u. prepare way, 62:10
20. sea, whose waters c. u. mire
Je 18 : 15. to walk in way not c. u.
50 : 26. c. her u. as heaps [27 : 30.
La. 2 : 10. c. u. dust upon heads, Eze.
Da. 11 : 15. king shall c. u. a mount

CASTAWAY.

1 Co. 9 : 27. lest I should be a c.

CASTEDST, EST, ETH.

Jb. 15 : 4. Yea, thou c-t off fear and
21 : 10. their cow c. not her calf
Ps. 50 : 17. c-dst my words behind
73 : 18. c-dst them into destruction
88 : 14. why c-t thou off my soul
147 : 6. L. c the wicked down
17. He c. forth his ice like morsels
Pr. 10 : 3. he c. away subst. of wick.
19 : 15. Slothfuln. c. into deep sleep
21 : 22. wise man c. down strength
26 : 18. mad man c. fire-brands
Is. 40 : 19. c. silver chains
Je. 6 : 7. so she c. out her wickedn.
Ho. 9 : †14. womb that c. the fruit
Mat. 9 : 34. He c. out devils, Mk 3 :
22. Lu. 11 : 15. [fear
1 Jn. 4 : 18. but perfect love c. out
3 Jn. 10. and c. them out of church
Re. 6 : 13. fig tree c. untimely figs

CASTING.

2 S. 8 : 2. he smote Moab, c. down
1 K. 7 : 37. bases, all had one c.
Ezr. 10 : 1. weeping and c. hims. down
Jb. 6 : 21. ye see my c. down
Ps. 74 : 7. by c. down dwelling pl.
89 : 39. profaned his crown by c. it
Eze. 17 : 17. c. up mounts, build'g forts
Mi. 6 : 14. thy c. down be in midst
Mat. 4 : 18. and Andr. c. net, Mk.1 : 16
27 : 35. garments c. lots, Mk. 15:24
Mk. 9 : 38. one c. out dev., Lu. 9 : 49
10 : 50. c. away garment, came to J.
Lu. 11 : 14. c. out a devil, dumb
21 : 1. rich men c. their gifts into

Lu. 21 : 2. saw poor widow c. in 2 mites
Ro. 11 : 15 if c. away be reconcil'g
2 Co 10 : 5. c. down imaginations
1 Pe. 5 : 7. c. all your care upon him

CASTLE.

1 Ch. 11 : 5. David took c. of Zion
7. David dwelt in c. city of David
Pr. 18 : 19. contentions like bars of c.
Ac. 21 : 34. com. Paul to be carried
into c., 37.-22 : 24.-23 : 10.
23 : 16. he ent. into c. told Paul | 32

CASTLES.

Ge. 25 : 16. Ishm.'s sons by their c.
Nu 31 : 10. they burnt their goodly c.
1 Ch. 6 : 54. priest's c. in their coasts
27 : 25. and in c. Jehonathan
2 Ch. 17 : 12. Jehosh. built in Jud c.
27 : 4. Jotham built c. and towers

CAS'TOR.

Ac. 28 : 11. sign, C. and Pollux

CATCH.

Ex. 22 : 6. if fire c. in thorns
Ju 21 : 21. c. you every man his wife
1 K. 20 : 33. men did hastily c. it
2 K. 7 : 12. we shall c. them alive
Ps. 10 : 9. in wait to c. poor, doth c.
35 : 8. let his net c. himself [poor
109 : 11. extortioner c. all he hath
Je. 5 : 26. they set a trap, they c. men
Eze. 19 : 3. learned to c. the prey, 6.
Hab. 1 : 15. they c. them in net
Mk. 12 : 13. to c. him in his words
Lu. 5 : 10. from hencef. shalt c. men
11 : 54. to c. someth out of his mou.

CATCHETH, ING.

Le. 17 : 13. who c-h any beast or fowl
Eze. 1 : †4. a fire c-g itself [sown
Mat. 13 : 19. devil c-h away what
Jn. 10 : 12. the wolf c-h the sheep

CATERPILLER, S.

1 K. 8 : 37. if be any c., 2 Ch. 6 : 28.
Ps. 78 : 46. gave their increase to c.
105 : 34. He spake, and c-s came
Is. 33 : 4. spoil like gathering of c.
Je. 51 : 14. fill thee with men as c-s
27. horses come up as rough c-s
Jo. 1 : 4. cankerworm left c. eaten
2 : 25. restore years c. hath eaten

CATTLE.

Ge. 1 : 25. G. made c. after th. kind
3 : 14. thou art cursed above all c.
7 : 21. all flesh died, of fowl and c.
8 : 1. God rem. Noah and c. in ark
9 : 10. I establish my cov. with c.
13 : 2. Ab. was very rich in c. silver
7. herd men of Ab.'s c.—Lot's c.
30 : 32 speckled and spotted c.
40. put them not to Laban's c.
41. stronger c. did conceive [ther
31 : 9. G. hath taken c. of your fa-
10. came to pass time c. conceived
18. carried away all his c., 2.
43. these c. are my c. all mine
34 : 5. his sons were with his c.
46 : 32. their trade been to feed c.
47 : 6. make them rulers over my c.
17. Jos gave bread in exch. for c.
Ex. 9 : 4. sever betw. c. of Isr. c.
6. all c. of E. died, but c. [of E.
7. not one of c. of Israel dead
20. made his servants and c. flee
21. left servants and c. in field
12 : 29. L. smote all firstb. of c.
Le. 1 : 2. shall bring your offer of c.
Nu 3 : 41 take c. of the Levites
20 : 19. if my c. drink, I will pay
32 : 1. beheld the place was for c.
4 land for c. thy serv'ts have c.
De. 2 : 35. c. we took a prey, 3 : 7.
Jos. 8 : 2. only c. take for a prey
27. only c. Israel took, 11 : 14.
1 K. 1 : 9. Adonijah slew c., 19, 25.
1 Ch. 28 : † 1. assem. stewards ov. c.
Jb. 1 : † 3. his c. was 7,000 sheep
† 10. his c. is increased in land
36 : 33. c. concerning the vapour
Ps 50 : 10. c. upon a thous. hills is

Ps. 104 : 14. he causeth grass for c.
148 : 10. beasts and all c. praise L.
Ec. 2 : 7. had great possessions of c.
Is. 7 : 25. for treading of lesser c.
43 : 23. not brought me small c.
46 : 1. their idols were upon c.
Je. 9 : 10. nor hear voice of c.
Eze. 34 : 17. betw. c. and c.,20, 22.
38 : 12. have gotten c. and goods
Jo. 1 : 18. herds of c. are perplexed
Hag. 1 : 11. for drought upon c.
Zch. 2 : 4. for mult. of men and c.
13 : 5. men taught me to keep c.
Lu. 17 : 7. having serv-t feeding c.
Jn. 4 : 12. Jacob drank, and his c.

Much CATTLE.

Ge. 30 : 43. Jac. incr. and had m.c.
Ex. 12:38. Isr. out of E. with m.c.
De. 3 : 19. I know ye have m. c.
Jos. 22 : 8. to tents with very m.c.
2 Ch. 26 : 10. Uzziah had m. c. in
Jon. 4:11. Nineveh,wherein is m.c.

Our CATTLE.

Ex. 10 : 26. o. c. shall go with us
17 : 3. to kill us, o. c. with thirst
Nu. 20 : 4. that we and o. c. die
32 : 16. build sheepfolds for o. c.
26. all o. c. shall be in cities of
Jos. 21 : 2. with suburbs for o. c.
Ne. 9 : 37. have dominion ov. o. c.
10 : 36. to bring firstborn of o. c.

Their CATTLE.

Ge. 34 : 23. Shall not t. c. be ours
36 : 7. not bear them bec. of t. c.
Nu. 31 : 9. slew Midianites, took t.c.
35 : 3. suburbs for t. c., Jos. 14:4.
Ju. 6 : 5. Midianites came with t.c.
1 S. 23 : 5. Dav. brought away t.c.
1 Ch. 5 : 9. bec. t. c. were multipli.
7 : 21. they came to take aw. t. c.
Ps. 78 : 48. he gave up t. c. to hail
107 : 38. suff. not t. c. to decrease
Je. 49 : 32. a booty, t. c. a spoil

Thy CATTLE.

Ge. 30 : 29. how t. c. was with me
31 : 41. I served six years for t. c.
Ex. 9 : 3. hand of Lord is upon t. c.
19. send now and gather t. c.
20 : 10. nor t. c. do work,De. 5:14.
34 : 19. firstling am. t. c. is mine
Le. 19 : 19. let not t. c. gender with
25 : 7. sab. of land be meat for t.c.
De. 11 : 15. send grass for t. c.
28 : 4. blessed be fruit of t. c. 11.-
30 : 9. [land
51. sh. eat fruit of t. c. and thy
Is. 30 : 23. shall t. c. feed in large

Your CATTLE. [pastu.

Ge.47:16.Give y.c., I give money for
Le. 26 : 22. will destroy y. c. [y.c.
De. 3 : 19. y. c. in cities, Jos. 1:14.
7 : 14. nor female barren am. y. c.
2 K. 3 : 17. may drink, ye and y. c.

CAUGHT.

Ge. 22 : 13. behind him a ram c. by
39 : 12. she c. him by garment
Ex. 4 : 4. put his hand, c. serpent
Nu. 31 : 32. rest of prey men had c.
Ju. 1 : 6. c. Adoni-bezek, and cut
8 : 14. c. young man of Succoth
15 : 4. Samson c. 300 foxes
21 : 23. took wives of them they c.
1 S. 17 : 35. I c. him by his beard
2 S. 2 : 16. c. every one his fellow
18 : 9. Abs.'s head c. hold of oak
1 K. 1 : 50.Adonijah c.hold alt., 51.
2 : 28. Joab c. hold horns of altar
11 : 30. Ahijah c. new garment
2 K. 4 : 27. Shunamite c. Elisha
2 Ch. 22 : 9. they c. Ahaziah.
Pr. 7 : 13. she c. him, and kissed
Je. 50 : 24. O Babylon, thou art c.
Mat. 14 : 31. Jesus c. Peter, and
21 : 39. the husbandmen c. him
Mk. 12 : 3. they c. serv. and beat
Lu. 8 : 29. oftentimes it c. him
Jn. 21 : 3. they that night c. noth.
Jn.21:10.bring of the fish ye have c.
Ac. 6 : 12. upon Stephen and c. him
8 : 39. Spirit of L. c. away Philip
16 : 19. they c. Paul and Silas
26 : 21. Jews c. me in the temple
27 : 15. when ship was c. we let
2 Co. 12 : 2. I knew a man c. up to
4. How he was c. up into para.
16. crafty, I c. you with guile
1 Th. 4 : 17. we sh. be c. up togeth.
Re. 12 : 5. her child was c. up to G.

CAUL, S.

Ex. 29 : 13. c. above liver, 22. Le.
3 : 4, 10, 15.-4 : 9.-7 : 4.-8 : 16,
25.-9 : 10, 19.
Is. 3 : 18. L. will take away their c-s
Ho. 13 : 8. will rend c. of their heart

CAUSE. [Noun.]

Ex. 22 : 9. c. of both before judges
23 : 2. nor speak in a c. to decline
3. Nor counten. poor man in c.
6. nor wrest judgm. of poor in c.
Nu. 16 : 11. for wh. c. thou and all
27 : 5. Moses brought c. before L.
De. 1 : 17. c.too hard for you, bring
Jos. 20 : 4. manslayer sh. declare c.
1 S. 17 : 29. Is there not a c. ?
25 : 39. L. hath pleaded c. of my
2 S. 13 : 16. There is no c. this evil
15 : 4. hath any c. come unto me
1 K. 8 : 45. maintain their c., 49,59.
2 Ch. 6 : 35, 39.
11 : 27. was the c. he lifted hand
12 : 15. c. from L., 2 Ch. 10 : 15.
1 Ch. 21 : 3. c. of trespass to Isr. ?
2 Ch. 19 : 10. what c. of your breth.
Ezr.4 : 15.for wh. c. city was destr.
Ne. 6 : 6. for which c. buildest wall
Jb. 5 : 8. unto G. will commit my c.
13 : 18. now, I have ordered my c.
23 : 4. would order my c. bef. him
29 : 16. c. I knew not, I searched
31 : 13. despise c. of my servant
Ps. 9 : 4. hast maintained my c.
35 : 23. awake to my c. my God
27. let be glad th. favour my c.
140 : 12. I know L. will maint. c.
Pr. 18 : 17. He first in his own c.
25 : 9. Debate thy c. with neighb.
29 : 7. righteous consid. c. of poor
31 : 8. open mouth for dumb in c.
Ec. 7 : 10. say not, What is c.
Is. 1 : 23. nor c. of widow come
41 : 21. Produce your c., saith L.
51 : † 8. who is master of my c.
51 : 22. G. that pleadeth c. of his
Je. 5 : 28. judge not c. of fatherless
11 : 20. to thee revealed my c.
20 : 12. unto thee opened my c.
22 : 16. He judged c. of poor
La. 3 : 36. to subvert in a c.
59. seen my wrong, judge c. [8.
Jon. 1 : 7. may know for whose c.,
Mat. 5 : 32. saving for c. of fornica.
19 : 3. to put away wife for ev. c.
Lu. 8 : 47. for what c. she touched
23 : 22. I have found no c. of death
Ac. 10 : 21. what is c. ye are come ?
13 : 28. tho. no c. of death in him
19 : 40. no c. we may give account
23:28. when I would have known c.
25 : 14. Festus declared Paul's c.
28 : 18. bec. no c. of death in me
Ro. 15 : 22. for wh. c. I been hindr.
2 Co. 4 : 16. For wh. c. we faint not
5 : 13. sober, it is for your c.
7 : 12. I did it not for his c. that
Ph. 2 : 18. For same c. do ye joy
2 Ti. 1 : 12. For which c. I suffer
He. 2:11. for wh. c.he is not asham.
1 Pe.2:†23. committed his c.to him

For this CAUSE.

Ex. 9 : 16. f. t. c. I raised Pha.
2 Ch. 32:20. f.t.c. Hez.and Is. pray
Da. 2 : 12. f.t.c. king was angry
Mat.19 : 5.f.t.c.man leave fa.cleave
to wife, Mk. 10 : 7. Ep. 5 : 31.
Jn. 12 : 18. f. t. c. people met him
27. f. t. c. came I unto hour
18 : 37. f. t. c. came I into world
Ac. 28 : 20. f.t.c.theref. have I suff.
Ro. 1 : 26. f. t. c. G. gave them up
13 : 6. f. t. c. pay ye tribute also
15 : 9. f. t. c. I will conf. to thee
1 Co. 4 : 17. f.t.c. have sent to you
Timothy [power
11 : 10.f.t.c.ought woman to have
30. f. t. c. many are weak
Ep. 3:1. f.t.c. I Paul, prisoner of C.
14. f. t. c. I bow my knees
Col. 1 : 9. f.t.c. since day we heard
1 Th. 2 : 13. f.t.c. thank we God
3 : 5. f.t.c. wh. no longer forbear
2 Th. 2 : 11. f.t.c. G. send delusion
1 Ti. 1 : 16. f.t.c. I obtained mercy
Tit. 1 : 5. f.t.c. left I thee in Crete
He. 9 : 15. f.t.c. he is the mediator
1 Pe. 4 : 6. f.t.c. was gospel preach.

Plead CAUSE.

1 S. 24 : 15. the Lord p. my c., Ps.
35 : 1.-43 : 1.-119 : 154.
Ps. 74 : 22. O God, p. thine own c.
Pr. 22 : 23. Lord will p. their c.
23 : 11. shall p. their c. with thee
31 : 9. p. the c. of poor, needy
Je. 30 : 13. is none to p. thy c.
50 : 34. Lord shall p. their c.
51 : 36. Behold, I will p. thy c.
Mi. 7 : 9. until he p. my c.

Without CAUSE.

1 S. 19 : 5. to slay David w. a c.?
Jb. 2 : 3. me to destroy him w. a c.
9 : 17. multipli. my wounds w. c.
Ps. 7 : 4. I delivered him that w.c.
25 : 3. ashamed that transgr.w.c.
35 : 7.w.c.hid net,digged pit w.c.
19. hate me w.c., 69: 4.Jn.15:25.
109 : 3. fought against me w. a c.
119 : 78. perversely with me w. c.
161. Princes persecuted me w. c.
Pr. 1 : 11. lurk for innocent w. c.
3 : 30. Strive not with a man w.c.
23 : 29. who hath wounds w. c.
24 : 28.not witness ag.neighb.w.c.
Is. 52 : 4. Assyrian oppr. them w.c.
La. 3 : 52. chased me sore w. c.
Eze. 14 : 23. have not done w. c.
Mat. 5:22. angry with his bro.w.c.

CAUSES.

Ex. 18 : 19. mayest bring c. to God
26. hard c. they brought to Mos.
De. 1 : 16. Hear c. betw. brethren
Je. 3 : 8. c. whereby backsli. Israel
La. 2 : 14. seen c. of banishment
3 : 58. hast pleaded c. of my soul
Ac. 26:21. For these c. Jews caught

CAUSE. [Verb.]

Ge. 7 : 4. c. it rain forty days
45 : 1. cried c. ev. man to go out
Ex. 8:5. c. frogs to come up upon E.
9 : 18. c. it to rain grievous hail
21 : 19. c. him to be healed
Le. 19 : 29. to c. her to be a whore
24 : 19. if man c. blemish in neigh.
26 : 16. and c. sorrow of heart
Nu. 8 : † 7. c. razor to pass over
16 : 5. Lord will c. him to come
35 : 30. ag. person to c. him to die
De. 1 : 38. shall c. Isr. to inherit it,
3 : 28.-31 : 7. Jos. 1 : † 6.
12 : 11. sh. choose to c. his name
24 : 4. not c. the land to sin
28 : † 61. them will L. c. to ascend
Ju. 6 : † 11. wheat to c. it flee
2 S. 13 : 13. whither c. my shame
1 K. 8 : 31. oath to c. him swear
2 K.19 : 7.will c.him to fall,Is.37:7.
Ne. 13 : 26. did women c. to sin
Es. 3 : 13. c. to perish, 7 : † 4.-8:11.
5 : 5. c. Haman make haste to do
6 : † 9. c. him to ride on horseback
Jb. 6 : 24. c. me to underst. wherein
† 27. c. to fall upon fatherless
20 : 2. my thoughts c. me to ans.

Jb. 34 : 11. c. ev. man to find acc. to
38:†37. c. to lie down bot. of heav.
Ps. 10 : 17. wilt c. thine ear to hear
67 : 1. c. face to shine, 80 : 3,7,19.
71 : 2. Deliv. and c. me to escape
76 : 8. didst c. judgm. to be heard
80 : 9. c. it to take deep root
90 : † 12. c. hearts to come to wisd.
143 : 8. c. me to hear, c. me to kn.
Pr. 4 : 16. unless c. some to fall
8 : 21. c. those love me to inherit
19 : † 18. not spare to c. him to die
23 : † 5. wilt c. thine eyes to flee
Ec. 2 : 20. to c. my heart to despair
5 : 6. to c. thy flesh to sin
Can. 8 : 13. c. me to hear it
Is. 3 : 12. who lead c. to err, 9 : 16.
10 : 30. c. it to be heard unto Laish
13 : 10. moon not c. light to shine
27 : 6. c. them of Jac. to take root
28 : 12. may c. the weary to rest
30 : 30. L. c. his voice to be heard
42 : 2. nor c. his voice to be heard
58 : 14. c. thee to ride upon high pl.
61 : 11. c. righteousness to spring
66 : 9. and not c. to bring forth ?
Je. 3 : 12. not c. mine anger to fall
7 : 3. c. you to dwell in this pl., 7.
12 : † 9. c. beasts of field to come
13 : 16. glory to L. bef. he c. darku.
15 : 11. c. the enemy to entreat
23 : 27. to c. my people forget my
25 : † 10. c. to perish the voice
31 : 2. wh. I went to c. him to rest
9. will c. them to walk by rivers
32 : 44. c. captiv. return, 33 : 26.
La. 3 : 32. tho. he c. grief, yet will
Eze. 20 : 37. c. you to pass und. rod
24 : 8. it might c. fury to come
34 : 15. I will c. them to lie down
36 : 12. c. men to walk upon you
Da. 8 : 25. he sh. c. craft to prosper
9 : 17. O our G., c. thy face to shine
† 18. not c. to fall our supplica.
11 : † 32. shall he c. to dissemble
Ho. 4 : † 9. I will c. to return
Jo. 3 : 11. c. thy mighty ones come
Am. 6 : 3. c. seat of violence come
8 : 9. c. sun to go down at noon
9 : † 9. c. to move Isr. am. nations
Na. 2 : † 8. none sh. c. them to turn
Ha. 1 : 3. why c. me behold griev-
Mat. 5:†29. if eye c. to offend [ance
6 : † 2. c. not trumpet to be sound.
10 : 21. ag. parents and c. th. put
to death, Mk. 13 : 12. Lu. 21:16.
Ro. 16 : 17. mark who c. divisions
Col. 4 : 16. c. that it be read in
church [away
Re. 12:15. might c. her to be carried
13 : 15. c. as many as not worship
CAUSE to cease. See CEASE.

CAUSED.
Ge. 2 : 5. L. G. not c. it to rain
21. God c. a deep sleep
20 : 13. God c. me to wander from
Ex. 14 : 21. L. c. sea to go back
Nu. 31 : 16. c. Israel to com. whored.
De. 34 : 4. land, I c. thee to see
Ju. 16:19. she c. him to shave locks
2 S. 7 : 11. c. thee to rest fr. enem.
22 : † 40. c. to bow, Ps. 18 : † 39.
1 K. 2 : 19. c. seat for k.'s mother
2 Ch. 34 : 32. he c. all to stand it
Ezr. 1 : † 1. Cyrus c. a voice to pass
6 : 12. G. that c. his name to dw.
Ne. 8 : 7. Lev. c. peo. to underst., 8.
Es. 5 : † 10. Haman c. his friends
14. Haman c. gallows made
Jb. 29 : 13. c. widow's heart to sing
31 : 16. c. eyes of widow to fail
39. c. owners thereof to lose life
37 : 15. c. light of cloud to shine
38 : 12. c. dayspring to know his pl.
Ps. 66 : 12. c. men to ride over heads
78 : 13. divided sea, and c. them
26. He c. an east wind to blow
Ps. 119 : 49. thou hast c. me to hope
Pr. 7 : 21. she c. him to yield
Is. 6 : † 7. c. it to touch my mouth
19 : 14. they have c. Egypt to err
43 : 23. I have not c. thee to serve
47 : † 10. thy wisd. c. thee to turn
63 : 14. Spirit of L. c. him to rest
Je. 3:†18. land I c. fathers to possess
12 : 14. c. my people Isr. inherit
13 : 11. c. to cleave to me Israel
23 : 13. c. my people Israel to err
29 : 31. S. c. you to trust in a lie
32 : 33. thou hast c. all this evil
34 : 11. c. servants to return, 16.
48 : 4. little ones have c. a cry
La. 2 : 17. c. enemy rejoice over thee
Eze. 16 : 7. c. thee to multiply
24 : 13. I have c. fury to rest upon
29 : 18. Neb. c. his army to serve
32 : 23. c. terror in la., 24, 25, 26.
39 : 28. c. th. to be led into captiv.
Da. 9 : 21. Gabriel being c. to fly
Ho. 4 : 12. whored-s c. them to err
Am. 2 : 4. their lies c. them to err
4 : 7. I c. rain upon one city, I c. not
Jon. 3 : 7. he c. it to be proclaimed
Zch. 3 : 4. c. thine iniquity to pass
Mal. 2 : 8. c. many to stumble
Jn. 11 : 37. c. th. man not have died
Ac. 15 : 3. c. great joy to brethren
2 Co. 2 : 5. But if any have c. grief

CAUSELESS.
1 S. 25 : 31. lust shed blood c.
Ps. 26 : 2. curse c. not come

CAUSEST.
Jb. 30 : 22. c. me to ride upon wind
Ps. 65 : 4. blessed is man th. c. appr.

CAUSETH.
Nu. 5 : 18. c. the curse, 19, 22, 24, 27.
Jb. 12 : 24. he c. them to wander
in wilderness, Ps. 107 : 40.
20 : 3. spirit of underst. c. me to
37 : 13. c. it to come for correc.
Ps. 104 : 14. He c. the grass to grow
135 : 7. He c. vapours to ascend,
Je. 10 : 13.—51 : 16.
147 : 18. c. his wind to blow
Pr. 10 : 5. son c. shame, 17:2.—19:26.
10. he that winketh c. sorrow
† 17. refuseth reproof c. to err
14 : 35. against him that c. shame
17:2. shall rule over a son c. shame
18 : 18. lot c. contentions to cease
19 : 27. instruction that c. to err
28 : 10. c. righteous to go astray
Is. 61 : 11. garden c. things sown
64 : 2. fire c. waters to boil
Eze. 26 : 3. sea c. waves to come up
44 : 18. that c. sweat
Da. 11 : † 20. c. an exactor of kingd.
Mat. 5 : 32. c. her to commit adult.
2 Co. 2 : 14. G., c. us to triumph
9 : 11. c. through us thanksg. to G.
Re. 13 : 12. c. earth to worship
16. c. all to receive a mark in

CAUSEWAY.
1 Ch. 26 : 16. lot came by the c.
18. Parbar westward four at c.
Pr. 15 : † 19. way of righteous as c.
Is. 7 : † 3. c. of fuller's field

CAUSING.
2 K. 2 : † 19. c. to miscarry
Can. 7 : 9. c. lips of those asleep
Is. 30 : 28. bridle c. them to err
Je. 29 : 10. in c. you to return
33 : 12. c. flocks to lie down
Eze. 39 : † 28. L. c. them to be led

CAVE, S.
Ge. 19 : 30. Lot dwelt in a c. he
23 : 9. may give me c. of Machpe.
17. c. made sure to Abraham, 20.
19. Ab. buried Sarah in the c.
25 : 9. buried him in c. of Mach.
49 : 29. bury me with father in c.
30. c. in field of Mach., 50 : 13.
32. purchase of field, and c.
Jos. 10 : 16. five kings hid in c., 17.
Ju. 6 : 2. Israel made c-s
1 S. 13 : 6. Israel did hide in c-s
22 : 1. David escaped to the c.
24 : 3. was a c. ; Saul went in
24 : 10. Lord delivered thee in c.
2 S. 23 : 13. unto c. of Adullam
1 K. 18 : 4. prophets hid in a c., 13.
19 : 9. Elijah came unto a c. and
Is. 2 : 19. into c-s for fear of Lord
Eze. 33 : 27. die that be in c-s
Jn. 11 : 38. the grave, It was a c.
He. 11 : 38. they wandered in c-s

CEASE.
Ge. 8 : 22. day and night not c.
Ex. 9 : 29. the thunder shall c.
23 : † 5. c. to leave thy business
Nu. 8 : 25. from age of fifty sh. c.
11 : 25. elders prophesied, not c.
17 : 5. to c. murmurings
De. 15 : 11. poor shall never c.
32 : 26. remem. of them to c.
Jos. 22 : 25. chil. c. from fearing L.
Ju. 15 : 7. avenged, after I will c.
20 : 28. go to battle, or shall I c.?
1 S. 7 : 8. c. not to cry unto L. for us
2 K. 23 : † 5. to c. idols. priests
2 Ch. 16 : 5. Baasha, let his work c.
Ezr. 4 : 23. made to c. by force
6 : † 8. they be not made to c.
Ne. 6 : 3. why should work c. ?
Jb. 3 : 17. wicked c. from troubling
10 : 20. my days few, c. then
14 : 7. tender branch will not c.
Ps. 37 : 8. c. from anger, and
46 : 9. He maketh wars to c. to
89 : 44. made his glory to c.
119 : † 119. causest wicked to c.
Pr. 19 : 27. c. to hear instruction
20 : 3. honour to c. from strife
22 : 10. and reproach shall c.
23 : 4. c. from thy wisdom
Ec. 12 : 3. grinders c. because few
Is. 1 : 16. c. to do evil
2 : 22. c. ye from man
10 : 25. and indignation shall c.
16 : 10. vintage shouting to c.
17 : 3. fortress c. from Ephraim
21 : 2. all sighing made to c.
33 : 1. c. to spoil shalt be spoiled
Je. 14 : 17. let tears run and not c.
17 : 8. nor c. from yielding fruit
31 : 36. then seed of Isra. shall c.
La. 2 : 18. let not apple of eye c.
Eze. 6 : 6. that your idols may c.
7 : 24. make pomp of strong to c.
12 : 23. I will make this proverb c.
23 : 27. make thy lewdness to c.
30 : 10. make multi. of Egypt to c
18. of her strength c., 33 : 28.
Ho. 7 : † 4. raiser c. from raising
Am. 7 : 5. O L., c., by shall whom
Jacob arise ?
Ac. 13 : 10. not c. to pervert right
1 Co. 13 : 8. tongues, they shall c.
Ep. 1 : 16. I c. not to give thanks
Col. 1 : 9. not c. to pray for you
2 Pe. 2 : 14. eyes cannot c. fr. sin

Cause, ed, eth, to CEASE.
Le. 26:†6. c. t. c. beasts, Eze. 34:25.
Ru. 4 : † 14. not c-d t. c. a kinsman
2 K. 23 : † 5. c. t. c. idolatrous priests
Ezr. 4:21. c. these men t. c., city be
5 : 5. they could not c. them t. c.
Ne. 4:11. slay them and c. work t.c.
Ps. 85:4. c. thine anger tow. us t.c.
Pr. 18 : 18. lot c-h contentions t.c.
Is. 13:11. c. arrogancy of proud t.c.
30 : 11. c. the Holy One of Israel t.c.
Je. 7 : 34. c. mirth t. c., Ho. 2:11.
16 : 9. I will c. t. c. out of this pla.
36 : 29. c. t. c. man and beast
48 : 35. I will c. t. c. him that offereth
Eze. 16 : 41. c. thee t. c. from playing harlot
23 : 48. thus will I c. lewdness t.c
26 : 13. I will c. noise of thy songs t.c
30 : 13. c. images t. c. out of Noph

Eze.34: 10. c. them t. c. fr. feed-g flock
Da. 9: 27. he shall c. oblation t. c.
11: 18. c. reproach off. by him t. c.
Ho.1: 4. will c. t. c. kingd. of Israel

CEASED.

Ge. 18: 11. it c. to be with Sarah
Ex. 9: 33. thunders and hail c.
34. when Pha. saw thunders c.
Jos. 5: 12. manna c. on morrow
Ju. 2: 19. they c. not from doings
5: 7. inhabi. of villages c. in Israel
1 S. 2: 5. they that were hungry c.
25: 9. spake in name of Da. and c.
Ezr. 4: 24. then c. work of h. of G.
Jb. 32: 1. three men c. to ans. Job
Ps. 35: 15. did tear me and c. not
77: 2. my sore ran in night c. not
Is. 14: 4. oppressor c. golden city c.
La. 5: 14. elders have c. from gate
15. The joy of our heart is c.
Jon. 1: 15. Jonah, sea c. raging
Mat. 14: 32. wind c., Mk. 4: 39.–6: 51.
Lu. 7: 45. not c. to kiss my feet
8: 24. they c. and was a calm
11: 1. as he was praying when he c.
Ac. 5: 42. they c. not to preach Jes.
20: 1. aft. uproar was c. Paul called
31. three years I c. not to warn
21: 14. he not be persuaded we c.
Ga. 5: 11. then is offence of cross c.
He. 4: 10. c. from his own works
10: 2. they not have c. to be offer.
1 Pe. 4: 1. who suff. in flesh, c. fr. [sin

CEASETH.

Ps. 12: 1. help, L., godly man c.
49: 8. redempt. precious, it c. for
Pr. 26: 20. where is no tale-bearer [strife c.
Is. 16: 4. the spoiler c.
24: 8. mirth c. joy of the harp c.
33: 8. the way-faring man c.
La. 3: 49. mine eye trickleth c. not
Ho. 7: 4. c. fr. raising aft. he kneaded
Ac. 6: 13. c. not speak blasphemous

CEASING.

Ex. 21: † 19. pay for c. of his time
1 S. 12: 23. sin in c. to pray for you
Is. 6: † 9. Hear ye without c. but
Ac. 12: 5. prayer made without c.
Ro. 1: 9. without c. I make mention, 1 Th. 1: 3.
1 Th. 2: 13. we thank G. without c.
5: 17. Pray without c. in ev. thing
2 Ti. 1: 3. without c. I have remem.

CEDAR.

2 S. 7: 2. said, I dwell in house of c.
7. Why build ye not me a h. of c.?
1 K. 4: 33. he spake fr. c. to hyssop
5: 8. I will do all thy desire conc. c.
6: 9. and boards of c., 15, 16.
10. on house with timber of c.
18. c. of house was carved (2)
1 K. 6: 20. covered altar of c.
36. row of c. beams, 7: 12.
7: 2. c. pillars with c. beams upon
3. was covered with c., 7. [pil.
2 K. 14: 9. thistle sent to c., 2 Ch. 25: 18. [c.
Jb. 40: 17. Behemoth moveth tail like
Ps. 92: 12. righteous grow like c.
Can. 1: 17. beams of our house are c.
8: 9. inclose her with boards of c.
Is. 41: 19. will plant in wildern. c.
Je. 22: 14. is ceiled with c. painted
15. bec. thou closest thyself in c.
Eze. 17: 3. took highest branches of c.
22. take of highest branch of c.
23. it shall bear fruit a goodly c.
27: 24. chests made of c. among the
31: 3. Assyrian was a c. in Leban.
Zph. 2: 14. shall uncover c. work
Zch. 11: 2. Howl, for c. is fallen

CEDAR trees.

Nu. 24: 6. Israel's tabernacles as c. t.
2 S. 5: 11. Hiram sent c. t. to David
1 K. 5: 6. they hew me c. t. out of Leb.
10. so Hiram gave Sol. c. t., 9: 11.
2 K. 19: 23. I will cut down tall c. t.
1 Ch. 22: 4. David prepared c. t.
2 Ch. 1: 15. c. t. as sycamore, 9: 27.
2: 8. send me c. t. out of Lebanon
Ezr. 3: 7. gave money to bring c. t.

CEDAR wood.

Le. 14: 4. take c. w., 6, 49, 51, 52.
Nu. 19: 6. the priest shall take c. w.
1 Ch. 22: 4. bro-t much c. w. to Da.

CEDARS.

1 K. 7: 11. meas. of stones and c.
10: 27. c. made he as sycamore trees
1 Ch. 14: 1. timber of c. with masons
17: 1. I dwell in a house of c.
6. Why ye not built me h. of c.
2 Ch. 2: 3. didst send Da. c. to build
Ps. 29: 5. voice of L. breaketh c.
80: 10. boughs were like goodly c.
148: 9. praise him all c. and fruitf.
Can. 5: 15. his countenance as the c.
Is. 9: 10. change sycamores into c.
37: 24. I will cut down the tall c.
44: 14. He heweth him down c.
Je. 22: 7. sh. cut down thy choice c.
23. O Leb., makest thy nest in c.
Eze. 31: 8. c. in garden not hide him
Am. 2: 9. Amorite, height as c.
Zch. 11: 1. Leb., fire devour thy c.

CEDARS of Lebanon.

Ju. 9: 15. of bramble devour c. o. L.
Ps. 104: 16. c. o. L. wh. he planted
Is. 2: 13. day of L. upon all c. o. L.
14: 8. c. o. L. rejoice at thee
Eze. 27: 5. c. fr. L. to make masts

CEDRON.

Jn. 18: 1. went over brook C.

CEILED, ING.

1 K. 6: 15. he built walls with c-g
2 Ch. 3: 5. he c-d greater house with fir [painted
Je. 22: 14. c-d with cedar and
Eze. 41: 16. c-d fr. ground | † c-g with wood [houses
Hag. 1: 4. time to dwell in c-d

CELEBRATE.

Le. 23: 32. even to even shall c. sab.
41. a statute, ye shall c. it in 7th
Is. 38: 18. death cannot c. thee

CELESTIAL.

1 Co. 15: 40. are c. bodies, glory of c.

CELLARS.

1 Ch. 27: 28. over c. of oil was Joash

CEN'CHREA.

Ac. 18: 18. Paul having shorn his head in C. [at C.
Ro. 16: 1. Phebe servant of church

CENSER, S.

Le. 10: 1. sons of Aaron took c-s
16: 12. take c. full of burning coals
Nu. 4: 14. put upon it ves. even c-s
16: 6. Take ye c-s | 17. ev. man c.
39. Eleazar took the brazen c-s
46. Moses said, Take c. [4: 22.
1 K. 7: 50. c-s of pure gold, 2 Ch.
2 Ch. 26: 19. Uzziah had a c. in
Eze. 8: 11. with every man his c.
He. 9: 4. holiest had the golden c.
Re. 8: 3. angel, having a golden c.
5. angel took the c. and filled it

CENSURE.

2 Co. 2: † 6. sufficient is this c.

CENTURION, S.

Mat. 8: 5. there came unto him a c.
8. c. said, Lord, I am not worthy
13. Jes. said unto c., Go thy way
27: 54. when c. saw earthquake
Mk. 15: 39. c. saw he so cried, 44, 45.
Lu. 7: 2. c. servant was sick
6. c. sent friends to him
23: 47. when c. saw what was done
Ac. 10: 1. Cornelius was a c. of
22. Cornelius the c. a just man
21: 32. who immediately took c-s
22: 25. Paul said to c., 27: 31.
26. When c. heard that, he
23: 17. then Paul called one of c.
23. he called unto him two c.
24: 23. he com. a c. to keep Paul
Ac. 27: 1. deliv. Paul unto Julius a c.
6. there c. found a ship
11. c. bel. master more than Paul
43. c. willing to save Paul, kept
28: 16. c. delivered the prisoners

CE'PHAS.

Jn. 1: 42. shalt be called C. stone
1 Co. 1: 12. ev. one saith, I am of C.
3: 22. whether Paul, or C. or life
9: 5. as brethren of Lord, and C.
15: 5. that he was seen of C. then
Ga. 2: 9. Ja., C. and John, pillars

CEREMONIES.

Nu. 9: 3. keep passover acco. to c.
He. 9: † 1. first covenant had also c.

CERTAIN. [Some.]

Ex. 16: 4. gather c. rate ev. day
Nu. 16: 2. Korah rose with c. of
De. 13: 13. c. men chil. of Belial
25: 2. wicked beaten by c. number
2 Ch. 8: 13. aft. c. rate offering
Ne. 1: 2. Hanani and c. men of Jud.
4. I mourned c. days, and fasted
11: 23. a c. portion be for singers
13: 25. I smote c. of them, and
Je. 41: 5. came c. from Shechem
52: 15. capt. carried away c. poor
Da. 8: 27. I Daniel was sick c. days
11: 13. king come after c. years
Mat. 8: 19. a c. scribe came and said
18: 23. likened to c. king, 22: 2.
20: 20. sons desiring a c. thing
Mk. 12: 42. a c. widow, Lu. 21: 2.
14: 57. arose c. bare false witness
Lu. 5: 12. when he was in c. city
17. came to pass on c. day as teach.
8: 20. told him by c., Thy mother
10: 38. into a c. village, 17: 12.
11: 27. a c. woman lifted voice
37. c. Pharisee besought him
18: 9. parable to c. who trusted
23: 19. Who for a c. sedition
24: 1. and c. others with them
22. c. women made us astonished
24. c. with us went to sepulchre
Jn. 5: 4. angel went at c. season
Ac. 9: 19. Saul was c. days with
10: 48. Peter to tarry c. days
12: 1. to vex c. of the church
15: 2. Bar. and c. other of them
24. c. which went from us
17: 28. as c. of your own poets
19: 13. c. of vagabond
31. c. of the chief of Asia that
23: 17. hath c. thing to tell him
Ro. 15: 26. c. contribu. for saints
Ga. 2: 12. bef. c. came from James
He. 2: 6. one in a c. place testified
4: 4. spake in c. place of 7th day
7. he limited a c. day, saying
10: 27. a c. fearful looking for
Jude 4. there are c. men crept in

A CERTAIN Man.

See MAN.

CERTAIN. [Sure.]

De. 13: 14. and the thing c., 17: 4
1 K. 2: 37. know for c. thou die, 42.
Je. 26: 15. know for c. if ye put
Da. 2: 45. the dream is c. and
Ac. 25: 26. no c. thing to write
1 Co. 4: 11. no c. dwelling-place
1 Ti. 6: 7. it is c. we can carry

CERTAINLY.

Ge. 18: 10. I will c. return to
26: 28. We saw c. Lord with thee
43: 7. could we c. know he would
44: 15. man as I can c. divine?
50: 15. will c. requite us evil
Ex. 3: 12. c. I will be with thee
22: 4. If theft be c. found in his
Le. 5: 19. he hath c. trespassed
24: 16. the congre. sh. c. stone him
Jos. 9: 24. it was c. told thy serv-ts
Ju. 14: 12. c. declare the riddle
1 S. 20: 3. thy father c. knoweth
9. if I knew c. evil were determ.
23: 10. c. heard Saul will come

1 S. 25 : 28. c. make a sure house
1 K. 1 : 30. so will I c. do this day
2 K. 8 : 10. thou mayest c. recover
2 Ch. 18 : 27. if c. return in peace
Pr. 23 : 5. riches c. make wings
Je. 8 : 8. Lo, c. in vain made he it
13 : 12. not c. know every bottle
25 : 28. Ye shall c. drink [land
36 : 29. k. of Bab. shall c. destroy
40 : 14. c. know Baal is sent?
42 : 19. know c. I have admonish.
22. c. ye shall die by sword
44 : 17. c. do what goeth out of
La. 2 : 16. c. day looked for
Da. 11 : 10. one shall c. come, 13.
Zch. 11 : † 11. poor c. knew it was
Lu. 23 : 47. c. this a righteous man

CERTAINTY.

Jos. 23 : 13. for c. L. will no more
1 S. 23 : 23. come to me with c.
Pr. 22 : 21. c. of words of truth
Da. 2 : 8. c. ye would gain time
Lu. 1 : 4. know c. of those things
Ac. 21 : 34. could not know the c.
22 : 30. would have known the c.

CERTIFY, IED.

2 S. 15 : 28. word fr. you to c. me
Ez. 4 : 14. we sent and c-d king
16. c-d king, if city be built
5 : 10. their names to c. thee
7 : 24. we c. you to impose no
Es. 2 : 22. Esth. c-d king in Mordecai's name [preached of me
Ga. 1 : 11. I c. you that gospel wh. was

CE'SAR.

Mat. 22 : 17. Is it lawful to give tribute to C.? Mk. 12 : 14. Lu. 20 : 22.
21. Render to C. things, Mk. 12 : 17. Lu. 20 : 25.
Lu. 2 : 1. went out a decree fr. C.
3 : 1. in 15th year of Tiberius C.
23 : 2. forbidding tribute to C.
Jn. 19 : 12. If thou let this man go, not C.'s friend : speaketh ag. C.
15. ans., We have no king but C.
Ac. 11 : 28. in days of Claudius C.
17 : 7. do contrary to decrees of C.
25 : 8. nor ag. C. have I offended
11. I appeal unto C.
21. till I might send him to C.
26 : 32. if he had not appeal. to C.
27 : 24. thou must be bro-t bef. C.
28 : 19. I was constr. to appeal to C.
Ph. 4 : 22. they th. are of C. househ.

CE'SAREA.

Mat. 16 : 13. Jesus came into C.
Mk. 8 : 27. Jes. went into towns of C.
Ac. 8 : 40. prea., till he came to C.
9 : 30. breth. brought Paul to C.
10 : 24. morrow aft. they ent. into C.
11 : 11. Cornelius sent 3 men fr. C.
12 : 19. Herod went down to C.
18 : 22. when he had landed at C.
21 : 16. went with us of disci. of C.
23 : 23. ready 200 soldi. to go to C.
25 : 1. after 3 days he ascen. fr. C.
4. ans., Paul should be kept at C.

CE'SIL. [38 : † 31.

Jb. 9 : † 9. wh. maketh Arcturus C. |

CHAFED.

2 S. 17 : 8. they be c. in their minds

CHAFF.

Jb. 21 : 18. wicked as c. that storm
Ps. 1 : 4. like c. which wind
35 : 5. Let them be as c. bef. wind
Is. 5 : 24. as flame consumeth c.
17 : 13. nations be chased as c.
29 : 5. terrible ones shall be as c.
33 : 11. Ye shall conceive c. and
41 : 15. thresh mts., hills as c.
Jo. 23 : 28. What is c. to wheat?
Da. 2 : 35. like c. of threshing floor
Ho. 13 : 3. as c. which is driven
Zph. 2 : 2. before day pass as c.
Mat. 3 : 12. burn up c., Lu. 3 : 17.

CHAIN. [16, 29.

Ge. 41 : 42. gold c. ab. his neck, Da. 5 : 7,
Ps. 73 : 6. pride compasseth as a c.
Can. 4 : 9. ravished me with one c.
La. 3 : 7. hath made my c. heavy
Eze. 7 : 23. Make a c. land is full of
16 : 11. I put a c. on thy neck [c.
Ac. 28 : 20. I am bound with this
Ep. 6 : † 20. I an ambassador in a c.
2 Ti. 1 : 16. was not asham. of my c.
Re. 20 : 1. angel and c. in hand

CHAIN work.

1 K. 7 : 17. wreaths of c. w. for pillars

CHAINS.

Ex. 28 : 14. fasten wreathen c., 22, 24, 25.—39 : 15, 17, 18.
39 : 15. made on breast-plate c.
Nu. 31 : 50. for atonement, c. and
Ju. 8 : 26. c. about camels' necks
1 K. 6 : 21. c. of gold bef. oracle
2 Ch. 3 : 5. set palm trees and c.
16. made c. as in oracle
Ps. 149 : 8. To bind kings with c.
Pr. 1 : 9. instruction be c. ab. neck
Can. 1 : 10. neck comely with c.
Is. 3 : 19. L. will take away thy c.
40 : 19. and casteth silver c.
45 : 14. shall come after thee in c.
Je. 40 : 4. I loose thee from thy c.
Eze. 19 : 4. bro-t him with c. into E.
9. they put him in ward in c.
Mk. 5 : 3. bind him, no not with c.
4. c. oft plucked asunder
Ac. 12 : 7. Peter's c. fell off fr. his
2 Pe. 2 : 4. to hell, delivered into c.
Jude 6. reserved in everlasting c.
See Bound.

CHALCEDONY.

Re. 21 : 19. third founda. was a c.

CHAL'COL = CAL'COL.

1 K. 4 : 31. Sol. was wiser than C.
1 Ch. 2 : 6. the sons of Zerah ; C.

CHALDE'A. [L.

Je. 50 : 10. C. shall be a spoil, saith
51 : 24. render to inhab. of C. evil
35. blood be upon inhab. of C.
Eze. 16 : 29. multipli. fornica. to C.
23 : 16. sent messengers into C.

CHALDE'AN.

Ezr. 5 : 12. gave into hand of Neb. C.
Da. 2 : 10. asked such at any C.

CHALDEANS.

Jb. 1 : 17. C. made out three bands,
Is. 23 : 13. land of C. Assyr. founded
43 : 14. have brought down all C.
47 : 1. is no throne O dau. of C.
5. into darkness O daughter of C.
48 : 14. his arm shall be on the C.
20. flee ye from the C.
Je. 21 : 4. wherewith ye fight ag. C.
9. that falleth to C. sh. live, 38 : 2.
25 : 12. punish land of C., 50 : 1, 45.
32 : 5. tho. ye fight with C. sh. not
24. city is giv. into hand of C., 43.
29. C. shall set fire on this city
33 : 5. come to fight with the C.
37 : 8. the C. shall fight ag-st city
9. saving, C. shall depart from us
10. tho. ye had smitten army of C.
14. said Jere., I fall not away to C.
38 : 19. afraid of Jews fall. to the C.
23. shall bring out thy chil. to C.
39 : 8. C. burnt king's house, and
40 : 9. said, Fear not to serve the C.
10. dwell at Mizpah, to serve C.
41 : 3. Ishmael slew C. at Mizpah
43 : 3. sett. thee on to deliv. us to C.
50 : 35. A sword is upon the C.
45. Lord hath purposed ag. C.
51 : 4. slain shall fall in land of C.
52 : 8. army of C. pursued Zed.
Eze. 12 : 13. I will bring him to C.
23 : 14. she saw the images of C.
Da. 1 : 4. might teach tongue of C.
2 : 2. then king com. to call the C.
3 : 8. certain C. accused the Jews
4 : 7. came in C. and soothsayers
5 : 7. king cried to bring in the C.
11. thy father made master of C.
Da. 9 : 1. Darius made king over C.
Ha. 1 : 6. lo, C. that hasty nation
Ac. 7 : 4. Abr. came out of land of C.

CHAL'DEES.

2 K. 24 : 2. L. sent ag. bands of C.
25 : 4. the C. were against the city
10. army of C. brake down walls
26. to Egypt, were afraid of C. [C.
2 Ch. 36 : 17. bro-t upon them k. of
Is. 13 : 19. Babylon the beauty of C.
See Ur.

CHALK-STONES.

Is. 27 : 9. maketh stones of altar as c.

CHALLENGETH.

Ex. 22 : 9. another c. to be his

CHAMBER.

Ge. 43 : 30. Joseph entered into c.
Ju. 15 : 1. to my wife into the c.
16 : 9. liers in wait in c., 12.
2 S. 13 : 10. Bring meat into the c.
18 : 33. went up to c. and wept
1 K. 1 : 15. went unto king into c.
14 : 28. into guard c., 2 Ch. 12 : 11.
17 : 23. brought him out of c.
2 K. 4 : 11. Elisha turned into the c.
23 : 11. c. of Nathan-melech
Ezr. 10 : 6. went into c. of Johanan
Ne. 13 : 4. oversight of c. of house
5. prepared for Tobiah a c.
7. preparing him c. in courts
8. cast household stuff out of c.
Jb. 37 : † 9. out of c. whirlwind
Ps. 19 : 5. as bridegroom out of c.
Can. 3 : 4. c. of her th. conceived me
Je. 35 : 4. into c. of sons of Hanan
36 : 10. read the book in the c.
20. laid up roll in c. of Elishama
Eze. 40 : 45. c. whose prospect
46. c. whose prospect tow. north
41 : 7. fr. lowest c. to highest
42 : 1. c. over against separate place
Da. 6 : 10. windows open in his c.
Jo. 2 : 16. bridegroom go forth of c.
See Bedchamber, Guardchamber, Guestchamber.

Inner CHAMBER.

1 K. 20 : 30. Benhadad fled, into i. c.
22 : 25. into i. c. to hide, 2 Ch. 18 : 24.
2 K. 9 : 2. carry Jehu into i. c.

Little CHAMBER.

2 K. 4 : 10. make a l. c. on wall
Eze. 40 : 7. l. c. was one reed long
13. the gate from roof of one l. c.

Side CHAMBER, S.

Eze. 41 : 5. breadth of s. c. 4 cubits
6. the s. c-s were three, one over
9. thickness of wall for s. c. five

Upper CHAMBER, S.

2 K. 1 : 2. fell thro. a lattice in u. c.
23 : 12. altars on top of u. c. Josiah
2 Ch. 3 : 9. and he overlaid the u. c-s with gold
Eze. 42 : 5. u. c-s were shorter for
Ac. 9 : 37. laid Dorcas in an u. c.
39. Peter, when come into u. c.
20 : 8. many lights in u. c. where

CHAMBERS.

De. 32 : † 25. terror from the c.
1 K. 6 : 5. against wall he built c., 10.
1 Ch. 9 : 26. porters over c., 23 : 28.
33. who in c. were free
28 : 12. of all c. round about
2 Ch. 31 : 11. Hez. com-d prepare c.
Ezr. 8 : 29. until ye weigh them in c.
Ne. 10 : 37. c. of h. of our G., 38, 39.
12 : 44. app-d over c. for treasures
13 : 9. and they cleansed the c.
Jb. 9 : 9. maketh c. of the south
Ps. 104 : 3. beams of his c. in waters
13. He watereth hills from his c.
105 : 30. frogs in c. of their king
Pr. 7 : 27. going down to c. of death
24 : 4. by knowledge c. be filled
Can. 1 : 4. k. brought me into his c.
Is. 26 : 20. enter thy c. and shut
Je. 22 : 13. buildeth his c. by wrong
14. build wide house, large c.

Je. 35 : 2. bring Rechabites into c.
Eze. 8 : 12. in c. of his imagery
21:14.sword entereth privy c. [36.
40 : 7. little c.,10, 12, 16,21, 29,33,
17. thirty c. upon pavement
44. c. of singers in inner court
42 : 4. bef. c. was a walk
13. holy c. where priests
44 : 19. lay them in the holy c.
45 : 5. a possession for twenty c.
46 : 19. into holy c. of priests
Mat.24 : 26. behold he is in secret c.

CHAMBERING.

Ro. 13 : 13. walk not in c. and

CHAMBERLAIN, S.

2 K. 9 : † 32.to Jehu two or three c.
23 : 11. of Nathan-melech the c.
Es. 1 : 10. seven c. that served k.
12. at king's command by c., 15.
2 : 3. Hege k's c. | 14.Shaashgaz c.
15. Hegai king's c. appointed
21. two of king's c. were wroth
4 : 4. Esther's maids and c.came
5. Hatach one of the king's c.
6 : 14. came king's c. and hasted
7 : 9. Harbonah one of k's c. said
Ac. 12 : 20. Blastus the king's c.
Ro. 16 : 23. Erastus c. of city

CHAMELEON.

Le. 11 : 30. these be unclean, c.

CHAMOIS.

De. 14 : 5. these ye shall eat, c.

CHAMPAIGN.

De. 11 : 30. who dwell in the c.
Eze. 37 : † 2. many bones in open c.

CHAMPION.

1 S. 17 : 4. went a c. out of camp
23. came up c. Philistine of G
51. Philis. saw their c. was dead

CHA'NAAN. See CA'NAAN.

CHANCE, [Noun.]

1 S. 6 : 9. c. that happened to us
2 S. 1:6. I happ. by c. upon Gilboa
Ec. 9 : 11. time and c. happeneth
Lu. 10 : 31. by c. a priest came

CHANCE, ETH.

De. 22 : 6. if a bird's nest c. to be
23 : 10. uncleanness that c-h him
1 Co. 15 : 37. it may c. of wheat

CHANCELLOR.

Ezr. 4 : 8. Rehum c. wrote, 9, 17.

CHANGE, S. [5 c-s

Ge. 45:22. each he gave c-s, to Benj.
Le. 27 : 33. it and c. be holy
Ju. 14 : 12. give 30 c. of raiment, 13.
19. gave c-s of garm. unto them
2 K. 5 : 5. he took ten c. of raiment
22. give them, two c. of garm.
23. bound two c. of garments
Jb. 10 : 17. c-s and war are ag. me
11 : † 10. make c. who can hinder?
14 : 14. wait till my c. come
Ps. 55: 19.have no c-s they fear not
Pr. 24 : 21. with them given to c.
Zch. 3 : 4. clothe with c. of raiment
He. 7 : 12. of necessity a c. of law

CHANGE. [Verb.]

Ge. 35 : 2. and c. your garments
Le. 27 : 10. he shall not c. it
33. nor c. it, if he c.
Jb. 17 : 12. They c. night into day
Ps. 102 : 26. as vesture c. them
Is. 9 : 10. will c. them into cedars
40 : † 31. wait upon L. c. strength
Je. 2 : 36. so much to c. thy way?
13 : 23. Can Ethiopian c. his skin?
Da. 7 : 25. shall think to c. times
Ho. 4 : 7. c. glory into shame
Ha. 1 : 11. Then shall his mind c.
Mal. 3 : 6. I am the Lord, I c. not
Ac. 6 : 14. shall c. the customs
Ro. 1 : 26. women did c. use
Ga. 4 : 20. desire to c. my voice
Ph. 3 : 21. Christ, shall c. vile body
He. 12 : † 17. no way to c. his mind

CHANGEABLE.

Is. 3 : 22. take c. suits of apparel

CHANGED.

Ge. 31 : 7. father c. my wages, 41.
41 : 14. Joseph c. his raiment, and
Le. 13 : 16. if raw flesh be c.
55. if plague not c. his colour
Nu. 32 : 38. names being c.
1 S. 21 : 13. he c. his behaviour
2 S. 12 : 20. David c. his apparel
2 K.24 : 17. k. c. his name to Zedek.
25 : 29. c. prison garm., Je. 52 : 33.
Es. 2 : † 9. he c. her to best place
Jb. 29 : † 20. bow was c. in my
30 : 18. by disease is my garm. c.
Ps.102 : 26.as vesture be c.,He.1:12.
106 : 20. they c. their glory into
Ec. 8:1.boldness of face be c. [an ox
Is. 24 : 5. c. the ordinance
Je. 2 : 11. c. their gods my peo. c.
48 : 11. and his scent is not c.
La. 4 : 1. how is fine gold c.?
Eze. 5 : 6. she hath c. my judgm.
Da. 2 : 9. speak, till the time be c.
3 : 19. visage was c. ag-st Shadrach
27. nor coats c. nor smell of fire
28. have c. the king's word
4 : 16. let his heart be c. fr. man's
6 : 8. sign writing that it be not c.
15. that no decree may be c.
17. that purpose might not be c.
Mi. 2 : 4. c. portion of my people
Ac. 28 : 6. barbarians c. their minds
Ro.1:23. c. glory of uncorrupt. God
25. Who c. truth of God into lie
1 Co. 15 : 51. we shall all be c., 52.
2 Co. 3 : 18. c. into same image
He. 7 : 12. priesthood being c.

CHANGED, EST,
countenance. [him

Jb. 14 : 20. thou c-t his c., sendest
Da. 5 : 6.king's c. was c. in him, 9.
10. nor let thy c. be c.
7 : 28. my c. c. in me

CHANGERS.

Pr. 24:†21. meddle not with c.
Mat. 21:12. Jes. overthrew tables of
money-c.,Mk.11:15.Jn.2:14,15.

CHANGETH, ING.

Ru. 4 : 7. manner in Isr. conc. c-g
Ps. 15:4. swear. to his hurt, c-h not
Da. 2 : 21. he c-h times and seasons

CHANNEL, S.

2 S. 22 : 16. c-s of sea app.,Ps.18:15.
Jb. 31 : † 22. arm broken fr. c. bone
Ps. 18 : 15. c-s of waters were seen
Is. 8 : 7. shall come up over his c-s
27 : 12. beat off from c. of river

CHA'NOCH. [C.

Ge. 4 : † 17. she conceived and bare

CHANT.

Am. 6 : 5. c. to sound of viol

CHAPEL.

Am. 7 : 13. it is [illegible] king's c.

CHAPITER, S.

Ex. 36 : 38. overlaid c-s, 38 : 28.
38 : 17. overlay. of c. were silv., 19.
1 K. 7 : [illegible]. made two c. of brass
17. c-s upon top of pillars, 18,19.
41, 42. 2 Ch. 4 : 12, 13.
2 K. 25 : 17. c. was brass, Je. 52:22.
Am. 9 : † 1. smite the c. of the door
Zph. 2 : † 14. the bittern shall lodge

CHAPMEN. [in c.

2 Ch. 9:14. besides what c. brought

CHAPPED.

Je. 14 : 4. because ground is c.

CHAR'ASHIM.

1 Ch. 4 : 14. father of valley of C.

CHARGE. [Noun.]

Ge. 26 : 5. Abraham kept my c.
28 : 6. Isaac gave Jacob a c.
Ex. 6 : 13. gave Moses and Aa. a c.
Nu. 3 : 28. keeping c. of sanc., 38.
31. their c. shall be the ark
4 : 31. c. of burden in tabernacle
8 : 26. Levites, touching their c.
9 : 19. Israel kept c. of Lord, 23.,
27 : 23. Joshua a c., De. 31 : 23.
Nu. 31 : 47. kept c. of tabernacle
De.21:8.lay not blood unto peo.'s c.
Jos. 22 : 3. Reubenites kept c. of L.
2 S. 17 : † 23. Ahithophel gave c.
18 : 5. king gave c. conc. Absalom
1 K. 4 : 28. ev. man accord. to his c.
11 : 28. Jerob. ruler over all c.
2 K. 7 : 17. lord to have c. of gate
1 Ch. 9 : 27. bec. c. was upon them
28. c. of ministering vessels
26 : † 30.of Hebronites 1700 over c.
2 Ch.30 : 17.had c. of killing passo.
Ne. 7 : 2. Hanani c. over Jerusalem
Es. 3 : 9. that have c. of business
Jb.34 : 13. Who hath given him a c.?
Ps. 35 : 11. they laid to my c.
109 : † 8. let another take his c.,
Ac. 1 : † 20.
Je. 39 : 11. king gave c. conc. Jere.
47 : 7. given it a c. ag-st Ashkelon
52 : 25. had c. of men of war
Eze.9 : 1.them that have c. ov. city
44 : 8. not kept c. of holy things
15. that kept c. of my sanctuary
48 : 11. priests kept my c. who
Ac. 7 : 60. lay not sin to their c.
8 : 27. eunuch, had c. of all treas.
12:†25.B. and Saul fulfill. their c.
16 : 24. having receiv. c. thrust
23 : 29. noth. laid to his c. worthy
Ro.8 : 33.who lay to c. of God's elect
1 Co. 9 : 18. make gosp. without c.
1 Ti.1:18.This c.I commit unto thee
2 Ti. 4 : 16. not be laid to their c.

Give CHARGE.

Nu. 27 : 19. and g. Joshua a c.
De. 31 : 14. call Josh. that I g. a c.
2 S. 14 : 8. I will g. c. conc. thee
2 K. 20 : † 1. g. c. concern. house,
Is. 38 : † 1. [dom and c.
1 Ch. 22:12. only the L. g. thee wis-
Ps. 91 : 11. g. his angels c., Mat.
4 : 6. Lu. 4 : 10.
Is. 10 : 6. g. him c. to take spoil
1 Ti. 5 : 7. these things g. in c.
6 : 13. I g. thee c. in sight of God

KEEP CHARGE.

See KEEP.

CHARGES. [c.

2 Ch. 8 : 14.appoin. Levites to their
31:17.from 20 years in their c.,16.
35 : 2. set priests in c. and encour.
Ac. 21 : 24. be at c. with them
1 Co. 9 : 7. warfare at his own c.?

CHARGE. [Verb.]

Ex. 19 : 21. Go down, c. the people
Nu. 5 : 19. priest sh. c. her by oath
De. 3 : 28. c. Joshua and encour.
Ne. 10 : 32. to c. ourselves yearly
Es. 4 : 8. c. Esther that she go in
Can. 2 : 7. I c.you, O ye daughters,
3 : 5.–5 : 8.–8 : 4. [c. us?
5 : 9. What thy beloved, thou dost
Mk. 9 : 25. I c. thee come out
1 Th. 5 : 27. c. you epistle be read
1 Ti. 1:3. c. th. they teach no other
5 : 21. I c. thee bef. G., 2 Ti. 4 : 1.
6 : 17.c.them are rich in this work

CHARGEABLE.

2 S. 13 : 25. not all go, lest we be c.
Ne. 5 : 15. governors were c. to peo.
2 Co. 11 : 9. with you, I was c. to no
1 Th. 2 : 9. bec. we would not be c.
2 Th. 3 : 8. might not be c. to any

CHARGED.

Ge. 26 : 11. Abimelech c. his people
28 : 1. Isaac called Jacob, c. him
40 : 4. captain c. Jo. with them
49 : 29. Jacob c. his sons, and said
50 : † 16. c. a messenger to Joseph
Ex. 1 : 22. Pharoah c. all his peo.
De. 1 : 16. I c. your judges
24 : 5. nor be c. with any business
27 : 11. Moses c. people same day
Jos.18 : 8.c.them went to desc. land
22 : 5. Moses serv. of Lord c. you
Ru. 2 : 9. Have I not c. young men

1 S. 14: 27. Saul c. people, 28.
2 S. 11: 19. c. messenger, saying
18: 12. in our hearing king c. thee
1 K. 2: 1. David c. Solomon his son
43. com-t that I have c. thee with
13: 9. so was it c. me by Lord
2 K. 17: 15. conc. whom L. had c.
35. made cov. and c. them [Ezr. 1:2.
2 Ch. 36: 23. Lord c. me to build,
Ne. 13: 19. c. gates not be opened
Es. 2: 10. as Mordecai c. her, 20.
Jb. 1: 22. nor c. God foolishly
4: 18. his angels he c. with folly
Je. 32: 13. I c. Baruch bef. them
35: 8. obeyed Jonadab in all he c.
Mat. 9: 30. Jes. straitly c. that no
man know, Mk. 5: 43. Lu. 9: 21.
12: 16. Jesus c. not to make him
known, Mk. 3: 12.
16: 20. c. he his disciples
17: 9. c. th. Tell vision to no man
Mk. 1: 43. c. him, sent him away
7: 36. c. not to tell, 8: 30.–9: 9.
Lu. 5: 14.–8: 56.
8: 15. c. them, Take heed
10: 48. c. him he sho. hold peace
Ac. 23: 22. young man dep. and c.
Ro. 3: †9. we have c. Jews and [him
1 Th. 2: 11. we c. ev. one as a fa.
1 Ti. 5: 16 let not church be c.

CHARGEDST, EST, ING.

Ex. 19: 23. thou c-dst us, Set bounds
2 S. 3: 8. c-est with fault conc. wom.
Ac. 16: 23. c-g jailer to keep them
2 Ti. 2: 14. c-g strive not about [words

CHARGER, S.

Nu. 7: 13. offering 1 silver c., 19, 25,
31, 37, 43, 49, 61, 67, 73, 79.
84. dedication of altar, twelve c.
85. each c. of silver 130 shekels
Ezr. 1: 9. this is number 1000 c.
Mat. 14: 8. Bapt. head in c., Mk. 6: 25.
11. head bro-t in c., Mk. 6: 28.

CHARIOT.

Ge. 41: 43. he made him ride in c.
Ex. 14: 25. L. took off c. wheels
1 K. 7: 33. like work of c. wheel
10: 29. c. came and went out of E.
18: 44. Prepare thy c. and get down
20: 25. number thee c. for c. and
33. caused him to come into c.
22: 35. blood ran into the c.
38. one washed c. in pool of Sa.
2 K. 2: 11. there appeared c. of fire
12. My father, c. of Isr., 13: 14.
5: 21. from c. to meet Gehazi
9: 16. Jehu in c. | 27. Smite in c.
28. carr. him in a c. to Jerus., 23: 30.
10: 15. took him up into c.
1 Ch. 28: 18. gold for pattern of c.
2 Ch. 1: 17. out of E. c. for 600 shek.
2 Ch. 35: 24. serv. took him out of c.
Ps. 46: 9. burneth the c. in fire
76: 6. c. and horse cast into sleep
Can. 3: 9. c. of wood of Lebanon
Is. 21: 7. c. with horsem. c. of asses
9. here cometh a c. of men with
43: 17. Who bringeth forth the c.
Je. 51: 21. will I break in pieces c.
Mi. 1: 13. bind c. to swift beast
Zch. 6: 2. first c. red horses, sec. c.
3. in third c. white horses
9: 10. I will cut off c. fr. Ephr.
Ac. 8: 29. Go join thyself to his c.
38. he com-d the c. to stand still

His CHARIOT.

Ge. 46: 29. Joseph made ready h. c.
Ex. 14: 6. Pha. made ready h. c.
Ju. 4: 15. Sisera lighted off h. c.
5: 28. Why h. c. so long in coming?
1 K. 12: 18. king speed to h. c., 2
Ch. 10: 18.
22: 34. to driver of h. c. Turn hand
35. Ahab was stayed up in h. c.
2 K. 5: 9. Naaman came with h. c.
26. when man turned from h. c.
9: 21. h. c. ready, went each in h. c.
2 K. 9: 24. Jehor. sunk down in h. c.
10: 16. they made him ride in h. c.
2 Ch. 18: 34. king of Israel stayed
himself in h. c.
Ps. 104: 3. maketh clouds h. c.
Ac. 8: 28. sitting in h. c. read Esaias

CHARIOT cities.

2 Ch. 1: 14. horsemen he placed in c. c.
8: 6. Sol. built c. c. and store cities
9: 25. bestowed in c. c. and with k.

CHARIOT horses.

2 S. 8: 4. houghed all c. h., 1 Ch. 18: 4.
2 K. 7: 14. They took theref. 2 c. h.

CHARIOT man.

2 Ch. 18: 33. said to c. m. Turn hand

CHARIOTS.

Ge. 50: 9. went up with Joseph c.
Ex. 14: 7. Pha. took 600 c. all the c.
17. will get honour upon his c., 18.
28. the waters covered all the c.
15: 4. Pha.'s c. hath he cast into sea
19. horse of Pha. went in with c.
Jos. 17: 16. c. of iron, 18. Ju. 1: 19.
Ju. 4: 13. Sisera gath-d his c. [–4: 3.
4: 15. L. discomfited Sisera and c.
16. Barak pursued after c.
5: 28. why tarry wheels of his c.?
1 S. 8: 11. k. will appoint for his c.
13: 5. Philis. to fight ag. Isr. 30,000 c.
2 S. 1: 6. c. and horsem. foll. Saul
8: 4. Da. took 1000 c. (2) 1 Ch. 18: 4.
10: 18. David slew men of 700 c.
1 K. 1: 5. prepared c. and horsem.
10: 26. Sol. had 1400 c., 2 Ch. 1: 14.
16: 9. Zimri capt. of half his c.
22: 31. th. had rule over c. [18: 31.
32. capt-s of c. saw Jehos., 2 Ch.
33. capt-s of c. perceiv., 2 Ch. 18: 32.
2 K. 13: 7. left but ten c. and fifty
18: 24. trust on E. for c., Is. 36: 9.
19: 23. mult. of my c. I am come
23: 11. burned c. of the sun
Ps. 68: 17. c. of G. are 20,000 [mina.
Can. 6: 12. my soul like c. of Am-
Is. 2: 7. nor is any end of their c.
22: 7. choicest valleys full of c.
18. c. of thy glory be shame
31: 1. woe to them trust in c.
37: 24. by mult. of c. am I come
66: 15. L. with c. like whirlwind,
Je. 4: 13. Da. 11: 40.
Je. 4: 13. his c. be as a whirlwind
47: 3. at rushing of his c.
Ez. 23: 24. come ag. thee with c.
26: 10. walls shake at noise of c.
27: 20. merch. in prec. clothes for c.
Jo. 2: 5. Like noise of c. leap
Mi. 5: 10. I will destroy thy c.
Na. 2: 3. c. shall be with torches
4. c. shall rage in streets and jos.
13. I will burn her c. in smoke
Hag. 2: 22. I will overthrow c.
Zch. 6: 1. four c. from between two
Re. 9: 9. sound of wings as of c.

CHARIOTS with horses.

Ex. 14: 9. all the h. and c. of Pha.
De. 11: 4. he did unto h. and c. [23.
20: 1. seest h. and c. fear not
Jos. 11: 4. h. and c. very many
6. hough their h. burn c.
9. Josh. houghed h. burnt their c.
2 S. 15: 1. Abs. prepared h. and c.
1 K. 20: 1. ag. Sama. with c. and h.
2 K. 6: 14. sent he horses and c.
17. mt. was full of c. and h.
7: 6. to hear a noise of h. and c.
10: 2. are with you c. and h.
Ps. 20: 7. some trust in c. some in h.
Can. 1: 9. compar. to h. in Pha. c.
Is. 66: 20. bring breth. upon h. in c.
Je. 17: 25. enter princes in c. 22: 4.
46: 9. Come up, ye h. rage, ye c.
50: 37. sword is upon h. and c.
Eze. 26: 7. upon Tyrus Neb. with c.
39: 20. at my table with h. and c.
Na. 3: 2. prancing h. jumping c.
Ha. 3: 8. ride on h. and c. of salv.
Re. 18: 13. no man buys h. and c.

CHARITABLY.

Ro. 14: 15. now walkest not c.

CHARITY.

Ro. 14: † 15. now walkest thou not
1 Co. 8: 1. but c. edifieth [ace. to c.
13: 1. and have not c., 2, 3.
4. c. suff. long, c. envieth not
8. c. never faileth: but whether
13. faith, hope, c. greatest is c.
14: 1. Follow c. desire spiritual
16: 14. Let all be done with c.
Col. 3: 14. above all put on c.
1 Th. 3: 6. good tidings of your c.
2 Th. 1: 3. c. toward each other
1 Ti. 1: 5. end of comm. is c.
2: 15. if continue in faith and c.
4: 12. be an example in c. in
2 Ti. 2: 22. follow righteousness, c.
3: 10. known my life, faith, c.
Tit. 2: 2. aged men be sound in c.
1 Pe. 4: 8. fervent c. cover sins
5: 14. Greet with a kiss of c.
2 Pe. 1: 7. to brotherly-kindness c.
3 Jn. 6. borne witness of thy c.
Jude 12. spots in your feasts of c.
Re. 2: 19. I know thy works, c.

CHARMED, ING.

Ps. 58: 5. c-g never so wisely
Je. 8: 17. serpents wh. not be c.

CHARMER, S.

De. 18: 11. not be found am. you a c.
Ps. 58: 5. not heark. to voice of c-s
† not hearken to c. be the c. never
Is. 19: 3. seek to idols and to c-s

CHARRAN.

Ac. 7: 2. before Abr. dwelt in C., 4.

CHASE.

Le. 26: 7. shall c. all your enemies
8. five of you shall c. a hundred
36. sound of leaf shall c. them
De. 32: 30. one c. 1000, Jos. 23: 10.
Ps. 35: 5. angel of L. c. them

CHASED, ETH, ING.

De. 1: 44. Amorites c-d you as bees
Jos. 7: 5. c-d them fr. bef. gate
8: 24. wilderness they c-d them
10: 10. c-d th. along way to Beth-
11: 8. smote and c-d unto Zidon
Ju. 9: 40. Abim. c-d him, he fled
20: 43. Benjamites and c-d them
1 S. 17: 53. Isr. returned from c-g
Ne. 13: 28. I c. him from me [Phil.
Jb. 18: 18. he be c. out of world
20: 8. be c. away as a vision of
Pr. 19: 26. c-h away his mother
Is. 13: 14. it shall be as the c-d roe
17: 13. they shall be c. as the chaff
La. 3: 52. enemies c-d me sore
1 Th. 2: † 15. killed proph., and c. us

CHASTE.

2 Co. 11: 2. present you as c. virgin
Tit. 2: 5. that young women be c.
1 Pe. 3: 2. behold your c. conversa.

CHASTEN.

2 S. 7: 14. I will c. him with rod
Ps. 6: 1. nor c. me in hot, 38: 1.
Pr. 9: 18. c. thy son while hope
Da. 10: 12. didst c. thyself bef. God
Re. 3: 19. As many as I love I c.

CHASTENED.

De. 21: 18. they have c. him, he
Jb. 33: 19. He is c. also with pain
Ps. 69: 10. I c. my soul with fast.
73: 14. plagued, and c. ev. morn.
118: 18. Lord hath c. me sore, he
He. 7: † 15. though I have c. they
1 Co. 11: 32. c. th. we be not condemn.
2 Co. 6: 9. as c. and not killed
He. 12: 10. for a few days c. us

CHASTENEST, ETH, ING.

De. 8: 5. c-d his son, so L. c. thee
Jb. 5: 17. despise not c. of Almighty,
Pr. 3: 11. He. 12: 5.
Ps. 94: 12. Blessed is man thou c.
Pr. 13: 24. loveth him c-d betimes
Is. 26: 16. prayer when c. upon them

He. 12: 6. whom the L. loveth he c.
7. If ye endure c. what son whom father c. not?
11. no c. seemeth joyous

CHASTISE.

Le. 26: 28. will c. you for sins
De. 22: 18. elders shall c. him
1 K. 12: 11. I will c. you with scorpions, 14. 2 Ch. 10: 11, 14.
Ho. 7: 12. I will c. them as their
10: 10. my desire that I c. them
Lu. 23: 16. I will c. him, 22.

CHASTISED, ETH.

1 K. 12: 11. father hath c. you with whips, 14. 2 Ch. 10: 11, 14.
Ps. 94: 10. c-h heathen, he correct?
Je. 31: 18. hast c. me, and I was c.

CHASTISEMENT.

De. 11: 2. chil. hath not seen the c.
Jb. 34: 31. I have borne c. I will
Ps. 73: † 14. my c. was ev. morning
Is. 53: 5. c. of our peace upon him
Je. 30: 14. with c. of a cruel one
He. 12: 8. without c. then not sons

CHATTER.

Is. 38: 14. like crane did I c.

CHE'BAR.

Eze. 1: 1. by the river of C., 3. | 3: 15, 23.-10: 15, 20, 22.-43: 3.

CHECK.

Jb. 20: 3. heard c. of my reproach

CHECKER work.

1 K. 7: 17. Hiram made nets of c. w.

CHEDORLA'OMER.

Ge. 14: 1. C. king of E. | 4, 5.

CHEEK. [Ch. 18: 23.

1 K. 22: 24. smote Micaiah on c., 2
Jb. 16: 10. smitten me on c.
La. 3: 30. c. to him that smiteth
Mi. 5: 1. shall smite judge upon c.
Mat. 5: 39. smite thee on thy right c.
Lu. 6: 29. unto him smiteth one c.

CHEEK bone. [offer

Ps. 3: 7. smitten enemies on c. b.

CHEEK teeth.

Jo. 1: 6. nat., hath c. t. of great lion

CHEEKS.

De. 18: 3. give unto priest the two c.
Can. 1: 10. thy c. are comely with
5: 13. His c. are as a bed of spices
Is. 50: 6. I gave my c. to them that
La. 1: 2. her tears are on her c.

CHEER. [Verb.]

De. 24: 5. shall c. up his wife he
Ec. 11: 9. let heart c. thee in youth

Good CHEER.

Pr. 17: † 1. full of g. c. with strife
Mat. 9: 2. Son, be of g. c. thy sins
14: 27. Be of g. c. it is I, Mk. 6: 50.
Jn. 16: 33. be of g. c. I have overc.
Ac. 23: 11. said, Be of g. c. Paul
27: 22. I exhort you to be of g. c.
25. sirs, Be of g. c. for I believe G.
36. then were they all of g. c.

CHEERETH.

Ju. 9: 13. wine, wh. c. G. and man

CHEERFUL.

Pr. 15: 13. maketh c. countenance
Zch. 8: 19. be to Judah c. feasts
9: 17. corn sh. make young men c.
2 Co. 9: 7. God loveth a c. giver

CHEERFULLY.

Ac. 24: 10. I do more c. answer

CHEERFULNESS.

Ro. 12: 8. sheweth mercy with c.

CHEESE, S.

1 S. 17: 18. carry ten c. to captain
2 S. 17: 29. Barzil. brought c. to Da.
Jb. 10: 10. not curdled me like c.?

CHE'LAL.

Ezr. 10: 30. sons of Pahath-moab, C.

CHEL'LUH.

Ezr. 10: 35. of sons of Bani, C.

CHE'LUB. [27: 26.

1 Ch. 4: 11. C. ho. of Shuah, begat

CHELU'BAI.

1 Ch. 2: 9. sons of Hezron, C.

CHEM'ARIM.

Zph. 1: 4. I will cut off name of C.

CHE'MOSH.

Nu. 21: 29. art undone, O peo. of C.
Ju. 11: 24. wilt possess what C. giv.?
1 K. 11: 7. Solomon built a high place for C., 33.
Je. 48: 7. C. shall go into captivity
13. Moab shall be ashamed of C.
46. O Moab, peo. of C. perisheth

CHEN'AAN.

Ge. 9: † 18. Ham is the father of C.

CHENA'ANAH.

1 K. 22: 11. Zedekiah son of C., 24.
1 Ch. 7: 10. 2 Ch. 18: 10, 23.

CHEN'ANI.

Ne. 9: 4. stood upon stairs C.

CHENANI'AH.

1 Ch. 15: 22. C. was for song, 27.
26: 29. C. and sons for judges

CE'PHAR-HAAM'MONAI.

Jos. 18: 24. cities tribe of Benj. C.

CHEPHI'RAH.

Jos. 9: 17.-18: 26. Ezr. 2: 25. Ne. [7: 29.

CHE'RAN.

Ge. 36: 36 chil. of Dishon C., 1 Ch. 1: [41.

CHER'ETHIM.

Eze. 25: 16. behold, I will cut off C.

CHER'ETHITES.

1 S. 30: 14. invasion upon south of C.
2 S. 8: 18. Benaiah the son of Jehoiada was over C., 20: 23. 1 Ch. 18: 17.
15: 18. all C. passed before king
Zph. 2: 5. Woe unto nation of C.

CHERISH, ED, ETH.

1 K. 1: 2. let her c. him, and lie in
4. damsel fair and c-d the king
Ep. 5: 29. c-h his own flesh, as L. the
1 Th. 2: 7. as a nurse c-h children

CHE'RITH.

1 K. 17: 3. by the brook C., 5.

CHE'RUB. [Place.]

Ezr. 2: 59. went up fr. C., Ne. 7: 61.

CHERUB.

Ex. 25: 19. c. on one end, and c., 37: 8.
2 S. 22: 11. rode upon c., Ps. 18: 10.
1 K. 6: 25. other c. was ten cubits
26. height of one c. ten cubits
Eze. 9: 3. glory of God from c., 10: 4.
10: 7. one c. stretched forth hand
14. first face was the face of a c.
28: 14. Thou art the anointed c.
16. will destr. thee, O covering c.
41: 18. betw. c. and c.: every c. had

CHERUBIM.

Ge. 3: 24. at east of the garden c.
Ex. 25: 18. make two c. of gold
26: 1. c. of cunning work, 31.-36:
37: 7. made two c. of gold [8, 35.
1 K. 6: 23. within oracle two c.
25. both the c. of one measure
27. set c. within inner house
28. overlaid c. with gold
8: 7. c. covered the ark, 2 Ch. 5: 8. He. 9: 5.
2 Ch. 3: 10. in holy house two c.
Eze. 10: 5. sound of c. wings was
8. c. the form of man's hand
15. the c. were lifted up
16. c. went, the wheels went
19. c. lifted up their wings, 11: 22.
20. I knew they were the c.

Between CHERUBIM.

Ex. 25: 22. meet thee from b. two c.
Nu. 7: 89. from b. two c. spake
1 S. 4: 4. ark of L. dwelleth b. c., 2 S. 6: 2. 2 K. 19: 15. Is. 37: 16.
Ps. 80: 1. dwelleth b. c. shine forth
99: 1. he sitteth b. c. let earth
Eze. 10: 2. coals of fire from b. c., 6.
7. hand from b. c. to fire b. c.

CHES'ALON.

Jos. 15: 10. mt. Jearim which is C.

CHE'SED.

Ge. 22: 22. Milcah's chil., C.

CHE'SIL.

Jos. 15: 30. utterm. cities of Jud., C.

CHESNUT tree, s.

Ge. 30: 37. Jacob took rods of c. t.
Eze. 31: 8. c. t-s not like his branches

CHEST, S.

2 K. 12: 9. Jehoi. took c. bored hole
10. saw was much money in c.
2 Ch. 24: 8. at king's com. made c.
10. bro-t in and cast into c.
11. high-pr.'s officer emptied c.
Eze. 27: 24. merchants in c-s of rich

CHESUL'LOTH.

Jos. 19: 18. their border toward C.

CHEW, ED, ETH.

Le. 11: 3. c-h cud, 5, 6. De. 14: 6.
4. that c. cud, De. 14: 7. [c-h
7. c-h not cud, De. 14: 8. | 26. nor
Nu. 11: 33. ere flesh was c-d wrath

CHE'ZIB.

Ge. 38: 5. Shelah bare C.

CHICKENS.

Mat. 23: 37. hen gathereth her c.

CHIDE.

Ex. 17: 2. people did c. why c. you?
Ju. 8: 1. Ephr. did c. with Gideon
Ps. 103: 9. He will not always c.

CHIDING.

Ex. 17: 7. Meribah, bec. of c. Is.

CHI'DON.

1 Ch. 13: 9. threshing floor of C.

CHIEF.

Ge. 37: † 36. sold Jo. to c. marshal
40: 2. c. of butlers c. of bakers
9. c. butler told his dream to
21. restored c. butler unto his butl.
22. hanged c. baker as Joseph
Nu. 3: 32. Eleazar be c. over c. of
4: 34. c. of cong. numbered
46. c. of Israel numbered
De. 1: 15. I took c. of your tribes
33: 15. c. things of ancient mounts.
Ju. 20: 2. c. of people, 1 S. 14: 38. Ne. 10: 14.
1 S. 15: 21. peo. took c. of things
2 S. 23: 18. Abishai was c. am. three
1 K. 9: 23. were c. of the officers
14: 27. c. of guard wh. kept door
1 Ch. 5: 2. of Jud. came c. ruler
9: 26. Levites four c. porters
11: 6. smiteth Jebusites first be c., Joab went first and was c.
18: 17. sons of David were c.
26: 10. his father made him c.
29: 22. to be the c. governor
2 Ch. 8: 10. c. of king Sol.'s officers
Ezr. 9: 2. rulers c. in this trespass
Ne. 11: 3. these are c. of province
Jb. 12: 24. taketh away heart of c.
29: 25. I chose their way, sat c.
40: 19. behemoth c. of ways of G.
Ps. 78: 51. he smote c., 105: 36.
137: 6. Jerus. above my c. joy
Pr. 1: 21. Wisdom crieth in c. place
8: † 26. c. part of dust of the world
16: 28. separateth c. friends
Can. 4: 14. orchard with c. spices
Is. 14: 9. hell stirreth up c. ones
Je. 13: 21. hast taught them as c.
31: 7. shout among c. of nations
49: 35. of Elam, c. of their might
50: † 36. sword is upon c. stays
51: † 59. Seraiah c. chamberlain
La. 1: 5. Her adversaries are the c.
Eze. 4: † 2. set c. leaders ag. Jerus.
20: † 40. I require c. of your obla.
44: † 30. c. of first fruits priest's
Da. 2: † 14. Arioch c. marshal
48. c. of gov-rs over wise men
11: 41. c. of chil. of Ammon esca.
Am. 6: 1. named c. of nations
6. anoint thems. with c. ointments
Mat. 20: 27. whoso. will be c. am.
23: 6. love c. seats, Mk. 12: 39.
Mk. 6: 21. supper to his c. estates
Lu. 11: 15. casteth out devils thro. c.
14: 1. house of one of c. Pharis.
7. they chose the c. rooms, 20: 46.
19: 2. c. among the publicans

Lu. 19:47. c. of peo. sought to dest.
22 : 26. c. as he that doth serve
Jn.12:42. am. c. rulers many believ.
Ac. 14 : 12. Paul was the c. speaker
16 : 12. which is c. city of that
17 : 4. of c. women not a few
18 : 8. c. ruler of synagogue, 17.
19 : 31. c. of Asia sent unto him
25 : 2. c. of Jews, 28 : 17.
Ep.2:20.J.C.c.corner-st., 1 Pe. 2 : 6.
1 Ti. 1 : 15. sinners, of whom I c.
1 Pe. 5 : 4. c. Sheph. shall appear

CHIEF captain.

Ge. 21 : 22. Phicol c. c., 32.–26 : 26.
2 S. 5 : 8. smiteth he sh. be c. and c.
Ac. 21 : 31. tidings came to the c. c.
32. saw c. c. they left beating
23:17.Bring this young man to c.c.
24 : 7. c. c. Lysias came upon us, [21 : 31.–22 : 24.–23 : 10.
22. c. c. shall come, I will know

CHIEF captains.

2 S. 23 : 8. Adino sat c. among c.
1 Ch.27:3. c. of all c. for first month
2 Ch. 8 : 9. Isr. were c. of Sol.'s c.
Ac. 25 : 23. Agrippa was with c. c.
Re. 6 : 15. rich men and c. c. hid

CHIEF fathers.

Nu. 31 : 26. c. f. of congregation
32 : 28. c. f. of tribes [1. 2 Ch.5:2.
36 : 1. c. f. of chil. of Isr., 1 K. 8 :
1 Ch. 9 : 9. c. of f. in house of
34. These c. f. of Levites
15 : 12. c.f. of Levites, 5,6,7,8,9,10.
24 : 31. c. f. of priests and Levites
26 : 32. 2700 c. f. Da. made rulers
2 Ch. 26 : 12. whole number of c.f.
Ezr. 1 : 5. rose up c. of f. of Judah
Ne. 7 : 70. c. of f. gave to work, 71.
12 : 22. were recorded c. of f.

CHIEF house.

Nu. 3 : 24 c. of h. of Gershonites
30. c. of h. of the Kohathites
35. c. of h. of the Merarites
25 : 14. Zimri was of c. h. among
15. Cozbi, of a c. h. in Midian
Jos.22 : 14.out of each c.h. a prince
1 Ch. 5 : 15. c. of h. of fathers

CHIEF man, or men.

Le. 21 : 4. not defile hims. a c. m.
1 Ch. 7 : 3. sons of Uzzi, c. m.
8 : 28. by generations c. m.
11 : 10. c. of mighty m.
24 : 4. more c. m. of Eleazar, than
Ezr. 5 : 10. names of m. were c.
7 : 28. I gathered c. m. to go up
Is. 41 : 9. I called thee from c. m.
Ac. 13 : 50. Jews stirred up c. m.
15 : 22. Judas and Silas, c. m.
28 : 7. of c. m. of the island

CHIEF priest. [52:24.

2 K. 25 : 18. took Seraiah c. p., Je.
1 Ch. 27 : 5. Benaiah a c. p. was
29 : 22. anointed Zadok c. p.
2 Ch. 19 : 11. Amariah c. p. is over
26 : 20. Azariah c.p. looked,31:10.

CHIEF priests.

2 Ch. 36 : 14. all c. of p. and peo.
Ezr. 8 : 24. separated 12 of c. of p.
29. weigh them before c. of p.
10 : 5. made c. p. and Isr. swear
Ne. 12 : 7. c. p. in days of Joshua
Mat. 2 : 4. gath-d c. p. and scribes
16 : 21. suffer many things of c.p.
26 : 14. Judas went to c.p.,Mk.14:
10. [c.p., Mk.14:43.
47. a multitude with staves from
27 : 12. when he was accused of c.
p., Mk. 15 : 3. Lu. 23 : 10.
41. c. p. mocking, Mk. 15 : 31.
62.c.p. and Phari. came to Pilate
Mk. 8 : 31. be rejected of c. p.
14 : 1. c. p. sought to take him,
55. Mat. 26 : 59. Lu. 9 : 22.–19:
47.–22 : 2.
Lu. 23 : 4. said Pilate to c. p.
23. voices of c. p. prevailed

Jn. 7 : 32. c. p. sent officers, 18 : 3.
18 : 35. c. p. have delivered thee
19 : 15. c. p. ans., we have no k.
Ac. 9 : 14. authority fr. c.p., 26:10.
22 : 30. commanded c. p. to appear

CHIEF prince, s.

1 Ch. 5 : † 2. of Judah came c. p.
7 : 40. chil. of Asher, c. of p-s
Eze. 38 : 2. Gog c. p. of, 3.–39 : 1.
Da. 10 : 13. Michael one of c. p-s

CHIEF singer, s.

Ne. 12 : 46. in days of Da. c. of s-s
Ha. 3 : 19. to c. s. on instruments

CHIEFEST.

1 S. 2 : 29. fat with c. offerings
9 : 22. made them sit in c. place
21 : 7.Doeg, c. of herdmen to Saul
2 Ch. 32 : 33. Hez. in c. of sepul.
Can. 5 : 10. beloved c. am. 10,000
Mk. 10 : 44. will be c. shall be serv.
2 Co. 11 : 5. behind c. apos., 12 : 11.

CHIEFLY. [mit.

Ro. 3 : 2. c. bec. to them were com-
Ph. 4 : 22. c. of Cesar's household
2 Pe. 2 : 10. c. that walk aft. flesh

CHILD. [shrubs

Ge. 21 : 15. Hagar cast c. under
16. Let me not see death of c.
37 : 30. c. is not, whi. shall I go?
42 : 22. spake I, Do not sin ag. c.?
Ex. 2 : 8. maid called c's mother
10.c.grew she bro-t him unto Pha.
22 : 22. sh. not afflict fatherless c.
Ju. 11 : 34. Jephthah's dau. only c.
13 : 5. c. shall be a Nazarite, 7.
13 : 8.teach what we sh.do unto c.
24. c. grew and Lord blessed him
1 S. 1 : 25. they brought c. to Eli
3 : 8. Eli perceiv. L. had called c.
2 S. 12 : 14. c. that is born sh. die
15. L. struck c. Uriah's wife bare
16. David besought G. for the c.
19. David perceiv. c. was dead
22. while c. was alive I fasted
1 K.3 : 25.Divide the living c. in two
14 : 3. tell what shall become of c.
12. feet ent. city, c. shall die, 17.
17 : 21. stretched himself upon
c., 2 K. 4 : 34.
22. soul of c. came again
2 K. 4 : 29. lay staff upon face of c.
4 : 31. told him c. is not awaked
32. behold c. was dead and laid
35. c. sneezed, c. opened eyes
Pr. 23 : 13. withh. not correct. fr.c.
Ec. 4 : 8. he hath c. nor brother
15. with second c. in his stead
Is. 3 : 5. c. shall behave proudly
7 : 16.bef.c.know to refuse the evil
8 : 4.bef.c.knowl.to cry, My father
11:8.c.put hand on cockatrice' den
65 : 20. c. shall die 100 years old
Je. 4 : 31. bringeth forth her first c.
31 : 20.Is Ephr.my son? a pleas.c.
44 : 7. to cut off man, woman, c.
Mat.10 : 21. fa. sh. deliv. c. to death
17 : 18. c. was cured fr. that hour
23 : 15. twofold more c. of hell
Mk. 9 : 24. father of c. cried out
Lu.1:59. they came to circumcise c.
66.What manner of c. sh. this be
76. c. shalt be called Prophet of
80. c. grew, waxed strong, 2 : 40.
2 : 21. for circumcising of c.
27. parents brought in c. Jesus
43. c. Jesus tarried behind in
9 : 38. Master, he is my only c.
42. Jes. healed c. deliv.him to fa.
Jn. 4 : 49. come down ere my c. die
16 : 21. as soon as is deliv. of c.
Ac. 4 : 27. of a truth ag. c. Jesus
Ac.4:30. signs done by name c. Jes.
13 : 10. Saul said, thou c. of devil
Re.12 : 4.devour her c. soon as born
5. her c. was caught up to God

A CHILD. [100 yrs.

Ge. 17 : 17. a c. born unto him is
Ge.18:13.sh.I bear a c. who am old
44 : 20.a fa., and a c. of his old age
Ex. 2:2. he was a goodly c., He.11 :
Le. 12 : 5.if she bear a maid c. [23.
1 S. 2 : 18. Sam., a c. girded with
linen [her
1 K. 3 : 17. I was deliv. of a c. with
13 : 2. a c. sh. be born to h. of Da.
Jb.33:25.his flesh fresher than a c.
Ps. 131 : 2. as a c. as a weaned c.
Pr. 20 : 11. a c. is known by doings
22 : 6. Train up a c. in the way he
15. Foolishness is in heart of a c.
23:24.begetteth a wise c. have joy
29 : 15.a c. left bringeth to shame
21. bringeth up servant fr. a c.
Ec. 4 : 13. Better is a wise c. than
10 : 16.Woe, O land,when k.is a c.
Is. 9 : 6. For to us a c. is born
10:19.trees few,a c. may write th.
Je.1 : 6.cannot speak, I am a c., 7.
20 : 15. a man c. is born to thee
Ho.11:1. when Isr. a c. I loved him
Mk. 9 : 21.how long? he said of a c.
36. took a c. set him, Lu. 9 : 47.
1 Co. 13 : 11. when a c. I spake as
a c., underst. as a c. thought
Ga. 4 : 1. heir as long as he is a c.
2 Ti. 3:15. fr. a c. known scriptures
He.11 : 11.S-h deliv.of a c.past age
Re. 12 : 5. a man c. to rule nations

Little CHILD.

Ge. 47 : † 12. nourish his father's
house as a l. c. [to go
1 K. 3 : 7. I am a l. c. I know not
11 : 17. Hadad fled,being yet a l.c.
2 K. 5 : 14. came like flesh of l. c.
Is. 11 : 6. a l. c. shall lead them
Mat. 18 : 2.Jesus called a l.c. unto
4. humble hims.as this l.c. [him
5. who shall receive one such l.c.
Mk. 10:15.whoso. not receive kingd.
of G. as a l. c., Lu. 18 : 17.

No CHILD.

Ge. 11 : 30. Sarai barren, had n. c.
Le.22 : 13.if priest's dau. have n.c.
De. 25 : 5.if one bro. die, have n.c.
2 S. 6 : 23. Michal had n. c. unto
the day of death
2 K. 4:14. ans. Verily she hath n.c.
Lu. 1 : 7. they had n.c. bec.Elisab.
Ac.7 : 5.promised when he had n.c.

Sucking CHILD.

Nu. 11 : 12. as father beareth s. c.
Is. 11 : 8. s. c. play on hole of asp
49:15.Can a woman forget her s.c.
La.4 : 4.tongue of the s.c. cleaveth

This CHILD.

Ex. 2 : 9. take t. c. and nurse him
Lu. 2 : 17. which was told conc.t.c.
34. t. c. is set for fall and rising
9 : 48. whosoever shall receive t. c.
in my name, receiveth

With CHILD.

Ge. 16 : 11. Hagar, thou art w. c.
19:36.dau-s of Lot were w.c.by fa.
38 : 24. Tamar thy dau. is w. c.
25. By the man whose these are,
am I w. c. [c.
Ex. 21 : 22. if men hurt woman w.
1 S.4 : 19. Phinehas' wife, was w.c.
2 S.11:5.Bath-sheba said, I am w.c.
2 K.8:12.rip up women w.c., 15:16.
Ec.11:5.grow in womb of her w. c.
Is.26:17.wom.w.c.th.draweth near
18. We have been w. c. in pain
54:1.Sing, that didst not trav.w.c.
Je.30:6.whe. man doth travail w.c.
31 : 8. bring fr.north women w.c.
Ho. 13 : 16.wom. w.c. sh.be ripped
Am.1:13. they ripped up women w.
Mat.1:18.found w.c.of H.Ghost [c.
23. a virgin shall be w. c. and
24 : 19. woe to them are w. c. in
those days, Mk.13:17.Lu.21:23.
Lu.2:5.with Mary,being great w.c.
1 Th.5:3. as travail upon wom.w.c.

Re. 12 : 2. and she being w. c. cried

Young CHILD.

1 S. 1 : 24. she bro-t him, c. was y.
Mat.2:8.search diligently for y.c.,9,
13. take y.c. and his mother ⌊11.
14. he took y. c. and his mother
20.dead which sought y. c. life

CHILDBEARING.

1 Ti. 2 : 15. she shall be saved in c.

CHILDHOOD.

1 S.12:2. have walked bef. you fr. c.
Jb.33 : † 25.flesh be fresher than c.
Ec. 11 : 10. c. and youth are vanity

CHILDISH.

1 Co.13 : 11.man, I put aw.c. things

CHILDLESS.

Ge. 15 : 2. what give me, I go c. ?
Le.20:20.bear sin, they sh. die c.,21.
1 S. 15 : 33.As thy sword made wom.
c. thy mother be c. am. wom.
Je. 22 : 30. Write ye this man c.
Lu. 20 : 30. second took her, died c.

CHILDREN.

Ge. 3 : 16. in sorrow bring forth c.
16 : 2. may be I obtain c. by her
25 : 22. c. struggled within her
29 : † 1. into land of c. of east
30 : 1. said, Give me c. or I die
33 : 5. c. God hath given thy serv.
49:8.thy fa.'s c. shall bow bef.thee
Ex. 12 : 37. 600,000 men besides c.
20 : 5. visiting iniq. of fathers upon
c., 34 : 7. Nu. 14 : 18. De. 5 : 9.
21 : 4. wife and c. be her master's
Nu.13 : 28. we saw c. of Anak there
17 : † 10.for token ag.c.of rebellion
26 : 11.notwi. c. of Korah died not
De. 2 : 9. given Ar to c. of Lot, 19.
9 : 2. who stand bef. c. of Anak ?
13 : 13. c. of Belial are gone out
14 : 1. Ye are the c. of the Lord
21:15.borne him c.belov.and hated
23 : 8.c. begotten of them sh. enter
24 : 16. fa-s not be put to death for
c. nor c. for fa-s, 2 Ch. 25 : 4.
32 : 20.c. in whom there is no faith
33 : 24.Let Asher be blessed with c.
Jos. 17 : 2. the male c. of Manasseh
22 : 9. c. of Reub. and Gad, 10, 11.
Ju. 4 : 6. men of c. of Naphtali
8 : 18. each resembled c. of a king
14 : 16. put riddle unto c. of peo.
20 : 13. deliv. us the c. of Belial
1 S. 2 : 5. hath many c. is feeble
10:27.c. of Belial said, How save us
2 S. 3 : † 34. falleth bef. c. of iniq.
7 : 10. neither c. of wickedn. afflict
them any more, 1 Ch. 17 : 9.
1 K.21 : 13. came 2 men, c.of Belial
2 K. 2 : 24. two she-bears tear 42 c.
9 : 1. Elisha called one of c. of pro.
10 : 13. c. of king, c. of queen
14 : 6. c. of murderers he slew not,
as is written, 2 Ch. 25 : 4.
17 : 34.nor do as L. com-d c. of Jac.
19 : 3. c. come to birth, Is. 37 : 3.
1 Ch. 2 : 30. Seled died without c.
32. and Jether died without c.
4 : 27. Shimei's breth. not many c.
16 : 13. O ye c. of Jac., Ps. 105 : 6.
2 Ch.13:7.gath. to Jerob.c.of Belial
25 : 7. L. not with all c. of Ephr.
11. Amaziah smote of c. of Seir
Ezr. 2 : 1. c. of province, Ne. 7 : 6.
10 : 44. some had wives by wh. c.
Ne. 9 : 23. c. multipliedst as stars
Jb. 19 : 17. I entreated for c. sake
30 : 8. c. of fools, c. of base men
41 : 34. a king over all c. of pride
Ps. 17 : 14. they are full of c.
34:11.Come, ye c. hearken unto me
69 : 8. an alien to my mother's c.
72 : 4. he shall save c. of needy
78 : 6. c. wh. be born might know
82 : 6. all of you c. of Most High
83 : 8. they have holpen c. of Lot
102 : 28. c. of thy serv-ts continue
Ps. 113:9.barren a joyf. mother of c.
127 : 3. Lo c. are a heritage of L.
4. As arrows in hand, so are c.
137:7.Remember, O L., c. of Edom
148 : 12.let old men and c.praise L.
149 : 2. let c. of Zion be joyful
Pr. 4 : 1. Hear, ye c. instruction,
5 : 7.-7 : 24.-8 : 32.
17 : 6. glory of c. are their fathers
31 : 28. her c. call her blessed
Ec. 6 : 3. If a man beget 100 c.
Can. 1 : 6. my mother's c. angry
Is. 1 : 2. I bro-t up c. they rebelled
4. c. that are corrupters ⌈gers
2 : 6. please thems. in c. of stran-
3 : 4.will give c. to be their princes
12. c. are their oppressors
8:18.I and c. L. hath giv.,He.2:13.
13 : 18. no pity, eye not spare c.
21 : 17. mighty of c. of Kedar be
23 : 4. I trav. not, nor br. forth c.
30 : 1. Woe to rebellious c. saith L.
9. lying c.,c. th. will not hear law
38 : 19. father to c. make known
47 : 8.neith. shall I know loss of c.
9. in one day loss of c. widowh.
49 : 20. c. thou shalt have, sh. say
54 : 1. more are c. of desolate than
c. of marr. wife, Ga. 4 : 27.
57:4.are ye not c. of transgr.,a seed
5. slaying the c. in the valleys
63 : 8. my peo. c. that will not lie
66:8.as Zion trav.she bro-t forth c.
Je. 3 : 14.turn, O backsliding c., 22.
19. How shall I put thee am. c.?
4 : 22. my people are sottish c.
6 : 11. pour it upon c. abroad ⌈dle
7 : 18. c. gather wood, fathers kin-
9 : 21. death entered to cut off c.
15 : 7. I will bereave them of c.
31 : 15. Rachel for her c.,Mat.2:18.
29. c. teeth on edge, Eze. 18 : 2.
48 : † 45. sh. devour crown of c.
La. 2 : 20. wom. eat c. span long ?
5 : 13. c. fell under the wood
Eze. 2 : 4. for they are impudent c.
20 : 21. c. rebelled ag. me, walked
23 : † 17.c. of Babel to her into bed
33 : 30. c. still are talking ag. thee
44:†7.into my sanct.c.of a stranger
47:22.to strangers that sh.beget c.
Da. 1 : 4. c. in whom no blemish
15.countenances fairer than all c.
17. these four c. G. gave knowl.
2 : † 25. found a man of the c. of
the captivity
12 : 1. Michael shall stand for c. of
Ho. 1 : 2. take c. of whoredoms
2 : 4. not mercy upon her c. for c.
10 : 9. battle ag. c. of iniq. did not
14. mother in pieces upon her c.
11 : 10. c. shall tremble from west
13 : 13.in pl.of breaking forth of c.
Jo. 2 : 16. gath. c. and those that
23. Be glad then ye c. of Zion
Am. 9 : 7.Are ye not as c. of Ethio.
Mi. 1 : 16. poll thee for delicate c.
Zph. 1 : 8. I will punish king's c.
Mal. 4 : 6. turn heart of fathers to
c. heart of c. to, Lu. 1 : 17.
Mat.2:16.Herod slew all c. in Beth.
18. Rachel weeping for her c.
3 : 9. of stones to raise c., Lu. 3:8.
5 : 45.ye may be the c. of your Fa.
8 : 12. c. of kingd. sh. be cast out
9 : 15. Can c.of bridecham. mourn
while? Mk. 2 : 19. Lu. 5 : 34.
10 : 21.c.rise ag.parents,Mk.13:12.
11:19.is justified of her c.,Lu.7:35.
13 : 38. good seed are c. of kingd.,
tares are c. of wicked one
15 : 26. to take c. bread, Mk. 7:27.
17 : 26. Jesus saith to him, Then
are the c. free ⌈10 : 29.
19 : 29. forsak. c. for my sake, Mk.
20 : 20. came mother of Zeb's. c.
21 : 15. scribes saw c. cry. in tem.
Mat. 23:31. c. of th. killed prophets
27 : 56. mother of Zebedee's c. followed Jesus ⌈filled
Mk. 7 : 27. said, Let the c. first be
28. dogs eat of the c. crumbs
9 : 37. receiv. one of such c. in my
name, 41. ⌈trust
10 : 24. c. how hard for them that
30. receive houses, breth., and c.
Lu. 1 : 17. turn hearts of fa-s to c.
5 : 34. make c. of bride-cham. fast
7 : 32. c. setting in market-place
6 : 35. ye shall be c. of Highest
16 : 8.c.of this world wiser than c.
18 : 29. left c. for kingd. of G. sake
20 : 29. the first died without c.
34. the c. of this world marry
Jn. 8 : 39. if Ab.'s c. ye would do
21 : 5. saith, c. have ye any meat?
Ac. 3 : 25. ye are c. of the prophets
13 : 26. c. of stock of Abraham
21 : 5.on our way with wives and c.
Ro. 8 : 17. if c. then heirs, heirs of
God ⌈they all c.
9 : 7. neither bec. seed of Ab. are
11. c. being not yet born ⌈ice c.
1 Co.14:20.not c.in underst.,in mal-
2 Co. 12 : 14. c. ought not to lay up
for parents, but parents for c.
Ga. 3 : 7. the same are the c. of Ab.
4 : 3. we, when c. were in bondage
25. Jerusa. in bondage with her c.
27. desolate hath many more c.
31. we are not c. of bondwoman
Ep. 1 : 5. predesti. to adoption of c.
2 : 2. spirit in c. of disobedience
3. were by nature c. of wrath
4 : 14. we be no more c. tossed to
5 : 1. be followers of G. as dear c.
6.wrath upon c. of disob.,Col.3:6.
6 : 1. c. obey parents, Col. 3 : 20.
1 Th. 2 : 7. nurse cherisheth her c.
1 Ti. 5 : 4. if any widow have c.
10. if she hath brought up c. if
14.younger women marry,bear c.
Ti. 1 : 6. having faithful c.
He. 2 : 13. Behold I and c. wh. God
2 : 14. as c. are partakers of flesh
12 : 5. exhortation unto you as c.
1 Pe. 1 : 14. As obedient c. not fash.
2 Pe. 2 : 14. full of adult., cursed c.
2 Jn. 1. elder unto elect lady and c.
13. c. of thy elect sister greet
Re. 2 : 23. will kill her c. with death
See AMMON, CAPTIVITY.

CHILDREN of Benjamin.

Nu. 1 : 37. of the c. o. B., 35,400
Ju. 1 : 21. c. o. B. not drive Jebus.
20 : 13. c. o. B. would not heark.
2 S. 2 : 25. c. o. B. gathered after
Abner ⌈Ne. 11 : 4.
1 Ch. 9 : 3. in Jerusalem c. o. B.,
12 : 16. came of c. o. B. to David
Je. 6 : 1. O c. o. B. gather to flee

Children's CHILDREN.

Ge. 45 : 10. near me, thou and c. c.
Ex. 34 : 7. iniq. of fathers on c. c.
De. 4 : 25. when beget c. and c. c.
2 K.17:41. served images c.and c.c.
Ps. 103 : 17. his righte. unto c. c.
128 : 6.shalt see thy c.c. and peace
Pr. 13 : 22. an inherit. to his c. c.
17 : 6.c.c.crown of old, glory of c.
Je. 2 : 9. with your c.c. will I plead
Eze. 37 : 25. sh. dwell, and th. c.c.

Fatherless CHILDREN.

Ps. 109 : 12. nor any to favour f.c.
Je. 49 : 11.Leave f.c.I will preserve

CHILDREN of God.

Mat. 5 : 9. peacemakers the c. o. G
Lu. 20:36. c. o. G. being c. of resur
Jn. 11:52. sho. gath. in one c.o. G
Ro. 8 : 16.witness th. we are c.o.G.
21. into glorious liberty of c.o.G.
9 : 8. c. of the flesh, not c. o. G.
26. shall be called c. o. living G.
Ga. 3 : 26. ye all c. o. G. by faith

1 Jn.3:10.c.o. G. manifest c. of de.
5: 2. by this know we love c.o.G.

His CHILDREN.

Ge. 18: 19. Abr., I know will command h. c. [all h. c.
37: 3. Israel loved Jo. more than
De. 17: 20. prolong days and h. c.
32: 5. th. spot is not spot of h. c.
† not h. c. that is their blot
33: 9. nor knew h. own c.
1 S. 30: 22. save his wife and h. c.
2 S. 12: 3. ewe lamb grew with h. c.
2 K. 8: 19. give him light and h.c.
2 Ch. 28: 3. burnt h. c. aft. heath.
33: 6. h. c. to pass through fire
Jb. 5: 4. h. c. are far from safety
17: 5. eyes of h. c. shall fail
20: 10. h. c. seek to please poor
21: 19. layeth up iniq. for h. c.
27: 14. If h. c. be multiplied, it is
Ps. 89: 30. If h. c. forsake my law
103:13. like as a fath. pitieth h. c.
109: 9. Let h. c. be fatherless
10. Let h. c. be vagabonds
Pr. 14: 26. h. c. shall have refuge
20: 7. h. c. are blessed after him
Is.14: 21.Prepare slaught. for h.c.
29: 23. when he seeth h. c. in
Ho.9:13. Ephr.sh. bring forth h.c.
Mat. 18: 25. h. wife and c. be sold
Lu. 14: 26. any man hate not h.c.
Jn. 4: 12. h. c. drank thereof
1 Th. 2: 11. charged you as fa.h.c.
1 Ti. 3: 4. having h. c. in subject

CHILDREN of Israel.

Ge. 50: 25. Jo. took oath of c. o. I.
Ex. 1: 7. the c. o. I. were fruitful
12. grieved bec. of the c. o. I.
2: 23. c. o. I. sighed
25. God looked on c. o. I.
4: 31. heard L. had visited c. o. I.
6: 5. heard groaning of the c.o.I.
13. c.o. I. out of E, 26,27.-12:51.
9: 4. nothing die that is c. o. I.
12: 37. c. o. I. 600,000 on foot
29: 43. I will meet with c. o. I.
31: 17. sign betw. me and c. o. I.
Le. 17: 13. whoso. he be, c.o.I. or
25: 55. to me c. o. I. are servants
Nu. 14: 10. glory of L. bef. c. o. I.
Jos. 7:12.c.o.I. not stand bef. ene.
1 S. 11: 8. c. o. I. were 300,000
2 S. 21: 2. Gibeonites not of c.o.I.
2 K. 17: 24. them instead of c.o.I.
Ne. 8: 17. had not c. o. I. done so
Ps. 103: 7. his acts to c. o. I.[him
148: 14. c.o. I. a people near unto
Is. 27: 12. gath-d one by one, O ye c. o. I. [45: 11.
Eze. 44: 15. c. o. I. went astray,
Am. 2: 11. Is it not thus, O c.o. I.
4: 5. this liketh you, O ye c.o.I.
Mat. 27: 9. they of c.o.I. did value
Lu. 1: 16. many of c. o. I. sh. turn
Ac. 5: 21. all the senate of the c.o.
7: 23. to visit breth. c. o. I. [I.
37. Moses which said to c. o. I.
9: 15. to bear my name bef. c.o.I.
10: 36. word God sent to c. o. I.
Ro.9:27. tho. c. o. I. be as the sand
2 Co. 3: 7. c.o.I.not behold face of
13. c. o. I. not look to the end
He. 11: 22. mention of departing of c. o. I. [c. o. I.
Re. 2: 14. stumbling-block before
7: 4. sealed 144,000 of c. o. I.
21: 12. names of 12 tribes of c.o.I.

CHILDREN of Judah.

Nu. 1: 26. c. o. J. by their genera.
Jos. 14: 6. c. o. J. came to Joshua
2 S. 1: 18. teach c. o. J. use of bow
2 Ch. 13:18. c. o. J. prevailed [cap.
25: 12. 10,000 did c. o. J. carry
28: 10. to keep under the c. o. J.
Je. 32: 32. all the evil of c. o. J.
50: 4. they and c. o. J. weeping
33.Isr.and c.o. J. were oppressed
Jo. 3: 19. the violence ag. c. o. J.

CHILDREN of light.

Lu. 16: 8. wiser than c. o. l.
Jn. 12: 36. that ye may be c. o. l.
Ep. 5: 8. light in L., walk as c.o.l.
1 Th. 5: 5. Ye are all c. o. l.

Little CHILDREN.

Nu. 16: 27. l. c. stood in the door
2 K. 2: 23. came l. c. and mocked
Es. 3: 13. in one day to destroy l.c.
Eze. 9: 6. Slay utterly maids, l. c.
Mat. 18: 3. except become as l. c.
19: 13. there brought to him l. c.
14. suffer l. c. to come unto me,
Mk. 10: 14. Lu. 18: 16.
Jn. 13: 33. l. c. yet a little while I
Ga. 4: 19. l. c. of whom I travail
1 Jn. 2: 1. my l. c. I write, 12, 13.
18. l. c. it is the last time
28. now l. c. abide in him
3: 7. l. c. let no man deceive
18. l. c. not love in word
4: 4. are of God, l. c. and have
5: 21. l. c. keep yours. from idols

CHILDREN of men.

Ge. 11: 5. tower wh. c.o.m. built
1 S. 26: 19. if c. o. m. cursed they
2 S. 7: 14. with stripes of c. o. m.
1 K. 8: 39. hearts of c.o.m., 2 Ch. [6:30.
Ps. 11:4. eyelids try c.o. m.
12:1.faithful fail from am. c. o.m.
14:2. fr. heaven upon c.o.m., 53:2.
36:7. c.o.m.put trust und. shadow
45: 2. Thou art fairer than c.o.m.
90: 3. sayest, Return ye c. o. m.
107: 8. works to c. o. m.15,21, 31.
115: 16.earth give not the c.o.m.
Pr. 15: 11. more then hearts c.o.m.
La.3:33. he doth not grieve c.o.m.
Da. 2: 38. wherever c. o.m. dwell

Men CHILDREN. [18.

Ex. 1: 17. midwives saved m. c.,
34:23. all m.c. shall appear bef.L.

Men, Women, and CHILDREN.

De. 3:6.in Bashan we destr.m.w.c.
31: 12. gather m. w.c.to hear and
1 S. 22: 19. smote Nob,m.w.c. and
Ezr. 10:1. a great cong. of m.w. c.
Je. 40: 7. unto Gedaliah m. w. c.
Mat. 14: 21. had eaten, were about
5000 m. beside w. c., 15: 38.

My CHILDREN.

Ge. 30: 26. Give me m. c. for whom
31: 43. these c. are m. c. these
42: 36. ye have bereaved of m. c.
43: 14. If I be bereaved of m. c. I
Ex. 13: 15. firstb. of m.c. I redeem
21: 5.I love master, wife, and m.c.
1 K. 20: 7. he sent to me for m. c.
Jb. 29: 5. that I were as when m.c.
Is. 49: 21. seeing I have lost m. c.
Je. 10: 20. m. c. are gone forth of
La. 1: 16. m. c. are desolate [me
Eze. 16: 21. thou hast slain m. c.
Lu. 11: 7. m. c. are with me in bed
2 Co. 6: 13. I speak as unto m. c.
3 Jn. 4. that m. c. walk in truth

No CHILDREN.

Ge. 16: 1. Sarai Ab.'s wife bare n.c.
30: 1. Rachel saw she bare n. c.
Nu.3: 4. Nadab and Abihu n. c.
1 S. 1: 2. Hannah had n. c. [12:19.
Mat. 22: 24. die having n. c., Mk.
Lu. 20: 31. seven took her, left n.c.

Our CHILDREN.

Ge. 31. 16. riches are ours and o. c.
Ex. 17: 3.to kill us, and o.c. and o.
Nu. 14: 3. that o. c. be a prey
De. 29: 29. belong to us and to o.c.
Jos. 22:24. o. might speak unto o.c.
25. c. make o. c. cease fearing L.
Ne. 5: 5. o. c. as their c. [o.c.
Mat.27:25.His blood be on us and on

CHILDREN of promise.

Ro. 9:8. c.o.p. are counted for seed
Ga. 4: 28. we, as Isaac, are c. o. p.

Strange CHILDREN.

Ne. 9: 2. Israel separated fr. s.c.
Ps. 144: 7. rid me from s. c., 11.
Ho. 5: 7. they have begotten s. c.

Their CHILDREN.

Ge. 31: 43. what can I do unto t. c.
De. 4: 10. that they may teach t. c.
5: 29.might be well with t.c.ever
31: 13. t. c. may learn to fear L.
Jos. 5: 7. t. c. Joshua circumcised
1 K. 9: 21. of t.c. did Sol. levy trib.
2 K. 8: 12. thou wilt dash t. c. and
17: 31. burnt t. c. to the gods
41. t. c. served images as did fa-
2 Ch. 20: 13. before L. with t. c.
25: 4. he slew not t. c. but did
Ne. 9: 23. t. c. thou multipliedst as
13: 24. t.c. spake half in speech of
Jb. 21: 11. little ones, t. c. dance
24: 5. wilder. yieldeth food for t.c.
Ps. 78: 4. not hide them from t. c.
6. arise and declare them to t. c.
90:16.let thy glory appear unto t.c.
132:12. t. c. sh. sit upon thy thro.
Is. 13: 16. t. c. shall be dashed
Je. 17: 2. whilst t. c. remem. altars
18: 21. deliver up t. c. to famine
30: 20. t. c. shall be as aforetime
32: 18. iniquity into bosom of t.c.
39. for good of them and of t. c.
47: 3. fathers not look back to t.c.
La. 4: 10. women have sodden t. c.
Eze. 20: 18. I said to t. c. in wilder.
23: 39. had slain t. c. to idols
37: 25. they and t. c. shall dwell
Da. 6: 24. cast t. c. into den of lions
Ho. 9: 12. tho. bring up t. c. yet I
Jo. 1: 3. your c. tell t. c. and t. c.
Mi. 2: 9. from t. c. taken my glory
Zch.10: 7.t. c. sh. see it and be glad
9. they shall live with t. c. and
Mat. 17: 25. tribute of t. own c. or
Ac. 13: 33. fulfilled unto us t. c.
21: 21. not to circumcise t. c.
1 Ti. 3: 12. deacons ruling t. c. well
Tit. 2: 4. young women to love t.c.

Thy CHILDREN.

Ex.13: 13.firstb.among t.c. redeem
De. 4: 40. well with t. c., 12:25,28.
6: 7. shalt teach diligently to t. c.
30: 2. thou and t. c. shall obey
Jos. 14: 9. land be thine and t. c.
1 S. 16: 11. said, Are here all t.c.?
1 K. 2: 4. if t. c. take heed to way
8: 25. t. c. take heed, 2 Ch. 6: 16.
20: 3. thy wives and t.c. are mine
2 K. 4: 7. live thou and t.c. of the
10: 30. t.c. sh. sit on throne [rest
2 Ch. 21: 14. Lord will smite t. c.
Jb. 8: 4.If t.c.have sinned ag. him
Ps.45: 16.Instead of fathers be t.c.
73: 15.offend ag.generation of t.c.
128: 3. t. c. like oliveplants about
132: 12. If t. c. will keep my cov.
147: 13. he hath blessed t. c.
Is. 49: 17. t. c. shall make haste
25. I will contend, will save t. c.
54: 13. all t. c. shall be taught of L., great be peace of t. c.
Je. 5: 7. t. c. have forsaken me
31: 17. hope t.c.shall come again
38:23.shall bring out t.c.to Chald.
Eze. 16: 36. by blood of t. c. didst give
Ho. 4: 6. I will also forget t. c.
Mat. 23: 37. would I gathered t. c.
as a hen gath., Lu. 13: 34.
Lu. 19: 44. sh. lay t.c. within thee
2 Jn. 4. of t. c. walking in truth

Young CHILDREN.

Jb. 19: 18. y. c. despised me, they
La. 4: 4. y. c. ask bread, no man
Na. 3: 10. her y.c. were dashed in
Mk.10:13.bro-t y.c.to him to touch
Ac. 7: 19. so that they cast out y. c.

Your CHILDREN.

Ex. 12: 26. when y. c. shall say

Ex. 22:24. widows, and y. c. fatherl.
Le. 25 : 46. take as inherit. for y. c.
26:22. beasts shall rob you of y. c.
Nu.14:33. y.c.sh. wander in wildern.
De. 1 : 39. y. c. shall go in thither
11 : 2. I speak not with y. c. who
19. my words, ye shall teach y. c.
21. that days of y.c. be multiplied
29 : 22. gene. to come of y.c.sh. say
32 : 46. shall com. y.c. to observe
Jos. 4 : 6. when y.c. ask fathers, 21.
22. then ye shall let y. c. know
1 K. 9 : 6. if y. c. turn fr. foll. me
1 Ch.28 : 8. inherit. to y.c., Ezr. 9:12.
2 Ch. 30 : 9. y.c. shall find compas.
Ps. 115 : 14. L. shall increase y. c.
Je. 2 : 30. in vain have I smit. y.c.
Mat. 7 : 11. gifts to y. c., Lu.11:13.
12 : 27. by whom do y.c. cast out?
Lu. 23 : 28. weep for yours. and y.c.
Ac.2:39. promise unto you and y.c.
1 Co. 7 : 14. else were y. c. unclean
Ep. 6:4. provoke not y.c., Col.3:21.

CHIL'EAB.

2 S. 3 : 3. David's second son C.

CHIL'ION. See MAH'LON.

CHIL'MAD.

Eze. 27 : 23. and C. thy merchants

CHIM'HAM.

2 S.19 : 37. C. let him go over, 38, 40.
Je. 41 : 17. dwelt in habita. of C.

CHIMNEY.

Ho. 13 : 3. be as smoke out of c.

CHIN'NERETH, CHIN'NEROTH, CIN'NEROTH.

Nu.34 :11. side of sea of C. | De.3:17.
Jos. 11:2. plains south of C. | 12:3.–
13 : 27.–19 : 35. 1 K. 15 : 20.

CHI'OS.

Ac. 20 : 15. came next day over ag. [C.

CHIS'LEU.

Ne. 1 : 1. in the month C., Zch. 7:1.

CHIS'LON.

Nu. 34 : 21. Elidad son of C.

CHIS'LOTH-TA'BOR.

Jos. 19 : 12. border went to C.

CHIT'TIM = KIT'TIM.

Nu. 24 : 24. ships shall come fr. C.
Is. 23 : 1. fr. land of C. it is revealed
12. pass over to C. there no rest
Je. 2 : 10. for pass over isles of C.
Eze.27:6. ivory bro't out of isles of C.
Da. 11 : 30. ships of C. sh. come ag.

CHI'UN.

Am. 5 : 26. Moloch and C. images

CHLO'E.

1 Co. 1 : 11. them of house of C.

CHODE.

Ge. 31:36. Jac. wroth, c. with Laban
Nu. 20 : 3. people c. with Moses and

CHOICE. [Noun.]

Ge. 23 : 6. in c. of our sepul. bury
Ac. 15 : 7. God made c. among us

CHOICE. [Adjective.]

Ge. 49 : 11. binding colt to c. vine
De.12 : 11. sh. bring all your c. vows
1 S. 9 : 2. Saul, a c. young man
2 S. 10 : 9. of c. of Israel, 1 Ch.19:10.
2 K. 3 : 19. smite every c. city
19 : 23. c. firtrees, Is. 37 : 24.
1 Ch. 7 : 40. c. and mighty men
2 Ch. 25 : 5. found 300,000 c. men
Ne. 5 : 18. for me daily six c. sheep
Pr.8 : 10. knowl. rather than c. gold
19. my revenue better than c. silv.
10 : 20. tongue of just is as c. silv.
Can. 6 : 9. she is the c. one of her
Je. 22 : 7. shall cut thy c. cedars
48 : † 15. c. of Moab are gone down
Eze.23:†7. whored. with c. of Asher
24 : 4. fill it with the c. bones
5. Take the c. of flock and burn
31:16. trees of Eden, the c. and best
Ac. 15 : 7. God made c. among us

CHOICEST.

Is. 5 : 2. planted with the c. vine
22 : 7. thy c. valleys full of chariots

CHOKE, ED.

Mat.13:7. thorns c-d, Mk.4:7. Lu.8:7.
22. care of world, deceitfulness of
riches c. word, Mk. 4 : 19.
Mk. 5 : 13. were c. in sea, Lu. 8:33.
Lu.8:14. are c. with cares and riches

CHOLER.

Da. 8 : 7. a he goat moved with c.
11:11. k. of south be moved with c.

CHOOSE. [As an act of God.]

Nu. 16 : 7. the man the L. doth c.
17 : 5. man's rod I shall c. sh. blos.
De. 7 : 7. L. did not c. you because
12 : 5. place L. shall c., 11, 14, 18, 26.
–14 : 23, 24, 25.–15 : 20.–16 : 2,
6, 7, 15, 16.–17 : 8, 10.–18 : 6.–
26 : 2.–31 : 11. Jos. 9 : 27.
17 : 15. him king, wh. L. shall c.
1 S. 2 : 28. I c. him of all tribes
2 S. 16 : 18. L. and this people c.
21 : 6. hang in Gibeah wh. L. did c.
1 K. 14 : 21. city the L. did c.
Ne. 9 : 7. God who didst c. Abram
Ps. 25 : 12. teach in way he shall c.
47 : 4. He shall c. our inheritance
Is. 14 : 1. Lord will yet c. Israel
49 : 7. Holy One of Isr. sh. c. thee
66 : 4. I will c. their delusions
Zch. 1 : 17. L. will c. Jerus., 2 : 12.

CHOOSE.

Ex. 17 : 9. c. us out men, and fight
De. 23 : 16. dwell in place ho sh. c.
30 : 19. c. life that thou may live
Jos. 24 : 15. c. this day wh. serve
1 S. 17 : 8. c. you a man for you
2 S. 17 : 1. Let me c. 12,000 men
19 : † 38. what shalt c. that I do
24 : 12. c. one of them, 1 Ch.21:10.
1 K. 18 : 23. c. one bullock, 25.
Jb. 9 : 14. c. my words to reason
34 : 4. Let us c. to us judgment
33. whether thou refuse, or c.
Ps. 84 : † 10. I c. to sit at threshold
Pr. 1 : 29. did not c. fear of Lord
3 : 31. and c. none of his ways
Is. 7 : 15. may know to c. good, 16.
56 : 4. eunuchs c. things please me
65 : 12. c. that I delighted not
Eze. 21 : 19. c. a place, c. it at the
Ph. 1 : 22. what I shall c. I wot not

CHOOSEST, ETH, ING.

Jb. 7 : 15. my soul c. strangling
15 : 5. thou c. tongue of crafty
Ps. 65 : 4. Blessed is man thou c.
Is. 40 : 20. he c. tree will not rot
41 : 24. abomination is he c. you
He. 11 : 25. c-g to suffer affliction

CHOP.

Mi. 3 : 3. break bones and c. them

CHOR-A'SHAN.

1 S. 30 : 30. sent spoil to them in C.

CHORA'ZIN.

Mat. 11 : 21. woe unto C., Lu.10:13.

CHOSE.

Ge. 6 : 2. wives of all wh. they c.
13 : 11. Lot c. plain of Jordan
Ex. 18 : 25. Moses c. able men
De. 4 : 37. he c. their seed, 10 : 15.
Jos. 8 : 3. Jos. c. 30,000 mighty
Ju. 5 : 8. They c. new gods, then
1 S. 13 : 2. Saul c. three thousand
17 : 40. c. him five smooth stones
2 S. 6 : 21. L. c. me bef. thy father
10 : 9. c. of choice men, 1 Ch.19:10.
1 K. 8 : 16. I c. no city to build a
house, 2 Ch. 6 : 5.
11 : 34. for David, whom I c.
1 Ch. 28 : 4. Lord c. me before all
Jb. 29 : 25. I c. out their way
Ps. 78 : 67. c. not tribe of Ephraim
68. But c. the tribe of Judah
70. he c. David also his servant
Is. 66 : 4. c. that I delighted not
Eze. 20 : 5. In the day when I c. Isr.
Lu. 6 : 13. of his disciples he c. 12
14 : 7. how they c. chief rooms
Ac.6 : 5. c. Stephen man full of faith
Ac.13:17. God of Isr. c. our fathers
15 : 40. Paul c. Silas and departed

CHOSEN.

Ex. 15 : 4. c. captains drowned
Nu. 16 : 5. him c. cause to come
Jos. 24 : 22. ye have c. you the L.
Ju 10:14. cry unto gods ye have c.
1 S. 8 : 18. king ye have c., 12 : 13.
20 : 30. thou hast c. son of Jesse
1 K. 3 : 8. hast c. a great people
8 : 44. city c., 48. 2 Ch. 6 : 34, 38.
1 Ch. 16 : 13. chil. of Jacob his c.
Jb. 36 : 21. c. rather than affliction
Ps. 33 : 12. people he hath c. for
89 : 3. made a cove. with my c.
19. exalted one c. out of people
105 : 6. ye chil. of Jacob his c.
26. Aaron whom he had c.
43. brought his c. with gladness
106 : 5. may see the good of thy c.
23. had not Moses his c. stood
Pr. 16 : 16. understanding to be c.
22 : 1. good name is to be c.
Is. 43 : 20. to give drink to my c.
65 : 15. name a curse to my c.
66 : 3. have c. their own ways
Je. 8 : 3. death be c. rather than
49 : 19. who is a c. man, 50 : 44.
Mat. 20 : 16. but few c., 22 : 14.
Mk. 13 : 20. elect's sake he hath c.
Lu. 10 : 42. Mary c. good part
Jn. 6 : 70. Have not I c. you twelve
Ac. 1 : 2. apostles whom he had c.
24. whether of these hast c.
9 : 15. for he is a c. vessel to me
10 : 41. to witnesses c. before
Ro. 16 : 13. Salute Rufus c. in Lord
2 Co. 8 : 19. c. of churches to travel
1 Ti. 5 : † 9. let not a widow be c.
2 Ti. 2 : 4. c. him to be a soldier
1 Pe. 2 : 9. ye are a c. generation
Re. 17 : 14. they are called c. and

God hath CHOSEN. [11.

De. 12:21. G. h. c. to put name, 16:
21 : 5. them G. h. c. to minister
1 Ch. 29 : 1. Sol. G. h. c. is young
Ac. 22 : 14. G. of fathers h. c. thee
1 Co. 1 : 27. G. h. c. foolish things,
G. h. c. weak things
28. things despised G. h. c.
2 Th. 2 : 13. G. fr. beginn. h.c. you
Ja. 2 : 5. h. not G. c. the poor

CHOSEN of God.

Lu. 23 : 35. if he be Christ, c. o. G.
Ac. 10 : 41. witnesses c. bef. o. G.
1 Pe. 2 : 4. a living stone, c. o. G.

I have CHOSEN.

1 K. 11 : 13. for Jerus.'s sake I h.c.,
2 K. 21 : 7.–23 : 27. 2 Ch. 6 : 6.
32. city I h. c. out of all tribes
1 Ch. 28 : 6. I h. c. him to be son
2 Ch. 7 : 16. h. I c. and sanc. house
Ne. 1 : 9. place I h. c. to set name
Ps. 119:30. I h.c. way of truth, 173.
Is. 41 : 8. Jacob whom I h. c.
9. I h. c. thee, and [Mat. 12:18.
43 : 10. my servant whom I h. c.,
44 : 1. Israel whom I h. c.
2. Jeshurun whom I h. c.
48 : 10. I h. c. thee in furnace
58 : 5. this fast that I h. c.? 6.
Ha. 2 : 23. I h. c. thee, saith Lord
Jn. 13 : 18. I know whom I h. c.
15 : 16. not c. me, I h. c. you
19. I h. c. you out of the world

Lord hath CHOSEN.

De. 7 : 6. L. h. c. thee people, 14 : 2.
18 : 5. L. h.c. him out of all tribes
1 S. 10 : 24. See him whom L. h. c.
16 : 8. Neither h. the L. c. this
10. Sam. said, L. h. not c. these
1 Ch. 15 : 2. them L. h. c. to carry
28 : 4. L. h. c. Judah ruler [ark
5. L. h. c. Solo. to build hou., 10.
2 Ch. 29 : 11. L. h. c. you to serve
Ps. 33 : 12. whom he h. c. for inher.
105 : 26. Aaron whom he h. c.

Ps.132:13. L. h.c. Zion | 135:4. Jac.
Je. 33 : 24. two families L. h. c.
Zch. 3 : 2. L. th. h. c. Jeru. rebuke
Mk. 13 : 20. elect's sake wh. he h. c.
Ep. 1 : 4. Acc. as he h. c. us in him

CHOSEN men.

Ju. 20 : 16. 700 c. m. left-handed
1 S. 24 : 2. Saul took 3,000 c. m.,
2 S. 6:1. Da. gath. all c. m. [26:2.
1 K.12 : 21.180,000 c.m.,2 Ch.11:1.
2 Ch. 13 : 3. Abijah set the battle in array with 400,000 c. m., Jeroboam with 800,000 c. m.
Ps. 78 : 31. smote c. m. of Israel
Ac. 15 : 22. c. m. of their company, [25.

CHOZE'BA.

1 Ch. 4 : 22. C. had dominion in

CHRIST.

Mat. 1 : 17. unto C. are 14 genera.
2 : 4. where C. should be born
16 : 16. thou art C. the Son of God
23 : 8. your Master, even C., 10.
24 : 5. many shall come, saying, I am C., Mk. 13 : 6. Lu. 21 : 8.
26:68. Prophesy C. who smote thee?
Mk. 9 : 41. because ye belong to C.
12 : 35. say scribes C. is son of Da., Lu. 20 : 41.
15 : 32. Let C. descend from cross
Lu. 2 : 26. not die, bef. had seen C.
4 : 41. devils, knew he was C.
23 : 35. save himself, if he be C.
39. If C. save thyself and us
24 : 26. Ought not C. to have suff.?
46. thus it behooved C. to suffer
Jn. 4 : 25. Messias, wh. is called C.
7 : 27. when C. cometh, no man kn.
31. C. cometh, will he do more?
41. Shall C. come out of Galilee?
42. C. cometh of seed of David
9 : 22. if any confess he was C.
12 : 34. heard C. abideth for ever
Ac. 2 : 30. would raise up C. to sit
36. made Jesus both Lord and C.
3 : 18. G. bef. shewed C. sho. suffer
8 : 5. Philip preached C. unto them
9 : 20. he preached C. in synagog.
17 : 3. that C. must needs have suff.
26 : 23. that C. should suffer
Ro. 5 : 6. in due time C. died
8. while sinners C. died for us
6 : 4. as C. was raised from dead
9. C. being raised, dieth no more
7 : 4. dead to law by body of C.
8 : 9. if any have not Spirit of C.
10. if C. be in you, body is dead
11. he that raised up C. fr. dead
9 : 3. wish myself accursed fr. C.
5. C. came, who is over all, God
10 : 4. C. is end of law for righte.
6. to bring C. down from above
7. to bring up C. from dead
14 : 9. to this end, C. died, and rose
15. Destr. not him for wh. C. died
18. he that serveth C. is accept.
15 : 3. even C. pleased not himself
7. as C. received us, to glory
18. wh. C. not wrought by me
20. not where C. was named
16 : 5. Epenetus firstfruits to C.
1 Co. 1 : 17. C. sent me not to bap.
23. we preached C. crucified
24. C. the power of God, and the
3 : 23. ye are C. and C. is God's
5 : 7. C. our passover is sacrificed
8 : 11. bro. perish, for wh. C. died
9 : 21. under law to C. th. I might
10 : 4. and that rock was C. [gain
9. Nor let us tempt C. as some of
15 : 3. I deliv. to you, how C. died
12. if C. be preached that he rose
15 : 15. testif. that he raised up C.
16. if rise not, is not C. raised
17. if C. not raised, faith is vain
23. man in his order, C. firstfruits
2 Co. 2 : 12. to Troas to pr. C.'s gosp.
3 : 4. such trust have we thro. C.
5 : 16. tho. known C. after flesh
6 : 15. concord C. with Belial?
11 : 2. as a chaste virgin to C.
Ga. 2 : 20. not I, but C. liv. in me
21. then C. is dead in vain
3 : 13. C. hath redeemed us fr. curse
24. schoolmaster, to bring us to C.
29. if ye C. then are Abr.'s seed
4 : 7. then heir of God through C.
19. I travail, until C. be formed in
5 : 1. liberty whw. C. made us free
2. if circ., C. shall profit nothing
4. C. is become of no effect
24. that are C. have crucifi. flesh
Ep. 2 : 12. ye were without C.
3 : 17. That C. may dwell in your
4 : 15. may grow in him, even C.
20. ye have not so learned C.
5 : 2. as C. also loved us, and hath
14. C. shall give thee light
23. husb., as C. is head of church
24. as church is subject unto C.
25. love wives, as C. loved church
32. I speak conc. C. and church
6 : 5. singleness of heart as unto C.
Ph. 1 : 15. some preach C. of envy
16. the one pr. C. of contention
18. C. is preached, I rejoice
20. C. be magnified in my body
3 : 8. but dung, th. I may win C.
4 : 13. can do all through C. who strengtheneth [after C.
Col. 2 : 8. rudiments of world, not
3 : 1. C. sitteth on right hand
4. C. who is our life shall appear
11. but C. is all and in all
13. as C. forgave you, so do ye
24. for ye serve the Lord C.
He. 3 : 6. C. as son over own house
5 : 5. C. glorified not himself
9 : 11. C. a high priest of good
24. C. not enter. into holy places
28. C. was once off. to bear sins
1 Pe. 2 : 21. C. also suffered for us
3 : 18. C. hath once suffer. for sins
4 : 1. as C. suffered for us in flesh
Re. 11 : 15. kingd-s of L and his C.
12 : 10. kingd. of G. power of his C.
See BLOOD, PREACH.

Against CHRIST.

Ac. 4 : 26. kings gathered a. his C.
1 Co. 8 : 12. sin ag. breth. sin a. C.
1 Ti. 5 : 11. wax wanton a. C.

By CHRIST.

2 Co. 1 : 5. consola. aboundeth b.C.
Ga. 2 : 17. we seek to be justifi. b.C.
Ep. 3 : 21. glory in church b. C.

For CHRIST. [bapt.

1 Co. 1 : 17. f. C. sent me not to
4 : 10. fools f. C. sake, ye are wise
2 Co. 5 : 20. ambassadors f. C. [in
12 : 10. in distresses f. C. sake
Ep. 4 : 32. God f. C. sake forgiven
Ph. 3 : 7. those I counted loss f. C.
2 Th. 3 : 5. to patient waiting f. C.
He. 11 : † 26. esteem. reproach f. C.

Jesus with CHRIST. [22.

Mat. 1 : 16. J. who is call. C., 27 : 17,
16 : 20. tell no man he was J. the C.
Jn. 1 : 17. but grace came by J. C.
17 : 3. know thee, and J. C. whom
20 : 31. might believe J. is the C.
Ac. 2 : 38. bapt. in name of J. C.
3 : 6. In name of J. C. rise up
20. send J. C. who was preached
4 : 10. by J.C. doth this man stand
5 : 42. ceased not to preach J. C.
8 : 12. preaching conc. name of J.C.
37. I believe J. C. is Son of God
9 : 34. J. C. maketh thee whole
10 : 36. preaching peace by J. C.
16 : 18. in name of J.C. come out
17 : 3. J. I preach to you is C.
18 : 5. Paul testified that J. was C.
28. showing by script. J. was C.
19 : 4. th. should believe on C. J.
Ro. 1 : 1. a serv. of J. C., Ph. 1 : 1.
Ro. 1:3. Conc. his Son J. C. our Lord
6. are ye the called of J. C.
8. I thank my God through J. C.
2 : 16. judge secrets of men by J.C.
3 : 22. righteousn. by faith of J.C.
24. through redemption in J. C.
5 : 15. gift by grace, by one man J.
17. reign in life by one J. C. [C.
6 : 3. as were baptized into J. C.
8 : 1. no condem. to them in C. J.
2. Spi. of life in C. J. made me free
15 : 8. J.C. was minister of circum.
16 : 3. Aquila, my helpers in C. J.
1 Co. 1 : 1. Paul apostle of J. C., 2 Co. 1 : 1. Ep. 1 : 1. [J. C.
2. with all that call upon name of
4. grace given you by J. C.
30. but of him are ye in C. J.
2 : 2. to know any thing, save J.C.
3 : 11. that is laid, wh. is J. C.
4 : 15. in C. J. have I begott. you
2 Co. 1 : 19. J. C. who was preached
4 : 6. knowl. of G. in face of J. C.
5 : 18. hath reconciled us by J. C.
13 : 5. know ye not J. C. is in you
Ga. 1:1. neith. by man, but J.C., 12.
2 : 16. justified by faith of J. C.
3 : 14. blessing on Gent. thro. J.C.
26. chil. of G. by faith in C. J.
28. ye are all one in C. J.
4 : 14. rec. me as an angel, as C. J.
5 : 6. in J. C. neither circum., 6:15.
Ep. 1 : 5. adop. of children by J. C.
2 : 6. in heavenly places in C. J.
10. created in J.C. unto good works
13. in C. J. ye who were far off
20. J. C. being chief corner stone
3 : 9. G. who created all by J. C.
21. glory in church by C. J.
Ph. 1 : 6. perform it until day of J.C.
8. I long in bowels of J. C.
11. fruits of righteousness by J.C.
19. supply of Spirit of J. C.
2 : 5. mind in you, was in C. J.
11. J. C. is L., to glory of G. the
21. seek not things are J. C. [Fa.
3 : 3. rej. in C.J. and have no conf.
3 : 8. all loss for excellency of C.J.
12. I am apprehended of C. J.
14. prize of high calling in C. J.
4 : 19. riches in glory by C. J.
21. salute every saint in C. J.
Col. 2 : 6. as rec. C.J. so walk in him
1 Ti. 1 : 15. C. J. came to save sinn.
16. in me first J. C. might shew
2 : 5. mediator, man C. J. [fession
6:13. C. J. who witn-d a good con-
2 Ti. 1 : 1. promise of life in C. J.
9. acc. to grace given us in C. J.
10. sav. J.C. who hath abol. death
13. in faith and love, in C. J.
2 : 1. strong in grace in J. C.
8. J. C. of seed of Da. was raised
10. obtain salva. which is in C. J.
3 : 12. live godly in C. J. sh. suffer
Tit. 2 : 13. appearing of G. and Sav.
3 : 6. on us abund. thro. J.C. [J. C.
Phm. 1. P. a prisoner of J. C., 9, 23.
He. 3 : 1. High P. of our profess. C.J.
10 : 10. off. of body of J.C. once for
13 : 8. J. C. the same yesterday
21. pleasing in his sight thro. J.C.
1 Pe. 2 : 5. sacr. accep. to G. by J.C.
4 : 11. G. be glorified through J.C.
5 : 10. called us to glory by C. J.
14. Peace be with you all in C. J.
1 Jn. 1:3. fellowship wi. Fa. and Son
7. blood of J. C. cleanseth [J. C.
2 : 1. we have an advocate, J. C.
4 : 2. spirit th. confesses J.C. is come
3. confesseth not J. C. is come
5 : 1. believeth that J. is the C.
6. came by water and blood, J. C.
20. in him, even in his Son, J. C.
Re. 1 : 9. kingd. and patience of J.C.

Lord Jesus CHRIST.

Ac. 11 : 17. who believed on L. J. C.

Ac. 15: 11. through grace of L. J. C.
26. name of L.J.C., 2 Th. 1: 12.-
3: 6. [be saved
16: 31. Believe on L. J.C., thou sh.
20: 21. testifying faith tow. L.J.C.
Ro. 5: 1. peace through L. J. C.
11. joy in God, through L. J. C.
6: 11. alive unto G. thro. J.C. our L.
23. gift is eternal life thro. L.J.C.
7: 25. I thank G. thro. J.C. our L.
8: 39. sepa. fr. love of G. in C. J.
13: 14. put ye on L. J. C. [our L.
16: 18. such serve not our L. J.C.
20. grace of L. J. C. be with you,
24. 2 Co. 13: 14. Ga. 6: 18. 2
Th. 3: 18. Re. 22: 21.
1 Co. 1: 7. for coming of L. J. C.
8: 6. one L.J.C. by whom all things
9: 1. Have I not seen J. C. our L.
15: 57. victory thro. our L. J. C.
16: 22. If any love not L. J. C.
2 Co. 1: 2. peace from G. and L. J.
C., Ga. 1: 3. Ep. 1: 2. Col. 1: 2.
8: 9. know grace of our L. J. C.
Ga. 6: 14. save in cross of L. J. C.
Ep. 1: 3. blessed be Fa. of L. J. C.
17. God of L. J. C. give spirit of
3: 11. purposed in C. J. our L.
14. bow knees unto Fa. of L. J. C.
6: 24. grace with all love L. J. C.
Ph. 3: 20. look for Saviour L. J. C.
Col. 2: 6. rec-d C. J. the L., so walk
1 Th. 1: 3. patience of hope in L.J.C.
2: 19. our joy in pres. of L. J. C.
3: 11. our L. J. C. direct our way
13. estab. at coming of L. J. C.
5: 9. obtain salvation by L. J. C.
23. preserved unto coming of L.
J. C. [J. C.
2 Th. 2: 1. beseech by coming of L.
16. L. J. C. given us consolation
1 Ti. 1: 12. I thank C. J. our L.
5: 21. I charge thee bef. L. J. C.,
2 Ti. 4: 1. [spirit
2 Ti. 4: 22. the L. J. C. be with thy
Ja. 2: 1. faith of L. J. C. the L. of
2 Pe. 1: 8. knowl. of L. J. C., 2: 20.
11. into kingdom of L. J. C.
16. power and coming of L. J. C.
3: 18. grow in knowl. of L. J. C.
Jude 4. denying our L. J. C.
21. looking for mercy of L. J. C.

In; or into CHRIST.

Ac. 24: 24. heard conc. faith i. C.
Ro. 9: 1. I say the truth i. C.
12: 5. many are one body i. C.
16: 7. who were i. C. before me
9. Salute Urbane, our helper i.C.
10. salute Apelles approved i. C.
1 Co. 3: 1. I speak as unto babes i.C.
4: 10. we fools, ye are wise i. C.
15. tho. 10,000 instruct. i. C.
17. ways wh. be i. C. as I teach
15: 18. asleep i. C. are perished
19. if in this life only have hope i.
22. i. C. shall all be made alive [C.
2 Co. 1: 21. wh. establisheth us i. C.
2: 14. causeth us to triumph i. C.
17. in sight of G. speak we i. C.
3: 14. vail is done away i. C.
5: 17. i. C. he is a new creature
19. G. was i. C. reconcil. world
20. we pray you i. C. stead, be
11: 3. simplicity that is i. C.
12: 2. I knew a man i. C. above
19. i. C. we do all things [14 yrs.
Ga. 1: 22. unto ch-s of Judea i. C.
3: 17. cov. confirmed of God i. C.
27. as many as been bapt. i-o C.
Ep. 1: 3. with spiritual bless-gs i. C.
10. gather in one all things i. C.
12. glory, who first trusted i. C.
20. wrought i. C. wh. he raised
3: 6. partakers of promise i. C.
Ph. 1: 13. my bonds i. C. manifest
2: 1. If be any consolation i. C.
Col. 1: 2. and faithful breth. i. C.
Col. 2: 5. steadfastn. of y-r faith i.C.
1 Th. 4: 16. dead i. C. sh. rise first
1 Ti. 2: 7. I speak the truth i. C.
Phm. 8. might be much bold i. C.
1 Pe. 3: 16. good conversa. i. C.

Is CHRIST.

Mat. 24: 23. Lo, here i.C., Mk. 13: 21.
Mk. 12: 35. C. i. son of Da., Lu. 20:
Lu. 2: 11. Saviour who i. C. [41.
23: 2. saying, that he i. C. a king
Jn. 7: 41. others said, This i. C. [C.
Ac. 9: 22. Saul, proving this i. very
17: 3. Jesus I preach to you i. C.
Ro. 8: 34. it i. C. that died, yea
1 Co. 1: 13. i. C. divided? was Paul
7: 22. being free, i. C. servant
11: 3. head of every man i. C.
12: 12. many are 1 body, so i. C.
15: 13. dead rise not, i. C. not risen,
20. now i. C. risen fr. dead [16.
2 Co. 10: 7. if any trust he i. C.'s
Ga. 2: 17. i. C. minister of sin?
3: 16. to thy seed, which i. C.
Ph. 1: 21. For to me to live i.C. but
Col. 1: 27. i. C. in you, the hope
1 Jn. 2: 22. denieth J. i. the C.

Of CHRIST.

Mat. 11: 2. John heard works o. C.
22: 42. What think ye o. C.?
Ro. 8: 9. if any man have not the
Spirit o. C.
35. who separate us fr. love o. C.
14: 10. bef. judgment seat o. C.
15: 19. fully preached gospel o. C.
16: 16. churches o. C. salute you
1 Co. 1: 6. testim. o. C. confirmed
12. I of Cephas, and I o. C.
17. lest cross o.C. be of none effect
2: 16. we have the mind o. C.
4: 1. ministers o. C. and stewards
6: 15. bodies are members o. C.
10: 16. cup, communion of bl. o. C.
br. communion of body o. C.
11: 1. followers of me, as I am o.C.
3. head of wom. is man, head o.C.
12: 27. now ye are the body o. C.
2 Co. 1: 5. as suff. o. C. abound in us
2: 10. forgave I it in person o. C.
15. are a sweet savour o. C.
3: 3. ye are the epistle o. C.
4: 4. lest light of gospel o.C. shine
5: 14. love o. C. constraineth us
8: 23. breth. they are glory o. C.
10: 1. beseech by gentleness o. C.
5. ev. thought to obedience o. C.
14. preaching the gospel o. C.
11: 10. As truth o. C. is in me
23. Are they ministers o. C. [10.
12: 9. power o. C. upon me, Re. 12:
13: 3. proof o. C. speaking in me
Ga. 1: 6. grace o. C. unto anoth. gosp.
7. would permit gospel o. C.
10. if pleased men, not. serv. o.C.
2: 16. be justified by faith o. C.
6: 2. so fulfil law o. C.
12. persecution for cross o. C.
Ep. 2: 13. made nigh by blood o.C.
3: 4. my knowl. in mystery o. C.
8. the unsearchable riches o. C.
19. know love o. C. which passeth
4: 7. acc. to measure of gift o. C.
12. edifying of body o. C.
13. stature of fulness o. C. [C.
5: 5. hath any inheri. in kingd. o.
6: 6. as servants o. C. doing will
Ph. 1: 10. offence till day o. C.
29. unto you given in behalf o.C.
2: 16. I may rejoice in day o. C.
30. for work o.C. nigh unto death
3: 9. righteousness thro. faith o. C.
18. they enemies of cross o. C.
Col. 1: 7. a faithful minister o. C.
24. behind of afflictions o. C.
2: 2. mystery of God, and o. C.
11. sins of flesh by circum. o. C.
17. shadow of thi., body is o. C.
3: 16. Let word o. C. dwell in you
Col. 4: 3. door, to speak mystery o. C.
12. a serv. o. C. saluteth you
2 Th. 2: 2. day o. C. is at hand
3: 5. you into patience o. C.
2 Ti. 2: 19. that nameth name o. C.
He. 3: 14. partakers o. C. if we hold
6: 1. principles of doctrine o. C.
9: 14. much more bl. o. C. purge
11: 26. reproach o.C. greater riches
1 Pe. 1: 11. Spirit o. C. did signify
19. redeem. with preci. blood o.C.
4: 13. as ye are partakers o.C. suff-gs
14. if reproached for name o. C.
5: 1. witness of sufferings o. C.
2 Jn. 9. in the doctrine o. C. (2)
Re. 20: 6. be priests of G. and o. C.

That CHRIST.

Jn. 1: 25. if be not t. C. nor Elias
6: 69. we are sure thou art t. C.

The CHRIST.

Mat. 16: 20. tell no man he was t. C.
26: 63. tell whether thou be t. C.
Mk. 8: 29. Pe. saith, Thou art t.C.
14: 61. Art t. C. Son of Blessed?
Lu. 3: 15. John, whe. he were t. C.
9: 20. Pe. said, Thou art t. C. of G.
22: 67. scribes, say., Art thou t. C.
Jn. 1: 20. confessed, I am not t. C.
41. found Messias, which is t. C.
3: 28. I said, I am not t. C. but
4: 29. told me all, is not this t. C.
42. we know this is t. C., 7: 26.
7: 41. others said, This is t. C.
10: 24. if be t. C. tell us plainly
11: 27. I believe thou art t. C.
20: 31. might believe Jes. is t. C.
1 Jn. 2: 22. that denieth Jes. is t.C.
5: 1. whoso believeth Jesus is t. C.

With CHRIST.

Ro. 6: 8. if we be dead w. C. we
8: 17. if chil. then joint heirs w. C.
Ga. 2: 20. I am crucified w. C.
Ep. 2: 5. G. hath quickened us w.C.
Ph. 1: 23. to depart and be w. C.
Col. 2: 20. if dead w. C. fr. world
3: 1. If risen w. C. seek things abo.
3. your life is hid w. C. in God
Re. 20: 4. reigned w. C. 1000 years

CHRISTS.

Mat. 24: 24 arise false C., Mk. 13: 22.

CHRISTIAN, S.

Ac. 11: 26. first called C. at Antioch
26: 28. almost persua. me to be a C.
1 Pe. 4: 16. if any man suffer as a C.

CHRONICLES. [in C.

1 K. 14: 19. rest of acts of Jerob.
1 Ch. 27: 24. nor number put in C.
Es. 6: 1. to bring the book of C.

CHRYSOLITE.

Re. 21: 20. seventh foundation a c.

CHRYSOPRASUS.

Re. 21: 20. tenth founda. of city a

CHUB. [c.

Eze. 30: 5. C. shall fall by sword

CHUN.

1 Ch. 18: 8 fr. Tibhath and C. cities

CHURCH. [my c.

Mat. 16: 18. upon this rock build
18: 17. tell it to the c., if he neglect
Ac. 2: 47. Lord added to c. daily
5: 11. great fear came upon all c.
8: 1. great persecution ag. c. at J.
11: 26. they assembled with c.
14: 23. ordained elders in every c.
27. when they had gathered c.
15: 3. brought on way by the c.
22. it pleased elders with c. to
18: 22. when he had saluted c.
Ro. 16: 5. greet c. in their house
1 Co. 4: 17. as I teach in every c.
14: 4. prophesieth edifieth c.
5. that c. may receive edifying
23. if c. be come into one place
16: 19. salute c. in their house
Ep. 1: 22. head over all to the c.
3: 10. be known by c. wisd. of G.
5: 24. as c. is subject unto C. so

Ep.5:25. as Christ loved c. and gave
27. present a glorious c.
29. cherisheth it, as L. the c.
32. I speak conc. Christ and c.
Ph. 3 : 6. persecuting the c. [me
4 : 15. no c. communicated with
Col. 1 : 18. is head of body the c.
24. for his body's sake, the c.
4 : 15. salute c. in Nymphas' hou.
1 Th. 1 : 1. c. of Thess., 2 Th. 1 : 1.
1 Ti. 5 : 16. let not c. be charged
Phm. 2. Paul, to c. in thy house
He. 12 : 23. to c. of firstborn in
1 Pe. 5 : 13. c. at Bab. saluteth you
3 Jn. 6. of thy charity before c.
9. I wrote unto c. but Diotrephes

In the CHURCH.

Ac. 7 : 38. was i. t. c. in wildern.
13 : 1. prophets i. t. c. at Antioch
1 Co. 6 : 4. are least esteemed i.t.c.
11 : 18. ye come together i. t. c.
12 : 28. God hath set some i. t. c.
14 : 19. i. t. c. I had rather speak
28. let him keep silence i. t. c.
35. for women to speak i. t. c.
Ep. 3 : 21. unto him be glory i.t.c.
Col. 4 : 16. cause it to be read i.t.c.

Of the CHURCH.

Ac. 8 : 3. Saul, made havoc o. t. c.
11:22.tid-gs came unto ears o.t.c.
12 : 1. Herod vexed certain o.t.c.
5. prayer was made o.t.c. for Pe.
15 : 4. they were received o. t. c.
20 : 17. Paul sent elders o. t. c.
Ro. 16 : 1. Phebe, a servant o. t. c.
23. Gaius mine host and o. t. c.
1 Co. 14 : 12. to edifying o. t. c.
Ep. 5 : 23. as Christ is head o. t. c.
He. 2 : 12. in midst o. t. c. I sing
Ja. 5 : 14. call elders o. t. c.
3 Jn. 10. Diotr. casteth th. o. t. c.
Re. 2 : 1. to angel o. t. c. of Ephes.
8. c. in Smyrna | 12. Pergamos
18. c. of Thyatira | 3 : 1. Sardis
7. c. of Phila. | 14. Laodicea

CHURCH of God.

Ac. 20 : 28. feed the c.o.G. which he
1 Co. 1 : 2. c. o. G. at Corinth
10 : 32. none offence to c. o. G.
11 : 22. or despise ye the c. o. G.
15:9.I persecuted c.o.G., Ga.1:13.
2 Co.1 : 1. unto the c.o.G. which is
1 Ti. 3 : 5. how take care of c.o.G.
15. the c. o. the living G.

CHURCHES.

Ac. 9 : 31. Then had the c. rest
15 : 41. Paul went confirming c.
16 : 5. were c. establish. in faith
19 : 37. are neither robbers of c.
Ro. 16 : 4. to whom c. give thanks
16. The c. of Christ salute you
1 Co. 7 : 17. so ordain I in all c.
11 : 16.we no such custom, neith.c.
14 : 33. author of peace as in all c.
34. Let women keep silence in c.
16 : 1. as given order to c. of Gala.
19. c. of Asia salute you [Mace.
2 Co. 8 : 1. grace bestowed on c. of
18. gospel throughout all c.
19. chosen of c. to travel with us
23. they are messengers of c.
24. before c. proof of your love
11 : 8. I robbed other c. taking
28. daily the care of all c. [wages
12 : 13. wherein ye inferior to c.?
Ga. 1 : 2. unto the c. of Galatia
22. unknown by face to c.
1 Th. 2 : 14. followers of c. of God
2 Th. 1 : 4. we glory in you in c.
Re. 1 : 4. John to seven c. in Asia
11. send it to seven c. in Asia
20. seven stars are angels of c.
candlesticks are seven c.
2 : 7. hear what Spirit saith unto
c., 11, 17, 29.-3 : 6, 13, 22.
23. c. know I am he searcheth
22 : 16. testify these things in c.

CHURL.

Is. 32 : 5. nor c. be said bountiful
7. instruments of the c. are evil

CHURLISH.

1 S. 25 : 3. Nabal was c. and evil

CHURNING.

Pr. 30 : 33. c. of milk bring. butter

CHU'S'HAN-RISHATHA'IM.

Ju. 3 : 8. c. king of Mesopota., 10.

CHU'ZA.

Lu. 8 : 3. C. Herod's steward

CIELED, ING. See CEILED.

CILIC'IA.

Ac. 6 : 9. they of C. disputed with S.
15 : 23. breth. of the Gentiles in C.
41. he went through C. confirm.
21 : 39. Tarsus city in C.22 : 3. | 23 : 34.
27 : 5. sailed over sea of C.
Ga. 1 : 21. came into regions of C.

CI'MAH.

Jb. 9 : † 9. maketh Arcturus and C.

CINNAMON.

Ex. 30 : 23. take of sweet c.
Pr. 7 : 17. perfum. my bed with c.
Can. 4 : 14. plants are an orch. of c.
Re. 18 : 13. no man buyeth her c.

CIN'NEROTH.

See CHIN'NEROTH.

CIRCLE.

Pr. 8 : † 27. set a c. on depth
Is. 40 : 22. sitteth on c. of earth

CIRCUIT, S. [c.

1 S. 7 : 16. went from year to year in
Jb. 22 : 14. walketh in c. of heaven
Ps. 19 : 6. his c. unto ends of earth
Ec. 1 : 6. wind retur. acc. to his c-s

CIRCUMCISE.

Ge. 17 : 11. ye shall c. foreskins
De. 10 : 16. c. foreskin of heart
30 : 6. Lord will c. thine heart
Jos. 5 : 2. c. again chil. of Israel
4. is cause why Joshua did c.
Je. 4 : 4. c. yourselves to Lord,
Lu. 1 : 59. they came to c. child
Jn. 7 : 22. ye on sab. c. a man
Ac. 15 : 5. needful to c. them
21 : 21. ought not to c. their chil.

CIRCUMCISED.

Ge. 17 : 10. Every man child be c.
12.eight days old sh.be c.,Le.12:3.
13. he bought with thy money, be
c., Ex. 12 : 44.
14.not c.that soul be cut off
23. Abraham c. flesh of foreskin
26. that day Ab. was c. and Ish.
21 : 4. c. Isaac 8 days old, Ac.7 : 8.
34 : 15. if as we be eve. male be c.
24. eve. male was c., Ex. 12 : 48.
Jos. 5 : 3. Joshua c. chil. of Israel
7. had not c. them by the way
† 8. people made an end to be c.
Je. 9 : 25. punish all c. with uncir.
Ac. 15 : 1. Except c. not saved, 24.
16:3. Paul c. Tim. bec. of Jews [c.
Rom. 4 : 11. father of all though not
1 Co. 7 : 18. Is any called being c.?
let him not become uncir-d. Is
called in uncir.? let him not be
Ga. 2 : 3. Tit. compelled to be c. [c.
5 : 2. if c. Christ profit you noth.
3. to every man that is c.
6 : 12. constrain you to be c.
13. neither they c. keep law
Ph. 3 : 5. c. eighth day, of stock
Col. 2 : 11. In whom also ye are c.

CIRCUMCISING.

Jos. 5 : 8. had done c. people
Lu. 2 : 21. days accom. for c. child

CIRCUMCISION.

Jn. 7 : 22. Moses gave unto you c.
23. If on sabbath receive c.
Ro. 2 : 25. c. profiteth, if keep law;
if break law, thy c. is uncir.
26. uncircum. be counted for c.
27. by letter and c. dost transgr.
28. nor is that c, wh. is outward

2 : 29. c. is that of the heart
3 : 30. shall justify c. by faith
4 : 9. blessedness then on c. only?
10. How was it reckoned? when
he was in c.? not in c.
1 Co. 7 : 19 c. is keeping of com-ts
Ga. 2 : 9. should go unto c. [6 : 15.
5 : 6. in J. C. neither c. availeth,
11. if I preach c. why do I
Ep. 2 : 11. that called c. in flesh
Ph. 3 : 3. we c. worship G. in
Col.2:11.c. without hands, by c. of
3 : 11. neither c. nor uncir. but C.

Of CIRCUMCISION.

Ex. 4 : 26. bloody husb. beca. o. c.
Ac. 7 : 8. gave Ab. covenant o. c.
10 : 45. they o. c. were astonished
11:2. they o.c. contended with Pe.
Ro. 3 : 1. what profit is there o. c.?
4 : 11. he received the sign o. c.
12. fa. o. c. to them not o. c.
15 : 8. Jes. C. was a minister o. c.
Ga. 2 : 7. gospel o. c. com. to Pe.
8. in Peter to apostleship o. c.
12. them, which were o. the c.
Col. 4 : 11. and Justus o. c. sal. you
Tit. 1 : 10. unruly, espec. they o.c.

CIRCUMSPECT.

Ex. 23 : 13. in all things, be c.

CIRCUMSPECTLY.

Ep. 5 : 15. See that ye walk c. not

CIS = KISH.

Ac. 13 : 21. Saul the son of C.

CISTERN, S.

2 K. 18 : 31. drink every one water
of his c., Is. 36 : 16.
2 Ch. 26 : † 10. Uzziah cut out c-s
Ne. 9 : † 25. houses full of c-s
Pr. 5 : 15. Drink out of thine own c.
Ec. 12 : 6. wheel broken at c.
Je. 2 : 13. hewed out c-s broken c-s

CITIES.

Ge. 19 : 29. when God destroyed the
c. of the plain
35 : 5. terror of God upon c.
41 : 48. Joseph laid up food in c.
47 : 21. people he removed to c.
Le. 25 : 32. c. of Levites redeemed
26 : 25. within your c. send pesti.
Nu. 13 : 19. what c. they dwell in
28. c. walled and gr., De. 1 : 28.
21 : 2. I will utterly destroy c.
32 : 24. c. for your little ones
35 : 8. every one shall give of his
c. to Levites, Jos. 14 : 4.-21 : 2.
De. 2 : 37. nor to c. in mountains
3 : 12. c. gave I unto Reubenites
19. abide in c. I have given
4 : 41. severed 3 c. this side Jor.
6 : 10. to give thee goodly c.
19 : 5. flee unto one of these c.,
4 : 42. Jos. 20 : 4.
21 : 2. c. round about him slain
Jos. 9 : 17. Isr. came unto their c.
10 : 19. suff. them not to enter c.
11 : 13. as for c. that stood still
18 : 9. described it by c. in book
Ju. 12 : 7. was buried in one of c.
20 : 48. men of Isr. set on fire c.
21 : 23. they repaired the c. and
1 S. 7 : 14. c. Philistines had taken
31 : 7. Israelites forsook c. and
fled, 1 Ch. 10 : 7.
2 S.10:12.c. of our G., 1 Ch.19:13.
1 K. 9 : 12. Hiram came to see c.
13. What c. hast given me?
19. c. of store Solomon had
20 : 34. c. father took I restore
2 K. 13 : 25. recovered c. of Israel
1 Ch. 2 : 22. Jair had 23 c. in Gilead
4 : 31. These were their c. to
2 Ch. 28 : 18. invaded c. of low coun.
34 : 6. did he in c. of Manasseh
Ezr. 3 : 1. Isr. in their c., Ne. 7 : 73.
Ne. 9 : 25. took strong c., a fat land
11 : 1. nine parts in other c.
Es. 9 : 2. Jews gath., togeth. into c.

Jb. 15: 28. dwelleth in desolate c.
Ps. 9: 6. thou hast destroyed c.
Is. 6: 11. ans-d Until c. be wasted
14: 21. nor fill world with c.
17: 9. strong c. be as forsaken
19: 18. In that day sh. five c. in E.
33: 8. he hath despised the c.
42: 11. wilder. and c. thereof, 14: 17.
54: 3. c. to be inhab., Eze. 36: 10.
64: 10. Thy holy c. a wilderness
Je. 2: 15. his c. are burned
28. acc. to number of c., 11: 13.
5: 6. leopard shall watch over c.
13: 19. c. of south be shut up
20: 16. be as c. L. overthrew
31: 21. turn, O Isr., to these thy c.
33: 13. c. of mts.-c. of vale, c. of
48: 28. Moab leave c., dwell in rock
49: 13. c. be perpetual wastes
18. Gomorr. and neighb-r c., 50: 40.
50: 32. fire in c. | 51: 43. c. a desola.
Eze. 25: 9. c. on his frontiers
26: 19. like c. not inhabited
30: 7. in midst of c. wasted
17. these c. into captivity
35: 9. thy c. shall not return
36: 4. c. which became a prey
Ho. 8: 14. send fire upon his c.
11: 6. sword shall abide on his c.
Am. 4: 8. three c. to one for water
Ob. 20. possess c. of the south
Mi. 5: 11. I will cut off the c.
14. so will I destroy thy c.
7: 12. fr. Assyria and fortified c.
Zph. 3: 6. their c. are destroyed
Zch. 1: 17. My c. shall yet spread
Mat. 10: 23. not have gone over c.
11: 1. to preach in their c.
20. began he to upbraid c. [c.
Lu. 4: 43. preach kingd. of G. to other
19: 17. have author-y over ten c., 19.
Ac. 5: 16. out of c. round about
14: 6. Lystra and Derbe c. of
16: 4. they went through the c.
26: 11. I persecuted to strange c.
2 Pe. 2: 6. c. of Sod. and Go. to ashes
Jude 7. c. in like manner
Re. 16: 19. c. of the nations fell

All CITIES. [See BUILT.]
Nu. 21: 25. Isr. took a. these c. and dwelt in c., De. 2: 34.-3: 4. Jos. 10: 39.
31: 10. burnt a. their c., Ju. 20: 48.
35: 7. a. c. of Lev. 48 c., Jos. 21: 41.
De. 20: 15. thus do unto a. c. afar
Jos. 11: 12. a. c. of kings destroyed
21: 19. a. c. of Aaron were 13 c.
33. a. c. of Gershonites 13 c.
40. a. c. of Merari by lot 12 c.
1 S. 18: 6. women came out of a. c.
2 S. 12: 31. did he to a. c. of Ammon
24: 7. came to a. c. of Hivites
1 K. 22: 39. a. c. Ahab built are
2 Ch. 14: 14. Asa smote a. the c.
Ne. 8: 15. proclaim in a. their c.
10: 37. have tithes in a. the c. of
Je. 4: 26. a. the c. were brok. down
33: 12. in a. c. a habita. of sheph.
34: 1. Jerus. and ag. a. c. thereof
49: 13. a. the c. be perpet. wastes
Ho. 13: 10. save thee in a. thy c.
Mk. 6: 33. ran afoot out of a. c.
Ac. 8: 40. preached in a. c. till he

Defenced CITIES.
Is. 36. 1: Sennacherib ag. d. c.
37: 26. be to lay waste the d. c.
Je. 4: 5. assemble, let us go into the d. c., 8: 14.
34: 7. these d. c. remained of Jud.

Fenced CITIES.
Nu. 32: 17. little ones dwell in f. c.
De. 3: 5. c. were f. with high walls
9: 1. c. f. up to heaven, Jos. 14: 12.
Jos. 10: 20. rest entered into f. c.
2 S. 20: 6. lest he get him f. c.
2 K. 18: 13. king of Assyria come ag. all f. c., 2 Ch. 32: 1. Is. 36: 1.
2 K. 19: 25. be to lay waste f. c.
2 Ch. 12: 4. Shishak took f. c., 11: 10.
14: 6. Asa built f. c. in Jud. [19.
17: 2. Jehosh. placed forces in f. c.
19: 5. set judges through all f. c.
21: 3. Jehosh. gave his sons f. c.
33: 14. capts. of war in all f. c.
Je. 5: 17. sh. impoverish thy f. c.
Eze. 36: 35. ruined c. are become f.
Da. 11: 15. k. of north take f. c.
Ho. 8: 14. Judah multiplied f. c.
Zph. 1: 16. day of alarm ag. f. c.

CITIES of Judah.
2 S. 2: 1. Shall I go up to c. o. J.?
1 K. 12: 17. children of Israel which dwelt in c. o. J., 2 Ch. 10: 17.
2 K. 23: 5. burnt incense in c. o. J.
8. brought priests out of c. o. J.
1 Ch. 6: 57. to sons of Aa. c. o. J.
2 Ch. 14: 5. c. o. J. the high places,
17: 7. to teach in c. o. J. [31: 1.
13. business in c. o. J.
19: 5. set judges in the c. o. J.
20: 4. out of c. o. J. came to seek L.
23: 2. gather Levites out of c. o. J.
24: 5. Go unto c. o. J. gath. money
31: 6. Isr. in c. o. J. brought tithes
33: 14. put captains in c. o. J.
Ne. 11: 3. in c. o. J. dwelt ev. one, 20.
Ps. 69: 35. God will build c. o. J.
Is. 40: 9. to c. o. J. behold your G.
44: 26. to c. o. J. Ye sh. be built
Je. 1: 15. of north ag. c. o. J., 34: 7.
4: 16. give their voice ag. c. o. J.
7: 17. what they do in c. o. J. [22.
9: 11. c. o. J. desolate, 10: 22.-34:
11: 6. Proclaim words in c. o. J.
12. shall c. o. J. cry to gods
17: 26. they sh. come from c. o. J.
32: 44. take witness in c. o. J.
33: 10. without man in c. o. J.
13. in c. o. J. shall flocks pass
40: 5. governor over c. o. J.
44: 6. my fury kindled in c. o. J.
21. incense ye burned in c. o. J.
La. 5: 11. ravished maids in c. o. J.
Zch. 1: 12. not mercy on c. o. J.

CITIES of refuge.
Nu. 35: 6. be six c. o. r., 13, 14.
11. appoint c. o. r., Jos. 20: 2.
1 Ch. 6: 67. sons of Kohath c. o. r.

Six CITIES.
Nu. 35: 6. s. c. for refuge, 13, 15.
Jos. 15: 59. in mts. of Judah s. c.

CITIES with Suburbs.
Le. 25: 34. s. of c. may not be sold
Nu. 35: 2. give to Levites s. for c.
Jos. 21: 3. gave to Levites c. and s.
41. c. of Levites 48 with their s.
1 Ch. 6: 64. gave Levites c. with s.

CITIES with Villages.
Jos. 15: 36. c. with the v., 32.-13: 23, 28.-16: 9.-18: 24.-19: 6.
1 S. 6: 18. c. and country v.
1 Ch. 27: 25. storehou. in c. and v.
Mat. 9: 35. Jesus went about all c. and v. teaching, Lu. 13: 22.
Mk. 6: 56. he entered into v. or c.

CITIES with Waste.
Le. 26: 31. will make your c. w., 33.
Is. 61: 4. they shall repair the w. c.
Je. 4: 7. thy c. be laid w., Eze. 12: 20.
Eze. 6: 6. in your dwellings c. be w.
19: 7. laid w. c. | 35: 4. lay c. w.
29: 12. c. laid w. sh. be deso. 40 yrs.
36: 35. w. c. are become fenced
38. w. c. be filled with men
Am. 9: 14. they shall build the w. c.

Your CITIES.
Is. 1: 7. y. c. are burned with fire
Je. 40: 10. dwell in y. c. ye have tak.
Am. 4: 6. cleanness of teeth in y. c.

CITIZEN, S.
Lu. 15: 15. prodigal joined a c.
19: 14. his c-s hated him, and
Ac. 21: 39. a c. of no mean city
Ep. 2: 19. but fellow c-s with saints

CITY.
Ge. 4: 17. Cain builded a c.
11: 4. let us build us a c. and a
5. Lord came down to see the c.
8. and they left off to build c.
18: 26. if I find fifty righte. within
28. destroy c. for lack of five? [c.
19: 15. lest consumed in iniq. of c.
24: 13. dau-s of c. to draw water
34: 24. heark-d that went out of c.
25. came upon the c. boldly [c.
44: 13. ev. man his ass and ret. to
Nu. 21: 28. flame is gone out fr. c.
22: † 39. Balaam to c. of streets
De. 2: 36. not one c. too strong
3: 4. was not a c. we took not
13: 15. surely smite inhab. of c.
20: 10. c. to fight ag. it, then pro-
19. besiege a c. a long time [claim
21: 3. c. next to slain man, 6.
Jos. 3: 16. very far from c. Adam
6: 3. compass c. six days, 7.
24. they burnt c., De. 13: 16. Jos. 8: 8, 19. Ju. 1: 8.-18: 27.
8: 2. ambush for c. behind it
17. they left c. open, pursued
20. smoke of c. ascend. to heav.
11: 19. was not a c. made peace
Jos. 15: 13. c. of Arba, wh. c. is Heb.
19: 50. gave Joshua c. be asked
20: 4. shall stand at entry of c.
Ju. 1: 16. c. of palm-trees, 3: 13. 2 Ch. 28: 15.
6: 27. he feared men of the c.
8: 17. Gideon slew the men of c.
9: 45. beat down c. and sowed it
51. all they of the c. fled
20: 40. flame of c. ascended up to
Ru. 1: 19. all the c. was moved
3: 11. for c. of my people know
1 S. 1: 3. out of c. yearly to worsh.
4: 13. told it, all c. cried out
5: 9. hand of L. against the c.
11. destruction through all the c.
8: 22. Go every man unto his c., 1 K. 22: 36. Ezr. 2: 1. Ne. 7: 6.
9: 10. c. where man of God was
15: 5. Saul came to c. of Amalek
23: 10. to destroy c. for my sake
28: 3. Isr. buried him in own c.
30: 3. came to c. and it was burned
2 S. 10: 3. to search c. and spy it
11: 16. obser-d c. assigned Uriah
12: 1. two men in one c. one rich
12: 26. took royal c. | 27. c. of waters
15: 2. Of what c. art thou? [river
17: 13. c., we will draw it into
19: 37. I may die in mine own c.
20: 19. seekest to destroy a c. and
1 K. 1: 45. so that c. rang again
11: 32. Jerus. c. I have chosen, 36.
2 K. 6: 19. neither is this the c.
10: 25. went to c. of house of Baal
11: 20. and the c. was in quiet
24: 10. c. Jerus. besieged, 25: 2.
2 Ch. 15: 6. c. was destroyed of c. for
19: 5. he set judges c. by c. [G.
30: 10. posts passed from c. to c.
32: 18. that they might take the c.
Ezr. 4: 12. building rebellious c.
Ne. 2: 3. not sad, when c. waste, 5.
11: 9. Judah was second over c.
Es. 3: 15. c. Shushan was perplex
8: 15. c. of Shushan rejoiced
Ps. 48: 2. c. of great King, Mat. 5: 35
59: 6. go round the c., 14.
72: 16. they of c. shall flourish
107: 4. they found no c. to dwell in
122: 3. Jerus. as a c. compact
127: 1. except Lord keep the c.
Pr. 8: 3. wisdom at entry of c. [c.
9: 3. crieth upon highest places of
10: 15. wealth his strong c., 18: 11.
11: 10. well with righte. c. rejoic-
11. by upright c. is exalted [eth.
16: 32. than he that taketh a c.
18: 19. harder to be won than str. c.

Pr. 21 : 22. wise scaleth c. of mighty
25 : 28. is like a c. broken down
29 : 8. Scornful bring c. into snare
Ec. 9 : 14. There was a little c. and
15. poor wise man delivered c.
10:15.Knoweth not how to go to c.
Can. 3 : 3. watchmen that go about
c., 5 : 7. [ful c., 21.
Is. 1 : 26. c. of righteousness, faith-
14 : 31. Howl, O gate, cry, O c.
17 : 1. Damascus from being a c.
19 : 2. shall fight, c. against c.
24 : 10. c. of confusion is broken
25 : 2. of a c. a heap, to be no c.
26 : 1.We have strong c., salv. will
32 : 19. c. sh. be low in low place
33 : 20. Zion, c. of solemnities
60 : 14. shall call thee c. of Lord
62 : 12. be called c. not forsaken
Je. 3 : 14. will take you one of a c.
4 : 29. c. shall flee for the noise
19 : 12. make this c. as Tophet
23 : 39. forsake you, and c. I gave
25 : 29. evil on c. called by my na.
29 : 7. And seek peace of c.
32 : 24.come unto c. and c. is given
39 : 2. c. was broken up, 52 : 7.
46 : 8. I will destroy the c. [joy
49 : 25. c. of praise not left, c. of
51 : 31. of Bab. th. his c. is taken
La. 1 : 1. How doth c. sit solitary
2 : 15. is this c. men called perfec.
Eze. 4 : 1. portray upon it c. Jerus.
7 : 23. ch. the c. is full of violence
9 : 1. that have charge over c.
4. Go through midst of c. Jerus.
9. c. is full of perverseness
10 : 2. scatter fire over the c.
27 : 32. What c. is like Tyrus?
33 : 21. one saying, c. is smitten
48 : 35. name of c. be, L. is there
Da. 9 : 18. c. called by thy na., 19.
Ho. 6 : 8. c. of them work iniquity
Am. 4 : 7.rain upon one c. not ano.
5 : 3. c. that went out by a thous.
Mi. 6 : 9. Lord's voice crieth unto c.
Ha. 2 : 12. establish-h a c. by iniq.
Zph. 3 : 1. woe to oppressing c.
Zch 8 : 3. Jerus. a c. of truth
5. streets of c. be full of boys
21. of one c. shall go to another
14 : 2. not be cut off from c.
Mat. 2 : 23. c. Nazareth, Lu. 2:4,39.
5 : 14. c. that is set on a hill
35. Jerus the c. of great King
8 : 34. c. came out to meet Jesus
9 : 1. and came into his own c.
10 : 11. whatsoever c. ye enter
15. than for th.c.,Mk.6:11.Lu.10:
21 : 10. all the c. was moved [12.
22 : 7. king burnt up their c.
23:34. persecute them from c. to c.
Mk. 1 : 33. all the c. was gathered
5 : 14. told it in c., Lu. 8 : 34.
Lu. 1 : 26. a c. of Galilee, 4 : 31.
2 : 3. taxed, every one to his c.
7 : 12. much people of c. with her
9:10.belonging to c. called Bethsa.
19 : 41. he beheld the c. and wept
23 : 51. Arimathea, c. of Jews
Jn. 1 : 44. the c. of Andrew and Pe.
4 : 5. cometh he to a c. of Samaria
39. many of that c. believed
19 : 20. crucified nigh to c.
Ac. 8 : 5. went down to c. of Sama.
8. was great joy in that c. [hear
13 : 44. came almost whole c. to
14 : 13. which was before their c.
21. preached gospel to that c.
16 : 12. in that c. certain days
20. exceedingly trouble our c.
17 : 5. set all the c. in an uproar
16. saw c. wholly given to idol.
19 : 29. c. filled with confusion
35. how that c. of Ephesians
21 : 30. all the c. was moved
27 : 8. whereunto was c. of Lasea

2 Co. 11 : 32. kept c. of Damascenes
He. 11 : 10. c. that hath founda.
16. hath prepared for them a c.
12 : 22. come to c. of living God
13 : 14.here we no continuing c.
Ja. 4 : 13. we will go into such a c.
Re. 11 : 13. tenth part of c. fell
20 : 9. they compassed beloved c.
21 : 14. wall of c. had twelve
15. golden reed to measure c.
16. the c. lieth four square
18. c. was pure gold, like glass
23. c. had no need of the sun
See BUILD, ED, BUILT.

Bloody CITY.

Eze. 22 : 2. wilt thou judge b. c.
24 : 6. Woe to b. c., 9. Na. 3 : 1.

CITY of David.

2 S.5 : 9.called it c. o. D.,1 Ch.11:7.
6 : 10. not remove ark into c.o.D.
12. bro-t ark into c. o. D., 16. 1
Ch. 13 : 13.-15 : 29.
1 K. 3 : 1. Sol. brought her into c.
o. D., 9 : 24. 2 Ch. 8 : 11.
8 : 1. ark out of c. o. D.,2 Ch.5:2.
11 : 43. Sol. buried in c. o. D., 2
Ch. 9 : 31. [c.o.D.
1 Ch. 11 : 5. castle of Zion, wh. is
2 Ch. 24 : 16. buried Jehoi.in c.o.D.
Is. 22 : 9. seen breaches of c. o. D.
29 : 1. Ariel, c. where D. dwelt
Lu. 2 : 4. Jo. went unto c. o. D.
11. born in c. o. D. a Saviour
See BURIED in City of David.

Defenced or Fenced CITY.

2 K. 3 : 19. ye sh. smite every f. c.
10 : 2. with you f. c. and armour
17 : 9. from tower of watchmen to
f. c., 18 : 8.
2 Ch. 11 : 23. he dispersed of all his
children unto every f. c.
Is. 25 : 2. hast made of d. c. a ruin
27 : 10. the d. c. shall be desolate
Je. 1 : 18. made thee this day a d.c.

Elders with CITY.

De. 19 : 12. e. of his c. sh.fetch him
21 : 6. e. of that c. next to slain
20. say to e. of c. son is stubborn
22 : 17. spread cloth bef. e. of c.
25 : 8. e. of his c. shall call him
Jos. 20 : 4. declare cause to e. of c.
Ju. 8 : 16. Gideon took e. of c.
Ru.4:2. Boaz took 10 men of e.of c.
Ezr. 10 : 14. with them e. of ev. c.

Every CITY.

De. 2 : 34. of e. c. we left none,3:6.
Ju. 20 : 48. smote men of e. c.
2 Ch. 11 : 12. in e. c. put shields
28: 25. in e.c. he made high places
31 : 19. of sons of Aaron in e. c.
Je. 4 : 29. e. c. shall be forsaken
48 : 8. spoiler shall come upon e.c.
Mat. 12 : 25. e. c. divided ag. itself
Lu.8 : 1.e.c. and vill.preaching | 4.
10 : 1. two and two into e. c.
Ac. 15:21. in e.c. them that preach
36. Let us visit our breth. in e.c.
20:23. H. Ghost witnesseth in e.c.
Tit.1:5.shouldest ordain eld. in e.c.

CITY of God, or Lord.

Ps. 46:4. streams make glad c.o.G.
48 : 1. greatly to be praised in c.o.
8. c.o.G.God will establish it [G.
87:3. Glo. things of thee,O c. o.G.
101 : 8. wicked doers from c. o. L.
Is. 60 : 14. call thee, The c. o. L.
He. 12 : 22. come to c. o. living G.
Re. 3 : 12. upon him name of c. o.

Great CITY. [my G.

Ge.10:12.Asshur build. Resen, g. c.
Jos. 10:2. feared, bec. Gibeon a g.c.
Ne.7:4. now c. was large and g.but
Je. 22 : 8 why L. thus to this g. c.
Jon. 1 : 2. go to Nineveh, that g.c.,
3 : 3. Nin.,an exceeding g. c. [3:2.
4 : 11. not spare Nineveh that g.c.
Re. 11 : 8. dead bodies in str.of g.c.

Re.14:8.Bab.th.g.c.,18:10,16,19,21.
16:19.g.c. was divided into 3 parts
17:18.woman thou saw.is that g.c.
18:18. What c.like unto this g. c.
21 : 10. shewed me that g.c.Jerus.

Holy CITY. [h.c.

Ne. 11:1.cast lots to dwell in Jerus.
18.all the Levites of the h.c.were
Is.48:2.call thems. of the h.c. [384
52 : 1. put on beaut. garm. O h.c.
Da. 9 : 24. seventy weeks upon h.c.
Mat. 4 : 5. devil tak. him into h.c.
27 : 53. into h.c. and app. to many
Re. 11 : 2. the h. c. shall they tread
21:2.I John saw h.c. coming fr. G.
22 19.sh. take his part out of h.c.

In, or Into CITY.

Ge. 19 : 12. whatso. hast i. c. bring
34 : 28. i. c. and that in field
De. 20 : 14. all that is i. c. take
22 : 23. a man find her i. c., 24.
28 : 3. Blessed shalt thou be i. c.
16. Cursed shalt thou be i. c.
Jos. 6 : 20. that the peo. went i. c.
21. they destroyed all i. c.
8:19. entered i. c. and set it on fire
20:6. dwell i.c. until he stand bef.
Ju. 1 : 24. shew us entrance i. c.
8:27.Gideon put the ephod i.his c.
19 : 12. turn aside i. c. of stranger
1 S. 4 : 13. man came i. c. and told
9:14.were come i.c.behold Samuel
20:29.our family hath sacr. i. c.
2 S.12:1.two men i. one c., one rich
15 : 25 Carry back ark i. c.
27. return i. c. and your sons
19 : 3. gat them by stealth i. c.
37. I may die i. my own c.
1 K. 13 : 25. they told it i. c.
14:11.dieth of Jerob. i. c. dogs eat
12. when thy feet enter i. c.
16 : 4. dieth of Baasha i. c. dogs
20 : 30. i. c. into an inner cham.
21 : 24. dieth i. c. dogs eat
2 K. 7 : 4. say, We will enter i. c.
12. catch them, and get i. c.
20 : 20. Heze. brought water i. c.
25 : 3. famine prevailed i. c.
Ps. 31 : 21. kindness i. a strong c.
55 : 9. I have seen violence i. c.
60:9. bring me i. strong c.,108:10.
Pr. 1 : 21. i. c. wisdom uttereth
Ec. 7 : 19. ten mighty men i. c.
8 : 10. wicked forgotten i. c.
Is. 24 : 12. i. c. is left desolation
32 : 13. houses of joy i. joyous c.
Je. 14 : 18. If I enter i. c. then
38 : 9. there is no more bread i. c.
52 : 6. famine was sore i. c.
La. 1 : 19. gave up ghost i. c.
Eze. 7 : 15. i. c. famine devour
9 : 7. went forth and slew i. c.
Ho. 11 : 9. I will not enter i. c.
Jo. 2 : 9. shall run to and fro i. c.
Am. 3 : 6. trumpet be blown i. c.
shall there be evil i. a c.?
7 : 17. Thy wife be a harlot i. c.
Jon. 3 : 4. Jonah to enter i. c.
Mat. 9 : 1. he came i. his own c.
10 : 5. i. c. of Samaria enter not
11. i. whatsoever c. ye enter
21 : 18. as he returned i. c.
26 : 18. Go i. c. to such a man
28 : 11. some of watch came i. c.
Mk. 1 : 45. openly enter i. the c.
5 : 14. told it i. the c., Lu. 8 : 34.
14 : 13. Go i. c., Ac. 9 : 6.
16. came i. the c. and found
Lu. 1:39. with haste i. a c. of Jud.
2 : 3. taxed, every one i. his c.
5 : 12. when he was i. a certain c.
7 : 11. he went i. a c. called Nain
37. a woman i. c. a sinner
18 : 2. There was i. a c. a judge
3. was a widow i. that c.
22 : 10. when ye are entered i. c.
24 : 49. tarry ye i. c. of Jerus.

Jn. 4 : 8. disciples were gone i. c.
28. and went her way i. the c.
11 : 54. i. a c. called Ephraim
Ac. 8 : 8. was great joy i. that c.
9. i. same c. used sorcery
9 : 6. Arise and go i. the c.
11 : 5. I was i. c. of Joppa
14 : 20. he rose up and came i. c.
16 : 12. we were i. that c. abiding
21 : 29. Trophimus with him i. c.
24 : 12. in synagogues nor i. c.
2 Co. 11 : 26. been in perils i. c.
Ja. 4 : 13. we will go i. such a c.
Re. 22 : 14. enter through gates i. c.

Out of the CITY.

Ge. 44 : 4. when gone o. o. c. [c.
Ex. 9 : 29. soon as I am gone o. o.
33. and Moses went o. o. c.
Le. 14 : 45. shall carry them o. o. c.
Jos. 8 : 22. other side issued o.o.c.
Ju. 1 : 24. saw a man come o. o. c.
9 : 43. people come forth o. o. c.
20 : 38. flame with smoke rise o.o.c.
1 S. 1 : 3. went up o. o. c. yearly
2 S. 18 : 3. better succour us o.o.c.
20 : 16. cried a wise woman o.o.c.
1 K. 21 : 13. carried Naboth o. o. c.
2 K. 2 : 23. little chil. o.o.c. mocked
7 : 12. when they come o. o. c.
9 : 15. said, let none escape o.o.c.
1 Ch. 20 : 2. bro-t much spoil o.o.c.
2 Ch. 33 : 15. Josiah cast idols o.o.c.
Jb. 24 : 12. Men groan from o.o.c.
Je. 39 : 4. Zede. went o.o.c., 52 : 7.
Eze. 48 : 30. are goings o. o. c.
Mi. 4 : 10. shalt thou go o. o. c.
Mat. 10 : 14. depart o.o. house or c.
21 : 17. he went o. o. c.
Mk. 11 : 19. even come he went o.o.c.
Lu. 4 : 29. they thrust him o. o. c.
8 : 4. come to him o. o. c.
27. o. o.c. man which had devils
9 : 5. go o. o. that c. shake dust
Jn. 4 : 30. then they went o. o. c.
Ac. 7 : 58. cast Stephen o. o. c.
14 : 19. stoned Paul, drew him o. o. c.
16 : 13. sabbath we went o. o. c.
39. depart o. o. the c.
21 : 5. brought us, till were o.o.c.

CITY of refuge.

Nu. 35 : 25. restore him to c. o. r.
26. without border of c. o. r., 27.
28. sh. have remained in c. o. r.
32. him that is fled to c. o. r.
Jos. 21 : 13. Hebron c. o. r., 1 Ch.
21. Shechem c.- | 27. Golan [6:57.
32. Kedesh c.o.r. | 38. Ramoth

This CITY.

Ge. 19 : 14. for L. will destroy t. c.
20. t. c. is near to flee unto
21. I will not overthrow t. c.
Jos. 6 : 26. cursed he buildeth t. c.
Ju. 19 : 11. let us turn in unto t.c.
1 S. 9 : 6. in t. c. a man of God
2 K. 2 : 19. situa. of t. c. pleasant
6 : 19. neither is t. the c. : follow me
18 : 30. t.c. not be deliv., Is. 36 : 15.
19 : 32. into t. c., 33. Is. 37 : 34.
34. I will defend t. c., 20 : 6. Is. 37 : 35.-38 : 6.
23 : 27. I will cast off t. c. Jerus.
2 Ch. 6 : 34. they prayed tow. t. c.
Ezr. 4 : 13. if t. c. be builded, 16.
15. t. c. is a rebellious city
19. t. c. of old made insurrection
21. t. c. be not builded, until
Ne. 13 : 18. G. bring evil upon t.c.?
Je. 6 : 6. t. is the c. to be visited
17 : 25. t. c. shall remain for ever
19 : 8. I will make t. c. desolate
11. Even so will I break t. c.
12. even make t. c. as Tophet
15. bring upon t. c. all the evil
20 : 5. I will deliver strength of t.c.
21 : 9. abideth in t. c. die by sw.
10. set my face ag. t. c. for evil
Je. 22 : 8. why L. done thus unto t.c.?
26 : 6. I will make t. c. a curse
11. he hath prophesied ag. t. c.
15. bring innocent blood upon t.c.
27 : 17. wherefore t.c. be laid waste?
32 : 3. give t. c. to Chal., 28.-34 : 2.-38 : 3, 18. [cation
31. t. c. been to me as a provo-
36. t. c. ye say, It shall be deliv.
33 : 5. for wick. I hid face fr. t. c.
34 : 22. cause them to return to t.c.
38 : 17. t. c. shall not be burnt
23. shalt cause t. c. to be burnt
39 : 16. my words on t. c. for evil
La. 2 : 15. t. c. men call perfection
Eze. 11 : 2. give wick. counsel in t.c.
3. t. c. is the caldron, and we, 7.
11. t. c. shall not be your caldron
Mat. 10 : 23. persecute in t. c. flee
Ac. 18 : 10. I have much peo. in t.c.
22 : 3. I was brought up in t. c.

Without the CITY.

Ge. 19 : 16. men set Lot w. t. c.
Le. 14 : 40. an uncl. place w.c., 41.
Nu. 35 : 5. shall measure from w.t.c.
2 Ch. 32 : 3. stop fountains w. t. c.
Re. 14 : 20. wine press trodden w.t.c.

CLAD. [new garm.

1 K. 11 : 29. Jerob. c. himself with
Is. 59 : 17. was c. with zeal as cloak

CLAMOROUS.

Pr. 9 : 13. a foolish woman is c.

CLAMOUR.

Ep. 4 : 31. anger and c. be put away

CLAP hands.

Jb. 27 : 23. Men shall c. h. at him
Ps. 47 : 1. c. your h., all ye people
98 : 8. Let floods c. their h., let hills be joyful
Is. 55 : 12. trees of field shall c. h.
La. 2 : 15. pass by c. h. at thee
Na. 3 : 19. hear bruit of thee c. h.

CLAPPED, PETH.

2 K. 11 : 12. c-d their hands, and
Jb. 34 : 37. he c-h his hands among us
Eze. 25 : 6. hast c. thine hands

CLAU'DA.

Ac. 27 : 16. island called C.

CLAU'DIA.

2 Ti. 4 : 21. Eubulus greeteth C.

CLAU'DIUS. See CESAR.

CLAU'DIUS LYS'IAS.

Ac. 23 : 26. C. greeting to Felix

CLAVE. [Cleft.]

Ge. 22 : 3. Ab. c. wood for burnt-off.
Nu. 16 : 31. ground c. asunder
Ju. 15 : 19. G. c. hollow in jaw
1 S. 6 : 14. they c. wood of cart
Ps. 78 : 15. He c. rocks, Is. 48 : 21.

CLAVE. [Adhered.]

Ge. 34 : 3. his soul c. unto Dinah
Ru. 1 : 14. Ruth c. unto mother in l.
2 S. 20 : 2. Judah c. unto their king
23 : 10. until his hand c. unto sword
1 K. 11 : 2. Sol. c. unto these in love
2 K. 18 : 6. Hezekiah c. to Lord
Ne. 10 : 29. They c. to brethren
Ac. 17 : 34. certain men c. unto Paul

CLAWS.

De. 14 : 6. the cleft into two c.
Da. 4 : 33. his nails like birds' c.
Zch. 11 : 16. he shall tear their c.

CLAY.

Jb. 4 : 19. that dwell in houses of c.
10 : 9. hast made me as the c.
13 : 12. are like to bodies of c.
27 : 16. prepare raiment as c.
33 : 6. I am formed out of c.
38 : 14. It is turned as c. to seal
Ps. 40 : 2. me out of the miry c.
Is. 29 : 16. esteemed as potter's c.
41 : 25. as potter treadeth the c.
45 : 9. c. say to him fashioneth it?
64 : 8. we are c. thou our potter
Je. 18 : 4. vessel made of c. was
6. as c. is in potter's hand
43 : 9. stones, hide them in c.
Da. 2 : 33. his feet, part c., 34, 42
35. c. broken in pieces, 45.
41. feet and toes part potter's c.
Na. 3 : 14. go into c. and tread
Ha. 2 : 6. that ladeth hims. with c.
Jn. 9 : 6. he made c. of spittle, and anointed eyes with c.
14. sab. day when Jesus made c.
15. he put c. on mine eyes
Ro. 9 : 21. potter power over c.?

CLAY ground. [4 : 17.

1 K. 7 : 46. vessels in c. g., 2 Ch.

CLEAN. [Adverb.]

Le. 23 : 22. not make c. riddance
Jos. 3 : 17. c. over Jordan, 4 : 1, 11.
Ps. 77 : 8. Is his mercy c. gone?
Is. 24 : 19, earth is c. dissolved
Jo. 1 : 7. he hath made it c. bare
Zch. 11 : 17. his arm shall be c. dried
2 Pe. 2 : 18. that were c. escaped [up

CLEAN. [Adjective.]

Ge. 7 : 2. of ev. c. beast shalt take
8. c. beasts, and beasts not c.
8 : 20. took of ev. c. beast and c.
35 : 2. be c. change garments
Le. 4 : 12. unto a c. place, 6 : 11.
7 : 19. all that be c. shall eat
10 : 10. difference betw. c., 11 : 47.-20 : 25. Eze. 22 : 26.-44 : 23.
14. eat in a c. place, Nu. 19 : 9.
13 : 6. wash his clothes and be c., 34.-14 : 8, 9. Nu. 19 : 9.
14 : 4. take two birds alone and c.
8. that he may be c., 9. Nu. 19 : 19.
11. priest maketh him c. shall
16 : 30. ye may be c. from your sins
22 : 4. not eat of holy things until c.
23 : 22. c. riddance of corners of field
Nu. 8 : 7. so make themselves c.
19 : 12. on 7th day he shall be c.
18. c. person shall take hyssop
19. c. person sprinkle upon uncl.
De. 12 : 15. and c. may eat, 22.-15 : 22.
14 : 11. c. birds eat | 20. c. fowls eat
23 : 10. amo. you any man, not c.
1 S. 20 : 26. not c. he is not c. [14.
2 K. 5 : 10. flesh come again, be c.,
12. may I wash and be c.
13. to thee, Wash and be c.? [c.
2 Ch. 30 : 17. passovers for ev. one not
Jb. 11 : 4. I am c. in thine eyes
14 : 4. c. thing out of unclean
15 : 14. man that he should be c.
15. heavens not c. in his sight
25 : 4. he be c. born of woman?
33 : 9. I am c. without transgres.
Pr. 16 : 2. ways of a man are c. in
Ec. 9 : 2. things alike to c. and uncl.
Is. 1 : 16. wash ye, make you c.
28 : 8. so there is no place c.
30 : 24. oxen eat c. provender
52 : 11. be c. that bear vessels [sel
66 : 20. bring an offering in c. ves-
Je. 13 : 27. Jerusa. wilt be made c.?
Eze. 36 : 25. sprinkle c. wat. upon you
Mat. 8 : 2. thou canst make me c., Mk. 1 : 40. Lu. 5 : 12. [5 : 13.
3. I will, be thou c., Mk. 1 : 41., Lu.
23 : 25. c. the outside, 26. Lu. 11 : 39.
27 : 59. wrapped it in a c. linen
Lu. 11 : 41. all things are c. to you
Jn. 13 : 10. c. every whit : ye are c.
11. Ye are not all c.
15 : 3. now ye are c. through word
Ac. 18 : 6. blood upon heads, I am c.
Re. 19 : 8. fine linen, c. white, 14.

CLEAN hands.

Jb. 9 : 30. make h. never so c.
17 : 9. hath c. h. sh. be stronger
Ps. 24 : 4. He that hath c. h.

CLEAN heart.

Ps. 51 : 10. Create in me a c. h. [h.
73 : 1. G. good to such as are of c.
Pr. 20 : 9. I have made my h. c.?

Is CLEAN.

Le. 13 : 13. he i. c., 17, 37, 39.
40. yet i. he c.? 41.

Le.14:57. teach when it i. unc. and c.
15: 8. spit upon him that i. c.
Nu. 9: 13. man that i. c., 19: 9.
18: 11. ev. one that i. c. in hou., 13.
Ps. 19: 9. fear of the Lord i. c.
Pr. 14: 4. no oxen are, crib i. c.
Jn. 13: 10. but i. c. every whit

Pronounce CLEAN.

Le. 13: 6. shall p. him c., 13, 17, 23, 28, 34, 37.-14: 7.
59. to p. it c. 14: 48.

Shall be CLEAN.

Le. 11: 36. a fountain s. b. c.
12: 8. she s. b. c., 15: 28. [23.
13: 58. it s. b. c., 14: 53. Nu. 31:
14: 9. he s. b. c., 20.-15: 13.-17: 15.-22: 7. Nu. 19: 12, 19.
Nu. 31: 24. ye s. b. c., Eze. 36:25.
Ps. 51: 7. Purge me, I s. b. c.

CLEANNESS.

2 S. 22:21. c. of my hands, Ps.18:20.
25. c. in his eyesight, Ps. 18:24.
Am. 4: 6. given you c. of teeth

CLEANSE.

Ex. 29: 36. c. the altar, Le. 16:19.
Le. 14: 49. to c. house, 2 birds, 52.
16: 19. seven times, and c. it
30. make atonement, to c. you
Nu. 8: 6. Take the Levites and c. them, 7.-15, 21.
2 Ch. 29: 15. c. house of Lord, 16.
Ne. 13: 22. Levites sh. c. themsel.
Ps. 19: 12. c. from secret faults
51: 2. and c. me from my sin
119: 9. young man c. his way?
Je. 4: 11. a dry wind not to c.
33: 8. c. from iniq., Eze. 37: 23.
Eze. 36: 25. from idols will I c.
39:12. that they may c. land, 14, 16.
43: 20. shalt c. and purge it, 22.
45: 18. and c. the sanctuary
Jo. 3:21. I will c. their blood that I
Mat. 10: 8. Heal sick, c. lepers
23: 26. c. first that is within cup
2 Co. 7: 1. c. ours. fr. all filthiness
Ep. 5: 26. c. it with washing
Ja. 4: 8. c. your hands, ye sinners
1 Jn. 1: 9. c. us from unrighte.

CLEANSED.

Le. 11: 32. until even, so it be c.
12: 7. she shall be c. from issue
14: 4. him to be c., 7, 8, 14, 17, 18, 19, 25, 28, 29, 31.
Nu. 35: 33. land cannot be c. [day
Jos. 22: 17. we are not c. until this
2 Ch. 29: 18. c. all house of Lord
30: 18. for many had not c. themselves, yet did eat
19. prepareth heart, tho. not c.
34: 5. Josiah c. Judah and Jerus.
Ne. 13: 9. they c. the chambers
30. I c. them from strangers
Jb. 35: 3. what profit, if I be c.?
Ps. 73: 13. c. my heart in vain
Is. 3: † 26. she being c. shall sit
Eze. 22: 24. art land not c.
36: 33. sh. have c. you fr. iniquity
44: 26. after he is c. reckon 7.
Da. 8: 14. then sanctuary be c.
Jo. 3: 21. cleanse blood I not c.
Mat. 8: 3. his leprosy was c.
11: 5. lepers are c., Lu. 7: 22.
Mk. 1: 42. and he was c.
Lu. 4: 27. none c. save Naaman
7: 22. lepers c. the deaf hear
17: 14. lepers went they were c.
Lu. 17: 17. were not ten c. but
Ac. 10: 15. What G. hath c., 11: 9.

CLEANSETH, ING.

Le. 13: 7. seen of priest for c-g
14: 2. leper in day of c-g, 23, 32.
15: 13. number seven days for c-g
Jb. 37: 21. wind passeth and c. them
Nu. 6: 9. shave his head in his c-g
Pr.20: 30. blueness of a wound c-h
Mk. 1: 44. offer for thy c-g, Lu.5,14.
1 Jn.1:7. blood of Jes.C. c-h us fr. sin

CLEAR. [Verb.]

Ge. 44: 16. how sh. we c. ourselves?
Ex. 34: 7. by no means c. guilty
Ec. 3: † 18. that they might c. G.

CLEAR. [Adjective.]

Ge. 24: 8. c. from my oath, 41.
2 S. 23: 4. by c. shining after rain
Ps. 51: 4. be c. when thou judgest
Can. 6: 10. fair as moon, c. as sun
Is. 18: 4. like a c. heat upon herbs
Am. 8: 9. darken earth in a c. day
Zch. 14: 6. the light shall not be c.
2 Co.7: 11. approved yourse. to be c.
Re. 21: 11. light c. as crystal, 22: 1.
18. city pure gold, like c. glass

CLEARER.

Jb. 11: 17. age shall be c. than noon

CLEARING.

Nu. 14: 18. by no means c. guilty
2 Co. 7: 11. what c. of yourselves.

CLEARLY.

Jb. 33:3. my lips sh. utter knowl. c.
Mat. 7: 5. c. to pull mote, Lu.6:42.
Mk. 8: 25. and saw every man c.
Ro. 1: 20. from creation are c. seen

CLEARNESS.

Ex. 24: 10. as body of heav. in c.

CLEAVE. [Divide.]

Le. 1: 17. he shall c. it with wings
Ps. 74: 15. thou didst c. fountain
Ha. 3: 9. didst c. earth with rivers
Zch. 14: 4. mount shall c. in midst

CLEAVE. [Adhere.]

Ge. 2: 24. a man shall c. unto his wife, Mat. 19: 5. Mk. 10: 7.
De. 4: 4. ye that did c. unto the L.
10: 20. him serve, to him shalt c.
11: 22.-13: 4.-30: 20. Jos. 22: 5.
13: 17. shall c. naught of cursed th.
28: 21. pestil. c. unto thee, Jos. 22:
60. they shall c. unto thee [5.
Jos. 23: 8. but c. unto L. your G.
† if ye will c. unto the L. your G.
12. c. unto remnant of nations
2 K.5:27. leprosy of Naaman c. unto
Jb.38:38. clods c. fast together [thee
Ps. 101: 3. hate work, not c. to me
102: 5. my bones c. to my skin
137: 6. let my tongue c. to roof of
Is.14: 1. shall c. to the house of Jac.
Je.13: 11. caused to c. unto me Israel
42:†16. famine shall c. aft. you in E.
Eze. 3: 26. make tongue c. to roof
Da. 2: 43. shall not c. one to ano.
11: 34. c. to them with flatteries
Ac.11:23. purpose of heart c. unto L.
Ro. 12: 9. c. to that which is good

CLEAVED. [sins

2 K. 3: 3. Jehoram c. unto Jerob.'s
Jb.29:10. their tongue c. to the roof
31:7. if blot have c. to mine hands

CLEAVETH. [Adhereth.]

Jb. 19: 20. my bone c. to my skin
Ps. 22:15. my tongue c. to my jaws
41: 8. An evil disease c. unto him
44: 25. our belly c. unto earth
119: 25. My soul c. unto the dust
Jer. 13: 11. as girdle c. to loins
La. 4: 4. tongue of sucking child c.
8. their skin c. to their bones [us
Lu. 10: 11. dust of your city c. on

CLEAVETH. [Divideth.]

De. 14: 6. beast that c. the cleft
Jb. 16: 13. he c. my reins asunder
Ps. 141: 7. when one c. wood
Ec. 10:9. c. wood sh. be endangered

CLEFT. [Verb.]

Mi. 1: 4. valleys shall be c. as wax

CLEFT, S.

Ex. 33: 22. will put thee in a c.
De. 14: 6. that cleaveth the c. into two claws [c-s
Can. 2: 14. O my dove, that art in
Is. 2: 21. to go into c-s for fear
57: 5. slaying chil. under c-s of rocks
Je.49: 16. that dwellest in c-s, Ob. 3.
Am.6: 11. smite little house with c-s

CLEMENCY.

Ac.24: 4. that thou hear us of thy c.

CLEM'ENT.

Ph.4:3. C., and other my fellow lab.

CLE'OPAS, CLE'OPHAS.

Lu. 24: 18. whose name was C.
Ju. 19: 25. Mary, wife of C. stood

CLERK. See TOWNCLERK.

CLIFF, S.

2 Ch. 20: 16. they come by c. of Ziz
Jb. 30: 6. To dwell in c-s of valleys

CLIFT. See CLEFT, S.

CLIMB, ED, ETH.

1 S. 14:13. Jona. c-d up upon hands
Je. 4: 29. they shall c. up rocks
Jo. 2: 7. sh. c. wall like men of war
9. they shall c. upon houses
Am. 9: 2. they c. up to heaven
Lu. 19: 4. Zaccheus c-d up sycam.
Jn. 10: 1. c-h up some other way.

CLIPPED. [be c.

Je. 48: 37. head bald, every beard

CLOAK.

Is.59: 17. he was clad with zeal as c.
Mat. 5:40. take coat let him have c.
Lu. 6: 29. taketh thy c. forbid not
Jn. 15: 22. no c. for their sin
1 Th. 2: 5. a c. of covetousness
2 Ti. 4: 13. c. I left at Troas bring
1 Pe. 2: 16. a c. of maliciousness

CLODS.

Jb.7: 5. flesh clothed with c. of dust
21: 33. c. of the valley be sweet
38: 38. the c. cleave fast together
Is.28: 24: doth ploughman break c.
Ho. 10: 11. Jac. shall break his c.
Jo.1:17. seed is rotten under their c.

CLOKE. See CLOAK.

CLO'PAS.

Jn.19:†25. Mary, wife of C. and Mary

CLOSE.

Nu. 5: 13. kept c. from husband
2 S. 22: 46. of c. places, Ps. 18: 45.
1 Ch. 12: 1. David kept himself c.
Jb. 28: 21. kept c. from fowls
41: 15. as with a c. seal
Je. 42: 16. famine follow c.
Da. 8: 7. him come c. to ram
Am. 9: 11. c. up the breaches
Lu. 9: 36. kept it c. and told no
Ac. 27: 13. they sailed c. by Crete

CLOSED.

Ge. 2: 21. Lord c. up the flesh
20: 18. c. up all the wombs
Nu. 16: 33. earth c. upon them
Ju. 3: 22. fat c. upon the blade
Is. 1: 6. they have not been c.
29: 10. Lord hath c. your eyes
Da. 12: 9. the words are c. up
Jon. 2: 5. the depth c. me round
Mat. 13: 15. eyes c., Ac. 28: 27.
Lu. 4: 20. he c. book, and gave it

CLOSER.

Pr. 18: 24. friend that sticketh c.

CLOSEST.

Je. 22: 15. c. thyself in cedar

CLOSET, S.

Jo. 2: 16. let bride go out of her c.
Mat. 6: 6. prayest, enter into thy c.
Lu. 12: 3. spoken in the ear in c-s

CLOTH, S.

Ex. 31: 10. c-s of service, 35: 19.-39: 1, 41.
Nu. 4:8. c. of scarlet | 13. purple c., 12. in c. of blue, 6, 7, 9, 11.
De. 22: 17. spread c. before elders
1 S. 19: 13. covered image with c.
21: 9. sword is wrapt in a c.
2 S. 20: 12. and cast a c. upon him
2 K. 8: 15. Hazael took a thick c.
Is. 30: 22. away as a menstruous c.
Mat.9:16. a piece of new c., Mk.2: 21.
27: 59. wrapped it in a linen c.
Mk.14:51. a linen c. about body | 52.

CLOTHE. [coats

Ex. 40: 14. bring sons and c. with
Es. 4: 4. raiment to c. Mordecai

CLOUDS.
De. 4 : 11. c. and thick darkness
Ju. 5 : 4. c. also dropped water
2 S. 22 : 12. about him thick c. of the skies, Ps. 18 : 11, 12.
23 : 4. be as a morning without c.
1 K. 18 : 45. heaven was black wi. c.
Jb. 20:6. tho. his head reach unto c.
22 : 14. Thick c. are a covering
26 : 8. He bindeth up waters in c.
35:5. c. wh. are higher than thou
36 : 28. c. do distil upon man
29. understand spreadings of c.?
32. With c. he covereth the light
37 : 16. knowest balancings of c.?
38 : 37. Who number c. in wisdom?
Ps. 36:5. faithfuln. reacheth unto c.
57:10. thy truth unto the c., 108:4.
68 : 34. his strength is in the c.
77 : 17. c. poured out water, skies
78 : 23. Tho. he com. c. fr. above
97 : 2. c. and darkness about him
104 : 3. maketh c. his chariot
147 : 8. covers heaven with c.
Pr. 3 : 20. c. drop down dew
8 : 28. When he established the c.
25 : 14. is like c. without rain
Ec. 11 : 3. c. be full of rain, empty
4. regardeth c. shall not reap
12 : 2. nor c. return after the rain
Is. 5 : 6. com. c. that they rain not
14 : 14. I will ascend above the c.
Je. 4 : 13. he shall come up as c.
Da. 7 : 13. Son of Man came with c.
Jo. 2 : 2. a day of c., Zph. 1 : 15.
Na. 1 : 3. c. are the dust of his feet
Zch. 10 : 1. Lord sh. make bright c.
Mat. 24 : 30. see Son of Man coming in c., 26 : 64. Mk. 13:26.-14:62.
1 Th. 4 : 17. sh. be caught up in c.
2 Pe. 2 : 17. they are c. carried with
Jude 12. c. they are without water
Re. 1 : 7. Behold he cometh with c.

CLOUDY.
Ex. 33 : 9. the c. pillar descended
10. all the people saw c. pillar
Ne. 9 : 12. leddest by c. pillar
Ps. 99 : 7. He spake in c. pillar
Eze. 30 : 3. day of Lord, a c. day
34 : 12. been scattered in c. day

CLOUTED.
Jos. 9 : 5. took old shoes and c.

CLOUTS.
Je. 38:11. Ebed-me. took old cast c.
12. Put c. under armholes

CLOVEN.
De. 14 : 7. divide the c. hoof
Ac. 2 : 3. appeared c. tongues

CLOVENFOOTED.
Le. 11 : 3. c. that shall ye eat
7. tho. swine be c. he is unclean
26. not c. are unclean to you

CLUSTER.
Nu. 13 : 23. a branch with one c.
24. Eschol, bec. of c. of grapes
Can. 1 : 14. as a c. of camphire
Is. 65 : 8. new wine is found in c.
Mi. 7 : 1. there is no c. to eat

CLUSTERS.
Ge. 40 : 10. c. brought ripe grapes
De. 32 : 32. grapes of gall, c. bitter
1 S. 25 : 18. Abigail bro-t 100 c. of
30 : 12. gave Egyptian two c.
Can. 7 : 7. thy breasts like c., 8.
Re. 14 : 18. gather c. of the vine

CNI'DUS.
Ac. 27 : 7. sailed over against C.

COACHES. [in c.
Is. 66:†20. bring breth. upon horses,

COAL.
2 S. 14 : 7. so shall quench my c.
Is. 6 : 6. seraphim having a live c.
47 : 14. sh. not be a c. to warm at
La. 4 : 8. visage blacker than a c.

COALS.
Le. 16 : 12. take censer full of c.
De. 32 : † 24. devoured with c.
2 S. 22 : 9. c. kindled, 13. Ps. 18 : 8.
1 K. 19 : 6. a cake baken on the c.
Jb. 41 : 21. His breath kindleth c.
Ps.18:12. hail stones and c. of fire, 13.
120 : 4. arrows with c. of Juniper
140 : 10. Let burning c. fall upon
Pr. 6:28. go on hot c. not be burned
25 : 22. heap c. of fire, Ro. 12 : 20.
26 : 21. As c. are to burning c.
Can. 8 : 6. c. thereof are c. of fire
Is. 44 : 12. smith worketh in the c.
19. I have baked bread upon c.
54 : 16. smith that bloweth the c.
Eze. 1 : 13. appearance like c.
10:2. fill thine hand with c. of fire
24 : 11. then set it empty upon c.
Ha. 3 : 5. burning c. at his feet
Jn.18 : 18. servants made a fire of c.
21 : 9. saw fire of c. and fish laid

COAST.
Ex. 10 : 4. bring locusts into thy c.
Nu. 24 : 24. ships fr. c. of Chittim
34 : 11. c. sh. go from Shepham to
De. 2 : 4. c. of your breth, chil. of
3 : 17. Jordan, and the c. thereof
11 : 24. to utterm. sea your c. be
16 : 4. no leav. bread in all thy c.
19 : 8. if Lord enlarge thy c.
Jos. 1 : 4. down of sun be your c.
15 : 4. goings out of c. were at sea
18 : 5. Jud. shall abide in their c.
Ju. 1 : 18. Judah took Gaza with c.
36. c. of Amorites was from
11:20. trusted not Isr. to pass c.
1 S. 6:9. if it go by its own c.
7 : 13. no more into c. of Israel
17 : † 1. pitched in c. of Dammim
27 : 1. to seek me in c. of Israel
30 : 14. invasion on c. of Judah
2 K. 14:25. Jerob. restored c. of Isr.
1 Ch. 4:10. bless me, enlarge my c.
Zph. 2 : 7. c. be for remnant of Jud.

Sea COAST.
Eze. 25:16. destroy remnant of s. c.
Zph. 2 : 5. Woe to inhab. of s. c.
6. s. c. sh. be dwellings for sheph.
Mat. 4:13. Jes. in Caper. upon s. c.
Lu. 6 : 17. mult. from s. c. came

South COAST.
Jos. 15 : 1. Zin. utterm. part of s. c.
4. at sea, this shall be your s. c.
18 : 19. of Jordan, this was s. c.

COAST of the Tribe.
Jos. 13 : 16. c.- Reuben | 25. Gad
30. c.- Manasseh, 17 : 7, 9.
15 : 4. c.- Judah, 12.
16:3. c.-Joseph | 18:11. Benjamin
19 : 22. c.- Issachar | 29. Asher
33. c.- Naphtali | 41. Dan

COASTS.
Ex.10:14. locusts in all c. of Egypt
16. not one locust in all c. of Egypt
Nu.34:2. land of Canaan with c., 12.
De. 2 : 4. to pass thro. c. of breth.
19 : 3. shalt divide c. of thy land
28 : 40. olive trees thro. all thy c.
Jos. 18:5. Jo. shall abide in their c.
Ju. 11 : 22. possessed c. of Amorites
18 : 2. Dan sent five men from c.
19:29. sent concubine into c. of Isr.
1 S. 5 : 6. even Ashdod and c.
7 : 14. c. did Israel deliver out of
11 : 3. messengers into c. of Isr., 7.
2 S. 21 : 5. be destr. from c. of Isr.
1 K. 1 : 3. fair damsel through all c.
2 K. 10 : 32. Hazael smote in all c.
1 Ch. 21 : 12. angel destroy. thro. c.
2 Ch. 11 : 13. resorted to him out c.
Ps. 105 : 31. lice in all their c.
33. he brake trees of their c. [c.
Je. 25 : 32. whirlwind be raised fr.
50 : 41. kings raised fr. c. of earth
Eze. 33 : 2. if take man of their c.
Jo. 3 : 4. me, all c. of Palestine?
Mat. 2 : 16. Herod slew chil. in all c.
8 : 34. out of their c., Mk. 5 : 17.
15 : 21. Jes. depart. into c. of Tyre
Mat. 15 : 22. woman out of same c.
39. came into c. of Magdala
16 : 13. came into c. of C. Philip.
19 : 1. into c. of Judæa, Mk. 10:1.
Mk. 7 : 31. departing from c. of Tyre
Ac. 13 : 50. expelled Paul out of c.
19 : 1. thro. upper c. to Ephesus
26 : 20. shewed thro. all c. of Jud.
27 : 2. to sail by c. of Asia

COAT.
Ge. 37 : 3. c. of colours, 23, 31, 32.
32. whether thy son's c., 33.
Ex. 28 : 4. for Aaron broidered c.
39. embroider c. of linen
29 : 5. shalt put upon Aaron the c.
Le. 8 : 7. he put upon him the c.
16 : 4. he sh. put on holy linen c.
1 S. 2 : 19. made him a little c.
17 : 5. Goliath with c. of mail, 38.
2 S. 15 : 32. Hushai with c. rent
Jb. 30:18. bindeth as collar of my c.
Can. 5 : 3. I have put off my c. how
Mat. 5 : 40. if any take away thy c.
Lu. 6 : 29. forbid not to take thy c.
Jn. 19 : 23. c. was without seam
21 : 7. Peter girt his fisher's c.

COATS.
Ge. 3 : 21. God made c. of skins
Ex. 28 : 40. for Aa.'s sons make c.
29 : 8. sons, put c. on them, 40:14.
39 : 27. c. linen of woven work
Le. 8 : 13. put c. upon Aaron's sons
10 : 5. they carried them in their c.
Da. 3 : 21. were bound in their c.
27. nor were their c. changed
Mat. 10 : 10. neither provide two c.
Mk. 6:9. put not on two c., Lu. 9:3.
Lu.3:11. hath two c. let him impart
Ac. 9 : 39. shewing c. Dorcas made

COCK.
Mat. 26 : 34. this night bef. c. crow,
75. Mk. 14 : 30, 72. Lu.22:34, 61.
74. the c. crew, Lu.22:60. Jn.18:27.
Mk. 13 : 35. if master at c.-crowing
14:68. he went out the c. crew, 72.
Jn. 13 : 38. c. shall not crow till thou hast denied me thrice

COCKATRICE, S.
Pr. 23 : † 32. last it stingeth like c.
Is. 11 : 8. child put hand on c. den
14 : 29. of serpent's root come a c.
59 : 5. They hatch c. eggs, weave
Je. 8 : 17. I will send c-s am. you

COCKCROWING.
Mk. 13 : 35. at midnight or at the c.

COCKLE.
Jb. 31:40. c. grow instead of barley

COFFER.
1 S. 6 : 8. put the jewels in a c.
11. they laid ark and c. upon cart
15. Levites took down the c.
Ezr. 6 : † 2. was found in a c. a roll

COFFIN.
Ge. 50 : 26. Joseph was put in a c.
Lu. 7 : † 14. he touched c. and said

COGITATIONS.
Da. 7 : 28. my c. much troubled me

COLD. [Noun.]
Ge. 8:22. c. and heat shall not cease
Jb.24 : 7. naked have no cover. in c.
37 : 9. c. cometh out of the north
Ps. 147 : 17. who stand bef. his c.?
Pr. 20:4. not plough by reason of c.
25 : 13. As c. of snow in harvest
Ac. 28 : 2. received us because of c.
2 Co. 11 : 27. in c. and nakedness

COLD. [Adjective.] [ther
Pr. 25:20. taketh garment in c. wea-
25. As c. waters to a thirsty soul
Je. 18 : 14. sh. c. waters be forsaken
Na. 3 : 17. camp in hedges in c. day
Mat. 10 : 42. give a cup of c. water
24 : 12. love of many shall wax c.
Jn. 18 : 18. made a fire, for it was c.
Re. 3 : 15. art neither c. nor hot, 16.

COLHO'ZEH.
Ne. 3 : 15. Shallum son of C., 11 : 5.

COLLAR, S.
Ju. 8: 26. earrings, beside c-s
Jb. 30: 18. disease bindeth me as c.
COLLECTION.
2 Ch. 24: 6. to bring in the c., 9.
1 Co. 16: 1 conc. c. for the saints
COLLEGE.
2 K. 22: 14. dwelt in c., 2 Ch. 34: 32.
COLLOPS.
Jb. 15: 27. c. of fat on his flanks
COLONY.
Ac. 16: 12. Philippi chief city and c.
COLOS'SE.
Col. 1: 2. Paul, to the saints at C.
COLOUR.
Le. 13: 35. if plague not changed c.
Nu. 11: 7. c. as c. of bdellium
Es. 1: † 6. and stone of blue c.
Pr 23: 31. when wine giveth his c.
Eze. 1: 4. as the c. of amber, 27.-8: 2.
7. c. of burnished brass, Da. 10: 6.
16. wheels like c. of beryl, 10: 9.
22. firmament as c. of crystal
Ac. 27: 30. under c. as though they
Re. 17: 4. woman in scarlet c.
COLOURS.
Ge. 37: 3. Jac. made coat of many
c., 23, 32. [of needlework (3)
Ju. 5: 30. to Sisera prey of divers c.
2 S. 13: 18. had garm. of divers c., 19.
1 Ch. 29: 2. prep-d stones of divers c.
Is. 54: 11. lay stones with fair c.
Eze. 16: 16. high pla. with divers c.
17: 3. eagle with divers c. to Leb-
COLOURED. [anon
Re. 17: 3. upon a scarlet c. beast
COLT, S.
Ge. 32: 15. Thirty camels with their
49: 11. binding ass's c. to vine [c.
Ju. 10: 4. 30 sons rode on 30 ass c.
12: 14. sons and neph. on 70 ass c.
Jb. 11: 12. though man born like c.
Zch. 9: 9. riding upon a c. the foal
of an ass, Mat. 21: 5. Jn. 12: 15.
Mat. 21: 2. Go, ye shall find ass
tied, c. with her, Mk. 11: 2. Lu.
19: 30. [11: 7.
7. brought ass and c. and set, Mk.
Mk. 11: 4. found c. tied by door, 7.
11: 5. what do you loosing c.? Lu.
19: 33. [set Jesus
Lu. 19: 35. cast garm. on c. and
COME.
Ge. 6: 20. two of every sort shall c.
7: 1. c. thou, and house into ark
8: † 9. caused her to c. into ark
19: 32. c. let us make fa. drink wine
: 27. Wherefore c. ye to me
: 33. c. for my hire
: 44. c. let us make a covenant
: 8. If Esau c. to company
: 14. until I c. unto Seir
: 16. c. to Ephrath, 48: 7.
37: 10. c. to bow down to thee
13. c. I will send thee unto
37: 20. c. let us slay him, and cast
27. c. sell him to Ishmaelites
41: † 21. when c. to inward parts
29. c. seven years of plenty, 35.
54. 8 yrs. of dearth began to c.
42: 7. said, Whence c. ye, Jos. 9: 8.
45: 18. fa. and households and c.
19. bring your father and c.
49: 10. not fr. Judah until Shiloh c.
Ex. 3: 13. wh. I c. to chil. of Isr.
18: 16. have a matter they c.
19: 9. I c. unto thee in cloud
20: 24. where my name I will c.
21: 14. c. presump. upon neigh.
23: 27. destr. peo. to whom thou c.
Nu 10: 29. c. thou with us we
22: 6. c. curse me this people, 11.
24: 19. shall c. he shall have domin.
De. 18: 6. if Levite c. with desire
28: 2. these blessings sh. c. on thee
15. these curses c. upon, 45.
32: 35. things that sh. c. upon them

Ju. 13: 5. no razor c., 1 S. 1: 11.
1 S. 2: 34. c. upon thy sons in 1 day
9: 13. peo. will not eat until he c.
10: 8. shalt tarry, till I c. to thee
17: 45. I c. to thee in name of L.
20: 21. c. thou, for there is peace
2 S. 6: 9. How shall ark of L. c. to me
15: † 2. when any c. to the king
17: 2. I c. upon him while weary
19: 33. c. thou over with me
1 K. 8: 31. oath c. bef. thine altar
20: 33. if any th. would c. fr. him
22: 27. feed this fellow until I c.
2 K. 5: 8. let him c. now to me
6: † 19. not the way, c. ye aft. me
18: 32. Until I c. and take you
away, Is. 36: 17. [of thee
1 Ch. 29: 12. riches and honour c.
14. all things c. of thee, and of
2 Ch. 8: 11. whereto ark of L. hath c.
Es. 1: 12. Vashti refus. to c. at k.'s
17. deed of queen shall c. abroad
5: † 10. Haman caused friends to c.
8: 6. how see evil c. unto my peo.?
Jb. 3: 7. Let no joyful voice c. there.
13: 13. let c. on me what will
14: 14. wait till my change c.
21. his sons c. to honour, and he
22: 21. be at peace, good shall c.
23: 3. I might c. to his seat
37: 13. causeth it to c. for correc.
38: 11. Hitherto shalt thou c. but
Ps. 40: 7. Lo, I c., He. 10: 7, 9.
42: 2. when shall I c. before God?
50: 3. G. sh. c. not keep silence
65: 2. unto thee shall all flesh c.
80: 2. stir up thy strength, and c.
86: 9. all nations sh. c. and worsh.
90: † 12. cause heart to c. unto wisd.
101: 2. O wh. wilt thou c. unto me
109: 17. he loved cursing, let it c.
119: 41. Let thy mercies c., O L., 77
Pr. 6: 11. so thy poverty c., 24: 34
10: 24. fear of the wicked shall c.
26: 2. curse causeless shall not c.
Ec. 1: 11. to c. with thi. that sh. c.
9: 2. All things c. alike to all
Can. 2: 10. my love, c. away, 13.
4: 8. c. with me, my spouse
16. and c. thou south, blow
Is. 5: 19. let counsel of holy One c.
10: 3. desolation which shall c.
13: 5. they c. from a far country
6. day of L., it shall c. as destruc
21: 12. inquire ye; return, c.
26: 20. c. my peo., enter chambers
27: 6. th. c. of Jacob to take root
35: 4. God will c. with veng. (2)
10. and c. to Zion with songs
40: 10. Lord will c. with a strong
41: 25. raised up one, and he sh. c.
44: 7. coming, and sh. c., 47: 13.
45: 20. Assemble, c. draw near
24. even to him shall men c.
47: 9. two things shall c. to thee
51: 11. redeemed sh. c. unto Zion
55: 1. c. ye to waters, c. ye, c. buy
3. c. unto me, hear, your soul
59: 20. Redeemer shall c. to Zion
60: 3. Gentiles shall c. to thy
light, 4, 5. Je. 16: 19. [fire
66: 15. behold, Lord will c. with
Je. 2: 31. we will c. no more unto
3: 22. we c. unto thee, thou art G.
9: 17. mourning women, may c.
13: 22. Whf. c. these thi. upon me?
17: 15. where word of L.? let it c.
27: 7. serve until time of land c.
31: 9. they shall c. with weeping
38: 25. if the princes hear, and c.
40: 4. if seem good to c., if ill to c.
46: 18. as Carmel, shall he c.
49: 4. Who shall c. unto me?
50: 41. a peo. shall c. from north
La. 1: 4. none c. to solemn feasts
22. let all their wick. c. bef. thee
Eze. 12: 16. abom. whither they c.

Eze. 13: 18. will ye save souls that c.?
21: 19. sword may c., 20.-32: 11.
27. until he c. whose right it is
33: 3 when he seeth sword c., 6.
31. they c. unto thee as people
33. lo it will c. then shall know
36: 8. they are at hand to c.
37: 9. c. from four winds, O breath
Ho. 6: 1. c. let us return unto the L.
3. he shall c. unto us, as the rain
10: 12. time to seek the L. till he c.
Jo. 1: 15. day of L. as destruc. shall
2: 31. bef. terrible day of L. c. [c.
Jon. 1: 7. c. let us cast lots
Mi. 4: 8. shall it c. kingd. shall c.
Ha. 2: 3. it will surely c. not tarry
Zph. 2: 2. bef. fierce anger of L. c.
Zch. 1: 21. What c. these to do?
14: 5. G. shall c. and all saints
Mal. 3: 1. L. shall c. to his temple
4: 6. lest I c. and smite the earth
Mat. 2: 6. out of thee sh. c. a Gov.
8 I may c. to worship him also
3: 7. from wrath to c., Lu. 3: 7.
1 Th. 1: 10.
5: 24. first be reconciled, then c.
6: 10. Thy kingdom c., Lu. 11: 2.
7: 15. false prophets c. to you in
8: 7. Jes. saith, I will c. and heal
8. not worthy thou shouldest c.
9. c. and he cometh, Lu. 7: 8.
11. many sh. c. fr. east and west
10: 13. worthy, let your peace c.
11: 3. he that sho. c.? Lu. 7: 19, 20.
28. c. all ye that labour
14: 28. bid me c. to thee on water, 29.
16: 24. If any man will c. after me
27. Son of man shall c. in glory
17: 10. Elias must first c.? 11.
Mk. 9: 11.
18: 7. needs be offences c., Lu. 17: 1.
19: 21. go, sell, and c., Lu. 18: 22.
22: 4. c. unto the marriage, 3.
23: 35. upon you c. all righte. blood
24: 5. many shall c. in my name,
and deceive, Mk. 13: 6. Lu. 21: 8.
14. gospel preached, then end c.
42. know not hour L. doth c.
50. c. in day he looketh not, Lu.
12: 46. [9: 26.
25: 31. S. of man c. in glory, Lu.
34. c. ye blessed of my Father
27: 49. whether Elias will c. to
save him [you fishers
Mk. 1: 17. c. ye after me, I will make
4: 22. nothing kept secret, but that
it should c. abroad, Lu. 8: 17.
7: 23. these evil things c. fr. within
8: 34. if any will c. after me, Lu.
9: 23.-14: 27.
9: 1. kingdom of G. c. with power
10: 14. suffer little chil. to c. unto
me, Mat. 19: 14. Lu. 18: 16.
21. and c., take up the cross
12: 7. c. let us kill him, Lu. 20: 14.
Lu. 1: 35. H. G. shall c. upon thee
7: 7. neith. tho. myself worthy to c.
10: 1. place whither he would c.
12: 38. c. in sec. watch, or c. in third
13: 7. three years I c. seeking fruit
14. are six days, in them c. and
14: 17. c. for all things ready
20. married a wife I cannot c.
27. not bear cross, and c. after me
17: 20. when kingdom should c.
19: 13. he said, Occupy till I c.
20: 16. c. and destroy husband.
21: 34. day c. unawares, 35.
22: 18. until kingd. of G. shall c.
Jn. 1: 39. He saith, c. and see, 46.
3: 26. baptizeth, and all men c.
5: 14. lest worse thing c. unto
40. ye will not c. to me, that ye
43. I am c. in my Father's name
6: 37. all that Fa. giveth me shall c.
44. No man can c. exc. Fa., 65.
7: 34. where I am, ye cannot c.

Jn.7:37. If any man thirst, let him c.
8 : 14. ye cannot tell whence I c.
21. I go ye can-t c., 22.-13 : 33.
12 : 35. lest darkness c. upon you
13 : 19. I tell bef. it c. that when it is c. [will c.
14 : 18. not leave you comfortless, I
23. we will c. unto him
17 : 11. are in world, I c. to thee, 13
18 : 4. Jes. knowing all th. should c.
21 : 22. If I will he tarry till I c.
Ac. 1 : 11. this Jes. shall so c. as ye
2 : 20. before great day of Lord c.
3 : 19. when times of refreshing c.
7 : 34. c. I will send thee into E.
8 : 24. Pray none of these things c.
27. had c. to Jerus. to worship
9 : 38. not delay to c. to them
10 : 28. c. unto one of anoth. nat.
13 : 40. lest that c. upon you that
16 : 9. c. over into Macedonia
19 : 4. believe on him that sho. c.
24 : 23. forbid no acquaintance to c.
26 : 7. our twelve tribes hope to c.
22. than Moses say should c.
Ro. 3 : 8. say, do evil, that good c.
9 : 9. at this time, will I c.
15 : 29. c. in fulness of gospel
1 Co. 1 : 7. ye c. behind in no gift
4 : 5. judge nothing until Lord c.
21. c. with a rod or in love
11 : 26. shew L.'s death till he c.
34. will I set in order when I c.
14 : 6. c. speaking with tongues
15 : 35. with what body do they c.?
16 : 2. no gatherings when I c.
10. if Timothy c. see he be, 11.
12. Apollos, I desired him to c.
2 Co. 1 : 15. I was minded to c. bef.
12 : 20. fear when I c. I not find
Ga. 2 : 21. if righte. c. by law, then
3 : 14. blessing of Ab. c. on Gent.
19. till seed should c. to whom
Ep. 4 : 13. all c. in unity of faith
2 Th. 1 : 10. shall c. to be glorified
2 : 3. not c. except c. a falling aw.
1 Ti. 2 : 4. c. unto knowl. of truth,
2 Ti. 3 : 7. [wh. is to c.
4 : 8. life that now is, and of that
13. Till I c. give attendance to
2 Ti. 3 : 1. perilous times shall c.
4 : 3. time will c. will not endure
9. Do diligence to c. shortly, 21.
Tit. 3 : 12. be diligent to c. unto me
He. 4 : 16. Let us c. boldly unto throne
7 : 25. able to save them th. c. to G.
10 : 37. he that shall c. will c.
Ja. 2 : 2. c. man with gold ring
4 : 1. whence c. wars, c. they not
5 : 1. miseries that shall c. upon you
1 Pe. 1 : 10. proph-d of grace sho. c.
2 Pe. 3 : 9. all should c. to repent.
10. day of Lord will c. as a thief,
Re. 3 : 3.-16 : 15.
1 Jn. 2 : 18. heard, antichrist shall c.
3 Jn. 10. if I c. I will remember
Re. 2 : 5. repent, else I will c., 16.
25. that ye have, hold fast till I c.
3 : 10. temptation c. upon all world
11. I c. quickly, 22 : 7, 12, 20.
6 : 1. saying, c. and see, 3, 5, 7.
15 : 4. all nations sh. c. and worship
18 : 10. in one hour is thy judgm. c.
22 : 17. and let him athirst c.

COME again. [See DAYS.]

Ge. 28 : 21. so that I c. a. to fath.'s
Ex. 14 : 26. waters may c. a. on E.
Le. 14 : 43. if the plague c. a.
Ju. 6 : 18. will tarry until thou c. a.
8 : 9. When I c. a. in peace I
13 : 8. let man of G. c. a. unto us
2 S. 19 : 30. c. a. in peace to own
1 K. 2 : 41. Shimei was c. a. [house
12 : 5. depart 3 days, c. a., 2 Ch. 10 : 5.
12. c. to me a., 2 Ch. 10 : 5, 12.
20. Israel heard Jerob. had c. a.
17 : 21. O L., let child's soul c. a.
2 K. 5 : 10. thy flesh shall c. a.
2 Ch. 30 : 9. they sh. c. a. into land
Ezr. 6 : 21. Israel c. a., Ne. 8 : 17.
Ps. 126 : 6. sh. c. a. with rejoicing
Pr. 3 : 28. Say not, Go and c. a.
Je. 31 : 16. c. a. fr. land of ene., 17.
37 : 8. Chal. shall c. a. and fight
La. 1 : † 11. make their soul c. a.
Lu. 10 : 35. I c. a. I will repay
Jn. 14 : 3. I will c. a. and receive
28. how I said, I go away and c. a.
2 Co. 2 : 1. not c. a. in heaviness
12 : 21. lest, when I c. a. God will
13 : 2. if I c. a. I will not spare

COME down.

Ge. 45 : 9. saith Jo. c. d. unto me
Ex. 3 : 8. I am c. d. to deliver
19 : 11. Lord will c. d. upon Sinai
32 : 1. Moses delayed to c. d.
Nu. 11 : 17. I will c. d. and talk
De. 28 : 24. from heaven it sh. c. d.
43. thou shalt c. d. very low
Ju. 1 : 34. not suffer to c. d. to val.
7 : 24. c. d. against Midianites
15 : 12. we are c. d. to bind thee
1 S. 6 : 21. c. d. and fetch ark up
23 : 11. Saul c. d.? he will c. d.
20. c. d. acco. to desire of thy soul
2 K. 1 : 4. not c. d. fr. bed, 6, 16.
9. Thou man of God, c. d.
10. let fire c. d., 11, 12. [c. d.
Ne. 6 : 3. doing great work, I cannot
Ps. 7 : 16. c. d. upon his own pate
72 : 6. He shall c. d. like rain
144 : 5. Bow heavens, O Lord c. d.
Is. 31 : 4. c. d. to fight for mt. Zion
34 : 5. sword, sh. c. d. upon Idumea
47 : 1. c. d., O virgin daughter
64 : 1. O, that thou wouldest c. d.
Je. 13 : 18. principalities shall c. d.
21 : 13. Who shall c. d. against us?
48 : 18. c. d. fr. thy glory and sit
Eze. 26 : 16. princes of sea sh. c. d.
27 : 29. pilots shall c. d. fr. ships
30 : 6. pride of her power sh. c. d.
34 : 26. shower to c. d. in season
Da. 5 : † 20. he was made to c. d.
Jo. 2 : 23. c. d. for you the rain
3 : 11. thy mighty ones to c. d.
Mat. 24 : 17. on housetop not c. d.
27 : 40. If Son of G. c. d. from the cross, 42. Mk. 15 : 30.
Lu. 9 : 54. command fire to c. d.?
19 : 5. Jesus said, Zaccheus, c. d.
Jn. 4 : 49. c. d. ere my child
Ac. 7 : 34. am c. d. to deliver them
8 : 15. when were c. d. prayed
14 : 11. gods are c. d. to us [18 : 1.
Re. 10 : 1. angel c. d. from heaven,
12 : 12. devil is c. d. to you
13 : 13. maketh fire c. d. fr. heav.
20 : 1. angel c. d. having key of

Come forth.

Ge. 15 : 4. c. f. out of thy bowels
1 S. 14 : 11. Hebrews, c. f. out of
1 K. 2 : 30. thus saith k. c. f. [holes
8 : 19. c. f. out of loins, 2 Ch. 6 : 9.
2 K. 10 : 25. slay, let none c. f.
Jb. 23 : 10. I shall c. f. as gold
Ps. 17 : 2. Let my sentence c. f.
88 : 8. shut up, and I cannot c. f.
Pr. 25 : 4. c. f. a vessel for finer
Ec. 7 : 18. feareth God shall c. f.
Is. 11 : 1. c. f. a rod out of Jesse
14 : 29. of serp. c. f. cockatrice
34 : 1. world, all that c. f. of it
48 : 1. art c. f. of waters of Judah
Je. 4 : 4. lest my fury c. f. like
37 : 5. Pha.'s army was c. f., 7.
46 : 9. let mighty men c. f.
48 : 45. a fire c. f. out of Heshbon
Eze. 5 : 4. fire c. f. into hou. of Isr.
21 : 19. twain c. f. of one land
Da. 3 : 26. ye servants of God, c. f.
9 : 22. O Dan., I am c. f. to give
Jo. 3 : 18. a fountain shall c. f.
Mi. 5 : 2. out of thee c. f. ruler
Zch. 2 : 6. c. f. flee from north
Mat. 13 : 49. angels shall c. f. and
15 : 18. c. f. from heart, defile,
Mk. 9 : 29. kind c. f. by prayer
Lu. 12 : 37. will c. f., and serve
Jn. 5 : 29. shall c. f. they good
11 : 43. he cried, Lazarus c. f.
Ac. 7 : 7. shall c. f. and serve me

COME hither.

Ge. 15 : 16. fourth gen. shall c. h.
Jos. 3 : 9. c. h. hear words of Lord
Ju. 16 : 2. Samson is c. h.
Ru. 2 : 14. At meal-time c. thou h.
1 S. 10 : 22. if the man should c. h.
16 : 11. not sit down till he c. h.
2 S. 14 : 32. c. h. that I may send
20 : 16. say unto Joab, c. h. that I
2 K. 8 : 7. The man of God is c. h.
Pr. 25 : 7. better it be said, c. up h.
Da. 3 : 26. ye servants of G. c. h.
Mat. 8 : 29. art c. h. to torment us
Jn. 4 : 15. neither c. h. to draw
16. call thy husband and c. h.
Ac. 17 : 6. turned world are c. h.
25 : 17. Thf. when they were c. h.
Re. 4 : 1. voice said, c. up h., 11 : 12.-17 : 1.-21 : 9.

Come in, or into.

Ge. 6 : 18. thou shalt c. i. the ark
19 : 31. not a man to c. i. to us
24 : 31. c. i. thou blessed of Lord
Ex. 12 : 23. not suffer destroy. to c. i.
28 : 43. when they c. i. unto tab.
Le. 16 : 3. Aaron c. i. holy place
26. shall c. i. camp, 28. Nu. 19 : 7.-31 : 24.
Nu. 27 : 21. at his word shall c. i.
34 : 2. When ye c. i. land, 15 : 18.
Le. 19 : 23. [c. i.
De. 31 : 2. I can no more go out and
Jos. 14 : 11. so my strength to c. i.
28 : † 1. Joshua c. i. days
1 S. 4 : 7. said, G. is c. i. camp
1 K. 1 : 14. I will c. i. after thee
42. c. i.; for thou art valiant
3 : 7. I know not how to c. i.
14 : 6. c. i. thou wife of Jeroboam
15 : 17. not suffer any c. i.
2 K. 4 : 4. when c. i. shut door
11 : 9. took each his men to c. i.
1 Ch. 24 : 19. to c. i. house of Lord
2 Ch. 1 : 10. go out and c. i.
16 : 1. might let none c. i. to Asa
23 : 6. none c. i. house save priests
Ne. 2 : 7. till I c. i. Judah
4 : 11. neith. see till we c. i. midst
Es. 5 : 12. Esther Let no man c. i.
6 : 5. king said, Let Haman c. i.
Ps. 5 : 7. c. i. thy hou. in thy mercy
24 : 7. King of glory shall c. i., 9.
69 : 1. waters are c. i. my soul
79 : 1. heathen are c. i. thy inher.
96 : 8. and c. i. his courts
109 : 18. so let it c. i. his bowels
Can. 4 : 16. beloved c. i. garden
Is. 19 : 1. Lord shall c. i. Egypt
23. Assyrian shall c. i. Egypt
24 : 10. ev. hou. shut, no man c. i.
52 : 1. no more c. i. the uncirc.
59 : 19. enemy sh. c. i. like flood
Je. 17 : 19. gate, kings of Judah, c. i.
51 : 50. let Jerus. c. i. your mind
51. strangers are c. i. sanctuary
Eze. 11 : 5. that c. i. your mind
38 : 8. in latter years c. i. land
10. shall things c. i. thy mind
Mi. 5 : 5. Assyr. sh. c. i. our land
Mat. 10 : 12. c. i. house, salute it
16 : 27. Son of man sh. c. i. glory
24 : 5. many shall c. i. my name, Mk. 13 : 6. Lu. 21 : 8.
25 : 31. Son of man sh. c. i. glory
Lu. 8 : 41. besought c. i. his house
11 : 33. they wh. c. i. may see light
12 : 38. c. i. second watch, or c. i.
46. c. i. a day when he looketh not
14 : 23. go compel them to c. i.

Lu.16:28.lest they c. i. this torment
Jn. 3 : 19. light is c. i. the world
5 : 43. I am c. i. my Fa.'s name,
if ano. c. i. his own [11:27.
6 : 14. prophet that sho. c. i. wor.,
Ac. 7 : 3. c. i. land I shall shew
16 : 15. Lydia, saying, c. i. house
Ro. 11 : 25. fulness of Gent. be c. i.
1 Co. 14 : 23. c. i. those unlearned
24. c. i. one that believeth not
Ja. 2 : 2. there c. i. a poor man
Re. 3 : 20. I will c. i. to him and

COME near. [sup
Ge. 12 : 11. Abram was c. n. to E.
20 : 4. Abimelech had not c.n. her
27 : 21. Isaac said unto Jac. c. n.
45 : 4. Jo. said unto brethren, c.n.
Ex. 12 : 48. let him c. n. and keep it
16 : 9. say unto Isr. c. n. bef. L.
19 : 22. priests which c. n. to L.,
De. 21 : 5.
28:43. when they c.n. altar, 30:20.
Nu. 16 : 5. will cause him to c. n.
40. that no stranger c.n. to offer
Jos. 3 : 4. c. not n. unto the ark
10 : 24. c. n. put your feet upon
1 S. 10 : 20. caused tribes to c. n.
2 S. 20 : 16. unto Joab, c. n. hither
1 K. 18 : 30. Elijah to all peo. c. n.
Ps. 32 : 9. be held in, lest c. n.
119 : 169. Let my cry c.n. bef. thee
Is. 34 : 1. c. n. ye nations, to hear
41:1. let us c.n. together to judgm-t
† 21. cause to c. n. your cause
48 : 16. c. ye n. unto me, hear ye
50 : 8. adversary ? let him c.n. me
54 : 14. it shall not c. n. thee
65 : 5. say, c. not n. me
Eze. 18 : 6. nor c. n. to menstruous
40 : 46. c. n. L. to minister, 44 :
15, 16.–45 : 4.
44 : 13. they shall not c.n. unto me
Am. 6 : 3. which cause the seat of
violence to c. n.
Mal. 3:5. I will c. n. you to judgm-t
Lu. 19 : 41. was c.n. he beheld city
Ac. 23 : 15. or he c. n. are ready to

COME nigh. [kill
Ex. 24 : 2. they shall not c. n. nor
34 : 30. afraid to c. n. him [n.
Le. 10 : 3. be sanctified in all that c.
21:21. no man hath blemish c. n.,
Nu. 8 : 19. Isr. c. n. unto sanc. [23.
18 : 4. stranger not c. n.
De. 20 : 2. when c. n. to battle
Ps. 32 : 6. floods shall not c.n. him
91 : 7. it shall not c. n. thee
10. neither plague c.n. thy dwell.
Pr. 5:8. c. not n. door of her house
Mk. 2:4. not c. n. for press, Lu. 8:19.
Lu. 10 : 9. kingd. of God is c.n., 11.

COME not.
Ge. 49 : 6. O my soul c. n. thou
Ex. 19 : 15. c. n. at your wives
Nu. 14 : 30. shall n. c. into land
16 : 12. said, We will n. c. up, 14.
18 : 3. they shall n.c. nigh vessels
De. 23 : 10. unclean shall n. c.
Jos. 23 : 7. That ye c. n. among
nations [mine
Ju. 16 : 17. hath n. c. a razor upon
2 S. 5 : 8. lame n. c. into house
14 : 29. Joab he would n. c. (2)
1 K. 13 : 22. carcass n.c. to sepulc.
2 K. 19:32. king of Assyr. n. c. into
city, 33. Is. 37 : 33, 34.
1 Ch. 11 : 5. Thou shalt n.c. hither
2 Ch. 35 : 21. I c. n. against thee
Ezr. 10 : 8. whosoever would n. c.
Ne. 13 : 1. Moabite n.c. into congr.
Jb. 3 : 6. n.c. into num. of months
13 : 16. hypocrite n. c. bef. him
Ps. 69:27. them n.c. into thy righte.
132 : 3. I will n. c. into tabern.
Pr. 26 : 2. curse causeless shall n.c.
Is. 7 : 17. days that have n. c.
25. shall n. c. the fear of briers
Is. 28:15. scourge shall n.c. unto us
32 : 10. gathering shall n. c.
Je. 37 : 19. king of Bab. shall n. c.
Eze. 9 : 6. c. n. near man upon
whom is the mark
16 : 16. like things shall n. c.
Ho. 4 : 15. c. n. ye unto Gilgal
9 : 4. soul shall n.c. into h. of L.
Zch. 14 : 17. whoso. will n. c. up
18. if family of E. c. n., 19.
Mat. 22 : 3. and they would n. c.
Jn. 5 : 24. shall n. c. into condem.
40. ye will n. c. to me that ye
11:56. think ye he will n.c. to feast
15 : 22. if I had n. c. they not sin
16 : 7. if I go not Comforter n. c.
1 Co. 4 : 18. as tho. I would n. c.

COME out.
Ge. 15 : 14. c. o. with substance
17 : 6. kings sh. c.o. of thee, 35:11.
24 : 13. daughters of city c. o.
Ex. 17 : 6. smite rock, c. water o.
Le. 16 : 17. until he c. o. and have
Nu. 1 : 1. after they were c. o. of
Egypt, 9 : 1.–33 : 38. 1 K. 6 : 1.
11 : 20. eat until it c.o. at nostrils
12 : 4. c. o. ye three to tabernacle
20:18. lest I c.o. ag. thee with sw.
22 : 5. is a people c.o. of Egypt, 11
33 : 38. Aa. died 40th year aft. Isr.
De. 28 : 7. c.o. one way, and [c.o.
Jos. 8 : 6. c.o. after us till we
Ju. 9 : 15. let fire c. o. of bramble
29. Increase army and c. o.
21 : 21. if daughters c. o. to dance
1 S. 2 : 3. let not arrogancy c. o.
11 : 3. to-morrow will c. o., 10.
17 : 8. c. o. to set battle in array
24 : 14. After whom is king c. o.?
2 S. 16 : 7. c. o., c.o., bloody man
1 K. 6 : 1. after Israel were c. o.
20 : 17. are men c. o. of Samaria
18. c. o. for peace, c.o. for war
2 K. 5 : 11. He will c. o. to me
18 : 31. agreem. and c.o., Is.36:16.
19 : 9. he is c. o. to fight thee
Ps. 14:7. O that salv. were c.o. of Z
68 : 31. Princes shall c. o. of E.
Pr. 12 : 13. just sh. c. o. of trouble
Is. 34 : 3. their stink shall c. o. of
Na. 1 : 11. c. o. th. imagineth evil
Mat. 5 : 26. c.o. till thou hast paid
26 : 55. Are ye c. o. as ag. thief
with swords, Mk. 14:48. Lu. 22:52.
Mk. 1 : 25. c. o. of him, Lu. 4 : 35.
5 : 8. c. o. unclean sp., Lu. 8 : 29.
7 : 15. c. o. of him they defile
Lu. 4 : 36. unclean spirits and they
c. o., Mat. 8 : 32. Mk. 9 : 25.
Jn. 1 : 46. can any good c.o. of Naz.
7 : 41. Shall Ch. c. o. of Galilee?
Ac. 16 : 18. in name of Jesus c. o.
Ro. 11 : 26. c.o. of Z. the Deliverer
2 Co. 6 : 17. c.o. from among them
He. 7 : 5. c. o. of loins of Abraham
Re. 16 : 13. spirits c. o. of dragon
18 : 4. c. o. of her, my people

COME short.
Ro. 3:23. all have c.s. of glory of G.
He. 4 : 1. lest any seem to c.s. of it

COME to pass.
Ex. 4 : 8. c. t. p. if not believe, 9.
Nu. 11 : 23. wheth. my word c.t.p.
17:5. c.t.p. the man's rod I choose
De. 7 : 12. shall c.t.p., 11:13.–28:1.
13 : 2. sign or wonder c.t.p.
18 : 19. c.t.p. that whoso. will not
hearken, 28 : 15.
22. thing follow not, nor c. t. p.
Jos. 23:14. all are c. t. p., no good
Ju. 13 : 12. let thy words c. t. p.
17. when thy sayings c. t. p. we
21 : 3. O L. why is this c. t. p.
1 K. 13 : 32. saying shall c. t. p.
18 : 12. c. t. p. soon as I gone
Is. 2 : 2. c.t.p. in last days, Mi. 4:1.
7 : 7. nor shall it c.t.p. [Ac. 2:17.
Is. 14:24. as I thought, so it c.t.p.
42 : 9. former things are c.t.p.
Je. 17:24. shall c.t.p. if ye diligently
28 : 9. word of prophet c. t. p.
32 : 24. hast spoken, is c. t. p.
Eze. 12 : 25. word I speak c. t. p.
24 : 14. I have spoken, it sh. c.t.p.
Da. 2 : 29. known what sh. c. t. p.
Ho. 1 : 5. c. t. p. I will break bow
Jo. 2 : 32. c. t. p. that whosoever
shall call, Ac. 2 : 21.
Am. 8 : 9. c. t. p. I will cause sun
Zch. 6 : 15. this sh. c.t.p. if ye obey
7 : 13. it is c.t.p. as he cried
13:3. c.t.p. wh. any sh. prophecy
Mat. 24 : 6. things must c.t.p., Lu.
21 : 9. [t. p.
Mk. 11 : 23. things he saith shall c.
13 : 29. see these c.t.p., Lu. 21:31.
Lu. 2 : 15. this thing wh. is c.t.p.
21:7. sign when these sh. c. t. p., 28.
36. escape all that shall c. t. p.
24 : 12. wond. at what was c. t. p.
18. not known things c. t. p.
Jn. 13 : 19. when it is c.t.p., 14:29.
Ac. 3 : 23. c. t. p. that every soul
Re. 1 : 1. must shortly c.t.p. [22:6.

COME together.
Jb. 9 : 32. should c.t. in judgment
19 : 12. his troops c. t. against me
Je. 3 : 18. c.t. out of land of north
50 : 4. and Jud. shall c. t. going
Ac. 1 : 6. When were c.t., 28 : 17.
10 : 27. found many c. t.
19 : 32. knew not wherefore c. t.
21 : 22. multitude must needs c.t.
1 Co. 7:5. c.t. again, that Sat. tempt
11 : 17. you c. t. not for better
18. when ye c.t., 20, 33.–14 : 26
34. ye c. not t. to condemnation
14 : 23. If whole church be c. t.

COME up.
Ex. 19 : 13. trumpet soundeth they
shall c. u. [De. 10 : 1
24. c. u. thou and Aaron, 24 : 1
24 : 12. c.u. to me into the mount
33:5. I will c.u. into midst of thee
34 : 2. c. u. in morning to Sinai
3. no man shall c. u. with thee
Nu. 20 : 5. made us c. u. out E.
Jos. 4 : 16. priests c.u. out of Jor.,
10 : 4. c. u. and help me [17, 18.
6. c. u. to us quickly, save us
Ju. 1 : 3. c. u. with me into my
12 : 3. whf. are ye c. u. this day
15 : 10. Why are ye c. u. ag. us?
16 : 18. saying, c. u. this once
1 S. 14 : 10. if they say c. u. unto us
17 : 25. seen this man that is c.u.
1 K. 1 : 35. Then ye c.u. after him
45. c. u. from thence rejoicing
20 : 22. king will c. u. ag. thee
33. caus. him to c. u. into chari.
2 K. 16:7. c.u. and save me from k.
18:25. Am c. u. without L. Is. 36:10.
19 : 23. c. u. to height, Is. 37 : 24.
28. tumult is c. u., Is. 37 : 29.
2 Ch. 20 : 16. c. u. by cliff of Ziz
Jb. 7 : 9. to grave, c. u. no more
Pr. 25 : 7. better be said, c. u. hith.
Is. 5 : 6. there shall c. u. briars and
thorns, 32 : 13.–34 : 13.
8 : 7. c. u. over all his channels
14 : 8. no feller is c. u. ag. us
55 : 13. of thorn c. u. fir trees (2)
60 : 7. c. u. with accept. on altar
Je. 4 : 13. he shall c. u. as clouds
9 : 21. death is c. u. into windows
46 : 9. c. u. ye horses; rage ye
49 : 19. shall c. u. like lion, 50 : 44.
22. c. u. and fly as the eagle
50 : 9. c. u. ag. Bab. an assembly
51 : 27. horses to c. u. as caterpil.
42. sea is c. u. upon Babylon
La. 1 : 14. and c. u. upon my neck
Eze. 24 : 8. might cause fury to c. u.
26 : 3. nations to c. u. against thee

Eze. 37 : 12. to c. u. out of graves
38 : 16. shalt c. u. ag. my people
18. my fury c. u. in my face
39 : 2. thee to c. u. fr. north parts
47 : † 12. on bank shall c. u. trees
Ho. 1 : 11. shall c. u. out of land
10 : 8. thistle c. u. on altars
13 : 15. wind of Lord shall c. u.
Jo. 1 : 6. nation c. u. upon laud
2 : 20. his stink shall c. u.
3 : 9. let all men of war c. u.
12. Let heathen c. u. to valley of
Am. 4 : 10. stink of camps to c. u.
Ob. 21. saviours sh. c. u. on Zion
Jon. 1 : 2. wickedness is c. u. bef. me
4 : 6. L. made a gourd to c. u.
Mi. 2 : 13. breaker is c. u. before
Na. 2 : 1. dasheth in pieces is c. u.
Zch. 14 : 17. that who so. will not c. u.
18. if family of E. go not u., c. not
Ac. 8 : 31. he desired Philip to c. u.
39. were c. u. out of water
10 : 4. Corne., thy alms are c. u.
Re. 4 : 1. c. u. hither, 11 : 12.

COME. [Passive.]

Ge. 6 : 13. end of all flesh is c.
18 : 5. theref. are c. to your serv.
21. acc. to cry wh. is c. unto me
42 : 9. to see land ye are c.
21. therefore is this distress c.
47 : 4. to sojourn are we c.
Ex. 2 : 18. How is it ye are c. so soon
3 : 9. cry of Israel is c.
20 : 20. for G. is c. to prove you
Nu. 22 : 11. is peo. c. out of Egypt
De. 4 : 30. tribulation and all are c.
31 : 11. all Israel is c. to appear
17. Are not these evils c. upon us
Jos. 5. 14. as captain am I c.
Ju. 16 : 2. Samson is c. hither
1 S. 4 : 7. God is c. into camp
9 : 16. peo. bec. their cry is c. unto me
2 S. 1 : 9. anguish is c. upon me
19 : 11. speech of Isr. is c. to king
1 K. 17 : 18. c. to call my sin
2 K. 4 : 1. creditor c. to take sons
5 : 6. when this letter is c. unto thee
22. be c. to me from mt. Ephr.
8 : 7. the man of God is c. hither
1 Ch. 12 : 17. If ye be c. peaceably
Ezr. 9 : 13. aft. all that is c. upon us
Jb. 3 : 25. thing I feared is c., 4 : 5.
Ps. 44 : 17. All this is c. upon us
53 : 6. O that salvation were c.
55 : 5. Fearf. and trembling are c.
69 : 2. I am c. into deep waters
102 : 13. yea the set time is c.
Is. 10 : 28. He is c. to Aiath, he is
51 : 19. two things are c. unto thee
56 : 1. for my salvat. is near to c.
60 : 1. Arise, shine, for thy light is c.
63 : 4. year of my redeemed is c.
Je. 40 : 3. sinned, theref. this is c.
46 : 21. day of their calam. was c.
47 : 5. Baldness is c. upon Gaza
50 : 27. woe to them, their day is c.
31. day is c. I will visit thee [c.
51 : 13. dwellest on wat., thy end is
La. 3 : 47. Fear and a snare is c.
4 : 18. days fulfilled, end is c.
5 : 1. O L., what is c. upon us
Eze. 7 : 2. end is c. upon land, 3, 6.
5. an only evil, behold is c.
7. morn. is c. upon thee, O thou
10. day, behold, it is c., 39 : 8.
17 : 12. king of Bab. is c. to Jerus.
21 : 25. prince whose day is c., 29.
Da. 9 : 13. all this evil is c. upon u.
Ho. 9 : 7. days of visita. are c. (2)
Am. 8 : 2. The end is c. on Israel
Mi. 1 : 9. he is c. to gate of my peo.
Mat. 3 : 7. to flee from wrath to c.?
12 : 28. kingd. of G. is c. Lu. 11 : 20.
44. is c. he findeth it empty
17 : 12. Elias is c., Mk. 9 : 13.
18 : 11. Son of man is c. to save
26 : 50. Friend, wheref. art thou c.
Mk. 1 : 24. art c. to destr. us, Lu. 4 : 34.
4 : 29. puts sickle, bec. harvest is c.
14 : 8. she is c. aforehand to anoint
41. Sleep on now, the hour is c.
Lu. 7 : 34. Son of man is c. eating
15 : 27. brother is c. fa. killed calf
19 : 9. salvation c. to this house
10. Son of man is c. to seek lost
Jn. 3 : 19. that light is c. into world
4 : 25. when he is c. he will tell us
11 : 28. Master is c. and calleth
12 : 23. hour is c. Son be glori., 17 : 1.
13 : 1. wh. J. knew his hour was c.
3. he was c. from God
15 : 26. when Comforter is c.
16 : 8. when he is c. he will reprove
13. Spirit of truth is c. he guide
21. wom. sorrow bec. hour is c.
17 : 1. Father, the hour is c.
Ac. 1 : 8. aft. H. G. is c. upon you
2 : 1. day of Pentecost was c.
Ro. 11 : 11. salva. is c. unto Gentiles
16 : 19. your obedience is c. am. all
1 Co. 10 : 11. upon whom ends of
world are c. [is c.
13 : 10. when that which is perfect
Ga. 3 : 25. after that faith is c. we
Col. 1 : 6. Which gospel is c. to you
1 Th. 2 : 16. wrath is c. upon them
He. 9 : 11. Christ being c. an high pr.
12 : 22. ye are c. unto mt. Zion
1 Jn. 4 : 2. that J. C. is c. in flesh
3. confesseth not C. is c., 2 Jn. 7.
5 : 20. we know Son of God is c.
Re. 6 : 17. day of his wrath is c.
11 : 18. thy wrath is c. and time
12 : 10. Now is c. salva. and strength
14 : 7. hour of his judgment is c.
18 : 10. in 1 hour is thy judg. c.
17. great riches is c. to nought
19 : 7. marriage of the Lamb is c.

I am or I am not COME.

Ex. 18 : 6. I Jethro, a. c. unto thee
Nu. 22 : 38. Balaam said, I a. c.
De. 26 : 3. I a. c. into country the L.
Jos. 5 : 14. as capt. of host a. I c.
1 S. 16 : 2. I a. c. to sacrifice, 5.
2 S. 14 : 15. I a. c. to speak of this
32. Wheref. a. I c. from Geshur?
19 : 20. I a. c. to meet my lord
Ps. 69 : 2. I a. c. into deep waters
Ec. 1 : 16. I a. c. to great estate
Can. 5 : 1. I a. c. into my gar. my sis.
Da. 9 : 23. I a. c. to shew, 10 : 14.
10 : 12. I a. c. for thy words [destr.
Mat. 5 : 17. Think not I a. c. to
9 : 13. I a. n. c. to call righteous
10 : 34. not I a. c. to send peace
35. I a. c. to set man at variance
Lu. 12 : 51. that I a. c. to give peace?
Jn. 1 : 31. theref. a. I c. baptizing
5 : 43. I a. c. in my Father's name
7 : 28. I a. n. c. of myself, he
9 : 39. Jes. said, For judgm. I a. c.
10 : 10. I a. c. they might have life
12 : 46. I a. c. a light into world
16 : 28. I a. c. into world, again I

COME joined with time.

Ge. 30 : 33. righte. answer in t. to c.
Ex. 13 : 14. son ask. in t. to c., What
is this? De. 6 : 20. Jos. 4 : 6, 21.
Jos. 22 : 24. in t. to c. chil. speak, 28.
1 S. 1 : 20. t. was c. after Hannah
Ps. 102 : 13. t. to favour Zion is c.
Pr. 31 : 25. she sh. rejoice in t. to c.
Can. 2 : 12. t. of singing of birds is c.
Is. 13 : 22. her t. is near to c.
30 : 8. note in a book for t. to c.
42 : 23. who will hear for t. to c.
Je. 27 : 7. until very t. of land c.
Eze. 7 : 7. t. is c. day of trouble, 12.
22 : 3. blood that her t. may c.
Hag. 1 : 2. t. is not c. L.'s house be
Lu. 9 : 51. t. c. he be received up
13 : 35. until t. c. wh. ye shall say
Jn. 7 : 6. My t. is not yet c., 8.
16 : 4. when t. sh. c. ye may remem.
Ga. 4 : 4. when fulness of t. was c.
1 Ti. 6 : 19. good founda. ag. t. to c.
2 Ti. 4 : 3. t. c. they not endure
1 Pe. 4 : 17. t. is c. that judgm. must

Yet COME.

De. 12 : 9. ye are not y. c. to rest
Jn. 2 : 4. my hour is not y. c.
7 : 6. my time is not y. c., 8.
30. his hour was not y. c., 8 : 20.
11 : 30. Jes. was not y. c. into town
Re. 17 : 10. five fallen, other not y. c.

COMELINESS.

Is. 53 : 2. he hath no form nor c.
Eze. 16 : 14. was perfect thro. my c.
27 : 10. they of Lud set forth thy c.
Da. 10 : 8. my c. into corruption
1 Co. 12 : 23. have more abund. c.

COMELY.

1 S. 16 : 18. David, a c. person
Jb. 41 : 12. his c. proportion
Ps. 33 : 1. praise is c. for. 147 : 1.
Pr. 30 : 29. yea, four are c. in going
Ec. 5 : 18. it is c. for one to eat
Can. 1 : 5. I am black but c.
10. cheeks are c. with jewels
2 : 14. and thy countenance is c.
4 : 3. like scarlet, thy speech is c.
6 : 4. Thou art c. O my love, as
Is. 4 : 2. fruit of earth shall be c.
Je. 6 : 2. dau. of Zion to c. woman
1 Co. 7 : 35. speak for that wh. is c.
11 : 13. is it c. a woman pray uncov.?
12 : 24. our c. parts have no need

COMERS.

Is. 44 : † 19. fall down to the c. of tree
He. 10 : 1. never make c. perfect

COMEST.

Ge. 10 : 19. as thou c. to Gerar
13 : 10. as thou c. to Zoar
24 : 41. when thou c. to my kindred
De. 2 : 19. c. nigh chil. of Ammon
20 : 10. c. nigh to city to fight it
23 : 24. c. into neigh.'s vineyard
25. c. into corn of neighbour
28 : 6. Blessed when thou c. in
19. Cursed when thou c. in
Ju. 17 : 9. Whence c. thou? 19 : 17.
1 S. 16 : 4. c. peaceably? 1 K. 2 : 13.
17 : 43. I a dog, thou c. with staves.
45. Thou c. to me with a sword
2 S. 1 : 3. Da. said, whence c. thou
3 : 13. bring Michal when c.
1 K. 19 : 15. when c. anoint Hazael
2 K. 5 : 25. Whence c. thou, Gehazi?
Jb. 1 : 7. c. thou? Satan ans., 2 : 2.
Je. 51 : 61. When thou c. to Bab.
Jon. 1 : 8. What occupa.? whence c.?
Mat. 3 : 14. needed to be baptized of
thee, c. thou to me?
Lu. 23 : 42. when c. into thy kingd.

COMETH.

Ge. 30 : 11. troop c. | 37 : 19. dreamer c.
Ex. 29 : 30. when he c. into tab.
Le. 11 : 34. such water c. is unclean
De. 18 : 8. c. of sale of patrimony
28 : 13. cover that which c. from thee
Ju. 13 : 14. not eat that c. of vine
1 S. 4 : 3. when ark c. may save us
9 : 6. all man of G. saith c. to pass
20 : 27. Whf. c. not son of Jesse?
29. Therof. he c. not to k.'s table
2 S. 18 : 27. c. with good tidings
1 K. 14 : 5. when she c. in will feign
2 K. 9 : 18. but he c. not again, 20.
11 : 8. with k. as he c. in, 2 Ch. 23 : 7.
12 : 4. c. into any man's heart to
1 Ch. 29 : 16. c. of thine hand
2 Ch. 20 : 9. when evil c. upon us
Jb. 3 : 21. long for death, it c. not
27 : 9. G. hear cry when troubl. c.?
28 : 20. Whence c. wisdom, where
Ps. 30 : 5. but joy c. in morning
62 : 1. upon G., fr. him c. my salv.
75 : 6. promotion c. not from east
78 : 39. wind passeth and c. not
96 : 13. bef. L., for he c. to judge
the earth, 98 : 9. 1 Ch. 16 : 33.

Ps. 118: 26. Blessed that c. in name of
121: 1. hills, fr. whence c. my help
2. My help c. from L. who made
Pr. 1: 26. mock when your fear c.
27. your destruc. c. as whirlw.
2: 6. out of mouth c. knowledge
11: 2. When pride c. then c. shame
13: 5. wicked man c. to shame
18: 3. When wicked c. c. contempt
29: 26. man's judgm. c. from L.
Ec. 1: 4. and another generation c.
6: 4. he c. in with vanity
11: 8. live many yrs., all c. is vanity
Can. 2: 8. he c. leaping upon mts.
Is. 13: 9. day of L. c. with wrath
30: 13. whose breaking c. suddenly
27. name of Lord c. from far
62: 11. say to Zion, thy salv. c.
63: 1. Who is this that c. fr. Edom?
Je. 6: 20. what purpose c. to me inc.
17: 6. he sh. not see when good c.
8. shall not see when heat c.
43: 11. when c. he shall smite E.
La. 3: 37. Who saith, and it c. to
5: † 4. our wood c. for price
Eze. 14: 4. c. to a prophet, 7.
20: 32. c. in your mind sh. not be
21: 7. because it c. behold it c.
24: 24. when this c. know I am L.
33: 31. come unto thee as people c.
33. when this c. to pass, then
47: 9. shall live whither river c.
Da. 11: 16. c. ag. him do exploits
12: 12. Blessed that c. to 1335 days
Ho. 7: 1. thief c., and robbers
Jo. 2: 1. day of the L. c., Zch. 14: 1.
1 Th. 5: 2. [when he c.
Mi. 5: 6. sh. deliver us from Assyrian
7: 4. day of thy visitation c.
Mal. 4: 1. day c. that shall burn,
day that c. shall burn them
Mat. 3: 11. that c. aft. me is mightier than I, Mk. 1: 7. Lu. 3: 16. Ac. 13: 25.
5: 37. is more than these c. of evil
8: 9. I say, Come, he c., Lu. 7: 8.
13: 19. then c. the wicked one
18: 7. man by whom offence c.
21: 5. Behold, thy King, c. unto thee, Jn. 12: 15. Zch. 9: 9.
9. Blessed he th. c. in name of L., Hosanna, 23: 39. Mk. 11: 9, 10. Lu. 13: 35.-19: 38. Jn. 12: 13.
24: 44. S. of man c., 25: 13. Lu. 12: 40.
46. lord when he c., Lu. 12: 43.
25: 6. Behold bridegroom c.
19. lord of those servants c.
26: 40. c. unto disciples findeth th. asleep, 45. Mk. 14: 37, 41.
Mk. 4: 15. Satan c. imme., Pr. 8: 12.
6: 48. he c. unto them upon the sea
8: 38. be ash. when he c. in glory
9: 12. Elias c. first, and restoreth
13: 35. when master of house c.
14: 43. while he yet spake c. Judas
Lu. 6: 47. Whoso. c. to me, and hear.
11: 25. c. he findeth it swept [ing
12: 37. when he c. sh. find watch-
40. c. at an hour ye think not
43. when he c. sh. find so doing
54. c. a shower and so it is
55. will be heat, and it c. to pass
15: 6. c. home, calleth friends
17: 20. kingd. c. not with observa.
18: 8. S. of man c. sh. he find faith
Jn. 1: 9. lighteth ev. man that c.
15. c. after me is preferred, 30.
3: 8. canst not tell whence it c.
20. nor c. to the light, lest deeds
21. doeth the truth, c. to light
31. that c. fr. heav. is above all
4: 21. Woman, hour c., 23.-16: 32.
25. I know that Messias c.
5: 44. honour that c. from G. only
6: 35. he that c. never hunger, 37.
45. hath learned of Fa. c. unto me
7: 27. Christ c. no man knoweth, 31.
Jn. 7: 42. Christ c. of seed of David
9: 4. night c. no man can work
14: 6. no man c. unto Fa. but by [me
30. prince of this world c.
16: 2. time c. that whoso. kill. you
25. time c. I no more speak in [prov.
32. hour c. ye sh. be scatt-d
Ac. 10: 32. when he c. shall speak
Ro. 4: 9. c. this blessedn. on circumc.
10: 17. So then, faith c. by hearing
1 Co. 15: 24. Then c. the end
2 Co. 11: 4. c. preacheth another Jes.
11: 28. which c. upon me daily
Ga. 5: 8. persuasion c. not of [3: 6.
Ep. 5: 6. c. the wrath of God, Col.
1 Th. 5: 2. day of L. c. as a thief
3. safety; sudden destruction c.
1 Ti. 6: 4. words, whereof c. envy
He. 10: 5. c. into world, he saith
11: 6. that c. to G. must believe
Jude 14. L. c. with 10,000 saints
Re. 1: 7. he c. with clouds, every
11: 14. third woe c. quickly
17: 10. he c. he must continue

COMETH down.

Is. 55: 10. rain c. d. from heaven
Jn. 6: 33. bread of G. is he c. d., 50.
Ja. 1: 17. every good gift c. d.
Re. 3: 12. Jerus. which c. d. from [God

COMETH forth.

Ge. 24: 43. virgin c. f. to draw water
Ex. 4: 14. he c. f. to meet thee
8: 20. lo, he c. f. to the water
Ju. 11: 31. whatso. c. f. of doors
1 S. 11: 7. Whoso. c. not f. aft. Saul
Jb. 5: 6. afflic. c. not f. of dust
14: 2. He c. f. like a flower, and
Is. 28: 29. This c. f. from Lord
Eze. 33: 30. hear word c. f. from L.
Mi. 1: 3. L. c. f. out of his place

COMETH nigh.

Nu. 1: 51. stranger that c. n. be put to death: 3: 10, 38.-18: 7.

COMETH out.

Ex. 28: 35. be heard when he c. o.
Nu. 12: 12. consum. when he c. o.
De. 28: 57. evil tow. young that c. o.
1 K. 8: 41. stranger that c. o. of far
Jb. 20: 25. and c. o. of the body
37: 22. fair weather c. o. of north
Can. 3: 6. Who c. o. of wilderness?
Is. 26: 21. L. c. o. of his place to
42: 5. earth, and that w. c. o. of it
Je. 46: 20. destruc. c. o. of north
Eze. 4: 12. dung that c. o. of man
Mat. 15: 11. c. o. of mouth, this defileth a man, Mk. 7: 20.
24: 27. lightning c. o. of east

COMETH up.

1 S. 28: 14. An old man c. u. covered
Can. 8: 5. Who c. u. from wildern.?
Is. 24: 18. he that c. u. out of pit
Je. 46: 7. Who c. u. as a flood?
50: 3. out of north c. u. a nation
Ha. 3: 16. when he c. u. to people
Mat. 17: 27. take up fish first c. u.

COMFORT, S.

Jb. 6: 10. Then should I have c.
10: 20. alone, that I may take c.
Ps. 94: 19. thy c-s delight my soul
119: 50. This my c. in affliction
76. let merciful kindn. be my c.
Is. 57: 6. Sh. I receive c. in these?
18. I will also restore c-s unto him
Eze. 16: 54. thou art a c. unto them
Mat. 9: 22. be of good c., Lu. 8: 48.
Mk. 10: 49. Be of good c. rise
Ac. 9: 31. walking in c. of H. G.
Ro. 15: 4. through c. of scriptures
1 Co. 14: 3. speaketh unto men to c.
2 Co. 1: 3. Blessed be God, of all c.
4. c. wherewith we are comforted
7: 4. of you, I am filled with c.
13. we were comforted in your c.
13: 11. brethren, be of good c.
Ph. 2: 1. if there be any c. of love
19. that I may be of good c.
Col. 4: 11. these only, been c. to me

COMFORT. [Verb.]

Ge. 5: 29. sh. c. us conc. our work
18: 5. c. ye your hearts, after that
27: 42. Esau doth c. himself
37: 35. sons and dau-s rose to c. him
Ju. 19: 5. c. heart with bread, 8.
2 S. 10: 2. Da. to c. him, 1 Ch. 19: 2.
1 Ch. 7: 22. breth. came to c. him
19: 2. serv. of Da. to Hanun to c. him
Jb. 2: 11. his friends came to c. him
7: 13. When I say, My bed sh. c. me
9: 27. If I say, I will c. myself
21: 34. How then c. ye me in vain
Ps. 23: 4. thy rod thy staff, they c.
71: 21. shalt c. me on every side
119: † 76. let merciful kindn. c. me
82. When wilt thou c. me?
Can. 2: 5. c. me with apples
Is. 22: 4. labour not to c. me
40: 1. c. ye, c. ye my people
51: 3. L. shall c. Zion, c. her waste
19. by whom shall I c. thee?
61: 2. sent me to c. all th. mourn
66: 13. so will I c. you, in Jerus.
Je. 8: 18. When I would c. myself
16: 7. nor sh. men tear to c. them
31: 13. I will c. them, make rejoi.
La. 1: 2. am. lovers, none to c. her, 17.
21. there is none to c. me
2: 13. equal to thee, that I may c.?
Eze. 14: 23. c. when see their ways
Zch. 1: 17. Lord shall yet c. Zion
10: 2. diviners, they c. in vain
Jn. 11: 19. to c. them conc. broth.
2 Co. 1: 4. we be able to c. them
2: 7. ye ought rather to c. him
Ep. 6: 22. might c. your hearts, Col. 4: 8. [faith
1 Th. 3: 2. to c. you concerning
4: 18. c. one ano. with these words
5: 11. Wherefore c. yours. together
14. c. feeble-minded, support
2 Th. 2: 17. L. Jes. c. your hearts

COMFORTABLE, BLY.

2 S. 14: 17. word of Lord be c.
19: 7. speak c-y to thy servants
2 Ch. 30: 22. spake c-y to Levites
32: 6. he set captains and spake c-y
Is. 40: 2. Speak ye c-y to Jerusalem
Ho. 2: 14. I will speak c-y to her
Zch. 1: 13. ans. angel with c. words

COMFORTED, EST.

Ge. 24: 67. Isaac was c. after his
37: 35. Jac. refused to be c. for
38: 12. Jud. was c. and went up to
50: 21. Joseph c. his brethren
Ru. 2: 13. fav. for thou hast c. me
2 S. 12: 24. David c. Bath-sheba
13: 39. he was c. conc. Amnon
Jb. 42: 11. breth. c. him over all evil
Ps. 77: 2. my soul refused to be c.
86: 17. bec. thou, Lord, hast c. me
119: 52. I rem. judgm-s, have c. mys.
Is. 12: 1. anger is turned thou c-t [me
49: 13. G. hath c. peo., 52: 9.
54: 11. Oh. thou afflicted, not c.
66: 13. ye shall be c. in Jerus.
Je. 31: 15. Rachel refused to be c.
Eze. 5: 13. fury to rest, I will be c.
14: 22. be c. concerning the evil
31: 16. all that drink water be c.
32: 31. Pharaoh shall be c.
Mat. 2: 18. not be c. bec. were not
5: 4. mourn for they shall be c.
Lu. 16: 25. he is c. thou tormented
Jn. 11: 31. The Jews which c. her
Ac. 16: 40. seen brethren c. them
20: 12. young man alive, were c.
Ro. 1: 12. that I be c. with you
1 Co. 14: 31. all learn and be c.
2 Co. 1: 4. wherew. we are c. of G
6. whether we be c. it is
7: 6. God c. us by coming of Tit.
7. consola. he was c. in you
13. we were c. in your comfort
Col. 2: 2. that hearts might be c.

1 Th. 2: 11. ye know how we c. you
3: 7. we were c. in all our afflict.

COMFORTER, S. [19: 3.
2 S. 10: 3. he hath sent c-s, 1 Ch.
Jb. 16: 2. miserable c-s are ye all
Ps. 69: 20. I looked for c-s but
Ec. 4: 1. oppressed, had no c.
La. 1: 9. she had no c. [far fr. me
16. c. that sho. relieve my soul is
Na. 3: 7. whence shall I seek c-s?
Jn. 14: 16. give you another C.
26. C. which is H. G. shall teach
15: 26. when the C. is come
16: 7. C. will not come

COMFORTETH.
Jb. 29: 25. one that c. mourners
Is. 51: 12. I am he that c. you
66: 13. As one whom mother c.
2 Co. 1: 4. Who c. us in tribula.
7: 6. God that c. cast down

COMFORTLESS.
Jn. 14: 18. I will not leave you c.

COMING, S.
Ge. 30: 30. blessed thee since my c.
43: † 20. O sir, c. down to buy food
Le. 14: † 48. if priest c. in shall look
Nu. 22: 16. let nothing hinder fr. c.
Ju. 5: 28. Why chariot long in c.?
1 S. 16: 4. elders trembled at his c.
29: 6. c. in with me, since day of c.
2 S. 3: 25. to know thy c. in
2 K. 13: 20. invaded at c. in of yr.
19: 27. I know thy c. in, Is. 37: 28.
Ps. 19: 5. brideg. c. out of his cham.
37: 13. seeth his day is c.
121: 8. L. shall preserve thy c. in
Is. 14: 9. hell to meet thee at c.
44: 7. things c. let them shew
Je. 8: 7. observe time of their c.
Eze. 43: 11. goings out and c-s in
Da. 4: 23. holy one c. from heaven
Mi. 7: 15. acc. to days of c. out of E.
Mal. 3: 2. who abide day of c.?
4: 5. bef. c. of the great day
Mat. 16: 28. see Son of man c.,
24: 3 what be sign of thy c.?
27. c. of Son of man be, 37, 39.
30. Son of man c. in clouds, 26:
64. Mk. 13: 26.-14: 62. Lu. 21: 27.
48. My lord delayeth c., Lu. 12: 45.
25: 27. at c. received my own, Lu.
Mk. 6: 31. many c. going [19: 23.
13: 36. c. suddenly find you sleep.
Lu. 2: 38. she c. in gave thanks
9: 42. was c. devil tare him
18: 5. lest by contin. c. she weary
21: 26. wh. are c. on the earth
23: 29. c. in wh. they shall say
Jn. 1: 27. c. after me is preferred
5: 7. while I am c. anc. steppeth
25. hour is c., 28. | 10: 12. wolf c.
Ac. 1: † 8. power of Holy Ghost c.
7: 52. shewed bef. of c. of Just One
9: 28. he was with them c. in and
10: 3. angel of God c. in to him
25. Peter was c. in, Corne. met
13: 24. John preached bef. his c.
1 Co. 1: 7. waiting for c. of our L.
15: 23. that are Christ's at his c.
16: 17. I am glad of c. of Stephanas
2 Co. 7: 6. God comf. us by c. of Tit.
7. not by his c. only, but by conso.
13: 1. third time I am c. to you
Ph. 1: 26. more abundant by my c.
1 Th. 2: 19. our rejoicing at L.'s c.
3: 13. unblameable at c. of our L.
4: 15. we wh. remain unto c. of L.
5: 23. blameless unto c. of Lord
2 Th. 2: 1. beseech you by c. of L.
8. destroy with brightness of c.
9. whose c. is aft. working of Satan
Ja. 5: 7. Be patient unto c. of Lord
8. c. of Lord draweth nigh
1 Pe. 2: 4. c. as unto a living stone
2 Pe. 1: 16. make known c. of L. J.
3: 4. Where is promise of his c.?
12. hasting unto c. of day of God

9

1 Jn. 2: 28. not be asha. at his c.
Re. 13: 11. another beast c. up
21: 2. new Jerus. c. down from G.

COMMAND. [Noun.]
2 S. 23: † 23. set Benaiah at his c.
Jb. 39: 27. eagle mount at thy c.?

COMMAND. [Verb.]
Ge. 18: 19. Ab. will c. his children
50: 16. father did c. before he died
Ex. 8: 27. sacrifi. as G. shall c. us
18: 23. if do, and God c. thee so
27: 20. c. the chil. of Isr., Le. 24: 2.
Nu. 5: 2.-28: 2.-34: 2.-35: 2.
De. 2: 4. Jos. 1: 11.
Le. 6: 9. c. Aaron and his sons
13: 54. priest shall c., 14: 4, 36.
Nu. 9: 8. I will hear what L. c.
36: 6. This is the thing L. doth c.
De. 28: 8. L. c. blessing upon thee
32: 46. c. your chil. to observe
Jos. 3: 8. c. priests bear ark, 4: 16.
11: 15. so did Moses c. Joshua
Ps. 42: 8. L. will c. his loving-k.
44: 4. O God, c. deliver. for Jacob
Is. 45: 11. conc. work of hands, c. me
Je. 27: 4. c. them to say to masters
La. 1: 10. didst c. they sho. not enter
Mat. 4: 3. c. stones be br., Lu. 4: 3.
19: 7. Why Moses c. to give writing
27: 64. c. sepulchre be made sure
Mk. 10: 3. What did Moses c. you?
Lu. 8: 31. not c. them to go into deep
9: 54. wilt thou we c. fire to come
Ac. 5: 28. Did not we straitly c. you
15: 5. to c. to keep law of Moses
2 Th. 3: 4. ye do, and will thi. we c.
6. we c. you breth. in name of L.
12. such we c. and exhort by L.
1 Ti. 4: 11. These things c. and

I COMMAND.
Ex. 7: 2. speak all I c. Je. 1: 7, 17.
34: 11. Observe what I c., De. 12: 28.
Le. 25: 21. I will c. my bless. upon
De. 4: 2. not add unto word I c.
7: 11. com. I c. thee, 8: 11.-10:
13.-11: 8, 27.-13: 18.-30: 8.
24: 18. I c. thee to do this, 22.
30: 16. I c. this day to love Lord
Is. 5: 6. I will c. clouds that
Je. 11: 4. do all which I c. you
34: 22. I will c. and cause
Am. 9: 3. thence will I c. serpent
4. thence I c. the sword
9. I will c. and sift Israel
Jn. 15: 14. if ye do what I c. you
17. I c. you, ye love one another
Ac. 16: 18. I c. thee in name
1 Co. 7: 10. to the married I c.

COMMANDED.
Ge. 45: 19. thou art c. this do ye
50: 12. Joseph's sons did as he c.
Ex. 1: 17. midw. not as king c.
Le. 10: 13. eat it, for so I am c.
De. 1: 18. I c. you at, 3: 18, 21.
31: 29. turn from way I have c.
Jos. 4: 8. Israel did as Joshua c.
8: 8. fire, See I have c. you
22: 2. obeyed my voice in all I c.
Ju. 13: 14. all I c. let her observe
1 S. 20: 29. bro. c. me to be there
21: 2. king c. me a business
2 S. 13: 28. have not I c. you
21: 14. they performed all king c.
2 K. 11: 9. acc. to all Jehoiada c.
16: 16. did accord-g to all Ahaz c.
1 Ch. 21: 17. Is it not I c. people
2 Ch. 8: 14. so had David c.
14: 4. Asa c. Judah to seek Lord
32: 12. Hezekiah | 33: 16. Manas.
Ne. 13: 19. I c. gates be shut
22. I c. Levites to cleanse thems.
Es. 3: 2. for the king had so c.
12. written acc. to all Haman c.
4: 17. Mordecai did as Esther c.
8: 9. written acc. to all Mord. c.
Jb. 38: 12. Hast thou c. morning
Is. 48: 5. molten image hath c.
Je. 35: 6. Jonadab c. us, Ye shal.
drink no wine, 10, 14, 16, 18
Eze. 12: 7. I did so as c., 37: 7.
Da. 3: 4. to you it is c. O people
19. c. they should heat furnace
6: 16. king c. they bro-t Daniel
24. king c. they bro-t those men
Am. 2: 12. c. prophets
Mat. 10: 5. Jes. c. Go not into way
14: 9. c. it be given, Mk. 6: 27.
19. c. mult. sit, 15: 35. Mk. 6: 39.
18: 25. lord c. him to be sold
21: 6. disciples did as Jesus c.
27: 58. Pilate c. body to be deliv.
28: 20. teaching to obs. all I c.
Mk. 5: 43. c. something be given
her to eat, Lu. 8: 55. [ney
6: 8. c. should take noth. for jour-
8: 6. c. peo. to sit down on ground
7. blessed fishes, and c. to set th.
10: 49. Jes. c. blind man called
11: 6. said even as Jesus had c.
13: 34. c. the porter to watch
Lu. 8: 29. he c. unclean spirit to
9: 21. c. them to tell no man
17: 9. thank serv. did things c., 10.
18: 40. Jes. c. him to be brought
19: 15. he c. serv-ts to be called
Ac. 4: 15. c. to go out of council
18. c. not speak in name, 5: 40.
5: 34. Gama. c. to put apos. forth
8: 38. he c. chariot to stand
10: 48. he c. them to be baptized
12: 19. Herod c. they be put to dea.
16: 22. magis. c. to beat them
18: 2. Claudius c. all Jews to dep.
21: 33. captain c. him to be bound
34. c. him carri. into castle | 22: 24.
22: 30. c. chief pr. and council to
23: 10. capt. c. soldiers go down, 31.
35. c. him kept in Herod's hall
24: 23. c. a centu. to keep Paul
25: 6. next day Festus c. Paul
17. I c. man to be brought forth
27: 43. c. they which could swim
1 Co. 14: 34. c. to be under obedi-
1 Th. 4: 11. work as we c. you [ence
2 Th. 3: 10. c. you if any not work
He. 12: 20. could not endure that c.
Re. 9: 4. c. them not to hurt grass

God COMMANDED.
Ge. 2: 16. G. c. man, Of every tree
6: 22. acc. to all G. c. did he [eat
7: 9. into ark as G. had c., 16.-
21: 4. De. 20: 17. Jos. 10: 40.
De. 5: 15. G. c. thee to keep sab.
5: 32. observe to do as G. c. you
33. walk in all ways G. c. you
6: 1. G. c. to teach you, 20.-13: 5.
26: 16. This day G. c. thee to keep
Ju. 4: 6. G. c. to go toward Tabor
1 Ch. 14: 16. David did as G. c. him
2 Ch. 35: 21. G. c. me make haste
Ezr. 7: 23. Whatsoever is c. by G.
Ps. 68: 28. G. hath c. thy strength
Mat. 15: 4. G. c. Honour thy fa.
Ac. 10: 33. to hear all c. of G.
2 Co. 4: 6. G. who c. light to shine

Lord COMMANDED.
Ge. 7: 5. Noah did acc. to all L. c.
Ex. 7: 6. Aaron did as L. c., 10, 20.
-12: 28, 50. Nu. 17: 11.
16: 16. this is the thing L. c., 32.-
35: 4. Nu. 30: 1.
34. As L. c. Moses, 34: 4.-39: 1,
5, 7. &c.-40: 19, &c. Le. 8: 9.-
9: 10. [Nu. 20: 27.-27: 11.
Le. 8: 4. Moses did as L. c. him,
Nu. 36: 2. L. c. my lord to give
De. 6: 24. L. c. us to do statutes
9: 16. out of way L. c. you
10: 5. tables, as the L. c. me
1 S. 13: 14. L. c. him to be captain
2 S. 17: † 14. L. c. to defeat counsel
24: 19. David went up, as L. c.
1 Ch. 21: 27. L. c. the angel, he
24: 19. as L. G. of Israel c. him

Ps. 106 : 34. conc. whom L. c. them
133 : 3. for there L. c. blessing
Je. 13 : 5. I hid it as L. c. me
La. 1 : 17. L. hath c. conc. Jacob
Ac. 13 : 47. turn to Gent., so L. c.

COMMANDED.
[By God or Lord.]

Ge. 3 : 11. eaten of tree I c. not, 17.
Ex. 23 : 15. as I c. in time appoint.
Lev. 7 : 38. in the day he c. Israel
10:1.offered fire wh. he c. them not
De. 17 : 3. served gods, I have not
c., 18 : 20. Je. 19 : 5.-23 : 32.-
Jos. 1 : 9. have I not c. thee? [29:23.
7:11.transg. covenant I c., Ju.2:20.
13 : 6. by lot, as I have c. [17 : 6.
2 S. 7 : 7. c. to feed my peo., 1 Ch.
11. time I c. judges, 1 Ch. 17 : 10.
1 K. 11 : 10. had c. Sol. conc. this
17 : 4. c. ravens to feed thee [thing
9. c. a widow to sustain thee
1 Ch. 16 : 15. mindful of word he c.
to thousand gene., Ps. 105 : 8.
40. written in law, wh. he c. Israel
Ps. 7 : 6. awake to the judgment c.
33 : 9. he c. and it stood fast
111 : 9. hath c. his coven. for ever
119 : 4. c. us to keep thy precepts
138. testimo. hast c. are righte.
148 : 5. he c. and they were created
Is. 13 : 3. have c. my sanctified ones
34 : 16. for my mouth it hath c.
45 : 12. heavens and host I c.
Je. 7 : 23. this thing c. I them, Obey
31. wh. I c. not, 19 : 5.-32 : 35.
11 : 8. all words I c. them to do
17 : 22.hallow sab.,as I c. your fa-s
50 : 21. do acc. to all I have c. thee
La. 2 : 17. word he c. in days of old
Eze. 9 : 11. I have done as thou c.
24 : 18. in morn. as I was c., 37:10.
Zch. 1 : 6. words I c. did they not
Mal. 4 : 4. Rem. law I c. in Horeb
Lu. 14 : 22. L. it is done as thou c.
Ac. 10 : 42. he c. us to preach

Moses COMMANDED.

Nu. 16 : 47. Aaron took as M. had c.
De. 31:25. that M. c. Levites, saying
33 : 4. M. c. us a law, even the
Jos. 1 : 7. observe acc. to all M. c.
22 : 2. ye have kept all M. c. you
1 Ch. 15 : 15. M. c. acc. to word of L.
Mat. 8 : 4. offer gift that M. c. for a
Mk.1:44.offer things M. c., Lu. 5:14.
Jn. 8 : 5. M. c. such sh. be stoned

COMMANDEDST, EST.

Jos. 1 : 16. all thou c-t us we do
18. not hearken in all thou c t
Ne. 1 : 7. wh. thou c-dst Moses, 8.
9 : 14. thou c-dst them precepts
Je. 32 : 23. done nothing thou c-dst
Ac. 23 : 3. c-t me to be smitten?

COMMANDER.

Is. 55 : 4. given him for c. to peo.

COMMANDETH.

Nu. 32 : 25. will do as my lord c.
Jb. 9 : 7. G. c. sun, it riseth not
36 : 10. he c. that they ret. fr. iniq.
32. light, and c. it not to shine
37 : 12. may do whatever he c.
Ps. 107 : 25. he c. the stormy wind
La. 3 : 37. cometh, when L. c. not?
Am. 6 : 11. L. c. great horse
Mk. 1 : 27. he c. spirits, Lu. 4 : 36.
Lu. 8 : 25. he c. winds, they obey
Ac. 17 : 30. c. all men to repent

COMMANDING.

Ge. 49 : 33.Jac.an end of c. his sons
Mat. 11 : 1. end of c. disciples
Ac. 24 : 8. c. his accusers to come
1 Ti. 4 : 3. c. to abstain from meats

COMMANDMENT.

Ex. 34:32. gave in c. all L. had spok.
Nu. 15 : 31. broken c., sh. be cut off
23 : 20. I have received c. to bless
27:14. ye rebelled against my c. in
De. 30 : 11. this c. I command
1 K. 2 : 43.why hast not kept the c.
2 K. 18 : 36. king's c., ans. not, Is
1 Ch. 12 : 32. were at their c. [36:21.
28 : 21. people will be at thy c.
2 Ch. 8 : 13. offering acc. to c. of Mo.
† 14. so was the c. of David
19 : 10. what cause betw. law and c.
30 : 12. one heart to do the c. of k.
31 : 5. as soon as the c. came, Isr.
Ezr. 8 : 17. I sent with c. to Iddo
10 : 3. that tremble at c. of God
Ne. 11 : 23. was king's c. conc. them
13 : † 5. wine and oil, was c. of Lev.
Es. 1 : 12. Vashti refused king's c.
2 : 20. Esther did c. of Mordecai
3 : 3. Why transgressest king's c.?
9 : 1. when king's c. drew nigh to
Jb. 23 : 12. nor gone back fr. the c.
Ps. 119 : 96. c. is exceeding broad
147 : 15. sendeth his c. upon earth
Pr. 6 : 23. the c. is a lamp, and
8 : 29. waters sho. not pass his c.
13 : 13. feareth c. be rewarded
19 : 16. keepeth c. keepeth his soul
Ec. 8 : 5. keepeth c. feel no evil thing
Je. 35 : 14. obey fa. Jonadab's c.
Da. 3 : 22. king's c. was urgent
9 : 23. c. came, and I am come to
Ho. 5 : 11. he walked after the c.
Mal. 2 : 1. O priests, this c. is for you
4. I have sent this c. unto you
Mat. 8 : 18. Jes. gave c. to depart
22 : 36. Master, wh. is the great c.?
38. This is great c., Mk. 12 : 30.
Mk. 12 : 28. Which is first c. of all
31. is no other c. greater than these
Lu. 15 : 29. nei. transgr-d I thy c.
23 : 56. rested sabbath acc. to c.
Jn. 10 : 18. This c. I receiv. of Fa.
11 : 57. had given c. that if any kn.
12 : 49. gave a c. what I sho. say
50. I know that his c. is life
14:31.as Fa. gave me c. even so I do
15 : 12. c. That ye love one ano.,
1 Jn. 3 : 23. [such c.
Ac. 15 : 24. to whom we gave no
17 : 15. c. unto Silas to come to him
23 : 30. gave c. to his accusers
25 : 23. at Festus' c. Paul was bro-t
Ro. 7 : 8. sin taking occa. by c., 11.
9. when c. came, sin revived
10. c. which was ordained to life
12. c. is holy, and just, and good
13. sin by c. become exceeding
13 : 9. if be any other c. it is
1 Co. 7 : 6. I speak this, not of c.
2 Co. 8 : 8. I speak not by c. but
Ep. 6 : 2. is first c. with promise
1 Ti. 1 : 5. end of the c. is charity
He. 7 : 5. have a c. to take tithes
16. not after law of a carnal c.
18. is a disannulling of the c.
11 : 22. Jo. gave c. conc. his bones
23. they were not afraid of k.'s c.
2 Pe. 2 : 21. to turn from holy c.
3 : 2. mindful of c. of us apostles
1 Jn. 2 : 7. an old c. which ye heard
3 : † 11. this is c. ye heard fr. begin.
23. his c., That we should believe
4 : 21. this c. have we from him
2 Jn. 4. we received c. from Father
6. This is the c., That as ye heard

Give or given COMMANDMENT.

Ex. 25 : 22. things I will g. in c.
De. 1 : 3. L. had g. him in c. unto
Ezr.4:21. g. c. to cease until ano. c.
Ps. 71 : 3. hast g. c. to save me
Is. 23:11. L. hath g. c. against city
Na. 1 : 14. L. hath g. c. conc. thee
Jn. 11:57. g. c. if any knew where he

COMMANDMENT of God.

Mat. 15 : 3. Why transgress c. o. G.
6. ye made c. o. G. of none effect
Mk. 7:8. laying aside the c. o. G. ye
9. Full well ye reject c. o. G.
Ro. 16 : 26. acc. to c. o. everl. G.
1 Ti.1:1. by c. o. G. our Sav., Tit. 1:3.

Keep COMMANDMENT.
See KEEP.

COMMANDMENT of the Lord.

Ex. 17 : 1. journeyed acc. to c. o.
L., Nu. 9 :18, 20.-10 : 13.
Nu. 3 : 39. Mo. numbered at c. o. L.
24 : 13. I cannot go bey. c. o. L.
33:38. Aa. went up to Hor. at c. o. L.
Jos. 22 : 3. ye kept charge of c. o. L.
1 S. 12 : 14. not rebel ag. c. o. L.
15. if not obey, but rebel ag. c. o. L.
13 : 13. thou hast not kept c. o. L.
15:13.Saul said, I performed c. o. L.
24. I have transgressed c. o. L.
2 S. 12 : 9. Whf. hast despised c. o. L.
2 K. 24 : 3. at c. o. L. came this
upon Judah
2 Ch. 29:25. was c. o. L. by prophets
Ps. 19 : 8. the c. o. L. is pure
1 Co. 7 : 25. conc. virgins no c. o. L.

New COMMANDMENT.

Jn. 13 : 34. a n. c. I give unto you
1 Jn. 2 : 7. Breth., I write no n. c.
8. a n. c. I write unto you [c.
2 Jn. 5. not as though I wrote a n.

Rebelled against COMMANDMENT. [Zin.

Nu. 27 : 14. ye r. a. my c. in des. of
De. 1 : 26. ye r. a. c. of your G., 43.
9:23. ye r. a. c. of L. and believ. not
La. 1 : 18. I have r. a. his c.

COMMANDMENTS.

Ge.26:5.that Abraham kept my c. [c.
Ex. 15 : 26.if thou wilt give ear to his
34 : 28. he wrote upon tables the
ten c., De. 4 : 13.-10 : 4.
Le. 4 : 13. have done ag. any c., 27.
5 : 17. commit sin forbid. by c. of L.
27 : 34. These are c. the L. comm.
Nu. 15 : 39. remember all c. of L.
De. 8 : 11. in not keeping c. [3 : 4.
11 : 13. if hearken to c., 28 : 13. Ju.
27. if ye will obey the c. of L.
28. if ye will not obey the c. of L.
1 S. 15 : 11. Saul not perform. c.
1 K. 11 : 34. bec. he hath kept my c.
14 : 8. David who kept my c.
18 : 18. in that ye have forsaken c.
2 K. 17 : 16. they left c. of L.
19. Jud. kept not the c. of L.
18 : 6. kept his c. which he com.
2 Ch. 7 : 19. if ye forsake my c.
24 : 20. Why transgress ye the c.
Ezr. 9 : 10. we have forsaken thy c.
14. Should we again break thy c.
Ps. 89 : 31. if they keep not my c.
111 : 7. all his c. are sure
112 : 1. blessed is he delight. in c.
119 : 6. respect unto all thy c.
10. let me not wander from c.
19. hide not thy c. from me
21. which do err from thy c.
32. run the way of thy c.
35. to go in path of thy c.
47. I will delight in thy c.
66. for I have believed thy c.
73. that I may learn thy c.
86. c. are faithful | 151. c. truth
98. thro. c. hast made me wiser
127. I love thy c. | 131. I longed c.
143. c. delights | 172. c. righte.
166. done c. | 176. not forget c.
Pr. 2 : 1. if thou wilt hide my c.
7 : 1. lay up my c. with thee
10 : 8. wise in heart will receive c.
Is. 48 : 18. hadst hearkened to c.
Mat. 5 : 19. whoso. break least c.
15 : 9. teach. c. of men, Mk. 7 : 7.
22 : 40. On these two c. hang law
Mk.10:19. knowest c., Lu. 18 : 20.
12 : 29. first of all c. is, Hear O Isr.
Lu. 1 : 6. walking in c. blameless
Jn. 14 : 21. He that hath my c.
15 : 10. If keep my c. as Father's c.
1 Co. 7 : 19. nothing, but keeping c.

1 Co.14:37. things I write you,are c.
Ep. 2: 15. law of c. contained
Col. 2: 22. c. and doctrines of men
4: 10. touching whom ye rec-d c.
1 Th. 4: 2. ye know what c. we gave
Tit. 1: 14. c. of men, that turn
1 Jn. 2: 4. keepeth not c. is a liar
3: 24. keepeth his c. dwell. in him
5: 3. his c. are not grievous
2 Jn. 6. is love, th. we walk after c.

Do COMMANDMENTS.

Nu. 15: 40. d. all my c. be holy
De. 6: 25. observe to d. all c., 15:
5.-28: 1, 15.-30: 8.
1 Ch. 28: 7. if constant to d. my c.
Ps.103: 18.remem. his c. to d.them
111: 10. understanding that d. c.
Re. 22: 14. Blessed they that d. c.

Not do COMMANDMENTS.

Le. 26: 14. if ye will n. d. c.
15. so that ye will n. d. all my c.

Keep COMMANDMENTS.

[See KEEP.]

COMMEND.

Lu. 23: 46. thy hands I c. my spirit
Ac. 20: 32. breth. I c. you to God
Ro. 3: 5. if unrighte c. righte. of G.
16: 1. I c. unto you Phebe our
2 Co. 3: 1. Do we begin to c. ours.?
5: 12. For we c. not ourselves
10: 12. compare with some that c.

COMMENDATION.

2 Co. 3: 1. need we, epistles of c.

COMMENDED.

Ge. 12: 15. princes c. Sarai before
Pr. 12: 8. man be c. acc. to wisd.
Ec. 8: 15. Then I c. mirth, bec.
Lu. 16: 8. lord c. unjust steward
Ac. 14: 23. c. them to L. on whom
2 Co. 12: 11. I ought to have been c.

COMMENDETH, ING.

Ro. 5: 8. God c-h his love tow. us
1 Co. 8: 8. meat c-h us not to G.
2 Co. 4: 2. c-g ours. to every man's
6: † 4. in all c-g ours. as ministers
10: 18.not he that c-h hims.is appr.

COMMISSION, S.

Ezr. 8: 36. delivered the king's c-s.
Ac. 26: 12. I went with c. fr. chief

COMMIT.

Ex. 20: 14. not c. adultery, De. 5:
18. Mat. 5: 27.-19: 18.Ro.13: 9.
Le. 5: 17. sin, and c. things forbid.
18: 26. not c. any abomina., 30.
29. who shall c. any abomina.
Nu. 5: 6. if c. any sin that men c.
De. 19: 20. c. no more evil
Ju. 13: † 1. ad led to c. evil in sight
2 Ch. 21: 11. Jerus. to c. fornication
Jb. 5: 8. unto G. I c. my cause
Ps. 31: 5. thine hand c. my spirit
37: 5. c. thy way unto the Lord
Pr. 16: 3. c. thy words unto Lord
12. abom. to kings to c. wickedn.
Is. 22: 21. I will c. thy governm.
23: 17. c. fornic. with kingdoms
Je. 37: 21. c. Jeremiah to prison
44: 7. Why c. ye this great evil
Eze. 8: 17. c. abom. they c. here
16: 43. shalt not c. this lewdness
22: 9. midst of thee c. lewdness
Ho. 6: 9. priests c. lewdness
7: 1. for they c. falsehood [stripes
Lu 12: 48. did c. things worthy of
16: 11. who c. to your trust riches
Jn. 2: 24. Jesus did not c. himself
Ro. 1:32. c. things worthy of death
2: 2. is ag. them c. such things
22. dost thou c. sacrilege?
1 Co. 10: 8. Neither c. fornication
1 Ti. 1: 18. charge I c. unto thee
2 Ti. 2: 2. same c. to faithful men
Ja. 2: 9. respect to persons ye c. sin
1 Pe. 4: 19. c. keeping of souls
1 Jn. 3: 9. born of G. not c. sin
Re. 2: 14. taught Isr. to c. fornica.
Re.2:20.my servants to c.fornication
See ADULTERY.

COMMIT iniquity.

2 S. 7: 14. If c. i. I will chasten
Jb. 34: 10. Al., that he should c.i.
Je. 9: 5. weary thems. to c. i.
Eze. 3: 20. turn and c. i., 33: 13.

COMMIT trespass.

Le. 5: 15. if c. t. thro. ignorance
6: 2. c. a t. against the Lord
Nu. 5: 12. if a man's wife c. t.
31: 16. caused Israel to c.t. ag. L.
Jos. 22: 20. Achan c.t. in accur. th.

COMMIT whoredom, s.

Le. 20: 5. that c. w. with Molech
Nu. 25: 1. c.w. with dau-s of Moab
Eze. 16: 17. didst c.w. with images
34. none followeth thee to c. w-s
20: 30. c. ye w. after their abom.
23: 43. will they c. w-s with her
Ho.4: 10.shall c.w. and not increase
13. your daughters shall c.w., 14.

COMMITTED.

Ge. 39: 8. c. all he hath to my hand
22. keeper c. to Jo. the prisoners
Le. 4: 35. atonement for sin he c.
18: 30. abom. customs wh. were c.
20: 23. c. these things, and I abhor.
Nu. 15: 24. if aught be c. by ignor.
De. 17: 5. bring forth man that c.
21: 22. if c. sin worthy of death
Ju. 20: 6. have c. folly in Israel
1 K. 8: 47. we have c. wickedness
14: 22. provoked him with sins c.
27. shields c. he to, 2 Ch. 12: 10.
1 Ch. 10: 13. died for transgr. he c.
2 Ch. 34: 16. c. to thy serv-ts they
Je. 2: 13. my peo. c. two evils [do
5: 30. horrible thing is c. in land
16: 10. what is our sin we have c.
29: 23. have c. villainy in Israel
40: 7. c. unto him men, women
44: 3. c. to provoke to anger, 9.
Eze. 16: 26. thou hast c. fornica.
51. Nor Sama. c. half thy sins
52. sins thou hast c. more abom.
18: 21. turn from sins he c., 22, 28.
27. his wickedness he hath c.
20: 43. loathe yours. for evils c.
23: 3. they c. whoredoms in E.
7. she c. whoredoms with them
33: 16. None of sins c. be mention.
Ho. 1: 2. land c. great whoredom
4: 18. c. whoredom continually
Mk. 15: 7. who had c. murder in
Lu. 12: 48. to whom men c. much
Ju. 5: 22. Fa. c. all judgm. unto Son
Ac. 8: 3. haling wom. c. to prison
25: 11. c. thing worthy of death
25. c. nothing worthy of death
27: 40. they c. thems. to the sea
28: 17. I have c. nothing ag. peo.
Ro. 3: 2. were c. the oracles of G.
1 Co.9: 17. gospel c. unto me, Tit.1:3.
10: 8. Nor fornication as some c.
2 Co. 5: 19. c. unto us word of recon-
11: 7. Have I c. an offence in [cil.
12: 21. lasciviousness wh. they c.
Ga. 2: 7. gospel of uncirc. c. unto me
as gos.of circ. unto Pe., 1 Ti.1: 11.
1 Ti. 6: 20. O Tim. keep what is c.
2 Ti. 1: 12. able to keep that I c.
14. good thing c. unto thee keep
Ja. 5: 15. if he have c. sins, they
1 Pe. 2: 23. c. himself to him that
Jude 15. ungodly deeds they have c.
Re. 17: 2. kings c. fornication, 18: 3, 9.
See ABOMINATION, S, ADULTERY.

COMMITTED iniquity.

Ps. 106: 6. we have c. i. we have
Eze. 33: 13. for his i. c. he shall
die, 18. [wickedly
Da. 9: 5. we have c. i. and done

COMMITTED trespass.

Le. 5: 7. bring for his t. he c. two
turtledoves [thing
Jos. 7: 1. Israel c. a t. in accursed
Jos. 22: 16. What t. is this ye have c.
31. bec. have not c. this t. ag. L.
Eze. 15: 8. bec. they c. a t. I will
20: 27. in that they c. a t. ag. me

COMMITTEST, ETH, ING.

Ps 10: 14. poor c-h hims. unto thee
Eze. 8: 6. great abom. that Isr. c-h
33: 15. walk without c-g iniquity
18. righte. c-h sh. die, 18: 24, 26.
Ho. 4: 2. by lying, and c-g adultery
5: 3. O Ephr. thou c-t whoredom
Jn. 8: 34. c-h sin is servant of sin
1 Co. 6: 18. c-h fornication sinneth
against body [law
1 Jn. 3: 4. whoso. c-h sin transgr.
8. he that c-h sin is of the devil

COMMODIOUS.

Ac. 27: 12. the haven was not c.

COMMON.

Nu. 16: 29. if these die c. death of
De. 20: † 6. vineyard, not made it c.
28: † 30. not use it as c. meat
1 S. 21: 4. There is no c. bread
5. the bread is in a manner c.
Ec. 6: 1. there is an evil, it is c.
Je. 31: 5. sh. eat them as c. things
Eze. 23: 42. with men of c. sort
Mat. 27: 27. took Jes. into the c. hall
Mk. 7: † 2. eat bread with c. hands
Ac. 2: 44. had all things c., 4: 32.
5: 18. put apostles in c. prison
10: 14. never eaten anyth. c., 11: 8.
15. G. cleansed call not c., 11: 9.
28. should not call any man c.
Ro. 14: † 14. nothing c. of itself;
esteem. anything to be c.
1 Co. 10: 13. no temptation but c. to
Tit. 1: 4. Titus my son, aft. c. faith
Jude 3. to write to you of c. salvation

COMMON people.

Le. 4: 27. any of c. p. sin thro. igno.
Je. 26: 23. body into graves of c. p.
Mk. 12: 37. c. p. heard him gladly

COMMONLY.

Mat. 28: 15. saying c. reported

COMMONWEALTH.

Ep. 2: 12. being aliens fr. c. of Isr.

COMMOTION, S. [to c.

2 Ch. 29: † 8. L. hath deliv. them
Je. 10: 22. a great c. out of north
Lu. 21: 9. hear of c-s be not terri.

COMMUNE.

Ge. 34: 6. Hamor went out . . to c.
Ex. 25: 22. there I will c. with thee
1 S. 18: 22. c. with David secretly
19: 3. I will c. with my fa. of thee
Jb. 4: 2. If we assay to c. with thee
Ps. 4: 4. c. with your own heart
64: 5. they c. of laying snares
77: 6. in night I c. with heart

COMMUNED, ING.

Ge. 18: 33. Lord left c-g with Ab.
23: 8. Ab. c. | 34: 8. Hamor c.
42: 24. Joseph | Ju. 9: 1. Abim. c.
Ex 31: 18. end of c-g upon Sinai
1 S. 9: 25. Samuel c. | 25: 39. David c.
1 K. 10: 2. q. of S. c. wi. Sol., 2 Ch. 9: 1.
2 K. 22: 14. they c. with Huldah
Ec. 1: 16. I c. with mine own heart
Da. 1: 19. and king c. with them
Zch. 1: 14. angel that c. with me
Lu 6: 11. they c. what do to Jesus
22: 4. Judas c. to betray Jesus
24: 15. while c. Jesus drew near
Ac. 24: 26. Felix c. oftener with

COMMUNICATE. [Paul

Ga. 6: 6. Let him that is taught c.
to him that teacheth
Ph. 4: 14. that ye did c. with my
affliction [ing to c.
1 Ti. 6: 18. that they do good, will-
He. 13: 16. and to c. forget not

COMMUNICATED.

Ga. 2: 2. I c. to them that gospel
Ph. 4: 15. no church c. with me

COMMUNICATION, S.

2 S. 3: 17. Abner had c. with eld.

2 K. 9 : 11. ye know man and his c.
Mat. 5 : 37. let your c. be Yea
Lu. 24 : 17. What manner of c.
1 Co. 15 : 33. evil c. corrupt
Ep. 4 : 29. no corrupt c., Col. 3 : 8.
Phm. 6. c. of thy faith effectual

COMMUNION.

1 Co. 10 : 16. c. of blood, c. of body
2 Co. 6 : 14. what c. light with ?
13 : 14. c. of H. G. be with you

COMPACT, ED.

Ps. 122 : 3. Jerusalem is a city c.
Ep. 4 : 16. body fitly joined and c-d

COMPANIED.

Ac. 1 : 21. which have c. with us

COMPANIES.

Ju. 7 : 16. 300 men into three c.
20. three c. blew trumpets
9 : 34. wait ag. Shechem in four c.
43. he divided them into three c.
1 S. 11 : 11. Saul put people in 3 c.
13 : 17. spoilers came in three c.
2 K. 5 : 2. Syrians had gone by c.
11 † 7. two c. shall keep watch
Ne. 12 : 31. two c. gave thanks, 40.
Jb. 6 : 19. c. of Sheba waited for th.
Is. 21 : 13. O ye travelling c. of
57 : 13. let thy c. deliver thee
Mk. 6 : 39. to make all sit down by [c.

COMPANION.

Ex. 32 : 27. go slay ev. man his c.
Ju. 14 : 20. Samson's wife giv. to c., [15:6.
1 Ch. 27 : 33. Hushai k.'s c.
Jb. 30 : 29. I am a c. to owls
Ps. 119 : 63. a c. to all th. fear thee
Pr. 13 : 20. c. of fools be destroyed
28 : 7. c. of riotous shameth father
24. same is c. of destroyer
Can 1 : † 15. my c. thou art fair
Mal. 2 : 14. she is thy c. wife of thy
Ph. 2 : 25. Epaphroditus my c.
Re. 1 : 9. I John, your c. in tribu- [lation

COMPANIONS.

Ju. 11 : 38. with her c. and bewailed
14 : 11. thirty c. to be with him
Ezr. 4 : 7. rest of c. unto Artax.
6 : 13. c., acc. to that wh. Darius
Jb. 35:4. I will ans. thee and thy c.
41:6. sh. c. make banquet of him?
Ps. 45 : 14. her c. shall be brought
122 : 8. for my c. sake, I will say
Can. 1 : 7. aside by flocks of thy c.
8 : 13. c. hearken to thy voice
Is. 1:23. thy princes are c. of thieves
Eze. 37 : 16. for Jud. and Isr. his c.
Da. 2 : 17. made thing kno. to his c.
Ac. 19:29. caught Paul's c. in travel
He. 10 : 33. c. of them so used

COMPANY. [Noun.]

Ge. 30 : † 11. his name Gad, a c.
32 : 8. If Esau come to one c.
21. lodged that night in c.
35 : 11. a c. of nations be of thee
37 : 25. c. of Ishm. from Gilead
Nu. 16 : 6. Korah and all his c.
16. Be thou and thy c. before L.
40. be not as Korah and c.
22 : 4. this c. lick up all that are
26 : 9. in c. of Korah, 27 : 3.
Ju. 9 : 37. c. come by the plain
44. Abimelech and c. with him
18 : 23. thou comest with such c. ?
1 S. 10 : 5. meet c. of prophets, 10.
19 : 20. c. of prophets prophesying
30 : 15. Canst bring me to this c.?
2 K. 5 : 15. his c. came to Elisha
9 : 17. spied c. of Jehu, I see c.
2 Ch. 24 : 24. Syrians with small c.
Ne. 12:38. other c. that gave thanks
Jb. 16 : 7. made desolate all my c.
34 : 8. c. with workers of iniquity
Ps. 55 : 14. unto house of God in c.
68 : † 27. princes with their c.
30. Rebuke the c. of spearmen
84 : † 7. c. to c. every one in Zion
106 : 17. earth cov. c. of Abiram
18. fire was kindled in their c.
Pr. 24 : † 19. not c. with wicked
29 : 3. keepeth c. with harlots
Can. 1 : 9. to c. of horses in Pha.'s
6 : 13. As it were c. of two armies
Eze. 16 : 40. shall bring c. ag. thee
23 : 46. I will bring a c. upon them
47. c. shall stone them
27 : 34. thy c. in midst shall fall
32 : 22. Ashur is there and her c.
38 : 7. prepare, thou and thy c.
Ho. 6 : 9. so c. of priests murder
Lu. 2 : 44. supposing him in c.
6 : 17. he came, and c. of his disci.
22. separate you from their c.
9 : 14. sit down by fifties in a c.
38. a man of the c. cried out
11 : 27. woman of c. lifted voice
12 : 13. one of c. said, Master
24 : 22. woman of our c. made us [aston.
Ac. 4 : 23. went to own c.
10 : 28. unlawful for Jew to keep c.
13 : 13. when Paul and his c.
15 : 22. to send chosen men of c.
17 : 5. Jews gath. a c. and set city
21 : 8. we of Paul's c. departed
Ro. 15:24. if I be filled with your c.
1 Co. 5:11. not to keep c. with fornica.
2 Th. 3 : 14. have no c. with him
He. 12 : 22. to innum. c. of angels
Re. 18 : 17. all c. in ships afar off

Great COMPANY.

Ge. 50 : 9. went with Jo. a g. c.
2 Ch. 9:1. queen of Sheba with g.c.
20 : 12. no might against this g.c.
Ps. 68 : 11. g. c. of those th. pub- [lished
Je. 31 : 8. a g. c. sh. return
Eze. 17 : 17. nor Pha. with g. c.
Lu. 5 : 29. a g. c. of publicans
23 : 27. foll'd him, g. c. of people
Jn. 6 : 5. saw g. c. come unto him
Ac. 6 : 7. g. c. of priests obedient

COMPANY. [Verb.]

1 Co. 5:9. not to c. with fornica., 11.

COMPARABLE.

La. 4 : 2. sons of Zion c. to gold

COMPARE, ED, ING.

Ps. 89:6. who in heav. be c. unto L.?
Pr. 3:15. not to be c. unto wisd., 8:11.
Can. 1 : 9. have c. thee, O my love
Is. 40 : 18. likeness will ye c. unto [him?
46 : 5. to wh. will ye c. me?
Mk. 4:30. what comparison sh. we c.
Ro. 8 : 18. are not worthy to be c.
1 Co. 2 : 13. c-g spiritual things
2 Co. 10 : 12. c-g ourselves with
some, and c-g thems. amongst [thems.

COMPARISON.

Ju. 8:2. what I done in c. of you? 3.
Hag. 2:3. is it not in c. of it as noth.?
Mk. 4:30. with what c. sh. we comp.?

COMPASS. [Noun.]

Ex. 27 : 5. put net und. c. of altar
38 : 4. he made a grate und. the c.
Nu. 34 : 5. sh. fetch a c., Jos. 15:3.
2 S. 5 : 23. fetch a c. behind them
1 K. 7 : 35. top was a round c.
2 K. 3:9. fetched c. of 7 days' journey
Pr. 8 : 27. set a c. on face of depth
Is. 44 : 13. he marketh it with c.
Ac. 28 : 13. we fetched c. to Rhegium

COMPASS. [Verb.]

Nu. 21 : 4. to c. the land of Edom
Jos. 6 : 3. ye sh. c. city, all ye men
4. seventh day c. city 7 times
2 S. 24 : † 2. c. the tribes of Israel
1 K. 7:23. 30 cubits did c., 2 Ch. 4:2.
2 K. 11 : 8. c. the king, 2 Ch. 23 : 7.
Jb. 16 : 13. His archers c. me round
40 : 22. willows of brook c. him
Ps. 5 : 12. with favour wilt c. him
7 : 7. congregation c. thee
17 : 9. deadly enemies who c. me
26 : 6. hands, so will I c. thine alt.
32 : 7. c. me with songs of deliv.
10. trusteth in L. mercy c. him
49 : 5. iniq. of my heels sh. c. me
140 : 9. head of those that c. me
Ps. 142:7. the righte. sh. c. me about
Pr. 4 : † 9. she sh. c. thee with crown
Is. 50 : 11. c. yours. with sparks
Je. 31 : 22. a woman shall c. a man
52 : 21. fillet of 12 cubits did c.
Ha. 1 : 4. wicked doth c. righteous
Mat. 23 : 15. woe to you, ye c. sea
Lu. 19 : 43. enemies shall c. thee

COMPASSED.

Ge. 19 : 4. men of Sodom c. house
De. 2 : 1. we c. Seir many days
Jos. 6 : 11. ark of the Lord c. city
15 : 10. border c. from Baalah
Ju. 11 : 18. they c. land of Edom
16 : 2. c. Samson in, and laid wait
1 S. 23 : 26. Saul men c. D. and men
2 S. 22 : 5. waves of death c. me,
Ps. 18 : 4.-116 : 3. [with horses
2 K. 6 : 15. behold a host c. city
2 Ch. 21 : 9. smote Edomites whi.c.
Jb. 19 : 6. God c. me with his net
26 : 10. hath c. waters with bounds
Ps. 17 : 11. have c. us in our steps
22 : 12. bulls c. me | 16. dogs c.
Ec. 7 : † 25. heart c. to know wisd.
La. 3 : 5. he hath c. me with gall
Zch. 14 : † 10. land be c. as plain
Lu. 21 : 20. when ye see Jerus. c.
He. 5 : 2. he is c. with infirmity

COMPASSED about.

De. 32 : † 10. lo wildern. he c. them a.
2 S. 18 : 15. young men c. Abs. a.
22 : 6. sorrows of hell c. me a., Ps. [18:5.
2 K. 6 : 14. Syrians c. city a.
8:21. smote Edomites wh. c. him a.
2 Ch. 18 : 31. they c. a. Jehosh.
Ps. 40 : 12. innum. evils c. me a.
88 : 17. they c. me a. together,
109 : 3.-118 : 11, 12.
118 : 10. All nations c. me a.
Jon. 2:3. floods c. me a. thy billows
He. 11 : 30. fell, after c. a. 7 days
12 : 1. c. a. with cloud of witnes.
Re. 20 : 9. they c. camp of saints a.

COMPASSEST, ETH, ING.

Ge. 2 : 11. c-h Havilah | 13. Ethio.
1 K. 7:24. c-g the sea (2), 2 Ch. 4:3.
Ps. 73 : 6. pride c-h them as chain
139 : 3. Thou c-t my path and
Ho. 11 : 12. Ephr. c-h me with lies

COMPASSION.

1 K. 8 : 50. give them c. bef. them
2 Ch. 30 : 9. children shall find c.
Mat. 9 : 36. Jesus moved with c.,
14 : 14. Mk. 6 : 34.
18 : 27. lord was moved with c.
Mk. 1 : 41. Jesus moved with c. put
1 Pe. 3 : 8. having c. one of another
1 Jn. 3:17. shutteth his bowels of c.

Full of COMPASSION.

Ps. 78 : 38. he being f. o. c. forgave
86 : 15. thou art a G. f. o. c., 111:
4.-112 : 4.-145 : 8.

Have or Had COMPASSION.

Ex. 2 : 6. babe wept, and she h. c.
De. 13 : 17. L. may h. c. upon thee
30 : 3. then L. will h. c. upon thee
1 S. 23:21. blessed for ye h. c. on me
1 K. 8 : 50. may h. c. on them.
2 K. 13:23. L. was gracious and h.c.
2 Ch. 36 : 15. he h. c. on his people
17. Chaldees h. no c. upon young
Is. 49 : 15. h. c. on son of womb
Je. 12 : 15. I will h. c. on them
La. 3 : 32. will he h. c., Mi. 7 : 19.
Mat. 15:32. h. c. on multi., Mk. 8:2.
18 : 33. h. c. on fellow servant
20:34. Jes. h. c. on them and touch.
Mk. 5 : 19. how L. h. c. on thee
9 : 22. if thou canst, h. c. on us
Lu. 7 : 13. when L. saw her, he h.c.
10 : 33. Samaritan h. c. on him
15 : 20. father h. c. ran and fell
Ro. 9:15. h. c. on whom I will h.c.
He. 5 : 2. can h. c. on ignorant
10 : 34. ye h. c. of me in my bonds

Jude 22. of some h. c. making diff.

COMPASSIONS.

La. 3 : 22. because his c. fail not
Zch. 7 : 9. shew c. every man to bro.

COMPEL.

Le. 25 : 39. not c. him to serve
Es. 1 : 8. drinking ; none did c.
Mat. 5 : 41. c. thee to go a mile
Mk. 15 : 21. c. one Simon to bear
Lu. 14 : 23. c. them to come in

COMPELLED, EST.

1 S. 28 : 23. his servants c. Saul
2 Ch. 21 : 11. Jehoram c. Judah
Mat. 27 : 32. Simon, they c. to bear
Ac. 26 : 11. I c. them to blaspheme
2 Co. 12:11. glorying, ye have c. me
Ga. 2 : 3. was c. to be circumcised
14. why c-t Gent. to live as Jews?

COMPLAIN, ED, ING.

Nu. 11 : 1. people c-d it displeased
Ju. 21 : 22. breth. come to us to c.
Jb. 7 : 11. I will c. in bitterness
31 : 38. furrows thereof c.
Ps. 77 : 3. I c-d and my spirit was
144 : 14. be no c-g in our streets
La. 3 : 39. doth a living man c?

COMPLAINERS.

Nu. 11 : † 1. when people were c. it
Jude 16. these are murmurers, c.

COMPLAINT, S.

1 S. 1 : 16. out of abund. of my c.
Jb. 7 : 13. couch shall ease my c.
9 : 27. If I say, I will forget my c.
10 : 1. I will leave c. upon myself
21 : 4. As for me, is my c. to man?
23 : 2. Even to-day is my c. bitter
Ps. 55 : 2. I mourn in my c.
142 : 2. I poured out my c.
Ac.25:7.c-s ag. Paul, they not prove
Col. 3 : † 13. if any have c. ag. any

COMPLETE.

Le. 23 : 15. seven sabbaths be c.
Col. 2 : 10. ye are c. in him who
4 : 12. that ye may stand c. in all

COMPOSITION.

Ex. 30 : 32. like it after the c., 37.

COMPOUND, ETH.

Ex. 30 : 25. an ointment c. after art
33. Whoso. c-h anything like it

COMPREHEND, ED.

Jb. 37 : 5. things we cannot c.
Is. 40 : 12. hath c. dust of the earth
Jn. 1 : 5. darkness c-d it not
Ro. 13:9. is briefly c. in this saying
Ep. 3 : 18. able to c. with saints

CONANI'AH.

2 Ch. 35 : 9. C. and chief of Levites

CONCEAL, ED, ETH.

Ge. 37:26. if slay bro. and c. his bl.
De. 13 : 8. not spare, neither c. him
Jb. 6 : 10. I have not c. words
27 : 11. what with Al. will I not c.
41 : 12. I will not c. his parts nor
Ps.40:10.I have not c. thy loving-k.
Pr. 11 : 13. faithful spirit c-h matter
12 : 23. A prudent man c-h knowl.
25 : 2. glory of God to c. a thing
Je. 50 : 2. declare ye, and c. not

CONCEIT, S.

Pr. 18 : 11. as a high wall in c.
26 : 5. lest he be wise in his own c.
12. Seest man wise in own c.?
16. sluggard is wiser in own c.
28 : 11. rich is wise in own c.
Ro. 11 : 25. lest wise in your c.
12 : 16. be not wise in own c-s

CONCEIVE, ING.

Ge. 30 : 38. c. when came to drink
Nu. 5 : 28. free, and shall c. seed
Ju. 13 : 3. shalt c. and bear a son,
5, 7. Lu. 1 : 31.
Jb. 15 : 35. c. mischief, Is. 59 : 4.
Ps. 51 : 5. in sin did mother c. me
Is. 7 : 14. a virgin shall c. a son
33 : 11. Ye shall c. chaff
59 : 13. c-g words of falsehood
Eze. 38 : † 10. c. mischiev. purpose

He. 11:11. Sarah rec. strength to c.

CONCEIVED.

Ge. 4 : 1. Eve c. | 17. Cain's wife c.
16 : 4. Hagar c. | 21 : 2. Sarah c.
25:21. Rebek.c. |29:32. Leah c.,33.
30:5. Bilhah c. | 23.Rach. c. a son
39. the flocks c., 31 : 10.
38 : 3. Shuah c., 4, 5. [c.
18. Tamar c. |Ex. 2 : 2. Jochebed
Le.12:2.c.seed and borne a man-ch.
Nu. 11 : 12. Have I c. all this peo.?
1 S. 1 : 20. Hannah c. and, 2 : 21.
2 S. 11:5. Bathsheba c., told David
2 K. 4 : 17. Shunammite c.
Jb. 3 : 3. There is a man child c.
Ps. 7 : 14. c. mischief, brought
Can. 3 : 4. chamber of her c. me
Is. 8 : 3. prophetess c.
Je. 49 : 30. c. a purpose against you
Ho. 1 : 3. Gomer, which c. and
2 : 5. she that c. them done shamef.
Mat. 1 : 20. that c. in her is of H. G.
Lu. 1 : 36. Elisab. hath c. son in age,
2 : 21. named before he was c. [24.
Ac. 5 : 4. why hast c. this thing?
Ro. 9 : 10. when Rebekah had c.
Ja. 1 : 15. when lust hath c., it

CONCEPTION.

Ge. 3 : 16. I will multiply thy c.
Ru. 4 : 13. the Lord gave her c.
Ho. 9 : 11. glory flee from c.

CONCERN, ETH.

Ps. 138 : 8. L. perfect that c-h me
Eze. 12 : 10. This burden c-h prince
Ac. 28 : 31. things which c. L. J. C.
2 Co.11: 30.which c. my infirmities

CONCERNING.

Ge. 19 : 21. accepted thee c. this
42 : 21. We are guilty c. our bro.
Ex. 6 : 8. c. which I did swear to
give, Nu. 14 : 30.
Le. 4 : 2. c. things which ought not
to be done, 13, 22, 27.
26. atonem. for him c. sin, 5 : 6.
6 : 3. what was lost, lieth c. it
Nu. 10 : 29. spoken good c. Israel
1 K. 11 : 10. com. him c. this thing
2 K. 20 : † 1. c. thy house, Is.38:†1.
Ne. 1 : 2. c. Jews that escaped [22.
13 : 14. Remem. me, O G., c. this,
Ps.90: 13.thee c. thy serv., 135:14.
Ec. 1 : 13. c. all done under heaven
7 : 10. not inquire wisely c. this
Is. 5 : † 20. say c. evil, It is good
30 : 7. theref. have I cried c. this
45 : 11. ask me c. my sons, c. work
Je. 16 : 3. c. sons, c. daughters, c.
mothers, c. fathers
18 : 7. speak c. nations, c. kingd.
27 : 19. c. pillars, sea, bases, (4)
Eze. 14 : 22. comforted c. evil, c. all
21 : 28. saith L. c. Ammonites
47 : 14. c. which I have lifted my
Da.2 : 18.mercies of G. c. this secret
6 : 17. purpose not changed c. Dan.
Mat. 11 : 7. unto mult c. John, Lu.
16 : 11. I speak not c. bread [7:24.
Mk. 5 : 16. that saw, told c. swine
7 : 17. disciples asked c. parable
Lu. 2 : 17. told them c. this child
18 : 31. by proph. c. Son of man
24 : 19. c. Jesus of Naz. which was
27. expounded things c. himself
44. written in psalms c. me [bro.
Jn. 11 : 19. comfort them c. their
Ac. 1 : 16. c. Judas which was guide
8 : 12. things c. kingdom of God
13 : 34. as c. he raised him up
19 : 39. inquire c. other matters
25 : 16. c. crime laid against him
28 : 22. as c. this sect, we know
23. persua-g them C.Jesus,Ro.1:3.
Ro. 9 : 5. as c. flesh Christ came
27. Esaias crieth c. Israel
11 : 28. As c. gospel, are enemies
16 : 19. wise to good, simple c. evil
1 Co. 7 : 25. c. virgins, I no com-t

1 Co. 8 : 4. c. eating things offered to
12 : 1. c. spiritual gifts [idols
16 : 1. c. collection for the saints
2 Co. 11 : 21. I speak as c. reproach
Ep. 5 : 32. but I speak c. Christ
Ph. 3 : 6. c. zeal, persecu-g church
4 : 15. as c. giving and receiving
1 Th. 3 : 2. to comfort you c. your
faith, 1 Ti. 1 : 19.
1 Ti. 6 : 21. some erred c. the faith
2 Ti. 2 : 18. who c. truth have erred
3 : 8. reprobates c. the faith
He. 7 : 14. speak noth. c. priesthood
11 : 20. blessed Jacob c. things to
22. command, c. his bones
1 Pe. 4 : 12. c. the fiery trial [YOU.
See HIM, ME, THEE, THEM, US,

CONCISION.

Jo. 3 : † 14. in the valley of c.
Ph. 3 : 2. beware of the c.

CONCLUDE, ED. [c.

Ac. 21 : 25. touching Gent. we have
Ro. 3 : 28. we c. a man is justified
11 : 32. hath c. them in unbelief
Ga. 3 : 22. hath c. all under sin

CONCLUSION.

Ec. 12 : 13. hear c. of matter

CONCORD.

2 Co. 6 : 15. c. Christ with Belial?

CONCOURSE.

Pr. 1 : 21. crieth in place of c.
Ac. 19 : 40. give account of this c.

CONCUBINE.

Ju. 19 : 2. his c. played the whore,
1, 9, 10, 24, 25, 27.
29. his c. and divided her, 20 : 6.
20 : 4. I and my c. to lodge
2 S. 3 : 7. Why in unto my fa.'s c.?
21 : 11. What Rizpah c. of Saul

CONCUBINES.

Ge. 25 : 6. unto sons of c. Ab. gave
2 S. 5 : 13. Da. took him more c.
16 : 22. Absalom went in to fa.'s c.
19 : 5. have saved lives of thy c.
20 : 3. the king put his c. in ward
1 K. 11 : 3. Solomon had 300 c.
2 Ch. 11. 21. Rehob. took 60 c.
Es 2 : 14. Shaashgaz who kept the c.
Can. 6 : 8. are 60 queens and 80 c.
9. yea, the c. and they praised her
Da. 5 : 3. his c. drank in them, 23.

CONCUPISCENCE.

Ro.7:†7.I had not kno. c. except law
8. sin wrought all manner of c.
Col. 3 : 5. mortify members, evil c.
1 Th. 4 : 5. Not in the lust of c.

CONDEMN.

Ex. 22 : 9. whom judges shall c.
De. 25 : 1. judges shall c. the wicked
Jb. 9 : 20. my mouth shall c. me
10 : 2. say to G. Do not c. me
34 : 17. c. him that is most just?
40 : 8. wilt thou c. me, that
Ps. 37 : 33. nor c. him when judged
94 : 21. they c. innocent blood
109 : 31. from those c. his soul
Pr. 12 : 2. wicked devices he c.
Is. 50 : 9. who is he shall c. me?
54 : 17. every tongue shall c.
Mat. 12 : 41. shall c., Lu. 11 : 32.
42. queen of south shall rise up
in judgment and c. it, Lu.11:31.
20 : 18. c. him to death, Mk. 10 : 33.
Lu. 6 : 37. c. not, and ye not be con.
Jn. 3 : 17. not his Son to c. world
8 : 11. neither do I c. thee, go
2 Co. 7 : 3. I speak not to c. you
1 Jn. 3 : 20. if our heart c. us
21. if our heart c. us not, then

CONDEMNATION.

Lu. 23 : 40. thou art in the same c.
Jn.3 : 19. this is c. that light is come
5 : 24. believeth sh. not come into c.
Ro. 5 : 16. judgment by one to c.
18. as by one, judgm. came to c.
8 : 1. there is no c. to them in C.
1 Co. 11 : 34. come not togeth. to c.

2 Co. 3 : 9. if ministra. of c. be glori.
1 Ti. 3 : 6. lest fall into c. of devil
Ja. 3 : 1. shall receive greater c.
5 : 12. be nay, lest ye fall into c.
Jude 4. of old ordained to this c.

CONDEMNED.

2 Ch. 36 : 3. c. land in 100 talents
Jb. 32 : 3. yet c. Job
Ps. 109 : 7. judged, let him be c.
Am. 2 : 8. drink the wine of c.
Mat. 12 : 7. not have c. guiltless
37. by thy words shalt be c.
27 : 3. Judas, saw he was c.
Mk. 14 : 64. all c. him to be guilty
Lu. 6 : 37. cond. not, ye not be c.
Lu. 24 : 20. delivered him to be c.
Jn. 3 : 18. He that believeth not c., believeth not is c. already
8 : 10. hath no man c. thee?
Ro. 8 : 3. for sin c. sin in flesh
1 Co. 11 : 32. not be c. with world
Tit. 2 : 8. speech that cannot be c.
3 : 11. sinneth, being c. of hims.
He. 11 : 7. by which he c. world
Ja. 5 : 6. Ye c. and killed just
9. grudge not, lest ye be c.
2 Pe. 2 : 6. God c. them with an [wicked

CONDEMNEST, ETH, ING.

1 K. 8 : 32. and judge servants c-g
Jb. 15 : 6. own mouth c-h thee
Pr. 17 : 15. he that c. just, is abom.
Ac. 13 : 27. fulfilled them in c-g him
Ro. 2 : 1. judgest ano. thou c-t thys.
8 : 34. Who is he that c.?
14 : 22. c-h not hims. in th. allow.

CONDESCEND.

Ro. 12 : 16. but c. to men of low

CONDITION, S.

1 S. 11 : 2. On this c. will make cov.
Da. 11 : † 17. enter with equal c-s
Lu. 14 : 32. he desireth c-s of peace

CONDUCT, ED.

2 S. 19 : 15. c. king over Jordan, 31.
40. people of Judah c-d king
Ac. 17 : 15. that c-d Paul bro-t him
1 Co. 16 : 11. but c. him in peace

CONDUIT.

2 K. 18 : 17. stood by c., Is. 36 : 2.
20 : 20. how he made a pool and c.
Is. 7 : 3. meet Ahaz at end of c.
Eze. 31 : † 4. sent out her c. unto

CONEY, IES.

Le. 11 : 5. c. cheweth, De. 14 : 7.
Ps. 104 : 18. a refuge for the c-s
Pr. 30 : 26. the c-s a feeble folk

CONFECTION.

Ex. 30 : 35. make a c. after art

CONFECTIONARIES.

1 S. 8 : 13. take your dau-s to be c.

CONFEDERACY.

Is. 8 : 12. c. to whom people say c.
Ob. 7. men of thy c. brought thee

CONFEDERATE.

Ge. 14 : 13. these were c. with Ab.
Ps. 83 : 5. they are c. against thee
Is. 7 : 2. Syria is c. with Ephraim

CONFERENCE.

Ga. 2 : 6. in c. added nothing

CONFERRED.

1 K. 1 : 7. Adonijah c. with Joab
Ac. 4 : 15. they c. saying, What do, to
25 : 12. Festus, when he had c.
Ga. 1 : 16. I c. not with flesh and

CONFESS.

Le. 5 : 5. he shall c. he hath sinned
16 : 21. Aaron sh. c. over goat iniq.
26 : 40. If they shall c. their iniq.
Nu. 5 : 7. they shall c. their sins
1 K. 8 : 33. Isr. c. thy name, 2 Ch. 6 : 24.
35. c. thy name and, 2 Ch. 6 : 26.
Ne. 1 : 6. c. sins of chil. of Israel
Jb. 40 : 14. c. thy hand can save
Ps. 18 : † 49. I will c. to thee
32 : 5. I said, I will c. my transgr.
Mat. 10 : 32. whoso. shall c. me bef. men, him will I c. bef., Lu. 12 : 8.
Jn. 9 : 22. if did c. he was Christ
12 : 42. rulers did not c. him, lest
Ac. 23 : 8. no resurrec. Pharis. c. both
24 : 14. c. that after way they call
Ro. 10 : 9. c. with mouth L. J.
14 : 11. every tongue shall c. to G.
15 : 9. I will c. to thee am. Gentiles
Ph. 2 : 11. ev. tongue c. J. is L.
Ja. 5 : 16. c. your faults one to ano.
1 Jn. 1 : 9. If we c. our sins, he is faith.
4 : 15. Whoso. c. J. is Son of G.
2 Jn. 7. who c. not that J. C. is come
Re. 3 : 5. c. his name bef. my Fa.

CONFESSED, ETH, ING.

Ezr. 10 : 1. Ezra had c. weeping
Ne. 9 : 2. Isr. stood and c. their sins
Pr. 28 : 13. whoso c-h and forsaketh
Da. 9 : 20. while c-g my sin and
Mat. 3 : 6. were baptized c-g their sins
Jn. 1 : 20. John c-d I am not C.
Ac. 19 : 18. many c. and shewed deeds
He. 11 : 13. c-d they were strangers
13 : † 15. our lips c-g to his name
1 Jn. 4 : 2. Ev. spirit th. c-h C. is come
3. ev. spirit that c-h not J. C. is [come

CONFESSION.

Jos. 7 : 19. glory to G. make c. to him
2 Ch. 30 : 22. offering and making c.
Ezr. 10 : 11. Now make c. unto L. G.
Da. 9 : 4. I prayed and made c.
Ro. 10 : 10. with mouth c. is made
1 Ti. 6 : 13. witnessed a good c.

CONFIDENCE.

Ju. 9 : 26. put their c. in Gaal
2 K. 18 : 19. What c. is this? Is. 36 : 4.
Jb. 4 : 6. Is not this thy fear, thy c.?
18 : 14. His c. shall be rooted out
31 : 24. to fine gold, Thou art my c.
Ps. 65 : 5. art c. of all the earth
118 : 8. L. than to put c. in man
9. in L. than to put c. in princes
Pr. 3 : 26. for L. shall be thy c.
14 : 26. in fear of L. is strong c.
21 : 22. casteth down strength of c.
25 : 19. c. in an unfaith. man is like
Is. 30 : 15. in c. be your strength
Je. 48 : 13. asha. of Beth-el their c.
Eze. 28 : 26. they shall dwell with c.
29 : 16. E. be no more c. of Israel
Mi. 7 : 5. put ye not c. in a guide
Ac. 28 : 31. preaching with all c.
2 Co. 1 : 15. in this c. I was minded
2 : 3. c. in you, that my joy is joy
7 : 16. I have c. in you in all things
8 : 22. great c. wh. I have in you
10 : 2. c. wherew. I think to be bold
11 : 17. foolishly in c. of boasting
Ga. 5 : 10. I have c. in you thro. L.
Ep. 3 : 12. access with c. by faith
Ph. 1 : 25. having c. I shall abide with
3 : 3. we have no c. in flesh
4. Though I might have c. in flesh
2 Th. 3 : 4. c. in Lord touching you
Phm. 21. Having c. in thy obedience
He. 3 : 6. if we hold fast c. and hope
14. if hold begin. of our c. steadfast
10 : 35. Cast not away your c.
11 : † 1. faith is c. of things hoped
1 Jn. 2 : 28. he appear, we may have c.
3 : 21. then have we c. toward G.
5 : 14. and this is the c. we have

CONFIDENCES.

Je. 2 : 37. Lord hath rejected thy c.

CONFIDENT.

Ps. 27 : 3. tho. war rise, will I be c.
Pr. 14 : 16. fool rageth and is c.
Ro. 2 : 19. art c. thou art a guide
2 Co. 5 : 6. we are always c. knowing
8. we are c. willing to be absent
9 : 4. be ashamed in same c. boasting
Ph. 1 : 6. Being c. of this very thing
14. many of breth. waxing c. by

CONFIDENTLY.

1 K. 4 : † 25. Judah and Isr. dwelt c.
Ps. 16 : † 9. flesh sh. dwell c. in hope
Eze. 38 : † 11. I will go to them that dwell c., 39 : † 6.
Lu. 22 : 59. c. affirmed, this fellow was

CONFIRM.

Ru. 4 : 7. manner to c. all things
1 K. 1 : 14. I will c. thy words
2 K. 15 : 19. c. kingd. in his hand
Es. 9 : 29. Es. wrote to c. letter of
31. to c. these days of Purim
Ps. 68 : 9. didst c. thine inherit.
Is. 35 : 3. and c. feeble knees
Eze. 13 : 6. that they would c. word
Da. 9 : 27. c. cove. for one week
11 : 1. even I stood to c. him
Ro. 15 : 8. to c. the promises made
1 Co. 1 : 8. shall c. you to the end
2 Co. 2 : 8. that ye would c. your love

CONFIRMATION.

Ph. 1 : 7. in c. of the gospel
He. 6 : 16. an oath of c. is an end

CONFIRMED.

2 S. 7 : 24. hast c. to thyself Israel
2 K. 14 : 5. as soon as kingd. was c.
1 Ch. 14 : 2. Lord had c. him king
16 : 17. c. same to Jac., Ps. 105 : 10.
2 Ch. 25 : † 3. when kingd. c. he slew
Es. 9 : 32. Esther c. matters of Purim
Da. 9 : 12. c. words he spake ag. us
Ac. 15 : 32. exhorted breth. and c. th.
1 Co. 1 : 6. testimony of C. was c.
Ga. 3 : 15. if c. no man disannull.
17. covenant c. before of God
He. 2 : 3. was c. unto us by them
6 : 17. he c. it by an oath

CONFIRMETH, ING.

Nu. 30 : 14. bonds upon her, he c.
De. 27 : 26. Cursed he c-h not words
Is. 44 : 26. c-h word of his servant
Mk. 16 : 20. c-g word with signs
Ac. 14 : 22. c-g souls of the disciples
15 : 41 thro. Syria c-g churches

CONFISCATION.

Ezr. 7 : 26. judgm. he executed to c.

CONFLICT.

Ps. 39 : † 10. I am consumed by c.
Ph. 1 : 30. same c. ye saw in me
Col. 2 : 1. knew c. I have for you

CONFORMABLE.

Ph. 3 : 10. made c. to his death

CONFORMED.

Ro. 8 : 29. c. to image of his Son
12 : 2. be not c. to this world, but

CONFOUND.

Ge. 11 : 7. c. their language, 9.
Je. 1 : 17. lest I c. thee bef. them
1 Co. 1 : 27. to c. wise, to c. things

CONFOUNDED.

2 K. 19 : 26. inhab. were c., Is. 37 : 27.
Jb. 6 : 20. c. bec. they had hoped
Ps. 35 : 4. be c. that seek my soul
69 : 6. let not those seek thee be c.
71 : 13. be c. adversaries to my soul
24. are c. that seek my hurt
83 : 17. Let them be c. forever
97 : 7. c. be all that serve images
129 : 5. let all be c. that hate Zion
Is. 1 : 29. c. for gardens ye have
19 : 9. that weave net works be c.
37 : 27. their inhabitants were c.
Je. 9 : 19. c. because forsaken land
10 : 14. founder c. by image, 51 : 17.
17 : 18. be c. that persecute me
46 : 24. dau. of E. c. | 48 : 20. Moab c.
49 : 23. Hamath c. | 50 : 2. Bel c.
50 : 12. Your mother be sore c.
51 : 47. Bab. her whole land be c.
51. c. bec. we heard reproach
Eze. 16 : 52. be thou c., 54, 63.
Mi. 7 : 16. nations be c. at might
Zch. 10 : 5. riders on horses be c.
Ac. 2 : 6. the multitude were c.
9 : 22. Saul c. the Jews at Damas.

Ashamed and CONFOUNDED. [70 : 2

Ps. 40 : 14. a. a. c. that seek my soul,
Is. 24 : 23. moon be c. a. sun a.
41 : 11. incensed ag. thee be a. a. c.
45 : 16. idol makers sh. be a. a. c.
54 : 4. shall not be a. neither c.

Je. 14 : 3. nobles were a. a. c.
15 : 9. hath borne 7 been a. a. c.
22 : 22. then shalt thou be a.a.c.
31 : 19. I was a. yea c. bec. I did
Eze. 36 : 32. be a.a.c. for your ways
Mi. 3 : 7. seers a. a. diviners c.

Not CONFOUNDED.

Ps. 22 : 5. our fathers were n. c.
Is. 45 : 17. nor c. world with. end
50 : 7. God will help, I n. be c.
1 Pe. 2 : 6. believeth shall n. be c.

CONFUSED.

Is. 9 : 5. battle is with c. noise
Ac. 19 : 32. the assembly was c.

CONFUSION.

Ge. 11 : † 9. is the name of it c.
Le. 18 : 23. a beast to lie thereto is c.
20:12. they have wrought c. ⌈c. (2)
1 S. 20 : 30. chosen Da. to thine own
Ezr. 9 : 7. delivered to c. of face
Jb. 10 : 15. I am full of c. see mine
Ps. 35 : 4. to c. th. devise my hurt
44 : 15. My c. is continu. before me
70. 2. to c. that desire my hurt
71 : 1. let me never be put to c.
109 : 29. cover thems. with own c.
Is. 24 : 10. city of c. is broken
30 : 3. in shadow of Egypt your c.
34 : 11. be stretch upon it line of c.
41 : 29. their molten images are c.
45 : 16. makers of idols sh. go to c.
61 : 7. for c. they shall rejoice in
Je. 3 : 25. and our c. covereth us
7 : 19. do they provoke thems. to c.
20 : 11. everl. c. never be forgot.
Da. 9 : 7. belongeth c. of faces, 8.
Ac. 19 : 29. city was filled with c.
1 Co. 14 : 33. God is not author of c.
Ja. 3 : 16. where envying there is c.

CONGEALED.

Ex. 15 : 8. depths were c. in sea

CONGRATULATE.

1 Ch. 18 : 10. of his welfare and c.

CONGREGATION.

Le. 4 : 21. it is a sin off. for c., 14.
10 : 17. given it you to bear iniq.
16 : 33. an atonem. for all c. ⌊of c.
Nu. 1 : 16. these the renowned of c.
10 : 7. when c. is to be gath. blow
14 : 27. How long sh. I bear evil c.
35. do it unto this evil c.
15 : 15. One ordinance sh. be for c.
16:21. Separate yours. from c. that
33. perished from am. c., 26 : 9.
45. Get you up from am. this c.
46. go unto c. make atonement
47. Aaron ran into midst of c.
19 : 9. c. of children of Israel for
20. soul shall be cut off from c.
20 : 2. no water for c., 27 : 14.
12. shall not bring c. into land
27 : 16. let L. set a man over c.
31 : 43. half that pertained unto c.
35 : 12. manslayer die not, until stand bef. c., 24, 25. Jos. 20 : 6.
De. 33 : 4. even inheritance of the c.
Jos. 9:27. drawers of water for the c.
Ju. 20 : 1. c. was gath. as one man
21 : 5. came not with c. to Lord
1 K. 12 : 20. they called Jerob. to c.
2 Ch. 29 : 31. c. bro-t in sacrifices
30 : 17. many in c. not sanctified
24. Hez. did give to c. 1000 bullocks
Ezr. 10 : 8. himself separated fr. c.
Ne. 8 : 2. priest bro-t law before c.
13 : 1. Moabite not come into c.
Jb. 15 : 34. c. of hypocrites be deso.
30 : 28. I stood up and cried in c.
Ps. 1 : 5. nor sinners in c. of righte.
7 : 7. c. of people compass thee
22 : 22. in c. will I praise thee
26 : 5. I hated c. of evil doers
58 : 1. Do ye speak righte., O c.?
68 : 10. Thy c. hath dwelt therein
74:2. Rem. c. thou hast purchased
19. forget not c. of thy poor
75 : 2. when receive c. I will judge
Ps. 82:1. G. standeth in c. of mighty
89 : 5. thy faithf. in c. of saints
107 : 32. let them exalt him in c.
111 : 1. I will praise the L. in c.
Pr. 5 : 14. in all evil in midst of c.
21 : 16. remain in c. of dead ⌈c.
Is. 14 : 13. I will sit upon m-t of the
Je. 6 : 18. know, O c. what is among
30 : 20. c. be established bef. me
La. 1 : 10. they not enter into thy c.
Ho. 7 : 12 chastise as c. hath heard
Jo. 2 : 16. gather people sanctify c.
Ac 13 : 43. when c. was broken up

All the CONGREGATION.

Le. 8 : 3. gather a. c. unto door of
9 : 5. a. c. drew near bef. L. ⌊tab.
16 : 17. make atonement for a. c.
24:14. a. c. stone him, 16. Nu. 15:35.
Nu. 1 : 2. Take ye sum of a. c., 26:2.
14 : 10. a. c. bade stone them
16 : 3. seeing a. c. are holy ⌈c.
22. one sin, thou be wroth with a.
20 : 27. up in sight of a. c., 25 : 6.
27 : 19. set him before a. c., 22.
Jos. 8 : 35. Josh. read not bef. a. c.
9 : 18. a. c. murmured ag. princes
22 : 20. wrath fell on a. c. of Isr.
1 K. 8 : 14. king blessed a. c., 55.
1 Ch. 29 : 20. a. c. blessed the L. G.
2 Ch. 6 : 13. upon knees bef. a. c.
23 : 3. a. c. made cov. with the k.
29 : 28. a. c. worshipped. singers
30 : 2. a. c. to keep passover ⌊sang
Ne. 5:13. a. c. said, Amen, and praised
8 : 17. a. c. that made booths

Elders of the CONGREGATION.

Le. 4 : 15. e. o. c. shall lay hands
Ju. 21:16. e. o. c. said, How for wives

Great CONGREGATION.

1 K. 8 : 65. Sol. held a feast, all Isr. a g. c., 2 Ch. 7 : 8.–30 : 13.
Ezr. 10:1. assembl. out of Isr. a g. c.
Ps. 22 : 25. my praise of thee in g. c.
35 : 18. give thee thanks in g. c.
40 : 9. preached righte. in g. c.
10. not concealed truth fr. g. c.

CONGREGATION of Israel

Ex. 12 : 6. c. o. I. kill it in even-g
19. soul be cut off from c. o. I.
47. c. o. I. shall keep passover
Le. 4:13. if c. o. I. sin thro. ignorance
Nu. 16 : 9. L. separ. you from c. o. I.
2 Ch. 5 : 6. c. o. I. sacrificed sheep
24 : 6. acc. to com-t of c. o. I.

CONGREGATION of the Lord.

Nu. 16:3. why lift you above c. o. L.
20 : 4. c. o. L. into this wilder.
27 : 17. c. o. L. not as sheep that
31:16. plague am. c. o. L., Jos. 22:17.
De. 23 : 1. not enter into c. o. L., 2. 3.
8. enter into c. o. L. in 3d gene.
Jos. 22 : 16. saith whole c. o. L.
1 Ch. 28 : 8. in sight of c. o. L. keep
Mi. 2:5. cast a cord in c. o. L. ⌊com.

Tabernacle of the CONGREGATION.

Ex. 29 : 10. bullock bef. t. o. c.
44. I will sanctify t. o. c.
31 : 16. service of the t. o. c.
26. thou shalt anoint t. o. c.
33 : 7. called it t. o. c. went to (2)
35 : 21. work of t. o. c., Nu. 4 : 3, 23, 25, 30, 35, 39, 43.
Le. 1 : 1. spake out of t. o. c.
3 : 8. kill it before t. o. c., 13.
4 : 5. priest sh. bring it to t. o. c.
6 : 30. bro-t into t. o. c. to recon.
10:7. not go out from door of t. o. c.
9. no wine wh. ye go into t. o. c.
16:16. do for t. o. c. | 33. atonem. for
Nu. 8 : 9. bring Levites bef. t. o. c.
12 : 4. Come out ye three to t. o. c.
14 : 10. glory of Lord in t. o. c.
17 : 4. lay up in t. o. c. ⌈23:32.
18 : 4. keep charge of t. o. c., 1 Ch.
Nu 19 : 4. of her blood bef. t. o. c.
25 : 6. weeping bef. door of t. o. c.
De. 31 : 14. present yours. in t. o. c.
Jos. 18 : 1. at Shiloh set up t. o. c.
1 K. 8 : 4. bro-t t. o. c., 2 Ch. 5 : 5.
2 Ch. 1 : 3. there was the t. o. c.
See DOOR.

Tent of the CONGREGATION.

Ex. 39 : 32. t. o. c. finished
40 : 2. set up t. o. c.
40:22. table in t. o. c. | 24. candlest.
26. he put golden altar in t. o. c.
34. a cloud covered t. o. c.
35. Moses not able to enter t. o. c.

Whole CONGREGATION.

Ex. 16 : 2. w. c. of Isr. murmured
Le. 4 : 13. w. c. sin thro. ignorance
Nu. 3 : 7. sh. keep charge of w. c.
14 : 2. w. c. said, Would G. that we
Jos. 22 : 18. will be wroth with w. c.
Ju. 21 : 13. w. c. sent to Benjamin
2 Ch. 6 : 3. king blessed the w. c.
Ezr. 2 : 64. w. c. 42,360, Ne. 7 : 66.
Pr. 26 : 26. wick. be shewed bef. w. ⌊c.

CONGREGATIONS.

Ps. 26 : 12. in c. will I bless Lord
68 : 26. Bless ye God in the c.
74 : 4. Thine enemies roar in thy c.

CONI'AH.

Je. 22:24. though C. were signet upon ⌈hand
28. is this man C. broken idol?
37 : 1. Zed. reigned instead of C.

CONONI'AH.

2 Ch. 31 : 12. C. the Levite ruler, 13.

CONQUER, ING.

Re. 6 : 2. he went forth c. and to c.

CONQUERORS.

Ro. 8:37. in all we are more than c.

CONSCIENCE, S.

Ec. 10 : † 20. curse not king in c.
Jn. 8 : 9. convicted by their own c.
Ac. 23 : 1. I have lived in good c.
24 : 16. a c. void of offence
Ro. 2 : 15. their c. bearing witness
9 : 1. my c. bearing me witness
13 : 5. be subject for c. sake
1 Co. 8 : 7. with c. of idol eat it, and c. weak is defiled
10. weak c. be embold. to eat?
12. wound weak c. ye sin ag. C.
10 : 25. no question for c. sake, 27.
28. eat not, for his and c. sake
29. c. I say, not thine own
2 Co. 1 : 12. testimony of our c.
4 : 2. commending to ev. man's c.
5 : 11. made manifest in your c-s
1 Ti. 1 : 5. out of a good c.
19. Holding faith and good c.
3 : 9. mystery of faith in pure c.
4 : 2. c. seared with a hot iron
2 Ti. 1 : 3. whom I serve with c.
Tit. 1 : 15. mind and c. is defiled
He. 9 : 9. perfect, as pertain-g to c.
14. purge c. from dead works
10 : 2. had no more c. of sins
22. hearts sprinkl. from evil c.
13 : 18. trust we have a good c.
1 Pe. 2 : 19. if for c. endure grief
3 : 16. Having a good c. as they
21. the answer of a good c.

CONSECRATE.

Ex. 28 : 3. c. Aaron | 41. c. A's sons
29 : 9. c. Aaron and sons, 30 : 30.
35. seven days c., Le. 8 : 33.
32 : 29. c. yours. this day to L.
Le. 16 : 32. c. to minis. in priest's
Nu. 6:12. c. unto L. days of separa.
1 Ch. 29:5. to c. his service unto L.
2 Ch. 13 : 9. to c. himself with a
Eze. 43 : 26. they shall c. thems.
Mi. 4 : 13. I will c. their gain unto ⌊L.

CONSECRATED.

Le. 21 : 10. c. to put on garments
Nu. 3 : 3. whom he c. to minister
Jos. 6 : 19. vessels of brass, are c.
Ju. 17 : 5. Micah c. one of sons, 12.

1 K. 13: 33. whoso. would, Jorob. c.
2 Ch. 26: 18. c. to burn incense
29: 31. have c. yourselves unto L.
33. c. things were 600 oxen
31: 6. tithe of holy things c.
Ezr. 3: 5. all feasts that were c.
He. 7: 28. Son, who is c. for everm.
10: 20. By a living way he hath c.

CONSECRATION, S.

Ex. 29: 22. it is a ram of c., Le. 8: 22.
34. if flesh of c-s remain
Le. 7: 37. this is the law of the c-s
8: 28. c-s for a sweet savour unto
31. eat bread in basket of c-s [L.
33. days of your c. be at an end
Nu. 6: 7. c. of his G. upon his head
9. defiled the head of his c.

CONSENT, ED, EDST, ING.

Ge. 34: 15. But in this will we c.
23. only let us c. unto them, they
De. 13: 8. shalt not c. unto him
Ju. 11: 17. sent to k., but not c.
1 K. 20: 8. said. Hearken not, nor c.
2 K. 12: 8. c. to receive no more mon.
Ps. 50: 18. sawest a thief, thou c.
Pr. 1: 10. if sinners entice, c. not
Da. 1: 14. so he c-d to them, and
Lu. 23: 51. had not c. to the deed of
Ac. 8: 1. Saul c-g unto his dea., 22: 20.
18: 20. to tarry longer, he c-d not
Ro. 1: † 32. not only do, but c. with
7: 16. I c. unto law that it is good
1 Ti. 6: 3. c. not to wholesome words

CONSENT. [Noun.] [c.

1 S. 11: 7. they came out with one
Ps. 83: 5. consulted with one c.
Hos. 6: 9. the priests murder by c.
Zph. 3: 9. L. to serve with one c.
Lu. 14: 18. with one c. to make excuse
1 Co. 7: 5. except with c. for a time

CONSIDER.

Ex. 33: 13. c. this nation is thy peo.
Le. 13: 13. priest sh. c. the leprosy
De. 4: 39. c. it in thine heart
8: 5. c. in heart, as man chasteneth
32: 7. c. the years of many gene.
29. wise to c. their latter end
Ju. 18: 14. c. what ye have to do
19: 30. c. of it, take advice
1 S. 12: 24. c. how great things done
25: 17. c. what thou wilt do
Jb. 11: 11. will he not then c. it?
23: 15. when I c. I am afraid of
34: 27. would not c. of his ways
37: 14. c. wondrous works of God
Ps. 5: 1. O Lord c. my meditation
8: 3. When I c. thy heavens
9: 13. O Lord, c. my trouble
13: 3. c. me | 25: 19. c. my enem.
37: 10. shalt diligently c. his place
45: 10. Hearken O dau. and c.
48: 13. c. her palaces, that ye tell
50: 22. c. this, ye that forget God
64: 9. shall wisely c. of his doing
119: 95. will c. thy testimonies
153. c. mine affliction, deliver me
159. c. how I love thy precepts
Pr. 6: 6. go to the ant, c. her ways
23: 1. with a ruler c. what is bef. thee
24: 12. that pondereth heart c. it?
Ec. 5: 1. c. not that they do evil
7: 13. c. the work of God, who
14. but in day of adversity c.
Is. 1: 3. my people doth not c.
5: 12. neither c. operation of his
14: 16. shall narrowly c. thee
18: 4. will c. in my dwelling-place
41: 20. see, and know, and c.
43: 18. nor c. the things of old
52: 15. had not heard sh. they c.
Je. 2: 10. c. if be such a thing
23: 20. in latter days c. it, 30: 24.
La. 1: 11. c.; for I am become vile
2: 20. c. to whom hast done this
5: 1. O Lord, c. our reproach
Eze. 12: 3. it may be they will c.
Da. 9: 23. underst., and c. the vision
Ho. 7: 2. they c. that I remember
Ha. 1: 5. saith L., c. your ways, 7.
2: 15 I pray you, c. fr. this day, 18.
Mat. 6: 28. c. the lilies, Lu. 12: 27.
Lu. 12: 24. c. the ravens, they
Jn. 11: 50. Nor c. it is expedient
Ac. 15: 6. elders came to c. of this
2 Ti. 2: 7. c. and L. give underst.
He. 3: 1. brethren, c. the Apostle
7: 4. c. how great this man was
10: 24. let us c. one ano. to provoke
12: 3. c. him endured contradic.

CONSIDERED, EST.

1 K. 3: 21. when I c. in morning
5: 8. I have c. things thou sentest
Jb. 1: 8. Hast thou c. Job? 2: 3.
Ps. 31: 7. thou hast c. my trouble
77: 5. I have c. the days of old
Pr. 24: 32. I saw and c. it well
Ec. 4: 1. I c. all oppressions done
4. I c. all travail and every work
15. I c. all the living which walk
9: 1. for all this I c. to declare
Je. 33: 24. c-t not what peo. have
Da. 7: 8. I c. the horns [spoken
Mat. 7: 3. c-t not beam in own eye
Mk. 6: 52. they c. not the miracle
Ac. 11: 6. I c. and saw beasts
12: 12. when Peter had c. thing
Ro. 4: 19. he c. not his own body

CONSIDERETH, ING.

Ps. 33: 15. he c. all their works
41: 1. Blessed is he that c. the poor
Pr. 21: 12. righte. man. c. house of
† 29. upright, he c. his way [wick.
28: 22. c. not poverty shall come
29: 7. righte. c. cause of poor [it
31: 16. She c. a field, and buyeth
Is. 44: 19. none c. in his heart to
57: 1. none c. that righte. is taken
Eze. 18: 14 c-h and doeth not, 28.
Da. 8: 5. as I was c-g, a he goat
Ga. 6: 1. c-g thyself, lest be tempted
He. 13: 7. c-g end of their conversa.

CONSIST, ETH.

Lu. 12: 15. life c-h not in abund.
Col. 1: 17. by him all things c.

CONSOLATION, S.

Jb. 15: 11. Are c-s of God small?
21: 2. and let this be your c-s
Is. 66: 11. satisfi. with breasts of c-s
Je. 16: 7. nor give them cup of c.
Lu. 2: 25. Simeon, waiting for c.
6: 24. rich, ye have receiv. your c.
Ac. 4: 36. which is, the son of c.
15: 31. they rejoiced for the c.
Ro. 15: 5. God of c. grant you to be
2 Co. 1: 5. our c. aboundeth by C.
6. afflicted, for your c. and salva.
comforted for your c.
7. shall ye be partakers of c.
7: 7. by c. wh. he was comforted
Ph. 2: 1. If any c. in C., fulfil ye
2 Th. 2: 16. hath given us everl. c.
Phm. 7. have great c. in thy love
He. 6: 18. we might have a strong c.

CONSORTED.

Ac. 17: 4. c. with Paul and Silas

CONSPIRACY.

2 S. 15: 12. Absa.'s c. was strong
2 K. 12: 20. his servants made a c.
14: 19. c. ag. Amaziah, 2 Ch. 25: 27.
15: 15. acts of Shallum and his c.
30. Hoshea made a c. ag. Pekah
17: 4. king of Assyria found c. in
Je. 11: 9. c. found am. men of Jud.
Eze. 22: 25. is a c. of her prophets
Ac. 23: 13. forty had made this c.

CONSPIRATORS.

2 S. 15: 31. Ahithophel is among c.

CONSPIRED.

Ge. 37: 18. c. against Jo. to slay
1 S. 22: 8. all have c. against me
13. why have ye c. ag. me, thou
1 K. 15: 27. Baasha c. ag. Nadab
16: 9. Zimri c. ag. Elah and slew, 16.
2 K. 9: 14. Jehu c. against Joram
10: 9. I c. ag. my master and slew
15: 10. Shallum c. ag. Zach., and
25. Pekah c. ag. Pekahiah, and
21: 23. serv. of Amon c., 2 Ch. 33: 24.
24. slew all c. ag. Amon, 2 Ch. 33: 25.
2 Ch. 24: 21. they c. ag. Jehoiada
25. serv. of Joash c. ag him, 26
Ne. 4: 8. c. all of them to fight
Am. 7: 10. Amos hath c. ag. thee

CONSTANT, LY.

1 Ch. 28: 7. if he be c. to do my com.
Ezr. 9: † 8. us a c. abode in holy
Ps. 51 † 10. renew c. spirit within
Pr. 21: 28. that heareth, speaketh, c.
Ac. 12: 15. Rhoda c. affirmed it
Tit. 3: 8. these things affirm c.

CONSTELLATIONS.

2 K. 23: † 5. that burnt incense to c.
Is. 13: 10. c. shall not give th. light

CONSTRAIN, ED, ETH.

2 K. 4: 8. woman c. him to eat
Jb. 32: 18. spirit within me c-h
Mat. 14: 22. J. c. disciples, Mk. 6: 45
Lu. 24: 29. c-d him, saying, Abide
Ac. 16: 15. Lydia c. us to come
28: 19. I was c. to appeal to Cesar
2 Co. 5: 14. love of Christ c-h us
Ga. 6: 12. c. you to be circumcised

CONSTRAINT.

1 Pe. 5: 2. the oversight. not by c.

CONSULT, ED, ETH.

1 K. 12: 6. Rehob. c. with old, 8.
1 Ch. 13: 1. David c. with captains
2 Ch. 20: 21. Jehosh. c. with people
Ne. 5: 7. then I c-d with myself
Ps. 62: 4. only c. to cast him down
83: 3. c-d against thy hidden ones
5. have c. with one consent
Eze. 21: 21. king of Bab. c. images
Da. 6: 7. presidents and capt. c-d
Mi. 6: 5. remember what Balak c.
Ha. 2: 10. c-d shame to thy house
Mat. 26: 4. c-d might take Jesus
Lu. 14: 31. c-h whe. with 10,000
Jn. 12: 10. c-d to put Laz. to death

CONSULTATION.

Mk. 15: 1. chief priests held a c.

CONSULTER.

De. 18: 11. a c. with spirits

CONSUME.

Ge. 41: 30. famine shall c. land
Ex. 33: 3. lest I c. thee in way, 5.
Le. 26: 16. ague shall c. eyes
De. 5: 25. this fire will c. us
7: 16. thou shalt c. all peo. which
28: 38. locust shall c. it, 42.
32: 22. a fire in anger c. earth
Jos. 24: 20. c. after done you good
1 S. 2: 33. man be to c. thine eyes
2 K. 1: 10 let fire c. thee, 12.
Jb. 15: 34. fire c. tab. of bribery
20: 26. a fire not blown c. him
24: 19. heat c. snow waters
Ps. 37: 20. c. into smoke c. away
39: 11. his beauty to c. away
49: 14. their beauty c. in grave
78: 33. days did he c. in vanity
Is. 7: 20. it shall c. beard
10: 18. c. glory of his forest
27: 10. shall calf c. branches [dad
Je. 49: 27. fire c. palaces of Ben-ha-
Eze. 4: 17. c. away for iniquity
13: 13. great hailstones to c. it
21: 28. sword is furbished to c.
22: 15. I will c. thy filthiness
24: 10. kindle fire, c. the flesh
35: 12. are given us to c.
Da. 2: 44. it shall c. these kingd-s
7: 26. domin., to c. and destroy it
Ho. 11: 6. sword c. his branches
Zph. 1: 2. I will c. all off land
3. I will c. man and beast
Zch. 5: 4. remain in house c. it
14: 12. eyes, tongue shall c. away
2 Th. 2: 8. Wicked, whom L. sh. c.
Ja. 4: 3. may c. it on your lusts

CONSUME them.
Ex. 32: 10. wax hot I may c.t.,12.
Nu. 16: 21. c. t. in a moment, 45
De. 7: 22. not c. t. at once
1 S. 15: † 18. Amal. tell thou c. t.
2 Ch. 18:†10. push Syria until c.t.
Ne. 9: 31. didst not utterly c. t.
Es. 9: 24. Haman cast lot to c. t.
Ps. 59: 13. c. t. in wrath, c. t.
Je 8: 13. I will surely c. t. saith
14: 12. I will c. t. by sword
Eze. 20:13. fury upon them to c. t.
Lu. 9: 54. fire to c. t. as Elias did

CONSUMED.
Ge. 19: 15. lest be c. in iniquity
17. to mountain, lest be c.
31: 40. in day drought c. me
Ex. 3: 2. behold, bush was not c.
15: 7. wrath c. them as stubble
22: 6. if corn be c. therewith [off.
Le. 6: 10. fire hath c. with burnt
9: 24. c. upon altar burnt off.
Nu. 11: 1. c. them in uttermost
12: 12. of whom flesh is half c.
16: 26. lest ye be c. in their sins
35. fire c. the 250 men
21: 28. fire hath c. Ar of Moab
25: 11. that I c. not chil. of Israel
32: 13. generation done evil was c.
De. 2: 16. men of war were c.
Jos. 5: 6. men of war, of E. were c.
Ju. 6: 21. fire out of rock c. flesh
1 S. 27: † 1. I shall one day be c.
2 S. 18 †39. soul of David was c.
21: 5. The man that c. us
22: 39. I have c. them
1 K. 18: 38.fell and c. sac.,2 Ch.7:1.
2 K. 1: 10. fire c. his fifty, 12.
7: 13. as all Israelites that are c.
2 Ch. 8: 8. whom chil. of Isr. c. not
Ne. 2: 3. gates thereof are c., 13.
Jb. 1: 16. fire of God c. sheep
4: 9. by breath of his nostrils c.
6: 17. snow and ice are c.
7: 9. cloud is c. and vanisheth
19: 27. reins c. | 33: 21. flesh is c.
Ps. 6: 7. Mine eye c., 31: 9.
10. my bones c., 102: 3.
39: 10. c. by blow of thy hand
64: † 6. c. by that they searched
71: 13. let them be c. that are
73: 19. utterly c. with terrors
78: 63. fire c. their young men
90: 7. we are c. by thine anger
104: 35. Let sinners be c. out of
119: 87 they had almost c. me
139. My zeal hath c. me, because
Pr. 5: 11. flesh and body are c.
Is. 16: 4. oppressors c. out of land
29: 20. the scorner is c. and all
64: 7. c. us because of iniquities
Je. 5: 3 c. they refused correction
6: 29. lead is c. | 12: 4. beasts
20: 18. days be c. with shame
36: 23. until all the roll was c.
44: 18. we have been c. by sword
La.2: 22. those I swaddled enemy c.
3: 22. of Lord's mercies we not c.
Eze. 19: 12. rods fire c., 22: 31.
24: 11. scum of it may be c.
43: 8. wherefore I have c. them
Mal. 3: 6. sons of Jacob are not c.
Ga. 5: 15. ye be not c. one of ano.

Shall be CONSUMED.
Nu. 14: 35. in wilder. s. they b. c.
17: 13. s. we b. c. with dying?
1 S. 12: 25. ye s. b. c. and king
Pr. 22: † 8. with his anger he s.b.c.
Is. 1: 28. that forsake L. s. b. c.
66: 17. eat swine's flesh, s. b. c.
Je. 14: 15. by famine s. proph. b. c.
16: 4. s. b. c. by sword,44:12, 27.
Eze. 5: 12. with famine s. b. c.
13: 14. it shall fall and ye s. b. c.
34: 29. s. b. no more c. with hung.
47: 12. nor s. fruit thereof b. c.
Da. 11: 16. land which s. b. c.

CONSUMED,
with **till** or **until.**
De. 2: 15. destroy u. c., Jos. 5: 6.
28: 21. u. he have c. thee [c.
Jos. 8: 24. edge of sw. u. they were
10: 20. slaying them t. c.
1 S. 15: 18. fight u. they be c.
2 S. 22: 38. I turned not u. I had
c. them, Ps. 18: 37.
1 K. 22: 11. push Syrians u. c. th.,
2 K. 13: 17, 19. 2 Ch. 18: 10.
Ezr. 9: 14. angry t. hadst c. us
Je. 9: 16. send sword t. I have c.
them, 24: 10.-27: 8.-49: 37.

CONSUMETH, ING.
De. 4: 24. G. is a c. fire, He. 12:29.
9: 3. L. goeth before thee as c. fire
Jb. 13: 28. he c. as a garment
22: 20. remnant of them fire c.
31: 12. fire that c. to destruction
Is. 5: 24. as the flame c. chaff

CONSUMMATION.
Da. 9: 27. make desolate until c.

CONSUMPTION.
Le. 26: 16. appoint over you c.
De. 28: 22. L. smite thee with c.
Ju. 20: † 40. whole c. of the city
Is. 10: 22. c. decreed shall overflow
23. the Lord shall make a c.
28:22. I have heard from Lord a c.

CONTAIN.
1 K. 8: 27. heaven of heav. cannot
c. thee, 2 Ch. 2: 6.-6: 18.
18: 32. as would c. 2 meas. of seed
Eze. 45: 11. bath may c. tenth
Jn. 21: 25. world not c. the books
1 Co. 7: 9. if cannot c. let th. marry

CONTAINED, ETH, ING.
1 K. 7: 26. c-d 2,000 baths
38. one laver c-d 40 baths
Eze. 23: 32. sister's cup c-h much
Jn. 2: 6. six water-pots c-g two
Ro. 2: 14. by nature thi. c-d in law
Ep. 2: 15. abol. law c. in ordinan-
1 Pe. 2: 6. it is c. in scripture [ces

CONTEMN, ED, ETH.
Ps. 10: 13. Wheref. do wicked c. G.
15: 4. In eyes a vile person is c.
107: 11. c-d counsel of Most High
Can. 8: 7. substance would be c.
Is. 16: 14. glory of Moab be c.
Eze. 21: 10. it c-h rod of my son
13. what if sword c. rod?

CONTEMPT.
Ge. 38: † 23. lest we become a c.
Es. 1: 18. Thus arise too much c.
Jb. 12: 21. c. on princes, Ps.107:40.
31: 34. c. of families terrify me
Ps. 119: 22. Remove from me c.
123: 3. we are filled with c.
4. soul filled with c. of proud
Pr. 18: 3. wicked cometh, then c.
Is. 23: 9. into c. the honourable
Da. 12: 2. shall awake to everl. c.

CONTEMPTIBLE.
Mal. 1: 7. say, table of Lord is c.
12. meat c. | 2: 9. I made you c.
2 Co. 10: 10. his speech c.

CONTEMPTUOUSLY.
Ps. 31: 18. speak c. ag. righteous

CONTEND.
De. 2: 9. neither c. in battle, 24.
Jb. 9: 3. If c. he cannot ans. one
13: 8. will ye c. for God?
Pr. 28: 4. such as keep the law c.
Ec. 6: 10. nor may he c. with him
Is. 49: 25. I will c. with him
50: 8. who will c. with me?
57: 16. I will not c. forever
Je. 12: 5. how c. with horses?
18: 19. to voice of them that c.
Am. 7: 4. Lord called to c. by fire
Mi. 6: 1. c. thou bef. the mountain
Jude 3. earnestly c. for the faith

CONTENDED.
Ne. 13: 11. c. I with rulers, 17.
25. I c. with them and cursed

Jb. 31: 13. servants when they c.
Is. 41: 12. not find them that c.
Ac. 11: 2. of circum. c. with him

CONTENDEST, ETH, ING.
Jb. 10: 2. shew me wherefore c-t
40: 2. that c-h with Almighty
Pr. 29: 9. If wise c-h with foolish
Jude 9. when c-g with the devil

CONTENT. [Adjective.]
Ge. 37: 27. sell him breth. were c.
Ex. 2: 21. Moses c. to dwell
Le. 10: 20. heard that, he was c.
Jos. 7: 7. would we had been c.
Ju. 17: 11. Levite c. to dwell
19: 6. Be c. and tarry all night
2 K. 5: 23. Naaman said, Be c.
6: 3. one said, Be c. and go with
Jb. 6: 28. Now therefore be c.
Pr. 6: 35. neither will he rest c.
Lu. 3: 14. be c. with your wages
Ph. 4: 11. in every state to be c.
1 Ti. 6: 8. raiment, let us be c.
He. 13: 5. be c. with such things
3 Jn. 10. not c. with prating

CONTENT. [Verb].
Mk. 15: 15. Pilate willing to c.

CONTENTION.
Ge. 26: † 20. he called the well c.
Ps. 95: † 8. harden not as in c.
Pr. 13: 10. by pride cometh c.
17: 14. leave off c. bef. it be med.
18: 6. fool's lips enter into c.
22: 10. Cast out scorner, c. sh. go
Is. 41: † 12. not find men of thy c.
Je. 15: 10. borne me a man of c.
Ha. 1: 3. there are that raise up c.
Ac. 15: 39. the c. was so sharp
Ph. 1: 16. The one preach Ch. of c
1 Th. 2: 2. to speak gospel with c.

CONTENTIONS.
Pr. 18: 18. lot causeth c. to cease
19. c. like bars of castle [15.
19:13. c. of wife are a dropping, 27:
21: † 9. than with woman of c.
23:29. Who hath woe? who hath c.
1 Co. 1: 11. there are c. am. you
Tit. 3: 9. avoid c. and strivings

CONTENTIOUS.
Pr. 21: 19. than with c. woman
26: 21. c. man to kindle strife
27: 15. dropping and c. woman
Ro. 2: 8. unto them that are c.
1 Co. 11: 16. if any seem to be c.

CONTENTMENT.
1 Ti. 6: 6. godliness with c. is gain

CONTINUAL.
Ex. 29: 42. be a c. burnt offering
Nu. 4: 7. the c. bread shall be
2 Ch. 2: 4. house for c. shewbread
Ne. 10: 33. for the c. meat offering
Pr. 15: 15. merry heart c. feast
19: 13. conten-s of wife a c. drop.
27: 15. A c. dropping in rainy day
Is. 14: 6. smote with a c. stroke
Je. 48: 5. c. weeping shall go up
52: 34. c. diet giv. him, 2 K.25:30.
Eze. 39: 14. men of c. employment
Lu. 18: 5. lest by c. coming she
Ro. 9: 2. c. sorrow in my heart
See BURNT OFFERING.

CONTINUALLY.
Ge. 6: 5. imagination was evil c.
8: 3. waters ret. from off earth c.
Ex. 28: 30. upon heart bef. Lord c.
29: 38. two lambs day by day c.
Le. 24: 2. oil to cause lamps to burn
8.set it in order bef. the L. c. [c.
Jos. 6:13. horns bef. ark went on c.
1 S. 18: 29. Saul Da.'s enemy c.
2 S. 9: 7. eat br. at my table c.
13. did eat c. at king's table
15: 12. peo. increased c. with Abs
1 K.10:8.serv. c. bef. thee, 2 Ch.9:7
2 K. 4: 9. man of G wh. passeth c.
25: 29. Jehoi. eat br. c., Je.52:33.
1 Ch. 16:6. priests with trumpets c.
11. seek L., seek his face c.

1 Ch. 16:37. to minister before ark c.
2 Ch. 12 : 15. wars betw. Jerob. c.
24 : 14. burnt off. in house of L. c.
36 : † 15. sent to them, rising up c.
Jb. 1:5. sanct. sons. Thus did Job c.
Ps. 34 : 1. his praise be c., 71 : 6.
35 : 27. c. the L. be magnified, 40: 16.=70 : 4.
38 : 17. sorrow c. before me
40 : 11. truth c. preserve me
42 : 3. c. say, Where is thy God?
44 : 15. My confusion c. before me
50 : 8. burnt offerings c. before me
52 : 1. goodn. of God endureth c.
58 : 7. melt as waters wh. run c.
69:23. make their loins c. to shake
70 : 4. say c., Let G. be magnified
71 : 3. whereunto I may c. resort
6. my praise be c. of thee
14. I will hope c. and yet
72:15. prayer sh. be made for him c.
73 : 23. I am c. with thee
74 : 23. tumult increaseth c.
109:10. Let his chil. be c. vagabonds
15. Let them be before Lord c.
119:44. So shall I keep thy law c.
109. My soul is c. in my hand
117. respect unto thy statutes c.
140 : 2. c. are gathered for war
Pr. 6 : 14. deviseth mischief c.
21. Bind them c. upon thy heart
Ec. 1:6. whirleth about c., and wind
Is. 21 : 8. c. upon watch tower
49 : 16. thy walls are c. before me
51 : 13. hast feared c. because
52 : 5. my name c. is blasphemed
58 : 11. Lord shall guide thee c.
60 : 11. thy gates shall be open c.
65 : 3. provoketh me to anger c.
Je. 6 : 7. before me c. is grief
33 : 18. to do sacrifice c.
Eze. 46 : 14. meat off. c. to the L.
Da. 6 : 16. God whom servest c., 20.
Ho. 4 : 18. committed whored. c.
12 : 6. and wait on thy God c.
Ob. 16. so shall heathen drink c.
Na. 3 : 19. thy wickedness passed c.
Ha. 1 : 17. not spare c. to slay na.?
Zch. 8 : † 21. let us go c. and pray
Lu. 24 : 53. c. in temple praising G.
Ac. 6 : 4. ourselves c. to prayer
10 : 7. waited on Cornelius c.
Ro. 13 : 6. c. upon this very thing
He. 7 : 3. abideth a priest c.
10 : 1. sacrifices year by year c.
13 : 15. the sacrifice of praise c.

CONTINUANCE.

De. 28 : 59. plagues and of long c.
Ps. 139 : 16. in c. were fashioned
Is. 64 : 5. in those is c.
Eze. 39 : † 14. sever out men of c.
Da. 1 † 10. liking than children of c.
Ro. 2 : 7. patient c. in well doing

CONTINUE.

Ex. 21 : 21. if he c. day or two
Le. 12 : 4. c. in the blood, 5.
1 S. 12 : 14. c. following the Lord
13 : 14. thy kingdom not c.
2 S. 7 : 29. that it may c. for ever
1 K. 2 : 4. L. may c. word he spake
Jb. 15 : 29. neither substance c.
17 : 2. eye c. in their provocation?
Ps. 36 : 10. O c. thy lovingkindness
49 : 11. that their houses shall c.
72 : † 17. shall be as a son to c.
102 : 28. chil. of thy servants c.
119 : 91. c. acc. to thy ordinances
Is. 5 : 11. c. until night, till wine
65 : † 22. elect make them c. long
Je. 32 : 14. may c. many days
Da. 11 : 8. c. more years than king
Mat. 15 : 32. c. now three days
Jn. 8 : 31. If ye c. in my word
15 : 9. c. ye in my love
Ac. 13 : 43. to c. in grace of God
14 : 22. exhorting to c. in faith
26 : 22. I c. unto this day
Ro. 6 : 1. Shall we c. in sin, th. grace
11 : 22. thou c. in his goodness
Ga. 2 : 5. truth of gospel might c.
Ph. 1 : 25. I shall c. with you all
Col. 1 : 23. If ye c. in the faith
4 : 2. c. in prayer, and watch
1 Ti. 2 : 15. if they c. in faith
4 : 16. doctrine ; c. in them
2 Ti. 3 : 14. c. in things learned
He. 7 : 23. not suffer to c. by death
13 : 1. Let brotherly love c.
Ja. 4 : 13. c. there a year and buy
2 Pe. 3 : 4. all things c. as they were
1 Jn. 2 : 24. ye shall c. in the Son
Re. 13 : 5. power to c. 42 months
17 : 10. he must c. a short space

CONTINUED.

Ge. 40 : 4. he served them, and c.
1 S. 1 : 12. as she c. praying before
1 K. 22 : 1. c. 3 years without war
2 Ch. 29 : 28. c. till burnt off. was
Ne. 5 : 16. I c. in the work of wall
Jb. 27 : 1. Job c. his parable, 29 : 1
Ps. 72 : 17. his name be c. as sun
Je. 31 : † 32. sho. I have c. a husb.
Da. 1 : 21. Dan. c. to year of Cyrus
Mat. 20 : † 12. last have c. one hour
Lu. 6 : 12. c. all night in prayer
22 : 28. ye c. with me in tempta.
Jn. 2 : 12. c. there not many days
8 : 7. c. asking, he lifted up
11 : 54. there c. with disciples
Ac. 1 : 14. These c. in prayer
2 : 42. c. in apostles' doctrine
8 : 13. Simon c. with Philip
12 : 16. But Peter c. knocking
15 : 35. Paul and Barnabas c.
18 : 11. c. there a year and 6 mos.
19 : 10. c. by space of two years
20 : 7. Paul c. speech until midn.
27 : 33. c. fasting, having taken
He. 8 : 9. c. not in my covenant
1 Jn. 2 : 19. no doubt c. with us

CONTINUETH, ING.

Jb. 14 : 2. as shadow, and c-h not
Je. 30 : 23. a c. whirlwind, it
Ac. 2 : 46. c-g daily with one accord
Ro. 12 : 12. c-g instant in prayer
Ga. 3 : 10. Cursed c-h not in all thi.
1 Ti. 5 : 5. c-h in supplications
He. 7 : 24. because he c. ever
13 : 14. we have no c. city, but
Ja. 1 : 25. perfect law, c-h in it

CONTRADICTING.

Ac. 13 : 45. with envy c. blasphe-g

CONTRADICTION.

He. 7 : 7. without c. less is blessed
12 : 3. endured such c. of sinners

CONTRARIWISE.

2 Co. 2 : 7. c. ye ought to forgive
Ga. 2 : 7. c. when saw gospel was
1 Pe. 3 : 9. railing, but c. blessing

CONTRARY.

Le. 26 : 21. walk c., 23, 27, 40.
26 : 24. will I walk c., 28, 41.
Es. 9 : 1. though turned to c.
Eze. 16 : 34. c. is in thee, art c.
Mat. 14 : 24. for the wind was c.
Mk. 6 : 48. winds were c., Ac. 27 : 4.
Ac. 17 : 7. these do c. to decrees
18 : 13. to worship God c. to law
23:3. com-st me be smitten c. to law
26 : 9. c. to name of Jesus
Ro. 11 : 24. graffed c. to nature
16 : 17. c. to doctrine ye learned
Ga. 5 : 17. c. one to the other
Col. 2 : 14. handwriting c. to us
1 Th. 2 : 15. and are c. to all men
1 Ti. 1 : 10. c. to sound doctrine
Tit. 2 : 8. he of c. part be ashamed

CONTRIBUTION.

Ro. 15 : 26. c. for poor saints

CONTRITE.

Ps. 34 : 18. such as of c. spirit
51 : 17. c. heart, not despise
Is. 57 : 15. that is of c. spirit, to revive heart of c. ones
Is. 66 : 2. of c. spirit and trembleth

CONTROVERSY, IES.

De. 17 : 8. being matters of c.
19 : 17. betw. whom c. is, sh. stand
21 : 5. by their word c. be tried
25 : 1. If there be c. between men
2 S. 15 : 2. that had a c. came
2 Ch. 19 : 8. he set Levites for c-s
Is. 34 : 8. of recomp. for c. of Zion
Je. 25 : 31. L. hath c. with nations
Eze. 44 : 24. in c. they shall stand
Ho. 4 : 1. L. hath a c. with inhab.
12 : 2. L. hath a c. with Judah
Mi. 6 : 2. L. c. with his people [tery
1 Ti. 3 : 16. without c. great is mys-

CONVENIENT, LY.

Pr. 30 : 8. with food c. for me
Je. 40 : 4. it seemeth c. to go, 5.
Mk. 6 : 21. a c. day was come
14 : 11. might c-y betray him
Ac. 24 : 25. when a c. season, I will
Ro. 1 : 28. to do things not c.
1 Co. 16 : 12. when have c. time
Ep. 5 : 4. talking, nor jesting, c.
Phm. 8. to enjoin thee that c.

CONVERSANT.

Jos. 8 : 35. strangers c. amo. them
1 S. 25 : 15. long as we were c.

CONVERSATION.

Ps. 37 : 14. as be of upright c.
50 : 23. ordereth his c. aright
2 Co. 1 : 12. in sincerity we had c.
Ga. 1 : 13. ye have heard of my c.
Ep. 2 : 3. had our c. in times past
4 : 22. concerning the former c.
Phm. 1 : 27. c. as becometh gospel
3 : 20. For our c. is in heaven
1 Ti. 4 : 12. be an example in c.
He. 13 : 5. c. be without covetous.
7. considering end of their c.
Ja. 3 : 13. shew out of a good c.
1 Pe. 1:15. holy in all manner of c.
18. not redeemed from vain c.
2 : 12. c. honest among Gentiles
3 : 1. may be won by c. of wives
2. while they behold chaste c.
16. falsely accuse your good c.
2 Pe. 2 : 7. vexed with the filthy c.
3 : 11. ought ye to be in all holy c.

CONVERSION.

Ac. 15 : 3. declaring c. of Gentiles

CONVERT, ED.

Ps. 51 : 13. sinners be c. unto thee
Is. 6 : 10. lest c. and be healed
60 : 5. abundance of sea be c.
Mat. 13:15. be c. and heal, Mk. 4:12.
18 : 3. c-d and become as children
Lu. 22 : 32. c. strengthen brethren
Jn. 12 : 40. be c. and I, Ac. 28 : 27.
Ac. 3 : 19. Repent ye and be c.
Ja. 5 : 19. do err, and one c. him

CONVERTETH, ING.

Ps. 19 : 7. law is perfect, c-g soul
Ja. 5 : 20. he which c-h a sinner

CONVERTS.

Is. 1 : 27. her c. be redeemed with

CONVEY, ED.

1 K. 5 : 9. I will c. them by sea
Ne. 2 : 7. c. me over till I come
Jn. 5 : 13. Jesus c-d himself away

CONVICTED.

Jn. 8 : 9. c. by their conscience

CONVINCE, ED, ETH.

Jb. 32 : 12. none of you c-d Job
Jn. 8 : 46. Wh. of you c-h me of sin?
16 : † 8. when come he will c.
Ac. 18 : 28. mightily c-d the Jews
1 Co. 14 : 24. he is c. of all, he
Tit. 1 : 9. be able to c. gainsayers
Ja. 2 : 9. c-d of law as transgressors
Jude 15. to c. all that are ungodly

CONVOCATION.

Ex. 12 : 16. a holy c., Le. 23 : 2, 3, 4, 7, 8, 21, 24, 27, 35, 36, 37. Nu. 28 : 18, 25.=29 : 1, 7, 12.
Nu. 28 : 26. day of first-fr. holy c.

CONY, IES. See CONEY.

COOK, S.

Ge. 40 : † 17. was work of a c.
1 S. 8 : 13. daughters to be c-s
9 : 23. Samuel said to c. Bring
24. c. took up the shoulder

COOL. [Noun.]

Ge. 3 : 8. walking in c. of day

COOL. [Adjective.]

Pr. 17 : † 27. is of a cool spirit

COOL. [Verb.]

Lu. 16 : 24. and c. my tongue

CO'OS.

Ac. 21 : 1. we came unto C.

COPIED.

Pr. 25 : 1. men of Hezekiah c.

COPING.

1 K. 7 : 9. from foundation unto c.

COPPER.

Ezr. 8 : 27. two vessels of fine c.

COPPERSMITH.

2 Ti. 4 : 14. Alex. the c. did evil

COPULATION.

Le. 15 : 16. seed of c. go out
17. skin whereon is seed of c.
18. with whom lie with seed of c.

COPY.

De. 17 : 18. write him c. of law
Jos. 8 : 32. c. of law of Moses
Ezr. 4 : 11. c. of letter sent, 5 : 6.
23. c. of Artax. letter was read
7 : 11. this is c. of letter Artax.
Es. 3 : 14. c. of a writing for, 8 : 13.
4 : 8. Mordecai gave Hatach a c.

COR.

Eze. 45 : 14. of a bath out of the c.

CORAL.

Jb. 28 : 18. No mention made of c.
Eze. 27 : 16. Syria thy merch. in c.

CORBAN.

Mk. 7 : 11. It is C. that is, a gift

CORD.

Jos. 2 : 15. let spies down by a c.
Jb. 30 : 11. he hath loosed my c.
41 : 1. draw out tongue with a c.?
Ec. 4 : 12. threefold c. not broken
12 : 6. Or ever silver c. be loosed
Mi. 2 : 5. a c. by lot in the congr.

CORDS.

Ex. 35 : 18. court and their c., 39 : 40. Nu. 3 : 26, 37.-4 : 26, 32.
Ju. 15 : 13. Samson with new c.
14. c. upon arms became as flax
Es. 1:6. c. of fine linen and purple
Jb. 36 : 8. if holden in c. of afflic.
Ps. 2 : 3. let us cast away their c.
118 : 27. bind the sacrifice with c.
129 : 4. hath cut c. of wicked
140 : 5. proud have hid c. for me
Pr. 5 : 22. holden with c. of his sins
Is. 5 : 18. that draw iniq. with c.
33 : 20. nor any of c. be broken
54:2. lengthen c.strengthen stakes
Je. 10 : 20. spoiled, my c. broken
38 : 6. they let down Jere. with c.
12. let them down by c.
13. they drew up Jere. with c.
Eze. 27 : 24. chests bound with c.
Ho. 11 : 4. I drew with c. of man
Jn. 2 : 15. a scourge of small c.

CORE.

Jude 11. in gainsaying of C.

CORIANDER.

Ex. 16 : 31. like c. seed, Nu. 11 : 7.

COR'INTH.

Ac. 18:1. aft. these Paul came to C.
19 : 1. pass while Apollos was at C.
1 Co. 1 : 2. ch. of God at C. them sanctified in C. J., 2 Co. 1 : 1.
2 Co. 1 : 23. I came not as yet to C.
2 Ti. 4 : 20. Erastus abode at C.

CORIN'THIANS.

Ac. 18 : 8. many of the C. believed
2 Co. 6 : 11. O ye C. our mouth is

CORMORANT.

Le. 11 : 17. have in abom. little owl, c. and great owl, De. 14 : 17.
Is 34. 11. c. possess it, Zph. 2:14.

CORN.

Ge. 41 : 49. Jo. gath. c. as sand, 35.
57. came to Joseph to buy c.
42 : 2. heard was c. in E., Ac.7:12.
19. carry c. for famine of your
43 : 2. when they had eaten c.
Ex. 22 : 6. stacks of c. be consumed
Le. 2 : 16. priest burn beaten c.
23 : 14. eat bread nor parched c.
Nu. 18 : 27. as c. of threshing floor
De. 16 : 9. begin-t to put sickle to c.
25 : 4. not muzzle ox treadeth out c., 1 Co. 9 : 9. 1 Ti. 5 : 18.
Jos. 5 : 11. did eat of the old c., 12.
Ru. 2:14. he reached her parched c.
3:7. Boaz to lie down at heap of c.
1 S.17:17.Take for breth.parched c.
25 : 18. Abigail took of parched c.
2 S. 17:28. they brought parched c.
2 K. 19:26. as blasted c., Is.37 : 27.
Ne. 5 : 2. we take up c. for them
3. that we might buy c.
10. might exact of them c.
Jb. 5 : 26. as a shock of c. cometh
24 : 6. reap ev. one his c. in field
39:4. Their young grow up with c.
Ps. 65 : 9. preparest them c.
13. valleys are covered with c.
72:16. be handful of c. in the earth
78 : 24. given of the c. of heaven
Pr. 11 : 26. withhold. c. peo. curse
Is. 17 : 5. harvest man gathereth c.
28 : 28. Bread c. is bruised
62:8. no more give thy c. to enem.
Eze. 36 : 29. I will call for the c.
Ho. 2 : 9. I will take away my c. in
10:11. Ephr. loveth to tread out c.
14 : 7. they shall revive as the c.
Jo. 1 : 10. for the c. is wasted
17. barns broken, c. is withered
Am. 8:5. new moon gone may sell c.
9 : 9. I will sift Isr. as c. is sifted
Mk. 4 : 28. after that the full c.
Jn. 12 : 24. Exc. a c. of wheat fall

Ears of CORN.

Ge. 41 : 5. seven e.o.c. came up
Le. 2 : 14. offer green e. o. c. dried
Ru. 2 : 2. glean e. o. c. after him
2 K. 4 : 42. brought full e. o. c. in
Jb. 24 : 24. are cut off as e. o. c.
Mat. 12 : 1. to pluck e. o. c., Mk. 2 : 23. Lu. 6 : 1.

CORN fields.

Mk. 2 : 23. went through c. on sabbath day, Mat. 12 : 1. Lu. 6 : 1.

CORN with floor.

Is. 21 : 10. my threshing and c. of my f. [c. f.
Ho. 9 : 1. loved a reward on every

Standing CORN.

Ex. 22 : 6. that s. c. be consumed
De. 23:25. come into s.c. of neighb.
Ju. 15 : 5. foxes into s.c. burn s.c.

CORN and wine.

Ge. 27:28. G. give plenty of c.a.w.
37. with c.a.w. I sustained him
De. 7 : 13. will bless thy c. a. w.
11:14. mayest gath. in thy c.a.w.
12:17.not eat tithe of c.a.w.,14:23.
16:13. after hast gath. thy c.a.w.
18 : 4. give firstfr. of thy c. a. w.
28:51. shall not leave thee c.w. or
33:28. Jac. be upon land of c.a.w.
2 K. 18:32. land of c.a.w.,Is.36:17.
2 Ch. 31 : 5. bro-t firstfr. of c. a.w.
32 : 28. Storehouses for c. a. w.
Ne. 5 : 11. restore part of c. w. a.
10:39.offer. of c.of new w.,13:5,12.
Ps. 4 : 7. than in time c.a.w. incr.
La. 2 : 12. say, Where is c. a. w.?
Ho.2:8. knew not I gave her c.a.w.
22. earth shall hear the c.a.w.
7 : 14. they assemble for c.a.w.
Jo. 2 : 19. I will send you c. a. w.
Hag. 1 : 11. for drought on c.a.w.
Zch. 9:17. c. shall make young men cheerful, a. new w. the maids

CORNELIUS.

Ac. 10 : 1. man in Cesarea called C, 3, 17, 21, 22, 24, 30.
7. angel which spake to C.
25. C. met Peter, fell at his feet
31. C. thy prayer is heard

CORNER.

Le 21 : 5. neith. shave c. of beard
2 Ch. 28 : 24. made altars in ev. c.
Ps. 118 : 22. become head stone of c.
Pr. 7 : 8. Passing near her c.
12. she lieth in wait at every c.
21 : 9. better to dwell in c., 25:24.
Is. 30 : 20. thy teachers not into c.
Je. 31:38. city be built to gate of c.
48 : 45. devour the c. of Moab
51 : 26. shall not take stone for a c.
Eze. 46 : 21. in every c. of court
Am. 3 : 12. in Sama. in c. of a bed
Zch. 10 : 4. Out of him came c.
Mat. 21 : 42. stone rejected, same is become head of c., Ps. 118 : 22. Mk. 12 : 10. Lu. 20:17. Ac. 4:11. 1 Pe. 2 : 7.
Ac. 26 : 26. this was not done in a c.

CORNER gate.

2 K. 14 : 13. from gate of Ephraim unto the c. g., 2 Ch. 25 : 23.
2 Ch. 26:9. towers at Jerus. at c.g.
Zch. 14 : 10. land be inhab. to c.g.

CORNER stone, s.

Jb. 38 : 6. who laid the c. s. thereof
Ps. 144:12.our dan-s may be as c.s-s
Is. 28 : 16. precious c.s., 1 Pe. 2:6.
Ep. 2 : 20. C. being the chief c.s.

CORNERS.

Ex. 25 : 12. put rings in four c. of ark, 26.-27 : 4.-37 : 3, 13.
26 : 23. boards make for c., 36:28.
27 : 2. horns upon four c., 38 : 2.
Le. 19 : 9. shalt not reap c., 23 : 22.
27.sh. not round c. of your heads
Nu. 24 : 17. smite the c. of Moab
De. 32 : 26. I will scatter th. into c.
1 K. 7 : 30. c. had under setters, 34.
1 S. 14 : † 38. ye c. of the people
Ne. 9 : 22. didst divide th. into c.
Jb. 1 : 19. smote four c. of house
Is. 11 : 12. gath. dispersed fr. 4 c.
Je. 9 : 26. I will punish all in uttermost c., 25 : 23. -49 : 32.
Eze. 7 : 2. end is come upon four c.
45 : 19. blood upon 4 c., 43 : 20.
46 : 21. pass by four c. of court
Zph. 3 : † 6. their c. are desolate
Zch. 9 : † 15. as c. of the altars
Mat. 6 : 5. they love to pray in c.
Ac. 10 : 11. sheet knit at 4 c., 11:5.
Re. 7 : 1. angels standing on four c.

CORNET, S.

Ex. 19 : † 13. c. sound. long come
2 S. 6 : 5. David played on c-s
1 Ch. 15 : 28. ark with sound of c.
2 Ch. 15 : 14. shouting with c-s
Ps. 98 : 6. with c. make joyful noise
150 : † 3. Praise him with c.
Da. 3 : 5. what time ye hear c., 15.
10. made decree, ev. man hear c.
Ho. 5 : 8. Blow ye the c. in Gibeah
Jo. 2 : † 1. Blow ye the c. in Zion

CORPSE, S.

2 K. 19 : 35. all dead c-s, Is. 37:36.
Na.3:3.no end of c-s, stumble on c-s
Mk. 6 : 29. disci. took John's c.

CORPULENT.

Je. 50 : † 11. grown c. as a heifer

CORRECT.

Ps. 39 : 11. dost c. man for iniquity
94 : 10. chasti. heathen, sh. not he
Pr. 29 : 17. c. thy son, and he [c.?
Je. 2 : 19. own wickedn. sh. c. thee
10:24. O L. c. me, but with judgm.
30 : 11. c. thee in measure, 46:28.

CORRECTED, ETH.

Jb. 5:17. happy is man whom G.c-h
Pr. 3 : 12. whom L. loveth, he c-h
29 : 19. serv. not be c. by words

He. 12 : 9. had fathers which c-d us

CORRECTION.

Jb. 37 : 13. rain, whether for c. or
Pr. 3 : 11. my son despise not his c.
7 : 22. He goeth as a fool to the c.
15 : 10. c. griev. to him th. forsak.
† 32. refuseth c. despiseth soul
22 : 15. rod of c. drive it from him
23 : 13. Withhold not c. fr. child
Je. 2 : 30. your chil. received no c.
5 : 3. they refused to receive c.
7 : 28. This nation receiveth not c.
Ho. 5 : † 2. I have been c. of them
Ha. 1 : 12. hast establ. them for c.
Zph. 3 : 2. she received not c.
2 Ti. 3 : 16. scripture profita. for c.

CORRUPT. [Adjective.]

Ge. 6 : 11. earth also was c., 12.
Ju. 2 : † 19. was dead they were c.
Jb. 17 : 1. My breath is c. my
Ps. 14 : 1. They are c., 53 : 1.-73 : 8.
38 : 5. My wounds are c.
Pr. 25 : 26. as a c. spring
Eze. 20 : 44. according to c. doings
23 : 11. c. in her inordinate love
Da. 2 : 9. prepared c. words
Mal. 1 : 14. cursed th. sacri. c. thing
Mat. 7 : 17. c. tree bring evil fruit
18. nor c. tree good fr., Lu. 6:43
12 : 33. make tree c. and fruit c.
Ep. 4 : 22. put off the old man c.
29. let no c. communication
1 Ti. 6 : 5. disputings of c. minds
2 Ti. 3 : 8. men of c. minds

CORRUPT. [Verb.]

De. 4 : 16. lest ye c. yourselves, 25.
31 : 29. after my death ye will c.
Da. 11 : † 17. give him the dau. to c.
32. shall he c. by flatteries
Mal. 2 : 3. I will c. your seed
Mat. 6:19. moth and rust doth c., 20.
1 Co. 15 : 33. evil communica. c.
2 Co. 2 : 17. many that c. the word
Jude 10. in those things they c.
Re. 11 : † 18. them that c. earth
19 : 2. great whore did c. earth

CORRUPTED, ETH, ING.

Ge. 6 : 12. for all flesh had c. his
Ex. 8 : 24. the land was c.
32 : 7. get thee down, thy people
have c., De. 9 : 12.-32 : 5.
Ju. 2 : 19. c-d more than fathers
Eze. 16 : 47. wast c. more than
28 : 17. thou hast c. thy wisdom
Da. 11 : 17. give him dau. c-h her
Ho. 9 : 9. have deeply c. thems. as
Am. 1 : † 11. and c-d his compassions
Zph. 3 : 7. they rose early and c.
Mal. 2 : 8. ye have c. cov. of Levi
Lu. 12 : 33. where no moth c-h
2 Co. 7 : 2. we have c. no man
11 : 3. lest minds be c. fr. simplic.
Ja. 5 : 2. your riches are c.

CORRUPTERS.

Is. 1 : 4. children that are c.
Je. 6 : 28. iron, they are all c.

CORRUPTIBLE.

Ro. 1 : 23. image like to c. man
1 Co. 9 : 25. to obtain a c. crown
15 : 53. this c. must put on incor.
1 Pe. 1 : 18. not redeemed with c.
23. born again not of c. seed
3 : 4. in that which is not c.

CORRUPTION.

Le. 22 : 25. their c. is in them
2 K. 23 : 13. on right of mount of c.
Jb. 17 : 14. to c. Thou my father
Ps. 16 : 10. neither suffer Holy One
to see c., Ac. 2 : 27.-13 : 35.
49 : 9. live for ever, and not see c.
Is. 38 : 17. hast deliv. from pit of c.
Da. 10 : 8. my comeliness into c.
Jon. 2:6. hast brought my life fr. c.
Ac. 2:31. neither his flesh did see c.
13 : 34. no more to return to c.
36. David laid to his fa-s saw c.
37. whom God raised saw no c.
Ro. 8 : 21. deliv. from bondage of c.
1 Co. 15 : 42. is sown in c. raised in
50. neither c. inherit incorrup.
Ga. 6 : 8. shall of all flesh reap c.
2 Pe. 1 : 4. escaped the c. that is
2 : 12. perish in their own c.
19. they are the servants of c.

CORRUPTLY.

2 Ch. 27 : 2. the people did yet c.
Ne. 1 : 7. We have dealt c. ag. thee

CO'SAM.

Lu. 3 : 28. Addi son of C.

COST. [Noun.]

2 S. 19:42. eaten at all of king's c.?
1 Ch. 21:24. nor burnt off. without c.
Lu. 14 : 28. and counteth c.

COST. [Verb.]

2 S. 24 : 24. nor offer that c. noth.

COSTLINESS.

Re. 18:19. ships made rich by her c.

COSTLY.

1 K. 5 : 17. they brought c. stones
7 : 9. All these were of c. stones
10. foundation was of c. stones
11. and above were c. stones
Jn. 12 : 3. took spikenard, very c.
1 Ti. 2 : 9. not with c. array

COTES.

2 Ch. 32:28. Hez. made c. for flocks

COTTAGE, S.

Is. 1 : 8. dau. of Zion is left as a c.
24 : 20. earth be removed like c.
Zph. 2:6. sea coast be c-s for sheph.

COUCH, ES.

Ge. 49 : 4. Reuben went to my c.
Jb. 7 : 13. I say, my c. shall ease
Ps. 6 : 6. I water my c. with tears
Am. 3 : 12. in Damascus in a c.
6 : 4. that stretch upon their c-s
Lu. 5 : 19. let him down with his c.
24. Arise, take up thy c. and go
Ac. 5 : 15. they laid sick on c-s

COUCH, ED.

Ge. 49 : 9. Judah c-d as a lion
Nu. 24 : 9. He c-d he lay as a lion
Jb. 38 : 40. When they c. in dens

COUCHETH, ING.

Ge. 49 : 14. Issa., ass c-g down
De. 33:13. for deep that c-h beneath
Eze. 25 : 5. make Ammonites a c-g [place

COULD, EST.

Ge. 27 : 1. Isaac old, he c. not see
Ex. 8 : 18. to bring lice, but c. not
1 S. 3 : 2. Eli's eyes dim, he c. not
1 K. 14 : 4. Ahijah c. not see [see
2 K. 3 : 26. break to k. but c. not
1 Ch. 21 : 30. Da. c. not go bef. it
2 Ch. 13:7. Rehob. c. not withs. th.
Ps. 37 : 36. but he c. not be found
Is. 5:4. c. been done more to viney.?
Je. 3 : 5. hast done evil as thou c-t
15 : 1. my mind c. not be tow. peo.
Eze. 16 : 28. c-t not be satisfied
Jon. 1 : 13. bring it to land, but c.
Mk. 6 : 19. Herodias would have
killed him but she c. not
9 : 18. and they c. not, Lu. 9 : 40.
14 : 8. She hath done what she c.
Jn. 21 : 25. world c. not contain
Ac. 13:39. c. not be justified by law

COULTER, S.

1 S. 13 : 20. Isr. to sharpen each his
21. they had a file for their c. [c.

COUNCIL, S.

2 S. 23:† 23. Da. set Benaiah over c.
Ps. 68 : 27. princes of Judah and c.
Mat. 5 : 22. Raca in danger of c.
10 : 17. deliv. up to c-s, Mk. 13 : 9.
12 : 14. Pharisees held a c.
26:59. c. sought false wit., Mk. 14:
Mk. 15 : 1. c. bound Jesus [55.
Lu. 22:66. led Jesus into their c.
Jn. 11:47. priests gath. c., Ac. 5:21.
Ac. 4 : 15. com-d to go out of c.
5 : 27. and set them before c.
34. stood up in c. a Pharisee
41. departed from c. rejoicing
Ac. 6 : 12. brought Stephen to c.
15. all in c. looking on him
22 : 30. com-ed their c. to appear
23 : 1. Paul beholding the c.
6. he cried out in c. Men
15. ye with c. signify to captain
20. Paul to morrow into c.
28. brought him into their c.
24 : 20. evil in me, while before c.
25 : 12. Festus conferred with c.

COUNSEL.

Ex. 18 : 19. I will give thee c.
Nu. 27 : 21. Eleazar ask c. for him
31 : 16. c. of Balaam to trespass
De. 32 : 28. a nation void of c.
Jos. 9 : 14. asked not c. at Lord
Ju. 20 : 7. give here your c.
2 S. 15:31. c. of Ahith. foolishness
34. mayest defeat the c. of A.
16 : 23. all c. of Ahith. with Da.
17 : 14. L. defeated c. of Ahith.
20 : 18. sh. surely ask c. at Abel
1 K. 1 : 12. let me give thee c.
12 : 8. forsook c. of old men, 13.
2 Ch. 10 : 8, 13.
14. c. of the young men, 9.
28. took c. made calves of gold
2 K. 6:8. took c. with his servants
18 : 20. c. for war, Is. 36 : 5.
1 Ch. 10 : 13. Saul died for ask. c.
2 Ch. 22 : 5. Ahaziah after their c.
25 : 16. Art made of king's c.
30:2. king taken c. to keep passo.
23. assembly took c. to keep
32 : 3. Hez. took c. with princes
Ezr. 10 : 3. acc. to c. of my lord
10 : 8. according to c. of princes
Ne. 4 : 15. brought c. to nought
Jb. 5 : 13. c. of froward headlong
10 : 3. shine on c. of wicked
12 : 13. he hath c. and underst.
21 : 16. c. of wick. is far, 22 : 18.
38 : 2. darkeneth c. by words?
42 : 3. hideth c.. without knowl.?
Ps. 1 : 1. not in c. of ungodly
14 : 6. shamed the c. of poor
16 : 7. bless L. hath given me c.
20 : 4. the Lord fulfil all thy c.
31 : 13. while they took c. ag. me
33 : 10. c. of heathen to naught
55 : 14. We took sweet c. together
64 : 2. from secret c. of wicked
73 : 24. shalt guide me with thy c.
83 : 3. crafty c. against thy people
106 : 13. waited not for his c. but
43. provoked him with their c.
107 : 11. contemned c. of M. High
Pr. 8 : 14. c. is mine, and wisdom
11 : 14. Where no c. is peo. fall
12 : 15. hearkeneth to c. is wise
15 : 22. With. c. purposes disapp.
19:20. Hear c. receive instruction
20 : 5. c. in man like deep water
18. Every purpose establ. by c.
21 : 30. no wisdom nor c. ag. L.
24 : 6. by wise c. shalt make war
27: 9. sweet. of friend by hearty c.
Is. 5 : 19. c. of H. One draw nigh
7 : 5. taken evil c. against thee
11 : 2. spirit of c. rest upon him
19 : 3. I will destroy c. of Egypt
11. c. of counsellors brutish
23:8. taken this c. against Tyre?
28:29. L. which is wonderful in c.
29 : 15. seek deep to hide c. fr. L.
40 : † 13. who of his c. taught
14. With whom took he c.
44:26. performeth c. of his messen.
Je. 18 : 18. nor c. perish from wise
23. knowest all their c. ag. me
19 : 7. make void the c. of Judah
32 : 19. mighty God, great in c.
38 : 15. if I give c. wilt not thou
49 : 7. is c. perished from prudent
30. king of Bab. taken c. ag. you
Eze. 7 : 26. c. perish from ancients
11 : 2. give wicked c. in this city

Eze. 18 : †9. not be in c. of my peo.
Da. 2 : 14. Daniel answered with c.
Ho. 4 : 12. my peo. ask c. at stocks
Mi. 4:12. neither understand his c.
Zch. 6 : 13. c. of peace betw. both
Mat. 22 : 15. Pharisees took c. how
27 : 1. chief priests and elders of
people took c. against Jesus
7. took c. and bought potter's
28 : 12. taken c. they gave money
Mk. 3 : 6. took c. ag. Jes., Jn. 11:53.
Lu. 23 : 51. not consented to c. of
Jn. 18 : 14. now Caiaphas gave c.
Ac. 4 : 28. thy c. determined bef.
5 : 33. they took c. to slay them
38. if this c. of men, it will come
9 : 23. Jews took c. to kill him
27 : 42. soldiers c. to kill prisoners
Ep. 1 : 11. after c. of his own will
He. 6 : 17. immutability of his c.

COUNSEL of God, or Lord.

Ju. 18 : 5. they said, Ask c. o. G.
20:18. chil. of Isr. asked c.o.G., 23.
1 S. 14 : 37. Saul asked c. o. G.
Ps. 33 : 11. c. o. L. stand, Pr. 19:21.
Is. 19 : 17. because of the c. o. L.
Je. 23:18. who hath stood in c.o.L.
49 : 20. Theref. hear c.o.L., 50:45.
Lu. 7 : 30. Lawyers rejected c.o.G.
Ac. 2 : 23. by determinate c. o. G.
20 : 27. to declare all c. o. G.

My COUNSEL. [c.

2 Ch. 25:16. not hearkened unto m.
Jb. 29:21. men kept silence at m.c.
Ps. 119 : † 24. the men of m. c.
Pr. 1 : 25. set at nought m. c.
30. they would none of m. c.
Is. 46 : 10. m.c. shall stand, I will
11. execu. m.c. from far country
Je. 23:22. if they had stood in m.c.
Da. 4 : 27. O king, let m. c. be

Own COUNSEL.

Jb. 18 : 7. his o. c. cast down
Ho. 10:6. Isr. be ashamed of his o.c.

Take COUNSEL.

Ne. 6 : 7. Come now, let us t. c.
Ps. 2 : 2. rulers t. c. against Lord
13 : 2. How long t. c. in my soul
71 : 10. that wait for my soul, t. c.
Is. 8 : 10. t. c. it come to nought
16 : 3. t. c. execute judgment
30 : 1. that t. c. but not of me
45 : 21. Tell ye, let them t. c.

COUNSELS.

Jb. 37 : 12. it is turned by his c.
Ps. 5 : 10. let them fall by own c.
81 : 12. walked in their own c.
Pr. 1 : 5. shall attain unto wise c.
12 : 5. c. of wicked are deceit
22:20. I writ. excellent things in c.
Is. 25 : 1. c. of old are faithfulness
47 : 13. wearied in mult. of thy c.
Je. 7 : 24. in c. of their evil heart
Ho. 11 : 6. devour bec. of own c.
Mi. 6 : 16. in c. of house of Ahab
1 Co. 4 : 5. make manif. c. of heart

COUNSEL, LED.

2 S. 16 : 23. which Ahithophel c-d
17 : † 7. that Ahith. c-d is not good
11. I c. that all Israel be gath.
15. Ahith. did c. and thus I c-d, 21.
2 Ch. 25:†16. G. hath c. to destroy
Jb. 26 : 3. How hast thou c. him
Ps. 32 : † 8. I will c. thee
Ec. 8:2. I c. thee to keep king's com-t
Re. 3:18. I c. thee to buy of me gold

COUNSELLOR.

2 S. 15 : 12. David's c., 1 Ch. 27 : 33.
1 Ch. 26 : 14. Zechariah a wise c.
27 : 23. Jonathan was a c.
2 Ch. 22 : 3. Athaliah was his c.
Is. 3 : 3. Lord taketh away c.
9 : 6. be called Wonderful, C.
40 : 13. who being his c. hath
41 : 28. for I beheld, was no c.
Mi. 4 : 9. is thy c. perished?
Na. 1 : 11. out of thee a wicked c.
Mk. 15 : 43. Joseph a c., Lu. 23:50.
Ro. 11 : 34. who hath been his c.

COUNSELLORS.

2 Ch. 22 : 4. c. after father's death
Ezr. 4 : 5. hired c. against them
7 : 14. art sent of king and his c.
15. king and c. fully offered
28. extended mercy to me bef. c.
8 : 25. gold king and c. offered
Jb. 3 : 14. at rest with c. of earth
12 : 17. leadeth c. away spoiled
Ps. 119 : 24. thy testimonies my c.
Pr. 11 : 14. multi. of c. safety, 24: 6.
12 : 20. to c. of peace is joy
15 : 22. in multi. of c. established
Is. 1 : 26. restore thy c. as at begin.
19 : 11. wise c. of Pha. brutish
Da. 3 : 24. said to c. Did we not cast
27. the king's c. saw these men
4 : 36. my c. sought unto me
6 : 7. all the c. have consulted

COUNT. [Noun.]

Ex. 12 : 4. your c. for the lamb

COUNT. [Verb.]

Le. 19 : 23. c. fruit as uncircum.
23 : 15. c. from morrow after
25 : 27. let c. years of sale, 52.
Nu. 23 : 10. can c. dust of Jacob
1 S. 1 : 16. c. not me dau. of Belial
Jb. 19 : 15. maids c. me stranger
31 : 4. Doth not be c. all my steps
Ps. 87 : 6. L. c. when he writeth
139 : 18. If I c. th. more than sand
22. I c. them my enemies
Mi. 6 : 11. Shall I c. them pure
Ac. 20 : 24. neither c. I my life dear
Ph. 3 : 8. I c. all loss, c. but dung
13. I c. not to have apprehended
2 Th. 1 : 11 c. you worthy of call.
3 : 15. c. him not as an enemy
1 Ti. 6 : 1. c. masters worthy of
Phm. 17. If thou c. me a partner
Ja. 1 : 2. c. it joy when ye fall
5 : 11. we c. happy which endure
2 Pe. 2 : 13. c. it pleasure to riot
3 : 9. as some men c. slackness
Re. 13 : 18. c. number of beast

COUNTED.

Ge. 15:6. c. it to him for righte, Ps.
106 : 31. Ro. 4 : 3. Ga. 3 : 6.
30 : 33. be c. stolen with me
31 : 15. Are we not c. strangers
Le. 25 : 31. c. as fields of country
Nu. 18 : 30. c. unto Lev. as increase
1 K. 1 : 21. I and Sol. be c. offend.
3 : 8. cannot be c. for multitude
1 Ch. 21 : 6. Benjamin c. he not
23 : 24. c. by names by their polls
Ne. 13 : 13. were c. faithful
Jb. 18 : 3. Wheref. we c. as beasts
41 29. Darts are c. as stubble
Ps. 44 : 22. we are c. as sheep
88 : 4. c. with them go to the pit
Pr. 17 : 28. hold. peace is c. wise
27 : 14. be c. a curse to him
Is. 5 : 28. hoofs be c. like flint
32 : 15. field be c. for a forest
33 : 18. where is he c. towers
40 : 15. nations c. as small dust
17. nations c. less than nothing
Ho. 8 : 12. were c. as strange thing
Mat. 14:5. c. him proph., Mk. 11:32.
Lu. 21 : 36. be c. worthy to escape
Ac. 5 : 41. rejoicing were c. worthy
19 : 19. burned books, c. price
Ro. 2 : 26. uncir. be c. for circum.
4 : 3. c. unto him for righteousness
5. his faith is c. for righteousness
9 : 8. children of prom. c. for seed
Ph. 3 : 7. those I c. loss for Christ
2 Th. 1 : 5. be c. worthy of kingd.
1 Ti. 1 : 12. that he c. me faithful
5 : 17. elders c. worthy of double
He. 3 : 3. c. worthy of more glory
7 : 6. he whose descent is not c.
10 : 29. c. blood of cov. unholy
See ACCOUNTED.

COUNTETH, ING.

Jb. 19 : 11. c-h me of enem. 33:10
Ec. 7 : 27. c-g one by one, to find
Lu. 14 : 28. first, and c-h the cost

COUNTENANCE. [Verb.]

Ex. 23 : 3. Neither c. a poor man

COUNTENANCE, S.

Ge. 4:5. Cain was wroth, c. fell
24 : † 6. damsel was of good c.
31 : 2. Jacob beheld c. of Laban
5. father's c. not toward me
Nu. 6 : 26. L. lift his c. upon thee
De. 28 : 50. a nation of fierce c.
Ju. 13 : 6. his c. like c. of angel
1 S. 1 : 18. her c. no more sad
16:7. Look not on his c. or height
12. Da. was of beautiful c., 17:42.
25 : 3. Abigail | 2 S. 14 : 27. Tamar
2 S. 23 : † 21. slew a man of c.
2 K. 5 : † 1. Naaman lifted in c.
8 : 11. settled his c. on Hazael
Ne. 2 : 2. Why is thy c. sad
3. why not c. sad, when city
Jb. 14 : 20. thou changest his c.
29 : 24. light of my c. cast not d-n
Ps. 4 : 6. lift light of thy c. upon us
10 : 4. thro. pride of c. not seek G.
11 : 7. c. doth behold upright
21 : 6. made him glad with thy c.
42 : 5. praise him for help of c.
11. who is health of my c., 43 : 5.
44 : 3. light of thy c. did save them
80 : 16. perish at rebuke of thy c.
89 : 15. walk, O L. in light of thy c.
90 : 8. secret sins in light of thy c.
Pr. 15 : 13. maketh a cheerful c.
16 : 15. In light of king's c. is life
25 : 23. so angry c. a backbiting
27 : 17. so man sharpeneth c. of
Ec. 7 : 3. by sadness of c. heart is
Can. 2 : 14. see c. thy c. is comely
5 : 15. his c. is as Lebanon
Is. 3 : † 3. man eminent in c.
9. c. doth witness against them
Eze. 27 : 35. be troubled in their c.
Da. 1:13. let our c-s be looked upon
15. their c-s appeared fairer
5 : 6. king's c. was changed
8 : 23. king of fierce c. stand up
Mat. 6 : 16. as hypocrites, of sad c.
28 : 3. c. like lightning, Lu. 9:29.
Ac. 2 : 28. full of joy with thy c.
2 Co. 3 : 7. not behold Moses, for c.
Re. 1 : 16. c. was as sun shineth
See CHANGED.

COUNTERVAIL.

Es. 7 : 4. not c. king's damage

COUNTRIES.

Ge. 26 : 3. unto thy seed these c., 4.
41 : 57. all c. came to buy corn
Jos. 13:32. c. wh. Moses did distrib.
14 : 1. c. chil. of Israel inherited
2 K. 18 : 35. Who among all c. that
1 Ch. 22:5. house of glory through c.
2 Ch. 20 : 29. fear of G. on all those c.
34 : 33. abom. out of all the c.
Ezr. 3:3. fear, because of people of c.
4:20 kings which ruled over all c.
Ps. 110 : 6. wound over many c.
Is. 8 : 9. give ear ye of far c.
Je. 23 : 3. I will gather my flock
out of all c., 8.–32 : 37.
28 : 8. prophesied against many c.
Eze. 5 : 5. Jerusalem in midst of c.
6. changed statutes more than c.
6 : 8. when scattered through c.
11:16. tho. I scattered them among
c. little sanctuary in c. [34:41.
17. assemble you out of c., 20 :
12 : 15. disperse them in the c.,
20 : 23.–29 : 12.–36 : 19, 24.
20 : 32. as families of the c.
22 : 4. a mocking to all c.
25:7. cause thee to perish out of c.
29 : 12. disperse through c., 36:19.
35 : 10. These two c. shall be mine
Da. 9 : 7. all the c. whither driven

Da. 11 : 40. he shall enter into c.
41. many c. be overthrown
42. forth his hand upon the c.
Zch. 10 : 9. remember me in far c.
Lu. 21 : 21. that are in c. enter

COUNTRY.

Ge. 19 : 28. smoke of c. went
24 : 4. thou shalt go unto my c.
29 : 26. not be so done in our c.
30 : 25. that I may go unto my c.
34 : 2. Shechem prince of c.
36 : 6. into c. from face of Jacob
42 : 33. lord of c. said unto us
Nu. 15 : 13. all born in c. shall do
32 : 4. c. Lord smote before Israel
De. 4 : 43. Beser in the plain c.
26 : 3. come into c. Lord sware
Jos. 2 : 2. to search out the c., 3.
6 : 27. fame noised through all c.
7 : 2. Go up and view the c.
19 : 51. made end of dividing c.
Ju. 8 : 28. c. in quietness 40 years
11 : 21. Israel possessed that c.
16 : 24. the destroyer of our c.
Ru. 1 : 2. came into c. of Moab
22. returned out of c. of Moab
2 S. 15 : 23. all the c. wept
18 : 8. battle scattered over all c.
21 : 14. Saul buried they in c.
1 K. 20 : 27. Syrians filled the c.
2 K. 3 : 20. c. filled with water
18 : 35. deliv. c. out of mine hands
Ne. 12 : 28. out of the plain c.
Is. 1 : 7. c. is desolate, cities burnt
20 : † 6. inhabitants of this c.
22 : 18. like a ball in a large c.
Je. 2 : 7. bro-t you into plentiful c.
22 : 10. not see his native c.
26. into c. wh. ye were not born
31 : 8. bring them from north c.
48 : 21. judgment upon plain c.
50 : 9. an assembly from north c.
51 : † 49. slain of all the c.
Eze. 20 : 38. bring them forth of c.
25 : 9. glory of c. Beth-jeshimoth
32 : 15. c. shall be destitute [c.
47 : 22. be unto you as born in the
Jon. 4 : 2. when yet in my c.
Mi. 1 : † 11. inhab. of c. of flocks
Mat. 8 : 28. c. of the Gergesenes
9 : 31. his fame in all that c.
14 : 35. into all that c.
Mk. 5 : 1. c. of Gadarenes, Lu. 8 : 26.
5 : 10. not send them out of c.
14. told it in the c., Lu. 8 : 34.
6 : 36. into c. round, Lu. 9 : 12.
5, 6. into villages or c.
15 : 21. coming out of c., Lu. 23 : 26.
16 : 12. walked and went into c.
Lu. 2 : 8. in the same c. shepherds
3 : 3. into all the c. about Jordan
4 : 37. place of c. round about
8 : 37. c. of Gadarenes round a-
15 : 15. joined to citizen of that c.
Jn. 11 : 54. unto c. near wilderness
55. many went out of the c.
Ac. 4 : 36. Levite of c. of Cyprus
12 : 20. their c. was nourished
18 : 23. over all c. of Galatia
27 : 27. they drew near to some c.
He. 11 : 9. as in a strange c.
14. plainly that they seek a c.
15. been mindful of that c.
16. desire better c. a heavenly

Far COUNTRY.

Jos. 9 : 6. We be come from f. c., 9.
1 K. 8 : 41. out of a f. c., 2 Ch. 6 : 32.
2 K. 20 : 14. They are come from a
f. c. even Babylon, Is. 39 : 3.
Pr. 25 : 25. so good news from f. c.
Is. 13 : 5. from f. c. to destr. land
46 : 11. executeth counsel fr. f. c.
Je. 4 : 16. watchers come from f. c.
6 : 20. sweet cane from a f. c.
8 : 19. them that dwell in f. c.
Mat. 21 : 33. househ. went into a f.
c., Mk. 12 : 1. Lu. 20 : 9
Mat. 25 : 14. is as man trav-g into f. c.
Lu. 15 : 13. his journey into f. c.
19 : 12. nobleman went into f. c.

Own COUNTRY.

Le. 16 : 29. whether one of your o.
c., 17 : 15.–24 : 22.
1 K. 10 : 13. she went to her o. c.
11 : 21. that I may go to my o. c.
22 : 36. proclam. ev. man to his o. c.
Je. 51 : 9. every one into his o. c.
Mat. 2 : 12. depart. into their o. c.
13 : 54. into his o. c. he taught,
Mk. 6 : 1. [Lu. 4 : 24.
57. save in his o. c., Mk. 6 : 4.
Mk. 6 : 1. he came into his o. c.
Jn. 4 : 44. proph. no honour in his [o. c.

Thy COUNTRY.

Ge. 12 : 1. Abram, get thee out of
t. c., Ac. 7 : 3.
32 : 9. Return to t. c. and kindred
Nu. 20 : 17. Let us pass thro. t. c.
Jon. 1 : 8. what is t. c.? of what
Lu. 4 : 23. do also here in t. c.

COUNTRY villages.

1 S. 6 : 18. of fenced cities and c. v.

COUNTRYMEN.

2 Co. 11 : 26. in perils by mine own c.
1 Th. 2 : 14. suff. things of your c.

COUPLE.

2 S. 13 : 6. make me c. of cakes
16 : 1. met Da. with a c. of asses
Is. 21 : 7. with c. of horsemen, 9.

COUPLE. [Verb.]

Ex. 26 : 6. shalt c. the curtains, 9.
11. taches to c. tent, 36 : 18.
39 : 4. shoulder pieces to c. ephod

COUPLED, ETH.

Ex. 26 : 3. the five curtains be c.,
36 : 10, 13, 16.
10. of curtain wh. c-h the second
24. two boards sh. be c., 36 : 29.
39 : 4. by two edges was it c.
1 Pe. 3 : 2. conversa. c-d with fear

COUPLING, S.

Ex. 26 : 4. fr. selvedge in c., 36 : 11.
4. in c. of second, 36 : 11, 12.
10. is outmost in the c., 36 : 17.
28 : 27. over ag. other c., 39 : 20.
2 Ch. 34 : 11. buy timber for c-s

COURAGE.

Jos. 2 : 11. nor any c. in any
2 Ch. 15 : 8. took c. put away idols
19 : † 11. take c. and do, and L.
Is. 44 : † 14. he taketh c. for hims.
Da. 11 : 25. stir up his c. against k.
Ac. 28 : 15. thanked God, took c.

Good COURAGE.

Nu. 13 : 20. be of g. c. and bring
De. 31 : 6. Be strong, and of g. c., 7, 23.
Jos. 1 : 6, 9, 18.–10 : 25. 1 Ch.
22 : 13.–28 : 20.
2 S. 10 : 12. of g. c. let us play the
men, 1 Ch. 19 : 13. Ezr. 10 : 4.
Is. 41 : 6. [31 : 24.
Ps. 27 : 14. Wait on L., be of g. c.,

COURAGEOUS, LY.

Jos. 1 : 7. be c., 23 : 6. 2 Ch. 32 : 7.
2 S. 13 : 28. fear not, be c. valiant
2 Ch. 19 : 11. Deal c-y and L. shall be
Am. 2 : 16. he that is c. shall flee

COURSE.

1 Ch. 27 : 1. chief fathers of ev. c.
28 : 1. ministered to king by c.
2 Ch. 5 : 11. priests not wait by c.
Ezr. 3 : 11. they sung togeth. by c.
Ps. 82 : 5. foundations out of c.
Je. 8 : 6. ev. one turned to his c.
23 : 10. their c. is evil, and their
Lu. 1 : 5. Zach. was of the c. of
8. executed in order of his c.
Ac. 13 : 25. as John fulfilled his c.
16 : 11. came with straight c., 21 : 1.
20 : 24. finish my c. with joy
21 : 7. when we had finished our c.
1 Co. 14 : 27. by three, that by c.
Ep. 2 : 2. acc. to c. of this world
2 Th. 3 : 1. word may have free c.
2 Ti. 4 : 7. I have finished my c.
Ja. 3 : 6. on fire the c. of nature

COURSES.

Ju. 5 : 20 stars in their c. fought
1 K. 5 : 14. Leb 10,000 a month by c.
1 Ch. 23 : 6. the Levites into c.
27 : 1. served k. in any matter of c.
28 : 13. c. of priests, 21. 2 Ch. 35 : 4.
2 Ch. 8 : 14. Sol. appoi. c. of priests
23 : 8. Jehoiada dismissed not c.
31 : 2. Hez. appoi. c. of the priests
35 : 10. Levites stood in their c.
Ezr. 6 : 18. set Levites in their c.
See WATERCOURSE, S.

COURT.

Ex. 27 : 9. c. of tabern. hangings
for c., 35 : 17.–38 : 9.–39 : 40.
12. breadth of c., 13. | 18. length
19. pins of c., 35 : 18.–38 : 20, 31.
40 : 8. thou shalt set up the c.
Le. 6 : 16. in c. of tab. shall eat it, 26.
2 S. 17 : 18. man had well in his c.
1 K. 8 : 64. king hallow middle of c.
2 K. 20 : 4. afore Is. was gone into c.
2 Ch. 4 : 9. made c. of the priests
20 : 5. Jehosh. stood before new c.
24 : 21. they stoned Zech. in c. of L.
29 : 16. brought uncleann. into c.
Es. 5 : 1. Esther stood in inner c.
6 : 4. k. said, Who is in the c.?
5. Behold Haman standeth in c.
Is. 34 : 13. dragons, a c. for owls
35 : † 7. shall be a c. for reeds [hou.
Je. 19 : 14. Jere. stood in c. of L.'s
26 : 2. Stand in c. of L.'s house
32 : 2. Jere. prophet was shut in c.
of prison, 33 : 1.–39 : 15. [13.
38 : 6. Jere. into the dungeon in c.,
Eze. 8 : 7. bro-t me to door of c., 16.
10 : 3. cloud filled the inner c.
40 : 17. outward c., 42 : 1.–46 : 21.
28. brought me to inner c., 43 : 5
44 : 19. go forth into outer c.
21. ent. into inner c., 17, 27.
45 : 19. put blood upon gate of c.
46 : 21. in ev. corner of c. was c.
Am. 7 : 13. it is the king's c.
Ac. 16 : † 19. drew Paul into the c.
17 : † 22. Paul stood in c. of Areopa.
19 : † 38. the c. days are kept
Ph. 1 : † 13. bonds in Cæsar's c.
Re. 11 : 2. c. without the temple

COURTS.

2 K. 21 : 5. built altars for host of
heaven in two c., 2 Ch. 33 : 5.
23 : 12. altars in 2 c. Josiah brake
1 Ch. 23 : 28. office to wait in c.
28 : 6. Solomon shall build my c.
12. gave Solomon pattern of c.
2 Ch. 23 : 5. all people be in c.
Ne. 13 : 7. chamber in c. of house of
Ps. 65 : 4. that he dwell in thy c.
84 : 2. soul fainteth for c. of Lord
92 : 13. flourish in c. of our God
96 : 8. bring off. come into his c.
100 : 4. Enter his c. with praise
116 : 19. pay my vows in c. of L.'s
135 : 2. Ye that stand in c. of God
Is. 1 : 12. this to tread my c.?
62 : 9. sh. drink in c. of my holi.
Eze. 9 : 7. fill the c. with the slain
Zch. 3 : 7. judge my house, keep my c.
Lu. 7 : 25. live delica. in king's c.

COURTEOUS, LY.

Ac. 27 : 3. Julius c-y entreated Paul
28 : 7. Publius lodged us c-y
1 Pe. 3 : 8. breth., be pitiful, be c.

COURTIER.

Jn. 4 : † 46. a certain c. whose son

COUSIN, S.

Lu. 1 : 36. thy c. Eliz. hath conceiv.
58. her c-s heard how L.

COVENANT.

Ge. 9 : 12. This is the token of the
c., 13, 17.–17 : 11.
17 : 4. my c. is with thee
13. my c. shall be in your flesh

Ge.17:14. soul cut off, broken my c.
Ex. 31 : 16. sab. for a perpetual c.
34 : 28. wrote upon tables the c.
Le. 26 : 15. but ye break my c.
Nu. 25 : 12. I give my c. of peace
13. c. of an overl. priesthood
De. 4 : 13. he declared his c.
23. lest ye forget c. of the Lord
31. Lord not forget c. of fathers
9 : 9. to receive tables of c.
11. Lord gave me tables of c.
15. two tables of the c. were
29 : 1. These are the words of c.
12. thou shouldest enter into c.
21. acc. to all the curses of c.
25. ye have forsaken the c.
31 : 20. they will break my c.
Ju. 2 : 1. I will never break my c.
1 S. 20 : 8. servant into c. of Lord
1 K. 19 : 10. Israel forsaken c., 14.
20 : 34. I will send thee with this c.
2 K. 13 : 23. bec. of his c. with Ab.
23 : 3. to perform c., and all the people stood to c., 2 Ch. 34:31.
1 Ch. 16:15. Be ye mindful of his c.
2 Ch. 15:12. ent-d into c. to seek L.
23:1. Jehoi. took into c. with him
34 : 32. inhab. did acc. to c. of G.
Ne. 13 : 29. defiled c. of priesthood
Ps. 25 : 14. he will shew them his c.
44:17. neith. dealt falsely in thy c.
50 : 16. take my c. in thy mouth
55 : 20. he hath broken his c.
74 : 20. respect to c. for dark plac.
78:37.their heart not right, neither were they steadfast in his c.
89 : 28. c. sh. stand fast with him
34. My c. will I not break, nor
39. made void c. of thy servant
111 : 5. ever be mindful of his c.
9. commanded his c. for ever
Pr. 2 : 17. forgetteth c. of her God
Is. 28 : 18. c. with death be disan.
33 : 8. broken c. despised cities
42 : 6. give for c. of people, 49 : 8.
54:10. nei. c. of my peace removed
56 : 4. eunuchs hold of my c., 6.
59 : 21. As for me, this is my c.
Je. 11 : 2. Hear ye words of c., 6.
3. Cursed be man obeyeth not c.
8. bri. upon them all words of c.
14 : 21. break not thy c. with us
22 : 9. bec. they have forsaken c.
31 : 32. which my c. they brake
33 : 20. break my c. of day and c.
21. may c. be broken with David
25. If my c. be not with day
34 : 10. peo. which had ent. into c.
18. who have not performed c.
50 : 5. us join to L. in perpetual c.
Eze. 16 : 8. I ent. into c. with thee
59. oath in breaking c., 17 : 18.
61. give for dau-s, not by thy c.
17 : 15. he break c. and be deliv.?
16. oath he despised, c. brake
19. my c. he hath broken
20 : 37. bring you into bond of c
44 : 7. they have broken my c.
Da. 9 : 27. confirm c. for one week
11 : 22. broken, also prince of c.
28. his heart shall be ag. holy c.
30. have indignation ag. holy c.
32. such as do wickedly ag. c.
Ho. 10 : 4. swear. falsely in mak. c.
Zch. 11 : 10. I might break my c.
Mal. 2 : 4. my c. be with Levi, 5.
8. ye have corrupted c. of Levi
10. by profaning c. of our fathers
14. yet she is the wife of thy c.
3 : 1. messen. of c. ye delight in
Ac. 3 : 25. ye chil. of c. God made
7 : 8. he gave him c. of circumc.
11 : 27. this is my c. when I take
Ga. 3 : 15. tho. it be but man's c.
17. the c. confirmed bef. of God
He. 8 : 6. mediator of a better c.
7. if first c. had been faultless

He.8:9. they continued not in my c.
9 : 1. first c. had also ordinances
4. and the tables of the c.
See ARK, BLOOD, BREAK.

Book of the COVENANT.

Ex. 24 : 7. Moses took the b. o. c.
2 K. 23:2. Josiah read all the words of b. o. c., 2 Ch. 34 : 30.
21. keep passover as in b. o. c.

Establish, ed, COVENANT.

Ge. 6 : 18. with thee e. my c., 9 : 9.
17 : 7. e. c. betw. me and Abraham
19. e. c. with Isaac, and seed, 21.
Ex. 6 : 4. I have e-d my c. with th.
Le. 26 : 9. multiply and e. my c.
De. 8 : 18. that he may e. his c.
Eze. 16 : 60. e. to thee an everl. c.
62. I will e. my c. with thee

Everlasting COVENANT.

Ge. 9 : 16. that I may remem. e. c.
17 : 13. be in your flesh for e. c.
19. c. with Isaac for an e. c.
Le. 24 : 8. taken from Isr. by e. c.
2 S. 23 : 5. an e. c. ordered in all
1 Ch. 16 : 17. confirmed to Israel for an e. c., Ps. 105 : 10.
Is. 24 : 5. have broken e.c. [32:40.
55 : 3. e. c. with you, 61 : 8. Je.
Eze. 37 : 26. be e. c. with them
He. 13 : 20. through blood of e. c.

Keep, eth, ing, or kept COVENANT.

Ge. 17 : 9. Thou shalt k. my c.
10. is my c. which ye shall k.
Ex. 19 : 5. if ye will k. my c.
De. 7 : 9. he is G. which k. c., 12. 1 K. 8 : 23. 2 Ch. 6 : 14. Ne. 1 : 5.-9 : 32.
29 : 9. k. words of this c. and do
33 : 9. they have k. thy c.
1 K. 11:11. hast not k. c., Ps. 78:10.
Ps. 25 : 10. to such as k. c., 103:18.
132 : 12. If thy children k. my c.
Eze. 17 : 14. by k. of c. it might
Da. 9 : 4. k. c. and mercy to them

Made COVENANT.

Ge. 15 : 18. day L. m. c. with Ab.
21 : 27. Ab. and Abim. m. c., 32.
Ex. 34 : 27. I have m. c. with Isr.
De. 5 : 2. Lord m. a c. in Horeb
3. m. not c. with fa-s, He. 8 : 9.
29 : 1. besides c. he m. in Horeb
31 : 16. will break my c. I m.
Jos. 24 : 25. Josh. m. c. with peo.
1 S.18:3.Jona. and Da. m.c., 23:18.
20 : 16. Jona. m. c. with h. of Da.
1 K. 8 : 9. m. c. with Isr., 2 Ch. 6 : 21 ark wh-n is c. of L. he m. [11.
20 : 34. Ahab m. c. with Benjam.
2 K. 11 : 4. Jehoi. m. c. with rulers
17. m. c. betw. Lord and king
17 : 15. rejected c. m. with fa-s
35. with whom L. had m. c.
38. c. m. with you not forget
23 : 3. Josiah m. c., 2 Ch. 34 : 31.
1 Ch. 11 : 3. Da. m. c. with elders
16:16. be mindful of c. be m. with Abraham, Ne. 9 : 8. Ps. 105 : 9.
2 Ch. 5 : 10. at Horeb when L. m. a
21 : 7. of c. he m. with David [c.
23 : 3. cong. m. a c. with k. Joash
Jb. 31 : 1. m. a c. with mine eyes
Ps. 50 : 5. m. c. with me by sacri.
89 : 3. m. a c. with my chosen
Is. 28 : 15. have m. c. with death
57:8. enlarged thy bed and m. c.
Je. 11 : 10. broke c. I m. with fa-s
31:32. not acc. to c. I m., He. 8:9.
34 : 8. Zed. m. c. with people, 15.
13. I m. c. with your fathers
15. ye had m. c. before me
18. performed not c. ye had m.
Eze. 17 : 13. and m. a c. with him

Make COVENANT.

Ge. 17 : 2. m. c. betw. me and thee
26 : 28. let us m. c., 31 : 44. Ezr.
Ex. 23:32. m. no c., De. 7:2. [10:3.

Ex. 34:10. I m.c. before thy people
12. lest m. c. with inhab., 15.
De. 29 : 14. Neither with you only
1 S. 11 : 1. m. a c. with us [m. c.
2. On this condition I m. c.
2 Ch. 29 : 10. in my heart to m. c.
Ne. 9 : 38. we m. a sure c.
Jb. 41 : 4. will he m. a c. with thee?
Je. 31 : 33. this is the c. I will m., He. 8 : 10.-10 : 16.
Eze. 34 : 25. m. c. of peace, 37 : 26.
Ho. 2 : 18. m. c. with beasts
12 : 1. they do m. c. with Assyr.

New COVENANT.

Je. 31 : 31. n. c. with Isr., He. 8:8.
He. 8 : 13. a n. c. the first old
12 : 24. mediator of the n. c.

Remember, ed, COVENANT.

Ge. 9 : 15. I will r. my c., Le. 26 : 42. Eze. 16 : 60.
Ex. 2 : 24. r-d his c. with Abraham
6 : 5. I have r-d my c.
Le. 26 : 45. for their sakes r. c.
Ps. 105:8. he hath r. his c., 106:45.
Am. 1 : 9. r-d not brotherly c.
Lu. 1 : 72. and to r. his holy c.

COVENANT of SALT.

Le. 2 : 13. s. o. c. to be lacking
Nu. 18 : 19. it is c. o. s. for ever
2 Ch. 13 : 5. to David by c. o. s.

Trangressed, ing COVENANT.

De. 17 : 2. wickedn. in t-g his c.
Jos. 7 : 11. they have t-d my c.
7 : 15. bec. he t. c. of the Lord, Ju. 2 : 20. 2 K. 18 : 12.
23 : 16. When ye have t. c. of L.
Je. 34 . 18. give men that t. my c.
Ho. 6 : 7. they like men t. the c.
8 : 1. because they have t. my c.

COVENANTS.

Ro. 9 : 4. to whom pertaineth c.
Ga. 4 : 24. two c. one from Sinai
Ep. 2:12. strangers from c. of prom

COVENANT-BREAKERS.

Ro. 1:31. without understanding, c.

COVENANTED.

2 Ch. 7 : 18. as I have c. with Da.
Hag. 2:5. acc. to word I c. with you
Mat. 26 : 15. c. for thirty pieces
Lu. 22 : 5. c. to give him money

COVER.

Ex. 10 : 5. locusts shall c. earth
21 : 33. dig a pit and not c. it
25 : 29. c. withal, 37 : 16. Nu. 4 : 7.
28 : 42. to c. their nakedness
33 : 22. I will c. thee while I pass
40 : 3. thou shalt c. the ark
Le. 13 : 12. leprosy c. all the skin
16 : 13. clouds of incense c.
17 : 13. pour out blood, and c.
Nu. 22 : 5. they c. face of earth
De. 23 : 13. c. wh. cometh fr. thee
33 : 12. Lord shall c. him all day
1 S. 24 : 3. Saul went to c. his feet
1 K. 7 : 18. to c. chapiters, 41, 42. 2 Ch. 4 : 12, 13.
Ne. 4 : 5. c. not their iniquity
Jb. 16 : 18. O earth, c. not my bl.
21 : 26. worms shall c. them [34.
22 : 11. abun. of waters c. thee, 38:
40 : 22. The shady trees c. him
Ps. 91 : 4. c. thee with feathers
104 : 9. turn not to c. earth
109 : 29. c. with own confusion
139 : 11. Surely darkness sh. c. me
140 : 9. mischief of lips c. them
Is. 11 : 9. as waters c. sea, Ha. 2:14.
14 : 11. worms c. thee
22 : 17. Lord will surely c. thee
26 : 21. earth no more c. her slain
30 : 1. c. with a covering, but
58 : 7. naked, that thou c. him
59 : 6. nor c. thems. with works
60 : 2. darkness shall c. earth
6. multitude of camels sh. c. thee

Je. 46 : 8. I will c. the earth
Eze. 7 : 18. horror shall c. them
12 : 6. thou shalt c. thy face
12. he shall c. his face, that
24 : 7. poured it not on ground to
17. c. not thy lips, eat not ⌊c.
22. ye shall not c. your lips
26 : 10. horses, their dust c. thee
19. when waters shall c. thee
30 : 18. as for her a cloud c. her
32 : 7. I will c. the heaven
37 : 6. c. you with skin and
38 : 9. like cloud to c. land, 16.
Ho. 2 : 9. flax to c. her nakedness
10 : 8. say to mts. c. us, Lu. 23:30.
Ob. 10. shame shall c. thee
Mi. 3 : 7. shall all c. their lips
7 : 10. shame c. her th. said unto
Ha. 2 : 17. violence of Leb. c. ⌊me
Mk. 14 : 65. to spit, c. his face
1 Co. 11 : 7. man not to c. head
1 Pe. 4 : 8. charity c. mult. of sins

COVERED.

Ge. 7 : 19. mountains were c., 20.
9 : 23. c. nakedness of their fa.
24 : 65. Rebekah c. herself
38 : 14. Tamar c. her with vail
Ex. 8 : 6. frogs c. land of E.
14 : 28. the waters c. chariots
15 : 5. The depths c. them
10. the sea c. them, Jos. 24 : 7.
16 : 13. quails c. the camp
24 : 15. a cloud c. the mount, 16.
37 : 9. c. with wings mercy seat
40 : 21. vail c. ark of testimony
34. a cloud c. the tent of the
Le. 13 : 13. leprosy c. all his flesh
Nu. 4 : 20. when holy things c.
9 : 15. c. the tab., 16.-16 : 42.
De. 32 : 15. art c. with fatness
Ju. 4 : 18. Jael c. Sisera, 19.
1 S. 19 : 13. Michal c. the image
28 : 14. old man cometh up c.
1 K. 1 : 1. c. David with clothes
6:9. c. house with beams, and, 7:3.
15. c. floor | 20. c. the altar
35. c. them with gold
8 : 7. cherubim c. the ark, 1 Ch. 28 : 18. 2 Ch. 5 : 8.
2 K. 19 : 1. Hezekiah c. himself with sackcloth, Is. 37 : 1.
2. c. with sackcloth, Is. 37 : 2.
2 Ch. 3 : † 6. Solomon c. the house
Jb. 23 : 17. nor c. darkn. from face
31 : 33. if I c. my transgressions
Ps. 44 : 15. shame of face c. me
19. c. us with shadow of death
: † 5. and horror hath c. me
: 13. valleys c. over with corn
: 13. wings of dove c. with silver
: 13. c. with reproach th. seek
: † 53. sea c. enemies, 106 : † 11.
: 10. hills c. with shadow of it
: 45. hast c. him with shame
106 : 17. c. company of Abiram
139 : 13. c. me in mother's womb
Pr. 26 : 23. a potsherd c. with
26. Whose hatred is c. by deceit
Ec. 6 : 4. his name c. with darkn.
Is. 6 : 2. with twain he c. his face
22 : † 17. L. who c. with excellent
25 : † 7. destr. covering c. over peo.
29 : 10. the seers hath he c.
51 : 16. I have c. thee in shadow
61 : 10. c. me with robe of righte.
Je. 51 : 42. she is c. with waves
La. 2 : 1. c. daughter of Zion with
3 : 16. he hath c. me with ashes
43. hast c. with anger, and perse.
44. c. thyself with a cloud
Eze. 1 : 11. two wings c. bodies, 23.
16 : 8. and c. thy nakedness
10. I c. thee with silk
18 : 7. and hath c. the naked, 16.
24 : 8. her blood should not be c.
27 : 7. blue and purple c. thee
31 : 15. I c. the deep for him
Eze. 37 : 8. and skin c. them above
Jon. 3 : 6. k. of Nin. c. with sackcl.
8. and beast be c. with sackcloth
Ha. 3 : 3. His glory c. heavens
Mat. 8 : 24. ship was c. with waves
10 : 26. nothing c. that shall not be revealed, Lu. 12 : 2.
1 Co. 11 : 6. if woman be not c.

COVERED face, s.

Ge. 38 : 15. Tamar had c. her f.
Ex. 10 : 15. locusts c. f. of earth
2 S. 19 : 4. but David c. his f.
Es. 7 : 8. they c. Haman's f.
Ps. 69 : 7. shame hath c. my f.
Pr. 24 : 31. nettles c. f. thereof
Is. 6 : 2. with twain he c. his f.
Je. 51 : 51. shame hath c. our f-s

Head, s COVERED.

2 S. 15 : 30. David had his h. c.
Es. 6 : 12. Haman, his h. c.
Ps. 140 : 7. c. my h. in battle
Je. 14 : 3. and c. their h-s, 4.
1 Co. 11 : 4. ev. man praying, h. c.

COVERED sin.

Ps. 32 : 1. whose s. is c., Ro. 4 : 7.
85 : 2. thou hast c. all their s.

COVERER.

Na. 2 : † 5. c. shall be prepared

COVEREDST, EST.

De. 22 : 12. vesture wherewith c-est
Ps. 5 † 11. about because thou c-est
104 : 2. c-est thyself with light
6. c-dst it with the deep as garm.
Eze. 16 : 18. broid. garm. and c-dst

COVERETH.

Ex. 29 : 13. fat that c. inwards, 22. Le. 3 : 3, 9, 14.-4 : 8.-7 : 3.-9 : 19.
Nu. 22 : 11. people c. face of earth
Ju. 3 : 24. Surely he c. his feet
Jb. 9 : 24. he c. faces of judges
15 : 27. c. his face with fatness
36 : 30. he c. bottom of the sea
32. With clouds he c. the light
Ps. 73 : 6. violence c. as garment
84 : † 6. Baca, rain c. the pools
109 : 19. be as garment wh. c. him
147 : 8. c. heaven with clouds
Pr. 10:6. violence c. the mouth, 11.
12. love c. all sins
12 : 16. prudent man c. shame
17 : 9. c. a transgr-n seeketh love
28 : 13. c. his sins, sh. not prosper
Je. 3 : 25. our confusion c. us
Eze. 28 : 14. art cherub that c.
Mal. 2 : 16. for one c. violence
Lu. 8 : 16. lighted candle c. it

COVERING. [Part. and adj.]

Ex. 25 : 20. c. mercy seat with
Nu. 4 : 5. shall take down c. vail
Eze. 28 : 16. destr thee, O c. cherub
Mal. 2 : 13. c. altar with tears

COVERING, S.

Ge. 8 : 13. Noah removed c. of ark
20 : 16. to thee a c. of the eyes
Ex. 22 : 27. his c. for his skin
26 : 7. to be a c. upon tab., 36:11.-39 : 34. Nu. 3 : 25.
14. c. for tent of ram's skins, 36 : 19.-39 : 34.-40 : 19.
35 : 12. vail of c., 39:34.-40:21.
Le. 13 : 45. leper put c. upon lip
Nu. 16 : 38. broad plates for c.
19 : 15. vessel which hath no c.
2 S. 17 : 19. c. over well's mouth
Jb. 22 : 14. Thick clouds c. to him
24 : 7. naked have no c. in cold
26 : 6. destruction hath no c.
31 : 19. seen any poor, without c.
Ps. 105 : 39. He spread cloud for c.
Pr. 7 : 16. bed with c-s of tapestry
31 : 22. maketh c-s of tapestry
Can. 3 : 10. he made c. of purple
Is. 4 : † 5. upon the glory be a c.
22 : 8. he discovered c. of Judah
† 17. covered thee with excel. c.
25 : 7. face of c. cast over all peo.
28 : 20. c. narrower, than can wrap
Is. 30 : 1. cover with c. not of my Spi
22. ye shall defile c. of images
50 : 3. I make sackcloth their c.
Eze. 28 : 13. precious stone thy c.
1 Co. 11 : † 10. wom. ought to have a
15. hair is given her for c. ⌊c.
See Badgers' Skin, s.

COVERS.

Ex. 25 : 29. make c., 37 : 16.
Nu. 4 : 7. put c. to cover withal

COVERT.

1 S. 25 : 20. Abigail came by c.
2 K. 16 : 18. c. for the sabbath
Jb. 38 : 40. when lions abide in c.
40 : 21. behemoth lieth in c. of
Ps. 61 : 4. trust in c. of thy wings
Is. 4 : 6. a tabernacle for a c.
16 : 4. be thou a c. from spoiler
32 : 2. man be c. from tempest
Je. 25 : 38. forsaken his c. as lion

COVET.

Ex. 20 : 17. Thou shalt not c., De 5 : 21. Ro. 7 : 7.-13 : 9.
Mi. 2 : 2. they c. fields and take
1 Co. 12 : 31. But c. the best gifts
14 : 39. c. to prophesy

COVETED, ETH.

Jos. 7 : 21. then I c. them, and
Pr. 21 : 26. c-h all the day long
Ha. 2 : 9. Woe to him c-h evil covet
Ac. 20 : 33. I c. no man's silver
1 Ti. 6 : 10. while some c. after

COVETOUS.

Ps. 10 : 3. wicked blesseth c.
Lu. 16 : 14. Pharisees who were c.
1 Co. 5 : 10. yet not altog. with c.
11. c. with such not to eat
6 : 10. nor c. inherit kingd., Ep. 5 : 5.
1 Ti. 3 : 3. bishop must not be c.
2 Ti. 3 : 2. in last times men c.
2 Pe. 2 : 14. exerc. with c. practices

COVETOUSNESS.

Ex. 18 : 21. able men hating c.
Ps. 119 : 36. Incline not heart to c.
Pr. 28 : 16. hateth c. shall prolong
Is. 57 : 17. for his c. was I wroth
Je. 6 : 13. ev. one given to c., 8 : 10.
22 : 17. eyes are not but for thy c.
51 : 13. and measure of thy c.
Eze. 33 : 31. their heart goeth aft. c.
Ha. 2 : 9. that coveteth an evil c.
Mk. 7 : 22. out heart proceedeth c.
Lu. 12 : 15. he said, Beware of c.
Ro. 1 : 29. being filled with all c.
2 Co. 9 : 5. as a matter not of c.
Ep. 5 : 3. c. let it not be named
Col. 3 : 5. mortify c. which is idola.
1 Th. 2 : 5. nor used cloak of c.
He. 13 : 5. conversa. be without c.
2 Pe. 2 : 3. thro. c. make merchan.

COW.

Le. 22 : 28. c. shall not kill it
Nu. 18 : 17. firstl. of c. not redeem
Jb. 21 : 10. their c. casteth not
Is. 7 : 21. man nourish a young c.
11 : 7. c. and the bear shall feed
Eze. 4 : 15. given thee c. dung for
Am. 4 : 3. ev. c. at that before her

COZ.

1 Ch. 4 : 8. C. begat Anub and

COZ'BI.

Nu. 25 : 15. woman slain was C.
18. beguiled you in matter of C.

CRACKLING.

Ec. 7 : 6. c. of thorns under pot

CRACKNELS.

1 K. 14 : 3. take with thee c.

CRAFT.

Da. 8 : 25. shall cause c. to prosper
Mk. 14 : 1. take him by c. and put
Ac. 18:3. because he was of same c.
19 : 25. by this c. have our wealth
27. not only our c. is in danger
Re. 18 : 22. of whatsoever c. he be

CRAFTILY.

Ju. 9 : † 31. he sent messengers to Abimelech c.

CRAFTINESS.
Jb. 5 : 13. wise in c., 1 Co. 3 : 19.
Lu. 20 : 23. he perceived their c.
2 Co. 4 : 2. not walking in c. nor
Ep. 4 : 14. carried by cunning c.
CRAFTSMAN.
De. 27 : 15. the work of the c.
Re. 18 : 22. no c. be found more
CRAFTSMEN.
2 K. 24 : 14. carried away c., 16.
1 Ch. 4 : 14. for they were c.
Ne. 11 : 35. Ono, the valley of c.
Ho. 13 : 2. all of it the work of c.
Ac. 19 : 24. no small gain to c.
38. c. have matter against any
CRAFTY.
Jb. 5 : 12. he disapp. devices of c.
15 : 5. thou choosest tongue of c.
Ps. 83 : 3. c. counsel ag. thy people
2 Co. 12 : 16. being c. I caught you
CRAG.
Jb. 39 : 28. eagle abideth on c.
CRANE.
Is. 38 : 14. Like c. so did I chatter
Je. 8 : 7. c. observe time of coming
CRASHING.
Zph. 1 : 10. be great c. from hills
CRAVED, ETH.
Pr. 16 : 26. for his mouth c-h it
Mk. 15:43. Joseph c-d body of Jesus
CREATE.
Ps. 51 : 10. c. in me a clean heart
Is. 4 : 5. c. upon ev. dwell.-p. cloud
45 : 7. c. darkness, I c. evil
57 : 19. I c. the fruits of the lips
65 : 17. I c. new heavens and new
18. rejoice in that which I c.
CREATED, ETH.
Ge. 1:1. In beginning G. c. heaven
21. God c. great whales
27. G. c. man in his own image, male and female, 5 : 1, 2.
2 : 3. in it rested from all he c.
6 : 7. I will destroy man I have c.
De. 4 : 32. since day God c. man
Ps. 89 : 12. north and south hast c.
102 : 18. peo. to be c. shall praise
104 : 30. send spirit they are c. [c.
148 : 5. commanded and they were
Is. 40 : 26. who hath c. these things
41 : 20. Holy One of Israel c. it
42 : 5. he that c. the heavens
43 : 1. Lord that c. thee, O Jacob
7. I have c. him for my glory
45 : 8. I the Lord have c. it
12. I have c. man upon it
18. he c. it not in vain [ning
48:7. They are c. now, not fr. begin-
54 : 16. I have c. smith, c. waster
Je. 31 : 22. L. hath c. a new thing.
Eze. 21 : 30. judge where wast c.
28 : 13. in day thou wast c.
15. perfect from day thou wast c.
Am. 4 : 13. he that c-h wind, L. is
Mal. 2 : 10. hath not one God c. us
Mk. 13 : 19. begin. of creation G. c.
1 Co. 11 : 9. man c. for the woman
Ep. 2:10. workmanship c. in Christ
3 : 9. who c. all things by J. C.
4:24. after God is c. in righteousn.
Col. 1:16. by him were all things c.
3 : 10. after image of him c. him
1 Ti. 4 : 3. meats G. c. to be rec-d
Re. 4:11. hast c. all things, for thy pleasure are and were c.
10 : 6. who c. heaven and the
CREATION.
Mk. 10 : 6. from c. male and female
13 : 19. as was not from the c.
Ro. 1 : 20. from c. are clearly seen
8 : 22. that whole c. groaneth
2 Pe. 3 : 4. continue as from c.
Re. 3 : 14. beginning of c. of God
CREATOR.
Ec. 12 : 1. remember C. in youth
Is. 40 : 28. C. of ends of earth
43 : 15. I am the Lord, C. of Israel

Ro. 1 : 25. creature more than C.
1 Pe. 4 : 19. as to a faithful C.
CREATURE.
Ge. 1 : 20. bring forth moving c.
Le. 11 : 46. law of ev. c. that mov.
Nu. 16 : † 30. if L. create a new c.
Mk. 16:15. gospel to ev. c., Col. 1 : 23.
Ro. 1:25. served c. more than Crea.
8 : 19. earnest expectation of the c.
20. c. made subject to vanity
21. c. be delivered from bondage
† 22. c. groaneth and travaileth
39. nor c. able to separate us
2 Co. 5 : 17. if in C., he is a new c.
Ga. 6 : 15. nor unci., but a new c.
Col. 1 : 15. firstborn of every c.
1 Ti. 4 : 4. every c. of G is good
He. 4 : 13. nor any c. not manifest
Re. 5 : 13. every c. in heaven heard
Living CREATURE.
Ge. 1 : 21. God created every l. c.
24. Let earth bring forth the l. c.
2:19. whats. Adam called every l. c.
9 : 10. establish cov. with every l. c.
12. token betw. me and ev. l. c., 15.
Le. 11 : 46. the law of every l. c.
Eze. 1 : 20. spirit of l. c., 21.—10 : 17.
10 : 15. l. c. I saw by Chebar, 20.
CREATURES.
Is. 13 : 21. be full of doleful c.
Ja. 1 : 18. kind of firstfr. of his c.
Re. 8 : 9. c. in the sea died
Living CREATURES.
Eze. 1 : 5. likeness of four l. c.
13. it went among the l. c.
14. l. c. ran, return. as lightning
15. l. c. one wheel by l. c.
19. when l. c. went wheels went
3 : 13. noise of wings of l. c.
CREDITOR, S.
De. 15 : 2. Every c. that lendeth it
1 S. 22 : † 2. ev. one that had a c.
2 K. 4 : 1. c. to take my two sons
4 : † 7. go, sell oil, and pay the c.
Is. 50 : 1. to which of c-s sold you?
Lu. 7 : 41. a certain c. had 2 debtors
CREEK, S.
Ju. 5 : † 17. Asher continued on c-s
Ac. 27 : 39. they discov. a certain c.
CREEP.
Le. 11 : 20. All fowls that c.
31. uncl. to you am. all that c.
Ps. 104 : 20. beasts of forest c. forth
Eze 38 : 20. all things that c.
2 Ti. 3 : 6. they who c. into houses
CREEPETH, ING.
Ge. 1 : † 20. bring forth c-g creature
25. G. made ev. thing that c., 26.
† 28. dominion over thing that c.
30. given to every thing c. herb
7 : 8. c. went in two and two, 14.
21. all flesh died that c. upon
8 : 17. Bring forth every thing c.
19. whatso. c. went out of ark
Le. 11 : 41. every thing that c. be an abomination, 43, 44.—20 : 25.
De. 4 : 18. likeness of thing that c.
Ps. 69 : † 34. Let ev. thing that c. praise
CREEPING thing, s.
Ge. 1 : 26. domin. over every c. t.
7 : 14. every c. t. went into ark
Le. 5 : 2. carcass of unclean c. t.
11 : 21. may eat, of every c. t.
22 : 5. whoso. toucheth any c. t.
De. 14 : 19. c. t. that flieth uncl.
1 K. 4 : 33. spake of beasts, c. t-s
Ps 104 : 25. in sea are c. t-s innumer.
148 : 10. all c. t-s praise the L.
Eze. 8 : 10. form of c. t-s portrayed
38 : 20 c. t-s shall shake at my
Ho. 2 : 18. a covenant with the c. t-s
Mi. 7 : † 17. out of holes like c. t-s
Ha. 1 : 14. makest men as c. t-s
Ac. 10 : 12. Peter saw c. t-s, 11 : 6
Ro. 1 : 23. an image like c. t-s
CREPT.
Jude 4. certain men c. in unawares

CRES'CENS.
2 Ti. 4 : 10. C. is departed to Galatia
CRETE, CRETES.
Ac. 2 : 11. C-s we hear in our tongues
27 : 7. sailed under C. | 13. close by C.
12. attain Phenice, a haven of C.
21. and not have loosed from C.
Tit. 1 : 5. this cause left I thee in C.
CRE'TIANS.
Tit. 1 : 12. the C. are always liars
CREW.
Mat. 26 : 74. immediately the cock c., Mk. 14:68. Lu. 22:60. [18:27.
Mk. 14 : 72. second time cock c., Jn.
CRIB.
Jb. 39 : 9. unicorn abide by thy c.?
Pr. 14 : 4. no oxen the c. is clean
Is. 1 : 3. ass knoweth his master's c.
CRIED.
Ge. 27 : 34. Esau c. with great cry
39 : 15. heard that I c. [knee
41 : 43. they c. before him, Bow
55. people c. to Pha. for bread
45 : 1. he c. Cause ev. man to go
Ex. 2 : 23. they c. and cry came up
5 : 15. the officers c. to Pharaoh
Nu. 11:2. peo. c. to Moses. he pray.
14 : 1. c. and peo. wept that night
De. 22:24. stone damsel, bec. c. not
27. damsel c. and none to save
Ju. 5:28. Sisera's moth. c. thro. lat.
7 : 20. c., sword of L. and of Gid.
21. all the host c. and fled
10 : 12. ye c. to me, I deliv. you
15 : † 19. The well of him that c.
1 S. 14 : † 20. peo. were c. together
17 : 8. Goliath c. to armies of Isr.
20 : 37. Jonathan c. after lad, 38.
24 : 8. c. aft. Saul, saying My lord
26 : 14. Da. c. to peo. and Abner
2 S. 20 : 16. Then c. a wise woman
22 : 7. I c. to G., and he did hear
1 K. 18 : 2. he c. ag. altar, 4, 32.
18 : 28. c. aloud, and cut thems.
2 K. 2 : 12. Elisha c. My father, my
4 : 1. there c. a certain woman
8 : † 21. Moabites were c. together
6 : 5. he c. Alas, for it was borrow
8:5. woman c. to king for her hou.
11:14. Athaliah c. Treason, treason
1 Ch. 5 : 20. they c. to God in battle
2 Ch. 32 : 20. Isaiah c. to heaven
Ne. 9 : 27. they c. thou heardest, 28.
Jb. 17 : † 14. I have c. to corruption, my father
29 : 12. Bec. I deliv-d poor that c.
30 : 5. they c. as after a thief
Ps. 18:6. in my distress I c. unto G.
41. they c. but was none to save
22 : 5. they c. and were delivered
24. wh. he c. unto him he heard
30 : 2. I c. unto thee, and thou
8. I c. to thee, O L., made suppli.
31:22. heardest supplica. when I c.
34 : 6. poor man c. and L. heard
66 : 17. I c. unto him with, 77 : 1.
88:1. O L., I have c. day and night
13. unto thee have I c. [146, 147.
119:145. I c. with my whole heart |
130 : 1. Out of the depths have I c.
138 : 3. In day I c. thou answ.
Is. 6 : 3. one c. unto another, Holy
4. moved at voice of him that c.
21 : 8. he c. A lion : My lord
30:7. theref. have I c. conc. [is c.
Je. 4 : 20. Destruc. upon destruc.
12 : † 6. thy brethren c. after thee
La. 4 : 15. c. unto them, Depart ye
Eze. 9:8. I fell upon my face and c.
10 : 13. it was c. to them, O wheel
Da. 4:14. c. and said, Hew down tree
6 : 20. he c. O Daniel
Hos. 7 : 14. not c. with heart [god
Jon. 1:5. mariners c. ev. man to his
2 : 2. I c. by reason of afflic. out of the belly of hell c. I
Zch. 7 : 7. L. hath c. by proph., 1:4

Zch. 7: 13. as he c. and they not hear, so they c. and I not hear
Mat. 14: 30. Peter c. Lord save me
15: 22. c. saying, Have mercy on me
20: 31. c. the more, Have mercy on us, Mk. 10: 48. Lu. 18: 39.
21: 9. c. Hosanna, Mk. 11: 9. Jn. 12: 13.
Mk. 3: 11. c., Thou art Son of God
9: 26. spirit c. and rent him
Lu. 8: 8. c., He that hath ears to hear
16: 24. c., Father Ab., have mercy
18: 38. c., Jesus have mercy, 39.
23: 21. they c. saying, Crucify him
Jn. 7: 28. c. Jesus in temple
37. Jesus c. If any man thirst
12: 44. Jes. c. He that believeth
18: 40. c. all, Not this man
Ac. 16: 17. c., These men serv-s of G.
19: 32. some c. one thing, 21: 34.
22: 24. know whf. they c. so ag. him
24: 21. I c. standing among them
Re. 10: 3. he c. 7 thunders uttered
12: 2. she with child, c. travailing
14: 18. c. to him that had sickle
18: 2. he c. mightily, saying
18. c. when they saw the smoke
19. they c. weeping and wailing

CRIED out.

1 S. 4: 13. told it, all the city c. o.
5: 10. Ekronites c. o.
1 K. 22: 32. Jehosh. c. o., 2 Ch. 18: 31.
2 K. 4: 40. c. o., is death in pot
Je. 20: 8. I c. o., I cried violence
Mat. 8: 29. spirits c. o., Lu. 4: 33.
14: 26. disci. c. o. for fear, Mk. 6: 49.
20: 30. blind man c. o., Have mercy
Mk. 1: 23. with unclean spirit c. o.
9: 24. the father c. o., Lu. 9: 38.
15: 13. c. o. again, Crucify him, 14. Mat. 27: 23. Lu. 23: 18. Jn. 19: 6, 15.
39. centurion saw that he so c. o.
Lu. 8: 28. saw Jesus he c. o.
Jn. 19: 12. c. o., If let this man go
Ac. 19: 28. c. o., Great is Diana, 34.
22: 23. they c. o., and threw dust
23: 6. Paul c. o., I am a Pharisee

CRIED unto the Lord.

Ex. 8: 12. Moses c. u. L., 15: 25.—17: 4. Nu. 12: 13.
14: 10. Isr. c. u. L., Ju. 3: 9, 15.—4: 3.—6: 7.—10: 10.
Nu. 20: 16. when we c. u. L. he heard, De. 26: 7.
Jos. 24: 7. c. u. L. he put darku.
1 S. 7: 9. Samuel c. u. L., 15: 11.
12: 8. your fathers c. u. L., 10.
1 K. 17: 20. Elijah c. u. L., 21.
2 K. 20: 11. Isaiah c. u. L.
2 Ch. 14: 11. Asa c. u. L.
2 Ch. 13: 14. they c. u. L., Ps. 107: 6, 13. Jon. 1: 14.
Ps. 3: 4. I c. u. L., 120: 1.—142: 1.
La. 2: 18. heart c. u. L. O daughter of Zion

CRIED with a loud voice.

Ge. 39: 14. lie with me, I c. w.—
1 S. 28: 12. woman at Eu-dor c. w.—
2 S. 19: 4. David c. w.— O Absalom
2 K. 18: 28. Rabshakeh c. w.— in the Jews' language, Is. 36: 13.
2 Ch. 32: 18. c. w.— in Jew's speech
Ne. 9: 4. of the Levites, c. w.—
Eze. 11: 13. fell upon my face, c. w.—
Mat. 27: 46. about ninth hour Jesus c. w.—, 50. Mk. 15: 34, 37. Lu. 23: 46. Jn. 11: 43.
Mk. 1: 26. evil spirit c. w.—
5: 7. c. w.— What have I to do
Lu. 4: 33. man had unclean devil, c. w.— [c. w.—
Ac. 7: 57. they (Stephen's enemies)
60. Steph. kneel. down and c. w.—
16: 28. Paul c. w.—
Re. 6: 10. they c. w.— How long, O
7: 2. angel c. w.—, 10: 3.—19: 17.
Re. 7: 10. mult. stood bef. Lamb c. w.—

CRIES. See Cry.

CRIEST, ETH.

Ge. 4: 10. voice of broth.'s blood c.
Ex. 14: 15. Wheref. c-t thou to me?
22: 27. when he c. I will hear
1 S 26: 14. Who thou th. c-t to k.?
Jb. 24: 12. soul of wounded c.
Ps. 72: 12. deliver needy when he c.
84: 2. my flesh c. out for living G.
Pr. 1: 20. Wisdom c., 23, 8: 3.—9: 3.
2: 3. if thou c-t after knowledge
Is. 26: 17. as woman that c. in pangs
40: 3. voice of him th. c. in wilder.
57: 13. Wh. c-t let companies deliv.
Je. 12: 8. my heritage c. ag. me
30: 15. Why c-t for thine affliction?
Mi. 6: 9. Lord's voice c. to city
Mat. 15: 23. her away, she c. aft. us
Lu. 9: 39. he c. out, it teareth him
Ro. 9: 27. Esaias also c. conc. Israel
Ja. 5: 4. the hire of labourers, c.

CRIME, S.

Jb. 31: 11. this is a heinous c.
Eze. 7: 23. land is full of bloody c-s
Ac. 25: 16. to answer conc. c. laid
27. not to signify the c. laid ag.

CRIMSON. [c., 14.

2 Ch. 2: 7. man cunning to work in
3: 14. he made the vail of blue, c.
Is. 1: 18. tho. your sins be red like c.
Je. 4: 30. Tho. clothest thyself with

CRIPPLE. [c.

Ac. 14: 8. being a c. from womb

CRISPING pins.

Is. 3: 22. L. will take away c. p.

CRIS'PUS.

Ac. 18: 8. C. ruler of synag. believ.
1 Co. 1: 14. baptized none but C.

CROOKBACKED.

Le. 21: 20. man c. sh. not approach

CROOKED.

De. 32: 5. they are a c. generation
Ju. 5: † 6. walked through c. ways
Jb. 26: 13. formed the c. serpent
Ps. 125: 5. as turn to their c. ways
Ec. 1: 15. c. not be made straight,
Pr. 2: 15. Whose ways are c. [7: 13.
Is. 27: 1. leviathan, c. serpent
40: 4. c. be straight, 42: 16. Lu. 3: 5.
45: 2. I will make c. pla. straight
59: 8. they have made c. paths
La. 3: 9. he hath made my paths c.
Ph. 2: 15. in midst of c. nation

CROP. [Noun.]

Le. 1: 16. shall pluck away his c.

CROP, PED.

Eze. 17: 4. c-d top of young twigs
22. c. off from the top of twigs

CROSS. [14: 27.

Mat. 10: 38. taketh not his c., Lu.
16: 24. take up his c. and follow me, Mk. 8: 34.—10: 21. Lu. 9: 23.
27: 32. Simon, they compel. to bear his c., Mk. 15: 21. Lu. 23: 26.
40. If Son of G., come down from c., 42. Mk. 15: 30, 32.
Jn. 19: 17. he bearing his c. went
19. wrote title, put it on c.
25. stood by c. his mother
31. bodies not remain upon c. on
1 Co. 1: 17. lest c. be of none effect
18. preaching of c. foolishness
Ga. 5: 11. offence of c. ceased
6: 12. persecution for c. of Christ
14. forbid I sho. glory, save in c.
Ep. 2: 16. reconcile both by c.
Ph. 2: 8. obedient unto death of c.
3: 18. are enemies of c. of Christ
Col. 1: 20. made peace thro. blood of
2: 14. nailing it to his c. [c.
He. 12: 2. for joy endured c.

CROSSWAY.

Ob. 14. nor have stood in the c.

CROUCH, ETH.

1 S. 2: 36. c. to him for piece of silv.
Ps. 10: 10. He c-h and humbleth

CROW, ING. See Cock.

CROWN. [Noun.]

Ex. 25: 25. golden c. to the border
29: 6. put holy c. upon the mitre
30: 4. golden rings under c., 37: 27.
39: 30. plate of the c. of pure gold
Le. 8: 9. upon his forefront the c.
21: 12. c. of anointing oil upon him
2 K. 11: 12. c. upon Joash, 2 Ch.
Es. 1: 11. Vashti with c. [23: 11.
Jb. 31: 36. bind it as a c. to me
Ps. 89: 39. thou hast profaned his c.
132: 18. upon himself c. flourish
Pr. 4: 9. c. of glory sh. she deliver
12: 4. virtuous woman is c. to hus.
14: 24. c. of wise is their riches
16: 31. hoary head is c. of glory
17: 6. chil.'s chil. c. of old men
27: 24. c. endure to ev. generation?
Can. 3: 11. behold k. Sol. with c.
Is. 28: 1. Woe to the c. of pride
5. Lord shall be for a c. of glory
62: 3. shalt also be a c. of glory
Je. 13: 18. c. of glory come down
Eze. 21: 26. diadem, take off c.
Zch. 9: 16. they sh. be as stones of c.
Jn. 19: 5. J. wearing a c. of thorns
1 Co. 9: 25. obtain corruptible c.
Ph. 4: 1. dearly belov. my joy and c.
1 Th. 2: 19. what is our c. of rejoic.
2 Ti. 4: 8. laid up for me a c. of
Ja. 1: 12. he shall receive c. of life
1 Pe. 5: 4. ye shall receive c. of glory
Re. 2: 10. I will give a c. of life
3: 11. that no man take thy c.
6: 2. c. given unto him, and went

CROWN of gold.

Ex. 25: 11. make upon it a c. o. g., 24.—30: 3.—37: 2, 11, 12, 26.
Es. 8: 15. Mord with great c. o. g.
Ps. 21: 3. settest c. o. g. on his head

CROWN with head.

Ge. 49: 26. shall be on c. of Jo.'s h.
De. 33: 20. teareth arm with c. of h.
2 S. 1: 10. I took the c. upon his h.
12: 30. k.'s c. from h., 1 Ch 20: 2.
14: 25. from sole to c. of h., Jb. 2: 7.
Es. 2: 17. king set the c. upon her h.
6: 8. c. royal which is upon his h.
Jb. 19: 9. hath taken c. from my h.
Is. 3: 17. smite with scab the c. of h.
Je. 2: 16. have broken c. of thy h.
48: 45. c. of h. of tumultuous ones
La 5: 16. c. is fallen fr. our h. [h.
Eze. 16: 12. beautiful c. upon thine
Mat. 27: 29. c. of thorns, and put it on his h., Mk. 15: 17. Jn. 19: 2.
Re. 12: 1. upon her h. c. of 12 stars
14: 14. having on his h. a golden c.

CROWNS.

1 Ch. 2: † 54. c. of house of Joab
Eze. 23: 42. beautif. c. on their heads
Zch. 6: 11. make c. | 14. c. to Helem
Re. 4: 4. elders had c. of gold
10. cast their c. before the throne
9: 7. on locusts' heads c. like gold
12: 3. a red dragon having seven c.
13: 1. having upon his horns ten c.
19: 12. on his head were many c.

CROWN, ED.

Ps. 5: † 12. with favour wilt c. him
8: 5. thou hast c-d him with glory
Pr. 14: 18. prudent c-d with knowl
Can. 3: 11. crown his mother c-d him
Na. 3: 17. Thy c-d are as locusts
2 Ti. 2: 5. not c-d except he strive
He. 2: 9. we see J. c-d with glory

CROWNEDST, EST.

Ps. 65: 11. c-est year with thy goodn
He. 2: 7. thou c-dst him with glory

CROWNETH, ING.

Ps. 103: 4. c-h thee with loving-k.
Is. 23: 8. against Tyre the c-g city

CRUCIFY.

Mat. 20: 19. deliv. to Gent. to c. him
23: 34. some of them ye shall c.
27: 31. away to c. him, Mk. 15: 20

Mk. 15 : 13. cried again, c. him, 14.
27. with him they c. two thieves
Lu. 23 : 21. they cried, c. him, c. him, Jn. 19 : 6, 15.
Jn. 19 : 10. I have power to c. thee
He. 6 : 6. they c. Son of G. afresh

CRUCIFIED. [24:7.
Mat. 26 : 2. betrayed to be c., Lu.
27:22. Let him be c., 23. Lu.23:23.
26. Pilate delivered him to be c., Mk.15:15.Jn.19:16. [Jn.19:23.
35. c. him and parted, Mk.15:24.
38. thieves c. with him, 44. Mk. 15 : 32. Lu. 23:33. Jn. 19:18,32.
28:5.seek Jes.who was c.,Mk.16:6.
Mk. 15 : 25. third hour they c. him
Lu.24:20. to death and have c. him
Jn. 19 : 20. where Jesus was c., 41.
Ac. 2:23. by wick. hands ye have c.
36. made J. whom ye c. L., 4:10.
Ro. 6:6. our old man is c. with him
1 Co. 1 : 13. was Paul c. for you?
23. we preach C. c. unto Jews
2 : 2. know thing, save J. C. him c.
8. would not have c. L. of glory
2 Co. 13 : 4. tho. he was c. through
Ga. 2 : 20. I am c. with C. [weakn.
3 : 1. C. been set forth, c. among you [flesh
5 : 24. they that are C.'s have c.
6:14. by whom world is c. unto me
Re. 11 : 8. Egypt, where our L. was [c.

CRUEL.
Ge. 49 : 7. their wrath, for it was c.
Ex. 6 : 9. hearkened not for c.bond.
De. 32 : 33. wine as c. venom of asps
Jb. 30:21.Thou art become c. to me
Ps. 25 : 19. hate me with c. ha'red
71 : 4. deliv. out of hand of c. man
Pr. 5 : 9. lest give thy years to c.
11:17. that is c. troubleth his flesh
12:10. mercies of the wicked are c.
17:11. c. messenger be sent ag. him
27:4. Wrath c. | Can. 8:6. jealousy
Is. 13 : 9. day of L. cometh, c. [c.
19 : 4. Egyp-s will I give to c. lord
Je. 6 : 23. they are c., 50 : 42.
30 : 14. with chastisement of c. one
La. 4:3. daughter of my people is c.
He. 11 : 36. had trial of c. mockings

CRUELLY.
Eze. 18 : 18. because he c. oppressed

CRUELTY.
Ge. 49 : 5. instruments of c. in their
Ju. 9 : 24. c. done to sons of Jerub.
Ps. 27 : 12. such as breathe out c.
74 : 20. are full of habitations of c.
Pr. 27 : † 4. Wrath is c. anger is
Eze. 34 : 4. with c. ye ruled them

CRUMBS.
Mat. 15 : 27. dogs eat c., Mk. 7 : 28.
Lu. 16:21. to be fed with c. wh. fell

CRUSE.
1 S. 26:11. take spear and c. of wat.
12. so Da. took spear and c., 16.
1 K. 14 : 3. take c. of honey and go
17 : 12. I have but little oil in a c.
14. nor c. of oil fail, till Lord, 16.
19 : 6. Elijah had c. of water at his
2 K. 2:20. Bring me new c. put salt

CRUSH. [c.
Jb. 39 : 15. forgetteth her foot may
La. 1 : 15. to c. my young men
3 : 34. to c. under feet all prisoners
Am. 4 : 1. kine of Bashan c. needy

CRUSHED.
Le. 22 : 24. not offer to L. what is c.
Nu. 22 : 25. ass c. Balaam's foot
De. 28:33. be only oppressed and c.
Ju. 10 : † 8. Philis. c. chil. of Isr.
2 Ch.16:†10.Asa c. some of the peo.
Jb. 4 : 19. which are c. bef. moth
5 : 4. his chil. are c. in the gates
20 : † 19. Bec. he hath c. the poor
34:†25. he overturneth they are c.
Is. 59 : 5. is c. breaketh into a viper
Je. 51 : 34. Nebuchadn. hath c. me

CRY, CRIES.
Ge. 18 : 21. acc. to c. wh. is come up
Ex. 2 : 23. c. came up unto G., 3:9.
3 : 7. I have heard their c. I know
Nu.16:34. Isr. fled at the c. of them
Ju. 4 : † 13. gath. by c. his chariots
1 S. 5 : 12. c. of city went to heaven
9:16. bec. their c. is come unto me
2 S. 22 : 7. my c. did enter his ears
1 K. 8 : 28. to hearken unto the c. and to the prayer, 2 Ch. 6 : 19.
Ne. 5 : 6. angry wh. I heard their c.
9 : 9. heardest their c. by Red sea
Es. 4 : 1. Mord. cried with bitter c.
9 : 31. matters of fastings and c.
Jb. 16 : 18. let my c. have no place
34 : 28. cause c. of poor to come, he heareth c. of afflicted
Ps. 5:2. Hearken unto my c. my K.
9 : 12. forgetteth not c. of humble
17 : 1. O Lord, attend unto my c.
18 : 6. my c. came before him [c.
34:15. his ears are open unto their
39:12. O Lord, give ear unto my c.
40:1. he inclined, and heard my c.
88:2. incline thine ear unto my c.
102 : 1. O L., let my c. come unto
106 : 44. regarded, wh. he heard c.
119 : 169. Let my c. come bef. thee
142 : 6. Attend unto c. I am low
Pr. 21 : 13. stopp. ears at c. of poor
Ec. 9 : 17. than c. of him th. ruleth
Is. 5 : 7.looked for righte., behold c.
15 : 5. raise up c. of destruction
8.c.is gone round borders of Moab
30 : 19. he will be gracious at thy c.
43 : 14. Chald. whose c. is in ships
Je. 7:16. neith. lift c. for them, 11:14.
8 : 19. Behold voice of c. of my peo.
14 : 2. c. of Jerusalem is gone up
18:22. Let c. be heard from houses
25 : 36. c. of shepherds be heard
46 : 12. thy c. hath filled the land
48 : 4. little ones caused c. heard
5. enemies heard c. of destruction
34. From c. of Hesh. unto Elealeh
49 : 21. is moved at the c. of Edom
50 : 46. c. heard at taking of Bab.
51 : 54. sound of a c. from Bab.
La.3 : 56. hide not ear at my c.
Eze. 27 : 28. shake at c. of pilots
Zph. 1 : 10. be a c. from fish gate
Mat.25:6. at midnight was a c. made
Ja. 5 : 4. c-s of th. that reaped are
Re. 14 : 18. loud c. to him with sickle

Great CRY.
Ge. 18 : 20. c. of Sodom is g., 19:13.
27 : 34. Esau cried with a g. c.
Ex.11:6.shall be a g. c. thro. Egypt
12 : 30. there was a g. c. in Egypt
Ne.5:1.was g. c. of people and wives
Ac. 23 : 9. so said, arose a g. c.

Hear or Not hear CRY.
Ex. 22 : 23. I will surely h. their c.
Jb.27:9.Will G. h. his c. when trou.
Ps. 61 : 1. h. my c. O God, attend
145 : 19. he will h. their c. and save
Je. 14 : 12. they fast, I will n. h. c.
20 : 16. let him h. c. in morning

CRY. [Verb.]
Ex. 5:8. they are idle, theref. they c.
22 : 23. If thou afflict, and they c.
32:18. nei. is it voice of them that c.
Le. 13 : 45. cov. lip, and c. unclean
Ju. 10 : 14. Go c. unto the gods ye
2 S.19:28.What right I to c. to king
2 K. 8 : 3. went to c. for her house
2 Ch.20:9. c. in our afflic.,thou hear
Jb. 30 : 20. I c., thou dost not hear
24. tho. they c. in his destruction
35 : 9. oppressed to c. they c. out
12. they c. but none giveth ans.
36 : 13. they c.not when he bindeth
38:41.when his young ones c. to G.
Ps. 22 : 2. I c. in daytime, thou
27 : 7. Hear, O L., when I c.,28 : 2.
28:1.unto thee will I c., my rock, 2.
Ps. 34 : 17. The righteous c. and L. heareth [turn back
56 : 9. When I c. mine enemies
57 : 2. I will c. unto G. Most High
61 : 2. From end of earth will I c.
86 : 3. Be merciful, for I c. daily
89 : 26. sh. c., Thou art my father
141 : 1. Lord, I c., make haste
147 : 9. food to young ravens wh.c.
Pr. 8 : 1. Doth not wisdom c. ?
21 : 13. he shall c. but not be heard
Is.8:4. bef. child knowl. to c. My fa.
10 : † 30. c. shrill, O dau. of Gallim
13:22.wild beasts of island shall c.
14 : 31. c. O city, thou Palestina
15 : 4. Heshbon sh. c. and Elealeh
33 : 7. their valiant ones shall c.
34 : 14. satyr shall c. to his fellow
40 : 2. c. to Jerus., her warfare
6. said, c. he said,What sh. I c.?
42:2.he shall not c. nor cause voice
13. he sh. c. yea. prevail ag. enem.
14. will I c. like travailing woman
46 : 7. one shall c., he not answer
58 : 9. shalt c. and he say, Here I
65:14.ye shall c.for sorrow of heart
Je. 2 : 2. Go and c. in ears of Jerus.
3:4.Wilt thou not from this time c.
4 : 5. Blow ye trumpet, c. gather
11:11. tho. they c.,I will not heark.
12. c. unto gods to wh. they offer
14. not hear when they c., Eze. 8:
22:20. Go up to Leb., and c. fr. [18.
25 : 34. Howl ye shepherds and c.,
48 : 20. Eze. 21 : 12. [c.
31 : 6.watchmen upon Ephraim sh.
46 : 17. c. there, Pha. is but a noise
47 : 2. men shall c. and all inhab.
49 : 3. c. ye daughters of Rabbah
29. shall c. Fear is on every side
La. 3 : 8. when I c. he shutteth out
Eze. 9 : 4. that c. for abomina. done
24:17.Forbear to c.make no mourn.
26 : 15. isles shake, wh. wounded c.
27:30. they sh. c. bitterly for Tyrus
Hos. 8 : 2.Isr. shall c.,We know thee
Jo. 1 : 19. O Lord, to thee will I c.
20. beasts c. also unto thee
Jon.3:8.let man and beast c.unto G.
Mi. 3 : 5. prophets c. Peace
Na. 2 : 8. th. c. but none look back
Zph. 1 : 14. mighty shall c. bitterly
Zch. 1 : 14. angel said c. thou, 17.
Mat.12 :19.He shall not strive,nor c.
Lu. 18:7. not G. avenge elect, wh. c.
Ro. 8 : 15.whereby we c. Abba, Fat.
Ga. 4 : 27. c. thou that travailest not

CRY against. [15.
De. 15 : 9. he c. unto L. a. thee, 24 :
2 Ch.13:12.priests to c. alarm a.you
Jb. 31 : 38. If my land c. a. me
Jon. 1 : 2. go to Nineveh, and c. a.it

CRY aloud.
1 K. 18 : 27. Elijah said, c. a. for he
Jb. 19 : 7. I c. a. but is no judgm.
Ps. 55 : 17. at noon will I c. a.
Is. 24 : 14. they shall c. a. from sea
54 : 1.break forth into singing,c.a.
58 : 1. c. a. spare not, lift voice
Ho. 5 : 8. c. a. at Beth-aven
Mi. 4 : 9. why c. a.? is there no king

CRY out.
1 S. 2 : † 24. make L.'s people c. o.
4 : † 19.was with child, near to c.o.
8 : 18. ye shall c. o. bec. of your k.
Jb. 19 : 7. I c. o.of wrong, but I am
35 : 9.c.o. by rea. of arm of mighty
Is. 12 : 6 c.o. thou inhabit. of Zion
15 : 4. soldiers of Moab shall c. o.
5. My heart shall c. o. for Moab
29 : 9. and wonder, c. o. and cry
Je. 48 : 31. I will c.o . for Moab
La. 2 : 19. Arise c. o. in the night,
Am. 3 : 4. young lion c. o. of den?
Ha. 1 : 2. I c.o.to thee,but thou not
2 : 11. the stone shall c.o. of wall
Mk.10:47.began to c. o. Have mercy

Lu. 19 : 40. stones would c. o.

CRY unto the Lord.

1 S. 7 : 8. Cease not to c. u. L.
Ps. 107 : 19. c. u. L. in trouble, 28.
Is. 19 : 20. c. u. L. bec. of oppressors
Jo. 1 : 14. sanctify a fast c. u. L.
Mi. 3 : 4. shall c. u. L. but he not

CRYING.

1 S. 4 : 14. Eli heard noise of c.
2 S. 13 : 19. Tamar went on c.
Jb. 39 : 7. nei. regard-h c. of driver
Ps. 69 : 3. I am weary of my c.
Pr. 19 : 18. not soul spare for his c.
30 : 15. horsel. two dau-s c. give
Is. 22 : 5. a day of c. to mountains
24 : 11. is a c. for wine in streets
65 : 19. c. be no more heard in her
Je. 48 : 3. c. sh. be from Horonaim
Zch. 4 : 7. bring forth head st. with c.
Mal. 2 : 13. covering altar with c.
Mat. 3 : 3. voice of one c. in wilder., Prepare, Mk. 1 : 3. Lu. 3 : 4. Jn. 1 : 23.
9 : 27. c., Thou Son of D. have mercy
21 : 15. saw chil. c. in the temple
Mk. 5 : 5. c. and cutting hims. with [stones
15 : 8. the mult., c. aloud
Lu. 4 : 41. devils c. Thou art Christ
Ac. 8 : 7. spirits c. came out of many
14 : 14. ran among people, c. out
17 : 6. rulers of the city c.
21 : 28. c. out, Men of Israel
36. mult. foll., c. Away with him
25 : 24. c. that he ought not to live
Ga. 4 : 6. your hearts c. Abba Fath.
He. 5 : 7. off. prayers with strong c.
Re. 14 : 15. Angel c. with loud voice
21 : 4. be no more death nor c.

CRYSTAL.

Jb. 28 : 17. and c. cannot equal it
Eze. 1 : 22. as colour of terrible c.
Re. 4 : 6. was a sea of glass like c.
21 : 11. light of city was clear as c.
22 : 1. pure river of life, clear as c.

CUBIT.

Ge. 6 : 16. in a c. shalt finish ark
De. 3 : 11. breadth of it a ft. c. of man
1 K. 7 : 24. the knops, ten in a c.
2 Ch. 4 : 3. ten in a c. compassing sea
Ez. 43 : 13. c. is a c. and hand br.
Mat. 6 : 27. add c. to stature? Lu. [12 : 25.

CUBITS.

Ge. 6 : 15. of ark 300 c. breadth 50 c.
7 : 20. fifteen c. upw. did waters
Ex. 25 : 10. two c. and half the ark
1 S. 17 : 4. Goliath's height six c.
1 K. 6 : 2. length 60 c. breadth 20
23. each of cherubim ten c.
7 : 38. ev. laver was four c. high
2 K. 14 : 13. Jehoash brake walls of Jerus., 400 c., 2 Ch. 25 : 23.
Eze. 6 : 3. height 60 c. breadth 60
Es. 5 : 14. gallows 50 c. high, 7 : 9.
Eze. 40 : 23. from gate to gate 100 c.
47. he measured the court, 100 c.
42 : 17. the settle shall be 14 c. long
41 : 2. breadth of door was ten c.
9. thickness of wall was five c.
43 : 16. altar shall be twelve c. long
Da. 3 : 1. height of image 60 c.
Zch. 5 : 2. length of flying roll 20 c.
Jn. 21 : 8. fr. land as it were 200 c.
Re. 21 : 17. wall of the city 144 c.

CUCKOO.

Le. 11 : 16. c. in abomina., De. 14 : 15.

CUCUMBERS.

Nu. 11 : 5. we remember the c.
Is. 1 : 8. as lodge in garden of c.

CUD. See CHEW and CHEWETH.

CUMBERED, ETH.

Lu. 10 : 40. Martha was c. about
13 : 7. why c-h it the ground?

CUMBRANCE.

De. 1 : 12. How can I bear your c.

CUMI.

Mk. 5 : 41. Jes. said unto her Talitha [c.

CUMMIN.

Is. 28 : 25. doth he not scatter c.
28 : 27. nor is cart wheel turned upon c. but c. is beaten
Mat. 23 : 23. ye pay tithes of c.

CUNNING, LY.

Ge. 25 : 27. grew, and Esau was a c. hunter [8, 35.
Ex. 26 : 1. cheru. of c. work, 31.-36:
28 : 15. make breastpl. of c. work
31 : 4. To devise c. works
35 : 33. to make any c. work
38 : 23. Aholiab a c. workman, 35 : 35.
39 : 8. made breastpl. of c. work
1 S. 16 : 16. c. player on a harp
18. son of Jesse is c. in playing
1 K. 7 : 14. c. to work in brass
1 Ch. 22 : 15. c. men for every work
25 : 7. all c. in songs, were 288
2 Ch. 2 : 7. c. to work in gold
13. have sent c. man of Huram
14. c. men of David thy fa., 7.
26 : 15. engines invented by c. men
Ps. 58 : † 5. be charmer never so c.
137 : 5. my right hand forget her c.
Pr. 19 : † 25. and simple will be c.
Can. 7 : 1. joints, work of c. workm.
Is. 3 : 3. take away the c. artificer
40 : 20 he seeketh a c. workman
Je. 9 : 17. send for c. women that
10 : 9. they are all work of c. men
Da. 1 : 4. chil. c. in knowledge
Hos. 6 : † 8. Gil. is a city c. for bl.
Ep. 4 : 14. carried by c. craftiness
2 Pe. 1 : 16. not followed c-y devised [fables

CUP.

Ge. 40 : 11. Pha.'s c. in mine hand, 13.
44 : 2. put silver c. in sack's mouth
12. c. was found in Benj. sack, 16.
2 S. 12 : 3. it drank of his own c.
1 K. 7 : 26. like brim of c., 2 Ch. 4 : 5.
Ps. 11 : 6. be portion of their c.
16 : 5. L. is the portion of my c.
23 : 5. my c. runneth over
73 : 10. waters of full c. are wrung
75 : 8. in hand of Lord is a c.
116 : 13. I will take the c. of salv.
Pr. 23 : 31. giveth its colour in c.
Is. 51 : 17. hast drunk at hand of L. the c. dregs of c. of trembling
22. taken the c. of trembling
Je. 16 : 7. nor give c. of consolation
25 : 15. Take wine-c. of this fury
17. took I c. at Lord's hand
28. if they refuse c. at thine hand
49 : 12. judgm. not to drink c.
51 : 7. Bab. hath been a golden c.
La. 4 : 21. c. sh. pass thro. unto thee
Eze. 23 : 31. her c. into thine hand
32. shalt drink of thy sister's c., 31.
33. c. of astonish. | c. of Samaria
Ha. 2 : 16. c. of L.'s hand be turned
Zch. 12 : 2. Jerus. a c. of trembling
Mat. 10 : 42. c. of cold wat., Mk. 9 : 41.
20 : 22. Are ye able to drink of c.? Mk. 10 : 38. [39.
23. Ye sh. drink of my c., Mk 10:
23 : 25. clean outside of c., Lu. 11: [39.
26. cleanse first th. within c.
26 : 27. he took c. gave thanks, Mk. 14 : 23. Lu. 22 : 17, 20. 1 Co. 11 : 25.
39. if possible, let this c. pass from me, Mk. 14 : 36. Lu. 22 : 42.
42. if this c. may not pass fr. me
Lu. 22 : 20. this c. is new testament in my blood, 1 Co. 11 : 25.
Jn. 18 : 11. c. my Fa. hath giv. me
1 Co. 10 : 16. c. of blessing we bless
21. not drink c. of L. c. of devils
11 : 26. as often as ye drink of c.
27. drink c. of Lord unworthily
28. so let him drink of that c.
Re. 14 : 10. without mixture into c.
16 : 19. unto her c. of his wrath
17 : 4. woman having a golden c.
18 : 6. in c. she filled, fill double

CUPS.

2 S. 17 : † 28. Barzillai brought c.
1 Ch. 28 : 17. Da. gave gold for c.
Is. 22 : 24. on Eliakim vessels of c.
Je. 35 : 5. set pots full of wine and c.
52 : 19. Chal. took spoons and c.
Mk. 7 : 4. as the washing of c., 8.

CUPBEARER, S.

1 K. 10 : 5. queen saw c-s, 2 Ch. 9 : 4.
Ne. 1 : 11. For I was the king's c.

CURDLED.

Jb. 10 : 10 Hast c. me like cheese?

CURE, S.

Je. 33 : 6. I will bring it c.
46 : † 11. dau. of E., no c. be to thee
Lu. 13 : 32. I do c-s to-day and

CURE, ED.

Je. 33 : 6. I will c. them and will
46 : 11. O dau. of E., thou not be c.
Ho. 5 : 13. not c. you of wound
Mat. 17 : 16. disci. could not c. him
18. child was c. from that hour
Lu. 7 : 21. same hour he c. many
9 : 1. them power to c. diseases
Jn. 5 : 10. Jews said to him th. was c.

CURIOUS, LY.

Ex. 28 : 8. c. girdle, 27, 28.-29 : 5. -39 : 5. Le. 8 : 7.
35 : 32. devise c. works in gold
Ps. 139 : 15. c-y wrought in lowest
Ac. 19 : 19. many that used c. arts

CURLED.

Can. 5 : † 11. his locks are c. and

CURRENT.

Ge. 23 : 16. c. money with merch.

CURSE. [Noun.]

Ge. 27 : 12. I shall bring a c. on me
13. moth. said, Upon me be thy c.
Nu. 5 : 18. priest have bitter water that causeth c., 19, 22, 24, 27.
27. woman be a c. among people
De. 11 : 26. I set before you this day blessing and c., 30 : 1.
28. a c. if you will not obey com.
29 shalt put c. upon Ebal
21 : † 23. he hanged is c. of God
23 : 5. c. into a blessing, Ne. 13 : 2.
29 : 19. heareth words of this c.
Jos. 6 : 18. make camp of Isr. a c.
Ju. 9 : 57. came c. of Jotham
1 K. 2 : 8. me with a grievous c.
2 K. 22 : 19. that they become a c.
Ne. 10 : 29. they entered into a c.
Jb. 31 : 30. to sin by wishing c.
Pr. 3 : 33 c. of L. in house of wick.
26 : 2. c. causeless shall not come
27 : 14. it be counted a c. to him
28 : 27. hideth eyes have many a c.
Is. 24 : 6. c. devoured the earth
34 : 5. come upon people of my c.
43 : 28. theref. given Jacob to c.
65 : 15. leave your name for a c.
Je. 24 : 9. deliver them to be a c., 25 : 18.-29 : 18.-42 : 18.-44 : 8, 12.
26 : 6 I will make city c. to na.
29 : 22. be taken up a c. by all
44 : 22. theref. is your land a c.
49 : 13. sworn Bozrah shall bec. a c.
La. 3 : 65. Give thy c. unto them
Da. 9 : 11. the c. is poured upon us
Zch. 5 : 3. This is the c. that goeth
8 : 13. as ye were c. amo. heathen
Mal. 2 : 2. if not hear, I will send c.
3 : 9. cursed with c. for ye robbed
4 : 6. lest I smite earth with a c.
Ac 23 : 12. bound under a c., 14.
Ga. 3 : 10. as are of the works of law, are under c. [a c.
13. C. redeemed fr. c. being made
Re. 22 : 3. shall be no more c.

CURSES.

Nu. 5 : 23. priest sh. write these c.
De. 28 : 15. these c. shall come, 45.
29 : 20. all the c. that are written in this book, 27. 2 Ch. 34 : 24.
21. according to all c. of cove.
30 : 7. will put these c. upon enem.

CURSE. [Verb.]

Ge. 8 : 21. I will not c. ground

Ge.12:3. will c. him th. curseth thee
Ex. 22:28. shalt not c. ruler of peo.
Le. 19 : 14. shalt not c. the deaf
Nu. 22 : 6. Come, I pray thee, c. me this people, 17.
11. Balak said, come, c. me them, 23 : 7, 13, 27.
12. Balaam, Thou sh. not c. peo.
23 : 8. How shall I c. whom G. not?
11. I took thee to c. enem., 24:10.
25. Neither c. them at all, nor
De. 23 : 4. hired Balaam to c., Ne.
27:13. stand upon Ebal to c. [13:2.
Jos. 24:9. Balak called Balaam to c.
Ju. 5 : 23. c. Meroz, c. ye bitterly
2 S. 16:9. Why this dead dog c. king?
10. let him c. bec. L. said, c., 11.
Jb. 1 : 11. c. thee to thy face, 2 : 5.
2 : 9. said wife, c. God and die
3 : 8. Let them c. it that c. the day
Ps. 62 : 4. bless with mouth, but c.
109 : 28. Let them c. but bless thou
Pr. 11:26. withh. corn, peo. shall c.
24 : 24. him shall the people c.
30 : 10. Accuse not serv., lest he c.
Ec. 7 : 21. lest hear servant c. thee
10 : 20. c. not the king, c. not rich
Is. 8 : 21. c. their king and God
Je. 15 : 10. every one doth c. me
Mal. 2 : 2. I will c. your blessings
Mat. 5 : 44. bless them that c. you, Lu. 6 : 28. [14 : 71.
26 : 74. then began he to c., Mk.
Ro. 12 : 14. bless and c. not
Ja. 3 : 9. therewith c. we men

CURSED.

Ge. 3 : 14. serp. c. | 17. c. is ground
4 : 11. Cain c. | 9:25. c. be Canaan
5 : 29. bec. of ground Lord hath c.
27 : 29. c. be ev. one curseth, Nu.
49 : 7. c. be their anger, for [24:9.
Le. 20 : 9. hath c. father or mother
24 : 11. blasphemed the name of the Lord and c. [23.
14. Bring forth him th. hath c.,
Nu. 22 : 6. he wh. thou cursest is c.
23 : 8. How curse, whom G. not c.
De. 27 : 15. c. be he, 16, 17, 18, 19, 20, 21, 22, 23, 24, 25, 26.
28 : 16. c. in city, c. in field
17. c. sha. be thy basket and store
18. c. be fruit of thy body
19. c. when comest in, when goest
Jos. 6 : 26. c. be man build. Jeric.
9 : 23. Now ye Gibeonites are c.
Ju. 9 : 27. did drink, and c. Abim.
21:18. c. he that giv. wife to Benj.
1 S.14:24. c. th. eateth till even., 28.
17 : 43. Philis. c. David by his gods
26 : 19. but if men, c. be they
2 S. 16 : 5. Shimei c. still, 7, 13.
19 : 21. bec. he c. L.'s anointed
1 K. 2 : 8. Shimei who c. me with
2 K. 2 : 24. c. them in name of L.
9 : 34. Go see now this c. woman
Ne. 13 : 25. I contend. and c. them
Jb. 1 : 5. may be my sons have c. G.
3 : 1. then Job c. his day
5 : 3. suddenly I c. his habitation
24 : 18. their portion is c. in earth
Ps. 37 : 22. they c. of him be cut off
119 : 21. rebuked proud that are c.
Ec. 7 : 22. thyself hast c. others
Je. 11 : 3. c. be man obey. not cov.
17 : 5. c. be man trusteth in man
20 : 14. c. be day I was born
15. c. man who bro-t tidings to fa.
48 : 10. c. that doeth L.'s work deceitfully, c. that keepeth
Mal. 1 : 14. but c. be the deceiver
2 : 2. I have c. your blessings
3 : 9. Ye are c. with a curse, for ye
Mat. 25 : 41. Depart from me ye c.
Jn. 7 : 49. knoweth not law are c.
Ga. 3 : 10. c. that continueth not
13. c. that hangeth on tree
2 Pe. 2:14. c. chil. who have forsak.

CURSED thing.

De. 7 : 26. lest be c. t. for it is c.t.
13 : 17. nought of c.t. to thy hand

CURSEDST, ETH.

Ge. 12 : 3. curse him that c. thee
27 : 29. cursed be every one that c. thee, Nu. 24 : 9.
Ex. 21 : 17. that c. his fa. be put to death, Le. 20 : 9. Pr. 20 : 20.
Le. 24 : 15. whoso. c. his G. sh. bear
Nu. 22 : 6. whom thou c-t is cursed
Ju. 17 : 2. silver which thou c-t
Pr. 30 : 11. genera. that c. father
Mat. 15 : 4. that c. fa. or mother, let him die death, Mk. 7 : 10.
Mk.11:21. fig tree thou c-t is wither.

CURSING, S. [c.

Nu. 5 : 21. charge wom. with oath of
De. 27 : † 13. stand for a c. on Ebal
28 : 20. L. shall send upon thee c.
30 : 19. set bef. you blessing and c.
Jos. 8 : 34. he read blessings and c-s
2 S.16:12. requite me good for his c.
Ps. 10 : 7. mouth full of c., Ro.3:14.
59 : 12. c. and lying they speak
109 : 17. he loved c. so let it come
18. he clothed himself with c.
Pr. 29:24. heareth c. bewrayeth not
Je. 23 : † 10. bec. of c. land mourn.
He. 6 : 8. bear. thorns is nigh unto
Ja. 3 : 10. out of same mouth c. [c.

CURTAIN.

Ex. 36 : 9. length of one c. was, 15.
12. loops made he in c., 11, 17.
Ps. 104 : 2. who stretchest out the heavens like a c., Is. 40 : 22.

CURTAINS.

Ex. 26 : 1. tab. with ten c., 2.-36:8.
Nu. 4 : 25. Gershonites bear c.
2 S. 7:2. ark within c., 1 Ch. 17:1.
Can. 1 : 5. am comely as c. of Sol.
Is. 54:2. stretch forth c. of thy hab.
Je. 4 : 20. tents spoiled, and my c.
10 : 20. none to set up my c.
49 : 29. they shall take their c.
Ha. 3 : 7. c. of Midian did tremble

CUSH.

Ge. 10:6. sons of Ham, C., 1 Ch.1:8.
7. sons of C. Seba and Havilah
8. C. begat Nimrod, 1 Ch. 1:9, 10.
Is. 11 : 11. recover remn. left fr. C.

CU'SHAN.

Ha. 3 : 7. tents of C. in affliction

CU'SHI. [seen

2 S. 18 : 21. C. tell king what hast
23. Ahimaaz overran C.
Je. 36 : 14. all princes sent son of C.
Zph. 1 : 1. word to Zph. son of C.

CUSTODY.

Nu. 3 : 36. c. of sons of Merari
Es. 2 : 3. virgins to c. of Hege, 8.
14. to c. of Shaashgaz the king's

CUSTOM.

Ge. 31 : 35. c. of women is upon me
Ju. 11 : 39. and it was a c. in Isr.
1 S. 2 : 13. priests' c. with peo. was
Ezr. 3 : 4. acc. to the c., Je. 32 : 11.
4 : 13. then will they not pay c.
20. been kings, and c. was paid
7:24. sh. not impose c. upon priests
Ps. 119 : † 132. be merciful acc. to c.
Mat. 9 : 9. Jes. saw Matthew at receipt of c., Mk. 2 : 14. Lu.5:27.
17 : 25. of whom do kings take c.?
Lu. 1 : 9. acc. to c. of priest's office
2 : 27. to do for him after c. of law
42. to Jerusalem after c. of feast
4:16. as Jesus c., he went into syn.
Jn. 18 : 39. a c. that I release one
Ro. 13 : 7. render c. to wh. c. is due
1 Co. 11 : 16. we have no such c.

CUSTOMS.

Le. 18 : 30. none of these abom. c.
Je. 10 : 3. c. of the people are vain
Ac. 6 : 14. change c. Moses deliv-d
16 : 21. teach c. not lawful
21 : 21. ought not to walk after c.

Ac. 26:3. I know thee expert in all c.
28:17. tho. I commit-d nothing ag. [c.

CUT.

Ex. 39 : 3. c. it in wires to work it
Le. 1 : 6. shall c. the burnt off., 12.
8:20. c. ram into pieces, Ex. 29:17.
22 : 24. shall not offer what is c.
De. 14 : 1. ye sh. not c. yourselves
Ju. 20:6. concu. and c. her in pieces
1 K. 18 : 23. c. bullock in pieces, 33.
28. c. thems. after their manner
2 K. 24 : 13. be c. in pieces all vessels of gold, 2 Ch. 28 : 24.
1 Ch. 20 : 3. he c. them with saws
2 Ch. 2 : 8. skill to c. timber, 10, 16.
Ps. 58 : 7. let them be as c. in pieces
107 : 16. c. bars of iron, Is. 45 : 2.
Is. 9 : † 20. he shall c. on the right
51 : 9. art thou th. hath c. Rahab
Je. 16 : 6. lament, nor c. thems.
34 : 18. when they c. calf in twain
36 : 23. he c. roll with penknife
41 : 5. clothes rent, having c. th.
47 : 5. how long wilt c. thyself?
Eze. 16 : 4. thy navel was not c.
Da. 2 : 5. if ye will not, shall be c.
3 : 29. who speak ag. G. shall be c.
Am. 9 : 1. c. them in the head
Ha. 3 : † 16. c.'th. with his troops
Zch. 12:3. burden thems. with it be
Ac. 5:33. were c. to heart, 7 : 54. [c.
27 : † 40. when had c. anchors

CUT asunder.

Ps. 129 : 4. c. a. cords of wicked
Je. 50 : 23. hammer of earth c. a.
Zch.11:10. staff Beauty, and c. it a.
14. then I c. a. my other staff
Mat. 24:51. shall c. him a., Lu.12: [46.

CUT down.

Ex. 34:13. ye shall c.d. their groves, De. 7 : 5. 2 K. 18 : 4.-23 : 14.
Le. 26 : 30. I will c.d. your images
Nu. 13 : 23. c. d. a branch, 24.
De. 19 : 5. stroke with axe to c. d.
20 : 19. trees for meat not c. d.
20. trees not for meat shalt c. d.
Jos. 17 : 15. wood country and c.d.
Ju. 6:25. c.d. grove that is by it, 30.
9 : 48. c. d. bough from trees
2 K. 6 : 4. to Jor. they c. d. wood
6. c. d. stick and cast it in
19 : 23. I will c.d. cedars, Is.37:24.
2 Ch. 15 : 16. and Asa c.d. her idol
34 : 7. Josiah c.d. all idols in the
Jb. 8 : 12. in his greenness, not c.d.
14:2. forth like flower, and is c.d.
7. hope of a tree if it be c. d.
22 : 16. wicked c. d. out of time
20. our substance is not c. d.
Ps. 37 : 2. they shall soon be c. d.
80:16. branch is burned, it is c.d.
90 : 6. in the evening it is c. d.
Is. 9 : 10. sycamores are c. d. but
10 : 34. c. d. thickets in forests
14 : 12. how art th. c.d. to ground
18 : 5. c. d. the branches
22 : 25. the nail shall be c. d.
Je. 22 : 7. sh. c.d. thy choice cedars
25 . 37. peaceable habita. are c.d.
46 : 23. c.d. her forest, saith Lord
48 : 2. shalt be c. d. O Madmen
Eze. 6 : 6. that images may be c.d.
39 : 10. neith. c. d. out of forests
Na. 1 : 12. tho. many, shall be c.d.
Zph. 1 : 11. merchant peo. are c.d.
Mat. 21 : 8 c.d. branches, Mk.11:8.
Lu. 13 : 7. c. it d. why cumbereth
9. after that thou shalt c. it d.

CUT off.

Ge. 9 : 11. neith. all flesh be c. o.
17 : 14. uncirc. child shall be c.o.
41:†36. land be not c.o. thro. fam.
Ex. 4 : 25. c. o. foreskin of son
8 : † 9. to c.o. the frogs from thee
9 : 15. thou sh. be c.o. from earth
12 : 15. soul sh. be c. o., 19.-31 : 14. Nu. 15 : 30, 31.-19 : 13.

x. 23 : 23. and I will c. them o.
30 : 33. shall be c.o. from peo..38.
Le. 7 : 20, 21, 25, 27.-17 : 4, 9.-
19 : 8.-23 : 29. Nu. 9 : 13.
e. 17:10. I will c. him o. fr. people,
18 : 29.-20 3, 6, 18. Nu. 19:20
14. whoso. eateth blood be c. o.
20 : 17. be c. o. in sight of people
22 : 3. that soul shall be c. o. fr.
25 : † 23. not sold to be quite c. o.
Nu. 4 : 18. c. not o. Kohathites
15:31. th. soul sh. utterly be c. o.
De. 12 : 29. God shall c. o. nations
19:1. hath c. o. nations, Jos 23:4.
23 : 1. hath privy member c. o.
25 : 12. thou shalt c.o. her hand
Jos. 3:13. Jordan be c. o., 16.-4:7.
7 : 9. c. o. our name from earth
9 : † 23. not c.o. fr. being bondm.
11 : 21. Joshua c. o. the Anakims
Ju. 1 : 6 c. o. thumbs, and toes
21 : 6. there is one tribe c. o.
Ru. 4 : 10. name of dead not c. o.
1 S. 2 : 31. I will c. o. thine arm
33. man whom I shall not c. o.
5 : 4. Dagon's hands were c. o.
17 : 51. David c. o. Goliath's head
20 : 15. shalt not c. o. thy kindn.
not when L. hath c. o. enem.
24 : 4. Da. c. o. skirt of Saul's, 5.
21. Swear thou wilt not c. o. my
1 S. 24 : † 7. so David c.o. his servants with these words [robe
11. for in that I c.o. skirt of thy
28 : 9. how Saul hath c.o. wizards
31 : 9. and they c. o. Saul's head
2 S. 4:12. slew them and c.o. hands
7 : 9. c.o. thy enem. out of sight
10 : 4. Hanan took Da.'s servants,
and c. o. garments, 1 Ch. 19:4.
20 : 22. they c. o. head of Sheba
21 : † 5. man that c. us o. [man
1 K. 8 : † 25. not be c. o. to thee a
9 : 7. will I c. o. Isr. out of land
11 : 16. had c.o. ev. male in Edom
13 : 34. c.o. Jerob.'s house, 14:14.
14:10. I will c.o. from Jerob. him
18 : 4. when Jezebel c.o. prophets
21 : 21. I will c.o. from Ahab him
that pisseth, 2 K. 9 : 8.
2 K. 16 : 17. Ahaz c.o. borders of the
18 : 16. Hez. c. o. gold from doors
1 Ch. 17:8. have c.o. all thine enem.
2 Ch. 22 : 7. to c. o. house of Ahab
32:21. he was c. o. fr. house of L.
32 : 21. angel to c. o. mighty men
Jb. 4 : 7. where righteous c. o.?
6 : 9. let loose his hand, and c. me
8:14 whose hope shall be c.o. [o.
10:† 1. my soul is c. o. while I live
11 : 10. if he c. o. who hinder?
14 : † 10. man dieth, and is c. o.
18 : 16. shall his branch be c. o.
21 : 21. num. of his months is c. o.
23:17 I was not c.o. bef. darkness
24 : 24. c.o. as tops of ears of corn
30 : 20. when people are c. o.
Ps. 12 : 3. c. o. all flattering lips
31 : † 17. let the wicked be c. o.
22. I am c. o. before thine eyes
34 : 16. to c. o. remembr. of them
37 : 9. for evil doers shall be c. o.
22. they that be cursed be c. o.
28. seed of wicked shall be c. o.
34. wicked c. o., thou sh. see it
38. end of wicked shall be c. o.
54 : 5. c. them o. in thy truth
75 : 10. horns of wicked I c. o.
76 : 12. c. o. the spirit of princes
83 : 4. Come, let us c. them o.
88 : 5. are c. o. from thy hand
16. terrors have c. me o.
90 : 10. soon c.o. and we fly away
94 : 23. shall c. them o. in wick.
101 : 5. that slander-h will I c. o.
8. c. o. wicked doers from city
109 : 13. let his posterity be c. o.
Ps. 109 : 15. L. may c. o. mem. of th.
118 : † 10. in name of L. I will c.o.
119 : † 139. zeal hath c. me o.
143 : 12. of thy mercy c.o. enemies
Pr. 2 : 22. wicked shall be c. o.
23 : 18. expecta. not be c.o.,24:14.
Is. 6 : † 5. then said I, Woe is me,
for I am c. o.
9 : 14. L. will c. o. head and tail
10 : 7. to c. o. nations not a few
11 : 13. adversaries of Jud. be c.o.
14 : 22. c. o. from Bab. the name
15 : † 1. Moab c.o. | 2. beard c.o.
18 : 5 c. o. sprigs with pruning
22 : 25. a burden shall be c. o.
29 : 20. watch for iniq. are c. o.
38 : 12. c. me o. with pining sickn.
48:9. refrain, that I c. thee not o.
19. his name not have been c. o.
53 : 8. he was c. o. out of living
55 : 13. sign that shall not be c.o.
56 : 5. name, that sh. not be c. o.
66 : 3. as if he c. o. a dog's neck
Je. 7:28. truth is c.o. from mouth
29. c.o. thine hair, O Jerus. cast
9:21. to c. o. chil. and young men
11 : 19. let us c. him o. from living
44 : 7. to c.o. man and woman out
8. might c. yours. o. be a curse
11. my face ag. you to c.o. Jud.
46 : † 28. I not utterly c. thee o.
47 : 4. c.o. fr. Tyrus | 5. Ashkelon
48 : 2. c. it o. from being a nation
25. the horn of Moab is c. o.
49 : 26. men of war be c. o.,50:30.
50 : 16. c. o. sower from Babylon
51 : 6. be not c. o. in her iniquity
62. spoken ag. this place to c. it o.
La. 2 : 3. c.o. in anger horn of Isr.
3 : 53. c.o. my life in dungeon, 54.
Eze. 14:8. c. him o. from my people
13. c.o. man and beast, 17,19,21.
-25 : 13.-29 : 8.
17 : 9. shall he not c. o. fruit?
17. forts to c. o. many persons
21:3. c.o. righteous and wicked, 4.
25 : 7. I will c. thee o. fr. people
16. I will c. o. the Cherethim
30 : 15. I will c. o. multitude of No
31 : 12. terri. of nations c. him o.
35 : 7. c. o. from Seir him that
37 : 11. we are c. o. for our parts
Da. 4 : 14 tree c. o. his branches
9 : 26. Messiah shall be c. o., but
Ho. 4 : † 5. c. o. mother | † 6. peo.
8:4. idols, that may be c. o. [c.o.
10 : 7. Samaria, her k. is c. o., 15.
Jo. 1 : 5. the new wine is c. o., 9.
16. is meat c. o. before our eyes?
Am. 1 : 5. c. o. inhab. from Aven
8. c. o. inhabitant from Ashdod
2 : 3. I will c. o. judge fr. midst
3 : 14. horns of altar be c. o.
Ob. 5. how art thou c. o.
9. ev. one of Esau may be c. o.
10. thou shalt be c. o. for ever
14. c. o. those that did escape
Mi. 5 : 9. enemies shall be c. o.
10. horses | 11. cities c. o.
12. witchcrafts | 13. images c. o.,
Na. 1 : 15. wicked is c. o. [Na. 1:14.
2 : 13. c. o. thy prey from earth
3 : 15. sword shall c. thee o.
Ha. 3 : 17. tho. flock shall be c. o.
Zph. 1 : 3. c. o. man from land
4. c. o. remnant of Baal
11. that bear silver c. o.
3 : 6. I have c. o. the nations
7. so dwelling not be c. o.
Zch. 5 : 3. one th. sweareth be c.o.
9 : 6. c. o. pride of Philistines
10. c. o. chariot from Ephraim
11 : 8. three shepherds I c. o.
9. is to be c. o., let it be c. o.
16. not visit those that be c. o.
13 : 2. I will c. o. names of idols
8. two parts shall be c. o. and die
Zch. 14:2. residue shall not be c. o.
Mal 2 : 12. L. will c. o. man doeth
Mat. 5 : 30. if right hand offend, c.
it o., 18 : 8. Mk. 9 : 43, 45.
Mk. 14 : 47. c. o. his ear, Lu. 22 :
50. Jn. 18 : 10, 26. [boat
Ac. 27 : 32. soldiers c. o. ropes of
Ro. 11 : 22. thou shalt also be c. o.
2 Co. 11 : 12. I may c. o. occasion
Ga. 5 : 12. were c. o. that trouble

CUT out. [you

2 Ch. 26 : † 10. Uzziah c. o. cisterns
Jb. 33 : † 6. I am c. o. of the clay
Pr. 10 : 31. froward tongue be c. o.
Da. 2 : 34. c. o. without hands, 45.
Ro. 11 : 24 if c. o. of olive tree

CUT short.

2 K. 10 : 32. L. began to c. Isr. s.
Ro. 9 : 28. c. it s. in righteousness

CUT up.

Jb. 30 : 4. Who c. u. mallows by
Is. 33:12 as thorns c. u. be burned

CUTH, CU'THAH.

2 K. 17 : 30. men of C. made Nergal,

CUTTEST, ETH. [24.

De. 24 : 19. When thou c-t harvest
Jb. 28 : 10. he c. rivers am. rocks
Ps. 29 : † 7. voice of L. c. flames of
46 : 9. he c. the spear in sunder
141 : 7. as when one c. wood
Pr. 26 : 6. that sendeth message by
fool, c. off the feet
Je. 10 : 3. one c. tree out of forest
22 : 14. and c. him out windows

CUTTING, S.

Ex. 31 : 5. in c. of stones, 35 : 33.
Le. 19:28. not any c-s for dead,21:5.
25 : † 23. land not sold for c. off
De. 24 : † 1. write her bill of c. off
Is. 38 : 10. in the c. off. of my days
Je. 30 : † 23. a c. whirlwind, it sh.
48 : 37. upon all hands shall be c-s
Eze. 7 : † 25. c. off cometh
16 : † 3. thy c. out is of Canaan
Jon. 2 : † 6. I went to c-s of mount
Ha. 2:10. shame by c. off many peo.
Mk. 5 : 5. crying and c. hims. with

CYMBAL, S. [stones

1 Ch. 15 : 19. sound with c-s, 16:42.
16 : 5 Asaph with c-s, Ezr. 3 : 10.
2 Ch. 5 : 13. with c-s praised Lord
Ps 150 : 5. Praise him upon c-s [c.
1 Co 13 : 1. I am become as tinkling

CYMBALS, psalteries, harps

2 S. 6 : 5. all Israel played on h., p.,
c., 1 Ch. 13:8.-15:28.[2 Ch.5:12.
1 Ch. 15:16. singers with p., h., c.,
25 :1. sho. prophesy wi h., p., c.. 6.
2 Ch. 29 : 25. Levites with c., p., h.,

CYPRESS. [Ne. 12:27.

Can. 1:†14. unto me as cluster of c.
4 : † 13. fruits, c. with spikenard
Is. 44 : 14. he taketh c. and oak

CY'PRUS.

Ac. 4 : 36. Joses of country of C.
11 : 19. travelled as far as C.
20. some of them were men of C.
13 : 4. Seleucia they sailed to C.
15 : 39. took Mark and sailed to C.
21 : 3. when we had discovered C.
16. they bro-t one Mnason of C.
27 : 4. launched, we sailed und. C.

CYRE'NE.

Mat. 27 : 32. found man of C. Simon
Ac. 2 : 10. parts of Libya about C.
11 : 20. some were men of C.
13 : 1. Lucius of C. was in church

CYRE'NIAN, S.

Mk. 15:21. Simon a C to, Lu.23:26
Ac. 6 : 9. called synagogue of C-s

CYRE'NIUS.

Lu. 2 : 2. when C. was gov. of Syria

CY'RUS.

2 Ch. 36 : 22. first year of C. Lord
stirred up spirit of C., Ezr. 1 : 1.
23. thus saith C. king, Ezr. 1 : 2.
Ezr. 1 : 7. C. bro-t vessels, 8.-5 : 14

Ezr.3:7.acc. to grant they had of C.
4 : 3. will build as C. hath com. us
5 : 13. C. a decree to build, 17.-6:3.
Is. 44 : 28. of C., He is my shepherd
45 : 1. Lord to his anointed, to C.
Da. 1 : 21. continu. to 1st year of C
6 : 28. Dan. prosp-d in reign of C.
10:1. 3d yr. of C. thing was reveal.

D.

DAB'AREH.
Jos. 21 : 28. D. with her suburbs
DAB'BASHETH.
Jos. 19 : 11. their border reached to
DAB'ERATH. [D.
Jos. 19 : 12. then goeth out to D.
1 Ch. 6 : 72. out of Issachar, D.
DAGGER.
Ju. 3 : 16. Ehud made him **a d.** | 21.
22. could not draw **d.** out of belly
DA'GON. [god
Ju. 16 : 23. a sacrifice unto D. their
1 S. 5:2 ark into house of D (2) [off (3)
3. D. fallen (2), 4. | 4. head of D cut
5. nei. priests of D. into D.'s h. (8)
7. hand sore upon us and D. [of D.
1 Ch.10:10. Saul, his head in temple
DAILY. [straw, 19.
Ex.5:13. Fulfil your **d.** tasks as when
16:5. twice as much as gathered **d.**
Nu.4:16. **d.** meat offering, Eze.46:13.
28 : 24. this manner ye offer **d.**
29:6. beside **d.** burnt-off., Ezr. 3:4.
Ju. 16 : 16. she pressed him **d.**
2 K. 25 : 30. allowance was **a d.** rate
Ne. 5 : 18. was prepared for me **d.**
Es. 3:4. when they spake **d.** heark.
Ps. 13:2. sorrow in my heart **d.** [G.?
42 : 10. say **d.** unto me, Where thy
56:1. he fighting **d.** oppresseth me
2. enemies would **d.** swallow me
61:8. that I may **d.** perf. my vows
68: 19. Lord who **d.** loadeth us
72 : 15. and **d.** shall he be praised
74 : 22. foolish reproacheth thee **d.**
86 : 3. I cry **d.** | 88:9. I called **d.**
88 : 17. came round me **d.** like wat.
Pr. 8 : 30. I was **d.** his delight
34. watching **d.** at my gates
Is. 58 : 2. Yet they seek me **d.** and
Je. 7 : 25. **d.** rising up early and
20 : 7. I am in derision **d.**, 8.
37 : 21. give him **d.** price of bread
Eze. 30:16. Noph have distressed **d.**
45 : 23. Kid **d.** for sin offering
Da. 1 : 5. appointed **a d.** provision
8 : 11. by him the **d.** sacrifice was
taken away, 11 : 31.-12 : 11.
Ho. 12 : 1. Ephr. **d.** increaseth lies
Mat. 6 : 11. our **d.** bread, Lu. 11:3.
26 : 55. I sat **d.** with you in tem.,
Mk. 14 : 49. Lu. 19 : 47.-22:53.
Lu.9:23. let him take up his cross **d.**
Ac. 2 : 46. continuing **d.** with one
47. Lord added to the church **d.**
3 : 2. laid **d.** at gate of the temple
5 : 42. **d.** in temple and ev. house
6 : 1. widows neglected in **d.** minis.
16:5. churches incr. in number **d.**
17 : 11. Bereans searched scrip. **d.**
17. in the market **d.** [Tyr.
19 : 9. disputing **d.** in school of
1 Co. 15 : 31. I die **d.**
2 Co. 11:28. upon me **d.** care of ch-s
He. 3 : 13. but exhort one ano. **d.**
7 : 27. needeth not **d.** to offer
10 : 11. every priest standeth **d.**
Ja. 2 : 15. sister destitute of **d.** food
DAINTY, IES.
Ge. 49 : 20. Asher yield royal **d-s**
Jb. 33 : 20. soul abhorreth **d.** meat
Ps. 141 : 4. me not eat of their **d-s**
Pr. 23 : 3. not desirous of his **d-s**
6. neither desire his **d.** meats
Ha. 1 : † 16. is fat, their meat **d.**
Re. 18 : 14. all thi. **d.** are departed

DALAI'AH.
1 Ch. 3 : 24. sons of Elioenai, D.
DALE.
Ge. 14 : 17. valley of Shaveh, k.'s **d.**
2 S. 18 : 18. a pillar in king's **d.**
DALMANU'THA. [D.
Mk. 8 : 10. be with disci. came into
DALMA'TIA.
2 Ti. 4 : 10. Titus is departed unto D.
DAL'PHON.
Es. 9 : 7. in Shushan Jews slew D.
DAM. [22 : 27.
Ex. 22 : 30. seven days with **d.**, Le.
De. 22 : 6. not take **d.** with young
7. But thou shalt let the **d.** go
DAMAGE.
Ezr. 4 : 22. why **d.** grow to hurt of
Es. 7 : 4. not countervail king's **d.**
Pr. 26 : 6. and drinketh **d.**
Da. 6 : 2. king should have no **d.**
Ac. 27 : 10. voyage will be with **d.**
2 Co. 7 : 9. rec. **d.** by us in nothing
DAM'ARIS.
Ac. 17:34. woman named D. believ.
DAMASCENES. [D.
2 Co. 11 : 32. Aretas k. kept city of
DAMAS'CUS.
Ge. 15 : 2. steward is Eliezer of D.
2 S. 8 : 6. in Syria of D., 1 Ch. 18:6.
1 K. 11 : 24. Rezon reigned in D.
19 : 15. return to wilderness of D.
20 : 34. make streets for thee in D.
2 K. 5 : 12. Abana, Pharpar, rivers
8 : 7. Elisha came to D. [of D.?
14 : 28. Jerob. how he recovered D.
16 : 9. king of Assyria went ag. D.
10. king Ahaz saw an altar at D.
1 Ch. 18 : 5. Syrians of D. came to
2 Ch. 24:23. sent spoil unto k. of D.
28:5. a great mult. of captiv. to D.
23. Ahaz sacrifi. unto gods of D.
Can. 7 : 4. Lebanon, looketh tow. D.
Is. 7:8. head of Syria D. head of D.
8 : 4. riches of D. be taken away
10 : 9. saith, is not Samaria as D.?
17 : 1. the burden of D., Je. 49:23.
3. kingdom shall cease from D.
Je. 49 : 24. D. is waxed feeble and
27. will kindle fire in wall of D.
Eze. 27 : 18. D. thy merch-t in wine
Am. 1 : 3. for 3 transgressions of D.
5. I will break also the bar of D.
3 : 12. that dwell in D in a couch
5 : 27. to go into captiv. beyond D.
Zch. 9 : 1. D. shall be the rest [3, 8.
Ac. 9 : 2. Saul desired letters to D.,
10. a disciple at D. Ananias
19. was Saul with disciples at D.
22. Saul confounded Jews at D.
27. how he preached boldly at D.
22 : 5. I received letters, went to D.
6 And as I was nigh unto D., 26:12.
10. Lord said, Arise, go into D. [D.
11. not see, being led, I came into
26 : 20. I shewed first unto th. of D.
Gal. 1 : 17. returned again unto D.
DAM'MIM.
1 S. 17 : † 1. pitched in coast of D.
DAMNABLE.
2 Pe. 2 : 1. bring in **d.** heresies
DAMNATION.
Mat. 23 : 14. ye shall receive greater
d., Mk. 12 : 40. Lu. 20 : 47.
33. how escape **d.** of hell?
Mk. 3 : 29. in danger of eternal **d.**
Jn. 5 : 29. to resurrection of **d.**
Ro. 3 : 8. whose **d.** is just
13 : 2. shall receive to thems. **d.**
1 Co. 11 : 29. eateth and drink. **d.**
1 Ti. 5 : 12. **d.** because cast off faith
2 Pe. 2 : 3. their **d.** slumbereth not
DAMNED.
Mk. 16 : 16. believeth not sh. be **d.**
Ro. 14 : 23. doubteth is **d.** if he eat
2 Th. 2 : 12. be **d.** who believ. not
DAMSEL, S. [pitcher
Ge. 24 : 14. **d.** to wh. I say, Let down

Ge. 24 : 16. **d.** very fair to look upon
28. **d.** told them of mother's hou.
55. Let **d.** abide with us few days
57. We will call **d.** and inquire
61. Rebekah arose and her **d-s**
34 : 3 loved **d.**, spake kindly unto
4. Get me this **d.** to wife, 12. [**d.**
De. 22 : 15. Then shall mother of **d.**
bring tokens of **d.**-'s virginity
16. **d.**-'s father sh. say unto elders
19. 100 shekels give unto fa. of **d.**
20. if virginity not found for **d.**
21. shall bring out **d.**, stone her
23. If a **d.**, a virgin, be betrothed
24. stone **d.** because she cried not
25. if a man find **d.** and force her
26. unto **d.** thou shalt do nothing;
in **d.** no sin worthy of death
27. betrothed **d.** cried, none to save
28. If man find a **d.** not betrothed
29. he sh. give **d.**-'s fa. 50 shekels
Ju. 5 : 30. to every man a **d.** or two
19 : 3. when father of **d.** saw him
4. the **d.**-'s father retained him
5. **d.**-'s father said, Comfort, 8.
6. **d.**-'s father had said, tarry, 9.
Ru. 2 : 5. said Boaz, Whose **d.** is this?
6. It is the Moabitish **d.** th. came
1 S. 25 : 42. Abigail rode with 5 **d-s**
1 K. 1 : †2. sought for k. young **d.**, 3.
4. **d.** was very fair, cherished k-g
Ps. 68 : 25. among them **d-s** playing
Mat. 14 : 11. John Baptist's head in
a charger, given to **d.**, Mk. 6:28.
26 : 69. **d.** came unto him saying,
Thou also wast with Jesus, Jn.
Mk. 5 : 39. **d.** is not dead [18 : 17.
40. he entereth where **d.** was (2)
41. he took the **d.** by the hand,
said, **d.** (I say unto thee) arise
42. straightway the **d.** arose and
6 : 22. king said unto **d.**, Ask of me
28. head, **d.** gave it to mother (2)
Ac. 12 : 13. door, **d.** came to hearken
16 : 16. a **d.** possessed with a spirit
DAN. [Person.] [D.
Ge. 30 : 6. th. called she his name
35 : 25. sons of Bilhah; D., Naphta-
46 : 23. sons of D., Nu. 26:42 (2). [li
49 : 16. D. shall judge his people
17. D. sh. be a serpent by the way
Ex. 1 : 4. chil. of Israel which came
into Egypt, D., Gad, 1 Ch. 2 : 2.
DAN. [Tribe or Territory.]
Nu. 1 : 12. Of D.; Ahiezer the son of
2 : 25. standard of D. on the north
31. All in camp of D. were 157,600
26:42. the sons of D.: families of D.
De. 27 : 13. upon Ebal to curse; D.
33 : 22. of D. said, D is lion's whelp
Ju 5 : 17. why D. remain in ships?
13 : 25. Spirit to move him in c. of D.
1 Ch. 27 : 22. ruler. Of D.; Azareel
2 Ch 2 : 14. of woman of dau-s of D.
Eze 48 : 1. east, west; portion for D.
2. border of D., portion for Asher
32. one gate of Benjamin, one of D.
Children of DAN. [tions
Nu. 1 : 38. Of the - of D by genera-
2 : 25. capt. of - D., Ahiezer, 7 : 66.
10 : 25. standard of - D. set forward
34 : 22. prince of the - D., Bukki
Jos. 19 : 40. seventh lot came for - D.
47. coast of - D. went out too little; - D. went to fighting. Lesh-
48. This is inheritance of - D. [em
Ju. 1 : 34. Amorites forced the - D.
18 : 2. - D. sent of their family five
16. 600 men of - D. stood by gate
22. men in houses overtook - D.
23. they cried unto the - D. [heard
25. - D. said, Let not thy voice be
26. And the - D. went their way
30. - D. set up the graven image
Tribe of DAN.
Ex. 31 : 6. I have given with him
Aholiab of - D., 35 : 34.-38 : 23.

e. 24 : 11. daughter of Dibri, of - D.
Nu. 1 : 39. numbered of - D. 62,700
13 : 12. Send men. Of - D., Ammiel
34 : 22. princes of the - D. to divide
os. 19 : 40. seventh lot for - D., 48.
21 : 5. had out of - D. cities, 23.
u. 18 : 30. were priests to - D. until

DAN. [Place.] [to D.
Ge. 14 : 14. Abram pursued them un-
De. 34 : 1. shewed Mos Gilead unto D.
Jos. 19 : 47. called Leshem D., after D. their father, Ju. 18 : 29.
K. 12 : 29. calves of gold, one in Beth-el, other in D., 2 K. 10 : 29.
30. peo. went to worship unto D. [4.
15 : 20. Ben-hadad smote D., 2 Ch. 16 :
Je. 4 : 15. a voice declareth from D.
8 : 16. snorting of horses heard fr. D.
Eze. 27 : 19. D. occupied in thy fairs
Am. 8 : 14. say, Thy God, O D., liveth

DANCE, S. [with d-s
Ex. 15 : 20. women went aft. Miriam
Ju. 11 : 34. dau-r to meet him with
21 : 21. if come to dance in d-s [d-s
1 S 21 : 11. sing of him in d-s, 29 : 5.
Ps. 150 : 4. Praise him with d., 149 : 3.
Je. 31 : 4. thou shalt go forth in the
13. shall virgin rejoice in d. [d-s
La. 5 : 15. our d. turned into mourn-

DANCE, ED. [ing
Ju. 21 : 21. if daughters come to d.
23. took wives of them that d-d
2 S. 6 : 14 David d-d before the Lord
Jb. 21 : 11. little ones, their chil. d.
Ec. 3 : 4. a time to mourn, time to d.
Is. 13 : 21. satyrs shall d. there [32.
Mat 11 : 17. ye have not d-d, Lu. 7 :
14 : 6. dau-r of Herodias d-d, Mk.

DANCING. [6 : 22.
Ex. 32 : 19. he saw the calf and d.
1 S. 18 : 6. women came d. to meet S.
30 : 16. drinking, d. bec. of spoil
2 S. 6 : 16. she saw David d., 1 Ch.
Ps. 30 : 11. mourning into d. [15 : 29.
Lu. 15 : 25. as he came heard music,

DANDLED. [d.
Is. 66 : 12. ye be d. upon her knees

DANGER. [22.
Mat. 5 : 21. sh. be in d. of judgment,
22. in d. of council, d. of hell fire
Mk. 3 : 29. in d. of eternal damnation
Ac. 19 : 27. not only our craft is in d.
40. in d. to be called in question

DANGEROUS.
Ac. 27 : 9. when sailing was now d.

DAN'IEL.
1 Ch. 3 : 1. sons of David, second D.
Ezr. 8 : 2. of sons of Ithamar D.
Ne. 10 : 6. those that sealed, D., Ba.
Eze. 14 : 14 Though D. and Job in it,
28 : 3. thou art wiser than D [20.
Da. 1 : 6. were of child-n of Judah, D.
7. unto D. the name of Belteshazzar
8. D purposed he would not defile
9. God had brought D. into favour
10. prince of eunuchs said unto D.
11. said D to Melzar, set over D.
7 : 1. I D had a dream

DAN'ITES. [of D.
Ju. 13 : 2. a man of Zorah, of family
18 : 1. tribe of D. sought inherit-e
11. went of family of D. 600 men
1 Ch. 12 : 35. of D expert in war,

DAN-JA'AN. [28,600
2 S. 24 : 6. to D. and about to Zidon

DAN'NAH. [D.
Jos. 15 : 49 cities in the mountains;

DA'RA[1] **or DAR'DA.**[2]
1 K. 4 : 31. Solomon wiser than D.[2]
1 Ch. 2 : 6. sons of Zerah ; Calcol, D.[1]

DARE. [† D.[2]
Jb. 41 : 10. None that d. stir him up
Ro 5 : 7. some would even d. to die
15 : 18. I will not d. to speak of any
1 Co. 6 : 1. d. any of you go to law
2 Co. 10 : 12. we d. not make ourselves of the number, or compare

DARI'US.
Ezr. 4 : 5. frustrate, until reign of D.,
5 : 5. till matter came to D., 6, 7. [24.
6 : 1. then D., made decree, 12.
15. was finished in 6th year of D.
Ne. 12 : 22. priests to reign of D.
Da. 5 : 31. D. took the kingdom
6 : 9. whf. D. signed the writing
25. king D. wrote to all people
9 : 1. 1st year of D. the Mede, 11 : 1.
Hag. 1 : 1. in second year of D., 15,-
2 : 10. Zch. 1 : 7.
Zch. 7 : 1. 4th yr. of D. word came

DARK.
Ge. 15 : 17. when it was d.
Ex. 9 : † 32. wheat and rye were d.
Le. 13 : 6. if the plague be somewhat d. the priest sh., 21, 26, 28, 56.
Nu. 12 : 8. speak not in d. speeches
Jos. 2 : 5. when d. men went out
2 S. 22 : 12. d. waters, Ps. 18 : 11.
Ne. 13 : 19. gates began to be d.
Jb. 3 : 9. Let stars of twilight be d.
12 : 25. They grope in the d.
18 : 6. light sh. be d. in his taber.
22 : 13. can he judge thr. d. cloud?
24 : 16. In d. they dig thro. houses
30 : † 3. they were d. as night
Ps 35 : 6. Let their way be d.
49 : 4. open d. saying on harp
74 : 20. d. places of earth are full
78 : 2. utter d. sayings of old
88 : 12. wonders be known in d.?
105 : 28. sent darkness made it d.
Pr. 1 : 6. wise and their d. saying
7 : 9. in the black and d. night
Is. 5 : † 30. sh. be d. in the destruo.
29 : 15. their works are in the d.
45 : 19. not spoken in a d. place
Je. 13 : 16. feet stumble on d. mts.
La. 3 : 6. hath set me in d. places
Eze. 8 : 12. what Israel do in d.
32 : 7. I will make the stars d.
8. lights of heaven will make d.
34 : 12. been scattered in d. day
Da. 8 : 23. underst-g d. sentences
Jo. 2 : 10. sun and moon be d.
Am. 5 : 8. maketh day d., 20.
Mi. 3 : 6. d. to you, day sh. be d.
Zch. 14 : 6. light not clear, nor d.
Lu. 11 : 36. body having no part d.
Jn. 6 : 17. and it was now d.
20 : 1. Mary came when yet d.
2 Pe. 1 : 19. shineth in a d. place

DARKEN, ED, ETH.
Ex. 10 : 15. so that land was d.
Jb. 38 : 2. Who that d-h counsel
Ps. 69 : 23. Let eyes be d., Ro. 11 : 10.
139 : † 12. darkness d-h not fr. thee
Ec. 12 : 2. sun, or stars be not d.
3. that look out of windows be d.
Is. 5 : 30. the light is d.
9 : 19. Through wrath of L. land is d.
13 : 10. sun d., Jo. 3 : 15.
24 : 11. all joy is d., mirth is gone
Eze. 30 : 18. At Tehaphn. day be d.
Am. 8 : 9. d. earth in clear day
Zch. 11 : 17. his right eye be d.
Mat. 24 : 29. sun be d., Mk. 13 : 24.
Lu. 23 : 45. and the sun was d.
Ro. 1 : 21. foolish heart was d.
Ep. 4 : 18. having underst-g d-d
Re. 8 : 12. so as third part was d.
9 : 2. sun and air were d.

DARKISH.
Le. 13 : 39. bright spots in skin d.

DARKLY.
1 Co. 13 : 12. we see thro. a glass d.

DARKNESS.
Ge. 1 : 2. d. was upon the deep
5. light day, d. he called night
18. to divide the light from d.
15 : 12. a horror of d. fell upon Ab.
Ex. 10 : 21. there may be d. over E.
22. thick d. in all E. three days
14 : 20. was d. to them, but light
20 : 21. Moses drew near unto d.
De. 4 : 11. mountain burned with d.
5 : 22. words Lord spake out of d.
Jos. 24 : 7. d. betw. you and Egyp.
2 S. 22 : 10. d. und. his feet, Ps. 18 : 9.
12. he made d. his pavilions
29. will enlighten my d., Ps. 18 : 28.
Jb. 3 : 5. Let d. and shadow of death
6. As for th. night, let d. seize it
5 : 14. meet with d. in daytime
10 : 22. a land of d. as d. itself
19 : 8. he hath set d. in my paths
20 : 26. All d. be hid in his secret pl.
22 : 11. Or d. that canst not see
23 : 17. I was not cut off bef. d. neith. hath he covered the d.
28 : 3. an end to d. the stones of d.
34 : 22. no d. where workers of iniq.
37 : 19. cannot order our speech by reason of d.
38 : 9. thick d. a swaddling band
19. as for d. where is the place?
Ps. 18 : 11. made d. his secret pla.
35 : † 6. let their way be d. and
88 : 18. mine acquaintance into d.
97 : 2. Clouds and d. are round him
104 : 20. makest d. and it is night
105 : 28. sent d. and made it dark
139 : 11. Surely d. shall cover me
12. d. hideth not from thee
Pr. 2 : 13. to walk in ways of d.
4 : 19. way of the wicked is as d.
Ec. 6 : 4. name be covered with d.
Isa. 5 : 30. if look to land, behold d.
8 : 22. they sh. look, and behold d.
45 : 3. give thee treasures of d.
47 : 5. get thee into d. O dau. of
60 : 2. d. shall cover the earth, and gross d. the people
Je 13 : 16. before he cause d. and make light gross d.
Eze. 32 : 8. will set d. upon thy land
Jo. 2 : 2. day of d. and of thick d.
31. sun be turned into d., Ac. 2 : 20.
Am. 4 : 13. maketh the morning d.
Na. 1 : 8. d. sh. pursue his enemies
Mat. 6 : 23. body full of d., Lu. 11 : 34.
8 : 12. into outer d., 22 : 13.-25 : 30.
27 : 45. fr. sixth hour d., Mk. 15 : 33.
Lu. 22 : 53. is hour and power of d.
23 : 44. was d. over all the earth
Ac. 13 : 11. fell on him mist and d.
Ep. 5 : 8. ye were sometime d.
11. no fellowsh. with works of d.
6 : 12. ag. rulers of d. of this world
Col. 1 : 13. deliv-d us fr. power of d.
1 Th. 5 : 5. we not of night nor d.
He. 12 : 18. ye are not come to d.
2 Pe. 2 : 4. delivered into chains of d.
17. to whom mist of d. is reserv.
1 Jn. 2 : 11. d. hath blinded his eyes
Jude 6. in everl. chains under d.
13. is reserved blackness of d.
Re. 16 : 10. kingd. was full of d.

DARKNESS with day.
Jb. 3 : 4. Let that d. be d. let not
15 : 23. that d. of d. is at hand
Ec. 11 : 8. let him remem. d. of d.
Is. 58 : 10. thy d. be as the noon-d.
Jo. 2 : 2. a d. of d. and, Zph. 1 : 15.
Am. 5 : 20. Shall not d. of Lord be d.?

In DARKNESS.
De. 28 : 29. thou shalt grope i. d.
1 S. 2 : 9. wicked sh. be silent i. d.
1 K. 8 : 12. Lord said he would dwell i. the thick d., 2 Ch. 6 : 1.
Jb. 17 : 13. have made my bed i. d.
Ps. 11 : † 2. may i. d. shoot at upright
82 : 5. they walk on i. d.
88 : 6. hast laid me i. d. in deeps
91 : 6. pestilence that walketh i. d.
107 : 10. such as sit i. d. and
143 : 3. enemy made me dwell i. d.
Pr. 20 : 20. his lamp be put out i. d.
Ec. 2 : 14. the fool walketh i. d.
5 : 17. eateth i. d. | 6 : 4. departeth
Is. 42 : 7. bri. them that sit i. d. out
49 : 9. to them i. d. shew yours

Is. 59 : 9. for light, but walk i. d.
Je. 23 : 12. be as slippery ways i. d.
Da. 2 : 22. knoweth what is i. d.
Mat. 4 : 16. peo. wh. sat i. d. saw
Jn. 8:12. that foll. me not walk i.d.
12 : 35. walketh i. d. knoweth not
46. believeth, sho. not abide i. d.
Ro. 2:19. light of them wh. are i.d.
1 Th. 5 : 4. ye, breth., are not i.d.
1 Jn. 1 : 6. and walk i. d. we lie
2 : 9. hateth his brother, is i. d.
walketh i. d., 11.

Land of DARKNESS.

Jb. 10 : 21. bef. I go to l. o. d.
22. a l. o. d. as d. itself, and
Je. 2 : 31. been unto Isr. a l. o. d.?

DARKNESS with light.

Ge. 1:4. God divided the l. from d.
18. great lights to divide l. fr. d.
Jb. 10 : 22. land where l. is as d.
17 : 12. the l. is short bec. of d.
18 : 18. He be driven fr. l. into d.
26 : † 10. until end of l. with d.
29 : 3. by his l. I walked thro. d.
30 : 26. I waited for l., came d.
Ps.112:4. unto upright aris-h l. in d.
139 : 12. d. and l. are both alike
Ec. 2 : 13. as far as l. excelleth d.
Is. 5 : 20. put d. for l., l. for d.
9 : 2. peo. in d. seen great l., upon
them l. shined, Mat. 4 : 16.
42 : 16. make d. l. before them
45 : 7. I form l. and create d.
50 : 10. walketh in d. hath no l.
Je. 13 : 16. look for l., he make it d.
La. 3 : 2. bro-t me into d. not l.
Am. 5 : 18. day of L. is d. not l.
Mi. 7 : 8. when I sit in d. L. be l.
Mat. 6 : 23. l. in thee be d. how
great is that d.! [12 : 3.
10 : 27. tell in d., speak in l., Lu.
Lu. 1:79. l. to them that sit in d., and
the shadow of death, Ro. 2 : 19.
11 : 35. that l. in thee be not d.
Jn. 1 : 5. light shineth in d. d.
comprehended it not
3 : 19. men loved d. rather than l.
12 : 35. Walk while have l., lest d.
Ac. 26 : 18. turn them fr. d. to l.
Ro. 13 : 12. works of d. put on l.
1 Co. 4 : 5. to l. hidden things of d.
2 Co. 4:6. com-d l. to shine out of d.
6 : 14. what commun. l. with d.?
1 Pe. 2 : 9. out of d. into marvell. l.
1 Jn. 1 : 5. God is l., in him is no d.
2:8. d. is past, true l. now shineth

Out of DARKNESS.

De. 5:22. ye heard voice o.o.d., 23.
Jb. 12 : 22. He discov. deep things
o. o. d. [o. o. d.
15 : 22. believeth not he sh. return
30. He shall not depart o. o. d.
Ps.107:14. He brought them o.o.d.
Is. 29 : 18. eyes of blind see o.o.d.

DAR'KON.

Ezr. 2 : 56. chil. of D., Ne. 7 : 58.

DARLING.

Ps. 22 : 20. Deliver my d. from dog
35 : 17. L., rescue my d. fr. lions

DART, S.

2 S. 18 : 14. Job took three d.
2Ch.32:5. Heze. made d-s and shields
Jb. 41 : 26. the d. cannot hold
29. d. are counted as stubble
Pr. 7 : 23. Till d. strike thro. liver
Jo. 2:†8. fall upon d. not be wound.
Ep. 6 : 16. fiery d-s of the wicked
He. 12:20. be thrust thro. with a d.

DASH.

2 K. 8 : 12. thou wilt d. their chil.
Ps. 2 : 9. d. in pieces like potter's
91 : 12. lest thou d. thy foot ag. a
stone, Mat. 4 : 6. Lu. 4 : 11.
Is. 13 : 18. bows sh. d. young men
Je. 13:14. I will d. one ag. another

DASHED, ETH.

Ex. 15 : 6. O Lord, hath d. in pieces
Ps.137 : 9. d-h little ones ag. stones
Is. 13 : 16. Their chil. shall be d.
in pieces, Ho. 13 : 16. Na. 3:10.
Ho. 10 : 14. moth. was d. upon chil
Na. 2 : 1. He that d. in pieces is

DATES.

2 Ch. 31 † 5. chil. of Isr. brought d.

DA'THAN.

Nu. 16 : 12, 24, 27. See ABIRAM.

DAUB, ED, ING.

Ex. 2 : 3. she d-d ark with slime
Eze. 13 : 10. d-d it with untempered
11. Say to th. which d. it, it shall
12. Where is d-g whw. ye d-d it.?
14. break down wall ye have d.
22 : 28. her prophets have d. them

DAUGHTER.

Ge. 20:12. d. of my fa., not d. of m.
24 : 23. Whose d. art thou? 47.
24. I am d. of Bethuel, 47.
48. master's bro.'s d. to son
34 : 7. folly in lying with Jacob's d.
8. Shechem longeth for your d., 3.
17. will take our d. and be gone
19. he had delight in Jacob's d.
Ex. 1 : 16. if a d. she shall live
2 : 5. d. of Pha. came to wash
21 : 31. have gored a son or a d.
Le. 12 : 6. days fulfilled for a d.
14 :† 10. ewe-lamb, d. of her year
18 : 17. nor take her dau.'s d.
21 : 9. d. of priest, if she profane
22:12. if priest's d. be married to a
13. if priest's d. be a widow or
Nu. 27 : 9. if no d. give inheritance
36 : 8. d. that possesseth inherit.
De. 27 : 22. Cursed he that lieth with
d. of father or d. of mother
28 : 56. eye be evil toward her d.
Ju. 11 : 34. Jeph.'s d. came to meet
40. to lament Jeph.'s d. four days
1 S. 1 : 16. not handm. d. of Belial
18 : 19. Saul's d. should been giv.
2 S. 6 : 16. Saul's d. looked thro.
window, 1 Ch. 15 : 29.
23. Michal d. of Saul had no child
12 : 3. little ewe-lamb as d.
1 K. 3 : 1. Solo. took Pharaoh's d.
11 : 1. loved many, with d. of Pha.
2 K. 8 : 18. d. of Ahab was Jeho.'s
9 : 34. bury Jezebel, she is a k.'s d.
1 Ch. 2 : 49. d. of Caleb was Achsah
Es. 2 : 7. took uncle's d. for his d.
Ps.45:10. Hearken, O d. and consid.
13. king's d. is glorious within
Can. 7:1. how beautif., O prince's d.
Je. 31 : 22. backsliding d., 49 : 4.
46 : 19. O d. in E., furnish thyself
48 : 18. d. that dost inhabit Dibon
Eze. 14:20. deliv. son nor d.
16 : 44. As is mother, so is her d.
45. art moth.'s d. that loatheth
27 : † 6. d. of Ashurites made thy
44 : 25. for son or d. may defile
Da. 11 : 6. k.'s d. of south come
17. shall give him the d. of wom.
Hos. 1 : 6. conc. again, and bare d.
Mi. 5 : 1. gather, O d. of troops
7:6. d. riseth up against her mother, Mat. 10 : 35. Lu. 12 : 53.
Zph. 3 : 10. d. of my dispersed
Mal. 2 : 11. married d. of strange
Mat. 9 : 22. Jesus said, d. be of good
comf., Mk. 5 : 34. Lu. 8 : 48.
10 : 37. loveth d. more than [6:22.
14 : 6. d. of Herodias danced, Mk.
15 : 28. her d. was made whole
Mk. 7:25. wh. young d. had an uncl.
26. cast devil out of her d.
30. found her d. laid upon bed
Lu. 2 : 36. d. of Phanuel of tribe of
42. he had one only d. 12 years
13:16. this woman, being d. of Ab.
Ac. 7:21. Pharaoh's d. took him up
He. 11:24. refus. to be son of Pha.'s d.

DAUGHTER of Babylon.

Ps.137:8. O d. o. B. to be destroyed
Is. 47 : 1. O d. o. B., sit on ground
Je. 50:42. battle ag. thee, O d. o. B.
51 : 33. d. o. B. is like threshing f.
Zch. 2:7. O Zi., dwellest with d.o.B.

DAUGHTER of the Chaldeans.

Is. 47 : 1. is no throne, O d. o. C.
5. get thee into darkness, O d.o.C.

DAUGHTER of Edom.

La. 4 : 21. and be glad, O d. o. E.
22. will visit thine iniq., O d.o.E.

DAUGHTER of Egypt.

Je. 46 : 11. go into Gilead, d. o. E.
24. The d. o. E be confounded

DAUGHTER of Gallim.

Is. 10 : 30. Lift up voice, O d. o. G.

His DAUGHTER.

Ge. 29 : 6. Rachel h. d. cometh
24. gave unto h. d. Leah, 46:18.
29. gave to Rachel h. d., 46 : 25.
Ex. 2:21. gave Moses Zipporah h.d.
21 : 7. if sell h. d. to be servant
Le. 21:2. for h. d. he may be defiled
Nu. 27:8. inherit. unto pass to h.d.
30 : 16. statutes betw. fa. and h.d.
De. 7 : 3. nor h. d. take to thy son
18 : 10. not one that maketh h.d.
to pass thro. fire, 2 K. 23 : 10.
Ju. 11:34. h. d. came with timbrels
21 : 1. not any give h. d. to Benj.
1 S. 17 : 25. k. will give him h. d.
18 : 27. Saul gave him h. d.
1 Ch. 2 : 35. Sheshan gave h. d. to
Es. 2 : 7. whom Mord. took for h.d.

DAUGHTER of Jerusalem.

2 K. 19 : 21. d. o. J. hath shaken
her head at thee, Is. 37 : 22.
La. 2 : 13. what liken to thee, d.o.J.
15. they wag head at d. o. J.
Mi. 4: 8. kingd. shall come to d.o.J.
Zph. 3:14. rejoice with heart, d.o.J.
Zch. 9 : 9. d.o.J. thy king cometh

DAUGHTER of Judah.

La. 1 : 15. L. hath trodden d. o. J.
2 : 2. down strong holds d. o. J.
5. increased in d.o. J. mourning

DAUGHTER in law [i.l.

Ge. 38 : 16. he knew not she was d.
24. Tamar thy d. i. l. played the
Le. 18 : 15. nakedn. of thy d. i. l.
20 : 12. if a man lie with his d. i.l.
Ru. 1 : 22. Naomi, Ruth her d. i.l.
4 : 15. d. i. l. which loveth thee,
1 S. 4 : 19. d. i. l. was with child
1 Ch. 2 : 4. Tamar his d. i. l. [i.l.
Eze. 22 : 11. another defileth his d.
Mi. 7 : 6. for the d. i. l. riseth aga.
the mother in law, Mat. 10 : 35.
Lu. 12 : 53.

My DAUGHTER.

De. 22 : 16. gave m. d. to this man
17. tokens of m. d. virginity
Jo. 15 : 16. give m. d., Ju. 1 : 12.
Ju. 11 : 35. m.d. hast bro-t me low
19 : 24. here is m. d. a maiden
Ru. 2 : 2. and she said, Go m. d.
3 : 1. m. d. shall I not seek rest
10. Blessed be thou of L. m. d.
16. Who art thou m. d.
18. Sit still m.d. until thou know
Mat. 9 : 18. m. d. is even now dead
15 : 22. m. d. is vexed with devil
Mk. 5 : 23. m. d. at point of death

DAUGHTER of my people,

Is. 22 : 4. bec. of spoiling of d.o.p.
Je. 4 : 11. dry wind tow. d. o. p.
6 : 14. healed d.o.p. slightly, 8:11.
26. O, d. o. p. gird with sackc.
8 : 19. voice of cry of d. o. p.
21. for hurt of d.o.p. am I hurt
22. why is not health of the d.
o. p. recovered
9 : 1. weep for slain of d. o. p.
7. how shall I do for d. o. p.
14 : 17. virgin d. o. p. is broken
La. 2 : 11. destruct. of d.o.p., 3:48.
4 : 3. d. o. p. is become cruel

La. 4 : 6. iniq. of d. o. p. is greater
10. in destruction of d. o. p.

DAUGHTER of Tarshish.

Is. 23 : 10. pass thro. as river d. o. T.

Thy DAUGHTER.

Ge. 29 : 18. serve 7 years for t. d.
Ex. 20 : 10. nor t. d., De. 5 : 14.
Le. 18 : 10. nakedn. of t. dau.'s d.
19 : 29. Do not prostitute t. d.
De. 7 : 3. t. d. not give to his son
12 : 18. rejoice and t. d., 16 : 11, 14.
13 : 6. if t. d. entice thee
22 : 17. I found not t. d. a maid
2 K. 14 : 9. Give t. d., 2 Ch. 25 : 18.
Mk. 5 : 35. t. d. is dead, Lu. 8 : 49.
7 : 29. devil is gone out of t. d.

DAUGHTER of Tyre.

Ps. 45 : 12. d. o. T. shall be there

DAUGHTER of Zidon.

Is. 23 : 12. O oppressed d. o. Z.

DAUGHTER-S of Zion.

2 K. 19 : 21. The virgin, the d. o. Z. hath despised thee, Is. 37 : 22.
Ps. 9 : 14. praise in gates of d. o. Z.
Is. 1 : 8. d. o. Z. as a cottage
4 : 4. washed away filth of d. o. Z
10 : 32. ag. mount of d. o. Z., 16 : 1.
52 : 2. loose thyself O d. o. Z.
62 : 11. d. o. Z., thy salva. cometh
Je. 4 : 31. heard voice of d. o. Z.
6 : 2. likened d. o. Z. to comely
23. men of war ag. thee, d. o. Z.
La. 1 : 6. fr. d. o. Z. beauty is dep.
2 : 1. L. covereth d. o. Z. with a cloud
4. slew in taber. of d. o. Z.
8. L. to destroy wall of d. o. Z.
10. elders of d. o. Z. sit on
13. I equal to thee, O d. o. Z. ?
18. O wall of d. o. Z. let tears
4 : 22. punish-t accompli., O d. o. Z.
Mi. 1 : 13. the beginn. of sin to d. o. Z.
4 : 8. strong hold of d. o. Z.
10. be in pain, O d. o. Z.
13. Arise and thresh, O d. o. Z.
Zph. 3 : 14. Sing, O d. o. Z.
Zch. 2 : 10. rejoice, O d. o. Z., 9 : 9.
Mat. 21 : 5. Tell d. o. Z. king com.
Jn. 12 : 15. Fear not d. o. Z. thy k.

DAUGHTER of Zur.

Nu. 25 : 15. was Cozbi d. o. Z.

DAUGHTERS.

Ge. 6 : 1. d. were born unto them
2. sons of God saw d. of men
6 : 4. sons of G. came unto d. of men
19 : 14. them wh. married his d.
36. both d. of Lot with child
24 : 3. not wife of d. of Canaanites, 37.-28 : 1, 6.
13. d. came to draw water
27 : 46. weary of life bec. of d. of Heth
28 : 8. d. of Ca. pleased not Isaac
30 : 13. d. will call me blessed
31 : 26. hast carried away my d.
43. d. are my d. | 50. if affl. d.
34 : 1. Dinah went out to see d.
9. give your d., and take our d.
16. our d. unto you, take y-r d., 21.
49 : †22. a bough whose d. run over
Ex. 2 : 16. priest of Mid. had 7 d.
6 : 25. Aa.'s son took one of d. of
21 : 9. deal with her aft. manner of d.
34 : 16. d. go a whoring aft. gods
Le. 26 : 29. flesh of d. shall ye eat
Nu. 21 : † 25. in Heshbon and d.
26 : 33. names of d., 27 : 1. Jos. 17 : 3.
27 : 7. d. of Zeloph. speak right
36 : 10. so did d. of Zeloph., 11.
De. 23 : 17. be no whore of d. of Isr.
Ju. 3 : 6. took d. to be their wives
21 : 7. we will not give our d.
18. may not give th. wives of our d.
Ru. 1 : 11. Turn again, my d., 12.
13. nay, my d. it grieveth me
1 S. 8 : 13. d. to be confectionaries
2 S. 13 : 18. were king's d. virgins
Ne. 3 : 12. Shallum, and his d.
5 : 5. our d. are bro-t into bondage
7 : 63. one of d. of Barzil., Ezr. 2 : 61.
10 : 30. not give our d. to people
Jb. 42 : 15. no wom. so fair as d. of Jb.
Ps. 45 : 9. King's d. amo. hon. wom.
144 : 12. d. may be as corner stone
Pr. 31 : 29. Many d. have done virtu.
Can. 2 : 2. so is my love among d.
6 : 9. The d. saw and blessed her
Is. 13 : † 21. d. of owl dw., 34 : † 13
32 : 9. ye careless d. give ear
43 : † 20. d. of owl sh. honour me
60 : 4. d. be nursed at thy side
Je. 9 : 20. Teach your d. wailing
29 : 6. give your d. to husbands
49 : 2. her d. shall be burned
3. Cry, ye d. of Rabbah, gird ye
La. 3 : 51. bec. of d. of my city
Eze. 13 : 17. set face ag. d. of thy peo.
16 : †31. in d. is thine eminent place
46. Sama., her d. Sod., and her d.
48. Thou and thy d., 55.
49. idleness in her and her d.
53. bring back captiv. of her d.
55. sister Sodom and d. return
61. give them unto thee for d.
23 : 2. two women, d. of one moth.
26 : 6. her d. shall be slain, 8.
30 : 18. her d. shall go into captiv.
32 : 16. d. of nations lament her
18. d. of the famous nations
Ho. 4 : 13. d. sh. commit whoredom
14. I will not punish your d.
Mi. 1 : † 8. mourning as d. of owl
Lu. 1 : 5. wife was of d. of Aaron
Ac. 2 : 17. your d. shall prophesy
21 : 9. same had four d. virgins
1 Pe. 3 : 6. whose d. long as ye do

DAUGHTERS of Israel.

De. 23 : 17. be no whore of d. o. I.
Ju. 11 : 40. d. o. I. yearly to lament
2 S. 1 : 24. Ye d. o. I., weep over Saul

DAUGHTERS of Jerusalem.

Can. 1 : 5. black, but comely, d. o. J.
2 : 7. I charge you, O d. o. J., 3 : 5.-5 : 8.-8 : 4.
3 : 10. paved with love for d. o. J.
5 : 16. this my beloved, O d. o. J.
Lu. 23 : 28. d. o. J. weep not for me

DAUGHTERS of Judah.

Ps. 48 : 11. let d. o. J. be glad
97 : 8. and the d. o. J. rejoiced

DAUGHTERS in law.

Ru. 1 : 6. she arose with her d. i. l., 7.
8. Naomi said to her two d. i. l.

DAUGHTERS of Moab.

Nu. 25 : 1. Isr. whoredom with d. o. M.
Is. 16 : 2. d. o. M. be at fords of Arnon

DAUGHTERS of music.

Ec. 12 : 4. d. o. m. be brought low

DAUGHTERS of the Philistines.

Ju. 14 : 1. saw woman of d. o. P.
2. woman of d. o. P. get her for me
2 S. 1 : 20. publish it not lest d. o. P.
Eze. 16 : 27. deliv-d thee to d. o. P.
57. d. o. P. which despise thee

DAUGHTERS of Shiloh.

Ju. 21 : 21. if d. o. S. come to dance, catch every man a wife (2)

DAUGHTERS, with sons.

Ge. 5 : 4. he begat s. and d., 7, 10, 13, 16.-11 : 11.
19 : 12. thy s. and d. bring out
31 : 28. not suff. me to kiss s. and d.
55. he kissed his s. and d.
37 : 35. s. and d. rose to comf. him
46 : 15. souls of s. and d. were
Ex. 3 : 22. put them on s. and d.
10 : 9. with s. and d. will we go
21 : 4. have borne him s. or d.
32 : 2. earrings of s. and d. bring
34 : 16. take of their d. unto thy s.
Le. 10 : 14. thou, s. and d., shall eat in holy place, Nu. 18 : 11, 19.
Nu. 21 : 29. he hath given his s. and d. into captivity
26 : 33. Zelophehad had no s., but d., Jos. 17 : 3.
De. 12 : 12. ye and s. and d. rejoice
31. s. and d. they have burnt, 2 K. 17 : 17. Je. 7 : 31.-32 : 35.
28 : 32. s. and d. given to ano. peo.
41. beget s. and d. but not enjoy
53. shalt eat flesh of s. and d.
32 : 19. provoking of his s. and d.
Jos. 7 : 24. bro-t Achan, s. and d.
17 : 6. d. of Manas. inherit. amo. s.
Ju. 3 : 6. gave their d. to their s.
12 : 9. Ibzan took d. for his s.
1 S. 1 : 4. her s. and d. portions
2 : 21. Hannah bare 3 s. and 2 d.
30 : 3. s. and d. were tak. captives
6. grieved, ev. man for s. and d.
19. nothing lacking, s. nor d.
2 S. 5 : 13. there were yet s. and d. born to David, 1 Ch. 14 : 3.
19 : 5. saved lives of thy s. and d.
1 Ch. 2 : 34. Sheshan no s. but d.
4 : 27. Shimei had 16 s. and 6 d.
23 : 22. Eleazar had no s. but d.
25 : 5. G. gave Heman 14 s. and 3 d.
2 Ch. 11 : 21. Reho. had 28 s. 60 d.
13 : 21. Abijah begat 22 s. and 16 d.
24 : 3. Jehoiada begat s. and d.
28 : 8. captive 200,000 wom., s. and d.
29 : 9. our s. d. wives are in captiv.
31 : 18. genealogy of their s. and d.
Ezr. 9 : 2. have tak. d. for their s.
12. not d. to their s., Ne. 13 : 25.
Ne. 4 : 14. fight for s., d., and wives
5 : 2. We, our s. and d. are many
5. bring into bondage s. and d.
10 : 28. s. and d. clave to breth.
30. nor d. for our s., Ezr. 9 : 12.
Jb. 1 : 2. born to Job 7 s. 3 d., 42 : 13.
13. his s. and d. were eating, 18.
Ps. 106 : 37. sac. s. and d. unto devils
38. shed blood of their s. and d.
Is. 43 : 6. bring my s. fr. far, and my d.
49 : 22. bring thy s. in arms, and d.
56 : 5. name better than s. and d.
Je. 3 : 24. shame devoured s. and d.
5 : 17. eat that s. and d. sho. eat.
11 : 22. s. and d. sh. die by famine
14 : 16. have none to bury s. and d.
16 : 2. neith. shalt have s. nor d.
3. saith L. concerning s. and d.
19 : 9. to eat flesh of s. and d.
29 : 6. Take wives, beget s. and d.
35 : 8. we, s. and d. drink no wine
48 : 46. s. and d. are taken captiv.
Eze. 14 : 16. deliver neith. s. nor d., 18.
22. remnant, both s. and d.
16 : 20. s. and d. and sacri. them
23 : 4. mine, and bare s. and d.
10. took s. and d., slew her, 25.
47. they shall slay their s. and d.
24 : 21. s. and d. fall by sw., Am. 7 : 17.
25. when I take their s. and d.
Jo. 2 : 28. s. and d. prophesy, Ac. 2 : 17.
3 : 8. will sell your s. and d.
2 Co. 6 : 18. be my s. and d. saith L.

DAUGHTERS of Syria.

Eze. 16 : 57. time of thy reproach of the d. o. S.

Two DAUGHTERS.

Ge. 19 : 8. I have t. d. let me bring th.
15. take thy wife and thy t. d.
30. Lot dw. in cave, he and t. d.
29 : 16. Laban had t. d., Leah, and
31 : 41. served 14 y-s for thy t. d.
Ru. 1 : 7. Naomi went out with t. d.
1 S. 2 : 21 Hannah bare t. d.
14 : 49. Saul's t. d. were Merab and
Pr. 30 : 15. horseleech hath t. d.

DAUGHTERS of the uncircumcised.

2 S. 1 : 20. lest d. o. u. triumph

DAUGHTERS of Zion.

Can. 3 : 11. Go forth, O ye d. o. Z
Is. 3 : 16. d. o. Z. are haughty
17. with scab the head of d. o. Z.
4 : 4. washed away filth of d. o. Z

DA'VID. [Lu. 3 : 31.
Ru. 4 : 22. Jesse begat D., Mat. 1 : 6.
1 S. 16 : 13. Spirit of L. came upon D.
19. Send me D. | 21. D. came
23. D. took harp and played, 18 :
17 : 14. D. youngest [10.-19 : 9.
15. D. returned from Saul
23. D. heard words of Goliath
28. Eliab's anger kindled ag. D.
38. S. armed D. | 42. Goliath saw
43. Philistine cursed D. [D.
50. D. prevailed over the Philis.
57. as D. fr. slaughter of Philis.
18 : 1. soul of Jona. was knit to D.
3. Jona. and D. made a covenant
5. D. went whither Saul sent him
7. D. slain his ten thous., 29 : 5.
9. Saul eyed D. from that day
14. D. behaved himself wisely
16. all Israel and Judah loved D.
24. said, On this manner spake D.
26. pleased D. to be k.'s son in law
28. Saul saw the L. was with D.
29. Saul became D.'s enemy
19 : 1. S. spake to servants to kill D.
5. wilt sin against innocent blood to slay D.? [escaped, 18.
10. Saul sought to smite D. but D.
12. Michal let D. thro. window
19. D. is at Naioth | 22. where D.?
20 : 6. D. asked to run to Beth-le., 28.
17. Jonathan caused D. to swear
24. D. hid | 25. D. place empty, 27.
34. Jona. was grieved for D. [exc.
41. wept one with ano. until D.
21 : 1. Ahim. afraid at meeting of D.
10. D. fled to Achish for fear of S.
11. is not this D. the king? 29 : 3.
22 : 1. D. escaped to cave Adullam
3. D. went thence to Mizpeh
5. D. came into forest of Hareth
14. who is so faithful as D.?
17. because their hand is with D.
23 : 2. D. inquired of L., 4.-30 : 8.
2 S. 2 : 1.-3 : 19, 22.-21 : 1.
5. D. and men went to Keilah
9. D. knew Saul practised misch.
15. D. was in wilderness of Ziph
24. D. and men in wilderness
28. Saul retur. from pursuing D
24 : 1. D. in wilderness of En-gedi
5. D. heart smote him
7. So D. stayed his servants
16. Is this thy voice, my son D.?
26 : 17. [Paran
22. D. sware unto S. | 25 : 1. D. to
25 : 5. D. sent out ten young men
22. more do G. unto enemies of D.
26 : 1. doth not D. hide in hill
5. D. beheld where Saul lay
12. D. took spear and cruse of
17. And Saul knew D. voice
21. said S. return, my son D.
27 : 1. D. said, I shall perish by S.
4. D. fled to Gath | 8. D. invaded
7. D. dwelt in country of Philis.
11. saying, so did D., so will be
28 : 17. L. given it to thy neighb., D.
29 : 3. Is this D.? | 6. called D.
30 : 1. D. and men to Ziklag
5. D. two wives taken captives
10. D. pursued, he and 400 men
17. smote them from twilight
18. D. recovered all that Am., 19.
20. D. took all the flocks and herds
2 S. 1 : 11. D. took hold on clothes
15. D. called one of young men
17. D. lamented over Saul and
2 : 5. D. sent messen. to Jabesh-gil.
10. house of Judah followed D.
3 : 1. house of D. waxed stronger
2. unto D. sons born in Hebron
9. exc. as L. hath sworn to D.
17. ye sought for D. to be king
20. Abner came to D. to Hebron
28. D. said, I and kingdom are
5 : 1. came all tribes of Isr. to D.
2 S. 5 : 6. thinking, D. cannot come in
7. D. took strong hold of Zion
10. D. grew great, L. with him
12. D. perceiv. L. had established
17. D. went down to the hold
20. to Baal-per. D. smote them
21. D. burned images
6 : 2. D. went to bring up ark of G.
5. D. all Israel played bef. the L.
9. D. was afraid of L. that day
10. D. would not remove the ark
12. D. brought up the ark of G., 2,
14. D. danced | 15. D. bro-t ark [15.
7 : 20. can D. say more? 1 Ch. 17 : 18.
8 : 1. D. smote Philis. | 3. Hadadezer
6. Lord preserve D., 14. [18 : 7.
7. D. took shields of gold, 1 Ch.
13. D. gat him a name [18 : 14.
15. D. reigned over all Isr., 1 Ch.
15. D. reigned, executed judgm.
10 : 2. D. sent to Hanun, 1 Ch. 19 : 2.
3. thinkest thou that D. doth honour thy father, 1 Ch. 19 : 3.
18. D. slew men of 700 chariots
11 : 3. D. inquired after woman
6. D. sent for Uriah | 14. D. wrote
27. D. had done displeased Lord
12 : 1. L. sent Nathan unto D., 7.
5. D. anger was kindled ag. man
13. D. said, I have sinned ag. L.
16. D. besought God for the child
19. D. perceived child was dead
24. D. comforted Bath-sheba
29. D. fought against Rabbah
30. their k.'s crown on D. head
13 : 7. D. sent to Tamar
30. tidings came to D.
15 : 30. D. went up by Olivet [D.
16 : 6. cast stones at D. | 10. Curse
17 : 1. I will pursue after D.
16. tell D. | 22. D. arose [for D.
27. D. was come, 24. | 29. honey
18 : 1. D. numbered peo. with him
24. D. sat between the two gates,
19 : 43. we have more right in D.
20 : 1. We have no part in D.
3. D. came to his house at Jerus.
11. he for D. let him go aft. Joab
21 : 16. thought to have slain D.
22 : 51. mercy unto D., Ps. 18 : 50.
23 : 1. these the last words of D.
8. mighty wh. D. had, 1 Ch. 11 : 10.
15. D. longed and said Oh, that
24 : 10. D. heart smote him, aft. he
25. D. built there an altar unto
1 K. 1 : 11. D. our lord knoweth it
2 : 10. D. slept with his fathers [not
32. slew th., my fa. D. not know.
44. knowest what thou didst to D.
3 : 14. if walk as thy fa. D., 9 : 4.
5 : 7. who hath given D. a wise son
8 : 16. I chose D. to be over Israel
20. I am risen up in room of D.
9 : 5. estab. throne as I prom. to D.
11 : 38. build thee as I built for D.
11 : 39. I will afflict seed of D.
12 : 16. what portion we in D.? see to own house D., 2 Ch. 10 : 16.
15 : 4. for D.'s sake did L. give
1 Ch. 6 : 31. whom D. set over service of song, 23 : 6.
10 : 14. Lord turned kingd. to D.
11 : 3. D. made a cov. with them
12 : 18. thine are we, D. then D.
21. they helped D. against rovers
14 : 17. fame of D. went into all
15 : 27. D. clothed with fine linen
16 : 1. set ark in tent D. had pitch.
43. D. returned to bless his house
21 : 21. Ornan saw D. bowed to D.
22 : 5. D. prepared abun. bef. death
23 : 1. so when D. was old and
28 : 11. D. gave to Sol. the pattern
29 : 10. D. blessed L. bef. congre.
2 Ch. 1 : 8. shewed gr. mercy unto D.
9. promise unto D. be established
34 : 3. he began to seek aft. G. of D.
Ezr. 8 : 2. of sons of D. Hattush was
Ne. 3 : 16. place over ag. sepul. of D.
12 : 24. com-t of D. man of God
36. with musical instru. of D.
Ps. 72 : 20. prayers of D. are ended
89 : 35. I will not lie unto D.
49. lovingk. wh. swarest unto D.
132 : 1. L. remem. D. and his afflic.
11. the Lord hath sworn unto D.
17. will I make horn of D. bud
Can. 4 : 4. thy neck like tower of D.
Is. 9 : 7. upon throne of D., 16 : 5.
29 : 1. woe to Ariel, where D. dw.
55 : 3. sure mercies of D., Ac. 13 : 34.
Je. 17 : 25. kings upon throne of D.
23 : 5. raise to D. a righte. branch
33 : 15. branch to grow up unto D.
17. D. shall never want a man to
36 : 30. upon throne of D., 22 : 30.
Am. 6 : 5. instru. of music like D.
9 : 11. raise up tab. of D., Ac. 15 : 16.
Zch. 12 : 8. feeble as D. and D. as G.
Mat. 1 : 1. J. C. the son of D., 6, 17.
20. thou son of D. fear not to
9 : 27. Thou son of D. have mercy, 15 : 22.-20 : 30, 31. Mk. 10 : 47, 48. Lu. 18 : 38, 39.
12 : 3. not read what D. did a hungered? Mk. 2 : 25. Lu. 6 : 3
23. said, Is not this the son of D?
21 : 9. Hosanna to son of D., 15.
22 : 42. C. is son of D., Mk. 12 : 35.
45. if D. call him L., how is he son, 43. Mk. 12 : 36, 37. Lu. 20 : 41, 42, 44.
Mk. 11 : 10. bless. be the kingd. of D.
Lu. 1 : 32. give him throne of D.
3 : 31. Nathan the son of D.
Jn. 7 : 42. C. cometh of seed of D.
Ac. 1 : 16. by the mouth of D. spake
2 : 25. D. speaketh concerning him
29. me speak of patriarch D.
34. D. is not ascend. into heaven
13 : 22. he raised D. to be their k.
34. give you sure mercies of D.
36. D. fell on sleep, and saw
15 : 16. build again tabernacle of D.
Ro. 1 : 3. C. of seed of D., 2 Ti. 2 : 8.
4 : 6. as D. describeth blessedness
11 : 9. D. sd., Let th. table be snare
He. 4 : 7. saying, in D., To day, if
11 : 32. fail me to tell of D. [22 : 16.
Re. 3 : 7. key of D. | 5 : 5. root of D.,
See CITY of David, FATHER.

Days of DA'VID.
2 S. 21 : 1. was a famine in **d. o.** D.
1 K. 2 : 1. **d. o.** D. nigh that he die
1 Ch. 7 : 2. number was in **d.** o. D.
Ne. 12 : 46. in **d. o.** D. were singers
Ac. 7 : 45. drave out unto **d. o.** D.

Hand of DA'VID. [D.
1 S. 20 : 16. let L. require it at **h.o.**
2 S. 3 : 8. not deliv-d th. into **h.o.**D.
18. by **h. o.** D. I will save Israel
21 : 22. fell by **h. o.** D., 1 Ch. 20 : 8.

House of DA'VID.
1 S. 20 : 16. Jonathan made covenant with **h. o.** D. [D., 6.
2 S. 3 : 1. war betw. **h. o.** Saul and
7 : 26. let **h. o.** D. be established
1 K. 12 : 19. so Isr. rebelled ag. **h. o.** D. unto this day, 2 Ch. 10 : 19.
20. none follow. **h. o.** D. but Jud.
26. shall kingd. return to **h.o.**D.
13 : 2. a child be born to **h. o.** D.
14 : 8. rent kingdom from **h.o.**D., 2 K. 17 : 21. [o. D.
2 Ch. 21 : 7. L. not destroy the **h.**
Ps. 122 : 5. thrones of the **h. o.** D.
Is. 7 : 2. it was told the **h. o.** D.
13. hear ye, O **h.o.** D., Je. 21 : 12.
22 : 22. key of **h. o.** D. I will lay
Zch. 12 : 7. glory of **h.o.** D. not mag.
8. and the **h. o.** D. shall be as G.
10. pour upon **h.o.D.** spi. of grace
12. family of **h.o.** D. mourn apart
13 : 1. a fountain opened to **h.o.D.**

Lu. 1:27. name was Jo., of h.o.D.
69. raised horn of salv. in h.o.D.
2 : 4. bec. he was of the h. o. D.

DA'VID with king.

1 S. 21:11. is not this D. k. of land?
2 S. 2 : 4. anointed D. k. over Jud.
11. time that D. was k. in Hebron
3 : 31. and k. D. followed the bier
5 : 3. k. D. made league, anointed D. k., 1 Ch. 11 : 3.-12 : 31, 38.
8 : 11. which k. D. did dedicate to L. with the gold, 1 Ch. 26 : 26.
20:21. lift. his hand ag. k., even D.
1 K. 1:37. than throne of lord k.D.
47. k. s serv-ts came to bless k. D.
1 Ch. 29 : 9. D. the k. rejoiced with great joy [son
2 Ch. 2 : 12. given to D. k. a wise
29:27. ordained by D. k., Ezr. 3:10.
Je. 30 : 9. shall serve L. and D. k.
Ho. 3 : 5. shall seek L. and D. k.
Mat. 1:6. begat D. k., and D.the k.
Ac. 13 : 22. raised up D. to be k.

DA'VID with servant.

2 S. 3 : 18. by hand of my s. D. I
7 : 5. tell my s. D. thus saith L., 8.
26. let house of thy s. D. be estab. before thee, 1 Ch. 17 : 24.
1 K. 3:6. shew. thy s. D. gr. mercy
8 : 24. kept with thy s. D. th. thou promisedst [6 : 16.
25. keep with thy s. D., 26. 2 Ch.
66.goodn. he had done for D.his s.
11 : 13. for D. my s.'s sake, 32, 34.
Ps 132 : 10. Is. 37 : 35.
36.that D. my s. may have a light
38. statutes, as my s. D. did,14:8.
2 Ch.6:42.remem. mere. of D. thy s.
Ps. 78 : 70. he chose D. also his s.
89 : 3. I have sworn unto D. my s.
20. I have found D. my s.
144:10. who deliv-h D. s. fr. sword
Je. 33 : 21. cov.broken with D.my s.
22. will multiply seed of D. my s.
26. cast away seed of D. my s.
Eze. 34 : 23. my s. D. sh. feed them
24. my s. D. shall be a prince am.
37:24. D. my s. shall be k. over th.
25. my s. D. shall be their prince
Lu. 1 : 69. salv. in house of his s. D.
Ac. 4 : 25. who by mouth of s. D.

DAWN. [Verb.]

Mat. 28 : 1. as it began to d. tow.
2 Pe. 1 : 19. until the day d. and

DAWNING.

Jos. 6 : 15. rose about d. of day
Ju. 19 : 26. came woman in d. of
Jb. 3 : 9. neither let it see d. of day
7 : 4. I am full of tossings unto d.
Ps. 119 : 17. I prevented the d.

DAY.

Ge. 1 : 5. God called the light d.
16. greater light to rule d.
3 : 8. walking in gard. in cool of d.
18 : 1. tent door in heat of d.
32 : 24. wrestled with him until d.
26. Let me go, for d. breaketh
Ex. 21 : 21. if he continue a d. or
40:37. Journ. not, till d. it was tak.
Le. 23 : 37. every thing upon his d.
Nu. 3 : 13. d. I smote firstb., 8:17.
7:11. ea. prince sh. offer on his d.
14 : 34. each d. sh. bear your iniq.
30 : 8. if husb. disal. her on d., 12.
De. 4 : 10. d. thou stoodest bef. L.
15. manner of similitude on d.
9 : 7. fr. d. didst depart out of E.
24. rebellious fr. d. I knew you
21 : 15. At his d. give him his hire
Jos. 6 : 10. until d. I bid you shout
9 : 12. d. we came to go to you
10 : 13. sun hasted not about a d.
14. was no d. like that bef. or aft.
Ju. 16 : 2. when d. we kill Samson
18 : 30. until d. of cap. of land
19 : † 8. they tarried till d. declin.
11. by Jebus, d. was far spent

Ju.19:30.from d.Isr.came out of E.
Ru. 4:5. d. thou buyest field of Na.
1 S. 9 : 15. L. told Sam. a d. before
24 : 4. Behold d. of wh. Lord said
26 : 10. or his d. shall come to die
2 S. 3 : 35. while yet d., Je. 15 : 9.
13 : 32. from d. he forced his sister
19 : 24. fr. d. king departed, till d.
1 K. 2:37. on d. thou goest out, 42.
8 : † 59. thing of a d. in his d.
17:14. until the d. L. sendeth rain
2 K. 4:8. fell on a d. Elisha, 11, 18.
Ne. 4 : 2. they make an end in a d.
22. night a guard, labour on d.?
Es. 9 : 17. it a day of feasting, 18,19.
Jb 1 : 4. feasted every one his d.
6. a d. when sons of G., 13.-2 : 1.
3 : 3. d. perish wh-n I was born
14 : 6. till he accomplish his d.
18 : 20. sh. be astonished at his d.
19 : 25. stand at latter d. upon ear.
21 : 30. reserved to d. of destruc.
Ps. 19 : 2. d. unto d. utter. speech
37 : 13. he seeth his d. is coming
78 : 42. nor remem-d d. he deliv-d
84 : 10. a d. in thy courts is better
119 : 164. Seven times a d. I praise
Pr. 4:18. th. shineth unto perfect d.
7 : 20. come home at d. appointed
27 : 1. knowest not what a d. may
Can 2:17. Until d. break,4:6. [bri.
Is. 7 : 17. from d. Ephr. departed
30 : † 8. may be for the latter d.
43 : 13. bef. the d. was, I am he
49 : 8. in d. of salv. have I helped
58 : 5. a d. to afflict his soul? wilt call this acceptable d.
61 : 2. d. of vengeance of G., 63:4.
Je. 6:4. Woe unto us! the d. goeth
12:3.d. of slan-r | 17:16.woeful d.?
20 : 14. Cursed be d. I was born
27:22.there be until d. I visit them
32 : 31. from d. they built it, unto this d. [unto this d.
36 : 2. fr. d. I spake unto thee even
38 : 28. until d. Jerus. was taken
47 : 4. of d. that cometh to spoil
50 : 27. woe, for th. d. is come, 31.
Eze. 4 : 6. thee each d. for a year
7:10. Behold the d. it is come [29.
21 : 25. prince, whose d. is come,
28 : 15. from d. thou wast created
30 : 2. Woe worth the d. [d.
3. For d. is near, even the cloudy
18. At Tehaphnehes d. be dark
34 : 12. scattered in the dark d.
Da. 6 : 10. petition 3 times a d., 13.
Ho. 9 : 5. What do in solemn d.?
Jo. 2 : 2. a d. of darkness and
Am. 5 : 8. him that mak. d. dark
8 : 10. make end as a bitter d.
Mi. 3 : 6. d. be dark over them
7 : 4. the d. of thy watchmen
Zph. 2 : 2. the d. pass as the chaff
3 : 8. until d. I rise up to the prey
Zch. 4:10. despis. d. of sma. things?
Mal. 3 : 2. abide d. of his coming?
4 : 1. d. cometh that shall burn
Mat. 6 : 34. Sufficient unto the d.
20 : 2. agreed for a penny a d.
12. burden and heat of d.
24 : 38. marrying until d. Noe entered into ark, Lu. 17 : 27.
50. lord of servant come in d. he looketh not, Lu. 12: 46.
25 : 13. ye neither know d. nor
Mk. 1:35.rising a great while bef. d.
6:21.when convenient d. was come
Lu. 1:20. until d. these be perform.
80. child grew till d. of his shewing
4 : 42. when d. he departed [ing
5 : 17. on a certain d. as he was teaching, 8 : 22.
6 : 13. when it was d. he called
9 : 12. when the d. began to wear
17 : 4. trespass seven times in a d.
24. so Son of Man be in his d.

Lu.22:7. the d. of unleavened bread
66. soon as was d., Ac. 12 : 18.
24 : 29. the d. is far spent
Jn. 6 : 39. raise it again at last d.
40. raise him at last d., 44, 54.
8:56. fa. Ab rejoiced to see my d.
9 : 4. I must work while it is d.
11 : 24. resurrection at last d.
12 : 7. against d. of my burying
Ac. 1 : 2. Until d. he was taken up
2 : 1 the d. of Pentecost, 20 : 16.
15. is but third hour of the d.
12 : 21. on set d. Herod sat upon
16 : 35. when it was d., 23:12.-27:
17 : 31. hath appointed a d. [39.
21 : 26. next d. purifying himself
27 : 29. cast anchors, wished for d.
28 : 23. appointed him a d.
Ro. 2: 5. wrath against d. of wrath
13 : 12. d. is at hand, let us
14 : 6 regardeth d. reg. it to Lord
1 Co. 3 : 13. for d. shall declare it
4 : † 3. judged of you or man's d.
2 Co. 6 : 2. now is the d. of salva..
Ep. 4:30. sealed unto d. of redemp.
Ph. 1:6. perform it until d. of J C.,
Col. 1:6. since d. ye heard it, 9. [10.
1 Th. 5 : 5. Ye are chil. of the d.
8. who are of the d. be sober
2 Th. 2 : 2. the d. of Ch. is at hand
He. 4 : 7. he limiteth a certain d.
8. would he have spok. of ano. d.?
10 : 25. more as ye see d. approa-g
2 Pe. 1 : 19. until the d. dawn [G.
3:12. hasting unto coming of d. of
Re. 8 : 12. d. shone not for 3d part
9 : 15. were prepared for a d.

See ATONEMENT, BATTLE, CALAMITY, DARKNESS, EVIL, HOLY, LAST.

All the DAY.

Ps. 25 : 5. on thee do I wait a.t. d.
71 : 15. shew thy salva. a. t. d.
89 : 16. in thy name rejoice a.t.d.
102 : 8. enem. reproach me a. t. d.
119 : 97. law my meditation a.t.d.
Is. 28:24. ploughm. plough a. t. d.
65 : 2. spread out my hands a.t.d.
5. these are a fire burneth a.t.d.
La. 1 : 13. made me desolate a.t.d.
3 : 3. turneth hand ag. me a. t. d.
14. derision to my people a. t. d.
62. heard device ag. me a. t. d.
Mat. 20:6. Why stand a. t. d. idle?

All the DAY long.

De. 28 : 32. fail with longing a.d.l.
33 : 12. L. shall cover him a. d. l.
Ps. 32 : 3. thro. my roaring a. d.l.
35 : 28. speak of thy praise a.d. l.
38 : 6. I go mourning, a. d. l.
12. they imagine deceits a. d. l.
44 : 8. In God we boast, a. d. l.
22. sake we are killed a. d. l.
71 : 24. shall talk of thy righteousness a. d. l.
73:14. a. d. l. have I been plagued
Pr.21 : 26. coveteth greedily a. d. l.
23 : 17. be in the fear of L. a. d. l.
Ro. 8 : 36. we are killed a. d. l.
10 : 21. a. d. l. I stretched hands

DAY of Death.

Ge. 27 : 2. I know not d. o. my d.
Ju. 13 : 7. be Nazarite to d. o. d.
1 S. 15 : 35. Sam. came no more to see Saul until d. o. d. [d.
2 S. 6 : 23. had no child unto d.o.
20 : 3. concu. shut up unto d.o.d.
2 K. 15 : 5. Uzziah was a leper unto d. o. d., 2 Ch. 26 : 21. [birth.
Ec. 7 : 1. d. o. d. better than d. of
8:8.neith.hath he power in d.o.d.
Je. 52: 11. in prison till d. o. his d.
34.ev. day a portion, until d.o.d.

By DAY, and DAY by day.

Ge. 39 : 10. she spake to Jo. d.b.d.
Ex. 13 : 21. L. went bef. them b.d.
22. took not pillar of cloud b. d.

Ex. 29 : 38. offer two lambs d. b. d. continually, Nu. 28 : 3.
40 : 38. cloud of the Lord was upon tabernacle b. d., Nu. 9 : 16.
Nu. 10 : 34. cloud of L. upon them b. d., 14:14. De. 1:33. Ne. 9:19.
Ju. 6 : 27. he could not do it b. d.
2 S. 21 : 10. nor birds on them b. d.
1 Ch. 12 : 22. d. b. d. came to Da.
2 Ch. 21:15. reason of sickn. d.b.d.
24 : 11. d. b. d. and gath-d money
30 : 21. priests praised L. d. b. d.
Ezr. 6 : 9. let it be given d. b. d.
Ne. 8 : 18. d. b. d. he read in law
Ps. 91 : 5. nor arrow that flieth b.d.
121 : 6. sun not smite thee b. d.
136 : 8. The sun to rule b. d. for
Is.60:19.sun no more thy light b.d.
Je. 31 : 35. sun for a light b. d.
Eze. 12 : 3. remove b. d. in sight
7. brought forth my stuff b. d.
Lu. 11 : 3. Give us d. b. d. bread
2 Co. 4 : 16. is renewed d. b. d.
Re. 21 : 25. gates not be shut b. d.

Every DAY.

Ge. 6 : † 5. the thoughts evil e. d.
Ex. 16 : 4. gather certain rate e. d.
29 : 36. shalt offer a bullock e. d.
1 S. 23 : 14. Saul sought Da. e. d.
2 S. 13 : 37. Da. mourned son e. d.
2 K. 25 : 30. a daily rate for e. d.
1 Ch. 16 : 37. as e. d. work required
2 Ch. 8 : 13. aft. certain rate e. d.
14. duty of e. d. requir., Ezr.3:4.
Ne. 11 : 23. for singers, due e. d.
12 : 47. porters e. d. his portion
Es. 2 : 11. Mord. walked e. d. bef.
Ps.7:11. G. angry with wicked e.d.
56 : 5. e. d. they wrest my words
145 : 2. e. d. will I bless thee
Is. 51 : 13. and hast feared e. d.
52 : 5. my name e. d. blasphemed
Eze. 43 : 25. prepare e. d. a goat
Lu. 16 : 19. fared sumptuously e.d.
Ro. 14 : 5. esteemeth e. d. alike

Feast DAY.

Ps. 81 : 3. blow trumpet on f. d.
Mat. 26:5. Not on the f.d.,Mk.14:2.
Jn. 2 : 23. in f. d. many believed in

First DAY.

Ge. 1 : 5. evening and morning f.d.
8:5. f. d. of month mts. were seen, 13. Ex. 40 : 2, 17. Le. 23 : 24.
Ex. 12 : 15. f. d. ye shall put away leaven, whoso eateth fr. f. d. to
16. in f. d. a holy convoca., Le. 23 : 7, 35. Nu. 28 : 18.-29 : 1.
Le. 23 : 39. f. d. shall be a sabbath
40. shall take on f. d. boughs of
Nu. 1:1.L. spake unto Moses on f.d.
18. assem-d congregation on f. d.
33:38.in f. d. Aaron to Mount Hor
De. 16:4.flesh sacri. f.d. not remain
Ju. 20 : 22. in array the f. d.
2 Ch. 29:17. began on f.d. to sanct.
Ezr. 3 : 6. fr. f. d. began they to off.
7:9. upon f. d. began to go fr. Bab. on f. d. came to Jerusalem
10 : 16. sat down in f. d. of tenth
17. by f. d. of first month they
Ne.8:2. Ezra brought law upon f.d.
18. f. unto last d. he read in law
Eze. 26:1. in f. d. word of L. came, 29 : 17.-31 : 1.-32 : 1. Hag. 1:1.
45 : 18. in f. d. shalt offer bullock
Da. 10 : 12. from f. d. didst set thy heart [14 : 12.
Mat. 26:17. f. d. of unleav. br., Mk.
Ac. 20:18. fr. f. d. I came into Asia
Ph. 1 : 5. fellowship from f.d. until [now
See WEEK.

Second DAY.

Ge. 1 : 8. evening and morning s. d.
Ex. 2 : 13. when he went out s. d.
Nu. 7 : 18. on s. d. Nethaneel
29 : 17. on s. d. offer 12 bullocks
Jos. 6 : 14. s. d. compassed city
Jos.10:32. took Lachish on the s.d.
Ju. 20 : 24. Isr. came ag. Benj. s.d.
1 S.20:34.Jona.did eat no meat s.d.
2 Ch. 3 : 2. he began to build s. d.
Ne. 8 : 13. on s. d. were gathered
Es. 7 : 2. king said to Esther s. d.
Je.41:4.s.d. aft.he had slain Gedali.
Eze. 43:22. s. d. thou shalt offer kid

Third DAY.

Ge. 1:13. evening and morning t. d.
22 : 4. t. d. Ab. saw the place afar off [Jacob was
31 : 22. was told Laban on t. d.
34 : 25. t. d. when they were sore
Ex. 4:†10. nor since t.d., Jos. 3:†4.
19 : 11. be ready ag. t. d. for t. d. L. will come upon Sinai, 15.
Le. 7 : 17. flesh of sacrifice on t. d. be burnt, 19 : 6.
Nu. 19:12. purify hims. t.d.,31 : 19.
19. clean sprinkle uncl. on t. d.
29 : 20. on t. d. eleven bullocks
De. 19 : † 4. hated not from t. d † 6.
Jos. 9:17. Isr. came unto cities t. d.
Ju. 20:30. Isr. went ag. Benj. t. d.
1 S. 4 : † 7. not such a thing t. d.
19 : † 7. was in his presence as t.d.
20 : 5. hide in field until t. d., 12.
2 S. 3 : † 17. Ye sought Da. t. d.
1 K. 12 : 12. Jerob. came to Rehob. t. d., 2 Ch 10 : 12.
2 K. 13 : † 5. Israel dwelt as t. d.
20 : 5. t. d. go unto house of L., 8.
1 Ch. 11 : † 2. t. d. wast he that leddest out Israel
Ezr. 6 : 15. house finished on t. d.
Es.5:1. t.d. Es.put on royal apparel
Ho. 6:2. in t. d. he will raise us up
Mat. 16 : 21. be killed, and raised again t. d., 17 : 23. Lu. 9 : 22.
20 : 19. t. d. he shall rise, Mk. 9 : 31.-10 : 34. Lu. 18 : 33.-24:7,46.
27:64. sepul. made sure until t. d.
Lu. 13:32. t. d. I shall be perfected
24 : 21. today is t. d. since these things [Cana
Jn. 2 : 1. t. d. was a marriage in
Ac. 10 : 40. raised up the t. d.
27 : 19. t. d. we cast out tackling
1 Co. 15 : 4. that he rose again t.d.

Fourth DAY.

Ge. 1:19. evening and morning f.d.
Nu. 29:23. on the f. d. ten bullocks
2 Ch. 20 : 26. f. d. they assembled
Ezr.8:33.f.d.silver and gold weighed
Zch. 7 : 1. word unto Zech. in f. d.

Fifth DAY.

Ge. 1 : 23. evening and morning f.d.
Nu. 29:26. on the f.d. nine bullocks
Eze. 1 : 1. f. d. of month, 2.-8 : 1.
33 : 21. in f. d. one came unto me

Sixth DAY.

Ge. 1:31. evening and morning s. d.
Ex.16:5.s.d.gath.twice as much,22.
29. giveth s. d. bread of two days
Nu. 7 : 42. s. d. Eliasaph offered
29 : 29. on s. d. eight bullocks

Seventh DAY.

Ge. 2 : 2. s. d. God ended his work
3. G. blessed s. d., Ex. 20 : 11.
Ex.12:15. leaven first d. until s. d.
16. s. d. shall be a holy convocation, Le. 23 : 8. Nu. 28 : 25.
13 : 6. s. d. shall be a feast
16 : 26. but s. d. is the sabbath, 20 : 10. Le. 23 : 3. De. 5 : 14.
27. went out some on the s. d.
29. no man go out of his place s.d.
24 : 16. s. d. he called unto Moses
31:17. on s. d. God rested, He.4:4.
34 : 21. on s. d. thou shalt rest
35:2. on s.d. shall be holy d. to you
Le. 13 : 5. priest sh. look on him s. d., 6, 27, 32, 34, 51.-14 : 39.
14 : 9. s. d. he sh. shave, Nu. 6:9.
Nu. 19 : 12. s. d. he shall be clean
19. on s. d. purify hims., 31 : 19.
Nu.31:24.wash your clothes on s.d.
De. 16 : 8. on s. d. a sol. assembly
Jos. 6 : 4. s. d. compass city, 15.
Ju. 14 : 15. s. d. said unto Sams.'s [wife
17. on the s. d. he told her
2 S. 12 : 18. on s. d. child died
1 K.20:29. in s. d. battle was joined
2 K. 25 : 8. on s. d. came Nebuzar-
Es. 1 : 10. on s.d. Ahasu. was merry
Eze. 30 : 20. in s. d. word came
45 : 20. so do s. d. of month
He. 4 : 4. spake of s. d. on this wise, God did rest the s. d.

Eighth DAY.

Ex. 22 : 30. on e.d. shalt give it me
Le. 9 : 1. e. d. Moses called Aaron
12 : 3. e. d. flesh of foreskin be
14 : 10. e.d. sh. take two he lambs
23. turtledoves on e. d., 15 : 14. Nu. 6 : 10.
22 : 27. fr. e. d. it shall be accepted
23 : 36. on e. d. be holy convoca.
39. on e. d. shall be a sabbath
Nu. 29 : 35. on e. d. a sol. assembly, 2 Ch. 7 : 9. Ne. 8 : 18.
1 K. 8 : 66. e. d. he sent peo. away
Eze. 43 : 27. e. d. make burnt off-g
Lu. 1 : 59. on e. d. came to circum. child, Ac. 7 : 8. Ph. 3 : 5.

Ninth DAY.

Le. 23 : 32. shall afflict souls in n.d.
2 K. 25 : 3. n. d. famine prevailed in the city, Je. 52 : 6.
Je. 39 : 2. n. d. city was broken up

Tenth DAY.

Ex.12:3. t. d. of this mo. take lamb
Le. 16:29. on t. d. shall afflict your souls, 23 : 27. Nu. 29 : 7.
25 : 9. on t. d. trumpet of jubilee
Jos. 4:19. peo. came out of Jor. t.d.
2 K 25 : 1. in t. d. Neb. came ag. Jerus., Je. 52 : 4. Eze. 24 : 1.
Je.52:12. in t.d. Neb. burned house
Eze. 20 : 1. in t. d. elders came
40 : 1. in t. d. hand of L. was

Eleventh DAY.

Nu. 7 : 72. on e. d. Pagiel offered

Twelfth DAY.

Nu. 7 : 78. on t. d. Ahira offered
Ezr. 8:31. departed on t.d. unto Jer.
Eze. 29 : 1. t. d. word came unto [Eze.

Thirteenth DAY.

Es. 3:12. scribes were called on t.d.
13. letters to destroy Jews upon t. d., 8 : 12.-9 : 1.
9 : 17. on t.d. of Adar they rested
18. Jews at Shushan assemb. on [t.d.

Fourteenth DAY.

Ex. 12 : 6. sh. keep lamb until f.d.
18. on f. d. eat unleav. bread
Le. 23 : 5. in f. d. is L.'s passover
Nu. 9 : 3, 5.-28 : 16. Jos. 5 : 10.
2 Ch. 30 : 15.-35 : 1. Ezr. 6 : 19.
Eze. 45 : 21.
Nu. 9 : 11. f. d. at even sh. eat it
Es. 9 : 15. Jews gathered on f. d.
17. on f. d. of same rested they
Ac. 27:33. is f. d. ye contin. fasting

Fifteenth DAY.

Ex.16:1. unto wildern. of Sin on f.d.
Le 23 : 6. on f.d. is feast, Nu.28:17.
34. f. d. of seventh month, 39. Nu. 29 : 12. Eze. 45 : 25.
Nu.33:3.depart. fr. Rameses on f.d.
1 K. 12 : 32. ord. feast on f. d., 33.
Es.9:18. Jews f. d. rested yearly, 21.
Eze. 32 : 17. f. d. word of Lord unto [Eze.

Sixteenth DAY.

2 Ch. 29 : 17. s.d. they made an end

Seventeenth DAY.

Ge. 7 : 11. in s. d. fount. broken up
8 : 4. ark rested s. d. upon Ararat

Twentieth DAY.

Nu. 10:11. on t. d. cloud was taken
Ezr. 10:9. on t. d. peo. sat in streets

One and twentieth DAY.

Ex. 12 : 18. eat unl. bread until o.d.

Hag. 2 : 1. in -d. word to Haggai.

Three and twentieth DAY.

2 Ch. 7 : 10. -d. Sol. sent peo. away
Es. 8 : 9. on -d. written as Morde.

Four and twentieth DAY.

Ne. 9 : 1. -d. Israel assembled
Da. 10 : 4. in -d. I was by river
Hag. 1 : 15. -d. L. stirred Zeruh.
2 : 10. in -d. word by Haggai, 20.
18. consider fr. t. d. of 9th month
Zch. 1 : 7. upon -d. word unto Zech.

Five and twentieth DAY.

Ne. 6 : 15. wall was finish. in -d.
Je. 52 : 31. -d. Evil-mer. lifted

Seven and twentieth DAY.

Ge. 8 : 14. on -d. was earth dried
2 K. 25 : 27. on -d. Evil-mer.

Good DAY.

1 S. 25 : 8. we come in a g. d.
Es. 8 : 17. Jews had a g. d., 9 : 19.
9 : 22. from morning into a g. d.

Great DAY.

Je. 30 : 7. alas, that d. is g.
Ho. 1 : 11. g. shall be d. of Jezr.
Jo. 2 : 11. d. of L. is g. and terri.
31. g. and terrible d. of L., Ac. 2 : 20.
Zph. 1 : 14. g. d. of L. is near
Mal. 4 : 5. bef. coming of g. d. of L.
Jn. 7 : 37. g. d. of feast, Jesus cried
Jude 6. unto judgment of the g. d.
Re. 6 : 17. g. d. of wrath is come
16 : 14. gather to battle of g. d.

In the DAY.

Ge. 2 : 4. i. d. L. made the earth
17. i. d. thou eatest shalt die
3 : 5. i. d. ye eat, eyes be open.
31 : 40. i. d. drought consum. me
35 : 3. answ. i. d. of my distress
Ex. 32 : 34. i. d. when I visit
Le. 6 : 5. i. d. of trespass offering
20. offer i. d. when, 7 : 36.
7 : 35. i. d. he presented them
14 : 2. i. d. of his cleans-g, Nu. 6 : 9.
† 57. i. d. of clean and unclean
Nu. 7 : 10. altar i. d. anointed, 84.
25 : 18. slain i. d. of plague
28 : 26. i. d. of first fruits
30 : 5. fa. disallow i. d. he heareth
7. husband held peace i. d. 16.
De. 9 : 10. i. d. of assembly, 10 : 4.-18:
Jos. 10 : 12. i. d. L. deliv-d Amori.
14 : 11. strong as i. d. Mo. sent me
1 S. 20 : † 19. didst hide i. d.
21 : 6. hot bread i. d. it was taken
2 S. 22 : 1. i. d. L. had deliv. him
1 K. 2 : 8. cursed me i. d. I fled
Ne. 9 : 12. led i. d. by cloudy pillar
Ne. 13 : 15. i. d. they sold vict.
Es. 9 : 1. i. d. enem. of Jews hoped
Jb. 20 : 28. flow away i. d. of wrath
Ps. 95 : 8. i. d. of tempta., He. 3 : 8.
102 : 2. Hide not face i. d. of trouble, i. d. when I call
110 : 3. willing i. d. of thy power?
5. shall strike kings i. d. of wrath
137 : 7. Remem. Edom i. d. of Jeru.
: 3. i. d. I cried thou answ-dst
138 : 34. not spare i. d. of veng.
Pr : 4. Riches profit not i. d. of wra.
24 : 10. If faint i. d. of adversity
Ec. 7 : 14. i. d. of prosperity be joyful, i. d. of adversity consider
8 : 8. neith. power i. d. of death
12 : 3. i. d. wh. keepers sh. tremble
Can. 3 : 11. crowned him i. d. of espousals and i. d. of gladness
8 : 8. i. d. wh. she shall be spoken for
Is. 9 : 4. as i. d. of Midian
10 : 3. what do i. d. of visitation?
11 : 16. i. d. he came out of E., Ho. 2 : 15.
13 : 13. i. d. of anger
14 : 3. i. d. L. shall give thee rest
17 : 11. i. d. shalt make thy plant grow i. d. of grief
27 : 8. rough wind i. d. of east w.
30 : 25. i. d. of great slaughter
26. i. d. L. bindeth up breach
Is. 58 : 3. i. d. of fast find pleasure
Je. 7 : 22. i. d. I bro-t them out
11 : 4, 7.-31 : 32.-34 : 13.
Je. 16 : 19. refuge i. d. of affliction
17 : 17. art my hope i. d. of evil
18 : 17. shew back i. d. of calamity
36 : 30. dead body be cast out i. d.
La. 1 : 12. afflic. me i. d. of his anger
2 : 1. remem. not footst. i. d. of anger
21. slain them i. d. of anger
3 : 57. drewest near i. d. I called
Eze. 7 : 19. gold not deliv. i. d. of wrath
16 : 4. i. d. thou wast born, 5.
56. Sod. not menti. i. d. of pride
24 : 25. i. d. I take their strength
27 : 27. fall i. d. of thy ruin
30 : 9. great pain as i. d. of Egypt
31 : 15. i. d. he went to the grave
32 : 10. for his life i. d. of thy fall
33 : 12. i. d. he turneth fr. wick.
not able to live i. d. he sinneth
36 : 33. i. d. sh. have cleansed you
Ho. 2 : 3. as i. d. she was born
4 : 5. Theref. shalt thou fall i. d.
5 : 9. Ephr. desolate i. d. of rebuke
Am. 1 : 14. i. d. of a whirlwind
8 : 9. will darken earth i. clear d.
Ob. 11. i. d. stoodest on other side
12. nor rejoic. i. d. of their destr.
14. did remain i. d. of distress
Mi. 7 : 11. i. d. thy walls be built
Mal. 4 : 3. i. d. that I shall do this
Lu. 17 : 30. i. d. the Son is revealed
Jn. 7 : 37. i. last d. of the feast
11 : 9. walk i. d. he stumbl-h not
12 : 48. judge him i. last d.
Ro. 2 : 16. i. d. G. sh. judge secrets
13 : 13. walk honestly as i. d.
1 Co. 1 : 8. be blameless i. d. of L.
2 Co. 6 : 2. i. d. of salv. I succoured
Ep. 6 : 13. to withstand i. evil d.
Ph. 2 : 16. may rejoice i. d. of C.
He. 8 : 8. i. d. of temptation in the
8 : 9. i. d. I took them by hand
1 Pe. 2 : 12. glorify God i. d. of vis.

DAY of Judgment.

Mat. 10 : 15. tolerable for Sodom in d. o. j., 11 : 24. Mk. 6 : 11.
11 : 22. tolerable for Tyre in d. o. j.
12 : 36. shall give account in d. o. j.
2 Pe. 2 : 9. reserve unjust to d. o. j.
3 : 7. reserved unto fire ag. d. o. j.
1 Jn. 4 : 17. have boldn. in d. o. j.

DAY of the Lord.

Is. 2 : 12 d. o. L. be upon proud
13 : 6. d. o. L. is at hand, Jo. 1 : 15. Zph. 1 : 7.
9. d. o. L. cometh, Jo. 2 : 1. Zch. 14 : 1.
34 : 8. it is d. o. L.'s vengeance
Je. 46 : 10. this is d. o. L. of hosts
La. 2 : 22. in d. o. L.'s anger none
Eze. 13 : 5. battle in d. o. L. Ob. 15.
30 : 3. d. o. L. is near, Jo. 3 : 14.
Am. 5 : 18. Woe that desire d. o. L.
20. sh. not d. o. L. be darkness, 18.
Zph. 1 : 8. in d. o. L.'s sacrifice
18. deliver in d. o. L.'s wrath
2 : 2. bef. d. o. L.'s anger come
3. be hid in d. o. L.'s anger
Mal. 4 : 5. bef. coming of d. o. L.
1 Co. 5 : 5. spirit saved in d. o. L.
2 Co. 1 : 14. ye are ours in d. o. L.
1 Th. 5 : 2. d. o. L. cometh as a thief, 2 Pe. 3 : 10.
Re. 1 : 10. in the Spirit on t. L.'s d.

See GREAT DAY.

Next DAY.

Mat. 27 : 62. n. d. that followed
Lu. 9 : 37 n. d. when they were come
Jn. 1 : 29. n. d. John seeth Jesus
35. n. d. John and two of his
12 : 12. n. d. much peo. were come
Ac. 4 : 3. them in hold until n. d.
14 : 20. n. d. he depart. with Barna.
20 : 15. n. d. we came to Miletus (3)
21 : 8. the n. d. we departed
25 : 6. n. d. sitting on judgm. seat
Ac. 27 : 3. n. d. we touched at Sidon
28 : 13 came n. d. to Puteoli

DAY with Night.

Ge. 1 : 14. lights to divide d. fr. n.
18. to rule over the d. and n.
8 : 22. d. and n., shall not cease
31 : 39. whether stolen by d. or n.
Ex. 10 : 13. an east wind d. and n.
13 : 21. give light to go by d. and n.
Le. 8 : 35. at door of tab. d. and n.
Nu. 11 : 32. peo. stood d. and all n.
De. 28 : 66. shalt fear d. and n.
Jos. 1 : 8. thou shalt meditate there. in d. and n., Ps. 1 : 2.
1 S. 19 : 24. lay naked all d. and n.
25 : 16. a wall unto us by n. and d.
1 K. 8 : 29. eyes be opened tow. this house n. and d., 2 Ch. 6 : 20.
Ne. 1 : 6. which I pray d. and n.
4 : 9. set a watch ag. them d. and n.
Es. 4 : 16. eat nor drink n. or d.
Jb. 17 : 12. They change n. into d.
26 : 10. until d. and n. come to end
Ps. 32 : 4. d. and n. thy hand heavy
42 : 3. my tears my meat d. and n.
55 : 10. d. and n. th. go upon walls
74 : 16. d. is thine, n. also thine
88 : 1. O Lord, I have cried d. and n.
139 : 12. the n. shineth as the d.
Ec. 8 : 16. d. nor n. seeth sleep
Is. 4 : 5. smoke by d. fire by n.
27 : 3. I L. will keep it d. and n.
28 : 19. sh. it pass over by d. and n.
34 : 10. not be quenched d. nor n.
38 : 12. pining sickness; fr. d. to n.
13. d. to n. wilt make end of me
60 : 11. gates, not be shut d. nor n.
62 : 6. never hold peace d. nor n.
Je. 9 : 1. weep d. and n. for slain
14 : 17. tears d. and n., La. 2 : 18.
16 : 13. serve other gods d. and n.
33 : 20. should not be d. nor n.
25. If my cov. be not with d. and n.
Am. 5 : 8. maketh d. dark with n.
Zch. 14 : 7. it shall be one day known to Lord, not d. nor n.
Mk. 4 : 27. sleep and rise n. and d.
5 : 5. d. and n. he was in mts.
14 : 30. this d. this n. before cock crow
Lu. 2 : 37. with prayers n. and d.
18 : 7. elect. which cry d. and n.
Ac. 9 : 24. watched gates n. and d.
20 : 31. cease not to warn n. and d.
26 : 7. instantly serving G. d. and n.
2 Co. 11 : 25. suff. shipwreck, a n. and a d. been in the deep
1 Th. 2 : 9. labouring d. and n. bec.
3 : 10. n. and d. praying, 1 Ti. 5 : 5.
2 Th. 3 : 8. but wrought n. and d.
2 Ti. 1 : 3. I have remem. of thee in prayers n. and d.
Re. 4 : 8. they rest not d. and n.
7 : 15. serve him d. and n. in tem.
8 : 12. d. shone not, and the n.
12 : 10. accused them d. and n.
14 : 11. they have no rest d. nor n.
20 : 10. tormented d. and n. for ever

One DAY.

Ge. 27 : 45. depriv. of both in o. d.?
33 : 13. overdrive o. d. flock die
Le. 22 : 28. kill it and young in o. d.
Nu. 11 : 19. Ye shall not eat o. d.
1 S. 2 : 34. in o. d. shall die both
27 : 1. I shall o. d. perish by Saul
1 K. 4 : 22. Solo.'s provision for o. d.
20 : 29. Isr. slew 100,000 in o. d.
2 Ch. 28 : 6. slew 120,000 in o. d.
Ezr. 10 : 13. neither work of o. d.
Es. 3 : 13. kill chil. in o. d., 8 : 12.
Is. 9 : 14. branch and rush in o. d.
10 : 17. devour his thorns in o. d.
47 : 9. two things sh. come in o. d.
66 : 8. earth to bring forth in o. d.?
Zch. 3 : 9 remove iniquity in o. d.
14 : 7. be o. d. which sh. be kno.
Ac. 21 : 7. abode with breth. o. d.
28 : 13. after o. d. south wind

Ro. 14: 5. esteem. o. d. above ano.
1 Co. 10:8. fell in o. d. 23,000
2 Pe. 3:8. o. d. with L. as 1000 yrs.
Re. 18:8. her plagues come in o. d.

Sabbath DAY.

Ex. 16: 26. seventh d. is s.,20: 10.
20: 8. Remember s. d. to keep it,
De. 5: 12. Je. 17: 24, 27.
11. Lord blessed the s. d.
31:15.whoso.doeth work upon s.d.
35: 3. sh. kindle no fire upon s.d.
Nu.15:32.gathered sticks upon s.d.
28: 9. offer upon s. d. two lambs
De. 5: 15. God com-d to keep s. d.
Ne.10:31.if peo. sell victuals on s.d.
13: 15. burdens to Jerus. on s. d.
17. evil ye do, and profane s. d.
19. no burden be bro-t in on s.d.
22. keep gates to sanctify s. d.
Je. 17: 21. bear no burden on s. d.
22. nor carry burden on s. d.
Eze. 46:4. prince shall offer in s. d.
Mat. 12: 1. Jesus went on the s.d.
through the corn, Mk. 2: 23.
8. Son of Man is Lord of s. d.
11. fall into pit on s. d., Lu.14:5.
24:20. pray your flight be not s. d.
Mk. 2: 24. why do they on s. d.
that is not lawful, Mat. 12: 2.
3:2. would heal on s.d., Lu. 6: 7.
6:2. he went into synagogue on s.
d., Lu. 4: 16. Ac. 13: 14.
Lu. 13: 16. loosed fr. bond on s. d.
14: 1. went to eat bread on s. d.
3. Is it lawful to heal on s. d.
23: 56. spices, and rested the s. d.
Jn.5:10.s.d.it is not lawful to carry
16. bec.he had done these on s.d.
7: 22. ye on s. d. circumc. a man.
9: 14. it was s.d. Jesus made clay
16. he keepeth not the s. d.
19: 31. bodies not upon cross s.d.
Ac. 13: 27. read every s. d., 15: 21.
44. next s. d. came whole city

Same DAY.

Ge. 7:11. s. d. were fountains brok.
15:18. In s. d. Lord made a cove.
Ex.19:1 s. d. came they into wilder.
Le.7: 15. flesh eaten the s. d., 16.-
19: 6.-22: 30.
23:28. ye shall do no work in s.d.
29.that sh.not be afflicted in s. d.
Nu. 6: 11. hallow his head s. d.
1 K. 8: 64. s. d. king hallow court
13: 3. he gave a sign the s. d.
Is. 7: 20. s. d. L. shave with razor
Eze. 23:38. defiled sanct., s. d., 39.
24:2. write name of this s. d.: king
of Babylon ag. Jerus. s. d.
Zph. 1: 9. s. d. will I punish those
Zch. 6: 10. and come the s. d.
Mat. 13: 1. s. d. went Jesus out
22: 23. s. d. came to him Saddu.
Mk. 4:35. s. d. when even was come
Lu. 13:31. s. d. came certain Phari.
17: 29. s. d. Lot went out of Sod.
23: 12. s. d. Pilate and H. friends
24: 13. went s. d. to a village
Jn. 5: 9. on s. d. was sabbath
20: 19. s. d. at even., J. in midst
Ac. 1: 22. unto s. d. he was tak. up
2: 41. s.d. were added 3,000 souls

Selfsame DAY.

Ge. 7: 13. the s. d. entered Noah
17: 26. s. d. was Ab. circumcised
Ex. 12: 17. s. d. I bro-t armies, 51.
Le.23:14. no parched corn until s.d.
De. 32:48. L. spake unto Moses s.d.

Since the DAY.

Ex. 10: 6. s. d. they on earth
De. 4: 32. s. d. God created man
1 S. 8: 8. s. d. I brought them out
of E., 1 K. 8: 16. 1 Ch. 17: 5.
2 Ch. 6: 5.
29:6. evil in thee s.d. of thy coming
2 K. 8: 6. s. d. she left land
21: 15. anger s. d. fathers came

Je. 7: 25. s. d. your fathers came
Col. 1: 6. s. d. ye heard of it
9. s. d. we heard it, not cease

That DAY.

Ge 33:16. Esau ret. t. d. on his way
Ex. 8:22. sever in t. d. land of Gos.
10: 13. east wind on land all t.d.
28. t. d. seest my face, shalt die
13: 8. shalt shew thy son in t. d.
14: 30. Thus L. saved Israel t. d.
32: 28. there fell t. d. 3,000
Le.16:30. t.d.sh. priest make atone.
Nu. 9: 6. not keep passover t. d.
30: 14. he held his peace in t. d.
De.1:39. chil. in t. d. had no knowl.
21: 23. in any wise bury him t.d.
31: 18. will hide my face in t. d.
Jos. 6: 15. t. d. compassed city
9: 27. made them t. d. hewers of
wood [kims
14: 12. heardest in t. d. how Ana-
Ju. 3: 30. Moab was subdued t. d.
6: 32. t. d. he called him Jerub.
20: 26. Isr. fasted t. d., 1 S. 7: 6.
1 S.3: 12.t.d. I will perform ag. Eli
8: 18. ye sh. cry out in t. d. Lord
will not hear you in t. d.
9: 24. Saul did eat with Sam. t.d.
10:9. those signs came to pass t.d.
12: 18. sent thunder and rain t.d.
14: 23. So L. saved Israel t. d.
31. they smote Philistines t. d.
37. Saul asked, he answ. not t.d.
16:13. Spirit of L. upon Da. fr. t.d.
18: 9. Saul eyed David from t. d.
20: 26.Saul spake not t. d.
21: 10. Da. fled t. d. for fear of S.
27: 6. Achish gave him Zik. t. d.
2 S. 6: 9. Da. was afraid of L. t. d.
11: 12. Uriah abode in Jerus. t.d.
19:2.Victory t.d.turned into mour
1 K. 14:14. cut off h. of Jerob. t.d.
22: 25. see in t. d., 2 Ch. 18: 24.
35. battle incr. t. d., 2 Ch.18:34.
2 Ch. 15: † 11. offered t.d. 700 oxen
Ne. 8: 17. to t. d. Isr. not done so
13: 1. t. d. read in book of Moses
Es. 3: 14. be ready ag. t. d., 8: 13.
Jb. 3: 4. Let t. d. be darkness
Ps. 146: 4. in t. d. his tho-ts perish
Pr.12:†16.fool's wrath is in t.d. kn.
Is.2:11.L. alone be exalt. in t.d.,17.
10: 32. sh. he remain at Nob t.d.
11: 10. in t. d. a root of Jesse
12:4. t.d. ye sh. say, Praise the L.
19:21. Egyp. shall know L. in t.d.
24:21. in t. d. L. shall punish host
26:1. t.d. this song be sung in Jud.
29: 18. t.d. shall deaf hear words
52: 6. shall know t. d. I am he
Je.39:†10. Neb. gave vineyards t.d.
16. they shall be accompl. t. d.
17. I will deliver thee in t. d.
Eze. 29: 21. in t. d. Isr. be exalted
38: 19. in t.d. be a great shaking
39: 22. know I am L. from t. d.
48: 35. name of city fr. t. d. be
Ho. 2: 18. t. d. will I make a cov.
Jo. 3: 18. t.d. mts. shall drop wine
Am. 2: 16. flee away nak. in t. d.
8:3. the songs be howlings in t. d.
Ob.8. not in t.d. destroy wise men?
Zph. 1: 15 t. d. is a day of wrath
Zch. 2: 11. nations joined to L.t.d.
9: 16. God shall save them t. d.
11: 11. my cov. it was broken t.d.
12: 8. feeble at t. d. be as David
11. In t. d. be great mourning
13: 1. In t. d. be fountain opened
14: 4. feet sh. stand t. d. on m-t
9. in t. d. shall there be one L.
Mal. 3: 17. t. d. I make up jewels
Mat. 7: 22. Many will say in t.d.L.
22: 46. nei. durst fr. t.d. ask him
24: 36. of t. d. knoweth no man,
• Mk. 13: 32. [14: 25.
26:29. till t.d. I drink it new, Mk.

Lu. 6: 23 Rejoice ye in t. d.
10: 12. more toler. t.d. for Sodom
17: 31. In t. d. he upon housetop
21: 34. so t. d. come unawares
23: 54. t. d. was the preparation
Jn. 1: 39. they abode wi. him t. d.
11: 53. fr. t. d. they took counsel
14: 20. t. d. sh. know I am in Fa.
16:23. t.d. ye shall ask me noth.
26. t. d. ye sh. ask in my name
1 Th. 5: 4. t.d. overtake as a thief
2 Th. 1:10. testim. believed in t. d.
2: 3. t. d. shall not come, except
2 Ti.1:12. committed unto him ag.t.
18. find mercy of Lord in t.d.[d.
4:8. crown L. sh. give me at t. d.

This DAY.

Ge. 4: 14. hast driven me out t. d.
24: 12. send me good speed t. d.
42. I came t. d. unto the well
25:31. Sell me t.d. thy birthright
33. Swear to me t. d. and he sw.
35:20.pillar of Ra.'s grave unto t.d.
41: 9. I remem. my faults t. d.
42:13.youngest t.d.with our fa.,32.
48: 15. God who fed me unto t.d.
Ex. 12: 14. t. d. be for memorial
17. observe t.d. in your genera.
13: 3. Remem. t.d. ye came out, 4.
De. 1: 10. you are t.d. as stars
2:25. t.d. will I put dread of thee
4:4. alive ev. one t. d, 5: 3.[man
5: 24. seen t. d. G. doth talk with
6: 24. as at t. d., 8: 18. Ezr. 9: 7.
7: 11. statutes I com. thee t.d.
4: 40.-6: 6.-8: 1, 11.-10: 13.-
30: 2, 8. [perish
8: 19. I testify ag. you t.d. ye sh.
11: 8. com-ts I command you t.d.,
13, 27, 28.-13: 18.-15: 5.-19:
9.-27: 1, 4.
26. bef. you t. d. a blessing and
32. statutes I set before you t.d.
12: 8. not do aft. things ye do t.d.
26:17. avouched t.d. the L. thy G.
18. L. hath avouched thee t. d.
27:9. t. d. art become people of L.
29:4. not given you ears unto t.d.
10. Ye stand t. d. all before L.
18. heart turn-h aw. t.d.fr.L.[19.
30:15. bef. thee t.d. life and death,
16. I com. thee t. d. to love L.
31: 27. while I am yet alive t. d.
34:6. no man kn. his sepul. to t.d.
Jos. 3: 7. t. d. will I magnify thee
4: 9. stones are there unto t. d.
5: 9. t. d. rolled away reproach
7: 25. L. shall trouble thee t. d.
14: 10. I am t. d. 85 years old
11. am as strong t.d. as when Mos.
22: 16. to turn t. d. from foll-g L.
17. we not cleansed until t. d.
22. in rebellion save us not t. d.
23: 8. cleave to L. as unto t. d.
14. t. d. I am going way of all
24: 15. choose you t. d. wh. serve
Ju. 1: 26. Luz is name unto t. d.
10: 15. deliver us only we pray t. d.
19: 30. since Is. came out of land
Eg. to t. d., 1 S. 8: 8. 2 S. 7: 6.
2 K. 21:15. 1 Ch.17:5. Je.7:25.
Ru. 4: 9. ye are witnesses t. d.,10.
1 S. 10: 19. t. d. rejected your G
11: 13. not a man be put to death
12:5. anointed is witn. t. d.[t. d.
14: 45. Jona. wrought with G.t.d.
15: 28. rent kingd. from thee t.d.
17: 10. I defy armies of Isr. t. d.
18: 21. shalt t. d. be my son in l-
21: 5. tho. it were sanctified t. d.
22: 8. to lie in wait as at t. d., 13.
25: 32. sent thee t. d. to meet me
33. t. d. fr. coming to shed blood
26: 19. driven me out t. d. from
21. my soul was precious t. d.
24. thy life was much set by t.d.
30:25. an ordin. for Isr. unto t. d

S. 3 : 38. a great man fallen t. d.
39. I am t. d. weak, though king
: 3. were sojourners until t. d.
18 : 20. not bear tidings t. d.
K.2:24.Adou.be put to death t.d.
: 61. to keep com-ts as at t. d.
K. 2 : 22. waters healed unto t. d.
: 9. t. d. day of good tidings [41.
17 : 34. t.d. do aft.former manner,
Ch. 5 : 9. there it is unto t. d.
35 : 21. I come not ag. thee t. d.
e. 1 : 11. prosper thy servant t. d.
: 9. t. d. holy unto the L., 10.
: 36. we are servants t. d.
s. 2 : 7. my son t. d. have I begotten thee, Ac. 13:33. He. 1:5.
118 : 24. t. is the d. L. hath made
119 : 91. continue t.d. acc. to thy
r. 7 : 14. t. d. I paid my vows
22 : 19. made known to thee t. d.
s. 38 : 19. living praise as I do t.d.
56 : 12. tomorrow shall be as t.d.
58 : 4. sh. not fast as ye do t. d.
e. 1 : 10. t.d. set thee over nation
25 : 18. a curse as at t. d., 44 : 22.
35 : 14. unto t. d.they drink none
36 : 2. fr. days of Josiah unto t. d.
44 : 2. t. d. they are a desola., 6.
10. are not humbled unto t. d.
a. 2 : 16. t. is d. we looked for
ze. 39 : 8. t. is d. I have spoken
a. 9 : 7. confusion of faces, as t.d.
ag. 2 : 15. consider from t. d., 18.
19. from t. d. will I bless you.
at. 6 : 11.Give us t. d. daily bread
11:23. Sod. have remain. until t.d.
27:8.called field of blood unto t.d.
19. I have suffered t. d. in dream
28:15.reported am. Jews until t.d.
k. 14 : 30. t. d. ye shall deny me
u. 2 : 11. is born t. d. a Saviour
4 : 21. t. d. is this scripture fulfi.
19 : 9. t. d. is salv. come to this h.
42. hadst kn. at least in t. thy d.
22 : 34. not crow t. d. bef. thou
c. 2:29. sepul. is with us unto t.d.
4 : 9. If we t. d. be examined
13 : 33. t.d. begotten thee, He.1:5.
19 : 40. called in question for t. d.
20 : 26. I take you to record t. d.
22 : 3. zealous as ye are all t. d.
23 :1. in good conscience till t. d.
24 : 21. am called in question t. d.
26 : 2. answer for myself t. d.
22. continue t. d. witnessing
29. I would all that hear me t.d.
o. 11 : 8. sho. not hear unto t. d.
Co. 3:14.until t. d.remain.vail,15.

To DAY or Day to DAY.

e. 21 : 26. heard I of it but t. d.
30:32. will pass thro.thy flock t.d.
40 : 7. Whf. look ye so sadly t.d.
x. 2:18.how are come so soon t.d.
5 : 14. in making brick t. d.
14: 13.salva. he will shew you t.d.
16 : 23. which you will bake t. d.
25. Eat t. d. : t. d. is sabbath
19 : 10. sanctify people t. d.
32 : 29. Consecrate yours. t. d. to
e. 9 : 4. for t. d. L. will appear
10 : 19. if eaten sin-offering t. d.
e. 15 : 15. I com. thee this t. d.
29 : 13. may eat. thee t.d. for peo.
s. 22 : 18. ye rebel t. d. aga. L.
. 21 : 3. be t. d. one tribe lacking
u. 2 : 19. Where hast gleaned t.d.
S. 4 : 3. Whf. L. smitten us t.d.
: † 13. for t. d. ye shall find him
† 27. stand still t. d. that I shew
1 : 13. t. d. Lord wrought salva.
2 :17.Is it not wheat harvest t.d.
4 : 30. people eaten t. d. of spoil
4: 10.L.had deliv.thee t.d., 26:23.
S. 6 : 20. How glorious king t. d.
1 : 12. Tarry here t. d. also
3 : 4. Why lean from d. t. d.
6 : 3. t. d. house of Isr.restore me

1 K. 18 : 15. I will shew myself t.d.
22:5. inquire of L. t.d., 2 Ch.18:4.
2 K. 2: 3. take master fr. head t.d.,
4 : 23. Whf. wilt go to him t.d. [5.
6:28.Give son we may eat him t.d.
1 Ch. 16 : 23. shew fr. d. t. d. his salvation, Ps. 96 : 2.
Es. 3 : 7. cast lot from d. t. d.
Jb. 23:2. t.d. is my complaint bitter
Ps. 95 : 7. t. d. if ye will hear his voice, He. 3 : 7,15.-4:7.
Je. 34 : † 15. ye were t. d. turned
Zch. 9 : 12. t. d. do I declare, that
Mat. 6: 30. grass wh. t.d. is tomor. into oven, Lu. 12 : 28.
16 : 3. foul weather t.d. sky is red
21 : 28. go work t. d. in vineyard
Lu. 5 : 26. seen strange things t. d.
13 : 32. do cures t. d. and to mor.
33. I must walk t. d. and day fol.
19:5. t. d. I must abide at thy hou.
23 : 43. t. d. be wi. me in paradise
24 : 21. t. d. is the third day
He. 3 : 13. while it is called t. d.
5 : 5. t. d. have I begotten thee
13 : 8. Jes. C., same yester. t. d.
Ja. 4 : 13. ye that say, t. d. or to morrow [t. d.
2 Pe. 2:8. Lot vexed his soul from d.

DAY of trouble.

2 K. 19 : 3. This is d. o. t., Is. 37:3.
Ps. 20 : 1. L. hear thee in d. o. t.
50 : 15. call upon me in d. o. t.
59 : 16. been my refuge in d. o. t.
77 : 2. In d. o. t. I sought L.
86:7. In d.o.t. I will call upon thee
Is. 22 : 5. it is d. o. t., and treading
Je. 51 : 2. in d. o. t. shall be ag.her
Eze. 7:7. time is come, d. o. t. near
Na. 1 : 7. L. is strong hold in d.o.t.
Ha. 3 : 16. might rest in d. o. t.
Zph. 1 : 15. that day is a d. o. t.

DAYS.

Ge. 4 : † 3. at end of d. Cain bro-t
8 : 3. after 150 d. waters abated
24 : † 1. Ab. old and gone into d.
27 : 41. d. of mourning for my fa.
29 : † 14. Jac. abode a month of d.
47 : 9. d. of my pilg. are 130 years
† 28. d. of years of his life 147 yrs.
50:4.wh. d. of mourning were past
Nu. 11 : † 20. eat of it a month of d.
14 : 34. num. of d. ye search. land
De. 4 : 32. ask now of d. past
10 : 10. I stayed in mount forty d.
Jos. 23 : † 1. Josh. come into d.
Ju. 11 : † 4. aft. d.Ammon made war
1 S. 13 : 11. Samuel came not within
18 : 26. d. were not expired [d.
27:†7. Da. with Philis. a year of d.
29 : 3. hath been with me these d.
1 K. 2 : 11. d. Da. reigned over Isr.
3:2.no h.built unto L.until those d.
14 : 20. d. Jerob. reigned 22 years
30. war between Rehoboam and Jeroboam all their d.
15:16.bet. Asa and B.all their d.,32.
2 K. 10 : † 36. d. Jehu reigned were
13 : 3. hand of Ben-h. all their d.
15 : † 13. reigned a month of d.
18:4. to those d. Isr. did burn inc.
23 : 22. from d. of the judges, not
1 Ch. 23 : 1. Da. old and full of d.
29 : 15. our d. as shadow, Jb. 8 : 9.
28. he died full of d. riches and
2 Ch. 24 : 15. Jehoi. was full of d.
Ezr. 4 : 2. d. Esar-h. bro-t us up
9 : 7. since d. fa-s we in trespass
Ne. 1 : 4. I mourned certain d.
8:17. since d. of Joshua, unto that
Es. 9 : 22. As d. the Jews rested
26. they called these d. Purim
28.that these d.should be remem.
Jb. 1 : 5. when d. of feasting gone
3 : 6. not be joined unto d. of year
7 : 1. his d. like d. of a hireling?
10 : 5. Are thy d. as d. of man

Jb. 12 : 12. in length of d. unders-g
21 : 13. spend their d. in wealth
30 : † 1. that are of fewer d. than I
16. d. of affic. taken hold on me
27. d. of affliction prevented me
32 : † 4. for they were elder for d.
7. I said, d. should speak
33 : 25. return to d. of his youth
36 : 11. spend their d. in prosper.
42 : 17. So Job died, full of d.
Ps. 21 : 4. gavest him length of d.
23:†6. in L.'s house to length of d.
37 : 18. L. knoweth d. of upright
44 : 1. work thou didst in their d.
55 : 23. not live half their d.
61 : † 6. add d. to d. of the king
77 : 5. I have considered d. of old
78 : 33. their d. did he consume
89 : 29. throne as d. of heaven
45. d. of his youth shortened
90 : 9. all our d. are passed away
10. d. of our y-s are threescore
12. So teach us to number our d.
90 : 14. we may be glad all our d.
91 : † 16. With length of d. satisfy
93 : † 5. holiness to length of d.
94 : 13. give rest fr. d. of adversity
119 : 84. How many d. of servant?
139:†16.what d. they sh-ld be fash.
143 : 5. I remember the d. of old
Pr. 3 : 2. length of d. sh. they add
16. Length of d. is in her right
Ec. 5 : 20. not much remem. d. of
7 : 10. that former d. were better
8 : 15. abide wi. him d. of his life
11 : 8. let him remem. d. of darku.
12 : 1. while the evil d. come not
Is. 7 : 17. d. that have not come
23 : 7. antiquity is of ancient d.
15. according to d. of one king
51 : 9. awake, as in ancient d.
60 : 20. d. of mourning be ended
65 : 20. sh. be no more infant of d.
22. as d. of tree d. of my people
Je.2:32. forgot. me d.without num.
6 : 11. aged, with him full of d.
28 : † 3. in two years of d. will I
31 : 33. After those d. put my law
32 : † 39. that they fear me all d.
35 : 8. drink no wine all our d.
36:2. fr. d. of Josiah unto this day
La. 4 : 18. our d. are fulfilled
Eze. 4 : 4. acc. to number of d.,5,9.
12 : 23. d. at hand, effect of vision
16 : 22. not remem. d. of youth,43.
Da. 7 : 9. Ancient of d. sit, 13, 22.
8 : 14. unto 2300 d. sanctuary be
10 : † 2. mourning 3 weeks of d.
12:11. abom. set up, sh. be 1290 d.
12. he that waiteth to 1335 d.
13. stand in thy lot at end of d.
Ho. 2:13. visit upon her d. of Baalim
9 : 7. d. of visitation, d. of recomp.
10 : 9. sinned from d. of Gibeah
Am. 4 : † 4. tithes after 3 yrs. of d.
5 : † 21. not smell your holy d.
Mi. 5 : † 2. from d. of eternity
7 : 15. acc. to d. of thy coming.out
Hag. 2 :16. Since those d. when one
Zch. 8:†4.with staff for multi. of d.
9. ye that hear in these d.
10. bef. these d. no hire for man
11. I will not be as in former d.
15. thought in these d. to do well
Mal. 3 : 7. d. of fathers ye are gone
Mat. 11 : 12. fr. d. of John Baptist
24 : 22. exc. those d. be shortened no flesh saved, Mk. 13 : 20.
29. after tribulation of those d.
37. as d. of Noe, so coming of Son
Mk. 2 : 1. into Caper. after some d.
Lu. 1 : 23. soon as d. of his ministra.
24. aft. those d. Elisa. conceived
2 : 6. when d.were accompl., 21, 22.
43. when they had fulfilled d.
5 : 35. the d. will come, 17 : 22.
19 : 43. the d. sh. come upon, 21:6.

Lu. 21: 22. these be d. of vengeance
23: 29. the d. are coming in wh.
24: 18. come to pass in these d.
Ac. 3: 24. foretold of these d.
5: 36. bef. these d. rose Theudas
37. in the d. of the taxing [16: 12.
9: 19. Then was Saul certain day,
10: 48. Peter to tarry certain d.
11: 27. in these d. came prophets
12: 3. were d. of unleav. bread
15: 36. some d. after Paul said
16: 12. city abiding certain d.
19: † 38. if matter ag. any, court d.
20: 6. sailed aft. d. of unleav. br.
21: 5. accomplished those d., 26.
15. after those d. we took
38. bef. these d. madest uproar
24: 24. aft. certain d. Felix | 25: 13.
Ga. 4: 10. Ye observed d. months
Ep. 5: 16. because the d. are evil
He. 7: 3. neith. beginn. of d. nor end
8: 8. Behold d. come [10: 16.
10. house of Isr. after those d.,
10: 16. cov. I will make aft. t. d.
32. call to remembrance former d.
1 Pe. 3: 10. he th. would see good d.
Re. 11: 3. shall prophesy 1260 d.
12: 6. should feed her 1260 d.
See DAVID, LAST, OLD, JOURNEY.

All the DAYS.

Ge. 3: 14. dust shalt thou eat a.t.d.
5: 5. a. d. Adam lived 930 years
8. a. d. of Seth | 11. of Enos
14. d. of Cainan | 23. Enoch
27. a. d. of Methuselah, 969 yrs.
9: 29. a. d. of Noah 950 years
Le. 13: 46. a. d. the plague sh. be
15: 25. a. d. of her issue uncl., 26.
Nu. 6: 4. a. d. of his separ., 5, 6, 8.
De. 4: 9. depart fr. thy heart a. d.
10. to fear me a. d., 1 K. 8: 40.
12: 1. to possess it a. d. ye live
Jos. 4: † 24. might fear L. a. d.
24: 31. Israel served L. a. d. of
Joshua and a. d., Ju. 2: 7.
Ju. 2: 18. a. d. of the judge [life
1 S. 1: 11. give him unto L. a. d. of
7: 13. ag. Philistines a.d. of Samuel
15. Sam. judged Isr. a. d. of life
1 K. 4: 25. dw. safely a. d. of Sol.
11: 25. Rezon advers. a. d. of Sol.
2 K. 13: 22. Hazael oppr Isr. a.d.
23: 22. nor in a. d. of the kings
2 Ch. 24: 2. a. d. of Jehoiada, 14.
Ezr. 4: 5. frustrate purposes a. d.
Jb. 1: † 5. Thus did Job a.d. [of Cy.
14: 14. a. d. of my appointed time
Ps. 23: 6. mercy follow me a. d.
27: 4. dwell in house of L. a. d.
Pr. 15: 15. a. d. of afflic. are evil
31: 12. him good, a. d. of her life
Ec. 2: 3. do a. d. of their life
9: 9. a. d. of life of thy vanity
Is. 38: 20. str. instruments a.d. of life
63: 9. carried them a. d. of old
Lu. 1: 75. in holiness a. d. of our life
See His LIFE, Thy LIFE.

DAYS come.

Ec. 12: 1. while evil d. c. not [c.
Is. 7: 17. sh. bring upon thee d.
Je. 23: 5. Behold the d. c., 7.-30:
3.-31: 27, 31, 38.
Am. 4: 2. d. c. that he will take you
Mat. 9: 15. d. sh. c. when bridegr.
taken, Mk. 2: 20. Lu. 5: 35.
Lu. 17: 22. d. c. when ye sh. desire
19: 43. d. c. thy enem. cast trench
21: 6. d. c. there shall not be left
He. 8: 8. d. c. I will make new cov.

Few DAYS.

Ge. 24: 55. Let damsel abide f. d.
27: 44. tarry f. d. till bro.'s fury
29: 20. seemed unto him but f. d.
47: 9. f. and evil are d. of my pil.
Nu. 9: 20. cloud was a f. d. on tab.
Jb. 14: 1. born of woman is of f. d.
32: † 6. Elihu said, I am of f. d.
Ps. 109: 8. Let his d. be f., let ano.
Da. 11: 20. within f. d. he be destr.
He. 12: 10. for a f. d. chastened us

His DAYS.

Ge. 6: 3. yet h. d. shall be 120 yrs.
10: 25. in h. d. earth divid., 1 Ch.
1: 19. [h. d., 29.
De. 22: 19. he sh. not put her aw. all
1 K. 1: † 6. not displeas. him fr. h. d.
15: 14. perfect all h.d., 2 Ch. 15: 17.
16: 34. In h. d. build Jericho
21: 29. not bring the evil in h. d.
2 K. 8: 20. In h.d. Edom, 2 Ch. 21: 8.
12: 2. Jehoash did right all h. d.
15: 18. depart. not all h. d. fr. sins
1 Ch. 22: 9. and quietness in h. d.
2 Ch. 34: 33. all h. d. they dep. not
Jb. 14: 5. Seeing h.d. are determined
15: 20. wick. travaileth all h. d.
24: 1. Why do they not see h. d.?
Ps. 72: 7. In h. d. righte. flourish
103: 15. man, h. d. are as grass
144: 4. h. d. are as a shadow
Pr. 28: 16. hateth covet. prolong h.d.
Ec. 2: 23. all h. d. are sorrows
5: 17. All h.d. he eateth in darkn.
8: 12. though h. d. be prolonged
13. wicked sh. not prolong h. d.
Is. 65: 20. that hath not filled h. d.
Je. 17: 11. leave in midst of h. d.
22: 30. man that not prosper in h.d.
23: 6. In h. d. Jud. shall be saved

In the DAYS.

Ge. 26: 1. fam. that was i. d. of Ab.
30: 14. Reub. i. d. of wheat har.
Ju. 5: 6. i. d. of Shamgar, i. d. of
8: 28. in quietness i. d. of Gideon
1 S. 17: 12. for old man i. d. of Saul
2 S. 21: 1. was a famine i. d. of David
9. were put to death i. d. of harv.,
i. first d. of barley
1 K. 10: 21. silver was nothing i.
d. of Solomon, 2 Ch. 9: 20.
22: 46. Sodomites i. d. of Asa
1 Ch. 4: 41. these came i. d. of Hez.
13: 3. inquired not i. d. of Saul
2 Ch. 26: 5. sought God i. d. of Zech.
32: 26. came not i. d. of Hezekiah
Jb. 29: 2. as i. d. God preserv. me
4. As I was i. d. of my youth
Ps. 37: 19. i. d. of famine be satis.
49: 5. Wheref. I fear i. d. of evil?
Ec. 2: 16. i. d. to come be forgot.
11: 9. heart cheer thee i.d. of youth
12: 1. Remem. thy Creator i. d. of
Je. 26: 18. Micah prophe. i. d. of Hez.
La. 1: 7. Jerus. remem. i.d. of her affl.
Eze. 16: 60. will remem. my cov. i.d.
22: 14. or hands be strong i. d. I
Da. 2: 44. i. d. of these kings God
5: 11. i. d. of thy fa., light was
Hos. 2: 15. sing as i. d. of her youth
9: 9. corrupted as i. d. of Gibeah
12: 9. as i. d. of solemn feast
Jo. 1: 2. this been i. d. of fathers?
Mat. 2: 1. Jesus was born i. d. of
Herod, Lu. 1: 5.
23: 30. if been i. d. of our fathers
24: 38. as i. d. before the flood
Mk. 2: 26. i. d. of Abiathar
Lu. 1: 25. hath L. dealt with me i. d.
4: 25. many widows i. d. of Elias
17: 26. as i. d. of Noe | 28. of Lot
Ac. 5: 37. rose Judas i. d. of taxing
11: 28. to pass i. d. of Claudius Ce.
He. 5: 7. Who i. d. of his flesh
1 Pe. 3: 20. G. waited i. d. of Noah
Re. 10: 7. i. d. of seventh angel
11: 6. rain not i. d. of prophecy

In those DAYS.

Ge. 6: 4. giants in the earth i. t. d.
De. 17: 9. unto judge i. t. d., 19: 17.
26: 3. unto priest that sh. be i.t.d.
Ju. 17: 6. i.t.d. there was no king
in Israel, 18: 1.-21: 25.
20: 27. ark of G. was there i.t.d.
1 S. 3: 1. word of L. precious i.t.d.
2 S. 16: 23. he counselled i.t.d.
2 K. 20: 1. i. t. d. was Hez. sick
unto death, 2 Ch. 32: 24. Is. 38: 1.
Je. 33: 16. i.t.d. shall Jud. be sav.
50: 4. i.t.d. Isr. shall seek God
20. i.t.d. iniq. shall be sought for
Da. 10: 2. i.t.d. I Dan. was mourn.
Jo. 2: 29. i.t.d. will pour out my
Spirit upon the, Ac. 2: 18.
Mat. 3: 1. i. t. d. came John the
Baptist, Mk. 1: 9.-2: 20.
24: 19. Woe that give suck i.t.d.,
Mk. 13: 17. Lu. 21: 23.
Mk. 1: 9. i.t.d. Jes. came fr. Naz.
2: 20. then shall they fast i. t. d.
13: 19. i. t. d. shall be affliction
Lu. 1: 39. Mary arose i. t. d.
20: 1. on one of t.d. as he taught
Ac. 7: 41. they made a calf i. t. d.
Re. 2: 13. not denied my faith i.t.d.
9: 6. i.t.d. shall men seek death

Latter DAYS.

Nu. 24: 14. peo. do to peo. in l. d.
De. 4: 30. in l.d. if thou turn to L.
31: 29. evil will befall you in l. d.
Je. 23: 20. in l.d. consider it, 30: 24.
48: 47. bring captiv. of Moab in l.d.
49: 39. captivity of Elam in l. d.
Eze. 38: 16. come ag. my peo. in l.d.
Da. 2: 28. mak. kn. what be in l.d.
10: 14. what befall thy peo. in l.d.
Ho. 3: 5. shall fear L. in l. d.

Many DAYS. [d.

Ge. 37: 34. Jac. mourned for son m.
47: † 8. How m. are d. of thy life?
Jos. 22: 3. not left brethren m. d.
2 S. 19: † 34. Barzillai said, How
m. d. are years of my life
1 K. 2: 38. Shimei dw. at Jerus. m.
3: † 11. hast not asked m. d. [d.
17: 15. she, and he, did eat m.d.
1 Ch. 7: 22. Ephr. mourned m. d.
Ps. 34: 12. What is he loveth m.d.
119: 84. How m. are d. of servant
Ec. 6: 3. so d. of his years be m.
11: 1. shalt find it after m. d.
Is. 24: 22. aft. m.d. be visited, Eze.
32: 10. m.d. ye be troubled | 38: 8
Je. 32: 14. continue m.d., 35: 7.
37: 16. Jere. had remained m. d.
Eze. 12: 27. vision that he seeth is
for m. d., Da. 8: 26.-10: 14.
Da. 11: 33. shall fall by captiv. m.d.
Ho. 3: 3. shalt abide for me m. d.
4. Isr. abide m.d. without a king
Lu. 15: 13. not m.d. after, younger
Jn. 2: 12. continued not m.d. [son
Ac. 1: 5. be bapt. not m. d. hence
9: 23. after m.d. Jews took counsel
43. tarried m. d. in Joppa
13: 31. he was seen m.d. of them
16: 18. this did she m. d. Paul
21: 10. tarried m.d. in Cesarea
25: 14. they had been there m.d.
27: 7. had sailed slowly m. d.
20. nor sun in m. d. appeared

My DAYS.

Ge. 29: 21. Give me my wife, for m.
d. are fulfilled [d:
2 K. 20: 19. good if truth be in m.
Jb. 7: 6. m.d. swifter than shuttle
16. let alone, m. d. are vanity
9: 25. m.d. are swifter than a post
10: 20. Are not m. d. few, cease
17: 1. m. d. are extinct, graves
11. m.d. are past, my purposes
27: † 6. not reproach me for m.d.
29: 18. multiply m.d. as the sand
Ps. 39: 4. know measure of m.d.
5. made m. d. as a handbreadth
102: 3. m. d. are consumed like
11. m.d. are like a shadow [smo.
23. he shortened m. d.
24. take me not in midst of m.d.
116: † 2. will call upon him in m.d.
Is. 38: 10. in cutting off of m. d.
39: 8. be peace and truth in m.d.

Je. 20:18. m.d.consum.with shame
Prolong, ed, eth, DAYS.
De. 4: 26. not p. your d. upon it,
40. mayest p.thy d.,22:7. [30:18.
5: 16. that thy d. be p., 6: 2.
33. that ye may p. your d., 11:9.
17:20.to end that he may p. his d.
32: 47. ye sh. p. your d. in land
Pr. 10: 27. fear of Lord p-h d.
28: 16. hateth covetousn. p. his d.
Ec. 8: 12. tho. a sinner's d. be p.
13. neith. shall wicked p. his d.
Is. 13: 22. her d. shall not be p.
53: 10. seed, he shall p. his d.
Eze. 12: 22. d. are p. vision faileth
Sabbath DAYS.
Mat. 12: 5. on s. d. priests profane
10. is it lawful to heal on s. d.?
12. lawful to do well on s. d.
Mk. 3: 4. lawful to do good on s. d., Lu. 6: 9.
Lu. 4: 31. he taught them on s. d.
6: 2. is not lawful to do on s. d.
Ac. 17: 2. three s.d. reasoned with
Col. 2: 16. judge in respect of s. d.
Thy DAYS.
Ex. 20: 12. Honour fa. that t. d.
23: 26. number of t. d. will fulfil
De. 12: † 19. forsake not Lev. t. d.
23: 6. not seek peace all t. d.
25: 15. that t. d. be lengthened
30:20. he is thy life, length of t.d.
31: 14. t.d. appro. thou must die
33: 25. as t. d. so thy strength be
1 S. 25: 28. evil not found all t.d.
2 S. 7: 12. when t. d. be fulfilled
1 K. 3: 13. not be any like all t. d.
14. then I will lengthen t. d.
11: 12. in t. d. I will not do it [5.
2 K.20:6.I will add unto t.d., Is.38:
1 Ch. 17: 11. when t. d. be expired
Jb. 10: 5. Are t. d. as days of man
38: 12. Hast com-d morning since
21. number of t.d. is great [t.d.
Pr. 9: 11. by me t. d. be multipl.
Eze. 22: 4. caused t.d. to draw near
Two DAYS.
Ex. 16: 29. sixth day bread of t.d.
Nu. 9: 22. whether t. d. or month
11:19. Ye sh. not eat one, nor t.d.
2 S. 1: 1. Da. abode t. d. in Ziklag
Ezr. 10: 13. nor is this work of t.d.
Es. 9: 27. would keep these t. d.
Ho. 6: 2. After t. d. will revive us
Mat. 26: 2. after t. d. is feast, Mk.
Jn. 4: 40. he abode t.d. [14:1.
43. after t.d. he departed thence
11: 6. he abode t.d. in same place
Three DAYS.
Ge. 40: 12. three branches are t.d.
13.within t.d. Pha. lift thy head,
18. three baskets are t. d. [19.
42: 7. put them all into ward t.d.
Ex. 3: 18. let us go t.d.journey into wil., 5: 3.-8: 27.-15: 22.
10: 22. thick darkness in E. t. d.
23. nor rose any from place t. d.
Jos. 1: 11. within t. d. pass over
2: 16. hide there t. d., 22. [Jord.
Ju. 19: 4. abode with him t. d.
1 S. 9: 20. asses lost t. d. ago
21: 5. women been kept fr. us t.d.
30: 12. he had eaten no bread t.d.
13.bec. t.d. agone I fell sick [t.d.
2 S.20:4.Assemble me men of Jud.in
24:13.be t.d.pestilence,1 Ch.21:12.
1 K.12:5.Depart for t.d.,2 Ch.10:5.
2 K. 2:17. sought him t.d. but not
1 Ch. 12: 39. with Da. t. d. eating
2 Ch. 20: 25. were t. d. gath. spoil
Ezr. 8: 15. we abode in tents t. d.
32. to Jerus. abode t.d.,Ne.2:11.
10: 8. whoso. not come in t.d., 9.
Es. 4: 16 eat nor drink t.d.[12:40.
Jon. 1: 17. Jonah in fish t.d., Mat.
Mat. 15:32. on mult. bec. they continue with me t. d., Mk. 8: 2.

Mat. 26: 61. to destroy temple of G. and build it in t. d., 27: 40.
Mk. 14: 58.-15: 29. Jn. 2: 19.
27:63. aft. t.d. I will rise, Mk.8:31.
Lu. 2: 46. aft. t. d. found in tem.
Jn. 2: 20. wilt thou rear it in t. d.
Ac.9:9.Saul was t.d. without sight
25: 1. after t. d. he ascended
28:7.Publius lodged us t.d. court.
12. we tarried there t. d.
17. after t. d. Paul called chief of
Re. 11: 9. bodies t. d. and a half
11. after t.d. spirit of life entered
Four DAYS.
Ju. 11:40. lament dau.of Jeph. f.d.
Jn. 11: 17. Laz. lain in grave f. d.
39. stinketh, for been dead f. d.
Ac. 10: 30. f. d. ago I was fasting
Five DAYS.
Nu. 11: 19. nor f. d. nor ten days
Ac. 20: 6. we came to Troas in f.d.
24:1.after f.d. Ananias high priest
Six DAYS.
Ex. 16: 26. s. d. ye shall gather it
20: 9. s. d. shalt thou labour, 23: 12.-34: 21. De. 5: 13.
11.in s.d. Lord made heav. 31:17.
24: 16. cloud covered Sinai s. d.
31: 15. s. d. may work be done,
35: 2. Le. 23: 3.
De. 16: 8. s.d. shalt eat unleav. br.
Jos. 6: 3. round city, Thus do s.d.
14. compassed city once, so s. d.
Eze. 46: 1. gate shut s. working d.
Mat. 17: 1. after s.d. Jesus taketh Peter, Mk. 9: 2.
Lu. 13: 14. s. d. ought to work
Jn. 12:1. Jesus s.d. bef.passo.came
Seven DAYS.
Ge. 7: 4. s.d. I will cause it to rain
8: 10. Noah stayed s. d., 12.
50:10. Jo. mourned for his fa.s.d.
Ex. 12: 15. s. d. ye shall eat unl. bread, 13: 6, 7.-23: 15.-34: 18.
Le. 23: 6. Nu. 28: 17. De 16:3.
19. s.d. shall no leav., De. 16: 4.
22:30. s.d. be with dam, Le.22:27.
29:30. priest sh. put them on s. d.
35. s.d. shalt consecrate,Le.8:33.
37. s. d. shalt make atonement
Le. 12: 2 she shall be unclean s.d.
13: 5. then priest shalt shut him up s.d. more, 21, 26, 33,50,54.
14: 8. tarry out of his tent s. d.
15: 19. issue, she be put apart s.d.
23: 8. an off. by fire unto L. s. d.
39. gath-d fruit ye shall keep feast s. d., 40, 41. Nu. 29: 12.
Nu. 12:14. Miriam not be asha.s.d.
15. Miriam shut out fr camp s.d.
19: 14. all in tent be unclean s.d.
De. 16:13. observe feast of tab. s.d.
Ju.14:12. if ye can decla. within s.d.
17. she wept bef. him the s. d.
1 S. 10: 8. s. d. shalt thou tarry
11: 3. said, Give us s. d. respite
13: 8. tarried s. d. acc. to time
31: 13. fasted s. d., 1 Ch. 10: 12.
1 K. 8: 65. Sol. held a feast s. d.
16: 15. Zimri did reign s. d. in
2 Ch. 7:9. kept dedica. of altar s.d.
30: 21. chil. of Isr. kept feast of unl. bread s.d., 35:17.Ezr.6:22.
23.took counsel to keep other s.d.
Ne. 8: 18. kept the feast s. d. [d.
Es. 1: 5. feast unto great and sm. s.
Jb 2: 13. sat upon ground s. d.
Is. 30: 26. light of sun, as of s. d.
Eze. 3: 15. I remained aston. s. d.
43:26. s. d. shall they purge altar
Ac. 20: 6. where we abode s. d.
Ac. 21: 4. we tarried s. d., 28: 14.
27. s. d. were almost ended
He. 11: 30. fell aft. compassed s.d.
Eight DAYS. [4.
Ge. 17:12. e.d. old be circumc., 21:
2 Ch. 29:17. sanctify h. of L. in e.d.

Lu. 2:21. when e. d. were accompl
9: 28. e. d. after he took Peter
Jn. 20: 26. after e. d. Jesus came
Ten DAYS.
Nu. 11: 19. ye shall not eat t. d.
1 S. 25:38. t.d. after L. smote Nabal
Ne. 5: 18. once in t. d. all wine
Je. 42: 7. aft. t.d. word of L. came
Da. 1: 12. Prove thy serv-ts t. d.
15. at end of t.d. counten. fairer
Ac. 25: 6. tarried more than t. d.
Re. 2: 10. sh. have tribula. t. d.
Eleven DAYS.
De. 1: 2. e. d. journey bet. Horeb
Twelve DAYS.
Ac. 24:11. but t. d. since I went up
Fourteen DAYS.
1 K. 8: 65. Sol. held a feast f. d.
Fifteen DAYS.
Ga. 1: 18. I abode with Peter f. d.
Twenty DAYS.
Nu. 11: 19. sh. not eat flesh t. d.
One and Twenty DAYS.
Da. 10: 13. withstood me -d.
Thirty DAYS.
Nu. 20: 29. mourned for Aa. t. d.
De. 34: 8. Isr. wept for Moses t. d.
Es. 4: 11. not called to king t. d.
Da. 6: 7. whoso. ask for t.d., 12.
Three and thirty DAYS.
Le. 12:4. in blood of her purify. -d.
Forty DAYS.
Ge. 7: 4. to rain upon earth f. d.
50: 3. f. d. were fulfilled for
Ex. 24: 18. Moses in mount f. d.,
34: 28. De. 9: 9.-10: 10.
Nu. 13:25. returned aft. f. d.,14:34.
De. 9: 25. I fell down bef. L. f. d.
1 K.19:8. strength of that meat f.d.
Eze.4:6.shalt bear iniq. of Jud. f.d.
Jon.3:4.f.d.and Nineveh be overth.
Mat. 4: 2. when he had fasted f.d.
Mk. 1: 13. Jes. was f.d. in wil.,Lu.
Ac. 1: 3. seen of them f. d. [4: 2.
Fifty and two DAYS.
Ne. 6: 15. wall was finished in -d.
Your DAYS.
De 11: 21. y. d. may be multiplied
Je. 16: 9. to cease in y. d. mirth
35:7.all y.d. ye shall dwell in tents
Eze. 12: 25. in y.d. will I say word
Jo. 1: 2. Hath this been in y. d.
Ha. 1: 5. a work in y. d.,Ac.13:41.
DAYSMAN.
Jb. 9: 33. neith. any d. betwixt us
DAYSPRING.
Jb. 38: 12. d. to know his place
Lu.1:78. d. from on high visited us
DAYSTAR.
2 Pe. 1: 19 d. arise in your hearts
DAYTIME. [d.
Jb. 5:14. They meet with darkn. in
24: 16. houses they marked in d.
Ps. 22: 2. I cry in d. hearest not
42: 8. L. command lovingk. in d.
78:14.in d. he led them with cloud
Is. 4:6. be a tab. for a shadow in d.
21: 8. upon watchtower in d.
Lu. 21:37. in d. he was teaching in
2 Pe. 2: 13. pleasure to riot in d.
DEACON, S.
Ph. 1: 1. to the saints with the d-s
1 Ti. 3: 8. the d-s must be grave
10. let them use office of d., 13.
12. d-s be husbands of one wife
DEAD.
Ge. 20: 3. Thou art but a d. man
23: 3. Ab. stood up fr. bef. his d.
Ex. 4: 19. d. which sought thy life
9: 7. not one of Isr-s' cattle d.
12: 30. not a house wh. not one d.
33. Egyp. said, We be all d. men
14: 30. saw Egyptians d. on shore
21: 34. d. beast shall be his, 36.
35. d. ox they shall divide
Le. 22: 4. toucheth anything uncl. by the d., 11: 31, 32. Nu.19:18.

Nu. 5 : 2. whoso. is defiled by **d.**
6 : 11. for that he sinned by the **d.**
12 : 12. Let her not be as one **d.**
16 : 48. stood betw. **d.** and living
De. 25 : 5. wife of **d.** not marry a
Ju. 3 : 25. their lord was fallen **d.**
4 : 22. behold, Sisera lay **d.**, 5 : 27.
16 : 30. **d.** Samson slew at his dea.
Ru. 1 : 8. as ye have dealt with **d.**
4 : 5. to raise up name of **d.**, 10.
1 S. 4 : 17. Hoph. and Phin. are **d.**
19. father in l. and husb. were **d.**
24 : 14. dost pursue? after a **d.** dog,
31 : 7. Saul his sons **d.**, 1 Ch. 10 : 7.
2 S. 1 : 4. Saul and Jona. are **d.**, 5.
9 : 8. sho. look upon **d.** dog as I
11 : 24. some of king's serv-ts be **d.**
13 : 33. to think all k.'s sons are **d.**
16 : 9. Why **d.** dog curse my lord
19 : 28. all of fa.'s house **d.** men
1 K. 3 : 22. living mine, **d.** thy son, 23.
13 : 31. When **d.** bury me in sepul.
21 : 15. Arise, for Naboth is **d.**
Es. 2 : 7. her father and mother **d.**
Jb. 1 : 19. young men, they are **d.**
26 : 5. **d.** things formed fr. under wat.
Ps. 31 : 12. I am forgot. as **d.** man
76 : 6. chariot and horse into **d.**
88 : 5. free amo. **d.** like slain [sleep
10. Wilt shew wonders to **d.**?
106 : 28. they ate sacrifices of **d.**
115 : 17. **d.** praise not the Lord
143 : 3. in darkn. as those long **d.**
Pr. 2 : 18. her paths unto the **d.**
9 : 18. knoweth not **d.** are there
21 : 16. remain in congr. of the **d.**
Ec. 4 : 2. I praised **d.** which are **d.**
9 : 3. after that they go to the **d.**
4. living dog better than **d.** lion
5. the **d.** know not any thing
10 : 1. **d.** flies cause the ointment
Is. 8 : 19. for the living to the **d.**
14 : 9. it stirreth up the **d.** for thee
22 : 2. not slain nor **d.** in battle
26 : 14. They are **d.** [body
19. **d.** men sh. live, with my **d.**
59 : 10. desolate places as **d.** men
La. 3 : 6. in dark as they **d.** of old
Eze. 44 : 25. at no **d.** person to defile
Mat. 2 : 20. are **d.** th. sought child's
8 : 22. let **d.** bury their **d.** [life
9 : 24. maid is not **d.** but sleepeth,
Mk. 5 : 39. Lu. 8 : 52.
10 : 8. heal the sick, raise the **d.**
11 : 5. **d.** are raised up, Lu. 7 : 22.
22 : 31. resurr. of **d.**, Mk. 12 : 26.
32. G. is not the God of the **d.**,
Mk. 12 : 27. Lu. 20 : 38.
23 : 27. full of **d.** men's bones
28 : 4. keepers became as **d.** men
Mk. 9 : 26. as one **d.** many said He is **d.**
12 : 26. as touch-g **d.** th. they rise
15 : 44. Pilate marv. if he were **d.**
Lu. 7 : 12. a **d.** man carried out
10 : 30. leaving him half **d.**
24 : 5. Why seek living among **d.**?
Jn. 5 : 21. as Father raiseth up **d.**
25. **d.** sh. hear voice of Son of G.
6 : 49. eat manna, and are **d.**, 58.
11 : 25. tho. he were **d.** shall he live
41. where the **d.** was laid
12 : 1. Laz. was which had been **d.**
Ac. 2 : 29. patriarch David is both **d.**
5 : 10. young men found her **d.**
10 : 42. ordained of G. to be Judge
of quick and **d.**, 2 Ti. 4 : 1.
14 : 19. supposing he had been **d.**
20 : 9. Eutychus was taken up **d.**
26 : 8. Why incred. G. sho. raise **d.**?
28 : 6. fallen down **d.** suddenly
Ro. 4 : 17. G. who quickeneth **d.**
19. consid-d not his body now **d.**
5 : 15. thro. offence of one many be **d.**
6 : 2. we that are **d.** to sin, live?
8. if we be **d.** with C. we believe
11. reckon yours. to be **d.** unto sin
7 : 2. if husb. be **d.**, 3. 1 Co. 7 : 39.

Ro. 7 : 4. ye also are **d.** to law, 6. Ga. 2 :
14 : 9. be lord of **d.** and living [19.
1 Co. 15 : 15. if so be **d.** rise not
16. if **d.** rise not then, 29, 32.
35. some say, How are **d.** raised?
52. **d.** sh. be raised incorruptible
2 Co. 1 : 9. trust in G. who raiseth **d.**
5 : 14. died for all, then were all **d.**
Ep. 2 : 1. **d.** in trespasses, 5. Col. 2 : 13.
Col. 2 : 20. if **d.** with C., 2 Ti. 2 : 11.
3 : 3. ye are **d.** and your life is hid
1 Th. 4 : 16. **d.** in C. shall rise first
He. 6 : 1. repentance from **d.** works
9 : 14. purge conscience fr. **d.** works
17. testa. of force after men **d.**
11 : 4. he being **d.** yet speaketh
12. sprang of one, as good as **d.**
35. Wom. received their **d.** raised
1 Pe. 2 : 24. we being **d.** to sins sho.
4 : 5. to judge quick and **d.** [live
6. the gosp. preached to th. are **d.**
Jude 12. twice **d.** plucked by roots
Re. 1 : 5. Jesus firstbegottten of **d.**
17. saw him, I fell as **d.**
3 : 1. hast name thou livest art **d.**
11 : 18. time of the **d.** is come
14 : 13. Blessed are **d.** die in L.
16 : 3. sea as blood of **d.** man
20 : 5. rest of **d.** lived not again
Re. 20 : 12. I saw the **d.** stand bef.
G.; **d.** were judged out of books
13. sea gave up **d.** wh. were in it
See BODY, BURY, CARCASS,
CORPSE, RESURRECTION.

For the DEAD.

Le. 19 : 28. not make cuttings **f. t. d.**
21 : 1. sh. none be defiled **f. t. d.**
De. 14 : 1. not make baldness **f. t. d.**
26 : 14. not giv. aught **f. t. d.** [t. d.
2 S. 14 : 2. as wom. th. mourned **f.**
Jer. 16 : 7. not tear to comf. **f. t. d.**
22 : 10. Weep ye not **f. t. d.** [t. d.
Eze. 24 : 17. make no mourning **f.**
1 Co. 15 : 29. what do who are bapt.
f. t. d. why bapt. **f. t. d.**?

From the DEAD. [28 : 7.

Mat. 14 : 2. John B., is risen **f. t. d.**,
Mk. 9 : 10. what rising **f. t. d.** mean?
Lu. 16 : 30. if one went unto th. **f. t. d.**
31. persua., tho. one rose **f. t. d.**
24 : 46. rise **f. t. d.** 3d day, Jn. 20 : 9.
Ac. 10 : 41. after he rose **f. t. d.**
26 : 23. be first that sho. rise **f. t. d.**
Ro. 6 : 13. as those alive **f. t. d.**
10 : 7. that is, to bring up C. **f. t. d.**
11 : 15. rec. of them be life **f. t. d.**
1 Co. 15 : 12. preached he rose **f. t. d.**
Ep. 5 : 14. arise **f. t. d.** C. shall give
Col. 1 : 18. who is firstborn **f. t. d.**
He. 11 : 19. able to raise him **f. t. d.**
13 : 20. bro-t again **f. t. d.** our L. J.
See RAISED, RISEN.

Is DEAD.

Ge. 42 : 38. for his bro. **i. d.**, 44 : 20.
De. 25 : 6. in name of bro. that **i. d.**
Jos. 1 : 2. Moses my servant **i. d.**
Ju. 20 : 5. they forced that she **i. d.**
2 S. 2 : 7. Saul **i. d.**, 4 : 10.
11 : 21. Uriah the Hittite **i. d.**, 24.
12 : 18. if tell him child **i. d.**, 19.
23. now he **i. d.** wheref. should I
13 : 32. Amnon only **i. d.** [fast
14 : 5. and my husb. **i. d.**, 2 K. 4 : 1.
18 : 20. no tidings bec. k.'s son **i. d.**
19 : 10. Absalom **i. d.**
1 K. 21 : 14. Naboth is stoned and **i. d.**
Eze. 44 : 31. not eat that **i. d.** of its.
Mat. 9 : 18. My daughter **i. d.**, Mk.
5 : 35. Lu. 8 : 49.
Mk. 9 : 26. that many said, He **i. d.**
Jn. 8 : 52. Ab. **i. d.** and proph., 53.
11 : 14. said Jesus, Lazarus **i. d.**
Ac. 2 : 29. Da. **i.** both **d.** and buried
Ro. 6 : 7. that **i. d.** is freed fr. sin
8 : 10. if C. be in you, body **i. d.**
Ga. 2 : 21. if righteousn. by law, C.
i. d. in vain

1 Ti. 5 : 6. liveth in pleasure, **i. d.**
Ja. 2 : 17. faith, if not works **i. d.**, 20.
26. as body without spirit **i. d.** so

Was DEAD. [w. d.

Ge. 50 : 15. Jo.'s breth saw their fa.
Nu. 20 : 29. cong. saw Aaron **w. d.**
Ju. 2 : 19. when the judge **w. d.**
8 : 33. as soon as Gideon **w. d.**
9 : 55. when Isr. saw Abim. **w. d.**
1 S. 17 : 51. P-s saw champion **w. d.**
25 : 39. Da. heard Nabal **w. d.**
28 : 3. Sam. **w. d.**, all Isr. lamen.
31 : 5. saw Saul **w. d.**, 1 Ch. 10 :
2 S. 4 : 1. son heard Abner **w. d.** [.
11 : 26. Bathsheba heard husb. w.
12 : 19. Da. perceived child **w. d.**
13 : 39. Amnon, seeing he **w. d.**
1 K. 3 : 21. to give child suck, it **w. d.**
11 : 21. Hadad heard Joab **w. d.**
21 : 15. Jezebel heard Naboth **w. d.**
2 K. 3 : 5. when Ahab **w. d.** Moab
4 : 32. behold, child **w. d.** and laid
11 : 1. saw her son **w. d.**, 2 Ch. 22 : 10.
Mat. 2 : 19. But when Herod **w. d.**
Lu. 7 : 15. he that **w. d.** sat up
8 : 53. knowing that she **w. d.**
15 : 24. my son **w. d.** and is alive
32. thy brother **w. d.** and is alive
Jn. 11 : 39. sister of him that **w. d.**
44. he that **w. d.** came forth
19 : 33. saw Jesus **w. d.** brake not
Ac. 7 : 4. thence when his fa. **w. d.**
25 : 19. of one Jesus which **w. d.**
Ro. 7 : 8. without law sin **w. d.**
Re. 1 : 18. I am he liveth, and **w. d.**
2 : 8. which **w. d.** and is alive

DEADLY.

1 S. 5 : 11. **d.** destruction thro. city
Ps. 17 : 9. deliver me fr. **d.** enemies
Eze. 30 : 24. **d.** wounded man [hurt
Mk. 16 : 18. if drink **d.** thing, it not
Ja. 3 : 8. tongue, full of **d.** poison
Re. 13 : 3. **d.** wound healed, 12.

DEADNESS.

Ro. 4 : 19. neith. **d.** of Sarah's womb

DEAF.

Ex. 4 : 11. or who maketh the **d.**?
Le. 19 : 14. Thou shalt not curse **d.**
1 S. 10 : † 27. Saul was as though **d.**
Ps. 38 : 13. I as a **d.** man heard not
58 : 4. they are like the **d.** adder
Is. 29 : 18. in that day **d.** hear words
35 : 5. ears of **d.** be unstopped
42 : 18. Hear, ye **d.**; look, ye blind
19. who is **d.** as my messenger?
43 : 8. Bring **d.** that have ears
Mi. 7 : 16. their ears shall be **d.**
Mat. 11 : 5. the **d.** hear, Lu. 7 : 22
Mk. 7 : 32. brought unto him one **d.**
37. He maketh the **d.** to hear
9 : 25. Thou **d.** spirit, come out.

DEAL. [Verb.]

Ge. 19 : 9. will we **d.** worse with thee
24 : 49. if ye **d.** truly with my mas.
32 : 9. Return, I will **d.** with thee
34 : 31. **d.** with sister as harlot?
Ex. 1 : 10. let us **d.** wisely with th.
8 : 29. let not Pha. **d.** deceitfully
21 : 9. **d.** wi. her aft. manner of dau-s
23 : 11. in like man. **d.** with viney.
Le. 19 : 11. not steal, nor **d.** falsely
Nu. 11 : 15. if **d.** thus, kill me
De. 7 : 5. thus **d.** with them [20 : 8.
Jos. 2 : 14. **d.** kindly, Ru. 1 : 8. 1 S.
2 S. 18 : 5. **d.** gently with young man
2 Ch. 2 : 3. didst **d.** with Da., so **d.**
19 : 11. **d.** courageously [with me
Jb. 42 : 8. lest I **d.** after your folly
Ps. 75 : 4. I said, **d.** not foolishly
105 : 25. heart to **d.** subtilely
119 : 17. **d.** bountif. with thy servant, 142 : 7. [to thy mercy
124. **d.** with thy servant acc. un-
Pr. 12 : 22. **d.** truly are his delight
Is. 26 : 10. in land he will **d.** unjust.
52 : 13. my serv. shall **d.** prudently
58 : 7. Is it not to **d.** br. to hungry?

s. 18. 23. d. thus in thine anger
21 : 2. if so be that L. d. with us
ze. 8 : 18. Theref. will I d. in fury
16 : 59. I will d. with thee as thou
18 : 9. to d. truly ; he is just
22 : 14.strong in days I d. wi. thee
23 : 25. d. furiously with thee
29 d. with thee hatefully
31 : 11. he sh surely d. with him
a. 1 : 13. seest, d. with thy serv-ts
5 : † 20. hardened to d. proudly
11 : 7. sh. d. ag. them and prevail
Co. 2 : † 17. d. deceitfully with
See TREACHEROUSLY. [word

DEAL. [Noun.]

x. 29 : 40. a tenth d. of flour, Le.
14 : 21. Nu. 15 : 4.-29 : 4.
Nu. 28 : 13. a several tenth d., 21,
29.-29 : 10, 15. [lished
Mk. 7:36. more a great d. they pub-
10 : 48. he cried more a great d.

DEALS. [9.

e. 14 : 10. take 3 tenth d., Nu. 15:
23 : 13. two tenth d. for, Nu. 28:9.
17. wave loaves of two tenth d.
24 : 5. two tenth d. be in one cake
Nu. 15 : 6. two tenth d. of flour, 28:
20, 28.-29 : 3, 9, 14.
28 : 20. three tenth d. to a bullock,
28.-29 : 3, 9, 14.

DEALER, S.

s. 21 : 2. treacherous d.dealeth
24 : 16. treacherous d-s have dealt

DEALEST, ETH.

x. 5:15.Whf. d-t thus with serv-s?
u. 18 : 4. thus d. Micah with me
S. 23 : 22. told me he d. subtilely
Pr. 10:4. poor th. d. with slack ha.
13:16. prudent man d. with knowl.
14 : 17. He soon angry d. foolishly
21 : 24. who d. in proud wrath
s. 21:2. treach. dealer d. treach-ly
33 : 1. Woe to thee d-t treach-ly
Je. 6:13. fr. proph. even unto priest
every one d. falsely, 8 : 10.
He. 12 : 7. God d. with you as sons

DEALING, S.

e. 6 : † 2. If lie to neighbour in d.
S. 2 : 23. I hear of your evil d-s
Ps.7:16.violent d. upon his own pate
Jn. 4 : 9. Jews no d-s with Samari.

DEALT.

Ge. 16 : 6. Sarai d. hardly with her
33:11. God hath d. graci. with me
43 : 6. Whf. d. ye so ill, as to tell
Ex. 1 : 20. G. d. well with midwiv.
14:11. whf. hast d. thus with us
18 : 11. in thing they d. proudly
21 : 8. he hath d. deceitf. with her
Ju. 9 : 16. if ye d. well with Jerub.
19. if ye have d. truly, rejoice in
Ru. 1 : 8. as ye have d. with dead
20. Alm. hath d. bitterly with me
1 S. 14 : † 33. Ye have d. treacher.
24 : 18. thou hast d. well with me
25 : 31. when L. have d. well with
my lord [1 Ch. 16 : 3.
2 S. 6 : 19. he d. among all people,
1 K. 12 : 15. they d. faithf., 22 : 7.
21 : 6. Manasseh d. with wizards, 2
Ch. 33 : 6. [Ammon
1 Ch. 20 : 3. so d. Da. with cities of
2 Ch. 6 : 37. we have d. wickedly
11 : 23. Rehob. d. wisely, and
Ne. 1 : 7. We have d. corruptly ag.
9:10.knewest they d. proudly, 16, 29.
Jb. 6:15. My breth. have d. deceitf.
Ps. 13 : 6. Lord d. bountif. with me
44 : 17. nor d. falsely in thy cove.
78 : 57. d. unfaithf. like fathers
103:10. not d. with us aft. our sins
116 : 7. L. d. bountif. with thee
119 : 65. hast d. well with servant
78. they d. perversely with me
147 : 20. not d. so with any nation
Is. 24 : 16. have d. very treach., Je.
3 : 20.-5 : 11.-12 : 6. La. 1 : 2.
Is. 33 : 1. d. not treacherously with
Eze. 22 : 7. in thee d. by oppression
25 : 12. Edom hath d. ag-t Judah
by vengeance [by revenge
15. Because Philistines have d.
Jo. 2 : 26. God hath d. wondrously
Zch. 1 : 6. as Lord thought, so he d.
Lu. 1 : 25. Thus hath L. d. with me
2 : 48. Son, why thus d. with us?
Ac. 7 : 19 d. subtilely with kindred
25 : 24. this man about whom the
Jews have d. with me [ev. man
Ro. 12 : 3. acc-g as God hath d. to
See TREACHEROUSLY.

DEAR.

Je. 15 : † 7. bereave of what is dear
31 : 20. Is Ephraim my d. son?
Lu. 7:2. serv. who was d. unto him
Ac. 20 :24. neith. count I my life d.
Ep. 5 : 1. followers of G. as d. chil.
Ph. 2 : † 20. For I have no man so
d. unto me [servt.
Col. 1 : 7. Epaphras our d. fellow-
13. into kingdom of his d. son
1 Th. 2 : 8. bec. ye were d. to us

DEARLY beloved.

Je. 12:7. have giv. d. b. into ha. of
Ro. 12 : 19. d. b., avenge not [ene.
1 Co.10:14.my d.b.,Ph.4:1.2 Ti.1:2.
2 Co. 7:1.d. b., 12 : 19. 1 Pe. 2 : 11.
Phm. 1. Philemon our d. b.

DEARTH.

Ge. 41:54. d. began, d. in all lands
2 K 4 : 38. there was d. in land
2 Ch. 6:28. if there be a d., or mil-
Ne. 5 : 3. buy corn bec. of d. [dew
Je. 14 : 1. word to Jere. concern. d.
Ac. 7 : 11. came a d. over all E.
11 : 28. there should be a great d.

DEATH.

Ge. 21 : 16. Let not see d. of child
24 : 67. Isaac comf. after mo.'s d.
25 : 11. after d. of Ab., G. blessed
27 : 7. bless thee bef. my d. [Isaac
10. that he bless thee bef. his d.
Ex. 10 : 17. may take fr. me this d.
Nu.16:29. die common d. of all men
23 : 10. Let me die d. of righteous
35:25. slayer abide unto d. of high
priest, 28, 32. Jos. 20 : 6. [d.
31. for life of murderer guilty of
De. 30 : 15. I have set bef. you life
and d., 19. Je. 21 : 8.
31:27. much more rebel aft. my d.
29. aft. my d. will corrupt yours.
33 : 1. Moses blessed Isr. bef. his d.
Jos. 1 : 1. aft. d. of Moses serv. of
Ju. 1 : 1. after d. of Jos. chil. of Isr.
5 : 18. jeoparded lives unto the d.
16 : 16. his soul was vexed unto d.
30. dead he slew at his d. more
Ru. 1:17. if aught but d. part thee
2 : 11. hast done since d. of husb.
1 S. 4 : 20. about time of her d.
15:32. the bitterness of d. is past
20 : 3. but a step betw. me and d.
22 : 22. occasi. d. of thy fa.'e hou.
26 : † 16. are sons of d. ye kept not
2 S. 1 : 1. after d. of Saul when Da
23. in their d. were not divided
15 : 21. in d. or life, their serv. be
19 : † 28. all fa.'s house men of d.
22 : 5. when waves of d. compassed
me, Ps. 18 : 4.-116 : 3.
6. snares of d., Ps. 18 : 5. [Sol.
1 K. 11 : 40. Jerob. in E until d. of
2 K. 2:21. shall not be any more d.
4 : 40. man of G., d. is in pot
2 K. 20 : 1. was Hezekiah sick unto
d., 2 Ch. 32 : 24. Is. 38 : 1.
1 Ch.22:5. Da. prepared bef. his d.
2 Ch. 22:4. counsellors aft. d. of fa.
32:33. Jud. did Heze. honour at d.
Ezr. 7 : 26. unto d. or to banishm.
Jb. 3 : 21. long for d. it cometh not
7:15. So that my soul chooseth d.
18 : 13. firstb. of d. sh. devour his
Jb.27:15.remain sh. be buried in d.
28:22. Destruction and d. say, We
30:23.know thou wilt bri. me to d.
Ps. 6 : 5. in d. is no remem. of thee
7 : 13. prepared instruments of d.
13 : 3. lest I sleep the sleep of d.
22 : 15. bro-t me into dust of d.
48:14. G. will be our guide, unto d.
49 : 14. d. shall feed on them
55 : 4. terrors of d. fallen upon me
15. Let d. seize upon them
73 : 4. are no bands in their d.
79 : † 11. reserve children of d.
89 : 48.What man shall not see d.?
102 : 20. loose those appoi to d.
116: 15. Precious is d. of his saints
118:18. not given me over unto d.
Pr. 2 : 18. her house inclineth unto
5 : 5. Her feet go down to d. [d.
7 : 27. down to chambers of d.
8 : 36. they that hate me love d.
11 : 19. pursueth it to his own d.
12 : 28. in pathway there is no d.
13 : 14. from snares of d., 14 : 27.
14 : 12. end are ways of d., 16 : 25.
14 : 32. righteous hope in his d.
16 : 14. wrath of k. as messen.of d.
18 : 21. d. in power of tongue
21 : 6. to and fro of them seek d.
24:11. forbear to deliv.drawn unto
26 : 18. madman casteth d. [d.
Ec. 7 : 26. more bitter than d.wom.
Can. 8 : 6. for love is strong as d.
Is. 25 : 8. swallow up d. in victory
38 : 18. d. cannot celebrate thee
53 : 9. with the rich in his d.
12. poured out his soul unto d.
Je. 8 : 3. d. chosen rather than life
9:21. d. is come up into windows
15 : 2. as are for d. to d., 43 : 11.
18 : † 23. their counsel for d.
26: † 11. judgm of d.is for this man
La. 1 : 20. at home there is as d.
Eze. 18 : 32. I have no pleasure in
d. of wicked, 33 : 11.
31 : 14. are all delivered unto d.
Ho. 13 : 14. O d. I will be plagues
Jon. 4 : 9. well to be angry unto d.
Ha. 2 : 5. is as d. cannot be satis.
Mat. 2 : 15. there until d. of Herod
10:21. deliver bro. to d.,Mk.13:12.
15 : 4. curseth fa. or mother, let
him die the d., Mk. 7 : 10.
16 : 28. some not taste of d. till
see Son, Mk. 9 : 1. Lu. 9 : 27.
20 : 18. they shall condemn him to
d., Mk. 10 : 33. [Mk. 14 : 34
26 : 38. sorrowful even unto d.,
66 He is guilty of d., Mk. 14: 64.
Mk. 5 : 23. My dau. at point of d.
Lu. 2:26. not see d. bef. had seen C.
22 : 33. I will go with thee both d.
23 : 22. have found no cause of d.
24 : 20. to be condemned to d.
Jn. 4:47. heal his son at point of d.
8 : 51. shall never see d., 52.
11 : 4. This sickness is not unto d.
13. Jesus spake of his d.
12:33. signifying what d., 18 : 32.
21:19.by what d. he sho. glorify G.
Ac. 2 : 24. having loosed pains of d.
8:1.S.consent-g unto his d.,22:20.
13:28. found no cause of d. in him
22 : 4. I persecu. this way unto d.
28 : 18. was no cause of d. in me
Ro. 5 : 10. reconciled to G. by d. of
his Son, much more, Col. 1:22.
12. d. by sin, so d. passed upon
14. d.reigned fr. Adam to Mo.,17.
21. as sin hath reigned unto d.
6 : 3. so many as were baptized into
J. C., were baptized into his d.?
4. buried by baptism into d.
5. planted in likeness of his d.
9. d. hath no domin. over him
16. his serv.,wheth. of sin unto d.
21. end of those things is d.

Ro. 6:23. For the wages of sin is d.
7: 5.sin work to bring fruit unto d.
10. com-t of life I found unto d.
13.Was good made d. to me? [d.?
24. who deliv. me fr. body of this
8: 2. free from law of sin and d.
6. to be carnally minded is d.
38. nor d. nor life separate us
1 Co. 3: 22. life or d. all are yours
4: 9. G., as it were appointed to d.
11: 26. ye do shew the Lord's d.
15:21.since by man came d.by man
26. last enemy be destroyed is d.
54. d. is swallowed up in victory
55. O d. where is thy sting! [sin
56. sting of d. is sin, strength of
2 Co.1:9. had sentence of d. in ours.
10. who deliv. us fr. so great a d.
2: 16. To one savour of d. unto d.
3: 7. if ministra. of d. glorious
4:11.are deliv. unto d. for Jes. sake
12. So then d. worketh in us
7: 10. sorrow of world worketh d.
Ph. 1: 20. whether by life or by d.
2: 8. obedient unto d. d. of cross
27. Epaph. sick nigh unto d. [d.
30. Bec.for work of C. he was nigh
3:10.made conformable unto his d.
2 Ti. 1: 10. who hath abolished d.
He. 2: 9. Jesus for suffering of d.
crowned, that he taste d. for
14. through d. destroy him that
had the power of d.
15.deliver th. who thro. fear of d.
7:23.not suffered to continue,by d.
9: 15. by means of d. for redemp.
16. must be d. of testator
11: 5. that he should not see d.
Ja. 1: 15. sin bringeth forth d.
1 Jn. 3:14. loveth not abideth in d.
5: 16. sin unto d. | 17. not unto d.
Re. 1: 18. keys of hell and of d.
2: 10. Be faithful unto d. I will
11. not be hurt of second d.
6: 8. his name that sat was d.
9:6. men sh. seek d. and d.sh.flee
12: 11. loved not lives unto the d.
13: 3. of heads, as wounded to d.
18:8. her plagues come one day,d.
20: 6. second d. hath no power
13. d. and hell delivered up dead
14. d. cast into lake, this sec. d.
21: 4. there shall be no more d.
8. which is the second d.
See DAY.

From DEATH.

Jos. 2: 13. deliver our lives f. d.
Jb. 5: 20. In fam. redeem thee f.d.
Ps.33:19 To deliver their soul f. d.
56: 13. hast deliv. soul f.d.,116:8.
68: 20. unto L. belong issues f. d.
78: 50. spared not their soul f. d.
Pr. 10: 2. righte. deliv. f. d., 11:4.
Ho. 13: 14. will redeem them f. d.
Jn.5:24. is passed f. d., 1 Jn. 3: 14.
He. 5: 7. to him able to save f. d.
Ja. 5:20. know he sh. save soul f.d.

Gates of DEATH.

Jb. 38: 17. Have the g. o. d. been
opened unto thee?
Ps. 9: 13. liftest me from g. o. d.
107:18.they draw near unto g.o.d.

Put to DEATH.

Ge.26:11.touch. this man, be p.t.d.
Ex. 21: 29. his owner be p. t. d.
35:2.whoso.work on sab. be p.t.d.
Le. 19:20. not p. t. d. bec. not free
20: 11. both shall surely be p.t.d.
24: 21. killeth be p.t.d., Nu.35:30.
Nu.1:51. stranger that cometh nigh
be p. t. d., 3: 10,38.-18: 7.
De. 13: 5. that dreamer be p. t. d.
9.hand upon him to p.t.d.,17:7.
17: 6. of one witness not p. t. d.
21: 22. he be p. t. d. and thou
hang him on a tree
24: 16. fathers shall not be p. t.
d. for children, neither chil.
p. t. d. for fathers, 2 K. 14: 6.
Jos. 1: 18. rebel ag. com-t be p.t.d.
Ju. 6: 31. plead. for Baal be p.t.d.
20:13. may p.them t.d.,1 S.11:12.
1 S. 11: 13. not be p.t.d.,2 S.19:22.
2 S. 8: 2. with two lines to p. t. d.
19: 21.Shall not Shimei be p.t.d.?
21: 9. were p.t.d. in days of harv.
1 K. 2: 8. I will not p. thee t. d.
24. Adonijah shall be p. t. d.
26. not at this time p. thee t. d.
2 Ch. 15:13. not seek L. be p. t. d.
23: 7. cometh into h., be p. t. d.
Es. 4: 11. is one law to p. him t.d.
Je. 18: 21. their men be p. t. d.
26: 15. know if ye p. me t. d.
19. did Judah p. him at all t. d.?
21.Jehoi.sought to p. Urijah t.d.
38: 4. let this man be p. t. d.
15. wilt thou not p. me t. d.?
16. I will not p. thee t. d., 25.
43: 3. Chald. that might p.us t.d.
52:27. and p. them t.d. in Riblah
Mat. 10: 21. chil. cause them to be
p.t.d., Mk. 13:12. Lu. 21: 16.
14: 5. would p. him t. d. he fe r.
26: 59. false witness ag J. to p.
him t. d., 27: 1. Mk. 14: 55.
Mk. 14: 1. to take him and p. t.d.
Lu.18:33. they shall p.him t.d.,31.
23:32. two malefact. to be p. t. d.
Jn. 11: 53. counsel to p. him t. d.
12: 10. might p. Lazarus t. d.
18: 31. not lawful to p. any t. d.
Ac.12:19.com-d keepers to be p.t.d.
26: 10. when p. t. d. I gave voice
against them [ened
1 Pe. 3:18. p.t.d.in flesh,but quick-
See SURELY.

Shadow of DEATH.

Jb. 3:5.Let darkn. and s.o. d. [22.
10: 21. land of darkn. and s.o.d.,
12: 22. bringeth to light s. o. d.
16: 16. on my eye-lids is s. o. d.
24:17.morning is to them as s.o.d.
28: 3. He searcheth out s. o. d.
34: 22. There is no darkn. nor s.
o. d. where sinner may hide
38: 17. hast seen doors of s. o. d.
Ps. 23:4. walk thro. valley of s.o.d.
44:19. hast covered us with s.o.d
107: 10. sit in darkn. and s. o. d.
14. them out of darkn.and s.o.d
Is.9:2. dwell in land of the s. o. d.
Je.2:6. bro-t us thro. land of s.o.d.
13: 16. light he turn into s. o. d.
Am. 5: 8. s. o. d. into morning
Mat.4: 16. peo. that sat in s. o. d.
Lu.1:79.give light to them in s.o.d.

With DEATH.

Is. 28: 15. we have made cov. w. d.
18. cov. w. d. shall be disannull.
Re. 2: 23. will kill her chil. w d.
6: 8. power given to kill w d.

Worthy of DEATH.

De. 17: 6. w.o.d. shall be pt t to d.
19: 6. whereas he was not w.o.d.
21: 22. have com. a sin w. o. d.
22: 26. in damsel no sin w. o. d.
1 K.2:26.Abiathar, thou art w.o.d.
Lu. 23: 15. nothing w.o.d. is done
Ac.23:29.noth. to his charge w.o d.
25:11.if I have com. thing w.o d
25. he had com. nothing w.o.d
26:31. man doeth nothing w.o d
Ro. 1:32. com-t such things w.o.d.

DEATHS.

Je. 16:4. They sh. die of grievous d.
Eze.28:8.die d. of them slain in sea-
10. shalt die d. of uncircumcised
2 Co. 11: 23. frequent. in d. oft

DEBASE.

Is. 57: 9. didst d. thyself unto hell

DEBATE. [Verb.]

Pr. 25:9. d. cause with thy neighb.
Is.27:8. in measure, thou wilt d.

DEBATE, S.

Is. 58:4. ye fast for strife and d.
Ro. 1: 29. full of envy, murder, d.
2 Co. 12:20. I fear lest there be d-s

DE'BIR. [Person, Place.]

Jos. 10: 3. D. king of Eglon
38. Israel with him to D., 39.
11: 21. and cut off Anakims fr. D
12: 13. the king of D.
13: 26. the border of D.
15: 7. border went up toward D.
15. name of D. was, 49. Ju. 1: 11.
21:15. D. with suburbs, 1 Ch.6:58.

DEB'ORAH.

Gen. 35: 8. D. Rebekah's nurse died
Ju. 4: 4. D. a prophetess judged
5: 1. Then sang D. saying
7. until I D. arose mother in Isr.
12. Awake, awake, D.
15. princes of Issachar with D.

DEBT, S.

1 S. 22: 2. ev. one in d. went to D.
2 K. 4:7. Go, sell the oil, pay thy d
Ne. 10:31. leave exaction of ev. d.
Pr. 22:26. Be not of sureties for d-s
Mat. 6:12. forgive us our d-s as w
18: 27. and forgave him the d.
30. cast into prison till be pay d.
32. lord said, I forgave thee d.
Ro. 4:4.reward not of grace but d.

DEBTOR.

Eze. 18: 7. restored to d. pledge
Mat. 23:16. swear by gold is a d.
† 18. sweareth by gift, he is d.
Ro. 1: 14. I am d. to the Greeks
Ga. 5: 3. is a d. to do whole law

DEBTORS.

Mat. 6: 12. as we forgive our d.
Lu. 7: 41. a creditor had two d.
13: † 4. think ye they d. above all?
16: 5. called ev. one of his lord's d.
Ro. 8: 12.breth , we are d. not to flesh
15: 27. and their d. they are

DECAP'OLIS.

Mat.4:25.multitudes foll.him fr D.
Mk. 5: 20. began to publish in D.
7: 31. thro. midst of coast of D.

DECAY. [Noun.]

Le. 25: 35. if bro. be fallen in d.
Ro. 11: † 12. d. of them riches of

DECAYED, ETH.

Ne. 4: 10. strength of bearers d-d
Jb. 14: 11. as flood d-h and drieth
Ec. 10: 18. By slothf. building d-h
Is. 44:26. I will raise up d-d places
He. 8:13. wh. d-h is ready to vanish

DECEASE.

Lu. 9: 31. spake of his d. at Jerus.
2 Pe. 1:15. aft. my d. to have in re-

DECEASED. [mem.

Is. 26: 14. are d. they sh. not rise
Mat. 22:25. first, when he marri. d.

DECEIT, S.

Jb. 15:35. their belly prepareth d.
27: 4. nor my tongue utter d.
31: 5. or if my foot hasted to d.
Ps. 5: † 6. L. abhor man of d.
10:7. His mouth full of cursing, d.
36: 3. Words of his mouth are d.
38: 12. imagine d-s all day
43: † 1. O deliv. me fr. man of d.
50: 19. thy tongue frameth d.
55: 11. d. and guile depart not
† 23. men of d. sh. not live half
72:14.sh. redeem their soul from d.
101: 7. worketh d. not dw. in my
109: † 2. mouth of d. is open. ag.
119: 118. their d. is falsehood | me
Pr. 11: † 1. balances of d. are abom
12: 5. counsels of wicked are d.
17. false witness sheweth d.
20. d. in them. th. imagine evil
14: 8. but the folly of fools is d.
20: 17. Bread of d. is sweet to man
† 23. balances of d. are not good
26: 24. he that hateth, layeth up d.
26. Whose hatred is covered by d.

s. 30: 10. speak smooth, proph. d-s
33: † 15. that despiseth gain of d-s
53: 9. neith. any d. in his mouth
Je. 5: 27. so are houses full of d.
8: 5. they hold fast d. they refuse
9: 6. thro. d. refuse to know me
8. tongue, it speaketh d.
14: 14. prophesy d. of their heart
23: 26. they are prophets of d. of
42: † 20. used d. ag. your souls
Eze. 22: † 7. have they dealt by d.
† 29. people of land have used d.
Ho. 11: 12. Isr. compass. me with d.
12: 7. balances of d. in his hands
Am. 8: 5. falsifying balances by d.
Zph. 1: 9. fill master's hou. with d.
Mk. 7: 22. out of heart proceed d.
Ro. 1: 29. full of murder, d.
3: 13. with tongues have used d.
Col. 2: 8. lest spoil you thro. vain d.
1 Th. 2: 3. our exhortation not of d.

DECEITFUL.

Ps. 5: 6. the Lord will abhor d. man
35: 20. devise d. matters ag. them
43: 1. O deliver me from d. man
52: 4. devouring words, d. tongue
55: 23. d. men shall not live half
78: 57. turned aside like d. bow
109: 2. mouth of d. opened ag. me
120: 2. deliv. my soul fr. d. tongue
Pr. 11: 18. worketh a d. work
12: † 24. d. shall be under tribute
14: 25. a d. witness speaketh lies
23: 3. his dainties they are d. meat
27: 6. kisses of an enemy are d.
29: 13. poor and d. meet together
31: 30. Favour is d. and beauty
Je. 17: 9. heart is d. above all things
Ho. 7: 16. they are like a d. bow
Mi. 6: 11. with bag of d. weights
12. tongue is d. in their mouth
Zph. 3: 13. nor d. tongue be found
2 Co. 11: 13. such are d. workers
Ep. 4: 22. corrupt acc. to d. lusts

DECEITFULLY.

Ge. 34: 13. sons ans. Hamor d.
Ex. 8: 29. let not Pha. deal d. any
21: 8. seeing he dealt d. with her
Le. 6: 4. thing he hath d. gotten
Jb. 6: 15. breth. dealt d. as a brook
13: 7. Will ye talk d. for God?
Ps. 24: 4. not lift soul nor sworn d.
52: 2. tongue like razor, working d.
Je. 48: 10. that doeth work of L. d.
Da. 11: 23. after league, he work d.
2 Co. 2: † 17. that deal d. with word
4: 2. nor handling word of God d.

DECEITFULNESS.

Mat. 13: 22. and the d. of riches
choke the word, Mk. 4: 19.
He. 3: 13. hardened thro. d. of sin

DECEIVABLENESS.

2 Th. 2: 10. with all d. of unrighte.

DECEIVE.

2 S. 3: 25. Abner came to d. thee
1 K. 22: † 20. Who shall d. Ahab?
2 K. 4: 28. did not I say, do not d.
18: 29. let not Hezekiah d. you,
2 Ch. 32: 15. Is. 36: 14.
19: 10. let not thy God d., Is. 37: 10.
Pr. 24: 28. and d. not with lips
Is. 58: † 11. spring wh. waters d. not
Je. 9: 5. will d. ev. one his neighb.
29: 8. your diviners in midst d. you
37: 9. saith L. d. not yourselves
Ho. 12: † 7. merch. he loveth to d.
Zch. 13: 4. wear rough garm. to d.
Mat. 24: 4. no man d. you, Mk 13: 5.
5. I am C. d. many, 11. Mk. 13: 6.
24. they shall d. the very elect
Ac. 5: † 3. why Sat. filled heart to d.
Ro. 16: 18. by fair speeches d. simple
1 Co. 3: 18. Let no man d. himself
Ep. 4: 14. they lie in wait to d.
5: 6. Let no man d. you, 2 Th. 2:
3. 1 Jn. 3: 7.
1 Jn. 1: 8. if say we no sin, we d.

Re. 20: 3. d. the nations no more
8. go to d. nations in four quar.

DECEIVED.

Ge. 31: 7. father hath d. me and
Le. 6: 2. if soul sin or d. neighbour
De. 11: 16. heed that heart be not d.
1 S. 19: 17. Why hast d. me? 28: 12.
2 S. 19: 26. my servant d. me
Jb. 12: 16. d. and deceiver are his
15: 31. not him d. trust in vanity
31: 9. If heart been d. by woman
Pr. 20: 1. whosoever is d. thereby
Is. 19: 13. the princes of Noph are d.
44: 20. d. heart hath turned him
Je. 4: 10. hast greatly d. this peo.
20: 7. O L. hast d. me, I was d.
49: 16. Thy terriblen. hath d. thee
La. 1: 19. my lovers, they d. me
Eze. 14: 9. if proph. be d. I d. him
Ob. 3. pride of heart hath d. thee
7. men at peace have d. thee
Lu. 21: 8 take heed ye be not d.
Jn. 7: 47. Phari. ans. Are ye also d
Ro. 7: 11. sin taking occasion d. me
1 Co. 6: 9. Be not d., 15: 33. Ga. 6: 7.
1 Ti. 2: 14. Adam was not d. but
2 Ti. 3: 13. deceiving and being d.
Tit. 3: 3. d. serving divers lusts
Re. 18: 23. by sorceries nations d.
19: 20. he d. them th. receiv. mark
20: 10. devil that d. them was cast

DECEIVER, S.

Ge. 27: 12. seem to my fa. as d.
Jb. 12: 16. deceived and d. are his
Mal. 1: 14. cursed be d. who in flock
Mat. 27: 63. remem. that that d. said
2 Co. 6: 8. as d-s and yet true
Tit. 1: 10. many d-s especi. of circ.
2 Jn. 7. confess not Jes. this is a d.
many d-s are entered

DECEIVETH, ING. [d.

2 K. 18: † 32. not unto Hez. when he
Pr. 26: 19. So is man th. d. neighb.
Is. 3: † 16. daughters d-g with eyes
Jn. 7: 12. said, Nay, he d. the peo.
Ga. 6: 3. when nothing, he d. hims.
2 Ti. 3: 13. evil men wax worse, d-g
Ja. 1: 22. d-g your own selves
26. but d. his own heart
Re. 12: 9. called the devil, which d.
13: 14. d-h them on the earth

DECEIVINGS.

2 Pe. 2: 13. sporting with their d.

DECENTLY.

Ro. 13: † 13. Let us walk d. as in day
1 Co. 14: 40. Let all things be done

DECIDED. [d.

1 K. 20: 40. said, Thyself hast d. it

DECISION.

Jo. 3: 14. multitudes in valley of d.

DECK, ED.

Jb. 40: 10. d. thyself with majesty
Pr. 7: 16. I have d. my bed with
Is. 63: † 1. who is this that is d.
Je. 10: 4. They d. it with silver
Eze. 16: 11. I d-d thee with ornam.
13. Thou wast thus d. with gold
Ho. 2: 13. she d-d with her ear rings
Re. 17: 4. woman was d. with gold
18: 16. Alas, that city that was d.

DECKEDST.

Eze. 16: 16. and d. high places
23: 40. d. thyself with ornaments

DECKEST, ETH.

Is. 61: 10. as bridegroom d-h hims.
Je. 4: 30. tho. thou d-t with orna.

DECLARATION.

Es. 10: 2. d. of greatness of Mord.
Jb. 13: 17. hear my d. with ears
Lu. 1: 1. to set forth in order a d.
2 Co. 8: 19. to d. of ready mind

DECLARE.

Ge. 41: 24. none could d. it to me
De. 1: 5. in Moab began Moses to d.
Jos. 20: 4 d. cause in ears of elders
Ju. 14: 12. if ye can-t d. it me, 13.
15. may d. unto us the riddle

1 K. 22: 13. prophets d. good unto
the king, 2 Ch. 18: 12.
1 Ch. 16: 24. d. his glory among
the heathen, Ps. 96: 3.
Es. 4: 8. shew copy and d. it unto E
Jb. 12: 8. fishes shall d. unto thee
21: 31. Who d. way to his face?
28: 27. Then did he see it, and d. it
31: 37. I would d. num. of my steps
38: 4. d. if thou hast underst-g
18. breadth of earth, d. if knowest
40: 7. d. thou unto me, 42: 4.
Ps. 9: 11. d. amo. peo. his doings
19: 1. heavens d. the glory of G.
22: 31. d. his righte., 50: 6.-97: 7.
30: 9. Shall dust d. thy truth?
40: 5. if I w-ld d. them, th. are more
50: 16. What thou to d. my statutes
64: 9. men shall d. work of God
73: 28. that I may d. all thy works
75: 1 thy wondrous works d.
78: 6. and d. them to their chil.
102: 21. To d. name of L. in Zion
107: 22. d. his works with rejoic.
118: 17. live and d. works of L.
145: 4. shall d. thy mighty acts
Ec. 9: 1. I considered to d. all this
Is. 3: 9. they d. their sin as Sodom
12: 4. d. his doings amo. people
21: 6. watchman, let him d. what
41: 22. let them d. things to come
42: 9. new things do I d. bef. they
12. d. his praise in the islands
43: 9. who can d. this, and shew?
26. d. th. thou mayest be justif.
44: 7. who, as I, shall d. it?
45: 19. I L. d. things th. are right
48: 6. will not ye d. it? [8: 33.
53: 8. who shall d. his gene.? Ac.
66: 19. sh. d. my glory amo. Gent.
Je. 5: 20. d. this in house of Jacob,
9: 12. L. spok., that he may d. it
31: 10. d. it in isles afar off
38: 15. If I d. it wilt put to death?
25. d. what thou said unto king
42: 20. what G. shall say, d. unto us,
50: 28. d. in Zion vengeance of L.
51: 10. let us d. in Z. work of L.
Eze. 12: 16. d. their abomi., 23: 36.
40: 4. d. all thou seest to Israel
Da. 4: 18. d. the interpretation [sion
Mi. 3: 8. d. unto Jac. his transgres-
Zch. 9: 12. I d. that I will render
Mat. 13: 36 d. the parable of tares
15: 15. said Peter d. this parable
Ac. 13: 32. we d. glad tidings
41. in no wise bel. tho. man d. it
17: 23. Whom ye ignorantly worship, him d. I unto you
20: 27. not shunned to d. couns.
Ro. 3: 25. set to d. his righte., 26.
1 Co. 3: 13. work, the day sh. d. it
11: 17. in this I d. I praise you not
15: 1. I d. unto you the gospel
Col. 4: 7. my state sha. Tychicus d.
He. 11: 14. d. plainly they seek
1 Jn. 1: 3. that we have seen d. we
5. this is message we d. unto you

I will DECLARE.

Jb. 15: 17. that I have seen I w. d.
Ps. 2: 7. I w. d. decree [He. 2: 12.
22: 22. I w. d. name to brethr.,
38: 18. I w. d. mine iniquity
66: 16. I w. d. what done for soul
75: 9. I w. d. for ever, I will sing
145: 6. I w. d. thy greatn. [to G.
Is. 57: 12. I w. d. thy righte. and thy
Je. 42: 4. I w. d. it, I will keep
Jn. 17: 26. declared thy name, and

DECLARE ye. [w. d.

Is. 48: 20. voice of singing d. y.
Je. 4: 5. d. y. in Judah, publish in
46: 14. d. y. in E. publish in Mig.
50: 2. d. y. among nations, publish
Mi. 1: 10. d. y. it not at Gath

DECLARED.

Ex. 9: 16. that my name may be d.

Le. 23: 44. Moses d. to chil. of Isr.
Nu. 1: 18. they d. their pedigrees
15: 34. in ward, bec. it was not d.
De. 4:13. he d. to you his covenant
2 S. 19: 6. thou hast d. this day
Ne. 8: 12. understood words d.
Jb. 26: 3. hast plentifully d. thing
Ps. 40: 10. I have d. thy faithfulln.
71: 17. have I d. thy wondr. works
77:14. d. thy strength amo. people
88: 11. thy lovingkl. be d. in grave
119: 13. have I d. thy judgments
26. I have d. my ways, and thou
Is. 21: 2. griev. vision is d. unto me
10. that I heard of G. have I d.
41: 26. hath d. from beginn. 45: 21.
43: 12. I have d., 44: 8.–48: 5.
48: 3. I have d. former things fr.
14. which hath d. these things?
Je. 36: 13. Micaiah d. all words
42: 21. I have this day d. it to you
Lu. 8: 47. she d. him bef. all people
Jn. 1: 18. No man seen G., Son d.
17: 26. I have d. to them thy name
Ac. 9: 27. he d. how he had seen L.
10: 8. when he had d. these things
12: 17. he d. how L. bro-t him out
15: 4. d. all G. had done with them
14. Simeon d. how G. did visit
21: 19. d. what things G. wrought
25: 14. Festus d. Paul's cause unto [k.
Ro. 1: 4. d. to be the Son of G.
9: 17. name might be d. thro. earth
1 Co. 1: 11. been d. unto me of you
2 Co. 3: 3. ye are d. to be epis. of C.
Col. 1: 8. Who d. your love in Spirit
Re. 10: 7. be finished as he d.

DECLARETH, ING.

Is. 41: 26. there is none that d-h.
46:10. d-g end from the beginning
Je. 4: 15. a voice d-h from Dan
Ho. 4: 12. their staff d-h unto them
Am. 4: 13. d-h unto man his tho-t
Ac. 15: 3. d-g conversion of Gent.
12. d-h what miracles G. wrought
1 Co. 2: 1. d-h unto you testim. of [G.

DECLINE.

Ex. 23: 2. nor speak, to d. after
De. 17: 11. shalt not d. fr. sentence
Ps. 119: 157. not d. fr. thy testimo.
Pr. 4: 5. neith. d. fr. words of my
7: 25. Let not heart d. to her ways

DECLINED, ETH.

Ju. 19: † 8. tarried till day d.
2 Ch. 34: 2. d-d neither to right ha.
Jb. 23: 11. way I kept and not d.
Ps. 44: 18. nor steps d. fr. thy way
102: 11. days like shadow that d-h
109: 23. gone like shadow when it [d-h
119: 51. have I not d. fr. law

DECREASE, ED, ING.

Ge. 8: 5. waters d-d continually
† the waters were in d-g until
Ps. 107: 38. suffer not cattle to d.
Jn. 3:30. He must incr., I must d.

DECREE, S.

2 Ch. 30: 5. So they established a d.
Ezr. 4: † 21. d. to cause to cease
5:13. Cyrus made a d. to build, 17.
6: 1. Darius made a d., 12.
7: 21. I Artaxerxes made a d., 13.
Es. 1: 20. king's d. wh. he sh. make
2: 8. king's command. and d., 9: 1.
3: 15. d. in Shushan, 8: 14.–9: 14.
4: 3. d. came, was gr. mourning
8: 17. his d. came, Jews had joy
9:32. d. of Esther confirmed these
Jb. 20: † 29. heritage of his d. fr. G.
28: 26. When he made d. for rain
38: † 10. established my d. upon it
Ps. 2: 7. declare d. L. hath said
148: 6. a d. which shall not pass
Pr. 8: 29. he gave to sea his d.
Is. 10: 1. that decree unrighte. d-s
Je. 5:22. bound of sea by perpet. d.
Da. 2: 9. there is but one d. for you
13. d. went that wise men, 4: 6.
Da. 2:15. Why is d. so hasty fr. king
3: 10. Thou, O king hast made d.
29. I make d., That every people
4: 17. This is by d. of watchers
24. this is d. of Most High
6: 8. O k., establish d., 7, 9, 12.
13. Dan. regardeth not thee, nor d.
26. I make d., That in ev. domin.
Jon. 3: 7. by d. of king and nobles
Mi. 7: 11. that day d. be far remov.
Zph. 2:2. Before the d. bring forth
Lu. 2: 1. went out a d. from Cæsar
Ac. 16: 4. delivered d-s to keep
17: 7. do contrary to d-s of Cæsar

DECREE. [Verb.]

Jb. 22: 28. shalt d., and it shall be
Pr. 8: 15. By me princes d. justice
Is. 10: 1. Woe to them that d. unrighteous decrees

DECREED.

Es. 2:1. what was d. against Vashti
9:31. as had d. for thems. and seed
Jb. 38: 10. brake up my d. place
Is. 10: 22. consump. d. sh. overfl.
1 Co. 7: 37. so d. that he will keep

DE'DAN.

Ge. 10: 7. sons of Raamah, Sheba, D., 25:3. 1 Ch. 1:9. Eze. 38:13.
1 Ch. 1: 32. sons of Jokshan, D.
Je. 25: 23. I made D. to drink
49: 8. dwell deep, O inhab. of D.
Eze. 25: 13. of D. sh. fall by sword
27: 15. D. were thy merchants, 20.

DED'ANIM.

Is. 21: 13. O ye companies of D.

DEDICATE.

De. 20: 5. die and ano. man d. it
2 S. 8:11. which Da. did d. unto L.
1 Ch. 26:27. Out of spoils did th. d.
2 Ch. 2: 4. I build h. to d. it to G.

DEDICATED.

De. 20: 5. built new h. hath not d.
Ju. 17: 3. wholly d. silver unto L.
1 K. 7: 51. things which Da. his fa. had d., 1 Ch. 18:11. 2 Ch. 5:1.
8: 63. and Isr. d. house, 2 Ch. 7:5.
15: 15. Asa bro-t things his fa. d., himself d., 2 Ch. 15: 18.
2 K. 12: 4. All money of d. things
18. things kings of Judah had d.
1 Ch. 26: 20. over d. things, 26.
26. what the captains had d.
28. all Sam., and Joab had d.
28: 12. treasures of d. things
2 Ch. 24: 7. d. things upon Baalim
31:12. bro-t in d. things faithfully
Eze. 44: 29. ev. d. thing be theirs
He. 9:18. nor first testa. d. without [blood

DEDICATING.

Nu. 7: 10. offered for d. of altar
11. each prince for d. of altar

DEDICATION.

Nu. 7: 84. d. of the altar, 88.
2 Ch. 7: 9. they kept d. of altar
Ezr. 6:16. chil. of captiv. kept the d.
17. offered at d. of this house
Ne. 12: 27. d. of wall of Jerusalem
Da. 3:2. to d. of image k. set up, 3.
Jn. 10:22. was at Jerusa. feast of d.

DEED. [done?

Ge. 44: 15. What d. this ye have
Ex. 9: 16. in very d. I raised thee
Ju. 19: 30. There was no such d.
1 S. 25: 34. in very d. except thou
26: 4. Saul was come in very d.
2 S. 12: 14. by d. given occasion
Es. 1: 17. d. of queen come abroad
Ps. 137: † 8. that recomp-h thy d.
Pr. 19: † 17. his d. will he pay
Lu. 23: 51. Jo. not consented to d.
24: 19 Jes. who was mighty in d.
Ac. 4:9. this day examin. of good d.
Ro. 15: 18. make Gent. obed. by d.
1 Co. 5:2. hath done this d. be tak.
3. conc. him th. hath done this d.
2 Co. 10:11. in d. when we are pres.
Col. 3:17. whatso. ye do in word or d.
Ja. 1: 25. shall be blessed in his d.
1 Jn. 3:18. not love in word, but in [d.

DEEDS.

Ge. 20:9. done d. ought not be done
1 Ch. 11: † 22. a man, great of d.
16: 8. his d. am. peo., Ps. 105: 1.
2 Ch. 35: 27. his d., are written
Ezr. 9: 13. come upon us for evil d.
Ne. 6: 19. they reported his good d.
13: 14. wipe not out my good d.
Ps. 28: 4. Give th. acc. to their d.
Is. 59: 18. acc. to d. he will repay
Je. 5: 28. overpass d. of wicked
25: 14. will recompense acc. to d.
Lu. 11: 48. ye allow d. of fathers
23: 41. receive reward of our d.
Jn. 3: 19. loved darkn. bec. d. evil
20. lest his d. should be reprov.
21. that his d. be made manifest
8: 41. Ye do d. of your father
Ac. 7: 22. Moses was mighty in d.
9: 36. Dorcas was full of alms-d.
19: 18. many shewed their d.
24:2 by thy provi. worthy d. done
Ro. 2:6. render to ev. man acc. to d.
3: 20. by d. of law no flesh justifi.
28. justified by faith without d.
8: 13. if ye mortify d. of body
2 Co. 12: 12. wrought in mighty d.
Col. 3: 9. put off old man with d.
2 Pe. 2: 8. vexed with unlawful d.
2 Jn. 11. is partaker of his evil d.
3 Jn. 10. I will remember his d.
Jude 15. convince of ungodly d.
Re. 2: 6. hatest d. of Nicolaitans
22. tribulation, exc. repent of d.
16: 11. they repented not of d.

DEEMED.

Ac. 27: 27. shipmen d. they drew [near

DEEP, S.

Ge. 1: 2. darkness upon face of d.
7: 11. fountains of d. were broken
8: 2. fountains of d. were stopped
49: 25. bless with bless. of the d.
De. 33: 13. d. th. coucheth beneath
Jb. 38: 30. face of d. is frozen
41: 31. maketh d. to boil like a
32. would think d. to be hoary
Ne. 9: 11. persec-s threwest into d.
Ps. 36: 6. judgments are great d.
42: 7. d. calleth unto d. at noise
69: 15. neith. let d. swallow me
Ps. 88: 6. hast laid in the d.
104: 6. coveredst it with the d.
107: 24. see his wonders in the d.
148: 7. Praise the Lord all d.
Pr. 8: 28. strengt-d fountains of d.
Is. 44: 27. saith to the d., Be dry
51:10. wh. dried waters of great d.
63: 13. that led them thro. the d.
Eze. 26:19. I sh. bring d. upon thee
31:4. d. set him on high wi. rivers
15. I covered the d. for him
Am. 7: 4. it devoured the great d.
Jon. 2: 3. hadst cast me into the d.
Ha. 3: 10. the d. uttered his voice
Zch. 10: 11. d-s of river sh. dry up
Lu. 5: 4. Launch out into the d.
8:31. not com. them to go into d.
Ro. 10: 7. or who descend into d.?
2 Co. 11: 25. a night and day in d.

DEEP. [Adjective.]

Jb. 12: 22. He discovereth d. things
Ps. 64: 6. thought and heart is d.
69: 2. I sink in d. mire, d. wa-s
14. let me be deliv. out of d. wa-s
80: 9. didst cause it to take d. root
92:5. L., thy thoughts are very d.
95: 4. In his hand are d. places
135:6. did he in seas and d. places
140: 10. them be cast into d. pits
Pr. 18: 4. words are as d. waters
20: 5. Counsel is like d. water
22: 14. of strange wom. is a d. pit
23: 27. For a whore is a d. ditch
Ec. 7: 24. exceed-g d. who find it?
Is. 7: † 11. make thy petition d.

Is. 29:15. seek **d.** to hide th. couns.
30 : 33. he hath made Tophet **d.**
Je. 49 : 8. dwell **d.** O inhab. of De.
Eze. 3 : † 5. to a peo. **d.** of lips, † 6.
23 : 32. drink of thy sister's cup **d.**
32 : 14. will I make their wa-s **d.**
34 : 18. to have drunk **d.** waters
Da. 2 : 22. He revealeth **d.** things
Lu. 6 : 48. digged **d.** laid founda. on
Jn. 4 : 11. the well is **d.** ⌊rock
1 Co.2:10.searcheth **d.** things of G.
2 Co. 8 : 2. **d.** poverty abounded

DEEP sleep. ⌈Adam
Ge. 2 : 21. God caused **d. s.** upon
15 : 12. a **d. s.** fell upon Abram
1 S. 26 : 12. **d. s.** was upon th. ⌈15.
Jb. 4 : 13. **d. s.** falleth on men, 33:
Pr. 19:15. Slothf. casteth into **d. s.**
Is. 29 : 10, L. poured spirit of **d. s.**
Da. 8 : 18. I was in a **d. s.**, 10 : 9.
Ac. 20:9. Eutychus fallen into **d.s.**

DEEPER.
Le. 13 : 3. plague **d.** than sk.,25,30.
4. if spot not **d.**, 31, 32, 34.
Jb. 11 : 8. it is **d.** than hell, canst?
Is. 33 : 19. a people of **d.** speech

DEEPLY.
Is. 31 : 6. Israel have **d.** revolted
Hos. 9 : 9. They have **d.** corrupted
Mk. 8 : 12. Jes. sighed **d.** in spirit

DEEPNESS.
Mat. 13 : 5. they had no **d.** of earth

DEER.
De. 14 : 5. ye shall eat the fallow **d.**
1 K. 4 : 23. Solomon had fallow **d.**

DEFAMED, ING.
Je. 20 : 10. for I heard **d-g** of many
1 Co. 4 : 13. Being **d.** we intreat

DEFEAT. ⌈17 : 14.
2 S. 15 : 34. **d.** counsel of Ahitho.,

DEFENCE. ⌈with us
Nu. 14 : 9. their **d.** is depart., Lord
2 Ch. 11:5. Rehob. built cities for **d.**
Jb. 22 : 25. Almighty sh. be thy **d.**
Ps. 7 : 10. My **d.** is of G. wh. saveth
31 : 2. be thou for a house of **d.**
59 : 9. I will wait, G. is my **d.**, 17.
16. thou hast been my **d.** ⌈ed, 6.
62:2. G. is my **d.** I sh. not be mov-
89:18. L. is our **d.** Holy One of Isr.
94 : 22. L. is my **d.** and G. rock of
Ec. 7 : 12. wisd. is a **d.** money a **d.**
Is. 4 : 5. upon glory shall be a **d.**
19 : 6. brooks of **d.** sh. be emptied
33:16. his **d.** be munition of rocks
Na. 2 : 5. **d.** shall be prepared
Ac. 19 : 33. would have made his **d.**
22 : 1. hear my **d.** which I make
Ph. 1 : 7. and in **d.** of the gospel
17. knowing I am set for **d.** of gos-

DEFENCED. ⌊pel
Zch. 11 : † 2. **d.** forest is come down
See **Defenced CITIES, CITY.**

DEFEND, ED.
Ju. 10 : 1. Tolah arose to **d.** Israel
2 S. 23 : 12. Shammah **d-d** ground
2 K. 19 : 34. I will **d.** this city, 20 :
6. Is. 37 : 35.-38 : 6.
Ps. 20 : 1. name of God of Jacob **d.**
59 : 1. **d.** fr. them th. rise ag. me
82 : 3. **d.** the poor and fatherless
Is. 31 : 5. so will Lord **d.** Jerus.
Zch. 9:15. L. of hosts shall **d.** them
12:8. in that day shall L. **d.** inhabi.
Ac. 7 : 24. he **d-d** him and avenged

DEFENDEST, ING.
Ps. 5: 11. shout, bec. thou **d.** them
Is. 31:5. **d-g** Jerus. he will deliver it

DEFER.
Ec. 5 : 4. vowest, **d.** not to pay it
Is. 48 : 9. will I **d.** mine anger
Da. 9 : 19. **d.** not for own sake

DEFERRED, ETH.
Ge. 34 : 19. the young man **d-d** not
Pr. 13 : 12. Hope **d-d** maketh sick
19 : 11. discretion **d-h** anger
Ac. 24:22. Felix heard these he **d-d**

DEFIED. See DEFY.

DEFILE.
Le. 11 : 44. nei. **d.** yours., 18:24,30.
15 : 31. when they **d.** my taberu.
18:20. **d.** thyself with neighb.'s wi.
23. Neith. lie with any beast to **d.**
28. land spue not when ye **d.** it
20 : 3. to Molech, to **d.** my sanct.
21 : 4. not **d.** hims., a chief man
11. nor **d.** hims. for fa. or moth.
22 : 8. he shall not eat to **d.** hims.
Nu. 5 : 3. that they **d.** not camps
35 : 34. **d.** not land ye sh. inhabit
2 K. 23:13. high places did king **d.**
Can. 5 : 3. washed my feet, how **d.**
Is. 30:22. sh. **d.** covering of images
Je. 32 : 34. in the house to **d.** it
Eze. 7 : 22. robbers shall **d.** it
9:7. **d.** house, fill courts with slain
20 : 7. **d.** not yours. with idols, 18.
22 : 3. maketh idols to **d.** herself
28 : 7. they sh. **d.** thy brightness
33:26. ye **d.** ev. man neighb.'s wife
37:23. Nor sh. **d.** thems. any more
43 : 7 my name sh. Isr. no more **d.**
44:25. at no dead pers. to **d.** thems.
Da. 1:8. would not **d.** with k.'s meat
Mat. 15 : 18. and they **d.** the man,
20. Mk. 7 : 15, 23.
Mk. 7:18. into man, it cannot **d.** him
1 Co. 3:17. If any man **d.** tem. of G.
1 Ti. 1 : 10. law is for them that **d.**
Jude 8. filthy dreamers **d.** the flesh

DEFILED.
Ge. 34 : 2. lay with Dinah, **d.** her
5. Jacob heard he had **d.** Dinah
13. because he had **d.** Dinah, 27.
Le. 5 : 3. uncleanness a man be **d.**
11 : 43. that he sho. be **d.** thereby
13 : 46. plague in him he sh. be **d.**
15: 32. law of him is **d.** by his seed
18 : 24. in all these nations are **d.**
25. land is **d.** I visit iniq., 27.
19 : 31. nor seek wizards to be **d.**
21 : 1. shall none be **d.** for dead
3. for sister a virgin, may he be **d.**
Nu. 5 : 2. whoso. is **d.** by dead
13. she be **d.**, 27. | 14. if not **d.**, 28.
20. instead of husb. and be **d.**, 29.
6 : 9. hath **d.** head of consecration
12. because his separation was **d.**
9 : 6. who were **d.** by dead body, 7.
19 : 20. bec. he hath **d.** sanctuary
De. 21 : 23. that land be not **d.**
22 : 9. lest fruit of vineyard be **d.**
24 : 4. husb. not take her after **d.**
2 K. 23 : 8. Josiah **d.** high places
10. **d.** Topheth in the valley
1 Ch. 5 : 1. as he **d.** his father's bed
Ne. 13 : 29. bec have **d.** priesthood
Jb. 16 : 15. **d.** my horn in dust
Ps. 74 : 7. **d.** dwellingplace, 79 : 1.
106 : 39. were **d.** with own works
Is. 24 : 5. earth is **d.** under inhabit.
59:3. your hands are **d.** with blood
Je. 2 : 7. when ye ent-d, ye **d.** land
3:9. thro. her whored. she **d.** land
16 : 18. bec. they have **d.** my land
19 : 13. houses of kings sh. be **d.**
Eze. 4 : 13. shall Isr. eat **d.** bread
5 : 11. bec. thou hast **d.** my sanct.
7 : 24. their holy places shall be **d.**
18 : 6. neith. **d.** neighb.'s wife, 15.
11. hath even **d.** neighbour's wife
20 : 43. doings wherein ye been **d.**
22 : 4. **d.** thyself in idols, 23 : 7.
11. another lewdly **d.** dau.inlaw
23 : 13. I saw that she was **d.**
17. Babylonians **d.** her with
38. **d.** my sanctuary in same day
28 : 18. hast **d.** thy sanctuaries
36:17. they **d.** it by their own doings
43 : 8. they have **d.** my holy name
Ho. 5 : 3. and Israel is **d.**, 6 : 10.
Mi. 4 : 11. that say, Let her be **d.**
Mk. 7:2. disciples eat with **d.** hands
Jn. 18 : 28. went not in, lest be **d.**
1 Co. 8 : 7. conscience weak is **d.**
Tit 1 : 15. to them **d.** is nothing
pure, mind and conscience **d.**
He. 12 : 15. thereby many be **d.**
Re. 3 : 4. a few who not **d.** garm
14 : 4. who are not **d.** with women

DEFILEDST, ETH.
Ge. 49:4. to fa.'s bed, then **d-t** thou
Ex. 31:14. **d-h** sab., be put to death
Nu. 19:13. purifi-h not hims., **d.** tab.
35 : 33. not pollute land, blood **d.**
Mat. 15 : 11. Not which goeth into
mouth **d.** ⌈**d.** not
20. to eat with unwashen hands
Mk. 7 : 20. wh. cometh out **d.** man
Jn. 3 : 6. tongue, it **d.** whole body
Re. 21 : 27. in no wise enter that **d.**

DEFRAUD, ED.
Le. 19: 13. shalt not **d.** thy neighb.
1 S. 12:3. whom have I **d.**? whom?
4. they said, Thou hast not **d.**
Mi. 2 : † 2. so they **d.** a man and
Mal. 3 : † 5. ag. those th. **d.** hireling
Mk. 10 : 19. false witness, **d.** not
1 Co. 6 : 7. why not suff. to be **d.**
8. you do wrong, and **d.** brethren
7:5. **d.** not, except it be with consent
2 Co. 7 : 2. we have **d.** no man
1 Th. 4 : 6. that no man **d.** his bro.

DEFY, IED.
Nu. 23:7. curse me Jac., **d.** Israel
8. how **d.** whom L. not **d-d**?
1 S. 17 : 10. I **d.** the armies of Isr.
25. to **d.** Israel is he come up
26. that he should **d.** armies of G.
36. he hath **d.** the armies of God
45. God of Israel thou hast **d.**
2 S.21:21. when he **d.** Isr., Jonathan
slew him, 1 Ch. 20 : 7.
23:9. **d-d** Philis. gathered to battle

DEGENERATE.
Je. 2: 21. art turned into **d.** plant!

DEGREE, S.
2 K. 20 :9. shadow go forward 10 **d-s**,
or back ten **d-s**? Is. 38 : 8 (4).
10. a light thing to go down ten
d-s ; let shadow return ten **d-s**
11. Lord brought shadow ten **d-s**
backw., which it had gone down
in **d-s** † of Ahaz.
Is 38 : 8 (4). shadow of the **d-s**

DEHA'VITES. ⌈D.
Ezr. 4 : 9. Then wrote Dinaites and

DE'KAR. See MAKAZ.

DELAI'AH. ⌈D.
1 Ch. 24 : 18. three and 20th lot to
Ezr 2 : 60 The chil. of D., Ne. 7:62.
Ne. 6 :10. I unto Shemaiah son of D.
Je. 36 : 12. princes sat there, D. and
25. D. made intercession to king

DELAY. [Noun.]
Ac.25:17. without **d.** I sat on judgm.

DELAY, ED, ETH.
Ex. 22 : 29. not **d.** to offer firstfruits
32:1. that Moses **d-d** to come down
Ps. 119:60. **d-d** not to keep com-ts
Mat. 24 : 48. My lord **d-h**, Lu.12:45
Ac. 9 : 38. he would not **d.** to come

DELECTABLE.
Is. 44 : 9. their **d.** things not profit

DELICACIES.
Re.18:3. merchants rich thro. her **d.**

DELICATE.
De. 28 : 54 **d.** man or woman, 56.
Is. 47: 1. thou no more be called **d.**
Je. 6 : 2. likened Zion to **d.** woman
Mi. 1 : 16. thee bald for **d.** children

DELICATES.
Je. 51:24 filled his belly with my **d.**

DELICATELY.
1 S. 15 : 32. Agag came to him **d.**
Pr. 29:21. **d.** bringeth up servant
La. 4 : 5. that did feed **d.** are desol.
Lu. 7 : 25 live **d.** are in k.'s courts
1 Ti. 5 : † 6. she th. liveth **d.** is dead

DELICATENESS.
De. 28 : 56. foot upon ground for **d.**

DELICIOUSLY.
Re. 18 : 7. how she lived d., 9.
DELIGHT. [Noun.]
Ge. 34 : 19. had d. in Jacob's dau.
De. 10:15. L.had a d. in thy fathers
21 : 14. if thou have no d. in her
1 S. 15 : 22. L. as great d. in off-gs?
18 : 22. say, king hath d. in thee
2 S. 15 : 26. if say, I no d. in thee
Jb. 22 : 26. shalt have d. in Almi.
Ps. 1 : 2. his d. is in law of Lord
16 : 3. excellent, in wh. is my d.
27 : † 4. to behold the d. of the L.
119: 24. Thy testimonies are my d.
77. live, for thy law is my d.,174.
Pr. 8:30. I was daily his d.rejoicing
11 : 1. just weight is the Lord's d.
20. upright in their way are his d.
12 : 22. that deal truly are his d.
15 : 8. prayer of upright is his d.
16 : 13. Righte. lips are d. of kings
18 : 2. fool hath no d. in underst.
19 : 10. d. is not seemly for a fool
24 : 25. that rebuke him sh. be d.
29:17. give d. unto thy soul [of d.
Ec. 12 : † 10. preacher sought words
Can. 2 : 3. under shadow with gr.d.
Is. 58 : 2. take d. in appros. to God
13. if thou call the sabbath a d.
62 : † 4. called, My d. is in her
Je. 6 : 10. have no d. in word of L.
Da. 11 : † 41. enter into land of d.
† 45. plant tabern. in mount of d.
DELIGHTS.
2 S. 1: 24. who clothed you with d.
Ps. 119 : 92. Unless law been my d.
143. yet thy com-ts are my d.
Pr. 8 : 31. my d. with sons of men
Ec. 2 : 8. I gat me the d. of men
Can. 7 : 6. pleasant thou, for d.
DELIGHT. [Verb.]
Nu. 14 : 8. If L. d. in us, will bring
1 S. 24 : 3. why king d. in this?
Jb. 27 : 10. Will he d. in Almighty?
34 : 9. that he should d. with God
Ps. 22 : † 8. let him deliv., if he d.
37 : 4. d. thyself also in the Lord
11. meek sh. d. in abund.of peace
40: 8. I d. to do thy will, O my G.
49 : † 13. posterity d. in th. mouth
62 : 4. d. in lies | 68: 30. d. in war
94 : 19. thy comforts d. my soul
119:16. I will d. in thy statutes,35.
47.d.in thy com. | 70.d.in thy law
Pr. 1 : 22. How long scorners d.
2 : 14. d. in frowardness of wick.
Ec. 2 : † 24. d. his senses in good
Is. 1 : 11. d. not in bl. of bullocks
13 : 17. as for gold, sh. not d. in
55 : 2. let your soul d. in fatness
58 : 2. they d. to know my ways
14. shalt d. thyself in the L.
Je. 9 : 24. In these things I d. saith
Mal. 3 : 1. messen. of cov. ye d. in
Ro. 7 : 22. I d. in law aft. inw. man
DELIGHTED.
1 S. 19 : 2. Jona. d. much in David
2 S. 22 : 20. he d. in me, Ps. 18:19.
1 K. 10 : 9. L. d. in thee, 2 Ch. 9:8.
Ne. 9 : 25. d. in thy great goodn.
Es. 2 : 14. except king d. in her
Ps. 22:8. deliv. seeing he d. in him
109 : 17. he d. not in blessing
Can. 2 : † 3. I d. under his shadow
Is. 65 : 12. wherein I d. not, 66: 4.
66 : 11. d. with abund. of her glo.
DELIGHTEST, ETH.
Es. 6 : 6. k. d. to honour, 7, 9, 11.
Ps. 37:23. by L. and he d.in his way
51 : 16. thou d. not in burnt-off.
112 : 1. that d. greatly in his com.
147 : 10. he d. not in str. of horse
Pr. 3 : 12. the son in whom he d.
Is. 42 : 1. elect, in wh. my soul d.
62 : 4. called Hephzi-b. for L. d.
66:3.their soul d.in abomina. [cy.
Mi.7:18.retain.not anger, d. in mer-
Mal. 2 : 17. say, G. d. in that do evil
DELIGHTSOME.
Mal. 3 : 12. ye shall be a d. land
DELI'LAH.
Ju. 16 : 4. a woman in Sorek, D.
6. D. said, Tell me, 10, 13, 18.
12.D. took new ropes bound Sams.
DELIVER.
Ge. 40:13. thou shalt d. Pha.'s cup
Ex. 5 : 18. yet sh he d. the bricks
22 : 7. If man d. unto neighb., 10.
26. d. it by sun goeth down
23 : 31. I will d. inbah. of land
Nu. 21 : 2. If wilt d. this people
35 : 25. shall d. the slayer out
De. 7 : 24. d. kings into thy hand
23 : 15. not d. unto mas. the serv.
25 : 11. to d. her husb. out of hand
32: 39. any th. can d., Is. 43 : 13.
Jos. 2 : 13. will d. our lives fr.death
8 : 7. G. will d. it into your hand
20 : 5. they shall not d. the slayer
Ju. 7 : 7. d. Mid. into thine hand
10 : † 1. arose Tola to d. Israel
11 : 30. if thou sh. d. Ammon into
13 : 5. Samson sh. begin to d. Isr.
1 S. 7 : 14. the coasts did Israel d.
12 : 21. aft. things which cannot d.
23: 4. I will d. Philis., 2 S. 5 : 19.
24 : 4. d. enemy into thine hand
28 : 19. L. will d. Israel to Philis.
2 S. 14:16. k. will hear to d. handm.
20 : † 6. let Sheba d. hims. from
1 K. 18 : 9. Wouldst d. serv. to Ahab
20 : 13. I will d. this mult., 28.
22 : 6. L. shall d. it into king's
hand, 12, 15. 2 Ch. 18 : 5, 11.
2 K. 3 : 18. he will d. the Moabites
12 : 7. d. it for breaches of house
18:35. that L. d. Jerus., Is. 36 : 20.
22: 5. d. into hand of workmen
2 Ch. 25 : 15. could not d. own peo.
28 : 11. and d. captives again
32 : 13. were gods able to d. lands?
14. your G. be able to d. you, 17.
15. no god able to d. his people
Ezr. 7 : 19. those d. thou bef. G. of
Jb. 10:7. none can d. out of thy ha.
22: 30. sh. d. island of innocent
33 : 28. d. soul from going into pit
Ps. 6 : 4. O Lord, d. my soul, 17 : 13.
-22 : 20. 116 : 4.-120 : 2.
7:2. while th. is none to d., 50:22.
33 : 17. nor d. by his gr. strength
19. To d. their soul from death
56 : 13. wilt d. my feet fr. falling?
72 : 12. d. needy when he crieth
74 : 19. d. not soul of turtledove
82 : 4. d. poor out of hand of wick.
89 : 48. sh. he d. his soul fr. grave?
Pr. 4 : 9. a crown sh. she d. to thee
6 : 3. Do this, my son, d. thyself
5. d. thyself as a roe fr. hunter
23 : 14. shalt d. his soul from hell
Ec. 8 : 8. nor wickedness d. those
Is. 5 : 29. none shall d. it [learned
29 : 11. which men d. to one that is
31 : 5. defending also he will d. it.
43 : 13. none can d. out of my ha.
44 : 20. he cannot d. his soul
46 : 2. they could not d. burden
47:14. shall not d. thems. fr. flame
50 : 2. have I no power to d.
Je. 15 : 9. residue will I d. to sword
18 : 21. d. their chil. to the famine
20 : 5. I will d. strength of city
21 : 7. I will d. Zedekiah fr. sword
22:3. d. the spoiled out of the hand
43 : 11. d. such as are for death
51 : 6. d. every man his soul, 45.
Eze. 13 : 21. I will d. my people, 23.
14 : 14. d. their own souls, 20.
16. shall d. sons nor dau-s, 18,20.
33 : 5. taketh warning sh. d. soul
34 : 10. will d. my flock fr. mouth
Da. 3 : 29. no god can d. aft. this sort
8 : 4. nor was any could d. fr. ram
Da.8:7. none th. could d. ram out of
Ho. 2 : 10. none shall d. her out of
Am. 2 : 14. neith. mighty d. hims.
15. swift of foot sh. not d. hims.
6 : 8. I will d. city with all that is
Mi. 5 : 8. teareth and none can d.
6 : 14. shalt take hold, but not d.
Zch. 2 : 7. d. thyself, O Zion
11:6.d.ev. one into neighb.'s hand
Mat. 10 : 21. bro. d. bro. to death
Ac. 25 : 16. not Romans to d. man
1 Co. 5 : 5. d. such one unto Satan
2 Co. 1 : 10. from death, and doth d.
2 Pe. 2 : 9. Lord kn. how to d. godly
DELIVER him.
Ge. 37 : 22. to d. h. to his father
42 : 37. d. h. into my hand, I will
Ex. 21 : 13. G. will d. h. into his
De. 2 : 30. might d. h. into thy
3 : 2. I will d. h. and people into
19 : 12. d. h. into hand of avenger
24 : 13. thou shalt d. h. the pledge
Ju.4:7. I will draw Sisera and d. h.
1 S. 23:20. our part shall be to d. h.
2 S. 14:7. d. h. that smote his bro.
20 : 21. d. h. and I will depart
Jb. 33 : 24. d. h. from going to pit
Ps.22:8.would d. h., let him d. h.
41 : 1. L. d. h. in time of trouble
2. wilt not d. h. unto will of ene.
71 : 11. there is none to d. h. [h.
91 : 14. love upon me, thf. will I d.
15. I will be with him, will d.h.
Pr. 19:19. if d. h., must do it again
Je. 21 : 12. d. h. spoiled fr. oppress.
Eze. 33:12. righteousn. of righteous
shall not d. h.
Da. 6 : 14. heart on Dan. to d. h.
Jon. 4 : 6. shadow to d. h. fr. grief
Mat. 20 : 19. d. h. to Gent. to crucify, Mk. 10 : 33. Lu. 20 : 20.
Ac. 21 : 11. [I will d. h.
26 : 15. What will ye give me, and
27 : 43. let him d. h. now, if he
DELIVER me.
Ge. 32 : 11. d. m. I pray fr. Esau
1 S.17:37.will d.m.out of h.of Goli.
23 : 11. men of Keilah d. m.? 12.
24 : 15. the L. be judge, and d.m.
26:24.let him d.m.out of all tribu
30 : 15. nor d. m. into ha. of mas.
2 S. 3 : 14. d. m. my wife Michal
1 K. 20 : 5. shalt d. m. thy silver
Jb. 6:23. d. m. from enemy's hand,
Ps. 31 : 15.-59 : 1.
Ps. 7 : 1. O L., save me and d. m.
25 : 20. keep my soul, and d. m.
27 : 12. d. m. not unto will of ene.
31 : 2. Bow ear, d. m. speedily
39 : 8. d. m. fr. my transgressions
40 : 13. Be pleased to d. m.
43 : 1. O d. m. fr. deceitful man
51 : 14. d. m. fr. bloodguiltiness
59 : 2. d. m. from workers of iniq.
69 : 14. d. m. out of the mire
18. Draw nigh unto my soul, d.
70 : 1. make haste to d. m. [m.
71 : 2. d. m. in thy righte., 31 : 1.
4. d. m. out of hand of wicked
109 : 21. bec. mercy is good d. m.
119:134.d.m.fr.oppression of man
153. Consider affliction, and d.m.
154. Plead my cause, and d. m.
170. d. m. accord. to thy word
140 : 1. d. m. O L. from evil man
142 : 6. d. m. from my persecutors
143 : 9. d. m. from mine enemies
144 : 7. d. m. out of great waters
11. d. m. from strange children
Is. 44 : 17. d. m., thou art my God
Je. 38:19. Afraid of Jews, lest d. m.
Ac. 25 : 11. no man may d. m.
Ro.7:24.who d.m.fr. body of death?
2 Ti. 4 : 18. L. d. m. fr. evil work
DELIVER thee.
De. 7 : 16. people L. shall d. t.
23 : 14. L. walketh in camp to d. t.

Ju. 15 : 12. to bind, that we d. t., 13.
1 S. 17 : 46. L. will d. t. into mine
23 : 12. L. said, They will d. t. up
1 K. 18 : 23. d. t. 2,000 horses
20 : 6. will d. t. and city, Is. 38 : 6.
Jb. 5 : 19. he shall d. t. in six troub.
36 : 18. great ransom cannot d. t.
Ps. 50 : 15. I will d. t., thou glori-
91 : 3. d. t. fr. snare of fowler [fy
Pr. 2 : 12. d. t. fr. way of evil man
16. To d. t. from strange woman
Is. 57 : 13. let thy companies d. t.
Jer. 1 : 8. I am with thee to d. t.,
19.–15 : 20, 21.
38 : 20. Jere. said, They sh. not n. t.
39 : 17. I will d. t. in that day
18. I will surely d. t.
Eze. 21 : 31. d. t. into hand of brutish
23 : 28. d. t. to them thou hatest
25 : 4. I will d. t. to men of the east
7. I will d. t. for spoil to heathen
Da. 6 : 16. thy God will d. t.
20. thy G. able to d. t. fr. lions?
Ho. 11 : 8. how shall I d. t., Isr.?
Mat. 5 : 25. judge d. t. to, Lu. 12 : 58.

DELIVER them.

Ex. 3 : 8. am come to d. t., Ac. 7 : 34.
De. 7 : 2. when L. sh. d. t., 23.
Jos. 11 : 6. will I d. t. up all slain
Ju. 11 : 9. if L. d. t. before me
20 : 28. to morrow I will d. t. into
1 S. 14 : 37. wilt thou d. t., 2 S. 5 :
19. 1 Ch. 14 : 10.
1 K. 8 : 46. d. t. to enemy, 2 K. 21 : 14.
2 K. 3 : 10. to d. t. into Moab, 13.
1 Ch. 14 : 10. L. said, I will d. t. into
2 Ch. 6 : 36. and d. t. over bef. enem.
25 : 20. of G., that he might d. t.
Ne. 9 : 28. many times didst d. t.
Jb. 5 : 4. neither is any to d. t.
Ps. 22 : 4. trusted, and thou didst d. t.
37 : 40. L. shall help, and d. t.
106 : 43. Many times did he d. t.
Pr. 11 : 6. righte. of upright sh. d. t.
12 : 6. mouth of upright sh. d. t.
24 : 11. forbear to d. t. drawn to
Is. 19 : 20. send Saviour and d. t.
Je. 24 : 9. I d. t. to be remov., 29 : 18.
29 : 21. d. t. into hand of Nebu., 46 : 26
Eze. 7 : 19. gold not d. t., Zph. 1 : 18.
34 : 12. seek my sheep, and d. t.
Am. 1 : 6. they carried to d. t. to Edom
Zch. 11 : 6. out of hand I not d. t.
Ac. 7 : 25. that God would d. t.
He. 2 : 15. d. t. who thro. fear of

DELIVER us.

De. 1 : 27. to d. u. into hand, Jos. 7 : 7.
Ju. 10 : 15. d. u. only this day
20 : 13. d. u. the chil. of Belial
1 S. 4 : 8. Woe unto us, who shall d. u.
12 : 10. d. u. out of hand of ene.
2 K. 18 : 30. L. will d. u., 32. Is. 36 : 15, 18
1 Ch. 16 : 35. d. u. from heathen
2 Ch. 32 : 11. saying, The L. sh. d. u.
Ps. 79 : 9. d. u., purge away sins
Je. 43 : 3. d. u. into hand of Chal.
La. 5 : 8. none that doth d. u.
Da. 3 : 17. our G. is able to d. u.,
and he will d. u.
Mi. 5 : 6. thus sh. he d. u. fr. Assyr.
Mat. 6 : 13. d. u. fr. evil, Lu. 11 : 4.
2 Co. 1 : 10. we trust he will yet d. u.
Ga. 1 : 4. might d. u. fr. evil world

DELIVER you.

Ge. 42 : 34. so will I d. y. your bro.
Le. 26 : 26. d. y. bread by weight
Ju. 10 : 11. Did not I d. y. fr. Egyp.?
13. forsak. me, I will d. y. no more
14. let them d. y. in tribulation
1 S. 7 : 3. he will d. y. fr. Philis.
2 K. 17 : 39. shall d. y. fr. all enem.
18 : 29. shall not be able to d. y.
2 Ch. 32 : 14. be able to d. y. out of
15. how much less your God d. y.
Is. 36 : 14. Hez. not be able to d. y.
46 : 4. I will carry, and will d. y.
Je. 42 : 11. save and d. y. from his
Eze. 11 : 9. d. y. into hands of stran.
Da. 3 : 15. who G. that shall d. y.?
Mat. 10 : 17. they will d. y. up,
19.–24 : 9. Mk. 13 : 9, 11.

DELIVERANCE, S.

Ge. 45 : 7. G. save your lives by gr. d.
Ju. 15 : 18. hast given this great d.
1 S. 11 : † 9. to morrow have d.
2 S. 19 : † 2. d. into mourning
2 K. 5 : 1. L. had given d. unto Syria
13 : 17. arrow of L.'s d. of d. from
1 Ch. 11 : 14. L. saved th. by great d.
2 Ch. 12 : 7. I will grant th. some d.
Ezr. 9 : 13. hast given us such a d.
Es. 4 : 14. then d. arise to Jews
Ps. 18 : 50. Great d. giveth he to
32 : 7. compass me with songs of d.
44 : 4. command d-s for Jacob
Is. 26 : 18. we have not wrought d.
Jo. 2 : 32. in Zion in Jerus. sh. be d.
Ob. 17. upon mount Zion be d.
Lu. 4 : 18. preach d. to the captives
He. 11 : 35. not accepting d.

DELIVERED.

Ge. 9 : 2. ev. beast, into your hand d.
14 : 20. G. who d. thine enemies
25 : 24. her days to be d. fulfilled
Ex. 1 : 19. d. ere midwives come
5 : 23. neith. hast d. thy peo. at all
12 : 27. smote Egyp., d. our houses
18 : 10. who hath d. peo. from Egypt
Nu. 31 : 5. d. out of thousands of Isr.
De. 2 : 36. the L. d. all unto us
3 : 3. G. d. into our hands king of
9 : 10. L. d. two tables of stone
31 : 9. Moses d. law unto priests
Jos. 21 : 44. L. d. enemies into their
Ju. 1 : 4. he d. Canaanites into
3 : 31. Shamgar, he d. Israel
5 : 11. are d. fr. noise of archers
8 : 7. when L. hath d. Zebah
11 : 21. Lord d. Sihon into hand
16 : 23. Our god hath d. Samson, 24.
1 S. 4 : 19. Phinehas' wife to be d.
17 : 35. d. it out of his mouth
30 : 23. d. company came ag. us
2 S. 21 : 6. Saul's sons be d. unto us
1 K. 3 : 17. d. of child with her
18. after I was d. this woman d.
2 K. 19 : 11. thou be d.? Is. 37 : 11.
1 Ch. 11 : 14. d. that parcel and slew
16 : 7. that day Da. d. this psalm
2 Ch. 23 : 9. Jehoiada d. shields
34 : 9. d. money bro-t into h. of G.
15. Hilkiah d. book to Shaphan
Ezr. 5 : 14. vessels were d. unto Shesh.
8 : 36. they d. k.'s commissions
Jb. 22 : 30. d. by pureness of hands
23 : 7. be d. for ever fr. my judge
29 : 12. Because I d. t. poor that cried
Ps. 22 : 5. They cried, and were d.
33 : 16. mighty man not d. by str.
55 : 18. hath d. my soul in peace
56 : 13. hast d. my soul from death,
86 : 13.–116 : 8.
60 : 5. That thy belov. be d., 108 : 6.
69 : 14. be d. fr. them that hate me
78 : 61. d. his strength into captiv.
Pr. 11 : 8. righte. is d. out of troub.
9. thro. knowledge sh. just be d.
21. seed of righte. shall be d.
28 : 26. walketh wisely shall be d.
Ec. 9 : 15. poor wise man d. city
Is. 20 : 6. to be d. fr. king of Assyr.
29 : 12. book d. to him not learned
36 : 19. have they d. Samaria
38 : 17. hast d. it fr. pit of corrup.
49 : 24. shall lawful captive be d.?
25. prey of terrible shall be d.
66 : 7. she was d. of a man child
Je. 7 : 10. are d. to do these abom.
20 : 13. for he hath d. soul of poor
32 : 16. d. evidence unto Baruch
Eze. 3 : 19. hast d. thy soul, 21.–33 : 9.
14 : 16. they only shall be d., 18.
17 : 15. sh. he break cov. and be d.?
31 : 14. they are all d. unto death
Eze. 32 : 20. she is d. to the sword
Da. 3 : 28. d. servants that trusted
6 : 27. who d. Daniel from lions
12 : 1. that time thy peo. sh. be d.
Jo. 2 : 32. call on Lord shall be d.
Am. 9 : 1. that escapeth not be d.
Mi. 4 : 10. to Bab., there thou be d.
Ha. 2 : 9. be d. from power of evil
Mal. 3 : 15. that tempt G. are d.
Mat. 11 : 27. All things are d. unto
me of my Fa., no, Lu. 10 : 22.
25 : 14. serv-ts and d. unto th. goods
27 : 58. Pilate comm. body to be d.
Mk. 7 : 13. tradition wh. ye have d.
9 : 31. d. into hands of, Lu. 24 : 7.
10 : 33. sh. be d. unto chief priests
15 : 15. released Barabbas unto
them, and d. Jesus, Lu. 23 : 25.
Lu. 1 : 57. time came she be d., 2 : 6.
74. Being d. out of hand of ene.
4 : 6. that is d. unto me, I give it
17. was d. unto him book of Esaias
9 : 44. Son of man shall be d. into
12 : 58. give diligence th. thou be d.
18 : 32. he shall be d. unto Gent.
Jn. 16 : 21. soon as she is d. of child
18 : 35. priests have d. thee unto me
36. that I not be d. to Jews
19 : 16. d. he him to be crucified
Ac. 2 : 23. d. by counsel of God
15 : 30. Judas and Silas d. epistle
23 : 33. they d. epistle to governor
27 : 1. they d. Paul to one Julius
28 : 16. centurion d. prisoner
17. was I d. prisoner fr. Jerus.
Ro. 4 : 25. was d. for our offences
6 : 17. form of doct. wh. was d.
7 : 6. now we are d. from the law
8 : 21. creature sh. be d. fr. corrup.
15 : 31. I be d. fr. them not believ.
2 Co. 4 : 11. are always d. to death
2 Th. 3 : 2. be d. from unreas. men
1 Ti. 1 : 20. wh. I have d. unto Satan
2 Ti. 4 : 17. I was d. out of mouth
He. 11 : 11. by faith Sarah was d.
2 Pe. 2 : 7. and d. just Lot, vexed
21. to turn fr. com-t d. unto them
Jude 3. for faith once d. unto saints
Re. 12 : 2. and pained to be d.
4. woman wh. was ready to be d.
See HAND, HANDS.

DELIVERED him.

Ge. 37 : 21. Reuben d. h. out of
Le. 6 : 2. wh. was d. h. to keep, 4.
De. 2 : 33. our God d. h. bef. us
1 K. 13 : 26. thf. Lord d. h. unto lion
17 : 23. Elijah d. h. unto his moth.
Ps. 7 : 4. d. h. that is mine enemy
Mat. 18 : 34. d. h. to the tormentors
27 : 2. and d. h. to Pilate, Mk. 15 : 1.
18. for envy had d. h., Mk. 15 : 10.
26. d. h. to be crucifi., Jn. 19 : 16.
Lu. 7 : 15. Jesus d. h. to his mother
9 : 42. Jesus healed child and d. h.
24 : 20. how our rulers d. h. to
Jn. 18 : 30. we would not have d. h.
Ac. 7 : 10. God d. h. out of afflic.
12 : 4. Herod d. h. to four quatern.

DELIVERED me. [Pha.

Ex. 18 : 4. God d. m. from sword of
Ju. 12 : 3. when I saw ye d. m. not
1 S. 17 : 37. L. that d. m. from lion
2 S. 22 : 18. d. m. fr. ene., Ps. 18 : 17.
20. he d. m. bec. delighted in
me, Ps. 18 : 19. [Ps. 18 : 43.
44. d. m. fr. strivings of people,
49. hast d. m. fr. violent, Ps. 18 : 48.
2 K. 22 : 10. Hilkiah d. m. a book
Jb. 16 : 11. G. d. m. to the ungodly
Ps. 34 : 4. Lord d. m. from my fears
54 : 7. hath d. m. out of all trou.
Jn. 19 : 11. that d. m. greater sin
Ac. 12 : 11. d. m. out of ha. of Herod
2 Ti. 3 : 11. out of all Lord d. m.

DELIVERED thee.

1 S. 24 : 10. L. d. t. to day into my ha.
2 S. 12 : 7. I d. t. out of hand of

Ps. 81: 7. in trouble, and I d. t.
Eze.16:27. I d. t. to them that hate
Jn. 18: 35. priests d. t. unto me

DELIVERED them.

Ex. 18: 8. Moses told how L. d. t.
De. 5: 22. tables of stone, and d.t.
Ju. 3: 9. L. raised deliv-r who d.t.
2 K. 19: 12. gods d. t., Is. 37: 12.
2 Ch. 29: 8. hath d. t. to trouble
Ps. 78: 42. he d. t. from enemy
107: 6. he d.t. out of distresses
20. he d. t. from destructions
Is. 34: 2. hath d. t. to slaughter
Eze. 16: 21. d. t. to pass thro. fire
Lu. 1:2. they d. t. unto us eye wit.
19: 13. d. t. ten pounds, and said
Ac. 16: 4. they d.t. decrees to keep
1 Co. 11: 2. keep ordin. as I d. t.
2 Pe.2:4. d.t. into chains of darkn.

DELIVERED up.

Nu. 21: 3. L. d. u. Canaanites
Jos. 10: 12. L. d. u. Amorites
2 S. 18:28. d.u. men that lift hand
Am. 1:9. they d.u. captiv.to Edom
Ob. 14. nor d.u. those that remain
Mat. 4: † 12. heard that John was
d. u. into prison [ye d. u.
Ac. 3: 13. glorified his Son whom
Ro. 8:32. spared not Son d. him u.
1 Co. 15:24. shall have d.u. kingd.
Re. 20:13. death and hell d.u. dead

DELIVERED us, or you.

Ex. 2:19. Egyp. d.u. fr. shepherds
Ac. 6:14. change customs Mo. d.u.
Ro. 6:17. obeyed doctrine was d. y.
1 Co. 11:23. I rec. that I d.y.,15:3.
2 Co. 1: 10. d.u. fr. so great death
Col. 1: 13. d.u. fr. power of darku.
1 Th. 1:10. Jes. who d.u. fr. wrath

DELIVEREDST, EST.

Ne. 9: 27. thou d. them to enemies
Ps. 35: 10. d. poor fr. him spoileth
Mi. 6: 14. what d. I give to sword
Mat. 25:20. d. unto me five talents
22. L. thou d. unto me 2 talents

DELIVERER.

Ju. 3: 9. raised up d. to Israel, 15.
18: 28. there was no d., 2 S. 14: †
6. Ps. 7: † 2.
2 S. 22: 2. L. is my d., Ps.18: 2.
Ps. 40: 17. thou art my d., 70: 5.
144: 2. my fortress and my d.
Ac. 7: 35. did God send to be a d.
Ro. 11: 26. come out of Sion the d.

DELIVERETH.

Jb. 36: 15. He d. poor in his afflic.
Ps. 18: 48. He d. me from enemies
34: 7. that fear him, and d. them
17. L. d. them out of troubles, 19.
97: 10. d. out of hand of wicked
144: 10. who d. Da. from sword
Pr. 10: 2. righte. d. fr. death, 11:4.
14: 25. A true witness d. souls
31: 24. she d. girdles unto merch.
Is. 42: 22. for a prey, and none d.
Da. 6: 27. God d. and rescueth
Am. 3: † 12. sheph. d. out of mouth

DELIVERING.

Ex. 5: † 23. d. thou hast not deliv.
Lu. 21:12. d. you up to synagogues
Ac. 22: 4. d. into prisons both men
26: 17. d. thee from the Gentiles

DELIVERY.

Is. 26: 17. near time of her d.

DELUSION, S.

Is. 66: 4. I will choose their d-s
2 Th. 2: 11. send them strong d.

DEMAND. [Noun.]

Da. 4: 17. the d. by word of holy

DEMAND, ED.

Ex. 5: 14. d-d Wherefore have ye
not fulfilled your task
2 S. 11: 7. David d-d of Uriah
Jb.38:3. I will d. of thee, 40:7.-42:4.
Da. 2: 27. secret which king d-d
Mat. 2: 4. he d. where C be born
Lu. 3:14. soldiers d-d, What sh. we
Lu. 17:20. when he was d. of Phari.
Ac. 21: 33. captain d. who he was

DE'MAS.

Col. 4:14. and D. greet you, Phm. 24.
2 Ti. 4: 10. D. hath forsaken me

DEME'TRIUS.

Ac. 19: 24. D. a silversmith, who
38. if D. have a matter ag. any
3 Jn. 12. D. hath good report of all

DEMONSTRATION.

1 Co. 2: 4. but in d. of the Spirit

DEN, S.

Ju. 6: 2. chil. of Israel made d-s
Jb. 37: 8. Then beasts go into d-s
38: 40. When they couch in d-s
Ps. 10: 9. he lieth as lion in his d.
104: 22. lay thems. down in d-s
Can. 4: 8. look from the lions' d-s
Is. 11: 8. hand on cockatrice's d.
32: 14. towers be for d-s
Je. 7:11. is this house d. of robbers
9: 11. make Jerus. d. of dragons
10:22. cities of Jud. a d. of dragons
Da. 6: 7. into d. of lions, 12, 16, 24.
17. laid upon mouth of d.
19. king went in haste to d.
23. take Daniel out of the d.
Am. 3: 4. young lion cry out of d.?
Na. 2: 12. filled d-s with ravin
Mat.21:13. my house ye ha. made d.
of thieves, Mk. 11:17. Lu.19:46.
He. 11: 38. they wandered in d-s
Re 6: 15. bondm. and freem. in d-s

DENIED.

Ge. 18:15. Sarah d. saying, I laugh.
1 K. 20: 7. sent and I d. him not
Jb. 31: 28. I should have d. God
Mat. 26: 70. Peter d. 72. Mk. 14:68,
70. Lu. 22:57. Jn. 18: 25, 27.
Lu. 8: 45. all d. they touched him
12: 9. be d. before angels of God
Jn. 1: 20. John d. not, I am not C.
13: 38. till thou hast d. me thrice
Ac. 3: 13. ye d. in pres. of Pilate
14. ye d. Holy One and just
1 Ti. 5: 8. he hath d. the faith
Ro. 2: 13. and hast not d. my faith
3:8. kept my word, not d. my name

DENIETH.

Lu. 12: 9. he that d. me before men
1 Jn. 2: 22. liar, that d. Jesus is C.?
antichrist, that d. Fa. and Son
23. whoso. d. Son, same hath not

DENOUNCE. [Father

De. 30: 18. I d. this day that ye sh.

DENY, ING. [perish

Jos.24:27. witness, lest ye d. your G.
1 K. 2: 16. I ask d. me not, Pr.30:7.
Jb. 8: 18. his place, it shall d. him
Pr 30: 9 Lest I be full and d. thee
Mat. 10:33. whoso-r d. me, him I d.
16: 24. If come after me, let him d.
himself, Mk. 8: 34. Lu. 9: 23.
26: 34. bef. cock crow shalt d. me,
75. Mk. 14:30, 72. Lu. 22:34, 61.
35. die, yet not d. thee, Mk. 14:31.
Lu. 20: 27. d. is any resurrection [it
Ac. 4: 16. manifest, and we can-t d.
2 Ti. 2: 12. if we d. him, he d. us
13 faithful: he cannot d. hims.
3: 5. form of godliness, d-g power
Tit. 1: 16. but in works they d. him
2: 12. d-g ungodliness and lusts
2 Pe. 2: 1. d-g Lord th. bought them
Jude 4. and d-g the only Lord God

DEPART. [hand

Ge. 13: 9. if thou d. to the right
Ex. 18: 27. Moses let fath. in law d.
33: 1. Moses, d. thou and people
Nu. 10: 30. I will d. to mine own la.
De. 9: 7. from day didst d. out of Eg.
Jos. 24: 28. Josh. let people d. into
Ju. 19: 5. rose to d., 7, 8, 9. [inherit-e
1 S. 22: 5. Abide not in the hold; d.
29: 10. as soon as ye be up, d. [d.
11. So David and his men rose to
30: 22. may lead them away and d.
2 S. 11: 12. I will let thee d.
15: 14. make speed to d. lest he
1 K. 11: 21. to Pha. Let me d.
12: 5. d. for three days, then
24. to d. acc. to word of the Lord
Jb. 20: 28. incr. of his house sh. d.
Is. 11: 13. envy of Ephraim sh. d.
52: 11. d. ye, d. ye. go, La. 4:15.
54: 10. the mountains shall d.
Je. 50: 3. shall d. both man and
Mi. 2: 10. d. this is not your rest
Zch. 10: 11. sceptre of E. shall d.
Mat. 8: 18. to d. unto other side
34. d. out of coasts, Mk. 5: 17.
10: 14. when ye d. out of house
shake off, Mk. 6: 11. Lu. 9: 4.
Lu. 2: 27. lettest serv-t d. in peace
13: 31. d. Herod will kill thee
21: 21. let them in midst d. out
Jn. 7: 3. said d. go into Judea
13:1. when Jes. knew he should d.
16: 7. but if I d. I will send him
Ac. 16: 36. now d. and go in peace
39. desir. them to d. out of city
20: 7. Paul preached ready to d.
22: 21. d. I will send thee to Gent.
23: 22. capt. let young man d.
25: 4. he would d. shortly thither
27: 12. more part advised to d.
1 Co. 7: 11. if she d. let her remain
15. if unbelieving d. let him d.
Ph. 1: 23. to d. and to be with C.
Ja. 2: 16. say to them, d. in peace

DEPART from.

Ex. 8: 11. frogs shall d. f. thee
29. swarms of flies may d.f. Pha
21: 22. woman, so fruit d. f. her
Le. 25: 41. shall he d. f. thee
Nu. 16: 26. d. f. tents of wicked
De. 4: 9. lest they d. f. thy heart
Ju. 7: 3. let him d. f. Gilead
1 S. 15: 6. d. f. Amalekites, lest I
2 S.12:10. sword never d.f. thy hou.
20: 21. deliver Sheba, I will d. f.
1 K. 15:19. may d. f. me, 2 Ch.16:3.
2 Ch. 18: 31. moved them to d. f.
Jb. 21:14. unto God, d.f. us, 22:17.
28: 28. to d. f. evil is underst-g
Ps. 6: 8. d. f. me, workers of iniq.,
Mat. 7: 23. Lu. 13: 27.
34: 14. d. f. evil, do good, 37: 27.
101: 4. frow. heart shall d. f. me
119: 115. d. f. me, ye evil doers
139: 19. d. f. me ye bloody men
Pr. 3: 7. fear the Lord, d. f. evil
13: 14. d. f. snares of death, 14:27.
19. abom. to fools to d. f. evil
15: 24. may d. f. hell beneath
16: 6. by fear of L. men d. f. evil
17. highway is to d. f. evil
Is. 14: 25. burden d. f. shoulders
Je. 6: 8. lest my soul d. f. thee
17: 13. that d. f. me be written
31: 36. if ordinances d. f. bef. me
37: 9. Chal. shall surely d. f. us
Eze. 16: 42. my jealousy d. f. thee
Ho. 9: 12. woe when I d. f. them
Mat. 25: 41. d. f. me ye cursed
Mk. 6: 10. abide, till ye d. f. place
Lu. 5: 8. d. f. me, I am sinful man
8: 37. besought him to d. f. them
Ac. 1: 4. should not d. f. Jerus.
18:2. com-d all Jews to d.f. Rome
1 Co. 7: 10. let not wife d. f. husb.
2 Co. 12: 8. besought L. it might d.
1 Ti. 4: 1. some shall d.f. faith [f.
2 Ti. 2: 19. nameth C. d. f. iniq.

Not DEPART.

Ge. 49: 10. sceptre d. n. from Jud.
Jos. 1: 8. book of law shall n. d.
Ju. 6:18. n. d. hence, until I come
2 S. 7: 15. my mercy shall n. d.
22:23. statutes, I did n.d. fr. them
2 Ch. 35:15. might n. d. fr. service
Jb. 7: 19. How long n. d. from me
15: 30. He sh. n. d. out of darku.
Ps. 55: 11. guile d.n. from streets

. 3:21. n. d. from thine eyes, 4:21.
: 7. d. n. fr. words of my mouth
7:13. evil shall n. d. fr. his house
2:6. when he is old he will n. d.
7: 22. yet will n. his foolishn. d.
. 54: 10. my kindness shall n. d.
9: 21. my Spirit, and words, n. d.
. 32: 40. they shall n. d. from me
7:9. Chaldeans, for they sh. n. d.
it. 14: 16. need n. d. give to eat
i. 4: 42. stayed him, that he d. n.
2: 59. shalt n. d., till hast paid

DEPARTED.

3. 12: 4. Ab. d. as L. had spoken
4: 12. took Lot and d.
1:14. Hagar d. | 24:10. Eleazer d.
6: 17. Isaac d. | 31:55. Laban d.
7: 17. man said, They are d.
2: 26. laded their asses and d.
5: 24. sent breth. away, they d.
u. 12: 9. anger kindled, and he d.
2: 7. and the elders of Moab d.
s. 2: 21. sent spies, and they d.
1. 9: 55. d. ev. man, 2 S. 6: 19.
8: 7. Then the five men d., 21.
9: 10. Levite d. | 21:24. Israel d.
S. 6: 6. let Isr. go, and they d.?
0: 42. David arose and d., 22:1, 5.
S. 12: 15. so Nathan d.
.7: 21. d., they came out of well
.9: 24. from day the king d.
K. 12: 5. people d., 2 Ch. 10: 5.
16. So Israel d. unto their tents
.4: 17. Jerob.'s wife d. to Tirzah
19:19. Elijah d. and found Elisha,
0: 9. messengers d. [2 K. 1: 4.
38. prophet d. and waited for k.
K. 5:5. Naam. d. | 10:12. Jehu, 15.
24. let men go, and they d.
19: 36. Sennacherib d., Is. 37: 37.
Ch. 16: 43. people d. every man
21: 4. Joab d. and went thro. Isr.
Ch. 21: 20. Jehoram d. without
s. 105: 38. E. glad when they d.
. 38: 12. Mine age is d. and
. 41:10. Ishm. d. to go to Ammo.
a. 1: 6. Zion all her beauty is d.
at. 2:9. heard king, wise men d., 12.
13. when they were d. behold
14. Joseph and Mary d. into E.
: 12. Jesus d., 9: 27.-11: 1.-12:
9.-13: 53.-14: 13.-15: 21, 29-
16: 4.-19: 15. Mk. 1: 35.-6:46.
-8: 13. Lu. 4: 42. Jn. 4: 3, 43.
-6: 15.-12: 36.
: 7. d. to his house, Lu. 5: 25.
31. were d. spread abroad fame
11: 7. as they d., Jes. began to say
7:5. Judas d. and hanged himself
60. sepul. and d., 28:8. Lu. 24:12.
k. 6: 32. d. into a desert place
:30. d. and passed through Gali.
u. 1: 23. Zach. d. to his house
7: 24. messengers of John were d.
:35. out of wh. devils were d., 38.
: 6. d. and went through towns
10: 30. thieves wounded him d.
35. morr. when the Samaritan d.
24: 12. beheld clothes laid and d.
n. 5: 15. man d. and told the Jews
c. 10:7. angel d. | 11:25 Barna. n.
12: 17. Peter d. | 18:4. they n. to
14: 20. Paul d. [der
15:39. Paul and Barnabas d. asun-
40. Paul chose Silas and d.
16: 40. Paul and Silas d.
17: 15. to come with speed they d.
18: 7. Paul d., 23.-20: 1, 11.
21: 5. d. our way, 8.-28: 10, 11.
28: 25. when agreed not, they d.
29. he said these words, Jews d.
Ti. 4:10. Demas forsaken me, is d.
h. 15. he therefore d. for season
e. 6: 14. heaven d. as a scroll

DEPARTED from.

e. 26:31. they d. f. Isaac in peace
31: 40. sleep d. f. mine eyes
Ex. 19:2. d. f. Rephidim, Nu. 33:15.
35: 20. all Israel d. f. Moses
Le. 13: 58. if plague be d. f. them
Nu. 10: 33. they d. f. mount of L.
12: 10. cloud d. f. off tabernacle
14: 9. their defence is d. f. them
33:3. d. f. Rameses | 6. d. f. Succo.
8. d. f. Pi-hai. | 13. d. f. Dophkah
15. And they d. f., 17, 18, 19, 20,
27, 30, 31, 35, 41, 42, 43, 44, 45, 48.
De. 1: 19. when we d. f. Horeb
Jos. 22: 9. d. f. chil. of Isr. out of
Ju. 16: 20. wist not L. was d. f. him
1 S. 4: 21. glory is d. f. Israel, 22.
10: 2. When d. f. me, thou sh. find
15: 6. Kenites, d. f. Amalekites
16: 14. Spirit of L. d. f. Saul, 18:12.
23. and evil spirit d. f. him
28: 15. G. is d. f. me, and ans. not
16. seeing L. is d. f. thee
1 K. 20:36. soon as thou art d. f. me
2 K. 3: 27. they d. f. him to own
5: 19. d. f. Elisha a little, 8: 14.
19:8. Senna. d. f. Lachish, Is. 37:8.
2 Ch. 24:25. they were d. f. him
Ezr. 8: 31. Then we d. f. Ahava
Ps. 18:21. not wickedly d. f. my G.
Is. 7: 17. day Ephraim d. f. Jud.
Je. 29: 2. smiths were d. f. Jerus.
37:5. Chal-s heard they d. f. Jerus.
Eze. 6:9. whorish heart hath d. f. me
10: 18. glory of L. d. f. threshold
Da. 4: 31. kingdom is d. f. thee
Ho. 10: 5. glory of Sama. is d. f. it
Mat. 15: 29. and Jesus d. f. thence
19: 1. finished, he d. f. Galilee
20: 29. as they d. f. Jericho
24: 1. Jesus d. f. the temple
28: 8. they d. quickly f. sepul.
Mk. 1:42. leprosy d. f. him, Lu. 5:13.
Lu. 1: 38. angel d. f. Mary
4: 13. devil d. f. him for season
9: 33. as they d. f. him, Pet. said
Ac. 5: 41. they d. f. the council
12: 10. forthwith angel d. f. him
13: 14. when they had d. f. Perga
15: 38. John d. f. Pamphylia
17: 33. Paul d. f. them, 18: 1.-
19: 9. Ph. 4: 15.
19: 12. diseases d. f. them
22: 29. straightway they d. f. him
Re. 18: 14. fruits lusted after are d.
f. thee, things dainty are d.

DEPARTED not from.

2 S. 22: 22. I have n. wickedly d.
f. my God, Ps. 18: 21.
2 K. 3:3. he d. n. f. sins of, 13: 2
10:29. Jehu d. n. f. sins of Jerob.,
31.-13: 6, 11.-14: 24.-15: 9,
18.-17: 22.
18: 6. Heze. d. n. f. following L.
2 Ch. 8: 15. d. n. f. com-t of king
20: 32. Jehosh. d. n. f. way of Asa
34: 33. they d. n. f. following L.
Ne. 9: 19. cloud d. n. f. them by
Ps. 119: 102. I d. n. f. thy judgm.
Lu. 2: 37. Anna d. n. f. the temp.

DEPARTED out, or not out.

Ge. 12:4. old when he d. o. of Haran
Ex. 33: 11. Joshua d. n. o. of tab.
Nu. 14: 44. ark d. n. o. of camp
De. 24: 2. when she is d. o. of house
Ju. 6: 21. angel d. o. of his sight
17: 8. Levite d. o. of Beth-lehem
1 S. 23: 13. David d. o. of Keilah
2 S. 11: 8. Uriah d. o. of king's h.
Mal. 2: 8. ye are d. o. of the way
Mat. 17:18. rebuk. devil, and he d. o.

DEPARTETH.

Jb. 27: 21. wind carrieth, and he d.
Pr. 11: † 22. wom. who d. fr. discret.
14: 16. A wise man d. from evil
Ec. 6: 4. in with vanity, d. in dark.
Is. 59: 15. he that d. fr. evil a prey
Je. 3:20 as a wife treacherously d.
17:5. man whose heart d. from L.
Na. 3: 1. woe to city, prey d. not
Lu. 9: 39. bruising him hardly d.

DEPARTING.

Ge. 35:18. as her soul was in d. she
Ex. 16: 1. after their d. out of E.
Is. 59: 13. in d. away from God
Da. 9:5. sinned, by d. fr. precepts, 11.
Ho. 1:2. have com. whored. d. fr. L.
Mk. 6: 33. the people saw them d.
7: 31. and d. from coast of Tyre
Ac. 13:13. John d. fr. them, return.
20: 29. aft. my d. sh. wolves enter
He. 3: 12. evil heart, in d. fr. God
11: 22. mention of d. of Israel

DEPARTURE.

Eze. 26: 18. isles be troub. at thy d.
2 Ti. 4: 6. time of my d. is at hand

DEPEND.

Jb. 22: † 2. doth his good success d.

DEPOSED.

Da. 5: 20. he was d. from throne

DEPRIVED, ING.

Ge. 27: 45. why be d. of both in
Jb. 39:17. God hath d. her of wisd.
Ps. 35: † 12. to the d-g of my soul
Is. 38: 10. am d. of residue of yrs.

DEPTH.

Jb 28: 14. d. saith it is not in me
38: 16. walked in search of d.?
Ps. 33: 7. he layeth up the d. in st.
69: † 2. I sink in the mire of d.
Pr. 8:27. set a compass upon the d.
25:3. heav. for height, earth for d.
Is. 7: 11. ask it either in the d. or
Jon. 2: 5. the d. closed me round
Mat. 18:6. better drowned in the d.
Mk. 4: 5. no d. of earth, it withered
Ro. 8: 39. nor d. separate us fr. love
11: 33. O the d. of the riches both
Ep. 3: 18. what is d. of love of C.

DEPTHS.

Ex. 15: 5. d. have covered them
8. d. were congealed in the sea
De. 8: 7. d. th. spring out of hills
Ps. 68: 22. bring my peo. fr. the d.
71: 20. sh. bring me fr. d. of earth
77: 16. the d. were troubled
78: 15. gave drink as out of gr. d.
106: 9. he led them thro. the d. as
107: 26. they go down again to d.
130: 1. Out of the d. have I cried
Pr. 3:20. By his knowl. d. are broken
8:24. When no d. I was bro-t forth
9: 18. her guests are in d. of hell
Is. 51: 10. made d. of sea a way
Eze. 27: 34. shalt be broken in d.
Mi. 7: 19. will cast their sins into d.
Re. 2: 24. not known d. of Satan

DEPUTED.

2 S. 15: 3. is no man d. of the k.

DEPUTY, IES.

1 K. 22: 47. in Edom, a d. was k.
Es. 8: 9. it was written to d-s
9: 3. and the d-s helped the Jews
Ac. 13: 7. a sorcerer with the d.
8. seeking to turn d. fr. the faith
12. d. when he saw believed
18: 12. Gallio was d. of Achaia
19: 38. are d-s let them implead

DER'BE. [D. | 20.

Ac. 14:6. They fled unto Lystra and
16: 1. Then came he to D. | 20: 4.

DERIDE, ED.

Ha. 1:10. shall d. every strong hold
Lu. 16: 14. Pharisees d-d him
23: 35. rulers with the peo. d-d him

DERISION.

Jb. 30: 1. younger, have me in d.
Ps. 2: 4. L. shall have them in d.
44: 13. d. to them about us, 79:4.
59: 8. shalt have heathen in d.
119: 51. proud have had me in d.
Je. 20: 7. in d. daily | 8. a d. daily
48: 26. Moab shall be in d., 39.
Je. 48:27. was not Isr. a d. to thee?
La. 3: 14. I was a d. to my people
Eze. 23: 32. drink and be in d.

Eze.36:4. to cities which became a d.
Ho. 7: 16. this sh. be their d. in E.

DESCEND.

Nu. 34:11. border shall d. unto sea
1 S. 26: 10. he shall d. into battle
Ps. 49: 17. glory sh. not d. aft. him
65: † 10. caus. rain d. into furrows
104: † 8. to ascend, valleys d., 10.
Is. 5: 14. rejoiceth sh. d. into it
Eze. 26:20. that d. into pit, 31: 16.
Mk. 15: 32. Let C. d. from cross
Ac. 11: 5. I saw vision, vessel d.
Ro. 10: 7. Who shall d. into deep?
1 Th. 4: 16. L. shall d. from heaven

DESCENDED.

Ex. 19: 18. Lord d. upon Sinai in [fire
33: 9. the cloudy pillar d.
34: 5. L. d. in the cloud
De. 9: 21. brook that d. out of mt.
Jos. 2: 23. two men d. fr. mountain
17: 9. coast d. unto river Kanah
18: 13. the border d., 16, 17.
Ps. 133:3. as dew that d. upon Zion
Pr. 30: 4. Who hath asc. up, or d.?
Mat. 7: 25. rain d. floods came, 27.
28: 2. angel d. from heaven
Lu. 3: 22. H. G. d. in bodily shape
Ac. 24: 1. Ananias high-priest d.
Ep. 4: 10. he that d. is the same, 9.

DESCENDETH, ING.

Ge. 28: 12. angels d-g, Jn. 1: 51.
Is. 15: † 3. ev. one shall howl d-g
Mat. 3:16. saw Spirit d-g, Mk.1:10.
Jn. 1: 32. saw Spirit d-g like dove
33. Upon whom sh. see Spirit d-g
Ac.10:11. vessel d-g as sheet [above
Ja. 3: 15. This wisd. d-h not from
Re. 21: 10. city d-g out of heaven

DESCENT.

Mi. 1: † 4. as waters down a d.
Lu. 19: 37. at d. of mount of Olives
He. 7: 3. Melchisedec without d.
6. whose d. is not counted fr. them

DESCRIBE, ED, ETH.

Jos. 18: 4. thro. land and d. it, 6, 8.
8. Joshua charged them that went to d. the land [book
9. and they d-d it by cities in a
Ju. 8:14. he d-d unto him princes
Ro. 4: 6. as Da. d-h blessedness
10: 5. Moses d-h righteousn. of law

DESCRIPTION.

Jos. 18: 6. ye shall bring d. to me

DESCRY.

Ju. 1: 23. sent to d. Beth-el

DESERT.

Ex. 3: 1. flock to back side of d.
5: 3. three days' journey into d.
19: 2. were come to d. of Sinai
23: 31. bounds from d. unto river
Nu. 20: 1. Isr. came into d. of Zin
27: 14. ye rebelled in d. of Zin
33: 16. removed from d. of Sinai
2 Ch. 26: 10. built towers in the d.
Jb. 24: 5. as wild asses in d. go
Ps. 75: † 6. promotion not from d.
78: 40. how oft grieve him in d.?
102: 6. I am like an owl of d.
106: 14. tempted God in the d.
Is. 13: 21. wild beasts of d. shall lie there, 34: 14. Je. 50: 39.
21: 1. as whirlwinds, so fr. the d.
35: 1. d. rejoice | 6. streams in d.
40:3. make straight in d. high-way
41: 19. I will set in d. the fir-tree
43: 19. even make rivers in d., 20.
51: 3. make her d. like garden of
Je. 17: 6. sh. be like heath in d.
25:24. that dwell in d. shall drink
50: 12. Chaldea shall be a d.
Eze. 47: 8. these waters go into d.
Mat. 24: 26. Behold, he is in d.
Jn. 6: 31. did eat manna in the d.
Ac. 8: 26. Jerus. to Gaza, wh. is d.

DESERT land.

De. 32: 10. He found him in a d. l.
Pr. 21: † 19. better dwell in l. of d.

DESERT place.

Mk. 6: 31. Come ye into a d. p.
32. depart. into a d. p., Mat. 14: 13. Lu. 4: 42. [Lu. 9: 12.
35. This is a d. p., Mat. 14. 15.
Lu. 9: 10. went privately into d. p.

DESERTS.

Is. 48:21. when he led them thro. d.
Je. 2:6. L. led us thro. a land of d.
5: † 6. wolf of d. shall spoil
Eze. 13: 4. prophets like foxes in d.
Lu. 1: 80. John was in the d. till
He. 11: 38. they wandered in d.

DE'SERT, S. [Deserving.]

Ps. 28: 4. render them their d.
Eze.7:27. acc. to their d-s will I judge

DESERVE, ETH, ING.

Ezr. 9:13. less than our iniquities d.
Jb. 11: 6. exact. less than iniq. d-h
Ju. 9: 16. done to him acc. to d-g

DESIRABLE.

Ge. 27: † 15. Rebek. took d. raiment
1 K. 20: † 6. d. in thy eyes
Ezr. 8: † 27. of copper d. as gold
Is. 44: † 9. d. things sh. not profit
La. 1: † 7. remem. all her d. things
† 10. his hand upon her d. things
2: † 4. slew all the d. of the eye
Eze. 23: 6. all d. young men, 12, 23.
Jo. 3: † 5. into temp. my d. things

DESIRE. [Noun.]

Ge. 3: † 6. tree was d. to the eyes
16. thy d. shall be to thy husb.
4: 7. to thee shall be his d. thou
De. 18: 6. with all d. of his mind
21:11. hast a d. to have her to wife
1 S. 9: 20. on whom is d. of Israel?
23: 20. acc. to all d. of thy soul
2 S. 23: 5. all my salva., all my d.
1 K. 5: 8. do thy d. conc. timber
9. accompl. my d. in giving food
10. acc. to all Solomon's d., 9: 11.
9: 1. Sol. had finished all his d.
† 19. d. of Sol. which he desired
10: 13. Sol. gave queen of Sheba all her d., 2 Ch. 9: 12.
2 Ch. 15: 15. sought with whole d.
21: † 20. Jeho. departed without d.
32: † 27. for instruments of d.
36: † 10. took vessels of d. to Bab.
Jb. 9: † 26. my days as ships of d.
14: 15. wilt have a d. to work of
31: 16. If withheld poor from d.
35. my d. is that Al. would ans.
33: † 20. soul abhorreth meat of d.
34: 36. My d. is Job be tried to
Ps. 10: 3. wicked boasteth of d.
17. hast heard d. of humble
21: 2. hast given him heart's d.
38: 9. L. all my d. is before thee
54:7. seen d. upon enemies, 92: 11.
59:10. G. sh. let me see d. upon ene.
78: 29. he gave them their own d.
92: 11. hear my d. of the wicked
106: † 24. despised a land of d.
112: 8. until he see his d. on ene.
10. d. of wicked shall perish
118:7. sh. see my d. on th. hate me
145:16. satisfiest d. of ev. living th.
19. fulfil d. of them fear him
Pr. 10:24. d. of righte. be granted
11: 23. d. of righteous is only good
13: 12. d. cometh, it is tree of life
19. d. accomplished is sweet
18:1. Thro. d. a man having separ.
19: 22. d. of a man is his kindn.
21: 25. d. of slothful killeth him
Ec. 6: 9. than wandering of d.
12: 5. d. shall fail, bec. man goeth
Can. 7: 10. his d. is toward me [d.
Is. 2: † 16. of L. on all pictures of
26: 8. d. of soul is to thy name
32: † 12. lament for fields of d.
Je. 2:† 24. snuffeth wind at d. of her
3: † 19. how give thee land of d.?
12: † 10. portion of d. a wildern.
25: † 34. fall like a vessel of d.
Je. 44: 14. to wh. ye have d. to ret.
Eze. 24: 16. take d. of thine eyes
21. profane d. of your eyes, 25.
26: † 12. destroy houses of thy d.
Da. 11: † 8. into E. ves. of their d.
37. neith. he regard d. of women
Ho. 10: 10. my d. I should chastise
13: † 15. treasure of vessels of d.
Am. 5: † 11. vineyards of d.
Mi. 7: 3. uttereth mischievous d.
Na. 2: † 9. end of vessels of d.
Ha. 2: 5. enlargeth his d. as hell
Hag. 2:7. d. of all nations sh. come
Zch. 7: † 14. laid land of d. desol.
Lu. 22: 15. With d. I desir. to eat
Ro. 10: 1. my heart's d. to G. for
15: 23. having a great d. to come
2 Co. 7: 7. told us your earnest d.
11. what fear, what vehement d.
Ph. 1: 23. having a d. to depart
1 Th. 2: 17. to see your face with d.

DESIRES.

Ge. 6: † 5. d. of his heart are evil
Ps. 37: 4. sh. give d. of thy heart
140: 8. grant not, d. of wicked
Da. 9: † 23. a man of d., 10: † 11.
10: † 3. I ate no bread of d.
Ho. 9: † 16. slay d. of their womb
Ep. 2: 3. fulfilling d. of flesh

DESIRE. [Verb.]

Ex. 10: 11. serve the L.; ye did d.
34: 24. neith. sh. any d. thy land
De. 5: 21. Neith. d. neighb.'s wife
7: 25. thou shalt not d. the silver
Ju. 8: 24. Gideon said, I would d.
1 K. 2: 20. I d. one small petition
2 K. 4: 28. Did I d. a son of my
Ne. 1: 11. servants who d. to fear
Jb. 13: 3. I d. to reason with God
21: 14. d. not knowl. of thy ways
33: 32. for I d. to justify thee
36: 20. d. not night when people
Ps. 40: 6. offering didst not d.
45: 11. k. greatly d. thy beauty
65: † 9. after hast made it d. rain
70: 2. to confusion th. d. my hurt
73: 25. none on earth I d. besides
Pr. 3:15. all thou canst d. not to be
23: 6. neither d. his dainty meats
24: 1. evil men, nor d. to be with
Is. 53: 2. no beauty we sho. d. him
Je. 22: 27. land they d. to return
42: 22. die in place ye d. to go
Da. 2: 18. I would d. mercies of G.
Am. 5: 18. Woe that d. day of L.
Mk. 9: 35. If any man d. to be first
10: 35. do for us whatso. we sh. d.
11: 24. What ye d. when ye pray
15: 8. d. him to do as he done
Lu. 17: 22. d. to see one of the days
20: 46. d. to walk in long robes
Ac. 23: 20. Jews agreed to d. thee
28:22. d. to hear what thou think.
1 Co. 14: 1. and d. spiritual gifts
2 Co. 11: 12. them wh. d. occasion
12: 6. tho. I would d. to glory, I
Ga. 4: 9. ye d. to be in bondage
20. I d. to be present with you
21. ye that d. to be under law
6: 12. as d. to make a fair shew
13. d. to have you circumcised
Ep. 3: 13. I d. ye faint not [fruit
Ph. 4: 17. not bec. I d. gift, I d.
Col. 1:9. d. ye be filled with knowl.
1 Ti. 2: † 1. I d. supplica. be made
3: 1. If man d. office of a bishop
He. 6: 11. d. ev. one to show dili.
11: 16. they d. a better country
Ja. 4: 2. ye d. to have, and cannot
1 Pe. 1:12. wh. angels d. to look into
2: 2. As babes d. the sincere milk
Re. 9: 6. men shall d. to die, and

DESIRED.

Ge. 3: 6. tree d. to make wise
1 S. 12: 13. behold king wh. ye d.
1 K. 9:19. which Sol. d., 2 Ch. 8:6.
2 Ch. 11: 23. Rehob. d. many wives

2 Ch.21: 20. departed with-t being d.
Es. 2: 13. whatso. she d. was given
Jb. 20: 20. not save of that he d.
Ps. 19: 10. More to be d. than gold
27: 4. One thing I d. of Lord
39:† 11. that wh. is to be d. in him
107: 30. bringeth unto their d. ha-
132: 13. d. Zion for habitation [ven
14. here will I dw., for I have d.
Pr. 8: 11. all d. not to be compar.
21: 20. There is a treasure to be d.
Ec. 2: 10. what my eyes d. I kept
Is. 1: 29. asha. of oaks ye have d.
26: 9. have I d. thee in night
Je. 17: 16. neither I d. woeful day
Da. 2: 16. Dan. d. of the king time
23. made kn. what we d. of thee
11: † 38. honour G. with things d.
Ho. 6: 6. I d. mercy not sacrifice
Mi. 7: 1. my soul d. first ripe fruit
Zph. 2: 1. gather, O nation, not d.
Mat. 13: 17. righte. have d. to see
16: 1. d. he would shew a sign
Mk. 15:6. prisoner whomsoever they
d., Lu. 23: 25. [to eat
Lu. 7: 36. one of the Phari. d. Jes.
9: 9. who is this, he d. to see him
10: 24. many kings have d. to see
22: 15. I have d. to eat this pass.
31. Satan hath d. to sift you as
23: 25. released whom they d.
Jn.12: 21. d. him, Sir we wo. see Jes.
Ac. 3: 14. d. a murderer to be grant.
7: 46. d. to find a tab. for the G.
8: 31. the eunuch d. Philip to come
9: 2. Paul d. of high priest letters
12: 20. they of Sidon d. peace
13: 7. Sergius Paulus d. to hear
21. afterward they d. a king
28. d. Pilate that he be slain
16: 39. d. them to depart out
18: 20. d. him to tarry longer
25: 3. d. favour ag. Paul that he
28: 14. were d. to tarry 7 days
1 Co.16: 12. d. him to come unto you
2 Co. 8: 6. we d. Titus to finish
12: 18. I d. Titus, with him I sent
1 Jn. 5: 15. have petitions we d.

DESIREDST. [of God

De. 18: 16. Accord. to all thou d.
Mat. 18: 32. I forgave, bec. thou d.

DESIREST.

Ps. 51: 6. d. truth in inward parts
16. thou d. not sacrifice, else

DESIRETH.

De. 14: 26. for whatso. thy soul d.
1 S. 2: 16. as much as thy soul n.
18: 25. say to Da., k. d. not dowry
20: 4. d. I will do, 1 K. 11: 37.
2 S. 3: 21. reign over all heart d.
Jb. 7: 2. As a serv-t d. the shadow
23: 13. soul d. that he doeth
Ps. 17: † 12. lion that d. to ravin
34: 12. what man is he that d. life
68: 16. hill God d. to dwell in
Pr. 12: 12. wicked d. net of evil
13: 4. sluggard d. and hath not
21: 10. soul of wicked d. evil
Ec. 6: 2. wanteth nothing he d.
Lu. 5: 39. drunk old wine d. new
14: 32. he d. conditions of peace
1 Ti. 3: 1. bishop, d. a good work

DESIRING. [47.

Mat. 12: 46. d. to speak with him,
20: 20. d. a certain thing of him
Lu. 8: 20. brethren d. to see thee
16: 21. d. to be fed with crumbs
Ac. 9: 38. d. him he wo. not delay
19: 31. d. him th. he not advent.
25: 15. d. to have judgm. ag. him
2 Co. 5: 2. d. to be clothed upon
1 Th. 3: 6. d. greatly to see us
1 Ti. 1: 7. d. to be teachers of
2 Ti. 1: 4. Greatly d. to see thee

DESIROUS.

Pr. 23: 3. Be not d. of his dainties
Zph. 2: † 1. gather, O nation not d.
Lu. 23: 8. Herod was d. to see him
Jn. 16: 19. kn. they were d. to ask
2 Co. 11: 32. d. to apprehend me
Ga. 5: 26. not be d. of vainglory
1 Th. 2: 8. affectionately d. of you

DESOLATE.

2 S. 13: 20. Tamar remain. d. in ho.
2 Ch. 36: 21. lay d. she kept sab.
Jb. 15: 28. dwelleth in d. cities
16: 7. made d. all my company
30: 3. wildern. in former time d.
38: 27. To satisfy the d. ground
Ps. 25: 16. have mercy, for I am d.
40: 15. Let them be d. for a reward
69: 25. Let their habitation be d.
143: 4. my heart within me is d.
Is. 1: 7. Your country is d. your
3: 26. she d. sh. sit upon ground
7: 19. shall rest all in d. valleys
13: 22. beast sh. cry in d. houses
24: 6. that dwell therein are d.
49: 8. to inherit d. heritages
21. lost my children, and am d.
54: 1. more are chil. of d., Ga. 4: 27.
3. make d. cities to be inhabited
Je. 2: 12. be ye very d. saith Lord
6: 8. lest I make thee d. a land
9: † 10. habita. of wildern. are d.
11. I will make cities of Judah d.,
10: 22.-33: 10.-44: 6.
10: 25. have made his habita. d.
12: 11. made it d. and d. it mourn.
19: 8. I will make this city d.
32: 43. It is d. without man, 33: 12.
49: 20. sh. make habita. d., 50: 45.
La. 1: 4. all her gates are d.
13. made me d. all day, 3: 11.
16. my children are d. the enemy
4: 5. that did feed delicately are d.
5: 18. Bec. of mt. of Zion wh. is d.
Eze. 6: 6. that your altars be d.
19: 7. he knew their d. palaces
20: 26. that I might make them d.
25: 13. I will make Edom d.
26: 19. I shall make thee a d. city
29: 12. in the countries d., 30: 7.
30: 14. I will make Pathros d.
35: 3. Seir, I will make thee d., 7.
12. They are d. given us to con-
14. I will make thee d. [sume
15. didst rejoice, because it was d.
36: 3. bec. they have made you d.
4. saith the Lord to d. wastes
35. d. cities are become fenced
36. know I the L. plant th. was d.
Da. 9: 17. shine on sanct. th. is d.
27. for abom. he shall make it d.
11: 31. abom. that mak. d., 12: 11.
Ho. 2: † 12. I will make d. her vines
13: 16. Samaria shall become d.
Jo. 1: 17. the garners are laid d.
18. flocks of sheep are made d.
Mi. 1: 7. all the idols will I lay d.
6: 13. making thee d. bec. of sins
Zph. 3: 6. their towers are d. [35.
Mat. 23: 38. house left d., Lu. 13:
Ac. 1: 20. Let his habitation be d.
1 Ti. 5: 5. a widow indeed and d.
Re. 17: 16. hate whore, and make d.
18: 19. in one hour is she made d.

Land DESOLATE.

Ge. 47: 19. that the l. be not d.
Ex. 23: 29. lest the l. become d.
Le. 26: 34. l. enjoy sab. long as lieth
d., 35, 43. 2 Ch. 36: 21.
Is. 6: 11. Until the l. be utterly d.
13: 9. day of L. cometh to lay l. d.
62: 4. neither l. be termed d.
Je. 4: 7. is gone to make l. d.
27. L. said, whole l. shall be d.
7: 34. cease mirth, for l. sh. be d.
12: 11. the whole l. is made d.
18: 16. to make their l. d. and a
25: 38. l. is d. bec. of his anger
32: 43. l. whereof ye say it is d.
50: 3. nation shall make her l. d.
Eze. 6: 14. make l. d. yea more d.
Eze.12: 19. her l. may be d. from all
20. cities waste, the l. shall be d.
14: 16. l. shall be d., Mi. 7: 13.
15: 8. and I will make the l. d.
19: 7. l. was d. and the fullness
25: 3. l. of Israel when it was d.
29: 9. l. of E. shall be d., 10, 12.-
30: 7.-32: 15. [and the pomp
33: 28. for I will lay the l. most d.
29. I am L., when laid l. most d.
36: 34. n. l. be tilled, it lay d.
35. l. that was d. is like Eden
Jo. 2: 20. will drive him unto a l. d.
Zch. 7: 14. l. was d. they laid l. d.

DESOLATE places.

Jb. 3: 14. built d. p. for thems.
Ps. 109: 10. seek bread out of d. p.
Is. 49: 19. d. p. sh. be too narrow
59: 10. we are in d. p. as dead
Eze. 6: 6. and high p. shall be d.
26: 20. when I sh. set thee in p. d.
38: 12. to turn hand upon d. p.
Am. 7: 9. high p. of Isaac sh. be d.
Mal. 1: 4. will ret., and build d. p.

Shall be, or shalt be DESOLATE.

Le. 26: 22. and your highways s. b. d.
33. your land s. b. d. and cities
Jb. 15: 34. cong. of hypocrites s. b. d.
Ps. 34: 21. that hate righte. s. b. d.
22. none th. trust in him s. b. d.
Is. 5: 9. many houses s. b. d.
15: 6. of Nimrim s. b. d., Je. 48: 34.
27: 10. Yet defenced city s. b. d.
Je. 26: 9. this city s. b. d. without
33: 10. place ye say s. b. d. [habi.
46: 19. Noph s. b. d. without in-
48: 9. Moab for the cities s. b. d.
49: 2. Rabbah s. b. a d. heap
50: 13. Babylon s. b. wholly d.
51: 26. thou s. b. d. for ever
Eze. 6: 4. your altars s. b. d.
29: 12. cities of E. s. b. d. 40 years
33: 28. Mountains of Isr. s. b. d.
35: 4. O mount Seir, thou s. b. d., 15.
Ho. 5: 9. Ephr. s. b. d. in the day

DESOLATE wilderness.

Je. 12: 10. my pleas. portion a d. w.
Jo. 2: 3. behind them it is a d. w.
3: 19. E. and Edom sh. be a d. w.

DESOLATION. [d.

Le. 26: 31. bring your sanct. unto
32. I will bring the land into d.
Jos. 8: 28. Joshua made Ai a d.
2 K. 22: 19. they should become a d.
2 Ch. 30: 7. who gave them to d.
Jb. 30: 14. in d. they rolled upon me
Ps. 73: 19. brought into d. in mo.
Pr. 1: 27. When fear cometh as d.
3: 25. be not afraid of d. of wick.
Is. 6: † 11. until land desol. with d.
17: 9. in that day there shall be d.
24: 12. in the city is left d.
47: 11. d. shall come upon thee sud.
51: 19. two things are come, d.
64: 10. Zion is a wild., Jerus. a d.
Je. 9: † 11. cities of Jud. a d., 34: 22.
22: 5. this house sh. become a d.
25: 11. this whole land sh. be a d.
18. to make Jerusa. and Jud. a d.
† 38. forsak. covert their land is d.
44: 2. behold, this day they are d.
22. is your land a d. [Hazor
49: 13. Bozrah a d. | 17. Edom | 33.
50: 23. how is Bab. become a d.
51: 29. to make land of Bab. a d.
43. her cities are a d. a dry land
La. 3: 47. snare is come upon us d.
Eze. 7: 27. prince clothed with d.
23: 33. sh. be filled with cup of d.
33: † 28. will lay the land d. and d.
35: † 7. make mt. Seir d. and d.
Da. 8: 13. conc. the transgr. of d.
Ho. 12: 1. Ephr. daily increas-h d.
Jo. 3: 19. E. and Edom sh. be a d.
Mi. 6: 16. that I make thee a d.
Zph. 1: 13. houses sh. become a d.

Zph. 1:15. day is a day of wrath, d.
2 : 4. Ashkelon be a d. | 9. Moab d.
13. he will make Nineveh a d.
14. d. shall be in thresholds
15. Nine. become a d. for beasts
Mat. 12 : 25. Every kingd. divid. ag. itself is brought to d., Lu. 11:17.
24 : 15. see abomi. of d., Mk. 13:14.
Lu. 21:20. then know d. is nigh

DESOLATIONS.

Ezr. 9 :9. reviving, and to repair d.
Ps. 46 : 8. what d. he hath made
74 : 3. Lift up feet to perpetual d.
Is. 15 :†6. for the waters of Nimrim shall be d., Je. 48 : †34.
49:†6. serv. to restore d. of Israel
61 : 4. they shall raise up former d. the d. of many generations
Je. 25: 9. make nations perpetual d.
12. make land of Chal. perpet. d.
51 : † 26. Bab. shall be everl. d., †62,
Eze. 35 : 9. make Seir perpetual d.
Da. 9 : 2. seventy years in d. of J.
18. O my God behold our d.
26. to end of war d. are determ.

DESPAIR. [Noun]

2 Co. 4 : 8. perplexed, but not in d.

DESPAIR, ED.

1 S. 27 : 1. and Saul shall d. of me
Ec. 2 : 20. to cause my heart to d.
2 Co. 1 : 8. that we d-d even of life

DESPERATE, LY.

Jb. 6:26. reprove speeches of one d.
Is. 17 : 11. in day of d. sorrow
Je. 2 :†25. thou saidst Is the case d.
17 : 9. heart of man is d-y wicked

DESPISE.

Le. 26 : 15. if ye d. my statutes
1 S. 2 : 30. d. me sh. be lightly est.
2 S. 19 : 43. Why then did ye d. us?
Es. 1 : 17. shall d. their husbands
Jb. 5 : 17. d. not thou chastening of the Al., Pr. 3 : 11. He. 12:5.
9 : 21. tho. perf., I would d. life
10 : 3. thou d. work of thine
31 : 13. If I d. cause of manserv.
Ps. 51:17. contrite heart, wilt not d.
73 : 20. shalt d. their image
102 : 17. will not d. their prayer
Pr. 1 : 7. but fools d. wisdom
3:11. d. not chast-g of L., He. 12:5.
6 : 30. Men do not d. a thief, if he
23 : 9. a fool will d. the wisdom
22. d. not thy mother when old
Is. 18 : † 2. whose land the rivers d.
30 : 12. Because ye d. this word
Je. 4:30. thy lovers will d. thee [me
23 : 17. They say unto them th. d.
La. 1 : 8. all that honoured, d. her
Eze. 16 : 57. dau-s of Philis. d. thee
28:26. judgm. upon all th. d. them
Am. 5 : 21. I d. your feastdays
Mal. 1:6. O priests, th. d. my name
Mat. 6 : 24. d. the other, Lu. 16:13.
18 : 10. ye d. not one of little ones
Ro. 14:3. let not him eateth, d. him
1 Co. 11 : 22. or d. ye church of G.
16 : 11. let no man theref. d. him
1 Th. 5 : 20. d. not prophesyings
1 Ti. 4 : 12. Let none d. thy youth
6 : 2. not d. them, bec. they breth.
Tit. 2 : 15. Let no man d. thee
2 Pe. 2 : 10. chiefly that d. govern.
Jude 8. d. dominion, speak evil

DESPISED.

Ge. 16 : 4. Hagar's mistress was d.
5. saw she had conceiv., I was d.
25 : 34. Esau d. his birthright
Le. 26 : 43. bec. they d. my judgm.
Nu. 11 : 20. bec. ye have d. Lord
14 : 31. sh. know land ye have d.
15 : 31. Bec. ye d. word of the L.
De. 32 : † 19. L. saw it, he d. them
Ju. 9 : 38. is this the peo. thou d.?
1 S. 10 : 27. they d. him and bro-t
2 S. 6 : 16. she d. him, 1 Ch. 15:29.
12:9. Why hast thou d. com. of L.?
2 S. 12:10. bec. hast d. me, tak. wife
2 K. 19 : 21. dau-r of Zion hath d. thee, and laughed, Is. 37 : 22.
2 Ch. 36 : 16. but they d. his words
Ne. 2 : 19. they laughed and d. us
4 : 4. Hear, O our G., for we are d.
Jb. 12 : 5. he is a lamp d. of him
19 : 18. Yea, young chil. d. me
Ps. 22 : 6. am d. of peo., Is. 53 : 3.
24. not d. affliction of afflicted
53 : 5. to shame, bec. G. hath d.
106 : 24. they d. the pleasant land
119 : 141. I am small and d. yet
Pr. 1 : 30. they d. all my reproof
5 : 12. How my heart d. reproof?
12 : 8. he of perverse heart be d.
9. He that is d. and hath a serv.
Ec. 9 : 16. poor man's wisd. is d.
Can. 8 : 1. yea I should not be d.
Is. 5 : 24. d. word of the Holy One
33 : 8. he hath d. the cities
53 : 3. He is d. and reject. of men, he was d. and we esteemed not
60 : 14. all that d. thee shall bow
Je. 22 : 28. man Coniah a d. idol
33 : 24. they have d. my people
49:15. will make thee small and d.
La. 2 : 6. he hath d. in the indigna.
Eze. 16 : 59. which hast d. the oath, 17 : 16, 18, 19.
20:13. they d. my judgments, 16.
24. but had d. my statutes
22 : 8. hast d. mine holy things
28 : 24. round them that d. them
Am. 2 : 4. bec. they d. law of Lord
Ob. 2. thou art greatly d.
Zch. 4 : 10. d. day of small things?
Mal. 1:6. Wherein we d. thy name?
Lu. 18 : 9. righteous, and d. others
Ac. 19 : 27. tem. of Diana sh. be d.
1 Co. 1 : 28. things d. hath G. chos.
4 : 10. ye honourable, we are d.
Ga. 4 : 14. my tempta. ye d. not
He. 10 : 28. that d. Moses' law, died
Ja. 2 : 6. But ye have d. the poor

DESPISERS.

Ac. 13:41. ye d. wonder, and perish
2 Ti. 3 : 3. fierce, d. of those good

DESPISEST, ING.

Eze. 24:†13. they belong to d-g rod?
Ro. 2 : 4. d-t riches of his goodness?
He. 12 : 2. endured cross d-g shame

DESPISETH.

Jb. 36 : 5. G. is mighty, d. not any
Ps. 69 : 33. L. d. not his prisoners
Pr. 11 : 12. that is void of wisdom d. his neighbour [stroyed
13:13. Whoso d. word shall be de-
14 : 2. He that is perverse d. him
21. He that d. his neighb. sinneth
15 : 5. fool d. his fa.'s instruction
20. a foolish man d. his mother
32. refuseth instruct. d. his soul
19 : 16. he th. d. his ways sh. die
30 : 17. eye that d. to obey mother
Is. 33 : 15. d. gain of oppressions
49 : 7. saith L. to him wh. man d.
Eze. 21 : † 10. rod of my son, it d.
Lu. 10 : 16. d. you, d. me; d. me, d. him that sent me [but G.
1 Th. 4 : 8. He that d. d. not man

DESPITE.

Ne. 4 : † 4. hear, for we are a d.
Eze. 25 : 6. with thy d. ag. Judah
He. 10 : 29. done d. unto Spirit of

DESPITEFUL, LY.

Eze. 25 : 15. vengeance wi. d. heart
36 : 5. with d. minds to cast it out
Mat. 5 : 44. d-y use you, Lu. 6:28.
Ac. 14 : 5. an assault to use th. d-y
Ro. 1 : 30. haters of G. d. proud

DESTITUTE. [ter

Ge. 24:27. hath not left d. my mas-
Ps. 102 : 17. regard prayer of d.
141 : 8. leave not my soul d.
Pr. 11 : † 12. d. of heart, despiseth
15:21. Folly joy to him d. of wisd.
Eze. 32 : 15. d. of that it was full
1 Ti. 6 : 5. men d. of the truth
He. 11:37. wandered, being d. afflic.
Ja. 2 : 15. If a bro. or sister be d.

DESTROY. [ed?

Ge. 18:23. Wilt d. rightte. with wick-
24. Wilt thou d. the place?
28. wilt d. city for lack of five?
19 : 13. will d. place | 14. d. city
Ex. 15 : 9. my hand shall d. them
34 : 13. sh. d. their altars, De. 7:5.
Le. 26 : 22. send beasts to d. cattle
Nu. 24 : 17. shall d. chil. of Seth
19. d. him th. remaineth of city
32 : 15. ye shall d. all this people
33 : 52. shall d. their pictures and
De. 4 : 31. not forsake neith. d. thee
6 : 15. lest Lord thy G. d. thee
7 : 2. utterly d. them, 20 : 17. Jos. 11 : 20. Ju. 21 : 11. 1 S. 15 : 18.
23. L. shall d. them with mighty
24. thou shalt d. their name from
9 : 3. sh. d., and bring them down
14. Let me alone, that I d. them
25. L. hath said he would d. you
12 : 2. Ye shall d. all the places
3. their gods, and d. names of th.
20 : 20. trees not for meat shalt d.
31:3. L. thy G. will d. these nat-s
32 : 25. sh. d. young man and vir-
33 : 27. shall say, d. them [gin
Jos. 7 : 12. except ye d. accursed fr.
1 S. 15 : 3. smite Amalek utterly d.
6. depart, lest I d. you with th.
2 S. 14 : 7. we will d. the heir also
11. not suffer revengers to d. any more, lest they d. my son
16. that would d. me and my son
20 : 20. far be it fr. me, I should d.
22:41. d. them hate me, Ps. 18:40.
1 K. 16:12. Zimri d. the h. of Baasha
2 K. 10 : 19. d. worshippers of Baal
18:25. Go ag. land, d. it. Is. 36:10.
Ezr. 6 : 12. d. kings that shall put
Es. 7 : 4. sold, that they should d.
Jb. 8 : 18. If he d. him fr. his place
10 : 8. made me, yet dost d. me
19:26. aft. my skin, worms d. body
Ps. 5 : 6. d. them speak leasing
10. d. them, O G. let them fall
21 : 10. Their fruit shalt thou d.
28 : 5. sh. d. them, and not build
52 : 5. God shall d. thee for ever
55:9. d. O L., divide their tongues
69 : 4. th. would d. me are mighty
74 : 8. said, Let us d. them togeth.
106:23. d. them had not Mo. stood
127 : † 5. they shall d. the enemies
143 : 12. d. all that afflict my soul
144 : 6. shoot arrows and d. them
145 : 20. all the wicked will he d.
Pr. 1:32. prosp. of fools sh. d. them
11 : 3. perversen. of transgr. sh. d.
15 : 25. L. will d. house of proud
21 : 7. robberies of wicked d. them
Ec. 5:6. wh. G. d. work of thine ha.?
7 : 16. why shouldest d. thyself?
Is. 3 : 12. d. the way of thy paths
11 : 9. nor d. in holy mt., 65 : 25.
15. d. tongue of Egyptian sea
13 : 9. he sh. d. sinners out of it
25 : 7. will d. in this mt. the face
Je. 5 : 10. Go ye upon walls and d.
6 : 5. let by night d. her palaces
11:19. Let us d. the tree with fruit
12 : 17. I will d. that nation
13 : 14. I will not spare, but d. th.
15:6. will stretch hand and d. thee
17 : 18. d. them with double destr.
23:1. Woe unto pastors th. d. sheep
36 : 29. king of Bab. sh. d. this la.
48 : 18. he sh. d. thy strong holds
49 : 9. thieves by night they will d.
50:21. waste, utterly, d. after them
50 : 26. d. Babylon utterly
51 : 3. d. ye utterly all her host
La. 3 : 66. Persecute and d. them

Eze. 9: 8. wilt d. residue of Israel?
25: 16. d. remnant of seacoast
26: 4. they sh. d. walls of Tyrus
12. shall d. thy pleasant houses
Da. 2: † 18. they should not d. Dan.
4: 23. Hew the tree down and d. it
8: 24. d. wonderfully, and d. mighty
25. by peace sh. he d. many
9: 26. peo. shall d. city and [him
11: 26. that feed of his meat sh. d.
Ob. 8. sh. I d. wise men of Edom?
Mi. 2: 10. polluted, it shall d. you
Zph. 2: 13. ag. north, and d. Assyria
Mat. 12: 14. how they might d. him,
Mk. 3: 6.–11: 18. [men
21: 41. will miserably d. those wick.
27: 20. ask Barabbas, and d. Jes.
Mk. 12: 9. d. husbandm., Lu. 20: 16.
Jn. 2: 19. Jesus said, d. this tem.
Ac. 6: 14. this Jes. sh. d. this place
1 Co. 3: † 17. if any man d. the temple of God, him sh. God d.
6: 13. G. sh. d. both it and them
2 Th. 2: 8. shall d. with brightness
He. 2: 14. d. him had power of
1 Jn. 3: 8. d. works of devil [death
Re. 11: 18. d. them wh. d. the earth

I will, or will I DESTROY.

Ge. 6: 7. I w. d. man I created
13. I w. d. them with the earth
7: 4. ev. living substance w. I d.
Ex. 23: 27. I w. d. all the people
Le. 23: 30. same soul w. I d.
26: 30. I w. d. high-pla., Eze. 6: 3.
Nu. 21: 2. I w. utterly d. cities
Ps. 101: 8. I w. early d. the wick.
118: 10. in name of L. w. I d., 11, 12.
Is. 19: 3. I w. d. the counsel
42: 14. I w. d. and devour at once
Je. 15: 7. I w. d. my people since
25: 9. nations, I w. utterly d. th.
46: 8. I w. d. the city, and inhabi.
49: 38. I w. d. king and princes
51: 20. with thee w. I d. kingdoms
Eze. 14: 9. I w. d. that prophet
25: 7. I w. d. thee, shalt know I am L., 28: 16. Zph. 2: 5.
30: 13. saith Lord, I w. d. idols
32: 13. I w. d. also all the beasts
34: 16. I w. d. fat and the strong
Ho. 2: 12. I w. d. her vines and
4: 5. fall, and I w. d. thy mother
Am. 9: 8. I w. d. the sinful kingd.
Mi. 5: 10. I w. d. thy chariots
14. so w. I d. thy cities
Ha. 2: 22. I w. d. the kingdoms
Mk. 14: 58. say, I w. d. this tem.
1 Co. 1: 19. I w. d. wisd. of wise

See UTTERLY.

Not DESTROY.

Ge. 18: 28. if find 45 I will n. d. it
31. n. d. it for twenty's sake
32. he said, I will n. d. Sodom
De. 9: 26. d. n. thy peo. and inher.
10: 10. Lord would n. d. thee
20: 19. thou shalt n. d. the trees
1 S. 15: 9. would n. utterly d. th.
24: 21. swear wilt n. d. my name
26: 9. And David said d. him n.
2 K. 8: 19. n. d. Jud. for Da.'s sake
13: 23. would n. d. nor cast out
2 Ch. 12: 7. thf. I will n. d. them
12. that the L. would n. d. him
21: 7. L. would n. d. house of Da.
35: 21. forbear fr. G. that he d. n.
Ps. 106: 34. They did n. d. nations
Is. 65: 8. d. it n. a blessing is in it; so that I may n. d. them [d. it
Eze. 22: 30. in gap, that I should n.
Da. 2: 24. d. n. wise men of Bab.
Am. 9: 8. I will n. d. house of Jac.
Mal. 3: 11. he shall n. d. fruits of
Ro. 14: 15. d. n. him with thy meat
20. For meat d. n. work of God

To DESTROY.

Ge. 6: 17. bring a flood t. d. all flesh
9: 11. nor any more a flood t. d., 15.
Ge. 19: 13. L. hath sent us t. d. it
Ex. 8: 9. entreat for thee t. d. frogs
12: 13. plague not upon you t. d.
Le. 26: 44. neither abhor them t. d.
De. 1: 27. Lord hath brought us out of Egypt t. d. us, Jos. 7: 7.
2: 15. hand of L. t. d. them from
7: 10. that hate him t. d. them
9: 19. Lord was wroth t. d. you
28: 63. L. will rejoice t. d. you
Jos. 9: 24. t. d. all the inhabitants
22: 33. t. d. land wh. Reubenites
Ju. 6: 5. Midianites t. d. the land
1 S. 23: 10. Saul seeketh t. d. city
26: 15. came in one t. d. the king
2 S. 1: 14. not afraid t. d. L.'s anoin.
14: 11. not suffer revengers t. d.
20: 19. seekest t. d. city and a moth.
24: 16. hand upon Jerusalem t. d.
1 K. 9: 21. Isr not able utterly t. d.
13: 34. sin to house of Jerob. t. d. it
2 K. 24: 2. sent against Jud. t. d. it
1 Ch. 21: 15. an angel to Jerus. t. d.
Ezr. 6: 12. t. d. this house of G.
2 Ch. 20: 23. of Seir, utterly t. d. every one helped t. d. another
25: 16. G. hath determined t. d.
Es. 3: 6. Haman sought t. d. Jews, 13.–4: 7, 8.–8: 5.–9: 24.
† 9. let it be written t. d. them
8: 11. t. d. all power of the peo.
Jb. 2: 3. thou movedst me t. d. him
6: 9. would please God t. d. me
Ps. 40: 14. seek my soul t. d., 63: 9.
119: 95. wicked waited t. d. me
Is. 10: 7. it is in his heart t. d.
13: 5. come from far t. d. land
23: 11. L. hath given com-t t. d.
32: 7. wicked devices t. d. poor
51: 13. as if oppressor ready t. d.
54: 16. I have created waster t. d.
Je. 1: 10. set thee t. d., 18: 7.–31: 28.
15: 3. appoint beasts t. d.
51: 11. device is ag. Bab. t. d. it
La. 2: 8. The L. purposed t. d. wall
Eze. 5: 16. famine, I will send t. d.
21: 31. brutish men skillful t. d.
22: 27. t. d. souls, to get dishon.
25: 15. t. d. it for old hatred
30: 11. nations brought t. d. land
43: 3. when I came t. d. the city
Da. 2: 12. t. d. wise men of Bab., 24.
7: 26. t. d. his dominion unto end
11: 44. he shall go with fury t. d.
Ho. 11: 9. will not return t. d. Ephr.
Zch. 12: 9. I will seek t. d. nations
Mat. 2: 13. Herod seek child t. d.
5: 17. Think not that I am come t. d., I am not come t. d. but
10: 28. fear him able t. d. both soul
26: 61. said, I am able t. d. temp.
Mk. 1: 24. come t. d. us? Lu. 4: 34.
9: 22. into waters t. d. him
Lu. 6: 9. on sab to save life or t. d.
9: 56. not come t. d. men's lives
19: 47. the chief sought t. d. him
Jn. 10: 10. thief cometh t. d.
Ja. 4: 12. is one lawgiv. able t. d.

DESTROYED.

Ge. 7: 23. ev living subst. was d.
13: 10. before the Lord d. Sodom
19: 29. when G. d. cities of plain
Ex. 8: † 24. the land was d. by flies
10: 7. knowest not yet E. is d.
De. 1: 44. chased as bees and d. you
2: 12. d. from bef. them, 22: 23.
21. the L. d. them, 4: 3.–11: 4.
2 K. 21: 9. 2 Ch. 33: 9.
7: 20. hide thems from thee, be d.
23. with a mighty destruction until they be d. [d.
24. able to stand until thou have
9: 8. L. was angry to have d. you
12: 30. after that they be d.
28: 20. until th. be d., 24, 45, 51, 61.
48. yoke upon neck until he have
31: 4. unto land of them he d. [d.
Jos. 24: 8. I d. them fr. bef. you d.
Ju. 5: † 27. where he bowed, there he fell down d.
20: 21. Benj. d. of Isr. 22,000, 25.
35. chil. of Isr. d. 25,100 of Benj.,
2 S. 21: 5. devised that we be d. [42.
24: 16. to angel that d., 1 Ch. 21: 15.
1 K. 15: 13. Asa d. her idol and
2 K. 8: † 23. the kings are surely d.
10: 28. Jehu d. Baal out of Isr.
11: 1. d. all seed royal, 2 Ch. 22: 10.
19: 12. wh. my fa-s d., Is. 37: 12.
18. they have d. them, Is. 37: 19.
21: 3. high places Hez. had d.
1 Ch. 5: 25. people whom God d.
21: 12. or three months to be d.
2 Ch. 14: 13. they were d. bef. L.
15: 6. nation was d. of nation
24: 23. d. all princes of people
34: 11. houses which k-s of Judah
36: 19. d. all the goodly vessels [d.
Ezr 4: 15. for cause was this city d.
5: 12. Neb-r, Chaldean, d. this hou.
6: † 11. sh. alter word, let him be d.
Es. 3: 9. be written that they be d.
9: 6. Jews slew and d. 500 men
Jb. 19: 10. He hath d. me on ev. side
† 26. though this body be d. yet
Ps. 9: 5. hast d. wick. | 6. d. cities
11: 3. If founda. be d. what righte.
73: 27. d. all that go a whoring
78: 45. sent frogs, which d. them
47. He d. their vines with hail, and
137: 8. O dau. of Bab., to be d.
Pr. 13: 23. is d. for want of judgm.
Is. 14: 17. Lucifer d. cities thereof
20. because thou hast d. land
26: 14. theref. hast thou d. them
48: 19. name not have been d.
Je. 12: 10. pastors have d. viney.
48: 4. Moab is d. | 51: 8. Bab. is d.
51: 55. d. out of Bab. the gr. voice
La. 2: 5. L. hath d. his strong holds
6. he hath d. places of assembly
9. he hath d. and broken her bars
Eze. 26: 17. How art thou d., th. was
27: 32. Tyrus, like the d. in sea
43: † 3. prophesy that city be d.
Da. 7: 11. beast slain, his body d.
Ho. 13: 9. O Isr. thou hast d. thys.
Am. 2: 9. d. I Amorite, I d. his
Mat. 22: 7. sent and d. murderers
Lu. 17: 27. flood came, and d. all
29. it rained fire fr. heav. and d. all
Ac. 9: 21. Is not this he th. d. them
13: 19. d. seven nations in Chana.
19: 27. her magnif. should be d.
Ro. 6: 6. that body of sin be d.
1 Co. 10: 9. some d. of serpents
10. some d. of the destroyer
Ga. 1: 23. preacheth faith wh. he d.
2: 18. if I build again things I d.
He. 11: 28. lest he that d. firstborn
2 Pe. 2: 12. as beasts made to be d.
Jude 5. L. d. them that believed not
Re. 8: 9. part of the ships were d.

Are DESTROYED.

Ju. 21: 16. women a. d. out of Benj.
Jb. 4: 20. a. d. from morn. to night
34: 25. he overturn. so they a. d.
Is. 9: 16. that are led of them a. d.
Je. 22: 20. for all thy lovers a. d.
Ho. 4: 6. a. d. for lack of knowl.
Zph. 3: 6. their cities a. d. there

Not DESTROYED.

Ju. 21: 17. That a tribe be n. d.
2 Ch 20: 10. n. them d., Ps. 78: 38.
Da. 7: 14. his kingdom n. be d.
2 Co. 4: 9. cast down, but n. d.

Shall be DESTROYED.

Ge. 34: 30. I s. b. d. and my hou.
Es. 4: 14. thy fa.'s house s. b. d.
Ps 37: 38. transgressors s. b. d.
92: 7. It is that they s. b. d. for
Pr. 13: 13. despiseth word s. b. d.
20. companion of fools s. b. d.
29: 1. hardeneth his neck s. b. d.

Is. 10: 27. the yoke s. b d. bec. of
Je. 48:8. valley perish, plain s. b. d.
42. Moab s. b. d. fr. being peo.
Eze. 30: 8. when her helpers s. b. d.
32: 12. mult. thereof s. b. d. [6:26.
Da. 2: 44. a kingd. s. never b. d.,
11: 20. within few days he s. b. d.
Ho. 10: 8. the sin of Isr. s. b. d..
Ac. 3: 23. th. will not hear s. b. d.
1 Co. 15:26. last enemy that s. b. d.

Utterly DESTROYED.

Ex. 22:20. sacrificeth unto any God, save unto L., shall be u. d.
Nu. 21: 3. they u. d. Canaanites
De. 2: 34. we u. d. Sihon and peo.
3:6. we u. d. cities of Og, Jos. 2: 10.
4:26. if corrupt yours. sh. be u. d.
Jos. 6: 21. they u. d. all in Jericho
8: 26. had u. d. inhab. of Ai, 10: 1.
10: 28. Joshua took . . and u. d. all the souls therein, 35, 37, 39, 40. Joshua u. d. all that breathed
11: 12. cities and kings he u. d., 21.
Ju. 1: 17. Judah, Simeon, u. d. Zep-h
1 S. 15: 9. ev. thing vile, refuse u. d.
15. spared best; rest we have u. d.
20. I have u. d. the Amalekites, 8.
21. spoil should have been u. d.
1 Ch. 4: 41. d. them u. unto this day
2 Ch. 32: 14. nations my fa-s u. d.
Is. 34: 2. all nations, L. hath u. d.
See UTTERLY destroy, ed.
See UNTIL destroyed.

DESTROYER, S.

Ex. 12: 23. not suffer d. into hou.
Ju. 16: 24. deliv. d. of our country
Jb. 15: 21. in prosperity d. come
33: 22. life draweth near to d-s
Ps. 17: 4. kept me fr. paths of d.
Pr. 28: 24. is companion of a d.
Is. 49: 17. thy d-s go forth of thee
Je. 4: 7. d. of Gent. is on his way
22: 7. will prepare d-s against thee
50: † 9. arrows be as of a mighty d.
11. O d-s of my heritage
1 Co. 10: 10. were destroyed of d.
Re. 9: † 11. king hath his name a d.

DESTROYEST, ETH.

De. 8: 20. As nations which L. d.
Jb. 9: 22. He d. perfect and wick.
12: 23. increaseth nations, and d.
14: 19. thou d. the hope of man
Ps. 18: † 47. it is God that d. peo.
Pr. 6: 32. doeth it, d. own soul
11: 9. hypoc. with mouth d. neighb.
31: 3. not ways to that d. kings
Ec. 7: 7. and a gift d. heart
9: 18. sinner d. much good
Je. 51: 25. O mt., which d. the earth
Mat. 27: 40. that d-t temp., Mk. 15: 29.

DESTROYING.

1 Ch. 21: 12. angel of L. d. thro. Isr.
15. as he was d. L. repented
Pr. 28: † 24. is companion of man d.
Is. 28: 2. strong one, as a d. storm
Je. 2: 30. devoured like a d. lion
18: † 14. not have mercy fr. d. them
51: 1. will raise ag. Bab. a d. wind
25. I am ag. thee, O d. mountain
La. 2: 8. not withdr. hand fr. d.
Eze. 9: 1. with d. weapon in hand
20: 17. mine eye spared fr. d. them
See UTTERLY

DESTRUCTION.

Ex. 12: † 13. plague not upon you for a d. [place, Utter d.
Nu. 21: † 3. called the name of the
24: † 20. his latter end sh. be to d.
De. 7: 23. L. sh. destr. with mighty d.
32: 24. be devour. with bitter d.
1 S. 5: 9. L. was ag. city with gr. d.
11. was a deadly d. through city
1 K. 20: 42. I appointed to d. [ano.
2 Ch. 20: † 23. one helped for d. of
22: 4. were his counsellors to d.
7. d. of Ahaziah was of God
26: 16. heart was lifted up to his d.
Es. 8:6. how endure d. of my kindr.?
9: 5. Jews smote enemies with d.
Jb. 5: 21. neither be afraid of d.
22. At d. and fami. shalt laugh
18: 12. d. sh. be ready at his side
21: 17. how oft cometh their d.?
20. his eyes shall see his d.
30. wicked is reserved to d.
26: 6. d. hath no covering
28: 22. d. death say, We heard
30: 12. raise ag. me ways of their d.
24. tho. they cry in his d.
31: 3. Is not d. to the wicked?
12. is fire that consumeth to d.
23. d. from God was terror to me
29. if rejoi. at d. of him th. hated
Ps. 35: 8. Let d. come unawares, into that d. let him fall
55: 23. shalt bring into pit of d.
73: 18. thou castedst them into d.
88: 11. faithfuln. be declar. in d.?
90: 3. Thou turnest man to d.
91: 6. d. that wasteth at noon-d.
103: 4. redeemeth thy life from d.
Pr. 1: 27. d. cometh as whirlwind
10: 14. mouth of foolish is near d.
15. d. of poor is their poverty
29. d. to workers of iniq., 21: 15.
13: 3. that openeth lips sh. have d.
14: 28. want of peo. is d. of prince
15: 11. Hell and d. are bef. the L.
16: 18. Pride goeth before d.
17: 19. exalteth his gate seeketh d.
18: 7. A fool's mouth is his d.
12. Bef. d. the heart is haughty
19: † 18. let not soul spare to his d.
24: 2. their heart studieth d.
27: 20. Hell and d. are never full
31: 8. such as are appointed to d.
Is. 1: 28. d. of transgr. and sinners
10: 25. mine auger cease in their d.
13: 6. it shall come as a d. fr. Al.
14: 23. I will sweep Bab. with d.
15: 5. shall raise up a cry of d.
19: 18. one be called city of d.
24: 12. gate is smitten with d.
49: 19. land of thy d. too narrow
51: 19. and d. are come unto thee
59: 7. and d. are in their paths
60: 18. d. no more heard in bord.
Je. 4: 6. from north a great d., 6: 1.
20. d. upon d. is cried, for land
17: 18. destr. them with double d.
46: 20. d. cometh out of the north
48: 3. a voice from Horonaim, d.
5. enem. have heard cry of d.
50: 22. sound of gr. d. is in land
51: 54. great d. from Chaldeans
La. 2: 11. d. of dau. of my peo., 3: 48.
3: 47. and d. is come upon us
4: 10. in d. of the daughter of my
Eze. 5: 16. send famine for their d.
7: 25. d. cometh, they seek peace
9: † 6. slay to d. old and young
32: 9. when I bring d. am. nations
Ho. 7: 13. d. because they transgr-d
9: 6. they are gone, because of d.
13: 14. O grave, I will be thy d.
Jo. 1: 15. as d. fr. Al. it sh. come
Ob. 12. neith. rejoiced in their d.
Mi. 2: 10. destroy you with sore d.
Zch. 14: 11. sh. be no more utter d.
Mat. 7: 13. broad way leadeth to d.
Ro. 3: 16. d. and misery in th. ways
9: 22. vessels of wrath fitted to d.
1 Co. 5: 5. unto Satan for d. of flesh
2 Co. 10: 8. not for your d., 13: 10.
Ph. 3: 19. many Whose end is d.
1 Th. 5: 3. then sudden d. cometh
2 Th. 1: 9. punished with everl. d.
1 Ti. 6: 9. lusts wh. drown men in d.
2 Pe. 2: 1. bring upon thems. swift d.
3: 16. unstable wrest unto own d.

DESTRUCTIONS.

Ps. 9: 6. d. are come to perpet. end
35: 17. rescue my soul fr. their d.
107: 20. delivereth from their d.
Is. 5: † 30 it shall be dark in the d.

DETAIN, ED.

Ju. 13: 15. let us d. thee until we
16. Tho. thou d., I will not eat
1 S. 21: 7. Doeg was that day d-d

DETERMINATE.

Ac. 2: 23. by d. counsel of God

DETERMINATION.

Zph. 3: 8. my d. is to gath. nations

DETERMINE.

Ex. 21: 22. shall pay as judges d.

DETERMINED.

1 S. 20: 7. sure evil is d. by him
9. if I knew evil were d. by fa.
33. Jona. knew it was d. of fa.
25: 17. evil is d. ag. our master
2 S. 13: 32. by Abs. this been d.
2 Ch. 2: 1. Solo. d. to build a house
25: 16. G. hath d. to destroy thee
Es. 7: 7. he saw evil d. against him
Jb. 14: 5. seeing his days are d.
Is. 10: 23. a consumption d., 28: 22.
19: 17. counsel of L. hath d. ag. it
Da. 9: 24. Seventy weeks are d.
26. unto end of war desola. are d.
27. that d. shall be poured upon
11: 36. that is d. shall be done
Lu. 22: 22. Son goeth as it was d.
Ac. 3: 13. Pilate d. to let him go
4: 28. to do what thy counsel d.
11: 29. disciples d. to send relief
15: 2. d. th. Paul and B. go to Jerus.
37. Barnabas d. to take John
17: 26. d. times bef. appointed
19: 39. be d. in a lawful assembly
20: 16. Paul had d. to sail by Eph.
25: 25. d. to send Paul to Augus.
27: 1. d. we should sail into Italy
Ro. 1: † 4. d. to be the Son of God
1 Co. 2: 2. I d. not to kn. any thing
5: † 3. present in spirit I have d.
2 Co. 2: 1. I d. this with myself
Tit. 3: 12. I have d. there to winter

DETEST.

De. 7: 26. thou shalt utterly d. it.

DETESTABLE.

Je. 16: 18. defiled land with d. thi.
Eze. 5: 11. defiled sanct. with thy d.
7: 20. made images of d. things
11: 18. shall take away d. things
21. heart walketh after d. things
37: 23. Nei. defile with d. things

DEU'EL or REU'EL.

Nu. 1: 14. Eliasaph the son of D., † R., 7: 42, 47.—10: 20.—2: 14. † R.

DEVICE.

2 Ch. 2: 14. to find out every d.
Es. 8: 3. to put away his d. that
† 5. to reverse the d. by Haman
9: 25. his d. ret. upon his head
Ps. 21: 11. imagined mischievous d.
140: 8. further not his wicked d.
Ec. 9: 10. no work nor d. in grave
Je. 18: 11. I devise a d. against you
51: 11. d. is ag. Bab. to destroy it
La. 3: 62. their d. ag. me all day
Ac. 17: 29. stone grav. by man's d.

DEVICES.

Jb. 5: 12. disappoint-h d. of crafty
11: † 3. d. make men hold peace?
21: 27. d. ye wrongfully imagine
Ps. 10: 2. let them be tak. in d. they
33: 10. d. of people of none effect
37: 7. bringeth wicked d. to pass
Pr. 1: 31. be filled with own d.
12: 2. man of wicked d. condemn
19: 21. many d. in man's heart
Is. 32: 7. wicked d. to destr. poor
66: † 4. I also will choose their d.
Je. 11: 19. had devised d. ag. me
18: 12. we will walk after own d.
18. let us devise d. ag. Jeremiah
Da. 11: 24. he shall forecast his d.
25. they shall forecast d. ag. him
2 Co. 2: 11. not ignorant of his d.

DEVIL.

Mat. 4: 1. Jes. to be tempted of d.

Mat.4:5. d. taketh him into holy city
8. d. taketh him up into a high
11. Then d. leaveth him [mt.
9: 32. a dumb man with d., 12:22.
11: 18. say He hath a d., Lu. 7:33.
13: 39. enemy that sowed is the d.
15:22. dau. grievously vexed wi. d.
17: 18. Jes. rebuked d. he depar.
25: 41. fire, prepared for the d.
Mk. 5:15. him posses. with d., 16, 18.
7: 29. d. is gone out of dau., 26, 30.
Lu. 4: 2. forty days tempted of d.
3. d. said unto him, 6.
5. d. taking him up into high mt.
13. when d. had ended tempta.
33. had a spirit of an unclean d.
35. when d. had thrown him
8: 12. cometh d. and taketh word
29. driven of d. into wilderness
9: 42. coming d. threw him down
11: 14. And he was casting out d., when d. was gone out
Jn. 6:70. and one of you is a d.
7: 20. said, Thou hast a d., 8: 48.
8: 44. Ye are of your father d.
49. I have not a d. | 52. hast a d.
10: 20. many said, He hath a d.
21. not words of him hath a d.
13: 2. d. having put into Judas
Ac. 10: 38. healing all oppr. of d.
13: 10. thou child of the d.
Ep. 4: 27. Neither give place to d.
6: 11. able to stand ag. wiles of d.
1 Ti. 3: 6. fall into condem. of d.
7. he fall into snare of d.
2 Ti. 2: 26. recov. out of snare of d.
He. 2: 14. power of death, that is d.
Ja. 4: 7. Resist n. and he will flee
1 Pe. 5: 8. your adversary the d.
1 Jn. 3: 8. commit. sin is of d. that might destroy works of d.
10. chil. of the d. are manifest
Jude 9. Michael, contending with d.
Re. 2: 10. d. shall cast into prison
12: 9. old serpent called the d.
12. d. is come having power
20: 2. old serpent, which is the d.
10. d. th. deceiv. was cast into fire

DEVILS. [d.

Le. 17: 7. no more offer sacr. unto
De. 32: 17. they sacrificed unto d.
2 Ch. 11: 15. ord. him priest for d.
Ps. 106:37. sacr. their sons unto d.
Mat. 4: 24. those possessed with d., 8:16, 28, 33. Mk. 1:32. Lu. 8:36.
8:31. so d. besought, Mk. 5: 12.
9:34. He casteth out d. thro. prince of d., 12:24. Mk. 3:22. Lu. 11:15.
Mk. 1:34. he suffered not d. to speak
9:38. Master, we saw one casting out d. in thy name, Lu. 9: 49. [ing
Lu. 4: 41. d. came out of many, say-
8: 2 Mary M., out of whom seven d.
27. certain man which had d. long
30. Legion; bec. many d. into him
33. Then went d. out of the man
35 out of whom d. were departed,
36 he that was possessed of d. [38.
9: 1. gave them power over all d.
10: 17. even d. are subject unto us
13: 32. tell that fox, I cast out d.
1 Co. 10: 20. Gentiles sacrifice to d.; not ye have fellowship with d.
21. Ye cannot drink cup of Lord and cup of d... of table of d. [d.
1 Ti. 4: 1. giving heed to doctrines of
Ja. 2: 19. d. also believe, and tremb.
Re. 9: 20. they should not worship d.
16: 14. they are spirits of d. work-g
18: 2. Bab-n is become habitation [of d.
See CAST out.

DEVILISH.

Ja. 3: 15. This wisdom is sensual, d.

DEVISE.

Ex. 31: 4. To d. cunning works in gold and silver, 35: 35. [brass
35: 32. to d. curious works in gold,
2 S. 14: 14. he d. that his banished
Ps. 35: 4. to confusion, th. d. hurt
20. d. deceitful matters ag. them
41: 7. ag. me do they d. my hurt
Pr. 3: 29. d. not evil. ag. neighbour
14: 22. do they err that d. evil? mercy to them d. good
16: 30. shutt. eyes to d. froward
Je. 18: 11. I d. a device against you
18. let us d. devices ag Jeremiah
Eze. 11: 2. are men that d. mischief
Mi. 2: 1. Woe to them that d. iniq.
3. ag. this family do I d. an evil

DEVISED.

2 S. 21: 5. consumed us d. ag. us
1 K. 12: 33. in month which he d.
Es. 8: 3. he had d. ag. Jews, 9: 24, 25
5. to reverse letters d. by Haman
Ps. 31: 13. d. to take my life
Je. 11: 19. knew not they d. devices
48: 2. in Heshbon have d. evil
51: 12. L. both d. and, La. 2: 17.
2 Pe. 1: 16. cunningly d. fables

DEVISETH.

Ps. 36: 4. he d. mischief on his bed
52: 2. Thy tongue d. mischi f
Pr. 6: 14. he d. mischief continually
18. heart th. d. wicked imagina.
16: 9. man's heart d. his way
24: 8. d. evil be called mischiev.
Is. 32: 7. he d. to destroy poor
8. the liberal d. liberal things

DEVOTE, ED.

Le. 27: 21. holy unto L. as field d.
28. no d-d thing a man shall d. unto L. be sold: ev d. thi. holy
Nu. 18: 14. Ev. thing d. be thine
De. 13: † 17. cleave nothing of d.
Jos. 6: † 17. city shall be d. [thing
Ezr. 10: † 8. his substance sh. be d.
Ps. 119: 38. who is d. to thy fear
Eze. 44: † 29. ev. d. thing sh. be [theirs

DEVOTIONS.

Ac. 17: 23. For as I beheld your d.

DEVOUR.

Ge. 49: 27. morning sh. d. prey
De. 32: 42. and my sword d. flesh
2 S. 2: 26. Shall sword d. for ever?
18: † 8. wood multiplied to d.
2 Ch. 7: 13. command locusts to d.
Jb. 18: 13. firstb. of death sh. d. his
Ps. 80: 13. wild beast doth d. it
Pr. 30: 14. jawteeth as knives to d.
Is. 1: 7. your land strangers d.
9: 12. sh. d. Isr. with open mouth
18. wickedness shall d. briers
31: 8. the sword shall d. him
42: 14. I will destr. and d. at once
56: 9. all ye beasts of field come to d., Je. 12: 9.-15: 3.
Je. 2: 3. that d. Israel shall offend
12: 12. sword shall d., 46: 10, 14.
30: 16. that d. thee be devoured
48: 45. shall d. corner of Moab
Eze. 7: 15. famine shall d. him
34: 28. neither shall the beasts d.
35: † 12. mts. are given us to d.
36: 14. shalt thou d. men no more
Da. 7:5. d. flesh | 23. d. whole earth
Ho. 5: 7. shall a month d. them
11: 6. sword sh. d. his branches
13: 8. will I d. them like a lion
Am. 1: 4. fire d. palaces, 7, 10, 12.
Ob. 18. shall kindle in them, and d.
Na. 2: 13. sword d. young lions
Ha. 3: 14. rejoi-g was as to d. poor
Zch. 9: 15. shall d. and subdue
12: 6. they shall d. all the people
Mat. 23: 14. for ye d. widows' houses, Mk. 12: 40. Lu. 20: 47.
2 Co. 11: 20. suffer, if man d. you
Ga. 5: 15. if bite and d. one another
He. 10: 27. shall d. adversaries
1 Pe. 5: 8. seeking wh. he may d.
Re. 12: 4. to d. her child soon as

Fire DEVOUR.

Ju. 9: 15. let f. d. cedars of Leb.
Ju. 9: 20. let f. d. men of Shechem
Ps. 21: 9. and f. shall d. them
50: 3. God come, f. shall d. bef.
Is. 26: 11. f. of enemies sh. d. them
33: 11. breath as f. shall d. you
Eze. 15: 7. another f. sh. d. them
28: 37. to pass thro. f. to d. them
Am. 5: 6. break out like f. and d. it
Na. 3: 13. the f. shall d. thy bars
15. there shall the f. d. thee
Zch. 11: 1 that f. may d. thy cedars

It shall DEVOUR.

Jb. 18: 13. i. s. d. strength of his sk.
Is. 10: 17. i. s. d. his thorns
Je. 5: 14. words fire, i. s. d. them
17: 27. i. s. d. palaces of Jerus.,
21: 14. i. s. d. all things, 50: 32.
Eze. 20: 47. i. s. d. ev. green tree
28: 18. i. s. d. I will bring to ashes
Ho. 8: 14. i. s. d. palaces of Judah
Am. 1: 14. i. s. d. palaces of Rabbah
2: 2. fire, i. s. d. palaces of Kirioth
5. fire i. s. d. palaces of Jerus.

DEVOURED. [money

Ge. 31: 15. he hath quite d. our
37: 20. Some evil beast d. him, 33.
41: 7. seven thin ears d. rank, 24.
Le. 10: 2. went fire fr. L. and d.
Nu. 26: 10. time fire d. 250 men
De 31: 17. will hide, they sh. be d.
32: 24. be d. with burning heat
2 S. 18: 8. wood d. more than sw. d.
22: 9. out of his mouth n., Ps. 18: 8.
Ps. 78: 45. divers sorts of flies wh. d.
79: 7. For they have d. Jacob
105: 35. the locusts d. the fruit of
Is. 1: 20. rebel, ye be d. with sw.
24: 6. hath the curse d. the earth
Je 2: 30. your sword d. prophets
3: 24. shame hath d. the labour
8: 16. for they have d. the land
10: 25. have eaten Jac. and d. him
30: 16. that devour thee sh. be d.
50: 7. All that found d. them
17. king of Assyria hath d. him
51: 34. Nebuchadrezzar d. me
La. 4: 11. it hath d. foundations
Eze. 15: 5. less when fire hath d. it
16: 20. hast sacri. sons to be d.
19: 3. to catch prey, it d. men, 6.
14. fire gone out, wh. d. her fruit
22: 25. like lion, they d. souls
23: 25. residue be d. by fire
33: 27. give to beast to be d., 39: 4.
Da. 7: 7. d. and break in pieces, 19.
Ho. 7: 7. have d. their judges
9. Strangers have d. his strength
Jo. 1: 19. fire d. pastures, 20.
Am. 4: 9. fig trees, palmerworm d.
7: 4. and it d. the great deep
Na. 1: 10. shall be d. as stubble
Zph. 1: 18. land be d. by jealousy
3: 8. earth be d. with my jealousy
Zch. 9: 4. Tyrus sh. be d. with fire
Mat. 13: 4. fowls came and d. them, Mk. 4: 4. Lu. 8: 5.
Lu. 15: 30. son who d. thy living
Re. 20: 9. fire came and d. them

DEVOURER.

Mal. 3: 11. I will rebuke the d.

DEVOUREST, ETH.

2 S. 11: 25. sword d. one as ano.
Pr 19: 28. mouth of wick. d. iniq.
20: 25. man who d. that wh. is holy
Is. 5: 24. as fire d. stubble, Jo. 2: 5.
La. 2: 3. like flaming fire which d.
Eze. 15: 4. fire d. both ends of it
36: 13. Thou land d-t up men
Jo. 2: 3. A fire d. before them
Ha. 1: 13. wicked d. more righte.
Re. 11: 5. fire d. their enemies

DEVOURING.

Ex. 24: 17. his appear. like d. fire
Ps. 52: 4. Thou lovest all d. words
Is. 29: 6. visited with d. fire, 30: 30.
30: 27. his tongue is as a d. fire
33: 14. Who dwell with d. fire?

DEVOUT.

Lu. 2 : 25. Simeon was just and d.
Ac.2:5. were at Jerus.Jews, d. men
8 : 2. d. men carried Ste. to burial
10:2. Cornel. d. man | 7.d. soldier
13 : 50. Jews stirred up d. women
17 : 4. of d. Greeks a great mult.
17. Paul disputed with d. persons
22 : 12. Ananias a d. man

DEW.

Ge. 27 : 28. God give thee of d., 39.
Ex. 16 : 13. d. lay round the host
14. when d. that lay was gone
Nu. 11 : 9. when d. fell on camp
De. 32 : 2. my speech sh. distil as d.
33 : 13. blessed is Jo 's land for d.
28. his heaven sh. drop down d.
Ju. 6 : 37. If d. be on fleece only
38. wringed d. out of fleece
39. let there be d. | 40. was d.
2 S. 1 : 21. let be no d. upon you
17:12.we will light upon him as d.
1 K. 17 : 1. there shall not be d.
Jb. 29 : 19. d. lay upon my branch
38 : 28. who hath begotten the d.?
Ps. 110 : 3. hast d. of thy youth
133 : 3. As d. of Hermon, as the d.
Pr. 3 : 20. clouds drop down d.
19 : 12. favour as d. upon grass.
Can. 5 : 2. my head is filled with d.
Is. 18 : 4. like cloud of d. in heat
26 : 19. thy d. is as the d. of herbs
Da. 4:15. wet with d. of heaven, 23,
33 body wet with d., 5 : 21. ⌊25.
Ho. 6 : 4. goodness as early d., 13:3.
14 : 5. I will be as d. to Israel
Mi. 5 : 7. Jacob shall be as the d.
Hag. 1:10. heaven is stayed from d.
Zch. 8:12. heavens sh. give their d.

DIADEM.

Jb. 29 : 14. my judgm. was as a d.
Is. 28 : 5. and for a d. of beauty
62 : 3. a royal d. in hand of God
Eze. 21 : 26. Remove the d. take

DIAL.

2 K. 20 : 11. in d. of Ahaz, Is.38:8.

DIAMOND.

Ex. 28 : 18. second row a d., 39:11.
Je. 17:1. sin of Jud. written with d.
Eze.28:13. d. was covering of Tyrus

DIAN'A.

Ac. 19 : 24. made silv. shrines for D.
27. temple of great goddess D.
28. they cried, Great is D. of, 34.
35. Ephesus is worshipper of D.

DIB'LAIM.

Ho. 1 : 3. Hosea took dau. of D.

DIB'LATH.

Eze. 6 : 14. than wilderness tow. D.

DI'BON.

Nu. 21 : 30. perished even unto D.
32 : 34. children of Gad built D.
Jos. 13:17.Mo. gave D. unto Reuben
Ne. 11 : 25. chil. of Jud. dwelt at D.
Is. 15 : 2. up to D. the high place
Je. 48 : 18. dau. that dost inhab. D.
22. judgment is come upon D.

DI'BON-GAD.

Nu. 33:45. pitched in D. | 46. fr. D.

DIB'RI.

Le. 24 : 11. Shelometh dau. of D.

DID.

Ex. 13 : 8. bec. of th. L. d. unto me
18 : 24. father in law d. all he said
De 4:3. what L. d. bec. of Baal-pe.
Jos. 9:10. all he d. to 2 k-s of Amo.
24 : 5. acc. to that I d. am. them
1 S. 12:7. wh. he d. to you and fa-s
30 : † 21. Da. asked how they d.
2 S. 3 : 36. whatso. k. d. pleased all
1 K. 2 : 5. d. to me and d. to capt-s
11 : 25. mischief that Hadad d.
2 K. 18:3. d. right acc. to all David
Ne. 2 : 16. knew not what I d. ⌊d.
Es.2:11. walked to know how Es. d.
9 : 5. d. what they would unto
Je.7:12. what I d. to it for wickedn.
Je.15:4.wh. he d. in Jerus. ⌈Lu.6:3.
Mat. 12 : 3. not read what Da. d.?
21 : 15. saw wonderful things he d.
Mk. 3 : 8. heard great things he d.
Jn. 2 : 23. miracles he d., 6 : 2, 14.
4 : 29. told me all ever I d., 39.
9 : 26. said, What d. he to thee?
15 : 24. works none other man d.
Ac. 2 : 22. which G. d. by him in
3 : 17. ye d. it, as d. your rulers
11 : 30. wh. they d. and sent it
10 : 18. And this d. she many days
26:10. Which thing I d. in Jerus.
2 Co. 8 : 5. d. not as we hoped
He. 7 : 27. he d. once when he off-d
1 Pe. 2 : 22. Who d. no sin, nor

DID joined with as.

Ge.21:1. L. d. unto Sarah a. he had
43 : 17. the man d. a. Joseph bade
50:12.sons d. unto him a. he com.
Ex. 7 : 6. d. a. Lord commanded,
10, 20.-12 : 28, 50.-39 : 32. Le.
8 : 4.-16 : 34.-24 : 23. Nu. 1 :
54.-2 : 34.-20:27.-27:22.-31:31.
Le. 4:20. a. he d. wi. bullock, 16:15.
Nu. 23 : 2. d.a. Balaam had spok.;
De. 2:12. a. Isr. d. unto land ⌊30.
22. a. he d. to Esau | 3:6. Sihon
Jos.4:18. over banks a. they d. bef.
23. a. L. your God d. to Red sea
10 : 28. d. to king of Makkedah a.
11 : 9. Joshua d. a. Lord bade
Ju. 6 : 27. Gideon d. a. L. had said
15 : 11. a. they d. unto me, so I
2 S. 3:36. a. what the k. d. pleased
5 : 25. Da. d. so a. Lord com-d
1 K. 21:11. elders d.a. Jezebel sent
26. Ahab d. a. d. the Amorites
2 K. 8 : 18. Jehoram, a. d. Ahab
17:11. a.d. heathen the L. carried
41. a.d. their fathers, so do they
1 Ch. 14 : 16. Da. d. a. God com-d
2 Ch.25:4. d. a. it is written in law
Is. 58:2. a. a nation that d. righte.
Da. 6:10. Dan. gave thanks a. he d.
Mat. 1:24. Jo. d. a. angel had bid.
21 : 6. d. a. Jesus com-d, 26 : 19.
28:15.watch d.a. they were taught
Lu. 9 : 54. consume a. Elias d.
Ac. 3 : 17. through ignorance a. d.
your rulers ⌈thers d.
7 : 51. ye resist H. Gh. a. your fa-
11 : 17. like gift, a. he d. unto us
He. 4:10. ceased fr. works a. God d.

DID with evil.

Ge. 50 : 15. will requite us e. we d.
17. forgive breth. for they d. e.
Ju. 2 : 11. d. e. in sight of Lord, 3:
7, 12.-4 : 1.-6 : 1.-10 : 6.-13 : 1.
1 K. 14 : 22.-15 : 26, 34.-16 : 7,
30. 2 K. 8 : 27.-13 : 2, 11.-14 :
24.-15 : 9, 18, 24, 28.-17 : 2. 2
Ch. 22 : 4. ⌈of L.
1 K. 11 : 6. Solomon d. e. in sight
2 K. 21 : 2. Manas. d. e., 2 Ch.33:2.
23 : 32. Jehoahaz d. e. | 37. Jehoi.
24:9.Jehoiachin d.e. | 19.Zed.d.e
2 Ch. 12 : 14. Rehoboam d. e.
33 : 22. Amon d. e. as his father
Ne 9 : 28. after had rest they d. e.
13:7. understood the e. Eliashib d.
Is. 65:12. d.e. bef. mine eyes, 66:4.
2 Ti. 4 : 14. coppersmith d. me

DID not. ⌊much e.

Ex.1:17. midwives d.n. as k. com-d
2 K.16:2.Ahaz d.n. right, 2 Ch.28:1.
Ne. 13 : 18. d. n. your fa-s thus (2)
Je.11:8.words com-d th. d. them n.
Jon. 3 : 10. repented of evil, d. it n.
Mat. 13 : 58. he d.n. many mighty
25 : 45. d. it n. to one of these (2)
Jn. 8 : 40. to kill me, this d.n. Ab.
2 Co. 7 : 12. I d. it n. for his cause

DID so.

Ge. 6:22. Noah, as G. com-d s.d. he
29 : 28. Jac. d.s. fulfilled her week
42 : 20. bring bro. And they d. s.
Ex. 7 : 6. as tho L. commanded s.
d. they, 10.-12 : 28, 50.-39 : 32.
-40 : 16. Nu. 1 : 54.
22. magicians d. s., 8 : 7, 18.
8 : 24. Lord d. s. and a swarm of
17 : 6. Moses d. s. | 10. Joshua
Nu. 8:3. Aa-n d.s.; he lighted lamps
36 : 10. s. d. the dau-s of Zelophe.
Jos. 6:14. compassed city, s. they d.
11 : 15. s. d. Moses, s. d. Joshua
Ju. 2 : 17. they d. not s. | 6 : 40. G.
1 S. 1 : 7. he d. s. yr. by yr. ⌊d. s.
2 : 14. s. they d. in Shiloh to Isr.
27 : 11. s. d. Da. and so will be his
1 K. 12 : 32. s. d. he in Beth-el
14 : 4. Jerob.'s wife d. s. ⌈d.not I
Ezr. 6 : 13. s. they d. | Ne. 5:15. s.
Is. 20:2. Isaiah d.s. walking naked
Je.38:12.Jere.d.s. | Eze.12:7.I d.s.
Mat. 9:19. Jes. arose, s.d. his disci.
Lu. 6:10. Stretch forth ha., he d. s.
26. s. d. their fa-s to false proph.
Jn. 18 : 15. foll. Jes. and s. d. ano.
Ac. 19 : 14. seven sons of Sheva who

Thus DID. ⌊d.s.

Ge. 42 : 25. to fill sacks. t. d. he
Ex. 36 : 29. t.d. he to both of them
40:16. t.d. Moses acc. as L. com-d
Nu. 32 : 8. t. d. your fathers
2 S. 12:31. t.d. he unto all the cities
2 K. 16 : 16. t. d. Urijah the priest
2 Ch. 24 : 11. t. they d. day by day
31 : 20. t.d. Hezekiah thro. Judah
Ne. 13 : 18. d. not your fathers t..
Jb. 1 : 5. sanctified them, t.d. Job

DIDST.

Ge. 20 : 6. d. this in the integrity
Nu. 21:34. as d. unto Sihon, De.3:2.
Jos. 8 : 2. as thou d. unto Jericho
2 S. 12 : 12. for thou d. it secretly
13:16. other that thou d. unto me
1 K. 2 : 44. that thou d. to David
8:18. d. well it was in heart, 2 Ch.
Ne. 9 : 17. wonders thou d. ⌊6 : 8.
Ps. 39 : 9. dumb, bec. thou d. it
44 : 1. told work thou d. in days
137:†8. the deed wh. thou d. to us
Is. 64 : 3. When d. terrible things
Ac. 7 : 28. kill me as thou d. Egyp.

DID'YMUS.

Jn. 11 : 16. Thomas who is called
D., 20 : 24.-21 : 2.

DIE.

Ge. 6 : 17. ev. thing in earth sh. d.
33 : 13. if overdrive, flock will d.
44 : 9. let him d. | 22. fa. would d.
46 : 30. let me d. | 47:29. Isr. must
Ex. 7 : 18. fish in river shall d. ⌊d.
9 : 4. nothing sh. d. that is of Isr.
19. hail sh. come they shall d.
10 : 28. seest my face thou shalt d.
11:5.firstb. in E. shall d. ⌈they d.
21 : 28. ox gore man or woman th.
22 : 10. beast to keep, and it d.
14. borrow of neighb. and it d.
28 : 43. when they come to altar,
bear not iniq., and d., Le. 22:9.
Le. 11 : 39. if any beast d.
20 : 20. they shall d. childless
Nu. 4 : 15. not touch holy thing,
lest they d.
20. are covered, lest they d.
6:7. for bro. or sister when they d.
9. If any man d. very suddenly
14:35. in this wildern. they sh. d.
16 : 29. if these d. common death
17 : 13. cometh near tab. shall d.,
18:3. nei. they, nor you, d. ⌊18:22.
20:26. strip Aa., he shall d. there
23 : 10. let me d. death of righte.
27:8. If a man d. and have no son
De.17:5. stone th. they d., 22:21, 24.
12. man sh. d. | 18 : 20. prophet
22:22. both sh. d. | 25. man only d.
24:3. if latter husb. d. | 7. thief d.
25:5. if d. and no chil, Mk.12:19.
31 : 14. days approach th. thou d.

De. 32:50. behold Canaan, and d. in
Ju. 16: 30. Let me d. with Philis.
1 S. 2: 23. increase of house sh. d.
34. thy two sons in one day sh. d.
14: 45. peo. said, Shall Jona. d.?
2 S. 18: 3. nor if half of us d.
1 K. 14: 12. enter city, child sh. d.
2 K. 20: 1. thou shalt d., Is. 38:1.
2 Ch. 25: 4. not d. for chil., every
man d. for his sin, Je. 31: 30.
Jb. 2: 9. wife said, Curse G. and d.
4: 21. they d. without wisdom
12: 2. wisdom shall d. with you
14: 8. tho. stock d. in the ground
14. If man d. shall he live again?
34: 20. In a moment shall they d.
36: 12. if obey not, they shall d.
14. they d. in youth, their life is
Ps. 49: 10. that wise men d. also
104: 29. takest breath, they d.
Pr. 10:21. fools d. for want of wisd.
Ec. 7: 17. why d. before thy time?
9: 5. living know they shall d.
Is. 22: 18. in large country, shalt d.
51:6. th. that dwell therein sh. d.
12. afraid of man that shall d.
65: 20. child d. a hundred yrs. old
Je. 11: 22. young men shall d. by
sword, dau-s shall d. by famine
16: 4. They sh. d. of griev. deaths
6. great and the small shall d.
20: 6. come to Bab. and there d.
21: 6. shall d. of great pestilence
28: 16. This year thou shalt d.
34: 5. But thou shalt d. in peace
42: 17. unto E. to sojourn; they
shall d., 44: 12. [33: 8.
Eze. 3: 18. wick. d. in his iniquity,
5: 12. d. with pestil., 6:12.-33:27.
18: 4. soul sinneth, shall d., 20.
28: 8. thou shalt d. death of
10. Thou shalt d. the deaths of
the uncircumcised
Am. 2: 2. Moab sh. d. with tumult
6:9. if ten men in one h. th. sh. d.
7: 11. Jerobo. shall d. by sword
17. shalt d. in a polluted land
9:10. sinners of peo. sh. d. by sw.
Zch. 11: 9. that that dieth, let it d.
13: 8. saith L., two parts shall d.
Mat. 15:4. that curseth fa. or moth.,
let him d., Mk. 7: 10. [28.
22: 24. d. having no seed, Lu. 20:
Lu. 20: 36. neith. can d. any more
Jn. 4: 49. Sir, come ere my child d.
8: 21. shall seek me and d., 24.
11:26. believ-h in me sh. never d.
50. that one d. for peo., 18: 14.
51. that Jesus d. for that nation
12:24. exc. corn of wheat d. if it d.
Ro. 5:7. for righte. man will one d.
1 Co. 15: 22. For as in Adam all d.
36. is not quickened except it d.
He. 7: 8. men that d. rec. tithes
Re. 14:13. Blessed that d. in the L.

He DIE.

Ge. 38: 11. Lest h. d. as his breth.
44:31. lad is not with us, h. will d.
Ex. 21: 12. smiteth man, that h. d.
14. sh. take him fr. altar, th. h. d.
20. smite his servant, and h. d.
35. ox hurt another's that h. d.
22: 2. if thief be smitten th. h. d.
Nu. 35: 16. if he smite him that h.
d., 20, 21, 23. De. 13: 10.-19:
5, 11.-21: 21. [De. 19:12.
17. wherew. h. may d., 18, 23.
De. 20: 5. lest h. d. in battle. 6, 7.
Ju. 6: 30. Bring out son that h. d.
2 S. 11: 15. from Uriah that h. d.
1 K. 1: 52. if wickedness h. sh. d.
2: 1. days of Da. nigh that h. d.
19:4. Elijah requested h. might d.
21: 10. stone him that h. may d.
Ps. 41: 5. When shall h. d. and
Pr. 5:23. h. shall d. without instr.
15:10. h. that hateth reproof sh. d.
Pr. 19: 16. h. th. despiseth ways sh. d.
Je. 21: 9. h. abideth in city shall
d., 38: 2. [him captive
22:12. h. shall d. whither they led
38: 10. take up Jere. before h. d.
Eze. 3: 19. if warn wicked, h. shall
d. in iniq., 20.-18: 18, 24, 26.-
33: 9, 13, 18.
12: 13. not see it, tho. h. d. there
17: 16. in Babylon h. shall d.
Lu. 20: 28. h. d. without children,
Mk. 12: 19. [18: 32.
Jn. 12:33. what death h. should d.,

I DIE.

Ge. 19:19. lest evil take me, and I d.
26: 9. I said, lest I d. for her
27:4. my soul may bless thee bef. I
30: 1. said, Give me chil., or I d. [d.
45: 28. I will see him before I d.
48: 21. Israel said to Joseph, I d.
50:5. lo, I d. | 24. Joseph said, I d.
De. 4: 22. I must d. in this land
Ju. 15: 18. now sh. I d. for thirst
Ru. 1:17. Where thou diest, will I d.
1 S. 14: 43. taste, and lo, I must d.
2 S. 19: 37. that I d. in own city
1 K. 2: 30. Nay, but I will d. here
Jb. 27:5. till I d. I will not remove
29: 18. I said, I sh. d. in my nest
Pr. 30:7. deny me th. not bef. I d.
Je. 37:20. not ret., lest I d. [14:31.
Mat. 26: 35. Tho. I should d., Mk.
1 Co. 15: 31. I protest, I d. daily

Not DIE. [47: 19.

Ge. 42:2. may live and n. d., 43:8.-
20. so words verified, ye sh. n. d.
Ex. 21: 18. d. n., but keepeth his
28:35. be heard, th. he d. n. [bed
30: 20. wash, that they d. n., 21.
Le. 8: 35. keep charge th. ye d. n.
15:31. that they d. n., Nu. 4:19.-
17: 10. [that he d. n.
16:2. th. he come not at all times,
13. cover mercy seat, th. he d. n.
Nu. 35: 12. manslayer, d. n., Jos.
20: 9. [more that I d. n.
De. 18: 16. nei. see great fire any
33: 6. Let Reuben live and n. d.
Ju. 6: 23. thou shalt n. d., 1 S.
20: 2. 2 S. 12: 13.-19: 23. Je.
38: 24. [we d. n.
1 S. 12:19. Pray for thy serv-ts that
20: 14. shew me kindn. th. I d. n.
2 K. 18: 32. that ye live and n. d.
2 Ch. 25: 4. fathers n. d. for chil.
Ps. 118: 17. I shall n. d. but live
Pr. 23: 13. if beatest him with rod,
he shall n. d., Eze. 18: 17, 21,
28.-33: 15. Jn. 21: 23.
Is. 51: 14. that he n. d. in pit
66: 24. their worm shall n. d.
Je. 11: 21. thou n. d. by our hand
34: 4. Zed., Thou n. d. by sword
Eze. 13:19. slay souls that sho. n. d.
Ha. 1: 12. we shall n. d. L. thou
Jn. 6:50. that a man eat, and n. d.
21: 23. that that disciple sho. n. d.

Surely DIE.

Ge. 2: 17. thou shalt s. d., 20: 7.
1 S. 14: 44.-22: 16. 1 K. 2:37,
42. Je. 26:8. Eze. 3:18.-33:8, 14.
3: 4. serp. said, Ye shall not s. d.
Nu. 26:65. L. said, They shall s. d.
Ju. 13: 22. We shall s. d. bec. we
1 S. 14: 39. tho. in Jona. my son,
he sh. s. d., 20: 31. 2 S. 12: 5.
2 K. 8: 10. Eze. 18: 13.
2 S. 12: 14. child born shall s. d.
2 K. 1: 4. not come, but s. d., 6, 16.

To DIE.

Ge. 25: 32. I am at the point t. d.
Ex. 14: 11. t. d. in wilderness, Nu.
21: 5. [bear sin t. d.
Nu. 18: † 22. come nigh, lest they
35: 30. testify, to cause him t. d.
† 31. for him who is faulty t. d.
Jos. 2: † 14. instead of you t. d.
1 S. 26: 10. his day shall come t. d.
16. ye are worthy t. d. bec. ye
28: 9. a snare, to cause me t. d.
2 Ch. 32: 11. yours. t. d. by famine
Ps. 79: 11. that are appointed t. d.
88: 15. I am afflic. and ready t. d.
Pr. 19: † 18. spare, to cause him t. d.
Ec. 3: 2. to be born, time t. d.
Je. 26: 11. This man worthy t. d.
16. man not worthy t. d.
38: 9. he is like t. d. for hunger
26. return to Jona.'s house t. d.
Jon. 4:3 it is better for me t. d., 8.
8. Jonah fainted, and wished t. d.
Lu. 7: 2. servant was ready t. d.
Jn. 19: 7. by our law he ought t. d.
Ac. 21: 13. I am ready also t. d.
25: 11. if worthy I refuse not t. d.
16. not of Romans to deliver t. d.
Ro. 5: 7. for good man some would
even dare t. d.
1 Co. 9: 15. were better for me t. d.
2 Co. 7: 3. you in our hearts t. d.
Ph. 1. 21. to live is C. t. d. is gain
He. 9:27. appoint. to men once t. d.
Re. 3: 2. things th. are ready t. d.
9:6. desire t. d. and death sh. flee

We DIE.

Ge. 47: 15. why w. d. in thy, 19.
Ex. 14: 12. than that w. d. in wilderness [De. 5: 25.
20: 19. let not G. speak, lest w. d.,
Nu. 17:12. Behold, w. d. we perish
20: 4. that w. and cattle d. there
1 S. 12: 19. Pray that w. d. not
2 S. 14: 14. for w. must needs d.
1 K. 17: 12. me and my son that w.
may eat it and d. [d.? 4.
2 K. 7: 3. Why sit we here until w.
4. if kill us, w. sh. but d. [15:32.
Is. 22: 13. to morrow w. d., 1 Co.
Jn. 11: 16. go that w. d. with him
Ro. 14: 8. whether w. d. w. d. un-

Ye DIE. [to L.

Ge. 3: 3. neither touch it lest y. d.
Le. 10: 6. neith. rend clothes, lest
7. not go out, lest y. d., 9. [y. d.
Nu. 18: 32. nor pollute, lest y. d.
Ps. 82: 7. But y. shall d. like men
Is. 22: 14. not be purged till y. d.
Je. 22: 26. there shall y. d., 42: 16.
27: 13. Why will y. d.? Eze. 18:
31.-33: 11. [sword
42: 22. know that y. sh. d. by the
Jn. 8: 21. and y. sh. d. in sins, 24.
Ro. 8: 13. if live after flesh y. d.

DIED. [Haran

Ge. 7: 21. all flesh d., 22. | 11: 28.
11: 32. Terah d. | 23: 2. Sarah d.
25:8. Abraham d. | 17. Ishmael d.
35: 8. Deborah the nurse d. [d.
18. Rachel d., 19.-48:7. | 29. Isaac
36: 33. Belah d. | 34. Jobab d.
35. Husham d. | 36. Hadad d., 1
37. Samlah d. [Ch. 1: 51.
38. Saul d. | 39. Baal-hanan d.
38:12. Jud.'s wife d. | 46:12. Er d.
50:16. Thy fa. did command bef. he
26. So Joseph d., Ex. 1: 6. [d.
Ex. 2: 23. k. of E. d. | 7:21. fish d.
8: 13. frogs d. | 9:6. cattle of E. d.
16: 3. Would to G. we had d. in
E., Nu. 14: 2.-20: 3.-26: 10.
Le. 10: 2. Nadab and Abihu d., 16:
1. Nu. 3: 4.-26:61. 1 Ch. 24:2.
Nu. 14: 37. searchers of the land d.
20: 28. Aaron d., 33: 38, 39. De.
10: 6.-32: 50. [them th. d.
16: 49. now they that d. beside
20:1. Miriam d. | 21:6. much peo. d.
25: 9. that d. in plague 24.000
26: 11. the chil. of Korah d. not
27: 3. dau-s of Zeloph. said, Our fa.
d. in wilder. but d. in own sin
De. 34:5. Mos. d. | 7. 120 when he d.
Jos. 5: 4. all the men of war d.
10: 11. they were more which d.

Jos. 24: 29. Josh. d., Ju. 2: 8. [22.
33. Eleazar son of Aa. d., 1 Ch. 23:
Ju. 1: 7. Adonibezek d.
2: 21. nations Jos. left when he d.
8: 11. Othniel d. | 8:32. Gideon d.
9: 49. all the men of Shechem d.
10: 2. Tola d. | 5. Jair d.
12:7. Jephthah judged 6 yrs. then
10. Ibzan d. | 12. Elon d. [d.
15. Abdon d. | Ru. 1: 3. Elim. d.
5. Mahlon and Chilion d. both
1 S. 4: † 11. Eli's sons d.
5: 12. that d. were not smit. with
25:1. Sam. d. | 37. Nabal's heart d.
31: 5. armourbearer fell upon his sword and d. with him, 6. 1 Ch. 10: 5, 13. [men d.
2 S. 2:23. Asahel d. | 31. So that 360
3: 33. d. Abner as a fool [13: 10.
6:7. there Uzzah d. bef. L., 1 Ch.
10:1. king of Ammon d., 1 Ch. 19:1.
18. Shobach d. | 11:17. Uriah d.
12: 18. on 7th day child d. [d.
17:23. Ahithophel hang. hims. and
18: 33. would G. I had d. for thee,
19: 6. all we had d. this day [Abs.
24: 15. d. of people, even fr. Dan
1 K. 3:19. this woman's child d. in
14: 17. came to threshold child d.
16: 18. Zimri d. | 22. Tibni d.
22: 35. Ahab d., 37. [then d.
2 K. 4: 20. on her knees till noon
9:27. Ahaziah to Megiddo d. there
13:14. Elisha d. 20. | 24. Hazael d.
23:34. Jehoahaz to E. and d. there
1 Ch. 2: 30. Seled d. without chil.
32. Jether d. | 2 Ch. 16:13. Asa d.
18:34. time of sun going down he d.
24: 15. Jehoiada full of days d.
22. wh. he d. he said, The L. look
35: 24. Josiah d. and was buried
Jb. 3: 11. Why d. I not fr. womb?
42: 17. so Job d. being old and
Is. 6:1. in year k. Uzziah d. I saw L.
14: 28. In year that king Ahaz d.
Je. 28:17. Hananiah the prophet d.
Eze. 11: 13. Pelatiah d.
24: 18. at even my wife d.
Ho. 13: 1. offended in Baal, he d.
Mat. 22:27. and last of all the woman d. also, Mk. 12:22. Lu. 20:32.
Mk. 12: 21. second took her, and d.
Lu. 16: 22. beggar d. rich man d.
20: 31. they left no chil. and d.
Jn. 11: 21. if here, bro. not d., 32.
37. caused that man not have d.
Ac. 7: 15. Jac. went into E. and d.
9: 37. Dorcas was sick and d.
Ro. 5: 6. in due time Christ d., 8.
7: 9. sin revived, and I d.
8: 34. it is Christ that d. [and
14: 9. to this end C. both d. rose
15. destr. not him with thy meat for whom C. d., 1 Co. 8: 11.
1 Co. 15: 3. how C. d. for our sins
2 Co. 5: 14. if one d. for all, all d.
15. live unto him wh. d. for them
1 Th. 4: 14. if we believe Jesus d.
5: 10. Who d. for us that we live
He. 10: 28. despised Moses' law d.
11: 13. These d. in faith, not hav.
22. By faith Joseph when he d.
Re. 8: 9. third part of creatures d.
11. many d. of waters bitter
16: 3. every living soul d. in sea

And he, So he, That he DIED.

Ge. 5: 5. of Adam 930 yrs. a. h. d.
9:29. Noah's were 950 yrs. a. h. d.
Nu. 15: 36. stoned him a. h. d., 1 K. 12: 18.-21:13. 2 Ch. 10: 18.
Ju. 4: 21. Jael smote nail, s. h. d.
9: 54. thrust him thro. a. h. d.
1 S. 4: 18. Eli's neck brake a. h. d.
14: 45. rescued Jona. t. h. d. not
25: 38. Lord smote Nabal t. h. d.
2 S. 1: 15. he smote him t. h. d.
2 S. 3: 27. t. h. d. for bl. of his bro.
11: 21. smote Abim. t. h. d. [d.
20: 10. struck him not again a. h.
1 K. 2:25. fell upon him t. h. d., 46.
12: 18. stoned Adoram t. h. d., 2 Ch. 10: 18. [of L.
2 K. 1: 17. s. h. u. accord. to word
7: 17. peo. trod upon him a. h. d.,
8: 15. cloth on face, t. h. d. [20.
12: 21. his servants smote Joash a. h. d., 2 Ch. 24: 25.
25: 25. smote Gedaliah, t. h. d.
1 Ch. 29: 28. a. h. d. in good old age
2 Ch. 13:20. L. struck Jerob. a. h. d.
21: 19. bowels fell out s. h. d. [30.
Lu. 20: 29. a. h. d. without chil.,
Ac. 7:15. Jac. d. in E., h. a. our fa.
Ro. 6: 10. in t. h. d. h. d. unto sin
2 Co. 5:15. t. h. d. for all, th. they

DIEST.

Ru. 1: 17. Where thou d. will I die

DIET.

Je. 52: 34. his d. was continual d.

DIETH.

Le. 7:24. fat of beast th. d. of itself
22: 8. d. of its. shall not eat, De. 14: 21. [man d.
Nu. 16: † 29. If these d. as every
19: 14. when a man d. in tent
2 S. 3: 33. Died Abner as a fool d.?
1 K. 14:11. th. d. in city sh. dogs eat
16: 4. d. in field fowls eat, 21: 24.
Jb. 14: 10. man d. and wast. away
21: 23. One d. in his full strength
25. ano. d. in bitterness of soul
36:† 14. their soul d. in youth, life
Ps. 49: 17. when he d. he sh. carry
Pr. 11:7. wicked man d. his expecta.
Ec. 2: 16. how d. the wise man?
3: 19. as one d. so d. the other
Is. 50: 2. their fish d. for thirst
59: 5. he that eat. of their eggs d.
Eze. 4: 14. nor eaten that d. of its.
18: 26. committeth iniq., and d. in them [that d.
32. no pleasure in death of him
Zch. 11: 9. that that d. let it d.
Mk. 9:44. their worm d. not, 46, 48.
Ro. 6:9. C. being raised d. no more
14:7. none liv. no man d. to hims.

DYING. See after DYED.

DIFFER, ETH, ING.

Ro. 2: † 18. triest the things th. d.
12: 6. gifts d-g acc. to grace given
1 Co. 4: 7. who maketh thee to d?
15: 41. one star d-h from another
Ga. 4: 1. heir when child d-h noth.
Phi. 1:† 10. may try things that d.

DIFFERENCE, S.

Ex. 11:7. L. put a d. betw. Egyp. and
Le. 10:10. a d. betw. holy and unho.
11: 47. to make a d. betw. uncl.
20: 25. put a d. betw. clean beasts
Eze. 22: 26. put no d. shewed no n.
44: 23. teach my peo. d. betw. holy
Ac. 15: 9. no d. betw. us and them
Ro. 3:22. that bel., for there is no d.
10: 12. is no d. betw. Jew and Gr.
14: † 23. putteth a d. betw. meats
1 Co. 7:34. d. betw. wife and a virgin
12: 5. d-s of administrations
Jude 22. compassion making a d.

DIFFICULT.

Zch. 8: † 6. if it be d. in the eyes

DIG.

Ex. 21: 33. if a man d. a pit, and
De. 8: 9. hills thou mayest d. brass
23: 13. have paddle, and d. therew.
Jb. 3: 21. d. for it more than treas.
6: 27. ye d. a pit for your friend
11: 18. thou shalt d. about thee
24:16. in dark they d. thro. houses
39: † 21. His feet d. in the valley
Eze. 8: 8. Son of man, d. in wall
12: 5. d. thou thro. the wall, 12.
Am. 9: 2. Though they d. into hell
Lu. 13:8. L., let it alone, till I d. about
Lu. 16: 3. I cannot d., to beg I am [ash.

DIGGED.

Ge. 21: 30. witness that I d. this well
26: 15. wells servants had d., 18.
19. servants d. in valley, 21, 22, 25.
32. told Isaac of well they d.
49: 6. in selfwill d. down a wall
50: 5. in grave I had d. bury me
Ex. 7: 24. all Egypt-s d. for water
Nu. 21: 18. princes d., nobles d.
De. 6: 11. wells d., Ne. 9: 25.
2 K. 19: 24. I have d. and drunk strange waters, Is. 37: 25.
2 Ch. 16: † 14. sepulchres he had d.
26: 10. Uzziah d. wells for cattle
Ps. 7: 15. made pit and d. it, 57: 6.
35: 7. they d. a pit for my soul
40: † 6. mine ears hast thou d.
94: 13. until pit be d. for wicked
119: 85. proud have d. pits for me
Is. 5: 6. it sh. not be pruned nor d.
7: 25. on hills be d. with mattock
51: 1. hole of pit whence ye are d.
Je. 13:7. I went to Euphrates and d.
18: 20. d. a pit for my soul, 22.
Eze. 8: 8. when I had d. in wall
12: 7. I d. thro. wall with hand
Jon. 1:† 13. d. hard to bri. it to land
Mat. 21: 33. d. a winepress in it
25: 18. d., and hid lord's money
Mk. 12: 1. d. place for winefat
Lu. 6:48. d. and laid founda. on rock
Ro. 11: 3. d. down thine altars

DIGGEDST, ETH, ING.

De. 6: 11. wells wh. thou d-t not
Pr. 16: 27. ungod. man d-h up evil
26: 27. d-h a pit shall fall, Ec. 10:8.
Je. 2: † 34. have not found it by d-g

DIGNITY, IES.

Ge. 49: 3. Reuben, excellency of d.
Es. 6: 3. what d. done to Mord.?
Ec. 10: 6. Folly is set in great d.
Ha. 1: 7. d. shall proceed of thems.
2 Pe. 2: 10. speak evil of d-s, Jude [8.

DIK'LAH.

Ge. 10:27. Joktan begat D., 1 Ch. 1:21.

DIL'EAN.

Jos. 15: 38. D. Mizpeh, cities

DILIGENCE.

Pr. 4:23. Keep thy heart with all d.
Lu. 12: 58. as art in way, give d.
Ro. 12: 8. that ruleth with d.
2 Co. 8: 7. as ye abound in all d.
2 Ti. 4: 9. Do thy d. to come, 21.
He. 6:11. that ev. one shew same d.
2 Pe. 1: 5. giving all d. add to faith
10. give d. to make calling sure
Jude 3. gave all d. to write of salva.

DILIGENT.

De. 19: 18. sh. make d. inquisition
Jos. 22:5. take d. heed to do com-ts
Ps. 64: 6. accomplish d. search
77: 6. my spirit made d. search
Pr. 10: 4. hand of d. maketh rich
12: 24. hand of d. shall bear rule
27. substance of d. is precious
13: 4. soul of d. shall be made fat
21:5. thoughts of d. tend to plenty
22: 29. Seest man d. in business?
27: 23. Be d. to know thy flock
2 Co. 8:22. whom we have oft. proved d. but now much more d.
2 Tit. 3:† 10. hast been a d. follower
Ti. 3: 12. be d. to come unto me
2 Pe. 3:14. be d. th. ye be found of him

DILIGENTLY.

Ex. 15: 26. If thou wilt d. hearken to, De. 11: 13.-28: 1. Je. 17:24.
Le. 10: 6. Moses d. sought the goat
De. 4: 9. Only keep thy soul d.
6: 7. shalt teach them d. to chil.
17. ye shall d. keep com-ts, 11: 22.
13: 14. ask d. and if it be truth
17: 4. inquired d., behold it true
24:8. take heed th. thou observe d.
1 S. 20: † 19. thou shalt go down d.
1 K. 20: 33. the men did d. observe

zt. 7 : 23. be d. done for house of G.
b 13 : 17. Hear d. my speech, 21 : 2.
s. 37 : 10. shalt d. consider his pls.
119 : 4. com-ded to keep precepts d.
r 7 : 15. came I d. to seek thy face
11 : 27. He that d. seeketh good
23 : 1. consider d. what is before
s. 21 : 7. he hearkened d. ⌊thee
55 : 2. hearken d. unto me and eat
e. 2 : 10. consider d., see if be such
12 : 16. if they d. learn ways of peo.
ch. 6 : 15. if ye will d. obey the L.
Mat. 2 : 7. inquired d. time star app.
8. Go, search d. for young child
16. had d. inquired of wise men
Mk. 7 : †3. exc. they wash hands d.
Lu. 15 : 8. and seek d. till she find it
Ac. 18 : 25. taught d. things of Lord
Ti. 5 : 10. if d. followed every good
Ti. 1 : 17. in Rome he sought me d.
Tit. 3 : 13. bri. Apollos on journey d.
He. 11 : 6. rewarder of them d. seek
12 : 15. Looking d. lest any fail of
Pe. 1 : 10. prophets have searched
DILL. Mat. 23 : †23. ⌊d.

DIM.

Ge. 27 : 1. Isaac was old, his eyes d.
48 : 10. eyes of Isr. were d. for age
De. 34 : 7. Moses, his eye was not d.
S. 3 : 2. Eli's eyes to wax d., 4 : 15.
Jb. 17 : 7. Mine eye is d. by sorrow
s. 32 : 3. eyes that see sh. not be d.
La. 4 : 1. How is gold become d.?
5 : 17. for these things our eyes are d.

DIMINISH, ED, ING.

Ex. 5 : 8. ye shall not d. aught th-f
11. nor aught of work be d-d, 19.
21 : 10. her duty of marriage, he not
30 : †15. the poor shall not d. ⌊d.
Le. 25 : 16. acc. to yrs. d. price of it
Nu. 26 : †54. to few d. inherit-e, 33 :
De. 4 : 2. nei. d. aught, 12 : 32. ⌊†54.
Pr. 13 : 11. Wealth by vanity be d-d
Is. 21 : 17. mighty of Kedar be d-d
Je. 10 : †24. anger, lest thou d. me
26 : 2. all I command d. not a word
29 : 6. ye may be increased, not d-d
48 : †37. ev. head bald, beard d-d.
Eze. 5 : 11. defiled sanct-y, I d. thee
16 : 27. I d-d thine ordinary food
29 : 15. I will d. them, sh. no more
Ro. 11 : 12. if d-g of them be riches
DIMLY. Is. 42 : †3.

DIM'NAH.

Jos. 21 : 35. D. with her suburbs

DIMNESS.

Is. 8 : 22. behold trouble, d. of anguish
9 : 1. d. not be as was in her vexat-n

DI'MON. ⌈(2)

Is. 15 : 9. waters of D. be full of blood
DIMO'NAH. See KINAH.

DI'NAH. ⌈46 : 15.

Ge. 30 : 21. Leah a dau. D., 34 : 1, 3.-
34 : 13. bec Shechem had defiled D.,
25. D.'s breth. slew Shechem, 26 ⌊5.
DI'NAITES. See DEHAVITES.

DINE, ED.

Ge. 43 : 16. shall d. with me at noon
Lu. 11 : 37. Phari. besought him to d.
Jn. 21 : 12. Jesus saith, Come and d.
15. had d-d, Jesus saith to Simon

DIN'HABAH.

Ge. 36 : 32. his city was D., 1 Ch. 1 :

DINNER. ⌊43.

Pr. 15 : 17. Better is a d. of herbs
Mat. 22 : 4. I have prepared my d.
Lu. 11 : 38. had not washed before d.
14 : 12. when makest a d., call not

DIONYS'IUS. ⌊friends

Ac. 17 : 34. believed; D. the Areopa-

DIOT'REPHES. ⌊gite

3 Jn. 9. D., who loveth preëminence

DIP.

Ex. 12 : 22. d. it in blood in basin
Le. 4 : 6. shall d. his finger, 17.-14 : 16.
14 : 6. d. living bird in blood, 51.
Nu. 19 : 18. clean person sh. d. hyssop
De. 33 : 24. let Asher d. foot in oil
Ru. 2 : 14. d. thy morsel in vinegar
Lu. 16 : 24. Lazarus that he d. his
DI'PHATH. 1 Ch. 1 : †6. ⌊finger

DIPPED, PETH.

Ge. 37 : 31. they d-d coat in the blood
Le. 9 : 9. Aaron d-d finger in blood
Jos. 3 : 15. feet of priests were d-d in w.
1 S. 14 : 27. d-d end of rod in honeyco.
2 K. 5 : 14. Naaman d. in Jordan
8 : 15. Hazael d-d cloth in water
Ps. 68 : 23. foot d-d in blood of ene-s
Mat. 26 : 23. He that d-h his hand
with me in dish, Mk. 14 : 20.
Jn. 13 : 26. when he had d-d sop (2)
Re. 19 : 13. with vesture d-d in blood

DIRECT, ED, ETH. ⌈en

Ge. 46 : 28. to d. his face unto Gosh-
Jb. 32 : 14. not d-d his words ag-t me
37 : 3. He d-h it und. whole heaven
Ps. 5 : 3. in morning I d. my prayer
119 : 5. O that my ways were d-d
141 : †2. let my prayer be d-d as inc.
Pr. 3 : 6. acknowledge him, he sh. d.
11 : 5. righteousness of perfect shall
16 : 9. the Lord d-h his steps ⌊d.
21 : 29. for upright, he d-h his way
Ec. 10 : 10. wisdom is profitable to d.
Is. 40 : 13. Who hath d-d Spirit of
45 : 13. I will d. all his ways ⌊L.?
61 : 8. I will d. their work in truth
Je. 10 : 23. not in man to d. his steps
1 Th. 3 : 11. L. d. our way unto you
2 Th. 3 : 5. L. d. hearts into love of G.

DIRECTION. ⌈giver

Nu. 21 : 18. digged well by d. of law-
Ps. 19 : †4. Their d. is gone out thro.

DIRECTLY. ⌈tabern.

Nu. 19 : 4. sprinkle blood d. before
Eze. 42 : 12. way d. before the wall

DIRT. ⌈out

Ju. 3 : 22. the fat closed, d. came
Ps. 18 : 42. I did cast them out as d.
Is. 57 : 20. whose waters cast up d.

* **DISALLOW, ED.**

Nu. 30 : 5. if father d. her; because
her father d-d her ⌈her not
8. if husband d-d her | 11. if d-d
1 Pe. 2 : 4. d-d of men, but chosen of
7. stone which the builders d-d is

DISANNUL, LED, LETH.

Jb. 40 : 8. Wilt thou d. my judgm.?
Is. 14 : 27. L. hath purposed, who d.
28 : 18. covenant with death be d-d
Ga. 3 : 15. covenant no man d-h ⌈d.
17. covenant in Chr., law cannot

DISANNULLING. ⌈ment

He. 7 : 18. is verily a d. of command-

DISAPPOINT, ED, ETH.

Jb. 5 : 12. He d-h devices of crafty
Ps. 17 : 13. Arise, O Lord, d. him
Pr. 15 : 22. Without counsel purposes

DISCERN. ⌊are d-d

Ge. 31 : 32. d. what is thine with me
38 : 25. she said, d. whose are these
2 S. 14 : 17. so is my lord to d. good
19 : 35. can I d. between good and
1 K. 3 : 9. I may d. between good and
11. asked underst-g to d. judgment
Ezr. 3 : 13. could not d. noise of joy
Jb. 4 : 16. I could not d. the form
6 : 30. my taste d. perverse things
Eze. 44 : 23. d. between unclean and
Jon. 4 : 11. not d. betw. right hand
Mal. 3 : 18. d. betw. righte. and wicked
Mat. 16 : 3. ye can d. face of sky; but
can ye not d. times? Lu. 12 : 56.
He. 5 : 14. senses exercised to d. good

DISCERNED. ⌈hairy

Ge. 27 : 23. d. him not, his hands
1 K 20 : 41. king of Israel d. he was
Ne. 13 : †24. d. not to speak in Jews'
Pr. 7 : 7. I d. among the youths a y.
1 Co. 2 : 14. they are spiritually d.
†15. yet he himself is d. of no man

DISCERNER.

He. 4 : 12. is a d. of the thoughts

DISCERNETH, ING.

Ec. 8 : 5. a wise man's heart d-h time
Ro. 14 : †23. that d-h betw-n meats
1 Co. 2 : †15. he that is spiritual d-h
11 : 29. not d-g the Lord's body ⌊all
12 : 10. to another is given d-g of

DISCHARGE. ⌊spirits

Ec. 8 : 8. there is no d. in that war

DISCHARGED.

1 K. 5 : 9. will cause them to be d.

DISCIPLE. ⌈Lu. 6 : 40.

Mat. 10 : 24. d. not above master,
25. enough for d. he be as master
42. cup of water in name of a d.
27 : 57. Joseph, who was Jesus' d.
Lu 14 : 26. If any man hate not his
life he cannot be my d. ⌈my d.
27. doth not bear cross cannot be
33. forsaketh not all cannot be my
Jn. 9 : 28. Thou his d.; we Moses' ⌊d.
18 : 15. Pet. followed, so did anoth.
d.; d. known unto high priest
16. Then went out that other d.
19 : 26. d. standing by whom he lov.
27. saith to the d., Behold thy
mother! that d. took her unto
38. being a d. secretly ⌊his home
20 : 2. d. whom Jesus loved, 21 : 7, 20.
3. Peter went and that other d.
4. the other d. did outrun Peter
8. went in that other d., he saw
21 : 23. that that d. should not die
24. This is the d. which testifieth
Ac. 9 : 10. was a certain d. Ananias
26. they believed not he was a d.
36. at Joppa a d. named Tabitha
16 : 1. a certain d. named Timoth-s
21 : 16. Mnason of Cyprus, an old d.

DISCIPLES.

Is 8 : 16. seal the law among my d.
Mat. 9 : 14. came to him d. of John
12 : 1. thy d. do that is not lawful
13 : 10. d. said, Why speakest in p.
14 : 26. d. saw him walking on sea
15 : 2. Why do thy d. transg. tradition of elders? Mk. 7 : 5. ⌈afraid
17 : 6. d. heard it, they were sore
13. d. underst-d he spake of John
16. thy d., they could not cure him
19. came d. to Jesus apart ⌈est
18 : 1. came d., saying, Who great-
19 : 13. d. rebuked them, Mk. 10 : 13.
20 : 17. Jesus took twelve d. apart
21 : 1. Jesus sent two d., saying,
Go, Mk. 11 : 1. Lu. 19 : 29. ⌈ed
6. d. went, did as Jesus command-
20. when d. saw it they marvelled
22 : 16. Phari. sent unto him their
24 : 3. the d. came privately ⌊d.
26 : 17. d. to Jesus, saying, Where
18. I will keep passover with my
d., Mk. 14 : 14. Lu. 22 : 11.
19. d. did as Jesus had appointed
26 Jesus took bread, gave it to d.
35. Likewise also said all the d.
36. saith unto d., Sit here while I
40. cometh unto d., findeth asleep
56. all d. forsook him, and fled
28 : 16. eleven d. went into Galilee
†29. Go ye, make d. of all nations
Mk. 2 : 18. d. of John and Pharisees
fast; they say, Why do d. of
Pharisees fast, but thy d. fast
not? Mat. 9 : 14. Lu. 5 : 33. ⌈bread
8 : 14. the d. had forgotten to take
9 : 14. I spake to thy d. that they
cast him out; cou. not, Lu. 9 : 40.
10 : 24. d. astonished at his words
Lu. 7 : 18. d. of Jn. shewed him of all
9 : 16. loaves, gave to d. to set bef.
multitude, Jn. 6 : 11 (2). ⌈sible
17 : 1. said he unto d., It is impos-
22. he said unto d., The days will
19 : 37. the d. began to praise God
39. Phari. said, Master, rebuke thy
Jn. 1 : 37. the two d. followed Jes. ⌊d.
3 : 25. between John's d. and Jews
4 : 1. Pharisees heard Jesus baptized more d. than John ⌈any
33. said d. one to another, Hath

Jn. 7 : 3. **d.** may see works thou do-
8 : 31. then are ye my **d.**, 13:35. ⌊est
9 : 28. Thou his, but we Moses' **d.**
13 : 5. he began to wash the **d.**' feet
22. Then **d.** looked one on anoth.
15 : 8. bear fruit, so sh. ye be my **d.**
18 : 17. Art not one of this man's **d.**?
20 : 10. **d.** went aw. unto own home
18. Mary told **d.** she had seen L.
19. doors were shut where **d.** were
20. **d.** glad when they saw Lord
25. other **d.** said, We have seen L.
21 : 1. Jesus shewed himself to **d.**
4. but **d.** knew not it was Jesus
8. other **d.** came in a little ship
12. none of the **d.** durst ask him
Ac. 1 : 15. Peter stood in midst of **d.**
6 : 1. number of **d.** multiplied, 7.
2. the twelve called **d.** unto them
9 : 1. Saul breathing slaughter ag.
19. Saul certain days with **d.** ⌊**d.**
25. **d.** let him down in a basket
26. Saul assayed to join the **d.** ⌈th.
38. Joppa, **d.** had heard Peter was
11 : 26. **d.** called Christians first in
29. **d.**, every man to send relief
13 : 52. **d.** were filled with joy and
14 : 20. as **d.** stood about he rose
22. Confirming the souls of the **d.**
28. they abode long time with **d.**
15 : 10. to put yoke upon neck of **d.**
18 : 23. Paul strengthening the **d.**
27. exhorting **d.** to receive him
19 : 1. Paul to Ephesus finding **d.**
9. Paul separated the **d.** ⌈not
30. Paul would, **d.** suffered him
20 : 1. Paul called **d.**, embraced th.
7. When **d.** came to break bread
30. to draw away **d.** after them
21 : 4. finding **d.**, we tarried 7 days
16. went with us certain **d.** of Ce-

His DISCIPLES. ⌊sarea

Mat. 5 : 1. when he was set, **h. d.** ca.
8 : 21. another of **h. d.** said unto h.
23. into a ship, **h. d.** followed him,
Mk. 8 : 10. Lu. 8 : 22. ⌈save us
25. **h. d.** awoke him, saying, Lord,
9 : 10. many sinners came and sat
with him and **h. d.**, Mk. 2 : 15.
11. the Pharisees said unto **h. d.**,
Why eateth, Mk. 2:16. Lu. 5:30.
19. Jes. followed, and so did **h. d.**
37. saith he unto **h. d.**, The harv.
10 : 1. called unto him **h.** twelve **d.**,
gave them power ag-t, Lu. 9 : 1.
11 : 1. end of commanding **h.** 12 **d.**
2. John sent two of **h. d.**, Lu. 7:19.
12 : 1. **h. d.** began to pluck ears of
corn, Mk. 2 : 23. Lu. 6 : 1. ⌈**h. d.**
49. he stretched forth hand toward
13 : 10. **h. d.** came, said unto h., 36.
14 : 12. **h. d.** came and took up the
body and buried it, Mk. 6 : 29.
15. evening, **h. d.** came to him, saying, This is desert pl., Mk. 6:35.
19. gave loaves to **h. d.** and **d.** to
mult., 15:36 (2). Mk. 6:41.-8:6.
22. Jesus constrained **h. d.** to get
into a ship, Mk. 6:45. ⌈Phari.
15 : 12. **h. d.** said, Knowest that
23. **h. d.** besought, Send her aw.
32. Jesus called **h. d.**, Mk. 8 : 1.
33. **h. d.** say, Whence so much
16 : 5. when **h. d.** were come ⌊bread
13. he asked **h. d.**, Whom do men
say, that I am? Mk. 8 : 27.

DISCIPLINE.

Jb. 36 : 10. He openeth their ear to
d., and commandeth that they

DISCLOSE.

Is. 26 : 21. earth shall **d.** her blood

DISCOMFITED. ⌈peo.

Ex. 17 : 13. Joshua **d.** Amalek and
Nu. 14.45. Canaanites **d.** them
Jos. 10 : 10. Lord **d.** them bef. Israel
Ju. 4 : 15. Lord **d.** Sisera bef. Barak
8 : 12. Gideon took kings, **d.** host
1 S. 7 : 10. thund. upon Philis. and **d.**
2 S. 22 : 15. and **d.** them, Ps. 18 : 14.
Is. 31 : 8. his young men sh. be **d.**

DISCOMFITURE.

1 S. 14 : 20. was a very great **d.**

DISCONTENTED.

1 S. 22 : 2. ev. one **d.** gath. unto Da.

DISCONTINUE.

Je. 17 : 4. shalt **d.** from heritage

DISCORD.

Pr. 6 : 14. mischief, he soweth **d.**
19. that soweth **d.** among breth.

DISCOURAGE, ED.

Nu. 21 : 4. soul of people was **d.**
32 : 7. why **d.** ye hearts of people?
9. they **d-d** heart of chil. of Isr.
De. 1 : 21 fear not, nor be **d.**
28. brethren have **d.** our heart
Is. 42 : 4. He not be **d.** till he set
Col. 3 : 21. provoke not chil. lest be

DISCOVER. ⌊**d.**

De. 22 : 30. sh. not **d.** his fa.'s skirt
1 S. 14 : 8. will **d.** ours. to them
Jb. 41 : 13. Who **d.** face of garm.?
Pr. 18 : 2. his heart may **d.** itself
25 : 9. **d.** not secret to another
Is. 3 : 17. L. **d.** their secret parts
Je. 13 : 26. will **d.** thy skirts, Na. 3 : 5.
La. 4 : 22. he will **d.** thy sins
Eze. 16 : 37. I will **d.** thy nakedn.
Ho. 2 : 10. I will **d.** her lewdness
Mi. 1 : 6. I will **d.** the foundation

DISCOVERED.

Ex. 20 : 26. that nakedn. be not **d.**
Le. 20 : 18. he hath **d.** her fountain
1 S. 14 : 11. **d.** thems unto garrison
22 : 6. Saul heard David was **d.**
2 S. 22 : 16. foundations of the world
were **d.**, Ps. 18 : 15.
Is. 22 : 8. he **d.** covering of Judah
57 : 8. hast **d.** thyself to another
Je. 13 : 22. for iniq. are thy skirts **d.**
La. 2 : 14. have not **d.** thine iniq.
Eze. 13 : 14. foundation shall be **d.**
16 : 36. nakedn. **d.** thro. whored.
57. Before thy wickedness was **d.**
21 : 24. in that your transgr. are **d.**
22 : 10. have **d.** their fa.'s nakedn.
23 : 10. These **d.** her nakedness
18. she **d.** her whoredoms, and **d.**
her nakedness
29. of thy whoredoms shall be **d.**
Ho. 7 : 1. iniq. of Ephraim was **d.**
Ac. 21 : 3. when we had **d.** Cyprus
27 : 39. they **d.** a certain creek

DISCOVERETH, ING.

Jb. 12 : 22. he **d-h** deep things out
Ps. 29 : 9. voice of Lord **d-h** forest
Ha. 3 : 13. by **d-g** founda. unto neck

DISCREET, LY. ⌈**d.**

Ge. 41 : 33. let Pha. look out a man
39. none so **d.** and wise as thou
Mk. 12 : 34. Jes. saw he answ. **d-y**
Tit. 2 : 5. teach young wom. to be **d.**
† 6. young men exhort to be **d.**

DISCRETION.

Ps. 112 : 5. will guide affairs with **d.**
Pr. 1 : 4. to the young man **d.**
2 : 11. **d.** shall preserve thee
3 : 21. my son, keep wisd. and **d.**
5 : 2. thou mayest regard **d.**
11 : 22. a fair woman without **d.**
19 : 11. **d.** deferreth his anger ⌈**d.**
Is. 28 : 26. G. doth instruct him to
Je. 10 : 12. stretched heav-s by his **d.**

DISDAINED.

1 S. 17 : 42. Goliath saw Da. he **d.**
Jb. 30 : 1. fathers I **d.** to set with

DISEASE. ⌊dogs

2 K. 1 : 2 whe. I recov. of this **d.**
8 : 8. Shall I recover of this **d.**? 9.
2 Ch. 16 : 12. Asa diseased until his
d. was great, yet in his **d.** he
21 : 15. great sickn. by **d.** of bowels
18. L. smote him with incur. **d.**
Jb. 30 : 18. by **d.** is my garm. chang.
Ps. 38 : 7. my loins with loaths. **d.**
Ps. 41 : 8. evil **d.** cleaveth unto him
Ec. 6 : 2. this is vanity, an evil **d.**
Mat. 4 : 23. healing of **d.**, 9:35.-10:1.
Jn. 5 : 4. made whole of whatso. **d.**

DISEASES. ⌈7 : 15.

Ex. 15 : 26. none of **d.** upon thee, De.
De. 28 : 60. bring upon thee **d.** of E.
2 Ch. 21 : 19. he died of sore **d.**
24 : 25. they left him in great **d.**
Ps. 103 : 3. who healeth all thy **d.**
Ha. 3 : † 5. burning **d.** at his feet
Mat. 4 : 24. bro-t all sick peo. with
divers **d.**, Mk. 1 : 34. Lu. 4 : 40.
Lu. 6 : 17. to be healed of their **d.**
9 : 1. gave them power to cure **d.**
Ac. 19 : 12. **d.** departed from them
28 : 9. which had **d.** in island, came

DISEASED.

1 K. 15 : 23 Asa **d.** in feet, 2 Ch. 16 : 12.
Eze. 34 : 4. **d.** have ye not strength-d
21. have push. **d.** with your horns
Mat. 9 : 20. woman **d.** with issue
14 : 35. brought all **d.**, Mk. 1 : 32.
Jn. 6 : 2. miracles he did on **d.**

DISFIGURE.

Mat. 6 : 16. hypocrites **d.** their faces

DISGRACE.

Je. 14 : 21. do not **d.** the throne

DISGUISE, ED, ETH.

1 S. 28 : 8. And Saul **d.** himself
1 K. 14 : 2. Jerob. said, **d.** thyself
20 : 38. one of sons of prophets **d.**
22 : 30. Ahab said, I will **d.** myself,
and he **d.** hims., 2 Ch. 18 : 29.
2 Ch. 35 : 22. Josiah **d.** hims. to fight
Jb. 24 : 15. adulterer **d-h** his face

DISH, ES. ⌈16.

Ex. 25 : 29. shalt make thee **d-s**, 37 :
Nu. 4 : 7. and put thereon the **d-s**
Ju. 5 : 25. bro-t butter in lordly **d.**
2 K. 21 : 13. as man wipeth a **d.**
Mat. 26 : 23. dippeth in **d.**, Mk. 14 :

DI'SHAN. ⌊20.

Ge. 36 : 21, 28, 30. 1 Ch. 1 : 38, 42.

DI'SHON.

Ge. 36 : 21, 25, 26, 30. 1 Ch. 1 : 38, 41.

DISHONEST. See GAIN.

DISHONESTY.

2 Co. 4 : 2. renounced things of **d.**

DISHONOUR. [Noun.]

Ezr. 4 : 14. not meet to see king's **d.**
Ps. 35 : 26. clothed with **d.**, 71 : 13.
69 : 19. thou hast known my **d.**
Pr. 6 : 33. and **d.** shall he get
Ro. 9 : 21. one vessel, another to **d.**
1 Co. 15 : 43. sown in **d.** is raised
2 Co. 6 : 8. By honour and **d.** by
2 Ti. 2 : 20. are vessels, some to **d.**

DISHONOUR, EST, ETH.

Mi. 7 : 6. For the son **d-h** father
Jn. 8 : 49. I honour Fa. ye **d.** me
Ro. 1 : 24. to **d.** their own bodies
2 : 23. thro. breaking law, **d-t** God
1 Co. 11 : 4. man cover-d **d-h** head
5. woman uncov-d **d-h** her head

DISINHERIT.

Nu. 14 : 12. will **d.** them and make

DISJOINTED.

Je. 6 : † 8. lest my soul be **d.** from
Eze. 23 : † 17. her mind was **d.** fr.

DISMAYED. ⌊them

De. 31 : 8. fear not, nor be **d.**, Jos.
1 : 9.-8 : 1.-10 : 25. 1 Ch. 22 :
13.-28 : 20. 2 Ch. 20 : 15, 17.-
32 : 7. ⌈26. Is. 37 : 27.
1 S. 17 : 11. they were **d.**, 2 K. 19 :
Is. 21 : 3. I was **d.** at seeing of it
41 : 10. fear not, be not **d.**, Je. 1 :
17.-10 : 2.-23 : 4.-30 : 10.-46 :
27. Eze. 2 : 6.-3 : 9.
23. that we may be **d.** and
Je. 8 : 9. wise men are **d.**, 10 : 2.
17 : 18. let them be **d.**, not me be **d.**
46 : 5. Wheref. have I seen them **d.**
48 : 1. Misgab is confounded, **d.**
49 : 37. will cause Elam to be **d.**
50 : 36. mighty of Bab. shall be **d.**

. thy mighty men shall be **d.**

DISMAYING.

}: 39. Moab shall be a **d.**

32: † 23. caused **d.** in the land

DISMISSED.

23: 8. priest **d.** not courses

5:30. **d.** they came to Antioch

41. spoken he **d.** assembly

DISOBEDIENCE.

: 19. by one man's **d.** many

10: 6. readiness to revenge **d.**

: 2. worketh in children of **d.**

wrath upon chil. of **d.**, Col. 3:6.

2. ev. **d.** received just recomp.

11. lest any fall by the same

xample of **d.**

DISOBEDIENT.

13: 26. man of G. who was **d.**

: 26. they were **d.** against me

: 17. turn **d.** to wisd. of just

3:19. not **d.** unto heav-y vision

: 30. **d.** to parents, 2 Ti. 3: 2.

1. stretched hands unto **d.** peo.

31. delivered from **d.** in Judea

1: 9. the law was made for **d.**

.: 16. deny him, being **d.**

. we also were sometimes **d.**

1: † 31. perished not with **d.**

2:7. them wh. be **d.** the stone

stumble at word, being **d.**

o. spirits in prison, which **d.**

DISOBEYED.

13: 21. as thou hast **d.** Lord

DISORDERLY.

5: † 14. warn them that are **d.**

3: 6. withdraw fr. brother **d.**

we behaved not ourselves **d.**

some who walk amo. you **d.**

DISPATCH, ED.

10: † 14. till this matter be **d**-d

23:47. sh. **d.** them with swords

DISPENSATION.

9: 17. a **d.** of gos. is commit.

: 10. **d.** of fulness of times

. ye heard of **d.** of grace

l: 25. minister acc. to **d.** of G.

DISPERSE.

14:34. Saul said, **d.** yourselves

5: 7. lips of wise **d.** knowl.

12: 15. **d.** them in countries,

20: 23.-29: 12.-30: 23, 26.

15. will **d.** thee in countries

DISPERSED.

11: 23. Rehob. **d.** of children

: 8. certain peo. **d.** amo. peo.

12: 9. He hath **d.**, 2 Co. 9: 9.

: 16. Let thy fountains be **d.**

: 12. shall gather **d.** of Judah

36: 19. were **d.** thro. countries

3: 10. dau. of my **d.** shall bri.

: 35. will he go unto the **d.**

: 37. many as obeyed were **d.**

DISPERSER.

l: † 1. **d.** is come bef. thy face

DISPERSIONS.

5:34. days of **d.** accomplished

DISPLAYED.

): 4. banner that it may be **d.**

DISPLEASE.

1: 35. Let it not **d.** my lord

2:34. if **d.** thee, I will get back

9: 7. return, **d.** not the lords

11: 25. Let not this **d.** thee

4: 18. Lest L. see, and it **d.**

DISPLEASED.

8: 10. thing he did **d.** the L.

7. hand on head of Ephr. it **d.**

1:1. peo. complained, it **d.** L.

anger of L. kindled, Mo. was **d.**

: 6. But the thing **d.** Samuel

8. Saul was wroth, saying **d.**

:8. David was **d.**, 1 Ch. 13: 11.

27. thing Da. had done **d.** L.

l: 6. his father had not **d.** him

43. went to his house **d.**, 21: 4.

21: 7. G. was **d.** with this

): 1. thou hast been **d.** O turn

Is. 59: 15. it **d.** him was no judgm.

Da. 6: 14. king sore **d.** with hims.

Jon. 4: 1. But it **d.** Jonah exceed.

Ha. 3: 8. Was L. **d.** against rivers?

Zch. 1: 2. L. sore **d.** with fathers

15. I am very sore **d.** with heath

for I was but a little **d.**

Mat. 21: 15. scribes saw, were **d.**

Mk. 10: 14. Jesus saw, he was **d.**

41. to be much **d.** with Ja. and Jn.

Ac. 12: 20. Herod was highly **d.**

DISPLEASING.

1 K. 9: † 13. called them land of **d.**

DISPLEASURE.

De. 9: 19. I was afraid of the hot **d.**

Ju. 15: 3. though I do them a **d.**

Ps. 2: 5. shall vex them in sore **d.**

6: 1. chasten me in hot **d.**, 38: 1.

Zch. 1: † 2. Lord hath been with **d.**

DISPOSED, ETH.

Jb. 34: 13. who **d.** whole world?

37: 15. Dost know when G. **d.** th.?

Ps. 50: † 23. that **d**-h his way aright

Ac. 18: 27. **d.** to pass into Achaia

1 Co. 10: 27. feast and ye be **d.** to go

DISPOSING, S.

Pr. 16: † 1. **d**-s of the heart in man

33. whole **d.** is of the Lord

DISPOSITION.

Ac. 7: 53. receiv-d law by **d.** of angels

DISPOSSESS, ED.

Nu. 32: 39. Machir **d**-d Amorite

33: 53. ye shall **d.** inhabi. of land

De. 7: 17. how can I **d.** them?

Ju. 11: 23. Lord hath **d.** Amorites

DISPUTATION, S. [d.

Ac. 15: 2. Paul and B. had no small

Ro. 14: 1. but not to doubtful **d**-s

DISPUTE. [Noun.]

Mk. 9: 34. had **d.** who be the greatest

DISPUTE, ED.

Jb. 23: 7. righte. might **d.** with him

Mk. 9: 33. What was it that ye **d**-d

Ac. 9: 29. Saul **d**-d ag. the Grecians

17: 17. Paul **d**-d in synagogue

Jude 9. Michael **d**-d ab. body of Mo.

DISPUTER.

1 Co. 1: 20. where **d.** of this world?

DISPUTEST, ING.

Ac. 6: 9. them of Asia **d**-g with Ste.

19: 8. **d.** the things of God, 9.

24: 12. they neither found me **d.**

Ro. 9: † 20. who thou **d**-t with G.?

DISPUTING, S.

Ac. 15: 7. had been much **d.** Pe. rose

Ph. 2: 14. Do all things without **d**-s

1 Ti. 6: 5. Perverse **d**-s of men

DISQUIET, ED.

1 S. 28: 15. Why hast thou **d.** me?

Ps. 39: 6. surely they are **d.** in vain

42: 5. why cast down, O my soul?

why art thou **d.**? 11.-43: 5

Pr. 30: 21. For 3 things earth is **d.**

Je. 50: 34. **d.** inhabit. of Babylon

DISQUIETNESS.

Ps. 38: 8. I have roared by rea. of **d.**

DISSEMBLED, ETH.

Jos. 7: 11. they have stolen and **d.**

Pr. 26: 24. He that hateth **d**-h with

Je. 42. 20. For ye **d.**, when ye sent

Ga. 2: 13. other Jews **d.** likewise

DISSEMBLERS.

Ps. 26: 4. nor will I go in with **d.**

DISSENSION. [d.

Ac. 15: 2. Paul and B. had no small

23: 7. a **d.** betw. Pharis. and Sad.

10. arose a great **d.**, the chief cap-

DISSIMULATION. [tain

Ro 12: 9. Let love be without **d.**

Ga. 2: 13. Barna. carried with th. **d.**

DISSOLVE, ED, EST.

Jb. 30: 22. thou **d**-t my substance

Ps. 65: † 10. **d**-t earth with showers

75: 3. earth and all inhabi. are **d.**

Is. 14: 31. thou Palestina art **d.**

24: 19. the earth is clean **d.**

34: 4. all host of heav. sh. be **d.**

Da. 5. 16. thou canst **d.** doubts

Na. 2: 6. the palace shall be **d.**

2 Co. 5: 1. if h. of this tab. were **d.**

2 Pe. 3: 11. all these shall be **d.**

12. heavens on fire shall be **d.**

DISSOLVING. [Noun.]

Da. 5: 12. **d.** of doubts was in Dan.

DISTAFF.

Pr. 31: 19. her hands hold the **d.**

DISTANCES.

Is. 33: † 17. behold land of far **d.**

DISTANT.

Ex. 36: 22. two tenons equally **d.**

DISTIL.

De. 32: 2. my speech shall **d.** as dew

Jb. 36: 28. clouds **d.** upon man abun.

DISTINCTION.

1 Co. 14: 7. exc. give **d.** in sounds

DISTINCTLY.

Ne. 8: 8. they read in law of God **d.**

DISTINGUISHETH.

1 Co. 4: † 7. who **d.** thee from ano.?

DISTRACTED.

Ps. 88: 15. thy terrors, I am **d.**

DISTRACTION.

1 Co. 7: 35. attend on L. without **d.**

DISTRESS. [Noun.]

Ge. 35: 3. G. who ans. me in my **d.**

42: 21. theref. is this **d.** upon us

Ju. 11: 7. ye come when in **d.** [Da.

1 S. 22: 2. ev. one in **d.** gath-d unto

2 S. 22: 7. In my **d.** I called upon

L., Ps. 18: 6.-118: 5.-120: 1.

1 K. 1: 29. redeem-d soul out of all **d.**

2 Ch. 28: 22. in **d.** Ahaz tresp. more

Ne. 2: 17. Ye see **d.** we are in

9: 37. and we are in great **d.**

Ps. 4: 1. hast enlarged me in **d.**

Pr. 1: 27. mock when **d.** cometh

Is. 5: † 30. if look to land, behold **d.**

25: 4. thou strength to needy in **d.**

53: † 8. he was taken away by **d.**

La. 1: 20. Behold, O L., I am in **d.**

Ob. 12. nor spoken proudly in **d.**

14. nor delivered those in **d.**

Zph. 1: 15. that day is a day of **d.**

17. I will bring **d.** upon men

Lu. 21: 23. sh. be great **d.** in land

25. upon the earth **d.** of nations

Ro. 8: 35. sh. **d.** separate us from?

1 Co. 7: 26. good for present **d.**

1 Th. 3: 7. we comforted in your **d.**

DISTRESSES.

Ps. 25: 17. O bring me out of **d.**

107: 6. he deliv-d them out of **d.**

13. he saved them out of **d.**, 19.

28. he bringeth them out of **d.**

Eze. 30: 16. Noph sh. have **d.** daily

2 Co. 6: 4. approving ourselves, in **d.**

12: 10. I take pleasure in **d.** for C.

DISTRESS, ED.

Ge. 32: 7. Then Jac. was greatly **d.**

Nu. 22: 3. Moab was **d.** [ites

De. 2: 9. **d.** not Moabites | 19. Ammon

28: 53. enemies **d.** thee. 55, 57.

Ju. 2: 15. Israel greatly **d.**, 10: 9.

1 S. 13: 6. peo. were **d.**, did hide

14: 24. men of Isr. **d.** | 28: 15. Saul **d.**

30: 6. David was greatly **d.**

2 S. 1: 26. I am **d.** for thee, Jona.

2 Ch. 28: 20. k. of Assyr. **d.** Ahaz.

Is. 29: 2. Yet I will **d.** Ariel

7. that **d.** her sh. be as a dream

Je. 10: 18. I will **d.** inhabi. of land

2 Co. 4: 8. We are troubl., yet not **d.**

DISTRIBUTE.

Jos. 13: 32. Moses did **d.** for inherit.

2 Ch. 31: 14. Kore to **d.** oblations

Ne. 13: 13. office was to **d.** unto breth.

Lu. 18: 22. sell all, **d.** unto poor

Ep. 4: † 28. to **d.** to him that needeth

1 Ti. 6: 18. rich to be ready to **d.**

DISTRIBUTED.

Jos. 14: 1. Eleazar and Joshua **d.**

1 Ch. 24: 3. Da. **d.** them, 2 Ch. 23: 18

Jn. 6: 11. Jes. **d.** to the disciples

1 Co. 7: 17. as G. **d.** to every man

1 Co. 10: 13. to rule G. hath d. to us

DISTRIBUTETH, ING.

Jb. 21: 17. G. d-h sorrows in anger
Ro. 12: 13. d-g to necess. of saints

DISTRIBUTION.

Ac. 4: 35. d. was made unto ev. one
2 Co. 9: 13. for your liberal d.
He. 2: † 4. witness, with d. of H. G.

DITCH, ES. [Jezreel

1 K. 21: † 23. eat Jezebel by d. of
2 K. 3: 16. Make this valley full of d-s
Jb. 9: 31. thou plunge me in the d.
Ps. 7: 15. fallen into d. he made
Pr. 23: 27. a whore is a deep d.
Is. 22: 11. a d. betw. two walls
Da. 9: † 25. d. in troublous times
Mat. 15: 14. both into d., Lu. 6: 39.

DIVERS.

De. 22: 9. not sow viney. with d. seeds
11. not wear garment of d. sorts
25: 13. not have in bag d. weights
14. in thy house d. measures
Ju. 5: 30. a prey of d. colours
2 S. 13: 18. had garm. of d. colours, 19.
1 Ch. 29: 2. stones of d. colours
2 Ch. 16: 14. bed with d. kinds of [spice
21: 4. Jeho. slew d. of princes
30: 11. d. of Asher humbled them.
Ps. 78: 45. he sent d. sorts of flies
105: 31. there came d. sorts of flies
Pr. 20: 10. d. weights and d. meas.
23. d. weights are an abom. unto L.
Ec. 5: 7. are also d. vanities [ours
Eze. 16: 16. high places with d. col-
17: 3. great eagle had d. colours
Mat. 4: 24 brought sick with d. diseases, Mk. 1: 34. Lu. 4: 40.
24: 7. famines, earthq. in d. places, Mk. 13: 8. Lu. 21: 11.
Mk. 8: 3. d. of them came far
Ac. 19: 9. when d. were hardened
1 Co. 12: 10. d. kinds of tongues
2 Ti. 3: 6. wom. led away with d. lusts
Tit. 3: 3. deceived, serving d. lusts
He. 1: 1. who in d. manners spake
2: 4. G. witness with d. miracles
9: 10. d. washings | 13: 9. d. doctr.
Ja. 1: 2. when fall into d. tempta.

DIVERSE. [d.

Le. 19: 19. nor let cattle gender with
Es. 1: 7. vessels d. one fr. another
3: 8. their laws are d. fr. all people
Da. 7: 3. beasts came d. one fr. ano.
7. a 4th beast d. fr. all beasts, 19.
23. d. fr. all kingd-s | 24. d. fr. first.

DIVERSITIES.

1 Co. 12: 4. d. of gifts | 6. operations
28. set in church d. of tongues

DIVIDE.

Ge. 1: 6. let firmament d. waters
14. be lights, to d. the day, 18.
49: 27. at night he shall d. spoil
Ex. 14: 16. stretch over sea and d. it
21: 35. d. the money, d. dead ox
26: 33. vail shall d. betw. holy and
Le 1: 17. cleave it, but not d., 5: 8.
11: 4. that d. the hoof, 7. De. 14: 7.
Nu. 31: 27. d. prey into two parts
33: 54. d. land by lot, 34: 17, 18, 29.
De. 19: 3. d. coasts into three parts
Jos. 1: 6. d. for inherita., 13: 6, 7.
18: 5. they shall d. into 7 parts
22: 8. d. the spoil with brethren
2 S. 19: 29. Thou and Ziba d. land
1 K. 3: 25. d. the living child, 26.
Ne. 9: 11. didst d. sea, Ps. 74: 13.
22. didst d. them into corners
Jb. 27: 17. innocent shall d. silver
Ps. 55: 9. O L., d. their tongues
Pr. 16: 19. to d. spoil with proud
Is. 9: 3. rejoice when d. spoil
53: 12. shall d. spoil with strong
Eze. 5: 1. take balances d. hair
45: 1. d. land by lot, 47: 21, 22.
48: 29. this is land ye shall d.
Da. 11: 39. he sh. d. land for gain
Lu. 12: 13. he d. inherit. with me
Lu. 22: 17. Take this, d. it amo. yours.

I will DIVIDE.

Ge. 49: 7. I w. d. them in Jacob
Ex. 15: 9. said I w. d. the spoil
Ps. 60: 6. I w. d. Shechem, 108: 7.
Is. 53: 12. theref. w. I d. him a portion

DIVIDED.

Ge. 1: 4. G. d. light | 7. d. waters
10: 5. were isles of the Gentiles d.
25. was the earth d., 1 Ch. 1: 19.
32. were nations d. aft. the flood
14: 15. Ab. d. himself ag. them
15: 10. Ab. d. them, birds d. he not
32: 7. Jacob d. people with him
33: 1. he d. the chil. unto Leah and
Ex. 14: 21. and waters were d. [Ra.
Nu. 26: 53. land sh. be d. for inher.
56. by lot sh. the possession be d.
31: 42. d. from men that warred
De. 4: 19. which the Lord hath d.
29: † 26. not d. to them any portion
32: 8. Most High d. to the nations
Jos. 14: 5. they d. the land, 18: 10.-19: 51.-23: 4.
Ju. 5: 30. have they not d. prey
7: 16. he d. the 300 men into three
9: 43. Abime. d. them into three
19: 29. Levite d. her into 12 pieces
2 S. 1: 23. in death were not d.
1 K. 16: 21. Then were peo. of Isr. d.
18: 6. Ahab and Ob. d. the land
2 K. 2: 8. waters were d. hither
1 Ch. 23: 6. Da. d. them into courses
24: 4. chief men, were d. by lot, 5.
2 Ch. 35: 13. they d. other offerings
Jb. 38: 25. Who d. a water-course
Ps. 68: 12. she at home d. spoil
78: 13. He d. the sea and caused
55. d. them an inheri., Ac. 13: 19.
136: 13. To him wh. d. Red sea
Is. 33: 23. prey of great spoil d.
34: 17. his hand hath d. it by line
51: 15. I am the L. that d. the sea
La. 4: 16. anger of L. d. them
Eze. 1: † 11. wings were d. above
37: 22. nor be d. into two kingd.
Da. 2: 41. kingdom shall be d. but
5: 28. kingd. is d. given to Medes
11: 4. kingd. be d. tow. four winds
Hos. 10: 2. Their heart is d.
Am. 1: † 13. they d. the mountains
7: 17. thy land shall be d. by line
Mi. 2: 4. he hath d. our fields
Zch. 14: 1. thy spoil be d. in midst
Mat. 12: 25. kingd. or house d. not stand, Mk. 3: 24, 25. Lu. 11: 17.
26. he is d. against himself, Mk. 3: 26. Lu. 11: 18.
Mk. 6: 41. the two fishes d. he
Lu. 12: 52. be five in one house d.
53. The father shall be d. ag. son
15: 12. d. unto them his living
Ac. 13: 19. d. their land by lot
14: 4. multitude was d., 23: 7.
1 Co. 1: 13. Is Christ d.? was Paul?
Re. 16: 19. the great city was d.

DIVIDER.

Lu. 12: 14. who made me d. over [you?

DIVIDETH.

Le. 11: 4. but d. not the hoof, 5, 6.
26. of every beast which d. hoof
De. 14: 8. swine, bec. it d. hoof
Jb. 26: 12. d. sea with his power
Ps. 29: 7. voice of Lord d. flames
Je. 31: 35. d. sea when waves roar
Mat. 25: 32. d. his sheep fr. the goats
Lu. 11: 22. taketh armour, d. spoils

DIVIDING.

Jos. 19: 49. made an end of d. land
51. made an end of d. country
Is. 63: 12. led them, d. water bef.
Da. 7: 25. until a d. of time
1 Co. 12: 11. d. to ev. man severally
2 Ti. 2: 15. rightly d. word of truth
He. 4: 12. d. asunder of the joints

DIVINATION, S.

Nu. 22: 7. rewards of d. in hand
Nu. 23: 23. neith. is any d. ag. Isr.
De. 18: 10. useth d., 2 K. 17: 17.
1 S. 15: † 23. rebellion is as sin of d.
Pr. 16: † 10. d. is in lips of king
Je. 14: 14. they prophesy d.
Eze. 12: 24. nor flattering d. in Isr.
13: 6. They have seen lying d.
7. have ye not spoken lying d.?
23. sh. see no more divine d-s
21: 21. k. of Bab. stood to use d.
22. At right hand was d. of Jerus.
23. sh. be unto them as a false d.
Ac. 16: 16. a damsel with a spirit [of d.

DIVINE. [Verb.]

Ge. 44: 15. such a man as I can d.?
1 S. 28: 8. d. by familiar spirit
Eze. 13: 9. on prophets that d. lies
21: 29. while they d. a lie unto
Mi. 3: 6. be dark that ye sh. not d.
11. the prophets d. for money

DIVINE. [Adjective]

Pr. 16: 10. d. sentence in lips of k.
Eze. 13: 23. see no more d. divinat.
He. 9: 1. had ordinan. of d. service
2 Pe. 1: 3. as d. power hath given
4. be partakers of the d. nature

DIVINER, S.

De. 18: 14. nations hearkened unto
Jos. 13: † 22. Balaam the d. [d-s
1 S. 6: 2. Philis. called for the d-s
Is. 44: 25. that maketh d-s mad
Je. 27: 9. hearken not to your d-s
29: 8. Let not your d-s deceive you
Mi. 3: 7. and the d-s confounded
Zch. 10: 2. the d-s have seen a lie

DIVINETH, ING.

Ge. 44: 5. is this whereby he d.?
Eze. 22: 28. and d-g lies unto them
Mi. 3: † 6. be dark unto you from d-g

DIVISION. [Ch. 1: † 19.

Ge. 10: † 25. name of the one, D., 1
Ex. 8: 23. a d. betw. my peo. and thy
2 Ch. 35: 5. acc. to d. of Levites
Can. 2: † 17. hart on mts. of d.
Lu. 12: 51. I tell you, Nay, but d.
Jn. 7: 43. there was a d. among the people, 9: 16.-10: 19.
1 Co. 12: † 25. sho. be no d. in body

DIVISIONS.

Jos. 11: 23. to Isr. acc. to their d., 12: 7.-18: 10. 2 Ch. 35: 5, 12.
Ju. 5: 15. For the d. of Reuben, 16.
1 S. 23: † 28. called place rock of d.
1 Ch. 23: † 6. Da. divided into d.
24: 1. these are d. of sons of Aa.
26: 1. Conce. d. of porters, 12, 19.
Ezr. 6: 18. set priests in d., Ne. 11: 36.
Ro. 16: 17. mark them wh. cause d.
1 Co. 1: 10. that there be no d. amo. you
3: 3. whereas there is amo. you d.
11: 18. I hear, that be d. amo. you

DIVORCE.

Je. 3: 8. I had given a bill of d.

DIVORCED.

Le. 21: 14. high pr. not take d. woman
22: 13. if priest's dau. be wid. or d.
Nu. 30: 9. ev. vow of her that is d.
Mat. 5: 32. whoso. sh. marry her d.

DIVORCEMENT.

De. 24: 1. write her a bill of d., 3.
Is. 50: 1. Where bill of mother's d.
Mk. 10: 4. Moses suffered bill of d.
See WRITING.

DIZ'AHAB.

De. 1: 1. in plain betw. Paran D. and

DO.

Ge. 16: 6. Ab. said, d. to her as it
18: 25. Judge of all earth d. right?
19: 22. I cannot d. any thing till
31: 16. now what G. hath said d.
32: 12. I will surely d. thee good
41: 25. G. shewed what he is to d., 28.
Ex. 4: 15. teach you what ye sh. d.
12: † 47. all congregation shall d.
15: 26. if wilt d. that wh. is right De. 6: 18.-12: 25.-13: 18.-21: 9.
18: 20. shew work they must d.

Ex. 19: 8. all L. hath spok. we will d.
20: 9. six days d. all thy work, 23:
12. De. 5: 13.
29: 35. thus shalt thou d. to Aaron
Le. 18: 4. ye shall d. my judgments
19: 37.-20: 22.-Eze. 36: 27.
5. which if man d., Ne. 9: 29.
Eze. 20: 11, 13, 21.
25: 18. ye shall d. my statutes, 20:
8.-22: 31. De. 17: 19.-28: 16.
Nu. 15: 14. as ye d. so he sh. d.
22: 20. word I say unto thee, sh. d.
24: 14. what this peo. d. to thy peo.
32: 25. Thy serv. will d., as my lord
De. 5: † 1. ye may keep to d. them
27 speak and we will d. it [22.
7: 11. keep com-ts to d. them, 11:
17: 10. d. acc. to the sentence, 11.
19: 19. d. to him as he thought to
20: 15. shalt thou d. unto cities [d.
27: 26. words of law to d. them
30: 12. may hear it and d. it, 13.
31: 4. L. sh. d. unto them as Sihon
32: 6. d. ye thus requite the Lord
Jos. 6: 3. Thus shalt thou d. six days
7: 9. what d. unto thy great name?
10: 25. shall L. d. to your enemies
22: 24. What have ye to d. with G.?
23: 6. to d. all written in law of
Moses, 1 Ch. 16: 40. 2 Ch. 34: 21.
Ju. 7: 17. that as I d. so sh. ye d.
8: 3. able to d. in compa. of you?
18: 14. consider what ye have to d.
18. said priest, What d. ye? [d.
Ru. 3: 4. will tell thee what thou sh.
1 S. 16: 3. shew thee what shalt d.
22: 3. till kn. what G. will d. for me
26: 25. thou shalt d. great things
2 S. 3: 18. Now then d. it [17: 23.
7: 25. d. as thou hast said, 1 Ch.
15: 4. judge, I would d. him justice
26. let him d. as seemeth good
21: † 4. is not silver we have to d.
24: 12. d. it unto thee, 1 Ch. 21: 10.
1 K. 2: 6. d. acc. to thy wisdom
31. d. as he hath said, fall upon
8: 32. d. and judge thy servants
39. forgive, and d., 2 Ch. 6: 23.
11: 33. d. that is right, 38.-14: 8.
18: 34. d. it the sec. time d. it third
2 K. 9: 18. thou to d. with peace? 19.
17: 34. they d. after former manners
18: 12. would not hear nor d. them
20: 9. L. will d. as he hath spoken
1 Ch. 4: † 10. wouldest d. me fr. evil
17: 2. said, d. all in thine heart
21: 8. d. away iniq. of thy serv-t
2 Ch. 9: 8. thee king, to d. judg.
19: 6. judges, Take heed what ye d.
7. now take heed and d. it
9. Thus shall ye d. in fear of L.
20: 12. nor know we what to d.
25: 8. if thou wilt go, d. it
Ezr 4: 2 we seek God, as ye d.
7: 10. to seek law of L. and d. it
18. that d. after will of your G.
Ne. 2: 12. G. put in my heart to d.
5: 12. sho. d. acc. to this promise
9: 24. d. with them as they would
Jb. 7: 20. sinned, what shall I d.?
11: 8. high as heav. what canst d.?
13: 20. d. not two things unto me
Ps. 40: 8. I delight to d. thy will
50: 16. to d. to declare my statutes
83: 9. d. unto them as unto Midi.
109: 21. But d. thou for me, O G.
119: † 112. inclined my heart to d.
132. be merciful as usest to d. to
143: 10. teach me to d. thy will
Pr. 3: 27. power of hand to d. it
Ec. 9: 10. d. it with thy might
Is. 10: 3. d. in day of visitation?
28: 21. d. his strange work
45: 7. I the L. d. all these things
Je. 2: 18. what thou to d. in E.? (2)
4: 30. spoiled what wilt thou d.?
5: 31. what will ye d. in the end?

Je. 7: 17. Seest not wh. th. d. in Jud.
11: 4. Obey my voice and d. them
15. beloved to d. in mine house?
12: 5. how d. in swelling of Jordan
14: 7. O Lord d. it for name's sake
18: 6. can-t I d. with you as potter
39: 12. d. to him as he shall say
42: 3. may shew thing we may d.
50: 15. hath done, d. unto her, 29.
La. 1: 22. d. unto them as unto me
Eze. 8: 6. seest thou what they d.?
16: 5. No eye pitied thee, to d. any
18: 5. but if a man d. that which
is right, 21. 33: 14, 19.
24: 22. ye shall d. as I have done, 24.
31: † 11. in doing sh. d. unto him
36: 37. Inquired of to d. it for th.
Da. 9: 19. O Lord hearken and d.
11: 3. sh. d. acc. to his will, 16, 36.
39. Thus sh. he d. in strong holds
Ho. 9: 5. What d. in solemn day?
10: 3. what should king d. to us?
Jo. 2: 21. L. will d. great things
3: 4. what to d. with me, O Tyre?
Am. 3: † 6. shall not L. d. somewhat
7. L. will d. nothing but reveal.
Jon. 4: 9. I d. well to be angry
Mi. 6: 8. to d. justly and to love
Zch. 1: 6 Like L. thought to d. unto
21. What come these to d.? [us
8: 16. These are things ye shall d.
Mat. 5: 19. whoso. shall d. and teach
47. what d. ye more than others?
8: 29. What have we to d. with
thee? Mk. 1: 24. Lu. 4: 34.
12: 50. whoso. shall d. the will of
my Fa. in heav., Mk. 3: 35.
20: 15. lawful to d. with mine own
32. What will ye I d.? Mk. 10: 36.
21: 24. by what authority I d. these
thi., 27. Mk. 11: 29, 33. Lu. 20: 8.
40. what will he d. unto those husbandm.? Mk. 12: 9. Lu. 20: 15.
23: 3. works they d. to be seen
27: 19. nothing to d. with just man
Mk. 3: 35. whoso. sh. d. will of G.
6: 5. could there d. no mighty
7: 8. many such things ye d., 13.
12. suffer him no more to d. for fa.
10: 35. should d. whatso. we desire
11: 28. who gave authority to d.
Lu. 4: 23. done, d. in thy country
6: 2. Why d. that not lawful to d.?
11. what they might d. to Jesus
31. would men d. to you, d. ye
7: 4. worthy for whom he d. this
8: 21. who hear word and d. it
10: 37. Go and d. thou likewise
13: 32. I d. cures to day and
16: 4. I am resolved what to d.
17: 10. done that was duty to d.
19: 48. not find what th. might d.
22: 23. wh. of them shall d. this
23: 31. if d. these in green tree
34. they know not what they d.
Jn. 2: 5. Whatso. he saith, d. it
4: 34. my meat is to d. will of him
5: 30. I can of own self d. nothing
36. works that I d. bear witness
6: 6. he knew what he would d.
28. What shall we d.? Ac. 2: 37.-
38. not to d. mine own will [16: 30.
7: 4. If thou d. these shew thyself
17. If any man will d. his will
8: 28. I d. nothing of myself
29. I d. always things please him
39. ye would d. works of Ab.
9: 33. if not of G., he d. nothing
10: 25. works that I d. in my Fa.'s
11: 47. Phari. said, What d. we?
13: 7. What I d. knowest not now
15. ye should d. as I have done
17. happy are ye if ye d. them
14: 12. works I d. sh. he d. also
14. ask in my name, I will d. it
15: 14. my friends, if ye d. whatsoever I command

Jn. 15: 21. will they d. unto you, 16: 3.
17: 4. work thou gavest me to d.
21: 21. what shall this man d.?
Ac. 1: 1. of all Jesus began to d.
4: 28. to d. whatso. thy counsel
5: 35. intend to d. touching men
9: 6. What wilt thou have me to d.
10: 6. tell what thou oughtest to d.
14: 15. Why d. ye these things?
15: 36. breth., and see how they d.
16: 28. d. thyself no harm, for
17: 7. these d. contrary to Cesar
19: 36. be quiet d. nothing rashly
26: 9. that I ought to d. many things
20. d. works meet for repentance
Ro. 1: 32. not only d. the same
2: 3. judgest them d. such things
14. d. by nature things in law
7: 15. that I d. I allow not, what
I would that d. I not, (3) 19.
16. If I d. that I would not
17. it is no more I that d. it, 20.
12: 8. let him d. it with simplicity
1 Co. 7: 36. let him d. what he will
9: 17. if I d. this thing willingly
10: 31. whatso ye d., d. all to glory
16: 10. worketh work of L. as I d.
2 Co. 8: 10. not only to d., but to be
13: 7. ye sho. d. that is honest
Ga. 2: 10. which I was forward to d.
14. to live as d. the Jews (2)
3: 10. written in law to d. them
5: 17. ye can-t d. things ye would
21. d. such things shall not inherit
Ep. 6: 9. d. same things to serv-ts
21. kn. my affairs, and how I d.
Ph. 2: 13. God worketh both to d.
4: 9. things seen in me, d.
Col. 3: 17. whatso. ye d., d. all in
23. whatso. ye d., d. it heartily
1 Th. 3: 12. in love, even as we d.
4: 10. ye d. it toward all brethren
11. to d. your own business
5: 6. let us not sleep as d. others
11. edify, even as also ye d.
24. Faithful, who also will d. it
2 Th. 3: 4. ye both d. and will d.
2 Ti. 4: 5. d. work of an evangelist
9. d. thy diligence to come, 21.
Phm. 21. wilt d. more than I say
He. 4: 13. him with wh. we have to d.
10: 7. Lo, I come to d. thy will, 9.
13: 6. I not fear what man shall d.
21 make you perfect to d. his will
1 Pe. 4: 11. d. it as of ability G. giv-h
2 Pe. 1: 10. if d. these, ye sh. never fall
3: 16. wrest, as they d. other Script.
1 Jn. 1: 6. If . . lie and d. not truth
2: 3. we d. know that we know
3: 22. bec. we d. things pleasing in

Can or Canst DO. [dau-s
Ge. 31: 43. what c. I d. with my
De. 3: 24. what God c. d. acc. to thy
1 S. 28: 2. sh. know what serv. c. d.
Jb. 11: 8. high as heav.; what c-t d.?
15: 3. speeches, he c. d. no good
22: 17. what c. Almighty d. for th.?
42: 2. I know thou c-t d. every thi.
Ps. 11: 3. what c. the righteous d.?
56: 4. I not fear what flesh c. d., 11.
118: 6. I not fear: what c. man d.?
Ec. 2: 12. what c. man d. aft. king?
Je. 38: 5. king, not he c. d. ag. you
Mk. 9: 22. if c-t d., have compassion
Lu. 12: 4. have no more they c. d.
Jn. 3: 2. no man c. d. these miracles
5: 19. Son c. d. nothing of hims., 30.
15: 5. without me ye c. d. nothing
2 Co. 13: 8. we c. d. noth. ag truth
Ph. 4: 13. I c. d. all things thro. Ch.
See Do COMMANDMENTS.

DO with evil. [d. e.
Ex. 23: 2. not follow multitude to
Le. 5: 4. or if a soul swear to d. e.
De. 4: 25. shall d. e. in sight of Lord
31: 29. bec. ye will d. e. in sight [e.
1 S. 20: 13. if please father to d. thee

2 S. 12 : 9. why despised L. to d.e.
2 K. 8 : 12. I know e. thou wilt d.
17 : 17. sold themselves to d. e.
21 : 9. Manas.seduced to d. more e.
Ne. 9 : † 28. they returned to d. e.
13 : 27. hearken to d. this gr. e.
Ps. 34 : 16. face of L. ag. them d.e.
37 : 8. fret not thyself to d. e.
Pr. 2 : 14. Who rejoice to d. e.
24 : 8. He that deviseth to d. e.
Ec. 5 : 1. consider not they d. e.
8 : 11. heart of men fully set to d.e.
12. Tho. sinner d. e. 100 times
Is. 1 : 16. wash ye, cease to d. e.
41 : 23. d. good or e., that we may
Je. 4 : 22. my peo. are wise to d. e.
10 : 5. not afraid, cannot d. e.
13:23. that are accustomed to d.e.
18 : 10. If it d. e. in my sight
Eze. 6 : 10. that I would d. this e.
Mi. 7 : 3. may d.e. with both hands
Zph. 1 : 12. L. not do good, nor d.e.
Mk. 3 : 4. lawful to d. e.? Lu. 6 : 9.
Ro. 3 : 8. say, Let us d. e. that
13 : 4. But if thou d. e., be afraid
2 Co. 13 : 7. I pray that ye d. no e.
1 Pe.3:12. face of L. is ag. them d.e.

DO with good.

Ge. 19 : 8. d. as is g. in your eyes
27:46. What g. shall my life d.me?
32 : 12. I will surely d. thee g.
Le. 5 : 4. soul, pronouncing to d.g.
Nu. 10 : 29. and we will d. thee g.
24 : 13. to d. g. or bad of my own
De. 1 : 14. spoken is g. for us to d.
8 : 16. prove, to d. thee g. at end
28 : 63. L. rejoiced to d. you g.
30 : 5. and he will d. thee g.
Ju.10:15.d. unto us whats.seem. g.
17:13. know I that L. will d. me g.
19 : 24. d. with them what seem.g.
1 S. 1:23. d. what seemeth thee g.,
14 : 36, 40. 2 S. 19 : 27, 37.
3 : 18. It is L.; let him d. what
seemeth him g., 2 S. 10 : 12.
2 K.10 : 5. d.that is g. in thine eyes
1 Ch. 19 : 13. L. d. what is g. in his
21 : 23. king d. that is g.in his eyes
Ne. 5 : 9. It is not g. that ye d.
Jb. 15:3. with speeches can d.no g.
Ps. 34 : 14. d. g., 37 : 3, 27.-51:18.
-125 : 4. Mat. 5 : 44. Lu.6:9,35.
36 : 3. he hath left off to d. g.
Pr. 31 : 12. She will d. him g.
Ec. 3 : 12. for man to d. g. in life
Is. 41 : 23. yea d. g. or do evil
Je. 4 : 22. to d.g. have no knowl.
10 : 5. neith. is it in them to d. g.
13 : 23. may ye d.g. that are accus.
26 : 14. d. with me as seemeth g.
29 : 32. nor behold the g. I will d.
32:40. not turn away to d.them g.
41. I will rejoice to d. them g.
33 : 9. hear all the g. I d. them
Mi. 2 : 7. do not my words d. g. to
Zph. 1:12. say,The L. will not d. g.
Mk. 3 : 4. saith, Is it lawful to d. g.
on sabbath-days, or to do evil?
Lu. 6 : 9.
14 : 7.the poor, ye may d. them g.
Lu. 6:33. if d. g. to them which d.
g. to you what thank
Ro. 7:19. g. that I would, I d. not
21. when I would d.g.evil is pres.
13:3. d. g., thou shalt have praise
Ga. 6 : 10. let us d.g. unto all men
1 Ti.6:18. charge rich, th. they d.g.
He. 13:16.to d.g. and communicate
Ja. 4 : 17. knoweth to d. g., doeth
1 Pe. 3 : 11. eschew evil, d. g. ⌊not

Have I to DO. ⌈19:22.

2 S.16:10.What h. I t. d. with you?
1 K. 17 : 18. What h. I t. d. with
thee? 2 K. 3 : 13. 2 Ch. 35 : 21.
Mk. 5 : 7. Lu. 8 : 28. Jn. 2 : 4.
Ho.14:8. What h. I t.d. with idols?
1 Co. 5:12. what h. I t.d. to judge

I shall, or I will DO.
Will I, shall I, would I DO.

Ge. 27 : 37. what s. I d. unto thee
47 : 30. I w. d. as thou hast said
Ex. 3 : 20. which I w.d. in midst
6 : 1. sh. see what I w. d. to Pha.
17 : 4. What s. I d. to this people?
33 : 17. unto Mos. I w. d. this thi.
34 : 10. I w. d. marvels (2)
Nu.14:35. I w. surely d. it to cong.
22 : 17. I w.d. whatso.thou sayest
33 : 56. I s. d. to you as I thought
Ru. 3 : 5. All thou sayest I w. d.
11. I w.d. to thee all thou requir.
13. then w. I d. the part of a
kinsman to thee
1 S. 3 : 11. I w. d. a thing in Israel
10 : 2. What s. I d. for my son
20 : 4. thy soul desireth, I w. d. it
28 : 15. make known what I s. d.
2 S. 12 : 12. I w. d. this before Isr.
18 : 4. What seemeth best I w. d.,
19 : 38. ⌈d. for you
21 : 3. to the Gibeonites, What s. I
4. What you sh. say, that w.I d.
1 K. 5 : 8. I w. d. all thy desire
20 : 9. All didst send for, I w. d.
2 K. 2 : 9. Ask what I s. d. for thee
4:2. unto her,What s.I d.for thee?
Es. 5:8. I w.d. to morrow as the k.
Jb. 7 : 20. What s. I d. unto thee
31 : 14. What s. I d. when G. riseth
34:32. done iniq., I w. d. no more
Pr. 24:29. I w.d. to him as he hath
Is. 5 : 5. tell what I w. d. to viney.
42 : 16. These w. I d., not forsake
43 : 19. I w. d. a new thing
46 : 10. I w. d. all my pleasure
11. I have purposed it, I w. d. it
48 : 11. for own sake w. I d. it
Je.7:14. thf. w. I d. unto this house
9 : 7. how s. I d. for dau. of peo.?
19:12. Thus w. I d.unte this place
25 : 6. and I w. d. you no hurt
29:32. good I w. d. for my people
51:47. I w.d. judgm. upon images
Eze. 5 : 9. I w. d. in thee what I
7 : 27. I w. d. after their way
22 : 14. I have spoken, and w. d.
it, 24 : 14.-36 : 36.
35 : 11. I w. d. acc. to thine anger
36:11. I w.d. better unto you than
Ho. 6 : 4. O Ephraim, what s. I d.
unto thee?
Am. 4 : 12. w. I d. unto thee, Isr.
Mat. 19 : 16. Master, what good
thing s. I d.? ⌈with Jesus
27 : 22. Pilate saith, What s. I d.
Lu. 12 : 17. What s. I d., no room
16:3. What s. I d.? 20:13.Ac.22:10.
18 : 18. What s. I d. to inherit
Jn. 14:13. ye sh. ask, that w. I d.
14. if ask in my name I w. d. it
2 Co. 11 : 12. what I do,that I w.d.
Phm.14.without thy mind w-d I d.
See JUDGMENT. ⌊noth.

Must DO.

Ex. 18 : 20. shew work they m. d.
Nu. 23 : 26. All L. speaketh,I m.d.
Ezr. 10 : 12. As hast said m. we d.
Pr. 19 : 19. if deliver, m.d. it again
Ac.16:30. What m.I d.to be saved?

DO with no, or not.

Ge. 18 : 29. I will n. d. it for forty's
30. I will n. d. it if I find thirty
34:19. young man deferred n.to d.
Ex.20:10. is the sabbath, in it shalt
n. d. work, Le. 23 : 31.
21 : 11. if he d.n. these 3 unto her
23 : 24. shalt n. d. aft. their works
Le. 16 : 29. and d. n. work, 23 : 3,
28. De. 15 : 19. Je. 17 : 24.
18:3. after their doings ye sh.n.d.
19:15.d.n.unrighte. in judgm.,35.
23 : 7. d. n. servile work, 8, 21,25,
35, 36. Nu. 28 : 18, 25, 26.
26 : 14. if will n. d. my com-ts, 15.

Nu. 8 : 26. fr. age of 50 d.n. service
23:19. and shall he n. d. it? ⌈8.
29:7. n. d. any work, De. 5:14.-16:
De. 12 : 8. n. d. after things we do
13 : 11. shall d. n. such wickedn.
17:13. d. n. more presumptuously
Ju. 6:27. feared, he could n. d. it
19 : 23. my brethren, d.n.this folly
24. unto this man d. n. so vile
Ru. 3:13. if n. d. part of a kinsman
1 S.26:21.I will n.more d.thee harm
1 K.11:12.I will n.d.it for Da.'s sake
2 K. 7 : 9. lepers said, We d.n.well
17 : 15. L. charged n. d. like them
18 : 12. not hear them, n. d. them
Ezr. 7 : 26. whoso will n.d. the law
Jb. 13 : 20. Only d. n. two things
34 : 12. God will n. d. wickedly
41 : 8. remember battle, d.n.more
Ps. 119:3.they d. n. iniq. they walk
Je. 22:3. d. n. wrong to stranger (2)
42 : 5. L. be a witness, if we d. n.
Eze. 5 : 9. I will n. d. any more like
23:48. taught n. to d. after lewdn.
33:31.hear words, but will n.d. th.
32. hear thy words, but d. th. n.
Zph. 3:5. just L., he will n. d. iniq.
13. remnant of Isr. n.d.iniq. ⌈47.
Mat.5:46. d.n. publicans the same?
6:1. d. n. your alms before men
12:2. d. that n. lawful on sabbath
19 : 18. Thou shalt d. n. murder
20:13. Friend, I d. thee n. wrong
23 : 3. n.d. after their works, they
say and d. n. ⌈work
Mk. 6 : 5. could there d.n. mighty
Lu. 6 : 46. d. n. the things I say
Jn. 6 : 38. n. to d. mine own will
10 : 37. if I d. n. works of my Fa.
Ro. 7 : 15. would, that d. I n., 19.
8 : 3. for what the law could n. d.
1 Jn. 1 : 6. we lie, and d. n. truth
Re. 19 : 10. See thou d. it n., 22:9.

Observe with DO.

De.5:32.ye shall o. to d. as L. com.
you, 8 : 1.-11 : 32.-12 : 1.-24 :
8. 2 K. 17 : 37.
6 : 3. o. to d., 12 : 32.-28 : 13, 15,
58.-31 : 12.-32 : 46.
25. if we o. to d. these com-ts
15 : 5. to o. to d. all these com-ts
16 : 12. shalt o. and d. these stat.
17:10 shalt o. to d. as they inform
Jos. 1:7 mayest o. to d. all the law
2 K. 21:8. if they will o. to d. acc
Ne.10:29. into an oath to o. and d.
Eze. 37:24. they sh. o. and d. them
Mat. 23 : 3. what bid you, o. and d.

Shall we DO. We shall DO.

Ju. 13 : 8. what w.s.d. unto child
12. order, how s.w.d. unto him?
21 : 7. how s.w.d. for wives, 16.
1 S. 5:8. What s.w.d. with the ark
6:2. What s.w.d. to the ark of L.
2 S. 16 : 20. Give counsel what s.w.
17 : 6. s.w.d. after his saying? ⌊d.
2 K. 6 : 15. Alas, master, how s.w.
d. ⌈talents
2 Ch. 25 : 9. what s. w. d. for 100
Es.1:15. What s.w.d. unto Vashti?
Ps. 60:12. w.s.d. valiantly, 108:13.
Can.8:8. what s.w.d. for our sister
Jon. 1 : 11. they said, What s. w.
d. to thee? ⌈12, 14.
Lu. 3 : 10. asked, What s. w. d.?
Jn. 6 : 28. What s. w. d. that we
might work works of God?
Ac. 2:37. Men, breth. what s.w.d.
4 : 16. What s.w.d. to these men?

DO with so.

Ge. 18 : 5. s. d. as thou hast said
19:7. d. not s. wickedly, Ju.19:23.
44 : 17. God forbid that I sho.d.s.
Ex. 8 : 26. It is not meet s. to d.
Le. 4 : 20. s. shall be d., 16:16. Nu.
9 : 14.-15 : 14.
8 : 34. s. Lord commanded to d.

Nu. 14 : 28. s. will I d., 32 : 31. Is.
65 : 8. Eze. 35 : 15.
15 : 12. s. shall he d. to every one
22 : 30. I wont to d. s. unto thee
32 : 23. if will not d.s. ye sinned
De. 3 : 21. s. shall L. d. unto kings
4 : 5. ye should d. s. in land ye go
12:4. Ye shall not d.s. unto L., 31.
30. nations serve gods? s. I d.
18:14. L. not suffered thee s. to d.
22 : 3. s. shalt d. with his raim.
5. all that d. s. are abomination
Ju. 7:17. that as I d. s. shall ye p.
11 : 10. if we d. not s. acc. to thy
14:10. s. used the young men to d.
Ru. 1 : 17. L. d.s. to me, 1 S. 14:44.
1 S. 3 : 17. God d. s. to thee [thee
8 : 8. served gods, s. d. they unto
20 : 13. L. d. s. and more to Jona.
25 : 22. s. d. God unto enemies
30:23. Ye shall not d.s. my breth.
2 S. 3:9. s.d. God to Abner, s.I d.
35. God d. s. to me, 19 : 13. 1 K.
2 : 23.-20 : 10. 2 K. 6 : 31. [d.
9 : 11. said Ziba, s. shall thy serv.
1 K. 1:30. s. will I certainly d. [d.
2:38. as k. said, s. will thy servant
19 : 2. s. let the gods d. to me
22 : 22. go and d. s., 2 Ch. 18:21.
2 K. 17 : 41. as did fathers, s. d.
1 Ch.13:4. cong. said they would d.s.
Ezr. 10 : 12. said, s. must we d.
Ne. 5 : 12. they said, s. will we d.
6 : 13. I sho. be afraid, d.s. and sin
13 : 21. if ye d. s. again I will lay
Es. 6 : 10. d. s. to Mordecai
7 : 5. who durst presume to d. s.?
Jb. 13 : 9. d. ye s. mock him?
Pr. 20 : 30. s. d. stripes the belly
24 : 29. Say not, I will d.s. to him
Is. 10:11. s. d. to Jerus. and idols?
65 : 8. s. will I d. for serv.'s sake
Je. 28:6. Lord d. s., perform words
Eze. 45 : 20. s. shalt d. 7th day
Da. 11:30. s. sh. he d., return [you
Ho. 10 : 15. s. shall Beth-el d. unto
Mat. 5 : 47. d. not publicans s.?
7:12. men should d. to you d. ye s.
18:35. s. shall my Fa. d. unto you
Jn. 14 : 31. as Fa. gave com-t s. I d.
Ac. 7 : 51. as fathers did, s. d. ye
1 Co. 16 : 1. giv. order, even s.d. ye
Col. 3:13. as C. forgave you, s.d. ye
1 Ti. 1 : 4. which is in faith, s. d.
Ja. 2 : 12. s. d. as they th. be judg.

DO with this.

Ge. 11 : 6. t. they begin to d.
39 : 9. can I d. t. great wickedn.
41 : 34. Let Pha. d. t. and appoint
42 : 18. Joseph said, t. d. and live
43 : 11. If it must be so now, d. t.,
45 : 17. t. d. ye, 19.
Le. 26 : 16. I will d. t. to you
Nu. 16 : 6. t. d., Take you censers
Jos. 9 : 20. t. we will d. to the Gib.
Ju. 19 : 23. brethren, d. not t. folly
2 S. 13 : 12. brother d. not t. folly
23 : 17. far from me that I d. t.
2 K. 19:31. zeal of L. d. t., Is.37:32.
2 Ch. 19 : 10. t. d. ye sh. not tresp.
Ezr. 4 : 22. that ye fail not to d. t.
Pr. 6 : 3. d. t. now, my son
Is. 38:19. praise thee, as I d.t. day
Je. 32 : 35. should d. t. abomina.
Eze. 6 : 10. I would d. t. evil [32.
36 : 22. I d. not t. for your sakes,
Am.4:12. bec. I will d. t. unto thee
Mal. 4 : 3. in day that I shall d. t.
Mat. 8 : 9. d. t. he doeth it, Lu. 7:8.
9 ; 28. Bel. ye I am able to d. t.?
21 : 21. if faith, sh. not only d. t.
Mk. 11 : 3. if any say, Why d. t.?
Lu. 7 : 4. worthy for whom he sho.
10:28. t. d. thou shalt live [d.t.?
12:18. t. will I d., I will pull down
22:19. is my body t. d. in remem.
of me, 1 Co. 11 : 24, 25.

Ac. 21 : 23. d. t. that we say to thee
1 Co. 9 : 17. if I d. t. thing willing.
23. t. I d. for the gospel's sake
He. 6 : 3. t. will we d. if G. permit
13 : 19. I beseech you to d. t.
Ja. 4 : 15. if L. will, d. t. or that
See THIS, THING.

Will we DO. We will DO.

Ex. 19 : 8. L. said w.w.d., 24: 3,7.
Nu. 10 : 32. same goodness w.w.d.
De. 5 : 27. w. w. hear it and d. it
Jos. 1:16. all thou com. us w.w.d.
Ju. 20 : 9. thing w.w.d. to Gibeah
2 K. 10 : 5. w.w.d. all thou sh. bid
Je. 18 : 12. w. w. every one d. the
imagination
42:20. so declare, and w. w. d. it
44:17. w.w.d. whatever proceedeth

DO well.

Is. 1 : 17. evil. Learn to d. w.
Jon. 4 : 9. I d. w. to be angry
Zch. 8 : 15. to d. w. unto Jerus. and
Mat. 12:12. lawful to d. w. on sab.
Jn. 11 : 12. if he sleep, he sh. d.w.
Ac. 15 : 29. if keep yours., sh. d.w.
Ja. 2 : 8. if fulfil royal law, ye d.w.
1 Pe. 2 : 14. praise of them th. d.w.
20. if ye d. w. and suffer for it
3 : 6. dau-s ye are long as ye d.w.
2 Pe. 1 : 19. d.w. that ye take heed
3 Jn. 6. whom if bring, shalt d.w.

DOCTOR, S.

Lu. 2 : 46. Jesus in midst of the d-s
5 : 17. were d-s of law sitting by
Ac. 5 : 34. Gamaliel, d. of the law

DOCTRINE.

Ps. 19 : † 7. d. of the L. is perfect
Is. 28 : 9. make to understand d.
† 19. a vexation to understand d.
29 : 24. that murm. shall learn d.
53 : † 1. who hath believed our d.
Je. 10 : 8. stock is d. of vanities
Mat. 7 : 28. astonished at his d., 22:
33. Mk. 1 : 22.-11:18. Lu. 4:32.
16 : 12. beware of d. of Pharisees
Mk. 1:27. saying, What new d. this
4 : 2. said to them in his d., 12:38.
Jn. 7 : 17. if do will, shall kn. of d.
18 : 19. priest asked Jesus of his d.
Ac. 2 : 42. continued in apostle's d.
5 : 28. filled Jerus. with your d.
13 : 12. being astonished at the d.
17 : 19. know what this new d. is?
Ro. 6 : 17. obeyed that form of d.
16 : 17. contrary to d. ye learned
1 Co. 14 : 6. except I speak by d.
26. every one of you hath a d.
Ep. 4 : 14. carried with ev. wind of d.
1 Ti. 1 : 3. they teach no other d.
4:13. till I come, give attend. to d.
16. Take heed unto thyself, and d.
5 : 17. who labour in the word and
6 : 1. his d. be not blasphemed [d.
3. the d. according to godliness
2 Ti. 3:16. scripture is profita. for d.
4 : 2. exhort, with long suff. and d.
Tit. 2 : 7. in d. shewing incorruptn.
10. adorn d. of G. our Saviour
He. 6 : 1. principles of d. of Christ
2. Of d. of baptisms, and hands
2 Jn. 9. abideth not in d. of C.; he
that abideth in d. hath Father
Re. 2 . 14. that hold d. of Balaam
15. that hold d. of Nicolaitanes

Good DOCTRINE. [sake

Pr. 4 : 2. I give you g. d. not for-
1 Ti. 4 : 6. nourished in words of g.

My DOCTRINE. [d.

De. 32 : 2. m. d. shall drop as rain
Jb. 11 : 4. m. d. is pure, and I am
Jn. 7 : 16. m. d. is not mine, but
2 Ti. 3 : 10. hast fully known m.d.

Sound DOCTRINE.

1 Ti. 1 : 10. that is contrary to s.d.
2 Ti. 4 : 3. will not endure s. d.
Tit. 1 : 9. by s. d. to exhort
2 : 1. speak things become s. d.

This DOCTRINE.

2 Jn. 10. If any bring not t. d.
Re. 2 : 24. as many as have not t. d.

DOCTRINES. [Mk.7:7.

Mat. 15 : 9. for d. comm-ts of men,
Col 2:22. why after com-ts, d. of men
1 Ti. 4 : 1. giving heed to d. of devils
He. 13 : 9. not with divers strange d.

DO'DAI. See DODO.

DODA'NIM or RODA'NIM.

Ge. 10 : 4.† sons of Javan, D., 1 Ch.

DODA'VAH. [1: 7.†

2 Ch. 20 :37. Eliezer son of D. prophe-

DO'DO [1] or DO'DAI.[2] [sied

Ju. 10 : 1. of Puah, son of D.[1] [12.
2 S. 23 : 9. Eleazar son of D.[1], 1 Ch. 11:
24. Elhanan son of D.[1] of Beth-lehem, 1 Ch. 11 : 26. [D.[2],† D.[1]
1 Ch. 27 : 4. over course of sec. month

✱ DO'EG. [22.

1 S. 21 : 7. D., an Edomite, 22 : 9, 18,
22 : 18. priests, D. slew th. day 85(2)
22. I knew D. wou. surely tell Saul
Ps. 52.✱ D. the Edomite told Saul

DOER.

Ge. 39 : 22. Joseph was the d. of it
2 S. 3 : 39. L. shall reward d. of evil
Ps. 31 : 23. Lord rewardeth proud d.
Pr. 17 : 4. A wicked d. heed to false
Ja. 1 :23. If a hearer of word not a d.
25. not forgetful hearer but a d.
4 : 11. thou art not a d. of the law

DOERS.

2 K. 22 : 5. give it to d. of the work
Ps. 101 : 8. may cut off all wicked d.
Ro. 2 :13. d. of law shall be justified
Ja. 1 : 22. Be ye d. of the word, not
See EVIL doer, s.

DOEST.

Ge. 4 : 7. If d. well, if d. not well
21 : 22. G. with thee in all thou d.
Ex. 18:14. What this thou d. to peo.
17. thing that thou d. is not good
De. 12 : 28. when thou d. good
15:18. God sh. bless in all thou d.
Ju. 11:27. thou d. me wrong to war
2 S. 3 : 25. to know all that thou d.
1 K. 2 : 3. prosper in all thou d.
19 : 9. What d. thou here, Elij.? 13.
20 : 22. mark, see what thou d.
Jb 9 : 12. who say, What d. thou?
35:6. sinnest what d. thou ag. him?
Ps. 49:18 praise thee, when d. well
77 : 14. Thou art G d. wonders
86 : 10. and d. wondrous things
119 : 68. art good, and d. good
Ec. 8 : 4. or say, What d.? Da.4:35.
Je. 11 : 15. d. evil, thou rejoicest
15:5. who go to ask how thou d.?
Eze. 12:9. house said, What d. thou?
16 : 30. seeing thou d. all these
24 : 19. tell what there are thou d.
Jon. 4 : 4. d. well to be angry? 9.
Mat.6:2. when thou d. thine alms, 3
21 : 23. By what authority d. thou
these, Mk. 11 : 28. Lu. 20 : 2
Jn. 2:18. see-g thou d. these things?
3 : 2. no man do miracles thou d.
7 : 3. disci. may see works thou d.
13:27. said, Th. thou d. do quickly
Ac. 22 : 26. Take heed what thou d.
Ro. 2:1. judgest, d. same things, 3.
Ja. 2 : 19. believest, thou d. well
3 Jn. 5. d. faithf. whats. d. to breth.

DOETH.

Ge. 31:12. seen all Laban d. to thee
Ex. 31 : 14. whoso. d. work therein
that be cut off, 15. Le. 23 : 30.
Le. 4 : 27. while he d. against any
6 : 3. all these a man d. sinning [ly
Nu. 15:30. soul th. d. presumptuous-
24 : 23. who live when God d. this?
Jb. 5 : 9. which d. great things, 9:
10.-37 : 5. Ps. 72 : 18.-136 : 4.
23 : 13. soul desireth, that he d.
24 : 21. He d. not good to the widow
Ps. 1 :3. whatso-r he d. shall prosper

P. 14 : 1. there is none d. good, 3.
53 : 1, 3. Ro 3: 12.
15 : 3. nor d. evil to neighbour
5. d. these, shall never be moved
106:3. blessed is he that d. righte.
118 : 15. of L. d. valiantly, 16.
Pr. 6 : 32. d. it, destroyeth his soul
11 : 17. d. good to his own soul
17 : 22. A merry heart d. good like
Ec. 2 : 2. said of mirth, What d. it?
3:14. whatsoever God d. sh. be for
ever, God d. it that men fear
7 : 20. there is not a man d. good
8 : 3. he d. whatso pleaseth him
Is. 56 : 2. Blessed is the man d. this
Je. 48 : 10. d. work of L. deceitf
Eze. 17 : 15. shall he escape that d.
18 : 10. that d. the like to any one
11. d. not any of those duties
14. consid-h and d. not such
24. d. acc. to all the abomina-s
27. d. that which is lawful and
Da 4 : 35. d. acc. to will in heaven
9 : 14. L. is righteous in all he d.
Am. 9 : 12. saith the L. that d. this
Mal.2:12.L. will cut off man d. this
17. say, Ev. one d. evil is good
Mat. 6 : 3. not left ha. know right d.
7 : 21. he that d. will of my Fa.
24. whoso. hear. sayings. and d.
26. heareth and d. not, Lu. 6 : 49
8 : 9. Do this, he d. it, Lu. 7 : 8.
Lu. 6 : 47. hear. my sayings and d.
Jn 3 : 20. every one that d. evil
21. d. truth cometh to the light
5 : 19 what things he d. d. Son
20. sheweth him all himself d.
7 : 4. no man d. any thi. in secret
51. bef. it know what he d.
9 : 31. d. his will, him he heareth
14 : 10. Fa. in me, he d. works
15 : 15. knoweth not what lord d.
16 : 2. will think he d. G. service
Ac. 15 : 17. L. who d. all those thi.
26 : 31. d. noth. worthy of death
Ro. 2 : 9. anguish upon soul d. evil
10 : 5. man that d. these shall live
by them, Ga. 3 : 12.
13 : 4. wrath upon him that d. evil
1 Co. 6 : 18. Every sin a man d. is
7 : 37. will keep his virgin, d. well
38 giveth her in marriage d. well,
giveth her not d. better
Ga 3 : 5. d. be it by works of law
Ep. 6 : 8. whatso good thing any d.
Col. 1 : 6. forth fruit, as it d. in you
3 : 25. he that d. wrong sh. receive
1 Th. 2 : 11. as father d. his chil.
Ja. 4 : 17. kno to do good, d. it not
1 Jn. 2 : 17. d. will of God abideth
29. d. righteousn. is born of him,
3 Jn. 10. remember deeds he d. [3:7.
11 that d. evil hath not seen God
Re. 13 : 13. he d. great wonders; so

DOG.

Ex. 11:7. ag. Isr. sh. not a d. move
De. 23:18. not price of d. into hou.
Ju. 7 : 5. lappeth as d. lappeth
1 S. 17:43. Philis. unto D., Am I a d.?
24 : 14. whom dost pursue ? a d. ?
2 S. 3 : 8. said, Am I a d.'s head?
9 : 8. look upon such dead d. as I
16 : 9. this dead d. curse my lord?
2 K. 8:13. Haz. said, Is thy serv. a d.
Ps. 22 : 20. darling fr. power of d.
59 : 6. make a noise like a d., 14.
Pr. 26 : 11. As a d. returneth to his
vomit, 2 Pe. 2 : 22.
17. that taketh a d. by the ears
Ec. 9 : 4. living d. is better than
Is. 66 : 3. as if he cut off d.'s neck

DOGS.

Ex. 22 : 31. flesh torn, cast it to d.
Mat. 15 : 26. Mk. 7 : 27.
1 K. 14:11. sh. d. eat, 16 : 4.-21:24.
21 : 19. place d. licked blood of Naboth, d. lick thy blood [36.
23. d. sh. eat Jezebel, 2 K. 9 : 10

1 K. 22:38. d. licked up Ahab's blood
Jb. 30 : 1. I disdained to set with d.
Ps. 22 : 16 d. have compassed me
68 : 23. and the tongue of thy d.
Is. 56 : 10. dumb d. | 11. greedy d.
Je. 15 : 3. sword to slay, d. to tear
Mat. 7 : 6. Give not holy unto d.
15 : 27. d. eat of crumbs, Mk. 7:28
Lu. 16 : 21. the d. licked his sores
Ph. 3 : 2. Beware of d. beware of
Re. 22 : 15. without are d. and

DOING. [Participle.]

Ex. 15 : 11. like thee d. wonders
1 K. 22 : 43. d. right, 2 Ch. 20 : 32.
1 Ch. 22 : 16. Arise and be d., L. be
Ezr. 9 : 1. d. acc. to their abomina-s
Ne. 6 : 3. I am d. great work, I
Mat. 24 : 46. find so d., Lu. 12 : 43.
Ac. 10 : 38. went about d. good
Ep. 6 : 6. d. will of God from heart
1 Ti. 5:21. d. nothing by partiality
He. 13 : † 21 d. that is well pleas.

DOING. [Noun.]

Ge 31 : 28. done foolishly in so d.
44 : 5. ye have done evil in so d.
Nu. 20:19. without d. any thing else
De. 9 : 18. ye sinned in d. wicked.
1 K. 16 : 19. Zimri sinned in d. evil,
2 K. 21. 16.
Jb. 32 : 22. in so d. my Mak. would
Ps. 64 : 9. wisely consider of his d.
66 : 5. he is terrible in d. toward
118 : 23. This is Lord's d. marvel-
lous, Mat. 21 : 42. Mk. 12 : 11.
Is. 56 : 2. keepeth hand fr. d. evil
58 : 13. fr. d. thy pleasure on my
Je. 32:†19. in counsel, mighty in d.
Eze. 31:†11. in u. he sh. do unto him
Lu. 12:43. Blessed serv-t L. find so d.
Ac. 24 : 20. if found evil d. in me
Ro. 12 : 20. in so d. shalt heap coals
2 Co 8 : 11. Now perform d. of it
1 Ti 4 : 16. in d. this sh. save thys.
Ja. 1 : † 25. sh. be blessed in his d.

Well DOING.

Ro 2 : 7. patient continu. in w. d.
Ga. 6:9. not weary in w. d., 2 Th. 3:13
1 Pe. 2:15. with w. d. put to silence
3 : 17. better that ye suff. for w. d.
4 : 19. commit their souls in w. d.

DOINGS.

Le. 18 : 3. After d. of E., after d. of
Canaan, shall ye not do
De. 28 : 20. of wickedn. of thy d.
Ju. 2 : 19. ceased not fr. their own d.
1 S. 25 : 3. Nabal was evil in his d.
2 Ch. 17:4. walked not aft. d. of Isr.
Ps. 9 : 11. declare his d., Is 12 : 4.
77 : 12. I will talk of thy d.
Pr. 20 : 11. child is known by his d.
Is. 1 : 16. put away evil of your d.
3 : 8. bec. their d. are ag. the L.
10. shall eat the fruit of their d.
Je. 4 : 4. my fury burn, bec. of your
d., 21 : 12.-26 : 3.-44 : 22.
18. thy d. have procured these
7 : 3. Amend d., 5.-26 : 13.-35 : 15.
11 : 18. thou shewedst me their d.
17:10. acc. to fruit of his d., 21:14.
18 : 11. return, make your d. good
23 : 2. will visit evil of your d.
22. fr. evil of d., 25 : 5. Zch 1 : 4.
32 : 19. give acc. to fruit of his d.
Eze. 14 : 22. ye sh. see their d., 23.
20 : 43. there shall ye remem. d.
44. nor acc. to your corrupt d.
21 : 24. in all your d. sins appear
24 : 14. acc. to thy d. they judge
36 : 17. defiled it by their own d.
19. acc. to d. I judged them
31. sh. remem. your d. not good
Ho. 4 : 9. I will punish their d. [G.
5 : 4. will not frame d. to turn unto
7 : 2. own d. have set them about
9 : 15. for wick. of d. I will drive
12 : 2. acc. to his d. will he recom.
Mi. 2 : 7. are these his d.?

Mi 3:4. have behaved ill in their d.
7 : 13. be desolate for fruit of d.
Zph. 3 : 7. corrupted all their d.
11. not be ashamed for thy d.?
Zch. 1 : 6. acc. to our d. so dealt

DOLEFUL.

Is 13 : 21. full of d. creatures
Mi. 2 : 4. lament with d. lamenta.

DOMINION, S.

Ge. 1 : 26. have d. over fish, 28.
27:40. when thou shalt have the d.
37 : 8. thou have d. over us?
Nu. 24 : 19. of Jac. he that sh. have
Ju. 5 : 13. have d. over nobles [d.
14 : 4. Philis had d. over Israel
1 K. 4 : 24. Sol. had d. over all the
9 : 19. to build in his d., 2 Ch. 8:6.
2 K. 20 : 13. noth. in all his d. that
Hez. shewed not, Is. 39 : 2.
1 Ch. 4 : 22. who had d. in Moab
18 : 3. as he went to stablish d.
2 Ch. 21:8. Edomites fr. Judah's d.
32 : † 9. Sennacherib and his d.
Ne. 9 : 28. they had d. over them
37. they have d. over our bodies
Jb. 25 : 2. d. and fear are with him
38 : 33. canst thou set d. thereof
Ps. 8 : 6. to have d. over the works
19 : 13. sins, let them not have d.
49 : 14. the upright shall have d.
72 : 8. have d. from sea to sea [d.
103 : 22. bless L. in all pla. of his
114 : 2. Jud. his sanct. Isr. his d.
119 : 133. let not any iniq have d.
145 : 13. thy d. endureth thro. all
Is. 26 : 13. other lords had d.
Je. 2 : † 31. whf. say peo., We have
34 : 1. all the kingd-s of his d. [d.
51 : 28. rulers and land of his d.
Da. 4 : 3. his d. is from genera. to
22. d. reacheth to end of earth
34. d. is an everlasting d., 7 : 14
6 : 26. in ev. d. men fear bef. G. of
Daniel, and his d. shall
7 : 6. beast, and d. was given to it
12. beasts had d. taken away
14. was given him d. and glory
26. they shall take away his d.
27. d. shall be given to the saints
all d-s shall serve him
11:3. king shall rule with great d.,
4. not acc. to d. wh. he ruled [5.
Mi. 4 : 8. unto thee even the first d.
Zch. 9 : 10. his d. be fr. sea to sea
Mat. 20 : 25. princes exercise d.
Ro. 6 : 9. death hath no more d.
14. sin sh. not have d. over you
7 : 1. law d. over a man as long
2 Co. 1 : 24. Not d. over your faith
Ep. 1 : 21. above all power, and d.
Col. 1 : 16. whether thrones or d-s
1 Pe. 4 : 11. God, to whom be praise
and d. for ever, 5 : 11. Re. 1:6.
2 Pe. 2:†10. that despise d., Jude 8.
Jude 25. to only wise God be d.

DONE. [had d.

Ge. 9 : 24. Noah knew what his son
18 : 21. have d. acc. to cry of it
24 : 66. told Isaac all he had d.
26 : 29. we have d. nothing but
29 : 26. not be d. in our country
34:7. folly, wh. ought not to be d.
44 : 5. ye have d. evil in so doing
15. What deed this ye have d.?
Ex. 1 : 18. Why have ye d. this
2 : 4. sister stood to wit what be d.
3 : 16. seen that d. to you in E.
12:16. no work be d. in them, save
what be eat, that only be d.
13 : 8. this d. bec. of that L. did
18 : 1. heard of all G. had d. for Mo
8. all L. had d. unto Pharaoh
9. goodness Lord had d. to Israel
21 : 31. acc. to this judgm it be d.
31 : 15. Six days may work be d.
35 : 2. Le. 23 : 3. [com-d (2
39 : 43. they had d. it as Lord had

Le. 5: 17. things forbidden to be d.
8: 5. L. com-d to be d., De. 26:14.
11:32. vessel, wherein work is d.
18: 27. these abom-s have men d.
24: 19. so shall it be d. to him
20. so shall it be d. to him
Nu. 5: 7. they shall confess sin d.
12: 11. we have d. foolishly [him
15: 34. not declared what be d. to
22:2. Balak saw all that Isr. had d.
27:4. Why name of our fa. be d. aw.?
32:13. that had d. evil were consu.
De. 3: 21. G. hath d. unto two k-s
10: 21. is thy G. that hath d.
19: 19. thought to have d. unto brother [build
25: 9. So be d. unto man will not
29: 24. say, Whf. hath L. d. thus unto land? 1 K. 9: 8. 2 Ch. 7: 21 Je. 22: 8. [10:1.
Jos. 9: 3. Jos. had d. unto Jericho,
10: 32. had d. to Libnah, 39.
35. d. to Lachish | 37. to Eglon
22: 24. if not rather d. it for fear
24: 31. all he had d. for Israel
Ju. 2: 10. works he had d. for Isr.
3: 12. because they had d. evil in
9: 16. if ye have d. truly and d.
24. cruelty d. to 70 sons of Jeruh.
19: 30. There was no such deed d.
Ru. 3: 16. told her all man had d.
1 S. 4: 16. said, What is d. my son
11: 7. so sh. it be d. unto his oxen
17: 26. What be d. to man killeth
27. So be d. to man th. killeth him
25: 30. L. shall have d. to my lord
28: 17. d. as he spake, Eze. 12:28.
2 S. 11:27. Da. had d. displeased L.
13: 12. no such thi. ought to be d.
24: 17. but these sheep, what have they d.? 1 Ch. 21: 17.
1 K. 8:66. goodn. L. had d. for Da.
14:22. abo. all their fathers had d.
19: 1. Ahab told all Elijah had d.
22: 53. acc. to all his fa. had d., 2 K. 15: 3, 9, 34.-23: 32. [14.
2 K. 4: 13. What to be d. for thee?
8: 4. great things Elisha hath d.
10: 10. L. hath d. that he spake by Elijah, Is. 38: 15. Je. 40: 3.
19: 11. thou hast heard what kings of Assyria have d. to lands, 2 Ch. 32: 13. Is. 37: 11
21: 15. have d. evil, 2 Ch. 29: 6.
23: 19. all acts he had d. in Beth-
2 Ch. 24: 16. he had d. good in Isr.
29: 36. for thing was d. suddenly
32:25. not acc. to benefit d. to him
31. to inquire of wonder th. was d.
Ezr. 6: 12. let it be d. with speed
9: 1. these were d. princes came
10: 3. be d. according to law
Ne. 6: 8. no such things d. as thou
9: 33. we have d. wickedly, Ps. 106:6. Da. 9:5, 15. [she had d.
Es. 2: 1. remem. Vashti, and what
4: 1. Mordecai perceived all was d.
6: 6. What shall be d. unto the man? [to honour
9. be d. to man wh. k. delighteth
Jb. 21: 31. who repay what he d.?
34: 29. whether it be d. ag. na or
Ps. 33: 9. he spake and it was d.
71: 19. who hath d. great things,
106: 21.-126: 2, 3. [tongue
120: 3. what be d. unto thee, false
Pr. 3:30. if he have d. thee no harm
4:16. except they have d. mischief
Ec. 1: 9. that d. is that sh be d.
13. conc. all d. under heaven
14. seen works are d. under sun,
4: 1, 3.-8: 9, 17.-9. 3, 6.
2: 12. wh. hath been already d.
Is. 3:†11. reward of his hands, be d.
41: 4. Who hath d. it? I Lord
44: 23. Sing, for Lord hath d. it
48: 5. say, Mine idol hath d. them

Je. 3: 6. what backsli. Isr. hath d.
16. neither shall that be d.
5:13. thus shall it be d. unto them
7: 13. bec. ye have d. all these
30. chil. of Judah have d. evil
11: 17. they have d. ag. thems.
30: 24. not ret. until have d. it
34: 15. had d. right in my sight
35:10. d. all th. Jonadab com-d, 18.
38: 9. these have d evil to Jere.
44: 17. we have d. and our fa-s
48: 19. ask him fleeth, What is d.
50: 15. as she hath d. do unto, 29.
51: 35. violence d. to me
La. 2: 17. Lord hath d. that [my
Eze. 23: 39. thus have they d. in
39: 8. it is come, it is d. saith L.
43: 11. if asha. of all they have d.
44: 14. for all that shall be d.
Da. 11: 36. that determ. shall be d.
Zph. 3: 4. d. violence to the law
Mat. 6: 10. Thy will be d., 26: 42. Lu. 11: 2.-22: 42. [unto thee
8: 13. as hast believed, so be it d.
11: 20. mighty works were d., 23.
11: 21. if mighty works d. in you been d. in Tyre, Lu. 10: 13.
17: 12. have d. whatso. they listed
18: 19. thing they ask, it sh. be d.
31. fellow-serv-ts saw what was d.
21: 21. cast into sea, it sh. be d.
23: 23. ought ye to have d., Lu.11:
25: 21. Well d. good, 23. [42.
40. as ye have d. it unto one of least have d. it unto me
27: 54 things th. were d., 28: 11.
Mk. 4: 11. things d. in parables
5: 14. to see what was d., Lu.8:35.
19. tell how great things L. hath d. for thee, 20. Lu. 8: 39.
33. knowing what was d. in her
6: 30. told him what they had d.
9: 13. d. unto him whatso. listed
13: 30. gene. not pass, till all be d.
14: 8. She hath d. what she could
15: 8. him to do, as he had ever d.
Lu. 1: 49. he hath d. great things
3: 19. for the evils Herod had d.
8: 34. fed them saw what was d.
56. to tell no man what was d.
9: 7. Herod heard of all was d.
10. apostles told all they had d.
10:13. d. in Ty. and S. wh. d. in you
13: 17. glorious things d. by him
14: 22. L. it is d. as thou com-d
17: 10. when have d. all have u. that was our duty
23: 8. some miracle d. by him
15. noth. worthy of death is d.
31. tree, what shall be d. in dry?
47. centurion saw what was d.
48. beholding things d., smote
24: 21. 3d day, since these were d.
35. told things d. in the way
Jn. 1: 28. These things d. in Beth.
5: 29. that have d. good unto life, that have d. evil, unto damna.
15: 7. ask, it shall be d. unto you
19: 36. things were d. that scrip.
Ac. 2: 43. many signs were d. by
4: 9. good deed d. to impotent
16. notable miracle hath been d.
21. glorified G. for that was d.
28. counsel determ. bef. to be d.
30. signs may be d., 8: 13.
5: 7. wife, not know. what was d.
12: 9 wist not it was true was d.
13: 12. deputy saw what was d.
14: 3. wonders d. by their hands
27. rehearsed all God d., 15: 4.
21: 14. The will of the Lord be d.
33. capt. deman-d what he had d.
24: 2. very worthy deeds are d.
Ro. 9: 11. neith. having d. good or
1 Co. 9: 15. nor be so d. unto me
13: 10. that in part sh. be d. away
14: 26. Let all be d. unto edifying

1 Co. 14: 40. Let all be d. decently
16: 14. Let all be d. with charity
2 Co. 3: 7. glory to be d. away
14. old test. wh. vail is d. away
9: 11. if that d. away is glorious
5: 10. receive things d. in body, according to that he hath d.
Ep. 5:12. things wh. are d. in secret
6: 13. and having d. all to stand
Ph. 2: 3. Let noth. be d. thro. strife
4:14. well d. that ye communicate
Col. 4:9. make kn. all things are d.
Tit. 3: 5. not by works we have d.
He. 10: 29. hath d. despite to Spirit
Re. 16: 17. saying, It is d., 21: 6.
22: 6. things wh. must shortly be

Hast thou DONE. [d.

Ge. 4: 10. he said, What h. t. d.? 31: 26. Nu. 23: 11. 1 S. 13: 11. 2 S. 3: 24. Jn. 18: 35.
20: 9. What h. t. d.? Ju. 15: 11.
2 S. 7: 21. acc. to thy heart h.t.d.
16: 10. Wherefore h. t. d. so?
1 K. 1: 6. saying, Why h. t. d. so?
1 Ch. 17: 19. O Lord, h. t. d. this
Ps. 50: 21. These things h. t. d.
Jon. 1: 10. said, Why h.t.d. this?

Hath he DONE. [d.?

1 S.20:32. Whf. be slain? what h.h.
Mat. 27: 23. gov. said, Why, what evil h.h.d.? Mk.15:14. Lu.23:22.
Ac. 9: 13. evil h.h.d. to thy saints

Have I DONE.

Ge. 20: 5. in innocency h. I d. this
40:15. here h. I d. noth. to put me
Nu. 22: 28. What h. I d.? 1 K. 19: 20. Mi. 6: 3.
Jos. 7: 20. sinned, thus h. I d.
Ju. 8: 2. What h. I d.? 1 S. 17:29.-20: 1.-26:18.-29: 8. Je. 8:6.
15: 11. did unto me so h. I d.
Eze. 39: 24. acc. to transgr. h. I d.
Da. 6: 22. O king h. I d. no hurt
Ac.25:10. to Jews h. I d. no wrong

He hath DONE.

Ex. 5: 23. h.h.d. evil to this peo.
Le. 5:16. amends for harm h.h.d.
8:34. As h.h.d. so L. commanded
19: 22. atonem. for sin h. h. d.
24:19. as h.h.d. so be done to him
Jos. 24: 20. after h.h.d. you good
Ju. 15: 10. do to him as h. h. d.
1 S. 6: 9. h.h.d. us this great evil
12:24. consider great things h.h.d.
1 Ch. 16: 12. remem. marvell. works h. h. d., Ps. 78:4.-98:1.-105:5.
Ps. 66:16. will declare what h. h. d.
115: 3. G h. d. whatso. h. pleased
Pr. 24: 29. to him as h. h. d. to me
Is. 12: 5. h. h. d. excellent things
Eze. 3: 20 righte. h. h. d., 18: 24.
17:18. h.h.d. these, sh. not escape
18: 13. h. h. d. all these abom.
14. seeth fa.'s sins h. h. d.
22. in righte. that h. h. d. sh. live
26. for iniquity that h. h. d.
24: 24. acc. to all h. h.d. sh. ye do
33: 16. h. h. d. that is lawful
Jo. 2:20. bec. h. h. d. great things
Mk. 7: 37. h. h. d. all things well
2 Co.5:10. receive acc. to that h.h.d.
Col. 3:25. receive for wrong h. h. d.

I have DONE.

Ge. 8: 21. nor smite ev. as I h. d.
21: 23. acc. to kindn. I h.d. thee
27: 19. I h. d. as thou badest me
28:15. until I h.d. that I have spo.
30:26. knowest service I h. d. thee
Ex. 10: 2. signs I h. d. am. them
Jos. 24: 7. eyes seen what I h. d.
Ju. 1: 7. as I h. d. so G. requit. me
9: †48. what I h. d. make haste, do as I h. d. [d. unto th.
15: 11. as they did unto me, so h. I
2 S. 14: 21. now I h. d. this thing
24: 10. sinned in that I h. d. I h. d. very foolishly, 1 Ch. 21:8.

2 S. 24:17. sinned, I h. d. wickedly
1 K. 3:12. I h. d. acc. to thy word
18:36. I h. d. at thy word [d. it?
2 K. 19:25. not heard, how I h.
20:3. I h. d. that is good, Is. 38:3.
Ne. 5:19. all I h. d. for this peo.
13:14. that I h. d. for h. of G.
Jb. 34:32 if I h. d. iniquity, I will
Ps. 7:3. O Lord, if I h. d. this
119:121. I h. d. judgm. and justice
Pr. 30:20. I h. d. no wickedness
Is. 10:11. as I h. d. unto Sama.
13. by the str. of hand I h. d it
33:13. Hear far off what I h. d.
37:26. hast heard how I h. d. it?
Je. 7:14. fa-s as I h. d. to Shiloh
30:15. sins incr-d I h. d. these
Je. 42:10. repent of evil I h. d.
Eze. 12:11. I h. d. as thou com-d
12:11. as I h. d. be done unto th.
14:23. know I h. not d. without
17:24. I L. have spok. and h. d. it
24:22. ye shall do as I h. d.
Da. 6:22. O king, h. I d. no hurt
Zch. 7:3. weep, as I h. d. many yrs.
Jn. 7:21. I h. d. one work, and
13:12. Know ye what I h. d. to you?
15. should do as I h. d. to you

Not DONE.

Ge. 20:9. done deeds ought n. be d.
34:7. thing ought n. to be d.
Nu. 16:28. I n. d. of own mind
De. 32:27. say, L. hath n. d. this
2 K 5:13. wouldest n. have d. it?
Ne. 6:9. fr. work, that it be n. d.
8:17. fr. Joshua, Isr. had n. d. so
Is. 5:4. done, that I have n. d.
Eze. 5:9. in thee that I have n. d.
Da. 9:12. n. been d. as upon Jerus.
Jn. 15:24. if I had n. d. works?
Ac. 26:26. was n. d. in a corner

DONE with this.

Ge 20:5. in innocency have I d. t.
42:28. What is t. God hath d.
44:15. What deed is t. ye have d.?
Ex. 13:8. t. is d. bec. of that the L.
14:5. said, Why have we d. t. [did
De. 32:27. lest say, L. hath not d.
Ju. 2:2. Why have ye d. t.? [all t.
15:6. Philis. said, Who hath d. t.?
7. Tho. ye have d. t. I be avenged
20:12. What wickedness is t. is d.?
1 K. 11:11. Forasmuch as t. is d. of
Ps. 7:3. O Lord, if I have d. t. [thee
22:31. shall declare he hath d. t.
Is. 41:20. may know L. hath d. t.
Eze. 23:38. t. they have d. unto me
Jon 1:10. Jonah, why hast d. t.
Mal. 2:13. And t. have ye d. again
Mat. 1:22. all t. was d., 21:4.-26:56.
13:28. An enemy hath d. t. [14:8.
26:13. t. that woman hath d. Mk.
Lu. 5:6 had d. t. they inclosed a
Ac. 4:7. By what power have ye d.
10:16. t. was d. thrice, 11:10. [t.?
28:9. t. was d. others were healed
See THIS. [Pro.] **This THING.**
DONE with this thing. [d.-?
Ge. 20:10. What sawest, that hast
21:26. I wot not who hath d.-
22:16. bec. hast d.-, not withheld
Ex. 1:18. Why have ye d.- [son
Jos. 9:24. we afraid of you, have d.-
Ju. 6:29. Gideon hath d.- (2) [me
11:37. she said, Let t. t. be d. for
1 S. 28:18. Lord hath d.- unto thee
2 S. 2:6. requite bec. ye have d.-
12:5. man that hath d.- sh. die
14:20. hath thy servant Joab d.-
21. king said unto Joab I have d.-
1 K. 1:27. Is t. t. d. by the king?
1 Ch. 21:8. sinned bec. I have d.-
2 Ch. 11:4. return, t. t. is d. of me
Mk. 5:32. to see her that had d.-

Thou hast DONE.

Ge. 3:13. What is this that t. h. d.?
12:18.-26:10.-29:25. Ju. 8:1.-
15:11. 2 S. 12:21. [Ch. 25:16.
Ge. 3:14. Bec. t. h. d. this, 22:16. 2
20:9. t. h. d. deeds ought not to be
27:45. he forget that t. h. d. to
31:28. t. h. now d. foolishly, 1
S. 13:13. 2 Ch. 16:9. [14:43.
Jos. 7:19. tell what t. h. d., 1 S.
Ru. 2:11. been shewed me all t. h. d.
1 S. 24:19. t. h. d. unto me
26:16. thing not good t. h. d.
1 K. 14:9. t. h. d. evil above all
2 K. 2:10. t. h. d. hard in asking
10:30. t. h. d. well in executing
23:17. t. h. d. ag. altar of Beth.
Ne. 9:33. t. h. d. right, but we
Ps. 40:5. wonderful works t. h. d.
52:9. praise thee, bec. t. h. d. it
109:27. may know that t. h. d. it
Pr. 30:32. If t. h. d. foolishly
Is. 25:1. for t. h. d. wonder. works
Je. 2:23. way, know what t. h. d.
3:5. t. h. d. evil things
La. 1:21. they are glad t. h. d. it
22. do unto them as t. h. d. unto
2:20. consid. to whom t. h. d. this
Eze. 16:48. Sod. not done as t. h. d.
51. in all abom. which t. h. d.
54. confounded in all t. h. d.
59. will deal with thee as t. h. d.
63. I am pacified for all t. h. d.
Ob. 15. as t. h. d. it sh. be done to
Jon. 1:14. t. h. d. as it pleaseth
Ac. 10:33. t. h. d. well, art come

DOOR.

Ge. 4:7. not well, sin lieth at d.
6:16. d. of ark shalt set in side
19:9. they came near to break d.
11. wearied themselves to find d.
Ex. 12:23. L. will pass over the d.
21:6. master sh. bring him to d.
26:36. hanging for the d., 35:
15, 17. Nu. 4:26.
Nu. 2:36. curtain for d. of court
De. 15:17. thrust it thro. ear unto d.
2 S. 13:17. bolt the d. after her
18. brought her out, and bolted d.
1 K. 6:8. d. for mid. chamber was
33. made he for d. of temple
34. two leaves of d. were folding
14:6. sound, as she came in at d.
17. to threshold of d. child died
2 K. 4:15. she stood in the d.
9:3. Then open the d. and flee
10. And he opened d. and fled
12:9. priests that kept d.
Es. 2:21. which kept the d., 6:2.
Jb. 31:9. if laid wait at neigh.'s d.
34. fear, that I went not out of d.
Ps. 141:3. O L., keep d. of my lips
Pr. 26:14. As d. turn. upon hinges
Can. 5:4. in hand by hole of d.
8:9. if she a d. we will inclose her
Eze. 8:3. to d. of the inner gate, 7.
8. digged in wall, behold a d.
16. behold at d. of temple of L.
10:19. stood at d. of east gate
11:1. at d. of the gate 25 men
40:13. d. ag. d. | 41:2. breadth of
41:11 one d. toward the north
24. for 1 d., 2 leaves for other d.
Eze. 42:2. north d. | 12 d. in head of
46:3. people sh worship at the d.
Da. 3:26. Neb. came to d. of furna.
Ho. 2:15. valley of Achor d. of hope
Am 9:1. Smite the lintel of the d.
Mat. 27:60. he rolled stone to d. of
sepulchre, Mk. 15:46.
Mat 28:2. angel rolled stone from d.
Mk. 1:33. city was gath. at the d.
2:2. was no room, not about the d.
11:4 found colt tied by the d.
16:3. Who shall roll us stone fr. d.?
Jn. 10:1. ent. not by d. is a thief
2. that entereth in by the d.
7. I am the d., 9.
18:16. But Peter stood at the d.
17. saith damsel that kept the d.
Ac. 5:9. feet at d. to carry thee out
12:6. keepers bef. d. kept prison
13. as Peter knocked at the d.
16. when had opened d. and saw
14:27 opened d. of faith to Gen.
1 Co. 16:9. a great d. is opened
2 Co. 2:12. d. was opened unto me
Col. 4:3. open a d. of utterance
Ja. 5:9. judge standeth bef. the d.
Re. 3:8. I set bef. thee an open d.
20. I stand at d. and knock, if
any man open the d.
4:1. behold a d. open in heaven

DOOR with house.

Ge. 19:11. smote them at d. of h.
43:19. they communed at d. of h.
Ex. 12:22. none go out at d. of h.
Le. 14:38. priest sh. go to d. of h.
De. 22:21. damsel to d. of her fa.'s h.
Ju. 19:22. beset h. beat at d.
26. fell at d. of man's h., 27.
2 S. 11:9. Uriah slept at d. of k.'s h.
1 K. 14:27. kept d. of king's h.
2 K. 5:9. Naaman stood at d. of h.
Ne. 3:20. d. of h. of Eliashib
21. Merimoth repaired fr. d. of h.
Pr. 5:8. come not nigh d. of h.
9:14 she sitteth at the d. of her h.
Je. 26:10. princes sat at d. of L.'s h.
36:10. Baruch read at d. of L.'s h.
Eze. 8:14. me to d. of L.'s h., 47:1.

Keeper, s of DOOR.

2 K. 22:4. silver, k-s o. d. gathered
23:4. k-s o. d. to bring vessels of
25:18. captain of guard took three
k-s o. d., Je. 52:24 [hands on
Es. 6:2. k-s o. d. sought to lay
Je. 35:4. chamber of Maaseiah k. o.
See DOORKEEPER, s. [d.

DOOR with post, s. [p.

Ex. 12:7. blood, strike it on upper d.
21:6. master bring him unto d. p.
De. 11:20. write them upon d. p-s
Is. 6:4. p-s of d. moved at voice of
Eze. 41:3. measured p. of d. (3, 16.,

DOOR with shut. [d. p-s

Ge. 19:6. s. the d. after him
10. and s. to the d.
2 K. 4:4. thou sh. s. the d. upon thee
5. s. the d. upon her
21. s. the d. upon him
33. s. the d. upon them twain
Mat. 6:6. when thou hast s. the d.
25:10. And the d. was s.
Lu. 11:7. The d. is now s.
13:25. risen up, and hath s. to the d.

Tabernacle DOOR.
See **HANGING, S.**

DOOR of tabernacle of congregation.

Ex. 29:4. Aaron and his sons bring
unto the d.-, wash th., 40:12.
11. kill the bullock before Lord by
d.-, 32. Le. 1:3, 5.-3:2.-4:4.
42. continual burnt-offer-g at d.-
33:9. cloudy pillar stood at d.-, 10.
38:8. women wh. assembled at d.-
30. he made sockets to the d.-
40:6. set the altar before the d.-,
29. Le. 4:7, 18.-17:6. [to d.-, 4.
Le. 8:3. gather all congregation un-
31. Boil the flesh at d.- [10:7.
33. not go out of d.- 7 days, 35.
12:6. she shall bring a pigeon or
turtledove unto d.- [Jos. 19:51.
14:11. before Lord at d.-, 16:7.
23 two pigeons he shall bring unto d.-, 15:14, 29. Nu. 6:10.
17:4. bringeth it not unto d.-, 9.
5. bring sacrifices unto d.-, 19:21.
Nu. 6:13. Nazarite unto d.-, 13.
10:3. trumpets blow, assemble at
12:5. Lord stood in d. o. t. [d.-
16:18. in d.- with Moses, 19 [50.
20:6. Mos., Aa., unto d.-, fell upon
25:6. were weeping bef. d.- [faces
27:2. daughters of Zelophehad by d.-

De. 31 : 15. pillar of cloud over d. -
1 S. 2 :22 lay with the women at d.-
1 Ch. 9 :21. Zech-h was porter of d. -

DOOR with tent, s. [day

Ge. 18 : 1. Abr. sat in t. d. in heat of
2. he ran to meet them from t. d.
10. Sarah heard it in the t. d. [t.
Ex. 26 : 36. make hanging for d. of
33 : 8. stood every man at his t. d.
10. worship-d ev. man at his t. d.
Nu. 11: 10. weep every man in d. of t.
16 : 27. Dathan and Abiram came
out, stood in d. of their t-s
Ju. 4 : 20. said, Stand in d. of t s

DOORS.

Jos. 2 : 19. whoso. sh. go out of d.
Ju. 3 : 24. d. of parlour locked, 23.
25. he opened not d. of parlour
11 : 31. cometh of d. I will offer
16 : 3. Samson took d. of the city
19 : 27. her lord opened the d.
1 S. 3 : 15. Samuel opened d. of h.
21 : 13. David scrabbled on d.
1 K. 6:31. d. of olive, 32. | 34 d. of fir.
7 : 5. all the d. were square
50. for d. of inner h., 2 Ch. 4:22.
2 K. 18:16. Hezekiah cut gold fr. d.
2 Ch. 3 : 7. d. thereof with gold
4 : 9. d. for court and overlaid d.
23 : 4. Levites be porters of d.
29 : 3. Hez. opened d. of house
34 : 9. Levites wh. kept d. gath-d
Ne. 3 : 1. Eliashib set up d., 3, 6,
13, 14, 15.-6 : 1.-7 : 1.
Jb. 31 : 32. op-d my d. to traveller
38 : 10. I set bars and d. to sea
17. seen d. of shadow of death?
41 : 14. Who open d. of his face?
Ps. 24 : 7. lifted up, ye everl. d., 9.
78 : 23. tho. he had op-d d. of heav.
Pr. 8 : 3. Wisdom crieth at the d.
34. waiting at posts of my d.
Is. 57:8. behind d. hast set up remem.
Eze. 33 : 30. still talking in the d.
41 : 11. d. of side cham. toward
23. temple and sanc. had two d.
24. d. had two leaves apiece
25. on d. of temple cherubim
42 : 4. d. toward north
11. according to their d., 12.
Mi. 7 : 5. keep d. of mouth fr. her
Zch. 11 : 1. Open thy d. O Lebanon
Mat. 24 : 33. near, at d., Mk. 13 :29.
Ac. 5 : 19. angel opened prison d.
23. keepers standing bef. the d.
16 : 26. immedi. all d. were open.
27. keeper seeing prison d. open

DOORS, with shut.

Ju. 3 : 23. Ehud s. d. of parlour
2 Ch. 28 : 24 Ahaz s. d. of L.'s hou.
29 : 7. fathers have s. d. of porch
Ne. 6 : 10. let us s. d. of temple
7 : 3. let them s. d. and bar them
Jb. 3 : 10. s. not d. of moth.'s womb
38 : 8. who s. up the sea with d.?
Ec. 12 : 4. d. shall be s. in streets
Is. 26 : 20. enter, and s. thy d.
Mal. 1 : 10. who s. d. for nought?
Jn. 20 : 19. d. were s. Jes. came, 26.
Ac. 21 : 30. forthwith d. were s.

DOORKEEPER, S.

1 Ch. 15 :23. Berechiah, Elkanah d-s
24. and Jehiah d-s for the ark
Ps. 84:10. I had rather be d. in hou.

DOPH'KAH. [D.

Nu. 33 : 12. encamped in D. | 13. from

DOR. [Ch. 7 : 29.

Jos. 11 : 2 D., 12 : 23 (2). - 17 : 11. 1
Ju. 1 : 27. Manasseh drive inhab-ts
1 K 4 : 11. in the region of D. [of D.

DOR'CAS, DOE or ROE.

Ac. 9 : 36.† Tabitha, by interpr-n D.
39. shewing the garments D. made

DOTE, DOTED. [sh. d.

Je. 50 : 36. sword upon liars; they
Eze. 23 : 5. Aholah d-d on lovers [d.
7. whoredoms wi. all on whom she
Eze. 23 : 12. She d-d upon Assy-s, 9.
16. as she saw, d-d upon th,
20. she d-d upon their paramours

DO'THAN. [(2)

Ge 37 : 17. Joseph found them in D.
2 K 6 : 13. Elisha, behold, he is in D.

DOTING. [words

1 Ti. 6 : 4. but d. about questions of

DOUBLE. [Adj.]

Ge. 43 : 12. And take d. money, 15.
Ex. 22 : 4. If theft, he sh. restore d.
7. let him pay d. | 9. sh. pay d.
39 : 9. they made breastplate d.
De. 15 : 18. worth a d. hired serv.
21 : 17. by giving him a d. portion
Ju. 17 : † 10. a d. suit of apparel
1 S. 1 : † 5. to Hannah d. portion
2 K. 2 : 9. let d. portion of thy spi.
1 Ch. 12 : 33. were not of d. heart
Jb. 11 : 6. they are d. to that wh. is
41 : 13. who come with d. bridle?
42 : † 10. L. added to Job unto d.
Ps. 12 : 2. with d. heart do speak
Pr. 31 : † 21. clothed with d. garm.
Is. 40 : 2. receiv. d. for all her sins
61 : 7. for your shame sh. have d.
in their land sh. possess d.
Je. 16 : 18. will recomp. their sin d.
17 : 18. destr. with d. destruction
Zch. 9:12. I will render d. unto thee
1 Ti. 5:17. counted worthy of d. hon.
Re. 18 : 6. d. unto her, d. acc. to
works, in cup she filled, fill d.

DOUBLE, ED.

Ge. 41 : 32. dream was d-d to Pha.
Ex. 26 : 9. shalt d. sixth curtain
28 : 16. Foursquare, being d.
39 : 9. a span breadth being d-d
2 S. 20 : † 10. Joab d-d not stroke
Eze. 21 : 14. sword be d. 3d time
Re. 18 : 6. reward and d. unto her

DOUBLEMINDED. [d.

Ja. 1 : 8. A d. man is unstable in his
4 : 8. purify your hearts, ye d.

DOUBLE-TONGUED.

1 Ti. 3 : 8. deacons must be not d.

DOUBT, S.

Ge. 37 : 33. Jo. is without d. rent
De. 28 : 66. thy life shall hang in d.
Jb. 12 : 2. No d. ye are the people
Da. 5 : 12. dissolving of d-s in Dan.
16. heard thou canst dissolve d-s
Lu. 11:20. no d. kingd. of G. is come
Ac. 2 : 12. were in d. saying, What
28 : 4. No d. this man is murderer
1 Co. 9 : 10. our sakes, no d. writt.
Ga. 4 : 20. for I stand in d. of you
1 Jn. 2 : 19. would no d. have continued with us

DOUBT, ED, ETH.

Mat. 14:31. said, wht. didst thou d.
21 : 21. if ye have faith, and d. not
28 : 17. worsh. him, but some d-d
Mk. 11 : 23. sh. not d. in his heart
Jn. 10 : 24. How long make us d.?
Ac. 5 : 24. d-d wher-to would grow
10 : 17. while Peter d-d of vision
25:20. bec. I d-d of such questions
Ro. 14 : 23. d-h is damned if he eat

DOUBTFUL.

Lu. 12 : 29. neith. be of d. mind
Ac. 25:†20. I was d. how to inquire
Ro. 14 : 1. not to d. disputation

DOUBTING.

Jn. 13 : 22. d. of whom he spake
Ac. 10 : 20. go, nothing d., 11 : 12.
1 Ti. 2 : 8. men pray without d.

DOUBTLESS.

Nu. 14 : 30. d. not come into land
2 S. 5 : 19. I will d. deliv. Philis.
Ps. 126 : 6. d. come again, rejoicing
Is. 63 : 16. d. thou art our Father
1 Co. 9 : 2. yet d. I am to you
2 Co. 12 : 1. not expo. d. to glory
Ph. 3 : 8. Yea d. I count all but loss

DOUGH.

Ex. 8 : † 3. frogs shall come into d.
Ex. 12:†34. peo. took d. bef. leavened
d. being in clothes
39. baked unleav. cakes of the d.
Nu. 15 : 20. offer a cake of d., 21.
De. 28 : † 5. blessed sh. be thy d.
Ne. 10 : 37. br. firstfruits of our d.
Je. 7 : 18. women knead their d.
Eze. 44 : 30. give priests first of d.
Ho. 7 : 4. aft. he hath kneaded the

DOVE. [d.

Ge. 8:8. Noah sent forth a d., 10. 12.
9. d. found no rest for foot
11. d. came in to him in evening
Ps 55 : 6. that I had wings like d.
68 : 13. ye sh. be as wings of a d.
Can. 1 : 15. thou hast d. eyes, 4 : 1.
2:14. my d. let me see thy counte.
5 : 2. Open to me, my love, my d.
6:9. My d. my undefiled is but one
Is. 38 : 14. I did mourn as a d.
Je. 48 : 28. dwell in rock like d.
Ho. 7 : 11. Ephr. is like a silly d.
11 : 11. they shall tremble as a d.
Mat. 3:16. Spirit of G. descend like
a d., Mk. 1 : 10. Lu. 3 : 22. Jn.

DOVES. [1:32.

2 K. 6 : 25. of a cab of d. dung
Can 5:12. His eyes are as eyes of d.
Is. 59 : 11. we mourn sore like d.
60 : 8. flee as d. to their windows
Eze. 7 : 16. be like d. of valleys
Na. 2 : 7. lead as with voice of d.
Mat. 10 : 16. harmless as d.
21 : 12. them th. sold d., Mk. 11:15.
Jn. 2 : 14. found those th. sold d.
16. said unto them sold d., Take
See TURTLEDOVE.

DOWN. [Egypt

Ge. 37 : 25. balm, to carry it d. to
43 : 11. take fruits, carry d. present
49 : 14. Issachar is ass couching d.
Le. 22 : 7. when sun is d., De. 23:11.
Nu. 33:52. pluck d. their high places
De. 23:†13. when sittest d. abroad
Jos. 8 : 29. sun was d., Joshua commanded to take his carcass d.
Ju. 4 : 15. Sisera lighted d. off chari.
2 S. 3 : 35. if I taste aught till sun d.
2 K. 5 : 21. Naaman lighted d. from
Ps. 17 : 11. set eyes bowing d. to ea.
44 : 5. thro. thee push d. our ene-s
78 : 31. smote d. the men of Israel
102 : 19. he hath looked d. from the height.

DOWNSITTING.

Ps. 139 : 2. Thou knowest my d.

DOWNWARD.

2 K. 19 : 30. take root d., Is. 37:31.
Ec. 3 : 21. spirit of beast goeth d.
Eze 1 : 27. appearance of loins d.,

DOWRY. [8:2.

Ge. 30:20. endued me with good d.
34 : 12. Ask me never so much d.
Ex. 22 : 17. pay acc. to d. of virgins
1 S. 18:25. king desireth not any d.

DRACHMA.

Lu. 15 : † 8. what woman having 10

DRAG. [d.

Ha. 1 : 15. gather them in their d.
16. they burn incense unto their

DRAGGING. [d.

Jn. 21 : 8. d. the net with fishes

DRAGON.

Ps. 91 : 13. d. shalt thou trample
Is. 27 : 1. sh. slay d. in the sea
51 : 9. cut Rahab, and wounded d.
Je. 51:34. Neb. swallowed me like d.
Eze. 29 : 3. Pharaoh, the great d.
Re. 12 : 3. behold, a great red d.
4. the d. stood | 7. d. fought
12 : 9. d. was cast out, 13.
16. flood wh. d. cast out of mouth
17. d. was wroth with woman
13 : 2. the d. gave him his power
4. they worshipped the d.
11. he spake as a d.
16 : 13. like frogs come out of d.

Re. 20 : 2. hold on d. that old ser- [pent
DRAGON well.
Ne. 2 : 13. I went out, even bef. d.
DRAGONS. [w.
De. 32 : 33. Their wine is poison of
Jb. 30:29. I am a brother to d. [d.
Ps. 44 : 19. broken us in place of d.
74 : 13 thou breakest heads of d.
148:7 Praise L. ye d. and all deeps
Is. 13 : 22. d. in pleasant palaces
34 : 13. be habitation for d., 35:7.
43 : 20. d. and owls sh. honour me
Je. 9 : 11. make Jerus. a den of d.
10 : 22. make cities of Jud. den of
14 : 6. snuffed wind like d. [d.
49 : 33. Hazor | 51 : 37. Bab. for d.
Mi. 1 : 8. will make wailing like d.
Mal. 1 : 3. laid heritage waste for d.
DRAMS.
1 Ch. 29 : 7. gave of gold 10,000 d.
Ezr. 2 : 69. gave 61,000 d. of gold
8 : 27. basins of gold, of 1,000 d.
Ne. 7:70. gave to treasure 1,000 d.
71. gave 20,000 d. of gold, 72.
DRANK.
Ge. 9 : 21. Noah d. was drunken
24:46. I d. she made camels drink
27 : 25. bro-t him wine and he d.
43:†34. they d. largely, were merry
Nu. 20 : 11. cong. d. and beasts
De. 32 : 38. d. wine of drink off-g
2 S. 12 : 3. d. of his own cup [water
1 K. 13 : 19. eat bread in h. and d.
17 : 6. and he d. of the brook [d.
Da. 1 : 5. k. appoin. of wine wh. he
8. not defile hims. with wine he
5 : 1. Belshazzar d. bef 1,000 [d.
3. his concubines d. in them
4. they d. wine, praised gods
Mk. 14:23. he gave and they all d.
Lu. 17 : 27. they d. they marri, 28.
Jn. 4 : 12. our fa. Jac. who d. thereof
1 Co. 10 : 4. drink : for they d. of
that spiritual Rock that
DRAUGHT. [ual rock
Mat 15:17. cast out in d., Mk. 7:19.
Lu. 5:4. let down your nets for a d.
9. astonished at d. of the fishes
DRAUGHT house.
2 K. 10 : 27. made Baal's house a d.
DRAVE. [h.
Ex. 14 : 25. they d. them heavily
Jos. 16 : 10. d. not out Canaanites
24 : 12 d. them out bef. you, Ju. 6:9.
18. L. d. out bef. us all people
Ju. 1:19. Judah d. out inhabitants
1 S. 30 : 20. d. before other cattle
2 S. 6 : 3. d. the cart, 1 Ch. 13 : 7.
2 K. 16:6. Rezin d. Jews from Elath
17 : 21. Jerob. d. Isr. from foll-g L.
Ac. 7 : 45. whom G. d. out bef. our
18 : 16. Gallio d. them fr. judgm.
See DROVE. [seat
DRAW.
Ge. 24 : 44. I will d. for thy camels
Ex. 15 : 9. I will d. my sword
Ju. 4 : 6. d. toward mount Tabor
7. I will d. unto thee Sisera capt.
5 : † 14. they that d. with the pen
9 : 54. Abim. said, d. sword and
slay me, 1 S. 31 : 4. 1 Ch. 10:4.
20 : 32. d. from city to highways
2 S. 17 : 13. d. the city into river
Jb. 21 : 33. ev. man sh. d. after him
Ps. 28 : 3. d. me not with wicked
Ec. 2:† 3. to d. my flesh with wine
Can. 1 : 4. d. me, we will run after
Is. 5:18 Woe unto them d. iniq. with
66 : 19. send unto nations th. d. bow
Eze. 21:3. I will draw my sword out
28 : 7. strangers sh. d. their swords
30 : 11. sh. d. their swords ag. E.
32 : 20. d. her, and all her multi.
Jn. 4 : 11. hast nothing to d. with
15. thirst not, nor come hither to
6:44. except the Father d. him [d.
12 : 32. If I be lifted up, d. all men
13
Jn. 21:6. they were not able to d. it
Ac. 20 : 30. to d. away disciples
Ja. 2:6. d. you bef. judgment-seats
DRAW back. [a hook
Eze. 39 : † 2. I will d. thee b. with
He. 10:38 by faith, but if any d. b.
39. not who d. b. to perdition
DRAW near. [cities
Ju. 19 : 13. let us d. n. to one of
1 S. 14 : 36. Let us d. n. unto God
38. d. ye n. hither all the chief
Ps 73 : 28. it is good to d. n. to G.
107 : 18. th. d. n. unto gates of death
Is. 29:13. this peo. d. n. with lips
45 : 20. d. n., ye that are escaped
57 : 3. d. n., ye sons of sorceress
Je. 30 : 21. I will cause him to d. n.
46 : 3. order buckler, d. n. to bat.
Eze. 9 : 1. charge over city to d. n.
22 : 4. caused thy days to d. n.
Jo. 3 : 9. let all men of war d. n.
He. 10 : 22. d. n. with a true heart
DRAW nigh.
Ex. 3 : 5. he said, d. not n. hither
Ps. 69 : 18. d. n. to my soul
119 : 150. d. n. that fol. mischief
Ec. 12 : 1. nor years d. n. when
Is. 5 : 19. counsel of Holy One d. n.
He. 7 : 19. by wh. we d. n. unto G.
Ja. 4 : 8. d. n. to G., he will d. n.
DRAW out. [to you
Ex. 12:21. d. o. and take you lamb
Le. 26 : 33. I will d. o. a sword [ly
Ju. 3:22 not d. dagger o. of his bel-
Jb. 41:1. d. o. leviathan with hook?
Ps. 35 : 3. d. o. also the spear
36 : † 10. d. o. thy lovingkindn.
85 : 5. d. o. thine anger to all gen.
Pr. 20 : 5. of underst. will d. it o.
Is. 57:4. ag. wh. do ye d. o. tongue?
58 : 10. if d. o. soul to hungry
Je. 49 : 20. Surely the least of flock
shall d. them o., 50 : 45.
La. 4 : 3. sea monsters d. o. breast
Eze. 5 : 2. third part sh. scatter, I
will d. o. a sword, 12.—12 : 14.
Hag. 2 : 16. came to d. o. 50 vessels
Ju. 2 : 3. d. o. now, and bear unto
DRAW up. [gov.
Jb. 40:23. that he can d. u. Jordan
DRAW water, s. [43.
Ge. 24 : 11. that women go to d. w.,
13. daughters come out to d. w.
20. Rebekah ran again to d. w.
1 S. 9 : 11. maidens going to d. w.
Is. 12 : 3 with joy shall ye d. w. of
Na. 3 : 14. d. w-s for siege [salva.
Jn. 4 : 7. woman of Sama. to d. w.
DRAWER, S.
De. 29 : 11. fr. hewer to d. of water
Jos. 9 : 21. be d-s of water, 23, 27.
DRAWETH.
De. 25 : 11. wife of one d. near
Ju. 19 : 9. day d. towards evening
Jb. 24 : 22. He d. also the mighty
33 : 22. his soul d. near unto grave
Ps. 10 : 9. catch the poor when he
d. him into his net
88 : 3. my life d. nigh unto grave
Pr. 8:† 13. happy man th. d. unders.
Is. 26 : 17. d. near her delivery
Eze. 7 : 12. the day d. near
Am. 9 : † 13. overtak. him d. seed
Mat. 15 : 8. peo. d. nigh with lips
Lu. 21 : 8. I am C., time d. near
28. for your redemption d. nigh
Ja. 5 : 8. coming of the L. d. nigh
DRAWING.
Ju. 5 : 11. in the places of d. water
8 : † 10. fell 120,000 d. sword
Jn. 6 : 19. see Jesus d. nigh ship
DRAWN.
Ex. 2 : † 10. called his name d. out
Nu. 22 : 23. ass saw angel, his sword
d., 31. Jos. 5 : 13. 1 Ch. 21:16.
De. 21 : 3. a heifer, not d. in yoke
30 : 17. d. away, and worsh. gods
Jos. 8 : 6. till d. them from city
16. were d. from city, Ju. 20:31.
15 : 9. And the border was d., 11.
Ru. 2 : 9. drank wh. young men d.
Jb. 20 : 25. It is d. and cometh out
Ps. 37:14. wicked have d. sword
55:21. softer than oil yet d. swords
Pr. 24:11. deliv. that are d. unto dea.
Is 21 : 15. they fled from d. swords
28 : 9. that are d. from breasts
Je. 22 : 19. d. and cast forth beyond
31 : 3. with lovingkindn have I d.
La. 2 : 3. hath d. back right hand
Eze. 21 : 5. I L. have d. sword, 28.
Ac. 11:10. all d. again into heaven
Ja. 1 : 14. d. away of his own lusts
DREAD. [Noun.]
Ge. 9 : 2. d. of you on every beast
Ex. 15 : 16. d. shall fall upon them
De. 2:25 d. of thee upon nat-s, 11:25.
Jb. 13 : 11. sh. his d. fall upon you?
21. let not thy d. make me afraid
Is. 8 : 13. let him be your d.
DREAD. [Verb.]
De. 1 : 29. I said unto you, d. not
1 Ch. 22 : 13. be strong, d. not
DREADFUL.
Ge. 28 : 17. How d. is this place!
Jb. 15 : 21. A d. sound in his ears
Eze. 1 : 18. rings, they were d.
Da. 7 : 7. behold, a 4th beast d., 19.
9 : 4. O Lord, the great and d. G.
Ha. 1 : 7. the Chaldeans are d. [fen
Ma. 1 : 14. my name d. am. heath-
4 : 5. coming of gr. and d. day of
DREAM. [Noun] [L.
Ge. 20 : 3. G. to Abim. in a d., 6.
31 : 10. Jac. saw in a d. the rams
11. angel spake unto Jac. in a d.
24. God came to Laban in a d.
40:5. butler and baker dreamed d.
9. butler told his d. to Joseph
16. said unto Jo., I was in my d.
41:7. behold, it was a d., 1 K. 3:15.
8. Pharaoh told them his d.
12. interpret to each acc. to d.
15. thou canst understand a d.
17. In d. I stood upon bank
22. I saw in my d. seven ears
25. The d. of Pharaoh is one, 26.
32. d. was doubled unto Pharaoh
Nu. 12 : 6. I L. will speak in a d.
Ju. 7 : 13. told a d. unto his fellow
15. when Gideon heard the d.
1 K. 3 : 5. L. appear. to Solo. in d.
Jb. 20 : 8. He shall fly away as a d.
33 : 15. In d. openeth ears of men
Ps. 73 : 20. As d. when one awaketh
Ec. 5 : 3. d. cometh thro. business
Is. 29 : 7. fight ag. Ariel be as a d.
Je. 23 : 28. hath d. let him tell a d.
Da. 2 : 3. troubled to know the d.
4. tell serv-s d. | 6. if shew d.
5. not make kn. unto me d., 9.
26. Art able to make known d.
28. Thy d., and visions of head
36. is d. we will tell interpreta.
45. d. is certain and the interp.
4 : 5. saw d. made me afraid, 18.
6. make known interpreta-n of d.
7. I told d., 8. | 9. tell me my d. [6.
19. d. be to them that hate thee (2)
7 : 1. Daniel had a d.; he wrote d.
Mat. 1 : 20. angel unto Joseph in a
d., saying, Fear not, 2 : 13, 19.
2 : 12. warned of God in a d., 22.
27 : 19. I suffered many things in a
See DREAMED. [d.
DREAMS. [† 19.
Ge. 37 : 8. they hated him for his d.,
20. see what will become of his d.
41 : 12. Hebrew interpreted our d.
1 S. 28:6. Lord answ-d nei. by d., 15.
Jb. 7 : 14. thou scarest me with d.
Ec. 5 : 7. in d. are divers vanities
Je. 23 : 27. to forget my name by d.
32. am ag. them prophesy false d.

Da. 1 : 17. had underst·g in **d.**,5:12.
2 : 2. magicians to show king his **d.**
Zch. 10 : 2. diviners have told false
See DREAM, ED, DREAMER. [**d.**

DREAM., [Verb.]

Ps 126. 1. we were like them that **d.**
Jo. 2:28. your old men sh. **d.** dreams, [Ac.2:17.

DREAMED.

Ge 28 : 12. Jacob **d.**, behold a ladder
41 : 11. we **d.** dream in one night (2)
15. Pha. said, I have **d.** a d-m, 1,5.
42 : 9. Jos-h remembered dream he
Ju. 7 : 13. Behold, I **d.** a dream [**d.**
Je. 23 : 25. I **d.**, I have **d.** [27 : † 9.
29 : 8. nei. hearken to dreams **d.**,
Da. 2 : 1. Neb·r **d.** dreams, troubled
3. the king said, I have **d.** a dream
See DREAM. [Noun.]

DREAMER, S.

Ge. 37 : 19. Behold, this **d.** cometh
De. 13 : 1. If arise a **d.** of dreams
3. not hearken unto **d.** of dreams
5. that **d.** of d-ms be put to death
Je. 29 : †24. Thus speak to Shemaiah
Jude 8. those filthy **d**-s defile [the **d.**

DREAMETH, ING.

Is. 29 : 8. hungry man **d**-h, thirsty
56 : †10. watchmen are **d**-g [man **d**-h

DREGS.

Ps. 75:8. the **d.** wicked shall drink
Is. 51:17. drunken **d.** of the cup, 22.

DRESS.

Ge. 2 : 15. man into garden to **d.** it
18 : 7. y-g man, he hasted to **d.** it
De. 21:†12. shave head, **d.** her nails
28 : 39. plant vineyards, **d.** them
2 S. 12 : 4. to **d.** for wayfaring man
13 : 5. Tamar **d.** meat in my sight
7. Amnon's house, **d.** him meat
1 K. 17 : 12. that I may **d.** it for me
18 : 23. I will **d.** the other bullock
1 K. 18 : 25. Elijah said, **d.** it first

DRESSED.

Ge. 18 : 8. Abr. took calf he had **d.**
Le. 7 : 9. all that is **d.** be the priest's
1 S. 25 : 18. Abigail took five sheep **d.**
2 S. 12 : 4. took poor man's lamb, **d.** it
19 : 24. Mephib-h had nei. **d.** his feet
1 K. 18 : 26. **d.** bullock, called on B-l
He. 6 : 7. herbs for them by whom **d.**

DRESSER, DRESSETH.

Ex. 30 : 7. Aaron, when he **d**-h lamps
Lu. 13 : 7. said he unto **d**-r of viney.

DREW.

Ge. 24 : 20. Rebekah **d.** water, 45.
37 : 28. they **d.** up Jos. out of pit
38 : 29. Zarah **d.** back his hand
Ex. 2 : 10. I **d.** him out of water
16. Jethro's daughters **d.** water
19. Egyp. **d.** water enough for us
Jos. 8 : 26. Josh. **d.** not hand back
Ju. 8 : 10. fell 120,000 th. **d.** sword
20. the youth **d.** not his sword
20 : 2. of Isr. 400,000 **d.** sword, 17.
15. of Benj. 26,000 that **d.** sword
25. all these **d.** the sword, 35.
37. liers in wait **d.** thems. along
46. fell of Benj. 25,000 th. **d.** sw.
Ru. 4 : 8. So he **d.** off his shoe
1 S. 7 : 6. to Mizpeh, and **d.** water
17 : 51. David **d.** Goliath's sword
2 S. 22 : 17. he took me, he **d.** me out of many waters, Ps. 18 : 16.
23 : 16. three mighty men **d.** water out of well of Beth., 1 Ch 11 : 18.
24 : 9. in Isr. 800,000 th. **d.** sword
1 K. 22 : 34. man **d.** a bow at a venture, 2 Ch. 18 : 33.
2 K. 3 : 26. took 700 that **d.** sword
9 : 24. Jehu **d.** bow with full str.
1 Ch. 19 : 16. they **d.** forth Syrians
21 : 5. Isr. were 1,100,000 that **d.** sword, Judah, 470,000
2 Ch. 5 : 9. **d.** out staves, 1 K. 8 : 8.
14 : 8. of Benj. **d.** bows, 280,000
Je. 38 : 13. **d.** up Jere. with cords
Ho. 11 : 4. I **d.** with cords of a man
Mat. 13 : 48. they **d.** to shore, Mk. 6 : 53. [47. Jn. 18 : 10.
26 : 51. Peter **d.** his sword, Mk. 14:
Lu. 23 : 54. and the sabbath **d.** on
Jn. 2 : 9. servants **d.** water knew
21 : 11. **d.** the net full of fishes
Ac. 5 : 37. **d.** away much people
14 : 19. **d.** Paul out of the city
16 : 19. **d.** Paul into marketplace
27. the jailer **d.** his sword, and
17 : 6. **d.** Jason and certain breth.
19 : 33. they **d.** Alex. out of mul.
21 : 30. Paul and **d.** him out of tem.
Re. 12 : 4. tail **d.** third part of stars

DREW near.

Ge. 18 : 23. Ab. **d. n.** said, Wilt thou
Ex. 20 : 21. Mos. **d. n.** to thick darkn.
Le. 9 : 5. cong. **d. n.** before Lord
1 S. 7 : 10. Philis. **d. n.** to battle
9 : 18. Saul **d. n.** to Sam. in gate
17 : 16. Goliath **d. n.** morn. and,
40. Dav. **d. n.** to Goliath [41, 48.
2 S. 18 : 25. Ahimaaz came and **d.n.**
Es. 5 : 2. Esther **d. n.** and touched
9 : 1. k.'s decree **d. n.** to oxeen-n
Zph. 3 : 2. she **d.** not **n.** to her G.
Mat. 21 : 34. time of fruit **d. n.**
Lu. 15 : 1. **d. n.** publicans to hear
22 : 47. Judas **d. n.** to Jes. to kiss
24 : 15. Jes. **d. n.**, and went with
Ac. 7 : 31. Moses **d. n.** to behold
27 : 27. they **d. n.** some country

DREW nigh.

Ge. 47 : 29. time **d. n.** that Isr. die
Ex. 14 : 10. Pha. **d. n.** Isr. cried
Jos. 8 : 11. the people **d. n.** bef. Ai
2 S. 10 : 13. Joab **d. n.** ag. Syrians
1 K. 2 : 1. days of Da. **d. n.** he sho.
1 Ch. 19 : 14. **d. n.** bef. Syrians [dic
Mat. 21 : 1. they **d. n.** to Jerusalem
Lu. 15 : 25. elder son as he **d. n.**
22 : 1. feast of unleav. bread **d. n.**
24 : 28. they **d. n.** to the village
Ac. 7 : 17. time of promise **d. n.**
10 : 9. as they **d. n.** unto city, Peter

DREWEST.

La. 3 : 57. **d.** near in day I called

DRIED.

Ge. 8 : 7. until waters were **d.**, 13.
14. on 27th day was the earth **d.**
Le. 2 : 14. offer green ears of corn **d.**
Nu. 6 : 3. nor moist grapes or **d.**
11 : 6. our soul is **d.** away
Jos. 2 : 10. how Lord **d.** up Red sea
4 : 23. Lord **d.** up Jordan, as Red sea, wh. he **d.** up before us
5 : 1. heard L. had **d.** up Jordan
Ju. 16 : 7. with withs never **d.**, 8.
1 K. 13 : 4. Jerob.'s hand **d.** up
17 : 7. brook **d.** bec. been no rain
2 K. 19 : 24. with sole of feet have I **d.** all the rivers, Is. 37 : 25.
Jb. 18 : 16. His roots shall be **d.** up
28 : 4. they are **d.** up are gone aw.
Ps. 22 : 15. My strength is **d.** like
69 : 3. my throat is **d.** eyes fail
106 : 9. rebuked Red sea, it was **d.**
Is. 5 : 13. mult. **d.** up with thirst
19 : 5. the river shall be **d.** up
6. brooks of defence shall be **d.** up
51 : 10. Art thou not it hath **d.** sea
Je. 23 : 10. pleas. places of wild. **d.** up
50 : 38. her waters they sh. be **d.** up
Eze. 17 : 24. that I **d.** up green tree
19 : 12. east wind **d.** up her fruit
37 : 11. they say, Our bones are **d.**
Ho. 9 : 16. their root is **d.** up, they
13 : 15. his fountain shall be **d.** up
Jo. 1 : 10. the new wine is **d.** up
12. vine is **d.** up | 20. rivers are **d.**
Zch. 11 : 17. arm sh. be clean **d.** up
Mk. 5 : 29. fountain of her bl. **d.** up
11 : 20. they saw figtree **d.** up [**d.**
Re. 14 : † 15. harvest of the earth is
16 : 12. of Euphrates was **d.** up

DRIEDST, ETH.

Jb. 14 : 11. and as the flood **d.** up
Ps. 74 : 15. **d**-t up mighty rivers
Pr. 17 : 22. broken spirit **d.** bones
Na. 1 : 4. L. makes sea dry, **d.** up [rivers

DRINK, S.

Ge. 21 : 19. Hagar gave the lad **d.**
24 : 14. will give thy camels **d.**, 46.
18. she gave him **d.**, 19.
Le. 11 : 34. all **d.** that may be drunk
Nu. 20 : 8. thou shalt give cong. **d.**
Ju. 4 : 19. she gave Sisera **d.**
2 S. 23 : 15. Oh that one would give me **d.** of well of Be., 1 Ch. 11 : 17.
Ezr. 3 : 7. gave **d.** to them of Zidon
Es. 1 : 7. gave **d.** in vessels of gold
Ps. 78 : 15. gave **d.** as out of depths
102 : 9. mingled my **d.** with weep.
104 : 11. They give **d.** to ev. beast
Is. 32 : 6. cause **d.** of thirsty to fail
43 : 20. rivers, to give **d.** to my peo.
Da. 1 : † 5. the king appointed them of the wine of his **d.**, 10.
Ho. 2 : 5. lovers that give me **d.**
4 : 18. Their **d.** is sour, they have
Ha. 2 : 15. Woe th. giveth neighb **d.**
Hag. 1 : 6. ye are not filled with **d.**
Mat. 25 : 35. thirsty, ye gave me **d.**
37. gave thee **d.** | 42. gave me no **d.**
Jn. 4 : 9. a Jew, askest **d.** of me
6 : 55. my blood is **d.** indeed
Ro. 12 : 20. if enemy thirst, give **d.**
14 : 17. kingd. of G. not meat and **d.**
1 Co. 10 : 4. drink same spiritual **d.**
Col. 2 : 16. let no man judge you in **d.**
He. 9 : 10. stood only in meats, **d**-s

DRINK offering.

Ge. 35 : 14. Jacob poured a **d. o.**
Ex. 29 : 40. wine for a **d. o.** Nu. 15 : 5.
41. shalt do acc. to the **d. o.**
30 : 9. nor sh. ye pour **d. o.** thereon
Le. 23 : 13. **d. o.** shall be of wine
Nu. 6 : 17. the priest sh. offer his **d. o.**, 29 : 22, 25, 28, 31, 34, 38.
15 : 7. **d. o.** 3d part of hin of wine
10. for a **d. o.** half a hin of wine
24. his **d. o.** acc. to the manner
28 : 7. the **d. o.** thereof, 8, 9.
10 besides the continual **d. o.**, 15 : 24 -29 : 16
2 K. 16 : 13 poured his **d. o.** [a **d. o.**
Is. 57 : 6. to them hast thou poured
65 : 11 that furnish **d. o.** to that number [of Lord
Jo. 1 : 9. **d. o.** is cut off fr. house
13. **d. o.** is withhol. house of God
2 : 14. if he return and leave a **d. o.**

DRINK offerings.

Le. 23 : 18. they shall be for a burnt off. with **d. o.**, 37. Nu. 6 : 15.
28 : 31.-29 : 6, 11, 18, 19, 21, 24, 30, 33, 37, 39. [of wine
Nu. 28 : 14. **d. o.** sh. be half a hin
29 : 39. for your **d. o.** and peace off.
De. 32 : 38. drank wine of their **d. o.**
1 Ch. 29 : 21. with their **d. o.** 2 Ch.
Ezr. 7 : 17. buy speedily **d. o.** [29 : 35.
Ps. 16 : 4. **d. o.** of blood will I not
Je. 7 : 18. pour **d. o.** to other gods to provoke me, 19 : 13 -32 : 29.
44 : 17. **d. o.** to queen of, 18, 19, 25.
Eze. 20 : 28. there they poured **d. o.**
45 : 17. princes part to give **d. o.**

Strong DRINK.

Le. 10 : 9. Do not drink **s. d.** when
Nu. 6 : 3. Nazarite separate fr. **s. d.**
De. 14 : 26. bestow that money for what soul lusteth, **s. d.** [years
29 : 6. nor have ye drunk **s. d.** 40
Ju. 13 : 4. wife not drink **s. d.**, 7, 14.
1 S. 1 : 15. I drunk wine nor **s. d.**
Ps. 69 : †12. song of drinkers of **s. d.**
Pr. 20 : 1. mocker, **s. d.** is raging
31 : 4. not for princes to drink **s. d.**
6. Give **s. d.** to him ready to perish
Is. 5 : 11. may follow **s. d.** woe to them
22. woe unto men of strength to mingle **s. d.** [it
24 : 9. **s. d.** be bitter to them drink

Is. 28:7. they have erred thro. s.d.
they are out of way thro. s. d.
29 : 9. stagger, but not with s. d.
56 : 12. we will fill ours. with s.d.
Mi. 2:11. will prophesy s. d. [s. d.
Lu. 1 : 15. Jn. not drink wine nor

DRINK. [Verb.]

Ge. 24 : 17. Let me d., 14, 45.
18. she said, d. my lord, 19, 46.
30 : 38. set rods flocks came to d.
Ex. 15:24. murm., What sh. we d.?
32 : 20. made chil. of Isr. d. of it
Le. 10 : 9. not d. wine lest ye die
De. 32 : 14. d. pure blood of grape
Nu. 6 : 3. neith. d. liquor of grapes
Ju. 7:5. down upon his knees to d.
Ru. 2 : 9. when athirst, go and d.
2 S. 16 : 2. such as be faint may d.
23 : 16. drew water, but Da. would
not d., 17. 1 Ch. 11 : 18, 19.
1 K. 17 : 4. thou shalt d. of brook
Es. 3 : 15. k. and Haman sat to d.
7 : † 1. k. came to d. with Esther
Jb. 21 : 20. d. wrath of Almighty
Ps. 36:8. d. of river of thy pleasures
50 : 13. or d. blood of goats
60 : 3. made us d. wine of aston.
69 : 21. they gave me vinegar to d.
75 : 8. wicked of earth sh. d. them
78 : 44. rivers into bl. could not d.
80 : 5. gavest them tears to d.
110 : 7. He shall d. of the brook
Pr. 4 : 17. d. wine of violence
31 : 5. Lest they d. and forget law
7. let him d. and forget poverty
Can. 5 : 1. d. yea, d. abundantly
Is. 24 : 9. str. drink bitter to them
51 : 22. shalt no more d. it [d. it
62 : 9. shall d. it in courts of my
65 : 13. my servants sh. d. but ye
Je. 16 : 7. nor cup of consola. to d.
23 : 15. make them d. wat. of gall
25 : 15. cause nations to d. it
16. they shall d. and be moved
17. took cup made nations to d.
26. k. of Sheshach shall d. after
27. d. ye, be drunken, and spue
28. saith L., Ye shall certainly d.
35:14. unto this day they d. none
49:12. whose judgm. not to d. not
go unpun. shalt surely d.
Eze. 4 : 11. d. by measure, from
time to time shalt d.
23:32. Thou shalt d. of sister's cup
34 : 19. d. that wh. ye have fouled
39 : 18. d. bl. of princes of earth
19. d. blood till ye be drunken
Da. 5 : 2. his concubines might d.
Am. 4 : 1. say to masters, let us d.
Ob. 16. so shall all heathen d. continually, shall d. and swallow
Ha. 2 : 16. d. thou, let thy foreskin
Hag. 1 : 6. ye d. but are not filled
Zch. 9 : 15. sh. d. and make noise
Mat. 10 : 42. give to d. one of these
20:22. are ye able to d. of the cup
that I shall d. of? Mk. 10 : 38.
23. ye sh. d. of my cup, Mk. 10:39.
26 : 27. cup, saying, d. ye all of it
29. I will not d. until day when
I d. it new, Mk. 14:25. Lu. 22:18.
42. if cup may not pass except I
27:34. gave him vinegar to d. [d.
48. sponge, put it on a reed, gave
him to d., Mk. 15 : 36.
Mk. 16 : 18. if d. any deadly thing
Jn. 4 : 10. who saith, Give me to d.
6 : 53. exc. d. his bl. ye no life [7.
7 : 37. thirst, let him come and d.
18:11. cup fa. given me, sh. I not d.?
1 Co. 10 : 4. all d. same spiritual d.
21. cannot d. cup of L. and devils
11:25. do, as oft as ye d. in remem.
12 : 13. all made to d. into one Spi.
Re. 16 : 6. hast given them bl. to d.

DRINK water, s.

Ge. 24 : 43. give w. of pitcher to d.
Ex. 7 : 18. shall loathe to d. w., 21.
24. digged about river for w. to d.
15 : 23. could not d. w-s of Marah
17 : 1. was no w. for people to d.
2. Give us w. that we may d.
6. w. out of it, that they may d.
Nu. 5:24. he shall cause the woman
to d. bitter w., 26. 27.
20 : 5. neither any w. to d., 33:14.
17. nor will we d. w. of wells, 21:
19. I and cattle d. of thy w. [22.
De. 2:6. buy w. that ye may d., 28.
Ju. 4 : 19. Give me a little w. to d.
7:6. rest bowed upon knees to d. w.
1 S. 30 : 11. they made Egyp. d. w.
2 S. 23 : 15. give me to d. of w. of
well of Beth-le., 1 Ch. 11 : 17.
1 K. 13 : 8. nor bread, nor d. w., 9.
18. d. w. But he lied unto
17:10. Elijah said, Fetch a little w.
that I may d. [may d.
2 K. 3 : 17. valley with w. that ye
18 : 31. d. every one w-s of his
cistern, Is. 36 : 16.
Jb. 22:7. not given w. to weary to d.
Pr. 5 : 15. d. w-s out of own cist.
25 : 21. enemy thirsty, give w. to
Je. 2:18. to d. the w-s of Sihor [d.
8:14. given us w. of gall to d., 9:15.
23 : 15. will make th. d. w. of gall
Eze. 4:11. shalt d. w. by meas., 16.
12 : 18. d. thy w. with trembling
19. sh. d. their w. with astonish.
31 : 14. their trees that d. w., 16.
Da. 1 : 12. pulse to eat, and w. to d.
Am. 4 : 8. wandered to d. w. but
Jon. 3 : 7. let them not d. w.
Mk. 9:41. give you a cup of w. to d.
Jn. 4:7. Jes. saith, Give me w. to d.
1 Ti. 5 : 23. d. no longer w., but

DRINK with wine.

Ge. 19:32. make our father d. w., 34.
33. they made their fa. d. w., 35.
Le. 10 : 9. Do not d. w. when ye go
into tabernacle
Nu. 6 : 3. Nazarite shall d. no w.
20. after that Nazarite may d. w.
De. 28:39. shalt plant vineyards, but
shalt not d. of the w., Am. 5:11.
Ju. 13:4. Man.'s wife d. no w., 7, 14.
2 S. 16 : 2. w., such as faint may d.
Ps. 60 : 3. made us d. w. of aston.
Pr. 4 : 17. they d. w. of violence
9 : 5. d. of w. I have mingled
31 : 4. it is not for kings, to d. w.
Ec. 9 : 7. d. thy w. with a merry
Can. 8 : 2. cause to d. of spiced w.
Is. 5 : 22. Woe to mighty to d. w.
24 : 9. shall not d. w. with a song
62:8. sons of stranger not d. thy w.
Je. 35 : 2. give Rechabites w. to d.
5. set pots and said d. ye w.
6. We will d. no w., Ye sh. d. no w.
8. charged us to d. no w.
14. com-d his sons not to d. w.
Eze. 44:21. Neith. sh. any priest d. w.
Da. 1 : 16. took w. they should d.
Jo. 3 : 3. sold a girl for w. to d.
Am. 2 : 8. d. w. of the condemned
12. ye gave Nazarites w. to d.
6:6. That d. w. in bowls, and anoint
9 : 14. sh. plant vineyards, d. w.
Mi. 6 : 15. shall not d. w., Zph. 1:13.
Mk. 15:23. d. w. mingled with myrrh
Lu. 1 : 15. John shall d. neither w.
Ro. 14 : 21. It is not good to d. w.
Re. 14 : 8. she made all na. d. of w.
10. shall d. of w. of wrath of G.

DRINKERS.

Ps. 69 : † 12. the song of the d.
Jo. 1 : 5. and howl, all ye d. of wine

DRINKETH. [d.?

Ge. 44 : 5. Is this it in wh. my lord
De. 11 : 11. land d. water of rain
Jb. 6 : 4. poison d. up my spirit
15 : 16. man, d. iniq. like water!
34 : 7. like Job who d. scorning
Jb. 40 : 23. he d. up a river
Pr. 26:6. sendeth by fool, d. damage
Is. 29 : 8. he d. but he awaketh
44 : 12. the smith, he d. no water
Mk. 2 : 16. he d. with publicans?
Jn. 4 : 13. d. of this water sh. thirst
14. whoso. d. of water I sh. give
6 : 54. d. my bl., hath eternal life
56. d. my blood dwelleth in me
1 Co. 11:29. d. unworthily d. damna.
He. 6 : 7. earth wh. d. in the rain

DRINKING.

Ge. 24 : 19. for camels until done d.
22. camels had done d. the man
Ru. 3 : 3. until Boaz had done d.
1 S. 30 : 16. they were eating and d.
1 K. 4 : 20. Jud. and Isr. many, d.
10 : 21. Sol.'s d. vessels, 2 Ch. 9 : 20.
16:9. Elah d. | 20:12. Benha. d., 16.
1 Ch. 12 : 39. with Da. three days d.
Es. 1 : 8. d. was acc. to the law
Jb. 1:13. his sons and dau-s d., 18.
Is. 22 : 13. eating flesh, and d. wine
Mat. 11 : 18. John came neither
eating nor d., Lu. 7 : 33.
19. Son of man came d., Lu. 7:34.
24:38. eating and d. until flood ca.
Lu. 10 : 7. d. such thi. as they give
Col. 2:† 16. no man judge you for d.

DRIVE.

2 K. 4 : 24. d.; slack not riding
Jb. 18 : 11. Terrors sh. d. to his feet
† 18. he sh. d. him fr. light into
24 : 3. d. away ass of fatherless
Ps. 68 : 2. As smoke, so d. them aw.
Pr. 22:15. rod of correction sh. d. it
Is. 22 : 19. I d. thee fr. thy station
Je. 24 : 9. curse whither I d. them
46:15. stood not, bec. L. did d. them
Eze. 4 : 13. am. Gent., whi. I will d.
Da. 4 : 25. shall d. thee fr. men, 32.
Jo. 2 : 20. I will d. northern army
Ac. 27 : 15. ship, we let her d.
Ga. 5 : † 7. who did d. you back?

DRIVE out.

Ex. 6 : 1. with str. hand d. them o.
23 : 28. hornets, sh. d. o. Hivite
29. I will not d. o. in one year
30. By little I will d. them o.
31. and thou shalt d. them o.
33 : 2. I will d. o. the Canaanite
34 : 11. behold I d. o. Amorite
Nu. 22 : 6. that I may d. them o.
33 : 52. shall ye d. o. all inhabi.
55. if ye will not d. o. inhabi.
De. 4:38. to d. o. nations from bef
thee greater, 9 : 4, 5. Jos. 3 : 10.
9 : 3. so shalt thou d. them o.
11 : 23. then will L. d. o. nations
18:12. L. doth d. them o. bef. thee
Jos. 13 : 6. them will I d. o.
14 : 12. I sh. be able to d. them o.
15 : 63. chil. of Jud. could not d. o.
17 : 12. chil. of Manas. not d. o.
13. not utterly d. o., Ju. 1 : 28.
18. shalt d. o. Canaanites
23 : 5. L. shall d. o. of your sight
13. no more d. o., Ju. 2 : 3, 21.
Ju. 1:19. Jud. could not d. o. inhabit.
21. Benj. did not d. o. Jebusites
27. Neither did Manasseh d. o.
29. Ephr. | 30. Zebulun not d. o.
31. Asher | 33. Naphtali not d. o.
32. they did not d. them o.
11 : 24. whom L. G. shall d. o.
2 Ch. 20 : 7. didst d. o. inhabi.
Ps. 44 : 2. How didst d. o. heathen
Je. 27:10. that I sho. d. you o., 15.
Ho. 9 : 15. d. them o. of my house
Zph. 2 : 4. d. o. Ashdod at noonday

DRIVEN.

Ge. 4 : 14. hast d. me out this day
Ex. 10 : 11. d. from Pha.'s presence
22 : 10. beast be d. away, no man
Le. 26 : † 36. sound of a d. leaf
Nu. 32:21. until he have d. o. enem.
De. 4:19. lest be d. to worship them

De. 30 : 1. whither L. hath d. thee
4. if any of thine be d. out
Jos. 23 : 9. L. d. out great nations
1 S. 26 : 19. d. me out this day
Jb. 6 : 13. is wisdom d. from me?
13 : 25. break leaf d. to and fro?
18 : 18. He sh. be d. fr. light into
30 : 5. They were d. fr. among men
Ps. 40 : 14. let them be d. backward
68 : 2 As smoke is d. away, so
114 : 3. Jordan was d. back, 5.
Pr. 14 : 32. wicked is d. away in
Ec. 3 : † 15. G. requireth wh. is d. aw.
Is. 8 : 22. they sh. be d. to darkn.
19 : 7. thing sown by brooks be d.
41 : 2. as d. stubble to his bow
Je. 8 : 3. places whi. I have d. them,
23 : 3, 8.–29 : 14, 18.–32 : 37.
16 : 15. fr. lands whi. he had d. them
23 : 2. ye have d. them away, and
12. they shall be d. on and fall
40 : 12. out of all places whi. were
d., 43 : 5. [d. thee
46 : 28. end of nations whi. I have
49 : 5. ye shall be d. out ev. man
50 : 17. Isr. lions have d. him away
Eze. 31 : 11. I have d. him out for
34 : 4. nor bro. wh. was d. away, 16.
Da. 4 : 33. was d. from men, 5 : 21.
9 : 7. countries whi. thou hast d.
Ho. 13 : 3. as chaff d. with whirlw.
Mi 4 : 6. her that was d., Zph. 3 : 19.
Lu. 8 : 29. he d. of devil into wildern.
Ac. 27 : 17. strake sail, so were d.
27. d. up and down in Adria
Ja. 1 : 6. is like wave d. with wind
3 : 4. ships are d. of fierce winds

DRIVER.

1 K. 22 : 34. Ahab said unto d. of his
Jb. 39 : 7. nei. regard-h crying of d.

DRIVETH, ING.

Ju. 2 : 23. without d. them out
hastily [for he d-h furiously
2 K. 9 : 20. d. is like d. of Jehu,
1 Ch. 17 : 21. by d. out nations bef.
Ps. 1 : 4. ungodly like chaff wind d-h
Pr. 25 : 23. northwind d-h aw. rain
Mk. 1 : 12. spirit d-h him into wilde.

DROMEDARY, IES.

1 K. 4 : 28. they bro-t barley for d-s
Es. 8 : 10. sent letters on young d-s
Is. 60 : 6. d-s of Midian cover thee
Je. 2 : 23. thou art a swift d.

DROP, S. [water

Jb. 36 : 27. maketh small the d-s of
38 : 28. who begotten d-s of dew?
Can. 5 : 2. locks with d-s of night
Is 40 : 15. nations as d. of bucket
Lu. 22 : 44. sweat as great d-s of blood

DROP. [Verb.]

De. 32 : 2. doctrine shall d. as rain
33 : 28. heavens sh. d. dew, Pr. 3 : 20.
Jb. 36 : 28. Which clouds do d.
Ps. 65 : 11. and thy paths d. fatness
12. d. on pastures of wilderness
Pr. 5 : 3. lips of strange woman d. as
Can. 4 : 11. Thy lips d. as honeycomb
Is. 45 : 8. d. down, ye heavens
Eze. 20 : 46. d. thy word tow. south
21 : 2. d. thy word tow. holy places
Jo. 3 : 18. mountains shall d. down
new wine, Am. 9 : 13.
Am. 7 : 16. d. not thy word ag. Isaac
Mi. 2 : †6. d. not, say they to them

DROPPED, ETH, ING.

Ju. 5 : 4. heavens d-d clouds d-d
1 S. 14 : 26. behold the honey d-d
2 S. 21 : 10. until water d. upon th.
Jb. 29 : 22. my speech d-d upon th.
Ps. 68 : 8. heavens d-d at pres. of G.
119 : †28. my soul d-h for heaviness
Ec. 10 : 18 thro. idleness house d-h
Can. 5 : 5. my hands d-d with myrrh
13. his lips d-d myrrh

DROPPING, S.

Pr. 19 : 13. are continual d., 27 : 15.
Am. 6 : †11. will smite house with d-s

DROPSY.

Lu. 14. 2. a man bef. him, wh. had d.

DROSS.

Ps. 119 : 119. puttest aw. wick. like d.
Pr. 25 : 4. Take d. from the silver
26 : 23. like a potsherd with silver d.
Is. 1 : 22. thy silver is become d.
25. I will purge away thy d.
Eze. 22 : 18. house of Isr. is become d.;
they are even the d. of silver
19. Because ye are all become d.

DROUGHT.

Ge. 31 : 40. in the day d. consu. me
De. 8 : 15. fiery serpents and d. [d.
28 : † 22. Lord shall smite thee with
Jb. 24 : 19. d. consume snow-waters
Ps. 32 : 4. my moisture into d. of
Is. 58 : 11. L. satisfy thy soul in d.
Je. 2 : 6. L. bro-t us thro. land of d.
17 : 8. not be careful in year of d.
50 : 38. A d. is upon her waters
Ho. 13 : 5. know thee in land of gr. d.
Hag 1 : 11. I called for a d.

DROVE, S.

Ge. 32 : 16. every d. by themselves,
put a space betwixt d. and d.
19. so com-d he all that fol. the d-s
33 : 8. what meanest by all this d.?

DROVE. [Verb.]

Ge. 3 : 24. So God d. out the man
15 : 11. fowls came, Ab. d. them aw.
Ex. 2 : 17. shepherds d. them away
Nu. 21 : 32. they d. out the Amorite
Jos. 15 : 14. Caleb d. sons of Anak
1 Ch. 8 : 13. who d. inhab. of Gath
Ha. 3 : 6. he d. asunder nations
Jn. 2 : 15. he d. them out of temple

DROWN, ED.

Ex. 15 : 4. capt-s are d. in Red sea
Can. 8 : 7. neither can floods d. it
Am. 8 : 8. be d. as by flood of, 9 : 5.
Mat. 18 : 6. better he were d. in sea
1 Ti. 6 : 9. d. men in perdition
He. 11 : 29. Egypt. assaying were d.

DROWSINESS.

Pr. 23 : 21. d. sh. clothe with rags

DRUNK. [Adj.]

De. 32 : 42. mine arrows d. with bl.
1 S. 30 : 12. nor d. water three days
2 S. 11 : 13. David made Uriah d.
1 K. 16 : 9. Elah was drinking hims. d.
20 : 16. Benhadad drinking hims. d.
Is. 43 : † 24. nor hast made me d.
63 : 6. make them d. in my fury
Je. 46 : 10 sw. be d. with their bl.
51 : 57. I will make d. her princes,
Ep. 5 : 18. be not d. with wine
Re. 17 : 2. d. with wine of fornica.

DRUNK, EN. [Verb.]

Le. 11 : 34. all drink that may be d.
De. 29 : 6. eaten bread nor d. wine
Ju. 15 : 19. Sams, had d., his spirit ca.
Ru. 3 : 7. when Boaz had d. he went
1 S. 1 : 9. after they d. in Shiloh
15. I have d. neither wine nor
1 K. 13 : 22. and hast eaten and d.
2 K. 6 : 23. eaten and d. sent them
19 : 24. d. strange waters, Is. 37 : 25.
Can. 5 : 1. d. my wine with milk
Is. 51 : 17. hast d. cup of fury (2)
Je. 49 : 12. they have assuredly d-n
51 : 7. nations have d-n of her wine
La. 5 : 4. We have d-n wat for money
Eze. 34 : 18. to have d. of deep wat-s
Da. 5 : 23. thy wives d. wine in them
Ob. 16. as ye d. upon my holy mt.
Lu. 5 : 39. No man having d. old w.
13 : 26. We have d. in thy presence
17 : 8. and serve me till I have d-n
Jn. 2 : 10. when men have well d.
Re. 18 : 3 all nations have d. of wrath

DRUNKARD, S. [a d.

De. 21 : 20. This our son, a glutton,
Ps. 69 : 12. I was the song of the d-s
Pr. 23 : 21. d. shall come to poverty
26 : 9. As a thorn into hand of a d.
Is. 24 : 20. The earth sh. reel like a d.

Is. 28 : 1. Woe to d-s of Ephr., 3.
Eze. 23 : † 42. d-s were bro-t fr. wil.
Jo. 1 : 5. Awake, ye d-s and weep
Na. 1 : 10. while drunken as d-s
1 Co. 5 : 11. with bro. is a d. eat not
6 : 10. nor d-s inherit kingd. of G

DRUNKEN. [Adj.]

Ge. 9 : 21. Noah was d. and uncov-d
De. 29 : † 19. to add d. to thirsty
1 S 1 : 13. Eli thought Hannah d.
14. said unto her, How long be d.?
25 : 36. Nabal's heart merry, for he
was very d. [Ps. 107 : 27.
Jb. 12 : 25. stagger like a d. man,
Is. 19 : 14. as d. man staggereth
29 : 9. d. but not with wine, 51 : 21.
34 : † 7. land shall be d. with blood
49 : 26. sh. be d. with own blood
Je. 23 : 9. I am like a d. man
25 : 27. be d. and spue, and fall
48 : 26. Make d. for he magnified
51 : 7. Bab. that made all earth d.
39. make d. that they may sleep
La. 3 : 15. me d. with wormwood
4 : 21. thou shalt be d., Na. 3 : 11.
Eze. 39 : 19. drink bl. till ye be d.
Na. 1 : 10. while d. as drunkards
Ha. 2 : 15. his neighb., makest d.
Mat. 24 : 49. shall begin to eat and
drink with d., Lu. 12 : 45.
Ac. 2 : 15. are not d. as ye suppose
1 Co. 11 : 21. one hungry, ano. is d.
1 Th. 5 : 7. they d. are d. in night
Re. 17 : 6. woman d. with bl. of saints

DRUNKENNESS.

De. 29 : 19. to add d. to thirst
Ec 10 : 17. princes eat not for d.
Je 13 : 13. fill inhabi. of Jeru. with d.
Eze. 23 : 33. shalt be filled with d.
Lu. 21 : 34. lest overcharg. with d.
Ro. 13 : 13. let us walk, not in d.
Ga. 5 : 21. works of flesh murders, d.

DRUSIL'LA.

Ac. 24 : 24. Felix came with wife d.

DRY. [Adj.]

Le. 7 : 10. meat off. with oil and d.
13 : 30. it is a d. scall, a leprosy
Jos. 9 : 5. bread d. and mouldy, 12.
Ju. 6 : 37. be d. upon all the earth
39. Let it be d. only upon fleece, 40.
Jb. 13 : 25. pursue the d. stubble?
Ps. 105 : 41. they ran in d. places
Pr. 17 : 1. Better is a d. morsel
Is. 25 : 5. as heat in a d. place
32 : 2 man be as rivers in d. place
44 : 27. Be d. I will dry up
56 : 3. eunuch say, I am d. tree
Je. 4 : 11. A d. wind, not to fan
51 : 36. will make her springs d.
Eze. 17 : 24. made d. tree flourish
20 : 47. it shall devour ev. d. tree
30 : 12 I will make the rivers d.
37 : 2. the bones were very d.
4. O ye d. bones
Ho. 9 : 14. L. give them d. breasts
13 : 15. his spring shall become d.
Na. 1 : 4. rebuketh sea; maketh it d.
10. be devoured as stubble d.
Zph. 2 : 13. will make Nineveh d.
Mat. 12 : 43. thro. d. places, Lu. 11 : 24.
Lu. 23 : 31. what shall be done in d.?

DRY ground.

Ge. 8 : 13. the face of the g. was d.
Ex. 14 : 16. sh. go on d. g. in sea, 22.
Jos. 3 : 17. priests on d. g., Israelites
passed over on d. g.
2 K. 2 : 8. Elisha went over on d. g.
Ps. 107 : 33. watersprings into d. g.
35. turneth d. g. into watersp.
Is. 44 : 3. pour floods upon d. g.
53 : 2. grow as a root out of d. g.
Eze. 19 : 13. she is planted in a d. g.

DRY Land. See LAND.

DRY. [Verb]

Jb. 12 : 15. the waters and they d.
15 : 30. flame shall d. his branches
Is. 42 : 15. will d. up herbs, d. pools

Is. 44:27. d. up thy rivers | 50:2.sea
Je. 51: 36. saith, I will d. up her sea
Zch. 10 : 11. deeps of river sh. d.up

DRYSHOD.

Is. 11 : 15. and make men go d.

DUE, DUES. [N. and adj.]

Le. 10:13. thy d. and son's d., 14.
De. 18:3. this shall be the priest's d.
1 Ch.15:13. sought not aft. d. order
16 : 29. the glory d. to his name,
Ps. 29 : 2.-96 : 8.
Ne. 11 : 23. for singers, d. ev. day
Pr. 3 : 27. Withhold not to whom d.
Mat. 18:34. till he pay all th. was d.
Lu. 23 : 41. we receive d. reward
Ro. 13 : 7. Render to all their d-s,
tribute to whom tribute is d.
1 Co.7:3. husb. unto wife d. benevo-
lence

DUE season.

Le. 26 : 4. rain in d. s., De. 11 : 14.
Nu. 28 : 2. observe to offer in d. s.
Ps. 104 : 27. their meat in d.s.,145:
15.
Pr. 15:23. word spoken in d. s.
Ec. 10:17. when princes eat in d.s.
Mat. 24:45. meat in d.s., Lu.12:42.
Ga. 6 : 9. in d. s. reap if faint not

DUE time.

De. 32 : 35. foot shall slide in d. t.
Ro. 5:6. in d.t. C. died for ungodly
1 Co. 15 : 8. one born out of d. t.
1 Ti. 2 : 6. be testified in d. t. [word
Tit. 1 : 3. in d. t-s manifested his
1 Pe. 5:6. he may exalt you in d.t.

DUKE, S.

Ge 36:15.d-s of sons of Esau ; d. (4)
16.d. . . d. . . d. . . d-s of, 17, 18,
19.
29. d-s of Horites; d.(4) 21, 30 (3).
40. d-s that came of Esau ; d. . .
41, 42, 43. 1 Ch. 1:51, 52, 53, 54.
Ex. 15 : 15. d-s of Edom be amazed
Jos. 13 : 21. Zur, Hur, Reba, d-s of
Sihon

DULCIMER.

Da. 3 : 5. d. and all kinds, 10, 15.

DULL.

Mat. 13 : 15. their ears are d., Ac.
28:27.
He. 5:11. seeing ye are d.of hearing

DU'MAH.

Ge.25:14.sons of Ishm. D.,1 Ch.1:30.
Jos. 15 : 52. D. in Judah's inheri.
Is. 21 : 11. burden of D. he called

DUMB.

Ex. 4 : 11. or who maketh thee d.
Ps. 38 : 13. I was as d. man
39 : 2. I was d. with silence, 9.
Pr. 31 : 8. Open thy mouth for d.
Is. 35 : 6. tongue of d. shall sing
53 : 7. as sheep bef. shearers is d.
56 : 10. his watchmen are d. dogs
Eze. 3 : 26. be d. and not a reprov.
24 : 27. shalt speak, be no more d.
33 : 22. I was no more d.
Da. 10:15. face to ground, I became
d.
Ha. 2 : 18. to make him d. idols
19. that saith to d. stone, Arise
Mat.9:32. brought to him a d. man
33. the d. spake, Lu. 11 : 14.
12 : 22. one d. and he healed him
15 : 30. having with them those d.
31. saw the d. speak, Mk. 7 : 37.
Mk. 9 : 17. brought my son who
hath a d. spirit
25. Thou d. spirit, come out of
him
Lu. 1 : 20. thou shalt be d. until
Ac. 8 : 32. like lamb d. bef. shearer
1 Co. 12:2. carried aw. unto d. idols
2 Pe. 2 : 16. the d. ass speaking

DUNG. [Noun.]

Ex. 29:14. and d. shalt thou burn,
Le. 4 : 11.-8:17.-16:27.Nu.19:5.
1 K. 14:10. as man taketh away d.
2 K. 6 : 25. of a cab of doves' d.
9 : 37. carcass of Jezebel be as d.
18 : 27. may eat own d., Is. 36:12.
Jb.20:7. shall perish like his own d.
Ps. 83 : 10. they became as d.
Is. 5 : † 25. their carcasses were as
d., Je. 9 : 22.
Je.8:2.they sh. be for d. upon earth
16:4. sh. be as d. | 25:33 sh. be d.
Eze. 4 : 12. bake it with d. that
15.lo, given cow's d. for man's d.
Zph. 1 : 17. their flesh sh. be as d.
Mal. 2:3. I will spread d. upon your
faces, d. of your feasts
Ph. 3 : 8. count all things but d.

DUNG. [Verb.]

Lu. 13 : 8. till I dig ab. it, and d. it

DUNG gate.

Ne. 3 : 13. Hanun repaired valley
gate unto the d. g.
14. but the d.g. repaired Malchia
12 : 31. one company went tow.d.
g.

DUNG port.

Ne. 2:13. Nehemiah went to the d.
p.

DUNGEON.

Ge. 40 : 15. th. they put me into d.
41 : 14. bro-t Jo. hastily out of d.
Ex. 12 : 29. to firstborn in d.
Is. 24 : † 22. be gath. as prisoners in
d.
Je. 37 : 16. Jere. was ent. into d.
38 : 6. they cast him into d. was
no water in d., 7, 9.
10. take up Jeremiah out of d.
11. let them down into d. to Jere.
13. drew up Jeremiah out of d.
La. 3 : 53. cut off my life in d.
55. I called, O Lord, out of d.

DUNGHILL, S.

1 S. 2:8. lifteth beggar from d., Ps.
113:7.
Ezr. 6 : 11. let his house be a d.
Is. 25:10. as straw is trodden for d.
La. 4 : 5. in scarlet, embrace d-s
Da. 2 : 5. your houses be made d.
3 : 29. their houses be made a d.
Lu. 14:35. unsav. salt not fit for d.

DUNGY.

De. 29 : † 17. ye have seen d. gods

DU'RA.

Da. 3 : 1. image in plain of D.

DURABLE.

Pr. 8 : 18. d. riches are with me
Is. 23 : 18. shall be for d. clothing

DURETH.

Mat. 13 : 21. not root, d. for while

DURST.

Es. 7 : 5. that d. presume to do so
Jb. 32 : 6. I d. not shew mine opin.
Mat. 22 : 46. no man d. ask more
questions, Mk. 12:34. Lu.20:40.
Jn. 21 : 12. none of disciples d. ask
Ac. 5 : 13. d. no man join to them
7 : 32. Then Moses d. not behold
Ju. 9. he d. not bring railing accu.

DUST.

Ge. 3 : 14. d. shalt thou eat all life
19.d. thou art, and unto d. shalt
13 : 16. if can number d. of earth
18 : 27. who am but d. and ashes
Ex. 8 : 16. say to Aaron, smite d.
17. Aaron smote d. of earth
9 : 9. it shall become small d.
Le. 14 : 41. pour d. they scrape off
17 : 13. pour bl. cover it with d.
Nu. : † 17. take d. of heifer
23 : 10. Who count d. of Jacob ?
De. 9 : 21. d. into brook, 2 K.23:12.
28 : 24. make rain of thy land d.
Jos. 7 : 6. elders put d. upon heads
2 S. 16 : 13. cursed Da., and cast d.
1 K. 18 : 38. fire of L. consumed d.
20 : 10. if d. of Samaria suffice
2 Ch. 34 : 4. made d. of images
Jb. 2 : 12. sprinkled d. upon heads
7 : 5. flesh clothed with clods of d.
10 : 9. wilt bring me into d. again?
28 : † 2. iron is taken out of d.
6. the earth, it hath d. of gold
34 : 15. man sh. turn again unto d.
38 : 38. d. groweth into hardness
42 : 6. and repent in d. and ashes
Ps. 22:15. hast brought me into d.
30 : 9. Shall d. praise thee, shall it
72 : 9. his enemies shall lick d.
78 : 27. he rained flesh also as d.
Ps. 102 : 14. thy servants favour d.
103 : 14. he remem-h we are d.
Ec. 12 : 7. shall d. return to earth
Is. 2 : † 19. go into caves of d.
34 : 7. their d. shall be made fat
9. d. be turned into brimstone
40 : 12. who compreh. d. of earth?
49 : 23. shall lick up d. of thy feet
52 : 2. Shake thyself fr.d.O Jerus.
65 : 25. d. be serpent's meat
La.2:10.cast d. upon heads, Eze.27:
30.
Eze. 24 : 7. to cover it with d.
26 : 4. I will scrape her d. fr. her
10. horses, d. shall cover thee
12. thy d. in midst of water
Am. 2:7. That pant aft d. of earth
Mi. 7 : 17. They shall lick the d.
Na. 1 : 3. clouds are d. of his feet
Ha. 1 : 10. for they shall heap d.
Mat. 10 : 14. shake off the d. of
your feet, Mk. 6 : 11. Lu. 9 : 5.
Lu. 10 : 11. d. of your city we wipe
off
Ac. 13 : 51. they shook off d.
22 : 23. as they threw d. into air
Re. 18 : 19. cast d. on their heads

As the DUST.

Ge. 13 : 16. I will make thy seed a.
d. of earth, 28 : 14. 2 Ch. 1 : 9.
De. 9 : 21. stamped calf small a. d.
2 S. 22 : 43. I beat them as small a.
d., Ps. 18 : 42.
Jb. 22 : 24. shalt lay up gold a. d.
27:16.Tho. he heap up silver a.d.
Ps. 78 : 27. He rained flesh as d.
Is. 5 : 24. their blossom go up a.d.
40 : 15. nations a. small d. of balance
41:2.gave them a.d.to sword
Zph. 1 : 17. bl. be poured out a. d.
Zch. 9 : 3. heaped up silver a. d.

In the DUST.

Jb. 4 : 19. whose founda. is i. d.
7 : 21. now shall I sleep i. d.
16 : 15. have defiled my horn i. d.
17 : 16. our rest together is i. d.
20 : 11. sh. lie down with him i.d.
21 : 26. sh. lie down alike i. d.
39 : 14. eggs, warmeth them i. d.
40 : 13. Hide them i. d. together
42 : 6. I repent i. d. and ashes
Ps. 7 : 5. lay mine honour i. d.
Is. 2 : 10. hide thee i. d. for fear
26 : 19. sing, ye that dwell i. d.
47 : 1. Come, sit i. d. O virgin
La. 3 : 29. He putteth mouth i. d.
Da. 12 : 2. sleep i. d. shall awake
Mi. 1 : 10. weep not, roll thys. i.d.
Na. 3 : 18. nobles shall dwell i. d.

Like DUST.

2 K. 13:7. make l. d. by threshing
2 Ch. 1 : 9. a people l. d. of earth
Jb. 30 : 19. I am become l. d.
Is. 29 : 5. thy strangers be l. d.

Of the DUST.

Ge. 2 : 7. Lord formed man o. d.
Nu. 5 : 17. shall take o. d. in tab.
De. 32 : 24. poison of serpents o.d.
1 S. 2:8.the poor out o.d.,Ps.113:7.
1 K. 16 : 2. I exalted thee out o.d.
Jb. 5 : 6. affliction cometh not o.d.
14 : 19. things that grow out o.d.
Pr. 8:26. highest part o.d. of world
Ec.3:20.unto one place, all are o.d.
Is. 29 : 4. speech be low out o. d.

To or unto the DUST.

Ps. 22 : 29. all that go down t. d.
44 : 25. our soul is bowed t. d.
104 : 29. die and return t. their d.
119 : 25. My soul cleaveth u. d.
Ec. 3 : 20. all of d. and turn t. d.
Is. 25 : 12. sh. bring fortress t. d.
26 : 5. bringeth lofty city t. d.

DUSTED.

2 S. 16 : † 13. Shimei threw stones
and d. with dust

DUTY, IES.

Ex. 21 : 10. her d. of marriage sh.
he
De. 25 : 5. perf. d. of husb.'s bro.

25:7. will not perform the d. of my husband's brother
Ch. 8 : 14. as d. of every day required, Ezr. 3 : 4.
. 12 : 13. this is whole d. of man
e. 18 : 11. if he beget a son that doeth not those d-s
. 17:10. done that wh. was our d.
. 15:27. their d. is to minister in

DWARF.

. 21 : 20. d. sh. not come nigh to ⌊off.

DWELL.

. 4 : 20. fa. of such as d. in tents
: 27. Japhet d. in tents of Shem
: 12. shall d. in pres. of breth.
: 30. Lot feared to d. in Zoar
: 15. d. where it pleaseth thee
:3. of Canaanites, am. whom I d.
:20. will my husb. d. with me
: 10. land bef. you, d. and trade
16. we will d. with you, and ⌊(2)
22. men consent to d. with us, 23.
: 1. go to Beth-el, and d. there
: 13. Zeb. sh. d. at haven of sea
. 2 : 21. Moses was content to d. with the man ⌈29 : 46.
: 8. that I may d. among them,
: 45. I will d. am. chil. of Israel
. 13: 46. unclean shall d. alone
3 : 42. d. in booths, 43. Ne. 8 : 14.
. 5 : 3. camps, in midst I d.
3 : 29. Amo. d. in mts., Jos. 10 : 6.
3 : 9. lo, the people shall d. alone
2 : 17. shall d. in fenced cities
5 : 2. give unto Levites, cities to d. in, and suburbs round, 3. Jos. 14 : 4.-21 : 2.
34. I the L. d. among chil. of Isr.
. 11:30. d. in champaign ag. Gilg.
2 : 11. name d. there, Ezr. 6 : 12.
3 : 12. G. hath given thee to d.
3 : 16. serv. escaped shall d. with
3:12. he sh. d. betw. his shoulders
. 9 : 7. Peradv. ye d. am. us, 22.
0 : 4. place, that he d. am. them
6. he shall d. in that city
: 13. cities ye built not, ye d. in
. 9 : 41. Gaal not d. in Shechem
7 : 10. Mic. said to Lev. d. with me
11. Lev. was content to d. with
3 : 1. Danites sought inheri. to d.
. 27 : 5. that I d. there : for why should thy serv. d. in royal city
. 6 : 13. I will d. am. chil. of Isr.
: 12. he would d. in thick darkness, 2 Ch. 6 : 1.
: 9. get to Zarephath, and d.
. 4 : 13. I d. among own people
: 27. let them go and d. there
Ch. 8 : 2. caused chil. of Isr. to d.
: 10. brethren th. d. in cities
. 10 : † 10. ye have caused to d. strange wives, Ne. 13 : † 23.
. 3 : 5. let a cloud d. upon it
: 14. wickedness d. in thy tab.
: 15. shall d. in his tabernacle
: 6. to d. in the cliffs of valleys
. 5 : 4. neith. sh. evil d. with thee
: 1. who sh. d. in thy holy hill?
:†9. my flesh sh. d. in confidence
: 13. His soul shall d. at ease
: 27. depart from evil, and d.
: 4. that he may d. in thy courts
. They that d. in uttermost parts
: 16. hill God desireth to d. in, yea the Lord will d. in it
8. that L. might d. among them
: 25. let none d. in their tents
5. build Jud. that they may d.
: 9. that d. in wildern. sh. bow
: 55. made Isr. d. in their tents
: 10. than d. in tents of wick.
1 : 6. faithful that they may d.
7 : 4. they found no city to d. in
6. he maketh the hungry to d.
3 :†5. L. who exalteth hims. to d.
0 : 5. that I d. in tents of Kedar

Ps. 132:14. my rest, here will I d. for
139 : 9. if I d. in uttermost parts
140 : 13. upright sh. d. in thy pres.
143 : 3. made me to d. in darkness
Pr. 1 : 33. heark-h unto me shall d.
8 : 12. I wisdom d. with prudence
21:†7. robbery of wick. shall d.
9. better to d. in corner, 25 : 24.
19. it is better to d. in wildern.
Is. 6 : 5. I d. in midst of people of
11 : 6. wolf sh. d. with the lamb
13 : 21. owls shall d. there, satyrs
16:4. Let mine outcasts d. with th.
23 : 13. th. d. in wildern., Je. 9 : 26.
18. merch-e for them th. d. bef. L.
24 : 6. that d. therein are desolate
26 : 5. down them that d. on high
19. sing, ye that d. in the dust
30 : 19. the people sh. d. in Zion
32:16. judgment sh. d. in wildern.
18. my peo. d. in peaceful habi.
33 : 14. Who d. with devour. fire? who shall d. with burnings?
16. He shall d. on high, his place
24. that d. therein be forgiven
34:11. owl and raven shall d. in it
40 : 22. spreadeth as a tent to d. in
49 : 20. give place that I may d.
58 : 12. restorer of paths to d. in
65 : 9. my servants shall d. there
Je. 8 : 19. them th. d. in far coun.
25:24. mingled peo. that d. in des.
29 : 32. Shemaiah not a man to d.
31 : 24. d. in Judah husbandmen
35 : 7. all your days d. in tents
40 : 5. d. with him am. the people
10. I will d. at Mizpah to serve
42:14. into E., and there will we d.
44 : 14. have desire to return to d.
48 : 28. ye that d. in Moab, d. in
49 : 1. his peo. d. in cities ⌊rock
8. d. deep, O inhabitant of Dedan
18. nor shall a son of man d. in it, 33.-50 : 40.
31. d. alone | 51:1. d. in midst of
Eze. 2 : 6. thou dost d. am. scorp.
16 : 46. she and dau-s d. at thy left
17 : 23. under it shall d. all fowl
28 : 26. shall d. with confidence
36 : 33. cause you to d. in cities
39 : 6. am. them that d. carelessly
9. th. d. in cities of Israel shall
43 : 7. where I will d. in midst of Isr. for ever, 9. Zch. 2 : 10, 11.
Da. 2 : 38. whereso. chil. of men d.
Ho. 12 : 9. make thee d. in tabern.
14:7. They th. d. under his shadow
Jo. 3:20. But Judah sh. d. for ever
Am. 3 : 12. taken out that d. in Sa.
Mi. 4 : 10. thou shalt d. in the field
7 : 14. the flock which d. solitary
Na. 3 : 18. thy nobles sh. d. in dust
Hag. 1:4. time to d. in ceiled houses?
Zch. 8 : 4. women sh. d. in Jerus.
9 : 6. bastard shall d. in Ashdod
14 : 11. men sh. d. in it ⌈11 : 26.
Mat. 12 : 45. ent. and d. there, Lu.
Lu. 21:35. as a snare on all that d. on earth, Ac. 17 : 26. ⌈d.
Ac. 7 : 4. into land wherein ye now
28:16. Paul was suff. to d. by hims.
Ro. 8:9. if Spirit of G. d. in you, 11.
1 Co. 7 : 12. she be pleased to d.
2 Co. 6 : 16. G. said, I will d. in th.
Ep. 3 : 17. That C. d. in your hearts
Col. 1:19. in him sho. all fulness d.
3 : 16. Let word of C. d. in you
1 Pe. 3 : 7. ye husbands, d. with th.
1 Jn. 4 : 13. know that we d. in him
Re. 7 : 15. he on the throne shall d.
12 : 12. heavens, ye th. d. in them
13 : 6. ag. them that d. in heaven
21 : 3. with men, will d. with them

DWELL with **earth.**

1 K. 8 : 27. will God d. on e.? 2 Ch. 6 : 18. ⌈e., 6 : 25.
Da. 4 : 1. languages that d. in all

Re. 3:10. to try them th. d. upon e.
6 : 10. avenge bl. on them d. on e.
11:10. they that d. upon e. sh. rej.
13:8. that d. upon e. shall worship
14. deceiveth them th. d. on e.
14 : 16. to preach to them d. on e.
17 : 8. that d. on e. shall wonder

DWELL with **house,** s.

De. 28 : 30. shalt build a h., shalt not d. therein, Am. 5:11. ⌈17 : 1.
2 S. 7 : 2. I d. in a h. of cedar, 1 Ch.
5. build me a h. to d., 1 Ch. 17 : 4.
1 K. 2 : 36. Build h. in Jeru. and d.
8:17. I and this wom. d. in one h.
8:13. surely built thee h. to d. in
2 Ch. 2 : 3. cedars to build h. to d.
8 : 11. My wife not d. in h. of Da.
Jb. 4:19. them th. d. in h-s of clay
19 : 15. d. in h. count me a stran.
Ps. 23:6. I will d. in h. of L. for ev.
27 : 4. that I may d. in h. of L.
84:4. Blessed they th. d. in thy h.
101:7. worketh deceit, shall not d. within my h. ⌈in h.
113 : † 9. he maketh barren to d.
Pr. 21:9. d. in corner of a h., 25:24.
Je. 20 : 6. d. in thy h. go to captiv.
29:5. Build ye h-s, d. in them, 28.
35 : 9. Nor to build h-s for us to d.

DWELL with **Jerusalem.**

1 Ch. 23 : 25. that ye may d. in J.
Ne. 11 : 1. one of ten to d. in J.
2. willingly off-d thems. to d. at J.
Je. 33 : 16. and J. shall d. safely
35 : 11. for fear of Chal. we d. at J.
Zch. 8 : 3. I will d. in midst of J.
8. they shall d. in midst of J.
Ac. 2 : 14. all ye that d. at Jerus.
4:16. is manifest to all that d. in J.
13 : 27. that d. at J. have condom.

DWELL with **land.** ⌊him

Ge. 24:37. Canaani. in whose l. I d.
26 : 2. d. in l. I shall tell thee of
34 : 21. let them d. in the l., and
45 : 10. thou shalt d. in l. of Go.
46 : 34. that ye may d. in l. of Go.
47 : 6. in l. of Goshen let th. d., 4.
Ex. 8 : 22. l. in which my people d.
23 : 33. They shall not d. in thy l.
Le. 20 : 22. l. whi. I bring you to d.
25 : 18. ye sh. d. in the l. in safety
26 : 5. ye sh. d. in your l. safely
Nu. 13:19. what the l. is they d. in
28. peo. be strong that d. in l.
29. Amalekites d. in l. of south
33 : 55. shall vex you in l. ye d.
35 : 32. come again to d. in l.
34. defile not l. wherein I d.
De. 12 : 10. d. in l. the L. giv. you
30 : 20. that thou mayest d. in l.
Jos. 17 : 12. but the Canaani. would d. in that l., Ju. 1 : 27.
16. that d. in l. of the valley
24 : 15. the gods in whose l. d. ye, Ju. 6 : 10. ⌈25 : 5.-40 : 9.
2 K. 25 : 24. fear not, d. in l., Je.
Ps. 37 : 3. do good, so d. in the l.
68 : 6. rebellious d. in a dry l.
85 : 9. that glory may d. in our l.
Pr. 2 : 21. upright shall d. in l.
Is. 9 : 2. d. in l. of shadow of death
Je. 23 : 8. sh. d. in own l., 27 : 11.
24 : 8. that d. in l. of E., 44 : 1, 8, 13, 26. ⌈87 : 25.
35:15. ye sh. d. in l., Eze. 36:28.-
42 : 13. if say, We will not d. in l.
43 : 4. obeyed not L. to d. in l., 5.
50 : 3. l. desolate, none shall d.
Eze. 28 : 25. then sh. d. in their l.
38 : 12. the people that d. in the l.
Ho. 9 : 3. They sh. not d. in L.'s l.
Ha. 2 : 8. violence of l., and all th. d., 17. ⌈that d. in l.
Zph. 1 : 18. speedy riddance of all

DWELL with **place.** ⌈in

Ex. 15 : 17. p. thou hast made to d.
1 S. 12 : 8. made them d. in this p.

2 S. 7 : 10. d. in a p. of their own
2 K. 6 : 1. p. where we d. is strait
2. make us a p. where we may d.
1 Ch. 17 : 9. they sh. d. in their p.
Is. 57 : 15. I d. in high and holy p.
Je. 7 : 3 cause you to d. in this p.,

DWELL safely. [7.

Pr. 1:33. heark-h unto me sh. d. s.
Je. 23 : 6. in his days Isr. sh. d. s.,
Eze. 28 : 26.-34 : 25, 28.-38 : 8.
32 : 37. I will cause them to d. s.
Eze. 38:11. I will go to them th. d.

DWELL in safety. [s.

Le. 25 : 18. keep my judgm., ye sh.
d. i. s., 19.-26 : 5. De. 12 : 10.
De. 33 : 12. beloved of L. sh. d. i. s.
28. Isr. then shall d. i. s. alone
Ps. 4 : 8. L. only makest me to d. i.

DWELL therein. [s.

Le. 26 : 32. ene. wh. d. t. be aston.
Nu.14:30. I sware to make you d.t.
33 : 53. ye sh. d. t., De. 11:31.-17:
Ps. 24:1. world, they th. d. t. [14.
37 : 29. the righteous shall d. t.
69 : 36. that love his name sh. d.t.
107 : 34. for wickedn. of them th.
d. t., Je. 12 : 4. [Am. 9 : 5.
Is. 24 : 6. that d. t. are desolate,
33 : 24. peo. that d. t. are forgiven
34 : 17. fr. gener. to gen. sh. d. t.
51 : 6. they that d. t. shall die
Je. 4:29. city forsak., not man d.t.
8 : 16. devoured city, and all d. t.
47 : 2. overfl. land and that d. t.
48:9. the cities without any to d.t.
50 : 39. beasts and owls shall d.t.
Eze. 12 : 19. violence of them d. t.
32 : 15. shall smite them that d.t.
37 : 25. they and chil. shall d. t.
Mi. 7:13. desolate, bec. of them d.t.
Na. 1 : 5. world burnt, and all d.t.
Ac. 1 : 20. his habita., let no man d.
Re. 13:12. wh. d. t. to worship [t.

DWELL together.

Ge. 13 : 6. that they might d. t.,
substance great, so not d. t.
36:7. riches more than might d. t.
De. 25:5. if breth. d. t., and one die
Ps. 133 : 1. breth. to d. t. in unity

DWELLER, S. [tents

Ps.69:†25.let there not be a d. in th.
Is. 18 : 3. ye d-s on earth, see [ru.
Ac. 1:19. was known unto d-s at Je-
2 : 9. d-s in Mesopota., we do hear

DWELLEST.

De. 12 : 29. thou d. in their land
19 : 1. thou d. in their cities
26 : 1 possessest inhori. and d.
2 K. 19 : 15. O L. of Isr., which d.
betw. cherubim, Ps. 80:1. Is.37:
Ps.123:1.O thou th. d. in heav. [16.
Can. 8 : 13. that d. in the gardens
Is. 10 : 24. d. in Zion, be not afraid
47 : 8. hear this, that d. carelessly
Je. 49 : 16. that d. in clefts, Ob. 3.
51 : 13. O thou th. d. upon waters
La.4:21. Edom, th. d. in land of Uz
Eze. 7 : 7. d. in land, time is come
12 : 2. d. in midst of rebellious
Mi. 1 : † 11. thou that d. fairly
Zch. 2 : 7. d. with dau. of Babylon
Jn. 1 : 38. Master, where d. thou?
Re. 2 : 13. I know where thou d.

DWELLETH.

Le. 16 : † 16. that d. among them
19 : 34. stranger that d. with you
25 : 39. if bro. that d. be poor, 47.
De. 33 : 20. God d. as a lion [day
Jos. 6 : 25. Rahab d. in Isr. to this
22 : 19. wherein L.'s tabernacle d.
1 S. 4 : 4. ark of Lord, who d. betw.
cherubim, 2 S. 6 : 2. 1 Ch. 13:6.
27 : 11. he d. in country of Philis.
2 S. 7 : 2. ark d. within curtains
1 Ch. 23:†25. L. d. in Jeru. for ever
Jb. 15 : 28. he d. in desolate cities
38 : 19. Where way where light d.?
Jb. 39 : 28. She d. and abid. on rock
Ps. 9 : 11. Sing to L. who d. in Zion
26 : 8. place where thine honour d.
91 : 1. He that d. in the secret pl.
113:5. who like L. who d. on high?
135 : 21. blessed be L. d. at Jeru.
Pr. 3 : 29. he d. securely by thee
Is. 8 : 18. L. who d. in mount Zion
33 : 5. L. is exalted; he d. on high
Je. 29 : 16. of peo th. d. in this city
44 : 2. desola., no man d. therein
49 : 31. nation th. d. without care
51 : 43. land wherein no man d.
La. 1 : 3. Jud. d. among heathen
Eze. 16 : 46. sister d. at right hand
17 : 16. king d. that made him k.
38:14. day my peo. Israel d. safely
Da. 2 : 22. and light d. with him
Ho. 4 : 3. every one that d. therein
shall mourn, Am. 8 : 8. [Zion
Jo. 3 : 21. cleanse bl., for L. d. in
Mat. 23 : 21. sweareth by him th. d.
Jn. 6 : 56. drink my blood, d. in me
14 : 10. Fa. that d. in me, he doeth
17. the Spirit, for he d. in you
Ac. 7 : 48. d. not in temples made
with hands, 17:24. [d. in me, 20.
Ro. 7 : 17. no more I, but sin that
18. in my flesh d. no good thing
8:11. quicken, by Sp. th. d. in you
1 Co. 3 : 16. that Sp. of G. d. in you
Col. 2 : 9. in him d. fuln. of Godh.
2 Ti. 1 : 14. keep by H. Gh. d. in us
Ja. 4:5. spirit that d. in us lusteth
2 Pe. 3:13. earth wherein d. righte.
1 Jn.3:17. how d. love of G. in him?
24. th. keepeth com-ts, d. in him
4:12. if love one ano., G. d. in us
15. confess J. is Son of G., G. d.
16. he th. d. in love, d. in G. [in
2 Jn. 2. truth's sake wh. d. in us
Re. 2 : 13. slain am. you, where Sat.

DWELLING. [Part.] [d.

Ge. 25 : 27. Jacob was plain man d.
in tents [the country
Jos. 13 : 21. dukes of Sihon d. in
1 K. 21 : 8. in city d. with Naboth
Je. 6: † 2. Zion to wom., d. at home
46 : 19. O thou dau. d. in Egypt
Eze. 38 : 11. all d. without walls
Jo. 3 : 17. I am your G. d. in Zion
Ac. 2:5. there were d. at Jeru. Jews
19 : 17. Greeks d. at Ephesus
1 Ti. 6 : 16. d. in light no man
He. 11 : 9. d. in tabern. with Isaac
2 Pe. 2 : 8. Lot, th. righte. man d.

DWELLING. [Noun.] [am.

Ge. 10 : 30. their d. was fr. Mesha
27 : 39. thy d. shall be fatness
30 : † 20. she called his name d.
Nu. 21 : 15. that goeth to d. of Ar
2 K. 17 : 25. beginning of their d.
2 Ch. 6:2. I have built pl. for thy d.
Ps. 49 : 14. consume in grave fr. d.
91 : 10. nor any plague nigh thy d.
Pr. 21 : 20. oil in d. of the wise
24:15. lay not wait ag. d. of righte.
Je. 49 : 33. Hazor sh. be d. for drag-
Eze. 48:15. for the city, for d. [ons
Da. 2 : 11. gods, whose d. not with
flesh [32.-5 : 21.
4 : 25. thy d. be with the beasts,
Na 2 : 11. Where is d. of lions?
Zph. 3 : 7. their d. not be cut off
Mk. 5 : 3. had his d. among tombs

DWELLINGS. [d.

Ex. 10 : 23. chil. of Isr. had light in
Le. 3 : 17. perpetual statute thro.
your d., 23:14.-21, 31. Nu. 35:29.
7 : 26. ye shall eat no blood in d.
23 : 3. ye sh. do no work in d., 31.
Jb. 18:19. nor any remaining in d.
21. such are d. of wicked
39 : 6. made the barren land his d.
Ps. 55:15. wickedn in their d. [Jac.
87 : 2. gates of Z., than all d. of
Is. 32 : 18. peo. sh. dwell in sure d.
Je. 9 : 19. our d. have cast us out
Eze. 25 : 4. men of east make d. in
Zph. 2 : 6. coast be d. for shepherds

DWELLINGHOUSE.

Le. 25 : 29. if man sell d. in city

DWELLINGPLACE, S.

Nu. 24 : 21. said, Strong is thy d.
1 K. 8 : 30. hear in heaven thy d.
39, 43, 49. 2 Ch. 6 : 21, 30, 39.
1 Ch. 6:32. ministered bef. the d. of
54. Now these are their d-s [tab.
2 Ch. 30 : 27. prayer up to holy d.
36 : 15. L. had compass on his d.
Jb. 8:22. d. of wick. come to nought
21 : 28. where are d-s of wicked?
Ps. 49 : 11. their d-s to all genera.
52 : 5. G. sh. pluck thee out of d.
74 : 7. casting down d. of thy name
76 : 2. in Salem his tab., d. in Zion
79 : 7. they have laid waste his d.
90 : 1. L. thou hast been our d.
Is. 4:5. L. will create upon every d.
18 : 4. will consider in my d. [d-s
Je. 30 : 18. will have mercy on his
51 : 30. have burned her d-s, 27.
51:37. Bab. sh. become a d. for drag.
Eze. 6 : 6. In all d-s cities waste
37 : 23. I will save them out of d-s
Ha. 1 : 6. to possess d-s not their's
1 Co.4:11. naked, have no certain d.

DWELT.

Ge. 11 : 2. they d. there, 31.-26 : 17.
2 K.16:6. 1 Ch.4:43. 2 Ch.28:18.
19 : 29. overth. cities in wh. Lot d.
20:1. Ab. d. betw. Kadesh and Shur
23 : 10. Ephron d. am. chil. of Heth
25 : 11. Isaac d. by well Lahai-roi
18. they d. from Havilah unto
Le. 18 : 3. doings of E. wherein ye d.
26 : 35. not rest sab. when ye d.
Nu. 31: 10. wherein they d. a, 2 K. 17:
Ru. 1 : 4. they d. there ten yrs. [29
1 S. 12 : 11. G. deliv. and ye d. safe
1 K. 13:11. d. an old proph. in B., 25.
Jos. 9 : 16. neighb. and they that d.
24 : 2. Your fa-s d. on other side
Ju. 1 : 16. went and d. amo. peo.
18 : 7. peo. how they d. careless
1 K. 4 : 25. Jud. and Isr. d. safely
1 Ch. 4 : 23. that d. among plants
40. of Ham d. there of old
Ne.4:12. Jews wh. d. by them came
11 : 30. d. fr. Beer-she. unto Hin.
Jb. 29 : 25. I d. as a king in army
Ps. 74 : 2. Zion wherein thou hast d.
Is. 29 : 1. Ariel, city where David d.
Je.2:6. thro. land where no man d.
39 : 14. Jere. d. among the people
Ez. 3 : 15. th. d. by river of Chebar
31 : 6. his shadow d. nations, 17.
37 : 25. lands wherein fathers d.
Da. 4 : 21. under which beasts d.
Zph. 2 : 15. city that d. carelessly
Lu. 1 : 65. fear came on all that d.
Jn. 1 : 14. Word made flesh and d.
39. They saw where he d. and
Ac. 13 : 17. when they d. in Egypt
22 : 12. good report of all th. d.
28 : 30. Paul d. in hired house
Re. 11 : 10. tormented them d. on

DWELT at.

Ge. 22 : 19. Ab. d. a. Beer-sheba
Nu. 21 : 34. Amor. which d. a. Heshbon, De. 3 : 2.-4 : 46.
De. 1:4. d. a. Ashtaroth, Jos. 12 : 4.
Ju. 9 : 41. Abim. d. a. Arumah
1 K. 15:18. Benhadad d. a. Damas.,
2 Ch. 16 : 2. [37 : 37.
2 K. 19 : 36. Sennach. d. a. Nin., Is.
1 Ch. 2 : 55. scribes wh. d. a. Jabez
4 : 28. they d. a. Beer-sheba and
9 : 34. fathers of Levites d. a. Je.
2 Ch. 19 : 4. Jehosh. d. a. Jerus.
Ac. 9 : 22. Saul conf. Jews that d. a.
32. Pe. to saints who d. a. Lydda

DWELT in.

Ge. 4 : 16. d. i. land of Nod

Ge. 13 : 7. Perizzite **d. i.** land
12. Abram **d. i.** Canaan. Lot **i.** cities
18. **d. i.** plain of Mamre, 14 : 13.
16 : 3. aft. Ab. **d. i.** land of Ca.
19 : 30. **d. i.** mountain and his two
Nu. 20 : 15. we have **d. i.** E. long time
21 : 31. Isr. **d. i.** land of Amorites
De. 1 : 4. **d. i.** Heshbon, Jos. 12 : 2.
6. **d.** long enough **i.** mount
2 : 8. **d. i.** Seir thro. way, 12. [5 : 22.
12. **d. i.** their stead, 21, 22, 23. 1 Ch.
29 . 16. how we **d. i.** land of E.
33 : 16. good will of him **d. i.** bush
Ju. 8 : 11. way of them **d. i.** tents
29. Jerubbaal **d. i.** own house
21 : 23. repaired cities and **d. i.**
1 S. 19 : 18. Samuel **d. i.** Naioth
31 : 7. Philis. **d. i.** them, 1 Ch. 10 : 7.
2 S. 7 : 6. not **d. i.** house since I bro-t
Israel out of E., 1 Ch. 17 : 5.
9 : 12. all that **d. i.** house of Ziba.
13. So Mephibos. **d. i.** Jerusalem
14 : 28. Abs. **d.** two years in Jerus.
1 K. 2 : 38. Shimei **d. i.** Jerusalem
12 : 2. Jerob. fled fr. Sol., **d. i.** E.
13 : 11. **d.** an old prophet **i.** Beth-el
2 K. 13 : 5. Israel **d. i.** their tents
15 : 5. Ahaz. **d. i.** house, 2 Ch. 26 : 21.
17 : 24. pos. Samaria and **d. i.** cities
22 : 14. Huldah prophetess **d. i.**
Jerus. in college, 2 Ch. 34 : 22.
1 Ch. 4 : 41. these **d. i.** their rooms
5 : 10. fell and they **d. i.** their tents
8 : 28. chief men, **d. i.** Jerusalem
11 : 7. Dav. **d. i.** castle, 2 S. 5 : 9.
2 Ch. 11 : 5. Rehoboam **d. i.** Jerus.
Ezr. 2 : 70. priests, Levites, Nethinim,
d. i. cities, Ne. 3 : 26.–11 : 21.
Ne. 7 : 73. all Isr. **d. i.** their cities
Jb. 22 : 8. honourable men **d. i.** it
29 : 25. **d.** as a king **i.** the army
Ps. 94 : 17. soul almost **d. i.** silence
Is. 13 : 20. nor shall it be **d. i.** from
gener. to gener., Je. 50 : 39.
Je. 35 : 10. we have **d. i.** tents
41 : 17. **d. i.** habit. of Chimham
Eze. 36 : 17. when Isr. **d. i.** own la.
39 : 26. when **d.** safely **i.** their land
Da. 4 : 12. fowls **d. i.** the boughs
Mat. 2 : 23. Joseph **d. i.** Nazareth
4 : 13. Jesus **d. i.** Capernaum
Lu. 13 : 4. sinners ab. all **d. i.** Jerus.
Ac. 7 : 2. bef. Ab **d. i.** Charran, 4.
9 : 35. all th. **d. i.** Lydda and
11 : 29. relief unto breth. wh. **d. i.**
19 : 10. all they who **d. i.** Asia
2 Ti. 1 : 5. **d.** first **i.** thy grandmo.

DWELT therein. [d. t.
Nu. 32 : 40. Gilead unto Machir, he
De. 2 : 10. Emims **d. t.** | 20. giants **d.**
8 : 12. built goodly houses **d. t.** [t.
Jos. 19 : 47. poss-d and **d. t.**, 21 : 43.
50. built city **d. t.**, Ju. 18 : 28.
1 K. 11 : 24. Rezon to Damas. **d. t.**
12 : 25. Jerob. built Shechem, **d. t.**
2 Ch. 20 : 8. they **d. t.** built sanc.
Ne. 13 : 16. There **d.** men of Tyre **t.**
Ps. 68 : 10. Thy congr. hath **d. t.**

DWELT with.
Ru. 2 : 23. Ruth **d. w.** her mo. in l.
1 S. 22 : 4. mother **d. w.** k. of Moab
27 : 3. Da. **d. w.** Achish at Gath
1 Ch. 4 : 23. **d. w.** king for his work
9 : 32. these **d. w.** their breth., 9 : 38.
Ps. 120 : 6. My soul hath long **d. w.**
Je. 40 : 6. Jere. **d. w.** him am. peo.

DYED.
Ex. 25 : 5. take rams' skins **d.** red,
26 : 14.–35 : 7.–36 : 19.–39 : 34.
Is. 63 : 1. **d.** garments from Bozrah
Eze. 23 : 15. exceeding in **d.** attire
Na. 2 : † 3. the valiant in **d.** scarlet

DYING. [shalt die
Ge. 2 : † 17. when thou eatest, **d.** thou
Nu. 17 : 13. we be consum. with **d.**?
Mk. 12 : 20. the first **d.** left no seed
Lu. 8 : 42. Jairus' daughter lay a **d.**
2 Co. 4 : 10. in body the **d.** of L. J.
6 : 9. as **d.** and behold we live
He. 11 : 21. Jacob when **d.** bless. sons

E.

EACH.
Ge. 15 : 10. Ab. laid **e.** piece ag. ano.
34 : 25. Sim. Levi took **e.** his sword
40 : 5. **e.** man his dream [ment
45 : 22. to **e.** man changes of rai-
Ex. 18 : 7. asked **e.** other of welfare
30 : 34. of **e.** shall be a like weight
Nu. 1 : 44. **e.** one for house of fa-s
7 : 3. they brought for **e.** one an ox
16 : 17. and Aaron **e.** his censer
Jos. 22 : 14. **e.** chief h. a prince, **e.**
Ju. 8 : 18. **e.** resembled chil. of king
21 : 22. reserved not to **e.** his wife
Ru. 1 : 9. may find rest **e.** of you
1 K. 4 : 7. **e.** man his month in a year
22 : 10. kings, **e.** sat on his throne
2 K. 15 : 20. exacted of **e.** 50 shek.
Ps. 85 : 10. righte. and peace kissed **e.**
Is. 2 : 20. made **e.** for hims. to worsh.
6 : 2. seraphim, **e.** had six wings
35 : 7. where **e.** lay, shall be grass
57 : 2. **e.** walking in uprightness
Eze. 4 : 6. appoint. **e.** day for a year
Lu. 13 : 15. doth not **e.** on sab. loose
Ac. 2 : 3. cloven tongues upon **e.** [ox
Ph. 2 : 3. let **e.** esteem other better
2 Th. 1 : 3. charity toward **e.** other
Re. 4 : 8. beasts had **e.** six wings

EAGLE. [12.
Le. 11 : 13. **e.** have in abom., De. 14 :
De. 28 : 49. nation as swift as **e.**
32 : 11. As an **e.** stirreth up her nest
Jb. 9 : 26. as **e.** th. hasteth to prey
39 : 27. **e.** mount at thy command?
Pr. 23 : 5. riches fly away as an **e.**
30 : 19. way of an **e.** in the air is
Je. 48 : 40. fly as **e.** over Moab, 49 : 22.
49 : 16. tho. make nest high as **e.**
Eze. 1 : 10. had face of an **e.**, 10 : 14.
17 : 3. A great **e.** with gr. wings, 7.
Ho. 8 : 1. as an **e.** ag. house of L.
Ob. 4. Tho. thou exalt thyself as **e.**
Mi. 1 : 16. enlarge thy baldness as **e.**
Ha. 1 : 8. Chaldeans shall fly as **e.**
Re. 4 : 7. fourth beast like flying **e.**
12 : 14 to wom. wings of a great **e.**

EAGLES, 'S.
Ex. 19 : 4. how I bare you on **e.** wings
2 S. 1 : 23. were swifter than **e.**
Ps. 103 : 5. youth renewed like **e.**
Pr. 30 : 17. young **e.** shall eat it
Is. 40 : 31. mount with wings as **e.**
Je. 4 : 13. his horses swifter than **e.**
La. 4 : 19. persecu. swifter than **e.**
Da. 4 : 33. his hairs like **e.** feathers.
7 : 4. beast like lion, had **e.** wings
Mat. 24 : 28. **e.** be gather., Lu. 17 : 37.

EAR.
Ex. 21 : 6. sh. bore his **e.**, De. 15 : 17.
1 S. 9 : 15. L. had told Sam. in **e.**
20 : † 2. he will uncover mine **e.**
† 12. if I uncover thine **e.**
22 : † 8. none that uncov. mine **e.**
2 S. 7 : † 27. O Lord, hast opened **e.**
2 K. 19 : 16. bow down thine **e.**, Ps.
31 : 2.–86 : 1. [thy serv.
1 Ch. 17 : † 25. hast revealed **e.** of
Ne. 1 : 6. Let thine **e.** be attentive, 11.
Jb. 4 : 12. mine **e.** received little
12 : 11. Doth **e.** try words? 34 : 3.
13 : 1. mine **e.** hath heard and
29 : 11. When **e.** heard me, it bless.
21. Unto me men gave **e.** waited
32 : 11. I gave **e.** to your reasons
36 : 10. He openeth their **e.** to disci.
42 : 5. heard of thee by hear. of **e.**
Ps. 10 : 17. cause thine **e.** to hear
18 : † 44. at hearing of **e.** obey
31 : 2. Bow down thine **e.** to me
58 : 4. like adder, that stoppeth **e.**
77 : 1. I cried unto G., he gave **e.**
Ps. 94 : 9. He that planted **e.** sh. he
116 : 2. Bec. he hath inclined his **e.**
Pr. 5 : 1. bow **e.** to my underst-g
13. nor inclined my **e.** to them
15 : 31. **e.** that heareth reproof
17 : 4. liar giveth **e.** to a naughty
18 : 15. **e.** of wise seeketh knowl.
20 : 12. The hearing **e.** see-g eye
22 : 17. Bow **e.** hear words of wise
25 : 12. wise reprover an obed. **e.**
28 : 9. He that turneth away his **e.**
Ec. 1 : 8. nor is **e.** filled with hear.
Is. 48 : 8. time **e.** was not opened
50 : 4. he wakeneth my **e.** to hear
5. Lord hath opened mine **e.**
59 : 1. nei. is **e.** heavy it cannot hear
64 : 4. men not heard, nor perc. by **e.**
Je. 6 : 10. their **e.** is uncircumcised
7 : 24. nor inclined their **e.**, 26.–
11 : 8.–17 : 23.–25 : 4.–34 : 14.–44 : 5.
9 : 20. let your **e.** receive the word
35 : 15. ye have not inclined your **e.**
La. 3 : 56. hide not **e.** at my breath.
Am. 3 : 12. fr. lion a piece of an **e.**
Mat. 10 : 27. hear in the **e.** th. preach
26 : 51. smote off his **e.**, Mk. 14 : 47.
Lu. 12 : 3. wh. ye have spoken in **e.**
22 : 51. touched his **e.** and healed
Jn. 18 : 26. serv. whose **e.** Pe. cut off
1 Co. 2 : 9. not seen, nor **e.** heard
12 : 16. if **e.** say, Bec. I am not eye
Re. 2 : 7. that hath an **e.** let him hear,
11, 17, 29.–3 : 6, 13, 22.–13 : 9.

Give EAR.
Ex. 15 : 26. if wilt **g. e.** to his com.
De 1 : 45. L. would not **g. e.** unto
your voice, 2 Ch. 24 : 19. Ne. 9 : 30.
32 : 1. **g. e.** O heavens, I will sp.
Ju. 5 : 3. **g. e.** O ye princes [have kno.
Jb. 34 : 2. **g. e.** unto me, ye that
Ps. 5 : 1. **g. e.** to my words, 54 : 2.
17 : 1. **g. e.** unto my prayer, 55 : 1.–
39 : 12. **g. e.** to my cry, 141 : 1. [86 : 6.
49 : 1. **g. e.** all ye inhab., Joe. 1 : 2.
78 : 1. **g. e.** O peo. | 80 : 1. **g. e.** shep.
84 : 8. **g. e.** O God of Jacob
143 : 1. **g. e.** to my supplications
Is. 1 : 2. **g. e.** O earth, for L. hath
10. **g. e.** unto the law of our God
8 : 9. **g. e.** all ye of far countries
28 : 23. **g.** ye **e.** and hear [speech
32 : 9. careless dau-s **g. e.** to my
42 : 23. Who will **g. e.** to this?
51 : 4. **g. e.** unto me, O my nation
Je. 13 : 15. **g. e.** be not proud, the L.
Ho. 5 : 1. **g. e.** O house of king

Incline EAR.
Ps. 17 : 6. O G., **i.** thine **e.** unto me,
71 : 2.–88 : 2. Is. 37 : 17. Da. 9 : 18.
45 : 10. O daughter, **i.** thine **e.**
49 : 4. I will **i.** mine **e.** to parable
88 : 2. **i.** thine **e.** unto my cry
Pr. 2 : 2. that thou **i. e.** unto wisd.
4 : 20. my son, **i. e.** unto my say.
Is. 55 : 3. **i.** your **e.** and come

Right EAR.
Ex. 29 : 20. upon tip of **r. e.** of, Le.
8 : 23, 24.–14 : 14, 17, 25, 28.
Lu. 22 : 50. cut off **r. e.**, Jn. 18 : 10.

EAR, S. [of Corn]
Ge. 41 : 5. behold, 7 **e-s** came up, 22.
6. seven thin **e-s** blasted, 23, 27.
7. thin **e-s** devoured seven full
Ex. 9 : 31. for barley was in the **e.**
Le. 2 : 14. for meat offer. green **e-s**
23 : 14. nor eat green **e-s** until an
De. 23 : 25. mayest pluck the **e-s**
Ru. 2 : 2. let me glean **e-s** after him
2 K. 4 : 42. bro-t man of G. full **e-s**
Job 24 : 24. They are cut off as the
tops of the **e-s**
Is. 17 : 5. reapeth the **e-s** with arm
Mat. 12 : 1. disciples began to pluck
e-s of corn, Mk. 2 : 23. Lu. 6 : 1.
Mk. 4 : 28. **e.** the full corn in the **e.**

EARS. [chil.
Ge. 23 : † 10. Ephron ans. in **e.** of

Ge. 44 : 18. let speak in my lord's e.
50 : 4. speak, in the e. of Pharoah
Ex. 10 : 2. mayest tell in e. of son
17 : 14. rehearse it in e. of Joshua
Nu. 11 : † 1. it was evil in e. of L.
18. for you have wept in e. of L.
De. 31 : 30. M. spake in e. of cong.
Jos. 20 : 4. his cause in e. of elders
Ju. 9 : 2. e. of men of Shechem, 3.
1 S. 3:11. both e. of ev. one heareth tingle, 2 K. 21 : 12. Je. 19 : 3.
8 : 21. rehearsed them in e. of L.
18 : 23. servants spake in e. of Da.
25:†24. handmaid speak in thine e.
2 S. 3 : 19. spake in e. of Benjamin
7 : 22. accord. to all we have heard with e., 1 Ch. 17 : 20.
22 : 7. my cry did enter into his e.
Jb. 15:21. dreadf. sound is in his e.
28 : 22. heard fame with our e.
33 : 16. Then he openeth e. of men
Ps. 18 : 6. my cry came into his e.
34 : 15. e. are open unto their cry
44 : 1. We heard with our e. O G.
115:6. have e. but hear not, 135:17.
Pr.21:13. stoppeth e. at cry of poor
23 : 9. Speak not in the e. of a fool
26 : 17. taketh a dog by e. [e.
Is. 11:3. nei. reprove aft. hearing of
32 : 3. e. that hear shall hearken
33 : 15. stopp. his e. fr. hear. of bl.
35 : 5. e. of deaf sh. be unstopped
42:20. opening e. but he hear. not
43 : 8. bring deaf that have e.
Je. 2 : 2. Go cry in e. of Jerusalem
5 : 21. which have e. and hear not
29 : 29. Zeph. read in e. of Jere.
36 : 6. read them in e. of all Jud.
15. Sit now and read it in our e.
20. told all in e. of the king
21. Jehudi read it in e. of the k.
Mat. 28 : 14. if come to gov.'s e.
Mk. 7 : 33. he put fingers into his e.
35. straightway his e. were open.
8 : 18. having e. hear ye not?
Ac. 7 : 51. ye uncirc. in heart and e.
11:22. tidings came unto e. of ch-ch
17 : 20. bringest strange thi. to e.
Ro. 11:8. e. that they sho. not hear
2 Ti. 4 : 3. teachers, having itch. e.
Ja. 5 : 4. are entered into e. of L.
1 Pe. 3 : 12. his e. are open unto [prayers

EARS to hear.

De. 29 : 4. L. not given you e. t. h.
Eze. 12 : 2. have e. t. h., hear not
Mat. 11 : 15. He that hath e. t. h, let him hear, 13 : 9, 43. Mk. 4 : 9, 23.-7 : 16. Lu. 8 : 8.-14 : 35.

Mine EARS.

Nu. 14 : 28. as have spok. in m. e.
Ju. 17 : 2. silver speakest of in m. e.
1 S. 15 : 14. this bleating in m. e.?
2 K. 19 : 28. tumult into m. e., Is. 37 : 29. [prayer
2 Ch. 7 : 15. m. e. attent unto the
Jb. 33:† 8. thou hast spok. in m. e.
Ps. 40 : 6. m. e. hast thou opened
92 : 11. m. e. shall hear my desire
Is. 5 : 9. In m. e. said the Lord
22 : 14. revealed in m. e. by Lord
Eze. 8 : 18. tho. they cry in m. e.
9 : 1. He cried also in m. e.
Lu. 1 : 44. thy salutation in m. e.

EARS of the people.

Ex. 11 : 2. Speak now in the e. o. p.
De. 32 : 44. Moses spake in e. o. p.
Ju. 7 : 3. proclaim in the e. o. p.
1 S. 11:4. told tidings in the e. o. p.
2 K. 18 : 26. talk not in e. o. p., Is. [36:11.
Ne. 8 : 3. e. o. p. attentive
13 : † 1. day they read in e. o. p., Je. 28 : 7.-36 : 6, 10, 13, 14.

Their EARS.

Ge. 20 : 8. Abim. told these in t. e.
35 : 4. gave Jac. earrings in t. e.
Ex. 32 : 3. brake off earrings in t. e.
De. 31 : 28. speak words in t. e.
2 K. 23 : 2. he read in t. e. all the words, 2 Ch. 34 : 30. Je. 36 : 15.
Jb. 36:15. openeth t. e. in oppress.
Is. 6:10. t. e. heavy, lest they hear with t. e.. Mat. 13:15. Ac. 28:27.
Mi. 7 :16. nations, t. e. sh. be deaf
Zch. 7 : 11. stopped t. e., Ac. 7 : 57.
2 Ti. 4:4. sh. turn away t. e. fr. truth

Thine EARS.

1 S. 25:†24. let handm. speak in t. e.
2 Ch. 6 : 40. let t. e. be attent unto
Ps. 10 : 17. cause t. e. to hear [pray.
130:2. let t. e. be attentive to voice
Pr. 23 : 12. apply t. e. to knowl.
Is. 30 : 21. t. e. shall hear a word
49 : 20. chil. shall say in t. e.
Je. 28 : 7. hear word I speak in t. e.
Eze. 3 : 10. hear with t. e., 40 : 4.-
16 : 12. ear-rings in t. e. [44 : 5
23 : 25. they shall take away t. e.
24:26. to cause to hear with t. e.

Your EARS.

De. 5 : 1. hear statutes I speak in y. e.
Jb. 13 : 17. hear declara. with y. e.
Ps. 78 : 1. incline y. e. to the words
Je. 26 : 11. have heard with y. e.
15. L. sent me to speak in y. e.
Mat. 13 : 16. but blessed are y. e.
Lu. 4:21. this scrip. fulfilled in y. e.
9:44. Let these sayings sink in y. e.

EAR, ED.

De. 21:4. valley neither e-d nor sown
1 S. 8 : 12. k. set them to e. ground
Is. 30:24. oxen that e. the ground

EARING.

Ge. 45:6. sh. be neither e. nor harvest
Ex. 34 : 21. in e. time shalt rest

EARLY.

Ge. 19 : 2. ye shall rise e. and go
Ju. 7 : 3. fearful, let him depart e.
19:9. to morrow get you e. on way
2 K. 6:15. serv. of man of G. risen e.
Ps. 46 : 5. God shall help, right e.
57 : 8. I will awake e., 108 : 2.
63 : 1. my G., e. will I seek thee
78 : 34. they inquired e. after G.
90 : 14. satisfy us e. with thy mercy
101 : 8. I will e. destroy all wicked
Pr. 1 : 28. they shall seek me e.
8 : 17. that seek me e. sh. find me
Can. 7 : 12. get up e. to vineyards
Is. 26 : 9. with my spi. seek thee e.
Ho. 5 : 15. in afflict. will seek me e.
6 : 4. as the e. dew it goeth, 13 : 3.
Lu. 24 : 22. women e. at sepulchre
Jn. 18 : 28. led Jesus, and it was e.
20 : 1. first cometh Mary Mag., e.
Ja. 5 : 7. receive e. and latter rain
See AROSE, RISE, RISEN, RISING, ROSE, MORNING.

EARNEST. [Noun.]

2 Co. 1 : 22. given e. of Spirit, 5 : 5.
Ep. 1 : 14. e. of our inheritance

EARNEST. [Adj.]

Pr. 27 : † 6. kisses of enemy are e.
Ac. 12:†5. e. prayer unto G. for him
Ro. 8:19. e. expectation of creature
2 Co. 7 : 7. when he told e. desire
8 : 16. put same e. care into Titus
Ph. 1:20. Acc. to my e. expectation
He. 2:1. ought to give more e. heed

EARNESTLY.

Nu. 22 : 37. Did I not e. send
1 S. 20 : 6. Da. e. asked leave, 28.
Ne. 3 : 20. Baruch e. repaired piece
13 : † 6. I e. requested
Jb. 7 : 2. serv. e. desireth shadow
Je. 11:7. I e. protested unto fathers
31 : 20. I do e. remem. him still
Mi. 7 : 3. evil with both hands e.
Lu. 22 : 44. in agony he prayed e.
56. maid e. looked upon Peter
Ac. 3 : 12. why look ye so e. on us?
23 : 1. Paul e. beholding council
1 Co. 12 : 31. covet e. best gifts
2 Co. 5 : 2. we groan, e. desiring
Ja. 5 : 17. prayed e. it not rain
Jude 3. should e. contend for faith

EARNETH.

Hag. 1:6. e. wages, e. to put in bag

EARRING, S.

Ge. 24 : 22. man took a golden e.
30. when Laban saw e. on sister's
47. I put the e. upon her face
35 : 4. gave unto Jac. all their e.
Ex. 32 : 2. Break off golden e-s, 3.
35 : 22. bro-t e-s for their offerings
Nu. 31 : 50. bro-t e-s to make atone.
Ju. 8 : 24. give ev. man e-s of prey
Jb. 42 : 11. ev. one gave Job an e.
Pr. 25 : 12. As e. of gold, so a wise
Is. 3:20. t. L. will take away the e-s
Eze. 16 : 12. I put e-s in thine ears
Ho. 2 : 13. decked herself with her [e-s

EARTH.

Ge. 1 : 2. the e. was without form
10. God called the dry land e.
11. Let e. bring forth grass, 24.
12. e. brought forth grass and
28. replenish e. subdue it, 9 : 1.
6 : 11. e. was corrupt before God
13. the e. is filled with violence
7 : 17. ark was lifted above e.
8 : 14. in sec. month was e. dried
22. e. remain., seedtime not cease
9 : 11. nei. be flood to destr. the e.
13. token of cov. betw. me and e.
10:25. was the e. divided, 1 Ch. 1:19.
11 : 1. whole e. was of 1 language
18:18. nations of e. shall be blessed in him, 22:18.-26:4.-28:14.
26:15. stopped and filled th. with e.
27 : 28. God give thee fatness of e.
41:47. e. brought forth by handfuls
Ex. 8 : 22. I am L. in midst of e.
9 : 29. mayest know e. is L.'s, De. 10:14. Ps. 24:1. 1 Co. 10:26, 28.
10 : 5. cannot be able to see e.
15:12. stretchest hand, e. swallow.
20 : 24. altar of e. thou sh. make
Nu.16:30. if the e. open her mouth
32. e. opened her mouth and swallowed them up, 26 : 10. Ps. 106 : 17.
34. Lest e. swallow us also
De. 28 : 1. set thee above nat. of e.
23. e. under thee shall be iron
32 : 1. hear, O e. words of my
13. ride on high places of the e.
22. a fire shall consume the e.
1 S. 2 : 8. pillars of e. are Lord's
4:5. Isr. shouted, so that e. rang
14 : 15. trembled, and e. quaked
2 S. 1:2. with e. upon his head, 15:32.
22:8. then the e. shook, Ps. 18 : 7.
1 K. 1 : 40. so that the e. rent
2 K. 5 : 17. two mules' burden of e.
1 Ch. 16 : 31. let e. rejoice, Ps. 96 : 11.
33. bec. God cometh to judge the e., Ps. 96 : 13.-98 : 9.
Ezr. 5 : 11. of God of heaven and e.
Ne. 9 : 1. sackclothes and e. upon
6. hast made the e., Is. 45 : 12.
Jb. 5 : 25. offspring as grass of e.
9 : 6. shaketh e. out of her place
24. e. is given into hand of wick.
11 : 9. measure is longer than e.
12 : 15. waters they overturn the e.
15:19. Unto whom alone e. was giv.
16 : 18. O e. cover not my blood
18 : 4. sh. e. be forsaken for thee?
20 : 27. the e. sh. rise up ag. him
22 : 8. mighty man, he had the e.
24 : 4. poor of the e. hide thems.
26:7. he hangeth the e. upon noth.
28 : 5. out of the e. cometh bread
30 : 6. to dwell in caves of the e.
8. they were viler than the e.
34:13. Who giv. him charge over e.?
37 : 17. when he quieteth the e.
38 : 4. when I laid foundations of the e., Is. 24 : 18.-51 : 13, 16. Je. 31:37. Zch. 12 : 1. He. 1 : 10.
18. Hast perceived breadth of e.?

Ps. 2 : 8. give uttermost parts of e.
10. be instructed, ye judges of e.
10:18. man of e. no more oppress
12:6. as silver tried in furnace of e.
25 : 13. his seed sh. inherit the e.
33 : 5. e. is full of goodness of L.
14. looketh on all inbah. of e.
37:9. wait upon L. inherit e., 11.22.
46 : 2. not fear tho. e. be removed
6. uttered his voice, e. melted
47 : 9. shields of e. belong unto G.
48 : 2. joy of whole e. is Zion
60 : 2. hast made the e. tremble
63 : 9. sh. go into lower parts of e.
65 : 8. dwell in utterm. parts of e.
9. Thou visitest e. and waterest
67 : 6. e. yield increase, Eze. 34 : 27.
68 : 8. e. shook, heavens dropped
32. Sing unto G., kingdoms of e.
71 : 20. bring me fr. depths of e.
72:6. down as showers th. water e.
19. let whole e. be filled with
73 : 9. tongue walketh thro. the e.
74 : 12. working salv. in the e.
75 : 3. e. and all inhabi. are dissolved, Is. 24 : 19.
8. wicked of e. sh. wring them
76 : 8. e. feared | 77 : 18. trembled,
9. arose to save meek of e. ⌊97 : 4.
78 : 69. like e. wh. he hath establ.
82 : 8. Arise, O God, judge the e.
90 : 2. or ever hadst formed e.
94 : 2. Lift up thys. judge of the e.
97 : 1. L. reigneth, let e. rejoice
99 : 1. L. reigneth, let e. be moved
102 : 25. hast laid founda. of e.,
104 : 5. Pr. 8 : 29. Is. 48 : 13.
104 : 9. they turn not to cover e.
13. e. is satisfied with fruit of thy
24. O L., e. is full of thy riches
114 : 7. Tremble, O e. at pres. of L.
115 : 16. e. hath he given to chil.
119:64. e. O L., is full of thy mercy
90. hast established the e.
147 : 8. who prepareth rain for e.
148 : 13. his glory is above e.
Pr. 8:19. L. founded the e., Is. 24 : 1.
8:23. I was fr. everl., or ever e. was
26. as yet he had not made e.
10 : 30. wick. shall not inhab. e.
25 : 3. e. for depth is unsearchable
30 : 14. devour poor from off the e.
16. e. not filled with water
21. For 3 things e. is disquieted
Ec. 1 : 4. the e. abideth for ever
5 : 9. profit of the e. is for all
Is. 4 : 2. fruit of e. be excellent
5 : 8. be placed alone in the e.
6 : 3. whole e. is full of his glory
11 : 4. smiteth e. with his mouth
9. e. shall be full of knowl. of L.
13 : 13. e. sh. remove out of her pl.
14 : 7. The whole e. is at rest
9. even all chief ones of the e.
16. this the man made e. tremb.?
24 : 1. Lord maketh the e. empty
4. The e. mourneth, 33 : 9. ⌈tants
5. e. is defiled under the inhabi-
6. hath the curse devoured e.
19. e. is broken, e. is dissolved
20. e. reel | 26:19. e. cast out dead
26:21. e. shall disclose blood
34 : 1. let e. hear, and all therein
40:22. th. sitteth upon circle of e.
28. Creator of the ends of the e.
42 : 5. he that spread forth e.
44 : 24. spread abroad e. by myself
45 : 8. let skies pour, e. open
12. I have made e., Je. 27 : 5.
18. God that formed the e.
22. be ye saved all ends of the e.
49 : 8. cov. of people to establ. e.
13. and be joyful, O e.
51 : 6. look upon e., e. sh. wax old
54 : 5. G. of whole e. he be called,
Mi. 4 : 13. Zch. 4 : 14.
9. waters no more go over e.

Is. 55 : 10. watereth e. and maketh
61 : 11. as e. bringeth forth bud
66 : 1. saith L., e. is my footstool
8. e. bring forth in one day?
Je. 4:23. I beheld e. it without form
28. For this shall the e. mourn
6 : 19. Hear, O e., I will bring evil
10 : 10. at his wrath e. sh. tremble
22 : 29. O e. e. e. hear, Mi. 1 : 2.
26 : 6. a curse to nations of e.
33 : 9. an honour bef. nations of e.
46 : 8. I will go up and cover e.
49 : 21. e. is mov. at noise, 50 : 46.
51 : 15. made e. by his power
La. 2 : 15. The joy of the whole e.
Eze. 7 : 21. give it to wicked of e.
9 : 9. The Lord hath forsaken e.
34 : 27. e. shall yield her increase
35 : 14. When whole e. rejoiceth
43 : 2. e. shined with his glory
Da. 7 : 23. shall devour the whole e.
Ho. 2 : 21. heavens shall hear the e.
22. e. shall hear corn and wine
Jo. 2 : 10. e. shall quake bef. them
Am. 8 : 9. I will darken e. in clear
Jon. 2 : 6. e. with bars was ab. me
Mi. 6 : 2. hear, ye foundations of e.
7 : 17. they like worms of the e.
Na. 1 : 5. e. is burned at his pres.
Ha. 2:14. e. filled with knowl. of L.
3 : 3. e. was full of his praise
6. He stood and measured e.
9. didst cleave e. with rivers
Hag. 1 : 10. e. is stayed from fruit
Zch. 1 : 10. to walk to and fro thro.
e., 11.-4 : 10.-6 : 7.
4 : 10. eyes of L. run thro. the e.
Mal. 4 : 7. lest I smite e. with curse
Mat. 5 : 5. meek they shall inherit
13. Ye are the salt of the e. ⌊e.
35. swear not by e. for it is God's
12 : 40. three nights in heart of e.
42. uttermost parts of the e., Mk.
13 : 27. Lu. 11 : 31. Ac. 1 : 8.
13 : 5. had not much e., Mk. 4 : 5.
24 : 30. all tribes of e. mourn
27 : 51. the e. did quake
Mk. 4 : 28. e. bringeth forth fruit
Jn. 3 : 31. he that is of the e. is
earthly and speaketh of the e.
Ac. 3 : 25. in thy seed all e. be
4 : 26. kings of e. stood ⌊blessed
10 : 12. fourfoot. beasts of e., 11:6.
1 Co. 15 : 47. first man of e. earthy
Ep. 4:9. desc. into lower parts of e.
2 Ti. 2 : 20. vessels of wood and e.
He. 6 : 7. e. which drinketh in rain
11 : 38. in dens and caves of e.
12 : 26. Whose voice shook the e.
Ja. 5 : 7. for precious fruit of e.
18. e. brought forth her fruit
2 Pe. 3 : 5. e. standing out of water
3 : 10. e. and works sh. be burned
Re. 6 : 8. over fourth part of e.
7 : 1. angels on 4 corners of e.
3. Hurt not e. nor sea, 2.
9 : 4. not hurt grass of e.
11 : 4. olive trees bef. God of the e.
6. have power to smite the e.
18. destroy them which destr. e.
12 : 16. e. opened and swallowed
13 : 12. causeth e. to worsh. beast
14 : 15. harvest of the e. is ripe
18. gather of the vine of e.
17 : 5. harlots and abom. of e.
18 : 1. e. was lightened with glory
11. merchants of e. shall weep
23. thy merch-ts great men of e.
19 : 2. whore, which did corrupt e.
20 : 8. deceive nations in 4 quar.
9. upon breadth of e. ⌊of e.
11. from whose face the e. fled
See BEASTS, DUST, ENDS, FACE, KINGS, HEAVEN, PEOPLE, WHOLE.

All the EARTH.

Ge. 1 : 26. have dominion over a. e.
Ge. 7:3. to keep seed alive upon a. e.
11 : 9. confound language of a. e.
18 : 25. not Judge of a. e. do right
19:31. unto us aft. manner of a. e.
Ex. 9 : 14. is none like me in a. e.
16. my name thro. a. e., Ro. 9 : 17.
19 : 5. treasure ; for a. e. is mine
34 : 10. not been done in a. e.
Nu. 14:21. a. e. be filled with glory
Jos. 3 : 11. L. of a. e., 13. Zch. 6:5.
23 : 14. going way of a. e., 1 K. 2:2.
Ju. 6 : 37. if it be dry upon a. e.
1 S. 17 : 46. a. e. may kn. is a G.
30 : 16. upon a. e. eating and
1 K. 10 : 24. a. e. sought to Solomon
2 K. 5:15. no G. in a. e. but in Isr.
1 Ch. 16 : 14. his judgm. are in a.
e., Ps. 105 : 7.
23. Sing unto L. a. e., Ps. 96 : 1.
30. Fear before him a. e., Ps. 33 :
8.-96 : 9. ⌈a. e., 9.
Ps 8 : 1. excellent is thy name in
19 : 4. line gone out thro. a. e.
45 : 16. make princes in a. e.
47 : 2. L. k. over a. e., 7. Zch. 14:9.
57 : 5. let thy glory be above a. e.,
11.-108 : 5. ⌈98 : 4.-100:†1.
66 : † 1. Make a joyful noise a. e.,
4. a. e. shall worship thee
83 : 18. Most High over a. e., 97:9.
Is. 10 : 14. so have I gathered a. e.
12:5. excellent things, kn. in a. e.
25 : 8. rebuke of people, from a. e.
Je. 26 : 6. this city a curse to a. e.
33 : 9. be an honour bef. a. e.
51 : 7. cup, made a. e. drunken
25. O mount. wh. destroyest a. e.
49. at Bab. sh. fall slain of a. e.
Da. 2 : 39. a kingd. rule over a. e.
4 : 1. peo. th. dwell in a. e., 6 : 25.
11. sight to end of a. e., 20.
Ha. 2 : 20. let a. e. keep silence
Zph. 3 : 8. a. e. shall be devoured
Zch. 1 : 11. a. e. sitteth still and
5 : 6. resemblance through a. e.
Lu. 23 : 44. was darkness over a. e.
Ro. 10 : 18. sound went into a. e.
Re. 5 : 6. Spirits of G. sent into a. e.

From the EARTH.

Ge. 2 : 6. went up a mist f. e.
4 : 11. now art thou cursed f. e.
6 : † 13. I will destroy them f. e.
7 : 23. they were destroyed f. e.
8 : 11. waters were abated f. e.
Ex. 9:15. shalt be cut off f. e., Jos.
7 : 9. Ps. 109 : 15. Pr. 2:22. Na.
1 S. 28 : 13. Saul arose f. e. ⌊2:13.
2 S. 4 : 11. shall I not take you f. e.
12 : 17. went to raise him f. e.
20. David arose f. e. and washed
Jb. 18 : 17. His remem. perish f. e.
Ps. 21 : 10. destroy their fruit f. e.
34:16. cut off remem. of them f. e.
148 : 7. Praise L. f. e. ye dragons
Pr. 30 : 14. to devour poor f. e.
Je. 10 : 11. they sh. perish f. e. ⌈21.
Eze. 1 : 19. living creatures up f. e.,
10 : 16. wings to mount f. e., 19.
Da. 7 : 4. and it was lifted up f. e.
Am. 3 : 5. one take up a snare f. e.
Jn. 12 : 32. if I be lifted up f. e.
Ac. 8 : 33. for his life is taken f. e.
9 : 8. Saul arose f. e. saw no man
22 : 22. Away with such fellow f. e.
Re. 6 : 4. power giv. to take peace f.
14 : 3. 144,000 redeemed f. e. ⌊e.

In or into the EARTH.

Ge. 1 : 22. let fowl multiply i. e.
4 : 12. vagabond thou be i. e., 14.
6 : 5. wickedn. of man great i. e.
17. every thing i. e. shall die
10 : 8. Nimrod a mighty one i. e.
19 : 31. not a man i. e. to come in
45:7. preserve you a posterity i. e.
Ex. 20 : 4. is i. e. beneath, De. 5:8.
Jos. 7 : 21. they are hid i. e. ⌈i. e.
Ju. 18 : 10. no want of any thing is

2 S. 7 : 9. like name of great men i.
e., 1 Ch. 17 : 8. [Ch. 17 : 21.
23. what nation i. e. like Isr.? 1
14 : 20. to know all things i. e.
1 Ch. 29 : 11. all that is i. e. thine
2 Ch. 6 : 14. is no God like thee i. e.
Jb. 1 : 7. going to and fro i. e., 2:2.
8. is none like Job i. e., 2 : 3.
14 : 8. Though root wax old i. e.
24 : 18. their portion is cursed i. e.
38 : 33. canst set dominion i. e.?
39 : 14. ostrich, leaveth eggs i. e.
Ps. 16 : 3. to saints that are i. e.
46 : 8. desola. he hath made i. e.
10. be still, I will be exalted i. e.
58:11. he is a God th. judgeth i. e.
72 : 16. be a handful of corn i. e.
119 : 19. I am a stranger i. e. [e.
140:11. not evil speaker be estab. i.
Pr. 11 : 31. righte. be recomp. i. e.
Is 26 : 9. thy judgments are i. e.
18. not wrought deliverance i. e.
40 : 24. stock sh. not take root i. e.
42 : 4. till he have set judgm. i. e.
62:7. till he make Jerus. praise i. e.
65 : 16. who blesseth himself i. e.
and that sweareth i. e.
Je. 14 : 4. There was no rain i. e.
17:13. forsake thee, be written i. e.
23:5. exec. judgment and just. i. e.
31 : 22. L. created a new thing i. e.
Da. 4 : 15. leave stump i. e., 23.
Ho. 2 : 23. sow her unto me i. e.
Jo. 2 : 30. will shew wonders i. e.
Am. 5 : 7. who leave off righte. i. e.
Mat. 6 : 10. Thy will be done i. e.,
Lu. 11 : 2. [money
25 : 18. digged i. e. and hid lord's
25. afraid, hid thy talent i. e.
Mk. 4 : 31. mustard seed, sown i. e.
less than all seeds i. e.
Ac. 2 : 19. signs i. e. beneath
Ph. 2 : 10. things i. e., Col. 1 : 20.
1 Jn. 5:8. three that bear witn. i. e.
Re. 8 : 5. censer and cast it i-o e.
12 : 9. Satan was cast out i-o e.
14 : 19. thrust sickle i-o e.

On or upon the EARTH.

Ge. 6 : 6. repented L. he had made
man o. e. [rupt
12. God looked u. e. it was cor-
7 : 4. cause it to rain u. e. 40 days
12. the rain was u. e. 40 days, 17.
8:17. be fruitful and multiply u. e.
9 : 2. upon all that moveth u. e.
19:23. sun was risen u. e. when Lot
28 : 12. behold a ladder set up o. e.
Ex. 10 : 6. since they were u. e.
Le. 11 : 29. creep u. e., 42, 44. [19.
De. 4 : 10. days they live u. e., 12:1,
36. u. e. he shewed great fire
12 : 16. ye shall pour it u. e., 24.
2 S. 12 : 16. Da. lay all night u. e.
14 : 7. not leave name u. e. [6:18.
1 K. 8 : 27. will G. dwell o. e.? 2 Ch.
17 : 14. until L. sends rain u. e.
1 Ch. 29 : 15. our days o. e. as a
shadow, Jb. 8:9. [to man u. e.
Jb. 7:1. Is there not appointed time
19:25. stand at the latter day u. e.
20 : 4. since man was placed u. e.
37 : 6. saith to snow, Be thou o. e.
41 : 33. u. e. there is not his like
Ps. 7 : 5. let ene. tread my life u. e.
41 : 2. and he shall be blessed u. e.
67 : 2. Th. thy way be known u. e.
73:25. is none u. e. I desire besides
112 : 2. His seed be mighty u. e.
Pr. 30 : 24. four things little u. e.
Ec. 7:20. is not just man u. e. [e.
10 : 7. princes walking as serv-ts u.
11 : 2. not what evil be done u. e.
3. the clouds empty thems. u. e.
Can. 2 : 12. flowers appear o. e.
Is. 28 : 22. a consumption u. e.
51 : 6. lift up eyes, and look u. e.
Je. 9 : 3. not valiant for truth u. e.

La. 2 : 11. my liver is poured u. e.
Da. 2:10. not a man u. e. can shew
the matter [e.
Am. 3 : 5. Can bird fall in snare u.
9 : 9. shall not least grain fall u. e.
Mat. 6:19. Lay not up treasures u. e.
9 : 6. Son hath power o. e. to forgive, Mk. 2 : 10. Lu. 5 : 24.
10:34. not come to send peace o. e.
16 : 19. whatso. bind o. e., 18 : 18.
18:19. if two of you shall agree o. e.
23 : 9. call no man your fa. u. e.
35. all righte. blood shed u. e.
Mk. 9 : 3. as no fuller o. e. can
Lu. 2 : 14. Glory to God, o. e. peace
6:49. man that built a house u. e.
12:49. I am come to send fire o. e.
51. I am come to give peace o. e.?
18 : 8. shall he find faith o. e.?
21 : 25. u. e. distress of nations
26. things which are coming o. e.
Jn. 17 : 4. I have glorified thee o. e.
Ro. 9 : 28. short work L. make u. e.
Ep. 6 : 3. mayest live long o. e. [e.
Col. 3 : 2. affection not on things o.
5. mortify members wh. are u. e.
He. 8:4. if o. e. should not be priest
11 : 13. confes. were strangers o. e.
12:25. refused him that spake o. e.
Ja. 5:5. have lived in pleasure o. e.
17. it rained not o. e. for 3 years
Re. 3 : 10. try them dwell u. e. [e.
5 : 10. k-s, priests, we sh. reign o.
6 : 10. avenge bl. on them dwell o.
7 : 1. that wind not blow o. e. [e.
8 : 7. and they were cast u. e.
9 : 3. smoke of locusts u. e.
10 : 2. set his left foot u. e.
8. of angel wh. standeth u. e., 5.
11 : 10. they that dwell u. e., 13 :
8, 14.-14 : 6.-17 : 8.
14 : 16. thrust in sickle o. e.
16 : 1. pour vials of wrath u. e.
2. first poured out his vial u. e.
18 : 24. blood of all slain u. e.

Out of the EARTH.

1 S. 28 : 13. gods ascend. o. o. e.
2 S. 23 : 4. grass springing o. o. e.
Jb. 8 : 19. o. o. e. sh. others grow
28 : 2. Iron is taken o. o. e. and
5. for e., o. o. it cometh bread
Ps. 85 : 11. Truth sh. spring o. o. e.
104 : 14. he may bring food o. o. e.
35. Let sinners be consum. o. o. e.
Da. 7:17. four kings, sh. arise o. o. e.
Ho. 2 : 18. break the battle o. o. e.
Mi. 7 : 2. good man is perish. o. o. e.
Re. 13 : 11. beast coming up o. o. e.

To, or, unto the EARTH.

Ge. 24 : 52. he worship. bowing t. e.
37 : 10. to bow ours. to thee, t. e.?
42 : 6. bowed thems. t. e., 43 : 26.
48 : 12. he bowed with his face t. e.
Jos. 5 : 14. Joshua fell t. e., 7 : 6.
1 S. 5 : 3. Dagon upon his face t. e.
17 : 49. Goliath fell upon face t. e.
24 : 8. Da. stooped with face t. e.
25 : 41. she bowed t. e., 1 K. 1:31.
26 : 8. let me smite him t. e.
20. let not my blood fall t. e.
2 S. 1 : 2. came to Da. he fell t. e.
14:11. not hair fall t. e., 1 K. 1:52.
18:28. fell t. e. upon his face [of L.
2 K. 10 : 10. fall u. e. noth. of word
2 Ch. 20 : 24. dead bodies fallen t. e.
Jb. 12 : 8. speak t. e. it shall teach
Ps. 17 : 11. set eyes, bowing t. e.
44 : 25. our belly cleaveth u. e.
50 : 4. sh. call t. e, that he judge
146:4. breath goeth, he retur. t. e.
Ec. 3 : 21. spirit of beast goeth t. e.
12 : 7. Then shall dust return t. e.
Is. 8 : 22. they shall look u. e.
28 : 2. cast down t. e. with hand
63 : 6. I will bring down their
strength t. e. [whole e.
Je. 15 : 10. a man of contention t.

La. 2 : 1. cast from heaven u. e.
Ho. 6:3. latter and former rain u. e.
Lu. 24 : 5. bowed their faces t. e.
Ac. 9 : 4. Saul fell t. e. and heard
10 : 11. great sheet, let down t. e.
26 : 14. we were all fallen t. e.
Re. 6 : 13. stars of heaven fell u. e.
12:4. drew stars, did not cast th. t. e.
13. dragon saw he was cast u. e.

EARTHEN.

Le. 6 : 28. e. vessel wherein sodden
11:33. e. vessel whereinto any fall.
14 : 5. birds killed in e. vessel, 50.
Nu. 5 : 17. holy water in e. vessel
2 S. 17:28. Brought beds, e. vessels
Je. 19 : 1. get a potter's e. bottle
32 : 14. put evidences in e. vessel
La. 4 : 2. esteemed as e. pitchers
2 Co. 4:7. this treasure in e. vessels

EARTHLY. [things

Jn. 3 : 12. If I have told you e.
31. he that is of the earth is e.
2 Co. 5:1. if our e. house of tabern.
Ph. 3:19. walk, who mind e. things
Ja. 3 : 15. this wisdom is e., sensual

EARTHQUAKE, S.

1 K. 19 : 11. an e.; L. was not in e.
12. after e. a fire, L. not in fire
Is. 29 : 6. shalt be visited with e.
Am. 1:1. he saw two years before e.
Zch. 14 : 5. as ye fled from bef. e.
Mat. 24 : 7. shall be e-s in divers
places, Mk. 13 : 8. Lu. 21 : 11.
27 : 54. when centurion saw the e.
28:2. was great e. angel of L. came,
Ac. 16 : 26. Re. 6 : 12.-11 : 13.
Re. 8 : 5. thunderings and e., 11:19.
16 : 18. a great e. so mighty an e.

EARTHY.

1 Co. 15 : 47. first man is of earth e.
48. As is e. such are they th. are e.
49. as we have borne image of e.

EASE. [Noun.]

De. 28 : 65. am. nations find no e.
Ju. 20 : 43. trod Benjamites with e.
Jb. 12:5. thought of him th. is at e.
16:12. I was at e. | 21:23. dieth at e.
Ps. 25 : 13. His soul shall dwell at e.
123 : 4. scorning of those at e.
Pr. 1 : † 32. e. of simple slay them
Is. 32 : 9. rise up, ye women at e.
11. tremble, ye women at e.
Je. 46:27. Jac. shall return, be at e.
48 : 11. Moab been at e. fr. youth
49:†31. up unto nation th. is at e.
Eze. 23 : 42. a voice of a mult. at e.
Am. 6 : 1. Woe to them at e. in Z.
Zch. 1 : 15. displeased with heath.
Lu. 12 : 19. take thine e. eat [at e.

EASE, ED.

De. 23 : 13. when wilt e. thyself
2 Ch. 10 : 4. e. thou the yoke, 9.
Jb. 7 : 13. couch e. my complaint
16 : 6. I forbear, what am I e.?
Is 1 : 24. I will e. me of adversa.
38 : † 14. O L. I am oppr. e. me
2 Co. 8 : 13. other men be e. and ye

EASEMENT.

Ju. 3 : † 24. doeth his e. in summer

EASIER. [cham.

Ex. 18 : 22. so it be e. for thyself
Mat. 9:5. whe. is e. to say, thy sins
forgiv., Mk. 2 : 9. Lu. 5 : 23.
19 : 24. it is e. for a camel to go
thro. eye, Mk. 10:25. Lu. 18:25.
Lu. 16:17. it is e. for heaven to pass

EASILY. [voked

1 Co. 13 : 5. charity is not e. pro-
He. 12 : 1. sin which doth so e. be-

EAST. [Noun.] [set us

Ge. 3 : 24. at e. of garden, cherubim
4 : 16. Cain in Nod on e. of Eden
10 : 30. Sephar, a mount of the e.
11 :2. journeyed fr. e., found plain
12:8. Abram removed unto a mt. on
e. of Beth-el, Hai on e. [ed e.
13 : 11. Lot chose plain; journey-

Ge. 28 : 14. sh. spread to west and e.
29 : 1. Jacob into laud of peo. of e.
Nu. 3 :38. those that encamp tow. e.
23 : 7. Balak brought me out of e.
Jos. 11 : 3. sent to Canaanite on e.
12 : 1. Israel possessed plain on e.
3. from plain to Chinneroth on e.,
even salt sea on e. ⌈the e.
16 : 1. unto the water of Jericho on
6 border passed on e. to Janohah
17 : 10. they met in Issachar on e.
18 : 7. inherit-e beyond Jord. on e.
19 :13. border passeth on e. to Gitt.
Ju. 6:3. the children of the e. came
against them, 33.-7 : 12 ⌈e.
8 : 10. all left of hosts of chil. of the
11. dwelt in tents on e. of Nobah
1 K. 7 : 25. twelve oxen, three looking toward the e., 2 Ch. 4 : 4.
1 Ch. 9 : 24. porters toward e., west
12 :15. put to flight them toward e.
2 Ch. 31 : 14. Kore, porter toward e.
Ne. 3 : 36. water gate toward the e.
Jb. 1 : 3. greatest of all men of the e.
Ps 75 :6. promotion nei from e. nor
103 : 12. As far as e. is from west
107 : 3. he gathered them from e.
Is. 2 : 6. bec. replenished from the e.
11 : 14. spoil them of e., Je. 49 :28.
41 : 2. raised righteous man from e.
43 : 5. I will bring thy seed from e.
46 : 11. Calling ravenous bird fr. e.
Je. 31 : 40. unto horse gate tow. e.
Eze. 8 : 16. 25 men, faces toward e.;
worshipped sun toward e.⌈e., 10.
25 : 4. I will deliver thee to men of
39 : 11. unto Gog valley on e. of sea
40 : 6. unto the gate which looketh
toward the e., 22, 23.-42 : 15.-
43 : 1, 4.-44 : 1.-46 : 1, 12. ⌈e.
32. bro-t me into inner court tow.
41 : 14. separate place toward the e.
42 : 10. in wall of court tow. e., 12.
43 : 2. glory of God came fr. the e.
17. his stairs shall look toward e.
47 : 1. forefront of house toward e.
8. waters issue toward the e.
48 : 10. toward e. 10,000 in breadth
17. suburbs of city toward e., 250
Da. 8 : 9. horn waxed great tow. e.
11:44. tidings out of e. sh. trouble
Am. 8:12. sh. wander fr. north to e.
Zch. 14 : 4. mount of Olives before
Jerus. on the e.; sh. cleave tow. e.
Mat. 2:1. wise men from e. to Jerus.
2. we have seen his star in e., 9.
8 : 11. many come fr. e., west, Lu.
24:27. as lightning out of e.⌊13 :29
Re. 7 : 2. ano. angel ascending fr. e.
16 : 12. way of kings of e. prepared
21 : 13. On e. three gates, on north

EAST. (Adj) ⌈Gilead
1 Ch. 5 : 10. dwelt thro-t e. land of
2 Ch. 29 : 4. Levites into the e. street
Eze. 47 : 18. measure unto the e. sea
48 : 1. these his sides, e. and west
Jo. 2 : 20. will drive him tow. e. sea

EAST end. ⌈e.e.
2 Ch. 4 : 10. set sea on right side of
5 : 12. Levites stood at e.e. of altar

EAST gate.
Ne. 3:29. Shemaiah keeper of e. g.
Je. 19 : 2. valley of Hinnom by e. g.
Eze. 10 : 19. every one stood at e. g.
11 : 1. spirit brought me unto e. g.
40:44. one at e. g. having prospect

EAST part, s. ⌈ashes
Le. 1 : 16. crop, cast it on e. p. by
Nu. 10 : 5. alarm, camps on e. p-s
See **East SIDE, East WIND.**

EASTER. ⌈him
Ac. 12 :4. intending after E. to bring

EASTWARD. ⌈Eden
Ge. 2 : 8. God planted garden e. in
13:14. lift thine eyes e., De. 3 : 27.
Lev. 16:14. finger up. Mercy Seat e.
See Cubits, side.

EASY. ⌈unders.
Pr. 14 : 6. knowl. e. unto him that
Mat. 11 : 30. my yoke is e. my bur.
1 Co. 14:9. words e. to be understood
Ja. 3 : 17. wisd. is e. to be entreated

EAT.
Ge. 2 : 16. of ev. tree mayest e., 3:2.
3 : 5. in day ye e. eyes be opened
6. Eve did e. | 12. I did e., 13.
14. dust shalt thou e. all thy life
17. in sorrow shalt thou e. all thy
18. thou shalt e. herb of field ⌊life
22. take of tree of life and e.
18 : 8. angels, they did e., 19 : 3.
27 : 4. savoury meat, that I may e.,
19. e. of my venison, 25, 31. ⌊7, 10.
31 : 46. and they did e. there
40 : 17. birds did e. them out of
43 : † 16. these men sh. e. with me
32. Egyptians did e. by thems.
Ex. 10 : 5. locusts shall e. ev. tree
12. locusts may e. ev. herb, 15.
12 : 8. with bitter herbs shall e. it
16. no work, save that ev. man e.
43. no stranger sh. e., 48. Le. 22:13.
44. when circumc., then shall he e.
16 : 25. e. that to day, to day is a
35. chil. of Isr. did e. manna 40 y-s
until came, Jn. 6 : 31, 49, 58.
23 : 11. that poor of people may e.
29 : 32. Aaron and sons shall e.,
Le. 6 : 16.-8 : 31.-24 : 9.
34 : 15. and thou e. of his sacrifice
Le. 6 : 18. males shall e. it, 29.-7 : 6.
Nu. 18 : 10. ⌈shall e. it
26. priest that offereth it for sin
7 : 19. all clean shall e., Nu. 18 : 11.
24. but ye shall in no wise e. of it
10 : 12. e. it without leaven
11:21. these ye may e., 22. De. 14:20.
25 : 20. What shall we e. 7th year
26 : 16. sow in vain, enemies e. it
Nu. 11 : 5. remember fish we did e.
13. Give us flesh, we may e., 21.
23 : 24. not lie down until he e. of
25 : 2. peo. did e. of their sacrifices
De. 2 : 6. buy meat that ye may e.
12 : 15. e. in thy gates, 21.-15 : 22.
-26 : 12. ⌈22.-15 : 22.
15. the unclean and clean may e.,
18. must e. bef. L., 14 : 26. 15:20.
20. I will e. flesh, mayest e. flesh
27. and thou shalt e. the flesh
14:21. give unto stranger th. he e.
20 : 6. lest he die, and ano. e. of it
23 : 24. then thou mayest e. grapes
28 : 39. grapes, for worms sh. e. th.
53. e. fruit of own body, La. 2:20.
32 : 38. did e. fat of sacrifices
Jos. 5 : 11. they did e. of old corn
24 : 13. of vineyards and oliveyards
ye planted not, do ye e.
Ju. 13:7. nei e. any uncl. thing, 14.
19:8. they tarried, and did e. ⌈sad
1 S. 1 : 18 Hannah did e. no more
9:13. afterwards they e. that bidden
14 : 34. e. and sin not ag. Lord
20:34. Jona did e. no meat sec. day
28 : 22. e. that thou have strength
2 S 9 : 11. e. at my table, 1 K. 2:7.
12 : 3. it did e. of his own meat
13 : 6. I may e. at her hand, 5, 10.
19 : 28. did e. at thine own table
1 K. 14 : 11. dieth of Jerob. sh. dogs
e., 16 : 4.-21 : 23. 2 K. 9 : 10, 36.
17 : 12 that we may e. and die
15. she and he did e. many days
18 : 19. wh. e. at Jezebel's table
19 : 5. the angel said, Arise and e.,
7. Ac. 10 : 13.-11 : 7.
2 K. 4 : 43. they shall e. and leave
44. they did e. and left thereof
6 : 28. said, Give thy son that we e.
him, we will e. my son to-mor.
29. we boiled my son. did e. him
18:31. e. ev. man of vine, Is. 36:16.
2 Ch. 30 : 18. did e. passover
Ezr. 6 : 21. children of Israel did e.
Ne. 5 : 2. take up corn, that we e.
9 : 25. did e. were filled, Ps. 78:29.
Jb. 3 : 24. my sighing cometh bef.
31:8. let me sow, another e. ⌊I e.
Ps. 22 : 26. meek sh. e. be satisfied
22:29. All they that be fat shall e.
50 : 13. will I e. the flesh of bulls
78 : 25. man did e. angels' food
128:2. shalt e. labour of thine ha.
Pr. 1 : 31. e. fruit of own way, Is.
3 : 10. ⌈violence
13 : 2. soul of transgressors sh. e.
18 : 21. that love it sh. e. the fruit
24 : 13. My son e. thou honey
27:18. keepeth fig tree shall e. fruit
30 : 17. eye, young eagles sh. e. it
Ec. 2 : 25. who can e. more than I?
5 : 11. increased that e. them
12. sleep sweet, whe. he e. little
10 : 16. princes e. in the morning
17. when princes e. in due season
Can. 4 : †1. of goats that e. of Gilead
16. come into his garden e. fruits
Is. 4 : 1. We will e. our own bread
5 : 17. waste places sh. strangers e.
7 : 15. Butter and honey sh. he e.
22. Butter and honey sh. eve. one e.
9 : 20. e. on left hand, e. flesh of
11 : 7. lion shall e. straw, 65 : 25.
30:24. asses sh. e. clean provender
37 : 30. sow, plant vineyards, e.
the fruit, 65 : 21. Je. 29 : 5, 28.
Am. 9 : 14.
51 : 8. worm sh. e. them like wool
55 : 1. come ye, buy and e. yea
2. hearken unto me, e. that good
62 : 9. They th. gathered sh. e. it
65 : 4. a peo. which e. swine's flesh
13. my serv-ts sh. e. ye be hungry
22. they shall not plant and ano. e.
Je. 15:16. Thy words found, I did e.
19:9. shall e. flesh of friend in siege
31 : 5. plant and e. as common
Eze. 2 : 8. open thy mouth and e.
3 : 1. e. that thou findest, e. roll
4:10. e. by weight | 5:10. fa-s e. sons
16 : 13. thou didst e. fine flour
22 : 9. they e. upon the mountains
34 : 3. ye e. fat, clothe with wool
19. e. that trodden with feet
42 : 13. shall e. most holy things
Da. 1 : 13. that e. of king's meat, 15.
4 : 33. Neb. did e. grass as oxen
Ho. 4 : 10. they sh. e. and not have
enough, Mi. 6 : 14. Hag. 1 : 6.
9 : 3. they shall e. unclean things
4. that e. thereof sh. be polluted
Am. 6 : 4. that e. lambs of flock
Mi. 3 : 3. who e. flesh of my people
Zch. 11 : 9. rest e. one flesh of ano.
16. he shall e. the flesh of the fat
Mat. 12 : 4. how Da. did e. shew-br.
14 : 20. did all e. and were filled,
15 : 37. Mk. 6:42 -8:8. Lu. 9:17.
15:27. dogs e. of crumbs, Mk. 7:28.
38. they that did e. were 4,000.
26 : 21. And as they did e. he said,
Mk. 14 : 18, 22.
26. Jesus said, Take e., this is my
body, Mk. 14 : 22. 1 Co. 11 : 24.
Mk. 2:16. saw him e. with publicans
6:44. that did e. were above 5,000
11 : 14. No man e. fruit of thee
14 : 12. that thou mayest e. passover? 14. Lu. 22:8, 11. Jn. 18:28.
Lu. 6 : 1. and did e. rubbing them
7 : 36. desired he would e. with him
10 : 8. e. such things as are before
15 : 16. husks that swine did e.
23. killed fatted calf, let us e.
17 : 27. they did e. they drank
24 : 43. he did e. before them
Jn. 4 : 31. disci., saying, Master e.
6 : 26. bec. ye did e. of loaves and
50. th. a man may e. and not die
53. Exc. ye e. flesh of Son of man

Ac. 2 : 46. did e. meat with gladn.
11 : 3. thou didst e. with them
23 : 14. e. nothing until have slain Paul.
Ro. 14 : 2. believeth he may e. all.
23. doubteth is damned if he e.
1 Co. 8 : 7. for some e. it as a thing offered unto an idol
8. nei. if e. are we better, if e. not
13. I will e. no flesh while world
10 : 3. all e. same spiritual meat
18. who e. of sacrifices, partakers
25. whatso. sold in shambles, e.
27. e. asking no question for cons.
11 : 34. if any hunger, e. at home
2 Th. 3 : 10. if any work not, nei. e.
2 Ti. 2 : 17. word will e. as canker
Ja. 5 : 3. shall e. your flesh as fire
Re. 17:16. sh. e. her flesh, and burn
19:18. That ye may e. flesh of kings
See BLOOD, BREAD, FAT.

Did EAT.

Ge. 3: 6. Eve gave to husb. he d. e.
25 : 28. bec. he d. e. of his venison
27:25. brought it to Isaac, he d. e.
39 : 6. aught save bread he d. e.
1 S. 30:11. gave Egyp. bread he d. e.
2 S. 9 : 13. he d. e. at his table
12 : 20. set bread bef. him, he d. e.
Mk. 1 : 6. John d. e. locusts and
Lu. 4 : 2. those days he d. e. noth.
17 : 27. they d. e., drank, mar., 28.
Ga. 2 : 12. before he d. e. with Gent.

EAT with drink.

Ge. 24 : 54. they did e. and d., 26 : 30. Ex. 24 : 11. Ju. 9 : 27.-19 : 4.
Ex. 32:6. sat to e. and d., 1 Co. 10 : 7,
34 : 28. nor e. bread, nor d. water. De. 9 : 9, 18.
1 S. 30:11. Egyp. did e. bread and d.
2 S. 11 : 11. go into h. to e. and d.?
13. David called he did e. and d.
12: 3. e. of his meat d. of his cup
19 : 35. can thy servant taste what I e. or d.? [Adonijah
1 K. 1 : 25. they e. and d. before
13 ; 8. neither will I e. bread nor d. water, 9, 16, 17, 22.
18 : 41. Elijah said, e. and d. [d.
2 K. 6:22. set, that they may e. and
7 : 8. into 1 tent and did e. and d.
18 : 27. e. own dung and d. piss, Is. 36 : 12.
1 Ch. 29 : 22. e. and d. before Lord
2 Ch. 28: 15. gave them to e. and d.
Ezr. 10:6. Ezra did e. no br. nor d.
Ne. 8 : 10. e. the fat and d. sweet
12. all peo. went to e. and d.
Es. 4 : 16. nei. e. nor d. three days
Jb. 1 : 4. called sisters to e. and d.
Pr. 23 : 7. e. and d. saith he to thee
Ec. 2 : 24. noth. better than that he e. and d., 3 : 13.-5 : 18.-8 : 15.
Can. 5:1. e. O friends, yea d. abun.
Is. 21 : 5. e. d. ye princes, anoint
22: 13. let us e. and d., to morrow we die, 1 Co. 15 : 32.
Je. 16 : 8. sit with th. to e. and d.
22 : 15. did not thy fa. e. and d.?
Eze. 25 : 4. sh. e. thy fruit d. milk
39 : 17. may e. flesh and d. blood
Da. 1 : 12. pulse to e. water to d.
Zch. 7 : 6. when ye did e. and d.
Mat. 6 : 25. what ye shall e. or d., 31. Lu. 12 : 29. [Lu. 12 : 45.
24 : 49. to e. and d. with drunken,
Lu. 5: 30. Why e. and d. with publi.?
33. fast, but thy disciples e. and d.
12 : 19. take thine ease, e. d. and
17 : 8. afterward shalt e. and d.
22 : 30. may e. and d. at my table
Ac. 9 : 9. Saul did neither e. nor d.
10 : 41. did e. and d. with him aft.
23 : 12. e. nor d. till killed Paul, 21.
Ro. 14 : 21. e. flesh nor d. wine
1 Co. 9 : 4. not power to e. and d.?
10 : 7. peo. sat down to e. and d.
1 Co. 10 : 31. Whether thf. ye e. or d.
11 : 22. not houses to e. and d. in?
26. as ye e. this bread and d. cup
27. shall e. and d. unworthily
28. so let him e. and d. of that cup

EAT not.

Ge. 2 : 17. of tree of knowledge, thou shalt n. e. of it, 3 : 1, 3.
3 : 11. I com-ed thee n. to e.. 17.
9 : 4. blood sh. you n. e. Le. 19:26. De. 12 : 16, 23, 24, 25.-15 : 23.
24 : 33. n. e. until I have told errand
32 : 32. chil. of Isr. e. n. of sinew
43 : 32. Egyp-s n. e. with Hebr.
Ex. 12:9. e. n. of it raw, nor sodden
45. foreigner n. e. thereof, 29 : 33.
Le. 11 : 4. these n. e., De. 14 : 3, 7.
8. their flesh sh. ye n. e., 11. De.
42. creep, them ye n. e. [14 : 8.
22 : 4. leper n. e. of holy, 6, 10, 12.
8. that torn he sh. n. e. to defile
Nu. 11 : 19. ye shall n. e. one day
De. 12 : 17. mayest n. e. the tithe
14 : 10. hath not fins and scales n. e.
12. these ye shall n. e., eagle
21. ye shall n. e. anything that dieth of itself, Eze. 44 : 31.
28 : 31. ox be slain, thou shalt n. e.
Ju. 13 : 4. e. n. any unclean, 7, 14.
1 S. 1 : 7. she wept and did n. e.
9 : 13. peo. will n. e. until he come
28 : 23. Saul refused, I will n. e.
2 K. 4 : 40. could n. e. thereof
7 : 2. shalt see it but n. e. thereof, 19.
Ezr. 2 : 63. n. e. of most holy things, Ne. 7 : 65.
Ps. 141 : 4. let me n. e. of dainties
Pr. 23 : 6. e. n. bread of him that hath evil eye
Eze. 24 : 17. e. n. bread of men
Mk. 7:3. Jews, except wash, e. n. 4.
Lu. 22 : 16. I will n. e. thereof
1 Co. 5 : 11. with such no n. to e.
8 : 8. nei. if e. n. are we worse
10 : 28. e. n. for his sake th. shew- [ed

Shall EAT.

Ge. 45 : 18. ye s. e. the fat of land
Ex. 12:11. s. ye e. it, with loins girded ye s. e. it in haste, L.'s passo.
15. s. ye e. unleav. bread, 20.
18. first month ye s. e. unleav. br.
16 : 12. saying, At even ye s. e. flesh
22 : 31. nei. s. ye e. flesh torn
Le. 7 : 23. ye s. e. no fat, 24. [14.
26. ye s. e. no manner of bl., 17 :
10 : 13. ye s. e. it in holy place
14. wave breast s. ye e. in clean
11 : 2. beasts ye s. e., De. 14 : 4, 6.
3. cheweth cud that s. ye e., De. 14: 4, 6. [De. 14 : 9.
9. These s. ye e. of all in wat-s,
19 : 25. 5th year s. ye e. of fruit
23 : 14. ye s. e. neither bread nor
25 : 12. ye s. e. increase out of field
19. ye s. e. your fill, dwell in safe.
22. ye s. e. of old store, 26 : 10.
26 : 26. ye s. e. and not be satis.
29. ye s. e. flesh of sons and dau.
Nu. 11 : 18. L. give flesh, ye s. e.
18 : 31. and ye s. e. in every place
De. 12 : 7. there ye s. e. before L.
14 : 9. all that have fins s. ye e.
11. of all clean birds ye s. e. [day
1 S. 9 : 19. for ye s. e. with me to
2 K. 19 : 29. ye s. e. this year such things as grow, Is. 37 : 30.
Is 1 : 19. if obedient ye s. e. good of
61:6. ye s. e. the riches of the Gent.
Eze. 39 : 19. ye s. e. fat till full
Jo. 2: 26. ye s. e. in plenty, and be
Lu. 12 : 22. no thought what ye s. e.

To EAT.

Ex. 16:8. L. shall give you flesh t. e.
Nu. 11:4. Who give us flesh t. e.? 18.
De. 12: 20. thy soul longeth t. e. fle.
18 : 8. shall have like portions t. e.
1 S. 9 : 13. he go to high place t. e.
1 S. 20 : 24. king sat down t. e. meat
2 S. 3 : 35. came to cause David t. e.
9 : 10. master's son have food t. e.
13 : 9. bef. him, but he refused t. e.
16 : 2. summer fru. for young men
17 : 29. for peo. with him t. e. [t. e.
2 K. 4 : 40. poured out for men t. e.
2 Ch. 31 : 10. we ha. had enough t. e.
Ne. 9 : 36. land thou gavest, t. e. the
Ps. 78 : 24. rain. manna upon them t.
Pr. 23 : 1. sittest t. e. with ruler [e.
25 : 27. not good t. e. much honey
Ec. 5 : 19. given power t. e. thereof
6:2. God giveth him not power t. e.
Is. 23 : 18. them t. e. sufficiently
Je. 2 : 7. plentiful coun. t. e. fruit
19 : 9. cause t. e. flesh of sons
Eze. 3 : 2. caused me t. e. that roll
3. Son of man, cause belly t. e.
Da. 4:25. make thee t. e. grass, 32.
Mi 7 : 1. there is no cluster t. e.
Ha. 1 : 8. eagle th. hasteth t. e. [e.
Mat. 12 : 1. pluck ears of corn and t.
4. not lawful for him t. e., Mk. 2 : 26, Lu. 6 : 4. [37, Lu. 9 : 13.
14 : 16. give ye them t. e., Mk. 6 :
15 : 20. t. e. with unwashen hands
32. mult. nothing t. e., Mk. 8 : 1, 2.
26 : 17. where prepare t. e. passover?
Mk. 5 : 43. someth. be given her t. e.
6 : 31. no leisure so much as t. e.
Lu. 22 : 15. desired t. e. this passo.
Jn. 4 : 32. meat t. e. ye know not of
33. any brought him aught t. e.?
6 : 52. How give us his flesh t. e.?
Ac. 27 : 35. broken it, he began t. e.
1 Co. 8 : 10. emboldened t. e. things offered to idols
11 : 20. this is not t. e. L.'s supper
33. when ye come together t. e.
He. 13 : 10. an altar whereof they have no right t. e.
Re. 2 : 7. give t. e. of tree of life
14. t. e. things sacrificed, 20.
17. I will give t. e. of hid. manna

EAT up.

Ge. 41 : 4. lean did e. u. 7 fat, 20.
Le. 26:38. land of enemies e. you u.
Nu. 24 : 8. he shall e. u. nations
De. 28 : 33. a nation shall e. u. [fi.
Ps. 27 : 2. enem. came to e. u. my
105 : 35. did e. u. all the herbs in
Is 50:9. moth sh. e. them u., 51:8.
Je. 5 : 17. they shall e. u. harvest e. u. flocks, e. u. thy vines
22:22. wind sh. e. u. thy pastures
Ho. 4: 8. They e. u. sin of my peo.
Am. 7: 4. deep, and did e. u. a part
Mi. 5: †6. sh. e. u. land of Assyria
Na. 3 : 15. e. thee u. like cankerw.
Re. 10:9. angel said unto me, e. it u.

EATEN. [not?

Ge. 3 : 11. Hast thou e. of tree sho.
14:24. Save wh. young men have e.
27 : 33. I have e. all before thou
31: 38. rams of flock have I not e.
41 : 21. when they had e. them, not be known they had e.
43 : 2. when they had e. up corn
Ex. 12 : 46. in one house sh. it be e.
13 : 3. sh. no leavened br. be e., 7.
21 : 28. ox be stoned, flesh not be e.
22 : 5. if man cause field to be e.
29 : 34. sh. not be e. bec. it is holy
Le. 6 : 16. be e. in holy pl., 26.-7 : 6.
23. be wholly burnt, not e., 7 : 19.
30. no sin offering shall be e.
7 : 15. sh. be e. day it is offer., 16.
18. if sacri. of peace offering be e.
10 : 17. why ye not e. sin off-g?
18. ye should indeed have e. it
19. if I had e. sin offering to day
11 : 13. sh. not be e., 41. De. 14:19.
34. of meat which may be e.
47. beast that may not be e. (2)
17 : 13. catcheth beast th. may be e.
19:6. sh. be e. day ye offer, 22:30.

Le. 19 : 7. if it be e. on 3d day
23. uncirc. it sh. not be e. [45:21.
Nu. 28:17. unleav. bread be e., Eze.
De. 6:11. when thou shalt have e.,
12:22. Even as hart is e., [8:10,12.
20 : 6. planted viney. not e. of it
26 : 14. I have not e. in mourning
29:6. ye have not e. bread nor dr.
31 : 20. shall have e. and be filled
Jos. 5 : 12. after had e. of old corn
Ru. 3 : 7. when Boaz had e. and
1 S. 14 : 30. if people had e. freely
28 : 20. he had e. no bread all day
30:12. had e. his spirit came again
2 S. 19 : 42. have we e. of k.'s cost?
1 K.13:22. camest and hast e.bread
28. lion had not e. the carcass
2 K.6:23. when had e. he sent them
Ne. 5 : 14. have not e. bread of gov.
Jb. 6 : 6. unsavoury e. without salt
31 : 17. Or have e. morsel alone
39. If I have e. fruits without
money [hath e.me up,Ju.2:17.
Ps. 69:9. for the zeal of thine house
102 : 9. I have e. ashes like bread
Pr. 9 : 17. bread e. in secret pleas.
23 : 8. morsel e. shalt thou vomit
Can. 5 : 1. have e. my honeycomb
Is. 3:14.ye have e. up the vineyard
5 : 5. hedge thereof sh. be e. up
6 : 13. a tenth return and be e.
44 : 19. I have roasted flesh and e.
Je. 10 : 25. they have e. up Jacob
24 : 2. figs not be e., 3, 8.-29 : 17.
31 : 29. e. sour grapes, Eze. 18 : 2.
Eze. 4 : 14. not e. that which dieth
18 : 6. not e. upon mountains, 15.
11. even hath e. upon mountains
34:18. to have e. up good pasture
Ho. 10 : 13. ye have e. fruit of lies
Jo. 1 : 4. left cankerworm e.,2 : 25.
Mat. 14:21. they th. had e.,Mk.8:9.
Lu. 13 : 26. we have e. in thy pres.
17 : 8. till I have e. afterward thou
Jn.6:13. remained unto them had e.
Ac.10:10. he hungry,would have e.
14. I have never e. any common
12 : 23. he was e. of worms
20 : 11. when he had e. departed
27 : 38. e. enough they lightened
Re. 10 : 10. had e. it, my belly bit- [ter

EATER, S.

Ju. 14:14. Out of the e. came meat
Pr. 23 : 20. am. riotous e.s of flesh
Is. 55 : 10. that it give bread to e.
Na. 3 : 12. sh. fall into mouth of e.

EATEST.

Ge. 2 : 17. in day thou e. shalt die
1 S.1:8. said Elk., Why e. thou not
1 K. 21 : 5. Why so sad e. no bread

EATETH.

Ex. 12:15. e. leavened bread be cut
off, 19. [27.-17 : 10, 15.
Le. 7 : 18. the soul that e., 20, 25,
11 : 40. he that e. of carcass
14 : 47. he that e. in house
17 : 14. whoso. e. it shall be cut off
19 : 8. that e. shall bear his iniq.
Nu. 13 : 32. land e. up inhabitants
1 S. 14 : 24. Cursed man that e.,28.
Jb. 5 : 5. harvest the hungry e. up
21:25. ano. never e. with pleasure
40 : 15. behemoth e. grass as an ox
Ps. 106 : 20. an ox that e. grass
Pr. 13 : 25. righteous e. to satisfy-g
30 : 20. she e. and wipeth mouth
31:27. e. not the bread of idleness
Ec. 4 : 5. the fool e. his own flesh
5 : 17. all his days he e. in darkn.
6:2. a stranger e. it, this is vanity
Is. 28 : 4. while in his hand he e. it
29 : 8. he e. but awaketh hungry
44 : 16. and with part he e. flesh
59:5. he that e. of their eggs dieth
Je. 31 : 30. man that e. sour grape
Mat. 9 : 11. Why e. your master
with publi.? Mk.2:16. Lu.15:2.

Mk. 14 : 18. One of you who e. with
me, shall betray, Jn. 13 : 18.
Jn. 6:54. e. my flesh hath eter. life
56. e. my flesh dwelleth in me
57. he that e. me. sh. live by me
58. that e. of this bread sh. live
Ro. 14 : 2. another weak e. herbs
3. not him e. despise him e. not
6. that e. to the L., that e. not
to the L. e. not [offence
20. evil for that man who e. with
23. damned bec. he e. not of faith
1 Co. 9 : 7. who plant. viney. and e.
not of fruit? e. not of milk
11:29.e. unworthily, e. damnation

EATING.

Ge. 2 : † 16. of ev. tree e. thou eat
Ex. 12 : 4. take a lamb, every man
according to his e.,16:16,18,21.
Ju. 14 : 9. Samson went on e.
1 S. 14:34. sin not in e. with blood
30 : 16. spread upon all earth e.
1 K. 1:41. guests made an end of e.
2 K 4 : 40. as they were e. pottage
Jb. 20 : 23. rain it while he is e.
Is.66:17. e. swine's flesh, and abom.
Am. 7 : 2. made an end of e. grass
Mat. 26 : 26. were e. Jes. took bread
Ac. 1 : † 4. e. with them, com. them
1 Co. 8:4. conc e. of things sacrificed
11 : 21. in e. every one taketh own
See DRINKING. [supper

E'BAL.

Ge. 36 : 23. of Shobal, E.,1 Ch.1:40.
De. 11 : 29. shalt put curse upon E.
27 : 4. set up stones in mount E.
13. stand upon mount E. to curse
Jos. 8 : 30. Josh. built altar in E
33. half of them stood over-ag. E.
1 Ch. 1 : 22. And E. and Abimael

E'BED. [35.

Ju. 9 : 26. Gaal son of E., 28, 30, 31,
Ezr. 8 : 6. up from Babylon. E. son

E'BED-ME'LECH.

Je. 38 : 7 E. heard they put Jerem-h
8. E. went, spake to king [in prison
10. k commanded E. Take 30 men
11. E. took old rags, let down to J.
12. E. said unto Jere-h, Put these
39 : 16. Go, speak to E., Ethiopian

EB'EN-E'ZER.

1 S. 4 : 1 Israel pitched beside E.
5 : 1. Philistines brought ark fr E.
7 : 12. stone, Samuel called it E.

E'BER or HE'BER.

Ge. 10 : 21. Shem, fath. of chil. of E.
24. Salah begat E., 11 : 14, 15. 1
Ch. 1 : 18, 25. Lu. 3 : 35. H.
25. E. two sons, 1 Ch. 1 : 19. [17.
11 : 16 E. lived 34 yrs., begat Peleg,
1 Ch. 8 : 12. sons of Elpaal ; E., Mi.
Ne. 12 : 20. were priests ; of Amok, E.

E'BER. [People.] [E.

Nu.24:24.ships fr.Chittim sh. afflict

EBI'ASAPH=ABI'ASAPH

1 Ch. 6 :23. Elkanah, E. his son, Assir, 37.-9 : 19. | 1 Ch. 26 : † 1.

EBONY. [e.

Eze. 27 : 15. for a present, horns of

EBRO'NAH. [E.

Nu. 33 : 34. encamped at E. | 35. fr.

ECHO.

Eze. 7 : † 7. not e. of the mountains

ED. [E.

Jos. 22 : 34. chil. of Gad called altar

E'DAR. [E.

Ge. 35 : 21. spread tent by tower of

E'DEN. [Person.] [tified

2 Ch.29: 12. Levites ; Joah, E., sanc-
31 : 15. next him were E., Jeshua

E'DEN. [Place.]

Ge. 2 :8. Lord planted a garden in E.
10. a river out of E. to water garden
15. God took man put him in E.
3 : 23. G. sent him fr. garden of E.
24. placed at garden of E. flaming
4:16. Cain dwelt on east of E. [sword

Is. 51 : 3 make her wildern-s like E
Eze. 28 : 13. Thou in E., garden of G.
31 : 9 all trees of E envied him
16. trees of E. shall be comforted
18. art like among trees of E.? (2)
36 : 35. This land is like garden of E.
Jo. 2 : 3. land is as garden of E. bef.

E'DEN or BETH-E'DEN.

2 K. 19 : 12. delivered chil. of E. in
Thelasar? Is. 37 : 12. [merch-ts
Eze. 27 : 23. Haran. Canneh, E., thy
Am. 1 : 5 cut off from hou. of E., †B.

E'DER. [Person.] [30.

1 Ch. 23 : 23. sons of Mushi ; E, 24 :

E'DER. [Place.] [dah, E.

Jos. 15 : 21. uttermost cities of Ju-

EDGE, S.

Ex. 13 : 20. encamped in Etham in
e. of wilderness, Nu. 33 : 6.
26 : 4. make loops of blue upon the
e. of one certain (2), 5, 10
(2).-36 : 11, 12, 17 (2). [39 : 4.
28 : 7. shoulderpieces joined at 2 e-s,
Nu 33 :37. mount Hor in e. of Edom
Ju. 3 : 16. made a dagger, had 2 e-s
Jos 13 : 27. e. of sea of Chinnereth
Ec. 10 : 10. If he do not whet the e.
Eze. 43 : 13. border by e. be a span
Lu. 4 : † 29. led Jesus unto e. of hill
Re. 2 : 12. hath sharp sword with
See TEETH. [two e-s
See Edge of the SWORD,
Smite or Smote with edge
of SWORD.

EDGED.

See TWOEDGED.

EDIFICATION.

Ro. 15 : 2. please his neighbour to e.
1 Co. 14 : 3. speaketh unto men to e.
2 Co. 10 :8. authority given us for e.
13 :10. power Lord hath given me to [e.

EDIFIED.

Ac. 9 : 31. had churches rest, were e.
1 Co. 8 † 10. conscience of him weak
14 : 17. but the other is not e. [be e.

EDIFIETH. [ity e.

1 Co. 8 : 1. knowledge puffeth, char-
14 : 4. speaketh in unknown tongue
e. himself ; that prophesieth e.

EDIFY. [church

Ro. 14 : 19. things one may e. anoth-
1 Co. 10 : 23. all lawful, but e. not [er
Ep. 4 : † 29. that which is good to e.
1 Th. 5 : 11. e. one another as ye do

EDIFYING.

1 Co. 14 : 5. church may receive e.
12. seek that ye may excel to e.
14 : 26. Let all things be done unto
2 Co. 12 : 19. we do all for your e. [e.
Ep. 4 : 12. for e. of body of Christ
16. increase of the body unto e.
29. that which is good to use of e.
1 Ti. 1 : 4 questions rather than e.

E'DOM. [Person.] [E.

Ge. 25 : 30. therefore his name called
36 : 1. Esau, who is E., 8, 19, 43.

E'DOM.

[People or Country.]

Ge 32 : 3. of Seir the country of E.
36:16. dukes of Eliphaz in land of E.
17. dukes of Reuel in land of E.
21. children of Seir in land of E.
31. these are the kings th. reigned
in the land of E., 1 Ch.1 :43 [E.
32. Bela son of Beor reigned in
43. the dukes of E., 1 Ch. 1:51, 54.
† 43. he is Esau the father of E.
Ex. 15 :15. dukes of E. sh. be amazed
Nu. 20 : 14. Moses sent messengers
unto king of E., Ju. 11 : 17.
18. E. said, Thou shalt not pass,
20. E. came out ag. him [Ju.11:17.
21. E. refused to give Isr. passage
23. Hor, by coast of land of E. [E.
21 :4. by Red sea, to compass la. of
24 : 18. E. shall be a possession

Nu. 33 : 37. Hor in edge of land of E.
34 : 3. south quarter by coasts of E.
Jos. 15 : 1. lot of Judah, to bord. of E.
21. cities of Judah tow. coast of E.
Ju. 5 : 4. when marchedst out of E.
11 : 18. they compassed land of E.
1 S. 14 : 47. Saul fought against E.
2 S. 8 : 14. in E. ; throughout all E.
put he garrisons, they of E. bec.
David's servants, 1 Ch. 18 : 13.
1 K. 9 : 26. Eloth in la. of E., 2 Ch. 8 : 17.
11 : 14. he was of king's seed in E.
15. when Dav. was in E., and Joab
had smitten every male in E., 16.
22 : 47. then no king in E. : deputy
2 K. 3 : 8. way thro. wilderness of E.
9. So went the king of E. ⌈him
12. Elisha king of E. went down to
20. came water by the way of E.
26. to break through unto k. of E.
8 : 20. In his days E. revolted, 22.
14 : 7. He slew of E. in valley of salt
10. Thou hast indeed smitten E.
1 Ch. 18 : 11. gold that he bro-t from
2 Ch. 25 : 20. sought aft. gods of E. ⌊E.
Ps. 60.* smote of E. in valley of salt
8 over E. will cast my shoe, 108 : 9.
9. who lead me into E. ? 108 : 10.
83 : 6. confederate : tabernac-s of E.
137 : 7. Remember the child-n of E.
Is. 11 : 14. sh. lay their hand upon E.
63 : 1. Who is this cometh from E. ?
Je. 9 : 26. I will punish Judah and E.
25 : 21. I made the nations drink ; E.,
27 : 3. send them to king of E. ⌊Moab
40 : 11. when all Jews in E. heard
49 : 7. Conc. E., Thus saith the Lord
17. Also E shall be a desolation
20. hear counsel of Lord against E.
22. mighty men of E. as a woman
Eze. 25 : 12. Bec. E. dealt ag-t Judah
13. will stretch mine hand upon E.
14. will lay my vengeance upon E. :
shall do in E. acc. to mine anger
32 : 29. There is E. and her kings
Da. 11 : 41. these sh. escape, E., Moab
Jo. 3 : 19. E. shall be a wilderness
Am. 1 : 6. to deliver them up to E.
9. they delivered captivity to E.
11. For three transgressions of E.
2 : 1. burned bones of king of E.
9 : 12. may possess remnant of E.
Ob. 1. Thus saith God cone-g E. ⌈of E.
8. Sh. I not destroy wise men out
Mal. 1 : 4. E. saith, We are impover-

Daughter of E'DOM. ⌊ished

La. 4 : 21. Rejoice, be glad, O - E.
22. I will visit thine iniquity, O - E.

E'DOMITE, S.

Ge 36 : 9. Esau, father of the E-s, 43.
De. 23 : 7. not abhor an E. : thy bro.
1 K. 11 : 1. Sol-n loved women of E-s
14. Lord stirred up Hadad the E.
17. Hadad fled, he and certain E-s
2 K. 8 : 21. Joram rose by night, and
smote E-s, 2 Ch. 21 : 9. ⌈of salt
1 Ch. 18 : 12. Abishai slew E-s in v-y
13. E-s became David's servants
2 Ch. 21 : 8. E-s revolted fr. Jud., 10.
25 : 14. Amaziah fr. slaughter of E-s
19. Lo, thou hast smitten the E-s
28 : 17. E-s had come, smitten Ju-

ED'REI. ⌊dah

Nu. 21 : 33. Og went, and people, to
the battle at E., De. 3 : 1.
De. 1 : 4. and Og the king of Bashan,
dwelt at Astaroth in E., Jos. 12 : 4.
3 : 10. we took all Bashan unto E.
Jos. 13 : 12. Og reigned in E. ⌈chir
31. Ashtaroth, E., unto chil. of Ma-
19 : 37. Kedesh, E., cities of Naph-i

EFFECT. [Noun.] ⌈e.

Nu. 30 : 8. husband make vow of none
2 Ch. 34 : 22. spake to her to that e.
Ps. 33 : 10. devices of peo. of none e.
Is. 32 : 17. the e. of righteousness
Eze. 12 : 23. the e. of every vision ⌈e.
Mat. 15 : 6. made com-t of G. of none
Mk. 7 : 13. mak-g word of G. of none e.
Ro. 3 : 3. make faith of G. without e. ?
4 : 14. made the promise of none e.
9 : 6. Not as tho. word taken none e.
1 Co. 1 : 17. lest cross of Ch. ef none e.
Ga. 3 : 17. make promise of none e.
5 : 4. Christ is become of no e. unto

EFFECT. [Verb.] ⌊you

Je. 48 : 30. his lies shall not so e. it

EFFECTED.

2 Ch. 7 : 11. all into Sol-n's heart, he e.

EFFECTUAL.

1 Co. 16 : 9. For a great door and e.
2 Co. 1 : 6. is e. in enduring suffer-g
Ep. 3 : 7. grace unto me by e. working
4 : 16. acc. to e. working in ev. part
Phm. 6. Th. thy faith may become e.
Ja. 5 : 16. The e. prayer of righte-s

EFFECTUALLY. ⌊man

Ga. 2 : 8. he that wrought e. in Peter
1 Th. 2 : 13. word of God e. worketh

EFFEMINATE.

1 Co. 6 : 9. nor e. sh. inherit kingdom

EGG, S. ⌊of God

De. 22 : 6. If nest, whether young or
e-s, the dam upon young or e-s
Jb. 6 : 6. any taste in white of an e. ?
39 : 14. ostrich which leaveth e-s
Is. 10 : 14. as one gathereth e-s left,
have I gathered all the earth
59 : 5. They hatch cockatrice' e-s ;
he that eateth of their e-s dieth
Je. 17 : 11. as partridge sitteth on e-s
Lu. 11 : 12. if ask an e. will he offer

EG'LAH. ⌊scorpion ?

2 S. 3 : 5. E., David's wife, 1 Ch. 3 : 3.

EG'LAIM. ⌈E.

Is. 15 : 8. the howling thereof unto

EG'LON king of Moab.

Ju. 3 12. Lord strengthened E. -
14. Isr. served E. - 18 y-rs ⌊ag. Isr.
15. by Ehud Isr. sent present unto
17. E. was a very fat man ⌊E. -, 17.

EG'LON. [Place.]

Jos. 10 : 3. Adoni-zedek sent unto k.
of E., saying, Come and help me
5. five kings . . king of E. gathered
23. five kings out of cave, k. of E.
34. Joshua unto E., fought ag-t it
36 Joshua went from E. unto He-
37. acc. to all he had done E. ⌊bron
12 : 12. Joshua smote ; king of E. one
15 : 39. Lachish, Bozkath, and E.

E'GYPT. ⌈E.

Ge. 12 : 10. Abram went down into
14. Abram was come into E., 11.
15 : 18. given land from river of E.
25 : 18. sons of Ishmael dwelt from
Havilah unto Shur th. is before
26 : 2. said, go not down into E. ⌊E.
37 : 25. myrrh, to carry down to E.
28. they brought Joseph into E.
36. Midianites sold him into E.
39 : 1. Joseph was bro-t down to E.
41 : 8. called for all magicians of E.
57. all countries into E. to buy co.
42 : 1. when Jac. saw was corn in E.
2. I have heard there is corn in E.
3. brethren went to buy corn in E.
43 : 15. went to E., stood bef. Joseph
45 : 4. I am Joseph ye sold into E.
9. God hath made me Lord of E.
13. tell my father of my glory in E.
23. laden with good things of E.
46 : 3. I am God, fear not to go into
4. I will go with thee into E. ⌊E.
6. into E., Jacob and all his seed, 7.
8. the names of chil. of Israel wh.
came into E., Ex. 1 : 1. ⌈66
26. All souls which came into E.
27. sons of Joseph in E. were two,
all souls of hou. of Jac. into E. 70
47 : 21. removed from one end of E.
29. bury me not, I pray thee, in E.
Ge. 48 : 5. sons born bef. I came into E.
50 : 14. Joseph returned into E.
22. Joseph dwelt in E., father's h.
26. Joseph was put in coffin in E.
Ex. 1 : 5. Joseph was in E. already
8. king over E. which knew not J.
3 : 7. I have seen the affliction of
my people in E., Ac. 7 : 34. ⌈E.
16. I have seen that done to you in
17. bring you out of affliction of E.
20. will smite E. with my wonders
†22 jewels, raiment ; ye sh. spoil E.
4 : 18. return unto my breth-n in E.
19. L. said unto Moses, go into E.
21. into E., do wonders bef. Pha-h
6 : 27. to bring out Israel from E.
7 : 4. that I may lay hand upon E.
5. wh. I stretch forth hand upon E.
11. magicians of E. did in like, 22.
19. Say unto Aaron, stretch thine
hand upon waters of E., 8 : 6.
9 : 4. sever betw. cattle of Isr. and E.
6. all the cattle of E. died ⌈found-n
18. hail, such as not in E. since the
10 : 2. What things I wrought in E.
7. knowest thou not E. is destroyed
14. locusts rested in coasts of E.
19. not one locust in all coast of E.
11 : 1. yet one plague more upon E.
4. about midnight into midst of E.
12 : 12. ag-t all gods of E. judgment
27. passed over houses of Isr. in E.
30. Then was a great cry in E. ⌈E.
40. sojourning of Isr. who dwelt in
13 : 3. Remember this day in which
ye came out from E. ⌈from E.
14. By strength L. brought us out
17. Lest people repent, return to E.
14 : 7. he took all the chariots of E.
11. Bec. there were no graves in E.
12. the word we did tell thee in E.
23 : 15. Abib ; in it camest out fr. E.
Nu. 11 : 5. remember fish we did eat
18. it was well with us in E. ⌊in E.
13 : 22. Hebron built bef. Zoan in E.
14 : 3. not better to return into E. ?
4. they said, Let us return into E.
19. forgiven peo. fr. E. until now
22. wh. have seen my miracles in E.
20 : 15. How our fathers went into
E., and we have dwelt in E. long
22 : 5. is a people come out from E.
26 : 59. mother bare to Levi in E.
34 : 5. border from Azmon unto the
river of E., Jos. 15 : 4. ⌈34.
De. 1 : 30. all he did for you in E., 4 :
6 : 21. We Pharaoh's bondmen in E.
22. Lord shewed wonders upon E.
7 : 15. none of diseases of E. upon
18. what God did unto all E ⌊thee
10 : 22. Thy fa-s went down into E.
11 : 3. miracles he did in midst of E.
4. what he did unto the army of E.
16 : 12. shalt remember that thou
wast a bondman in E., 24 : 18.
17 : 16. nor cause peo. to return to E.
26 : 5. my father went down into E.
28 : 27. smite thee with botch of E.
60. will bring upon thee diseases of
68. bring them into E. again ⌊E.
Jos. 5 : 9. rolled away reproach of E.
9 : 9. fame of him and all he did in E.
13 : 3. from Sihor, wh. is before E.
15 : 47. Gaza unto the river of E.
24 : 4. Jacob and chil. went into E.
5. I sent out Moses and plagued E.
7. have seen that I have done in E.
14. gods your fathers served in E.
Ju. 6 : 8. I brought you up from E.
13. did not Lord bring us from E.
11 : 16. when Israel came up fr. E.
1 S. 2 : 27. house of thy father in E.
12 : 8. when Jacob was come into E.
15 : 2. laid wait when he came fr. E.
7. smote to Shur, over against E.
30 : 13. said, I am a young man of E.
2 S. 7 : 23. peo. thou redeemedst fr. E.

1 K. 4 : 21. Solomon reigned unto border of E., 2 Ch. 9 : 26 [of E.
30. Sol-'s wisdom excelled wisdom
8:65. a feast, all Israel from Hamath unto the river of E., 2 Ch. 7 : 8.
11 : 17. Hadad fled into E., 18.
21. Hadad heard in E. David slept
40. Jerob-m fled into E., in E. until death of Sol., 12 : 2. 2 Ch. 10 : 2.
2 K. 18 : 21. thou trustest upon a bruised reed, even E., Is. 36 : 6.
24. How put thy trust on E. Is. 36 : 9.
23 : 34. Jehoahaz: he came to E. and died, 2 Ch. 36 : 4. [of E.
24 : 7. Babylon had taken from river
25 : 26. captains of armies came to E.
1 Ch. 13 : 5. all Israel, fr. Shihor of E.
2 Ch. 26 : 8. his name spread to E.
Ne. 9 : 9. affliction of fathers in E.
Ps. 78 : 43. wrought his signs in E.
51. And smote all the firstborn in E., 135 : 8.-136 : 10. [pieces
89 : † 10. Thou hast broken E. in
105 : 23. Israel also came into E.
38. E. was glad when they departed
106 : 7. underst-d not wonders in E.
21. God had done gr. things in E.
135 : 9. sent wonders into thee, O E.
Pr. 7 : 16. my bed with fine linen of E.
Is. 7 : 18. shall hiss for the fly in E.
10 : 24. ag-t thee after manner of E.,
11 : 11. peo. left from Syria, E. [26.
19 : 1. The burden of E. Lord shall come into E.: idols of E. shall be moved, heart of E. shall melt
3. spirit of E. shall fail in midst
12. what L. hath purposed upon E.
13. they have also seduced E. [err
14. and they have caused E. to
15. Neither sh. be any work for E.
16. that day sh. E. be like women
17. Judah shall be a terror unto E.
21. And the Lord sh be known to E.
22. And the Lord shall smite E.
23. Assyrians shall come into E.
24. shall Israel be third with E.
25. Blessed be E. my people, and
20 : 3. for a sign and wonder upon E.
4. uncovered, to the shame of E.
5. sh. be ashamed of E. their glory
23 : 5. As report conc. E., so of Tyre
27 : 12. L. beat off unto stream of E.
30 : 2. That walk to go into E., and to trust in shadow of E.! [sion
3. trust in shadow of E. y-r confu-
31 : 1. Woe to th. that go down to
43 : 3. I gave E. for thy ransom [E.
45 : 14. labour of E. sh. come unto
52 : 4. My peo. went down into E.
Je. 2 : 18. what hast thou to do in E.
36. thou shalt be ashamed of E.
9 : 26. I will punish E., Judah and
26 : 21. Urijah afraid, fled into E.
22. Jehoiakim sent men into E. (2)
37 : 7. Pha-'s army sh. return to E.
41 : 17. they departed to go into E.
42 : 15. If ye set faces to enter E., 17.
16. famine shall follow you in E.
18. my fury upon you when ye en-
19. O Jud., Go ye not into E. [ter E.
43 : 2. Go not into E. to sojourn
12. fire in houses of the gods of E.
46 : 2. word of Lord to Jer-h ag. E.
8. E. riseth up like a flood [dol
14. Declare in E., publish in Mig-
19. O thou daughter dwelling in E.
20. E. is like a very fair heifer
25. I will punish No, E. with gods
Eze. 17 : 15. his ambassadors into E.
20 : 7. defile not with the idols of E.
8. neither did forsake idols of E.
23 : 3. committed whoredoms in E.
8. Neither left she her whoredoms brought from E.; for in youth
27. so thou not remember E. (2)
27 : 7. Fine linen from E. thy sail
29 : 2. Son of man, prophesy ag-t E.
Eze. 29 : 6. All E. shall know I am L.
14. will bring again captivity of E.
30 : 4. sword shall come upon E., gr. pain when slain sh. fall in E.
6. They that uphold E. shall fall
8. when I have set a fire in E., 16.
9. pain upon them as in day of E.
10 will make multitude of E. cease
11. they shall draw swords ag-t E.
15. my fury upon Sin, strength of
18. when I sh. break yokes of E. [E.
19. will I execute judgments of E.
32 : 12. they shall spoil pomp of E.
16. they shall lament for E. [of E.
18. Son of man, wait for multitude
Da. 11 : 8. carry captives into E. [E.
43. power over precious things of
Ho. 7 : 11. they call to E., go to As-
8 : 13. they shall return to E. [syria
9 : 3. Ephraim shall return to E.
6. E. sh. gather them up, Memphis
12 : 1. and oil is carried into E.
Jo. 3 : 19. E. shall be a desolation [E.
Am. 4 : 10. pestilence aft. manner of
8 : 8. drowned as by flood of E., 9 : 5.
Na. 3 : 9. Ethiopia, E. her strength
Zch. 10 : 11. sceptre of E. sh. depart
14 : 18. if family of E. go not up
19. This be the punishment of E.
Mat. 2 : 13. take child, flee into E., 14.
19. angel appear-h to Joseph in E.
Ac. 2 : 10. dwellers in E., we do hear
7 : 9. patriarchs sold Joseph into E.
10. made him governor over E.
12. when Jac. heard was corn in E.
15. So Jacob went into E. and died
17. people grew, multiplied in E.
34. come, I will send thee into E.
39. in hearts turned back into E.
He. 11 : 26. greater than treas. in E.
27. By faith he forsook E. [and E.
Re. 11 : 8. city wh. is called Sodom

Daughter of EGYPT.

Je. 46 : 11. take balm, O virgin, - E.
24. The - E. shall be confounded

King of EGYPT.

Ge. 40 : 1. butler of the - E. and his baker had offended their lord - E.
5. butler and baker of - E. in pris.
Ex. 1 : 15. - E. spake to Heb. midwives
17. did not as - E. commanded
18. - E. called for the midwives
2 : 23. in process of time - E. died
3 : 18. thou and elders unto - E.
19. I am sure - E. not let you go
5 : 4. - E. said, Whf. let people go
14 : 5. told the - E. the people fled
1 K. 11 : 40. J-m. fled unto Shishak - E.
14 : 25 Shishak - E. came up ag-t Jerusalem, 2 Ch. 12 : 2, 9.
2 K. 17 : 4. sent messeng-s to So - E.
24 : 7. - E. came not again . . had taken all that pertained to - E.
2 Ch. 36 : 3. - E. put him at Jerus-m
4. - E. made Eliakim his broth. k.

Pharaoh king of EGYPT.

Ex. 6 : 11. Go, speak unto P. - of E.
13. L. gave them charge unto P. - E.
27. are they wh spake unto P. - E.
29. speak unto P. - E. all that I say
14 : 8. hardened heart of P. - E.
De. 7 : 8. Lord hath redeemed you from hand of P. - E, 2 K. 17 : 7.
11 : 3. miracles he did unto P. - E.
1 K. 3 : 1. Sol-n affinity with P. - E.
9 : 16. For P. - E. had taken Gezer
11 : 18. Hadad came unto P. - E.
2 K. 18 : 21. so is P. - E. unto all that trust on him, Is. 36 : 6.
23 : 29. P.-nechoh - E. went ag-t the king of Assyria, 2 Ch. 35 : 20.
Je. 25 : 19. P. - E. and his servants
44 : 30. I will give P.-hophra - E. into the hand of his enemies
46 : 2. word of L. ag. P.-necho - E.
17. did cry P. - E. is but a noise
Eze. 29 : 2. set thy face ag-t P. - E.
3. saith Lord, I am ag. thee, P. - E.
30 : 21. I have broken arm of P. - E.
22. Behold, I am against P. - E.
31 : 2. Son of man, speak unto P. -
32 : 2. take up lament-n for P. - E. [E.
Ac. 7 : 10. favour in sight of P. - E.

Land of EGYPT. [est

Ge. 13 : 10. like - E., as thou com-
21 : 21. took him a wife out of - E.
41 : 19. such as I never saw in all -
29. plenty throughout all - E. [E.
30. plenty be forgotten in all - E.
33. a man wise, set him over - E.
34. take up fifth part of the - E.
36. ag-t famine which sh. be in - E.
41. I have set thee over all the - E.
43. he made him ruler over all - E.
44. without thee shall no man lift his hand or foot in all the - E.
45. Joseph went over all the - E.
46. Joseph went through-t all - E
48. seven years, which were in - E.
53. seven years of plenteousness
54. in all - E. was bread [in - E.
55. when all - E. was famished
56. the famine waxed sore in - E.
45 : 8. G. made me ruler thro-t - E.
18. I will give you good of all - E.
19. take you wagons out of - E.
20. the good of all the - E. is yours
26. Joseph is governor over - E.
46 : 20. unto Joseph in - E were b.
47 : 6. The - E. is before thee [in - E.
11. Joseph gave them possession
13. so the - E. and Canaan fainted
14. Joseph gathered money in - E.
15 when money failed in the - E.
20. Joseph bought all - E. for Pha.
26. made it a law over all the - E.
27. Israel dwelt in - E., in Goshen
28. Jacob lived in - E. 17 years
48 : 5. thy two sons, born in - E.
50 : 7. went up all elders of the - E.
Ex. 4 : 20. Moses he returned to - E.
5 : 12. scattered through-t all - E.
6 : 13. L. gave charge to bring children of Israel out of - E., 26.
28. Lord spake unto Moses in - E.
7 : 3. multiply wonders in the - E.
4. may bring my people out of - E.
19. may be blood thro-out all - E.
21. was blood throughout all - E.
8 : 5. cause frogs to come upon - E.
6. frogs came, covered the - E.
7. magicians bro-t frogs upon - E.
16. dust become lice thro-out - E.,
24. swarms of flies into all - E. [17
9 : 9. ashes become dust in all - E., a boil with blains thro-out - E.
22. may be hail in all the - E. upon every herb throughout - E.
23. Lord rained hail upon the - E.
24. was none like it in all the - E.
25. hail smote throughout all - E.
10 : 12. Stretch hand over - E. for locusts that they come upon - E.
13. Moses stretched rod over - E.
14. locusts went up over all - E.
15. not any green thing thro-t - E.
21. may be darkness over the - E.
22. thick darkness in - E. 3 days
11 : 3. Moses very great in the - E.
5. all firstborn in the - E. shall die
6. a great cry throughout all - E.
9. wonders be multiplied in - E.
12 : 1. Lord spake unto Moses in - E.
12. I will pass through the - of E., and smite all firstborn in - E. [E.
13. not destroy you when I smite -
17. I bro-t your armies out of - E.
29. Lord smote all firstborn in - E.
41. hosts of L. went out from - E.
42. for bringing them out from - E.
51. Lord did bring Isr. out of - E.
13 : 15 Lord slew firstborn in - E.
18. went up harnessed out of - E.

Ex. 16 : 1. after departing out of - E.
3. Would to God we had died in the - E, Nu. 14 : 2 [from - E.
6. ye sh. know Lord brought you
32. when I brought you from - E.
19 : 1. Israel were gone out of - E.
20 : 2. I the Lord which brought thee out of the - E., 29 : 46. Le. 19 : 36.-22 : 33.-25 : 38.-26 : 13 Nu. 15 : 41. De. 5 : 6. Ps. 81 : 10.
22 : 21. for ye were strangers in the - E., 23:9. Le. 19:34. De. 10 : 19.
32 : 1. this Moses that brought us out of - E., 23. [- E., 8
4 gods wh. brought thee out of
7. thy people thou broughtest out of - E. have corrupted themselves, 33 : 1. De. 9 : 12.
11. people which thou hast bro-t out of - E. with gr. power, De. 9 : 26.
Le. 11 : 45. bringeth you out of - E.
18 : 3. After the doings of the - E.
23 : 43. when I bro-t them out of - E.
25 : 42. are my servants which I brought out of the - E., 55.
26 : 45. ancestors whom I brought out of the - E. [E., 9 : 1.
Nu. 1 : 1. second year after . . out of -
3 : 13. on the day that I smote all the firstborn of the - E., 8 : 17.
14 : 2. we had died in the - E.
26 : 4. Israel which went forth out of the - E. 33 : 1 [- E.
33 : 38. 40th year after Israel out of
De. 1 : 27. hated us, bro-t us out of - E.
6 : 12. lest thou forget Lord which brought thee out of - E., 8 : 14.
9 : 7. day didst depart out of - E.
11 : 10. For the land is not as - E
13 : 5. to turn you away from God which bro-t you out of - E., 10.
15 : 15. remember that thou wast a bondman in - E., 5 : 15. -24 : 22.
16 : 3. camest out of - E. in haste remember. day camest out of - E.. 6.
20 : 1. God is with thee which bro-t thee out of - E. [in - E.
29 : 2. all Lord did before your eyes
29 : 16. know how we dwelt in - E.
25. when he bro-t them out of - E.
34 : 11. Lord sent him to do in - E.
Jos. 24 : 17. Lord, he it is brought us and fathers out of the - E.
Ju. 2 : 12. brought them out of - E.
19 : 30. from day children of Israel came out of - E. [- E.
1 S. 12 : 6. brought your fathers out
27 : 8. to Shur, even unto the - E.
1 K. 6 : 1. 480th year after Isr. were come out of the - E. [of - E., 21.
8 : 9. covenant when they came out
9 : 9. forsook L. who brought their fathers out of - E. [out of - E.
12 : 28. gods which brought thee
2 K. 17 : 7. sinned against God which had brought them out of - E.
36. who bro-t you up out of - E.
2 Ch. 6 : 5. Since day I brought my people out of the - E. [the - E.
7 : 22. God which bro-t them out of
20 : 10. when they came out of - E.
Ps. 78 : 12. Marvellous things in - E.
81 : 5. when he went through - E.
Is. 11 : 16. day he came up out of - E.
19 : 18. shall five cities in the - E. speak language of Canaan [E.
19. altar to the Lord in midst of -
20. it shall be for a witness in - E.
27 : 13. outcasts in - E. sh. worship
Je. 2 : 6. Neither said, Where is the Lord that brought us out of - E.
7 : 22. day that I brought them out of the - E., 11 : 4, 7. -34 : 13. [- E.
25. Since day fathers came out of
Je. 16 : 14. no more say, Lord liveth th. brought Isr. out of - E., 23 : 7.

Je. 24 : 8. give them that dwell in - E.
31 : 32. to bring them out of the - E.
32 : 20. Which hast set signs in - E.
21. brought thy people Israel out
42 : 14. we will go into - E. [of - E.
16. sword sh. overtake you in - E.
43 : 7. So they came into the - E.
11. he cometh, he shall smite - E
12. he sh. array himself with - E.
13. images of Beth-shemesh in - E.
44 : 1. Jews which dwell in - E. [E.
8. burning incense unto gods in -
12. Judah, that have set faces to go into - E., they shall fall in - E.
13. punish them that dwell in - E
14. none gone into - E. sh. escape
15. that dwelt in - E., answ-d Jer-h
24. Hear, all Judah, th. are in - E.
26. of any man of Judah in - E. [ed
27. all of Judah in - E. be consum-
28. small number sh. return out of - E ; that are gone into - E.
46 : 13. Neb. should smite all - E. [E.
Eze 19 : 4. him with chains unto -
20 : 5. day I made mys. known in - E.
6. In the day I lifted hand to bring them forth of the - E. [E.
8. my anger against them in the -
9. in bringing them out of the - E.
10. I caused them to go out of - E.
36 I pleaded with fathers in - E.
23 : 19. she played the harlot in - E.
27. thy whoredom bro-t from - E.
29 : 9. - E. shall be desolate, 10, 12.
19. I will give the - E. unto Neb-r
20. given him - E. for his labour
30 : 13. be no more a prince of - E. ;
I will put a fear in the - E. [- E.
25. sword he sh. stretch out upon
32 : 15. When I make - E. desolate
Da. 9 : 15. bro-t thy people out of -
11 : 42. the - E. shall not escape [E.
Ho. 2 : 15. when she came out of - E
7 : 16. this be their derision in - E.
11 : 5. He shall not return into - E.
12 : 9. I that am the Lord thy God from the - E., 13 : 4. [- E., 3 : 1.
Am. 2 : 10. I brought you up from
3 : 9. publish in the palaces in - E.
9 : 7. I brought Israel out of - E.
Mi. 6 : 4. I brought thee out of - E.
7 : 15. days of coming out of the - E.
Zch. 10 : 10. bring them again out of
Ac. 7 : 11. dearth over all - E [- E
36. aft. he shewed wonders in - E.
40. Mos. which bro-t us out of - E.
13 : 17. when strangers in the - E.
He. 8 : 9. to lead them out of - E.
Jude 5. saved people out of the - E.

Out of EGYPT.

Ge. 13 : 1. Abram went up - E. ; and
43 : 2. corn they had brought - E.
45 : 25. they went up - E. into Ca.
47 : 30. carry me - E, bury me in
Ex. 3 : 10. mayest bring my peo. - E.
11. Who am I . . bring Isr. - E. ?
12. When hast brought peo. - E.
12 : 39. dough which they bro-t - E. : bec. they were thrust - E. [E.
13 : 8. done unto me when I came -
9. for with a strong hand hath L. brought thee - E., 16. De. 4 : 37. -6 : 21.-9 : 26.-26 : 8. 1 K. 8 : 51.
17 : 3. Wherefore hast brought us - E. to kill us, 14 : 11. Nu 21 : 5.
18 : 1. heard L. had bro-t Israel - E.
34 : 18. in month Abib camest - E.
Nu. 11 : 20. wept, saying, Why came we forth - E. ? [- E.
20 : 5. wherefore made us to come
16. Lord, he hath brought us - E.
22 : 11. there is a people come - E.
23 : 22. God brought them - E
24 : 8. God brought him - E. [land
32 : 11. none that came - E. sh. see
De. 4 : 20 Lord brought you out of iron furnace, - E., 1 K. 8 : 51.

De. 4 : 45. statutes, aft. they came - E.
46. smote aft. they were come - E.
9 : 12. people which thou hast bro-t - E. have corrupted [night
16 : 1. Lord brought thee - E. by
6. at season that thou camest - E.
23 : 4. they met you not with bread when ye came - E [come - E.
24 : 9. unto Miriam after ye were
25 : 17. Remember what Amalek did when ye were come - E.
26 : 8. brought us - E. with signs
Jos. 2 : 10. how the Lord dried up the Red sea when ye came - E.
5 : 4. people that came - E., males died after they came - E. [cumc.
5. all born by the way - E. not cir-
6. till all men of war which came - E. were consumed [1 K. 8 : 53.
24 : 6. I brought your fathers - E.,
32. bones of Joseph Isr. bro-t - E.
Ju. 2 : 1. I made you to go - E. [- E.
11 : 13. took my land they came
1 S. 8 : 8. Since I brought them - E., 2 S. 7 : 6. 1 K. 8 : 16. [- E.
10 : 18. saith Lord, I brought Israel
12 : 8. M. brought your fathers - E.
15 : 6. kindn-s when they came - E.
1 K. 10 : 28. Sol. had horses brought - E., 2 Ch. 1 : 16.-9 : 28.
29. chariot came - E. for 600 shekels of silver, 2 Ch. 1 : 17.
2 K. 21 : 15. since fathers came - E.
1 Ch. 17 : 21. peo thou redeemed - E.
2 Ch. 5 : 10. covenant when they came
10 : 2. Jeroboam returned - E. [- E.
12 : 3. peo. with-t number came - E.
Ne. 9 : 18. calf, is G. that bro-t thee
Ps. 68 : 31. Princes sh. come - E. [- E.
80 : 8. Thou hast brought vine - E.
114 : 1. When Israel went - E., Jac.
Is. 19 : 23. be a highway - E. to As.
Je. 26 : 23. they fetched Urijah - E.
37 : 5. Pha-h's army was come - E.
Ho. 11 : 1. I called my son - E. [E.
11. They shall tremble as a bird -
12 : 13. by prophet L. bro-t Isr. - E.
Hag. 2 : 5. covenanted when ye came
Mat. 2 : 15. - E. called my son [- E.
He. 3 : 16. some, not all th. came - E.

EGYPTIAN.

Ge. 16 : 1. had a handmaid, an E., name Hagar, 3.-21 : 9.-25 : 12.
39 : 1. an E bought him of Ishm-s
2. Joseph in house of his mast., E
5. L. blessed E -'s house for Jos-h
Ex. 1 : 19. Hebrew women not as E.
2 : 11. Moses spied E. smiting a He-
12. he slew the E., Ac 7 : 24. [brew
14. kill me as thou killedst E. ?
19. An E. delivered us of sheph-ds
Le 24 : 10. whose father was an E
De. 23 : 7. thou shalt not abhor an E
1 S. 30 : 11. they found an E. in field
2 S. 23 : 21. Benaiah slew an E. ; E. had spear, he plucked spear out of E.'s hand, 1 Ch. 11 : 23.
1 Ch. 2 : 34. S. serv-t, an E., Jarha
Is. 11 : 15. destroy tongue of E. sea
19 : 23. shall come E. into Assyria
Acts 7 : 28. as thou diddest the E.
21 : 38. thou that E. madest up- [roar?

EGYPTIANS.

Ge. 12 : 12. when E. see thee, sh. say
14. E. beheld the woman was fair
41 : 55. Pha. said unto E.. Go unto
56. Joseph sold unto the E , 47 : 15.
43 : 32. bread for E. by themselves; because E. might not eat with Hebrews ; abomination unto E.
45 : 2. he wept aloud ; E heard
46 : 34. shepherd is abomin. unto E.
47 : 20. E. sold every man his field
50 : 3. E. mourned for him 70 days
11. this is grievous mourning to E.
Ex. 1 : 13. E. made Israel serve with
3 : 8. to deliver out of hand of E.

Ex. 3 : 9. wherewi. E. oppress them
21. will give this people favour in
sight of E., 11 : 3.-12 : 36 (2).
22. and ye shall spoil the E., 12 : 36.
6 : 5. Israel whom E. keep in bonda.
6. out from under burdens of E., 7.
7 : 5. E. shall know I am Lord ⌈21.
18. E. sh. loathe to drink of river,
24. E. digged about river for water
8 : 21. houses of E. be full of flies
26. we sacrifice abominat-n of E. (2)
9 : 11. the boil was upon all the E.
10 : 6. locusts shall fill houses of E.
11 : 7. difference between E. and Isr.
12 : 23. L. will pass thro. to smite E.
27. when he smote E. and deliv-d
30. Pha. rose up in night, and all E.
33. E. were urgent upon the people
35. they borrowed of the E. Jewels
36. and they spoiled the E. ⌊of gold
14 : 9. E. pursued after them, 10, 23.
12. been bet-r for us to serve E. (2)
13. E. seen today ye sh. see no more
17. I will harden hearts of the E.
20. cloud betw. camp of E. and Isr.
24. Lord looked unto host of E.
thro. pillar of fire, troubled E.
25. E. said, Let us flee from Isr.,
for the Lord fighteth against E.
26. that waters may come upon E.
27. L. overthrew E. in the sea (2)
30. L. saved Israel out of hand of
E.; Isr. saw E. dead upon shore
31. Israel saw work L. did upon E.
15 : 26. diseases wh. I bro-t upon E.
18 : 8. M. told all L. had done unto E.
9. delivered out of hand of E., 10 (2).
19 : 4. have seen what I did unto E.
32 : 12. Wherefore should E. say
Nu. 14 : 13. Moses said, E. sh. hear it
20 : 15. E. vexed us and our fathers
33 : 3. Israel went out in sight of E.
4. E. buried all their firstborn
De. 26 : 6. E. evil entreated us ⌈ers
Jos. 24 : 6. E. pursued aft. your fath-
7. put darkn. between you and E.
Ju 6 : 9. I delivered you out of the
hand of E., 1 S. 10 : 18. ⌈the E.
10 : 11. Did not I deliver you from
1 S. 4 : 8. are the Gods that smote E.
6 : 6. Wheref. harden hearts as E
and Pharaoh hardened hearts!
2 K. 7 : 6. hired E. to come upon us
Ezr. 9 : 1. acc. to abominations of E.
Is. 19 : 2. I will set E. against the E.
4. E. will I give unto hand of cruel
21 E. shall know Lord in that day
23. E. shall serve with Assyrians
20 : 4. shall lead away E. prisoners
30 : 7. E. shall help to no purpose
31 : 3. Now E. are men. and not God
Je. 43 : 13. gods of E. shall he burn
La 5 : 6. We have given hand to E.
Eze. 16 : 26. fornication with the E.
23 : 21. in bruising thy teats by E.
29 : 12. I will scatter E., 30 : 23, 26.
13 end of 40 years will I gather E.
Ac. 7 : 22. M. learned in wisdom of E.
He. 11 : 29. E. assaying, were drowned

E'HI=AHI'RAM.

Ge. 46 : 21. sons of Benjamin, Gera,
E., Rosh, Muppim, Nu. 26 : †38.

E'HUD. ⌈E.

Ju 3 : 15. Lord raised up a deliverer,
16. E. made a dagger, two edges
20. E. came unto him sitting in
parlour. E. said, I have a mes.
21 E. took dagger. thrust it into
23. E. went forth through porch
26. E. escaped while they tarried
4 : 1. Isr. did evil when E. was dead
1 Ch. 7 : 10. sons of Bilhab, Jeush, E.
8 : 6. And these are the sons of E.

EIGHT.

Ge. 22 : 23. these e. Milcah did bear
Ex 26 : 25. shall be e. boards, 36 : 30.
Nu. 7 : 8. Moses gave e. oxen unto
Nu. 29 : 29. on sixth day e. bullocks
1 S. 17 : 12. Jesse; he had e. sons
1 K. 7 : 10. was of stones of e. cubits
1 Ch. 24 : 4. e. among sons of Itha-r
Ec. 11 : 2. Give to seven, also to e.
Je. 41 : 15. Ishmael escaped with e.
Eze 40 : 9. porch of gate e. cubits
31. going up to it e. steps, 34, 37.
41. e. tables, whereupon slew sac.
Mi. 5 : 5. ag-t him e. principal men
1 Pe. 3 : 20. e. souls were saved by w.

See **Eight DAYS.**
See **Eight YEARS.**
See **Eight HUNDRED.**
See **Eight THOUSAND.**

EIGHTEEN.

1 K. 7 : 15. two pillars of brass of e.
cubits, 2 K. 25 : 17. Je. 52 : 21.
1 Ch. 26 : 9. had sons and brethren e.
2 Ch. 11 : 21 Rehoboam took e. wives
Ezr. 8 : 18. Sherebiah with breth. e.
Lu. 13 : 4. e. upon whom tower fell

See **Eighteen THOUSAND.**

EIGHTEENTH.

1 Ch. 24 : 15. lot came; e. to Aphses
25 : 25. they cast lots; e. to Hanani

See **Eighteenth YEAR.**

EIGHTH. ⌈liel

Nu. 7 : 54. On e. day offered Gama-
1 K. 6 : 38. in Bul, which is e. month
12 : 32. ordained feast in e. mo., 33.
1 Ch. 12 : 12. men of war, Johanan e.
24 : 10. lot came forth, e. to Abijah
25 : 15. cast lots, e. to Jeshaiah ⌈e.
26 : 5. sons of Obed-edom, Peulthai
27 : 11. e. captain for e. month was
2 Ch. 29 : 17. e. day came to porch
Zch. 1 : 1. In e. month word came
2 Pe. 2 : 5. saved Noah the e. person
Re. 17 : 11. beast that was is the e.
21 : 20. foundations; the e., beryl

See **Eighth DAY.**
See **Eighth YEAR.**

EIGHTIETH. See
Four HUNDRED eightieth.

EIGHTY. See HUNDRED.

EITHER. ⌈29.

Ge. 31 : 24. not to Jacob e. good or,
Le. 10 : 1. took e. of them his censer
13 : 49. if plague greenish e. in warp
or in woof, 51, 53, 57, 58, 59.
22 : 23. e. a bullock or a lamb that
25 : 49. e. his uncle or uncle's son
Nu. 6 : 2. e. a man or woman separ.
22 : 26. no way to turn, e. to right
24 : 13. to do e. good or bad of mine
De. 17 : 3. worshipped e. sun or m.
28 : 51. not leave e. corn or wine
Ju. 9 : 2. e. sons of Jerubbaal reign
1 S. 20 : 2. father will do nothing e.
25 : 31. e. thou hast shed blood ⌊gr.
30 : 2. slew not any, e. great or sm.
1 K. 7 : 15. did compass e. of them
10 : 19. stays on e. side on the seat
18 : 27. e. is talking or pursuing
1 Ch. 21 : 12. e. three years' famine
2 Ch. 18 : 9. sat e. of them on throne
Ec. 9 : 1. no man knoweth e. love or
11 : 6. whe. prosper, e. this or that
Is. 7 : 11. ask a sign, e. in depth or
17 : 8. neither respect e. groves or
Mat. 6 : 24. e. he will hate the one,
and love the other, Lu. 16 : 13.
12 : 33. e. make the tree good, or
Lu. 6 : 42. e. how say to thy brother
15 : 8. e. what woman having ten p.
Jn. 19 : 18. crucified, on e. side one
Ac. 17 : 21. e. to tell or to hear some
1 Co. 14 : 6. exc. I speak e. by reve-
Ph. 3 : 12. e. were already perfect ⌊la.
Ja. 3 : 12. bear berries, e. a vine figs?
Re. 22 : 2. e. side of river, tree of life

E'KER. ⌈Jamin

1 Ch. 2 : 27. sons of Ram, Maaz, E.,

EK'RON. ⌈of E.

Jos. 13 : 3. From Sihor unto borders
15 : 11. border went unto side of E.
Jos. 15 : 45. cities of Judah, E. with
19 : 43 of Dan; coast was Elon, E. ⌊16
Ju. 1 : 18. Judah took E. with coast
1 S. 5 : 10. sent ark of God to E. (2)
6 : 16. the five lords returned to E.
17. golden emerods, for E. one
7 : 14. cities restored fr. E. unto Ga.
17 : 52. pursued Philist. to gates of
E., wounded fell even unto E.
2 K. 1 : 2. Go, inquire of Baal-zebub,
god of E., 3, 6, 16. ⌈zab, E.
Je. 25 : 20. make them a curse, Az.
Am. 1 : 8. will turn mine hand ag E.
Zph. 2 : 4. E. shall be rooted up
Zch. 9 : 5. Gaza be sorrowful, and E
7. he be as governor, E. as Jebusite

EK'RONITES.

Jos. 13 : 3. remaineth; Gittites, E.
1 S. 5 : 10. ark, to Ekron, E. cried out

EL'ADAH. ⌈son

1 Ch. 7 : 20. Tahath his son, E. his

E'LAH. [Person.]

Ge 36 : 41. duke E., 1 Ch. 1 : 52.
1 K. 4 : 18. Shimei, son of E, in B.
16 : 6. Baasha slept, E. reigned in
8. In 26th year of Asa began E. to
13. sins of Baasha and sins of E.
14. rest of acts of E., are ⌈18 : 1, 9.
2 K. 15 : 30. Hoshea son of E., 17 : 1.-
1 Ch. 4 : 15. of Caleb; E.; sons of E.
9 : 8. E. son of Uzzi, son of Michri

Valley of E'LAH.

1 S. 17 : 19. Saul and Israel in - E.
fighting with Philistines, 22. ⌈E.
21 : 9. Goliath whom thou slewest in

E'LAM. [Person.] ⌈17.

Ge. 10 : 22. of Shem; E., 1 Ch. 1 :
1 Ch. 8 : 24. Hananiah, E, heads of
26 : 3. sons of Meleshemiah, E 5th
Ezr. 2 : 7. chil. of E. 1254, Ne. 7 : 12.
31. chil. of other E. 1254, Ne. 7 : 34.
8 : 7. up from Bab-n; of sons of E.
10 : 2. one of sons of E. unto Ez. ⌈E.
26. taken strange wives; of sons of
Ne. 10 : 14. chief of people; E., Bani
12 : 42. And the priests E. and Eger

E'LAM. [Place.]

Ge. 14 : 1. Chedorlaomer k. of E., 9.
Is. 11 : 11. recover his people from E.
21 : 2 Go up, O E.; besiege, O Media
22 : 6. E. bear quiver, with chariots
Je. 25 : 25. all kings of E. shall drink
49 : 34. word of L. came against E.
35. saith L., I will break bow of E.
36. upon E. the four winds; no
nation whither outcasts of E.
37. I will cause E. to be dismayed
38. I will set my throne in E.
39. will bring again captivity of E.
Eze. 32 : 24 is E. about her grave
Da. 8 : 2. Shushan in province of E.

E'LAMITES. ⌈E.

Ezr 4 : 9. wrote ag-t Jerusalem, the
Ac. 2 : 9. Parthians, E., we do hear

EL'ASAH. ⌊speak

Ezr. 10 : 22. sons of Pashur; E. ⌈phan
Je. 29 : 3. By hand of E. son of Sha-

E'LATH,[1] or E'LOTH.[2]

De. 2 : 8. thro. way of the plain fr. E.[1]
1 K. 9 : 26. E[2] on shore of Red Sea
in Edom, 2 Ch. 8 : 17. † E.[1]
2 K. 14 : 22. Azariah built E[1], restored it to Judah, 2 Ch. 26 : 2. E.[2]
16 : 6. Rezin recovered E.[1] to Syria,
and drave Jews from E.[1]: Syrians came to E.[1] and dwelt, † E.[2]

EL-BETH'-EL.

Ge 35 : 7. called place E., because

ELBOWS. Eze. 13 : † 8.

ELDA'AH.

Ge. 25 : 4. sons of Midian; Ephah,
and Epher, and E., 1 Ch. 1 : 33

EL'DAD.

Nu. 11 : 26. name of the one was E.
27. E. and Medad do prophesy

ELDER. [Adj.] ⌈the e.

Ge. 10 : 21. Shem, bro. of Japheth,

Ge.25:23.e. serve younger, Ro 9:12.
27: 42. words of Esau her e. son
29: 16. name of the e. was Leah
1 S. 18: 17. my e. daughter Merab
1 K. 2: 22. kingd. he mine e. bro.
Jb. 15: 10. very aged men, much e.
than thy father [the
32: 4. Elihu waited, they e. than
Eze. 16: 46. thy e. sister is Samaria
61. sisters thine e. and younger
23: 4. names were Aholah the e.
Lu.15:25.his e. son was in the field
1 Ti. 5: 2. entreat the e. women
1 Pe. 5:5. younger, submit unto the
ELDER. [A Ruler.] [e.
1 Ti. 5: 1. Rebuke not an e. but
19. Ag. an e. receive not an accu.
1 Pe. 5: 1. I exhort, who am an e.
2 Jn. 1. The e. unto the elect lady
3 Jn. 1. e. unto well-beloved Gaius

ELDERS.

Ge. 50: 7. e. of his house went
Ex. 24: 14. said unto e. Tarry ye
Le. 4: 15. e. of cong. sh. lay hands
Nu. 11:25. L. gave spirit unto 70 e.
22:4. e. of Midian, 7 | 7. e. of Moab
De. 21: 2. Then thy e. shall come
22: 16. damsel's fa. sh. say unto e.
25: 7. go up to gate unto the e.
9. in presence of e. and loose his
29:10. ye stand bef. the L. your e.
31: 28. Gather unto me all e. of
32: 7. ask fa. and e. they will tell
Jos. 23: 2. Jos. called for e. of Isr.
24: 31. Israel served L. all days of
Joshua and of e., Ju. 2: 7.
Ju. 8: 14. described e. of Succoth
11: 5. e. of Gilead, 7, 8, 9, 10, 11.
21: 16. Then e. of cong. said
1 S.11:3. e. of Jabesh said, Give us
16: 4. e. of the town trembled
30: 26. he sent of spoil unto e. of
Judah [Why ye last
2 S. 19: 11. Speak unto e. of Jud.,
1 K. 20: 7. k. of Isr. called the e.
8. all the e. said, Hearken not
21: 8. sent letters unto the e.
11. e. did as Jezebel had sent
2 K.6:32.Elisha sat in house, and e.
10: 1. Jehu sent to e. of Jezreel
19: 2. Hezekiah sent e., Is. 37: 2.
23: 1. gath-d unto him e. of Jud.
Ezr. 5: 5. eye of G. was upon the e.
6: 14. e. of the Jews builded and
10: 8. according to counsel of e.
Ps. 107: 32. praise in assembly of e.
Pr. 31: 23. husb. known am. the e.
Je. 26: 17. rose up certain of e.
29: 1. of e. wh. were carried away
La. 1: 19. e. gave up ghost in city
2:10.e. of Zion sit upon the ground
4: 16. favoured not e., 5: 12.
5: 14. e. have ceased from gate
Eze. 8:1. e. of Judah sat before me
Jo. 1: 14. a fast, gather the e., 2:16.
Mat. 15: 2. transg. tradition of e.?
16:21. suffer things of the e.,27:12
26: 57. when e. were assembled
59. e. sought false witness against
27:3. brought 30 pieces of sil. to e.
20. priests and e. persuaded mult.
41. priests mocking with e. said
28: 12. assembled with the e.
Mk. 7: 3. holding tradition of e., 5.
8: 31. be rejected of e., Lu. 9: 22.
11:27. to him e. as he was walking
14: 43. a great mult. from the e.
53. were assembled e. and scribes
15: 1. held a consulta. with the e.
Lu. 7: 3. sent unto him e. of Jews
20: 1. came upon Jes. with the e.
22: 52. Jesus said unto the e.
Ac. 4: 5. rulers and e. were gath-d
23. reported all the e. had said
6:12. they stirred up people and e.
11: 30. sent it to e. by Barnabas
14: 23. ordained e. in ev. church

Ac.15:2. apostles e. about question
4. they were received of the e.,22.
6. apostles and e. came
23. apostles, e. send greeting
16: 4. decrees ordained of the e.
20: 17. he called e. of the church
21: 18. all the e. were present
22: 5. estate of e. bear me witness
23: 14. said to e., We have bound
24: 1. Ananias descended with e.
25: 15. about whom e. inform. me
1 Ti. 5: 17. e. rule well be counted
Ti. 1: 5. ordain e. in every city
He. 11: 2. by faith e. obtained a
Ja. 5: 14. let him call for e. of ch-h
1 Pe. 5: 1. e. among you, I exhort
Re. 4: 4. I saw 24 e. 10. the 24 e.
fall, 5: 8, 14.-11: 16.-19: 4.
5: 5. one of e. saith, Weep not
6. in midst of e. stood a lamb
11. voice of many angels about e.
7: 11. all angels stood about the e.
13.one of e. ans., What are these?
14: 3. they sung a new song bef. e.

ELDERS with city.

De. 19:12. e. of his c. sh. fetch him
21: 3. e. of c. sh. bring heifer, 4.
6. e. of that c. shall wash hands
19. bring son unto e. of his c.
22: 15. father bring tokens of virginity unto e. of c., 17. [him
25: 8. e. of his c. shall speak unto
Jos. 20: 4. decla. cause in ears of e.
Ju. 8: 16. he took the e. of the c.
Ru. 4: 2. took ten men of e. of c.
Ezr. 10: 14. with them e. of ev. c.

ELDERS of Israel.

Ex. 3: 16. gather the e. o. I., 4:29.
18. come e. o. I. unto the king
12: 21. Moses called for all e. o. I.
17: 5. take with thee of e. o. I.
6. Mos. did so in sight of e. o. I.
18:12.e.o.I.came to eat with Jethro
24:1.seventy of e.o.I., 9, Nu.11:16.
Nu. 16: 25. e. o. I. followed him
De. 27: 1. e. o. I. commanded peo.
31:9.Moses deliv.this law unto e.o.
Jos. 7: 6. e. o. I. put dust upon [I.
24: 1. Joshua called for e. o. I.
1 S. 8: 4. all e. o. I. gath. thems.
2S.3:17.communication with e.o.I.
5: 3. all e. o.I.came to king, 1 K.
8: 3. 2 Ch. 5: 4.
17: 4. saying pleased e. o. I.
15. did Ahith. counsel e. o. I.
1 Ch. 11: 3.e.o. I.come to the king
21: 16. e.o. I.fell upon their faces
Eze. 14: 1. came e.o. I. unto me
20: 1. e. o. I. came to inquire of
3. Son of man speak to e. o. I.
Ac. 4: 8. Ye rulers and e. o. I.

ELDERS with people.

Ex. 19: 7. Moses called for e. of p.
Nu. 11: 16. knowest to be e. of p.
24. Moses gath. 70 of the e. of p.
Ru. 4: 4. buy it bef. e. of my p.
1 S. 15: 30. honour me bef. e. of p.
Mat.21:23. e. of p. came, Lu.22:66.
26: 3. e. of p. unto palace of pri
47. with a multitude fr. e. of p.
27: 1. e. of p. took counsel ag. J.
Ac.6:12.they stirred up the p.and e.

ELDEST.

Ge. 24: 2. Ab. said unto his e. serv.
27: 1. Isaac called Esau his e. son
15. goodly raiment of e.son Esau
44: 12. searched and began at e.
Nu. 1:20. Reuben, Isr's.e. son.26:5.
1 S. 17:13. three e. sons of Jesse,14.
28. Eliab his e. brother heard Da.
2 K. 3: 27. he took his e. son
2 Ch. 22: 1. band had slain e.
Jb.1:13. drinking in e. bro.'s h.,18.
Jn. 8:9.they went out beginning e.

E'LEAD. See Zabad.

ELEA'LEH. [E., 3.
Nu. 32:37. children of Reuben built

Is. 15: 4. Heshbon shall cry, and E.
16: 9. water with my tears, O E.
Je. 48: 34. cry of Heshbon unto E.

ELE'ASAH.

1 Ch.2:39. begat E. | 40.-8:37.-9:43.

ELEA'ZAR.

Ex. 6: 25. Aaron's son E., 28: 1.
Nu. 3: 2.-20: 25.-26: 60. 1 Ch.
6: 3.-24: 1. Ezr. 7: 5.-8: 33.
Le. 10:16. Moses was angry with E.
Nu. 3: 4. E. ministered in priest's
32. E. son of Aaron sh. be chief
4: 16. to office of E. pertaineth
16: 39. E. priest took censers
19: 3. shall give her unto E. priest
20: 26. put his garments upon E.
28. Moses and E. came fr. mount
26: 63. numbered by Moses and E.
27: 22. set Joshua before E. priest
31:12.bro-t spoil unto Moses and E.
26. Take sum of prey thou and E.
41. Moses gave tribute unto E.
34: 17. E. and Josh. shall divide
the land, Jos. 14: 1.-19: 51.
Jos. 17: 4. near E. | 24:33. E. died
1 S. 7: 1. they sanctified E. [12.
2 S. 23: 9. E. son of Dodo, 1 Ch. 11:
1 Ch. 9: 20. son of E. was ruler
23: 21. sons of Mahli; E., 24: 28.
22. E. died, had no sons, 24: 28.|
24: 4. more chief men of sons of E
5. governors were of sons of E.
Ne. 12:42. and E. priests, Ezr. 10:25.
Mat. 1: 15. Eliud begat E. and E.

ELECT.

Is. 42: 1. mine e. in whom my soul
45: 4. Israel mine e. I have called
65: 9. mine e. shall inherit it, and
22. mine e. shall long enjoy work
Mat. 24: 22. for e. sake those days
be shortened, Mk. 13: 20.
24. deceive very e., Mk. 13: 22.
31. angels, sh. gather his e. from
winds, Mk. 13: 27
Lu.18:7. shall not God avenge? [e.?
Ro. 8: 33. who lay to charge of G.'s
Col. 3:12. Put on as e. of G. bowels
1 Ti.5:21.I charge thee bef. e. angels
2 Ti. 2: 10. endure for e. sake [e.
Tit. 1:1. apostle acc. to faith of G's.
1 Pe. 1:2.e. acc. to foreknowl. of G.
2: 6. in Sion a corner-stone, e.
2 Jn. 1. The elder unto the e. lady
13. children of thy e. sister greet

ELECTED.

1 Pe. 5: 13. church at Bab. e.with

ELECTION.

Ro. 9: 11. purpose according to e.
11: 5. is a remn. acc. to e. of grace
7. e. hath obtained it, the rest
28. touching e. they are beloved
1 Th. 1: 4. Knowing your e. of G.
2 Pe. 1: 10. to make your e. sure

ELEGANTLY. [e.

Is. 32: † 4. of stammerers sh. speak

EL-ELO'HE-IS'RAEL.

Ge. 33: 20. Jacob called altar E.

ELEMENTS.

Ga. 4: 3. under e. of the world [e.
9. how turn to weak and beggarly
Col. 2:†8. after e. of the world, not
†20. dead with C. fr. e. of world
2 Pe. 3: 10. e. shall melt, 12.

E'LEPH.

Jos. 18: 28. Zelah, E Jerus. cities

ELEPHANT. [9:21.

1 K.10:†22. bringing e. teeth, 2 Ch.
Jb. 40: † 15. behold e. I have made

ELEVATION. [e.

Ju. 20 :†38. they should make great

ELEVEN.

Ge. 32: 22. Jacob took his e. sons
37: 9. e. stars made obeis. to me
Ex. 26: 7. e. curtains shalt make
8. e. curtains all of one measure
36: 14. e. curt. | 15. e. of one size
Nu. 29:20. on third day e. bullocks

De. 1: 2. e. days' journey fr. Horeb
Jos. 15: 51. e. cities with villages
Ju. 16:5. give e. hund. pieces of sil.
17: 2. I took e. hund. shekels of
3. restored e. hundred shekels to
2 K. 23: 36. Jehoi. reigned e. years
in Jerus., 2 Ch. 36:5. [Je. 52: 1.
24: 18. Zedek. e. yrs., 2 Ch. 36: 11.
Mat. 28:16. e. discip. went into Gal.
Mk. 16: 14. he appeared unto the e.
Lu. 24: 9. they told all these unto
33. found the e. gathered [the e.
Ac. 1: 26. numbered wi. e. apostles
2: 14. Peter standing with e. said

ELEVENTH.

De. 1: 3. in 40th year and e. month
1 K. 6: 38. e. year house finished
2 K. 9: 29. in e. yr. of Joram began
25: 2. Jerus. was besieged to e. yr.
of Zedekiah, Je. 52: 5.
1 Ch. 12: 13. Machbanai the e.
24: 12. e. lot came to Eliashib
25: 18. e. to Azareel, he, his sons
27: 14. e. captain for the e. month
Je. 1:3. Jere. proph-d e. yr. of Zed.
39: 2. e. year city was broken up
Eze. 26: 1. word of L. to Ezekiel in
the e. year, 30: 20.-31: 1.
Zch. 1: 7. e. month wh. is Sebat
Mat. 20: 6. about e. hour he went
9. that were hired about e. hour
Re. 21: 20. e. foundation of city

ELHA'NAN.

2 S. 21: 19. E. slew brother of Goliath, 1 Ch. 20: 5. [11: 26.
23: 24. E. the son of Dodo, 1 Ch.

E'LI.

1 S. 1: 25. they bro-t child to E.
2:11. child did minister bef. E., 3: 1.
12. sons of E. were sons of Belial
27. came a man of God unto E.
3: 5. Sam. ran unto E. said, 6: 8.
12. I will perform ag. E. all things
14. iniq. of E. house not be purged
15. feared to shew E. the vision
4:14. man came hastily told E., 16.
1 K. 2: 27. wh. he spake conc. E.

E'LI, or ELO'I,
lama sabachthani.

Mat. 27: 46. cried, E. E. l. s., Mk. [15: 34.

ELI'AB.

Nu. 1: 9. of Zebulun, E. son of Helon, 2: 7.-7: 24, 29.-10: 16.
16: 1. Dathan and Abiram sons of
E., 12.-26: 9. De. 11: 6.
26: 8. And sons of Pallu, E.
De. 11: 6. what did unto sons of E.
1 S. 16:6. when come he looked on E.
17: 28. E. heard, and his anger
1 Ch. 2: 13. Jesse begat firstb. E.,
1 S. 17: 13. 2 Ch. 11: 18.
6: 27. E. son of Nahath, the son
12: 9. E. captain of the Gadites
15: 18. E. porter, 20. | 16: 5. E.
2 Ch. 11: 18. Rehob. took dau. of E.

ELI'ADA.

2 S. 5: 16. E. son of Da., 1 Ch. 3: 8.
2 Ch. 17: 17. E. a mighty man

ELI'ADAH.

1 K. 11: 23. G. stirred up Rezon son [of E.

ELI'AH.

1 Ch. 8: 27. E. sons of Jeroh. | Ezr. [10: 26.

ELI'AHBA.

2 S. 23: 32. E. Shaalbonite, 1 Ch. 11: [33.

ELI'AKIM.

2 K. 18: 18. out to Rab-shakeh E., Is. [36: 3.
19: 2. sent E. to Isaiah, Is. 37: 2.
23: 34. made E. king. 2 Ch. 36: 4.
Ne. 12: 41. E. Maaseiah priests
Is. 22: 20. I will call my servant E.
Mat. 1: 13. Abiud begat E. and E.
Lu. 3: 30. Jonan, was son of E.

ELI'AM.

2 S. 11: 3. Bath-sheba dau. of E.
23: 34. E. the son of Ahithophel

ELI'AS = ELIJAH.

Mat. 11: 14. is E. wh. was to come
16: 14. some say E., Mk. 6: 15.-
8: 28. Lu. 9: 8, 19. [4. Lu. 9: 30.
17: 3. there appeared E., Mk. 9:
4. three tabernacles, one for E.,
Mk. 9: 5. Lu. 9: 33.
10. E. must first come, Mk. 9: 11.
11. E. sh. restore all, Mk. 9: 12.
12. E. come already, Mk. 9: 13.
27: 47. calleth for E., Mk. 15: 35.
49. whe. E. will come, Mk. 15: 36.
Lu. 1: 17. bef. him in power of E.
4: 25. many widows in days of E.
9: 54. command fire as E. did
Jn. 1: 21. Art thou E.? art thou
25. if not E. why baptizest thou?
Ro. 11: 2. what Scrip. saith of E.
Ja. 5: 17. E. was a man subject to

ELI'ASAPH.

Nu. 1: 14. E. son of Deuel | 2: 14.
-3: 24.-7: 42, 47.-10: 20.

ELI'ASHIB.

1 Ch. 3: 24. E. Pelaiah sons of
24: 12. 11th lot came to E. [12: 23.
Ezr. 10: 6. Johanan son of E., Ne.
24. E. singer | 27. E. son of, 36.
Ne. 3: 1. E. the high-priest
12: 10. Joiakim begat E. and E.
13: 4. E. was allied | 7. evil E. did
28. sons of Joiada, son of E.

ELI'ATHAH.

1 Ch. 25: 4. sons of Heman, E. | 27.

ELI'DAD.

Nu. 34: 21. E. the son of Chislon

E'LIEL.

1 Ch. 5: 24. heads of house of fa-s
E. and | 6: 34.-8: 20, 22.-11:
46, 47.-12: 11.-15: 9, 11. 2 Ch. [31: 13.

ELIE'NAI.

1 Ch. 8: 20. heads of fathers, E. and

ELIE'ZER.

Ge. 15: 2. steward of my house E.
Ex. 18: 4. Moses' son E., 1 Ch. 23: 15.
1 Ch. 7: 8. the sons of Becher, E.
15: 24. Benaiah and E. priests
23: 15. sons of Moses, E., Ex. 18: 4.
17. son of E. was Rehabiah
27: 16. ruler of Reubenites was E.
2 Ch. 20: 37. E. prophesied against
Jehoshaphat
Ezr. 8: 16. sent I for E. and Ariel
10: 18. E. had strange wives, 23, 31.
Lu. 3: 29. Jose, was the son of E.

ELIHOE'NAI.

Ezr. 8: 4. E. son of Zerahiah

ELIHO'REPH.

1 K. 4: 3. E. Ahiah, sons of Shisha

ELI'HU.

1 S. 1: 1. of Jehoram, son of E.
1 Ch. 12: 20. E. fell to David
26: 7. E. Shemachiah strong men
27: 18. E. one of breth. of David
Jb. 32: 2. wrath of E. was kindl., 5.
4. E. waited | 6. ans., 34: 1.-35: 1.

ELI'JAH = ELI'AS.

1 K. 17: 1. E. Tishbite said unto Ahab
15. she did acc. to saying of E.
22. Lord heard the voice of E.
23. E. took child and bro-t him
18: 2. E. to shew hims. unto Ahab
7. Art thou that my lord E?
8. E. is here [mocked them
16. Ahab went to meet E. | 27. E.
40. E. slew all prophets of Baal
46. hand of the Lord was on E.
19: 1. told Jezebel all E. had done
9. L. said, What doest here E.? 13.
20. Elisha left oxen ran aft. E., 21.
21: 20. said to E. Hast found me?
2 K. 1: 8. Ahaziah said, It is E.
10. E. ans-d, let fire come down, 12.
13. capt. fell on his knees bef E.
17. died acc. to word E. had spok.
2: 1. L. would take E. into heav.
8. E. took his mantle, wrapt it
11. E. went up by a whirlwind
14. Where is the Lord God of E.?
15. spirit of E. doth rest on Elisha
2 K. 3: 11. poured wat. on hands of E.
9: 36. wh. he spake by E., 10: 10, 17.
2 Ch. 21: 12. came a writing from E.
Ezr. 10: 21. Maaseiah E. sons of
Mal. 4: 5. I will send you E. prophet
See ELIAS.

EL'IKA.

2 S. 23: 25. Da. set over his guard E.

E'LIM.

Ex. 15: 27. came to E., Nu. 33: 9.
16: 1. their journey fr. E., Nu. 33: 10.

ELIM'ELECH.

Ru. 1: 2. man was E. | 3. E. died
2: 1. Boaz was of family of E. | 3.
4: 9. bought all th was E. of Naomi, [3.

ELIOE'NAI.

1 Ch. 3: 23. sons of Neariah, E.
24. sons of E. | 4: 36.-7: 8.-26:
3. Ezr. 10: 22, 27. Ne. 12: 41.

EL'IPHAL.

1 Ch. 11: 35. E. the son of Ur.

ELIPH'ALET.

2 S. 5: 16. E. David's son, 1 Ch. 14: 7.

EL'IPHAZ.

Ge. 36: 4. Adah bare to Esau, E., 10. [Ch. 1: 35
11. sons of E. 12, 15. 1 Ch. 1: 36.
Jb. 2: 11. E. came to mourn
4: 1. E. the Temanite, 15: 1.-22: 1.
42: 9. E. did as Lord com-d | 7.

ELIPH'ELEH.

1 Ch. 15: 18. breth. of sec. degree [| 21.

ELIPH'ELET.

2 S. 23: 34. E. son of Ahasbai | 1
Ch. 3: 6, 8.-8: 39. Ezr. 8: 13.-
See ELIPHALET. [10: 33.

ELIS'ABETH.

Lu. 1: 5. Zach.'s wife E. | 7. E. barren
24. E conceived, 36. | 40. salut. E.
41. E. was filled with Holy Ghost
57. E. full time that she be deliv.

ELISE'US.

Lu. 4: 27. many lepers in days of E.

ELI'SHA = ELISE'US.

1 K. 19: 16. anoint E. to be prophet
17. escaped fr. Jehu, sh. E. slay
19. Elijah found E. ploughing
2 K. 2: 5. the prophets came to E., 3.
12. E. saw it, and cried, My fa.
15. spirit of Elijah rest on E. | 9.
3: 11. Here is E. son of Shaphat
4: 1. cried a certain wom. unto E.
8. E. passed to Shunem, where
17. that season that E. had said
32. E. was come, child was dead
5: 9. so Naaman stood at door of E.
6: 12. E. telleth words thou speak.
17. chariots of fire about E.
18. E. prayed unto the Lord (2)
20. E. said, L. open eyes of these
31. if head of E. stand on him
8: 4. tell me things E. hath done
5. wom. whose son E. restored
14. said, What said E. to thee?
13: 14. Now E. was fallen sick
16. E. put hands upon k.'s hands
17. E. said, Shoot | 20. E. died
21. cast man into sepulchre of E.

ELI'SHAH.

Ge. 10: 4. sons of Javan, E., 1 Ch. [1: 7.
Eze. 27: 7. and purple fr. isles of E.

ELISH'AMA.

Nu. 1: 10. E. son of Ammihud, 2:
18.-7: 48, 53.-10: 22. 1 Ch. 7: 26.
2 S. 5: 16. E. David's son, 1 Ch. 3:
6, 8.-14: 7.
1 Ch. 2: 41. Jekamiah begat E.
2 Ch. 17: 8. he sent with them E.
Je. 36: 12. E. scribe sat there, 20.
41: 1. E. of the seed royal

ELISH'APHAT.

2 Ch. 23: 1. E. the son of Zichri

ELISH'EBA.

Ex. 6: 23. Aaron took E. to wife

ELISHU'A.

2 S. 5: 15. E. David's sons, 1 Ch. 14: 5.

ELI'UD.

Mat. 1: 14. begat E. | 15. E. begat

ELIZ'APHAN.
Nu. 3: 30. chief of Kohathites sh. be E. | 34: 25. 1 Ch. 15: 8. 2 [Ch.29:13.
ELI'ZUR.
Nu. 1: 5. E. the son of Shodeur | 2: 10.-7: 30, 35.-10: 18.
EL'KANAH.
Ex. 6: 24. sons of Korah, E.
1 S. 1: 1. his name was E.
21. E. went to offer yearly sac.
2: 11. E. to his h. | 20. blessed E.
1 Ch. 6: 23. son of E., 27, 34, 35.-9: 16. [hite
25. sons of E., 26. | 12:6. E. Kor-
15: 23. E. was doorkeeper for
2 Ch. 28: 7. E. next to the king
EL'KOSHITE.
Na. 1: 1. vision of Nahum the E.
EL'LASAR.
Ge. 14: 1. Arioch king of E., 9.
EL'MODAM.
Lu. 3: 28. Cosam, the son of E.
ELMS. [e.
Ho.4:13. upon hills under oaks and
EL'NAAM.
1 Ch. 11: 46. Joshaviah sons of E.
ELNA'THAN.
2 K. 24: 8. Nehushta dau. of E.
Ezr. 8: 16. I sent for E. and Jarib
Je. 26:22. Jehoia-m sent E. into E.
36: 12. E. son of Achbor sat
25. E. had made intercess. to king
ELO'I. See ELI.
E'LON. [Person, Place.]
Ge. 26: 34. Bashemath dau. of E.
36: 2. Esau took Adah dau. of E.
46: 14. sons of Zebulun; and E.
Jos. 19: 43. inheritance of Dan, E.
Ju.12:11. E. judged Isr. | 12.E.died
E'LON-BETH-HA'NAN.
1 K. 4: 9. the son of Dekar in E.
E'LONITES. [E.
Nu. 26: 26. of Elon, the family of
ELOQUENT.
Ex. 4: 10. Moses said, I am not e.
Pr.1:†6. to understand an e. speech
Is. 3: 3. L. doth take away e. orator
Ac. 18: 24. Apollos, an e. man
E'LOTH. See E'LATH.
EL'PAAL.
1 Ch. 8:11. begat E. | 12.sons of, 18.
EL'PALET.
1 Ch. 14: 5. chil. of David, E. and
EL'PARAN.
Ge. 14: 6. E. wh. is by the wildern.
ELSE.
Ge. 30: 1. Give me chil. or e. I die
Nu.20:19. without doing any th. e.
De. 4: 35. Lord he is God, there is none e., 39. 1 K. 8: 60. Is. 45: 5,6,14,18,21,22.-46:9. Joel 2:27.
Jos.23:12. e. if ye any wise go back
Ju. 7: 14. noth e. save sw. of Gid.
2 S. 3: 35. if I taste aught e. till
1 Ch. 21: 12. e. 3 days sw. of Lord
2 Ch. 23: 7. whoso. e. cometh in be
Ne. 2: 2. nothing e. but sorrow of
Ps.51:16. not sacri. e. would give it
Ec.2:25.who e. hasten more than I
Is.47:8. I am, none e. beside me,10.
Mat. 9:17.e. bottles break and wine
Mk. 2: 21. e. new piece tak. fr. old
22. e. new wine burst bottles
Lu. 14: 32. Or e. while other is yet
Jn. 14: 11. e. believe me for work's
Ac.17:21.noth. e. but to tell or hear
Ro. 2: 15. accusing, or e. excusing
1 Co. 7: 14. e. were your chil. uncl.
14: 16. e. when thou shalt bless
15:29. e. what sh. they do wh. are
Re. 2:5. repent or e. I will come,16.
EL'TEKEH. [23.
Jos. 19: 44. for tribe of Dan, E.,21:
EL'TEKON.
Jos. 15: 59. E., six cities with vil-
EL'TOLAD. [lages
Jos.15: 30. uttermost cities E.,19:4.

E'LUL.
Ne. 6: 15. wall finished month E.
ELU'ZAI.
1 Ch. 12:5. am. the mighty men, E.
EL'YMAS.
Ac. 13: 8. E. the sorcerer withstood
EL'ZABAD.
1 Ch.12:12.men of might E. the 9th
EL'ZAPHAN.
Ex. 6:22. sons of Uzziel, E.,Le.10:4.
EMBALM, ED.
Ge. 50: 2. Joseph com-d physicians to e. his fa.,physicians e-d Isr.
3. are fulfilled days of those e-d
26. they e-d Joseph in Egypt
EMBOLDENED, ETH.
Jb. 16: 3. what e-h that thou ans.
1 Co. 8:10. conscience of weak be e.
EMBRACE, ED, ING.
Ge. 29: 13. Laban e-d Jacob and
33: 4. Esau e-d Jacob and kissed
48: 10. Jacob e-d Joseph's sons
2 K. 4:16. this season shalt e. a son
Jb. 24: 8. they e. the rock for
Pr. 4: 8. honour, when dost e. her
5: 20. why e. bosom of a stranger
Ec. 3: 5. a time to e. and a time to refrain from e-g
Can. 2:6. right ha. doth e. me, 8:3.
La. 4: 5. in scarlet e. dunghills
Ac. 20: 1. Paul e-d disciples and departed [not yours.
10. Paul e-g Eutyc. said, Trouble
He. 11: 13. seen and e-d promises
EMBROIDER.
Ex. 28: 39. thou shalt e. the coat
EMBROIDERER.
Ex. 35: 35. to work all work of e.
38: 23. Aholiab, an e. in blue
EMERALD, S.
Ex. 28: 18. second row an e., 39:11.
Eze. 27: 16. Syria in thy fairs with
28: 13. ev. precious stone, e. [e-s
Re. 4: 3. was a rainbow like an e.
21:19. fourth foundation was an e.
EMERODS. [e.
De. 28: 27. L. will smite thee with
1 S. 5: 6. L. smote Ashdod with e.
9. men had e. in secret parts
12. men th. died not smit. with e.
6: 4. they ans. Five golden e., 17.
5. sh. make images of your e., 11.
E'MIMS.
Ge. 14: 5. Chedorlaomer smote E.
De. 2:10. E. dwelt there in past, 11.
EMINENT.
Jb. 22: † 8. e. man dwelt in earth
Is. 3: † 3. doth take e. in counte.
Eze. 16:24. hast built an e. pl., 31.
39. sh. throw down thine e. place
17: 22. I will plant it upon e. mt.
1 Ti. 2: † 2. pray for all in e. place
EMMAN'UEL.
Mat. 1: 23. they shall call his name
See IMMANUEL. [E.
EM'MAUS.
Lu. 24:13. two went same day to E.
EM'MOR.
Ac. 7: 16. Ab. bought of sons of E.
EMPIRE.
Es. 1: 20. be published thro. his e.
EMPLOY, ED.
De. 20: 19. not cut tree to e. in siege
†19. the tree is to be e-d in the siege
1 Ch.9:33.singers e-d day and night
Ezr. 10: 15. Jona. e-d about this
EMPLOYMENT. [matter
Eze. 39: 14. men of continual e.
EMPTIED.
Ge. 24: 20. Rebekah e. her pitcher
42: 35. to pass as they e. sacks
2 Ch. 24: 11. priest's officer e. chest
Ne. 5: 13. thus be he shaken and e.
Is.3:†26. she e. sh. sit upon ground
19: † 3. spirit of Egypt shall be e.
6. brooks of defence shall be e.
24: 3. The land shall be utterly e.

Je. 48: 11. Moab not been e.
Na. 2:2. emptiers have e. them out
EMPTIERS.
Na. 2: 2. e. have emptied them out
EMPTINESS. [e.
Is. 34: 11. stretch upon it stones of
EMPTY. [Adjective.]
Ge. 31: 42. had sent me away e.
37: 24. pit was e. no water in it
41: 27. the seven e. ears blasted
Ex. 3: 21. when ye go, not go e.
23: 15. in mouth Abib, none appear bef. me e.,34:20. De.16:16.
De. 15: 13. shalt not let him go e.
Ju. 7: 16. ev. man's hand e. pitch.
Ru. 1: 21. L. hath bro-t me home e.
3: 17. Go not e. unto mother in l.
1 S. 6: 3. send not ark away e.
20:18.bec.thy seat will be e., 25,27.
2 S. 1: 22. sw. of Saul returned not
2 K. 4: 3. go, borrow e. vessels [e.
Ne. 5:†13. thus be he shaken and e.
Jb. 11: † 12. for e. man would be
22: 9. hast sent widows away e.
26: 7. stretcheth north over e. pl.
Is. 24: 1. L. maketh the earth e.
29: 8. hungry man awak. soul is e.
32: 6. to make e. soul of hungry
Je. 14:3. retur. with their vessels e.
51: 34. k. of Bab. made me e. ves.
Eze. 24: 11. set it e. upon coals
Ho. 10: 1. Israel is an e. vine, be
Na. 2: 10. Nineveh is e. and void
Mat. 12:44. is come, he findeth it e.
Mk. 12: 3. they beat him, and sent him away e., Lu. 20: 10, 11.
Lu. 1: 53. rich he sent e. away
EMPTY, ING.
Le. 14: 36. that they e. the house
Ec. 11: 3. the clouds e. themselves
Je. 48: 12. wanderers sh. e. his ves.
51: 2. fanners shall e. her land
Ho. 10: † 1. vine e-g fruit it giveth
Ha. 1: 17. Shall they e. their net
Zch. 4: 12. which e. the golden oil
Mal. 3: † 10. if I will not e. a bless-
EMULATION, S. [ing
Ro. 11: 14. provoke to e. my breth.
Ga. 5: 20. works of the flesh are e-s
ENABLED. [me
1 Ti. 1: 12. I thank C. who hath e.
EN'AJIM.
Ge. 38: † 14. sat in door of E., 21.
E'NAM.
Jos. 15: 34. cities in the valley, E.
E'NAN.
Nu. 1: 15. renowned, Ahira son of E., 2: 29.-7: 78, 83.-10: 27.
ENCAMP.
Ex. 14: 2. e. before Pi-hahiroth
Nu.1:50. Levites shall e. about tab.
2: 17. as they e. so set forward
27. th. e. by him sh. be tribe of
3: 38. those that e. bef. tabern.
10: 31. how we are to e. in wilder.
2 S. 12: 28. e. ag. Rabbah, take it
Jb. 19: 12. his troops e. about tab.
Ps. 27: 3. Though a host e. ag. me
Zch. 9: 8. I will e. about mine hou.
ENCAMPED.
Ex. 13: 20. they e. in Etham
15:27. to Elim and e. by the waters
18: 5. Moses e. at the mount of G.
Nu. 33: 10. fr. Elim e. by Red sea
11. from Red sea, and e. in Sin
12. e. in 13, 24, 46.
14. e. at, 17, 26, 30, 32, 34, 35.
Jos. 4: 19. peo. e. in Gilgal, 5: 10.
10: 5. kings of Amorites e. before
31. e. against it and fought, 34.
Ju. 6: 4. Midianites e. ag. Israel
9: 50. Abimelech e. ag. Thebes
10:17. chil. of Ammon e. in Gilead and Israel e. at Mizpeh
1 S. 11: 1. Nahash e. ag. Jabesh-gil.
13: 16. Philistines e. in Michmash
2 S. 11: 11. servants are e. in fields

1 K.16:15.peo. e. ag. Gibbethon,16.
1 Ch. 11: 15. Philis. e. in valley
2 Ch. 32: 1 Sennacherib e. ag. cit.

ENCAMPETH, ING.

Ex. 14: 9. overtook them e-g by sea
2 K. 6: † 8. in such place be my e-g
Ps. 34: 7. angel of the L. e-h round
53:5. scat. bones of him e-h ag. thee

ENCHANTER, S.

De. 18: 10. shall not be found an e.
Je.27:9. hearken not to dreamer nor

ENCHANTMENTS. [e.

Ex. 7: 11. magicians with e., 22.-
8: 7, 18.
Le. 19: 26. nor shall ye use e.
Nu. 23: 23. there is no e. ag. Jacob
24: 1. Balaam went not to seek e.
2 K. 17:17. Isr. used divinat. and e.
21:6. Manasseh used e., 2 Ch.33:6.
Ec. 10:11. serpent will bite with. e.
Is.47:9. for great abnud. of thine e.
12. stand now with thine e.

ENCLOSE. See INCLOSE.

ENCOUNTERED. [him

Ac. 17: 18. certain philosophers e.

ENCOURAGE, ED.

De. 1: 38. e. him, he sh. cause,3:28.
1 S.30:6. Dav. e-d himself in L. God
2 S. 11: 25. say to Joab, and e. him
2 Ch. 17: † 6. his heart was e-d in
31: 4. that Levites be e-d [Lord
35:2. Josiah e-d them to service of
Ps. 64: 5. e. thems. in evil matter
Is. 41: 7. carpenter e-d goldsmith

END. [Verb.]

Mat. 10: † 23. ye shall not e. cities

END. [Noun.]

Ge. 6: 13. e. of all flesh is come
47: 21. one e. of E. to other e.
Ex. 23: 16. the e. of year, 34: 22.
25: 19. cherub on one e. on other
e. mercy seat, 37: 8. [other
26: 28. e. to e. | 36: 33. one e. to
De. 13: 7. one e. of earth to other
28:64. L. scatter fr. one e. of earth
32: 20. I will see what their e. be
Ju. 6: 21. angel put e. of his staff
19: 9. day groweth to an e. lodge
1 S. 14: 27. Jona. put e. of the rod
2 S. 14: 26. ev. yr.'s e. he polled it
2 K. 10: 21. house of Baal full fr. e.
21: 16. Jerus. with blood fr. one e.
2 Ch. 21:19. e. of 2 yrs., his bowels
Ezr. 9:11. unclean. fr. one e. to ano.
Jb. 6:11. what my e. th. I prol. life?
16: 3. Shall vain words have e.?
26: 10. until night come to an e.
28: 3. He setteth an e. to darku.
Ps. 7: 9. wickedness come to an e.
9: 6. are come to a perpetual e.
19:6. going forth is fr. e. of heaven
37: 37. the e. of that man is peace
38. e. of wicked shall be cut off
39: 4. make me to know mine e.
61:2. From e. of earth will, Is.5:26.
73: 17. then I understood their e.
102: 27. and thy years have no e.
107: 27. are at their wits' e.
119: 96. seen an e. of perfection
Pr.5:4. her e. bitter | 23:18. is an e.
14:12. e. thereof are ways of death
25: 8. know not what to do in e.
Ec. 4: 8. is no e. of all his labour
16. there is no e. of all the people
7: 2. e. of men | 8. better is the e.
10: 13. e. of his talk is madness
12: 12. of making books is no e.
† 13. let us hear e. of matter
Is. 2: 7. nor any e. of their treasures, nor any e. of chariots
9: 7. of his government be no e.
13: 5. they come fr. e. of heaven
16: 4. the extortioner is at an e.
23: 15. aft. e. of 70 years Tyre. 17.
42: 10. sing his praise fr. e. of the
45: 17. world without e. [earth
46: 10. Declaring e. fr. beginning

Je. 5: 31. what will ye do in the e.?
12: 12. fr. one e. other e., 25: 33.
17: 11. at his e. he shall be a fool
29: 11. to give you an expected e.
31: 17. there is hope in thine e.
44: 27. consumed, until be an e.
50: † 26. came ag. Bab. fr. the e.
51:13. that dwellest, thine e. come
31. that his city is taken at one e.
La. 4: 18. our e. near, our e. come
Eze. 7: 2. An e. the e. is come, 3,6.
21: 25. iniq. have an e., 29.-35: 5.
Da. 7: 28. is the e. of the matter
8: 17. time of e. shall be vision
19. at the time e. sh. be, 11: 27.
9: 26. e. be with flood, and to e.
11: 6. in e. of years they sh. join
35. purge them to time of e.
40. at time of e. king of south
45. come to his e. and none help
12: 4. seal the book even to the e.
8. O Lord, what shall be the e.?
9. words are closed up, till the e.
13. But go thou thy way till the e.
Am. 3: 15. houses shall have an e.
5: 18. to what e. desire the day?
8: 2. e. is come upon my people
10. I will make e. as bitter day
Na. 2: 9. there is none e. of store
3: 3. is none e. of their corpses
Mat. 13: 39. the harvest is the e.
of the world, 24: 3.-28: 20.
24: 3. what sign of e. of world?
14. gospel be preached, then e.
31. gather from one e. of heaven
26: 58. Peter sat to see the e.
28: 1. In e. of the sab. came Mary
Mk. 3: 26. cannot stand, hath an e.
Lu. 1: 33. of his kingd. be no e.
18: 1. parable unto them, to this e.
22: 37. things conc. me have an e.
Jn. 18: 37. To this e. was I born
Ro. 6:21. e. of those things is death
22. fruit of holin., e. everl. life
10: 4. Christ is the e. of the law
14: 9. to this e. Christ both died
1 Co. 15: 24. Then cometh the e.
2 Co. 2: 9. For to this e. did I write
11: 15. whose e. be acc. to works
Ep. 3: 21. glory world without e.
Ph. 3: 19. whose e. is destruction
1 Ti. 1: 5. e. of com-t is charity
He. 6: 8. whose e. is to be burned
16. an oath is an e. of all strife
7: 3. neither beginn. nor e. of life
9:26. once in the e. hath he appear.
13:7. consid-g e. of their conversa.
Ja. 5: 11. ye have seen e. of Lord
1 Pe. 1:9. Receiving e. of your faith
4: 17. what e. of them obey not
Re. 21: 6. I am Alpha and Omega,
beginn. and e., 22: 13.

At the END.

Ge. 4: † 3. a. e. of days Cain bro-t
8: 6. a. e. of 40 days Noah opened
41:1. a. e. of 2 years Pha. dreamed
Ex. 12:41. a. e. of 430 years, L.'s host
Le. 8: 33. consecration be a. an e.
D. 9: 11. a. e. of 40 days and 40
14: 28. a. e. of 3 years bring tithe
15: 1. a. e. of 7th year release
31:10. a. e. of 7th year read this law
Jos. 9: 16. a. e. of 3 days aft league
Ju. 11: 39. a. e. of two months she
Ru. 3: 7. Boaz lay a. e. of heap
2 S. 14:26. a. e. of year he polled it
24:8. Joab came a. e. of 9 months
1 K.2:39. a. e. of 3 ys. two of Shimei's
17: † 7. a. e. of days brook dried
2 K.8:3. a. e. of 7 yrs. woman retur.
18: 10. a. e. of 3 years took Sama.
2 Ch. 18: † 2. a. e. of years Jehosh.
20:16. sh. find them a. e. of brook
24:23. a. e. of yr. host of Syria came
Ne. 13: † 6. a. e. I obtained leave
Ps. 107: 27. and are a. their wits' e.
Is. 7:3. meet Ahaz a. e. of conduit

Je. 34:14. a. e. of 7 ys. let go ev. serv.
Eze. 3:16. a. e. of 7 days word of L.
Da. 1:5. a. e. might stand bef. king
15. a. e. of 10 days their counten.
18. a. e. of days the king had sd.
4:29. a. e. of 12 months he walked
34. a. e. of the days I Nebuchad.
11: † 13. a. e. of times shall come
12: 13. stand in lot a. e. of days
Ha. 2: 3. but a. e. it shall speak
Mat. 13: 49. So be a. e. of world, 40.

But the END.

Pr. 14: 12. way that seemeth right,
b. e. are ways of death, 16: 25.
20: 21. b. e. not be blessed [21:9.
Mat.24:6. b. e. is not yet, Mk.13: 7. Lu.
1 Pe. 4: 7. b. e. of all things is at

Last END. [hand

Nu. 23: 10. let my l. e. be like his
Je. 12: 4. He shall not see our l. e.
La. 1: 9. she remem. not her l. e.
Da. 8: 19. thee kn. what be in l. e.

Latter END.

Nu. 24: 20. l. e. be that he perish
De. 8: 16. to do thee good at l. e.
32: 29. would consider their l. e.
Ru. 3: 10. shewed kindness in l. e.
2 S. 2: 26. will be bitterness in l. e.
Jb. 8: 7. thy l. e. greatly increase
42: 12. L. blessed the l. e. of Job
Pr. 19:20. mayest be wise in thy l. e.
Is. 41:22. consider them, know l. e.
47:7. nei. didst remember l. e. of it
2 Pe. 2:20. l. e. is worse than begin.

Made an END.

Ge.27:30. Isaac had m. e. of blessing
49:33. Jacob m. e. of com. his sons
Le. 16: 20. m. e. of reconciling
Nu. 4: 15. m. e. of covering sanct.
16: 31. m. e. of speaking, De. 20:
9.-32: 45. Ju. 15: 17. 1 S. 18:
1.-24: 16. 2 S. 13: 36. 1 K. 1:
41.-3:1. Je. 26:8.-43:1.-51:63.
De. 26: 12. hast m. e. of tithing
31: 24. Moses had m. e. of writing
Jos. 5: † 8. had m. e. of circum-g
8: 24. had m. e. of slaying, 10:20.
19: 49. m. e. of dividing land, 51.
Ju. 3: 18. m. e. to offer, 1 S. 13: 10.
1 S. 10: 13. m. e. of prophesying
2 S. 11: 19. hast m. e. of telling
1 K. 7: 40. Hiram m. e. of work
8: 54. Solomon m. e. of praying,
2 Ch. 7: 1.
2 K. 10: 25. soon as he m. e. of
offering, 2 S. 6: 18. 1 Ch. 16: 2.
2 Ch. 29: 29. [Seir
2 Ch. 20:23. m. e. of inhabitants of
24:10. i to chest, until they m. e.
29: 17. 16th day of 1st mo. m. e.
Ezr. 10: 17. m. e. with all the men
that had taken strange wives
Eze. 42: 15. m. e. of measuring
43: 23. hast m. e. of cleansing it
Am. 7: 2. m. e. of eating the grass
Mat.11:1. m. e. of com. his disciples

Make an END.

1 S. 3:12. when I begin, I will m. e.
2 Ch.31:† 1. brake images, until m. e.
Ne. 4: 2. will they m. e. in a day
Jb. 18: 2. ere you m. e. of words?
Is. 33:1. shalt m. e. to deal treach.
38: 12. wilt thou m. e. of me, 13.
Eze. 20: 17. nor did I m. e. of them
Da. 9: 24. weeks, to m. e. of sins
Na. 1: 8. m. utter e. of place, 9.
Zph. 1: 18. by taking, I will m. e.?

Make a full END.

Je. 4: 27. land desolate, yet I not
m. f. e., 5: 18.-30: 11.-46: 28.
5:10. and destroy, but m. not f. e.
Eze. 11: 13. L., wilt thou m. f. e.?

To the END.

Ex. 8: 22. sever Goshen, t. e. thou
mayest kn. I am L., Eze. 20:26.
Le. 17: 5. t. e. Isr. may bring sacri.
De. 15: † 4. t. e. there be no poor

De. 17 : 16. t. e. he multiply horses
20. t. e. he may prolong his days
Jos. 18 : 16. border came t. e. of mt
1 S. 9 : 27. going down t. e. of city
Ne. 3 : 21. t. e. of house of Eliash.
Ps. 19 : 4. their words t. e. of world
30 12. t. e. my glory may sing
119 : 112. perform thy statutes t.e.
Ec. 3 : 11. find out from begin. t. e.
7 : 14. t. e. man find nothing after
Is. 48 : 20. utter it t. e. of earth
49 : 6. my salvation t. e. of earth
Je. 3 : 5. anger, will he keep it t.e.?
Eze. 31 : 14. t. e. none of trees exalt
Da. 4 : 11. sight t. e. of the earth
22. thy dominion t. e. of earth
12 : 6. How long t. e. of wonders
Ob. 9. t. e. every one be cut off
Mat. 10 : 22. that endureth t. e. sh. be saved, 24 : 13. Mk. 13 : 13.
Ac. 7 : 19. t. e. they might not live
Ro. 1 : 11. t. e. you may be establ.
4:16. t. e. the promise might be sure
2 Co. 1 : 13. you shall acknowl. t.e.
3 : 13. look t. e. of that abolished
1 Th. 3 : 13. t. e. he may estab. your
1 Pe. 1 : 13. be sober, and hope t.e.

Unto the END.

De. 11 : 12. begin-g u. e. of year
Jos. 15 : 5. was u. e. of Jordan
Ru. 2 : 23. glean u. e. of barley har.
Jb. 34 : 36. desire Job be tried u. e.
Ps. 46 : 9. wars to cease u. e. of earth
119 : 33. and I shall keep it u. e.
Is. 62 : 11. proclaimed u. e. of world
Je. 1 : 3. it came u. e. of 11th year
Da. 6 : 26. his dominion even u. e.
7 : 26. destroy his dominion u. e.
9 : 26. and u. e. of war desolations
Mat. 28 : 20. I am with you, even u. [e.
Jn. 13 : 1. he loved them u. e.
1 Co. 1 : 8. shall confirm you u. e.
He. 3 : 6. hold fast confidence u. e.
14. if hold begin-g stedfast u. e.
6 : 11. full assurance of hope u. e.
Re. 2 : 26. keepeth my works u. e.

ENDS.

Ex. 25 : 18. in two e. of mercy seat
De. 33 : 17. push people to e. of earth
1 S. 2 : 10. shall judge e. of earth
1 K. 8 : 8. e. of staves seen, 2 Ch. 5 : 9.
2 K. 10 : † 32. L. to cut off e. of Isr.
Jb. 28 : 24. looketh to e. of earth
37 : 3. his lightning unto e. of earth
38 : 13. take hold of the e. of earth
Ps. 19 : 6. his circuit to e. of it
22 : 27. e. of the world shall remem.
48 : 10. thy praise unto e. of earth
59 : 13. G. ruleth in Jac. to e. of earth
65 : 5. confidence of e. of earth
67 : 7. all e. of the earth sh. fear
72 : 8. from river unto e. of earth
98 : 3. e. of earth seen salv. of G.
135 : 7. vapours to ascend from e. of earth, Je. 10 : 13.–51 : 16.
Pr. 17 : 24. eyes of fool are in e. of
30 : 4. who estab-d e. of the earth?
Is. 26 : 15. remov. it unto e. of earth
40 : 28. Creator of e. of earth
41 : 5. e. of the earth were afraid
9. have taken fr. the e. of earth
43 : 6. bring my dau-s fr. e. of earth
45 : 22. look and be saved, all the e.
52 : 10. all e. shall see salv. of God
Je. 16 : 19. Gent. shall come fr. e. of
25 : 31. A noise to the e. of the earth
Eze. 15 : 4. fire devoureth both the e.
Mi. 5 : 4. he be gr. unto e. of earth
Zch. 9 : 10. his dominion to e. of the
Ac. 13 : 47. for salv. unto e. of earth
Ro. 10 : 18. words unto e. of the world
1 Co. 10 : 11. upon whom e. of world [are

ENDAMAGE.

Ezr. 4 : 13. shalt e. revenue of kings

ENDANGER, ED.

Ec. 10 : 9. cleaveth wood shall be e.
Da. 1 : 10. make me e. my head to

ENDEAVOUR, ED, ING.

Ac. 16 : 10. we e-d to go into Maced.
2 Co. 5 : †9. e. th. we may be accep.
Ep. 4 : 3. e-g to keep unity of Spirit
1 Th. 2 : 17. we e-d to see your face
2 Pe. 1 : 15. I will e. th. you be able

ENDEAVOURS.

Ps. 28 : 4. acc. to wickedness of e.

ENDED, ETH, ING.

Ge. 2 : 2. on seventh day God e. work
41 : 53. years of plenteousn. were e.
47 : 18. When that year was e.
De. 31 : 30. words until they were e.
34 : 8. days of mourning for Mos. e.
Ru. 2 : 21. until have e. harvest
1 S. 3 : †12. perform beginn. and e-g
2 S. 20 : 18. and so they e. the matter
1 K. 7 : 51. So was e. all the work
2 Ch. 29 : 34. help till work was e.
Es. 9 : † 28. nor memorial be e.
Jb. 31 : 40. The words of Job are e.
Ps. 72 : 20. prayers of David are e.
Is. 24 : 8. noise of them rejoice e-h
60 : 20. days of mourning sh. be e.
Je. 8 : 20. is past, summer is e.
Eze. 4 : 8. till thou hast e. siege
Mat. 7 : 28. Jesus had e., Lu. 7 : 1.
Lu. 4 : 2. when forty days were e.
13. when devil had e. tempta.
Jn. 13 : 2. supper being e. the devil
Ac. 19 : 21. Aft. these things were e.
21 : 27. when 7 days almost e.
Re. 1 : 8. I am the beginning and e-g

ENDLESS.

1 Ti. 1 : 4. heed to e. genealogies
He. 7 : 16. after power of an e. life

EN'DOR.

Jos. 17 : 11. Manasseh had E. and
1 S. 28 : 7. wom. at E. with spirit
Ps. 83 : 10. Jabin, wh. perished at E.

ENDOW.

Ex. 22 : 16. sh e. her to be his wife

ENDUED.

Ge. 30 : 20. e. me with good dowry
2 Ch. 2 : 12. to David, a wise son e. with prudence
13. have sent man e. with underst.
Lu. 24 : 49. until ye be e. with power
Ja. 3 : 13. Who is e. with knowl.?

ENDURE.

Ge. 33 : 14. as the chil. be able to e.
Ex. 18 : 23. thou shalt be able to e.
Es. 8 : 6. how can I e. to see evil
Jb. 8 : 15. fast, but it shall not e.
31 : 23. his highness I could not e.
Ps. 9 : 7. the L. shall e. for ever, 102 : 12, 26 –104 : 31.
30 : 5. weeping may e. for a night
72 : 5. sh. fear thee as long as sun e.
17. His name shall e. for ever
89 : 29. His seed to e. for ever, 36.
Pr. 27 : 24. crown e. to ev. genera.?
Eze. 22 : 14. Can thy heart e.?
Mat. 24 : 13. that shall e. unto the end, Mk. 13 : 13.
Mk. 4 : 17. and so e. but for a time
2 Th. 1 : 4. tribulations that ye e.
2 Ti. 2 : 3. e. hardness as a soldier
10. I e. all things for elects' sake
4 : 3. will not e. sound doctrine
5. But watch thou e. afflictions
He. 12 : 7. If ye e. chastening, G.
20. could not e. what was com-d
Ja. 5 : 11. count them happy which e.
1 Pe. 2 : 19. if for conscience e. grief

ENDURED.

Ps. 81 : 15. time sho. have e. for ev.
Ro. 9 : 22. if God e. with long suff.
2 Ti. 3 : 11. what persecutions I e.
He. 6 : 15. after he had patiently e.
10 : 32. ye e. a great fight of afflic.
11 : 27. Moses e. as seeing him who
12 : 2. e. cross | 3. e. contradiction

ENDURETH.

Ps. 15 : †3. nor e. reproach ag. neighb.
30 : 5. his anger e. but a moment
52 : 1. goodness of G. e. continually
Ps. 72 : 7. peace so long as the moon e.
100 : 5. his truth e. to all genera.
145 : 13. dominion e. thro. all gene.
Mat. 10 : 22. e. to the end be saved
Jn. 6 : 27. meat which e. unto life
1 Co. 13 : 7. charity, e. all things
Ja. 1 : 12. Blessed that e. tempta.

ENDURETH for ever.

1 Ch. 16 : 34. for his memory e. f. e., 41. 2 Ch. 5 : 13.–7 : 3, 6.–20 : 21. Ezr. 3 : 11. Ps. 106 : 1.–107 : 1.–118 : 1, 2, 3, 4.–136 : 1, 2, 3, etc.–138 : 8. Je. 33 : 11.
Ps. 111 : 3. his righte. e. f. e., 112 : 3, 9.
10. his praise e. f. e. | 117 : 2. truth
119 : 160. thy judgm. e. f. e.
135 : 13. Thy name, O Lord, e. f. e.
1 Pe. 1 : 25. word of the L. e. f. e.

ENDURING.

Ps. 19 : 9. fear of Lord clean, e. for [ever
2 Co. 1 : 6. effectual in e. same suff.
He. 10 : 34. in heaven e. substance

E'NEAS.

Ac 9 : 34. E. Ch. maketh thee whole

EN-EGLA'IM.

Eze. 47 : 10. sh. stand fr. En-gedi to E.

ENEMIES.

Jos. 10 : 13. avenged thems. upon their e.
Ju. 3 : 28. delivered your e. into your hand
1 S. 18 : 25. avenged of king's e.
20 : 15. when L. cut off e. of David
16. L. require it at hand of Da.'s e.
25 : 22. So do God, to e. of David
29 : 8. fight ag. e. of my lord
30 : 26. present of spoil of e. of L.
2 S. 12 : 14 occasion to e. to blasp.
18 : 32. The e. be as that young man
2 Ch. 20 : 29. L. fought ag. e. of Isr.
Es. 9 : 1. e. of Jews hoped power
Ps. 17 : 9. hide me from my deadly e.
37 : 20. e. of L. be as fat of lambs
45 : 5. arrows sharp in heart of k.'s e.
127 : 5. speak with the e. in gate
Je. 12 : 7. beloved into hands of e.
48 : 5. e. heard a cry of destruc.
La. 1 : 2. her friends are become e.
5. Her adversaries chief, e. prosp.
Mi. 7 : 6. man's e. are of own house
Ro. 5 : 10. if when e. were reconcil.
11 : 28. As conc. gospel, they are e.
1 Co. 15 : 25. till he put all e. under
Ph. 3 : 18. are e. of cross of Christ
Col. 1 : 21. e. in your mind by wick.

His ENEMIES.

Ge. 22 : 17. seed possess gate of h. e.
Nu. 24 : 8. sh. eat up nations h. e.
18. Seir be possession for h. e.
32 : 21. until he hath driven h. e.
De. 33 : 7. be a help from h. e.
1 S. 14 : 47. fought ag. all h. e.
2 S. 7 : 1. Lath given him rest fr. h. e.
18 : 19. how L. avenged him of h. e.
22 : 1. deliv. him out of hand of h. e.
1 Ch. 22 : 9. give him rest fr. h. e.
Jb. 19 : 11. counteth me one of h. e.
Ps. 10 : 5. all h. e. he puffeth at them
41 : 2 not deliv. unto will of h. e.
68 : 1. Let G. arise, let h. e. be scat.
21. G. shall wound head of h. e.
72 : 9. h. e. shall lick the dust
78 : 66. smote h. e. in hinder parts
89 : 42. hast made all h. e. rejoice
97 : 3. fire burneth up h. e.
112 : 8. see his desire upon h. e.
132 : 18. h. e. clothe with shame
Pr. 16 : 7. maketh h. e. to be at peace
Is. 9 : 11. L. shall join h. e. togeth.
42 : 13. he shall prevail ag. h. e.
59 : 18. repay recompence to h. e.
66 : 6. rendereth recompence to h. e.
Is. 66 : 14. indigna. be known tow. h. e.
Je. 44 : 30. Pha. into hand of h. e.
Na. 1 : 2. reserveth wrath for h. e.
8. darkness shall pursue h. e.
He. 10 : 13. till h. e. be made footst.

Mine ENEMIES.

Nu. 23 : 11. to curse m. e., 24 : 10.

e. 82: 41. vengeance to m. e.
S. 2:1. mouth enlarged over m.e.
14: 24. that I be avenged on m.e.
S. 5: 20. Lord hath broken forth upon m. e., 1 Ch. 14: 11.
22: 4. be saved fr. m. e., Ps. 18:3.
S. 22:38. pursued m. e., Ps. 18:37.
41. given necks of m.e., Ps. 18:40.
49. bringeth me forth from m.e.
Ch. 12: 17. to betray me to m.e.
's. 3:7. thou hast smitten all m.e.
5:8. lead me, O Lord, bec. of m.e.
6: 7. eye waxeth old bec. of m. e.
10. Let all m. e. be ashamed
7:6. arise, O L., bec. of rage of m.e.
9:3. When m. e. are turned, sh. fall
18:48. He delivereth me from m.e.
23: 5. prep. table in pres. of m.e.
25:2. let not m.e. triumph, 35: 19.
19. Consider m. e. they are many
27: 2. m. e. came to eat my flesh
6. head be lifted up above m. e.
11. in a plain path, bec. of m. e.
12. Deliv. not unto will of m. e.
31:11. I was a reproach amo. m. e.
15. deliver me from hand of m. e.
38:19. m. e. are lively, and strong
41: 5. m. e. speak evil of me.
42: 10. m. e. reproach me, 102: 8.
54:5. He sh. reward evil unto m.e.
7. seen his desire upon m.e, 59:10.
56: 2. m. e. would swallow me up
9. When I cry, then sh. m. e. turn
59:1. Deliver me from m. e., 143:9.
69: 4. they being m. e. wrongfully
18. deliver me because of m. e.
71: 10. m. e. speak against me
92:11. shall see my desire on m. e.
119:98. made me wiser than m. e.
139. m.e. have forgotten thy word
157. Many are m. e. yet do I not
138:7. stretch forth hand ag. m. e.
139:22. I hate, I count them m.e.
143: 12. of thy mercy cut off m.e.
s. 1: 24. I will avenge me of m. e.
a. 1:21. m.e. heard of my trouble
3: 52. m. e. chased me like a bird
u. 19:27. those m.e. bring and slay

Our ENEMIES.

Ex. 1: 10. they join also unto o. e.
De. 32:31. o. e. thems. being judges
S. 4: 3. save us out of ha. of o. e.
12:10. deliver us out of ha. of o.e.
S. 19: 9. out of hand of o. e., Ps. 44: 7. [unto us
Ne. 4:15. when o.e. heard it was kn.
5: 9. because of reproach of o. e.
6: 1. o. e. heard I had builded, 16.
Ps. 44: 5. will we push down o. e.
60:12. sh. tread down o. e., 108: 13.
80: 6. o. e. laugh among thems.
136: 24. hath redeemed us fr. o.e.
a. 3:46. o. e. opened their mouths
u. 1:71. That we be saved fr. o.e.
74. delivered out of hands of o.e.

Their ENEMIES. [e.

Ex. 32: 25. made them naked am. t.
e. 26: 36. send faintness in the land of t. e., 41. 1 K. 8: 48.
44. when they be in land of t. e.
os. 7:8. turneth backs bef. t. e., 12.
10:13. had aveng. thems. upon t.e.
21: 44. stood not a man of t. e. bef. them, L. deliv-d t.e. into ha.
23: 1. given rest fr. t. e., Es. 9:16.
u. 2:14. sold into the hand of t. e.
18: deliv. out of ha. of t. e., 8:34.
S. 14: 30. spoil of t. e. they found
K. 21: 14. deliver into hand of t. e., 2 Ch 6:36.–25:20. Ne. 9:27,28.
Ch. 6: 28. if t. e. besiege in cities
34. if peo. go to war ag. t. e. [e.
20:27. L. made them rejoice over t.
s. 8: 13. avenge thems. on t. e.
9: 5. Thus Jews smote all t. e.
22. Jews rested from t. e., 16.
s. 78: 53. sea overwhelmed t. e.
Ps. 81: 14. I sho. soon ha. subdu. t.e.
105: 24. made stronger than t. e.
106: 11. the waters covered t. e.
42. t. e. oppressed, he deliv. them
Je. 15: 9. deliver to sword bef. t. e.
19: 7. fall by sword bef. t. e., 20:4.
9. wherew. t. e. sh. straiten them
20: 5. treasures of k-s into hands of t.e., 34:20, 21.–21:7. Eze. 39:23.
49: 37. to be dismayed before t. e.
Eze. 39: 27. gath. out of t. e. lands
Am. 9: 4. tho. into captiv. bef. t.e.
Zch. 10: 5. men, tread down t. e.
Re. 11:5. if hurt, fire devoureth t.e.,
12. ascended, t. e. beheld them

Thine ENEMIES.

Ge. 14:20. delivered t.e. into thy ha.
49: 8. thy hand be in neck of t.e.
Ex. 23: 22. will be enemy to t. e.
27. I will make t. e. to turn backs
Nu. 10: 35. L., let t. e. be scattered
De. 6: 19. To cast out all t. e. bef.
20: 1. When thou goest ag. t. e.
14. shalt eat spoil of t. e. [21:10.
23: 9. When host goeth ag. t. e.
14. to give up t. e. [S. 7: 11.
25: 19. given thee rest fr. t. e., 2
28: 7. cause t. e. to be smitten
25. to be smitten before t. e.
31. sheep be given unto t. e.
48. Shalt thou serve t. e. [57.
28: 53. t. e. shall distress thee, 55,
30: 7. G. will put curses upon t. e.
33: 29. t. e. shall be found liars to
Jos. 7: 13. canst not stand bef. t. e.
Ju. 5: 31. So let all t. e. perish, O L.
11: 36. taken vengeance of t. e.
1 S. 25: 26. let t. e. be as Nabal
29. souls of t. e. sh. he sling out
2 S. 7: 9. cut off all t. e., 1 Ch. 17:8.
19:6. lovest t. e. hatest thy friends
24: 13. or flee 3 months bef. t. e.
1 K. 3: 11. nor asked life of t. e., 2 Ch. 1: 11.
1 Ch. 17: 10. I will subdue t. e.
21: 12. sword of t. e. overtaketh
Ps. 8: 2. ord-d strength bec. of t.e.
21: 8. Thine hand find out all t. e.
66: 3. thro. thy power t. e. submit
68: 23. foot dipped in blood of t.e.
74:4. t.e. roar | 83:2. make a tumult
23. Forget not the voice of t. e.
89:10. scattered t. e. with thy arm
51. Wherew. t. e. reproached, O L.
92: 9. lo, t. e. O L., t. e. sh. perish
110: 1. make t. e. thy footstool, Mat. 22: 44. Mk. 12: 36. Lu. 20: 43. He. 1: 13.
2. rule thou in the midst of t. e.
139: 20. t. e. take thy name in vain
Is. 26: 11. fire of t. e. shall devour
62: 8. no more give corn for t. e.
Je. 15: 14. make thee to pass with [t.e.
La. 2: 16. t. e. opened mouth
Da. 4: 19. interpretation be to t. e.
Mi. 4:10. L. shall redeem thee fr. t.e.
5: 9. all t. e. shall be cut off
† 14. so will I destroy t. e. [t. e.
Na. 3: 13. thy gate sh. be open unto
Lu. 19: 43. t. e. shall cast a trench

Your ENEMIES.

Le. 26: 7. ye shall chase y. e.
8. y. e. shall fall bef. you by sword
16. sow in vain, y. e. shall eat it
17. ye shall be slain before y. e.
32. y. e. shall be astonished
34. and ye be in y. e. land
37. no power to stand bef. y. e.
38. land of y. e. shall eat you
Le. 26: 39. pine away in y. e. lands
Nu. 10: 9. ye shall be saved fr. y.e.
14: 42. not smitten bef. y. e., De. [1: 42.
De. 12: 10. rest fr. all y. e.
20: 3. approach unto battle ag. y.e.
4. L. goeth to fight for you ag. y.e.
28: 68. ye shall be sold unto y. e.
Jos. 10: 19. but pursue after y. e.
Jos. 10:25. thus sh. Lord do to all y.e.
22:8. divide spoil of y.e. with breth.
1 S. 12: 11. Lord delivered you out of band of y. e., 2 K. 17: 39.
Mat. 5: 44. Love y. e., Lu. 6:27,35.

ENEMY.

Ex. 15: 6. thy right hand dashed e.
9. e. said, I will pursue [enemies
23: 22. I will be an e. unto thine
Nu. 10: 9. if you go to war ag e.
35: 23. was not his e. nor sought
De. 32: 27. I feared the wrath of e.
42. beginning of revenges upon e.
33:27. he shall thrust out e. [e., 24.
Ju. 16: 23. Our god hath deliv. our
1 S. 2: 32. shalt see e. in my habit.
18: 29. Saul became David's e.
24: 19. if find e. will he let him go
2 S. 22: 18. He deliv-d me from my strong e., Ps. 18: 17.
1 K. 8: 33. when peo. smitten before e. bec. sinned, 2 Ch. 6:24.
37. if their e. besiege them
44. If peo. go to battle against e.
46. if sin, and thou deliver to e.
2 Ch. 25: 8. make thee fall bef. e.
26: 13. to help king ag. the e.
Ezr. 8: 22. help us ag. e. in way
Es. 7: 4. e. could not countervail
6. The e. is this wicked Haman
8:1. Haman Jew's e., 8:10.–9:10,24.
Jb. 33: 10. counteth me his e.
Ps. 7: 5. Let e. persecute my soul
8: 2. mightest still e. and avenger
9: 6. O e. destructions to an end
42: 9. mourning bec. of e.? 43: 2.
44: 10. makest us turn back fr. e.
16. by reason of e. and avenger
55: 3. I mourn. bec. of voice of e.
12. not an e. that reproach me
61: 3. been a strong tower fr. e.
64: 1. preserve life from fear of e.
74: 3. all that e. hath done wick.
10. shall e. blaspheme for ever?
18. Remember e. hath reproached
78: 42. remembered not the day when he delivered from e.
89: 22. e. sh. not exact upon him
143: 3. e. hath persecuted my soul
Pr. 27: 6. kisses of an e. deceitful
Is. 59: 19. e. sh. come in like flood
63:10. he was turned to be their e.
Je. 6: 25. sword of e. on ev. side
15:11. cause e. to entreat thee well
18: 17. I will scatter them bef. e.
30: 14. thee with wound of an e.
31: 16. come again fr. land of e.
44:30. k. of Bab. his e. sought life
La. 1: 5. into captivity before e.
9. e. hath magnified himself
16. chil. desolate, bec. e. prevailed
2:3. hath drawn back hand bef. e.
4. He hath bent his bow like an e.
5. The Lord was an e. he hath
4: 12. that e. sho. have ent. gates
Eze. 36:2. e. had said ag. you, Aha
Ho. 8: 3. Isr. e. shall pursue him
Mi. 2:8. my peo. is risen up as an e.
Na. 3: 11. seek strength bec. of e.
Mat. 13:25. his e. came, sowed tares
28. He said, An e. hath done this
39. e. that sowed is the devil
Lu. 10: 19. over all the power of e.
Ac. 13: 10. thou e. of all righte.
1 Co. 15:26. last e. is death [truth?
Ga. 4: 16. Am I your e. bec. I tell
2 Th. 3: 15. count him not as an e.
Ja. 4: 4. friend of world e. of God

ENEMY'S hand.

Jb. 6: 23. Deliver me from e. h.
Ps. 78:61. deliv-d his glo. into e. h.

Hand of the ENEMY.

Le. 26: 25. pestilence, and ye shall be deliv. into h. o. e., Ne. 9:27.
Ezr. 8:31. he delivered us fr. h.o.e.
Ps. 31: 8. not shut me into h.o.e.
106:10. redeemed fr. h.o.e., 107:2.

La. 1 : 7. her peo. fell into h.o.e.
2 : 7. given into h. o. e. the walls

Mine ENEMY.

1 S. 19 : 17. why sent away m. e.?
1 K. 21:20. Hast found me, O m.e.
Jb. 16:9. m. e. sharpeneth his eyes
27 : 7. Let m.e. be as wicked, and
Ps. 7:4. I delivered him th. is m.e.
13 : 2. how long m. e. be exalted
4. Lest m.e. say, I have prevailed
41 : 11. because m. e. doth not triumph [e. consumed
La.2: 22. those I swaddled hath m.
Mi. 7:8 rejoice not ag. me, O m.e.
10. she that is m. e. shall see it

Thine ENEMY.

Ex. 23 : 4. If thou meet t. e.'s ox
De. 28 : 57. t. e. shall distress thee
1 S. 24 : 4. t. e. into thy hand, 26:8.
28 : 16. seeing L. is become t. e.
2 S. 4 : 8. head of Ish-bosheth t. e.
Jb. 13:24. Whf. holdest me for t.e.
Pr. 24:17. Rejoi. not when t.e. fall.
25 : 21. If t. e. hunger, Ro. 12:20.
La. 2 : 17. t. e. to rejoice over thee
Zph. 3 : 15. L. hath cast out t. e.
Mat.5:43. said, Thou shalt hate t.e.

ENFLAME. See INFLAME.

ENGAGED.

Je. 30 : 21. who is this th. e. his [heart

EN-GAN'NIM.

Jos. 15 : 34. cities E. | 19:21.-21:29.

EN'-GEDI.

Jos. 15 : 62. in wildern. of Jud. E.
1 S. 23 : 29. David dwelt in E., 24:1.
2 Ch. 20 : 2. mult. ag. Jehosh. in E.
Can. 1:14. camphire in viney. of E.
Eze. 47:10. fishers shall stand fr. E.

ENGINE, S. [e-s

2 Ch. 26:15. Uzziah made in Jerus.
Je. 6: † 6. e. of shot, Eze. 26 : † 8.
32: † 24. behold the e. of shot
Eze. 26 : 9. shall set e-s of war ag.

ENGRAFTED. [walls

Ja. 1 : 21. receive with meekness e.

ENGRAVE, EN. [word

Ex. 28 : 11. shalt e. the two stones
Zch. 3 : 9. I will e. graving thereof
2 Co. 3:7. ministration of death e-n

ENGRAVER.

Ex. 28 : 11. work of an e. in stone
35 : 35. all manner of work of e.
38 : 23. Aholiab, of tribe of Dan,

ENGRAVINGS. [an c.

Ex. 28 : 11. like e. of a signet, 21, 36.-39 : 14, 30.

EN-HAD'DAH.

Jos.19:21. Issachar's border tow. E.

EN-HAK'KORE.

Ju. 15 : 19. Samson called place E.

EN-HA'ZOR.

Jos. 19 : 37. fenced cities are E. and

ENJOIN, ED.

Es. 9 : 31. days of Purim as Es. had
Jb. 36:23. who e-d him his ways [e.
He. 9:20. blood God hath e. to you
Phm.8. to e. that wh. is convenient

ENJOY, ED. [43.

Le. 26:34. land sh. e. her sabbaths,
Nu. 36 : 8. that Isr. may e. inheri.
De. 28:41. beget sons, but not e. th.
Jos.1:15.sh.return unto land and e.
2 Ch. 36 : 21. until land e-d her sab.
Jb. 7:†7. mine eye no more e. good
Ec. 2 : 1. e. pleasure, this is vanity
24. his soul e. good, 3 : 13.-5:18.
9 : † 9. e. life with wife thou lovest
Is. 65 : 22. elect shall long e. work
Ac.24:2. by thee we e. great quietn.
1 Ti. 6:17. G. giveth us all thi. to e.
He. 11 : 25. than e. pleasures of sin

ENLARGE.

Ge. 9 : 27. G. shall e. Japhet, he
Ex. 34 : 24. I will e. thy borders
De. 12:20. When L. shall e. border
19 : 8. if the Lord e. thy coast as
1 Ch. 4:10. O that wouldest e. coast
Ps. 119 : 32. when shalt e. my heart
Is. 54 : 2. e. the place of thy tent
Am. 1 : 13. might e. their border
Mi. 1 : 16. e. thy baldness as eagle
Mat. 23 : 5. e. borders of garments

ENLARGED.

1 S.2:1. my mouth is e. over enem.
2 S. 22 : 37. e. my steps, Ps. 18:36.
Ps. 4 : 1. hast e. me in distress
25 : 17. troubles of my heart are e.
Is. 5 : 14. Theref. hell hath e. hers.
57 : 8. thou hast e. thy bed
60:5. thine heart sh. fear and be e.
2 Co. 6 : 11. O Corin. our heart is e.
13. for recompence be ye also e.
10 : 15. that we shall be e. by you

ENLARGETH, ING.

De. 33:20. blessed be he th. e. Gad
Jb. 12 : 23. he e. the nations, and
Eze. 41 : 7. was an e-g and winding
Ha. 2 : 5. who e. his desire as hell

ENLARGEMENT.

Es. 4 : 14. e. sh. arise fr. ano. place

ENLIGHTEN, ING.

Ps. 18 : 28. L. will e. my darkness
19 : 8. com-t is pure, e-g the eyes

ENLIGHTENED.

1 S. 14 : 27. Jona.'s eyes were e., 29.
Jb. 33 : 30. e. with light of living
Ps. 97:4. His lightnings e. the world
Is. 60:†1. be e. for thy light cometh
Ep. 1 : 18. eyes of understanding e.
He. 6 : 4. impossible for those once

EN-MISH'PAT. [c.

Ge. 14 : 7. they came to E. which is

ENMITY.

Ge. 3:15. e. betw. thee and woman
Nu. 35 : 21. Or in e. smite him [e.
22. But if he thrust him without
Lu. 23 : 12. for bef. they were at e.
Ro. 8 : 7. carnal mind is e. ag. God
Ep.2:15. abolished in his flesh the e.
16. by cross having slain the e.
Ja. 4 : 4. friendship of world is e.

E'NOCH. [with God

Ge.4:17. wife bare E. | 5:18. begat E.
5 : 22. E. walked with God, 24.
Lu. 3 : 37. Mathusala, which was son of E., Ge. 5 : 21.
He. 11 : 5. by faith E. was translat.
Jude 14. E. also prophesi. of these

E'NON.

Jn. 3 : 23. John was baptizing in E.

E'NOS = E'NOSH.

Ge. 4 : 26. Seth called son's name E | 5 : 6, 7, 9, 10, 11.
Lu. 3 : 38. Cainan was son of E.

E'NOSH.

1 Ch. 1 : 1. Adam, Sheth, E. Ge. 4 :

ENOUGH. [† 26.

Ge. 24 : 25. we have straw e.
33:9. Esau said, I have e. my bro.
11. Take my bless-g, bec. I have e.
34 : 21. land, behold, It is large e.
45 : 28. It is e. Joseph is yet alive
Ex. 9 : 28. Entreat the L. for it is e.
36: 5. peo. bring much more than e.
De.1:6. have dwelt long e. in mount
2 : 3. compassed this mt. long e.
Jos. 17:16. The hill is not e. for us
2 S. 24 : 16. It is e. stay hand, 1 K. 19 : 4. 1 Ch. 21 : 15. Mk. 14:41. Lu. 22 : 38.
2 Ch. 31 : 10. we have had e. to eat
Pr. 27:27. thou shalt have goats' milk e.
28 : 19. he shall have poverty e.
30 : 15. four things say not, It is e.
16. the fire that saith not, It is e.
Is.56:11. dogs, wh. can never have e.
Je.49:9. will destroy till they have e.
Ho. 4:10. shall eat, and not have e.
Ob. 5. would they have stolen till e.?
Na. 2 : 12. The lion did tear e.
Hag. 1:6. ye eat, but ye have not e.
Mal.3:10. sh. not be room e. to rec.
Mat. 10:25. e. for disciple to be as
25 : 9. lest be not e. for us [master
Lu. 15 : 17. hired servants have bread e. [ship
Ac. 27 : 38. eaten e. lightened the

ENQUIRE. See INQUIRE.

ENRAGED.

Pr. 26:†17. is e. with strife belonging not to him

ENRICH, ED, EST.

1 S. 17 : 25. king will e. him with great riches [God
Ps. 65 : 9. greatly e-t it with river of
Eze. 27 : 33. thou didst e. the kings
1 Co.1:5. Th. in ev. thing ye are e-d
2 Co. 9:11. Being e-d in ev. thing to

EN-RIM'MON.

Ne. 11 : 29. And at E. and Zareah

EN-RO'GEL.

Jos. 15 : 7. goings out at E. | 18:16.
2 S. 17 : 17. Jona. stayed by E.
1 K. 1:9. Adonijah slew sheep by E.

ENROLLED.

Lu. 2:†1. decree that all world be e.
He. 12 : † 23. of firstborn e. in heav.

ENSAMPLE, S. [e-s

1 Co. 10:11. happened unto them for
1 Th. 1 : 7. So that ye were e-s to all
Ph. 3 : 17. as ye have us for an e.
2 Th. 3 : 9. to make ourselves an e.
1 Pe. 5 : 3. not lords, but e-s to flock
2 Pe. 2 : 6. Sodom and Gom. an e.

EN'-SHEMESH. [17.

Jos. 15 : 7. toward waters of E. | 18:

ENSIGN, S.

Nu. 2 : 2. with e. of fathers house
Ps. 74 : 4. set up their e-s for signs
Is. 5 : 26. he will lift e. to nations
11 : 10. sh. stand for an e. to peo.
12. he sh. set up an e. for nations
18 : 3. see ye, when he lifteth up e.
30 : 17. till ye be left as e. on hill
31:9. his princes sh. be afraid of e.
Zch. 9 : 16. of a crown lifted as an e.

ENSNARE, ED.

Jb. 34 : 30. reign not, lest peo. be e.
Ps. 12:†5. in safety fr. him would e.

ENSUE.

1 Pe. 3 : 11. seek peace, and e. it

ENTANGLE, ED, ETH.

Ex. 14 : 3. say, They are e. in land
Mat. 22 : 15. how they might e. him
Ga.5:1. be not e. with yoke of bond.
2 Pe.2:20. they are e. and overcome
2 Ti. 2 : 4. e-h hims. with affairs of

EN-TAP'PUAH. [life

Jos. 17 : 7. unto inhabitants of E.

ENTER.

Ju. 18:9. not slothful to e. land [ge
Eze. 42 : 14. when priests e. then not
44 : 3. prince shall e., 46: 2, 8.
Da. 11:17. set face to e. wi. strength
24. e. peaceably upon fattest pl-s
Mk. 13:15. nei. e. to take any [roof
Lu. 7 : 6. not worthy sho. e. under
He. 4 : 6. remaineth that some must

ENTER in. [e.

Nu. 4 : 23. all that e. i. to perform
2 K. 11:5. 3d part that e. i. on Sab.
2 Ch. 23:19. that none unclean e. i.
Is. 26 : 2. righteous nation may e.i.
59 : 14. and equity cannot e. i.
Je. 7 : 2. e. i. at gates, 17:20.-22:2.
Eze.44:2. gate be shut, no man e.i.
17. when ye e. i. at gates
Jo. 2 : 9. like thief e. i. at windows
Mat. 7:13. e. i. at strait, Lu. 13:24.
12:45. they e.i. and dwell, Lu.11:26.
Lu. 8 : 16. wh. e. i. may see light
13 : 24. many will seek to e. i.
Jn. 10 : 9. if any e. i. he be saved
Ac. 20 : 29. grievous wolves sh. e. i.
Re. 22 : 14. may e. i. thro. gates

ENTER into.

Ge. 12 : 11 Ab. was near to e. i. E.
Ex. 40 : 35. Mo. not able to e. i. tent
Nu. 5 : 24. water sh. e. i. woman, 27.
De. 23 : 8. chil. shall e. i. congre.
29 : 12. That thou should. e. i. cov.

Jos. 10: 19. not to e. i. their cities
2 S. 22: 7. my cry did e. i. his ears
1 K. 14:12. when thy feet e. i. city
22:30. I will disguise and e. i. bat.
2 K. 7:4. If we e. i. city, then fam.
19: 23. I will e. i. lodgings of his borders, and, Is. 37: 24.
2 Ch. 30: 8. e. i. his sanctuary
Ne. 2: 8. the house that I sh. e. i.
Es. 4: 2. none might e. i. k.'s gate
Jb. 22: 4. will he e. i. Judgment?
34: 23. that he e. i. judgm. wi. G.
Ps. 37:15. sword sh. e. i. own heart
45: 15. they sh. e. i. king's palace
100: 4. e. i. his gates with thanksg.
118: 20. gate i. which righteous e.
Pr. 18:6. fool's lips e. i. contention
Is. 2: 10. e. i. the rock, and hide
3: 14. e. i. judgm. with ancients
26:20. my peo. e. i. thy chambers
57: 2. He shall e. i. peace
Je. 8:14. let us e. i. defenced cities
14: 18. if I e. i. city, behold fam.
17: 25. sh. e. i. gates kings, 22: 4.
21: 13. who shall e. i. our hab.?
41: 17. departed to go to e. i. E.
42: 15. If ye set faces to e. i. E.
La. 3:13. arrows to e. i. my reins
Eze. 7:22. robbers shall e. i. it and
13: 9. nor they e. i. land of Israel
26: 10. e. i. thy gates, as men e. i. city wherein a breach
37:5. will cause breath to e. i. you
44: 9. nor uncircum. e. i. sanct.
16. they shall e. i. my sanctuary
Da. 11: 7. shall e. i. the fortress
40. He shall e. i. the countries
41. He shall e. i. glorious land
Am. 5: 5. Beth-el, nor e. i. Gilgal
Jon. 3: 4. Jonah began to e. i. city
Zch. 5:4. flying roll e. i. h. of thief
Mat. 5: 20. in no case e. i. kingd.
6: 6. when prayest, e. i. closet
7: 21. not every one shall e. i.
10: 11. i. what city ye sh. e., Lu. 10: 8, 10. [Mk. 3: 27.
12: 29. e. i. a strong man's house,
18: 8. better for thee to e. i. life halt or maimed, Mk. 9:43,45,47.
19: 17. if thou wilt e. i. life, keep
23. a rich man shall hardly e. i.
24. for rich man to e. i. kingdom of G., Mk 10:23,24,25. Lu. 18:24,25.
25: 21. e. i. the joy of thy L., 23.
Mk. 1: 45. no more openly e. i. city
5: 12. may e. i. swine, Lu. 8: 32.
6:10. house ye e. i., Lu. 9:4.-10:5.
9: 25. and e. no more i. him
14:38. lest e. i. tempta., Lu. 22:46.
Lu. 24: 26. and to e. i. his glory?
Jn. 3: 4. can he e. i. womb again?
5. he cannot e. i. kingdom of G.
Ac. 14:22. thro. tribula. e. i. kingd.
He. 4: 3. do e. i. rest, if they shall e. i. rest, 5, 6.
11. Let us labour to e. i. that rest
10:19. to e. i. holiest by bl. of Jes.
Re. 15:8. no man able to e. i. temp.
21: 27. in no wise e. i. it th. defil.

ENTER not.

Ps. 143: 2. e. n. into judgm. with
Pr. 4: 14. e. n. path of wicked
23: 10. e. n. fields of fatherless
Je. 16: 5. e. n. house of mourning
Mat. 10: 5. any city of Samar. e. n.
26: 41. e. n. into temptation, Lu [22:40.

Not ENTER.

Nu. 20: 24. Aaron n. e. into land
De. 23: 1. sh. n. e. into cong., 2, 3.
2 Ch. 7: 2. priests n. e. into house
Ps. 95:11. they sho. n. e. my rest
La. 1: 10. shall n. e. thy congrega.
Eze. 20: 38. they shall n. e. land
Ho. 11: 9 I will n. e. into city
Mat. 18:3. n. e. kingd. of heaven
Mk. 10:15. n. e. therein, Lu. 18:17.
Lu. 21: 21. let n. them in coun-s e.
He. 3:11. sh. n. e. into my rest, 18.
19. they could n. e. bec. of un- [belief
See KINGDOM.

ENTERED.

Ge. 7: 13. the self-same day e. Noah
19: 3. angels e. into his house
23. sun risen when Lot e. Zoar
31: 33. Laban e. into Rachel's tent
43: 30. Jos. e. into his chamber
Ex. 33: 9. as Moses e. into tabern.
Jos. 2: 3. bring the men that are e.
8: 19. e. into city and took it
10:20. of them e. into fenced cities
Ju. 6: 5. e. into land to destroy it
9: 46. e. into a hold of god Berith
2 S. 10: 14. bef. Abishai and e. city
1 K. 1: † 1. David was e. into days
2 K. 7: 8. e. into another tent
9: 31. as Jehu e. in at gate, Jeze.
2 Ch. 12: 11. when king e. house
15: 12. e. into a cov. to seek the L.
27: 2. Jotham e. not temple of L.
32: 1. king of Assyr. e. into Jud.
Ne. 2: 15. turned and e. by gate
10: 29 they e. into a curse [sea?
Jb. 38: 16. Hast e. into springs of
22 e. into treasures of snow?
Je. 2: 7. when ye e. ye defiled land
9: 21. death is e. into our palaces
34: 10. which had e. into covenant
37: 16. When Jeremiah was e. into the dungeon
La. 1: 10. heathen e. her sanctuary
4: 12. enemy should have e. gates
Eze. 2: 2. spirit e. into me, 3: 24.
16: 8. I e. into a covenant wi. thee
36: 20. when they e. unto heathen
44:2. bec. God of Isr. hath e. in by
Ob. 11. day foreigners e. his gates
13. shouldest not have e. gate
Ha. 3: 16. rottenness e. my bones
Mat. 8: 5. when Jesus was e. into Capernaum, Mk. 2: 1. Lu. 7:1.
23. e. into a ship, 9:1. Mk. 4:1.-8: 10. Lu. 5: 3. Jn. 6: 17.-21: 3.
12: 4. How he e. house of God
24: 38. day Noah e. ark, Lu. 17:27.
Mk. 1: 21. he e. into syn., 3:1. Lu. 6: 6. Ac. 18: 19. [38.
29. e. into house of Simon, Lu. 4:
5: 13. spirits e. into swine, and were choked in sea, Lu. 8: 33.
6: 56. whith. he e. they laid sick
7: 17. e. into house fr. people, 24.
11: 2. soon as e., ye sh. find colt
11. and Jesus e. into Jerusalem
Lu. 1: 40. Mary e. house of Zach.
7: 44. I e. thine house, thou gav.
8: 30. devils were e. into him
9: 34. feared as they e. cloud
10: 38. e. a village, 9: 52.-17: 12.
11: 52. lawyers, ye e. not in yours.
19: 1. Jesus e. and passed through
22:3. e. Sat. into Judas, Jn. 13:27.
10. are e. city, shall meet you
24: 3. they e. found not body
Jn. 4: 38. ye are e. into th. labours
6: 22. no boat save 1 discip. were e.
18: 1. garden, into which he e.
33. Pilate e. into judgment hall
Ac. 3: 2. e. into temp., 8.-5: 21.-21: 26. [hands on him
9: 17. Ananias e. and putting
10: 24. after they e. into Cesarea
11: 8. nothing unc. e. my mouth
12. we e. into man's house
16: 40. e. into house of Lydia
18: 7. e. into man's house named
19:30. Paul wd. have e. unto peo.
21: 8. we e. house of Philip
23: 16. he e. into castle told Paul
25: 23. Agrippa was e. into place
28:8. to wh. Paul e. in, and prayed
Ro. 5: 12. sin e. world | 20. law e.
1 Co. 2: 9. nei. have e. heart of man
He. 4: 6. they e. bec. of unbelief
10. For he that is e. into his rest
He. 6:20. Whith. forerun. is for us e.
9: 12. he e. in once holy place, 24.
Ja. 5: 4. are e. into the ears of L.
2 Jn. 7. many deceivers are e.
Re. 11:11. Spirit of life e. into them

ENTERETH.

Nu. 4:30. numb. ev. every one e. into service of the taber., 35, 39, 43.
2 Ch. 31:16. ev. one that e. h. of L.
Pr. 2: 10. When wisdom e. heart
17: 10. reproof e. more into a wise
Eze. 21: 14. sword e. into th. privy
42: 12. tow. east as one e. [chamb.
46: 9. e. in by way of north gate
Mat. 15:17. whatso. e. in at mouth, goeth into belly, Mk. 7: 18.
Mk. 5: 40. e. where damsel was
7: 19. it e. not into his heart
Lu. 22: 10. into house where he e.
Jn. 10: 1. e. not by door into sheepf.
2. e. in by door, is shepherd
He. 6: 19. e. into that within vail
9: 25. as high priest e. every year

ENTERING, S.

Ex. 35: 15. at the e. in of the tab.
Jos. 8: 29. cast it at the e. of gate
20: 4 shall stand at e. of the gate
Ju. 9:35. Gaal stood in e. of gate, 40.
44. Abim. stood in e. of gate
18: 16. 600 men of Dan stood by e.
17. priest stood in the e. of gate
1 S. 23:7. by e. town th. hath gates
2 S. 10: 8. battle in array at e. in,
1 K. 6: 31. for e. of oracle [11: 23.
19:13. Elijah stood in e. in of cave
2 K. 7: 3. four leprous men at e. of
10: 8. lay heads in 2 heaps at e. of
23: 8. in e. of gate of Joshua
11 at e. in of house of Lord
1 Ch. 5: 9. unto e. in of wilderness
2 Ch. 18:9. sat at e. of gate of Sama.
23: 4. third part e. on sabbath
13. king at pillar by e. in [E.
15. e. of horse g. | 26: 8. e. in of
33: 14. to e. in at fish gate
Is. 23: 1. is no house, no e. in [27.
Je. 1: 15. set thrones at the e., 17:
Eze. 26:†10. acc. to e-s of city brok.
44: 5. mark well e. in of house
Mat. 23: 13. neither suffer ye them that are e. to go in, Lu. 11: 52.
Mk. 4: 19. lusts of other things e.
7: 15. noth. without e. can defile
8: 13. e. into ship again departed
16: 5. e. into sepulchre they saw
Lu. 19: 30. at your e. find colt tied
Ac 8: 3. Saul e. into every house
27: 2. e. into ship of Adram.
1 Th. 1: 9. manner of e. in we had
He. 4: 1. promise of e. his rest
See HAMATH, HEMATH.

ENTERPRISE.

Jb. 5: 12. hands cannot perf. their [e.

ENTERTAIN, ED.

He. 13:2. Be not forgetf. to e. strangers for some have e-d angels

ENTICE.

Ex. 22: 16. if a man e. a maid
De. 13: 6. if wife e. thee secretly
Ju. 14:15. e. husband, th. he declare
16: 5. lords said to Delilah, e. him
2 Ch. 18: 19. Who shall e. Ahab
20. I will e. him | 21. Thou shalt e.
Pr. 1: 10. if sinners e. consent not

ENTICED, ETH.

Jb. 31: 27. if heart been secretly e.
Pr. 16:29. A violent man e-h neighb.
20: † 19. meddle not with him e-h
Je. 20: † 7. hast deceived, I was e.
10. Peradventure he will be e.
Ja. 1: 14. is tempted when e.

ENTICING words.

1 Co. 2:4. preaching not with e. w.
Col. 2:4. lest any beguile with e. w.

ENTIRE.

Am. 1: † 6. with an e. captivity
Ja. 1: 4. that ye be perfect and e.

ENTRANCE, S.
Ju. 1: 24. Shew us e. into city
25. when he shewed them the e.
1 K.18:46.bef. Ahab to e. of Jezreel
22: 10. kings sat in e. of Samaria
1 Ch. 4: 39. went to e. of Gedor
2 Ch. 12:10. kept e. of king's house
Ps. 119:130. e. of thy words giveth
Eze. 40: 15. from face of gate of e.
Mi. 5: 6. land of Nimrod in e-s
1 Th. 2: 1. yourselves know our e.
2 Pe. 1: 11. so an e. shall be minis- [tered

ENTREAT.
Ge. 23: 8. e. for me to Ephron
Ex. 8:8. Pha. called for Moses, said, e. L., 28.-9: 28.-10: 17.
9. when shall I e. for thee
29. I will e. Lord
Ru. 1: 16. e. me not to leave thee
1 S. 2: 25. if man sin, who shall e.?
1 K. 13: 6. e. the face of the Lord
Jb. 11: † 19. many shall e. thy face
Ps.45:12. am. people, e. thy favour
Pr. 19: 6. will e. favour of prince
Je. 15:11. cause enemy e. thee well
Ac. 7: 6. e. them evil 400 years
1 Co. 4: 13. Being defamed, we e.
Ph. 4: 3. I e. thee also, yokefellow
1 Ti. 5: 1. but e. him as a father

ENTREATED. [sake
Ge. 12: 16. he e. Ab. well for her
25: 21. Isaac e. for wife, L. was e.
Ex. 5: 22. why hast evil e. people?
8: 30. Moses went and e. L.,10:18.
De. 26: 6. Egyptians evil e. us
Ju. 13: 8. Then Manoah e. the L.
2 S. 21:14. G. was e. for land,24:25.
1 Ch. 5:20. cried and he was e. [19.
2 Ch. 33: 13. prayed, and G. was e.,
Ezr. 8: 23. God, and he was e. of us
Jb. 19:16. I e. him with my mouth
17. tho. I e. for children's sake
Ps.119:58. e. thy favour with whole
Is. 19: 22. sh. be e. of them [18:32.
Mat. 22: 6. e. them spitefully, Lu.
Lu. 15: 28. came his fa. and e. him
20:11. e. him shamefully, and sent
Ac. 7: 19. same evil e. our fathers
27: 3. Julius courteously e. Paul
1 Th. 2: 2. we were shamefully e.
He. 12: 19. e. word not be spoken
Ja. 3: 17. wisdom is easy to be e.

ENTREATETH.
Jb. 24: 21. he evil e. the barren

ENTREATIES.
Pr. 18: 23. poor useth e. but rich
2 Co. 8:4. praying us with much e.

ENTRY, IES.
2 K. 16: 18. k.'s e. without turned
1 Ch. 9:19. fathers keepers of the e.
2 Ch. 4:22. doors of e. were of gold
Pr. 8: 3. wisdom crieth at e. of city
Je. 19: 2. is by e. of east gate
26: 10. e. of new gate of L.'s hou.
38: 14. Zed. took Jere. into 3d e.
43:9. hide stones at e. of Pha.'s h.
Eze. 8: 5. image of jealousy in e.
27: 3. e. of sea | 40: 11. e. of gate
40: 38. chambers and e-s were by
42:9. the e. on east side [posts
46: 19. After he brought me thro.

ENVIED. [e.
Ge. 26: 14. Philistines e. Isaac
30: 1. Rachel e. her sister, said
37: 11. Joseph's breth. e. him
Ps. 106: 16. They e. Moses in camp
Ec. 4: 4. a man is e. of his neighb.
Eze. 31: 9. trees in garden e. him

ENVIES. See ENVY.

ENVIEST, ETH.
Nu. 11: 29. e-t thou for my sake?
1 Co. 13: 4. charity suff. long, e-h [not

ENVIOUS.
Ps.37:1.nor be e. ag. workers of iniq.
73: 3. for I was e. at the foolish
Pr. 24: 1. be not e. ag. evil men
19. neither be thou e. at wicked

ENVIRON.
Jos. 7: 9. Canaanites shall e. us

ENVY, IES.
Jb. 5: 2. e. slayeth the silly one
Pr. 14: 30. e. is rottenness of bones
27: 4. who is able to stand bef. e.?
Ec. 4: † 4. e. of man fr. his neighb.
9: 6. hatred, and e. is perished
Is. 11: 13. e. of Ephr. shall depart
26:11. they sh. be asha. for their e.
Eze. 35: 11. acc. to thine e. [15:10.
Mat. 27: 18. for e. deliv. him, Mk.
Ac. 5: † 17. were filled with e. [Jo.
7:9. patriarchs moved with e. sold
13:45. Jews filled with e. spake ag.
17: 5. the Jews moved with e.
Ro. 1: 29. full of e. murder, debate
Ph. 1:15. Some preach C. even of e.
1 Ti. 6: 4. whereof cometh e. strife
Tit. 3: 3. living in malice and e.
Ja. 4: 5. spirit in us lusteth to e.
1 Pe. 2: 1. laying aside malice, e-s

ENVY. [Verb.]
Pr. 3: 31. e. thou not oppressor
23: 17. Let not heart e. sinners
Is. 11: 13. Ephraim sh. not e. Jud.

ENVYING, S.
Ro. 13: 13. walk honestly, not in e.
1 Co. 3: 3. is am. you e. and strife
2 Co. 12: 20. I fear lest there be e-s
Ga. 5: 21. works of the flesh are e-s
26. provoking one another, e.
Ja. 3: 14. But if ye have bitter e.
16. where e. is, there is confusion

EP'APHRAS.
Col. 1: 7. as ye learned of E. our
4: 12. E. a serv. of Christ, Phm.23.

EPAPHRODI'TUS.
Ph. 2: 25. to send to you E. | 4:18.

EPEN'ETUS.
Ro. 16: 5. salute my well belov. E.

E'PHAH. [Person.]
Ge. 25: 4. E. son of Midian, 1 Ch.
1 Ch. 2:46. E. Caleb's concu. [1:33.
47. Pelet, E. and Shaaph
Is. 60: 6. dromedaries of E. shall

EPHAH. [Measure.]
Ex. 16: 36. homer is 10th part of e.
Le. 5: 11. part of e. of flour, 6:20.
19: 36. have a just e., Eze. 45:10.
Nu. 5: 15. part of e. of barley meal
Ju.6:19. unleav. cakes of e. of flour
Ru. 2: 17. about an e. of barley
1 S. 1: 24. one e. of flour and
17: 17. take e. of parched corn
Is. 5: 10. seed of homer yield an e.
Eze. 45:11. e., bath be one measure
24. e. for bullock, e. for ram
46: 5. a hin of oil to an e., 7, 11.
Am. 8: 5. making the e. small
Zch. 5: 6. This is an e. that goeth
7. woman sitteth in midst of e.
8. he cast it into midst of the e.
9. lifted e. betw. earth and heav.
10. Whither do these bear e.?
See **Tenth** PART.

E'PHAI.
Je. 40: 8. E. the Netophathite

E'PHER. [1: 33.
Ge. 25: 4. sons of Midian, E., 1 Ch.
1 Ch. 4: 17. sons of Ezr. E. | 5: 24.

E'PHES-DAM'MIM. [†13.
1S.17:1.Philis.pitched in E.,1Ch.11:

EPHE'SIANS. [34.
Ac. 19:28. Great is Diana of the E.,
35. city of E. worshipper of Diana
21:29. with Paul Trophimus an E.

EPH'ESUS.
Ac. 18: 19. Paul came to E., 19: 1.
21. Paul sailed from E.
24. Jew named Apollos came to E.
19: 17. known to Greeks at E.
26. not alone at E. but all Asia
35. said Ye men of E.
1 Co. 16: 8. I will tarry at E.
20: 16. Paul determ. to sail by E.
17. sent to E. called the elders

1 Co.15:32. fought with beasts at E.
Ep. 1: 1. to saints which are at E.
1 Ti. 1: 3. besought to abide at E.
2 Ti. 1:18. ministered unto me at E.
4: 12. Tychicus have I sent to E.
Re.1:11. send unto E. | 2:1.angel at [E.

EPH'LAL.
1 Ch. 2:37. begat E. E. begat Obed

E'PHOD. [Person.]
Nu. 34:23. prince Hanniel son of E.

EPHOD. [Girdle.]
Ex. 25: 7. stones set in e., 35: 9, 27.
28: 4. they shall make an e., 6.
8. curious girdle of e., 27, 28.-39:
5, 20. Le. 8: 7. [of e., 25.
12. put them upon the shoulders
15. make it aft. work of e., 39: 8.
26. in the side of the e., 39: 19.
31. make robe of e. of blue, 39:22.
29: 5. upon Aa. the robe of the e.
39: 2. made e. of gold, blue
Le. 8: 7. he put the e. upon him
Ju. 8: 27. Gideon made an e.
17: 5. the man Micah made an e.
18:14.is in these hou.e.and teraph.
17. took image and e., 18, 20.
1 S. 2: 18. Sam. was girded with e.
28. choose him to wear e. bef. me?
14: 3. And Ahiah wearing an e.
21: 9. sword in a cloth behind e.
22:18. Doeg slew 85 th. did wear e.
23: 6. Abimelech fled with an e.
9. Da. said, Bring hither e., 30:7.
2 S. 6: 14. David was girded with a linen e., 1 Ch. 15: 27.
Ho. 3:4. Isr. many days without e.

EPH'PHATHA.
Mk. 7: 34. he saith to him e.

E'PHRAIM. [Person, People.]
Ge. 41: 52. Joseph's sec. son was E.
48:14. Isr. laid hand upon E. head
20. God make thee as E. and he set E. before Manasseh
Nu. 1: 10. the prince of E., 7: 48.
2: 18. on west be standard of E.
10: 22. standard of camp of E.
26: 35. the sons of E., 1 Ch. 7: 20.
De. 33: 17. are ten thousands of E.
Jos. 16: 9. the cities for E., 17: 9.
Ju. 1: 29. nor E. drive Canaanites
5: 14. Out of E. a root ag. Amal.
8:2. gleaning of grapes of E. better
12: 4. Jephthah fought with E.
2 S. 2: 9. Ish-bosheth king over E.
1 Ch. 7:22. E. their father mourned
9: 3. in Jerus. dwelt of chil. of E.
2 Ch. 15: 9. the strangers out of E.
17: 2. set garrisons in cities of E.
25: 10. separated army out of E.
28: 7. Zichri a mighty man of E.
30: 18. many of E. not cleansed
31: 1. all Isr. brake images in E.
Ps. 78: 9. chil. of E. being armed
80: 2. Bef. E. stir up thy strength
Is. 7: 2. Syria is confed. with E.
5. E. hath taken evil counsel
8. within 65 yrs. shall E. be brok.
9. the head of E is Samaria
17. fr. day E. departed fr. Judah
9: 9. E. that say in the pride and
21. Manas. sh. eat E. and E. Ma.
11: 13. E. shall not envy Judah, Judah shall not vex E.
17: 3. fortress shall cease from E.
28: 1. Woe to the drunkards of E.
3. drunkards of E. shall be trodd.
Je. 7: 15. cast out whole seed of E.
31:18. I have heard E. bemoaning
Eze. 37: 16. For Joseph, stick of E.
19. stick of Joseph in hand of E.
48:5. unto west side a portion for E.
Ho. 5:3. E. O E thou com. whored.
5. Isr. and E. sh. fall in their iniq.
9. E. shall be desolate
12. I will be unto E. as a moth
13. E. saw his sickness, E. went to
14. E. as lion | 6:4. O E. what do

5:10. there is the whoredom of E.
1. iniq. of E. was discovered
E. hath mixed amo. the people
9. E. hath hired lovers
. E. hath made altars to sin
3. E. shall eat unclean things
watchman of E. with my G.
:. As for E. their glory shall fly
1. E. bring forth chil. to murd.
: 6. E. shall receive shame
:. I will make E. to ride
: 3. I taught E also to go
How shall I give thee up E.?
I will not return to destroy E.
:. E. compasseth me with lies
: 1. E. feedeth on wind
E. said, Yet I am become rich
1. E. provoked him to anger
: 1. When E. spake trembling
:. iniquity of E. is bound up
8. E. sh. say, What I to do with
19. possess fields of E. ⌊idols?
. 9: 10. I cut off chariot fr. E.
1. When have filled bow with E.
: 7. E. sh. be like a mighty man

E'PHRAIM is.

60: 7. E. i. strength of, 108: 8.
31:9. fa. to Isr., E. i. my firstb.
). i. E. my dear son? is he a
4: 17. E. i. joined to idols
1. E. i. oppressed and broken
8. E. i. a cake not turned
1. E. i. like silly dove
16. E is smitten, root dried up
: 11. E. i. as a heifer taught

E'PHRAIM with tribe.

1: 33. numb. of t. of E. 40,500
: 8. Of t. of E. to spy land
: 24. of t. of E. to divide land
16: 8. inheritance of t. of E.
: 5. Kohathites had cities out of
t. of E., 20. 1 Ch. 6: 66.
78: 67. he chose not t. of E.

E'PHRAIM. [Place.]

13: 23. Baal-hazor beside E.
: 6. battle was in wood of E.
. 14: 13. the gate of E., 2 Ch.
25: 23. Ne. 8: 16.-12: 39.
11: 54. Jesus went into city E.

Mount, or Mountain of E'PHRAIM, or E'PHRON.

15: 9. border to cities of m.
15. if m. E. be too narrow ⌊E-n
7. Shechem in m. E., 21: 21.
2:9. buried Joshua in m. of E.
27. blew trumpet in m-n of E.
. palm tree of Deborah in m. E.
4. Gideon sent messengers thro.
m. E ⌈came to m. E.
: 1. Micah of m. E. | 8. Levite
13. Danites passed unto m. E.
1. Levite sojourning on m. E.
1: 1. Elkanah of m. E.
4. Saul passed through m. E.
20: 21. man of m. E., Sheba
5: 22. two men from m. E.
1: 15. publi. affliction fr. m. E.
: 6. watchman upon m. E.
19. Isr. sh. be satisfied upon m.

E'PHRAIMITE, S. ⌊E.

16: 10. Canaanites dwell am.
12:5. said, Art thou an E.? 4.⌊E-s
fell at that time of E-s 42,000

E'PHRAIN.

1. 13: 19. Abijah took E.

E'PH'RATAH. [Person.]

1. 2:50. Hur, firstborn of E., 4: 4.

EPH'RATAH. [Place.]

4: 11. do thou worthily in E.
132: 6. we heard of it at E.
5: 2. Beth-lehem E. tho. little

EPH'RATH. [Person, Place.]

35: 16. little way to come to E.
. Rachel buri. in way to E., 48: 7.
1. 2:19. Caleb took unto him E.,

EPH'RATHITE, S. ⌊50.

1: 2. Mahlon, Chilion, E-s of
1 S. 1: 1. Elkanah an E. | 17: 12. Jesse
1 K. 11: 26. Jeroboam an E. ⌊E.

E'PHRON. [Person.]

Ge. 23: 8. entreat for me to E.
16. Ab. heark. to E. silver to E.
25: 9. Ab. was buried in field of E.
49: 30. Ab. bought wi. field of E., 50:

E'PHRON. [Place.] ⌊13.

See MOUNT E'PHRAIM.

EPICU'REANS.

Ac. 17: 18. E. encountered Paul.

EPISTLE, S.

Ac. 15: 30. they delivered e., 23: 33.
Ro. 16: 22. I Tertius who wrote e.
1 Co. 5: 9. I wrote unto you in e.
2 Co. 3: 1. or need e-s of commenda.
2. Ye are our e. written in hearts
3. ye are declared to be e. of C.
7: 8. the same e. made you sorry
Col. 4: 16. when this e. is read,
likewise read e. fr. Laodicea
1 Th. 5: 27. this e. be read unto all
2 Th. 2: 15. taught by word or e.
3: 14. if obey not word by this e.
17. wh. is the token in every e.
2 Pe. 3: 1. This sec. e. I now write
16. as in all his e-s speaking in th.

EQUAL, S.

Es. 3: †8. not e. for k. to suffer them
Ps. 17: 2. thine eyes behold things e.
55: 13. But it was thou, mine e.
Pr. 26: 7. legs of lame are not e.
Is. 40: 25. to whom I be e.? 46: 5.
Eze. 18: 25. say, way of L. not e.,
Is not my way e.? 29.-33: 17, 20.
18: 29. O Isr. are not my ways e.?
33: 17. for them, their way is not e.
Da. 5: †: 21. his heart e. with beast
Mat. 20: 12. made them e. unto us
Lu. 20: 36. they are e. unto angels
Jn. 5: 18. making himself e. with G.
Ga. 1: 14. I profited above my e.
Ph. 2: 6. not robbery to be e. wi. G.
Col. 4: 1. give servants what is e.
Re. 21: 16. breadth, height of city e.

EQUAL, LETH. ⌈feet

2 S. 22: †34. e-h my feet with hinds'
Jb. 28: 17. gold, crystal cannot e. it
19. topaz of Ethiopia sh. not e. it
La. 2: 13. what shall I e. to thee, O

EQUALITY. ⌊virgin

2 Co. 8: 14. by an e., may be an e.

EQUALLY.

Ex. 36: 22. One board had two tenons

EQUITY. ⌊e. distant

Ps. 98: 9. he sh. judge peo. with e.
99: 4. thou dost establish e. thou
Pr. 1: 3. to receive instruction of e.
2: 9. then shalt thou understand e.
17: 26. not good to strike princes
Ec. 2: 21. labour is in e. ⌊for e.
Is. 11: 4. reprove with e. for meek
56: † 1. saith L. Keep e. do justice
59: 14. truth fallen, e. cannot enter
Mi. 3: 9. ye that pervert all e.
Mal. 2: 6. he walked with me in e.

ER.

Ge. 38: 3. his name E. | 6. wife for E.
7. E. was wicked, 1 Ch. 2: 3.
46: 12. E. died, Nu. 26: 19.
1 Ch. 4: 21. E the father of Lecah
Lu. 3: 28. Elmodam, son of E.

E'RAN, E'RANITES.

Nu. 26: 36. of E the family of E-s

ERAS'TUS.

Ac. 19: 22. Paul sent E. into Maced.
Ro. 16: 23. E. chamberlain of city
2 Ti. 4: 20. E. abode Corinth, Troph.

ERE.

Ex 1: 19. delivered e. midwives come
Nu. 14: 11. how long e. they believe
Jb. 18: 2. how long e. you make end
Je. 47: 6. O sw. how long e. quiet?
Ho. 8: 5. e. attain to innocency?
Jn. 4: 49. come e. my child die

E'RECH. ⌈E.

Ge. 10: 10. beginning of his kingd.

ERECTED.

Ge. 33: 20. Jacob e. there an altar

E'RI, E'RITES.

Ge. 46: 16 sons of Gad E. | Nu. 26: 16

ERR.

2 Ch. 33: 9. Manas. made Judah to e.
Jb. 5: † 24. shalt visit habit. and
not e.
Ps. 95: 10. that do e. in their heart
119: 21. which do e. fr. thy com-ts
118. hast trodden them that e.
Pr. 5: † 19. e. always in her love
10: † 17. refus. reproof, causeth to
14: 22. not e. that devise evil? ⌊e.
19: 27. instruction th. causeth to e.
Is. 3: 12. they which lead thee
cause thee to e., 9: 16.
19: 14. they have caused E. to e.
28: 7. they e. in vision, they stumb.
30: 28. bridle causing them to e.
35: 8. wayfaring men shall not e.
63: 17. why hast thou made us to e.
Je. 23: 13. the prophets caused my
people Israel to e., Mi. 3: 5.
32. cause my people to e. by lies
Ho. 4: 12. whored. caused them to
Am. 2: 4. lies caused them to e. ⌊e.
Mat. 22: 29. Jesus said, Ye do e.
not knowing Scrip., Mk. 12: 24, 27
He. 3: 10 do always e. in hearts
Ja. 1: 16. Do not e. my beloved
5: 19. if any of you do e. fr. truth

ERRAND.

Ge. 24: 33. not eat till told mine e.
Ju. 3: 19. I have a secret e. O king
2 K. 9: 5. I have an e. to thee, O capt.

ERRED.

Le. 5: 18. ignorance wherein he e.
Nu. 15: 22. ye have e. and not
1 S. 26: 21. I have e. exceedingly
Jb. 6: 24. underst. wherein I have e.
19: 4. be it indeed that I have e.
Ps. 119: 110. I e. not fr. thy precepts
Is. 28: 7. they have e. thro. wine
priest and prophet have e.
29: 24. that e. in spirit shall come
1 Ti. 6: 10. they have e. from faith
21. some have e. conc. the faith
2 Ti. 2: 18. Who conc. truth have e.

ERRETH.

Pr. 10: 17. refuseth reproof e.
Eze. 45: 20. shalt do for every one

ERROR, S. ⌊that e.

Nu. 35: † 11. that killeth any by e.
2 S. 6: 7. G. smote Uzzah for his e.
Jb. 19: 4. mine e. remaineth with mys.
Ps. 19: 12. Who can underst. his e-s
Ec. 5: 6. neither say, it was an e.
10: 5. an evil I have seen as an e.
Is. 32: 6. to utter e. ag. the Lord
Je. 10: 15. are the work of e-s, 51: 18.
Da 3: † 29. who speak e. ag. God of
4: † 27. if it be a healing of thine e.
6: 4. neither any e. found in him
Mat 27: 64. last e. be worse than 1st
Ro. 1: 27. recompense of their e.
Ja. 5: 20. converteth sinner from e.
2 Pe. 2: 18. escaped fr. them in e.
3: 17. ye led away with e. of wick.
1 Jn. 4: 6. hereby know we spi. of e.
He. 9: 7. he offered for e-s of peo.
Jude 11. greedily aft. e. of Balaam

ESA'IAS. See ISAIAH.

E'SAR HAD'DON.

2 K. 19: 37. E. reigned, Is. 37: 38.
Ezr. 4: 2. days of E. king of Assur

E'SAU.

Ge. 25: 25. they called his name E.
26. hand took hold E.'s heel
27. E. was a cunning hunter
28. Isaac loved E. | 29. E came fr.
34. E. despised his birthright
27: 11. E. my bro. is a hairy man
19. I am E. thy firstborn, 32.
21. whe. thou be my son E., 24.
41. E. hated Jacob bec. of bles.
42. words of E. told to Rebekah

Ge.28:9. went E. unto Ishmael, and
32: 3. Jac. sent messengers to E.
11. Deliver me, from hand of E.
18. present sent unto my lord E.
33: 4. E. ran to meet him, and
9. E. said, I have enough, bro.
35: 1. fleddest from E. thy bro.
29. sons E. and Jac. buried him
36: 1. the genera-s of E., 1 Ch. 1:35.
8. dwelt E. in mount Seir, De. 2:
4, 5, 12, 22. Jos. 24: 4.
43. he is E. father of Edomites
De. 2: 5. given Seir unto E., 12. Jos.
22. did to chil. of E. in Seir [24:4.
Jos. 24: 4. Jac. and E., 1 Ch. 1:34.
Je. 49: 8. br. calamity of E. on him
10. I have made E. bare, I have
Ob. 6. How things of E. searched
18. house of E. be for stubble
21. judge mount of E. | 8, 9, 19.
Mal. 1: 2. Was not E. Jacob's bro.
3. and I hated E., Ro. 9: 13.
He. 11:20. Isaac blessed Jac. and E.
12: 16. lest profane person, as E.

ESCAPE. [Noun]

Ps. 55: 8. hasten my e. from storm

ESCAPE. [Verb.]

Ge. 19: 17. e. for thy life, e. to mt.
19. I cannot e. to the mountain
20. O let me e. | 22. e. thither
32: 8. other company shall e.
Jos. 8: 22. they let none of them e.
1 S. 27: 1. e. into land of Philis.
2 S. 15: 14. let us flee, not else e.
20: 6. lest Sheba get cities and e.
1 K. 18: 40. let none e., 2 K. 9: 15.
2 K. 10: 24. if any of the men e.
19: 31. e. out of Zion, Is. 37: 32.
23: † 18. they let his bones e. with
Ezr. 9:8. grace to leave a remn. to e.
Es. 4: 13. Think not thou shalt e.
Jb. 11: 20. the wicked shall not e.
Ps. 56:7. Shall they e. by iniquity?
71: 2. Deliver me, cause me to e.
141: 10. let wicked fall whilst I e.
Pr. 19: 5. speaketh lies shall not e.
Ec. 7:26. pleaseth God sh. e. fr. her
Is. 20: 6. and how shall we e.
66:19. send those that e. unto na-s
Je. 11: 11. evil they not able to e.
25: 35. nor principal of flock to e.
32: 4. Zed. not e., 34:3.-38:18, 23.
42: 17. none into E. sh. e., 44:14.
44:14. none return but such as e.
28. Yet a small number th. e. sw.
46: 6. let not mighty man e.
48: 8. spoiler come, no city sh. e.
50: 28. voice of them th. e. out of
29. let none e. recomp. her [Bab.
Eze. 6: 8. some that shall e. sword
9. they that e. shall remem. me
7: 16. that e. sh. e., be like doves
17: 15. sh. he e. that doeth such
18. done these thi., he sh. not e.
Da. 11: 41. shall e. out of his hand
42. land of Egypt shall not e.
Jo. 2:3. and nothing shall e. them
Ob. 14. to cut off those that did e.
† 17. upon Zion sh. be they th. e.
Mat. 23:33. how e. damna. of hell?
Lu. 21: 36. accounted worthy to e.
Ac.27:42. to kill prisoners lest any e.
Ro. 2: 3. shalt e. judgm. of God?
1 Co. 10: 13. will make a way to e.
1 Th. 5:3. sudden destr., and not e.
He. 2:3. How e. if we neglect so gr.
12: 25. much more shall not we e.

ESCAPED.

Ge. 14: 13. there came one had e.
Ex. 10: 5. locust eat what is e.
Nu. 21: 29. hath given sons and
dau-s that e. into captivity
De. 23: 15. not deliver serv. e.
Ju.3:26. Ehud e. while they tarried
29. there e. not a man, 1 S. 30:17.
12: 5. Ephraimites wh. were e.
21:17. inherit. for them that be e.
1 S. 14: 41. Jona. taken, but peo. e.
19: 10. David e. that night, 12, 18.
17. sent away enemy he is e.?
22: 1. e. to cave of Adul. | 20. Abi
23: 13. told Saul, David was e.
2 S. 1: 3. Out of the camp am I e.
4: 6. Rachab and Baanah e.
1 K. 20: 20. Ben-hadad the king e.
2 K. 19: 30. remnant e. of Judah
shall take root, Is. 37: 31.
37. e. into Armenia, Is. 37: 38.
1 Ch. 4: 43. smote rest that were e.
2 Ch. 16:7. theref. is host of Syria e.
20: 24. fallen to earth, none e.
30: 6. will return to you th. are e.
36: 20. e. fr. sword carried he aw.
Ezr. 9: 15. for we remain yet e.
Ne. 1: 2. I asked conc. Jews had e.
Jb. 1: 15. I only am e., 16, 17, 19.
19:20. am e. with skin of my teeth
Ps. 124: 7. Our soul is e. as a bird
snare is broken and we are e.
Is. 4:2. shall be comely for them e.
10: 20. and such as are e. of Jacob
45: 20. draw near, ye that are e.
Je. 41: 15. Ishmael son of Neth. e.
51: 50. Ye that have e. remem. L.
La. 2:22. so th. none e. nor remain.
Eze. 24:27. mouth opened to him e.
33:21. th. had e. came unto me, 22.
Jn. 10: 39. he e. out of their hands
Ac. 27:44. so they all e. safe to land
28: 1. when e. then they knew
4. tho. he e. sea, yet vengeance
2 Co. 11: 33. I was let down and e.
He. 11:34. thro. faith e. edge of sw.
12: 25. if they e. not who refused
2 Pe. 1: 4. e. corruption in world
2:18. allure those th. were clean e.
20. aft. have e. pollutions of world

ESCAPER. [to tell

2 K. 9: † 15. let no e. go out of city

ESCAPETH.

1 K. 19: 17. e. sword of Hazael sh
Jehu slay; that e. Jehu shall
Is. 15:9. bring lions upon him th. e.
Je. 48:19. ask her e., What is done?
Eze. 24: 26. he th. e. sh. come unto
Am. 9:1. he that e. not be delivered

ESCAPING. [37:†31.

2 K.19:†30. e. of house of Judah, Is.
2 Ch. 20: † 24. they dead, not an e.
Ezr.9:14. so that there sho. be no e.
Is. 4: † 2. branch comely for e. of
37:†32. e. sh. go out of Zion [Isr.
Je. 25: † 35. e. fr. principal of flock

ESCHEW, ED, ETH.

Jb. 1: 1. feared G. e-d evil, 8.-2: 3.
1 Pe. 3: 11. Let him e. evil and do

E'SEK. [good

Ge. 26: 20. Isaac called well E.

ESH'-BAAL.

1 Ch. 8: 33. Saul begat E., 9: 39.

ESH'BAN. [Ch. 1:41.

Ge. 36: 26. chil. of Dishon; E., 1

ESH'COL. [Person, Place.]

Ge. 14: 13. Mamre, brother of E.
24. Aner, E., let th. take portion
Nu. 13: 24. was called brook E., 23.
32: 9. unto valley of E., De. 1: 24.

E'SHEAN.

Jos. 15: 52. cities in the mts. E.

E'SHEK.

1 Ch. 8: 39 sons of E. were Ulam

ESH'KALONITES.

Jos. 13: 3. E., the Gittites, Ekron-

ESH'TAOL. [ites

Jos. 15: 33. cities in the valley, E.
19: 41. coast of inheri. was E. |
Ju. 13: 25.-16: 31.-18:2, 8, 11.

ESH'TAULITES.

1 Ch. 2: 53. of them came the E.

ESH'TEMOA. [Person.]

1 Ch. 4:17. Ishbah father of E. | 19.

ESH'TEMOA. [Place.]

Jos. 21: 14. to chil. of Aaron, E., 1
Ch. 6: 57. | 1 S. 30: 28.

ESH'TEMOH.

Jos. 15: 50. in the mountains E.

ESH'TON.

1 Ch. 4: 11. fa. of E. | 12. E. begat

ES'LI.

Lu. 3: 25. Naum, the son of E.

ESPECIALLY.

Ps. 31: 11. reproach e. am. neigh-s
Ac. 26:3. e. bec. I know thee expert
Ga. 6: 10. e. the househ. of faith
1 Ti. 5: 17. e. who labour in word
2 Ti.4:13. bring, but e. parchments
See SPECIALLY.

ESPIED. See ESPY.

ESPOUSALS. [his e.

Can. 3: 11. crowned him in day of
Je. 2: 2. I remem. love of thine e.

ESPOUSED. [I e.

2 S. 3: 14. Deliver me Michal whom
Mat. 1:18. When Mary was e. to Jo.
Lu. 1: 27. To a virgin e. to a man
2: 5. Joseph went to be taxed with
Mary his e. wife
2 Co. 11: 2. e. you to one husband

ESPY, IED.

Ge.42:27. he e-d money in his sack's
Jos. 14: 7. Moses sent me to e. land
Je. 48: 19. e. ask him that fleeth
Eze. 20: 6. land I had e-d for them
See SPIED, SPY.

ES'ROM.

Mat. 1: 3. E. begat Aram, Lu. 3:33.

ESTABLISH.

Ge. 6: 18. with thee will e. my cov.,
9:9.-17: 7. Le. 26:9. Eze. 16:62.
17: 19. I will e. my covenant, 21.
Nu. 30: 13. ev vow, her husb. e. it
De 8: 18. that he may e. his cove.
28: 9. L. shall e. thee a holy peo.
29: 13. that he e. thee for a people
1 S. 1: 23. L. e. his word, 2 S. 7:25.
2 S. 7: 12. I will e. his kingd., 13.
1 Ch. 17: 11.-22: 10.-28: 7.
1 K. 7: † 21. called name of right
pillar, He sh. e., 2 Ch. 3: † 17.
9: 5. I will e. throne of thy kingd.
15: 4. to set up his son, and e.
2 Ch 9: 8. God loved Isr. to e. them
Jb. 36: 7. he doth e. them for ever
Ps. 7: 9. e. the just | 48:8. G. e. it
10: † 17. wilt e. heart of humble
87: 5. Highest himself sh. e. her
89: 2. thy faithfuln. shalt thou e.
4. seed will I e. for ever [in heav.
90: 17. e. thou work of our hands,
99: 4. thou dost e. equity [e. it
Pr. 15: 25. will e. border of widow
Is. 9: 7. to e. it with judgment
49: 8. give for cove. to e. the earth
62: 7. till he e. Jerus. a praise
Je. 33: 2. L. that formed it, to e. it
Eze. 16: 60. I will e. an everl. cov.
Da. 6: 7. consulted to e. royal stat.
8. O king, e. the decree
11: 14. exalt thems. to e. vision
Am. 5: 15. e. judgment in the gate
Ro. 3: 31. void? yea, we e. the law
10:3. going about to e. own righte.
1 Th. 3: 2. we sent Tim. to e. you
He. 10:9. takes first, that he e. sec.
See STABLISH.

ESTABLISHED.

Ge. 9: 17. token of cov. I have e.
41: 32. it is bec. thing is e. by G.
Ex. 6: 4. I have also e. my cov.
15: 17. in sanct. thy hands have e.
De. 32: 6. hath he not e. thee?
1 S. 3: 20. Samuel was e. a prophet
13:13. would L. have e. thy kingd.
20: 31. thou not be e. nor kingd.
2 S. 5: 12. perceived L. had e. him
7: 26. let the house of thy servant
Da. be e. for ever, 1 Ch. 17:24.
1 K. 2: 12. his kingd. was e. greatly
24. as L. liveth, wh. hath e. me
46. kingd. was e. in hand of Sol.

h. 17:23. thing be e. for ever, 24.
h. 1:9. O L., let thy prom. be e.
: 1. when Rehob. had e. kingd.
: 3. when kingd. was e. to him
: † 6. Jotham e. his ways bef. L.
): 5. e. a decree to keep passover
. 21 : 8. seed is e. in their sight
: † 10. when I e. decree upon it
. 24 : 2. hath e. it upon floods
: † 23. steps of a good man are e.
): 2. feet upon rock, e. my goings
: 5. he e. a testimony in Jacob
9 earth be e. for ever, 119 : 90.
: 2. throne is e.
1: † 7. telleth lies sh. not be e.
1: † 8. his cou[n]ts are e. for ever
2: 8. heart e. he not be afraid
0: 11. Let not evil speaker be e.
. 3: 19. Lord, hath e. the heav-s
: 26. and let all thy ways be e.
23. When he e. the clouds above
:3. man sh. not be e. by wickedn.
: 22. in mult. of counsell. are e.
: 12. throne is e. by righteousn.
:18. Ev. purpose is e. by counsel
: 3. by understanding is hou. e.
1: 4. who hath e. ends of earth
7 : 9. If not believe, not be e.
: 5. in mercy shall throne b. e.
:18. G. that made earth, hath e.
: 14. in righte. shalt thou be e.
10 : 12. e. world by wisd., 51 : 15.
. 4 : 36. I was e. in my kingdom
. 1 : 12. thou e. them for correct.
t. 18 : 16. two witn. ev. word e.
. 16 : 5. churches e. in the faith
. 1 : 11. some gift, that ye may be e.
. 8 : 6. e. upon better promises
: 9. it is good that heart be e.
e. 1 : 12. tho. e. in present truth
See STABLISHED.

all be ESTABLISHED.

25 : 30. house s. b. e. for ever, 2 S. 7 : 16.
19 : 15. of two or 3 witnesses s. matter b. e., 2 Co 13 : 1. [haud
. 24 : 20 kingd. s. b. e. in thine
. 7 : 16. thine house, and throne s. b. e. for ever, 1 K. 2 : 45.
h. 17 : 14. and his throne s. b. e. for everm., Ps. 89 : 37. [s. b. e.
h. 20 : 20. Believe in L. God, so
22 : 28. shalt decree, it s. b. e.
89:21. With wh. my hand s. b. e.
: 10. world s. b. e. th. it be e.
2:28. their seed s. b. e. bef. thee
12 : 19. the lip of truth s. b. e.
: 3. thy thoughts s. b. e.
: 5. his throne s. b. e. for ever,
29 : 14. [Mi. 4 : 1.
2 : 2. mt. of L.'s house s. b. e.,
: 5. in mercy s. throne b. e.
: † 8. by liberal things s. he b. e.
30 : 20. their congrega. s. b. e.
. 5 : 11. to build it a house, and it s. b. e.

ESTABLISHETH.

30 : 14. he e. all her vows
29 : 4. king by judgm., e. land
6 : 15. no decree which the king e. changed
See STABLISHETH.

ESTABLISHMENT.

. 32 : 1. After e. Sennach. came
89 : † 14. justice and judgment are e. of thy throne, 97 : † 2.

ESTATE, S.

. 17 : 17. e. of man of high deg.
1 : 19. let king give her royal e. unto another
22 : † 20. our e. is not cut down
136:23. remem. us in our low e.
1 : 16. I am come to great e.
18. conc. e. of the sons of men
16:55. Sama. retu. to former e.
11. I will settle you aft. old e-s

Da. 11 : 7. one stand in his e., 21.
20. stand in his e. raiser of taxes
38. in his e. honour G. of forces
Mk. 6 : 21. a supper to his chief e-s
Lu. 1:48. regarded low e. of handm.
Ac. 22:5. e. of elders d th bear witn.
Ro. 12 : 16. condes. to men of low e.
Col. 4:8. th. he might know your e.
Jude 6. angels wh. kept not first e.
See STATE.

ESTEEM.

Jb. 36 : 19. Will he e. thy riches?
Ps. 119 : 128. I e. all thy precepts
Is. 53 : 4. did e. him smitten of God
Ph. 2 : 3. each e. other better than
1 Th. 5:13. e. them highly for work's
1 Pe. 2 : † 17. e. all men, love broth.

ESTEEMED.

De. 32 : 15. lightly e. rock of salva.
1 S. 2 : 30. despise me be lightly e.
18 : 23. seeing I am lightly e.
Jb. 23 : 12. have e. words of mouth
Pr. 17 : 28. shutteth lips, e. man of understanding
Is. 29 : 16. sh. be e. as potter's clay
17. fruitful field be e. as a forest
53 : 3. despised, and we e. him not
La. 4 : 2. are e. as earthen pitchers
Lu. 16 : 15. e. am. men is abomi.
1 Co. 6 : 4. set to judge who least e.

ESTEEMETH, ING.

Jb. 41:27. He e. iron as straw, brass
Ro. 14:5. e-h one day above ano. (2)
14. that e. any thing to be unci.
He. 11 : 26. e-g the reproach of Ch.

ES'THER.

Es. 2 : 7. Hadassah, that is E.
17. k. loved E. | 18. king made E.
22. told it to E [feast
4:4. E. maids came, she sent raim.
9. told E. words of Mordecai
12. told to Mordecai E. words
17. Mordecai did all E. had com.
5 : 2. k. held out to E. sceptre, 8:4.
3. What wilt thou queen E., 6.
12. E. let no man come with king
7 : 2. What is thy petition qu. E.?
7. Haman to make request, to E.
8 : 2. E. set Mord. over Haman, 1.
3. E. spake again before the king
7. I have giv. E. house of Haman
9 : 29. E. wrote with all authority
32. decree of E. confirmed these

ESTIMATE.

Le. 27 : 14. priest shall e. it good or bad, as priest e. it, so stand

ESTIMATION, S.

Le. 5 : 15. bring a ram with thy e.
27 : 2. persons be for L., by thy e.
3. thy e. sh. be of male, | 4,5,6,7, 8,13,15,16,17,18,19,23, (2)27,(2)
25. all thy e-s according to shekel
Nu. 18:16. month old, acc. to thy e.
2 K. 12 : † 4. of the souls of his e.

ESTRANGED.

Jb. 19:13. mine acquaintance are e.
Ps. 58 : 3. wicked are e. from womb
78 : 30. were not e. from their lust
Je. 19 : 4. bec. they have e. this pl.
Eze. 14:5. they are all e. thro. idols

E'TAM.

Ju. 15 : 8. Samson dwelt in rock E.
11 3,000 men went to top of E.,
1 Ch. 4 : 3, 32. 2 Ch. 11 : 6.

ETERNAL.

De. 33 : 27. The e. G. is thy refuge
Is. 60 : 15. make thee e. excellency
Mk. 3 : 29. in danger of e. damna.
Ro. 1 : 20. e. power and Godhead
2 Co. 4 : 17. an e. weight of glory
18. things wh. are not seen are e.
5 : 1. have a house e. in heavens
Eph. 3 : 11. Acc. to e. purpose in C.
1 Ti. 1 : 17. unto King e. be honour
2 Ti. 2:10. obtain salva. wi. e. glory
He. 5 : 9. the author of e. salvation
6 : 2. the doctrine of e. Judgment
He. 9:12. obtained e. redemp. for us
14. thro. e. Sp. offered hims. to G
15. receive promise of e. inherit.
1 Pe. 5:10. called us unto his e. glory
Jude 7. suffering vengeance of e. fire

ETERNAL life.

Mat. 19:16. do th. I may have e. l.?
25 : 46. righteous sh. go into l. e.
Mk. 10 : 17. I do, that I may inherit e. l.? Lu. 10 : 25.–18 : 18.
30. receive in world to come e. l.
Jn. 3 : 15. believeth sho. have e. l.
4 : 36. gathereth fruit unto l. e.
5:39. Scriptures, for in th. have e. l.
6 : 54. drinketh my bl. hath e. l.?
68. thou hast words of e. l.
10 : 28. I give unto my sheep e. l.
12 : 25. hateth life, keep it to l. e.
17 : 2. sho. give e. l. to as many as
3. this is l. e. th. they might know
Ac. 13:48. many as ordained to e. l.
Ro. 2 : 7. who seek for glory, e. l.
5:21. so might grace reign unto e. l.
6 : 23. gift of G. is e. l. thro. J. C.
1 Ti. 6 : 12. O man, lay hold on e. l.,
Tit. 1 : 2 In hope of e. l. [19.
3 : 7. heirs acc. to hope of e. l.
1 Jn. 1 : 2. e. l. which was with Fa.
2:25. prom. he promised, even e. l.
3:15 no murderer hath e. l. abid.
5 : 11. God hath given to us e. l.
13. may know that ye have e. l.
20. This is the true God, and e. l.
Jude 21. for mercy of L. unto e. l.

ETERNITY.

1 S. 15 : † 29. e. of Isr. will not lie
Is. 57:15. lofty One th. inhabiteth e.
Je. 10 : † 10. L. is true G., King of e.
Mi. 5 : † 2. goings been fr. days of e.

E'THAM.

Ex. 13:20. encamped in E., Nu. 33:6.
Nu. 33:8. journ. in wildern. of E., 7.

E'THAN.

1 K. 4 : 31. Solomon wiser than E.
1 Ch. 2 : 6. sons of Zerah, E. | 8.–6: 42, 44.–15 : 17, 19.

ETH'ANIM.

1 K. 8:2. Israel assembled in mo. E.

ETH'BAAL.

1 K. 16 : 31. wife Jezebel dau. of E.

E'THER.

Jos. 15 : 42. Libnah, E. cities, 19 : 7.

ETHIO'PIA.

Ge. 2 : 13. compasseth land of E.
2 K. 19:9. Tirhakah k. of E., Is. 37:9
Es. 1 : 1. reigned fr. India to E., 8:9
Jb. 28 : 19. topaz of E. not equal it
Ps. 68 : 31. E. sh. stretch out hands
87 : 4. behold Tyre with E.; man
Is. 18:1. bey. rivers of E., Zph. 3:10.
20 : 3. walked baref. for sign on E.
5. they shall be ashamed of E.
43 : 3. I gave Egypt, E. for thee
45 : 14. merchan. of E. sh. come
Eze. 30:4. pain in E. | 5. E. fall, 38:5
Na. 3 : 9. E. the strength of No
Ac. 8 : 27. a man of E. a eunuch

ETHIO'PIAN.

Nu. 12 : 1. E. woman he married
2 Ch. 14 : 9. Zerah the E. came ag.
Je. 13 : 23. Can E. change his skin
38:7. Ebed-melech E., 10,12.–39:16.

ETHIO'PIANS.

2 Ch. 14 : 12. L. smote E., E. fled
16 : 8. Were not E. a huge host?
21 : 16. stirred Arabians near E.
Is. 20 : 4. shall lead E. captives
Je. 46 : 9. E. that handle shield
Eze. 30 : 9. make careless E. afraid
Da. 11 : 43. E. shall be at his steps
Am. 9 : 7. Are ye not as chil. of E.?
Zph. 2 : 12. Ye E. shall be slain
Ac. 8 : 27. Candace queen of E.

ETH'NAN.

1 Ch. 4 : 7. sons of Helah were E.

ETH'NI.

1 Ch. 6 : 41. son of E. son of Jerah

EUBU'LUS.

2 Ti. 4: 21. E. greeteth thee

EU'NICE.

2 Ti. 1: 5. faith wh. dwelt in mother E.

EUNUCH.

Ge. 37: †36. Potiphar an e. of Pha.'s
2 K. 8: †6. k. appointed e. to restore
23: † 11. Nathan-melech e.
25: †19. out of city took e., Je 52: 25.
Is. 56: 3. neit. e. say, I am a dry tree
Ac. 8: 27. an e. had come to Jerus.
34. e. said, of whom speaks proph.
36. e. said, what hinder me to be baptized?
38. went into the wat., both Philip and e.
39. that e. saw him no more

EUNUCHS.

1 S. 8: † 15. tenth of your seed to e.
2 K. 9: 32. looked out two or three e.
20: 18. thy sons shall be e. in palace of k. of Bab., Is. 39: 7.
24: †12. Jehoiachin went, he and e.
1 Ch. 28: † 1. Da. assembled the e.
2 Ch. 18: †8. Ahab called one of e.
Es. 1: †12. refused to come by his e.
4: †4. Est.'s maids and e. told her
Is. 56: 4. L. unto e. that keep my sab.
Je. 29: 2. aft. e. were depart. fr. Jerus.
34: 19. e. which passed betw. parts of
38: 7. Ebed-melech one of e. heard
41: 16. e. he brought from Gibeon
Da. 1: 3. spake unto master of his e.
7. prince of the e. gave names
8. Daniel requested of prince of e.
9. Dan. into favour with prince of e., 10, 11.
18. prince of e. brought them in before Neb.
Mat. 19: 12. some are e. born, some made e., some made thems. e.

EUO'DIAS.

Ph. 4: 2. I beseech E. and beseech

EUPHR'ATES.

Ge. 2: 14. the fourth river is E.
15: 18. unto great river E.
De. 1: 7. go unto gr. river E., Jos. 1: 4.
11: 24. yours fr. river E. unto sea
2 S. 8: 3. David smote Hadadezer at river E., 1 Ch. 18: 3.
2 K. 23: 29. Necho to E., 2 Ch. 35: 20.
24: 7. k. of Bab. took fr. Egypt to E.
1 Ch. 5: 9. Reuben inhab. from E.
Je. 13: 4. go to E. | 5. hid it by E.
7. I went to E. and digged
46: 2. word came ag. Pha. by E.
6. shall stumble and fall by E.
10. hath a sacrifice by E.
51: 63. shalt cast it into midst of E.
Re. 9: 14. angels bound in river E.
16: 12. poured out his vial upon E.

EUROCLYDON.

Ac. 27: 14. tempestu. wind called E.

EU'TYCHUS.

Ac. 20: 9. sat a young man named E.

EVANGELIST, S.

Ac. 21: 8. entered house of Philip e.
Ep. 4: 11. gave some apostles, e-s
2 Ti. 4: 5. watch, do work of an e.

EVE.

Ge. 3: 20. Adam called his wife's name E.
4: 1. Adam knew E. his wife
2 Co. 11: 3. as serpent beguiled E.
1 Ti. 2: 13. Adam first, then E.

EVEN. [Noun.]

Ge. 19: 1. two angels to Sodom at e.
Ex. 12: 18. 14th day at e., Jos. 5: 10.
16: 6. Moses said, at e. shall ye know
12. at e. eat flesh | 13. at e. quails
18: 14. stand by thee fr. morn. to e.?
29: 39. lamb offer at e., 41. Nu. 28: 4, 8.
30: 8. Aa. lighteth lamps at e.
Le. 11: 24. shall be unclean until e., 25, 27, 28, 31, 32, 39, 40.–14: 46.–15: 5, 6, 7, etc.–17: 15.
22: 6. Nu. 19: 7, 8, 10, 21, 22.
23: 5. of first month, at e. is L.'s passover, Nu. 9: 3. De. 16: 6.
32. ninth day at e. fr. e. unto e.
Nu. 9: 11. 14th of sec. month at e.
15. at e. there was upon tab.
21. cloud abode fr e. unto morning
19: 19. bathe, shall be clean at e.
De. 16: 4. thou sac. first day at e.
28: 67. say, Would God it were e.
Ju. 20: 23. they wept bef. L. until e.
26. they fasted until e., 2 S. 1: 12.
21: 2. people abode till e. before G.
Ru. 2: 17. gleaned in field until e.
1 S. 20: 5. hide unto third day at e.
2 S. 11: 13. at e. he went to lie on bed
1 K. 22: 35. Ahab died at e., 2 Ch. 18: 34.
1 Ch. 23: 30. praise L. every e.
Eze. 12: 4. thou shalt go forth at e.
7. in the e. I digged through wall
24: 18. and at e. my wife died
Mat. 8: 16. When e. was come, 20: 8.–26: 20.–27: 57. Mk. 4: 35.–6: 47.–11: 19.–15: 42.
Mk. 1: 32. at e. they bro-t diseased
13: 35. at e. at midnight, or at
Jn. 6: 16. when e. was come, disci.

EVEN. [Adverb.]

Ex. 27: 5. net be e. to midst of altar
1 K. 1: 48. mine eyes e. seeing it
Pr. 22: 19. made known e. to thee
Is. 44: 28. e. saying to Jerusa. thou
56: 5. e. to them will I give name
Eze. 20: 11. man do, he sh. e. live
21: 13. if sword contemn e. rod
Ro. 8: 23. e. we ourselves groan
1 Co. 11: 14. doth not e. nature teach
15: 24. kingd. to G., e. Father
2 Co. 1: 3. blessed be God, e. the Fa.
10: 13. a measure to reach e. unto
Ph. 2: 8. obedient unto death, e. death

EVEN. [Adjective.]

Jb. 31: 6. be weighed in e. balance
Ps. 26: 12. foot standeth in e. pla.
Can. 4: 2. teeth like sheep e. shorn
Lu. 19: 44. sh. lay thee e. with

EVENING. [Adjective.]

1 K. 18: 29. prophesied until e. sacr.
36. at time of offering of e. sacr.
2 K. 16: 15. Upon gr. altar burn e. off.
Ezr. 9: 4. astonished until e. sacr.
5. at e. sacr. I arose fr. my heavin.
Ps. 141: 2. prayer be as e. sacrifice
Da. 9: 21. about time of e. oblation
Ha. 1: 8. more fierce than e. wolves
Zph. 3: 3. her judges are e. wolves
Zch. 14: 7. at e. time shall be light

EVENING. [Noun.]

Ge. 8: 11. dove came in in the e.
24: 11. by well at time of e.
30: 16. Jac. came out of field in e.
Ex. 12: 6. Israel sh. kill it in the e.
16: 8. when L. sh. give you in e.
De. 23: 11. when e. cometh, sh. wash
Jos. 10: 26. hanging on trees until e.
Ju. 19: 9. now day draweth tow. e.
1 S. 14: 24. cursed that eateth until e.
30: 17. Da. smote them unto the e.?
Es. 2: 14. In the e. she went, and
Jb 7: †4. when shall e. be measured
Ps. 59: 6. They return at e. they
14. at e. let them return and
90: 6. in the e. it is cut down
104: 23. goeth to his labour until e.
Pr. 7: 9. went to her house in e.
Ec. 11: 6. in e. withhold not hand
Je. 6: 4. shadows of e. are stretched
Eze. 33: 22. hand of L. upon me in e.
46: 2. gate sh. not be shut until e.
Zph. 2: 7. shall lie down in the e.
Mat. 14: 15. was e. his discip. came
23. e. was come, he was alone
16: 2. When e. ye say, it will be fair
Mk. 14: 17. in e. cometh with the 12.
Lu. 24: 29. Abide, for it is tow. e.
Jn. 20: 19. same day at e. came Jes.

EVENING with morning.

Ge. 1: 5. the e. and m. were 1st day
8. e. and m. 2d day | 13. 3d day
19. e. and m. 4th day
23. e. and m. 5th day | 31. 6th
Ex. 18: 13. stood by Mo. from m. to e.
27: 21. order it fr. e. to m., Le. 24: 3
1 S. 17: 16. Philis. drew near m. e.
1 K. 17: 6. bro-t bread m. and e.
1 Ch. 16: 40. to offer burnt offerings m. and e., 2 Ch. 2: 4.–13: 11.–31: 3. Ezr. 3: 3.
Jb. 4: 20. are destroyed fr. m. to e.
Ps. 30: † 5. weeping in e. joy in m.
55: 17. e. m., and noon, will pray
65: 8. outgoings of m. and e. to rej.
Da. 8: † 14. unto 2,300 e. m. sanct.
26. vision of e. and m.
Ac. 28: 23. persuading from m. to e.

EVENINGS.

Ex. 12: † 6. sh. kill it betw. two e.
Nu. 9: †3. keep passover betw. two e.
28: †4. offer other lamb betw. two e.
Je. 5: 6. wolf of e. shall spoil them

EVENINGTIDE.

2 S. 11: 2. e. Da. walked upon roof
Is. 17: 14. behold at e. trouble

See EVENTIDE.

EVENT.

Ec. 2: 14. one e. happeneth to all, 9: 3.
9: 2. one e. to righteous and wick.

EVENTIDE.

Ge. 24: 63. Isaac to meditate at e.
Jos. 7: 6. Jos. fell upon face until e.
8: 29. king of Ai he hanged until e.
Mk. 11: 11. e. was come, Jes. went out
Ac. 4: 3. put them in hold, for now e.

EVER.

Le. 6: 13. fire shall e. be burning
Nu. 22: 30. e. since I was thine
De. 4: 33. did e. people hear God?
19: 9. and to walk e. in his ways
Ju. 11: 25. did he e. fight ag. Isr.?
1 K. 5: 1. Hiram was e. lover of Da.
Jb. 4: 7. who e. perished, innocent?
Ps. 5: 11. let them e. shout for joy
25: 6. tender mercies e. of old
15. mine eyes are e. toward L.
37: 26. he is e. merciful, and lend.
51: 3. and my sin is e. before me
90: 2. or e. formed earth, Pr. 8: 23.
111: 5. he will e. be mindful of cov.
119: 98. thy com-ts are e. with me
Can. 6: 12. e. I was aware, my soul
Is. 28: 28. will not e. be threshing
33: 20. not stakes e. be removed
Da. 6: 24. or e. they came at bottom
Jo. 2: 2. hath not been e. the like
Mat. 24: 21. was not, nor e. sh. be
Mk. 15: 8. to do as he had e. done
Lu. 15: 31. Son, thou art e. with me
Jn. 4: 29. told me all th. e. I did, 39.
8: 35. serv. abideth not, but Son e.
10: 8. all e. came bef. me thieves
18: 20. I e. taught in synagogue
Ac. 23: 15. e. he come ready to kill
Ep. 5: 29. no man e. hated his own
1 Th. 4: 17. so we e. be with Lord
5: 15. e. follow that. wh. is good
2 Ti. 3: 7. e. learning, never able
He. 7: 24. this man continueth e.
25. e. liveth to make intercession
Jude 25. to God be glory, now and e.

See ENDURETH.

For EVER.

Ge. 13: 15. to thee give it and seed f. e.
43: 9. let me bear blame f. e., 44: 32.
Ex. 3: 15. this is my name f. e.
12: 14. feast by ordinance f. e., 17.
24. an ordinance to thee f. e.
14: 13. shall see them no more f. e.
19: 9. people may believe thee f. e.
21: 6. and he shall serve him f. e.
31: 17. sign betw. me and Isr. f. e.
32: 13. land, they sh. inherit it f. e.
Le. 25: 23. land sh. not be sold f. e.
30. house sh. be established f. e.
46. be your bondmen f. e.
Nu. 10: 8. ordinance f. e., 15: 15.–18: 8.
18: 19. it is covenant of salt f. e.
24: 20. Amalek shall perish f. e.
24. Eber, he shall perish f. e.

De. 4:40. earth wh. God giv. thee f. e.
5: 29. be well with them f. e., 12:
13:16. it shall be a heap f. e. ⌊28.
15: 17. he sh. be thy servant f. e.
18: 5. God hath chosen him f. e.
23:6. sh. not seek their peace f. e.
28: 46. they sh. be for a sign f. e.
29:29. revealed belong unto us f. e.
Jos. 4:7. these stones memorial f. e.
24. that ye might fear Lord f. e.
8:28. burnt Ai, made it a heap f. e.
14:9. land sh. be thine inheri. f. e.
1 S. 1: 22. bef. Lord and abide f. e.
2:30. house should walk bef. me f. e.
32. not be an old man in hou. f. e.
35. walk bef. mine anointed f. e.
3: 13. I will judge his house f. e.
14. Eli's house not be purged f. e.
20: 15. shalt not cut off kind. f. e.
23. L. be betw. thee and me f. e.,
27:12. he sh. be my serv. f. e. ⌊42.
28:2. thee keeper of mine head f. e.
2 S. 2: 26. Abner said, Shall sword devour f. e.? ⌈f. e.
3:28. I and kingd. guiltless bef. L.
7: 24. confirmed Isr. to thee f. e.
26. let thy name be magnifi. f. e.
29. that his house continue f. e.
1 K. 8:13. settled place to abide f. e.
9: 3. house to put my name f. e.
10:9. bec. the Lord loved Isr. f. e.
11: 39. afflict Da.'s seed, not f. e.
12:7. be thy serv-ts f. e., 2 Ch. 10:7.
2 K. 5: 27. leprosy unto thee f. e.
1 Ch. 17: 22. didst make thine f. e.
23:13. he and sons f. e. to burn inc.
28: 9. if forsake him, he cast thee
29:18. O L. keep this f. e. ⌊off f. e.
2 Ch. 7: 16. my name be there f. e.
21:7. he promised to give light f. e.
30:8. his sanct. he hath sanctifi. f. e.
33:4. in Jerus. sh. my name be f. e.
Ne. 13: 1. not come into congr. of
Jb. 4:20. they perish f. e. ⌊God f. e.
14:20. thou prevailest f. e. ag. him
19: 24. with iron pen in rock f. e.
20:7. sh. perish f. e. like his dung
23: 7. delivered f. e. fr. my judge
36: 7. he doth establish them f. e.
Ps. 9: 7. the Lord sh. endure f. e.
18. expecta. of poor not perish f. e.
12:7. O L., thou preserve them f. e.
13: 1. how long forget me, O L.
19:9. fear of L. enduring f. e. ⌊f. e.?
21: 6. made him most blessed f. e.
23:6. will dwell in house of L. f. e.
28: 9. feed, and lift them up f. e.
29: 10. L. sitteth king f. e. ⌈13.
30: 12. I will give thanks f. e., 79:
33:11 counsel of L. standeth f. e.
37: 18. their inheri. shall be f. e.
28. his saints are preserved f. e.
29. righteous dwell in land f. e.
41:12. settest me bef. thy face f. e.
44: 8. we praise thy name f. e.
23. O Lord, cast us not off f. e.
45: 2. God blessed thee f. e. ⌈f. e.
49: 8. redemption of soul ceaseth
11. that their houses contin. f. e.
52: 5. God shall destroy thee f. e.
9. I will praise thee f. e. will wait
61:4. I will abide in thy taber. f. e.
7. he shall abide before God f. e.
8. sing praise unto thy name f. e.
66: 7. he ruleth by his power f. e.
68: 16. Lord will dwell in it f. e.
72: 17. his name shall endure f. e.
19. blessed be his glori. name f. e.
73: 26. God is my portion f. e.
74: 1. why hast cast us off f. e.?
10. shall enemy blaspheme f. e.?
19. forget not congr. of poor f. e.
75: 9. I will declare f. e. sing
77:7. will L. cast off f. e.? ⌊praises
8. is mercy clean gone f. e.?
79:5. how long, L., be angry? f. e.?
81:15. their time sho. endured f. e.
Ps. 83:17. let them be confound. f. e.
85: 5. wilt be angry with us f. e.?
89:1. will sing of mercies of L. f. e.
2. Mercy sh. be built up f. e. ⌈36.
29. his seed make to endure f. e.,
46. how long hide thyself? f. e.?
92: 7. it is that they be destr. f. e.
93:5. holiness becometh hou. f. e.
103: 9. neither keep anger f. e.
105:8. he hath remem. his cov. f. e.
110: 4. priest f. e. after order of Melch., He. 5:6.-6:20.-7:17, 21.
111:9. he hath com-ed his cov. f. e.
112: 6. he shall not be moved f. e.
119:89. f. e. O L., thy word is settled
125: 2. from hencef. f. e., 131: 3.
132:14. this is my rest f. e. ⌊Is. 9:7.
146: 6. L. who keepeth truth f. e.
10. Lord shall reign f. e.
Pr. 27: 24. for riches are not f. e.
Ec. 2: 16. no remem. of wise f. e.
3:14. whatso. G. doeth, sh. be f. e.
9: 6. nor have they more a portion
Is. 26: 4. Trust ye in L. f. e. ⌊f. e.
32:17. of quietn. and assurance f. e.
34:10. smoke thereof sh. go up f. e.
17. shall possess it f. e. from gen.
40: 8. word of God sh. stand f. e.
47: 7. saidst, I shall be lady f. e.
51:6. but my salvation sh. be f. e.
8. my righteousness shall be f. e.
57:16. I will not contend f. e., nor
59: 21. my words not depart f. e.
60:21. peo. shall inherit land f. e.
64: 9. nor remember iniquity f. e.
65: 18. rejoi. f. e. in what I create
Je. 3:5. will he reserve his anger f. e.?
12. I will not keep anger f. e.
17:4. ye kindle fire shall burn f. e.
25. Jerusalem shall remain f. e.
31:40. it sh. not be plucked up f. e.
32: 39. that they fear me f. e.
35: 6. Jonadab said, Ye shall drink no wine f. e.
19. Jonadab not want a man f. e.
49:33. Hazor be for desolation f. e.
50:39. no more inhab. f. e., 51:26,
La. 3:31. L. will not cast off f. e. ⌊62.
5: 19. thou, O L. remainest f. e.
20. whf. dost thou forget us f. e.?
Eze. 37: 25. Da. be their prince f. e.
43: 7. I will dwell in Isr. f. e., 9.
Da. 2: 44. kingd. shall stand f. e.
4:34. I praised him that liveth f. e.
6: 26. G. of Daniel, steadfast f. e.
7:18. saints sh. possess kingd. f. e.
12: 7. sware by him th. liveth f. e.
Ho. 2:19. will betroth thee unto me
Jo. 3:20. Jud. shall dwell f. e. ⌊f. e.
Am. 1: 11. Edom kept wrath f. e.
Ob. 10. Edom, thou be cut off f. e.
Jon. 2: 6. with bars about me f. e.
Mi. 2:9. ye have taken my glo. f. e.
4: 7. L. shall reign over them f. e.
7: 18. retaineth not anger f. e.
Mal. 1:4. ag. whom L. indigna. f. e.
Mat. 6: 13. thine is glory f. e.
21: 19. no fruit grow on thee f. e., Mk. 11: 14.
Lu. 1: 33. sh. reign over Jacob f. e.
55. spake to Ab. and seed f. e.
Jn. 8: 35. servant abideth not f. e.
12: 34. heard Christ abideth f. e.
14: 16. Comf. abide with you f. e.
Ro. 1:25. Creator, who is bless. f. e.
9: 5. Christ, God blessed f. e.
11:36. to whom be glory f. e., 16:27.
2 Co. 9: 9. his righte. remain. f. e.
Ph. 15. shouldest receive him f. e.
He. 10: 12. one sacri. for sins f. e.
14. perfected f. e. them sanctified
13: 8. J. C. same to day and f. e.
1 Pe. 1: 23. of God, wh. liveth f. e.
25. word of Lord endureth f. e.
2 Pe. 2: 17. darkness reserved f. e.,
3:18. glory now and f. e. ⌊Jude 13.
1 Jn. 2: 17. will of G. abideth f. e.
2 Jn. 2. truth's sake be with us f. e.
See ESTABLISH, ESTABLISHED.

For EVER and EVER.

Ex. 15: 18. L. shall reign f. e.
1 Ch. 16: 36. Blessed be God f. e. peo. said Amen, 29:10. Da. 2:20.
Ne. 9: 5. bless your God f. e.
Ps. 9: 5. hast put out name f. e.
10: 16. The Lord is king f. e.
21:4. gav. him length of days f. e.
45: 6. Thy throne, O G., is f. e.
17. people sh. praise thee f. e.
48: 14. this God is our God f. e.
52: 8. I trust in mercy of G. f. e.
111: 8. They stand fast f. e. are
119:44. So sh. I keep thy law f. e.
145:1. I will bless thy name f. e.
2. I will praise thy name f. e. 21.
148: 6. hath stablished them f. e.
Is. 30: 8. be for time to come, f. e.
34: 10. none sh. pass thro. it f. e.
Je. 7: 7. dwell in land I gave f. e.
25:5. L. given to you and fa-s f. e.
Da. 7: 18. shall possess kingd. f. e.
12: 3. they sh. shine as stars f. e.
Mi. 4: 5. walk in name of God f. e.
Ga. 1: 5. To whom be glory f. e. Ph. 4:20. 1 Ti. 1:17. 2 Ti. 4:18. He. 13: 21. 1 Pe. 5: 11. Re. 1:6.
He. 1:8. Thy throne, O God, is f. e.
1 Pe. 4: 11. praise and domin. f. e.
Re. 4: 9. sat on throne, who liveth f. e., 10.-5: 14.-10: 6.-15: 7.
5: 13. honour be to Lamb f. e.
7: 12. power be unto our G. f. e.
11: 15. Christ shall reign f. e.
14: 11. smoke ascendeth f. e.-19:3.
20: 10. shall be tormented f. e.
22: 5. and they shall reign f. e.

Live for EVER. ⌈e.

Ge. 3: 22. eat of tree of life and l. f.
De. 32: 40. lift ha. and say, I l. f. e.
1 K. 1: 31. Let king David l. f. e.
Ne. 2: 3. said unto k., Let k. l. f. e.
Ps. 22: 26. your heart shall l. f. e.
49: 9. that he should still l. f. e.
Da. 2: 4. O king, l. f. e., 3: 9.-5: 10.-6: 6, 21.
Zch. 1: 5. prophets, do they l. f. e.?
Jn. 6:51. if eat of this bread sh. l. f. e.,

Statute for EVER. ⌊58.

Ex. 27: 21. it shall be a s. f. e., 28: 43.-29:28.-30:21. Le. 6: 18.-7: 34, 36.-10: 9, 15.-16:31.-17:7.-23:14, 21, 31, 41.-24: 3. Nu. 18: 11, 19, 23.
Le. 6: 22. it is a s. f. e. unto Lord
Nu. 19: 10. unto the stranger for a

EVERLASTING. ⌊s. f. e.

Ge. 17: 8. Canaan for e. possession, 48: 4. ⌈26.
21: 33. e. God, Is. 40: 28. Ro. 16:
49: 26. utmost bound of e. hills
Ex. 40: 15. e. priesthood, Nu. 25:13.
Le. 16: 34. this be an e. statute
De. 33: 27. underneath are e. arms
Ps. 24:7. e. doors, 9. | 100:5. mercy e.
112: 6. righteous be in e. remem.
119: 142. Thy righteousn. is an e.,
139:24. and lead me in way e. ⌊144.
145:13. thy kingd. is an e. kingd., Da. 4: 3.-7: 27. 2 Pe. 1: 11.
Pr. 10: 25. righteous is e. founda.
Is. 9: 6. his name be called, e. Fa.
26: 4. in JEHOVAH is e. strength
33: 14. dwell with e. burnings?
35: 10. ransomed shall come with e. joy, 51: 11. | 61: 7. e. joy
45: 17. e. salva. | 54: 8. e. kindu.
55: 13. e. sign | 56: 5. e. name, 63:
60: 19. L. be an e. light, 20. ⌊12.
Je. 10: 10. God, he is an e. King
20: 11 e. confusion not be forgot.
23:40. bring e. reproach upon you
31: 3. loved thee with an e. love
51: † 26. thou shalt be e. desola-s
Da. 4: 34. domin. is e. domin., 7:14.

Da. 9 :24. to bring in e. righteousn-s
12 : 2. to shame and e. contempt
Ha. 3 :6. the e. mount-ns were scattered; his ways are e. [fire
Mat. 18 : 8. than to be cast into e.
25 : 41. Depart ye cursed into e. fire
46. shall go into e. punishment
Lu. 16 : 9. they may receive you into e. habitations [struction
2 Th. 1 : 9. be punished with e. de-
2 : 16. hath given us e. consolation
1 Ti. 6 : 16. to whom be honour e.
Jude 6. angels reserved in e. chains
Re. 14 : 6. having e. gospel to preach

See

Everlasting COVENANT.

From EVERLASTING.

Ps. 41:13. Blessed be G. f. e., 106:48.
90 : 2. f. e. to everl-g thou art God
93 : 2. throne of old: thou art f. e.
103 : 17. mercy of L. is f. e. to everl.
Pr. 8 : 23 I was set up f. e., or ever
Is 63 :16. O Lord, thy name is f. e.
Mi 5 :2. goings forth have been f. e.
Ha 1 : 12. Art thou not f. e., O Lord

EVERLASTING life.

Da. 12 : 2. awake, some to e. l., some
Mat. 19 : 29. and shall inherit e. l.
Lu. 18: 30. in the world to come l. e.
Jn. 3 : 16. Son, whosoever believeth in him should have e. l. [e. l.
36. He that believeth on Son hath
4 : 14. well springing up into e. l.
5 : 24. heareth my word hath e. l.
6 :27. meat wh. endureth unto e. l.
40. every one wh. seeth Son and believeth may have e. l. [e. l.
47. He that believeth on me hath
12 : 50. I know his comm-t is l. e.
Ac. 13 : 46 yours. unworthy of e. l.
Ro. 6 : 22. free fr. sin, have the end
Ga. 6 :8. sh. of Spirit reap l. e. ⌊e. l.
1 Ti. 1: 16. hereafter believe on him

EVERMORE. ⌊to l. e.

De. 28 : 29. thou shalt be spoiled e.
2 S. 22 : 51. sheweth mercy unto David and his seed for e., Ps. 18:50.
2 K. 17: 37. shall observe to do for e.
1 Ch. 17 : 14. his throne shall be established for e. [ures for e.
Ps. 16 : 11. at thy right hand pleas-
37 : 27. Depart fr. evil, dwell for e.
77 : 8. doth his promise fail for e.?
86 : 12. will glorify thy name for e.
89 :28. My mercy I keep for him for
52. Blessed be the Lord for e. ⌊e.
92: 8. thou, L., art most high for e.
105 : 4. Seek Lord, seek his face e.
106 :31. counted for righteousness, unto all generat-s for e. [for e.
113:2. Blessed be name of the Lord
115 : 18. we will bless Lord for e.
121:8. preserve thy going out for e.
132 :12. chil. sit upon throne for e.
133 : 3. Lord commanded life for e.
Eze. 37 : 26. I will set my sanctuary in the midst of them for e., 28.
Jn. 6: 34. Lord, e. give us this bread
2 Co. 11 : 31. Jes. Chr., blessed for e.
1 Th. 5 : 16. Rejoice e. Pray [e.
He. 7 : †25. he is able to save them
28. Son, who is consecrated for e.
Re. 1 : 18. behold, I am alive for e.

EVERY.

Ge. 1: 21. God created e. living creature, e. winged fowl aft. his kind
29. I have given you e. herb bearing seed, e. tree in which is fruit
30. to e. beast, to e. fowl I have given e. green herb for meat
2 : 5. God made e. plant of field (2)
16. Of e. tree of garden mayest eat
3 : 1. not eat of e. tree of garden?
4 : 22. an instructor of e. artificer
6 : 5. e. imaginat-n of his heart evil
7:2. Of e. clean beast take by sevens
4. e. living substance will destroy
Ge. 7 :14 e. beast aft. his kind, e. fowl, e. bird of e. sort went into ark
23. e. living substance destroyed
9 : 10. my covenant with e. living creature, e. beast of earth (3)
15. I will remember my covenant betw. me and e. creature, 12, 16.
17 : 10. e. man child be circumcised, 34 : 15, 22. [e. man child
12. eight days old be circumcised,
23. took e. male of Abr.'s house; and circumcised flesh [quarter
19 :4. compassed the house from e.
20: 13. at e. pl. say, He my brother
32: 16. into hand of serv-ts e. drove
34 : 23. Sh. not e. beast of theirs be
24. e. male was circumc-d ⌊ours?
46 : 34. e. shepherd is abomination
Ex. 1 : 22. e. son ye shall cast into river, e. daugh. save alive [beast
13: 12. unto the Lord e. firstling of a
13. e. firstling of an ass redeem
36 : 30. under e. board two sockets
Le. 6 : 23. e. meat off-g for priest be
11:15. not be eaten, e. raven ⌊burnt
46. is law of e. living creature (2)
15 : 4. e. bed wh-on he lieth uncl-n
12. e. vessel of wood sh. be rinsed
17. e. garment e. skin wh-on is seed
17 : 15. e. soul that eateth that wh.
19 : 10. neith. gather e. grape ⌊died
24 : 8. e. sabbath set it in order
27 : 28. e. devoted thing most holy
Nu. 1 : 4. with you be man of e. tribe
5 : 2. put out of the camp e. leper
13 : 2. of e. tribe shall send a man
18 :9. e. oblation, e. meat offering, e. sin offering shall be holy (4)
10. In holy place e. male sh. eat it
14. e. thing devoted in Isr. thine
19 : 15. e. open vessel is unclean
29 : 14. 3 tenth deals unto e. bull-k
36 :8. e. daughter be wife unto one
De. 15 : 1. end of e. 7 years a release
21 : 5. by their word sh. e. controversy, e. stroke be tried [work
30 : 9. G. make thee plenteous in e.
Jos. 3 : 12. take out of e. tribe a man
Ju. 21 :11. Ye shall destroy e. male, e. woman th. hath lain by man
1 S. 3 : 18. Samuel told him e. whit
2 S. 21 : 20. man that had on e. hand six fingers, on e. foot six toes
1 K. 7 : 30. e. base four wheels, undersetters at side of e. addition
38. brass: e. laver was four cubits
11 : 15. smitt. e. male in Edom, 16.
2 K. 3 : 19. ye shall fell e. good tree, mar e. good piece of land, 25.
16 : 4. incense under e. green tree
1 Ch. 9 :32. shewbread, prepare e. sab.
13 :1. Dav. consulted with e. leader
26 : 32. e. matter pertaining to God
2 Ch. 29 :35. drink off-gs for e. burnt
Ne. 10:31. leave exact-n of e. debt ⌊off.
Es. 1 : 22. he sent letters unto e. province, to e. people (4), 8 : 9.
2:12. when e. maid's turn was come
13. thus came e. maiden unto king
3 : 12. governors over e. province, rulers of e. peo. of e. prov-e (4)
9 : 28. days be kept throughout e. generat-n, e. family, e. prov-e (4)
Ps. 119 :101. my feet from e. evil way
104. tbf I hate e. false way, 128.
Pr. 2:9. shalt underst-d e. good path
7 : 12. she lieth in wait at e. corner
14 :1. e. wise woman build-h house
15. The simple believeth e. word
15 : 3. eyes of the L. are in e. place
20 : 3. e. fool will be meddling [sel
18. e. purpose establis-d by coun-
27: 24. crown endure to e. genera-
30 : 5. e. word of God is pure ⌊tion?
Ec. 3 : 17. there is a time for e. purpose and for e. work [work done
8 : 9. I applied my heart unto e.
Is. 2 : 15. day of Lord shall be upon e. high tower, and e. fenced wall
19 : 14. caused Eg. to err in e. work
21 : †8. I am in my ward e. night
24 : 10. e. house is shut up, no man
30:32. e. place where grounded staff
44 :23. singing, ye mts., and e. tree
45: 23. Unto me e. knee shall bow, e. tongue sh. swear, Ro. 14 : 11.
Je. 2 : 20. upon e. high hill, and under e. green, playing the harlot
9 : 4. e. brother will supplant, e. neighb. will walk with slanders
13 : 12. e. bottle be filled with wine
16 : 16. they shall hunt them from e. mountain, from e. hill [left
43: 6. took e. person Nebuzar-adan
51: 29. e. purpose of L. ag. Babylon
La. 4 : 1. are poured out in e. street
Eze. 8 : 10. e. form of creep-g things
12 : 14. will scatter tow. e. wind all
23 days at hand, effect of e. vision
16 :24. thee a high place in e. street
21 : 10. contemneth rod, as e. tree
39: 4 unto ravenous birds of e. sort
17. Speak unto e. feathered fowl
44 :5. mark e. going forth of sanct.
30. e. oblation of e. sort, priest's
46: 21. in e. corner of court a court
Da 3 : 29. e. people wh. speak amiss
6:26. in e. dominion men trembled
11 : 36. magnify hims. above e. god
Ho. 9 : 1. loved reward upon e. corn-
Am. 2 : 8. clothes by e. altar ⌊floor
4 :3. e. cow at that wh. is before her
8 : 3. many dead bodies in e. place
10. bring baldness upon e. head
Zch. 10:4. out of him e. oppres-r [14.
12:12. shall mourn, e. family apart,
Mal. 1:11. in e. place incense be off-d
Mat. 3 : 10. e. tree wh. bringeth not forth good fruit, 7 : 19. Lu. 3 :9.
4 : 4. by e. word out of mouth of G.
7 : 17. e. good tree bringeth forth
9 : 35. heal-g e. sickness, e. disease
12 : 25. e. kingdom, e. hou. divided ag-t itself, not stand, Lu. 11:17.
36. e. idle word that men sh. speak
13 :47. net that gathered of e. kind
52. e. scribe instructed unto [ted
15:13. e. plant wh. Father not plan-
18 : 16. two witnesses, e. word may be established, 2 Co. 13:1. [cause
19:3. lawful to put away wife for e.
Mk. 1 : 45. came to him fr. e. quarter
9: 49. e. sacrifice sh. be salted with
16: 15. preach gospel to e. creature
Lu. 2 :23. e. male th. openeth womb
41. his parents to Jerusalem e. yr.
3 : 5. e. valley shall be filled, e. mountain be brought low [of G.
4 : 4. not by bread, but by e. word
37. fame of him went into e. place
5 : 17. doctors of law out of e. town
6 : 44. e. tree is known by own fruit
16 : 19. fared sumptuously e. day
Jn. 15 : 2. e. branch that beareth not fruit, e. branch th. beareth fruit
19 :23. his garm-ts. to e. soldier part
Ac. 2 : 5. devout men out of e. nat-n
43. fear came upon e. soul [Proph.
3 : 23. e. soul which will not hear
5 : †15. brought the sick in e. street
42. in e. house ceased not to teach
8 : 3. made havoc, entering e. hou
10 : 35. in e. nation he that feareth
13 : 27. prophets are read e. sabb-h
14 : 23. ordained elders in e. church
15 : 21. Moses being read e. sabbath
18 :4. reasoned in synagogue e. sab.
22 : 19. I beat in e. synagogue them
26 :11. I punished them in e. syna.
Ro 2 : 9. upon e. soul th. doeth evil
3 : 2. what profit? Much e. way
19. That e. mouth may be stopped
8:†22. e. creature travaileth in pain
13 : 1. Let e. soul be subject unto

Ro 14 : 5. another esteemeth e. day
1 Co. 1 : 2. in e. place call upon Jes.
4 : 17 as I teach in e. church (2)
6 : 18. e. sin that a man doeth
7 : 2. let e. woman have own husb.
11 : 5. But e. woman that prayeth wi.
15 : 30. why we in jeopardy e. hour?
38 God giveth to e. seed own body
2 Co 2 : 14. savour by us in e. place
9 : 8. ye may abound to e. good w
10 : 5. into captivity e. thought
Ep. 1 : 21. set him far above e. name
4 : 14 carried with e. wind of doct.
16. e. joint in measure of e. part
Ph. 1 : 3. upon e. remembrance of
4. in e. prayer of mine [preached
18. What then? e. way Christ is
2 : 9. given him name above e. na.
10. at name of Jesus e. knee bow
11. that e. tongue should confess
4 : 21. Salute e. saint in Christ Jes.
Col. 1 : 10. fruitful in e. good work
15. Who is firstborn of e. creature
23. wh. was preached to e. creat.
1 Th. 1 : 8. in e. place your faith is
2 Th. 2 : 17. stablish you in e. good w.
3 : 6. e. brother th. walketh disor-
17. is token in e. epistle [derly
1 Ti. 4 : 4. e. creature of God is good
5 : 10. if she followed e. good work
2 Ti. 2 : 21. prepared unto e. good w
4 : 18. sh. deliver me fr. e. evil work
Tit. 1 : 16. unto e. good work repro-
3 : 1. be ready to e. good work [bate
He. 2 : 2. e. transgression rec-d just
3 : 4. e. house is builded by some
5 : 1. e. high priest taken [offer
8 : 3. e. high priest is ordained to
9 : 19. Moses had spoken e. precept
25. priest into holy place e. year
10 : 3. remembrance of sins e. year
11 e. priest standeth daily minist.
12 : 1. let us lay aside e. weight
6. scourgeth e. son he receiveth
13 : 21. you perfect in e. good work
Ja. 1 : 17. e. good gift and e. perfect
gift is from above [tamed
3 : 7. e. kind of beasts, of birds is
16 where envying, is e. evil work
1 Pe. 2 : 13. Submit to e. ordinance
1 Jn. 4 : 1. believe not e. spirit, but
2. e. spirit that confesseth Jesus
3. e. spirit th. confesseth not Jes.
Re. 1 : 7. and e. eye shall see him
5 : 9. redeemed us out of e. kindred
13. e. creature which is in heaven
6 : 14. e. mt., island were moved
15. e. bondman, e. free man hid
14 : 6. to preach to e. nation, peop.
16 : 3. e. living soul died in the sea
20. e. island fled away, and mts.
18 : 2. Babylon, the hold of e. foul
spirit, a cage of e. unclean bird
17. e. shipmaster stood afar off
21 : 21. e. gate was of one pearl
22 : 2. yielded her fruit e. month

See **Every BEAST,**
Every CITY, Every DAY.

EVERY man. [bail

Ex. 9 : 19. upon e. m. and beast,
12 : 44. e. m.'s servant when circ-d
16 : 16. an omer for e. m. : take ye
e. m. for them in his tents
32 : 29. e. m. upon his son and bro
35 : 22. e. m. offered gold unto L.
23. e. m. with whom was blue
24. e. m. with wh. shittim wood
36 : 1. wrought e. wise hearted m.
2. Moses called e. wise hearted m.
8. e. wise hearted m. made curt-s
Nu. 11 : 10. weep, e. m. in door of t.
33 : 54. e. m.'s inheritance be where
36 : 8. enjoy e. m. inheritance of
De. 1 : 41. girded on e. m. his weap-s
Ju. 7 : 21. stood e. m. in his place
9 : 55. departed e. m. unto his pla.
21 : 24. departed e. m. to his tribe;

Ju. 21 : 24 e. m. to his inheritance.
1 S. 10 : 25. S. sent e. m. to his house
13 : 2 Saul sent e. m. to his tent
20. to sharpen e. m. his axe and
14 : 34. peo. brought e. m. his ox (2)
27 : 3. dwelt e. m. with household
2 S. 2 : 3 did David bring up e. m.
19 : 8. Israel fled e. m. to his tent
20 : 2. e. m. of Israel went from Da.
1 K. 1 : 49 guests went e. m. his way
4 : 27. victuals for e. m. in his m.
28. brou-t e. m. acc. to his charge
22 : 17. let th. return, e. m. to his
house in peace, 2 Ch. 18 : 16. [sto.
2 K. 3 : 25. on good land cast e. m.
9 : 13. hasted, took e. m. his garm-t
11 : 8. ye shall compass king about,
e. m. with weapons, 2 Ch. 23 : 7.
9. the captains took e. m. his
men, came to priests, 2 Ch. 23 : 8.
11. the guard stood, e. m. with
weapons in his hand, 2 Ch 23 : 10.
12 : 5. e. m. of his acquaintance
1 Ch. 16 : 43. departed e. m. to house
2 Ch. 6 : 30. unto e. m. acc. to ways
10 : 16. e. m. to your tents, O Isr.
20 : 27. returned, e. m. of Judah
25 : 22. Judah fled e. m. to his tent
Jb. 42 : 11. e. m. gave him money
Pr. 13 : 16. e. prudent m. dealeth
Ec. 3 : 13. e. m. should eat, enjoy
Ca. 3 : 8. e. m. sword on his thigh
Je 22 : 8 sh. say e. m. to his neighb.
23 : 27. dreams, they tell e. m. to
31 : 30. e. m. that eateth sour grape
34 : 9. e. m. should let his manservant, e. m. his maidserv. go free
14 let ye go, e. m. his brother
16. ye caused e. m. his servant ;
e. m. his handmaid to return
37 : 10. rise e. m. in tent, burn city
49 : 5. ye shall be driven out e. m.
51 : 6. Flee, deliv. e. m. his soul, 45.
Eze. 14 : 4. e. m. that setteth up idols
38 : 21. e. m.'s sword ag-t brother
Zch. 7 : 9. shew mercy e. m. to bro.
Jn. 7 : 53. e. m. went unto own ho.
Ac. 2 : 6. e. m. heard them speak
1 Co. 3 : 8. e. m. receive acc. to lab-r
10. e. m. take heed how he build-
13. fire shall try e. m.'s work [eth
7 : 17. as God distributed to e. m.
9 : 25. e. m. th. striveth for mastery
11 : 4. e. m. praying, his head cov-d
12 : 11. dividing to e. m. as he will
2 Co. 9 : 7. e. m. acc. as he purposeth
Ga. 5 : 3. I testify to e. m. circumc-d
He. 8 : 11. they shall not teach e. m.
his brother, Know the Lord (2)
Re. 22 : 12. to give e. m. acc. as his
18. I testify unto e. m. that bear-
See **Every MAN.** [eth
See **Every MORNING.**

EVERY one. [me

Ge. 4 : 14. e. o. that findeth sh. slay
10 : 5. divided, e. o. after his tongue
27 : 29. cursed be e. o. curseth thee
30 : 33. e. o. not speckled spotted
35. e. o. that had some white in it
49 : 28. father blessed them e. o.
Ex. 14 : 7. chariots, captains e. o.
26 2. e. o. of curtains one measure
28 : 21. stones; e. o. with na., 39 : 14.
30 : 13. e. o. that passeth amo., 14.
31 : 14. sabbath, e. o. that defileth
33 : 7. e. o. which sought L. went
35 : 21 came e. o. whose heart stirred
him, e. o. wh spirit made, 3 : 2.
24. e. o. that did offer silver and
38 : 26. e. o. that went to be numb-d
Le. 6 : 18 off-gs, e. o. that toucheth
11 : 26. carcasses, e. o. that toucheth them unclean [iquity
19 : 8. e. o. that eateth it bear in-
20 : 9. e. o. that curseth his father
Nu. 1 : 4. e. o. head of house of fa-s
2 : 34. set forward e. o. aft. families

Nu. 4 : 19. Aaron shall appoint them
e. o. to his service. 39, 43, 47
49 numbered e. o. acc. to service
5 : 2. out of camp e. o. th. hath issue
13 : 2 Send thou men, e. o. a ruler
15 : 12. so do to e. o. acc. to num-
16 : 3. congregation holy e. o. [ber
17 : 2. take of e. o. of them a rod
6. e. o. of their princes gave a rod
18 : 11. e. o. clean shall eat of it, 13.
21 : 8. e. o. bitten, when he looketh
25 : 5. Slay ye e. o. his men [sh. live
26 : 54 to e. o. his inheritance acc-g
35 : 8. e. o. shall give of his cities
15. e. o. that killeth unawares may
36 : 7. e. o. shall keep to inheritance of the tribe, 9. [of you
De. 1 : 22. came near unto me e. o.
4 : 4. are alive e. o. of you this day
33 : 3. e. o. sh receive of thy words
Jos. 21 : 42. cities e. o. with suburbs
Ju. 7 : 5. e. o. that lappeth of water;
e. o. that boweth down to drink
16 : 5. give thee e. o. of us 1.100 p.
20 : 16. 700, e. o. could fling stones
1 S. 2 : 36. e. o. left in thine house
3 : 11. ears of e. o. shall tingle [o.
20 : 15. cut off enemies of David e.
22 : 2. e. o. in distress, e. o. in debt,
e. o. discontented .. unto him
7 will son of Jesse give e. o. fields
2 S. 2 : 16. they caught e. o. his fel.
27. gone e. o. from following bro.
6 : 19. e. o. cake of bread. So peo.
departed e. o. to hou., 1 Ch. 16 : 3.
18 : 17. Israel fled e. o. to his tent
20 : 12. he saw that e. o. stood still
1 K. 7 : 36. acc. to proportion of e. o.
38. upon e. o. of ten bases of laver
9 : 8 e. o. that passeth astonished
20 : 20. they slew e. o. his man
22 : 28. hearken, O people, e. o.
2 K. 12 : 4. money of e. o. th. passeth
18 : 31. eat ye e. o. of his fig tree,
drink ye e. o. of cistern, Is. 36:
23 : 35. e. o. acc. to taxation [16 (8).
2 Ch. 6 : 29. shall e. o. know his sore
7 : 21. house astonishment to e. o.
20 : 23. e. o. helped to destroy ano.
30 : 17. e. o. not clean, to sanctify
18. The good Lord pardon e. o.
31 : 16. e. o. that entereth hou. of L.
Ezr. 2 : 1. unto Jerus. and Judah, e.
o. unto his city. Ne. 7 : 6. [fered
3 : 5. and of e. o. that willingly of-
6 : 5. vessels restored e. o. to place
8 : 34. By number, by weight e. o.
9 : 4. e. o. that trembled at words
Ne. 3 : 28. e. o. over ag-t his house
4 : 15. we returned e. o. unto work
17. e. o. with one of hands wro-t
18. builders, e. o. had sword girded
22. Let e. o. lodge within Jerus-m
23. e. o. put them off for washing
5 : 7. Ye exact usury e. o. from bro.
7 : 3 e. o. in his watch, and e. o.
to be over against his house
8 : 16. booths, e. o. upon roof of h.
10 : 28. e. o. having knowledge
11 : 3. dwelt e. o. in his possession
20. Levites, e. o. in his inherit-ce
13 : 10. were fled e. o. to his field
30. Levites e. o. in his business
Jb. 1 : 4. sons feasted e. o. his day
2 : 11. Job's friends e. o. fr. own pl.
12. wept and rent e. o. his mantle
24 : 6. They reap e. o. corn in field
40 : 12. Look on e. o. that is proud,
bring him low, 11. [gold
42 : 11. gave him e. o. an earring of
Ps. 12 : 2. They speak vanity e. o.
with his neighbour [his glory
29 : 9. in temple doth e. o. speak of
32 : 6. For this sh. e. o. godly pray
49 : 14. grave a habitation to e. o.
63 : 11. king, e. o. that sweareth by
64 : 6. the thought of e. o. is deep

Ps. 68 : 30. till e. o. submit, with silver
71 : 18. until I ha. shewed thy power
to e. o. that is to come ⌈mighty
78 : † 25. e. o. did eat bread of the
115 : 8. so is e. o. that trusteth in
them, 135 : 18. ⌈endureth
119 : 160. e. o. of thy judgments
128 : 1. Blessed, e. o. feareth Lord
Pr. 8 : 18. happy e. o. th. retaineth
16 : 5. e. o. proud is abomination
20 : 6. proclaim e. o. own goodness
21 : 5. e. o. that is hasty, to want
Ec. 10 : 3. Yea, a fool saith to e. o.
that he is a fool ⌈e. o. of them
15. labour of the foolish wearieth
Can. 4 : 2. e. o. bear twins, 6 : 6.
8 : 11. e. o. for fruit to bring 1,000
Is. 1 : 23. princes, e. o. loveth gifts
2 : 12. day of the Lord shall be upon e. o. proud, e. o. lifted up
3 : 5. people sh. be oppressed, e. o.
by another, e. o. by neighbour
4 : 3. e. o. am-g the living in Jerus.
7 : 22. honey shall e. o. eat in land
9 : 17. for e. o. is a hypocrite ⌈land
13 : 14. shall flee e. o. into his own
15. e. o. found be thrust thro.; e.
o. joined unto them fall by sw.
14 : 18. kings, lie in glory, e. o. in h.
15 : 3. in their streets e. o. sh. howl
16 : 7. for Moab e. o. shall howl
19 : 2. shall fight, e. o. ag. brother,
e. o. ag-t his neighbour ⌈afraid
17. e. o. that maketh mention,
34 : 15. vultures, e. o. wi. her mate
41 : 6. helped e. o. his neighbour;
e. o. said to brother, . . courage
43 : 7. e. o. called by my name ⌈ter
47 : 15 sh. wander e. o. to his quar-
53 : 6. have turned e. o. to own
55 : 1. Ho e. o. that thirsteth ⌊way
56 : 6. e. o. that keepeth sabbath
11. look to own way, e. o. for gain
Je. 1 : 15. sh. set e. o. throne at gates
5 : 6. e. o. that goeth out be torn
8. e. o. neighed aft. neighb.'s wife
6 : 3. shall feed e. o. in his place
13. e. o. is given to covetousness;
e. o. dealeth falsely, 8 : 10.
8 : 6. e. o. turned to his course, as
9 : 4. Take heed e. o. of neighbour
5. will deceive e. o. his neighbour
20. O ye women, teach e. o. her
neighbour lamentation ⌈of evil
11 : 8. walked e. o. in imagination
15 : 10. e. o. of them doth curse me
16 : 12. walk e. o. after imaginat-ns
18 : 11. return ye e. o. from evil way
12. we will e. o. do imagination of
16. e. o. that passeth sh. wag head
19 : 8. e. o. that passeth thereby
sh. hiss, 49 : 17.–50 : 13. ⌈friend
9. shall eat e. o. the flesh of his
20 : 7. daily e. o. mocketh me ⌈ons
22 : 7. ag-t thee, e. o. wi. his weap-
23 : 17. they say unto e. o., No evil
30. steal my words e. o. fr. neighb.
35. say e. o. to neighbour, e. o. to
bro., what hath L. answ-d? ⌈way
25 : 5. Turn ye now e. o. fr. his evil
31 : 30. e. o. sh. die for own iniqu-y
32 : 19. to give e. o. acc. to his ways
34 : 10. e. o. should let manservant,
e. o. his maidservant go free
17. in proclaiming liberty e. o. to
36 : 7. may be return e. o. from evil
50 : 16. sh. turn e. o. to his people,
flee e. o. to his own land ⌈battle
42. e. o. in array like a man to
51 : 9. let us go e. o. into own coun-
56. e. o. of their bows broken ⌊try
Eze. 1 : 6. e. o. had four faces, and
e. o. four wings, 10 : 21. ⌈10 : 22
9. went e. o. strai-t forward, 12.–
11. two wings of e. o. were joined
23. wings, e. o. had two, which
covered on this side; e. o. had

Eze. 7 : 16. mourning, e. o. for ini-
10 : 14. e. o. had four faces ⌊quity
19. e. o. stood at east gate of L.'s
14 : 7. e. o. wh. separateth from me
16 : 15. thy fornications on e. o.
25. opened thy feet to e. o. that
44. e. o. that useth proverbs use
18 : 30. I will judge you, O Israel, e.
o. according to ways, 33 : 20.
20 : 39. Go, ye, serve e. o. his idols
22 : 6. princes, e. o. to shed blood
33 : 26. defile e. o. neighbour's wife
30. e. o. to brother, saying, Come
45 : 20. so do for e. o. that erreth
Da. 12 : 1. delivered e. o. writ. in book
Ho. 4 : 3. e. o. therein shall languish
Jo. 2 : 7. sh. march e. o. on his ways
8. shall walk e. o. in his path ⌈in?
Am. 8 : 8. Sh. not e. o. mourn there-
Ob. 9. e. o. of m-t of Esau be cut off
Jon. 1 : 7. said e. o., let us cast lots
3 : 8. turn e. o. from his evil way
Mi. 4 : 5. e. o. in name of his god
Zph. 2 : 11. worship e. o. fr. his place
15. e. o. that passeth by sh. hiss
Hag. 2 : 22. e. o. by sword of brother
Zch. 5 : 3. e. o. that stealeth and e.
o. that sweareth sh. be cut off
8 : 10. I set e. o. ag-t his neighbour
10 : 1. L. sh. give to e. o. grass in
11 : 6. e. o. into neighbour's hand
9. rest eat e. o. flesh of another
13 : 4. ashamed e. o. of his vision
14 : 13. e. o. on hand of neighbour
16 e. o. shall go to worship King
Mal. 2 : 17. When ye say, e. o. that
doeth evil is good ⌈Lu. 11 : 10.
Mat. 7 : 8. e. o. th. asketh receiveth
21. Not e. o. that saith, Lord
26. e. o. th. heareth these sayings
18 : 35. if forgive not e. o. his broth.
19 : 29. e. o. th. hath forsaken hou.
25 : 29. For unto e. o. that hath sh.
be given, Lu. 19 : 26. ⌈is it I?
26 : 22. began e. o. to say, Lord,
Mk. 7 : 14. Hearken unto me e. o.
9 : 49. e. o. shall be salted with fire
Lu. 2 : 3. taxed, e. o. into own city
4 : 40. he laid hands on e. o., healed
6 : 40. e. o. perfect be as his master
9 : 43. while they wondered e. o. at
11 : 4. we forgive e. o. indeb-d to us
16 : 5. called e. o. of lord's debtors
18 : 14. e. o. that exalteth himself
Ju. 3 : 8. so is e. o. born of Spirit
20. e. o. th. doeth evil hateth light
6 : 7. that e. o. may take a little
40. e. o. wh. seeth the Son, may h.
18 : 37. e. o. th. is of truth heareth
21 : 25. many things, if writt. e. o.
Ac. 2 : 38 Repent, be baptized e. o.
3 : 26. e. o. of you fr. his iniquities
5 : 16. and they were healed e. o.
16 : 26. e. o.'s bands were loosed
17 : 27. tho. he not far fr. e. o. of us
20 : 31. I ceased not to warn e. o.
21 : 26. until an offering for e. o.
28 : 2. kindled fire, received us e. o.
Ro. 1 : 16. gospel is unto salvation to
e. o. that believeth ⌈believeth
10 : 4. righteousness to e. o. that
12 : 5. e. o. members one of another
14 : 12. So e. o. of us sh. give acc-t
15 : 2. Let e. o. please his neighb-r
1 Co. 1 : 12. e. o. of you saith, I am of
7 : 17. as L. hath called e. o. ⌊Paul
11 : 21. e. o. taketh bef. other his
12 : 18 members e. o. in body ⌊sup.
14 : 26. e. o. of you hath a psalm
16 : 2. let e. o. lay by him in store
16. submit to e. o. that helpeth
2 Co. 5 : 10. that e. o. receive things
done in the body ⌈tinueth not
Ga. 3 : 10. Cursed is e. o. that con-
13. Cursed is e. o. hangeth on tree
Ep. 4 : 7. unto e. o. of us grace acc-g
5 : 33. let e. o. of you so love wife

1 Th. 2 : 11. we charged e. o. of you
4 : 4. e. o. sh. know how to possess
2 Th. 1 : 3. charity of e. o. abound-h
2 Ti. 2 : 19. Let e. o. th. nameth name
He. 5 : 13. e. o. that useth milk is
6 : 11. th. e. o. shew same diligence
1 Jo. 2 : 29. e. o. th. doeth righteousn.
4 : 7. e. o. that loveth is born of G.
5 : 1. e. o. that loveth him th. begat
Re. 2 : 23. to e. o. acc. to your works
5 : 8. 24 elders, having e. o. harps
6 : 11. white robes given unto e. o.

See Every SIDE.
See Every THING.
See THING, S, with
creep, creepeth, or creeping.
See Every WAY,
Every WHERE.

E'VI. ⌈13 : 21.
Nu. 31 : 8. slew kings, E., Zur, Jos.

EVIDENCE, S.
Je. 32 : 10. I subscribed the e. and
11. I took the e. of the purchase
12. I gave the e. unto Baruch
14. Take these e-s, this e. which
is sealed, this e. which is open
16. when I deliv-d e. of purchase
44 sh. buy fields and subscribe e-s
He. 11 : 1. faith is the e. of things not

EVIDENT. ⌊seen
Jb. 6 : 28. for it is e. unto you if I lie
Ga. 3 : 11. that no man is justified by
the law, it is e. ⌈perdition
Ph. 1 : 28. which is an e. token of
He. 7 : 14. e. our Lord sprang out of
15. it is yet far more e. ⌊Judah

EVIDENTLY.
Ac. 10 : 3. saw in a vision e. an angel
Ga. 3 : 1. Chr. hath been e. set forth

EVIL. [Adj.] ⌈8 : 21.
Ge. 6 : 5. every imagination only e.,
28 : † 8. dau-s of Canaan e. in eyes
37 : 20. e. beast hath devoured. 33.
48 : † 17. Jos-h saw, it was e. in his
Ex. 5 : 19. see they were in e. case
21 : † 8. If she be e. in eyes of master
33 : 4. people heard these e. tidings
Le. 26 : 6. I rid e. beasts out of land
Nu. 11 : † 1. it was e. in ears of Lord
14 : 27. How long bear e. congreg.
35. I will do it unto this e. cong-n
20 : 5. to bring us unto this e. pla.
22 : † 34. if it be e. in thine eyes, I
De. 1 : 35. not one of this e. genera.
6 : † 22. Lord shewed signs, great
and e. upon Egypt ⌈upon thee
7 : 15. put none of the e. diseases
15 : 9. lest eye e. ag-t poor brother
22 : 14. an e. name upon her, 19.
28 : 54. eye shall be e. toward wife
56. her eye sh. be e. tow. husband
Jos. 24 : 15. if it seem e. to serve L.
1 S. 2 : 23. I hear of your e. dealings
18 : † 8. say-g was e. in Saul's eyes
25 : 3. Nabal was churlish and e.
2 S. 11 : † 25. not be e. in thine eyes
† 27. thing David had done was e.
in eyes of Lord, 1 Ch. 21 : † 7.
1 K. 5 : 4. given me rest, is neither
adversary nor e. occurrent ⌈16.
2 K. 21 : 15. have done that wh. was e.,
1 Ch. 2 : 3. Er was e. in sight of Lord
2 Ch. 21 : 6. Jehoram, that wh was e.
29 : 6. fathers have done that was e.
Ezr. 9 : 13. come upon us for e. deeds
Ps. 41 : 8. An e. disease cleaveth ⌈ter
64 : 5. encourage thems. in e. mat-
78 : 49. trouble by sending e. angels
112 : 7. sh. not be afraid of e. tidings
140 : 11. Let not e. speaker be establ.
Pr. 6 : 24. To keep thee fr. e. woman
24 : † 18. lest it be e. in eyes of Lord
Ec. 5 : 14. riches perish by e. travail
6 : 2. this is vanity, and e. disease
9 : 12. as fishes taken in an e. net
Is. 7 : 5. Ephr. have taken e. counsel
32 : 7. instruments of churl are e.

Je. 49:23. they have heard e. tidings
Eze. 5 : 16. send e. arrows of family
17. will I send upon you e. beasts
6 : 11. Alas, for all e. abom. of Isr.
34:25. will cause e. beasts to cease
38 : 10. shalt think an e. thought
Ha.2:9. coveteth an e. covetousness
Mal. 1 : 8. if ye offer blind for sacri.
is it not e. [good
Mat. 5: 45. sun to rise on e. and
7: 11. If ye being e., Lu. 11 : 13.
17. corrupt tree bringeth forth e.
18. good tree cannot bri. forth e.
12 : 34. how being e. speak good
39. An e. gene. seeketh sign, Lu.
11 : 29. [murders, Mk. 7 : 21.
15 : 19. out of heart e. thoughts,
24:48. if e. servant say in his heart
Lu. 6 : 22. cast out your name as e.
35. kind to the unthankful and e.
45.e.treasure of heart, Mat.12:35.
Jn. 3:19. loved darkn. bec. deeds e.
Ac. 24: 20. if found e. doing in me
1 Co. 15:33. e. communicat. corrupt
Ga.1:4.might deliver us fr. e. world
Ep. 4:31. let e. speaking be put aw.
Ph. 3 : 2. beware of e. workers
Col. 3 : 5. mortify e. concupiscence
1 Ti. 6 : 4. cometh e. surmisings
Tit. 1: 12. Cretians are e. beasts
He.10:22.sprinkled fr. e. conscience
Ja. 2 : 4. are judges of e. thoughts
4 : 16. boastings, all such rejoic-g e.
1 Pe. 2 : 1. laying aside e. speakings
2 Jn. 11. partaker of his e. deeds
Re. 2 : 2. canst not bear them are e.

EVIL day, s.

Ge.47:9. e. have d-s of my life been
Pr. 15 : 15. All d-s of afflicted are e.
Ec. 12 : 1. while the e. d-s come not
Am. 6 : 3. that put far away e. d.
Ep. 5:16. Redeem-g time, bec. d-s e.
6:13. be able to withstand in e. d.

Day of EVIL. See EVIL. [Noun.]

EVIL doer, s.

Jb. 8 : 20. nei. will he help e. d-s
Ps. 26:5. I hated the congr. of e.d-s
37:1. Fret not thyself bec. of e.d-s
9.e.d-s shall be cut off, but those
94 : 16. Who will rise up ag. e.d-s
119 : 115. Depart fr. me, ye e. d-s
Is. 1 : 4. ah, sinful nation, seed of
9 : 17. every one is an e.d. [e. d-s
14:20.seed of e.d-s never renowned
31 : 2. will arise ag. house of e.d-s
Je. 20: 13. deliv. soul from e. d-s
23 : 14. strengthen hands of e. d-s
2 Ti. 2 : 9. I suffer trouble as e. d.
1 Pe. 2 : 12. speak ag. you as e. d-s
14. are sent for punishm. of e.d-s
3 : 16. speak evil of you as e. d-s
4:15. let none of you suffer as an e.
See DOINGS, Evil EYE. [d.

EVIL-favouredness.

Deut. 17 : 1. bullock wherein is e. f.

EVIL heart.

Ge. 8:21. imagina. of man's h. is e.
Je. 3 : 17. nor walk after imagination of e. h.
7 : 24. walked in imagina. of e. h.
11 : 8. ev. one in imagina. of e. h.
16:12. ev. one aft. imagina. of e.h.
18:12. ev. one do imagina. of e.h.
He. 3 : 12. lest be an e.h. of unbe-

EVIL man. [lief

Ps. 10:15. Break thou arm of e.m.
140:1. Deliver me, O L. from e.m.
Pr. 2:12. To deliver fr. way of e.m.
17 : 11. An e.m. seeketh rebellion
24 : 20. sh. be no reward to e. m.
29:6. In transgr. of e.m. is a snare
Mat. 12 : 35. an e. m. out of evil
treasure bringeth evil, Lu.6:45.

EVIL men. [e. m.

Jb. 35 : 12. none ans. bec. of pride of
Pr. 4 : 14. go not in way of e. m.
12:12. wicked desireth net of e.m.

Pr. 24 : 1. be not envious ag. e. m.
19. fret not thyself bec. of e.m.
28:5. e.m. understand not judgm.
2 Ti. 3 : 13. e. m. shall wax worse
See REPORT.

EVIL spirit, s.

Ju. 9 : 23. sent e. s. betw. Abim.
1 S. 16:14. an e.s. troubled him,15.
16. when the e. s. is upon thee
23. and e. s. departed from him
18 : 10. e. s. came upon Saul,19 : 9.
Lu. 7 : 21. he cured many of e. s-s
8 : 2. woman been healed of e. s-s
Ac. 19 : 12. e. s-s went out of them
13.to call over them wh. had e.s-s
15. e. s. said, Jesus I know, Paul
16. man in whom the e. s. was

EVIL thing.

Ge. 38 : † 10. the t. he did was e.
2 K. 4 : † 41. was no e. t. in the pot
Ne. 13 : 17. What e. t. this ye do?
Ps. 141 : 4. Incline not my heart to
Ec. 8 : 3. stand not in an e.t. [e.t.
5. keepeth com-t, sh. feel no e.t.
12 : 14. every secret t. good or e.
Je. 2 : 19 it is an e. t. and bitter
Ti.2:8. having no e. t. to say of you

EVIL things.

Jos. 23 : 15. bring upon you all e.t.
Pr. 15 : 28. wicked poureth out e.t.
Je 3 : 5. hast done e.t. as couldest
Mat. 12 : 35. evil man bring. forth
Mk.7:23. e. t. come fr. within [e. t.
Lu. 16 : 25. likewise Lazarus e. t.
Ro. 1 : 30. proud, inventors of e.t.
1 Co. 10 : 6. should not lust after e.

EVIL time. [t.

Ps.37:19. sh. not be ashamed in e.t.
Ec. 9 : 12. so men are snared in e.t.
Am. 5:13. keep silence, it is an e.t.
Mi. 2 : 3. nor go haughtily, t. is e.

EVIL way, s. [e.w.

1 K. 13 : 33. Jerob. returned not fr.
2 K.17:13.Turn fr.e.w-s, Eze.33:11.
Ps. 119:101. refrained from ev. e.w.
Pr. 8 : 13. fear of L. is to hate e.w.
28:10. righte. to go astray in e. w.
Je. 18 : 11. return ev. one from e.
w., 25 : 5.-26:3.-35:15.-36:3,7.
23:22. sho. have turned th. fr.e.w.
Eze. 36 : 31. remem. your e. w-s
Jon. 3 : 8. turn ev. one from e. w.
10. saw they turned from e. w.
Zch. 1 : 4. turn ye now fr. your e.

EVIL work, s. [w-s

Ec. 4 : 3. who hath not seen e. w.
8 : 11. Bec. sentence ag. an e. w.
Jn. 7:7. I testify w-s are e. [but e.
Ro. 13 : 3. not terror to good w-s
2 Ti. 4:18. deliver me fr. every e.w.
Ja.3:16. confusion, and every e. w.
1 Jn.3:12. Bec. his own w-s were e.

EVIL. [Adverb.]

Ex. 5 : 22. why so e. entreated peo.
De. 26 : 6. Egyp. e. entreated us
1 Ch. 7 : 23. went e. with his house
Jb. 24 : 21. He e. entreateth barren
Mk. 9 : 39. lightly speak e. of me
Jn. 18 : 23. If spoken e. bear witn.
Ac.7:6.sho. entreat them e. 400 y-rs
19. same e. entreated our fathers
14 : 2. minds e. affected ag. breth.
19 : 9. spake e. of that way bef.
23 : 5. not speak e. of ruler [mult.
Ro.14:16. not your good be e. spok.
1 Co. 10:30. why am I e. spoken of
Tit. 3 : 2. To speak e. of no man
Ja. 4 : 11. Speak not e. one of ano.,
speaks e. of bro., speaks e. of
1 Pe. 3 : 16. they speak e. of you
17. better suffer for well than e.
4 : 4. speaking e. of you [doing
14. their part he is e. spoken of
2 Pe. 2 : 2. way of truth be e. spok.
10. to speak e. of dignities,Jude 8.
12. as beasts, speak e. of things
they understand not, Jude 10.

EVIL. [Noun.]

Ge. 19:19. lest e. take me and I die
28 : † 8. dau-s of Canaan e. in eyes
44 : 5. ye have done e. in so doing
34. lest I see e. shall come on my
50:15. requite us all e. we did [fa.
20. ye thought e. against me
Ex. 5 : 23. he hath done e. to peo.
10:10. look to it, for e. is bef. you
21 : † 8. if she be e. in eyes of mas.
32:14. L. repented of e. he thought
to do, 2 S. 24 : 16. 1 Ch. 21 : 15.
Nu. 11 : † 1. was e. in ears of Lord
22 : † 34. if it be e. in thine eyes
De. 19: 20. commit no more such e.
29:21. L. shall separate him unto e.
30 : 15. set bef. thee death and e.
31 : 29. e. befall you in latter days
Jos. 24 : 15. if it seem e. to serve L.
Ju. 2:15. hand of L. ag. them for e.
9 : 57. e. of Shechem did G. render
20 : 34. they knew not e. was near
41. they saw e. was come upon
1 S. 20 : 7. be sure e. is determined
9. if I knew e. were determined
24:11. e. nor transg. in mine hand
17. whereas I rewarded thee e.
25:17. e. is determined ag. our mas.
26. that seek e. to my lord, be as
28. e. hath not been found in thee
26 : 18. what e. is in my hand?
29 : 6. I have not found e. in thee
2 S. 3 : 39. L. sh. reward doer of e.
12 : 11. I will raise up e. ag. thee
16 : † 8. behold thee in thy e.
19 : 7. worse than all e. that befel
1 K. 14 : 9. hast done e. ab. all bef.
16 : 25. wrought e. in eyes of L.,
2 Ch. 21 : 6.-29 : 6. Je. 52 : 2.
17 : 20. hast bro-t e. upon widow
22 : 23. a lying spirit, Lord hath
spoken e. cone. thee,2 Ch.18:22
2 K. 21:12. bringing e. upon Jerus.
22:20. thine eyes sh. not see all e.
1 Ch. 21 : † 7. was e. in eyes of L.
17. it is I th. have done e. indeed
2 Ch. 20:9. If when e. cometh upon
Es. 7 : 7. he saw was e. determ. [us
8:6. endure to see e. unto my peo.?
Jb. 1:1. one that eschewed e.,8.-2:3.
5:19. in seven sh. no e. touch thee
31:29. or lift up when e. found him
42:11. they comfort. him ov. the e.
Ps. 5:4. nei. shall e. dwell with thee
7 : 4. If I rewarded e. unto him at
15 : 3. nor doeth e. to his neighb.
21 : 11. they intended e. ag. thee
23 : 4. I will fear no e., thou art
34:21. e. sh. slay wicked [with me
36 : 4. he abhorreth not e.
40:14. be put to shame wish me e.
41:†1. L. deliver him in day of e.
5. speak e. of me | † 7. devise e.
49 : 5. Whf. I fear in days of e.?
50:19. Thou givest thy mouth to e.
54:5. sh. reward e. unto mine ene.
56 : 5. their thoughts ag. me for e.
90:15.years wherein we have seen e.
91:10. no e. befall thee, Je. 23:17.
97:10. Ye that love the L., hate e.
109 : 20. that speak e. ag. my soul
140 : 11. e. shall hunt violent man
Pr. 1 : 16. feet run to e., Is. 59 : 7.
33. shall be quiet from fear of e.
3:29. Devise not e. ag. thy neighb.
5:14. I was almost in all e. in cong.
11:19. pursueth e. pursu. it to his
12:20.Deceit in them th. imagine e.
21. shall no e. happen to the just
13 : 21. e. pursueth sinners
14 : 22. not err that devise e.?
16 : 4. the wicked for the day of e.
27. An ungodly man diggeth up e.
30. moving his lips he bringeth e.
19:23. he sh. not be visited with e.
20:8. a king scatt-h e. with his eyes
22. Say not, I will recompense e.

Pr.20:30.blue.of wound cleanseth e.
21 : 10. soul of wicked desireth e.
22 : 3. prudent foreseeth e., 27:12.
24 : † 18. lest it be e. in eyes of L.
30 : 32. if hast thought e. lay hand
Ec. 2 : 21. This is vanity, and gr. e.
5 : 13. is a sore e. I have seen, 16.
6 : 1. an e. wh. I have seen, 10 : 5.
9:3. This is an e. am. things done,
heart of men full of e. [earth
11 : 2. knowest not what e. be upon
Is. 3 : 9. rewarded e. unto thems.
13 : 11. I will punish world for e.
33:15. shutteth eyes from seeing e.
45 : 7. I make peace and create e.
47:11. Thf. shall e. come upon thee
56 : 2. keepeth hand from doing e.
57:1. righteous is taken from the e.
Je. 1 : 14. Out of north an e., 6 : 1.
2 : 3. e. shall come upon them
†28. if can save thee in time of e.
4 : 4. lest fury, bec. of e. of your
doings,21:12. 23:2.-26:3.-44:22.
5 : 12. neither sh. e. come upon us
7 : 30. chil. of Judah have done e.
11:†12. not save them in time of e.
†14. not hear when they cry for e.
15. doest e. then rejoicest [of Isr.
17. pronounced e. ag. thee for e.
15 : 11. entreat thee well in time of
17:17. art my hope in day of e. [e.
18. bring upon them the day of e.
18 : 8. nation turn from e. I will repent of e., 26:3, 13, 19.-42:10.
11. I frame e. ag. you and devise
19:15. bring e. I have pronounced
21:10. set my face ag. this city for e.
25 : 32. e. shall go from na. to na.
28 : 8. prophets prophesied of e.
29 : 11. I think of peace not of e.
32 : 30. chil. of Judah only done e.
32. Bec. of all e. of chil. of Israel
35 : 17. will bring upon Jud. the
e. I have pronounced, 36 : 31.
36 : 3. house of Jud. will hear all e.
38:9. these men have done e. in all
41:11. all the e. Ishmael had done
44 : 2. seen all the e. I have bro't
11. will set my face ag. you for e.
17. we had plenty, and saw no e.
27. I will watch over them for e.
29. my words stand ag. you for e.
48 : 2. in Heshbon they devised e.
51 : 24. I will render to Bab. all e.
60. wrote e. sho. come upon Bab.
Eze. 7:5. An e. an only e. it is come
14:22. ye sh. be comforted conc. e.
Da. 9 : 14. L. hath watched upon e.
Jo.2:13. Lord repenteth him of the e.
Am.3:6. be e. in city, L. not done it?
9:10. who say, e. sh. not overtake us
Jon. 3 : 10. God repented of e., 4 : 2.
Mi. 1:12. but e. came down from L.
2 : 1. that work e. upon their beds
3. ag. this family do I devise an e.
3 : 11. Is L. among us ? none e. can
Na. 1 : 11. that imagineth e. ag. L.
Ha. 1 : 13. purer eyes than to behold e. [power of e.
2:9 that he may be delivered from
Zph. 3:15. shalt not see e. any more
Zch. 7:10. let none imagine e., 8: 17.
Mal. 1 : 8. ye offer sick, is it not e.?
2 : 17. ev. one that doeth e. is good
Mat. 5 : 11. all manner of e. ag. you
37. more than these, cometh of e.
39. I say, that ye resist not e.
6 : 34. Sufficient unto the day is e.
9 : 4. Whf. think ye e. in your
27 : 23. Pilate said, what e. hath
he done ? Mk. 15 : 14. Lu. 23:22.
Mk. 9: 39. lightly speak e. of me
Lu. 6 : 45. e. man bringeth forth e.
Jn. 3:20. doeth e. hateth the light
5:29. that have done e. to resurrec.
18:23. If spoken e. bear witn. of e.
Ac. 9:13. how much e. he hath done

15

Ac. 28:9. we find no e. in this man
Ro. 2:9 upon ev. soul that doeth e.
7 : 19 the e. I would not, that I do
12 : 9. abhor that wh. is e. cleave
17. Recompense to no man e. for e.
21. be not overcome of e. overc. e.
13 : 4. wrath upon him doeth e.
14 : 20. it is e. for man who eateth
16 : 19. have you simple conc. e.
1 Co. 13 : 5. charity thinketh no e.
1 Th.5:15. that none render e. for e.
22. Abstain fr. all appearance of e.
1 Ti.6:10. love of money is root of e.
Tit. 3:2. mind to speak e. of no man
Ja. 1:13. G. can-t be tempted with e.
3 : 8. the tongue is an unruly e.
1 Pe. 3:9. Not rendering e. for e. or
3 Jn. 11. that doeth e. not seen G.

Bring EVIL. [all e.

Jos. 23 : 15. L. shall b. upon you
2 S. 15 : 14. lest b. e. upon us [Abs.
17 : 14. that L. might b. e. upon
1 K.14:10. will b. e. on hou. of Jerob.
21 : 21. I will b. e. upon thee
29. not b. e. in his days, but in
2 K. 22 : 16. saith L., I will b. e.
upon this place, 2 Ch. 34 : 24.
2 Ch. 34:28. nor eyes see e. I will b.
Is.31:2. I will b. e. and not call back
Je. 4 : 6. I will b. e. from north
6 : 19. I will b. e. upon this people
11 : 11. I will b. e. upon them
23. I will b. e. upon Anathoth
19:3. I will b. e. upon this place, 15.
23 : 12. I will b. e. year of visita.
25 : 29. I begin to b. e. on the city
35 : 17. will b. upon Jud. e., 36:31.
39:16. b. my words upon city for e.
42:17. escape fr. e. I b. upon them
45 : 5. I will b. e. upon all flesh

Did EVIL. See DID.

Do EVIL. See DO.

From EVIL.

Ge. 48:16. who redeemed me f. all e.
1 S. 25 : 39. hath kept his serv. f. e.
1 Ch. 4 : 10. wouldst keep me f. e.
Jb. 28:28. to depart f. e. is underst.
Ps. 34 : 13. Keep thy tongue f. e.
14. Depart f. e., 37 : 27. Pr. 3 : 7.
121:7. L. shall preserve thee f. all e.
Pr. 4 : 27. remove thy foot f. e.
13:19. abomi. to fools to depart f. e.
14 : 16. A wise man departeth f. e.
16:6. by fear of L. men depart f. e.
17. of upright is to depart f. e.
Is. 59:15. departeth f. e. hims. a prey
Je. 9 : 3. they proceed f. e. to e.
23 : 22. should have turned f. e.
51:64. Babylon not rise f. e. way
Mat. 6 : 13. deliver us f. e., Lu. 11 : 4.
Jn. 17 : 15. shouldst keep them f. e.
2 Th.3:3. stablish, and keep you f. e.
1 Pe. 3 : 10. refrain his tongue f. e.

EVIL with good.

Ge. 2 : 9. knowl. of g. and e., 17.
3:5. as gods knowing g. and e., 22.
44 : 4. Whf. ye rewarded e. for g.?
De. 1:39. no knowl. betw. g. and e.
1 S. 25 : 21. requited me e. for g.
2 S. 19:35. discern betw. g. and e.?
1 K. 22 : 8. Micaiah not prophesy g.,
but e., 18. [but e.
2 Ch. 18 : 7. never prophesieth g.
17. not prophesy g. to me but e.
Jb. 2 : 10. we receive g., and not e.?
30 : 26. I looked for g., e. came
Ps. 35 : 12. rewarded me e. for g.,
109 : 5. [adversaries
38:20. that render e. for g. are mine
52 : 3. Thou lovest e. more than g.
Pr. 15 : 3 L. beholding e. and g.
17 : 13. Whoso rewardeth e. for g.
31:12. She will do him g. and not e.
Ec. 12 : 14. whether it be g. or e.
Is.5:20. Woe to them call e. g. and g.
7:15. to refuse e. choose g., 16. [e.
Je. 18 : 20. Sh. e. be recomp for g.?

Je.39:16. upon city for e. not for g.
42:6. Whe. g. or e. we will obey L.
La. 3 : 38. proceedeth not e. and g.
Am. 5 : 14. Seek g. and not e. that
15. Hate the e. and love the g.
9:4. set eyes upon them for e. not g.
Mi. 3 : 2. Who hate g., and love e.
Mal.2:17. say, Ev. one doeth e. is g.
Mat. 5 : 45. sun to rise on e. and g.
Ro. 7 : 21. would do g., e. present
9:11. neither having done g. nor e.
12 : 9. Abhor e. cleave to that g.
21. overcome e. with g. (2)
16 : 19. wise unto that which is g.,
simple conc. e. [and e.
He. 5 : 14. exercised to discern g.
1 Pe. 3 : 11. him eschew e. and do g.
3 Jn. 11. follow not e. but g.

Great EVIL. See GREAT.

Put away EVIL.

De. 13:5. p. e. a. from midst of thee
17 : 7. shalt p. e. a. from am. you,
19 : 19.-21 : 21.-22:21, 24.-24:7.
12. p. e. a. from Israel, 21 : 21.
Ju. 20 : 13.
Ec. 11 : 10. p. a. e. from thy flesh
Is. 1 : 16. wash ye, p. a. e. of doings

EVIL in sight of the Lord.

Nu. 32 : 13. had done e. i.-, Ju.3:12.
Ju. 2 : 11. Israel did e. i.-, 3 : 7, 12.
-4 : 1.-6 : 1.-10 : 6.-13 : 1. 1 K.
11 : 6.-14 : 22.-15 : 26, 34.-16:
7, 30.-22 : 52. 2 K. 8 : 18, 27.-
13 : 2, 11.-14 : 24.-15 : 9, 18, 24,
28.-17 : 2.-21 : 2, 20. 2 Ch. 22 :
4.-33 : 2, 22.-36 : 5, 9, 12.
1 S. 15 : 19. thou didst e. i.-
1 K. 16 : 19. in doing e. i.-
21 : 20. sold to work e. i.-
2 K. 3 : 2. he wrought e. i.-
17 : 17. sold themselves to do e. i.-
21 : 16. to sin, in doing that which
was e. i.-, 23:32, 37.-24 : 9, 19.
1 Ch. 2 : 3. Er was e. i.- [i.
2 Ch.33:6. Manas. wrought much e.

This EVIL.

E .32:12. repent of t. e. ag. thy peo.
1 . 6 : 9. he hath done us t. gr. e.
1 : 19. added t. e. to ask a king
2 . 13:16. t. e. in sending me away
1 . 9:9. L. brought upon them t. e.
2 K. 6 : 33. he said, Behold, t. e. is
of the Lord [them
2 Ch. 7 : 22. thf. brought t. e. upon
Ne. 13:18. did not our G. bring t. e.?
27. Sh. we hearken to do t. great e.?
Jb. 2:11. Job's friends heard of t. e.
Ps. 51 : 4. done t. e. in thy sight
Je.16:10 L. pronounced t. e. ag. us
32 : 23. thou hast caused all t. e.
42. as I brought t. e. upon peo.
40 : 2. G. hath pronounced t. e.
44 : 7. Whf. commit ye t. great e.
23. thf. t. e. is happened unto you
Da. 9 : 13. all t. e. is come upon us
Jon. 1 : 7. whose cause t. e. is upon

EVILS. [us, 8.

De. 31:17. many e. shall befall, will
say, are not these e. come
18. for e. they sh. have wrought
21. when many e. are befallen
Ps. 40 : 12. innum. e. compassed
Je. 2 : 13. people have commit. 2 e.
Eze. 6 : 9. shall loathe thems. for e.
20:43. loathe yours. for all your e.
Ho. 7 : † 1. e. of Samar. were discov.
Lu. 3 : 19. for all e. Herod had done
Ja. 1 : † 13. God cannot be tempted
with e.

E'VIL-MERO'DACH.

2 K. 25:27. E. king of Bab., Je.52:31.

EWE or EWES.

Ge.21:28. Ab. set 7 e. lambs by thems.
29. What mean seven e. lambs ?
30. these 7 e. lambs sh. thou take
31:38. e-s have not cast their young
32 : 14. two hundred e. for Esau

Le. 14 : 10. take one e. lamb of
22 : 28. whe. cow or e. not kill it
2 S. 12 : 3. noth. save one e. lamb
Ps. 78:71. took him fr. following e-s

EXACT.

De.15:2.shall not e. it of his neighb.
3. Of foreigner mayest e. it
Ne. 5 : 7. You e. usury one of bro.
10. I likewise might e. money
11. restore 100th of money ye e.
Ps. 89 : 22. enemy not e. upon him
Is. 58 : 3. in fasts e. your labours
Lu. 3 : 13.e.no more than is appoin.

EXACTED, ETH.

2 K. 15 : 20. Menahem e-d money
23 : 35. Jehoiakim e-d silver and
Jb. 11 : 6. God e-h less than thine iniquity deserveth

EXACTION, S.

Ne. 10 : 31. leave e. of every debt
Eze. 45 : 9. take away your e-s from the e.

EXACTOR, S.

Jb.39:†7.nor regardeth he crying of
Is. 60:17. make thine e-s righteousn.

EXALT.

Ex. 15 : 2. father's G., and I will e. him
1 S. 2 : 10. shall e. horn of anoint.
Jb. 17 : 4. thf. shalt thou not e.them
Ps. 34 : 3. let us e. his name togeth.
37 : 34. shall e. thee to inherit la.
66 : 7. let not rebellious e. thems.
92 : 10. my horn shalt thou e. like
99 : 5. e. ye the Lord our God, 9.
107 : 32.Let them e.him in congr.
118 : 28. art my G., I will e. thee
140 : 8. lest the wicked e. thems.
Pr. 4 : 8. e. her, she shall promote
Is. 13 : 2. e. the voice unto them
14 : 13. I will e.my throne ab. stars
25 : 1. thou my God, I will e. thee
Eze. 21 : 26. e. him that is low
29 : 15. nor e. itself more above na.
31 : 14. to the end none of trees e.
Da. 11: 14. robbers of thy peo. sh. e.
36. king e. himself above ev. god
Ho. 11 : 7. none at all would e. him
Ob. 4. Though e. thyself as eagle
Mat. 23 : 12. whoso shall e. himself
2 Co. 11 : 20. if a man e. himself, if
1 Pe. 5 : 6. humble yours. that he e.

EXALTED.

Nu. 24 : 7. his kingdom shall be e.
1 S. 2 : 1. she said, mine horn is e.
2 S. 5:12.perceiv. L.had e.his kingd.
22: 47.e.be G.of my salv.,Ps.18:46.
1 K. 1 : 5. then Adonijah e. hims.
14 : 7. I e. thee from am.peo.,16:2.
2 K. 19 : 22. ag. whom hast thou e. thy voice, Is. 37 : 23.
1 Ch. 29 : 11. thou art e. as head
Ne. 9 : 5. is e. above all blessing
Jb. 5 : 11. who mourn be e.to safety
24 : 24. They are e. for a little wh.
36 : 7. doth establish, they are e.
Ps. 12: 8. when the vilest men are e.
13 : 2. how long enemy be e. ov.me
21 : 13. Be thou e. L., in own str.
46 : 10. I will be e. am. heathen, I will be e. in the earth [e.
47 : 9. belong unto G. he is greatly
57 : 5. Be e. O God, ab. heav., 11.
75:10. horns of righteous sh. be e.
89:16.in thy righte. shall they be e.
17. in thy favour our horn be e.
19. e. one chosen out of people
24. in my name sh.his horn be e.
97 : 9. L., art e. far above all gods
108 : 5. be thou e. O G., ab. heav.
112:9.his horn sh.be e.with honour
118 : 16. right hand of Lord is e.
140 : † 8. let not the wicked be e.
Pr. 11 : 11. By the upright city is e.
Is. 2 : 2. mountain of L.'s house be e. above hills, Mi. 4 : 1. [16.
11. L. be e. in that day, 17. 5 :
12 : 4. mention that his name is e.
30 : 18. be e. that he have mercy

Is. 33 : 5. L. is e. | 10. will I be e.
40 : 4. Every valley shall be e.
49 : 11.my highways shall be e.[e.
52 : 13. behold my servant shall be
Eze. 17 : 24. L. have e. low tree
19 : 11. her stature was e., 31: 5.
Ho.† 11 : 7. together they e. not him
13 : 1. Ephraim spake, he e. hims.
6. filled, and heart was e.
Mat. 11: 23. Capernaum e. unto heaven, Lu. 10 : 15.
23 : 12.e. hims. be abased humble himself be e. Lu. 14: 11.-18:14.
Lu. 1 : 52. e. them of low degree
Ac. 2 : 33. by right hand of God e.
5 : 31. Him hath God e. with his
13 : 17. God of Isr. e. people in E.
2 Co. 11 : 7. abasing that you be e.
12 : 7. lest I be e. above meas., 7.
Ph. 2 : 9. God hath highly e. him
Ja. 1 : 9. bro. rejoice that he is e.

EXALTEST, ETH.

Ex. 9 : 17. e-t thyself ag. my peo.
Jb. 36 : 22. God e. by his power
Ps. 113 : † 5. God, who e. hims. to
148 : 14. He e. horn of his people
Pr. 3:† 35.glory, but shame e. fools
14 : 29. is hasty of spirit e. folly
34. Righteousness e.a nation,but
17 : 19. e.his gate seeketh destruc.
Lu. 14 : 11. e. hims. be abas.,18: 14.
2 Co. 10 : 5. down ev. thing e. itself
2 Th. 2 : 4. e. hims. above all G.

EXAMINATION.

Ac. 25 :26.that after e.had,I might write

EXAMINE.

Ez. 10 : 16. sat down to e. matter
Ps. 26 : 2. e. me, O Lord, prove me
1 Co. 9 : 3. Mine ans. to them e. me
11 : 28. let a man e. himself
2 Co. 13 : 5. e. yourselves, prove

EXAMINED, ING.

Lu. 23 : 14. I have e. him bef. you
Ac. 4 : 9. we be e. of good deed
12:19.Herod e-d keepers and com-d
22 : 24. should be e. by scourging
29.departed who sho. have e. him
24 : 8.by e-g of whom thou mayest
28:18. e-d me would have let me go

EXAMPLE, S.

Mat. 1 : 19. not willing to make her an e.
Jn. 13 : 15. I have given you an e.
Ro. 15: † 5. like minded aft. e. of C.
1 Co.10:6. these things were our e-s
1 Ti. 4 : 12. be thou an e. of believ.
He. 4 : 11. lest any fall aft. same e.
8 : 5. serve unto e. of heavenly
Ja.5: 10. prophets for e. of suffering
1 Pe. 2: 21. C. suffered leaving an e.
Jude 7.set forth for an e.suffer.veng.
See ENSAMPLE, S.

EXCEED.

De.25:3.Forty stripes and not e.lest if he e. bro. seem vile
Mat. 5 :20.exc.your righte. e.scribes
1 Co. 3 : 9. ministration doth e. in

EXCEEDED, EST, ETH.

1 S. 20 : 41. they wept until Da. e-d
1 K.10: 7. thy wisdom e-h the fame
23. Solomon e-d all for riches
2 Ch. 9 : 6. thou e-t fame I heard
Jb.36 : 9.sheweth transgr. they e-d

EXCEEDING.

Ge. 15 : 1. I am thy e. great reward
17 : 6. I will make thee e. fruitful
27 : 34.Esau cried with e.bitter cry
Ex. 1 : 7. Israel waxed e. mighty
19 : 16. voice of trumpet e. loud
Nu. 14 : 7. land we passed is e. good
1 S. 2 : 3. Talk no more e. proudly
2 S. 8 : 8. Da. took e. much brass
12 : 2.rich man had e.many flocks
1 K. 4: 29.G.gave Sol.wisd. e.much
7 : 47. vessels unweighed, e. many
1 Ch.20:2. he brought e.much spoil
22 : 5. house must be e. magnifical
2 Ch. 11 : 12. made cities e. strong

2 Ch. 14 : 14. e. much spoil in them
16: 12.Asa, his disease was e.great
32 : 27. Hez. had e. much riches
Ps.21:6.thou hast made him e.glad
43 : 4. will I go unto G. my e. joy
119 : 96. thy com-t is e. broad
Pr. 30 : 24. four things are e. wise
Ec. 7 : 24. that e. deep, who find it
Je.48:29.pride of Moab,he is e.proud
Eze. 9 : 9. iniquity of Isr. is e. great
16 : 13. eat oil, and wast e. beauti.
23 : 15.e.in dyed attire upon heads
37 : 10. stood up an e.great army
47 : 10. as fish of great sea, e.many
Da. 3 : 22. bec. furnace was e. hot
6 : 23. Then was king e. glad
7 : 19. fourth beast was e. dreadful
8:9.little horn which waxed e.great
Jon. 3 : 3. Nin. was e. great city
4 : 6. Jonah was e. glad of gourd
Mat. 2 : 10. rejoiced with e. gr. joy
16. Herod, mocked, was e. wroth
4 : 8. taketh up into e. high mt.
5 : 12. Rejoice and be e. glad
8:28. possessed with devils,e.fierce
17 : 23. And they were e. sorry
26 : 22. were e. sorrowful [14:34.
38. My soul is e. sorrowful, Mk.
Mk. 6 : 26. the king was e. sorry
9 : 3. his raiment e. white as snow
Lu. 23:8.Herod saw Jes.was e. glad
Ac. 7 : 20. Moses was born, e. fair
Ro. 7 : 13. that sin become e. sinful
2 Co. 4 : 17. an e. weight of glory
7:4. I am e. joyful in all our tribu.
9 : 14. for e. grace of God in you
Ep. 1 : 19. e. greatness of his power
2 : 7. might shew e. riches of grace
3 : 20. is able to do e. abundantly
1 Ti. 1:14. grace of L. was e. abun.
1 Pe. 4 : 13. be glad with e. joy
2 Pe. 1 : 4. unto us e. great promises
Jude 24. you faultless with e. joy
Re. 16 : 21. the plague was e. great

EXCEEDINGLY.

Ge. 7 : 19. the waters prevailed e.
13 : 13. men of Sodom sinners e.
16 : 10. I will multiply thy seed e.
17:2. make cov. and multiply thee
20. I will multiply Ishmael e. [e.
27:33. And Isaac trembled very e.
30 : 43. Jacob increased e., 47:27.
1 S. 26 : 21. I have erred e.
2 S. 13 : 15. Amnon hated her e.
2 K. 10 : 4. elders of Sama. e. afraid
1 Ch. 29 : 25. L. magnified Sol. e.,
2 Ch.17:12.waxed great e.[2 Ch.1:1.
26:8. Uzziah strengthened hims. e.
Ne. 2 : 10. heard of it, grieved them
Es. 4 : 4. queen was e. grieved [e.
Jb. 3 : 22. rejoi. e. when find grave
Ps. 68 : 3. let righteous e. rejoice
106:14. lusted e. in the wilderness
119:167.testimonies, I love them e.
123 : 3. are e. filled with contempt,
Is. 24 : 19. earth is moved e. [4.
Da. 7 : 7. a fourth beast strong e.
Jon. 1 : 10. men were e. afraid
16. Then the men feared the L. e.
4 : 1. But it displeased Jonah e.
Mat. 19 : 25. they were e. amazed
Mk. 4 : 41. they feared e. and said
15 : 14. cried out more e. Crucify
Ac. 16 : 20. These men e. trouble
26 : 11. e. mad against them [city
27 : 18. e. tossed with a tempest
2 Co.7:13. and e. the more joyed we
Ga. 1 : 14. e. zealous of traditions
1 Th.3:10.night and day praying e.
2 Th. 1 : 3. your faith groweth e.
He. 12 : 21. Moses said, I e. fear

EXCEL.

Ge. 49:4. Unstable as water, not e.
1 Ch. 15 : 21. harps on Shemi. to e.
Ps.103:20. angels, th. e. in strength
Is. 10:10. whose images did e. them
1 Co. 14 : 12. seek that ye may e.

EXCELLED, EST, ETH.
1 K.4:30. Sol.'s wisd. e-d wisd. of E.
Pr.31:29. done virtuously, thou e-t
Ec. 2: 13. wisdom e-h folly, as far as light e-h dark. [that e-h
2 Co. 3: 10. by reason of the glory

EXCELLENCY. [e.?
Ge.4:†7. doest well, shalt thou have
49: 3. e. of dignity, e. of power
Ex. 15: 7. in greatness of thine e.
De. 33: 26. who rideth in his e.
29. and who is the sword of thy e.
Jb. 4:21. Doth not their e. go away
13: 11. Sh. not his e. make afraid
20: 6. Tho. his e. mount to heav.
22:†20 their e. the fire consumeth
37: 4. thundereth with voice of e.
40: 10. Deck thyself now with e.
Ps. 47: 4. e. of Jac. whom he lov.
62: 4. consult to cast him down
68: 34. his e. is over Israel [fr. e.
Pr. 17: † 7. lip of e. becometh not
Ec. 2: † 13. I saw an e. in wisdom
7:12. e. of knowledge is, that wisd.
Is.13:19. beauty of the Chaldees' e.
35: 2. e. of Carmel, e. of our G.
60:15. make thee an etern. e. [of e.
Eze. 16: † 56. not mentioned in day
24:21. my sanct. e. of your strength
Am. 6: 8. I abhor the e. of Jacob
8: 7. L. hath sworn by e. of Jacob
Na. 2: 2. the e. of Jac. as e. of Isr.
Mal. 2: † 15. had he e. of the Spirit
1 Co.2:1. came not with e. of speech
2 Co. 4: 7. that e. of power be of G.
Ph. 3: 8. I count all loss for e. of C.

EXCELLENT. [esty
Es. 1: 4. Ahasu. shewed his e. maj-
Jb. 37: 23. Almighty is e. in power
Ps. 8: 1. how e. is thy name in! 9.
16: 3. e. in whom is all my delight
36: 7. How e. is thy lovingkindn.
76: 4. thou art more e. than mts.
141: 5. reprove, it sh. be an e. oil
148: 13. Lord, his name alone is e.
150: 2. praise acc. to his e. greatn.
Pr. 8:6. speak of e. things [neighb.
12: 26. righteous more e. than
17: 7. e. speech becometh not fool
27. man of underst. is of e. spirit
22: 20. Have I not writt. e. things
Can. 5: 15. countenan. e. as cedars
Is. 4: 2. fruit of earth shall be e.
12:5. Sing to L. hath done e. things
22: † 17. L. covered with e. cover.
28: 29. L. of hosts e. in working
Eze. 16: 7. art come to e. ornam.
27:†24. thy merchants in e. things
Da. 2: 31. whose brightness was e.
4: 36. e. majesty added unto me
5: 12. e. spirit found in Dan., 6:3.
14. heard e. wisdom is found in
Lu. 1: 3. most e. Theophilus [thee
Ac. 23: 26. e. governor Felix
Ro. 2: 18. approvest things that are more e., Ph. 1: 10.
1 Co. 12: 31. shew I a more e. way
He. 1: 4. obtained more e. name
8:6. he obtained more e. ministry
11: 4. Abel offered more e. sacrifi.
2 Pe. 1:17. came a voice fr. e. glory

EXCEPT. [me
Ge. 31:42. e. G. of my fa. been with
32:26. not let go, e. thou bless me
42: 15. e. youngest bro. come, 43:
43: 10. e. we had lingered [3, 5.
47: 26. e. land of the priests only
Nu. 16: 13. e. make thyself prince
De. 32: 30. e. their Rock had sold
Jos. 7: 12. e. you destroy accursed
1 S. 25: 34. e. thou hasted to meet
2 S. 3: 9. e. as the L. hath sworn
13. e. thou first bring Michal
5: 6. e. thou take away the blind
2 K. 4:24. slack not riding, e. I bid
Es. 2: 14. e. king delighted in her
4: 11. e. king hold golden sceptre
Ps. 127:1. e. Lord build the house, e. the Lord keep the city
Pr. 4: 16. sleep not, e. done misch.
Is. 1:9. e. L. left remnant, Ro.9:29.
Da. 2: 11. none shew it, e. gods
3: 28. nor worship god, e. own G.
6: 5. e. find it conc. law of his G.
Am. 3: 3. can two walk e. agreed?
Mat. 5: 20. e. righteousn. exceed
12: 29. e. bind str. man, Mk.3:27.
18: 3. I say, e. ye be converted and
19: 9. put aw. wife, e. for fornica.
24:22. e. days be short., Mk.13:20.
26: 42. if cup not pass, e. I drink
Mk 7: 3. Phari. e. wash oft, eat
Lu. 9: 13. e. we buy meat [not, 4.
13: 3. e. ye repent, ye sh. perish, 5.
Jn.3:2. miracles, e. G. be with him
3. e. a man be born again, he
5. e. a man be born of water
27. receive nothing, e. it be given
4: 48. e. ye see signs and wonders
6: 44. e. Father draw him
53. e. ye eat flesh of Son of man
65. e. it were given him of my Fa.
12: 24. e. a corn of wheat fall into
15: 4. can-t bear fruit, e. ye abide
19: 11. no power, e. it were given
20: 25. e. I see prints of the nails
Ac. 8: 1. all scattered, e. apostles
31. e. some man sho. guide me?
15: 1. e. ye be circum. ye cannot
24: 21. e. it be for this one voice
26: 29. all as I am, e. these bonds
27: 31. Paul said, e. abide in ship
Ro. 7: 7. not kn. lust, e. law said
10: 15. how preach, e. they be sent
1 Co. 7:5. defraud not one the other e. with consent [interpret
14: 5. speaketh with tongues, e. he
6. e. I shall speak by revelation
7. e. give a distinction in sounds
9. e. ye utter words easy to be
15: 36. is not quickened, e. it die
2 Co. 12:13. e. I was not burdenso.
13: 5. C. in you, e. be reprobates?
2 Th. 2: 3. e. come a falling away
2 Ti. 2:5. not crowned, e. he strive
Re.2:5. remove candlest. e. thou rep.
22. into tribulation, e. they repent

EXCEPTED.
1 Co. 15:27. he is e. who did put all

EXCESS.
Mat. 23: 25. within are full of e.
Ep. 5: 18. with wine, wherein is e.
1 Pe.4:3. walked in lusts, e. of wine
4. that ye run not to same e.

EXCHANGE. [Noun.]
Ge. 47: 17. Joseph gave bread in e.
Le. 27: 10. it and the e. sh. be holy
Jb. 20: † 18. acc. to substance of e.
28:17. e. of it sh. not be for jewels
Mat. 16: 26. what shall a man give in e. for his soul? Mk. 8: 37.

EXCHANGE. [Verb.]
Eze. 48:14. not sell nor e. firstfruits

EXCHANGERS. [to e.
Mat. 25: 27. oughtest to put money

EXCLUDE, ED.
Ro. 3:27. Where is boasting? it is e.
Ga. 4: 17. they would e. you, that

EXCOMMUNICATED.
Jn.9:†34. dost teach us? they e. him

EXCUSE. [Noun.]
Lu. 14: 18. they began to make e.
Jn. 15:†22. they no e. for their sin
Ro. 1: 20. so that they are without

EXCUSE, ED, ING. [e.
Lu.14:18. pray thee have me e-d, 19.
Ro. 2:15. thoughts accusing or e-g
2 Co. 12: 19. think you we e. ours.

EXECRATION.
Je. 42: 18. and ye shall be an e.
44:12. shall be an e. and reproach
Ac. 23:†12. bound thems. with oath

EXECUTE. [of e.
Ex. 12: 12. e. judgm. ag. gods of E.
Nu. 5: 30. priest shall e. upon her
8:11. th. they may e. service of L.
De.10:18. He doth e. judgm. of wid.
1 K. 6:12. if thou wilt e. my judgm.
Ps.119:84. when wilt thou e. judgm.
149:7. To e. vengeance upon heath.
9. To e. upon them judgm. written
Is. 16:3. Take counsel, e. Judgment
Je. 7: 5. e. judgm. betw. man and
21:12. e. judgment in the morning
22:3. e. judgm. and righteousness
23:5. branch sh. e. judgm., 33:15.
Eze: 5:8. will e. judgm. in thee, 10.
15. when I sh. e. judgm. in thee
11: 9. I will e. Judgments am. you
16:41. shall e. judgments upon thee
25:11. I will e. judgm. upon Moab
17. I will e. vengeance upon them
30: 14. I e. judgments in No
19. Thus will I e. judgm. in E.
45: 9. e. judgment and justice
Ho.11:9. I will not e. the fierceness
Mi. 5: 15. I will e. veng. in anger
7: 9. until he e. judgment for me
Zch.7:9. e. true judgm. shew mercy
8: 16. e. the judgment of truth
Jn.5:27. given authority to e. judgm
Ro. 13: 4. minister of G. to e. wrath
Jude 15. to e. judgment upon all

EXECUTED.
Nu. 33:4. upon gods Lord e. judgm
De. 33:21. he e. justice of the Lord
2 S. 8:15. Da. e. judgm., 1 Ch. 18:14.
1 Ch. 6: 10. that e. priest's office
24:2. and Ithamar e. priest's office
2 Ch. 24: 24. e. judgm. ag. Joash
Ezr. 7: 26. let judgm. be e. speedily
Ps. 106:30. Then Phinehas, e. judg.
Ec.8:11. bec. sentence is not e. speed.
Je. 23:20. anger not ret. until he e.
Ez. 11:12. nei. e. my judgm., 20: 24.
18:8. e. true judgm. betw. man, 17.
23:10. they had e. judgm. upon her
28: 22. when I have e. judgm., 26.
39: 21. heath. see judgm. I have e.
Lu. 1: 8. while Zach. e. pr.'s office

EXECUTEDST, EST.
1 S. 28:18. nor e-dst his fierce wrath upon Amalek
Ps. 99:4. thou e-est judgm. in Jacob

EXECUTETH. [e.
Ps. 9:16. L. is known by judgm. he
103: 6. Lord e. righteousness and
146: 7. L. e. judgment for oppres.
Is. 46: 11. man that e. my counsel
Je. 5:1. any e. judgm., I will pardon
Jo. 2: 11. he is strong that e. word

EXECUTING.
2 K. 10: 30. well in e. that is right
2 Ch.11:14. Jerob. cast them off fr. e.
22: 8. Jehu e. judgm. upon Ahab's

EXECUTION. [h.
Es. 9: 1. decree near to be put in e.

EXECUTIONER, S.
Mk. 6: 27. king sent an e. and com.
Ge. 37: † 36. Potiphar, chief of e-s
Je.39:†9. Nebuz. chief of e-s, 52:†12.
Da. 2: † 14. Arioch chief of the e-s

EXEMPTED.
1 K. 15:22. made proclama., none e.

EXERCISE. [Noun.]
1 Ti. 4: 8. bodily e. profiteth little

EXERCISE. [Verb.]
Ps.131:1. nor do I e. in thi. too high
Je. 9: 24. L. which e. lovingkindn.
Mat. 20: 25. princes of Gentiles e. dominion they that are great e. authority, Mk. 10:42. Lu.22:25.
Ac. 24:16. e. myself to have consci.
1 Ti. 4: 7. e. thyself unto godliness

EXERCISED, ETH.
Ec. 1: 13. sore travail, to be e., 3:10.
Eze. 22: 29. peo. of land e. robbery
He. 5: 14. senses e. to discern good
12: 11. fruit of righte. to them e.
2 Pe. 2: 14. heart e. with covetous
Re. 13:12. he e-h power of first beast

EXHORT.

Ac. 2:40. with many words did he e.
27:22. I e. you to be of good cheer
2 Co. 9:5. thought it necessary to e.
1 Th. 4: 1. we beseech you, e. you
† 18. e. one ano. with these words
5:†11. whf. e. yourselves togeth.
14. we e. you, warn unruly
2 Th. 3:12. such we command, and e.
1 Ti. 2: 1. I e. that 1st of all, prayer
6: 2. These things teach and e.
2 Ti. 4: 2. e. with all longsuffering
Tit. 1:9. be able to e. and convince
2:6. Young men e. to be sobermind-
9. e. servants to be obedient ⌊ed
15. speak, e. and rebuke with
He. 3: 13. e. one another daily
1 Pe. 5: 1. elders among you, I e.
Jude 3. needful for me to e. you

EXHORTATION.

Lu. 3:18. many things in e. preached
Ac. 13: 15. if ye have word of e. say
15: † 31. they rejoiced for the e.
20: 2. when Paul had giv. much e.
Ro. 12: 8. exhorteth, him wait on e.
1 Co. 14: 3. speaketh unto men to e.
2 Co. 8:17. indeed he accepted the e.
1 Th. 2: 3. our e. was not of deceit
1 Ti. 4: 13. give attendance to e.
He. 12: 5. ye have forgotten e.
13: 22. beseech, suffer word of e.

EXHORTED, ETH.

Ac. 11: 23. Barna. e. th. they cleave
15:32. e-d breth. with many words
Ro. 12: 8. he that e-h let him
1 Th. 2:11. As you know how we e-d

EXHORTING.

Ac. 14: 22. e. to contin. in the faith
18: 27. brethren wrote, e. disciples
He. 10: 25. but e. one another, and
1 Pe. 5:12. by Silva. I have written e.

EXILE.

2 S. 15: 19. art stranger, and an e.
Is. 51: 14. e. hasteneth to be loosed

EXORCISTS.

Ac. 19:13. certain vagabond Jews, e.

EXPANSION.

Ge. 1:†6. let there be an e. in waters

EXPECTATION.

1 Ch. 29:†15. shadow, there is no e.
Jb. 6: † 8. O that G. would grant e.
Ps. 9: 18. e. of poor shall not perish
62:5. wait upon G., my e. is fr. him
Pr. 10: 28. e. of wick. perish, 11: 7.
11: 23. e. of the wicked is wrath
23: 18. e. sh. not be cut off, 24: 14.
Is. 20: 5. sh. be ashamed of their e.
6. shall say, Behold, such is our e.
Je. 29:†11. I think to give you an e.
Zch. 9: 5. her e. shall be ashamed
Lu. 3: 15. as peo. were in e. Jn. said
Ac. 12: 11. deliv-d me fr. e. of Jews
Ro. 8: 19. e. of creature waiteth for
Ph. 1: 20. Acc. to my earnest e.

EXPECTED, ING.

Jb. 32: † 4. Elihu had e. till Job
Je. 29: 11. think to give you e. end
Ac. 3: 5. e-g to receive something
He. 10: 13. e-g till his enemies be
made his footstool

EXPEDIENT. ⌈die

Jn. 11: 50. e. for us that one man
16:7. it is e. for you that I go away
18: 14. e. that one man die for peo.
1 Co. 6: 12. all things not e., 10:23.
2 Co. 8:10. e. for you who have begun
12: 1. not e. for me to glory

EXPEL, LED.

Jos. 13: 13. Isr. e-d not Geshurites
23:5. God shall e. them before you
Ju. 1: 20. he e-d three sons of Anak
11:7. Did not ye e. me out of hou.?
2 S. 14: 14. his banished be not e.
Ac. 13: 50. they e-d them out of coasts

EXPENSES.

Ezr. 6: 4. e. be given out of k.'s house
8. I decree e. be given to these men

EXPERIENCE.

Ge. 30: 27. by e. that L. hath bles.
Ec. 1: 16. my heart had great e. of
Ro. 5: 4. patience worketh e. and e.
He. 5: † 13. useth milk hath no e.

EXPERIMENT.

2 Co. 9:13. by e. of this ministration

EXPERT.

1 Ch. 12: 33. of Zeb. 50,000 e. in
35. of Danites | 36. of Asher e.
Can. 3: 8. all hold swords, e. in war
Je. 50: 9. arrows sh. be as of e. man
Ac. 26: 3. I kn. thee to be e. in cus-

EXPIATION. ⌊toms.

Nu. 35:†33. can be no e. for the land

EXPIRED.

1 S. 18: 26. the days were not e.
2 S. 11: 1. year was e., 1 Ch. 20: 1.
1 Ch. 17: 11. come when days be e.
2 Ch. 36:10. when year e. Neb. sent
Es. 1: 5. when days e. king made
Eze. 43:27. when days are e. it sh. be
Ac. 7: 30. when forty years were e.
Re. 20:7. 1000 years e. Sat. be loosed

EXPLOITS.

Da. 11:28. to his land he shall do e.
32. people shall be strong and do e.

EXPOSED.

Ju. 5: † 18. and Naphtali a peo. e.

EXPOUND, ED.

Le. 24:†12. in ward, to e. mind of G.
Ju. 14: 14. could not e. riddle ⌈dle
19. garments to them who e-d rid-
Mk. 4:34. when alone, he e-d all thi.
Lu. 24: 27. he e-d to them Script.
Ac. 11: 4. but Peter e-d it by order
18:26. Aq. and Pris. e-d to him way
28:23. Paul e-d kingd. of G. ⌊of G.

EXPRESS.

He. 1: 3. being e. image of person

EXPRESS, ED.

Nu. 1: 17. took men e-d by names
1 Ch. 12: 31. Manas. 18,000, e-d by
16: 41. were e-d by name ⌊name
2 Ch. 28: 15. men e-d took captives
31: 19. men e-d to give portions
Ezr. 8: 20. Nethinim e-d by name
Jb. 6:†3. want words to e. my grief

EXPRESSLY.

1 S. 20: 21. If I e. say unto the lad
Eze. 1: 3. word came e. to Ezekiel
1 Ti. 4: 1. Now the Spirit speaketh

EXPULSIONS. ⌊e.

Eze. 45: † 9. take away your e.

EXTEND, ED, ETH.

Ge. 39: † 21. L. e-d kindness to Jo.
Ezr. 7: 28. hath e-d mercy unto me
9: 9. our G. hath e. mercy unto us
Ps. 16:2. my goodn. e-h not to thee
109: 12. Let be none to e. mercy
Is. 66: 12. I will e. peace like river
Je. 31: † 3. I have e-d lovingkind-

EXTINCT. ⌊ness

Jb. 17:1. my days are e. the graves
Is. 43: 17. they are e. are quenched

EXTINGUISH, ED.

Jb. 6:†17. when it is hot, they are e.
Eze. 32: † 7. when I shall e. thee

EXTOL, LED.

Ps. 30: 1. I will e. thee, O Lord
66: 17. was e-d with my tongue
68: 4. e. him rideth upon heavens
145:1. I will e. thee, my God, O K.
Is. 52: 13. my servant shall be e.
Da. 4: 37. I Neb. e. the King of

EXTORTION.

Eze. 22: 12. thou hast gained by e.
Mat. 23: 25. within they full of e.

EXTORTIONER, S.

Ps. 109: 11. let e. catch all he hath
Is. 16: 4. the e. is at an end
Lu. 18: 11. I am not as other men e.
1 Co. 5: 10. not altogether with e-s
11. if any man be an e.
6: 10. nor e-s inherit kingd. of G.

EXTREME.

De. 28:22. L. smite with e. burning

EXTREMITY.

Jb. 35: 15. ye kno. it not in gr. e.

EYE.

Ge. 45: † 20. let not e. spare stuff
Ex. 10: † 5. locusts cover e. of the
earth ⌈21. Mat. 5: 38.
21:24. e. for e., Le. 24:20. De. 19:
26. if man smite e. of serv. (2)
Le. 21: 20 hath a blemish in his e.
Nu. 11: †7. e. of manna was as the
e. of bdellium
De. 28: 54. his e. sh. be evil tow. bro.
56. her e. shall be evil tow. husb.
32: 10. kept him as apple of his e.
34: 7. his e. was not dim, nor his
Ezr. 5: 5. e. of G. was upon elders
Jb. 7:8. e. that hath seen me, shall
10:18. giv. up ghost, no e. had seen
20: 9. e. wh. saw him sh. no more
24:15. e. of adulterer wait. for twilight, saying, No e. shall see
28: 7. a path which the vulture's
e. hath not seen
10. e. seeth every precious thing
29: 11. e. saw me, it gave witness
Ps. 33: 18. e. of L. upon them that
35: 19. nei. let them wink with e.
21. Aha, aha! our e. hath seen it
94: 9. formed e. shall he not see?
Pr. 10:10. that winketh with the e.
20: 12. seeing e. Lord hath made
22: 9. hath a bountiful e. be bles.
30: 17. e. that mocketh at father
Ec. 1:8. e. is not satisfi. with seeing
4: 8. neither e. satisfi. with riches
Is. 13: 18. e. shall not spare chil.
52: 8. for they shall see e. to e.
64: 4. nei. hath e. seen, 1 Co. 2:9.
La. 2: 4. slew all pleasant to e.
Eze. 9: 5. let not your e. spare
16: 5. None e. pitied, to do these
Mi. 4: 11. let our e. look upon Zion
Mat. 6: 22. The light of the body is
the e., Lu. 11: 34.
7:3. beholdest mote in bro.'s e., not
beam in own e., Lu. 6: 41, 42.
18: 9. if e. offend, pluck it out
19: 24. camel to go thro. e. of needle than, Mk. 10:25. Lu. 18:25.
Mk. 9:47. kingdom of G. with one e.
1 Co. 12: 16. Bec. I am not the e. I
am not of the body ⌈can-t say
17. If whole body an e. | 21. e.
15: 52. in twinkling of an e.
Re. 1: 7. and every e. shall see him

Evil EYE. ⌈e.

Pr. 23:6. bread of him that hath e.
28:22. hasteth to be rich hath e. e.
Mat. 6: 23. if e. be e., Lu. 11: 34.
20:15. Is thine e. e. bec. I am good?
Mk. 7: 22. out of heart proceedeth

Mine EYE. ⌊e. e.

1 S. 24: 10. bade kill m. e. spared
Jb. 7:7. m. e. sh. no more see good
13: 1. m. e. hath seen all this
16:20. m. e. poureth tears unto G.
17:2. m. e. continue in provoca.?
7. m. e. is dim by reason of sorr.
42: 5. now m. e. seeth thee
Ps. 6: 7. m. e. is consumed, 31: 9.
32: 8. I will guide thee with m. e.
54: 7. m. e. hath seen his desire
88:9. m. e. mourneth by affliction
92: 11. m. e. shall see my desire
Je. 13: 17. m. e. shall weep sore
40:†4. come to Babylon I will set
m. e. on thee ⌈3: 48.
La. 1: 16. m. e., m. e. runneth,
3: 49. m. e. trickleth down and
51. m. e. affecteth my heart
Eze. 5:11. neither shall m. e. spare,
7: 4, 9.–8: 18.–9: 10.
20: 17. Nevertheless m. e. spared

Right EYE.

Zch. 11: 17. sword be on his r. e.,
his r. e. be darkened
Mat. 5: 29. if r. e. offend, pluck it

Thine EYE.

De. 7: 16. t. e. shall not pity, 13:
8.-19: 13, 21.-25: 12.
15: 9. t. e. be evil ag. poor bro.
Mat. 6:22. if t. e. single, Lu. 11:34.
7:3. beam that is in t. own e., 4, 5.
Lu. 6: 41, 42. ⌈out, Mk. 9: 47.
18: 9. if t. e. offend thee, pluck it
See APPLE.

EYES.

Ge. 3: 6. and pleasant to the e.
7. e. of them both were opened
16: 4. her mistress was despised in
5. I was despised in her e. ⌊e.
20: 16. he is to thee covering of
21: 19. God opened Hagar's e.
28:†8. daughters of Canaan evil in
e. of Isaac ⌈e. of the cattle.
30: 41. Jacob laid the rods bef. the
39: 7. master's wife cast e. upon
Joseph ⌈raoh, 45: † 16.
41: 37. was good in the e. of Pha-
48:10. e. of Israel were dim for age
Ex. 5: 21. abhorred in e. of Pha.
21:†8. if evil in e. of master ⌈Isr.
24: 17. glory of L. like fire in e. of
Le. 4:13. if thing be hid from the e.
of assembly, Nu. 15: † 24.
26: 16. burning ague consume e.
Nu. 5:13. hid from e. of hush. ⌈e.
10: 31. mayest be to us instead of
16:14. wilt thou put out e. of th.?
20: 12. to sanctify me in e. of Isr.
22: 31. Lord opened e. of Balaam
24: 3. man whose e. are open, 15.
De. 16:19. gift doth blind e. of wise
28: 65. L. give thee failing of e.
29: 4. L. not given you e. to see
Ju. 16: 28. I be avenged for my e.
1 S. 8: † 6. thing evil in e. of Sam.
16: † 7. man looketh on the e., L.
† 12. David was ruddy, fair of e.
18: † 8. saying evil in e. of Saul
29: † 6. art not good in e. of lords
†7. thou do not evil in e. of lords
2 S. 6:20. uncovered in e. of handm
17: † 4. saying right in e. of Abs.
24:3. that the e. of king may see it
1 K. 1:20. e. of all Isr. are upon thee
2 K. 6:17. L. opened e. of young man
20. said, L., open e. of these men
9: † 30. Jez. put her e. in painting
25: 7. put out e. of Zedekiah, Je.
39: 7.-52: 11. ⌈the peo.
1 Ch. 13: 4. was right in e. of all
2 Ch. 30: † 4. thing was right in e.
of king and cong., Es. 1: † 21.
Ne. 8: † 5 Ezra opened book in e.
Jb. 10: 4. Hast e. of flesh? ⌊of peo.
11: 20. e. of the wicked shall fail
17: 5. even e. of his chil. shall fail
22: † 29. sh. save him hath low e.
28:21. Seeing it is hid fr. e. of liv-
29: 15. I was e. to the blind ⌊ing
31: 16. caused e. of widow to fail
39: 29. and her e. behold afar off
Ps. 15: 4. In whose e. a vile person
19: 8. com-t enlightening the e.
115:5. e. but they see not, 135:16.
123: 2. e. of serv-ts, eye of maiden
145: 15. e. of all wait upon thee
146: 8. L. openeth e. of the blind
Pr. 1: † 17. in vain net in e. of bird
6:†17. haughty e. are abomination
10: 26. as smoke to e. so sluggard
15: 30. light of e. rejoiceth heart
17:8. as precious stone in e. of him
24. e. of a fool in ends of earth
23: 29. who hath redness of e.?
27: 20. e. of man are never satisfi.
Ec. 2: 14. wise man's e. in head
6: 9. Better the sight of e. than
11:7. pleasant for e. to behold sun
Can. 1:15. thou hast dove's e., 4:1.
Is. 3: 8. to provoke e. of his glory
16. dau-s of Zion with wanton e.
5: 15. e. of lofty shall be humbled
Is. 29: 18. e. of the blind shall see
32: 3. e. that see shall not be dim
35: 5. Then e. of blind be opened
42:7. To open the blind e., to bring
43:8. Bring forth blind that have e.
52: 10. made bare his arm in e. of
59:10. we grope as if we had no e.
Je. 4: † 30. rentest e. with paint-g
5: 21. e. and see not, Eze. 12: 2.
34:3. sh. behold e. of king of Bab.
Eze. 1:18. their rings were full of e.
10: 12. the wheels were full of e.
23: 16. soon as saw with her e.
38: 23. be known in e. of nations
Da. 7: 8. in horn e. like e. of man
20. horn that had e. and a mouth
Ha. 1: 13. purer e. than to behold
Zch. 3:9. upon one stone be 7 e. ⌊evil
8: 6. If marvellous in e. of remu.
9:1. when e. of man sh. be tow. L.
Mat. 18: 9. rather than having 2 e.
to be cast into hell fire, Mk.9:47.
Mk. 8: 18. Having e. see ye not?
Lu. 4: 20. e. of all fastened on him
10:23. Blessed are the e. which see
Jn. 9: 6. he anointed e. of blind
32. any opened e. of one born bli.
10: 21. Can devil open e. of blind?
11:37. Could not man, wh. opened
Ac. 9:40. Dorcas opened her e. ⌊e.?
Ro. 11: 8. giv. e. they sho. not see
Ga. 3: 1. bef. whose e. C been set
Ep. 1: 18. e. of your understanding
He. 4: 13. all things open to e. of
2 Pe. 2: 14. e. full of adultery
1 Jn. 2: 16. lust of the e. and pride
Re. 4:6. in throne 4 beasts full of e.
8. had six wings, and were full of
5: 6. a Lamb, having seven e. ⌊e.

His EYES.

Ge. 27: 1. Isaac old, h. e. were dim
49: 12. h. e. sh. be red with wine
Nu.24:4.trance,hav-g h.e. open,16.
De. 24:1. she find no favour in h. e.
Ju. 16: 21. Philistines put out h.e.
1 S. 3: 2. Eli, h. e. wax dim, 4:15.
14: 27. h. e. were enlightened
18: † 20. thing was right in h. e.
2 S. 19: † 18. to do the good in h.e.
22: † 25. my cleanness bef. h. e.
1 K. 9: † 12. were not right in h.e.
14:4. Ahijah not see, h. e. were set
2 K. 4:34. he lay upon child and put
h. e. upon h. e. ⌈h. e.
35. child sneezed 7 times opened
6: 17. open h. e. that he may see
25: 7. they slew sons of Zedekiah
before h. e., Je. 39: 6.-52: 10.
1 Ch. 21: 23. let k. do good in h. e.
Es. 8: 5. if I pleasing in h. e.
Jb. 16: 9. enemy sharpeneth h. e.
21: 20. h. e. shall see his destruc.
24: 23. h. e. are upon their ways
27:19. the rich man openeth h. e.
34:21. h. e. are upon ways of man
36:7. He withdraweth not h. e. fr.
40: 24. He taketh it with h. e.
41: 18. h. e. like eyelids of morn.
Ps. 10: 8. h. e. privily set ag. poor
11: 4. h. e. behold chil. of men
36: 1. is no fear of God bef. h. e.
66: 7. h. e. behold the nations
Pr. 6: 13. He winketh with h. e.
16: 30. He shutteth h. e. to devise
20:8. a king scatt-h evil with h.e.
21: 10. neighb. findeth no favour
in h. e. ⌈h. e.
24: † 18 L. see it, and it be evil in
28: † 11: rich is wise in h. own e.
27. hideth h. e. shall have curse
Ec. 8: 16. nor sleepeth with h. e.
Can.5:12. h. e. are as eyes of doves
8:10. in h. e. as one found favour
Is. 11:3. not judge aft. sight of h.e.
17: 7. h. e. shall have respect to
Holy One ⌈evil
33: 15. shutteth h. e. from seeing
Is.59:†15.evil in h.e. was no judgm.
Je. 32: 4. h. e. shall behold h. e.,
Eze. 12: 12. see not ground wi. h.e.
20: 7. cast ye away abomi. of h.e.
Da. 8: 5. notable horn betw. h. e.
10: 6. h. e. as lamps of fire ⌊21.
Mk. 8:23. when he had spit on h.e.
25. After he put hands upon h.e.
Jn. 9:14. made clay, and open. h.e.
21. or who hath opened h. e.
Ac. 9:4. Pe. fasten-g h. e upon him
9: 8. when h. e. were opened he
18. there fell from h. e. scales
13: 9. then Saul set h. e. on him
1 Jn. 2: 11. bec. darkn. hath blinded h. e. ⌈fire, 2: 18.-19: 12.
Re. 1: 14. h. e. were as a flame of

Lift or lifted up EYES.

Ge. 13: 10. Lot l-d u. his e. and
14. l. u. now thine e. and look, 31:
12. De. 3:27. 2 K. 19:22. Ps. 49:18.-
60: 4. Je. 3:2. Eze. 8:5. Zch. 5:5.
18:2. and Ab. l-d u. his e., 22:4, 13.
24:63. Isaac | 64. Reb. l-d u. her e.
31: 10. Jac., 33: 1. | 43:29. Joseph
33: 5. l-d u. e. and saw wom. and
37: 25. eat bread: th y l-d u. e.
Ex. 14: 10. l-d u. their e. Egyp-s
Nu. 24: 2. Balaam l-d u. his e.
De. 4: 19. lest thou l. u. e. unto
Jos. 5:13. Josh. l-d u. his e. ⌊heav.
Ju. 19:17. the old man l-d u. his e.
1 S. 6: 13. l-d u. their e. saw ark
2 S. 13: 34. young man l-d u. his
e., 18: 24.
1 Ch. 21: 16. David l-d u. his e.
Jb. 2: 12. they l-d u. e. and knew
Ps. 121: 1. I will l. u. e. unto hills
123: 1. unto thee l. I u. mine e.
Is. 37: 23. ag. whom hast l-d u. e.?
51: 6. l. u. your e., Eze. 33: 25.
Jn. 4: 35.
Eze. 18:6. nor l-d u. e. to idols, 15.
12. hath l-d u. his e. to idols
23:27. thou shalt not l. u. thine e.
Da. 4: 34. I Neb. l-d u. mine e.
8: 3. I l-d u. mine e., 10: 5. Zch.
1: 18.-2: 1.-5: 1, 5, 9.-6: 1.
Mat. 17: 8. had l-d u. e. saw no
Lu. 6: 20. Jesus l-d u. his e., Jn.
6: 5.-11: 41.-17: 1. ⌈ing
16: 23. in hell he l-d u. his e. be-
18: 13. not l. u. so much as his e.

EYES of the Lord. ⌈L.

Ge. 6: 8. Noah found grace in e. o.
38: † 10. thing was evil in e. o. L.
De. 11: 12. e. o. L. are always upon
13: 18. do what is right in e. o. L.
1 S. 26: 24. life set by in e. o. L.
2 S. 11:†27. thing David did was evil
in e. o. L., 1 Ch. 21: † 7.
15: 25. if I find favour in e. o. L.
1 K. 15: 5. bec. David did right in
e. o. L., 11.-22: 43. 2 Ch. 14: 2.
2 Ch. 16: 9. the e. o. L. run to and
fro thro. whole earth, Zch. 4:10.
Ps. 34:15. e. o. L. are upon righteous, and his ears, 1 Pe. 3: 12.
Pr. 5: 21. ways of man bef. e. o. L.
15: 3. e. o. L. are in every place
22: 12. e. o. L. preserve knowl.
Is. 49:5. sh. I be glorious in e. o. L.
Am. 9:8. e. o. L. upon sinf. kingd.

Mine EYES.

Ge. 31: 40. sleep depart. from m. e.
44: 21. that I may set m. e. upon
Ju. 14: † 3. get her, she is right in
m. e. ⌈blind m. e.?
1 S. 12: 3. have I received bribe to
14:29. see how m. e. been enlight.
26:24. thy life much set by in m.e.
1 K. 1: 48. one to sit, m. e. seeing
9: 3. hallowed house, m. e. shall
be there perpetually, 2 Ch. 7:16.
10:7. until m. e. seen it, 2 Ch. 9:6.
11:33. not walked, to do that right
in m. e., 14: 8. 2 K. 10: 30.

!Ch. 7 : 15. now m. e. sh. be open
Jb. 3:10. it hid not sorrow fr. m.e.
4 : 16. an image was before m. e.
19 : 27. m. e. sh. behold, and not
31:1. I made covenant with m. e.
7. mine heart walked after m. e.
Ps. 13 : 3. lighten m. e. lest I sleep
25 : 15. m. e. are ever tow. the L.
26:3.thy lovingkindn. is bef. m. e.
38:10.as for light of m.e. it is gone
69:3.m.e.fail,whilst I wait for God
73:†16. that it was labour in m. e.
77 : 4. Thou holdest m. e. waking
101:3. set no evil thing bef. m. e.
6. m. e. shall be upon the faithf.
116 : 8. hast deliv. m. e. fr. tears
119:18.Open m.e. | 37.Turn m.e.
82. m. e. fail for thy word
123. m. e. fail for thy salv. [e.
136. Rivers of wat-s run down m.
148. m. e. prevent night watches
131:1.not haughty, nor m.e. lofty
132:4. I will not give sleep to m.e.
141 : 8. m. e. are unto thee, O G.
Ec. 2 : 10. whatsoever m.e. desired
Is. 1 : 15. I will hide m. e. fr. you
16. put away evil doings fr. m.e.
6 : 5. m. e. have seen the King
38 : 14. m. e. fail with look. upw.
65 : 12. did evil bef. m. e., 66 : 4.
16. because they are hid fr. m.e.
Je. 9 : 1. m. e. were fount. of tears
13:17. m. e. sh. weep sore [tears
14 : 17. Let m. e. run down with
16 : 17. m. e. are on their ways,
nor is iniquity hid from m. e.
24 : 6. set m. e. upon them good
La. 2 : 11. m. e. do fail with tears
Ho. 13 : 14. repent. be hid fr. m.e.
Am. 9:4. I will set m. e. upon them
Mi. 7 : 10. m. e. shall behold her
Zch. 8:6.sho. it be marvell. in m.e.
9 : 8. now have I seen with m. e.
12 : 4. open m. e. upon h. of Jud.
Lu. 2:30. m. e. have seen thy salv.
Jn. 9 : 11. Jesus anointed m. e.,15.
30. yet he hath opened m. e.
Ac.11:6. when I had fastened m. e.

Our EYES. [e.

Nu. 11 : 6. noth. but manna bef. o.
De. 6 : 22. L. shewed signs bef. o.e.
21 : 7. blood, nor have o.e. seen it
2 S.20:†6. Sheba deliv. hims.fr.o.e.
2 Ch.20:12.O G., o.e. are upon thee
Ezr. 9 : 8. that our G. lighten o. e.
Ps. 118:23. L.'s doing, it is marvell.
in o. e., Mat. 21:42. Mk. 12:11.
123 : 2. o. e. wait upon L. our G.
Je. 9 : 18. o. e. may run with tears
La. 4 : 17. o. e. as yet failed
5:17. for these things o.e. are dim
Jo. 1 : 16. Is not meat cut bef. o.e.
Mat. 20 : 33. L., that o. e. be open.
1 Jn. 1 : 1. we have seen with o. e.

Own EYES.

Nu. 15 : 39. seek not after your o.e.
De. 12 : 8. not do, whatso. is right
in his o. e., Ju. 17 : 6.-21 : 25.
2 S. 4 : † 10. in o. e. bringer of good
Ne. 6 : 16. enem. cast down in o. e.
Jb. 32:1. bec. righteous in his o. e.
Ps. 36 : 2. flattereth hims. in o. e.
Pr. 3 : 7. Be not wise in thine o. e.
12 : 15. way of fool is right in o.e.
16:2. ways of man are clean in o.e.
21 : 2. way of man right in o. e.
26 : † 5. answer a fool, lest he be
wise in o. e. [o. e.
30 : 12. a generation th. are pure in
Is. 5 : 21. Woe to them wise in o.e.
Ga. 4 : 15. would have plucked out

Right EYES. [o. e.

1 S. 11 : 2. may thrust out all your

Their EYES. [r. e.

Ge. 42 : 24. he Simeon before t. e.
Ex. 8 : 26. abomi. of E-ns bef. t. e.
Le. 20 : 4. do any ways hide t. e.
Nu. 20 : 8. speak unto rock bef. t.e.
27 : 14. sanctify at water bef. t. e.
Jos.22:†30.was good in t.e.,2S.3:†36
2 K.6:20.L.opened t.e.and they saw
Ezr. 3 : 12. foundation laid bef. t. e.
Es. 1 : 17. despise husbands in t. e.
Jb. 21 : 8. their offspring bef. t. e.
Ps. 17 : 11. have set t. e. bow. down
69 : 23. Let t. e. be darkened
73 : 7. t. e. stand out with fatness
Pr. 29 : 13. L. lighteneth both t. e.
30:13. a gen., O how lofty are t. e.
Ec. 5 : 11. beholding them wi. t. e.
Is. 6:10. shut t. e. lest they see wi.
t. e., Mat. 13 : 15. Ac. 28 : 27.
13:16. children be dashed bef. t. e.
44 : 18. shut t. e. they cannot see
Je. 14:6. t. e. did fail, bec. no grass
Eze. 6 : 9. t. e. which go whoring
20 : 8. not cast away abomi. of t.e.
24. t. e. were after father's idols
21 : 6. with bittern. sigh bef. t. e.
22:26. have hid t. e. fr. my sabb-s
24 : 25. take fr. them desire of t.e.
36 : 23. I sh. be sanctified bef. t.e.
37 : 20. sticks in thy hand bef. t.e.
38 : 16. sanctified, O G., bef. t. e.
Zch. 14 : 12. t. e. sh. consume aw.
Mat. 9 : 29. touched he t. e. saying
30. t. e. were opened, and Jesus
13:15.t. e. they have closed [sight
20:34. Jes. touched t. e. t. e. rec.
26:43. t. e. were heavy, Mk.14:40.
Lu. 24 : 16. t. e. were holden
31. t. e. were opened, they knew
Jn. 12 : 40. he hath blinded t. e.
Ac. 26 : 18. To open t. e. and turn
Ro. 3:18. is no fear of God bef. t.e.
11:10. Let t.e. be darkened [21:4.
Re. 7 : 17. wipe all tears from t. e.,

Thine or thy EYES.

Ge. 16 : † 6. do that is good in t. e.
20 : † 15. dwell as is good in t. e.
30 : 27. if I found favour in t. e.
46:4.Jo. sh. put his hand upon t.e.
47 : 19. Whf. shall wo die bef. t.e.?
Ex. 13 : 9. for memorial betw. t. e.
16. for frontlets betw. t.e.,De.6:8.
Nu. 22 : † 34. if it be evil in t. e. I
will go back [the L.
De. 3 : 21. t. e. have seen all that
27. lift up t. e. behold it wi. t.e.
4 : 9. forget things t. e. have seen
7 : 19. temptations t. e. saw, 29:3.
10 : 21. terrible thi. t. e. have seen
28 : 31. Thine ox be slain bef. t.e.
32. t. e. shall look, and fail [67
34. shalt be mad for sight of t. e.,
34 : 4. caused thee to see it wi. t. e.
Ju. 10 : † 15. we have sinned, do to
us whatso. is good in t. e., 2 K.
Ru. 2 : 9. Let t. e. be on field [10:5.
10. Why found grace in t. e.?
1 S. 2 : 33. sh. be to consume t. e.
20 : 3. I have found grace in t. e.
29. If I have found favour in t.e.
24 : 10. t. e. seen how L. deliv-d
25 : 8. let y. men find favour in t.e.
26 : 21. my soul was prec. in t. e.
27:5.If I have found grace in t. e.
2 S. 10 : † 3. said unto Hanun, in t.
e. doth David honour thy father, 1 Ch. 19 : † 3.
11:†25. let not thing be evil in t.e.
12:11. will take thy wives bef. t.e.
19 : 27. do thf. what is good in t.e.
22 : 28. t. e. are upon the naughty
1 K. 8 : 29. that t. e. be open tow.
this house, 52. 2 Ch. 6 : 20, 40.
20 : 6. whatso. is pleasant in t. e.
21 : † 2. if it be good in t. e. I will
2 K. 7 : 2. thou shalt see it wi. t. e.
10 : 5. do what is good in t. e.
19:16. open, Lord, t. e., Is. 37:17.
22 : 20. t. e. shall not see all evil
1 Ch.17:17. this small thing in t. e.
2 Ch. 34 : 28. nor t. e. see all evil
Ne. 1 : 6. ear be attentive, and t. e.
Jb. 7 : 8. t. e. are upon me [open
11 : 4. I am clean in t. e.
14 : 3. dost open t. e. upon such
15 : 12. what do t. e. wink at?
Ps. 5:†5. foolish not stand bef. t. e.
17 : 2. let t. e. behold things equal
31 : 22. I am cut off from bef. t.e.
50:21. and set th. in order bef. t. e.
91 : 8. Only with t. e. shalt behold
139 : 16. t. e. did see my substance
Pr. 3 : 21. not depart fr. t. e., 4 : 21.
4 : 25. Let t. e. look right on
6 : 4. Give not sleep to t. e. nor
20:13. open t. e. and thou be satis.
23 : 5. Wilt set t. e. upon that is
26. let t.e. observe my ways [not?
33. t. e. behold strange women
25 : 7. prince whom t. e. have seen
Ec. 11 : 9. O young man, walk in the
sight of t. e.
Can. 4 : 9. ravished heart with t. e.
6 : 5. Turn away t. e. from me
7:4 t. e. like fish pools in Heshb.
Is. 30 : 20. t. e. shall see teachers
33 : 17. t. e. shall see the King in
his beauty; and the land
20. t. e. see Jerus. a quiet habi.
Je.5:3. L., are not t. e. upon truth?
20 : 4. fall by sword, t. e. behold it
22 : 17. t. e. are not but for covet-
31:16 refrain t. e. fr. tears [ousn.
32 : 19. t. e. open upon ways of
34 : 3. t. e. sh. behold k of Bab.
39 : † 12. take Jere., set t. e. upon
42:2. few, as t. e. behold us [him
Eze.23:40.for whom paintedst t-y e.
24 : 16. take desire of t. e. [44 : 5.
40:4. Son of man, behold wi. t.e.,
Da. 9 : 18. open t. e. behold desola.
Lu. 19:42. now they are hid fr. t.e.
Jn. 9:10.How were t. e. opened? 26.
17. sayest he hath opened t. e.?
Re. 3 : 18. anoint t. e. with eyesalve

Your EYES.

Ge. 3 : 5. day ye eat y. e. be opened
19 : 8. do to them as is good in y.e.
34 : 11. Let me find grace in y.e.
45 : † 9. nei. let be anger in y. e.
12. y. e. and eyes of my brother
50:4. If I have found grace in y.e.
Nu. 33 : 55. those ye let remain be
pricks in y. e., Jos. 23 : 13.
De. 1 : 30. did bef. y. e.,4:34.-29:2.
4 : 3. y. e. seen what Lord did bec.
of Baal-peor, 11 : 7. Jos. 24 : 7.
9 : 17. I brake two tables bef. y.e.
11 : 18. be as frontlets betw. y. e.
14 : 1. not make baldn. betw. y.e.
1 S. 12:16. what L. will do bef. y. e.
2 Ch. 29 : 8. hissing, as ye see with
Is.29:10. L. hath closed y.e. [y.e.
40 : 26. Lift y. e., Je. 13:20. [y.e.
Je. 7 : 11. house a den of robbers in
16 : 9. cease out of this pla. in y.e.
29 : 21. he sh. slay them bef. y. e.
Eze. 24:21. desire of y. e. and what
Zph. 3 : 20. turn captiv. bef. y. e.
Hag. 2 : 3. in y. e. in comparison
Zch. 11 : † 12. If good in y. e. [nif.
Mal. 1 : 5. y. e. sh. see, E. be mag-
Mat.13:16. blessed are y. e. for they

EYEBROWS. [see

Le. 14 : 9. he sh. shave all his hair

EYED. [off his e.

1 S. 18 : 9. Saul e. Da. fr. that day

Tender EYED.

Ge. 29 : 17. Leah was t. e. Rachel

EYELIDS.

Jb. 3 : † 9. nor see e. of morning
16 : 16. on mine e. is shadow of
41 : 18. his eyes like e. of morning
Ps. 11 : 4. his e. try chil. of men
132 : 4. or slumber to mine e.
Pr. 4 : 25. let thine e. look straight
6 : 4. or slumber to thine e. [e.
25. nei. let her take thee with her

Pr. 30 : 13. their e. are lifted up
Je. 9 : 18. that our e. may gush wi.

EYESALVE. [wat.
Re. 3:18. anoint thine eyes with e.

EYESERVICE.
Ep. 6 : 6. not with e.. Col. 3: 22.

EYESIGHT.
2 S. 22 : 25. recomp. accord. to my cleanness in his e., Ps. 18 : 24.

EYEWITNESSES.
Lu. 1 : 2. from beginning were e.
2 Pe. 1 : 16. were e. of his majesty

EZ'BAI.
1 Ch. 11 : 37. Naarai the son of E.

EZ'BON.
Ge. 46:16. sons of Gad, E., 1 Ch. 7:7.

EZEKI'AS. [begat
Mat. 1 : 9. Achaz begat E., | 10. E.

EZE'KIEL.
Eze. 1 : 3. word of L. came unto E.
24 : 24. E. is unto you a sign

E'ZEL.
1 S. 20:19. shalt remain by stone E.

E'ZEM.
1 Ch. 4 : 29. And they dwelt at E.

E'ZAR = E'ZER.
1 Ch. 1:38. the sons of Seir; E. and

E'ZER.
Ge.36:21. Dishon, E. dukes, | 27,30.
1 Ch. 4:4.-7:21. Ne.3:19.-12:42.
1 Ch. 12:9. men of might, E. the 1st

E'ZION-GA'BER.
Nu.33:35. encamped at E., | 36. De.
2 Ch. 20:36. made ships at E. [2:8.

E'ZION-GE'BER.
1 K. 9:26. ships in E., | 22:48. 2 Ch.

EZ'NITE. [8: 17.
2 S. 23:8. mighty men, Adino, the E.

EZ'RA.
1 Ch. 4 : 17. sons of E. Jether and
Ezr. 7:10. E. had prepared his heart
12. Artaxerxes k. unto E., 11.
25. thou, E. aft. wisdom of thy G.
10:1. when E. had prayed and conf.
Ne. 8 : 2. E. bro-t law before cong.
6. E. blessed the great God
12 : 1. these are priests, Jere., E.
13. of E. Meshullam was priest
26. were in days of E. scribe
36. E. the scribe before them

EZ'RAHITE.
1 K. 4 : 31. wiser than Ethan the E.

EZ'RI.
1 Ch 27:26. over them th. did work E.

F.

FABLES.
1 Ti. 1 : 4. Nor give heed to f.
4:7. refuse profane and old wives' f.
2 Ti. 4:4. they sh. be turned unto f.
Tit. 1:14. Not giving heed to Jewish
2 Pe. 1:16. cunningly devised f. [f.

FACE. [firma.
Ge. 1 : † 20. fowls may fly in f. of
3 : 19. In sweat of f. shalt eat br.
16 : 8. I flee fr. f. of mistress Sarai
19 : 1. bowed f. tow. the ground
† 21. I have accepted thy f. conc.
Ge. 24:47. I put earrings upon her f.
30 : 33. for my hire before thy f.
32 : † 20. peradv. will accept my f.
† 30. called place, The f. of G.
35:1. when fleddest fr. f. of Esau, 7.
36:6. Esau went fr. f. of bro. Jacob
43:31. washed his f. and went out
46:28. Jo. to direct his f. to Goshen
48:12. Jo. bowed with his f. to earth
Ex. 2:15. Moses fled from f. of Pha.
14:19. cloud went from bef. their f.
25. said, Let us flee fr. f. of Isr.
25:†37. may give light ag. f. of it?
34:29. skin of his f. shone, 30, 35.
33. till done, he put a vail on his f.
Le. 13:41. hath hair fallen tow. his f.
19:32. shalt honour f. of old man
Nu. 12:14. if fa. had but spit in her f.
Nu.19:3. one sh. slay heifer bef. his f.
De. 1:17. not be afraid of f. of man
7:10. repayeth them hate him to f.
† 23. L. sh. deliver bef. thy f., and destroy them, 9 : 3.-28 : 7.
8 : 20. L. destroyeth bef. your f.
25 : 2. wicked be beaten bef. his f.
9. sh. loose shoe, and spit in his f.
28:31. ass sh. be taken bef. thy f.
† 50. a nation strong of f. which
31:5. sh. give them up bef. your f.
Jos. 7:10. wheref. liest upon thy f.?
Ju. 11: † 3. Jeph. fled fr. f. of breth.
1 S. 5:3. Dagon was fallen upon f., 4.
17:†24. they fled from Goliath's f.
19 : † 8. Philistines fled from his f.
24 : 8. Da. stooped with f. to earth
25 : 41. Abigail bowed on her f.
28 : 14. Saul stooped with f. to gr.
2 S.2:22. how hold up my f. to Joab?
7 :†9. have cut off enem. fr. thy f.
14:33. Abs. bowed on f. to ground
17: † 11. that thy f. go to battle
24 : 20. Araunah bowed hims. bef. king on his f., 1 Ch. 21 : 21.
1 K. 1 : 23. Nathan bowed himself with his f., 2 Ch. 20 : 18.
31. Bath-sheba bowed with her f.
2:†16. I ask one, turn not aw. my f.
8:14. king turned his f., 2 Ch. 6:3.
10: † 24. all earth sought f. of Sol.
18 : 42. Elijah put f. betw. knees
19:13. wrapped his f. in mantle [f.
20:38. prophet with ashes upon his
21 : 4. Ahab turned away his f.
2 K. 4:29. lay staff upon f. of child
31. Geha. laid staff upon f. of child
8 : 15. Hazael spread it on his f.
9 : 30. Jezebel painted her f.
32. Jehu lift up his f. to window
13 : 14. Joash wept over his f.
† 20. nei. cast be them fr. his f.
18 : 24. turn away f., Is. 36 : 9. [2.
20:2. Hez. turned f. to wall, Is. 38:
21: † 13. wipeth turneth it upon f.
25 : † 19. saw king's f., Je. 52:†25.
2 Ch. 6:42. O Lord, turn not aw. f. of thine anointed, Ps. 132 : 10.
30: 9. Lord will not turn f. fr. you
32:†2. Hez. saw his f. was to war
21. he returned with shame of f.
34 : † 4. strewed upon f. of graves
35:22. Josiah would not turn his f.
Ezr. 9 : 6. I blush to lift up my f.
7. to confusion of f., Da. 9:8. [5.
Jb. 1:11. will curse thee to thy f., 2:
4 : 15. a spirit passed before my f.
6:†28. for it is bef. your f. if I lie
11 : 15. shalt lift f. without spot
†19. yea, many sh. entreat thy f.
16 : 8. leanness beareth witn. to f.
16. My f. is foul with weeping
21 : 31. Who declare way to his f.?
22 : 26. shalt lift up thy f. unto G.
24 : 15. and disguiseth his f.
26:9. He holdeth back f. of throne
30 : 10. spare not to spit in my f.
41:13. Who discover f. of his garm.?
14. Who can open doors of his f.?
42 : † 8. for his f. will I accept
† 9. Lord accepted the f. of Job
Ps. 5:8. thy way straight bef. my f.
17 : † 13. O Lord, prevent his f.
15. I will behold thy f. in righte.
21:12. make ready arrows ag. f. of
41:12. thou settest me bef. thy f. [th.
45 : † 12. rich shall entreat thy f.
68 :†1. that hate him flee fr. his f.
84 : 9. look upon f. of anointed
89:14. mercy and truth sh. go bef. f.
23. will beat down foes bef. his f.
119 : † 58. I entreated thy f. with
Pr. 6 : † 35. not accept f. of ransom
7:13. and with an impudent f. said
21:29. wicked man hardeneth his f.
Ec. 8 : 1. boldness of f. be changed
Is. 5 : † 21. woe unto prudent bef. f.
Is. 16 : 4. covert fr. f. of the spoiler
21:†15. they fled from f. of sword
24 : † 1. L. perverteth f. of earth
25 : 7. he will destr. f. of covering
28:25. he hath made plain f. thereof
29 : 22. nei. shall his f. wax pale
49 :23. they sh. bow to thee with f.
65: 3. that provoked me to my f.
Je. 1 : 13. f. thereof tow. the north
† f. was from f. of the north
2 : 27. turned back not f., 32 : 33.
4 : 30. rentest f. with painting
13 : 26. discover skirts upon thy f. that shame appear, Na. 3 : 5.
18 :17. I will shew back and not f.
22 : 25. fr. them whose f. thou fear.
32:31. remove it from before my f.
La. 3:35. to turn the right of a man before f. of Most High
Eze. 1:10. f. of man, f. of lion, f. of ox, f. of eagle, 10 : 14.-41 : 19.
2: † 4. they are hard of f. and stiff
3:8. I made thy f. strong ag. their
7 : 22. My f. will I turn fr. them
14 : 3. stumblingblock bef. f., 4, 7.
38 : 18. fury sh. come up in my f.
41 : 21. squared and the f. of sanc.
Da.8:18. was in sleep on my f., 10:9.
10 : 6. his f. as lightning
11: 18. he sh. turn his f. unto isles
19. turn his f. toward fort [10
Ho. 5:5. of Isr. testifieth to his f., 7:
7 : 2. doings, they are bef. my f.
Jo. 2:6. Bef. their f. peo. be pained
20. will drive him with his f. tow.
Na. 2 : 1. that dasheth, come bef. f.
Zph. 1 : † 2. consume fr. f. of land
Mal. 1 : † 9. I pray beseech f. of G.
Mat. 6 : 17. anoint head, wash thy f.
11 : 10. I send my messenger bef. thy f., Mk. 1 : 2. Lu. 7 : 27.
18 : 10. angels behold f. of my Fa.
26 : 67. then did they spit in his f.
Lu.2: 31. hast prepared bef. f. of all
9 : 52. sent messengers bef. f., 10:1.
53. his f. as tho. he would go to J.
22 : 64. struck him on f.
Jn. 11:44. his f. bound with napkin
Ac. 2 : 25. I foresaw L. bef. my f.
7:45. G. drave out bef. f. of our fa-s
1 Co. 14 : 25. falling down on his f.
2 Co.3:7. could not behold f. of Moses
13. Moses who put vail over his f.
18. we all with open f. beholding
4 : 6. glory of God, in f. of J. C.
5 : † 12. which glory in f. and not
11 : 20. if man smite you on the f.
Ga. 1:22. unknown by f. unto ch-s
2 : 11. I withstood him to the f.
Ja. 1:23. behold. natural f. in glass
Re. 4 : 7. 3d beast had f. as man
6 : 16. hide us from f. of him that
10 : 1. his f. was as it were the sun
12 : 14. nourished fr. f. of serpent
20 : 11. from whose f. heaven fled

FACE of the country.
2 S 18:8. battle scattered over f. o. c.
See SEEK, SET, SHINE, SKY, WATERS, WILDERNESS, WORLD.

FACE with cover, ed, eth.
Ge. 38 : 15. a harlot, bec. she c-d f.
Ex.10:5. locusts sh. c. f. of earth, 15.
Nu. 22:5. they c. f. of earth, 11.
2 S. 19 : 4. king c. his f. and cried.
Es. 7 : 8. they c-d Haman's f.
Jb. 15:27. c-h his f. with his fatness
23 : 17. nor c-d darkness fr. my f.
Ps.44:15. shame of my f. hath c-d me
69:7. for thy sake shame c-d my f.
Pr. 24: 31. nettles had c-d f. thereof
Is. 6 : 2. with twain c-d f. and feet
Ez. 12:6. thou shalt c. thy f. that
12. the prince shall c. his f.
Mk.14: 65. spit on him, and c. his f.

FACE of the deep, or depth.
Ge. 1 : 2. darkness upon f. o. d-p.

Jb. 38: 30. the f. o. d-p is frozen
Pr. 8:27. set compass upon f.o.d-h

FACE of the earth.

Ge. 1: 29. ev. herb upon f. o. e.
4: 14. hast driven me fr. f. o. e.
6:1. began to multiply on f. o. e.
7: 3. keep seed alive upon f. o. e.
4. will destroy fr. off f.o. e., 6: 7
De. 6:15. 1 K. 13: 34. Am. 9: 8.
8: 9. waters on f. o. whole e.
11: 4. scattered upon f. o. e., 8,9.
41: 56. famine over all f. o. e.
Ex. 32: 12. consume them fr. f.o.e.
33: 16. fr. all people upon f. o. e.
Nu. 12: 3. meek ab. all upon f. o. e.
De. 7: 6. ab. all people upon f.o.e.
1 S. 20: 15. cut off ev. one fr. f.o.e.
2 S. 14: † 7. remainder upon f. o.e.
Ps. 104: 30. thou renewest f. o. e.
Is.23:17. with kingdoms on f. o. e.
Je. 8:2. for dung upon f.o.e., 16:4.
28: 16. I will cast thee fr. f. o. e.
Eze. 34: 6. scattered upon all f.o.e.
38: 20. all upon f. o. e. shake
39:14. remain upon f.o.e. to cleanse
Da. 8: 5. he goat came on f. o. e.
Am. 5: 8. poureth upon f.o.e., 9:6.
Zch. 5: 3. curse goeth over f. o. e.
Lu. 12: 56. ye can discern f. o. e.
21: 35. that dwell on f. o. whole e.
Ac. 17: 26. to dwell on all f. o. e.

FACE to face.

Ge. 32: 30. for I have seen G. f.t.f.
Ex. 33: 11. L. spake to Moses f.t.f.
Nu. 14:14. thou, L. art seen f. t. f.
De. 5: 4. L. talked with you f. t. f.
34:10. Moses, whom L. knew f.t.f.
Ju.6: 22. I have seen an angel f.t.f.
Pr. 27: 19. in water f. answ-h t. f.
Eze. 20: 35. there I will plead f.t.f.
Ac. 25:16. he have accusers f. t. f.
1 Co. 13: 12. thro. glass, then f.t.f.
2 Jn. 12. I trust to speak f. t. f.
3 Jn. 14. trust to see and speak f.t.f.

Fell before, on, or upon, FACE, S. [17.

Ge. 17: † 3. Abram f.o. his f. and,
50: 1. Joseph f. u. his father's f.
18. brethren f. down b. his f.
Le. 9:24. peo. saw, they f.o. their f-s
Nu. 14:5. Moses and Aaron f. o.f-s
16: 22, 45.-20: 6.
16: 4. Moses | 22: 31. Balaam f.o.f.
Jos. 5: 14. Joshua f. o. his f., 7:6.
Ju. 13: 20. Manoah and wife f.o.f-s
Ru. 2: 10. Then she f. o. her f.
1 S. 17:49. Goliath | 20:41. Da.f.o.f.
25:23. Abig. | 2 S.9:6. Mephib.f.o.f.
2 S. 14: 4. wom. of Tekoah f. o. f.
22. Joab | 18:28. Ahimaaz f. u. f.
1 K. 18:7. Obad. | 39. peo. f. o. f-s
1 Ch. 21:16. Da. and elders f. u. f-s
Eze.1:28. when I saw it I f.u.my f.
3: 23.-9: 8.-11: 13.-43: 3.-44:
4. Da. 8: 17.
Da. 2: 46. Neb. f. u. his f. [o. f.
Mat. 17: 6. disciples | 26:39. Jesus f.
Lu. 5: 12. man full of leprosy f.o.f.
17: 16. f. o. f., was a Samaritan
Re. 7: 11. f. before throne o. f-s.
11: 16. the 24 elders f. u. f-s

FACE of the field.

Le. 14: † 7. bird loose upon f. o. f.
2 K.9:37. Jezebel as dung upon f.o.f.
Eze. 29: † 5. fall upon f. o. f.
39:†5. Gog shall fall upon f. o. f.

FACE of the gate.

Eze. 40: 15. from f.o.g. of entrance

FACE of the ground.

Ge. 2:6. mist watered whole f.o.g.
7: 23. destr-d th. was upon f.o.g.
8: 8. were abated from off f. o. g.
13. behold f. o. g. was dry

Hide, est, eth, or hid FACE.

Ge. 4: 14. from thy f. shall I be h.
Ex. 3: 6. Moses h. his f. afraid
De. 31: 17. will h. my f., 18.-32:20.
Jb. 13:24. Whf. h-t f. and holdest
me enemy? Ps. 44: 24.-88:14.
34: 29. when h-h f. who behold?
Ps. 10: 11. h-h f. he will never see
13:1. how long wilt thou h. thy f.?
22:24. nei. hath h. his f. from him
27:9. h. not f., 69:17.-102:2.-143:7.
30: 7. thou didst h. thy f., 104:29.
51: 9. h. thy f. from my sins
Is. 8:17. h-h his f. fr. house of Jac.
50: 6. I h-d not my f. fr. shame
54:8. In a little wrath I h-d my f.
59: 2. your sins have h. his f.
64: 7. hast h. thy f. from us [f.
Je. 16: 17. thy ways not h-d fr. my
33:5. I have h-d my f. fr. this city
Eze. 39: 23. h. I my f. fr. them, 24.
29. Nor will I h. my f. any more
Mi. 3: 4. he will h. f. at that time
Re. 6:16. h. us fr. f. of him that sit- [teth

FACE of the house.

Eze. 41: 14. breadth of the f.o.h.

FACE with look, ed.

2 K. 14: 8. saying, Come, let us l.
one ano. in f., 2 Ch. 25: 17.
11. they l-d one ano. in the f.

FACE of the Lord.

Ge. 19: 13. the cry great bef. f.o.L.
Ex. 32: † 11. Mo. entreated f. o. L.
1 S. 26: 20. not my blood fall bef. f.
1 K. 13:6. Entreat now f.o.L. [o.L.
Ps. 34: 16. The f. o. L. is against
them that do evil, 1 Pe. 3: 12.
Je. 26: † 19. Hez. besought f. o. L.
La. 2:19. pour out heart bef. f.o.L.
4: † 16. f. o. L. hath divided them
Lu. 1: 76. thou shalt go bef.f.o.L.

FACE of the porch.

Eze. 40: 15. f. o. p. were 50 cubits
41:25. were thick planks on f.o.p.

FACE with see, saw, seen.

Ge. 32: 20. afterw. I will s. his f.
33: 10. therefore have I s. thy f.
43:3. Ye sh. not s. my f., 5.-44:23.
44: 26. may not s. man's f. except
46:30. let me die, since I have s.f.
48:11. had not thought to s. thy f.
Ex.10:28. Pha. said, s. my f. no more
29. Mo. said, I will s. thy f. no more
33: 20. Thou canst not s. my f.
23. back, but my f. shall not be s.
34: 35. chil. of Isr. s. f. of Moses
2 S.3:13. not s. my f. exc. bring Mi.
14:24. k. said, Let him not s. my f.
28. Abs. two years s. not king's f.
32. now thf. let me s. king's f.
2 Ch. 25: 21. they s. one ano. in f.
Es.1:14. seven princes who s. k.'s f.
Jb. 33: 26. he sh. s. his f. with joy
Ac. 6: 15. s. f. as f. of an angel
20:25. ye shall s. my f. no more, 38.
Col. 2:1. many as have not s. my f.
1 Th.2:17. endeavoured to s. your f.
3:10. praying, we might s. your f.
Re. 22: 4. shall s. his f. and name

Seek FACE. [105:4.

1 Ch. 16: 11. s. his f. contin-y, Ps.
2 Ch. 7: 14. if my people s. my f.
Ps. 24:6. gene. that s. thy f. O Jac.
27: 8. saidst, s. my f. my heart
said, thy f. Lord will I s.
Pr. 7:15. came diligently to s. thy f.
29: † 26. many s. f. of a ruler
Ho. 5: 15. return till they s. my f.

Set FACE.

Ge. 31:21. Jac. s. his f. tow. Gilead
Le. 17: 10. s. my f. ag. soul, 20:6.
20:3. s.f. ag. that man, 5. Eze.14:8.
26: 17. s. my f. ag. you, Je.44:11.
Nu. 24:1. Balaam s.f. tow. wildern.
2 K. 12: 17. Hazael s. f. to Jerus.
1 Ch.19:†10. Joab saw f. of battle s.
2 Ch.20:†3. Jehosh. s. f. to seek L.
Is. 50:7. I have s. my f. like a flint
Je. 21: 10. I have s. my f. ag. city
Eze. 4: 3. s. thy f. ag. it, besieged
7. shalt s. f. tow. siege at Jerus.
Eze.6:2. s. thy f. tow. mts. of Israel
13:17. s. thy f. ag. dau-s of my peo.
15: 7. I will s. my f. against them
20:46. Son of man, s.f. tow. south
21:2. Son of man, s.f. tow. Jerus.
16. go thee whitherso. thy f. is s.
25: 2. Son of man, s. f. ag. Amm.
28:21. f. ag. Zidon | 29:2. f. ag. Pha.
35:2. f. ag. mt. Seir | 38:2. f. ag. Gog
Da. 9: 3. I s. my f. unto L. God
10: 15. I s. my f. toward ground
11: 17. he shall s. his f. to enter
Lu. 9: 51. he s. f. to go to Jerus.

FACE with shine. [thee

Nu. 6:25. L. make his f. to s. upon
Ps. 31: 16. Make thy f. to s. upon
thy servant, 119: 135. [us
67: 1. God cause his f. to s. upon
80: 3. cause f. to s. we saved, 7:19.
104: 15. oil to make his f. to s.
Ec. 8:1. wisdom maketh his f. to s.
Da.9:17. cause f. to s. on thy sanc.
Mat. 17: 2. his f. did s. as the sun

FACE of the sky.

Mat. 16: 3. O ye hypocrites, ye can
discern the f. o. s., Lu. 12:56.

FACE of the water, s.

Ge.1:2. Spi. of God moved upon f.o.
7:18. ark went upon f.o.w-s [w-s
Ec. 11: †1. cast bread upon f.o.w.
Ho. 10: † 7. off as foam on f.o.w.

FACE of the wilderness.

Ex.16:14. on the f. o.w. lay manna

FACE of the world.

Jb.37:12. he commandeth on f.o.w.
Is. 14:21. nor fill f.o.w. with cities
27: 6. Israel shall fill f.o.w. with [fruit

FACES.

Ge. 9: 23. their f. were backward
18: 22. men turned f. fr. thence
30: 40. f. of flocks tow. ring-str.
40: †7. whf. are your f. evil to day
42: 6. bowed with their f. to earth
Ex. 19: 7. Moses laid before their f.
20:20. his fear may be bef. your f.
25: 20. f. sh. look one to another
37:9. mercyseatward were f. of cher.
De.1:†17. not acknowl. f. in judgm.
Ju. 18:23. turned their f. and said
2 S. 19: 5. hast shamed f. of serv-ts
1 K. 2: 15. all Isr. set their f. on me
1 Ch. 12: 8. f. were like f. of lions
2 Ch. 3: 13. their f. were inward
7: 3. f. to ground upon pavement
29: 6. our fa-s have turned aw. f.
Ne. 8: 6. worsh-d with f. to ground
Jb. 9: 24. he covereth f. of judges
40: 13. and bind their f. in secret
Ps. 34: 5. their f. were not asham.
83:16. Fill their f. with shame, O L.
Is. 3: 15. that ye grind f. of poor
13: 8. their f. shall be as flames
25: 8. G. will wipe tears fr. all f.
53: 3. hid as it were our f. fr. him
Je. 1: 8. Be not afraid of their f.
17. be not dismay. at their f. lest
5: 3. their f. harder than a rock
7: 19. to confusion of their f.
30:6. all f. are turned into paleness
42: 15. f. to enter E., 17.-44: 12.
50: 5. to Zion with f. thitherward
51: 51. shame hath covered our f.
La. 5: 12. f. of elders not honoured
Eze. 1: 6. and every one had four
f., 10, 11, 15.-10: 21, 22.
3: 8: thy face strong ag. their f.
7: 18. shame shall be on their f.
8: 16. men, with their f. tow. east
14: 6. turn your f. from all abom.
20: 47. all f. sh. be burned therein
41: 18. every cherub had two f.
Da. 1: 10. why see your f. worse
9: 7. but unto us confusion of f.
Jo. 2: 6. all f. shall gather blackn.
Na. 2: 10. f. of all gather blackn.
Ha. 1: 9. f. sh. sup up as east wind
Mal. 2:3. spread dung upon your f.

Mal. 2 :†9. ye have accepted f. in law
Mat. 6:16. for hypocrites disfigure f.
Lu. 24 :5. they bowed f. to the earth
Re. 7 : 11. angels fell before throne
9 : 7. locusts, f. as f. of men⌊on f.
See **Fell on FACE, S.**

FACTIONS.

1 Co. 3 : † 3. there is among you f.

FADE.

Ex. 18 : † 18. fading thou wilt f. aw.
2 S. 22 : 46. shall f. away, Ps.18:45.
Ps. 1 : † 3. his leaf also shall not f.
Is. 64 : 6. and we all do f. as a leaf
Je. 8 : 13. I will consume, leaf sh. f.
Eze. 47 : 12. whose leaf shall not f.
Ja. 1:11. so rich man shall f. away

FADETH.

Jb. 14 : † 18. the mountain falling f.
Is. 1 : 30. be as oak, whose leaf f.
24 : 4. The earth f. the world f.
40 : 7. grass withereth, flower f.,8.
1 Pe. 1 : 4. inheri. that f. not away
5 : 4. crown of glory that f. not

FADING. ⌊away

Is. 28:1. glorious beauty a f. flower
4. glorious beauty be a f. flower

FAIL. [Noun.]

Jos. 3:10. with-t f. drive Canaanites
Ju. 11 : 30. with-t f. deliver Ammon
1 S. 30 : 8. shalt with-t f. recover all
Ezr. 6:9. given day by day with-t f.

FAIL. [Verb.]

Ge. 47 : 16. Give cattle, if money f.
De.28:32. thine eyes f. with longing
31 : 6. Lord doth go, he will not f.
thee, 8. Jos. 1: 5. 1 Ch. 28 : 20.
1 S. 2 : 16. them not f. to burn fat
17 : 32. Let no man's heart f. him
20 : 5. I sho. not f. to sit with k.
2 S. 3:29. let not f. fr. hou. of Joab
1 K.2:4. not f. thee man on throne,
8 : 25.-9 : 5. 2 Ch. 6 : 16.-7:18.
17:14. neither sh. cruse of oil f.,16.
Ezr. 4 : 22. that ye f. not to do this
Es. 6 : 10. let noth. f. of all spoken
9:27. not f. to keep days of Purim,
Jb.11:20. eyes of wicked sh. f. ⌊28.
14 : 11. As waters f. from the sea
17 : 5. even eyes of his chil. sh. f.
31 : 16. caused eyes of widow to f.
Ps. 12 : 1. faithful f. from am. men
69 : 3. mine eyes f. while I wait
77 : 8. doth his prom. f. for everm.
89:33. nor suffer my faithfuln. to f.
119 : 82. Mine eyes f. for thy word
123. Mine eyes f. for thy salvation
Pr. 22 : 8. rod of his anger shall f.
Ec. 12 : † 3. the grinders f. because
5. desire shall f. bec. man goeth
Is. 9 : 3. the spirit of E. shall f. in
5. waters f. | 21:16. glory of Ke.f.
31 : 3. they all shall f. together
32 : 6. cause drink of thirsty to f.
10. for the vintage shall f.
34 : 16. no one of these shall f.
38 : 14. mine eyes f. with looking
42 : 4. not f. nor be discouraged
51:14. that his bread should not f.
57 : 16. spirit should f. before me
58 : 11. spring whose waters f. not
Je. 14:6. eyes did f. bec. was no grass
15 : 18. unto me as waters that f.?
48 : 33. caused wine to f., Ho. 9 : 2.
La. 2 : 11. Mine eyes f. with tears
3 : 22. bec. his compassions f. not
Am. 8 : 4. make poor of land to f.
Ha. 3 : 17. altho. labour of olive f.
Lu. 16 : 9. when ye f. they may rec.
17. than one tittle of law to f.
22:32. prayed that thy faith f. not
1 Co. 13 : 8. prophecies they shall f.
He. 1 : 12. same, thy years sh. not f.
11 : 32. time f. to tell of Gideon
12 : 15. lest any man f. of grace of

FAILED. ⌊G.

Ge. 42 : 28. their heart f. them
47 : 15. money f. in land of E.
Jos. 3 : 16. waters f. were cut off
21 : 45. f. not any good thing wh.
L. prom., 23 : 14. 1 K. 8 : 56.
Jb. 19 : 14. My kinsfolk have f.
Ps. 142 : 4. refuge f., no man cared
Can. 5:6. my soul f. when he spake
Je.51:30. their might f. they as wom.
La. 4 : 17. our eyes as yet f. for

FAILETH.

Ge. 47 : 15. why die? for money f.
Le. 25 : † 35. if thy brother's hand f.
Jb. 21:10. bull gendereth and f. not
Ps. 31 : 10. strength f. me, 38 : 10.
40 : 12. my heart f. me, 73 : 26.
71:9. forsake me not when strength
109 : 24. my flesh f. of fatness ⌊f.
143 : 7. Hear me, O L., my spirit f.
Ec. 10 : 3. walketh, his wisd. f. him
Is. 15 : 6. grass f. is no green thing
40 : 26. for he is strong, not one f.
41 : 17. their tongue f. for thirst
44 : 12. is hungry his strength f.
59:15. truth f. and he that depart.
Eze. 12 : 22. prolonged ev. vision f.
Zph. 3 : 5. judgm. to light, he f. not
Lu. 12 : 33. a treasure that f. not
1 Co. 13 : 8. Charity never f.

FAILING.

De. 28 : 65. L. shall give f. of eyes
Lu. 21 : 26. Men's hearts f. for fear

FAIN.

Jb. 27 : 22. would f. flee out of hand
Lu. 15 : 16. f. have filled belly with

FAINT. [Adj.] ⌊husks

Ge. 25:29. Esau came, and was f.,30.
De. 25 : 18. smote thee when wast f.
Ju. 8 : 4. f. yet pursuing them
5. give loaves of bread to the
people, for they be f.
1 S. 14 : 28. people were very f., 31.
30:10. so f. they could not go ov.,21.
2 S. 16 : 2. such as be f. may drink
21 : 15. David fought and waxed f.
Is. 1 : 5. head sick, whole heart is f.
13 : 7. Theref. shall all hands be f.
29 : 8. awaketh, and behold he is f.
40 : 29. He giveth power to the f.
44 : 12. he drinketh no water, is f.
Je. 8:18. comfort myself, heart is f.
La. 1 : 22. sighs many, my heart f.
5 : 17. For this our heart is f.
Zph. 3 :† 16. Zion, let not hands be f.

FAINT. [Verb.]

De. 20 : 3. let not your hearts f.
8. lest his brethren's heart f.
Jos. 2 : 9. the inhabitants of land f.
24. inhabi. of country f. bec. of us
Pr. 24 : 10. If f. in day of adversity
Is. 40 : 30. youths sh. f., Am. 8:13.
31. not be weary, walk and not f.
Je. 51 : 46. And lest your hearts f.
La. 1 : 13. hath made me f. all day
2 : † 11. sucklings f. | 19. chil. f.
Eze.21:7. ev. spirit shall f. knees sh.
15. their heart may f. and ruins
Mat. 15 : 32. not fasting lest they f.
Mk. 8 : 3. if send fasting, they will f.
Lu. 18 : 1. always to pray, not to f.
2 Co. 4 : 1. as recei. mercy we f. not
16. For which cause we f. not
Ga. 6 : 9. we shall reap, if we f. not
Ep.3:13. that ye f. not at my tribu.
2 Th. 3 : † 13. f. not in well doing
He. 12 : 3. lest ye be wearied and f.
5. nor f. when art rebuked of him

FAINTED.

Ge. 45 : 26. Jacob's heart f. for
47 : 13. land of Canaan f. by famine
Ps. 27 : 13. f. unless I had believed
107 : 5. thirsty, soul f. in them
Is. 51 : 20. sons f. they lie at head
Je. 45 : 3. I f. in my sighing
Eze. 31 : 15. trees of field f. for him
Da. 8 : 27. I Daniel f. and was sick
Jon. 2:7. When soul f. I remem. L.
4 : 8. f. and wished in hims. to die
Mat. 9 : 36. compassion bec. th. f.
Re. 2 : 3. laboured and hast not f.

FAINTEST, ETH. ⌈f.

Jb. 4:5. now come upon thee, thou
Ps. 84 : 2. soul f. for courts of L.
119 : 81. My soul f. for thy salva.
Is. 10 : 18. when standardbearer f.
40 : 28. Creator of ends of earth f.

FAINTHEARTED. ⌊not

De. 20 : 8. who is f. let him return
Is. 7 : 4. nor be f. for the two tails
Je. 49:23. Hamath and Arpad are f.

FAINTNESS.

Le. 26 : 36 send f. into their hearts

FAIR.

Ge. 6 : 2. saw dau-s of men were f.
12 : 11. Sarah was f., 14. | 24 : 16.
Rebekah f., 26 : 7. ⌈17 : 42.
1 S. 16 : † 12. David was f. of eyes,
2 S. 13 : 1. Tamar was f., 14 : 27.
1 K. 1 : 4. Abishag a f. damsel, 3.
Es. 1 : 11. Vashti f. | 2 : 7. Esther f.
2:2 Let f. young virgins be sought
3. may gather f. young virgins
Jb. 37 : 22. f. weather out of north
42:15. no wom. so f. as Job's dau-s
Pr. 7 : 21. with f. speech she caused
11 : 22. f. wom. without discretion
26:25. speaketh f. believe him not
Can. 1 : 15. thou art f., 16.-4 : 1, 7.
2 : 10. Rise, my love, my f. one,13.
4 : 10. How f. is thy love, my sis.
6 : 10. f. as moon | 7:6. f. art thou
Is. 5 : 9. many houses great and f.
54 : 11. lay stones with f. colours
Je. 4:30. in vain shalt make thys. f.
11 : 16. olive tree f. of goodly fruit
12 : 6. though they speak f. words
46 : 20. E. is like a very f. heifer
Eze. 16 : 17. hast taken f. jewels
39. shall take f. jewels, 23 : 26.
31 : 3. cedar in Leb. with f. bran-s
7. was he f. in his greatness
9. I have made him f. by branches
Da. 4 : 12. leaves f. fruit much, 21.
Ho.10:11. pass. over upon her f. neck
Am. 8 : 13. f. virgins shall faint
Zch. 3 : 5. let them set a f. mitre
Mat. 16 : 2. it will be f. weather for
Ac. 7 : 20. Moses was exceeding f.
Ro. 16 : 18. by f. speeches deceive
Ga. 6 : 12. to make f. shew in flesh

FAIRER, EST.

Ju.15:2. is younger sis. f-r than she?
Ps. 45 : 2. art f-r than chil. of men
Can. 1 : 8. f-t am. women, 5:9.-6:1.
Da. 1 : 15. countenances app. f-r.

FAIR HAVENS.

Ac. 27:8. to a place called the F. H.

FAIRLY.

Mi. 1 : † 11. thou that dwellest f.

FAIRS. ⌈16,19,22.

Eze. 27:12. they traded in thy f.,14,
27. Thy riches and f. sh. fall into

FAITH. ⌊seas

De. 32 : 20. chil. in whom is no f.
Mat.6:30. O ye of little f., 8 : 26.-14:
31.-16 : 8. Lu. 12 : 28. ⌈17 : 9.
8 : 10. so great f. not in Isr., Lu.
17 : 20. f. as a grain of mustard
21 : 21. if f. ye sh. not only do this
23 : 23. omitted judgm. mercy, f.
Mk. 4 : 40. how is it ye have no f.?
11 : 22. Jesus saith, Have f. in G.
Lu. 17 : 5. said, L. Increase our f.
6. if had f. ye might say to tree
18:8. Son of man cometh, he find f.?
Ac. 3:16. f. by him, giv. soundness
6 : 5. Stephen, a man full of f., 8.
7. priests were obedi. to the f.
11 : 24. Barnabas good, full of f.
13 : 8. seeking to turn deputy fr. f.
14:9. perceiv. he had f. to be heal
22. exhorting to continue in f.
27. had opened door of f. to Gen
16 : 5. churches were establ. in
17:†31. hath offered f. unto all m
20 : 21. f. tow. our L. Jesus Chr

Ac.24:24. Felix heard Paul conc. f.
Ro. 1: 5. grace for obedience to f.?
17. righte. of G. revealed fr. f. to f.
3: 3. make f. of G. without effect?
27. boasting? It is excluded by f.
4: 5. f. is counted for righte., 9.
11. circum. a seal of righte. of f.
12. walk in steps of f. of Abraham
13. was through righteousn. of f.
14. if they of law heirs, f. void
16. it is of f. wh. is of f. of Ab.
9: 30. righte., which is of f., 10: 6.
10: 8. word of f. wh. we preach
17. f. cometh by hearing, hearing
12: 3. acc. as G. dealt measure of f.
6. prophesy acc. to propor. of f.
14: 22. Hast f.? have it to thyself
23. eateth not of f. not of f. is sin
16: 26. for the obedience of f.
1 Co. 12: 9. To ano. f. by same Spi.
13: 2. tho. I have all f. and not
13. now abideth f. hope, charity
2 Co. 4: 13. having same Spir. of f.
Ga. 1:23. f. which once he destroyed
3: 2. works, or by hearing of f., 5.
7. that they which are of f., 9.
12. law is not of f. but, The man
23. bef. f. came | 25. aft. f. is come
5: 6. f. which worketh by love
22. fruit of Spirit is love, joy, f.
6: 10. who are of household of f.
Ep. 4:5. One L., one f., one baptism
13. all come in unity of the f.
6:16. Above all, taking shield of f.
23. Peace to breth., with f. fr. G.
Ph. 1: 25. furtherance and joy of f.
27. striving tog. for f. of gospel
1 Th. 1: 3. remembering work of f.
5: 8. putting on breastplate of f.
2 Th. 1: 4. we glory for your f.
11. fulfil work of f. with power
3: 2. for all men have not f.
1 Ti.1:5. f. unfeigned | 5:8. denied f.
14. grace exceeding abun. with f.
19. Holding f. and good conscience;
some conc. f. made shipwreck
3: †6. not one newly come to f.
9. holding the mystery of f. in
4: 1. some shall depart from the f.
6. nourished up in words of f.
5: 12. have cast off their first f.
6: 10. they have erred from f., 21.
11. follow f. | 12. Fight fight of f.
2 Ti. 1: 5. unfeigned f. in thee
2: 18. overthrow f. of some [f.
22. follow f. | 3:8. reprobate conc.
3: 10. thou hast fully known my f.
4: 7. my course, I have kept the f.
Tit. 1: 1. acc. to f. of God's elect
4. Titus own son, aft. common f.
Phm. 5. Hearing of thy f. tow. L.
He.4:2. not profit, not mixed with f.
6: 1. not laying foundation of f.
10: 22. heart in full assurance of f.
23. hold fast profession of our f.
11: 1. f. is subst. of things hoped
6. without f. impos. to please G.
12: 2. author and finisher of our f.
13: 7. whose f. follow, considering
Ja. 2: 1. f. with respect of persons
14. say he hath f. can f. save him?
17. f. without works dead, 20, 26.
18. say, Thou hast f. I have works
22. how f. wrought with works,
by works was f. made perfect
5: 15. prayer of f. shall save sick
2 Pe. 1: 1. obtained like precious f.
1 Jn. 5: 4. overcometh world, our f.
Jude 3. earnestly contend for the f.
20. building yours. on most holy f.
Re.2:13. thou hast not denied my f.
19. I know thy works, and f.
13: 10. patience and f. of saints
14:12. are they that keep f. of Jes.

By FAITH.

Ha. 2:4. the just shall live b. his f.,
Ro. 1: 17. Ga. 3: 11. He. 10: 38.
Ac.15:9. purifying their hearts b. f.
26: 18. sanctified b. f. is in me
Ro. 1: 12. may be comforted b. the
mutual f. both of you and me
3: 22. righteousness of God b. f.
28. justified b. f., 5: 1. Ga. 2: 16.
30. justify circum. b. f. [-3:24.
5: 2. By wh. we have access b. f.
9: 32. Bec. they sought it not b. f.
11: 20. standest b. f., 2 Co. 1: 24.
2 Co. 5: 7. we walk b. f. not sight
Ga. 2: 20. I live b. f. of Son of G.
3: 22. that promise b. f. be given
26. ye are the chil. of God b. f.
5: 5. wait for hope of righte. b. f.
Ep. 3: 12. in wh. have access b. f.
17. that C. dwell in hearts b. f.
Ph. 3: 9. righte. wh. is of G. b. f.
He. 4: † 2. were not united b. f.
11: 4. b. f. Abel | 5. b. f. Enoch
7. b. f. Noah | 8. b. f. Ab., 9, 17.
20. b. f. Isaac | 21. b. f. Jacob
22. b. f. Joseph made mention
23. b. f. Moses, 24, 27. | 31. Rahab
29. b. f. they passed thro. Red sea
30. b. f. walls of Jericho fell
Ja. 2: 24. by works justified, not b.

In FAITH. [f. only

Ro. 4: 19. being not weak i. f.
20. staggered not, strong i. f.
14: 1. Him weak i. f. receive you
1 Co.16:13. Watch, stand fast i. the f.
2 Co. 8: 7. as ye abound i. f.
13: 5. Examine whe. ye be i. the f.
Col. 1: 23. If ye continue i. the f.
2: 7. rooted, stablished i. the f.
1 Ti. 1: 2. Tim. my son i. the f.
4. godly edifying wh. is i. f.
2: 7. teacher of the Gentiles i. f.
15. saved, if they continue i. f.
3: 13. purchase boldness i. the f.
4: 12. be example of believers i. f.
2 Ti. 1: 13. hold fast the form i. f.
Tit. 1: 13. be found i. the f., 2: 2.
3: 15. Greet them love us i. the f.
He. 11: 13. These all died i. f.
Ja. 1: 6. But let them ask i. f.
2: 5. chosen poor of world, rich i. f.
1 Pe. 5: 9. Whom resist, steadfast i.

Their FAITH. [the f.

Mat.9:2. Jes. seeing t. f., Mk.2:5. Lu.

Through FAITH. [5:20.

Ac. 3:16. t. f. in his name this man
Ro. 3:25. propitiation t. f. in blood
30. who justify uncircum. t. f.
31. Do we make void law t. f.?
Ga. 3: 8. would justify heath. t. f.
14. receive promise of Spirit t. f.
Ep. 2: 8. grace are ye saved t. f.
Ph. 3: 9. that righte. which is t. f.
Col. 2: 12. risen t. f. of opera. of G.
2 Ti. 3: 15. wise unto salva. t. f.
He. 6:12. who t. f. inherit promises
11:3. t. f. we underst. worlds fram-
11. t. f. Sara receiv. strength [ed
11: 28. t. f. he kept the passover
33. Who t. f. subdued kingdoms
39. obtained a good report t. f.
1 Pe. 1: 5. kept by power of G. t. f.

Thy FAITH.

Mat. 9: 22. t. f. made thee whole,
Mk. 5: 34.-10:52. Lu. 8:48.-17:
15: 28. O woman, great is t. f. [19.
Lu. 7: 50. t. f. saved thee, 18: 42.
22: 32. I prayed that t. f. fail not
Phm. 6. communi. of t. f. effectual
Ja. 2: 18. shew t. f. without works

Your FAITH.

Mat. 9: 29. Acc. to y. f. be it unto
Lu. 8: 25. he said, Where is y. f.?
Ro. 1: 8. y. f. is spok. thro. world
1 Co. 2: 5. y. f. not stand in wisd.
15: 14. and y. f. is also vain, 17.
2 Co. 1: 24. Not dominion over y. f.
10: 15. hope when y. f. is increased
Ep. 1: 15. aft. I heard of y. f. in L.
Ph. 2: 17. offered upon serv. of y. f.
Col. 1: 4. Since heard of y. f. in C.
2: 5. beholding steadfastn. of y. f.
1 Th. 1:8. y. f. to God-ward is spr.
3: 2. to comfort you conc. y. f.
5. I sent to know y. f. lest
6. Tim. brought us tidings of y. f.
7. we were comforted by y. f.
10. perfect what is lacking in y. f.
2 Th. 1: 3. y. f. groweth exceed-g
Ja. 1: 3. trying of y. f. worketh pa.
1 Pe. 1: 7. trial of y. f. more prec.
9. Rec-g end of y. f. even salva.
21. that y. f. might be in God
2 Pe.1:5. add to y. f. virtue, to vir-

FAITHFUL. [tue

Nu. 12: 7. Moses is f., He. 3: 2, 5.
De. 7: 9. f. God who keepeth cov.
1 S. 2: 35. I will raise up f. priest
3:†20. Samuel was f. to be a proph.
22: 14. said, who is so f. as David?
2 S. 20: 19. I one of them f. in Isr.
Ne. 7: 2. Hananiah was a f. man
9: 8. foundest his heart f. bef. thee
13: 13. counted f. to distribute
Jb. 12: † 20. he removeth lip of f.
Ps. 12: 1. f. fail from among men
31: 23. love L., for L. preser-h f.
89: 37. as a f. witness in heaven
101: 6. Mine eyes sh. be on the f.
119:86. All thy command-ts are f.
138. thy testimonies are very f.
Pr. 11:13. f. spirit concealeth matter
13: 17. f. ambassador is health
14: 5. A f. witness will not lie
20: 6. a f. man who can find?
25: 13. as snow, so is a f. messen.
27: 6. f. are the wounds of a friend
28:20. f. man sh. abound wi. bl-gs
Is. 1:21. How is f. city become har-
26. shalt be called the f. city [lot!
8: 2. I took unto me f. witnesses
49:7. k-s sh. see, bec. of L. th. is f.
Je. 42: 5. L. be f. witness betw. us
Da. 6: 4. forasmuch as he was f.
Ho. 11: 12. Judah is f. with saints
Mat. 24: 45. Who then is f. serv.?
25:21. Well done, good and f. serv.
23. been f. in a few things. Lu.
Lu.12:42. Who is f. steward? [19:17.
16:10. f. in the least is f. in much
11. not been f. in unrighte mam.
12. not f. in what is ano. man's
Ac. 16: 15. If ye have judged me f.
1 Co. 1: 9. G. is f. by whom, 10:13.
4: 2. in stewards, that a man be f.
17. sent you Tim. f. in the Lord
7:25. obtained mercy of L. to be f.
Ga. 3: 9. are blessed with f. Ab.
Ep. 1: 1. to saints and f. in C. J.
6: 21. Tychicus a f. minister in L.
Col. 1: 2. To saints and f. breth. in
7. Epaphras, a f. minister, 4: 7.
4: 9. Onesimus, a f. brother
1 Th. 5:24. f. is he that calleth you
2 Th. 3: 3. L. is f. who sh. stablish
1 Ti. 1: 12. thank C., counted me f.
15. This is f. saying, 4: 9. Ti. 3:8.
3: 11. their wives must be f. in all
6: 2. do them service bec. are f.
2 Ti. 2: 2. same commit to f. men
11. a f. saying | 13. abideth f.
Tit. 1: 6. blameless having f. chil.
9. Holding fast the f. word, as
He. 2: 17. he might be a f. high pr.
3: 2. f. to him that appointed him
10:23. he is f. th. promised, 11:11.
1 Pe. 4:19. souls, as unto a f. Crea.
5:12. written by Silvanus a f. bro
1 Jn. 1: 9. he is f. to forgive us
Re. 1: 5. C. the f. witness, 3: 14.
2: 10. be f. unto death, I will give
13. was my f. martyr [f.
17: 14. they with him, called, and
19: 11. sat upon him was called f.
21: 5. words are true and f., 22:6.

FAITHFULLY.

2 K. 12: 15. for they dealt f., 22:7.

2 Ch. 19 : 9. Thus do in fear of L. f.
31 : 12. they brought offerings f.
34 ; 12. the men did the work f.
Pr. 29 : 14. k. that f. judgeth poor
Je. 23:28. let him speak my word f.
3 Jn. 5. thou doest f. to brethren

FAITHFULNESS.

1 S. 26 : 23. L. render to ev. man his [f.
Ps. 5 : 9. is no f. in their mouth
36 : 5. thy f. reacheth unto clouds
40 : 10. I have declared thy f.
88 : 11. f. be declared in destruo. ?
89 : 1. I will make known thy f.
2. f. shalt thou establish in heav.
5. thy f. also in congr. of saints
8. who like to thy f. about thee?
24. my f. and mercy be with him
33. nor suffer my f. to fail
92 : 2. good to shew f. every night
119 : 75. thou in f. has afflict me
† 86. all thy commandments are f.
90. Thy f. is unto all generations
† 138. thy testimonies are very f.
143 : 1. hear; in thy f. answer me
Is. 11 : 5. f. be girdle of his reins
25 : 1. thy counsels of old are f.
La. 3 : 23. mercies new, gr. thy f.
Ho. 2 : 20. I will betroth thee in f.

FAITHLESS.

Mat. 17 : 17. O f. generation, Mk. 9 : 19. Lu. 9 : 41.
Jn. 20 : 27. be not f. but believing

FALL. [Noun.]

Pr. 16 : 18. a haughty spirit bef. a f.
29 : 16. righteous sh. see their f.
Je. 49:21. earth moved at noise of f.
Eze. 26 : 15. isles shake at their f.
18. isles shall tremble in thy f.
31 : 16. to shake at sound of his f.
32:10. ev. man for his life in thy f.
Mat. 7:27. house fell, gr. was the f.
Lu. 2 : 34. child is set for f. and ris.
Ro. 11:11. thro. their f salv. is come
12. if f. of them be riches of world

FALL. [Verb.]

Ge. 2 : 21. deep sleep to f. upon [Adam
43 : 18. seek occa. and f. upon us
45:24. See ye f. not out by the way
49 : 17. so his rider sh. f. backw.
Ex. 15 : 16. Fear and dread shall f.
21 : 33. if man dig pit, and ass f.
Le. 11 : 32. upon whatso. any f.
37. if carcass f. on any seed, 38.
19 : 29. lest land f. to whoredom
26 : 7. they shall f. before you, 8.
36. shall f. when none pursueth
37. they shall f. one upon ano.
Nu. 5:†21. L. doth make thigh to f.
6 : † 12. days that were bef. shall f.
11:31. and let them f. by the camp
14 : 29. carcasses sh f. in wildern.,
34 : 2. is land sh. f. unto you [32.
De. 22 : 8. if any man f. fr. thence
Ju. 8:21. Rise thou, and f. upon us
15:12. Swear ye will not f. upon me
18. and f. into hand of uncircum.
Ru. 2 : 16. let f. some handfuls
† 22. that they f. not upon thee
3 : 18. know how matter will f.
1 S. 3 : 19. none of words f. to gro.
14 : 45. not hair of head f. to gro., 2 S. 14:11. 1 K. 1:52. Ac. 27:34
18 : 25. to make Da. f. by Philis.
22:17. would not f. upon the priests
18. Turn thou, and f. upon priests
26 : 20. let not my blood f. to earth
2 S. 1 : 15. f. on him, 1 K. 2:29, 31.
24 : 14. let us f. into hand of God, not f. into hand, 1 Ch. 21 : 13.
1 K. 22 : 20. who persuade Ahab to go f. at Ramoth-g.? 2 Ch. 18:19.
2 K. 7:4. let us f. unto host of Syr.
10 : 10. sh. f. noth. of word of L.
14 : 10. why meddle, that thou should. f. and Jud? 2 Ch. 25:19.
1 Ch. 12 : 19. will f. to master Saul
2 Ch. 21 : 15. until bowels f. out
2 Ch. 25:8. G. make thee f. bef. enemy
Es. 6 : † 10. suffer not a whit to f.
13. bef. whom hast begun to f. (2)
Jb. 6 : † 27. cause to f. upon fatherl.
12 : † 3. I f. not lower than you
13 : 11. not his dread f. upon you?
31:22. let arm f. fr. shoulder blade
Ps. 5:10. let f. by own counsels [ish
9 : 3. mine enemies sh. f. and per-
10 : 10. poor may f. by strong ones
35 : 8 into that destruo. let him f.
37 : 24. Tho. f. not be utterly cast
45 : 5. arrows, whereby people f.
64:8. make tongue to f. upon thems.
78 : 28. he let it f. in their camp
82 : 7. ye sh. f. like one of princes
91:7. A thousand sh. f. at thy side
106 : † 27. their seed f. am. nations
118 : 13. hast thrust th. I might f.
140 : 10. Let burning coals f. upon
141:10. Let wicked f. into own nets
145 : 14. Lord upholdeth all that f.
Pr. 4 : 16. unless cause some to f.
10 : 8. a prating fool shall f., 10.
11:5. wicked sh. f. by his wickedn.
14. Where no counsel the peo. f.
28. trusteth in his riches shall f.
22 : 14. he abhorred of the L. sh. f.
24 : 16. wicked sh. f. into mischief
26:27. diggeth a pit sh. f., Ec. 10:8.
28:10. astray sh. f. into his own pit
14. hardeneth his heart shall f.
18. that is perverse sh. f. at once
Ec. 4 : 10. if f. one will lift fellow
11 : 3. if the tree f. toward south
Is. 8 : 15. many among them sh. f.
10 : 4. they sh. f. under the slain
34. Leb. shall f. by a mighty one
22 : 25. nail fastened in sure pla. f.
24 : 18. fleeth from fear f. into pit
20. earth shall f. and not rise
28 : 13. that they might f. backw.
30 : 13 iniq. as breach ready to f.
25. in slaughter, when towers f.
40 : 30. young men shall utterly f.
47 : 11. mischiefs shall f. upon thee
54 : 15. sh. f. for thy sake [on you
Je. 3 : 12. not cause anger to f. up-
6 : 15. sh. f. am. them th. f., 8:12.
21. fa-s and sons sh. f. upon them
8 : 4. Shall they f. and not arise?
9 : 22. carcasses of men f. as dung
15 : 8. I have caused him to f.
23:12 they sh. be driven on and f.
19. a whirlw. f. upon head, 30:23.
25:27. be drunken, and spue, and f.
34. ye shall f. like pleasant vessel
37 : 14. I f. not away to Chaldeans
† 20. let my supplica. f. bef. thee
42:†2. let our supplica. f. bef. thee
44 : 12. shall all f. in land of E.
46 : 6. they shall stumble and f.
16. He made many to f. yea one
48 : 44. fleeth shall f. into pit [30.
49 : 26. young men f. in streets, 50:
50 : 32. And the most proud sh. f.
51 : 4. slain f. in la. of Chal. 47, 49.
44. yea, wall of Babylon shall f.
49. Bab. caused slain of Isr. to f.
La. 1 : 14. made my strength to f.
Eze. 6 : 7. slain shall f. in midst
13 : 11. say unto them it shall f. and ye, O gr. hailstones, sh. f.
14. founda. sh. be discov. and f.
24:6. by piece, let no lot f. upon it
27 : 27. all thy company sh. f., 34.
29:5. shalt f. upon open fields, 39:5.
30 : 4. when slain shall f. in Egypt
6. They that uphold Egypt sh. f.
22. cause sword to f. out of his ha.
32:12. by swords cause mult. to f.
33:12. not f. in day th. he turneth
35 : 8. in all thy rivers sh they f.
36:†14. nor cause to f. thy nations
38 : 20. steep places f. ev. wall f.
39:3. arrows to f. | 4. f. upon mts.
44 : 12. caused Isr. to f. into iniq.
Eze. 45 : † 1. ye cause land to f. by lot
47:14. land sh. f. to you for inheri.
Da. 9 : † 18. not our supplica. to f.
11 : 14. robbers of thy peo. shall f.
19. but he shall stumble and f.
34. they sh. f. | 35. some f. to try
Ho. 4 : 5. thf. shalt thou f. in the day, prophet also shall f.
14. peo. that not underst. shall f.
5 : 5. Ephr. shall f. Judah shall f.
10: 8. sh. say to the hills, f. on us
14 : 9. transgressors sh. f. therein
Am. 3 : 5. Can bird f. where no gin
14. horns of altar sh. f. to ground
8 : 14. they shall f. and never rise
9 : 9. sh. not least grain f. to earth
Mi. 7 : 8. rejoice not, O enemy, wh. [I f.
Na. 3:12. sh. f. into the mouth
Mal. 2 : † 8. have caused many to f.
Mat. 10:29. not 1 sparrow f. to gro.
12:11. if it f. into a pit on sabbath
15:14. both f. into ditch, Lu. 6:39.
27. crumbs wh. f. fr. masters' table
21 : 44. whoso. f. on this stone be brok., on whomso. it sh. f., Lu. 20 : 18. [13 : 25.
24:29. stars sh. f. from heav., Mk.
Lu. 10:18. I beheld Sa. as lightn. f.
23 : 30. to say to mts., f. on us
Jn. 12 : 24. exc. a corn f. into grou.
Ac. 27 : 17. lest they f. into quicks.
32. soldiers cut ropes let her f. off
34. sh. not a hair f. from the head
Ro. 11:11. stumbled that they sho. f.
14 : 13. put occasion to f. in bro.'s [way
1 Co. 10:12. take heed lest he f.
1 Ti. 3:6. f. into condemna. of dev.
7. lest he f. into reproach [tation
6:9. that will be rich f. into temp-
He. 4:11. lest any f. aft. same exam.
10:31. fearful to f. into hands of G.
Ja. 1:2. joy, wh. ye f. into tempta.
5:12. swear not, lest ye f. into con- [dem.
2 Pe. 1:10. if do these never f.
3 : 17. lest ye f. from steadfastness
Re. 6 : 16. said to the mts., f. on us
9 : 1. I saw a star f. from heaven

FALL away.

Lu. 8:13. in time of temptation f. a.
He. 6:6. If they f. a. to renew them

FALL down.

De. 22:4 see thy brother's ass f. d.
Jos. 6 : 5. wall of city sh. f. d. flat
1 S. 21 : 13. Da. let his spittle f. d.
Ps. 72:11. all kings sh. f. d. bef. him
Is. 13: † 7. thf. shall all hands f. d.
31 : 3. that is holpen shall f. d.
34 : 4. their host shall f. d. as leaf
44 : 19. sh. I f. d. to stock of tree?
45:14. Sabeans sh. f. d. unto thee
46 : 6. they f. d., they worship
Eze. 30:25. arms of Pharaoh sh. f. d.
Da. 3:5. ye f. d. worship image, 10.
15. if ye f. d. and worship image
11 : 26. many shall f. d. slain
Mat. 4 : 9. if wilt f. d. worship me,
Re. 4:10. the 24 elders f. d. [Lu. 4:†7.

FALL with sword.

Ex. 5 : 3. lest he f. upon us with s.
Le. 26:7. they sh. f. bef. you by s., 8.
Nu. 14:3. us unto this land to f. by s.
43. ye shall f. by s. [32 : † 21.
2 K. 19 : 7. Sennach f. by s., 2 Ch.
Ps. 63:10. they sh. f. by s., Eze. 6:
Is. 3 : 25. men shall f. by s. [11.
13 : 15. every one sh. f. by the s.
31:8. Then sh. Assyrian f. with s.
37 : 7. I will cause him to f. by s. in own land, Je. 19 : 7.
Je. 20:4. Pashur's friends sh. f. by s.
39 : 18. thou shalt not f. by the s.
Eze. 5 : 12. third part shall f. by s.
6:11. shall f. by s., by the famine
12. he that is near shall f. by s.
11 : 10. Ye shall f. by the s., I will
17 : 21. his fugitives shall f. by s.
23:25. thy remnant sh. f. by the s.

Eze. 24 : 21. sons and dau-s sh. f. by
25:13. they of Dedan sh. f. by s. [s.
30:5. men in the league sh. f. by s.
6. fr. tower of Syene, sh. f. by s.
17. young men shall f. by the s.
22. will cause s. to f. out of his ha.
33 : 27. they in wastes sh. f. by s.
Da. 11:33. that underst. sh. f. by s.
Ho. 7 : 16. princes sh. f. by the s.
13 : 16. Samaria shall f. by the s.
Jo. 2:8. f. upon s. not be wounded
Am. 7:17. thy sons and dau-s f. by s.
Lu. 21:24. they sh. f. by edge of s.

FALLEN. [uance f.?
Ge. 4 : 6. Cain, why is thy counte-
Le. 13 : 41. that hath his hair f. off
25 : 35. if thy bro. be f. in decay
Jos. 8 : 24. all Ai were f. on sword
Ju. 3:25. their lord was f. down dead
18:1. inherit. had not f. unto them
19 : 27. the woman was f. at door
1 S. 5 : 3. Dagon was f. upon face
26:12. deep sleep fr. L. f. upon them
31:8. Saul and sons f., 1 Ch. 10:8.
2 S. 1:10. could not live aft. he was f.
12. mourned, bec. they were f.
3 : 38. is a great man f. this day
17 : † 9. when some be f. at first
1 K. 8:†56. not f. one word of prom.
20:†25. army like army th. was f.
2 K. 13 : 14. Now Elisha was f. sick
25 : 11. f. did the captain carry
2 Ch. 20:24. dead bodies f. to earth
29:9. our fathers have f. by sword
Es. 7 : 8. Haman was f. upon bed
Ps. 20 : 8. are brought down and f.
36 : 12. are the workers of iniq. f.
Is. 14:12. How art thou f., O Luci.!
26 : 18. nor inhabi. of the world f.
Eze. 32 : 22. all f. by sw., 23, 24.
Ho. 14 : 1. thou hast f. by iniquity
Zch. 12:†8. f. at that day be as Da.
Lu. 14:5 shall have an ox f. into pit
Ac. 8:16. H. Ghost was f. upon none
20:9. Eutychus f. into a deep sleep
26 : 14. when were all f. I heard
27:29. lest sho. have f. upon rocks
28:6. when Paul sho. have f. dead
Ph. 1 : 12. f. to furtherance of gos.
Re. 2:5. Remem. whence thou art f.

Are FALLEN.
2 S. 1 : 4. many of the people a. f.
19. how a. the mighty f.! 25. 27.
22 : 39. a. f. under feet, Ps. 18:38.
Ps. 16:6. lines a. f. in pleasant pla.
55:4. terrors of death a. f. upon me
57:6. into midst whereof they a. f.
69:9. the reproaches of them a. f.
Is. 9 : 10. The bricks a. f. down
Je. 38 : 19. Jews that a. f. to Chal.
46:12. mighty men, they a. f. both
50:15. Babylon's foundations a. f.
La. 2 : 21. my virgins a. f. by sw.
Eze. 31 : 12. his branches a. f.
32:27. not lie with mighty that a. f.
Ho. 7:7. all their kings a. f., none
1 Co. 15 : 6. some a. f. asleep, 18.
Ga. 5:4. justifi. by law, ye a. f. fr. grace
Re. 17 : 10. seven kings, five a. f.

Is FALLEN.
Le. 13:40. whose hair i. f. off [Jor.
Nu. 32:19. our lot i. f. on this side
Jos. 2 : 9. I know your terror i. f.
Jb. 1:16. fire of G. i. f. from heav.
Ps. 7 : 15. and i. f. into the ditch
Is. 3:8. Jerus. ruined, and Jud. i. f.
16 : 9. shouting for thy fruits i. f.
21 : 9. Bab. i. f., i. f., Re. 14 : 8.–
59:14. truth i. f. in streets [18:2.
Je. 48 : 32. spoiler i. f. upon fruits
51 : 8. Babylon i. suddenly f.
La. 5:16. crown i. f. from our heads
Eze. 13 : 12. Lo, when the wall i. f.
Am. 5 : 2. virgin of Isr. i. f. [i. f.
9 : 11. I will raise up taberu. that
Zch. 11 : 2. Howl, for the cedar i. f.
Ac. 15:16. build tab. of Da. which i. f.

FALLER.
Je. 46 : †16. he multiplied the f.

FALLEST.
Je. 37 : 13. Thou f. away to Chal.

FALLETH.
Ex. 1 : 10. whe . f. out any war
Le. 11 : 33. vessel whereinto any f.
35. thing whereupon carcass f.
Nu. 33:54. inheri. be where his lot f.
2 S. 3 : 29. not fail one th. f. on sw.
34. as a man f. bef. wicked men
17:12. will light upon him as dew f.
Jb. 4: 13. when deep sleep f., 33:15.
Pr. 13 : 17. wick. messen. f. into
17: 20. perverse tongue f. into
24 : 16. a just man f. seven times
17. Rejoice not when ene. f. [f.
Ec. 4:10. woe to him alone when he
9:12. snared when it f. upon them
11 : 3. where tree f. there sh. it be
Is. 34 : 4. as the leaf f. off vine
44:15. mak. image, and f. down, 17.
Je. 21:9. that f. to Chal-s shall live
Da. 3 : 6. whoso f. not down, 11.
Mat. 17: 15. ofttimes he f. into fire
Lu. 11 : 17. a house divided f. [me
15 : 12. portion of goods that f. to
Ro. 14 : 4. to master he stand. or f.
Ja. 1 : 11. flower thereof f., 1 Pe. 1:

FALLING. [Part.] [24.
Nu. 24 : 4. f. into a trance, 16.
De. 19:†16. testify ag. him f. away
Jb. 4:4. words upholden him was f.
14 : 18. mt. f. cometh to nought
Ps. 56 : 13. deliver feet fr. f., 116:8.
Pr. 25:26. righte. man f. bef. wick
Is. 34 : 4. as a f. fig from fig tree
Lu. 8 : 47. came trembling f. down
22 : 44. gr. drops of blood f. down
Ac. 1 : 18. and Judas f. headlong
27:41. f. into place where two seas
1 Co. 14:25. so f., he will worsh. G.

FALLING, S.
Jb. 41:†23. f-s of his flesh are joined
2 Th. 2 : 3. except there come a f.
Jude 24. that is able to keep fr. f.

FALLOW.
Je. 4 : 3. Break up f. ground, Ho.
See DEER. [10 : 12.

FALSE.
Ex. 23 : 1. shalt not raise f. report
7. Keep thee far from a f. matter
2 K. 9 : 12. said, It is f. tell us now
Jb. 36 : 4. my words shall not be f.
Ps. 119: 104. I hate ev. f. way, 128.
120:3. be done unto thee f. tongue?
Pr. 11 : 1. A f. balance is an aboni.
17:4. wicked giveth heed to f. lips
20 : 23. a f. balance is not good
25 : 14. whoso boasteth of a f. gift
Je. 8 : † 8. f. pen of scribes worketh
14 : 14. they prophesy a f. vision
23:32. ag. them prophesy f. dreams
37:14. said Jere., It is f. I fall not aw.
La. 2 : 14. seen for thee f. burdens
Eze. 21:23. shall be unto them as f.
Zch. 8:17. love no f. oath [divination
10:2. diviners have told f. dreams
Mal. 3:5. swift witness ag. f. swearers [f. prophets, Mk. 13: 22.
Mat. 24:24. shall arise f. Christs and
Lu. 19:8. taken any thi. by f. accusa.
2 Co. 11: 13. such are f. apostles
26. been in perils among f. breth.
Ga. 2 : 4. bec. of f. breth. unawares
2 Ti. 3 : 3. f. accusers [brought in
Tit. 2:3. aged wom., be not f. accu-
2 Pe. 2:1. shall be f. teachers [sers
See False PROPHET, S.

FALSE witness, es.
Ex. 20 : 16. sh. not hear f. w. ag. thy
neighbour, De. 5 :20. Mat. 19:18.
Mk. 10:19. Lu. 18 : 20. Ro 13.9.
De. 19 : 16. If a f. w. rise up ag. man
18 if witness be f. w. do unto him
Ps. 27 : 12. f. w-s are risen up ag. me
35 : 11. f. w-s did rise; laid to my
Pr. 6 : 19. f. w. that speaketh lies
12:17. a f. w. sheweth deceit, 14:5.
19:5. f. w. shall not be unpun., 9.
21 : 28. a f. w. shall perish
25:18. that beareth f. w. is a maul
Mat. 15 : 19. of heart proceed f. w.
26:59. elders sought f. w. ag. Jes.
60. tho. many f. w-s came, found
they none, at last 2 f. w-s
Mk. 14 : 56. bare f. w. ag. him, 57.
Ac. 6 : 13. set up f. w-s, who said
1 Co. 15:15. we are found f. w-s of G.

FALSEHOOD. [life
2 S. 18: 13. have wrought f. ag. my
Jb. 21 : 34. in answers remaineth f.
Ps. 7 : 14. he hath bro-t forth f.
119:118. trodden them, deceit is f.
144:8. hand is right hand of f., 11.
Pr. 20 : † 17. bread of f. is sweet
25:†14. whoso boasteth in gift of f.
Is. 28 : 15. under f. have we hid
57:4. seed of f.? | 59:13. words of f.
Je. 3:†10. she turned to me but in f.
8:†8. false pen of scribes work. for f.
10 : 14. molten image is f., 51 : 17.
13 : 25. thou hast trusted in f.
37 : † 14. said Jeremiah, It is a f.
Ho. 7 : 1. they commit f. and thief
Mi. 2 : 11. If a man walking in f.

FALSELY. [f.
Ge. 21: 23. swear thou wilt not deal
Le. 6:3. found lost, and sweareth f.
5. all about wh. he hath sworn f.
19 : 11. neither deal f. nor lie
12. sh. not swear by my name f.
De. 19 : 18. if witness testified f.
Ps. 35 : † 19. let not enem. f. rejoi.
44:17. nor have we dealt f. in cov.
Je. 5:2. tho. say, L. liveth, swear f.
31. prophets prophesy f., 29 : 9.
6 : 13. every one dealeth f., 8 : 10.
7:9. will ye steal, murder, swear f.?
40:16. thou speakest f. of Ishmael
43:2. speakest f., L. not sent thee
Ho. 10:4. swearing f. in making cov.
Mi. 2 : † 11. if a man walk with the
wind and lie f.
Zch. 5 : 4. curse enter house swear-
Mat. 5:11. say evil ag. you f. [eth f.
Lu. 3 : 14. nor accuse f. be content
1 Ti. 6 : 20. of science, f. so called
1 Pe. 3:16. f. accuse your good con-

FALSIFYING. [versa.
Am. 8 : 5. f. balances by deceit

FAME. [house
Ge. 45 : 16. f. was heard in Pha.'s
Nu. 14 : 15. nations heard f. of thee
Jos. 6 : 27. Joshua's f. was noised
9:9. we heard f. of G., what he did
1 K. 4 : 31. his f. was in all nations
10 : 1. heard f. of Sol., 2 Ch. 9 : 1.
7. wisd. exceedeth f., 2 Ch. 9 : 6.
1 Ch. 14:17. f. of Da. unto all lands
22:5. house must be of f. and of glo.
Es. 9 : 4. Mord.'s f. thro. provinces
Jb. 28 : 22. heard f. with our ears
Is. 66 : 19. isles th. not heard my f.
Je. 3 : † 9. thro. f. of her whoredom
6 : 24. we have heard the f.
Zph. 3 : 19. get them f. in ev. land
Mat. 4:24. f. of Jesus went abroad,
Mk. 1 : 28. Lu. 4 : 14, 37.–5 : 15.
9 : 26. f. thereof went abroad
31. they spread abroad his f.
14 : 1. Herod heard of f. of Jesus

FAMILIAR friend, s.
Jb. 19 : 14. f. f-s have forgott. me
Ps. 41 : 9. f. f. hath lifted up heel

FAMILIAR spirit. [ag. me
Le. 20 : 27. man or woman of a f. s.
1 S. 28 : 7. Seek me a woman that
hath a f. s.; a f. s. at Endor
8. divine to me by the f. s. and
1 Ch. 10 : 13. Saul died also for
asking of one had f. s.
2 Ch. 33:6. Manasseh dealt with f. s.
Is. 29 : 4. voice as of one hath f. s.

FAMILIAR spirits. [s.

Le. 19:31. Regard not them have f.
20:6.ag.soul that turneth after f.s.
De. 18 : 11. nor consulter with f. s.
1 S.28:3.Saul put aw. those had f. s.
9. hath cut off those have f. s.
2 K. 21:6. Manasseh dealt with f.s.
23 : 24. workers with f. s. Josiah
Is. 8 : 19. say unto you, Seek f. s.
19 : 3. shall seek to them have f.s.

FAMILIARS. [ing

Je. 20 : 10. f. watched for my halt-

FAMILIES.

Ge. 8 : † 19. creepeth, after their f.
10 : 5. isles of Gent. divided aft. f.
18. were f. of Canaanites spread
20.Ham.aft.theirf. | 31.f.ofShem
12 : 3. all f. of earth be blessed,28:
36:40. dukes of Esau acc. to f. [14.
47:12. Jo. nourished breth. with f.
Ex. 6:14. these be the f. of Reuben,
Nu. 26 : 7. Jos. 13 : 15, 23.
15. these are the f. of Simeon,
Nu. 26 : 12, 14. Jos. 19 : 1, 8.
17. f. of Gershon, Nu. 3 : 18, 21.
-4:22, 24, 38, 40, 41. Jos. 21:33.
19. f. of Levi, 25. Nu. 4 : 46.-26 :
57, 58. Jos. 21 : 27. 1 Ch. 6 : 19.
12:21.take you lamb acc. to your f.
Le. 25 : 45. of f. of strangers buy
Nu. 1 : 2. sum of Isr. after their f.
2 : 34. every one after their f.
3 : 19. sons of Kohath by f., 27,29,
30.-4 : 37. Jos. 21 : 4, 10.
20. sons of Merari, by their f.,33,
35.-4 : 33, 42, 44, 45. Jos. 21 :
34, 40. 1 Ch. 6 : 63.
23. f. of Gershonites shall pitch
4 : 18. Cut not off f. of Kohathites
11 : 10. heard weep thro. their f.
26 : 15. the f. of Gad, 18, Jos. 13 :
24, 28. [1, 12,20.
20. the f. of Judah, 22. Jos. 15 :
23. sons of Issachar after their f.,
25. Jos. 19 : 17, 23.-21:6. 1 Ch.
6 : 62.-7 : 5.
26.f.of Zebulun, 27. Jos.19:10,16
28. sons of Joseph after f., 36 : 1.
34. the f. of Manasseh, 36 : 12.
Jos. 13 : 29.-17 : 2.
35. of Ephr. aft. their f., 37. Jos.
16 : 5, 8.-21 : 5, 20. 1 Ch. 6 : 66.
38. sons of Benj. aft. their f., 41.
Jos. 18 : 11, 20, 21. 1 S. 10 : 21
42. sons of Dan aft. their f., Jos.
19 : 40, 48. [19 : 24, 31.
44. sons of Asher aft. their f.,Jos.
48. sons of Naphtali aft. their f.,
50. Jos. 19 : 32. [nas.'s f.
27 : 1. dau-s of Zelophehad of Ma-
33:54 divide your land am. your f.
36 : 1. chief fa-s of f. of Gilead
Jos. 6 : † 23. bro-t Rahab and her f.
7:14. tribe L. taketh come acc. to f.
13:31.to chil of Machir, by their f.
19 : 40. tribe of Dan acc. to f., 48.
1 S. 9 : 21. least of all f. of Benj.
1 Ch. 2:53. the f. of Kirjath-jearim
55. f. of the scribes at Jabez
4 : 2. are the f. of the Zorathites
8. f. of Aharhel, son of Harum
21. the f. that wrought fine linen
38. these were princes in their f.
5 : 7. brethren by their f.
2 Ch.35:5. acc. to divisions of f.,12.
Ne. 4 : 13. set people after their f.
Jb.31:34.contempt of f. terrify me?
Ps. 68 : 6. G. setteth solitary in f.
107 : 41. maketh him f. like flock
Je. 1 : 15. will call all f. of north
2 : 4. hear, ye f. of house of Israel
10:25.fury upon f. call not on name
15 : † 3. appoint over them four f.
25 : 9. I will take all f. of north
31 : 1. be God of all f. of Israel
33 : 24. two f. which L. hath chos.
Eze. 20 : 32. be as f. of countries
Am.3:2. You have I known of all f.
Na. 3 : 4. selleth f. thro. witchcrafts
Zch. 12:†12. land shall mourn, f. f.
14. f. that remain, ev. fam. apart
14:17. whoso will not come of all f.

FAMILY.

Le.20:5. I will set my face ag. his f.
25:10. return ev. man to his f.,41.
47. to the stock of stranger's f.
49. any of his f. may redeem him
Nu. 3 : 21. Of Gershon was the f. of
27. of Kohath was f. of Amram.
26 : 5. f. of Hanochites, f. of Pall.
6. the f. of, 12, 13, 15, 16, 17, 20,
21, 23, 24, 26, 29, 30, 31, 32, 35,
36, 38, 39.40, 44,45,48,49,57,58.
27 : 4. why fa.'s name done aw fr.
11. his inheri. unto next of f. [f.
36 : 6. marry to f. of fa.'s tribe, 8,
De. 29 : 18. lest a f. turn fr. L. [12.
Jos. 7:14. f. which the Lord taketh
17. he took the f. of Zarhites
Ju. 1 : 25. let go the man all his f.
6 : 15. my f. is poor in Manasseh
9:1. communed with f. of mother's
13 : 2. Manoah of f. of the Danites
17:7.a yo. man, Levite of f. of Jud.
18 : 2. Danites sent of their f., 11.
19. thou be priest to a f. in Isr.
21 : 24. departed, ev. man to his f.
Ru. 2 : 1. kinsman of f. of Elimel.
1 S. 9 : 21. my f. the least of Benj.
10 : 21. f. of Matri was taken
18 : 18. what is my fa.'s f. in Isr.?
20 : 6. yearly sacr. for all the f.,29.
2 S.14:7.whole f. is risen ag. handm.
16 : 5. a man of the f. of Saul
1 Ch. 4 : 27. neither did f. multiply
6:61. to f. of Kohath cities giv.,70.
71. given out of f. of half tribe
13 : 14. ark with f. of Obed-edom
Es. 9 : 28. of Purim kept by ev. f.
Je. 3 : 14. one of a city, two of a f.
8:3. death be chosen by this evil f.
Am. 3:1. ag. the f. I bro-t out of E.
Zch. 12 : 12. every f. apart, 13, 14.
14 : 18. if the f. of Egypt go not up
Ep.3:15. whole f. in heav. and earth

FAMINE.

Ge. 12 : 10. f. was grievous in land
26:1. f. in land, besides the first f.
41:27. empty ears sh. be 7 y-rs of f.
30. the f. shall consume the land
31. plenty not be kno. by rea. of f.
36. against the seven years of f.
50. unto Joseph two sons bef. f.
56. f. over all face of earth
47:13. land fainted by reason of f.
Ru. 1 : 1. Judges ruled, there was f.
2 S. 21 : 1. a f. in days of David
24:13. Shall seven years of f. come
1 K. 8:37. If there be f., 2 Ch.20:9.
18 : 2 sore f. in Samaria, 2 K.6:25.
2 K. 7 : 4. then the f. is in the city
8 : 1. the Lord hath called for a f.
25 : 3. the f. prevailed in Jerus.
1 Ch.21:12. Either three years f. or
2 Ch. 32:11. persuadeth to die by f.
Jb. 5:20. In f. he shall redeem thee
22. At destruc. and f. shalt laugh
30:3.For want and f. were solitary
Ps. 33 : 19. keep them alive in f.
37:19. in days of f. sh. be satisfied
105:16. he called for a f. upon land
Is. 5 : † 13. their glory are men of f.
14 : 30. I will kill thy root with f.
51 : 19. destruc. f. sword, are come
Je. 5:12. nor sh. we see f., 14:13,15.
14:15. by f. prophets be consumed
16. people be cast out bec. of f.
18.behold them th. are sick with f.
15 : 2. such as are for f. to the f.
18 : 21. deliver up their chil. to f.
21 : 7. deliver from the f. to Neb.
24 : 10. send f. am. them, 29 : 17.
27 : 8. nation will I punish with f.
29 : 18. I will persecute with f.
Je.32:24.city is giv. to Chal. bec. of f.
34 : 17. I procl. liberty for you to f.
42 : 16. f. shall follow close after
52 : 6. the f. was sore in the city
La. 5 : 10. skin black, bec. of f.
Eze. 5:12. 3d part consumed with f.
16 I send on them arrows of f.
17. So will I send on you f.,14:13.
7 : 15. f. within, f. and pestilence.
12 : 16. leave a few men fr. the f.
14:21.judg-ts upon Jerus. sw. and f.
36 : 29. I will lay no f. upon you
30. rec. no more reproach of f.
Am.8:11. I will send f. not of bread
Lu. 4 : 25. when great f. thro. land
15 : 14. arose mighty f. in that la.
Ro. 8 : 35. f. separate fr. love of C.?
Re.18:8.plagues in one day, death, f.

By, or by the FAMINE.

2 Ch. 32 : 11. give yours. to die b.f.
Je. 11:22. sons dau-s shall die b. f.
14 : 12. consume them b. t. f., 15.
16 : 4. they shall be consumed b.
f., 44 : 12, 18, 27. [die b. t. f.
21 : 9. that abideth in city shall
27 : 13. why will ye die b. t. f.?
32:36.be deliv. to king of Bab. b.t.f.
38:2.in city sh. die b.t.f., Eze.6:12.
42:17. they sh. die b.t.f. and pesti.
22. certainly ye shall die b. t. f.
44 : 13. as I punished Jerus. b.t.f.
Eze. 6 : 11. they shall fall b. t. f.

FAMINES.

Mat. 24 : 7. there shall be f. pesti-
lences, Mk. 13 : 8. Lu. 21 : 11.

FAMISH, ED.

Ge.41:55. when all land of E. was f.
Pr. 10 : 3. L. not suffer righte. to f.
Is. 5 : 13. their honoura. men are f.
Zph. 2 : 11. will f. all gods of earth

FAMOUS.

Nu. 16:2. princes f. in congr., 26:9.
Ru. 4:11. be thou f. in Beth-lehem
14.that his name may be f. in Isr
1 Ch. 5 : 24. were f. men, 12 : 30.
Ps. 74 : 5. A man f. as he lifted axes
136 : 18.To him which slew f. kings
Eze. 23 : 10. became f. amo. women
32 : 18. daughters of the f. nations

FAN. [Noun.] [f.

Is. 30 : 24. provender winnowed wi.
Je. 15 : 7. I will fan them with a f.
Mat. 3 : 12. Whose f. is in his hand,

FAN. [Verb.] [Lu.3:17.

Is. 41 : 16. shalt f. them, wind carry
Je. 4 : 11. A dry wind, not to f., nor
See FAN [Noun]. FANNERS.

FANNERS. [her

Je. 51 : 2. unto Bab-n f. that sh. fan

FAR. [eous (2)

Ge. 18 : 25. f. fr. thee to slay right-
Ex. 8 : 28. ye sh. not go very f. away
23 : 7. keep thee f. fr. false matter
De. 12 : 21. if place be too f., 14:24.
29:22. the stranger come fr. f. land
Jos. 3:16. waters very f. fr. the city
8 : 4. go not very f. from city
9 : 22. saying, We are f. from you
Ju. 9 : 17. father adventured life f.
18 : 7. were f. fr. Zidonians, 28.
19 : 11. they by Jebus, day f. spent
1 S. 20 : 9. Jona. said, f. be it from
1 K. 8 : 46. carry away f. or near
2 Ch. 26 : 15. his name was spread f.
Ezr. 6 : 6. thf. be ye f. from thence
Ne. 4 : 19. we are separated one f.
Es. 9 : 20. Jews both nigh and f.
Jb. 5:4. His chil. are f. from safety
11 : 14. put iniquity f. away, 22:23.
34:10. f. be it fr. G. to do wickedn.
Ps. 10 : 5. judgm. f. out of sight
22 : 1. why so f. fr. helping me?
73 : 27. they f. fr. thee sh. perish
97:9. L. art exalted f. abo. all gods
103 : 12. f. as east from west, so f.
109 : 17. let blessing be f. fr. him
119:150. foll. mischief are f. fr. law

Ps.119:155. Salvation is f. fr. wicked
Pr. 4 : 24. perverse lips put f. from
5 : 8. Remove thy way f. from her
15 : 29. L. is f. from the wicked
19 : 7. do his friends go f. fr. him
22 : 5. keep soul, sh. be f. fr. them
15. the rod shall drive it f. fr. him
31:10. her price is f. above rubies
Ec. 2 : 13. f. as light excel-h darkn.
8 : † 5. time to be f. fr. embracing
Is. 6 : 12. L. have removed men f.
19 : 6. shall turn rivers f. away
26 : 15. hast removed nations f.
46:12. hear ye th. are f. fr. righte.
49:19. swallowed thee sh. be f. aw.
54 : 14. shalt be f. fr. oppression
59 : 9. Thf. is judgment f. fr. us
Je. 12 : 2. thou art f. fr. their reins
25 : 26. all the kings f. and near
27:10. to remove you f. fr. your la.
48 : 24. cities of Moab f. or near
47. Thus f. is judgm. of Moab
51 : 64. Thus f. are words of Jere.
La.1:17. removed my soul f. fr. pea.
Eze. 7 : 20. have I set it f. fr. them
11 : 15. said, Get ye f. from Lord
22 : 5. those f. from thee sh. mock
Da. 11 : 2. 4th k. f. richer than all
Jo.3:6. remove them f. from border
Am. 6 : 3. that put f. aw. evil day
Mi. 7:11. shall decree be f. removed
Mat. 16:22. said, Be it f. fr. thee, L.
Mk. 6 : 35. day was now f. spent (2)
12 : 34. art not f. fr. kingd. of G.
13 : 34. as a man taking f. journey
Lu. 7 : 6. he was not f. fr. house
22:51. Jesus said, Suffer ye thus f.
24 : 29. Abide, for day is f. spent
50. led them out f. as Bethany
Jn. 21 : 8. were not f. from land
Ac. 11:19. travelled as f. as Phenice
22. should go as f. as Antioch
17 : 27. he be not f. from ev. one
22:21. send thee f. hence unto Gent.
28 : 15. meet us as f. as Appii Fo.
Ro. 13 : 12. night is f. spent [glory
2 Co. 4 : 17. f. more exc-g weight of
10 : 14. we are come as f. as to you
Ep. 1 : 21. f. above all principality
4:10. ascended up f. abo. all heav.
Ph. 1 : 23. with C. wh. is f. better
He. 7 : 15. it is yet f. more evident
See COUNTRIES, COUNTRY.

From FAR.

28 : 49. nation against thee
De. f. f., Je. 5 : 15.
Is. 5 : 26. he will lift up ensign f. f.
10:3. desolation wh. shall come f.f.
22 : 3. bound which are fled f. f.
30 : 27. name of the L. cometh f.f.
43:6. bring my sons f.f., and,60:9.
49 : 1. hearken, ye people, f. f.
12. Behold, these shall come f. f.
60 : 4. sons shall come f. f. and daughters
Eze. 23 : 40. for men to come f. f.
Ha. 1 : 8. horsemen shall come f.f.
Mk. 8 : 3. divers of them came f. f.
See AFAR.

FAR from me.

1 S. 2:30. Lord saith, be it f. f. m.,
22 : 15. 2 S. 20 : 20.–23 : 17.
Jb. 13 : 21. Withdraw hand f.f.m.
19 : 13. hath put my breth. f.f.m.
21 : 16. counsel of wick. is f.f.m.,
30 : 10. they flee f.f.m. [22:18.
Ps. 22:11. O Lord, be not f. f. m.,
19.–35 : 22.–38 : 21.–71 : 12.
27 : 9. Hide not thy face f. f. m.
88 : 8. hast put acquaintance f. f. m. [f. m.
18. Lover and friend hast put f.
Pr. 30 : 8. Remove f. f. m. vanity
Ec. 7 : 23. wise, but it was f. f. m.
Is. 29:13. remov. their heart f.f.m.
Je.2:5. are gone f.f.m., become vain
La. 1:16. bec. comforter is f. f. m.

Eze. 43 : 9. the carcasses of their kings f. f. m.
44 : 10. Lev. that are gone f. f. m.
Mat. 15:8. heart is f. f. m., Mk.7:6.

FAR off.

Ge. 44 : 4. when gone, and not f. o.
Nu. 2:2. shall pitch f. o. about tab.
De. 13:7. not cousent to serve gods
20:15. thus do unto cities f.o. [f.o.
30 : 11. nei. is commandment f.o.
2 S. 15 : 17. the king tarried f. o.
2 Ch. 6 : 36. captives to a land f. o.
Ps. 55 : 7. Lo, would I wander f. o.
Pr. 27:10. is better than a bro. f. o.
Ec. 7 : 24. That f. o. who find out?
Is. 17 : 13. they shall flee f. o. and
33 : 13. Hear, ye f. o. what I done
17. sh. behold land that is f. o.
46:13. my righteousness not be f.o.
57 : 9. didst send messengers f. o.
19. peace to him f. o. and near
59 : 11. for salvation, but it is f. o.
Eze. 6:12. He f. o. sh. die of pestil.
8 : 6. that I go f. o. fr. my sanct.
11:16. altho. I have cast them f.o.
12:27. he prophesieth of times f.o.
Da.9:7. confus. to Isr. near and f.o.
Jo. 2 : 20. remove f. o. north. army
3 : 8. sell them to Sabeans f. o.
Mi. 4 : 7. make her cast f. o. a na.
Zch.6:15 they f.o. sh. build in tem.
Ep.2:13. ye f.o. are made nigh by C.

FARE. [Noun.] [it
Jon. 1 : 3. he paid the f., went into

FARE, ED.

1 S. 17:18. look how thy brethren f.
Lu.16:19. rich man f-d sumptuously

FARE ye well.

Ac. 15 : 29. ye shall do well. f.y.w.

FAREWELL.

Lu. 9:61. let me bid them f. at home
18 : 21. Paul bade them f. saying
23 : 30. what they had ag. him, f.
2 Co. 13 : 11. Finally, breth., f. Be

FARM.

Mat. 22 : 5. their ways, one to his f.

FARTHER. See FURTHER.

FARTHING, S.

Mat.5:26. till hast paid uttermost f.
10 : 29. two sparrows sold for f.?
Mk.12:42. she threw in 2 mites a f.
Lu. 12 : 6. five sparrows for two f.?

FASHION, S.

Ge. 6 : 15. f. thou shalt make ark
Ex. 26 : 30. f. of tabern. as shewed
37 : 19. bowls after f. of almonds
1 K. 6 : 38. acc. to f. of the house
2 K. 16 : 10. Ahaz sent f. of altar
Eze. 42 : 11. goings acc. to their f-s
43 : 11. shew them the form and f.
Ha. 2 : † 18. the fashioner of his f.
Mk. 2:12. We never saw it on this f.
Lu. 9 : 29. f. of his countenance
Ac. 7 : 44. taberu. acc. to f. seen
1 Co.7:31. f. of world passeth away
Ph. 2:8. being found in f. as a man
Ja. 1 : 11. grace of f. of it perisheth

FASHION, ED.

Jb.31:15. did not one f. us in womb?
Ex. 32 : 4. Aaron f-d the calf with
1 K. 7 : † 15. f-d 2 pillars of brass
Jb. 10 : 8. Thine hands f. me, Ps. 119 : 73.
Ps. 139 : 16. in continuance were f.
Is. 22 : 11. nei. respect unto him f-d
Eze. 16 : 7. thy breasts are f. [it
Ph. 3 : 21. f. like his glorious body

FASHIONETH, ING.

Ps. 33 : 15. He f-h their hearts alike
Is.44:12. smith f-h it with hammers
45 : 9. clay say to him f-h it
1 Pe. 1:14. not f-g yourse. to former

FAST. [Adj. and adv.] [lusts
Ge. 20 : 18. had f. closed-up wounds
Ju. 4 : 21. Sisera was f. asleep
15 : 13. but we will bind thee f.
16:11. If bind me f. with new ropes

Ru. 2 : 8. abide f. by my maidens
21. Boaz said, keep f. by yo. men
2 K. 6 : 32. hold him f. at the door
Jb. 2 : 3. holdeth f. his integrity
Ps. 65 : 6. strength setteth f. mts.
33:9. he commanded and it stood f.
Pr. 4 : 13. take f. hold of instruc.
Je.48 : 16. afflict. of Moab hasteth f.
50 : 33. took captives held them f.
Jon. 1 : 5. he lay in ship, f. asleep
Ac. 16 : 24. made feet f. in stocks
27 : 41. forepart stuck f. remained

FAST. [Noun.]

2 S. 12 : † 16. David fasted a f.
1 K. 21 : 9. Proclaimed a f. and set
12. they proclaimed a f. [Naboth
2 Ch. 20 : 3. Jehosh. proclaimed a f.
Ezr. 8 : 21. Ezra proclaimed a f.
Is. 58 : 3. in f. you find pleasure
5. such a f.? wilt thou call this f.
6. is not this the f. I have chosen?
Je. 36 : 9. proclaimed a f. bef. L.
Jo. 1 : 14. Sanctify a f. call, 2 : 15.
Jon. 3 : 5. of Nin. proclaimed a f.
Zch. 8 : 19. f. of 4th month of (4)
Ac. 27 : 9. f. was now already past

FAST. [Verb.]

2 S.12:21. didst f. and weep for child
23. he is dead, whf. should I f.?
Es. 4:16. f. ye for me, I and maidens will f. [not f.
Is. 58 : 4. ye f. for strife, ye shall
Je. 14 : 12. When they f. I not hear
Zch. 7 : 5. did ye at all f. unto me
Mat. 6 : 16. when f. be not as hypocrites th. they may appear to f.
18. thou appear not unto men to f.
9 : 14. why do we f. disciples f. not,
Mk. 2 : 18. [Lu. 5 : 35.
15. then shall they f., Mk. 2 : 20.
Mk. 2 : 18. disci. of Jn. used to f.
19. Can chil. of bridechamber f.?
they cannot f., Lu. 5 : 34, 35.
Lu. 5:33. why disci. of Jn. f. often?
18 : 12. I f. twice in the week

FASTED, EST.

Ju. 20 : 26. the people f. that day
1 S. 7 : 6. drew water, f. that day
31 : 13. f. seven days, 1 Ch. 10:12.
2 S. 1 : 12. mourned f. for Saul
12:16. David f. | 22. child alive I f.
1 K. 21:27. Ahab f. | Ezr. 8:23. we f.
Ne. 1 : 4. Neh. f. and prayed
Is. 58 : 3. Whf. have we f. say they
Zch. 7 : 5. when ye f. in fifth month
Mat. 4 : 2. Jesus f. forty days and
6 : 17. when thou f-t anoint head
Ac. 13 : 2. As they ministered to the Lord and f.
3. had f. they laid hands on them

FASTEN.

Ex. 28 : 14. f. chains to ouches, 25.
39 : 31. to f. the plate on high
Is. 22 : 23. I will f. him as a nail
Je. 10 : 4. they f. it with nails and

FASTENED.

Ex. 10 : † 19. f. locusts into Red sea
39:18. chains they f. in two ouches
40 : 18. Moses f. his sockets
Ju. 4 : 21. Jael f. nail into ground
16 : 14. Delilah f. it with a pin
1 S. 31 : 10. they f. Saul's body
2 S. 20:8. with swo. f. upon his loins
1 K. 6 : 6. that beams sho. not be f.
1 Ch. 10:10. f. head in tem. of Dag.
2 Ch. 9 : 18. six steps f. to throne
Es. 1 : 6. hangings f. with cords
Jb. 38 : 6. are the foundations f.
Ec. 12:11. as nails f. by the masters
Is. 22 : 25. nail f. in sure place
41:7. f. that it should not be moved
Eze. 40 : 43. within were hooks f.
Lu. 4 : 20. eyes of all f. on him
Ac. 11 : 6. when I had f. mine eyes
28:3. viper out of heat f. on his ha.

FASTENING. [ans.

Ha. 2 : † 11. f. of the timber shall

Ac. 3:4. Peter f. his eyes upon him

FASTING, S.

Ne. 9 : 1. were assembled with f.
Es. 4 : 3. decree came, there was f.
9 : 31. the matters of the f-s and
Ps. 35 : 13. I humbled soul with f.
69 : 10. chastened my soul with f.
109:24. my knees are weak thro. f.
Je. 36 : 6. read words of L upon f.
Da. 6 : 18. king passed night f. ⌊day
9 : 3. Daniel set hims. to seek by f.
Jo. 2 : 12. turn ye with f. weeping
Mat. 15 : 32 not send them away f.
17 : 21. not out but by f., Mk.9:29.
Mk. 8 : 3. if I send them away f.
Lu. 2 : 37. Anna served G. with f-s
Ac. 10 : 30. Four days ago I was f.
14:23. ord. elders, and prayed with f.
27 : 33. is 14th day ye continued f.
1 Co. 7 : 5. ye may give yourse. to f.
2 Co. 6 : 5. approving ours. in f-s
11:27. in f-s often, in cold and nak.

FAT. [Adjective.]

Ge. 41 : 4. did eat seven f. kine, 20.
† 5. seven ears of corn came up f., † 7.
49:20. Out of Asher his bread be f.
Nu. 13 : 20. what the land is, f. or
De 31 : 20. waxen f. then they turn
32 : 15. But Jeshurun waxed f.
and kicked, thou art waxen f.
Ju. 3 : 17. Eglon a very f. man
1 S. 2 : 29. make you f. with off-s
28 : 24. woman had a f. calf
1 K. 1 : 9. Adoni. slew f. cattle, 19, 25.
4 : 23. for one day was ten f. oxen
1 Ch. 4 : 40. they found f. pasture
Ne. 9 : 25. they took f. la. became f.
35. not served thee in f. land
Ps. 22:29. that be f. on earth sh. eat
37 : 20. enem. of L. as f. of lambs
92:14. they shall be f. and flourish.
119 : 70 Their heart as f. as grease
Pr. 11 : 25. liberal soul be made f.
13 : 4. soul of diligent be made f.
15:30 good report maketh bones f.
28 : 25. trusteth in L. be made f.
Is. 5 : 17. waste places of f. ones
6 : 10. Make heart of this peo. f.
10:16. sh. send amo. f. ones leanness
25:6. feast of f. thi. full of marrow
28 : 1. on head of f. valleys
4. beauty on head of f. valley
30 : 23. bread be f. and plenteous
34 : 6. sword of Lord is made f.
7. their dust be f. with fatness
58 : 11. L. shall make f. thy bones
Je. 5 : 28. are waxen f. they shine
50 : 11. ye are grown f. as heifer
Eze. 34:14. in a f. pasture shall feed
16. I will destroy f. and strong
20. judge betw. f. cattle and lean
45 : 15. one lamb out of f. pastures
Am. 5:22. nor regard off. of f. beasts
Ha. 1:16. by them their portion is f.

FAT. [Noun.]

Ge. 4 : 4. Abel bro-t of f. of flock
Ex. 23 : 18. nor f. of sacri. remain
29 : 13. take f. covereth inwards,
and f. upon kidneys, 22. Le. 3 :
3, 4, 9, 10, 14, 15.—4 : 8.—7:3, 4.
Le. 1:8. lay head and f. in order, 12.
3:16. for sweet savour, f. is Lord's
4 : 8. take off f. of bullock, 31, 35.
26. burn his f., 6 : 12.—7 : 3, 31.—
17 : 6. Nu. 18 : 17.
7 : 24. f. of beast dieth of itself, or
30. the f. with the breast, it
33. he that offereth f. shall have
8 : 20. Moses burnt f. of the ram
26. took wafer and put on f.
9 : 10. f. he burnt upon altar, 20.
19. f. of bullock and of ram
24. fire from L. consumed the f.
10 : 15. offerings made by fire of f.
16: 25. f. of sin offering shall burn
Nu. 18 : † 12. f. of oil have I given
Nu. 18:† 29. offering of Lord of all f.
De. 32 : 14. f. of lambs f. of kidneys
Ju. 3 : 22. f. closed upon blade
† 29. slew of Moab 10,000 all f.
1 S. 2 : 15. before they burnt f.
16. Let them not fail to burn the f.
15:22. to hearken is better than f.
2 S. 1 : 22. from f. of mighty, bow
1 K. 8 : 64. altar to little to rec. f.
2 Ch. 7 : 7. the f. of peace off., 29:35.
35 : 14. priest busied in offering f.
Jb. 15 : 27. collops of f. on flanks
Ps. 17 : 10. inclosed in own f.
20 :† 3. L. make f. thy burnt sacri.
23 : † 5. L. makest f. my head with
37:20. enem. of L. be as f. of lambs
73 : † 4. but their strength is f. no
81 :† 16. fed with f. of wheat, 147 :
Is. 1:11. full of f. of fed beasts ⌊† 14.
34 : 6. made f. with f. of kidneys
43:24. nor filled me with fat of sac.
Eze. 44 : 7. when ye offer f. and bl.
15. sh. stand to offer unto me the f.

Eateth FAT.

Ge. 45 : 18. ye shall e. f. of land
Le. 3 : 17. that ye e. no f. nor bl.,
7 : 25. whoso e. f. be cut off ⌊7:23.
De. 32 : 38. did e. f. of their sacri.
Ne. 8 : 10. e. the f. and drink sweet
Eze. 34 : 3. Ye e. f. and clothe you
39 : 19. ye shall e. f. till ye be full
Zch. 11 : 16. he sh. e. flesh of the f.
See PRESSFAT, WINEFAT.

FATFLESHED.

Ge. 41 : 2. came up seven kine f.

FATHER.

Ge. 4:20. Jabal f. of such as in tents
21. Jubal f. of all handle harp
9 : 18. Ham is f. of Canaan
17:4. be f. of many na., 5. Ro. 4:17, 18.
44:19. Have ye a f.? | 20. we have a
45 : 8. God made me f. to Pha. ⌊f.
Le. 24 : 10. whose f. was an Egyp.
Nu. 11 : 12. as a nursing f. beareth
30 : 16. statutes betw. f. and dau.
De. 22 : 15. f. sh. bring forth tokens
29. sh. give damsel's f. 50 shekels
Ju. 9 : 1. of house of his mother's f.
17 : 10. unto me a f. and priest
18 : 19. be to us a f. and a priest
19 : 3. f. of the damsel saw him
4. damsel's f. retained him
1 S. 9 : 3. Kish f. of Saul, 14 : 51.
1 Ch. 2 : 51. Salem f. of Beth-leh.
55. Hemath, f. of h. of Rechab
4 : 14. f. of valley of Charashim
8 : 29. dwelt f. of Gibeon, 9 : 35.
Es. 2 : 7. Es. had nei. f. nor mother
Jb. 29 : 16. I was a f. to the poor
31:18. bro-t up with me, as with a
38 : 28. Hath the rain a f.? or ⌊f.
Ps. 68 : 5. f. of fatherless, is God
103 : 13. as f. pitieth his children
Pr. 3:12 L. correcteth, as f. the son
4 : 1. Hear the instruction of a f.
10 : 1. wise son mak. glad f., 15:20.
17 : 21. the f. of a fool hath no joy
23 : 24. f. of righteous sh. rejoice
Is. 9 : 6. be called the everlasting F.
22 : 21. Eliakim be f. to inhab. of
38 : 19. f. to chil. make kno. truth
Je. 31 : 9. for I am a f. to Israel
Eze. 18:4. as soul of f. so of the son
19. doth not son bear iniq. of f.?
20. son sh. not bear iniq. of the f.
22 : 7. In thee they set light by f.
44 : 25. for f. or mother they may
Mi. 7 : 6. son dishonoureth f. ⌊defile
Mal. 1:6. if I a f. where mine honour
2 : 10. Have we not all one f.?
Mat. 10:21. f. deliv. child, Mk. 13 : 12.
37. He th. loveth f. more than me
11:25. Jes. said, I thank thee, O F.
26. Even so F. it seemed good,
Lu. 10 : 21. Jn. 11 : 41.
27. no man knoweth Son but F.
15 : 4. curseth f. him die, Mk. 7 : 10.
Mat. 19 : 5. leave f. cleave to his wife
29. that hath forsaken f. for my
name's, Mk. 10 : 29.
28 : 19. baptizing in name of F.
Mk. 5 : 40. he taketh f. of the damsel, Lu. 8 : 51.
9 : 24. f. of child cried, I believe
13:32. that day kn. no man, but F.
14 : 36. Abba, F. all things possible
15 : 21. Simon, f. of Alexander
Lu. 10:22. no man knows who F. is
11:11. If son shall ask bread of a f.
12:53. f. be divided against son, and
son against the f. ⌈18.
15 : 21. son said, f. I have sinned,
22. f. said, Bring forth best robe
16:27. f. send to my father's house
22 : 42. F. if willing, remove cup
23:34. F. forgive them, they kn. not
46. F. into thy hands, I commend
Jn. 1 : 14. as of only begotten of F.
18. Son which is in bosom of F.
3:35. the F. loveth the Son, 5 : 20.
4 : 21. nor at Jerus. worship the F.
23. shall worship the F. in spirit
53. f. knew it was at same hour
5 : 19. do noth. but he seeth F. do
21. as F. raiseth up dead, so Son
22. F. judgeth no man, but hath
23. Son, as they honour F., honour-h not Son, honour-h not F.
26. as the F. hath life in himself
30. not mine own, but will of F.
36. works F. hath given me to finish bear witn. F hath sent me
37. F. wh. hath sent me, 8 : 16.—
12 : 49.—14 : 24. 1 Jn. 4 : 14.
45. think not I will accuse you to
6 : 27. him God F. sealed ⌊F.
37. All that F. giveth me sh. come
39. is F.'s will, that I lose noth.
42. is not this Jes., whose f. we kn.
44. come, except F. draw him
45. learned of F. cometh unto me
46. not that any hath seen F. (2)
57. F. sent me, I live by F.
8 : 16. not alone, but I and F. that
18. the F. beareth witness of me
27. understood not he spake of F.
29. F. hath not left me alone
41. we have one F. even God
44. devil is a liar, and f. of it
10:15. As F. knoweth me, so I the
36. whom F. hath sanctified ⌊F.
38. believe F. is in me, I in him
12 : 27. F. save me from this hour
28. F. glorify thy name; a voice
50. as F. said unto me, so I speak
13:1. J. kn. he should dep. unto F.
3. knowing F. had given all things
14 : 6. man cometh unto F. but by
8. Lord, shew us the F. and it ⌊me
9. hath seen me, hath seen the F.
11. I in F. F. in me, 10.—17 : 21.
13. that F. be glorified in Son
16. will pray F. for you, 16 : 26.
26. Comforter whom F. will send
28. bec. I said I go unto the F.
31. I love the F. as F. gave com-t
15 : 9. As F. loved me, so I you
16. whatso. ye sh. ask of F., 16:23.
26. Comforter I will send you fr.
F. the Spi. who proceedeth fr. F.
16 : 3. have not known F. nor me
15. All things F. hath are mine
16. sh. see me, bec. I go to F., 17.
25. I sh. shew you plainly of F.
27. F. loveth you, bec. ye loved
28. I came fr. F. and go to F. ⌈me
32. am not alone, bec. F. is with
17:1. F., hour is come, glorify Son
5. O F. glorify me with own self
11. Holy F. keep those given me
24. F. I will that be where I am
25. O F. world hath not known
Ac. 1 : 4. wait for promise of the F.
7. seasons F. put in own power

Ac. 2:33. rec-d of F. promise of H.G.
28 : 8. the f. of Pub. lay sick
Ro. 4 : 11. be f. of all that believe
12. f. of circumc. to them who are
16. faith of Ab. who is f. of us all
6:4. as C. was raised fr. dead by F.
8:15. Spirit whereby we cry, Abba, F.
11 : 28. are beloved for F.s' sake
15 : 6. glorify G. F. of our L., 2 Co.
1: 3.-11 : 31. Ep. 1:3. 1 Pe.1:3.
1 Co. 8:6. to us is but one G. the F.
15:24. have deliv-d up kingd. to F.
2 Co. 1:3. F. of mercies, G. of comf.
6: 18. I will be a F. unto you, ye
Ga. 1 : 1. Paul an apostle by Jes. C. and G. the F. [Tit. 1 : 4.
3. peace from G. the F., 2 Ti. 1:2.
4. acc. to will of God and our F.
4:2. until time appointed of the F.
6. sent Spirit, crying, Abba F.
Ep. 1 : 17. God of Jes. F. of glory
2 : 18. access by one Spirit unto F.
3 : 14. I bow my knees unto the F.
4: 6. One God and F. of all, ab. all
5 : 20. Giving thanks unto the F., Col. 1 : 3, 12 -3 : 17.
6 : 23. love with faith fr. G. the F.
Ph. 2 : 11. Jes. is L. to glory of F.
22. as son with f. he hath served
Col. 1:19. pleased F. that all fulness
2:2. acknowl. of mystery of the F.
1 Th.1:1. church wh. is in G. the F.
2:11. we charged you, as a f. doth
1 Ti. 5 : 1. elder, entreat him as a f.
He. 1:5. will be to him a F. he shall
7: 3. Melchisedec without f. moth.
12 : 7. what son f. chasteneth not?
9. be in subjection unto F. of spirits
Ja. 1:17. ev. good gift cometh fr. F.
27. Pure religion bef. G. and F.
3: 9. bless we God, even the F.
1 Pe. 1 : 2. foreknowledge of God F.
17. if ye call on F. who judgeth
2 Pe. 1 : 17. received fr. F. honour
1 Jn. 1:2. eter. life, wh. was with F
3. our fellowship is with the F.
2 : 1. we have an Advocate with F.
13. I write bec. ye have known F.
15. if love world, love of F. is not
16. pride of life is not of the F.
22. he antichrist that denieth F.
23. denieth Son, hath not F. (2)
24. sh. continue in Son and in F.
3:1. what manner of love F. bestow.
4 : 14. the F. sent the Son to be
5 : 7. three bear record, F. Word
2 Jn. 3. mercy and peace fr. F. and from L. J. C. Son of F.
4. as we received a com-t from F.
9. he that abideth in C. hath the F.
Jude 1. are sanctified by God the F.
See ABRAHAM, HOUSE.

Her FATHER.

Ge.19:33. the firstborn lay with h.f.
29:9. Rachel came with h.f.'s sheep
12. was h. f.'s bro., she told h.f.
31:19. Rachel stolen images h.f.'s
35. to h. f. Let it not displease
34 : 11. Shechem said unto h. f.
38 : 11. Tamar dwelt in h.f.'s hou.
Ex. 22 : 17. if h. f. utterly refuse
Le. 21 : 9. profaneth h. f. be burnt
22:13. if returned unto h. f.'s hou. she shall eat of h. f.'s meat
Nu. 12 : 14. If h. f. had spit in face
30 : 3. if woman vow in h. f.'s h.
4. h. f. hear, and hold his peace
5. if h. f. disallow her in the day
16. yet in her youth in h.f.'s hou.
36 : 8. wife unto one of tribe of h. f.
De. 21 : 13. bewail h. f. a month
22 : 21. bring to door of h. f.'s house, bec. play whore in h. f.'s house [f.
Jos. 6:23. spies bro-t Rahab and h.
25. he saved h. f.'s household
15 : 18. ask of h. f. field, Ju. 1:14.
Ju.11:37. unto h.f. Let this be done
39. in two months return. to h.f.
15 : 1. h. f. not suffer him to go in
6. Philis. burnt her and h. f.
19 : 3. bro-t him into h. f.'s house
Es. 2:7. when h. f. and moth. dead

His FATHER.

Ge. 2 : 24. sh. man leave h. f. and cleave to wife, Mk.10:7. Ep.5:31.
9 : 22. Ham saw nakedness of h.f.
11:28. Haran died bef. h. f. Terah
22 : 7. Isaac spake unto Ab. h. f.
26:15. wells h.f. serv-ts digged, 18.
18. names h. f. called them
27:14. savoury meat h.f. loved, 31.
19. Jacob said unto h. f., 18.
22. near unto Isaac h. f.
26. h. f. Isaac said, 32, 39.
30. scarce gone from presence of h. f. [38.
34. Esau heard words of h.f., (2)
41. blessing whw. h. f. blessed
28:7. Jacob obeyed h.f. and moth.
8. dau-s of Canaan pleased not h.f.
31:53. Jacob sware by fear of h.f.
34:4. h. f. saying, Get me damsel
35 : 18. h. f. called him Benjamin
37 : 1. wherein h. f. was stranger
2. Jo. bro-t to h. f. their report
10. told dream to h.f. h.f. rebuk.
11. but h. f. observed saying
22. rid him, to deliv. him to h.f.
35. Thus h. f. wept for him
42 : 37. unto h. f. saying, Slay my sons [Send lad
43 : 8. Jud. said unto Israel h. f.,
44 : 20. loveth him and h. f.
22. the lad cannot leave h. f.
45 : 23. meat for h. f. by the way
46 : 1. sacrifices unto God of h. f.
29. Joseph went to meet Isr. h.f.
47 : 7. h. f. and set him bef. Pha.
12. Jo. nourished h.f. and breth.
48:9. Jo. unto h. f., They my sons
17. h.f. laid his right hand, 18.
19. h.f. refused, and said, I know
50 : 1. Jo. fell upon h.f.'s face and
2. Jo. com-d to embalm h. f.
50 : 10. mourning for h. f. 7 days
Ex. 6 : 20. Amram took h.f.'s sister
21:15. smiteth h. f. be put to dea.
17. curseth h. f. sh. die, Le.20:9.
Le. 19 : 3. sh. fear every man h. f.
20 : 11. man th. lieth with h. f.'s
17. if man take h. f.'s dau. [wife
21 : 2. of Aa. may be defil. for h.f.
11. high pr. not defile for h. f.
Nu. 6 : 7. not make unclean for h.f.
27 : 10. inheri. unto h. f.'s breth.
11. if h. f. no breth unto his
De. 21:18. which will not obey h.f.
19. sh. h.f. bring him unto elders
22 : 30. A man shall not take h.f.'s wife (2), 27 : 20. [h. f.
27:16. cursed be he setteth light by
22. Cursed lieth with dau. of h.f.
33 : 9. said to h. f. I not seen him
Ju.6:27. Gideon feared h.f.'s househ
8 : 32. Gideon in sepul. of h. f.
9 : 56. wickedness he did unto h. f.
14 : 4. h. f. knew not it was of L.
6. told not h. f., 1 S. 14:1. [man
10. So h. f. went down unto wo-
1 S. 14:27. when h. f. charged peo.
17 : 15. Da. to feed h. f. sheep
19 : 4. spake good of Da. unto h.f.
20 : 33. determ. of h. f. to slay Da.
34. h. f. had done him shame
2 S. 2 : 32. Asahel in sepul. of h. f.
7 : 14. I will be h.f. he be my son
10:2. h.f. shewed kindn., 1 Ch 19:2.
16:22. Abs. went in to h.f.'s concu.
17:23. Ahithophel in sepul of h.f.
21 : 14. Saul in sepul. of Kish h.f.
1 K. 1 : 6. h. f. had not displeased him [statutes of
2 : 12. throne of Da. h. f. | 8 : 3.
1 K. 5: 1. king in room of h. f., 2 K. 14 : 21.-23 : 30, 34. 1 Ch. 29:23. 2 Ch. 26 : 1.-36 : 1. Je. 22 : 11. Mat. 2 : 22.
7 : 14. h. f. was of Tyre, 2 Ch.2:14.
51. which h. f. had dedicated, 15: 15. 2 Ch. 5 : 1.-15 : 18. [f.
11:4. not perfect as heart of Da. h.
6. Sol. went not aft. the Lord, as did David h. f., 15: 11. 2 K. 18 : 3. 2 Ch. 28 : 1.-29:2. [him
17. Edomites of h. f. serv-ts with
33. not as Da. h. f., 2 K. 14 : 3.-16 : 2. [10 : 6.
12 : 6. stood bef. Sol. h. f., 2 Ch.
15 : 3. walked in all sins of h. f.
26. Nadab walked in way of h.f.,
22 : 43, 52. 2 K. 21 : 21.-22 : 2.
22 : 46. sodomites which remained in days of h. f.
53. all h. f. had done, 2 K. 15 : 3, 34.-24 : 9. 2 Ch. 26 : 4.-27:2.
2 K.3:2. Jehoram evil, not like h.f.
4:19. said unto h. f., My head, 18.
9 : 25. I and thou after Ahab h.f.
10 : 3. on h. f. throne and fight
13 : 25. cities out of hand of h. f.
14 : 5. Amaziah slew servants who had slain h. f., 2 Ch. 25 : 3.
21 : 3. high places which Hez. h. f. destroyed, 2 Ch. 33 : 3.
24:17. h.f.'s bro. king in his stead
1 Ch. 5 : 1. Reub. defiled h.f.'s bed
17 : 13. I will be h. f., 22:10.-28:6.
19 : 2. comfort him conc. h. f.
26 : 10. not firstborn yet h. f. made him the chief
2 Ch.3:1. L. appeared unto Da. h.f.
8:14. acc. to order of David h. f.
17 : 3. walked in 1st ways of h. f.
4. Jehosh. sought God of h.f. [Da.
20 : 32. walked in way of Asa h. f.
21 : 4. Jeho. risen to kingd. of h.f.
22:4. counsellors aft. death of h.f.
24 : 22. kindness Jehoi. h. f. had done [himself
33 : 23. Manasseh h. f. humbled
34:2. walked in ways of Da. h.f., 3.
Ps. 72:†17. to continue h.f.'s name
Pr. 13 : 1. wise son heareth instruc.
15:5. fool despiseth h. f.'s [of h.f.
17:25. foolish son is a grief to h.f.
19 : 13. fool. son is calam. of h. f.
26. wasteth h. f. causeth shame
20 : 20. curseth h. f. lamp put out
28 : 7. compau. of riotous shameth
24. Whoso robbeth h. f. or [h.f.
29:3. loveth wisdom, rejoiceth h.f.
30 : 17. eye th. mocketh h. f., ravens sh. [unto h. f.
Is. 45 : 10. Woe unto him th. saith
Eze. 18 : 14. son seeth all h.f.'s sins
17. shall not die for iniq. of h. f.
18. As for h. f. bec. he oppressed
22 : 11. humbled h. f.'s daughter
Da. 5 : 2. golden vessels h. f. had taken [same maid
Am. 2 : 7. man and h. f. in unto
Zch. 13 : 3. h. f. thrust him thro.
Mal. 1 : 6. A son honoureth h. f.
Mat.10:35. man at variance ag. h.f.
15:5. say to h. f. It is gift, Mk.7:11.
6. honour not h.f. he shall be free
16 : 27. Son of man shall come in glory of h. F., Mk. 8 : 38. Lu. 9 : 26.
21 : 31. Whether did will of h. f.?
Mk.7:12. no more do aught for h.f.
9 : 21. asked h. f. how long ago
10 : 7. man leave h. f., Ep. 5 : 31.
Lu. 1:32. L. sh. give throne of h.f.
59. called him after name of h.f.
62. they made signs unto h. f.
67. h. f. Zach. filled with H. G.
9 : 42. Jesus delivered him to h. f.
14 : 26. If come, and hate not h.f.
15 : 12. the younger said to h. f.

Lu. 15 : 20. came to **h. f.**, **h. f.** saw
28. came **h. f.** and entreated him
29. to **h. f.**, Lo, these many years
Jn. 5 : 18. said, that God was **h. F.**
Ac. 7 : 4. **h. f.** was dead he removed
14. Joseph called **h. f.** Jac. to him
16 : 1. son of Jewess, **h. f.** Greek, 3.
1 Co. 5 : 1. that one have **h. f.**'s wife
He. 7 : 10. he was yet in loins of **h. f.**
Re. 1 : 6. made us kings and priests
unto God and **h. F.** [in foreheads
14 : 1. 144,000 having **h. F.**'s name
See **HOUSE, S,** with **father, s.**

FATHER in law. [nath
Ge. 38:13. thy **f. i. l.** goeth to Tim-
25. when bro-t, sent to her **f. i. l.**
Ex. 3 : 1. Jethro his **f. i. l.**, 4 : 18.
18:1. Moses' **f. i. l.**, 6, 7, 8, 12, 14,
15, 17, 24, 27. Ju. 1 : 16.-4 : 11.
27. Moses let his **f. i. l.** depart
Nu. 10 : 29. Raguel, Moses' **f. i. l.**
Ju. 19 : 4. his **f. i. l.** retained him
7 rose to depart, his **f. i. l.** urged
1 S. 4:19. heard **f. i. l.** was dead, 21.
Jn. 18 : 13. **f. i. l.** to Caiaphas

My FATHER. [m.f.
Ge. 19 : 34. I lay yesternight with
20 : 12. she is dau. of **m. f.** not of
22 : 7. **m. f.**, Here am I, 27 : 18.
27:12. **m. f.** peradven. will feel me
31. Let **m. f.** eat of son's venison
34. Esau cried, bless me, O **m. f.**
38. one bless-g **m. f.**? bless me O
41. mourning for **m. f.** [m. f.
31:5. G. of **m. f.**, 42.-32:9. Ex. 18:
44 : 24. thy serv. **m. f.**, 27, 30. [4.
32. surety for lad unto **m. f.**, 34.
45 : 3. doth **m. f.** live? | 9. Haste
13. tell **m. f.** [to go to **m. f.**
47:1. **m. f.** and brethren are come
48:18. not so, **m. f.**, this is firstb.
50 : 5. **m. f.** made me swear, let
me go up and bury **m. f.**
Ex. 15 : 2. **m. f.**'s G. I will exalt
De. 26 : 5. ready to perish was **m. f.**
Jos. 2 : 13. ye will save alive **m. f.**
Ju. 9 : 17. **m. f.** fought for you
11 : 36. **m. f.** hast opened mouth
14 : 16. I have not told it **m. f.** nor
1 S. 9 : 5. lest **m. f.** leave the asses
14:29. said, **m. f.** troubled the land
18 : 18. and what is **m. f.**'s family?
19 : 2. Saul **m. f.** seeketh to kill
3. commune with **m. f.** of thee
20:2. **m. f.** will do noth. but show
9. determ-d by **m. f.** | 12. sounded
13. L. be with thee, as wi. **m. f.**
22 : 3. Let **m. f.** be with you
23:17. Saul **m. f.** sh. not find thee
24 : 11. **m. f.** yea, see skirt of robe
2 S. 3:7. gone in unto **m. f.**'s concu.
16 : 3. restore me kingd. of **m. f.**
19 : 37. be buried by grave of **m. f.**
1 K. 2 : 24. on throne of Da. **m. f.**
26. barest ark of L. bef. Da. **m.**
f., in all **m. f.** was afflicted
32. **m. f.** Da. not knowing thereof
44. wickedness didst to Da. **m. f.**
3 : 6. thou hast shewed Da. **m. f.**
great mercy, 2 Ch. 1 : 8. [f.
7. made thy serv. k. instead of **m.**
5:3. **m. f.** could not build a house
5. as Lord spake to David **m. f.**,
8 : 15, 18. 2 Ch. 6 : 4, 8.
8 : 17. it was in the heart of David
m. f. to build, 2 Ch. 6 : 7. [10.
20. in room of Da. **m. f.**, 2 Ch. 6:
24. hast kept with David **m. f.**
8 : 26. word spakest unto **m. f.**, 2
Ch. 6 : 16.
12 : 10. My little finger be thicker
than **m. f.**'s loins, 2 Ch. 10 : 10.
11. **m. f.** lade you, 2 Ch. 10 : 11.
14. **m. f.** chastised you, 2 Ch. 10 : 14.
15 : 19. league betw. **m. f.** thy fa.,
2 Ch. 16 : 3. [m. f.
19 : 20. Let me, I pray thee, kiss

16

1 K. 20:34. cities **m. f.** took I restore
2 K. 2 : 12. Elisha cried, **m. f. m. f.**
5:13. **m. f.** if proph. had bid thee
6 : 21. **m. f.** shall I smite them?
13 : 14. Joash said, O **m. f. m. f.**
the chariot of Israel
1 Ch. 28 : 4. L. chose me before all
hou. of **m. f.** amo. sons of **m. f.**
2 Ch. 2 : 3. didst deal with **m. f.** so
7. whom Da. **m. f.** did provide
Jb. 17 : 14. I said to corrupt., **m. f.**
34 : † 36. **m. f.** let Job be tried
Ps. 27 : 10. **m. f.** and moth. forsake
89:26. He cry, Thou art **m. F.** my G.
Pr. 4:3. for I was **m. f.**'s son, tend.
Is. 8:4. the child knowl. to cry, **m. f.**
Je. 2 : 27. Saying to a stock, **m. f.**
3:4. Wilt thou not cry, **m. F.**? 19.
20:15. Cursed who brought tidings
to **m. f.** [Jewry?
Da. 5 : 13. **m. f.** brought out of
Mat. 7:21. doeth will of **m. F.**, 12:50.
8 : 21. to go bury **m. f.**, Lu. 9:59.
10:32. him will I confess bef. **m. F.**
33. him will I also deny bef. **m. F.**
11:27. delivered of **m. F.**, Lu. 10:22.
15:13. plant **m. F.** hath not plant.
16 : 17. **m. F.** in heav. revealed it
18 : 10. angels behold face of **m. F.**
19. it shall be done of **m. F.**
35. So **m.** heaven. **F.** do unto you
20:23. for whom prepared of **m. F.**
24 : 36. day kno. no man but **m. F.**
25 : 34. Come ye blessed of **m. F.**
26:29. dr-k it new in **m. F.**'s kingd.
39. O **m. F.**, let this cup pass me
42. **m. F.**, thy will be done
53. that I cannot pray to **m. F.**?
Lu. 2 : 49. be about **m. F.**'s busin.
15 : 17. How many hired serv-ts of
18. arise, and go to **m. f.** [m. f.
16 : 27. send him to **m. f.**'s house
22 : 29. as **m. F.** hath appointed
24:49. I send the promise of **m. F.**
Jn. 5 : 17. **m. F.** worketh hitherto
30. not my own, but will of **m. F.**
43. I am come in **m. F.**'s name
6 : 32. **m. F.** giveth you true bre.
65. except it be given of **m. F.**
8 : 19. Ye nei. know me, nor **m. F.**
28. as **m. F.** hath taught me I sp.
38. which I have seen with **m. F.**
49. I honour **m. F.** ye dishonour
54. it is **m. F.** th. honoureth me
10:17. Theref. doth **m. F.** love me
18. This com-t I received of **m. F.**
25. works I do in **m. F.** name bear
29. **m. F.** is greater than all, none
is able to pluck out of **m. F.**'s
30. I and **m. F.** are one [hand
32. Many good works from **m. F.**
37. if I do not the works of **m. F.**
12:26. serve me, him **m. F.** honour
14 : 7. if known me, known **m. F.**
12. bec. I go unto **m. F.**, 16 : 10.
20. ye shall know I am in **m. F.**
21. loveth me, be lov. of **m. F.**, 23.
28. I go unto Fa., **m. F.** is great.
15 : 1. I vine, **m. F.** is husbandm.
8. Herein is **m. F.** glorified, that
10. as I have kept **m. F.**'s com-ts
15. all I heard of **m. F.** I made kn.
23. hateth me, hateth **m. F.**, 24.
18 : 11. cup **m. F.** given, sh. I not
20 : 17. not yet asc. to **m. F.** say
unto them, I ascend unto **m.**
F. and your Father
21. as **m. F.** sent me, so send I
Re. 2 : 27. as I received of **m. F.**
3:5. will conf. his name bef. **m. F.**
21. set down with **m. f.** on throne

Our FATHER.
Ge. 19 : 31. **o. f.** is old
32. make **o. f.** drink wine
31:1. Jac. taken all th. is **o. f.**, 16.
42 : 13. youngest is with **o. f.**, 32.
43 : 28. **o. f.** is in good health
Ge. 44:25. **o. f.** said, Go again, buy us
31. **o. f.** with sorrow to grave
Nu. 27 : 3. **o. f.** died in the wildern.
4. Why name of **o. f.** be done aw.?
1 Ch. 29 : 10. thou, L. G. of Isr. **o. f.**
Is. 63:16. Doubtless, thou art **o. F.**
64 : 8. O L., thou art **o. F.** we clay
Je. 35 : 6. **o. f.** com-d us drink no
8. obeyed voice of **o. f.**, 10. [wine
Mat. 8:9. think not to say, We have
Ab. to **o. f.**, Lu. 3:8. Jn. 8:39.
6 : 9. **o. F.** in heaven, Lu. 11 : 2.
Mk. 11:10. Blessed be kingd. of **o. f.**
Lu. 1 : 73. oath he sware to **o. f.** Ab.
Jn. 4 : 12. greater than **o. f.**? 8:53.
Ac. 7 : 2. God appeared unto **o. f.**
Ro. 1 : 7. grace to you, and peace fr.
God **o. F.** and L. J. C., 1 Co. 1:
3. 2 Co. 1 : 2. Ep. 1:2. Ph. 1:2.
Col. 1 : 2. 1 Th. 1:1. 2 Th. 1 : 2.
1 Ti. 1 : 2. Phm. 3.
9:10. conceived by one, **o. f.** Isaac
Ga. 1 : 4. acc. to will of G., **o. F**
Ph. 4 : 20. unto God **o. F.** be glory
1 Th. 1 : 3. in sight of G. and **o. F.**
3:11. G. **o. F.** direct our way [o. F.
13. stablish you in holin. bef. G.
2 Th. 1 : 1. unto church in G. **o. F.**
2 : 16. **o. F.** comfort your hearts

Their FATHER.
Ge. 9:23. cover-d nakedn. of **t. f.** (2)
19 : 33. they made **t. f.** drink wine
36. Lot's dau-s with child by **t. f.**
37 : 12. went to feed **t. f.**'s flock
32. they brought coat to **t. f.** [29.
42:35. **t. f.** saw bundles of money,
36. **t. f.** said, Me have ye bereav.
45:27. the spirit of Jac. **t. f.** reviv.
46 : 5. carried Jac. **t. f.** and little
49:28. **t. f.** spake and blessed them
50 : 15. **t. f.** was dead they said
Ex. 2 : 16. to water **t. f.**'s flock
18. Reuel **t. f.** said, How is it
40 : 15. as thou didst anoint **t. f.**
Nu. 3 : 4. in the sight of Aaron **t. f.**
27 : 7. inheritance among **t. f.**'s
breth., 36 : 12. Jos. 17 : 4.
36:6. to tribe of **t. f.** sh. th. marry
Jos. 19:47. after Dan **t. f.**, Ju. 18:29.
1 S. 2 : 25. hearkened not unto **t. f.**
10 : 12. said, But who is **t. f.**? [12.
1 K. 13:11. prophet's sons told **t. f.**,
1 Ch. 7 : 22. Ephr. **t. f.** mourned
24 : 2. and Abihu died bef. **t. f.**
19. under Aaron **t. f.** as Lord
25 : 3. hands of **t. f.** Jeduthun, 6
2 Ch. 21 : 3. **t. f.** gave great gifts
Jb. 42 : 15. **t. f.** gave them inheri.
Pr. 30 : 11. generation th. curs. **t. f.**
Je. 16:7. cup of consola. for **t. f.** [16.
35:14. Jonadab's sons obeyed **t. f.**'s,
Eze. 22 : 10. discov-d **t. f.s'** nakedn.
Mat. 4:21. in ship with Zebedee **t. f.**
22. left **t. f.** foll-d him, Mk. 1:20
13:43. righte. shine in kingd. of **t. f.**

Thy FATHER.
Ge. 12 : 1. Get thee fr. **t. f.**'s house
27 : 6. heard **t. f.** speak unto Esau
9. savoury meat for **t. f.**
10. bring it to **t. f.** that he eat
38 : 11. Remain a widow at **t. f.**'s
46 : 3. I am God of **t. f.** fear not
47 : 5. **t. f.** thy breth. are come, 6.
48 : 1. Behold **t. f.** is sick
49 : 4. thou wentest to **t. f.**'s bed
8. **t. f.**'s chil. shall bow down
25. by the G. of **t. f.** who help
26. blessings of **t. f.** prevailed
Ge. 50:16. **t. f.** com-d bef. he died, 6.
17. forgive servants of G. of **t. f.**
Ex. 20 : 12. Honour **t. f.** and moth.,
De. 5 : 16. Mat. 15 : 4.-19 : 19.
Le. 18 : 7. nakedn. of **t. f.**, not uncover, 8, 9, 11, 12, 14.-20 : 19.
Nu. 18:2. breth. of tribe of **t. f.** bri.
De. 32 : 6. is he **t. f.** bought thee?
7. ask **t. f.** he will shew thee

Ru. 2 : 11. how thou hast left t. f.
1 S. 10:2. t. f. hath left care of asses
14 : 28. t. f. straitly charged peo.
20:1. and what is my sin bef. t. f.?
3. t. f. certainly knoweth
6. If t. f. at all miss me, then say
8. why shouldest bring me to t. f.
10. what if t. f. ans. thee roughly
2 S. 6 : 21. L. chose me before t. f.
9 : 7. kindness for Jona. t. f. sake
10:3. Da. honour t. f., 1 Ch. 19:3.
13:5. when t. f. cometh to see thee
15:34. as I have been t. f.'s serv-t
16 : 19. as I served in t. f.'s pres.
21. t. f.'s concu. abhorr. of t. f.
17 : 8. t. f. is a man of war (2), 10.
1 K. 3:14. as t. f. Da. did walk, 9:4.
6 : 12. words which I spake unto David t. f., 9 : 5. 2 Ch. 7 : 18.
12 : 4. t. f. made yoke grievous, 9, 10, 2 Ch. 10 : 4. [t. f.
15 : 19. league betw. my fath. and
20 : 34. cities my fa. took fr. t. f.
2 K. 3:13. get thee to proph-s of t. f.
20 : 5. Thus saith, the God of Da. t. f., 2 Ch. 21 : 12. Is. 38 : 5.
1 Ch. 28:9. my son, know G. of t. f.
2 Ch. 7 : 17. if wilt walk as t. f.
2 : 14. cunning men of David t. f.
Jb. 15 : 10. men much elder th. t. f.
Pr. 1 : 8. instruction of t. f., 28:22.
6 : 20. My son, keep t. f.'s com-t
23 : 25. t. f. and moth. sh. be glad
27 : 10. t. f.'s friend forsake not
Is. 43 : 27. t. first f. hath sinned
58 : 14. with heritage of Jac. t. f.
Je. 12:6. house of t. f. dealt treach.
22 : 15. did not t. f. eat, drink?
Eze. 16 : 3. t. f. was an Amorite
Da. 5 : 11. in days of t. f. king (2)
18. God gave t. f. a kingdom
Mat. 6 : 4. t. F. seeth in secret, 6, 18.
6. shut thy door, pray to t. F.
Mk. 7 : 10. Moses said, Honour t. f., 10 : 19. Lu. 18 : 20. Ep. 6 : 2.
Lu. 2 : 48. t. f. and I sought thee
15 : 27. t. f. hath killed fatted calf
Jn. 8 : 19. they said, Where is t. f.?

Your FATHER.

Ge. 31 : 5. I see y. f.'s countenance
6. with all my power served y. f.
7. y. f. hath deceived me, and
9. cattle of y. f. and given them
29. God of y. f. spake unto me
43 : 7. y. f. alive? have ye bro.?
23. G. of y. f. hath given treasure
44 : 17. get up in peace unto y. f.
45 : 18. y. f. and households, come
19. bring y. f. and come
49 : 2. hearken unto Israel y. f.
Je. 35 : 18. ye obeyed Jonadab y. f.
Eze. 16 : 45. mother a Hittite, y. f.
Mat. 5:16. may glorify y. F. in heav.
45. may be chil. of y. F. in heav.
48. Be ye perfect, as y. F. in heav.
6 : 1. otherwise no reward of y. F.
8. y. F. knoweth what things ye have need of, 32. Lu. 12 : 30.
14. if ye forgive, y. F. will forgive
15. if ye forgive not, neither will y. F. forgive. Mk. 11 : 25, 26.
26. y. heavenly F. feedeth them, 32.
7 : 11. y. F. in heaven give good
10 : 20. spirit of y. F. speaketh in
29. not sparrow fall without y. F.
18 : 14. not will of y. F. one perish
23:9. call no man y. f. upon earth, one is y. F. which is in heaven
Lu. 6 : 36. be ye merciful, as y. F.
11 : 13. y. heavenly F. give H. Sp.
12:32. y. F.'s pleas. to give kingd.
Jn. 8 : 38. do what seen with y. f.
41. Ye do the deeds of y. f.
42. Jes. said, If G. were y. F. ye
44. Ye are of y. f. the devil, lusts of y. f. ye will do
20:17. I ascend to my F. and y. F.

FATHERS.

Ex. 6 : 14. these are the heads of their f. houses, 25. Jos. 14 : 1.-19:51.-21:1. 1 Ch. 8:10, 13, 28.
20:5. visiting iniq. of f. upon chil., 34 : 7. Nu. 14 : 18. De. 5 : 9.
De. 24:16. f. sh. not be put to death for the chil. nei. chil. for the f., 2 K. 14 : 6. 2 Ch. 25 : 4.
2 Ch. 35 : 5. divis. of families of f.
Jb. 30 : 1. f. I would have disdained
Pr. 19 : 14. riches are inher. of f.
Is. 49:23. kings sh. be thy nursing f.
Je. 6:21. f. sh. fall upon them, 13 : 14.
7 : 18. chil. gather, f. kindle fire
31 : 29. f. have eaten sour grapes, Eze. 18 : 2. [om of chil.
32:18. recomp. iniq. of f. into bos-
47 : 3. f. sh. not look back to chil.
Eze. 5 : 10. the f. shall eat the sons
Mal. 4 : 6. turn heart of f. to chil., and chil. to f., Lu. 1 : 17.
Jn. 7:22. not bec. of Mo., but of f.
Ac. 3 : 22. Mo. truly said unto the f.
7 : 2. Men, and f. hearken, 22 : 1.
13 : 32. promise unto f., Ro. 15 : 8.
22 : 3. perf. manner of law of the f.
Ro. 9 : 5. Whose are the f. of whom
11 : 28. beloved for the f. sakes
1 Co. 4:15. instructors, not many f.
Ep. 6:4. f. provoke not chil., Col. 3:21.
1 Ti. 1 : 9. for murderers of f.
He. 1:1. spake in times past unto f.
12 : 9. we had f. who corrected us
2 Pe. 3 : 4. since the f. fell asleep
1 Jn. 2 : 13. I write unto you f., 14.
See BURIED, CHIEF.

His FATHERS.

Le. 25:41. unto posses-n of h. f. ret.
Nu. 1:4. to head of house of h. f., 44.
36:8. may enjoy inheri. of h. f., 7.
1 K. 1 : 21. king sh. sleep with h. f.
15 : 12. he removed the idols h. f. made [had dedicated
2 K. 12 : 18. took the things h. f.
15 : 9. he did evil as h. f. [10.
21:22. forsook G. of h. f., 2 Ch. 21:
23 : 32. acc. to all h. f. had done, 37.-24 : 9.
2 Ch. 21 : 19. like burning of h. f.
28:25. Ahaz provoked God of h. f.
30:19. prepareth to seek G. of h. f.
33:12. humbled hims. bef. G. of h. f.
Ps. 49:19. shall go to gene. of h. f.
109:14. Let iniq. of h. f. be remem.
Da. 11 : 24. do what h. f. not done
37. Neither regard God of h. f.
38. a god whom h. f. knew not
Ac. 13 : 36. David was laid to h. f.

My FATHERS.

Ge. 47:9. not attained years of m. f.
30. I will lie with m. f. carry me
48 : 16. name of m. f. be named
49:29. bury me with m. f. in cave
Ex. 15 : 2. he is m. f. God, I will
1 K. 19:4. I am no better than m. f.
21:3. inheri. of m. f. unto thee, 4.
2 K. 19 : 12. have gods deliv-d them m. f. destr.? 2 Ch. 32:14. Is. 37:12.
2 Ch. 32:13. what I and m. f. done
15. out of the hand of m. f.
Ne. 2 : 3. place of m. f. sepul., 5.
Ps. 39 : 12. sojourner as m. f. were
Da. 2:23. I praise thee, O G. of m. f.
Ac. 24 : 14. so worship I G. of m. f.
Ga. 1:14. zealous of traditions of m. f.

Our FATHERS.

Ge. 46 : 34. we and also o. f., 47 : 3.
Nu. 20 : 15. How o. f. went into E.
36 : 3. inheritance of o. f., 4.
De. 5:3. not cov. with o. f.. 1 K. 8:21.
6:23. he sware unto o. f., 26:3, 15.
26 : 7. cried unto the God of o. f.
Jos. 22 : 28. of the altar o. f. made
24 : 17. brought o. f. out of E.
Ju. 6:13. where miracles o. f. told?
1 K. 8:40. land thou gavest unto o. f.
1 K. 8 : 53. broughtest o. f. out of E.
57. God be with us, as with o. f.
58. statutes, he com. o. f., Ps. 78:5.
2 K. 22:13. o. f. have not hearkened
1 Ch. 12 : 17. God of o. f. rebuke it
29 : 15. we sojourners, as all o. f.
18. O L. G. of o. f., keep for ever in the thoughts, 2 Ch. 20 : 6.
2 Ch. 6 : 31. wh. gavest o. f., Ne. 9:
29 : 6. o. f. have trespassed [36.
9. o. f. have fallen by the sword
34 : 21. o. f. have not kept word
Ezr. 5 : 12. after o. f. provoked G.
7 : 27. Blessed be the God of o. f.
9:7. Since o. f. in a great trespass
Ne. 9 : 9. didst see affliction of o. f.
16. o. f. dealt proudly, and hard-d
32. on o. f. and on all thy peo.
34. nor o. f. kept thy law
Ps. 22 : 4. o. f. trusted in thee
44 : 1. o. f. told thou didst, 78 : 3.
106 : 6. We have sinned with o. f.
7. o. f. understood not wonders
Is. 64 : 11. where o. f. praised thee
Je. 3 : 24. devoured labour of o. f.
25. o. f. have not obeyed voice
14 : 20. iniq. of o. f. we have sinn.
16 : 19. o. f. have inherited lies
44 : 17. as we have done, and o. f.
La. 5 : 7. o. f. have sinned, are not
Da. 9 : 6. o. f. and to all peo. of land
8. confusion of face to o. f.
16. for the iniquities of o. f.
Mi. 7 : 20. sworn to o. f. from old
Mal. 2 : 10. profaning cov. of o. f.
Mat. 23 : 30. If been in days of o. f.
Lu. 1:55. As he spake to o. f. to Ab.
72. mercy promised to o. f. [mt.
Jn. 4 : 20. o. f. worshipped in this
6 : 31. o. f. did eat manna
Ac. 3 : 13. God of o. f. hath glorifi.
25. of cov. God made with o. f.
5 : 30. God of o. f. raised up Jesus
7 : 11. o. f. found no sustenance
12. he sent out o. f. first
15. Jacob died, and o. f.
19. and evil entreated o. f. and
38. this is he wh. spake with o. f.
39. To wh. o. f. would not obey
44. o. f. had tabern. of witness
45. o. f. that came after
13 : 17. God of Israel chose o. f.
15 : 10. a yoke o. f. nor we able to
22:14. G. of o. f. hath chosen thee
26 : 6. of promise made unto o. f.
28 : 17. noth. ag. customs of o. f.
25. well spake H. G. unto o. f.
1 Co. 10 : 1. o. f. were under cloud

Slept with his FATHERS.

1 K. 2 : 10. so David s.-f., 11 : 21.
1.43. Solomon s.-f., 2 Ch. 9 : 31.
14 : 20. Jeroboam s.-f., 2 K. 14:29.
31. Rehoboam s.-f., 2 Ch. 12:16.
15 : 8. Abijam s.-f., 2 Ch. 14 : 1.
24. and Asa s.-f., 2 Ch. 16 : 13.
16 : 6. Baasha s.-f. | 28. Omri
22 : 40. Ahab s.-f.
50. Jehosh. s.-f., 2 Ch. 21 : 1.
2 K. 8:24. Joram s.-f. | 10:35. Jehu
13 : 9. Jehoahaz s.-f.
13. Joash s.-f., 14 : 16. [26 : 2.
14 : 22. after that king s.-f., 2 Ch.
15 : 7. Azariah s.-f. | 22. Menahem
38. Jotham s.-f., 2 Ch. 27 : 9.
16 : 20. Ahaz s.-f., 2 Ch. 28 : 27.
20 : 21. Hezekiah s.-f., 2 Ch. 32:33.
21 : 18. Manasseh s.-f., 2 Ch. 33:20.
24 : 6. Jehoiakim s.-f.
2 Ch. 26 : 23. Uzziah s.-f.

Their FATHERS.

Ex. 4 : 5. God of t. f. hath appeared
6 : 14. heads of t. f., 25. Jos. 14:1.-19 : 51.-21 : 1. 1 Ch. 5 : 24.-7: 2, 7.-8 : 6.-9 : 9, 13.
Le. 26:39. in iniq. of t. f. pine away
40. if they confess iniq. of t. f.
Nu. 1:16. princes of tribes of t. f.

Nu.11:12. land thou swarest to give to t. f., 14 : 23. De. 10 : 11.-31: 20. Jos. 1 : 6.-5 : 6.-21 : 43, 44. Je. 32 : 22.
13:2. of ev. tribe of t.f. sh. ye send
26 : 55. of t. f. they shall inherit
De. 29:25. have forsaken cov. of t.f.
Jos. 4 : 6. when chil. ask t. f., 21.
22:14. each a head of house of t.f.
Ju. 2 : 10. gene. were gath. to t. f.
12. they forsook the God of t. f.
17. out of the way t. f. walked in
19. they corrupted more than t.f.
20. my cov. which I com-d t. f.
22. if keep way of L., as t.f. kept
3:4. he commanded t. f. by Moses
21 : 22. when t. f. or breth. come
1 K. 8:34 again to land thou gavest to t. f., 48. 2 Ch. 6 : 25, 38.
9 : 9. who brought t. f. out of E.
14: 15. land which he gave to t. f. 2 K. 21 : 8. Je 16: 15.-24: 10.
22. provoked above all t. f. done
2 K. 17 : 14. neck of t.f. th. did not
15. covenant he made with t. f.
41. as did t. f. so do they
21:15. since day t.f.came out of E.
1 Ch. 4 : 38. house of t. f. increased
5 : 25. transgressed ag. God of t. f.
6 : 19. Levites according to t. f.
9 : 19. t. f. being over host of L.
29 : 20. blessed the God of t. f.
2 Ch. 7 : 22. forsook God of t. f., 24 : 24.-28 : 6.
11 : 16. to sacri. unto God of t. f.
13:18. they relied upon G. of t. f.
14:4. com-d to seek G.of t.f.,15:12.
19 : 4. bro-t back unto G. of t. f.
20 : 33. not prepared hearts unto God of t. f.
30 : 7. wh. trespassed ag.G.of t. f.
22. confession to God of t. f.
34:32. acco. to cove. of God of t.f.
33. from foll-g the God of t. f.
36 : 15 G. of t. f. sent by messen.
Ne. 9 : 2. confessed iniq. of t. f.
23. land thou promised to t. f.
Jb. 8 : 8. prepare to search of t. f.
15 : 18. wise men have told fr. t.f.
Ps. 78 : 8. And might not be as t.f.
12. Marvel. things in sight of t.f.
57. dealt unfaithfully like t. f.
Pr. 17 : 6. glory of chil. are t. f.
Is. 14 : 21. slaughter for iniq.of t.f.
Je. 7 : 26. did worse than t. f.
9 : 14. aft. Baalim, wh. t.f. taught
16. nor t. f. have known, 19 : 4.
16 : 3. conc. t. f. that begat them
23:27. as t.f. have forgot. my name
31 : 32. not acc. to cov. I made with t. f.. 11 : 10. He. 8 : 9.
50:7. sinned ag. L., the hope of t.f.
Eze. 2:3. t. f. have transgressed
5 : 10. fathers eat sons, sons eat t.f.
20 : 4. cause to know abomi. of t.f.
24. their eyes were aft. t. f. idols
22 : 10. they discov-d t. f. nakedu.
Am. 2 : 4. lies, aft. wh. t. f. walked
Mal. 4 : 6. turn heart of chil. to t.f.
Lu. 6 : 23. in like manner did t. f.
26. so did t. f. to false prophets

Thy FATHERS.

Ge. 15 : 15. shalt go to t. f. in peace
31 : 3. Return unto land of t. f.
49:8. t. f. chil. shall bow bef. thee
Ex. 10 : 6. t. f. nor t. f.'s fa-s seen
13 : 5. into land which he sware to t. f., 11. De. 6 : 10, 18.-7 : 12, 13.-8 : 18.-9 : 5.-13 : 17.-19 : 8. -28 : 11.-29 · 13.-30 : 20.
De. 1:21. possess it, as G. of t.f.said
4 : 31. nor forget covenant of t. f.
37. bec. he loved t. f., 10 : 15.
6 : 3. G. of t. f. hath promised
8 : 3. neither did t. f. know, 16.
10 : 22. t. f. went into E with 70
12 : 1. land G. of t. f. giveth

De. 13:6. gods thou nor t.f. known, 28 : 64. [3.
19:8. land wh. he promised t.f.,27:
28 : 36. nation thou nor t.f.known
30 : 5. and multiply thee above t.f.
9. as he rejoiced over t. f. [12.
31:16. shalt sleep with t.f., 2 S. 7 :
1 K. 13 : 22. not unto sepul. of t. f.
2 K 20:17. t. f.laid up be carried aw.
22:20. gather thee to t. f., 2 Ch.34:
1 Ch. 17 : 11 go to be with t.f. [28.
Ezr. 4 : 15. search the records of t.f.
Ps. 45 : 16. Instead of t. f. thy chil.
Pr.22:28.remove not land-mark t.f.
Is. 39:6. wh. t.f. have laid up [set
Je. 34 : 5. with burnings of t. f.
Ac. 7:32. I am God of t. f. G. of Ab.

Your FATHERS. [y.f.

Ge. 48 : 21. bring you unto land of
Ex. 3 : 13. The God of y. f. hath sent me, 15, 16. De. 1 : 11.-4:1. Jos. 18 : 3. 2 Ch. 28 : 9.-29 : 5.
Nu. 32 : 8. Thus did y.f., Ne. 13:18.
14. ye are risen up in y. f. stead
33 : 54. acc. to tribes of y. f.
De. 1 : 8. land Lord sware unto y.f., 35.-7: 8.-8:1.-11 : 9, 21. Ju.2:1.
32:17. sacri. to gods y.f. feared not
Jos. 24 : 2. y.f. dwelt on other side
6. I brought y. f. out of Egypt
14. put away gods y. f. served
15. whether gods y. f. served
1 S. 12 : 7. acts the L. did to y. f.
8. y. f. cried, L. bro-t forth y. f.
15. hand of L. ag. you as y. f.
2 K. 17:13. law which I com-d y.f.
2 Ch. 13:12. fight not ag. G. of y.f.
30 : 7. be not like y.f., 8. Zch 1:4.
33: 8. out of land appoint for y.f.
35 : 4. prepare by the house of y.f.
Ezr. 8:28. offering unto God of y. f.
10 : 11. confession unto G. of y. f.
Ps. 95 : 9. y. f. tempted me, He 3:9.
Is. 65 : 7. your and iniq. of y. f.
Je. 2 : 5. iniq. y. f. found in me?
3:18. to land I have given unto y.f.
7 : 7. dwell in the land I gave to y. f., 14.-23 : 39.-25 : 5.-35:15. Eze. 20 : 42.-36 : 28.-47 : 14.
22. I spake not to y. f. in day I
25. Since day y. f. came out of E.
11 : 4. Which I com-d y.f., 17: 22.
7. earnestly protested unto y. f.
16 : 11. Because y. f. forsaken me
12. worse than y. f. | 13.nor y.f.
34:13. I made a cov. with y. f.
14. y. f. hearkened not unto me
44 : 3. knew not, nei. they nor y.f.
9. ye forgotten wickedn. of y. f.?
10. in my statutes I set bef. y. f.
21. the incense ye, y. f. burn
Eze. 20 : 18. not in statutes of y. f.
27. in this y. f. blasphemed me
30. polluted aft. manner of y. f.
36. Like as I pleaded with y. f.
37 : 25. dwell in land y. f. dwelt
Ho. 9:10. y.f. as first ripe of fig tree
Jo. 1 : 2. this been in days of y. f.?
Zch. 1 : 2. L. displeased with y. f.
4. Be not as y. f. unto whom
5. y. f. where are they?
6. my words take hold of y. f.?
8 : 14. when y. f. provoked me
Mal. 3 : 7. fr. days of y. f. are gone
Mat 23:32. Fill up measure of y.f.
Lu. 11 : 47. prophets, y. f. killed
48. that ye allow deeds of y. f.
Jn. 6 : 49. y. f. did eat manna
58. not as y. f. did eat manna
Ac. 7 : 51. resist H. G. as y. f. did
52. have not y. f. persecuted
1 Pe. 1 : 18. by tradition from y. f.

FATHERLESS.

Ex. 22 : 22. not afflict any f. child
24. your wives be widows, chil. f.
De. 10 : 18. He doth execute the judgm.of the f.,Ps.82:3.Is 1:17.

Jb. 6 : 27. ye overwhelm the f.
22 : 9. arms of f. have been brok.
24 : 3. They drive away ass of f.
9. They pluck the f. from breast
29 : 12. because I delivered the f.
31 : 17. f. have not eaten thereof
21. if I lifted up my hand ag. f.
Ps. 10 : 14. thou art helper of f.
18. To judge f. and oppressed
68 : 5. A father of the f. a judge
109 : 9. let his children be f. his
12. nor let any favour his f. chil.
Pr. 23 : 10. enter not fields of f.
Is. 1 : 23. judge not f., Je. 5 : 28.
9:17. L. not have mercy on their f.
10 : 2. that they may rob the f.
Je. 49 : 11. Leave thy f. chil., I will
La. 5 : 3. We are orphans and f.
Eze. 22 : 7. in thee have vexed the f.
Ho. 14 : 3. in thee f. findeth mercy
Mal. 3 : 5. witness ag. those oppr. f.
Ja. 1 : 27. pure religion is to visit f.

FATHERLESS
with stranger or strangers.

De. 14 : 29. s., f. and widow shall eat, 24 : 19, 20, 21.-26 : 12, 13.
16:11. s.and f.rejoice with thee,14.
24 : 17. pervert judgm. of s. nor f.
27:19. perverteth judgm.of s.and f.
Ps. 94 : 6. slay s. and murder the f.
146 : 9. Lord preserveth s. and f.
Je. 7 : 6. if ye oppressed not the s., f. and widow, 22:3. Zch. 7 : 10.

FATHOMS.

Ac. 27:28. found it 20 f. again 15 f.

FATLING, S.

1 S. 15 : 9. Saul spared best of f-s
2 S. 6 : 13. David sacri. oxen f-s
Ps.66:15. offer burnt sacrifices of f-s
Is. 11:6. young lion, and f. together
Eze. 39 : 18. all f-s of Bashan
Mat. 22 : 4. f-s are killed, all ready

FATNESS.

Ge. 27 : 28. God give thee of the f.
39. thy dwelling be f. of earth
De. 32 : 15. art covered with f.
Ju. 9 : 9. said, Sho. I leave my f.?
Jb. 15: 27. covereth face with his f.
36 : 16. on thy table be full of f.
Ps. 36 : 8. satisfi. with f. of house
63:5.My soul be satisfied as with f.
65 : 11. all thy paths drop f.
73 : 7. eyes stand out with f.
109 : 24. my flesh faileth of f.
Is. 17:4. f. of his flesh sh. wax lean
34 : 6. sword of L. is fat with f.
7. their dust be made fat with f.
55 : 2. let your soul delight in f.
Je. 31:14. the soul of priests with f.
Ro. 11 : 17. partakest of f. of olive

FATS.

Jo. 2:24. f. shall overflow with wine
3 : 13. press is full, the f. overflow

FATTED.

1 K. 4 : 23. ten oxen, and f. fowl
Je. 46:21. hired men like f. bullocks
Lu. 15 : 27. killed f. calf, 23, 30.

FATTER, FATTEST.

Ps. 78 : 31. wrath of G. slew f-t
Da. 1 : 15. counten. appeared f-r
11 : 24. shall enter on f-t places

FAULT, S.

Ge. 41:9. I remember my f. this day
Ex. 5 : 16. f. is in thine own peo.
De. 25 : 2. to be beaten acc. to his f.
1 S. 29 : 3. have found no f. in him
2 S. 3 : 8. chargest me with a f.
Ps. 19 : 12. cleanse me fr. secret f.
59 : 4. prepare without my f.
Da. 6 : 4. could find no f. in him
Mat. 18:15. bro. trespass, tell him f.
Mk. 7 : 2. eat unwashen, found f.
Lu. 23 : 4. said, I find no f. in this man, 14. Jn. 18 : 38.-19 : 4, 6.
Ro. 9 : 19 say,Why doth he yet find
1 Co.6:7. is utterly a f. am. you [f.
Ga. 6 : 1. if man be overtak. in a f.

He. 8 : 8. For, finding f. with them
9 : † 14. off-d hims. without f. to G.
Ja. 5:16. Confess your f. one to ano.
1 Pe. 2 : 20. if when buffeted for f.
Re. 14 : 5. are without f. bef. throne

FAULTLESS.

He. 8 : 7. if first cov. had been f.
Jude 24. him able to present you f.

FAULTY.

Nu. 35 : † 31. no satisfaction for a murderer f. to die
2 S. 14 : 13. k. doth speak as one f.
Ho. 10 : 2. now shall they be found [f.

FAVOUR. [Noun.]

Ge. 39 : 21. Joseph f. in sight of
Ex. 3 : 21. I will give peo. f. in sight of Egyp., 11 : 3.-12 : 36.
De. 28 : 50. sh. not shew f. to young
33:23. O Naphtali, satisfied with f.
Jos. 11 : 20. they might have no f.
1 S. 2 : 26. Samuel was in f. with L.
Jb. 10 : 12. granted me life and f.
Ps. 5 : 12. with f. wilt compass him
30 : 5. his f. is life, weeping may
7. by f. hast made mount. stand
44 : 3. bec. hadst a f. unto them
45 : 12. even rich sh. entreat thy f.
89 : 17. in thy f. our horn exalted
106 : 4. remember me with the f.
112 : 5. A good man sheweth f.
119 : 58. I entreated thy f. with
Pr. 11:27. seeketh good procureth f.
13 : 15. Good underst-g giveth f.
14 : 9. am. righteous there is f.
35. king's f. is tow. wise servant
16 : 15. his f. is as a cloud of rain
19 : 6. Many entreat f. of prince
12. k.'s f. is as dew upon grass
22 : 1. loving f. rather to be chosen
29 : 26. Many seek the ruler's f.
31 : 30. f. is deceitful, and beauty
Ec. 9 : 11. nor f. to men of skill
Is. 26 : 10. Let f. be shewed to wick.
27 : 11. who formed will shew no f.
60 : 10. in my f. I had mercy
Je. 16 : 13. where I not shew you f.
31 : † 9. with f. will I lead them
Da. 1 : 9. G. had bro-t Dan. into f.
Lu. 2 : 52. Jesus increased in f.
Ac. 2 : 47. having f. with all people
7 : 10. gave Mos. f. in sight of Pha.
25 : 3. high priest desired f. ag. him

Find, eth, or found FAVOUR.

Ge. 18 : 3. if now I have f. f. in thy sight, 30 : 27. Nu. 11 : 15. 1 S. 20 : 29. Ne. 2 : 5. Es. 5 : 8.-7 : 3.-8 : 5.
Nu. 11 : 11. whf. have I not f. f.?
De. 24 : 1. it come to pass she fi. no f.
Ru. 2 : 13. Let me fi. f. in thy sight
1 S. 16 : 22. David hath f. f. in my
25 : 8. let the young men fi. f.
2 S. 15 : 25. if I fi. f. in eyes of L.
1 K. 11 : 19. Hadad f. f. in sight of
Pr. 3 : 4. shalt fi. f. in sight of G.
21 : 10. his neighbour f-h no f.
28 : 23. fi. more f. than he that
Can. 8:10. I was as one th. f. f. [flatt-th
Lu. 1 : 30. thou hast f. f. with G.
Ac. 7 : 46. David f. f. before God

Obtain, ed, eth. FAVOUR.

Es 2 : 15. Esther o-d f., 17.-5 : 2.
Pr. 8:35. findeth me, shall o. f. of L.
12:2. A good man o-h f. of the Lord
18 : 22. findeth a wife, o-h f. of L.

FAVOUR. [Verb.]

1 S. 29 : 6. the lords f. thee not
Ps. 35 : 27. that f. my righte. cause
102 : 13. set time to f. her is come
14. thy servants f. dust thereof
109 : 12. any to f. his fatherl. chil.

FAVOURABLE.

Ju. 21 : 22. Be f. for our sakes
Jb. 33 : 26. God will be f. unto him
Ps. 77 : 7. will the L. be f. no more?
85 : 1. thou hast been f. to thy la.

FAVOURED. [is not f.

Pr. 21 : † 10. w.cked; his neighbour
La. 4 : 16. they f. not the elders
Lu. 1 :28. Hail, thou th. art highly f.

Ill or Well FAVOURED.

Ge. 29:17. Rachel w. f. | 39 : 6. Jos-
41 : 2. w. f. kine, 4, 18. [eph w. f.
3. 7 other kine, i. f., 4, 19. 21, 27.
Da 1 : 4. Children w. f. and skilful
Na. 3 : 4. whoredoms of w. f. harlot

See EVILFAVOUREDNESS.

FAVOUREST, ETH. [go

2 S. 20 : 11. He that f-h Joab, let him
Ps. 41 : 11. By this I know th. f-t me
86 : † 2. I am one whom thou f-t

Evil FAVOUREDNESS.

De. 17 : 1. bullock wherein is e. f.

FEAR.

Ge. 9 : 2. f. of you be upon ev. beast
31 : 42. f. of Isaac had been with me
53. Jac. sware by the f. of Isaac
Ex. 15 : 16. f. shall fall upon them
23 : 27. I will send my f. before thee
De. 2 : 25. put f. of thee upon nations
11 : 25. L. sh. lay f. of you upon land
28 : 67. f. of thine heart whw. fear
1 Ch. 14 : 17. L. bro-t f. of him upon
Ezr. 3 : 3. f. upon them bec. of peo.
Ne. 6 : 14. them th. put me in f., 19.
Es. 8 : 17. f. of Jews fell upon, 9 : 2.
9 : 3. bec. f. of Mord. fell upon th.
Jb. 3 : † 25. I feared a f. and it came
4 : 6. Is not this thy f., thy confid.?
14. f. came upon me and trembl.
6 : 14. he forsaketh f. of Almighty
9 : 34. let not his f. terrify me
15 : 4. yea, thou castest off f. and
21 : 9. houses safe from f. nor rod
22 : 10. sudden f. troubleth thee
25 : 2. Dominion and f. are with him
39 : 22. He mocketh at f. is not
Ps. 5 : 7. in thy f. will I worship tow.
9 : 20. put them in f., O Lord, that
14 : 5. There were they in great f.
31 : 11. I was a f. to acquaintance
13. f. was on every side
48 : 6. f. took hold upon them there
53 : 5. were in f. where no f. was
64 : 1. preserve my life fr. f. of ene.
90 : 11. acc. to thy f. so thy wrath
105 : 38. f. of them fell upon them
119 : 38. thy serv., devoted to thy f.
Pr. 1 : 26. mock when your f. cometh
27. When your f. cometh as desola.
33. shall be quiet from f. of evil
3 : 25. Be not afraid of sudden f.
10 : 24. f. of wicked come upon him
20 : 2. f. of k. is as roaring of lion
29 : 25. f. of man bringeth snare
Can. 3 : 8. sword bec. of f. in night
Is. 7 : 25. sh. not come f. of briers
8 : 12. neither f. ye their f. nor be
13. the Lord, let him be your f.
14 : 3. L. shall give thee rest fr. f.
21 : 4. night of pleasure into f.
24 : 17. f. and the pit are upon thee
18. that fleeth from f., Je. 48 : 44.
29 : 13. their f. is taught by men
63 : 17. hardened heart from thy f.
Je. 2 : 19. that my f. is not in thee
6 : 25. f. is on every side, 20 : 10.
20 : † 3. L. hath called thy name f.
30 : 5. We have heard a voice of f.
32 : 40. put my f. in their hearts
46 : 5. f. was round about
48 : 43. f. and pit be upon thee
49 : 5. I will bring a f. upon thee
24. f. hath seized on Damascus
29. shall cry, f. is on every side
La. 3 : 47. f. and a snare is come
Eze. 21 : † 15. f. of sword ag. gates
30 : † 4. great f. shall be in Ethiopia
13. I will put a f. in land of E.
Mal. 1 : 6. if master, where is my f.?
Lu. 1 : 12. Zach. saw, f. fell upon him
65. f. came on all, 7 : 16. Ac. 2 : 43.
-5 : 5, 11.-19 : 17. Re. 11 : 11.
3 : † 14. to soldiers, Put no man in f.

Ro. 13 : 7. render f. to whom f. is due
1 Co. 2 : 3. I was with you in f.
2 Co. 7 : 11. what f.! what desire!
2 Ti. 1 : 7. not given us spirit of f.
Col. 2 : † 1. knew what great f. I have
He. 2 : 15. them who thro. f. of death
12 : 28. may serve God with godly f.
1 Pe. 1 : 17. pass time of sojourn. in f.
3 : 15. answer with meekn. and f.
1 Jn. 4 : 18. no f. in love, love cast.

For FEAR. [out f.

De. 28 : 67. f. the f. thou shalt fear
Jos. 22 : 24. not done it f. f. of thing
Ju. 9 : 21. dwelt f. f. of Abimelech
1 S. 21 : 10. fled that day f. f. of Saul
23 : 26. haste to get away f. f. of Saul
Jb. 22 : 4. reprove thee f. f. of thee?
Ps. 119 : 120. My flesh trembleth f. f.
Is. 31 : † 8. shall flee f. f. of sword
9. he shall pass to strong hold f. f.
Je. 35 : 11. f. f. of army of Chal.
Je. 37 : 11. army broken up f. f. of Pharaoh's army [Baasha
41 : 9. which Asa had made f. f. of
50 : 16. f. f. of oppressing sword
Mal. 2 : 5. f. f. whw. he feared me
Mat. 14 : 26. disciples cried out f. f.
28 : 4. f. f. of him keepers did shake
Lu. 21 : 26. hearts failing f. f.
Jn. 7 : 13. no man spake openly f. f.
19 : 38. a disciple, but secretly f. f.
20 : 19. assembled f. f. of the Jews
Re. 18 : 10. f. f. of her torment, 15.

FEAR of God.

Ge. 20 : 11. f. o. G. is not in this place
2 S. 23 : 3. just, ruling in f. o. G.
2 Ch. 20 : 29. f. o. G. on all kingd-s
Ne. 5 : 9. ought to walk in f. o. G.?
15. so did not I, bec. of f. o. G.
Ps. 36 : 1. no f. o. G. bef. his eyes
Ro. 3 : 18. no f. o. G. bef. their eyes
2 Co. 7 : 1. perf-g holiness in f. o. G.
Ep. 5 : 21. submitting in f. o. G.

FEAR of the Lord.

1 S. 11 : 7. f. o. L. on peo., 2 Ch. 17 : 10.
2 Ch. 14 : 14. f. o. L. came upon them
19 : 7. let the f. o. L. be upon you
9. do, in the f. o. L., faithfully
Jb. 28 : 28. said, f. o. L. is wisdom
Ps. 19 : 9. f. o. L. is clean, enduring
34 : 11. chil., I will teach f. o. L.
111 : 10. f. o. L. is beginn. of wisd.
Pr. 1 : 7. f. o. L. beginn. of knowl.,
29. did not choose f. o. L. [9 : 10.
2 : 5. shalt understand f. o. L.
8 : 13. f. o. L. is to hate evil
10 : 27. f. o. L. prolongeth days
14 : 26. In f. o. L. is strong confide.
27. f. o. L. is fountain of life
15 : 16. Better is little with f. o. L.
33. f. o. L. is instruc. of wisdom
16 : 6. by f. o. L. men depart fr. evil
19 : 23. f. o. L. tendeth to life
22 : 4. by the f. o. L. are riches and
23 : 17. be in f. o. L. all day long
Is. 2 : 10. hide in dust for f. o. L.
19. sh. go into caves for f. o. L.
21. into clefts of rocks for f. o. L.
11 : 2. spirit of knowl., and f. o. L.
3. of quick underst-g in f. o. L.
33 : 6. f. o. L. is his treasure
Ac. 9 : 31. walking in f. o. L. and

With FEAR.

Ps. 2 : 11. Serve the Lord w. f.
Jon. 1 : † 10. were the men w. great f.
Mat. 28 : 8. they departed w. f. and
Lu. 5 : 26. they were all filled w. f.
8 : 37. Gadarenes taken w. great f.
2 Co. 7 : 15. how w. f. you receiv. him
Ep. 6 : 5. obedient to masters w. f.
Ph. 2 : 12. work out salvation w. f.
He. 11 : 7. Noah w. f. prepared ark
1 Pe. 2 : 18. be subject to masters w. f.
3 : 2. chaste conversat. coupled w. f.
Jude 23. others save w. f. pulling

Without FEAR. [f.

Jb. 39 : 16. her labour is in vain w.

Jb.41:33. is not his like, is made w. f.
Lu. 1:74. we might serve him w. f.
1 Co. 16:10. may be with you w. f.
Ph. 1: 14. bold to speak word w. f.
Jude 12. they feast, feeding thems. [w. f.

FEARS.

Jb. 15: † 21. sound of f. in his ears
Ps. 34:4. L. deliv-d me fr. all my f.
Ec. 12: 5. when f. be in the way
Is. 66: 4. will bring f. upon them
2 Co.7:5. were fightings, within were [f.

FEAR. [Verb.]

Le. 19:3. ye sh. f. ev. man his moth.
Nu. 14: 9. neither f. people of land
De. 4: 10. they may learn to f. me
5: 29. O that they would f. me
28:58. f. this glorious name, the L.
66. thou shalt f. day and night
67. for the fear whw. thou shalt f.
Ju. 7: 10. if thou f. to go down
1 K. 8: 40. may f. thee, 2 Ch. 6:31.
43. name to f. thee. 2 Ch. 6: 33.
2 K. 17: 38. neither f. other gods
39. Lord your God ye shall f. [9.
1 Ch. 16:30. f. bef. him earth, Ps. 96:
Ne. 1: 11. desire to f. thy name
Jb. 31: 34. Did I f. a great multi.?
Ps. 23: 4. I will f. no evil, for
27:1. L. is my salv., whom sh. I f.?
31:19. goodness for them th. f. thee
40: 3. many shall see it, and f.
49:5. Whf. sho. I f. in days of evil?
52: 6. righteous shall see, and f.
60:4. given banner to them that f.
61:5. heritage of those f. thy name
64: 9. all sh. f. and declare work
72:5. f. thee long as sun endureth
86:11. unite my heart to f. thy na.
102: 15. So heathen f. thy name
119:39. Turn aw. reproach wh. I f.
63. companion of all that f. thee
74. that f. thee be glad when see me
79. Let those f. thee turn unto me
Ec 3: 14. men should f. bef. him
Is. 8: 12. neither f. ye their fear
19:16. Egypt shall be afraid and f.
25: 3. city of terrible nations sh. f.
44:11. workmen sh. f. be ashamed
59: 19. So shall f. name of Lord
60: 5. heart sh f. and be enlarged
Je. 10: 7. who would not f. thee, O
23:4. and they sh. f. no more [K.?
32: 39. one heart that may f. me
33:9. they sh. f. for all the goodn.
51: 46. lest ye f. for rumour
Da. 1: 10. prince said, I f. king
6: 26. that men f. bef. G. of Dan.
Ho. 10: 5. inhabi. of Sama. shall f.
Mi. 7: 17. move as worms, and f.
Zph. 3: 7. Surely thou wilt f. me
Hag. 1: 12. people did f. bef. Lord
Zch. 9: 5. Ashkelon sh. see it and f.
Mal. 4:2. that f. my name shall sun
Mat. 21:26. if say, Of men, we f. peo.
Lu. 12: 5. forewarn whom ye sh. f.
Ro. 8: 15. spirit of bondage to f.
11:20. Be not high-minded, but f.
2 Co. 11: 3. I f. lest as the serpent
12:20. I f. lest I shall not find you
1 Ti.5:20. rebuke, that others may f.
He. 4: 1. let us f. lest promise
12:21. Moses said, I exceedingly f.
Re. 2: 10. f. none of those things
11:18. reward to them f. thy name

FEAR God.

Ge. 42:18. This do, and live, I f. G.
Ex. 18: 21. provide such as f. G.
Le. 19: 14. but shalt f. thy G., 32.
25: 17. shalt f. thy G., 36, 43.
Jb. 1:9. Doth Job f. G. for nought?
Ps. 66: 16. hear, all ye that f. G.
Ec. 5: 7. are vanities, f. thou G.
8: 12. be well with them that f. G.
12: 13. f. G., and keep his com-ts
Is. 29: 23. shall f. the G. of Israel
Lu. 23: 40. saying, Dost not f. G.?
Ac. 13: 16. that f. G. give audience

1 Pe. 2: 17. honour men, f. G.
Re. 14: 7. f. G., give glory to him

Hear and FEAR.

De. 13: 11. Isr. sh. h. a. f., 21:21.
17: 13. all people shall h. a. f.
19:20. which remain shall h. a. f.

FEAR him.

Ge. 32: 11. deliver fr. Esau, I f. h.
De. 13: 4. walk after G., and f. h.
2 K. 17:36. h. sh. ye f., him worsh.
Jb. 37: 24. Men therefore f. h.
Ps. 22: 23. f. h. ye seed of Israel
25. pay my vows bef. them f. h.
25:14. secret of L. with them f. h.
33: 18. eye of L. upon them f. h.
34:7. angel encamp. about th. f. h.
9. is no want to them that f. h.
67: 7. all ends of earth shall f. h.
85:9. salv. is nigh them that f. h.
103:11. great mercy tow. them f. h.
13. so L. pitieth them that f. h.
17. mercy of L. upon them th. f. h.
111:5. given meat unto them f. h.
145:19. fulfil desire of them th. f. h.
147:11. tak. pleasure in them f. h.
Mat. 10:28. f. h. who is able to destroy, Lu. 12: 5.
Lu. 1: 50. mercy on them f. h.
Rev. 19:5. praise God, ye that f. h.

FEAR the Lord.

De. 6:2. thou mightest f. L. [17:39.
13. thou shalt f. L., 10:20. 2 K.
24. to f. L. for our good always
10:12. f. L., walk in his ways [13.
14: 23. learn to f. L., 17:19-31:12,
Jos. 4: 24. that ye f. L. your God
24: 14. now therefore f. L., and
1 S. 12: 14. if ye will f. L., and
24. Only f. L. and serve him [1.
1 K. 18:12. I thy serv. f. L., 2 K. 4:
2 K. 17: 28. taught them how f. L.
Ps. 15: 4. honoureth them f. L.
22: 23. Ye that f. L., praise him
33: 8. Let all the earth f. L.
34: 9. O f. L. ye his saints
115: 11. Ye that f. L. trust in L.
13. He will bless them that f. L.
118: 4. that f. L.. say, his mercy
135: 20. ye that f. L. bless L.
Pr. 3: 7. f. L., and depart fr. evil
24: 21. My son, f. L., and king
Je. 5: 24. neither say, Let us f. L.
26: 19. not f. L., and besought
Ho. 3: 5. afterward sh. Israel f. L.
Jon. 1: 9. I f. L., God of heaven

FEAR not.

Ge. 15: 1. f. n., Abraham, I am thy shield
21: 17. f. n., God hath heard lad
26:24. f. n., I am with thee [f. n.
35: 17. midwife said unto Rachel,
43: 23. said, Peace be to you, f. n.
46: 3. f. n. to go down into E. [I
50: 19. Joseph said, f. n., for am
21. f. n., I will nourish you and
Ex. 14:13. f. n., stand and see salv.
20: 20. Mo. said, f. n., G. is come
Nu. 14: 9. L. with us, f. them n.
21:34. L. said unto Moses, f. him n.
De. 1: 21. go possess land, f. n.
3: 2. f. n. Og, 22. | 20: 3. enemies
31: 6. f. n. Canaani., Jos. 10:8, 25.
8. Lord doth go bef. thee, f. n.,
Jos. 8: 1. 1 Ch. 28: 20. [f. n.
Ju. 4: 18. Turn in, my lord, to me,
6: 10. f. n. gods of Amorites
23. Peace, f. n., thou shalt not die
Ru. 3: 11. now, my daughter, f. n.
1 S. 4:20. women said unto her, f. n.
12: 20. Sam. said unto peo., f. n.
22: 23. Abide thou with me, f. n.
23:17. Jona. said unto David, f. n.
2 S. 9:7. Da. said unto Mephib., f. n.
13: 28. he said, kill Amnon, f. n.
1 K. 17: 13. said unto widow, f. n.
2 K. 6:16. f. n., more with us than
17:34. unto this day, they f. n. L.

2 K. 25:24. f. n. to serve Chal., Je. 40:9.
2 Ch. 20: 17. L. with you, f. n. [G.
Ps. 55: 19. no changes, they f. n.
64: 4. they shoot at him, and f. n.
Is. 7: 4. f. n. tails of firebrands
35: 4. to them of fearf. heart, f. n.
41:10. f. n., I am with thee, 43:5.
13. I the Lord will hold my right hand, saying unto thee, f. n.
14. f. n., thou worm Jacob
43: 1. f. n., I have redeemed thee
44: 2. f. n., O Jacob my servant, Je. 30: 10.-46: 27, 28.
8. f. ye n., have not I told thee?
51: 7. f. n. the reproach of men
54: 4. f. n., shalt not be ashamed
Je. 5: 22. f. ye n. me? saith L.
La. 3: 57. thou saidst, f. n. [looks
Eze. 3: 9. f. n., nor be dismayed at
Da. 10:12. said unto me, f. n., Dan.
19. O man greatly beloved f. n.
Joel 2: 21. f. n., O land, be glad
Zph. 3:16. it be said to Jerus., f. n.
Hag. 2:5. Spirit remaineth am. you,
Zch. 8:13. be a blessing, f. n. [f. n.
15. I will do well to Jud., f. ye n.
Mal. 3:5. witness ag. them f. n. me
Mat. 1: 20. f. n. to take thee Mary
10:26. f. them n., is nothing covered
28. f. n. them wh. kill the body
31. f. n., ye are of more value, Lu. 12: 7.
28:5. angel said, unto women, f. n.
Lu. 1:13. f. n. Zach. | 30. f. n. Mary
2:10. angel said to shepherds, f. n.
5: 10. Jesus said unto Simon, f. n.
8: 50. Jairus, f. n.
12: 32. f. n., little flock
18: 4. Tho. I f. n. God, nor regard
Jn. 12: 15. f. n., daughter of Sion
Ac. 27: 24. f. n., Paul, thou must
Re. 1: 17. f. n., I am the first and [last

Not FEAR.

Ex. 9: 30. know ye will n. f. L.
2 K. 17: 35. sh. n. f. other gods, 37.
Jb. 9: 35. would I speak, n. f. him
11: 15. steadfast thou shalt n. f.
Ps. 27: 3. tho. a host encamp, n. f.
46:2. we n. f. tho. earth be remov.
56:4. n. f. what flesh can do, 118:6.
Is. 54: 14. far fr. oppression, n. f.
Je. 10:7. Who would n. f. thee, O K.?
Am. 3: 8. lion roared, who n. f.?
Lu. 23:40. said, Dost n. thou f. G.?
He. 13:6. n. f. what man do unto me
Re. 15:4. Who shall n. f. thee, O L.

FEARED.

Ge. 19: 30. Lot f. to dwell in Zoar
26:7. Isaac f. to say, She is my wife
Ex. 2:14. Moses f. and said, this th.
9:20. He that f. the word of the L.
De. 25: 18. Amalek smote f. not G.
32: 17. to new gods your fa-s f. n.
27. Were it not that I f. wrath of
Jos. 4:14. f. Joshua as they did Mo.
Ju. 6: 27. Gideon f. | 8:20. Jether f.
1 S. 3: 15. Sam. f. to shew vision
14: 26. for the peo. f. the oath
15: 24. because I f. the people
2 S. 3: 11. Ish-bosheth f. Abner
10: 19. Syrians f. to help Ammon
12: 18. David's serv. f. to tell him
1 K. 1: 50. Adonijah f. bec. of Sol.
3:28. all Isr. heard judgm., f. king
2 K. 17:7. f. other gods | 25. f. not L.
1 Ch. 16:25. to be f. above all gods, Ps. 96: 4. [a fast
2 Ch. 20: 3. Jehosh. f. proclaimed
Jb. 32: † 6. I f. to shew mine opin.
Ps. 14: † 5. f. a great fear, 53: † 5.
76:7. Thou art to be f. | 8. earth f.
11. presents to him ought to be f.
78: 53. led them safely, so f. not
130: 4. forgiveness, that thou [be f.
Is. 41: 5. isles saw it and f.
51: 13. hast f. continually ev. day
57: 11. whom hast f. that hast lied

Je. 8 : 8. her sister Judah f. not
42 : 16. sword ye f. shall overtake
44 : 10. not humbled, nor have f.
Eze. 11 : 8. Ye have f. the sword
Da. 5 : 19. all nations f. before him
Mal. 2 : 5. for fear whw. he f. me
Mat. 14 : 5. Herod f. mult., 21 : 46.
Mk. 4 : 41. And they f. exceedingly
6 : 20. Herod f. John, knowing he
11 : 18. and the chief priests f. Jes.
32. if say, of men, they f. peo., 12:
12. Lu. 20 : 19.-22 : 2. Ac. 5:26
Lu. 9 : 34. f. as they ent. into cloud
45. f. to ask him of that saying
18 : 2. in city a judge wh. f. not G.
19 : 21. I f. thee bec. austere man
Jn. 9 : 22. spake thus, bec. f. Jews
Ac. 16 : 38. magistrates f. when they
He. 5 : 7. C. was heard in that he f.

FEARED God.

Ex. 1:17. midwives f. G., saved chil.
21. bec. they f. G., he made houses
Ne. 7:2. faithful and f. G. ab. many
Jb. 1 : 1. Job was one that f. God
Ac. 10 : 2. Cornelius was one f. G.

FEARED greatly.

Jos. 10 : 2. the Canaanites f. g.
1 S. 12 : 18. all the peo. g. f. the L.
1 K. 18 : 3. Obadiah f. the L. g.
Jb. 3 : 25. thing I g. f. is come
Ps. 89:7. G. is g. to be f. in assem.
Mat. 27:54. centurion and they f. g.

FEARED the Lord.

Ex. 14:31. people f. L. and bel. Mo.
2 K. 17 : 32. So they f. L., 33, 41.
Ho. 10:3. no king, bec. we f. not L.
Jon. 1 : 16. men f. L. exceedingly
Mal. 3:16. f. L. spake oft one to ano.,
book of remem. for them f. L.

FEAREST.

Ge. 22 : 12. now I know thou f. G.
Is. 57 : 11. and thou f. me not?
Je. 22 : 25. into hand of them thou [f.

FEARETH.

1 K. 1 : 51. Adonijah f. king Sol.
Jb. 1 : 8. Job, one that f. G., 2 : 3.
Ps. 25 : 12. What man is he f. L.?
112 : 1. Blessed is the man f. L.
128 : 1. Blessed is every one f. L.
4. the man be blessed that f. L.
Pr. 13 : 13. f. com. t be rewarded
14 : 2. walketh in uprightn. f. L.
16. wise man f. depart. fr. evil
28 : 14. Happy is man f. always
31 : 30. woman f. L. be praised
Ec. 7 : 18. f. G. shall come forth of
8 : 13. bec. wicked f. not before G.
9 : 2. as he that f. an oath
Is. 50 : 10. Who am. you f. the L.?
Ac. 10 : 22. just, and one that f. G.
35. he that f. him, is accepted
13 : 26. whosoever amo. you f. G.
1 Jn. 4 : 18. that f. is not perf. in [love

FEARING.

Jos. 22 : 25. our chil. cease fr. f. L.
Mk. 5 : 33. the woman f. came
Ac. 23:10. capt. f. lest Paul be pull.
27 : 17. f. lest fall into quicks., 29.
Ga. 2 : 12. f. them of circumcision
Col. 3:22. in singleness of heart f. G.
He. 11 : 27. not f. wrath of king

FEARFUL, LY.

Ex. 15:11. who like thee, f. in praises
De. 20:8. f. let him return. Ju. 7 : 3.
28 : 58. mayest fear this f. name
Is. 35 : 4. say to them of a f. heart
Mat. 8:26. Why f. O of little faith?
Mk. 4 : 40. said, Why are ye so f.?
Lu. 21 : 11. f. sights in divers plac.
He. 10 : 27. f. looking for of judgm.
31. f. to fall into hands of God
Re. 21 : 8. f. shall have part in lake
Ps. 139:14. f-y wonderfully made

FEARFULNESS.

Ps. 55:5. f. and trembling are come
Is. 21 : 4. f. affrighted me
33 : 14. f. surprised hypocrites

FEAST.

Ge. 19:3. Lot made a f. | 21:8. Ab. a f.
26 : 30. Isaac f. | 29 : 22. Laban
40:20. Pha. made a f. unto his serv-ts
Ex. 5 : 1. hold a f. unto me, 10 : 9.
12 : 14. shall keep it a f., Le. 23:39,
13 : 6. seventh day be a f. [41.
23:14. Three times keep a f. in year
16. the f. of harvest, (2) 34 : 22.
32 : 5. Aa. said, To-morrow is a f.
Nu. 28 : 17. the 15th day is the f.
29 : 12. ye shall keep a f. to the L.
De. 16 : 14. shalt rejoice in thy f.
Ju. 14 : 10. Samson made f.
12. declare it within 7 days of f.
17. she wept while their f. lasted
21 : 19. a f. of L. in Shiloh yearly
1 S. 9 : † 12. f. to day in high place
20 : † 6. yearly f. for all the family
25 : 36. Nabal held a f. like a king
2 S. 3 : 20. David made Abner a f.
1 K. 3 : 15. Sol. made a f., 8 : 65.
8:2. all men of Isr. assembled at f.
12:32. Jerob. ordained f. like unto f.
33. ordained a f. to chil. of Isr.
2 Ch. 5:3. f. in 7th month, Ne. 8:14.
7:8. Sol. kept the f. seven days, 9.-
30 : 22. Ne. 8 : 18. Eze. 45 : 25.
Es. 1 : 3. Ahas. made a f., 5.-2 : 18.
9. Vashti made a f. | 8 : 17. Jews
Pr. 15 : 15. merry heart a contin. f.
Ec. 10 : 19. f. is made for laughter
Is. 25 : 6. L. make to all peo. a f.
Je. 16 : † 5. enter not mourning f.
Eze. 45:21. f. of 7 days : unleav. bread
23. seven days of f. he sh. prepare
Da. 5 : 1. Belshazzar made a gr. f.
Mat. 27:15. at that f. gov. was wont
to release prisoner, Mk. 15 : 6.
Lu. 2 : 42. went up aft. custom of f.
5 : 29. Levi made him a great f.
14 : 13. when makest f. call poor
23 : 17. must release one at the f.
Jn. 2 : 8. bear to governor of the f.
9. When ruler of f. tasted water
4 : 45. Galileans having seen all he
did at f., for they unto f.
5 : 1. Aft. this was a f. of the Jews
6 : 4. the passover a f. of the Jews
7:8. Go ye up unto this f. I go not
10. then went he up unto the f.
11. the Jews sought him at the f.
14. about midst of f. Jes. taught
37. In last day, th. gr. day of f.
10 : 22. it was at f. of dedication
11:56. think ye, he not come to f.?
12:12. much peo. th. were come to f.
20. certain Greeks th. came to f.
13 : 29. buy we have need of ag. f.
Ac. 18 : 21. I must keep this f.
1 Co. 5:8. keep f. not with old leav.
10 : 27. if any believe not bid you [to f.

FEAST day, days.

Ho. 2 : 11. cause her f. d-s to cease
9:5. what will ye do in d. of the f.
Am. 5:21. I hate, despise your f. d-s
Mat. 26:5. Not on the f. d., Mk. 14:2.
Jn. 2:23. in the f. d. many believed

FEAST of the passover.

Ex. 34 : 25. nor sacrif. of f. o. p.
be left [p., Mk. 14 : 1.
Mat. 26 : 2. after two days is f. o.
Lu. 2 : 41. ev. year at f. o. p. his
parents [his hour
Jn. 13 : 1. bef. f. o. p. Jesus knew

Solemn FEAST.

De. 16:15. Seven days shalt keep s. f.
Ps. 81:3. blow trumpet on s. f. day
La. 2 : 7. noise is in the s. f. day
Ho. 12 : 9. dwell as in days of s. f.

FEAST of tabernacles.

Le. 23 : 34. day shall be f. o. t.
De. 16 : 13. Thou shalt observe f.
o. t. seven days
16. three times appear in f. o. t.,
31 : 10. 2 Ch. 8 : 13.
Ezr. 3:4. kept f. o. t. as it is written
Zch. 14:16. sh. go up to keep f. o. t.
18. heathen that come not to
keep f. o. t., 19.
Jn. 7:2. Jews' f. o. t. was at hand

FEAST of unleavened bread.

Ex. 12 : 17. ye shall observe f. o.
u. b., 23 : 15.-34 : 18.
Le. 23 : 6. on 15th day is f. o. u. b.
De. 16 : 16. appear in f. o. u. b., 2
Ch. 8 : 13. [keep f. o. u. b.
2 Ch. 30 : 13. people assembled to
21. children of Isr. kept f. o. u. b.
35 : 17. f. o. u. b. sev. days, Ezr.
6 : 22. Eze. 45 : 21.
Mat. 26 : 17. first day of f. o. u. b.
disciples came
Mk. 14 : 1. was f. o. u. b., Lu. 22:1.

FEAST of weeks.

Ex. 34 : 22. shalt obs. f. o. w., De.
16 : 10. [o. w.
De. 16 : 16. all males appear in f.
2 Ch. 8 : 13. offered burnt off. in f.

FEASTS. [o. w.

Le. 23 : 2. these are my f., 4, 37, 44.
Ps. 35 : 16. hypocrit. mockers in f.
Is. 5 : 12. pipe, and wine in their f.
Je. 51:39. In heat I will make f.
Eze. 45 : 17. prince's part off-gs in f.
46 : 11. in f. meat off. be an ephah
Am. 8 : 10. your f. into mourning
Zch. 8 : 19. shall be joy, cheerful f.
Mat. 23 : 6. they love the upperm.
rooms at f. and, Mk. 12 : 39.
Lu. 20 : 46.
Jude 12. spots in your f. of charity

Appointed FEASTS.

Is. 1 : 14. your a. f. my soul hateth

Set FEASTS. [s. f.

Nu. 29 : 39. these ye sh. do in your
1 Ch. 23 : 31. offer on s. f., Ezr. 3:5.
2 Ch. 31 : 3. k.'s portion for s. f.
Ne. 10:33. charged for off-gs for s. f.

Solemn FEASTS.

Nu. 15 : 3. when make offer. in s. f.
2 Ch. 2 : 4. build h. for off-g on s. f.
8:13. offering on s. f. 3 times a yr.
La. 1 : 4. bec. none come to the s. f.
2 : 6. caused s. f. to be forgotten
Eze. 36:38. as flock of Jerus. in s. f.
46 : 9. peo. come bef. Lord in s. f.
Ho. 2 : 11. cause to cease her s. f.
Na. 1 : 15. O Judah, keep thy s. f.
Mal. 2 : 3. even dung of your s. f.

FEAST, ED.

Jb. 1 : 4. his sons f-d in their houses
2 Pe. 2 : 13. sporting, while they f.
Jude 12. spots, when they f. wi. you

FEASTING.

Es. 9 : 17. made it a day of f., 18.
22. should make them days of f.
Jb. 1 : 5. when days of f. were gone
Ec. 7:2. than to go to the hou. of f.
Je. 16 : 8. not go into house of f.

FEATHERED. See FOWL.

FEATHERS.

Le. 1 : 16. pluck his crop with his f.
Jb. 39 : 13. gavest f. to ostrich?
Ps. 68 : 13. f. covered with gold
91 : 4. sh. cover thee with his f.
Eze. 17 : 3. an eagle, full of f., 7.
Da. 4 : 33. his hairs like eagles' f.

FED.

Ge. 30 : 36. Jacob f. Laban's flock
36 : 24. as he f. asses of Zibeon
41:2. seven kine f. in meadow, 18.
47 : 17. he f. them with bread
48 : 15. God who f. me all my life
Ex. 16 : 32. bread wherew. I f. you
De. 8 : 3. he f. thee with manna
16. Who f. thee in the wilderness
2 S. 20 : 3. put concubines and f.
1 K. 18 : 4. he f. them wi. bread, 13.
1 Ch. 27 : 29. herds th. f. in Sharon
Ps. 37 : 3. verily thou shalt be f.
78 : 72. he f. them, acc. to integ.
81:16. f. them with finest of wheat

Is. 1: 11. am full of fat of f. beasts
Je. 5: 7. when I had f. them to full
8. were as f. horses in morning
Eze. 16: 19. honey wherew. I f. thee
34: 3. ye eat fat kill them are f.
8. sheph-s fed thems., f. not flock
Da. 4: 12. all flesh was f. with it
5: 21. they f. Neb. with grass, like
Zch. 11: 7. staves, and I f. flock
Mat.25:37.when saw we and f. thee?
Mk. 5: 14. f. swine fled, Lu. 8: 34.
Lu. 16: 21. to be f. with crumbs th.
1 Co. 3: 2. I have f. you with milk

FEE.

Da. 2: † 6. ye shall receive of me f.
5: † 17. give thy f. to another, yet

FEEBLE, FEEBLER.

Ge. 30:42. cattle f. he put not in, so
the f-r were Laban's
De. 25: 18. Amalekites smote all f.
1 S. 2: 5. hath many children, is f.
2 S.4:1. Ish-bosheth's hands were f.
2 Ch. 28:15.carried all f. upon ass-s
Ne. 4: 2. What do these f. Jews?
Jb. 4: 4. strengthened the f. knees
Ps. 38: 8. I am f. and sore broken
105: 37. not f. person am. tribes
Pr. 30: 26. conies are but a f. folk
Is. 16: 14. remnant shall be very f.
35:3.weak hands, confirm f. knees
Je. 6:24. heard fame, our hands wax
49: 24. Damascus is waxed f. [f.
50:43. k. of Bab.'s hands waxed f.
Eze. 7: 17. All hands sh. be f.,21:7.
Zch. 12: 8. he that is f. be as David
1 Co. 12: 22. members which seem
He. 12: 12. lift up f. knees [more f.

FEEBLEMINDED.

1 Th. 5: 14. brethren comfort the f.

FEEBLENESS.

Je. 47: 3. fa-s not look back for f.

FEED. [Verb.]

Ge. 37: 12. went to f. fa.'s flock,13.
16. tell me, where they f. flocks
46: 32. their trade been to f. cattle
Ex. 22: 5. f. in another man's field
34: 3. nei. let flocks f. bef. mount
1S.17:15 fr. Saul to f. his fa.'s sheep
2 S. 5: 2. shalt f. my people Israel
7:7. I com-d to f. Israel,1 Ch 17:6.
1 K. 17: 4. com-d ravens to f. thee
Jb. 24: 2. take away flocks and f.
20. worms sh. f. sweetly on him
Ps. 28: 9. f. them, and lift up
49:14. in grave, death sh. f. on th.
78: 71. he bro-t David to f. Jacob
Pr. 10: 21. lips of righteous f. many
Can. 4: 5. roes which f. am. lilies
6: 2. beloved gone to f. in gardens
Is. 5: 17. lambs f. aft. their manner
11: 7. cow and the bear shall f.
14: 30. firstb. of the poor shall f.
27: 10. shall calf f. and lie down
30: 23. cattle sh. f. in large past.
40: 11. sh. f. his flock as sheph.
49: 9. They shall f. in the ways
58:14. f. thee with heritage of Jac.
61: 5. strangers sh. f. your flocks
65:25. wolf and lamb sh. f. togeth.
Je.2:†16. chil. of Noph f. on crown
3: 15. pastors who shall f. you
6: 3. sh. f. every one in his place
23: 2. ag. pastors that f. my peo.
4. will set up shepherds sh. f. th.
50: 19. Israel shall f. on Carmel
La. 4: 5. f. delicately are desolate
Eze. 34:2. Woe to sheph-s f. thems.
3. ye eat fat, but f. not flock
10. nei. shall shepherds f. thems.
13. f. them upon mts. of Isr., 14.
23. my serv. David shall f. them
Da. 11: 26. f. of his meat destr. him
Ho. 4: 16. L. will f. them as a lamb
9: 2. flour and winepress not f. th.
Jon. 3: 7. let them not f. nor drink
Mi. 5: 4. sh. f. in strength of Lord
7: 14. let them f. in Bashan

Zph. 2: 7. they shall f. thereupon
3:13. they sh. f. none make afraid
Zch. 11: 9. said I, I will not f. you
16. shall not f. that th. standeth
Mat. 2: † 6. of thee a Gov. th. sh. f.
Lu. 15: 15. he sent him to f. swine
Ac. 20: 28. take heed to f. church
1 Co.9:†13.they f.of things of temple
13:3. tho. I give my goods to f. poor
Re. 7: 17. Lamb shall f. them
12:6. should f. her there 1260 days

FEED. [Imperatively.]

Ge. 25: 30. f. me with red pottage
29: 7. water ye sheep, and f. them
1 K. 22: 27. f. him with bread and
water of affliction, 2 Ch. 18: 26.
Pr. 30: 8. f. me with food conven.
Can. 1: 8. f. thy kids beside tents
Mi. 7: 14. f. thy peo. with thy rod
Zch. 11: 4. f. flock of slaughter [17.
Jn.21:15.f. my lambs | 16. f. sheep,
Ro. 12: 20. if enemy hunger f. him
1 Pe. 5:2. f. the flock of G. am. you

I will FEED.

Ge. 30: 31. I w. again f. thy flock
2 S. 19: 33. I w. f. thee in Jerusa.
Is. 49:26. I w. f. them oppress thee
58: 14. I w. f. thee with heritage
Je.9:15 I w. f. with wormw..23:15.
Eze. 34:13. I w. f. them upon mt-s
14. I w. f. them in a good past.
15. I w. f. my flock, and cause
16. I w. f. the fat with judgment
Zch. 11: 7. I w. f. flock of slaugh.
9. Then said I, I w. not f. you

FEEDER.

Ge. 4:† 2. Abel was f. of sheep, Cain

FEEDEST, ETH.

Ps. 80: 5. f-t with the bread of tears
Pr. 15: 14. the mouth of fools f. on
28:†7. he that f. glutt-s, shameth
Can. 1: 7. tell me where thou f-t
2: 16. my belov. f. am. lilies, 6: 3.
Is. 44:20. He f. on ashes, a deceived
Ho. 12: 1. Ephraim f. on wind
Mat. 6: 26. heavenly Fath. f. them
Lu. 12: 24. ravens sow not, God f.
1 Co. 9: 7. who f. flock, eateth not

FEEDING. [milk

Ge. 37: 2. Joseph was f. his flock
Jb. 1: 14. oxen ploughing, asses f.
Eze. 34:10. them to cease fr. f. flock
Na. 2: 11. where f. place of lions?
Mat. 8:30.swine f.,Mk.5:11.Lu.8:32.
Lu. 17: 7. having servant f. cattle
Jude 12. f. thems. with. fear, clouds

FEEL.

Ge. 27: 12. My father will f. me
21. Come, th. I may f. thee, son
Ju. 16: 26. th. I may f. the pillars
Jb. 20: 20. he shall not f. quietness
Ps. 58: 9. Bef. pots can f. thorns
Ec. 8:5. keepeth com-t sh. f. no evil
Ac.17:27. if haply they might f. aft.

FEELING.

Ep. 4: 19. being past f. given thems.
He. 4: 15. with f. of our infirmities

FEET. [f.

Ge. 29: † 1. then Jac. lifted up his
49: 10. lawgiver fr. betw. his f.
33. Jacob gathered up f. in bed
Ex. 3: 5. shoes off thy f., Ac.7:33.
11: † 8. get out, and peo. at thy f.
12: 11. eat passo. with shoes on f.
Le. 11: 21. have legs above their f.
23. creeping things wh. have 4 f.
42. whatsoever hath more f.
De. 2: 28. will pass thro. on my f.
11: † 6. all substance at their f.
28: 57. young one fr. betw. her f.
33: 3. and they sat down at thy f.
Jos.3:15. f. of priests dipped in Jor.
4: 3. priests' f. stood firm, 9. [f.
9: 5. old shoes, clouted upon their
10:24. put f. upon necks of kings
14: 9. land thy f. have trodden
Ju. 1: † 7. thumbs and f. cut off

Ju. 3: 24. surely he covereth his f.
4:15. Sisera fled away on his f., 17.
5: † 15. Barak was sent on his f.
27. at her f. bowed, at her f. dead
Ru. 3:4. uncover his f. lay down, 7.
8. behold a woman lay at his f.
1 S. 2: 9. will keep f. of his saints
14:13.Jona. climbed on han. and f.
24: 3. Saul went in to cover his f.
25: † 27. young men th. walk at f.
†42. Abig. with five damsels at f.
2 S. 2: † 18. Asahel was light of f.
3: 34. nor thy f. put into fetters
4: 4. was lame of his f., 9: 3, 13.
12. cut off their hands and f.
19: 24. Mephi. had not dressed f.
22:34. he maketh my f. like hind's
f., Ps. 18: 33. Ha. 3: 19. [36.
37. so my f. did not slip, Ps. 18:
1 K. 2:5. blood of war in shoes on f.
14: 6. Ahijah heard sound of her f.
12. f. enter city, child shall die
15:23.diseased in his f.,2 Ch.16:12.
2 K. 3: † 9. no wat. for cattle at f.
4: 27. she caught him by the f.
6:32.sound of his mast.'s f. behind
9:35. found no more of her than f.
13: 21. dead man stood upon his f.
18:†27. may drink water of their f.
21:8. nor f. of Isr. move any more
1 Ch. 28: 2. Da. stood upon his f.
Ne. 9: 21. not old, f. swelled not
Jb. 12: 5. ready to slip with his f.
13: 27. my f. in stocks, 33: 11.
27. a print upon heels of my f.
18: 8. cast into net by his own f.
11. terrors sh. drive him to his f.
29:15.to blind, f. was I to the lame
30: 12. youth, push away my f.
39: † 21. his f. dig in the valley
Ps. 22: 16. pierced my hands and f.
25: 15. he sh. pluck my f. out of
31: 8. set my f. in a large room
40:2. he set my f. upon rock, and
56:13.wilt deliver my f. fr. falling?
66:9. suff-h not our f. to be moved
73: 2. my f. were almost gone
74: 3. Lift up thy f. unto desolat-s
105: 18. f. they hurt with fetters
115: 7. f. have they, but walk not
116: 8. hast deliv. my f. fr. falling
119:59.turned my f. unto testimo.
101. I refrained my f. fr. evil way
105. Thy word is lamp unto my f.
122:2.f. sh. stand within thy gates
Pr. 1:16. f. run to evil, 6:18. Is. 59:
4: 26. Ponder path of thy f. [7.
5: 5. her f. go down to death
6:13. wicked man speak. wi. his f.
28. go upon coals f. not be burn.?
7: 11. her f. abide not in her hou.
19: 2. hasteth with f. sin-h [age
26: 6. cutteth off f. drinketh dam-
29: 5. flatterer spreadeth net for f.
Can. 7: 1. How beautiful are thy f.
Is. 3: 16. making tinkling with f.
18. take aw. ornaments about f.
6: 2. with twain he covered his f.
7: 20. Lord shall shave hair of f.
23:7. her own f. sh. carry her afar
26: 6. f. of poor sh. tread it down
32: 20 that send forth f.of the ox
41:3.way he had not gone with his
49:23. sh. lick up dust of thy f. [f.
52: 7. the f. of him that bringeth
good tidings, Na. 1: 15.
60:13. make place of my f. glorious
Je. 13:16. bef. f. stumble upon mts.
14: 10. have not refrained their f.
18: 22. digged pit, hid snares for f.
38: 22. thy f. are sunk in the mire
La. 1: 13. he spread a net for my f.
Eze. 1: 7. their f. were straight f.
2:1.said,Son of man, stand upon f.
2. Spirit set me upon my f., 3:24.
16:25. hast opened thy f. to ev.one
24: 17. put thy shoes upon thy f.

Eze. 24 : 23. tires shall be on your heads, shoes upon your f.
25:6. bec. hast stamped with the f.
32: 2. troublest waters with thy f.
34:18 foul the residue with your f.
19. what ye have fouled with f.
37 : 10. lived and stood upon f.
Da. 2 : 33. his f. part of iron, 42.
34. stone smote image upon his f.
41. thou sawest f. part of clay
7 : 4. made stand upon f. as man
7. stamped the residue with f. of it, 19. [Re. 1 : 15.-2 : 18.
10 : 6. his f. like polished brass,
Na. 1 : 3. clouds are dust of his f.
Zch. 14:4. his f. upon mt. of Olives
12. consume while stand upon f.
Mat. 10 : 14. when ye depart shake off dust of f., Mk.6:11. Lu. 9:5.
15 : 30. cast the lame at Jesus' f.
18:8. than having two f. to be cast
28 : 9. held him by f. and worsh.
Lu. 1:79. to guide our f. into way of
7 : 38. she kissed his f. and anoint.
45. woman not ceased to kiss my f.
8:35. found man sitting at f. of Jes.
41. Jairus fell down at f. of Jesus
10 : 39. Mary, who sat at Jesus' f.
15:22. ring on hand, shoes on his f.
24:39. Behold my hands and my f.
40. he shewed them his f. [3.
Jn. 11:2. wiped his f. with hair, 12:
12:3. Mary anointed the f. of Jesus
13:9. Lord, not my f. only but ha.
20 : 12. angel at head, other at f.
Ac. 3 : 7. his f. received strength
4:35. at apostles' f., 37.-5:2. [husb.
5 : 9. f. of them who buried thy
7:58. laid clothes at a yo. man's f.
13:25. shoes of f. not worthy to loose
51. shook off dust of their f.
14 : 8. sat a man impotent in his f.
10. Paul said, Stand upright on f.
16 : 24. made f. fast in stocks
21 : 11. Agabus bound his own f.
22 : 3. bro-t up at f. of Gamaliel
26 : 16. rise, and stand upon thy f.
Ro. 3 : 15. f. are swift to shed blood
10 : 15. f. of them that preach gos.
1 Co. 12:21. nor head to f. I no need
Ep. 6:15. your f. shod with prepara.
He. 12 : 13. straight paths for f.
Re. 3 : 9. them worship bef. thy f.
10 : 1. angel, his f. as pillars of fire
11 : 11. two witn. stood upon f.
13 : 2. his f. were as f. of bear [f.
22:8. I fell down to worship bef his

At his FEET. [a.h.f.

Ex. 4:25. Zipporah cast the foreskin
Ju. 4 : 10. Barak with 10,000 **a.h.f.**
Ru. 3 : 14. she lay **a.h.f.** until the
1 S. 25 : 24. Abigail fell **a.h.f.** and
2 K. 4:37. wom. of Shunem fell **a.h.f.**
Es. 8:3. Es. fell **a.h.f.** and besought
Ha. 3:5. burning coals went **a.h.f.**
Mat. 18 : 29. fellow serv. fell **a.h.f.**
Mk. 5 : 22. Jairus. fell **a. h. f.**
7:25. Syrophe-n woman fell **a.h.f.**
Lu. 7 : 38. she stood **a.h.f.** behind
Jn. 11 : 32. Mary fell down **a. h. f.**
Ac. 5 : 10. Sapphira fell **a.h.f.** and
10 : 25. Cornelius fell down **a.h.f.**
Re. 1 : 17. saw, I fell **a.h.f.** as dead
19:10. I fell **a.h.f.** to worship him

FEET with sole, s.

De. 11:24. s-s of f. tread sh. be yours
Jos. 3:13. soon as s-s of priests' f., 4 : 18. [f.
1 K. 5:3. L. put them und. s-s of his
2 K. 19 : 24. s. of my f. have dried, Is. 37 : 25.
Is. 60 : 14. sh. bow at s-s of thy f.
Eze. 1 : 7. s. of f. like calf's [filed
43 : 7. pla. of s-s of f. no more de-
Mal. 4:3. be ashes under s-s of your

Under FEET. [f.

Ex. 24:10. u. his f. a sapphire stone
2 S. 22:10. darkness **u. f.**, Ps. 18: 9.
39. they are fallen **u.** my f.
Ps. 8:6. hast put all things **u.** his f., 1 Co. 15 : 27. Ep. 1 : 22.
47 : 3. sh. subdue nations **u.** our f.
91 : 13. dragon thou trample **u.** f.
Is. 14 : 19. as carcass trodden **u.** f.
28 : 3. drunkards sh. be trodd. **u.f.**
La. 3 : 34. crush **u.** f. all prisoners
Mat. 7 : 6. lest trample them **u.** f.
Ro. 16 : 20. bruise Satan **u.** your f.
1 Co. 15: 25. put all enem. **u.** his f.
He. 2 : 8. put all in subjee. **u.** his f.
Re. 12:1. clothed with sun, moon **u.f.**

FEET with wash, ed.

Ge. 18 : 4. water be fetched, **w.** f.
19 : 2. tarry all night, **w.** your f.
24:32. Laban gave wat. to **w.** his f.
43:24. gave wat., they **w-d** their f.
Ex. 30 : 19. Aaron and sons shall **w.** their hands and f., 21.-40:31.
Ju. 19 : 21. Lev. and concu. **w-d** f.
1 S. 25 : 41. to **w.f.** of servants of
2 S. 11 : 8. Uriah, Go, **w.** thy f.
Ps. 58 : 10. **w.f.** in blood of wicked
Can. 5:3. have **w-d** my f. how shall I
Lu. 7 : 38. to **w.** his f. with tears
44. she hath **w-d** my f. with tears
Jn. 13:5. he began to **w.** disciples' f.
6. Lord dost thou **w.** my f.?
8. saith, Thou shalt never **w.** my f.
10. needeth not save to **w.** his f.
12. So after he had **w-d** their f. he said to them [your f.
14. If I your Master have **w-d**
1 Ti. 5:10. if she have **w-d** saints' f.

FEIGN.

2 S. 14 : 2. f. thyself a mourner
1 K. 14:5. sh. f. herself another wom.
Lu. 20 : 20. sho. f. thems. just men

FEIGNED, EST.

1 S. 21 : 13. David f. himself mad
2 S. 22 : † 45. strangers shall yield f. obedience, Ps. 18 : † 44.
1 K. 14 : 6. why f-t thou thyself to be another? [heart
Ne. 6 : 8. thou f-t them out of own
Ps. 17 : 1. prayer goeth not of f. lips
66 : † 3. enemies sh. yield f. obedi.
81 : † 15. haters of L yielded f. obedience [andise
2 Pe. 2:3. with f. words make merch-

FEIGNEDLY. [f.

Je. 3 : 10. hath turned unto me but

FE'LIX. [F.

Ac. 23:24. may bring Paul safe unto
26. Lysias to excellent gov. F.
24:3. we accept it, most noble F., 22.
24. when F. came with his wife
25. as Paul reasoned, F. trembled
27. F. left Paul bound, 25 : 14.

FELL.

Ge. 4:5. Cain wroth, his counten. f.
14 : 10. kings of Sod. and Gom. f.
15 : 12. a deep sleep f. upon Abram
25 : † 18. Ishm. f. in presence of
33 : 4. Esau f. on his bro.'s neck
44:14. Joseph's brethren f. bef. him
45:14. Joseph f. upon Benj.'s neck
46 : 29. Jacob f. on Joseph's neck
Ex. 32 : 28. f. of people 3000 men
Le. 16:9. goat upon wh. L.'s lot f., 10.
Nu. 11 : 4. multitude f. a lusting
9. dew f. upon camp, manna f.
14 : 5. Moses and Aaron f., 16: 22. 45.-20 : 6. [12,000
Jos. 8 : 25. all that f. that day, were
11:7. Josh. came and f. upon them
16:1. lot of chil. of Jo. f. fr. Jord.
17:5. there f. 10 portions to Manas.
22 : 20. wrath f. on congr. [ra f.
Ju. 4:16. Sisera's host f. | 5:27. Sise-
7 : 13. a cake smote tent that it f.
8 : 10. for there f. 120,000 men
12: 6. f. of Ephraimites 42,000
16 : 30. the house f. upon the lords
20 : 44. f. of Benj. 18,000 men
1 S. 4 : 10. f. of Isr. 30,000 footmen
18. Eli f. from his seat backward
11 : 7. fear of Lord f. on people
14 : 13. Philistines f. bef. Jona.
19 : † 24. Saul prophesied, and f.
22 : 18. Doeg f. upon the priests
25 : 24. Abigail f. at David's feet
28:20. Saul f. straightw on the earth
29 : 3. no fault since he f. unto me
30 : 13. three days agone I f. sick
31:4. Saul took a sword f. upon it
5. his armourbearer f., 1 Ch. 10 : [4, 5.
2 S. 4:4. Mephibosheth f.
11 : 17. f. some of people of David
13 : 2. Amnon f. sick for his sister
20 : 8. Joab's sword f. out, as he
21 : 9. they f. all seven together
22. f. by hand of Da., 1 Ch. 20:8.
1 K. 2:25. Benaiah f. upon Adonijah
32. f. upon two men more righte.
34. Benaiah f. upon Joab
46. upon Shimei [David
12 : † 19. so Israel f. from house of
14 : 1. Abijah son of Jerob. f. sick
17:17. the son of the woman f. sick
18:38. fire of Lord f. and consumed
20 : 30. a wall f. upon 27,000 men
2 K. 1 : 13. captain f. on knees before Elijah and besought him
2:13. took mantle of Elijah that f.
4 : 8. it f. on day Elisha passed, 11.
18. it f. on a day the child went
37. Shunammite f. at his feet and bowed herself
6:5. the axe head f. into the water
6. man of G. said, Where f. it?
7 : 20. so it f. peo. trode upon him
25 : 11. fugitives that f. away to k.
1 Ch. 5 : 10. Hagarites, who f. by
12 : 19. f. some of Manas. to Da.
21 : 14. f. of Israel 70,000 men
26 : 14. lot eastw. f. to Shelemiah
27 : 24. f. wrath for it against Isr.
2 Ch. 15 : 9. f. to Da. out of Israel
17:10. fear of L. f. upon all kingd-s
20 : 18. inhabi. of Jerus. f. bef. L.
21 : 19. his bowels f. out by sicko.
25 : 13. soldiers of Israel f. upon
Ezr. 9 : 5. I f. upon my knees [9:2.
Es. 8:17. fear of Jews f. upon them,
9:3. fear of Mordecai f. upon them
Jb. 1: 15. Sabeans f. upon the asses
17. Chaldeans f. upon camels, and carried them away
19. the house f. upon young men
Ps. 27:2. foes to eat my flesh, they f.
78 : 64. Their priests f. by sword
105 : 38. fear of Israel f. on Egypt
Je. 39 : 9. f. away, that f. to him,
46:16. one f. upon another [52:15.
La. 1:7. her peo. f. into hand of ene.
5 : 13. children f. under the wood
Eze. 8:1. hand of L. f. upon me, 11:5.
39 : 23. f. they all by the sword
Da. 4 : 31. f. a voice from heaven
7 : 20. came, before whom three f.
10: 7. great quaking f. upon them
Jon. 1:7. and the lot f. upon Jonah
Mat. 7 : 25. the house f. not | 27 it f., Lu. 6:49. [4:4. Lu. 8:5.
13:4 seed f. by the wayside, Mk.
5. some f. upon stony places, Mk. 4:5. Lu. 8:6. [4:7. Lu. 8:7, 14.
7. And some f. among thorns, Mk.
8. f. into good gro., Mk. 4 : 8. Lu.
Mk. 5 : 22. Jairus f. at his feet [8:8.
7:25. Syroph-n woman f. at his feet
9 : 20. he f. on ground wallowed
14 : 35. Jesus f. on the ground
Lu. 1 : 12. fear f. upon Zacharias
8 : 23. as sailed, Jesus f. asleep
10 30. a man f. among thieves, 36.
13: 4. upon wh. tower in Siloam f.
15 : 20. his father f. on his neck
16 : 21. crumbs which f. from rich
Jn. 18 : 6. went backward and f.
Ac. 1 : 25. Judas by transgression f.

Ac.1:26.lots,and lot f.upon Matthias
7: 60. had said this, he f. asleep
9:4. Saul f. to the earth and heard
18. f. from his eyes as scales
10: 10. Peter f. into a trance
44. H.Ghost f. on them all,11:15.
12: 7. chains f. off Peter's hands
13: 11. there f. on him a mist
36 Da. f. on sleep saw corruption
19: 17. fear f. on all Jews at Eph.
20: 10. Paul f. on Eutychus
37. they all f. on Paul's neck
22: 7. I f. unto the ground, and
Ro. 11: 22. on them wh. f. severity
15: 3. reproaches of them f. on me
1 Co. 10: 8. f. in one day 23,000
He. 3:17. whose carcasses f. in wild.
2 Pe. 3: 4. since fathers f. asleep
Re. 1: 17. I f. at his feet as dead
6: 13. And the stars of heaven f.
8: 10. f. a great star from heaven
11: 11. great fear f. upon them wh.
13. tenth of city f. by earthquake
16: 2. there f. a grievous sore
19. divided,and cities of nations f.
21. f. upon men great hail out of
19: 10. I f. at his feet to worship
See FACE, FACES.

FELL down. [f.d.

Nu. 22: 27. when ass saw angel, she
De.9: 18. And I f.d. bef. Lord, 25.
Jos.6:20. peo. shouted the wall f.d.
Ju. 5: 27. bowed there he f.d. dead
19:26. concubine f. d. at door of h.
1 S.17: 52. Philis. f. d. by the way
31:1. Isr. f.d. in Gilboa, 1 Ch.10:1.
2 S. 2: 16. so they f. d. together
23. Asahel f.d. there, and died
18:28.Ahimaaz f.d. | 19:18.Shimei
2 K. 1:2. Ahaziah f.d. thro. lattice
1 Ch. 5: 22. there f. d. many slain
2 Ch.13:17. f.d. of Isr. 500,000 men
Es. 8: 3. Esther f.d. at Ahas-s' feet
Jb. 1: 20. Job f.d.and worshipped
Ps. 107: 12. they f.d., none to help
Da. 3:7. all nations f.d. and worsh.
23. these 3 f.d. bound in furnace
Mat.2:11. wise men f.d. and worsh.
18: 26. The serv. f.d. saying, 29.
Mk. 3: 11. uncl. spirits f.d.bef.him
5: 33. woman with issue f. d.
Lu. 5: 8. Peter f.d. at Jesus' knees
8: 28. man which had devils f. d.
41. Jairus f.d. | 17:16. Samaritan
Jn. 11: 32. Mary f.d. at his feet
Ac.5:5. Ananias f.d. | 10. Sapphira
10:25. Cornelius f.d. | 16:29.jailer
19:35. image which f.d.fr. Jupiter
20: 9. Eutychus f. d. from loft
He. 11: 30. walls of Jericho f. d.
Re.5:8.elders f.d. bef.Lamb,14 | 19:
22: 8. John f. d. before angel [4.

FELL, ED.

2 K. 3: 19. ye shall f. ev. good tree
25. and they f-d all the good trees

FELLER.

Is.14:8. no f. is come up against us

FELLEST, ING.

2 S.3:34. man bef.wicked so f-t thou
2 K. 6: 5. as one was f-g a beam

FELLOES.

1 K.7:33. f. and spokes were molten

FELLOW.

Ge. 19:9. This one f. came to sojourn
Ex. 2:13. Whf. smitest thou thy f.?
18:†16.I judge betw. man and his f.
Ju.7:13. man told dream to his f.,14.
22. L. set ev. man's sword ag. his
f. thro. host, 1 S. 14: 20.
1 S. 21: 15. brought this f. to play
madman; this f. come into my
25: 21. in vain kept all this f.hath
29: 4. Make this f. return, go to
2 S. 2: 16. caught every one his f.
1 K.22:27. f. in prison, 2 Ch. 18:26.
2 K. 9: 11. whf. came this mad f.?
Ec. 4: 10. if fall, one will lift his f.
Is. 34: 14. satyr shall cry to his f.
Jon. 1: 7. said one to his f. cast lots
Zch. 11: †9. eat flesh of his f. [f.
13:7.awake,O sword, ag. man is my
Mat. 12: 24. f. not cast out dev. but
26: 61. f. said, I am able to destroy
71. This f.was with Jes.,Lu.22:59.
Lu. 23: 2. found this f. perverting
Jn. 9: 29. as for this f. we know not
11: 16. Didymus said unto his f.
disciples [say?
Ac. 17: †18. what will this base f.
18: 13. f. persuadeth to worship G.
22: 22. Away with such a f.
24: 5. found this man pestilent f.

FELLOW citizens.

Ep.2:19. f.c.with saints and househ.

FELLOW heirs.

Ep.3:6. That Gentiles should be f.h.

FELLOW helper, s.

2 Co. 8:23. Titus my f.h. conc. you
3 Jn.8. that we be f.h-s to the truth

FELLOW labourer, s.

1 Th. 3: 2. sent Timotheus our f. l.
Ph.4:3. Clement,with other my f.l-s
Phm. 1. Paul unto Philemon f. l.
24. Marcus, Lucas, my f. l-s

FELLOW prisoner, s.

Col.4: 10. Aristarchus f.p. saluteth
Phm. 23. Epaphras my f. p. in C.
Ro. 16: 7. Andron. and Junia my f.

FELLOW servant, s. [p-s

Mat. 18:28. found f.s.who owed him
29. his f. s. fell down at his feet
31. when f. s-s saw what was done
33. have had compassion on f. s.
24: 49. sh. begin to smite his f.s-s
Col.1: 7. learned of Epaph. our f.s.
4: 7. Tychicus, who is a f. s. in L.
Re. 6:11. till f.s-s should be fulfilled
19:10. do it not, I am thy f.s., 22:

FELLOW soldier. [9.

Ph. 2: 25. to Epaphroditus my f.s.
Phm. 2. Paul to Archippus our f.s.

FELLOW workers.

Col. 4: 11. These only my f. w. to

FELLOWS. [kingd.

Ju. 11: 37. bewail virginity, I and f.
18: 25. lest angry f. run upon thee
20: †11. all Isr.were gath. f. as one
2 S. 6: 20. as one of vain f. uncov-h
Ps.45:7.oil of gladness ab. f..He.1:9.
Is. 44: 11. all his f. sh. be ashamed
Eze. 37:19. take tribes of Isr. his f.
Da. 2:13. Dan. and his f. to be slain
18. Dan. and his f.sho. not perish
Da.7:20.look was more stout than f.
Zch. 3: 8. thou and thy f. that set
Mat. 11: 16. chil. calling to their f.
Ac. 17: 5. Jews took lewd f. of

FELLOWSHIP.

Le. 6:2. deliv. him to keep, or in f.
Ps. 94: 20. throne of iniq. f. with
Ac.2:42. they contin. in apostles' f.
1 Co. 1: 9. called unto f. of his Son
10:20. not th. ye have f.with devils
2 Co.6:14.what f.righteousness with.
8: 4. f. of ministering to saints
Ga. 2: 9. gave me right hand of f.
Ep. 3: 9. men see f. of the mystery
5:11. no f. with works of darkness
Ph. 1: 5. for your f. in gospel
2: 1. if there be any f. of Spirit
3:10. may know f. of his sufferings
1 Jn. 1: 3. that ye have f. with us
our f. is with Father, and
6. if we say we have f. with him
7. if we walk in light, we have f.

FELT. [him

Ge. 27: 22. Jac. near, and Isaac f.
31: †34. Laban f. all the tent, but
Ex. 10: 21. darkness that may be f.
Pr. 23: 35. beaten me, I f. it not
Mk. 5: 29. she f. she was healed
Ac.28:5. shook off beast f. no harm

FEMALE. [5:6.

Le. 4: 28. f. without blemish, 32.-
Le.27:4.if a f.thy estimation 30 shek.
5.thy estimation for f. 10 shek.,7.
6. for f. fr. month old, 3 shek.

FEMALE with male.

Ge. 1:27. m. and f. created he, 5:2.
6: 19. two of every sort, m. and f.
7: 2. take by sevens, m. and f., 3.
9. went in two and two, m. and f.
16. that went, went in m. and f.
Le. 3: 1. if he offer it, m. or f.
6. if offering be of flock, m. or f.
12: 7. law for her borne a m. or f.
Nu. 5: 3. m. and f. sh. ye put out
De. 4:16. image, likeness of m. or f.
7: 14. sh. not be m. or f. barren
Mat.19:4. made m. and f.,Mk.10:6.
Ga. 3: 28. in C. is neither m. nor f.

FENCE. [Noun.]

Ps. 62: 3. ye be as a tottering f.

FENCED. [f.

2 S. 23: 7. that touch them must be
Jb. 10:11. he hath f. me with bones
19: 8. He hath f. up my way that
Is. 5:2. beloved hath viney. he f. it

FENCED city.

2 K. 3: 19. ye sh. smite every f. c.
10:2. there are with you a f.c. and
17: 9. from tower to f. c., 18: 8.

FENCED cities.

Nu. 32: 17. little ones sh. dwell in
36. f.c. and folds for sheep [f.c.
De. 3:5. these c. were f. with walls
9: 1. to possess c. f. up to heaven
Jos. 10: 20. rest entered into f. c.
14:12. that the c.were great and f.
19: 35. f. c. are Ziddim, Zer, and
1 S. 6: 18. golden mice, acc. to f.c.
2 S. 20: 6. pursue, lest he get f. c.
2 K. 18: 13. Sennach. came up ag.
f. c. of Jud. and took,2 Ch. 12:
19:25. shouldest lay waste f.c. [4.
2 Ch.8:5. Sol. built f. c. with walls
11: 10. in Benjamin f. c., 23.
12:4.Shishak took the f.c. of Jud.
14: 6. Asa built f.c. land had rest
17:2. Jehosh. placed forces in f.c.,
19. [Judah
19: 5. set judges thro-t all f. c. of
21: 3. Jehosh. gave them f. c. in
32: 1. encamped ag. the f.c. [Jud.
33: 14. put captains of war in f.c.
Je. 5: 17. shall impoverish thy f.c.
Eze. 36:35. ruined c. are become f.
Da. 11: 15. king sh. take most f.c.
Ho. 8:14. Jud. hath multiplied f.c.
Zph. 1: 16. day of alarm ag. f. c.

FENCED place.

2 K.19:†24. rivers of f.p., Is.37:†25.
Ha. 2: †1. I will set me upon f. p.

FENCED wall, s.

De. 28: 52. until f. w-s come down
Is. 2:15. day of L. upon every f.w.
Je. 15: 20. I will make thee a f.w.

FENS. [of f.

Jb. 40:21. Behemoth lieth in covert

FERRET.

Le. 11: 30. f. and lizard unclean

FERRY boat.

2 S.19:18.went a f.b.for k.'s househ

FERVENT, LY.

Ac. 18:25. Apollos, being f. in spirit
Ro. 12: 11. f. in spirit, serving L.
2 Co.7:7. told your f. mind tow. me
Col. 4: 12. labouring f-y for you in
Ja. 5:16. f. prayer of righteous man
1 Pe 1:22.love with a pure heart f-y
4: 8. ab. all things have f. charity
2 Pe. 3:10. sh. melt with f. heat,12.

FES'TUS.

Ac. 24:27. F. came into Felix' room
25: 1. Now when F. was come in,
9.F. to do the Jews pleasure [12,22.
13. Agrippa came to salute F.
14. F. declared Paul's cause
23. at F. com-t Paul was brought
24.F. said King Agrippa,26:24,32.
26: 25. I am not mad, noble F.

FETCH.

Ge. 18:5. I will f. a morsel of bread
27 : 9. go f. me two good kids, 13.
45. then I will f. thee fr. thence
Ex. 2 : 5. ark, she sent maid to f. it
Nu. 20 : 10. f. water out of rock.?
34 : 5. border sh. f. a compass fr.
De. 19 : 12. the elders shall f. him
24 : 10. not go to f. his pledge, 19.
30 : 4. from thence will L. f. thee
Ju. 11 : 5. elders went to f. Jeph.
20 : 10. take men to f. victuals for
1 S. 4 : 3. Let us f. ark of the cov.
6 : 21. come f. it up to you [31.
16 : 11. said unto Jesse, f. Saul, 20:
26 : 22. let us come and f. spear
2 S. 5 : 23. f. a compass behind th.
14 : 13. not f. home his banished
20. To f. about this form of speech
1 K. 17 : 10. f. me a little water
11. she going to f. it, he called
2 K. 6 : 13. go spy that I may f. him
2 Ch. 18 : 8. f. quickly Micaiah
Ne. 8 : 15. f. olive branches, pine
Jb. 36 : 3. I will f. knowl. fr. afar
Is. 56 : 12. say they, I will f. wine
Je. 36 : 21. k. sent Jehudi to f. roll
Ac. 16 : 37. let them come and f. us

FETCHED, ETH.

Ge. 18 : 4. Let a little water be f.
7. Ab. f. a calf tender and good
27 : 14. Jacob f. kids to his mother
De. 19 : 5. hand f-h a stroke with axe
Jos. 15 : 3. f-d a compass to Karkaa
Ju. 18 : 18. they f. carved image
1 S. 7 : 1. men f. up ark of the L.
10 : 23. they ran and f. Saul thence
2 S. 4 : 6. tho. would have f. wheat
9 : 5. k. David f. Mephibosheth
11 : 27. Da. f. Bath-sheba to his h.
14 : 2. Joab f. fr. Tekoah wise wom.
1 K. 7 : 13. Sol. f. Hiram out of Tyre
9 : 28. they f. from Ophir gold
2 K. 3 : 9. f. compass of 7 days' jour.
11 : 4. Jehoiada f. rulers over hundr.
2 Ch. 1 : 17. f-d from E. chariot and
12 : 11. guard came and f. shields
Je. 26 : 23. they f. Urijah out of E.
Ac. 28 : 13. fr. thence we f. a com- [pass

FETTERS.

Ju. 16 : 21. bound Samson with f.
2 S. 3 : 34. nor thy feet put into f.
2 K. 25 : 7. put out eyes of Zed.
bound with f., Je. 39 : †7.-52 : †11.
2 Ch. 33 : 11. Manas. bound with f.
36 : 6. bound Jehoi. in f. to
Ps. 105 : 18. feet they hurt with f.
149 : 8. bind nobles with f. of iron
Mk. 5 : 4. bound with f., Lu. 8 : 29.

FEVER. [f.

De. 28 : 22. L. shall smite thee with
Mat. 8 : 14. saw Peter's wife's mother sick of a f., Mk. 1 : 30. Lu. 4 : 38.
15. rebuked the f. it left her, Mk.
1 : 31. Lu. 4 : 39.
Jn. 4 : 52. at 7th hour the f. left him
Ac. 28 : 8. fa. of Publius sick of a f.

FEW. [days

Ge. 24 : 55. Let damsel abide a f.
27 : 44. tarry a f. days till bro.'s fury
34 : 30. I being f. they will slay me
47 : 9. f. and evil have days been
Le. 26 : 22. I will make you f., De.
4 : 27.-28 : 62. [the taberu.
Nu. 9 : 20. cloud was a f. days on
13 : 18. see peo. whether they be f.
26 : 54. to f. give less inheri., 35 : 8.
56. poss. divid. betw. many and f.
De. 26 : 5. fa. sojourned with a f.
33 : 6. Reub. let not his men be f.
1 S. 14 : 6. to save by many or f.
17 : 28. with whom left f. sheep?
1 Ch. 16 : 19. even a f. and strangers
2 Ch. 29 : 34. priests were too f.
Ne. 2 : 12. I arose, I and some f.
7 : 4. city large, but people were f.
Jb. 10 : 20. Are not my days f.? cease
Jb. 14 : 1. man is of f. days, and full
16 : 22. When a f. years are come
32 : †6. I am f. of days, ye are old
Ps. 109 : 8. Let his days be f. and ano.
Ec. 5 : 2. G. in heav., let words be f.
9 : 14. was a little city, f. men in it
12 : 3. grinders cease, bec. are f.
Is. 10 : 19. rest of the trees sh. be f.
24 : 6. inhabi. burned, f. men left
41 : † 14. fear not Jac. ye f. men
Eze. 5 : 3. shalt take f. in number
12 : 16. I will leave f. men fr sword
Da. 11 : 20. within f. days be destr.
Mat. 7 : 14. f. there be that find it
9 : 37. labourers are f., Lu. 10 : 2.
15 : 34. a f. little fishes, Mk. 8 : 7.
20 : 16. but f. are chosen, 22 : 14.
25 : 21. been faithful in a f. things, 23.
Mk. 6 : 5. laid hands on a f. sick folk
Lu. 12 : 48. be beaten with f. stripes
13 : 23. are there f. that be saved?
Ac. 24 : 4. wouldest hear us f. words
Ep. 3 : 3. as I wrote afore in f. words
He. 12 : 10. for a f. days chastened us
13 : 22. writ. unto you in f. words
1 Pe. 3 : 20. wherein f. that is, 8 souls
Re. 2 : 14. a f. things ag. thee, 20.
3 : 4. hast a f. names even in Sardis

But FEW.

Ge. 29 : 20. seemed to him b. a f. days
Le. 25 : 52. if there remain b. f. years
Jos. 7 : 3. men of Ai are b. f. [12.
1 Ch. 16 : 19. When ye b. f., Ps. 105 :
Je. 42 : 2. we are left b. a f. of many

Not FEW.

2 K. 4 : 3. borrow empty vessels n. a f.
Is. 10 : 7. cut off nations n. a f.
Je. 30 : 19. multiply they shall n. be f.
Ac. 17 : 4. chief women n. a f. | 12. of [men

FEWER, EST.

Nu. 33 : 54. to f-r give less inheri.
De. 7 : 7. ye were the f-t of all peo.
Jb. 30 : † 1. are of f-r days than I

FEWNESS.

Le. 25 : 16. acc. to f. of years diminish

FIDELITY.

Tit. 2 : 10. servants shewing good f.

FIELD.

Ge. 23 : 11. the f. give I thee, 9, 17.
13. will give money for f., 25 : 10.
20. f. and cave made sure unto Ab.
25 : 29. Esau fr. f. | 27 : 3. to f., 5.
27 : 27. smell of my son as of a f.
31 : 4. Rachel and Leah to the f.
33 : 19. bought parcel of a f.
47 : 20. sold every man his f.
49 : 30. in f. wh. Ab. bought, 50 : 13.
Ex. 22 : 5. if a man cause f. eaten
6. so that corn or f. be consumed
Le. 19 : 9. reap corners of f., 23 : 22.
19. not sow f. with mingled seed
25 : 3. Six years shalt sow thy f.
4. in 7th year shalt not sow thy f.
34. f. of suburbs not be sold [f.
27 : 16. sanctify unto L some part of
17. if he sanctify his f., 18.
20. if not redeem f. or if sold f.
22. unto L. a f. | 24. f. sh. return
De. 5 : 21. nei. covet thy neighb's f.
14 : 22. f. bringeth forth year by y.
Jos. 15 : 18. to ask f., Ju. 1 : 14.
Ru. 2 : 8. Go not to glean in ano. f.
9. Let thine eyes be on f. that
22. meet thee not in any other f.
4 : 5. What day buyest f. of Naomi
2 S. 2 : † 16. called f. of strong men
14 : 30. Joab's f. is near mine
31. Why serv-s set my f. on fire?
2 K. 18 : 17. pool, wh. is in highway
of fuller's f., Is. 7 : 3.-36 : 2.
Ne. 13 : 10. Lev. fled ev. one to his f.
Ps. 96 : 12. Let f. be joyful
Pr. 24 : 30. I went by f. of slothful
27 : 26. and goats are the price of f.
31 : 16. She consid. a f. and buyeth
Ec. 5 : 9. k. himself is served by f.
Is. 5 : 8. woe to them th. lay f. to f.
Is. 16 : 10. joy is taken out of plentiful
f., Je. 48 : 33.
Je. 4 : 17. As keepers of f. are they ag.
12 : 4. how long herbs of f. wither?
26 : 18. Zion be ploughed like a f.,
Mi. 3 : 12. [8, 9, 25.
32 : 7. Buy thee my f. in Anathoth,
35 : 9. nei. have we viney. not f.
Eze. 17 : † 8. was planted in a good f.
Jo. 1 : 10. f. is wasted, land mourn.
Mat. 13 : 24. good seed in his f. 27, 31.
38. f. is the world, good seed chil.
44. is like unto treasure hid in f.
he selleth and buyeth that f.
27 : 7. they bought potter's f., 10.
8. f. called f. of blood, Ac. 1 : 19.
Lu. 17 : 7. will say, when come fr. f.
Ac. 1 : 18. this man purchased a f.
See BEAST, S, GRASS, HERB, S,
TREE, S.

Fruitful FIELD.

2 K. 19 : † 23. I will enter his f. f.,
Is. 37 : † 24.
Is. 10 : 18. consume glory of his f. f.
29 : 17. Leb. shall be turned into a f.
32 : 15. until wilderness be a f. f.
and f. f. be counted a forest
16. and righteousness in the f. f.
Eze. 17 : 5. he planted seed in a f. f.

In the FIELD.

Ge. 4 : 8. to pass when they were i. f.
24 : 63. Isaac went to meditate i. f.
65. What man walketh i. f.
29 : 2. be looked, behold well i. f.
30 : 14. Reuben found mandrakes i. f.
34 : 28. took that in city and i. f.
37 : 15. Joseph was wandering i. f.
39 : 5. all he had in house and i. f.
Ex. 1 : 14. all manner of service i. f.
9 : 19. gather all thou hast i. f., 3, 21.
25. hail smote all i. f.
16 : 25. to day ye sh. not find it i. f.
23 : 16. wh. thou hast sown i. f.
De. 21 : 1. if found slain, lying i. f.
22 : 25. if a betrothed damsel i. f.
24 : 19. hast forgot a sheaf i. f.
28 : 3. blessed shalt thou be i. f.
16. cursed shalt thou be i. f.
Jos. 8 : 24. slaying inhab. of Ai i. f.
Ju. 9 : 32. lie in wait i. f., 43.
13 : 9. angel came unto woman i. f.
Ru. 2 : 3. gleaned i. f., 17.
1 S. 4 : 2. slew of the army i. f.
6 : 18. stone remaineth i. f. of Josh.
14 : 15. trembling in the host i. f.
19 : 3. stand beside my father i. f.
20 : 5. hide myself i. f., 24.
30 : 11. they found an Egyp. i. f.
2 S. 10 : 8. were by thems. i. f.
14 : 6. sons they two strove i. f.
17 : 8. bear robbed of whelps i. f.
1 K. 11 : 29. they two were alone i. f.
14 : 11. that dieth of Jeroboam i. f.
21 : 24. him that dieth of Ahab i. f.
2 K. 7 : 12. camp to hide thems. i. f.
1 Ch. 19 : 9. kings were i. f.
27 : 26. that did the work i. f.
2 Ch. 26 : 23. i. f. of the burial wh.
Jb. 24 : 6. They reap every one i. f.
Ps. 78 : 12. marvellous thi-s i. f., 43.
Pr. 24 : 27. make it for thyself i. f.
Je. 14 : 5. the hind calved i. f.
17 : 3. O my mountain i. f. I will
41 : 8. have treas-s i. f. of wheat
Eze. 7 : 15. he i. f. sh. die by sword
26 : 6. sh. slay thy dau-s i. f., 8.
Mi. 4 : 10. thou shalt dwell i. f.
Zch. 10 : 1. give to ev. one grass i. f.
Mal. 3 : 11. nor vine cast fruit i. f.
Mat 24 : 18. Neith. let him i. f. re-
turn, Mk. 13 : 16. Lu. 17 : 31.
40. shall two be i. f., Lu. 17 : 36.
Lu. 2 : 8. shepherds abiding i. f.
12 : 28. clothe the grass which is i. f.
15 : 25. Now his elder son was i. f.

Into the FIELD.

Nu. 22 : 23. ass turned, and went i. f.

Nu. 23:14. bro-t him i. f. of Zophim
Ju. 9: 42. people went out i. f.
1 S. 6: 14. cart came i. f. of Josh.
20: 11. Jona. said, Come let us go
35. Jona. went out i. f. [i. f.
2 S. 11: 23. men came unto us i. f.
18: 6. went out i. f. against Israel
20: 12. he removed Amasa i. f.
2 K. 4: 39. i. f. and gather. gourds
Can. 7: 11. beloved, let us go i. f.
Je. 6: 25. Go not i. f. nor walk by
14:18. if I go i. f. behold the slain

Of the FIELD.

Ge. 2: 5. God made ev. plant o. f.
23: 19. cave o. f. of Mach., 49:30.-
25:27. cunning hunter o. f. [50:13.
30: 16. Jac. came out o. f. in ev-g
34: 7. sons of Jac. came out o. f.
41:48. food o. f. | 49:32. purchase
47: 24. four parts for seed o. f.
Ex 23: 16. gath. thy labours o. f.
Le. 25: 12. increase onto o. f., 2 Ch.
26: 4. trees o. f. sho. yield [31: 5.
27:28. no devoted thing o. f. be sold
De. 20: 19. tree o. f. is man's life
Ju. 5: 4. when marchedst out o. f.
18. death in high places o. f.
19: 16. came an old man out o. f.
Ru. 2: 3. o. f. belonging to Boaz
1 S. 11: 5. after the herd out o. f.
2 K. 8: 6. fruits o. f., La. 4: 9.
9: 25. in portion o. f. of Naboth
37. carcass as dung upon face o. f.
18: 17. highway o. fuller's f., Is.
7: 3.-36: 2. [o. f.
1 Ch. 27: 26. over them did the work
Jb. 5:23. in league with stones o. f.
Ps. 103: 15. as a flower o. f. so he
Pr. 27: 26. goats are the price o. f.
Can. 2: 7. charge by roes o. f., 3: 5.
Is. 16: 10. joy out o. plentiful f.
37: 27. inhabit. were as grass o. f.
40: 6. is grass, and as flower o. f.
43: 20. beast o. f. sh. honour me
55: 12. trees o. f. shall clap hands
Je. 4: 17. as keepers o. f. are they
18: 14. snow of Leb. fr. rock o. f.
Eze. 16: 7. to multiply as bud o. f.
17: 24. trees o. f. sh. know that I
20: 46. against forest o. south f.
31: 4. rivers unto all trees o. f.
34: 27. tree o. f. sh. yield her fruit
36: 30. will multiply increase o. f.
39: 10. shall take no wood out o. f.
Da. 4: 15. in tender grass o. f. and
Ho. 10: 4. hemlock in furrows o. f.
Jo. 1:11. harv-t o. f. is perish. [o. f.
12. all trees o. f. are withered
19. flame burned all trees o. f.
Mi. 1: 6. Samaria as a heap o. f.
Mat. 6: 28. Consider the lilies o. f.
30. if God so clothe the grass o. f.
13: 36. Declare parable of tares o. f.
See BEAST, S, of the field.

Open FIELD.

Le. 14:7. let living bird loose into o. f.
17: 5. bring sac. they offer in o. f.
Je. 9: 22. men's carcasses upon o. f.
Eze. 16:5. thou wast cast out in o. f.
32: 4. I will cast thee upon o. f.
33: 27. him in o. f. will give to
39: 5. Thou shalt fall upon the o. f.

FIELDS.

Ex. 8: 13. the frogs died out of f.
Le. 25:31. shall be counted as the f.
27: 22. not of f. of his possession
Nu. 16:14. not given us inher. of f.
20: 17. will not pass thro. f., 21:22.
De. 11:15. will send grass into thy f.
32: 13. he might eat increase of f.
32. as vine of the f. of Gomorrah
Jos. 21: 12. f. gave they to Caleb
Ju. 9: 27. went into f. and gather-d
44. people in f. and slew them
1 S. 8:14. he will take your f. and
22:7. will son of Jesse give each f.?
25: 15. in f. were a wall unto us

2 S. 1: 21. rain upon you nor f. of
1 K. 2: 26. Get thee to thine own f.
16: 4. that dieth of Baasha in f.
2 K. 23: 4. f. of Kidron and carried
1 Ch. 6:56. f. of the city and villages
16: 32 let the f. rejoice, and all
27: 25. over storehouses in the f.
2 Ch. 26: † 10. vinedr-s in fruitf f.
31: 19. priests wh. were in the f.
Ne. 11: 25. villages with their f.
30. Lachish and f. [out of f.
12: 29. f. of Geba | 44. gath. tithes
Jb. 5: 10. sendeth waters upon f.
Ps. 107: 37. sow thee f. and plant
132: 6. we found it in f. of wood
Pr. 8: 26. as yet had not made f.
23: 10. enter not f. of fatherless
Is. 16: 8. for f. of Heshbon languish
32: 12. shall lament for pleasant f.
Je. 6: 12. f. be turned unto others,
13:27. seen thine abom-s in f. [8: 10.
31: 40. all f. unto brook Kidron
32: 15. f. shall be possessed again
43. f. bought | 44. Men sh. buy f.
39: 10. Nebuzar-adan gave them f.
40: 7. capts. of forces in the f., 13.
Ho. 12: 11. altars as heap in f.
Ob. 19. shall possess f. of Ephraim
Mi. 2: 2. they covet f. and take them
4. turning, he hath divided our f.
Ha. 3: 17. alth. f. yield no meat
Mk. 2:23. went thro. corn f., Lu. 6:1.
Lu. 15: 15. into his f. to feed swine
Jn. 4: 35. lift up eyes, look on f.
Ja. 5: 4. labourers, wh. reaped your

Open FIELDS. [f.

Le. 14:53. let go living bird into o. f.
Nu. 19: 16. slain with sword in o. f.
2 S. 11: 11. serv-ts encamped in o. f.
Eze. 29: 5. shalt fall upon o. f.

FIERCE. [f.

Ge. 49: 7. cursed be their anger, it
De. 28: 50. a nation of a f. counten.
Jb. 4: 10. the voice of f. lion and
10: 16. Thou huntest me as f. lion
28: 8. nor f. lion passed by it
41: 10. None is so f. dare stir [th.
Is. 19: 4. a f. king shall rule over
33: 19. Thou shalt not see f. people
Da. 8: 23. a king of f. countenance
Ha. 1: 8. horses more f. than wolves
Mat. 8: 28. with devils, exceeding f.
Lu. 23: 5. they were more f. saying
2 Ti. 3: 3. incontinent, f., despisers
Ja. 3: 4. ships driven of f. winds
See ANGER, WRATH.

FIERCENESS. [f.

Jb. 39: 24. swalloweth ground with
Je. 25:38. land desol. for f. of oppres.
See ANGER, WRATH. [sor

FIERCER.

2 S. 19: 43. words of Judah were f.

FIERY.

Nu. 21: 6. the L. sent f. serpents
8. Make thee a f. serpent, and
De. 8: 15. wherein were f. serpents
33: 2. fr. right hand went a f. law
Ps. 21: 9. make them as a f. oven
Is. 14: 29. fruit be a f. flying serp.
Da. 3: 6. into f. furnace, 11, 15, 21.
17. able to deliver us fr. f. furnace
23. three men fell into f. furnace
26. near to mouth of f. furnace
7: 9. his throne was like f. flame
10. A f. stream issued and came
Na. 2: † 3. chariots with f. torches
Ep. 6: 16. able to quench the f. darts
He. 10: 27. judgm., and f. indigna.
1 Pe. 4:12. not strange conc. f. trial

FIFTEEN.

Ge. 7: 20. f. cubits upw. did waters
Ex. 27: 14. hangings f. cubits, 15.
-38: 14, 15.
See DAYS, FATHOMS, FURLONGS, HUNDRED PIECES, SHEKELS, YEARS

FIFTEENTH.

See DAY, LOT, YEAR.

FIFTH.

Re. 9: 1. f. angel sounded and I saw
16: 10 f. angel poured out his vial
21: 20. f. foundation a sardonyx
See DAY, LOT, MONTH, PART, RIB, SEAL, SON, TIME, YEAR.

FIFTIES.

Ex. 18: 21. rulers of f., 25. De. 1:15.
1 S. 8: 12. appoint captains over f.
2 K. 1:14. burnt two captains of f.
Mk. 6: 40 sat down by f., Lu. 9: 14.

FIFTIETH.

Le. 25: 10. ye shall hallow f. year
11. A jubilee shall that f. year be
2 K. 15:23. In the f. year of Azariah
27. In the 2 and f. year of Azariah

FIFTY.

Ge. 6: 15. breadth of ark f. cubits
18: 24. not spare for f. righte.? 26.
Ex. 26: 5. f. loops, 10.-36: 12, 17.
27: 12. hangings of f. cubits, 38:12.
Le. 23:16. after 7 sab. number f. days
Nu. 31: 30. portion of f. for Levites
47. Moses took one portion of f.
1 K. 7: 2. breadth of house f. cubits
18: 4. hid them by f. in cave, 13.
2 K. 1: 9. capt. of f. with f., 11, 13.
10. let fire consume thy f., 12.
Es. 5:14. gallows f. cubits high, 7:9.
Is. 3: 3. L. will take capt. of f.
Eze. 40: 15. unto face of porch f.
cubits [33, 36.-42: 7.
21. the length f. cubits, 25, 29,
42: 2. breadth of door f. cubits
Lu. 7: 41. 500 pence, the other f.
16: 6. sit down quickly, write f.
See BASINS, HORSEMEN, HUNDRED, MALES, MEN, PILLARS, SHEKELS, TACHES, THOUSAND, VESSELS, Fifty YEARS.

FIFTY and two, five, or six.

Ezr. 2: 22. men of Netophah, f. a. s.
29. chil. of Nebo f. a. t., Ne. 7: 33.
Ne. 6: 15. wall finished in f. a. t. days
See Fifty and two YEARS.
See Fifty and five YEARS. [days

FIG, S.

Ge. 3: 7. sewed f. leaves for aprons
Nu. 13: 23. they brought of the f-s
20: 5. it is no place of seed, or f-s
1 S. 25: 18. Abig. took 200 cakes f-s
30:12. gave the Egyp. a cake of f-s
2 K. 20:7. Take lump of f-s., Is. 38:21.
1 Ch. 12:40. that were nigh bro-t f-s
Ne. 13:15. on sab. some brought f-s
Can. 2:13. fig tree putteth green f-s
Is. 34: 4. falling f. from fig tree
Je. 8: 13. shall be no f-s on figtree
24: 1. two baskets of f. set bef. tem.
2. One bask. good f-s naughty f-s
3. f-s; the good f-s very good
5. Like these good f-s so will I
8. evil f-s that cannot be eaten
29: 17. I will make them like vile f-s
Am. 7: †14. I a gath-r of wild f-s
Na. 3:12. fig trees with first ripe f-s
Mat. 7: 16. f-s of thistles? Lu. 6:44.
Mk. 11: 13. the time of f-s was not
Ja. 3:12. figtree bear berries, vine f-s?
Re. 6: 13. as fig tree casteth her f-s

FIG tree.

Ju. 9:10. trees said to f. t., reign, 11.
1 K. 4: 25. safely und. f. t., Mi. 4:4.
2 K. 18:31. eat ev. one of f. t., Is. 36:16.
Pr. 27:18. keepeth f. t. sh. eat fruit
Ho. 9:10. fathers as first ripe in f. t.
Jo. 1: 7. he hath barked my f. t.
12. vine is dried, f. t. languisheth
2: 22. f. t. and vine yield strength
Ha. 3:17. Altho. f. t. sh. not blos.
Hag. 2: 19. f. t. hath not bro-t forth
Zch. 3:10. call ev man und. f. t. [11:13
Mat. 21:19. he saw f. t. in way, Mk.
20. is f. t. withered! Mk. 11:20, 21.
21. do wh. is done to the f. t.
24: 32. parable of f. t., Mk. 13:28.

Lu. 13:6. a man had a f. t. planted
7. I come, seeking fruit f. t. on
21: 29. Behold f. t. and all trees
Jn. 1:48. under f. t., I saw thee, 50.
Ja. 3: 12. Can f. t. bear olive
Re. 6: 13. as f. t. casteth untimely

FIG trees.

De. 8: 8. a land of vines, and f. t.
Ps. 105: 33. he smote vines and f.t.
Je. 5:17. shall eat thy vines and f.t.
Ho. 2: 12. I will destroy her f. t.
Am. 4: 9. when gard-s and f.t. incr.
Na. 3: 12. strong holds be like f. t.

FIGHT. [Noun.]

1 S. 17: 20. as host was going to the [f.
1 Ti. 6: 12. Fight good f. of faith
2 Ti. 4: 7. I have fought a good f.
He 10: 32. endured gr. f. of afflic-
11: 34. waxed valiant in f. [tions

FIGHT. [Verb.]

De. 1: 41. said, we will go up and f.
42. nor f. for I am not am. you
2:32. Sihon and his peo. came to f.
Ju. 11: 12. are come ag. me to f.
1 S. 4: 9. quit yours. like men, f.
17:10. give me man that we may f.
2 S. 11: 20. so nigh when ye did f.?
1 K. 22:31. f. not small, 2Ch. 18:30.
2 Ch. 18:31. compassed Jehosh. to f.
20: 17. Ye shall not need to f.
35:22. came to f. in valley of Megid.
Ps. 144: 1. teacheth fingers to f.
Je. 51: 30. mighty forborne to f.
Zch. 10: 5. sh. f. bec. L. is wi. them
14: 14. Judah sh. f. at Jerusalem
Jn. 18: 36. then would my serv-s f.
1 Co. 9: 26. f. I, not as beateth air
1 Ti. 6: 12. f. good fight of faith
Ja. 4: 2. ye kill, ye f. and war

See Battles

FIGHT against.

Ex. 1:10. lest join our enem. f. a. us
De. 20: 10. come nigh city to f. a.
Jos. 10: 25. enemies a. whom ye f.
11: 5. they pitched to f. a. Israel
19: 47. Danites went to f. a. Lesh.
Ju. 1: 1. who go up first to f. a. th.?
3. that we may f. a. Canaanites, 9.
10: 9. Ammon to f. a. Judah
18. f. a. chil. of Ammon, 11: 32.
11: 8. Jeph. to f. a. Ammon, 9.
25. strive ag. Isr. or f. a. them f.
12: 3. why come ye to f. a. me?
20:20. Isr. set thems. to f. a. Benj.
1 S. 15: 18. f. a. Amalekites until
23: 1. Philistines f. a. Keilah
29:8. that I not f. a. enemies of k.
1 K. 12: 21. Rehob. assembled all
Judah to f. a. Isr., 2 Ch. 11:1.
24. not f. a. your breth., 2 Ch. 11:4.
20:23. let us f. a. them in plain, 25.
26. to Aphek to f. a. Israel
22: 32. turned to f. a. Jehosh.
2 K. 3: 21. kings were come to f. a.
19: 9. he is come out to f. a. thee
2 Ch. 13: 12. O Isr. f. not a. Lord
32:2. Senn. purposed to f. a. Jerus.
35:20. Necho came to f. a. Carche.
Ne. 4: 8. conspired to f. a. Jerus.
Ps. 35: 1. f. a. them that f. a. me
56: 2. they be many that f. a. me
Is. 19: 2. sh. f. ev. one a. his bro.
29: 7. all nations f. a. Ariel
8. nations that f. a. mount Zion
Je. 1: 19. shall f. a. thee, 15: 20.
21: 4. whw. ye f. a. king of Bab.
5. I will f. a. you with str. arm
32:24. given into hand of Chal. th.
f. a. it, 29.-34: 22.-37: 8.
37: 10. smitten Chal. th. f. a. you
Zch. 14:3. L. sh. f. a. those nations
Ac. 5: 39. lest found to f. a. God
23: 9. if angel, let us not f. a. God
Re. 2: 16. f. a. them with sword of

FIGHT for.

Ex. 14:14. L. shall f. f. you, De. 1:
30.-3:22.-20: 4.
2 K. 10:3. f. f. your master's house
Ne. 4: 14. f. f. your brethren; sons
20. resort ye, our G. shall f. f. us
Is. 31: 4. L. shall come to f. f. Zion

FIGHT with.

Ex. 17: 9. go out, f. w. Amalek
Jos. 9: 2. Canaanites to f. w. Josh.
Ju. 8: 1. to f. w. Midianites
9: 38. go out and f. w. Abimelech
11:6. that we f. w. chil. of Ammon
1 S. 13: 5. Philis. to f. w. Isr., 28:1.
17: 9. If he be able to f. w. me
32. will go and f. w. this Philis., 33.
2 Ch. 35:22. Josiah disguised to f. w.
Is. 30: 32. in battles will he f. w. it
Je. 32: 5. though ye f. w. Chald.
33: 5. They came to f. w. Chald.
41:12. took men, went to f. w. Ishm.
Da. 10: 20. return to f. w. prince
11: 11. king of the south f. w. him

FIGHTETH, ING.

Ex. 14:25. L. f-h for them ag. Egyp-s
Jos. 23:10. L. G., he it is f-h for you
1 S. 17: 19. Isr. were f-g Philistines
25: 28. my lord f-h battles of Lord
2 Ch. 26: 11. had a host of f-g men
Ps. 56:1. O God, he f-g oppres-h me

FIGHTING, S.

Nu. 22: † 11. peradv. I prevail in f.
2 Co. 7: 5. without f-s within fears
Ja. 4: 1. whence come wars and f.

FIGURE, S.

De. 4: 16. lest make similitude of f.
1 K. 6: 29. he with carved f-s of
Is. 44: 13. maketh it aft. f. of man
Ac. 7: 43. f-s he made to worship
Ro. 5: 14. is f. of him was to come
1 Co. 4:6. I have in a f. transferred
10:†6. now these things were our f-s
He. 9: 9. was f. of time then pres.
24. which are f-s of the true
11: 19. whence receiv. him in a f.
1 Pe. 3:21. The like f. even baptism

FIGURED.

Le. 26: † 1. nei. set up any f. stone

FILE.

1 S. 13: 21. had f. for mattocks

FILL. [Noun.]

Le. 25: 19. sh. eat your f. in safety
De. 23: 24. mayest eat grapes thy f.
Pr. 7: 18. let us take our f. of love

FILL. [Verb.]

Ge. 1: 22. and f. waters in the seas
42: 25. Jo. com-d to f. sacks, 44: 1.
Ex. 10: 6. locusts sh. f. thy houses
16: 32. f. a homer of it to be kept
32:†29. f. your hands to day to L.
Le. 16: †32. priest, he sh. f. his ha
1 S. 16: 1. f. thine horn with oil
1 K. 1: † 14. I will f. up thy words
18: 33. f. four barrels with water
1 Ch. 29:†5. who willing to f. hand?
2 Ch. 13: † 9. cometh to f. his hand
Jb. 8: 21. f. thy mouth wi. laugh-g
15:2. should a wise man f. his belly
20: 23. When about to f. his belly?
23: 4. would f. mouth with argu-s
38: 39. f. appetite of young lions
41:7. f. his skins with barbed irons?
Ps. 81: 10. open mouth, I will f. it
83: 16. f. their faces with shame
110: 6. f. places with dead bodies
Pr. 1: 13. we shall f. our houses
8: 21. I will f. their treasures
Is. 8: 8. wings f. breadth of land
14:21. nor f. face of world wi. cities
27: 6. Isr. shall f. face of world
56: 12. f. ours. with strong drink
Je. 13:13. f. inhabit. with drunkenn.
23:24. Do not I f. heaven and earth
33:5. is to f. them with dead bodies
51: 14. f. thee with men as caterpillars [roll
Eze. 3: 3. f. thy bowels with this
7:19. not satisfy souls nor f. bowels
9: 7. f. the courts with the slain
10: 2. f. hand with coals of fire
Eze. 24:4. f. it with the choice bones
30: 11. they sh. f. land with slain
32:4. I will f. beasts of whole earth
5. f. valleys with thy height
35: 8. I will f. mts. with the slain
43: † 26. shall purge altar, and f.
hands [house
Zph. 1: 9. who f. their masters'
Hag. 2: 7. I will f. house with glory
Zch. 9: † 15. they shall f. both bowls
Mat. 9: 16. wh. is put in to f. it up
15: 33. whence bread to f. mult.?
23: 32. f. ye up measure of fa-s
Jn. 2: 7. f. waterpots with water
Ro. 15:13. G. of hope f. you with joy
Ep. 4:10. that he might f. all things
Col. 1:24. f. up behind of suff-gs of C.
1 Th. 2:16. Jews, to f. up their sins
Re. 18: 6. cup she filled f. double

FILLED.

Ge. 6: 13. earth is f. with violence
21: 19. Hagar f. bottle with water
24: 16. Rebekah f. her pitcher
26: 15. Philis. f. wells with earth
Ex. 1:7. the chil. of Isr. f. the land
2: 16. they f. the troughs to water
28: 3. I have f. with wisd., 35:35.
31: 3. f. him with Sp of G., 35:31.
40: 34. glory of L. f. tabern., 35.
De. 26: 12. they may eat and be f.
31: 20. when eaten and f. thems.
Jos. 9: 13. bottles we f. were new
1 K. 8: 10. cloud f. house of the L.
11. glory of L. f. the house, 2 Ch.
5: 14.-7: 1, 2.
18: 35. he f. the trench with wat.
20: 27. Syrians f. the country
2 K. 3:25. ev. man his stone and f. it
21: 16. f. Jerus. with blood, 24:4.
23: 14. Josiah f. places with bones
Ezr. 9: 11. f. it fr. one end to ano.
Jb. 3:15. princes f. houses with silv.
16: 8. hast f. me with wrinkles
22: 18. Yet he f. houses with good
Ps. 38:7. loins are f. with loathsome
71: 8. mouth be f. with praise
72: 19. let earth be f. with glory
80: 9. to take deep root, it f. land
104:28. openest hand, f. with good
123: 3. we are f. with contempt
4. Our soul is exceedingly f. with
Pr. 5: 10. strangers be f. wi. wealth
25: 16. Lest thou be f. with honey
30: 16. earth is not f. with water
22. fool when he is f. with meat
Ec. 1: 8. nor is ear f. with hearing
6: 3. his soul be not f. with good
7. yet appetite is not f.
Can. 5: 2. my head is f. with dew
Is. 6: 1. and his train f. the temple
21: 3. are my loins f. with pain
33: 5. L. hath f. Zion with judgm.
34: 6. sword of L. is f. with blood
43: 24. nor f. me with fat of sacri.
65: 20. that hath not f. his days
Je. 15: 17. hast f. me with indigna.
16: 18. f. inheri. with carcasses
19: 4. f. place with blood of inno-
41:9. Ishm. f. pit with slain [cents
46: 12. thy cry hath f. the land
51: 34. f. his belly with delicates
La. 3: 15. f. me with bitterness
30. he is f. full with reproach
Eze. 8: 17. f. land with violence
10: 3. cloud f. the inner court
11: 6. ye have f. streets with slain
28: 16. they f. thee with violence
36: 38. waste cities be f. with men
43: 5. glory of L. f. house, 44: 4.
Da. 2: 35. stone cut out f. earth
Na. 2: 12. lion f. holes with prey
Ha. 2: 16. Thou art f. with shame
Hag. 1: 6. ye are not f. with drink
Zch. 9:13. I have f. bow with Ephr.
Mat. 27:48. one of them f. a sponge
with vinegar, Mk. 15:36. Jn. 19:
Mk. 2: 21. new piece that f. it [29.

Mk.7:27.said,Let the chil.first be f.
Lu. 1: 53. He hath f. the hungry
2: 40. Jesus f. with wisdom
5: 7. they came and f. both ships
14:23. compel that my house be f.
15:16. fain have f. belly wi. husks
Jn. 2: 7. they f. them up to brim
6:13. f. 12 baskets with fragments
16: 6. sorrow hath f. your heart
Ac. 2: 2. mighty wind f. the house
4: 8. Peter, f. with Holy Ghost
5:3. why hath Satan f. thine heart
28. have f. Jerus. with your doc.
9: 17. mightest be f. with H. G.
13: 9. Paul, f. with H. G. set
Ro. 1: 29. f. with all unrighteousn.
15: 14. that ye are f. with knowl.
24. somewh. f. with your company
2 Co. 7: 4. I am f. with comfort
Ep. 3: 19. might be f. with fulness
5: 18. not with wine, f. with Spi.
Ph. 1: 11. f. with fruits of righte.
Col.1:9. might be f. with the knowl.
2 Ti. 1: 4. th. I may be f. with joy
Ja. 2: 16. be ye warmed and f.
Re.8:5. angel f. the censer with fire
15: 1. is f. up the wrath of God
18:6. in cup she hath f. fill double

Shall, or shalt be FILLED.

Ex.16:12.in morn.s.b.f. with bread
Nu.14:21.earth s.b.f. wi.glory of L.
2 K. 3: 17. valley s.b.f. with water
Pr. 1: 31. s.b.f. with own devices
3:10. s. thy barns b.f. with plenty
12:21. wicked s.b.f. with mischief
14: 14. backslider s. b. f. with his
18:20. with incr. of lips s. he b. f.
20:17. his mouth s.b.f. with gravel
24: 4. by knowl. s. chambers b.f.
Je.13:12. bottle s.b.f. with wine,12.
Eze. 23:33. s-t b. f. with drunken.
39: 20. thus ye s.b.f. at my table
Hab.2:14. earth s.b.f. with knowl.
Zch. 9: 15. they s. b. f. like bowls
Mat. 5:6. that hunger, they s. b. f.
Lu. 1: 15. John s. b. f. with H. G.
3: 5. Every valley s. b. f.
6:21. blessed th. hunger, ye s.b.f.

Was FILLED

Ge. 6: 11. earth, w. f. with violence
1 K. 7: 14. Hiram w. f. with wisd.
2 K. 3: 20. country w.f. with wat.
2 Ch. 5: 13. house w.f. with cloud
16:14. bed w. f. with sweet odours
Ps. 126: 2. mouth w.f. with laugh.
Is. 6: 4. house w. f. with smoke
Je. 51: 5. tho. laud w. f. with sin
Eze. 10: 4. house w. f. with cloud
Lu 1: 41. Elisab. w. f. with H. G.
67. Zacharias w. f. with H. G.
Jn.12:3. house w.f. with the odour
Ac. 19:29. city w.f. with confusion
Re. 15:8. temple w. f. with smoke

Were FILLED.

Ho. 13: 6. Acc. to pasture so w. f.
they w. f. and heart exalted
Lu. 4: 28. they w. f. with wrath
5: 26. glorified G. and w. f. with
6: 11. w.f. with madness [fear
8: 23. they w. f. with water
Jn. 6: 12. when they w. f. he said
26. bec. ye eat of loaves and w.f.
Ac. 2: 4. w. all f. with H. G., 4:31.
3: 10. they w. f. with wonder
5: 17. and w. f. with indignation
13: 45. the Jews w. f. with envy
52. disciples w. f. with joy
Re. 19: 21. all fowls w.f. with flesh
See EAT.

FILLEDST, EST.

De. 6:11. houses full, wh. thou f-dst [not
Ps. 17: 14. whose belly thou f-est
with tress. [f-dst many people
Eze. 27: 33. when wares went forth

FILLET, S.

Ex. 27: 10. and their f-s shall be of
silver, 11.–38: 10, 11, 12, 17, 19.
Ex. 36:38. overlaid chapiters and f.
Je. 52: 21. a f. of twelve cubits

FILLETED.

Ex. 27: 17. all be f. with silver, 38: [17.
38: 28. overlaid chapiters and f.

FILLETH, ING.

Jb. 9: 18. he f. me with bitterness
Ps. 84: 6. rain also f. pools
107:9. f-h hungry soul with goodn.
129: 7. Wh. mower f. not his hu.
147: 14. he f. with finest wheat
Ac. 14: 17. f-g our hearts with food
Ep. 1: 23. fulness of him that f. all [them

FILTH.

Le. 1: † 16. pluck away his crop
with f. thereof
Is. 4: 4. When L. washed f. of Zion
Na. 3: 6. I will cast abominable f.
1 Co. 4: 13. we as the f. of world
1 Pe. 3: 21. not putting away f. of [flesh

FILTHINESS.

2 Ch. 29: 5. carry f. out of holy pl.
Ezr.6:21. separated from f. of heath.
9: 11. uncl. land with f. of people
Pr. 30: 12. yet not washed from f.
Is. 28: 8. tables full of vomit and f.
Je.5:†30. and f. is committed in land
23:†14. I have seen f. in prophets
La. 1: 9. her f. is in her skirts
Eze. 16: 36. thy f. was poured out
22: 15. and I will consume thy f.
24: 11. that f. of it may be molten
13. in thy f. is lewdness; shalt
not be purged from thy f.
36: 25. from f. will I cleanse you
2 Co. 7: 1. cleanse fr. all f. of flesh
Ep. 5: 4. Nor let f. be once named
Ja. 1: 21. Wherefore lay apart all f.
Re. 17: 4. cup full of f. of fornica- [tion

FILTHY.

Jb.15:16. How much more f. is man
Ps. 14: 3. altog. become f., 53: 3.
Is. 64: 6. all our righte. as f. rags
Zph. 3: 1. Woe to her that is f.
Zch.3:3.Josh. clothed with f. garm.
4. Take away f. garments fr. him
Col. 3:8. you put off f. communicat.
1 Ti. 3: 3. nor greedy of f. lucre, 8.
Tit. 1: 7. not given to f. lucre
11. for f. lucre's sake, 1 Pe. 5: 2.
2 Pe.2:7.Lot vexed with f. conversa
Jude 8. these f. dreamers defile flesh
Re. 22: 11. that is f. let him be f. [still

FINALLY.

2 Co. 13: 11. f. brethren, farewell,
Ep. 6: 10. Ph. 3: 1.–4:8. 2 Th:
3: 1. 1 Pe. 3: 8.

FIND.

Ge. 19:11. wearied thems. to f. door
32:19. speak unto Esau when ye f.
Nu. 32: 23. your sin sh. f. you out
35:27. the revenger of blood f. him
De. 22:25. f. damsel and lie, 23, 28.
Ju. 14:12. f. it out, then will I give
17:8. sojourn where he could f., 9.
Ru. 1: 9. L. grant ye may f. rest
1 S. 20: 21. Go, f. out arrows, 36.
24: 19. if a man f. his enemy
1 K. 18: 5. peradv. we may f. grass
2 Ch. 2: 14. to f. out every device
32: 4. why Assyria f. much water
Jb. 23: 3. Oh, that I might f. him
34:11. cause man to f. acc. to ways
Ps. 10:15. wickedn. till thou f. none
Pr. 2: 5. shalt f. knowl. of God
4:22. my words life to those f. them
8: 9. right to them that f. knowl.
12. I f. out knowl. of witty inven.
Ec. 7: 14. should f. noth. aft. him
27. one by one to f. out account
12: 10. f. out acceptable words
Can. 5:8. if f. my beloved, tell him
Is. 34: 14. screech owl sh. f. rest
58: 3. in day of fast you f. pleas.
Je. 10:18. distress, that they f. it so
La. 1:6. like harts th. f. no pasture
2: 9. her prophets f. no vision
Da 6:4. princes sought to f. occasion
ag. Dan., but could f. none
5. not f. except we f. conc. law of
Mat. 7: 14. few there be that f. it
18: 13. if so be he f. it, he rejoic-h
Mk. 11:13. if haply he might f. any
13:36. Lest coming, he f. you slee .
Lu. 6:7. might f. an accusa. ag. him
12:38. f. them so, blessed are serv-s
13: 7. I come seeking fruit f. none
15:4. go af. that is lost until he f. it
8. seek diligently till she f. it?
Jn. 10:9. in and out and f. pasture
Ac. 7: 46. desired to f. a tab. for G.
17:27. might feel after and f. him
23: 9. We f. no evil in this man
Ro. 9:19. Why doth he yet f. fault?
2 Co. 9: 4. and f. you unprepared
2 Ti. 1:18. he may f. mercy of the L.
See FAVOUR.

Can or canst FIND.

Ge. 41: 38. c. we f. such a one as
Ex. 5: 11. get straw where c. f. it
Ezr. 7: 16. all gold thou c-t f.
Jb. 3:22. glad when they c. f. grave
11: 7. c-t by searching f. out G.?
c-t f. out Alm. unto perf.?
Pr. 20: 6. faithful man who c. f.?
31: 10. Who c. f. a virt. woman?
Ec. 3: 11. no man c. f. out work G.
7: 24. exc-g deep, who c. f. it?
Je.5:1. if ye c. f. man seeketh truth

Cannot FIND.

Ge. 38: 22. retur. said, I c. f. her
1 K.18:12. if c. f. thee, will slay me
Jb. 17: 10. I c. f. one wise man am.
37: 23. Alm., we c. f. him out
Ec. 8: 17. man c. f. out the work

FIND grace.

Ge. 32: 5. I may f. g. in thy sight,
Ex. 33: 13.
33: 8. to f. g. in sight of my lord
15. let me f. g., 34: 11. [my lord
47: 25. let us f. g. in the sight of
Ru. 2: 2. in whose sight I sh. f. g.
1 S. 1: 18. Let thy handmaid f. g.
2 S.16:4. may f. g. in thy sight, O k.
He. 4: 16. f. g. to help in time of

I FIND.

Ge. 18: 26. If I f. in Sodom fifty
28. If I f. there 45 | 30. if I f. 30.
Ps. 132: 5. Until I f. place for L.
Ec.7:26. I f. more than death wom.
Can. 8:1. when I sho. f. thee, I kiss
Je. 45: 3. sighing, and I f. no rest
Lu. 23: 4. Pilate said, I f. no fault
in this man, Jn. 18:38.–19: 4, 6.
Ro. 7: 18. that is good, I f. not
21. I f. law, when I would do good

Not FIND or FIND not.

Ex. 16: 25. to day ye shall n. f. it
Le. 12: † 8. if hand f. n. suffic-y
1 S. 23: 17. Saul shall n. f. thee
2 S.17:20. sought, could n. f. them
Pr. 1: 28. shall seek me early, but
sh. n. f. me, Ho. 5: 6. Jn. 7:
Ec.7:28. seeketh, but I f. n. [34, 36.
Can. 5: 6. but I could n. f. him
Is. 41: 12. shalt n. f. them, Ho.2:7.
Da. 6: 5. n. f. occasion ag-t Daniel
Ho. 2:6. that she sh. n. f. her paths
Am. 8: 12. run to seek word, and
n. f. it [him
Lu. 5: 19. n. f. way might bring
19: 48. n. f. what might do to Jes.
Jn. 7:35. go, that we sh. n. f. him?
Ro. 7: 18. how to do good, I f. n.
2 Co.12:20. n. f. you such as I would
Re.9:6. seek death, and shall n. f. it

Shall, or shalt FIND.

Ge. 44:†34. see evil that s. f. my fa.
De. 4: 29. if seek L. thou s-t f. him
28:65. s-t f. no ease am. these nat-s
Ju. 9: 33. do as thou s-t f. occasion
1 S. 9: 13. ye s. f. him bef. he eat
10:2. s. f. two men by Ra.'s sepul.
† 7. shalt do as thy hand s. f.

2 K. 7: † 9. tarry, we s. f. punish.
2 Ch. 20: 16. s. f. them at end of
20: 9. chil. s. f. compas. [brook
Ezr. 4: 15. s. f. in book of records
Ps.17:3.tried me, and s-t f. nothing
21:8.Thy hand s. f. out all enem.
Pr. 1: 13.We s. f. all precious substance [29: 13.
8: 17. seek me early, s. f. me, Je.
Pr. 16: 20. matter wisely, s. f. good
19: 8. keepeth underst. s. f. good
Ec. 11: 1. s-t f. it after many days
Je. 2:24. in her mouth they s. f. her
6: 16. ye s. f. rest, Mat. 11: 29.
29: 13. s. f. me, when ye search
Ho. 12:8. in labours s. f. none iniq.
Mat. 7:7. seek and ye s. f., Lu.11:9.
10: 39. loseth life for my sake s. f. it, 16: 25.
17:27. thou s-t f. a piece of money
21: 2. ye s. f. an ass tied, and a colt, Mk. 11: 2. Lu. 19: 30.
22: 9. as ye s. f. bid to marriage
24:46. s. f. so doing, Lu. 12:37,43.
Lu. 2: 12. Ye s. f. babe wrapped in
18:8.cometh s.he f. faith on earth?
Jn. 21: 6. on right side, ye s. f.
Re.18:14. thou s-t f. them no more

FINDEST.

Ge. 31:32.With whomso. f. thy gods
Eze. 3: 1. eat that thou f. eat this

FINDETH.

Ge. 4: 14. that f. me shall slay me
De.19:†5.slippeth and f.his neighb.
Jb. 33: 10. he f. occasions ag. me.
Ps. 119:162. I rejoice, as one f. spoil
Pr. 3: 13. Happy is man f. wisd.
8:35.whoso f. me, f. life, shall obt.
14: 6. scorner seeketh wisd. f. not
17: 20. a froward heart, f. no good
18: 22. Whoso f. a wife f. a good
21: 10. his neighbour f. no favour
21. followeth aft. mercy f. life
Ec. 9:10.Whatso. thy hand f. to do
La. 1: 3. am. heathen, she f. no rest
Ho. 14: 3. in thee fatherl. f. mercy
Mat. 7: 8. he seeketh f., Lu. 11:10.
10:39. He that f. his life sh. lose it
12:43.dry pla., seeking rest, f.none
44. f. it empty, swept, Lu. 11:25.
26: 40. f. disci. asleep, Mk. 14:37.
Jn. 1: 41. first f. own bro. Simon
43. Jesus f. Philip
45. Philip f. Nathanael
5:14.Afterw. Jesus f. him in tem- [ple

FINDING.

Ge. 4: 15. lest any f. Cain kill him
Jb. 9: 10. doeth things past f. out
Ps. 32: † 6. shall pray in time of f.
Is. 58: 13. f. thine own pleas. nor
Lu. 11:24. seeking rest, and f. none
Ac.4:21.f. noth. how might punish
19: 1. Paul f. certain disci., 21: 4.
21:2.f.ship sailing over to Phenicia
Ro. 11: 33. and his ways past f. out
He. 8: 8. For, f. fault with them

FINE. [Verb.]

Jb. 28: 1. place for gold where they [f. it

FINE. [Adj.]

Ge. 18:6. three measures of f. meal
Ezr. 8: 27. vessels of f. copper, as
Jb. 28:†15.f.gold not given for wisd.
Is. 19: 9. they that work in f. flax
Re. 1:15. feet like unto f. brass, 2:18.

FINE flour.

Le. 2: 1. offering be of f. f., 24: 5.
4. cakes of f. f. mingled with oil,
5, 7.-7: 12.-14: 10, 21.-23: 13.
Nu. 6: 15.-7: 13, 19, 25, 31, 37,
43, 49, 55, 61.-8: 8.
5: 11. part of ephah of f. f., 6: 20.
1 K. 4: 22. thirty measures of f. f.
2 K.7:1. measure of f. f. for, 16,18.
1 Ch. 9: 29. to oversee f. f., 23: 29.
Eze. 16: 13. thou didst eat f. f.
19. I gave thee f. f., and oil
46: 14. oil to temper with f. f.

Re. 18: 13. none buyeth her f. f.

FINE gold.

2 Ch. 3: 5. he overlaid with f. g., 8.
Jb. 28: † 15. f. g. not be given for
17. not be for jewels of f.g. [wisd.
31:24. to f. g. Thou my confidence
Ps. 19: 10. to be desired than f. g.
119: 127. I love com-ts above f. g.
Pr. 3: 14. gain of wisdom than f.g.
8: 19. My fruit is better, than f.g.
25: 12. as ornam. of f. g., so is a
Ca. 5: 11. His head is as most f. g.
15. pillars upon sockets of f. g.
Is. 13:12. man more prec. than f.g.
La. 4: 1. how most f. g. changed!
2. sons of Z. comparable to f. g.
Da. 2: 32. This image's head f. g.
10: 5. girded with f. g. of Uphaz
Zch. 9:3.Tyrus heaped f. g. as mire

FINE linen.

Ge. 41: 42. Pha. in vest-s of f. l.
Ex. 25: 4. offering ye sh. take, f. l.
26: 1. ten curtains of f. twined l.
31. vail of f. l., 36: 35. 2 Ch. 3:14
36. hanging of f. twined l., 27: 9,
16, 18.-36: 37.-38: 9, 16, 18.
28:5. gold and f. l. to make garm.
6. ephod of f. l., 39: 2.
8. girdle f. l., 39: 5, 29.
15.breastplate of f.twined l.,39:8.
39. shalt embroider coat of f. l.,
and make mitre of f. l.
35: 6. let him bring off-g of f. l.
23. every man with whom f. l.
25. the women brought of f. l.
35. wisd. to work all manner of
work and f.l., 38:23. 2 Ch. 2:14.
36: 8. wrought curtains of f. l.
39: 27. made coats of f. l. for Aa.
28. mitre of f. l., bonnets of f. l.
1 Ch.4:21. families that wrought f.l.
15: 27. David with robe of f. l.
Es. 1:6. hangings with cords of f. l.
8:15. Mord. went with garm. of f.l.
Pr. 7: 16. decked my bed with f. l.
31: 24. maketh f. l., and selleth it
Is. 3: 23. Lord will take away f. l.
Eze. 16: 10. I girded thee with f. l.
13. thy raiment was of f. l. and
27: 7. f. l. from E. to be thy sail
16. Syria occupied with f. l.
Mk. 15: 46. Joseph bought f. l. [l.
Lu. 16:19. rich man in purple and f.
Re.18:12.merchandise of f. l.depart.
16. city in f. l. come to nought
19:8. granted to be arrayed in f. l.
14. armies in heav. clothed in f.l.

FINER. [Noun.]

Pr. 25:4. come forth a vessel for the [f.

FINEST.

Ps. 81:16. fed thee with f. of wheat
147: 14. filleth with f. of wheat

FINING.

Pr. 17: 3. f. pot is for silver, 27:21.

FINGER.

Ex. 8:19. said, This is the f. of God
29:12. put blood upon altar with f.
31:18.written with f. of G..De.9:10.
Le. 4: 6. priest dip f. in bl., 17, 25,
30, 34.-8: 15.-9: 9.-16: 14, 19.
14:16. priest sh. dip right f. in oil,
and sprinkle with his f., 27.
Nu. 19: 4. take of her bl. with his f.
1 K. 12: 10. little f. thicker, 2 Ch.
Is. 58:9. putting forth of f. [10:10.
Lu. 11: 20. if I wi. f. of G. cast out
16: 24. may dip tip of his f. in wa.
Jn. 8: 6. with f. wrote on ground
20:25. put my f. into print of nails
27. Reach hither thy f. and behold

FINGERS. [20: 6.

2 S. 21:20. on ev. hand six f., 1 Ch.
Ps. 8:3. consider heav-s, work of thy
144:1. L., teach. my f. to fight [f.
Pr. 6: 13. wicked teacheth with f.
7: 3. Bind them upon thy f. write
Can. 5: 5. f. with sweet myrrh

Is. 2: 8. which own f. made, 17: 8.
59:3.hands with blood, f. with iniq
Je. 52: 21. thickness of pillar 4 f.
Da. 5: 5. came f. of a man's hand
Mat. 23: 4. burdens, will not move
them with one of f., Lu. 11:46.
Mk. 7:33. he put his f. into his ears

FINISH.

Ge. 6: 16. in cubit shalt thou f. it
Da. 9: 24. to f. transgression, and
Zch. 4: 9. Zerub.'s hands shall f. it
Mat. 10: † 23. sh. not f. cities of Isr.
Lu. 14: 28. whe. sufficient to f. it
29. founda., and is not able to f. it
30. began to build, not able to f.
Jn. 4: 34. my meat is to f. his work
5:36. works Fa. hath given me to f.
Ac. 20: 24. I might f. my course
Ro. 9: 28. For he will f. the work
2 Co.8:6. would f. in you same grace
Ph. 1: † 6. hath begun, will f. it

FINISHED.

Ge. 2: 1. heavens and earth were f.
Ex. 39: 32. all the work f., 40: 33.
De. 31: 24. end of writing until f.
Jos 4:10. stood until ev. thing was f.
Ru.3:18.not rest, until have f. thing
1 K. 6: 9. Sol. built house and f. it,
14. 22, 38. 2 Ch. 5: 1.-7: 11.
7: 1. Sol. f. all his house, 9: 1, 25.
2 Ch. 8: 16.
22. work of the pillars f.
1 Ch.27:24. to number, but he f. not
28:20. L. not fail thee, until hast f.
2 Ch. 4: 11. Huram f. the work
24: 14. when had f. repairing
29: 28. sang, until burnt off. was f.
31: 1. when all was f. all Israel
7. they f. heaps in seventh month
Ezr. 4: † 12. Jews have f. the walls
5: 16. building, and yet it is not f.
6: 14. elders of Jews built f. it, 15.
Ne. 6:15. wall was f. in 52 days
Da. 5:26. G. numb-d kingd. and f.
12: 7. all these things sh. be f.
Mat.13:53.when Jes. had f. parables
19: 1. Jes. had f. sayings, 26: 1.
Jn.17:4. I have f. work thou gavest
19:30. said, It is f. and bowed head
Ac. 21: 7. f. our course from Tyre
2 Ti. 4: 7. I have f. my course
He. 4: 3. works f. fr. foundation
Ja. 1: 15. sin, f. bringeth death
Re. 10: 7. mystery of G. sh. be f.
11: 7. witn-s shall have f. testimo.
20: 5. lived not. until 1,000 years f.

FINISHER. [faith

He. 12: 2. Jes., author and f. of our

FINS. [14: 9.

Le. 11: 9. whatever hath f. eat, De.
10. hath not f. be an abomi., 12.

FIR.

1 K.5:8. do all conc. timber of f.
6: 15. cov-d floor with planks of f.
Can. 1: 17. cedar, our rafters of f.

FIR tree.

1 K. 6: 34. two doors were of f. t.
2 Ch. 3:5. house he ceiled with f. t.
Is. 41:19. I will set in desert the f.t.
55: 13. Instead of thorn come f. t.
60: 13. f. t. the pine tree, and box
Hos. 14: 8. I am like a green f. t.
Zch. 11: 2. Howl, f. t.

FIR trees. [11.

1 K. 5: 10. Hiram gave Sol. f.t., 9:
2 K. 19: 23. cut tall f.t., Is. 37: 24.
2 Ch. 2: 8. Send me f. t.
Is. 14: 8. the f. t. rejoice
Ps. 104:17. for stork f. t. her house
Eze. 27:5. made ship boards of f. t.
31:8. f. t. were not like his boughs
Na. 2:3. f. t. sh. be terribly shaken

FIR wood. [f. w.

2 S. 6: 5. Isr. played on instru-s of

FIRE.

Ge. 15:†17. a lamp of f. passed betw.
22:6. Ab. took f. in hand, and knife

Ge.22:7. my fa., Behold f. and wood
Ex. 3: 2. the bush burned with f.
9: 23. Lord sent hail and the f.
24. there was hail, and f.mingled
12: 8. eat flesh that night roast
19:18. L. upon Sinai in f. [wi.f.,9.
22: 6. If f. break out, and catch in
32: 24. cast gold into f. came calf
40: 38. f. was on tabern. by night,
Nu. 9: 16. De. 1: 33. [(2)
Le. 1:7. sons of priest put f. on alt.,
8. upon wood in f., 12, 17.-3: 5.
2:14. green ears of corn dried by f.
6:9. f. of altar burning, 10, 12, 13.
9: 24. came a f. out fr. bef. Lord
10: 1. sons of Aa. put f. in censers
2. out f. from L. and devoured
16: 13. shall put incense upon f.
18: 21. not let thy seed pass thro.
f., De. 18:10. 2 K. 17:17.-23:10.
22: 22. nor make an offering by f.
Nu. 6: 18. take hair, put it in f.
9:15. as it were appearance of f.,16.
11: 2. Moses prayed, f. quenched
16: 7. take ye censers, put f., 18.
37. take censers, and scatter f.
46. Take censer,and put f.therein
18: 9. holy things reserved fr. f.
21: 28. is f. gone out fr. Heshbon
31:10. their goodly castles with f.
23. that may abide f. go thro. f.
De. 4: 11. mount. burned with f.,
36. shewed thee his great f. [9:15.
5: 5. for ye afraid by reason of f.
18: 16. nor let me see great f. more
33: † 2. fr. hand went a f. of law
Jos.7:25. Isr. burned Achan with f.
Ju. 6: 21. rose up f. out of rock
9: 15. let f. come out of bramble
16: 9. of tow when it toucheth f.
1 K. 18: 23. put no f. under, 25.
24. God that answereth by f.
38. f. of Lord fell, 2 Ch. 7: 1, 3.
19: 12. aft. earthquake a f. but L.
not in f. after f. a voice [14.
2 K. 1: 10. then let f. come down,
12. f. of G. came down from heav.
2:11. app-d chariot and horses of f.
6:17. mount. full of chariots of f.
16:3. Ahaz made son to pass thro. f.
19: 18. have cast gods into f.
21: 6. made son pass thro. f., 2
Ch. 33: 6. [f.
23:10. no man make son pass thro.
1 Ch. 21:26. L. ans. from heav. by f.
2 Ch. 35:13. roasted passover with f.
Ne. 2: 3. gates consumed wi. f.,13.
Jb. 1:16. f. of God is fallen fr. heav.
18: 5. spark of his f. not shine
28: 5. is turned up as it were f.
41: 19. and sparks of f. leap out
Ps. 39: 3. while musing f. burned
46: 9. he burneth chariot in f.
66:12. went thro. f. and wa. [wick.
68: 2. as wax melteth bef. f. let
74: 7. have cast f. into thy sanct.
78: 14. all night with light of f.,
83:14. As f. burneth wood [105:39.
97: 3. A f. goeth before him [f.
105: 32. he gave hail and flaming
118:12. quenched as f. of thorns
140:10. let them be cast into the f.
148: 8. f. and hail, stormy wind
Pr. 6: 27. Can man take f. in bos.
16: 27. in his lips is as burning f.
26:20. Where no wood f. goeth out
21. as wood is to f. so is contentious [enough
30: 16. grave and f.; saith not,
Is. 9: 5. this sh. be with fuel of f.
18. wickedness burneth as f.
19. people shall be as fuel of f.
10: 16. sh. kindle a burning like f.
17. light of Isr. shall be for a f.
30: 14. not a sherd to take f. from
33. pile is f. and much wood
31: 9. saith L., whose f. is in Zion
Is. 37:19. kings cast their gods into f.
43: 2. walkest thro. f. not burned
44: 16. He burneth part in f., and
saith, Aha, I have seen the f.
47:14. as stubble, f. sh. burn them
50: 11. walk in light of your f.
64: 2. as when melting f. burneth,
f. causeth waters to boil
65: 5. these are a f. all the day
66: 15. the Lord will come with f.
16. by f. will L. plead with all flesh
24. worm not die,nei. f. be quench.
Je. 4: 4. lest my fury come like f.
5: 14. my words in thy mouth f.
20: 9. his word as a f. in my bones
21: 12. lest my fury go out like f.
22: 7. sh. cast choice cedars in f.
29:22. whom k. of Bab. roasted in f.
32: 35. sons to pass thro. f. to Molech, Eze. 16: 21.-20: 26, 31.
36: 22. there was a f. on hearth
23. Jehudi cut roll, cast it into f.
48: 45. f. sh. come out of Heshbon
51: 58. folk shall labour in the f.
La. 2: 3. ag. Jac. like flaming f.
4. he poured out his fury like f.
Eze.1: 4. behold, a f. infolding its.
13. f. bright, out of f. lightning
10: 6. Take f. from betw. wheels
7. cherub stretched hand unto f.
15: 6. forests given to f. for fuel
7. go out from one f. and anoth.
19: 14. f. is gone out of rod of her
21:31. will blow ag. thee in f.,22:21.
32. Thou shalt be for fuel to f.
22: 20. to blow f. upon it, to melt
24: 9. I will make pile for f. great
12. her scum shall be in f.
28:18. will bring f. fr. midst of thee
36:5. in the f. of my jealousy,38:19.
Da. 3: 27. upon whose bodies f. no
power, nor smell of f. passed
7: 9. his wheels like burning f.
10: 6. his eyes as lamps of f.
Ho. 7: 6. in morning as a flaming f.
Jo. 2: 30. blood, f. and, Ac. 2: 19.
Am.5:6. lest break like f. in h. of Jo.
7:4. L. God called to contend by f.
Ob. 18. house of Jac. shall be a f.
Mi.1:4. molten und. him as wax bef.
Na. 1:6. fury poured out like f. [f.
Ha. 2:13. peo. shall labour in very f.
Zch. 2: 5. be unto her a wall of f.
3: 2. is not this a brand out of f.?
12:6. gov-s of Jud. like hearth of f.
13: 9. bring 3d part thro. f. [(2)
Mal. 3: 2. he is like a refiner's f.
Mat. 3: 10. tree bringeth not good
fruit cast into f., 7: 19. Lu. 3:
9. Jn. 15: 6.
11. with H. Ghost, and f., Lu.3:16.
13: 40. tares are burned in the f.
42. sh. cast into furnace of f., 50.
17: 15. oft. falleth into f., Mk.9:22.
18: 8. having hands to be cast
into everl. f., Mk.9:43,46,47,48.
25: 41. Depart, ye cursed, into
everlasting f.
Mk. 9: 44. f. is not quenched, 45.
49. ev. one sh. be salted with f.
14: 54. Peter warmed himself at f.
Lu. 9: 54. we command f. to come
17: 29. the same day it rained f.
22: 56. maid beheld him by the f.
Ac. 2: 3. cloven tongues, like as f.
28: 3. when Paul laid sticks on f.
5. he shook off the beast into f.
1 Co. 3: 13. it shall be revealed by
f. f. sh. try every man's work
15. he shall be saved, yet as by f.
2 Th.1:8. In flaming f. taking venge.
He. 1: 7. his ministers a flame of f.
11:34. Quenched the violence of f.
12: 18. mount that burned with f.
Ja. 3: 5. matter a little f. kindleth
6. tongue is a f. a world of iniq.
5: 3. eat your flesh as it were f.
1 Pe. 1:7. of gold, tho. tried with f.
2 Pe.3:7. reserved unto f. ag. judgm.
12. heavens on f. shall be dissol.
Jude 7. suffering veng. of eternal f.
23. save pulling them out of f.
Re. 3: 18. buy of me gold tried in f.
4: 5. seven lamps of f. bef. throne
8: 5. the angel filled censer with f.
7. hail and f. mingled with blood
8. as gr. mountain burning with f.
9:17. out of mouths issued f.,11:5.
18. third part was killed by the f.
13: 13. maketh f. come fr. heaven
14:18. angel wh. had power over f.
15: 2. as sea of glass mingled wi. f.
16: 8. power to scorch men with f.
20: 9. and f. came down from G.
10. devil was cast into lake of f.
14. and hell cast into lake of f.
15. not in book of life, cast into f.
21: 8. in lake wh. burneth with f.
See **BRIMSTONE, BURN, BURNED, BURNT, COALS, CONSUME, CONSUMING, DEVOUR, DEVOURED, DEVOURING, FLAME, HELL, MIDST.**

Kindle, ed, eth, FIRE.

Ex. 22: 6. k-d f. make restitution
35: 3. ye shall k. no f. on sabbath
De. 32: 22. a f. is k-d in my anger
and sh. burn, Je. 15: 14.-17:4.
2 S. 22: 13. bef. him coals of f. k-d
Ps. 78: 21. so f. was k-d ag. Jacob
106:18. f. was k-d in their company
Is. 10: 16. sh. k. a burning like f.
50: 11. behold, all ye that k. a f.
Je.7:18. gathered wood, fathers k-d f.
11: 16. he k-d f. upon green olive
17:27. then will I k. a f. in the gates
21: 14. I will k. a f. in the forest
43:12. I will k. f. in houses of gods
49: 27. I will k. a f. in the wall of
50: 32. I will k. a f. in his cities
La. 4: 11. L. hath k-d a f. in Zion
Eze. 20: 47. I will k. a f. in forest
24: 10. k. the f. consume the flesh
Am. 1: 14. will k. f. in wall of Rab.
Mal.1:10. nor k. f. on alt. for nought
Lu. 12: 49. I am come to send f.
what if it be k-d
22: 55. when had k-d f. in hall
Ac. 28: 2. the barbarians k-d a f.
Ja. 3: 5. great matter little f. k-h

Made by FIRE.

Ex. 29: 18. an offering m.b.f. unto
the L., 25, 41. Le. 1: 9, 13, 17.
-2: 2, 9, 16.-3: 3, 5, 9, 11, 14,
16.-7: 5, 25.-8: 21, 28.-21: 6.
-22: 27.-23: 8, 13, 18, 25, 27,
36, 37.-24: 7. Nu. 15: 3, 10, 13,
14.-18: 17.-28: 3.
Le. 2: 3. offerings of the L. m.b.f.,
10.-4: 35.-5: 12.-6: 17, 18.-7:
30, 35.-10: 12, 15.-21: 21.-24:
9. De. 18: 1. 1 S. 2: 28.
10: 13. sacrifices m. b. f., Nu.28:
2. Jos. 13: 14.
Nu. 15: 25. their sacrifice m. b. f.,
28: 6, 8, 13, 19, 24.-29:6,13,36.

Pillar, s of FIRE.

Ex. 13: 21. L. before them in p. o.
f., 22. -40: 38. Nu. 14: 14.
Ne. 9: 12, 19.
14: 24. L. looked thro. the p.o.f.
Re. 10: 1. and his feet as p-s o. f.

Send, or sent FIRE.

La. 1: 13. he s-t f. into my bones
Eze. 39: 6. I will s. f. on Magog
Ho. 8: 14. will s. f. upon his cities
Am. 1: 4. will s.f. into hou. of Ha-
7. I will s.f. on wall of Gaza [zael
10. will s. f. on Tyrus
12. I will s. f. upon Teman
2:2. I will s.f. upon Moab | 5.Jud.
Lu. 12: 49. come to s. f. on earth

Set or setteth FIRE.

De. 32:22. s. on f. founda-s of mts.

Jos. 8: 8. ye shall s. city of Ai on f.
19. they hasted, and s. city on f.
Ju. 1: 8. Judah had s. Jerus. on f.
9: 49. the people s. the hold on f.
15: 5. had s. the brands on f.
20: 48. they s. on f. cities of Benj.
2 S. 14: 30. s. Joab's field on f.
31. Why serv-ts s. my field on f.?
2 K. 8: 12. will s. strong holds on f.
Ps. 57: 4. I lie am. them are s. on f.
Pr. 29: †8. scornful men s. city on f.
Is. 27: 11. the women s. them on f.
42: 25. he hath s. him on f. round
Je. 6: 1. s. up sign of f. in Beth-hac.
32: 29. Chal-s shall s. on f. city
Eze. 30: 8. when I have s. f. in E.
14. I will s. f. in Zoan | 16. in E.
39: 9. s. on f. burn weapons of Gog
Ja. 3: 6. tongue is a fire, and s-h on
f. it is s. on f. of hell

Strange FIRE.

Le. 10: 1. Nadab and Abihu off-d s. f.
Nu. 3: 4. died when off-d s. f., 26: 61.

FIRES.

Is. 24: 15. glorify ye the L. in the f.

FIREBRAND, S.

Ju. 7: † 16. put f-s within pitchers
15: 4. Samson took f. and put f. in
Pr. 26: 18. As mad man casteth f-s
Is. 7: 4. tails of these smoking f-s
Am. 4: 11. ye were as a f. plucked

FIREPANS.

Ex. 27: 3. thou shalt make basins
and f. [sels of brass
38: 3. he made the f. and all ves-
2 K. 25: 15. f. carried he away, Je.
[52: 19.

FIRKINS.

Jn. 2: 6. containing two or three f.

FIRM.

Jos. 3: 17. priests stood f. on dry [ground
4: 3. where priests' feet stood f.
Jb. 41: 23. are f. in themselves
24. His heart is as f. as a stone
Ps. 73: 4. no bands, strength is f.
Da. 6: 7. consulted to make f. decree
He. 3: 6. rejoicing of hope f. unto [end

FIRMAMENT.

Ge 1: 6. Let be a f. in midst of water
7. G. made f. divided waters und.
f. from waters above f.
8. God called the f. Heaven
14. Let there be lights in f., 15.
17. and God set them in the f.
20. fowl that may fly ab. open f.
Ps. 19: 1. f. sheweth his handywork
150: 1. praise him in f. of power
Eze 1: 22. likeness of f. as crystal, 23.
25. was a voice from f.
26. ab. f. was likeness of throne
10: 1. in f. above the cherubim
Da. 12: 3. shall shine as brightness [of f.

FIRST.

Ge. 2: 11. The name of f. is Pison
25: 25. f. came out red all over
26: 1. a famine besides f. famine
38: 28. midwife said, This came f.
41: 20. did eat up f. 7 fat kine
Ex. 4: 8. if not hearken to f. sign
22: 29. delay to offer f. ripe fruits
23: 19. the f. of firstfruits bring
28: 17. f. row be sardine, 39: 10.
34: 1. two tables like unto the f., 4.
De. 10: 1, 2, 3.
Le. 4: 21. as he burned f., bullock
5: 8. offer what is for sin off. f.
9: 15. off-d it for sin, as the f.
Nu. 2: 9. These shall f. set forth
10: 13. f. took their journey, 14.
15: 20. offer cake of f. of your dough
for heave off., 21. Eze. 44: 30.
24: 20. Amalek was f. of nations
De. 10: 10. according to the f. time
11: 14. give thee f. and latter rain
13: 9. thine hand sh. be f. upon him
17: 7. hands of witn. be f. upon him
18: 4. the f. of the fleece give him
33: 21. provided f. part for hims.

Jos. 21: 10. theirs was f. lot, 1 Ch.
24: 7.-25: 9. [20: 18.
Ju. 1: 1. who shall go up f. to fight,
20: 39. Isr. smitten as in f. battle
1 S. 14: 14. f. slaughter was 20 men
35. was f. altar Saul built unto L.
2 S. 3: 13. except thou f. bring Michal
19: 20. am come f. this day to meet
43. advice should not be f. had
23: 19. captain he attained not unto
f. three, 23. 1 Ch. 11: 21, 25.
1 K. 17: 13. but make a little cake f.
18: 25. dress it f. for ye are many
20: 17. yo. men of princes went f.
1 Ch. 9: 2. f. inhabi. that dwelt [f.
11: 6. Whosoever smiteth Jebusites
16: 7. day Da. deliv. f. this psalm
2 Ch. 3: 3. length after f. measure
17: 3. walked in f. ways of Da.
Ezr. 3: 12. had seen glory of f. hou.
Es. 1: 14. which sat f. in kingdom
Jb 15: 7. Art thou f. man born?
Pr. 18: 17. that is f. in his own cause
Is. 41: 27. f. sh. say to Zion, Behold
43: 27. f. fa. hath sinned ag. me
60: 9. the ships of Tarshish f. to
Je. 4: 31. bringeth forth her f. child
16: 18. f. I will recomp. their iniq.
36: 28. write words were in f. roll
50: 17. f. king of Assyria devoured
Eze. 10: 14. f. face was of cherub
40: 21. f. gate, Zch. 14: 10.
Da. 6: 2. Dan., was f. president
7: 4. f. beast like lion, Re. 4: 7.
8. f. horns plucked up by
24. another shall be diverse fr. f.
8: 21. great horn betw. eyes is f. king
10: † 13 Michael f. came to help me
Ho. 2: 7. will return to my f. husb.
Am. 6: 7. sh. go with f. that go cap.
Mi. 4: 8. to thee the f. dominion
Hag. 2: 3. who saw house in f. glory
Zch. 6: 2. In f. chariot red horses
12: 7. L. sh. save tents of Jud. f.
Mat. 5: 24. f. be reconciled to thy bro.
6: 33. seek ye f. kingd. of G. [6: 42.
7: 5. f. cast beam out of eye, Lu.
8: 21. f. to bury my father, Lu. 9: 59.
10: 2. The f. Simon who is called Pe.
12: 29. f. bind strong man, Mk. 3: 27.
45. state worse than f., Lu. 11: 26.
13: 30. Gather ye f. the tares
17: 10. that Elias must f. come,
11. Mk. 9: 11, 12.
27. take up fish that f. cometh
20: 10. the f. came, they supposed
21: 28. he came to f. and said, Son
31. who of twain? They say, The f.
36. he sent other servants than f.
22: 25. f. when married, Mk. 12:
20. Lu. 20: 29. [30.
38. this is f. com., Mk 12: 28, 29,
23: 26. Phari. cleanse f. th. within
Mk. 4: 28. f. the blade, then the ear
7: 27. Let the children f. be filled
9: 35. if desire to be f. he be last
13: 10. gospel must f. be published
16: 9. he appeared f. to Mary Mag.
Lu. 1: 3. perfect understanding fr. f.
2: 2. f. made when Cyrenius gov.
6: 1. on second sabbath after f.
9: 61. let me f. go bid farewell
10: 5. f. say, Peace be to this hou.
11: 38. that he had not f. washed
12: 1. say unto disciples f. of all
14: 18. The f. said, I have bought
28. sitteth not down f. and count.
31. down f. and counteth the cost
16: 5. unto f., How much owest
17: 25. f. must he suffer many thi.
19: 16. came f. say-g L. thy pound
21: 9. these must f. come to pass
Jn. 1: 41. He f. findeth bro. Simon
5: 4. f. stepped in, was made whole
8: 7. without sin, let him f. cast sto.
10: 40. where John at f. baptized
18: 13. led him away to Annas f.

Jn. 19: 32. soldiers brake legs of the f.
20: 4. disci. came f. to sepul., 8.
Ac. 3: 26. unto you f. God sent him
7: 12. Jacob sent out our fathers f.
11: 26. called Christians f. in An-
12: 10. past f. and 2d ward [tioch
13: 24. Jn. had f. preached baptism
46. it sho. f. have been spoken to
16: † 12. Philippi f. city of Maced.
26: 20. f. unto them of Damascus
23. C. sho. be f. sho. rise fr. dead
27: 43. sho. cast thems. f. into sea
Ro 1: 8. f. I thank my God thro. C.
16. Jew f. and also to Greek
2: 9. of Jew f. and of Gentile, 10.
10: 19. f. Mo. saith, I will provoke
11: 35. who hath f. given to him?
15: 24. if f. I be somewhat filled
1 Co. 11: 18. f. of all when ye come
12: 28. f. apostles, secondarily
14: 30. let the f. hold his peace
15: 3. for I delivered f. of all that
45. f. man Adam made liv. soul
46. that not f. which is spiritual
47. f. man is of earth, earthy
2 Co. 8: 5. f. gave selves to the L.
12. if there be f. a willing mind
Ep. 1: 12. who f. trusted in Christ
4: 9. descended f. into lower parts
6: 2. wh. is f. com-t with promise
1 Th. 4: 16. dead in Ch. shall rise f.
2 Th. 2: 3. except a falling away f.
1 Ti. 1: 16. in me f. C. might shew
2: 1. exhort, f. of all supplications
13. Adam f. formed, then Eve
3: 10. let these also f. be proved
5: 4. f. to shew piety at home
12. they have cast off their f. faith
2 Ti. 1: 5. faith dwelt f. in grandm.
2: 6. husbandm. must be f. partaker
4: 16. At my f. ans. no man with me
Tit. 3: 10. after f. 2d admonition
He. 4: 6. to whom it was f. preached
5: 12. which be the f. principles
7: 2. f. being by interpr-n, King
27. offer f. for his own sins, then
8: 7. f. covenant, 13.-9: 1, 15, 18.
9: 2. f. taber, wher. shewbread, 6, 8.
10: 9. taketh aw. f. that he establ.
Ja. 3: 17 wisd from ab. is f. pure
1 Pe. 4: 17. if judgm. f. begin at us
2 Pe 1: 20. knowing this f., 3: 3.
1 Jn. 4: 19. love, bec. he f. loved
Jude 6. angels who kept not f. es.
Re. 2: 4. thou hast left thy f. love
5. repent, and do the f. works
4: 1 f. voice | 7. f. beast
8: 7. f. angel | 16: 2. f. poured vial
13: 12. exerciseth power of f. beast
20: 5. this is the f. resurrection, 6.
21: 1. f. heaven and f. earth passed
19. f. foundation was jasper
See DAY. LAST.

At the FIRST.

Ge. 13: 4. where Ab. made altar a. [f.
28: 19. city was called Luz a. f.
43: 18. bec. of money returned a. f.
20. we came a. f. to buy food
De. 9: 18. I fell bef. L. as a. f., 25.
Jos. 8: 5. when come ag. us as a. f.
6. say, They flee bef. us as a. f.
Ju. 18: 29. name of city Laish a. f.
20: 32. are smitten down as a. f.
2 S. 17: 9. some be overthr. a. f.
1 K. 20: 9. didst send for to serv. a. f.
1 Ch. 15: 13. bec. ye did it not a. f.
Ne. 7: 5. register of them came a. f.
Is. 1: 26. restore judges as a. f.
9: 1. a. f. he lightly afflicted land
Je. 7: 12. place I set my name a. f.
33: 7. I will build them as a. f.
11. return the captivity as a. f.
Da. 8: 1. which appeared unto me a. f.
Jn. 12: 16. disci. understood not a. f.
19: 39. a. f. came to Jesus by night
Ac. 15: 14. G. a. f. did visit Gent.
26: 4. was a. f. amo. mine own nat.

Ga. 4:13. I preached unto you, a.f.
He.2:3.a.f. began to be spoken by L.

FIRST month. See MONTH.

FIRST ripe.

Ex. 22 : 29. delay to offer f. r. fruits
Nu.13:20. the time of the f.r.grapes
18 : 13.whatso. is f. r. sh. be thine
Je. 24:2. even like figs that are f.r.
Ho. 9 : 10. f. r. in fig tree at her f.
Mi. 7 : 1. my soul desired f. r. fruit
Na. 3 : 12. trees with f. r. figs

FIRST year. See YEAR.

FIRSTBEGOTTEN.

He. 1 : 6. bringeth in f. into world
Re. 1:5. faithful wit. and f. of dead

FIRSTBORN. [34.

Ge. 19:31. f. said unto the younger,
33. f. went in, and lay with fa.
37. the f. bare a son and called
27:19. Jac. said, I am Esau, f.,32.
29 : 26. to give younger before f.
43 : 33. f. according to birthright
48 : 18. Not so father, this is the f.
Ex. 4:22. Isr. is my son, even my f.
23. I will slay thy son, even thy f.
11 : 5. all f. in land of E. shall die
12 : 12. I will smite all f. in land
29. smote all f. in E., 13: 13, 15.
13: 2. Sanctify unto me all the f.
22:29.f. of sons shalt give unto me
34:20. f. of sons redeem, Nu.18:15.
Le 27:†26. f. of beasts no man sanc.
Nu. 3 : 12. instead of all the f., 41,
45.-8 : 17, 18.
13. bec. all f. of Isr. are mine, I
hallowed all f. of Israel
40. number f. of males of Israel
42. Moses numbered f. of Isr.,43.
50. of f. of Israel took he money
33 : 4. Egyptians buried all their f.
De. 21:15. if the f. son be her's, 16.
17. for the right of f. is his
25 : 6. f. wh. she beareth, succeed
Jos. 6 : 26. sh. lay founda. in his f.
Ju. 8 : 20. Jether his f. Up slay
1 K. 16 : 34. founda. in Abiram f.
1 Ch. 2 : 3. Er f. of Jud. was evil
5 : 1. sons of Reuben the f. (2)
26:10. tho. not the f. yet his father
2 Ch. 21:3. Jehoram, bec. he was f.
Ne. 10 : 36. to bring f. to h. of God
Jb. 18 : 13. f. of death shall de- our
Ps. 78 : 51. he smote all the f. in
Egypt, 105:36.-135:8.-136:10.
89 : 27. my f. higher than kings
Is. 14 : 30. f. of the poor shall feed
Je.31:9.I a fa.to Isr. Ephr. is my f.
Mi. 6 : 7. give my f. for my transgr.
Zch. 12 : 10. in bitterness for his f.
Mat. 1 : 25. Mary her f. son,Lu.2:7.
Ro. 8 : 29. be f. am. many brethren
Col. 1 : 15. who is f. of ev. creature
18. is beginning, f. fr. the dead
He.11:28. lest he th. destr. f. touch
12 : 23. ye are come to church of f.

FIRSTFRUIT, S.

Ex. 23 : 16. f-s of thy lab. hast sown
19. f-s of thy land, 34:26. De.26:2.
34:22. least of f-s of wheat harvest
Le. 2 : 12. oblation of f-s sh. offer
14. meat off-g of f-s, green ears
23 : 10. bring a sheaf of the f-s
17. they are the f-s unto Lord
20. wave them with bread of f-s
Nu. 18 : 12. f. of oil, wine, wheat
28 : 26. in day of f-s when ye offer
De. 18 : 4. f-s of thy corn, wine, oil
26 : 10. I have brought f-s of land
2 K.4:42. brought the man of G. f-s
2 Ch. 31 : 5. brought in abnud. f-s
Ne. 10 : 35. bring f-s of our ground
37. should bring f-s of our dough
12:44. over chambers for f-s,13:31.
Pr. 3 : 9. honour Lord with the f s
Je. 2 : 3. Israel was f-s of his incr.
Eze. 20 : 40. will I require f-s
44 : 30. first of all f-s of all things

Eze.48:14. nor exchange f-s of land
Am. 6 : † 1. named the f-s of nations
Ro. 8 : 23. which have f-s of Spirit
11 : 16. if f. be holy, lump is holy
16:5. f-s of Achaia,1 Co.16:15. [23.
1 Co.15:20.C. f-s of them that slept,
Ja. 1 : 18. a kind of f-s of creatures
Re.14:4.being f-s unto G. and Lamb

FIRSTLING. [19.

Ex. 13:12. shalt set apart ev. f., 34:
13. f. of ass shalt redeem, 34 : 20.
Le. 27 : 26. L.'s f. no man sanctified
Nu. 18:15. f. of uncl. beasts redeem
17. f. of a cow not redeem
De. 15 : 19. all f. males sanctify
33 : 17. Jo.'s glory like f. of bul-k

FIRSTLINGS.

Ge. 4:4. Abel brought of f. of flock
Nu. 3:41. instead of all f. am. cattle
De. 12:6. sh. bring f. of your herds
17. not eat within thy gates f.
14:23. eat f. in place L. sh. choose
Ne. 10 : 36. f. of our herds to bring

FISH. [Noun.]

Ge. 1:26. dominion over f. of sea, 28.
Ex. 7 : 18. f. in river shall die, 21.
Nu. 11 : 5. the f. we did eat in E.
22. shall all f. of sea be gathered
De. 4 : 18. nor likeness of any f. [f.
Ne. 13:16. men of Tyre wh. brought
Ps. 8 : 8. hast put f. under his feet
105:29. into blood, and slew their f.
Is. 19 : 10. sluices and ponds for f.
50:2. their f. stinketh bec. no wat.
Eze. 29:4. f. to stick unto thy scales
5. I will leave thee, and all f.
47 : 9. sh. be a very gr. mult. of f.
10. f. shall be as f. of great sea
Jon.1:17.in belly of f.three days, (2)
2:1.prayed unto L.out of f.'s belly
10. L. spake to f., it vomited Jon.
Mat. 7:10. if he ask a f., Lu. 11:11.
17:27. take up f. that first cometh
Lu. 24 : 42. gave piece of broiled f.
Jn. 21 : 9. they saw f. laid thereon
10. Bring of f. ye have caught
13. bread, and giveth them, and f.
See GATE, SPEARS.

FISHES.

Ge. 9:2. fear of you sh. be on all f.
48 : † 16. let the lads grow as f. do
1 K. 4:33. of creeping things and f.
Jb. 12 : 8. f. of the sea sh. declare
Ec. 9 : 12. the f. taken in evil net
Eze. 38 : 20. So that f. of sea shake
Ho. 4 : 3. f. of sea be taken away
Ha. 1 : 14. makest men as f. of sea
Zph. 1 : 3. I will consume the f.
Mat. 14:17. but 5 loaves and 2 f.,19.
Mk.6:38,41. Lu.9:13, 16. Jn.6:9,
15:34.loaves and few f.,Mk.8:7. [11.
36. took seven loaves and the f.
Mk. 6 : 43. full of fragments and f.
Lu. 5 : 6. inclosed a gr. multi. of f.
9. was astonished at draught of f.
Jn. 21:6. not able to draw it for f.,8.
11. drew net to land full of gr. f.
1 Co. 15 : 39. flesh of beasts, ano.

FISH. [Verb.] [of f.

Je. 16 : 16. many fishers, they sh. f.

FISHER, S. [them

Is. 19 : 8. The f-s also shall mourn
Je. 16 : 16. I will send for many f-s
Eze. 47 : 10. f-s shall stand upon it
Mat.4:18.for they were f-s,Mk.1:16.
19. make you f-s of men, Mk.1:17.
Jn.21:7. Peter girt his f-'s coat unto

FISHERMEN. [him

Lu. 5 : 2. f. were gone out of them

FISHHOOKS.

Am. 4 : 2.take your poster'ty with f.

FISHING.

Jn. 21 : 3. Peter saith, I go a f.

FISHPOOLS. [bon

Can. 7 : 4.thine eyes like f. in Hesh-

FISHY. [only

1 S. 5 : † 4. f. part of Dagon was left

FIST, S.

Ex. 21 : 18. one smite anot. with f.
Pr. 30 : 4. who gath-d wind in f-s?
Is. 58 : 4. smite with f. of wickedn.
Mk. 7:†3. wash their hands with f.

FIT. [man

Le. 16 : 21. send him by hand of f.
1 Ch. 7:11. f. to go out to war, 12:8.
Jb.34:18.f. to say to k.,Thou wicked?
Pr. 24:27. work make it f. for thys.
Eze.15†5. vine made f. for no work
Lu.9:62.looking back,is f.for kingd.
14:35. not f. for land nor dunghill
Ac. 22 : 22. it is not f. he sho. live
Col. 3 : 18. wives, submit as f. in L.

FITCHES.

Is. 28 : 25. doth he not cast the f.?
27. f. not threshed, f. are beaten
Eze. 4 : 9. take barley, millet, f.

FITLY.

Pr. 25 : 11. A word f. spoken is like
Can. 5 : 12. his eyes washed with
milk, and f. set
Ep. 2 : 21. all building f. framed
4 : 16. whole body f. joined toget.

FITTED, ETH.

1 K. 6:35. gold f. upon carved work
Pr. 22 : 18. shall be f. in thy lips
Is. 44 : 13. carpenter f. with planes
Ro. 9 : 22. vessels of wrath f. to
He. 10 : † 5. body hast thou f. me

FIVE.

Ge. 18:28. wilt destroy for lack of f.?
47:2. presented f. of breth. to Pha.
Ex. 13:†18. Isr. went up f. in rank
26:3. other f. curtains, 9.-36: 10,16.
26. make f. bars, 27.-36 : 31, 32.
37. f. pillars, 36:38 [36:38. f.sock-
ets [broad
27:1. altar f. cubits long, f. cubits
18. height of hangings f. cubits,
38 : 1. f. cubits breadth, f. [38:18.
Le. 26 : 8. f. shall chase a hundred
Jos. 1 : † 14. pass marshalled by f.
Ju. 7:†11. to outside of ranks by f.
1 K. 6 : 6. f. cubits, 10, 24.-7: 16,23.
2 Ch. 3: 11,12.-4: 2.-6: 13.Je.52:
22. Eze. 40 : 7, 48.-41:2,9,11,12.
7 : 39. f. bases on right, f. on left
49. candlesticks f. on right side,f.
on left, 2 Ch. 4 : 6, 7, 8.
1 Ch. 7 : 3. f., all of them chief men
7. f. heads of house of fa-s
11:23. slew Egypt-n f. cubits high
Is. 17: 6. or f. in outmost branches
30 : 17. at rebuke of f. sh. ye flee
Mat. 25 : 2. f. of them wise, and f.
Lu.12:52. there sh.be f.in one house
19 : 19. Be thou also over f. cities
See BRETHREN, CITIES, DAMSELS, DAYS, EMERODS, GOATS, HORSES, HUNDRED, HUSBANDS, KINGS, LAMBS, LOAVES, LORDS, MEASURES, MEN, MICE, MONTHS, PIECES, PORCHES, POUNDS, RAMS, SHEEP, SONS, SPARROWS, STONES, TALENTS, THOUSAND, TIMES, TREES, WORDS, YEARS, YOKE.

FIVESQUARE. [f.

1 K.6:†31. lintel and side posts were

FIXED.

2 Ch.12:†14.Rehob. f. not his heart
Ps.57:7.heart is f. I will sing,108:1.
112 : 7. heart is f. trusting in L.
Lu. 16 : 26. betw. us and you a gulf

FLAG, S. [f.

Ex. 2 : 3. she laid the ark in the f-s
5. when she saw ark among f-s
Jb. 8 : 11. can f. grow without wat.
Is. 19 : 6. reeds and f-s shall wither

FLAGON, S.

2 S. 6 : 19. a f. of wine, 1 Ch. 16:3.
Can. 2:5. Stay me with f-s, comfort
Is.22:24.fr. cups, to all vessels of f-s
Ho.3:1. look to gods, love f-s of wine

FLAKES.
Jb. 41 : 23. f. of his flesh are joined
FLAME, S.
Ex. 3:2. angel in f. of fire, Ac.7:30.
Nu. 21 : 28. a f. from city of Sihon,
Je. 48 : 45. [in f.
Ju. 13: 20. f. went up, angel went
20 : 38. should make a great f. rise
40. f. of city ascended to heaven
Jb. 15: 30. f. sh. dry up branches
41 : 21. f. goeth out of his mouth
Ps. 29 : 7. voice of L. divideth f-s
83 : 14. f. setteth mount-s on fire
106 : 18. f. burned up the wicked
Pr.26:†18. madman who casteth f-s
Can. 8 : 6. fire hath a vehement f.
Is. 5 : 24. as f. consumeth chaff
10 : 17. Holy One shall be for a f.
13 : 8. amazed, faces sh. be as f-s
29 : 6. shalt be visited with f. of
30 : † 27. with grievousness of f.
30. L. shall shew his arm with f.
43 : 2. nei. sh. f. kindle upon thee
47:14.shall not deliver thems. fr. f.
66:15.render rebuke with f-s of fire
Eze.20:47. f. shall not be quenched
Da.3:22. f. slew men took Shadrach
7:9. his throne was like the fiery f.
11. till body given to burning f.
11:33. yet they shall fall by the f.
Jo. 1: 19. f. hath burned trees of
2:3.and behind them a f. burneth
5. like the noise of a f. of fire
Ob. 18. house of Joseph be a f.
Na. 3:†3. lifteth up the f. of sword
Lu. 16 : 24. am tormented in this f.
He. 1:7. maketh ministers f. of fire
Re.1:14.eyes were as f. of fire,2:18.-
FLAMING. [19:12.
Ge. 3:24. at garden of Eden f. sword
Eze. 20:47. f. flame not be quench.
Na. 2 : 3. chariots with f. torches
See FIRE.
FLANKS.
Le. 3 : 4. fat on them, which is by
f., 10, 15.-4 : 9.-7 : 4.
Jb. 15 : 27. collops of fat on his f.
FLASH.
Eze. 1:14. appear. of f. of lightning
FLAT.
Le. 2 : † 5. baken on f. plate, 7 : † 9.
21 : 18. hath a f. nose not appro.
Nu.22:31. Balaam fell f. on his face
Jos. 6 : 5. wall of city shall fall f.
20. people shouted, wall fell f.
FLATTER, ETH.
Ps. 5 : 9. they f. with their tongue
36:2. he f-h himself in his own eyes
78 : 36. they did f. him with mouth
Pr. 2 : 16. f-h with her words, 7 : 5.
20:19. meddle not with him th. f-h
28 : 23. more favour than he th.f-h
29 : 5. man that f-h spreadeth net
FLATTERIES.
Da. 11 : 21. sh. obtain kingd. by f.
32. do wickedly sh. he corrupt by
34. many shall cleave with f. [f.
FLATTERING.
Jb. 32 : 21. nei. let me give f. titles
22. I know not to give f. titles
Ps. 12 : 2. with f. lips and double
3. Lord shall cut off all f. lips
Pr. 7 : 21. with f. of lips she forced
26 : 28. a f. mouth worketh ruin
Eze. 12:24. be no more f. divination
1 Th. 2 : 5. neither used we f. words
FLATTERY.
Jb. 17: 5. speaketh f. to his friends
Pr. 6 : 24. keep fr. f. of strange wom
FLAX.
Ex. 9 : 31. f. was smitten, f. bolled
Jos. 2 : 6. she hid with stalks of f.
Ju. 15 : 14. cords became as f.
Pr. 31 : 13. She seeks wool and f.
Is. 19 : 9. work in fine f. confound.
42 : 3. smoking f. not quench, Mat.
Eze. 40 : 3. with a line of f. [12:20.

Ho. 2:5. aft. my lovers that give me
9. will recover my wool and f. [f.
FLAY, ED.
Le. 1 : 6. he sh. f. the burnt off-g
2 Ch.29:34. few, they could not f.all
35 : 11. blood, Levites f-d them
Mi. 3 : 3. f. their skins fr. off them
FLEA. [20.
1 S. 24 : 14. is k. come after a f.? 26:
FLED. [f.
Ge. 14 : 10. kings of Sod. and Gom.
16 : 6. Hagar f. | 31 : 22. Jacob f.,
Ho. 12 : 12. [12, 15, 18.
39 : 13. garm. in hand and was f.,
Ex. 2 : 15. Moses f. fr. Pha., 4 : 3.,
Ac. 7 : 29.
14 : 5. told king of E. that peo. f.
27. the Egyptians f. ag. the sea
Nu. 16:34. Isr. f. at the cry of them
De. 34 : † 7. nor natural force f.
Jos. 8 : 15. Israel f. by the way of
10 : 16. these five kings f. and hid
Ju. 1 : 6. Adoni-be. f. | 4:15. Sisera
7:21. all the host f., 22. [f. aw., 17.
8:12. Zalmunna f. | 9:21. Jotham f.
9 : 51. to the tower f. all men and
11:3. Jeph. f. | 20:45. Benj-s f., 47.
1 S. 4 : 16. I f. to day out of army
14 : 22. when heard that Philis. f.
17 : 24. men of Isr. f. fr. Goliath
19 : 10. David f. and escaped, 12,
18.-20 : 1.-21 : 10.-27 : 4.
22 : 20. Abiathar f. after Da., 23:6.
30 : 17. save four hundred wh. f.
31 : 1. Isr. f. from the Philis., 7.
2 S. 19 : 8.-23 : 11.
2 S. 1 : 4. peo. are f. from battle
4 : 3. Beerothites f. to Gittaim
4. nurse f. | 10:14. Syrians f., 18.
13 : 29. Abs. and k.'s sons f.,34,37,
18:17. all Isr. f. ev. one to tent [38.
1 K. 2:7. they came to me when I f.
28. Joab f. unto tab., 29.
11 : 17. Hadad f. to go into Egypt
11 : 23. Rezon f. | 40. Jeroboam f.
12 : 2. f. from Sol., 2 Ch. 10 : 2.
20 : 20. Syrians f., 1 Ch. 19 : 18. 2
30. rest f. to Aphek, f. [K. 7:7.
2 K. 8 : 21. people f. into their tents
9 : 10. prophet f. | 23. Joram f.
25 : 4. men f. by night, Je. 52 : 7.
1 Ch. 10 : 1. the men of Isr. f., 11 :
13. 2 Ch. 13 : 16. [and they f.
2 Ch. 14:12. Lord smote Ethiopians
Ne. 13 : 10. Levites f. every one
Es. 6 : † 1. king Ahasuerus' sleep f.
Ps. 31 : 11. they that did see me f.
114:3. sea saw it and f. Jordan was
Is. 21 : 14. prevented with br. him
22 : 3. all thy rulers are f. [that f.
33:3. At the noise of tumult peo. f.
Je. 4 : 25. all birds of heav-s were f.
9 : 10. the fowl and beast are f.
26:21. Urijah f. | 46:5. Egyp. are f.
46 : 21. her hired men are f. away
Jon.4:2. Thf. I f. bef. unto Tarshish
Zch. 14 : 5. flee as ye f. bef. earthq.
Mat. 8 : 33. they that kept them f.
26 : 56. disciples f., Mk. 14 : 50.
Mk. 16 : 8. they f. from sepulchre
Ac. 16:27. supposing prisoners had f.
He. 6 : 18. f. for refuge to lay hold
Re. 12:6. woman f. | 16:20. island f.
20 : 11. fr. face earth and heaven f.
He FLED.
Ge. 31 : 20. told him not that h. f.
21. So h. f. | 35 : 7. when h. f.
from brother [13, 15, 18.
39 : 12. h. left his garment and f.,
Jos. 20 : 6. slayer unto city whence
h. f., Nu. 35 : 25.
Ju. 9 : 40. Abim. chased Gaal. h. f.
1 S. 22 : 17. they knew when h. f.
2 K. 9 : 10. h. opened door and f.
27. Ahaziah fled, h. f. to Megiddo
14:19. h.f. to Lachish, 2 Ch.25:27.
Je. 26 : 21. Urijah heard it h. f.

Jon. 1 : 10. h. f. fr. pres. of the L.
Mk. 14 : 52. h. left linen cloth, f.
Is FLED. [naked
Nu. 35 : 32. no satisfac. for him th.
1 S. 4 : 17. Isr. i.f. bef. Philis. [i.f.
2 S. 19 : 9. Da. i. f. out of the land
Is.10:29. Ramah afraid, Gibeah i. f.
They FLED.
Ge 14:10. t. that remained f. to mts.
Jos. 7 : 4. t. f. bef. the men of Ai
10 : 11. as t. f. L. cast gr. stones
1 S. 4:10. Isr. smitten, t. f. ev. man
to tent, 2 K. 14:12. 2 Ch.25:22.
17:51. saw champion was dead t.f.
19 : 8. David slew Philis., and t. f.
2 S.10:13. Syrians ; t.f., 1 Ch.19:14,
2 K.3:24. smote Moabites, t. f. [15.
1 Ch. 10 : 7. all Israel saw that t.f.
Ps. 104 : 7. At thy rebuke t. f. they
Is. 21:15. t.f. fr. the swords [hasted
Je. 39 : 4. then t. f. forth of the city
48 : 45. t. th. f. stood und. shadow
La. 4 : 15. when t. f. and wandered
Da. 10:7. so that t. f. to save thems.
Ho. 7 : 13. Woe, for t. have f. fr. me
Lu. 8 : 34. saw what was done, t. f.
Ac. 14 : 6. t. were ware of it and f.
19:16. so t.f. out of house wounded
FLEDDEST. [Esau
Ge. 35 : 1. when thou f. fr. face of
Ps.114:5. ailed thee, O sea, thou f.?
FLEE.
Ge.16:8. I f.fr.face of mistress Sarai
19 : 20. this city is near to f. unto
27 : 43. arise, f. to Laban my bro.
Ex. 14 : 25. Let us f. fr. face of Isr.
21 : 13. appoint place whi. he sh.f.
Le.26:17. f.when none pursueth,36.
Nu.10:35. that hate thee f.,Ps.68:1.
24 : 11. now f. thou to thy place
35 : 6. cities, that manslayer may
f. thither, 11, 15. De. 4 : 42.-
19 : 3, 4, 5. Jos. 20 : 3, 4, 9.
De. 28 : 7. f. bef. thee 7 ways, 25.
Jos. 8 : 5. as at first we will f., 6.
20. no power to f. this way or that
Ju. 20 : 32. Let us f. and draw them
2 S. 4 : 4. nurse haste to f. she fell
15:14. f. else we not escape fr.Abs.
17 : 2. people with him shall f.
19:3. as men when they f. in battle
24:13.wilt thou f. 3 mos.bef.enem.?
1 K. 12 : 18. Rehob. made speed to
f. to Jerus., 2 Ch. 10 : 18.
2 K. 9:3. Then open door, and f.
Ne. 6:11. Should such a man as I f.?
Jb. 20 : 24. sh. f. from iron weapon
27:22. would fain f. out of his ha.
30:10. abhor, they f. far from me
41:28. arrow cannot make him f.
Ps. 11 : 1. how say ye, f. as bird to
68 : 1. let them th. hate f. bef. him
12. Kings of armies f. apace
139:7. whi. shall I f. fr. presence?
143:9. O L., I f. to thee to hide me
Pr. 28:1. wicked f. no man pursu.
17. he shall f. to the pit, let no
Is. 10:3. to wh. will ye f. for help?
31. inhab. of Gebim gather to f.
13 : 14. f. ev. one into own land
15 : 5. fugitives shall f. unto Zoar
17 : 13. they shall f. far off
20:6. expectation whi. we f. for help
30 : 16. for we will f. upon horses
17. at rebuke of five shall ye f.
31:8. f.fr.sword, his young men sh.
48 : 20. f. ye from the Chaldeans
Je. 4:29. city f. for noise of horsem.
6 : 1. gather to f. out of Jerusalem
25 : 35. shepherds no way to f.
48:6. f. save your lives, and be [f.
9. Give wings unto Moab, that it
49:8. Edom sh. f. | 24. Damascus
30. f. dwell deep, O ye of Hazor
50 : 16. sh. f. ev. one to own land
28.voice of them that f.from Bab.
Je. 51 : 6. f. out of Bab., Zch. 2 : 6.

Am. 5: 19. As if man did f. fr lion
Jon.1:3.Jonah rose to f.unto Tarsh.
Na. 3:7. that look on, sh. f. fr. thee
Zch. 2: 6. sh. f. from land of north
14:5. f. to valley of the mountains
Mat. 2: 13. take young child and f.
3: 7. f. from wrath? Lu. 3: 7.
10:23.persec.you in city f.into ano.
24: 16. Then let them in Judea f.
into mts , Mk. 13:14. Lu.21:21.
Jn. 10:5. stranger not follow, but f.
Ac. 27:30. shipmen were about to f.
1 Co. 6: 18. f. forn 10: 14. f. idol
1 Ti. 6: 11. O man of God, f. these
2 Ti. 2: 22. f. also youthful lusts
Ja. 4:7. Resist devil, and he will f.
Re. 9: 6. days death sh. f. fr. them
See FLY.

FLEE away. [cretly
Ge. 31: 27. Whf. didst thou f. a. se-
2 S. 18:3. if we f. a., they not care
Jb. 9:25. my days f. a., see no good
Ps. 64:8. all that see them shall f.a.
Can. 2: 17. Until shadows f. a.,4:6.
Is. 35: 10. sorrow and sighing f. a.
51: 11. sorrow and mourning f. a.
Je. 46: 6. Let not the swift f. a.
Am. 2: 16. he courageous shall f. a.
7:12.O seer,go f.a.into land of Jud.
9:1. he that fleeth shall not f. a.
Na. 2: 8. Nineveh sh. f. a. [f. a.
3:17. as grasshopp-s in hedges they

FLEECE.
De. 18: 4. the first of f. give Levites
Ju. 6: 37. put f. of wool in floor
38. Gideon wringed dew out of f.
39. let it be dry only upon f., 40.
Jb. 31: 20. if not warmed with f.

FLEEING. [sword
Le. 26: 36. they sh. flee as f. from
De. 4: 42. f. unto one of these cities
Jb. 27: † 22. in f. he would flee out
30: 3. for want and famine f. into

FLEETH. [wildern.
De. 19: 11. smite him mortally, f.
Jb. 14: 2. he f. as a shadow and
Is. 24: 18. who f. fr. noise of fear
Je. 48: 19. ask him that f. and her
44 he that f. fr. the fear, sh. fall
Am. 9:1. he that f. sh. not flee aw.
Na.3:16.cankerworm spoileth and f.
Jn. 10: 12. that is a hireling f., 13.

FLESH.
Ge. 2: 21. G. closed up f. instead
23. bone of my bones and f. of f.
24. cleave unto his wife, be one f.
6:3. not strive with man,for he is f.
9: 4. But f. with life thereof
17: 11. sh. circumcise f. of foresk.
13. My cov-t shall be in your f.
14.whose f. not circum. be cut off
23. Abr. circum. f. of their foresk.
37: 27. he is our bro. and our f.
Ex. 4:7. hand was turned as other f.
28: † 42. linen breeches to cover f.
29: 14. burn the f., Le. 9: 11.-16:
27. Nu. 19: 5. [be poured
30: 32. Upon man's f. shall it not
Le. 6:27.what touch f. shall be holy
7: 15. f. of sacr. of peace off-gs
19. as for f. all clean shall eat
8: 31. Boil the f. at door of taber.
12: 3. f. of his foreskin be circum.
13:10. if quick raw f., 14, 15, 16, 24.
18. The f. also even in the skin
38. if in skin of f. bright spots, 39.
15: 7. toucheth f. of him hath issue
19. if her issue in her f. be blood
21:5. nor make cuttings in their f.
Nu. 11:13. Whence I have f. to give
33. while f. was betw. their teeth
12: 12. of wh. f. is half consumed
18: 18. f. of them shall be thine
De. 32: 42. my sword sh. devour f.
Ju. 6: 19. the f. he put in a basket
20. Take f. and unleav. cakes
20:21 fire out of rock, consumed f.
1 S. 2: 13. while f. was in seething
15. Give f. to roast for priest [3.
2 S. 6: 19. dealt to each f., 1 Ch. 16:
1 K. 17:6. ravens bro-t him br. and
f. in morn., br. and f. in ev-g
19: 21. boiled their f. with instru.
2 K. 4: 34 f. of child waxed warm
2 Ch. 32:8. With him is an arm of f.
Ne. 5: 5. our f. is as f. of breth.
Jb. 10: 4. Hast thou eyes of f.? [f.
11. hast clothed me with skin and
Ps.56:4.will not fear what f. can do
78: 20. can he provide f. for peo.?
27.He rained f. upon them as dust
39. he rememb. they were but f.
79:2. f. of saints given unto beasts
Pr. 4: 22. my sayings health to f.
23: 20. not am. riotous eaters of f.
Is. 10:†18. the glory fr. soul to the f.
31: 3. their horses are f. not spirit
49:26. I will feed them with own f.
Je. 11: 15. holy f. is passed fr. thee
12: 12. no f. shall have peace
17:5.cursed man maketh f. his arm
Eze. 4:14. nor abomi. f. into mouth
10: † 12. their f. backs, full of eyes
11: 3. this city is caldron, we the f.
7. your slain, they are the f.
11. nor shall ye be the f. in midst
19. I will give heart of f., 36: 26.
16: 26. great of f. incr. whored-s.
Eze. 23: 20. whose f. is as f. of asses
24: 10. consume the f. spice it well
37: 6. will bring up f. upon you, 8.
40: 43. upon tables was f. offering
Da. 2:11. gods, dwelling not with f.
7: 5. said unto it, devour much f.
10:3. nei. f. nor wine in my mouth
Ho.8:13. they sacrifice f. for sacrif-s
Mi. 3: 2. pluck f. off their bones
3. as f. within the caldron
Zph. 1:17. their f. sh. be poured out
Hag. 2: 12. if one bear holy f.in skirt
Zch. 14: 12. their f. shall consume
Mat.16:17. f. and bl. not revealed it
19: 5. they twain shall be one f.,
6. Mk. 10:8. 1 Co. 6:16. Ep. 5:31.
24:22.sho.no f. be saved,Mk. 13:20.
26: 41. but f. is weak, Mk. 14: 38.
Lu.24:39.spirit hath not f.and bones
Jn. 1: 14. WORD was made f.
6: 63. Spir. quick-h, f. prof. noth.
Ac. 2: 30. seed of Da. acc. to f., Ro.
Ro. 3:20. sh. no f. be justified [1: 3.
4: 1. Ab. as pertaining to f. found
7: 25. with f. I serve law of sin
8: 3.in that law was weak thro. f.
Son in likeness of sinful f.
12. debtors, not to the f. to live
9: 3. for my kinsmen acc. to f.
5. of whom as conc. f. C. came
13: 14. make not provision for f.
1 Co. 1: 29. That no f. should glory
15:39. one f. of men, ano. of beasts
50.f.and bl. cannot inherit kingd.
2 Co.1:17. do I purpose acc.to the f.?
4: 11. life of Jes. be manifest in f.
7: 5. our f. had no rest, we troub.
10: 2. as if we walked acc. to f.
Ga. 1: 16. I conferred not with f.
2: 16. by works of law no f. justif.
3: 3. are ye made perfect by f.?
5: 13. liberty for an occasion to f.
17. f. lusteth ag. Spirit, Sp. ag. f.
24. th. are C.'s have crucified f.
Ep. 2:3. conversat. in lusts of our f.
6: 5. masters acc. to f., Col. 3: 22.
12. we wrestle not ag. f. and bl.
He. 2:14. children are partakers of f.
12: 9. fa-s of our f. who corrected
Jude 7. and going after strange f.
8. these filthy dreamers defile f.
23. hating garment spotted by f.
Re. 19: 18. may eat f. of captains,
f. of mighty men
21. fowls were filled with their f.
See EAT, EN, ETH, ING, BONE.

After the FLESH. [no
Jn. 8: 15. Ye judge a. t. f. I judge
Ro. 8: 1. in C., walk not a. t. f., 4.
5. that are a. t. f. mind things of
12. not debtors to live a. t. f. [f.
13. if ye live a. t. f. ye sh. die
1 Co. 1: 26. not many wise men a.
10: 18. Behold Israel a. t. f. [t. f.
2 Co. 5: 16. we know no man a. t.
f. tho. we have kno. Cr. a. f.
10: 3. we do not war a. t. f. [also
11: 18. seeing many glory a. t. f. I
Ga. 4: 23. Ishm.was born a.t.f.,29.
2 Pe. 2: 10. them that walk a. t. f.

All FLESH. [way
Ge. 6:12. for a. f. had corrupted his
13. God said, end of a. f. is come
17. destroy a. f. wherein is breath
19. of a. f. two of ev. sort, 7: 15.
7: 16. went in male fem. of a. f.
21. a. f. died that moved upon
8: 17. bring forth of a. f. both of
9: 11. nor sh. a. f. be cut off, 15.
16.covenant betw.me and a.f.,17.
Le. 17: 14. life of a. f. is the blood
Nu. 8: 7. let them shave a. their f.
16: 22. G. of spirits of a. f. 27:16.
18:15. that openeth matrix of a. f.
De. 5: 26. who of a. f. heard word
Jb.12:†10. in hand is breath of a. f.
34: 15. a. f. shall perish together
Ps. 65: 2. unto thee sh. a. f. come
136: 25. Who giveth food to a. f.
145: 21. let a. f. bless holy name
Is. 40: 5. a. f. shall see it together
6. a. f. is grass, 1 Pe.1:24. [21:5
49:26 a. f. sh. know I am Sav., Eze.
66: 16. by fire will L. plead with a.
23. a. f. shall come to worship [f.
24. sh. be an abhorring unto a. f.
Je. 25: 31. he will plead with a. f.
32:27. I am the L. the God of a. f.
45: 5. I will bring evil upon a. f.
Eze. 20:48. a. f. sh. see I have kindl.
21:4.my sword go ag a. f.fr south
Da. 4: 12. and a. f. was fed of it
Jo. 2: 28. my Spirit upon a. f.,
Ac. 2: 17.
Zch. 2:13. Be silent, O a. f. bef. L.
Lu. 3:6. a. f. shall see salva. of G.
Jn. 17:2. given him power over a. f.
1 Co. 15: 39. a. f. is not same flesh

His FLESH. [eaten
Ex. 21: 28. and h. f. shall not be
29: 31. seethe h. f. in [8: 17.
Le. 4: 11. burn all h. f. with head,
6: 10.lin.breeches upon h.f.,16: 4.
13: 2. a rising in skin of h. f.
3. look on plague in skin of h. f.
4. If bright spot be white in h. f.
11. It is an old leprosy in h. f.,13.
14:9. he shall wash h. f. in water,
15: 16.-16: 24, 28. Nu. 19: 7
15:2.hath running issue out of h.f.
3.whether h. f. run with his issue
17: 16. But if he wash not, nor
bathe h. f.
22:6. unclean, unless he wash h.f.
1 K. 21:27. Ahab put sackcl. on h.f.
2 K. 5: 14. h. f. came again [f.
6:30.Joram had sackcloth upon h.
Jb. 2: 5. touch his f. he will curse
14: 22. But h. f. shall have pain
31: 31. said not, O that we had of
33: 21. h. f. is consumed [h. f.
25. h. f. be fresher than a child's
41:23. the flakes of h. f. are joined
Pr.11: 17.cruel troubleth h.f. [h.f.
Ec. 4: 5. fool foldeth hands, eateth
Is. 17: 4. fatness of h. f. wax lean
Jn. 6: 52. can give h. f. to eat?
Ac. 2: 31. nei h. f. did see corrup.
Ga. 6:8. soweth to h. f. reap corrup.
Ep. 2: 15. abolished in h. f. enmity
5: 29. no man ever hated h. own f.
30. members of his body, of h. f.
Col. 1:22.reconciled in body of h. f.

He. 5 : 7. who in days of h. f. when
10 : 20. consecrated thro. vail, h.f.

In the FLESH or in FLESH.

Ge. 17 : 24. Ab. was circumc. i. t. f.
25. Ishmael circumcised i. t. f.
Eze.44 : 7. bro-t in uncircum. i. f.
9. uncirc. i. f. not enter sanctu.
Da. 1 : 15. counten. fairer fatter i.f.
Ro. 2 : 28. circum. outward i. t. f.
7:5.when i. t. f. the motions of sin
8: 3. for sin condemned sin i. t. f.
8. they i. t. f. cannot please God
9. ye are not i. t. f. but in Spirit
1 Co. 7 : 28. sh. have trouble i. t. f.
2 Co. 10:3. tho. walk i. t. f. not war
12 : 7. given to me a thorn i. t. f.
Ga. 2 : 20. life I now live i. t. f. is
6 : 12. to make fair shew i. t. f.
Ep. 2 : 11. in time past Gentiles i.
t. f. called circumc. i. t. f.
Ph. 1:22. if I live i. t. f. this is fruit
24. to abide i. t. f. is more needful
3 : 3. have no confidence i. t. f.
4. though I might have confidence i. t. f.
Col. 2:1. have not seen my face i.t.f.
5. tho. I be absent i. t. f. I am
1 Ti. 3:16. God was manifest i. t. f.
Phm. 16. more unto thee, both i.t.f.
1 Pe.3:18.C.being put to death i.t.f.
4 : 1. C. hath suff-d for us i. t. f.
for he th. suff-d i. t. f. hath
2. live the rest of his time i. t. f.
6. be judged acc. to men i. t. f.
1 Jn.4:2.denieth C. is come i.t.f., 3.
2 Jn. 7. confess not C. is come i.t.f.

My FLESH.

1 S. 25 : 11. shall I then take m. f.?
Jb.4:15. the hair of m. f. stood up
6: 12. of stones? or is m. f. brass?
7 : 5. m. f. is clothed with worms
13:14.Wh.f.I take m.f.in my teeth?
19: 20. my bone cleaveth to m. f.
22. and not satisfied with m. f.?
26. yet in m. f. shall I see G.
21 : 6. trembl. taketh hold of m. f.
Ps.16:9.m.f. shall rest in hope, Ac.
38:3.no soundness in m.f.,7. [2:26.
63 : 1. m. f. longeth for thee in a
73 : 26. m. f. faileth, but G. is my
84 : 2. and m. f. crieth out for G.
102 : † 5. my bones cleave to m. f.
109 : 24. m. f. faileth of fatness
119 : 120. m. f. trembleth for fear
Ec. 2 : † 3. to draw m. f. with wine
Je. 51 : 35. violence done to m. f.
La. 3 : 4. m. f. hath he made old
Jn. 6 : 51. bread I will give, is m. f.
54. eateth m. f. hath eter. life, 56.
55. m.f. is meat indeed, my blood
Ro. 7 : 18. in m. f. dw-h no good
11:14. provoke them wh. are m. f.
Ga. 4 : 14. my temptation in m. f.
Col. 1 : 24. of afflic-s of C. in m. f.

Of the FLESH. [f.

Ex. 12 : 46. not carry forth aught o.
29 : 34. if aught o. t. f. remain unto morn., Le. 8 : 32. [De. 16 : 4.
Le. 7 : 17. o. t. f. of sac., 18, 20, 21.
13:3. look on plague in skin o.t.f.
43. leprosy app-h in skin o. t. f.
17 : 11. life o. t. f. is in the blood
De. 28 : 55. nor give o. t. f. of chil.
Pr. 14 : 30. heart is life o. t. f.
Ec. 12 : 12. study is weariness o.t.f.
Jn. 1 : 13. born, not of will o. t. f.
3 : 6. which is born o. t. f. is flesh
Ro. 8 : 5. flesh do mind things o.t.f.
† 6. minding o. t. f. is death
† 7. minding o.t.f. is enmity ag. G.
9 : 8. They wh. are chil. o. t. f.
1 Co.5:5. unto Sat.for destruc.o.t.f.
2 Co. 7 : 1. from all filthiness o.t.f.
Ga. 4 : 13. through infirmity o.t.f.
5 : 16. ye sh. not fulfil lusts o.t.f.
19. works o. t. f. are manifest
6 : 8. soweth to f. shall o. t. f. reap

Ep. 2 : 3. in lusts o.t.f.desires o.t.f.
Col. 2 : 11. body of sins o. t. f. [f.
23. not in honour to satisfying o.t.
He. 9 : 13. to the purifying o. t. f.
1 Pe. 3:21. putting away filth o.t.f.
2 Pe. 2:18. allure thro. lusts o. t. f.
1 Jn. 2 : 16. the lust o. t. f. lust of

FLESH pots. [eyes

Ex. 16 : 3. when we sat by the f. p.

Thy FLESH.

Ge. 40 : 19. the birds shall eat t. f.
1 S. 17:44. will give t. f. unto fowls
2 S. 5 : 1. bone and t. f., 1 Ch.11:1.
2 K. 5 : 10. wash, t. f. shall come
Pr.5:11.mourn,when t.f.is consum.
Ec.5: 6. not mouth cause t. f. to sin
11 : 10. put away evil from t. f.
Is. 58:7. hide not thys. fr. t. own f.
Eze.32:5. I will lay t. f. upon mts.

Your FLESH.

Le. 19:28. not make cuttings in y. f.
Ju. 8 : 7. will tear y. f. with thorns
Eze. 36 : 26. stony heart out of y. f.
Ro. 6 : 19. bec. of infirmity of y. f.
Ga. 6:13. th. they may glory in y.f.
Col. 2 : 13. dead in uncircum. of y.f.
Ja. 5 : 3. rust shall eat y. f. as fire

FLESHED. [ED.

See FATFLESHED, LEAN FLESH-

FLESHHOOK, S.

Ex. 27 : 3. shalt make his f-s and
38 : 3. made vessels and the f-s
Nu. 4:14. put upon purple cloth, f-s
1 S. 2 : 13. priest's serv. with a f.
14. all that the f. brought up
1 Ch. 28 : 17. gave pure gold for f-s
2 Ch.4:16. he made pots and the f-s

FLESHLY.

2 Co. 1 : 12. not with f. wisdom
3 : 3. but in f. tables of the heart
Col. 2 : 18. puffed up by his f. mind
1 Pe. 2 : 11. abstain from f. lusts

FLEW.

1 S. 14 : 32. people f. upon the spoil
25 : † 14. our master f. upon them
Is. 6 : 6. Then f. one of seraphim

FLIES.

Ex. 8:21. will send swarms of f.,24.
22. no swarms of f. sh. be there
29. L. th. swarms of f. may dep.
31. removed swarms of f. fr. Pha.
Ps. 78 : 45. He sent divers sorts of f.
105 : 31. came divers sorts of f.
Ec. 10 : 1. Dead f. cause ointment to

FLIETH. [send

De. 4 : 17. likeness of any fowl th. f.
14:19. creeping thing that f. is uncl.
28 : 49. a nation as swift as eagle f.
Ps. 91 : 5. for arrow that f. by day
Na. 3 : 16. cankerworm spoileth and

FLIGHT. [f.

Le. 26:8. put 10,000 to f., De. 32:30.
1 Ch. 12 : 15. put to f. all of valleys
Jb. 11 : † 20. f. shall perish fr. wick.
Is. 52 : 12. not with haste nor by f.
Je. 46 : † 5. mighty ones are fled a f.
Da. 9 : † 21. Gabriel to fly with f.
Am. 2 : 14. f. shall perish fr. swift
Mat. 24:20. pray f. be not in winter,
Mk. 13 : 18. [aliens.
He. 11 : 34. turned to f. armies of

FLINT.

De.8:15. bro-t water out of rock of f.
Jb. 28 : † 9. he putteth hand upon f.
Ps. 114 : 8. turning f. into fountain
Is.5:28. hoofs shall be counted like f.
50 : 7. have I set my face like a f.
Eze. 3:9. harder than f. thy forehead

FLINTY.

De. 32 : 13. suck oil out of f. rock

FLIT.

Je. 49: † 30. flee. f. greatly, O inhabi.

FLOATS.

1 K. 5 : 9. convey in f., 2 Ch. 2 : 16.

FLOCK.

Ge. 4:4. Abel bro-t of firstlings of f.
21 : 28. Ab. set ewe lambs of f. by

Ge. 27:9. Go to f. and fetch two kids
29 : 10. Jacob watered the f.
30 : 31. I will feed and keep thy f.
32. I will pass thro. thy f. to day
40. separate all the brown in f.
31 : 38. rams of thy f. I not eaten
33 : 13. if overdrive f. will die
37 : 2. Joseph was feeding the f.
12. breth. went to feed their f., 13.
38 : 17. I will send thee a kid fr. f.
Ex. 2 : 16. troughs to water fa.'s f.
17. Moses helped, watered f., 19.
3 : 1. Moses led f. to back of desert
Le. 1 : 2. bring your offering of f.
3 : 6. Peace offering of the f.
5 : 6. he shall bring a female fr f.
18. ram without blemish out of f.
6 : 6. Ezr. 10 : 19. Eze. 43:23, 25.
27 : 32. conc. tithe of herd or of f.
Nu. 15 : 3. make sweet savour of f.
De. 12 : 17. firstlings of thy f.
21. thou shalt kill of thy f.
15 : 14. furnish liberally out of f.
19. firstling males of f. sanctify
16:2. shalt sacrifice unto L. of the f.
1 S. 17 : 34. lion took lamb out of f.
2 S. 12 : 4. spared to take of own f.
2 Ch. 35 : 7. Josiah gave of the f.
Jb. 30 : 1. to set with dogs of my f.
Can. 1 : 7. makest f. to rest at noon
8. go thy way by footsteps of f.
4 : 1. thy hair as f. of goats, 6 : 5.
2. teeth like f. of sheep, 6 : 6.
Is. 40:11. sh. feed his f. like sheph.
63 : 11. with the shepherd of his f.
Je.13:17. bec L.'s f. is carried captive
20. where f. given thee, beaut-l f.
23 : 2. Ye have scattered my f.
3. I will gather remn. of my f.
25 : 34 wallow, ye principal of f.
35. nor principal of f. to escape
36. howling of principal of the f.
31:10. keep him as shepherd his f.
12. shall sing for young of the f.
49 : 20. least of f. sh. draw, 50:45.
51 : 23. will break shepherd and f.
Eze. 24:5. Take the choice of the f.
34 : 3. ye eat fat, but feed not f.
6. my f. was scattered upon earth
8. my f. became prey, my f. meat
10. require my f. deliver my f.
12. As shepherd seeketh out his f.
15. I will feed my f. | 17. O my f.
19. my f. eat that trodden
22. Therefore will I save my f.
31. ye my f. f. of my pasture
36 : 38. as holy f. as f. of Jerus.
45 : 15. sh. offer one lamb out of f.
Am. 6 : 4. eat lambs out of f.
7 : 15. L. took me as I foll-d the f.
Jon. 3 : 7. let not herd nor f. taste
Mi. 2:12. as f. in the midst of their
4 : 8. thou, O tower of the f. [fold
7 : 14. feed thy people, f. of thine
Ha. 3:17. tho. f. be cut off fr. fold
Zch. 9 : 16. save them as f. of peo.
10 : 2. they went their way as a f.
3. L. of hosts hath visited his f.
11 : 4. Feed the f. of slaughter, 7.
7. poor of f. waited upon me, 11.
17. Woe to idol sheph. leaveth f.
Mal. 1 : 14. deceiver wh. hath in f.
Mat. 26 : 31. sheep of f. be scatt-d
Lu. 2:8. keeping watch over their f.
12 : 32. Fear not little f. it is Fa.'s
Ac. 20 : 28. take heed to all the f.
29. grievous wolves not sparing f.
1 Co. 9 : 7. who feedeth a f. and eat-
1 Pe. 5 : 2. Feed f. of G. [eth not
3. but being ensamples to the f.

Like a FLOCK. [a.f.

Jb. 21 : 11. send their little ones l.
Ps. 77 : 20. leddest thy peo. l. a. f.
78 : 52. guided them in wil. l.a.f.
80 : 1. leadest Joseph l. a. f.
107:41. maketh families l.a.f. [a.f.
Eze.36:37. increase them with men l.

FLOCKS.

Ge. 29 : 2. three f. of sheep by well, out of that watered the f.
3. thither were all f. gathered
8. We cannot, until all f. be gath-d
30 : 36. Jac. fed rest of Laban's f.
38. Jac. set rods before the f.
39. f. conceived before the rods
40. Jac. set faces of f. tow. ring-streaked, his own f. by thems.
32 : 5. I have oxen, asses, f. and
7. he divided the f. and herds
37 : 14. see whe it be well with f.
16. tell me where they feed f.
47 : 4. have no pasture for their f.
17. Jo. gave bread in exch. for f.
Le. 1 : 10. if his offering be of the f.
5 : 15. ram without blemish out of f.
Nu. 31 : 19. Isr. took spoil of all f.
30. shalt take one portion of f.
32 : 26. our wives, our f. sh. be there
De. 7 : 13. he will also bless the f.
28 : 4. blessed sh. be f. of thy sheep
18. cursed sh. be f. of thy sheep
51. who shall not leave the f.
Ju. 5 : 16. hear bleatings of the f.
1 K. 20 : 27. pitched like two little f.
1 Ch. 4 : 39. to seek pasture for f.
41. bec. was pasture for their f.
27 : 31. And over the f. was Jaziz
2 Ch. 17 : 11. Arabians bro-t him f.
32 : 28. stalls for beasts, cotes for f.
Jb. 24 : 2. violently take away f.
Ps. 8 : † 7. f. oxen all und. his feet
65 : 13. pastures are clothed with f.
78 : 48. gave f. to hot thunderbolts
Can. 1 : 7. aside by f. of companions
Is. 17 : 2. cities of Aroer sh. be for f.
32 : 14. palaces sh. be pasture of f.
60 : 7. All f. of Kedar sh. be gath-d
61 : 5. strangers shall feed your f.
65 : 10. Sharon shall be a fold for f.
Je. 6 : 3. shepherds with f. sh. come
10 : 21 all f. shall be scattered
31 : 24. in Ju. they that go with f.
33 : 12. shepherds causing f. to lie
13. f. shall pass ag in under rod
49 : 29. tents and f. sh. they take
50 : 8. be as he goats before the f.
Eze. 25 : 5. a couching place for f.
34 : 2. sho. not shepherds feed f.?
36 : 38. waste cities with f. of men
Jo. 1 : 18. f. of sheep are desolate
Mi. 1 : † 11. inhabitant of country of f.
5 : 8. a young lion am. f. of sheep
Zph 2 : 6. sea coast sh. be folds for f.
14. f. shall lie down in Nineveh

FLOCKS with herds.

Ge. 13 : 5 Lot also had f. and h.
24 : 35. L. hath given Ab. f. and h.
26 : 14. Isaac had poss-n of f. and h.
32 : 7. Jacob divided f. and h.
33 : 13. f. and h. with young are
45 : 10. be near me, thou, f. and h.
47 : 1. f. and h. are come, 46 : 32.
50 : 8. f. and h. left they in Goshen
Ex. 10 : 9. will go with our f. and h.
24. let your f. and h. be stayed
12 : 32. f. and h. and be gone, 38.
34 : 3. let f. nor h. feed bef. mount
Nu. 11 : 22. Sh. the f. and h. be slain
De. 8 : 13. when h. and f. multiply
12 : 6. firstlings of h. and f., 17.–14 : 23. Ne. 10 : 36.
1 S. 30 : 20. David took all f. and h.
2 S. 12 : 2. rich man had many f. and h.
2 Ch. 32 : 29. possessions of f. and h.
Pr. 27 : 23. know f. look well to h.
Je. 3 : 24. shame devoured f. and h.
5 : 17. nation shall eat thy f. and h.
Ho. 5 : 6. sh. go with f. and h. to seek L.

FLOOD.

Ge. 6 : 17. even I, bring a f. of wat.
7 : 6. when f. of waters upon earth
7. Noah went in bec. of waters of f.
10. after 7 days f. upon earth
Ge. 7 : 17. f. was 40 days upon earth
9 : 11. nei. be any more f. to destr., 15.
28. Noah lived aft. the f. 350 years
10 : 1. unto them sons born aft. f.
32. nations were divided after f.
11 : 10. begat Arphax. 2 y-rs aft. f.
Jos. 24 : 2. on other side of f., 3, 14, 15.
Jb. 14 : 11. as f. decayeth and drieth
22 : 16. founda. overthrown with a f.
28 : 4. f. breaketh out fr. inhabi.
Ps. 29 : 10. Lord sitteth upon f.
66 : 6. they went thro. the f. on foot
69 : 15. let not water-f. overfl. me
74 : 15. Thou didst cleave the f.
90 : 5. carriest them away as with f.
Is. 28 : 2. as a f. shall cast down
59 : 19. enemy sh. come in like a f.
Je. 46 : 7. Who this th. cometh as f.
8. Egypt riseth up like a f.
47 : 2. waters shall be an overfl-g f.
Da. 9 : 26. the end sh. be with a f.
11 : 22. with arms of a f. be overfl.
Am. 8 : 8. it sh. rise up as a f., 9 : 5.
9 : 5. sh. be drowned as by f. of E.
Na. 1 : 8. with an overrunning f.
Mat. 24 : 38. in days bef. f. were eat-g
39. not until f. came, Lu. 17 : 27.
Lu. 6 : 48. wh. f. arose stream beat
2 Pe. 2 : 5. bringing in f. upon world
Re. 12 : 15. dragon poured wat. as f.
16. the earth swallowed up the f.

FLOODS.

Ex. 15 : 8. f. stood upright as heap
2 S. 22 : 5. f. of ungodly, Ps. 18 : 4.
Jb. 20 : 17. He shall not see the f.
28 : 11. bindeth f. from overfl-g
Ps. 24 : 2. he hath establ d it upon f.
32 : 6. surely in f. of great waters
69 : 2. deep waters, where f. overfl.
78 : 44. had turned their f. into bl.
93 : 3. f. have lifted up, O L. f.
98 : 8. Let the f. clap their hands
Can. 8 : 7. nei. can the f. drown love
Is. 44 : 3. will pour f. upon dry gro.
Eze. 31 : 15. I restrained the f. thereof
Jon. 2 : 3. f. compassed me about
Mat. 7 : 25. f. came, winds blew, 27.

FLOODGATES.

Ge. 7 : † 11. f. of heav. were opened

FLOOR. [Verb.]

2 Ch. 34 : 11. for timber to f. houses

FLOOR, S.

Ge. 50 : 11. saw mourning in f. of Atad
Nu. 5 : 17. priests sh. take dust in f.
De. 15 : 14. shalt furnish out of f.
16 : † 13. aft. hast gathered in thy f.
Ju. 6 : 37. put a fleece of wool in f.
Ru. 3 : 2. he winnoweth in the f.
3. get thee down to the f., 6.
14. Let not be known a wom. came into f. [cov-d the f., 16.
1 K. 6 : 15. cedar both f. and walls, he
30. overlaid f. of hou. with gold
7 : 7. with cedar fr. one side of f. to
2 K. 6 : 27. out of barn-f. or winepr.
2 Ch. 18 : † 9. they sat in f. at ent-g
Is. 21 : 10. and the corn of my f.
Ho. 9 : 1. a reward upon ev. corn-f.
2. f. and winepress not feed them
13 : 3. chaff th. is driven out of f.
Jo. 2 : 24. f-s shall be full of wheat
Mi. 4 : 12 gather as sheaves into f.
Mat. 3 : 12. thoro. purge his f., Lu. 3 : 17.
See THRESHINGFLOOR, S.

FLOUR.

Ex. 29 : 2. of wheaten f. make them
Le. 2 : 2. take his handful of f., 6 : 15.
Nu. 28 : 5 tenth part of ephah of f. for off-g. 20, 28.–29 : 3, 9, 14.
Ju. 6 : 19. an ephah of f., 1 S. 1 : 24.
1 S. 28 : 24. f. and kneaded, 2 S. 13 : 8.
2 S. 17 : 28. bro-t f. parched corn
See DEAL, FINE.

FLOURISH.

Ps. 72 : 7. In his days shall righte. f.
16. they of city shall f. like grass
92 : 7. when all workers of iniq. f.
Ps. 92 : 12. righte. sh. f. like palmtree
13. they sh. f. in courts of our G.
132 : 18. upon hims. shall crown f.
Pr. 11 : 28. righteous f. as branch
14 : 11. taber. of upright shall f.
Ec. 12 : 5. when almond tree sh. f.
Can. 7 : 12. let us see if the vine f.
Is. 17 : 11. in morn. shalt make seed f.
66 : 14. your bones sh. f. like herb
Eze. 17 : 24. I L. made dry tree f.

FLOURISHED, ETH, ING.

Ps. 90 : 6. in the morning it f-h
92 : 14. in old age, they shall be f-g
103 : 15. as a flower of field, so he f-h
Can. 2 : † 9. he looketh forth, f-g through lattice
6 : 11. I went to see whe. vine f.
Da. 4 : 4. I was at rest, f-g in palace
Ph. 4 : 10. your care of me hath f.

FLOW.

Jb. 20 : 28. his goods shall f. away
Ps. 147 : 18. he causeth the waters f.
Can. 4 : 16. that the spices may f. out
Is. 2 : 2. all nations sh. f. unto it
48 : 21. caused wat-s f. out of rock
60 : 5. thou shalt see and f. togeth.
64 : 1. mts. might f. at thy presence
Je. 31 : 12. sh. f. to goodness of L.
51 : 44. nations not f. togeth. any
Jo. 3 : 18. that day hills f. wi. milk, rivers of Judah f. with waters
Mi. 4 : 1. people shall f. to mt. of L.
Jn. 7 : 38. out of belly f. living water

FLOWED.

Jos. 4 : 18. Jor. f. over all his banks
Ju. 5 : † 5. mountains f. before L.
Is. 64 : 3. mts. f. down at thy pres.
La. 3 : 54. Waters f. over mine head

FLOWER.

1 S. 2 : 33. shall die in f. of their age
1 Co. 7 : 36. if she pass f. of her age

FLOWER.

Ex. 25 : 33. and f. in one branch, 37 : 19.
Jb. 14 : 2. cometh as f. is cut down
15 : 33. he sh. cast f. as the olive
Ps. 103 : 15. as a f., so he flourisheth
Is. 18 : 5. sour grape ripening in f.
28 : 1. glorious beauty a fading f., 4.
40 : 6. goodliness thereof is as the f. of field [11. 1 Pe. 1 : 24.
7. f. fadeth, 8 Na. 1 : 4. Ja. 1 : 10,

FLOWERS.

Ex. 25 : 31. his f. be of same, 37 : 17.
37 : 20. made like almonds, his f.
Nu. 8 : 4. unto f. was beaten work
1 K. 6 : 18. cedar carved with knops and open f., 29, 32, 35.–7 : 26, 49.
2 Ch. 4 : 5. brim of cup with f. of lilies
21. f. lamps, and tongs of gold
Can. 2 : 12. The f. appear on earth
5 : 13. His cheeks are as sweet f.

Her FLOWERS.

Le. 15 : 24. if h. f. be upon him, he
33. of her that is sick of h. f.

FLOWETH, ING.

Ex. 3 : 8. to bring them to a land f-g with milk and honey, 17.–13 : 5.–33 : 3. Je. 11 : 5.–32 : 22. Eze. 20 : 6, 15.
Le. 20 : 24. a land that f-h wi. milk and honey, Nu. 13 : 27.–14 : 8.–16 : 13, 14. De. 6 : 3.–11 : 9.–26 : 9, 15.–27 : 3.–31 : 20. Jos. 5 : 6.
Pr. 18 : 4. wellspring of wisd. as f-g brook [stream
Is. 66 : 12. glory of Gent-s like f-g
Je. 18 : 14. sh. cold f-g wa-s be forsa.?
49 : 4. Wh. f. gloriest in f. valley?

FLUTE, S.

1 K. 1 : † 40. all peo. piped with f-s
Da. 3 : 5. when ye hear f., 7, 10, 15.

FLUTTERETH.

De. 32 : 11. as eagle f. over her young

FLUX.

Ac. 28 : 8. fa. of Publius sick of a f.

FLY. [Noun.]

Is. 7 : 18. L. shall hiss for f. in Eg.

FLY. [Verb.]
Ge. 1:20. fowl that may f. ab. earth
1 S. 15 : 19. didst f. upon the spoil
2 S. 22 : 11. upon cherub, did f. upon wings of wind, Ps. 18 : 10.
Jb. 5 : 7. trouble as sparks f. upw.
20 : 8. He sh. f. away as a dream
39 : 26. Doth hawk f. by thy wisd.?
Ps.55:6.would I f. away, be at rest
90 : 10. soon cut off, and we f. aw.
Pr. 23 : 5. riches f. away as eagle
Is. 6:2. six wings, wi. twain he did f.
11 : 14. f. upon shoulders of Philis.
60 : 8. Who these that f. as cloud
Je 48 : 40. he shall f. as an eagle
Eze. 13 : 20. hunt souls to make f.
Da.9:21.Gab. being caused f. swiftly
Ho. 9 : 11. glory sh. f. aw. like bird
Ha. 1 : 8. they shall f. as the eagle
Re. 12 : 14. might f. into wilderness
14 : 6. I saw ano. angel f. in heav.
19 : 17. to all fowls th. f. in midst of heaven
See FLEE, FLEETH.

FLYING.
Le. 11:21. may ye eat of ev. f. thing
23.all other f. things an abomina.
Ps. 148 : 10. and f. fowl, praise Lord
Pr. 26 : 2. as swallow by f. so curse
Is. 14 : 29. his fruit be fiery f. serp.
30:6. fr. whence come fiery f. serp.
31:5.As birds f. so L. defend Jerus.
Zch. 5 : 1. and behold, a f. roll, 2.
Re. 4 : 7. fourth beast like f. eagle
8:13. heard an angel f. thro. heav.

FOAL, S. [f-s
Ge. 32 : 15. Jacob took 20 asses, ten
49 : 11. Binding his f. unto the vine
Zch.9:9.upon f. of an ass, Mat.21:5.

FOAM. [Noun.]
Ho. 10 : 7. k. of Sama. is cut off as f.

FOAMETH, ING.
Mk. 9:18. f-h and gnasheth, Lu.9:39.
20. he fell on ground wallowed f-g
Jude 13. f-g out their own shame

FODDER.
Jb. 6:5. or loweth the ox over his f.

FOES. [thy f.
1 Ch. 21:12. or to be destroyed bef.
Es. 9 : 16. Jews slew of f. 75,000
Ps. 27 : 2. and f. came upon me
30 : 1. hast not made my f. to rej.
89 : 23. I will beat down his f. bef.
Mat. 10 : 36. man's f. be they of household [stool
Ac. 2 : 35. Until I make thy f. foot-

FOLD, S.
Nu. 32 : 24. build f-s for sheep, 36.
Ps 50 : 9. take no he goats out of f-s
Is. 13 : 20. shepherds make f. there
65 : 10. Sharon sh. be f. for flocks
Je.23 : 3. will bring them to their f-s
Eze. 34:14. upon mts. sh. their f. be
Mi. 2 : 12. as flock in midst of f.
Ha. 3 : 17. flock sh. be cut off fr. f.
Zph. 2 : 6. sea coast be f-s for flocks
Mat. 13 : 8. bro-t forth fruit, some 100, 60, 30, f., 23. Mk. 4 : 8, 20.
19:29. forsaken houses, rec. 100 f.
Jn. 10 : 16. other sheep I have, not of this f. there sh. be one f. and
See FOURFOLD, HUNDREDFOLD, SIXTYFOLD, TENFOLD, THIRTYFOLD, THREEFOLD, TWOFOLD.

FOLD, EN, ETH, ING.
1 K.6:34. leaves of one door were f-g
Pr. 6:10. f-g of hands to sleep, 24:33.
Ec.4:5.fool f-h his hands and eateth
Na. 1:10.while they be f-n as thorns
He. 1 : 12. as vesture shalt f. them

FOLK, S.
Ge. 33:15. leave with thee some of f.
Pr. 30 : 26. conies are but a feeble f.
Je. 51 : 58. the f. shall labour in fire
Mk. 6:5. laid hands upon few sick f.
Jn. 5 : 3. a multitude of impotent f.
Ac. 5 : 16. multitude, bringing sick [f-s

FOLLOW.
Ge. 24:8. if woman not willing to f.
44 : 4. Joseph said, Up, f. aft. men
Ex. 11 : 8. and people that f. thee
14 : 4. I will harden Pha. he sh. f.
17. Egyp-s shall f. them [chief f.
21: 22. if hurt woman, yet no mis-
23. if mischief f. then life for
23 : 2. not f. a multitude to do evil
De. 16:20. what is just shalt thou f.
18:22.if the thing f. not, nor come
Ju. 9:3. hearts inclined to f. Abim.
1 S. 25 : 27. be given young men, who f. my lord [David
30 : 21. so faint they could not f.
2 S. 17 : 9. am. people that f. Abs.
1 K.19:20.let me kiss fa.,then will f.
Ps. 38:20. bec. I f. thing th. good is
45:14. virgins her compan-s that f.
94 : 15. all the upright shall f. it
119:150. nigh that f. after mischief
Is. 5 : 11. they may f. strong drink
51 : 1. ye that f. aft. righteousness
Je.17:16.fr. being a pastor to f. thee
42 : 16. famine sh. f. close aft. you
Eze. 13:3. prophets th. f. own spirit
Ho. 2 : 7. shall f. after her lovers
6 : 3. know, if we f. on to know L.
Mat. 8:19. I will f. thee, Lu.9:57,61.
Mk. 16 : 17. these signs f. them
Lu. 17 : 23. go not aft., nor f. them
22 : 49. when saw what would f.
Jn. 10 : 5. stranger will they not f.
13:37.L.why cannot I f. thee now?
Ac. 3 : 24. prophets from Sam., and those that f. after
Ro. 14 : 19. f. things make for peace
1 Co. 14 : 1. f. after charity, desire
Ph. 3 : 12. f. after, if I may appre.
1 Th. 5 : 15. ever f. that wh. is good
2 Th.3:7.know how ye ought to f.us
9. ourselves an ensample to f. us
1 Ti. 5 : 24. some they f. after
6:11. O man of G., f. righte., 2 Ti.
He.12:14. f. peace wi. all men [2:22.
13 : 7. whose faith f. consid-g end
1 Pe. 1:11 testified glory th. sho. f.
2 : 21. an example, that ye sho. f.
2 Pe. 2 : 2. shall f. pernicious ways
3 Jn. 11. f. not that which is evil
Re. 14 : 4. are they th. f. the Lamb
13. and their works do f. them

FOLLOW him.
1 K. 18 : 21. if the L. be G., f. h.
Mk. 5 : 37. suffered no man to f.h.
6 : 1. he went, and his disci. f. h.
Lu.22:10. f. h. into hou.,Mk.14:13.
Jn. 10 : 4. he goeth bef., sheep f. h.

FOLLOW me. [39.
Ge. 24 : 5. wom. not willing to f. m.,
Ju. 3 : 28. Ehud said, f. after m.
8:5. give bread unto peo. th. f. m.
1 K. 20 : 10. handfuls for peo. that f. m. [to man
2 K. 6 : 19. f. m., I will bring you
Ps. 23:6. goodn. and mercy sh. f.m.
Mat. 4:19. Jesus saith, f. m. and I, 8 : 22.-9:9. Mk. 2:14. Lu. 5:27.
16 : 24. let him take up his cross f. m., Mk.8:34.-10:21. Lu.9:23.
19 : 21. sell that thou hast, f. m., Lu. 18 : 22. [21:19, 22.
Lu. 9:59. he said, f. m., Jn. 1:43.-
Jn. 10 : 27. my sheep hear and f.m.
12:26. If any will serve, let him f.
13:36. thou canst not f.m.now[m.
Ac. 12 : 8. garm. about thee, f. m.

FOLLOWED. [man
Ge. 24 : 61. Rebekah and damsels f.
Ge.32:19. com-d he all th. f. droves
Nu. 32 : 12. wholly f. L., De. 1 : 36.
De. 4 : 3. men that f. Baal-peor
11 :†6. swallowed substance wh. f.
Jos. 6 : 8. ark of covenant f. them
14 : 8. I wholly f. the Lord, 9, 14.
Ju. 2 : 12. forsook L. f. other gods
Ju.9:49.cut his bough, and f.Abim.
1 S. 14 : 22. they f. hard aft. Philis.
17 : 13. Jesse's 3 sons f. Saul, 14.
31 : 2. Philis. f. Saul, 2 S. 1 : 6. 1 Ch. 10 : 2.
2 S. 2 : 10. house of Jud. f. David
3 : 31. king Da. himself f. the bier
17:23. Ahith. saw his counsel not f.
20 : 2. Isr. f. Sheba son of Bichri
1 K. 12 : 20. none th. f. hou. of Da.
16 : 21. half f. Tibni, half f., 22.
18 : 18. forsak. L., hast f. Baalim
20 : 19. and the army wh. f. them
2 K. 3 : 9. no water for cattle th. f.
4 : 30. Elisha rose and f. her
5 : 21. So Gehazi f. after Naaman
9 : 27. Jehu f. after Ahaziah, and
13 : 2. Jehoahaz f. sins of Jerob.
17 : 15. f. vanity, and became vain
Ps.68:25.players on instrum-s f. aft.
Eze. 10:11. whi. head looked, they f.
Am. 7 : 15. L. took me as I f. flock
Mat. 8 : 10. said to them that f.
19 : 27. forsaken all and f. thee
21:9.th. f. cried Hosanna,Mk.11:9.
27 : 55. many women which f. Jes.
62. day that f. day of preparation
Mk. 10 : 28. we left all f. thee, Lu.
32. as they f. were afraid [18:28.
52. received sight and f. Jesus
Lu. 22 : 54. And Peter f. afar off
23:55. f. aft. and beheld sepulchre
Jn. 1 : 37. disci-s heard him and f.
11 : 31. f. She goeth unto grave
Ac.13:43.religious proselytes f. Paul
16 : 17. The same f. Paul and us
21 : 36. f. aft. crying, Away with
Ro. 9 : 30. Gent-s who f. not righte.
31. who f. aft. law of righteousn.
1 Co.10:4.drank of rock th. f. them
1 Ti. 5 : 10. if she have f. ev. good work [fables
2 Pe. 1:16. not f. cunningly devised
Re. 6 : 8. Death and Hell f. wi. him
8 : 7. f. hail and fire with blood
14 : 8. f. ano. angel, saying, Bab. is
9. third angel f. them, saying, If

FOLLOWED him. [f.h.
Nu. 16 : 25 Moses rose, elders of Isr.
Ju.9:4.hired light persons who f. h.
1 S. 13 : 7. all the peo. f.h. tremb.
2 S. 11:8. there f. h. a mess of meat
Mat. 4:20. left nets f. h., Mk. 1:18.
22. they left the ship and f. h.
25. there f. h. great multitudes of people, 8 : 1.-12 : 15.-19 : 2.-20: 29. Mk. 2 : 15.-5:24. Lu. 9 : 11, 23 : 27. Jn. 6 : 2. [Jn. 1 : 40.
8 : 23. his disci-s f. h., Lu. 22 : 39.
9 : 9. arose and f. h., Mk. 2 : 14.
19. Jesus arose and f. h. so did
27. two blind men f. h. crying
20:34. rec-d sight f. h., Lu. 18:43.
26 : 58. Peter f. h. afar, Mk. 14:54. Lu. 22 : 54.
Mk.1:36.Simon f. aft. h., Jn.18:15.
14 : 51. f. h. a certain young man
15 : 41. f. h. minist-d unto him
Lu. 5 : 11. forsook all and f. h., 28.
7 : 9. Jesus said unto peo. th. f.h.
23:49. women that f. h. fr. Galilee
Ac. 12 : 9. Peter went out and f. h.
Re. 19 : 14. armies in heaven f. h.

FOLLOWED me.
Nu. 14 : 24. Caleb hath f. m. fully
32 : 11. they have not wholly f.m.
1 K. 14 : 8. Da. f. m. wi. all heart
Ne. 4 : 23. men of guard wh. f. m.
Mat. 19 : 28. that f. m. in regenera.

FOLLOWEDST.
Ru. 3 : 10. thou f. not young men

FOLLOWER. [doc.
2 Ti. 3 : †10. been a diligent f. of my

FOLLOWERS. [3 : 17.
1 Co. 4 : 16. be f. of me, 11 : 1. Ph.
Ep. 5 : 1. be ye f. of G. as dear chil.
1 Th. 1:6. ye became f. of us and L.

1 Th.2:14. ye became f.of ch-s [faith
He. 6 : 12. be f. of them who thro.
1 Pe. 3:13. if ye be f. of that is good

FOLLOWETH.

2 K. 11 : 15. that f. her kill, 2 Ch.
Ps.63:8.My soul f. hard aft. [23:14.
Pr. 12: 11. f. vain persons, 28: 19.
15: 9. loveth him f. righte., 21:21.
Is. 1: 23. every one f. after rewards
Eze. 16:34.none f.to com. whored-s
Ho. 12: 1. Ephr. f. after east wind
Mat. 10: 38. taketh not cross and f.
Mk. 9: 38. he f. not us, Lu. 9: 49.
Jn. 8: 12. f. me shall not walk in

FOLLOWING. [darkn.

Ge. 41: 31. by reason of famine f.
De. 7: 4. turn aw. thy son fr. f. me
12: 30. thou be not snared by f.
Jos. 22:16. from f. Lord, 18, 23, 29.
1 S. 12: 20. 2 K. 17: 21. 2 Ch.
25: 27.-34: 33.
Ju. 2: 19. corrupted in f. other gods
Ru. 1: 16. or to return fr. f. thee
1 S. 12: 14. if ye continue f. the L.
14: 46. Saul went up fr. f. Philis.
15: 11. Saul is turned from f. me
24: 1. was returned from f. Philis.
2 S. 2: 19. Asahel turned not fr. f.
Abner, 21, 22, 30.
26. bid people return fr. f. breth.
7: 8. I took thee from f. the sheep,
to be ruler,1 Ch. 17:7.Ps.78:71.
1 K. 1: 7. and they f. Adonijah
9: 6. if you sh. at all turn from f.
21: 26. Ahab did abom. in f. idols
2 K. 18: 6. departed not fr. f. him
Ps. 48: 13. may tell it to genera. f.
78: 71. From f. ewes gr. wi. young
109: 13. in generation f. let name
be blotted [signs f.
Mk. 16:20. confirming the word with
Lu. 13: 33. walk to-morrow day f.
Jn. 1: 38. Jes. turned saw them f.
43. day f. | 6:22. day f. peo. saw
20: 6. Pe. f. him, went into sepul.
21: 20. seeth disciple Jes. loved f.
Ac. 21: 1. day f. unto Rhodes, 18.
23:11. night f. the L. stood by him
2 Pe. 2:15. astray, f. way of Balaam

FOLLY. [in Isr.

Ge. 34: 7. Shechem had wrought f.
De. 22: 21. f. by playing the whore
Jos. 7:15. Achan wrought f. in Isr.
Ju. 19:23. I pray you, do not this f.
† 24. do not the matter of this f.
20:6. they have committ. f. in Isr.
10. acc. to f. they wrought in Isr.
1 S. 25:25. Nabal is his name, and f.
2 S. 13:12. bro., do not thou this f.
Jb. 1:†22.Job attributed not f. to G.
4:18. his angels he charged with f.
24: 12. God layeth not f. to them
42:8. lest I deal wi. you aft. your f.
Ps. 49:13. This their way is their f.
85: 8. let them not turn again to f.
Pr. 5:23. in greatn. of f. he go astray
13: 16. fool layeth open his f.
14: 8. the f. of fools is deceitful
18. simple inheriters f. but pru-
24. foolishness of fools is f. [dent
29. he hasty of spirit exalteth f.
15:21.f.joy to him destitute of wisd.
16: 22. instruction of fools is f. [f.
17:12. let bear meet than fool in his
18: 13. bef. he heareth it, it is f.
26:4. Answer not a fool acc. to his f.
5. Ans. a fool accord. to his f., lest
11. so a fool returneth to his f.
Ec. 1:17. heart to know wisd. and f.
2: 3. I sought to lay hold on f.
12. turned to behold wisdom f.
13. wisdom excelleth f. far as light
7: 25. to know wickedness of f.
10: 1. so little f. him in reputation
6 f. is set in great dignity, rich sit
Is. 9:17. and ev. mouth speaketh f.
Je. 23:13. I have seen f. in prophets
Ho. 2: † 10. I will discover her f. in
2 Co. 11:1. bear wi. me little in my f.
2 Ti. 3:9. their f. sh. be made man-

FOOD. [ifest

Ge. 2:9. every tree that is good for f.
3:6. wom. saw tree was good for f.
6: 21. take thou unto thee of all f.
41: 35. gather all f. of good years
36. f. be for store to land, 48.
48. f. in cities f. of the field
42: 7. came to buy f., 10.-43:2, 4,
20, 22.-44: 25. [househ.
33. take f. for the famine of your
44:1. he com-d to fill sacks with f.
47:24. your f. and f. for little ones
Ex. 21: 10. her f. not be diminish.
Le. 3: 11. the f. of the offering, 16.
19:23. planted all manner of trees
21:†17. not appro. to offer f. [for f.
22:7. eat of holy things, bec. his f.
De. 10:18. stranger, in giving him f.
1 S.14:24.eateth f. until evening,28.
2 S. 9:10. that master's son have f.
1 K. 5:9. in giving f. for my househ.
11. Sol. gave Hiram wheat for f.
Ne.9:†25. poss-d trees of f. in abund.
Jb. 23: 12. thy words more than f.
24:5. wilderness yieldeth f. for th.
38: 41. provideth for raven his f.?
40:20.mountains bring him forth f.
Ps. 78:25. Man did eat angels' f. he
104:14. bring forth f. out of earth
136: 25. Who giveth f. to all flesh
146: 7. L. wh. giveth f. to hungry
147:9. He giveth to the beast his f.
Pr. 6: 8. ant gath-h f. in harvest
13:23. Much f. is in tillage of poor
27:27.goats' milk enough for thy f.
28:3. is like rain wh. leaveth no f.
30: 8. feed me with f. convenient
31: 14. she bringeth her f. fr. afar
Eze. 16: 27. thine ordinary f.
48: 18. the increase shall be for f.
Ac. 14: 17. seasons, filling hearts
with f.
2 Co. 9:10. minister bread for your f.
1 Ti. 6:8. having f. and raiment, let
Ja. 2: 15. if destitute of daily f.

FOOL. [erred

1 S. 26: 21. I have played f. and
Ps. 14: 1. f. said in his heart, 53:1.
49:10. f. and brutish person perish
92: 6. nei. doth a f. underst. this
Pr. 10: 8 prating f. shall fall, 10.
23. a sport to a f. to do mischief
11: 29. f. be servant to wise
12: 15. way of f. right in own eyes
16. f. wrath is presently known
13: 16. but f. layeth open his folly
14: 16. f. rageth and is confident
15:5. f. despiseth his fa.'s instruc.
17: 7. Excellent speech becometh
not a f. [into f.
10. reproof more than 100 stripes
12. let bear meet man rath. than f.
16. why is a price in hand of a f.?
21. He that begetteth a f. doth
28. f. when he holdeth his peace is
18: 2. f. no delight in underst-g
6. f. lips enter into contention
Pr. 18:7. f. mouth is his destruction
20: 3. every f. will be meddling
26: 4. answer not a f. | 5. ans. a f.
8. so he that giveth honour to f.
10. the great G. rewardeth the f.
11. as a dog so a f. returneth to
27: 3. f. wrath heavier than both
22. Though bray a f. in a mortar
29:11. f. uttereth all his mind, but
Ec. 2: 14. f. walketh in darkness
15. as it happeneth to f. so to me
16. no remem. of wise more than f.
19. who kno-h whe. he wise or f.?
4: 5. f. foldeth his hands together
5: 3. a f. voice known by multi. of
6:8. what hath wise more than f.?
10: 2. a f. heart is at his left hand
Ec.10:14.f.full of words,man cannot
Je. 17:11. at his end he be a f. [tell
Mat. 5: 22. whoso. sh. say, Thou f.
Lu. 12:20. f., this night thy soul sh.
1 Co. 3:18. a f. that he may be wise
15: 36. thou f., that thou sowest
2 Co. 11: 16. Let no man think me
a f. [shall not be a f.
12:6. tho. I would desire to glory,
11. I am become a f. in glorying

As a or the FOOL.

2 S. 3:33. Died Abner a. a f. dieth?
Pr. 7: 22. a. a f. to the stocks
Ec. 2: 16. how dieth wise? a. t. f.
2 Co. 11:16. yet a. a f. receive me
23. ministers? I speak a. a f. I
am more

For a or the FOOL. [a f.

Pr. 19: 10. Delight is not seemly f.
24: 7. Wisdom is too high f. a f.
26: 1. honour is not seemly f. a f.
3. bridle for ass, rod f. t. f. back
30: 22. f. a f. filled with meat

Is a FOOL.

Pr. 10: 18. uttereth a slander i. a f.
19: 1. is perverse in lips, and i.a f.
28:26. trusteth in own heart i. a f.
Ec. 10: 3. when he th. i. a f. walketh,he saith to ev. one he i. a f.
Ho. 9:7. prophet i. a f. the spiritual
1 Ti. 6: † 4. i. a f. and kno-h noth.

Of a or of the FOOL.

Pr. 12: 15. way o. a f. is right in
his own eyes
17: 21. father o. a f. hath no joy
24. eyes o. a f. in ends of earth
23:9. Speak not in the ears o. a f.
26:6. sendeth message by hand o.
12.more hope o. a f., 29:20. [a f.
Ec. 7:6. of thorns, so laughter o.t.f.
10: 12. lips o. a f. will swallow

FOOLS. [hims.

2 S. 13: 13. shalt be as one of the f.
Jb. 12: 17. he maketh the judges f.
30: 8. they were chil. of f. [ishly
Ps. 75: 4. said to f., Deal not fool-
94: 8. ye f., when will ye be wise?
107:17. f. bec. of transgr. are afflic.
Pr. 1: 7. f. despise wisdom and
22. how long, ye f., hate knowl.?
32. prosperity of f. shall destroy
3:35. shame sh. be promotion of f.
8: 5. f. be ye of underst-g heart
10: 21. f. die for want of wisdom
12:23. heart of f. procl-h foolishn.
13:19. abomi. to f. to depart fr. evil
20. companion of f. sh. be destr.
14: 8. folly of f. is deceit
9. f. make a mock at sin
24. foolishness of f. is folly
33. in midst of f. is made known
15: 2. mouth of f. pour. foolishn.
14 mouth of f.feedeth on foolishn.
16: 22. instruction of f. is folly
19: 29. stripes for the back of f.
26:7. so parable in mouth of f., 9.
Ec. 5:1. to hear, than give sacr. of f.
4. he hath no pleasure in f.
7:4. heart of f. is in house of mirth
5. than to hear the song of f.
9. anger resteth in the bosom of f.
9:17. cry of him that ruleth am. f.
Is. 19:11. princes of Zoan are f., 13.
35:8. way-f-g men, tho. f., not err
Mat. 23: 17. Ye f. and blind, 19.
Lu. 11:40. Ye f. did not he th. made
24:25. O f. and slow of heart to beli.
Ro. 1:22. to be wise, they became f.
1 Co.4:10. We are f. for Christ's sake
2 Co. 11: 19. for ye suffer f. gladly
Ep. 5: 15. See ye walk not as f.

FOOLISH.

De. 32: 6. thus requite L., O f. peo.?
21. provoke with f. na., Ro. 10:19.
Jb. 2:10. speakest as one of f. wom.
5: 2. for wrath killeth the f. man
3. I have seen the f. taking root

Ps. 5: 5. f. not stand in thy sight
39: 8. make me not reproach of f.
73: 3. for I was envious at the f.
22. So f. was I and ignorant
74: 18. f. people have blasphemed
22. rememb. how f. man reproach.
Pr. 9: 6. Forsake the f. and live
13. f. woman is clamorous
10: 1. f. son is heaviness of moth.
14. mouth of f. near destruction
14: 1. f. plucketh house down
3. In the mouth of the f. is a rod
7. Go from presence of a f. man
15: 7. heart of the f. doeth not so
20. f. man despiseth his mother
17: 25. A f. son is a grief to his fa.
19: 13. A f. son is calamity of fa.
21: 20. f. man spendeth a treasure
29: 9. If wise contendeth with a f.
Ec. 4: 13. wise child than a f. king
7: 17. Be not wicked, nei. be thou f.
10: 15. labour of f. wearieth every
Is. 44: 25. he maketh their knowl. f.
Je. 4: 22: for my people is f. they
5: 4. Surely these are poor, are f.
21. Hear now this, O f. people
10: 8. are altogether brutish and f.
La. 2: 14. proph. have seen f. things
Eze. 13: 3. saith L., Woe to f. prophets
Zch. 11: 15. instruments of f. sheph.
Mat. 7: 26. be likened unto a f. man
25: 2. five were wise, five f., 3.
8. f. said unto wise, Give us oil
Ro. 1: 21. f. heart was darkened
2: 20. An instructor of the f.
1 Co. 1: 20. G. made f. wisd. of world
Ga. 3: 1. O f. Galat-s, who bewitch.?
3. Are ye so f.? begun in Spirit
Ep. 5: 4. filthiness, nor f. talking
1 Ti. 6: 9. be rich fall into f. lusts
2 Ti. 2: 23. f. questions, Tit. 3: 9.
Tit. 3: 3. we were sometime f.
1 Pe. 2: 15. to silence ignor. of f. men

FOOLISHLY.

Ge. 31: 28. thou hast now done f. in so doing, 1 S. 13: 13. 2 Ch. 16: 9.
Nu. 12: 11. sin wherein done f.
2 S. 24: 10. done very f., 1 Ch. 21: 8.
Jb. 1: 22. sinned not, nor charged G. f.
Ps. 75: 4. said unto fools, Deal not f.
Pr. 14: 17. is soon angry dealeth f.
30: 32. If hast done f. in lifting thys.
2 Co. 11: 17. I speak it as it were f.
21. I speak f. I am bold also

FOOLISHNESS.

2 S. 15: 31. counsel of Ahith. into f.
Ps. 38: 5. wounds stink bec. of f.
69: 5. O God, thou knowest my f.
Pr. 12: 23. heart of fools procl-h f.
14: 24. but the f. of fools is folly
15: 2. mouth of fools poureth f.
14. mouth of fools feedeth on f.
19: 3. f. of man perverteth way
22: 15. f. is bound in heart of child
24: 9. The thought of f. is sin
27: 22. yet will not his f. depart
Ec. 7: 25. to know the wickedn. of f.
10: 13. beginning of the words is f.
Mk. 7: 22. pride, f. come fr. within
1 Co. 1: 18. cross to them that perish, f.
21. God by f. of preaching to save
23. we preach C., unto Greeks f.
25. Bec. f. of G. is wiser than men
2: 14. things of Spirit are f. to him
3: 19. wisd. of world is f. with G.

FOOT.

Ge. 41: 44. no man shall lift up his f.
Ex. 12: 37. about 600,000 on f. [21.
21: 24. shalt give f. for f., De. 19:
30: 18. a laver of brass and his f., 28.-31: 9.-35: 16.-38: 8.-39: 39.-40: 11. Le. 8: 11.
Le. 13: 12. if a leprosy fr. head to f.
Nu. 22: 25. ass crushed Balaam's f.
De 8: 4. nor thy f. swell 40 years
11: 10. wateredst it with thy f.
25: 9. she sh. loose shoe fr. his f.
De. 29: 5. shoe not waxen old upon f.
32: 35. their f. sh. slide in due time
33: 24. Let Asher dip his f. in oil
Jos. 1: 3. ev. place f. sh. tread upon
5: 15. Loose thy shoe from off thy f.
Ju. 5: 15. Barak was sent on f.
1 S. 23: † 22. where his f. shall be
2 S. 2: 18. Asahel was as light of f.
21: 20. on f. six toes, 1 Ch. 20: 6.
2 K. 9: 33. Jehu trod Jezebel und. f.
2 Ch. 33: 8. nor remove f. of Israel
Jb. 23: 11. My f. hath held his steps
28: 4. even waters forgotten of f.
31: 5. if f. hath hasted to deceit
39: 15. forgetteth f. may crush th.
Ps. 9: 15. in net they hid f. taken
26: 12. My f. standeth in even pla.
36: 11. Let not f. of pride ag. me
38: 16. when my f. slippeth
66: 6. they went thro. the flood on f.
68: 23. f. may be dipped in blood
91: 12. angels bear thee, lest dash f. ag. stone, Mat. 4: 6. Lu. 4: 11.
94: 18. I said my f. slippeth [moved
121: 3. will not suffer thy f. to be
Pr 1: 15. refrain f. fr. their path
3: 23. and thy f. shall not stumble
26. sh. keep thy f. fr. being taken
4: 27. turn not, remove f. fr. evil
25: 17. Withdraw thy f. fr. neighbour's [like f. out of joint
19. confidence in unfaith. men is
Ec. 5: 1. Keep f. when goest into house of God [f.
Is. 14: 25. upon mts. tread him und.
18: 7. a nation trodden under f.
20: 2. put off thy shoe from off f.
26: 6. the f. shall tread it down
41: 2. called righte. man to his f.
58: 13. If turn f. from my sabbath
Je. 2: 25. Withhold thy f. fr being
12: 10. trodden my portion und. f.
La. 1: 15. L. trodden und. f. mighty
Eze. 6: 11. stamp with f., say, Alas
16: †6. trodden und. f. I said, Live
25: † 6. bec. hast stamped with f.
29: 11. No f. of man, no f. of beast
32: 13. nei. f. of man trouble them
Da. 8: 13. host to be trodden und. f.
Am. 2: 15. swift of f. not deliver hims.
Mat. 5: 13. salt, trodden under f.
14: 13. people followed him on f.
18: 8. if f. offend thee, Mk. 9: 45.
22: 13. Bind him hand and f. cast
Jn. 11: 44. dead came bound hand and f.
Ac. 7: 5. not so much as to set his f. on
1 Co. 12: 15. if f. say, Bec I not ha.
He. 10: 29. trodden und. f. Son of G.
Re. 1: 13. clothed with a garm. to f.
11: 2. holy city shall they tread under f.

Left FOOT.

Re. 10: 2. he set his L. f. on earth

See RIGHT foot.

Sole of FOOT.

Ge 8: 9. dove found no rest for - f.
De. 28: 35. smite with botch fr. - f.
56. not set s. o. her f. upon ground
65. neither shall - f. have rest
Jos. 1: 3. Every place that - f. tread
2 S. 14: 25. fr. - f. to head no blem.
Jb. 2: 7. Job with boils fr. - f. unto
Is. 1: 6. -f. unto head no soundness
Eze. 1: 7. s. o. feet like s. o. calfs f.
See TOES.

FOOTBREADTH.

De. 2: 5. give, no, not so much as a f.

FOOTED.

See BROKENFOOTED, CLOVENFOOTED, FOURFOOTED

FOOTMEN.

Nu 11: 21. The people are 600,000 f.
Ju. 20: 2. 400,000 f. that drew sword
1 S. 4: 10. fell of Israel 30,000 f. [f.
15: 4. numbered in Telaim 200,000
22: 17. Saul said unto f., Slay priests
2 S. 8: 4. 20,000 f., 10: 6. 2 Ch. 18: 4.
1 K. 20: 29. slew of Syrians 100,000 f.
2 K. 13: 7. leave but 10,000 f.
1 Ch. 19: 18. 40,000 f. and killed
Je. 12: 5. if hast run with f. and th.

FOOTSTEPS.

Ps. 17: 5. goings that my f. slip not
77: 19. in sea, thy f. are not known
89: 51. reproached f. of anointed
Can. 1: 8. go by f. of the flock

FOOTSTOOL.

1 Ch. 28: 2. build house for f. of G.
2 Ch. 9: 18. to throne with f. of gold
Ps. 99: 5. worship at his f., 132: 7.
110: 1. until I make thine enemies thy f., Mat. 22: 44. Mk. 12: 36. Lu. 20: 43. Ac. 2: 35. He. 1: 13.
Is. 66: 1. and earth is my f., Ac. 7: 49.
La. 2: 1. remem-d not his f. [his f.
Mat. 5: 35. swear not by earth, it is
He. 10: 13. till enemies be made his f.
Ja. 2: 3. poor, s here under my f.

FOR.

De. 4: 7. things that we call on him
2 S. 11: 22. all Joab had sent him f.
Pr. 28: 21. f. piece of br. man transg.
Mat. 5: 45. Fa., f. he maketh his sun rise on the evil and the good
6: 7. think to be heard f. much sp-g
25: 35. f. I was hungry, ye gave, 42.
Jn. 1: 16. we received grace f. grace
Ro. 13: 6. f. f. this ye pay tribute
2 Co. 5: 1 f. we know, if this house
13: 8. f. we can do noth. ag. but f.
2 Pe. 3: 12. looking f. the coming of

FORASMUCH.

Ge. 41: 39. f. as God hath shewed
De. 12: 12. f. as he hath no inherit.
Ju. 11: 36. f. as L. taken vengeance
1 S. 20: 42. f. as we have sworn
2 S. 19: 30. f. as my lord is come
1 K. 13: 21. f. as thou hast disobeyed
1 Ch. 5: 1. f. as Reu. defiled fa.'s bed
Is. 29: 13. f. as this peo. draw near
Je. 10: 16. f. as none like unto thee
7. f. am. wise men none like thee
Da. 2: 40. f. as iron break. all things
Lu. 1: 1. f. as many have taken in hand
Ac. 11: 17. f. as G. gave like gift
15: 24. f. as we have heard that
17: 29. f. as we are offspr. of God
24: 10. f. as thou hast been a judge
1 Co. 11: 7. f. as he is image of G.
14: 12. f. as ye are zealous of
15: 58. f. as ye know your labour
He. 2: 14. f. as chil. are partakers
1 Pe. 1: 18. f. as ye know ye were
4: 1. f. as C. hath suffered for us

FORBADE.

De. 2: 37. nor unto whatso. L. f. us
Mat. 3: 14. but John f. him, saying,
Mk. 9: 38. we f. him, Lu. 9: 49.
2 Pe. 2: 16. ass f. madness of proph.

FORBARE.

1 S. 23: 13. and Saul f. to go forth
2 Ch. 25: 16. Then the prophet f.
Je. 41: 8. Ishmael f. and slew not

FORBEAR.

Ex. 23: 5. if see his ass, and would f. to help him [sin
De. 23: 22. if shalt f. to vow, be no
1 S. 11: †3. f. us seven days that we may send [Ch. 18: 5, 14.
1 K. 22: 6. shall I go, or f.? 15. 2
2 Ch. 25: 16. f. why be smitten?
35: 21. f. thee fr. meddling with G.
Ne. 9: 30. Yet many years didst f.
Jb. 16: 6. I f. what am I eased?
Pr. 24: 11. thou f. to deliver them
Je. 40: 4. if it seem ill unto thee f.
Eze. 2: 5. will hear or f., 7.-3: 11.
3: 27. he th. forbeareth, let him f.
24: 17. f. to cry, make no mourning
Zch. 11: 12. give me my price, if not, f.
1 Co. 9: 6. not power to f. working?
2 Co. 12: 6. f. lest any think of me ab

1 Th. 3: 1. wh. we could no longer

FORBEARANCE. [f., 5.

Ro. 2:4. or despisest riches of his f.?
3:25. remission of sins thro. f. of G.

FORBEARETH, ING.

Nu. 9:13. that f-h to keep passover
Pr. 25: 15. By long f-g is prince
Je. 20: 9. I was weary with f-g
Eze. 3: 27. that f-h let him forbear
Ep 4: 2. f-g one ano., Col. 3: 13.
6: 9. masters, f-g threatening
2 Ti. 2: † 24. serv. of L. must be f-g

FORBID.

Nu. 11: 28. My lord Moses, f. them
1 S. 24: 6. L. f. I do this thing
26: 11 L. f. I stretch forth mine ha.
1 K. 21:3. said to Ahab, L. f. it me
1 Ch. 11: 19. My God f. it me, that do
Mk. 9: 39. Jes. said, f. him not, Lu
9: 50. [19: 14. Lu. 18: 16.
10: 14. little chil. f. them not, Mat.
Lu. 6: 29. f. not to take coat also
Ac. 10: 47. Can any f. water,
24: 23 sho. f. none of his acquaint.
1 Co. 14: 39. f. not to speak with

God FORBID. [tongues

Ge. 44:7. G. f., 17. Jos. 22:29.-24:16.
1 S. 1 :23.-14:45.-20:2. Jb. 27:
5. Lu. 20:16. Ro. 3: 4. 6, 31.-6:
2, 15.-7:7, 13.-9:14.-11:1, 11. 1
Co. 6:15. Ga. 2:17.-3:21.-6:14.

FORBIDDEN.

Le. 5: 17. if soul commit things f.
De. 4: 23. or likeness of what L. f.
Ac. 16: 6. were f. to preach in Asia

FORBIDDETH, ING.

Lu. 23: 2. f-g to give trib. to Cesar
Ac. 28: 31. preaching no man f-g him
1 Th. 2: 16. f-g us to speak to Gen.
1 Ti. 4: 3. f-g to marry, command-g
3 Jn. 10. f-h them would recei. breth.

FORBORNE. [fight

Je. 51: 30. mighty men have f. to

FORCE. [Noun.] [by f.

Ge. 31:31. peradv. thou wouldest take
De. 34: 7. nor his natural f. abated
1 S. 2: 16. if not, I will take it by f.
Ezr. 4:23. th. made them cease by f.
Jo. 30:18. By great f. of my disease
40: 16. his f. is in navel of belly
Je. 18:21. pour out blood by f. of sw.
23: 10. is evil, their f. is not right
48:45. under the shadow, bec. of f.
Eze. 34:4. with f. have ye ruled th
35: 5. shed blood by f. of sword
Am. 2: 14. strong not strengthen f.
Mat. 11:12. violent take it by f. [f.
Jn. 6:15. perceived would take him by
Ac. 23:10. to take Paul by f. [dead
He. 9:17. testament is of f. aft. men

FORCES. [ies

2 Ch. 17:2. Jehosh. placed f. in cit-
Jb. 36: 19. he will not esteem all f.
Is. 60: 5. 11. f. of Gentiles.
Je. 40:7. captains of the f., 13.-41:
11, 13, 16.-42: 1, 8.-43: 4, 5.
Da. 11:10. assemble a mult. of gr. f.
38. shall he honour the God of f.
Ob. 11. strangers carried away his f.
† 13. shouldest not have laid hands

FORCE. [Verb.] [on their f.

De. 22:25. if man f. and lie with her
2 S. 13: 12. my bro. do not f. me
Es. 7: 8. Will he f. the queen also

FORCED.

Ju. 1: 34. Amorites f. chil. of Dan
20: 5. my concubine have they f.
1 S. 13: 12. I f. myself and offered
2 S. 13: 14. he being stronger f. her
22. hated Amnon, bec. f. his sister
32. determined fr. day he f. Tamar
Pr. 7: 21. with flattering she f. him

FORCIBLE.

Jb. 6: 25. How f. are right words!

FORCING. [axe

De. 20: 19. not destroy trees by f. an
Pr. 30: 33. f. of wrath bringeth strife

FORD, S.

Ge. 32: 22. Jacob passed over f.
Jos. 2:7. men pursued spies unto f-s
Ju. 3: 28. Isr. took f-s of Jordan
Is. 16:2. dau-s at the f-s of Arnon

FORECAST. [25.

Da. 11: 24. he shall f. his devices,

FOREFATHERS.

Je. 11: 10. are turned to iniq. of f.
2 Ti 1:3. G., whom I serve fr. my f.

FOREFRONT.

Ex. 26:9. sixth curtain in f. of taber.
28: 37. blue lace, upon f. of mitre
Le. 8:9. upon his f. the golden plate
1 S. 14:5. f. of one rock was situate
2 S. 11:15. Set Uriah in f. of battle
2 K. 16: 14. bro-t brazen altar fr. f.
2 Ch. 20: 27. Jehosh. in f. of them
Eze. 40: 19. f. of lower gate unto f.
47: 1. f. of house stood tow. east

FOREHEAD.

Ge. 24: † 22. man took Jewel for f.
Ex. 28:38. plate sh. be on Aaron's f.
Le. 13: 41. he is f. bald, yet clean
42. it is a leprosy in his bald f.
43. if rising be reddish in bald f.
† 55. whe. it be in the head or f.
1 S. 17: 49. D. smote Philis. in his
f., the stone sunk in his f.
2 Ch. 26: 19. leprosy in Uzziah's f.
20. behold, he was leprous in f.
Je. 3: 3. thou hadst a whore's f.
Eze. 3: † 7 Israel are stiff of f.
8. made thy f. strong ag. their
9. As an adamant have made thy f.
16: 12. I put a jewel upon thy f.
Re. 14:9. receive mark of beast in f.
17:5. upon her f. a name, Mystery

FOREHEADS. [f.

Eze. 3:8. thy forehead strong ag. their
9: 4. mark on f. of them that sigh
Re. 7: 3. sealed servants of G. in f.
9: 4. have not seal of God in f.
13: 16. all to receive a mark in f.
14: 1. having his Fa.'s name in f.
20: 4. nor received mark upon f.
22: 4. his name sh. be in their f.

FOREIGNER, S.

Ex. 12: 45. f. shall not eat
De. 15: 3. Of a f. exact it again
Ob. 11. in day f-s entered his gates
Ep. 2: 19. ye are no more f-s

FOREKNEW.

Ro. 11:2. G. not cast away peo. he f.

FOREKNOW.

Ro. 8: 29. whom he did f. he also

FOREKNOWLEDGE.

Ac. 2:23. being deliv-d by f. of God
1 Pe. 1:2. Elect acc. to f. of G. the Fa.

FOREMOST.

Ge. 32: 17. Jacob com-d f. saying
33: 2. he put handm-s and chil. f.
2 S. 18:27. running of the f. is like

FOREORDAINED.

Ro. 3: † 25. f. to be a propitiation
1 Pe. 1: 20. who verily was f. bef.

FOREPART. [20.

Ex. 28:27. two rings toward f., 39:
1 K. 6:20. oracle in f. was 20 cubits
Eze. 42: 7. wall on f. of chambers
Ac. 27: 41. the f. of ship stuck fast

FORERUNNER. [tered

He. 6: 20. Whither f. is for us en-

FORESAW. [face

Ac. 2: 25. I f. Lord always bef. my

FORESEEN. [thi.

He. 11: † 40. having f. some better

FORESEETH, ING.

Pr. 22: 3. man f-h the evil, 27: 12.
Ga. 3: 8. Scrip. f-g G. would justify

FORESHIP.

Ac. 27: 30. cast anchors out of f.

FORESKIN.

Ge. 17: 11. shall circumcise your f.
14. flesh of his f. is not circum.
23. circum-d flesh of f., 24, 25.
Ex. 4:25. Zipporah cut off f. of son

Le. 12: 3. flesh of his f. be circum
De. 10:16. Circum. f. of your heart
Ha. 2: 16. let thy f. be uncovered

FORESKINS.

Jos. 5: 3. circumcised at hill of f.
1 S. 18: 25. but 100 f. of Philis.
27. David brought their f. to king
2 S. 3: 14. I espoused for hund. f.
Je. 4: 4. take away f. of your heart

FOREST.

1 S. 22:5. Da. came into f. of Hareth
1 K. 7: 2. Sol. built house of the f.
10: 17. in house of f., 2 Ch. 9: 16.
21. vessels of ho. of f., 2 Ch. 9: 20.
2 K. 19: 23. f. of Carmel, Is. 37:24.
Ne. 2: 8. Asaph, keeper of king's f.
Ps. 50: 10. ev. beast of f. is mine
104: 20. beasts of f. do creep forth
Is. 9: 18. kindle in thickets of f.
10: 18. shall consume glory of f.
19. rest of trees of his f. be few
34. cut down thickets of f.
21: 13. In f. of Arabia ye lodge
22: 8. didst look to armour of f.
29: 17. field esteemed as a f., 32:15.
32: 19. hail, coming down on the f.
44. 14. cypress fr. among trees of f.
23. break forth into singing, O f.
56: 9. beasts of f. come to devour
Je. 5: 6. lion out of f. sh. slay them
10: 3. one cutteth a tree out of f.
12: 8. Mine heritage as a lion in f.
21: 14. I will kindle a fire in the f.
26: 18. high places of f., Mi. 3: 12.
46: 23. they shall cut down her f.
Eze. 15:6. vine tree am. trees of f., 2.
20: 46. prophesy ag. f. of the south
47. say unto f. of south, Hear
Ho. 2: 12. I will make them a f.
Am. 3: 4. Will lion roar in the f.
Mi. 5: 8. as a lion among beasts of f.
Zch. 11:2. f. of the vintage is come

FORESTS.

2 Ch. 27:4. Jotham built castles in f.
Ps. 29: 9. voice of L. discovereth f.
Eze. 39: 10. nei. cut down out of f.

FORETELL.

2 Co. 13: 2. I f. you as if present

FORETOLD.

Mk. 13: 23. I have f. you all things
Ac. 3:24. proph. have f. of these days

FOREWARN, ED.

Lu. 12: 5. f. you whom ye sh. fear
1 Th. 4: 6. as we also have f-d you

FORFEITED.

Ezr. 10:8. all his subst. should be f.

FORGAT. [him

Ge. 40: 23. not remem. Jo., but f.
Ju. 3: 7. chil. of Israel f. Lord
1 S. 12: 9. when they f. the Lord
Ps. 78: 11. and they f. his works
106: 13. soon f. works | 21. f. G. Sav.
La. 3:17. far fr. peace, I f. prosperity
Ho. 2: 13. went aft. her lovers and f.

FORGAVE, EST. [me

Ps. 32: 5. thou f-t iniq. of my sin
78: 38. he f. their iniquity
99: 8. wast G. that f-t them, tho.
Mat. 18: 27. he loosed, and f. debt
32. O wicked servant, I f. all
Lu. 7:42. noth. to pay, he frankly f.
43. that he to whom he f. most
2 Co. 2: 10. if I f. any thing to wh.
I f. it for your sakes f. I it in
Col. 3:13. as Christ f. you, so do ye

FORGED.

Ps. 119: 69. proud have f. a lie

FORGERS.

Jb. 13: 4. ye are f. of lies

FORGET. [done

Ge. 27: 45. till he f. that thou hast
41: 51. G. made me f. all my toil
De. 4:9. lest f. things eyes have seen
23. lest ye f. the covenant of Lord
31. L. will not f. cov. of fathers
6: 12. lest thou f. L., 8: 11, 14, 19.
9: 7. f. not how provokedst the L.

De. 25:19. blot out Amalek, not f. it
1 S. 1: 11. if not f. thine handm.
2 K. 17:38. cov. I made ye sh. not f.
Jb. 8: 13. so paths of all that f. G.
9: 27. I will f. my complaint
11: 16. thou shalt f. thy misery
24: 20. womb shall f. him, worm
Ps. 9: 17. all nations that f. God
10: 12. O Lord, f. not the humble
13: 1. How long wilt thou f. me
45: 10. f. also thine own people
50: 22. consider this, ye that f. G.
59:11. Slay them not, lest my peo. f.
74:19. f. not the congr. of thy poor
23. f. not voice of thine enemies
78: 7. might not f. works of God
102:4. so that I f. to eat my bread
103: 2. bless L., f. not his benefits
119: 16. I will not f. thy word
83. do I not f. statutes, 109, 141.
93. I will never f. thy precepts
153. deliv., for I do not f. thy law
176. I do not f. thy com-ts [hs. f.
137: 5. If I f. thee, O Jer., let my
Pr. 3: 1. My son, f. not my law
4: 5. get understanding, f. it not
31: 5. Lest they drink and f. law
7. Let him drink and f. poverty
Is. 49: 15. Can wom. f. her child?
may f. yet I not f. thee
65: 11. ye that f. my holy mount.
Je. 2:32. Can maid f. her ornaments
23:27. cause my peo. to f. my name
39. I, even I, will utterly f. you
La. 5: 20. Wherf. dost f. us for ever?
Ho. 4: 6. forgot t. law, I will f. chil.
Am. 8: 7. will never f. any of works
He. 6: 10. God is not unrighte. to f.
13: 16. to communicate f. not

FORGETFUL.

He. 13:2. not f. to entert. strangers
Ja. 1: 25. he be not a f. hearer

FORGETFULNESS. [of f.
Ps. 88: 12. thy righteousn. in land

FORGETTEST, ETH, ING.

Ge. 41: † 51. Jo. called firstborn f-g
Jb. 39: 15. f-h foot may crush them
Ps. 9: 12. he f-h not cry of humble
44: 24. wherf. f-t our affliction?
Pr. 2: 17. f-h the cov. of her God
Is. 51: 13. f-t the Lord thy maker
Ja. 1: 24. he f-h what man he was
Ph. 3: 13. f-g those things behind

FORGIVE.

Ge. 50: 17. f. trespass of thy breth.
f. trespass of serv. of G.
Ex. 10: 17. f. my sin only this once
32:32. now, if thou wilt f. their sin
Nu. 30: 5. Lord shall f. her, 8, 12.
Jos. 24:19. G., he will not f. your sins
1 S. 25:28. f. trespass of thy handm.
1 K. 8: 30. when hearest f., 39. 2
Ch. 6: 21, 30. [Israel
34. hear, and f. sin of thy people
36. f. the sin of thy servants, 2
Ch. 6: 25, 27, 39. [ag. thee
50. f. thy peo. that have sinned
2 Ch. 7:14. will I hear and f. their sin
Ps. 25: 18. upon my pain f. my sins
86:5. L., art good and ready to f.
Is. 2:9. mean man boweth, therf. f. not
Je. 18:23. f. not their iniquity nor
31: 34. for I will f. their iniquity
36: 3. that I may f. their iniquity
Da. 9: 19. O Lord hear, O Lord f.
Am. 7: 2. I said, O Lord God, f.
Mat. 6:12. f. us, as we f., Lu. 11: 4.
14. if ye f. men, your Fa. will f.
15. if ye f. not, nei. will Fa. f. you
9: 6. hath power to f. sin, Mk. 2:
10. Lu. 5: 24. [I f. him?
18:21. how oft my brother sin, and
35. if ye from your hearts f. not
Mk. 2: 7. who can f. sins, Lu. 5:21.
11: 25. f. that your Fa. may f. you
26. if ye do not f. your Fa. not f.
Lu. 6:37. f. and ye shall be forgiven
Lu. 17:3. if thy bro. repent, f. him, 4.
23:34. Fa., f. them, they know not
2 Co. 2: 7. ought rather to f. him
10. To wh. ye f. any thing, I f.
12: 13. was not burdensome. f. me
1 Jn. 1:9. he is faithful to f. our sins

FORGIVEN. [be f.

Ge. 4: † 13. iniq. greater than may
Le. 4: 20. make atone-t, and it sh.
be f. them, 26, 31, 35.–5: 10,
13, 16, 18.–6: 7.–19: 22. Nu.
15: 25, 26, 28. De. 21: 8.
Nu. 14: 19. pardon, as thou hast f.
Ps. 32:1. whose transgr. is f., Ro. 4:7.
85:2. Thou hast f. iniq. of thy peo.
Is. 33: 24. peo. be f. their iniquity
Mat. 9: 2. thy sins be f. thee, 5.
Mk. 2: 5, 9. Lu. 5:20, 23.–7: 48.
12: 31. all sin be f. but ag. H Gh.
not be f., 32. Mk. 3:28. Lu 12:10.
Mk. 4: 12. their sins sh. be f. them
Lu. 6: 37. forgive, ye sh. be f. [is f.
7: 47. Her sins f. to whom little
Ac. 8:22. thought of heart may be f.
Ep. 4:32. G. for C.'s sake hath f. you
Col. 2:13. having f. you all trespasses
Ja. 5: 15. sins, they shall be f. him
1 Jn. 2:12. I write, bec. your sins are

FORGIVENESS, ES. [f.

Ps. 130: 4. But there is f. with thee
that thou mayest be feared
Da. 9:9. To Lord our God belong f-s
Mk. 3:29. never f. but danger of hell
Ac. 5: 31. G. exalted to give f.
13: 38. is preached unto you f.
26: 18. that they may receive f.
Ep. 1:7. in wh. we have f., Col. 1:14.

FORGIVETH, ING.

Ex. 34: 7. f g iniquity, Nu. 14:18.
Ps. 103: 3. who f-h all iniquities
Lu. 7:49. to say, who is this f-h sins
Ep. 4: 32. f-g one another, Col. 3:13.

FORGOT.

De. 24: 19. hast f. sheaf in field

FORGOTTEN.

Ge. 41:30. all the plenty sh. be f.
De. 26: 13. not transgr-d nor I f.
31:21. song not be f. out of mouths
32: 18. hast f. G. that formed thee
Jb. 19:14. my familiar friends f. me
28: 4. even waters f. of the foot
Ps. 9: 18. needy sh. not always be f.
10: 11. said in heart, God hath f.
31: 12. I am f. as a dead man
42: 9. my rock, Why hast f. me?
44: 17. yet have we not f. thee
20. If we have f. name of our God
77: 9. Hath G. f. to be gracious?
119: 61. but I have not f. thy law
139. mine enemies f. thy words
Ec. 2: 16. in days to come all be f.
8: 10. wicked were f. in the city
9: 5. for the memory of them is f.
Is. 17: 10. hast f. G. of thy salva.
23: 15. Tyre shall be f. 70 years
16. thou harlot that hast been f.
44: 21. O Isr., thou shalt not be f.
49:14. Zion said, my L. hath f. me
65: 16. bec. former troubles are f.
Je. 2: 32. peo. have f., 13:25.–18:15.
3: 21. they have f. the Lord
20:11. confusion never be f., 23:40.
23: 27. to forget, as fathers have f.
30: 14. All thy lovers have f. thee
44: 9. Have ye f. wickedn. of fa-s
50: 5. join in cov. that not be f.
6. have f. their resting place
La. 2:6. caused sab. to be f. in Zion
Eze 22:12. thou hast f. me, saith L.
23: 35. saith L., Bec. hast f. me
Ho. 4: 6. seeing thou hast f. law
8: 14. for Israel hath f. Maker
13: 6. heart exalted, have f. me
Mat. 16: 5. f. to take br., Mk. 8:14.
Lu. 12: 6. not one of them is f.
He. 12:5. ye have f. the exhortation
2 Pe. 1: 9. f. that he was purged

FORKS.

1 S. 13: 21. they had a file for the f.

FORM. [Noun.]

Ge. 1: 2. the earth was without f.
Ju. 8: † 18. each acc. to f. of a k.
1 S. 28:14. unto her, What f. is he of?
2 S. 14: 20. fetch this f. of speech
2 Ch. 4: 7. candlesticks of gold acc.
Es. 2: † 7. maid was fair of f. [to f.
Jb. 4: 16. I could not discern the f.
Is. 52: 14. his f. more than sons of
53: 2. no f. nor comeliness [men
Je. 4: 23. lo, it was without f.
Eze. 8: 3. f. of an hand and took
10. every f. of creeping things
10: 8. appeared f. of a hand
43: 11. show them f. of the house
Da. 2: 31. f. thereof was terrible
3: 19. f. of his visage was changed
25. f. of 4th is like Son of God
Mk. 16:12. appeared in an o. f. to two
Ro. 2: 20. which hast f. of knowl.
6: 17. obeyed that f. of doctrine
Ph. 2: 6. Who being in the f. of G.
7. took upon him f. of a servant
2 Ti. 1:13. Hold fast f. of sound words
3: 5. Having f. of godliness

FORM. [Verb.]

Is. 45: 7. I f. the light and create

FORMED.

Ge. 2:7. God f. man of the dust, 8.
19. out of gro. God f. ev. beast
De. 32:18. forgotten God th. f. thee
2 K. 19:25. that I have f. it, Is. 37:26.
Jb. 26:5. Dead things are f. und. wat.
13 his hand hath f. crooked serp.
33: 6. I also am f. out of the clay
Ps. 90: 2. or ever hadst f. earth
94: 9. f. the eye, sh. he not see?
95:5. and his hands f. the dry land
Pr. 26: 10. God that f. all things
Is. 27:11. th. f. them shew no favour
43: 1. saith he that f. thee, O Isr.
7. I have f. him, yea, made him
10. bef. me no god f. nor aft. me
21. This peo. have I f. for myself
44: 2. and f. thee from the womb
10. Who hath f. a god, or image?
21. art my serv. I have f. thee
24. thus saith he that f. thee
45: 18. God that f. earth, he f. it
49:5. Lord that f. me to be his serv.
54: 17. No weapon f. ag. thee shall
Je. 1: 5. Before I f. thee in belly
33: 2. L. that f. it to establish it
Am. 7:1. behold, he f. grasshoppers
Ro. 9:20. thing f. say to him that f. it
Ga. 4:19. until Christ be f. in you
1 Ti. 2: 13. Adam was first f. then

FORMER. [Noun.] [Eve

Je. 10:16 he is the f. of all. 51: 19.

FORMER. [Adj.]

Ge. 40: 13. deliv. cup aft. f. manner
Nu. 21:26. fought ag. f. king of Moab
De. 24: 4. her f. husband which
Ru. 4: 7. in f. time of redeeming
1 S. 17:30. people ans-d aft. f. manner
2 K. 1: 14. two capt-s of f. fifties
17: 34. they do aft. f. manner, 40.
Ne. 5: 15. f. gov-s chargeable
Jb. 8: 8. inquire, I pray, of f. age
30: 3. wilderness in f. time waste
Ps. 79: 8. O remember not f. iniq.
89: 49. where thy f. lovingkindn.?
Ec. 1: 11. is no remem. of f. things
7: 10. that the f. days were better
Is. 41: 22. let shew f. things, 43: 9.
42: 9. f. things are come to pass
43: 18 Remember ye not f. things
46: 9. Remember f. things of old
48: 3. have declared f. things fr.
61: 4. sh. raise up f. desolations
65: 7. measure f. work into bosom
16. bec. f. troubles are forgotten
17. the f. shall not be rememb.
Je. 5: 24. Lord that giveth the f.
and latter rain, Ho. 6:3. Jo. 2:23.

Je.34: 5. f.kings wh.were before thee
36 : 28. write in it all the f. words
Eze.16:55. sisters return to f. estate
Da. 11:13. multitude greater than f.
29. it shall not be as f. or latter
Hag. 2:9. glory greater than of f. h.
Zch. 1 : 4. f. proph-s cried. 7:7, 12.
8 : 11. I will not be as in f. days
14 : 8. waters go half tow. f. sea
Mal. 3:4. be pleas. to L. as in f. y-rs
Ac. 1:1. The f. treatise have I made
Ep. 4 : 22. put off conc. f. conversa.
He.10:32. call to remem. the f. days
1 Pe. 1 : 14. not acc. to f. lusts
Re. 21 : 4. f. things are passed aw.

FORMETH.

Am. 4 : 13. lo, he that f. the mts.
Zch. 12 : 1. and f. the spirit of man

FORNICATION, S.

2 Ch.21:11. caused Jerus. commit f.
Is. 23 : 17. Tyre sh. commit f. with
Eze. 16 : 15. pouredst f-s on ev. one
26. f. with the Egyptians
29. multiplied thy f. in Canaan
Mat. 5 : 32. saving for the f., 19 : 9.
15 : 19. out of heart f-s, Mk. 7:21.
Jn. 8 : 41. We be not born of f.
Ac. 15 : 20. abstain fr. f.,29.-21:25.
Ro. 1 : 29. Being filled with all f.
1 Co.5:1 is f. amo. you, and such f.
6 : 13. body is not for f. but for L.
18. Flee f. | 7 : 2. to avoid f.
2 Co. 12:21. not repented of their f.
Ga. 5 : 19. works of the flesh, are f.
Ep. 5 : 3. f. let it not be once named
Col. 3 : 5. mortify therefore f. uncle.
1 Th.4:3.that ye should abstain fr. f.
Jude 7.cities giving thems.over to f.
Re. 2 : 21. space to repent of her f.
9 : 21. nei. repented they of their f.
14 : 8. drink wine of wrath of f.
17 : 2. drunk with wine of her f.
4. full of filthiness of her f.
5. Babylon the great,mother of f.
18:3. all nations drunk with her f.
19:2. did corrupt earth with her f.
See COMMIT, COMMITTED.

FORNICATOR, S.

1 Co. 5 : 9. not to company with f-s
10.Yet not altogether with the f-s
11. if any brother be a f. [kingd.
6 : 9. nor shall f-s inherit the
He. 12:16. Lest there be any f. or

FORSAKE.

De. 31 : 16. this people will f. me
17. in that day I will f. them
Jos. 24 : 16. God forbid we f. the L.
20. If ye f. the L., and serve gods
Ju. 9 : 11. Should I f.my sweetness
2 K. 21 : 14. I will f. remnant of my
1 Ch. 28 : 9. if f. him, will cast thee
2 Ch. 7 : 19. if ye f. my statutes
15 : 2. if ye f. him, he will f. you
Ezr. 8 : 22. wrath ag. them that f.
Ps.27:9. neither f. me O God of [him
10. When fa. and mother f. me
37 : 8. Cease from anger, f. wrath
89 : 30. If his children f. my law
94:14. nei.will he f. his inheritance
119 : 53. horror, bec. wicked f. law
Pr. 9 : 6. f. the foolish, and live, go
28 : 4. th. f. the law, praise wicked
Is. 1 : 28. that f. L. be consumed
55 : 7. Let wicked f. his way
65:11. ye are they that f. L. forget
Je. 17 : 13. f. L. shall be ashamed
23 : 33. I will even f. you, 39.
51 : 9. f. her, and let us go ev. one
La. 5 : 20. wh. dost f. us so long
Eze. 20 : 8. nei. did f. idols of E.
Da. 11 : 30. that f. the holy cov.
Jon. 2 : 8. f. their own mercy [Mo.
Ac. 21 : 21. teachest the Jews to f.

FORSAKE not.

De. 12 : 19. take heed f. n. Levite
Jb. 20 : 13. Though he spare wickedness and f. it n.

Ps. 38 : 21. f. me n. O L., 71:9, 18.
119 : 8. O f. me n. utterly
138 : 8. f. n. works of own hands
Pr. 1 : 8. f. n. law of mother, 6:20.
4:2.I give you good doctr. f. ye n.
6. f. her n. she sh. preserve thee
27 : 10. Thine and fa.'s friend f.n.

Not FORSAKE.

De. 4 : 31. he will n. f. thee, 31 : 6,
8. 1 Ch. 28 : 20.
14 : 27. Levite thou shalt n. f.
Jos.1:5. n. fail nor f. thee,He.13:5.
1 S. 12 : 22. L. will n. f., 1 K. 6:13.
1 K. 8 : 57. let him n. leave nor f. us
Ne.9:31.didst n.consume,nor f. them
10:39. we will n.f. house of our G.
Pr. 3 : 3. let n. mercy and truth f.
Is.41:17. I, God of Isr. will n.f. th.
42:16.These will I do, and n.f. th.

FORSAKEN.

2 Ch. 21 : 10. he had f. the Lord,
24 : 24.-28 : 6.
Ne. 13 : 11. Why is house of God f.?
Jb. 18 : 4. shall earth be f. for thee
Ps. 37 : 25. I not seen righteous f.
Is. 7 : 16. land be f. of both kings
17 : 2. the cities of Aroer are f.
9. sh. be as f. bough, and upper.
27 : 10. the habitation shall be f.
32 : 14. Bec. the palaces shall be f.
54 : 6. L. called thee as a woman f.
62:4. Thou sh. no more be termed
Je. 4 : 29. every city shall be f. [f.
18 : 14. shall cold waters be f.?
Eze. 36 : 4. saith Lord to cities f.
Am. 5 : 2. the virgin of Israel is f.
Zph.2:4.Gaza sh.be f. and Ashkelon

Had, hast, hath FORSAKEN.

De. 28 : 20. doings, whereby h-t f.
Ju. 6 : 13. now Lord h-h f. us [me
2 Ch.21:10. bec. he h-d f. G. of his
24 : 20. forsaken L. he h-h f. you
24. bec. they h-d f. Lord, 28 : 6.
Jb.20:19. h-h oppressed and f. poor
Ps. 22 : 1. My God, my God, why
h-t f.me? Mat. 27:46.Mk.15:34.
71:11. counsel. saying, God h-h f.
Is.2:6.thou h-t f. the house of Jac.
49:14. Zion said, The L. h-h f. me
60 : 15. Whereas h-t been f. and
hated [19.
Je. 2 : 17. in that thou h-t f. Lord,
7 : 29. Lord h-h f. the generation
15 : 6. thou h-t f. me, saith Lord
25:38. he h-h f. his covert as lion
Eze. 8 : 12. Lord h-h f. earth, 9 : 9.
Mat. 19 : 29. every one that h-h f.
2 Ti. 4:10. Demas h-h f. me [hou-s

Have FORSAKEN.

De. 29 : 25. Because h. f. the Lord,
Ju. 10 : 10. [other gods
Ju. 10 : 13. ye h. f. me and served
1 S. 8 : 8. works whw. they h.f. me
12:10. sinned, bec. we h. f. the L.
1 K. 11 : 33. bec. that they h.f. me
18 : 18. ye h.f. the com-ts of Lord
19:10.Israel h.f. thy covenant,14.
2 K. 22 : 17. because they h. f. me,
2 Ch. 34 : 25. Je. 16 : 11.-19:4.
2 Ch. 12:5. h.f. me, I have left you
13:11.charge of L. but ye h.f. him
24 : 20. bec. ye h. f. L., he f. you
29:6. fa-s h. done evil, and f. him
Ezr. 9 : 10. for we h. f. thy com-ts
Is. 1:4. they h. f. L. and provoked
54 : 7. For a moment h. I f. thee
Je. 1 : 16. h. f. me burnt incense
2 : 13. h.f. me, fountain of waters
5:7.how pardon? thy chil. h.f.me
19. answer, Like as ye h. f. me
9:13. saith, Bec. they h.f. my law
19. confounded. bec. ye h.f. land
12 : 7. I h.f. my house, I have left
17:13. they h.f. fountain of living
22 : 9. they h. f. the cov. of God
Mat. 19 : 27. we h. f. all foll-d thee

2 Pe. 2 : 15. Which h. f. the right

Not FORSAKEN. [way

2 Ch. 13 : 10. our God we have n.f.
Ezr. 9 : 9. God n. f. us in bondage
Ps. 9 : 10. n. f. them that seek thee
Is. 62 : 12. Sought out, A city n. f.
Je. 51 : 5. Israel hath n. been f.,nor
2 Co.4:9.Persecuted, but n. f. : cast

FORSAKETH.

Jb. 6 : 14. he f. fear of the Almighty
Ps. 37 : 28. Lord f. not his saints
40 : † 12. iniquities, my heart f. me
Pr. 2 : 17. Wh.f. guide of her youth
15:10.grievous unto him th. f. way
28 : 13. sins, whoso confes-h and f.
Lu. 14 : 33. whos-r f. not all he hath

FORSAKING.

Is. 6 : 12. Until there be a great f.
He. 10 :25. Not f.assembling of ours.

FORSOMUCH. [ham

Lu. 19 : 9. f. as he is a son of Abra.

FORSOOK, EST. [him

De. 32 : 15. he f. God which made
Ju. 2 : 12. they f. the L., 13.-10 : 6.
1 S. 31 : 7. men of Israel f. their cities, fled, 1 Ch. 10 : 7. [Ch. 7:22.
1 K. 9 : 9. Because they f. God, 2
12 : 8. Rehoboam f. counsel of old
men, and, 13. 2 Ch. 10 : 8, 13.
2 K. 21 : 22. Amon f. God of his fa-s
2 Ch. 12 : 1. Rehoboam f.law of Lord
Ne. 9 : 17. God slow to anger, f-t not
19. thou f-t them not in wildern-s
Ps. 78 : 60. he f. tabernacle of Shiloh
119 : 87. but I f. not thy precepts
Is. 58 : 2. f. not ordinance of God
Je. 14 : 5. hind calved and f. it, bec.
Mat.26:56.disciples f.him, Mk.14:50
Mk. 1 : 18. f. nets and followed him
Lu. 5 : 11. they f. all, followed him
2 Ti. 4 :16. none stood, all men f. me
He. 11 : 27. By faith Moses f. Egypt

FORSWEAR.

Mat. 5 : 33.Thou shalt not f.thyself

FORT, S.

2 S. 5 : 9. So David dwelt in the f.[4.
2 K. 25:1. built f-s ag. Jerus., Je. 52:
Is. 25 :12. high f. sh. he bring down
29 : 3. I will raise f-s against thee
32 : 14. f-s and towers be for dens
Eze. 4 :2. Jerus., build f. ag., 21:22.
17 : 17. building f-s to cut off many
26 : 8.Neb-r shall make a f. ag.thee
33:27.they in f-s and caves shall die
Da. 11 : 19.turn toward f. of his own

FORTH. [land

Ge. 38 :29.How hast thou broken f.?
39 : 13. when she saw he was fled f.
Ex. 12 : 31. get you f. fr. my people
See BRINGETH, BRINGING, LED, SEND, SHINE, SPRING, STAND.
See **BRING forth, BROUGHT forth, CAME forth, CARRY forth, CAST forth, COME forth, GO forth, GONE forth, Stretch, ed, forth HAND, PUT forth, SENT forth, SET forth, WENT forth, That TIME, This TIME.**

FORTHWITH.

Ezr. 6 : 8. f. expenses be given
these men
Mat.13:5.f.sprung up,bec.no deepn.
26 : 49. f. he came to Jes, said,Hail
Mk. 1 : 29. f. entered hou. of Simon
43. charged, and f. sent him away
5 : 13. devils, f. Jes. gave th.leave
Jn. 19 : 34. f. came blood and water
Ac. 9 : 18. he received sight f., and
12 : 10. f. angel departed from him
21 : 30.drew Paul out,f. doors were

FORTIETH. [shut

See **Fortieth YEAR.**

FORTIFIED. [holds

2 Ch. 11 : 11.Rehoboam f. the strong
26 : 9. Uzziah built towers, f. them

Ne. 3 : 8. f. Jerus. unto broad wall
Mi. 7 : 12. he sh. come fr. f. cities

FORTIFY.

Ju. 9 : 31. they f. the city ag. thee
Ne. 4 : 2. will feeble Jews f. thems.?
Is. 22 : 10. houses broken to f. wall
Je. 51 : 53. tho. she f. her strength
Na. 2 : 1. f. thy power mightily
3:14. Draw waters, f. strong holds

FORTRESS, ES.

2 S. 22 : 2. Lord is my f., Ps. 18 : 2.
-31 : 3.-71 : 3.-91 : 2.-144 : 2.
Pr. 12 : † 12. desireth f. of evil men
Is. 17 : 3. f. shall cease from Ephr.
25 : 12. the f. shall he bring down
34 : 13. brambles come up in f-s
Je. 6 : 27. I have set thee for a f.
10:17. gather wares, O inhabi. of f.
Je. 16 : 19. O L. my f. in affliction
Da. 11 : 7. enter into the f. of king
10. sh. be stirred up even to his f.
† 39. thus shall he do in the f-s
Ho. 10 : 14. thy f-s shall be spoiled
Am. 5:9. spoiled shall come ag. the f.
Mi. 7:12. he shall come to thee fr. f.

FORTUNA'TUS. [of F.

1 Co. 16 : 17. I am glad of coming

FORTY.

Ge. 18 : 29. Peradv. be f. found ; I
will not do it for f. sake
2 K. 8:9. Hazael took f. camels' burd.
Ac. 23:13. than f. made conspiracy, [21.

FORTY cubits.

1 K. 6:17. house bef. it was f. c. long
Eze. 41 : 2. he measured length f. c.
46 : 22. were courts joined of f. c.
See BATHS, DAYS, KINE, SHEKELS,
SOCKETS, SONS, STRIPES.

FORTY years. See YEARS.

FORTY and two.

Nu. 35:6. to cities of refuge add f. t.
2 K. 2 : 24. two bears tare f. t. chil.
10:14. took them alive, slew t. a. f.
2 Ch. 22 : 2. f. a. t. years old Ahaz.
Ezr. 2 : 24. chil. of Azmaveth f. a. t.
Ne. 7 : 28. of Beth-azmaveth f. a. t.
Re. 11 : 2. city tread f. a. t. mos.
13:5. power to continue f. a. t. mos.

FORTY and five, six.

Ge. 18 : 28. if I find f. a. f. not destr.
Jos. 14 : 10. L. kept me f. a. f. years
1 K. 7 : 3. beams that lay on f. a. f.
Jn. 2:20. f. a. s. years tem. in build.

FORTY and eight, nine.

Le. 25:8. space be unto thee f. a. n.
years [Jos. 21 : 41.
Nu. 35 : 7. cities of Levites f. a. e.,
See HUNDRED, THOUSAND.

FORWARD.

Nu. 32 : 19. we will not inherit f.
Je. 7 : 24. they went backw. not f.
Eze. 43:27. upon eighth day and so f.
Zch. 1 : 15. they helped f. the afflic.
2 Co 8:10. to do, but to be f. yr. ago.
17. more f. of his own accord
Ga. 2 : 10. same I also was f. to do
3 Jn. 6. if bring f. on their journey
See That DAY, GO, SET, WENT.

FORWARDNESS.

2 Co. 8:8. by occasion of f. of others
9 : 2. For I know f. of your mind

FOUGHT.

Ex. 17 : 8. Amalek f. with Israel
10. so Joshua f. with Amalek,
Nu. 21 : 1. then king Arad f. ag. Isr.
23. Sihon f. ag. Isr., Ju. 11 : 20.
26. Sihon f. ag. former k. of Moab
Jos. 10 : 14. L. f. for Isr., 42.-23 : 3.
29. Josh. and all Isr. f. ag. Libnah
31. f. against Lachish | 34. Eglon
36. f. against Hebron | 38. Debir
24 : 8. Amorites f. with you
11. men of Jericho f. against you
Ju. 1 : 5. Adoni-bezek and f. ag. him
8. Judah had f. ag. Jerusalem
5 : 19. then f. the kings of Canaan
20. They f. from heav., the stars f.
Ju. 9 : 17. my father f. for you and
39. Gaal went and f. with Abim.
45. Abim. f. ag. city all day, 52.
12 : 4. men of Gilead f. with Ephr.
1 S. 4:10. Philistines f., 31:1. 1 Ch. 10:1
12 : 9. hand of k. of Moab, they f.
14 : 47. Saul f. ag. all his enemies
15 : † 5. Saul f. against Amalek
19 : 8. So David f. with the Philistines, 23 : 5. 2 S. 21 : 15.
2 S. 2 : 28. people stood still, nor f.
8 : 10. f. ag. Hadadezer, 1 Ch. 18:10.
10 : 17. Syrians f. ag. Da., 1 Ch. 19:17.
11 : 17. men of city f. with Joab
12 : 26. f. against Rabbah, 27, 29.
2 K. 8 : 29. Joram f. against Hazael,
9 : 15. 2 Ch. 22 : 6.
12 : 17. Hazael f. against Gath
13 : 12. Joash f. ag. Amaziah, 14:15.
1 Ch. 19:18. 7000 men wh. f. in char-s
2 Ch. 20: 29. L. f. ag enemies of Isr.
27 : 5. He f. also with king of Am
Ps. 109 : 3. f. ag. me without a cause
Is. 20 : 1. Tartan f. against Ashdod
63:10. turned their enemy and f. ag.
Je. 34 : 1. peo. f. against Jerus., 7.
Zch. 14 : 3. as when he f. in battle
12. L. will smite them th. f. ag. Jeru.
1 Co. 15 : 32. I have f. with beasts
2 Ti. 4 : 7. I have f. a good fight
Re. 12 : 7. Michael f. ag. dragon

FOUL. [Adj.]

Jb. 16:16. My face is f. with weeping
Mat. 16:3. It will be f. weather to day
Mk. 9 : 25. he rebuked the f. spirit
Re. 18: 2. Bab. the hold of ev. f. spirit

FOUL, ED, EST.

Eze. 32 : 2. troublest waters f-t rivers
34 : 18. but ye must f. the residue
19. they drink that wh. yo have f-d

FOUND.

Ge. 2:20. for Adam not f. a helpmeet
8 : 9. dove f. no rest for her foot
11 : 2. f. a plain in land of Shinar
16 : 7. angel f. her by a fountain
19 : † 15. take thy dau-s. wh. are f.
26 : † 12. Isaac f. a hundred fold
19. Isaac's servants digged f. a well
32. serv-s said, We have f. water
27 : 20. How hast f. it so quickly?
30 : 14. Reuben f. mandrakes in f.
31 : 33. Laban went f. not images
37. what hast f. of all thy stuff?
36 : 24. Anah that f. the mules
37: 15. f. him | 17. f. them at Dothan
32. coat and said, This have we f.
38: 23. kid, thou hast not f. her, 20.
44 : 8. money wh. we f. in our sacks
16. God hath f. iniq. of servants
Ex. 15:22. three days and f. no water
16:27. to gather manna and f. none
18: † 8. told all travel th. had f. them
Le. 6 : 3. if f. that wh. was lost, 4.
† 5. in the day of his being f. guilty
25 : † 26. if hand hath f. sufficiency
Nu. 15:32. f. man that gath-d sticks
33. that f. bro-t him unto Moses
20 : † 14. the travel that hath f. us
31: † 50. bro-t what ev. man hath f.
De. 21 : † 17. double portion of all f.
22 : 3. with what hast f. do likew.
14. I f. her not a maid, 17.
27. f. her in field, damsel cried
24: 1. hath f. some uncleann. in her
32 : 10. He f. him in a desert land
Jos. 2 : 22. pursuers sought, f. not
10 : 17. five kings are f. hid in cave
Ju. 1 : 5. they f. Adoni-bezek [dle
14 : 18. if not wi. heifer, not f. rid-
15 : 15. f. new jawbone of an ass
21 : 12. they f. 400 young virgins
1 S. 9:4. thro. Shalisha, f. not asses
11. f. maidens going to draw wat.
20. thine asses are f., 10 : 2, 16.
12:5. have not f. aught in my hand
13 : 19. was no smith f. in Israel
22. no sword f. in hand of people
1 S. 14:30. of ene. they f., 2 Ch. 20:25.
25 : 28. evil not been f. with thee
29 : 3. I have f. no fault in him, 6.
8. what hast f. in thy servant
30 : 11. they f. Egypt-n in field
31 : 8. f. Saul and 3 sons fallen
2 S. 7 : 27. thy serv. f. in his heart
to pray this prayer, 1 Ch. 17:25.
1 K. 1:3. coasts of Isr. and f. Abish.
7:47. nor was weight of the brass f.
11 : 29. prophet Ahijah f. Jerob.
13 : 28. he f. his carcass in the way
18 : 10. oath that they f. thee not
19 : 19. Elijah departed f. Elisha
20 : 36. a lion f. him and slew him
37. f. ano. and said Smite [thee
21 : 20. hast f. me, O ene.? have f.
2 K. 2 : 17. sought Elijah, but f. not
4:39. gath. herbs, and f. wild vine
9 : † 21. f. Jehu in portion of Nab.
35. f. no more of her than skull
14:14. vessels f. in hou., 2 Ch. 25:24.
17 : 4. king of Assyr. f. conspiracy
19 : 8. f. king of Assyria warring
against Libnah, Is. 37 : 8.
22 : 8. I f. book of law in h. of the
L., 23 : 24. 2 Ch. 34 : 14, 15.
25 : 19. took 60 f. in city, Je. 52:25.
1 Ch. 4 : 40. they f. fat pasture
41. tents and habita. they were f.
10 : 8. f. Saul | 24 : 4. chief men f.
26 : 31. f. mighty men | 29 : 8. precious stones f. [f., 25 : 5.
2 Ch. 2 : 17. numbered ; they were
19 : 3. good things f. in thee
29: 16. uncleann. : they f. in temple
Ezr. 2 : 62. sought their register,
but they were not f., Ne. 7 : 64.
8 : 15. I f. none of sons of Levi
10:18. f. th. had tak. strange wives
Ne. 5 : 8. they f. nothing to answer
8 : 14. they f. written in law of L.
Es. 4 : † 16. all Jews f. in Shushan
Jb. 28:13. nor wisd. f. in la. of living
31: † 25. if I rejoi. bec. hand f. much
29. when evil f. mine enemy
32:3. wrath kindled, bec. f. no ans.
13. Lest say, We have f. out wisd.
33 : 24. I have f. a ransom [of Job
42 : 15. no women f. so fair as dau-s
Ps. 69:20. for comforters but f. none
76 : 5. none of men f. their hands
84 : 3. yea sparrow hath f. a house
89 : 20. I have f. David my servant
107 : 4. wandered and f. no city
116 : 3. I f. trouble and sorrow,
pains of hell f. me.
119 : † 143. and anguish have f. me
132 : 6. we f. it in fields of wood
Pr. 7 : 15. thy face, and I have f.
24 : 14. so wisd. be when hast f. it
25 : 16. Hast f. honey? eat suffici.
Ec. 7 : 27. Behold, this have I f.
28. one man am. thousand have I
f. a woman have I not f.
29. this only have I f. that G. made
Can 3: 1. I sought, but f. him not, 2.
3. watchmen f. me, 5 : 7.
4. I f. him whom my soul loveth
Is. 10 : 10. hath f. kingdoms of idols
14. my ha. hath f. riches of peo.
22 : 3. all f. in thee bound togeth.
24 : † 22. shall they be f. wanting
57 : 10. hast f. life of thine hand
65 : 1. f. of them sought me not
Je. 2: 5. What iniq. fathers f. in me?
34. In thy skirts is f. blood of poor
5 : 26. am. my peo. are f. wicked
14 : 3. they came to pits f. no wat.
15 : 16. Thy words were f. I did eat
23:11. in my h. have I f. their wick.
41 : 3. Chaldeans th. were f. there
8. ten f. that said, Slay us not
12. f. him by the great waters
50 : 7. all that f. have devoured th.
24. thou art f. and also caught
La. 2 : 16. this is day, we have f. it

Eze. 22 : 30. sought man, f. none
Da. 1 : 20. f. them ten times better
2 : 25. I have f. man of captives
5 : 12. excell. spirit was f. in Dan.
27. art weighed, and f. wanting
6 : 4. nor was any fault f. in Dan.
11. these men f. Daniel praying
Ho. 9 : 10. I f. Israel like grapes
12 : 4. he f. him in Beth-el, and
8. Ephr. said, I have f. substance
Jon. 1 : 3. he f. a ship for Tarshish
Mi. 1 : 13. transg-s of Isr. f. in thee
Mat. 2 : 8. when f. him bring word
8 : 10. not f. so great faith, Lu.7:9.
13 : 44. when hath f. he hideth it
46. f. one pearl of great price
18:28. f. one of his fellow servants
20:6. he f. others idle [13. Lu.13:6.
21:19. f. nothing thereon, Mk. 11 :
22 : 10. gathered all as they f.
26:43.he f. them asleep, Mk. 14:40.
Lu. 22 : 45. [none, Mk.14:55.
60. sought witnesses, yet f. they
27 : 32. they f. a man of Cyrene
Mk. 1 : 37. when had f. him [f.fault
7 : 2. eat with unwash. hands, they
30. when come, she f. devil gone
11 : 4. they f. the colt tied by door
Lu. 2 : 16. f. babe lying in manger
45. f. him not they turned back
46. aft. 3 days f. him in temple
4 : 17. f. place where it was writ.
7 : 10. returning f. servant whole
8 : 35. they f. man clothed and in
15 : 5. f. the sheep, he layeth it
6. Rejoice, for I have f. my sheep
9. when she hath f. the piece, she
17 : 18. are not any f. to give glory
19 : 32. they f. even as he had said
unto them, 22 : 13. Mk. 14 : 16.
23 : 2. f. this fellow perverting na.
14. I have f. no fault in this man
22. f. no cause of death, Ac.13:28.
24 : 2. they f. stone rolled away
3. they f. not body of Lord Jesus
23. when they f. not his body
24. f. it as woman had said
33. f. eleven gathered together
Jn. 1 : 41. We have f. Messias, 45.
2:14. Jes. f. in tem. that sold oxen
6 : 25. f. him on other side of sea
9 : 35. f. him sd. Dost thou believe
11:17.f.he had lain in grave 4 days
12:14.Jes.when he f.young ass, sat
Ac. 5 : 10. young men f. her dead
22. officers f. them not in prison
23. The prison truly f. we shut
7 : 11. our fathers f. no sustenance
9 : 2. that if he f. any of this way
33. f. a man named Eneas
10:27. Peter f. many come together
11:26. he f. bro-t him unto Antioch
12 : 19. Herod sought Pe., f. not
13 : 6. they f. a certain sorcerer
22. f. Da., a man aft. own heart
17 : 6. f. them not, drew Jason
23. I f. an altar with this inscrip.
18 : 2. f. a Jew | 19 : 19. f. it 50,000
24 : 5. f. this man pestilent fellow
12. nei. f. me in temple disputing
18. Jews f. me purified
20. if f. any evil doing in me
25 : 25. I f. noth. worthy of death
27:6.f.ship | 28. f. it 20 fathoms (2)
28:14. to Puteoli,where we f. breth.
Ro. 4:1.what Ab. our father hath f.
7:10. which was ordained to life, I
f. to be unto death
1 Co. 15 : 15. we are f. false witn-s
2 Co.2:13.Bec.I f. not Titus my bro.
Ga. 2 : 17. we also are f. sinners
Ph. 2 : 8. f. in fashion as a man
1 Ti. 3 : 10. being f. blameless
2 Ti. 1 : 17. Onesiph. sought f. me
He. 12 : 17. f. no place of repent.
1 Pe. 1 : 7. faith be f. unto praise
2 Jn. 4. I f. of thy chil. walking in

Re. 2 : 2. hast tried, hast f. them liars
3 : 2. I have not f. thy works perf.
12 : 8. nor their place f. in heaven
16 : 20. mountains were not f.
See FAVOUR.

Be FOUND. [32.

Ge. 18:29. Peradv. b. forty f., 30,31,
44 : 9. With whomso. it b. f.
Ex. 9 : 19. wh. shall b. f. in field
12:19.no leav. shall b. f. in houses
21:16. stealeth man, if b. f. in ha.
22 : 2. If thief b. f. breaking, 7, 8.
4. If theft b. certainly f. in hand
De. 17 : 2. If there b. f. am. you
18 : 10. not b. f. any th. maketh
21 : 1. If one b. f. slain in the land
22:20. tokens of virginity b. not f.
22. b. f. lying with woman marr.
28. lie with her, and they b. f.
24:7. b. f. stealing | 33:29.b.f.liars
1 S.10:21. sought, he could not b. f.
2 S.17:12.upon him where he sh.b.f.
13. there b. not one stone f.
1 K. 1 : 52. if wickedn. b. f. in him
2 K. 12:5. whereso. any breach b. f.
1 Ch. 28 : 9. if seek him, will b. f. of
thee, but if forsake, 2 Ch. 15 : 2.
Jb. 20:8. he sh. fly aw. and not b. f.
28 : 12. where shall wisdom b. f.?
Ps.32:6.shall pray when mayest b.f.
36 : 2. until his iniq. b. f. hateful
37 : 36. I sought, but he could not
Pr.6:31. if he b. f. sh. restore [b. f.
16 : 31. if it b. f. in way of righte.
30 : 6. lest reprove thou b. f. liar
10. lest curse, and thou b.f. guilty
Is. 30 : 14. shall not b. f. a sherd
35 : 9. nor any beast shall b. f.
51 : 3. joy and gladness shall b. f.
55 : 6. Seek L. while he may b. f.
Je. 29:14. I will b.f. of you, saith L.
50:20. sins of Judah shall not b. f.
Eze. 26 : 21. shalt thou never b. f.
Da. 11:19. he shall fall, and not b.f.
12:1. ev. one shall b. f. in the book
Ho. 10 : 2. shall they b. f. faulty
Zph. 3:13. nor deceitful tongue b.f.
Zch. 10 : 10. place not b. f. for them
Ac. 5:39. lest ye b. f. to fight ag-t G.
1 Co.4:2.that a steward b. f. faithful
2 Co. 5 : 3. we shall not b. f. naked
11 : 12. they may b. f. even as we
12 : 20. that I b. f. as ye would not
Ph.3:9. b. f. in him, not having own
2 Pe. 3:14. may b. f. of him in peace
Re. 18:21. Bab. b. f. no more at all
22. no craftsman sh. b. f. in thee

FOUND grace.

Ge. 6 : 8. Noah f. g. in eyes of L.
19 : 19. servant f. g. in thy sight
33 : 10. if I have f. g. in thy sight,
47 : 29.-50 : 4. Ex. 33: 12.-34:9.
Ju. 6 : 17. 1 S. 27 : 5.
39 : 4. Joseph f. g. in his sight
Ex. 33 : 12. thou hast also f. g., 17.
16. how known that I f. g.?
Nu. 32 : 5. if we have f. g. in thy
Ru. 2:10. why I f. g. in thine eyes?
1 S. 20 : 3. fa. knoweth I have f. g.
2 S.14: 22.serv.knoweth I have f.g.
Je. 31 : 2. people f. g. in the wilder.

Is FOUND.

Ge. 44 : 10. he with whom it i. f. be
my serv., 16. [ries
De. 20 : 11. peo. that i. f.be tributa-
1 K. 14 : 13. in him i. f. good thing
2 K.22:13. book th.i. f.,2 Ch.34:21.
Ezr. 4 : 19. it i. f. city been rebell.
Jb. 19:28. seeing root of matter i. f.
Pr. 10 : 13. in the lips wisdom i. f.
Is.13:15.Ev. one i. f.be thrust thro.
37 : † 4. prayer for remu. that i. f.
65 : 8. As new wine i. f. in cluster
Je. 2 : 26. As thief asha. when i. f.
34. in thy skirts i. f. the blood of
11 : 9. A conspiracy i. f. am. Jud.
Da. 5 : 14. wisdom i. f. in thee

Ho. 14 : 8. From me i. thy fruit f.
Lu. 15:24. son was lost and i. f.,32.
2 Co. 7 : 14. our boasting i. f. a tr.

Was FOUND.

Ge. 44:12. cup w. f. in Benj.'s sack
47 : 14. Jo. gath. money that w. f.
Ex. 35: 23. man with wh.w.f.purple
24. with wh. w. f. shittim wood
Ju. 20 : †48. smote all that w. f.
1 S.13:22. with Saul and Jona. w. f.
1 K.7: 47. nei. w. weight of brass f.
2 K.12:10. told the money that w.f.
20 : 13. shewed all that w. f. in
treasury, Is. 39 : 2.
22 : 9. gather the money that w.
f., 2 Ch. 34 : 17.
23:2.book which w. f., 2 Ch.34:30.
2 Ch. 15 : 4. he w. f. of them, 15.
21:17.carried aw.substance th.w.f.
36 : 8. that which w. f. in him
Ezr. 6 : 2. w. f. at Achmetha a roll
Ne. 13 : 1 w. f. written, Es. 6 : 2.
Es. 2 : 23. inquisition made, it w. f.
Ec. 9 : 15. w. f. in it poor wise man
Je. 48 : 27. w. he f. am. thieves?
Eze. 28 : 15. perfect till iniq. w. f.
Da. 1 : 19. none w. f. like Dan.
2:35. iron, clay brok.,no place w.f.
5 : 11. wisd. of gods w. f. in him
6 : 4. nei. w. any error f. in him
22. bec. innocency w. f. in me
23. no hurt w. f. upon him
Mat.1:18. w. f. with child of H.Gh.
Lu. 9:36. voice past, Jes. w. f. alone
Ac.8:40. But Philip w. f. at Azotus
Ro. 10: 20.I w.f.of them sought not
1 Pe.2:22. nei.w.guile f.in his mou.
Re.5:4. no man w.f. worthy to open
14 : 5. in mouth w. f. no guile
18 : 24. in her w. f. blood of proph.
20 : 11. w. f. no place for them

Was not FOUND.

Mal.2 : 6. iniq. w. n. f. in his lips
He. 11 : 5. Enoch w. n. f. bec. God
Re. 20 : 15. whoso. w. n. f. written

FOUNDATION. [in book

Ex. 9 : 18. not been in E. since f.
Jos. 6 : 26. shall lay f. in firstborn
1 K. 5 : 17. hewn stones to lay f.
6 : 37. in 4th year was f. of ho. laid
7 : 9. of costly stones from f., 10.
16 : 34. laid f. of Jericho in firstb.
2 Ch. 8 : 16.work prep. unto day of f.
23 : 5. 3d part at gate of the f.
31 : 7. they began to lay f. of heaps
Ezr. 3 : 6. f. of temple not yet laid
10. when the builders laid f., 12.
5 : 16. Sheshbazzar laid f. of house
7 : †9. upon first day was the f.
Jb. 4:19. in them whose f. is in dust
22 : 16. f. was overfl. with flood
Ps.87:1. His f. is in holy mountains
102 : 25.Of old thou hast laid the f.
137:7.Rase it, rase it, even to the f.
Pr. 10 : 25. righte. is an everl. f.
Is. 28 : 16. I lay in Zion for a f.
44:28. to temp. thy f. shall be laid
48 : 13. My hand hath laid the f.
Eze. 13 : 14. f. shall be discovered
Ha. 3 : 13. discov-g f. unto neck
Hag. 2 : 18. fr. day the f. was laid
Zch. 4 : 9. Zerubbabel hath laid f.
8 : 9. prophets when f. was laid
12 : 1. L. which layeth f. of earth
Lu. 6 : 48. and laid the f. on a rock
49.that without a f. built a house
14 : 29. lest after he hath laid the f.
Ro.15:20.Lest build on ano.man's f.
1 Co. 3 : 10. as masterbuild. I laid f.
11. for other f. can no man lay
12. if any man build upon this f.
Ep. 2 : 20. are built on f. of proph.
1 Ti. 6 : 19. Laying up a good f.
2 Ti. 2 : 19. f. of God standeth sure
He. 1 : 10. thou, L., hast laid the f.
6:1. not laying the f. of repentance
Re. 21 : 19. the first f. jasper; sec.

FOUNDATION of the World.

Mat. 13 : 35. kept secret fr. f. o. w.
25:34. kingdom prepared fr. f. o. w.
Lu. 11:50. the blood shed fr. f. o. w.
Jn.17:24. thou lovedstme bef. f. o. w.
Ep.1:4. chosen us in him bef. f. o. w.
He.4:3. works were finished fr. f. o. w
9:26. must have oft suff. since f. o. w.
1 Pe.1:20. foreordained bef. f. o. w.
Re. 13 : 8. Lamb slain fr. f. o. w.
17 : 8. names not written fr. f. o. w.

FOUNDATIONS.

De. 32 : 22. set on fire f. of mts.
2 S. 22 : 8. the f. of heaven moved
16. f. were discovered, Ps.18:7,15.
Ezr. 4 : 12. set up walls joined f.
6 : 3. let f. thereof be strongly laid
Jb.38:4. Where thou when I laid f.?
6. Whereupon are f. fastened
Ps. 11 : 3. If f. be destroyed, what
82 : 5. all f. of earth out of course
104 : 5. Who laid the f. of earth
Pr. 8 : 29. when he appointed the f.
Is.16:7. for f. of Kir-hareseth mourn
24 : 18. f. of the earth do shake
40 : 21. have ye not underst. of f.?
51 : 13. L. that laid f. of the earth
16. that I may lay f. of the earth
54 : 11. I will lay f. with sapphires
58:12. shalt raise f. of many gene-s
Je. 31 : 37. if f. can be searched
50:15. her f. are fallen, her walls are
51 : 26. not take of thee stone for f.
La. 4 : 11. it hath devoured the f.
Eze. 30 : 4. E.'s f. shall be broken
41 : 8. f. of side chambers were a
Mi. 1 : 6. and I will discover the f.
6 : 2. hear, O mts., and ye strong f.
Ac. 16 : 26. f. of prison were shaken
He. 11 : 10. looked for city hath f.
Re. 21 : 14. walls of city had 12 f.
19. f. garnished with preci. stones

FOUNDED.

1 Ch.9:†22. were porters wh. Dav. f.
2 Ch.3:†3. things wherein Sol. was f.
Ezr. 3 : †6. temple was not yet f.
Ps. 8 : †2. of babes hast f. strength
24:2. for he hath f. it upon the seas
78 : †69. like earth which he hath f.
89:11. world and fulness thou hast f.
104 : †5. f. earth upon her bases
8. to place thou hast f. for them
119 : 152. thy testimonies thou hast f. for ever
Pr.3:19. by wisdom hath f. the earth
Is. 14 : 32. That the L. hath f. Zion
23:13. people was till not Assy r. f. it
Am. 9 : 6. hath f. his troop in earth
Hab.1:† 12. O G'd, thou hast f. a rock
Mat.7: 25. it fell not was f. upon them
Lu. 6 : 48. for it was f. upon a rock

FOUNDER.

Ju. 17 : 4. mother gave them to f.
Is. 41 : †7. carpenter encouraged f.
Je. 6 : 29. bellows are burned, f. melteth in vain
10 : 9. work of the hands of the f.
14. every f. confounded, 51 : 17.

FOUNDEST, ING.

2 Ch.24:†27. conc. Joash f-g the hou.
Ne. 9 : 8. And f-t his heart faithful

FOUNTAIN.

Ge. 16 : 7. angel found Hagar by a f.
Le. 11 : 36. a f. shall be clean
20:18. he discovered her f. f. of bl.
De. 33 : 28. f. of Jacob be upon a land of corn
Jos. 15 : 9. border fr. hill unto the f.
1 S.29:1. the Israelites pitched by a f.
Ne. 2 : 14. gate of the f., 3:15.-12:37.
Ps. 36 : 9. For with thee is f. of life
68: 26. bless the Lord fr. f., of Isr.
74 : 15. Thou didst cleave the f.
114 : 8. turned flint into f. of water
Pr. 5 : 18. Let thy f. be blessed
13 : 14. The law of wise is f. of life
Pr.14:27. The fear of Lord is a f. of life
25 : 26. is as a troubled f.
Ec. 12 : 6. pitcher be broken at f.
Can.4:12. A f. sealed | 15. of gardens
Je. 2:13. forsaken f. of waters, 17:13.
6 : 7. As a f. casteth out her waters
9 : 1. Oh that mine eyes were a f.
Ho. 13 : 15. his f. shall be dried up
Jo. 3:18. f. sh. come forth of h. of L.
Zch. 13 : 1. In that day f. be opened
Mk. 5 : 29. f. of her blood was dried
Ja. 3 : 11. f. send forth sweet water?
12. no f. can yield salt water and
Re 21 : 6. I will give of f. of life.

FOUNTAINS.

Ge. 7 : 11. f. of deep were broken up
8 : 2 f. of the deep were stopped
De. 8 : 7. bringeth thee into la of f.
1 K. 18 : 5. Go unto all f. of water
2 Ch.32:3. counsel to stop wat-s of f.
4. much peo. who stopped all f.
Pr. 5 : 16. Let thy f. be dispersed
8:24. when no f. abounding with wat.
28. when he strength-d f. of deep
Is. 41 : 18. I will open f. in valleys
Re. 7 : 17. lead them unto living f.
8 : 10. star fell upon f. of waters
14:7. worship him that made the f.
16 : 4. angel poured his vial upon f.

FOUR.

Ex. 22 : 1. restore f. sheep for a
25 : 34. shall be f. bowls made like
26 : 2. the breadth of one curtain f. cubits, 8.-36:9, 15. De 3:11. 1K.7: 19, 27, 38. Eze. 41 : 5.-43 : 14.
27 : 16. pillars f. sockets f., 38 : 19.
37 : 20. and in candlestick f. bowls
Le.11:20. fowls going upon all f., 21.
27. that go on all f. unclean, 42.
Jos. 21 : 18. f. cities, 22, 24, 29, 31, 35, 37, 39.
2 S. 21 : 22. These f. born to giant
1 K. 7 : 30. f. corners, 34. Eze. 46 : 34. were f. undersetters [22, 23.
1 Ch. 26:17. Lev. northw. f. a day (2)
18. At Parbar, f. at causeway
Pr. 30:15. f. things say not, enough
18. be f. things wh. I know not
21. for f. things it cannot bear
24. be f. things little upon earth
30:29. f. things are comely in going
Is. 17:6. f. or 5 in outmost branches
Je.49:36. from Elam bring f. wind-(2)
Eze. 1 : 6. ev. one had f. faces, 15.-
10 : 14. ev. one had f. wings, 10 : 21.
16. they f. had one likeness, 10:10.
18. full of eyes round them f.
37 : 9. Come fr. f. winds, O breath
42 : 20. meas-d it by f. sides [20.
43:15. altar f. cubits, upw. f. horns,
Da. 7 : 2. f. winds strove on the sea
6. f. wings of fowl, f. heads
8 : 8. came f. horns tow. f. winds
11:4. kingd. divided tow. f. winds
Am. 1 : 3. for f. not turn aw. punishm., 6, 9, 11, 13.-2 : 1, 4, 6.
Zch. 2:6. spread you abr. as f. winds
Mat. 24:31. angels, they shall gather his elect fr. f. winds, Mk. 13:27.
Mk. 2 : 3. sick of palsy borne of f.
Ac. 27:29. they cast f. anchors out
Re. 6:6. voice in midst of f. beasts, 1.
7:1. f. angels, holding f. winds, 2.
9:14. f. angels bound in Euph., 15.
See BARRELS, BEASTS, CARPENTER, CHARIOTS, CHILDREN, COMPANIES, CORNERS, CREATURES, FOUR DAYS, ENDS, FINGERS, FOWL, GENERATIONS, HEADS, HORNS, HUNDRED, JUDGMENTS, KINDS, KINGS, LEAVES, MEN, MONTHS, OXEN, PARTS, PORTERS, QUARTERS, QUARTERNIONS, RINGS, ROWS, SIDES, SONS, SPIRITS, SQUARES, THOUSAND, TWENTY, WAGONS, WHEELS.

FOUR Times. See TIMES.

FOURFOLD.

2 S. 12 : 6. he shall restore lamb f.
Lu. 19:8. taken any thi., I restore f.
See TWENTY, HUNDRED, THOUSAND.

FOURFOOTED.

Ac. 10:12. f. beasts of the earth, 11:6.
Ro. 1 : 23. man, birds and f. beasts

FOURSCORE.

Ex. 7:7. Moses f. yrs. old, Aaron f. and 3 yrs. old, when spake unto [Pha.
Ju.3:30. land had rest f. y-rs
2 S. 19 : 32. Barzillai f. yrs. old, 35.
1 Ch. 15:9. Eliel the chief, and his f.
Ps. 90 : 10. and if they be f. years
Can. 6:8. queens, and f. concubines
Lu. 2:37. a widow f. and four years
16 : 7. Take thy bill, and write f.
See MALES, MEN, PIECES, PRIESTS.

FOURSCORE and five, six.

Ge. 16 : 16. Ab. was f. a. s. when Hagar bare Ishmael
Jos. 14:10. lo, I am f. a. f. yrs. old
1 S. 22 : 18. Doeg slew f. a. f. pers.

One or four hundred and FOURSCORE.

Gen. 35:28. days of Isaac were o. h. [f.
1 K.6:1. in f. h. f. yrs. aft. come out [of E.
See THOUSAND.

FOURSQUARE.

Ex. 27:1. altar sh. be f., 30:2.-38:1.
28 : 16. the breastplate f., 39 : 9.
1 K 6:†33. made posts of olive tree f.
7 : 31. gravings with borders f.
Eze. 40 : 47. he measured court f.
48 : 20. shall offer holy oblation f.
Re. 21 : 16. And the city lieth f.

FOURTEEN.

Jos. 15:36. in valley f. cities, 18:28.
1 K. 8 : 65. Sol. held feast f. days
Eze 43 : 17. settle be f. cubits long
See GENERATIONS, LAMBS, SONS, SOULS, THOUSAND, WIVES, YEARS.

FOURTEENTH.

See DAY, LOT, NIGHT, YEAR.

FOURTH.

Ge. 2 : 14. f. river is Euphrates
Eze. 10 : 14. f. had face of eagle
Da. 3:25. form of f. is like Son of G
7:23. The f. beast sh. be f. kingd.
11 : 2. the f. shall be far richer
Zch. 6:3. in f. chariot grisled horses
Re. 4 : 7. f. beast like flying eagle
16:8. f. angel poured vial upon sun
21 : 19. chalcedony ; f. an emerald
See ANGEL, BEAST, DAY, GENERATION, KINGDOM, LOT, MONTH, PART, ROW, SON, SEAL, WATCH, YEAR.

FOWL.

Ge. 1 : 20. f. that fly above earth
21. ev. winged f. | 22. f. multiply
7:23. f. of heav. was destroyed, 21.
8:17. bring forth of flesh, of f., 19, 20.
9:10. I establish my cov. with the f.
Le. 7:26. eat no blood, of f. or beast
11 : 46. This is law of beasts and f.
20 : 25. souls abom. by beasts or f.
De. 4 : 17. likeness of any winged f.
1 K. 4:23 fatted f. | 33. spake of f.
Jb. 28:7. path which no f. knoweth
Ps. 148:10. flying f. praise the Lord
Je. 9 : 10. f. of the heavens are fled
Eze. 17:23. und. it shall dwell all f.
39:17. Speak to every feathered f.
44:31. not eat thing torn, f. or beast
Da. 7 : 6. on back four wings of a f.

FOWL, S of the air.

Ge. 1:26. dominion over f. o. a., 28, 30. Ps. 8 : 8.
2:19. G. formed every f. o. a., 20.
6:7. L. said, I will destroy f-s o. a.
7 : 3. of f-s o. a. by sevens | 8.
9:2. fear of you be upon ev. f. o. a.

De. 28:26. carcass be meat unto f-s o. a. [46.
1 S. 17:44. give thy flesh to f-s o. a.,
1 K. 4:33. Sol. spake of beasts and f.
14 : 11. him dieth in fields f-s o. a.
should eat, 16:4. - 21:24. [thee
Jb. 12 : 7. ask f-s o. a., th. sh. tell
28 : 21. kept close from f-s o. a.
Mat. 6 : 26. f-s o. a., they sow not
Mk.4:4. f-s o. a. devoured it, Lu. 8:5
4:32. f-s o. a. may lodge, Lu. 13:19.
Ac. 10:12. sheet wh-n f-s o. a., 11:6.

FOWLS.

Ge. 6 : 20. f. after their kind
15 : 11. when f. came on carcasses
Le. 1 : 14. if burnt sacri. be of f.
11 : 13. these f. have in abomina.
20. All f. that creep, going upon
20:25. between f. unclean and clean
De. 14 : 20. But of clean f. may eat
Ne. 5:18. also f. were prepared for me
Ps. 50 : 11. I know all f. of mts.
78 : 27. he rained f. as sand of sea
Is. 18 : 6. shall be left to f. of mts.,
f. shall summer upon them
Da. 4:14. let f. get fr. his branches
Mat. 13:4. the f. devoured the seed
Lu. 12:24. how much better than f.
Re. 19 : 17. angel cried to all the f.
21. f. were filled with their flesh

FOWLS of heaven.

Jb. 28 : † 21. kept close fr. f. o. h.
35:11. maketh us wiser than f. o. h.
Ps. 79:2. of serv-ts meat unto f. o. h.
104:12. f. o. h. have their habita
Je. 7:33. carcasses of this peo. be meat
for f. o. h., 16:4. - 19:7. - 34:20.
15 : 3. appoint f. o. h. to destroy
Eze. 29:5. Pha. for meat to f. o. h.
31:6. f. o. h. made nests in Assyr.
13. Upon his ruin sh. f. o. h. remain
32:4. will cause f. o. h. to remain
38 : 20. f. o. h. shall shake at my
Da. 2:38. O k., f. o. h. given into thine
4:12. f. o. h. dwelt in boughs, 21.
Ho. 2:18. made a cov. with f. o. h.
4 : 3. shall languish with f. o. h.
7 : 12. bring them down as f. o. h.
Zph. 1 : 3. I will consume f. o. h.

FOWLER, S.

Ps. 91 : 3. deliver thee from snare of f.
124:7. soul esca-d out of snare of f-s
Pr. 6 : 5. deliver as a bird from f.
Je. 5 : †26. peo. pry as f-s lie in wait
Ho. 9 : 8. proph. is a snare of a f.

FOX, ES.

Ju. 15 : 4. Samson caught 300 f-s
Ne. 4 : 3. f. sh. break stone wall
Ps. 63 : 10 sh. be a portion for f-s
Can. 2 : 15. Take the f-s, little f-s
La. 5 : 18. Zion the f-s walk upon it
Eze. 13 : 4. thy prophets are like f-s
Mat. 8 : 20. f-s have holes, Lu. 9:58.
Lu. 13:32. tell that f. I cast out devils

FRAGMENTS.

Mat. 14 : 20. they took up the f. 12
bask-s, Mk. 6:43. Lu. 9:17. Jn. 6:13.
Mk. 8:19. how many baskets of f.? 20.
Jn. 6 : 12. Gather up f. that remain

FRAIL.

Ps. 39 : 4. may know how f. I am

FRAME, S.

Ps. 103 : 14. he knoweth our f.
Je. 7 : † 18. cakes to f. of heaven
18 : † 3. he wrought a work on f-s
44 : † 17. burn inc. unto f. of heav.
Eze. 40 : 2. was as the f. of a city

FRAME, ED, ETH.

Ju. 12: 6. could not f. to pronounce
Ps. 50 : 19. thy tongue f-h deceit
94 : 20. f-h mischief by a law
Is. 29:16. thing f-d say to him f-d it?
Je. 18 : 11. Behold I f. evil ag. you
Ho. 5:4. not f. doings to turn un. G.
Ep. 2 : 21. In whom all building f-d
He. 11 : 3. worlds f-d by word of G.

FRANKINCENSE.

Ex. 30 : 34. take spices with pure f.
Le. 2 : 1. put f., 15. - 5 : 11. - 24 : 7.
2. shall take oil with f. [Nu. 5:15.
16. priest burn oil with f., 6 : 15.
1 Ch. 9 : 29. appointed to oversee f.
Ne. 13 : 5 where they laid the f.
9. thi. brought I vessels and f.
Can. 3: 6. who this perfumed with f.
4 : 6. I will get me to hill of f.
14. cinnamon, with all trees of f.
Mat. 2:11. they presented unto him f.
Re. 18 : 13. no man buyeth their f.

FRANKLY.

Lu. 7 : 42. he f. forgave them both

FRAUD.

Ps. 10 : 7. His mouth is full of f.
Is. 30 : † 12. because ye trust in f.
Ja. 5 : 4. hire kept back by f. crieth

FRAY.

De. 28 : 26. f. them away, Je. 7: 33.
Zch. 1 : 21. these are come to f. them

FRECKLED.

Le. 13: 39. it is a f. spot th. groweth

FREE.

Ex. 21 : 2. Hebr. serv., 7th year he
sh. go out f., De. 15:12. Je. 34:9, 14.
5. if serv. say, I will not go out f.
11. sh. she go f. without money
26. sh. let him go f. for eye's sake
27. let him go f. for tooth's sake
Le 19 : 20. not be put to death bec.
not f. [ter water
Nu. 5 : 19. be thou f. from this bit-
28. if woman not defiled, be f.
De. 15 : 13. when sendest him out f.
18. not hard when sendest him f.
24 : 5. sh. be f. at home one year
1 S. 17 : 25. make his fa's house f.
1 K. 15: † 22. a proclam.; none was f.
1 Ch. 9 : 33. the singers who were f.
2 Ch. 26 : † 21. Uzziah in a f. house
29 : 31. as were of f. heart offered
Jb. 3 : 19. servant is f. from master
39: 5. Who hath sent out wild ass f.?
Ps. 51 : 12. uphold me with f. Spirit
88 : 5. f. am. dead, like slain in
105 : 20. the king let him go f.
Is. 58 : 6. to let oppressed go f.,
Je. 34:9. each sho. let serv. go f., 10.
11. caused them they let go f. to
Mat. 15 : 6. honour not fa, he be f.
17 : 26. Then are the children f.
Mk. 7:11. It is Corban, he shall be f.
Jn. 8 : 32. truth shall make you f.
33. how sayest, Ye sh. be made f.
36. if Son make you f. be f. ind.
Ac. 22 : 28. said, But I was f-born
Ro. 5 : 15. not as offence, so f. gift
16. f. gift is of many offences
18. f. gift upon all unto justifica.
6 : 18. Being made f. fr. sin, 22.
20. servants of sin f. fr. righteousn.
7:3. if husband be dead, she is f. fr.
8 : 2. Spi. of life made me f. fr. dea.
1 Co. 7 : 21. if mayest be made f.
† 22. he called in Lord is made f.
9 : 1. Am I not apos.? am I not f.?
19. though I be f. from all men
12:13. bapt. by one Spi., bond or f.
Ga. 3: 28. bond nor f., Col. 3 : 11
4 : 26. Jerus. which is above, is f.
31. not chil. of bondwom., but of f.
5 : 1. liberty wh w. C. made us f.
Ep. 6:8. sh. receive of L., bond or f.
2 Th. 3:1. word may have f. course
1 Pe 2 : 16. as f. not using liberty
Re. 13:16. causeth f. and bond, to rec.
19:18. may eat flesh of bond and f.

FREE offerings.

Ex. 36:3. brought f. o. ev. morning
Am. 4:5. proclaim and publish f. o.

FREE woman.

Ga. 4:22. two sons, by bondm., and f. w.
23. he of f. w. was by promise
30. not be heir with son of f. w.

FREED.

Jos. 9:23. shall none of you be f.
Ro. 6 : 7. he that is dead is f. fr. sin

FREEDOM. [given

Le. 19 : 20. lieth with wom., not f.
Eze. 27:†20. merchant in clothes of f.
Ac. 22 : 28. sum obtained I this f.

FREELY.

Ge. 2 : 16. of ev. tree mayest f. eat
Nu. 11:5. remem. fish we did eat f.
1 S. 14 : 30. if peo. eaten f. to day
Ezr. 2 : 68. chief fathers offered f.
7 : 15. which king hath offered f.
Ps. 54 : 6. I will f. sacrifi., O Lord
Ho. 14 : 4. I will love them f.
Mat. 10 : 8. f. ye have rec., f. give
Ac. 2 : 29. breth., let me f. speak
26 : 26. king, bef. whom I speak f.
Ro. 3 : 24. justified f. by his grace
8 : 32. will with him f. give us all
1 Co. 2 : 12. know things f. given us
2 Co. 11 : 7. preached gospel of G. f.
Re. 21 : 6. give of fount. of life f.
22 : 17. whoso. will, let him take f.

FREEMAN.

1 Co. 7:22. is called, is the Lord's f.
Re. 6 : 15. ev. bondman and f. hid

FREEWILL.

Ezr. 7 : 13. of their f. to go to Jerus.

FREEWILL offering.

Le. 22 : 21. offereth f. o. be perfect
23. bullock mayest offer for f. o.
Nu. 15 : 3. will make sacri. in f. o.
De. 16 : 10. with a tribute of f. o.
23 : 23. a f. o. shalt thou keep
Ezr. 1:4. help with beasts besides f. o.
3:5. willingly off-d a f. o. unto Lord
7 : 16. silver canst find with f. o.
8:28. silver and gold are a f. o. unto

FREEWILL offerings. [L.

Le. 22 : 18. offer oblation for f. o.
23 : 38. beside all f. o., Nu. 29 : 39.
De. 12 : 6. thither bring your f. o.
17. not eat within gates thy f. o.
2 Ch. 31:14. Kore was over f. o. of G.
Ps. 119:108. Accept f. o. of my mou.

FREQUENT.

Pr. 27 : † 6. kisses of enemy are f.
2 Co. 11 : 23. in prisons more f. in

FRESH, ER.

Nu. 11:8. taste of manna as of f. oil
Jb. 29 : 20. My glory was f. in me
33:25. His flesh be f-r than child's
Ps. 92 : 10. be anointed with f. oil
Ja. 3:12. can yield salt water and f.

FRET.

Le. 13:55. shalt burn, it is f. inward

FRET, TED, TETH, TING.

Le. 13 : 51. is f-g leprosy, 52. - 14:44.
1 S. 1 : 6. provoked to make her f.
Ps. 37 : 1. f. not, 7, 8. Pr. 24 : 19.
Pr. 19 : 3. his heart f-h ag. Lord
Is. 8 : 21. when hungry, they sh. f.
Eze. 16 : 43. hast f-d me in these

FRIED.

Le. 7:12. mingled with oil of flour f.
1 Ch. 23:29. to wait about that wh. [is f.

FRIEND.

Ge. 38:20. sent kid by hand of f., 12.
Ex. 33:11. to Mos. as man unto his f.
De. 13 : 6. or if thy f. entice thee
Ju. 14 : 20. whom he used as his f.
2 S. 13:3. Amnon had a f. Jonadab
15 : 37. Hushai David's f., 16 : 16.
16 : 17. Is this thy kindness to thy
f.? why wentest not with thy f.?
1 K. 4 : 5. Zabud was principal officer, the king's f.
2 Ch. 20:7. gavest to seed of Ab. thy f.
Jb. 6:14. pity be shewed from his f.
27. and ye dig a pit for your f.
16:†21. as a man pleadeth for his f.
Ps. 35:14. as tho. he had been my f.
41 : 9. familiar f. lifted up his heel
88:18. Lover and f. hast put fr. me
Pr. 6 : 1. if thou be surety for f.
3. in hand of f. make sure thy f.

Pr. 17 : 17. A f. loveth at all times
18. surety in presence of his f.
18 : 24. a f. closer than a brother
19 : 6. ev. man is f. to him giveth
22 : 11. the king shall be his f.
27 : 6. Faithful are wounds of a f.
9. so man's f. by hearty counsel
10. own f. thy fa.'s f. forsake not
14. blesseth f. with a loud voice
17. sharpeneth countenance of f.
Can. 5:16. This is my beloved, my f.
Is. 41 : 8. thou art seed of Ab. my f.
Je. 3 : † 20. as a wife departeth fr. f.
6 : 21. the neighb. and f. sh. perish
19 : 9. sh. eat ev. one flesh of his f.
Ho. 3:1. beloved of her f. adulteress
Mi. 7 : 5. Trust ye not in a f. put
Mat. 11:19. f. of publicans, Lu. 7:34.
20:13. ans-d, f. I do thee no wrong
22 : 12. f. how camest thou hither?
26:50. Jesus said, f. whf. art come?
Lu. 11:5. shall have f. and go at midnight and say, f. lend me 3 loaves
6. f. of mine in his journey is come
8. though he will not give him
because he is his f.
14 : 10. may say, f. go up higher
Jn. 3 : 29. f. of bridegr. rejoiceth
11 : 11. Our f. Laza. sleepeth ⌈f.
19 : 12. If let man go, not Cesar's
Ac. 12 : 20. having made Blastus f.
Ja. 2 : 23. Ab. was called f. of God
4 : 4. will be a f. of world, is ene. of

FRIENDS. ⌊God

Ge. 26:26. fr. Ahuzzath one of his f.
1 S. 30 : 26. Da. sent of spoil to f.
2 S. 3 : 8. shew kindness to Saul's f.
19 : 6. lovest enemies, hatest thy f.
1 K. 16 : 11. Zimri left not one of f.
Es. 5 : 10. Haman called for his f.
14. said wife and his f. unto him
6 : 13. Haman told his wife and f.
Jb. 2 : 11. when Job's 3 f. heard
16:20. My f. scorn me, but mine eye
17:5. He that speaketh flattery to f.
19 : 14. my familiar f. have forgot.
19. All my inw. f. abhorred me
21. Have pity upon me, O ye f.
32 : 3. ag. 3 f. Elihu's wrath kindl.
42:7. My wrath is kindl. ag. thy 2 f.
10. Lord turned captivity of Job
when he prayed for his f.
Ps. 38 : 11. my f. stand aloof from
Pr. 14 : 20. the rich hath many f.
16 : 28. whisperer separa. chief f.
17:9. repeateth a matter, sepa-h f.
18 : 24. hath f. must shew himself
19:4. Wealth mak. many f. ⌊friendly
7. much more do his f. go far
Can. 5:1. eat, O f. drink, yea, drink
Je. 20:4. make thee terror to thy f.
6. shalt be buried there, and f.
38 : 22. Thy f. have set thee on
La. 1 : 2. her f. have dealt treach.
Zch. 13:6. wounded in hou. of my f.
Mk. 3 : 21. when his f. heard of it
5 : 19. Jes. saith, Go home to thy f.
Lu. 7 : 6. centurion sent f. to him
12 : 4. f. Be not afraid of them kill
14 : 12. makest dinner, call not f.
15 : 6. he calleth together his f.
9. she calleth her f. and neighb-s
29. that I might make merry with
16 : 9. Make f. of the mammon ⌊f.
21 : 16. ye shall be betrayed by f.
23 : 12. Pilate and Herod made f.
Jn. 15 : 13. lay down life for his f.
14. Ye are my f. if ye do what I
15. but I have called you f.
Ac. 10 : 24. Cornelius called his f.
19 : 31. certain f. sent unto him
27:3. gave liberty to go unto his f.
Ro. 16 : † 10. them of Aristobu.'s f.
† 11. greet f. of Narcissus in L.
3 Jn. 14. Our f. salute thee, Greet f.

FRIENDLY.

Ju. 19 : 3. went to speak f. to her
Ru. 2:13. spoken f. to thine handm.
Pr. 18 : 24. must shew himself f.
Ho. 2 : † 14. I will speak f. to her

FRIENDSHIP.

Pr. 22:24. Make no f. with angry man
Ja. 4:4. f. of world is enmity with G.

FRINGE, S.

Nu. 15 : 38. make f-s put upon f. a
39. it shall be to you for a f.
De. 22:12. make f-s on 4 quarters

To and FRO.

Ge. 8 : 7. raven, which went t. a. f.
Ex. 29 : † 24. shake t. a. f. a wave off.
2 K. 4 : 35. Elisha walked in house
t. a. f. ⌈a. f., 2 : 2.
Jb. 1 : 7. Satan said, From going t.
7 : 4. I am full of tossings t. a. f.
13:25. thou break leaf driven t. a. f.
Ps. 107 : 27. they reel t. a. f.
Pr. 21 : 6. is a vanity tossed t. a. f.
Is. 24 : 20. earth shall reel t. a. f.
33 : 4. as running t. a. f. of locusts
49 : 21. and removing t. a. f.
Eze. 27 : 19. Dan also going t. a. f.
Zch. 1 : 10. Lord sent to walk t. a. f.
11. walked t. a. f. thro. earth
6 : 7. might walk t. a. f. through
earth, so they walked t. a. f.
Ep. 4 : 14. be no more chil. tossed
See RUN. ⌊t. a. f.

FROGS.

Ex. 8:2. I will smite borders with f.
3. shall bring forth f.
4. f. sh. come up on thee, 5, 6.
7. the magicians brought up f.
8. L. that he take away f., 9, 12.
11. f. sh. depart | 13. f. died
Ps. 78:45. he sent f. wh. destroyed
105 : 30. land brought forth f.
Re. 16 : 13. I saw uncl. spirits like f.

FROM. ⌈land

1 S. 6:5. hand f. off you, f. off your
Mat. 4:25. mult. f. Decapolis, f., (4)

FRONT. ⌈him

2 S. 10 : 9. Joab saw f. of battle ag.
2 Ch. 3 : 4. porch in f. of house

FRONTIERS.

Eze. 25 : 9. from cities on his f.

FRONTLETS.

Ex. 13 : 16. be for f. betw. eyes
De. 6 : 8. shall be as f., 11 : 18.

FROST. ⌈night

Ge. 31 : 40. drought by day, f. by
Ex. 16 : 14. as small as the hoar f.
Jb. 37 : 10. By breath of G. f. is giv.
38 : 29. f. of heav., who gendered
Ps. 78 : 47. sycamore trees with f.
147 : 16. he scattereth the hoar f.
Je. 36 : 30. Jehoi.'s body cast to f.

FROWARD.

De. 32 : 20. are a very f. generation
2 S. 22 : 27. with pure shew thys.
pure, with f. shew f., Ps. 18:26.
Jb. 5 : 13. counsel of f. is headlong
Ps. 101 : 4. A f. heart shall depart
Pr. 2 : 12. that speaketh f. things
15. and they f. in their paths
3 : 32. For the f. is abomi. to Lord
4 : 24. Put away fr. thee f. mouth
6 : 12. walketh with a f. mouth
8 : 8. there is nothing f. in them
13. and the f. mouth do I hate
10 : 31. f. tongue shall be cut out
11:20. of f. heart, are abomi. to L.
16 : 28. A f. man soweth strife
30. shutt. eyes to devise f. things
17:20. hath f. heart, findeth no good
21 : 8. The way of a man is f.
22 : 5. Thorns are in way of the f.
1 Pe. 2 : 18. subject to gentle, also

FROWARDLY. ⌊to f.

Is. 57:17. went f. in way of his heart

FROWARDNESS.

Pr. 2 : 14. delight in f. of wicked
4 : † 24. put from thee f. of mouth
6:14. f. is in his heart, he deviseth
10 : 32. mouth of wick. speaketh f.

FROWNED. ⌈them

1 S. 3:†13. sons vile, he f. not upon

FROZEN.

Jb. 38 : 30. face of the deep is f.

FRUIT.

Ge. 1:29. Behold, I have given you
every tree wherein is f.
4 : 3. Cain brought of f. of ground
30 : 2. hath withheld f. of the womb
Ex. 21 : 22. her f. depart from her
Le. 19 : 23. sh. count the f. uncirc.
24. in 4th year f. shall be holy
23 : 39. when ye have gath. in f.
†40. on first day f. of goodly trees
25 : 3. six years shalt gather in f.
27 : 30. the tithe of f. is the Lord's
Nu. 13 : 26. they shewed f. of land
27. we came to land, this is f. of
De. 1 : 25. took f. in their hands
7 : 13. he will bless f. of thy land
22 : 9. lest f. of thy seed, f. of thy
vineyard be defiled
26 : 2. shalt take of first of all f.
28:4. blessed shall be f. of thy body
11. plenteous in f. of body, 30 : 9.
18. cursed shall be f. of thy body
33. f. of thy land, and labours
40. thine olive shall cast his f.
42. all thy f. sh. locust consume
Ju. 9 : 11. should I forsake my f.?
2 S. 16 : 2. summer f. for young
Ne. 10:35. f. of all trees, year by yr.
Ps. 21:10. Their f. shalt thou destroy
58 : †11. verily is f. for the righte.
72 : 16. f. shall shake like Leb.
104 : 13. earth is satisfied with f.
105 : 35. the locusts devoured the f.
127 : 3. f. of womb is his reward
132 : 11. of f. of thy body will I set
Pr. 8 : 19. my f. is better than gold
10 : 16. f. of wicked tendeth to sin
11 : 30. f. of righte. tree of life
12 : 14. satis. by f. of mouth, 18:20.
31 : 16. with f. of hand she planteth
31. give her of f. of her hands
Can. 2 : 3. his f. sweet to my taste
8 : 11. f. to bri. 1000 pieces of sil.
12. those that keep the f. 200
Is. 3 : 10. shall eat f. of doings
4 : 2. f. of earth shall be excellent
10 : 12. will punish f. of stout heart
13 : 18. have no pity on f. of womb
14:29. his f. shall be a fiery serpent
27 : 6. fill face of the world with f.
9. this is f. to take away his sin
28 : 4. as the hasty f. bef. summer
57 : 19. I create f. of the lips, Peace
65 : 21. plant vineyards, and eat f.
Je. 6 : 19. bring f. of their thoughts
7 : 20. my fury upon f. of ground
11 : 16. olive tree, fair, goodly f.
19. let us destroy tree with the f.
17 : 10. acc. to f. of his doings, 21 :
Eze. 17 : 9. cut off the f. ⌊14.—32:19.
19 : 12. east wind dried up her f.
14. fire hath devoured her f.
25 : 4. eat thy f. drink thy milk
36 : 30. I will multiply f. of tree
47 : 12. nor shall f. be consumed
Da. 4:12. leaves fair and f. much, 21.
14. he cried, Scatter his f.
Ho. 9:†14. a womb th. casteth the f.
16. slay beloved f. of womb
10 : 1. mult. of his f. he hath incr.
13. ye have eaten the f. of lies
14 : 8. From me is thy f. found
Am. 2 : 9. I destroyed his f. from ab.
6 : 12. f. of righteousn. into hemlock
7 : 14. I, a gatherer of sycamore f.
8 : 1. a basket of summer f., 2.
Mi. 6 : 7. f. of body for sin of my soul
7 : 13. land desol. for f. of doings
Ha. 3 : 17. neither f. be in the vines
Hag. 1 : 10. earth is stayed fr. her f.
Zch. 8 : 12. the vine shall give her f.
Mal. 1 : 12. table is polluted, and f.
3 : 11. nor your vine cast her f.

Mat. 12: 33. make tree good, and f. good, tree is known by his f.
21: 19. Let no f. grow on thee for ev.
34. when time of f. drew near
26: 29. I will not drink of f. of vine until I, Mk. 14: 25. Lu. 22: 18.
Mk. 12: 2. might receive f. of viney.
Lu. 1: 42. blessed is f. of thy womb
6: 44. every tree known by his f.
13: 6. he sought f. and found none
7. I come seeking f. on fig tree
20: 10. that they sho. give him of f.
Jn. 4: 36. gathereth f. to life eter.
Ac. 2: 30. of f. of his loins raise
Ro. 1: 13. might have some f. amo. you
6: 21. What f. had ye in those thi.
22. ye have your f. unto holiness
15: 28. have sealed to them this f.
1 Co. 9: 7. viney. eateth not of f.
Ga. 5: 22. But f. of Spirit is love, joy
Ep. 5: 9. f. of Spi. is in all goodn.
Ph. 1: 22. this is the f. of my lab.
4: 17. I desire f. that may abound
He. 13: 15. let us offer f. of our lips
Ja. 3: 18. f. of righ'te. is sown in peace
5: 7. waiteth for precious f.
Jude 12. f. withereth, without f.

Bear, Bare, or Beareth FRUIT.

2 K. 19: 30. sh. b. f. upward, Is. 37: 31.
Eze. 17: 8. in good soil that it b. f.
23. in height of Israel it shall b. f.
Ho. 9: 16. root is dried shall b. no f.
Jo. 2: 22. not afraid, tree b-th f.
Mat. 13: 23. good gro. he who b-th f.
Lu. 8: 8. on good ground b-re f.
13: 9. if it b. f. well, if not, cut it
Jn. 15: 2. ev. branch in me th. b-th not f. ev. branch that b-h f.
4. as branch cannot b. f. of itself
8. that ye b. much f. be my disci.

Bring, eth, or Brought forth FRUIT.

Le. 25: 21. it shall b. f. f. for 3 years
Nu. 13: 20. and b. of the f. of the land
Ne. 10: 35. to b. the f. of all trees, 37.
Ps. 1: 3. that b-h f. f. in season
92: 14. They shall b. f. f. in old age
Can. 8: 11. every one for the f. was to b. silver
Je. 12: 2. wicked grow, b. f. f.
Eze. 36: 11. shall inc. and b. f. f.
47: 12. it sh. b. f. new f. for meat
Ho. 10: 1. Israel b-h f. f. to hims.
Mat. 3: 10. b-h not f. good f., 7: 19. Lu. 3: 9.
7: 17. ev. good tree b-h f. good f.
18. good tree cannot b. f. evil f.
13: 26. when blade b-t f. f., 8.
Mk. 4: 20. as hear word and b. f. f.
28. earth b-th f. f. of herself
29. when f. is b-t f. he putteth
Lu. 6: 43. b-h not f. corrupt f., nei. corrupt tree b. f. good f.
8: 14. and b. no f. to perfection
15. they b. f. f. with patience
Jn. 12: 24. if it die, it b-th f. much f.
15: 2. purgeth that it b. f. more f.
5. the same b-th f. much f., 8.
16. I ordained th. you sho. b. f. f.
Ro. 7: 4. that we sho. b. f. f. unto G.
5. did work to b. f. f. unto death
Col. 1: 6. gospel b-h f. f. in you
Ja. 5: 18. Elijah prayed, earth b-t f. f.
See EAT, FIRSTFRUIT, S.

FRUIT trees.

Ne. 9: 25. possessed f. t. in abund.

Yield, ed, eth, ing FRUIT.

Ge. 1: 11. the fruit tree y-g f., 12.
Le. 25: 19. And land shall y. her f.
26: 4. trees of field shall y. their f.
De. 11: 17. that land y. not her f.
Pr. 12: 12. root of righteous y-h f.
Je. 17: 8. nei. cease from y-g f.
Eze. 34: 27. tree of field sh. y. her f.
36: 8. y. your f. to my people Isr.
Mk. 4: 7. thorns choked it y-d no f.
8. on good ground and did y. f.
He. 12: 11. y-th peaceable f. of
Re. 22: 2. tree y-d her f. ev. month

FRUITS.

Ge. 43: 11. take of best f. in land
Ex. 22: 29. to offer first of thy ripe f.
23: 10. six years shalt gather in f.
Le. 25: 15. acc. to years of the f., 16.
22. till her f. come in, eat of old
26: 20. neither sh. trees yield their f.
De. 33: 14. precious f. brought forth
2 S. 9: 10. thy sons shall bring in f.
2 K. 8: 6. Restore all the f. of field
19: 29. plant vineyards, and eat f.
Jb. 31: 39. If eaten f. with money
Ps. 107: 37. fields, wh. may yield f.
Ec 2: 5. planted trees of all kind of f.
Can. 4: 13. orchard with pleasant f.
16. let my beloved eat pleasant f.
6: 11. I went to see f. of valley
7: 13. at our gates are all pleasant f.
Is. 33: 9. Carmel shake off their f.
La. 4: 9. pine away for want of the f.
Mal. 3: 11. he shall not destroy the f.
Mat. 3: 8. Bring f. meet for, Lu. 3: 8.
7: 16. Ye shall know them by their f., 20.
21: 34. th. they might rec. f. of it
41. who render f. in their seasons
43. to a nation bringing forth f.
Lu. 12: 17. no room to bestow my f.
18. there will I bestow all my f.
2 Co. 9: 10. incr. f. of your righto.
Ph. 1: 11. filled with f. of righte.
2 Ti. 2: 6. first partaker of the f.
Ja. 3: 17. wisdom is full of good f.
Re. 18: 14. f. thy soul lusted after
22: 2. tree of life bare 12 manner of f.

Summer FRUITS.

2 S. 16: 1. Ziba with 100 of s. f.
Is. 16: 9. thy s. f. are fallen
Je. 40: 10. gather wine and s. f.
12. Jews gathered wine and s. f.
48: 32. spoiler is fallen upon thy s. f.
Mi. 7: 1. as when they gath-d s. f.

FRUITFUL.

Ge. 1: 22. God blessed them, saying, Be f., 28.-8: 17.-9: 7.-35: 11.
17: 6. I will make thee exceeding f.
20. make Ishm. f. | 48: 4. Jac. f.
26: 22. made room, we shall be f.
28: 3. God Almighty make thee f.
41: † 52. God caused me to be f. (2)
49: 22. Joseph is a f. bough (2)
Ex. 1: 7. And chil. of Isr. were f.
Le. 26: 9. I will make you f. and
2 Ch. 26: †10. husbandm. in f. fields
Ps. 107: 34. f. land into barrenness
128: 3. Thy wife shall be as a f. vine
148: 9. Mts. and f. trees, praise L.
Is. 5: 1. hath a vineyard in f. hill
17: 6. in the outmost f. branches
32: 12. shall lament for f. vine
Je. 4: 26. f. place was a wilderness
23: 3. they sh. be f. and increase
Eze. 19: 10. she was f. and full of
Ho. 13: 15. Tho. he be f. an east wind
Ac. 14: 17. gave rain f. seasons
Col. 1: 10. being f. in every good work
See FIELD.

FRUSTRATE, ETH.

Ezr. 4: 5. hired to f. their purpose
Ps. 33: †10. L. maketh f. counsel of
Is. 44: 25. That f-h tokens of liars
Mk. 7: †9. full well ye f. com. of G.
Ga. 2: 21. I do not f. grace of God

FRYINGPAN.

Le. 2: 7. be a meat offering in the f.
7: 9. all dressed in f. be the priest's

FUEL.

Is. 9: 5. this shall be with f. of fire
19. people shall be as f. of fire
Eze. 15: 4. vine tree into fire for f., 6.
21: 32. Thou shalt be for f. to fire

FUGITIVE, S.

Ge. 4: 12. a f. shalt thou be
Ge. 4: 14. I sh. be a f. and a vagabond
Ju. 12: 4. Ye Gileadites are f-s
2 K. 25: 11. f-s that fell to the king
Is. 15: 5. his f-s shall flee to Zoar
Eze. 17: 21. his f-s shall fall by sword

FULFIL.

Ge. 29: 27. f. her week, and we will give
Ex. 5: 13. f. your daily task
23: 26. number of thy days I will f.
1 K. 2: 27. that he might f. word of L.
1 Ch. 22: 13. if takest heed to f. stat-s.
2 Ch. 36: 21. to f. threescore and ten years
Jb. 39: 2. Canst number months they f.?
Ps. 20: 4. L. grant to f. thy counsel
5. the Lord f. all thy petitions
145: 19. He will f. desire of them fear
Mat. 3: 15. becometh us to f. righte.
5: 17. not come to destroy, but f.
Ac. 13: 22. Da., who shall f. my will
Ro. 2: 27. uncirc. if it f. the law
13: 14. for the flesh, to f. the lusts
Ga. 5: 16. ye sh. not f. lusts of flesh
6: 2. burdens, and so f. law of C.
Ep. 4: †10. that he might f. all things
Ph. 2: 2. f. ye my joy, that ye be
Col. 1: 25. given to me, to f. word
4: 17. f. the ministry, 2 Ti. 4: † 5.
2 Th. 1: 11. f. all pleasure of his will
Ja. 2: 8. If ye f. the royal law
Re. 17: 17. in hearts to f. his will

FULFILLED.

Ge. 25: 24. when her days were f.
29: 21. give wife, my days are f.
28. and Jac. did so, and f. her week
50: 3. forty days were f. for him, so are f. the days
Ex. 5: 14. Wh. ye not f. your task?
7: 25. seven days f. aft. L. smitten
Le. 12: 4. until purification be f., 6.
Nu. 6: 13. when days of separa. f., 5.
32: †11. bec. they have not f. aft. me
De. 1: †36. Caleb f. to go after me
1 S. 18: †26. the days were not f.
2 S. 7: 12. when days be f. and
14: 22. king f. request of servant
1 K. 8: 15. hath with his hand f. it
24. f. it with thy hand, 2 Ch. 6: 15.
11: † 6. Sol. f. not after the Lord
2 Ch. 6: 4 L. hath f. that he spake
Ezr. 1: 1. word of L. might be f.
Jb. 36: 17. hast f. judgm. of wicked
Je. 44: 25. ye and your wives have f.
La. 2: 17. hath f. word he com-d
4: 18. our days are f. end is come
Eze. 5: 2. when days of siege are f.
Da. 4: 33. same hour was thing f.
10: 3. till three whole weeks f.
Mat. 1: 22 that it might be f., 2: 15, 23.-4: 14.-8: 17.-12: 17.-13: 35.-21: 4.-26: 56.-27: 35. Jn. 12: 38.-15: 25.-17: 12.-18: 9, 32.-19: 24, 28, 36.
2: 17. was f. that spoken, 27: 9.
5: 18. in no wise pass till all be f.
13: 14. is f. prophecy of Esaias
24: 34. shall not pass till all these things be f., Lu. 21: 32.
Mk. 1: 15. time is f. kingd. of God
13: 4. what sign when all sh. be f.?
Lu. 1: 20. my words sh. be f. in season
2: 43. had f. days, they returned
21: 22. that all are written may be f.
24. until times of Gentiles be f.
22: 16. not eat until be f. in k-m
24: 44. all must be f. spoken by Mos.
Jn. 3: 29. this my joy theref. is f.
17: 13. have my joy f. in thems.
Ac. 3: 18. what G. shewed, he so f.
9: 23. many days f. Jews took coun.
12: 25. Paul and Barna. f. ministry
13: 25. and as John f. his course
27. have f. them in condem-g him
29. when had f. all written of him
33. God hath f. the same unto us
14: 26. for the work which they f.
Ro. 8: 4. righte. law might be f. in us

Ro.13:8.that loveth ano. hath f.law
2 Co. 10 : 6. when obedience is f.
Ga. 5 : 14. the law is f. in one word
Re. 6:11. until killing of breth.be f.
15:8. till the seven plagues were f.
17:17. until the words of God be f.
20:3. deceive no more, till 1000 yrs.
See SCRIPTURE, S. [be f.

FULFILLING.

Ps. 148 : 8. stormy wind f. his word
Ro. 13 : 10. love is the f. of the law
Ep. 2 : 3. f. the desires of the flesh

FULL.

Ge.14:10.Siddim was f. of slime pits
15:16.iniq.of Amorites is not yet f.
35 : 29. Isaac being f. of days, died
41 : 7. thin devoured 7 f. ears, 22.
43:21.ev. man's money in f.weight
Ex. 8 : 21. houses shall be f. of flies
16 : 33. put a homer f. of manna
22 : 3. he sho. make f. restitution
Le.2:14. off. corn beaten out f. ears
16 : 12. censer f. of coals, hands f.
19 : 29. land became f. of wickedn.
Nu. 7 : 13. both f. of fine flour, 19,
25, 31, 37, 43, 49, 55, 61, 67, 73, 79
22 : 18. if house f. of silver, 24:13.
De.6:11.houses f. of all good things,
when thou shalt be f., 8:10,12.
11:15.grass, that thou mayest be f.
21 : 13. sh. bewail her fa. f. month
33:23. Naphtali f. of blessing of L.
34 : 9. Joshua was f. of the Spirit
Ju. 6 : 38. wringed dew, a bowl f.
16 : 27. house was f. of men and
Ru. 1 : 21. I went out f. and Lord
2 : 12. a f. reward be given thee
1 S. 2 : 5. that were f. hired out
18:27. gave them in f. tale to king
27 : 7. in country of Philis. f. year
2 S. 8 : 2. one f. line to keep alive
23 : 11. f. of lentiles, 1 Ch. 11 : 13.
1 K. 17 : † 15. she did eat a f. year
2 K. 3:16. Make valley f. of ditches
4 : 6 when vessels were f. she said
: 17. mountain was f. of horses
: 15. all way was f. of garments
9 : 24. Jehu drew bow with f. [to
strength
10:21. house of Baal f. fr. one end
1 Ch. 21 : 22. grant it for f. price
24. I will buy it for a f. price
Es. 3 : 5. was Haman f. of wrath
5 : 9. he was f. of indignation ag.
Jb.7:4.I am f. of tossings to and fro
10 : 15. I am f. of confusion, see
11 : 2. sho. man f. of talk be justi.
14 : 1. man of few days f. of troub.
20:11. His bones f. of sins of youth
21 : 23. one dieth in his f. strength
24. His breasts are f. of milk
32:18. I am f. of matter. the Spirit
36:16. that on table be f. of fatness
Ps. 17 : 14. they are f. of children
69 : 20. I am f. of heaviness
73:10.waters of a f. cup are wrung
74:20. dark places are f. of cruelty
78:25. angels' food, sent meat to f.
104:16.The trees of L. are f. of sap
127:5. Happy th.hath his quiver f.
144:13.That our garners may be f.
Pr. 17 : 1. than house f. of sacrifi.
25 : † 17. lest he be f. and hate thee
27 : 7. f. soul loatheth honeycomb
20. Hell and destruction never f.
30 : 9. lest I be f. and deny thee
Ec. 1:7. run into sea, yet sea not f.
8. All things are f. of labour
4:6.than both hands f. with travail
11 : 3.If clouds be f. they empty
Is. 1 : 11. I am f. of burnt off-gs
21. faithful city f. of judgment
11:9. earth sh. be f. of knowl. of L.
13 : 21. be f. of doleful creatures
22:2. f. of stirs | 7. f. of chariots
25 : 6. fat things, feast f. of marrow
28 : 8. For all tables are f. of vomit
Is.30:27.his lips are f.of indignation
Je. 4 : 12. a f. wind fr. those places
5 : 7. when I had fed them to the f.
35:5. bef. Rechabites pots f.of wine
La. 1 : 1. city solitary was f. of peo.
3 : 30. he is filled f. with reproach
Eze. 10 : 4. court f. of brightness of
17 : 3. eagle with wings f. of feath.
19 : 10. she fruitful f. of branches
28:12. f. of wisd. perfect in beauty
32 : 6. rivers shall be f. of thee
15. destitute of that it was f.
37 : 1. in valley wh. was f. of bones
39:19. sh. eat fat till ye be f. [to f.
Da. 8 : 23. when transg-rs are come
Jo. 2 : 24. floors sh. be f. of wheat
Mi. 3 : 8. I am f. of power by Spirit
6 : 12. rich men are f. of violence
Ha. 3 : 3. earth was f. of his praise
Zch. 8 : 5. streets be f. of boys and
Mat. 6 : 22. thy body shall be f. of
light, Lu. 11 : 34, 36.
23. whole body be f. of darkness
13 : 48. Which, when it was f. they
drew to shore
15:37.that was left seven baskets f.
23 : 25. within are f. of extortion
27. are f. of dead men's bones
28. within ye are f. of hypocrisy
Mk. 4 : 28. after th. f. corn in ear
37. beat into ship, so it was f.
7 : 9. f. well ye reject com-t
15 : 36. filled sponge f. of vinegar
Lu. 1 : 57. now Elizab. f. time came
5 : 12. behold a man f. of leprosy
6:25.Woe unto you f.ye sh.hunger
16 : 20. Lazarus at gate f. of sores
Jn. 1 : 14. dwelt am. us f. of grace
7:8. for my time is not yet f. come
15 : 11. your joy might be f.,16:24.
19 : 29. set a vessel f. of vinegar
21 : 11. drew net f. of gr. fishes
Ac. 2 : 13. These are f. of new wine
28. me f. of joy with thy counten.
6 : 5. Stephen f. of faith, 8.-7 : 55.
7 : 23. when Mo. f. forty years old
9 : 36. Dorcas f. of good works and
13:10.And said, O f. of all subtilty
19 : 28. f. of wrath and cried out
Ro. 1 : 29. being f. of envy, murder
15 : 14. persuad. ye are f. of goodn.
1 Co. 4 : 8. Now ye are f. now rich
Ph. 2:26. for he was f. of heaviness
4 : 12. I am instructed to be f. and
18. I have all and abound, I am f.
2 Ti. 4 : 5. f. proof of thy ministry
Ja. 3 : 8. tongue f. of deadly poison
17. wisd. fr. above is f. of mercy
1 Pe.1:8.joy unspeak.and f. of glory
2 Pe. 2 : 14. eyes f. of adultery
1 Jn. 1 : 4. that your joy may be f.
2 Jn. 8. that we receive f. reward
12. to face, that our joy may be f.
Re. 4 : 6. four beasts f. of eyes, 8.
5:8.having golden vials f.of odours
15:7. seven golden vials f. of wrath
16 : 10. his kingd. was f. of darkn.
17 : 3. wom. f. of names of blasph.
4.a golden cup f. of abominations
21 : 9. seven vials f. of 7 plagues
See AGE, ASSURANCE, BASKETS, BLOOD, COMPASSION, DAYS, END, EYES, FURY, HOLY GHOST, HOUSE, INCENSE, MONTH, WEEKS, YEAR, S.

Is FULL.

2 K. 4 : 4. shalt set aside that i. f.
Ps. 10 : 7. i.f. of cursing, Ro. 3:14.
26 : 10. right hand i. f. of bribes
29 : 4. voice of L. i. f. of majesty
33 : 5. earth i. f. of goodness of L.
48:10.thy right hand i.f.of righte.
65:9. river of God, wh. i.f. of wat.
75 : 8. wine is red, i. f. of mixture
88 : 3. my soul i. f. of troubles
104 : 24. the earth i.f. of thy riches
119:64. the earth i.f. of thy mercy
Ec. 9 : 3. heart of men i. f. of evil
10 : 14. A fool i. f. of words, man
Is. 2 : 7. i. f. of silv. i. f. of horses
8. their land i. f. of idols, they
6 : 3. whole earth i. f. of his glory
Je.5:27. as cage i.f. of birds, houses
6 : 11. with him that i. f. of days
23:10.For the land i.f.of adulterers
Eze.7:23.land i.f.of crimes, city i.f.
9 : 9. land i.f. of blood, city i.f. of
Jo. 3 : 13. press i. f. fats overflow
Am. 2 : 13. cart that i.f. of sheaves
Na. 3 : 1. it i. all f. of lies
Lu.11:34.i.f. of light, i.f. of darkn.
39. inward part i. f. of ravening

To the FULL.

Ex. 16:3. sat and did eat bread t. f.
8. when L. shall give bread t. f.
Le. 26 : 5. ye shall eat bread t. f.

FULLER, S.

2 K. 18 : 17. stood in the highway
of the f-s field, Is. 7 : 3.-36 : 2.
Mal. 3:2. like refiner's fire, f-s soap
Mk. 9 : 3. no f. on earth can white

FULLY.

Nu. 7 : 1. Mo. had f. set up tabern.
14 : 24. Caleb th. followed me f.
Ru.2:11. It hath f. been shewed me
1 K. 11 : 6. Sol. went not f. after L.
Ec.8:11. the heart is f. set to do evil
Je. 12 : † 6. they cried after thee f.
Na. 1:10. devoured as stubble f. dry
Ac. 2 : 1. day of Pente. was f. come
Ro. 4 : 21. being f. persuaded that
14:5. Let every man be f. persuad.
15 : 19. I have f. preached gospel
Col. 1 : † 25. a minister f. to preach
2 Ti. 3:10. hast f. known my doctr.
4:17. th. preaching might be f.kn.
Re. 14 : 18 thrust sickle, grapes f.

FULNESS. [ripe

Ge. 48 : † 19. his seed a f. of nations
Ex. 22:†29. not delay to offer thy f.
Nu. 18 : 27. as f. of the winepress
De. 22 : † 9. lest f. of thy seed be
33:16. prec. things of earth, and f.
1 S. 28 : † 20. Saul fell with f. of his
1 Ch. 16 : 32. let the sea roar and
the f., Ps. 96 : 11.-98 : 7.
Jb. 20 : 22. in f. shall be in straits
Ps. 16 : 11. in thy pres. is f. of joy
24 : 1. earth is the Lord's and its
f., 1 Co. 10 : 26, 28.
50:12. world is mine, and f.,89:11.
Is. 6 : † 3. his glory is f. of earth
8 :† 8. f. of the breadth of thy land
34 : † 1. let earth hear and the f.
42 :† 10. that go down to sea and f.
Je. 8:†16. have devoured la. and f.
47:†2.wat-s sh.overflow land and f.
Eze. 16 : 49. iniq. of Sod., f. of bread
12 : † 19. land was desolate and the
f., 19 : 7.-30 : † 12.
Am. 6:†8. will deliver up city, and f.
Mi. 1 : † 2. hearken, O earth, and f.
Jn. 1 : 16. of his f. have we received
Ro. 11 : 12. how much more their f.!
25. until f. of Gent. be come in
15 : 29. I shall come in f. of gospel
Ga. 4 : 4. when f. of time was come
Ep. 1 : 10. in f. of times might gath.
23. f. of him that filleth all in all
3:19. be filled with all the f. of God
4 : 13. come unto stature of f. of C.
Col. 1:19. in him should all f. dwell
2 :9. in him dwelleth f. of Godhead

FUNDAMENT.

Ju. 3:†22. dagger, it came out at f.

FURBISH, ED. [dines

Je. 46 : 4. f. spears, put on brigan-
Eze. 21:9. sw. is sharp. and f-d, 10.
11. given to be f-d | 28. sword f-d

FURIOUS.

Pr. 22 : 24. with f. man shalt not go
29:22.f.man aboundeth in transgr.
Eze. 5 : 15. judgm. in f. rebukes,
Da. 2 : 12. king was very f. [25 : 17.

Na. 1: 2. L. revengeth, and is f.

FURIOUSLY.

2 K. 9: 20. like Jehu, he driveth f.
Eze. 23:25. they sh. deal f. with thee

FURLONGS. [60 f.

Lu. 24: 13. Emmaus from Jerusa.
Jn. 6: 19. rowed 5 and 20 or 30 f.
11: 18. Bethany nigh Jerus. 15 f.
Re. 14: 20. blood by space of 1600 f.
21: 16. he measured city, 12,000 f.

FURNACE, S.

Ge. 15:17. smoking f. burning lamp
19: 28. went up as smoke of a f.
Ex. 9: 8. handfuls of ashes of f.
10. they took ashes of the f.
19: 18. smoke asc-d as smoke of f.
De. 4: 20. hath taken you out of f.
1 K. 8: 51. fr. midst of f., Je. 11: 4.
Ne. 3: 11. repaired tower of the f-s
12: 38. fr. tower of f-s unto wall
Ps. 12:6. as silver tried in f. of earth
Pr. 17: 3. for silv., f. for gold, 27:21.
Is. 31: 9. fire in Zion, his f. in Jerus.
48: 10. chosen thee in f. of afflic.
Eze. 22: 18. Isr. dross in midst of f.
20. will gather you as tin in f.
22. As silver is melted in f.
Da. 3: 6. be cast into fiery f., 11.
Mat. 13:42. cast th. into f. of fire, 50.
Re. 1: 15. feet, as if burned in a f.
9: 2. arose a smoke, as of great f.

FURNISH, ED.

De.15:14. Thou shalt f. him liberally
1 K.9:11. Hiram f-d Sol. with cedar
Ps. 78: 19. Can G. f. table in wild.?
Pr. 9: 2. hath f-d her table
Is. 65: 11. that f. the drink offering
Je. 46:19. f. thyself to go into captiv.
Mat. 22:10. wedding f-d with guests
Mk. 14:15. shew room f-d, Lu. 22:12.
2 Ti. 3: 17. f-d unto all good works

FURNITURE.

Ge. 31: 34. put them in camels' f.
Ex. 31: 7. taberu. and his f., 39:33.
8. table and his f. | 9. altar with f.
35: 14. the candlestick and his f.
Na. 2: 9. none end of pleasant f.

FURROW.

1 S. 14: †14. slew 20 within half a f.
Jb. 39:10. canst bind unicorn in f.?

FURROWS.

Jb. 31: 38. or the f. complain
Ps. 65: 10. thou settlest f. thereof
129: 3. they made long their f.
Eze. 17: 7. might water it by f. of
10. wither in f. where it grew
Ho. 10: 4. judgm. as hemlock in f.
10. bind thems. in their two f.
12: 11. their altars as heaps in f.

FURTHER. [Adv.]

Nu. 22: 26. angel went f. and [peo.
De. 20: 8. officers sh. speak f. unto
1 S. 10: 22. they inquired of L. f.
Jb. 38: 11. hitherto shalt come, no f.
40: 5. twice, I will proceed no f.
Ec. 8: 17. f. tho. a wise man think
12: 12. f., my son, be admonished
Mat. 26: 39. he went a little f. and
65. what f. need have we of witnesses? Mk. 14: 63. Lu. 22: 71.
Mk. 1: 19. when had gone little f.
5: 35. why troublest mast. any f.?
Lu. 24:28. as tho. he wo. have gone
Ac. 4: 17. spread no f. am. peo. [f.
21. when had f. threatened them
12: 3. Herod proceeded f. to take
21:28. f. he bro-t Greeks into tem.
24:4. I be not f. tedious unto thee
27: 28. gone little f. they sounded
2 Ti. 3: 9. they sh. proceed no f.
He. 7: 11. what f. need ano. priest

FURTHER, ED.

Ezr. 8:36. f-d people and house of G.
Ps. 140: 8. f. not his wicked device

FURTHERANCE.

Ph. 1: 12. happ-d unto f. of gospel
25. sh. abide with you for your f.

FURTHERMORE.

Ex. 4: 6. L. said f. to Moses, Put
Eze. 8: 6. Lord said f. to Ezekiel

FURY. [aw.

Ge. 27: 44. until thy bro.'s f. turn
Le. 26: 28. contrary to you in f.
Jb. 20: 23. G. shall cast f. of wrath
Is. 27:4. f. is not in me, who would
34: 2. his f. upon all their armies
51: 13. feared bec. of f. of oppressor; where is f. of oppressor?
17. O Jerus., hast drunk cup of f.
20. they are full of the f. of the L.
22. dregs of cup of f. no more dr.
59: 18. will repay f. to his adversa.
63: 3. I will trample them in my f.
5. bro-t salv., my f. it upheld me
6. will make them drunk in my f.
66: 15. to render his anger with f.
Je. 4: 4. lest my f. come like fire
6: 11. I am full of f. of the Lord
21: 5. I will fight against you in f.
12. lest my f. go out like fire
23: 19. whirlw. is gone in f., 30:23.
25: 15. Take the winecup of this f.
32:31. city been a provoca. of my f.
37. driven them in my f.
33: 5. whom I have slain in f.
36: 7. great is f. L. hath pronoun.
La. 4: 11. The L. hath accompl. f.
Eze.5:13. cause my f. to rest upon th.
know when I have accompl. f.
15. when execute judgm-ts in f.
6: 12. thus will I accomplish my f.
8: 18. thf. will I deal in f. my eye
13: 13. rend with a wind in my f.
16: 38. I will give thee blood in f.
42. make my f. tow. thee to rest
19:12. she was plucked up in my f.
20: 33. with f. will I rule over you
21: 17. I will cause my f. to rest
22: 20. so will I gather you in f.
24:8. That it might cause f. to come
13. till I have caused f. to rest
25: 14. do in Edom acc. to my f.
36: 6. I have spoken in my f.
38: 18. that my f. shall come up
Da. 3:13. Neb-r in his f. command-
19. Then was Neb-r full of f. [ed.
8:6. he ran unto him in f. of power
9:16. let thy f. be turned fr. Jerus.
11:44. he sh. go forth with great f.
Mi.5:15. will execute f. upon heath.
Na. 1: † 2. L. revengeth, th. hath f.
Zch. 8: 2. was jealous with great f.
See POUR, POURED, POURING.

G.

GA'AL.

Ju. 9:41. Zebul thrust out G. | 26, 28, 30, 31, 35, 36, 37, 39.

GA'ASH.

Jos. 24: 30. on north side of hill G., Ju. 2:9. 2 S. 23:30. 1 Ch. 11:32.

GA'BA.

Jos. 18: 24. cities of Benj. were G.
Ezr. 2: 26. chil. of G., 621. Ne. 7:30.

GAB'BAI.

Ne. 11: 8. And after him G.

GAB'BATHA.

Jn. 19:13. called pavement, in Heb.,

GA'BRIEL. [G.

Da. 8:16. G. make this man underst.
9:21. praying, man G. touched me
Lu. 1: 19. I am G. that stand in
26. G. was sent from God to Mary

GAD.

Ge. 30: 11. she called his name G.
35: 26. the sons of Zilpah; G.
46: 16. sons of G., Nu. 1: 24-26: 15, 18. 1 Ch. 12: 14.
49: 19. G. a troop shall overcome
Nu. 1: 14. prince of G., 2: 14.-7:42.
32: 1. G. had multitude of cattle
2. chil. of G. spake to Moses
29. if chil. of G. pass over Jordan
Nu. 32: 33. Moses gave to G. Sihon
34: 14. chil. of G. have received their inheri., Jos. 13: 28.-18: 7.
De. 27: 13. upon Ebal to curse G.
33: 20. Blessed be he enlargeth G.
Jos. 4: 12. chil. of G. passed over
22: 9. chil. of G. retur. out of Shi.
1 S. 13:7. Hebr-s went to land of G.
2 S. 24: 5. in midst of river of G.
Je. 49: 1. why king inherit G.?
Eze. 48: 27. portion for G.
34. one gate of G.

Tribe of GAD.

Nu. 1: 25. numb. t. o. G. 45,650
2: 14. t. o. G. shall set forward, capt. of G. shall be, 10: 20.
13: 15. of t. o. G. to spy land
34: 14. the t. o. G. have received their inherit., Jos. 13: 24.
Jos. 20: 8. out of t. o. G. Ramoth in Gil., 21:7, 38. 1 Ch. 6: 63, 80.
Re. 7: 5. of t. o. G. sealed 12,000

GAD. [The prophet.]

1 S. 22:5. prophet G. said unto Da.
2 S. 24: 11. G. David's seer, 1 Ch. 21: 9, 18.
14. G. I am in a great strait
1 Ch. 29:29. acts of Da. in book of G.
2 Ch. 29: 25. acc. to command of G.

GADARENES'.

Mk. 5:1. country of G., Lu. 8:26, 37.

GADDEST.

Je. 2:36. why g. thou about so much

GAD'DI.

Nu. 13: 11. G. the son of Susi

GAD'DIEL.

Nu. 13: 10. G. the son of Sodi

GA'DI.

2 K. 15:14. Menahem son of G., 17.

GAD'ITE, S.

De. 3: 12. land gave I unto G-s, 16.
Jos. 22: 1. Joshua called the G-s
2 S. 23: 36. Bani G. one of David's
2 K. 10: 33. Hazael smote the G-s
1 Ch. 12: 8. of G-s separated to Da.
26:32. David made rulers over G-s

GA'HAM. [G.

Ge. 22: 24. Reumah bare Tebah and

GA'HAR. [7: 49.

Ezr. 2:47. Nethinim; chil. of G., Ne.

GAIN, S.

Ju. 5:19. kings of Canaan took no g.
Jb. 22:3. is it g. to make way perf.?
Pr. 1:19. ways of ev. one greedy of g.
3:14. the g. is better than fine gold
15:27. th. is greedy of g. troubleth
28:8. that by unjust g. increaseth
Is. 33:15. despiseth g. of oppression
56:11. ev. one for his g. fr. quarter
Eze. 22:13. smitten at dishonest g.
27. like wolves to get dishonest g.
Da. 11: 39. sh. divide land for g.
Mi. 4:13. will consecrate g. unto L.
Ha. 2:†9. woe to him gaineth evil g.
Ac. 16: 16. bro-t masters much g.
19. saw hope of g-s was gone
19: 24. no small g. to craftsmen
2 Co. 12:17. Did I make a g. of you?
18. Did Titus make a g. of you?
Ph. 1:21. to live is C., and to die is g.
3: 7. what things were g. to me
1 Ti. 6: 5. supposing g. is godliness
6. godlin. with content is great g.
Ja. 4:13. there buy, sell, and get g.

GAIN. [Verb.]

Da. 2: 8. I know ye would g. time
Mat. 16:26. what profited if g. world, and lose? Mk. 8:36. Lu. 9:25.
1 Co. 9:19. that I might g. the more
20. might g. Jews | 22. g. weak
21. g. them that are without law

GAINED. [hath g.?

Jb. 27:8. what hope hypocrite, tho.
Eze. 22:12. greedily g. by extortion
Mat. 18: 15. thou hast g. thy bro.
25: 17. received two g. two, 22.
20. I have g. besides five talents

Lu. 19 : 15. how much every man g.
16. L., thy pound hath g. ten, 18.
Ac. 27 : 21. to have g. this harm
2 Jn. † 8. lose not things ye have g.

GAINSAY. [to g.
Lu. 21 : 15. adversaries not be able

GAINSAYERS.
Tit. 1 : 9. be able to convince the g.

GAINSAYING. [g.
Ac. 10 : 29. Theref. came I without
Ro. 10 : 21. hands unto g. people
Tit. 2 : † 9. to please masters, not g.
Jude 11. perished in the g. of Core

GA'IUS. [edonia
Ac. 19 : 29. having caught G. of Mac-
20 : 4. accompanied him G. of Derbe
Ro. 16 : 23. G., mine host, saluteth
1 Co. 1 : 14. I baptized none but G.
3 Jn. 1. elder unto well beloved G.

GA'LAL. [11 : 17.
1 Ch. 9 : 15. of Levites, G. | 16. Ne.

GALA'TIA, ANS. [18 : 23.
Ac. 16 : 6. gone thro-t region of G.,
1 Co. 16 : 1. to churches of G., Ga. 1 : 2.
Ga. 3 : 1. O fool-h G-s, who bewitched
2 Ti. 4 : 10. departed; Crescens to G.
1 Pe. 1 : 1. strangers throughout G.

GALBANUM. [g.
Ex. 30 : 34. Take sweet spices, stacte,

GAL'EED. [48.
Ge. 31 : 47. heap, Jacob called it G.,

GALILE'AN, S.
Mk. 14 : 70. thou art a G., Lu. 22 : 59.
Lu. 13 : 1. some told him of the G-s
2. these G-s sinners above all G-s?
23 : 6. Pilate asked wheth. man a G.?
Jn. 4 : 45. G-s received him, having
Ac. 2 : 7. are not these which speak

GAL'ILEE. [G-s?
Jos. 21 : 32. Kedesh in G. to be city
of refuge, 20 : 7. 1 Ch. 6 : 76.
1 K. 9 : 11. gave Hiram 20 cities in G.
2 K. 15 : 29. Tiglath-pileser took G.
Is. 9 : 1. grievously afflict her in G.
Mat 2 : 22. Joseph turned into G.
4 : 15. beyond Jordan, G. of Gentiles
25. multitudes from G., Mk. 3 : 7.
26 : 32. I will go before you into G.,
28 : 7.-Mk. 14 : 28.-16 : 7. [G.
69. Thou also wast with Jesus of
27 : 55. women wh. followed Jesus
from G., Mk. 15 : 41. Lu. 23 : 49, 55.
28 : 10. tell brethren go into G., 16.
Mk. 1 : 28. his fame about G. [4 : 44.
39. he preached throu-t G., Lu.
6 : 21. a supper to his lords of G.
9 : 30. passed through G., Lu. 17 : 11.
Lu. 1 : 26. Gabriel unto a city of G.
2 : 4. Joseph fr G. unto Beth-le. | 39.
4 : 31. of G., 8 : 26. Jn. 12 : 21.
5 : 17. doctors of every town of G.
23 : 5. all Jewry, beginning from G.
6. When Pilate heard of G. he ask-
24 : 6. how he spake when in G. [ed
Jn. 4 : 3. He departed into G., 43, 45.
7 : 9. he abode still in G [46, 47, 54.
41. Shall Christ come out of G.?
52. thou of G.? out of G. no proph.
Ac. 1 : 11. Ye of G. | 5 : 37. Judas of G.
9 : 31. had churches rest thro-t G.
10 : 37. word which began from G.
13 : 31. seen of them came from G.
See CANA, JESUS with Galilee
See HEROD, SEA, By the SEA.

GALL.
De. 29 : 18. lest be a root that bear g.
32 : 32. their grapes are grapes of g.
Jb. 16 : 13. he poureth out my g.
20 : 14. his meat is the g. of asps
25. sword cometh out of his g.
Ps. 69 : 21. They gave me g. for meat
Je. 8 : 14. G. hath giv. us water of g.
9 : 15. I will give water of g., 23 : 15.
La. 3 : 5. hath compassed me with g.
19. rememb-g wormwood and g.
Am. 6 : 12. have turned judgm. into g.
Mat. 27 : 34. vinegar mingled with g.
Ac. 8 : 23. thou art in g. of bitter- [ness

GALLANT.
Is. 33 : 21. nor sh. g. ship pass there- [by

GALLANTS.
Na. 2 : † 5. he shall recount his g.
Zch. 11 : † 2. bec. the g. are spoiled

GALLERY, IES.
Can. 1 : † 17. beams cedar, g-s of fir
7 : 5. king is held in the g-s
Eze. 41 : 15. he measured the g-s
42 : 3. was g. ag. g. in stories, 5.-41 : [16.

GALLEY.
Is. 33 : 21. wherein shall go no g.

GAL'LIM.
1 S. 25 : 44. Michal to Phalti of G.
Is. 10 : 30. lift voice, O dau. of G.

GAL'LIO.
Ac. 18 : 12. G. was deputy of Achaia
17. G. cared for none of those thi., [14.

GALLOWS.
Es. 5 : 14. g. be 50 cubits, 7 : 9.
6 : 4. spake to hang Mordecai on g.
7 : 10. hanged Haman on g., 8 : 7.
9 : 13. let H.'s sons be hanged on

GAMA'LIEL. [g., 25.
Nu. 1 : 10. G. son of Pedahzur, 2 :
20.-7 : 54, 59.-10 : 23.
Ac. 5 : 34. stood up a Pharisee G.
22 : 3. was brought up at feet of G.

GAM'MADIM.
Eze. 27 : 11. G. were in thy towers

GA'MUL.
1 Ch. 24 : 17. two and 20th lot to G.

GANGRENE. [a g.
2 Ti. 2 : † 17 word will eat as doth

GAP, S. [to g-s
Eze. 13 : 5. Ye have not gone up in-
22 : 30. a man that sho. stand in g.

GAPED, ETH.
Jb. 7 : † 2. as servant g-h aft. shadow
16 : 10. have g. upon me, Ps. 22 : 13.

GARDEN.
Ge. 2 : 8. L. G. planted g. eastward
9. tree of life in midst of g.
10. river out of Eden to water g.
15. God took man put him in g.
16. Of ev. tree of g. eat, 3 : 2. [3.
3 : 1. sh. not eat of ev. tree of g.,
8. voice of L. walking in g., 10.
3 : 23. Lord sent him forth fr. g.
24. at g. of Eden cherubim and
13 : 10. plain of Jordan as g. of L.
De. 11 : 10. and waterest it as a g.
1 K. 21 : 2. may have it for g. of herbs
2 K. 9 : 27. fled by way of g. house
21 : 18. buried in the g., 26.
25 : 4. by king's g., Ne. 3 : 15. Je. 39 : 4.-
Es. 7 : 7. palace g., 8.-1 : 5. [52 : 7.
Jb. 8 : 16. his branch shooteth in g.
Can. 4 : 12. A g. inclosed is my sister
16. blow upon g. let him come
5 : 1. I am come into my g. [into g.
6 : 2. My beloved is gone into g., 11.
Is. 1 : 8. dau. of Zion is as lodge in g.
30. ye be as g. hath no water
51 : 3. make desert like g. of God
58 : 11. shalt be like a watered g.
61 : 11. g. causeth things to spring
Je. 31 : 12. souls be as watered g.
La. 2 : 6. taken t-ber. as it were of g.
Eze. 28 : 13. been in Eden g. of God
31 : 8. cedars in g. of G. not hide him
9. trees in g. of God envied him
36 : 35. desol. land is like g. of Eden
Jo. 2 : 3. land is as the g. of Eden
Lu. 13 : 19. wh. a man cast into g.
Jn. 18 : 1. over Cedron, where was g.
26. did not I see thee in the g.
19 : 41. was a g. and in g. a sepul.

GARDENS.
Nu. 24 : 6. tents as g. by river side
Ec. 2 : 5. I made me g. and orchards
Can. 4 : 15. A fountain of g. a well
6 : 2. to feed in the g. gather lilies
8 : 13. thou in g. cause me to hear
Is. 1 : 29. ye sh. be confound. for g.
65 : 3. a people that sacrificeth in g.
Is. 66 : 17. that purify thems. in the g.
Je. 29 : 5. plant g. and eat fruit, 28.
Am. 4 : 9. blasting, when g. incr-d
9 : 14. they shall make g. eat fruit

GARDENER.
Jn. 20 : 15. She supposing he the g.

GA'REB. [Person, Place.]
2 S. 23 : 38. 1 Ch. 11 : 40. Je. 31 : 39.

GARLANDS.
Ac. 14 : 13. priest bro-t oxen and g.

GARLICK. [E.
Nu. 11 : 5. remem. g. we did eat in

GARMENT. [a g.
Ge. 9 : 23. Shem and Japhet took
25 : 25. first came red, like hairy g.
39 : 12. she caught Joseph by his
15. left his g. and fled, 18. [g., 13.
16. she laid up g. until lord came
Le. 6 : 10. shall put on his linen g.
27. sprinkled of blood upon any g.
13 : 47. g. wherein is leprosy, 49.
51. if plague be spread in the g.
52. burn g. | 53. not spread in g.
56. rend it out of g.
57. if it appear still in the g.
58. wash g. either warp or
59. law of leprosy in a g., 14 : 55.
15 : 17. g. wh-on is seed of [22 : 11.
19 : 19. nei. g. mingled upon thee. De.
De. 22 : 5. man not put on wom.'s g.
Jos. 7 : 21. a goodly Babylonish g.
24. Joshua took Achan, and g.
Ju. 8 : 25. spread g. cast earrings
2 S. 13 : 18. Tamar had a g. of divers
19. rent her g. and went crying
20 : 8. Joab's g. was girded unto
him [new g.
1 K. 11 : 29. Jerob. clad him-s. with
30. g. and rent it in 12 pieces
2 K. 4 : † 42. bro-t ears of corn in g.
9 : 13. took every man his g. and
Ezr. 9 : 3. I heard this I rent my g.
5. having rent g. I fell upon kne-s
Es. 8 : 15. Mord-i went with g. of pur.
Jb. 13 : 28. as a g. that is motheaten
30 : 18. by disease is my g. changed
38 : 9. when I made cloud the g.
14. they stand as a g.
41 : 13. Who discover face of his g.?
Ps 69 : 11. I made sackcl. my g.
73 : 6. violence cover-h them as g.
102 : 26. all shall wax old like a g.,
Is. 50 : 9.-51 : 6. He. 1 : 11.
104 : 2. coverest with light, as a g.
6. coveredst it with deep as a g.
109 : 18. clothed with cursing as g.
19. let it be unto him as g. [13.
Pr. 20 : 16. his g. th. is surety, 27 :
25 : 20. th. taketh g. in cold weath.
30 : 4. who bound waters in a g.?
Is. 51 : 8. moth sh. eat them like g.
61 : 3 give g. of praise for spirit of
Je. 43 : 12. as shepherd putteth on g.
Eze. 18 : 7. cov-d naked with g., 16.
Da. 7 : 9. whose g. white as snow
Mi. 2 : 8. ye pull off robe with g.
Hag. 2 : 12. holy flesh in skirt of g.
Zch. 13 : 4. wear a rough g. to deceive
Mal. 2 : 16. for one covereth violence
with his g. [2 : 21. Lu. 5 : 36.
Mat. 9 : 16. new cloth to old g., Mk.
20. touched hem of his g., 21.-
14 : 36. Mk. 5 : 27.-6 : 56. Lu 8 : 44.
22 : 11. had not on a wedding g., 12.
Mk. 10 : 50. Bartim. casting aw. his g.
13 : 16. not turn back to take g.
16 : 5. young man with a white g.
Lu. 22 : 36. let him sell g. and buy
Ac 12 : 8. Cast thy g. about thee
Jude 23. hating g. spotted by flesh
Re. 1 : 13. Son of man clothed with

GARMENTS. [a g.
Ge. 35 : 2. be clean, and change g.
38 : 14. Tamar put widow's g. off
49 : 11. washed his g. in wine [19.
Ex. 28 : 3. Aaron's g. to consecrate,
4.-29 : 5.-35 : 19.-39 : 41.

Ex. 29:21. sprinkle blood upon Aaron's g. upon g. of his sons (4), Le. 8 : 2, 30. [to make g.
31 : 10. I have given them wisdom
Le. 6 : 11. put off his g. put on other g., 16 : 23, 24.
21 : 10. consecrated to put on g.
Nu. 15 : 38. fringes in borders of g.
20 : 26. strip Aaron of g. put them
28. Moses stripped Aaron of g. put
Jos. 9:5. Gibeonites bro-t old g., 13.
Ju. 14:12. thirty change of g., 13, 19
17:†10. I will give thee order of g.
1 S. 18 : 4. Jona. gave David his g.
2 S. 10:4. cut off g. in middle, 1 Ch. 19.
13:31. David tare his g. and lay [4.
2 K. 5 : 22. give 2 changes of g., 23.
26. is it a time to receive g.?
7 : 15. all the way was full of g.
22: †14. Shallum, keeper of g. [33.
25:29. changed Jehoi.'s g., Je 52:
Ezr. 2: 69. they gave 100 priests' g.
Ne. 7 : 70. Tirshatha 530 priests' g.
72. people gave 67 priests' g.
Jb. 37 : 17. Dost know how thy g.
Ps. 22 : 18. They part my g. [warm
45 : 8. All thy g. smell of myrrh
133:2. ointment went to skirts of g.
Pr. 31 : † 21. clothed with double g.
Ec. 9:8. Let thy g. be always white
Can. 4 : 11. smell of thy g. like Leb.
Is. 9:5. battle is with g. rolled in bl.
52:1. put on beautiful g. O Jerus.
59:6. Their webs sh. not become g.
17. he put on g. of vengeance
61 : 10. clothed me with g. of salva.
63 : 1. cometh with dyed g. fr. Boz.?
2. g. like him treadeth in winefat.
3. blood be sprinkled upon my g.
Je. 36 : 24. not afraid, nor rent g.
La. 4 : 14. could not touch their g.
Eze. 16:18. tookest broid d g., 26:16.
42 : 14. lay g. they ministered in
44 : 17. sh. be clothed with linen g.
19. sh. not sanctify peo. with g.
Da. 3:21 bound in coats and other g.
Jo. 2 : 13 rend hearts, and not g.
Zch. 3:3. Josh. clothed wi. filthy g.
4. Take away filthy g. from him
5. clothed him with g. [11 : 8.
Mat. 21 : 8. spread g. in way, Mk.
23 : 5. enlarge borders of g. [24.
27 : 35. they parted his g., Mk. 15:
Mk. 11:7. cast g. upon colt, Lu. 19:35
Lu. 24 : 4. two men in shining g.
Jn. 13 : 4. laid his g. took a towel
12. taken his g. and was set
19 : 23. Jes. took g. made 4 parts
Ac. 9:39. coats and g. Dorcas made
Ja. 5 : 2. your g. are motheaten
Re 3 : 4. few names not defiled g.
16 : 15. Blessed is he that keepeth his g.

Holy GARMENTS.

Ex. 28 : 2. thou shalt make h. g. for Aaron, 4.-35 : 19.-39 : 1, 41.
29 : 29. h. g. of Aa. sh. be his sons
31 : 10. put wisdom to make h. g.
40 : 13. upon A. h. g. and anoint
Le. 16 : 4. h. g. he shall wash, 32.
Eze. 42 : 14. h. g. wherein they min- [ister

GAR'MITE.

1 Ch. 4:19. Nahum fa. of Keilah, G.

GARNER, S.

Ps. 144 : 13. our g-s may be full
Jo. 1 : 17. the g-s are laid desolate,
Mat. 3 : 12. his wheat into g., Lu. [3:17

GARNISH, ED.

2 Ch. 3:6. g. house with preci. stones
Jb. 26 : 13. By Spirit hath g. heav.
Mat. 12:44. swept and g., Lu. 11:25.
23 : 29. you g. sepul. of righteous
Re. 21:19. foundations of wall are g.

GARRISON, S.

1 S. 10:5. hill where is g. of Philis-s
13 : 3. Jonat. smote g. of Philist-s, 4.
23. g. of Philist-s, 14 : 11, 12. [6.
18. 14 : 1. let us go ov. to Phil's g., 4, 6.
15. g. and spoilers trembled
2 S. 8 : 6. g-s in Syria, 1 Ch. 18 : 6.
14. David put g-s, 1 Ch. 18 : 13.
23:14. g. of Philis. in, 1 Ch. 11:16.
2 Ch. 17 : 2. Jehosh. set g-s in Jud.
Eze. 26 : 11. thy strong g-s go down
2 Co. 11:32. gov. kept city with a g.

GASH'MU = GE'SHEM.

Ne. 6:6. reported and G. saith it, †1.

GAT.

Ge. 19:27. Ab. g. up early in morn.
Ex. 24:18. Moses g. him into mount
Nu. 11 : 30. g. him into the camp
14 : 40. g. them into top of mount
16:27. they g. up fr. tab. of Korah
Ju. 9 : 48. g. him up to mt. Zalmon
51. g. up to top of tower
19:28. rose, and g. him unto his pl.
1 S 13:15. g. him fr. Gilgal unto Gib.
24:22. Da. and men g. up into hold
26:12. they g. them away, 2 S. 4:7.
2 S. 8 : 13. David g. him a name
13 : 29. g. him upon his mule
17:23. g. home | 19:3. g. by stealth
1 K. 1:1. covered but he g. no heat
Ps. 116:3. pains of hell g. hold on me
Ec. 2:8. I g. men singers, and [lives
La. 5 : 9. We g. bread with peril of

GA'TAM. [Ch. 1:36.

Ge. 36 : 11. sons of Eliphaz, G., 1
16. Korah, G. these are the dukes

GATE. [60.

Ge. 22: 17. possess g. of enemies, 24:
28:17. Jac. said, this is g. of heav.
34 : 20. came to g. of the city
24. th. went out of g. of city
Ex. 27 : 16. g. of the court, 14.-38: 15, 18, 31.-39:40.-40:8, 33. Nu.
32:27. in and out fr. g. to g. [4:26.
De. 21:19. fa. sh. bring him unto g.
22:24. bring them both out unto g.
25 : 7. let bro.'s wife go up to g.
Jos. 2:7. gone out, they shut the g.
7 : 5. chased them from before g.
Ju. 16 : 3. Samson took doors of g.
18 : 16. 600 men by enter-g of g.
Ru. 4 : 1. Then went Boaz to the g.
10. name of dead be not cut off fr. [g.
1 S. 4 : 18. Eli fell by side of g.
21 : 13. scrabbled on doors of g.
2 S. 10 : 8. battle at entering of g.
15 : 2. Abs. stood beside the g.
18 : 4. by g. side | 24. over g.
33. k. went to chamber over g.
23:15. water of Beth-lehem by g., 16. 1 Ch. 11:18. [g. of the city
1 K. 17:10. when Elijah came to the
2 K. 7:3. leprous men at ent-g of g.
17. lord to have charge of g.
10 : 8. lay heads at entering of g.
11:19. the way of the g., 25:4. Je. 39:4.-52:7. Eze. 9:2.-44:1, 3, 4.-46 : 8, 9.-47 : 2.
14:13. g. of Ephr. corner g., 2 Ch. 25:23.-26:9. Ne. 12:39. Je. 31:38.
15 : 35. higher g. of house of L.
1 Ch. 26:13. they cast lots for ev. g.
2 Ch. 8:14. porters at ev. g., 35 : 15
32:6. street of g. of city [-12 : 37.
Ne. 2 : 14. g. of the fountain, 3:15.
12 : 39. old g. sheep g. prison g., 3 : 1, 6, 32.
Es. 4 : 2. Mord. before king's g., 6.-6 : 12.
5 : 1. king sat over ag g. of house
Jb. 29:7. When I went out to the g.
Ps. 118:20. this g. of L., righte. enter
Pr. 17 : 19. exalteth his g. seeketh
Can. 7 : 4. eyes like fishpools by g.
Is. 14 : 31. Howl, O g. cry, O city
24:12. g. is smitten with destruct.
28:6. that turn the battle to the g.
Je. 36:10. Baruch read at entry of g.
La. 5 : 14. elders have ceased fr. g.
Eze. 8 : 3. brought me to inner g.
9:2. six men came from higher g.
Eze. 11 : 1 at door of the g. 25 men
40:13. measured the g., 6, 7, 8, to 48.
43:4. glory of L. came by way of g.
44:2. This g. sh. be shut, none ent.
3. prince sh. enter by g., 46:2, 8.
45:19. put blood upon posts of g.
46:1. g. of inner court sh. be shut
2. g. sh. not be shut until evening
3. sh. worship at door of this g.
12. one shall open g. one shut g.
48 : 31. one g. of Reub., one g. of Judah, of Levi | 32, 33, 34.
Ob. 13. not ent-d g. of my people
Mi. 1:9. he is come into g. of my peo.
12. evil came fr. L unto g. of Jerus.
2:13. they have passed through g.
Zch. 14:10. Benj.'s g.—first g., (8)
Mat. 7:13. Enter in at the strait g. wide is the g., 14. Lu. 13 : 24.
Lu. 7 : 12. came nigh g. of city
16:20. beggar, Lazarus laid at his g.
Ac. 10:17. men fr. Cornel. stood bef. g.
12 : 10. came unto iron g. which opened [13.
14. Rhoda op-d not g. for gladn.,
He. 13:12. Jesus suffered without g.
Re. 21:21. every g. was of one pearl
See DUNG, EAST, ENTERING.

At the Gate. [18.

Ge. 23:10. that went in a. g. of city,
2 K. 9:31. as Jehu entered in a. g.
11:6. part sh. be a. g. of Sur, a third a. g. behind guard, 2 Ch. 23:5.
23 : 8. on a man's left hand a. g.
2 Ch. 24:8. set chest a. g. of h. of L.
Es. 5:13. Mord. a. king's g., 6 : 10.
Is. 22:7. horsemen set in array a. g.
Eze. 8 : 5. a. g. of altar this image
Ac. 3:2. they laid daily a. g. of tem.
10. who sat for alms a. g. Beautiful

Fish GATE.

2 Ch. 33:14 built on entering f. g.
Ne. 3 : 3. f. g. sons of Has. build
12 : 39. I after them from ab. f. g.
Zph. 1 : 10. noise of a cry fr. f. g.

High GATE. [g.

2 Ch. 23:20. they came thro. the h.
27:3. Jotham built h. g. of house
Je. 20:2. put Jere. in stocks in h. g.

Horse GATE. [h. g.

2 Ch. 23:15. she was come to ent-g of
Ne. 3:28. fr. h. g. repaired the priests
Je. 31 : 40. unto the corner of h. g.

In the GATE.

Ge. 19 : 1. Lot sat i. g. of Sodom
Ex. 32:26. Mos. stood i. g. of camp
De. 22 : 15. tokens of virginity unto elders i. g.
Ju. 16:2. laid wait for Samson i. g.
Ru. 4 : 11. peo. i. g. said, We wit.
1 S. 9 : 18. drew near to Sam. i. g.
2 S. 3 : 27. took Abner aside i. g.
19 : 8. king sat i. g. they told all
2 K. 7 : 1. for a shekel i. g., 18.
20. people trode upon him i. g.
1 Ch. 9 : 18. i. king's g., Es. 3:2, 3.
Es. 2:19. Mord. sat in king's g., 21.
5 : 9. Haman saw him i. king's g.
Jb. 5 : 4. his chil. are crushed i. g.
31 : 21. when I saw my help i. g.
Ps. 69:12. that sit i. g. speak ag. me
127:5. shall speak with enemies i. g.
Pr. 22:22. nor oppress afflicted i. g.
24 : 7. he openeth not mouth i. g.
Is. 29:21. snare for him reprov. i. g.
Je 7 : 2. Stand i. g. of L.'s house
17 : 19. stand i. g. of the people
37 : 13. when he was i. g. of Benj.
38 : 7. king sitting i. g. of Benj.
39 : 3. all princes of Bab. sat i. g.
Da. 2 : 49. Daniel sat i. g. of king
Am. 5:10. hate him th. rebuketh i. g.
12. turn aside poor i. g.
15. hate evil, establish judgm-t i. [g.

Old GATE.

Ne. 3:6. the o. g. repaired Jehoiada
12:39. priests went above the o. g.

Prison GATE.
Ne. 12: 39. they stood still in p. g.
Sheep GATE.
Ne.3:1. Eliash. and breth. built s.g.
32. going up of corner unto s. g.
12: 39. they went even unto s. g.
Jn. 5: † 2. by s. g. there is a pool
GATE with valley. [v.g.
2 Ch. 26: 9. Uzziah built towers at
Ne. 2: 13. I went out by g. of v.
15. I entered by the g. of v.
3: 13. the v. g. repaired Hanun
Water GATE. [w.g.
Ne. 3: 26. Nethinim dwelt over ag.
8:1. gathered into street bef. w.g.
3. he read in the law bef. w. g.
16. made booths in street of w.g.
12: 37. priests went even to w. g.
GATES.
De. 12: 12. rejoice, within your g.
Jos. 6:26. in son set up g., 1 K. 16:
Ju. 5: 8. new gods, war in g. [34.
11. people of Lord shall go to g.
2 K. 23: 8. brake high places of g.
2 Ch. 31:2. appointed to praise in g.
Ne. 1: 3. g. are burned, 2:3, 13, 17.
7:3. let not g. of Jerus. be opened
12:30. priests and Lev. purified g.
13:19. some of my serv-ts set I at g.
22. I com-d Levites to keep the g.
Ps. 9: 14. shew thy praise in g.
24:7. Lift up your heads, O ye g.,9.
87: 2. The Lord loveth g. of Zion
100: 4. Enter into his g. with thanksgiving
107: 16. he hath brok. g. of brass
118:19. Open to me g. of righteousn.
Pr. 1: 21. crieth in openings of g.,
8:34. watching daily at my g. [8:3.
14: 19. wicked at g. of the righte.
31: 23. Her husb. is known in g.
31. let own works praise her in g.
Can.7:13. at our g. all pleasant fruits
Is. 3: 26. And her g. shall lament
13: 2. may go into g. of nobles
26:2. Open ye g. that righte. may
38: 10. I sh. go to g. of the grave
45:1. to open bef. him two-leaved g.
2. will break in pieces g. of brass
62:10. go thro. g. prepare the way
Je. 1: 15. at entering of g. [2.
7: 2. enter in at the g., 17:20.-22:
14: 2. Jud. mourneth, g. languish
15:7. I will fan them with fan in g.
17:19. go and stand in g. of Jerus.
21. bear no burden on sab. by g.,
25. sh. enter into g., 22: 4. [24.
27. will kindle fire in g. of Jerus.
22: 19. shall be cast forth bey. g.
51: 58. her high g. sh. be burned
La. 1: 4. Zion's g. are desolate
2: 9. Her g. are sunk into ground
4: 12. adversary sho. have ent. g.
Eze. 21:15. set point of sword ag. g.
22. appoint battering rams ag. g.
26:2. she is brok. th. was g. of peo.
48:31 three g. aft. names of tribes,
32. at east side three g. [33. 34.
Ob. 11. day that foreigners ent. g.
Na. 2: 6 g. of rivers shall be op-d
3:13. g. of thy land sh. be set open
Zch.8:16. exec. judgm. of peace in g.
Mat.16:18. g. of hell sh. not prevail
Ac. 9: 24. watched g. to kill Paul
14: 13. priests bro-t oxen unto g.
Re.21:12. city 12 g. at g. 12 ang.
13. On east 3 g. on north 3 g.(4)
15. meas. city and g. thereof
21. twelve g. were twelve pearls
25. g. of it sh. not be shut at all
See BARS, DEATH.
Thy GATES. [5:14.
Ex. 20:10. stranger within t.g., De.
De. 6:9. shalt write on t. g., 11:20.
12:15. mayest eat flesh in t.g., 21.
17. not eat within t. g. tithe [g.
18. must eat, thou and Lev. in t.
De.14:21. give unto stranger in t.g.
27. Lev. within t. g. not forsake
28. shalt lay up tithe within t.g.
29. widow within t. g. shall eat
15:7. if be a poor man within t.g.
22. shalt eat firstling within t. g.
16:5. not sacrifi. passo. within t.g.
11 thou shalt rejoice thy son, and Lev. within t.g., 14.-26: 12.
18. officers shalt make in t. g.
17:5. bring man or wom. unto t.g.
18:6. if Lev. come from any of t.g.
23: 16. serv-t escaped dwell in t.g.
24:14. shalt not oppress within t.g.
28:52. he shall besiege thee in t.g.
55. enem. sh. distress thee in t.g.
31:12. gath. peo. within t.g. to hear
Ps.122:2. stand within t.g. O Jerus.
Is. 54: 12. make t. g. of carbuncles
60:11. t.g. sh. be open continually
18. thy walls salva. t. g. Praise
Eze. 26: 10. when he shall enter t.
GATH. [g. as men
1 S. 5: 8. let ark be carried unto G.
6: 17. golden emerods, for G. one
27: 4. told that Da. was fled to G.
2 S. 1:20. Tell it not in G., Mi.1:10.
15: 18. 600 men wh. came from G.
21:22. born to giant in G., 1 Ch.20:8.
1 K.2:39. serv-ts of Shimei ran unto
40. Shimei went to G. to seek [G.
2 K. 12: 17. Hazael fought ag. G.
1 Ch.7:21. whom the men of G. slew
8: 13. drove away inhab. of G.
18: 1. David took G. from Philis.
2 Ch 26: 6. Uzziah brake wall of G.
Am. 6: 2. go down to G. of Philis.
Mi. 1: 10. declare ye it not at G.
GATHER.
Ge. 6: 21. g. it: it be for food
31:46. he said, g. stones, they took
41: 35. g. all food of those years
Ex. 5:7. go g. straw | 12. g. stubble
9:19. g. cattle | 16:4. g. cert. rate, 16.
16: 5. g. twice as | 26. six days g.
27. 7th day for to g. found none
23:10. six y-rs sow and g., Le.25:3.
Le. 19: 9. not g. gleanings, 23: 22.
10. thou shalt not g. every grape
25:5. nor g. grapes of vine undr-d,
20. not sow, nor g. in incr. [11.
Nu. 10:4. if one trumpet, princes g.
11: 16. g. 70 men of elders of Isr.
19: 9. a man clean sh. g. the ashes
De. 11:14. rain that thou mayest g.
13: 16. thou shalt g. all the spoil
28:30 plant viney. not g. grapes, 39.
38. much seed out, g. little in
30:3. will g. thee fr. na-s, Eze.36:24.
31: 28. g. unto me all elders
Jos. 2: † 18. g. fa. and mo. home
1 S. 7: 5. g. all Israel to Mizpeh
2 S. 3: 21. g. all Isr. unto the king
1 K 18:19. g. all Isr. unto mt. Carmel
2 K.4:39. went into field to g. herbs
22:20. g. thee unto fa-s, 2 Ch.34:28.
1 Ch. 13: 2. send to brethren to g.
2 Ch. 24:5. g. money to repair h. of
Ne. 1: 9. will I g. them thence [L.
12: 44. appointed to g. for priests
Jb. 24: 6. they g. vintage of wick.
34:14. if he g. to himself his spirit
39: 12. will he bring seed and g. it
Ps. 26: 9. g. not soul with sinners
27:†10. when mo. forsake, L. will g.
39: 6. knoweth not who g. them
104: 28. That thou givest they g.
106:47. save g. us from am. heathen
Pr. 28: 8. g. for him th. pity poor
Ec. 2:26. travail to g. and heap up
Can. 6: 2 beloved gone to g. lilies
Is.10:31. of Gebim g. thems. to flee
34: 15. owl g. under her shadow
40:11. shall g. lambs with his arms
43:5 I will g. thee fr. the west [8.
52:†12. G. of Isr. will g. you up, 58:†
54:7. with gr. mercies will I g. thee
Is. 56: 8. Yet will I g. others to him
62: 10. cast up highway, g. stones
66: 18. I will g. all nations [wood
Je. 6: 1. g. to flee | 7: 18. chil. g.
9:22. none shall g. | 10:17. g. wares
23: 3. I will g. remnant of flock
29:14. I will g. you fr. all nations
31: 8. I will g. them fr. coasts of earth, 32:37.-Eze 20:34,41.-34:
10. He that scatt-d Isr. will g. [13.
40:10. g. ye wine and summer fruits
47: † 6. O sword, g. into scabbard
49: 5. none sh. g. him th. wand-h
51:11. bright the arrows; g. shields
Eze. 11: 17. I will g. you fr. people
16: 37. I will g. all thy lovers
22: 19. I will g. you into Jerus.
20 As g. silver, so will I g. you, 21.
24:4 g. pieces | 29:13. will g. Egyp-s
37: 21. I will g. them, 39: 17.
Ho. 8: 10. tho. hired am. nations, I
9:6. Egypt shall g. them up [will g.
Jo. 1:14. g. elders and inhabitants
2:6 peo. pained, faces sh. g. blackn.
16. g. people. g. chil. that suck
3: 2. I will g. all nations and bri.
Mi. 2: 12. I will g. remnant of Isr.
4:6. I will g. her driven, Zph.3:19.
12. he shall g. them as sheaves
5: 1. g. thyself in troops, O dau.
Na. 2: 10 faces of all g. blackness
Ha.1: 9. they shall g. the captivity
15. they g. them in their drag
Zph 3:8. determ-n is to g. nations
18 I will g. them th. are sorrowful
20. even in time that I g. you
Zch. 10: 8. I will hiss and g. them
10. I will g. them out of Assyria
14:2. will g. all nations ag. Jerus.
Mat. 3: 12. g. his wheat, Lu. 3: 17.
6: 26 nor do they g. into barns
7:16. g. grapes of thorns? Lu.6:44.
13: 28. Wilt thou that we g. them
29 lest while ye g. up the tares
30. burn tares, but g. the wheat
41. shall g. out of his kingd. all
25: 26. g. where I not strewed
Lu.13:34. as hen doth g. her brood
Jn. 6: 12. g. fragments th. remain
15: 6. men g. and cast into fire
Re. 14: 18. g. clusters of the vine
16: 14. g. them to battle of that
GATHER together. [day
Ge.34:30. I being few they shall g.t.
49:1. g. yours. t. ye sons of Jacob, 2.
Ex. 3:16. Go g. the elders of Isr. t.
Le. 8:3. g. cong. of Isr. t., Nu.8:9.
Nu.20:8. and g. thou the assembly t.
21:16. g. people t., De.4:10.-31:12.
2 S. 12: 28. g. the rest t. encamp
1 Ch. 16:35. save, O G. and g. us t.
22:2. David com-d to g.t. strangers
Ezr. 10:7. g. thems. t. unto Jerus.
Ne. 7:5. in my heart to g.t. nobles
Es. 2: 3. may g. t. all fair virgins
4: 16. g.t. Jews in Shushan, 8:11.
Jb. 11: 10. if he g. t. who hinder
Ps. 50: 5. g. my saints t. unto me
56:6. They g. thems. t. to mark my
94:21. they g. t. ag. the righteous
104: 22. The sun ariseth they g.t.
Ec. 3: 5. is a time to g. stones t.
Is. 11:12. sh. g.t. dispersed of Jud.
49: 18. these g. t. and come, 60:4.
54:15. they sh. g.t. but not by me
Je. 4: 5. blow trumpet, cry, g. t.
49:14. g. ye t. and come ag. Edom
Da. 3: 2. king sent to g. t. princes
Jo. 3: 11. g. yours. t. round about
Zph. 2: 1. g. t. yea, g. t. O nation
Mat. 13: 30. g. t. first the tares
24:31. shall g.t. his elect, Mk.13:27.
Jn.11:52. sho. g.t. in one, Ep.1:10.
Re. 19: 17. g. t. to supper of God
20: 8. to g. Gog and Magog t. to
GATHERED. [battle
Ge. 12:5. all substance they had g.

Ge. 25 : 8. Ab. was g. to his people
17.Ish.was g. | 35:29.Isaac was g.
41 : 48. g. food of the seven years
49:29. Jac. was g. to his peo., 33.
Ex.16:17.g.,some more, some ⌈8:15.
18. g. much. he th. g.little,2 Co.
21. g. it ev. morning, 18.Nu.11:8.
22. sixth day g. twice as much
23:16.when hast g. in thy labours
Le.23:39. when ye have g. in fruits
Nu.11:32.g. quails | 15:32.g. sticks
16:19.Korah g. cong.ag.Moses,42.
20:24. Aaron be g. to his peo., 26.
27 : 13. thou shalt be g. to thy
people, 31 : 2. De. 32:50. ⌈corn
De. 16 : 13. seven days after hast g.
Ju. 1 : 7. kings g. meat und. table
2 : 10. that genera. was g. to fa-s
6 : 34. Abiezer was g. after him
11 : 3. were g. vain men,2 Ch.18:7.
1 S. 5:8. they g. all lords of Philis.
22 : 2. ev. one in distress g. to Da.
2 S.14:14. as water spilt can-t be g.
2 K. 3 : 21. g. all able to put on ar-
4:39.g.wild gourds, lap full ⌊mour
22 : 20. Josiah be g. into grave in
peace, 2 Ch. 34:28. ⌈unto work
Ne. 5 : 16. all my servants were g.
Jb. 27 : 19. rich lie down, not be g.
Ps. 59 : 3. mighty are g. ag. me
107 : 3. he g. them out of lands
Pr. 27 : 25. herbs of mts. are g.
30 : 4. who hath g. wind in fists?
Ec. 2 : 8. I g. me silver and gold
Can. 5 : 1. I have g. my myrrh
Is. 5 : 2. he fenced it, g. out stones
10:14.as one gath-h eggs,I g. earth
27 : 12. ye shall be g. one by one
33:4. be g. like gath g of caterpil.
34:15. vultures be g. | 16 Spirit g.
49 : 5. Isr. be not g. yet I be glori.
56:8.others,besides those th.are g.
62 : 9. that have g. it shall eat it
Je. 3 : 17. nations sh. be g. unto it
8:2. they sh. not be g. nor, 25:33.
26 : 9. all people g. ag Jeremiah
40:15. Jews g. unto thee be scatt.
Eze.28:25.When I have g.h. of Isr.
29 : 5. thou shalt not be g.
38 : 8. is g. out of many people
12. people g. out of the nations
13. hast thou g. thy company
39:27.g.them out of enemies' lands
28.I have g. them unto own land
Ho. 10:10. people sh. be g.ag.them
Mi. 4 : 11. many nations g. ag. thee
7 : 1. I as when g. summer fruits
Mat. 13:40. as tares g. and burned
47. a net cast and g. of ev. kind
48. g. good into vessels, cast
25 : 32. bef. him be g. all nations
27 : 27. g. unto him whole band
Mk. 4 : 1. g. unto him peo., 5 : 21.
Jn. 11:47. g. chief priests a council
Ac 17 : 5. g. company, set city on
28 : 3. Paul g. a bundle of sticks
Re. 14 : 19. angel g. vine of earth

GATHERED together.

Ex.8:14.they g.them t. upon heaps
Le. 26 : 25. when g. t. within cities
Nu. 10 : 7. when cong. is to be g.t.
11:22. shall all fish of sea be g. t.
14 : 35. that are g. t. against me
Ju. 20 : 1. the congr. was g. t. as
one man, 11. Ezr. 3:1. Ne. 8:1
2 Ch.20:4.Jud.g.t. to ask help of L.
30 : 3. neith. had peo. g. thems. t.
Jb. 16:10. they g. thems. t. ag. me
30:7. under nettles were they g.t.
Ps. 35 : 15. the abjects g. t. ag. me
47 : 9. princes of people are g. t.
102 : 22. people are g.t.to serve L.
140:2. continually are g.t. for war
Pr. 30 : † 27. locusts go all g. t.
Is. 13 : 4. noise of nations g. t.
24 : 22. shall be g. t. as prisoners
43 : 9. Let all nations be g. t.
Is. 44 : 11. be g. t. let them stand
Ho.1:11.shall chil.of Judah be g.t.
Mi. 4 : 11. many na-s g. t. ag. thee
Zch. 12:3. tho. all peo. be g.t. ag.it
Mat. 2 : 4. g. priests and scribes t.
13 : 2. mult-s were g. t., Lu. 12:1.
18:20. where 2 or 3 are g. t.
22:10. g.t. as many as they found
34. Pharisees were g. t., 41.
23:37. how often would I have g.
chil. t. as hen, Lu. 13: 34.
24 : 28. eagles be g.t., Lu. 17 : 37
27:17. Jews were g. t. Pilate
Mk. 1 : 33. all the city was g. t.
2 : 2. many were g. t., Lu. 8 : 4
6 : 30. apostles g. t. unto Jesus
Lu. 11: 29. when people g. thick t.
15 : 13. younger son g. all t.
24 : 33. they found the eleven g.t.
Jn. 6:13. g. fragments t. and filled
Ac. 4 : 6. kin. of high priest g. t.
26. rulers were g.t. against Lord
27. people of Israel g. t.
12 : 12. many were g. t. praying
14:27.when they had g.the church
15:30. g. mult. t. deliv-d epis. ⌊t.
20:8. chamber where th. were g.t.
1 Co. 5:4. when g. t. and my spirit
Re. 16 : 16. g. t. into Armageddon
19 : 19. army g. t. to make war

GATHERER. ⌈fruit

Am 7 : 14. I was g. of sycamore
See GRAPEGATHERER, S.

GATHEREST, ING.

Nu 15:33.that found him g-g sticks
De.24:21.When thou g-t the grapes
1 K.17:10. widow g-g sticks, 12. ⌈ed
Mat.25:24.g-g where hast not strew-
Ac. 16:10. assuredly g-g L.called us

GATHERETH.

Nu. 19:10. that g. ashes shall wash
Ju. 19:†18. no man th. g. me to ho.
Ps. 33 : 7. He g. waters of the sea
41:6. his heart g. iniquity to itself
147 : 2. g. outcasts of Isr., Is.56:8.
Pr. 6 : 8. ant g. her food in harvest
10 : 5. g. in summer is a wise son
13:11. g. by labour shall increase
Is. 10:14. as one g. eggs th. are left
17 : 5. be as when harvestman g.
Je. 17 : † 11. as partridge g. young
Na. 3:18. people is scatt. no man g.
Ha. 2 : 5. g. unto him all nations
Mat.12:30. g. not scattereth,Lu 11:
23:37.as a hen g.her chickens ⌊23.
Jn. 4 : 36. he that reapeth g. fruit

GATHERING, S.

Ge. 1 : 10. g. of wat. called he Seas
49 : 10. to him shall g. of peo. be
Ex. 7 : † 19. hand upon g. of waters
Le. 11 : † 36. a g. of waters be clean
1 Ch. 26 : † 15. Obed-edom h. of g-s
2 Ch. 20:25. were 3 days in g. spoils
Is. 24:†22. with the g. of prisoners
32 : 10. vintage fail, g. not come
33:4. your spoil like g. of caterpil.
Eze. 22 : † 20. acc. to g. of silver
Mi. 7 : † 1. I am as g-s of sum. fruits
1 Co. 16 : 2. be no g-s when I come
2 Th. 2 : 1. by our g. togeth. unto

GATH-HE'PHER. ⌊him

2 K.14:25. Amittai the prophet of G.

GATH-RIM'MON.

Jos. 19 : 45.–21 : 24, 25. 1 Ch. 6:69.

GAVE.

Ge. 2 : 20. Adam g. names to cattle
3 : 12. woman g. me of the tree, 6.
14 : 20. g. him tithes, He. 7 : 2, 4.
25 : 5. Ab. g. all he had unto Isaac
28:4. land God g. unto Ab., 35:12.
39:21.shewed him mercy, g.favour
Ex. 6 : 13. Lord g. them a charge
11:3.L. g. the people favour,12:36.
14 : 20. the cloud g. light by night
Nu. 11 : 25. L. of spirit, g. unto 70
De. 9 : 11. L. g. me 2 tables, 10 : 4.
22 : 16. I g. my dau. to this man
Jos. 19 : 50. g. him city he asked
21 : 43. L. g. unto Israel all the
land, De. 2 : 12. ⌈30.
44. L. g. rest, 2 Ch. 15 : 15.–20 :
Ju. 6:9. I g. you their la., 2 K.21:8
Ru. 2 : 18. g. to her that reserved
4 : 13. Lord g. her conception
1 S. 10 : 9. G. g. Saul ano. heart
18 : 27. g. them in full tale
20 : 40. Jona. g. artillery unto lad
2 S. 12 : 8. I g. thee thy master's h.
1 K. 4:29. Lord g. Sol. wisdom, 5:12.
14 : 8. kingd. fr. house of Da. g. it
15. land wh. he g. their fathers
2 K. 13 : 5. Lord g. Israel a saviour
18 : 16. g. it to king of Assyr., 15.
1 Ch. 25 : 5. g. Heman 14 sons
2 Ch 13:5. g. kingd. to Da forever
32 : 24. g. Hez. a sign, 1 K. 13 : 3.
35 : 8. g. willingly unto people
Ezr. 2 : 69. g. aft. their ability
Ne. 8 : 8. read in law, g. the sense
Jb 1:21. L. g. and Lord hath taken
42 : 10. Lord g. Job twice as much
Ps. 18 : 13. Highest g. his voice
68:11. L. g. word, gr. was company
69:21. They g. me gall, g. vinegar
78 : 15. g. drink as out of depths
29. g. them their desire, 106 : 15.
46. g. increase unto caterpillar
50. g. life over to the pestilence
62. g. people over unto sword
99 : 7. ordinance that he g.
105 : 32. g. them hail for rain
44. g. them lands of the heathen
135 : 12. g. la. for heritage, 136:21
Pr. 8 : 29. When he g. sea his decr
Ec. 12 : 7. spirit unto God th. g. it
Is. 41 : 2. g. the nations bef. him
42 : 24. who g. Jacob for a spoil
43 : 3. I g. Egypt for thy ransom
50 : 6. I g. my back to the smiters
Je. 1 : † 5. g. thee a prophet unto
7 : 14. place wh. I g. to you ⌊nat-s
17 : 4. heritage I g. thee
23 : 39. forsake city I g. you
44 : 30. as I g. Zed. into hand of
Eze. 16 : 19. My meat wh. I g. thee
20 : 11. I g. them my statutes
12. also, I g. them my sabbaths
25. I g. them statutes not good
Da. 1 : 17. g. these four chil. knowl.
5 : 18. G. g. Nebuchad. thy fa., 19.
6 : 10. Daniel g. thanks bef. God
Ho. 2 : 8. not know I g. her corn
13 : 11. I g. thee a king in anger
Am. 2 : 12. ye g. the Nazarites wine
Mal. 2:5. I g. my cov. to Levi of life
Mat. 10 : 1. Jesus g. power ag. unclean spirits, Mk. 6 : 7. Lu.9:1.
14 : 19. brake and g. loaves to his,
15 : 36.–26 : 26. Mk. 6 : 41.–8 :
6.–14 : 22. Lu. 9 : 16.–22 : 19.
21 : 23. who g. thee authority?
Mk. 11 : 28. Lu. 20 : 2.
25 : 15. unto one he g. 5 talents
35. ye g. me meat, g. me drink
42. ye g. me no meat, g. me no
26 : 27. cup and g. thanks and g.
48. g. sign whomsoever I kiss
27 : 10. g. for the potter's field
34. g. him vinegar to drink
Mk. 2 : 26. g. shewbread to, Lu.6:4.
6 : 28. g. head to damsel
13 : 34. g. authority to his serv-s
14 : 23. g. cup to them and they
15 : 23. g. him to drink wine mingl.
45. g. body to Joseph, Jn. 19 : 38.
Lu. 4 : 20. g. again to minister
7 : 21. many blind he g. sight
10 : 35. two pence and g. to host
15 : 16. husks, and no man g.
18 : 43. all peo. g. praise unto G.
24 : 30. he took bread and g. them
42. g. broiled fish and honeycomb
Jn. 1 : 12. g. power to become sons
3 : 16. so loved world he g. his Son

Jn. 4 : 5. ground Jacob g. to son Joseph, 12.
6:31. He g. them bread from heav.
32. Mo. g. not that bread from
7:22.Mo. g. unto you circumcision
10 : 29. Fa. who g. them is greater
12 : 49. g. com-t what I sho. say
13 : 26. g. sop to Judas Iscariot
14 : 31. as Fa. g. me com-t, so I do
19 : 9. Jes. g. him no answer
Ac. 1 : 26. they g. their lots
2 : 4. as the Spirit g. utterance
7 : 5. he g. them no inheritance in
8. g. he him cov. of circum. [it
10.God g.Joseph favour and wisd.
8 : 6. peo. g. heed unto thi. Phil.
10. all g.heed unto Simon [spake
9 : 41. he g. her his hand and
10 : 2. Cornelius g. much alms
11:17. as God g. them the like gift
12 : 23. smote, bec. g. not G. glory
13 : 20. he g. unto them Judges
21. afterw. God g. them Saul
14 : 17. he did good, and g. us rain
15 : 24. we g. no such com-t [ag
26:10. put to death, I g. my voice
27 : 3. g. Paul liberty to go unto
Ro. 1:28. g. them to reprobate mind
1 Co. 3 : 5. as Lord g. to ev man
6. Apollos watered, God g. incr.
2 Co. 8 : 5. first g. own selves to L.
Ga. 1 : 4. g. hims. for our sins. Tit.
2:9. g. right ha. of fellowsh. [2:14.
20. loved me, g. himself for me
3 : 18. God g. it to Ab. by promise
Ep. 1 : 22. g. him to be head over
4:8. led captivity g. gifts unto men
11.And he g.some apostles; some
5 : 25.C.loved church,g.hims.for it
1 Th. 4:2. ye know com-t we g. you
1 Ti. 2 : 6.Who g. himself a ransom
He. 7 : 13. no man g. attendance at
12 : 9. corrected us, we g. reveren.
Ja. 5 : 18. prayed, heavens g. rain
1 Pe. 1:21. fr. dead and g. him glory
1 Jn. 3 : 23. love one ano. as he g.
5:10. beli-h not record G. g. [com.
Jude 3. g. all diligence to write
Re. 1 : 1. Revelation of J. C. God g.
2 : 21. I g. her space to repent of
11:13. remn. g. glory to G. of heav.
13 : 2. dragon g. him his power, 4
15 : 7. one of beasts g. unto 7 ang.

GAVE up.

Ge. 25 : 8. Ab. g. u. ghost, and died
17.Ishm. | 35:29. Isaac g.u.ghost
2 S. 24 : 9. Joab g. u. sum of num.
2 Ch.30:7.who g. them u. to desola.
Ps. 78 : 48. He g. u. cattle to hail
81 : 12. I g. them u. unto heart's lust
La. 1 : 19. my elders g. u. ghost
Mk. 15 : 37. Jes. cried, and g. u. ghost, 39. Lu. 23 : 46. Jn.19:30.
Ac. 5:5. Ananias g.u.the ghost. 10.
7 : 42. G. g. them u. to worship host [ghost
12 : 23.Herod eaten of worms g.u.
Ro. 1:24. G. g. them u. to unclean.
26. God g. them u. unto vile
Re. 20 : 13. sea g. u. the dead in it

GAVEST. [g.

Ge. 3 : 12. The woman whom thou
1 K. 8 : 34. land thou g. unto their fa-s, 40, 48. 2 Ch. 6 : 25, 31, 38. Ne. 9 : 35.
2 Ch. 20 : 7. g. it to seed of Ab.
Ne. 9 : 7. g. him the name of Ab.
13. thou g.them right judgments
15. g. them bread from heaven
20. Thou g. good Spirit, g. water
22. g. them kingdoms and nat-s
24. g. them into their hands, 30.
27. thou g. them saviours who
35. goodness g. land thou g., 36.
Jb. 39 : 13. g. goodly wings unto peacocks?
Ps. 21 : 4. He asked life; thou g. it
74 : 14. g. him to be meat to peo.
Lu. 7 : 44. g. me no water for feet
45. Thou g. me no kiss, this wom.
15:29. yet thou never g. me a kid
19 : 23. g. not money into bank
Jn. 17 : 4 finished work thou g. me
6.manifested unto men thou g.me thine they were, thou g. me
8. given them words thou g. me
12. those thou g. me I have kept
22. glory thou g. me, I have giv.
18 : 9. whom g. have I lost none

GAY.

Ja. 2 : 3. that weareth g. clothing

GA'ZA. [unto G.

Ge. 10 : 19. border of Canaanites
Ju. 1:18. Judah took G., Jos.15:47.
16 : 1. Samson went to G.
21. the Philis. bro-t Samson to G.
Je. 47 : 1. bef. Pharaoh smote G.
5. baldness is come upon G.
Am. 1: 6. three transgressions of G.
7. will send a fire on wall of G.
Zph. 2 : 4. G. shall be forsaken
Zch. 9 : 5. king shall perish from G.
Ac. 8:26. the way fr. Jerus. unto G.

GAZ'ATHITES, GAZ'ITES.

Jos. 13:3. G. Ashdothites, Ju. 16 : 2

GAZE, ING. [to g.

Ex. 19 : 21. lest break thro. to L.
Ac. 1 : 11. why stand g-g into heav.

GA'ZER.

2 S.5:25. smote Philis. to G., 1 Ch. [14 : 16.

GA'ZEZ.

1 Ch.2:46.Ephah, Caleb's conc. bare [G.

GAZINGSTOCK.

Na. 3 : 6. I will set thee as a g.
He. 10:33. whilst ye were made a g.

GAZ'ZAM.

Ezr. 2 : 48 the chil. of G., Ne. 7:51.

GE'BA. [6 : 60.

Jos. 21 : 17. G. with suburbs, 1 Ch.
1 S. 13 : 3. garrison of Philis. in G.
1 K. 15 : 22. Asa built G., 2 Ch. 16:6.
2 K. 23 : 8. defiled high places fr. G.
Is. 10 : 29. taken up lodging at G.
Zch. 14 : 10. sh be as a plain fr. G.

GE'BAL.

Ps. 83 : 7. G. Ammon confederate
Eze. 27 : 9. ancients of G. calkers

GE'BER. [19.

1 K. 4:13. son of G. in Ramoth-gil.,

GE'BIM.

Is.10:31. inhabi. of G. gather to flee

GEDALI'AH. [ruler

2 K.25:22. over them, made G. their
24. and G. sware to them, Je.40:9.
1 Ch. 25 : 3. sons of Jeduthun, G.
9. second lot came forth to G.
Ezr. 10 : 18. and G.taken stra. wives
Jer. 38 : 1. G. son of Pashur heard
40 : 14. G. son of Ahikam beli. not
41 : 2. Ishm. smote G., 2 K. 25: 25.
43 : 6. took all were left with G.
Zph.1:1.Zeph. son of Cushi son of G.
See AHIKAM.

GED'EON. See GID'EON.

GE'DER.

Jos. 12 : 13. the king of G. one

GEDE'RAH.

Jos. 15 : 36. Sharaim and G., cities

GEDE'RATHITE.

1 Ch. 12 : 4. Josabad the G.

GED'ERITE.

1 Ch. 27 : 28 over olive trees Baal-hanan, G.

GEDE'ROTH. [28 : 18.

Jos.15:41.G., Beth-dagon cities, 2 Ch.

GEDEROTHA'IM.

Jos. 15: 36.Sharaim, Gederah and G.

GE'DOR. [Person, Place.]

Jos. 15 : 58. Halhul, G. cities, 1 Ch. 4 : 39. [9 : 37.–12 : 7.
1 Ch. 4 : 4. Penuel of G. | 18.–8:31.–

GEHA'ZI.

2 K. 4: 12. Elisha said to G.call, 36.
2 K.4:27.G. came near to thrust her
5 : 21. so G. followed after Naaman
25.Elisha said, Whence comest G.?
8 : 4. king talked with G. servant

GEL'ILOTH.

Jos.18:17.and went forth toward G.

GEMAL'LI.

Nu. 13 : 12. Ammiel the son of G.

GEMARI'AH.

Je. 29 : 3. words Jere. sent by G.
36 : 10. in chamber of G., 11, 12.
25. G. made interces. not to burn

GENDER, ED, ETH.

Le.19:19. not let cattle g.wi. diverse
Ti. 2 : 23. that they do g. strifes
Jb.21: 10.Their bull g-h faileth not
38 : 29. the hoary frost who g-d it?
Ga.4:24. Sinai which g-h to bondage

GENEALOGIES.

1 Ch. 5 : 17. reckoned by g., 7 : 5, 7.
9 : 1. all Isr. were reckoned by g.
2 Ch.12:15.book of Shemaiah con. g.
31 : 19. portions to all reck-d by g.
1 Ti. 1:4.Nei. give heed to endless g.
Tit. 3:9. avoid foolish questions, g.

GENEALOGY.

1 Ch. 4 : 33. their g., 7 : 9. 2 Ch. 31 : 16, 17, 18. [right
5 : 1. g. not to be reck-d aft. birth-
7 : 40. g. of them apt to war
Ezr. 2 : 62. reckoned among those by g., 8 : 3. 1 Ch. 5 : 7.–9 : 22. Ne. 7 : 5, 64.
8 : 1. this is g. of them th. went up
Ne. 7:5. I found a register of the g.

GENERAL.

1 Ch. 27:34. g. of king's army Joab
He. 12 : 23. g. assembly and church

GENERALLY.

2 S. 17 : 11. that Isr be g. gathered
Je. 48:38. lamentation g. on house-

GENERATION. [tops

Ge. 7 : 1. thee righteous in this g.
15:16.in 4th g.they sh.come hither
Ex. 1:6. Joseph died, and all that g.
17:16.war with Amalek fr. g.to g.
20 : 5. visiting iniq. of fathers unto 4th g., 34 : 7. Nu. 14 : 18. De. 5 : 9. [ed, De. 2 : 14.
Nu. 32 : 13. until g. was consum-
De.1:35. not one of this g. see land
23:2.a bastard not enter to 10th g.
3. Ammonite to 10th g. not ent.
8. Egyp-ns in 3d g. shall enter
29:22. So that g. to come shall say
32 : 5. perverse and crooked g., 20.
†7.consider the years of g. and g.
Ju. 2 : 10. that g. were gath-d unto fa-s, there arose ano. g. aft.
2 K.10:30. thy chil. of 4th g., 15:12.
Es. 9 : 28. days shall be remem-d in every g. [and g.
Ps. 10 : † 6.not be moved unto g.
12:7.shalt preserve them fr. this g.
14 : 5. God is in g. of righteous
22 : 30. be accounted to L. for g.
24 : 6. This is g. of them seek him
48:13. th. ye may tell it to g. foll.
49 : 19. He sh. go to g. of fathers
71:18. shewed thy strength unto g.
73 : 15. offend ag. g. of thy chil.
77 : † 8. promise fail to g. and g.?
78 : 4. to g. to come praises of Ld.
6. That g. to come might know
8. might not be a rebellious g.
95:10.grieved with this g., He.3:10.
102 : 18. be written for g. to come
109:13.in g.foll.let name be blotted
112 : 2. g. of upright be blessed
145:4. One g. sh. praise thy works
Pr. 27 : 24. crown endure to ev. g.?
30 : 11. is a g. that curseth father
12. There is g. pure in own eyes
13. g. lofty | 14. g. whose teeth
Ec. 1:4.One g. passeth, ano. g.com.
Is.13:20.not dwelt in fr. g. to g., Je
34 : 10. fr. g. to g. waste [50 : 39.

Is.34:17.fr. g. to g. they shall dwell
51: 8. my salvation be fr. g. to g.
53: 8. who declare g.? Ac. 8: 33.
Je. 2: 31. O g. see ye word of L.
7:29. L. hath rejec. g. of his wrath
La.5:19. throne, remains fr. g. to g.
Da. 4:3. dominion is fr. g. to g.,34.
Jo.1:3. let their children tell ano. g.
3: 20. Jerus. shall dwell fr. g. to g.
Mat. 1: 1. The book of g. of J. C.
3: 7. O g. of vipers, 12: 34.-23: 33.
Lu. 3: 7 [Lu. 7: 31.
11:16.whereunto sh. I liken this g.?
12: 39. An adulterous g. seeketh
sign, 16: 4. Mk. 8: 12. Lu.11:29.
41.shall rise in judgment with this
g., Lu. 11: 32. [g., Lu. 11: 31.
42.queen of the south rise up with
45. be unto this wicked g. [9:41.
17: 17. O perverse g., Mk. 9:19. Lu.
23:36. All shall come upon this g.
24: 34. This g. shall not pass, Mk.
13: 30. Lu 21: 32. [sinful g.
Mk. 8: 38. shall be asha-d of me in
Lu. 1:50. mercy on them fr. g. to g.
11: 30. so Son of man be to this g.
50.bl.of proph-s required of g.,51.
16:8. chil. of world in their g. wiser
17:25.Son of man rejected of this g.
Ac. 2: 40. Save you fr. untoward g.
13:36. Da., after had served his g.
1 Pe. 2: 9. ye are a chosen g.
See FOURTH, THIRD.

GENERATIONS.

Ge. 2:4. these are g. of the heavens
5: 1. g. of Adam
6: 9. g. of Noah, 10: 1, 32.
6: 9. Noah perfect in his g.
9: 12. of cov. I make for perpet. g.
11: 10. g. of Shem | 27. g. of Terah
17:7.cov. betw. me and thy seed in g
9. thy seed in their g. [your g.
12. be circum., ev. manchild in
25:12. g. of Ishmael, 13. 1 Ch.1:29.
19. g. of Isaac | 36:1. g. of Esau, 9.
37: 2. These are the g. of Jacob
Ex. 3: 15. my memorial unto all g.
6: 16. sons of Levi acc. to g., 19.
12:17.sh. observe this day in your g.
42.night to be observed in their g.
16: 32. homer to be kept for g.,33.
27: 21. be a statute for ever unto
their g., 30: 21 Le. 3: 17.-6:
18.-7: 36 -10: 9.-17: 7.-23:14,
21, 31, 41.-24: 3. Nu. 18: 23.-
35: 29.
Le.21:17. of thy seed in their g. that
22: 3. be am. g. goeth unto holy
23: 43. your g. may know I made
24:3. statute for ev. in g., 15:14,21
Nu. 1:20. by g. aft. fam.,22, 24,&c.
3: 1. g. of Aaron and Moses
15: 15. ordinance forev. in your g.
23. henceforward among your g.
De. 7: 9. L. keepeth cov. to 1,000 g.
32: 7. consider years of many g.
Jos.22:27.witness betw. you and our
28. should say to our g. [g.
Ju. 3: 2. g. of Isr. might teach war
Ru. 4: 18 are the g. of Pharez
1 Ch.5:7. geneal. of g. was reck.,7: 2.
7: 2. men of might in their g., 4.
8: 28. by their g. chief men, 9: 9.
16: 15. his cov. word which he
com-d to a thous. g., Ps. 105:8.
26: 31. acc. to the g. of his fathers
Jb. 42:16. Job saw his sons, four g.
Ps.33:11. thoughts of heart to all g.
45:17.name to be remem-d in all g.
49:11.their dwellingplaces to all g.
61:6. prolong king's years as many
79:13.shew thy praise to all g. [g.
85: 5. draw out anger to all g.?
89:1.known thy faithfuln.to all g.
4. build up thy throne to all g.
90:1.been our dwellingplace in all g
100: 5. his truth endureth to all g.
Ps.102:12. thy remembr. unto all g.
106: 31. counted for righteousness
unto all g.
119: 90. faithfulness is unto all g.
146:10. thy G. shall reign to all g.
Is. 41: 4. calling the g. fr. beginn.
51: 9. awake, O arm, as in g. of old
58: 12. raise founda. of many g.
60: 15. make thee joy of many g.
61: 4. repair desola. of many g.
Jo. 2:2. even to the years of many g.
Mat. 1: 17. g. from Ab. to Da. are
14 g. carrying to Bab. 14 g., to
Christ 14 g.
Lu. 1: 48. all g. sh. call me blessed
Col. 1: 26. mystery been hid fr. g.

Throughout GENERATIONS.

Ex. 12:14. a feast to the L. t. your g.
29:42.contin.burnt off-g t. your g.
30:8.burn inc., 10. | 31.oil t. your g
31: 13. my sab-s sign t. your g.,16.
40: 15. everlasting priesthood t.
their g., Nu. 15: 38. 1 Ch. 9:34.
Le. 25: 30. that brought it t. his g.
Nu.10:8. ordinance t. your g. 18:23.
15: 38. fringes in border t. their g.
1 Ch.9.34.These were chief t. their g
Ps. 72: 5. they sh. fear thee t. all g.
102: 24. thy years are t. all g.
135:13. and thy memorial t. all g.
145:13. and thy dominion t. all g.

GENNES'ARET.

Mat.14:34.into land of G., Mk. 6:53.
Lu. 5: 1. Jesus stood by lake of G.

GEN'TILE.

Mk. 7: †26. the woman was a G.
Ro. 2: 9. of Jew first, also of G.,10.

GEN'TILES.

Ge. 10:5. By these isles of G. divided
Ju. 4: 2. in Harosheth of G.,13, 16
Is. 11: 10. to it shall the G. seek
42: 1. he shall bring judgm. to G.,
Mat. 12: 18.
6. for a light to G., 49: 6. Lu
2: 32. Ac. 13: 47.
49: 22. I will lift mine hand to G.
54: 3. thy seed shall inherit the G.
60: 3. And G. sh. come to thy light
5. forces of G. sh. come unto thee,
16. shalt suck milk of G. [11
61: 6. ye shall eat riches of the G.
9. their seed sh. be known am. G.
62: 2. G. shall see thy righteousn.
66: 12 glory of G. like flowing str.
19. shall declare my glory am. G.
Je. 4: 7. destroyer of G. on way
14:22.can vanities of G. cause rain?
16: 19. G. shall come from ends of
46:1. word came to Jere. against G
La 2: 9.her k. and princes among G.
Eze.4:13. eat defiled bread among G.
Ho.8:8. now shall they be among G.
Jo. 3:9. Proclaim ye this among G.
Mi. 5:8.remnant of Jacob be am. G.
Zch. 1: 21. to cast out horns of G.
Mal.1:11. my name be great am. G.
Mat.4:15. bey. Jordan, Galilee of G.
6: 32. after these things do G. seek
10:5. Go not into the way of the G.
18.testimony against them and G.
12:21.And in his name sh. G. trust
20: 19. deliv. him to G., Mk. 10: 33.
Lu. 18: 32. [Mk.10:42.Lu.22:25.
25. princes of G. exercise domin.,
Lu. 21: 24. Jerus. be trodden of G.
until times of G. be fulfilled
Jn 7:35. unto dispersed am. G and
teach G. [ed together
Ac.4:27. Pilate with G. were gather-
7:45.with Jes. into possession of G.
9: 15. to bear my name bef. the G.
10: 45. on G. was poured out gift
11:1. that G. received word of God
18.hath God to G. granted repent.
13: 42. G. besought words be prea.
46. Paul and B. said, We turn to G.
Ac.13:48.G. heard this, they were gl.
14:2.unbelieving Jews stirred up G.
5. an assault made of Jews and G.
27. opened door of faith to G.
15: 3. declaring conversion of G.
7. that G. should hear the word
12.wonders G. had wrought am. G.
14. how God at first did visit G.
17. G. upon whom my name is
called [among G.
19. we trouble not them, from
23.send greeting unto breth. of G.
18: 6. henceforth I will go unto G.
21:11.deliver Paul into hands of G.
19.G. wrought am. G. by his minis.
21. teachest Jews am. G to forsake
25. As touching G. which believe
22: 21. I will send thee far to G.
26: 17. Delivering thee from the G.
20.shewing the G. they sho. repent
23. that C. sho. shew light to G.
28:28.salvation is sent unto the G.
Ro.1:13. some fruit, as am. other G.
2: 14. G. which have not the law
24. God is blasphemed among G.
3:9. proved Jews and G. under sin
29. Is he not of G.? Yes, of G. also
9: 24. not of Jews only, but of G.
30. G. wh. foll. not after righte.
11:11.salvation is come unto the G.
12. dimin-g of them riches of G.
13. I speak to you G. as apostle
25. until the fulness of G. [of G.
15:9. that G. might glorify God, for
this I will confess among G.
10. Rejoice ye G. with his people
11. Praise Lord all ye G. and laud
12.to reign over G in him G. trust
16. that I be minister to the G.
that the offering up of G.
18. to make G. obedient by word
27. if G. have been made partakers
16:4. not I, but all churches of G.
1 Co. 5: 1. is not named among G.
10: 20. which G. sacrifice to devils
32. none offence, to Jews nor G.
12:2.know ye were G. carried away
13. one body, whether Jews or G.
Ga.2:2. that gospel I preach am. G.
8. same was mighty in me tow. G.
12. for he did eat with the G.
14. manner of G. why compell. G.
15. we Jews, and not sinners of G.
3: 14. blessing of Abra. on the G.
Ep. 2: 11. ye being in time past G.
3: 1. I prisoner of J. C. for you G.
6. that G. should be fellow heirs
8.preach am. G. unsearch. riches
4:17. that ye walk not as other G.
Col.1:27. glory of mystery among G.
1Th.2:16. Forbid-g us to speak to G.
4:5.Not in lust of concupisc., as G.
1 Ti. 2: 7. I am ordai-d teacher of G.
3: 16. preached unto G. believed on
2 Ti. 1: 11. an apostle teacher of G.
4: 17. that all the G. might hear
1 Pe.2:12.conversa. honest am.ong G.
4: 3. to have wrought will of G.
3 Jn. 7. went taking nothing of G.
Re.11:2. court is given unto the G.

GENTLE.

1 Th. 2: 7. we were g. among you
2 Ti. 2: 24. serv. of L must be g.
Tit. 3: 2. g. shewing all meekness
Ja. 3: 17. wisdom from above is g.
1 Pe.2:18.be subject to good and g.

GENTLENESS. [35.

2 S. 22:36. g. made me great, Ps. 18:
2 Co. 10: 1. I beseech by g. of C.
Ga. 5: 22. fruit of the Spirit is g.

GENTLY. [Abs.

2 S 18: 5. Deal g. with young man
Is.40: 11. g. lead those with young

GENU'BATH. [hold

1 K. 11: 20. G. was in Pha's house-

GE'RA. [G.

Ge. 46:21. sons of Benj. were Becher,

Ju. 3: 15. raised up Ehud son of G.
2 S. 16: 5. Shimei son of G., 19: 16,
18. 1 K. 2: 8.
1 Ch. 8: 3. Sons of Bela were G. | 5, 7.

GERAHS.

Ex 30: 13. shekel is 20 g., Le. 27:
25. Nu. 3: 47.-18: 16. Eze 45: 12.

GE'RAR. [est to G.

Ge 10: 19. fr. Sidon as thou come-
20: 1. Abraham sojourned in G.
2. Abimelech king of G., 26. 1, 26.
26: 6. Isaac in G., 17. | 20. herdm. of G.
2 Ch. 14: 13. Asa pursued them unto

GE'RED. [G., 14.

Ge. 5: † 15. Mehalaleel begat G.

GERGESENES'.

Mat. 8: 28. come into country of G.

GER'IZIM. [G.

De. 11: 29. shalt put blessing upon
27: 12. shall stand upon mount G.
Jos. 8: 33. half over against mount G.
Ju. 9: 7. Jotham stood in top of G.

GER'SHOM. [28: 15.

Ex. 2: 22. name of Moses son, G., 1 Ch.
18: 3. Zipporah and 2 sons, one G.
Ju. 18: 30. Jona. son of G. was priest
1 Ch. 26: 24. And Shebuel son of G.
Ezr. 8: 2. of sons of Phin. G. went up

GER'SHON.

Ge. 46: 11. sons of Levi, G., Ex. 6:
16. Nu. 3: 17. 1 Ch. 6: 1.-23: 6.
Ex. 6: 17. sons of G., Nu. 3: 18.
Nu. 3: 21. of G. was Libnites
25. charge of sons of G.
4: 22. Take the sum of sons of G., 38.
4: 28. service of sons of G.
7: 7. four oxen gave unto sons of G.
10: 17. sons of G. bearing taber.
Jos. 21: 6. cities chil. of G. had, 27.

GER'SHONITE, S. [26: 57.

Nu. 3: 21. families of G-s, 23.-4. 24.-
24. chief of G-s | 4: 27. service of G-s
Jos. 21: 33. All cities of G-s thirteen
1 Ch. 23: 7. Of the G-s, 2 Ch. 29: 12.
26: 21. sons of G. Laadan (2) | 29: 8.

GER'ZITES. See GEZRITES.

GE'SHAM. [ah

1 Ch. 2: 47. sons of Jahdai; G., Eph-

GE'SHEM = GASH'MU.

Ne. 2: 19. G. the Arabian, 6: 1, 2, † 6.

GE'SHUR. [3: 2.

2 S. 3: 3. Talmai king of G., 1 Ch.
13: 37. Absal. fled to king of G., 38.
14: 23. Joab to G. | 32. Whf. from G.?
15: 8. thy servant vowed while at G.
1 Ch. 2: 23. Jair took G., and Aram

GESH'URI, ITES. [2.

De. 3: 14. unto coasts of G., Jos. 13:
Jos. 12: 5. unto border of G., 13: 11.
13: 13. Israel expelled not G-s (2)
1 S. 27: 8. David invaded the G-s

GET.

Ge. 34: 4. g. me this damsel to wife
Ex. 1: 10. so g. them up out of land
14: 17. g. me honour upon Pha.
Le. 14: 21. if poor and can-t g. [31.
22. two pigeons, as able to g., 30,
32. whose hand is not able to g.
Nu. 6: 21. that that his hand sh. g.
22: 34. now I will g. me back again
De. 8: 18. giveth power to g. wealth
28: 43. strangers shall g. ab. thee
Ju. 14: 2. g. her for me to wife, 3.
1 S. 20: 29. let me g. away and see
23: 26. Da. made haste to g. away
2 S. 20: 6. Sheba g. fenced cities
1 K. 1: 2. that my lord may g. heat
12: 18. Rehob. made speed to g. up
to chariot to flee, 2 Ch. 10: 18.
2 K. 7: 12. catch alive, and g. city
Ps. 119: 104. Thro. thy precepts I
g. understanding
Pr. 4: 5. g. wisd., g. underst-g, 7.
6: 33. wound and dishonour he g.
16: 16. better it is to g. wisd. than
gold, to g. underst. rather than
17: 16. in hand of fool to g. wisd.
Pr. 22: 25. Lest learn ways g. a snare
Ec. 3: 6. there is a time to g.
Can. 4: 6. g. me to mts. of myrrh
7: 12. Let us g. early to vineyards
Je. 5: 5. I will g. me unto great men
19: 1. g. a potter's earthen bottle
46: 4. Harness horses, g. horsem.
48: 9. give wings, th. it may g. aw.
La. 3: 7. hedged me, I cannot g. out
Eze. 22: 27. to g. dishonest gain
Da. 4: 14. let beasts g. fr. under it
Zph. 3: 19. I will g. them praise
Mat. 10: † 9. g. neither gold nor silver
14: 22. to g. into ship, Mk. 6: 45.
Lu. 9: 12. lodge and g. victuals
Ac. 27: 43. into sea, and g. to land
2 Co. 2: 11. Lest Satan g. advantage
Ja. 4: 13. buy, sell, and g. gain

GET thee. [7: 3.

Ge. 12: 1. g. t. out of country, Ac.
22: 2. g. t. into land of Moriah
31: 13. g. t. out from this land
Ex. 7: 15. g. t. to Pha. in morning
10: 28. g. t. from me, take heed
11: 8. g. t. out, and all the people
19: 24. L. said to Moses, Away, g.
t. down, 32: 7. De. 9: 12. [32: 49.
Nu. 27: 12. g. t. up into Abarim, De.
De. 3: 27. g. t. up to top of Pisgah
17: 8. g. t. up to place L. choose
Jos. 7: 10. g. t. up, whf. liest thou?
17: 15. g. t. to wood country
Ju. 7: 9. Arise, g. t. unto the host
Ru. 3: 3. wash thyself, g. t. down
4: † 11. g. t. riches in Ephratah
1 S. 22: 5. g. t. into land of Judah
1 K. 1: 13. Go, g. t. in unto ki. Da.
2: 26. g. t. to Anathoth to own
14: 2. g. t. to Shiloh [fields
12. g. t. to thine own house
17: 3. g. t. hence | 9. to Zarephath
18: 41. Elijah said, g. t. up, eat
44. g. t. down, that rain stop not
2 K. 3: 13. g. t. to prophets of fa.
Ne. 9: 10. so didst thou g. t. name
Is. 22: 15. g. t. to this treasurer
30: 22. shalt say unto it, g. t. hence
40: 9. O Zion, g. t. into high mt.
47: 5. Sit silent, g. t. into darkn.
Je. 13: 1. g. t. a linen girdle [of Isr.
Eze. 3: 4. son of man, g. t. unto h.
11. go, g. t. to them of captivity
Mat. 4: 10. Jes. saith, g. t. hence, Sat.
16: 23. he said to Peter, g. t. behind me, Satan, Mk. 8: 33. Lu. 4: 8.
Lu. 13: 31. g. t. out, Herod will
Ac. 10: 20. Arise, g. t. down, go
22: 18. g. t. quickly out of Jerus.

GET you.

Ge. 19: 14. Lot said, Up, g. y. out
34: 10. trade, g. y. posses-s there
42: 2. g. y. down and buy for us
44: 17. g. y. up in peace unto fa.
Ex. 5: 4. g. y. unto your burdens
11. g. y. straw where can find
12: 31. g. y. from am. my people
Nu. 14: 25. g. y. into the wildern.
16: 24. g. y. up from about taber.
22: 13. Balaam said, g. y. into la.
De. 5: 30. g. y. into tents, Jos 22: 4.
Jos. 2: 16. g. y. to mountains, lest
Ju. 19: 9. g. y. early on your way
1 S. 9: 13. g. y. up, ye shall find
15: 6. g. y. down fr. Amalekites
25: 5. g. y. up to Carmel, and
Is. 30: 11. g. y. out of the way, turn
Je. 49: 30. g. y. far off, dwell deep
31. g. y. up to wealthy nation
Eze. 11: 15. said, g. y. far fr. the L.
Jo. 3: 13. g. y. down, press is full
Zch. 6: 7. g. y. hence, walk to and

GE'THER. [fro

Ge. 10: 23. chil. of Aram; G., 1 Ch. 1: 17.

GETHSEM'ANE.

Mat. 26: 36. place called G., Mk. 14: 32.

GETTETH. [chief

2 S. 5: 8. Whoso. g. up to gutter,
Pr. 3: 13. happy is man g. underst.
9: 7. reproveth a scorner g. shame,
rebuketh wicked g. a blot
15: 32. heareth reproof g. underst.
18: 15. heart of prudent g. knowl.
19: 8. g. wisdom loveth own soul
Je. 17: 11. g. riches, and not by right
48: 44. g. out of pit sh. be taken

GETTING. [g.

Ge. 31: 18. Jac. carried cattle of his
Pr. 4: 7. with thy g. get underst.
21: 6. g. of treasures by lying tongue

GEU'EL.

Nu. 13: 15. Of the tribe of Gad, G.

GE'ZER.

Jos. 10: 33. Horam king of G., 12: 12.
16: 10. Canaanites in G., Ju. 1: 29.
21: 21. G. with suburbs, 1 Ch. 6: 67.
1 K. 9: 16. king of E. taken G.
17. Sol. built G. and Beth-horon
1 Ch. 20: 4. war at G. with Philis.

GEZ'RITES = GER'ZITES.

1 S. 27: 8. David invaded the G. †

GHOST.

Ge. 49: 33. Jacob yielded up the g.
Jb. 10: 18. O that I had given up g.
11: 20. hope be as giving up of g.
14: 10. man giveth up the g. and
Je. 15: 9. hath borne 7, given up g.
Mat. 27: 50. Jes. cried, and yielded
up g., Mk. 15: 37. Lu. 23: 46.
Ac. 5: 10. Sapphira yielded up the g.
See GAVE UP, GIVE UP, HOLY.

GI'AH.

2 S. 2: 24. Ammah that lieth bef. G.

GIANT. [20: 4.

2 S. 21: 16. of sons of g., 18. 1 Ch.
20. born to g., 22. 1 Ch. 20: 8.
1 Ch. 20: 6. the son of the g.
Jb. 16: 14. he runneth upon me like

GIANTS. [g.

Ge. 6: 4. There were g. in those days
Nu. 13: 33. we saw g. sons of Anak
De. 2: 11. Emims were counted g.
3: 11. Og of Bashan remained of remnant of g., Jos 12: 4.-13: 12.
13. Bashan, called the land of g.
Jos. 15: 8. lot of Jud. at valley of g.
17: 15. get thee up to land of g.
18: 16. Benj. came to valley of g.

GIB'BAR = GIB'EON.

Ezr. 2: 20. chil. of G., 95. Ne. 7: 25.

GIB'BETHON.

Jos. 19: 44. the coast was G. | 21: 23.
1 K. 15: 27. smote at G. | 16: 15, 17.

GIB'EA. [of G.

1 Ch. 2: 49. Caleb's conc. bare fa.

GIB'EAH. [ties

Jos. 15: 57. Cain G. Timnah. 10 cit-
Ju. 19: 14. when they were by G.
16. an old man sojourned in G.
20: 9. this thing we will do to G.
13. deliv. us chil. of Belial in G.
29. liers in wait ab. G., 33, 36, 37.
30. put thems. in array ag. G.
1 S. 10: 26. Saul w. nt to G., 15: 34.
13: 15. Sam. gat him unto G., 16.
14: 2. Saul tarried in part of G.
2 S. 21: 6. will hang them in G.
Is. 10: 29. G. of Saul is fled
Ho. 5: 8. blow ye cornet in G. [of G.
9: 9. corrupted thems. as in days
10: 9. O Isr., hast sinned fr. days
of G. battle in G. not overtake

GIB'EATH.

Jos. 18: 28. G. and Kirjath: 14 cities

GIB'EATHITE.

1 Ch. 12: 3. sons of Shemaah the G.

GIB'EON.

Jos. 9: 3. inhabi of G. heard
10: 2. feared, bec. G. was great
4. help me, that we may smite G.
12. Sun, stand thou still upon G.
2 S. 2: 13. they met by pool of G.
3: 30. he had slain Asahel at G.
20: 8. were at great stone in G.
1 K. 3: 5. in G. the L. appeared, 9: 2

1 Ch. 8:29. at G. dw. fa. of G., 9:35.
21:29. altar of burnt offering at G.
Is. 28: 21. wroth as in valley of G.
Je. 28: 1. the son of Azur in G.
41:12. found Ishm. by waters in G.
See GIB'BAR.

GIB'EONITES.

2 S. 21: 1. Saul slew G. | 2, 3, 4.
9. he deliv-d into hands of G., 1 Ch. 12: 4. Ne. 3: 7.

GIB'LITES.

Jos. 13: 5. And the land of the G.

GIDDAL'TI.

1 Ch. 25:4. sons of Heman; G. | 29.

GID'DEL. [58.

Ezr. 2: 47. chil. of G., 56. Ne. 7:49,

GID'EON.

Ju. 6: 11. G. threshed wheat by
24. G. built an altar unto Lord
34. Spirit of Lord came upon G.
7: 1. Jeruh who is G. rose up
14. is nothing, save sword of G.
18. sword of L. and of G., 20.
8: 21. G. slew Zeba | 27. G. made
30. G. had 70 sons | 32. G. died
35. nor shewed kindn. to h. of G.
He. 11: 32. time fail me to tell of G.

GIDEO'NI.

Nu. 1: 11. prince of Benj. Abidan, son of G., 2:22.-7:60, 65.-10:24.

GI'DOM.

Ju. 20: 45. pursued hard unto G.

GIER eagle.

Le. 11: 18. in abomina., the g. e., [De. 14: 17.

GIFT.

Ge.34:12. Ask so much dowry and g.
Ex. 23: 8. take no g. a g. blindeth the wise, De. 16: 19. [6.
Nu. 8:19. given Levites as a g., 18:
18: 7. your office as a service of g.
11. the heaveoffering of their g.
De. 16: † 17. every man acc. to g.
2 S. 19: 42. hath he giv. us any g.?
Ps.45:12. dau of Tyre sh. be with g.
Pr. 17: 8. g. is as precious stone
23. wick. taketh g. out of bosom
18: 16. A man's g. maketh room
21: 14. g. in secret pacifieth anger
25: 14. whoso boasteth of false g.
Ec. 3: 13. it is the g. of God, 5:19.
7:7. and a g. destroyeth the heart
Eze. 46: † 5. meat off-g g. of his ha.
16. If a prince give a g. to sons
17. if he give a g. to one of serv-s
Mat. 5: 23. if bring thy g. to altar
24. Leave g. before altar and go
8: 4. offer the g. Moses com-d
15: 5. ye say, It is a g., Mk. 7:11.
23: 18. sweareth by g. guilty, 19.
Jn. 4:10. If thou knewest g. of God
Ac. 2: 38. receive g. of Holy Ghost
8: 20. tho-t g. of G. be purchased
10:45. on Gent. was poured the g.
11: 17. God gave them the like g.
Ro. 1:11. I may impart spiritual g.
5:15. so is free g. the grace of God and g. by grace abounded
16. so is g., free g. is of many of-
17. receive g. of righte. [fences
18. the free g. came upon all men
6: 23. the g. of God is eternal life
1 Co.1:7. th ye come behind in no g.
7:7. ev. man hath proper g. of God
13:2. tho. I have the g. of prophecy
16: † 3. to bring your g. to Jerus.
2 Co. 1:11. for g. bestowed upon us
8: 4. that we would receive g.
† 19. to travel with us with this g.
9:15. thanks unto G. for unspeak. g.
Ep. 2: 8. faith, it is the g. of God
3: 7. I made a minister, acc. to g.
4: 7. acc. to measure of g. of C.
Ph. 4:17. Not because I desire a g.
1 Ti. 4: 14. Neglect not g. in thee
2 Ti. 1: 6. stir up g. is in thee
He. 6:4. have tasted of heavenly g.
Ja. 1:17. ev. good g. and perf. g. is
1 Pe. 4: 10. every man received g.

GIFTS. [concu.

Ge. 25: 6. Ab. gave g. unto sons of
Ex. 28:38. Isr. sh. hallow in their g.
Le. 23: 38. your feasts, besides g.
Nu. 18: 29. of all g. offer the best
2 S.8:2. Syrians bro-t g., 6.1 Ch.18:2.
2 Ch.19:7. with L. is no taking of g.
21: 3. Jehosh. gave great g. of gold
26: 8. Ammonites gave g. to Uzziah
32: 23. many bro-t g. unto the L.
Es. 2: 18. Ahas-s made feast gave g.
9: 22. days of sending g. to poor
Ps. 16: † 4. that give g. to ano. god
68:18 thou hast received g. for men
72:10. k-s of Sheba and Seba offer g.
Pr.6: 35. not content, tho. givest g.
15: 27. he th. hateth g. shall live
19:6. man is friend to him giveth g.
29:4. receiveth g. overth-h judgm.
Is.1:23. every one loveth g. [lovers
Eze. 16: 33. give g. to whores, g. to
20: 26. I polluted them in their g.
31. when ye offer g. you pollute
39. pollute my name no more with
22: 12. taken g. to shed blood [g.
Da.2:6. shew dream, ye shall rec. g.
48. king gave Dan. many great g.
5: 17. said, Let thy g. be to thyself
Mat. 2: 11. presented unto him g.
7: 11. know how to give good g., Lu. 11: 13.
Lu. 21: 1. rich casting their g. into
5. temple was adorned with g.
Ro. 11: 29. g. of G. without repent.
12: 6. g. differing acc. to grace
1 Co. 12: 1. Now conc. spiritual g.
4. there are diversities of g. but
9. to ano. g. of healing, 28, 30.
31. But covet earnestly the best g.
14: 1. and desire spiritual g.
12. as ye are zealous of spirit-l g.
Ep. 4: 8. led captivity, gave g. unto
He. 2: 4. G. bearing witn. with g.
5: 1. th. he may offer g. and sacrif.
8: 3. high priest is ord-d to offer g.
4. there are priests that offer g.
9: 9. were off-d, both g. and sacri.
11: 4. God testifying of Abel's g.
Re. 11: 10. dwell upon earth shall [send g.

GI'HON.

Ge. 2: 13. name of sec. river is G.
1 K. 1: 33. bring Sol. down to G., 38.
45. have anointed him k. in G.
2 Ch. 32: 30. stop. watercourse of G.
33: 14. built wall on west of G.

GIL'ALAI.

Ne. 12: 36. G. with musical instru- [ments

GILBO'A.

1 S. 28: 4. all Israel pitched in G.
31: 1. Saul fell slain in mount G., 8. 2 S. 21: 12. 1 Ch. 10: 1, 8.
2 S. 1: 6. by chance upon mount G.
21. ye mountains of G. let no dew

GILDED.

Re.17:† 4. woman was g. with gold

GIL'EAD. [Person.]

Nu. 26: 30. are sons of G., 1 Ch.7:17.
27: 1. G. son of Machir, 26: 29.-36: 1. Jos. 17: 1, 3. 1 Ch. 2: 21, 23.-7: 14.
Ju. 11: 1. G. begat | 2. G's wife bare
1 Ch. 5: 14. son of G., son of Michael

GIL'EAD. [Place.]

Ge.31:21. and set his face toward mt.
37:25. company of Ishm-s fr. G. [G.
Nu. 32: 1. G. was a place for cattle
40. Moses gave G., De. 3: 15.
De. 34: 1. Lord shewed land of G.
Jos. 17: 1. Machir, had G. [G.
22: 13. Isr. sent Phineas into land of
Ju. 10: 18. head over inhab-s of G.
11: 11. Jephthah with elders of G.
2 S. 2:9. made Ishbosheth k. over G.
17: 26. Isr. pitched in land of G.
1 K. 17: 1. Elijah, who was of G.
Ps. 60: 7. G. is mine, 108: 8.
Can.4:1. thy hair as goats fr. G., 6:5.
Je. 8: 22. is there no balm in G.?
22: 6. art G. unto me
46: 11. go into G. O virgin
50: 19. soul satisfied upon G.
Ho. 6: 8. G. city of them work iniq.
12: 11. Is there iniquity in G.?
Am. 1: 3. they have threshed G.
13. ripped up women of G.
Ob. 19. Benjamin shall possess G.
Mi. 7: 14. let them feed in G.
Zch. 10: 10. bring them into land o. [G.
See RAMOTH.

GIL'EADITE, S.

Nu. 26: 29. of Gilead family of G.
Ju. 10: 3. Jair, a G. judged Israel
11: 1. Jephthah the G., 40.-12: 7.
12: 4. ye G. are fugitives of Ephr.
5. G-s took passages of Jordan
2 S. 17: 27. Barzil. G. brought beds,
2 K. 15: 25. 50 men of G. [19: 31
See BARZILLAI.

GIL'GAL.

Jos. 4: 19. people encamped in G.
9: 6. they went to Joshua at G.
10: 6. men of Gibeon sent to G.
Ju. 2: 1. an angel came up from G.
1 S. 7: 16. Samuel went to G.
10: 8. shalt go down bef. me to G.
11: 14. let us go to G. and
13: 7. Saul in G. | 8. Sam. not to G.
15: 33. Sam. hewed Agag in G.
Ho. 4: 15. come not ye unto G. nor
9: 15. their wickedness is in G.
12: 11. they sacrifice bullocks in G.
Am. 4: 4. at G. multiply transgres.
5: 5. enter not into G. for G. sh. go
Mi.6:5. Balaam ans. fr. Shittim to G.

GI'LOH.

Jos. 15: 51. G. G., 2 S. 15: 12.

GI'LONITE.

2 S. 15: 12. Ahithophel G., 23: 34

GIM'ZO.

2 Ch. 28: 18. Philis. had taken G.

GIN, GINS.

Jb. 18: 9. g. shall take him by heel
40: † 24. any bore his nose with g.?
Ps. 140: 5. they have set g-s for me
141: 9. g-s of workers of iniquity
Is. 8: 14. be for a g. to inhabitants of Jerusalem
Am.3:5. can bird fall where no g. is?

GI'NATH.

1 K. 16: 21. people followed Tibni the son of G., 22.

GIN'NETHO.

Ne. 12: 4. these are the priests G.

GIN'NETHON.

Ne. 10: 6. G., these priests, 12: † 4, 16.

GIRD.

Ge. 3: † 7. made things to g. about
Ex.29:5. g. him with curious girdle, 9
Ju. 3: 16. Ehud did g. his dagger
2 K. 3: † 21. were able to g. thems.
Is. 8: 9. g. yourselves [sweat
Eze.44:18. not g. with what causeth
Jo. 1: 13. g. yours., lament, priests
Lu. 12: 37. g. hims., make them sit
17: 8. g. thyself, and serve me
Jn. 21: 18. old, ano. shall g. thee
Ac. 12: 8. g. thyself bind on sandals
See LOINS, SACKCLOTH, SWORD.

GIRDED.

Le. 8: 7. he g. him with girdle
De.1:41. g. on ev. man his weapons
Ju. 18: 11. 600 g. with weapons
1 S.2:4. that stumbled are g. with str
18. Sam. g. with linen ephod
2 S. 6:14. Da. was g. with an ephod
20:8. Joab's garm. was g. unto him
22: 40. hast g. me with strength,
1 K.20:32. they g. sackcl. [Ps.18:39.
Ps.30: 11. hast g. me with gladness
65: 6. setteth fast mts. being g.
† 12. little hills are g. with joy
93: 1. strength whw. he hath g.
109: 19. girdle wherewith he is g.

Is. 45:5. I g. thee, tho. not kno. me
La.2:10.elders of Zi. g. with sackcl.
Eze.16:10. I g. thee with fine linen
23 : 15. Chaldeans g. with girdles
Jo. 1 : 8. like virgin g. with sackcl.
Jn. 13 : 4 he took towel g. himself
5. with towel wherewith he was g.
Re. 15 : 6. breasts g. with golden
See GIRT, LOINS, SWORD.

GIRDEDST, ETH, ING.

1 K. 20 : 11. that g-h on his harness
Jb.12 : 18. he g-h their loins with
Ps. 18 : 32. It is God that g-h me
Pr.31:17. she g-h her loins with str.
Is.3:24. instead of stomacher, g-g of sackcloth
22:12.L.did call to g-g with sackcl.
Jn. 21 : 18. When young thou g-t [thyself

GIRDLE.

Ex. 28 : 4. they shall make a g.
8. curious g. of ephod, 27, 28.-
29 : 5.-39 : 5, 20. Le. 8 : 7.
39. shalt make g. of needlework
39:29. made g. of fine twined linen
Le. 16 : 4. be girded with linen g.
1 S 18 : 4. gave Dav. his bow and g.
2 S.18 : 11. would have giv. thee a g.
20 : 8. upon it a g. with sw. fast-d
1 K.2 : 5. put bl. of war on his g.
2 K. 1 : 8. Elijah was girt with a g.
3 : † 21. that could gird with a g.
Jb.12:18. the loins of kings with a g.
†21. he looseth the g. of the strong
Ps. 109 : 19. g. whw. he is girded
Is. 3 : 24. instead of a g. be a rent
5 : 27. nor shall g. of loins be loosed
11 : 5. righteousn. be g. of his loins, faithfulness g. of his reins
22 : 21. strengthen Eliakim with g.
23:†10 O dau., there is no more g.
Je. 13 : 1. go, get thee a linen g., 2.
6. Euphra and take the g., 4, 7.
10. peo. as this g., good for noth.
11. as g. cleaveth to the loins
Mat. 3 : 4.Jn. a leathern a.,Mk.1:6.
Ac. 21 : 11. took Paul's g., said, Jews shall bind man owneth this g. [den g.
Re. 1 : 13. about the paps with gol-

GIRDLES.

Ex. 28:40. make for Aaron's sons g.
29 : 9.sh. gird Aa. and sons with g.
Le. 8 : 13. did gird Aa.'s sons with g.
Pr. 31: 24. deliv. g. unto merchant
Eze.23:15.images of Chald-s with g.
Da.5 : † 6. g. of his loins were loosed
Re.15:6.angels girded with golden g

GIR'GASHITE,[1] S, or GIR'GASITE.[2] [G.[1]

Ge. 10 : 16. begat the G.,[2] 1 Ch. 1:14.
15 : 21. Unto thy seed, G-s, Ne. 9:8.
De 7 : 1. when L. hath cast out G-s
Jos. 3 : 10. he will drive out the G-s
24 : 11. fought against you, the G-s

GIRL, S.

Jo. 3 : 3. they have sold a g. for wine
Zch. 8 : 5.streets full of boys and g-s

GIRT.

2 K. 1 : 8. g. with girdle of leather
Jn 21 : 7. Peter g. his fisher's coat
Ep. 6 : 14. loins g. about with truth
Re. 1 : 13.g. about paps with golden

GIS'PA. See ZIHA. [See LOINS.

GIT'TAH-HE'PHER.

Jos. 19 :13. passeth on the east to G.

GIT'TAIM. [11 : 33.

2 S. 4 : 3. Beerothites fled to G. | Ne.

GIT'TITE, S.

Jos 13 :3. G-s, Ekronites[Ch 13:13.
2 S. 6 : 10. Obed-edom the G., 11. 1
15:18.Pelethites, G-s, passed bef k.
19. send king to Ittai,G.,12.-18:2.
21 : 19. brother of Goliath G., 1 Ch.

GIT'TITH. [20 : 5.

Ps. 8 * To Musician upon G., 81,*

GIVE. [84.*

Ge. 15 : 2. what g. me, I go childless
7. out of Ur to g. thee this land
Ge. 23 : 11. field I g. and cave, 9, 13.
28 : 20. g. me bread and raiment
22. of all shall g. me. I g. the 10th
29 : 19. better I g. her thee, than g.
34:16. will we g. our dau-s unto you
38 : 16. What wilt g. me? 17, 18.
41 : 16 G. sh. g. Pha. ans. of peace
Ex.5:7.Ye sh. no more g. peo. straw
6 : 4. cov. with them to g. land
10 : 25. Thou must g. us sacrifices
21 : 23. thou shalt g., 22 : 29. Nu. 8 : 48.-7 : 5.-27 : 7. De. 2 : 28.- 14 : 21.-16 : 10.-18 : 4. Eze. 43 : 19. Mi. 1 : 14.
21 : 30. he shall g., 32, 34. Le. 15 : 14.-25 : 51, 52.-27 : 23. De. 22 : 29. 1 S. 2:10. Pr. 6: 31. Eze. 46 : 18. Da. 11 : 17. Mat. 26 : 53.Lu. 4 : 10.-20 : 16.
22 : 17. fa. utterly refuse to g. her
30. eighth day shalt g. it me
25:16.into ark, testimony I sh g., 21
30 : 12. shall g. ev. man a ransom
13. shall g. every one half a shekel, De. 18 : 3.-22 : 19. Is.7 : 22. Eze 45 : 8.
15. half shekel, when they g. off-g
Le. 5 : 16. fifth part g. it unto, 6: 5. -22 : 14. Nu. 5 : 7.
25 : 38. g. you land of Canaan
Nu. 3 : 9. shalt g. Levites unto Aa.
11:4. Who sh. g. us flesh to eat? 18.
15 : 21. ye sh. g., 18 : 28.-19 : 3.- 27 : 9, 10, 11.-32 : 29.-33:54.-35: 4, 6, 8, 13, 14. Le.7:32.Ju.14:13. Eze. 44 : 28, 30.-45 : 13.-47 : 23.
22 : 13. L. refuseth to g. me leave
18. If Balak g. me ho. full, 24: 13.
25 : 12. I g. to Phinehas my cov.
26 : 54. to many g. more inheri., to few g. the less, 33 : 54.
34:13. L. com-d to g. unto 9 tribes
35 : 2.ye shall g. to Levites suburbs
36 : 2. L. com-d lord to g. thee land
De.2:31.to g.Sihon | 4:38.g. thee la.
15 : 10.shalt g.him thine heart, 14.
16:17 g. as he is able, Eze.46:5, 11.
24 : 15. thou shalt g. him his hire
25 : 3. Forty stripes he may g. him
Jos. 17 : 4. L.com-d to g., 9:24.-21:2.
20 : 4. fleeth, they shall g. him pla.
Ju. 7 : 2. to g. Midianites into hands
8:25.ans , We will willingly g. them
1 S. 2 : 16. thou shalt g. it me now
28. did I g. unto house of thy fa. ?
32. wealth which G. shall g. Isr.
17 : 25. king will g. him his dau.
22 : 7. will son of Jesse g. fields ?
25 : 11. g. it to men wh. I know not?
2 S. 12 : 11. wives bef. eyes, and g.
23 : 15. Oh that one would g. me drink of well of Beth., 1Ch.11:17.
24 : 23. did Araunah g., 1Ch.21:23.
1 K. 3 : 5. Ask what I sh. g. thee. 2
8:32. g. acc. to his righte. [Ch.1:7.
11: 11.Kingdom fr thee and g., 35.
13 : 8. If thou wilt g. me half
21 : 3. L. forbid that I sho. g.
2 K.8:19. g. alway a light, 2 Ch.21: 7.
1 Ch. 29 : 12. make great and g.
2 Ch. 30 : † 8. g. hand unto L. [str.
12 hand of G. to g. them one heart
Ezr. 9 : 8. to g. us a nail in his holy
9. to g. us reviving, to g. us wall
Jb. 2:4. all a man hath g. for his life
14 : † 4. who g. clean out of uncl.?
32 : 22. not to g. flattering titles
Ps. 2 : 8. Ask, I shall g. thee heath.
14 : † 7. g. salv out of Zion, 53: †6.
37 : 4. sh. g. thee desires of heart
49 : 7. none can g. to God a ransom
51 : 16. not sacrifice, else would I g.
68 : † 33. doth g. out mighty voice
78: 20. can he g. bread also ? can be
91 : 11. g. his angels charge, Mat.
94 : 13. mayest g. him rest [4 : 6.
104 : 27. mayest g. them meat
Ps. 109 : 4. I g. myself unto prayer
111 : 6. g. th. heritage of heathen
120 : † 3. what deceitf. tongue g.
Pr. 29:15. rod and reproof g. wisd.
17. sh. d. thee rest, sh. g. delight
Ec.2:3. sought to g. mys. unto wine
26. may g. to him that is good
5 : 1. than to g. the sacr. of fools
Can. 8:7. g. substance of his house
Is. 30 : 23. then he shall g. rain
42 : 6. g. for cov. of peo., 49 : 8.
43 : 20. g. drink to my people
55 : 10. th. it may g. seed to sower
61 : 3. to g. beauty for ashes
62 : 8. no more g. thy corn to be
Je. 3 : 19. how g. thee pleasant la.
6 : 10. To whom sh. I g. warning?
9 : † 1. who will g. my head waters
16:7. nei. men g. th. cup of conso.
17:10. to g. man acc. to ways, 32:19.
25 : 31. g. wicked to the sword
29 : 11. to g. you expected end
38 : 15. if I g. counsel wilt thou
Eze. 2 : 8. open mouth, eat th. I g.
3 : 3. fill bowels with roll that I g.
16:36. by blood of thy chil. which didst g. them
20 : 28. brought them into land, I lifted up hand to g. it, 42.-47:
21:11. g. it into hand of slayer [14.
33 : 15. if wick. g. that he robbed
45:16. g. this oblation for the prince
46 : 11. as he sh. be able to g., 5.
16. If prince g. gift unto sons, 17.
Da. 9 : 22. I am come to g. skill
Mi.6:7. sh. I g. my firstb. for transgr.
Zch. 8 : 12. vine shall g. her fruit, ground shall g. increase, and the heavens g. their dew
Mat. 5 : 31. g. her a writing of
7 : 9. if ask br. will he g. stone?
10. fish, will he g. serp.? Lu.11:11.
11. how to g. gifts unto chil. so Fa. to g. them ask, Lu. 11:13.
10:42. g. cup of cold wat., Mk.9:41.
14 : 7. prom-d to g. what she ask
16 : 26. g. for his soul ? Mk. 8 : 37.
19 : 7. to g. a writing of divorc-t ?
20 : 23. sit on my right hand is not mine to g., Mk. 10 : 40.
28. g. life ransom for, Mk. 10:45.
22:17. lawful to g. tribute, Mk.12: 14. Lu. 20 : 22.-23 : 2.
24:45. to g. them meat in due sea.
26:15. what g. me, and I will deliv.
Mk.6:25. that th. g. me head of Jn.
12:9. g. viney. unto others, Lu.20:16
14:11. promised to g. him money
Lu. 1:77. To g. knowl. of salvation
4 : 6. whomso. I will I g. it
6 : 38. good measure shall men g.
8 : 55. com-d to g. her meat
10 : 7. eating such as they g.
19. I g. unto you power to tread
11 : 7. I cannot rise and g. thee
8. g. as many as he needeth
12 : 32. pleas. to g. you the kingd.
42. to g. their portion of meat
51. am come to g. peace on earth?
16 : 12. who g. you is your own ?
17:18. not found to g. glory to G.
18:12. g. tithes | 19 : 8. half of goods
20:10. sho. g. him fruit of viney.
16. sh. g. vineyard to others
22 : 5. covenan-d to g. him money
Jn.4:14. drinketh water I sh. g. him
6: 27. meat wh. Son of man sh g.
52. How can man g. us his flesh
7 : 19. Did not Moses g. the law
10 : 28. I g. to them eternal life
11 : 22. what thou ask, G. will g.
13 : 26. He it is to whom I g. a sop
29. that he sho. g. to the poor
34. a new com-t I g. unto you
14 : 16. he sh. g. you ano. Comf-r
27. my peace I g. unto you, not as world giv. g. I unto you

Jn.15:16.whatso.ye ask, he may g.
16:23. whatso. ye ask he will g. it
17: 2. that he sho. g. eternal life
Ac. 3: 6. such as I have g. I thee
5: 31. to g. repentance to Israel
6: 4. we will g. oursel. to prayer
7: 5. would g. it for a possession
38. received oracles to g. unto us
20: 32. able to g. you an inheri.
35. more blessed to g. than
Ro. 8: 32. freely g. us all things
14:12. ev. one g. account of hims.
1 Co. 7: 5. g. yourselves to fasting
25. yet I g. my judgm.,2 Co.8:10.
13: 3. though I g. my body to be burned ⌈sounds
14: 7. except g. distinction in
8. if trumpet g. uncertain sound
2 Co. 4:6. to g. light of the knowl.
5: 12. g. you occ. to glory on our
Ep. 1: 17. G. may g. you wisdom
4: 28. have to g. to him needeth
1 Ti. 5: 14. younger wom. g. none occasion ⌈tance
2 Ti. 2:25. if G. will g. them repen-
4: 8. righteous Judge shall g. me
He. 2: 1. to g. more earnest heed
1 Pe.3:15.ready always to g.an ans.
1 Jn. 5:16. g. life for them that sin
Re.11:18. shouldest g. reward unto
13: 15. power to g. life to image
† 16. to g. a mark in right hand
16:19. to g. her wine of his wrath
17: 13. sh. g. power unto beast
17. sh. g. kingdom unto beast
19: 7. Let us g. honour to him
22: 12. to g. ev. man acc. to work
See ACCOUNT, GLORY, SWARE.

GIVE.
[Imperative and optative.]
Ge. 14: 21. g. me the persons
27:28. God g. thee of dew of heav.
28: 4. g. thee the blessing of Ab.
29:21.g. me my wife | 30:1.g.chil.
30: 26. g. me my wives and chil.
43:14. G. Almighty g. you mercy
Ex. 17: 2. g. us water | Nu.11: 13.
Nu. 6: 26. L. g. thee peace ⌊flesh
27: 4. g. unto us a possession
Jos. 2: 12. and g. me a true token
14: 12. g. me this mt. ⌈Ju.1:15.
15:19.g. me a blessing, g. springs,
Ju. 20: 7. g. here your advice
1 S. 2: 20. g. thee seed of this wom.
8: 6. said, g. us a k. to judge us
11: 3. g. respite | 14:41.g.perf.lot
17: 10. g. me a man that we fight
21: 9. none like that, g. it me
25: 8. g. whatso. cometh to hand
27: 5. g. me place in some town
1 K. 3: 9. g. serv. unders-g heart
25. g. half to the one and half
26. g. her the living child, 27.
8: 39. g. ev. man acc. to his ways
50. g. them compassion bef. th.
17: 19. he said, g. me thy son
21:2. g. me thy vineyard
2 K.4:42.g.unto peo.th.may eat,43.
5:22.sons of proph-s g. th. I pray
6:28.g.thy son, th. we eat him,29.
10: 15. If it be, g. me thine hand
14:9. saying, g. thy daugh. to my son to wife. 2 Ch. 25: 18.
18: 23. g. pledges to my lord, Is.
22:5. g. it to doers of work ⌊36:8.
1 Ch. 16: 28. g. to L. ye kindreds, glory, 29. Ps. 29: 1, 2.-96:7, 8.
22:12.L.g. thee wisdom, underst-g
29:19. g. unto Sol. a perfect heart
2 Ch. 1:10. g. me now wisdom
Ne. 4:4. g. them for a prey in land
Jb. 6: 22. Did I say, g. a reward
32: 21. nor g. flattering titles
Ps. 28: 4. g. them acc. to deeds
60:11. g. help fr. trouble, 108:12.
72:1. g. king thy judgments, O G.
86: 16. g. strength to thy servant

Ps.119:34. g. me understanding, 73, 125, 144, 169. ⌈he be wiser
Pr. 9: 9. g. instruct. to wise man
23: 26. My son, g. me thine heart
25:21.hunger,g. him br.,Ro.12:20.
30:8.g. me nei. poverty nor riches
15. hath two dau-s, crying, g. g.
31: 6. g. strong drink unto him
31. g. her of fruit of her hands
Ec. 11: 2. g. a portion to seven
Is. 49: 20. g. place that I dwell
62:7. g. him no rest till he establ.
Je. 18: 19. g. heed to me, O Lord
35: 2. and g. them wine to drink
48: 9. g. wings unto Moab
La. 2: 18. let tears run, g. no rest
3: 65. g. them sorrow of heart
Eze. 3: 17. g. them warning fr. me
Da. 5: 17. g. thy rewards to ano.
Ho. 4: 18. her rulers do love, g. ye
9: 14. g. them, O L. what wilt g.
13:10. saidst, g. me k. and princes
14: † 2. take aw. iniq., g. good
Zch. 11: 12. g. me my price, if not
Mat. 5: 42. g. to him that asketh thee, Lu.6:30. ⌈bread, Lu.11:3.
6: 11. g. us this day our daily
9: 24. g. place | 10: 8. freely g.
14: 8. g. me John Baptist's head
16. g. ye them to eat, Mk. 6: 37. Lu. 9: 13. ⌈and thee
17: 27. and g. unto them for me
19: 21. g. to the poor, Mk. 10:21.
20:8. call labourers, g. their hire
25:8. g. us of your oil, our lamps
28. talent fr. him, g. it, Lu.19:24.
Lu. 6: 38. g. and it shall be given
11: 41. g. alms of such as, 12:33.
12: 58. to magistrate, g. diligence
14: 9. bade say, g. this man pla.
15:12. g. me portion of goods ⌈15.
Jn.4:7. Jes. saith, g. me to dri., 10,
6: 34. L. evermore g. us this br.
9:24.g. G.praise,this man a sinner
Ac. 8: 19. Simon said, g. me power
13: 16. Men of Israel g. audience
Ro. 12:19. rather g. pla. unto wrath
1 Co. 10: 32. g. none offence, nei.
2 Co.9:7. let him g. not grudgingly
Ep. 4: 27. Neitehr g. place to devil
Col. 4:1. g. unto serv-ts that is just
2 Th. 3:16. L. g. you peace always
1 Ti. 1: 4. neither g. heed to fables
4: 13. g. attendance to reading
15. g. thyself wholly to them
2 Pe. 1: 10. g. diligence to make
Re. 10: 9. g. me the little book
18: 7. torment and sorrow g. her
See CHARGE,EAR,GLORY,LIGHT.

I will GIVE.
Ge. 17:8. I w. g. unto thee,26:3,4.-48: 4. De. 34: 4.
16. I w. g. thee a son of her
28: 22. I w. g. tenth unto thee
34:11. sh. say unto me I w.g.,12.
45:18. I w. g. you good of the la.
Ex. 3: 21. And I w. g. peo. favour
24:12. I w. g. thee tables of stone
25: 22. wh. I w. g. thee in com-t
33:14.my presence I w.g.thee rest
Le. 26: 4. I w. g. rain, De. 11: 14.
6. I w. g. peace in the land
Nu. 10: 29. place L. said I w.g. it
11:21.w.g. flesh | 21:16.w.g.wat.
Jos. 8:18. I w.g. Ai into thine ha.
1 S. 1: 11. I w.g. him unto the L.
18: 21. I w. g. her, she be snare
2 S.12:11.I w.g.wives unto neighb.
1 K. 11: 13. I w. g. one tribe
31. I w. g. ten tribes to thee
13: 7. and I w. g. thee a reward
21:2. I w. g. thee better viney.,6.
7. I w. g. vineyard of Naboth
1 Ch.22:9.I w.g.rest, I w.g.peace
2 Ch. 1: 12. I w. g. thee riches
Ps. 30: 12. O Lord, I w.g. thanks
57: 7. I w. sing g. praise, 108: 1.

Pr. 3: 28. to morrow I w.g. when
Is. 3: 4. I w. g. chil. to be princes
41: 27. I w. g. to Jerus. one that bringeth good tidings ⌈49:8.
42: 6. I w. g. thee for covenant,
45: 3. I w.g. treasures of darkn.
49: 6. I w. g. thee for a light to
56: 5. I w. g. them everl. name
Je. 3: 15 I w. g. pastors acc. to
9: 15. I w. g. them gall to drink
14: 13. I w. g. you peace in land
15:†4.I w.g. them for a removing
17: 3. I w. g.substance to spoil
24: 7. I w. g. heart to know me
32: 39. I w. g. them one heart, Eze. 11: 19. ⌈transgr.
34:18. I w. g. the men that have
Eze. 7: 21. I w. g. it into hand of
11: 17. I w. g. you land of Israel
16: 38. I w. g. thee blood in fury
39. I w. g. thee into their hand
61. I w. g. them thee for dau-s
21:27. whose right it is, I w. g. it
23: 46. I w.g. them to be remov.
29:19. I w.g. land of E. unto Neb.
21. I w.g. thee opening of mouth
36: 26. I w. g. you heart of flesh
39: 4. w. g. thee unto rav. birds
11. w.g. unto Gog pla. of graves
Ho. 2:15. I w. g. her vineyards fr.
Zch. 3:7. w. g. thee places to walk
Mat. 11:28. come, I w. g. you rest
16: 19. I w.g. thee keys of kingd.
20:4. whatso. is right, I w.g. you
14. I w.g. unto last as unto thee
Mk. 6: 22. ask what wilt, I w. g.
Lu. 21: 15. I w. g. you a mouth
Jn. 6:51. bread I w.g. is my flesh, wh. I w. g. for life of world
Ac. 13:34. I w. g. mercies of David
He.8:†10.I w.g. my laws into mind
Re.2:10.be faithful, I w.g. a crown
17. I w. g. him a white stone
23. I w. g. ev. one acc. to works
28. I w.g. him the morning star
11: 3. I w. g. power to my witn.
21: 6. I w. g. to him athirst wat.

Lord GIVE. ⌊of life
Ex. 12: 25. land L. will g. you, Le. 14: 34.-23: 10.-25:2. Nu. 15:2.
16: 8. when L. g. you flesh to eat
Nu. 11:18. thf. L. will g. you flesh
14: 8. if L. delight he will g. it us
22: 13. L. refuseth to g. me leave
34: 13. L. com-d to g. the 9 tribes
36: 2. L. com-d to g. land by lot
De.1:25.good land L.doth g.,20.-20:
28:65. L. sh. g. trembl. heart ⌊16.
Jos.9:24. L. com-d Moses to g. land
17:4. L. com-d to g.us inheritance
21: 2. the L. com-d to g. us cities
Ru.4:12.L.shall g. thee of this wom.
1 K. 15: 4. L. his God did g. lamp
2 Ch. 25: 9. L. is able to g. much
Ps.29:11.L.will g.strength unto peo.
84: 11. L. will g. grace and glory
85: 12. L. shall g. that wh.is good
Is. 7: 14. L. shall g. you a sign
14: 3. the L. shall g. thee rest
30:20.tho. L. g. bread of adversity
Zch. 10:1. L. shall g. them showers
Lu.1:32. L. shall g. him the throne
2 Ti.1:16.L.g. mercy unto Onesiph.

Not GIVE or GIVE not.
Ge. 24:41. g. n. one, thou clear be
30:31.Jac.said,Thou shalt n.g.me
Ex. 5: 10. I will n.g. you straw
30:15.rich n.g.more,poor n.g.less
Le. 25: 37. n.g. money upon usury
De. 2: 5. will n. g. you of la., 9, 19.
7: 3. dau. thou n. g. to his son
28: 55. will n. g. of flesh of chil.
Ju. 21: 1. n. any of us g. dau. unto Benjamin to wife
7. sworn we will n. g. wives, 18.
1 S. 30: 22. will n.g. them of spoil
1 K. 21: 4. I will n. g. inheritance

Ezr. 4 : † 13. then **n.g.** toll, tribute
9:12.**g.n.**your dau-s,Ne.10:30.-13:
Ps.132:4. I will **n.g.** sleep eyes ⌊25.
Pr. 6 : 4. **g. n.** sleep to thine eyes
31:3.**g.n.** thy strength unto wom.
Ec. 7 : † 21. **g. n.** heart unto words
Is. 13 : 10. constellations **n.g.** light
42:8.my glory **n.g.** to ano., 48:11.
Je. 18 : 18. let us **n.g.** heed to any
26 : 24. **n. g.** Jeremiah into hand
Eze.32:7.I will cover sun, moon sh.
n.g.light,Mat.24:29.Mk.13:24.
Da. 11.21. **n.g.** honour of kingdom
Ho. 5:†4. **n.g.** their doings to turn
Jo.2:17. **g. n.** heritage to reproach
Mat.7:6.**g.n.**that is holy unto dogs
Mk. 12 : 15. give, or shall we **n. g.**
Ja. 2 : 16. **g. n.** things they need

GIVE thanks. ⌈18:49
2 S.22:50. I will **g.t.** unto thee, Ps.
1 Ch. 16:8. **g.t.** unto the L., 34.Ps.
105:1.-106:1.-107:1.-118:1,29.-
136 : 1, 3.
35. save us, O God, that we may
g. t. to holy name, Ps. 106:47.
41. expressed by name, to **g. t.**
25 : 3. sons with a harp to **g. t.**
2 Ch.31:2. Levites to **g.t.**,Ne.12:24.
Ps. 6 : 5. in grave who **g.** thee **t.**
30 : 4. Sing unto L. ye saints, **g. t.**
97 : 12. ⌈ever
12. O L., I will **g.t.** unto thee for
35:18. I will **g. t.**in the great cong.
42: † 5. I shall **g. t.** for help ⌈(2)
75 : 1. Unto thee, O G. do we **g. t.**
79 : 13. so we thy people will **g. t.**
92 : 1. good thing to **g. t.** unto L.
106 : 47. save us to **g.t.** unto name
119 :62. at midn. I will rise to **g.t.**
122 : 4. whi. tribes go up to **g. t.**
136 : 2. O **g. t.** unto God of gods
26. O **g.t.** unto the God of heaven
140 : 13. righte. shall **g. t.** to thy
Ro. 16 : 4. to whom not only I **g. t.**
1 Co. 10 : 30. that for which I **g. t.**
Ep. 1 : 16. I cease not to **g. t.** for you
Col.1: 3. We **g. t.** to God and the Fa.
1 Th. 1 : 2. We **g. t.** to God always
5 : 18. In every thing **g. t.**, this is
2 Th. 2 : 13. we are bound to **g. t.**
Re. 11 : 17. We **g.** thee **t.** L. G. Al.

GIVE up.
De. 23: 14.to **g. u.**thine enem.,31:5.
1 K.14 :16. he shall **g.** Isr.**u.** bec. of
Jb. 3:11.why did not I **g.u.**ghost ?
13 : 19. If hold tongue,I **g.u.**ghost
Is. 43 : 6. I will say to north, **g. u.**
Ho. 11 : 8. How **g.** thee **u.** Ephr. ?
Mi.5:3.Therefore will he **g.**them **u.**
6 : 14. that thou deliv. will I **g.u.**

Will I GIVE.
Ge. 12: 7. Unto thy seed **w.I g.**this
land.13:15.-24:7.-28:13.-35:12.
Ex. 32 : 13.-33 : 1.
De. 1 : 36. Caleb, to him **w. I g.**land
39. shall go in, to them **w. I g.**it
Jos.15: 16. **w. I g.** Achsah,Ju.1:12.
1 S 9 : 8. that **w. I g.**to man of G.
18 : 17. dau. Merab, **w. I g.** thee
1 K.11 : 36. unto son **w. I g.**1 tribe
1 Ch. 16:18. Unto thee **w. I g.** land,
the la. of Canaan, Ps. 105 : 11.
Ps. 18 : 49. **w. I g.** thanks to thee
Can. 7 : 12. **w. I G.** thee my loves
Is. 43 : 4. thf. **w. I g.** men for thee
56 : 5. unto them **w. I g.** in mine
Je. 4 : 12. **w. I g.** sentence ag. them
8 : 10.**w. I g.** their wives unto oth.
15 : 13. treasures **w. I g.** to speil
19 : 7. carcasses **w. I g.**to be meat
24 : 8. so **w. I g.** Zedekiah king
30:16.all th.prey upon thee **w.I g.**
45 : 5. thy life **w. I g.** for a prey
Eze. 15 : 6. **w. I g.** inhab of Jerus.
33 : 27. is in open field **w. I g.**
36 : 26. new heart also **w. I g.** you
Hag. 2 : 9. in this pla **w. I g.** peace

Mat. 4:9. devil said,All these **w. I g.**
Lu. 4 : 6. All this power **w. I g.**thee
Re. 2:7. overcometh **w. I g.**, 17, 26.

GIVEN.
Ge. 21 : 7. sho. have **g.** chil. suck
24 : 35. hath **g.** him flocks and
36. unto him **g.** all he hath
29 : 33. hath **g.** me this son also
30 : 6. heard my voice **g.** me a son
31 : 9. cattle of your fa. **g.** to me
Le.10:14. due, wh. are **g.**out of sac.
20 : 3. hath **g.** seed unto Molech
Nu. 3: 9. they are wholly **g.**, 8: 16.
18 : 6. are **g.** as a gift for L.
De. 12 : 15. acc. to blessing **g.**,16:17.
26 : 14. nor **g.** aught for the dead
Ru. 2 : 12. a reward be **g.**thee of L.
1 S. 2 : † 32. wealth wo. have **g.** Isr.
15 : 28. hath **g.** it to neigh.,28 : 17.
2 S.4 : 10. I would have **g.**a reward
12 : 8. I wo. have **g.** thee such thi.
18: 11. I would have **g.** ten shekels
19 : 42. hath king **g.** us any gift ?
1 K. 1 : 48. **g.** one to sit on throne
13 : 5. sign wh. man of G. had **g.**
2 K. 23: 11. kings of Jud.**g.**to sun
25 : 30. **g.** him of king,Je. 52 : 34.
1 Ch. 29 : 14. thine own have we **g.**
Ezr.6:9. let it be **g.**them day by day
9 : 13. **g.** us such deliv. as t is
Es. 3: 11. The silver is **g.** to thee
7:3.let my life be **g.**at my petition
Jb. 3 : 20. Whf. is light **g.** to him
23.Why is light **g.** to a man? ⌈**g.**
15:19. Unto whom alone earth was
24: 23. Tho. **g.** him to be in safety
33 : 4. breath of Alm. **g.** me life
34 : 13. Who hath **g.** him a charge
Ps. 78: 24. **g.**them of corn of heaven
79 : 2. dead bodies **g.** to be meat
111: 5. he hath **g.** meat unto them
112 : 9. hath **g.** to poor, 2 Co. 9:9.
115 : 16. earth hath he **g.** to men
Pr. 19 : 17. that he hath **g.**will pay
Ec. 8 : 8. neither shall wickedness
deliver those **g.** to it
12: 11. are **g.** from one shepherd
Is. 9 : 6. Child is born, unto us Son
47 : 8. that art **g.** to pleasure ⌊is**g.**
Je. 6 : 13. ev. one **g.** to covet.,8:10.
44 : 20. who had **g.** him that ans.
La.1:11.**g.** pleasant things for meat
5 : 6. We have **g.** hand to Egypt-s
Eze. 11 : 15. unto us land **g.**,33: 24.
16 : 17. my silver wh.I had **g.**thee
21 : 11. hath **g.** it to be furbished
35 : 12. they are **g.** to consume
Da. 2 : 38. fowls hath he **g.** in-o ha.
7 : 4. a man's heart was **g.** to it
6. dominion was **g.** to it, 14.
† 12. prolonging in life was **g.**
8 : 12. And an host was **g.** him
11 : 6. she shall be **g.** up and they
Mat. 13 : 11. **g.** unto you to know
mysteries, Mk.4 : 11.Lu. 8 : 10.
14 : 9. he com-d it to be **g.** her
19 : 11. save they to whom it is **g.**
21: 43. be **g.** to na. bringing fruits
22 : 30. are **g.** in marriage, Mk.12:
25. Lu. 20 : 35. ⌈poor,Mk. 14:5.
26:9. sold for much, and **g.** to the
28 : 18. All power is **g.** unto me in
Mk. 4 : 24. that hear more sh. be **g.**
5 : 43. com-d something be **g.** her
6 : 2. wisdom is this **g.** unto him
14:44. th. betrayed had **g.** a token
Lu. 12 : 48. much **g.** much required
19 : 15. called to whom **g.** money
22 : 19. my body wh. is **g.** for you
Jn. 1 : 17. law was **g.** by Moses
3 : 27. receive noth., exc. it be **g.**
35. **g.** all into his hand, 13 : 3.
4 : 10. wo. have **g.** thee living wat.
5 : 26. he hath **g.** to Son to have
27. hath **g.** him authority ⌊life
36. which the Fa. hath **g.** ⌈noth.
6 : 39. of all he hath **g.** me, I lose

Jn.6:65.no man come,exc.it were **g.**
11 : 57. Phari. had **g.** a com-t
13 : 3. knowing Fa. had **g.** all the
18 : 11. cup my Fa. hath **g.** sh. I
19:11.exc. it were **g.** thee fr. above
Ac. 3 : 16 faith **g.** him soundness
4 : 12. none other **g.** among men
8 : 18. hands Holy Ghost was **g.**
21 : 40. when had **g.** him licence
24 : 26. he hoped money be **g.** him
Ro. 5:5. by H. G. wh. is **g.** unto us
11:35. Or who hath first **g.** to him
12 : 3. grace **g.** us, 6. 1 Co. 1 : 4.
13. **g.** to hospitality, 1 Ti 3 : 2.
15 : 15. bec. of grace **g.** me of God
1 Co. 2:12. things freely **g.** us of G.
11 : 15. her hair is **g.** for cov-g
12:7. manif-n of Spirit **g.** to ev , 8
2 Co. 1 : 11. thanks be **g.** by many
22. **g.** us earnest of Spirit, 5 : 5.
5 : 18. **g.** us minis. of reconcilia.
12 : 7. **g.** me thorn in flesh ⌈**g.** life
Ga. 3 : 21. law **g.** which could have
22. promise **g.** to them th. believe
4 : 15. out eyes and **g.** them to me
Ep. 3:2.which is **g.** me to you-ward
8.Unto me who am least grace **g.**
4 : 7. is **g.** grace acc to measure
19. **g.** thems. over unto lasciviousness ⌈us
5 : 2. Ch. hath loved, **g.** hims. for
6 : 19. utterance may be **g.** me ⌈C.
Ph. 1: 29. unto you **g.** in behalf of
2 : 9 **g.** him a name ab. ev. name
Col. 1 : 25. acc. to dispensa. **g.** me
1 Ti. 4 : 14. gift **g.** thee by prophecy
2 Ti. 1 : 9. grace **g.** us by C. Jesus
He. 4:8. for if Jes. had **g.** them rest
2 Pe. 1:3. power hath **g.** unto us, 4.
3:15. wisd. **g.** unto him hath writ.
1 Jn. 3 : 24. by Spirit he hath **g.** us
4 : 13. bec. he hath **g.** us of Spirit
5:20. hath **g.** us an understand-g
Re. 6 : 2. crown was **g.** unto him
4. power was **g.** unto him (2), 8.
11. white robes were **g.** to ev. one
7:2.**g.** to hurt | 8:2.**g.** 7 trumpets
8 : 3. **g.** incense | 9 : 1. **g.** key
9 : 3. **g.** power | 5. **g.** not kill
11 : 1. **g.** reed | 2. **g.** unto Gent.
12:14. were **g.** 2 wings of gr. eagle
13 : 5. power **g.** to contin. 42 mos.
7. **g.** unto him to make war, (2)
20 : 4. judgm. was **g.** unto them

God or **Lord had GIVEN.**
2 K. 5 : 1. by him L. **h. g.** deliverance ⌈stance
2 Ch. 32 : 29. G. **h. g.** him sub-
Mat. 9:8. G. who **h. g.** such power
Jn. 6 : 23. after L. **h. g.** thanks

God or **Lord hath GIVEN.**
Ge. 24 : 35. the L. **h. g.** Ab. flocks
30:6. Rachel said, G. **h. g.** me son
18. Leah said, G. **h. g.** me hire
31:9. G. **h. g.** me your fa.'s cattle
33:5. chil. G. **h.** graciously **g.** me
43:23. G. **h. g.** you treas. in sacks
48:9. chil. G. **h. g.** me in this pla.
Ex. 16:15. bread which L. **h. g.** you
29. for L. **h. g.** you the sabbath
Le. 10 : 17. G. **h. g.** it to bear iniq.
Nu. 32 : 7. fr. going over into land
L. **h. g.**,9.De. 3:18.-28:52. Jos.
2 : 9, 14 -23 : 13, 15. Je. 25 : 5.
De. 12:15. blessing L. **h. g.**, 16:17.
13 : 12. cities wh. L. thy G. **h. g.**
26 : 11. good thing which L. **h. g.**
Jos. 6 : 16. Shout, for L. **h. g.** city
18 : 3. to possess land the L. **h. g.**
1 S. 1 : 27. L. **h. g.** me my petition
15:28. L. **h. g.** it to neighb., 28:17.
30 : 23. not so with what L. **h. g.**
2 Ch. 36: 23. kingd-s **h.** G. **g.**, Ezr.
Ps. 16:7. L. who **h.g.** counsel ⌊1:2.
Ec. 1:13. sore travail **h.** G. **g.**, 3:10.
5:19.man to wh G.**h.g.** riches.6:2.
Is. 8 : 18. I chil. L. **h. g.**, He. 2:13.

Is. 23 : 11. L. h. g. a com-t against
50:4. L. h. g. me tongue of learned
Je. 11 : 18. L. h. g. me knowledge
47 : 7. seeing L. h. g. it a charge
Da. 2 : 37. G. h. g. thee a kingdom
Jo. 2 : 23. G. h. g. you former rain
Na. 1:14. L. h. g. com-t conc. thee
Ac. 5:32. G. h. g. to them th. obey
17:31. G. h. g. assurance unto all
27 : 24. G. h. g. thee all that sail
Ro. 11:8. G. h. g. spirit of slumber
2 Co. 9 : 9. G. h. g. to the poor
10:8. L. h. g. us for edifica., 13:10.
1 Th. 4:8. G. who h. g. Holy Spirit
2 Th 2:16. G. h. g. everlast-g consola.
1 Jn. 5 : 11. this is record G. h. g.
See REST. ⌊us

I have or have I GIVEN.

Ge. 1:30. I h. g. ev. green herb, 29.
15:18. Unto thy seed h. I g. this la.
27:37. brethren h. I g. for servt-s
Le. 17 : 11. I h. g. it to you upon
Nu. 18:7. I h. g. priest's office ⌊alt.
20:12. land I h. g., 24.-27:12.-33:
53. De. 9:23. 1 K. 9:7. 2 Ch. 7:
20. Je. 35 : 15.
Jos. 1:3. tread upon th. I h. g. you
24 : 13. I h. g. you la. ye did not
1 K. 3:12. I h. g. thee a wise heart
13. I h. g. thee hast not asked
1 Ch. 29:3. I h. g. to house of my G.
Is. 43:28. I h. g. Jacob to the curse
55 : 4. I h. g. him for a witness to
Je. 8 : 13. things I h. g. shall pass
12 : 7. I h. g. dearly belov. of my
27 : 5. I h. g. it unto wh. it seem.
6. beasts of field h. I g. also
Eze. 4 : 15. I h. g. thee cow's dung
29 : 20. I h. g. him the land of E.
Am. 4:6. I h. g. you cleann. of teeth
9:15. no more pulled out of la. I h. g.
Jn. 13 : 15. I h. g. you an example
17:8. I h. g. words thou gavest, 14.
22. glory gavest me, I h. g. them
1 Co. 16:1. I h. g. order to churches

Not GIVEN. ⌈wife

Ge 38 : 14. she was n. g. him to
De. 26:14. I have n. g. aught for dead
29:4. L. hath n. g. you a heart
26. whom he had n. g. unto th.
1 Ch. 22:18. hath he n. g. you rest?
Ne. 13:10. portion of Lev. n. been g.
Jb. 22:7. hast n. g. water to weary
Ps. 78:63. maidens n. g. to marriage
118 : 18. n. g. me over unto death
124:6. who hath n. g. us as a prey
Is. 37:10. Jerus. n. be g. into hand
Je. 39:17. n. be g. into ha. of men
Eze. 3:20. bec. thou hast n. g. warn.
18:8. that hath n. g. upon usury
Mat. 13:11. given to you, to them n. g.
Jn. 7 : 39. for H. Gh. was n. yet g.
1 Ti. 3:3. bishop n. g. to wine, Tit.
8. deacons n. g. to much wine, ⌊1:7.
2 Ti. 1 : 7. God n. g. us spi. of fear
Tit. 2:3. aged women n. g. to wine

Shall be GIVEN. ⌈g.

Nu. 26 : 54. to ev. one s. inheri. b.
De. 28 : 31. thy sheep s. b. g. unto
enemies ⌈people
32. thy sons s. b. g. unto another
Ezr. 4 : 21. until ano. com-t s. b. g.
Es. 5:3. it s. b. g. to half of kingd.
Ps 72:15. s. b. g. of gold of Sheba
120:3. What s. b. g., false tongue?
Is. 3:11. reward of hands s. b. g. him
33:16. bread s. b. g. him, waters be
35:2. glory of Leb. s. b. g. unto it
Je. 21 : 10. city s. b. g. into hand
of king, he sh. burn it, 38:3,18.
Eze. 47:11. marishes, s. b. g. to salt
Da. 7:25. saints s. b. g. into his ha.
27. kingdom s. b. g. to the saints
Mat. 7:7. Ask, it s. b. g., Lu. 11:9.
10:19. it s. b. g. you in same hour,
Mk. 13:11. ⌈8:12. Lu. 11:29.
12 : 39. no sign s. b. g., 16:4. Mk.
Mat. 13:12. For whoso. hath, to him
s. b. g., 25:29. Mk. 4:25. Lu. 8:18.
-19:26. ⌈pared
20 : 23. it s. b. g. for whom pre-
21:43. kingd. of God s. b. g. to nation
Lu. 6 : 38. Give, and it s. b. g. you
Phm. 22 thro. prayers I s. b. g. you
Ja. 1:5. ask of God, and it s. b. g. him

Thou hast or hast thou GIVEN.

Ge. 15:3. Ab. said, t. h. g. no seed
De. 26 : 15. bless land t. h. g. us
Jos. 15:19. t. h. g. me south land,
Ju. 1 : 15. ⌈lot to inherit?
17 : 14. Why h. t. g. me but one
Ju. 15:18. t. h. g. this great deliv.
1 S. 22:13. t. h. g. him bread and sw.
2 S. 12 : 14. by deed t. h. g. occa.
22 : 36. t. h. g. me shield of thy
salva., Ps. 18 : 35. ⌈Ps. 18 : 40.
41. t. h. g. me necks of enemies,
1 K. 3:6. t. h. g. him a son to sit on
8 : 36. rain on land t. h. g., 2 Ch.
9:13. What cities t. h. g. me? ⌊6:27.
2 Ch. 20:11. out of posses-n t. h. g.
Ezr. 9 : 13. t. h. g. us deliverance
Ps. 21:2. t. h. g. his heart's desire
44:11. t. h. g. us like sheep for meat
60:4. t. h. g. a banner to them th.
61:5. t. h. g. me heritage of those
71 : 3. t. h. g. com-t to save me
Jn. 17:2. t. h. g. him power ov. all
7. that all t. h. g. me, are of thee
9. I pray for them wh. t. h. g. me
11. keep thro. name those t. h. g.
Re. 16:6. t. h. g. them bl. to drink

GIVER.

Is. 24:2. as with taker of usury, so g.
2 Co. 9 : 7. God loveth a cheerful g.

GIVEST. ⌈unto L.

De. 15 : 9. g. him nought, he cry
10. not be grieved thou g. him
Jb. 35:7. If righte., what g. thou him
Ps. 50:19. thou g. thy mouth to evil
80 : 5. thou g. them tears to drink
104:28. That g. them, they gather
145:15. thou g. them their meat in
Pr. 2 : † 3. if g. voice, for underst-g
6 : 35. neither will he rest content,
though thou g. many gifts
Eze. 3 : 18. g. not warning, to save
16:33. g. thy gifts to all thy lovers
34. g. reward, and no reward given
1 Co. 14:17. For thou g. thanks well

GIVETH.

Ge. 49:21. he g. goodly words ⌈two
Ex. 16 : 29. g. on 6th day bread of
20:12. days may be long in land L.
g., De. 4 : 40.-5 : 16.-25 : 15.
25 : 2. ev. man that g. it willingly
Le. 20:2. g. of his seed unto Molech, 4.
27 : 9. all that any man g. be holy
De. 2:29. into land which L. our G. g.
us, 4 : 1,21.-11:17,31.-12:1, 10.-
15:4, 7.-16:20 -17:14.-18:9.-19:
1,2,10, 14.-21:1,23.-24:4.-26 : 1,
2.-27 : 2, 3.-28 : 8. Jos. 1 : 11,15.
8:18. he g. thee power to get wealth
9:6. G. g. not land for thy righte.
12:10. g. you rest fr. enem , 25:19.
13 : 1. if a prophet g. thee a sign
16 : 5. gates wh. L. g., 18.-17 : 2.
2 S. 22 : † 48. it is God g. avengement for me, and, Ps. 18 : † 47.
1 K. 17:† 14. until the day L. g. rain
Jb 5:10. Who g. rain upon the earth
32:8. inspiration of Alm. g. underst.
33:13. he g. no account of his ways
34:29. g. quietness | 35:10. g. songs
36:6. g. right to poor | 31. g. meat
Ps. 18 : 50. deliverance g. he to ki.
37:21. righteous sheweth mercy g.
68:35. God of Isr. that g. strength
119:130. entrance of words g. light
127 : 2. so he g. his beloved sleep
136 : 25. Who g. food to all flesh,
146 : 7.-147 : 9.
Ps 144 : 10. g. salvation unto kings
147 : 16. He g. snow like wool
Pr. 2 : 6. L. g. wisd., out of mouth
3 : 34. he g. grace unto lowly, Ja.
4 : 6. 1 Pe. 5 : 5. ⌈your
13 : 15. Good understanding g. fa-
21:26. righte. g. spareth not, 22:9.
22:16. g. to rich sh. come to want
28: 27. g. unto poor shall not lack
Ec. 2 : 26. God g. to a man is good,
wisd., to sinner he g. travail
6 : 2. God g. him not power to eat
Is. 40 : 29. He g. power to the faint
42 : 5. g. breath | Je. 5 : 24. g. rain
Je. 31 : 35. g. the sun for a light
22:13. woe that g. not for his work
La. 3:30. g. cheek to him smiteth
Da. 2 : 21. he g. wisdom unto wise
4:17. g. it to whomso. he will, 25, 32.
Ho. 10 :† 1 vine emptying fruit it g.
Ha. 2:15. Woe unto him g. neighb.
Mat. 5:15. it g. light unto all ⌊drink
Jn. 3:34. God g. not Spirit by meas.
6:32. my Fa. g. you the true bread
33. who g. life unto the world
37. All the Fa. g. me shall come
10:11. good shepherd g. his life for
14 : 27. not as the world g. give I
21 : 13. taketh bread and g. them
Ac. 17 : 25. he g. to all life, breath
Ro. 12:8. g. let him with simplicity
1 Co. 3 : 7. God that g. the increase
7:38. th. g. in marriage doeth well
15:38. G. g. it a body as it pleased
2 Co. 3 : 6. letter killeth, Spi. g. life
1 Ti. 6 : 17. who g. us richly all
Ja. 1 : 5. ask of God, that g. to all
4 : 6. g. more grace, G. g. grace
1 Pe. 4 : 11. do it as of ability God g.
Re. 22 : 5. the L. God g. them light
See THANKS.

GIVING.

De. 10:18. loveth stranger in g. food
21 : 17. by g. him a double portion
Ru. 1:6. L. visited peop. in g. bread
1 K. 5:9. accompl. desire, in g. food
2 Ch. 6 : 23. g. him acc. to righte-s
Jb. 11 : 20. hope as g. up of ghost
Mat. 24 : 38. marrying and g. in
Ac. 8 : 9. g. out himself was some gr.
15 : 8. g. them the H. G. ⌈one
Ro. 4 : 20. in faith, g. glory to God
9 : 4. g. of law, and service of G.
1 Co. 14:7. g. sound | 16. g. thanks
2 Co. 6:3 g. no offence in any thing
Ph. 4:15. concerning g. and receiving
1 Ti. 4:1. g. heed to seducing spirits
Tit. 1:14. Not g. heed to Jew. fables
1 Pe. 3 : 7. g. honour to wife as to
2 Pe. 1 : 5. g. all diligence, add to
Jude 7. g. thems. over to fornica-
See THANKS. ⌊tion

GI'ZONITE.

1 Ch. 11:34. sons of Hashem the G.

GLAD.

Ex. 4 : 14. he will be g. in heart
Ju. 18 : 20. the priest's heart was g.
1 S. 11 : 9. men of Jabesh were g.
1 K. 8:66. went unto tents g. 2 Ch. 7:10
Es. 5:9. Haman g. | 8 : 15. Shushan
Jb. 3 : 22. g. when can find grave
22 : 19. righteous are g., Ps. 64:10.
Ps. 16:9. my heart is g. glory rejoi.
21:6. hast made him g. with coun.
34 : 2. humble shall be g., 69 : 32.
35 : 27. g. that favour my cause
45 : 8. they have made thee g.
46 : 4. streams make g. city of G.
67 : 4. let nations be g. and sing
90 : 15. Make us g.
92 : 4. thou L. hast made me g.
97:1. let isles be g. | 8. Zion was g.
104 : 15. wine maketh g. the heart
34. be g. in L. | 105 : 38. Egypt g.
107 : 30. are g. bec. they be quiet
119:74. they th. fear thee will be g.
122:1. g. when they said, Let us go

Ps. 126 : 3. done great things for us, we are g. ⌈15 : 20.
Pr. 10:1. wise son maketh g. father,
12 : 25. a good word maketh it g.
17 : 5. that is g. at calamities, not
23:25. Thy fa. and mother sh. be g.
24 : 17. not be g. when he stumbl.
27 : 11. My son, make my heart g.
Ec. 10 :†19. wine maketh g. the life
Is. 35 : 1. wilder. sh. be g. for th.
39:2. Hez. was g., and shewed th.
Je. 20 : 15. child is born, making g.
41 : 13. saw Johanan, then were g.
50 : 11. were g. O ye destroyers
La. 1 : 21. are g. thou hast done it
Da. 6 : 23. was king exceeding g.
Ho. 7 : 3. make king g. with wickedn.
Jon. 4 : 6. Jon. g. bec. of gourd
Zch. 10:7. chil. sh. see it and be g.
Mk. 14 : 11. were g. and promised money, Lu. 22 : 5. ⌈tidings
Lu. 1:19. I am sent to shew thee g.
8 : 1. shewing g. tidings of kingd.
15 : 32. was meet we should be g.
23:8. Her. saw Jes. he was exc. g.
Jn. 8:56. Ab. saw my day and was g.
11 : 15. g. for your sakes I was not
20:20. g. when they saw L. ⌊there
Ac. 11:23. had seen grace of G. was g.
13 : 32. decla. unto you g. tidings
48. Gentiles heard, they were g.
Ro. 10 : 15. bring g. tidings of good
16 : 19. I am g. on your behalf
1 Co. 16:17. g. of coming of Stepha.
2 Co. 2:2. who is he maketh me g.?
13 : 9. we are g. when we are weak
1 Pe. 4:13. glory revealed, ye may be

GLAD with rejoice, ed. ⌊g.

1 Ch. 16 : 31. let the heavens be g. and let the earth r., Ps. 96 : 11.
Es. 8:15. Shushan r-d and was g.
Ps. 9 : 2. I will be g. and r. in thee
14 : 7. Jacob r., Isr. be g., 53 : 6.
31 : 7. I will be g. and r. in mercy
32:11. Be g. and r., ye righte., 68:3.
40 : 16. seek thee be g. and r., 70:4.
48:11. let Zion r., dau-s of Jud. be g.
90 : 14. that we may be g. and r.
118:24. day, we will r. and be g. in it
Can. 1 : 4. we will be g. and r.
Is. 25 : 9. we will r. be g. in salv.
65 : 18. be you g. and r. for ever
66:10. r. ye with Jerus., and be g.
La. 4:21. r. and be g. O dau. of Edom
Jo. 2 : 21. O land, be g. and r.
23. Be g. ye chil. of Zion, r. in L.
Hab. 1 : 15. thf. they r. and are g.
Zph. 3 : 14. be g. and r. with heart
Mat. 5 : 12. r. be g. great is reward
Ac. 2:26. heart did r., tongue was g.
Re. 19:7. be g. and r., marriage come

GLADLY.

Mk. 6 : 20. Herod heard him g.
12 : 37. common peo. heard C. g.
Lu. 8:40. the people g. received him
Ac. 2 : 41. g. rec-d word were bapt.
21 : 17. brethren received us g.
2 Co. 11:19. ye suffer fools g. seeing
12 : 9. Most g. will I rather glory
15. I will very g. spend and be ⌊spent

GLADNESS.

Nu. 10 : 10. in day of g. ye sh. blow
De. 28 : 47. servedst not L. with g.
2 S. 6 : 12. Da. brought ark with g.
1 Ch. 16 : 27. and g. in his place
29:22. did eat that day with gr. g.
2 Ch. 29:30. they sang praises with g.
30 : 21. Israel kept feast with g.
23. kept other 7 days with g.
Ne. 8 : 17. there was very great g.
12 : 27. to keep dedication with g.
Es. 8:16. Jews had light, and g., 17.
9 : 17. day of feasting and g., 19.
Ps. 4 : 7. hast put g. in my heart
30 : 11. hast girded me with g.
43:†4. go unto G. the g. of my joy
45:7. anointed with oil of g., He. 1:9.
Ps. 45:15. With g. sh. they be bro-t
51 : 8. Make me to hear joy and g.
97 : 11. g. is sown for the upright
100 : 2. Serve the Lord with g.
105:43. he bro-t his chosen with g.
106 : 5. may rejoice in g. of nation
Pr. 10 : 28. hope of rights. be g.
Can. 3 : 11. in day of g. of his heart
Is. 16 : 10. joy and g. is taken away
22 : 13. joy and g. slaying oxen
30 : 29. have song and g. of heart
35:10. sh. obtain joy and g., 51:11.
51 : 3. joy and g. shall be found
Je. 7:34. cease voice of g., 16 : 9.–25:
31 : 7. Sing with g. for Jacob. ⌊10.
33 : 11. be heard voice of joy and g.
48 : 33. joy and g. taken from field
Jo. 1 : 16. joy and g. fr. house of G.
Zch. 8:19. to house of Jud. joy and g.
Mk. 4 : 16. who receive it with g.
Lu. 1 : 14. shalt have joy and g.
Ac. 2:46. did eat meat with g. of heart
12 : 14. she opened not gate for g.
14:17. filling hearts wi. food and g.
Ph. 2 : 29. Receive him in L. with all ⌊g.

GLASS, ES.

Is. 3 : 23. L. will take away the g-s
1 Co. 13:12. now we see thro. g. darkly
2 Co. 3 : 18. beholding as in a g.
Ja. 1:23. a man beholding face in g.
Re. 4 : 6. sea of g. like unto crystal
15 : 2. sea of g. mingled with fire
21 : 18. city pure gold, like clear g., ⌊21.
See LOOKING.

GLEAN, ED. ⌈24:21.

Le. 19 : 10. shalt not g. viney., De.
Ju. 1:†7. kings g-d their meat under
20:45. they g-d of th. in highways
Ru. 2 : 2. Let me now go to field and g. ears, 7, 8, 15, 16, 23.
3. she g-d after reapers, 17, 18, 19.
Je. 6 : 9. They shall throughly g. remnant

GLEANINGS.

Le. 19:9. gather g-s of harvest, 23:22.
Mi. 7:1. I am as grape g-s of vintage
See GRAPE, GRAPES.

GLEDE.

De. 14 : 13. ye shall not eat the g.

GLISTERING.

1 Ch. 29:2. I have prepared g. stones
Lu. 9 : 29. his raiment white and g.

GLITTER, ING.

De. 32 : 41. If I whet my g-g sword
Jb. 20 : 25. g-g sword cometh out
39 : 23. g-g spear rattleth ag. him
Eze. 21 : 10. furbished that it may g.
28. furbished to consu., bec. of g-g
Na. 3:3. horseman lifteth g-g spear
Ha. 3 : 11. shining of thy g-g spear

GLOOMINESS.

Jo. 2 : 2. day of darkness and g., Zph. 1 : 15.

GLORIEST, ETH.

Je. 9 : 24. let him that g., 1 Co. 1 : 31. 2 Co. 10 : 17.
49 : 4. Whf. g. thou in valleys?
Ja. 2 : †13. mercy g. ag. judgment

GLORIFIED.

Le. 10 : 3. bef. all peo. I will be g.
Is. 26 : 15. hast incr-d nation, art g.
44 : 23. Lord hath g. hims. in Isr.
49 : 3. O Isr., in whom I will be g.
55:5. H. One of Isr. hath g. thee, 60:9
60 : 21. work of hands, th. I be g.
61 : 3. planting of L. that he be g.
66 : 5. breth. said, Let the L. be g.
Eze. 28 : 22. I will be g. in midst
39 : 13. renown in day I sh. be g.
Da. 5 : 23. God hast thou not g.
Hag. 1 : 8. I will take pleasure in it, and be g. ⌈12. Lu. 5 : 26.
Mat. 9:8. marvelled, and g. G., Mk. 2:
15 : 31. they g. the God of Israel
Lu. 4:15. taught in synag-s, being g.
7 : 16. fear on all, and they g. God
13:13. she was made straight, g. G.
Lu. 17 : 15. the leper g. God
23:47. the centurion g. G. ⌈not g.
Jn. 7 : 39. H. Gh. not given, bec. Jes.
11 : 4. that Son of God might be g.
12:16. when J. was g. remem-d they
23. hour come Son of man be g.
28. I have g. it, and will glorify
13 : 31. is Son of man g. God is g.
32. G. be g. in him, God sh. glori.
14 : 13. that Fa. be g. in the Son
15:8. is my Fa. g. th. ye bear fruit
17 : 4. I have g. thee on earth
10. thine are mine, I am g. in th.
Ac. 3:13. G. of our fa-h hath g. Son
4 : 21. all g. G. for what was done
11 : 18. held their peace, and g. G.
13 : 48. Gentiles g. word of Lord
21 : 20. they of Jerusalem g. the L.
Ro. 1 : 21. they g. him not as God
8:17. if we suffer, that we be also g.
30. whom he justified, them he g.
Gal. 1 : 24. And they g. God in me
2 Th. 1 : 10. come to be g. in saints
12. that name of Jes. be g. in you
3 : 1. that word of Lord may be g.
He. 5 : 5. so Christ g. not himself
1 Pe. 4:11. G. in all things may be g.
14. but on your part he is g.
Re. 18:7. How much she hath g. hers.

GLORIFIETH, YING.

Ps. 50:23. Whoso off-h praise g-h me
Lu. 2 : 20. shepherds ret-d, g-g God
5 : 25. departed to own h., g-g God
18:43. blind man foll-d him., g-g G.

GLORIFY.

Ps. 22 : 23. all ye seed of Jac. g. him
50 : 15. I will deliver, thou shalt g.
86 : 9. all nations shall g. thy name
12. I will g. thy name for everm.
Is. 24 : 15. Whf. g. ye L. in the fires
25:3. Thf. shall strong peo. g. thee
60:7. I will g. house of my glory
Je. 30 : 19. multiply, I will g. them
Mat. 5 : 16. g. your Fa. in heaven
Jn. 12:28. Fa., g. thy name; I will ⌊g. it
13 : 32. G. shall g. him
16:14. He sh. g. me, for he sh. rece.
17:1. g. thy Son, that Son may g.
5. O Fa., g. me with own self
21:19. by what death he sho g. God
Ro. 15:6. one mind and mouth g. G.
9. that the Gentiles might g. God
1 Co. 6:20. g. G. in body and spirit
2 Co. 9:13. g. G. for your subjection
1 Pe. 2:12. g. G. in day of visitation
4 : 16. let him g. G. on this behalf
Re. 15 : 4. Who not fear, and g. thy ⌊name?

GLORIOUS.

Ex. 15:6. Thy right hand, O L., is g.
11. who like thee, O L., g. in holin.
De. 28:58. mayest fear this g. name
2 S. 6 : 20. How g. was king of Isr.
1 Ch. 29 : 13. we praise thy g. name
Ne. 9 : 5. blessed be thy g. name
Ps. 29 : † 2. worship the Lord in his g. sanctuary, 96 : † 9.
45 : 13. king's dau. is all g. within
66:2. sing forth, make his praise g.
72 : 19. blessed be his g. name
76:4. art more g. than mts. of prey
87 : 3. g. things are spoken of thee
111:3. His work honourable and g.
145 : 5. I will speak of g. honour
12. to make known g. majesty
Is. 4 : 2. branch of L. shall be g.
11 : 10. a root of Jesse, his rest g.
22 : 23. he shall be for a g. throne
28 : 1. g. beauty is a fading flower
4. g. beauty on head of fat valley
30:30. cause his g. voice to be heard
33 : 21. g. L. be place of streams
49 : 5. shall I be g. in eyes of L.
60 : 13. make place of my feet g.
63 : 1. who is this g. in apparel?
12. that led them with his g. arm
14. to make thyself a g. name
Je. 17:12. g. high throne fr. beginn.

Eze. 27 : 25. made very g. in the seas
Da. 11 : 16. he sh. stand in g. land
41. he shall enter into the g. land
45. betw. seas in g. holy mount.
Lu. 13:17. peo. rejoiced for g. things
Ro. 8:21. into g. liberty of the chil.
2 Co. 3 : 7. if ministration of death
engraven in stones g., 11.
8. ministration of Spirit be g., 10.
4 : 4. lest light of g. gospel shine
Ep. 5 : 27. might present it a g. ch
Ph. 3 : 21. be fashioned like his g.
body [power
Col. 1:11. strength-d acc. to his g.
1 Ti. 1 : 11. Acc-g to g. gospel of G.
Tit. 2:13. looking for the g. appearing

GLORIOUSLY.

Ex. 15:1. L., he hath triumphed g.
Is. 24:23. L. reign bef. his ancients g.

GLORY. [Noun.]

Ge. 31 : 1. of fa.'s gotten all this g.
Ex. 28:2. garments for Aa. for g., 40.
1 S. 2 : 8. make inherit throne of g.
4:21. g. is departed from Israel, 22.
†21. where is the g.? there is no g.
1 Ch. 22 : 5. house for L. must be
of g. [Mat. 6 : 13.
29 : 11. thine is power, and g.,
Es. 5:11. Haman told of g. of his
Jb. 39:20. g. of nostrils is terrible
40 : 10. and array thyself with g.
Ps. 24:7. King of g. shall come in, 9.
10. Who is this King of g.? The L.
29 : 3. the God of g. thundereth
49 : 16. when g. of house is incr-d
73 : 24. afterw. receive me to g.
79:9. help O G., for g. of thy name
85: 9. that g. may dwell in our la.
89:17. thou art g. of their strength
106 : 20. changed g. into similitude
145:11. speak of the g. of thy kingd.
149:5. Let the saints be joyful in g.
Pr. 3 : 35. The wise shall inherit g.
17 : 6. g. of chil. are their fathers
20:29. g. of young men is strength
25 : †6. set not out thy g. in pres.
27. men to search own g. is not g.
28:12. righte. rejoice there is g. [21.
Is. 2:10. hide for g. of his maj., 19,
4 : † 2. branch of L. be beauty and
5. the g. shall be a defence [g.
5 : † 13. their g. are men of famine
14. their g. and pomp sh. descend
10 : 3. where will ye leave your g.?
12. I will punish g. of high looks
18. sh. consume g. of his forest
11 : †10. root of Jesse, his rest be g.
13:19. Bab. g. of kingd. be as Sod.
14 : 18. all lie in g. each in his ho.
16 : 14. g. of Moab be contemned
17 : 3. be as g. of the chil. of Israel
4. g. of Jacob shall be made thin
20 : 5. sh. be ash-d of E. their g.
21:16. all g. of Kedar shall fail [ho.
22 : 24. hang upon him g. of fa.'s
23 : 9. to stain the pride of all g.
24: 16. songs, even g. to righte.
† 23. sh. be g. bef. his ancients
35:2. g. of Leb. shall be given unto
61 : 6. in their g. ye shall boast [it
66 : 11. delighted with abund. of g.
12. g. of Gent. as a flowing stream
Je. 2:11. peo. have changed their g.
13 : 11. might be to me for a g.
18. come down, crown of your g.
Eze. 20 : 6. is g. of all lands, 15.
24 : 25. take fr. them joy of their g.
25 : 9. I will open g. of country
26 : 20. I sh. set g. in land of living
31:18. To wh-m art thou like in g.?
Da. 2 : 37. given power and g., 7:14.
4 : 36. g. of my kingd. returned
11 : 20. in the g. of the kingdom
39. shall increase with g.
Ho. 4:7. change their g. into shame
9:11. As for Ephr, g. shall fly away
10:5. priests th. rejoiced for the g.

Mi. 1:15. unto Adullam the g. of Isr.
Na. 2 : 9. none end of store and g.
Ha. 2 : 16. filled with shame for g.
Hag. 2 : 3. saw this hou. in first g.?
7. I will fill this house with g.
9. g. of this latter house greater
Zch. 2 : 5. I will be g. in the midst
8. After the g. hath he sent me
6 : 13. build temple, sh. bear the g.
11:3. their g. is spoiled, a voice of
12:7. g. of hou. of Da., g. of Jerus.
Mat. 4 : 8. kingdoms, and g. of them
6 : 2. sound trumpet, that they
may have g. of men
16 : 27. shall come in the g. of his
Father, Mk. 8 : 38.
24 : 30. shall see Son coming with
great g., Mk. 13 : 26. Lu. 21:27.
Lu. 2:14. g. to God in highest, 19:38.
32. the g. of thy people Isr. [g.
4:6. All this power will I give, and
9:31. Who appeared in g. and spake
Jn. 17 : 5. with g. I had with thee
22. g. thou gavest, I have given
Ac. 7 : 2. G. of g. appeared unto fa.
12 : 23. bec. he gave not G. the g.
22:11. could not see for g. of light
Ro. 1 : 23. g. of the incorruptible
4 : 2. he hath whereof to g.
20. in faith, gi ing g. to God
6 : 4. raised by the g. of the Father
8:18. not worthy to be comp-d wi. g.
9:4. to wh. pertaineth g. and cov-s
23. he had afore prepared unto g.
11 : 36. to whom be g. for ever, Ga.
1:5. 2 Ti. 4:18. He. 13:21. 1 Pe. 5:11.
16:27. To G. only wise be g., 1 Ti. 1:17
1 Co. 2:7. G. hath ord d unto our g.
8. would not have crucified L. of g.
9 : 16. I have nothing to g. of
11 : 7. woman is the g. of the man
15. if wom. have long hair, it is g.
15:40. g. of celestial is one, g. of ter.
41. one g. of sun, ano. g. of moon
43. sown in dishonour, raised in g.
2 Co. 3 : 7. for g. of counten., wh. g.
9. if condemnation be g. righteousness exceed in g.
10. no g. by reason of g. excelleth
18. we are all changed fr. g. to g.
4:17. worketh eternal weight of g.
5 : 12. give you occasion to g.
8 : 19. administered to g. of same L.
23. messengers, and g. of Christ
Ep. 1 : 6. praise of g. of grace, 12, 14.
17. Fa. of g. may give your Spirit
18. know what is riches of g. [g.
3 : 13. my tribulations, wh. is your
21. Unto him be g. in church by C.
Ph. 1 : 11. fruits by C. unto g. of God
3 : 19. whose G. is in their shame
4:19. acc. to his riches in g. by C. J.
20. unto G. and our Fa. g. for ever
Col. 1 : 27. riches of g. of this mystery, C. in you, the hope of g.
3 : 4. sh. ye appear with him in g.
1 Th. 2 : 6. Nor of men sought we g.
12. who hath called you to his g.
20. For ye are our g. and joy
2 Th. 1 : 9. punished fr. g. of power
2 : 14. obtaining of the g. of our L.
1 Ti. 3 : 16. received up into g.
2 Ti. 2 : 10. salv. in C., with eter. g.
He. 2:10. bring-g many sons unto g.
3 : 3. counted worthy of more g.
9 : 5. cherubim of g. shadowing
Ja. 2 : 1. faith of our L., the L. of g.
1 Pe. 1 : 8. rejoice with joy, full of g.
11. it testified g. that sh. follow
21. that G. raised and gave him g.
24. all g. of man as flower of grass
2 : 20. what g. is it, if buffeted?
4 : 14. Spirit of g. resteth upon you
5 : 1. of g. that shall be revealed
10. called us unto eternal g. by C.
2 Pe. 1 : 3. that hath called us to g.
17. a voice to him fr. excellent g.

2 Pe. 3:18. To him be g. ever, Re. 1:6
Ju. 25. To only God our Sav. be g.
Re. 4 : 11. worthy to recei. g., 5 : 12.
7:12. Blessing and g. be unto our G.
11 : 13. remnant affrighted, gave g.
See CROWN, HONOUR, VAIN.

Give GLORY.

Jos. 7:19. My son, g. g. to the God
1 S. 6:5. ye shall g. g. unto God of
1 Ch. 16: 28. G. unto the Lord, g.
unto L. g., 29. Ps. 29 : 1, 2.-96:
7, 8. Je. 13 : 16.
Ps. 84 : 11. L. will g. grace and g.
115:1. Not unto us, unto thy name
g. g. for thy truth's sake
Is. 42 : 12. Let them g. g. unto L.
Mal. 2:2. not lay it to heart to g. g.
Lu. 17 : 18. returned to g. g. to G.
Re. 4 : 9. when those beasts g. g.
14 : 7. Fear God, and g. g. to him
16 : 9. and repented not to g. g.

GLORY of God.

Ps. 19 : 1. heavens declare g. o. G.
Pr. 25 : 2. g. o. G. to conceal thing
Eze. 8 : 4. g. o. the G. of Isr. there
9 : 3. g. o. G. was gone up fr. cherub
10: 19 g. o. G. was over them, 11:22.
43 : 2. g. o. G. came from the east
Jn. 11 : 4. this sickness for g. o. G.
40. believe, shouldest see g. o. G.
Ac. 7 : 55. Ste. looked saw g. o. G.
Ro. 3 : 23. all come short of g. o. G.
5 : 2. we rejoice in hope of g. o. G.
15 : 7. as C. also rec-d us to g. o. G.
1 Co. 10 : 31. drink, do all to g. o. G.
11 : 7. man is image and g. o. G.
2 Co. 1: 20. promises yea unto g. o. G.
4 : 6. light of knowl. of g. o. G.
15. thanksg. redound to g. o. G.
Ph. 1 : 11. are by Christ unto g. o. G.
2 : 11. that Jesus is L. to the g. o. G.
Re. 15 : 8. temple with smoke g. o. G.
21: 11. holy Jerus. Having g. o. G.
23. no need of sun, g. o. G. did

His GLORY.

De. 5 : 24. Lord hath shewed us h. g.
33: 17. h. g. like firstling of bullock
1 Ch. 16 : 24. Declare h. g., Ps. 96:3.
Ps. 21 : 5. h. g. is great in thy salv.
29 : 9. doth every one speak of h. g.
49: 17. h. g. descend aft. him [g.
72: 19. whole earth be filled with h.
78:61. delivered h. g. into enemies'
89 : 44. hast made h. g. to cease
97 : 6. all the people see h. g. [g.
102: 16. build Zion, sh. appear in h.
113:4. h. g. ab. the heavens, 148: 13.
Pr. 19: 11. h. g. to pass over transgr.
Is. 3 : 8. to provoke eyes of h. g.
6 : 3. whole earth is full of h. g.
8 : 7. k. of Assyria and h. g. come
10 : 16. under h. g. kindle a burning
59: 19. sh. fear h. g. from rising of
60 : 2. h. g. sh. be seen upon thee
Je. 22 : 18. not lament, Ah h. g..
Eze. 43 : 2. earth shined with h. g.
Da. 5 : 20. they took h. g. from him
Hab. 3 : 3. h. g. covered heavens
Mat. 6:29. Sol. and all h. g., Lu. 12:27.
19 : 28. Son of man sh. sit in h. g.
25:31. Son of man sh. come in h. g.,
Lu. 9 : 26. [saw h. g.
Lu. 9 : 32. when they were awake,
24 : 26. suff. and to enter into h. g.
Jn. 1 : 14. we beheld h. g. as the
2: 11. Jesus manifested forth h. g.
7: 18. seeketh h. g. that sent him
12 : 41. said Esaias, when he saw
h. g. [unto h. g.
Ro. 3 : 7. abounded through my lie
9 : 23. make known riches of h. g.
Ep. 1 : 12. be to praise of h. g., 14.
3 : 16. grant acc. to riches of h. g.
He. 1 : 3. being brightness of h. g.
1 Pe. 4 : 13. when h. g. be revealed
Jude 24. present bef. pres. of h. g.
Re 18 : 1. earth lightened with h. g.

GLORY of the Lord.
Ex 16:7.in morning ye sh.see g.o.L.
10.g.o. L. appeared in cloud, Le.
9:23. Nu. 14:10.-16:19,42.-20:6.
24:16. g.o.L. abode upon mt. Sinai
17. g. o. L. like devouring fire
40: 34. g.o.L filled tabernacle, 35.
Le. 9 : 6. g.o.L.sh. appear unto you
Nu.14:21.earth be filled with g.o.L.
1 K. 8 : 11. g. o. L. filled house,
2 Ch. 5 : 14.-7 : 1, 2, 3. Eze.
43 : 5.-44 : 4. [for ever
Ps. 104 : 31. g. o. L. shall endure
138 : 5. for great is the g. o. L.
Is. 35 : 2. they shall see the g.o.L.
40 : 5. g. o. L. shall be revealed
58 : 8. g.o. L. sh. be thy rereward
60 : 1. g. o. L. is risen upon thee
Eze.1:28. of the likeness of g. o. L.
3 : 12. Blessed be g.o.L.fr.his place
23. behold, g. o. L. stood there
10 : 4. g.o.L. went up from cherub
18. g.o. L. departed fr. threshold
11 : 23. g.o.L. went up fr. the city
43 : 4. g.o.L. came into the house
Ha.2: 14. filled with knowl.of g.o.L.
Lu.2: 9. g. o. L. shone about th.
2 Co. 3 : 18. as in glass g. o. L.

My or mine own GLORY.
Ge.45: 13.tell my father of all m.g.
Ex.29:43. tab.be sanctified by m.g.
33 : 22. while m. g. passeth by, I
Nu.14:22. men wh. have seen m.g.
Jb. 19 : 9. hath stripped me of m.g.
29 : 20. m. g. was fresh in me
Ps. 3 : 3. thou art m.g.and lifter up
4 : 2. how long turn m. g. into
shame? [g. may sing
16 : 9. m. g. rejoiceth | 30 : 12. m.
57 : 8. Awake up m. g.
62 : 7. in God is m. g.
108 : 1. I will give praise with m. g.
Is. 42 : 8. m. g. will I not give, 48: 11.
43 : 7. I have created him for m. g.
46 : 13. place salv. for Isr., m. g.
60 : 7. I will glorify house of m. g.
66 : 18. they sh.come and see m.g.
19. not seen m.g. declare m. g.
Eze. 39: 21. set m. g. am. heathen
Mi. 2 : 9. fr. chil. have ye tak.m.g.
Jn. 8 : 50. And I seek not m. o. g.
17 : 24. that they may behold m.g.

Thy GLORY.
Ex. 33 : 18. he said, Shew me t. g.
Ps. 8 : 1. hast set t. g. ab. heavens
45 : 3. gird thy sword with t. g.
57:5.let t.g.be ab. earth,11.-108:5.
63: 2.To see thy power and t.g.as I
90 : 16. let t. g. appear unto chil.
102 : 15. all kings of the earth t.g.
Is. 22 : 18. chariots of t.g. be shame
60 : 19. God t. g. | 62 : 2. k-s see t.
63: 15. behold fr.habita. of t.g. [g.
Je. 14 : 21. not disgrace throne of
48 : 18. come down fr. t. g. [t. g.
Ha. 2 : 16. spewing shall be on t.g.
Mk. 10 : 37. other on left ha.in t.g.

GLORY. [Verb.]
Ex. 8 : 9. Moses said g. over me
2 K. 14 : 10. g.of this, tarry at home
1 Ch. 16 : 10. g. ye in holy name,
Ps. 105 : 3.
35. we may give g. in thy praise
Ps. 63 : 11. sweareth by him sh. g.
64:10. all upright in heart sh. g.
106 : 5. that I may g. with inheri.
Is. 41:16. shalt g. in Holy One
45 : 25. in L. shall all seed of Isr. g.
Je. 4 : 2. and in him shall they g.
9 : 23. let not the wise.rich man g.
24. let him th. glorieth g. in this
Ro. 4 : 2.whereof to g.but not bef.G.
5 : 3. we g. in tribulations also
15 : 17. I have whereof I may g.
1 Co. 1 : 29. that no flesh g. in his
presence [10 : 17.
31.glorieth let him g.in L., 2 Co.
1 Co. 3 : 21. let no man g. in men
4:7.why g. as if hadst not rec.[g.
9 : 16. tho. preach, I have noth. to
2 Co.5 : 12.occa. to g. on our behalf
to them who g. in appearance
11:12.wherein g. they may be as we
18.many g. aft. the flesh, I will g.
30. If must g. will g. of infirm
12 : 1. not expedient for me to g.
5. Of such a one will I g., of myself will not g.[shall not be a f.
6. for tho. I would desire to g. I
9. I will rather g. in infirmities
Ga. 6 : 13. that they may g. in flesh
14. G. forbid I sho. g.save in cross
2 Th. 1 : 4. that we g. in you in ch-s
Ja. 1 : † 9. let bro. of low degree g.
3 : 14. if ye have envying g. not

GLORYING.
1 Co. 5 : 6. Your g. is not good
9:15.that any sho.make my g. void
2 Co. 7 : 4. great my g. of you
12 : 11. I am become a fool in g.
1 Th. 2 : † 19. what our crown of g.?

GLUTTON, S.
De. 21 : 20. this our son is a g.
Pr. 23 : 21. g. shall come to poverty
28 : † 7.feedeth g-s shameth his fa.

GLUTTONOUS.
Mat.11:19.Behold a man g.,Lu.7:34.

GNASH, ED, ETH.
Jb. 16 : 9. he g-h on me, Ps. 37 : 12.
Ps. 35 : 16. g-d upon me with teeth
112 : 10. he shall g. with his teeth
La. 2 : 16. enemies hiss and g. teeth
Mk. 9 : 18. he g-h with his teeth
Ac.7:54. they g-d on him with teeth

GNASHING.
Mat. 8 : 12. there shall be weeping
and g. of teeth, 13 : 42, 50.-22:
13.-24 : 51.-25 : 30. Lu. 13 : 28.

GNAT.
Mat.23:24. strain at a g.and swallow

GNAW, ED.
Zph.3:3.g.not the bones till morrow
Re.16:10. they g-d tongues for pain

GO.
Ge. 3:14. upon thy belly shalt thou
15:2. give seeing I g. childless [g.
16:8. whence camest? whi. wilt g.
24:38.thou g.unto my fa.'s hou.,4.
42. if thou prosper way wh. I g.
55. after that Rebekah shall g.
56. that I may g. to my master
58. Wilt thou g. with this man?
she said, I will g. [from us
26 : 16. Abim. said unto Isaac, g.
28 : 2. Arise, g. to Padan-aram
20. if G. will keep me in way I g.
30:25.that I may g.unto my place
32:26.Let me g. for day breaketh;
Jac. said, I will not let thee g.
37:30. child is not, whi. shall I g.?
43 : 8. Send lad, and we will g.
Ex. 3 : 11. that I sho. g. unto Pha.
19.k.of E.will not let you g.,4:21.
20. aft. that will let you g., 11:1.
21. when ye g. sh. not g. empty
4 : 12. g. I be with thy mouth,19.
23. Let my son g., if refuse to let
him g. I, 8 : 2, 21.-9 : 2.-10:4.
26. So he let him g. then she said
5:1.saith the G.of Isr., Let my peo.
g., 7 : 16.-8:1,20.-9:1,13.-10:3.
2. I know not L., nor let Isr. g.
6 : 1. with strong hand, let th. g.
8:8. I will let thy peo. g.,28.-9:28.
25. g. ye, sacrifice to your God
32. Pha., nei. would he let people
g., 7 : 14.-9 : 35.-10 : 26, 27.
10:7.let the men g. | 8.who sh.g.?
9. g. with our young and old
24. g. ye, serve L., 8, 11.-12 : 31.
13 : 21. light to g. by, Ne 9:12,19.
14 : 5. that we have let Israel g.
†25.wheels, made them g.heavily
17:5.said unto Mo. g. on bef. peo.
Ex.23:23.Angel sh.g.bef.thee,32:34.
32:23. gods to g. bef. us, Ac. 7:40.
33:14.My presence sh.g. with thee
34 : 9. if I found grace, g. am. us
Le. 14 : 53. let g. the living bird
16 : 22. let g. the goat, 10.
Nu. 10 : 32. be, if thou g. with us
20 : 17. will g. by k.'s highway,19.
22 : 13. refuseth to give leave to g.
22:18. I can-t g. bey. word, 24:13.
20. if men call thee, g., 35.
24:14. now, I g. unto my people
31:23.shall make it g.thro.fire and
32 : 6. shall your breth. g. to war
17. we will g. ready armed,20,21.
De. 1 : 33. to shew way ye sho. g.
4:5.land whi. ye g., 26.-6:1.-11:8,
34. G. assayed to g. [21.-30: 18.
40. g. well with thee,5:16.-19:13.
9 : 5. for uprightness dost g.
11 : 28. if ye g. after gods, 28 : 14.
14 : 25. g. unto place wh. L., 26:2.
20 : 5.let him g. to his hou., 6 7,8.
21:14. shalt let her g. whi.she will
22 : 7. in anywise let the dam g.
23 : 10. g. abroad out of camp
24 : 2. g. and be ano. man's wife
31:6. thy God, be it is doth g. wi.
7. thou must g. with this people
8. L. be it is doth g. before thee
16.land whi. they g. among them
21.I know imagina.they g. about
Jos. 1 : 16. whi. sendest we will g.
3 : 3. sh. remove, and g. after ark
4. may know way ye must g.
18 : 3. slack to g. to possess land
Ju. 1:25. they let g. man and fam.
4 : 8. If wilt g. with me, I will g.
6 : 14. Lord said, g. in thy might
7:4. say, This shall g. same sh.g.
11:8. to thee, that thou g. with us
12 : 1. not call us to g. with thee
16:17.if shaven,my stren-h will g.
18:5.whe. way we g.be prosperous
6. bef. Lord is way wherein ye g.
9. be not slothful to g. to possess
10. when ye g. | 19. g. with us
19 : 25. day began, they let her g.
Ru. 1 : 11. why will ye g. with me?
18. she was steadf minded to g.
2:2.let me g.and glean,g.my dau.
1 S. 5 : 11. let it g. to its own place
6 : 6. did they not let people g.?
8.ark,send it away, th. it may g.
9:6. let us g. he can shew our way
7. if g. what bring the man?
19.g.up,to morr.I will let thee g.
10:9. turned his back to g.fr.Sam.
12:21. sho. ye g. after vain things
16:2.How can I g.? if Saul hear it
17:33.art not able to g. ag. Philis.
37. g. and the Lord be with thee
39. and he assayed to g.
39.Da. said, I can-t g. with them
18 : 2. let him g. no more home
19 : 17. Let me g. why I kill thee?
20:5.let me g.that I may hide my s.
28. Da. asked leave to g., 29.
23 : 13. David went whi. could g.
25: 19. g. on before me, behold
26 : 19. saying, g. serve other gods
28 : 7. woman, that I may g. and
2 S. 12 : 23. I sh. g. to him, he not
13:13. whi. cause my shame to g.?
26. my bro. Am. g. — Why g.,27.
15:7. Abs. said, let me g. and pay
20. I g. whi. I may, return thou
17 : 11. g. to battle in thy person
19:36.Thy serv. will g. a little way
20:11.David, let him g. after Joab
1 K. 2 : 2. I g. way of all the earth
11:21.that I may g.to own country
22. let me g. in any wise
12:27.sh. kill me, and g. to Rehob.
13:17. nor g. by way thou camest
18 : 43. he said, g. again 7 times
20:42. hast let g. a man appointed

1 K.22:4. wilt g. with me to battle?
2 Ch. 18 : 3. [18 : 5, 14.
6.Sh.I g. ag. Ramoth-g.,15.2 Ch.
15. g. and prosper, 2 Ch. 18 : 14.
2 K. 3:7. g. with me against Moab?
4:23. Whf. thou g. to him to day?
6 : 22. set br. that they may g. eat
10:24.th. letteth him g. his life be
18:21.g.into ba.and pierce,Is 36:6.
2 Ch. 14:11. in thy name we g. ag.
25:7.let not army of Isr.g.wi. thee
8. if thou wilt g. do it, be strong
Jb.6:18. they g. to nothing [16:22.
10:21.Bef. I g. whence not return,
20:26. g. ill with him th. is left in tabernacle [g.
21:29. Have ye not asked them th.
27:6. my righte-n. I will not let g.
Ps. 32:8. teach thee in way shalt g.
38 : 6. I g. mourning all the day
39:13. bef. I g. hence, be no more
42:9.to G.why g.I mourning,43:2.
48:12. Walk about Zion, g. round
49:19.He sh. g. to gene. of his fa-s
59 : 6 g. round about city, 14.-55:
10. Can. 3 : 2. Is. 23 : 16.
84:7.Theyg.fr.strength to strength
85:13. Righte-n. sh. g. before him
89:14. mercy and truth sh. g. bef.
107:7.might g. to a city of habita.
129:8.g. by say-g, The bless. of L.
132 : 7. we will g. into his tabern.
139:7. whi. shall I g. fr. thy pres.
Pr. 2:19. None th. g. unto her ret.
3:28. g. and come again, to morr.
6 : 6. g. to the ant, thou sluggard
28.Can one g.upon hot coals,and
9 : 6. g. in way of understanding
14:7.g.fr. presence of foolish man
15:12.nei.will scorner g. unto wise
19 : 7. do his friends g. far fr. him
22:6. Train child in way he sho.g.
23 : 30. that g. to seek mixed wine
30 : 29. be 3 things which g. well
Ec.1:†7.rivers come,thither they g.
3 : 20. All g. unto one place, all
5:15. naked sh. g. as he came, 16.
6 : 6. do not all g. to one place?
7:2.better to g.to house of mourn.
9:3. aft. that, they g. to the dead
10:15.kno-th not how to g. to city
12:5.mourners g.about the streets
Can. 3 : 4. I would not let him g.
Is. 3 : 16. and mincing as they g.
6:8.whom send, who will g. for us
9. g. tell this peo., Ac. 28 : 26.
18 : 2. g. ye swift messengers
27 : 4. I would g. through them
28:13. that they might g. and fall
38 : 10. I shall g. to gates of grave
15. shall g. softly all my years
45 : 13. he sh. let g. my captives
16.g.to confusion,makers of idols
48:17. leadeth by way shouldest g.
58:8. thy righte. shall g. bef. thee
62:10. g. thro. g. thro. the gates
Je. 1: 7. shalt g. to all I send thee
7: 12. g. now unto my place
9:2. I might leave my peo. and g.
10 : 5. be borne bec. they can-t g.
12:†2. have taken root, they g. on
14:18. g. into land they know not
29:12.ye shall g.and pray unto me
31:22. How long g. about, O dau.
34 : 3. shalt g. to Bab., Mi. 4 : 10.
40:4.seemeth good to g.there d.,5.
5. he gave reward, and let him g.
15.Let me g.and I will slay Ishm.
42:22.die,in pla.whi.ye desire to g.
46 : 22. voice shall g. like serpent
48:†2. O Madmen, sword shall g.
50 : 4. they shall g. and seek L.
33. they refused to let them g.
La.4:18.we cannot g. in our streng.
Eze. 1:12. whi. Spirit was to g., 20.
8 : 6. I sho. g. far fr. sanctuary
9 : 4. g. thro. midst of the city, 5.

Eze. 13:20 and will let the souls g.
14 : 17. I say, Sword, g. thro. land
20:29. What is the high pla. ye g.?
21 : 16. g. thee one way or other
Ho.5:6.g.with flocks to seek the L.
7:11. call to E. they g. to Assyria
12. When they g. will spread my
11 : 3. I tau ht Ephraim to g.[net
Am.6:7. g. cap. with 1st th.g. cap.
Jon 1 : 2. g. to Nineveh, 3 : 2.
Mi. 2 : 3. nei. sh. ye g. haughtily
5: 8. if he g. thro. treadeth down
Zch. 6 : 7. the bay sought to g.
8. these g. toward north [uno.(2)
8:21. inhabit. of one city sh. g. to
23. g. with you, we have heard
9:14. g. with whirlwinds of south
Mat. 2:8. g. and search diligently
22. Jo. was afraid to g. thither
5:41.to g.a mile, g. twain,Lu.7:8.
8 : 9. and I say, g. and he goeth
32. said, g., they went into herd
9 : 6. take up thy bed and g.
13. g. ye learn what th. meaneth
10 : 6. g. rather to lost sheep of,7.
11. there abide till ye g.
13 : 28. that we g. and gath. them
14 : 22. get into ship and g. bef.
16 : 21. g. unto Jerus. and suffer
17 : 27. g. to the sea, cast hook
21:28. g. work | 30. ans-d I g. sir
25 : 9. g. rather to them that sell
26:36. Sit ye, while I g. and pray
28:7. g. quickly and tell disciples
10.g. tell breth.they g.into Gali.
19. g. ye and teach all nations
Mk.6:37.sh. we g. buy 200 pennyw.
5 : 19. g. home to thy friends
6 : 38. g. see | 45. g. to other side
10:25. camel to g. thro., Lu.18:25.
11 : 6. they let them g., bro-t colt
12 : 38. love to g. in long clothing
14:12. Where wilt thou that we g.
Lu. 1:17. shall g. bef. him in power
76. thou g. bef. face of the Lord
9 : 51. he set face to g. to Jerus.
60. g. and preach kingd. of God
10 : 37. said Jesus, g., do likewise
11 : 5. shall g. unto him at midn.
13 : 32. g. ye and tell that fox
14 : 4. healed him, let him g.
10. g. ye sit down in lowest
18.I bought ground must needs g.
15 : 4. g. after that which is lost
22 : 8. g. and prepare the passover
33. I am ready to g. to prison
68. you will not ans. nor let me g.
23:22. will chastise and let him g.
Jn. 4 : 4. must needs g. thro. Sam.
16. g. call thy husband, and
6 : 68. Lord, to whom shall we g.?
7 : 19. Why g. about to kill me?
33. I g. unto him that sent me
35. Whither will he g.—will he g.
8 : 11. g. and sin no more
14. but I know whither I g.
21. I g. my way, whither I g. ye
9 : 7. g. wash in the pool
11 : 11. g. that I may awake him
44. Loose him, and let him g.
13 : 36. Whi. I g. thou not follow
14 : 2. I g. to prepare a place for
4. whi. I g. ye know, way ye kn.
12. bec. I g. unto my Fa., 16:10.
28.bec.I said,I g.to Fa.,16:17,28.
15:16. ordained you that ye sho. g.
19 : 12. If thou let this man g.
20 : 17. but g. to my breth. and
21 : 3. I g. a fishing, they say, We also g. with thee
Ac. 1 : 25. might g. to his own pla.
3:13. when determ-d to let him g.
4:21.had threatened, they let th.g.
23.being let g.went to their comp.
5 : 20. g. speak in temple to peo.
40. not speak, and let them g.
8 : 26. Arise, g. toward south

Ac.10:20. g. doubting noth., 11:12
11 : 22. Barna. sho. g. far as Anti
16:35.sent,saying,Let those men g.
17:9. security of Jason, let them g.
14. Paul to g. to the sea
19:21.Paul purposed to g. to Jerus.
20 : 1. departed to g. into Macedo.
13. minded himself to g. afoot
22. I g. bound in the spirit unto Jerusalem
23:23.Make ready 200 soldiers to g.
32. left horsemen to g. with him
25 : 12. appealed to Cesar, shalt g.
20. whe. he would g. to Jerus.
27 : 3. Paul gave him liberty to g.
28 : 18. examined, would let me g.
Ro. 15: 25. now I g. unto Jerus.
1 Co. 6:1. you g. to law bef. unjust?
10 : 27. and ye be disposed to g.
16 : 4. if meet I g. they sh. g., 6.
6. my journey which I g.
2 Co. 9:5. exhort breth. th. they g.
Ph. 2 : 23. see how it g. with me
1 Th. 4 : 6. g. beyond or defraud
Re. 10 : 8. g. take little book
See FREE.

GO aside.

Nu. 5 : 12. if any man's wife g. a.
De. 28:14. shalt not g. a. fr. words
Je. 15:5. who shall g. a. to ask how
Ac. 4:15. they com-d them to g. a.

GO astray. [a.

De. 22 : 1. shalt not see bro.'s ox g.
Ps. 58:3. they g. a. as soon as born
Pr.5:23.in greatness of folly he g.a.
7 : 25. g. not a. into path [g. a.
28 : 10. Whoso causeth righte. to
Je.50:6. sheph-s caused th. to g.a.
Eze. 14:11. Isr. may g. no more a.

GO away.

Ex.8:28.you shall not g. very far a.
De. 15 : 13. not let him g. a. empty
16. if he say, I will not g. a.
1 S. 15 : 27. Sam. turned to g. a.
24:19. enemy, will he let him g.a.?
Jb. 4:21. doth not excellency g.a.?
15:30. by breath of mouth he g.a.
Je. 51 : 50. th. escaped sword, g.a.
Ho. 5 : 14. I, will tear and g. a.
Mat. 8 : 31. suffer us to g. a. into swine [ishment
25:46. these g. a. into everl. pun-
Jn. 6 : 67. said Jes., Will ye g. a.?
14:28. ye heard how I said, I g. a.,

GO back. [16 : 7.

Ex. 14 : 21. L. caused sea to g. b.
Jos. 23 : 12. if ye in any case g. b.
Ju. 11:35. I cannot g. b. [to thee?
1 K. 19:20. g. b., what have I done
2 K. 20 : 9. shall shadow g. b. ten
Ps. 80 : 18. so will not we g. b.
Je. 40 : 5. g. b. to Gedaliah, son of
Eze. 24: 14. I will not g. b., nor

GO down. [lang.

Ge. 11:7. let us g. d. and confound
18:21. I will g. d. and see whether
26 : 2. L. said, g. not d. into E.
37 : 35. I will g. d. into grave
43:5. if not send, we will not g.d.
44 : 26. cannot g. d., then will we g. d. [E.
46 : 3. fear not, Jac., to g. d. into
Ex.19:21. L. said, g. d., charge peo.
Nu. 16:30. they g. d. into pit [hire
De. 24 : 15. nei. sun g. d. upon his
Jos. 10 : 13. sun hasted not to g.d.
Ju. 5 : 11. peo. of L. g. d. to gates
7:10. if fear to g. d., go with Phu.
1 S.10:8.shalt g. d. bef. me to Gilg.
14: 36. Let us g. d. after Philis.
37. Shall I g. d. after Philistines
23:4. g. d. to Keilah, I will deliv.
26:6. Who g. d. with me to Saul?
29 : 4. let him not g. d. to battle
2 S. 11 : 8. Da. said, g. d. to thy h.
10. why not g. d. to house? [g.
15:20. sho. I make thee g. up and

1 K. 2:6. let not his hoar head **g.d.**
21: 18. **g. d.** to meet Ahab king
2 K. 1:15. **g. d.** wi. him, not afraid
20: 10. for shadow to **g.d.** 10 degrees
2 Ch. 20: 16. To morrow **g. d.** ag.
Jb. 17: 16. sh. **g. d.** to bars of pit
21: 13. in moment **g. d.** to grave
Ps. 22:29. all that **g. d.** to the dust
28:1. I like them th. **g.d.** into pit,
88: 4. Pr. 1: 12. ⌈I **g. d.**
30: 9. What profit in my bl. when
55:15. let them **g.d.** quick into hell
104: 8. they **g. d.** by the valleys
107:23. that **g.d.** to sea, Is. 42:10.
26. they **g. d.** to the depths
115: 17. nei. any **g. d.** into silence
143:7. like them th. **g. d.** into pit
Pr. 5: 5. Her feet **g. d.** to death
18: 8. **g. d.** into innermost parts
Is. 14:19. cast out, as those th. **g.d.**
30:2. Woe to children that walk to
g. d. into E., 31: 1.
38: 18. **g. d.** into pit cannot hope
60:20. sun sh. not **g.d.**, nor moon
Je. 18:2. **g.d.** to the potter's house
50:27. let them **g. d.** to slaughter
Eze. 24: † 16. nei. thy tears **g. d.**
26: 11. strong garrisons sh. **g. d.**
20. thee with them that **g. d.** to
pit, 31:14.–32:18, 24, 25, 29, 30.
47:8. these waters **g. d.** into desert
Am. 6: 2. **g. d.** to Gath of Philis.
8: 9. cause sun to **g. d.** at noon
Mi. 3: 6. sun **g. d.** over prophets
Mk.13:15. him on housetop not **g.d.**
Ac. 23: 10. com-d soldiers to **g. d.**
25: 5. are able to **g. d.** with me
Ep. 4:26. let not sun **g. d.** on your

GO forth. ⌊wrath

Ge. 8:16. **g.f.** of ark, thou and wif.
42:15. not **g. f.**, except bro. come
Le. 14: 3. priest shall **g. f.** of camp
Nu. 1:3. all able to **g. f.** to war, 20,
22, &c. 2 Ch. 25: 5.
De. 23: 12. shalt have place to **g. f.**
1 S. 23: 13. and he forbare to **g. f.**
2 S. 11:1. when kings **g.f.** to battle
13:39. Da. longed to **g.f.** unto Abs.
18: 2. I will **g. f.** with you, 3.
19:7. if thou **g.** not **f.**, will not tarry
1 K. 2: 36. **g.** not **f.** any whither
19: 11. **g. f.** stand upon mount
22:22. he said, I will **g.f.**; **g.f.** and
2 K. 9: 15. if your minds, let none
11: 7. all that **g. f.** on sab. ⌊**g. f.**
19: 31. out of Jerus. shall **g. f.** a
remnant, Is. 37: 32.
Jb. 24:5. as wild asses **g.** they **f.** to
39: 4. they **g. f.** and return not
Ps. 78: 52. he made his peo. to **g.f.**
108: 11. wilt **g. f.** with our hosts?
Pr. 25: 8. **g.** not **f.** hastily to strive
30:27. no king, yet **g. f.** by bands
Can. 3:11. **g. f.**, O ye dau-s of Zion
7:11. come, let us **g. f.** into villages
Is. 2: 3. out of Z. shall **g. f.** law,
Mi. 4: 2.
42:13. L. shall **g.f.** as mighty man
48: 20. **g. f.** of Bab., Je. 50: 8.
49:9. mayest say to prisoners, **g.f.**
17. made thee waste shall **g. f.**
62: 1. till righteousn. thereof **g.f.**
Je. 2:37. thou shalt **g. f.** from him
6: 25. **g.** not **f.** into the field
11: † 11. shall not be able to **g. f.**
14:18. if I **g.f.** into field, the slain
15:1. let them **g.f.** | 2. whi. we **g.f.**?
25: 32. evil shall **g.f.** fr. na. to na.
31:4. thou shalt **g.f.** in the dances
39. measuring line shall yet **g. f.**
38: 17. if wilt **g. f.** unto princes
18. if wilt not **g.f.** to princes, 21.
43:12. he sh. **g. f.** thence in peace
Eze. 8: 22. **g. f.** into plain and
9: 7. **g.** ye **f.** And they went **f.**
12: 4. **g. f.** as they that **g. f.** into
captivity | 12. prince **g. f.**

Eze. 20: 10. I caused them to **g. f.**
21: 4. my sword **g. f.**
30:9. that day messengers sh. **g.f.**
46: 8. he shall **g. f.** by the way
9. but he shall **g. f.** over ag. it
Da. 11: 44. he shall **g. f.** with fury
Jo. 2:16. let bridegr. **g. f.** of cham.
Mi. 4: 10. for now shalt thou **g. f.**
Ha. 1: 4. judgm. doth never **g. f.**
Zch.6:5. are the four spirits wh. **g.f.**
6. black horses **g.f.** into the north
9: 14. arrow **g. f.** as lightning
14: 3. shall Lord **g. f.** and fight
Mal. 4: 2. ye shall **g. f.** as calves
Mat.24:26. he is in the desert, **g.** not
Lu. 8: 14. **g. f.** and are choked ⌊**f.**
Ac. 16:3. Him would Paul have **g.f.**
He.13:13. Let us **g.f.** to him without
Re. 16: 14. spirits of devils wh. **g.f.**

GO forward. ⌈**g.f.**

Ex.14:15. speak unto Israel that they
Nu. 2: 24. they shall **g.f.** in, 10: 5.
2 K.20:9. sh. shadow **g.f.** 10 degrees
Jb. 23: 8. I **g.f.** bu the is not there

I will GO. ⌈to left

Ge. 13: 9. I **w. g.** to right, I **w. g.**
24: 58. go wi. this man? I **w. g.**
33:12. I **w. g.** bef. thee, Is. 45: 2.
45:28. son, I **w.g.** see him bef. I die
Nu. 20:19. I **w. g.** thro. on my feet
23: 3. stand by burnt off., I **w.g.**
De. 2: 27. I **w. g.** along highway
Ju. 1: 3. I **w. g.** with thee into lot
4: 8. if wilt go with me, **w.** I **g.**
9. said, I **w.** surely **g.** with thee
16:20. I **w. g.** out as at other times
Ru.1:16. whither thou goest, I **w.g.**
2 K. 6: 3. he answered, I **w.g.** ⌈tle
2Ch.18:29. he said, I **w.g.** to the bat-
Ps.43:4. then **w.** I **g.** unto altar of G.
71:16. I **w.g.** in strength of L. ⌈in
118:19. open gates of righte., I **w.g.**
Je.2:25. strangers, aft. them I **w.g.**
Eze. 38:11. I **w.g.** to them at rest
Ho. 2:5. said, I **w.g.** after my lovers
7. I **w. g.** to my first husband
5:15. I **w. g.** to my pl. till they seek
Mi. 1:8. I **w.g.** stripped and naked
Zch. 8: 21. go to seek L., I **w. g.**
Mat. 26:32. I **w.g.** bef. into Galilee,
Mk. 14: 28.
Lu. 15: 18. I **w. g.** to my father
Ac.18:6. hencef. I **w.g.** unto Gent.

GO in, into, or not GO in.

Ge. 11: 31. to **g.** i-o Canaan, 12: 5.
19: 34. make drink wine and **g. i.**
Ex. 4: 27. **g.** i-o wild. to meet Mo.
30: 20. When **g.** i-o tab. wash
32: 27. **g. i.** and out from gate to
Le. 10: 9. not wine, when ye **g.** i-o
tabern. ⌈to see plague
14:36. empty house, bef. priest **g.i.**
21: 11. nei. **g. i.** to any dead body
23. he shall **n. g. i.** unto the vail
Nu. 4:19. Aa. and his sons shall **g.i.**
20. not **g. i.** when holy things
8:15. after that sha. Levites **g.i.**, 24.
27:17. go out, and **g. i.** bef. them
32: 9. should **n. g. i.** the land
De. 1: 8. **g. i.** possess land, 27: 3.
Jos. 1: 11. Ne. 9: 15, 23.
37. thou shalt **n. g. i.**, 4: 21.
38. Joshua shall **g. i.** thither
39. betw. good and evil they sh. **g.i.**
4:1. that ye may **g. i.** possess, 8: 1.
6:18. that thou mayest **g.i.**, 10:11.
11:8. that ye be strong, and **g.i.**, 31.
24:10. **n. g.** i-o his house to fetch
Ju.15:5. let them **g.** i-o stand-g corn
19: 15. turned to **g. i.** and lodge
Ru. 3: 4. **g. i.** uncover his feet
2 S. 11:11. sha. I **g.** i-o house to eat?
1 K. 13:8. I will **n. g. i.** nor eat
16. I may not return, nor **g. i.**
17:12. may **g.i.** and dress it for me
22: 25. **g.** i-o inner chamber
2 K. 9: 2. look out Jehu and **g. i.**

2 K. 10: 25. **g. i.** and slay them, let
2 Ch. 18: 24. shalt **g.** i-o chamber
23:6. minister of Levites shall **g.i.**
Ne. 6: 11. who as I am would **g.** i-o
tem. to save life? I will **n. g. i.**
Es. 2:15. when Esther's turn to **g.i.**
4:8. to charge her that she **g. i.**
16. so will I **g. i.** unto the king
5:14. **g.** thou **i.** merrily with king
Jb. 34: †23. **g.** i-o judgm. with God
Ps. 26:4. nei. I **g. i.** wi. dissemblers
63: 9. **g.** i-o lower parts
66:13. I will **g.** i-o thy house with
118: 19. open gates, I will **g.** i-o
119:35. make me **g. i.** path of com.
132: 7. we will **g.** i-o his taberu.
Pr. 27: 10. **n. g.** i-o bro.'s house
Is.2:19. shall **g.** i-o holes of rocks, 21.
13: 2. may **g.** i-o gates of nobles
Je. 4: 5. let us **g.** i-o defenced cities
36: 5. I cannot **g.** i-o house of L.
42:14. we will **g.** i-o land of E., 17.
19. L. said, **g.** ye **n.** i-o Egypt
Eze.7:†17. knees **g.** i-o water, 21:†7.
46:10. when they **g. i.** sh. **g. i.**, 8.
Na. 3: 14. **g.** i-o clay, tread mortar
Zch. 6: 10. **g.** i-o house of Josiah
Mat.2:20. take child, and **g.** i-o Isr.
7: 13. many there be that **g. i.**
20:4. **g.** i-o vineyard, they went, 7.
21:2. **g.** i-o village over, Lu. 19:30.
31. harlots **g.** i-o kingd. bef. you
22: 9. **g.** i-o the highways, bid
23:13. nei. **g. i.** nei. suffer to **g. i.**
26: 18. **g.** i-o the city, Mk. 14:13.
32. will **g.** bef. you i-o Galilee,
28: 7. Mk. 14: 28.–16: 7.
28: 10. breth. that they **g.** i-o Gal.
Mk. 6: 36. that they may **g.** i-o the
country, Lu. 9: 12.
8:26. nei **g.**i-o the town, nor tell it
9:43. having 2 hands to **g.** i-o hell
14:14. sh. **g. i.** say ye to goodman
16: 15. **g.** i-o all the world, preach
Lu.5:24. take couch **g.**i-o thine hou.
8: 51. he suffered no man to **g. i.**
15: 28. angry, and would **n. g. i.**
19: 30. **g.** i-o village over
Jn.7:3. **g.** i-o Judea, that thy disci.
10:9. shall **g. i.** and out, and find
Ac. 1:11. as ye see him **g.** i-o heaven
3: 3. **g.** i-o temp., asked an alms
9:6. **g.** i-o city, be told thee, 22:10.
11. **g.** i-o street called Straight
16: 7. assayed to **g.** i-o Bithynia
Ja. 4:13. will **g.** i-o such a city
Re.13:10. leadeth i-o cap-y sh. **g.** i-o
17:8. the beast shall **g.** i-o perdition
See CAPTIVITY.

GO in peace.

Ge. 15:15. shalt **g.** to thy fa-s **i. p.**
Ex. 4: 18. said to Moses, **g. i. p.**
18:23. peo. sh. **g.** to their pl. **i. p.**
Ju. 18:6. priest to Danites, **g. i. p.**
1 S. 1:17. said to Hannah, **g. i. p.**
20: 42. Jonathan said to David,
g. i. p., 13.
25:35. Da. said unto Abigail, **g.i.p.**
29:7. Achish said unto Da., **g.i.p.**
2 S.15:9. king said unto Abs. **g.i.p.**
1 K. 2: 6. not hoary head **g.** down
i. p. ⌈**i. p.**
2 K. 5: 19. Elisha unto Naaman, **g.**
Is. 57: † 2. he shall **g. i. p.**, they
Mk. 5:34. **g. i. p.**, and be whole of
Lu. 7: 50. faith saved thee, **g.i.p.**,
Ac. 15: 33. were let **g. i. p.** ⌊8:48.
16: 36. now depart, **g. i. p.**

Go in to, or unto.

Ge. 16:2. Sarai said, **g.i.u.** my maid
19: 34. make drink wine, and **g.i.**
29:21. days, that I may **g.i.u.** her
30: 3. maid Bilhah, **g. i. u.** her
38: 8. **g. i. u.** thy brother's wife
Le.21:11. nei. **g. i. t.** any dead body
23. he shall not **g. i. u.** the vail
De. 21: 13. after shalt **g. i. u.** her

De.22:13.if take wife,and g.i.u.her
25: 5. husband's bro. g.i.u. her
Jos. 23: 12. marriages, g.i.u. them
Ju. 15: 1. I will g.i.t. my wife into
2 S. 16: 21. g.i.u. fa.'s concubines
1 K. 11:2. ye shall not g.i. t. them
Eze. 23: 44. to her as they g. i. t.
woman [maid
Am. 2:7. man and fath. g.i.t. same

Let us GO.

Ge. 33: 12. take our journey l.u.g.
37:17. them say, l. u.g.to Dothan
Ex.3:18.l. u. g. 3 days' journ., 5:3.
5:8. they say, l. u. g. sacrifice, 17.
13: 15. Pha. would hardly l.u.g.
Nu. 13: 30. l. u. g. at once and
possess [6: 14.
De. 13: 2. l. u. g. after other gods,
1 S. 9: 9. l. u. g. to the seer, 6, 10.
11: 14. l. u. g. to Gilgal, renew
14: 1. l. u. g. over to Philis., 6.
20: 11. l. u. g. out into field
2 K. 6:2. l. u. g. unto Jordan, take
Ps. 122: 1. l. u. g. into hou. of L.
Is. 2: 3. l.u.g. to mountain of L.
7: 6. l. u. g. ag. Judah and vex
Je. 4: 5.l.u. g. into defenced cities
6: 4. l. u. g. up at noon, Woe
5. l. u. g. and destroy palaces
35:11. l. u. g. to Jerus. for fear of
46: 16. l. u. g. again to our own
people [own country
51: 9. l. u. g., every one into his
Zch. 8: 21. l. u. g. to pray bef. L.
Mk. 1: 38. l. u. g. into next towns
14: 42. l.u.g., he that betrayeth
Lu. 2: 15. l.u.g. unto Bethlehem
8: 22. l. u. g. over the lake
Jn. 11: 7. l.u.g. into Judea again
15. l. u. g. unto him
16. l. u. g. that we may die
14: 31. Arise, l. u. g. hence
Ac. 15: 36. l. u. g. and visit breth.
He. 6:1. l.u.g. on unto perfection

GO near.

De. 5: 27. g. n. hear all L. says
2 S. 1: 15. Da. said, g.n. fall upon
Jb. 31: 37. as prince would I g. n.
Ac. 8: 29. g. n., join this chariot

GO not, or not GO.

Ge. 32:26. I will n. let thee g. exc.
Ex. 33: 15. If thy presence g. n.
Nu. 10: 30. Hobab said, I will n.g.
14: 42. g. n. up., De. 1: 42. 2 S.
5:23. 1 K. 12: 24. 1 Ch. 14: 14.
2 Ch. 11: 4.
20: 20. said, Thou shalt n. g.
22: 12. G. said unto Balaam, shalt
De. 1: 26. ye wo. n. g. up [n. g.
3: 27. thou shalt n. g. over this
Jordan, 4: 21, 22.-31: 13.
6: 14. sh. n. g. after other gods,
1 K. 11: 10.
24: 19. thou shalt n.g. to fetch it
32: 52. thou shalt n. g. thither
Jos. 8: 4. g. n. far from the city
Ju. 4: 8. n. g. with me, I n. g.
7:4. This sh. n. g., same sh. n.g.
20: 8. We will n. g. to his tent
Ru.3:17.g.n.empty unto thy moth.
1 S. 29: 8. that I may n. g. fight
ag. enemies, 9. [wo. n. g.
2 S. 13: 25. let n. all g. howbeit he
1 K. 2: 6. let n. his hoar head g.
down [g. n.?
2 K. 2: 18. Did I not say unto you,
1 Ch. 21: 30. Da. could n. g. bef. it
2 Ch. 25:13. soldiers that sho. n.g.
Ps. 30: 3. that I sho. n.g. down to
pit [n. g.
Pr. 4: 13. Take instruction, let her
14. g. n. into way of evil men
22:24.with furious man shalt n.g.
Is. 52: 12. shall n. g. out wi. haste
Je. 16: 8. n.g. into the house feast.
25:6. g. n. after other gods, 35:15.
27: 18. vessels left g. n. to Bab.

Je. 43: 2. g.n. into Egypt, 42: 19.
49:12. thou shalt n. g. unpunish.
Eze. 8: 25. Thou sh. n. g. out am.
42: 14. priests enter, sh. n.g. out
Mat. 10: 5. g. n. into way of Gent.
Lu. 10: 7. g. n. fr. house to house
17:23. see here or there, g. n. aft.,

GO out. [21: 8.

Ge. 9: 10. fr. all that g. o. of ark
24: 11. women g. o. to draw wat.
45:1. Cause ev. man to g.o. fr. me
Ex. 6: 11. he let chil. of Isr. g. o.
8: 29. Behold, I g. o. from thee
11: 4. will I g. o. into midst of E.
8. after that I will g. o.
10. would not let chil. of Isr.g.o.
12: 22. none of you g. o. at door
16:4. peo. shall g. o. gather a rate
29. let no man g. o. on 7th day
21: 2. in 7th year he sh. g.o. free
3. if by hims., sh. g.o. by hims.;
married, wife sh. g.o. with him
4. master's, he sh. g.o. by hims.
5. if serv. say, I will not g.o. free
7. a maidserv. not g. o. as mens.
11. then shall she g. o. free
Le. 6: 13. fire on altar never g. o.
8: 33. not g. o. of tab. in 7 days
10: 7. ye shall not g. o. at door
14: 38. priest sh. g. o. of house
15: 16. if seed of copulation g. o.
16: 18. shall g. o. to altar bef. L.
21: 12. Nei. g. o. of the sanctuary
25: 28. in jubilee it g. o., 31, 33.
30.not g.o. in jubil | 54.sh. g.o.
Nu. 27:17. Wh. may g.o. bef. them
21. at his word sh. they g. o.
De. 24: 5. taken wife, not g. o. to
28: 25. shalt g. o. one way [war
31: 2. I can no more g. o. and
Jos. 2: 19. who g.o. bl. be on head
14: 11. both to g. o. and come in,
1 K. 8: 7.
Ju. 9: 38. g.o. and fight with them
16:20.I will g. o. as at other times
20: 28. Shall I yet again g. o. to
battle [ens
Ru. 2:22. thou g. o. with his maid-
1 S. 8: 20. g. o. bef. us, and fight
19: 3. will g. o. and stand beside
20: 11. let us g. o. into the field
28: 1. said, thou shalt g.o. wi. me
2 S. 5: 24. L. sh. g. o. before thee
21: 17. shalt g. no more o. to bat.
1 K. 3: 7. I know not how to g. o.
8: 44. If g.o. to battle, 2 Ch 6:34.
15: 17. not suffer any to g. o., or
come in, 2 Ch. 16: 1. [o.
20: 31. put ropes on heads, and g.
1 Ch. 20: 1. time kings g.o. to bat.
2 Ch. 1: 10. knowl. th. I may g.o.
18:21. g.o. and be lying spirit,(2)
20: 17. to morrow g. o. ag. them
26: 18. g. o. of sanct., hast tresp-d
20. himself hasted also to g. o.
Jb. 15: 13. lettest such words g.o.
Ps.60:10. didst not g. o. wi. armies
109:†7. let him g. o. guilty [g.o.
Pr. 22: 10. out scorner, contention
Ec. 8: 3. not hasty to g.o. of sight
Is. 52: 11. depart ye, g. ye o. from
12. ye shall not g. o. with haste
55: 12. ye shall g. o. with joy
Je 21: 12. lest my fury g. o. like
51: 45. g. ye o. of midst of her
Eze. 15: 7. shall g. o. fr. one fire
44: 3. prince sh. g. o. same way
46: 9. shall g. o. by south gate
Am. 4: 3. sh. g. o. at the breaches
Zch. 14: 8. living waters g. o. from
Jerusalem
Mat.25:6.bridegr., g. ye o. to meet
Lu.8:31. not com. to g.o. into deep
9: 5. when g. o. of city shake off
14: 21. g. o. quickly into streets
23. g. o. into the highways and
1 Co.5:10.must needs g.o. of world

He. 11: 8. Ab., when called to g. o.
Re.3:12. overcometh, g. no more o.
20: 8. sh. g. o. to deceive nations

GO over.

De. 3: 25. let me g. o. and see land
28. Josh. g. o. bef. people, 31: 3.
4: 14. land whi. ye g. o., 26.-31:
13.-32: 47. [g. o.
22. I must not g. o. Jordan, ye
24:20. thou shalt not g.o. boughs
30: 13. Who shall g. o. sea for us?
31: 3. thy G. will g. o. bef. thee
34: 4. thou shalt not g.o. thither
Jos. 1: 2. arise, g. o. this Jordan
Ju. 12: 5. Ephr-s said, Let me g.o.
1 S. 14: 1. let us g. o. to Philis., 6.
30:10.so faint, they could not g.o.
2 S. 16:9. g.o. and take off his head
19:37. Chimham, let him g. o.,38.
Is. 8:7. come and g.o. his banks,8.
11: 15. make men g. o. dryshod
51:23. Bow down, th. we may g.o.
54:9. waters of Noah no more g.o.
Je. 41: 10. Ishm. to g. o. to Ammonites [side
Lu. 8: 22. Let us g. o. unto other

GO to.

Ge. 11: 3. g. t., let us make brick
4. g. t., let us build
7. g.t., let us confound languag.
38:16.g.t. I pray thee, let me come
Ju. 7: 3. g. t. procl. in ears of peo.
2 K. 5:5. King of Syr. said, g. t. go
Ec. 2:1. g. t. now, I will prove thee
Is. 5: 5. g. t., I will tell you what
Je.18:11. g.t., speak to men of Jud.
Ja. 4: 13. g. t., ye that say to day
5: 1. g. t. now, ye rich men, weep

GO up.

Ge. 35: 1. Arise, g. u. to Beth-el, 3.
44: 33. let lad g. u. with brethren
34. how I g. u. to father? 45: 9.
50: 6. Pha. said, g. u. bury fa.,5.
Ex.8:3. frogs g. u. come into house
19: 12. heed ye g. not u. into m-t
20: 26. g. u. by steps unto altar
24: 2. Nei. sh. people g.u. wi. him
32: 30. ye have sinned, I will g.u.
33: 1. g. u., thou and the people
3.I not g.u.in midst of thee [u.
34:24.desire la.when thou shalt g.
Le. 19:16. not g. u. as a talebearer
Nu. 13:30. let us g. u. and poss. it
31. we not able to g. u. ag. peo.
14: 40. Lo, we be here, and will g.
u., De. 1: 41. [u.
42.g. not u. | 44. presumed to g.
De. 1: 22. what way we must g. u.
28. Whither shall we g. u.
9: 23. g. u. possess land, 1: 21.
25:7. let his brother's wife g. u. to
30:12. Who sh. g. u. for us to heav.
Jos. 7: 3. let not all g. u., let 3000
men g. u., 8: 1, 3.
22:33. not intend to g. u. ag. them
Ju. 1: 1. who g. u. to fight them?
2. L. said, Judah sh. g. u., 20:18.
2:1. I made you g. u. out of Egypt
9: † 9. should I g. u. and down
for other trees? [mts.
11: 37. that I g. u. and down upon
18: 9. that we may g. u. ag. them
20: 9. will g. u. by lot ag. Gibeah
18. Which sh. g. u. first to battle?
23. Shall I g. u.? | 28. n. g. ag.
1 S.1:22.not g.u.until child weaned
6:20. to whom shall he g. u. from
us?
9: 13. find him bef. he g. u. to eat
14. Sam. to g. u. to high pla., 19
14: 9. if say, Tarry, we not g. u.
10. if say, Come up, we will g. u.
2 S. 2:1. said, Shall I g. u. into any
cities? L. said, g.u. to Hebron
5:19. shall I g. u. ag. Philistines?
15: 20. should I make thee g. u.
19:34. How long to live, that I g.u.

2 S. 24:18. g.u., rear altar, 1 Ch.21:
1 K.12:24. not g.u., 2 Ch.11:4. ⌊18.
27. If this people g. u. to do sacr.
28. too much to g. u. to Jerus.
18: 43. g. u., look toward the sea
22: 6. g. u., for L. shall deliver it
into ha. of king, 12. 2 Ch.18:11,14.
20. g. u. and fall, 2 Ch. 18:2, 19.
2 K. 1: 3. g. u., meet messengers
2: 23. g. u. thou bald head, g.u.
3: 7. wilt thou g. u. ag. Moab?
8. said, Which way sh. we g. u.
12:17. Hazael set to g. u. to Jerus.
18: 25. g. u. ag. land, Is. 36: 10.
20:5. third day shalt g.u. unto ho.
8. what sign th. I g. u.? Is.38:22.
22:4. g. u. to Hilkiah high priest
1 Ch. 14:10. sh. I g.u. | 14. g. not u.
2 Ch. 18:5. sh. we g.u. to Ramoth-?
36: 23. let him g. u., Ezr. 1: 3.
Ezr. 1:5. spirit G. raised to g.u. and
7: 9. began to g. u. from Bab.
13. all minded to g.u. go wi.me, 28.
Ne. 4: 3. if fox g. u. he sh. break
Ps. 104: 8. They g. u. by the mts.
132: 3. I will not g. u. into my bed
Can. 6:6. sheep that g.u. fr. washing
7: 8. I will g. u. to palm tree
Is. 2: 3. let us g. u. to mt. of L.,
Mi. 4: 2.
5: 24. blossom sh. g. u. as dust
7:6. let us g. u. ag. Judah and vex
15: 5. with weeping sh. they g.u.
21:2. g. u., O Elam | 34: 10. smoke
35:9. nor raven. beast g. u. ⌊g.u.
36: 10. g. u. ag. land, and destr.
Je. 5: 10. g. ye u. upon her walls
6:4. arise, and let us g. u. at noon
21: 2. that Nebuchad. may g. u.
22: 20. g. u. to Lebanon, and cry
31: 6. let us g. u. to Zion, unto L
46: 8. I will g. u. and cover earth
11. g. u. into Gilead, take balm
48:5. continual weeping shall g.u.
49: 28. g. u. to Kedar, and spoil
50: 21. g. u. ag. land of Meratha.
Eze. 38:11. g.u. to unwalled villages
40: 26. seven steps to g. u. to it
Ho. 4: 15. nei. g. u. to Beth-aven
Hag. 1: 8. g. u. to mt., bring wood
Zch. 14: 16. g. u. from year to y.
Mat. 20: 18. we g. u. to Jerus., Son
betrayed, Mk. 10:33. Lu. 18:31.
Lu. 14: 10. Friend, g. u. higher
Jn.7:8. g. ye u. unto feast, I g. not u.
Ac. 15:2. g. u. to Jeru. about ques.
21: 4. Paul sho. not g. u. to Jeru.
12. besought him not to g. u. to
25: 9. wilt thou g.u. to Jerusalem

GO his, or their way, s.

Ju.19:27. her lord rose up to g.h.w.
Pr.9:15. passengers who g. on t. w-s
Jn. 18:8. if ye me, let these g. t.w.

GO thy way.

Ge. 12:19. thy wife, take her, g.t.w.
1 S 20:22. g.t.w., L. hath sent thee
2 K. 4:29. take my staff, and g.t.w.
Ec. 9: 7. g. t. w. eat thy bread
Can. 1: 8. g. t. w. by footsteps of
Da. 12: 9. g. t. w., words are closed
13. g. t. w. till the end be
Mat. 5:24. g. t. w., be reconciled to
8: 4. g. t. w., shew thyself to the
priest, Mk. 1: 44.
13. g. t. w. as hast believ. so it
20: 14. Take thine, and g. t. w.
Mk. 7: 29. For this saying, g. t. w.
10: 21. g. t. w., sell whatsoever
52. g. t.w. faith made, Lu. 17:19.
Jn. 4: 50. g. t. w., thy son liveth
Ac. 9: 15. g. t. w., he is a chosen
24:25. Felix ans., g. t. w. for this

GO your way, s. ⌊time

Ge.19:2. ye sh. rise and g. on y.w-s
Jos. 2:16. afterw. g. y. w., Ju.19:5.
Ru. 1: 12. turn my dau-s, g. y. w.
Ne. 8:10. g. y.w. eat the fat, drink
Mat. 27:65. g. y. w. make it as sure
Mk. 11:2 g. y. w. into village over
16:7. g. y. w., tell his disciples th.
Lu. 7:22. g.y.w. tell Jn. what things
10:3. g.y.w-s, I send you as lambs
10. they receive you not, g. y.w-s
Re. 16: 1. g. y. w-s, pour out vials

GO a whoring. ⌊of wrath

Ex. 34:15. lest g.a.w. aft. their gods
16. sons g. a. w. after their gods
Le. 20: 5. cut off all g. a. w. after
him ⌈wizards
6. cut off such as g. a. w. after
Nu. 15: 39. ways, ye use to g. a. w.
De.31:16. peo. will g. a. w. after gods
2 Ch.21:13. Jeho. made Jud. g.a.w.
Ps. 73:27. destroyed all that g.a.w.
Eze.6:9. eyes which g. a. w. after idols

GOEST, ETH, ING.

See after GODWARD.

GOAD, S.

Ju. 3: 31. slew 600 with an ox g.
1 S. 13: 21. had file to sharpen g-s
Ec. 12: 11. words of the wise are as

GOAT. ⌊g-s

Ge. 15: 9. take she g. of 3 years
Ex. 22:†1. if a man steal a g.
Le. 3: 12. if his offering be a g.
4: 24. lay his hand upon head of g.
7: 23. he sh. eat no fat of ox, or g.
9: 15. g. wh. was sin off-g, 16:15,27.
10: 16. Mos. sought g. of sin off.
16: 9. Aaron shall bring the g., 10.
18. put blood of g. upon horns
20. he shall bring the live g.
21. hands upon live g.
22. let go the g. in wilderness
17: 3. whoso. killeth g. in camp
22: 27 when g. is bro-t 7 days
Nu. 15: 27. if sin thro. igno. bri. g.
18:17. firstling of a g. not redeem.
28: 22. one g. for sin off-g, to make
atonem., 29: 22, 28, 31, 34, 38.
De. 14: 4. ye shall eat the ox, g.
17:†1. not sac. g. wherein is blemish
Ju. 6: †4. Midianites left ox, or g.
Pr. 30:31. comely in going, a he g.
Eze. 43: 25. prepare ev. day a g.
Da.8:5. a he g. came from the west,
g. had a notable horn
8. the he g. waxed very great
21. rough g. is king of Grecia

Wild GOAT, S.

De 14:5. ye shall eat the w. g. ⌈g-s
1 S. 24:2. seek Da. upon rocks of w.
Jb. 39: 1. knowest thou when w. g-s
bring forth ⌈g-s
Ps. 104: 18. high hills refuge for w.

See SCAPEGOAT.

GOATS.

Ge. 4: †4. Abel bro-t firstling of g.
27: 9. fetch me two kids of the g.
16. put skins of g. upon his hands
30:32. spotted and speckled amo. g.
33. not speckled among g.
35. removed g. ringstreaked
31: 38. she g. not cast young
32:14. Two hundred she g. 20 he g.
37: 31. brethren killed a kid of g.
38: † 17. will send thee a kid fr. g.
Ex. 12: 5. ye shall take it out fr. g.
Le. 1: 10. his off. be of sheep or g.
4: 23. bring his off-g, kid of g., 28 -
9: 3. kid of g. for sin off-g ⌊5: 6.
16: 5. two kids of the g. | 7. two g.
8. Aaron sh. cast lots upon 2 g.
22: 19. offer a male of sheep or g.
† 21. a freewill off-g in beeves or g.
23: 19. shall sacrifice one kid of g.
for sin off-g, Nu. 7: 16, 28, 34,
40, 46, 52, 58, 64, 70, 76, 82.-15:
24.-28: 15,30.-29:5,11,16,19,25.
Nu. 7: 17. five rams, five he g., five
lambs, 23, 29, 35, 41, 47, 53, 59,
65, 71, 77, 83.
87. kids of g. for sin off-g, twelve
88. the he g. 60, the lambs sixty
Nu.31†:30. shalt take 1 portion of g.
De. 32: 14 he g. of breed of Bashan
Ju. 6: † 19. made ready a kid of g.
1 S. 25: 2. Nabal had a thousand g.
2 Ch. 17:11. Arab-s bro-t 7,700 he g.
29:21. bro-t 7 he g. for sin off-g, 23
Ezr.6:17. off-d at dedication 12 he g.
8:35. chil. of captiv. offered 12 he g.
Ps. 50: 9. I will take no he g. out
13. or will I drink blood of g.?
66:15. I will offer bullocks with g.
Pr. 27: 26. g. are price of thy field
27. thou shalt have g. milk enough
Can. 4:1. hair is as flock of g., 6: 5.
Is. 1:11. I delight not in bl. of he g.
14: † 9. stirreth up for thee all g.g.
34: 6. sword fat with blood of g.
Je.50:8. be as he g. bef. flocks ⌈g.
51: 40. slaughter like rams with he
Eze. 27: 21. Arabia occupied in g.
34: 17. judge betw. rams and he g.
39:18. ye sh. drink the blood of g.
43: 22. second day offer kid of g.
45: 23. kid of g. daily for sin off-g
Mi. 5: † 8. as a young lion am. g.
Zch.10:3. kindled, I punished the g.
Mat. 25: 32. divideth sheep from g.
33. he shall set g. on left hand
He.9:12. nor entered by blood of g.
13. if the blood of g. sanctifieth
19. he took blood of g. and sprinkl
10:4. not possi. blood of g. take sins

GOATS' hair.

Ex.25:4. offering ye shall take g.h.
26:7. shalt make curtains of g. h.
35: 6 willing, let him bring g. h.
23. man with wh. was found g.h.
26. and all the women spun g.h.
36: 14. she made curtains of g.h.
Nu. 31:20. purify all work of g. h.
1 S. 19:13. put a pillow of g. h., 16.

GO'ATH.

Je. 31:39. shall compass about to G.

GOATSKINS. ⌈g.

He.11:37. wandering in sheepskins,

GOB. ⌈†4.

2 S. 21:18. battle at G., 19. 1 Ch.20:

GOBLET.

Can. 7:2. thy navel is like round g.

GOD.

Ge. 6:5. G. saw wickedn. was great
16:13. name of L., Thou G. seest me
17:7. to be a G. unto thee and thy
31:13. I am the G. of Beth-el ⌊seed
42:28. What this G. done unto us?
45:8. not you sent me hither, but G.
48:21. I die, but G. sh. be with you
Ex.6:7. you to me, and be to you a G.
18: 19. and G. shall be with thee
Nu. 23:23. What hath G. wrought!
24:23. who live, when G. doeth this
De. 4: 7. what nation G. so nigh
29: 13. that he be unto thee a G.
1 S. 3: 17. G. do so and more also,
14:44.-25:22.-2 S.3:9,35.-19:13.
-1 K. 2: 23. 2 K. 6: 31.
17:46. all may know is a G. in Isr.
22: 3. till I know what G. will do
2 S.12:22. Who tell whe. G. be graci.
22:32. who is G. save L.? Ps. 18:31.
1 K. 18: 21. if L. be G. follow
39. The L., he is the G., L. he is
2 K.19:15. thou art G. alone ⌊the G.
2 Ch. 20: 6. O L. art not thou G. in
Ezr. 1: 3. G. be with him, he is G.
Ne. 9: 17. art a G. ready to pardon
Jb.22:13. How doth G. know? Ps.73:
Ps.4:1. call, O G. of my righte. ⌊11.
5:4. not G. hast pleas. in wickedn.
52: 7. made not G. his strength
57:2. G. that performeth all things
86:10. thou art G. alone, Is. 37:16.
140:7. O G. strength of my salva.
Is. 12:2. behold, G. is my salvation
44:8. Is a G. besides me? is no G.
45: 22. look unto me, I am G.
46:9. I am G. there is none like me

Je. 31 : 33. I will be their G., 32:38.
Eze. 28 : 2. said, I sit in seat of G.
9. thou shalt be man, and no G.
Ho. 8:6. workman made it, is not G.
11 : 9. I am G. and not man
Mi. 7:18. Who is a G. like unto thee
Mat. 1:23. name Emmanuel, wh. is
G. with us [mon, Lu. 16:13.
6:24. Ye cannot serve G. and mam-
19 : 17. is none good but one, that
is G., Mk. 10 : 18. Lu. 18 : 19.
Mk. 12:32. is one G. and none other
Jn. 1:1. the Word was with G. and
Word was G. [him
3: 2. can do miracles, exc. G. with
8:41. we have one Father even G.
42. I proceeded, and came fr. G.
17:3. know thee, the only true G.
Ac. 2 : 22. by wonders, wh. G. did
5 : 29. We ought to obey G. rather
7:9. sold Joseph, but G. with him
10 : 34. G. no respecter of persons
17 : 23. to the unknown G.
19 : 20. mightily grew word of G.
Ro. 3 : 4. let G. be true, man liar
8 : 31. If G. for us, who be ag. us?
15 : 5. G. of patience and consola.
1 Co. 8 : 6. is but one G. the Father
15:28. th. G. may be all in all
2 Co. 1:21. he wh. anointed us, is G.
13:11. G. of love and peace wi. you
Ep. 2 : 12. without G. in the world
2 Th. 2:4. above all called G. so that
he, as G. [flesh
1 Ti. 3 : 16. G. was manifest in the
Tit. 1:16. profess that they know G.
He. 3 : 4. that built all things is G.
4:10. ceased from works, as G. did
8 : 10. I will be to them a G. they
1 Jn. 1 : 5. G. is light, in him is no
4:12. No man seen G. at any time
Re. 21 : 3. G. shall be with them
4. G. shall wipe away all tears
7. I will be his G. he my son

Against GOD.

Ge. 39:9. how do this and sin **a.** G.?
Nu. 21 : 5. spake **a.** G., Ps. 78:19.
1 Ch. 5:25. they transgressed **a.** G.
2 Ch. 32 : 19. spake **a.** G. of Jerus.
Jb. 15 : 13. turnest thy spirit **a.** G.
25. stretcheth out his hand **a.** G.
34:37. multiplieth his words **a.** G.
Da. 3:29. speak **a.** G. of Shadrach
11:36. marvell. things **a.** G. of gods
Ho. 13 : 16. she hath rebelled **a.** G.
Ac. 5 : 39. lest found to fight **a.** G.
6:11. spoken blasphemous words **a.**
23 : 9. let us not fight **a.** G. [G.
Ro. 8 : 7. carnal mind enmity **a.** G.
9 : 20. who thou repliest **a.** G.
Re. 13 : 6. opened his mouth **a.** G.
See ALMIGHTY.

Before GOD.

Ge. 6 : 11. earth was corrupt **b.** G.
Ex. 18:12. eat with Moses' fa. **b.** G.
Jos. 24 : 1. presented thems. **b.** G.
Ju. 21:2. peo. abode till even **b.** G.
1 Ch. 13:8. Da. and Isr. played **b.** G.
10. and there Uzza died **b.** G.
16:1. offered burnt sacrifices **b.** G.
2 Ch. 33:12. Manas. humbled **b.** G.
34 : 27. Josiah's heart humbled **b.**
Ezr. 7:19. deliver **b.** G. of Jerus. [G.
Jb. 15 : 4. restrainest prayer **b.** G.
Ps. 42:2. when sh. I appear **b.** G.?
56:13. walk **b.** G. in light of living
61:7. He shall abide **b.** G. for ever
68 : 3. let righteous rejoice **b.** G.
84:7. ev. one in Z. appeareth **b.** G.
Ec. 2:26. give to him is good **b.** G.
5 : 2. heart hasty to utter **b.** G.
8 : 13. because he feareth not **b.** G.
Da. 2:18. desire mercies from **b.** G.
6 : 10. gave thanks **b.** G. as afore.
11. found making supplica. **b.** G.
26. that men tremble **b.** G. of Dan.
Lu. 1:6. were both righteous **b.** G.
Lu. 12:6. not one is forgotten **b.** G.
24:19. prophet mighty indeed **b.** G.
Ac. 7 : 46. Who found favour **b.** G.
10:4. thine alms for memorial **b.** G.
33. we all present **b.** G. to hear
23 : 1. in all good conscience **b.** G.
Ro. 2 : 13. not hearers just **b.** G.
3 : 19. world become guilty **b.** G.
4:2. whereof to glory, but not **b.** G.
14:22. faith? have it to thyself **b.** G.
2 Co. 12 : 19. we speak **b.** G. in C.
Ga. 1 : 20. behold, **b.** G. I lie not
1 Th. 3:13. stabl. your hearts **b.** G.
1 Ti. 5 : 4. good and accepta. **b.** G.
21. I charge thee **b.** G., 2 Ti. 4:1.
Ja. 1 : 27. Pure religion **b.** G.
Re. 3:2. not found works perf. **b.** G.
9:13. voice fr. horns of altar **b.** G.
12:10. which accused them **b.** G.
16:19. Bab. came in remem. **b.** G.
20 : 12. I saw dead, stand **b.** G.
See CALLED, CHOSEN, COMMANDED.

Eternal GOD.

De. 33 : 27. The **e.** G. is thy refuge

Everlasting GOD.

Ge. 21:33. Ab. called on name of **e.** G.
Is. 40 : 28. the **e.** G. fainteth not
Ro. 16:26. acc. to command-t of **e.** G.
See FATHER, FAVOUR, FEAR, FORBID, GAVE, GLORIFY.

High GOD. [7:1.

Ge. 14:18. priest of most **h.** G., He.
19. Blessed be Ab. of most **h.** G.
20. blessed be the most **h.** G. wh.
22. lifted hand unto most **h.** G.
Ps. 57:2. I will cry unto G. most **h.**
78:35. G. their rock, **h.** G. redeemer
56. they provoked the most **h.** G.
Da. 3:26. serv-ts of most **h.** G. come
4 : 2. wonders **h.** G. hath wrought
5 : 18. **h.** G. gave Neb. a kingdom
21. till he knew most **h.** G. ruled
Mi. 6:6. bow myself bef. most **h.** G.
Mk. 5:7. Son of most **h.** G., Lu. 8:28.
Ac. 16:17. are serv-ts of most **h.** G.

GOD of heaven.

2 Ch. 36:23. all kingd-s of earth hath
L. G. **o. h.** given me, Ezr. 1:2.
Ezr. 5 : 11. We servants of G. **o. h.**
12. our fathers provoked G. **o. h.**
6:9. for burnt off-gs of G. **o. h.**, 10.
7:12. scribe of law of G. **o. h.**, 21.
23. Whatever is com-d by G. **o. h.**
Ne. 1 : 4. I prayed bef. G. **o. h.**
2 : 4. So I prayed to G. **o. h.**
Ps. 136:26. give thanks unto G. **o. h.**
Da. 2:18. desire mercies of G. **o. h.**
19. Then Dan. blessed G. **o. h.**
44. G. **o. h.** shall set up a kingd.
Jon. 1 : 9. I fear the Lord, G. **o. h.**
Re. 11:13. remu. gave glory to G. **o.**
16 : 11. blasphemed G. **o. h.** [**h.**

Holy GOD.

Jos. 24 : 19. he is a **h.** G. a jealous
1 S. 6:20. Who stand bef. this **h.** G.?
Ps. 99 : 9. the Lord our G. is **h.**
Is. 5:16. G. that is **h.** be sanctified

GOD of hosts. [19.

Ps. 80:7. Turn us again, O G. **o. h.**,
14. Return, we beseech, O G. **o. h.**
89 : 8. G. **o. h.** who is strong L.
Ho. 12:5. G. **o. h.**; the L. is his memo.
Am. 4:13. The G. **o. h.** is his name
5:14. the G. **o. h.** shall be with you
27. Lord, whose name is G. **o. h.**
See LORD GOD.

GOD is or is not.

Ge. 21 : 22. G. **i.** with thee in all
31 : 50. G. **i.** witn. betwixt me and
Ex. 20 : 20. G. **i.** come to prove [lie
Nu. 23:19. G. **i.** not a man, that he
De. 3:24. what G. **i.** there in heaven
33:27. the eternal G. **i.** thy refuge
Jos. 24:19. G. **i.** a jealous G., Na. 1:2.
1 S. 4 : 7. G. **i.** come into the camp
10 : 7. G. **i.** with thee, 1 Ch. 17 : 2.
1 S. 28 : 15. G. **i.** departed from me
2 S. 22 : 33. G. **i.** my strength
1 Ch. 14:15. G. **i.** gone bef. thee to
2 Ch. 13:12. G. **i.** with us for capt.
Jb. 33 : 12. G. **i.** greater than man
36:5. G. **i.** mighty, despiseth not
26. G. **i.** great, we kno. him not
Ps. 7 : 11. G. **i.** angry with wicked
10:4. G. **i.** not in all his thoughts
14:5. G. **i.** in genera. of righteous
33 : 12. Blessed na. whose G. **i.** L.,
46:1. G. **i.** our refuge, 62:8. | 144:15.
5. G. **i.** in midst of her [**i.** King
47:5. G. **i.** gone up wi. shout | 7. G.
48 : 3. G. **i.** known in her palaces
50 : 6. G. **i.** judge himself, 75 : 7.
54 : 4. behold, G. **i.** my helper
56:9. this I know, for G. **i.** for me
59:9. I wait, G. **i.** my defence, 17.
62 : 7. In G. my salva., Is. 12 : 2.
68:5. a father of the fatherless **i.** G.
73 : 1. Truly G. **i.** good to Israel
26. G. **i.** strength of my heart
74 : 12. G. **i.** my King of old
89 : 7. G. **i.** greatly to be feared in
116:5. is the L. our G. **i.** merciful
118 : 27. G. **i.** L. that shewed light
Ec. 5:2. G. **i.** in heav., thou upon ea.
Is. 5:16. G. th. **i.** holy be sanctified
8 : 10. G. **i.** with us | 45:14. G. **i.** in
Zch. 8:23. heard G. **i.** with you [thee
Mat. 3:9. G. **i.** able of stones, Lu. 3:8.
22 : 32. G. **i.** not God of dead, but
Jn. 3 : 33. set to seal that G. **i.** true
4:24. G. **i.** a Spirit | 13:31. G. **i.** glori-
fied in him [sons
Ac. 10:34. G. **i.** no respecter of per-
Ro. 1 : 9. For G. **i.** my witness
11 : 23. G. **i.** able to graff them in
14:4. G. **i.** able to make him stand
1 Co. 1 : 9. G. **i.** faithful, by whom
10 : 13. G. **i.** faithf. will not suffer
14 : 25. and report th. G. **i.** in you
33. G. **i.** not author of confusion
2 Co. 1:18. as G. **i.** true our word was
9 : 8. G. **i.** able to make all grace
abound to you [mocked
Ga. 3 : 20. G. **i.** one | 6: 7. G. **i.** not
Ep. 2: 4. G. who **i.** rich in mercy
Ph. 1:8. G. **i.** my record, how I long
3:19. many whose G. **i.** their belly
1 Th. 2: 5. nor cloak, G. **i.** witness
He. 6:10. G. **i.** not unrighte. to forget your work of love
11 : 16. G. **i.** not asha. to be called
12 : 29. our G. **i.** a consuming fire
13 : 16. with such sacrifices G. **i.**
well pleased [love, 16.
1 Jn. 1: 5. G. **i.** light | 4: 8. G. **i.**
3 : 20. G. **i.** greater than our heart

GOD of Israel.

Ex. 24:10. went, and saw the G. **o.** I.
34 : 23. before L. G. the G. **o.** I.
Nu. 16 : 9. G. **o.** I. hath separ. you
Jos. 7:19. glory to G. **o.** I., 1 S. 6:5.
13 : 33. G. **o.** I. was their inherit.
22 : 16. what trespass ag. G. **o.** I.
24. What ye to do with G. **o.** I.
24 : 23. incline heart unto G. **o.** I.
Ju. 11:23. G. **o.** I. disposs-d Amor.
Ru. 2 : 12. reward be given of G. **o.** I.
1 S. 1:17. G. **o.** I. grant thy petition
5 : 11. Send ark of G. **o.** I. [6: 14.
1 K. 8:23. G. **o.** I. no G. like, 2 Ch.
14:13. some good thing tow. G. **o.** I.
1 Ch. 4 : 10. Jabez called on G. **o.** I.
17 : 24. L. of hosts is the G. **o.** I.
2 Ch. 15 : 13. who not seek G. **o.** I.?
Ezr. 7:15. freely offered unto G. **o.** I.
9 : 4. trembled at words of G. **o.** I.
Ps. 41 : 13. blessed be L. G. **o.** I. fr.
everl., 72 : 18. 106:48. Lu. 1:68.
Is. 41 : 17. G. **o.** I. will not forsake
45 : 3. I wh. call thee, am G. **o.** I.
48:2. they stay thems. upon G. **o.** I.
Eze. 8 : 4. glory of G. **o.** I. was there
Mat. 15 : 31. mult. glorified G. **o.** I.

Living GOD.
De. 5: 26. that heard voice of l. G.
Jos. 3:10. know the l. G. is am. you
1 S. 17: 26. defy armies of l.G., 36.
2 K. 19: 4. whom k. of Assyria sent
to reproach l.G.,16. Is. 37:4,17.
Ps. 42:2. My soul thirsteth for l. G.
84: 2. my heart crieth out for l. G.
Je. 10: 10. he is the l. G. everl. K.
23: 36. perverted words of l. G.
Da. 6:26. he is the l. G. and steadf.
Ho. 1:10. be said, Ye are sons of l.G.
Mat. 16:16. C., Son of l.G., Jn. 6:69.
26: 63. I adjure thee by l. G. tell
Ac. 14:15. turn fr. vanities unto l.G.
Ro. 9: 26. sh. be called chil. of l.G.
2 Co. 3: 3. with Spirit of the l. G.
6: 16. ye are the temple of l. G.
1 Th. 1: 9. from idols to serve l. G
1 Ti. 3: 15. which is church of l.G.
4: 10. we trust in the l. G., 6: 17.
He. 3:12. evil heart in dep. fr. l. G.
9:14. purge conscience to serve l.G.
10: 31. to fall into hands of l. G.
12:22. are come unto S. city of l.G.
Re. 7: 2. angel having seal of l. G.

Lord GOD, Lord his GOD, Lord my, our, their, your, GOD. See LORD.

Merciful GOD.
Ex. 34:6. The Lord G. m. gracious
De. 4: 31. Lord thy God is a m. G.
2 Ch. 30: 9. L. your G. is m. if ye
Ne. 9: 31. art a gracious and m.G.
Ps. 116: 5. gracious is L., G. is m.
Jon. 4: 2. I knew thou art a G. m.

Mighty GOD. [m.G.
Ge. 49: 24. bow abode by hands of
De. 7: 21. L. is am. you, a m. G.,
Ne. 9:32. our G. the m. G. [10: 17.
Jb. 36: 5. G. is m. despiseth not
Ps. 50: 1. m. G. the L. hath spok.
132: 2. how he vowed unto m. G.
5. Until I find habita. for m. G.
Is. 9: 6. name sh. be called m. G.
10: 21. remu. return unto m. G
Je. 32: 18. The m. G. is his name
Ha. 1:12. O m. G. thou hast estab.

My GOD. [them
Ge. 28:21. then sh. the L. be m. G.
Ex. 15: 2. he is m. G. m. fa.'s G.
Ru. 1:16. peo. my peo., thy G. m. G.
2 S. 22:7. I cried to m. G., Ps. 18:6.
22. not departed fr. m.G. Ps. 18:21.
30. by m. G. have I leaped over
a wall, Ps. 18: 29.
1 Ch. 28: 20. m. G. will be wi. thee
2 Ch. 18: 13. what m. G. saith, I
Ne. 5: 19. Think upon me, m. G.,
for good according to, 13: 31.
13: 14. Remember me, m. G., 22.
Ps. 22: 1. m. G. m. G. why hast
thou forsaken me? Mat. 27:46.
10. art m. G. fr. mother's belly
31: 14. I said, Thou art m. G.
38: 21. O m. G. be not far, 71:12.
42: 6. O m. G. my soul is cast do.
63: 1. m. G. early will I seek thee
89:26. cry, Thou art my Fa. m.G.
104:33. sing praise to m.G., 146:2.
118: 28. art m. G., I will praise
145: 1. I will extol thee, m. G.
Pr. 30:9. take name of m.G. in vain
Is. 7: 13. will ye weary m. G.?
40: 27. judgm. is passed fr. m. G.
44: 17. deliver me, thou art m.G.
61: 10. soul sh. be joyful in m.G.
Da. 6:22. m. G. hath sent his angel
Ho. 2: 23. say, Thou art m. G.,
Zch. 13: 9.
8: 2. Isr. sh. cry unto me, m. G.
9: 17. m. G. will cast them away
Mi. 7:7. I will wait, m. G. will hear
Jn. 20: 17. say, I ascend to m. G.
28. Thom. said, My L. and m.G.
Ro. 1:8. I thank m. G. for you all,
1 Co. 1:4.-14:18. Ph. 1:3. Phm. 4.
2 Co. 12: 21. lest, m. G. will
Ph. 4:19. m. G. sh. supply all need
Re. 3:12. will write upon him name of
See LORD **my God.** [m.G.

No GOD. [with me
De. 32: 39. I am he, there is n. g.
1 K. 8:23. n. G. like thee, 2 Ch. 6:14.
2 K. 1:16. is it bec. is n. G in Isr.?
5: 15. I know is n. G. in earth
2 Ch. 32: 15. n. g. of any na. able
Ps. 14: 1. fool said, There is n. G.,
Is. 43: 10. bef. me was n. G. [53:1.
44:6. besides me n. G., 8.-45:5,14,
Eze. 28: 9. shalt be man, n.G. [21.
Ho. 13:4. shalt know n. g. but me

O GOD.
Nu. 12: 13. heal her now, O G.
Ju. 16: 28. strengthen me, O G.
Ps. 4:1. hear me, O G. of my righte.
25: 22. redeem Isr O G. out of all
51: 14. Deliver fr. bloodguil. O G.
56:12. Thy vows are upon me, O G.
Is. 64: 4. nei. hath eye seen, O G.
He. 10: 7. I come to do thy will, O

Of GOD. [G., 9.
Ex. 9:†28. entreat be no voices o.G.
1 S. 14: † 15. was a trembling o.G.
1 Ch. 5: 22. slain bec. war was o.G.
2 Ch. 10: 15. the cause was o. G.
22:7. destruc. of Ahaziah was o.G.
24: 20. Amaz. not hear, for it o.G.
Ps. 7: 10. my defence is o. G.
Is. 29: † 1. Woe to the lion o. G.
53: 4. esteem him smitten o. G.
Mat. 16:23. savour. not o.G., Mk. 8:33.
Jn. 1:13. born not of man, but o.G.
6:46. he wh. is o. G. hath seen Fa.
7: 17. know of doctr. wheth. o.G.
8: 47. He that is o. G. heareth: ye
are not o. G. [not o. G.
9:16. this man not o. G. | 33. if he
12: 43. praise of men than o. G.
Ac. 5:39. if o. G. ye cannot overthr.
Ro. 2: 29. praise not of men, but o.
9:16. o. G. th. sheweth mercy [G.
13: 1. no power but o. G. powers
ordained o. G. [us wisd.
1 Co. 1: 30. who o. G. is made unto
2: 12. but the spirit which is o.G.
6: 19. have o. G. ye not your own
11: 12. all things o. G., 2 Co. 5:18.
2 Co. 2: 17. as o. G. in sight o. G.
3: 5. our sufficiency is o.G.[speak
Ph. 1:28. of salvation, and th. o.G.
3: 9. righteousness which is o. G.
He. 5: 4. called o. G. as was Aaron
1 Jn. 3:10. doeth not righto. not o.
4:1. try the spirits whe. o. G. [G.
3. confesseth not Christ is come,
is not o. G. [we are o. G.
6. We are o. G. | 5: 19. we know
3 Jn. 11. He th. doeth good is o.G.
See ADMONISHED, ANGEL, ARK, BORN, CHILDREN, CHOSEN, CHURCH, COUNSEL, FEAR, GLORY, GRACE, HAND, HATER, HOUSE, KINGDOM, KNOWLEDGE, LOVE, LOVERS, MAN, PEOPLE, POWER, SERVANT, SIGHT, SON, SONS, SPIRIT, TAUGHT, WILL, WORDS, WORK, WORKS, WORLD, WORSHIPPER, WRATH.

Our GOD.
Ex. 5:8. cry, Let us sacrifi. to o. G.
De. 31: 17. bec. o. G. is not among
32: 3. ascribe greatn. unto o. G.
Jos. 24: 18. will serve L., he is o.G.
Ju. 10: 10. bec. have forsak. o. G.
1 S. 2: 2. nei. is any rock like o.G.
2 S. 10: 12. let us play the men for
cities of o. G., 1 Ch. 19: 13.
22: 32. who rock, save o. G.? Ps
18: 31. [thee
1 Ch. 29: 13. Now o. G. we thank
2 Ch. 2: 5. great is o. G. ab. gods
14: 11. o. G. let not man prevail
2 Ch. 20:7. Art not o. G. who didst
Ezr. 9: 10. O o.G. what sh. we say?
Ne. 4: 4. Hear, O o. G.
20. o. G. shall fight for us
6: 16. this work wrought of o. G.
9: 32. o. G. the great, mighty G.
13:2. o. G. turned curse into bless.
Ps. 40:3. new song, praise unto o.G.
48: 14. this God is o. G. for ever
50: 3. o. G. shall not keep silence
67: 6. o. own G. shall bless us
68: 20. o. G. is the God of salva.
77: 13. who so great G. as o. G.?
95: 7. he is o. G. | 115:3. o. G. in
116: 5. o. G. is merciful [heav-s
Is. 25: 9. this is o. G. we have
55: 7. o. G. will abund-y pardon
59: 13. departing away from o. G.
61:2. proclaim day of veng. of o.G.
Da. 3: 17. o. G. is able to deliver
Zch. 9:7. that remaineth be for o.G.
1 Co. 6: 11. sancti. by Spi. of o. G.
He. 12: 29. o. G. is consuming fire
Re. 5: 10. made us to o. G. kings
7:10. Salvation to o. G. wh. sitteth
12. blessing, honour, be to o. G.
See PEACE, SERVE, SPEED.

GOD said.
Ge. 3: 1. G. s. ye shall not eat? 3.
17: 23. circum. same day, as G. s.
31: 16. whatsoev. G. hath s. do
De. 1: 21. as G. of thy fa. hath s.
2 Ch. 33:7. idol in house of wh. G.s.
Ac. 7: 7. nation will I judge s. G.
2 Co. 6:16. temple of G., as G. hath

GOD saith. [s.
2 Ch. 18: 13 G. s. that I will speak
24: 20. thus s. G. Why transgress
Ps. 50: 16. unto wicked G s. What
Is. 42:5. s. G., that created heav-s
54: 6. when wast refused, s. G.
57:21. no peace, s. my G., to wick.
66: 9. shut the womb, s. thy G.
Ac. 2: 17. to pass in last days, s.G.

GOD sent.
Ge. 45: 7. G. s. me before you
Ex. 3: 13. G. of your fa's s. me
15. the G. of Jacob hath s. me
Ju. 9: 23. G. s. evil spirit between
1 Ch. 21:15. G. s. angel unto Jeru.
Ne. 6: 12. I perceived G. not s. him
Je. 43:1. for which their G. s. him
2. G. hath not s. thee to say
Da. 6: 22. G. hath s. his angel
Jn. 3:17. G. s. not Son to condemn
34. he whom G. hath s. speaketh
Ac. 3: 26. G. raised his Son, s. him
10: 36. word wh. G. s. unto Isr.
Ga. 4: 4. G. s. forth Son made of
6. G. s. forth Spirit of his Son
1 Jn. 4:9. G. s. his only begott Son
10. G. s. Son to be propitiation
Re. 22: 6. G. s. his angel to shew

Servant, s of GOD.
Ge. 50:17. forgive s-s o.G. of thy fa.
1 Ch. 6: 49. as Mos. s. o. G. com-d
2 Ch. 24:9. collec., Mos. s. o. G. laid
Ezr. 5: 11. We are s-s o. G.
Ne. 10:29. law. given by Mo. s.o.G.
Da. 3: 26. ye s-s of most high G.
6: 20. O Daniel, s. o. living G.
9: 11. in the law of Moses s. o. G.
Ac. 16: 17. These are s-s o. high G.
Tit. 1:1. Paul a s. o. G., an apostle
Ja. 1: 1. James a s. o. G. and J.C.
1 Pe. 2: 16. liberty, but as s-s o. G.
Re. 7: 3. sealed the s-s o. our G.
15: 3. the song of Moses s. o. G.

Spoken with GOD.
Ge. 21: 2. time of wh. G. had s.
De. 26: 19. holy unto G. as he s.
Ps. 60: 6. G. s. in his holin., 108:7
62: 11. G. hath s. once, twice I
Mat. 22: 31. which was s. by G.
Ac. 3: 21. G. hath s. by prophets

Their GOD.
Ge. 17: 8. I will be t. G., Ex. 29:

45. Je. 24: 7.-31: 33.-32: 38.
Eze. 11: 20.-34: 24.-37: 23, 27.
Zch. 8: 8. 2 Co. 6:16. Re. 21:3.
Le. 21: 6. they sh. be holy unto t.
G., bread of t. G. they do offer
26: 45. that I be t. G., Eze.14:11.
2 S. 7:24. thou art t. G.,1 Ch.17:22.
Ezr. 5: 5. eye of t. G. upon elders
Ps. 79: 10. Where is t. G.? 115: 2.
Jo. 2: 17. [G.?
Is. 8: 19. sho. not peo. seek unto t.
21. shall curse king, and t. G.
58: 2. forsook not ordin. of t. G.
Je 5:4. know not judgm. of t.G.,5.
Da. 11: 32. people that know t. G.
Ho. 4: 12. gone a whor. from t. G.
5: 4. not frame doings unto t. G.
Zch. 12: 5. my strength in L. t. G.
He. 11:16. not ashamed to be called
See LORD their God. [t.G.

Thy GOD. [43.
Le. 19:14. shalt fear t. G., 25:17,36,
De. 10: 21. He is thy praise, t. G.
26:17. hast avouched L. to be t.G.
Ru. 1: 16. peo. my peo., t. G.my G.
2 K. 19: 10. Let not t. G. deceive,
thee, Is. 37: 10.
1 Ch. 12: 18. t. G. helpeth thee
2 Ch. 9: 8. because t. G. loved Isr.
Ezr. 7: 14. accord. to law of t. G.
25. aft. wisd. of t. G. laws of t.G.
Ne. 9: 18. t. G. that bro-t thee up
Ps.42:3.say unto me,Wheret.G.?10.
45: 7. t. G. anointed thee, He.1:9.
50: 7. O Israel, I am t. G.
68: 28. t. G. com-d thy strength
147: 12. praise t. G. O Zion [G.
Is. 41: 10. be not dismayed, I am t.
51: 20. are full of rebuke of t. G.
52: 7. unto Zion, t. G. reigneth
60: 19. L. a light, t. G. thy glory
62: 5. so sh. t. G. rejoice over thee
Da. 6:16 t. G. thou serv. will deliv.
20. is t. G. continually able?
10:12. to chasten thyself bef. t. G.
Ho. 4: 6. hast forgott. law of t. G.
9: 1. hast gone a whor. fr. t. G.
12: 6. turn to t. G. wait on t. G.
Am. 4: 12. prepare to meet t. G.
Jon. 1: 6. O sleeper, call upon t.G.
Mi. 6: 8. to walk humbly wi. t. G.
See LORD thy God.

To, or unto GOD.
Ge. 40:8.Do interpreta. belong t.G.?
Ex. 2: 23. their cry came up u. G.
Le. 21: 7. for he is holy u. his G.
De. 32:17. sac., not t. G., 1 Co. 10:
33:26.none like u.G. of Jeshu. [20.
Ju. 13: 5. Nazarite u. G.,7.-16:17.
1 S. 10: 3. meet thee 3 going t. G.
14: 36. Let us draw near u. G.
1 Ch. 26: 32. matter pertain-g t. G.
Jb. 22:2. Can man be profita. u.G.?
34: 31. it is meet to be said u. G.
Ps. 47: 9. shields of earth belong u.
62: 11. power belongeth u. G. [G.
68: 20. u. G. belong issues from
31. Ethio. stretch her hands u.G.
73: 28. is good to draw near t. G.
77: 1. I cried u. G. even u. G. wi.
Ec. 12: 7. spirit shall return u. G.
Is. 58:2. delight in approach-g t.G.
La. 3:41. let us lift our heart u. G.
Mat.22:21.render u. G.things which
are G.'s, Mk. 12:17. Lu. 20: 25.
Jn.13:3.was come from G. went t.G.
Ac. 4: 19. heark. more than u. G.
5: 4. hast not lied unto men, but
26:18.fr. power of Sat. u. G. [u.G.
20. turn t. G. and do works meet
Ro.6:10.liveth u.G. | 11. alive u.G.
13. yield yours u. G. as alive
7:4. that we bring forth fruit u.G.
12:1.your bodies a living sac. u.G.
14:12.account of hims. t.G. [u.G.
1 Co. 14: 2. speaketh not unto men
15: 24. sh.have deliv-d kingd. t.G.

Ph. 4:20. Now u. G. and our Father
be glory [u. G.
He. 7: 25. able to save them come
11:6.th. cometh t. G. must believe
12:23. ye are come t. G. the Judge
Ja. 4: 7. Submit yourselves t. G.
1 Pe. 3:18. C. suff-d, might bring us
4: 6. live acc. t. G. in Spirit [t.G.
Re. 5: 9. thou hast redeem. us t. G.
12:5. her child was caught up u.G.
14:4.firstfruits u.G. and the Lamb

True GOD.
2 Ch. 15: 3. Isr. been without t.G
Je. 10: 10. L. is the t. G., living G.
Jn. 17: 3. etern. life, to know t. G.
1 Th. 1: 9. fr. idols to serve t. G.
1 Jn. 5:20. this is t. G. and eternal

With GOD. [life
Ge. 5: 22. Enoch walked w. G., 24.
6: 9. and Noah walked w. G.
32: 28. as a prince hast pow. w.G.
Ex. 19: 17. bro-t peo. to meet w.G.
1 S. 14:45. wrought w. G. this day
2 S.23:5.Alth. my hou. not so w.G.
2 Ch. 35: 21. forbear meddl. w. G.
Jb. 9: 2. how man be just w. G.?
13: 3. I desire to reason w. G.
16:21. might plead for a man w.G.
25: 4. How man be justified w.G.?
27:13.port-n of a wicked man w.G.
34: 9. should delight hims. w. G.
23. sho. enter into judg.n. w. G.
37: 22. w. G. is terrible majesty
Ps. 78: 8. spirit is not steadf. w.G.
Ho. 11: 12. Judah yet ruleth w. G.
12: 3. Jacob had power w. G.
Mat. 19: 26. w. G. all things are
possible, Mk. 10: 27. Lu. 1:37.-
Lu.1:30. found favour w. G. [18:27.
2:52.Jes. increased in favour w.G.
Jn. 1:1. Word was w. G. was G., 2.
5: 18. himself equal w. G.,Ph.2:6.
Ro.2:11. no respect of persons w.G.
5: 1. by faith, we have peace w.G.
9:14. is there unrighteousn. w.G.?
1 Co. 3: 9. we are labourers w. G.
19. wisd. of world foolishn. w. G.
7: 24. ev. man therein abide w. G.
2 Th. 1:6. righte. w. G. to recomp.
Ja. 4: 4. friendship of world is enmity w. G. [cepta. w. G.
1 Pe. 2: 20. take patiently, this ac-

Would GOD.
Ex. 16: 3. w. G. we had died in E.
Nu. 14: 2. [were prophets
Nu. 11: 29. w. G. all L.'s people
20: 3. w. G. we died when breth.
De.28:67. w. G. it were even, w.G.
Jos. 7: 7. w. G. we dwelt on other
Ju. 9: 29. w. G. peo. were und. my
2 S. 18: 33. w. G. I had died for
2 K. 5: 3. w. G. my lord wi. proph.
Ac. 26: 29. w. G. all such as I am
1 Co. 4: 8. I w. to G. ye did reign
2 Co. 11: 1. w. to G. ye could bear

Your GOD. [wi. me
Ge. 43: 23. y. G. hath given you
Ex. 8: 25. go ye, sacrifice to y. G.
Le. 11: 45. bringeth out of E. to be
y.G., 22: 33.-25:38. Nu. 15:41.
26: 12. I will be y. G. ye my peo.,
Je. 7:23.-11:4.-30:22.Eze.36:28.
Nu. 10: 10. be a memorial bef.y.G.
15: 40. do my commandments, be
holy unto y. G.
Jos.24:27.witness, lest ye deny y.G.
1 S. 10: 19. this day rejected y. G.
2 Ch. 32: 14. th. y. G. deliver you
15.how much less y.G.deliv. you?
Ezr. 4:2. Let us build, we seek y.G.
Is. 35: 4. y. G. will come with veng.
40: 1. comfort my peo., saith y.G.
9. unto cities of Jud., Beho. y.G.
59:2. iniq-s separated between you
and y. G.
Eze. 34: 31. I am y. G. saith the L.
Da. 2: 47. y. G. is a God of gods

Ho. 1:9. not my peo., I not be y.G
Jn. 8: 54. ye say that he is y. G.
20:17. I ascend to my G. and y. G
See LORD your God.

GOD. [Referring to man.]
Ex.4:16.shalt be to Aa.instead of G.
7:1.I have made thee a g. to Pha.

GOD. [As idol.]
De.32:21.moved me to jealousy with
that which is not G.
39.I am he,there is no g.with me
Ju. 6:31. if he be a g. let him plead
8: 33. made Baal-berith their g.
9: 27. went into house of their g.
46. hold of house of g. Berith
11:24.wh. Chemosh thy g. giveth
16: 23. sacri-s unto Dagon g. (2)
24. Our g.hath deliv. into ha. (2)
1 S. 5:7. his hand is sore, on our g.
1 K. 11:33. Chemosh g. Milcom g.
18:27. he is a g. either talking, or
2 K. 1: 2. Baal-zebub the g. of Ekron, 3, 6, 16.
19: 37. worshipping in house of
Nisroch his g., 2 Ch. 32:21. Is.
37: 38. [deliv. his peo.
2 Ch.32:15. no g. of any na. able to
Ps. 16: 4. hasten after other g.
Is. 44:10. Who formed g. or image?
15. maketh g. worshippeth, 17.
45:20.pray unto a g. th.can-t save
46:6. maketh it a g. they worship
Ho. 13:4. shalt know no g. but me
Da. 1:2. vessels into house of his g.
4:8.Beltesh. acc. to name of my g.
11:36. magnify hims. above ev. g.
Am.2:8.wine of condem-d in h.of G.
5: 26. star of your g., Ac. 7: 43.
8:14. th.say, Thy g. O Dan, liveth
Jon.1:5.cried,every man unto his g.
Mi. 4:5. will walk in name of his g.
Ha. 1:11. imput. power unto his g.
Ac. 12:22. voice of a g. not of man

Any GOD.
Ex. 22:20. sacrifice to a. g. save L.
2 S.7:22.nor a.G.besides,1 Ch.17:20
Da.3:28. might not worsh.a.g. exc.
6:7.ask petition of a.G. or man,12.
11:37. neither shall he regard a.g.

Other GOD.
Ex. 34: 14. shalt worship no o. g.
Da. 3: 29. is no o. G. can deliver
1 Co. 8: 4. is none o. G. but one

Strange GOD.
De. 32: 12. was no s. g. with them
Ps.44:20. stretched hands to a s.g.
81:9.no s.g. be in thee,nei. worsh.
Is. 43: 12. no s.g. am. them [s.g.
Da. 11: 39. thus do with a s. g.
Mal. 2: 11. married dau. of a s. g.

GOD of this world.
2 Co.4:4.g.o.w. blinded the minds

GODS.
Ge. 3: 5. ye shall be as g. knowing
31:30. wh. hast stolen my g.? 32.
Ex.12:12.ag. all g. of E. I will exec.
20:23. shalt not make g. of silv.or
22:28. thou shalt not revile the g.
23: 24. shalt not bow to their g.
32. shalt make no cov. with their
g. [us, 23. Ac. 7: 40.
32: 1. up, make us g. to go before
4. These be thy g. O Israel, 8.
31. made them g. of gold [31:16.
34:15. whoring aft. their g.,16. De.
17. make no molten g., Le. 19: 4.
Nu. 25: 2. people to sacrifice g.
33:4.upon Egyptians' g.L. executed judgm.,Je.43:12,13.-46:25.
De. 7: 25. images of their g. burn
10:17. Lord your God is God of g.
12: 3. sh. hew down images of g.
30.thou inquire not after their g.
31.have done ev.abomi.unto their
g. burnt sons, dau-s to g.
13: 7. entice to g. of people round
20: 18. not to do as they unto g.

De. 29 : † 17. ye seen their dungy **g.**
32:37.sh. say, Where are their **g.**?
Jos. 22 : 22. L. G. of **g.** knoweth
23 : 7. nor make mention of **g.**
Ju. 2 : 3 their **g.** shall be a snare
5 : 8. They chose new **g.** then war
6 : 10. Fear not **g.** of Amorites
10:14. cry unto **g.** ye have chosen
17 : 5. Micah had a house of **g.**
18:24. Ye have taken away my **g.**
Ru.1:15.sis. in law is gone to her **g.**
1 S. 4 : 8. are G. that smote Egyp:.
6:5.will lighten his hand fr.your **g**
17:43. Philis. cursed Da. by his **g.**
28:13.I saw **g.** ascend.out of earth
2 S. 7:23. redeemest from E. and **g.**
1 K.11:2.will turn your heart aft.**g.**
8. Sol. sacrificed unto their **g.**
12:28.much to go up,behold thy **g.**
18:24. call on name of your **g.**,25.
19:2.let the **g.** do so to me, 20:10.
20 : 23. Their **g.** are **g.** of the hills
2 K. 17 : 29. every nation made **g.**
33. feared L. served own **g.**
18:33.Hath any of the **g.**delivered his land? 19:12. 2 Ch.32:13.14.
Is. 36:18.-37:12. [36:19.
34. Where the **g.** of Hamath? Is.
19:18. cast **g.** into fire, they no **g.**
1 Ch. 5 : 25. whoring aft. **g.** of land
10 : 10. armour in hou. of their **g.**
14:12.left their **g.**theywere burned
2 Ch.13:8.calves Jerob.made for **g.**
9. be priest of them th. are no **g.**
25:14. bro-t **g.** of Seir to be his **g.**
15. Why hast sought after **g.**,20.
28:23.sacrifi-d unto **g.**of Damas.(2)
32 : 17. **g.** of nations not delivered
19. against **g.** of people of earth
Ezr. 1:7. put vessels in h. of his **g.**
Ps. 82 : 1. G. judgeth among the **g.**
6.I have said,Ye are **g.**,Jn.10:34.
136:2. O give thanks unto G. of **g.**
138 : 1. before **g.** will I sing praise unto thee [broken
Is. 21 : 9. Babylon is fallen, her **g.**
41:23. that we may know ye are **g.**
42:17. say to images,Ye are our **g.**
Je. 2 : 11. changed her **g.** are no **g.**
28. where are **g.** thou hast made?
acc. to cities are thy **g.**, 11:13.
5:7. chil. sworn by them are no **g.**
10:11.**g.** th. have not made heav-s
11:12. cry unto **g.** unto wh. offer
16:20. man make **g.** and are no **g.**
48 : 35. burneth incense to his **g.**
Da. 2 : 11. can shew it, exc. the **g.**
47. that your God is a God of **g.**
4 : 8. in whom is spirit of holy **g.**
9. spirit of holy **g.** in thee,18.-5:
5 : 4. praised **g.** of gold, 23. [14.
11.wisdom like the wisd.of the **g.**
11:8. carry into E. **g.** with princes
36. speak marvell. things ag.G.of
Ho.14:3. nei. say,Ye are our **g.** [**g.**
Na. 1:14. out of the house of thy **g.**
Jn. 10 : 35. If he called them **g.**
Ac. 14 : 11. **g.** are come down to us
17 : † 23. I beheld **g.** you worship
19:26.they no **g.** made with hands
1 Co. 8:5. are called **g.** be **g.** many
Ga. 4 : 8. service unto them wh. are [no **g.**

All GODS.

Ex. 12 : 12. **a.** the **g.** of E. I will
18:11.the Lord is greater than **a.g.**
1 Ch.16:25.to be feared above **a.g.**,
Ps. 96:4. [Ps. 96:5.
26. **a. g.** of the people are idols,
2 Ch. 2:5. great is God above **a.g.**,
Ps. 135 : 5. [**a. g.**
Ps.95:3. Lord is a great King above
97:7.worsh. him **a.g.** | 9.above **a.**
Zph. 2:11. he will famish **a. g.** [**g.**

Among the GODS.

Ex.15:11.**a.g.** who is like thee,O L.
2 K. 18:35. who **a.g.** could deliver country ? 2 Ch. 32:14. Is. 36:20.
Ps.86:8.**a.g.** there is none like thee

Other GODS. [7.

Ex.20:3.have no **o.g.** bef. me,De.5:
23:13. make no mention of **o.g.**
De. 6:14. not go after **o.g.**, 11:28.-
28:14.1 K.11:10. Je.25:6.-35:15.
8 : 19. if thou walk after **o. g.**
13 : 2. Let us go after **o. g.**, 6 : 14.
18:20.prophet speak in name of **o.**
30:17.and worsh.**o.g.**,Je.22:9. [**g.**
31:18 in th day turned unto **o.g.**
20.then will they turn unto **o.g.**
Ju. 2 : 12. forsook L. foll-d **o. g.**
17. went a whoring after **o. g.**
19. in following **o.g.** to serve th.
1 K.9:9. hold upon **o.g.**,2 Ch.7:22.
11:4. wives turned heart aft. **o. g.**
14 : 9. hast gone and made **o. g.**
2 K. 5:17. I will not offer sac. unto
17:7. Isr. had feared **o. g.** [**o.g.**
35. Ye shall not fear **o. g.**,37,38.
22:17.have burned incense unto **o. g.**, 2 Ch. 34:25. Je. 1:16.-19:4.
2 Ch. 28:25. Ahaz to burn inc.unto
Je.7:6. aft.**o.g.** to your hurt [**o.g.**
9. after **o. g.** ye know not,13:10.
18. drink off. unto **o. g.**, 19:13.-
16:11.have walked aft.**o.g.** [32:29.
44:5.heark.not to burn no inc.unto
8.burn-g inc.unto **o.g.**,15. [**o.g.**
Ho. 3:1. look to **o.g.** and love wine

Serve, ed GODS.

Ex. 23 : 24. thou shalt not **s.** their **g.**, De. 6:14.-28:14. Jos. 23:7. 2 K. 17:35. Je.25:6.-35:15.
33. if thou **s.** their **g.** it be snare
De. 4:28. there ye sh. **s. g.** work of men's, 28:36,64. Je. 16:13.
12 : 2. nations s-d their **g.**
30. how did these nations **s. g.**?
29 : 18. turneth from God to **s.o.g.**
Da. 3 : 12. **s.** not **g.** nor worsh. ima.
14. do ye not **s.** my **g.**?
18. we will not **s.** thy **g.**

Serve, ed other GODS.

De.7:4. that they may **s.o.g.**,31:20.
8:19. if thou **s.o.g.**, 11:16. -30:17.
Jos. 24 : 20. 2 Ch. 7 : 19.
13 : 2. let us go **s. o. g.**, 6, 13.
17 : 3. hath s-d **o. g.**, 29 : 26, Jos.
23:16.Ju.10:13.1 S.8:8.Je.11:10.
Jos. 24:2. your fathers s-d **o. g.**, 15.
16. God forbid we **s. o. g.**
Ju. 2 : 19. they corrupted thems. to **s. o. g.**, Je. 11 : 10.-13 : 10.
10 : 13. have forsak. me s-d **o. g.**
1 S. 26:19. driven, saying, **s. o. g.**
1 K. 9:9. they s-d **o. g.**, 2 Ch.7:22.
Je.44:3. anger, th. they to **s. o. g.**

Strange GODS.

Ge. 35 : 2. Put away **s. g.**, 1 S. 7:3.
4. they gave Jac. **s. g.**,Jos.24:23.
De. 32:16. provoked him with **s. g.**
Jos. 24:20. if forsake L. serve **s. g.**
Ju. 10 : 16. they put away **s. g.**
2 Ch.14:3.Asa took aw.altar of **s.g.**
33:15. Josiah took away the **s. g.**
Je. 5:19. as ye served **s. g.** so serve
Ac.17:18.to be a setter forth of **s.g.**

GODDESS.

1 K. 11:5. Sol.went after **g.**of Zidon.
33.have worsh-dAshtoreth,the **g.**
Ac. 19 : 27. temple of great **g.** Diana
35. worshippers of the **g.** Diana
37.nor yet blasphemers of your **g.**

GODHEAD.

Ac.17:29. nor think G. is like to gold
Ro. 1 : 20. his eternal power and G.
Col.2:9.in him dwelleth fulness of G.

GODLINESS. [away

Is. 57 : † 1. and men of **g.** are taken
1 Ti. 2 : 2. lead a quiet life in all **g.**
10. becometh wom. professing **g.**
3 : 16. great is the mystery of **g.**
4:7. exercise thyself rather unto **g.**
8. **g.** profitable unto all things
6 : 3. to doctr. is according to **g.**
1 Ti. 6:5. corrupt, supp-g gain is **g.**
6. **g.** with contentment is gain
11. follow after righte., **g.** faith
2 Ti. 3 : 5. Having a form of **g.** but
Tit. 1 : 1. acknowl-g truth after **g.**
2 Pe.1:3.things that pertain unto **g.**
6. add to patience **g.** to **g.**, 7.
3 : 11. what persons ought to be in

GODLY. [**g.**

Ps.4:3.L.hath set apart him th.is **g.**
12:1.Help, L., for **g.** man ceaseth
32 : 6. For this ev. one **g.** pray
Mi. 7 : † 2. **g.** man is perished out of
Mal. 2 : 15. he might seek a **g.** seed
2 Co. 1 : 12. in **g.** sincerity our con-
7:9.sorry aft.a **g.**manner,11. [vers.
10. **g.** sorrow worketh repent.
11:2. jealous over you with **g.** jeal.
2 Ti. 3 : 12. all th. will live **g.** in C.
Tit. 2 : 12. that ye should live **g.**
He.12:28. let us serve G.with **g.** fear
2 Pe. 2 : 9. knoweth how to deliv. **g.**
3 Jn. 6. if bring forward aft. **g.** sort

GOD-WARD.

Ex. 18 : 19. Be thou for people to G.
2 Co. 3 : 4 have we thro. C. to G.
1 Th. 1 : 8. your faith to G. is spread

GOEST.

Ge.28:15.will keep thee whi.thou **g.**
32 : 17. whither **g.** thou? Ju. 19 : 17. Zch. 2 : 2. Jn. 13 : 36.-16 : 5.
Ex. 33 : 16. is it not in that thou **g.** with us? [thou **g.**
34 : 12. no cov. with inhabi. whi.
Nu. 14 : 14. **g.** bef. them by daytime
De.7:1.land thou **g.**to possess,11:29.
11:10. land whi. thou **g.** not as E.
12:29.G.cut off nations whi.thou **g.**
20:1.when thou **g.** to battle,21:10.
28 : 20. G. bless in all thou settest hand to, whi. thou **g.**, Jos., 1:7.
28 : 6. blessed when thou **g.** out
19. cursed when thou **g.** out
21. pestilence cleave whi. thou **g.**
63. plucked off land whi. **g.**,30:16.
32 : 50. die in mount whi. thou **g.**
Jos. 1:9. L. with thee whi. thou **g.**
Ju. 14 : 3 **g.** to take wife of Philis.
Ru. 1 : 16. for whi. thou **g.** I will go
1 S. 28 : 22. strength when thou **g.**
2 S. 15 : 19. whf. **g.** thou with us?
1 K.2:37.day thou **g.**over brook,42.
Ps. 44 : 9. but **g.** not wi. our armies
Pr.4:12.when **g.** steps not be strait.
6 : 22. when thou **g.** it sh. lead thee
Ec.5:1. keep foot when **g.** to h.of G.
9 : 10. nor wisd. in grave whi. **g.**
Je.45:5.give for a prey whi. thou **g.**
Mat. 8 : 19. follow whi. **g.**, Lu. 9:57.
Lu. 12 : 58. when **g.** with adversary
Jn. 11 : 8. to stone thee, **g.** again?
13 : 36. Lord whither **g.** thou?
14:5. L. we know not whi. thou **g.**
16:5. none asketh, whither **g.** thou

GOETH.

Ex. 7 : 15. he **g.** out unto the water
22 : 26. by that the sun **g.** down
28 : 29. Aaron bear when he **g.** in
30.upon Aa.'s heart when he **g.** in
35. sound heard when he **g.** in
Le.11:21.eat th. **g.** upon all four,42.
27. **g.** upon paws am. all beasts
14 : 46. he that **g.** into h. be uncl.
15 : 32.whose seed **g.** fr. him, 22 : 4.
16 : 17. none in tab. when he **g.** in
22 : 3. **g.** unto holy things having uncleanness [blee, holy
27 : 21. field, when it **g.** out in ju-
Nu. 5 : 29. law, when wife **g.** aside
De. 1:30.L. which **g.** bef. shall fight
9 : 3. thy God is he that **g.** bef.you
19:5. **g.** into wood with his neighb.
20:4.your G. is he that **g.**with you
23 : 9. when host **g.** ag. enemies
24 : 13. deliver pledge when sun **g.**
Ju.5:31. as sun when he **g.** in might
1 S. 6 : 9. if it **g.** up by way of coast

1 S.22:14. as Da., who g. at bidding
30: 24. his part that g. to battle
2 K.5:18. master g. into ho. of Rim.
11:8. with king as he g., 2 Ch.23:7.
Ezr. 5: 8. this work g. fast on and
Jb. 7: 9. that g. down to grave
9: 11. he g. by me, I see him not
16:†6. tho. forbear what g. fr. me?
34:8. when g. with workers of iniq.
37: 2. hear sound g. out of mouth
39:21. he g. on to meet armed men
41: 20. Out of nostrils g. smoke
21. a flame g. out of mouth
Ps. 17: 1. prayer g. not out of feigned lips
41: 6. when g. abroad, he telleth
68: 21. such as g. on in trespasses
88: 16. thy fierce wrath g. over me
97:3. fire g. bef. him, burneth enem.
104:23. man g. forth unto his work
126: 6. he th. g. forth and weepeth
146:4. his breath g. forth; he retur.
Pr. 6: 29. g. in to his neighb's wife
7:22. g. aft. her, as ox g. to slaugh.
11:10. g. well with rights., city rejoi.
16: 18. pride g. before destruction
20:19. that g. about as a talebearer
26:9. thorn g. into ha. of drunkard
20. where no wood is, fire g. out
31:18. her candle g. not out by night
Ec. 1: 5. sun g. down, hasteth
6. wind g. toward the south
3:21. spi. of man g. up, of beast g.
12:5. bec. man g. to his long home
Can. 7: 9. that g. down sweetly
Is. 28: 19. fr. the time it g. forth
30: 29. when one g. with pipe to
55: 11. my word be that g. forth
59:8. g. therein sh. not know peace
63: 14. as a beast g. into valley
Je. 5: 6. ev. one that g. out be torn
6: 4. woe unto us, for day g. aw.
21:9. g. out to Chal-s sh. live, 38:2.
22: 10. weep for him that g. away
30:23. whirlwind of L. g. with fury
44: 17. do what g. out of mouth
49:17. that g. by it be aston., 50:13.
Eze. 7: 14. but none g. to battle
33: 31. heart g. after covetousness
44: 27. in day he g. into sanctu.
Ho. 6: 4. goodn. as early dew, it g.
5. judgments as light th. g. forth
Zch. 5: 3. is the curse that g. forth
6. This is an ephah that g. forth, 5.
Mat. 8: 9. I say go, he g., Lu.7: 8.
12: 45. g. and taketh, Lu. 11: 26.
13:44. for joy g. selleth all ⌈fileth
15:11. not that g. into mouth de-
17:21. kind g. not out but by prayer
18:12. g. into the mts. and seeketh
26: 24. Son of man g. as it is written of him, Mk. 14:21. Lu.22:22.
28:7. g. bef. you into Gal., Mk.16:7.
Mk. 7: 19. g. into the draught
14: 45. he g. straightway to him
Jn. 3: 8. canst not tell whi. it g.
7: 20. who g. about to kill thee?
10: 4. he g. bef., sheep follow him
11: 31. she g. unto grave to weep
12: 35. not whi. he g., 1 Jn. 2:11.
1 Co. 6: 6. bro. g. to law with bro.
9:7. who g. warfare at own charges
Ja. 1: 24. beholdeth himself and g.
Re. 14: 4. follow Lamb whi. he g.
17:11. is of 7, and g. into perdition
19: 15. out of mouth g. a sword

GOG.

1 Ch. 5: 4. sons of Joel; G. his son
Eze. 38: 2. set thy face against G.
3. say, I am ag. thee, O G., 39:1.
16. when sanctified in thee, O G.
18. when G. come ag. land of Isr.
39: 11. unto G. place of graves
Re. 20: 8. G. and Magog, to gather

GOING. ⌈upon Ab.

Ge. 15:12. sun g. down, a sleep fell
25: † 32. Esau said, I am g. to die
Ex.17:12. steady, to g. down of sun
23:4. if meet enemy's ox g. astray
Le. 11: 20. fowls that creep g. upon
Nu.34:4. g. forth fr. south to Kadesh
De.16:6. passover at g. down of sun
33:18. Rejoice, Zebu., in thy g. out
Jos. 7: 5. smote them in g. down
10:11. were in g. down to Beth-horon
27. at g. down of sun carcasses tak.
23: 14. I am g. way of all earth
Ju.8:†30. 70 sons g. out of his thigh
19: 18. I am g. to house of L.
28. let us be g. but none answ.
1 S. 9: 27. g. down to end of city
10: 3. meet 3 men g. up to God
17: 20. as the host was g. to fight
2 S.2:19. in g. turned not fr. Abner
5:24. sound of g. in trees, 1 Ch.14: 15.
1 K. 17:11. as she was g. to fetch it
22:36. proclama. at g. down of sun
2 K. 2: 23. g. by way, chil. mocked
9: 27. smote Ahaziah at g. to Gur
1 Ch. 11: † 9. Da. in g. and incr-g
2 Ch. 18: 34. sun g. down, he died
Ezr. 7: † 9. founda. of g. from Bab.
Jb. 1: 7. g. to and fro in earth, 2:2.
33: 24. deliver fr. g. down to pit
28. deliver his soul fr. g. into pit
Ps. 19:6. g. forth is fr. end of heav.
50: 1. earth, fr. rising of sun to g. down, 113: 3. Mal. 1: 11.
104: 19. sun knoweth his g. down
144: 14. no breaking in, nor g. out
Pr. 7:27. g. down to cham. of death
14: 15. prudent looketh well to g.
30: 29. yea, four are comely in g.
Is. 13:10. sun be darkened in his g.
Je. 48: 5. in g. up of Luhith; in g. down of Horonaim
50: 4. g. and weeping sh. seek L.
Eze.40:31. g. up had 8 steps, 34, 37.
44: 5. ev. g. forth of sanctuary
46: 12. aft. g. forth, one shut gate
Da. 6: 14. laboured till g. down of
9: 25. fr. g. forth of com-t ⌊sun
Ho. 6: 3. his g. forth is prepared
Zch. 8: † 7. country of g. down of sun
† 21. g. speedily to entreat
Mat. 4: 21. g. on he saw other two
20: 17. g. up to Jerus., Mk.10:32.
25: † 8. oil, our lamps are g. out
26: 46. let us be g., he is at hand
28:11. were g. some of watch cam.
Lu. 14: 31. what king g. to war
Jn. 4: 51. as he was g. down
8: 59. g. through midst of them
Ac. 20: 5. g. bef., tarried at Troas
Ro.10:3. g. to establish own righto.
1 Ti. 5: 24. sins g. bef. judgment
He.7:18. disannulling of com. g. bef.
1 Pe. 2: 25. were as sheep g. astray
Jude 7. g. after strange flesh are
See COMING. ⌊set forth

GOINGS.

Nu. 33: 2. Moses wrote their g. out
34: 5. g. out of their borders, 8, 9, 12. Jos. 15: 4, 7, 11.—16: 3, 8.—18: 12, 14. ⌈his g.
Jb. 34: 21. upon man, he seeth all
Ps.17:5. hold up my g. in thy paths
37: † 31. none of his g. shall slide
40:2. upon a rock, establ-d my g.
44: † 18. nor have our g. declined
68: 24. seen thy g. even g. of G.
140: 4. purposed to overthr. my g.
Pr. 5: 21. he pondereth all his g.
20: 24. man's g. are of the Lord
Is. 59: 8. is no judgment in their g.
Eze. 42: 11. their g. out were ac. to
43: 11. shew them g. out thereof
48: 30. these are the g. out of city
Mi. 5: 2. g. forth been fr. of old

GO'LAN. See BASHAN.

GOLD. ⌈g.

Ge. 2: 11. whole land of Havilah is
Ge.2:12. the g. of that land is good
24: 22. ten shekels weight of g.
41:42. chain of g. about Jo.'s neck
Ex. 20:23. nor make you gods of g.
25:12. cast 4 rings of g. for ark, 26.—26:29.—28:23, 26, 27.—37:3, 13.
13. make staves of shittim wood overlay them with g., 28.—26: 29, 37.—30: 5.—37: 4, 15, 28.
18. make two cherubim of g., 37:7.
26:6. make fifty taches of g., 36:13.
32. hooks sh. be of g., 37.—36:38.
28: 5. sh. take g., 8, 15.—39: 5, 8.
6. ephod of g., 39:2. | 8. girdle of
11. ouches of g., 13.—39:6, 13, 16.
15. breastplate of g. | 20. set in g.
24. chains of g., 1 K. 6: 21.
33. thou shalt make bells of g.
32:24. Who g. let him break it off
31. peo. have made them gods of g.
35:22. bro-t jewels of g. off-g of g.
36: 34. overlaid boards with g. (2)
38. he overlaid chapiters with g.
38:24. all the g. that was occupied
39: 3. did beat g. into thin plates
40: 5. shalt set altar of g. bef. ark
Nu. 7:14. spoon of 10 shekels of g.,
84. at dedica. 12 spoons of g. ⌊20.
86. g. of spoons was 120 shekels
31:50. jewels of g. chains, 51, 52, 54.
Jos.7:21. a wedge of g. of 50 shekels
24. took Achan and wedge of g.
Ju. 8:26. earrings 1700 shekels of g.
1 S. 6: 8 jewels of g. in a coffer
11. they laid mice of g. on cart
15. took coffer with jewels of g.
2 S. 1: 24. put on ornaments of g.
8: 7. Da. took shields of g., 1 Ch. 18: 7. 2 Ch. 3: 7.
1 K. 6:22. house he overlaid with g.
28. cherubim with g., 2 Ch. 3:10.
30. floor overlaid with g.
32. cherubim overlaid with g., 35.
7: 48. made altar table of g., 6:21.
49. tongs of g. | 50. hinges of g.
9:11. Hiram king of Tyre furnished Sol. with g., 10:11. 2 Ch. 9:10.
10:2. queen of Sheba came with g., 2 Ch. 9: 1. ⌈2 Ch. 9: 13.
14. weight of g. came in 1 year,
16. Sol. made 200 targets of beat-
17. he made 300 shields of g. ⌊en g.
18. overlaid throne with best g.
12: 28. Jerob. made 2 calves of g.
14:26. took away shields of g. ⌈g.
22:48. Jehosh. made ships to go for
2 K. 18:16. Hez. cut off g. fr. doors
1 Ch. 21:25. for pla. 600 shek. of g.
28: 14. Da. gave of g. by weight for g., 15, 16, 17, 18.—29: 2, 5.
2 Ch. 3: 6. g. was g. of Parvaim
9. nails was 50 shekels of g.
4: 7. ten candlesticks of g., 13:11.
8. basons of g. | 22. spoons of g.,
9:18. steps with a footstool of g. ⌊21.
12:9. Shishak carried shields of g.
Ezr. 8: 27. basons of g. copper precious as g. ⌈drachms of g.
Ne. 7: 70. Tirshatha gave 1000
71. fa-s gave g. | 72. peo. gave g.
Jb. 3:15. Or with princes th. had g.
22: 24. lay up g. as dust, g. of
† 25. Almighty be thy g. ⌊Ophir
23: 10. tried, I sh. come like g.
28:6. earth, it hath the dust of g.
15. wisd. cannot be gotten for g.
16. It cannot be valued with g.
17. g. and crystal cannot equal
31: 24. If I made g. my hope, or said to fine g. ⌈not g.
36: 19. Will he esteem thy riches?
37:†22. g. cometh out of north ⌈g.
42:11. ev. one gave Job earring of
Ps.19:10. More to be desired than g.
45: 9. queen in g. of Ophir
13. her clothing is of wrought g.
72:15. to him given of g. of Sheba

Pr. 11: 22. jewel of **g.** in swine's
16:16. better to get wisdom than **g.**
20: 15. is **g.** and multi. of rubies
Can. 1:10. comely with chains of **g.**
5: 14. His hands are as **g.** rings
Is. 14:†4. exactress of **g.** ceased [**g.**
30: 22. ornament of thy images of
40: 19. spreadeth it over with **g.**
60: 6. they sh. bring **g.** and inc.
17. For brass I will bring **g.** for
Je. 4: 30. thou deckest thee with **g.**
10: 9. **g.** fr. Uphaz, the work of
La. 4:1 How is the **g.** become dim!
fine **g.** changed! [**g.**, 28: 13.
Eze. 27:22. merchants of Sheba with
Da.2:38. head of **g.** | 3:1. image of **g.**
5: 7. chain of **g.** about neck, 16.
23. hast praised the gods of **g.**
29. put a chain of **g.** about Dan-l's
Zch. 4: 2. a candlestick all of **g.**
13: 9. will try them as **g.** is tried
Mat. 2:11. they presented unto him
23:16. whoso swear by **g.** of tem. [**g.**
17. whe. greater, **g.** or temple
1 Ti. 2: 9. not with **g.** or pearls, 1
He.9:4. ark overlaid wi. **g.** [Pe.3: 3.
Ja. 2:2. if come a man with **g.** ring
1 Pe. 1: 7. faith more pree. than **g.**
Re. 3: 18. I counsel to buy **g.** tried
4: 4. elders had crowns of **g.**
9: 7. locusts had crowns of **g.**
17: 4. woman was decked with **g.**
18: 16. great city decked with **g.**
See BEATEN, CROWN, FINE.

Pure GOLD.

Ex. 25:11. shalt overlay the ark wi.
p. g., 24.–30: 3.–37: 2, 11, 26.
17. make mercy seat of **p. g.**, 37:6.
29. dishes, covers of **p. g.**, 37:16, 23.
31. a candlest. of **p. g.**, 37: 17. 1
K. 7:49. 2 Ch. 4:20. [Ch. 4:22.
38. snuffdishes **p. g.**, 1 K. 7:50. 2
28:14. two chains of **p. g.**, 22.–39:
15. [30.
36. shalt make plate of **p. g.**, 39:
1 K. 6: 20. oracle he overlaid wi. **p.**
g., 21. [2 Ch. 9: 20.
10:21. vessels of Lebanon of **p. g.**,
1 Ch. 28: 17. **p. g.** for fleshhooks,
2 Ch. 3:4. overlaid porch with **p. g.**
9: 17. overlaid throne with **p. g.**
Jb. 28:19. wisd. not valued wi. **p. g.**
Ps.21:3. a crown of **p. g.** on his head
Re.21:18. city **p. g.** | 21. street **p. g.**

GOLD with silver. [35.

Ge. 13:2. Ab. rich in **s.** and **g.**, 24:
24: 53. jewels of **s.** of **g.** [**g.**
44:8. steal out of lord's hou. **s.** or
Ex. 3: 22. jewels of **s.** and **g.**, 11:2.
20:23. gods of **s.** of **g.** [–12:35.
25:3. the off-g, take **s.** and **g.**, 35:5.
31:4. to work in **g. s.**, and, 35:32.
Nu.22:18. h. full of **s.** and **g.**, 24:13.
31:22. Only **g.** and **s.** abide the fire
De. 7: 25. shalt not desire **s.** or **g.**
8: 13. thy **s.** and **g.** multiplied
17:17. nei. greatly multiply **s.** and **g**
29: 17. seen their idols, **s.** and **g.**
Jos.6:19. **s.** and **g.** consecrated, 24.
22:8. ret. unto tents with **s.** and **g.**
2 S. 8: 11. **s.** and **g.** Da. dedicated,
1 K. 7: 51.
21:4. will have no **s.** nor **g.** of Saul
1 K.10:22. Tarshish bringing **g.** and
s., 2 Ch. 9: 21.
15:15. Asa brought into house of L.
s. and **g.**, 2 Ch. 15: 18.
18. Asa took **s.** and **g.**, 2 Ch.16:2.
19. I sent present of **s.** and **g.**, 2
Ch. 16: 3. [**s.** and **g.**
20:3. **s.** and **g.** is mine | 5. deliver
7. sent for my wives, **s.** and **g.**
2 K. 5:5. ten tal-ts of **s.** 6000 pieces
7:8. carried thence **s.** and **g.** [of **g.**
14:14. Jehoash took **g.** and **s.**, 2 Ch.
16:8. Ahaz took **s.** and **g.** [25:24.
18: 14. 300 talents of **s.** 30 of **g.**
2 K.20:13. Hez. shewed **s.** and **g.**, Is.
39: 2. [acted **s.** and **g.**
23:35. Jehoiak. gave **s.** and **g.** ex-
25:15. things of **g.** in **g.** of **s.** in **s.**,
Je. 52: 19. [and **s.**
1 Ch. 29: 3. of my own good, of **g.**
2 Ch. 1: 15. k. made **s.** and **g.** plenteous as stones
2:7. to work in **g.** and **s.**, 14.
9: 14. brought **g.** and **s.** to Sol.
21: 3. fa. gave gifts of **s.** and **g.**
32: 27. treasuries for **s.** and **g.**
Ezr.1:4. men help with **s.** and **g.**, 6.
9. 30 chargers of **g.** 1000 of **s.**
10. Thirty basins of **g.** and **s.**
2:69. gave **s.** and **g.** | 7:15. carry **s.**
8:25. weighed **s.** and **g.**, 33. [and **g.**
Es. 1: 6. beds were of **g.** and **s.**
Jb. 28: 1. vein for **s.** place for **g.**
15. not be gotten for **g.** nei. **s.**
Ps.68:13. cov-d wi. **s.** feathers wi. **g.**
105: 37. bro-t out with **s.** and **g.**
115:4. idols are **s.** and **g.**, 135:15.
119:72. law better than **g.** and **s.**
Pr.8:10. receive not **s.** knowl. rather
than **g.** [**g.**, 27: 21.
17: 3. fining pot for **s.** furnace for
22:1. loving favour than **s.** and **g.**
25:11. apples of **g.** in pictures of **s.**
Ec. 2: 8. I gathered me **s.** and **g.**
Can. 1:11. borders of **g.** studs of **s.**
3:10. the pillars of **s.** bottom of **g.**
Is. 2: 7. land is full of **s.** and **g.**
20. cast his idols of **s.** and **g.**, 31:7.
13: 17. not regard **s.**; as for **g.**
46:6. They lavish **g.** and weigh **s.**
60:9. to bring **s.** and **g.** with them
Je.10:4. They deck it with **s.** and **g.**
Eze. 7:19. cast aw. **s.** and **g.** **s.** and
g. not able to deliv, Zph. 1:18.
16:13. wast decked with **g.** and **s.**
17. fair jewels of my **g.** and **s.**
28: 4. gotten **g.** and **s.** into thy
38:13. carry aw. **s.** and **g.** [treas.
Da.2:35. **s.** and **g.** broken to pieces, 45
5:4. praised gods of **g.** and **s.**, 23.
11:38. god he honour with **g.** and **s.**
43. power over treas. of **g.** and **s.**
Ho. 2:8. I multiplied her **s.** and **g.**
8: 4. of their **s.** and **g.** made idols
Jo.3:5. ye have taken my **s.** and **g.**
Na. 2:9. take the spoil of **s.** and **g.**
Ha.2:19. it is laid over wi. **g.** and **s.**
Hag. 2: 8. **s.** is mine, **g.** is mine
Zch.6:11. **s.** and **g.** and make crowns
14:14. be gath. together **g.** and **s.**
Mal. 3: 3. purge them as **g.** and **s.**
Mat.10:9. Provide neither **g.** nor **s.**
Ac. 3: 6. **s.** and **g.** have I none
17: 29. we ought not think God-
head like unto **g.** or **s.**
20: 33. coveted no man's **s.** or **g.**
1 Co.3:12. if build on founda. **g. s.**
2 Ti.2:20. in gr. h. vessels of **g.** and **s.**
Ja. 5: 3. Your **g.** and **s.** cankered
1 Pe. 1: 18. not redeemed with corruptible things, as **s.** and **g.**
Re. 9: 20. not worship idols of **g.**, **s.**
See **SILVER with gold.**

Talent, s of GOLD.

Ex.25:39. Of **t. o. g.** shall he make it
37:24. of a **t. o.** pure **g.** made he it
2 S.12:30. crown a **t. o. g.**, 1 Ch.20:2.
1 K.9:14. Hiram sent Sol. 120 **t. o. g.**
28. sent from Ophir 420 **t. o. g.**
10:10. she gave Sol. 120 **t. o. g.**, 2
Ch. 9:9. [Ch. 9: 13.
14. to Sol. in 1 y-r 666 **t. o. g.**, 2
2 K.23:33. land to **t. o. g.**, 2 Ch.36:3.
1 Ch.22:14. Da. prep. 100,000 **t. o. g.**
29: 4. of my good 3000 **t. o. g.**
7. chief of fa-s gave 5000 **t. o. g.**
2 Ch. 8:18. from Ophir 450 **t. o. g.**
Ezr.8:26. I weighed **o. g.** vessels 100
Vessels of GOLD. [t.
2 S. 8:10. Toi sent to David **v. o. g.**,
1 Ch. 18: 10.
1 K. 10: 21. Solomon's drinking **v.**
o. g., 2 Ch. 9: 20. [9: 24.
25. brought present, **v. o. g.**, 2 Ch.
2 K.12:13. not for h. of L. **v. o. g.**
24:13. Neb. cut in pieces **v. o. g.**
2 Ch. 24:14. of money made **v. o. g.**
Ezr. 1:11. All **v. o. g.** and silv. 5400
5: 14. **v. o. g.** Cyrus delivered
8:26. weighed of **v. o. g.** 100 talents
Es. 1:7. gave them drink in **v. o. g.**
Da. 11:8. shall carry into E. **v. o. g.**
2 Ti.2:20. not only **v. o. g.** but wood
See **Vessels of SILVER.**

GOLDEN.

Ge. 24: 22. man took a **g.** earring
Ex. 25:25. a **g.** crown to the border
28:34. **g.** bell | 30:4. two **g.** rings,
32:2. Break off **g.** earrings [39:20.
Le. 8:9. upon forefront the **g.** plate
Nu.7:26. One **g.** spoon of ten shek.
86. **g.** spoons were twelve
Ju. 8: 24. had **g.** earrings, bec.
26. weight of **g.** earrings he requ.
1 S. 6:4. **g.** emerods, **g.** mice, 17, 18.
2 K. 10: 29. Jehu not fr. **g.** calves
1 Ch.28:17. for **g.** basins gave gold
2 Ch. 13: 8. are with you **g.** calves
Ezr. 6: 5. let **g.** vessels be restored
Es.4:11. hold out **g.** scep., 5:2.–8:4.
Ec.12:6. **g.** bowl be broken [wedge
Is. 13: 12. man more prec. than **g.**
14: 4. How hath **g.** city ceased
Je.51:7. Bab. hath been **g.** cup in L.'s
Da. 3: 5. worship **g.** image, 7, 10.
12. Jews, nor worsh. **g.** image, 14, 18
5:2. Belsh. com-d to bring **g.** vessels
3. bro-t **g.** vessels tak. out of tem.
Zch. 4: 12. **g.** pipes, empty **g.** oil
He. 9: 4. **g.** censer where was **g.** pot
Re.1:12. I saw seven **g.** candlesticks
13. one girt with **g.** girdle, 15:6.
20. mystery of 7 **g.** candlesticks
2: 1. in midst of **g.** candlesticks
5:8. **g.** vials, 15:7. | 8:3. **g.** censer
14:14. a **g.** crown | 17:4. a **g.** cup
21: 15. had a **g.** reed to meas. city
See **Golden ALTAR,** SPOON.

GOLDSMITH, S.

Ne. 3: 8. Uzziel of the **g**-s repaired
31. **g.**'s son | 32. repaired the **g**-s
Is. 40:19. **g.** spreadeth it with gold
41:7. carpenter encouraged the **g.**
46:6. hire a **g.** he maketh it a god

GOL'GOTHA.

Mat. 27: 33. were come to a place
called G., Mk. 15:22. Jn. 19:17.

GOLI'ATH.

1 S. 17: 4. G. of Gath went out, 23.
21: 9. sword of G. the Philistine
22:10. he gave him the sword of G.
2 S.21:19. slew bro. of G., 1 Ch.20:5.

GO'MER.

Ge. 10: 2. G. Magog, 1 Ch. 1: 5.
3. sons of G. Riphath, I Ch. 1:6.
Eze. 38: 6. G. and all his bands
Ho. 1: 3. took G. dau. of Diblaim

GOMOR'RAH. See SODOM.

GONE.

Ge.24:†1. Ab. old, and **g.** into days
31:30. thou wouldest needs be **g.**
34:17. take our dau. we will be **g.**
42: 33. food for househ. and be **g.**
Ex. 12: 32. take flocks and be **g.**
De. 32: 36. seeth their power is **g.**
1 S.14:3. peo. knew not Jona. was **g.**
17. and see who is **g.** from us
15:20. I have **g.** way Lord sent me
20: 41. soon as lad was **g.** David
2 S. 3: 7. whf. **g.** in unto my fa.'s
22. he was **g.** in peace, 23. [concu.
24. quite **g.** | 13:15. Arise, be **g.**
24:8. when they had **g.** thro. land
1 K. 2:41. Shimei had **g.** fr. Jerus.
13: 24. when **g.** a lion met him
14: 10. takes away dung till all **g.**
18: 12. soon as I am **g.** Spirit sh.
20: 40. as I was busy, he was **g.**

1 K. 22:13. th. was g. to call Micaiah
1 Ch. 17:5. have g. fr. tent to tent
Jb.7:4.When sh.I arise,night be g.
19:10. destroyed me, and I am g.
24:24.exalted for a while,but are g.
28 : 4. they are dried up and g.
Ps.38:10. light of mine eyes, it is g.
42:4.I had g. with mult.to h.of G.
73 : 2. me, my feet were almost g.
77:8. his mercy clean g. for ever?
103 : 16. wind passeth, and it is g.
109 : 23. I am g. like the shadow
Pr. 7: 19. good man is g. a long
20:14.when he is g. then boasteth
Ec. 8: 10. who had come and g. fr.
Can. 2: 11. the rain is over and g.
5 : 6. beloved had withdrawn, was
6:1. Whither is thy beloved g.⌊g.
Is.5:13.my people are g.into captiv.
24 : 11. the mirth of the land g.
41 : 3. by the way he had not g.
46 : 2. thems. are g. into captiv.
Je.2:5. what iniq. in me, th.they g.
23. I have not g. after Baalim?
5:23. this peo. are revolted and g.
9:10.beasts g. | 15:6.art g.backw.
44:14.none g. into E. sh. escape,8.
28.remnant that are g.shall know
48 : 11. nei. hath he g. into cap.
50:6. they have g. from mt.to hill
La. 1:3. Jud. g. | 5. Zion's chil. g.
6.g.with-t strength | 18.virg-s g.
Eze.37:21.Isr. from heathen whi.g.
Da.2:5. said, thing is g. from me,8.
Ho. 4: † 18. their drink is g. they
9 : 6. they are g. bec. of destruc.
Am.8:5. when will new moon be g.
Mi. 1 : 16. they are g. into cap. fr.
Mk. 1 : 19. g. a little further, saw
Lu. 2:15. angels were g. from them
19: 7. g. to be guest with sinner
24: 28. made as if wo. have g. fur-
Jn. 4:8. disci. g. to buy meat ⌊ther
12: 19. the world is g. after him
Ac.16:19. saw hope of gains was g.
20:25.am.wh. I have g. preaching
1 Pe. 3 : 22. who is g. into heaven
Jude 11.have g. in the way of Cain

GONE about.

1 S. 15: 12. Saul is g. a. to Gilgal
Jb. 1:5. days of feastings were g.a.
Is.15:8. cry is g.a.borders of Moab
Ac.24:6.hath g. a. to profane tem.

GONE aside.

Nu.5:19. hast not g. a. to unclean.
20.if g.a. to ano. instead of husb.
Ps. 14 : 3. are all g. a. are filthy
Ac. 26 : 31. when g. a. they talked

GONE astray.

Ps. 119 : 176. I have g. a. like lost sheep
Is. 53 : 6. We like sheep have g. a.
Mat.18:12. if 100 sheep, one be g.a.
(2) ⌈g. a.
2 Pe. 2:15 forsaketh right way, are

GONE away.

Ju. 18 : 24. are g. a., what have I
2 S. 23 : 9. men of Israel were g. a.
Jb. 28 : 4. waters were g. a. fr. men
Is. 1 : 4. they are g. a. backward
Eze. 44:10. Levites are g. a. fr. me
Mal.3:7. ye are g. a. fr. ordinances
Lu. 2 : 15. as the angels were g. a.
Jn. 4 : 8. his disciples were g. a.
6 : 22. disciples were g. a. alone

GONE back.

Ru. 1:15. thy sister in law is g. b.
Jb.23:12. Nei. have I g.b. fr.com-t
Ps.53:3. Ev. one is g. b. none good
Je. 40:5. while he was not yet g.b.

GONE down.

1 S. 15: 12. Saul is g. d. to Gilgal
1 K. 1:25. Adonijah is g.d. ⌈viney.
21:18.Ahab g.d. to possess Nab.'s
2 K.20:11. shadow had g.d. in dial
of Ahaz, Is. 38 : 8. ⌈garden
Can.6:2. My beloved is g.d.into his
Je. 15:9. her sun is g.d. while day
48:15.y-g men are g.d. to slaugh.
Eze.31:12. peo. g.d. fr. his shadow
32:21. the strong are g. d. ⌈d.
24.Elam | 27.Tubal | 30.Zidon g.
Jon. 1:5. Jon. was g.d. unto ship

GONE forth. ⌈Zoar

Ge.19:†23. sun g. f. when Lot ent.
Ex.19:1. month when Isr. was g.f.
2 K.6:15. when serv. of Elisha was
1 Ch.14:15.God is g.f.bef.thee ⌊g.f.
Is. 51 : 5. my salvation is g. f.
Je. 4 : 7. is g.f. to make land deso.
10:20. my children are g. f. of me
23 : 15. is profaneness g.f. into la.
19. a whirlwind of the L. is g. f.
29:16. breth. not g.f. into captiv.
Eze. 7:10. day come, morning g. f.
36:20. these are peo. of L. are g.f.
Da. 2 : 14. g. f. to slay wise men
10:20.when I am g.f. prince come
Mk. 10 : 17. when he was g. f. one

GONE out. ⌊came

Ge. 27 : 30. scarce g. o. fr pres. of
Ex.9:29.as soon as I am g.o.⌊Isaac
Nu. 16 : 46. wrath g. o. fr. Lord
21 : 28. is a fire g. o. of Heshbon
De. 13 : 13. certain men g. o.
23:23. That wh. is g.o. of thy lips
Ju. 4 : 14. is not the Lord g. o.?
Ru. 1 : 13. ha. of L. is g. o. ag. me
1 S. 9:†7. bread is g. o. of our ves.
25 : 37. when wine g. o. of Nabal
2 K.5:2.Syrians g.o. by companies
7 : 12. we hungry, thf. they g. o.
20:4.afore Isa. was g.o. into court
Ps. 19: 4. line is g. o. thro. earth
89:34. alter thing g. o. of my lips
Is. 45 : 23. word is g. o. of mouth
Eze. 19 : 14. fire is g. o. of a rod
24:6. pot, whose scum is not g. o.
Mi. 2 : 13. gate and are g. o. by it
Mat.12:43. When uncl. spi. is g.o.,
25:8.our lamps are g.o.⌊Lu.11:24
26 : 71. Pe. was g. o. into porch
Mk. 5: 30. that virtue had g. o. of
him, Lu. 8: 46. ⌈Lu. 11:14
7:29. devil is g.o. of daughter, 30.
Lu. 5 : 2. fishermen were g. o.
Jn. 13:31. when was g. o. Jes. said
Ac. 13 : 42. g. o. of the synagogue
Ro. 3:12. They are all g. o. of way
1 Jn. 4 : 1. many false prophets are

GONE over. ⌊g.o.

De. 27 : 4. g. o. Jordan, 2 S. 17:22.
Jos. 4 : 23. until we were g. o.
2 S. 17:20. They be g. o. the brook
2 K. 2 : 9. they were g. o., Elijah
Ps. 38 : 4. iniq. are g. o. my head
42 : 7. waves and billows g. o. me
124 : 4. stream had g. o. our soul
5.proud waters had g.o.our soul
Is. 10:29. they are g. o. the passage
16 : 8. are g. o. the sea, Je. 48:32.
Mat.10:23.not have g.o. cit-s of Isr.
Ac. 20: 2. when he had g. o. those

GONE up.

Ge. 49 : 9. my son, thou art g. u.
De.9:9. When I was g. u. into mt.
Ju. 20 : 3. Israel g. u. to Mizpeh
2 S. 2:27. g.u. ev. one fr. following
2 K.1:4. not off bed on wh. g.u.,6,
Ps.47:5.God is g.u.with shout ⌊16.
Is. 15: 2. he is g.u. to Bajith and
22 : 1. g. u. to the housetops
57:8.discovered to ano.and art g.u
Je 3 : 6. she is g. u. on every mt.
14 : 2. cry of Jerusalem is g. u.
34:21. k of Bab.'s army are g. u.
48:15.Moab is g.u.out of her cities
Eze.9:3.glory of G. of Isr. was g.u.
13: 5. Ye have not g.u. into gaps
Ho. 8 : 9. they are g. u. to Assyria
Jn. 7 : 10. when breth. were g. u.
Ac.18:22. when he had g.u. and sa-

GONE a whoring. ⌊lut.

Le. 17 : 7. after whom have g.a.w.
Eze. 23 : 30. bec. thou hast g. a. w.
Ho. 4 : 12. g. a. w. from their G.
9:1. thou hast g. a. w. fr. thy G.

GOOD. [Noun.] ⌈g.

Ge. 26:29. done unto thee noth. but
27:46. Reb. said. what g.my life do
32 : 12. saidst, I will do thee g.
45:18. I will give you g. of Egypt
20. g. of the land of E is yours
50:20. G. meant it unto g. to bring
Nu. 10: 29. L. spoken g. conc. Isr.
De. 28 : † 6. shalt not seek their g.
30:15. have set bef. thee life and g.
Jos.24:20. consume, after done you
1 S. 20:12. if be g. tow. David ⌊g.
24:17. hast rewarded me g. for evil
19. wh-f Lord rewarded thee g.
25 : 30. acc. to all g. he hath spok.
2 S. 14 : 32. g. for me to been there
16 : 12. L. requite g. for cursing
1 K. 22 : 13. words of prophets declare g. to the king,2 Ch.18:12.
1 Ch.29:3. prepared of mine own g.
2 Ch. 24:16. bec. had done g. in Isr.
Ezr. 9 : 12. be strong, eat g. of la.
Es. 7 : 9. who had spoken g. for k.
Jb. 2: 10. sh. we rec. g. at hand of
5 : 27. know thou it for thy g. ⌊G.
7 : 7. mine eye shall no more see g.
9 : 25. my days flee, they see no g.
15:3.with speeches he can do no g.
21 : 16. their g. is not in their ha.
22 : 21. be at peace, g. shall come
24 : 21. he doeth not g. to widow
Ps. 4 : 6. Who will shew us any g.?
14 : 1. none doeth g. not one, 3.–
53 : 1, 3. Ro. 3 : 12. ⌈g.
34:12.loveth many days,that he see
39:2.I held my peace even from g.
104:28.hand,they are filled with g.
106 : 5. may see g. of thy chosen
122 : 9. bec. of ho. of L. I will seek
128:5. sh. see g. of Jerus. ⌊thy g.
Pr. 3:27.Withhold not g. to wh.due
11:17.merciful doeth g.to own soul
27.diligently seeketh g.procureth
12 : 14. a man satisfied with g. by
13 : 2. sh. eat g. by fruit of mouth
21. to righteous g. be repaid
14 : 22. truth be to them devise g.
16 : 20. a matter wisely, sh. find g.
17:20.froward heart, findeth no g.
22. a merry heart doeth g. like
19 : 8. keepeth underst-g shall find
Ec. 2:3. that g. for sons of men ⌊g.
24. his soul enjoy g., 3:13.–5:18.
3:12. I know is no g. in them
4 : 8. and bereave my soul of g.?
5 : 11. what g. is there to owners
6 : 3. his soul be not filled with g.
6. tho. live 100 years seen no g.
7:20.not a just man, that doeth g.
9 : 18. one sinner destr-h much g.
Is. 1:19. ye shall eat g. of the land
52:7.th.bringeth good tidings of g.
Je.8:15.for peace, no g. came,14:19.
17 : 6. he not see when g. cometh
18: 10. if it do evil, I repent of g.
20. I stood bef. thee to speak g.
29 : 32. nei. be behold g. I will do
32:42.I will bring g. I have promi.
33 : 9. shall hear g. that I do them
La. 3: † 17. fr. peace, I forgat g.
Eze. 16: 50. took them as I saw g.
Ho. 14 : † 2. take aw. iniq., give g.
Zch. 1:†17. cities thro. g. be spread
11 : 12. if think g. give me price
Mat.13:48.gath-d the g.into vessels
26:24.been g. had not been born
Mk. 10 : † 42. think g. to rule over
Jn. 5:29. have done g. unto resurr.
Ac. 10:38. who went about doing g.
14 : 17. in that he did g. gave rain
Ro.2:10. honour to man worketh g.
1 Th. 3:1. g. to be left at Athens
1 Jn.3:17. who hath this world's g.
See BAD, DO, DOETH, EVIL.

For GOOD.

De. 6 : 24. to fear the L. f. our g.
10:13. command this day f. thy g.
28: † 11. thee plenteous f. g., 30:9.
30: 9. L. will rejoice over thee f. g.
Ezr. 8:22. ha. our G. upon all f. g.
Ne. 5: 19. Think upon me, O G., f.
Jb.5:27. know it f. thy g. ⌊g., 13:31.
Ps. 86: 17. Shew me a token f. g.
119:122. Be surety for thy serv. f. g.
Je. 14: 11. Pray not for peo. f. g.
21: 10. not f. g. saith the L.
24:5. I sent out of place f. their g.
6. set mine eyes upon them f. g.
32: 39. fear me, f. g. of them ⌈g.
Mi. 1: 12. Maroth waited carefully f.
Ro.8:28. all things work toget. f. g.
13: 4. minister of G. to thee f. g.
15:2. let ev. one please neighb. f. g.

GOOD. [Adjective.]

Ge.2:9. pleasant to sight, and g. for
21:16. Hagar sat down g. way off
24: 12. send me g. speed this day
† 17. Rebekah was g. of counten.
41: 5. g. ears, 24. | 26. g. kine
35. gather food of g. years
43: 28. our father is in g. health
46:29. Joseph wept g. while ⌈bush
De.33:16. g. will of him that dw. in
28: 12. L. open unto thee g. treas.
1 S.2:24. it is no g. report th. I hear
12: 23. I will teach you the g. way
25:15. men were very g. unto us
29:9. I know thou art g. in my sight
2 S. 14: 32. g. for me to have been
2 S. 15: 3. see thy matters are g.
17:14. defeat g. counsel of Ahith.
19:18. to do what the k. thought g.
1 K. 8:36. teach g. way, 2 Ch. 6:27.
56. not failed 1 word of g. promise
12: 7. speak g. words, 2 Ch. 10:7.
2 K. 20:19. g. is word of L., Is. 39:8.
2 Ch. 19:11. Lord sh. be with the g.
30:18. The g. Lord pardon ev. one
22. taught the g. knowl. of L.
Ezr. 7: 9. g. hand of his G., Ne.2:8.
8:18. by g. hand of our G. upon us
Ne. 9:13. gavest them g. statutes
20. gavest g. Spirit to instruct
Jb. 10:3. Is it g. that thou oppress?
13:9. Is it g. that he search you out?
22:†2. doeth his g. success depend
39: 4. Their young are in g. liking
Ps. 25: 8. g. and upright is the L.
37:23. steps of g. man ordered by L.
45:1. My heart is inditing a g. mat-
86:5. thou, L., art g., 119: 68. ⌊ter
112: 5. a g. man sheweth favour
119: 39. thy judgments are g.
66. Teach me g. judgm. and
68. Thou art g. and doest g.
133: 1. how g. and pleasant it is
Pr.2:9. shalt underst. every g. path
20. mayest walk in way of g. men
12: 25. g. word maketh heart glad
14: 19. The evil bow before the g.
15:23. word in season, how g. is it?
30. g. report maketh bones fat
20: 18. with g. advice make war
22:1. g. name is rather to be chosen
Ec. 4: 9. g. reward for their labour
5: 11. what g. is there to owners?
9: 2. one event to the g. and clean
11:6. whe. they both sh. be alike g.
Je. 6:16. where is g. way, and walk
24: 2. g. figs | 3. very g.
5. Like g. figs, so I
29: 10. I will perform my g. word
Eze. 17:8. planted in g. soil by wat.
24: 4. gather every g. piece, thigh
Da.4:2. I thought it g. to shew signs
Zch.1:13. L. ans. angel with g. words
Mal. 2: 13. receiveth it with g. will
Mat. 3: 10. not g. fruit, 7:19. Lu.3:9.
7: 11. to give g. gifts, Lu. 11 : 13.
17. g. tree bringeth g. fruit, 18.
12: 33. make tree g. and fruit g.

Mat. 13:8. fell in g. gro., 23, Mk. 4:8,
20. Lu. 8: 8, 15.
24. g. seed, 27, 37, 38.
19: 16. g. Master, what g. thing
17. Why callest thou me g.? none
g. but one, Lu. 18: 19. ⌈g.?
20: 15. Is thine eye evil bec. I am
25:21. Well done, thou g. serv., 23.
Lu. 2:14. on earth, g. will tow. men
6: 38. g. measure, pressed down
43. g. tree not corrupt fruit
10: 42. Mary hath chosen g. part
12: 32. your Fa.'s g. pleas. to give
Jn. 2: 10. hast kept g. wine until
10: 11. I am g. shepherd, the g.
shepherd, 14.
Ac. 15:7. ye know th. g. while ago
18: 18. Paul tarried a g. while
Ro. 7:12. com-t is holy, just, and g.
18. in me dwelleth no g. thing
11: 24. graffed into g. olive tree
12:2. that g. and perfect will of G.
16: 18. g. words and fair speeches
1 Co. 15: 33. corrupt g. manners
Ep. 1: 5. g. pleasure of his will
6: 7. g. will doing service
Ph. 1: 15. some also of g. will
1 Th. 3:6. ye have g. rememb. of us
2 Th. 2:16. conso. and g. hope thro.
1 Ti. 1: 18. mightest war a g. warf.
3:13. purchase to thems. a g. degree
4: 6. sh. be a g. minister of J. C.
6:12. Fight the g. fight, 2 Ti. 4:7.
13. witnessed a g. confession
19. laying up a g. foundation
2 Ti. 2:3. a g. soldier of Jes. Christ
3: 3. despisers of those g.
Tit. 1:8. bishop be lover of g. men
2: 5. g. obedient to husbands
10. shewing all g. fidelity
He. 6: 5. have tasted g. word of G.
11:12. sprang of him as g. as dead
Ja. 1: 17. ev. g. gift | 2:3. g. place
3: 17. full of mercy and g. fruits
1 Pe. 2:18. be subject not only to g.
3: 10. will love life, and see g. days

See BAD, CHEER, COMFORT, CONSCIENCE, COURAGE, DAY, DEED, S, DO, DOING, HEED, PLEASURE, REPORT, STEWARDS.
See OLD age, Good SUCCESS

Is GOOD.

Ge. 2: 12. gold of that land i. g.
16: † 6. do as i. g. in thine eyes,
19: 8.-20: † 15.
De. 6:18. do that i. g. in sight of L.
23:†16. he sh. dwell where it i. g.
Ju. 9:†2. speak whe. it i. g. for you
1 S. 29: 6. coming in with me i. g.
1 K. 2: 38. Shimei said, saying i. g.
42. word I have heard i. g., 18:†
22: 13. speak th. which i. g. ⌊24.
2 K. 20:3. done that i. g., Is. 38:3.
1 Ch. 16: 34. the Lord i. g., 2 Ch.
5:13.-7:3. Ezr. 3:11. Ps. 100:5.-
106: 1.-107: 1.-118:1, 29.-135:
3.-136:1.-145: 9. Je. 33:11. La.
3: 25. Na. 1: 7.
19:13. L. do that i. g. in his sight
Jb. 34:4. know am. ours. what i. g.
Ps. 34: 8. O taste and see L. i. g.
69: 16. for thy lovingkindn. i. g.
73:1. Truly G. i. g. to Isr., to such
85: 12. L. shall give th. wh. i. g.
109:21. bec. thy mercy i. g. deliv.
143: 10. Spirit i. g. lead me into
Pr.11:23. desire of righte. i. only g.
25: 25. so i. g. news fr. far coun.
31:18. perc. her merchandise i. g.
Ec. 2: 26. G. giveth to man that i.
g., may give to him i. g. bef. G.
6: 12. who kno-h what i. g. for
7:11. Wisdom i. g. with an inher.
† 26. that i. g. bef. G. sh. escape
9: 2. as i. the g. so is the sinner
Is. 55: 2. eat ye that which i. g.
Je. 13:10. this girdle i. g. for noth.

Ho. 4: 13. bec. shadow thereof i. g.
Mi. 6: 8. He shewed thee, what i. g.
Mal. 2: 17. ye say, Every one that
doeth evil i. g.
Mk. 9: 50. Salt i. g. but, Lu.14:34.
Lu. 6: 45. bringeth forth that i. g.
18:19. none i. g. save one, th. is G.
Ro. 7:13. Was that i. g. made death
18. how to perf. th. i. g. I find
12: 9. cleave to that which i. g.
16: 19. have you wise to that i. g.
1 Co. 7:26. this i. g. for the present
Ep. 4: 29. no communica. but i. g.
1 Th. 5: 15. follow that i. g., 3 Jn.
21. hold fast that which i. g. ⌊11.
1 Ti. 1: 8. we know the law i. g.
2: 3. this i. g. and acceptable in
4: 4. every creature of God i. g.
5: 4. that i. g. and accept. bef. G.
1 Pe. 3: 13. if followers of th. i. g.

It is GOOD.

Ru. 2:22. i. i. g. dau. that ⌈54: 6.
Ps. 52: 9. on thy name, for i. i. g.,
73: 28. i. i. g. to draw near to G.
92:1. i. i. a g. thing to give thanks
119:71. i. i. g. th. I have been af-
147:1. i. i. g. to sing praises ⌊flict
Pr. 24:13. eat honey, bec. i. i. g.
Ec. 5:18. i. i. g. for one to eat and d-k
7: 18. i. i. g. that thou take hold
Is. 41:†7. saying of the soder, i. i. g.
La. 3:26. i. i. g. th. man both hope
27. i. i. g. th. man bear yoke in
Mat. 5: 13. i. i. g. for noth ⌊youth
17:4. i. i. g. for us to be here, Mk.
9: 5. Lu. 9: 33. ⌈i. i. g.
Ro. 7: 16. I consent unto law, that
14: 21. i. i. g. neither to eat flesh
1 Co. 7: 1. i. i. g. for a man not to
touch a woman, 8.
26. I say, i. i. g. for man so to be
Ga. 4:18. i. i. g. to be zealously af-

GOOD land. ⌊fected

Ex. 3:8. bring them to g. l., De.8:7.
Nu. 14: 7. land we searched is g. l.
De. 1: 25. it is a g. l. the L. doth
35. none of that genera. see g. l.
3:25. let me go, and see g. l. ⌈g. l.
4: 21. L. sware I sho. not go unto
22. ye sh. go and possess g. l.
6: 18. mayest go in and poss. g. l.
8: 7. Lord bringeth thee into g. l.
10. shalt bless the Lord for g. l.
9:6. giveth not g. l. for thy righte.
11: 17. lest ye perish fr. off g. l.
Jos. 23:13. until ye perish fr. g. l.,
16. ye sh. quickly perish fr. g. l.,
Ju. 18:9. seen l., it is very g. ⌊15.
1 K. 14:15. sh. root Isr. out of g. l.
2 K. 3:19. mar ev. g. piece of l., 25.
1 Ch. 28: 8. that ye possess g. l.

GOOD with make. ⌈14.

Ex. 21:34. owner of pit m. it g., 22:
22:11. owner sh. not m. it g., 13, 15.
Le. 24:18. killeth a beast sh. m. it g.
Nu. 23: 19. sh. he not m. it g.?
Je. 18: 11. m. ways and doings g.

GOOD man or GOODMAN.

2 S. 18: 27. said, Ahimaaz is a g. m.
Ps. 37: 23. steps of a g. m. are order-
112: 5. A g. m. sheweth favour ⌊ed
Pr. 7: 19. For the g. is not at home
12: 2. A g. m. obtaineth favour of
13: 22. A g. m. leaveth inheritance
14: 14. A g. m. sh. be satisfied fr.
Mi. 7: 2. The g. m. is perished ⌊hims.
Mat. 12: 35. A g. m. out of treasure,
20: 11. murmured ag. g. ⌊Lu. 6:45.
24: 43. if g. of house had known
in what watch thief, Lu. 12: 39.
Mk. 14: 14. say ye to g. of house,
Lu. 23: 50. Joseph g. m. ⌊Lu. 22:11.
Jn. 7: 12. some said, He is a g. m.
Ac. 11: 24. Barnabas was a g. m.
Ro. 5: 7. for a g. m. some would die

Not GOOD.

Ge. 2: 18. n. g. that man be alone

1 S. 29:†6. art n. g. in eyes of lords
2 S. 17 : 7. the counsel is n. g. [g.
Ps. 36:4. setteth hims. in way is n.
Pr. 16 : 29. leadeth into way n. g.
17 : 26. to punish the just is n. g.
18:5. is n. g. to accept the wicked
19:2 th. soul be wi-t knowl. is n.g.
20 : 23. false balance n. g. [28:21.
24:23.n.g. to have respect of per-s,
25 : 27. n. g. to eat much honey
Is. 65 : 2. walketh in way is n. g.
Eze. 18 : 18. did that which is n. g.
20 : 25. I gave them statutes n. g.
36 : 31. remem. your doings n. g.
Mat. 19:10. if so, it is n.g. to marry
Ac. 15 : 38. Paul thought n. g. to,
1 Co. 5 : 6 Your glorying is n. g.

Seem, ed, eth GOOD.

Jos. 9 : 25. as it s-h g. to thee to do
unto us,do,Ju.10:15. 1 S.14:36,
40. Ezr. 7:18. Es. 3 : 11. Je. 26 :
14.-40 : 4.
Ju. 19 : 24. do to them what s-h g.
1 S. 1 : 23. do what s-h g., 3 : 18.-
11 : 10.-24 : 4. [to Isr. (2)
2 S. 3 : 19. Abner spake all s-d g.
10:12. L. do that s-h him g.,15:26.
19:37. do to Chim. what s. g., 38.
24 : 22. offer up what s-h g. unto
1 K. 21:2. if s. g. to thee, Je. 40:4.
1 Ch. 13:2. If it s. g. unto you, let
Ezr. 5 : 17. if it s. g. to k., Es. 5:4.
Je. 18 : 4. as s-d g. to the potter
Mat.11:26 so it s-d g. in sight, Lu.
Lu. 1 : 3. It s-d g. to me [10: 21.
Ac. 15 : 25. It s-d g. unto us
28. it s-d g. to the Holy Ghost

GOOD with thing. [g.

Ex. 18:17. t. that thou doest is not
De. 1 : 14. t. hast spoken is g.
26 : 11. shalt rejoice in every g. t.
Jos.21:45.failed not aught of any g.
1 S. 26 : 16. This t. is not g. [t.
1 K.14:13 in him is found some g.t.
2 K. 8:9. Hazael took of ev. g. t. of
Ps 34:10.that seek L. not want g.t.
38:20. bec. I follow the t. th. g. is
84 : 11. no g. t. will he withhold
92 : 1. it is a g. t. to give thanks
Pr. 18:22. findeth wife, find. a g.t.
Je. 33 : 14. will perf. g. t. I prom-d
Ho.8:3.hath cast off the t. th. is g.
Mat. 19 : 16. what g. t. do to inher-
it life? [Nazareth?
Jn.1:46.Can any g. t. come out of
Ro. 7 : 18. in my flesh, dwelleth no
g. t.
Ga. 4:18. zealously affected in a g.t.
Ep. 4 : 28. working t. which is g.
6:8. knowing what g.t. man doeth
2 Ti.1:14. Th. g. t.committed, keep
Phm. 6. acknowl-g ev. g. t. in you
He. 13 : 9. it is a g. t. heart be es-

GOOD things. [tabl.

Ge. 45:23. Ten asses laden wi. g. t.
De. 6 : 11. give houses full of g. t.
Jos. 23 : 14. not one failed of g. t.
15. as all g. t. are come upon you
2 K. 25:†28. he spake g.t. with him,
Je. 52 : † 32.
2 Ch. 12:†12. in Judah were g. t.
19 : 3. in Jehosh. there are g. t.
Jb. 22 : 18. he filled houses wi. g.t.
Ps. 103:5. satisfieth mouth wi. g.t.
Pr. 28 : 10. upright shall have g.t.
Je. 5 : 25. sins have withholden g.t.
12 :†6. believe not, tho. speak g.t.
Mat. 7 : 11. give g. t. to them that
12:34 how can ye evil speak g. t.?
35. good man bringeth forth g.t.
Lu 1:53.hath filled hungry wi. g.t.
16 : 25 in lifetime receivedst g. t.
Ro. 10 : 15. bri. glad tidings of g.t.
Ga. 6 : 6. communicate in all g. t.
Tit.2:3.aged women teachers of g.t.
3:8. these t. are g. and profitable
He.9:11. C. being a high pr. of g.t.
He.10:1.the law having a shadow of

GOOD tidings. [g. t.

2 S.4:10.thinking to have bro-t g.t.
18 : 27. good, and cometh wi. g. t.
1 K. 1:42. valiant, and bringest g.t.
2 K. 7 : 9. this day is a day of g. t.
Is 40:9. O Zion. th. bringest g. t.
41:27. Jerus. one th. bringeth g.t.
52:7. feet of him th. bringeth g.t.
61 : 1. anointed me to preach g t.
Na.1:15.feet of him who bring. g.t.
Lu. 2 : 10. I bring you g. t. of great
joy [faith
1 Th. 3 : 6. brought us g. t. of your

GOOD understanding.

1 S.25:3.Abigal was a wom. of g.u.
Ps. 111:10. g. u. have all that do
command-ts
Pr. 3:4. So shalt find fav. and g.u.
13 : 15. g. u. giveth favour

Was GOOD.

Ge. 1:4. God saw that it w. g., 10,
12, 18, 21, 25. [w. very g.
31. God saw ev. thing, behold it
3 : 6. woman saw the tree w. g.
40:16. baker saw interpreta. w. g.
41:37. thing w. g. in eyes of Pha.,
49:15. Issa. saw rest w.g. [45:†16.
Jos. 22 :†30. w. g. in eyes of Phin.
1 S. 15 : 9. Saul spared all th. w.g.
2 Ch. 14:2. Asa did th. which w.g.
31 : 20. Hez. wrought that w. g.
Ne. 2 : 18. hand of G. which w. g.
Ec. 2:3. see what w. th. g. for sons

GOOD work. [g.w.

Ne. 2:18. strengthen hands for this
Mat. 26 : 10. She hath wrought a g.
w., Mk. 14 : 6.
Jn. 10:33. For g. w. stone thee not
2 Co. 9 : 8. that ye abound to ev. g.
Ph. 1:6. wh. hath begun g. w. [w.
Col. 1 : 10. being fruitf. in ev. g.w.
2 Th 2:17 stablish you in ev. g. w.
1 Ti. 3 : 1. a bishop desireth a g.w.
5 : 10. if she diligently foll-d g.w.
2 Ti. 2:21. prepared unto ev. g. w.
Tit. 1 : 16. unto ev. g.w. reprobate
3 : 1. to be ready to every g. w.
He. 13:21. Make you perf. in ev. g.

GOOD works. [w.

1 S.19:4. his w. to thee-ward very g.
Mat. 5:16. they may see your g.w.
Jn.10:32. Many g. w. have I shew.
Ac. 9 : 36. Dorcas full of g. w.
Ro.13:3.rulers not a terror to g.w.
Ep. 2 : 10. created in C. unto g.w.
1 Ti. 2 : 10. I will that women adorn
themselves with g. w.
5:10. widow well reported for g.w.
25. g. w. of some manifest
6:18.rich, th. they be rich in g.w.
2 Ti. 3 : 17. furnished unto all g.w.
Tit. 2 : 7. thyself a pattern in g. w.
14. a peculiar peo., zeal. of g. w.
3 : 8. caref. to maintain g. w., 14.
He. 10 : 24. to provoke unto g. w.
1 Pe. 2:12. may by g. w. glorify G.

GOODLIER, EST.

1 S. 8 : 16. will take g-t young men
9 : 2. not in Israel a g-r person
1 K. 20 : 3. chil., even g-t are mine

GOODLINESS.

Is. 40 : 6. g. as flower of the field

GOODLY.

Ge. 27 : 15. Rebek. took g. raiment
39 : 6. Joseph was a g. person
49:21.Naph. a hind giveth g.words
Ex. 2 : 2. she saw he was g. child
39:28. made g. bonnets of fine lin.
Le. 23 : 40. first day boughs of g.
Nu. 24 5. g. are thy tents,O Jacob!
31:10.they burnt all their g.castles
De. 3:25. let me see that g. mount.
6 : 10. g. cities thou buildedst not
8:12. lest when hast built g. hous.
Jos. 7 : 21. I saw g. Bab-h garment
1 S. 9:2. Saul, a young man, and g.
1 S. 16:12. David g. to look to [man
2 S. 23 : 21. slew an Egyptian, a g.
1 K. 1 : 6. Adonijah a very g. man
2 Ch. 36:10. bro-t to Bab. g. vessels
19. destroyed the g. vessels [cocks?
Jb. 39:13 Gavest g. wings unto pea-
Ps. 16 : 6. I have a g. heritage
80 : 10. boughs were like g. cedars
Je. 3:19. how give thee g. heritage?
11 : 16. green olive tree, of g. fruit
Eze. 17:8. that it might be a g. vine
23. bear fruit, and be g. cedar
Da 11 : † 16. stand in g. land, † 41.
† 45. shall plant in g. holy mt.
Ho. 10 : 1. have made g. images
Jo. 3 : 5. into temple my g. things
Zch. 10 : 3. made them as g. horse
Mat. 13:45. seeking g. pearls [stones
Lu. 21 : 5. temple adorned with g.
Re. 18 : 14. all things g. are departed
See APPAREL, PRICE.

GOODMAN. See **GOOD** man,

GOODNESS.

Ex. 18 : 9. rejoiced for all g. L. had
33 : 19. will make my g. pass bef.
34 : 6. the L. God abundant in g.
Nu. 10:32. what g. L. shall do [26.
2 S.7:28.promisedst this g.,1 Ch.17:
1 K. 8:66. joyful for g., 2 Ch. 7:10.
10 : † 7. hast added g. to thy fame
2 Ch. 6 : 41. let saints rejoice in g.
32:32.Hez. his g. | 35:26.Josiah g.
Ne. 9:25. delighted thems. in thy g.
35. not served thee in thy gr. g.
Ps. 16 : 2. my g. extendeth not to
21:3.preventest with blessings of g.
23 : 6. g. and mercy sh. follow me
25 : 7. remem. me, for thy g. sake
† 13. his soul shall lodge in g.
27 : 13. had believ. to see g. of L.
31 : 19. O how great is thy g.
33 : 5. earth is full of g. of the L.
52 : 1. g. of God endureth contin.
65:4. be satisfied with g. of thy h.
11. crownest year with g.
68:10. prepared of thy g. for poor
107 : 8. praise L. for g., 15, 21, 31.
9. filleth hungry soul with g.
144 : 2. My g. and my fortress
145 : 7. sh. utter memory of thy g.
Pr. 20:6. will proclaim ev. one his g.
Is. 63:7. his great g. tow. h. of Isr.
Je. 2 : 7. I brought you to eat g.
31 : 12. sh. flow togeth. to g. of L.
14. people be satisfied with my g.
33:9. they sh. tremble for all the g.
Ho. 3:5. sh. fear the Lord and his g.
6:4. your g. is as a morning cloud
10:1.acc. to g. of land made images
Zch. 9 : 17. how great is his g. and
Ro. 2:4. despisest thou riches of his
g.,not knowi. g g. of G. leadeth
11 : 22. Behold, g. and severity of
G., tow. thee g. if contin. in g.
15:14. persuaded you are full of g.
Ga. 5:22. fruit of Spi. is g., Ep. 5:9.
2 Th.1:11. fulfil good pleas. of his g.

GOODS.

Ge. 14:16. Ab. bro-t back all the g.
21. give me persons, and take g.
24:10. g. of master were in his ha.
31:18. Jac. carried aw. his g., 46:6.
Ex.22:8.not hand unto neighb.'s g.,
Nu.16:32.earth swall-d their g. [11.
31:9. Isr. took spoil of Mid. and g.
35:3. suburbs for Levites' cattle,g.
De. 28 : 11. L. make plenteous in g.
2 Ch. 21 : 14. L. smite thy wives, g.
Ezr. 1 : 4. let men help him with g.
6. all strengthened hands with g.
6:8. of king's g. expenses be given
7 : 26. or to confiscation of g.
Ne. 9:25. poss-d houses full of all g.
Jb. 20 : 10. his hands sh. restore g.
21. thf. sh. no man look for his g.
28. g. shall flow away his wrath
Ec. 5:11. g. increase, they are incr

Eze.38:12.have gotten cattle and **g.**
38: 13. art come to take aw. **g.**?
Zph. 1: 13. **g.** sh. become a booty
Mat. 12:29. how enter strong man's
h., spoil his **g.** exc., Mk. 3: 27.
24:47.sh. make him ruler ov. his **g.**
25: 14. delivered unto them his **g.**
Lu. 6: 30. of him th. taketh thy **g.**
11:21. his **g.** are in peace [ask not
12:18. there will I bestow all my **g.**
19. thou hast much **g.** laid up
15: 12. give me the portion of **g.**
16:1. accused that he wasted his **g.**
19:8. half of my **g.** I give to poor
Ac. 2:45. sold **g.** parted them to all
1 Co. 13:3. tho. I bestow all my **g.**
He.10:34. joyfully spoil-g of your **g.**
Re.3:17.rich, and increased with **g.**

GOPHER wood.

Ge. 6: 14. Make an ark of **g. w.**

GORE, ED.

Ex. 21:28. if an ox **g.** man or wom.
31. whe. he have **g.** a son or dau.

GORGEOUS, LY. [g-y

Eze. 23:12. Assyrians clothed most
Lu. 7: 25. **g**-y apparelled in courts
23:11.Herod arrayed Jes.in **g.**robe

GO'SHEN.

Ge. 45:10. shalt dwell in land of G.,
46: 34.-47: 4, 6, 27.
Ex. 8: 22. will sever land of G.
9: 26. Only in land of G. no hail
Jos. 10: 41. smote country of G.
11: 16. Joshua took all land of G
15: 51. inheritance of Judah, G.

GOSPEL.

Mk. 1: 1. beginning of **g.** of J. C
15. Jes. came, saying, believe **g.**
8:35. whoso. sh. lose his life for **g.**'s
10:29.left hou.for my sake and **g.**'s
13:10. **g.** must be published am.
Ac.15:7.Gent.by my mouth hear **g.**
20: 24. to testify **g.** of grace of G.
Ro. 1: 1. apostle, separated unto **g.**
9. whom I serve in **g.** of [of G.
16. I am not ashamed of **g.** of C.
2:16. sh. judge secrets acc. to my **g.**
10: 16. have not all obeyed **g.**
11: 28. conc. the **g.** are enemies
15: 16. ministering the **g.** of God
29. fulness of blessing of **g.** of C.
16: 25. to stablish you acc. to **g.**
1 Co.4:15.I have begotten you thro.
9: 12. lest we hinder **g.** of C. [r.
17. dispensation of **g.** is commit.
18.preach **g.**I may make **g.**with-t
charge; th. I abuse not power
23. this I do for **g.**'s sake [in **g.**
2 Co. 4:3. if **g.** hid, hid to them lost
4. lest light of glori. **g.** sho. shine
8:18. bro. whose praise is in the **g.**
9:13.prof-d subjection unto **g.**of C.
11:4. if ye receive ano. **g.**, Ga. 1:6.
Ga. 1: 7. would pervert **g.** of C.
2: 2. I communicated **g.** I preach
5. that truth of **g.** might contin.
7. **g.** of uncirc. commit. unto me
14.not acc.to the truth of the **g.**
Ep. 1:13. word of truth **g.** of salva.
3:6 partakers of promise in C.by **g.**
6:15.shod wi.preparation of the **g.**
19. to make kno. mystery of **g.**
Ph. 1: 5. For your fellowship in **g.**
7. defence and confirma. of **g.**, 17.
12.fallen out to furtherance of **g.**
27. let conversation be as becometh **g.** striving for faith of **g.**
2: 22. hath served with me in **g.**
4:3. women who lab-d wi. me in **g.**
15. know that in beginning of **g.**
Col. 1:5. ye heard bef. of truth of **g.**
23. be not moved from hope of **g.**
1 Th. 1: 5. **g.** came not in word
2:2. we were bold to speak **g.** of G.
4.allowed to be put in trust wi. **g.**
8. to have imparted not **g.** only
9:2. Timothy our fellow lab. in **g.**

2 Th. 1: 8. that obey not **g.**, 1 Pe.
2:14 be called you by our **g.** [4:17.
1 Ti. 1: 11. acc. to **g.** of blessed G
2 Ti. 1: 8. partaker of afflic of **g.**
10. immortality to light thro. **g.**
2: 8. J. Chr. raised acc. to my **g.**
Phm.13.have minist-d unto me in **g.**

GOSPEL.
with preach, ed, ing.

Mat. 4: 23. Jes. went p-g **g.**, 9:35.
Mk. 1: 14. [7: 22.
11: 5. poor have the **g.** p-d, Lu.
24:14.**g.**sh.be p-d, 26:13. Mk.14:9.
Mk. 16:15. go, p. **g.** to ev. creature
Lu. 4:18. hath anointed me to p.**g.**
9: 6. departed, p-g **g.** and healing
20:1. as he taught, and p-d the **g.**
Ac. 8: 25. p-d the **g.** in villages
14: 7. And there they p-d the **g.**
21. when had p-d **g.** to that city
16: 10. L. had called us to p. **g.**
Ro. 1:15. am ready to p.**g.**at Rome
10:15. beautiful feet of them p. **g.**
15: 19. I have fully p-d **g.** of C.
20. so have I strived to p.**g.** [g.
1 Co. 1:17. not to baptize, but to p.
9:14. that p. **g.** sho. live of gospel
16.tho.I p.**g.**have noth.to glory,
woe to me if I p. not **g.** [pel
18.when I p.**g.** I may make gos-
15: 1. I declare to you **g.** I p-d
2 Co. 2:12. I came to Troas to p.**g.**
10:14.come to you in p-g the **g.**, 16.
11:7.bec.I p-d to you freely the **g.**
Ga. 1:8. tho. we p. any other **g.**, 9.
11. **g.** p-d of me is not after man
3: 8. p-d before the **g.** unto Ab.
4:13.thro.infirmity of flesh I p-d **g.**
1 Th. 2: 9. we p-d to you **g.** of G.
He. 4: 2. to us was **g.** p-d as them
1 Pe.1:12. by them that p-d **g.** unto
you [you
25. this is word by **g.** is p-d unto
4: 6. for this cause **g.** p-d to dead
Re. 14:6. having everlasting **g.**to p.

GOT.

Ge.39:12.Joseph fled and **g.**out, 15.
Ps. 44:3. **g.** not land by own sword
Ec. 2:7. **g.** me servt-s and maidens
Je. 13: 2. I **g.** a girdle acc. to word
4. take the girdle thou hast **g.**

GOTTEN.

Ge. 4:1. I have **g.** a man fr. the L.
12: 5. souls they had **g.** in Haran
31: 1. wh. was fa.'s hath he **g.** all
Ex. 14: 18. when I have **g.** honour
Le. 6:4. thing he hath deceitfully **g.**
Nu. 31: 50. what hath **g.** of jewels
De. 8: 17. my hand **g.** this wealth
2 S. 17: 13. if he be **g.** into a city
Jb.28:15.wisd.cannot be **g.** for gold
31:25.if I rejoic-d bec.hand **g.**much
Ps. 98: 1. arm hath **g.** victory
Pr. 13:11. Wealth **g.** by vanity sh.
20: 21. inherit. may be **g.** hastily.
31:†29. many dau-s have **g.** riches
Ec. 1: 16. **g.** more wisdom than all
Is. 15: 7. abun. **g.** they carry aw.
Je. 48:36. riches he hath **g.** are per.
Eze. 28: 4. with wisdom **g.** riches
38: 12. of nat-s wh. have **g.** cattle
Da. 9: 15. thou hast **g.** thee renown
Mat. 11:†12. kingd. is **g.** by force
Ac. 21: 1. **g.** from them and had
launched
Re. 15:2. I saw them had **g.** victory

GOURD, S.

1 K. 6:†18. cedar of house with **g**-s
2 K. 4: 39. one gathered wild **g**-s
Jon.4:6. prepared **g.** Jon. glad of **g.**
7. a worm smote the **g.**
9. well to be angry for the **g.**?
10. thou hast had pity on the **g.**

GOVERN.

1 K.21:7.Dost now **g.** kingd. of Isr.?
Jb. 34: 17. he th. hateth right **g.**?
Ps. 67: 4. thou shalt **g.** the nations

GOVERNMENT, S.

Is. 9:6. **g.** sh. be upon his shoulder
7. of increase of his **g.** be no end
22:21.I will commit **g.** into his ha.
1 Co. 12: 28. helps, **g**-s, diversities
2 Pe. 2: 10. chiefly them th. despise

GOVERNOR. [g.

Ge.42:6 Joseph was **g.** ov. la., 45:26.
1 K. 18:3.Ob.was **g.** over Ahab's ho.
22: 26. carry him unto Amon the
g., 2 Ch. 18: 25. [41: 2, 18.
2 K. 25:23. Gedaliah **g.**, Jer.40:5,7.-
1 Ch. 29: 22. anointed Sol. chief **g.**
2 Ch. 1: 2. to every **g.** in all Israel
28: 7. Azrikam **g.** of the house
34: 8. Maaseiah **g.** [Jews
Ezr.5:3.Tatnai **g.**, 6:6, 13. | 6:7 **g.** of
5:14. Cyrus deliv. vessels unto **g.**
Ne. 5: 14. I not eaten bread of **g.**
18. I required not the bread of **g.**
10:†1 sealed were, Neh. the **g.**
12: 26 Nehemiah the **g.**, 5: 14.
Ps. 22: 28. he is the **g.** am. nations
Je. 20: 1. chief **g.** in house of L.
30: 21. **g.** sh. proceed from them
40:5. Go back to Gedaliah the **g.**
41:2. Ishm. smote Gedaliah **g.**, 18.
Ha. 1: 14. L. stirred up Zeruh. **g.**, 1.
2:2.speak to Zerubbabel the **g.**, 21.
Zch. 9:7. he shall be as a **g.** in Jud.
Mal. 1: 8. offer it now unto thy **g.**
Mat. 2:6. out of thee sh. come a **g.**
27:2. deliv-d to Pontius Pilate the
g., 11, 14, 15, 21, 23, 27 Lu. 3:1.
28: 14. if this come to **g.**'s ears
Lu. 2: 2. Cyrenius was **g.** of Syria
20: 20. deliver unto power of **g.**
Jn.2:8. bear unto **g.** of the feast, 9
Ac. 7: 10. made him **g.** over Egypt
23: 24. unto Felix **g.**, 26, 33, 34.
24: 1. informed **g.** ag. Paul
10. aft. **g.** had beck-d unto him
26: 30. king rose up, and the **g.**
2 Co. 11: 32. the **g.** under Aretas
Ja. 3: 4. ships turned whi. **g.** listeth

GOVERNORS.

Ju. 5: 9. My heart tow. **g.** of Isr.
14. out of Machir came down **g.**
1 K.10:15. **g.** of country, 2 Ch.9:14.
1 Ch. 24:5. **g.** of sanc. **g.** of h. of G.
2 Ch. 23:20. the **g.** of the people
Ezr. 8: 36. k.'s commissions to **g.**
Ne. 2:7. let letters be given to **g.**
5:15. former **g.** chargeable to peo.
Es. 3: 12. **g.** over every province
Is.19:†13. have seduced **g.** of Egypt
Da. 2: 48. k. made Dan. chief of **g.**
3: 2. the princes, the **g.**, 27.-6: 7.
Zch.12:5.**g.** shall say in their heart
6.will make **g.** of Jud. like hearth
Mat. 10:18. ye shall be bro-t bef **g.**
Ga. 4:2. heir is under tutors and **g.**
1 Pe. 2: 14. submit yours. unto **g.**

GO'ZAN.

2 K. 17: 6. king placed Isr. by river
of G., 18: 11. 1 Ch. 5: 26.
19:12. have destr-d, as G., Is.37:12.

GRACE.

Ezr 9:8.for little space **g.**heen shew-
Es. 2: 17. Es. obtained **g.**in his [ed
Ps. 45: 2. **g.** is poured into lips
84: 11. Lord, be will give **g.** and
Pr. 1: 9. ornament of **g.** unto head
3: 22. so be life and **g.** to thy neck
34 giveth **g.** unto lowly, Ja. 4:6.
4:9.give to head ornam. of **g.**
22:11. for **g.** of lips king his friend
Ec. 10: †12. The words of a wise
man's mouth are **g.**
Zch. 4: 7. crying, **g. g.** unto it
12: 10. I will pour the Spirit of **g.**
Jn. 1: 14. begotten of Fa., full of **g.**
16. we have all receiv.. **g.** for **g.**
17. **g.** and truth came by Jes. C
Ac. 4:33. great **g.** was upon them all
14: 3. testimony unto word of **g.**
18:27. helped them belie-d thro. **g.**

Ac. 20:32. I commend to word of g.
Ro. 1 : 5. by whom we received g.
7. g. to you and peace fr. G., 1 Co. 1 : 3. 2 Co. 1 : 2. Ga. 1 : 3. Ep. 1 : 2. Ph. 1 : 2. Col. 1 : 2. 1 Th. 1 : 1. 2 Th. 1 : 2. Phm. 3.
3:24. being justified freely by his g.
4 : 4. reward is not reckoned of g.
16. of faith, th. it might be by g.
5 : 2. we have access into this g.
17. more who receive abun. of g.
20. where sin abound-d g. more
21. might g. reign thro. righte-n.
6 : 1. in sin, that g. may abound?
14. under g. | 15. bec. under g.?
11 : 5. remn. acc. to election of g.
6. if by g. then no more of works
12:3. I say, thro. g. given unto me
6. gifts differing acc. to g. given
15 : 15. bec. of g. given me of G.
1 Co. 10 : 30. if I by g. a partaker
15:10. his g. bestowed not in vain
2 Co. 1:† 15. might have a sec. g.
4 : 15. g. might redound to glory
8 : 6. would finish in you same g.
7. see ye abound in this g. [g.
19. chosen to travel wi. us with this
9:8. God is able to make g. abound
12 : 9. My g. is sufficient for thee
Ga. 1:6. fr. him who called you to g.
15. God, who called me by his g.
2 : 9. when Ja. perceived g. given
5:4. justified by law, fallen from g.
Ep. 1 : 6. To praise of glory of g.
7. forgiveness, acc. to riches of g.
2 : 5. by g. ye saved thro. faith, 8.
7. might shew riches of his g.
3 : 8. Unto me least of all is g. giv.
4 : 7. unto ev. one of us is given g.
29. minister g. unto hearers
6 : 24. g. be with all love our L. J.
Ph. 1 : 7. ye are all partakers of g.
Col. 3 : 16. singing with g. in hearts
4 : 6. Let speech be alway with g.
18. g. be with you, 2 Ti. 4 : 22. Tit. 3 : 15. He. 13 : 25.
2 Th. 2:16. given good hope thro. g.
1 Ti. 1:2. g. mercy, and peace from G. our Father and our L. J. Christ, 2 Ti. 1:2. Tit. 1:4. 2 Jn. 3.
14. g. of our Lord was abundant
6 : 21. g. be with thee. Amen
2 Ti. 1 : 9. called us acc. to his g.
2 : 1. be strong in g. that is in C.
Tit. 3 : 7. justified by his g. we heirs
He. 4 : 16. boldly unto throne of g.
10 : 29. done despite unto Spi. of g.
12 : 28. let us have g. to serve G.
13 : 9. good heart be establ. with g.
Ja. 1 : 11. the g. of the fashion of it perisheth [humble
4 : 6. giveth more g. giveth g. to
1 Pe. 1:2. g. be multiplied, 2 Pe. 1:2.
10. who prophes-d of g. to come
13. hope for the g. | 3 : 7. heirs of
5 : 5. God giveth g. to humble [g.
10. G. of g. who called us unto gl.
2 Pe. 3:18. grow in g. and knowl. of J.
Jude 4. g. of God into lasciviousn.
Re. 1 :4. g. from him wh. is and was

See FIND, FOUND.

GRACE of God.

Lu. 2 : 40. g. o. G. was upon him
Ac. 11:23. when he had seen g. o. G.
13:43. continue in g. o. G. [15:40.
14 : 26. recommended to g. o. G.,
20 : 24. to testify gospel of g. o. G.
Ro. 5 : 15. more g. o. G. abounded
1 Co. 1:4. g. o. G. given you by J. C.
3 : 10. acc. to g. o. G. given to me
15:10. by g. o. G. I am what I am, yet not I, but g. o. G. with me
2 Co. 1:12. by g. o. G. had our conver.
6 : 1. receive not g. o. G. in vain
8 : 1. of g. o. G. bestowed on ch-s
9:14. for exceeding g. o. G. in you
Ga. 2:21. I do not frustrate g. o. G.
Eph. 3:2. if heard of dispensa. of g.
7. acc. to gift of g. o. G. [o. G.
Col. 1 : 6. since ye knew g. o. G.
2 Th. 1:12. ye in him, acc. to g. o. G.
Tit. 2:11. g. o. G. th. bringeth salva.
He. 2:9. that he by g. o. G. taste death
12 : 15. lest any fail of the g. o. G.
1 Pe. 4:10. stewards of manif. g. o. G.
5 : 12. testifying this is true g. o. G.

GRACE of Lord Jesus.

Ac. 15:11. thro. g. o. L. J. we be saved
Ro. 16:20. g. o. our L. Jesus Christ be with you, 24. 1 Co. 16 : 23. Ph. 4 : 23. 1 Th. 5 : 28. 2 Th. 3 : 18.
2 Co. 8 : 9. ye know g. o. our L. J.
13:14. The g. o. our L. J. C. love of G. and commu. of H. Ghost
Ga. 6 : 18. g. o. L. J. C. be, Phm. 25.
Re. 22:21. g. o. L. J. C. be with you. [Amen

GRACIOUS.

Ge. 43:29. God be g. unto thee son
Ex. 22 : 27. I will hear, for I am g.
33:19. be g. to whom I will be g.
34 : 6. L. God, g., 2 Ch. 30 : 9. Ps. 103:8.-116:5.-145:8. Jo. 2:13.
Nu. 6:25. L. make his face shine, be g.
2 S. 12 : 22. Who tell whe. G. be g.?
2 K. 5:† 1. Naaman was g. with mas.
13:23. the Lord was g. unto them
Ne. 9 : 17. a God, g. merciful, 31.
Jb. 33 : 24. Then he is g. unto him
Ps. 4:† 1. be g. unto me, and hear
77:9. Hath God forgotten to be g.?
86 : 15. thou, O Lord, art G. g., 111 : 4.-112 : 4. [honour
Pr. 11 : 16. A g. woman retaineth
26:† 25. maketh voice g. believe not
Ec. 10:12. of wise man's mouth are g
Is. 30:18. L. will wait that he be g.
19. g. unto thee | 33 : 2. unto us
Je. 22:23. how g. when pangs come
Am. 5 : 15. may be Lord will be g.
Jon. 4 : 2. I knew thou art a g. G.
Mal. 1 : 9. beseech G. that he be g.
Lu. 4 : 22. wondered at g. words
1 Pe. 2 : 3. If tasted that Lord is g.

GRACIOUSLY.

Ge. 33:5. chil. G. hath g. given me
11. bec. G. hath dealt g. with me
Ps. 119 : 29. grant me thy law g.
Ho. 14:2. take away iniq. receive g.
Lu. 1:† 28. thou that art g. accepted

GRAFF, ED.

Ro. 11:17. thou wild olive tree wert g
19. branches brok. that I be g. in
23. they sh. be g. in, G. is able to g.
24. were g. much more these be

GRAIN, S. [g.

Jo. 1 : † 17. g-s rotten under clods
Am. 9:9. not least g. fall upon earth
Mat. 13 : 31. kingd. of heav. like g. of mustard, Mk. 4:31. Lu. 13:19.
17:20. if ye faith as a g. of mustard sh. say unto mountain, Lu. 17:6.
1 Co. 15:37. bare g. wheat, or other

GRANDFATHER. [g.

Da. 5:† 11. in days of thy g. in him whom thy g. [out of Jewry
† 13. that Daniel whom g. bro-t

GRANDMOTHER.

1 K. 15 : † 10. g.'s name Maachah
2 Ti. 1:5. faith wh. dwelt in g. Lois

GRANT. [Noun.]

Ezr. 3:7. acc. to g. they had of Cyrus

GRANT. [Verb.]

Le. 25:24. sh. g. a redemp. for land
Ru. 1:9. L. g. you th. ye may find rest
1 S. 1:17. God g. thee thy petition
1 Ch. 21:22. g. me place of thresh-ingfloor; shalt g. for the full
2 Ch. 12 : 7. I will g. them deliv.
Ne. 1 : 11. g. him mercy in sight of
Es. 5:8. if it please k. to g. petition
Jb. 6:8. that G. g. thing I long for
Ps. 20 : 4. g. acc. to own heart
85 : 7. O Lord, g. us salvation
119 : 29. g. me thy law graciously
Ps. 140:8. g. not desires of wick. [37.
Mat. 20:21. g. 2 sons may sit, Mk. 10
Lu. 1 : 74. g. unto us, that deliv-d
Ac. 4 : 29. g. wi. boldness we speak
Ro. 15:5. G. g. you be likeminded
Ep. 3:16. g. you to be strengthened
2 Ti. 1:18. L. g. he may find mercy
Re. 3 : 21. will I g. to sit in my

GRANTED. [throne

1 Ch. 4:10. God g. that he request.
2 Ch. 1:12. Wisd. knowl. is g. thee
Ezr. 7:6. k. g. him all his requests
Ne. 2:8. k. g. acc. to good hand of G.
Es. 5:6. what thy petition, shall be g., 7 : 2.-9 : 12.
8 : 11. Wherein king g. the Jews
9 : 13. let it be g. to Jews in Shu.
Jb. 10 : 12. hast g. life and favour
Pr. 10:24. desire of righte. sh. be g.
Ac. 3:14. desired murd-r be g. you
11:18. hath G. to Gent. g. repent.
14:3. g. signs to be done by hands
Re. 19 : 8. was g. she be arrayed in

GRAPE.

Le. 19:10. nor gath. ev. g. of viney.
De. 32 : 14. didst drink blood of g.
Jb. 15:33. shake off unripe g. as vine
Can. 2:13. vines with tender g. give
7:12. let us see whe. tender g. app.
Is. 18 : 5. sour g. is ripening in
Je. 31 : 29. fathers eaten a sour g.
30. ev. man that eateth sour g.
Mi. 7 : 1. I am as the g. gleanings

GRAPES.

Ge. 40:10. clusters bro-t forth ripe g.
11. g. pressed th. into Pha.'s cup
49 : 11. washed clothes in bl. of g.
Le. 25 : 5. nor g. of vine undressed
11. in Jubilee, nor gather the g.
Nu. 6 : 3. nor shall he eat moist g.
13:20. was time of first ripe g. [g.
23. cut branch with 1 cluster of
24. Eschol, bec. of the cluster of
De. 23:24. mayest eat g. thy fill [g.
24:21. When thou gatherest the g.
28:30. plant viney. not gather g.,
32:32. their g. are g. of gall [39.
Ju. 8 : 2. gleaning of g. of Ephr.
9 : 27. trode g. and cursed Abim.
Ne. 13 : 15. wine and g. on the sab.
Can. 2:15. our vines have tender g.
7 : 7. breasts like clusters of g.
Is. 5:2. looked it sho. bring forth g.
4. sho. bring g. brought wild g.
17 : 6. gleaning g. sh. be left in it
24:13. gleaning g. when vint. done
Je. 8 : 13. shall be no g. on vine
25:30. shout as they that tread g.
49:9. not leave gleaning g., Ob. 5.
Eze. 18 : 2. fathers eaten sour g.
Ho. 3 : † 1. and loved flagons of g.
9:10. I found Isr. like g. in wilder.
Am. 9 : 13. treader of g. overtake
Mat. 7:16. Do men gather g. of thorns
Lu. 6:44. nor of bramble bush gath.
Re. 14:18. her g. are fully ripe [g.

GRAPEGATHERER, S.

Je. 6 : 9. turn back thy ha. as a g.
49:9. if g-s come, would they, Ob. 5.

GRASS.

Ge. 1 : 11. Let earth bring forth g.
12. the earth brought forth g.
Nu. 22:4. as the ox licketh up the g.
De. 11:15. will send g. for thy cattle
29:23. not sown, nor any g. grow.
32:2. distil as showers upon the g.
2 S. 23:4. as the g. springing out of
1 K. 18 : 5. find g. to save horses
2 K. 19 : 26. were as g. of field, as g. on housetops, Is. 37 : 27.
Jb. 5 : 25. thine offspring as the g.
6 : 5. wild ass bray when hath g.?
40:15. behemoth eateth g. as an ox
Ps. 23:† 2. in pastures of tender g.
37 : 2. sh. soon be cut down like g.
72:6. come like rain upon mown g.
16. they of city sh. flourish like g.

Ps.90:5.in morning they are like g.
92:7.When wicked spring as the g.
102: 4. My heart is with-d like g.
11.a shadow, am withered like g.
103:15. As for man, his days as g.
104:14. causeth g. to grow for cat-
106:20.of an ox that eateth g. [tle
129: 6. as the g. upon housetops
147:8.maketh g.to grow upon mts.
Pr.19:12.k.'s favour as dew upon g.
27:25. the tender g. sheweth itself
Is. 15:6. g. faileth, is no green thi.
35: 7. in habita. of dragons be g.
40:6. cry, All flesh is g.,1 Pe.1:24.
7.g.withereth, the people is g.,8
44:4. they sh. spring up as am. g.
51: 12. son of man be made as g.
Je.14:5.forsook it bec. was no g.,6.
50: 11. grown fat as heifer at g.
Da. 4: 15. leave stump in g., 23.
25. eat g. as oxen, 32, 33.-5: 21.
Am.7:2. had made end of eating g.
Mi. 5: 7. as showers upon the g.
Zch.10:1. L. shall give every one g.
Mat. 6:30. if G. clothe g.,Lu.12:28.
14:19. to sit down on g., Mk. 6:39.
Jn. 6: 10. now there was much g.
Ja. 1: 10. as g. he shall pass away
11. sun risen, but it withereth g.
Re. 8: 7. all green g. was burnt up
9:4.that they sho. not hurt the g.

GRASSHOPPER, S.

Le. 11: 22. these ye may eat, the g.
Nu. 13: 33. were in our sight as g-s
Ju. 6:5. came as g-s for mult., 7:12.
Jb. 39:20. Canst make afraid as g.?
Ec. 12: 5. the g. shall be a burden
Is. 40: 22. inhabitants are as g-s
Je.46:23. bec. are more than the g-s
Am. 7: 1. he formed g. in beginn.
Na. 3: 17. capt-s are as great g-s

GRATE.

Ex. 27:4. for altar a g. of brass, 35:
16.-38: 4, 5, 30.-39: 39.

GRAVE. [Adjective.]

1 Ti.3:8.deacons be g. | 11.wives g.
Tit. 2: 2. Th. aged men be sober, g.

GRAVE. [Noun.]

Ge. 35: 20. Jac. set pillar upon her
g. th. is pillar of Rachel's g.
37: 35. go down into g. unto son
42:38. hairs wi. sorrow to g.,44:31.
50:5. bury me in g. I have digged
Nu.19:16. toucheth a g. is unclean
18.sprinkle upon him touched g.
1 S. 2: 6. L. bringeth down to g.
2 S.3:32. people wept at Abner's g.
19: 37. buried by g. of my father
1 K. 2: 6. not his head go to g. in
peace [g. with bl.
9. his hoar. head bring down to
13: 30. laid his carcass in own g.
14:13.he only of Jerob. come to g.
2 K. 22: 20. gath-d into thy g., 2
Ch. 34: 28. [the g.
Jb. 3: 22. glad when they can find
5: 26. shalt come to g. in full age
7:9.goeth to g.come no more [to g.
10: 19. sho. been carried fr. womb
14: 13. O that thou hide me in g.
17:13.If I wait, the g. is my house
21: 13. in moment, go down to g.
32. yet sh. be brought to the g.
24:19. so doth g. those have sinn.
30: 24. not stretch his hand to g.
33: 22. soul draweth near to g.
Ps. 6: 5. in g. who give thanks?
30: 3. hast bro-t my soul from g.
31:17.let wicked be silent in the g.
49: 14. laid in g. consume in g.
15.redeem my soul fr. power of g.
55:†15. let them go quick into g.
86:†13. hast deliv-d my soul fr. g.
88:3.my life draweth nigh unto g.
5. like slain that lie in the g.
11. thy lovingkindness in the g.
89:48.sh.he deliv. soul fr. ha.of g.
Ps. 141: 7. our bones at g.'s mouth
Pr. 1: 12. us swallow them as g.
30:16.g. and barren womb,say not
Ec. 9:10. no wisdom in the g. whi.
Can. 8: 6. jealousy is cruel as g.
Is. 14: † 9. g. is moved to meet thee
11. Thy pomp is bro-t down to g.
19. thou art cast out of thy g.
38: 10. I shall go to gates of g.
18. the g. cannot praise thee
53: 9. he made his g.with wicked
Je. 20: 17. th. my moth. been my g.
Eze. 31:15. day he went down to g.
32:23.company is round her g., 24.
Ho.13:14. I will ransom them fr. g.,
O g. I will be destruction
Jon. 2: † 2. out of belly of g. cried I
Na. 1: 14. I will make thy g.
Jn. 11: 17. had lain in g. 4 days
31. She goeth to g. to weep there
38. Jesus groaning, cometh to g.
12: 17. called Laz. out of g. [tory?
1 Co. 15: 55. O g. where thy vic-
Re. 20: † 13. death g. deliv. up dead

GRAVES.

Ex. 14: 11. Bec. were no g. in E.
Nu. 11: † 34. called pla. g. of lust
2 K. 23: 6. cast the powder upon n.
2 Ch. 34: 4. strewed it upon g. of
Jb. 17: 1. the g. are ready for me
21: † 32. yet shall he be bro-t to g.
Is. 65: 4. Which remain among g.
Je.8:1.bring priests' bones out of g.
26: 23. his dead body into g. [26.
Eze. 32: 22. his g. are about, 23, 25,
37: 12. will open g. cause you to
come out of g. [out of g.
13. when I have opened g. bro-t
39: 11. give Gog place of g. in Isr.
Mat. 27:52. g. were opened, saints
53.many bodies of saints out of g.
Lu. 11: 44. for ye are as g.
Jn. 5: 28. all in g. sh. hear voice
Re.11:9. not suffer bodies put in g.

GRAVE. [Verb.]

Ex. 28: 9. shalt g. on onyxstones
36. a plate of gold, and g. on it
2 Ch. 2:7. send man can skill to g.
14. have sent cunning man to g.

GRAVECLOTHES.

Jn. 11:44. Laz. came bound with g.

GRAVED, ETH.

1 K.7:36. on borders g-d cherubims
2 Ch. 3: 7. g-d cherubim on walls
Is. 22: 16. g-h habita. in a rock

GRAVEL. [g.

Pr. 20: 17. mouth sh. be filled with
Is. 48: 19. offspr. of bowels like g.
La. 3: 16. broken my teeth with g.

GRAVEN. [stones

Ex.32:16.writing of G. g.upon tables
39:6. g. as signets are g.wi. names
Jb.19:24. g. with iron pen [of Isr.
Is. 49:16. g. thee upon palms of ha-s
Je. 17:1. is g. upon table of heart
Ha.2:18. that the maker hath g. it
Ac. 17: 29. Godhead is like gold g.

GRAVEN image.

Ex. 20: 4. shalt not make unto thee
any g. i., Le. 26: 1. De. 5: 8.
De. 4:16. lest ye make a g.i., 23,25.
27: 15. cursed man maketh g. i.
Ju. 17: 3. silv. for son to make g.i.
4. to founder, who made a g. i.
18: 14. is in these houses a g. i.
17. the g.i. | 30. Dan set up g.i.,
2 K.21:7.Manasseh set up g.i.in[31.
Is. 40: 19. workman melteth g. i.
20. a workman to prepare a g. i.
44: 9. that make a g.i. are vanity
10.Who hath molten a g.i. [i.,15.
17. with residue he maketh g.
45: 20. set up wood of their g. i.
48: 5. my g. i. hath com-d them
Je.10:14. confounded by g.i.,51:17.
Na. 1: 14. I will cut off the g. i.
Ha. 2: 18.What profiteth the g.i.?

GRAVEN images.

De. 7:5. ye shall burn their g.i.,25.
12: 3. ye shall hew down the g. i.
Ju.3:†19. Ehud turned by the g. i.
2 K. 17:41. feared L. served g. i.
2 Ch.33:19. set up g. i. bef. he was
34:7. when he had beaten the g.i.
Ps.78:58. moved to jealousy wi.g.i.
97:7. Confounded all th. serve g.i.
Is. 10: 10. whose g. i. did excel
21: 9. Bab. is fallen, and all g. i.
30: 22. sh. defile covering of g. i.
42: 8. nei. give my praise to g. i.
17. be ashamed that trust in g.i.
Je. 8:19. provoked to anger wi. g.i.
50: 38. it is the land of g. i. [52.
51:47. I will do judgm. upon g.i.,
Ho. 11: 2. they burned inc. to g.i.
Mi. 1: 7. all g.i. be beaten to pieces
5: 13. Thy g. i. will I cut off

GRAVING.

Ex. 32: 4. golden calf with a g. tool

GRAVING, S.

1 K. 7:31. upon mouth of laver g-s
2 Ch. 2: 14. skilful to grave g., †7.
Zch. 3:9. I will engrave g., saith L.

GRAVITY.

1 Ti. 3:4. chil. in subjection with g.
Tit. 2: 7. in doctrine shewing g.

GRAY. See HAIRS, HEAD.

GRAYHEADED.

1 S. 12: 2. I am old and g. my sons
Jb. 15: 10.With us are g. and aged
Ps. 71: 18. when I am old and g.

GREASE.

Ps. 119:70. their heart is as fat as g.

GREAT.

Ge. 12: 2. I will make thy name g.
24:35. Ab. my master is become g.
26: 13. man waxed g. | 14. g.store
30:8.With g.wrestlings with sister
39: 9. how can I do this g. wick.
45: 7. your lives by a g. deliv.
48: 19. my son, he also sh. be g.
Ex.18:22. ev.g.matter they sh.bring
De. 3: 5. unwalled towns g. many
10: 17. L.G. is a g. G., 2 Ch. 2: 5.
11: 7. eyes seen g. acts of Lord
18: 16. nei. let me see this g. fire
29: 24. what meaneth g. anger?
Jos. 7: 9. what unto thy g. name?
14: 12. thou heardest cities were g.
22: 10. built a g. altar by Jordan
24: 17. he did those g. signs in our
Ju.5:15. g. thoughts of heart [sight
1 S. 12: 17. perceive wickedn. is g.
22: † 15. noth. of this, little or g.
2 S. 5: 10. Da. went on and grew g.
7: 9. I have made thee a g. name
22. thou art g. O L. God, none
12: 14. given g. occasion to enem.
19: 32. was a g. man, 2 K. 5: 1.
22: 36. gentleness made me g., Ps.
18: 35. [are g.
24: 14. in g. strait—his mercies
1 K.8:42. shall hear of thy g. name,
2 Ch. 6: 32.
19: 7. journey is too g. for thee
2 K.4:8.to Shunem,where g.woman
22: 13. g. is the wrath of the Lord
1 Ch. 16: 25. g. is L., greatly to be
praised, Ps. 48: 1.-96: 4.-135:
5.-145: 3.
21: 13. for very g. are his mercies
29: 12. in thine hand to make g.
2 Ch.2:5. house is g. for g.is our G.
9. h. I am to build be wonderf.g.
17:12. Jehosh-t waxed g. exceed-y
28:13.trespass is g. | 34:21.g.wrath
Ezr. 5: 8. to house of g. G. [cov.
Ne. 1: 5. g. and terrible G. keepeth
4: 14. remember the L. who is g.
8: 6. Ezra blessed the g. God
9:32.now our God,the g.mighty G.
Es. 1:20. published, for it is g.
Jb. 5: 25. that thy seed shall be g.
22: 5. is not thy wickedness g.?

Jb. 30:18. by g. force of my disease
35:15.knoweth it not in g. extrem.
36: 18. a g. ransom | 26. God is g.
38: 21. number of thy days is g.
39:11.Wilt trust,bec.strength is g.?
Ps.12:†3.tongue th. speak. g.things
14: 5. were they in g. fear, 53: 5.
19: 11. in keeping of them is g. re-
21: 5. His glory is g. in [ward
25: 11. pardon mine iniq., it is g.
31: 19. Oh how g. is thy goodness
86: 10. art g. doest wondrous
92: 5. how g. thy works
95: 3. L. is a g. God | 99: 2. L g.
103: † 8. g. of mercy [in Zion
135: 5. I know the L. is g. [th.
139: 17. O God, how g. is sum of
Pr. 26:10. The g. G. that formed all
Ec. 9: 13. this wisdom seemed g.
Is. 5: 9. houses even g. and fair
9:2. have seen g. light, Mat.4: 16.
12: 6. g. is the holy One of Israel
19:20. send a saviour and a g. one
53:12.will divide him portion wi.g.
54: 13. g. be peace of thy chil.
Je. 5: 27. are become g. and rich
10: 6. thou art g. thy name is g.
20: 17. her womb to be always g.
32: 18. The g. The Mighty God is
19. g. in counsel,mighty in work
44: 26. have sworn by my g. name
La. 3: 23. new, g. is thy faithfuln.
Eze. 16: 7. thou hast waxed g.
17: 3. g. eagle with g. wings, 7.
24: 9. I will make pile for fire g.
29: 18. a g. service against Tyrus
31: 4. The waters made him g.
36: 23. will sanctify my g. name
38: 19. in that day be g. shaking
Da. 2: 45. g. G. hath made known
4: 3. How g. his signs, mighty
8: 4. ram pushing, he became g.
10: 7. g. quaking fell upon them
Jo. 2: 13. of g. kindness, Jon. 4:2.
3: 13. for their wickedness is g.
Am. 6: 2. thence go to Hamath g.
Mi. 5: 4. be g. unto ends of earth
Zch. 9: 17. how g. his goodness,
how g. his beauty!
Mal. 1: 11. my name shall be g.
among Gentiles, 11.
Mat. 2: 18. In Rama g. mourning
5: 12. be exc-g glad, g. is your reward in heav., Lu. 6: 23, 35.
19. be called g. in kingd. of heav.
6:23.if darkness,how g.that darkn.
8: 24. arose g. tempest, Mk. 4: 37.
26. there was a g. calm
13: 46. pearl of g. price
15: 28. g. is thy faith
19: 22. g. possessions, Mk. 10: 42.
20:25. g.exercise authority [10:43.
26. whoso. be g.among you, Mk.
22:36. Master, wh. is g. com-t?
38. This is first and g. com-t
24: 21. g. tribula., Re. 2:22.-7:14
24. shew g. signs, Lu. 21: 11.
30. power and g. glory, Lu.21:27.
31. g. sound of a trumpet
28: 2. g. earthquake, Ac. 16: 26.
Re. 6: 12.-11: 13.-16: 18.
Mk. 4:32. shooteth out g. branches
5: 11. g. herd of swine feeding
42. with a g. astonishment
10:46.a g.number of peo.,Ac.11:21.
48. cried more a g. deal
Lu. 1: 15. be g. in sight of L., 32.
2: 36. she was of g. age and had
4: 25. g. famine thro-out land
38. was taken with g. fever
5: 29. Levi made a g. feast (2)
7: 16. a g. prophet is risen
8: 37. were taken with g. fear
9: 48. least amo. you, shall be g.
10:2. harvest g. but labourers few
13: 19. it waxed a g. tree
14: 16. man made a g. supper

Lu.16:26.betw. us and you is g.gulf
21: 23. there sh be g. distress,11.
Jn. 6: 18. by reason of a g. wind
21:11.net to la.full of g. fishes [11.
Ac. 5: 5. g. fear on all, 11. Re. 11:
6: 8. did g. wonders and miracles
7: 11. dearth and g. afflic. came
8: 1. there was a g. persecution
2. made g. lamentation
9. giving out he was g. one
10: 11. been a g. sheet, 11: 5.
11:28. be g. dearth thro-out world
19:27. of the g. goddess Diana, 35.
28. g. is Diana of Ephesi. 34.
22: 6. from heaven a g. light
Ro. 9: 2. I have g. heaviness
1 Co 16:9.for a g. door and effectual
g. is my boldness of speech
2 Co. 3: 12. we use g. plainness of
7: 4. g. is my boldness, g. is
8: 2. in a g. trial of affliction
22. upon the g. confid. I have
Ep. 2: 4. for his g. love wherewith
5: 32. This is a g. mystery: but
Col. 4: 13. he hath a g. zeal for you
1 Th.2:17. to see face with g. desire
1 Ti. 3: 13. g. boldness in the faith
16. n.is mystery of godliness
6: 6. with content-t is g. gain
2 Ti. 2: 20. in g. house vessels of
Tit. 2: 13. appearing of the g. God
He. 4: 14. have a g. high priest
7: 4. consider how g.this man was
10: 32. ye endured a g. fight
35. wh. hath g. recompence
13: 20. that g. Shepherd of sheep
Ja. 3: 5. how g. a matter a little
1 Pe. 3: 4. in sight of G. of g. price
Re. 1: 10. heard a g. voice, 11: 12,
15.-16: 1, 17.-19: 1 -21: 3.
6: 4. given unto him g. sword
8: 8. as it were a g. mountain
10. there fell g. star fr. heaven
9: 2. as smoke of a g. furnace
14. bound in g. river Euphrates
11: 19. earthquake and g. hail
12: 1. a g. wonder in heaven
3. g. dragon having seven heads
9. the g. dragon was cast out
12. g. wrath bec. he knoweth
14. two wings of a g. eagle
13: 2. dragon gave him g. author.
13. he doeth g. wonders, so th.
14: 2. as voice of a g. thunder
19. into g. winepress of wrath
Re 15: 1. ano. sign in heaven, g.
16: 9. scorched with g. heat
12. his vial upon g. river
19. g. Bab. came in remembr.
17: 5. Babylon the g. the mother
of harlots, 18: 2.
18: 21. stone like g. millstone
19: 2. judged the g. whore, 17: 1.
17. gather unto supper of g. G.
20: 1. a g. chain in his hand
11. I saw a g. white throne
21: 12. had a wall g. and high
See CITY, COMPANY, CONGREGATION, CRY, DAY, DESTRUCTION.

GREAT evil.

1 S. 6: 9. he hath done us g. e.
Ne. 13: 27. hearken to do this g.e.
Ec. 2: 21. This is vanity, and g. e.
Je. 16:10.Whf. L. pronounced g. e.
26:19. Thus might we procure g.e.
32: 42. I bro-t g. e. upon people
44:7.Whf. commit g. e. ag. souls?
Da. 9: 12. bringing upon us g. e.
See EXCEEDING, JOY.

GREAT king, s.

2 K. 18: 19. thus saith the g. k.,
28. Is. 36: 4, 13. [builded
Ezr. 5: 11. which a g. k. of Israel
Ps 47: 2. the Lord is g.K. over all
48: 2. is Zion, city of the g. K.
95: 3. L. is a g. K. above all gods
136:17. thanks to him smote g.k.

Ec. 9: 14 came a g. k. against it
Je.25:14. g.k-s serve thems., 27: 7.
Mal. 1: 14. I am a g. K., saith L.
Mat.5:35. Jeru-. is the city of g. K.

GREAT men. [17: 8

2 S. 7: 9. like name of g.m., 1 Ch.
2 K. 10: 6. Ahab's sons with g.m.
11. Jehu slew all Ahab's g. m.
Ne 11:14 Zabdiel,son of one of g.m.
Jb 32:9. g.m. are not always wise
Pr.18:16. a gift bringeth bef. g. m.
25: 6. stand not in place of g. m.
Je. 5: 5. I will get me unto g. m.
52: 13. houses of g. m. burned he
Eze. 21: 14. sword of g. m. slain
Jon. 3:†7. with consent of his g.m.
Na. 3: 10. all her g. m. in chains
Re. 6: 15. g. m. hid in dens rocks
18: 23. merchants g. m. of earth

GREAT multitude, s.

Nu. 32:1. Gad had a g.m. of cattle
1 K. 20:13. Hast thou seen all g.m.
28. will deliver g. m. into hand
2 Ch. 13: 8. ye be a g. m. ye have
20: 2. cometh a g. m. ag. thee
15. not dismayed by rea. of g.m.
28:5. carried g.m. capt. to Damas.
Jb. 31: 34. Did I fear a g. m.
Is.16:14.that g.m. sh. be contemn.
Je. 44:15. women stood by, a g.m.
Eze.47:9. sh.be a very g. m. of fish
Da. 11: 11. king shall set a g. m.
Mat. 4: 25. g. m-s followed him,
8: 1.-12: 15.-19: 2.-20: 29. Mk.
3: 7, 8.-4: 1. Jn. 6: 2.
8:18. when Jesus saw g. m-s, 14:
14. Mk. 9: 14.
13:2.g. m-s were gath-d,Lu.14:25.
15:30. g. m-s came, having lame,
33. bread to fill so g. m., Mk.8:1.
21:8. g. m. spread garm-ts in way
26:47.with Judas g. m.,Mk.14:43.
Lu. 5: 6. inclosed g. m. of fishes
15. g. m-s came to hear, 6: 17.
Jn. 5: 3. lay a g. m. of impotent
Ac. 14: 1. g. m. of Jews believed
17: 4. of the devout Greeks g. m.
Re. 7:9. g. m. no man could num.
19:6.heard as it were voice of g.m.

GREAT nation, s.

Ge. 12: 2. I will make of thee a g.
n., 18: 18.-46: 3. Ex. 32: 10.
17:20.will make Ishm. g.n.,21:18.
De 4: 6. this g. n. is a wise people
26: 5. became g. n. and mighty
Jos. 23: 9. hath driven out g. n-s
Ps. 135: 10. smote g. n-s, slew k-s
Je. 6: 22. a g.n. shall be raised fr.
50:9.ag. Bab. an assembly of g.n.
41. people from north, a g. n.
Eze. 31:6. und. his shadow all g.n.

GREAT people.

De. 2: 10. Emims dwelt, a p. g.
21. Zamzummims, a p. g. many
9:2. a p.g., chil. of Anakim[g. p.
Jos. 17: 14. why but one lot, I am
15.if be a g.p. | 17.Thou art g.p.
1 K.3:8.a g.p. th. cannot be numb.
9. who able to judge g. p.? 2 Ch.
5: 7. Da. wise son over g.p.[1:10.
Is. 13: 4. noise in mts. as of g. p.
Jo. 2: 2. a g. p. hath not been ever

GREAT power. [like

Ex. 32: 11. thy peo. out of E. with
g. p., 2 K. 17: 36. Ne. 1: 10.
Nu. 14:17. let p. of my lord be g.
Jos.17:17.art a great peo. hast g.p.
Jb. 23: 6. Will he plead with g.p.?
Ps. 147: 5. Great is our L., of g.p.
Je. 27: 5. I have made the earth,
man and beasts, by my g. p.,
32: 17. [out g. p.
Eze. 17:9. it shall wither even with-
Na. 1: 3. L. slow to anger, g. in p.
Mk.13:26.com-g in clouds wi. g. p.
Ac. 4: 33. with g. p. gave apostles
8: 10. This man is the g. p. of G.

Re. 11 : 17. hast taken thy g. p.
18:1. angel fr. heav., having g. p.
GREAT sea.
Nu. 34:6. ye the g. s. for border, 7.
Jos. 1 : 4. fr. wilderness unto g. s.
9 : 1. when kings in coasts of g. s.
15:12. west border was to the g. s.,
47. inheritance of Judah, to g. s.
23 : 4. I have cut off to the g. s.
Eze. 47 : 10. as fish of g. s. many
15. border of land from g. s.
19. river to the g. s., 20.-48 : 28.
Da. 7:2. four winds strove upon g. s.
See SIN.
GREAT slaughter.
Jos. 10 : 10. slew them with a g. s.
20. made end of slaying wi. g. s.
Ju. 11:33. smote Ammon-s wi. g. s.
15:8. Sams. smote Philis. wi. g. s.
1 S. 4:10. Philis. smote wi. g. s., 17.
6:19. L. had smitten peo. wi. g. s.
19 : 8. Da. slew Philis. with g. s.,
2 S. 18 : 7. a g. s. of 20,000 men [28:5.
1 K. 20 : 21. slew Syrians with g. s.
2 Ch. 13 : 17. slew Isr. with a g. s.
28 : 5. smote Ahaz wi. g. s. [fall
Is. 30:25. day of g. s. when towers
34 : 6. L. hath a g. s. in Idumea
GREAT, with small. [g.
Ge. 19 : 11. smote wi. blindn. s. and
De. 1 : 17. shall hear s. as g. [s.
25 : 13. not divers weights, g. and
14. not divers measures, g. and s.
1 S. 5 : 9. smote the men s. and g.
20 : 2. my fa. will do noth. g. or s.
30 : 2. slew not any either g. or s.
19. was noth. lack. nei. s. nor g.
1 K. 22 : 31. Fight not with s. nor
g., 2 Ch. 18:30. [2 Ch. 34:30.
2 K. 23:2. s. and g. went into ho[illegible]
25:26. all peo. s. and g. came to E.
1 Ch. 26:13. cast lots as well s. as g.
2 Ch. 15:13. be put to death, s. or g.
31:15. to give to breth., g. and s.
36:18. into hands vessels, g. and s.
Es. 1 : 5. made feast unto g. and s.
20. to husbands honour, g. and s.
Jb. 3 : 19. s. and g. are there
37 : 6. saith to s. rain, to g. rain
Ps. 104 : 25. thi. creeping, s. and g.
115 : 13. that fear the L., s. and g.
Ec. 2 : 7. I poss-s of g. and s. cattle
Je. 16 : 6. g. and s. shall die in la.
Am. 8 : 5. the ephah s., shekel g.
Ac. 26 : 22. witnessing to s. and g.
Re. 11:18. reward to them, s. and g.
13 : 16. s. and g. to receive a mark
19 : 5. praise our God, s. and g.
18. eat flesh of all men, s. and g.
20 : 12. I saw dead, s. and g. bef.
So GREAT. [God
Ex. 32:21. bro-t s. g. a sin upon th.
De. 4 : 7. nation s. g. hath G. ? 8.
1 K. 3 : 9. who judge s. g. peo.? 2
Ch. 1 : 10.
Ps. 77:13. who s. g. a G. as our G.?
103:11. s. g. his mercy tow. them
Mat. 8 : 10. not found s. g. faith in
Isr., Lu. 7 : 9. [titude
15:33. bread as to fill s. g. a mul-
2 Co. 1:10. deliv. us fr. s. g. a death
He. 2 : 3. if we neglect s. g. salva.?
12:1. seeing we are compassed about
with s. g. a cloud of witnesses
Ja. 3 : 4. ships tho. s. g. yet turned
Re. 16 : 18. an earthquake and s. g.
18 : 17. in one hour s. g. riches
come to nought
GREAT stone, s. [mouth
Ge. 29 : 2. g. s. was upon well's
De. 27 : 2. set up g. s-s and plaster
Jos. 10 : 11. L. cast g. s-s fr. heav.
18. Roll g. s-s upon mouth of
cave, 27. [und. an oak
24 : 26. Josh. took g. s., and set it
1 S. 6:14. cart came where was g. s.
15. Levites put them on the g. s.
1 S. 6:18. unto g. s. of Abel [g. s.
14 : 33. Ye have transgr-d, roll a
2 S. 20 : 8. were at g. s. in Gibeon
1 K. 5 : 17. g. s-s to lay foundation
7 : 10. founda. of g. s., Ezr. 5 : 8.
2 Ch. 26:15. engines to shoot g. s-s
Ezr. 6 : 4. three rows of g. s-s and
Je. 43 : 9. take g. s-s and hide them
Mat. 27:60. a g. s. to door of sepul.
Mk. 16 : 4. s. rolled aw., it was g.
GREAT thing, s. [g. t.
De. 4 : 32. whe. such thing as this
10 : 21. God that hath done g. t-s
1 S. 12 : 16. see this g. t. L. will do
24. consider how g. t-s he hath
26 : 25. shalt do g. t-s and prevail
2 S. 7 : 21. word's sake done g. t-s
23. do for you g. t-s and terrible
2 K. 5:13. if proph. bid do some g. t.
8 : 4. tell g. t-s Elisha hath done
13. dog, th. he sho. do this g. t.'
1 Ch. 17 : 19. making known g. t-s
Jb. 5 : 9. to God who doeth g. t-s,
9 : 10.-37 : 5. [thee
Ps. 71:19. hast done g. t-s who like
106:21. forgat G. who done g. t-s
126 : 2. Lord hath done g. t-s, 3
Je. 33 : 3. shew thee g. mighty t-s
45 : 5. seekest g. t-s for thyself?
Da. 7 : 8. a mouth speaking g. t-s,
20. Re. 13 : 5. [of my law
Ho. 8 : 12. I have writ. the g. t-s
Jo. 2 : 20. bec. he hath done g. t-s
21. fear not, L. will do g. t-s
Mk. 3 : 8. heard what g. t-s he did
5 : 19. tell how g. t-s Lord hath
done, 20. Lu. 8:39. [t-s
Lu. 1 : 49. he th. is mighty done g.
8 : 39. published how g. t-s Jesus
Ac. 9:16. shew g. t-s he must suffer
1 Co. 9 : 11. is it g. t. if we reap
carnal things? [ters be transf.
2 Co. 11 : 15. no g. t. if his minis-
Ja. 3 : 5. tongue boasteth g. t-s
Very GREAT.
Ge. 26:13. Isaac grew until he v. g.
Ex. 11:3. Mo. was v. g. in the land
Nu. 11:33. L. smote wi. v. g. plague
13 : 28. cities are walled and v. g.
22 : 17. promote unto v. g. honour
1 S. 2 : 17. sin of young men v. g.
4 : 10. there was a v. g. slaughter
5 : 9. ag. city with v. g. destruc.
14 : 15. v. g. trembling | 20. v. g.
25:2. Nabal a v. g. man [discomfit.
2 S. 18:17. laid v. g. heap upon Abs.
19 : 32. Barzillai was v. g. man
1 K. 10:2. q. of Sheba wi. v. g. train
1 Ch. 21 : 13. v. g. are his mercies
2 Ch. 16:14. a v. g. burning for Asa
24:24. L. deliv-d v. g. host [10:1.
30:13. assembled v. g. cong., Ezr.
33 : 14. raised wall a v. g. height
Ne. 8 : 17. there was a v. g. gladn.
Jb. 1 : 3. Job a v. g. household
2 : 13. they saw his grief was v. g.
Ps. 104 : 1. O my G., thou art v. g.
Eze. 47 : 9. sh. be v. g. mult. of fish
Da. 8 : 8. the he goat waxed v. g.
11:25. k. of south. with v. g. army
Jo. 2 : 11. camp v. g. he is strong
Zch. 14 : 4. shall be a v. g. valley
Mat. 21:8. v. g. mult. spread garm.
Mk. 8 : 1. mult. v. g. having noth.
16 : 4. stone was rolled away was v.
Was GREAT. [g.
Ge. 6 : 5. wickedness of man w. g.,
13:6. their substance w. g. so that
1 K. 3 : 4. Gibeon, that w. g. high
2 K. 3 : 27. w. g. indigna. ag. Isr.
Es. 4 : 3. decree came w. g. mourn.
9:4. Mord. w. g. in king's h., 10:3.
Jb. 31:25. If I rej. bec. wealth w. g.
Ec. 2:9. I w. g. and increas. more
La. 1 : 1. she w. g. among nations
Da. 4 : 10. the tree's height w. g.
Mat. 7:27. g. w. the fall of it, Lu. 6:49.
GREAT waters.
2 S. 22 : † 17. drew me out of g. w.,
Ps. 18 : † 16. [w.
Ps. 29 : † 3. voice of L. is upon g.
32 : 6. in g. w. sh. not come nigh
77:19. thy way in sea, path in g. w.
107 : 23. that do business in g. w.
144:7. send, deliv. me out of g. w.
Is. 23:3. by g. w. the seed of Sihor
Je. 41:12. found Ishm. by g. w. of
51 : 55. her waves roar like g. w.
Eze. 1 : 24. noise of wings like g. w.
17 : 5. he placed seed by g. w.
8. planted in a good soil by g. w.
26 : 19. when g. w. sh. cover thee
27:26. rowers bro-t thee into g. w.
31 : 7. fair, for his root by g. w.
15. the g. w. were stayed [w.
32 : 13. will destr. beasts beside g.
Ha. 3 : 15. didst walk thro. g. w.
GREAT while. [17.
2 S. 7:19. g. w. to come, 1 Ch. 17:
Mk. 1 : 35. rising g. w. before day
Lu. 10 : 13. had g. w. ago repented
Ac. 28 : 6 barbarians looked a g. w.
GREAT work, s.
Ex. 14 : 31. Isr. saw g. w. L. did
Ju. 2 : 7. had seen all g. w-s of L.
1 Ch. 29:1. son young, and w. is g.
Ne. 4 : 19. w. is g. we are separa.
6 : 3. I am doing a g. w., I can-t
Ps. 111:2. w-s of L. are g., Re. 15:3.
Ec. 2 : 4. I made g. w-s, I builded
GREATER. [houses
Ge. 1 : 16. g. light to rule the day
4:13. punishm. g. than I can bear
39 : 9. is none g. in this h. than I
41 : 40. only in throne will I be g.
48:19. younger bro. be g. than he
Ex. 18 : 11. I know L. is g. than all
Nu. 14:12. of thee g. na., De. 9:14.
De. 1 : 28. people is g. than we
4 : 38. drive nations g. than thou,
7 : 1.-9 : 1.-11 : 23. [Ai
Jos. 10:2. bec. Gibeon was g. than
1 S. 14 : 30. not been g. slaughter
2 S. 13 : 15. hatred g. than love
16. this evil is g. than other [47.
1 K. 1 : 37. his throne g. than Da.,
1 Ch. 11 : 9. David waxed g. and g.
2 Ch. 3 : 5. g. ho. he ceiled with fir
Es. 9 : 4. Mordecai waxed g. and g.
Jb. 33 : 12. ans., G. is g. than man
La. 4 : 6. g. than punishm. of Sod.
Eze. 8:6. shalt see g. abomina., 13, 15.
Da. 11 : 13. set forth mult. g. than
Am. 6:2. their border g. than your
Hag. 2 : 9. glory of latter house g.
Mat. 11:11. not risen g. than Jn.,
least in kingdom g., Lu. 7 : 28.
12:6. in this pla. one g. than tem.
41. g. than Jonas here. Lu. 11:32.
42. behold, a g. than Sol. is here,
Lu. 11 : 31. [40. Lu. 20:47.
23 : 14. receive g. damna., Mk. 12:
17. is g. the gold, or the temple?
19. is g. the gift, or the altar?
Mk. 4 : 32. sown, it becometh g.
12 : 31. is no com-t g. than these
Lu. 12:18. down barns, and build g.
22:27. g. he that sitteth or serveth?
Jn. 1:50. shalt see g. things, 5:20.-
4:12. Art thou g. than Jac.? [14:12
5 : 36. I have g. witn. than of Jn.
8 : 53. art thou g. than fa. Ab.?
10 : 29. My Fa. g. than all, 14:28.
13:16. serv. not g. than lord, 15:20.
15 : 13. g. love no man than this
19 : 11. that deliv. me hath g. sin
Ac. 15 : 28. to lay upon you no g.
burden [lesser
Ro. 9 : † 12. The g. shall serve the
1 Co. 14 : 5. g. is he th. prophesieth
15:6 of whom g. part remain unto
He. 6:13. bec. he could swear by no
16. For men verily swear by g. [g.
9 : 11. g. and more perfect taberna.

He.11:26.Est.reproach of C.g.riches
Ja. 3: 1. we sh. receive g. condem.
2 Pe.2:11.angels wh.are g.in power
1 Jn. 3:20. G. is g. than our heart
4: 4. g. he that is in you, than he
5:9.witness of G. is g. this is witn.
3 Jn. 4. I have no g. joy than to

GREATEST. [hear

1 Ch. 12:14. least over 100, g. over
29.g. part had kept ward of Saul
Jb. 1: 3. was g. of all in the east
Mat. 13:32. grown, is g. am. herbs
18:1. Who g. in kingd. of heaven
4. as this little child, same is g.
23: 11. he that is g. be your serv.
Mk. 9:34. disputed who be g.,Lu.9:
Lu. 22: 24. strife who be g. [46.
26. he that is g. be as younger
1 Co. 13: 13. g. of these is charity

GREATEST with least.

Je.6:13. fr. l. unto g. given to covetousness, 8:10. [g., He. 8:11.
31: 34. all know me, from l. unto
42:1. all people fr. l. unto g. came
8. Jere. called people fr. l. to g.
44:12. they shall die, fr. l. unto g.
Jon. 3: 5. on sackcl. from g. to l.
Ac. 8: 10. gave heed from l. to g.

GREATLY. [row

Ge.3:16. I will g. multiply thy sor-
7: 18. waters incr-d g. upon earth
19: 3. Lot pressed upon them g.
24: 35. L. hath blessed my master
27: † 33. Isaac trembled g. [g.
32: 7. Then Jacob was g. afraid
Ex. 19:18. whole mount quaked g.
Nu.11:10.anger of L. was kindled g.
14: 39. Mo. told, peo. mourned g.
De. 15: 4. Lord shall g. bless thee
17:17.nor sh. he g. multiply silver
Ju. 2:15. L. ag. them, g. distressed
6: 6. Israel was g. impoverished
1 S.11:6. Saul's anger was kindl. g.
15. men of Israel rejoiced g.
12: 18. the people g. feared the L.
16:21. he loved him g. became his
17:11.heard Philis., they g. afraid
28: 5 Saul, his heart trembled g.
30: 6. David was g. distressed
2 S. 10:5. men g. asha., 1 Ch. 19:5.
12:5. David's anger was g. kindled
13:†15.hated her with gr.hatred g.
† 36. king with gr. weeping g.
14:†25.not man in Isr. to praise g.
24:10. I have sinned g.,1 Ch.21:8.
1 K.2:12.Sol.'s kingd. was establ.g.
5: 7. Hiram heard, he rejoiced g.
18: 3. Obadiah feared the Lord g.
1 Ch. 4: 38. house of fa-s incr-d g.
16: 25. great is the Lord, g. to be
praised, Ps. 48: 1.-96:4.-145:3.
2 Ch.25:10.anger g.kindled ag.Jud.
33:12. Manasseh humbled hims.g.
Ezr. 10: † 13. we have g. offended
Jb. 8:7. latter end sho. g. increase
Ps.21:1. in thy salv. how g. rejoice
28:7. heart g. rejoi-h, I will praise
38:6.I am bowed down g.go mourn.
45: 11. So k. g. desire thy beauty
47:9.belong to God,he is g.exalted
62: 2. I shall not be g. moved
65: 9. g. enrichest it with river of
71:23.lips sh.g.rejoice when I sing
78: 59. he g. abhorred Israel
89:7.G.g. to be feared in assembly
105:24. incr-d his peo. g., 107:38.
109: 30. I will g. praise the Lord
112: 1. delighteth g. in his com-t
116: 10. I was g. afflicted
119:51. have had me g. in derision
Pr. 23: 24. fa. of righteous g. rejoi.
Is. 42: 17. g. asha. trust in images
61:10. I will g. rejoice in the Lord
Je. 3: 1. sh. land be g. polluted?
4: 10. thou hast g. deceived peo.
9: 19. we are g. confounded
20:11.persecutors shall be g. asha.
Eze. 20: 13. sab-s they g. polluted
25: 12. Edom hath g. offended
Dan. 5: 9. Belshazzar g. troubled
9: 23. art g. beloved, 10: 11, 19.
Ob. 2. small, thou art g. despised
Jon.4:†4.art g. angry?†9. | †9.I am
Zph. 1:14. day of L. hasteth g. [g.
Zch. 9: 9. Rejoice g. O dau. of Zion
Mat. 27: 14. governor marvelled g.
Mk. 5: 23. Jairus besought him g.
38. he seeth them th. wailed g.
9:15. beheld, they were amazed g.
12: 27. G. of living, ye do g. err
Jn.3:29.rejoiceth g.bec.of bridegr.'s
Ac.3:11.ran to porch, g. wondering
6:7.disciples multiplied in Jerus.g.
1 Co. 16:12. I g. desired Apollos to
Ph.1:8. how g. I long after you all
4: 10. I rejoiced g. that your care
1 Th. 3: 6. desiring g. to see us
2 Ti. 1: 4. g. desiring to see thee
4: 15. hath g. withst-d our words
1 Pe.1:6.ye g.rejoice tho.in heavin.
2 Jn.4. rejoi-d g. that I found chil.
3 Jn. 3. I rejoiced g. when breth.
See FEARED. [testi.

GREATNESS.

Ex. 15: 7. in g. of thy excellency
16. by g. of thine arm sh. be still
Nu. 14: 19. acc. unto g. of mercy
De.3:24. begun to shew serv. thy g.
5: 24. Lord hath shewed us his g.
9: 26. hast redeemed thro. thy g.
11: 2. chil. who have not seen g.
32:3. ascribe g. unto our G. [g.
1 Ch. 17:19. to own heart done this
21. to make thee a name of g.
29:11. Thine, O L. is the g.,power
2 Ch.9:6.g. of thy wisd. not shewed
24:27. g. of the burdens upon him
Ne.13:22.spare me acc.to g. of mer.
Es. 10: 2. declara. of g. of Mord.
Ps. 66: 3. by g. enem. submit to
71: 21. Thou shalt increase my g.
79:11. acc. to g. of power preserve
145: 3. g. is unsearchable
6. I declare thy g. [g.
150:2. praise him acc. to his excell.
Pr. 5: 23. in g. of folly go astray
Is.40:26. calleth by g. of his might
57: 10. wearied in g. of thy way
63: 1. trav-g in g. of his strength
Je. 13:22. For g. of iniq. thy skirts
Eze. 31: 2. Whom like in thy g.?
7. was he fair in his g. [heav.
Da. 4: 22. thy g. reacheth unto
7:27. g. of kingd. be giv. to saints
Ep. 1:19. exceeding g. of his power

GREAVES.

1 S. 17: 6. Goliath had g. of brass

GRE'CIA.

Da. 8: 21. rough goat is king of G.
10: 20. when I am gone king of G.
11:2.sh. stir up all ag. realm of G.

GRE'CIANS.

Jo. 3: 6. chil. of Jud. sold unto G.
Ac. 6: 1. arose murmuring of G.
9: 29. Paul disputed ag. the G.
11:20.who spake unto G.preaching

GREECE.

Zch.9:13.thy sons, O Zion, ag. sons,
Ac. 20: 2. Paul came to G. [O G.

GREEDILY.

Pr. 21: 26. He coveteth g. all day
Eze.22:12.g.gained of thy neighb-s
Jude 11. ran g. after error of Ba-

GREEDINESS. [laam

Ep. 4:19. work all unclean. with g.

GREEDY.

Ps. 17: 12. Like lion g. of his prey
Pr. 1: 19. so is ev. one g. of gain
15:27. He g. of gain troubl. house
Is.56:11.they are g. dogs, can never
1 Ti. 3: 3. not g. of filthy lucre

GREEK. [Language.] [20.

Lu. 23: 38. superscrip. in G., Jn. 19:
Ac.21:37.capt. said, Canst speak G.
Re.9:11. in G. hath name Apollyon

GREEK. [Race.]

Mk. 7: 26. The woman was a G.
Ac.16:1.father of Tim. a G., 3. [†10.
Ro. 1: 16. Jew first, also to G., 2:†9,
10: 12. there is no difference betw.
Jew and G., Ga. 3:28. Col.3:11.
Ga. 2: 3. nor Titus, being a G.

GREEKS.

Jn.7:†35. go unto dispersed am. G.?
12: 20. certain G. came to worship
Ac. 14:1. mult. of G. beli., 17:4, 12.
18: 4. he persuaded Jews and G.
17. G. took Sosthenes and beat
19: 10. Jews and G. heard word
17. was known to all G. at Eph.
20:21. Testifying to G. repentance
21: 28. he bro-t G. into temple
Ro. 1: 14. I am debtor both to G.
1 Co. 1: 22. G. seek after wisdom
23. Christ crucifi. to G. foolishn.
24. to called, Jews and G. Christ

GREEN.

Ge. 1:30. to beast have giv. g. herb
9:3. as g. herb have I giv. you all
30:37. Jac. took rods of g. poplar
Ex. 10:15. remained not any g. thi.
Le. 2:14. offer for firstfruits g. ears
23:14. eat no g. ears until an off-g
Ju.16:7.If bind me with 7 g. withs
8. brought to her 7 g. withs
2 K. 19:26. inhab. as g. herbs, Is.
Es.1:6.g. and blue hangings [37:27.
Jb. 8: 16. He is g. before the sun
15: 32. his branch shall not be g.
39:8.wild ass searcheth aft. g. thi.
Ps. 23:2.me lie down in g. pastures
37: 2. they sh. wither as g. herb
35. seen wicked like g. bay tree
92:†14. in old age they shall be g.
Can. 1: 16. art fair, our bed is g.
2:13. fig tree putteth forth g. figs
Is.15:6. grass faileth, is no g. thing
Je. 11: 16. L. called name g. olive
17: 8. as tree spread. roots, leaf be
Ho. 14: 8. I am like g. fir tree [g.
Am. 7: † 1. he formed g. worms in
Mk. 6:39. companies upon g. grass
Re. 8: 7. all g. grass was burnt up
9:4. com-d not to hurt any g. thi.

GREEN tree, s. [t.

De.12:2.nations served gods und.g.
1 K. 14:23. images und. every g.t.,
2 K. 17: 10. [t., 2 Ch. 28: 4
2 K. 16: 4. Asa sac. under every g
Ps.52:8.I am like g. olive t. in h. of
Is 57:5. inflaming yours. und. g.t.
Je. 2: 20. under g. t. wanderest
3:6.und. every g. t. played harlot
13.scattered thy ways under g.t.
17:2. chil. remem. grove by g. t-s
Eze.6:13.thy slain be und. ev. g.t.
17:24. know I have dried up g. t.
20: 47. it shall devour every g. t.
Lu. 23: 31. if do these things in a g.

GREENISH. [t.

Le.13:49.if plague be g. in garment
14: 37. if plague be with streaks g.

GREENNESS.

Jb. 8: 12. Whilst it is yet in his g.

GREET, ETH.

1 S. 25:5. go to Nabal g. him
Ro. 16: 3. g.Priscilla and Aquila
5. g. church | 6. g. Mary who
8. g. Amplias | 11. g. household
1 Co. 16: 20. breth. g. you, Ph.4:21.
20. g. ye one another, 2 Co.13:12.
1 Pe. 5: 14. [g. you
Col.4:14.Luke physician and Demas
1 Th. 5: 26. g. breth. with a kiss
2 Ti. 4: 21. Eubulus g-h thee
Tit. 3: 15. g. them that love us in
2 Jn. 13. chil. of elect sister g. thee
3 Jn. 14. g. the friends by name

GREETING, S.

Mat. 23:7. g-s in markets, and to be
called of men, Lu.11:43.-20:46.

Ac. 15 : 23. The apostles, and elders, and brethren, send g.
23:26. Lysias unto Felix sendeth g.
Ja. 1 : 1. to the 12 tribes scatt., g.

GREW.

Ge. 2 : 5. Lord made herb bef. it g.
19:25. overthrew that g. upon gro.
21:8. Isaac g., 26:13 | 21:20. Ishm.
25 : 27. boys g. | 47 : 27. Israel g.
Ex. 1 : 12. more afflicted, more g.
2:10. Moses g. | Ju. 11:2. his wife's sons g.
Ju. 13 : 24. Samson g.
1 S. 2 : 21. child Sam. g. bef. Lord, 26.—3:19.
2 S. 5:10. David g. great
12 : 3. it g. up together with him
Eze. 17 : 6. It g. and became a vine
Da. 4 : 11. tree g. was strong, 20.
Jon. 1 : † 11. sea g. more tempestu.
Mk 4: 7. thorns g. up and choked
5 : 26. nothing bettered, g. worse
Lu. 1:80. child g. waxed strong, 2:40.
13:19. it g. and waxed a gr. tree
Ac. 7:17. peo. g. and multipl. in E.
12 : 24. word of G. g. and multip.
19:20. So mightily g. word of God

GREYHOUND.

Pr. 30:31. four comely in going, a g.

GRIEF, S.

Ge. 26:35. wh. were a g. unto Isaac
1 S. 1 : 16. out of g. have I spoken
25 : 31. this sh. be no g. unto thee
2 Ch. 6:29. when ev. one know own g.
Jb 2:13. saw his g. was very great
6 : 2. Oh that my g. were weighed
† 3. want words to express my g.
16 : 5. moving of lips assuage g.
6. Tho. I speak, g. not assuaged
Ps. 6 : 7. consumed bec. of g., 31:9.
31 : 10. my life is spent with g.
69:26. talk to g. of those wounded
139 : † 24. see if there be g. in me
147 : † 3. he bindeth up their g.
Pr. 17:25. A foolish son g. to father
Ec. 1 : 18. in much wisd. much g.
2 : 23. his days sorrows, travail g.
Is. 1 : † 13. it is g. even meeting
17:11. harvest be heap in day of g.
53 : 3. a man acquainted with g.
4. he hath borne our g-s carried
10. it pleased L., he put him to g.
Je. 6 : 7. bef. me continually is g.
10 : 19. I said, Truly, this is a g.
45 : 3. L. added g. to my sorrow
La. 3:32. tho. cause g. he will have compassion
Eze. 32 : †9. will provoke peo. to g.
Jon. 4:6. gourd, to deliver him fr. g.
2 Co. 2:5. if g. hath not grieved me
He. 13 : 17. do it with joy not g.
1 Pe. 2 : 19. toward God endure g.

GRIEVANCE.

Ha. 1:3. why cause me to behold g.?
†13. purer eyes than to look on g.

GRIEVE.

1 S. 2:33. man be to g. thine heart
2 K. 3:†19. g. ev. good piece of land
1 Ch. 4 : 10. fr. evil, th. it not g. me
Ps. 78:40. how oft did they g. him
La. 3 : 33. doth not willingly g. men
Eph. 4:30. g. not Holy Spirit of God

GRIEVED.

Ge. 6:6. it repented L. he made man, g. him at his heart
34 : 7. Jacob's sons were g. and wroth
45 : 5. be not g. that ye sold me
49 : 23. archers have sorely g. him
Ex. 1 : 12. they were g. bec. of Isr.
De. 15:10. sh. not be g. when givest
Ju. 10:16. his soul g. for misery of Isr.
1 S. 1:8. why is thy heart g.?
15:11. it g. Sam., he cried unto L.
20 : 3. Let not Jona. know lest g.
34. Jona. arose, he was g. for Da.
30 : 6. bec. soul of all peo. was g.
2 S. 19 : 2. how king was g. for son
Ne. 2: 10. it g. them exceedingly
13 : 8. it g. me sore, I cast forth all
Es. 4 : 4. was queen exceedingly g.
Jb. 4 : 2. if we commune, thou g.?
30:25. was my soul g. for poor?
Ps. 73 : 21. Thus my heart was g.
95 : 10. 40 years was I g. wi. gene.
112 : 10. wicked shall see it, be g.
119:158. I beheld transgr-rs was g.
139:21. am not I g. wi. those ag. thee
Is. 54 : 6. L. called thee as wom. g.
57:10. therefore thou wast not g.
Je. 5 : 3. hast stricken, they not g.
Da. 7:15. I Dan. was g. in spirit
11 : 30. he shall be g. and return
Am. 6 : 6. not g. for afflict. of Jo.
Mk. 3 : 5. g. for hardness of hearts
10:22. he went away g. he had great
Jn. 21:17. Pe. was g. bec. he said
Ac. 4 : 2. g. that they taught peo.
9 : † 38. not be g. to come to them
16:18. Paul being g. said to spirit
Ro. 14:15. if bro. g. with thy meat
2 Co. 2 : 4. I wrote not th. ye be g.
5. caused grief, he hath not g. me
He. 3:10. I was g. with that genera.
17. with whom was he g. 40 years?

GRIEVETH, ING.

Ru. 1 :13. it g-h me for your sakes
Pr. 26:15. g-h to bring it to mouth
Eze. 28:24. no more a g-g thorn unto Isr.

GRIEVOUS.

Ge. 12 : 10. famine was g. in land
18 : 20. L. said, bec. their sin is g.
21:11. thing very g. in Ab.'s sight
12. Let it not be g. in thy sight
41 : 31. the famine shall be very g.
50:11. is g. mourning to Egypt-s
Ex. 8:24. came g. swarm of flies
9:3. g. murrain | 18. very g. hail, 24.
10:14. locusts were very g.
1 K. 2:8. Shimei, cursed wi. g. curse
12:4. g. service lighter. 2 Ch. 10:4.
Ps 10:5. His ways always g.
31 : 18. speak g. things ag. righte.
Pr. 15 : 1. g. words stir up anger
10. Correction g. unto him that forsaketh
Ec. 2:17. work und sun is g. to me
Is. 15:4. his life sh. be g. unto him
21:2. g. vision is declared unto me
Je. 6:28. they are all g. revolters
10:19. Woe is me, my wound is g.
14 : 17. broken with a g. blow
16:4. they shall die of g. deaths
23 : 19. a g. whirlwind on wicked
30:12. thy wound g., Na. 3 : 19.
Mat. 23:4. bind burdens g., Lu. 11:46.
Ac. 20:29. g. wolves enter am. you
25 : 7. Jews laid g. complaints ag. Paul
Ph. 3 : 1. to me is not g.
He. 12:11. no chast g joyous but g.
1 Jn. 5:3. his com-ts are not g.
Re. 16:2. g. sore upon men had mark

GRIEVOUSLY.

Is. 9:1. afterw. did more g. afflict her
Je. 23:19. it sh. fall g. upon wicked
La. 1 : 8. Jerus. hath g. sinned
20. heart is turned, I g. rebelled
Eze. 14:13. land sin-th by tresp-g g.
Mi. 1:†9. she is g. sick of wounds
Mat. 8 : 6. my serv. g. tormented
15 : 22. my daughter is g. vexed

GRIEVOUSNESS.

Is. 10:1. write g. they prescribed
21:15. they fled from the g. of war

GRIND.

Ju. 16: 21. Samson did g. in prison
Jb. 31:10. let my wife g. unto ano.
Ec. 12:†3. grinders cease g. little
Is. 3:15. what mean ye to g. poor?
47:2. Take millstones and g. meal
La. 5:13. took young men to g.
Mat. 21 : 44. g. him to powder, Lu. 20 : 18.

GRINDERS.

Jb. 29:†17. I brake g. of wicked
Ec. 12:3. g. cease, bec. they are few

GRINDING.

Ec. 12:4. when sound of g. is low
Mat. 24:41. two women g., Lu. 17:35.

GRISLED=GRIZZLED.

Ge. 31 : 10. rams speckled and g., 12.
Zch. 6 : 3. in chariot were g. horses
6. the g. go tow. south country

GROAN.

Jb. 24 : 12. Men g. fr. out of city
Je. 51:52. thro. land wounded sh. g.
Eze. 30 : 24. Pha. shall g. bef. him
Jo. 1:18. How do the beasts g. herds
Ro. 8 : 23. we ourselves g. within
2 Co. 5:2. we g. desiring to be clothed
4. we in this tabernacle do g.

GROANED, ETH, ING.

Jn. 11 : 33. he g-d in spirit, and
38 Jesus g-g, cometh to the grave
Ro. 8 : 22. we know whole creation g-h

GROANING, S.

Ex. 2 : 24. God heard their g.
6 : 5. I heard g. of Isr., Ac. 7 : 34.
Ju. 2 : 18. it repented L. bec. of g.
Jb. 23:2. my stroke heavier than g.
Ps. 6 : 6. I weary with g. all night
38 : 9. my g. is not hid from thee
102 : 5. By rea. of g. bones cleave
20 To hear the g. of the prisoner
Eze. 30:24. wi. g. of wounded man
Ro. 8:26. g-s that cannot be uttered

GROPE, ETH.

De. 28:29. g. at noon as blind g-h
Jb. 5:14. g. in noonday as night
12:25. g. in the dark without light
Is. 59:10. g. for wall like blind, we g.

GROSS.

Is. 60:2. g. darkness cover people
Je. 13:16. look for light, it g. darkn.
Mat. 13:15. heart is waxed g., Ac 28:27.

GROUND. [Noun.]

Ge. 2 : 5. not a man to till g., 3:23
7. God formed man of dust of g.
19. of g. L. formed every beast
3:17. cursed is g. for thy sake
4:2. but Cain a tiller of g.
10. bro.'s blood crieth unto me fr. the g.
12. When thou tillest the g.
5:29. bec. of g. the L. hath cursed
8:21. I will not again curse the g.
18:2. Ab. bowed himself tow. g.
19:1. Lot bowed with face tow. g.
Ex. 3:5. standest is holy g., Ac. 7:33.
8:21. g. shall be full of flies
Nu. 16 : 31 the g. clave und. them
De. 28:4 blessed be fruit of g., 11.
Ju. 4 : 21. Jael fastened nail into g.
1 S. 8 : 12. set them to ear his g.
26 : 7. his spear stuck in the g. at
2 S. 23:11. piece of g. full of lentiles
12. he stood in g. and defended it
2 K. 2:19. water is nought g. barren
9 : 26. cast him into plat of g.
1 Ch. 11:13. parcel of g. full of barley
2 Ch. 4:17. k. cast them in clay g.
Ne. 10 : 35. bring firstfruits of g.
37. bring tithes of g. unto Levites
Jb. 5:6. nor trouble spring out of g.
14 : 8. though stock die in g.
18 : 10. snare is laid for him in g.
38 : 27. To satisfy the waste g.
39 : 24. swallows g. with fierceness
Ps. 105:35. locusts devoured fruit of g.
107:33. waterspr-gs into dry g.
35. turneth dry g. into watersp.
Is. 28 : 24. he break clods of his g.?
29 : 4. thou shalt speak out of g.
30 : 23. seed thou shalt sow the g.
24. asses that ear the g. shall eat
35:7. parched g. sh. become pool
51 : 23. hast laid thy body as g.
Je. 4 : 3. Break fallow g., Ho 10:12
7 : 20. my fury upon fruit of g.
14 : 4. Bec. g. is chapped, no rain
La. 2 : 2. hath bro-t Jud. to the g.
9. Her gates are sunk into g.
Eze. 12 : 6. thou see not the g., 12.
41 : 16. ceiled fr. g. up to windows
Da. 8:5. goat came, touched not g.
18. Dan.'s face tow. g., 10: 9,15.

Ho.2:18.make cov.with things of g.
Hag. 1:11.upon that wh. g.bringeth
Zch. 8:12. g. shall give her incr.
Mal.3:11.sh.not destroy fruits of g.
Mat.13:8. fell into good g., Lu. 8:8.
23. seed into good g., Lu. 8: 15.
Mk.4:26. as if sho. cast seed into g.
Lu. 12:16. g. of a certain rich man
13: 7. why cumbereth it the g.?
14:18. I have bought a piece of g.
19: 44. they shall lay thee with g.
Jn. 4:5. near parcel of g. Jac. gave
12:24. Exc. corn of wheat fall into
1 Ti. 3:15. pillar and g. of truth [g.
He. 11:† 1. faith is g. of thi. hoped
See DRY, FACE.

On or upon the GROUND.

Ge.19:25.overthrew wh.grew u.t.g.
38:9.he spilled it o.t.g.lest he give
44:14. Jo.'s breth. fell bef. him o.
t. g. [o. t. g.
Ex. 4: 3. Cast rod o.t.g. he cast it
9:23. thunder, and fire ran u.t.g.
14:16.Isr. sh. go o. dry g.thro., 22.
16: 14. small as hoar frost o.t.g.
Le. 20:25. creepeth u.t.g., De.4:18.
De. 15: 23. pour blood u. t. g. as
22: 6. if a bird's nest be o. t. g.
28:56.woman th.not set foot u.t.g.
Ju. 6: 39. u. all t. g. let be dew
40. there was dew u. all t. g.
1 S. 14: 25. was honey u. t. g.
32. slew calves o. t. g. [u. t. g.
20: 31. long as son of Jesse liveth
2 S. 14:14. as water spilt o. t. g.
17:12. upon him as dew fall.o.t.g.
24: 20. bef. k. on his face u. t. g.
2 K.13:18. he said, Smite u. t. g.
Jb. 1:20. Job fell u.t.g.and worsh.
2: 13. sat down with him u. t. g.
16:13. poureth out my gall u.t.g.
Is. 3: 26. she desolate sh. sit u.t.g.
47: 1. O dau. of Bab., sit o. t. g.
Je. 25: 33. they sh. be dung u.t.g.
27: 5. made man and beast u.t.g.
La.2:10.elders of dau.of Z.sit u.t.g.
21. young and old lie o. t. g.
Eze. 24: 7.she poured it not u.t.g.
26: 16. all princes sh. sit u. t. g.
Mat. 10: 29. one sh. not fall o.t.g.
15:35. multi. sit o.t.g., Mk. 8: 6.
Mk. 4:5. fell o. stony g., 16. [15.
8. fell o. good g., 20. Lu. 8: 8,
9: 20. he fell o.t.g. and wallowed
14: 35. he fell o. t. g. and prayed
Jn. 8: 6. Jesus wrote o. t. g., 8.
9: 6. he spat o. t. g. made clay

To or unto the GROUND.

Ge. 3: 19. till thou return u. t. g.
33: 3. Jacob bowed himself t.t.g.
Ju. 13:20. Manoah and wife t.t.g.
20:21. destroyed t.t.g. 22,000 men
25. destroyed t.t.g. of Isr.18,000
Ru. 2: 10. Ruth bowed fell t. t. g.
1 S. 3:19. none of his words fall t.t.
5: 4. Dagon fallen t. t. g. [g.
14: 45. not one hair fall t. t. g.
20:41. David fell on his face t.t.g.
25:23. Abigail bowed t. t. g. bef.
28:14.Saul stooped with face t.t.g.
2 S. 2:22. whf. smite thee t. t. g.?
8: 2. smote Moab, casting t. t. g.
14:4.woman fell on her face t.t.g.
22.Joab fellt.t.g. | 33.Abs.bowed
18:11. why didst not smite t.t.g.?
20:10. shed Amasa's bowels t.t.g.
1 K. 1: 23. Nathan bowed t. t. g.
2 K. 2: 15. sons of prophets t.t.g.
4: 37. Shunammite bowed t. t. g.
1 Ch. 21: 21. Ornan bowed t. t. g.
2 Ch.7:3.Isr.bowed with faces t.t.g.
20:18. Jehosh. bowed t. t. g. [g.
Ne.8:6.worshipped L.with faces t.t.
Ps.74:7.dwelling-pla. of thy name t.
89:39.crown,by casting t.t.g.[t.g.
44. hast cast throne t. t. g.
143: 3. smitten my life t. t. g.
Ps. 147:6. he casteth wicked t.t.g.
Is. 14: 12.how art cut t. t. g.! [g.
21: 9. images he hath brok. t. t.
25: 12. bring t. t. g. even to dust
26:5. lofty city he layeth t. t. g.
Je. 14:2. her gates black t. t. g.
La. 2:2. strong holds of Jud. t.t.g.
10. virgins hang heads t. t. g.
Eze. 13: 14. will bring wall t. t. g.
19: 12. mother was cast t. t. g.
26: 11. thy garrison t. t. g.
28: 17. I will cast thee t. t. g.
Da. 8: 7. he cast ram down t. t.g.
10. it cast down stars t. t. g.
12. cast down truth t.t.g.
Am. 3: 14. horns of altar fall t.t.g.
Ob. 3. Who sh. bring me t. t. g.
Mat. 10: 29. one sh. not fall t.t.g.
Lu. 22:44. drops of bl.falling t.t.g.
Jn. 18: 6. backw., and fell t. t. g.
Ac. 22:7. I fell u. t. g. heard voice

GROUND. [Verb.] [21.

Ex. 32:20. g. calf to powder, De. 9:
Nu. 11: 8. peo. g. manna in mills

GROUND corn.

2 S. 17: 19. g. c. on well's mouth

GROUNDED.

Is. 30: 32. where g. staff shall pass
Eph. 3: 17. that ye being g. in love
Co. 1: 23. If ye continue in faith, g.

GROVE. [sheba

Ge. 21:33. Abr. planted g. in Beer-
De. 16:21. not plant a g. near altar
Ju. 6: 25. and cut down g. by it
28. g. cut down that was by it
1 S. 22: † 6. Saul abode under a g.
1 K. 15: 13. idol in g., 2 Ch. 15:16.
16:33. Ahab made g.to provoke G.
2 K. 13: 6. remained g. in Samaria
17: 16. Isr. made g. served Baal
21:3. Manas.reared altars, made g.
7. set graven image of g.
23:4. out vessels made for the g.
6. he brought g. from h. of Lord
7.women wove hangings for the g.
15.Josiah burned high pla.and g.

GROVES. [7: 5.

Ex. 34: 13. ye sh. cut down g., De.
De. 12: 3. ye shall burn their g.
Ju. 3:7. and served g., 2 Ch. 24:18.
1 K. 14: 15. shall root up Isr., bec.
they made g. [17: 10.
23. built g. on every hill, 2 K.
18: 19. prophets of the g. 400
2 K. 18: 4. Hezek. cut down g.
23: 14. Josiah cut g., 2 Ch.34:3,4.
2 Ch. 14: 3. Asa cut down g.
17: 6. Jehoshaphat took away g.
19: 3. in that hast taken away g.
31:1. all Israel cut down g. [up g.
33: 3. Manas. made g. | 19. set
34: 3. began to purge Jud. fr. g.
7. when he had broken down g.
Is. 17:8. nei. shall he respect the g.
27: 9. g. and images not stand
Je. 17: 2. whilst chil. remember g.
Mi.5:14. I will pluck up thy g. out

GROW.

Ge. 2:9. L. G. made every tree to g.
48: 16. let them g. into a multi.
Nu. 6: 5. let locks of his hair g.
De. 21: † 12. suffer her nails to g.
Ju. 16: 22. hair of head began to g.
2 S. 23: 5. tho. he make it not to g.
2 K. 19: 29. eat such things as g.
Ezr. 4: 22. why g. to hurt of kings?
Jb. 8: 11. rush g. up without mire?
19. out of earth shall others g.
14: 19. things that g. out of dust
31:40. Let thistles g. inst. of wheat
39: 4. they g. up with corn, they
Ps. 92:12. sh. g. like a cedar in Leb.
104:14. grass to g. for cattle,147:8.
Ec. 11: 5. how bones g. in womb
Is. 11: 1. Branch g. of his roots
17: 11. shalt make thy plant g.
53: 2. he shall g. as a tender plant
Je. 12: 2. they g. bring fruit [Ps.
33:15.Branch of right-n.to g.unto
Eze. 44: 20. nor locks to g. long
47: 12. by river shall g. all trees
Ho. 14: 5. he shall g. as the lily
7. they sh. revive, g. as the vine
Jon.4:10. nei. madest it g.wh.came
Zch.6:12.name is BRANCH,he sh.g.
9: † 17. corn make young men g.
Mal. 4:2. ye sh. g. up as calves [27.
Mat.6:28.lilies how they g., Lu. 12:
13:30. Let both g. tog. till harvest
21: 19. Let no fruit g. on thee
Mk. 4: 27. g. up, he kno. not how
Ac. 5:24. doubted whereunto wo.g.
Ep. 4: 15. may g. up into him in
1 Pe. 2: 2. milk of word, that ye g.
2 Pe. 3: 18. g. in grace and knowl.

GROWETH.

Ex. 10: 5. locusts eat tree that g.
Le. 13: 39. spot that g. in skin
25: 5. g. of its own accord, 11.
De. 29: 23. nor any grass g. therein
Ju. 19: 9. behold, day g. to an end
Jb. 38:38.When dust g. into hardn.
Ps. 37: † 35. wicked as tree that g.
90: 5. like grass which g. up, 6.
129: 6. wh. wither-h afore it g. up
Is. 37: 30. sh. eat such as g. of its.
Mk. 4: 32. when it is sown it g. up
Ep. 2: 21. g. unto a holy temple
2 Th. 1:3. bec. your faith g. exceed.

GROWN. [g.

Ge. 38:11. till Shelah be g. | 14.was
Ex. 2: 11. when Moses was g. he
9: 32. not smitten, for not g. up
Le. 13: 37. black hair g. up therein
De. 32: 15. thou art g. thick,cov-d
Ru. 1:13. ye tarry for them till g.?
2 S. 10: 5. tarry till beards g., 1
Ch. 19: 5. [men g., 10.
1 K. 12: 8. consulted with young
2 K. 4: 18. child was g., it fell sick
19: 26. as corn blasted bef. g., Is.
37: 27. [to heavens
Ezr. 9: 6. our trespass is g. up un-
Ps.144:12. our sons as plants g. up
Pr. 24: 31. all g. over with thorns
Je. 50: 11. ye are g. fat as heifer
Eze.16:7. breasts fashioned, hair g.
Da. 4: 22. thou art g. strong (2)
33. till hairs were g. like eagle's
Mat. 13: 32. when it is g.is greatest

GROWTH. [(2)

Am. 7: 1. shooting up of latter g.,

GRUDGE. [Noun.]

Le. 19: 18. nor bear g. ag. people
Mk. 6: † 19. Herodias had g.ag.Jn.

GRUDGE, ING.

Ps. 59: 15. let them g. if not satisfi.
Ja. 5: 9. g. not one ag. another
1 Pe. 4: 9. Use hospitality without

GRUDGINGLY. [g-g

2 Co. 9: 7. let him give not g. or

GUARD. [39: 1.

Ge. 37:36. Jo. sold unto capt. of g.,
41:12. a Hebr.,serv. to a capt.of g.
1 S. 22: † 17. king said unto g. slay
2 S.23:23.David set him over his g.,
1 Ch. 11: 25. [2 Ch. 12: 10.
1 K. 14:27. shields to captain of g.,
28. g. bare them, 2 Ch. 12: 11.
2 K.10:25. Jehu said to g.and capt
11: 4. with capt-s and the g., 19.
6. part at gate behind g. [ons
11. g. stood ev. man with weap-
13.Athaliah heard noise of the g.
25: 8. captain of g. came unto Jerus., Je. 52: 12. [Je. 52:14.
10. capt. of g. brake down walls,
11. people capt. of g.carried away
12. capt. of g. left of poor of land
Ne. 4:22. in night may be g. to us
23. nor men of g. put off clothes
Je. 39:11. charge to capt. of g.conc.
40: 1. capt. of g. had let him go
5. capt. of g. gave him victuals

Je.52:30. capt. of g. took cap. 4600
Eze. 38: 7. be prepared, be a g.
Da. 2: 14. Dan. ans-d capt. of the g.
Mk. 6: † 27. king sent one of his g.
Ac. 28: 16. prisoners to capt. of g.

GUARDCHAMBER.
1 K.14:28.bare them to g., 2 Ch.12:

GUD'GODAH. [11.
De. 10:7. journeyed unto G. (2)

GUEST. [ner
Lu. 19: 7. gone to be g. with sin-

GUESTS.
1 K. 1:41. Adonij. and g. heard
49. all g. with Adonijah afraid
Pr. 9:18.her g. are in depths of hell
Zph. 1:7. for the Lord hath bid g.
Mat. 22:10. wedding furnished wi. g.
11. when king came in to see g.

GUESTCHAMBER.
Mk.14:14.Where is the g.? Lu.22:11.

GUIDE, S.
Ps. 48: 14. our g. even unto death
55: 13. it was thou, a man, my g.
Pr. 2: 17. forsaketh g. of her youth
6: 7. Which having no g. overseer
Je. 3: 4. My father thou art the g.
Mi. 7: 5. put not confidence in g.
Mat. 23: 16. Woe, ye blind g-s, 24.
Ac. 1: 16. g. to them took Jesus
Ro. 2:19. art confident thou art a g.
He. 13:†7. remem. them wh. are g-s

GUIDE. [Verb.]
Jb. 38: 32. canst thou g. Arcturus
Ps. 25:9. meek will he g. in judgm.
31: 3. for thy name's sake g. me
32: 8. I will g. thee wi. mine eye
73: 24. shalt g. me with counsel
112: 5. g. his affairs with discret.
Pr. 11:3. integrity of upright sh. g.
23: 19. g. thine heart in the way
Is. 49:10. by springs of water g. th.
51: 18. There is none to g. her
58: 11. L. shall g. thee continu-y
Lu. 1: 79. to g. our feet into peace
Jn. 16: 13. will g. you into truth
Ac.8:31.How, exc. some man g.me?
1 Th. 3: † 11. now God g. our way
1 Ti. 5:14. younger women g. house
He. 13:† 17. obey them that g. you

GUIDED, ING.
Ge. 48: 14. Isr. g-g hands wittingly
Ex.15:13. hast g-d them in strength
2 Ch.32:22. L. g-d them on ev. side
Jb.31:18.I g-d her fr.moth.'s womb
Ps. 78:52. g-g them in the wildern.
72. hast g-d them by skilfulness

GUILE.
Ex. 21: 14. if a man slay with g.
Ps. 32: 2. in whose spirit is no g.
34:13. lips from speaking g., 1 Pe.
3: 10. [from her streets
55: 11. deceit and g. depart not
Jn. 1: 47. an Israelite, in wh. no g.
2 Co. 12: 16. I caught you with g.
1 Th. 2: 3. our exhorta. not in g.
1 Pe. 2:1. laying aside malice and g.
22. nor was g. found in his mouth
Re. 14:5. in their mouth was no g.

GUILT. [bl., 21: 9.
De. 19: 13. put aw. g. of innocent

GUILTINESS.
Ge. 26:10. thou shouldest have bro-t
g. upon us [heavens
Ezr. 9: † 6. our g. is grown unto
Ps. 51: 14. deliver me fr. blood-g.
69: † my g. is not hid from thee

GUILTLESS.
Ex. 20:7. not hold him g., De. 5:11.
Nu. 5:31. Then shall the man be g.
32:22. afterw. return and be g. bef.
Jos. 2: 19. his blood on him, he g.
1 S. 26: 9. ag. L.'s anointed and g.
2 S. 3: 28. I and kingd. g. of blood
14: 9. said, king and throne be g.
1 K. 2:9. hold him not g.; for thou
art a wise man [the g.
Mat.12:7 ye wo. not have condem-d

GUILTY. [bro.
Ge. 42: 21. We are verily g. conc.
Ex.34:7. will by no means clear g.,
Nu. 14: 18. [are g., 32, 27.
Le. 4:13. which should not be done,
5: 2. he shall be unclean and g.
3. when he knoweth, he be g., 4.
5.when g. he shall confess his sin
17. tho. he wist it not, yet is he g.
6: 4. sinned and is g. he restore
Nu. 35:27. tho. kill slayer not be g.
31. no satisf. for murd-r g. of death
Ju. 21:22. not give, that you be g.
Ezr. 10: 19. being g. offered a ram
Ps. 5:†10. to make g. let them fall
34: † 21. that hate righteous be g.
109: † 7. when judged, go out g.
Pr. 30:10. lest he curse, thou be g.
Eze. 22:4. art g. in blood shed [g.
Ho. 5: † 15. will return till they be
Zch.11:5.slay and hold thems. not g.
Mat. 23: 18. swear by gift, he is g.
26:66.He is g. of death, Mk. 14:64.
Ro. 3: 19. all world may become g.
1 Co. 11:27. g. of body and bl. of L.
Ja.2:10. offend in one point, g. of all

GULF. [gr. g.
Lu. 16: 26. betw. us and you is a

GU'NI, GU'NITES. [7:13.
Ge. 46: 24. sons of Naph. G., 1 Ch.
Nu.26:48.of G. family of G-s | 1 Ch.

GUR. [5:15.
2 K.9:27.smote Ahaziah at G.

GUR-BA'AL. [G.
2 Ch. 26: 7. Arabians that dwelt in

GUSH, ED.
1 K. 18: 28. till the blood g-d out
Ps. 78: 20. smote rock, waters g-d
105: 41. op-d rock, waters g-d out
Is. 48:21. clave rock, waters g-d out
Je. 9: 18. eye-lids g. out wi. waters
Ac. 1: 18. he burst, bowels g-d out

GUTTER, S. [cattle
Ge. 30: 38. Jac. set rods in g-s bef.
41. laid rods bef. cattle in the g-s
2 S. 5: 8. who getteth up to the g.

H.

HA. [h., h.!
Jb. 39: 25. He saith am. trumpets,

HAAHASH'TARI.
1 Ch. 4: 6. Naarah bare him H.

HABAI'AH.
Ezr. 2:61. the chil. of H., Ne. 7:63.

HAB'AKKUK. [of H
Ha. 1:1. burden of H. | 3:1. prayer

HABAZINI'AH.
Je. 35: 3. son of Jere. son of H.

HABERGEON, S.
Ex. 28: 32. as it hole of h., 39: 23
2 Ch. 26: 14. h-s Uzziah prepared
Ne. 4:16. half of my serv-s held h-s
Jb. 41:26. dart, the h. cannot hold

HABITABLE.
Pr. 8: 31. in h. part of his earth

HABITATION.
Ex. 15: 2. I will prepare him a h.
Le. 13:46. without the camp his h.
De. 12:5. even to his h. sh. ye seek
1 S. 2: 29. why kick at off-g com-d
32. shalt see ene. in my h. [in h.?
2 S. 15: 25. will shew me it and h.
2 Ch.6:2.built a house of h. for thee
29: 6. turned from the h. of L.
30: † 27. prayer up to h. of holin.
Ezr. 7:15. G. of Isr. whose h. in Jer.
Jb. 5: 3. but suddenly I cursed h.
24. shalt visit thy h. and not sin
8:6. h. of thy righteousn. prosper.
18: 15. brimstone scatt-d upon h.
Ps. 26: 8. I have loved h. of thy h.
33: 14. Fr. place of h. he looketh
49 :†14. the grave a h. for ev. one
69: 25. Let their h. be desolate
71:3. Be th. my strong h. whereun
89:14.judgm. h. of thy throne, 97:2.

Ps. 91: 9. made Most High thy h.
104: 12. the fowls have their h.
107: 7. might go to city of h., 36.
132:5. find a h. for the mighty G.
13. L. hath desired it for his h.
Pr. 3: 33. blessed h. of the just
Is. 22: 16 graveth a h. for himself
27: 10. and the h. sh. be forsaken
32: 18. peo. dwell in peaceable h.
33: 20. shall see Jerus. a quiet h.
34: 13. it shall be a h. of dragons
35:7 in h. of dragons sh. be grass
63:15. behold fr. h. of thy holiness
Je. 9: 6. h. is in midst of deceit
10: 25. have made his h. desolate
25:30. L. mightily roar upon his h.
31:23.L. bless, O h. of justice, 50:7.
33: 12. cities be a h. of shepherds
41:17. dwelt in the h. of Chimham
49:19. come ag. h. of strong, 50:44.
50:19. will bring Isr. again to his h.
45. he sh. make their h. desolate
Eze. 16:†3. thy h. is of Canaan [h.
29: 14. I will cause E. to return to
Da. 4: 21. fowls of heaven had h.
Am.6:†3 h. of violence to come near
Ob. 3. whose h. is high, that saith
Ha. 3:11. sun and moon stood in h.
Ac. 1: 20 Let his h. be desolate
17: 26. determined bounds of h.
Ep. 2: 22. h. of God, thro. Spirit
Jude 6. angels wh. left their own h.
Re. 18: 2. Bab. become h. of devils

Holy HABITATION. [h.
Ex. 15: 13. hast guided them to h.
De. 26:15. Look from thy h. h. [h.
Ps. 68:5. Judge of widows is G. in h.
Je. 25:30. L. sh. utter voice fr. h. h.
Zch. 2: 13. he is raised out of h. h.

HABITATIONS.
Ge. 36:43. dukes of Edom acc. to h.
49: 5. instruments of cruelty in h.
Ex. 12: 20. in h. eat unl. br. [Sab.
35: 3. kindle no fire thro. h. upon
Le. 23: 17. out of h. 2 wave loaves
Nu. 15:2. When ye be come into h.
1 Ch. 4: 33. These were their h.
41. h. that were found, destroyed
7: 28. their h. were Bethel and
Ps.74:20 places full of h. of cruelty
78:28. he let it fall round their h.
Is. 54: 2. stretch curtains of thy h.
Je. 9: 10. h. of wild. a lamentation
21:13.Who shall enter into our h.?
25: 37. peaceable h. are cut down
49:20. he sh. make their h. desola.
La. 2: 2. L. swallowed h. of Jacob
Eze. 6:14. in h. make land desolate
Ho. 10:†10. I sh. bind them in 2 h.
Jo. 1: † 10. fire hath devoured h.
Am. 1: 2. h. of shepherds sh. mourn
Lu.16:9. may receive you into everl.

HA'BOR. [h.
2K.17:6.carried Isr.aw., placed th. in
Halah and H., 18:11. 1 Ch. 5:26.

HACHALI'AH.
Ne. 1:1. words of Ne. son of H., 10:1.

HACH'ILAH.
1 S. 23: 19. David hid in H., 26: 1.
26: 3. Saul pitched in hill of H.

HACH'MONI, ITE.
1 Ch. 11:11. Jashobeam a H-e, chief
27: 32. Jehiel son of H. [of capts.

HAD.
Ge. 24: 2. serv. ruled over all he h.
39: 6. he knew not aught he h.
Ex. 16: 18. he that gath-d much h.
noth., 2 Co. 8: 15. [fathers
De. 10: 15. L. h. a delight in thy
Jos.6:25. saved Rahab and all she h.
7: 24. took Achan and all he h.
2 S. 6: 22. shall I be h. in honour
12: 6. he did this, and h. no pity
23:8. mighty men whom David h.
2 K. 9: 31. she said, h. Zimri peace
1 Ch. 13: 14. L. blessed all he h.
28: 2. I h. in my heart to build a

1 Ch.28:12.pattern of all that he **h.**
2 Ch. 1:12. such as none of kings **h.**
Jb. 3:26. not in safety, nei. **h.** rest
31:31.Oh that we **h.**of his flesh! [**h.**
42:10. L. gave twice as much as he
Ps. 55: 6. I said, O that I **h.** wings
84:10. I **h.** rather be a doorkeeper
89: 7. to be **h.** in reverence of all
119: 51. **h.** me greatly in derision
56. This I **h.** bec. I kept precepts
Ec. 4:1. they **h.** no comforter [ness
Is. 38: 17. for peace I **h.** gr. bitter-
59: 10. grope as if we **h.** no eyes
60: 10. have I **h.** mercy on thee
Je. 4:23. heavens, they **h.** no light
9: 2. Oh that I **h.** a lodging
39:10. peo. wh. **h.** nothing in land
44:17.then **h.**we plenty of victuals
La. 1: 7. her pleasant things she **h.**
9. wonderfully, **h.** no comforter
Eze. 29: 18. yet **h.** he no wages
36:21. **h.** pity for mine holy name
Ho. 12:3. Jacob **h.** power with God
4. he **h.** power over the angel
Zch. 1: 12. ag. which hast **h.** indig.
Mal. 2: 15. **h.** he residue of Spirit
Mat. 3: 4. **h.** raiment of camel's
12: 10. which **h.** his hand withered, Mk. 3: 1, 3. Lu. 6: 8.
13: 5. **h.** not much earth (2) Mk.
6. **h.** no root, Mk. 4: 6. [4: 5.
46. he sold all that he **h.**
18: 25. But as he **h.** not to pay
19:22. **h.** great poss-ns, Mk. 10:22.
22: 11. **h.** not on wedding garm.
28. whose wife of 7, all **h.** her?
Mk. 12: 22, 23. Lu. 20: 33.
27: 16. they **h.** a notable prisoner
Mk. 8: 7. they **h.** a few small fishes
14 nei. **h.** in ship more than loaf
12: 44. she did cast in all she **h.**
Lu. 4: 40. all they that **h.** any sick
7: 42. **h.** nothing to pay, he
13: 6. certain man **h.** fig tree
Jn. 4: 18. hast **h.** five husbands
5: 4. made whole of disease he **h.**
6. he **h.** been now a long time
11: 17. he **h.** lain in grave four
12: 6. Judas **h.** the bag, 13: 29.
15:22 if I **h.** not come they **h.** not
17:5. glory I **h.** with thee [**h.** sin
Ac. 2: 44. **h.** all things common
13: 5. **h.** John to their minister
18: 18. shorn head, he **h.** a vow
19: 13. over them **h.** evil spirits
24: 19. **h.** aught ag. me, 23: 30.
25: 26. that after examination **h.**
28:19. not th. I **h.** aught to accuse
29. Jews **h.** great reasoning
Ro. 4:11. faith **h.** being uncirc., 12.
6: 21. What fruit **h.** ye in things
1 Co. 7:29. wives be as tho. **h.** none
2 Co. 1: 9. we **h.** sentence of death
1 Th. 1:9. manner of ent-g in we **h.**
He. 7: 6. blessed him **h.** promises
9: 1. first cov-t **h.** ordinances
1 Jn. 2:7. com-t ye **h.** from begin-g
2 Jn. 5. wh. we **h.** from beginning
Re. 1: 16. he **h.** in hand 7 stars
4: 4. **h.** on their heads crowns
6: 5. **h.** a pair of balances
10: 2. **h.** in his hand little book
21: 14. wall of city **h.** 12 foundations
See **ALL THAT HE HAD, BEAST, CENSER, CHARGE, COMPASSION, DAUGHTER, DEVILS, DISEASES, FACE, FAITH, FATHERS, HAIR, HEADS, HORNS, INFIRMITY, KING, LEGION, MARK, NAME, NEED, NOTHING, OPPORTUNITY, PLAGUES, PLATES, POWER, QUESTIONS, REST, SHIPS, SICKLE, SISTER, SONS, SPIRIT, STEWARD, TABERNACLE, TRIAL, TRUMPETS, VOW, WALL, WINGS, WOUND.**

HA'DAD[1] or **HA'DAR**[2][1:30†
Ge. 25:15.† sons of Ishm.; H.[2], 1 Ch.
36: 35.H.[1] son of Bedad reigned.
36. H.[1] died, 1 Ch. 1:47.[1Ch.1:46.
39. H.[2] reigned in his stead, 1 Ch.

HA'DAD. [1: 50.†
1 K. 11: 14. adversary unto Sol., H.
17. H. fled; H. being a little child
19. H. found great favour in Pha.
21. H. heard in Eg. David slept (2)
25. mischief H. did, 1 Ch. 1: 51.

HADADE'ZER[1]
or **HADARE'ZER.**[2]
2 S. 8: 3.† David smote H.[1], 9, 10(2).
1 Ch. 18: 3, 9, 10. H.[2]
5. to succour H.[1], 1 Ch. 18:5. H.[2]
7. took shields of gold on servants
of H.,[1] 1 Ch. 18:7. H.[2][18:8.H.[2]
8. from cities of H.[1] brass, 1 Ch.
10. H.[1] had wars(2).1Ch.18:10.H.[2]
12.dedicated of spoil of H.[1] [19:16.
10: 16.H.[2] bro-t out Syrians, 1 Ch.
19. serv-ts to H.[2] smitten, 1 Ch.19:
1 K. 11: 23. Rezon fled from H.[1] [19.

HA'DAD-RIM'MON.
Zch.12: 11.as mourning of H. in val-

HA'DAR. See Hadad. [ley

HADARE'ZER.
See Hadadezer.

HAD'ASHAH. See Zenan.

HADAS'SAH. [dau.
Es. 2: 7. brought up H. his uncle's

HADAT'TAH. See Hazor.

HA'DID.
Ezr.2:33.with Z. chil. of H., Ne.7:37.

HAD'LAI. [-11: 34.
2 Ch. 28:12. Amasa son of H. stood

HADO'RAM.
Ge. 10: 27. begat H., 1 Ch. 1: 21.
1 Ch. 18: 10. Tou sent H. to David
2 Ch. 10: 18. Rehob. sent H. Isr.

HA'DRACH. [stoned
Zch. 9: 1. burden of the Lord on H.

HADST.
Ge.30:30. little thou **h.** bef. I came
Ps. 44:3. thou **h.** favour unto them
Je. 3: 3. thou **h.** whore's forehead
He.10:8. off-g for sin **h.** no pleasure

HAFT.
Ju. 3: 22. **h.** went in after blade

HA'GAB.
Ezr. 2: 46. Nethinim; chil. of H.

HAG'ABA, HAG'ABAH.
Ezr. 2:45. Nethinim; chil of H., Ne.

HA'GAR=A'GAR. [7:48.
Ge. 16:1. H. was Sarai's maid, 3, 8.
15. H. bare Ab. son, 16.-25: 12.
21: 9. Sarah saw son of H. mock.
14. Ab. gave H. bread, sent her
17. to H. What aileth thee, H.?

HAGARENES'.
Ps. 83: 6. H. are confederate

HA'GARITES.
1 Ch. 5: 10. made war with H., 19.
20. H. were deliv. into their hand

HA'GERITE.
1 Ch.27:31. over flocks Jaziz the H.

HAG'GAI.
Ezr. 5: 1. H. prophesied unto Jews
6:14.prospered thro. prophe. of H.
Hag. 1:1. Lord by H., 3.-2:1, 10,20.

HAGGED'OLIM.
Ne.11:†14.overseer Zabdiel son of H.

HAG'GERI.
1 Ch. 11: 38. Mibhar son of H.

HAG'GI, HAG'GITES.
Ge. 46: 16. sons of Gad, H. Shuni
Nu. 26: 15. of H. the family of H-s

HAG'GIAH. [son
1 Ch. 6: 30. Shimea his son, H. his

HAG'GITES. See Haggi.

HAG'GITH.
2 S. 3: 4. Adonijah the son of H., 1
K. 1: 5, 11.-2: 13. 1 Ch. 3: 2.

HA'I. See Ai.

HAIL. [Interj.]
Mat. 26: 49. Judas said, **h.**, Master
Mat. 27: 29. **h.** king of the Jews,
Mk. 15: 18. Jn. 19: 3.
28:9. Jes. met them, saying, All **h.**
Lu. 1:28. angel to Mary, and said,

HAIL. [Noun.] [**h.**
Ex.9:18.cause it to rain grievous **h.**
23. the L. sent thunder and **h.**
26. where chil. of Isr. were, no **h.**
29.nor any more **h.** | 33.**h.** ceased
10:5. wh. remaineth fr. **h.**, 12, 15.
Jb. 38: 22. seen treasures of **h.**?
Ps.18:12.**h.** stones and coals of fire,
78:47. destroyed vines with **h.** [13.
48. He gave up their cattle to **h.**
105: 32. He gave them **h.** for rain
148: 8. Fire, **h.** snow and vapour
Is. 28:2. as a tempest of **h.** sh. cast
17. **h.** shall sweep refuge of lies
Hag. 2: 17. I smote you with **h.**
Re. 8: 7. there followed **h.** and fire
11: 19. tem. opened, was great **h.**
16: 21. there fell upon men a great

HAIL. [Verb.] [**h.**
Is.32:19.peo. shall dwell when it **h.**

HAILSTONES.
Jos. 10: 11. more wh. died with **h.**
Is. 30:30. L. shew indigna. with **h.**
Eze. 13:11. ye, O great **h.** shall fall
13.there sh.be great **h.**in my fury
38:22. I will rain great **h.** fire, and
See Hail.

HAIR. [10, 20, 25.
Le. 13:3. when **h.** in plague white,
4. **h.** be not turned white, 26.
30.if a yellow **h.** | 31.no black **h.**
32. no yellow **h.**, 36. [off **h.**, 9.
37. black **h.** grown | 14: 8. shave
Nu.6:19. aft. **h.** is shaven [breadth
Ju. 20: 16. cou. sling stones at **h.**
2 S. 14: 11. not one **h.** of son fall
26. bec. **h.** was heavy on him he
1 K. 1:52. shall not a **h.** of him fall
Ne. 13: 25. I plucked off their **h.**
Jb. 4:15. spirit passed, **h.** stood up
Can. 4:1. **h.** as flock of goats, 6: 5.
Is. 3: 24. inst. of well set **h.** baldn.
7: 20. Lord sh. shave **h.** of feet
50: 6. cheeks to th. plucked off **h.**
Je. 7: 29. Cut off thy **h.** O Jerus.
Eze. 5:1. divide **h.** | 16:7. **h.** grown
Zch. 13: † 4. neither shall they wear
a garment of **h.**
Mat.3:4.raim. of camel's **h.**,Mk.1:6.
5: 36. not make one **h.** white or
Jn. 11: 2. wiped feet with **h.**, 12:3.
1 Co. 11: 14. if a man have long **h.**
15. if a woman have long **h.** it is
1 Ti. 2: 9. not with broidered **h.**
1 Pe. 3:3. not of plaiting the **h.** and
Re. 6:12. sun black as sackcl. of **h.**
9: 8. they had **h.** as the **h.** of wo-
See **GOATS, HEAD.** [men

HAIRS.
Ge. 42: 38. bring down my gray **h.**
with sorrow, 44: 29, 31.
Le. 13: 21. if be no white **h.** [**h.**
De.32:21.suckling with man of gray
Ru.4:†15. nourisher of thy gray **h.**
Ps. 40: 12. are more than **h.** of my
head, 69: 4. [sake me not
71:†18. now unto gray **h.** O G.for-
Is. 46:4. to hoar **h.** will I carry you
Da. 4:33. till **h.** like eagle's feath-s
Ho. 7:9. gray **h.** are here and there
Mat. 10: 30. **h.** of our head num-
bered, Lu. 12: 7. [head, 44.
Lu. 7:38. wipe them with **h.** of her
Re. 1: 14. His **h.** white like wool

HAIRY.
Ge.25:25.the first red, like **h.** garm.
27:11. Esau **h.** man | 23.hands **h.**
2 K. 1: 8. Elijah was a **h.** man and
Ps.68:21. the **h.** scalp of such a one

HAK'KATAN.
Ezr. 8: 12. Johanan son of H.

HAK'KOZ.
1 Ch. 24: 10. the seventh lot to H.

HAKU'PHA. ⌈7:53.
Ezr. 2:51. Nethinim, chil. of H., Ne.
HA'LAH. See HA'BOR.
HA'LAK. ⌈Seir, 12:7.
Jos. 11 : 17. mount H. goeth up to
HALE, ING.
Lu. 12:58. lest adversary **h.** to judge
Ac. 8 : 3. Saul h-g men and women
HALF. ⌈he
Ex. 24:6. Mo. took h. the blood, **h.**
30 : 23. take of sweet cinnamon **h.**
Le. 6 : 20. **h.** in morn. **h.** at night
Nu. 12 : 12. flesh is **h.** consumed
31:29. Take it of their **h.** and give
30. the chil. of Isr.'s **h.**, 42, 43, 47.
36. **h.** which was portion of them
Jos. 8:33. **h.** of them over ag. Ebal
1 S. 14 : 14. within **h.** acre of land
2 S. 10:4. shaved off one **h.** of beards
18 : 3. nor if **h.** die, will they care
19:40. **h.** peo. of Isr. conducted Da.
1 K. 3:25. **h.** of child to one, **h.** to oth.
10 : 7. **h.** was not told, 2 Ch. 9 : 6.
13:8. if wilt give me **h.** thine house
16 : 21. **h.** followed Tibni, **h.** Omri
Ne. 3 : 9. ruler of **h.** of Jerus., 12.
16. **h.** part of Bethzur
17. **h.** of Keilah, 18.
4 : 6. wall was joined unto the **h.**
16. **h.** of servs. wrought, **h.** held
12 : 32. **h.** of princes ⌊spears, 21.
38. **h.** of people upon the wall
40. **h.** of the rulers with me
13:24. spake **h.** in speech of Ashdod
Es. 5:3. to **h.** of kingd., 7:2. Mk. 6:23.
Ps. 55:23. shall not live **h.** their days
Eze. 16:51. Nei. Sama. committed **h.**
Da. 12 : 7. times, and **h.**, Re. 12:14.
Ho. 3 : 2. bought her for **h.** homer
Zch. 14:2. **h.** of city into captivity
4. **h.** of mount tow. north, **h.** tow. s.
8. **h.** toward former sea, **h.** hinder
Lu. 10 : 30. leaving him **h.** dead
19:8. **h.** of my goods I give to poor
Re. 8:1. silence about **h.** an hour
11:9. dead bodies 3 days and **h.**, 11.
See CUBIT, HIN, SHEKEL, TRIBE.
HA'LI.
Jos. 19:25. border of Asher was H.
HAL'KUL.
Jos. 15 : 58. in the mts. H. Gedor
HALL.
Mat. 27:27. took Jes. into common **h.**
Mk. 15 : 16. soldiers led him into **h.**
Lu. 22:55. had kindled a fire in the **h.**
See JUDGMENT.
HALLELU'IAH.
Ps. 105:†45.-106:†1, 48.-111:†1.-113:
†1.-146:†1.-148:†1.-149:†1.-
See ALLELUIAH. ⌊150:†1.
HALLO'HESH.
Ne. 10 : 24. chief of peo. H. and
HALLOW.
Ex. 28:38. with chil. of Isr. shall **h.**
29 : 1. **h.** them to minister unto me
40 : 9. sh. **h.** it, and all the vessels
Le. 16 : 19. cleanse it and **h.** it
22 : 2. things they **h.** unto me, 3.
32. I am the Lord who **h.** you
25 : 10. shall **h.** the fiftieth year
Nu. 6:11. shall **h.** his head that day
1 K. 8:64. king **h.** court.
Je. 17 : 22. **h.** ye sabbath, 24, 27.
Eze. 20:20. and **h.** my sabbaths, they
44 : 24. sh. keep laws and **h.** sab-s
HALLOWED.
Ex. 20:11. L. blessed sab. and **h.** it
29:21. Aa. sh. be **h.** and his garm.
Le. 12:4. she sh. touch no **h.** thing
19:8. hath profaned **h.** thing of L.
22 : 32. I will be **h.** am. chil. of Isr.
Nu. 3:13. I **h.** unto me all firstborn
5:10. ev. man's **h.** things be his
16 : 37. take censers, they are **h.**, 38.
18:8. of all **h.** things I have given
29. even **h.** part thereof out of it
De. 26 : 13. I have bro-t **h.** things
1 S. 21 : 4. no common, but **h.** br.
6. Ahim. priest gave him **h.** bread
1 K. 9 : 3. I have **h.** this house, 7.
2 K. 12 : 18. Jehoash took **h.** things
2 Ch. 36:14. polluted h. he had **h.**
Mat. 6:9. **h.** be thy name, Lu. 11:2.
HALO'HESH.
Ne. 3:12. repaired Shallum son of H.
HALT. [Adj.] ⌈9 : 45.
Mat. 18 : 8. to enter into life **h.**, Mk.
Lu. 14:21. bring hither **h.** and bli.
Jn. 5 : 3. **h.** waiting for moving of
HALT, ED, ETH, ING.
Ge. 32:31. Jac. passed, he **h**-d upon
1 K. 18:21. How long **h.** ye betw. two
Ps. 38:17. am ready to **h.** my sorrow
Je. 20:10. familiars watched my **h**-g
Mi. 4:6. I will assemble her th. **h**-h
7. will make her that **h**-d a rem.
Zph. 3 : 19. I will save her th. **h**-h
HAM.
Ge. 5 : 32. Noah begat Shem, H., 6:
10.-9 : 18.-10 : 1. 1 Ch. 1 : 4.
7 : 13. same day H. entered ark
9 : 18. H. fa. of Canaan, 22. ⌈8.
10:6. sons of H. Cush., 20. 1 Ch. 1 :
14 : 5. smote the Zuzims in H.
1 Ch. 4 : 40. they of H. had dwelt
Ps. 78:51. he smote in taber-s of H.
105 : 23. sojourned in land of H.
27. wonders in land of H., 106:22.
HA'MAN. ⌈of wrath
Es. 3:1. king promoted H. | 5. H. full
2. king's servants reverenced H.
6. H. sought to destroy all Jews
7. cast lot bef. H. | 4:7. H. promis.
15. the king and H. sat to drink
5 : 4. king and H. came unto banquet, 5 : 8.-6 : 14.-7 : 1.
9. went H. forth that day joyful
11. H. told them of his riches
14. pleased H. | 6 : 5. H. in court
6:6. H. thought | 11. H. took apparel
12. H. to his house mourning
13. H. told wife | 7 : 6. wicked H.
7 : 7. H. request | 8. H. was on bed
10. hanged H. | 8:1. gave Es. house
of H., 2, 7. ⌈vised by H.
8 : 3. mischief by H. | 5. letters de-
9:10. slew sons of H. | 14. hanged th.
HA'MATH = HE'MATH.
Nu. 13 : 21. as men come to H.
34:8. fr. mount Hor to entrance of
H., Jos. 13 : 5. Ju. 3 : 3. 1 K. 8:
65. 2 K. 14:25. 1 Ch. 13:5. 2 Ch.
7 : 8. Am. 6 : 14.
2 S. 8 : 9. Toi k. of H., 1 Ch. 18 : 9.
2 K. 14 : 28. Jerob. recovered H.
17 : 24. king brought men from H.
30. men of H. made Ashima god
18:34. Where gods of H.? Is. 36 : 19.
19:13. Where king of H.? Is. 37:13.
23:33. in bands in land of H., 25:21.
1 Ch. 18:3. Da. smote Hada. to H.
2 Ch. 8:4. Sol. built store cities in H.
Is. 10:9. is not H. as Arpad?
11:11. L. recover his peo. from H.
Je. 39:5. in H. where he gave judgm.,
49:23. H. is confounded ⌊52 : 9.
52 : 27. Riblah in land of H.
Eze. 47:16. border tow. north, H., 17.
20. till a man come over ag. H.
48:1. border northw. to coast of H.
Am. 6:2. thence go to H. the great
Zch. 9:2. H. shall border thereby
HAM'ATHITE. ⌈16.
Ge. 10:18. Canaan begat H., 1 Ch. 1:
HA'MATH-ZO'BAH.
2 Ch. 8:3. Sol. prevailed against H.
HAM'MATH.
Jos. 19 : 35. fenced cities are Zer, H.
HAMMED'ATHA. ⌈10, 24.
Es. 3:1. Haman, son of H., 10.-8:5.-9:
HAM'MELECH.
Je. 36:26. Jerahmeel son of H. | 38:6.
HAMMER, S.
Ju. 4:21. Jael took **h.** in her hand
Ju. 5 : 26. with **h.** she smote Sisera
1 K. 6 : 7. neither **h.** nor axe heard
Ps. 74:6. break carved work wi. **h**-s
Is. 41:7. that smootheth with **h.**
44 : 12. smith fashioned it wi. **h**-s
Je. 10:4. fasten it with nails and **h**-s
23 : 29. like **h.** that breaketh rock
50:23. **h.** of whole earth cut asund.
Na. 2 : †1. **h.** is come bef. thy face
HAMMOL'EKETH.
1 Ch. 7:18. his sister H. bare Ishod
HAM'MON. ⌈6 : 76.
Jos. 19:28. border goeth to H. | 1 Ch.
HAM'MOTH-DOR.
Jos. 21:32. out of Napht. H. with sub-
HAM'ONAH. ⌊urbs.
Eze. 39:16. name of the city sh. be H.
HA'MON-GOG.
Eze. 39:11. shall call it valley of H.
15. have buried it in valley of H.
HA'MOR.
Ge. 33 : 19. Jacob bought a field of
chil. of H., Jos. 24 : 32.
34:2. Shechem son of H. Hivite, 4.
6. H. went to commune wi. Jac., 8.
24. unto H. hearkened citizens
26. they slew H. and Shechem
Ju. 9 : 28. serve the men of H.
HAMU'EL.
1 Ch. 4:26. H. his son, Zacchur his
HA'MUL, HA'MULITES.
Ge. 46 : 12. sons of Pharez, H., 1 Ch.
2 : 5.
Nu. 26 : 21. of H. the family of H-s
HAMU'TAL.
2 K. 23:31. Jehoahaz; his moth. H.
24:18. Zedekiah, moth. H., Je. 52:1.
HANAM'EEL.
Je. 32 : 7. H. thine uncle's son, 8.
9. I bought the field of H.
12. I gave evidence in sight of H.
HA'NAN.
1 Ch. 8 : 23. Abdon, H. chief men
38. Azel had 6 sons, H., 9 : 44.-11:
43. Ezr. 2 : 46. Ne. 7 : 49.-8 : 7.
-10 : 10, 22, 26.-13 : 13. Je. 35:4.
HANAN'EEL.
Ne. 3:1. tower of H., 12 : 39. Je. 31:
38. Zch. 14 : 10.
HANA'NI.
1 K. 16 : 1. to Jehu son of H., 7.
1 Ch. 25 : 4. H. son of Heman | 25.
2 Ch. 16 : 7. H. the seer came to Asa
19:2. Jehu son of H. went to meet
20 : 34. in book of Jehu son of H.
Ezr. 10 : 20. of sons of Immer, H.
Ne. 1 : 2. H. one of my breth. came
7:2. my bro. H. charge over Jerus.
12 : 36. H. with musical instrum-s
HANANI'AH.
1 Ch. 3:19. sons of Zerubbabel; H.
21. sons of H. | 8 : 24. H. Benj-e
25:4. H. son of Heman | 23. lot to H.
2 Ch. 26 : 11. Uzziah a host und. H.
Ezr. 10:28. H. Zabbai strange wives
Ne. 3 : 8. H. son of an apothecary
7 : 2. I gave H. charge over Jerus.
10 : 23. H. sealed | 12 : 12. H. with
Je. 28:1. H. false proph. ⌊trum-s, 41.
11. H. spake in presence of peo.
12. H. had broken Jere.'s yoke, 10.
15. Hear now, H.; L. not sent
17. H. died that year ⌈chamb.
36:12. Zed. son of H. sat in scribe's
37:13. Irijah, son of H. took Jere.
Da. 1 : 6. of children of Judah, H.
7. to H. the name of Shadrach
11. Melzar set over Daniel, H.
19. among all none like Dan., H.
2 : 17. Daniel made thing kn. to H.
HAND.
Ge. 9 : 2. into **h.** are they delivered
16:12. every man's **h.** against him
19:16. **h.** of wife, h. of 2 daughters
39:6. left all he had in Joseph's **h.**
12. left his garment in her **h.**, 13.
22. commit to Jo.'s **h.** prisoners

Ge.41:35. under the **h.**, Nu.4:28,33.
-7:8.-83:1. Ju. 3: 30. 2 S.18:2.
1 Ch. 26:28. 2 Ch. 26:11.-31:13.
44:17. man in wh. **h.** cup is found
48: 17. he held up his fa.'s **h.** to
Ex. 6: 1. with strong **h.** drive out
13: 3. by strength of **h.L.** brought
14: 8. out with high **h.**, Nu. 33:3
† 31.Isr.saw gr. **h.L.**did upon E-s
17: † 16. **h.** upon throne of the L
18: 10. from under **h.** of, **2 K. 8**:
20, 22.-**13**:5.-**17**:7. **2 Ch. 21**:10.
19: 13. there sh. not a **h.** touch it
21:24. **h.** for **h.** foot for, De.19:21.
28: † 41. anoint, and fill **h.**, 29:†9.
34: 29. tables of testim. in Mo. **h.**
38:15. on this **h.** and that **h.** were
Le. 12: † 8. if **h.** find not suffic-y
14: 32. leprosy, whose **h.** not able
22: 25. Nei. fr. strangers **h.** sh. ye
25:14. buyest aught of neigh-s **h.**
28. in **h.** of him that bought it
Nu. 15:†30. doth aught wi. high **h.**
35: † 17. if smite with stone of **h.**
De. 13: 9. afterw. **h.** of all the peo.
24: 1. divorce-t and give in her **h.**
25: 11. putteth forth her **h.**
12. shalt cut off her **h.** pity not
32: † 36. seeth their **h.** is gone
Jos. 2: 19. his bl. on our head if **h.**
Ju. 1: 35. **h.** of h. of Jos. prevailed
4:9. sh. sell Sisera into **h.** of wom.
21. hammer in her **h.**
5: 26. She put her **h.** to the nail
24. **h.** of chil. of Isr. prospered
15: 18. fall into **h.** of uncirc-d
17:†5. Mic. filled **h.** of one of sons
20:48.smote all came to **h.**of Benj.
1 S. 12:3. of whose **h.** any bribe? 4.
13:22. nor spear found in **h.** of Isr.
17: 50. was no sword in **h.** of Da.
18:21. **h.** of Philis. may be ag. him
20: 19. didst hide when business
22: 17. their **h.** is with Da. [in **h.**
23: 17. **h.** of Saul not find thee
2 S. 13: 5. and eat it at her **h.**, 6.
14:19. is not **h.** of Joab with thee
21: 20. on every **h.** 6 fingers, 1 Ch.
20: 6. [men, 1 Ch. 21:13.
24: 14. let me not fall into **h.** of
1 K. 2:46. kingd. estab. in **h.** of Sol.
13: 6. k.'s **h.** was restored again
18: 44. ariseth cloud like man's **h.**
22: 6. go up, L. shall deliver it into k.'s **h.**, 12, 15. **2 Ch. 18**: 5.
2 K. 7: 2. lord on whose **h.** king leaned, 17.
13: 5. fr. und. **h.** of Syrians [†27.
19:†26. inhabi-s short of **h.**, Is. 37:
1 Ch. 29: † 24. gave **h.** under Sol.
2 Ch. 12: 5. left you in **h.** of Shi.
Ezr. 7:9.good **h.** of his G. upon him
9: 2. **h.** of princes chief in tresp.
Ne. 4:17. wi. other **h.** held weapon
Jb. 9: 24. earth into **h.** of wicked
12: 6. into whose **h.** G. bringeth
10. in whose **h.** is soul of ev. liv.
20: 22. **h.** of wick. come upon him
21:16. their good is not in their **h.**
34:20. mighty be taken without **h.**
37: 7. sealeth up **h.** of ev. man
Ps. 31: 8. not shut into **h.** of ene.
36: 11. not **h.** of wick. remove me
123:2. servt-s look unto **h.** of mas.
127: 4. as arrows in **h.** of mighty
149: 6. twoedged sword be in **h.**
Pr. 6:3.when come into **h.** of friend
10: 4. poor th. dealeth with slack **h.**, **h.** of diligent maketh rich
11: 21. tho. **h.** join **h.** wick., 16:5.
12: 24. **h.** of diligent sh. bear rule
17: 16. why a price in **h.** of a fool
26: 9. as thorn into **h.** of drunk-d
Ec. 4: † 1. on **h.** of their oppressors
Is. 10: 5. staff in **h.** is my indigna.
13: 2. shake **h.** th. they go into
19: 4. give into **h.** of cruel lord
Is. 28: 2. L. sh. cast down with **h.**
Je. 12: 7. beloved into **h.** of enem.
18:4. vessel marred in **h.** of potter
6. as clay in potter's **h.** so ye
21:5. with outstretched **h.** ag. you
26:24.**h.**of Ahikam with Jere., not to give him into **h.** of people
50: 15. Shout she hath given **h.**
La. 5: 6. we have given **h.** to E-s
12. princes are hanged up by **h.**
Eze. 2: 9. **h.** was sent me, a roll
8:3. he put forth form of **h.**, 10:8.
16:49. nor strengthen **h.** of needy
21: † 14. smite **h.** to **h.** together
24. ye shall be taken with the **h.**
28:9. no god in **h.** of him th. slay.
34:10. require my flock at their **h.**
37:19. take stick in the **h.** of Ephr.
40: 5. in **h.** a measuring reed
Da. 5:5. came fingers of a man's **h.**
23. God, in whose **h.** thy breath
24. was part of **h.** sent from him
8: 25. shall be broken without **h.**
10: 10. behold. a **h.** touched me
Jo. 3: 8. sell sons into **h.** of Judah
Mi. 2: 1. it is in power of their **h.**
Zch. 4:10. plummet in **h.** of Zeruh.
Mat. 8: 15. he touched her **h.**
22: 13. Bind him **h.** and foot
Mk. 3:1. had withered **h.**, 3.Lu.6:8.
14: 41. is betrayed into **h.**'s of sin-s
Lu. 1: 1. taken in **h.** to set forth
22:21. **h.** of him th. betrayeth me
Jn. 10: 39. escaped out of their **h.**
11: 44. dead came, bound **h.** and
Ac. 12:17. Peter beckoning to them wi. **h.**, 13: 16.-19: 33.-21: 40.
1 Co. 12: 15. bec. I am not the **h.** I
21. eye cannot say unto **h.** I no need [mediator
Ga. 3: 19. ord. by angels in **h.** of
Re. 10: 8 book open in **h.** of angel
17: 4. having golden cup in her **h.**
19:2. avenged bl. of serv-s at her **h.**

At HAND, or at the HAND.

Ge. 9: 5. **a. t. h.** of ev. beast **a.t. h.** of man, **a. t. h.** of brother
27: 41. days of mourn. for fa. **a.h.**
33: 19. field Jac. bought **a.t.h.** of
De. 15: 9. year of release is **a. h.**
32:35. day of their calam. is **a. h.**
1 S. 9: 8. I have **a. h.** 4th of shek.
20: 16. Let the Lord even require it **a. t. h.** of David's enemies
2 K. 9: 7. avenge blood **a. t. h.** of
Ne. 11:24. Pethahiah was **a. t.** k.'s **h.** in all [15.-2:1. Zph. 1:7.
Is. 13: 6. day of L. is **a. h.**, Jo. 1:
Je. 23:23. Am I a G. **a.h.** and not?
Eze. 12: 23. the days are **a. h.** and
33:6.bl. will I require **a.** watch's **h.**
36:8. fruit, they are **a. h.** to come
Jo. 2: 1. day of L., it is nigh **a. h.**
Mat. 3: 2. kingd. of heav. is **a. h.**,
4: 17.-10: 7. [hour is **a.h.**
26: 18. My time is **a. h.** | 45. the
46. he is **a. h.** that doth betray,
Mk. 14: 42. [Lu. 21: 31.
Mk. 1:15. kingdom of God is **a. h.**,
Lu. 21: 30. summer is nigh **a. h.**
Jn. 2:13.Jews' passover **a.h.**, 11:55.
7:2. Jews' feast of tab-s was **a. h.**
19: 42. sepulchre was nigh **a. h.**
Ro. 13:12. night far spent, day **a.h.**
Ph. 4:5. moderation, the L. is **a.h.**
2 Th. 2: 2. that day of C. is **a. h.**
2 Ti. 4:6. time of my depart. is **a.h.**
1 Pe. 4: 7. end of all things is **a.h.**
Re. 1:3.for the time is **a. h.**, 22:10.

HAND broad. [b.

Eze. 40: 43. within were hooks a **h.**

By the HAND.

Ge. 38:20. sent kid **b.t.h.** of friend
Ex. 4:13. send **b.t.h.** of him whom
35: 29. which L. com-d **b. t. h.** of Moses, Le. 8: 36.-10: 11.-26:
46. Nu. 4: 37, 45, 49.-9: 23.-
10: 13.-15: 23.-16: 40.-27:23.-
36: 13. Jos. 14: 2.-20:2.-21: 2,
8.-22: 9. Ju. 3: 4. 1 K. 8: 53,
56. 2 Ch. 33:8.-35:6. Ne. 9: 14.
Ps. 77: 20. [Ithamar
Ex. 38: 21. sum of tab. **b. t. h.** of
Le. 16: 21. send him **b.t.h** of fit
Jos. 20: 9. not die **b. t. h.** of aven.
Ju. 16:26. unto lad th. held **b.t.h.**
1 S 18: 25. make Da fall **b.t.h.** of
27:1. I sh. perish **b. t. h.** of Saul
2 S. 3: 18. **b.t.h.** of my serv-t Da.
10: 2. to comfort him **b. t. h.** of
11:14.letter,sent it **b.t.h.** of Uriah
12:25. he sent **b. t. h.** of Nathan
21:22. fell **b.t.h.** of Da., 1 Ch.20:8.
1 K. 2:25. Sol. sent **b.t.h.** of Benai.
14: 18. which he spake **b. t. h.** of
16:7. **b.t.h.** of Jehu came word of
2 K. 14:25. he spake **b.t.h.** of Jon.
27. saved them **b. t. h.** of Jerob.
2 Ch.10:15. e spake **b.t.h.** of Ahij.
12: 7. wrath **b. t. h.** of Shishak
24:11. **b.t.h.** of the Levites, 23:18.
Ezr. 1:8. bring out vessels **b.t.h.** of
8: 33. vessels weighed **b. t. h.** of
Jb. 8:†20. nor take ungodly **b.t.h.**
Pr. 26:6. a message **b.t.h.** of a fool
Is. 51:18. nor th. taketh her **b.t.h.**
Je. 27: 3. yokes **b. t. h.** of messen.
31:32. I took them **b.t.h.**, He.8:9.
38:23.be taken **b.t.h.** of k. of Bab.
Eze. 25:14. veng. upon Edom **b.t.h.**
30: 10. mult. of E. to cease **b.t.h.**
12. land waste **b.t.h.** of strangers
Ho. 12: † 10. similitudes **b.t.h.** of
Mat. 9: 25. he went in took her **b. t. h.**, Mk. 1:31.-5:41. Lu.8:54.
Mk. 8:23. he took blind man **b.t.h.**
9: 27. Jesus took him **b. t. h.**
Ac. 7: 35. deliverer **b.t.h.** of angel
9:8.but they led him **b.t.h.**, 22:11.
13:11. seeking some to lead **b.t.h.**
23:19. chief capt. took him **b.t.h.**
Col.4:18. saluta. **b.t.h.** of me, Paul

Deliver, ed, eth into, from or out of HAND.

Ge. 9: 2. **i.** your **h.** are they **d-d**
14: 20. **d-d** enemies **i.** thine **h.**
32: 11. **d.** me **f. h.** of bro. Esau
16. **d-d i. h.**, Jos. 10: 30,32.-11:
8.-Ju. 6:1.-11:21.-13:1. 1 S.14:
12. 2 S. 10:10.-16:8. 1 K. 15:18.
2 K.13:3.-17:20.-22:9. 1 Ch.16:
7. 2 Ch. 28: 5.-34:17. Ezr. 9:7.
Is. 36: 15. Je. 32:4, 36.-37:17.-
46: 24. Eze. 23: 9.-31: 11.
40:13.shalt **d.** Pha.'s cup **i.** his **h.**
Ex. 2:19. Egyp-n **d-d** us **o. o. h.**
3:8. to **d.** them **o.o.h.** of E-s, 14:30.
18: 9. **d-d o. o.** the **h.**, 10. Ju. 9:
17. 1 S. 10: 18.-12: 11. 2 K. 18:
33. Is. 36:18.Eze.34:27.Lu.1:74.
21: 13. God **d-d** him **i.** his **h.**
Nu. 21: 2. If wilt **d.** peo. **i.** my **h.**
35:25. **d.** him **o. o. h.** of revenger
De. 1: 27. **d. i. h.**, 19:12. Jos. 7:7.
Ju. 15: 12. 1 S. 14:37.-23:12,20.
-28:19. 1 K. 18:9.-22:6,12,15. 2
K.3: 10, 13 -21:14.-22:5. 2 Ch.
18:5,11.-25:20. Ne. 9:27. Je.21:
7.-29:21.-46:26. Eze. 21:31.-28:
28. Zch. 11: 6.
7: 24. shall **d.** kings **i.** thine **h.**
26:11. **d. o. o. h.**, 1 S 7:3.-12:10.
2 S. 14:16. 2 K. 17:39. 2 Ch. 32:
11, 15. [43:13.
32:39. nor any **d. o.o.** my **h.**, Is.
Jos. 9: 26. **d.** them **o. o. h.** of Isr.
10: 8. **d-d** kings of Ca. **i.** thine **h.**
20: 5. not **d.** slayer **i.** his **h.**
21: 44. **d-d i.** their **h.**, Ju. 1:4. 2
K. 22:7. 1 Ch. 5:20. 2 Ch.13:16
-24: 24.
22: 31. **d-d** Isr. **o. o. h.** of Lord
24: 10. I **d-d** you **o. o.** his **h.**

Ju. 1: 2. have **d**-d land **i.** his **h.**
2:16.judges wh. **d**-d them **o. o. h.**
23. nei. **d**-d them **i. h.** of, 1 S. 12:
4: 7. will **d.** Sisera **i.** thine **h.** ⌊9.
14. **d**-d Sisera **i.** thine **h.**, 7.
6: 9. I **d**-d you **o. o. h.** of Egyp-s
7: 7. I will **d.** Mid-s **i.** thine **h.**
14. **i.** his **h.** hath G. **d**-d Midian
8: 7. when L. **d**-d Zebah **i.** mine **h.**
22. hast **d**-d us **f. h.** of Midian
10: 12. I **d**-d you **o. o.** their **h.**
12: 3. Lord **d**-d them **i.** my **h.**
13: 5. **d.** Isr. **o. o. h.** of Philis.
15: 13. bind thee fast **d. i.** their **h.**
16: 23. hath **d**-d Samson **i.** our **h.**
20: 28. I will **d.** Benj. **i.** thine **h.**
1 S. 4: 8. who **d.** us **o. o. h.** of Gods
14: 10. **d**-d them **i.** our **h.**, 30: 23.
17: 37. will **d.** me **o. o. h.** of Philis.
46. Lord will **d. i.** mine **h.**
23: 4. I will **d.** Philis. **i.** thine **h.**, 2 S. 5: 19. 1 Ch. 14: 10.
7. G. hath **d**-d him **i.** mine **h.**
11. Keilah **d.** me **i.** his **h.**?
14. G. **d**-d him not **i.** his **h.**
24: 15. L. **d.** me **o. o.** thine **h.**
26: 23. L. **d**-d thee **i.** my **h.**, 24: 10.
2 S. 12: 7. **d**-d thee **o. o. h.** of Saul, 22: 1. ⌈**h.**, 28.
1 K. 20: 13. I will **d.** Syrians **i.** thine
2 K. 18: 30. city not be **d**-d **i. h.** of king of Assyr., 19: 10. Is. 36: 15.
34. Hath god **d**-d land **o. o. h.**
35. Who am. gods **d**-d country **o.** mine **h.** that L. **d.** Jerus. **o. h.**
20: 6. I will **d.** thee and city **o. o. h.** of king of Assyria, Is. 38: 6.
2 Ch. 16: 8. he **d**-d them **i.** thine **h.**
25: 15. not **d.** peo. **o. o.** thine **h.**
32: 15. no god able to **d. o. o.** mine **h.** much less your G. **d. o. o.** mine **h.** (3) 13, 14, 17.
Ps. 22: † 20. **d.** darling **f. h.** of dog
71: 4. **d.** me **o. o. h.** of wick., 82: 4.
89: 48. **d.** his soul **f. h.** of grave
97: 10. **d**-h them **o. o. h.** of wick.
144: 7. **d.** me **f. h.** of stra. chil., 11.
Pr. 6: 5. **d.** thyself **f. h.** of hunter
Is. 36: 19. **d**-d Sama. **o. o.** my **h.**?
20. that L. **d.** Jerus. **o. o.** my **h.**
Je. 15: 21. will **d. o. o. h.** of wicked
20: 13. **d**-d poor **f. h.** of evil doers
21: 12. **d.** him spoiled **o. o. t. h.** of the oppressor, 22: 3.
32: 4. Zed. shall be **d**-d **i. h.** of k.
38: 19. lest they **d.** me **i.** their **h.**
43: 3. to **d.** us **i. h.** of Chaldeans
La. 5: 8. none **d.** us **o. o.** their **h.**
Da. 6: † 27. **d**-d Dan. **f. h.** of lions
Zch. 11: 6. **o. o. h.** I will not **d.**
Ac. 12: 11. **d**-d me **o. o. h.** of Herod

See **Hand of the ENEMY.**
See **ENEMY'S hand.**

HAND with **enemies.**

Ge. 14: 20. deliv-d **e.** into thine **h.**
1 S. 4: 3. save us out of **h.** of **e.**, 7: 8. -9: 16.-12: 10. 2 S. 3: 18. 2 K. 16: 7.
12: 11. you out of **h.** of **e.**, 2 K. 17: 39.
2 S. 18: † 19. L. judged him fr. **h.** of **e.**
19: 9. k. saved us out of **h.** of **e.**
2 K. 21: 14. I will deliver them into **h.** of **e.**, 2 Ch. 25: 20. Ne. 9: 27.
Ne. 9: 28. leftest them in **h.** of **e.**
Ps. 31: 15. deliver me from **h.** of **e.**
Je. 20: 5. I will give this city into **h.** of **e.**, 21: 7.-34: 20, 21. Eze. 39: 23.
44: 30. I will give Pha. into **h.** of **e.**
Mi. 4: 10. redeem thee fr. **h.** of **e.**
Lu. 1: 74. deliv-d out of **h.** of our **e.**

From the HAND.

De. 7: 8 L. redeemed **f. h.** of Pha.
Ju. 6: 14. save Isr. **f. h.** of Midian
1 S. 25: 39. pleaded **f. h.** of Nabal
2 Ch. 32: 22. Jerus. **f. h.** of Sennach.
Jb. 5: 15. saveth poor **f. h.** of mighty
6: 23. redeem me **f. h.** of mighty
Ps. 49: † 15. redeem soul **f. h.** of grave
Ps. 106: 10. saved **f. h.** of him th. hated redeemed **f. h.** of enemy
Je. 31: 11. **f. h.** of him was stronger
Ho. 13: † 14. them **f. h.** of the grave
Lu. 1: 71. saved **f. h.** of all hate us

HAND of God.

1 S. 5: 11. **h. o. G.** was heavy there
2 Ch. 30: 12. **h. o. G.** to give 1 heart
Ezr. 7: 9. acc. to good **h. o. G.**, Ne. 2: 8: 18. good **h. o. G.** upon us ⌊8.
22. **h. o. G.** upon all for good that
31. **h. o. G.** is upon us ⌊seek
Ne. 2: 18. I told of **h. o. G.** upon me
Jb. 2: 10. receive good at **h. o. G.**
19: 21. **h. o. G.** hath touched me
27: 11. I will teach you by **h. o. G.**
Ec. 2: 24. saw it was from **h. o. G.**
9: 1. wise are in **h. o. G.** ⌈G.
Is. 62: 3. royal diadem in **h. o.** thy
Mk. 16: 19. sat on right **h. o. G.**, Ro. 8: 34. Col. 3: 1. He. 10: 12. 1 Pe. 3: 22
Ac. 2: 33. by right **h. o. G.** exalted
7: 55. saw Jesus on right **h. o. G.**, 56.
1 Pe. 5: 6. humble yours. und. **h. o.** ⌊G.

His HAND.

Ge. 3: 22. lest put **h. h.** take tree of
16: 12. **h. h.** will be ag. every man
19: 16. men laid hold upon **h. h.**
22: 6. took fire in **h. h.**
24: 9. serv. put **h. h.** under thigh
10. all goods of master in **h. h.**
25: 26. **h. h.** took hold on Esau's
32: 13. Jacob took of that to **h. h.**
38: 28. upon **h. h.** scarlet thread, (2) 29, 30.
39: 3. L. made all prosper in **h. h.**
4. all he had put into **h. h.**
41: 42. Pha. took the ring off **h. h.**
46: 4. Jo. sh. put **h. h.** upon eyes
Ex. 4: 4. forth **h. h.** it a rod in **h. h.**
6. **h. h.** was leprous as snow, 7.
20. Moses took rod of G. in **h. h.**
17: 11. held up **h. h.** let down **h. h.**
21: 16. if found in **h. h.**
20. he die under **h. h.**
22: 4. if theft be found in **h. h.**
8. whe. put **h. h.** unto goods, 11.
24: 11. upon nobles laid not **h. h.**
32: 15. tables of testim. in **h. h.**, 34: 4.
Le. 1: 4 **h. h.** upon head of burnt off-g
5: † 7. if **h. h.** can-t reach to suffic-y
16: † 32. priest wh. he sh. fill **h. h.**
Nu. 5: 18. priest in **h. h.** bitter wat.
6: 21. besides that **h. h.** shall get
21: 26. taken all land out of **h. h.**
22: 23. his sw. in **h. h.**, 31. 1 Ch. 21: 16.
25: 7. Phine. took a javelin in **h. h.**
De. 19: 5. **h. h.** fetcheth a stroke
Jos. 5: 13. man with sword in **h. h.**
8: 26. drew not **h. h.** until destr-d
Ju. 3: 10. and **h. h.** prevailed ag.
6: 21 put end of staff in **h. h.**
14: 6. rent kid, had noth. in **h. h.**
1 S. 5: 7. **h. h.** is sore upon us
6: 3. know why **h. h.** is not remov.
5. peradv. he will lighten **h. h.**
9. that is not **h. h.** th. smote us
14: 26. no man put **h. h.** to mou.
27. Jona. put **h. h.** to mouth (2)
16: 16. that he sh. play with **h. h.**
23. harp and play with **h. h.**, 18: 10.
17: 40. Da. took sling in **h. h.** ⌊10.
57. with head of Philis. in **h. h.**
19: 5. his life in **h. h.** and slew Philis.
9. with javelin in **h. h.** ⌈G.
23: 16. Jona. strengthened **h. h.** in
27: 1. shall I escape out of **h. h.**
2 S. 6: 6. put **h. h.** to ark, 1 Ch. 13: 10.
1 K. 8: 15. with **h. h.** fulfilled it
11: 34. nor take kingd. out of **h. h.**
13: 4. **h. h.** be put forth dried up
2 K. 5: 11. strike **h. h.** over place
10: 15. he gave **h. h.** took him up
11: 8. compass king ev. man with weapons in **h. h.**, 11. 2 Ch. 23: 7.
14: 5. kingd. confirmed in **h. h.**
15: 19. **h. h.** be to confirm kingd.
2 K. 18: 21. on wh. if man lean go into **h. h.**, Is. 36: 6. ⌈**h. h.**
29. not able to deliv. you out of
19: 19. I bes. save out of **h. h.** ⌈me
1 Ch. 28: 19. underst. by **h. h.** upon
29: † 5. who is willing to fill **h. h.**
2 Ch. 17: 5 L. stabl-d kingd. in **h. h.**
26: 19. Uzziah censer in **h. h.**
36: 17. he gave them all into **h. h.**
Ne 6: 5. with open letter in **h. h.**
Jb. 6: 9. he would let loose **h. h.**
15: 23. day of darkness at **h. h.**
26: 13. **h. h.** formed crooked serp.
27: 22. would fain flee out of **h. h.**
28: 9. put-h forth **h. h.** upon rock
Ps. 37: 24. L. upholdeth with **h. h.**
33. L. will not leave him in **h. h.**
78: 42. They remembered not **h. h.**
89: 25. I will set **h. h.** in the sea
95: 4. in **h. h.** are the deep places
7. sheep of **h. h.** if ye will hear
106: 26. he lifted **h. h.** ag. them
129: 7. mower filleth not **h. h.**
Pr. 7: † 20. bag of money in **h. h.**
19: 24. slothful hideth **h. h.**, 26: 15
Ec. 5: 14. begets son, noth. in **h. h.**
15. noth. carry away in **h. h.**
Can. 5: 4. my beloved put in **h. h.**
Is. 6: 6. seraphim, live coal in **h. h.**
10: 32. he sh. shake **h. h.** ag. Zion
11: 8. weaned child put **h. h.** on
11. L. shall set **h. h.** sec. time
15. he sh. shake **h. h.** over river
22: 21. commit thy gov-t into **h. h.**
28: 4. while in **h. h.** he eateth it
34: 17. **h. h.** divided it unto them
37: 10. O Lord, save us from **h. h.**
40: 12. measured waters in **h. h.**
44: 5. subscribe with **h. h.** unto L.
49: 2. in shadow of **h. h.** hid me
53: 10. pleas. of L. prosper in **h. h.**
56: 2. keepeth **h. h.** fr. doing evil
Je. 1: 9. L. put forth **h. h.** touched
27: 8. consumed them by **h. h.**
34: 3. not escape out of **h. h.**
42: 11. and deliv. you fr. **h. h.**
La. 1: 10. adversa. hath spread **h. h.**
14. yoke of transgr. bound by **h. h.**
2: 8. he hath not withdrawn **h. h.**
3: 3. he turneth **h. h.** against me
Eze. 8: 11. ev. man wi. censer in **h. h.**
9: 1. with destroying weap. in **h. h.**
17: 18. when lo, he had given **h. h.**
18: 8. **h. h.** fr. iniq. | 17. fr. poor
30: 22. sword to fall out of **h. h.**
24. I will put my sword in **h. h.**
40: 3. line of flax in **h. h.**, 47: 3.
46: 7. acc. as **h. h.** shall attain unto
Da. 1: 2. Jehoi-m k. of Jud. into **h. h.**
4: 35. none can stay **h. h.** or say
7: 25. into **h. h.** until a time
8: 4. nei. deliver out of **h. h.**, 7.
25. cause craft to prosp. in **h. h.**
11: 11. mult. sh. be given into **h. h.**
16. land by **h. h.** be consumed
41. these shall escape out of **h. h.**
Ho. 12: 7. balances of deceit in **h. h.**
Am. 7: 7. with plumbline in **h. h.**
Ha. 3: 4. horns coming out of **h. h.**
Zph. 2: 15. passeth her shall wag **h. h.**
Zch. 2: 1. a measuring line in **h. h.**
8: 4. every man with staff in **h. h.**
14: 13 **h. h.** rise ag. ha. of neighb.
Mat. 3: 12. fan in **h. h.**, Lu. 3: 17.
12: 10. man had **h. h.** withered, Mk. 3: 1, 3. Lu. 6: 6, 8.
26: 23. that dippeth **h. h.** with me
Mk. 3: 5. **h. h.** restored, Lu. 6: 10.
7: 32. beseech to put **h. h.** upon him
Lu. 9: 62. having put **h. h.** to plough
15: 22. put a ring on **h. h.** and
Jn. 3: 35. given all thi. into **h. h.**
18: 22. struck with palm of **h. h.**
Ac. 7: 25. how G. by **h. h.** wo. deliver
9: 12. putting **h. h.** on him.
41. gave her **h. h.** and lifted
28: 3. a viper fastened on **h. h.**, 4

Re. 6:5. a pair of balances in **h. h.**
10 : 2. had in **h. h.** a book open
14 : 9. mark in forehead, or **h. h.**
14. having in **h. h.** sharp sickle
20:1.angel came wi. chain in **h.h.**

Into the HAND.

Ju. 3:8. anger of L. ag. Isr. he sold
them **i.t.h.** of, 4:2, 9. 1 S. 12:9.
Ne.9:30. gavest them **i.t.h.** of peo.
Pr. 6 : 3. come **i.t.h.** of thy friend
Is. 37 : 10. not be given **i. t. h.** of k.
of Assyria, Je. 39 : 17.
51:23.**i.t.h.**of them th. afflict thee
Je. 20 : 5. give **i.t.h.**, 4.-22:25.-32:
3.-34:2, 20, 21.-38 : 16.-44 : 30.
Is. 19 : 4. Eze. 21 : 11. [deans
32:24. city is given **i.t.h.** of Chal-
Eze. 30:12. sell land **i.t.h.** of wick.
25. put my sword **i.t.h.** of the k.
Jo.3:8.sell your sons and daughters
See LAY, LAID. [**i.t.h.**

Left HAND.

Ge. 14:15. Hobah on **l.h.**of Damas.
Le. 14:15. pour oil into **l. h.**, 27.
Ju. 3 : 21. Ehud put forth **l. h.**
7 : 20. companies lamps in **l. h.**
2 K.23:8.on a man's **l.h.**at the gate
1 Ch. 6:44, sons of Merari on **l. h.**
Mat. 25:41. on **l. h.** Depart, cursed
Ac. 21: 3. Cyprus, we left it on **l.h.**
See **Right HAND** with **left.**
See **LIFT, LIFTED hand, s.**

Lord's HAND.

Nu.11:23.Is the L.'s **h.**waxed short?
Is. 40 : 2. received of L.'s **h.** double
59:1. L.'s **h.** is not shortened. that
Je. 25:17. took I cup at the L.'s **h.**
51:7. Bab. a golden cup in L.'s **h.**

HAND of the Lord.

Ex. 9: 3. **h. o.** L. is upon thy cattle
16:3. Wo. we had died by **h.o.** L.
De. 2 : 15. **h. o.** L. was ag. them to
Jos. 4:24. peo. know **h.o.**L.mighty
22:31. deliv-d Isr. out of **h. o.** L.
Ju. 2:15. the **h. o.** L. was ag. them
Ru. 1:13. **h. o.** L. is gone ag. me
1 S. 5:6. **h. o.** L. heavy upon Ash.
9. **h. o.** L. ag. city with destruc.
7 : 13. **h. o.** L. against the Philis.
12 : 15. then shall **h.o.**L.be ag.you
2 S. 24 : 14. fall into **h. o.** L., 1 Ch.
1 K.18:46. **h.o.**L. on Elijah [21:13.
2 K. 3:15. **h.o.**L. came upon Elisha
Ezr.7:6.k.granted acc.to **h.o.**L.,28.
Jb.12 : 9. **h.o.**L. wrought,Is.41:20.
Ps. 75 : 8. in **h.o.**L. there is a cup
Pr. 21 : 1. king's heart in **h. o.** L.
Is. 19 : 16. of shaking of **h. o.** L.
25:10. in this mount. **h. o.** L. rest
51 : 17. hast drunk at **h.o.** L. cup
62 : 3. a crown of glory in **h.o.** L.
66:14. **h.o.**L. be known tow.serv-s
Eze. 1 : 3. **h.o.**L. upon him [37:1.
3: 14. **h.o.**L. upon me, 22.-8 : 1.-
33:22. **h.o.**L. upon me in evening
40 : 1. same day **h. o.** L. with him
Lu. 1: 66. **h. o.** L. was with him
Ac. 11 : 21. **h. o.** L. was with them
13: 11. the **h. o.** L. is upon thee

Mighty HAND.

Ex. 3:19. not let you go,with **m.h.**
32:11. broughtest forth with **m.h.**
De. 3:24. began to shew serv. **m.h.**
4: 34. take him a nation by **m.h.**
5: 15. thee out of E. by **m. h.**, 6:
21.-7: 8, 19.-9: 26.-11: 2.-26:
8.-34: 12.
2 Ch. 6:32.wh. is come for thy **m.h.**
Eze. 20:33. with a **m.h.** will I rule
34. I will bring you out with **m.h.**
Da. 9: 15. bro-t peo. out of E. with
m. h. [G.
1 Pe. 5 : 6. humble under **m. h.** of

Mine HAND.

Ex. 7 : 17. smite with rod in **m. h.**
17 : 9. with the rod of G. in **m.h.**
33:22. I will cover thee with **m.h.**
Ex.33:23.I will take away **m.h.**and
Nu. 22:29. would were sw. in **m.h.**
De. 8:17. might of **m.h.**got.wealth
10 : 3. having two tables in **m. h.**
32:41. if **m.h.**take hold on judgm.
Ju. 6: 36. if save Isr. by **m.h.**, 37.
7 : 2. saying **m.** own **h.** saved me
1 S. 18:17.Let not **m.h.**be upon him
21:4.no common bread und. **m.h.**
24:6. **m.h.**ag.L 's anointed, 26:11.
11. skirt in **m.h.**no transg-n (2)
12. **m. h.** not be upon thee, 13.
25 : 33. avenging mys. with **m.h.**
26 : 18. done? what evil in **m. h.**
2 S. 18:12. not put forth **m. h.** ag.
Absalom [by **m. h.**
1 Ch. 14 : 11. broken in upon enem.
22 : 18. inhabi. of land into **m. h.**
Jb. 13: 14. Whf. put life in **m. h.**?
31:25. rejoiced bec.**m.h.**got.much
Is. 48:13. **m.h.**laid founds.of earth
50 : 11. this ye have of **m. h.**
51:16. in the shadow of **m.h.** [50.
66:2. all hath **m. h.** made, Ac. 7:
Je.16:21. cause them to know **m.h.**
18 : 6. so are ye in **m. h.** O Israel
Eze. 12:7. digged thro.wall in **m.h.**
13:9. **m.h.** shall be upon prophets
20 : 22. I withdrew **m. h.** and
22:13. smitten **m.h.**at thy dishon.
37 : 19. they shall be one in **m.h.**
Ho. 2 : 10. none deliv. out of **m. h.**
Am. 1 : 8. turn **m. h.** ag. Ekron
9:2. tho. into hell,sh.**m.h.**take th.
Zch.2:9.will shake **m.h.** upon them
13 : 7. turn **m.h.** upon little ones
1 Co. 16 : 21. the salutation of me
Paul with **m.** own **h.**, 2 Th. 3:
17. [4: 18. Phm. 19.
Ga. 6 : 11. written with **m.h.**, Col.

My HAND.

Ge. 21 : 30. ewe lambs take of **m.h.**
31:29. it is in **m.h.** to do you hurt
39. of **m. h.** didst thou require it
33 : 10. receive my present at **m.h.**
39 : 8. com. all he hath to **m. h.**
40 : 11. Pha.'s cup was in **m. h.**
42 : 37. deliver him into **m. h.**
43 : 9. of **m. h.** shalt require him
Ex. 15:9. **m. h.** shall destroy them
De. 32 : 40. I lift up **m. h.** to heav.
Ju. 9 : 29. wo. peo. were und.**m.h.**
17:3. dedic. silver unto L.fr. **m.h.**
1 S.12:5. not found aught in **m. h.**
28 : 21. put my life in **m. h.** [Isr.
2 S. 3 : 12. **m. h.** wi. thee to bring
1 K. 13 : 6. that **m. h.** be restored
2 K. 5:18. and he leaneth on **m.h.**
Jb.29:20. bow was renewed in **m.h.**
31:27. or my mouth kissed **m. h.**
33:7.nei. **m.h.** be heavy upon thee
Ps. 77 : † 2. **m. h.** ran in the night
81 : 14. turned **m. h.** ag. enemies
89 : 21. **m. h.** shall be established
119:109.My soul is contin.in **m.h.**
Is. 1: 25. I will turn **m.h.**upon me
10: 10. As **m. h.** found kingd. of
13.By **m.h.**I have done it [idols
14. **m. h.** found riches of people
50 : 2. Is **m. h.** shortened at all
Je.25:15. wine cup of fury at **m.h.**
Jn. 10: 28. nor pluck out of **m. h.**
20:25. exc. I thrust **m.h.**into side
Ac. 7:50. Hath not **m.h.** made all?

Our HAND.

Ge.37:27. let not **o. h.** be upon him
43:21. have bro-t it again in **o. h.**
Nu. 31:† 49. men of war und. **o. h.**
De. 32 : 27. lest say, **o. h.** is high
Je.11:21. that thou die not by **o.h.**
2 Co. 10 : 16. things ready to **o. h.**

Out of HAND, or out of the HAND.

Ge. 48 : 22. which I took **o. o. t.**
h. of Amorite, De. 3 : 8.
Nu.5:25. take off-g **o.o.**woman's **h.**
11:15. kill me, I pray thee,**o.o.h.**
2 S. 23 : 21. spear **o. o. t.** E-n's **h.**,
1 Ch. 11 : 23.
1 K.11:12.kingd. **o.o.t.h.** of Sol.,13.
22:3. we take it not **o. o. t. h.** of
the king of Syria [Ben-hadad
2 K. 13:25. took again **o. o. t. h.** of
Ps. 82:4.rid them **o.o.t. h.**of wick.
Je.32:4 not **o.o.t.h.** of Chal.,38:18,
Jn.10:29. none pl. **o.o.** Fa.'s **h.** [23.
39. he escaped **o. o.** their **h.**
Re. 8 : 4. ascended **o. o.** angel's **h.**,

Right HAND. [10: 10.

Ge. 35:†18. called him son of **r. h.**
48:14. **r. h.** upon Eph.'s head, 18
Ex. 15 : 6. Thy **r. h.** is glorious
12.stretchedst **r.h.**, earth swall-d
29 : 20. put bl. upon thumb of **r.**
h., Le. 8:23,24.-14:14,17,25,28.
De. 33 : 2. fr. **r. h.** went a fiery law
Ju. 5 : 26. her **r. h.** to hammer
2 S. 20:9. Joab took Amasa wi. **r.h.**
1 K. 2:19. Bath-sheba on Sol.'s **r.h.**
2 K. 23:13. on **r. h.** of the mount of
1 Ch. 6:39.Asaph,who stood on **r.h.**
Jb. 23:9 he hideth himself on **r. h.**
30 : 12. upon my **r. h.** rise youth
40:14. th. thine own **r. h.** can save
Ps. 16:8. he is at my **r. h.** I sh. not
11. at thy **r. h.** pleasures everm.
17:7. savest by **r. h.** them th.trust
18:35.thy **r. h.** hath holden me up
20:6. with sav-g strength of **r. h.**
21:8. thy **r. h.** find those th. hate
26 : 10. their **r. h.** is full of bribes
44 : 3. but thy **r. h.** saved them
45:4. **r. h.** shall teach thee terrible
9. on **r. h.** did stand qu. in gold
48 : 10. thy **r. h.** full of righte-n.
60:5. save with thy **r. h.** and hear
63:8. thy **r. h.** upholdeth me
73:23. hast holden me by my **r. h.**
74:11.Why withdrawest thy **r. h.**?
77:10. I will remem. years of **r. h.**
78:54. to mt. his **r. h.** purchased
80 : 15. viney. thy **r. h.** planted
17. ha. be upon man of thy **r. h.**
89 : 13. high is thy **r. h.**
25. I will set his **r. h.** in rivers
42. hast set up **r. h.** of adversa.
91:7. 10,000 shall fall at thy **r. h.**
98:1. his **r. h.** hath gotten victory
108 : 6. save with thy **r. h.**
109 : 6. let Sat. stand at his **r. h.**
31. he sh. stand at **r. h.** of poor
110 : 1. Sit thou at my **r. h.** until
I make enem. footstool, Mat.
22 : 44. Mk. 12 : 36. Lu. 20 : 42.
Ac. 2 : 34. He. 1 : 13.
5.L.at thy **r.h.**sh.strike thro. k-s
118:15. **r. h.** of L. doeth valiantly
16. **r. h.** of the Lord is exalted
121:5.L.is thy shade upon thy **r.h.**
137 : 5. let my **r.h.** forget her cun-
138:7. thy **r. h.** sh. save me [ning
139:10.there thy **r. h.** sh. hold me
142 : 4. on my **r. h.** none know
144:8. **r. h.** is a **r. h.** of falseh.,11.
Pr. 3:16. Length of days in her **r.h.**
27:16. ointm. of **r. h.** bewrayeth
Ec 10:2. wise man's heart at **r. h.**
Can. 2 : 6. **r. h.** doth embrace me
8 : 3. his **r.** hand sho. embrace me
Is.41:10.I will uphold thee wi. **r. h.**
13. I thy G: will hold thy **r. h.**
44 : 20. Is not a lie in my **r. h.**
45 : 1. Cyrus whose **r. h.** I have
48 : 13. **r. h.** hath spanned heav.
62:8. L. hath sworn by his **r. h.**
63:12. led by **r. h.** of Moses [**h.**
Je.22:24.tho. Coniah signet upon **r.**
La. 2:3.drawn his **r. h.** from enemy
4. with his **r. h.** as adversary
Eze. 21 : 22. At **r. h.** divination for
Jerusalem
Ha.2:16. cup of L.'s **r. h.** be turned
Zch. 3:1. Satan standing at his **r.h.**
Mat. 5 : 30. if thy **r. h.** offend thee

Mat.25:34. them on his **r. h.** Come ye
26:64. Son of man sitting on **r. h.**
27 : 29. and a reed in his **r. h.**
Mk.14:62. sh. see Son of man sitting
on **r. h.** of power, Lu. 22 : 69.
16:19. sat on **r. h.** of God, He. 1 :
3.-8:1.-10:12.-12:2. 1 Pe. 3 : 22.
Lu. 6 : 6. whose **r. h.** was withered
Ac. 2:25. he is on my **r. h.** I sh.not
33. by **r. h.** of G. exalted, 5 : 31.
3 : 7. took him by **r. h.** and lifted
7 : 55. Jesus on **r. h.** of God, 56.
Ro. 8 : 34. who is at **r. h.** of God
Eph. 1 : 20. set him at his **r. h.** in
Col. 3:1. Christ sitteth on **r. h.** of G.
He. 1:3. on the **r. h.** of the Majesty
12 : 2. **r. h.** of the throne of G.
Re.1:16. in **r. h.** seven stars, 20.-2:1.
17. laid **r. h.** upon me, saying
5 : 1. I saw in his **r. h.** a book, 7.
13:16. to receive mark in their **r. h.**

Right HAND with left.

Ge. 13 : 9. if take **l. h.** I to **r. h.**
24 : 49. th. I may turn to **r. h.** or **l.**
48 : 13. Jo. took Ephr. in **r. h.** tow.
Isr. **l. h.** and Manas. in **l. h.**, 14.
Ex. 14:22. wall on **r. h.** and left, 29.
Nu. 20: 17. we not to **r. h.** nor **l.**,
De. 2:27.-5:32.-17:11,20.-28:14.
22:26. no way to turn to **r. h.** or **l.**
Jos. 1:7. turn not from it to **r. h.** or
l., 23 : 6. 1 S. 6 : 12. Pr. 4 : 27.
Ju.16:29. Sams. with **r. h.** other wi. **l.**
2 S.2:19. turned not to **r. h.** nor **l.**, 21
14:19. none can turn to **r. h.** or **l.**
16:6. all mighty men on **r. h.** and **l.**
1 K. 22 : 19. host of heaven standing on his **r. h.** and his **l.**, 2
Ch. 18 : 18.
2 K. 22 : 2. Josiah not to **r. h.** or **l.**
1 Ch. 12 : 2. could use **r. h.** and **l.**
2 Ch.3:17. pillars, 1 on **r. h.** other on
l., called **r. h.** Jachin: that on **l.**
4:6. ten lavers, 5 on **r. h.** 5 on **l.**
7. five candlest. on **r. h.** 5 on **l.**
34 : 2. declined nei. to **r. h.** nor **l.**
Ne. 8:4. **r. h.**; on **l. h.** Pedaiah
Jb.23:9. **l. h.** work, hideth on **r. h.**
Pr.3:16. days in **r. h.**; on **l. h.** riches
Ec. 10 : 2. **r. h.**: fool's heart at **l.**
Can. 2:6. His **l. h.** is und. my head,
his **r. h.** doth embrace me, 8 : 3.
Is. 9:20. snatch on **r. h.**, be hungry,
eat on **l. h.**, not satisfied
30:21. This the way, when ye to **r.**
h. and **l.** [**h.** and **l.**
54: 3. thou shalt break forth on **r.**
Eze. 16 : 46. Samaria at thy **l. h.**,
at **r. h.** Sodom
21 : 16. go either on **r. h.** or **l.**
39:3. bow out of **l. h.**, arrows out
of **r. h.** [unto heaven
Da. 12:7. held up his **r. h.** and **l. h.**
Jon.4:11. discern betw. **r. h.** and **l. h.**
Zch. 12:6. devour peo. on **r. h.** and **l.**
Mat. 6:3. let not **l. h.** kn. **r. h.** doeth
20 : 21. one on **r. h.** other on **l.**,
Mk. 10 : 37. [Mk. 10 : 40.
23. to sit on **r. h.** and **l.** not mine.
25:33. set sheep on **r. h.** goats on **l.**
27:38. two thieves, one on **r. h.** other
on **l.**, Mk. 15 : 27. Lu. 23 : 33.
2 Co. 6 : 7. armour of right-n. on **r.**
h. and **l.**

Stretch, ed, eth, ing, forth or out HAND. [slay

Ge. 22 : 10. Abraham s-d **f. h.** to
Ex. 3:20. will **s. o.** my **h.**, smite E.,
7:5.-9:15. Je. 6:12.-15:6.-51:25.
8:5. **s. f.** thine **h.** ov. rivers, 9:22.
-10:12, 21. Mat. 12:13. Mk. 3:5.
6. Aaron **s-d o. h.** ov. waters, 17.
10:22. Moses s-d **f. h.** tow. heaven
14 : 16. **s. o. h.** over sea, 26, 7 : 19.
21. Moses s-d **o.** his **h.** ov. sea, 27.
1 S. 26:9. who can **s. f. h.** ag. Lord's
2 S. 1 : 14. wast not afraid to **s. f. h.**
2 S. 24:16. **s-d o.** his **h.** upon Jerus.
Jb.15:25. For he s-h **o.** his **h.** ag. God
30 : 24. not **s. o.** his **h.** to grave
Ps.138:7. will **s. f.** thy **h.** ag enemies
Pr. 1:24. I have s-d **o.** my **h.**, none
31 : 20. she s-h **o.** her **h.** to poor
Is. 5 : 25. his **h.** is s-d **o.** still, 9:12,
17, 21.-10: 4.-14 : 27.
14 : 26. this is the **h.** that is s-d **o.**
23:11. He s-d **o.** his **h.** over the sea
31 : 3. When the L. shall **s. o.**
his **h.**
Je. 6 : 12. will **s. o.** my **h.**, 15:6.-51:
25. Eze. 14 : 9, 13.-25 : 7, 13, 16.
-35 : 3. Zph. 1 : 4.
Eze.6:14. will I **s. o.** my **h.** upon th.
10 : 7. one cherub s-d **f.** his **h.**
14 : 9. will **s. o. h.** upon prophet
13. will I **s. o.** mine **h.** upon la.
25:7. I will **s. o. h.** upon Ammon-
13. I will **s. o. h.** upon Edom [ites
16. I will **s. o. h.** upon the Philis.
35 : 3. I will **s. o. h.** ag. mt. Seir
Da. 11 : 42. he shall **s. f.** his **h.** upon
the countries [scorners
Ho. 7 : 5. he **s-d o.** his **h.** with
Zph.1:4. I will **s. o. h.** upon Judah
2 : 13. will **s. o.** his **h.** ag. Assyria
Mat. 12 : 49. s-d **f.** his **h.** toward dis-
26:51. one with Jes. s-d **o. h.** [ciples
Lu.6:10. said unto man, **s. f.** thy **h.**
See STRETCH, STRETCHED.

Strong HAND.

Ex. 6:1. wi. **s. h.** let them go, 13:9.
Nu. 20: 20. Edom ag. him wi. **s. h.**
Ju. 6 : † 2. **h.** of Midian s. ag. Isr.
1 K.8:42. hear of thy name and **s. h.**
Ne 1 : 10. hast redeemed by **s. h.**
Job 30 : 21. with thy **s. h.** opposest
Ps.89:13. **s.** is thy **h.**, high thy right
136 : 12. With a **s. h.** and with a
stretched out arm, Je. 32 : 21.
Is. 8 : 11. L. spake to me wi. **s. h.**
40:10. Lord will come with a **s. h.**

Their HAND. [Lot

Ge. 19:10. put forth **t. h.** and pulled
35:4. strange gods wh. were in **t. h.**
Ex.5:21. put sword in **t. h.** to slay us
Nu. 22:7. rewards of divina. in **t. h.**
Ju. 7 : 6. lapped, putting **t. h.** to
mouth [put in **t. h.**
1 K. 20 : 6. whatso. pleasant, they
1 Ch.5:10. Hagarites who fell by **t. h.**
2 Ch. 26 : 13. And under **t. h.** was
an army [house
Ezr. 6:12. put to **t. h.** to alter this
Jb.21:16. Lo, their good is not in **t. h.**
Ps.106:42. into subjection under **t. h.**
149:6. and a twoedged sword in **t. h.**
Is.10:5. staff in **t. h.** is mine indigna.
La.5:12. Princes are hanged by **t. h.**
Eze.16:39. I will give thee into **t. h.**
34:10. will require my flock at **t. h.**
Mi. 2 : 1. it, bec. in power of **t. h.**
Jn.10:39. but he escaped out of **t. h.**

Thine HAND.

Ge. 21:18. lift lad hold him in **t. h.**
22 : 12. Lay not **t. h.** upon lad
Ex. 4 : 2. What is that in **t. h.**? rod
6. Put **t. h.** into thy bosom
17. take rod in **t. h.**, 7:15.-17:5.
21. wonders I have put in **t. h.**
13:9. it shall be for a sign on **t. h.**,
16. De. 6 : 8 [be witn.
23 : 1. put not **t. h.** with wick. to
De.2:24. I have given into **t. h.** Sihon
13:9. **t. h.** sh. be first upon him, to
17. cleave nought of cursed to **t. h.**
14 : 25. bind up money in **t. h.**
15:7. nor shut **t. h.** from poor bro.
8. open **t. h.** wide to thy bro., 11.
23:25. mayest pluck the ears wi. **t.**
28:32. sh. be no might in **t. h.** [**h.**
30 : 9. plenteous in work of **t. h.**
Jos. 6 : 2. given into **t. h.** Jericho
8 : 18. for I will give Ai into **t. h.**
9:25. we are in **t. h.** to do unto us
Ju.8:15. and Zalmunna in **t. h.**? 6.
18 : 19. lay **t. h.** upon mouth [**h.**
1 S.14:19. unto priest, Withdraw **t.**
21:3. what is under **t. h.**? give me
8. under **t. h.** spear or sword
24 : 18. unto **t. h.** killedst me not
20. kingd. of Isr. estab-d in **t. h.**
25:8. give whatso. cometh to **t. h.**
26. avenging with **t.** own **h.**
28 : 17. rent kingdom out of **t. h.**
2 S. 13 : 10. that I may eat of **t. h.**
24:16 stay **t. h.**, 1 Ch.21:15.
17. let **t. h.** be ag. me, 1 Ch.21.17.
1 K.8:24. hast fulfilled it with **t. h.**,
2 Ch. 6 : 15.
17: 11. bring morsel of br. in **t. h.**
2 K. 4 : 29. take my staff in **t. h.**
8:8. k. said, Take present in **t. h.**
9 : 1. Take this box of oil in **t. h.**
10 : 15. give me **t. h.** and he gave
13 : 16. Put **t. h.** upon the bow
1 Ch. 4 : 10. that **t. h.** be with me
29 : 12. in **t. h.** power; and **t. h.**
16. store for ho. cometh of **t. h.**
2 Ch.16:7. king of Syr escaped **t. h.**
20 : 6. in **t. h.** is there not power
Ezr. 7 : 14. law of thy G. is in **t. h.**
25. wisd. of God, that is in **t. h.**
Jb. 1:11. put forth **t. h.** touch, 2:5.
12. upon himself put not forth **t. h.**
2 : 6. he is in **t. h.** save his life
10 : 7. none can deliv. out of **t. h.**
11 : 14. If iniq. in **t. h.** put it far
13:21. Withdraw **t. h.** far from me
35 : 7. what receiveth he of **t. h.**?
Ps. 10 : 12. arise, O G. lift up **t. h.**
21 : 8. **t. h.** sh. find out all enem.
31 : 5. Into **t. h.** I commit my spi.
38 : 2. **t. h.** presseth me
39 : 10. by blow of **t. h.**
104 : 28. thou openest **t. h.**, 145:16.
119 : 173. Let **t. h.** help me
138 : 7. **t. h.** against wrath of ene
144:7. Send **t. h.** fr. above, rid n e
Pr. 3 : 27. when in power of **t. h.**
30 : 32. lay **t. h.** upon thy mouth
Ec. 7 : 18. fr. this withdr. not **t. h.**
11 : 6. in eve-g withhold not **t. h.**
Is. 42 : 6. I the Lord will hold **t. h.**
47 : 6. give my inheri. into **t. h.**
51:22. out of **t. h.** cup of trembling
57 : 10. hast found the life of **t. h.**
Je 6 : 9. turn **t. h.** as grapegath
25 : 28. if they refuse cup at **t. h.**
36:14. Take in **t. h.** the roll, wherein
40 : 4. chains wh. were upon **t. h.**
Eze. 3:18. bl. will I require at **t. h.**,
6:11. Smite with **t. h.** [20-33:8.
10 : 2. fill **t. h.** with coals of fire
23:31. I will give her cup into **t. h.**
27 : 15. isles merchandise of **t. h.**
37:17. they sh. become one in **t. h.**
20. sticks shall be in **t. h.**
38:12. to turn **t. h.** upon desolate
Da. 2 : 38. fowls given into **t. h.**
3:17. G. will deliver us out of **t. h.**
Mi.5:9. **t. h.** be lifted upon adversa.
12. cut off witchcrafts out of **t. h.**
Ac.4:30. stretching forth **t. h.** to heal

Thy HAND.

Ge. 4 : 11. thy bro.'s blood fr. **t. h.**
16 : 6. maid is in **t. h.**; do to her
24:2. put **t. h.** und. my thigh, 47:29.
49 : 8. **t. h.** be in neck of enemies
Nu. 21 : 34. delivered Og into **t. h.**
De.2:7. L. blessed in works of **t. h.**,
14:29.-15:10.-23:20.-28:8, 12, 20
3 : 2. I will deliver Og into **t. h.**
33 : 3. all the saints are in **t. h.**
Jos. 10 : 6. Slack not **t. h.** fr. serv-s
1 K.20:42. hast let go out **t. h.** a man
Ps. 10 : 14. to requite it with **t. h.**
17 : 14. From men which are **t. h.**
31 : 15. My times are in **t. h.**
32 : 4. day and night **t. h.** heavy
44 : 2. drive out heathen wi. **t. h.**
74:11. Why withdraweth thou **t. h.**

Ps.80:17.Let **t.h.** be upon man of t.
88:5. are cut off fr. **t.h.** [right h.
109:27. may know th. this is **t.h.**
139: 10. there shall **t. h.** lead me
Pr. 6:1. if stricken **t.h.** wi. stranger
Ec. 9:10. Whatso. **t. h.** find-h to do
Is. 3: 6. let this ruin be under **t.h.**
26: 11. when **t. h.** is lifted up
64: 8. we are the work of **t. h.**
Je. 15: 17. I sat alone bec. of **t. h.**
Eze. 29: 7. hold of thee by **t. h.**
Mat. 18:8. if **t. h.** offend, Mk.9:43.
Jn. 20:27.reach **t. h.** and thrust it
Ac. 4: 28. to do what. **t. h.** determ.

HAND weapon.

Nu. 35:18. if he smite with a **h. w.**

Your HAND.

Ge. 9:2. into **y. h.** are they deliv-d
43:12. take double money in **y. h.**
Ex.12:11.shoes on feet,staff in **y.h.**
23:31.the inhab-s of land into **y.h.**
De.11:18. bind for a sign upon **y.h.**
12: 7. rejoice in all ye put **y.h.** to
Jos.8:7.G.will deliv.it into **y.h.**,20.
10:19. L. hath delivered into **y.h.**
24:8. gave Amorites into **y.h.**, 11.
Ju.3:28.Moab-s into **y.h.**, 2 K.3:18.
7: 15. Midianites into **y. h.**
2 S.4:11. not require his bl.of **y.h.**
2 Ch. 18:14. sh. be deliv. into **y.h.**
28:9. G. delivered them into **y. h.**
Is. 1: 12. who required at **y. h.**?
Je. 26:14. I am in **y.h.** do with me
38: 5. Zede. said, he is in **y. h.**
44: 25. ye have fulfilled with **y.h.**
Eze. 13:21. sh. be no more in **y. h.**
23. will deliver peo. out of **y. h.**
Mal. 1: 10. nor accept off-g at **y.h.**
13. should I accept this of **y.h.**?
2: 13. receiveth with good will at [**y. h.**

HANDS.

Ge. 16:9.submit thyself und. her **h.**
27:22.the **h.** are the **h.** of Esau,23.
49:24. **h.** made strong by **h.** of G.
Ex. 17:12. but Moses' **h.** were heavy
26†17. two **h.** sh. be in one board
29: 24. shalt put all in **h.** of Aa.
32:†29. fill your **h.** to day to the L.
Le.8:27.Aa.'s **h.** and upon son's **h.**
Nu.5:18.off-g of memorial in her **h.**
6: 19. put upon **h.** of Nazarites
De. 4:28. serve gods, work of men's **h.**,27:15. 2 K.19:18. 2 Ch.32:19.
9:15.tables of cov. in my two **h.**
17. I cast them out of my two **h.**
17:7.**h.** of witn-s be first upon him
31:29. to provoke thro. work of **h.**
Ju. 2: 14. deliv-d into **h.** of spoilers
6: 13. into **h.** of Midianites
8: 3. deliv-d into your **h.** princes
6. **h.** of Zebah and Zalmunna, 15.
34. out of **h.** of ene., 1 S. 14: 48.
10:7. into **h.** of Philist., 1 S. 7: 14.
18:10. G. given Laish into your **h.**
19:27. her **h.** were upon threshold
1 S. 14:48. out of **h.** of them spoiled
30: 15. nor into **h.** of my master
2 S. 2:7. **h.** be strong, Zch. 8:9, 13.
16:21. **h.** of all with thee be stro.
21: 9. into **h.** of the Gibeonites
23:6. they cannot be taken with **h.**
1 K. 10: † 19. were **h.** on seat and 2 lions stood, 2 Ch. 9: † 18.
14: 27. **h.** of guard, 2 Ch. 12: 10.
2 K. 3:11. water on **h.** of Elijah
9:35. found skull and palms of **h.**
10:24. men I brought into your **h.**
1 Ch. 25: 2. under the **h.** of Asaph
3. under **h.** of Jeduthun [L.
6. **h.** of father for song in ho. of
2 Ch. 15:7. let not your **h.** be weak
23:†18. by the **h.** of Da., 29: † 27.
Ezr. 4: 4 weakened **h.** of people
Jb. 4: 3. hast strength-d weak **h.**
5: † 20. redeem fr. **h.** of the sword
16:11. turned me into **h.** of wicked
17: 3. who will strike **h.** with me?
Jb.17:9.hath clean **h.** sh. be stronger
Ps. 24: 4. He th. hath clean **h.** [h.
26:10. In **h.** is mischief | 47: 1. clap
58:2.ye weigh violence of your **h.**
63: † 10. run out by **h.** of sword
68:31. Ethiopia sh. stretch out **h.**
115: 4. idols, work of men's **h.**, 135: 15. Is. 37: 19.
7. **h.** but handle not
134:2. lift up your **h.** in sanctuary
140:4. Keep me, from **h.** of wicked
Pr. 6:10. a little folding of **h.**, 24:33.
17. L. hate **h.** shed innoc. blo.
12: 14. recompense of man's **h.**
14:1. foolish plucketh it wi. her **h.**
17: 18. striketh **h.** become surety
22:26. Be not of them strike **h.**
30: 28 spider taketh hold with **h.**
31: 13. worketh will-y with her **h.**
16. with fruit of **h.** she planteth
19. her **h.** to spindle, her **h.** hold
20. reacheth forth her **h.** to needy
31. Give her of the fruit of her **h.**
Ec. 4: 6. both **h.** full with travail
7: 26. her **h.** as bands
10: 18. idleness of **h.** [workman
Can. 7: 1. work of **h.** of a cunning
Is. 1: 15. spread **h.** I will hide my eyes; your **h.** full of blood
2:8. worship work of their own **h.**
13:7. Theref. shall all **h.** be faint
31: 7. idols your **h.** have made
33:†21. L. will be pla. broad of **h.**
35: 3. Strengthen ye the weak **h.**
45: 9. or work say, He hath no **h.**
59:3. **h.** are defiled with blood
Je. 4: 31. spreadeth **h.** saying, Woe
10: 3. a tree, work of the **h.** of
9. of **h.** of the founder, blue and
19:7. cause them to fall by **h.** that
21:4. turn weapons in your **h.**
23: 14. they strengthen **h.** of evil doers, none return, Eze. 13:22.
25:6. wi. works of your **h.**, 7.-44:8.
33:13.under **h.** of him telleth them
38: 4. weak-h **h.** of men of war, **h.**
48:37. upon all **h.** be cuttings
La. 1:17. Zion spreadeth her **h.**
4: 2. how esteemed as work of **h.**
6. overthrown and no **h.** stayed
10.**h.** of pitiful wom. have sodden
Eze. 1: 8. had **h.** of a man, 10: 21.
7: 17. All **h.** be feeble, 21: 7.
21. into **h.** of strangers, 11: 9.
27. **h.** of peo. shall be troubled
35:†5. hast shed blood by **h.** of sw.
Da. 2: 34. stone cut out with-t **h.**,45.
Mi. 7: 3. may do evil with both **h.**
Na. 3:19. all shall clap **h.** ov. thee
Hag.2:17. in labour of your **h.**,1:11.
Zch. 4:9. **h.** of Zerub. laid founda.
Mat. 15:20. unwashen **h.**, Mk.7:2,5.
17:22. be betrayed into **h.** of, 26: 45. Mk. 9: 31-14: 41. Lu. 9:44.
18:8. having two **h.** to be cast into fire,Mk.9:43. [anot.without **h.**
Mk. 14: 58. temple made with **h.**
Lu. 22: 53. stretched no **h.** ag. me
24:7. be deliv-d into **h.** of sinf. men
Ac. 2:23. by wicked **h.** have crucifi.
5:12.by **h.** of apostles were wonders
7:48. temples made with **h.**, 17:24.
8: 18. laying on of apostles' **h.**
11:30.sent to elders by **h.** of Barna.
17:25.Nei. worshipped wi.men's **h.**
19: 11. miracles by the **h.** of Paul
26. no gods wh. are made wi. **h.**
20: 34. that these **h.** have ministered unto my necessities
21:11. sh. deliver into **h.** of Gent.
28:17. into the **h.** of the Romans
2 Co. 5: 1. house not made with **h.**
Ep. 2: 11. circumc. in flesh by **h.**
Col. 2: 11. circumc. without **h.**
1 Th. 4: 11. study to work with **h.**
1 Ti. 2: 8. pray lifting up holy **h.**
4:14.**h.** of the presbytery, He.6:2.
He. 9:11. a greater tab. not with **h.**
24.C.not into holy pl. made wi. **h.**
10: 31. fearful to fall into **h.** of G.
Ja. 4:8. Cleanse your **h.** ye sinners
See **CLAP, CLAPPED hands**

His HANDS.

Ge. 27: 23. **h. h.** were hairy
48: 14. guiding **h. h.** wittingly
49: 24. arms of **h. h.** made strong
Ex.9:33.**h. h.** unto the L.: and the
17: 12. Aa. and Hur stayed **h. h.**
32:19. Mo. cast tables out of **h. h.**
Le. 7:30. **h.** own **h.** sh. bring off-g
15: 11 not rinsed **h. h.** in water
16: 12. **h. h.** full of sweet incense
21. **h. h.** upon head of live goat
Nu. 24: 10. Balak smote **h. h.** tog.
De. 33: 7. let **h. h.** be sufficient
11. L. accept the work of **h. h.**
34: 9. Moses laid **h. h.** upon Josh.
Ju. 9:16. acc. to deserving of **h. h.**
†24.strength-d **h.h.** to kill breth.
11: 32. L. deliv-d them into **h. h.**
1 S. 5: 4. palms of **h. h.** cut off
14: 13. Jonathan climbed up upon **h. h.**
2 S. 4: 1. heard, **h. h.** were feeble
1 K. 8: 22. Sol. spread forth **h. h.** tow. heaven, 38, 54. 2 Ch. 6: 12, 13, 29. [h.
16: 7. in provoking wi. work of **h.**
2 K. 4:34. he put **h. h.** upon **h.h.**
5: 20. in not receiving at **h. h.**
13:16. Elisha put **h.h.** upon king's
2 Ch. 6:4. who with **h. h.** fulfilled
Ne. 4: 17. wi. one of **h. h.** wrought
Jb. 1:10. hast blessed work of **h.h.**
5:18. and **h. h.** make whole
20:10. **h. h.** sh. restore their goods
34: 19. all are the works of **h. h.**
37. he clappeth **h.h.** among us
Ps. 9:16. snared in work of **h. h.**
28: 5. regard not opera. of **h. h.**
78:72. guided by skilfuln. of **h. h.**
81: 6. **h. h.** were deliv. from pots
95: 5. and **h. h.** formed dry land
111:7.The works of **h.h.** are verity
Pr. 21: 25. **h. h.** refuse to labour
Ec. 4: 5. fool foldeth **h. h.** togeth
Can. 5: 14. **h. h.** are as gold rings
Is. 3: 11. reward of **h. h.** be given
5:12. nor consider opera. of **h. h.**
17: 8. not to altars, work of **h. h.**
25:11. L. sh. spread forth **h. h.** as he th. swim-h spreadeth **h. h.**
33: 15. shaketh **h. h.** from bribes
Je.30:6.whf. with **h.h.** on his loins?
50:43. k. heard report, **h. h.** feeble
Ha. 3: 10. deep lifted up **h. h.**
Zch 4: 9. **h. h.** shall finish house
Mat. 19: 13. should put **h. h.** on them, Mk. 10: 16.
27: 24. washed **h. h.** bef. mult.
Mk.6:2.such mighty works by **h.h.**
8:23. had put **h. h.** upon him, 25.
Lu. 24:40. shewed **h. h.**, Jn. 20:20.
50. lifted up **h. h.** and blessed
Jn. 13:3. given all things into **h. h.**
20:25. exc. I see in **h. h.** the print
Ac. 9: 17. **h. h.** on him, said Saul
12:1. Herod stretched **h.h.** to vex
7. chains fell off **h. h.** [h.
21: 11. Paul's girdle and bound **h.**
2 Co.11:33.let down,and escap.**h.h.**
Ep. 4:28. working with **h. h.** th. is
See LAY, LAID, LIFT, LIFTED.

Mine HANDS.

Ju. 11:30. chil. of Am. into **m. h.**
1 Ch.12:17.seeing no wrong in **m.h**
Jb. 16:17. not for injustice in **m.h.**
31:7. if blot hath cleaved to **m.h.**
Ps. 26:6. will wash **m. h.** in inno.
Is.29:23. seeth work of **m.h.** in thee
Eze. 21:17. I will smite **m. h.** toget.

My HANDS.

Ge. 20:5. in innocency of **m. h.** I
31:42. God seen labour of **m. h.**

Ex. 9 : 29. I will spread abroad m.
h., Ezr. 9 : 5. ⌈m. 2 h.
De. 9 : 15. tables of covenant were in
17. cast tables out of m. two h.
Ju. 12 : 3. I put my life in m. h.
2 S. 22 : 21. acc. to clean. of my h.,
Ps. 18:20,24. ⌈18:34.-144:1.
35. He teacheth m. h. to war. Ps.
Ne. 6:9. Now, O G., strengthen m. h.
Jb. 9 : 30. if m. h. never so clean
Ps. 7 : 3. if there be iniq. in m. h.
22 : 16. pierced m. h. and my feet
73:13. in vain I have washed m. h.
88 : 9. I have stretched out m. h.
111:2. lifting up of m. h. as sacri.
143 : 6. I stretch m. h. unto thee
Ec. 2:11. all works m. h. wrought
Can. 5 : 5. m. h. drop-d wi. myrrh
Is. 19 : 25. Assyria work of m. h.
45:11. ask me conc. work of m. h.
12. m. h. stretched out heavens
49:16. graven upon palms of m. h.
60:21. thy peo. the work of m. h.
65: 2. m. h. all day unto rebelli.
Da. 3:15. to deliver you out of m. h.?
10:10. set me upon palms of m. h.
Lu. 24:39. Behold m. h., Jn. 20:27.
Jn. 13:9 but also m. h. and head
Ro. 10:21. All day stretched m. h.
2 Ti. 1 :6. by putting on of m. h.

Our HANDS.

Ge. 5:29. comf. us conc. toil of o. h.
43:22. oth. money have we in o. h.
De. 3 : 3. G. deliv-d into o. h. Og
21 : 7. o. h. not shed this blood
Jos. 2:24. L. into o. h. all the land
Ju. 13 : 23. not meat-off-g at o. h.
16:24. deliv-d into o. h. our enemy
1 S. 17 : 47. will give you into o. h.
Ps. 44 : 20. o. h. to a strange god
90:17. establish thou work of o. h.
Je. 6:24. heard same, o. h. wax fee.
La. 3:41. lift up heart with o. h.
Ho. 14 : 3. nei. say to work of o. h.
Ac. 24 : 7. took him out of o. h.
27 : 19. cast out with o. own h.
1 Co. 4:12. working wi. o. own h.
1 Jn. 1:1. o. h. handled Word of life

Right HANDS. ⌈r. h.

Le. 8:24. put blood upon thumbs of
Ju. 7 : 20. trumpets in their r. h.
Ga. 2 : 9. me and Bar. r. h. of fell-p

Their HANDS.

Ge. 37:21. deliv-d him out of t. h., 22.
Ex. 29:10. shall put t. h. on bullock
15. t. h. upon head of ram, 19.
25. receive th. of t. h., Le. 8 : 28.
30:19. Aa. and sons wash t. h., 21.
Nu. 8:10. shall put t. h. upon Lev.
12. Lev. shall lay t. h. upon bull-k
De. 1:25. they bro-t of fruit in t. h.
21:6. shall wash. t. h. over heifer
Ju. 7:2. to give Midian-s into t. h.
12:2. ye deliv-d me not out of t. h.
2 S. 4 : 12. cut off t. h. and feet
2 K. 11:12. clapped t. h. said, G. save
22 : 17. might provoke me with all
works of t. h., 2 Ch. 34 : 25.
Ezr. 1:6. strengt-d t. h. with vessels
5:8. work goeth fast prosp-h in t. h.
6:22. to strengthen t. h. in work
10:19. gave t. h. that they wo. put
Ne. 2:18. strengt-d t. h. for the work
6:9. t. h. shall be weakened from
8 : 6. Amen, with lifting up t. h.
9 : 24. gavest them into t. h. with
Jb. 5:12. t. h. can-t perform enterp.
30:2. strength of t. h. profit me?
Ps. 28 : 4. give aft. work of t. h.
76:5. men of might not found t. h.
91:12. angels sh. bear thee in t. h.
125:3. lest righte. put t. h. unto iniq
Is. 2 : 8. worship work of t. h.
25 : 11. toge. with spoils of t. h.
59 : 6. act of violence is in t. h.
65 : 22. elect enjoy work of t. h.
Je. 1 : 16. worship-d works of t. h.
Je. 5 : † 31. the priests take into t. h.
25:14. acc. to works of t. h., La. 3:64.
32:30. provok. wi. work of t. h. ⌈h.
La. 1 : 14. Lord delivered me into t.
2 : † 20. chil. swaddled with t. h.
Eze. 10:12. t. h. and wings full of eyes
23 : 37. blood is in t. h., 45.
43 : † 26. purge altar and fill t. h.
Jon. 3 : 8. turn fr. violence in t. h.
Hag. 2 : 14. ev. work of t. h. unci.
Mat. 4 : 6. with t. h. sh. bear thee,
Lu. 4 : 11.
15 : 2. wash not t. h. when eat
26 : 67. smote wi. t. h., Mk. 14:65.
Mk. 7 : 3. exc. wash t. h. eat not
Lu. 6:1. eat, rubbing them in t. h.
Jn. 19 : 3. smote him with t. h.
Ac. 7 : 41. rejoiced in works of t. h.
14:3. granted wonders to be done
Re. 7:9. with palms in t. h. ⌊by t. h.
9:20. repented not of works of t. h.
20 : 4. nor rec-d his mark in t. h.

Thine HANDS.

De. 16:15. Lord shall bless thee in
all works of t. h., 24 : 19.
20 : 13. deliv-d it into t. h., 21:10.
Ju. 7 : 11. afterw. t. h. strength-d
Jb. 10 : 3. good to despise work of t.
8. t. h. have fashioned me ⌊h.
11:13. stretch out t. h. toward him
14:15. have desire to work of t. h.
22:30. deliv-d by pureness of t. h.
Ps. 128:2. shalt eat labour of t. h.
138 : 8. forsake not works of t. h.
Ec. 5:6. why G. destroy work of t. h.
Eze. 21:14. prophesy and smite t. h.
22:14. t. h. be strong in day I deal?
25 : 6. Bec. hast clapped t. h. ⌈h.
Mi. 5:13 no more worship work of t.
Zph. 3:16. Zion, Let not t. h. be slack
Zch. 13 : 6. What wounds in t. h.?
He. 1 : 10. heavens works of t. h.

Thy HANDS.

Ex. 15:17. in sanct. t. h. have estab.
2 S. 3:34. t. h. were not bound
Ps. 8:6. dominion ov. works of t. h.
92:4. will triumph in works of t. h.
102 : 25. heavens are work of t. h.
119 : 73. t. h. have made me and
143 : 5. I muse on the work of t. h.
144:†7. send t. h. from ab., rid me
Je. 2:37. shalt go., t. h. on thy head
Lu. 23:46. into t. h. I commend my
Jn. 21 :18 shalt stretch forth t. h.
He. 2:7. didst set him ov. works of t.

HANDBREADTH. ⌊h.

Ex. 25 : 25. a border of a h., 37 : 12.
1 K. 7 : 26. sea h. thick, 2 Ch. 4 : 5.
Ps. 39:5. hast made my days as a h.
Eze. 40:5. six cubits long, and h.
43:13. The cubit is a cubit and a h.

HANDED.

2 S. 17 : 2. while weary and weak h.
See LEFTHANDED.

HANDFUL.

Le. 2 : 2. priest sh. take h. of flour,
5 : 12.-6 : 15.-9 : 17. Nu. 5 : 26.
1 K. 17 : 12. a h. of meal in a barrel
Ps. 72:16. be a h. of corn in the earth
Ec. 4:6. Better is h. with quietness
Je. 9 : 22. as h. after harvestman

HANDFULS.

Ge. 41:47. earth brought forth by h.
Ex. 9 : 8. Take to you h. of ashes
Ru. 2:16. let fall some h. of purpose
1 K. 20:10. dust of Sa. suffice for h.
Eze. 13:19. pollute for h. of barley?

HANDKERCHIEFS.

Ac. 19:12. fr. his body to the sick h.

HANDLE, ED. [Verb.]

Ge. 4:21. fa. of such as h. the harp
Jb. 5 : 14. h. the pen of the writer
1 Ch. 12:8. could h. spear, 2 Ch. 25:5.
Ps. 115 : 7. hands, but they h. not
Je. 2:8. th. h. the law knew me not
46 : 9. Libyans that h. the shield
Eze. 21:11. furbished, that it be h-d
Eze. 27 : 29. all that h. the oar
Mk. 12:4. sent him shamefully h-d
Lu. 24:39. h. me | Col. 2:21. h. not
1 Jn. 1 : 1. have h-d of word of life

HANDLETH, ING.

Pr. 16:20. He that h-h matter wisely
Je. 50:16. cut off him that h-h sickle
Eze. 38:4. all of them h-g swords
Am 2:15. Nei. stand th. h-h the bow
2 Co. 4:2. not h-g word of G. deceitf.

HANDLES.

Can. 5 : 5 with myrrh on h. of lock

HANDMAID, S. ⌈12.

Ge. 16:1. Sarai had a h. Hagar, 25:
29 : 24. Zilpah to be Leah's h., 35:
26. ⌈35 : 25.
29. Bilhah Rachel's h., 30 : 4 -
33 : 1. divided chil. to two h-s
2. he put h-s and chil. foremost
Ex 23 : 12. son of h. be refreshed
Ju. 19:19. bread and wine for thy h.
Ru. 2: 13. spoken friendly thy h.
3 : 9. ans-d, I am Ruth thine h.
1 S 1:11 if look on afflic. of thine h.
16. Count not thine h. dau. of Beli.
18. Let thy h. find grace in thy
25 : 24. let thy h. speak ⌊sight
28. forgive trespass of thine h.
31. remember thy h.
41. let thy h. wash feet of serv-s
28:21. thine h. hath obeyed voice
2 S. 6 : 20. uncov-d in eyes of h-s
14 : 6. thy h. had 2 sons, they
20:17. Hear the words of thy h.
1 K. 1 : 13. didst not swear unto h.?
17. swearest by Lord unto thy h.
3:20. took son while thine h. slept
2 K. 4:2. Thy h. hath not any thing
16. man of G., do not lie unto h.
Ps. 86 : 16. turn, save son of thy h.
116:16. I thy serv-t, son of thy h.
Pr. 30 : 23. h. heir to her mistress
Je. 34 : 11. caused h. to ret. for h.
16. ye caused his h. to ret.
Jo. 2:29. upon h-s pour my spi.
Lu. 1 : 38. Behold the h. of the L.

HANDMAIDEN, S.

Ru. 2:13. tho. not like one of thy h-s
Lu. 1 : 48. low estate of h.
Ac. 2 : 18. On my h-s I will pour

HANDSTAVES.

Eze. 39:9. sh. burn h. and spears

HANDWRITING.

Col. 2:14. blotting out h. of ordinan.

HANDYWORK.

Ps. 19:1. firmament sheweth his h.

HA'NES. ⌈43 : † 7.

Is. 30 : 4. his ambassadors to H., Je.

HANG. ⌈tree

Ge. 40 : 19. Pha-h shall h. thee on a
Ex. 26 : 13. curtain shall h. over, 12.
33. h. vail, 32. | 40 :8. h. hanging
Nu. 25 : 4. h. them before the Lord
De. 21 : 22. if thou h. him on a tree
28 : 66. thy life shall h. in doubt
2 S. 21 : 6. will h. them up unto L.
Es. 6: 4. speak unto k. to h. Mord
7 : 9. king said, h. him thereon
Can. 4:4. there h. a thous. bucklers
Is. 22:24. shall h. upon him glory
La. 2:10. the virgins h. their heads
Eze. 15:3. men take pin to h. vessel
Mat. 22:40. On these two h. the law
Ac. 28:4. saw beast h. on his hand
He. 12:12. lift up hands wh. h. down

HANGED. ⌈13.

Ge. 40 : 22. h. the chief baker, 41 :
De. 21 : 23. that is h. is accursed
Jos. 8:29. king of Ai he h. on a tree
10 : 26. five kings h. he on 5 trees
2 S. 4:12. Baanah h. over the pool
17 : 23. Ahithophel h. himself
18:10. I saw Absalom h. in an oak
21:9. 7 sons of Saul h. they in, 13.
Ezr. 6 : 11. being set, let him be h.
Es. 2 : 23. two chamberl-s were h.
5 : 14. Mord. may be h. thereon

Es. 7 : 10. So they **h.** Haman, 8 : 7.
9 : 14. they **h.** Haman's ten sons
Ps. 137 : 2. **h.** harps upon willows
La. 5 : 12. Princes **h.** by hands
Eze 27 : 10. they **h.** the shield, 11.
Mat. 18 : 6. better a millstone were
h. about neck, Mk. 9 : 42. Lu.
27 : 5. Judas went **h.** hims. [17:2.
Lu. 19 : † 48. peo. **h.** on him to hear
23 : 39 one of thieves **h.** railed on
Ac. 5:30. whom ye slew and **h.** 10:

HANGETH, ING. [39.

Jos. 10:26. **h-g** upon trees till even.
Jb. 26 : 7. he **h-h** earth upon noth.
Ga. 3:13. Cursed that **h-h** on a tree

HANGING, S.

Ex. 26 : 36. thou shalt make a **h.**
for door, Nu. 3:25, 31.-4:25,26.
37. shalt make for **h.** five pillars
27 : 9. **h-s** of 100 cubits, 11.-38 :
12. **h-s** of 50 cubits, 38:12. [9,11.
14. The **h-s** on one side of gate fifteen cubits, 15.-38 : 14, 15.
36 : 37. a **h.** for the tabernacle
door, 35 : 15.-39 : 38.-40 : 5, 28.
2 K. 23:7. women wove **h-s** for grove
Es. 1 : 6. blue **h-s** fastened wi. cords
See **COURT** with **hanging, s.**

HA'NIEL. See REZIA.

HAN'NAH. [child-n

1 S. 1 : 2. two wives, one H.; H. no
5. unto H. worthy portion; he
8. H., why weepest | 9,13. [loved H.
15. H. said, No, my lord [2: 21.
19. Elka. knew H. | 20. H. conceived
22. H. went not | 2 : 1. H. prayed

HAN'NATHON.

Jos. 19 : 14. border on n. side to H.

HAN'NIEL. [H.

Nu. 34 : 23. prince of chil. of Joseph,

HA'NOCH,[1] ITES,
or HE'NOCH.[2] [1 : 33.[2]

Ge. 25 : 4. sons of Midian; H.[1], 1 Ch.
46 : 9. sons of Reuben; H.[1], Ex. 6 :
14. Nu. 26 : 5. 1 Ch. 5 : 3. [H-s
Nu. 26: 25. H.[1], of whom family of

HA'NUN.

2 S. 10 : 1. H. his son reigned [19:2.
2. said Da., kindness unto H., 1 Ch.
3. princes said unto H., 1 Ch. 19:3.
4. H. took Dav.'s serv-ts, 1 Ch. 19:4.
1 Ch. 19:6. H. sent 1,000 talents to hire
Ne. 3 : 13. valley gate repaired H. [30.

HAP. [Boaz's field

Ru. 2 : 3. her **h.** was to light on

HAPHRA'IM.

Jos. 19:19. Issachar's border tow. H.

HAPLY.

1 S. 14:30. if **h.** people eaten freely
Mk. 11 : 13. if **h.** he might find fruit
Lu. 14:29. Lest **h.** after laid founda.
Ac. 5:39. lest **h.** found to fight ag. G.
17:27. if **h.** they might feel aft. him
2 Co. 9:4. Lest **h.** if they of Macedo.

HAPPEN.

1 S. 28:10. no punishm. **h.** to thee
Pr. 12 : 21. sh. no evil **h.** to the just
Is. 41:22. let them shew what **h.**
Mk. 10:32. to tell what things sho. **h.**

HAPPENED. [Boaz'

Ru. 2 : † 3. her hap **h.** to light on
1 S. 6 : 9. a chance that **h.** to us
2 S. 1:6. as I **h.** upon m-t Gilboa
20 : 1. **h.** to be a man of Belial
Es. 4 : 7. Mord-i told him all had **h.**
Je. 44:23. thf. this evil is **h.** unto you
Lu. 24 : 14. talked of all had **h.**
Ac. 3:10. wi. wonder at that wh. **h.**
Ro. 11 : 25. blindness is **h.** to Isr.
1 Co. 10 : 11. things **h.** for ensample
Ph. 1:12. things **h.** unto me have fall.
1 Pe. 4:12. as tho. strange thing **h.**
2 Pe. 2:22. **h.** to them acc-g to prov-

HAPPENETH. [erb

Ec. 2 : 14. one event **h.** to them all
15. As it **h.** to fool, so it **h.** to me
8:14. just men, wick. men to wh. it **h.**
Ec. 9:11. time and chance **h.** to them

HAPPIER. [all

1 Co. 7 : 40. she is **h.** if she abide

HAPPY.

Ge. 30 : 13. **h.** am I, for dau-s will
† 13. Leah called his name Asher,
De. 33:29. **h.** art thou, O Isr. [**h.**
1 K. 10:8. **h.** thy men, **h.** these thy
servants, 2 Ch. 9 : 7.
Jb. 5 : 17. **h.** is man G. correcteth
Ps. 127:5. **h.** man hath quiver full
128 : 2. **h.** shalt thou be, it be well
137 : 8. **h.** he be rewardeth thee, 9.
144:15. **h.** that peo. in such a case,
h. people whose God is Lord
146:5. **h.** is he hath G. of Jac. for
Pr. 3:13. **h.** is man findeth wisdom
18. **h.** is ev. one retaineth her
14:21. **h.** is he hath mercy on poor
16:20. whoso trusteth in L., **h.** is
28 : 14. **h.** is man feareth alway
29 : 18. keepeth the law, **h.** is he
Je. 12 : 1. whf. **h.** th. deal treach-y?
Mal. 3 : 15. now we call proud **h.**
Jn. 13 : 17. if know, **h.** if do them
Ac. 26 : 2. I think myself **h.** king A.
Ro. 14:22. **h.** he condem-h not hims.
Ja. 5 : 11. them **h.** who endure
1 Pe. 3:14. suffer for righte-n., **h.** ye
4:14. reproached for name of C. **h.**

HA'RA. [ye

1 Ch. 5 : 26. k. of Assyr. bro-t them

HAR'ADAH. [unto H.

Nu. 33:24. encamped in H. | 25. fr. H.

HA'RAN. [Person.]

Ge. 11:26. begat H., 27. | 28. H. died
29. Nahor's wife was dau. of H.
31. Terah took Lot son of H.
1 Ch. 2:46. Ephah bare H. H. begat
23 : 9. sons of Shimei; H.

HA'RAN. [Place.] [H.

Ge. 11 : 31. Terah to H. | 32 died in
12 : 4. Abram departed out of H.
5. took souls they had gotten in H.
27 : 43. flee to H. | 29:4. Of H. we
28:10. Jacob went tow. H. [37:12.
2 K. 19 : 12. fathers destroyed H., Is.
Eze. 27: 23. H. and Eden merchants

HA'RARITE.

2 S. 23 : 11, 33. 1 Ch. 11 : 34, 35.

HARBO'NA
HARBO'NAH.

Es. 1 : 10. H. one of chamberlains,

HARD. [Adj.] [7:9.

Ge. 18 : 14. any thing too **h.** for L.?
35 : 16. Rachel had **h.** labour, 17.
42:†7. Joseph spake **h.** things, †30.
Ex. 1:14. lives bitter with **h.** bond.
18 : 26. **h.** causes bro-t unto Mo.
De 1 : 17. cause too **h.** bri. unto me
15:18. it sh. not seem **h.** unto thee
17 : 8. if matter too **h.** for thee in
26:6. Egyp-s laid on **h.** bondage
Ju. 4 : † 24. ha. of Isr. **h.** ag. Jabin
1 S. 1:†15. I am a woman **h.** of spirit
2: † 3. let not **h.** come out of mou.
2 S. 3 : 39. sons of Zeruiah too **h.**
13 : 2. Amnon thought it **h.** to do
1 K. 10:1. with **h.** questions, 2 Ch. 9:1.
14 : † 6. I am sent with **h.** tidings
2 K. 2 : 10. hast asked a **h.** thing
Jb. 30:†25. not I weep for him was **h.**
41 : 24. **h.** as piece of millstone
Ps. 31 :†18. lips, wh. speak a **h.** thing
60 : 3. hast shewed peo. **h.** things
88 : 7. Thy wrath lieth **h.** upon me
94 : 4. How long wicked speak **h.**
Pr. 13 : 15. way of transgr-rs is **h.**
Is. 14: 3. give thee rest fr. **h.** bond.
21:†2. **h.** vision is decla-d unto me
Je 32 : 17. nothing too **h.** for thee
27. I am L. is any thi. too **h.** for
Eze 2:†4. are chil. **h.** of face [me?
3:5. not sent to peo. of **h.** lang., 6.
Da. 5 : 12. shewing **h.** sentences
Mat. 25:24. I knew thou art **h.** man
Mk. 10:24. **h.** for th. trust in riches
Jn. 6 : 60. This is a **h.** saying
Ac. 9:5. **h.** to kick ag. pricks, 26:14.
He. 5:11. many thi. **h.** to be uttered
2 Pe. 3:16. things **h.** to be underst.
Jude 15. all ungodly of **h.** speeches

HARD. [Adverb.]

Le. 3 : 9. rump off **h.** by backbone
Ju. 9 : 52. Abim. went **h.** unto door
20:45. Israel pursued **h.** aft. Benj.
1 S. 14 : 22. followed **h.** after Philis.
31 : 2. the Philistines followed **h.**
upon, 2 S. 1 : 6. 1 Ch. 10 : 2.
1 K. 21:1. had a vineyard **h.** by pal.
1 Ch. 19:4. cut garm. **h.** by buttocks
Ps. 63 : 8. soul foll-h **h.** after thee
Jon. 1:13. rowed **h.** to bri. to land
Ac. 18 : 7. house joined **h.** to synag.

HARDEN. [14:4.

Ex. 4 : 21. **h.** Pha.'s heart, 7 : 3.-
14 : 17. I will **h.** hearts of Egyp-s
De. 15:7. shalt not **h.** thy heart, nor
Jos. 11 : 20. of L. to **h.** their hearts
1 S. 6:6. Whf. do ye **h.** your hearts?
2 Ch. 30 : † 8. **h.** not your necks as
Jb. 6:10. would **h.** myself in sorrow
Ps. 95:8. **h.** not your heart, He. 3:
8, 15.-4 : 7.

HARDENED.

Ex. 7 : 13. Lord **h.** Pha.'s heart, 9:
12.-10 : 1, 20, 27.-11 : 10.-14:8.
14. Pha.'s heart is **h.** | 22. was **h.**,
8 : 19.-9 : 7, 35. [32.-9 : 34.
8:15. **h.** his heart and heark-d not,
De. 2:30. Lord thy G. **h.** his spirit
1 S. 6:6. as Egyp-s and Pha. **h.** hearts
2 K. 17:14. they **h.** their necks like
2 Ch. 36 : 13. Zedekiah **h.** heart
Ne. 9:16. fa-s **h.** their necks, 17, 29.
Jb. 9:4. who **h.** hims. and prospered
39:16. She is **h.** ag. her young ones
Is. 63 : 17. why hast **h.** our heart
Je. 7 : 26. heark-d not; but **h.** neck
19 : 15. **h.** their necks not to hear
Da. 5 : 20. mind was **h.** in pride
Mk. 6:52. consid. not, heart was **h.**
8 : 17. have ye your heart yet **h.**?
Jn. 12 : 40. blinded their eyes, **h.**
Ac. 19 : 9. But when divers were **h.**
Ro. 11 : † 7. and rest were **h.**
He. 3 : 13. lest any of you be **h.**

HARDENETH.

Pr. 21 : 29. wicked man **h.** his face
28 : 14. **h.** heart fall into mischief
29 : 1. being reproved **h.** his neck
Ro. 9 : 18. whom he will he **h.**

HARDER.

Pr. 18:19. bro. offended **h.** to be won
Je. 5 : 3. made faces **h.** than a rock
Eze 3:9. **h.** than flint thy forehead

HARDHEARTED.

Eze. 3 : 7. all house of Isr. are **h.**

HARDLY. [lied

Ge. 16 : 6. when Sarai dealt **h.** she
Ex. 13 : 15. Pha. would **h.** let us go
Is. 8 : 21. pass thro. it **h.** bestead
Mat. 19 : 23. rich man sh. **h.** enter
kingd. of G., Mk. 10:23. Lu. 18:24.
Lu. 9:39. spir. **h.** departeth fr. him
Ac. 27 : 8. **h.** passing it, we came

HARDNESS. [**h.**

Jb. 38 : 38. When dust groweth into
Ps. 81 : † 12. I gave them up to **h.**
Mat. 19:8. bec. of **h.** of hearts suff-d,
to put away wives, Mk. 10 : 5.
Mk. 3:5. grieved for **h.** of hearts
16:14. upbraided them wi. their **h.**
Ro. 2 : 5. **h.** and impenitent heart
11 : † 25. **h.** in part happen. to Isr.
2 Ti. 2 : 3. endure **h.** as a good sol

HARE. [dier

Le. 11 : 6. **h.** is unclean, De. 14 : 7.

HA'REPH.

1 Ch. 2:51. H. father of Beth-gader

HA'RETH.

1 S. 22:5. Da. came into forest of H

HARHAI'AH.

Ne. 3 : 8. repaired Uzziel, son of H

HAR'HAS, or HAS'RAH.
2 K. 22 : 14. son of H., 2 Ch. 34:22.
HAR'HUR. [7:53.
Ezr. 2:51. Nethinim, chil. of H., Ne.
HA'RID = HADID.
Ezr.2:†33. The chil. Lod, H. and Ono
HA'RIM.
1 Ch. 24 : 8. The third lot to H.
Ezr. 2 : 32. chil. of H., 39.-10:21,31.
Ne.3:11.-7:35,42.-10:5,27.-12:†3,15.
HA'RIPH = JORAH.
Ne.7:24. chil. of H., Ezr.2:†18. | 10:
HARLOT. [19.
Ge. 34 : 31. deal with sister as h.?
38:15. Jud. thought her to be a h.
21. Where is the h. that was, 22.
24. Tamar dau. in law played h.
Le. 21 : 14. high priest not take a h.
Jos. 2 : 1. spies came into a h.'s ho.
6 : 17. only Rahab h. shall live, 25.
22. Go into the h.'s house and
Ju. 11 : 1. Jeph. was son of a h.
16 : 1. Samson saw there a h. and
Pr. 7 : 10. woman with attire of h.
Is. 1 : 21. faithful city become h.!
23:15. aft. 70 yrs. Tyre sing as a h.
16. take a harp, thou h. th. hast
Je. 2 : 20. wanderest, playing h.
3 : 1. hast played h. with many
6. und. ev. green tree, played h.
8. Judah went and played h. also
Eze. 16 : 15. playedst the h., 16, 28.
31. thou hast not been as a h.
35. O h. hear the word [h.
41. cause thee to cease fr. playing
23 : 5. Aholah played h. when
19. days she had played the h.
44. a woman that playeth the h.
Ho. 2 : 5. mother hath played h.
3 : 3. thou shalt not play the h.
4:15. tho. Isr. play h. let not Jud.
Jo. 3 : 3. have given a boy for a h.
Am. 7 : 17. Thy wife sh. be a h. in
Mi. 1 : 7. return to hire of h. [city
Na. 3:4. whoredoms of wellfav-d h.
1 Co. 6 : 15. make th. memb. of h.
16. is joined to a h. is one body
He. 11 : 31. h. Rahab perished not
Ja. 2 : 25. Rahab h. justifi. by works
HARLOTS.
1 K. 3 : 16. came h. unto the king
Pr.29:3. th. keepeth company wi. h.
Je. 5 : 7. by troops in h. houses
Ho. 4:14. with whores, sacri. wi. h.
Mat. 21:31. h. go into kingd. of G.
32. publicans and h. believed him
Lu. 15 : 30. devoured living wi. h.
Re. 17 : 5. BAB., MOTHER OF H.
HARM. [Noun.]
Ge. 31 : 52. not pass ov. pillar for h.
Le. 5 : 16. sh. make amends for h.
Nu. 35 : 23. not ene., nei. sought h.
1 S. 26 : 21. no more do thee h.
2 S.20:6. Sheba more h. than Abs.
2 K. 4 : 41. was no h. in the pot
1 Ch. 16:22. do my prophets no h.,
Ps. 105 : 15. [no h.
Pr. 3:30. strive not, if he done thee
Je. 39 : 12. look well, do him no h.
Ac. 16 : 28. Do thyself no h.
27:21. gained h. | 28:5. felt no h.
28:6. saw no h. | 21. spake any h.
HARM. [Verb.]
Pe. 3:13. who will h. you, if good?
HARMLESS.
Mat. 10 : 16. be wise h. as doves
Ro. 16:† 19. have you h. conc. evil
Ph. 2 : 15. that ye be h. sons of G.
He. 7 : 26. is holy, h. undefiled
HAR'NEPHER. [H.
1 Ch.7 : 36. sons of Zophah ; Suah,
HARNESS. [Noun.]
1 K.20:11. Let n. him gird-h h. boast
22:34. betw. joints of h., 2 Ch.18:23.
2 Ch. 9 : 24. brought every man h.
HARNESS, ED. [E.
Ex. 13 : 18. Isr. went up h-d out of
Je. 46:4. h. horses, get up horsem.
HA'ROD.
Ju. 7 : 1. Gideon pitched beside H.
HA'RODITE. [11 : 27.
2 S. 23 : 25 Shammah H. (2) 1 Ch.
HAR'OEH = REAIH.
1 Ch.2:52. Shobal had sons H., 4:†2.
HA'RORITE.
1 Ch. 11 : 27. Shammoth the H.
HAR'OSHETH.
Ju. 4 : 2. Sisera in H. of Gentiles,
HARP. [13, 16.
Ge. 4 : 21. fa. of them th. handle h.
31:27. might have sent thee wi. h.
1 S. 10 : 5. meet prophets wi. a h.
16 : 16. man cunning player on h.
23. David took a h. and played
1 Ch. 25 : 3. six prophesied wi. a h.
Jb.21:12. They take timbrel and h.
30 : 31. My h. is turned to mourn.
Ps. 33 : 2. Praise L. with h., 150:3.
43 : 4. on the h. will I praise thee
49:4. open my dark saying upon h.
57:8. awake psaltery and h., 108:2.
71 : 22. I will sing with h., 92:3.-
98 : 5.-147 : 7.-149 : 3.
81 : 2. bring hither the pleasant h.
Is. 5 : 12. h. and viol in feasts [h.
16 : 11. my bowels sh. sound like a
23 : 16. Take a h. | 24:8. joy of h.
ceaseth [7, 10, 15.
Da. 3 : 5. at sound of h. fall down,
1 Co. 14 : 7. whether pipe or h. exc.
HARPS.
1 K. 10 : 12. the king made of almug
trees h. and psalteries, 2 Ch.9:11.
1 Ch. 15 : 21. with h. on Sheminith
16 : 5. Jelel with psalteries and h.
2 Ch.20:28. to Jerus. wi psalteries, h.
Ps. 137 : 2. hanged h. upon willows
Is.30:32. it sh. be with tabrets and h.
Eze. 26 : 13. sound of h. be no more
Re. 5 : 8. elders, having every one h.
14 :2. harpers harping with their h.
15 : 2. I saw them having h. of God
See **CYMBALS with harps.**
HARPED. [or h.?
1 Co. 14 : 7. how known what piped
HARPERS, HARPING.
Re.14 :2. I heard the voice of h-s h-g
18:22. voice of h-s be heard no more
HARROW. [Verb.]
Jb. 39 : 10. will he h. valleys after
HARROWS. [thee?
2 S. 12 : 31. put them und. h. of
1 Ch.20:3. cut them wi. saws and h.
HAR'SHA. [7:54.
Ezr. 2:52. Nethinim; chil. of H., Ne.
HART, S.
De. 12 : 15. eat of h-s, 14:5.-15:22.
1 K. 4:23. ten fat oxen, besides h-s
Ps. 42:1. As h. panteth aft. waterb.
Is. 35 : 6. sh. lame man leap as h.
La. 1:6. her princes become like h-s
See YOUNG.
HA'RUM. [of H.
1 Ch. 4 : 8. families of Aharhel son
HARU'MAPH.
Ne. 3:10. repaired Jedaiah son of H.
HARU'PHITE.
1 Ch. 12 : 5. to Da. at Ziklag the H.
HA'RUS. [of H.
2 K. 21 : 19. Amon, his moth. dau.
HARVEST. [cease
Ge. 8 : 22. earth remaineth h. not
30 : 14. went in days of wheat h.
45 : 6. in 5 yrs. nei. earing nor h.
Ex. 23 : 16. keep feast of h., 34:22.
34 : 21. in earing and h. shalt rest
Le. 19 : 9. when ye reap h., 23 : 10,
22. De. 24 : 19.
25 : 5. grows of own accord of h.
Ru. 1 : 22. in beginn. of barley h.
2:21. fast by yo. men until ended h.
23. fast by maidens until end of h.
1 S. 6 : 13. men reaping their h.
8 : 12. will set them to reap his h.
1 S. 12 : 17. Is it not wheat h. to day
2 S. 21 : 9. to death in h. barley h.
10. for her from beginning of h.
Jb. 5:5. Whose h. the hungry eat-h
Pr. 6 : 8. ant gathereth food in h.
10 : 5. sleep. in h. causeth shame
20 : 4. beg in h. and have nothing
26:1. rain in h. so honour for fool
Is. 9 : 3. they joy acc. to joy in h.
16 : 9. shouting for thy h. is fallen
17:11. h. be a heap in day of grief
18 : 4. cloud of dew in heat of h.
5. afore the h. when bud is perf.
23 : 3. h. of river is her revenue
Je. 5 : 17. they shall eat up thy h.
24. reserveth to us weeks of h.
8 : 20. h. is past, summer is ended
Ho. 6 : 11. O Jud., he hath set a h.
Jo. 1 : 11. h. of the field is perished
3 : 13. Put in sickle, for h. is ripe
Am. 4 : 7. were yet 3 months to h.
Mat. 9 : 37. The h. is plenteous, the
38. Pray the L. of the h. to send,
Lu. 10 : 2. [time of h.
13 : 30. Let grow tog. until h. in
39. h. is end of the world, reap-s
Mk. 4 : 29. put in sickle h. is come
Lu. 10 : 2. he said, h. truly is great
Jn. 4 : 35. cometh h. fields white to
Re. 14:15. the h. of earth is ripe [h.
HARVEST with time.
Jos.3:15. Jordan overfl-h all t. of h.
Ju. 15:1. in t. of wheat h. Samson
2 S. 23 : 13. chiefs to Da. in h. t.
Pr.25:13. as cold of snow in t. of h.
Je. 50 : 16. handleth sickle in h. t.
51 : 33. a little while t. of her h.
Mat. 13 : 30. in the t. of h. I will
HARVESTMAN.
Is. 17:5. as when h. gathereth corn
Je. 9 : 22. fall as the handf. after h.
HASADI'AH.
1 Ch. 3:20. sons of Zerub., Ohel, H.
HASENU'AH.
1 Ch. 9:7. Hodaviah son of H., chief
HASHABI'AH.
1 Ch. 6 : 45. on left hand H. | 9:14.
25 : 19. 12th lot to H. | 3. [our
26 : 30. H. and breth. men of val-
27 : 17. 2 Ch. 35:9. Ezr. 8 : 19. Ne
8 : 17.-10:11.-11:15,22.-12:21.
HASHAB'NAH.
Ne. 10 : 25. chief of people H. and
HASHABNI'AH.
Ne 3:10. repaired Hattush son of H.
HASHBAD'ANA.
Ne. 8 : 4. on Ezra's left hand H.
HA'SHEM.
1 Ch 11:34. valiant men, sons of H
HASHMO'NAH. [in H.
Nu. 33 : 29. p. Mithcah and pitched
HA'SHUB, or HAS'SHUB.
1 Ch. 9 : 14. Of Lev. Shemaiah son of
Ne. 3 : 11, 23.-10 : 23.-11 : 15. [H.
HASHU'BAH.
1 Ch. 3 : 20. sons of Zerub., H. and
HA'SHUM. [Ohel
Ezr. 2 : 19. came with Zerub , chil.
of H. [strange wives
10 : 33. am. sons of priests taken
Ne. 7 : 22.-8 : 4.-10 : 18.
HASHU'PHA [2:†43.
Ne. 7:46. Nethinim, chil. of H., Ezr.
HAS'MAAH. See SHEM'AAH
HAS'RAH. See HAR'HAS.
HASSENA'AH.
Ne. 3 : 3. fish gate sons of H. build
HAS'SHUB. See HA'SHUB.
HAST.
Ge. 19:12. said unto Lot h. any be-
sides? whatso. h. in city bring
out [ing, father?
27:38. Esau said, h. but one bless-
32:28. as a prince h. power wi. G.
33:9. Esau said, keep that thou h.
45 : 10. come thou, all th. thou h.
11. all thou h. come to poverty

Ex. 9 : 19. gath. all thou **h.** in field
13:12.ev. firstling thou **h.** the L.'s
De. 8 : 13. all thou **h.** is multiplied
12 : 26. holy things wh. thou **h.**
Ju. 18 : 3. what **h.** thou here ?
1 S. 25 : 6. Peace be unto all thou **h.**
2 S. 15 : 35. **h.** thou not Zadok ?
2 K. 4 : 2 tell me, what **h.** in hou.
Jb. 10 : 4. **h.** thou eyes of flesh, or
40 : 9. **h.** thou an arm like God?
Pr. 3 : 28. say not, Go, when **h.** it
22 : 27. If thou **h.** nothing to pay
Is. 22 : 16. What **h.** thou? whom **h.**
Mat. 19:21. sell all thou **h.**, Mk. 10:
21. Lu. 18 : 22.
25 : 25. thou **h.** that is thine
Jn. 4 : 11. whence **h.** living water ?
18. he thou now **h.** is not hush.
6 : 68. thou **h.** words of eter. life
7 : 20. Thou **h.** a devil, 8:48, 52.
13 : 8. If I wash thee not, **h.** no
Ac 8:21. Thou **h.** nei. part nor lot
Ro. 2 : 20. **h.** the form of knowl.
14 : 22. **h.** thou faith? have it to
1 Co. 4 : 7. what **h.** th. didst not
8:10.if man see thee wh. **h.** knowl.
Ja.2:18. Thou **h.** faith and I works
Phm. 5. faith thou **h.** toward L.
Re. 2 : 3. thou **h.** patience, and (3)
6. this thou **h.**, 14, 15.
3 : 1. **h.** a name to live, 4.
8. **h.** a little strength
11. hold what thou **h.**

HASTE. [Noun.]

Ex.10:16. Pha. called for Mos. in **h.**
12 : 11. ye sh. eat it in **h.** girded
33.send out of land in **h.**,De.16:3.
1 S. 21:8. k.'s business required **h.**
2 K. 7 : 15. Syrians cast away in **h.**
Ezr. 4 : 23. went up in **h.** to Jerus.
Ps. 31 : 22. said in **h.** I am cut off
116 : 11. I said in **h.** All men liars
Is. 52:12. ye sh. not go out with **h.**
Da. 2:25. bro-t Dan. bef. king in **h.**
3:24. king rose up in **h.** and spake
6:19. king in **h.** unto den of lions
Mk. 6:25. she came with **h.** to king
Lu.1:39. Mary into hill country wi.
2:16. shepherds came wi. **h.** [**h.**

HASTE. [Verb.]

Ge. 19 : 22. **h.** thee, escape thither
45 : 9. **h.** ye and go to my fa., 13.
1 S. 20:38. Jona. cried, **h.** stay not
23:27.**h.**thee,for Philis.have luvad.
Ps.22:19.O my strength, **h.** to help
See **MAKE** haste. [me

HASTED.

Ge.18:7.to yo.man, he **h.** to dress it
24:18. she said, Drink, and **h.**, 20.
Ex. 5 : 13. the taskmasters **h.** them
Jos. 4 : 10. people **h.** over Jordan
8 : 14. when king saw it, they **h.**
19. ambush **h.** set city on fire
10 : 13. sun **h.** not to go down a
whole day [upon Gibeah
Ju. 20 : 37. liers in wait **h.** rushed
1 S. 17:48. Da. **h.** | 25:23. Abig., 42.
25 : 34. except thou hadst **h.** and
28:24. the witch at En-dor **h.** and
2 S. 19:16. Shimei, of Bahurim, **h.**
1 K. 20 : 41. prophet **h.** took ashes
2 K.9:13.they **h.** and put garments
2 Ch. 26 : 20. himself **h.** to go out
Es. 6 : 12. Haman **h.** to his house
14.**h.**to bring Haman unto banq.
Jb. 31 : 5. if my foot **h.** to deceit
Ps.48:5. troubled and **h.** aw.,104:7.
Ac. 20 : 16. Paul **h.** to be at Jerus.

HASTEN.

1 K. 22 : 9. **h.** hither Micaiah
2 Ch. 24 : 5. see ye **h.** the matter
Ps. 16 : 4. **h.** after another god
55:8. I wo. **h.** my escape fr. storm
Ec.2:25.or who can **h.** more than I
Is. 5 : 19. let him **h.** his work that
60 : 22. I L. will **h.** it in his time
Je.1:12.I will **h.** my word to perf. it

HASTENED, ETH.

Ge. 18 : 6. Ab. h-d into the tent
19:15.angels h-d Lot, saying,Arise
2 Ch. 24 : 5. the Levites h-d it not
Es.8:15. posts went h-d by k., 8:14.
Is. 51 : 14. exile h-d to be loosed
Je. 17 : 16. I have not h-d fr. being

HASTETH. [pastor

Jb. 9 : 26. as eagle that **h.** to prey
40:23. drinketh up a river, and **h.**
Pr. 7:23. as a bird **h.** to snare [not
19: 2. he that **h.** with feet sinneth
28:22. **h.** to be rich, hath evil eye
Ec 1 : 5. sun **h.** to where he arose
Je. 48 : 16. afflic. of Moab **h.** fast
Ha. 1 : 8. fly as eagle that **h.** to eat
Zph. 1 : 14. great day of the L. **h.**

HASTILY.

Ge.41:14. Joseph **h.** out of dungeon
Ju.2:23. without driving th. out **h.**
9 : 54. Abim-h called **h.** unto armourbearer
1 S. 4 : 14. came in **h.** and told Eli
1 K. 20:33. the men did **h.** catch it
Pr. 20:21. inheri. may be gotten **h.**
25 : 8. go not forth **h.** to strive
Jn. 11:31. saw Mary th. she rose **h.**

HASTING.

Is. 16 : 5. judgm. and **h.** righte-n.
2 Pe. 3 : 12. **h.** unto day of the L.

HASTY.

Pr. 14:29. **h.** of spirit exalteth folly
21 : 5. one th. is **h.** only to want
29:20. seest a man **h.** in his words
Ec. 5:2. let not heart be **h.** to utter
7 : 9. Be not **h.** in spi. to be angry
8 : 3. Be not **h.** to go out of sight
Is. 28 : 4. as **h.** fruit bef. summer
32 : † 4. heart of **h.** shall underst.
35 : † 4. Say to them of **h.** heart
Da. 2 : 15. Why is the decree so **h.**
Ha. 1:6. Chaldeans, that **h.** nation

HASU'PHA=HASH'UPHA

Ezr. 2:43. Nethinim, chil. of H., Ne.

HA'TACH. [7:†46.

Es.4:5. H. one of k.'s chamberlains
6. H. went to Mord. unto street,

HATCH, ETH. [9,10.

Is. 34 : 15. owl shall **h.** and gather
59 : 5. They **h.** cockatrice' eggs
Je. 17:11. as partridge on eggs h-h

HATE. [not

Ge.24:60.possess gate of those th.**h.**
50 : 15. Joseph will peradv. **h.** us
Le. 19:17. shalt not **h.** thy brother
26:17.that **h.** you sh. reign ov. you
Nu. 10:35. let them th. **h.** thee flee
De. 7:10. repayeth them th. **h.** him
15.lay upon them th.**h.**thee,30:7.
19 : 11. if any man **h.** his neighb.
22 : 13. if take a wife, and **h.** her
24:3. if the latter husband **h.** her
33:11.smite thro. loins of them th.
2 Ch.19:2.love them that **h.** L. [**h.**
Jb 8:22.**h.**thee be clothed wi. shame
Ps. 21 : 8. hand find those **h.** thee
34:21. th. **h.** righte. shall be deso.
44 : 10. they which **h.** us spoil for
68 : 1. let them that **h.** him flee
83 : 2. **h.** thee have lifted up head
89 : 23. I will plague them **h.** him
97 : 10. Ye that love the L. **h.** evil
105:25. He turned heart to **h.** peo.
129:5. let be turned that **h.** Zion
Pr.1:22. how long, fools, **h.** knowl.
6 : 16. these six doth the Lord **h.**
8:13. fear of the Lord is to **h.** evil;
pride do I **h.** [**h.** thee
9 : 8. Reprove not a scorner lest he
19:7. All breth. of poor do **h.** him
25 : 17. lest be weary, and **h.** thee
29 : 10. bloodthirsty **h.** upright
Ec. 3 : 8. time to love, a time to **h.**
Eze.16:27. deliv-d unto them **h.**thee
Da. 4:19. dream to them th. **h.** thee
Am. 5:10.They **h.** him th. rebuketh
15. **h.** the evil, and love the good

Mi. 3 : 2. Who **h.** good and love evil
Mat.5:43.been said, love thy neighb.
h. enemy [Lu. 6:27.
44. do good to them that **h.** you,
6 : 24. will **h.** the one, Lu. 16:13.
24:10. sh. betray and **h.** one ano.
Lu. 1 : 71. saved fr. ha. of all **h.** us
6:22. Blessed are ye when men **h.**
14 : 26. **h.** not his fa. and mother
Jn. 7:7. world cannot **h.** you [3:13.
15:18.marvel not if world **h.**.1 Jn.
Re. 17:16. these shall **h.** the whore

I HATE.

1 K. 22:8. but I **h.** him, 2 Ch.18:7.
Ps.101:3.I **h.** work of them th.turn
119 : 104. I **h.** ev. false way, 128.
113. I **h.** vain thoughts, but
163. I **h.** and abhor lying
139 : 21. Do not I **h.** th. hate thee
22. I **h.** them with perfect hatred
Pr. 8 : 13. froward mouth do I **h.**
Is. 61:8. I **h.** robbery for burnt off.
Je. 44:4. do not this thing th. I **h.**
Am. 5 : 21. I **h.** your feast days
6 : 8. I **h.** his palaces, therefore
Zch. 8 : 17. are things I **h.** saith L.
Ro. 7 : 15. what I **h.** that do I
Re.2:6 deeds of Nicolaitanes I **h.**,15

HATE me.

Ge.26:27.Wh.come,seeing ye **h.m.**
Ex. 20:5. visiting iniq. unto 3d and
4th generation of them **h. m.**,
De. 5 : 9.
De. 32:41. will reward them **h. m.**
Ju. 11 : 7. Did not ye **h. m.**?
14 : 16. dost **h. m.** [Ps. 18 : 40.
2 S.22:41. destroy them that **h.m.**,
Ps 9:13. I suffer of them th. **h.m.**
25:19.they **h. m.** with cruel hatr.
35 : 19. let them wink that **h. m.**
38:19.**h.m.** wrongf-y are many,69:
41:7. **h. m.** whisper together [4.
55 : 3. cast iniq. in wrath **h. m.**
69:14. be deliv-d from them **h.m.**
86 : 17. which **h. m.** may see it
118:7. my desire upon them **h.m.**
Pr. 8 : 36. that **h. m.** love death

HATED.

Ge. 27 : 41. Esau **h.** Jacob, because
29 : 31. the L saw Leah was **h.**
33. L. hath heard that I was **h.**
37:4. breth. **h.** Jo. yet more, 5, 8.
49:23. archers shot at him **h.** him
De. 1:27. Bec. the Lord **h.** us, 9:28.
4:42. **h.** him not in times past, 19:
4, 6. Jos. 20 : 5. [the **h.**
21:15. another **h.** | 16. bef. son of
17. shall acknowledge son of **h.**
Ju. 15 : 2. I thought thou **h.** her
2 S. 5:8. lame and blind that are **h.**
13:15.Amnon **h.** Tamar | 22.Absalom **h.** Amnon [Ps. 18 : 17.
22 : 18. deliv-d me fr. them **h.** me,
Es. 9 : 1. had rule over them **h.** th.
5. did unto those that **h.** them
Jb 31:29. destruc-n of him th.**h.**me
Ps. 26:5. I have **h.** congr. of evil
31 : 6. **h.** them th. regard vanities
44 : 7. hast put to shame th. **h.** us
55 : 12. nei. was it he that **h.** me
106:10. saved them fr. him that **h.**
41. they that **h.** them ruled over
Pr. 1 : 29. they **h.** knowledge
5 : 12. How have I **h.** instruction
14 : 17. man of wick. devices is **h.**
20. poor is **h.** even of his neighb.
Ec. 2:17. **h.** life | 18. I **h.** labour
Is.60:15. hast been forsaken and **h.**
66 : 5. brethren that **h.** you said
Je. 12 : 8. th. have I **h.** heritage
Eze. 16:37. will gather all thou **h.**
35 : 6. since thou hast not **h.** blood
Ho. 9 : 15. I **h.** them for wickedn.
Mal. 1 : 3. I loved Jacob, and **h.**
Esau, Ro. 9:13. [13. Lu.21:17.
Mat. 10 : 22. ye shall be **h.**, Mk 13:
24:9. ye shall be **h.** of all nations

Lu. 19 : 14. his citizens h. him
Jn.15:18.th. it h. me bef. it h. you
24. seen and h. both me and Fa.
25. They h. me without a cause
17:14. world hath h. them, bec.
Ep. 5:29. no man h. own flesh
He. 1 : 9. Thou hast h. iniquity

HATEFUL.

Ps.36:2. until his iniq. be found h.
Tit. 3:3. we h. hating one another
Re. 18 : 2. a cage of every h. bird

HATEFULLY.

Eze. 23:29. shall deal with thee h.

HATERS.

Ps.81:15.h. of L. sho. have submit.
Ro. 1:30. Backbiters, h. of God

HATEST.

2 S. 19: 6. lovest enem. h. friends
Ps. 5 : 5. h. all workers of iniquity
45:7. lovest righte-n. h. wickedn.
50 : 17. thou h. instruction, and
Eze.23:28. into hand whom thou h.
Re. 2 : 6. h. deeds of Nicolaitanes

HATETH, ING.

Ex.18:21. provide men h-g covet-n.
23 : 5. if see ass of him th. h. thee
De. 7:10. L. not slack to him th. h.
12:31. ev. abom. he h. have they
16 : 22. nor set up image Lord h.
22:16.dau. unto this man,he h.her
Jb. 16 : 9. He teareth me who h. me
34 : 17. he that h. right, govern?
Ps. 11 : 5. loveth violence, soul h.
120:6. dwelt with him th. h. peace
Pr. 11:15. that h. suretysh. is sure
12 : 1. that h. reproof is brutish
13 : 5. a righteous man h. lying
24. He th. spareth rod h. his son
15:10. he that h. reproof shall die
27. but he that h. gifts shall live
26:24. th. h. dissembleth wi. lips
28. A lying tongue h. afflicted
28:16.th. h. covet-n. prolong days
29 : 24. partner wi. thief h. soul
Is.1:14. appointed feasts my soul h.
Mal. 2: 16. that he h. putting away
Jn. 3 : 20. that doeth evil h. light
7:7. me the world h. bec. I testify
12:25.that h. his life in this world
15 : 19. not of world, thf. h. you
23. he that h. me h. my Father
Tit. 3 : 3. hateful and h-g one ano.
Jude 23. h-g garm. spotted by flesh
1 Jn.2:9.th. h. bro. is in darkn.,11.
3:15. Whoso. h. bro. is murderer
4:20. if say, I love G. and h. bro. [is liar

HATH.

Ge. 24:36. him h. he giv. all he h.
39 : 8. all that he h. to my hand
Le.22:5. whatso. uncleanness he h.
27:28. no devoted thi. of all he h.
Nu. 23 : 22. h. strength of, 24:8.
27:4.Why name aw. bec. h. no son
De.10:9. Levi h. no part nor inheri.,
12: 12.-14: 27, 29. [h.
21 : 16. sons to inherit that he
17. firstb.double por-n of all he h.
Jos. 6:22. bring out wom. all she h.
7: 15. be burnt, he and all he h.
1 S. 15:22. h. L. delight in off-gs?
25: 21. kept all this fellow h.
2 K.4:2. handmaid h. not any thi.
14.Verily she h. no child, her
Jb. 1 : 10. hedge about all he h.
11. touch all he h.
12. all that he h. is in thy power
2: 4. all man h. give for his life
5: 16. So the poor h. hope
38 : 28. h. the rain a father?
21 : 21. what pleas. h. he in house
Ps.37:16. little that a righteous h.is
109: 11. extortioner catch all he h.
127:5. Happy is man h. quiver full
146: 5. Happy he that h. God of
Pr. 12: 9. he that h. a serv. better
13: 4. sluggard desireth, h. noth.
7. maketh hims. rich, yet h.noth.
Pr.16:22.und-g is life unto him h. it
17 : 8. stone in eyes of him h. it
19 : 23. h. it, shall abide satisfied
23:29.Who h.woe? who h. sorrow?
Ec. 4 : 8. h. nei. child nor bro. [(6)
10. for he h. not another to help
6:8. what h. wise more than fool?
8 : 8. nei. h. he power in day of
Can. 8 : 8. sister, she h. no breasts
Is. 29 : 8. and his soul h. appetite
45 : 9. h. no hands | 50:10.no light
53: 2. he h. no form nor comeliness
55:1. he th. h. no money, come ye
Je. 23:28. prophet that h. a dream,
tell, he that h. my word, let
49 : 1. h. Isr. no sons? h. no heir?
La.3:20.My soul h. them in remem.
Mal. 1:14 deceiver which h. in flock
Mat 5:23. thy bro.h. aught ag. thee
8 : 20. h. not to lay head, Lu.9:58.
11 : 15. he that h. ears to hear, let
him hear, 13 : 9, 43. Mk. 4 : 9,
Lu. 8 : 8.-14 : 35. Re. 2 : 7, 11,
17, 29.-3 : 6, 13, 22.
18. nor drinking, they say He h. a
devil, Lu. 7 : 33. Jn. 10 : 20.
13 : 12. whoso. h. to him be given,
who h. not, fr. him be taken
th. he h., 25 : 29. Mk. 4 : 25.
Lu. 8 : 18.-19 : 26.
21. Yet h. he not root in himself
27. whence then h. it tares
44. selleth all he h. buyeth field
56. Whence h. this man these?
Mk. 6:2. [3. Lu. 19 : 31, 34.
21 : 3. L. h. need of them, Mk.11:
25:28. unto him wh. h. 10 talents
Mk. 3 : 22. he h. Beelzebub, and
26. cannot stand but h. an end
29. h. never forgiveness but is
30. said, He h. an unclean spirit
9 : 17. my son, wh. h. a dumb sp.
14 : 8. She h. done what she could
Lu. 3 : 11. He that h. two coats, let
12 : 5. wh. after he h. killed h.
44. make him ruler ov. all he h.
14 : 33. th. forsaketh not all he h.
19:24. give it him H. 10 pounds,25.
20 : 24. Whose superscription h.it?
22 : 36. h. a purse, that h. no sw.
24:39. spirit h. not flesh and bones
Jn. 3 : 29. He that h. the bride, is
36. believeth h. everlasting life,
5 : 24.-6:47,54. [self, so h.given
5 : 26. as the Father h. life in him-
6 : 9. which h. five barley loaves
12:48.h.one judgeth him, the word
14 : 21. He that h. my com-ts and
30. prince of world h. noth. in me
15:13. Greater love h. no man than
16 : 15. All things Fa. h. are mine
21.woman h.sorrow bec. her hour
19 : 11. deliv-d thee, h. greater sin
Ac. 9 : 14. he h. authority fr. chief
15 : 21. h. in ev. city them preach
23:17. h. a certain thi. to tell, 18.
Ro. 3 : 1. What advantage h. Jew?
4 : 2. if by works, he h. to glory
9 : 21. h. not the potter power ov.
1 Co. 7 : 4. wife h. not power of own
7. ev. man h. his proper gift of G.
12. If any brother h. a wife, 13.
12 : 12. body is one and h. many
14 : 26. h. a psalm, h. a doctrine
2 Co. 6 : 14. what fellowsh.h.right-
cousu. with unright. ? (2)
15. what concord h. C.?
16. h. temple of God
8:12 accepted acc. to that man h.
Ga. 4:27. the desolate h. more chil.
Ep. 5:5. nor idolater h. any inherit.
Ph. 3 : 4. if any thinketh he h.
1 Ti. 6:16.Who only h. immortality
Col. 4 : 13. he h. a great zeal for
He.3:3.builder h. more honour than
7 : 24. h. an unchangeable priesth.
10:35.confidence, which h.recomp.
He. 11:10. city wh. h. founda-s [17.
Ja. 2 : 14. tho. man say he h.faith,
1 Jn. 2 : 23. denieth Son, h. not Fa.
3 : 3. every man that h. this hope
15. no murderer h. eternal life
17.whoso h.this world's good,and
4 : 16. believed love God h. to us
18.no fear in love, fear h.torment
5:10. believeth on Son h. the witn.
12. h. Son h. life, h. not Son h.
2 Jn. 9.abideth not in doctr.of C h.
not G., abideth h. Fa. and Son
Re. 2:12. he wh. h. the sharp sword
18. Son of G. who h. his eyes like
3 : 1. he that h. the seven Spirits
7. that h. key of David opens
12 : 6. wildern. where she h. a place
12.knoweth he h.but a short time
13:18. Let him th.h.underst.count
16 : 9. God which h. power over
17:7.beast which h.the seven heads
9. here is mind which h. wisdom
20:6. on such 2d death h.no power

HA'THATH.

1 Ch. 4 : 13. sons of Othniel, H.

HATI'PHA. [7:56.

Ezr. 2:54. Nethinim; chil. of H., Ne.

HAT'ITA. [Ne. 7:45.

Ezr. 2 : 42. of porters; chil. of H.,

HATRED.

Ge. 26 : † 21. ano. well, called it h.
Nu 35 : 20. if he thrust him of h.
2 S. 13 : 15. h. wherewith he hated
Ps. 25 : 19. hate me with cruel h.
109 : 3. compassed me about wi.h.
5. rewarded me h. for love
139:22. I hate them with perf h.
Pr. 10 : 12. h. stirreth up strifes
18. hideth h. with lying is fool
15:17. Better than a stalled ox,and
26 : 26. h. is cov-d by deceit [h.
Ec. 9 : 1. no man kno-h love or h.
6. their h. and envy is perished
Eze. 25 : 15. to destroy it for old h.
35 : 5. Bec. hast had perpetual h.
11. acc. to envy used out of h.
Ho. 9 : 7. for iniq., and for great h.
8. prophet is h. in ho. of his God
Ga. 5 : 20. witchcraft, h. works of [flesh

HATS.

Da. 3: 21. bound in hosen and h.

HAT'TIL.

Ezr. 2 : 57. of Sol.'s serv-s chil. of H.

HAT'TUSH.

1 Ch. 3 : 22. sons of Shemaiah : H.,
Ezr. 8 : 2. Ne. 3 : 10.-10:4.-12:2.

HAUGHTILY.

Mi. 2 : 3. nei. sh. ye go h. this time

HAUGHTINESS.

Pr. 21 : † 4. the h. of eyes is sin
Is. 2 : 11. h. of men be bowed down
17. h. of men sh. be made low
13 : 11. will lay low h. of terrible
16:6. heard of h. of Moab,Je.48:29.

HAUGHTY.

2 S. 22: 28. thine eyes are upon h.
Ps. 131 : 1. Lord, my heart is not h.
Pr. 6 : †17. the Lord hateth h. eyes
16 : 18. h. spirit goeth bef. a fall
18 : 12. Bef. destruc. heart is h.
21 : 24 h. scorner is his name
Is. 3 : 16. Bec. dau-s of Zion are h.
10:33. and h. shall be humbled
24 : 4. h. peo. of earth languish
Eze. 16 : 50. h. bef. me, I took away
Zph.3:11.no more h. bec.of holy mt.

HAUNT. [Noun.]

1 S. 23 : 22. go see where his h. is

HAUNT. [Verb.]

1 S. 30:31. Da. and men wont to h.
Eze.26:17. terror to be on all th.h.it

HAU'RAN.

Eze. 47 : 16. is by coast of H., 18.

HAVE.

Ge. 11 : 6. they h. all one languag.
33 : 9. Esau said I h. enough, 11.
43 : 7. h. ye another brother

Ge. 44: 19. h. ye father?
46: 32. brought all they h., 47: 1.
Ex. 20: 3. h. no other gods, De. 5:7.
22: 3. if h. noth., he sh. be sold
Le. 7:7. pri. maketh atone-t h.it, 8.
10.ev.meat off-g sons of Aa. sh.h.
19: 36. a just hin shall ye h.
22: 13. if priest's daughter h. no child, Nu. 27: 8, 9.
25: 26. if man h. none to redeem
Nu. 11:13. Whence should I h.flesh
18: 20. h. no inheritance (2), 23, 24. De. 18: 1, 2. Jos. 18: 7.
22: 38. h. I now any power at all
25: 13. covenant of peace he sh.h.
35: 8. them th. h. many, th h.few
De. 5: 26. who heard G., as we h.?
Jos. 2: 13. alive fa. and all they h.
17:18. though they h. iron chariots
22:24. What h. you to do with L
Ju. 14: 15. h. ye called us to take that we h.? ⌈what h. I more
18: 24. Ye h. taken my gods, and
Ru. 1:12. I am too old to h. a husb.
1 S.8:19. will h. a king over us ⌊(2)
9: 7. is not a present; what h.we?
15: 3. utterly destroy all they h.
18: 8. can he h. more but kingd.?
21: 15. h. I need of madmen (2)
2 S. 13:9. said, h. out all men fr.me
15: 36. h. with them their 2 sons
16:10.What h. I to do with you,ye
18:18. I h.no son to keep my name
19: 28.What right h. I to cry unto
34. How long h. I to live? ⌊king
43. said, We h. ten parts in king
20: 1. We h. no part in David (2)
1 K. 8:28. h. respect unto prayer of
12:16.What portion h. we in David
17:12. I h. not a cake, but handful
20: 4. O king, I am thine, all I h.
21:2. that I may h. it for a garden
22:17. Isr. as sheep h. no shepherd
2 K. 11: 15. h. her forth, 2 Ch. 23:
20:9. This sign shalt h. of L. ⌊14.
2 Ch. 1: 12. nei. shall any h. like
16:9. hencef. shalt h. wars ⌈comp.
20: 12. we h. no might ag. this
35: 21. What h. I to do with thee
23. he said, h. me away, for I am
Ezr.4:16. sh. h. no portion,Ne.2:20.
Ne. 5: 5. other men h. our lands
Jb. 3: 9. look for light but h. none
6: 8.Oh that I might h.my request
10. Then should I yet h. comfort
21:15. what profit h. if we pray to
30:13. mar my path, h. no helper
35: 3. What profit I h. if cleansed
Ps. 2: 4. L. shall h. them in deris.
14:4.h.workers of iniq.uo knowl-e?
16: 6. I h. goodly heritage ⌊53: 4.
35: 25. not say, Ah, so wo. we h.it
73: 7. h. more than heart co. wish
25. Whom h. I in heaven but
104:33.to my G.while I h.my being
111:10. good uuderst-g h. all that
115: 5. h. mouths; eyes h. they
6. h.ears; noses h.,7.-135:16, 17.
119: 42. shall I h. whw. to ans.
165. Great peace h. they wh. love
146:2. sing praises while I h. being
149:9. this honour h. all his saints
Pr. 1: 14. let us all h. one purse
20:4. slugg. beg in harvest h.noth.
28: 19. tilleth land sh. h. plenty
29: 21. sh. h. him become his son
30: 2. I h. not the understanding
3.nor h.I the knowl. of the Holy
Ec.3:19.yea, they h.all one breath
7:12. wisd. giveth life to them h.it
9: 5. nei. h. any more a reward
6. nei. h. they any more portion
Can. 8:8.We h. a little sister and she
12. thou, O Sol., must h. a thous.
Is.5:13. are gone, bec. h. no knowl.
23: 12. there shalt thou h. no rest
26: 1. We h. a strong city, salvation
Is.30:29.Ye sh. h. a song as in night
40:29. th. h. no might, he incr-h
43:8. that h. eyes, deaf that h. ears
45: 21. h. not I the Lord? is no G.
24. say, In the L h.I righteousn.
49: 20. chil. thou shalt h. sh. say
50: 2. h. I no power to deliver?
11. this h. of mine ha., lie down
52: 5. what h. I here, saith the L.
56:11.dogs,wh.can never h.enough
61: 7. For shame you sh.h.double
Je. 5: 21. h. eyes see not, h. ears
31. my people love to h. it so
12: 12. no flesh shall h. peace
16: 2. nei. shalt h. sons nor dau-s
23:17. L. said, Ye sh.h.peace, 29:7.
35: 7. not plant viney., nor h.any
36: 30. h. none to sit upon throne
38: 2. he sh. h. his life for a prey
44: 14. they h. a desire to return
49: 9. will destroy till h. enough
31. nation which h. nei. gates nor
La. 3: 21. this I recall, thf. h. hope
Eze. 5: 11. nei. will I h. pity, 7: 4.
-8: 18.-9: 10. ⌈pity
9: 5. let not eye spare, nei. h. ye
18: 23. h. I pleas. that wicked die?
32.I h.no pleas. in death of,33:11.
21: 25. when iniq. shall h.end,29.
Da. 2: 30. for any wisdom that I h.
3: 25. I see 4 men, they h. no hurt
5: 7. shall h. a chain of gold, 16.
6: 2. king should h. no damage
Ho.10:3. they sh. say We h. no king
Mi. 3:6. night unto you, not h. vis.
Zph. 2:10. This h. for their pride
Hag. 1: 6. eat, but ye h.not enough
Mal. 2: 10. h. we not all one father?
Mat. 3: 9. We h. Abraham to our father? Lu. 3: 8.
5: 40. take coat, let him h. cloak
46. love th., what reward h. ye?
6: 2. They h. their reward, 5: 16.
8: 20. foxes h. holes (2), Lu. 9:58
29. What h. we to do with thee, Jesus? Mk. 1: 24. Lu. 4: 34.
13:12. shall h. more abund.,25:29.
14:4. not lawful to h. her,Mk.6:18.
15:33.Whence h.so much br.in wil.
34. How many loaves h. ye? Mk.
6:38.-8:5. ⌈tard, 21:21. Lu.17:6.
17:20. If h. faith as a grain of mus-
18: 12. man h. an hundred sheep
19: 16. that I may h. eternal life?
21. thou sh. h. treasure in heav.
27. foll-d thee, what shall we h.?
26: 11. ye h. the poor always, me h. not, Mk. 14: 7. Jn. 12: 8.
65. what need h. we of witnesses?
27:19.h. noth. to do with just man
43. let him deliv..if he will h.him
65. Ye h. a watch; go your way
Mk. 2:17.whole h. no need of phys.
19. as long as they h. the bridegr.
3: 15. to h. power to heal sick
4:17. h. no root in thems.,Lu.8:13.
23. if any h. ears, 7: 16. Re. 13:9.
40. how is it ye h. no faith? ⌈17.
8: 16. It is bec. we h. no bread,
9:50. h. salt in yourselves,h.peace
10:21. h. treas. in heav., Lu.18:22.
23. sh. they th. h. riches enter
11: 22. h. faith in God
23. shall h. whatsoever be saith
24. believe ye receive, ye shall h.
25. if ye h. aught against any
Lu. 6:32. what thank h. ye? 33, 34.
7: 40. I h. somewhat to say unto
8: 18. taken what he seem. to h.
9: 3. neither h. two coats
11:5.which of you shall h.a friend
6. I h. nothing to set bef. him
41. give alms of such as ye h.
12: 4. h. no more th. they can do
17. I h. no room where to bestow
24. which neither h. storehouse
33. Sell that ye h. and give alms
Lu.12:50.I h.baptism to be bapt.wi.
14: 18. I pray h. me excused, 19.
28. whether he h. suffi. to finish
15: 31. ever with me, all I h. is
16:28. For I h. five brethren ⌊thine
29. They h. Moses and prophets
18: 24. shall they that h. riches
19: 14. will not h. this man reign
17. h. thou author. over ten cities
22: 31. Sat. hath desired to h. you
37. things cone-g me h. an end
24:17.What communications ye h.
39.spirit not flesh, as ye see me h.
41. h. ye any meat? Jn. 21: 5.
Jn. 2:3. moth.of J. said, h. no wine
4. Wom., what h. I to do wi.thee?
3:15. not perish, h. everl. life, 16.
4: 17. woman said, I h. no husb.
32. I h. meat to eat ye know not
5: 7. I h. no man to put me into
26. hath given Son to h. life in
36.I h.greater witness than of Jn.
38. ye h. not his word abiding
39. think ye h. eternal life, and
40. to me that ye might h. life
42. I know ye h. not love of God
6: 40. beli-h, may h. everl. life
53. exc. ye eat his fl., h. no life
8: 6. th. they might h. to accuse
12. foll-h me, sh. h. light of life
26.I h. many things to say,16:12.
41. h. one father even God
49. I h. not a devil
9: 41. If blind, ye sho. h. no sin
10: 10. I am come that they h.life
16. other sheep I h. not of this
18. I h. power to lay it down, and
12: 35. Walk while he h. light, 36.
13:35. if ye h. love one to another
16:22. ye now h. sorrow, but I will
33. that in me ye might h. peace, ye sh. h. tribulation,I h.overc.
17: 13. that they might h. my joy
18:39. ye h. a custom I sho.release
19:7.We h. a law | 15.We h. no k.
10. knowest not I h. power, 11.
20: 31. that beli-g ye might h. life
Ac. 3:6. Silv. and gold h. I none (2)
9:6. L.,what wilt thou h. me to do?
16: 3. Him wo. Paul h. go wi. him
17: 28. in him we h. our being
18: 10. I h. much peo. in this city
19: 25. by this craft h. our wealth
38. h. a matter against any man
21:23. We h. 4 men wh. h. a vow
23:29. to h.noth. laid to his charge
24: 15. And h. hope toward God
16. to h. a conscience void
23. to let him h. liberty
25. when I h. a convenient season
25: 16. h. the accusers face to face
26.I h.no certain thi. to write (3)
Ro. 1:13. that I might h.some fruit
2: 14. Gentiles, wh. h. not the law
5: 2. by wh. h. access, Ep. 2: 18.
6: 22. ye h. your fruit unto holin.
8: 9. if any h. not Spirit of Christ
23. ours. also wh. h. firstfruits
9: 2. I h. great heaviness
9. I will come, Sarah sh. h. a son
10: 2. they h. a zeal of God but
12: 4. members h. not same office
13: 3. thou sh. h. praise of same
14:22. Hast thou faith? h. to thys.
15: 4. that we might h. hope
17. I h. whereof I may glory
1 Co. 2: 16. we h. the mind of C.
4:11. h. no certain dwellingplace
15. yet h. ye not many fathers
5: 1. that one sho. h. his fa.'s wife
6:4. If then ye h. judgm. of things
19. H. G. in you, wh. ye h. of G.
7: 2. let ev. man h. his own wife, every woman h. own husband
25. I h. no com-t of the Lord
28. such sh. h. trouble in the flesh
29. they that h. wives be as tho.

2 Co.7:32. wo h. you with-t carefuln.
40. I think I h. the Spirit of God
8: 1. know, we all h. knowledge
9: 4. h. we not power to eat, 5, 6.
16. I h. nothing to glory of
17. do this willingly I h. a reward
11: 10. ought wom. to h. power on
14. if a man h. long hair [head
15. if a woman h. long hair, it is
16. we h. no such custom, nei.
22. What! h. ye not houses to eat
12: 21. eye not to ha., I h. no need
23. h. more abun. comeliness 24.
25. sho. h. same care one for ano.
30. h. all the gifts of healing?
13: 1. h. not charity, I am become
2. tho. I h. all faith and h. not, 3.
15: 31. rejoi-g I h. in Christ Jesus
34. some h. not knowl. of God
2 Co.1:15. ye might h. a second bene.
2: 3. I sho. h. sorrow, Ph. 2: 27.
4. love I h. abundantly unto you
3: 4. such trust h. we thro. C.
12. Seeing we h. such hope
4: 1. seeing we h. this ministry
7. But we h. this treas. in earthen
5: 1. we h. a building of God, a
12. ye may h. somewhat to ans.
8: 11. out of that ye h.
Ga. 2: 4. liberty we h. in C. Jesus
6: 4. sh. he h. rejoicing in hims.
10. As we h. oppor. let us do good
Ep. 1: 7. In whom we h. redemption, Col. 1: 14. [4: 17.
3:12. In whom we h. boldness, 1 Jn.
Ep. 4:28. h. to give to him needeth
5: 11. h. no fellowship with unfr.
Ph. 1: 7. I h. you in my heart
4: 18. but I h. all and abound
20. I h. no man likeminded
3: 4. I might also h. confidence,
1 Jn. 2: 28.-3: 21.
17. as ye h. us for an ensample
Col. 1: 4. love ye h. to all saints
18. he might h. the preëminence
2: 1. what gr. conflict I h. for you
23. Wh. things h. a shew of wisd.
3: 13. if any man h. a quarrel ag.
4: 1. knowing ye h. a Master in
1 Th. 2: 14. ye suffered, as they h.
3:6. that ye h. good remembrance,
2 Ti. 1: 3.
4: 12. ye may h. lack of nothing
13. as others which h. no hope
5: 1. ye h. no need that I write
2 Th. 3: 2. for all men h. not faith
9. not bec. we h. not power [saved
1 Ti. 2: 4. Who will h. all to be
3: 7. he must h. a good report
5: 4. if any widow h. children
16. wom. th. believeth h. widows
6: 2. they that h. believing masters
Phm. 7. we h. great joy and conso.
He.4:13. him with whom we h. to do
14. Seeing that we h. a high pri.
15. we h. not a high priest
5: 12. ye h. need that one teach
14. by use h. senses exercised
6: 18. we might h. a strong conso.
19. hope we h. as an anchor
7: 5. h. a com-t to take tithes
28. high priests wh. h. infirmity
8: 1. We h. such a high priest, set
3. that this man h. somewhat
10:34. h. in heaven a better subst.
36. ye h. need of patience
12: 9. we h. had fa-s of our flesh
28. let us h. grace whereby we may
13: 5. content with such as ye h.
10. we h. an altar they h. no right
14. here h. we no continuing city
18. h. a good consci , 1 Pe. 3: 16.
Ja. 1: 4. let patience h. her perfect work
2: 1. h. not faith of C. with respect
14. h. not works, can faith save?
18. Thou hast faith, and I h. works
Ja. 3: 14. if ye h. bitter envy, strife
4: 2. Ye lust and h. not, desire to
h. and war, yet h. not
1 Pe. 4:8. ab. all h. fervent charity
2 Pe.1:15. h. these always in remem
19. we h. a more sure word of
2:14. a heart they h. exercised with
1 Jn. 1: 3. may h. fellowship, 6, 7.
1 Co 10: 20.
8. if we say, we h. no sin
2: 1. we h. an Advocate with Fa.
20 we h. unction fr. Holy One
4: 21. this com-t h. we from him
5: 13. may know ye h. eter. life
14. this is confidence we h. in him
15. know we h. the petitions we
3 Jn. 4. I h. no greater joy than
9. who loveth to h. pre-eminence
Re. 1: 18 I h. keys of hell
2:4 I h. somewhat ag. thee
10. ye shall h. tribulation
14. I h. a few things ag. thee, 20.
24. as many as h. not this doctr.
25. what ye h. already, hold fast
3: 17. and h. need of nothing
9: 4. which h. not the seal of God
11:6 These h. power to shut heav
12: 17. h. the testimony of Jes. C.
14: 11. they h. no rest day nor night
17:13. these h. one mind, and give
19:10. that h. testimony of Jesus
21:8. liars sh. h. their part in lake
22: 14. may h. right to tree of life
See COMPASSION, DOMINION.

HAVEN, S. [of ships
Ge. 49: 13 Zebu dwell at h. a h.
Ps 107:30. bring-h unto desired h.
Ac. 27:12 h. not commodious, a h.
See FAIR HAVENS.

HAV'ILAH. [Person, Place]
Ge. 2: 11. la. of H. is gold, 25: 18.
10:7. sons of Cush. H., 29. 1 Ch.1:9.
1 S. 15:7. smote Amal-s fr. H. [23.

HAVING. [22: 3.
Le. 7: 20. h. uncleann. upon him,
20:18. h. her sicko. | 22:22. h. wen
Nu.24:4. trance, but h. eyes open, 16.
Ru.1:13. stay for them fr. h. husb-s?
1 Ch. 21: 16. h. a drawn sword in
2 Ch. 11: 12. h. Judah and Benj.
Es. 6: 12 h. his head covered
Pr. 6: 7. wh. h. no guide, overseer
Eze. 38: 11. h. nei. bars nor gates
Mi. 1: 11. h. thy shame naked
Zeh. 9: 9. thy k. cometh h. salva.
Mat 7:29. taught as one h. author.
8: 9. h. soldiers under me, Lu.7:8.
9:36. sheep h. no sheph, Mk. 6:34.
15:30 mult. came h. with th. lame
18: 8. h. two hands or
9. h. two eyes, Mk 9: 43, 45, 47.
22:12. not h. a wedding garment
24. If die, h. no chil., Lu 20: 28.
25. h. no issue, left wife to bro.
26: 7. h. alabaster box, Mk. 14:3.
Mk. 8: 1. h. nothing to eat, Jesus
18. h. eyes, see ye not? h. ears
11:13. h. leaves | 12: 6. h. one son
Lu. 8:43. woman h. an issue of bl.
11:36 full of light h. no part dark
15:4. What man h. a hund. sheep?
8. what wom. h. 10 pieces of sil.?
17:7. which h. a serv. ploughing
Jn 5: 2 Bethesda h. five porches
7: 15. letters, h. never learned
18: 10. Peter h. a sword drew it
Ac. 2:47. h. favour with all the peo.
4:37. h. land, sold it, and bro-t the
22: 12. h. a good report of Jews
24: 22. h. more perfect knowl. of
Ro. 2: 14. h. not the law, are a law
12: 6. h. then gifts differing acc. to
15: 23. h. no more place in these
1 Co. 6: 1. h. a matter against ano.
7: 37. stedfast, h. no necessity
11: 4. h. his head covered
2 Co. 4:13. we h. same spirit of faith
2 Co.6:10. as h. noth., yet poss-g all
7: 1. h. these promises, beloved
9: 8. ye always h. all sufficiency
10: 6. h. in a readiness to revenge
15. h. hope, when faith is incr-d
Ep. 2: 12. h. no hope | 5: 27. not
h. spot
6: 14. h. your loins girt about
Ph. 1:23. h. a desire to depart, and
25. h. this confidence, I know
30. h. same conflict which ye saw
2: 2. likeminded, h. same love
3: 9. not h. my own righteousness
Col. 1:20. h. made peace thro. blood
2: 19. h. nourishment ministered
1 Ti. 3:4. h. his chil. in subjection
4: 8. h. the promise of the life th.
5: 12. h. damnation, bec. they cast
6: 8. h. food and raiment, let us
2 Ti. 2: 19. h. this seal, L. know-h
3: 5. h. a form of godliness, but
4:3. heap teachers, h. itching ears
Tit. 1: 6. h. faithful children
2: 8. h. no evil to say of you
He. 7:3. h. neith. beginning of days
10: 1. the law h. a shadow of good
19. h. therefore breth. boldness
1 Pe. 2:12. h. conversation honest
3: 16. h. a good conscience, they
2 Pe. 2: 14. h. eyes full of adult-y
2 Jn. 12. h. many things to write
Jude 19. sensual, h. not the Spirit
Re. 5:6. h. 7 horns | 8. h. harps
7:2. h. the seal of the living God
8: 3. h. a golden censer
9: 17. h. breastplates [wrath
12: 3. h. 7 heads | 12. h. great
13:1. h. seven heads and ten, 17:3.
14: 6. h. the everl. gospel to preach
14. h. on his head a golden crown
17. also h. a sharp sickle
15:1. angels h. seven last plagues, 6.
2. h. the harps of God | 17: 4. h.
a golden cup [key of the pit
18: 1 h. great power | 20: 1. h.
21:11. holy Jerus., h. glory of God

HAVOC.
Ac. 8: 3. Saul, he made h. of ch-h

HA'VOTH-JA'IR.
Nu.32:41. towns called H., Ju. 10:4.
See BASHAN-HAVOTH-JAIR.

HAWK. [dom?
Jb. 39: 26. Doth h. fly to thy wis-
See NIGHTHAWK.

HAY.
Pr. 27: 25. The h. appeareth, grass
Is. 15: 6. h. is withered, grass fail-h
1 Co. 3: 12. if build upon this foun-

HAZ'AEL. [dation h.
1 K. 19: 15. Go, anoint H. king [slay
17. escapeth sword of H sh. Jehu
2 K. 8: 8. H., 12.-9: 14.-12: 17(2), 18.
9. So H. went to meet Elisha
13. H. said, Is thy servant a dog
15. Ben-hadad died, H. reigned
28. to war ag. H., 29.-9: 15. 2 Ch.
10: 32. H. smote them [22: 5, 6.
12: 17. H. set face to go to Jerus-m
13: 3. delivered Isr. into hand of H.
22. H. oppressed Isr. | 24. H. died
25. out of hand of son of H. cities
Am. 1: 4. I send a fire into house of

HAZA'IAH. [H.
Ne. 11: 5. chil. of Judah; H. son of

HA'ZAR-AD'DAR. [H.
Nu. 34: 4. your border sh. go on to

HAZARDED.
Ac. 15: 26. h. lives for name of Chr.

HA'ZAR-E'NAN. [10.
Nu. 34: 9. border, goings out at H.,
Eze. 47: 17. border fr. sea be H., 48:1.

HA'ZAR-GAD'DAH.
Jos. 15: 27. cities toward Edom, H.

HA'ZAR-HAT'TICON.
Eze. 47: 16. H. is by coast of Hauran

HA'ZAR-MA'VETH. [20.
Ge.10: 26. Joktan begat H, 1 Ch.1:

HA'ZAR-SHU'AL.
Jos. 15 : 28. cities of Judah were H.
19 : 3. H., 1 Ch. 4 : 28. Ne. 11 : 27.
HA'ZAR-SU'SAH or SU'SIM
Jos. 19 : 5. in inherit-e, H., 1 Ch. 4 : 31.†
HAZ'AZON-TA'MAR.
2 Ch. 20 : 2. they in H., wh. is Engedi
HAZEL.
Ge. 30 : 37. Jacob took rods of h.
HA'ZELELPO'NI. [H.
1 Ch. 4 : 3. name of their sister was
HAZE'RIM. See AVIM, ITES.
HAZE'ROTH. [33:17.
Nu. 11 : 35. people abode at H. (2),
12 : 16. people removed fr. H., 33 : 18.
De. 1 : 1. plain betw-n Paran and H.
HAZ'EZON-TA'MAR. [H.
Ge. 14 : 7. Amorites which dwelt in
HA'ZIEL. See HARAN. [Per.]
HA'ZO. See CHESED.
HA'ZOR. [2, 17.
Jos. 11 : 1. Jabin king of H., Ju. 4 :
10. H. head of kingd-s | 11. burnt H.,
12 : 19. Josh. smote king of H. [13.
15 : 23. cities of Judah, H., and, 25.
19 : 36. H. inheritance of Naphtali
1 S. 12 : 9. Sisera capt. of host of H.
1 K. 9 : 15. levy Sol. raised to build H.
2 K. 15 : 29. king of Assyria took H.
Ne. 11 : 33. chil. of Benj. dwelt at H.
Je. 49 : 28. cone-g kingdoms of H.
30. Flee, O ye inhabitants of H.
33. H. be a dwelling for dragons
HA'ZOR-HADAT'TAH.
Jos. 15 : 25. cities of Judah, H., and
HE.
Ge. 3 : 16. h. shall rule over thee
6 : 3. not strive wi. man, h. is flesh
44 : 10. h. with wh. found be serv.
48 : 19. y-ger bro. be greater than h.
49 : 8. h. whom breth. shall praise
Ex. 4 : 16. h. sh. be thy spokesman (2)
9 : 34. hardened his heart, h. and
35 : 34. h. hath put in his heart (2)
Le. 7 : 33. h. am. sons of Aa. that
25 : 54. sh. go out in jubilee, h.
Nu. 24 : 9. cursed is h. curseth thee
De. 3 : 1. h. and all peo. to battle
8 : 18. h. giveth pow. to get wealth
27 : 16. cursed be h., 16, 17, 18, 19,
20, 21, 22, 23, 24, 25, 26.
31 : 6. h. wi. thee, will not fail, 8.
32 : 6. is not h. Fa. that bought?
39. I am h., and there is no God
wi. me, Is. 41 : 4.–43 : 10, 13.–46 :
4.–48 : 12. [10.
Jos. 23 : 3. G. is h., fought for you,
Ju. 10 : 18. man is h. to fight?
1 S. 4 : 16. I h. came out of army
9 : 2. not goodlier person than h.
16 : 12. Arise, anoint, this is h.
25 : 25. as name so is h. [h.
1 K. 2 : 32. upon 2 men better than
17 : 15. she h. and her house did
18 : 17. thou h. th. troubleth Isr.?
2 K. 18 : 22. h. whose places, Is. 36 : 7.
2 Ch. 29 : 3. h. in first year of reign
Jb. 9 : 24. where, and who is h.?
13 : 19. Who is h. will plead wi. me?
14 : 10. man dieth, and where is
h.? 20 : 7. Is. 63 : 11. [of womb
Ps. 22 : 9. thou art h. took me out
60 : 12. h. it is tread down ene.,
68 : 20. h. that is our G. is [108 : 13.
100 : 3. h. is G., it is h. th. made
144 : 10. it is h. giveth salv. [29 : 18.
Pr. 16 : 20. trust. in L. happy h.,
Ec. 5 : 8. h. th. is higher than high-t
6 : 3. untimely birth is bet-r than h.
Is. 40 : 22. it is h. sitteth on circle
51 : 12. I am h., comforteth, 52 : 6.
Jn. 18 : 5, 6, 8. Re. 1 : 18.–2 : 23.
Je. 5 : 12. belied L., said, It is not h.
14 : 22. Art not thou h., O L. our G.
38 : 5. k. is not h. can do any thi.
48 : 26. h. also sh. be in derision
Eze. 38 : 17. h. of wh. I have spok.?
Ha. 1 : 13. is more righte. than h.
Mat. 2 : 2. Where is h. th. is born k.
8 : 3. this is h. that was spoken of
11 : 3. Art thou h. that should
come? Lu. 7 : 19, 20.
12 : 30. h. not with me is ag. me,
and h., Lu. 11 : 23.
22 : 42. of C.? whose son is h.?
24 : 26. h. in desert, h. in chamb.
26 : 48. same is h. hold him, Mk.
Mk. 12 : 32. is none but h. [14 : 44.
Lu. 10 : 22. h. to whom Son reveal
11 : 7. h. from within shall answer
20 : 2. who is h. gave thee author.?
22 : 27. h. th. sitteth, or h. that
24 : 6. said, h. is not here, but risen
21. trusted h. sho. have redeemed
Jn. 1 : 15. h. of wh. I spake, 30.
4 : 26. I that speak to thee, am h.
7 : 11. Jews said, here is h.?
25. Is not this h. [shall die
8 : 24. if believe not I am h., ye
28. shall ye know I am h.
9 : 8. Is not this h. that begged?
9. This is h., but h. said, I am h.
36. Who is h. | 37. h. th. talketh
13 : 19. th. ye may believe I am h.
Ac. 3 : 10. knew it was h. who sat
7 : 38. This is h. was in church in
9 : 21. Is not this h. th. destroyed
10 : 21. Pe. said, I am h. ye seek
42. h. that was ordained of God
13 : 25. think ye I am? I am not h.
Ro. 2 : 28. h. not a Jew that is one
29. h. a Jew th. is one inwardly
14 : 18. h. that in these serveth C.
1 Co. 10 : 22. we stronger than h.?
2 Co. 10 : 7. as h. is C.'s. so are we
Christ's [you
1 Th. 5 : 24. Faithful is h. th. calleth
2 Th. 2 : 7. h. who letteth will let
He. 12 : 7. what son is h. the fa.
10. h. for our profit, th. we might
1 Pe. 1 : 15. h. which called you
1 Jn. 1 : 7. light, as h. is in the
2 : 6. to walk as h. walked [light
28. when h. sh. appear, we may
3 : 7. righte., even as h. is righto.
24. dwel-h in him, h. in him, 4 : 15.
4 : 4. greater h. in you, than h. in
17. as h. so are we in this [world
5 : 12. h. that hath Son, hath life
3 Jn. 11. h. that doeth good is of G.
Re. 20 : 6. holy is h. th. hath part
22 : 11. h. th. is unjust, h. that is
See BLESSED, CALLED, DID, DIE,
DIED, DO, EAT, FLED, IS, SAID,
SAITH, SENT, WAS, WENT.
HEAD.
Ge. 3 : 15. it sh. bruise thy h. thou
40 : 13. Pha. sh. lift up thy h., 19.
48 : 17. right ha. upon h. of Ephr.
49 : 26. blessings be on h. of Jos.,
and top of h., De. 33 : 16.
Ex. 12 : 9. roast his h. wi. his legs
29 : 6. mitre upon his h., Le. 8 : 9.
10. Aa. and sons put hands upon
h. of bullock, Le. 4 : 4.–8 : 14.
15. put hands upon h. of ram, 19.
Le. 8 : 18, 22. [offerings
Le. 1 : 4. put hand upon h. of burnt
3 : 2. lay hand on h. of his offer-g
4 : 29. hand upon h. of sin off-g, 33.
8 : 20. Moses burnt h. and pieces
13 : 44. his plague is in his h.
45. clothes be rent, his h. bare
14 : 18. h. of him to be cleans., 29.
16 : 21. hands upon h. of live goat
21 : 5. sh. not make baldn. upon h.
10. shall not uncover his h. nor
24 : 14. lay their hands upon his h.
Nu. 5 : 18. priest uncover wom.'s h.
6 : 5. sh. no razor upon Nazarite's h.
7. consecration of G. is on his h.
9. shall shave h., 18. De. 21 : 12.
11. shall hallow his h. that day
Jos. 2 : 19. upon his h. bl. on our h.
Ju. 5 : 26. she smote off Sisera's h.
13 : 5. no razor shall come on his
h., 16 : 17. 1 S. 1 : 11.
1 S. 5 : 4. h. of Dagon and both palms
17 : 57. Goliath's h. | 31 : 9. cut off
Saul's h. [own h.
25 : 39. wickedn. of Nabal upon his
28 : 2. make thee keeper of my h.
2 S. 1 : 2. earth upon his h., 15 : 32.
16. Thy bl. upon thy h., 1 K., 2 : 37.
2 : 16. ev. one his fellow by the h.
3 : 8. Abner said, Am I a dog's h.?
29. Let it rest on the h. of Joab
4 : 8. h. of Ish-bosh. unto David
14 : 26. polled his h. ev. year (2)
16 : 9. let me go ov., take off his h.
18 : 9. his h. caught hold of oak
20 : 21. his h. sh. be thrown to thee
2 K. 2 : 3. master fr. thy h. to day
4 : 19. said unto fa., My h. my h.
6 : 25. ass' h. sold for 80 pieces
31. if h. of Elisha stand on him
32. son of murd. to take mine h.
19 : 21. dau. of Jerus. hath shaken
h. at thee, Is. 37 : 22. [52 : 31.
25 : 27. did lift up h. of Jehoi-n, Je.
2 Ch. 6 : 23. way upon own h., 1 K.
Ezr. 9 : 6. Iniq-s incr-d over h. [8 : 32,
Ne. 4 : 4. turn reproach on own h.
Es. 9 : 25. device return upon own h.
Jb. 1 : 20. Job shaved his h. and
10 : 15. yet will not I lift up my h.
16 : 4. I could shake my h. at you
20 : 6. his h. reached unto clouds
Ps. 3 : 3. the lifter up of mine h.
7 : 16. His mischief ret. on own h.
22 : 7. shoot out lip, shake the h.
23 : 5. anointest my h. with oil
27 : 6. now sh. my h. be lifted up
38 : 4. iniq-s are gone over mine h.
44 : 14. a shaking of h. am. people
60 : 7. Ephr. strength of mine h.,
Jud. my lawgiver, 108 : 8.
68 : 21. G. sh. wound h. of enem-s
83 : 2. hate thee, have lifted h.
110 : 7. theref. sh. he lift up the h.
140 : 9. h. of those compass me
141 : 5. oil, wh. shall not break h.
Pr. 10 : 6. Blessings upon h. of just
11 : 26. upon h. of him selleth corn
20 : 29. beauty of old men gray h.
25 : 22. shalt heap coals of fire upon his h., Ro. 12 : 20.
Ec. 2 : 14. wise man's eyes in h.
Can. 2 : 6. left hand under my h.,
5 : 2. my h. is filled with dew [8 : 3
11. His h. as most fine gold
7 : 5. Thine h. is like Carmel
Is. 1 : 5. whole h. is sick heart
51 : 11. everl. joy be upon their h.
58 : 5. is it to bow down his h.?
59 : 17. helmet of salva. upon his h.
Je. 2 : 37. go, thine hands upon h.
9 : 1. O that my h. were waters
18 : 16. aston-d and wag his h.
23 : 19. upon h. of wicked, 30 : 23.
La. 2 : 15. wag h. at dau. of Jerus.
3 : 54. Waters flowed over mine h.
Eze. 9 : 10. recomp. way upon h.
17 : 19. will I recomp. upon his h.
29 : 18. every h. was made bald
33 : 4. blood be upon his own h.
Da. 2 : 38. Thou art this h. of gold
Jo. 3 : 4. recomp. upon your h., 7.
Am. 2 : 7. dust on the h. of poor
8 : 10. will br. baldness upon ev. h.
9 : 1. Cut them in h. all of them
Ob. 15. reward ret. upon thine h.
Jon. 2 : 5. weeds wrapped ab. my h.
Mi. 2 : 13. the L. on the h. of them
Zch. 1 : 21. no man did lift his h.
6 : 11. set crowns upon h. of Josh.
Mat. 5 : 36. Nei. swear by thy h.
6 : 17. when fast-st anoint h.
8 : 20. where to lay his h., Lu. 9 : 58.
14 : 8. John Bapt.'s h., 11. Mk. 6 : 28.
26 : 7. ointment on his h., Mk. 14 : 3

Mat. 27 : 30. smote him on **h.**, Mk.
37. set up over his **h.** this [15:19.
Mk. 6 : 24. **h.** of John Baptist, 25.
27. com-d his **h.** to be brought
12 : 4. wounded him in the **h.**
Lu. 7 : 46. My **h.** didst not anoint
Jn. 13:9. but also my hands and **h.**
20 : 7. napkin, was about his **h.**
12. one at **h.** and other at feet
Ac. 18 : 18. having shown his **h.** at
1 Co.11:4 **h.** cov'd, dishon-h his **h.**,
5. **h.** uncov. dishonoureth her **h.**
10. ought to have pow. on her **h.**
12 : 21. **h.** to feet, I have no need
Ep. 1:22. put all und. his feet, gave
his as **h.** to ch., 4:15. Col. 1:18.
Col. 2:19. not holding the **h.** from
Re. 19 : 12. on his **h.** many crowns
See BEARD, BALD, BOW, BOWED,
COVER, COVERED, CROWN.

HEAD with axe. [peth
De. 19:5. stroke with **a.** and **h.** slip-
See **AXE head.**

Bed's HEAD. [b. h.
Ge. 47 : 31. Isr. bowed himself upon

HEAD of the corner.
Mat. 21 : 42. is become the **h.** -, Mk.
12 : 10. Lu. 20 : 17. Ac. 4 : 11.

HEAD with hair, s. [1 Pe.2:7.
Le.13:40. whose **h.** is fallen off **h.**, 41.
14 : 9. leper shave all **h.** off his **h.**
Nu. 6 : 5. let locks of **h.** of **h.** grow
18. take **h.** of **h.** of his separation
Ju.16:22. **h.** of his **h.** began to grow
1 S. 14 : 45. not a **h.** of his **h.** sh. fall
2 S. 14 : 26. **h.** of **h.** at 200 shekels
Ezr. 9 : 3. plucked off **h.** of my **h.**
Ps. 40:12. more than **h.**-s of **h.**, 69 :
Can. 7 : 5. **h.** of **h.** like purple [4.
Da. 3 : 27. nor **h.** of **h.** singed
7 : 9. **h.** of his **h.** like pure wool
Mat.10:30. **h.**-s of your **h.** are num-
bered, Lu. 12 : 7. [44.
Lu.7:38. did wipe with **h.**-s of her **h.**,
21 : 18. not a **h.** of your **h.** perish
Ac. 27 : 34. not a **h.** fall from the **h.**
Re. 1 : 14. his **h.** and **h.**-s were white

Hoar, or hoary HEAD.
Le.19:32. Thou shalt rise bef. **h.**-y **h.**
1 K. 2: 6. let not his **h.** **h.** go down
Pr. 16:31. **h.**-y **h.** is a crown of glory

Spear's HEAD.
1 S. 17 : 7. Goliath; his s. **h.** weighed 600 shekels of iron, 2 S.21:†16.

HEADstone, HEADSTONE
Ps 118 : 22. is become **h. s.** of corner
Zch 4 :7. sh. bring **h.** with shoutings

HEAD. [As Ruler, Governor.]
Nu. 1:4. ev. one **h.** of house of fas.
17 : 3. one rod sh. be for **h.** of hou.
25 : 15. he was **h.** over a people of
De. 28 : 13. L. will make thee the **h.**
44. he be **h.** and thou sh. be tail
Jos. 11 : 10. Hazor was the **h.** of all
22 : 14. each one a **h.** of house of
Ju. 10 : 18. **h.** over all Gilead, 11:8.
11:9. I be your **h.**? | 11. made him
1 S.15:17. wast made **h.** of Isr.? [**h.**
2 S. 22 : 44. hast kept me to be **h.**
of the heathen, Ps. 18 : 43.
1 Ch. 11 : † 6. smiteth, shall be **h.**
29 : 11. art exalted as **h.** above all
Is. 7 : 8. **h.** of Damas. Rezin (2), 9.
9 : 14. cut off fr. Isr. **h.** and tail
15. ancient and honour. he is **h.**
19 : 15. work **h.** or tail, may do
Je. 22 : 6. Gilead to me, **h.** of Leb.
Ho. 1 : 11. shall app. thems. one **h.**
Ha. 3 : 13. woundedst **h.** of hou. of
14. didst strike thro. **h.** of villa-s
1 Co. 11 : 3. **h.** of ev. man is C., **h.**
of wom. is man, **h.** of C is G.
Eph. 5 : 23. husband is **h.** of wife,
even as C. is **h.** of church
Col.2:10. who is **h.** of all principal.

HEAD. [As Chief, Top.]
Ps. 137 : † 6. Jerus. bef. **h.** of my joy
Is. 28 : 1. are on **h.** of fat valleys, 4.
51 : 20. they lie at **h.** of all streets
Eze. 16:25. high places at **h.** of way
21 : 19. choose it at the **h.** of way
21. king stood at **h.** of two ways

HEADS.
Ge. 2 : 10. parted and became 4 **h.**
43 : 28. bowed their **h.**, Ex. 4 : 31.
2 Ch. 29 : 30.-Ne. 8 : 6.
Le. 10 : 6. Uncover not your **h.** lest
19 : 27. not round corners of **h.**
Jos. 7 : 6. dust upon **h.**, Jb. 2 : 12.
Ju. 7 : 25. the **h.** of Oreb and Zeeb
8 : 28. lifted up their **h.** no more
9 : 57. all the evil upon their **h.**
1 S. 29:4. sho. it not wi. **h.** of these
1 K. 20 : 31. let us put ropes on **h.**
32. put ropes on their **h.** and
2 K. 10 : 6. take **h.** of master's sons,
8. have bro. **h.** of king's sons [7.
1 Ch.12 : † 19. fall to Saul on our **h.**
Ps. 24 : 7. Lift up **h.** O ye gates, 9.
66:12. caused men to ride ov. our **h.**
74 : 13. brakest **h.** of the dragons
14. Thou breakest **h.** of leviathan
109:25. on me, they shaked their **h.**
Is. 15 : 2. on **h.** shall be baldness
35:10. to Zion everl. joy upon their
Je.14:3. they covered their **h.**, 4. [**h.**
La. 2:10. virgins of Jerus. hang **h.**
Eze. 7 : 18. baldness be on their **h.**
11:21. recomp-se on their **h.**, 22:31.
23 : 15. dyed attire upon their **h.**
42. crowns upon their **h.**, Re.4:4.
24: 23. tires shall be upon your **h.**
32 : 27. laid swords under their **h.**
44 : 18. linen bonnets on their **h.**
20. they shall poll their **h.**
Da. 7 : 6. beast had also four **h.**
Mat.27:39. wagging their **h.**, Mk.15:
Lu.21:28. look up, lift your **h.** [29.
Ac.18:6. Your blood upon your own
21:24. that they may shave **h.** [**h.**
Re. 9 : 7. and on their **h.** as crowns
17. **h.** of horses, **h.** of lions
19. tails like to serpents, had **h.**
12 : 3. red dragon having 7 **h.** [**h.**
13:1. beast having 7 **h.** and on his
3 I saw one of his **h.** as wounded
17 : 3. scarlet coloured beast, 7 **h.**
9. seven **h.** are seven mountains
18 : 19. they cast dust on their **h.**

HEADS. [As Governors.]
Ex. 18:25. made them **h.** over peo.,
De. 1 : 15.-33 : 5, 21.
Nu. 1:16. **h.** of thou-s in Isr., 10:4.
13:3. **h.** of chil. of Isr., 1 Ch.12:32.
25 : 4. take all **h.** of peo. hang th.
30:1. **h.** of tribes, De. 5:23. 1 K.8:1.
Jos. 22 : 21. and Gad ans-d **h.**, 30.
23:2. Joshua called for their **h.** and
2 Ch. 5:2. Sol. assembled all the **h.**
28:12. certain of **h.** of Ephr. stood
Ps. 110:6. wound **h.** over countries
Is. 29:†10. proph. and **h.** be cov-d
Mi. 3 : 1. Hear, O **h.** of Jacob, 9.
11. **h.** judge for reward, priests
See FATHERS. [teach

HEADBANDS.
Is. 3 : 20. L. will take away the **h.**

HEADLONG.
Jb. 5 : 13. counsel of froward is **h.**
Lu. 4 : 29. might cast him down **h.**
Ac.1:18. falling **h.** he burst asunder

HEADY.
2 Ti.3:4. men sh. be **h.** highminded

HEAL.
Nu. 12 : 13. **h.** her now, O God, I
De. 32 : 39. I kill, I wound, I **h.**
2 K. 20 : 5. I will **h.** thee, and add
8. What sign that L. will **h.** me?
2 Ch. 7:14. I will forgive and **h.** la.
Ps. 6:2. **h.** me, my bones are vexed
41:4. **h.** my soul, for I have sinned
60:2. **h.** the breaches for it shaketh
Ec. 3 : 3. time to kill, a time to **h.**
Is. 19 : 22. shall smite and **h.** it (2)
Is.57:18. seen ways, will **h.** him, 19.
Je. 3 : 22. I will **h.** your backslid-s
17:14. **h.** me, O L., I sh. be healed
30:17. I will **h.** thee of thy wounds
La.2:13. thy breach gr., who can **h.**
Ho. 5 : 13. yet could he not **h.** you
6 : 1. he hath torn, and will **h.** us
14 : 4. I will **h.** their backsliding
Zch. 11 : 16. he sh. not **h.** broken
Mat. 8 : 7. I will come and **h.** him
10:1. to **h.** all sickness, Mk. 3 : 15.
8. **h.** the sick, Lu. 9 : 2.-10 : 9.
12 : 10. Is it lawful to **h.** on sabbath day? Lu.14:3. [Ac. 28:27.
13:15. I should **h.** them, Jn.12:40.
Mk. 3:2. whe. he **h.** on sab., Lu.6:7.
Lu.4:18. sent me to **h.** brokenheart.
23. say, Physician, **h.** thyself
5:17. power of Lord present to **h.**
7:3. beseeching he would **h.** his serv
Jn.4:47. th. he wo come **h.** his son
Ac.4:30. stretching thine hand to **h.**

HEALED.
Ge. 20 : 17. God **h.** Abim. and wife
Ex.21:19. he sh. cause him to be **h.**
Le. 13 : 18. bile is **h.** | 37. scall **h.**
14:3. if plague of leprosy be **h.**, 48.
De. 28:27. with itch, canst not be **h.**
35. sore botch that cannot be **h.**
1 S. 6 : 3. offering, then he be **h.**
1 K.2:21. **h.** waters | 22. wat. were **h.**
8:29. king Joram went to be **h.** in
9:15. returned to be **h.**, 2 Ch.22:6
2 Ch. 30:20. L. heark-d and **h.** peo.
Ps. 30 : 2. I cried to thee, thou **h.**
107 : 20. sent his word, and **h.** th.
Is. 6 : 10. lest they see, and be **h.**
53:5. and with his stripes we are **h.**
Je. 6 : 14. **h.** hurt slightly, 8 : 11.
15:18. my wound refuseth to be **h.**
17:14. Heal me, O L., and I sh. be **h.**
51:8. take balm, if so be she be **h.**
9. We wo. have **h.** Bab., she not **h.**
Eze.30:21. not be bound up to be **h.**
34 : 4. nei. have ye **h.** sick [9.
47:8. bro-t into sea, waters sh. be **h.**,
11. marshes thereof sh. not be **h.**
Ho.7:1. When I would have **h.** Isr.
11 : 3. they knew not that I **h.** th.
Mat.4:24. had palsy and he **h.** them,
15:30.-19:2.-21:14. Mk. 6:5, 13.
Lu. 4 : 40.-9 : 11. [7 : 7.
8:8. speak, my serv. be **h.**, 13. Lu.
16. **h.** all were sick, Mk. 1 : 34.-3:
10.-6 : 5. [14 : 14.
12:15. multi. followed, he **h.** them,
22. blind and dumb he **h.** him
Mk. 5 : 23. that she may be **h.** and
29. she was **h.** of that plague
Lu. 5 : 15. hear and be **h.** by him
6:17. **h.** of their diseases, Ac.8:7.-
28 : 9. [5 : 16.
18. had uncl. spirits were **h.**, Ac.
19. virtue out and **h.** them all
8 : 2. women **h.** of evil spirits, 36.
43. neither could be **h.** of any
47. how she was **h.** immediately
9 : 42. **h.** child and delivered him
13 : 14. come and be **h.** not on sab.
14 : 4. and **h.** him. Ac. 3 : 11.-8:7.
17: 15. saw he was **h.** turned back
22:51. touched his ear, and **h.** him
Jn. 5 : 13. **h.** wist not who it was
Ac.4:14. beholding man who was **h.**
5 : 16. they were **h.** every one
14 : 9. that he had faith to be **h.**
28 : 8. Paul **h.** father of Publius
He. 12 : 13. but let it rather be **h.**
Ja. 5 : 16. pray that ye be **h.** [**h.**
1 Pe.2:24. by whose stripes ye were
Re. 13:3. deadly wound was **h.**, 12.

HEALER.
Is. 3 : 7. saying, I will not be a **h.**

HEALETH.
Ex.15:26. I am the L. that **h.** thee
Ps.103:3. L. who **h.** all thy diseases
147 : 3. He **h.** the broken in heart

Is. 30 : 26. be h. stroke of wound
HEALING. [Noun.]
2 Ch.24:†13. h. went up upon work
36:†16. wrath of L. till was no h.
Pr. 15 : †4. h. of tongue is a tree
Je. 14:19. There is no h. for us (2)
Da. 4 : † 27. if it a h. of thy error
Na. 3 : 19. is no h. of thy bruise
Mal. 4:2. arise with h. in his wings
Lu. 9:11. healed th. had need of h.
Ac. 4: 22. miracle of h. was shewed
1 Co.12:9. to ano. the gift of h., 28.
30. Have all the gifts of h.?
Re. 22 : 2. leaves for h. of nations
HEALING.
Je.30:13. thou hast no h. medicine
Mat. 4 : 23. went about h. all sickn.
9:35. h. every sickness and disease
Lu. 9 : 6. preaching gospel, and h.
Ac. 10:38. h. all oppressed of devil
HEALTH.
Ge. 43 : 28. our father is in good h.
2 S. 20: 9. Art thou in h. my bro.?
Ps. 38:†3. nei. any h. in my bones
42: 11. h. of my counten., 43 : 5.
67:2. thy saving h. may be known
Pr. 3 : 8. It sh. be h. to thy navel
4 : 22. are h. to all their flesh
12:18. the tongue of the wise is h.
13: 17. a faithful ambassador is h.
16 : 24. sweet to soul, h. to bones
Is. 58 : 8. thy h. shall spring forth
Je. 8 : 15. looked for a time of h.
22.why not h. of people recov-d?
30 : 17. I will restore h. unto thee
33 : 6. I will bring it h. and cure
Ac. 27 : 34. take meat, this for h.
3 Jn.2. mayest be in h. as thy soul
HEAP. [Noun.]
Ge. 31 : 46. made h. did eat on h.
52. This h. be witness, 48, 51.
Ex. 15 : 8. floods stood upright as a
h., Jos.3:13,16. Ps.33:7.-78:13.
De. 13 : 16. shall be a h. for ever
Jos.7:26.over him a gr. h. of stones
8:28. Josh. burnt Ai, made it a h.
29. on king of Ai gr. h. of stones
11:†13. cities th. stood on their h.
Ju. 15 : † 16. jawbone of ass, a h.
Ru. 3 : 7. to lie down at h. of corn
2 S. 18 : 17. laid great h. upon Abs.
Jb.8:17.His roots are wrapped ab.h.
21 : † 32. shall he watch in the h.
30 : † 24. not stretch hand to h.
Pr. 26 : † 8. precious stone in a h.
Can. 7:2. thy belly like h. of wheat
Is. 17 : 1. Damas. be a ruinous h.
11. harvest shall be a h. in grief
25 : 2. hast made of a city a h.
Je. 30:18. city be builded upon own
49:2.Rabbah be a desolate h. [h.
Mi. 1: 6. Samaria as a h. of field
Ha.3:15.walk thro.h. of great wat-s
Hag.2:16.came to h. of 20 measures
HEAPS.
Ex. 8 : 14. gathered them upon h.
Ju.15:16.jawbone of ass, h.upon h.
2 K. 10 : 8. Lay ye them in two h.
19:25. cities into ruinous h.,Is.37:
2 Ch.31:6.tithe, laid th. by h. [26.
7. 3d month began to lay h.
8. when the princes saw the h.,9.
Ne. 4 : 2. revive stones out of h.?
Jb. 15:28. ho-s ready to become h.
Ps. 79 : 1. have laid Jerus. on h.
Je. 9:11. will make Jerus. h.,26:18.
31:21.Set way-marks,make high h.
50 : 26. cast Babylon up as h. and
51:37. And Babylon sh. become h.
Ho. 12 : 11. their altars are as h.
Mi. 3 : 12. Jerus. shall become h.
HEAP. [Verb.]
De. 32:23. I will h. mischiefs upon
Jb. 16 : 4. co. h. up words ag. you
27:16. tho. he h. up silver as dust
36:13.hypoc. in heart, h. up wrath
Pr.25:22. h. coals of fire, Ro.12:20.

Ec. 2 : 26. to gather and to h. up
Eze. 24:10. h. on wood, kindle fire
Hab. 1 : 10. sh. h. dust and take it
2 Ti. 4:3. h. to themselves teachers
HEAPED, ETH.
Ps. 39 : 6. he h-h up riches, and
Ha. 2 : 5. he h-h unto him all peo.
Zch.9:3. Tyrus h-d up silver as dust
Ja. 5:3. Ye have h-d treasure toge.
HEAR.
Ge. 21:6. th. h. will laugh with me
23 : 6. h. us my lord, art mighty
37 : 6. h. I pray you, this dream
49 : 2. h. ye sons of Jac. hearken
Ex. 19:9. that peo. h. when I speak
32:18.noise of them th.sing do I h.
Nu. 16 : 8. h. ye sons of Levi
23 : 18. Rise up, Balak, and h.
30 : 4. father h. her vow and bond
De. 1:16. h. causes betw. brethren
4:10. I will make th. h. my words
5 : 1. h. Israel the statutes, 6 : 3.-
9:1.-20:3. Is. 48:1. Mk. 12:29.
27.h. all the L. our God doth say
12:28.h.all words I command thee
30:12.bring it, that we may h.,13.
31:12. h. and fear L., 13. Je. 6:10.
Jos. 3 : 9. h. the words of the Lord
6:5. when ye h. sound of trumpet,
shout, Ne. 4 : 20. Da. 3 : 5, 15.
Ju. 5 : 3. h. O ye kings, give ear
16.Why abodest, to h. bleatings?
14 : 13. riddle, that we may h. it
1 S. 2:23. I h. of your evil dealings
24. sons, no good report I h.
13 : 3. saying, Let the Hebrews h.
15:14. lowing of the oxen wh. I h.
16 : 2. if Saul h. it, will kill me
25:24.h.words of handm.,2 S.20:17
26:19.let my lord the k.h.words of
2 S.14: † 17. so my lord to h. good
15 : 3. no man deputed of k. to h.
10. soon as ye h. the trumpet
36. send unto me ev. thing ye h.
17:5. let us h. what Hushai saith
20:16. wom. cried out of city, h.h.
22:45.soon as h. obedi-t, Ps.18:44.
1 K. 3 : † 11. asked underst-g to h.
4 : 34. to h. wisd. of Sol., 10:8,24.
2 Ch.9:7,23.Mat.12:42.Lu.11:31
8:30.h.thou in heaven and forgive,
32,34,36,39,43,45,49. 2 Ch.6:21,
23, 25, 27, 30, 33, 35, 39.
18:26. called, saying, O Baal,h. us
2 K. 7:6. host to h. noise of chariot
18 : 28. h. word of the great king,
Is. 36 : 13. [Is. 37 : 17.
19 : 16. h. words of Sennacherib,
Ne. 1 : 6. mayest h. prayer of serv.
4 : 4. h. O G. for we are despised
8:2. all that co. h. with underst-g
Jb. 5 : 27. h. it, know it for good
13:17. h. dilig-y my speech, 21:2.
27 : 9. Will God h. his cry?
34 : 2. h. my words
38:1. Job, I pray, h. my speeches
42:4. h. I beseech thee, I will spe.
Ps. 4:1. h. my prayer, O G., 39:12.
-54:2.-84:8.-102:1.-143:1.
17 : 1. h. the right, O L., attend
20 : 1. L. h. thee in day of trouble
9. Save, Lord, let the king h. us
27:7. h. O L. when I cry wi. voice,
28:2.-64:1.-119:149.-130:2.140:
30 : 10. h. O L. have mercy [6.
49 : 1. h. this, all ye peo., give ear
50 : 7. h. O peo. I will speak, 81:8.
51:8.Make me to h. joy and gladn.
59:7. for who, say they, doth h.?
61 : 1. h. my cry, O God, attend
66:16. Come, h. all ye th. fear G.
102 : 20. h. groaning of prisoner
138:4.when h. words of thy mouth
143:8.Cause me to h.thy lovingki.
Pr.1:8. h. instruction of thy father
4 : 1. h. ye chil. instruc. of a fa.
10. h. O my son, receive, 19: 20.

Pr. 8:6. h. I will speak of excellent
33. h. instruction, and be wise
19:27. cease to h. instruction, that
22 : 17. h. the words of the wise
23 : 19. h. thou, my son, be wise
Ec. 5:1. more ready to h. than give
7 : 5. better to h. rebuke of wise
21. lest thou h. serv. curse thee
12:13.Let us h. conclusion of mat.
Can. 8 : 13. voice, cause me to h. it
Is. 1 : 2. h. O heavens, give ear
6:9. h. ye, underst. not, Mk. 4:12.
18:3. when bloweth trump., h. ye
33 : 13. h. ye that are afar off
34 : 1. let earth h. and all therein
42:18. h. ye deaf | 23. who will h.
43 : 9. let them h. say, It is truth
48:14. assemble yourselves and h.
16. h. ye this, I not spoken in se-
55 : 3. h. soul live, Jn. 5:25. [cret
Je. 4 : 21. shall I h. the trumpet?
6 : 10. give warning that they h.
18. h. ye nations | 19. h. O earth
10 : 1. h. word which L. speaketh
11 : 2. h. ye words of covenant, 6.
10. forefa-s refused to h., 13 : 10.
13 : 15. h. ye, for L. hath spoken
18 : 2. cause thee to h. my words
20 : 16. let him h. cry in morning
23:22. caused my peo. to h. words
38 : 25. if princes h. I have talked
42 : 14. nor h. sound of trumpet
49:20. h. the counsel of the L.,50:
La. 1:18. h. I pray you, all peo. [45.
Eze. 2 : 8. h. what I say unto thee
3 : 17. h. word at my mouth, 33:7.
27. He that heareth, let him h.
13:19. to my peo., th. h. your lies
33 : 30. h. word that cometh forth
31. h. thy words, but not do, 32.
36:15. h. in thee shame of heathen
Da. 5:23. hast praised gods of silver
wh. see not nor h., Re. 9: 20.
9 : 17. h. prayer of thy servant
19. h. O Lord, forgive, and do
Ho. 5 : 1. h. ye this, O priests, and
Jo.1:2.h. this, ye old men, give ear
Am.3:1.h.this word L.hath spoken,
4 : 1.-5 : 1.-8 : 4.
13. h. and testify in house of Jac.
Mi. 1 : 2. h. all ye people, hearken
3 : 1. h. O heads of Jacob, 9.
6:2 h.ye, O mts. | 9. h. ye the rod
Na. 3: 19. h. bruit of thee sh. clap
Zch. 7 : 12. lest they h. the law
8 : 9. h. in these days these words
Mat.10:14. nor h.your words, Mk.6:
11:4. shew John things ye h. [11.
5. deaf h., Mk. 7: 37. Lu. 7: 22.
13 : 17. h. things ye h., Lu. 10:24.
18. h. ye the parable, 21: 33.
15 : 10. he said unto mult. h. [7.
17:5. beloved Son, h. him, Mk. 9:
18:17. he neglect to h. them, to h.
church
Mk. 4:12. may h. and not underst.
18.such as h.word,20.Lu.8:12,13.
24.Take heed what ye h.you th.h
33. as were able to h. it [word
Lu. 5 : 1. pressed upon him to h.
15. multitudes came tog. to h.
6:17. came to h., and to be healed
27. unto you wh. h. Love enem.
8 : 18. Take heed theref. how ye h.
21. wh h. word and do it, 11:28.
9 : 9. who is this of whom I h.?
15:1. publicans and sinn. to h. him
16 : 2. How is it I h. this of thee?
29. have Mo. and proph., let th.h.
18 : 6. h. what unjust judge saith
19 : 48. peo. very attent. to h. him
21 : 38. came in temple to h. him
Jn. 5 : 25. they that h. shall live
30. as I h. I judge | 6:60. who can
h. it? [bef. it h. him?
7 : 51. Doth our law judge a man
8 : 43. bec. ye cannot h. my word

Jn. 9:27. whf. would ye h. it again
10:3. sheep h. his voice, he calleth
20. is mad; why h. ye him?
12: 47. if any h. and believe not
14:24. word wh. ye h. is not mine
Ac.2:8.h. ev. man in own toug.,11.
22. men of Isr. h. these words
33. shed forth this, ye now h.
10: 22. and to h. words of thee
33. to h. all things com-d thee
13: 7. desired to h. word of God
44. city came to h. word ⌈word
15: 7. Gent. by my mouth sho. h.
17: 21. to tell or h. some new thi.
19:26. ye h. Paul hath turned peo.
22: 1. h. ye defence I make now
24: 4. h. us of thy clemency
25: 22. I would h. man myself
28: 22. to h. what thou thinkest
Ro. 11:8. that they sho. not h. unto
1 Co. 11: 18. I h. there be divisions
Ph. 1: 27. may h. of your affairs
2 Th. 3:11. h. some walk disorderly
1 Ti. 4: 16. shalt save them h. thee
2 Ti. 4: 17. that all Gent. might h.
Ja. 1:19. let every one be swift to h.
1 Jn. 5: 15. we know th. he h. us
3 Jn. 4. h. my chil. walk in truth
Re. 1: 3. Blessed that h. prophecy
9: 20. which nei. can see nor h.
See EAR, EARS.

HEAR me.

Ge. 23:8. h. m. and entreat, 11,13.
Ex 6: 12. how shall Pha. h. m.?
1 K. 18: 37. h. m., O L, h. m.
1 Ch. 28: 2. h. m., my brethren
2 Ch. 13:4. h. m., thou Jeroboam
15:2. h. m., Asa | 20:20 h. m., O Judah
28: 11. h. m. and deliv. captives
29: 5. h. m., ye Levites, sanctify
Jb. 15: 17. I will shew thee, h. m.
31: 35. O that one would h. m.
Ps. 4: 1. h. m. when I call, O G.
13: 3. Consider, and h. m., O L.
17:6. called upon thee, wilt h. m.
38:16. said, h. m., lest they rejoi.
55: 2. Attend unto me, and h. m.
60: 5. save with right ha., h. m.
69: 13 in multitude of thy mercy h. m.
16. h. m., O L., for thy lovingk.
17. h. m. speedily, 143: 7.
119: 145. I cried, h. m., O Lord
Pr. 5: 7. h. m. now, O ye chil.
Mi. 7: 7. wait, my God will h. m.
Ac. 26: 3. I beseech thee to h. m.
29. all th. h. m. were such as I
1 Co. 14:21. yet will they not h.m.

HEAR not, or not HEAR.

De. 28:†49. tongue thou shalt n.h.
30:17.n.h.but worship other gods
1 S. 8: 18. Lord will n. h. you
Jb. 30:20. I cry, thou dost n. h. me
35:13. Surely G. will n. h. vanity
Ps. 66:18. If I regard iniq.. L. n.h.
94: 9. planted ear, shall he n. h.?
Is. 1:15.prayers, I will n.h.,Je.7:16.
11:14-14:12. Eze.8:18. Am.5:23.
30:9. chil. that will n. h. law of L.
59: 2. he will n. h. | 65:12. I spake ye did n. h. ⌈1: 4.
66:4. I spake, they did n. h., Zch.
Je. 5: 21. have ears and h. n., Eze.
12: 2. Mk. 8: 18. ⌈2: 2.
13:17.But if ye will n.h..22:5. Mal.
17:23. that they might n. h.,19 15.
Zch. 7: 11. ⌈will n. h.
22: 21. I spake, but thou saidst, I
Mi. 3:4. sh. cry to L., he will n. h.
Ha.1:2.how long sh.I cry,thou n.h.
Zch. 7: 7. n. h. words L. cried
Mat. 13: 13. h. n. nei. understand
18:16.if he will n.h. thee, take one
Lu. 16:31. If they h. n. Moses and
Jn.8:47.ye h.them n.,bec.not of G.
9: 27. I told you, ye did n. h.

Jn.10:8.but the sheep did n.h.them
Ac. 3: 23. soul wh. n. h. be destr.
1 Co. 14: 21. for all that they n. h.
Ga. 4: 21. und. law, do ye n.h. law

HEAR now, or now HEAR.

Nu. 12: 6. h. n. my words, 20: 10.
1 S. 22:7,12. Jb. 13:6. Je. 28:7.
Eze. 18: 25.
1 S. 22: 7. Saul said, h. n., Benj-s
12. h. n., thou son of Ahitub
Jb. 13:6. h. n., my reasoning
Pr. 5: 7. h. me n., O ye children
Is. 7: 13. h. ye n., O house of David
44: 1. yet n. h. O Jacob my serv.
47:8. h. n., thou given to pleasures
51: 21. h. n. this thou afflicted
Je. 5: 21. h. n. this, O foolish peo.
28: 15. h. n. Hananiah
37:20. h. n., I pray thee,O my lord
Mi. 6: 1. h. ye n. what L. saith
Zch.3:8.h.n.O Josh. the highpriest
Ac. 2: 33. shed forth this ye n. h.
Ph. 1:30.wh. ye saw in me, and n.h.

Shall or shalt HEAR.

Ex. 15:14. peo. s. h. and be afraid,
De. 13:11.-17:13.-19:20.-21:21.
Nu. 14:13.Then the Egypt-s s. h. it
De. 1: 17. ye s. h. small as great
2:25. who s. h. report of thee, and
4:6. which s. h. all these statutes
13: 12. If thou s. h. in 1 of cities
Jos. 7: 9. inhabitants s. h. of it
Ju. 7: 11. thou s. h. what they say
2 S. 15:35. thing whatso. thou s. h.
16:21. Isr. s. h. thou art abhorred
1 K.8:42. they s. h. of thy gr. name
2 K. 19: 7. s. h. rumour, Is. 37: 7.
1 Ch. 14:15.when s-t h. sound going
Jb. 22:27. prayer unto him, he s.h.
Ps. 34: 2. humble s. h. thereof
55:17. I will cry, he s. h. my voice
19. God s. h. and afflict them
92: 11. ears s. h. desire of wicked
141: 6. they s. h. my words, for
Is. 29: 18. in that day s. deaf h.
30: 19. when he s. h. will ans. thee
21. ears s. h. word behind thee
Je. 33: 9. s. h. all good that I do
Da. 3: 10. s. h. sound of cornet
Ho. 2:21. heaven s. h. the earth
22. earth s. h. corn and wine
Mat. 13: 14. By hearing, ye s. h.,
Ac. 28: 26. ⌈bro.
18: 15. if he s. h. thou hast gained
24: 6. ye s. h. of wars, Mk. 13: 7.
Lu. 21: 9. ⌈God, 28.
Jn. 5:25. dead s. h. voice of Son of
16:13. whatso. he s. h. that speak
Ac. 3: 22. him s. ye h. in all, 7:37.
25:22. Tomorrow. thou s. h. him
Ro.10:14. how s. h. with-t preacher

HEAR voice.

Ge. 4:23. h. my v. ye wives of Lam.
Le. 5: 1. sin and h. v. of swearing
De. 4:33. ever peo.h.v.of G.and live
36. out of heav. made thee h. v.
5: 25. if h. v. of G.. we shall die
18: 16. me not h. again v. of L.
33:7. he said,h. Lord the v.of Jud.
2 S.19:35.can I h.v. of singing men?
22:7. did h.my v. out of his temple
Jb. 3: 18. h. not v. of oppressor
37:2. h. attentively noise of his v.
Ps 5:3.My v.shalt thou h.in morn.
55:17. I will cry he shall h. my v.
95: 7. to day if ye will h. his v. harden not your, He. 3: 7, 15.-
4: 7. ⌈is thy v.
Can. 2:14. let me h. thy v. for sweet
Is. 32: 9. h. my v. careless dau-s
Je. 9: 10. nei. men h. v. of cattle
Mi. 6: 1. let the hills h. thy v.
Mat. 12: 19. nei. any man h. his v.
Jn.5:25.dead h.v. of Son of God,28.
10 :3.and the sheep h.his v.,16,27.
Ac. 22 :14.Just One, h. the v. of his
See Hear VOICE. ⌊mouth

Will HEAR. ⌈27.

Ex. 20: 19. speak, we w. h., De. 5:
22:23. they cry, I w. surely h., 27.
Nu. 9:8. I w. h. what L. will com.
De. 1: 17. bring it and I w. h. it
2 S. 14: 16. king w. h. to deliver
2 K. 19:4 may be G. w. h. words,
Is. 37: 4. ⌈Ps. 20: 6.
2 Ch.7:14. then w. I h. from heav.,
20: 9. then thou w. h. and help,
Ps. 38: 15. ⌈h. me
Ps. 4:3. Lord w. h. | 17:6. thou w.
85: 8. I w. h. what G. will speak
145:19. he w.h. their cry, and save
Pr. 1: 5. wise man w. h. and incre.
Is. 41: 17. the Lord w. h. them
65:24. while yet speaking, I w. h.
Je. 36:3. It may be ho. of Jud.w.h.
Eze. 2:5.whe.w. h. or forb.,7.-3:11.
Ho. 2: 21. I w. h. the heavens
Mi. 7:7. I will wait for G., G. w. h.
Zch. 10:6. am G. and w. h., 13: 9.
Ac. 17: 32. We w. h. thee again
21: 22. w. h. that thou art come
23:35. I w. h. thee,when accusers
28:28. salva. sent to Gent., they w.
HEAR ⌊h.
the word of the Lord.
1 K.22:19. h. th-f. w.- L., 2 Ch.18:
18. Je. 29: 20.-42: 15. Am. 7:16.
2 K.7:1. Then Elisha said h.- L., Je.
17: 20.-21: 11.
20:16.said unto Hez..h.-L.,Is.39:5.
Is. 1:10. h.- L., ye rulers of Sodom
28: 14. h.- L., ye scornful men
66: 5 h.- L., that tremble at his
Je.2:4.h.- L.,O house of Jacob,10:1.
7: 2. h.- L., all ye of Judah
9: 20. yet h.- L., O ye women
19:3. h.- L., O kings of Jud., 22:2.
22: 29. O earth, earth, h.- L.
31: 10. h.- L., O ye nations
34:4.yet h.- L.,O Zedekiah,king of
44: 24. h.- L., all Judah, 26.
Eze.6:3.ye mts.of Isr.,h.- L.,36:1,4.
13: 2. say unto prophets h.- L.
16:35. Wherefore, O harlot, h.- L.
20: 47. forest of the south, h.- L.
25: 3. say to Ammonites, h.- L.
34: 7. ye shepherds, h.- L., 9.
37: 4. say, O ye dry bones, h.- L.
Ho. 4:1. h.- L., ye children of Isr.
Am.7:16. Amaziah, h. thou w.- L.

Would or wouldest not HEAR.

Ge. 42:21. he besought, we w.n.h.
22. not sin ag. child, ye w. n. h.
Ex. 7:16. hitherto, thou w-t n. h.
De. 1:43. Israel w. n. h., 3:26. 2 K.
17: 14. ⌈25: 20.
2 K.14:11. Amaziah w. n. h., 2 Ch.
18: 12. Israel w. n. h., Ne. 9: 29.
Zch. 7: 13. ⌈h.
Is. 28:12. refreshing, yet they w.n.
Je.13:11. praise,they w.n.h.,29:19.
36:25.w.n.h. | Zch. 7:13. I w. n.

HEARD. ⌊h.

Ge. 16:11. bec. L. hath h.thy afflic.
18: 10. Sarah h. it in tent door
21: 26. neither yet h. I of it, but
27: 6. I h. thy fa. speak unto E.
29:33. L. hath h. that I was hated
45: 2. Jo. wept aloud, Egyp-s h.
Ex. 2: 24. God h. their groaning
4: 31. when they h. L. had visited
16:9. he hath h. your murmurings
18: 1. h. all G. had done for Mo.
23:13. nei. be h. out of thy mouth
28:35. sh. be h. when he goeth in
33: 4. when people h. evil tidings
Le. 10: 20. Mo. h. he was content
24: 14. let all h. him lay hands
Nu. 11:1. peo. complained, L. h. it
10. Moses h. the people weep
12:2. Miriam spake ag. Mo., L. h.it
14: 14. h. thou art am. this peo
15. nations have h. of thee

Nu. 30 : 7. held peace at her in the day he h. it [h. it, 12, 15.
8. disallowed her on the day he
33:40. h. of coming of chil. of Isr.
De. 4 : 32. anything been h. like it
Jos. 2: 11. as we h., hearts did melt
5: 1. h. L. had dried up waters
9 : 16. h. they were neighbours
1 S. 2 : 22. h. all that his sons did
4 : 14. Eli h. noise of the crying
7: 9. Samuel cried, Lord h. him
14 : 27. Jona. h. not when his fa.
23 : 11. will Saul come, as serv. h.
1 K. 1 : 11. not h. Adoni. doth reign
6 : 7. nor tool of iron h. in house
10:7. thy wisd. exceedeth the fame which I h. ? 1, 6.-2 Ch. 9 : 6.
19:13. Elijah h. he wrapped face in mantle [ago, Is. 37 : 26.
2 K. 19 : 25. Hast thou not h. long
2 Ch. 5:13. sound to be h. in prais-g
33 :.13. he was entreated and h.
Ezr. 3 : 13. the noise was h. afar
Ne. 12 : 43. joy of Jerusalem h. afar
Jb. 13 : 1. mine ear hath h. and
15:8. Hast thou h. the secret of G.?
19:7. I cry out of wrong, but not h.
26:14. how little portion h. of him
29 : 11. When ear h. me, it blessed
Ps. 6:9. L. hath h. my supplication
10 : 17. hast h. desire of humble
22:21. save me, for thou hast h. me
24. but when he cried he h., 34: 6.-40:1.-120:1. [me
34 : 4. I sought the L., and he h.
38 : 13. But I as a deaf man h. not
61 : 5. thou, O G. hast h. my vows
66 : 19. Verily God hath h. me, he
76 : 8. cause judgm. to be h. from
78 : 21. L. h. this and was wroth
59. when God h. this, was wroth
81: 5. h. a langu. I understood not
97 : 8. Zion h. and was glad, and
106 : 44. regarded afflic., when h.
118 : 21. thou hast h. me, and art
132:6. Lo, we h. of it at Ephratah
Pr. 21:13. he sh. cry, but not be h.
Is. 10:30. cause it to be h. unto Laish
40 : 21. have ye not h.? [not
28. hast not h. everl. God fainteth
48 : 6. Thou hast h. see all this
52:15. wh. they not h. sh. consid.
60:18. Violence sh. no more be h.
64:4. not h. what he hath prepar.
65 : 19. weeping sh. be no more h.
66 : 8. Who hath h. such a thing?
19. isles, that not h. my fame
Je. 4 : 19. hast h. sound of trumpet
6:7. casteth out wickedn., spoil is h.
7 : 13. rising early, but ye h. not
8 : 6. h. but they spake not aright
18 : 13. ask heathen, who h. such
22. let cry be h. from houses
20 : 10 I h. the defaming of many
25 : 36. howling of flock sh. be h.
26:11. hath proph-d as ye have h.
34:10. h. sho. let his manserv-t go
35 : 17. I have spoken, they not h.
46:12. nations have h. of thy shame
50 : 46. cry is h. am. the nations
51: 46. rumour shall be h. in land
La. 1 : 21. They have h. th. I sigh
3:61. Thou hast h. their reproach
Eze. 19 : 4. The nations h. of him
26:13. thy harp sh. be no more h.
33 : 5. He h. sound of the trumpet
Da. 12 : 8. h. but I understood not
Ho. 7:12. chastise, as cong. hath h.
Jon. 2:2. I cried unto L., he h. me
Mi. 5 : 15. fury, such as they not h.
Ha. 3 : 16. I h. my belly trembled
Mal. 3 : 16. L. hearkened and h. it
Mat. 2:3. When Her. the king had h., Mk. 6 : 14, 16, 20.
9. When had h. k. they departed
22. h. that Archelaus did reign
4 : 12. Jes. had h. John was cast
Mat. 5:21. h. it was said, 27, 33, 38, 43
6 : 7. be h. for much speaking
8:10. When Jes. h. it, 9 : 12.-14 : 13. Mk. 2 : 17. Lu. 7 : 9.-8 : 50.-18: 22, 23. Jn. 9 : 35.-11 : 4, 6.
11 : 2. when Jn. had h. in prison
12 : 24. when Pharis. h., 21 : 45.-22:34. Jn. 4 : 1.-7 : 32.-9 : 40.
13:17. have not h. them, Lu. 10:24.
14 : 1. the tetrarch h. of, Lu. 9 : 7.
15 : 12. were offended aft. they h.
17 : 6. when disciples h., 19 : 25.-20:24. Mk. 6:29.-10:41.-11:14.-16:11. Jn. 1:37.-6:60.-7:40. Ac.
19 : 22. yo. man h. he went [9:38.
20 : 24. when the ten h. it, 10 : 41.
30. blind men h. Jesus passed
21 : 45. when ch. had h., 22 : 34.
22:7. when k. h. he was wroth [11.
33. when mult. h., Mk. 3:8. Lu. 19:
26:65. h. his blasphemy, Mk. 14:64.
27:47. Some that h. said, Mk. 15:35.
Mk. 3 : 8. h. what gr. things he did
21. when his friends h. of it
4 : 15. when have h., Sat. cometh
5 : 27. had h. of Jes. came in press
6:14. when Herod h. of him, 16:20.
20. did many things h. gladly
55. carried sick where they h.
7 : 25. had unc. spirit h. of him
10 : 47. he h. it was Jes. cried out
11 : 18. chief priests h., Ac. 5 : 24.
12 : 28. having h. them reasoning
37. common people h. him gladly
14 : 11. when h. it they were glad
58. We h. him say I will destroy
15 : 35. when they h. said, Behold
16 : 11. when they h. he was alive
Lu. 1:13. thy prayer is h., Ac. 10:31.
41. Elizabeth h. salutation
58. cousins h. how L. shewed
66. th. h. laid them up, 2:18, 47.
2 : 20. praising G. for all they h.
47. all th. h. him were astonish-d
4 : 28. they in syn. when they h.
7 : 3. centu. when he h. of Jesus
22. things ye have h.
29. peo. that h., Jn. 12:12, 18, 29.
12 : 3. what spoken, be h. in the
14 : 15. one that sat at meat h.
15 : 25. he h. music and dancing
16 : 14. covetous, h. these things
19:11. as they h. he spake parable
18 : 26. they that h. it said, Who
20 : 16. h. it, they said, God forbid
23:6. When Pilate h., Jn. 19:8, 13.
8. had h. many things of him
Jn. 1 : 40. One of the two wh. h.
3 : 32. hath h. that he testifieth
4 : 1. Phari. had h. that Jesus
47. nobleman h. Jes. was come
6 : 45. ev. man that hath h. of Fa.
60. when they h. saying, 7 : 40.
8 : 6. wrote on gro., as tho. h. not
9. they wh. h. being convicted
9 : 32. since world began not h.
11:41. I thank that thou hast h. me
12 : 12. when they h. that Jesus
29. th. h. it said it thundered
14 : 28. Ye have h. how I said
18 : 21. ask them which h. me
19 : 8. Pilate h. that saying, 13.
21 : 7. when Peter h. it was the L.
Ac. 1 : 4. wait for prom. ye have h.
2:6. ev. man h. them speak, 10:46.
37. when h. this, they were pricked
4 : 4. many wh. h. word believed
24. when they h. they lifted voice, 5: 21, 33.-7: 54.-11: 18.-17: 8.-19: 5, 28.-21 : 12, 20
5 : 5. fear came on all them that h.
7 : 12. Jac. h. there was corn [1.
8:14. Apos. h. Sama. had rec-d, 11:
30. Philip h. him read Esaias
9 : 21. all that h. were amazed
10:46. h. them speak with tongues
13 : 48. when Gent. h. they glad
Ac. 14:9. the same h. Paul speak, who
14. Barna. and Paul h. they rent
16:14. wom. which worsh-d G., h.
25. sang praises, the prisoners h.
38. feared when h. they were Ro.
17 : 32. when they h. of resurrec.
18:26. when Aqui. and Pris. had h.
19 : 5. h. this, they were baptized
22 : 2. they h. he sp. in Hebrew
15. shalt witness of what hast h.
26. When centu. h. that, he went
23 : 16. when Paul's sister's son h.
24 : 22. When Felix h. these things
24. h. him conc-g faith in Christ
28 : 15. breth. h. of us they came
Ro. 10 : 14. in him of whom not h.
18. Have they not h.? Yes, verily
15 : 21. have not h. shall underst.
1 Co. 2 : 9. Eye not seen, nor ear h.
Ga. 1 : 13. have h. of my conversa.
23. h. only That he wh. persecu.
Ep. 1 : 13. after ye h. word of truth
15. aft. I h. of your faith in L.J.
3 : 2. If ye have h. of dispensa. of
4 : 21. if so be ye have h. him and
Ph. 2 : 26. ye had h. he been sick
4 : 9. those things ye have h., do
Col. 1 : 4. Since we h. of your faith
6. since ye h., and knew grace of
9. since day h. not cease to pray
23. gospel which ye have h.
2 Ti. 2 : 2. thi. thou hast h. of me
He. 2 : 3. confirmed by them h. him
3 : 16. some had h. did provoke
4:2. not mixed wi. faith in them h.
5 : 7. off-d prayers, and was h.
Ja. 5:11. have h. of patience of Job
1 Jn. 2 : 18. h. that antichrist, 4:3.
24. h. fr. beginn., 3 : 11. 2 Jn. 6.
Re. 3 : 3. Remem. how thou hast h.
5 : 13. all that are in them h. I
6 : 1. I h. as it were noise of
3. I h. sec. beast | 5. 3d beast
7 : 4. I h. number of them sealed
8 : 13. I h. an angel flying
9 : 16. I h. number of horsemen
16 : 5. I h. the angel of waters say
7. I h. another out of altar say
18:22. trumpeters sh. be h. no more
23. the voice of bride be h. no more [I h.
22 : 8. I saw these, h. them, when

I have HEARD.

Ge. 17 : 20. for Ishmael I h. h. thee
41:15. I h. h. say of thee thou canst interp. dreams, Da. 5 : 14, 16.
42 : 2. I h. h. there is corn in E.
Ex. 3 : 7. I h. h. their cry | 6 : 5. I h. h. groaning [Nu. 14:27.
16 : 12. I h. h. the murmuring,
De. 5:28. I h. h. voice of your words
1 S. 25:7. I h. h. thou hast shearers
1 K. 2 : 42. word I h. h. is good
9 : 3. I h. h. thy prayer bef. me, 2 K. 20 : 5. 2 Ch. 7:12. Is. 38:5.
2 K. 19:20. that thou prayed I h. h.
22 : 19. I h. h. thee, saith L., 2 Ch. 34 : 27.
Jb. 16 : 2. I h. h. many such things
20 : 3. I h. h. check of my reproach
42 : 5. I h. h. of thee by the ear
Ps. 31 : 13. I h. h. slander of many
62 : 11. twice I h. h. this, power
Is. 21 : 10. that which I h. h. of L.
28:22. I h. h. fr. L. a consumption
49 : 8. in acceptable time h. I h., 2 Co. 6 : 2.
Je. 23 : 25. I h. h. what prophets
31:18. I h. h. Ephraim bemoaning
42:4. I h. h. you, I will pray unto L.
49 : 14. I h. h. a rumour from L.
Eze. 35:12. I h. h. thy blasph-s, 13.
Ho. 14 : 8. I h. h. and observed him
Ha. 3 : 2. O L. I h. h. thy speech
Zph. 2:8. I h. h. reproach of Moab
Jn. 8 : 26. speak things I h. h. of
40. truth, which I h. h. of God

Jn.15:15.all things I h.h.of my Fa.
Ac. 7: 34. I h. h. their groaning
9: 13. L. I h. h. by many of this
2 Co. 6: 2. I h. h. thee in a time

HEARD with voice.

Ge. 3:8. they h. v. of L. in garden
10. I h. thy v., and was afraid
21: 17. God h. the v. of the lad
30: 6. h. my v. given me a son
39: 15. when he h. th. I lifted v.
Nu.7:89. he h. the v. of one speak.
20:16. we cried, he h. our v., sent
De. 1: 34. L. h. v. of your words
4: 12. no similitude, only he h. v.
33. hear v. of G. as hast h., 5:26.
5: 23. ye h. the v. out of darkness
24. we have h. his v. out of fire
28. Lord h. the v. of your words
26: 7. we cried, the Lord h. our v.
Ju. 18:25. Let not thy v. be h. am.
1 S. 1: 13. lips moved, v. was not h.
1 K. 17: 22. L. h. the v. of Elijah
2 Ch. 30:27. v. was h. prayer came
Jb. 4: 16. there was silence, I h.v.
33: 8. have h. v. of thy words
37: 4. not stay them when v. is h.
Ps.3: 4. unto L. with my v., he h.
6: 8. L. hath h. v. of my weeping
18:6. he h. my v. out of his temp.
19:3. no speech where v. is not h.
28:6.hath h.v. of my supplications
66: 8. make v. of praise to be h.
116: 1. I love L., bec. he h. my v.
Can. 2:12. the v. of the turtle is h.
Is. 6: 8. also I h. the v. of the L.
15:4.their v. sh. be h. unto Jahaz
30: 30. L. sh. cause glorious v. h.
42:2. nor cause v. h. in the street
58:4. to make your v. h. on high
65:19. v. of weeping no more be h.
Je. 3:21. a v. was h. upon high pla.
4: 31. I have h. a v. as of a wom.
9: 19. v. of wailing h. out of Zion
30: 5. We have h. a v. of trembl-g
31: 15. v. was h. in Ramah, Mat. [2:18.
La. 3:56. Thou hast h. my v.
Eze. 1:28.I h. a v. of one th. spake
3: 12. I h. behind me v. of great
19: 9. th. his v. no more be h.
27: 30. sh. cause their v. to be h.
Da.8:16.I h. man's v. betw. banks
10: 9. h. I the v. of his words (2)
Na. 2:13.v. of messeng. no more h.
Jn. 5: 37. Ye have neither h. his v.
Ac. 9: 4. h. a v. saying, Saul, 22: 7.-26: 14.
11: 7. I h. a v. saying, Arise
22: 9. h. not v. of him that spake
He. 12: 19. which v. they that h.
2 Pe. 1: 18. v. from heaven we h.
Re. 1: 10. I h. a great v., 16:1.-19: 1.-21: 3.
: 1. first v. I h. as of a trumpet
5: 11. I h. the v. of many angels
6: 6. I h. v. in midst of 4 beasts
7. I h. a v. of the 4th beast say
9: 13. I h. a v. from four horns
10: 4. I h. a v. from heaven, 8.-14: 2, 13.-18: 4.
12: 10. I h. a loud v. saying in
14: 2. I h. the v. of harpers harp.
19:6.I h. as it were v. of gr. mult.

We have HEARD.

Jos. 2: 10. w. h. h. how L. dried
9: 9. w. h. h. the fame of him and
2 S. 7: 22. none like thee accord. to all w. h. h., 1 Ch. 17: 20.
1 K. 20: 31. w. h. h. kings of Isr.
Jb. 28: 22. w. h. h. fame, Je.6:24.
Ps. 44:1. w. h.h. wi. our ears, our
48: 8. As w. h. h. so have we seen
78: 3. dark sayings which w.h.h.
Is. 16: 6. w.h.h. of pride of Moab, Je. 48: 29. [righteous
24: 16. w. h. h. songs, glory to
Je. 30: 5. w.h.h. voice of trembl.
51: 51. confounded, w.h.h. repr.

Ob. 1. w. h. h. rumour from Lord
Zch. 8: 23. w. h. h. G. is with you
Mk. 14: 58. w. h. h. him say, I
Lu. 4: 23. whatever w. h. h. done
22: 71. w. h.h. of his own mouth
Jn. 4: 42. we believe, w. h. h. him
12: 34. w. h. h. out of law that
Ac. 4: 20. can-t but speak w. h. h.
6: 11. w. h. h. him speak blasph.
14. w. h. h. him say, this Jesus
15:24. w.h.h. certain have troub.
19: 2. w. h. not h. whe. be H. G.
He. 2: 1. give heed to thi. w.h.h.
1 Jn. 1: 1. that which w. h. h., 3.
5. This is the message w.h. h. of

HEARD with word, s.

Ge. 24: 30. when he h. w-s of Re- [bek.
52.when Ab.'s serv-t h.w-s
27: 34. when Esau h. w-s of fa.
31: 1. Jac. h. w-s of Laban's sons
39: 19. master h. w-s of his wife
Nu.24:4.said, which h.w-s of G.,16.
Jos. 22:30. when heads of Isr. h.w-s
24: 27. it hath h. all w-s of Lord
Ju. 9: 30. Zebul h. w-s of Gaal
1 S. 8: 21. Sam. h. w-s of people
17: 11. and Isr. h. Goliath's w-s
23. acc. to same w-s Da. h. them
31. when w-s were h. which Da.
1 K. 2: 42. w. that I have h. is
5: 7. when Hiram h. Sol.'s w-s
21: 27. Ahab h. those w-s, rent
2 K.6:30.when king h. w-s of wom.
19: 6. be not afraid of w-s thou hast h., Is. 37: 6.
22: 11. king had h. w-s of book of law, he rent his, 18. 2 Ch. 34: 19. [courage
2 Ch.15:8.Asa h. these w-s he took
34: 26. conc. w. thou hast h.
Ne. 1: 4. I h. these w-s, I wept
5: 6. angry when I h. these w-s
8: 9. peo. wept, when h. w-s of
Jb.33:8. I have h. voice of thy w-s
Ec. 9:16. poor man's w-s are not h.
17.w-s of wise men are h. in quiet
Is. 37:4. reprove w-s wh.G. hath h.
Je. 23: 18. marked, and h. his w.
25:8. Bec. ye have not h. my w-s
26: 12. ag. city all w-s ye have h.
21. k. and all princes h. his w-s
36: 13. declared all w-s he had h.
16. h. all the w. men afraid [w-s
24. were not afraid that h. these
38:1. Pashur h. the w-s Jere. had
Da.6:14.Darius h.w-s was displeas.
10:12. thy w-s were h. I am come
Mat. 22: 22. h. w-s they marvelled
Mk. 5: 36. soon as Jesus h. the w.
Lu. 8: 15. having h. the w. keep it
10: 39. Mary sat and h. his w.
Ac. 10: 44. H. G. fell on them who
2 Co.12:4.h.unspeakable w-s [h.w.
Ep. 1:13. aft. ye h. the w. of truth
Col. 1: 5. ye h. in w. of the gospel
1 Th. 2: 13. received w. ye h. of us
2 Ti.1:13. form of sound w-s hast h.
He. 12:19. that h. entreated th. w.
1 Jn.2:7. w. ye have h. fr. beginn.

HEARDEST.

De. 4: 36. h. his words out of the
Jos. 14:12. h. in th. day how Anak.
2 K. 22: 19. when thou h. what I spake ag. this pla., 2 Ch.34:27.
Ne. 9: 9. h. their cry by Red sea
27. they cried, thou h. them, 28.
Ps. 31:22. h. voice of my supplica.
119: 26. I declared ways, thou h.
Is. 48:7. bef. day thou h. them not
8. thou h. not, yea, knewest not
Jon. 2:2. out of hell I cried, thou h.

HEARER, S.

Ro. 2: 13. not h-s of law are justifi.
Ep. 4: 29. minister grace unto h-s
2 Ti. 2: 14. to subverting of h-s
Ja. 1:22. be doers, and not h-s only
23. if any be a h. of the word

Ja.1:25. he being not a forgetful h.

HEAREST.

Ru.2:8.Boaz unto Ruth, h. thou not, my daughter?
1 S. 24: 9. Whf. h. men's words?
2 S. 5: 24. when h. sound in mul- berry trees [6:21.
1 K. 8: 30. when h. forgive, 2 Ch.
Ps. 22: 2. I cry in daytime, thou h.
65:2.thou th. h. prayer, unto thee
Mat. 21:16. h. thou what these say?
27:13. h. thou not how many thi.
Jn. 3: 8. wind bloweth, and thou h.
11: 42. I knew thou h. me always

HEARETH. [8.

Ex. 16: 7. he h. your murmurings,
Nu.30:5.if fa. disallow in day he h.
De. 29: 19. when h. words of curse
1 S.3:9.Speak, L., thy serv-t h., 10.
11. at wh. ears of ev. one that h. sh. tingle, 2 K. 21: 12. Je.19:3.
2 S. 17:9.h. it will say, is slaughter
Jb. 34:28. he h. cry of afflicted
Ps. 34: 17. The righteous cry, L. h.
38: 14. I was as man that h. not
69: 33. L. h. poor, despiseth not
Pr. 8:34. Blessed is man that h. me
13: 1. wise son h. fa.'s instruc.
8. but the poor h. not rebuke
15: 29. he h. prayer of the righte.
31. ear that h. reproof of life, 32.
18:13. th. ans-th matter bef. he h.
21: 28. the man that h. speaketh
25:10.Lest th. h. put thee to shame
29:24. h. cursing, bewrayeth not
Is. 41: 26. is none th. h. your words
42: 20 opening ears, but h. not
Eze. 3: 27. He that h. let him hear
33: 4. whoso. h. sound of trump.
Mat. 7: 24. whoso. h. sayings, 26. Lu. 6: 47, 49. [kingd.
13: 19. When any h. word of the
20. same is he h. word, 22, 23.
Lu. 10: 16. He that h. you h. me
Jn. 3: 29. who h. him rejoiceth
5: 24. h. my word, and believeth
8: 47. He th. is of G. h. G.'s words
9: 31. God h. not sinners, if any man doeth his will, him he h.
18: 37. Ev. one that is of truth, h.
2 Co. 12:6. think of me ab. that he
1 Jn. 4:5. of world, world h. th. [h.
6. he that knoweth God h. us
5:14. If ask acc. to his will, he h.us
Re. 22: 17. let him th. h. say, Come
18. I testify to every man that h.

HEARING. [Noun.]

Ge. 29: † 13. Laban heard h. of Jac.
† 33. name Simeon, that is, h.
De. 31: 11. read this law in their h.
2 S. 18:12. in our h. king charged
2 K. 4: 31. was neither voice nor h.
Ne. 8: † 2. all that understood in h.
Jb. 33: 8. thou hast spok. in my h.
37: † 2. hear in h. noise of voice
42: 5. I have heard of thee by h.
Ps. 18: † 44. at h. of ear will obey
Pr. 28: 9. that turneth ear fr. h. law
Ec. 1: 8. nor is ear filled with h.
Is. 6:† 9. hear ye in h. underst. not
11:3.nei. reprove aft. h. of his ears
21: 3. I was bowed at h. of it
28: † 9. whom make underst. h.?
33: 15. he that stoppeth ears from h. of blood [Ro. 10: † 16.
53: † 1. Who hath believed our h.?
Eze. 9:5. said in my h. Go after him
10:13. was cried unto th. in my h.
16: † 56. sister Sodom was not for h.
Am. 8: 11. fam. of h. word of L.
Ha. 3: † 2. O L. I have heard thy h.
Mat. 13: 13. and h. they hear not
14.By h. ye sh. hear, and not un- derst., Mk. 4: 12. Lu. 8: 10. Ac. 28: 26.
15. dull of h., Ac. 28:27. He.5:11.
Mk. 6: 2. many h. were astonished

Ac. 25: 21. reserved to h. of Augus.
23. was entered into place of h.
Ro.10:17. faith cometh by h. and h.
1 Co.12:17. where were the h.?
Ga. 3: 2. or by the h. of faith, 5.
He.5:11.hard,seeing ye are dull of h.
2 Pe.2:8. Lot in seeing and h.vexed

HEARING. [Adj. and Part.]

1 K. 3:†9. Give thy serv. a h. heart
Pr. 20: 12. h. ear, L. hath made
Eze.33:†4.he that h.heareth trump.
Mat. 13: 13. and h. they hear not
Lu.2:46. h. them and asking questi.
18: 36. h. mult. pass by, asked
Ac. 5: 5. Ananias h. these words
8: 6. h. seeing miracles he did
9: 7. h. a voice, but seeing no man
18: 8. many of Corin-s h. believed
Phm. 5. h. of thy love and faith

HEARKEN.

Ex. 6: 30. how shall Pha. h. to me?
De.7:12. if ye h. to these judgments
11: 13. if ye h. dilig-y unto com-ts
15:5. if h.unto voice of L., Je.17:24.
18: 15. Prophet, unto him h.
28:13. if h. unto com-ts,1 K.11:38.
Jos. 1: 17. so will we h. unto thee
1 S. 15: 22. to h. than fat of rams
30: 24. who h. unto you in this
1 K. 8: 28. have thou respect to h.
29. mayest h. unto the prayer,
52. 2 Ch. 6: 19, 20. [do this?
Ne. 13: 27. Shall we h. unto you to
Ps. 81: 8. O Israel, if thou wilt h.
Pr. 29: 12. If a ruler h. to lies
Is. 32: 3. ears of them that hear h.
42:23. who will h. for time to come
Je. 26: 3. If so be will h. and turn
5. To h. to prophets wh. I sent
29:12.ye sh.pray unto me, I will h.
35:13.Will ye receive instruc. to h.
37: 2. nor people of land did h.
Zch. 7: 11. they refused to h.
Ac.4:19.to h.unto you more than G.
12: 13. a damsel came to h.

HEARKEN. [Imperatively.]

Ge. 4: 23. wives, h. unto my speech
23:15. h. unto me | 49:2. unto Isr.
Nu.23:18. h. unto me, son of Zippor
De. 4: 1. h. O Isr., unto statutes
27: 9. Take heed, and h. O Israel
Ju. 9:7. h. unto me, men of Shech.
1 K.8:30. h. to supplica., 2 Ch. 6:21.
22: 28. he said, h. O peo., ev one
2 Ch. 18: 27. he said, h. all ye peo.
20:15.h.ye all Jud., and ye inhabi.
Jb. 13: 6. h. to pleadings of lips
32: 10. h. to me, 33: 31.
33: 1. h. to my words [standing
34: 10. h. unto me, men of under-
34. wise man h. | 37: 14. h. unto
this, O Job [h. O dau.
Ps. 34: 11. h. I will teach | 45: 10.
Pr. 7: 24. h. unto me, O chil., 8:32.
23: 22. h. unto fa. th. begat thee
Is. 28: 23. h. and hear my speech
34:1. h. ye people, 49:1. [Ho. 5:1.
46:3.h. unto me, O h. of Jac., 48:12.
12. h. unto me, stouthearted
51: 1. h. to me, ye th. follow after
4. h. unto me, my peo. [righte-n.
7.h.unto me,ye th.know righte-n.
55:2. h. diligently unto me, eat th.
Je. 6: 17. h. to sound of trumpet
Da. 9: 19. O Lord, h. and do
Mi. 1:2. h. O earth, and all therein
Mk. 4: 3. h. there went out a sower
7: 14. h. unto me, every one of you
Ac. 2: 14. men of Judea, h. to my
7: 2. men, breth., and fathers, h.
15:13. Men and breth., h. unto me
Ja. 2: 5. h. my beloved brethren

HEARKEN with **not.**

Ge. 34: 17. if n. h. to be circumc.
Ex. 7: 4. Pha. n. h. unto you, 22.
-11: 9. [me, 18, 21, 27.
Le. 26: 14. But if ye will n.h. unto
De. 13: 3. shalt n. h. unto dreamer
8. n. h. unto him, nei. eye pity
17:12.man th.will n.h. unto priest
18:19. whoso. n. h. unto my words
21: 18. chastened, he will n. h.
23: 5. n. h. unto Balaam, Jos.24:
Jos. 1:18. n. h. unto thy words [10.
Ju. 2: 17. would n. h. unto Judges
11: 17. king of Edom would n. h.
19: 25 men of Gibeah n.h. to him
20: 13. chil. of Benj. would n. h.
2 S. 13: 14. wo. n. h. unto her, 16.
1 K.20:8. elders said, h.n. unto him
2 K.17:40. n. h. but did aft.manner
18: 31. h. n. to Heze., Is. 36: 16.
2 Ch. 10: 16. Rehob. would n. h.
33: 10. L. spake, they would n. h.
Jb. 33: 33. If n. h. hold thy peace
Je. 6:10. ear is uncirc., they n. h.
17. said, We will n. h., 44: 16.
7: 27. they will n. h. unto thee
11:11.tho. cry unto me, I will n.h.
16:12. aft. evil heart, th. they n.h.
17: 27. if ye will n. h. unto me,
26: 4. Eze. 20: 39.
23: 16. h. n. unto prophets, 27:
9, 14, 16, 17.-29: 8.
38:15. if I give counsel, wilt n. h.
Eze. 3: 7. n. h. unto thee, will n.
20:8. rebelled,wo.n.h. [h.unto me
Ho.9:17. did n.h.unto him, Zch.1:4.
See **VOICE** with **hearken, ed.**

HEARKENED.

Ge. 23: 16. Abr. h. unto Ephron,
and weighed [h. to Rachel
30:17. God h. unto Leah | 22. God
34: 24. unto Hamor h. all th.went
39: 10. Joseph h. not unto her
Ex. 6: 9. h. not unto Mo., 16: 20.
12. chil. of Israel have not h. unto me [19.-9: 12.
7: 13. Pha. h. not unto th., 8: 15,
De. 9: 19. Lord h. unto me, 10: 10.
18: 14. h. unto observers of times
34: 9. Israel h. unto, Jos. 1: 17.
Ju. 11:28. king h. not unto Jepht.
1 S. 28: 21. woman of Endor h.un-
to Saul's words [16. 2 Ch.10:15.
1 K. 12: 15. king h. not unto peo.,
24. They h. to the word of the L.
15: 20. Ben-hadad h. unto king
Asa, 2 Ch. 16: 4.
2 K. 13: 4. L. h. unto Jehoahaz
16: 9. k. of Assyria h. unto Asa
20:13. Hezekiah h. unto messen-
21: 9. Israel h. not [gers fr. Bab.
22: 13. our fa-s h. not unto words
2 Ch. 24:17.Joash h. unto princes of
25:16. Amazi. h. not unto counsel
30: 20. L. h. to Hez., healed peo.
35:22. Josiah h. not unto Pha-nec.
Ne. 9: 16. our fathers h. not to thy
com-ts, 29, 34 Je. 34: 14.
Es.3:4. when Morde.h.not unto th.
Ps. 81: 13. O that my peo. had h.
Is. 21: 7. he h. diligently with
48: 18. O that thou hadst h. to
my commandments
Je. 6: 19. have not h. unto my
words, 7: 24, 26.-25: 3, 4, 7.-
26: 5.-29: 19.-32: 33.-34: 17.-
35: 14, 15, 16.-36: 31.-44: 5.
37: 14. Irijah h. not to Jeremiah
Eze. 3: 6. would have h. unto thee
Da. 9:6. Nei. have we h. unto serv-s
Mal. 3: 16. the Lord h., Je 8: 6.
Ac. 27: 21. Sirs, ye should have h.
unto me

HEARKENEDST, ETH, ING. [of L.

De. 28: 45. bec. h-t not unto voice
Ps. 103:20. ye angels h-g unto voice
Pr. 1:33. whoso. h-h dwell safely
12: 15. be th. h-h unto counsel is

HEART. [wise

Ge. 31: † 20. Jac. stole h. of Laban
34:†3.Shech.spake unto h.of Dinah
Ge. 45: 26. Jacob's h. fainted
Ex. 23: 9. ye know h. of stranger
28:30. they sh. be upon Aaron's h.
35:5. is of a willing h. let him bri.
35. hath filled with wisdom of h.
Le. 26: 16. shall cause sorrow of h.
Nu. 32:7. whf. discourage h. of Isr.
9. discouraged h. of chil. of Isr.
De. 5:29. O were such a h. in them
28:28. smite with astonishm. of h.
47. servedst not L. with gladn. of
65. L. sh. give trembling h. [h.
29:4.L. not given you h. to percei.
Jos. 14: 8. made h. of people melt
Ju. 5:15. were great thoughts of h.
16. were great searchings of h.
18:20. the priest's h. was glad [h.
1 S. 1:13. Hannah, she spake in her
4: †20. ans-d not, nei. set her h.
10: 9. so that G. gave another h.
16: 7. the Lord looketh on the h.
17: 32. Da. said, Let no man's h.
24:5.Da.'s h. smote him,2 S.24:10.
25:31. nor offence of h. unto lord
36. Nabal's h. was merry [15:29.
2 S. 6: 16. despised him in h., 1 Ch.
13:28. when Ammon's h. is merry
14: 1. king's h. was tow. Absalom
18:14.thrust darts thro. h. of Abs.
19:† 7. go speak to h. of thy serv-s
14. bowed h. of all men of Judah
1 K. 3: 9. Give an understand-g h.
12. I have giv. thee underst-g h.
4: 29. G. gave Sol. largeness of h.
8: 17. was in h. of Da., 2 Ch. 6:7.
66. peo. went unto tents glad of
h., 2 Ch. 7: 10. [2 Ch. 9: 1.
10: 2. communed of all in her h.,
11:4. perfect, as was the h. of Da.
12:27.then sh. h. of this peo. turn
2 K. 6: 11 h. of king was troubled
12:4. cometh into man's h., 2 Ch.
1 Ch.12:33.not of double h. [29:31.
† 33. were without a h. and a h.
16: 10. let the h. of them rejoice
Ps. 105: 3. [Je. 11: 20
29: 17. I know thou triest h., 18.
2 Ch.7:11.all th. came into Sol.'s h.
30: † 22. Hez. spake to h. of Lev.
Ezr. 6: 22. turned h. of k. of Assy.
7: 27. put such as this in k.'s h.
Ne. 2: 2. is noth. but sorrow of h.
Es. 1: 10. when h. of king merry
5: 9. Haman went with a glad h.
Jb.9:4. He is wise in h. and mighty
12: † 3. I have a h. as well as you
24. He taketh away h. of chief
29:13. I caused widow's h. to sing
34:†10.hearken unto me,men of h.
† 34. let men of h. tell me
36:13. hypocrites in h. heap wrath
37: 24. respecteth not wise of h.
38: 36. hath given underst-g to h.
Ps. 12:2. with double h. they speak
19: 8. statutes of L., rejoicing h.
34: 18. L. is nigh them of brok. h.
44: 21. he knoweth secrets of h.
45: 5. arrows sharp in h. of ene.
58: 2. in h. you work wickedness
64: 6. thought and h. is deep
73: 7. have more than h. co. wish
101: 4. froward h. shall depart
5. a proud h. will not I suffer
104: 15. wine, th. maketh glad h.,
bread, wh.strength-h man's h.
Pr. 6:18. a h. that deviseth wicked
† 32. com-h adultery, lacketh h.
7:10.met him a woman subtile of h.
8:5.fools, be ye of an underst-g h.
10:8. wise in h. will receive com-ts
20. h. of wicked is little worth
11:20.they of froward h. are abom.
29. fool be serv. to wise of h.
12:8. he of perverse h. be despis.
20. Deceit is in h. of them who
23. h. of fools procl-h foolish-n.
25. heaviness in h. mak. it stoop

Pr.13:12.Hope deferred mak.**h.** sick
14: 10. **h.** knoweth own bitterness
13. in laughter **h.** is sorrowful
14. backslider in **h.** be filled with
30. A sound **h.** is the life of flesh
33. Wisdom resteth in **h.** of him
15: 7. **h.** of foolish doeth not so
13. A merry **h.** maketh cheerful
countenance. but by sorrow of **h.**
14. **h.** of him that hath underst.
15. merry **h.** hath a contin. feast
28. **h.** of righteous studieth to
30. light of eyes rejoic. **h.** ⌊answ.
† 32. heareth reproof poss-h a **h.**
16: 1. preparation of **h.** fr. Lord
5.ev.one proud in **h.** is an abomi.
9. a man's **h.** deviseth his way
23. **h.** of wise teacheth his mouth
17: 16. a price in ha., hath no **h.**
20. froward **h.** findeth no good
22. A merry **h.** doeth good like a
18: 12. Before destruct. **h.** of man
15. **h.** of prudent getteth knowl.
19: 21. many devices in man's **h.**
20: 5. Counsel in **h.** like deep wat.
21: 1. king's **h.** is in hand of Lord
4. A high look, a proud **h.** is sin
22: 11. loveth pureness of **h.** the
15. Foolishn. bound in **h.** of child
24:12.th. pondereth **h.** consider it?
25: 3. **h.** of kings is unsearchable
20. th. singeth songs to heavy **h.**
26:23. wicked **h.** is like a potsherd
27: 9. Ointm. and perfume rej. **h.**
19. so **h.** of man anew-h to man
28: 25. proud **h.** stirreth up strife
31: 11. **h.** of husband doth trust
Ec. 7:3. by sadness the **h.** is better
4. **h.** of wise in ho. of mourning,
h. of fools in house of mirth
7. a gift destroyeth the **h.**
8:5. wise man's **h.** discerneth time
11. **h.** of men is set to do evil
9: 3. **h.** of sons of men full of evil
7.and drink thy wine wi.merry **h.**
10: 2. a wise man's **h.** is at right
ba.,fools **h.**at left ⌈15.Ac.28:27.
Is. 6:10. make their **h.** fat, Mat. 13:
9: 9. that say in stoutness of **h.**
10: 12. will punish stout **h.** of k.
13: 7. every man's **h.** shall melt
19: 1. **h.** of Egypt shall melt
30: 29. ye sh. have gladness of **h.**
32:4. **h.** of the rash shall underst.
35: 4. Say to them of fearful **h.**
40: † 2. Speak ye to **h.** of Jerus.
42:25. burned, he laid it not to **h.**
44: 20. deceived **h.** turned him
57: 1. no man layeth it to **h.**, Je.
15. revive **h.** of contrite ⌈12: 11.
59: 13. fr. the **h.** words of falseh.
65: 14. my serv-s sh. sing for joy
of **h.** ye sh. cry for sorrow of **h.**
† 17. former heavens not upon **h.**
Je. 2: † 24. wind at desire of her **h.**
3: † 16. nei. shall it come upon **h.**
4: 9. **h.** of the king shall perish
5: 23. this peo. hath a rebell. **h.**
9: 8. in **h.** he layeth his wait
26. Isr. are uncircumcised in **h.**
11:20. O L., th. triest reins and **h.**
17: 9. The **h.** is deceitful above all
10. I the L. search **h.** I try reins
20: 12. O Lord, that seest **h.**
23:26.How long this in **h.** of proph.
24: 7. I will give a **h.** to know me
48: 41. be as **h.** of a woman,49:22.
La. 3: 65. Give them sorrow of **h.**
Eze. 6: 9. with their whorish **h.**
11: 19. I will take stony **h.** out
13: 22. wi. lies made **h.** of righte.
18: 31. make you a new **h.** ⌊sad
21: 7. every **h.** sh. melt, all hands
25:6. rejoiced in **h.** wi. thy despite
15. vengeance with despiteful **h.**
27: 31. weep with bitterness of **h.**
36: 26. I will give you **h.** of flesh

Eze.44:7. uncirc-d in **h.**, 9. Ac.7:51.
Da. 4: 16. let a beast's **h.** be given
7: 4. a man's **h.** was given to it
Ho. 2: † 14. I will speak to her **h.**
4:11.Whored. and wine take aw.**h.**
7: 11. Ephr. silly dove without **h.**
Na. 2: 10. **h.** melteth, knees smite
Zph. 2: 15. city that said in her **h.**
Mal. 2: 2. if ye will not lay it to **h.**,
a curse, bec. do not lay it to **h.**
4: 6. turn **h.** of fa-s, **h.** of chil.
Mat. 11: 29. I am meek lowly in **h.**
12:34.out of abnud. of **h.**,Lu.6:45.
35. out of treas. of **h.**, Lu. 6: 45.
15: 18. come fr. **h.** and defile ⌈21.
19. out of **h.** evil thoughts,Mk.7:
Mk. 16:14. upbraided wi. hardn. of
Lu. 2: 19. Mary pondered in **h.** ⌊**h.**
51. mother kept sayings in her **h.**
8: 15. in a good **h.** having heard
24:25. O fools, slow of **h.** to believe
Jn. 13: 2. devil put into **h.** of Jud.
Ac.2:46. meat with singleness of **h.**
5: 33. heard, were cut to **h.**, 7:54.
11: 23. wi. purpose of **h.** cleave to
Ro. 2: 5. after thy impenitent **h.**
29. circumcision is that of the **h.**
6: 17. have obeyed from **h.** doctr.
10: 10. with the **h.** man believeth
1 Co. 2:9. nei. have entered into **h.**
7: 37. hath so decreed in his **h.**
2 Co. 2: 4. anguish of **h.** I wrote
3: 3. written in fleshly tables of **h.**
5: 12. in appearance, not in **h.**
8: 16. earnest care in **h.** of Titus
Ep. 6: 6. doing will of God from **h.**
Col. 3: 22. in singlen. of **h.** fear. G.
1 Th.2:17. fr. you in pres. not in **h.**
He. 4: 12. is a discerner of the **h.**
10:22.Let us draw near wi. true **h.**
13: 9. it is good the **h.** be establ.
1 Pe. 3: 4. the hidden man of **h.**
2 Pe. 2: 14. **h.** exercised wi. covet.
Re. 18: 7. saith in her **h.**, I sit a q.
See APPLY, BROKEN, CLEAN,
EVIL, HARDEN, HARDENED.

HEART. [Inner part.]

Ex. 15: 8. congealed in **h.** of sea
De. 4: †11. burned unto **h.** of heav.
Ps. 46: † 2. mts. be carried into **h.**
Pr. 23: †34. lieth down in **h.** of sea
30: † 19. ship in **h.** of sea
Mat. 12:40. Son of man be in **h.** of

HEART with all. ⌊earth

De. 11: 13. to serve him wi. **a.** your
h., Jos. 22: 5. 1 S. 12: 20, 24.
13:3. love L. your G. with **a.** your
h. and soul, 6: 5, 30: 6. Mat.
22:37. Mk. 12: 30, 33. Lu. 10:27.
26: 16. shalt do them with **a. h.**
30: 2. unto L. with **a.** thine **h.**,
10. Jo. 2: 12. ⌈18.
Ju. 16: 17. Samson told her **a. h.**,
1 K. 2: 4. If thy children walk before me with **a. h.**, 8: 23.
8:48. return unto thee wi. **a.** their
h., 2 K. 23: 25 2 Ch. 6: 38.
14:8.Da., followed me wi. **a.** his **h.**
2 K. 10: 31. Jehu took no heed to
walk in land of L., with **a. h.**
23: 3. made covenant to walk bef.
L. with **a.** their **h.**, 2 Ch. 34:31.
2 Ch. 15: 12. seek G. of fa-s with **a.**
15. sworn with all **t. h.** ⌊**h.**
22: 9. Jehosh. sought L. wi. **a. h.**
31: 21. he did it with **a.** his **h.**
Ps.86:12. praise thee, O L., wi **a.h.**
Pr. 3:5. Trust in L. with **a.** thy **h.**
Je. 29: 13. when ye search wi **a.h.**
Eze 36:5. joy of **a.** their **h.** to cast
Zph. 3:14.be glad wi. **a. h** O Jerus.
Ac. 8: 37. if believest with **a. h.**

His HEART.

Ge. 6:5. imagina. of **h. h.** only evil
6. it repented the Lord at **h. h.**
8: 21. L. said in **h. h.** | 17:17. Ab.
27:41. Esau said in **h. h.** ⌊in **h.h.**

Ex.4:14. seeth thee, be glad in **h.h.**
7: 23. nei. did he set **h. h.** to this
25: 2. giveth willingly with **h. h.**
28: 29. breastplate of judgm. upon
h. h. ⌈may teach
35: 34. he hath put in **h. h.** th. he
De. 2: 30. L. made **h. h.** obstinate
17: 17. wives, th. **h. h.** turn not
20. **h. h.** be not lifted abo. breth.
19: 6. avenger pursue, while **h.h.**
20:8. breth.'s heart faint as **h. h.**
24: 15. is poor, setteth **h.h.** upon
29:19. that he bless hims. in **h. h**
Ru. 3: 7. **h. h.** was merry, he went
1 S. 4: 13. **h. h.** trembled for ark
21:12. David laid up words in **h.h.**
25: †25. Let not lord lay it to **h.h.**
37. it came to pass th. **h. h.** died
within him ⌈**h. h.** trembled
27: 1. David said in **h. h.** | 28: 5.
2 S. 7: 27. serv. hath found in **h.h.**
to pray this, 1 Ch. 17: 25. ⌈**h.**
13:33. let not lord take thing to **h.**
19: 19. th. k. sho. take it to **h.h.**
1 K. 10: 24. G. put in **h. h.**, 2 Ch.
11:3.wives turned **h. h.**,4,9. ⌊9:23.
12: 26. Jerob. said in **h. h.** the
2 K. 9: 24. arrow went out at **h.h.**
2 Ch.12:14.bec. he prep-d not **h. h.**
17: 6. **h. h.** was lifted up in ways
of L. ⌈tion
26:16.**h.h.**was lifted up to destruc-
30: 19. prepareth **h. h.** to seek G.
32: 25. **h. h.** was lifted up, theref.
26. humbled for pride of **h. h.**
31. he might know all in **h. h.**
Ezr. 7:10. Ezra prep-d **h.h.** to seek
Ne. 9: 8. foundest **h. h.** faithful
Es. 6: 6. Haman thought in **h. h.**
7: 5. durst presume in **h. h.** to do
Jb. 34:14. If he set **h. h.** upon man
41: 24. **h. h.** is as firm as a stone
Ps. 10:3.wicked boasteth of **h. h.**'s
6. said in **h. h.**, 11, 13 -14: 1.-
15:2.speaketh truth in **h.h.** ⌊53:1.
21: 2. hast given him **h.h.**'s desire
33: 11. thoughts of **h. h.** to all
37: 31. law of his God is in **h. h.**
41: 6. **h. h.** gathereth iniq. to it.
55: 21. words smooth, war in **h.h.**
78:72. fed acc. to integrity of **h.h.**
112: 7. **h. h.** is fixed, trust. in L.
8. **h. h.** is establ., not be afraid
Pr. 6: 14. Frowardness in **h. h.**
18: 2. that **h. h.** may discover its.
19: 3. **h. h.** fretteth agst. the L.
23:7.as thinketh in **h. h.** so is he;
but **h. h.** is not with thee
26: 25. are seven abomi. in **h. h.**
28: 14. hardeneth **h. h.** sh. fall
Ec. 2: 23. **h. h.** taketh not rest,22.
5: 20. God ans-th in joy of **h. h.**
7: 2. living will lay it to **h. h.**
Can. 3: 11. day of gladn. of **h. h.**
Is. 7: 2. **h. h.** moved, and **h.** of
10:7. neither doth **h. h.** think so,
it is in **h. h.** to destroy and
32: 6 **h. h.** will work iniquity
44: 19. none considereth in **h. h.**
57: 17. frowardly in way of **h. h.**
Je. 9: 8. in **h. h.** he layeth wait
23: 20. till perf. thoughts of **h.h.**
30:21. **h. h.** to approach unto me
24. until perf-d intents of **h. h.**
48: 29. heard haughtiness of **h.h.**
Eze. 14: 4. setteth idols in **h. h.**,7.
31: 10. **h. h.** lifted up, Da. 5: 20.
Da. 1: 8. Daniel proposed in **h. h.**
4: 16. Let **h. h.** be changed.5:21.
6: 14. the king set **h.h.** on Daniel
8:25. shall magnify hims. in **h. h.**
11: 12. **h. h.** shall be lifted up
28. **h. h.** shall be ag. holy cov-t
Ob. 3. saith in **h. h.**,Who bring me
Mat. 5: 28. com-d adultery in **h.h.**
13:19. catcheth that sown in **h.h.**
24: 48. if say in **h. h.**, Lu. 12:45.

Mk. 7 : 19. it ent-h not into h. h.
11 : 23. not doubt in h. h. but
Lu. 6 : 45. out of good treas. of h.
h. evil man out of evil of h.h.
Ac. 7 : 23. into h. h. to visit breth.
1 Co. 7:37. standeth steadf. in h.h.
14:25.secrets of h. h. made manif.
2 Co. 9 : 7. as he purposeth in h.h.

Mine HEART.

Ge. 24:45. done speaking in m. h.
De.29:19.I walk in imagin. of m.h.
Jos. 14:7. word as it was in m. h.
1 S.2:35.sh. do acc. to that in m.h.
1 K.9:3. mine eyes and m. h. shall
be there perpetually, 2 Ch.7:16.
2 K.5:26. went not m.h. with thee
10:30.hast done acc. to all in m.h.
1 Ch.12:17.m.h. be knit unto you
28:2.I had in m.h. to build house
2 Ch.29:10 in m.h. to make a cov-t
Jb.31:7.m.h. walked aft. mine eyes
9.if m. h. been deceived by wom.
Ps. 17 : 3. Thou hast proved m. h.
119 : 11. word have I hid in m. h.
112.inclined m.h.to perform stat
Ec. 2:1. I said in m.h. Go to now,
I will prove, 15.–3 : 17, 18.
3. sought in m. h. to wine yet
acquainting m.h. wi. wisdom
Is. 63 : 4. day of veng. is in m. h.
Je. 8:15. you pastors acc. to m. h.
12:3. hast seen me and tried m.h.
15:16.thy word the rejo-g of m.h.
20 : 9. his word in m. h. as fire
23 : 9. m. h. within me is broken
48:31. m. h. shall mourn for men
36. m. h. shall sound for Moab
La.1:20. m.h. is turned within me
3 : 51. Mine eye affecteth m. h.
Ho.11:8 m.h. is turned within me
Ac. 13:22. Da. man aft. m. own h.
21:13. What mean ye break m.h.?

My HEART.

Ge.20:5.in integrity of m. h.I have
Ju. 5 : 9. m. h. is tow. governors
1 S. 2 : 1. said, m.h. rejoi-h in L.
2 K. 10 : 15. Is thine h. right as m.
h. is with thy h.?
Ne. 2:12. G. put in m.h. to do,7:5.
5:†7. then m. h. consulted in me
Jb.17:11. thoughts of m.h. broken
23 : 16. God maketh m. h. soft
27:6. m.h. shall not reproach me
31:27 m.h. been secretly enticed
33:3. words be of uprightn of m.h.
37:1. At this also m.h. trembleth
Ps. 4:7. hast put gladness in m.h.
13:2.counsel, sorrow in m.h.daily
5. m.h. shall rejoice in thy salv.
16 : 9. m. h. is glad [ceptable
19 : 14 meditation of m.h. be ac-
22 : 14. m. h. like wax
26 : 2. try my reins and m. h.
25:17.troubles of m.h. are enlarg.
27:3. m.h. shall not fear tho. war
8. m. h. said Thy face, L. I seek
28:7. m.h. trusted in him, m.h.
36 : 1. transgr-n of wicked saith in
38:8. disquietness of m.h. [m.h.
10. m. h. panteth, Is. 21 : 4.
39 : 3. m. h. was hot within me,
40:8. yea, thy law is within m. h.
10. not hid thy righte-n. within
12. thf. m.h. faileth me [m.h.
45:1. m.h. is inditing good matter
49 : 3. meditation of m. h. be of
55:4.m.h.is sore pained within me
57:7.m.h. is fixed, O G.,(2) 108:1.
61 : 2. when m. h. is overwh-d
66:18.If I regard iniquity in m.h.
69:20.Reproach hath broken m.h.
73:13. have cleansed m.h. in vain
21. m.h. was grieved [m. h.
26.m.h. faileth, G. is strength of
84:2. m.h. crieth out for living G.
86:11.unite m.h. to fear thy name
102:4. m.h. is smitten and with-d
Ps.109:22. m.h. is wounded within
119:32.wh.thou shalt enlarge m.h
36. Incline m.h.to thy testimon.
80. m. h. be sound in statutes
111.Thy testimo. rejoi-g of m.h.
131:1. Lord, m.h. is not haughty
139:23.Search me,and know m.h.
141:4.Incline not m.h.to any evil
143:4. m.h. within me is desolate
Pr. 5 : 12. m. h. despised reproof?
20:9. Who say, made m.h. clean?
23 : 15. if heart wise, m.h. rejoice
27 : 11. be wise make m. h. glad
Ec. 1 : 13. I gave m. h. to seek
16. m. h. had great experience
17. I gave m.h. to know wisdom
and madness
2:10. withheld not m.h. fr. joy (2)
20. cause m. h. to despair
9:1. all this I considered in m.h.
Can.4:9. ravished m. h. my sis., 9.
5 : 2. I sleep, but m. h. waketh
Is. 15 : 5. m. h. shall cry for Moab
Je. 4:19. am pained at m.h. m.h.
7 : 31. neither came it into m. h.
8 : 18. comfort mys. m. h. faint
La.1:22.my sighs many, m.h. faint
Da. 7 : 28. I kept matter in m. h.
Ac. 2 : 26. Theref. did m.h. rejoice
Ro. 9 : 2. continual sorrow in m.h.
10 : 1. m.h.'s desire to God for Isr.
Ph. 1 : 7. bec. I have you in m. h.
See APPLIED.

One HEART.

2 Ch.30:12. hand of G. to give o.h.
Je.32:39.give them o.h., Eze.11:19.
Ac. 4 : 32. multitude were of o. h.

Our HEART.

De. 1 : 28. breth. discouraged o. h.
Ps. 33 : 21. For o. h. shall rejoice
44 : 18. o. h. is not turned back
La. 3 : 41. lift up o. h. with hands
5 : 15. joy of o. h. is ceased
17. o. h. is faint [in us
Lu. 24:32. Did not o. h. burn with-
2 Co. 6 : 11. open, o. h. is enlarged
1 Jn. 3 : 20 if o. h. condemn us
21. if o. h. condemn us not, we

Own HEART.

Nu. 15 : 39. seek not aft. your o.h.
1 S. 13:14. man aft. o.h., Ac 13: 2.
2 S. 7 : 21. acc. to thine o. h. hast
done these things, 1 Ch. 17:19.
1 K. 8 : 38. man plague of his o.h.
12 : 33. which he devised of o. h.
Ne. 6 : 8. feignest them out of o.h.
Ps. 4 : 4. commune with your o.h.
20 : 4. Grant acc. to thine o. h.
37 : 15. sword shall enter o. h.
77 : 6. I commune with my o. h.
Pr. 28:26. trusteth in o.h. is a fool
Ec. 1 : 16. communed with o. h.
7:22. o.h. kn-th thou hast cursed
Je.9:14. aft. imagina. of o.h.,23:17.
23:16. speak a vision of their o.h.
26. deceit of their o.h.,Eze.13:17.
Eze. 14 : 5. take ho. of Isr. in o. h.
Ja. 1 : 26. but deceiveth his o. h.

Perfect HEART.

1 K.8:61.Let your h. be p. with L.
11 : 4. his h. not p. with L., 15:3.
15 : 14. Asa's h. was p. with the
Lord all his days, 2 Ch. 15:17.
2 K. 20:3. Hez. said, remem. how I
walked with p. h., Is. 38 : 3.
1 Ch.12:38.with p.h. to make Da.k.
28:9.my son, serve G. with a p.h.
29 : 9. with p. h. offered willingly
19. give unto Sol. my son p. h.
2 Ch. 16:9. of them whose h. is p.
19 : 9. do in fear of L. with p. h.
25:2. did right, but not with p.h.
Ps. 101:2. will walk in my ho. with

Pure HEART. [p.h.

Ps.24:4.who ascend? th. hath p.h.
Mat.5:8.Blessed are p. in h. [p.h.
1 Ti.1:5.end of com-t charity out of
2 Ti. 2 : 22. call on L. out of p. h.
1 Pe.1:22.love one ano. with a p.h.

Their HEART.

Ge. 42 : 28. t. h. failed them
Jos. 5 : 1. kings heard t. h. melted
2 S.18:†3.they will not set t.h.on us
1 K. 8:†47. if they bring back to t.
h., 2 Ch. 6 : † 37.
18:37. thou hast turned t.h. back
1 Ch. 29:18. prepare t.h. unto thee
Jb. 8 : 10. utter words out of t. h.?
17:4. hast hid t. h. from underst.
Ps. 10 : 17. thou wilt prepare t. h.
78:8.gene. that set not t.h. aright
18. tempted God in t. h.
37. t. h. was not right with him
95: 10. a people th. do err in t. h.
105:25.turned t.h. to hate his peo.
107 : 12. he brought down t. h.
119 : 70. t. h. is as fat as grease
140:2. Wh. imagine mischiefs in t.
Pr.24:2. t.h. studieth destruc. [h.
Ec. 3:11. he hath set world in t. h.
9 : 3. madness in t. h. while live
Is. 6 : 10. lest underst. with t. h.,
Mat. 13:15. Ac. 28:27. [Mk.7:6.
29:13.t.h.is far from me,Mat.15:8.
Je.5:24. Nei. say in t. h. let us fear
13:10. wh. walk in imagina.of t.h.
14:14. prophesy the deceit of t. h.
17:1. sin of Jud. graven upon t.h.
La. 2 : 18. t. h. cried unto the L.
Eze. 14:3. set up their idols in t.h.
20:16. t. h. went after their idols
21 : 15. that t. h. may faint
33 : 31. t. h. goeth aft. covetousn.
Ho. 4 : 8. set t.h. on their iniquity
7 : 6. made ready t. h. like oven
14. not cried unto me with t. h.
10:2.t.h.divided | 13:6.t.h.exalted
13 : 8. I will rend caul of t. h.
Zph. 1:12. punish men say in t. h.
Zch. 10 : 7. t. h. shall rejoice in L.
12:5. gov-s shall say in t. h.
Mk.6:52. t. h. was hard-d, Ro.1:21.
Lu.9:47. perceiving thought of t.h.
Jn. 12 : 40. hardened t. h. th. they
not understand with t. h.
Ac. 3 : 37. were pricked in t. h.
2 Co.3:15.Moses is read vail on t.h.
Ep. 4 : 18. bec. of blindness of t. h.
He 3:10. They do always err in t.h.

Thine HEART.

Ex.9:14. all my plagues upon t. h.
Le.19:17.shalt not hate bro. in t.h.
De. 4 : 39. consider it in t. h., 8:5.
6 : 5. shalt love L. with all t. h.
6. these words shall be in t. h.
7 : 17. If say in t. h. nations more
than I, 8 : 17.–18 : 21. Je.13:22.
8 : 2. led thee, to kn. what in t.h.
14. then t. h. be lifted up
9:4. Speak not thou in t. h. after
5. not for uprightness of t. h.
15 : 10. t. h. not be grieved when
28:67. for the fear of t. h. [givest
30 : 6 circumcise t. h. and h. of
17. if t. h. turn so that not hear
Ju. 16 : 15. when t.h. not with me
19:6. t.h. be merry, 9. 1 K. 21 : 7.
8. damsel's fa. said, Comfort t.h.
1 S. 2:33. the man be to grieve t.h.
9 : 19. I will tell thee all in t. h.
14 : 7. Do all in t.h.; I am wi. thee
acc.to t.h., 2 S.7:3. 1 Ch. 17 : 2.
17 : 28. I know naughtiness of t.h.
2 S. 3 :21.reign over all t.h. desireth
13 : † 20. bro.; set not t.h. on this
1 K. 2 : 44. Thou knowest all the
wickedn-s t. h. is privy to
8 : 18.in t. h. to build, 2 Ch.–6:8(2).
2 K. 10 : 15.Jehu said, Is t. h. right,
as my h. is with thy h. [25 : 19.
14 : 10. t. h. hath lifted thee, 2 Ch.
22 : 19. Because t. h. was tender,
and hast humbled, 2 Ch. 34 :27.
2 Ch. 19 : 3. prepared t.h. to seek G.

Jb.7:17.shouldest set t.h.upon him
10:13. these hast thou hid in t.h.
11 : 13. If thou prepare t. h. and
15:12.Why doth t.h.carry thee aw.
22 : 22. lay up his words in t. h.
Ps. 27 : 14. he sh. strengthen t. h.
37:4. sh. give thee desires of t. h.
Pr. 2 : 10. wisdom ent-h into t. h.
3 : 1. son, let t.h. keep my com-ts
3. write upon table of t. h., 7: 3.
4:4. Let t. h. retain my words,21.
6:21.Bind them contin-y upon t.h.
25.Lust not aft. her beauty in t.h.
7 : 25. Let not t. h. decline to her
23 : 15. if t. h. wise, my h. rejoice
17. Let not t. h. envy sinners
19. my son, guide t. h. in the
26. My son, give me t. h. [way
33.t.h.shall utter perverse things
24:17. not t.h. be glad he stumbl.
Ec. 5 : 2. not t.h. hasty to utter
7:†21. give not t.h. unto all words
11 : 9. walk in ways of t. h.
Can. 8:6. Set me as seal upon t. h.
Is. 14:13. said in t.h. I will ascend
33 : 18. t.h. shall meditate terror
47:8. that sayest in t.h. I am, 10.
49:21. shalt say in t. h. who hath
60:5. t.h. sh. fear and be enlarged
Je. 4:14. O Jerus. wash t. h. from
18.bitter, bec. it reach. unto t.h.
22: 17. t.h. is not but for covet-s
31 : 21. set t. h. toward highway
49:16.pride of t.h. deceived, Ob.3.
La. 2 : 19. pour out t. h. like water
Eze. 3 : 10. my words receive in t. h.
16 : 30. How weak is t.h., saith L.
22 : 14.Can t. h. endure in the days
28 : 2. Bec. t. h. is lifted up for, 5.
6. hast set t. h. as heart of God
17. t. h. lifted up bec. of beauty
40 : 4. set t. h. upon all I sh. shew
Da.5:22.Belshaz-r not humbled t.h.
10 : 12.didst set t.h. to understand
Ac. 5 : 3. why Satan filled t. h. to lie
4.why conceived this thi. in t. h.
8 : 22. thought of t. h. be forgiven
37.If believest with all t. h.[cend
Ro. 10 : 6. Say not in t. h., Who as-
9. shalt believe in t. h. G. raised

Thy HEART. [t. h.

Ge. 20 : 6. didst this in integrity of
De. 4 : 9. lest they depart from t. h.
29. find, if seek him with all t. h.
10 : 12. to serve Lord with all t. h.
15: 9. not a thought in t. wicked h.
30 : 14. word is very nigh, in t. h.
1 S 1 : 8.why is t. h. grieved ?[Job ?
Jb. 1 : †8. Satan, hast set t. h. on
Pr. 4 : 23. Keep t. h. with all dili-
27 :†23.set t.h. to thy herds[gence
Ec. 11 :9.let t. h. cheer thee in days
10. remove sorrow from t. h. [11.
Is. 47 : 7. not lay things to t.h., 57:
Da. 2 : 30. know thoughts of t. h.
Ac. 8 : 21. t. h. not right in sight of
Ro. 10 : 8. in t. h. the word of faith
See APPLY, HEART with all,
UPRIGHTNESS of heart.

Upright in HEART, S.

2 Ch. 29 : 34. Levites were more - h.
Ps. 7 :10. God, which saveth the - h.
11 : 2. may privily shoot at the - h.
32 : 11. shout for joy all ye - h.
36:10.continue righteousn-s to - h.
64 : 10. all the - h. shall glory
94 : 15. all the - h. shall follow it
97 :11. is sown, gladness for the - h.
125 :4. Do good unto them are - h-s

Whole HEART.

Ps. 9 : 1. I will praise thee, O Lord,
with w. h., 111 : 1.-138 : 1. [h.
119:2.Blessed th. seek him with w.
10. With my w. h. I sought thee
34. I shall observe it with w. h.
58. I entreated favour with w. h.
69.I will keep precepts with w.h.
Ps. 119 : 145. I cried wi. w. h., hear
Is. 1 : 5. head is sick, w. h. is faint
Je. 3:10. not turned with w. h. but
24:7. they shall return with w. h.
32 : 41. I will plant them with w.

Whose HEART. [h.

Ex. 35 : 21. w. h. stirred, 29.-36:2.
26.all the women, w.h.stirred th.
De. 29 : 18. w. h. turneth from L.
2 S. 17:10. w. h. is as heart of lion
1 K. 8:39.w.h.knowest, 2 Ch. 6:30.
2 Ch. 16 : 9. them w. h. is perfect
Ps. 84:5. in w. h. are ways of them
Ec. 7:26. the woman w. h. is snares
Is. 51 : 7. peo., in w. h. is my law
Je. 17 : 5. w. h. departeth from L.
Eze. 11:21. w. h. walketh after the
heart of detestable things
Ac. 16 : 14. w. h. the Lord opened

Your HEART.

De. 10:16. foreskin of y. h., Je. 4:4.
11 : 16. that y. h. be not deceived
18. sh. lay up my words in y. h.
Jos. 24 : 23. incline y. h. unto L.
1 K. 11:2. they will turn away y.h.
1 Ch. 22 : 19. set y. h. to seek Lord
Ps. 22 : 26. y. h. shall live for ever
31 : 24. he shall strengthen y. h.
62 : 8. pour out y. h. before him
10. if riches increase, set not y.h.
69:32. y. h. shall live that seek G.
Is. 66:14. see this, y. h. sh. rejoice
Je. 51 : 46. And lest y. h. faint
Jo. 2 : 13. rend y. h. not garments
Zch. 7 : 10. let none of you imagine
evil in y. h. [Lu. 12:34.
Mat. 6 : 21. there will y. h. be also,
Mk. 8:17. have ye y. h. hardened?
10:5. For hardn. of y. h. he wrote
Jn.14:1. Let not y.h. be troubl.,27.
16:6. I said this, sorrow filled y.h.
22. will see you, y. h. sh. rejoice
Ep. 5 : 19. making melody in y. h.
6:5.in singleness of y.h. as unto C.

HEARTS.

Ex. 31 : 6. in the h. of all wise
Jos. 7 : 5. wherefore h. of people
melted
1 S.10:26.men, whose h. G. touched
2 S. 15 : 6. so Abs. stole h. of Israel
13. h. of Israel are after Abs.
1 K. 8 : 39. thou only knowest the
h., 2 Ch. 6 : 30. [all h.
1 Ch. 28 : 9. for the Lord searcheth
Ps. 7:9. God trieth the h., Pr. 17:3.
Pr. 15 : 11. much more h. of men
21 : 2. Lord pondereth the h. [h.
31:6.Give wine unto those of heavy
Je. 48:41. mighty men's h. of Moab
Eze. 32 : 9. I will vex the h. of peo.
Da. 11:27. k-s' h. be to do mischief
Lu. 1 : 17. turn the h. of fathers to
2 : 35. thoughts of h. be revealed
21 : 26. signs ; Men's h. failing th
Ac. 1 : 24. knowest h. of men, 15:8.
Ro. 8 : 27. he th. searcheth the h.
16:18. deceive the h. of the simple
1 Co. 4 : 5. manifest counsels of h.
Re. 2 : 23. I am he th. searcheth h.

Our HEARTS.

Jos. 2:11. we heard, o. h. did melt
1 K. 8:58. Th. he may incline o. h.
Ps.90:12. apply o. h. unto wisdom
Ac. 14 : 17. filling o. h. with food
Ro. 5 : 5. love shed abroad in o. h.
2 Co. 1:22. earnest of Spirit in o.h.
3:2. Ye are epistle written in o. h.
4 : 6. God hath shined in o. h.
7:3. you are in o.h. to die and live
1 Th. 2 : 4. God, who trieth o. h.
He. 10:22. o. h. sprinkled fr. an evil
1 Jn. 3:19. assure o. h. before him

Their HEARTS.

Le. 26:36. send a faintness into t.h.
41. if t. uncirc-d h. be humbled
Ju.9:3.t.h.inclined to follow Abim.
16:25. t. h. were mer... ...ey said
Ju. 19:22. were making t. h. merry
2 Ch.6:14.walk bef. thee wi.all t.h.
11 : 16. as set t. h. to seek the L.
20 : 33. not prepared t. h. to God
Jb. 1 : 5. may be sons have cursed
G. in t. h.
Ps. 28 : 3. mischief is in t. h.
33 : 15. He fashioneth t. h. alike
35:25.Let them not say in t.h.,Ah
74: 8. said in t. h., Let us destroy
81 : 12. I gave up to t. h.'s lust
125:4. them th. are upright in t.h.
Is. 44:18. hath shut t. h. they can-t
Je. 31:33. my law in t. h., He. 8:10.
32 : 40. I will put my fear in t. h.
Eze. 13 : 2. prophesy out of t. h.
Ho. 7 : 2. they consider not in t. h.
Zch. 7 : 12. made t. h. as adamant
Mk. 2 : 6. and reasoning in t. h.
3 : 5. grieved for hardness of t. h.
4:15. word sown in t. h., Lu. 8:12.
Lu. 1 : 51. scattered proud in t. h.
66. heard laid them up in t. h.
3:15. all men mused in t. h. of Jn.
Ac.7:39.in t.h. turned back into E.
15 : 9. purifying t. h. by faith
Ro. 1 : 24. thro. the lust of t. h.
2 : 15. shew law written in t. h.
Col. 2 : 2. That t. h. be comforted
10 : 16. put my laws into t. h.
Re. 17 : 17. G. hath put in t. h. to

Your HEARTS. [fulfil

Ge. 18 : 5. comfort ye y. h.
De 20:3. O Isr., let not y. h. faint
32 : 46. Set y. h. to all the words
Jos. 23:14. know in y. h. and souls
1 S. 6 : 6. wherefore ye harden
y. h.?
7 : 3. if return unto L. with all y.
h. and prepare y. h. unto L.
Je. 42:20.dissembled in y.h. [y.h.
Zch. 8 : 17. let none imagine evil in
Mat. 9 : 4. Whf. think evil in y.h.?
18:35. if ye from y. h. forgive not
19:8.of hardness of y. h. ye suff-d
Mk.2:8.Why reason things in y. h.
Lu.5:22 said, What reason ye in y.
16 : 15 God knoweth y. h. [h.?
21:14. Settle in y. h. not to medi-
34.lest y.h. be overcharged [tate
24:38.why thoughts arise in y.h.?
Ga. 4 : 6. God sent Spirit into y. h.
Ep. 3:17. That C. may dwell in y.h.
6:22. that he might comfort y. h.
Ph. 4:7. shall keep y.h. and minds
Col. 3 : 15. let peace rule in y.h.
16. with grace in y. h.
4 : 8. know estate, comfort y. h.
1 Th. 3 : 13. he may establish y. h.
2 Th. 2:17. Comfort y.h. and estab.
3 : 5. the Lord direct y.h. into love
He. 3:8. Harden not y. h., 15.-4:7.
Ja. 3 : 14. if ye have strife in y. h.
4:8. purify y. h. ye doubleminded
5 : 5. wanton, ye have nourished
8. be patient, stablish y.h. [y.h.
1 Pe. 3 : 15. sanctify Lord in y. h.
2 Pe. 1:19. and daystar arise in y.h.

HEARTED.

Ex. 35 : 22. many as were willing h.
See BROKENHEARTED, FAINT-
HEARTED, HARDHEARTED,
MERRYHEARTED, STOUT-
HEARTED, TENDERHEARTED.

Wise HEARTED.

Ex. 28 : 3. speak unto all are w.h.
31 : 6. in hearts of all th. are w.h.
35:10. every w.h. am. you sh. come
25. all the women w. h. did spin
36 : 1. wrought every w. h. man,

HEARTH. [2. 8.

Ge. 18 : 6. make cakes upon h. [h.
Ps. 102 : 3. my bones are burned as
Is. 30 : 14. sherd to take fire fr. h.
Je. 36 : 22. a fire on the h. bef. him
23. cast the roll into fire on the h.
Zch. 12: 6. governm of Jud. like h.

HEARTILY.

Lu. 22:†15. **h.** desired to eat passo.
Col. 3 : 23. whatso. ye do, do it **h.**as

HEARTY.

Pr. 27 : 9. of a friend by **h.** counsel

HEAT. [Noun.]

Ge. 8 : 22. cold, **h.** summer, winter
18 : 1. in tent door in **h.** of the day
Ex. 11:†8. went out in **h.** of anger
De 29:24. what meaneth **h.** of this
32:24.be devoured with burning **h.**
1 S. 11 : 11. slew until **h.** of the day
2 S. 4 : 5. And sons came about the **h.** of the day [**h.**
1 K. 1 : 1. he gat no **h.** | 2. lord get
Jb. 6 : † 17. ice snow vanish in **h.**
24 : 19. Drought and **h.** consume
30 : 30. my bones are burned wi.**h.**
Ps. 19 : 6. nothing hid from the **h.**
Ec. 4 : 11. if two together, have **h.**
Is. 4 : 6. a shadow from **h.**, 25 : 4.
18 : 4. like clear **h.** upon herbs, like a cloud of dew in **h.**of harv.
25 : 5. as **h.** in dry place, even **h.**
49 : 10. nei. shall **h.** nor sun smite
Je. 17 : 8. not see when **h.** cometh
36 : 30. dead body be cast out to **h.**
51:39.In **h.** I will make their feasts
Eze. 3:14 I went in **h.** of my spirit
Ho. 7 : † 5. have made him sick with **h.** [day
Mat. 20 : 12. burden and **h.** of the
Lu.12:55.south wind blow,will be **h.**
Ac. 28 : 3. came viper out of **h.**
Ja. 1:11. sun risen with burning **h.**
2 Pe. 3:10. melt with fervent **h.**,12.
Re. 7 : 16. sun on them, nor any **h.**
16 : 9. scorched with great **h.** and

HEAT, ED.

Da. 3:19. **h.** the furnace one 7 times more than wont to be **h**-d
Ho. 7:4. are adulterers, as oven **h**-d

HEATH.

Je. 17:6. shall be like the **h.**, 48 : 6.

HEATHEN.

Le. 25:44. bondmen shall be of **h.**
26 : 45. bro-t forth i sight of **h.**
2 S.22:44.to be head of **h.**, Ps.18:43.
2 K. 16 : 3. walked acc. to abomi. of **h.**, 17 : 15.-21 : 2. 2 Ch. 28 : 3. -36 : 14.
17 : 8. Isr. walked in statutes of **h.**
11. as did **h.** Lord carried away
1 Ch. 16 : 35. deliver us from the **h.**
2 Ch. 20:6. rulest over kingd-s of **h.**
33 : 2. did like unto abomi. of **h.**
9. made Jud. to do worse than **h.**
Ezr.6:21.separated fr.filthiness of **h.**
Ne. 5:8. redeemed Jews sold unto **h.**
9. bec. of the reproach of the **h.**
6 : 16. all the **h.** about us saw [25.
Ps. 2 : 1. Why do **h.** rage? Ac. 4:
8. shall give thee **h.** for inheri.
9 : 5. Thou hast rebuked the **h.**
15. **h.** are sunk in pit they made
19. let **h.** be judged in thy sight
10:16. **h.** are perished out of his la.
33:10. counsel of **h.** to nought
44:2. How thou didst drive out the
46:6. **h.** raged, the kingd-s [**h.**
47 : 8. God reigneth over the **h.**
59 : 5. thf., awake to visit all the **h.**
8. shalt have all **h.** in derision
78 : 55. He cast out **h.** also, 80 : 8.
79 : 1. **h.** into thine inheri. [25.
6. Pour wrath upon **h.**, Je. 10:
10.Whf.**h.** say, Where their God? be known among **h.**, 115 : 2.
94:10. th. chastiseth **h.**shall not he
98 : 2. openly shewed in sight of **h.**
102:15. **h.** shall fear name of Lord
105 : 44. gave them lands of the **h.**
106 : 41. gave them into ha. of **h.**
111 : 6. give them heritage of **h.**
135:15. The idols of the **h.**are silver
149 : 7. execute vengeance upon **h.**
Is. 16 : 8. lords of **h.** have broken

Je. 10 : 2. Learn not way of the **h.**, the **h.** are dismayed at them
49 : 14. ambassador is sent unto **h.**
La 1 : 10. **h.** entered into her sanct.
Eze. 7 : 24. I will bring worst of **h.**
11 : 12. done after manners of **h.**
20:9.not be polluted bef. **h.**, 14, 22.
32. ye say, We will be as the **h.**
41. I will be sanct. bef. **h.**, 28:25.
22 : 4. thee a reproach unto the **h.**
16. thine inheri. in sight of **h.**
23 : 30. gone a whoring after **h.**
25 : 7. I will deliver thee to the **h.**
8. house of Jud.is like unto all **h.**
30 : 3. it shall be the time of the **h.**
31:11. into ha. of mighty of the **h.**
17. und. his shadow in midst of **h.**
34 : 28. no more be a prey to **h.**
29. nei. bear shame of **h.** more
36 : 3. possession unto residue of **h.**
4. a derision to residue of **h.**
5. spoken against residue of **h.**
6. bec. borne shame of **h.**, 7, 15.
20. when they entered unto the **h.** whither [28.-38 : 16.-39 : 7.
23. **h.** know I am Lord, 36.-37 :
39 : 21. **h.** sh. see my judgm., 23.
Jo. 2:17. th. **h.** sho. rule over them
3 : 11. come all ye **h.** and gather
12. Let the **h.** be wakened, and come, will I sit to judge all **h.**
Am. 9 : 12. possess remn-t of all **h.**
Ob. 15. day of L. near upon all **h.**
16. so sh. all **h.** drink continually
Mi. 5 : 15. will execute fury upon **h.**
Ha. 3 : 12. didst thresh **h.** in anger
Zph. 2 : 11. isles of **h.** shall worship
Hag. 2 : 22. will destr. strength of **h.**
Zch. 1 : 15. am sore displeased wi. **h.**
9 : 10. he sh. speak peace unto **h.**
14 : 14. wealth of **h.** shall be gath-d
18. plague whw. Lord smite **h.**
Mat. 6 : 7. use not repetitions as **h.**
18:17. let him be to thee as **h.** man
2 Co. 11 : 26. in perils by the **h.** in
Ga. 2:9. that we sho. go unto the **h.**
3 : 8. that God would justify the **h.**

Among the HEATHEN.

Le. 26 : 33. I will scatter you **a. t. h.**, Je. 9:16. Eze. 20:23.-22:15.
38. And ye shall perish **a. t. h.**
De. 4 : 27. left few in number **a.t.h.**
2 S. 22:50. I will give thanks to thee, O Lord, **a. t. h.** Ps. 18 : 49.
1 Ch.16:24.his glory **a.t.h.**,Ps.96:3.
Ne. 5:17. that came to us fr. **a.t.h.**
6:6. reported **a.t.h.** Gashmu saith
Ps. 44 : 11. hast scatt-d us **a. t. h.**
14. makest us byword **a. t. h.**
46:10. God, I will be exalted **a.t.h.**
79 : 10. let him be known **a. t. h.**
96:10.Say **a.t.h.** the Lord reigneth
106 : 35. they were mingled **a.t.h.**
47. O L., and gather us fr. **a.t.h.**
110 : 6. He shall judge **a. t. h.**
126:2. said **a. t. h.** L.done gr. things
Je.18:13.Ask **a.t.h.** who heard such
49: 15. make thee small **a. t. h.**
La. 1:3. she dwelleth **a.t.h.** [journ
4: 15. said **a.t.h.** They no more so-
20. Und. his shadow live **a. t. h.**
Eze. 11:16. tho. cast them far **a.t.h.**
12 : 16. may declare abomi. **a.t.h.**
16 : 14. thy renown went **a. t. h.**
36 : 19. I did scatter them **a. t. h.**
21. Israel profaned **a.t.h.**, 22, 23.
24. take you from **a.t.h.**, 37 : 21.
30. no reproach of fam. **a. t. h.**
39 : 21. will set my glory **a. t. h.**
28. to be led into captiv., **a. t.h.**
Jo. 2 : 19. no more reproach **a.t.h.**
Ob. 1. ambassador is sent **a. t. h.**
2. I have made thee small **a.t.h.**
Ha. 1 : 5. Behold ye **a.t.h.** regard
Zch. 8 : 13. ye were a curse **a. t. h.**
Mal. 1 : 11. my name be gr. **a. t.h.**
14. my name is dreadful **a. t. h.**

Ga. 1 : 16. might preach him **a.t.h.**

HEAVE.

See OFFERING, S, SHOULDER.

HEAVE, ED. [tion

Ex. 29 : 27. **h**-d of ram of consecra-
Nu. 15 : 20. as heave off-g so **h.** it
18 : 30. When ye have **h**-d best, 32.

HEAVEN.

Ge. 1 : 1. God created **h.** and earth
8. God called the firmament **h.**
14.lights in firmament of **h.**, 15, 17
20. fowl that fly in firma. of **h.**
7 : 11. windows of **h.** were opened
8 : 2. windows of **h.** were stopped
14:19.G.possessor of **h.** and earth,
19:24.rained fire fr.L.out of **h.**[22.
21 : 17. called to Hagar out of **h.**
22:11.called unto Ab.out of **h.**, 15.
27:28.G. give thee of dew of **h.**, 39.
28 : 17. said, This is the gate of **h.**
49 : 25. bless thee with bl-gs of **h.**
Ex. 20: 11. days L. made **h.**, 31:17.
24 : 10. as it were the body of **h.**
Le. 26 : 19. I make your **h.** as iron
De. 4 : 11. burned unto midst of **h.**
26.I call **h.** and earth to witness, 30 : 19.-31 : 28.
32.ask fr.one side of **h.** unto oth.
36. Out of **h.** he made thee hear
10:14 **h.**and **h.**of heav-s,Ps.115:16.
11 : 11. drinketh wat. of rain of **h.**
17. he shut up **h.**, 1 K. 8 : 35. 2 Ch. 6 : 26.-7 : 13.
21. be multiplied as days of **h.**
28 : 12. open **h.** to give thee rain
23. **h.** over thy head sh. be brass
30 : 4. most part of **h.**, Ne. 1 : 9.
33:13.for the precious things of **h.**
26.G.of Jeshurun rideth upon **h.**
1 S. 2 : 10. out of **h.** he thunder
2 S.18:9.taken up betw. **h.** and ear.
21:10. until wat. dropped out of **h.**
22:8. the foundations of **h.** moved
1 K.8:27 **h.** and **h.** of heavens cannot contain thee,2 Ch.2:6.-6:18
35. when **h.** is shut up, is no rain
18 : 45. **h.** was black with clouds
2 K.19:15. art G. hast made **h.** and earth. 2 Ch. 2 : 12. Ne. 9 : 6.
1 Ch.21:16. angel betw. **h.** and ear.
Jb. 11:8. It is high as **h.** what do?
20:27. **h.** shall reveal his iniquity
22 : 12. Is not God in height of **h.**?
14. he walketh in circuit of **h.**
26 : 11. pillars of **h.** tremble
38:29. frost of **h.** who gendered it?
33. Knowest ordinances of **h.**?
37. who can stay bottles of **h.**?
Ps. 19 : 6. His going is fr. end of **h.**
20 : 6. will hear him from holy **h.**
69:34. Let **h.** and earth praise him
78 : 23. tho. he opened doors of **h.**
24. had giv. them of corn of **h.**
89:29. his throne to endure as the days of **h.**
103 : 11. as **h.** is high above earth
105:40. satis. them with br. of **h.**
115:15. the Lord who made **h.** and earth, 121 : 2.-124 : 8.-134 : 3.-146:6. Is. 37:16. Je.32:17. Ac.4: 24.-14 : 15. Re. 14 : 7.
147:8. Who covereth **h.** with clouds
148 : 13. his glory is above the **h.**
Pr. 25 : 3. **h.** for height, earth for
Is. 13 : 5. They come fr. end of **h.**
40 : 12. who hath meted out **h.**
66 : 1. **h.** my throne, Ac. 7 : 49.
Je. 7 : 18. cakes to the queen of **h.**
10 : 2. not dismayed at signs of **h.**
23 : 24. Do not I fill **h.** and earth
31 : 37. If **h.** ab. can be measured
33 : 25. if I have not appointed ordinances of **h.** [**h.**, 18, 19, 25.
44 : 17. to burn inc. unto queen of
49 : 36. winds fr. 4 quarters of **h.**
51:15. stretched out the **h.** by his
48.**h.** and earth sh. sing for Bab.

La. 4 : 19. swifter than eagles of h.
Eze. 8 : 3. Spi. lifted me betw. earth
32:7. I will cover the h. [and h.
8. lights of h. will I make dark
Da. 4:15. dew of h., 23,25,33.-5:21.
35. acc. to his will in army of h.
37. Now I honour King of h.
5:23. lifted up thyself ag. L. of h.
7:2. four winds of h. strove upon
13. Son of man wi. clouds of h.
8 : 8. tow. four winds of h., 11:4.
Am. 9:6. buildeth his stories in h.
Hag. 1 : 10. h. is stayed from dew
Zeb. 2:6. spread you as winds of h.
5:9. ephah between earth and h.
Mal.3:10.if not open windows of h.
Mat. 5 : 18. Till h. and earth pass
34. nor swear by h.; it is God's
throne,Ja.5:12. [of h.,Lu.10:21
11:25. I thank thee, Father, Lord
23:22. swear by h. sweareth by G.
24 : 30. sign of Son of man coming
in clouds of h.,26:64.Mk.14:62.
31. gather elect fr. 1 end of h. to
35. h. earth sh. pass away, Mk.
13:31. Lu. 21:33. [Fa. only
36. no, not angels of h. but my
Mk.13:27.from uttermost part of h.
Lu. 3:21. Jes. praying, h. was op-d
4: 25. when h. was shut 3 years
15:18.Fa. I have sinned ag. h.,21.
16:17.easier for h. and ear. to pass
21:26 powers of h. sh. be shaken
Jn.1:51.Hereaft. ye sh. see h. open
Ac.3:21.Whom the h. must receive
10:11. I saw h. opened, Re. 19:11.
17:24. seeing that he is Lord of h.
Ja. 5 : 18. he prayed, h. gave rain
Re. 3 : 12. cometh down out of h.
6 : 14. h. departed as a scroll
8 : 13. angel flying thro. h., 14:6.
10 : 6. who created h. and things
11:6. These have power to shut h.
16:17. voice out of tem. of h.,21:3.
21. there fell great hail out of h.
18 : 20. Rejoice over her, thou h.
19 : 17. to all fowls that fly in h.
20 : 9. fire came from G. out of h.
11. earth and h. fled away [h.
21:1.I saw a new h. and earth, first
10. holy Jerus. descending out of
See **FOWL, S of heaven.** [h.

From HEAVEN.

Ge. 8 : 2. rain f. h. was restrained
Ex. 16 : 4. I will rain bread f. h.
20:22.I have talked with you f.h.,
Ne. 9:13. [La. 3 : 50.
De.26:15. Look down f.h., Is.63:15.
28 : 24. as dust f.h. shall it come
Jos. 10:11. L. cast great stones f.h.
Ju. 5 : 20. fought f.h. stars fought
2 S. 22 : 14. Lord thundered f. h.
2 K. 1 : 10. let fire come down f. h.
there came fire f. h., 12, 14.
1 Ch. 21:26. ans-d him f. h. by fire
2 Ch. 6 : 21. hear f.h., 23, 27, 30.
7:1. fire came f. h. and consumed
14. will I hear f. h. and forgive
Ne. 9 : 15. gavest them bread f. h.
9:27. thou heardest them f.h., 28.
Jb. 1 : 16. fire of G. is fallen f. h.
Ps. 14 : 2. L. looked f. h., 53 : 2.
33:13. The Lord looketh f. h. and
57: 3. shall send f. h. and save me
76:8.didst cause judgm. heard f.h.
80 : 14. O God, look down f. h.
85:11. righteousn. look down f. h.
102 : 19. f. h. did L. behold earth
Is. 14:12. How art thou fallen f. h.
55:10. as snow falleth f.h., [Lucif.
La. 2 : 1. L. cast f.h. beauty of Isr.
Da. 4:13. watcher came down f. h.
23. holy one coming down f. h.
31.fell a voice f.h. saying, kingd.
is departed, Mat. 3:17.Mk 1:11.
Lu. 3:22. Jn. 12:28. 2 Pe.1:18.
Mat. 16 : 1. shew them a sign f. h.
Mat 21:25. bapt. of John, f. h. or of
men? Mk.11:30,31. Lu. 20:4, 5.
28 : 2. earthq. for angel descended
f. h., Re. 10 : 1.-18:1.-20:1.
Mk. 8 : 11. a sign f. h., Lu. 11:16.
Lu. 9 : 54. we commanded fire f.h.
10:18. Satan as lightning fall f. h.
17:29.rained fire and brimstone f.h
21:11.great signs sh. there be f.h.
22 : 43. an angel f.h. strength-g
Jn. 1 : 32. saw Spirit desc-g f. h.
3 : 13. that came down f.h., 6: 33.
27. receive noth. exc. given f. h.
31. that cometh f. h. is above all
6 : 31. He gave them bread f. h.
32. Mo. gave you not bread f. h.
38. f. h. not to do own will, 42.
41. bread down f. h., 50, 51, 58.
Ac. 2 : 2. suddenly a sound f. h.
9:3. a light f. h. shined, 22:6.-26:
11:5. a great sheet let f.h. [13.
9. voice ans-d me again f. h.
14 : 17. did good, gave rain f. h.
Ro. 1:18. wrath of G. revealed f. h.
1 Co. 15:47. 2d man is Lord f. h.
2 Co. 5 : 2. clothed wi. house f. h.
Ga. 1 : 8. angel f. h. preach other
1 Th. 1 : 10. wait for his Son f. h.
4 : 16. the L. shall descend f. h.
2 Th. 1 : 7. L. J. be revealed f. h.
He. 12:25. from him speaketh f. h.
1 Pe. 1:12. preached with H.G. f.h.
Re. 8 : 10. fell a great star f. h.
9:1. I saw star fall f.h. unto earth
10: 4 I heard a voice f. h. saying,
Seal up,8.-11:12.-14:2,13.-18:4.
18:13. maketh fire come down f.h.
See **GOD of Heaven.**

Host, s of HEAVEN.

De. 4 : 19. seest h.o.h. to worship
17 : 3. hath worshipped h. o. h.
1 K. 22 : 19. I saw the Lord sitting
and h.o.h. by him,2 Ch.18:18.
2 K. 17:16. Isr. worshipped h.o.h.
21 : 3. Manasseh worshipped h. o.
h., 2 Ch. 33 : 3. [2 Ch 33 : 5.
5. he built altars for the h.o.h.,
23:4.burned vessels made for h.o.
5.them burned inc. to h.o.h. [h.
Ne.9:6.made the h. of heavens with
h., h. o. h. worship-h thee
Is. 34 : 4. h.o.h. shall be dissolved
Je.8:2. sh. spread them bef. h.o.h.
19:13. burnt inc. unto all h. o. h.
33 : 22. h.o.h. cannot be numb-d
Da. 8 : 10. great, even to h. o. h.
Zph 1:5.cut off them worsh. h.o.h.
Ac.7:42.gave them to worsh. h.o.h.

In HEAVEN.

Ex. 20 : 4. nor likeness of anything
i. h., De. 5 : 8. [works?
De.3:24. what god i. h. do like thy
4 : 39. that the Lord he is G. i. h.
30:12. It is not i. h. shouldest say
Jos. 2 : 11. your G. he is God i. h.
1 K. 8:23. is no God like thee i. h.,
2 Ch. 6 : 14. [43, 45, 49.
30. hear thou i. h., 32, 34, 36,39,
2 K. 7:2. if make windows i.h., 19.
1 Ch. 29: 11. all i. h. and ea. thine
2 Ch. 20 : 6. art not thou God i. h.
Jb. 16:19. behold, my witn. is i. h.
Ps 11:4. the Lord's throne is i. h.
73:25. Whom have I i.h. but thee
77 : 18. voice of thy thunder i. h.
78 : 26. an east wind to blow i. h.
89:6. who i. h. compared unto L.?
37. establ-d as faithful witn. i.h.
113:6.humbleth to behold thi. i.h.
119:89. L. thy word is settled i.h.
135:6. that did he i. h. and earth
Ec. 5:2. G. is i.h. thou upon earth
Is. 34:5. sword shall be bathed i.h.
Je. 8:7. stork i. h. kno-h her times
Da. 2 : 28. a God i.h. th. revealeth
6:27.worketh signs and woud. i.h.
Am. 9 : 6. buildeth his stories i. h.
Mat. 5:12. great is your reward i.h.
16. glorify your Father i. h.
45. chil. of your Fa. who is i. h.
48. Be perfect as your Fa. i. h.
6 : 9. pray ye; Our Fa. which art
i. h., Lu. 11:2. [i.h., Lu. 11:2.
10. will be done on earth as it is
20. But lay up treasures i. h.
7 : 11. shall Fa i. h. give good thi.
21. doeth will of my Fa. i.h., 12:
10:32. confess bef. my Fa. i.h. [50.
33. him will I deny bef. Fa. i. h.
16 : 17. Fa. wh. is i. h. revealed
19. bound i.h. loosed i.h., 18:18.
18 : 10. i. h. angels always behold
face of my Fa. i. h. [i. h.
19. done for them of my Father
19 : 21. thou shalt have treasure i.
h., Mk.10:21. Lu.18:22. [12:25.
22 : 30. as angels of G. i. h., Mk.
23 : 9. one is your Fa. who is i. h.
24 : 30. sign of Son of man i. h.
28:18. All power giv. unto me i.h.
Mk. 11:26. nor Fa. i. h. forgive, 25.
13 : 25. powers i. h. be shaken
32. no, not angels which are i.h.
Lu. 6 : 23. your reward is great i.h.
10 : 20. your names are writt. i.h.
15 : 7. joy be i. h. over one sinner
19 : 38. peace i. h. and glory in
Jn. 3 : 13. Son of man who is i. h.
Ac. 2 : 19. I will shew wonders i.h.
1 Co. 8 : 5. gods. i. h. or earth
Ep. 1 : 10. gather in one, things i.h.
3 : 15. whole family i. h. is named
6 : 9. your Master is i. h., Col.4:1.
Ph. 2 : 10. knee bow, of things i.h.
3 : 20. our conversation is i. h.
Col. 1:5. hope laid up for you i. h.
16. by him all things th. are i. h.
20. by him to reconcile thi. i. h.
He. 10 : 34. i. h. a better substance
12 : 23. the firstborn written i. h.
1 Pe. 1 : 4. an inheri. reserved i. h.
1 Jn. 5:7. three th. bare record i.h.
Re. 4 : 1. a door was opened i. h.
2. a throne was set i. h. one sat
5:3. no man i. h. able to open book
13. every creature i. h. saying
8:1.silence i. h. | 11:15.voices i.h.
11 : 19. tem. of G. was opened i. h.
12:1. appeared gr. wonder i.h., 3.
7. there was war i. h. Michael
8. nei. place found more i. h.
10. I heard a voice, i. h., 19 : 1.
13 : 6. to blaspheme them i. h.
14 : 17. angel out of temple i. h.
15 : 1. I saw another sign i. h.
5. tabernacle of testimony i. h.
19 : 14. armies in h. follo-d him

Into HEAVEN.

2 K. 2 : 1. Lord wo. take Elijah i.h.
11. Elijah went by whirlw. i. h.
Ps. 139 : 8. If I ascend i. h.
Pr. 30 : 4. Who asc-d i.h.? Ro. 10:6
Is. 14 : 13. said, I will ascend i. h.
Mk. 16 : 19. Lord was rec-d i. h.
Lu. 2 : 15. angels were gone i. h.
24 : 51. he was carried up i. h.
Ac. 1 : 11. gazing up i.h. taken i.h.
as have seen him go i. h.
7 : 55. Step. looked steadf-y i. h.
10:16.vessel received up i.h.,11:10.
He. 9 : 24. i. h., to appear for us
1 Pe. 3 : 22. gone i. h. on right ha.
See **KINGDOM of heaven.**

HEAVEN with star, s.

Ge. 1:17. G. set s-s in firmam. of h.
15 : 5. Look tow. h. tell the s-s
22 : 17. thy seed as s-s of h., 26:4.
Ex.32:13. 1 Ch. 27:23. Ne. 9:23.
De. 1:10. you are as s-s of h.,10:22.
28:62.ye were as s-s of h. for mult.
Is. 13 : 10. s-s of h. not give light
Eze. 32:7. cover h. make s-s dark
Na. 3 : 16. merchants as s-s of h.
Mat. 24 : 29. s-s shall fall from h.,
Mk. 13 : 25.

Re.6:13. s-s of **h.** fell unto the earth
9: 1. I saw a s. fall from **h.**, 8:10.
12: 4. tail drew part of s-s of **h.**

To or unto HEAVEN.

Ge. 11: 4. a tower may reach **u. h.**
28:12. ladder, top of it reached **t. h.**
De. 1: 28. cities walled **t. h.**, 9: 1.
4: 19. lest lift up thine eyes **u. h.**
30:12. Who shall go up for us **t. h.**
32:40. for I lift up my hand **t. h.**
Jos. 8:20. smoke of the city up **t. h.**
Ju. 20:40. flame of the city up **t. h.**
1 S. 5: 12. cry of city went up **t. h.**
1 K. 8: 54. with hands spread **t. h.**
2 Ch. 28:9. rage th. reacheth **u. h.**
30: 27. their prayer came **u. h.**
32: 20. Isa. prayed and cried **t. h.**
Ps. 107: 26. They mount up **t. h.**
Je. 51:9. her judgm. reacheth **u. h.**
53. Tho. Bab. should mount **t. h.**
Da. 4: 11. the tree reached **u. h.**, 20.
22. thy greatness reacheth **u. h.**
34. eyes **u. h.** and underst-g retu.
12: 7. held up his left hand **u. h.**
Am. 9: 2. tho. they climb up **t. h.**
Mat. 11:23. Capernaum, art exalted
u. h., Lu. 10:15. [6:41. Lu. 9:16.
14: 19. and looking up **t. h.**, Mk.
Mk. 7: 34. looking up **t. h.** sighed
Lu. 18: 13. not lift his eyes **u. h.**
Jn. 3: 13. no man ascended up **t. h.**
17: 1. Jes. lifted up his eyes **t. h.**
2 Co. 12:2. one caught up **t.** third **h.**
Re. 10: 5. angel lifted hand **t. h.**
11: 12. ascended up **t. h.** in cloud
18: 5. For her sins have reached **u.**

Toward HEAVEN. [h.

Ge. 15: 5. Look **t. h.** tell the stars
Ex. 9: 8. let Mo. sprinkle it **t. h.**
10. Moses sprinkled it up **t. h.**
22. Stretch forth hand **t. h.**, 10:21.
23. Moses stretched his rod **t. h.**
10:22. Mo. stretched his hand **t. h.**
Ju. 13:20. when flame went **t. h.**
1 K. 8: 22. Sol. spread hands **t. h.**,
2 Ch. 6: 13. [t. h.
Jb. 2:12. sprinkled dust upon heads
Pr. 23: 5. fly away as eagle **t. h.**
Ac. 1: 10. they looked steadfastly **t.**

Under HEAVEN. [h.

Ge. 1: 9. Let waters **u. h.** be gath.
6: 17. flood to destroy all fr. **u. h.**
7:19. high hills **u.** whole **h.** cover-d
Ex. 17: 14. put out remem. of Amalek fr. **u. h.**, De. 25:19. [u. h.
De. 2: 25. fear of thee upon nat-s
4:19. G. divided unto all nat-s **u. h.**
7: 24. destroy name fr. **u. h.**, 9:14.
29:20. L. blot out his name fr. **u. h.**
2 K. 14:27. blot name of Isr. fr. **u. h.**
Jb. 28: 24. for G. seeth **u.** whole **h.**
37: 3. He directeth it **u.** whole **h.**
41: 11. whatso. **u.** whole **h.** is mine
Ec. 1: 13. to search all done **u. h.**
2: 3. that good they sho. do **u. h.**
3: 1. time to ev. purpose **u. h.** [h.
Lu. 17: 24. light-h out of 1 part **u.**
Ac. 2: 5. devout of every nat. **u. h.**
4: 12. none other name **u. h.** given
Col. 1:23. gospel to ev. creature **u. h.**

HEAVENS.

Ge. 2:1. Thus **h.** and earth finished
4. generations of **h.** and earth in day Lord made **h.**
De. 32: 1. Give ear, O **h.**, Is. 1: 2.
33: 28. his **h.** shall drop down dew
Ju. 5: 4. earth trembled, **h.** drop-d
2 S. 22: 10. He bowed **h.**, Ps. 18:9.
1 K. 8: 27. **h.** cannot contain thee
1 Ch. 16: 26. but the L. made the **h.**, Ne. 9: 6. Ps. 96: 5.-102: 25.-136: 5.
31. Let the **h.** be glad, earth rejoi.
2 Ch. 6:25. hear fr. the **h.**, 33, 35, 39.
Ezr. 9: 6. trespass grown unto **h.**
Jb. 9: 8. Which alone spreadeth **h.**
14: 12. riseth not till **h.** no more
Jb. 15:15. **h.** are not clean in his sight
20: 6. Tho. excellency mount to **h.**
26: 13. By spirit he garnished **h.**
35: 5. Look unto **h.** behold clouds
Ps. 8:1. hast set glory abo. **h.**, 113:4.
3. When I consider thy **h.** the work
19:1. The **h.** declare the glory of G.
33: 6. By word of L. were **h.** made
50: 4. sh. call to the **h.** from above
6. **h.** shall declare his righteousn.
57: 5. Be thou exalted, O God, above **h.**, 11 -108: 5.
10. For thy mercy is great unto the **h.**, 108: 4.
68:4. extol him rideth upon **h.**, 33.
8. **h.** dropped at presence of God
73: 9. They set mouth ag. the **h.**
89:5. **h.** sh. praise thy wonders, L.
11. The **h.** are thine, earth also
96: 11. Let the **h.** rejoice, Re. 12:12.
97: 6. **h.** declare his righteousness
104: 2. stretchest out **h.**, Is. 40:22.
108:4. thy mercy is great above **h.**
115:16. The heaven, even **h.** are L.'s
144: 5. Bow thy **h.** O Lord, come
148: 1. Praise ye the L. fr. **h.** [h.
4. Praise him, ye **h.** of **h.** waters ab.
Pr. 3: 19. by underst-g estab-d **h.**
8: 27. When he prepared the **h.** I
Is. 13:13. will shake **h.**, Hag. 2:6, 21.
34: 4. **h.** sh. be rolled tog. as scroll
42: 5. he that created **h.**, 45: 18.
44:23. Sing, O ye **h.** L. hath done it
24. L., that stretcheth forth **h.**
45: 12.-51: 13. Je. 10: 12. Zch.
45:8. Drop down ye **h.** from [12:1.
48: 13. my right hand spanned **h.**
49:13. Sing, O **h.**; be joyful, O earth
50: 3. I clothe **h.** with blackness
51: 6. Lift up your eyes to **h.** look,
h. sh. vanish aw. like smoke
16. that I may plant **h.** and lay
55: 9. as **h.** are higher than earth
64: 1. that thou wouldest rend **h.**
65: 17. behold, I create new **h.** and
66: 22. as new **h.** I will make
Je. 2: 12. Be astonished, O ye **h.**
4:23. I beheld **h.** they had no light
25. all the birds of **h.** were fled
28. for this shall **h.** ab. be black
9: 10. fowl of **h.** and beast are fled
10: 11. gods that have not made **h.** sh. perish, and from und. **h.**
14: 22. or can the **h.** give showers?
La. 3:66. destroy them fr. under **h.**
Eze. 1: 1. **h.** were opened Mat. 3:16.
Da. 4: 26. known that **h.** do rule
Ho. 2:21. I will hear **h.** they sh. hear
Jo. 2: 10. **h.** shall tremble, sun
3: 16. **h.** and the earth sh. shake
Ha. 3: 3. G. came, glory cov-d **h.**
Zch. 6: 5. These are 4 spirits of **h.**
8: 12. the **h.** shall give their dew
Mat. 24: 29. powers of **h.** be shaken
Mk. 1: 10. he saw **h.** opened
Ac. 2: 34 David not ascended into **h.**
7: 56. I see the **h.** opened, and Son
Ep. 4: 10. far above all **h.** that he
He. 1: 10. **h.** work of thine hands
4: 14. priest th. is passed into **h.**
7: 26. high priest higher than **h.**
2 Pe. 3: 5. by word of God **h.** were
7. **h.** wh. are now, kept in store
10. **h.** shall pass aw. with noise
12 **h.** being on fire sh. be dissolved
13. look for new **h.** new earth.

In the HEAVENS.

Ps. 2: 4. sitteth **i. t. h.** shall laugh
18: 13. The L. thundered **i. t. h.**
36:5. Thy mercy, O Lord, is **i. t. h.**
89:2. faithfuln. shalt establ. **i. t. h.**
103:19. prepared his throne **i. t. h.**
115:3. God is **i. t. h.** he hath done
123:1. O thou that dwellest **i. t. h.**
Is. 5: 30. light is dark-d **i. t. h.**
Je. 10: 13. of waters **i. t. h.**, 51:16.
La. 3:41. our hearts unto G. **i. t. h.**
Jo. 2: 30. shew wonders **i. t. h.**
Lu. 12: 33. a treasure **i. t. h.** wh.
2 Co. 5: 1. house eternal **i. t. h.**
He. 8: 1. throne of Majesty **i. t. h.**
9: 23. patterns of things **i. t. h.**

HEAVENLY.

Mat. 6: 14. **h.** Fa. will forgive you
26. your **h.** Father feedeth them
32. **h.** Fa. knoweth ye have need
15:13. ev. plant **h.** Fa. not planted
18: 35. so my **h.** Fa. do unto you
Lu. 2: 13. multi. of **h.** host praising
11: 13. **h.** Fa. shall give Spirit
Jn. 3: 12. how beli., if I tell of **h.**
Ac. 26: 19. not disobed. unto **h.** vis.
1 Co. 15: 48. as is **h.** such are **h.**
49. we sh. bear image of the **h.**
Ep. 1: 3. blessings in **h.** places in C.
20. set him in **h.** places, 2: 6.
3:10. now unto powers in **h.** places
2 Ti. 4:18. preserve me to **h.** kingd.
He. 3: 1. partakers of **h.** calling
6:4. and have tasted of the **h.** gift
8: 5. serve unto shadow of **h.** thi.
9:23. **h.** things wi. better sacrifices
11:16. **h.** country | 12:22. **h.** Jerus.

HEAVIER.

Jb. 6: 3. it would be **h.** than sand
23: 2. stroke **h.** than my groaning
Pr. 27: 3. fool's wrath is **h.** than

HEAVILY.

Ex. 14: 25. wheels, so that drave **h.**
Ps. 35: 14. I bowed down **h.** as one
Is. 47: 6. upon ancient **h.** laid yoke

HEAVINESS.

Ezr. 9: 5. at sacri. I rose fr. my **h.**
Jb. 9: 27. if say, I will leave off **h.**
Ps. 69: 20. brok. heart, I full of **h.**
119: 28. My soul melteth for **h.**
Pr. 10: 1. foolish son **h.** of mother
12: 25. **h.** in heart mak. it stoop
14: 13. the end of that mirth is **h.**
Is. 1: † 4. a people of **h.** with iniq.
29: 2. there sh. be **h.** and sorrow
30: † 27. his anger, and burd. is **h.**
61:3. garm. of praise for spir. of **h.**
Ro. 9: 2. I have great **h.** and sor.
2 Co. 2: 1. I would not come in **h.**
Ph. 2:26. Epaph. my bro. full of **h.**
Ja. 4: 9. let joy be turned into **h.**
1 Pe. 1: 6. for a season, ye are in **h.**

HEAVY.

Ge. 41: † 31. famine sh. be very **h.**
48: † 10. eyes of Isr. were **h.** for
Ex. 5: †9. let work be **h.** upon men
17: 12. Moses' hands were **h.** they
18:18 this thing is too **h.** for thee
Nu. 11:14. not able, bec. it is too **h.**
Ju. 1: †35. hand of ho. of Jo. was **h.**
1 S. 4: 18. Eli an old man and **h.**
5:6. ha. of L. **h.** upon Ashdod, 11.
2 S. 14:26. bec. hair was **h.** on him
1 K. 12: 4. thy fa.'s **h.** yoke lighter, 10, 11, 14. 2 Ch. 10:4, 10, 11, 14.
14: 6. sent to thee with **h.** tidings
20: 43. Ahab went to ho. **h.**, 21:4.
2 K. 6: †14. k. sent a **h.** host [host
18: †17. Sennach. sent to Hez. a **h.**
Ne. 5: 18. bondage **h.** upon people
Jb. 33: 7. nei. shall my hand be **h.**
Ps. 32:4. thy hand was **h.** upon me
38: 4. as **h.** burden, too **h.** for me
Pr. 25:20. sing-h songs to **h.** heart
27: 3. stone is **h.**, but fool's wrath
31:6. wine unto those of **h.** hearts
Is. 6: 10. make their ears **h.**
24: 20. transgr-n sh. be **h.** upon it
30: 27. the burden thereof is **h.**
46: 1. your carriages **h.** loaden
58:6 fast, to undo the **h.** burdens?
59: 1. nei. ear **h.** th. it can-t hear
La. 3: 7. hedged me, made chain **h.**
Mat. 11: 28. all ye th. are **h.** laden
23: 4. for they bind **h.** burdens
26: 37. to be sorrowf., and very **h.**
43. eyes very **h.**, Mk. 14: 33, 40.

Lu. 9 : 32 Pet. and they h. wi. sleep

HE'BER, ITES. [7 : 31.

Ge. 46 : 17. sons of Beriah ; H., 1 Ch.
Nu. 26 : 45. of H. family of H-s [5 : 24.
Ju. 4 : 11. H. the Kenite, 17 (2), 21.-
1 Ch. 4 : 18. wife bare H. fa. of Socho
5 : 13. of chil-n of Gad, Jachan, H
7 : 32. H. begat Japhlet, Shomer
8 : 22. Ishpan, H. were chief men, 17.
See EBER or HEBER.

HE'BREW. [Language.]

Lu. 23 : 38. over him in H., Jn. 19 : 20
Jn. 19 : 13. called in H., Gabbatha
17. the place called in H., Golgotha
See TONGUE. [Language.]

HE'BREW. [Race.] [H

Ge. 14 : 13. came one told Abram the
39 : 14. brought in a H. to mock us
41 : 12. with us a young man, a H.
Ex. 2 : 11. an Egyptian smiting a H.
Je. 34 : 9. should let a H. go free, 14.
Jon. 1 : 9. he said unto them, I am a
Ph. 3 : 5. I am a H. of the Heb-s [H.

HE'BREW.

man, midwives, or servant.

Ge 39 : 17. H. s. came in to mock me
Ex 1 : 15. king of Eg. spake to H. m-s
21 : 2. If thou buy a H. s., six years
De 15 : 12. And if a H. m. be sold
See Heb. WOMAN, WOMEN

HE'BREWS.

Ge 40 : 15. I stolen out of land of H.
43 : 32. Egyptians not eat with H.
Ex. 2 : 6. This is one of H.' children
13. two men of the H. strove [3.
3 : 18. God of the H. met with us, 5:
7 : 16. God of H. hath sent me [3.
9 : 1. saith G. of H., Let peo., 13.-10.
1 S 4 : 6. great shout in camp of H.?
9. that ye be not servants unto H.
13 : 3. Saul blew, Let the H. hear
7. some of H. went over Jordan
19. Lest H make swords or spears
14 : 11. the H. come out of the holes
21. H with the Philistines turned
29 : 3. What do these H. here? [H.
Ac. 6 : 1. murmuring of Grecians ag.
2 Co. 11 : 22. Are they H.? so am I
Ph. 3 : 5. I am a Hebrew of the H.

HE'BREWESS.

Je. 34 : 9. man should let a H. free

HE'BRON. [Place.] [19.

Ge 13 : 18 Mamre which is in H., 23:
23 : 2. Kirjath-arba, the same is H.,
35 : 27. Jos. 14 : 15.-15 : 13, 54.-
20 : 7.-21 : 11. Ju. 1 : 10. [of H.
37 : 14. Jacob sent Jos. out of vale
Nu. 13 : 22. H. was built bef. Zoan (2)
Jos. 10 : 3. king of H., 5, 23.-12 : 10.
39. as to H. so he did to Debir, 36.
11 : 21. Josh. cut off Anakim fr. H.
14 : 13. gave Caleb H., 14.-15 : 13.
19 : 28. for chil. of Asher H. [Ju. 1 : 20.
21 : 13. to chil. of Aaron H., city of
refuge, 11.-20 : 7. 1 Ch. 6 : 55, 57.
Ju. 1 : 10. Judah ag. Canaanites in H.
16 : 3. took doors to top of hill bef.
1 S. 30 : 31. sent spoil to th. in H. [H.
2 S. 2 : 1. Whither I go? Unto H. [3.
11. David king in H. seven years,
5 : 5. 1 K. 2 : 11. 1 Ch. 29 : 27.
32. Joab and his men came to H.
3 : 5. born to Da. in H., 2. 1 Ch. 3 : 1, 4.
20. Abn. came to Da. to H., 19, 22, 27.
32. buried Abner in H. | 4 : 1.
4 : 8. head of Ish-bosheth to H., 12.
12. hanged them over pool in H.
5 : 1. all the tribes to Dav. unto H.,
3 (2) 1 Ch. 12 : 23, 38. 11 : 1, 3 (2).
13. more wives aft. he. . come fr. H.
15 : 7. let me go pay my vow in H., 9.
10. sh say, Absal. reigneth in H.
2 Ch. 11 . 10. Rehoboam built H. in

HE'BRON. [Per.] [Judah

Ex. 6 : 18 sons of Kohath ; H., Nu.
3 . 19 1 Ch 6 2, 18.-23 : 12. [H.
1 Ch. 2 . 42. sons of Mareshah fa. of
1 Ch. 2 : 43. sons of H., 15 : 9.-23 : 19.-

HE'BRONITES. [24 : 23.

Nu. 3 : 27. the family of the H., 26 :
58. 1 Ch. 26 : 23, 30, 31.

HEDGE. [Noun.] [him?

Jb. 1 : 10. Hast not made h. about
Pr. 15 : 19. way of slothful is a h.
Ec. 10 : 8. breaketh a h. serp. bite
Is. 5 : 5. I will take away the h.
La. 2 : †6. violently taken aw. his h.
Eze. 13 : 5. nei. made up h. for Isr.
22 : 30. man that sho. make up the h.
Mi. 7 : 4. the upright sharper than h.
Mk. 12 : 1. he set a h. about it

HEDGES.

1 Ch. 4 : 23. those that dwelt amongst
plants and h.
Ps. 80 : 12. hast broken her h.? 89 : 40.
Je. 49 : 3. run to and fro by the h.
Na. 3 : 17. as grasshoppers in h.
Lu. 14 : 23. Go into highways and h.

HEDGE, ED.

Jb. 3 : 23. whom God hath h. in
19 : †11. thou hast h. me wi. bones
La. 3 : 7. He hath h. me about
Eze. 13 : †5. have not h. up for Isr.
Ho. 2 : 6. I will h. thy way wi. thorns
Mat. 21 : 33. planted a viney. and h. it

HEED.

De. 2 : 4. take good h., 4 : 15. Jos. 23 : 11.
2 S. 20 : 10. Amasa took no h. to sw.
2 K. 10 : 31. Jehu took no h. to walk
Ps. 119 : 9. taking h. acc. to word
Pr. 17 : 4. A wick. giveth h. to false
Ec. 12 : 9. preacher gave good h. [lips
Is. 21 : 7. he hearkened wi. much h.
Je. 18 : 18. not give h. to his words
19. Give h. to me, O Lord, and
Ac. 3 : 5. he gave h. unto them
8 : 6. people of Samaria gave h.
10. gave h. to Simon [1 : 14.
1 Ti. 1 : 4. Nei. give h. to fables, Tit.
4 : 1. some giving h. to seducing
spirits [earnest h.
He. 2 : 1. we ought to give more
See TAKE.

HEEL, S.

Ge. 3 : 15. thou shalt bruise his h.
25 : 26. hold on Esau's h., Ho. 12 : 3.
49 : 17. Dan an adder biteth horse's
Jb. 13 : 27. print upon h. of feet [h.
18 : 9. The gin shall take him by h.
Ps. 41 : 9. lifted h. ag. me, Jn. 13 : 18.
49 : 5. iniq. of h. compass me
Je. 13 : 22. for iniq. thy h. made bare

HE'GAI or HE'GE.

Es. 2 : 3. H. the k.'s chamberlain, 8,

HEIFER. [15.

Ge. 15 : 9. Take me a h. of 3 years,
Nu. 19 : 2. bring red h. without spot
5. one shall burn the h., 6.
9. gather ashes of h., 10, 17.
De. 21 : 3. elders shall take a h.
4. elders shall strike off h. neck
6. elders sh. wash hands over h.
Ju. 14 : 18. if not ploughed wi. my h.
1 S. 16 : 2. the Lord said, Take a h.
Is. 15 : 5. cry out for Moab as a h.
Je. 46 : 20. Egypt is like a fair h.
48 : 34. uttered their voice as a h.
50 : 11. bec. ye are grown fat as h.
Ho. 4 : 16. Isr. as backsliding h.
10 : 11. Ephraim is as h. taught
He. 9 : 13. ashes of h. sprinkling uncl.

HEIGHT.

Ge. 6 : 15. h. of ark be 30 cubits
Ex. 25 : 10. ark of shittim wood, cubit and a half be h., 23.-37 : 1, 10
27 : 1. h. of altar 3 cubits, 38 : 1.
18. h. of court 5 cubits, 38 : 18.
30 : 2. h. of altar 2 cubits, 37 : 25.
1 S. 16 : 7. look not on h. of stature
17 : 4. Goliath's h. was six cubits
1 K. 6 : 2. h. of ho. of G. 30 cubits
20. oracle 20 cubits in the h.
26. h. of one cherub 10 cubits
7 : 2. h. of house of Leb. 30 cubits
1 K. 7 : 16. h. of one chapiter 5 cubits
23. h. of molten sea 5 cubits
27. h. of one base 3 cubits
32. h. of wheel was cubit and
2 K. 19 : 23. With chariots am come
to h. of mts., Is. 37 : 24.
25 : 17. The h. of one pillar was
eighteen cubits, Je. 52 : 21.
2 Ch. 33 : 14. raised it very great h.
Ezr. 6 : 3. h. of G.'s ho. 60 cubits
Jb. 22 : 12. Is not God in h. of heav.?
and behold h. of stars
Ps. 102 : 19. L. looked fr. h. of sanct.
Pr. 25 : 3. The heaven for h. earth
Is. 7 : 11. ask it in depth, or in h.
Je. 31 : 12. shall sing in h. of Zion
49 : 16. O thou that holdest the h.
51 : 53. tho. fortify h. of her strength
Eze. 17 : 23. In mt. of h. of Isr., 20 :
19 : 11. she appeared in her h. [40.
31 : 5. his h. was exalted ab. trees
10. thou hast lifted up thys. in h.
14. none of trees exalt thems. for
32 : 5. fill valleys with thy h. [h.
41 : 8. I saw the h. of the house
Da. 3 : 1. image whose h. 60 cubits
4 : 10. I saw tree whose h. was gr.
11. h. reached unto heaven, 20.
Am. 2 : 9. h. was like h. of cedars
Ro. 8 : 39. Nor h. nor depth be able
Ep. 3 : 18. what h. of love of Christ?
Re. 21 : 16. breadth and h. of city

HEIGHTS. [equal

Jb. 9 : † 8. treadeth upon h. of sea
11 : † 8. it is h. of heav. what do?
Ps. 95 : † 4. h. of the hills are his
148 : 1. Praise Lord, praise in h.
Ec. 10 : † 6. folly is set in great h.
Is. 14 : 14. I will asc. ab. h. of clouds
33 : †16. he sh. dwell on h. his place

HEINOUS.

Jb. 31 : 11. for this is a h. crime

HEIR, S.

Ge. 15 : 3. one born in my h. is h.
4. saying, This not be thine h.
21 : 10. Ishm. sh. not be h. wi. son
Ju. 18 : † 7. was no h. of restraint
2 S. 14 : 7. we will destroy the h.
Pr. 30 : 23. handmaid h. to mistress
Je. 49 : 1. Hath Isr. no sons? no h.
2. Isr. be h. unto th. were his h-s
Mi. 1 : 15. will I bri. an h. unto thee
Mat. 21 : 38. This is the h., Mk. 12 : 7.
Lu. 20 : 14. [the world
Ro. 4 : 13. that he should be h. of
14. if they wh. are of law be h-s
8 : 17. if chil. then h-s, h-s of God,
and joint h-s with Christ
Ga. 3 : 29. ye h-s acc. to promise
4 : 1. That h. as long as he a child
7. if a son, then an h. of God
30. son of bondwom. not be h.
Ep. 3 : 6. Gent. should be fellow h-s
Tit. 3 : 7. h-s acc. to hope of eternal
He. 1 : 2. appointed h. of all things
14. them who sh. be h-s of salva.
6 : 17. to shew unto h-s of promise
11 : 7. became h. of the righteousn.
9. Jac. h-s with him of promise
Ja. 2 : 5. h-s of kingd. he promised
1 Pe. 3 : 7. as h-s toge. of grace of life

HE'LAH. [7.

1 Ch. 4 : 5. Asher had two wives, H. |

HE'LAM.

2 S. 10 : 16. came to H. and Shobach,

HEL'BAH. [17.

Ju. 1 : 31. Nei. Asher drive out chil.

HEL'BON. [of H.

Eze. 27 : 18. in the wine of H.

HELD.

Ge. 48 : 17. Joseph h. his fa.'s hand
Ex. 17 : 11. when Moses h. up ha. Isr.
36 : 12. loops h. one curtain to ano.
Ju. 7 : 20. h. lamps in left hands
16 : 26. Samson said unto lad h. him
Ru. 3 : 15. when she h. it, he meas-d
1 S. 25 : 36. Nabal h. a feast in ho.

2 S. 18 : 16. Joab h. back the peo.
1 K. 8 : 65. that time Sol. h. feast
1 Ch.11:†10. h. strongly with Da.
2 Ch. 4 : 5. the sea h. 3000 baths
Ne.4:16. the half h. both spears,21.
17. with other ha. be h. weapon
Es. 5 : 2. king h. out the sceptre
7 : 4. if sold, I had h. my tongue
Jb. 23 : 11. My foot h. his steps
Ps. 32:9. whose mouth must be h.
Ps.94:18. thy mercy, O L. h.me up
Pr.16:†5. hand join in ha. not be h. innocent, 17:†5 -19:†5.
Can. 3: 4. I h. him, and not let go
7:5. the king is h. in the galleries
Je. 50:33. took captives, h. th. fast
Da. 12:7. h. up right ha. and sware
Mat. 12:14. h. a council, Mk. 15:1.
Lu. 22:63. men th. h. Jes. mocked
Ac. 3 : 11. that was healed, h. Pe.
14:4. part h. with Jews, part with
Ro. 7 : 6. dead wherein we were h.
Re. 6:9. slain for testimony they h.

HELD peace. [p.
Ge.24:21. man wondering at her,h.
34 : 5. Jacob h. his p. until they
Le. 10 : 3. And Aaron h. his p.
Nu.30:7. her husb. h. his p.,11,14.
1 S. 10 : 27. despised Saul, he h. p.
2 K. 18 : 36. But people h. their p.
Ne.5:8. they h. p. and found noth.
Jb.29:10. nobles h. p. their tongue
Ps. 39 : 2. I was dumb, I h. my p.
Is. 36:21. they h. their p., Mk.3:4.-9: 34. [of old
57 : 11. have not I h. my p., even
Mat.26:63.Jesus h.his p.,Mk.14:61.
Lu. 14 : 4. they h. their p., 20:26. Ac. 11 : 18. [answered
Ac. 15 : 13. they h. their p. James

HEL'DAI.
1 Ch.27:15.capt.for 12th mo.was H.
Zch.6:10.take of the capt.even of H.

HE'LEB or HE'LED.
2 S.23:29 H.son of Baanah,1 Ch.11: [30.†

HE'LEK, ITES.
Nu. 26:30. of H. family of H-s, Jos. [17:2.

HE'LEM.
Zch. 6 : 14. crowns be to H. | 1 Ch. [7:35.

HE'LEPH.
Jos. 19 : 33. their coast was fr. H.

HE'LEZ.
2 S.23:26.H.the Paltite | 1 Ch.2:39.
1 Ch. 27 : 10. capt. of 7th mo. H. | [11:27.

HE'LI.
Lu. 3 : 23. which was the son of H.

HELIOP'OLIS=A'VEN.
Eze 30:†17. yo. men of H. shall fall

HEL'KAI.
Ne. 12 : 15. of Meraioth, H.

HEL'KATH.
Jos.19:25.their border was H.,21:31.

HEL'KATH-HAZ'ZURIM.
2 S. 2: 16. that place was called H.

HELL.
De. 32:22. sh. burn unto lowest h.
2 S. 22:6. sorrows of h. compassed, [Ps.18:5.
Jb. 11 : 8. deeper than h.
26 : 6. h. is naked before him
Ps. 9 : 17. wicked be turned into h.
16:10. thou wilt not leave my soul in h., Ac.2:27. [er of h., 86:13.
49:†15. redeem my soul from pow-
55: 15. let them go quick into h.
116:3.pains of h.gat hold upon me
139: 8. if bed in h. thou art there
Pr. 5 : 5. her steps take hold on h.
7 : 27. Her house is the way to h.
9:18.her guests are in depths of h.
15 : 11. h. and destruction bef. L.
24. that he may depart from h.
23: 14. shalt deliver his soul fr. h.
27 : 20. h. and destruc. never full
Is. 5 : 14. h. hath enlarged herself
14:9. h. is moved for thee to meet
15. shalt be brought down to h.
28:15. wi. h. are we at agreement
Is. 28:18. agreement wi. h.not stand
57:9. didst debase thyself unto h.
Eze. 31 : 16. I cast him down to h.
17. they went down unto h. with
32: 21. sh. speak to him out of h.
27. going down to h. wi. weapons
Am. 9 : 2. Though they dig into h.
Jon. 2 : 2. out of belly of h. cried I
Ha. 2 : 5. enlargeth his desire as h.
Mat.5:22 sh. be in danger of h. fire
29. whole body cast into h., 30.
10:28. to destroy soul and body in h., Lu. 12: 5. [to h.,Lu.10:15.
11 : 23. Capernaum brought down
16:18.the gates of h.sh.not prevail
18:9. having 2 eyes to be cast into h. fire, Mk. 9:47. [child of h.
23 : 15. make him twofold more
33. how escape damna. of h.?
Mk. 9 : 43. having two hands to go into h., 45.
Lu. 16 : 23. in h. lifted up his eyes
Ac. 2 : 31. his soul not left in h.
1 Co. 15:†55. O h. where victory?
Ja. 3 : 6. tongue is set on fire of h.
2 Pe. 2:4. if G. cast angels do. to h.
Re. 1 : 18. keys of h. and of death
6: 8. name was Death, h. followed
20 : 13. death and h. deliv-d dead
14. death and h. were cast into [lake

HELM.
Ja.3:4.are turned about with small [h.

HELMET, S.
1 S.17:5. h. of brass upon head, 38.
2 Ch. 26 : 14. Uzziah prepared h-s
Is. 59 : 17. a h. of salv. upon head
Je. 46:4. stand forth wi. your h-s
Eze. 23 : 24. set ag. shield and h.
27:10. they hanged the h. in thee
38:5.all of them with shield and h.
Ep. 6 : 17. take h. of salvation
1 Th. 5 : 8. for h. hope of salvation

HE'LON.
Nu. 1 : 9. of Zebulon, Eliab son of H., 2 : 7.-7 : 24, 29.-10 : 16.

HELP, S.
Ge. 2 : 18. make a h. meet for him
20. was not found a h. meet for
Ex. 18:4. G. of my fa. was my h.
De. 33:7. be thou a h. to him from
26. rideth upon heaven in thy h.
29. saved by L. shield of thy h.
Ju. 5 : 23. came not to h. of Lord
1 S. 11 : 9. sun be hot, ye have h.
2 Ch. 20 : 4. gath-d to ask h. of L.
Jb 6 : 13. Is not my h. in me?
31 : 21. when I saw my h. in gate
Ps. 3 : 2. say of my soul, is no h.
20 : 2. L. send h. from sanctuary
27:9. thou hast been my h. O God
33:20.Our soul waits for L. our h.
35:2. stand up for mine h., 44:26.
40 : 17. my h. and deliverer, 70:5.
42:5. praise him for h. of counten.
46 : 1. God is a very present h. in
60:11.Give us h.vain is h. of man,
63:7.Bec.hast been my h. [108:12.
71: 12. O G. make haste for my h.
89:19. I have laid h. upon mighty
94 : 17. Unless L. had been my h.
115:9.he their h. and shield,10,11.
121:1.unto hills, fr. whence my h.
2. My h. cometh from Lord wh.
124 : 8. Our h. is in name of Lord
146:3. trust not in man, in wh. no
5.Happy th. hath God for h. [h.
Is. 10 : 3. to whom ye flee for h.?
20:6.we flee for h. to be deliv.fr.k.
30:5.nor be h. nor profit,but shame
31:1. Woe to them go to E. for h.
2. ag. h. of them that work iniq.
La. 4 : 17. eyes failed for vain h.
Da. 11 : 34. be holpen with little h.
Ho.13:9. destroyed thys. in me is h.
Ac. 26:22. Having obtained h.of G.
27 : 17. h-s undergirding the ship
1 Co. 12 : 28. gifts of healings, h-s

HELP. [Verb.] [thee
Ge. 49:25. G. of thy fa. who sh. h.
Ex. 23 : 5. wouldest forbear to h. him, shalt h. him, De. 22: 4.
De. 32:38. let them rise and h. you
Jos.1:14. pass bef. breth. and h. th.
10 : 4. Come unto me and h. me
6. come up to us quickly, h. us
33. Horam came up to h. Lachish
2 S. 10 : 11. thou shalt h. me; then I will h. thee, 1 Ch. 19 : 12.
19. Syrians feared to h. chil. of Ammon, 1 Ch. 19 : 19.
14 : 4. said, h. O king, 2 K. 6 : 26.
2 K. 6 : 27. If L. not h. shall I h.
1 Ch. 12:17. if ye be come to h. me
22. day by day to Da. to h. him
18 : 5. Syrians to h. Hadarezer
22:17. Da. commanded to h. Sol.
2 Ch. 14 : 11. it is noth. with thee to h., h. us, O Lord [ly
19:2. Shouldest thou h. the ungod-
20 : 9. If we cry, then thou wilt h.
25 : 8. for God hath power to h.
26:13.mighty power to h. the king
28 : 16. unto k-s of Assyria to h.
23.gods h. them, th.they h. me
29:34. breth. Levites did h. them
32 : 3. his mighty men did h. him
8. with us is L. our G. to h. us
Ezr.1:4. let men of his place h. him
8 : 22. to require horsemen to h.
Jb. 8 : 20. nei. will he h. evil doers
29:12.I deliv-d him had none to h.
Ps.12:1. h. Lord | 22:11. none to h.
22:19.haste thee to h. me, 38:22.-40 : 13.-70 : 1.
37 : 40. Lord shall h. them
46 : 5. God shall h. her
59 : 4. awake to h. me
79:9.h.us, O God of salv. [Is.63:5.
107: 12. fell, there was none to h.,
109 : 26. h. me, O L. my G. save
118: 7. L. taketh part wi. th.h. me
119:86. h. me | 173. let ha. h. me
175. and let thy judgments h. me
Ec. 4 : 10. hath not ano. to h. him
Is. 30 : 7 Egyp-s shall h. in vain
41 : 10. I will h. thee, 13,14.-44:2.
50 : 7. Lord God will h. me, 9.
Je. 37:7. army, which is come to h.
La. 1 : 7. people fell, none did h.
Eze. 12:14. scatter all ab. him to h.
32:21. out of hell with th. that h.
Da. 10 : 13. one of princes to h. me
11:45. to his end, none sh. h. him
Mat. 15 : 25. worsh-d saying, L. h.
Mk. 9 : 22. have compassion h. us
24. L. I believe, h. mine unbelief
Lu. 5:7. they beckon. that they h.
10 : 40. bid her that she h. me
Ac. 16 : 9. Come into Mace. h. us
21:28. Crying out, Men of Isr. h.
Ph. 4 : 3. h. women that labored
He. 4 : 16. find grace to h. in need

HELPED.
Ex. 2 : 17. Moses stood up and h.
1 S.7:12.Hitherto hath the L. h. us
1 K. 1 : 7. foll-g Adonijah, h. him
20 : 16. thirty and two k-s that h.
1 Ch. 5 : 20. they were h. ag. them
12:19. h. them not, for lords sent
21. they h. David ag. the rovers
15:26.when God h. the Levites th.
2 Ch. 18 : 31. the Lord h. Jehosh.
20 : 23. ev. one h. to destroy ano.
26 : 7. God h. him ag. Philistines.
15. for he was marvellously h.
28: 21. king of Assyria h. him not
Ezr. 10:15. Shabbethai Lev. h. th.
Es. 9 : 3. officers of king h. Jews
Jb. 26 : 2. How hast h. him that is without power [the L. h. me
Ps. 28:7. and I am h. | 118:13. but
116 : 6. I was bro-t low, he h. me
Is.41:6.They h. ev. one his neighb.
49:8.in day of salv. have I h. thee

Zch. 1:15. they h. forward affliction
Ac. 18: 27. he was come, h. them
Re 12:16. the earth h. the woman

HELPER.

2 K. 14 : 26. nor any h. for Israel
Jb.30:13. mar my path, have no h.
Ps. 10 : 14. art h. of the fatherless
22:†11.Be not far, there is not a h.
30:10. L. be my h. | 54:4. G.my h.
72 : 12. deliver him hath no h.
Je. 47:4. cut off fr. Tyrus every h.
Ro. 16 : 9. Salute Urbane our h.
He. 13: 6. L. is my h. I will not fear

HELPERS. [the war

1 Ch. 12: 1. am. mighty men h. of
18. and peace be to thine h.
Jb. 9 : 13. proud h. do stoop under
Eze. 30:8. all her h. sh. be destr.
Na. 3: 9. Put and Lubim thy h.
Ro. 16 : 3. Priscilla, Aquila my h.
2 Co. 1 : 24. but are h. of your joy
See **FELLOW helper, s.**

HELPETH, ING.

1 Ch. 12 : 18. for thy God h-h thee
Ezr. 5 : 2. prophets of G. h-g them
Ps 22:1. why so far from h-g me?
Is. 31:3. both he that h-h shall fall
Ro. 8:26. Spirit h-h our infirmities
1 Co.16:16.ye submit to ev.one h-h
2 Co.1:11.Ye also h-g toge.by pray.

HELVE.

De. 19 : 5. head slippeth from h.

HEM, S.

Ex. 28:33. upon h. of it shalt make
pomegranates, 34.-39: 25, 26.
39 : 24. made upon h-s of the robe
Mat.9:20.touched h.of garm.,14:36.

BE'MAM = HO'MAM.

Ge.36:22.chil of Lotan,H.,1 Ch.1:39.

HE'MAN.

1 K. 4 : 31. Sol. was wiser than H.
1 Ch. 2 : 6. the sons of Zerah; H.
6:33. H. a singer, son of Joel, son
of, 15 : 17, 19.-16 : 41, 42.
25: 1. David appoin. of sons of H.,
4, 6. 2 Ch. 5:12.-29:14.-35:15.
5. sons of H. God gave H. 14 sons

HE'MATH. See HA'MATH.

1 Ch.2: 55. Kenites that came of H.

HEM'DAN = AM'RAM.

Ge.36:26. chil. of Dishon, H., 1 Ch.

HEMLOCK. [1:41.

Ho.10:4. judgm. springeth up as h.
Am. 6:12. fruit of righte-n. into h.

HEN. [13:34.

Mat. 23:37. h. gath-h chickens, Lu.

HEN.

Zch. 6: 14. crowns to Helem and H.

HE'NA. [for

2 K. 18 : 34. where are gods of H.
19:13.where is king of H.,Is.37:13.

HEN'ADAD.

Ezr.3:9.sons of H.,Ne.3:18,24.-10:9.

HENCE.

Ge. 37 : 17. They are departed h.
42 : 15. by Pha. ye not go h. [19.
50 : 25. carry my bones h., Ex. 13:
Ex. 11 : 1. he will let you go h.
33: 1. Depart, go up h. thou and
15.If thy pres.not,carry us not h.
De. 9 : 12. Arise, get thee down h.
Jos. 4 : 3. Take h. twelve stones
Ju. 6:18. Depart not h. I pray thee
Ru. 2: 8. nei. go h. but abide fast
by my maidens [Mat. 4: 10.
1 K. 17 : 3. Get thee h., Is. 30 : 22.
Ps. 39 : 13. O spare, before I go h.
Je.38:10 saying, Take fr. h. 30 men
Zch. 6 : 7. Get h. walk to and fro
Mat.17:20.Remove h. to yonder pl.
Lu.4:9.If Son of G. cast thys. fr. h.
13:31.Get thee out, and depart h.
Jn. 7 : 3. [cannot
16 : 26. would pass from h. to you
Jn. 2:16. Take these things h. [h.
14:31.let us go h. | 18:36.kingd.not
20 : 15. if have borne him h. tell me
Ac.1:5.with H.G. not many days h.
22:21. send thee far h. unto Gent.
Ja. 4:1. come they not h.' of lusts

HENCEFORTH.

Ge. 4:12. ground not h. yield thee
Nu.18:22.Nei.Isr. h. come nigh tab.
De 17:16. h. ret. no more that way
19 : 20. h. commit no more evil
Ju.2:21. I will not h. drive out any
2 K.5:17. h. not offer to other gods
2 Ch. 16:9. h. thou shalt have wars
Ps.125:2. L. about his peo. from h.
131:3.Isr.hope in the Lord from h.
Is.9:7.to estab. it with justice fr. h.
52:1. h. shall no more come uncl.
59:21. mouth of thy seed's seed h.
Eze. 36:12. no more h. bereave th.
Mi.4:7. L. shall reign in Zion fr. h.
Mat. 23 : 39. Ye shall not see me h.
26 : 29. I will not drink h. of vine
Lu.1:48 h. all gene-s call me bless-
5 : 10. h. shalt catch men [ed
12:52.h. shall be five in one house
Jn. 14:7. h. ye know him, and seen
15 : 15. h. I call you not servants
Ac. 4:17. they speak h. to no man
18: 6. h. I will go unto Gentiles
Ro. 6 : 6. h. we sho. not serve sin
2 Co. 5 : 15. sho. not h. live unto
16.h.know we no man(2) [thems.
Ga. 6:17. h. let no man trouble me
Ep. 4 : 14. we h. be no more chil.
17. that ye h. walk not as Gent.
2 Ti.4:8.h. is laid up for me a crown
He. 10:13. h. expecting till enemies
Re. 14:13. blessed who die in L., fr.

HENCEFORWARD. [h.

Nu. 15:23. h. am. your generations
Mat.21:19. no fruit grow on thee h.

HE'NOCH. See ENOCH.

HE'NOCH. See HANOCH.

HE'PHER. [Place.] [H.

Jos. 12 : 17. Joshua smote king of
1 K.4 :10.son of Hesed, to him all H.

HE'PHER, ITES.

Nu. 26 : 32. of H , the family of H-s
33. Zelophehad son of H. had no
sons, but dau-s, Jos 17:3.[of H.
27 : 1. came dau-s of Zeloph-d son
Jos. 17 : 2. was a lot for child-n of H.
1 Ch. 4 : 6. Naarah bare Ahuzam, H.
11 : 36. valiant men, H., Mechera-

HEPH'ZI-BAH. [thite

2 K. 21 : 1. Manasseh, mother's na.
Is. 62 : 4. thou shalt be called H.[H.

HER or SHE. [s.

Ge. 2 : 23. s. be called Woman bec.
3: 6. gave unto husband wi h., 12.
12 : 15. princes commended h. (2)
19. I might have taken h. to w.(2)
16 : 3. Sarai gave h. to Abr. to wife
6. Abram said; do to h. as pleaseth
7. angel found h. by fount-n[thee
17 : 16. I will bless h., s. shall be a
mother of nations (4) [breth.
20 : 5. s., even s. said, He is my
6. suffered I thee not to touch h.
12. my sister, s. became my wife
29:19. better th.I give h. to thee(2)
34 : 8. I pray give h. him to wife
38 : 14. s. covered h. with vail, sat
15. Judah thought h. a harlot +
26. s. been more righteous than I
39:10.Jos-h heark-d not unto h.(3)
Ex. 3 : 22. borrow of h. sojourneth
15 : 20. women after h. wi. timbrels
18 : 2. Moses' wife after he sent h.
6. thy wife, two sons with h.[back
21 : 8. he dealt deceitfully wi h.(4)
9. shall deal with h. after manner of daughters (2) [shall go
11. if he do not these unto h., s.
22. hurt so that fruit depart fr. h.
22 : 16. if lie with h. sh. endow h.
17. if father refuse to give h. unto
Le 12 : 7. atonem-t for h., 8.-15:30.
15 : 19. toucheth h. be unclean +
Le. 15 : 29. sh take unto h. 2 turtles
33. law of h. that is sick of (2)
18 : 18. Neither take a wife to vex h.
20. neighbour's wife to defile wi. h.
19 : 20. s. shall be scourged : s. not
Nu. 5 : 13. If no witness ag-t h. +
30. sh. execute upon h. this law
12 : 13. Moses cried, Heal h., O G.
30 : 5. if h. father disallow h., the
Lord shall forgive h. (3), 8, 12.
7. if h. husband held his peace at
h., 11 (2), 14 (2). [stand ag. h.
9. every vow of h. divorced shall
De. 20 : 7 he die, another take h. (2)
21 : 11 wouldest have h. to wife (2)
14. if no delight in h. let h. go;
not sell h., bec. humbled h. (5)
22 : 13. If a man take a wife and
hate h. (2) + [h. (4)
14. and bring an evil name upon
16. I gave my dau-r, he hateth h.
17. occasions of speech ag. h., 14.
19. not put h. away all his days, 29.
21. s. hath wrought folly in Isr.
27. found h., was none to save h.
29. his wife bec. he humbled h.(3)
24 : 1. found unclean-s in h. (4) +
3. if latter husband hate h. (4)
4 former husb. may not take h.(2)
25 : 5. husband's bro. sh. take h. (3)
8. If he say, I like not to take h.
12. Then thine eye sh. not pity h.
Jos. 6 : 17. Rahab shall live, s. and
all with h., bec. s. hid. 25.[day
25. s. dwelleth in Israel unto this
Ju. 4 : 5. Israel to h. for judgm-t +
18. s. covered him with a mantle
5 : 24. blessed sh. s. be above wom.
25. He asked water; s. gave him
milk (2) + [nor dau-r +
11 : 34. beside h. he had neith. son
39. father did with h. acc. to vow
13 : 9. Manoah, husb., not with h.
13. Of all I said, let h. beware [(3)
14. nei. let h. drink wine or strong
14 : 3. Get h. for me, s. pleas-h, 2, 7.
17. told h. bec. s. lay sore upon h.
15 : 2. I thought thou hatedst h.(4)
6. Philistines burnt h. and father
16 : 8. to h. 7 withs, s. bound him +
16. s. pressed him daily with words
17. he told h. all his heart (2), 18.
19. s. began to afflict him (4)
19 : 3. husband went after h. (3) +
25. man brought h. unto them (4)
20 : 6. I cut h. in p eces, 19 : 29.
Ru. 1 : 18. minded to go with h. +
2 : 14. s. sat beside reapers (3) +
3 : 6. acc-g to all h. mother bade h.
16. told h. all man had done to h.
1 S. 1:6. adversary provoked h.(2), 7.
10. s. in bitterness of soul wept, 7.
4 : 19. for h. pains came upon h.
18 : 21. that s. be a snare to him
25 : 42. Abigail with damsels aft. h.
2 S. 3 : 16. husb. weeping behind h.
13 : 1. fair sister; Amnon loved h.
14. stronger than s., forced h. +
1 K. 2 : 19. s. sat on his right hand
3 : 17. I was delivered of a child
with h. + [child, 26.
27. king said, Give h. the living
10 : 1. s. came to prove Solomon +
3. not any thing which he told h.
not (2), 2 Ch. 9 : 1 (2). + [gold
10 s. gave the king 120 talents of
2 K. 4 : 5. s. shut door upon h. (2) +
12. had called h., s. stood bef. him,
14. What is to be done for h.?[15.
27. Let h. alone, h. soul vexed (2)
9 : 30. s. painted h. face + [wall
33. Throw h. down; h. blood on
34. cursed woman, bury h.: s. is
king's daughter, 35 (2). [wi. h.
22 : 14. Huldah, they communed
2 Ch. 23 : 14. Slay h. not in house of
15. laid hands on h., slew h.[L.(3)

Es. 2 : 1. what was decreed ag-t **h.**
7. **s.** had nei. fath. nor mother +
17. made **h.** queen instead of Vas.
4 : 4. Esther's maids told it **h.** +
5. Hatach appointed to attend **h.**
5 : 12. am I invited unto **h.** wi. king
8 : 1. E. told what Mord. was unto **h.**
Jb. 31 : 10. let others bow upon **h.**
Ps. 45 : 14. **s.** sh. be bro-t unto King
46 : 5. God is in midst of **h.**, **s.** (3)
68 : †14. Almi. scattered kings for **h.**
80 : 11. **s.** sent boughs unto the sea
12. all they wh. pass do pluck **h.**
87 : 5. This man was born in **h.** (2)
Pr. 1 : 21. **s.** crieth in chief place of concourse (2), 20.–8 : 2, 3.–9 : 1.
2 : 4. If thou seekest **h.** as silver (2)
19. None that go unto **h.** return
3 : 15. **s.** more precious than rubies
18. happy ev. one retaineth **h.** (2)
4 : 6. Forsake **h.** not; love **h.** ⌈**h.** (2)
8. honour, when thou dost embr.
13. Let **h.** not go; for **s.** is thy life
5 : 8. Remove thy way far from **h.**
19. Let **h.** be as the loving hind
6 : 25. nei. let **h.** take thee wi. eyelids
29. whoso. toucheth **h.** not be inno.
7 : 11. **s.** is loud and stubborn +
13. So **s.** caught him, kissed him
21. flatter-g of lips **s.** forced him (2)
26. many strong been slain by **h.**
9 : 1. **s.** hath hewn seven pillars +
2. **s.** hath mingled **h.** wine (3)
14. **s.** sitteth at door of **h.** house
16. **s.** saith, Stolen waters sweet
17 : 25. bitterness to **h.** that bare
23 : 28. **s.** lieth in wait as for prey
27 : 16. hideth **h.** hideth the wind
31 : 11. husb. doth safely trust in **h.**
12. **s.** will do him good, not evil +
31. **h.** works praise **h.** in gates (2)
Ec. 7 : 26. sinner be taken by **h.** (2)
Can. 6 : 9. choice one of **h.** that bare
10. Who is **s.** fair as morn ⌊**h.** (7)
8 : 9. will build upon **h.** palace (2)
Is. 9 : 1. did afflict **h.** by way of sea
23 : 3. and **s.** is a mart of nations
7. own feet shall carry **h.** afar off
27 : 2. sing ye unto **h.** of red wine
29 : 7. that distress **h.** be as dream
30 : †7. I cried to **h.**, Their strength
51 : 18. There is none to guide her (2)
52 : 11. go ye out of midst of **h.**; be clean, Je. 51 : 45. ⌈is in **h.**
62 : †4. shalt be called, My delight
66 : 10. be glad with **h.** ye that love
12. will extend peace to **h.** ⌊**h.** (4)
Je. 2 : 24 that seek **h.**, not weary (3)
3 : 1. wife, shall he return unto **h.**?
6 : 3. shepherds sh. come unto **h.**
3. against **h.**, 4.–12 : 9.–46 : 22.–49 : 14.–50 : 3, 9, 15, 26.–51 : 2, 27, 28.
6. in the midst of **h.**, 46 : 21.–50 : 37.–51 : 47. Eze. 24 : 7.
7. violence and spoil is heard in **h.**
8 : 19. Zion? is not her king in **h.**?
44 : 19. cakes to worship **h.** (4) 18.
48 : 19. ask **h.** that escapeth ⌈44 (2).
49 : 19. make him run fr. **h.** (2), 50:
50 : 12. **s.** that bare you be ashamed
14. shoot at **h.**, spare no ⌈(3), 29 (2).
15. as **s.** hath done, do unto **h.**,
26. Cast **h.** up as heaps, and (4)
51 : 2. fanners that shall fan **h.** +
9. **s.** is not healed; forsake **h.**
33. Baby-n; it is time to thresh **h.**
64. shall not rise fr. evil upon **h.**
La. 1 : 1. how is **s.** become as widow!
2. none to comfort **h.**, 17. ⌊(3) +
2 : 16. We have swallowed **h.** up
4 : 6. and no hands stayed on **h.** ⌈**h.**
Eze. 16 : 49. abundance of idleness in
19 : 2. **s.** lay down among lions +
22 : 10. in thee they humbled **h.** +
23 : 5. harlot, when **s.** was mine (2) +
17. Babylonians came to **h.** (2) ⌈**h.**
18. my mind was alienated from

Eze. 24 : 12. scum went not out of **h.**
26 : 4. I will scrape dust fr. **h.** (2)
28 : 23. I send into **h.** pestilence (3)
30 : 18. as for **h.**, cloud cover **h.** (3)
32 : 16. the nations shall lament **h.** (3), 18. ⌈wife, nei. +
Ho. 2 : 2. plead: for **s.** is not my
3. Lest I strip **h.** naked, set **h.** (5) +
8 **s.** did not know I gave **h.** corn
14. I will speak comfortably unto
3 : 2. I bought her for 15 pieces ⌊**h.**
4 : 19. wind hath bound **h.** up in
9 : 2. new wine sh. fail in **h.** ⌊wings
Jo. 3 : 17. no strangers pass thro. **h.**
Am. 4 : 3. every cow at that bef. **h.**
5 : 2. there is none to raise **h.** up
Ob. 1. let us rise against **h.** in battle
Mi. 1 : 13. **s.** the beginning of sin to Z.
4 : 7. make **h.** that was cast off a strong nation (2), 6 (3). Zph. 3 : 19.
11. that say, Let **h.** be defiled, and
7 : 5. fr. **h.** that lieth in thy bosom
10. shame sh. cover **h.** which said
Na. 2 : 7. lead **h.** as wi. voice of doves
3 : 7. Nineveh, who bemoan **h.**?
Zph. 3 : 1. Woe to **h.** that is filthy
2. **s.** drew not near to **h.** God (4)
Zch. 2 : 5. I will be unto **h.** wall of
8 : 2. I was jealous for **h.** ⌊fire (2)
Mat. 1 : 6. David begat Sol. of **h.** that
20. th. conceived in **h.** is of H. Gh.
25. knew **h.** not till **s.** bro-t forth
5 : 28. looketh to lust after **h.** (2)
31. give **h.** writing of divorcem-t, 9:
32. whoso, marry **h.** divorced ⌊19.
8 : 15. touched hand, fever left **h.**, Mk. 1 : 31 (3). Lu. 4 : 39 (2). ⌈5 : 23.
9 : 18. lay hand upon **h.** **s.** sh., Mk.
12 : 42. **s.** came from utterm-t parts
14 : 4. It is not lawful to have **h.** +
7. an oath to give **h.** whatsoever **s.** would ask, 9. Mk. 6 : 23, 26.
15 : 23. Send **h.** away; for **s.** crieth after us + ⌈put **h.** away?
19 : 7. why did Moses command to
21 : 2. find an ass and colt with **h.**
22 : 28. whose wife shall **s.** be? all had **h.**, Mk. 12 : 21, 22, 23. Lu. 20 : 30, 31, 33. ⌈Mk. 14 : 9.
26 : 13. th s be for a memorial of **h.**,
Mk. 1 : 30. sick; they tell him of **h.**, Lu.
5 : 26. spent all that **s.** had ⌊4 : 38.
42. damsel walked: **s.** was of 12 yrs.
6 : 17. Philip's wife; he married **h.**
7 : 30. **s.** found the devil gone out
12 : 44. **s.** cast in all **s.** had, Lu. 21 : 4.
14 : 3. **s.** brake the box, poured it
5. And they murmured against **h.**
6. why trouble ye **h.**? (2) Jn. 12 : 7.
8. **s.** hath done what **s.** could ⌈**h.**
16 : 11. alive, and had been seen of
Lu. 1 : 29. **s.** was troubled at saying
36. this is 6th month with **h.** ⌊38.
45. blessed is **s.** that believed (2)
56. Mary abode with **h.** 3 months
58. neighbours rejoiced with **h.** (2)
2 : 38. **s.** was of great age, and ⌈**h.**
7 : 12. **s.** a widow, much people with
13. Lord had compassion on **h.** (3)
44. **s.** washed my feet with tears
47. sins forgiven; **s.** loved much
8 : 42. only daugh.; **s.** lay a dying
47. **s.** came trembling, declared (4)
52. all wept, and bewailed **h.**; he said, **s.** is not dead, 53, 55. ⌈sat
10 : 39 **s.** had a sister Mary which
40. Lord, bid **h.** that **s.** help me
42. good part not be taken from **h.**
13 : 12. Jesus saw **h.**, called **h.** to
13. laid his hands on **h.** ⌊him (3)
Jn. 4 : 27. or, Why talkest with **h.**?
8 : 3. when they had set **h.** in midst
7. let him first cast the stone at **h.**
11 : 20. **s.** heard Jes. was coming +
31. Jes. with **h.**, comforted **h.** (3)
33. When Jesus saw **h.** weeping (2)
19 : 27. that hour disciple took **h.**

Jn. 20 : 11. as **s.** wept **s.** stooped do. +
12. say unto **h.**, why weepest +
Ac. 5 : 10. found **h.** dead, buried **h.** (3)
9 : 37. laid **h.** in an upper chamber
40. when **s.** saw Peter, **s.** sat up (3)
41. called saints, presented **h.** al.
Ro. 16 : 2. receive **h.** in the Lord, assist **h.**; **s.** a succourer of many
1 Co. 7 : 11. But and if **s.** depart +
28. if virgin marry **s.** hath not sin.
36. if **s.** pass the flower of **h.** age
11 : 6. not covered, let **h.** be shorn (2)
15. long hair, it is a glory to **h.** (2)
13 : 5. Charity seeketh not **h.** own
Re. 2 : 21. I gave **h.** space to repent
22. I will cast **h.** into a bed (2)
12 : 2. **s.** being with child, cried
5. **s.** brought forth a man child
6. should feed **h.** there 1260 days
15. **h.** to be carried away of flood
17 : 6. when I saw **h.** I wondered ⌊7.
16. shall make **h.** desolate, burn **h.**
18 : 3. committed fornication wi. **h.**
4. voice saying, Come out of **h.**
6. Reward **h.** as she rewarded (3)
7. so much torm-t, sorrow give **h.**
9. kings who lived deliciously wi. **h.** sh. bewail **h.**, lament for **h.**
11. merchants sh. mourn over **h.**
20. God hath avenged you on **h.** (2)
24. in **h.** found blood of prophets
19 : 8. to **h.** granted th. **s.** be arrayed

See **LAY with, LIE with, LIETH with, She SAID.**

Said or Saith to or unto HER. ⌈tress

Ge. 16 : 9. angel – **h.**, Return to mis-
10. angel – **h.**, I multiply thy seed
11. angel – **h.**, Thou art with child
20 : 13. I – **h.**, This is thy kindness
Ex. 2 : 8. Pha-h's daughter – **h.**, Go
9. Pha-h's dau. – **h.**, Take child
Jos. 2 : 17. men – **h.**, We be blamel.
Ju. 4 : 8. Barak – **h.**, If go with me
19. Sisera – **h.**, Give me water, 20.
13 : 3. angel – **h.**, Thou art barren
14 : 16. Samson – **h.**, I not told fa.
16 : 5. Philistines – **h.**, Entice him
7. Samson – **h.**, If they bind me, 11.
13. he – **h.**, If thou weavest 7 locks
17. he – **h.**, not a razor upon head
19 : 28. he – **h.**, Up, let us be going
Ru. 1 : 10. – **h.**, We return with thee
2 : 14. Boaz – **h.**, At mealtime come
19. – **h.**, Where gleaned to day? ⌊20.
3 : 5. – **h.**, All thou sayest I will do
1 S. 1 : 8. – **h.**, Hannah, why weep-t
4 : 20. women by **h.** – **h.**, Fear not; **s.**
28 : 13. king – **h.**, Be not afraid
14. Saul – **h.**, What form is he of?
2 S 13 : 11. he – **h.**, lie with me (2) +
20. Abs. – **h.**, Amnon been wi. thee
14 : 2. Joab – **h.**, feign thys. mourner
5. king – **h.**, What aileth, 2K. 6 : 28
1 K. 2 : 20. king – **h.**, Ask on, moth.
17 : 13. Elijah – **h.**, Fear not, do as
2 K. 4 : 2. Elisha – **h.**, What sh. I do +
6 : 29. I – **h.** next day, Give thy son
Es. 5 : 3. king – **h.**, What wilt, Esth.
Eze. 23 : 43 I – **h.** old in adulteries
Ho. 3 : 3. I – **h.**, Thou shalt abide
Mat. 15 : 28. Jesus – **h.**, Great is thy
20 : 21. – **h.**, What wilt thou ⌊faith
Mk. 5 : 34. he – **h.**, thy faith saved
41. he – **h.**, Damsel (I say), arise
7 : 27. Jes. – **h.**, Let chil. be filled 29.
Lu. 1 : 30. angel – **h.**, Fear not, Mary
35. angel – **h.**, H. Ghost sh. come
61. they – **h.**, is none by this name
7 : 13. the Lord – **h.**, Weep not ⌈en
48. and he – **h.**, Thy sins are forgiv-
8 : 48. he – **h.**, be of good comfort
10 : 41. Jes. – **h.**, thou art carefu.
13 : 12. he – **h.**, thou art loosed (3)
Jn. 4 : 7. – **h.**, Give me to drink +
8 : 11. Jes. – **h.**, Nei. do I condemn
20 : 15. Jesus – **h.**, why weepest +

Ac. 5 : 9. Peter - h., How is it ye
12 : 15. they - h., Thou art mad
Ro. 9 : 12. it was - h., The elder sh.
See **WENT in unto**, TOLD,
WIFE, WITHIN, WOMAN, ZION.

HERALD. [you
Da. 3 : 4. Then a h. cried aloud, To

HERB. [12.
Ge. 1 : 11. Let earth bring forth h.,
29. given you ev. h. bearing seed,
2 : 5. made every h. bef. it grew[30.
3 : 18. thou shalt eat the h. of field
9 : 3. as h. have I given you all
Ex. 9 : 25. hail smote every h., 22.
10 : 15. locusts did eat every h., 12.
De. 29 : † 18. beareth poisonful h.
32 : 2. as small rain upon tender h.
2 K. 19 : 26. they were as the green
h., as corn blasted, Is. 37 : 27.
Jb. 8 : 12. flag withereth before any h.
38 : 27. to cause bud of h. to spring
Ps. 37 : 2. they sh. wither as green h.
104 : 14. grass for cattle, h. for man
Is. 66 : 14. your bones shall flourish

HERBS. [like an h.
Ex. 10 : 15. not any green thing in h.
12 : 8. with bitter h. eat, Nu. 9 : 11.
De. 11 : 10. wateredst as garden of h.
1 K. 21 : 2. have it for garden of h.
2 K. 4 : 39. one went out to gather h.
Ps. 105 : 35. And did eat up all the h.
Pr. 15 : 17. Better is a dinner of h.
27 : 25. h. of mount-s are gathered
Is. 18 : 4. like a clear heat upon h.
26 : 19. thy dew is as the dew of h.
42 : 15. I will dry up all their h.
Je. 12 : 4. How long shall h. wither
Mat. 13 : 32. greatest amo. h., Mk. 4:
Lu. 11 : 42. tithe all manner of h.[32.
Ro. 14 : 2. ano. who is weak eateth h.
He. 6 : 7. bringeth forth h. meet for

HERD, S. [calf
Ge. 18 : 7. Abr. ran unto h. fetched
47 : 17. gave bread in exchange for
18. my lord also hath our h-s[h-s
Le. 1 : 2. bring your offering of the
3. If his offering be of h., 3 : 1.[h.
27 : 32. conc-g tithe of h. or flock
Nu. 15 : 3. sweet savour unto L. of h.
De. 12 : 21. thou shalt kill of thy h.
15 : 19. firstling males of h. sanctify
16 : 2. sacrifice unto Lord of the h.
1 S. 11 : 5. Saul came after the h.[h.
2 S. 12 : 4. spared to take of his own
1 Ch. 27 : 29. over h-s in Sharon, h-s
Is. 65 : 10. Achor a place for the h-s
Je. 31 : 12. flow tog. for young of h.
Jo. 1 : 18. h-s of cattle are perplexed
Jon. 3 : 7. Let not h. taste any thing
Ha. 3 : 17. shall be no h. in the stalls
Mat. 8 : 30. a h. of swine feeding,
Mk. 5 : 11. Lu. 8 : 32. [swine
31. suffer us to go into the h. of
32. whole h. ran violently into
the sea (2), Mk. 5 : 13. Lu. 8 : 33.
See **FLOCKS with herds.**

HERDMAN. [h.
Am. 7 : 14. I was no prophet, but a

HERDMEN.
Ge. 13 : 7. strife betw-n h. of Abr.'s
cattle and h. of Lot's [thy h.
8. Let be no strife betw. my h. and
26 : 20. h. of G. did strive wi. Isaac's
1 S. 21 : 7. Doeg the chiefest of h.[h.
Am. 1 : 1. Amos was among h. of

HERE. [Tekoa
Ge. 16 : 13. Have I h. looked aft. him
19 : 12. Hast thou h. any besides [15.
21 : 23. Now swear unto me h. by G.
31 : 37. set it h. before my brethren
40 : 15. h. also have I done nothing
42 : 33. leave one of your brethren
47 : 23. lo, h. is seed for you, sow[h.
Ex. 24 : 14. Tarry ye h. for us until
33 : 16. wherein be known h. that
Nu. 14 : 40. Lo, we be h. and will go
22 : 8. Lodge h. this night, 19. [up
Nu. 23 : 1. Build h. altars, prepare h.,
32 : 16. will build sheepfolds h.[29
De. 5 : 3. who are all of us h. alive
12 : 8. after all the things we do h.
29 : 15. covenant with him that
standeth h., and him not h.
Jos. 18 : 6. I may cast lots for you h.,
Ju. 4 : 20. Is there any man h.? [8.
18 : 3. what hast h.? | 19 : 9. lodge h.
19 : 24. h. is my daugh., a maiden
20 : 7. give h. your advice, counsel
1 S. 1 : 26. I am the woman stood h.
9 : 8. I have h. part of shekel of sil-
11. and said, Is the seer h.? [ver
14 : 34. ox, sheep, slay h. and eat
16 : 11. Jesse, Are h. all thy child-n
21 : 8. is not h. a spear or sword?
9. sword of Goliath; it is h. (2)
23 : 3. Behold, we be afraid h. in Jud.
29 : 3. What do these Hebrews h.?
2 S. 20 : 4. Amasa, be thou h. present
24 : 22. behold, h. be oxen for sacrif.
1 K. 2 : 30. Nay; but I will die h.
18 : 8. tell thy lord, Elijah is h., 11, 14
19 : 9. Wh. doest h. Elijah? 13.
20 : 40. as serv-t, busy h. and there
22 : 7. Is there not h. a prophet of
the Lord, 2 K. 3 : 11. 2 Ch. 18 : 6.
2 K. 3 : 11. h. is Elisha | 7 : 3. Why sit we
7 : 4. leprous said, if we sit h. [h.
10 : 23. be h. none of servants of L.
1 Ch. 29 : 17. seen with joy people h.
Jb. 38 : 11. h. shall thy proud waves
35. lightnings may say, h. we are?
Ps. 132 : 14. my rest; h. will I dwell
Is. 21 : 9. h. cometh chariot of men
22 : 16. What hast h., whom h. (3)
28 : 10. h. a little, there a little, 13.
52 : 5. Now, what have I h., saith L.
Eze. 8 : 6. Israel committeth h., 17.
Ho. 7 : 9. gray hairs are h. and there
Mat. 12 : 41. a greater than Jonas is
h., Lu. 11 : 32. [Lu. 11 : 31.
42. a greater than Solomon is h.,
Mat. 14 : 8. Give me h. John B.'s head
17. h. but five loaves [Lu. 9 : 27.
16 : 28. some standing h., Mk. 9 : 1.
17 : 4. L., it is good for us to be h.: let
us make h., Mk. 9 : 5. Lu. 9 : 33.
24 : 2. shall not be left h. one stone
23. Lo, h. is Christ, Mk. 13 : 21.
26 : 36. Sit ye h. while I go and
pray yonder, Mk. 14 : 32.
28 : 6. He is not h., Mk. 16 : 6. Lu.
Mk. 6 : 3. are not his sisters h.? [24 : 6.
8 : 4. with bread h. in wilderness?
13 : 1. see what buildings are h.!
Lu. 4 : 23. do also h. in thy country
9 : 12. we are h. in a desert place
17 : 21. Nei. say, Lo h. or lo there!
23. say to you, See h. or see there
19 : 20. behold, h. is thy pound
22 : 38. Lord, h. are two swords
24 : 41. said, Have ye h. any meat?
Jn. 6 : 9. There is a lad h. which
11 : 21. L., if thou hadst been h., 32.
Ac. 8 : 36. h. is water | 9 : 10. I am h.,
9 : 14. h. he hath authority [L.
10 : 33. are we all h. before God[h.
16 : 28. Do thyself no harm, we are
24 : 19. Who ought to have been h.
20. let these h. say if they found
25 : 24. king Agrippa and all h. (2)
Col. 4 : 9. make known things done h.
He. 7 : 8. h. men that die receive
13 : 14. h. have we no contin-g city
Ja. 2 : 3. Sit h. in good pls., or sit h.
1 Pe. 1 : 17. your sojourning h. in fear
Re. 13 : 10. h. is patience of saints,
18. h. is wisdom; let him[14 : 12.
14 : 12. h. are they that kept com-ts
17 : 9. h. is mind which hath wis-
See ABIDE, SIT, TARRY. [dom
See **STAND here.**

HEREAFTER.
Is. 41 : 23. shew things to come h.
Eze. 20 : 39. Go, serve ye idols, h.
Da. 2 : 29. what come to pass h., 45.
Mat. 26 : 64. h. sh. ye see Son of man
Mk. 11 : 14. No man eat of thee h.
Lu. 22 : 69. h. shall Son of man sit
Jn. 1 : 51. h. ye sh. see heaven op-d
13 : 7. knowest not now, sh. know h.
14 : 30. h. I not talk much with you
1 Ti. 1 : 16. to them which h. believe
Re. 1 : 19. Write things shall be h.
4 : 1. I will shew things must be h.
9 : 12. there come two woes more h.

HEREBY.
Ge. 42 : 15. h. ye shall be proved
33. h. shall I know ye are true
Nu. 16 : 28. h. know Lord sent me
Jos. 3 : 10. h. know God is amo you
1 Co. 4 : 4. yet am I not h. justified
1 Jn. 2 : 3. h. do know we know him
5. h. know we that we are in him
3 : 16. h. perceive we love of God
19. h. know we are of the truth
24. h. we know he abideth in us
4 : 2. h. know ye the Spirit of God
6. h. know we the spirit of truth
13. h. know we that we dwell in

HEREIN. [him
Ge. 34 : 22. only h. will men consent
2 Ch. 16 : 9. h. hast done foolishly
Jn. 4 : 37. h. is that saying true, One
9 : 30. h. is a marvellous thing
15 : 8. h. is my Father glorified [to
Ac. 24 : 16. h. do I exercise myself
2 Co. 8 : 10. h. I give my advice[lov.
1 Jn. 4 : 10. h. is love, not that we
17. h. is our love made perfect

HEREOF.
Mat. 9 : 26. fame h. went abroad
He. 5 : 3. by reason h. he ought to

HE'RES. [offer
Ju. 1 : 35. Amorites would dwell in H.

HE'RESH. [Galal
1 Ch. 9 : 15. of the Levites; H. and

HERESY, IES.
Ac. 24 : 14. after the way they call h.
1 Co. 11 : 19. must be h-s amo. you
Ga. 5 : 20. works of flesh, wrath, h-s
2 Pe. 2 : 1. who bring in damnable h-s

HERETIC. [tion
Tit. 3 : 10. a h. after second admoni-

HERETOFORE. [h.
Ex. 4 : 10. I am not eloquent. neith.
5 : 7. no straw to make brick as h.
8. bricks which they did make h.
14. task in making brick as h.?
Jos. 3 : 4. ye not passed this way h.
Ru. 2 : 11. peo. thou knewest not h.
1 S. 4 : 7. not been such a thing h.
2 Co. 13 : 2. I write to them wh. h.

HEREUNTO. [sinned
Ec. 2 : 25. who else can hasten h.?
1 Pe. 2 : 21. even h. were ye called

HEREWITH. [h.
Eze. 16 : 29. thou wast not satisfied
Mal. 3 : 10. prove me now h., saith L.

HERITAGE, S.
Ex. 6 : 8. land, I will give it for h.
Jb. 20 : 29. h. appointed unto him
27 : 13. h. of oppressors they receive
Ps. 16 : 6. yea, I have a goodly h.
61 : 5. given me h. of those fear thy
94 : 5. They afflict thine h. [name
111 : 6. given them h. of heathen
119 : 111. Thy testimonies as an h.
127 : 3. Lo, chil. are an h. of the L.
135 : 12. Who gave their land for a
h. unto Israel (2), 136 : 21, 22.
Is. 49 : 8. to inherit desolate h-s[L.
54 : 17. This is h. of servants of the
58 : 14. feed thee with h. of Jacob
Je. 2 : 7. made mine h. abomination
3 : 19. How shall I give thee a good-
12 : 7. I have left mine h. [ly h.
8. Mine h. is as a lion [led bird
9. Mine h. is unto me as a speck-
15. I will bring ev. man to his h.
17 : 4. shalt discontinue fr. thine h.
50 : 11. O ye destroyers of mine h.

2 Ch.29 :20. H. gathered rulers | 18.
27. H. commanded to offer b. off-g
30. H. commanded to sing praises
31. H. said, Now bring sacrifices
36 H. rejoiced that G. prepared p.
30 : 1. 11. sent to all Israel. Judah
18. H. prayed, The L. pardon ev.
20. Lord hearkened to H. [one
22. H. spake comfortably unto all
24. H. did give to cong. 1,000 bul-
31 : 2. H. appointed courses [locks
8. when H. saw heaps, blessed God
9. H. questioned with priests cone.
11. H. commanded to prep cham-
13. overseers at com-t of H. [bers
20. thus did H. thro-t all Judah
32 : 8. peo. rested upon words of H.
9. Sennach-b send serv-ts unto H.
11. Doth not H. persuade you to d.
16. servants spake ag. Lord and H.
17. sh. not God of H. deliver peo-
20. for this cause H. prayed [ple
22. Lord saved H. fr. Sennacherib
23. And many bro-t presents to H.
25. H. rendered not acc. to benefit
26. H. humbled hims. for pride (2)
27. H. had exceeding much riches
30. This same H. stopped watercourse. H. prospered in works
Ezr. 2 : 16. The children of Ater of
H. 98, Ne. 7 : 21. [of H. copied
Pr. 25 : 1. proverbs of Sol. wh men
Is. 1 : 1. vision of Isaiah in days of H.
36 : 18. Beware lest H. persuade you
38 : 2. H. turned his face tow. wall
39 : 1. writing of H. when recovered
Je. 15 : 4. bec. of Manasseh son of H.
26 : 18. Micah prophesied in the
days of H., saying, Mi. 1 : 1. [d.
19. H. and all Judah put Micah to
Ho 1 : 1. word to Hosea in days of H.
Mat. 1:9. Achaz begat E. | 10. E. begat

HE'ZION.

1 K 15 : 18. son of H. king of Syria

HA'ZIR. [H.

1 Ch. 24 : 15. lot; came forth. 17th to
Ne. 10 : 20. those th. sealed were H.

HEZ'RAI[1] or **HEZ'RO.**[2]

2 S. 23 : 35. H.[1], Carmelite, 1 Ch. 11:

HEZ'RON. [Place.] [37.[2] †

Jos. 15 : 3. Judah, border passed to
25. cities of Judah, H., wh is [H.

HEZ'RON, ITES.

Ge. 46 : 9. the sons of Reuben; H.,
Carmi, Ex. 6 : 14. 1 Ch. 5 : 3.
12. sons of Pharez H., Hamul, Ru.
4 : 18. 1 Ch. 2 : 5.-4 : 1. [21.
Nu. 26 : 6. Of H., family of the H-s,
Ru. 4 : 19. H. begat Ram, Ram begat
1 Ch. 2 : 9. sons of H Ram, Chelubai
18. Caleb son of H. begat chil. of
21. H. went in to dau-r of Machir
24. after H. was dead, Abiah. H.'s
wife, bare him Ashur [of H.
25. sons of Jerahmeel, firstborn

HID. [thems.

Ge. 3 : 8. and Adam and his wife h.
10. I was naked and I h. myself
35 : 4. Jacob h. them under oak
Ex. 2 : 2. she h. Moses three months
12. Moses slew Egyptian, h. him
3 : 6. Moses h. his face, was afraid
Jos. 2 : 4. Rahab took men, h. th. ,6.
6 : 17. bec. she h. messengers. 25.
10 : 16. five kings h. thems. in cave
Ju. 9 : 5 Jotham was left; h. hims.
1 S. 3 : 18. Sam-l told Eli, h. nothing
10 : 22. he hath h. hims. amo. stuff
14 : 11. out of holes where h. thems.
22. men which h. thems. in mt. E.
20 : 24. David h. himself in the field
1 K. 18 : 4. Obadiah h. 100 proph-s, 13.
2 K. 4 : 27. Lord hath h. it from me
6 : 29. Give thy son; she h. her son
7 : 8. lepers carried gold, h. it (2)
11 : 2. h. him and nurse, 2 Ch. 22 : 11.
Jb. 3 : 10. nor h. sorrow fr mine eyes
Jb. 10 : 13. these h. in thine heart
17 : 4. h. their heart from underst-g
23 : † 12. I have h. words of his mou.
Ps. 9 : 15. in net they h. is own foot
35 : 7. have h. from me their net
8. let net he hath h. catch himself
55 : 12. would have h. myself fr. him
119 : 11. word ha. I h. in mine heart
140 : 5. proud have h. snare for me
Is. 28 : 15 under falsehood h. ours.
49 : 2 in shadow of his hand hath
h. me; in his quiver he h. me
53 : 3. we h. our faces from him [he
57 : 17. I h. me and was wroth, and
65 : 16. bec. they are h. fr. mine eyes
Je. 13 : 5. So I h. it by Euphrates
7. I took girdle from where I h. it
18 : 22. have h. snares for my feet
36 : 26. Baruch, Jeremiah, Lord h.
43 : 10. throne upon stones I ha. h.
Eze. 22 : 26. h. their eyes fr. sabb-hs
Mat. 11 : 25. because thou hast h.
these things fr wise, Lu. 10 : 21.
13 : 33. h. in 3 measures, Lu. 13 :
25 : 18. he h. his lord's money [21.
25. I h. thy talent in the earth
Lu. 1 : 24. Elisabeth h. herself five
See **Hide** or **Hid FACE.** [m.

HID
himself or **themselves.**

Ge. 3 : 8. Adam and wife h. t. fr. God
Jos. 10 : 16. these kings h. t. in cave
Ju. 9 : 5. Jotham was left, he h. h.
1 S. 10 : 22. Saul h. h. | 20 : 24. Da. h.
14 : 11. out of holes where h. t. [h.
22. men wh. h. t. in m-t Ephraim
1 Ch. 21 : 20. Ornan and 4 sons h. t.
Jb. 29 : 8. young men saw me, h. t.
Jn. 8 : 59. Jesus h. h. and went out
Re. 6 : 15. kings and great men h. t.

HID. [Passive.]

De. 33 : 19. suck of treas. h. in sand
Jos. 7 : 21. they are h. in my tent
22. behold, it was h. in his tent
10 : 17. kings are found h. in cave, 27.
2 S. 17 : 9. he is h. now in some pit
18 : 13. no matter h. from king, 1
K. 10 : 3. 2 Ch. 9 : 2. [12.
2 K. 11 : 3. h. in house of G., 2 Ch. 22:
2 Ch. 22 : 9. Ahaziah was h. in Sama.
Jb. 3 : 21. dig more than for h. treas.
23. Why light to man wh. way is
6 : 16. brooks, wh-n snow is h. [h.?
28 : 11. thing h. bringeth he forth
21. is h. from eyes of all living
29 : † 10. voice of nobles was h.
38 : 30. waters h. as with a stone
Ps. 17 : 14. belly fillest with h. treasure
19 : 6. nothing is h. from the heat
Pr. 2 : 4. searchest as for h. treasures
Is. 40 : 27. My way is h. from the L.
42 : 22. are h. in prison houses
65 : 16. they are h. from mine eyes
Je. 16 : 17. nor iniq. h. from mine eyes
32 : † 17. is nothing h. from thee
Ho. 13 : 12. sin of Ephraim is h.
Mat. 10 : 26. nothing h. that sh. not
be known, Mk. 4 : 22. Lu 8 : 17.
13 : 44. like treas. h. in field [-12 : 2.
Lu. 9 : 45. this saying was h., 18 : 34.
19 : 42. they are h. fr. thine eyes
Ep. 3 : 9. fr. beginning been h. in G.
Col. 1 : 26. mystery been h. fr. ages
2 : 3. are h. all treasure of wisdom
3 : 3. your life is h. with C. in God
He. 11 : 23. By faith Moses was h.

Be HID.

Ge. 4 : 14. from thy face shall I b. h.
Le. 4 : 13. b. h. from assembly, 5 : 3, 4.
Nu. 5 : 13. it b. h. from her husb.
Jb. 5 : 21. b. h. from scourge of tong.
20 : 26. darkness shall b. h. in his
Is. 29 : 14. underst. of prudent b. h.
Ho. 13 : 14. repentance shall b. h.
Am. 9 : 3. tho. they b. h. from my sight
Na. 3 : 11. shalt be drunken, b. h.
Zph. 2 : 3. ye shall b. h. in the day
2 Co. 4 : 3. if gospel b. h., it is h. to

Cannot be or **Could not be HID.** [h.

Mat. 5 : 14. A city set on a hill c-t.
Mk. 7 : 24. into house; but he c-d. h.
1 Ti. 5 : 25. that are otherw. c-t. h.

Not HID. [h. it

Jb. 15 : 18. wise men told, have n.
Ps. 32 : 5. mine iniquity have I n. h.
38 : 9. my groaning is n. h. fr. thee
40 : 10. I have n. h. thy righteousn.
69 : 5. my sins are n. h. from thee
139 : 15. My substance was n. h.
Je. 16 : 17. they are n. h. fr. my face
Ho. 5 : 3. and Israel is n. h. from me
Lu. 8 : 47. woman saw she was n. h.

HID'DAI[1] or **HU'RAI.**[2]

2 S. 23 : 30. H.[1] of brooks of G., 1 Ch.

HID'DEKEL. [11 : 32.†

Ge 2 : 14. name of third river is H.
Da. 10 : 4. as I was by great river H.

HIDDEN.

Ex. 9 : † 32. wheat and rye were h.
Le. 5 : 2. h. fr. him, he shall be unel.
De. 30 : 11. it is not h. from thee
Jb. 3 : 16. as an h. untimely birth
15 : 20. number of years is h. to the
18 : † 10. The snare is h. for him
24 : 1. times are not h. from thee
Ps. 51 : 6. in h. part make know wisd.
83 : 3. consulted against thy h. ones
Pr. 28 : 12. wicked rise. a man is h.
Is. 45 : 3. I will give thee h. riches
48 : 6. I have shewed thee h. things
Je. 33 : †3 I will shew thee h. things
Ob. 6. how are h. things sought up!
Zch. 11 : † 16. not visit th. who be h.
Ac. 26 : 26. none of these h. fr. him
1 Co. 2 : 7. h. wisdom God ordained
4 : 5. to light h. things of darkn.
2 Co. 4 : 2. h. things of dishonesty
1 Pe. 3 : 4. be h. man of the heart
Re. 2 : 17. give to eat of h. manna

HIDE. [Noun.]

Le. 8 : 17. h. and flesh be burnt, 9 : 11.

HIDE. [Verb.]

Ge. 18 : 17. Sh. I h. from Ab. what I?
47 : 18. We will not h. it fr. my lord
Ex. 2 : 3. could not longer h. him
Le. 20 : 4. any ways h. their eyes
De. 22 : 1. go astray, and h., 4.
3. thou mayest not h. thyself
Jos. 2 : 16. and h. there three days
7 : 19. tell, h. it not from me
Ju. 6 : 11. to h. wheat from Midian.
1 S. 3 : 17. h. it not fr, 2 S. 14 : 18
19 : 2. abide in secret place, and h.
20 : 2. why father h. this from me?
5. me go, that I may h. in field
19. to pla. where thou didst h.
1 K. 17 : 3. h. by brook Cherith
22 : 25. chamber to h., 2 Ch. 18 : 24.
Jb. 13 : 20. I not h. myself from thee
14 : 13. O wouldest h. me in grave
20 : 12. tho. h. it under his tongue
33 : 17. and h. pride from man
40 : 13. h. them in the dust together
Ps. 17 : 8. h. me under thy wings
27 : 5. time of trouble he shall h. me
in tab. shall he h. me
30 : 7. didst h. face I was troubled
31 : 20. shalt h. them in thy presence
55 : 1. h. not from supplication
64 : 2. h. me from counsel of wicked
78 : 4. not h. them from children
89 : 46. How long, L., h. thyself?
119 : 19. h. not thy commandments
143 : 9. O L., I flee unto thee to h.
Pr. 2 : 1. h. my com-s with thee [me
Is. 1 : 15. I will h. my eyes from you
2 : 10. and h. thee in the dust
3 : 9. h. not sin | 16 : 3. h. outcasts
26 : 20. h. thyself for a moment
29 : 15. seek deep to h. their couns
58 : 7. h. not from thine own flesh
Je. 13 : 4. h. it in hole of the rock
6. girdle I commanded thee to h.

Je. 36:19. Go, h. thee, thou, and Jere.
38 : 14. I will ask h. noth. fr. me
25. h. it not | 43 : 9. h. them in
La. 3:56. h. not ear at my breathing
Eze. 28 : 3. is no secret they can h.
31 : 8. cedars could not h. him
39:29. neither h. my face any more
Ja. 5: 20. shall h. multitude of sins
Re. 6:16. h. us fr. him that sitteth
See FACE.

HIDE himself.

1 S. 23:19. Doth not Da. h. h.? 26:1.
Je. 23:24. any h. h. in secret pla ?
49 : 10. shall not be able to h. h.
Jn. 12:36. Jesus did h. h. from them

HIDE themselves.

De. 7:20. till they that h. t. be destr.
1 S. 13 : 6. people did h. t. in caves
2 K. 7 : 12. Syrians gone to h. t. in
Jb. 24 : 4. poor of the earth h. t.
34 : 22. workers of iniq. may h. t.
Ps. 56:6. they h. t. mark my steps
Pr. 28:28. When wicked rise, men h. t.
Da. 10 : 7. so that they fled to h. t.
Am. 9:3. they h. t. in top of Carmel

HIDEST.

Jb. 13: 24. Whf. h. face ? Ps. 44:24 -
Ps. 10:1. Why h. in trouble? [88:14.
104 : 29. h. thy face they troubled
Is. 45 : 15. art a G. that h. thyself

HIDETH.

1 S. 23 : 23. find places where he h.
Jb. 23:9. he h. hims. on right hand
34:29. wh. h. face who behold him
42 : 3. Who is he that h. counsel
Ps. 10:11. h. his face, will never see
139:12. darkness h. not from thee
Pr. 10:18. h. hatred with lying lips
19:24. slothful h. his hand, 26:15.
22:3. prudent man h. hims., 27:12.
27 : 16. Whosoever h. her h. wind
28:27. h. his eyes sh. have a curse
Is. 8 : 17. h. face from Jacob
Mat. 13 : 44. wh. a man hath found

HIDING. [he h.

Jb. 31:33. h. mine iniq. in my bosom
Ps. 32 : 7. art my h. place, 119:114.
Is. 28:17. waters overfl. the h. place
32:2. a man shall be as a h. place
Ha. 3 : 4. was the h. of his power

HI'EL.

1 K. 16 : 34. H. Bethelite built Jeri-

HIERAP'OLIS. [cho

Col. 4 : 13. them that are in H.

HIGGAI'ON.

Ps. 9 : 16. H. Selah | 92 : †4.

HIGH.

Ge. 29 : 7. Lo, it is yet h. day
Ex. 14:8. Isr. with h. hand, Nu. 33:3.
Nu. 11 : 31. quails as two cubits h.
De. 3 : 5. cities fenced with h. walls
12 : 2. served gods upon h. mts.
26 : 19. thee h. above all nations
28:43. stranger above thee very h.
52. till thy h. walls come down
32 : 27. lest say, Our hand is h.
1 K. 9 : 8. at this house wh. is h.
be aston. 2 Ch. 7 : 21. [degree
1 Ch. 17 : 17. estate of a man of h.
Ne. 3:25. tower out fr. king's h. hou.
Es. 5: 14. gallows 50 cubits h., 7:9.
Jb. 11 : 8. h. as heaven, what do ?
21 : 22. judgeth those that are h.
22: 12. behold the stars, how h.
38 : 15. h. arm shall be broken
41 : 34. He beholdeth all h. things
Ps. 18:27. wilt bring down h. looks
49 : 2. give ear : Both low and h.
62 : 9. men of h. degree are a lie
71:19. thy righte. O. G. is very h.
78:69. built sanct. like h. palaces
89 : 13. h. is thy right hand
97:9. thou, L. art h., 99:2.-113:4.
101 : 5. him that hath a h. look
103:11. as heav. is h. above earth
131:1. nor exercise in things too h.
138:6. Tho. L. be h. yet hath respect
Ps. 139 : 6. Such knowledge, it is h.
149:6. h. praises of G. be in mouth
150 : 5. on h. sounding cymbals
Pr. 18:11. h. wall in his own conceit
21:4. h. look, a proud heart, is sin
24:7. wisdom is too h. for a fool
Ec. 12:5. be afraid of that wh. is h.
Is. 2 : 13. day of L. upon cedars h.
14. upon all h. mountains and
6:1. upon throne h. and lifted up
10 : 12. punish glory of h. looks
33. h. ones shall be hewn down
24 : 21. punish h. ones on h.
25:12. h. fort shall he bring down
30 : 13. as a breach in a h. wall
52:13. my servant shall be very h.
57:15. thus saith h. and lofty One
Je. 17:12. A glorious h. throne from
31 : 21. waymarks, make h. heaps
49:16. tho. makest nest h. as eagle
51:58. her h. gates sh. be burned
Eze. 1 : 18. their rings were so h.
17:24. I have brought down h. tree
21 : 26. exalt low, abase him h.
31 : 3. Assyrian was of h. stature
34:14. I will feed them on h. mts.
41:22. The altar of wood 3 cubits h.
Da. 8 : 3. the two horns were h.
Ob. 3. whose habitation is h.
Zph. 1 : 16. of alarm ag. h. towers
Jn. 19 : 31. that sab. was a h. day
Ac. 13:17. with a h. arm brought he
Ro. 12 : 16. Mind not h. things
13 : 11. it is h. time to awake
2 Co. 10:5. casting down ev. h. thing
Ph. 3 : 14. prize of h. calling of G.
Re. 21 : 12. Jerus. had a wall h.
See GATE, GOD, HILL, HILLS.

Most HIGH.

Nu. 24 : 16. knowledge of the M. H.
De. 32 : 8. M. H. divided to nations
2 S. 22 : 14. M. H. uttered his voice
Ps. 7:17. will sing praise to name of
L. m. h., 9:2.-92:1. [moved
21:7. thro. mercy of M. H. not be
46 : 4. holy place of tab. of M. H.
47 : 2. the Lord m. h. is terrible
50:14. and pay thy vows to M. H.
56 : 2. that fight ag. me, O M. H.
57 : 2. I will cry unto God m. h.
73:11. is there knowledge in M. H.?
77:10. years of right hand of M. H.
78:17. by provoking the M. H., 56.
82 : 6. all of you chil. of M. H.
83 : 18. art M. H. over all earth
91 : 1. in secret place of M. H.
9. hast made M. H. thy habita.
92 : 8. But thou, Lord, art M. H.
107:11. contemned counsel of M. H.
Is. 14 : 14. I will be like the M H.
La. 3 : 35. turn before face of M. H.
38. out of M. H. proceed. not evil
Da. 4:17. M. H. ruleth in kingdom
24. this is decree of the M. H.
25. M. H. rules in kingd. of men, 32.
34. and I blessed the M. H.
7 : 18. saints of M. H. take kingd.
22. judgm. given to saints of M. H.
25. speak great words ag. M. H.
27. to people of saints of M. H.
Ho. 7 : 16. return, but not to M. H.
11 : 7. they called them to M. H.
Ac. 7:48. M. H. dwelleth not in temp.
See MOUNTAIN.

On HIGH.

Ex. 25:20. stretch wings o. h., 37:9.
39:31. lace of blue, to fasten it o. h.
De. 28 : 1. God will set thee o. h.
2 S. 22: 49. hast lifted me up o. h.
23:1. man who was raised up o. h.
1 K. 21:9. Naboth o. h. am. peo., 12.
2 K. 19 : 22. against whom hast lifted thine eyes o. h.? Is. 37 : 23.
1 Ch. 14:2. his kingd. was lifted o. h.
2 Ch. 20:19. stood up to praise G. o. h.
34 : 4. images o. h. he cut down
Jb. 5:11. set o. h. those th. be low
Jb. 16 : 19. and my record is o. h.
31:2. what inherit. of Al. from o. h.
39:18. she lifteth up herself o. h.
27. Doth eagle make her nest o. h.?
Ps. 7:7. for their sakes return o. h.
68 : 18. Thou hast ascended o. h.
69 : 29. O God, set me up o. h.
75:5. Lift not up your horn o. h.
91:14. I will set him o. h. bec. he
93:4. Lord o. h. is mightier than
107 : 41. setteth he the poor o. h.
113:5. Who like G. who dwell. o. h.
Is. 22 : 16. heweth out sepul. o. h.
24:18. windows from o. h. are open
21. punish host of high ones o. h.
26 : 5. bringeth down them o. h.
32 : 15. Spirit be poured from o. h.
33:5. dwelleth o. h. | 16. sh. dwell
40 : 26. Lift up your eyes o. h.
58:4. make your voice heard o. h.
Je. 25 : 30. L. shall roar from o. h.
Eze. 31:4. deep set him up o. h. [h.
Ha. 2:9. that he may set his nest o.
3:10. deep lifted up his hands o. h.
Lu. 1:78. day-spring from o. h. hath
24 : 49. endued with power fr. o. h.
Ep. 4:8. When he ascended up o. h.
He. 1:3. right hand of Majesty o. h.
See PLACE, S, PRIEST, TOWER.

HIGHER.

Nu. 24:7. king sh. be h. than Agag
1 S. 9:2. Saul h. than any of, 10:23.
2 K. 15 : 35. Jotham built h. gate
Ne. 4:13. on h. places, I set the peo.
Jb. 35:5. clouds, wh. are h. than thou
Ps. 61:2. lead me to rock that is h.
89:27. will make him h. than kings
Ec. 5 : 8. and there be h. than they
Is. 55 : 9. as heavens h. than earth
my ways h. than your ways
Je. 36 : 10. read Baruch in h. court
Eze. 9 : 2. came from way of h. gate
42 : 5. galleries were h. than these
43 : 13. this be h. place of altar
Da. 8 : 3. one horn h. h. came last
Lu. 14 : 10. say, Friend, go up h.
Ro. 13 : 1. be subject to h. powers
He. 7:26. h. priest h. than heavens

HIGHEST. [sepul.

2 Ch. 32 : † 33. buried Hez. in h. of
Ps. 18 : 13. the H. gave his voice
87 : 5. H. himself sh. establish her
Pr. 8 : 26. nor h. part of the dust
9 : 3. crieth upon h. places of city
Ec. 5 : 8. higher than h. regardeth
Eze. 17 : 3. took h. branch of cedar
22. will take of h. branch of cedar
41 : 7. from lowest chamber to h.
Mat. 21:9. Hosanna in h., Mk. 11:10.
Lu. 1 : 32. called Son of the H.
35. power of H. sh. overshadow
76. be called prophet of the H.
2:14. Glory to God in the h., 19:38.
6 : 35. ye shall be chil. of the H.
14:8. sit not down in the h. room
20:46. love h. seats in synagogues

HIGHLY.

Lu. 1:28. said, thou art h. favoured
16:15. wh. is h. esteemed am. men
Ac. 12:20. Herod was h. displeased
Ro. 12:3. not think of hims. more h.
Ph. 2 : 9. God hath h. exalted him
1 Th. 5:13. esteem them very h. in

HIGHMINDED. [love

Ro. 11 : 20. Be not h., 1 Ti. 6 : 17.
2 Ti. 3:4. Traitors, h. lovers of pleas.

HIGHNESS.

Jb. 31:23. his h. I could not endure
Is. 13:3. them that rejoice in my h.

HIGHWAY, S.

Le. 26 : 22. h-s be desolate [2 : 27.
Nu. 20:17. king's h., 19.-21:22. De.
Ju. 5 : 6. days of Jael h-s unoccu.
20 : 31. began to kill peo. in h-s
32. Let us draw them unto h-s
20:45. gleaned in the h-s 5000 men
21 : 19. h. th. goeth fr. Bethel to

S.6:12. kine went along **h.** lowing
S.20: 12. wallowed in bl. in **h.**, 13.
K. 18: 17. **h.** of fuller's field, Is.7:
3.-36: 2.
r. 16: 17. **h.** of upright to depart
s. 11: 16. a **h.** for his people
19:23.a **h.** out of Egypt to Assyria
33: 8. **h**-s lie waste, wayfaring
35: 8. And a **h.** shall be there
40: 3. make in desert a **h.** for God
49: 11. my **h**-s shall be exalted
62: 10. cast up **h.** gather stones
e. 31: 21. set thine heart tow. **h.**
m. 5: 16. say in all the **h**-s, Alas
Mat.22:9. Go into **h**-s, 10 Lu.14:23.
Mk. 10:46. Bartimeus sat by the **h.**

HI'LEN = HI'LON.

Ch.6:58.H. with suburbs | 15: †51.

HILKI'AH.

K. 18: 18. Eliakim son of H., 26,
37; Is. 22: 20.-36: 22.
22: 4. Go up to H. high priest
8. H. gave book, 10. 2 Ch. 34:15.
12. king com-d H. to inquire of
the L., 2 Ch. 34: 20. [22.
14. H. went to Huldah, 2 Ch. 34:
23:4.com-d H. to bring vessels | 24.
Ch.6:13.Shallum begat H. and H.
45.H.son of Amaziah | 9:11.H.son
26: 11. H. sec. son of Hosah
Ch.34:9.H.the priest, 14,18.-35:8.
Ezr. 7: 1. H. son of Shallum
Ne. 8: 4. H. stood on Ezra's right
11: 11. Seraiah son of H. dwelt
12: 7. H. priest went with Zerub.
21. of H. Hashabiah was
s. 22:20. call my servant son of H.
e. 1: 1. words of Jere. son of H.
29: 3. Gemariah son of H. to Bab.

HILL.

Ex. 24: 4. Mo. built altar under **h.**
Nu. 14: 45. Canaanites dwelt in **h.**
e. 1: 41. ready to go up into **h.**, 43.
os. 5: 3. at the **h.** of foreskins
17: 16. The **h.** not enough for us
18:14. **h.** th. lieth bef. Beth-ho., 13.
24:30. buried on **h.** Gaash, Ju.2:9.
33. Eleazar was buried in a **h.**
u. 7: 1. were by the **h.** of Moreh
S. 7: 1. house of Abinadab in **h.**
9: 11. Saul and serv-ts went up **h.**
10: 5. shalt come to **h.** of G., 10.
23: 19. in **h.** of Hachilah, 26: 1, 3.
25: 20. Abig. came by covert of **h.**
S.2:24. were come to **h.** of Ammah
13: 34. much people came by **h.**
16: 13. Shimei went on **h.**'s side
21: 9. they hanged them in the **h.**
K. 11: 7. Solomon built in **h.** for
Chemosh [built on **h.**
16: 24. Omri bought **h.** Samaria,
K. 4: 27. to man of G. to the **h.**
s. 24: 3. Who ascend into **h.** of L.
42: 6. remember thee fr. **h.** Mizar
68: 15. **h.** of G. is as **h.** of Bashan
16 is **h.** G. desireth to dwell in
Can. 4: 6. get to **h.** of frankincense
Is. 5:1. vineyard in very fruitful **h.**
10:32. shake hand ag. **h.** of Jerus.
30: 17. be left as ensign on **h.**
31: 4. Lord shall fight for the **h.**
40:4. every mt. and **h.** be made low
Je. 16: 16. hunt them from every **h.**
31: 39. line upon the **h.** Gareb
49: 16. that holdest height of **h.**
50:6.they have gone from mt. to **h.**
Eze.34:26 places ab. my **h.** a bless-g
Mat. 5:14. A city that is set on a **h.**
Lu. 3:5. ev. **h.** shall be brought low
4: 29. led him to brow of the **h.**
9: 37. were come down from **h.**
Ac. 17: 22. Paul in midst of Mars **h.**

HILL country.

[out
Jos.13:6. inhab-s of **h.c.** will I drive
21:11. to sons of Aa., Arba in **h.c.**
Lu. 1:39. Mary went down into **h.c.**
65. were noised thro. all the **h.c.**

High HILL, S.

Ge. 7: 19. all **h. h**-s were covered
1 K.14:23.groves on **h.h.**,2 K.17:10.
Ps. 68: 15. **h. h.** as hill of Bashan
16.Why leap,ye **h.h**-s? this is hill
104:18. **h. h**-s are refuge for goats
Is. 30:25. upon **h. h.** rivers of wat.
Je. 2:20. upon **h. h.** wanderest.
17: 2. remem. groves upon **h. h**-s
Eze. 6:13. slain am. idols upon **h.h.**
20: 28. then they saw every **h. h.**
34: 6. sheep wandered upon ev. **h.**

Holy HILL.

[h.
Ps.2:6. set my king upon **h.h.**of Zi.
3: 4. L., he heard me out of **h. h.**
15: 1. L., who dwell in thy **h. h.**?
43: 3. bring me unto thy **h. h.**
99: 9. worsh. at his **h.h.** L. is holy

HILL, with top.

Ex. 17: 9. I will stand on **t.** of **h.**
10. Moses, Aaron, went to **t.** of **h.**
Nu. 14: 44. presumed to go to **h.t.**
Jos. 15: 9. border drawn fr. **t.** of **h.**
Ju. 16: 3. Samson carried to **t.**of **h.**
1 S. 26: 13. Da. stood on **t.** of **h.**
2 S. 2: 25. Abner stood on **t.** of **h.**
16: 1. Da. a little past **t.** of **h.**
2 K. 1: 9. Elijah sat on **t.** of **h.**

HILLS.

[h.
Ge. 49: 26. utmost bound of everl.
Nu. 23: 9. fr. the **h.** I behold him
De. 8:7. spring out of valleys and **h.**
9. out of whose **h.** dig brass
11: 11. it is land of **h.** and valleys
12: 2. upon **h.** und. ev. green tree
33:15. precious things of lasting **h.**
Jos. 10:40. Jos. smote country of **h.**
11: 16. Joshua took all, the **h.**
1 K. 20: 23. are gods of the **h.**, 28.
22: 17. saw Isr scattered upon **h.**
2 K. 16: 4. sacrificed and burnt incense on **h.**, 2 Ch. 28: 4.
Jb. 15: 7. wast thou before **h.**?
Ps. 18: 7. foundations of **h.** moved
50: 10. cattle upon thous. **h.** mine
65: 12. little **h.** rejoice on ev. side
72: 3. the little **h.** by righteousn.
80: 10. **h.** were covered by shadow
95: 4. strength of the **h.** is his
97: 5. **h.** melted like wax at pres.
98: 8. let **h.** be joyful together
104: 10. springs, which run am. **h.**
13. watereth **h.** from chambers
32. toucheth **h.** and they smoke
114: 4. **h.** skipped like lambs, 6.
121: 1. will lift mine eyes unto **h.**
148:9. Mountains and **h.** praise L.
Pr. 8:25. bef. **h.** was I bro-t forth
Can. 2:8. cometh skipping upon **h.**
Is. 2:2. shall be exalted above **h.**
2: 14. day of L. shall be upon **h.**
5:25 **h.**did tremble, their carcasses
7: 25. on all **h.** not come fear
40:12. Who weighed **h.** in balance?
41: 15. shalt make the **h.** as chaff
42: 15. I will make waste mts. **h.**
54: 10. mts. depart, **h.** be remov.
55: 12. **h.** break forth into singing
65: 7. blasphemed me upon the **h.**
Je. 3: 23. salva. hoped for from **h.**
4: 24. lo, the **h.** moved lightly
13: 27. seen thy abomina. on **h.**
Eze. 6: 3. saith L. to the **h.**, 36: 4.
35: 8. with his slain men in thy **h.**
36: 6. say to the **h.** to the rivers
Ho. 4: 13. they burn inc. upon **h.**
10: 8. shall say to **h.** Fall on us
Jo. 3: 18. **h.** shall flow with milk
Am. 9: 13. all the **h.** shall melt
Mi. 4: 1. shall be exalted above **h.**
6: 1. let the **h.** hear thy voice
Na. 1: 5. **h.** melt, earth is burned
Ha. 3: 6. the perpetual **h.** did bow
Zph. 1: 10. great crashing from **h.**
Lu.23:30. begin to say to **h.**Cover us

HIL'LEL.

Ju. 12: 13. Abdon son of H., 15.

HIM.

Ge.41:13. me restored **h.** he hanged
Ex.32:33. sinned, **h.** I will blot out
Le. 26: 46. laws betw. **h.** and Isr.
Nu. 14: 24. Caleb, **h.** will I bring
16:5.**h.**wh.he hath chosen[into la.
De. 10: 20. **h.** serve, to **h.** cleave
18: 5. L. hath chosen **h.** and sons
1 S.10:24. See ye **h.** L. hath chosen
20:36.Jona. shot arrow beyond **h.**
1 K.14:11. **h.** that dieth in city,16:
4.-21: 24. [wall, 2 K. 9: 8.
21: 21. **h.** that pisseth against the
2 K. 11:2. they hid **h.** even **h.** and
15. and **h.** that followed her, kill
17:36. **h.** shall ye fear, **h.** worship
Ne. 13: 26. **h.** did outlandish wom.
Es. 8: 7. **h.** they have hanged on
Jb.15:31.Let not **h.** that is deceived
29: 12. I deliv-d **h.** had none to
36:22.who teacheth like **h.**[help **h.**
40: 9. canst thou thunder like **h.**?
42: 8. Job, for **h.** will I accept
Ps. 4: 3. set apart **h.** that is godly
25: 12. **h.** should he teach in way
45: 11. worship **h.**
72: 12. **h.** no helper
101:5.**h.**hath high look, not suffer
Pr. 24:24.**h.** shall the people curse
Ec. 10: 1. little folly **h.** in reputa.
Je. 48: 35. **h.** that off-h in high
Eze. 35: 7. cut off from it **h.** that
Da.11:5.be strong ab.**h.**have domin.
Am. 1: 5. **h.** that holdeth sceptre
Mal. 2:12. will cut off **h.** that off-h
3:18.sh.discern betw.**h.** serveth G.
Mat. 4: 10. **h.** only serve, Lu. 4:8.
10: 32. **h.** will I confess, Lu. 12:8.
33. **h.** will I deny before my Fa.
40. receiveth **h.** that sent me,
Mk. 9: 37. [Ac. 3:22.-7:37.
17: 5. This is my Son, hear ye **h.**,
18:15. go tell **h.** betw. **h.** and thee
24:18.Nei. let **h.** in field,Mk.13:16.
27: 32. **h.** compelled to bear cross
Mk. 13: 14. let **h.** readeth unders.
15.let **h.** that is on the housetop
Lu. 23:25. **h.** that for sedition and
24: 24. as wom. said, **h.** saw not
Jn.1:3. with-t **h.**not any thi. made
5: 38. sent, **h.** ye believe not
43. in own name, **h.** ye will rec.
6: 27. **h.** hath God the Fa. sealed
37. **h.** that cometh to me, I will
in no wise cast out [my Fa.hon.
9:31. **h.** he heareth | 12:26.**h.** will
13:32. G. shall glorify **h.** in hims.
Ac.2:23. **h.** deliv-d | 5:31.**h.**exalted
10: 40. **h.** G. raised up third day
16:3.**h.** wo. Paul have to go wi **h.**
17:23.Wh. ye worship, **h.** declare I
Ro. 14: 1. **h.** that is weak in faith
3.Let not **h.**th. eateth, despise **h.**
1 Co. 3:17. defile tem. **h.** G. destroy
10:12.let **h.**that thinketh he stand.
2 Co. 5:21. made **h.** to be sin for us
Ga.6:6. Let **h.** th.is taught in word
Ep. 4:28. Let **h.** stole steal no more
Ph.2:23.**h.** I hope to send presently
29. Receive **h.** in the Lord
2 Th.2:9.**h.** whose coming is aft.the
He. 2:14. destroy **h.** hath power of
11: 12. and **h.** as good as dead

About HIM.

1 S. 22: 6. serv-s standing **a. h.**, 7.
17. said to footmen stood **a. h.**
1 K. 5: 3. for wars which were **a.h.**
2 Ch. 18: 31. they compassed **a. h.**
Jb. 1: 10. Hast made a hedge **a. h.**?
Ps.76:11. let all **a.h.** bring presents
89: 7. in reverence of all **a. h.**
Je. 48:17. all ye **a. h.** bemoan him
39. Moab a dismaying to all **a.h.**
50: 32. it shall devour all **a. h.**
La. 1: 17. adversaries shall be **a. h.**
Eze. 12. 14. scatter all that are **a.h.**
32:22. his graves are **a. h.**, 25, 26.

Mat.8:18.Jesus saw great mult **a.h.**
Mk. 8 : 32. the multitude sat **a. h.**
Jn. 10 : 24. Then came Jews **a. h.**
Re. 4:8. beasts each 6 wings **a. h.**

After HIM.

Ge. 17 : 19. and with his seed **a. h.**
18:19. will command househ. **a.h.**
Ex. 28:43. statute for his seed **a.h.**
29:29.holy garments be son's **a.h.**
Le. 20:5. all th. go a whoring **a. h.**
Nu. 32 : 15. if yo turn from **a. h.**
Jos. 20 : 5. if avenger pursue **a. h.**
Ju. 1:6. Adoni. they pursued **a. h.**
3 : 28 went **a. h.** and took fords
6:34. Abiezer was gath-d **a.h.**, 35.
1 S. 14 : 13. armourbearer **a. h.**
17:35. I went out **a. h.** and smote
26 : 3. David saw Saul came **a. h.**
2 S. 1 : 6. horsemen followed **a. h.**
15:17. king went and people **a. h.**
23 : 10. the people returned **a. h.**
1 K. 1:20. throne of my lord **a. h.**,
15:4. to set up his son **a.h.** [27.
2 K. 5:20. I will run **a.h.** and take
9:27. Jehu followed **a.h.** and said
14:19. sent **a.h.** to Lachish, 2 Ch.
25:27. [him, 23:25.
18: 5. so that **a.h.** was none like
1 Ch. 27 : 7. Zebadiah his son **a.h.**
2 Ch. 26 : 17. Azariah went in **a.h.**
Ne.3:16.**a. h.** repaired, 17,18,20, 21,
22, 23, 24, 30, 31.
Jb. 18 : 20. they **a. h.** be astonied
21:21.what pleasure in house **a.h.**
33. every man shall draw **a. h.**
41:32. maketh path to shine **a. h.**
Ps. 49:17. glory not descend **a. h.**
Pr. 20:7. his chil. are blessed **a. h.**
Ec. 3:22. to see what be **a.h.**, 6:12.
7:14. man sho. find nothing **a. h.**
10 : 14. **a. h.** who can tell him?
Eze. 9 : 5. go ye **a. h.** thro. city
Lu. 19 : 14. sent a messenger **a. h.**
Jn. 12 : 19. the world is gone **a. h.**
Ac. 5 : 37. drew much people **a. h.**
7: 5. to him. and to his seed **a. h.**
17:27.if haply they might feel **a.h.**
19:4. him which should come **a.h.**

Against HIM.

Ge. 16: 12. every man's hand **a. h.**
32: 25. saw he prevailed not **a.h.**
37: 18. they conspired **a.h.**, 1 K.
15:27.-16:9. 2 K. 14:19.-15: 10,
25.-21:23.
Ex. 16: 8. Lord heareth your murmurings **a.h.**,Nu.14:36.-16:11.
Nu. 22 : 22. for an adversary **a. h.**
De 19 : 11. if any man rise **a. h.**
16. if a false witness testify **a. h.**
33:11.smite thro.loins th. rise **a.h.**
Jos. 5: 13. stood a man over **a. h.**
Ju 14: 5. young lion roared **a. h.**
15: 14. Philistines shouted **a. h.**
20: 23. Lord said, Go up **a. h.**
2 S. 10: 9. front of battle was **a.h.**
1 K. 13: 4. hand he put **a. h.** dried
21:10.sons of Belial to bear witness
2 K 23:29. Josiah went **a.h.** [a.h.
24:2. sent **a. h.** bands of Chaldees
2 Ch. 32: 17. and to spe k **a. h.**
Es. 6: 13. shalt not prevail **a. h.**
Jb. 2: 3. altho. movedst me **a. h.**
8:4. if thy chil. have sinned **a. h.**
9 : 4. who **a. h.** and prospered?
14: 20. prevailest for ever **a. h.**
33:13. Why dost thou strive **a.h.**?
35:6. if sinnest. what doest **a. h.**?
Ps. 78 : 17. sinned yet more **a. h.**
Pr. 17 : 11. a cruel messenger **a. h.**
Ec. 4: 12. and if one prevail **a. h.**
Is. 10 : 15. axe boast **a. h.** heweth?
or the saw magnify itself **a. h.**
31:4.when mult. of sheph-s is **a.h.**
45 : 24. all incensed **a. h.** be asha.
59 : 19. sh. lift up a standard **a.h.**
Je 20 : 10. enticed we prevail **a. h.**
31:20.since I spake **a.h.** I remem.
Je.51:3.**a.h.**th. bendeth, let archer
Eze. 29 : 2. prophesy **a. h.**, 38 : 2.
38:21. I will call for a sword **a.h.**
22. I will plead **a. h.** with pestil.
Da. 9 : 11. we have sinned **a. h.**
11:16.he that cometh **a.h.** shall do
Mi. 3 : 5. they prepare war **a. h.**
7 : 9. bec. I have sinned **a. h.**
Ha. 2 : 6. these take parable **a. h.**
Mat. 12:14. a counsel **a.h.**, Mk.3:6.
Lu.14:31. to meet him cometh **a.h.**
Ac. 22 : 24. whf. cried so **a. h.**
23:30.bef. thee what they had **a.h.**
25 : 3. priest desired favour **a. h.**
15. Jews, desiring judgm. **a. h.**
Jude 9. durst not bring **a.h.** rail-g
15. ungodly sinners spoken **a.h.**
Re. 19 : 19. war **a. h.** sat on horse

At HIM.

Ge. 49 : 23. The archers shot **a. h.**
1 S. 20:33. Saul cast a javelin **a. h.**
2 S.16:13. Shimei threw stones **a.h.**
Jb. 27:23. Men sh. clap hands **a.h.**
Ps. 12:5. fr. him that puffeth **a. h.**
37:13. The Lord shall laugh **a. h.**
52: 6. righteous shall laugh **a. h.**
64:4. suddenly do they shoot **a.h.**
Is. 52:15. k-s sh. shut mouths **a.h.**
Da. 11:40. king of south push **a.h.**
Na. 1: 5. mountains quake **a. h.**
Mk. 6 : 3 they were offended **a. h.**
12: 4. **a. h.** they cast stones, and
17.they marvelled **a.h.**[ed about
Lu.7:9.he marvelled **a.h.** and turn-
8:19. not come **a. h.** for the press
Jn.6:41. Jews then murmured **a.h.**
8: 59. took they up stones to cast [a.h.

Before HIM.

Ge. 24:33. there was set meat **b. h.**
32:3. Jacob sent messengers **b. h.**
21. went the present over **b. h.**
41: 43. they cried **b. h.** Bow knee
43:33. sat **b.h.** | 44:14. fell **b.h.**
Ex. 34: 6. Lord passed by **b. h.**
Nu. 11: 20. and have wept **b. h.**
Jos. 6: 5. ascend up ev. man **b. h.**
22:27. might do service of L. **b.h.**
Ju. 9: 40. Abim. chased, fled **b.h.**
14:16.Samson's wife wept **b.h.**,17.
1 S. 16: 6. L.'s anointed is **b. h.**
21. David to Saul and stood **b.h.**
17: 7. one bearing a shield **b. h.**
2 S. 10: 13. fled **b. h.**, 1 Ch. 19:14.
11:13. Uriah did eat and dri. **b.h.**
12:20. required, they set br. **b. h.**
15:1. 50 men to run **b.h.**,1 K.1:5.
22:24.I upright **b.h.**,Ps.18:23. [h.
1 K.3:16.Then came two harlots **b.**
16:25. worse than all **b. h.**, 30, 33.
21: 10. two, sons of Belial, **b. h.**
2 K. 2: 15. bowed to ground **b. h.**
4:12. the Shunammite stood **b.h.**
38. sons of prophets sitting **b. h.**
6: 32. king sent a man from **b. h.**
10:4. k-s stood not **b.h.**how sh.we
17: 2. not as kings of Israel **b. h.**
18: 5. nor any **b.h.** were like him
21: 11. as the Amorites did **b. h.**
23:25. like to Josiah no king **b. h.**
25:29 did eat bread **b.h.**,Je.52:33.
1 Ch. 16:29. bring off-g come **b. h.**
30. Fear **b.h.**, Ps.96:9. Ec.3:14.-
29:25. not any **b.h.** like Sol.[8:12.
2 Ch. 2:4. to burn **b. h.** incense, 6.
14: 5. kingdom was quiet **b. h.**
29 : 11. chosen you to stand **b. h.**
Ne.2:1. it came that wine was **b.h.**
Es. 4: 8. request **b.h.** for her peo.
6: 9. proclaim **b. h.**, 11.
13. thou shalt fall **b. h.** [h.
Jb.13:15. will maintain my ways **b.**
16. hypocrite sh. not come **b. h.**
21:33. as there are innumera.**b.h.**
23: 4. I wo. order my cause **b. h.**
26:6. Hell is naked **b.h.** and destr.
35:14. judgment is **b.h.** thf. trust
41:22.sorrow is turned into joy **b.h**
Ps. 18:6. my cry came **b. h.**
12. at brightness that was **b. h.**
22:29. go to the dust sh. bow **b.h.**
50 : 3. a fire shall devour **b. h.**
62: 8. peo. pour out heart **b. h.**
68 : 1. let that hate him flee **b. h.**
4. Sing unto God, rejoice **b. h.**
72:9 They in wildern. sh. bow **b.h.**
11. kings shall fall **b. h.** nations
85:13. Righteousness sh. go **b.h.**
96:6.Honour and majesty are **b.h.**
9. worship the Lord, fear **b. h.**
97:3.A fire goeth **b.h.**and burneth
106:23. had not Moses stood **b. h.**
142: 2. I shewed **b. h.** my trouble
Pr. 8: 30. rejoicing always **b. h.**
17:24.Wisdom is **b.h.**hath underst
Is. 40:10. and his work **b.h.**,62:11.
17. All nations **b.h.** are as noth.
41:2. Who gave the nations **b. h.**
45:1. holden to subdue na-s **b. h.**
Je. 42: 9. your supplications **b. h.**
Eze.28:9.Wilt say **b.h.** slayeth thee
30:24.shall groan **b.h.**[stood **b.h.**
Da. 7: 10. ten thous. times 10,000
8: 4. that no beasts stand **b. h.**
7. no power in ram to stand **b.h.**
11: 16. none shall stand **b. h.**
22. they shall be overflown **b. h.**
Mi. 6: 6. I come **b. h.** with off-gs?
Ha. 2: 20. earth keep silence **b. h.**
3:5. **b.h.** went the pestilence and
Mal. 3:16. a book of remem. **b. h.**
Mat.25:32. **b. h.** he gath-d nations
27:29. they bowed the knee **b. h.**
Mk. 3: 11. fell down **b.h.**, 5: 33.
Lu. 1:17. **b.h.** in the spirit of Elias
75. In holiness and right-s **b. h.**
5:18. sought means to lay **b. h.**
11: 6. a friend, I have noth. to set
Jn. 3: 28. I am sent **b. h.** [b. h.
Ac. 28: 33. presented Paul **b. h.**
Ro. 4: 17. **b. h.** whom he believed,
Ep. 1:4. holy, without blame **b. h.**
He. 12: 2. for the joy set **b. h.**
1 Jn. 2: 28. not be ashamed **b. h.**
3: 19. sh. assure our hearts **b. h.**
Re. 13:12. power of first beast **b.h.**
19:20. that wrought miracles **b.h.**

See **BEFORE him.**

Behind HIM. [b. h.

Ge.18:10.Sarah heard it in tent door
2 S. 2: 23. spear came out **b. h.**[h.?
2 K. 6: 32. sound of master's feet **b.**
Jo. 2: 14. and leave a blessing **b. h.**
Zch. 1:8.**b. h.** red horses, speckled
Mat. 9: 20. a woman diseased came
b. h., touched, Lu. 8:44.[b. h.
Mk. 12: 19. if brother die, leave wife

See **BEHIND him.**

Beside HIM.

De. 4: 35. L. is God, is none **b. h.**
2 S. 15: 18. serv-s passed on **b. h.**
Ne. 8: 4. **b. h.** stood Mattithiah

By HIM.

De.2:30. Sihon not let us pass **b.h.**
33:12. beloved of L. sh. dwell **b.h.**
Ju. 3:15. **b. h.** chil. of Isr. sent a
19. all that stood **b. h.** went out
1 S. 2:3. **b. h.** actions are weighed
20:7. that evil is determined **b.h.**
1 K. 22:19. the host of heaven **b.h.**
2 K. 3: 11 inquire of L. **b.h.**, 8:8.
5:1.**b.h.** the Lord had given deliv.
1 Ch.11:11.three hundred slain **b.h**
Ne. 2:6. the queen also sitting **b.h.**
4: 3. Tobiah Ammonite was **b. h.**
Ps. 63: 11. ev. one sweareth **b. h.**
Is. 27:7. slaughter of th. slain **b.h.**
Da. 8:11. **b.h.** daily sacr. was tak.
12: 7. sware **b. h.** that, Re. 10:6.
Na.1:6.rocks are thrown down **b.h.**
Mat. 23: 21. sweareth **b. h.** who
22. sweareth **b. h.** that sitteth
Lu.3:19.Herod being reproved **b.h.**
Lu.9:7.Her.heard all was done **b.h.**
13: 17. glorious things done **b. h.**
Jn. 1:3. All things were made **b. h.**

Jn. 1:10. the world was made b.h.
Ac. 2:22. by miracles God did b.h.
8:16. the faith which is b. h.,4:10.
13:39. b. h. all that believe justif.
23 : 11. night foll-g L. stood b. h.
1 Co.1:5.in ev. thing enriched b.h.
8 : 6. by wh. all things, we b. h.
Ep.4:21.and have been taught b.h.
Col. 1:16. For b. h. were all things
17.bef. all,b.h. all things consist
20.b.h. to reconcile all thi., b.h.
3 : 17. giving thanks to God b. h.
2 Ti. 2 : 26. are taken captive b. h.
He. 7 : 25. that come to God b. h.
13 : 15. b.h. let us offer the sacri.
1 Pe. 1 : 21. b. h. do believe in God
2:14.are sent b.h. for punishment

Concerning HIM.

Ju. 21 : 5. made an oath c. h. that
2 K.19:21.hath spoken c.h.,Is.37:22
Es. 3 : 2. king had so com-d c. h.
Da. 5:29. a proclamation c. h. [32.
Jn. 7:12.murmuring am. peo. c.h.,
9 : 18. Jews did not believe c. h.
Ac. 2 : 25. David speaketh c. h.
23 : 15. ye would inquire c. h.
1 Co.5:3.c.h.that hath so done this
See FEAR.

For HIM. [h., 20.

Ge. 2:18. I will make a help meet f.
37 : 35. Joseph's father wept f. h.
43 : 9. I will be surety f. h. of
Ex. 22 : 2. blood shed f. h. | 3.
Le. 1 : 4. shall be accepted f. h. to
make atonement f. h., 4:26,31.
-5:13.-14:18, 19, 20,31.-15:15.-
19 : 22. Nu. 5 : 8.-6:11.-15:28.
Nu.27:21. who sh. ask counsel f.h.
35:32.ye shall take no satisf-n f.h.
De. 19:11. lie in wait f. h. and rise
33:7.let his hands be sufficient f.h.
Ju. 6 : 31. he that will plead f. h.
1 S. 2 : 25. if sin, who entreat f. h.
15:2. how he laid wait f.h. in way
17 : 31. rehearsed, Saul sent f. h.
22 : 10. inquired of L. f. h., 15.
27 : 4. sought no more again f. h.
2 S. 9 : 10. shall till the land f. h.
1 K. 2 : 22. ask f. h. the kingd. (2)
13:23. saddled f. h. the ass, to wit
14:13. all Israel shall mourn f. h.
2 Ch. 16:14. made gr. burning f.h.
21:19. peo. made no burning f. h.
Es. 5 : 4. banquet I prepared f. h.
9. Haman saw he moved not f.h.
6:3. said, There is noth. done f.h.
4. hang on gallows prep. f. h.
Jb. 13 : 7. talk deceitfully f. h.?
30:25.Did not I weep f.h. in trou
Ps. 3 : 2. say, There is no help f.h.
37 : 7. and wait patiently f. h.
49 : 7. nor give to G. ransom f. h.
72:15. prayer be made f.h. contin.
Pr. 9:4. f.h. wanteth underst-g.16.
28:8. gather it f. h. will pity poor
Can. 5 : 4. bowels were moved f. h.
Is. 8 : 17. wait upon L. look f. h.
25 : 9. we have waited f. h., 9.
29:21. a snare f.h. that reproveth
30:18. blessed they that wait f. h.
40:10. Lord, his arm sh. rule f. h.
64 : 4. prepared f. h. waiteth f.h.
Je. 22 : 18. sh. not lament f.h.,18.
31:20. my bowels are troubl. f. h.
La.3:25.L.is good unto th.wait f.h.
Eze. 17 : 17. Nei. Pha. f. h. in war
31 : 15. I caused Leb. to mourn f.
h. trees of field fainted f.h. (3)
45 : 20. so do f. h. that is simple
Da. 11 : 17. nei. shall she be f. h.
Am. 3:5. where no gin is f.h. [f.h.
Zph. 1:6. not sought L. nor inqui-d
Zch.12:10.f.h. in bitterness f. h.(2)
Mat. 12 : 4. not lawful f. h. to eat
18:6.better f.h.that millstone,Mk.
9 : 42. Lu. 17 : 2. [12 : 46.
24:50. when looketh not f.h., Lu.
Mk. 5:20. things Jes. had done f.h.
Lu. 2: 27. child Jes. to do f. h. aft.
8 : 40. they were all waiting f. h.
9 : 52. went to make ready f. h.
Ac. 12 : 5. prayer was made f. h.
1 Co.16:11. I look f. h. with breth.
Col. 1 : 16. all things created f. h.
He. 9:28. unto them that look f.h.

From HIM.

Ge. 35 : 13. and God went up f. h.
Le. 5 : 3. be hid f.h. when he kn-h
Ju. 3 : 19. all by him, went f. h.
16 : 19. his strength went f. h.
1 S. 3 : 18. Sam. hid noth. f.h. [h.
2 S.11:15. retire f. h. | 13:9.went f.
1 K. 20:33. whe. any thi. come f.h.
2 K. 25 : 5. his army scatt-d f. h.
2 Ch.12:12. wrath of L. turned f.h.
Jb.14:6. Turn f. h. th. he may rest
Ps. 22 : 24. nei. hid his face f. h.
35 : 10. poor f. h. spoileth him
55 : 12. wo. have hid myself f. h.
62 : 1. f. h. cometh my salvation
Is. 5 : 23. right-s of righteous f. h.
53 : 3. we hid our faces f. h.
Je. 3 : 1. she go f. h. become ano.
Da.5:24.part of ha. sent f.h.[man's
Am. 5 : 11. ye take f.h. burdens
Jon. 3 : 6. he laid his robe f. h.
Mat. 5 : 42. f. h. th. would borrow
13:12.f.h. shall be taken, Mk.4:25.
Lu. 8 : 18. [Lu. 19 : 26.
25:29. f. h. hath not sh. be taken,
Mk. 14 : 35. prayed, hour pass f.h.
Lu. 11:22. taketh f. h. his armour
Jn. 7:29. I am f.h. | 10:5. flee f. h.
Ga. 1 : 6. are so soon removed f.h.
He. 12:25. if turn f. h. that speak.
1 Jn.3:17.shutteth compassion f.h.
4 : 21. this com-t have we f. h.
Re. 1 : 4. peace f. h. which is
See DEPART, DEPARTED.

In HIM. [h.

Ge. 18 : 18. nations sh. be blessed i.
Ex. 23:21. Beware, my name is i.h.
Ju. 9 : 26. put confidence i. h.
1 S. 28 : 20. was no strength i. h.
29 : 3. no fault i. h., Jn. 19 : 4, 6.
2 S. 22:3. i. h. will trust, Ps. 91:2.
31. buckler to all trust i. h., Is.
1 K. 1:52. if wickedn. be i. h. [36:6.
3:28. saw wisdom of God was i. h.
14 : 13. bec. i. h. is some good thi.
17:17. there was no breath left i.h.
1 Ch. 5:20. they put their trust i.h.
Jb. 13:15. slay, yet will I trust i.h.
35:14. judgm. bef. him, trust i. h.
Ps. 2:12. Blessed th. put trust i.h.
18 : 30. buckler to all trust i. h.
28:7. my heart trusted i. h. and I
am helped [66 : 6.-149 : 2.
33:21. our heart shall rejoice i.h.,
34:8. blessed is man trusteth i. h.
22. none th trust i. h. be desol.
37:5.trust i.h. | 40 bec. trust i.h.
62 : 8. Trust i. h. at all times
64 : 10. righteous shall trust i. h.
72 : 17. men shall be blessed i. h.
92:15. no unright-s i. h., Jn. 7:18.
Pr. 14 : 7. not i. h. lips of knowl.
30:5. shield to them put trust i.h.
Ec. 4 : 16. come after not rej. i. h.
Je. 4 : 2. nations bless thems. i. h.
46:25. Pha. and all th. trust i. h.
48 : 11. his taste remained i. h.
La. 3:24. therefore will I hope i. h.
Da. 3:28. deliv-d serv-ts who trusted
6:4. nei. any fault found i. h. [i.h.
Ob. 7. is none understanding i. h.
Na. 1 : 7. kno-h them trust i. h.
Ha. 2:4. his soul is not upright i.h.
Mat. 13:57. they were offended i.h.
14 : 2. mighty works do shew i. h.
Lu. 23:22. fo. no cause of death i.h.
Jn. 1 : 4. i. h. was life, life was
3 : 15. whosoever believeth i. h.
should not perish, 16. Ac. 10:43.
Jn.4:14.shall be i.h.a well of water
6:56. in me, and I i. h., 10:38.-15:5.
7 : 5. nei. did breth. believe i. h.
8:44. bec. there is no truth i. h.
9 : 3. made manifest i. h.
11:10. no light i.h. [glorified i.h.
13:31. God is glorified i. h. | 32. if
Ac. 17:28. i. h. we live, move. and
Ro. 10:14. How believe i. h. of wh.
15:12. i. h. sh. the Gentiles trust
1 Co. 2:11. spirit of man wh. is i.h.
8:6.of wh.are all,we i.h., 1 Jn.5:20.
2 Co. 1:19.nay. but i.h.was yea,20.
5:21. made righteousn. of God i.h.
13:4. we are weak i. h. but [i. h.
Ep. 1:4. chosen us i. h. | 10. gather
Ph. 3:9. win C., and be found i. h.
Col. 1:19. i. h. sho. all fulness, 2:9.
2:6. walk ye i. h. | 7. rooted i. h.
9.i.h.dwelleth fulness of Godhead
10. ye are complete i. h.
He. 2:13. I will put my trust i. h.
10 : 38. sh. have no pleasure i. h.
1 Jn. 2:4. liar, the truth is not i.h.
5. i. h. is love of G. perfected (2)
6. abideth i. h. ought to walk
8. which is true i. h. and in you
10. none occa. of stumbling i. h.
15. love of Fa. is not i. h., 3 : 17.
27.taught, ye shall abide i. h.,28.
3 : 3. ev. man that hath hope i. h.
5. i. h. no sin | 6 i. h. sin-h not
9. seed remaineth i. h. can-t sin
15. no murd-r life abiding i. h.
24. keepeth com-ts dwelleth i.h.,
and he i. h., 4 : 13, 15, 16
5 : 14. confidence we have i. h.

Into HIM.

1 K. 17 : 21. child's soul come i. h.
22. soul of the child came i. h.
Lu.8:30.many devils were ent-d i.h.
Jn. 13:27. aft. sop, Satan ent-d i.h.
Ep. 4 : 15. may grow up i. h. in all

Of HIM.

Ge. 25:21. Lord was entreated o.h.
Ex. 23 : 21. Beware o. h. and obey
32:1. not what is become o. h., 23.
Le. 15 : 7. toucheth flesh o.h., 33.
25 : 36. Take thou no usury o. h.
Nu. 35 : 33. by blood o. h. shed it
De. 18 : 19. I will require it o. h.
22. not be afraid o. h., 2 K. 1:15.
1 S. 17 : 32. Let no man's heart fail
because o. h.
2 K.5:20.I will take somewhat o. h.
10 : 24. his life sh. be for life o. h.
1 Ch. 5:2. o.h. came the chief ruler
2 Ch. 28 : 23. they were ruin o. h.
33 : 13. he was entreated o. h., 19.
Ezr. 8 : 21. to seek o. h. right way
Jb.7:8.eye o. h. sh. see me no more
12:5. despised in the thought o.h.
18:21.place o. h. knoweth not God
23 : 15. consider, I am afraid o. h.
Ps.37:7.fret not bec.o.h.who prosp.
Pr. 16 : 26. mouth craveth it o. h.
23:24. beget-h wise child, have joy
26:12.of fool than o.h.,29:20.[o.h.
27:13. pledge o.h. for stra. woman
Is. 29 : 16 shall work say o. h.
52 : 7. feet o. h. bringeth good
tidings, Na. 1 : 15.
Je. 20 : 9. not make mention o. h.
42:11. Be not afraid o. h. saith L.
Eze. 14:10. as the punishment o.h.
17:13. k. of Bab. taken oath o. h.
18 : 32 no pleasure in death o. h.
19:4. The nations also heard o. h.
28:9. in ha. o. h. that slayeth thee
Zch. 8:23. skirt o. h. that is a Jew
9:8. will encamp bec. o.h. [14:21.
Mat. 26:24. written o.h., Mk. 9:13.-
27 : 19. suff-d in dream, bec. o. h.
Mk.8:30.they sho. tell no man o.h.
38. o. h. be asha-d. Lu. 9 : 26.
Lu. 6:30. o.h. that taketh thy goods
12:48. much given, o. h. sh. much

Jn. 10:36. o. h. whom Fa. sanctif.
Ro. 3:26. justifier o. h. that beli-h
9:11. not of works but o. h. that
16. it is not o.h. that willeth, but
11:36. For o.h. and thro. him are
1 Co. 1:30. But o. h. are ye in C.
1 Pe. 2:9. shew forth praises o. h.
2 Pe. 3:14. that ye be found o. h.
1 Jn. 1:5. message we heard o. h.
2:27. anointing we have rec-d o.h.
29 that doeth right-s is born o.h.
Re. 1:7. all kindr. shall wail bec. o.h.

On, or upon HIM.

Ex. 21:30. whatso. is laid u. h.
Le. 7:20. having his uncleann. u.h.
15:24. if her flowers be u. h. he
19:17. thou shalt not suffer sin u.h.
20:9. cursed fa., his bl. be u. h.
21:12. anoi-g oil of his G. is u. h.
Nu. 11:25. took of the spirit u. h.
15:31. his iniquity shall be u. h.
35:23. cast it u. h. that he die
De. 18:9. thine hand be first u. h.
17:7. hands of wit-s be first u. h.
29:20. curses in this book lie u.h.
Jos. 2:19. if any hand be u. h.
Ju. 3:10. Spirit of L. u. h., 14:6,
19.-15:14. Nu. 24:2. 1 S. 10:10.
1 S. 18:17. of Philis. be u.h. [-19:23.
2 S. 17:2. I will come u. h. weary
1 K. 8:31. oath u. h., 2 Ch. 6:22.
13:4. forth, saying, Lay hold o.h.
2 K. 4:21. she shut the door u. h.
6:31. if head of Elisha stand o. h.
7:17. people trode u. h. in gate, 20.
2 Ch. 32:25. there was wrath u. h.
Ezr. 7:6. hand of the Lord u. h., 9.
Jb. 7:17. shouldest set heart u. h.
15:21. destroyer shall come u. h.
20:22. hand of wick. come u. h.
23. and shall rain it u. h. while
25. sword cometh, terrors u. h.
27:9. will G. hear, when troub. u.h.?
Ps. 116:2. will call u. h. as long
145:18. L. is nigh unto all call u.h.
Is. 44:3. water u. h. th. is thirsty
53:5. the chastisement was u. h.
55:6. call ye u. h. while he is near
7. return he will have mercy u.h.
Je. 31:20. I will have mercy u. h.
Eze. 12:13. net will I spread u. h.
18:20. right-s of righte. be u. h.
wickedness of wick. be u. h.
Ho. 7:9. gray hairs are here u. h.
12:14. he sh. leave his blood u. h.
Mat. 12:18. I will put my Sp. u.h.
27:30. they spit u. h. and smote
Lu. 23:26. o. h. laid cross [o. h.
Jn. 1:32. abode u. h. | 33. remaining
8:18. beli-h o. h. is not condem-d,
5:24.-6:40. Ro. 9:33. 1 Pe. 2:6.
19:37. o. h. whom they pierced
Ac. 13:9. Then Saul set his eyes o.h.
Ph. 1:29. not only to believe o. h.
2:27. mercy o. h. not o. h. only
He. 2:16. not o. h. nature of ang.
Re. 6:2. he th. sat o. h., 5,8.-19:11.
20:3. and he set a seal u. h.

Over HIM.

Ge. 4:7. thou shalt rule o. h.
Le. 16:21. confess o. h. all iniq-s
25:43. not rule o. h. wi. rigor, 53.
2 S. 3:34. all the peo. wept o. h.
1 K. 13:30. they mourned o. h.
16:18. burnt the king's house o.h.
Ps. 109:6. set a wicked man o. h.
Eze. 19:8. spread their net o. h.
Da. 4:16. let seven times pass o.h.,
Ac. 8:2. made lament-n o. h. [23.
Ro. 6:9. death no dominion o. h.
Ja. 5:14. Is sick? let them pray o. h.

Through HIM.

Jn. 1:7. that all t. h. might believe
3:17. that world t. h. be saved
Ro. 5:9. be saved from wrath, t. h.
8:37. more than conquerors t. h.
11:36. of him, t. h. to him, are all
Ep. 2:18. t. h. we have access unto
1 Jn. 4:9. Son th. we might live t.h.

To, or unto HIM.

Ge. 4:26. to Seth, t. h. born a son
12:7. Lord, who appeared u. h.
17:17. child be born u. h. is old?
21:2. time of wh. G. spoken t. h.
24:36. u. h. hath he given all
49:10. u. h. shall gath-g of peo.
Ex. 4:16. be t. h. instead of God
22:25. not be t. h. as an usurer
28:43. statute for ever u. h., 30:21.
De. 1:36. t. h. will I give the land
18:15. Prophet, u.h. ye sh. hearken
Ju. 15:10. t. h. as he hath done
1 S. 28:17. L. hath done t. h. as he
2 S. 3:9. to Da., even so I do t. h.
2 K. 4:23. Whf. go t. h. today?
7:20. so it fell out u. h. peo. trode
2 Ch. 13:5. even t. h. and his sons
34:26. king, so shall ye say u. h.
Jb. 6:14. t. h. that is afflicted, pity
35:6. If sinnest, what doest u. h.?
Ps. 68:33. t. h. rideth on heavens
72:15. t. h. be given of gold of
136:7. t. h. that made great lights
17. t. h. that smote great kings
Ec. 9:2. one event t. h. that sacrifi-h,
and t. h. sacrifi-h not [smiteth
Is. 9:13. people turneth not u. h.
31:6. Turn u. h. from whom Isr.
40:17. counted t. h. less than
18. what will ye compare u. h.?
45:24. even t. h. shall men come
49:7. saith L. t. h. man despiseth
57:19. Peace t. h. afar off (2)
66:2. I will look, t. h. that is poor
Mat. 7:8. t. h. that knocketh, it
Lu. 6:29. u. h. that smiteth thee
8:18. hath, t. h. shall be given
12:10. u. h. blasphemeth ag. H. G.
20:38. G. of living, all live u. h.
Jn. 7:33. I go u. h. sent me, 16:5.
10:3. t. h. the porter openeth
Ac. 5:40. t. h. they agreed, and
8:11. t. h. they had regard, bec.
10:43. t. h. give all prophets witn.
Ro. 4:4. now t. h. that worketh
5. t. h. worketh not, but beli-h
7:4. t. h. who is raised from dead
11:36. and t. h. are all things
14:14. t. h. that esteemeth, t. h.
16:25. Now t. h. that is of power
1 Co. 14:11. I be u. h. barbarian
Ga. 3:6. it t. h. for righteousness
Ep. 3:21. u. h. be glory in church
He. 1:5. I will be t. h. a Father
5:7. u. h. that was able to save
Ja. 2:23. imputed u. h. for righte.
4:17. t. h. knoweth, t. h. it is sin
Re. 1:5. u. h. that loved us
2:7. t. h. overcometh, 17.-3:21.
26. t. h. will I give power ov. na-s
21:6. I will give u. h. is athirst

Toward HIM.

Ge. 31:2. it was not t. h. as before
Ju. 8:3. anger was abated t.h. [h.
2 Ch. 16:9. whose heart is perfect t.
Jb. 11:13. stretch thine hands t.h.
La. 2:19. Lift up thy hands t.h. for
Eze. 17:6. branches turned t. h.
2 Co. 2:8. wo. confirm your love t.h.

Under HIM.

Ex. 17:12. took stone put it u. h.
2 S. 18:9. the mule u. h. went away
Jb. 9:13. proud helpers stoop u. h.
Is. 58:5. to spread sackcloth u. h.
Eze. 17:6. roots thereof were u. h.
1 Co. 15:27. all put u. h., 28. He.

With HIM. [2:8.

Ge. 39:3. master saw L. was w. h.
Ex. 31:6. w. h. Aholiab, 38:23.
Nu. 12:8. w. h. will speak, Je. 32:4.
23:21. Lord his God is w. h.
De. 29:15. w. h. that standeth here,
w. h. that is not here
32:12. was no strange god w. h.
1 S. 3:19. Lord was w.h., 16:18. 18:
25:25. folly w.h. [12,14. 1 Ch. 11:9.
2 S. 16:18. and w. h. will I abide
1 K. 8:65. Sol. held a feast, and all
Israel w. h., 2 Ch. 7:8.
2 K. 3:12. word of the L. is w. h.
15:19. th. his hand might be w.h.
18:7. L. was w. h., he prospered,
1 Ch. 9:20. 2 Ch. 1:1.-15:9.
2 Ch. 15:2. L. wi. you, while ye w.h.
26:17. w. h. fourscore priests of L.
32:7. be more with us than w.h.
8. w. h. is an arm of flesh, wi. us
36:23. the L. be w. h., Ezr. 1:3.
Ezr. 8:3. w. h. 150 males
4. w. h. 200 males
6. w. h. 50 males
Jb. 12:13. w. h. is wisdom, 16.
18:6. candle be put out w. h.
22:21. Acquaint thyself w. h.
Ps. 89:24. my mercy be w. h.
91:15. I will be w. h. in trouble
130:7. w. h. is plenteous redemp.
Pr. 8:30. I as one bro-t up w. h.
Ec. 8:15. abide w. h. of his labour
Is. 3:10. righte., it sh. be well w.h.
11. wicked, it shall be ill w. h.
40:10. his reward is w. h., 62:11.
57:15. w. h. that is of contrite
Je. 22:15. it was well w. h., 16.
Eze. 31:11. mighty, he sh. deal w.h.
Mal. 2:5. cov. was w. h. of life
Mat. 5:25. while art in way w. h.
Mk. 3:14. ord-d 12, th. they be w.h.
5:18. prayed might be w. h., Lu.
Lu. 1:66. ha. of L. was w.h. [8:38.
22:56. maid said, This man w.h.
Jn. 3:2. miracles, exc. God w. h.
14:23. will make our abode w. h.
Ac. 7:9. but God was w. h., 10:38.
10:35. feareth is accepted w. h.
21:36. multi. crying, Away w.h.
Rom. 6:4. are buried w.h., Col. 2:12.
8. live w. h., 2 Co. 13:4. 1 Th. 5:
10. 2 Ti. 2:11. [us all
8:32. how shall he not w. h. give
1 Th. 4:14. will God bring w. h.
2 Ti. 2:12. we sh. reign w. h., Re.
He. 11:9. heirs w. h. [20:6.
2 Pe. 1:18. when w. h. in the mt.
Re. 3:20. I will sup w. h. and he
14:1. w. h. 144,000 having Fa.'s
17:14. they w. h. are called

Within HIM.

Jb. 14:22. soul w. h. shall mourn
20:14. his meat gall of asps w.h.
Pr. 26:24. layeth up deceit w. h.
Is. 63:11. put his Holy Spirit w.h.
Zch. 12:1. formeth spir. of man w.h.

HIMSELF.

Ge. 48:32. they set on for him by h.
Ex. 21:3. If he came in by h. he
shall go out by h. [16:6, 11.
Le. 9:8. sin offering which is for h.,
16:11. an atonement for h., 17,24.
Nu. 16:9. to bring you near to h.
31:53. taken spoil, every man for h.
De. 7:6. L. hath chosen thee to be
a peo. to h., 14:2.-28:9.-29:13.
2 S. 7:23.
33:21. he provided 1st part for h.
Jos. 22:23. let Lord h. require it
Ju. 3:19. he h. turned fr. quarries
1 S. 30:6. David encouraged h.
1 K. 19:4. Elijah h. went day's jour.,
requested for h. might die
2 Ch. 13:12. God h. is with us
26:20. yea, h. hasted to go out
Ezr. 10:8. h. separated fr. congr.
Jb. 1:12. only upon h. put not ha.
22:2. wise may be profitable to h.
27:10. Will he delight h. in Alm.?
32:2. bec. justified h. rather than
34:9. th. he sho. delight h. wi. G.
41:25. raiseth h. mighty afraid
Ps. 4:3. him that is godly for h.
10:14. poor commit-h h. unto thee

Ps. 35: 8. let his net catch h.
36: 4. setteth h. in way not good
50: 6. for God is judge h.
87: 5. Highest h. shall estab. her
132: 18. on h. his crown flourish
135:4. L. hath chosen Jacob to h.
Pr. 5:22. own iniq-s take wicked h.
11: 25. watereth be watered h.
13: 7. maketh h. rich, maketh h.
14: 14. good man be satisfied fr. h.
16: 4. Lord made all things for h.
26. laboureth, laboureth for h.
21: 13. shall cry h. not be heard
22: 3. foreseeth, hideth h., 27: 12.
29: 15. child left to h. bringeth
Can. 5: 6. beloved withdrawn h.
Is. 7: 14. L. h. sh. give you a sign
38: 15. spoken, h. hath done it
44: 5. ano. call h. by name Jacob
59:15. from evil, maketh h. a prey
63: 12. to make h. everl. name
Je. 10: 23. way of man is not in h.
29: 26. mad, maketh h. a prophet
51: 14. L. sworn by h., Am. 6: 8.
Eze. 45:22. sh. prince prepare for h.
Da. 9:26. Messiah be cut off, not for
Ho. 5: 6. hath withdrawn h. [h.
10:1 Israel bringeth forth fruit to
Am. 2: 14. mighty deliver h. [h.
15. swift of foot not deliver h.
Mat. 6:4. h. sh. reward thee openly
8: 17. h. took our infirmities
13:21. hath he not root in h., but
27:42.h.he cannot save, Mk.15:31.
Mk.3:21.said, He is beside h. [9:23.
8:34.let him deny h..Mat.16:24.Lu.
12: 33. to love his neighbour as h.
Lu.7:39.spake within h.,16:3.-18:4.
9: 25. whole world and lose h.
10: 1. whither he h. would come
11:26. 7 spirits more wick. than h.
12:47. kn. lord's will, prep-d not h.
15:17. when he came to h. he said
19:12. went to rec. for h. a kingd.
23: 2 saying, that he h. is Christ
51. who h. waited for kingd. of G
24: 27. expounded things conc. h.
36. Jesus h. stood in the midst of
Jn. 4: 2. tho. Jesus h. baptized not
5:18. making h. equal with G. [h.
19. I say, Son can do nothing of
26. as Father hath life in h., so
6: 6. h. knew what he would do
61. When Jes. knew in h. th. his
7: 4. he h. seeketh to be known
18. speaketh of h. seek. his own
8: 22. said Jews, Will he kill h.?
9: 21. ask him, he speak for h.
11:51. this spake he not of h., but
13: 32. God shall glorify him in h.
16: 13. he sh. not speak of h., but
27. the Father h. loveth you, bec.
19: 7. made h. the Son of God
12. whoso.maketh h. a king, sp-h
21: 1. Jesus shewed h. again, 14.
Ac. 5: 13. durst no man join h. to
36. Theudas, boasting h. to be
8: 9. giving out h. was great one
34. of wh. speaketh proph.? of h.?
10: 17. while Peter doubted in h.
12: 11. when Peter was come to h.
14:17. he left not h. without witn
25: 8. while he ans-d for h., 26: 1.
26:24.as he spake for h.Festus said
28: 16. Paul suff-d to dwell by h.
Ro. 12: 3. not to think of h. more
14:7. liveth to h., no man dieth to
12. give account of h. [h.
15: 3. even Christ pleased not h.
Co. 2: 15. h. is judged of no man
3: 15. he h. shall be saved, yet so
18. Let no man deceive h.
11: 28. But let a man examine h.
15:28. sh. Son h. be subject to [19.
Co.5:18.reconciled us to h.by Jes.,
10: 7. If trust to h. let him of h.
11: 20. ye suffer if a man exalt h.

Ga. 1: 4. who gave h. for our sins
2:20.gave h. | 6:3.think h.someth.
6: 4. have rejoicing in h. alone
Ep. 2: 15. to make in h. of twain
20. Jes. h. being chief corner st.
5: 2. hath given h. | 25. gave h.
27. present it to h. glorious ch
28. loveth h. | 33. wife, even as h.
Col.1:20.reconcile all things unto h.
2:†15. triumphing over them in h.
2 Th. 2: 4. shewing h. he is God
1 Ti. 2: 6. gave h. ransom for all
Tit. 2: 14. gave h., to purify to h.
3: 11. being condemned of h.
He. 1: 3. had by h. purged sins
2: 14. h. took part of the same
18. in that he h. hath suffered
5: 2. h. is compassed wi. infirmity
3. so also for h. to offer for sins
4. no man taketh this hon. to h.
5. C. glorified not h. to be made
6: 13. by no greater, sware by h.
7: 27. when he offered h., 9: 25.
9:26.to put aw. sin by sacrifice of h.
12: 3. contradic. of sinners ag. h.
1 Pe. 2:23. committed h. to him th.
1 Jn. 2: 6. ought h. to walk, as he
3: 3. hath this hope, purifieth h.
5: 10. believeth hath witness in h.
3 Jn. 10. nor h. receive brethren
Re. 19:12. name no man kn. but h.
21: 3. God h. shall be with them
See BOWED, HIDE.

HIN.

Ex. 29: 40. with the fourth part of
h. of oil, Le. 23:13. Nu. 15:4,5.
-28: 5, 7, 14.
30: 24. take also of oil olive a h.
Le. 19: 36. a just h. shall ye have
Nu. 15:5. fourth part of h. of wine
6. third part of h. | 9. half a h.
Eze. 4:11. sixth part of h. of water
45:24.h.of oil for ephah. 46:5,7,11.
46: 14. h. of oil to temper with

HIND, S.

Ge. 49: 21. Napht. is a h. let loose
2 S. 22: 34. he maketh my feet like
h-s' feet, Ps. 18: 33. Ha. 3: 19
Jb.39:1.canst mark when h-s calve?
Ps.29:9.voice of L.maketh h-s calve
Pr. 5: 19. Let her be as loving h.
Can. 2: 7. I charge you by h-s, 3:5.
Je. 14: 5. the h. calved in the field

HINDER end or sea.

2 S. 2:23. smote with h. e. of spear
Zch. 14: 8. half of th. toward h. s.

HINDER part, s. [4:4

1 K.7:25.h. p-s were inward, 2 Ch.
Ps. 78: 66. smote enemies in h. p-s
Jo. 2: 20 h. p. toward utmost sea
Mk. 4: 38. Jes. was in h. p. of ship
Ac. 27:41. h. p. broken with waves

HINDER. [Verb.]

Ge. 24:56. h. me not, seeing L. hath
Nu. 22:16. let noth. h. thee coming
Ne. 4: 8. fight, and h. the building
Jb.9:12.he taketh,who can h.him?
11:10.if he shut up,who can h.him?
Ac. 8:36. what h. me to be baptiz.?
1 Co. 9: 12. lest we h. gospel of C.
Ga. 5:7. run well, who did h. you?

HINDERED, ETH.

Ezr. 6:8. given, that they be not h.
Is. 14:6. ruled is persecut., none h-h
Lu. 11:52. them entering in, ye h-d
Ro. 15: 22. h-d from coming to you
1 Th. 2: 18. we would, but Sat. h-d
1 Pe.3:7.that your prayers be not h.

HINDERMOST.

Ge. 33:2. put Rachel and Joseph h.
Je. 50:12. h. of nations be wildern.

HINDMOST.

Nu. 2:31. sh. go h. with standards
De. 25:18. and smote the h. of thee
Jos. 10: 19. and smite the h. of them

HINGES.

1 K. 7: 50. the h. of gold for doors

Pr. 26:14. as door turneth upon h.

Valley of HIN'NOM.

Jos. 15: 8. border went by v. o. H.
18:16.and descended to the v.o.H.
2 K. 23:10. Tophet, wh. is in v.o.H.
2 Ch. 28:3. burnt incense in v.o.H.
33:6.chil.to pass thro.fire in v.o.H
Ne. 11:30. unto v. o. H.,Je.7:21, 32.
Je. 19:2. go forth to v.o.H. [-19:6.
32: 35. built high pla. in v. o. H.

HIP.

Ju. 15: 8. smote them h. and thigh

HI'RAH.

Ge. 38: 1. Adullamite, name H. 12.

HI'RAM = HU'RAM.

2 S.5:11. H. k. of Tyre sent messengers to Da.,1 Ch.14:1. [Da., 8.
1 K. 5:1. H. k. of Tyre was lover of
2. Sol. to H. | 7. H. heard
10. H. gave Sol. cedar trees
11. Sol. gave H. 20,000 meas-s of
12. was peace betw H. and Sol.
18.H.'s builders did hew | 9:11,14
7: 13. Sol. fetched H. out of Tyre
40. H. made lavers, H. made, 45.
9: 12. H. came to see cities Sol.
27. H. sent in navy his shipmen
10: 11. navy of H. bro-t almug tr.
22. at sea navy, with navy of H.

HIRE, S.

Ge. 30: 18. G. hath given me my h.
† called his name a h.
32. amo. goats, of such be my h.
33. when it sh. come for thy h.
31: 8. ringstreaked shall be thy h.
Ex. 22: 15. hired thing, for his h.
De. 23: 18. not bring h. of a whore
24: 15. At his day give him his h.
1 K. 5: 6. to thee will I give h.
Is. 23: 17. she shall turn to her h.
18. her h. shall be holiness to L.
Eze. 16:31. not as harlot scornest h.
41. shalt give no h. any more
29: † 20. I have giv. E. for his h.
Mi. 1: 7. all the h-s sh. be burned;
she gath-d it of h. of harlot
3: 11. priests teach for h. [beast
Zch. 8: 10 no h. for man, nor h.for
Mat. 20: 8. give them their h.
Lu. 10:7. labourer worthy of his h.
Ja. 5:4. h. of labourers is kept back

HIRE. [Verb]

1 Ch. 19:6. silver to h. th., chariots
Is 46:6.h.goldsmith, he maketh god
Mat. 20:1. went out to h. labourers

HIRED, EST.

Ge. 30:16. h. with son's mandrakes
Ex.22:15. if it be a h. thing it came
Le. 19: 13. wages of him that is h.
De.23:4.h.ag.thee Balaam, Ne.13:2.
Ju. 9: 4. Abim. h. vain persons
18: 4. Micah h. me, I his priest
1 S. 2: 5. th. were full, have h. out
2 S. 10: 6. h. Syrians, 1 Ch. 19: 7.
2 K. 7:6. king of Isr. hath h. ag us
2 Ch. 24: 12. h. masons, carpenters
25: 6. Amaziah h. 100,000 mighty
Ezr. 4: 5. h. counsellors ag. them
Ne. 6:12. Sanballat had h. him, 13.
Is.7:20.L.shave with razor that is h.
Je.46:21.h.men like fatted bullocks
Ho 8: 9. Eph. hath h. lovers
10. tho. they have h. am. nations
Mat. 20:7 Bec. no man hath h. us
9.came that were h.ab.11th hour
Ac.28:30.Paul two years in h.house

HIRED servant, s. [10.

Ex.12:45.h.s.not eat thereof,Le.22:
Le. 25:6. sab. shall be meat for h.s.
40. as a h. s. he shall be wi. thee
50. acc. to time of h. s. sh. it be
53. as yearly h. s. he be with him
De. 15:18 been worth double h.s.
24:14.Thou shalt not oppress h. s.
Mk.1:20. left Zeb. in ship with h.s-s
Lu. 15:17. how many h.s-s have br.
19. make me as one of thy h. s-s

HIRELING.
Jb. 7:1 are not his like days of h.?
2. as h. looketh for rew. of work
14:6. accomplish as a h. his day
Is.16:14. three y-s as y-s of h.,21:16.
Mal. 3:5. ag. those that oppress h.
Jn. 10:12. a h. and not shepherd
13. The h. fleeth, because he is a h.

HIREST.
Eze. 16:33. h. them that they come

HIS.
Ge. 38:9. Onan knew seed not be h.
Ex. 21:34. dead beast shall be h.
22:9. another challengeth to be h.
Le.27:15 add 5th part, and it be h.
Nu. 5:10. hallowed things be h.
16:5. the Lord will shew who are h.
23:10. let my last end be like h.
De. 21:17. right of firstborn is h.
2 S. 16:18. h. will I be, with him
1 K. 2:15. it was h. from the Lord
2 K. 15:25. capt. of h. conspired
Es. 4:11. is one law of h. to put
Jb. 12:16. deceived and deceiver are
18:15. bec. it is none of h. [h.
Ps. 30:4. sing, all ye saints of
95:4. the strength of the hills is h.
103:21. ye ministers of h. that do
Can. 2:16. beloved is mine, I h.
Eze.16:15. that passeth by, h. it was
46:17. it be h. to year of liberty
Da. 2:20. wisdom and might are h.
Ob. 14 to cut off h. th. did escape,
nor deliv-d up h. that remain
Ha. 2:6. increaseth that is not h.
Jn.7:16. doctrine is not mine, but h.
Ac. 16:33. was baptiz., he and all h.
Ro 8:9. if not Spi., is none of h.
2Ti.2:19. the L. knoweth them are h.
He.4:10. ceased fr. works, as G. fr. h.
See ANGELS, ANOINTED, BLOOD, BONES, BRETHREN, BROTHER, CHARIOT, DAUGHTER, DAYS, DISCIPLES, ENEMIES, EYES, FATHER, S, FLESH, GLORY, HAND, S, INIQUITY, ETC.

HISKIJA'HU.
1 Ch. 3:† 23. sons of Azariah, II.

HISS.
1 K. 9:8. this house ev. one sh. h.
Jb. 27:23. shall h. him out of place
Is 5:26. h. to them fr. end of earth
7:18. L. shall h. for the fly in E.
Je. 19:8. passeth thereby shall h.,
49:17.-50:13.
La 2:15. they h. at the dau of Jerus.
16. thy enemies h. gnash teeth
Eze. 27:36. merchants h. at thee
Zph. 2:15. ev one passeth by her sh.
Zch. 10:8. I will h. for them [h.

HISSING. [h.
2 Ch 29:8. he hath deliv-d them to
Je. 18:16. their land a perpet. h.
19:8. I will make this city a h.
25:9. I will make them a h., 18.-29:
51:37. Bab. shall be a h. [18.
Mi. 6:16. sho. make inhabitants a h.

HIT.
1 S. 31:3. archers h. him, 1 Ch.10:3.

HITHER.
Ge. 45:5. be not angry ye sold me h.
8. not you that sent me h. but G.
13. sh. haste and bring my fa. h.
Ex. 3:5. not nigh h. put off shoes
Jos 2:2. came men in h. to night
18:6. ye sh. bring description h.
Ju 18:3. said, Who brought thee h.?
19:12. We will not turn h. into city
1 S. 13:9. bring h. a burnt off-g to
14:18. said, Bring h. the ark of G.
34. Bring me h. every man his ox
36. let us draw near h. unto God
15:32. Bring h. Agag
17:28. Why camest h.
23:9 Bring h. ephod, 30:7.
2 S. 1:10. I have brought them h.
1 K. 22:9. Hasten h. Micaiah
2 K. 2:8. Jordan divided h. and, 14.
2 Ch. 28:13. not bring in captives h.
Ezr. 4:2. k. of Assur, bro-t us h.
Ps. 73:10. Thf. his people return h.
81:2. a psalm, bring h. timbrel
Pr.9:4. simple, let him turn in h., 16.
Is. 57:3. h. ye sons of sorceress
Mat.14:18. said, Bring them h. to me
17:17. Bring him h., Lu. 9:41.
22:12. Friend, how camest in h.?
Mk. 11:3. straight he will send him
Lu. 14:21. bring in h. poor and
15:23. bring h. fatted calf and kill
19:27. bring h. slay them bef. me
30. shall find a colt, bring him h.
Jn. 6:25. Rabbi, when camest h.?
20:27. Reach h. finger, reach h. ha.
Ac. 9:21. came h. for that intent
10:32. call h. Simon, wh. surname
19:37. ye have bro-t h. these men
See COME.

HITHERTO.
Ex.7:16. h. thou wouldest not hear
Nu. 14:† 19. hast forgiven peo. h.
Jos. 17:14. as L. hath blessed me h.
Ju. 16:13. h. thou hast mocked me
1 S. 1:16. out of grief spoken h.
7:12. h. hath the Lord helped us
2 S.7:18. hast bro-t me h., 1Ch.17:16.
15:34. been thy father's serv. h.
1 Ch. 9:18. h. waited in k.'s gate
12:29. h. greatest part kept ward
Jb. 38:11. h. shalt thou come
Ps.71:17. h. have I decla-d thy works
Is. 18:2. terrible from beginn. h.., 7.
Jn. 5:17. My Father worketh h.
16:24. h. have ye asked nothing
Ro. 1:13. to come, but was let h.
1 Co. 3:2. h. ye not able to bear it

HIT'TITE.
Ge. 23:10. Ephron the H. answ-d
25:9. in the field of Ephron the H.
26:34. Esau took dau-r of Beeri H.,
dau-r of Elon the H., 36:2. [H.
49:29. bury me in field of Ephron,
30. which Abr. bought of E. the
H. for buryingplace, 50:13. [H.
Ex. 23:28. hornets sh. drive out the
33:2. I will drive out the H., 34:11.
Jos. 9:1. H., Amorite, gathered to
fight with Joshua, 11:3. [the H.
1 S. 26:6. David said to Abimelech
Eze. 16:3. Jerusalem; thy mother
See URIAH. [a H., 45.

HIT'TITES.
Ge. 15:20. I given land of H., Jos.1:4.
Ex. 3:8. H., Amorites, Hivites, 17.-
13:5.-23:23. De. 7:1.-20:17.
Jos. 3:10.-12:8.-24:11. Ju. 3:
5. 1 K. 9:20. Ne. 9:8.
Nu. 13:29. the H. dwell in mts.
Ju. 1:26. man went into land of H.
3:5. chil. of Isr. dwelt among H.
1K.10:29. for all k-s of H., 2 Ch.1:17.
11:1. Sol. loved women of H.
2 K. 7:6. Isr. hired kings of H.
2 Ch. 8:7. H. Sol. made pay tribute
Ezr. 9:1. done after abom-s of H.

HI'VITE. [15.
Ge. 10:17. H. and Arkite, 1 Ch. 1
34:2. Hamor H. | 36:2. Zibeon,
Ex. 23:28. drive out H., 33:2.-34:11.
Jos. 9:1. H. and Jebusite heard
11:3. H. under Hermon in Mizpeh

HI'VITES.
Jos. 9:7. men of Isr. send unto H.
11:19. save H. inhab. of Gibeon
Ju. 3:3. H. that dwelt in mt. Leb.
2 S. 24:7. to all cities of H.
2 Ch. 8:7. of people left of the H.
See HIT'TITES.

HIZKI'AH. [Josiah
Zph. 1:1. son of H. in the days of

HIZKI'JAH.
Ne. 10:17. Ater, H., Azzur sealed

HO. [down
Ru. 4:1. he said, h. such a one, sit
Is.55:1. h. every one that thirsteth
Zch. 2:6. h. h. come forth, flee

HOAR, HOARY.
See FROSTS, HAIRS, HEAD.

HOARY.
Jb. 41:32. think the deep to be h.

HO'BAB. [4:11.
Nu. 10:29. Moses said to H. | Ju.

HO'BAH. [Damas.
Ge. 14:15. H. on the left hand of

HOD. [Zophah
1 Ch. 7:37. Bezer and H. sons of

HODAI'AH.
1Ch. 3:24. sons of Elioenai, H. and

HODAVI'AH[1] HODE'VAH[2]
1 Ch. 5:24. H.[1], Jahdiel, mighty men
9:7. son of H.[1] son of Hasenuah
Ezr. 2:40. † of chil. of H, Ne. 7:43.†
3:† 9. sons of H.[1] to set forward the

HO'DESH. [bab
1 Ch.8:9. Shaharaim begat of H., Jo-

HODE'VAH. See HODAVIAH.

HODI'AH. [ham
1 Ch. 4:19. his wife H. sister of Na-

HODI'JAH. [stand
Ne. 8:7. H caused people to under-
9:5. H. said, Stand up, bless the L.
10:10. that sealed were; H., 13, 18.

HOG'LAH.
Nu. 26:33. dau-s of Zelophehad, Mah-
lah, H., 27:1.-36:11. Jos.17:3.

HO'HAM. [brou
Jos. 10:3. sent unto H. king of He-

HOISED.
Ac. 27:40. h. mainsail to the wind

HOLD, S. [Noun.] [rith
Ju. 9:46. entered an h. of ho. of Be-
49 put them to h., set h. on fire
1 S. 22:4. David in the h., 24:22.
2 S. 5:17.-23:14. 1 Ch. 11:16.
5. Abide not in the h. [of war, 16.
1 Ch. 12:8. unto David into h., men
Je. 51:30. mighty remained in h-s
Eze.19:9. they brought him into h-s
41:6. h., but had not h. in the wall
Ac. 4:3. put th. in h. unto next day
Re.18:2 Bab-n h. of every foul spirit
See CAUGHT, GAT, LAID, LAY.

Strong HOLD, S.
Nu. 13:19. whe. in tents or s. h-s
Ju. 6:2. Isr. made caves and s. h-s
1 S. 23:14. David abode in s. h-s.
19. Doth not Da. hide in s. h-s
29. Da. dwelt in s. h-s at En-gedi
2 S. 5:7. David took s. h. of Zion
24:7. they came to s. h. of Tyre
2 K. 8:12. s. h-s wilt thou set on fire
2 Ch. 11:11. Rehob. fortified s. h-s
Ps. 89:40. hast bro-t his s. h-s to ruin
Is. 23:11. to destroy s. h-s
31:9. he shall pass over to his s. h.
Je. 48:18. spoiler destroy thy s. h-s
41. Kerioth is taken, s. h-s are surprised [of Jud. Mi. 5:11.
La. 2:2. he hath thrown down s. h-s
5. L. hath destroyed his s. h-s
Da.11:24. forecast devices ag. s. h-s
39. thus sh. he do in most s. h-s
Mi. 4:8. s. h. of the dau. of Zion
Na. 1:7 L. is a s. h. in trouble
3:12. thy s. h-s be like fig trees
14. Draw waters, fortify thy s. h-s
Ha. 1:10. they sh. deride ev. s. h.
Zch 9:3 Tyrus did build a s. h.
12. Turn to s. h. ye pris-rs [h-s
2 Co 10:4. mighty to pulling down s.
See TAKE, EN, ETH, TOOK hold.

HOLD. [Verb.]
Ge. 21:18. lift up the lad, h. him
Ex. 5:1. that they may h. a feast
9:2. refuse to let go, wilt h. them
10:9. we must h. a feast unto L.
20:7. Lord wilt not h. him guiltless, De. 5:11. [h. of her
De. 22:† 25. if the man take strong
Ru. 3:15. bring the vail and h. it

2 S. 2 : 22. how **h.** my face to Joab
1 K. 2: 9. Now **h.** him not guiltless
Es. 4 : 11. king **h.** out golden seep.
Jb. 6 : 24. and I will **h.** my tongue
9 :28.thou wilt not **h.** me innocent
13:19.if **h.** my tongue give up ghost
17 :9. righte. shall **h.** on his way
41 : 26. the habergeon cannot **h.**
Ps. 17 : 5. **h.** up my goings in paths
119 : 53. Horror taken **h.** upon me
117. **h.** thou me up, I shall be safe
139: 10.thy right hand shall **h.** me
Pr. 31 : 19. her hands **h.** the distaff
Can. 3 : 8. They all **h.** swords expert
Is. 41: 13. I L. will **h.** thy right ha.
42: 6.I will **h.** thine hand,and keep
Je. 2: 13. cisterns, can **h.** no water
50 : 42. They sh. **h.** bow and lance
Eze. 30: 21.make it strong to **h.** swo.
41 : 6. th. they have **h.** had not **h.**
Am. 6 : 10. he say, **h.** thy tongue
Zch. 11: 5. slay **h.** thems.not guilty
Mat. 6 : 24. else will **h.** to one, Lu.
21: 26. all **h.** Jn.as a proph. [16:13.
Mk. 7 : 4. other things rec. to **h.**
8. ye **h.** tradition of men, as
Ro. 1 : 18. **h.** truth in unrighte-s
Ph. 2: 29. and **h.** such in reputation
2 Th. 2: 15.**h.** the traditions ye have
He.3:14. if we **h.** beginn. of confid.
Re. 2 : 14. that **h.** doctr. of Balaam
15.that **h.** doctrine of Nicolaitanes

HOLD fast.

Jb. 8 : 15. sh. **h.** it **f.** but not endure
27 : 6. My righteousness I **h. f.**
Je. 8: 5. they **h. f.** deceit, refuse
Mat. 26 : 48. same is he, **h.** him **f.**
1 Th. 5: 21. prove, **h. f.** that is good
2 Ti. 1:13. **h. f.** form of sound words
He. 3 : 6. if we **h. f.** the confid. and
4: 14. **h. f.** our profession, 10 : 23.
Re. 2 : 25. that ye have already **h. f.**
3:3. **h. f.** repent | 11. **h. f.** thou hast

HOLD peace.

Ex. 14:14. L.shall fight,ye sh. **h. p.**
Nu. 30: 4. if her father **h.** his **p.**
14.if her husband **h.** his **p.** at her
Ju. 18 : 19. **h. p.** lay ha. upon mouth
2 S. 13 : 20. **h.** thy **p.** my sister, he is
2 K. 2: 3. I know it,**h.** you your **p.** 5.
7: 9. good tidings, and we **h.** our **p.**
Ne. 8 : 11. **h.** your **p.** day is holy
Jb. 11 : 3. Sho. lies make men **h. p.**
13: 5. that ye would **h.** your **p.**
13. **h.** your **p.** let me alone
33 : 31. **h.** thy **p.** and I will speak
33. **h.** thy **p.** I will teach wisdom
Ps. 83:1. O God,**h.** not thy **p.**.109:1.
Is. 62 : 1. For Zion's sake not **h. p.**
6. never **h.** their **p.** day nor night
64 : 12. wilt **h. p.** and afflict us
Je. 4 : 19. pained, I cannot **h.** my **p.**
Zph. 1 : 7. **h.** thy **p.** at pres. of L.
Mat. 20:31.rebuked bec.they sho.**h.**
p. Mk. 10 : 48. Lu. 18 : 39.
Mk. 1:25.**h.** thy **p.** come out Lu.4:35.
Lu. 19 : 40. if **h.** their **p.** the stones
Ac. 12 : 17. beckoning to **h.** their **p.**
18 : 9. Be not afraid, **h.** not thy **p.**
1 Co. 14: 30. let the first **h.** his **p.**

HOLDEN.

2 K.23:22. not **h.** such a passo.,23.
Jb. 36:8. if **h.** in cords of affliction
Ps. 18 : 35. right hand hath **h.** me
71 : 6. By thee have I been **h.** up
73:23. hast **h.** me by my right ha.
Pr.5:22.be **h.** with cords of his sins
Is. 42 : 14. have long **h.** my peace
45 : 1. whose right hand I have **h.**
Lu.24:16. eyes **h.** that they not kn.
Ac. 2:24. not possible he be **h.** of it
Ro. 14:4. he shall be **h.** up for God

HOLDEST.

Es. 4 : 14. if **h.** thy peace this time
Jb.13:24. whf. **h.** me for thine ene.
Ps. 77 : 4. thou **h.** my eyes waking
Je.49:16.O Thou that **h.** the height
Ha. 1:13. **h.** thy tong. when wicked
Re. 2 : 13. thou **h.** fast my name

HOLDETH.

Jb. 2 : 3. he **h.** fast his integrity
26:9.He **h.** back face of his throne
Ps. 66:9. G who **h.** our soul in life
Pr. 11:12. man of underst. **h.** peace
17:28. fool **h.** his peace is counted
Da. 10 : 21. none **h.** but Michael
Am. 1 : 5. cut off him **h.** sceptre, 8.
Re. 2 : 1. **h.** stars in his right hand

HOLDING.

Is.33:15.shaketh hands fr.**h.** bribes
Je. 6 : 11. I am weary with **h.** in
Mk. 7 : 3. **h.** tradition of the elders
Ph. 2 : 16. **h.** forth the word of life
Col. 2 : 19. not **h.** the Head
1 Ti. 1 : 19. **h.** faith and good consc.
3 : 9. **h.** mystery of faith in pure
Tit. 1 : 9. **h.** fast faithful word
Re. 7 : 1. I saw 4 angels **h.** 4 winds

HOLE.

Ex.28:32. be a **h.** in top of it,39:23.
2 K.12:9.Jehoid. bored **h.** in the lid
Can. 5 : 4. in hand by **h.** of door
Is. 11:8. child sh. play on **h.** of asp
51 : 1. look to **h.** of pit whence
Je. 13 : 4. hide it in a **h.** of rock
Eze. 8 : 7. behold a **h.** in the wall
Ja. 3 : † 11. at same **h.** sweet water

HOLES.

Ge. 40:†16. I had baskets full of **h.**
1 S. 14:11. Hebrews come out of **h.**
Is. 2 : 19. go into **h.** of rocks, 7:19.
42 : 22. they are all snared in **h.**
Je. 16:16. hunt them out of the **h.**
48 : 28. maketh nest in sides of **h.**
Mi. 7 : 17. shall not move out of **h.**
Na. 2 : 12. lion filled **h.** with prey
Hag. 1 : 6. put it in a bag with **h.**
Zch. 14:12. eyes consume in th. **h.**
Mat. 8 : 20. foxes have **h.**, Lu.9:58.

HOLIER, EST.

Is. 65 : 5. for I am **h**-r than thou
He. 9 : 3. tabern. is called the **h**-t
8. way into **h**-t not yet manifest
10:19. enter **h**-t by blood of Jesus

HOLILY.

1 Th. 2 : 10. how **h.** we behaved

HOLINESS.

Ex. 15:11. like thee, glorious in **h.**?
28:36. H. TO THE LORD, 36:†2.-
39 : 30. Zch. 14 : 20, 21.
1 Ch. 16:29. worship Lord in beauty of **h.**, Ps. 29 : 2.-96 : 9. [h.
2 Ch. 8 : 11. Sol. said, bec. places are
20 : 21. singers praise beauty of **h.**
31 : 18. sanctified themselves in **h.**
Ps. 30:4. rememb. of his **h.**, 97:12.
47:8. G. sitteth upon throne of **h.**
48 : 1. praised in mount. of his **h.**
60:6.G. hath spok. in his **h.**,108:7.
89 : 35. sworn by my **h.** I not lie
93:5. **h.** becometh thine ho. O L.
110 : 3. willing, in beauties of **h.**
Is. 23 : 18. her hire sh. be **h.** to L.
35:8. sh. be called, The way of **h.**
62 : 9. drink it in courts of my **h.**
63:15. behold fr. habita. of thy **h.**
18. people of thy **h.** possessed it
Je. 2 : 3. Israel was **h.** unto the L.
23 : 9. bec. of the words of his **h.**
31:23.L. bless thee, O mount.of **h.**
Am. 4 : 2. L. G. hath sworn by **h.**
Ob. 17. upon Zion shall be **h.**
Mal.2:11.Jud.hath profaned **h.** of L.
Lu. 1 : 75. might serve him in **h.**
Ac. 3 : 12. as tho. by **h.** made man
Ro. 1 : 4. acc. to Spirit of **h.** [walk
6:19. yield members serv-s unto **h.**
22. ye have your fruit unto **h.**
2 Co.7:1. perfecting **h.** in fear of G.
Ep. 4 : 24. new man created in **h.**
1 Th.3:13.stablish your hearts in **h.**
4:7.not called us to uncl.but to **h.**
1 Ti. 2 : 15. if they continue in **h.**
Tit. 2:3. in behaviour as becom. **h.**
He. 12 : 10. we partakers of his **h.**
14.Follow peace with men and **h.**

HOLLOW.

Ge. 32:25. touched **h.** of thigh, 32.
Ex. 27:8. shalt make altar **h.**, 38:7.
Le. 14 : 37. in walls with **h.** streaks
Ju. 15 : 19. † **h.** placed in the jaw
Is.40:12.meas. waters in **h.** of hand
Je. 52 : 21. conc. pillar it was **h.**

HO'LON = HI'LEN.

Jos. 15:51.H.cities of Jud. | 21:15.†
Je.48:21.judgment is come upon H.

HOLPEN.

Ps. 83 : 8. have **h.** children of Lot
86:17. bec. thou, Lord, hast **h.** me
Is. 31 : 3. that is **h.** shall fall down
Da. 11 : 34. be **h.** with a little help
Lu. 1 : 54. hath **h.** his servant Isr.

HOLY.

Ex. 3:5. place whereon thou standest **h.** ground, Jos.5:15.Ac.7:33.
16:23.to morrow is the **h.** sabbath
19:6. unto me **h.** nation, 1 Pe.2:9.
20:8.Remem.sab. day to keep it **h.**
28 : 38. hallow in all their **h.** gifts
29 : 6. put **h.** crown upon mitre
33. they are **h.** | 34. it is **h.**
30 : 25. make it an oil of **h.** oint.
32.it is **h.** and sh. be **h.** unto you
35. a perfume, pure and **h.**
31:14.keep sabbath, for it is **h.**,15.
Le. 8 : 9. put upon Aa. **h.** crown
10: 10. difference betw. **h.** and un.
16 : 4. He sh. put on **h.** linen coat
33.sh.make atonem. for **h.** sanct
19:2. I the L. your G. am **h.**,21:8.
20:7.be ye **h.** | 21:7. he **h.** unto G.
27:14. man sanctif. his house to be
30. tithe of land is **h.** unto L.[**h.**
Nu. 5:17. priest shall take **h.** water
6 : 8. All days of separa. he is **h.**
20. this is **h.** for the priest
15 : 40. remem. and be **h.** unto G.
16 : 3. seeing all congr. are **h.**
5.Lord shew who his, and who **h.**
18:17.not redeem them,they are **h.**
31 : 6. Phinehas with **h.** instrum.
1 S. 2:2. There is none **h.** as the L.
21 : 5. vessels of young men are **h.**
1 K. 8 : 4. they brought up ark and
all **h.** vessels, 2 Ch. 5 : 5.
2 K. 4 : 9. this is a **h.** man of God
1 Ch.22:19.**h.** vessels into hou.of G.
29 : 3. have prepared for **h.** house
2 Ch. 23 : 6. go in, for they are **h.**
35 : 3. said unto Levites wh. were
h. Put **h.** ark into ho. wh. Sol.
13. **h.** offerings sod they in pots
Ezr. 8:28. Ye **h.** to L. vessels are **h.**
9 : 2. **h.** seed mingled with people
Ne.9:14. madest known thy **h.** sab.
Ps. 20 : 6. hear him fr. **h.** heavens
22 : 3. art **h.** O thou that inhabit.
28:2. lift my hands tow. **h.** oracle
86:2.Preserve my soul, for I am **h.**
98:1. his **h.** arm hath got. victory
99 : 5. worsh. at footstool, he is **h.**
9. Exalt L. worship at his **h.** hill
105:42. he rememb. his **h.** promise
145 : 17. L. is **h.** in all his works
Pr.9:10.knowl. of the **h.** is underst.
20:25. devoureth that which is **h.**
30 : 3. nor have I knowl. of the **h.**
Is. 4 : 3. remain. in Jerus. he called
6:3. **h. h. h.** is the L. of hosts [**h.**
13.**h.** seed shall be the substance
27:13.sh.worship in the **h.** mount.
30:29. when a **h.** solemnity is kept
52 : 10. L. hath made bare **h.** arm
58:13. call sabbath the **h.** of the L.
64:10.Thy **h.** cities are a wilderness
11. **h.** and beautif. ho. is burned
Je. 11:15. **h.** flesh is passed fr. thee
Eze.22:26.no diff. betw. **h.** and pro-
36:38. incr. them as **h.** flock [fane
42 : 13. **h.** chambers, priests eat
14. their garments, they are **h.**

Eze.44:19.lay them in **h.** chambers
23.teach diff.betw.**h.** and profane
45 : 1. offer **h.** portion of land, 4.
6. obla. of **h.** portion, 7.-48 : 18.
46:19. into **h.** chambers of priests
48 : 10. for priests sh. be **h.** obla.
14. not sell firstfruits, for it is **h.**
20. shall offer the **h.** oblation,21.
Da. 4:8. Daniel in whom is spirit of
h. gods, 9, 18.-5 : 11.
11:28.his heart shall be ag. **h.** cov.
30. indignation ag. **h.** covenant ;
with them that forsake **h.** cov.
Hag.2:12. If one bear **h.** flesh, skirt
touch bread, shall it be **h.**?
Zch.2:12. shall inherit Jud.in **h.** la.
13. L. is raised out of **h.** habita.
Mat.7:6.Give not th. is **h.**unto dogs
25:31. sh. come, **h.** angels wi. him
Mk. 6:20. he was a just man and **h.**
8:38.with **h.** angels, Lu. 9:26. [21.
Lu. 1:70. mouth of **h.** proph.,Ac.3:
72. to remem. his **h.** covenant
2: 23. Ev. male he called **h.** to L.
Jn. 17 : 11. **h.** Fa. keep those given
Ac. 4 : 27. ag. thy **h.** child Jesus
30. wonders by name of **h.** child
7: 33 place thou standest is **h.**
10:22. warned fr. God by **h.** angel
Ro. 1 : 2. promised in **h.** Scriptures
7: 12. com-t is **h.** just, and good
11 : 16. if firstfruit **h.** if root **h.**
12:1. present your bodies a **h.** sacr.
16:16.Salute with **h.** kiss, 1 Co.16:
20. 2 Co. 13 : 12. 1 Th. 5 : 26. 1
Pe. 5 : 14.
1 Co. 3:17. the temple of God is **h.**
7:14.now are **h.** | 34. th. she be **h.**
Ep.1:4. **h.** and without blame,5:27.
3: 5. unto his **h.** apostles and
Col. 1: 22. present you **h.** unblam.
3: 12. as elect of G. **h.** and belov.
1 Th.5:27.be read unto all **h.** breth.
1 Ti. 2 : 8. lifting up **h.** hands
2 Ti.1:9.hath called us wi.**h.** calling
3:15.thou hast known **h.**Scriptures
Tit. 1 : 8. bishop must be sober, **h.**
He. 3 : 1. **h.** brethren, partakers of
7: 26. priest became us, who is **h.**
1 Pe.1:15.be ye **h.** in all conver.,16.
2 : 5. a **h.** priesthood to offer sacr.
3 : 5. **h.** women who trusted in G.
2 Pe.1:18.when wi. him in **h.**mount
21. **h.** men spake as moved by
2: 21. than to turn fr. **h.** com-t,
3 : 2. spoken bef. by **h.** prophets
11. persons in all **h.** conversa.
Re. 3:7. write ; These saith he is **h.**
4 : 8. saying, **h.h.h.** L. God Alm
6:10. How long, O L. **h.** and true
14:10. tormented in pres.of **h.**ang.
15:4. Who not fear thee? thou **h.**
18:20.Rejoice ov. her,ye **h.**apostles
20:6. **h.** is he th. hath part in first
21 : 10. he shewed me **h.** Jerus.
22 : 6. Lord God of the **h.** prophets
11. that is **h.** let him be **h.** still
See CITY, CONVOCATION.

HOLY day.

Ex. 35 : 2. seventh shall be a **h. d.**
Ne.8:9.This **d.** is **h.** unto L., 10,11.
10:31. not buy it on sab. or **h. d.**
Is. 58:13. doing pleas. on my **h. d.**
See GARMENTS, HOLYDAY.

HOLY Ghost.

Mat.1:18. found with child of H.G.
20. conceived in her is of H. G.
3:11. baptize you with H.G.,Mk.1:
8. Lu. 3:16. Jn. 1:33. Ac. 1:5.
12:31. blasphemy ag. H. G. not be
forgiven, Mk. 3 : 29. Lu. 12:10.
32. whoso. speaketh ag. H. G.
28 : 19. bapt. in name of Fa., H.G.
Mk.12:36.Da.said by H.G., Ac.1:16.
13:11. not ye th. speak, but H. G.
Lu. 1 : 15. Jn. be filled with H. G.
35. H. G. shall come upon thee

Lu.1:41.Elisab.was filled with H.G.
67. Zacharias filled with H. G.
2:25.name Simeon, H.G.upon him
26. revealed unto him by H. G.
3 : 22. H. G. descended in a bodily
4 : 1. Jesus being full of the H. G.
12:12.H.G.shall teach you in same
Jn. 7 : 39. H. G. was not yet given
14 : 26. Comforter, who is H. G.
20:22. Receive ye H. G., Ac. 2:38.
Ac. 1 : 2. he thro. H. G. had given
8. after H. G. is come upon you
2 : 4. all filled with H. G., 4 : 31.
33. received promise of H. G.
4 : 8. Peter, filled with H. G. said
5:3. Sat. filled heart to lie to H.G.
32. we witnesses, so is H. G.
6 : 3. look out men full of H. G.
5. Stephen, a man full of H. G.
7 : 51. ye always resist the H. G.
55. Ste. full of H. G. looked up to
8:15. prayed they might rec. H.G.
17. hands on them, rec-d H. G.
18. when Simon saw H. G. given
19.I lay hands, he may rec. H.G.
9:17. mightest be filled with H. G.
31. walking in comfort of H. G.
10:38.G. anointed Jesus with H.G.
44. H. G. fell on all heard word
45. on Gent. was poured H. G.
47. have rec. H. G. well as we
11 : 15. H. G. fell on th. as on us
16. ye sh. be baptized with H. G.
24. Barnabas, full of the H. G.
13 : 2. H. G. said, Separate Barna.
4. being sent forth by the H. G.
9. Paul, filled with H. G. set eyes
52. disciples filled with H. G.
15 : 8. giving H. G. as did unto us
28. it seemed good to the H. G.
16:6. forbidden of H. G. to preach
19: 2. have ye received H. G.? not
heard whether be any H. G.
6. the H. G. came on them
20:23. Save that H. G. witnesseth
28. H. G. made you overseers
21 : 11. saith H. G. So shall Jews
28:25. Well spake H. G. by Esaias
Ro.5:5. love shed in hearts by H.G.
9:1. conscience bearing witn. in H.
14:17.kingd. of G. joy in H.G. [G.
15:13. abound in hope thro. H. G.
16. being sanctified by H. G.
1 Co. 2 : 13. words H. G. teacheth
6 : 19. your body is tem. of H. G.
12 : 3. say Jes. is L. but by H. G.
2 Co. 6 : 6. by H. G. by love
13:14.communion of H.G. wi. you
1 Th. 1 : 5. gospel came in H. G.
6. rec-d word with joy of H. G.
2 Ti.1:14. good thing keep by H.G.
Tit. 3:5. saved by renewing of H.G.
He. 2:4. witness with gifts of H. G.
3:7. as H. G. saith, To day if hear
6 : 4. made partakers of H. G.
9 : 8. The H. G. this signifying
10 : 15. Whereof H. G. is witness
1 Pe. 1 : 12. with H. G. sent down
2 Pe. 1:21. spake as moved by H.G.
1 Jn. 5:7. Father, Word, and H. G.
Jude 20. beloved, praying in H. G.
See GOD, HABITATION, HILL.

Most HOLY. [h.

Ex. 26:33. betw. holy place and **m.**
34. ark of testim. in **m. h.** place
29 : 37. be an altar **m. h.**, 40 : 10.
30: 10. it is **m.h.** | 29. may be **m.**
36. perfume be to you **m. h.** [h.
Le. 2 : 3. remnant of meat offering,
it is **m. h.**, 10.-6 : 17.-10 : 12.
6:25. sin off-g is **m. h.**, 29 -10:17.
7:1.trespass off-g is **m.h.**,6.-14:13.
21 : 22. eat of **m. h.** and holy
24:9. cakes of fine flour are **m. h.**
27 : 28. ev. devoted thing is **m. h.**
Nu. 4 : 4. service about **m. h.** thi.
19. when approach **m. h.** things

Nu. 18:9. off-g to me shall be **m.h.**
10. In **m. h.** place shalt eat it
1 K. 6 : 16. built for **m. h.** place
7:50. made vessels for **m. h.** place
8:6.ark unto **m.h.** place,2 Ch.5:7.
1 Ch. 6 : 49. sons for work of **m.h.**
23:13. Aaron to sanctify **m.h.** thi.
2 Ch. 3 : 8. Sol. made **m. h.** house
10. **m. h.** house made 2 cheru.
4 : 22. inner doors for **m. h.** place
31 : 14. Kore to distribute **m. h.**
Ezr.2:63. not eat of **m. h.**, Ne.7:65.
Eze. 43 : 12. whole limit be **m. h.**
44 : 13. not come near in **m.h.** pl.
45 : 3. be sanctu. and **m. h.** place
48:12.oblation sh. be a thing **m.h.**
Da. 9 : 24. 70 weeks to anoint **m.h.**
Ho. 11 : 12. is faithful with **m. h.**
Jude 20. building on your **m. h.**

HOLY mountain, s.

Ps. 87 : 1. His founda. is in **h. m**-s
Is. 11:9. nor destr. in **h. m.**, 65:25.
56:7.them will I bring to my **h.m.**
57 : 13. he shall inherit my **h. m.**
65:11. ye are they forget my **h.m.**
66:20. on swift beasts to my **h.m.**
Eze. 20:40. in **h. m.** they sh. serve
28 : 14. wast upon **h. m.** of God
Da. 9:16. anger be turned fr. **h. m.**
20. presenting supplica. for **h.m.**
11:45.plant taber.in glorious **h.m.**
Jo. 2 : 1. sound alarm in **h. m.**
3:17.I am the L. in Zion my **h.m.**
Ob.16.drunk upon my **h.m.**[**h.m.**
Zph. 3:11. no more haughty bec. of
Zch. 8:3. **m.** of L. called the **h.m.**

HOLY name. [n.

Le. 20:3. Molech, to profane my **h.**
22:2. that they profane not **h. n.**
32. nei. shall ye profane my **h.n.**
1 Ch. 16 : 10. Glory ye in his **h. n.**,
Ps. 105 : 3. [Ps. 106 : 47.
16:35. we give thanks to thy **h. n.**,
29 : 16. to build ho. for thy **h. n.**
Ps. 33 : 21. we trusted in his **h. n.**
99:3. praise terrible **n.**, for it is **h.**
103:1. bless L., bless **h. n.**, 145:21.
111 : 9. **h.** is his **n.**, Lu. 1 : 49.
Is. 57:15. lofty One, whose **n.** is **h.**
Eze. 20:39. pollute you my **h. n.** no
36 : 20. they profaned my **h. n.**
21.But I had pity for mine **h.n.**
22. not your sakes, but my **h. n.**'s
39:7. make my **h. n.** known in Isr.
not let them pollute **h. n.**
25. I will be jealous for my **h. n.**
43:7. my **h. n.** Isr. no more defile
8. they defiled my **h. n.** [**h. n.**
Am. 2:7. in to maid, to profane my

HOLY One, or one, s.

De. 33 : 8. Urim be with thy **h. o.**
Jb.6:10.not concealed words of H.O.
Ps. 16 : 10. nor suffer thine H. O. to
see corruption, Ac. 2:27.-13:35.
89:19. spakest in vis. to thy H. O.
Is. 10:17. H. O. shall be for a flame
29 : 23. they shall sanctify H. O.
40:25. To whom equal? saith H.O.
43 : 15. I am the Lord your H. O.
49:7. Redeemer of Isr., his H. O.
Da. 4:13. a H. O. came fr. heav.,23.
17. the demand by word of **h.o**-s
Ho. 11 : 9. I am H. O. in midst of
Ha. 1:12. from everl. O L. my H. O.
3 : 3. the H. O. came from Paran
Mk. 1:24.I know thee who thou art,
the H. O. of God, Lu. 4 : 34.
Ac. 3 : 14. But ye denied the H. O.
1 Jn.2:20.have an unction fr. H. O.

HOLY One of or in Israel.

2 K. 19:22. thou hast lifted thy eyes
against H. O. **o.** I., Is. 37 : 23.
Ps. 71 : 22. unto thee will I sing, O
thou H. O. **o.** I.
78:41. they limited the H. O. **o.** I.
89 : 18. H. O. **o.** I. is our King
Is. 1 : 4. have provoked H. O. **o.** I

Is.5:19. let counsel of H.O.o.I.nigh
24. despi ed word of H. O. o. I.
10:20. stay on the L., the H.O.o.I.
12:6. great is the H.O.o. I. in thee
17 : 7. eyes respect to H. O. o. I.
29 : 19. poor sh. rejoice in H. o. I.
30 : 11. cause H. O. o. I. to cease
12. thus saith H. O. o. I., 15.
31 : 1. look not unto H. O. I.
41:14. saith Redeemer, H. O. o. I.
16. shalt glory in H. O. o. I.
20. H. O. o. I. hath created it
43: 3. I am the L. the H. O. o. I.
14. saith Redeemer, H. O. of I.
45:11.the L.the H.O.o.I.,and Mak.
47:4. L. is his name, the H. O.o.I.
48:17. Redeemer, H. O. o. I., 54:5.
49:7. Redeemer of I. and his H. O.
55 : 5. nations unto thee, for H. O.
60:9. bri. gold to H. O. o.I. [o.I.
14. call thee Zion of H. O. o. I.
Je. 50 : 29. proud ag. H. O. o. I.
51 : 5. land with sin ag.H. O. o. I
Eze. 39 : 7. I am the L., H. O. i. I.

HOLY oil.
See **ANOINTED with oil** and **ANOINTING oil.**

HOLY people.
De. 7:6. art a h. p. unto L.,14:2,21.
26:19. mayest be a h.p.unto the L.
28:9. L. shall establish thee a h.p.
Is. 62:12. shall call them the h. p.
Da. 8:24. prosper, and destroy. h.p.
12: 7. to scatter power of h. p.

HOLY place.
Ex. 28:29. goeth in unto h. p., 35.
43. to minister in h. p., 29: 30.
29:31. shalt seethe his flesh in h.p.
31 . 11. sweet incense for h. p.
35 : 19. service in h. p., 39 : 1, 41.
38:24. gold in all the work of h.p.
Le. 6:16.with unl. bread it be eaten
in h. p., 26.-7:6.-10:13.-24:9.
27. thou shalt wash that in h.p.
30. to reconcile withal in h. p.
10:17.have ye eaten sin off.i 1 h.p.?
18. blood not bro-t in within h.p.
14:13. slay burnt offering in h. p.
16:2. come not all times into h. p.
3. sh. Aaron come into the h. p.
16. make atonement for h. p.,17,
20. end of reconciling h. p. [27.
16: 23. when he went into h. p.
24. shall wash his flesh in h. p.
Jos. 5: 15. p. whereon standest is h.
1 K. 8 : 8. staves were seen in h. p.
10. pr-ts come out of h. p.,2 Ch.5:
1 Ch.23:32.keep charge of h.p.[11.
2Ch.29:5.carry filthiness out of h.p.
7. nor off-d burnt off-gs in h. p.
30:27. prayer to his h. dwelling-p.
35:5.stand in h.p.acc. to divisions
Ezr. 9 : 8. to give us a nail in h. p.
Ps. 24 : 3. who stand in his h. p.?
46: 4. streams make glad h. p.
68 : 17. L. am. them in the h. p.
Ec. 8. 10. who had gone fr. p. of h.
Is. 57 : 15. I dw. in high and h. p.
Eze 41:4. said,This is the most h.p.
42 : 13. p. is h.
14. not go out of h. p.
45 : 4. it shall be a h. p. for sanc.
Mat. 24: 15. ye see abomi-n in h. p.
Ac. 6: 13. blasph-s words ag. h. p.
21:28. man hath polluted this h.p.
He. 9 : 12. C. entered into h. p.
25. the high priest ev. year into

HOLY places. [h. p.
2 Ch. 8 : 11. because the p. are h.
Ps. 68 : 35. art terrible out of h. p.
Eze. 7 : 24. their h. p. be defiled
21 : 2. drop thy word tow. h. p.
He. 9:24. C.is not entered into h.p.

Shall be HOLY.
Ex. 22: 31. ye s.b. h. men unto me
29:37. toucheth altar s. b. h. [18.
30:29. toucheth them s.b. h.Le. 6.
Ex.30:32. holy,s.b.h.unto you, 37.
40 : 9. annoint tab. and it s. b. h.
Le. 6: 27 shalt touch flesh s. b. h.
11 : 44. ye s. b.h. for I am holy,45.
-19 : 2.-20 : 26.
19:24. fruit s. b.h. to praise the L.
21: 6.priests s.b. h.unto their G.,8.
23:20.they s. b. h.to the Lord for
25: 12. jubilee, it s. b. h. unto you
27 : 9. man giveth unto L. s. b. h.
10. exchange thereof s. b. h., 33.
21. in jubilee it s. b. h. to the L.
32. the tenth s. b. h. unto the L.
Nu. 6 : 5. Nazarite s. b. h. unto L.
16 : 7. man L. doth choose s. b. h.
18: 10.ev.male shall eat it, it s.b.h.
De. 23: 14. thf. s. thy camp b. h.
Je. 31 : 40. gate tow. east s. b. h.
Eze.45:1 portion s. b. h. in borders
Jo. 3: 17. then s. Jerusalem b. h.

HOLY Spirit.
Ps. 51: 11, take not thy h. S. fr. me
Is. 63 : 10. rebelled and vexed h. S.
11. where is he that put his h. S
Lu. 11: 13. heavenly Fa. give h. S.
Ep. 1: 13. sealed with h. S. of prom.
4 : 30. grieve not the h. S. of God
1 Th. 4: 8. hath given unto us h. S.

HOLY temple.
Ps. 5: 7. I will worship tow. h. t.,
11: 4. The Lord is in his h.t.[138:2.
65: 4. satisfied with goodn. of h. t.
79: 1. h. t. have they defiled
Jon. 2 : 4. I will look tow. thy h. t.
7. my prayer came into thy h. t.
Mi. 1: 2. L. from his h. t. be witn.
Ha. 2 : 20. the Lord is in his h. t.
1 Cor.3:17.t. of G. is h. wh. t. ye are
Ep. 2: 21. groweth to h. t. in the L.

HOLY thing.
Le. 5: 16.harm he hath done in h.t.
22 : 10. no stranger sh. eat of h. t.
14. if a man eat of h. t. unwitt.
27: 23. thy estimation as a h. t.
unto the Lord [t.
Nu. 4 : 15. they shall not touch h.
Eze. 48 : 12. oblation a t. most h.
Lu. 1: 35. that h. t. born of thee

HOLY things. [t.
Ex. 28: 38.Aa. may bear iniq. of h.
Le. 5: 15. sin thro.ignorance in h.t.
22: 2. separate from the h.t.of Isr.
3. whoso. goeth unto the h. t.
4. not eat of h.t.until clean, 6, 12.
7. be clean, and shall eat of h. t.
15. sh. not profane h. t. of Isr.
16. to bear iniq. when eat h. t.
Nu. 4 : 20. not see when h. t. cov-d
5: 9. every off-g of h.t.be his,18: 19.
18 : 32. nei. shall ye pollute h. t.
De. 12 : 26. thy h. t. take and go
1 Ch. 23 : 28. office in purifying h.t.
2 Ch. 31 : 6. bro-t in tithe of h. t.
Ne. 10: 33. made ordinances for h.t.
12 : 47. sanctified h. t. to Levites
Eze. 20 : 40. will require your h. t.
22:8.Thou hast despised mine h.t.
26. priests have profaned my h.t.
44 : 8. not kept charge of my h. t.
13. not come near to my h. t.
1 Co. 9 : 13.minister about h. t., He.
See **Most holy THINGS.** [8:2.

HOLYDAY. [h.
Ps. 42 : 4. with multitude that kept
Col. 2 :16. judge you in respect of h.

HO'MAM. See HEMAM.

HOME. [came h.
Ge. 39 : 16. garment until his lord
43: 16.Bring these men h., sh.dine
26. Joseph h., they bro-t present
Ex. 9 : 19. man not bro-t h. sh. die
De. 21 : 12.bri.her h. to thine house
24 : 5. he shall be free at h. one yr.
Jos. 2 :18. bring thy fath.,moth.,h.
Ju. 11 : 9. If ye bring me h. to fight
19 :9.early, that thou mayest go h.
Ru.1 : 21.L. hath bro-t me h. empty
1 S. 2 : 20. they went unto own h.
6 : 7. bring their calves h. fr. them
10. men shut up their calves at h.
10: 26. Saul went h. to Gibeah, 24:
18 : 2. let him go no more h. [22.
2 S. 13 : 7. Da. sent h. to Tamar
14 : 13. king not fetch h. banished
17 : 23. Ahithophel gat him h. to
1 K. 5: 14. a month in Leb.two at h.
13: 7. Come h. with me refresh, 15.
2 K. 14: 10. tarry at h. 2 Ch. 25: 19.
1 Ch. 13 : 12. bring ark of God h.
13. So Da. brought not the ark h.
2 Ch.25 : 10. separ. army of Ephr. to
go h. returned h. in anger
Es. 5 : 10. when Haman came h.
Jb. 39 : 12. that he bri. h. thy seed
Ps. 68 : 12. th. tarried at h. divided
Pr. 7: 19. the goodman is not at h.
20. will come h. at day appoi.
Ec. 12:5. man goeth to long h. [h.
Je. 6 : † 2. Zion to wom dwelling at
39 : 14. Gedaliah sho. carry him h.
La. 1 : 20. at h. there is as death
Ha. 2 : 5. proud, nei. keepeth at h.
Hag. 1 : 9. when ye bro-t it h. I did
Mat. 8: 6. my servant lieth at h. sick
Mk. 5: 19. go h. to thy friends [h.
Lu. 9: 61. first bid them farewell at
15 : 6. cometh h. he calleth friends
Jn. 16 : †32. scatt-d every man h.
19 : 27. disciple took her to his h.
20 : 10. disciples went to own h.
Ac. 2: †46. breaking bread at h.
21: 6. ship, they returned h. again
1 Co. 11:34. if hunger eat at h. [h.
14: 35. let them ask husbands at
2 Co. 5: 6. whilst we at h. in body
1 Ti. 5 : 4. learn to show piety at h.
Tit. 2 : 5. to be discreet,keepers at h.

Born at HOME,
or HOMEBORN. [ger
Ex. 12 :49, One law to h. and stran-
Le. 18 : 9. of thy sister, whether she
be b. a. h. or abroad [slave?
Je. 2 : 14. Is Israel a servant? a h.

HOMER, S.
Le. 27 : 16. a h. of barley seed at
Nu.11:32. th.gath-d least had 10 h-s
Is. 5 : 10. seed of a h. yield ephah
Eze. 45 : 11. measure be after the h.
13. sixth part of ephah of a h. of
14. for ten baths are a h. [wheat
Ho. 3 : 2. I bought her for h. and

HONEST. [half h.
Lu. 8: 15. in an h. and good heart
Ac. 6 : 3. look out 7 men of h. report
Ro. 12 : 17. things h. in sight of all
2 Co. 8 : 21. h. things in sight of L.
13 : 7. ye should do that wh. is h.
Ph. 4 : 8. whatso. things are h. just
Tit. 3 : †14. learn to profess h. trades
1 Pe. 2: 12. having our conversa-

HONESTLY. [tion h.
Ro. 13 : 13. Let us walk h. as in day
1 Th. 4 : 12. h. tow. them without
He. 13 : 18. in all things willing to

HONESTY. [live h.
1 Ti. 2 : 2. lead peaceable life in h.

HONEY.
Ge. 43 : 11. carry a little h. spices
Ex. 16 : 31. like wafers made with h.
Le. 2 : 11. sh. burn no leaven nor h.
De. 8 : 8. a land of h., 2 K. 18 : 32.
32 : 13. suck h. out of the rock.
Ju. 14 : 8. h. in carcass of lion, 9.
18. What sweeter than h.? what
1 S. 14 : 25. was h. upon ground
26. h. dropped | 29. I tasted h.,43.
2 S. 17 : 29. brought h. to David
1 K. 14 : 3. take cruse of h. to him
2 Ch.31:5. Isr. bro-t first fruits of h.
Jb. 20 : 17. sh. not see brooks of h.
Ps. 19 : 10. judgments sweeter than
h., 119: 103. [satis. thee
81 : 16. with h. out of rock have
Pr. 24 : 13. My son, eat h., 25 : 16.

Pr. 25:27. not good to eat much **h.**
Can. 4:11. **h.** milk under tongue
5:1. eaten honeycomb with my **h.**
Is. 7:15. Butter and **h.** sh. he eat
22. butter and **h.** shall ev. one eat
Je. 41:8. we have treasures of **h.**
Eze. 3:3. it was in my mouth as **h.**
16:13. thou didst eat fine flour, **h.**
27:17. Jud. traded in **h.** and balm
Mat. 3:4. John the Baptist's meat was locusts and wild **h.**, Mk. 1:6.
Re. 10:9 be in thy mouth sweet as **h.**
10. was in my mouth sweet as **h.**
See FLOWETH, FLOWING.

HONEYCOMB.

1 S. 14:27. put forth rod dipped in [h.
Ps. 19:10. sweeter also than **h.**
Pr. 5:3. lips of strange woman as **h.**
16:24. Pleasant words are as a **h.**
24:13. eat **h.** sweet to thy taste
27:7. The full soul loatheth a **h.**
Can. 4:11. Thy lips, O spouse, as a **h.**
5:1. eaten my **h.** with my honey
Lu. 24:42. gave him a piece of **h.**

HONOUR, S.

Ge. 49:6. mine **h.** be not thou united
Ex. 8:†9. said, Have this **h.** ov. me
14:17. I will get me **h.** upon Pha.
18. when gotten me **h.** upon Pha.
Nu. 22:17. promote thee unto **h.**, 37.
24:11. L. hath kept thee back fr. **h.**
27:20. shalt put some **h.** upon him
De. 26:19. make thee high in **h.**
Ju. 4:9. journey not be for thine **h.**
13:17. come to pass, we do thee **h.**
2 S. 6:22. of them I be had in **h.**
1 K. 3:13. have given thee riches, **h.**
1 Ch. 16:27. Glory and **h.** in his pres.
17:18. What Da. say for **h.** of serv.
29:12. riches and **h.** come of thee
28. Da. died, full of riches and **h.**
2 Ch. 1:11 hast not asked riches or **h.**
12. I will give thee riches and **h.**
17:5. Jehosh-t **h.** in abun., 18:1.
26:18. nei. shall it be for thy **h.** fr.
32:27. Hez. had much riches and **h.**
33. inhabi. of Jerusalem did him **h.**
Es. 1:4. shew **h.** of his majesty
20. all wives sh. give to hush-s **h.**
6:3. What **h.** hath been done Mord.
†6. in whose **h.** king delighteth
8:16. Jews had light, joy and **h.**
Jb. 14:21. His sons come to **h.**
Ps. 7:5. ene. lay mine **h.** in dust
8:5. crowned him wi. **h.**, He. 2:7.9.
21:5. **h.** and majesty upon him
26:8. I loved place where thine **h.**
29:†2. Give unto L. **h.** of his name
49:12. man being in **h.** abideth not
20. Man that is in **h.** and understandeth not
66:2. Sing forth **h.** of his name
71:8. my mouth be filled with thy **h.**
96:6. **h.** and majesty are bef. him
104:1. thou art clothed with **h.**
112:9. horn sh. be exalted with **h.**
145:5. I will speak of **h.** of thy
149:9. this **h.** have all his saints
Pr. 3:16. in her left hand riches **h.**
4:8. exalt her, she bring thee to **h.**
5:9. Lest give thine **h.** unto oth.
8:18. Riches and **h.** are with me
11:16. graci. woman retaineth **h.**
14:28. In mult. of people is king's **h.**
15:33. bef. **h.** is humility, 18:12.
20:3. It is an **h.** to cease fr. strife
21:21. followeth mercy, findeth **h.**
22:4. By fear of L. are riches **h.**
25:2. **h.** of kings is to search out
26:1. **h.** is not seemly for a fool
8. so is he th. giveth **h.** to a fool
29:23. **h.** sh. uphold the humble
31:25. Strength **h.** are her clothing
Ec. 6:2. to whom G. hath given **h.**
10:1. him that is in reputa. for **h.**
Je. 33:9. be to me an **h.** bef. nat-s
Da. 2:6. ye shall receive great **h.**
Da. 4:30. built for **h.** of my majesty
36. mine **h.** and brightness retu-d
5:18. G. gave thy father glory **h.**
11:21. not give **h.** of the kingd.
Mal. 1:6. if fa., where is mine **h.**?
Mat. 13:57. prophet not without **h.** save in, Mk. 6:4. Jn. 4:44.
Jn. 5:41. I receive not **h.** fr. men
44. receive **h.** one of ano., and seek not **h.** cometh from God
8:54. If honour mys., **h.** is noth.
Ac. 28:10. honoured us wi. many **h-s**
Ro. 2:7. in well doing seek for **h.**
10. **h.** to ev. man worketh good
9:21. of same lump one vessel to **h.**
12:10. in **h.** preferring one anot.
13:7. Render **h.** to whom **h.** is due
1 Co. 12:23. bestow more abun. **h.**, 24.
2 Co. 6:8. By **h.** and dishonour
Col. 2:23. not in any **h.** to satisfying
1 Th. 4:4. to possess his vessel in **h.**
1 Ti. 1:17. unto only wise G. be **h.**
5:17. counted worthy of double **h.**
6:1. count mas. worthy of all **h.**
16. to whom be **h.** power [ho., 21.
2 Ti. 2:20. some to **h.** some to dis-
He. 3:3. hath more **h.** than the hou.
5:4. no man taketh this **h.** unto
1 Pe. 1:7. found to praise, **h.** [hims.
2:†7. Unto you that believe, an **h.**
3:7. **h.** to wife as to weaker vessel
2 Pe. 1:17. he received from G. **h.**
Re. 4:9. when those beasts give **h.**
11. Thou art worthy to rec. glory and **h.**, 5:12. [12.-19:1.
5:13. **h.** and glory be unto him, 7.
19:7 Let us be glad, give **h.** to him
21:24. kings bring glory, **h.** into it

HONOUR. [Verb.]

Ex. 20:12. **h.** thy fa. and thy moth., [26.
De. 5:16. Mat. 15:4.-19:19. Mk. 7:10.-10 19. Lu. 18:20. Ep. 6:2.
Le. 19:15. not **h.** person of mighty
32. shalt **h.** the face of old man
Ju. 9:9. by me they **h.** G. and man
1 S. 2:30. them that **h.** me I will **h.**
15:30. yet **h.** me now, bef. elders
2 S. 10:3. thinkest Dav. doth **h.** thy fa., he sent unto thee? 1 Ch. 19:3.
Es. 6:6. k. delighteth to **h.**, 7, 9, 11.
Ps. 91:15. I will deliv. and **h.** him
Pr. 3:9. **h.** L. with thy substance
Is. 29:13. people with lips do **h.** me
43:20. beast of field shall **h.** me
58:13. **h.** him, not doing own ways
Da. 4:37. I extol and **h.** K. of heav.
11:38. sh. **h.** god of forces, a god his fa-s knew not, shall he **h.**
Mat. 15:6. and **h.** not fa. or moth.
Jn. 5:23. that all **h.** Son as **h.** Fa.
8:49. I **h.** my Fa., ye dishon. me
54. If I **h.** myself my **h.** is noth.
12:26 serve me, him will Fa. **h.**
1 Ti. 5:3. **h.** widows th. are widows
1 Pe. 2:17. **h.** all men, **h.** the king

HONOURABLE.

Ge. 34:19. Shechem was more **h.**
Nu. 22:15. sent princes more **h.** than
1 S. 9:6. a man of G., he is **h.** man
22:14. Da., who is **h.** in thy house
2 S. 23:19. Was he not most **h.** of three? thf. their capt., 1 Ch. 11:21.
23. was more **h.** than the thirty
2 K. 5:1. Naaman **h.** with master
1 Ch. 4:9. Jabez was more **h.** than
11:25. Behold, was **h.** am. thirty
Jb. 22:8. and the **h.** man dwelt in it
Ps. 45:9. King's dau.'s am. **h.** wom.
111:3. His work is **h.** and glorious
Is. 3:3. L. doth take aw. **h.** man
5. base behave proudly ag. **h.**
5:13. their **h.** men are famished
9:15. ancient and **h.** he is head
23:8. whose traffickers are the **h.**
9. into contempt all **h.** of earth
42:21. magnify law make it **h.** [L. **h.**
43:4. hast been **h.** | 58:13. holy of
Na. 3:10. lots for her **h.** men
Mk. 15:43. Joseph **h.** counsellor
Lu. 14:8. lest more **h.** man be bid.
Ac. 13:50. Jews stirred up **h.** wom.
17:12. **h.** women not a few beli-d
1 Co. 4:10. we are weak, ye are **h.**
12:23. members we think less **h.**
He. 13:4. Marriage is **h.** and bed

HONOURED.

Ex. 14:4. I will be **h.** upon Pha.
Pr. 13:18. regardeth reproof be **h.**
27:18. waiteth on master sh. be **h.**
Is. 43:23. nei. **h.** me with sacrifi.
La. 1:8. all that **h.** her, despise her
5:12. faces of elders were not **h.**
Da. 4:34. I **h.** him th. liveth for ev.
Ac. 28:10. **h.** us wi. many honours
1 Co. 12:26. or one member be **h.**

HONOUREST.

1 S. 2:29. **h.** thy sons above me

HONOURETH.

Ps. 15:4. he **h.** them that fear L.
Pr. 12:9. better than he th. **h.** hims.
14:31. he that **h.** him hath mercy
Mal. 1:6. A son **h.** his fa., where is my
Mat. 15:8. **h.** me wi. lips. Mk. 7:6.
Jn. 5:23. **h.** not the Son, **h.** not Fa.
8:54. it is my Father that **h.** me

HOODS.

Is. 3:23. I will take away the **h.**

HOOF.

Ex. 10:26. shall not a **h.** be left
Le. 11:3. Whatever parteth **h.** and
4. of them that divide **h.** (2)
5. divideth not **h.**, 4, 6. De. 14:7.
7. swine, tho. divide **h.**, De. 14:8.

HOOFS.

Ju. 5:22. were the horse **h.** broken
Ps. 69:31. please L. better than ox wi.
Is. 5:28. their horses **h.** like flint [h.
Je. 47:3. noise of stamping of **h.**
Eze. 26:11. Wi. **h.** of horses sh. tread
32:13. nei. **h.** of beasts trouble th.
Mi. 4:13. I will make thy **h.** brass.
See HORSEHOOFS.

HOOK.

2 K. 19:28. my **h.** in thy nose, Is. 37: [29.
Jb. 41:1. draw leviathan with **h.**? 2.
Mat. 17:27. cast a **h.** take up fish

HOOKS.

Ex. 26:32. **h.** shall be of gold, 37.- [36:36.
27:10. **h.** of pillars be of silver, 11, 17.-38:10, 11, 12, 17, 19, 28.
Eze. 29:4. put **h.** in thy jaws, 38:4.
40:43. within were **h.** a hand broad
See FISHHOOKS, PRUNINGHOOKS.

HOPE. [Noun.]

Ru. 1:12. If I should say, I have **h.**
Ezr. 10:2. is **h.** in Isr. conc. this
Jb. 4:6. Is not this thy fear, thy **h.**
5:16. poor hath **h.** iniquity stoppeth
7:6. My days are spent without **h.**
8:13. hypocrite's **h.** sh. perish, 14.
11:18. shalt be secure, bec. is **h.**
20. their **h.** as giving up of ghost
14:7. is **h.** of a tree if it be cut do.
19. thou destroyest the **h.** of man
27:8. what is **h.** of hypocrite tho.
41:9. the **h.** of him is in vain
Ps. 78:7. might set their **h.** in God
146:5. Happy he whose **h.** is in L.
Pr. 10:28. **h.** of righte. be gladness
11:7. **h.** of unjust men perisheth
13:12. **h.** defer-d maketh heart sick
14:32. righte. hath **h.** in his death
19:18. Chasten son while there is **h.**
26:12. **h.** of fool than him, 29:20.
Ec. 9:4. to him joined to living, is **h.**
Is. 57:10. is no **h.**, Je. 2:25.-18:12.
Je. 14:8 O the **h.** of Israel, 17:13.
17:7. Blessed is man wh. **h.** the L.
31:17. is **h.** in the end, saith L.
50:7. the L., the **h.** of their fa-s
La. 3:21. This I recall, thf. have **h.**
29. if so be there may be **h.**
Eze. 19:5. saw that her **h.** was lost
37:11. say, Our bones dried, **h.** lost

Ho. 2:15. valley of Achor door of h.
Jo. 8 : 16. L. will be h. of people
Zch. 9 : 12. Turn ye prisoners of h.
Ac. 16 : 19. saw h. of gains was gone
23 : 6. of h. and resur. of the dead
24:15. h. tow. G. which they allow
26 : 6. judged for h. of the promise
7. For wh. h. sake, I am accused
27 : 20. all h. th. we be saved gone
28:20. for h. of Israel I am bound
Ro. 5 : 4. patience ; experience, h.
5. h. maketh not ashamed, bec.
8:24. saved by h. h. seen is not h.
15:4. thro. patience might have h.
13. that ye may abound in h.
1 Co. 9:10. th. he be partaker of h.
13:13. now abideth faith, h. charity
15:19. If in this life only we have h.
2 Co. 1 : 7. our h. of you is steadf.
3:12. Seeing that we have such h.
10 : 15. h. when your faith is incr.
Ga. 5 : 5. we thro. Spirit wait for h.
Ep. 1 : 18. what is h. of his calling
2:12. having no h. and without G.
4 : 4. as ye are called in one h.
Col. 1:5. h. laid up for you in heav.
23. be not moved fr. h. of gospel
27. is Christ in you, h. of glory
1 Th. 1:3. your patience of h. in Jes.
2:19. For what is our h. or joy?
4:13. even as others who have no h.
5 : 8. for a helmet h. of salvation
2 Th. 2 : 16. hath given us good h.
1 Ti. 1 : 1. L. Jesus, who is our h.
Tit. 2:13. Looking for th. blessed h.
3 : 7. heirs acc. to h. of eternal life
He. 3:6. rejoicing of h. firm unto end
6 : 11. full assur. of h. unto end
18. have fled to lay hold upon h.
19. Which h. we have as anchor
7 : 19. bringing in of better h. did
1 Pe. 1:3. begotten us to a lively h.
21. that your h. might be in G.
3 : 15. asketh a reason of h. in you
1 Jn. 3:3. ev. man that hath this h.

In HOPE. [2: 26.

Ps. 16:9. my flesh sh. rest i. h., Ac.
Ro. 4:18. Who. ag. hope beli-d i. h.
5 : 2. rejoice i. h. of glory of God
8 : 20. hath subjected same i. h.
12:12. Rejoicing i. h. patient in trib.
15 : 13. that ye may abound i. h.
1 Co. 9:10. plougheth i. h. thresheth
Tit. 1 : 2. i. h. of eternal life [i. h.

Mine or my HOPE.

Jb. 17:15. where m. h.? as for m. h.
19 : 10. m-e h. hath he removed
31:24. If I have made gold m. h.
Ps. 39:7. wait I for? m. h. is in thee
71:5. thou art m. h. O L., Je. 17:17.
119:116. let me not be asha. of m.
La. 3 : 18. m. h. is perished [h.
Ph. 1:20. acc. to m. h. that in noth.

HOPE. [Verb.] [I h.?

Jb. 6:11. What is my strength, th.
Ps. 22 : 9. thou didst make me h.
31 : 24. courage, all ye th. h. in L.
33:18. th. h. in his mercy, 147:11.
22. thy mercy acc. as we h. in thee
38:15. For in thee, O Lord, do I h.
42:5. cast down? h. in G., 11.-43:
71 : 14. I will h. continually [5.
119:49. thou hast caused me to h.
81. I h. in thy word, 114.-130:5.
130:7. Let Isr. h. in the L., 131:3.
Is. 38 : 18. they in pit cannot h.
La. 3 : 24. portion, thf. will I h.
26. good th. man both h. and wait
Eze. 13 : 6. have made others to h.
Lu. 6:34. if lend to th. of wh. ye h.
Ac. 26:7. to wh. promise our tribes h.
Ro. 8:24. seeth, why doth he h. for
25. if we h. for what we see not
Ph. 2:23. Him I h. to send presently
1 Pe. 1:13. Whf. be sober, h. to end

HOPED. [power

Es. 9 : 1. enem. of Jews h. to have
Jb. 6:20. confounded bec. they had h.
Ps. 119:43. I have h. in thy judgm.
74. bec. I have h. in thy word, 147.
166. L. I have h. for thy salva.
Je. 3:23. in vain is salvation h. for
Lu. 23 : 8. h. to have seen miracle
Ac. 24:26. h. money sho. been given
2 Co. 8 : 5. this did, not as we h.
He. 11:1. substance of things h. for

HOPETH, ING.

Lu. 6:35. lend, h-g for nothing again
1 Co. 13 : 7. charity h-h all things
1 Ti. 3 : 14. I write, h-g to come

HOPH'NI. [shortly

1 S. 1 : 3. two sons of Eli, H., 4 : 4.
2:34. H. and Phin. die in one day
4 : 11. H. and Phin. were slain, 17.

Mount HOR.

Nu. 20 : 22. and came unto m. H.
23. L. spake unto Mo. and Aa. in
25. bring th. into m. H. [m. H.
27. Mo. and Aa. went into m. H.
21:4. journeyed fr. m. H., 33:37, 41.
33 : 38. Aa. went into m. H., 39.
34:8. From m. H. sh. point border, 7.
De. 32 : 50. Aaron died in m. H.

HO'RAM.

Jos. 10:33. H. king of Gezer came up

HO'REB.

Ex. 3:1. Moses came to H., 1 K. 19:8.
17:6. stand bef. thee upon rock in
33:6. stripped of ornam. by H. [H.
De. 1 : 2. are 11 days journey fr. H.
6. the L. spake unto us in H., 4:15.
19. when we departed fr. H.
4 : 10. when stoodest bef. L. in H.
5 : 2. L. made a cov. in H., 29 : 1.
9 : 8. in H. ye provoked the Lord
18 : 16. thou desiredst of L. in H.
1 K. 8 : 9. noth. save tables Moses
put in ark at H., 2 Ch. 5 : 10.
Ps. 106 : 19. they made a calf in H.
Mal. 4:4. I com-d unto Moses in H.

HO'REM. [Naph.

Jos. 19 : 38. Migdal-el H. cities of

HOR-HAGID'GAD.

Nu. 33 : 32. encamped at H. | 33.

HO'RI. [1:39.

Ge. 36:22. chil. of Lotan, H., 1 Ch.
30. dukes came of H. | Nu. 13 : 5.

HO'RIM.

De. 2: 12. H. dwelt in Seir bef. | 22.

HO'RITE, S.

Ge. 14 : 6. H-s in mount Seir
36:21. are the dukes of the H-s, 29.
20. these sons of Seir the H.

HOR'MAH.

Nu. 14 : 45. discomfited them to H.
21 : 3. and he called the place H.
De. 1: 44. destroyed you even to H.
Jos. 12 : 14. the king of H. one
15 : 30. cities of Judah, H.
19 : 4. Simeon had out of Jud. H.
Ju. 1 : 17. name of the city was H.
1 S. 30:30. a present to them in H.
1 Ch. 4 : 30. Shimei's sons at H.

HORN.

Ex. 21 : 29. if ox push with his h.
1 S. 2:1. mine h. is exalted in the L.
10. shall exalt h. of his anointed
16 : 1. fill thine h. with oil, go, I
13. Samuel took the h. of oil and
2 S. 22 : 3. h. of my salv., Ps. 18:2.
1 K. 1 : 39. Zadok took a h. of oil
1 Ch. 25:5. in words of G. to lift h.
Jb. 16 : 15. I have defiled my h.
Ps. 75:4. wicked, lift not up h., 5.
89 : 17. in thy favour h. exalted
24. in my name his h. exalted
92:10. my h. shalt thou exalt like
112:9. his h. shall be exalted [h.
132 : 17. make h. of David to bud
148:14. He exalteth h. of his peo.
Je. 48 : 25. h. of Moab is cut off
La. 2 : 3. hath cut off h. of Israel
17. he hath set up h. of adversa.
Eze. 29 : 21. cause h. of Isr. to bud
Da. 7 : 8. a little h. in this h., 20.
11. great words which h. spake
21. same h. made war with saints
8 : 5. goat had a notable h. betw.
8 : 8. strong, great h. was broken
9. out of one of th. came little h.
21. great h. that is between eyes
Mi. 4 : 13. I will make thine h. iron
Zch. 1:21. lift up their h. over land
Lu. 1:69. hath raised up a h. of salv.

HORNS.

Ge. 22 : 13. a ram caught by his h.
Ex. 27 : 2. make h. of it upon 4 corners, his h. of same, 30 : 2.-37:
25.-38 : 2.
29:12. put of the blood upon h. of
altar, Le. 4:7. 18, 25, 30, 34.-
8 : 15.-9 : 9.-16 : 18.
30:3. with pure gold overlay h., 37:
10. atonem. upon h. of it [26.
De 33:17. h. are like h. of unicorns
Jos. 6:4. seven priests bear 7 trumpets of rams' h., 6, 8, 13.
1 K. 1 : 50. caught hold on h. of
altar, 51.-2 : 28.
2 : 28. Joab caught hold on h. of
altar
22 : 11. Zedekiah made h. of iron,
2 Ch. 18 : 10.
Ps. 22 : 21. heard me fr. h. of uni-
69:31. bullock that hath h. [corns
75 : 10. h. of wicked will I cut off,
the h. of righte. sh. be exalted
118:27. bind sacri. unto h. of altar
Je. 17:1. heart and upon h. of altars
Eze. 27:15. for a present h. of ivory
34:21. ye pushed diseased with h.
43 : 15. fr. altar and upw be 4 h.
Da. 7:7. 4th beast had ten h., 20, 24.
8. I considered the h. three h.
were plucked up [Re. 17:12, 16.
24. ten h. are 10 k.'s that sh. arise,
8 : 3. ram had 2 h. 2 h. were high
6. goat came to ram had 2 h.
7. smote ram, brake his two h.
20. two h. are kings of Media and
Am. 6:13. Have we not taken h. by
Ha. 3:4. he had h. out of ha. [our
Zch. 1 : 18. I saw, behold, four h.
19. h. which have scatt-d Jud., 21.
21. to cast out h. of Gentiles
Re. 5 : 6. stood Lamb having 7 h.
9:13. voice fr. 4 h. of golden altar
12 : 3. having 7 heads and ten h.,
17 : 3, 7. [h.
13:1. beast having 10 h. and upon
11. ano. beast had 2 h. like lamb
See ALTAR, S.

HORNET, S.

Ex. 23: 28. I will send h-s bef. thee
De. 7: 20. L. will send h. am. them
Jos. 24 : 12. I sent the h. bef. you

HORONA'IM.

Is. 15 : 5. in the way of H. a cry
Je. 48 : 3. crying shall be from H.
5. in going down of H. a cry
34. fr. Zoar to H. uttered voice

HOR'ONITE.

Ne. 2:10. Sanballat H. heard, 19. |

HORRIBLE. [18:38.

Ps. 11:6. Upon wicked rain h. temp.
40 : 2. He bro-t me out of h. pit
Je. 5 : 30. A h. thing is committed
18:13. virgin of Isr. done h. thing
23:14. seen in prophets a h. thing
Ho. 6:10. I have seen a h. thing in

HORRIBLY. [Isr.

Je. 2:12. be h. afraid, O ye heavens
Eze. 32: 10. kings shall be h. afraid

HORROR. [fell

Ge. 15 : 12. an h. of great darkness
Jb. 18 : † 20. they laid hold on h.
Ps. 55:5. h. hath overwhelmed me
119 : 53. h. taken hold upon me
Eze. 7 : 18. h. shall cov. them, and

HORSE. [shame

Ge. 49:17. an adder biteth h. heels

Ex. 15 : 21. h. and rider he thrown
1 K. 10: 29. h. for 150 shek., 2 Ch.1:
20:20. Benhadad escaped on h.[17.
25. num. like army lost, h. for h.
Es. 6 : 8. h. king rideth on be bro-t
9. h. be deliv-d to one of princes
10. take h. as thou hast said
11. Haman the apparel and h.
Jb. 39:18. she scorneth h. and rider
19. Hast thou given h. strength?
Ps. 32 : 9. Be ye not as h. or mule
33: 17. h. is vain thing for safety
76:6. chariot and h. cast into sleep
147:10. delighteth not in str. of h.
Pr. 21:31. h. is prepared ag. battle
26: 3. A whip for h. rod for fool's
Is. 43:17. Which bringeth forth h.
63 : 13. led them thro. deep, as h.
Je. 8 : 6. as h. rusheth into battle
51:21. break in pieces h. and rider
Am. 2:15. nei. th. rideth h. deliver
Zch. 1:8. a man riding upon red h.
9:10. I will cut off h. from Jerus.
10: 3. them as goodly h. in battle
12:4. will smite ev. h. with blindn.
14:15. so sh. be the plague of the h.
Re. 6 : 2. I saw white h., 19 : 11.
4. red h. | 5. black h. | 8. pale h.
14:20. blood came unto h. bridles
19: 19. war ag. him that sat on h.
21. slain with sw. of him sat upon [h.

HORSE gate.
See Horse GATE.

HORSES.

Ge. 47:17. bread in exchange for h.
Ex. 9 : 3. hand of L. is upon h. [(2)
De. 17:16. not multiply h. to hims.
1 K. 4 : 28. Barley and straw for h.
10:25. they brought h. and mules,
2 Ch. 9 : 24. [16,17.-9:28.
28. Sol. had h. out of E., 2 Ch.1:
18:5. may find grass to save the h.
22: 4. my h. as thy h., 2 K. 3 : 7.
2 K. 2:11. there appeared h. of fire
5:9. Naaman came wi. h. and chari.
7: 7. they left h. and fled for life
10. h. tied | 13. take five of h.
9: 33. Jezebel's blood on the h.
11:16. way by wh. h. came into k.'s
14:20. Amaziah on h., 2 Ch. 25:28.
18: 23. deliver 2000 h., Is. 36 : 8.
23: 11. took away h. given to sun
Ezr. 2:66. Their h. were 736, Ne 7:68.
Ec. 10:7. I have seen serv-s upon h.
Is. 2 : 7. their land is full of h. and
5 : 28. their h. hoofs be like flint
30:16. No, for we will flee upon h.
31: 1. stay on h. trust in chariots
3. their h. are flesh, and not spirit
Je. 4:13. h. are swifter than eagles
5:8. They were as fed h. in morn
6: 23. they ride on h. set in array
8:16. snorting of his h. was heard
12: 5. how canst contend with h.?
46: 4. Harness the h. and get up.
47: 3. stamping of hoofs of his h.
50:42. ride upon h. in array
51:27. cause h. to come as caterpill.
Eze. 17 : 15. give him h. and peo.
23:6. horsemen riding upon h., 12.
20. issue is like the issue of h.
23. renowned, all upon h., 38:15
26: 10. of the abundance of his h.
11. With hoofs of h. sh. he tread
27:14. traded in thy fairs with h.
38:4. I will br. forth thy army h.
Ho. 1:7. I will not save by battle nor
14: 3. we will not ride on h. [h.
Jo. 2: 4. as appearance of h. and
Am. 4: 10. I have taken your h.
6:12. Shall h. run upon the rock?
Mi. 5: 10. that I will cut off thy h.
Ha. 1: 8. Their h. are swifter than
3:8. thou didst ride upon thine h.
15. didst walk thro. sea with h.
Hag. 2 : 22. I will overthr. h. and
Zch. 1: 8. behind him red h.[riders

Zch. 6:2. 1st chariot red h. 2d black
3. in 3d white h. in 4th bay h.
6. black h. go forth into north
10 : 5. riders on h. be confounded
14:20. in that day upon the bells of
h. HOLINESS TO THE LORD
Ja. 3 : 3. we put bits in h. mouths
Re. 9 : 7. locusts were like h.
17. I saw h. heads of h. as of lions
18: 13. buyeth merchandise of h.
19:14. armies foll-d upon white h.
18. may eat flesh of kings and h.
See CHARIOT, S.

HORSEBACK.

2 K. 9 : 18. one on h. to meet Jehu
19. Then he sent out second on h.
Es. 6 : 9. bri. him on h. thro. city
11. Haman bro-t him on h. thro.
8: 10. sent letters by posts on h.

HORSEHOOFS.

Ju. 5 : 22. Then were h. broken by

HORSELEECH.

Pr. 30 : 15. h. hath two daughters

HORSEMAN.

2 K. 9: 17. Joram said, Take a h.
Na. 3:3. h. lifteth up the bright sw.

HORSEMEN. [h.

Ge. 50 : 9. with Joseph chariots and
Ex. 14 : 9. h. of Pha. pursued, 23.
17. honour upon Pha. and h., 18.
26. that waters come upon E-ns
and h., 28. [24: 6.
15 : 19. Pha. and h. into sea, Jos.
1 S. 8 : 11. your sons to be his h.
13 : 5. Philis. gathered 6000 h. ag.
2 S. 1: 6. the h. followed hard
8:4 Da. took from Hadadezer 700 h.
10 : 18. David slew 40,000 h.
1 K. 1: 5. Adonijah prepared h.
4: 26. Sol. had 12,000 h., 10: 26.
9 : 19. Sol. had cities of store for
chariots, h., 22. 2 Ch. 8 : 6, 9.
20: 20. Ben-hadad escaped wi. h.
2 K. 2:12. chariot of Isr. and the h.
13: 7. leave to Jehoahaz but 50 h.
14. Joash said, O my father! the
chariot of Israel, and the h.
18: 24. put thy trust in E. for h.
2 Ch. 12: 3. Shishak with 60,000 h.
16: 8 Ethiopians with many h.
Ezr. 8:22. asham. to ask h. to help
Ne. 2 : 9. king had sent h. with me
Is. 21:7. he saw chariot with h., 9
22: 7. h. shall set thems. in array
28: 28. will not bruise it wi. his h.
31: 1. trust in h. bec. they strong
36:9. How put thy trust on E. for h.
Je. 4: 29. city sh. flee for noise of h.
46: 4. get up ye h. and stand with
Eze. 23: 6. h. riding upon horses, 12.
26:7. bring Neb-ar ag. Tyrus wi. h.
10. walls shake at noise of h.
27 : 14. of Togarmah traded wi. h.
38:4. Gog I will bring thee and h.
Da. 11:40. k. of north sh. come wi. h.
Ho. 1:7. not save by horses, nor by h.
Jo. 2: 4. as h. so shall they run
Ha. 1:8. their h. shall spread thems.,
their h. shall come from far
Ac. 23:23. ready h. threesc. and 10.
32. On morrow they left the h.
Re. 9:16 number of army of h. were
See THOUSAND.

HO'SAH. [Person, Place.]

Jos. 19:29. and the coast turn-h to H.
1 Ch. 16: 38. Obed-edom H porters
26:10. H. of chil. of Merari 11,16.

HO'SAI. [the H.

2 Ch. 33 : †19. am. the sayings of

HOSANNA.

Mat. 21: 9. h. to son of Da., h. in
highest, 15 Mk. 11:9,10. Jn. 12:

HO'SEA = O'SEE. [13.

Ho. 1 : 1. word of L unto H., 2.
Ro. 9 : 25. As he saith unto O.

HOSEN.

Da. 3:21. men were bound in their h.

HOSHAI'AH.

Ne. 12 : 32. after them went H.
Je. 42 : 1. Jezaniah son of H., 43:2.

HOSH'AMA.

1 Ch. 3 : 18. sons of Jeconiah, H.

HOSHE'A.

De. 32 : 44 he and H. spake to peo
2 K. 15:30. H made conspiracy, 17:4.
17 : 1. H. began to reign in Sama.
3. H. became k. of Assyria's serv.
6. year of H. Samaria tak., 18:10.
18:1. 3d yr. of H. | 9. 7th yr. of H.
1 Ch. 27 : 20. ruler of Ephr. was H.
Ne. 10: 23. H. sealed the covenant

HOSPITALITY.

Ro. 12 : 13. given to h., 1 Ti. 3 : 2.
Tit. 1: 8. lover of h. lover of good
1 Pe. 4:9. Use h. one to ano. [men

HOST. [h.

Lu. 10:35. two pence, gave them to
Ro 16 : 23. Gaius mine h. saluteth

HOST. [you

Ge. 2 : 1. earth finished, and all h.
21:22. Phichol chief cap. of h., 32.
32:2. Jac. said, This is God's h. [17.
Ex. 14:4. honoured upon all his h.,
24. L. looked unto h. of E-s thro.
pillar of fire, and troubled the h
28. waters covered h. of Pha.
16 : 13. in morn. dew lay round h.
Nu. 2 : 4. his h. and those numbered, 6, 8, 11, 13, 15, 19, 21, 23.
4:3. all th. enter into h. to do work
10: 14. h. of Judah | 15. Issachar
16. h. of Zebulun | 18. Reuben
19. h. of Simeon | 20, 22, 23, 24,
25, 26, 27.
31: 14. wroth with officers of h.
48. officers of h. came unto Mo.
De. 2 : 14. men of war wasted fr. h.
15. to destroy them from am. h.
23: 9. When h. goeth ag. enemies
Jos. 1 : 11. Pass thro. h. command
3:2. officers went thro. h. [peo.
5:14. as capt. of h. of L. am come,
8: 13. h. th. was on north of city [15.
18:9. came to Josh. to h. at Shiloh
Ju. 4 : 2. captain of h. was Sisera
16. all h. of Sisera fell upon sw.
7 : 8. h. of Midian in valley, 1, 11.
9. God said, Get thee unto h., 10,
13. cake of bread tumbled into h.
14. G. deliv-d Midian and h., 15, 22.
21. all the h. ran, and cried [cure
8 : 11. Gideon smote h. the h. se-
12. Gideon discomfited all h.
1 S. 11 : 11. Saul came into the h.
14:15. there was trembling in the h.
19. noise of the h. went on and
48. gath-d h. and smote Amalek
50. capt. of Saul's h. was Abner, 17:
55.-26: 5. 2 S. 2: 8.
17:20. Da. came as the h. was going
46. carcasses of h. of Philis.
28: 5. when Saul saw h. of Philis.
19. L. shall deliver h. of Isr. to
29: 6. coming in with me in h. is
good [19: 8.
2 S. 3: 23. Joab and h., 10:7. 1 Ch.
5: 24. L. smite h. of Philistines
8:9. When Toi heard Da. had smitten h. of Hadadezer, 1 Ch. 18:9.
10:18. Da. smote Shobach capt. of
h. who died, 16. 1 Ch. 19 : 18.
17:25. Abs. made Amasa capt. of h.
19: 13. if thou be not capt. of h.
20:23. Joab was over all h., 8:16.-
24:2 1 K. 1:19.-11:15, 21. 1 Ch.
18: 15. [h., 1 Ch. 11:18.
23: 16. these three brake thro. the
1 K. 2:32. Abner capt. of the h. Isr.
Amasa capt. of h. of Judah
35. k. put Benaiah over h., 4: 4.
16:16. made Omri captain of h.
20:1. Ben-hadad gathered all h.
22: 34. carry me out of the h.
36. a proclamation thro-t the h.

2 K. 3: 9. there was no water for **h.**
4:13. be spoken for to capt. of **h.**?
6:14. sent he horses and great **h.**, 15.
24. Ben-hadad gathered his **h.** and
7:4. let us fall unto **h.** of Syrians
6. L. made **h.** to hear noise of **h.**
14. king sent after **h.** of Syrians
9:5. the captains of **h.** were sitting
11: 15. Jehoi-a com-d officers of **h.**
18: 17. Sennach. sent a gr. **h.** ag.
25:1. Neb. and his **h.** ag. Jerusal.
19. principal scribe of **h.**, Je. 52: 25.
1 Ch. 9:19. fa-s over **h.** of the L.
11:15. **h.** of Philis. encamped
12:22. great **h.** like the **h.** of God
27:3. was chief of captains of **h.**
5. 3d capt. of **h.** was Benaiah
2 Ch. 14:9. ag them Zerah with a **h.**
16:7. thf. the **h.** of Syria escaped
8. Were not Lubims a huge **h.**?
18: 33. carry me out of the **h.**
24:24. L. delivered a great **h.** into
26:11. Uzziah had a **h.** of fighting
28:9. Oded went out bef. **h.** ⌊men
Ps. 27:3. Tho. a **h.** should encamp
33:6. **h.** of th. by breath of mouth
16. no k. is saved by mult. of a **h.**
136: 15. overthrew Pha. and **h.**
Is. 13:4. L. of hosts mustereth the **h.**
24:21. L. sh. punish **h.** of high ones
40:26. bring-h out their **h.** by num.
45:12. all their **h.** have I com-d
Je. 51: 3. destroy ye utterly all **h.**
Eze. 1:24. speech, as the noise of a **h.**
Da. 8:10. cast down some of **h.** ⌈**h.**
11. magnified hims. to prince of
12. an **h.** was given ag. daily sacri.
13. **h.** to be trodden under foot
Ob. 20. the captivity of this **h.**
Lu. 2:13. multitude of heavenly **h.**
See **Host, s of HEAVEN.**
See **CAPTAIN, S. HOSTS.** ⌈**h.**
Ge. 32: †2. called name of place, Two
Ex. 12: 41. **h.** of L. went out of E.
Jos. 10:5. k-s of Canaan and **h.**, 11:4.
Ju. 8:10. and Zalmunna with **h.** ⌈**h.**
1 K. 15: 20. sent the captains of the
Ps. 103: 21. Bless L., all ye his **h.**
108:11. wilt not, O G., go with **h.**?
148: 2. praise ye him, all his **h.**
Je. 3: 19. heritage of **h.** of nations
See **GOD of hosts, LORD of hosts.**

HOSTAGES.

2 K. 14: 14. Jehoash took gold and **h.** and returned to Sama., 2 Ch. ⌊22: 24.

HOT.

Ex. 16: 21. sun waxed **h.** it melted
Le. 13:24. flesh, whereof **h.** burning
De. 9:19. I was afraid of **h.** displeas.
19:6. lest pursue, while heart is **h.**
Jos. 9:12. This our bread we took **h.**
Ju. 2:14. anger of L. was **h.** against Israel, 20.-3: 8.-10: 7.
6:39. Gid. said, Let not anger be **h.**
9: † 30. heard Gaal, anger was **h.**
1 S. 11: 9. by the time sun be **h.**
21:6. put **h.** bread day it was tak.
1 K. 3: †26. her bowels **h.** upon son
Ne. 7: 3. be opened till sun be **h.**
Jb. 6:17. when **h.** they are consum.
Ps. 6:1. in thy **h.** displeasure, 38:1.
39:3. My heart was **h.** within me
78: 48. flocks to **h.** thunderbolts
85: †3. turned anger fr. waxing **h.**
Pr. 6:28. Can one go on **h.** coals?
Eze. 24:11. that brass of it may be **h.**
Da. 3:22. bec. furnace was exc-g **h.**
Ho. 7:7. They are all **h.** as an oven
1 Ti. 4: 2. seared with a **h.** iron
Re. 3:15. thou art nei. cold nor **h.**, I would thou wert cold or **h.**, 16.
See WAX. [Verb.]

HO'THAM.

1 Ch. 7: 32. Heber begat Shomer, ⌊and H.

HO'THAN.

1 Ch. 11:44. sons of H. the Aroerite

HO'THIR. ⌈28.

1 Ch. 25:4. sons of Heman, H. and,

HOTLY. ⌈me

Ge. 31: 36. hast so **h.** pursued after

HOTTEST. ⌈battle

2 S. 11:15. Uriah in forefront of **h.**

HOUGH, ED.

Jos. 11:6. said, Thou shalt **h.** horses
9. **h**-d horses, burnt chariots
2 S. 8:4. Da. **h**-d all the chariot horses

HOUR, S.

Da. 4: 19. Dan. astonied for one **h.**
Mat. 9:22. wom. made whole fr. th. **h.**
15: 28. dau. whole from that **h.**
17: 18. child was cured fr. that **h.**
20: 3. he went out about third **h.**
5. about 6th and 9th **h.** ⌈**h.**
6. about 11th **h.** | 9. hired 11th
12. These last wrought but one **h.**
24:36. that **h.** knoweth no man, 42. Mk. 13: 32. ⌈Lu. 12: 40, 46.
44. such an **h.** as ye think not, 50.
25: 13. ye know nei. day nor **h.**
26:40. could ye not watch one **h.**? Mk. 14:37. ⌈betrayed, Mk. 14:41.
45. **h.** is at hand, Son of man is
27:45. fr. sixth **h.** was darkness to ninth **h.**, Mk. 15:33. Lu. 23:44.
46. about 9th **h.** Jes. cried, Mk. 15:
Mk. 13:11. sh. be given you th. **h.** ⌊34.
14:35. if possible the **h.** might pass
15:25. third **h.**, and th. cruci. him
Lu. 10: 21. In that **h.** Jes. rejoiced
12:39. known **h.** thief would come
22:14. And when the **h.** was come
53. but this is your **h.** and power
59. about the space of one **h.** aft.
Jn. 1: 39. for it was about tenth **h.**
2: 4. Jes. saith, Mine **h.** is not yet
4: 6. it was about sixth **h.**, 19: 14.
21. believe me, the **h.** cometh, 23.
52. Then inquired he the **h.**, at seventh **h.** fever left him
5: 25. **h.** is co ing, 28.-16: 32.
7: 30. his **h.** not yet come, 8: 20.
11: 9. Are not twelve **h**-s in day?
12:23. The **h.** is come, 17: 1.
27. Fa., save me fr. this **h.**: but for this cause came I to this **h.**
13: 1. wh. Jes. knew **h.** was come
16:21. sorrow, bec. her **h.** is come
19:27. fr. that **h.** disciple took her
Ac. 2:15. seeing it is third **h.** of day
3: 1. at **h.** of prayer being 9th **h.**
5: 7. wife came in about 3 **h**-s aft.
10: 3. saw about 9th **h.** angel
9. Pet. went to pray about 6th **h.**
30. I was fasting until this **h.** ⌈is
19: 34. all cried about 2 **h**-s, Great
23: 23. Make ready at the third **h.**
1 Co. 4:11. to this present **h.** hunger
8:7. conscience of idol unto this **h.**
15:30. why we in jeopardy ev. **h.**?
Ga. 2: 5. gave place, not for an **h.**
Re. 3: 3. not know **h.** I will come
10. will keep thee fr **h.** of tempta.
8: 1. was silence about half an **h.**
9: 15. prepared for an **h.** a day
14: 7. the **h.** of his judgm. is come
17:12. receive power as kings one **h.**
18:10. in one **h.** is thy judgm. come
17. in **h.** great riches to nought
19. great city in one **h.** desolate

Same HOUR. ⌈15.

Da. 3: 6. **s. h.** be cast into furnace,
4:33. **s. h.** was thing fulfilled upon
5:5. In the **s. h.** came forth fingers
Mat. 8: 13. serv. was healed **s. h.**
Mat. 10: 19. given you that **s. h.** what ye shall speak, Lu. 12: 12.
26:55 In **s. h.** said Jesus to multi.
Lu. 7:21. **s. h.** cured many of plagues
20: 19. scribes **s. h.** sought to lay
24: 33. they **s. h.** returned to Jer.
Jn. 4: 53. father knew it was **s. h.**
Ac. 16: 18. spirit came out the **s. h.**
33. he took them **s. h.** of the night
Ac. 22:13. **s. h.** I looked up upon him
Re. 11: 13. **s. h.** was gr. earthquake

HOUSE. ⌈**h.**

Ge. 19: 4. men of Sodom compassed
24: 27. L. led me to **h.** of master's
31. prepared **h.** room for camels
28: 2. go to the **h.** of Bethuel, thy
39: 5. L. blessed the Egyptian's **h.**
45: 2. Egyp-s and **h.** of Pha. heard
Ex. 3: 22. sojourneth in her **h.**
12: 3. a lamb acc. to **h.** of fathers
30. not **h.** where not one dead
46. In one **h.** sh. passo. be eat. not carry flesh out of the **h.**
13: 3. day ye came out of **h.** of bond., 14. De. 5: 6.-6: 12. ⌈21.
20: 17. not covet neigh-s **h.**, De. 5:
22: 7. out of man's **h.**; if thief
Le. 14: 36. command they empty **h.**
38. priests go out of **h.** and shut
41. **h.** be scraped | 42. plaster **h.**
45. break down **h.** mortar of **h.**
46. goeth into **h.** be unclean, 47.
49. shall take to cleanse **h.**, 52.
53. atonement for the **h.** ⌈33.
25: 29. sell dwelling-**h.** in city, 30,
Nu. 30: 10. vowed in husb-d's **h.**
De. 7: 8. out of the **h.** of bondmen
8: 14. brought you out of **h.** of bondage, 13: 5, 10. Jos. 24: 17. Jud. 6: 8. Je. 34: 13. Mi. 6: 4.
22: 8. buildest new **h.** then thou
25: 10. **h.** of him hath shoe loosed
Jos. 2: 15. her **h.** upon town wall
Ju. 8. 35. nei. shewed kindn. to **h.** of
9: 6. **h.** of Millo made Abim. king
20. let fire come from **h.** of Millo
10: 9. Am. fought ag. **h.** of Ep.
16: 26. pillars whereon **h.** standeth
27. **h.** was full of men and wom.
30. **h.** fell upon the lords
17: 5. Micah had a **h.** of gods
18: 13. came unto the **h.** of Micah
19: 18. no man th. recei. me to **h.**
22. sons of Belial beset **h.**, 20: 5.
1 S. 3: 14. I have sworn unto **h.** of
9: 18. Tell me where seer's **h.** ⌊Eli
18: 10. he proph-d in midst of **h.**
25: 3. Nabal was of the **h.** of Caleb
28. L. will make my lord sure **h.**
2 S. 3: 1. war betw. **h.** of Saul **h.** of
8. do shew kindn-s unto **h.** of Saul
29. let not fail fr. **h.** of Joab one
4: 5. came to **h.** of Ishbosheth, 6, 7.
6: 12. L. blessed **h.** of Obed-e, Da. ark fr. **h.**, 1 Ch. 13: 14.-15: 25.
7: 6. not dwelt in **h.**, 1 Ch. 17: 5.
11. Lord he will make thee a **h.**
29. bless **h.** of thy serv., 1 Ch. 17.
9: 1. Is any left of **h.** of Saul? ⌊27.
12: 8. I give thee thy master's **h.**
13: 7. Go now to bro. Amnon's **h.**
15: 16. concu-s to keep **h.**, 16: 21.,
16: 5. man of **h.** of Saul ⌊20: 3.
1 K. 2: 24. who made me a **h.** as
27. spake conc. the **h.** of Eli
3: 17. I and this wom. dwell in 1 **h.**
5: 17. stones to lay founda. of **h.**
6: 22. **h.** he overlaid with gold
9: 25. so Solomon finished the **h.**
11:18. unto Pha. who gave him a **h.**
12: 31. Jerob. made **h.** of high pla.
14:10. bri. evil upon **h.** of Jerob., 14.
15: 29 Baasha smote **h.** of Jerob.
16: 11. Zimri slew all **h.** of Baasha
17: 15. she and **h.** eat many days
21: 22. make thy **h.** like **h.** of Jerob.
22: 39. ivory **h.** he made ⌈**h.**
2 K. 8: 3. to cry unto king for her
18. as did the **h.** of Ahab, 27. 2 Ch. 21: 6.-22: 3, 4. ⌈perish
9: 8. the whole of **h.** of Ahab shall
10: 3. fight for your master's **h.**
21. **h.** of Baal was full from one
27. made **h.** of Baal draught **h.**
12: 12. all that was laid out for **h.** to repair it, 22: 5, 6. 2 Ch. 34: 10.

2 K. 20: 13. Hez. shewed h. of precious things, h. of armour, Is. 39: 2.
23: 27. h. of wh. I said my name sh.
25: 9. ev. great man's h. he burnt
1 Ch. 2: 54. Ataroth the h. of Joab
26: 15. his sons, the h. of Asuppim
2 Ch. 3: 5. the greater h. he cieled
6. garnished h. with precious
3: 8. made the most holy h. [stones
7: 1. glory of L. filled h., Eze. 43: 4, 5.
12. chosen this place for h. of sacri.
22: 9. h. of Ahaziah had no power
34: 8. purged land and the h.
35: 21. ag. h. wherewith I have war
Ezr 5: 8. we went to h. of great God
6: 3. Let h. be builded at Jerus.
Ne. 12: 37. wall above the h. of David
Es. 2: 3. to h. of women, 9, 11, 13, 14.
8: 1. did give h. of Haman to Es., 7.
Jb. 1: 13. drinking wine in bro.'s h.
19. a wind smote corners of h. [18.
20: 19. taken aw. h. he builded not
21: 28. Where is the h. of the prince?
30: 23. h. appointed for all living
38: 20. shouldest know paths to h.
39: 6. whose h. I made wilderness
Ps. 31: 2. my rock be h. of defence
68: †6. G. setteth solitary in a h.
84: 3. the sparrow hath found a h.
104: 17. stork, fir trees are her h.
Pr. 2: 18. her h. inclineth to death
7: 8. y-g man went way to her h.
11. her feet abide not in her h.
Pr. 7: 27. Her h. is the way to hell
12: 7. h. of righteous shall stand
14: 11. h. of wicked be overthr.
15: 25. L. will destroy h. of proud
17: 1. h. full of sacri. with strife
19: 14. h. and riches are inheritance
21: 12. righteous consid. h. of wicked
25: 17. Withdraw fr. thy neighb.'s h.
Ec. 7: 2. to h. of mourning, than h. of
10: 18. thro. idlen. h. droppeth thro.
12: 3. keepers of h. shall tremble
Can. 1: 17. beams of our h. cedar
2: 4. brought me to banqueting h.
Is. 5: 8. Woe unto them join h. to h.
6: 4. the h. was filled with smoke
14: 17. opened not h. of prisoners
22: 15. over h. | 18. of thy lord's h.
23: 1. is no h. | 24: 10. ev. h. shut
31: 2. will arise ag. h. of evil doers
36: 3. Hilkiah's son wh. was over h.
42: 7. sit in darkness out of pris. h.
60: 7. I will glorify h. of my glory
64: 11. holy and beautif. h. burned
Je. 18: 2. go down to potter's h., 3.
21: 11. h. of the king of Jud., 22: 1.
26: 18. mt. of h. as high places
35: 2. Go unto the h. of Rechabites
37: 20. not ret. to h. of Jona. 38: 26.
Eze. 2: 5. for they are a rebellious h., 6.–3: 9, 26, 27.–12: 2, 3.
8. Be not rebellious like that h.
9: 6. ancient men before the h.
7. he said unto them, Defile h.
12: 2. dwellest in midst of rebell. h.
9. rebell. h. said, What doest thou?
25. in your days, O rebellious h.
17: 12. Say now to the rebellious h.
24: 3. utter parable unto rebell h.
43: 11. show them form of the h.
12. This is the law of h. (2)
21. burn it in appoin. place of h.
45: 20. so shall ye reconcile the h.
Da. 1: 2. he carried to h. of his god
Ho. 1: 4. avenge blood on h. of Jehu
Am. 1: 5. hold-h sceptre fr. h. of Eden
3: 15. smite winter h. wi. summer
6: 9. remain ten men in one h. [h.
11. will smite great h. little h.
7: 9. I will rise against h. of Jerob.
16. drop not word ag h. of Isaac
Ob. 18. h. of Esau be for stubble
Mi. 3: 12. Jerus. heaps, mt. of h. be as high places of forest
4: 2. let us go up to the h. of God

Mi. 6: 16. works of h. of Ahab kept
Na. 1: 14. out of the h. of thy gods
Ha. 3: 13. woundest head out of h.
Zec. 12: 12. the family of the h. of Nathan apart [Lu. 6: 48, 49.
Mat. 7: 25. beat upon that h., 27.
10: 12. when come into h. salute it, Mk. 6: 10. Lu. 9: 4. [Lu 10: 5.
13. if h. worthy, let peace come,
14. out of h. shake off dust
25. have called master of h.
12: 25. every h. divided against itself, Mk. 3: 25. Lu. 11: 17.
13: 1. same day went Jes. out of h.
20: 11. murmured ag. goodman of h.
23: 38. h. is left unto you desolate, Lu. 13: 35. [watch, Lu. 12: 39.
24: 43. if goodman of h. kn. what
Mk. 5: 38. cometh to the h. of ruler
7: 30. when she was come to her h.
10: 29. left h. or breth., Lu. 18: 29.
13: 35. when master of h. cometh
14: 14. goodman of h., Lu. 22: 11.
Lu. 7: 6. not far fr. h. centu. sent
10. ret-g to h. found serv. whole
8: 27. nei. in any h. but tombs
10: 7. in the same h. remain. Go not from h. to h.
12: 52. five in one h. divided
14: 21. master of h. being angry
15: 8. light candle and sweep h.
25. nigh h. he heard music
Jn. 12: 3. h. was filled with odour
Ac. 2: 2. sound fr. heaven filled h.
46. breaking bread fr. h. to h. [J
5: 42. in ev. h. ceased not to preach
10: 6. Simon tanner, h. by seaside
17. made inquiry for Simon's h.
11: 11. men unto h. where I was
12: 12. he came to the h. of Mary
17: 5. Jews assaulted h. of Jason
18: 7. h. joined hard to synagogue
19: 16. they fled out of that h. naked
20: 20. I taught you from h. to h.
Ro. 16: 5. greet church in their h.
1 Co. 16: 19. Col. 4: 15. [Chloe
1 Co. 1: 11. by them wh are of h. of
16: 15. ye know the h. of Stephanas
2 Co. 5: 1. if earthly h. be dissolved, we have a h.
2. clothed upon with h. fr. heaven
1 Ti. 5: 13. wandering from h. to h.
14. that younger women guide h.
2 Ti. 1: 16. mercy to h. of Onesiph.
2: 20. in great h. are vessels of gold
He. 3: 3. built h. more honour than h.
4. every h. is built by some man
6. whose h. are we, if we hold fast
See AARON, BORN, BUILD or BUILT, BUILDED, BUILDETH, BUILDING, CHIEF, DAVID, DOOR, DWELL.

HOUSE with father, s.

Ge. 12: 1. L. said, Get thee fr. f.'s h.
20: 13. caused me to wander fr. f.'s
24: 7. G. took me fr. f.'s h. [h.
23. is room in thy f.'s h. for us
38. to my f.'s h. and take a wife
40. wife for my son of my f.'s h.
28: 21. ag. to my f.'s h. in peace
31: 14. any portion for us in f.'s h.'
30. sore longedst after f.'s h.
38: 11. Remain widow at thy f.'s h.
Tamar dwelt in her f.'s h.
41: 51. G. made me forget f.'s h.
46: 31. breth. and f.'s h. are come
50: 22. Jo. dwelt in E., he and f.'s
Ex. 12: 3. a lamb, acc. to h. of f.'s [h.
Le. 22: 13. if returned to her f.'s h.
Nu 1: 2. sum of Isr. by h. of f-s, 18, 20, 22, 24, 28. ✝ [Jos. 22: 14.
4. ev. one head of h. of his f-s, 44.
26. h. of their f-s, 30, 32, 34, 36, 38, 40, 42.–2: 32, 34.–4: 2, 29, 34, 40, 42.–7: 2.–26: 2.–34: 14. Jos. 22: 14. 1 Ch. 5: 13. 2 Ch. 31: 17.
45. were numbered by h. of f-s

Nu. 2: 2. pitch with ensign of f.'s h.
3: 15. number of chil. of Levi after h. of f-s, 20.–4: 46. [of f-s
4: 38. Gershon | 42. Merari after h.
17: 2. acc. to h. of their f-s, 3.
18: 1. thou and f.'s h. bear iniquity
30: 3. woman vow in f.'s h., 16.
34: 14. Reub., Gad, acc. to h. of f-s
De. 22: 21. play whore in f.'s h.
Jos. 2: 12. ye shew kindn. to f.'s h.
Ju. 6: 15. I am least in my f.'s h.
9: 18. ye are risen up ag. my f.'s h.
11: 2. not inherit in our f.'s h., 7.
14: 15. lest we burn thee and f.'s h.
16: 31. all h. of his f. buried him
19: 2. concu. went to his f.'s h.
3. brought him into her f.'s h.
1 S. 2: 27. Did I appear unto h. of f.
28. I give unto h. of thy f. off-gs
30. I said h. of f. shall walk
31. cut off arm of thy f.'s h.
9: 20. is it not on all thy f.'s h.?
17: 25. k. will make his f.'s h. free
18: 2. go no more home to f.'s h.
22: 11. k. sent to call all his f.'s h.
16. thy f.'s h. sh. die, 22. [f.'s h.
24: 21. destroy my name out of
2 S. 3: 29. on Joab and his f.'s h.
14: 9. iniquity be on me, and f.'s h.
19: 28. all of my f.'s h. were dead
24: 17. let thy hand be ag. me and f.'s h. 1 Ch. 21: 17. [h. of f.
1 K. 2: 31. innocent bl. fr. me and
18: 18. thou and f.'s h. troubled Isr.
1 Ch. 2: 55. Hemath f. of h. of Rech.
4: 38. h. of their f-s incr-d greatly
5: 15. chief of house of f-s h., 24.–7: 2, 7, 9, 40.–9: 9, 13.–12: 30.
7: 4. with them after h. of f-s
12: 28. Zadok of f.'s h., 22 capt.
28: 4. G. chose me bef. h. of my f.
2 Ch. 21: 13. slain breth. of thy f.'s h.
Ezr. 2: 59. not shew f.'s h. Ne. 1: 6.
10: 16. chief of h. of f-s to exam.
Ne. 1: 6. I and my f.'s h. have sinned
Es. 4: 14. thou and f.'s h. be destroy.
Ps. 45: 10. forget peo. and f.'s h.
Is. 3: 6. hold of bro. of h. of f.
7: 17. bring upon thy f.'s h. days th.
22: 23. be for glori. throne to f.'s h.
24. hang upon him glory of f.'s h.
Je. 12: 6. the h. of f. dealt treach-sly
Lu. 16: 27. send him to my f.'s h.
Jn. 2: 16. not F.'s h. house of merch.
14: 2. In my F.'s h. many mansions
Ac. 7: 20. Moses was nourished in [f.'s h.

HOUSE of God.

Ge. 28: 17. none other but h. o. G.
22. this stone I set be G.'s h. [G.
Jos. 9: 23. drawers of wat. for h. o.
Ju. 18: 31. time h. o. G. in Shiloh
20: 18. Isr. went up to h. o. G.
26. peo. came unto h. o. G., 21: 2.
31. highway, one goeth to h. o. G.
1 Ch. 9: 11. ruler of h. o. G., Ne. 11: 11.
24: 5. governors of h. o. G. were sons
29: 2. for h. o. my G. the gold
3. set affection to h. o. my G.
2 Ch. 5: 14. glory of L. filled h. o. G
22: 12. hid in the h. o. G. six years
24: 13. they set h. o. G. in his state
33: 7. Manas. set image in h. o. G.
36: 19. they burnt the h. o. G.
Ezr. 5: 8. we went to h. o. great G.
15. let h. o. G. be builded, 6: 7.
7: 20. what so needful for h. o. G.?
23. let it be done for the h. o. G.
Ne. 6: 10. Let us meet in h. o. G.
13: 11. Why is h. o. G. forsaken?
Ps. 42: 4. I went to h. o. G., 55: 14.
52: 8. I like olive tree in h. o. G.
84: 10. be doorkeeper in h. o. G.
Ec. 5: 1. Keep foot when to h. o. G.
Is. 2: 3. let us go to h. o. G., Mi. 4: 2.
Ho. 9: 8. prop. hated in h. o. G.
Jo. 1: 13. off-g withholden fr. h. o. G
16. gladness cut off fr. h. o. G.

Zch. 7:2.unto h. o. G. men to pray
Mat. 12:4. How ent-d h. o. G. and
eat shewbr., Mk. 2:26. Lu.6:4.
1 Ti. 3:15. How to behave in h.o.G.
He. 10:21. high priest over h. o. G.
1 Pe. 4:17. judgm. must begin at h.
His HOUSE. [o. G.
Ge.12:17.L. plagued Pha. and h.h.
17:27. men of h. h. were circum.
39:4. him overseer over h. h., 5.
45:8. me lord of all h. h., Ac.7:10.
Le. 16:6. an atonement for h.h.,11.
27:14. when a man sanctify h. h.
15. if he will redeem h. h.
Nu. 22:18. If give h. h. full of silv.,
I cannot go beyo. word, 24:13.
De. 20:5. return to h. h., 6, 7, 8.
24:1. let him send her out of h.h.
10. shalt not go into h.h. to fetch
Ju. 8:27. became a snare to h. h.
9:16. well with Jerub. and h.h,19.
1 S.3:12. I have spoken conc-g h.h.
13. I will judge h. h. for ever
7:17. to Ramah, for there was h.h.
25:1. Isr. buried Samuel in h. h.
2 S.6:19. every one to h.h.,1 S.10:25.
21. chose me bef. thy fa.and h.h.
7:1. when king sat in h. h. [23.
25. spoken conc-g h. h., 1 Ch. 17:
11:9. Uriah went not to h. h., 10.
27. David fetched her to h.h. [13.
19:11. why last to bri. k. to h. h.?
21:1. It is for Saul and h. bloody h.
4. have no gold of Saul, nor of h.h.
1 K. 2:33. upon h. h. shall be peace
7:1. Sol. building, finished h. h.
12:24. return ev. man to h. h., 22:
17. 1 Ch. 16:43. 2 Ch. 11:4.-18:
13:19. did eat bread in h. h. [16.
16:7. sword ag. Baasha and h.h.,3.
20:43. king to h. h. heavy, 21:4.
21:29. will I bring evil upon h. h.
2 K. 6:32. Elisha sat in h. h. [not
20:13. noth. in h. h. Hez. shewed
1 Ch. 7:23. it went evil with h. h.
10:6. Saul, all h. h. died together
13:14. the ark remained in h. h.
2 Ch. 24:16. good tow. G. and h.h.
Ezr. 6:11. h. h. be made dunghill
Ne. 3:28. repaired over ag. h. h.
5:13. G. shake ev. man from h.h.
7:3. ev. one to be over ag. h. h.
Jb. 1:10. Hast hedge about h. h.?
7:10. sh. return no more to h. h.
8:15. He shall lean upon h. h. it
20:28. incr. of h. h. shall depart
21:21. what pleas. hath he in h.h.
27:18. He buildeth h.h. as a moth
Ps.49:16. when glory of h.h. is incr.
105:21. He made him Lord of h.h.
112:3. Wealth shall be in h. h.
Pr.6:31. substance of h. h., Can.8:7.
17:13. evil not depart from h. h.
Je. 23:34. I will even punish h. h.
Mi. 2:2. oppress a man and h. h.
Ha. 2:9. an evil covetousn. to h. h.
Zch. 5:4. it shall remain in h. h.
Mat. 9:7. he arose and departed to
h. h., Lu. 1:23.-5:25.
12:29. then he will spoil h. h., Mk.
3:27. [h., Mk. 13:15.
24:17. to take anything out of h.
43. not suffered h.h. to be broken
Mk. 8:26. he sent him away to h.h.
Lu. 8:41. th. he wo. come into h.h.
18:14. this went to h. h. justified
Jn. 4:53. hims. believed and h. h.
Ac. 7:10. over Egypt and all h. h.
10:2. feared God with all h. h.
22. warned to send for thee into h.
11:13. had seen angel in h. h. [h.
16:32. spake unto him all in h. h.
34. the jailer bro-t them into h.h.,
believing in G. with h.h., 18:8.
Col. 4:15. salute church in h. h.
He. 3:2. Moses faithful in h. h., 5.
11:7. prepared ark for sav. of h.h.

In the HOUSE.
Ge 27:15. took raiment of Esau i.h.
34:29. they spoiled all i. h.
39:5. blessing of L. upon all i. h.
8. wotteth not what wi. me i. h.
45:16. fame was heard in Pha.'s h.
Le.14:35. It seemeth plague i.h.,34.
43. if plague break out i. h.
44. if the plague be spread i. h.
47. that eateth i. h. shall wash
48. plague hath not spread i. h.
Jos.2:19. whoso. with thee i. h. blo.
6:17. Rahab live, all with her i. h.
Ju. 17:4. were i. h. of Mic., 12.
Ru. 1:9. rest, each i. h. of husb.
2:7. she tarried a little i. h.
1 S. 28:24. wom. had fat calf i. h.
31:9. to publish it i. h. of idols
10. put his armour i. h. of Ashta.
1 K. 3:17. deliv-d of child i. h.
6:7. not tool of iron heard i. h.
10:17. i. h. of forest of Lebanon
14:13. some good i.h. of Jeroboam
16:9. himself drunk i. h. of Arza
2 K. 4:2. what hast thou i. h.? (2)
35. he walked i. h. to and fro
5:18. I bow i. h. of Rimmon
24. he bestowed them i. h.
19:37. worsh-g i. h. of Nisroch, Is.
21:7. graven image i. h., 4. [37:38.
2 Ch. 36:17. slew young men i. h.
of sanctuary
Ezr. 1:7. put them i. h. of his gods
6:1. search made i. h. of the rolls
Es. 7:8. Will he force queen i. h.?
9. gallows standeth i.h. of Haman
Ps.119:54. my songs i.h. of pilgrim.
Pr. 3:33. curse of L. is i. h. of wick.
5:10. labours be i. h. of stranger
15:6. i. h. of righte. is treasure
Ec.7:4. heart of wise i.h. of mourn.;
heart of fools i. h. of mirth
Is. 44:13. maketh idol remain i. h.
Je. 7:30. abominations i. h., 32:34.
34:15. ye made cov-t bef. me i. h.
37:15. put him i. h. of Jonathan
Mi.1:10. i.h. of Aphrah roll in dust
6:10. treasures of wickedness i. h.
Zch. 13:6. wounded i. h. of friends
Mat. 5:15. light unto all are i. h.
9:10. Jes. sat at meat i. h., Lu.7:37.
26:6. i. h. of Simon, Mk. 14:3. Lu.
Mk. 2:1. noised he was i. h. [4:38.
9:33. being i. h. he asked them
10:10. i. h. disciples asked of mat.
Lu. 17:31. stuff i. h. let him not
Jn.8:35. the servant abideth not i.h.
11:20. Mary sat still i. h.
31. Jews with her i. h. saw Mary
Ac. 9:11. inquire i. h. of Judas
10:32. Pe. is lodged i. h. of Simon
1 Co. 16:19. church in their h.
Into HOUSE.
Ex. 8:3. frogs shall come i. h.
Le. 14:46. goeth i. h. be unclean
1 S.5:2. brought ark i. h. of Dagon
5. nor any come i. Dagon's h.
7:1. ark i. h. of Abinadab
2 S. 5:8. blind and lame not i. h.
Ne. 2:8. for h. I shall enter i.
Pr. 27:10. i. bro.'s h. in calamity
Can. 3:4. till I had bret. him i. h.
8:2. bring thee i. my mother's h.
Je. 16:5. ent. not i. h. of mourning
8. not go i. h. of feasting with th.
Am. 1:4. send fire i. h. of Hazael
5:19. went i. h. and leaned hand
Zch. 5:4. it sh. ent. i. h. of thief (2)
Mat.2:11. when they were come i.h.
8:14. Jes. was come i. Peter's h.
9:23. Jes. came i. ruler's h.
28. i. h. blind men foll-d, 17:25.
10:12. i. an h. salute it, Mk. 6:10.
Lu. 9:4. [h., Mk. 3:27.
12:29. how enter i. strong man's
13:36. Jes. i. h., Mk. 7:17.-9:28. Lu.
7:36.-8:51.-14:1.-22:54.

Mk. 1:29. ent-d i. h., 3:19. Mk. 7:
24. Ac. 9:17.
Lu. 1:40. ent. i. h. of Zacharias
10:38. Martha rec-d him i. her h.
22:10. follow him i. h. where ent-h
Ac. 8:3. ent-g i. ev. h. and haling
11:12. we ent-d i. man's h.
21:8. i. h. of Philip evang-t
2 Jn. 10. received him not i. h.
HOUSE of Israel.
Le. 10:6. let h.o.I. bewail burning
17:3. What man there be of h. o.
I. killeth ox or, 8. 10.-22:18.
Nu.20:29. all h.o.I. mourned for Aa.
1 S.7:2. h.o.I. lamented after the L.
2 S. 1:12. they mourned for h.o.I.
6:5. all h. o. I. played bef. Lord
15. David and h.o.I. bro-t up ark
12:8. I gave thee h.o.I. and Jud.
16:3. shall h.o.I. restore kingd.
1 K. 20:31. kings of h.o.I merciful
Ps. 98:3. rememb-d his truth tow.
115:12. he will bless h.o.I. [h.o.I.
135:19. Bless ye the L. O h. o. I.
Is. 5:7. vineyard of L. is h. o. I
14:2. the h.o.I. shall possess them
46:3. remnant of the h.o.I. hearken
63:7. goodness toward h. o. I.
Je. 2:4. Hear, all families of h.o.I
26. As thief, so is h. o. I. asham.
3:18. ho. of Jud. walk with h.o.I.
20. dealt treach-ly, O h.o.I.,5:11.
9:26. all h.o.I. are uncircumcised
11:10. h.o.I. have broken my cov.
17. pronounced evil of h. o. I.
13:11. cleave unto me whole h.o.I.
18:6. ye in mine hand h. o. I.
23:8. Lord who led the h. o. I.
31:27. sow h.o.I. with seed of man
31. new covenant with h.o.I.,33.
33:14. I promised unto h. o. I.
48:13. h.o.I. was asha. of Beth-el
Eze.3:1. speak unto h.o.I., 4.-17:2.
-20:27,30.-24:21.-33:10.-36:22.
5. thou art sent to the h. o. I.
7. h.o.I. will not hearken unto me
h. o. I. are impudent
17. watchman unto h.o.I., 33:7.
4:3. This sh. be a sign to h. o. I.
4. lay iniq. of h. o. I. upon it
5. shalt bear iniquity of h. o. I.
5:4. a fire sh. come into h. o. I.
6:11. abomina-s of h. o. I., 8:6.
8:10. idols of h.o.I. are portrayed
11. men of ancients of h.o.I.,12.
9:9. iniq. of h. o. I. exc-g great
11:5. Thus have ye said, O h. o. I.
15. all the h.o.I. wholly are they
12:6. thee for sign unto h. o. I.
9. hath not h.o.I. said,27.-18:29.
24. nor more divination within h.
13:5. nei. hedge for h.o.I. [o. I.
9. in the writing of the h. o. I.
14:4. of h.o.I. that sett. up idols,7.
5. take h.o.I. in their own heart
11. Th. h.o.I. go no more astray
18:6. nei. eyes to idols of h.o.I.,15.
25. O h.o.I. is not my way equal
30. judge you, O h. o. I., 33:20.
31. why will ye die, O h.o.I.?33:11.
20:13. But h.o.I. rebelled ag. me
39. O h. o. I. go ye, serve idols
40. there shall h. o. I. serve me
44. acc. to corrupt doings, h.o.I.
22:18. h. o. I. is to me dross
28:24. a pricking briar to h. o. I.
25. When have gath-d h. o. I.
29:6. a staff of a reed to h. o. I.
16. be no more confid. of h. o. I.
21. cause horn of h. o. I. to bud
34:30. even h. o. I. are my people
36:10. I will multiply all h. o. I.
17. h. o. I. dwelt in own land
21. my name wh. h.o.I. profaned
22. for your sakes, O h. o. I.
32. be ashamed, O h. o. I.
37. I will be inquired of by h.o.I

Eze. 37:11. bones are whole **h. o. I.**
16.for the **h.o.I.** his companions
39:12. seven mo-s **h.o.I.** burying
22. **h. o. I.** shall know I am L.
23. **h. o. I.** went into captivity
25. mercy upon whole **h. o. I.**
29. poured Spirit upon **h. o. I.**
40:4. declare all thou seest to **h.o.**
43:10. shew house to **h. o. I.** [I.
44:6. to rebellious, even to **h.o.I.**
12. caused **h. o. I.** to fall into
22. take maidens of **h. o. I.** [I.
45:6. possession be for whole **h.o.**
8. land shall they give to **h. o.I.**
17. reconciliation for **h. o. I.**
Ho. 1:4. to cease kingd. of **h. o. I.**
6. no more mercy upon **h. o. I.**
5:1. hearken, ye **h. o. I.** give ear
6:10. a horrible thing in **h. o. I.**
11:12. **h. o. I.** compasseth me
Am. 5:3. city leave ten to **h. o. I.**
4. saith L. unto **h. o. I.** Seek me
25. sacrifices 40 years, O **h. o. I.**
6:1. nations, to wh. **h. o. I.** came
14. ag. you a nation, O **h. o. I.**
7:10. conspired ag. thee in **h.o.I.**
9:9.I will sift **h.o. I.** am. nations
Mi 1:5. for sins of **h. o. I.** is this
3:1. Hear, ye princes of **h. o.I.**, 9.
Zch. 8:13. ye were curse, O **h. o. I.**
Mat.10:6.lost sheep of **h.o.I.**,15:24.
Ac. 2:36. let all **h. o. I.** know
7:42.**h.o.I.** have ye off-d to beasts
He. 8:8. new cov. with **h.o.I.**, 10.

HOUSE of Jacob.

Ge. 46:27. souls of **h. o. J.** seventy
Ex. 19:3. Thus shalt say to **h.o.J.**
Ps.114:1.**h.o.J.**from peo.of strange
Is.2:5.O **h. o. J.** walk in light of L.
6. hast forsaken people **h. o. J.**
8:17.L.hideth his face from **h.o.J.**
10:20. are escaped of **h. o. J.**
14:1. they shall cleave to **h. o. J.**
29:22. saith Lord cone-g **h.o. J.**
46:3. Hearken unto me, O **h. o. J.**
48:1. Hear ye this, O **h. o. J.**
58:1. spare not, shew **h.o.J.** sins
Je. 2:4. Hear word of L. **h. o. J.**
5:20. Declare this in the **h. o. J.**
Eze. 20:5. I lifted hand to **h. o. J.**
Am.3:13. Hear ye, testify in **h.o.J.**
9:8. not utterly destroy **h. o. J.**
Ob.17. **h.o.J.** shall possess poss-ns
18. **h. o. J.** shall be a fire
Mi. 2:7. O thou named **h. o. J.**
3:9. Hear this, ye heads of **h.o.J.**
Lu. 1:33. he reign over **h. o. J.**

HOUSE of Joseph.

Ge.43:17.bro-t men into J.'s **h.**,18.
Jos.17:17. Josh. spake unto **h.o.J.**
18:5. **h. o. J.** shall abide in coast
Ju. 1:22. **h. o. J.** went ag. Bethel
23. **h.o.J.** sent to destroy Beth-el
35. hand of **h. o. J.** prevailed
2 S. 19:20. first of all the **h. o. J.**
1 K.11:28.over the charge of **h.o.J.**
Am.5:6.break out like fire in **h.o.J.**
Ob. 18. **h. o. J** shall be a flame
Zch. 10:6. I will save the **h. o. J.**

HOUSE of Judah.

2 S. 2:4. anointed David king over
h. o. J., 7, 11. 1 Ch. 28:4.
12:8. I gave thee **h. o. J.** and Isr.
1 K. 12:21. he assembled **h. o. J**
23.Speak unto all **h.o.J.**and Benj.
2 K.19:30. remnant of **h.o.J.** shall
take root, Is. 37:31.
2 Ch. 19:11. Zebadiah of **h. o. J.**
22:10. destr-d seed royal of **h.o.J.**
Ne. 4:16. rulers behind **h. o. J.**
Is. 22:21. shall be fa. to **h. o. J.**
Je.3:18.**h. o. J.** walk with h.of Isr.
5:11. **h.o.J.** hath dealt treach-ly
11:10.**h.o.J.** hath broken my cov.
17. for evil of **h. o. J.** they done
12:14.I will pluck **h.o. J.** fr. them
13:11. to cleave unto me **h. o. J.**

Je. 31:27. I will sow **h. o. J.**
31. make new cov. with **h. o. J.**
33:14.good I promised unto **h.o.J.**
36:3. may be **h. o. J.** will hear all
Eze.4:6. bear iniq. of **h.o.J.**40 days
8:17. Is it light thing to **h. o. J.**?
9:9. iniquity of the **h.o.J.** is great
25:3.Ammon-s said,Aha,ag.**h.o.J.**
8. **h.o.J.** is like unto all heathen
12. Edom hath dealt ag. **h. o. J.**
Ho. 1:7. have mercy upon **h. o. J.**
5:12. be to **h. o. J.** as rottenness
14. I be as a y-g lion to **h. o. J.**
Zph.2:7. coast for remn-t of **h.o.J.**
Zch. 8:13. curse, O **h. o. J.**
15. to do well unto **h. o. J.**
19. the fast shall be to **h.o.J.**joy
10:3. L. hath visited the **h. o. J.**
6. I will strengthen the **h. o. J.**
12:4. I will open eyes unto **h.o.J.**
He.8:8. make new cov. with **h.o.J.**

HOUSE with king. [h.

2 S.11:2. Da. walked on roof of **k.'s**
8. Uriah departed out of **k.'s h.**
9. Uriah slept at door of **k.'s h.**
15:35. shalt hear out of **k.'s h.**
1 K 9:1.when Sol. finished **k.'s h.**
14:26. took away treasure of **k.'s**
h., 15:18.2 K.12:18.-14:14.-16:
8.-18:15.-24:13. 2 Ch. 12:9.-25:
16:18.Zimri burnt **k.'s h.** [24.
2 K. 7:11. told it to **k.'s h.** [13.
25:9.he burnt **k.'s h.**,Je.39:8.-52:
2 Ch. 23:5. third part be at **k.'s h.**
26:21. Jotham was over **k.'s h.**
28:21.took portion out of **h. of k.**
Ezr. 6:4. expenses be out of **k.'s h.**
Es.2:9.seven maidens out of **k.'s h.**
4:13.Think not thou esca.in **k.'sh.**
9:4. Mord. was great in **k.'s h.**
Je. 22:6. thus saith L. unto **k.'s h.**
Ho. 5:1. give ye ear, O **h. of the k.**

HOUSE of Levi.

Ex. 2:1. went a man of **h.** of L.
Nu. 17:8. rod of Aaron for **h. o. L.**
Ps. 135:20. Bless L. O **h. o. L.**
Zch. 12:13. family of **h. o. L.** apart

HOUSE with Lord.

Ex. 23:19. firstfruits shalt bring into **h.** of L., 34:26. Ne. 10:35.
De. 23:18. not price of dog into **h.**
Jos. 6:24. treasury of **h.** of L. [of L.
Ju. 19:18. I am going to **h.** of L.
1 S. 1:7. she went up to **h.** of L.
24. Hannah brought him unto **h.**
of L., 2 K. 12:4, 9, 13.-22:4. 2
Ch. 34:14.
2 S. 12:20. Da. came into **h.** of L.
1 K 8:1. end of building **h.** of L.
6:37. foundation of **h.** of L. laid,
2 Ch. 8:16. Ezr. 3:11. Zch. 8:9.
7:40. work for **h.** of L., 45, 48, 51.
2 Ch. 4:16.-5:1.-24:14.
8:10. cloud filled **h.** of L., 11. 2
Ch. 5:13.-7:2. Eze. 44:4.
63. so Israel dedicated **h.** of L.
10:5. went unto **h.** of L., 2 Ch.9:4.
2 K. 11:3. hid in **h.** of L. six years
4. he took an oath in **h.** of L.
15. let her not be slain in **h.** of
L.,2 Ch. 23:14. [L.,2 Ch.23:18.
18. appointed officers over **h.** of
19. they bro-t fr. **h.** of L., 23:6.
12:10. found in **h.** of the L., 14:
14.-16:8.-18:15.-22:8.-23:2, 24.
11. had oversight of **h.** of L.
16. tresp. money not into **h.** of L.
16:18.entry, turned he fr. **h.** of L.
19:14. Hez. into **h.** of L.,1.Is.37:1.
20:5. third day go up unto **h.** of L.
8. what sign that I shall go up
into **h.** of L., Is. 38:22.
23:2. words of cov. found in **h.** of
L., 24. 2 Ch. 34:15, 17, 30.
7.houses of sodomites by **h.** of L.
11. horses at ent-g in of **h.** of L.
25:9. burnt **h.** of L., Je. 52:13.

1 Ch. 6:31. of song in **h.** of L.,25:6.
22:1. Da. said, This is **h.** of L.
11. son, build **h.** of the L. thy G.
14. have prepared for **h.** of L.
23:4. forward work of **h.** of L.
26:12. to minister in **h.** of the L.
2 Ch.8:16.**h.** of the L.was perfected
26:21.was cut off from **h.** of L.,Jo.
29:5.Levites, sanctify **h.** of L.[1:9.
15. they came to cleanse **h.** of L.
33:15.Manas. took idol out of **h.**of
34:15. book of law in **h.** of L. [L.
36:14. priests polluted **h.** of L.
Ezr. 7:27. to beautify **h.** of the L.
Ps. 23:6. I will dwell in **h.** of L.
27:4. may dwell in **h.** of L. my life
92:13. that be planted in **h.** of L.
116:19.I will pay my vows in L.'s **h.**
118:26. blessed you out of **h.** of L.
122:1. said, Let us go into **h.** of L.
9.Bec. of **h.** of L. I seek thy good
134:1. th. stand in **h.** of L., 135:2.
Is. 2:2. L.'s **h.** be established in top
of the mts., Mi. 4:1.
37:14. Hez. went up into **h.** of L.
Je. 17:26. of praise unto **h.** of L.
20:1. was governor in **h.** of L.
2. gate, which was by **h.** of L.
26:2. come to worship in L.'s **h.**
7. speaking words in **h.** of L.
28:1. spake unto me in **h.** of L.
5. people that stood in **h.** of L.
29:26. sho. be officers in **h.** of L.
35:2. Rechabites into **h.** of L.
36:5. I cannot go into **h.** of L.
6.read in L.'s **h.** upon fasting day
38:14. entry that is in **h.** of L.
41:5. to bring them to **h.** of L.
51:51. into sanctuaries of L.'s **h.**
La. 2:7. made a noise in **h.** of L.
Jo. 3:18. fountain come of **h.** of L
Hag. 1:2. time L.'s **h.** sho. be built
14. did work in **h.** of L.
Zch. 11:13. to the potter in **h.** of L.
See COURT, DOOR, GATE, TREASURES, VESSELS.

Mine HOUSE.

Nu. 12:7. Moses faithf. in all **m.h.**
De.26:13. hall-d things out of **m.h.**
Jn. 19:23. man is come into **m. h.**
2 S. 11:11. sh. I go into **m. h.** to eat
2 K. 20:15. all things that are in **m.**
h. have they seen, Is. 39:4.
1 Ch.17:14.I will settle him in **m.h.**
Jb. 17:13. if I wait, grave is **m. h.**
Is. 56:5. will I give in **m. h.** name
7. **m. h.** be called **h.** of prayer,
Mat.21:13. Mk. 11:17. Lu.19:46.
Je.11:15.what my beloved do in **m.**
12:7. I have forsaken **m. h.** [h.
Eze. 8:1. as I sat in **m. h.** elders
23:39. thus have th. done in **m.h.**
Da.4:4.I, Neb., was at rest in **m.h.**
Ho. 9:15. will drive th. out of **m.h.**
Hag.1:9.Bec. of **m. h.** that is waste
Zch. 9:8. I will encamp about **m.h.**
Mal.3:10.th.there be meat in **m. h.**

My HOUSE.

Ge. 15:2. steward of **m. h.** Eliezer
3. one born in **m. h.** mine heir
34:30. I sh. be destr-d, and **m. h.**
41:40. thou shalt be over **m. h.**
Jos. 24:15. as for **m. h.**will serve L.
Ju. 11:31. forth of doors of **m. h.**
1 S.20:15.not cut off kindn.fr.**m.h.**
21:15. sh. fellow come into **m.h.**?
2 S.7:18.Who am I, and what is **m.**
h. that thou hast, 1 Ch. 17:16.
23:5. Altho. **m. h.** be not so wi. G.
1 K. 21:2. give it me,bec.near **m.h.**
Ps. 101:2. in **m. h.** with perf. heart
132:3. not come into tab. of **m. h.**
Pr.7:6. at window of **m.h.** I looked
Is. 3:7. in **m. h.** is neither bread
7. will make th. joyful in **m. h.**
Je. 23:11. in **m. h.** found wickedn.
Eze.44:7.in sanct.to pollute it,**m.h.**

Zch.8:7.then thou shalt judge **m.h.**
Mat.12:44.I will return into **m.h.**,
Lu. 11: 24. [**m. h.**
Lu. 9:61. let me bid them farewell at
14:23. compel, that **m. h.** be filled
Ac.10:30.9th hour I prayed in **m.h.**
16 : 15. come into **m. h.** and abide

Own HOUSE.

Ge.14:14.armed servt-s born in **o.h.**
30:30.when sh. I provide for **o. h.**
De. 22:2. shalt bring it unto **o. h.**
Jos. 20 : 6. shall come unto **o. h.**
Ju. 8 : 29. Jerubb. dwelt in **o. h.**
2 S. 4 : 11. slain righteous in **o. h.**
12:11.raise evil ag.thee out of **o.h.**
14 : 24. Let him turn to his **o. h.**,
so Abs. returned to **o. h.**
19:30.king is come in peace to **o.h.**
1 K. 2 : 34. Joab buried in his **o.h.**
3:1. made end of building his **o.h.**
7:1. Sol. building his **o.h.** 13 years
9:15. Sol. raised a levy to build his
o. h. [16.
12:16. see to thine **o. h.**, 2 Ch. 10:
14 : 12. get thee into thine **o. h.**
2 K. 21:18. Manasseh was buried in
garden of **o. h.**, 2 Ch. 33 : 20.
23.slew king in **o.h.**, 2 Ch. 33:24.
2 Ch.7:11. in heart to make in **o.h.**
8 : 1. built house of L. and **o. h.**
Es. 1:22. ev. man bear rule in **o.h.**
Pr. 11 : 29. he that troubleth **o. h.**
15:27. greedy of gain troubl-h **o.h.**
Is.14:18. lie in glory,ev.one in **o.h.**
Mi. 7 : 6. enemies are of **o. h.**
Hag.1:9. ye run ev. man unto **o.h.**
Mat. 13 : 57. proph. is not without
honour, save in **o. h.**, Mk. 6:4.
Lu. 1:23. he departed to **o. h.**,5:25.
56. Mary returned to her **o. h.**
5 : 29. Levi made gr. feast in **o. h.**
8:39. Return to thy **o.h.** and shew
Jn. 7:53. every man unto his **o. h.**
Ac. 28 : 30. Paul two years in **o. h.**
1 Ti. 3:4. One that ruleth well **o.h.**
5. if know not how to rule **o. h.**
5 : 8. especially for those of **o. h.**
He. 3 : 6. Christ as a Son over **o.h.**

This HOUSE.

Ge.39:9.none greater in **t.h.** than I
40 : 14. and bring me out of **t. h.**
1 K. 6:12. conc. **t. h.** thou building
8 : 27. less **t. h.** that I builded
29. eyes be opened toward **t. h.**,
2 Ch. 6 : 20. [Ch. 6 : 22.
31. before thine altar in **t. h.**, 2
33. sh. make supplica. unto thee
in **t. h.**, 42. 2 Ch. 6 : 24, 32.
38. spread hands toward **t. h.**
9:3. I have hallowed **t. h.**, 7. 2 Ch.
7 : 16, 20. [Ch. 7 : 21.
8. at **t. h.** every one shall hiss, 2
2 K. 21:7.**t.h.** I chosen, 2 Ch. 33:7.
2 Ch. 6:29. sh. spread hands in **t.h.**
20:9. If we stand bef. **t. h.** for thy
name is in **t. h.**
Ezr. 3:12. founda. of **t. h.** was laid
5 : 12. Neb. who destroyed **t. h.**
6:15. **t. h.** finished on third of Adar
Je. 7:10. come stand bef. me in **t.h.**
11. Is **t. h.** become a den of rob.
14.will I do unto **t.h.** as to Shiloh
22:4. enter in by the gates of **t. h.**
5. **t. h.** shall become a desolation
26:6. will I make **t. h.** like Shiloh
9. **t. h.** shall be like Shiloh
12.L.sent me to prophesy ag. **t.h.**
Hag.1:4.in houses, **t. h.** lie waste?
2:3.Who left that saw **t.h.** in glory?
7. I will fill **t. h.** with glory
9. glory of **t.** latter **h.** greater
Zch.4:9.Zerub. laid founda. of **t. h.**
Lu. 10:5. first say, Peace be to **t.h.**
19:9.This day is salv. come to **t.h.**

Thine HOUSE.

Ex. 8 : 3. frogs sh. come into **t. h.**
De. 6 : 7. talk when in **t.h.**, 11 : 19.
De.7:26.Nei. bring abomi. into **t.h.**
15 : 16. he loveth thee and **t. h.**
21:12. shalt bring her home to **t.h.**
13. remain in **t. h.** bewail father
22:8. bring not blood upon **t. h.**
25 : 14. not in **t. h.** divers meas.
26 : 11. thing G. given unto **t. h.**
Jos. 2:3. Bring men ent-d into **t.h.**
Ju. 12 : 1. we will burn **t. h.**
19 : 22. Bring man came into **t. h.**
Ru.4:11.woman th. is come into **t.h.**
1 S.2:31.not be an old man in **t. h.**
33.incr.of **t.h.** die in flower of age
36. ev. one in **t. h.** crouch to him
22 : 14. Da., is honourable in **t. h.**
25 : 6. peace to **t. h.** and unto all
35. Da. said, Go in peace to **t. h.**
2 S. 7 : 16. **t. h.** shall be establ-d
11:10. why didst not go unto **t.h.**?
12:10. sword never depart fr. **t. h.**
14 : 8. the king said, Go to **t. h.**, 1
K. 1 : 53.
1 K. 13 : 8. if thou give half **t. h.**
18. Bring him back into **t. h.**
20 : 6. serv-s, shall search **t. h.**
2 K.20:1.Set **t. h.** in order, Is.38:1.
15. What seen in **t. h.**? Is. 39:4.
17. all in **t.h.** be carried, Is. 39:6.
Ps. 69:9. zeal of **t.h.** eaten, Jn.2:17.
93:5. holiness becometh **t. h.**, O L.
128:3.wife as a fruitful vine by **t.h.**
Je. 38:17. thou shalt live and **t. h.**
Eze. 3:24. shut thyself within **t. h.**
44 : 30. blessing to rest in **t. h.**
Mat. 9:6. Arise, go to **t. h.**, Mk. 2 :
11. Lu. 5 : 24.
Lu. 7:44. I ent-d **t. h.** gavest no wat.

Thy HOUSE.

Ge. 7:1.Come,and all **t. h.** into ark
31 : 41. I been 20 years in **t. h.**
Nu. 18:11. ev. one clean in **t.h.**, 13.
De. 6 : 9. write upon posts of **t. h.**,
11 : 20. [of **t. h.**
Jos. 2 : 19. whoso. go out of doors
Ru.4:12.let **t.h.** be like **h.** of Pharez
1 S. 2 : 30. that **t. h.** walk bef. me
2 S. 11:8. Go to **t.h.** wash feet [22.
1 K. 16:3. **t.h.** like **h.** of Jerob., 21:
Ps. 5 : 7. to **t. h.** in mult. of mercy
26 : 8. I have loved habita. of **t.h.**
36 : 8. satisf. with fatness of **t. h.**
50 : 9. no bullock out of **t. h.**
65:4. we satisf. with goodn. of **t.h.**
66 : 13. into **t. h.** with burnt off.
Is. 58 : 7. poor th. are cast to **t. h.**
Ha. 2 : 10. consulted shame to **t. h.**
Mat. 26:18. will keep passo. at **t. h.**
Lu. 19 : 5. to day I abide at **t. h.**
Ac. 11:14. all **t. h.** be saved, 16:31.
Phm. 2. to church in **t. h.**; Grace

HOUSE with top. [26.

1 S. 9 : 25. communed on **t.** of **h.**,
2 S. 16:22. Abs. a tent upon **t.** of **h.**

See HOUSETOP, s.

HOUSES. [h.

Ge. 42 : 19. corn for famine of your
Ex. 1 : 21. he made midwives **h.**
6:14. These be heads of fathers' **h.**
8:9. to destroy frogs fr. thy **h.**, 11.
13. the frogs died out of the **h.**
21.swarms of flies into thy **h.**, 24.
9:20.He made his serv-s flee into **h.**
10 : 6. locusts shall fill thy **h.** and
h. of thy serv-s, **h.** of all E-s
12:7. on upper doorposts of **h.** [h.
13. blood be for a token upon the
15. put aw. leaven out of your **h.**
19.be no leaven found in your **h.**
23. L. not suffer destroyer in **h.**
27.who delivered our **h.** in Egypt
Le. 25:31. **h.** of villages be counted
32. **h.** of their pose-n, 33. [40.
Nu. 4:22. sum of Gershon thro. **h.**,
16 : 32. earth swall-d them and **h.**
17:6.each prince,acc.to fathers' **h.**
32:18.We will not ret. unto our **h.**
De. 6 : 11. to give **h.** full of good
De.8:12. when hast built goodly **h.**
19:1.dwellest in their **h.**, Ne. 9:25.
Jos. 9 : 12. hot provision out of **h.**
Ju 18:14.Do ye kn. ephod is in **h.**?
22. men in **h.** near Micah's
1 K. 13:32. cried ag. **h.** of high pla.
20 : 6. sh. search **h.** of thy serv-s
2 K. 17:29. in **h.** of the high places
32. sacrificed in **h.** of high places
23 : 7. brake **h.** of sodomites
19. **h.** of high pla. Josiah took
25:9. burnt **h.** of Jerus., Je 52:13.
1 Ch. 15 : 1. Da. made **h.** in city
28 : 11. gave to Sol. pattern of **h.**
29 : 4. to overlay the walls of **h.**
2 Ch. 34: 11. buy timber to floor **h.**
35 : 4. prepare yours. by **h.** of fa-s
Ne. 4:14. fight for wives and **h.** [h.
5:3. We have mortgaged lands and
11. Restore to them their **h.**
7 : 4. people few, **h.** not builded
10 : 34. we cast lots after **h.** of fa-s
Jb. 1 : 4. sons feasted in their **h.**
3: 15. who filled their **h.** wi. silver
4:19. them that dwell in **h.** of clay
15:28.dwelleth in **h.** no man inhab.
21 : 9. Their **h.** are safe from fear
22 : 18. he filled **h.** with good thi.
24:16.In the dark they dig thro. **h.**
Ps. 49:11. that their **h.** sh continue
83 : 12. Let us take the **h.** of God
Pr. 1 : 13. sh. fill our **h.** with spoil
30 : 26. yet make their **h.** in rocks
Ec. 2:4. I builded me **h.**, I planted
Is. 3 : 14. spoil of poor is in your **h.**
5:9. many **h.** sh be desolate, 6:11.
8 : 14. rock of offence to **h.** of Isr.
13 : 16. **h.** spoiled, wives ravished
21. their **h.** sh. be full of doleful
22. beasts cry in desolate **h.**
15 : 3. on tops of **h.** ev. one howl
22 : 10. have numb-d **h.** of Jerus.,
h. have ye broken to fortify
32 : 13. upon all **h.** of joy in city
42:22. in prison **h.**: they are prey
65 : 21. shall build **h.** and inhabit
Je. 5:7. by troops in the harlots' **h.**
27. As cage,are their **h.** full of dec.
6:12. their **h.** shall be unto others
17:22. burden out of **h.** on sabbath
18 : 22. Let cry be heard from **h.**
19 : 13. **h.** of Jerus. **h.** of k-s as To-
29 : 5. Build ye **h.** dwell, 28. [phet
32 : 15. **h.** and fields sh. be pose-d
29.**h.** upon whose roofs they off-d
33:4.**h.** of this city,and **h.** of kings
39 : 8. Chal. burned **h.** of people
43:12.a fire in **h.** of gods of E., 13.
La. 5 : 2. our **h.** are turned to aliens
Eze. 7 : 24. heathen sh. possess **h.**
11:3.It is not near, let us build **h.**
16:41.they sh.burn thine **h.**, 23:47.
26: 12. sh. destroy thy pleasant **h.**
28:26. they sh. build **h.** and plant
33 : 30. talking against thee in **h.**
45 : 4. holy portion be for their **h.**
Da 2:5. your **h.** be made a dunghill
3 : 29. **h.** shall be made dunghill
Ho.11:11.I will place th. in their **h.**
Jo. 2:9. they sh. climb up upon **h.**
Am. 3 : 15. **h.** of ivory sh. perish,
great **h.** shall have an end
Mi.1:14. **h.** of Achzib be a lie to k-s
2 : 2. they covet **h.** and take them
9. women ye cast fr. pleasant **h.**
Zph. 1:9. masters' **h.** with violence
13. their **h.** sh. become a desola.,
sh. build **h.** but not inhabit
2 : 7. in **h.** of Ashkelon lie down
Hag. 1: 4. for you to dwell in ceiled
Zch. 14 : 2. **h.** shall be rifled [h.?
Mat. 11:8. wear soft cloth. in ki.'s **h.**
19:29.that hath forsaken **h.** or wife,
Mk. 10 : 30. [40. Lu. 20 : 47.
23:14. devour widow's **h.**, Mk. 12:
Mk. 8: 3. if send them fasting to **h.**
Lu. 16 : 4. may receive me into **h.**

Ac. 4:34. possessors of h. sold [in?
1 Co. 11: 22. have ye not h. to eat
1 Ti. 3: 12. deacons ruling h. well
2 Ti.3:6. are they wh. creep into h.
Tit. 1: 11. who subvert whole h.

HOUSEHOLD, S.

Ge. 18: 19. he will command his h.
35:2. Jac. unto his h. put aw.gods
42:33. food for famine of your h-s
45:11. last thy h. come to poverty
18. take your h-s come unto me
47:12.Joseph nourished his fa.'s h.
24. four parts food for your h-s
Ex. 1: 1. ev. man and his h. came
12:4. if h. be too little for the lamb
Le. 16: 17. made atonem. for his h.
Nu.18:31. shall eat it and your h-s
De.6:22.shewed wonders upon his h.
11: 6. earth swall-d them and h-s
14: 26. shalt rejoice, and h., 12:7.
15: 20. eat it bef. L. thou and h.
Jos. 2: 18. bring thy fa.'s h. home
6: 25. saved Rahab her father's h.
7: 14. the family shall come by h.
18.he brought his h.man by man
Ju. 6:27. bec. he feared his fa.'s h.
18:25.thou lose thy life, wi. thy h.
1 S. 25: 17. evil determined ag. h.
27:3. ev. man with his h., 2 S. 2:3.
2 S. 6: 11. L. blessed him and h.
20.David returned to bless his h.
15: 16. king went forth and all h.
16: 2. asses for king's h. to ride
17:23.put h.in order,hanged hims.
19:18. boat to carry over king's h.
41.Why Judah brought k.and h.
1 K. 4: 6. Abishai was over the h.
7.provided victual for king and h.
5: 9. in giving food for my h.
11. Sol. gave Hiram wheat for h.
11: 20. Genubath was in Pha.'s h.
2 K. 7: 9. may go and tell king's h.
8:1. go and thine h. to sojourn, 2.
18:18. Eliakim son of Hilkiah who
was ov.h.,19:2. Is. 36:22.-37:2.
1 Ch. 24: 6. principal h. for Eleaz.
Jb. 1: 3. 3,000 camels and great h.
Pr. 27: 27. goats' milk for thy h.
31:15.She riseth giveth meat to h.
21. not afraid of snow for her h.,
all her h. clothed with scarlet
27.looketh well to ways of her h.
Mat. 10:25. much more th.of his h.
36. a man's foes they of own h.
24:45.ruler over his h., Lu. 12:42.
Ac. 16: 15. she was bapt. and her h.
Ro. 16: 10. Salute them of Aristo.h.
11. Greet them of h. of Narcissus
1 Co. 1:16. I baptized h. of Stepha.
Ga. 6:10. who are of the h. of faith
Ep.2:19. no more strangers, but fel-
low-citizens wi. saints and of h.
Ph.4:22.that are of Cesar's h.[of G.
2 Ti. 4: 19. Salute h. of Onesiph.

HOUSEHOLD servants.

Ac. 10:7. Cornelius called two h.s.

HOUSEHOLD stuff.

Ge. 31:37. what hast found of h.s.?
Ne. 13: 8. I cast out h. s. of Tobiah

HOUSEHOLDER.

Mat. 13:27. servants of the h. came
52. like a man that is a h., 20: 1.
21: 33. certain h. planted a viney.

HOUSETOP, S.

2 K. 19: 26. as green herb as grass
on h-s, Ps. 129: 6. Is. 37: 27.
Ps. 102: 7. as sparrow alone on h.
Pr.21:9.dwell in corner of h.,25:24.
Is. 22:1. art wholly gone up to h-s
Je.48:38.lamenta.upon h-s of Moab
Zph. 1:5. worsh. host of heav. upon
Mat.10:27. preach ye upon h-s [h-s
24:17. Let him on the h. not come
down, Mk. 13:15. Lu. 17:31.
Lu.5:19. upon h. let him down [h-s
12:3. in closets be proclaim. upon
Ac.10:9. Pet. went upon h. to pray

HOW.

Ge.26:9.h. saidst thou, She my sist.
27:20. h. hast found it so quickly
28: 17. h. dreadful is this place
39:9.h. can I do this gr. wickedn.
44:8.h. then sho. we steal of lord's
16.h.shall we clear ourselves [ho.
34. h. sh. I go to my fa. lad not
Ex. 2:18. h. is ye are come so soon
6:12. h. then shall Pha. hear me
30. h. sh. Pha. hearken unto me
18:8.Moses told h. L. deliv-d them
19:4. seen h. I bare you, De. 1:31.
Nu. 10:31. h. we are to encamp in
23:8.h. shall I curse? h.sh I defy?
24:5.h.goodly are thy tents,O Jac.
De. 1:12. h. can I bear cumbrance?
7: 17. h. can I dispossess them?
11:6.h.the earth opened her mouth
12: 30. h. did nations serve gods
25: 18. h. he met thee by the way
29:16. we know h. we dwelt in E.
h. we came through nations
32:30.h. should one chase a thous.
Jos. 9: 7. h. shall we make league
Ju. 13:12. h. sh. we order child (2)
16: 15. h. canst say, I love thee?
20: 3. Tell us, h. this wickedness
21:7. h. do for wives for them, 16
Ru. 3: 18. until h. matter will fall
1 S. 10:27. h. sh. this man save us?
14:29. h. mine eyes been enlight-d
16: 2. h. can I go? if Saul hear
2 S. 1: 4. h. went matter, tell me
5. h. knowest that Saul be dead?
19. h. are mighty fallen! 25, 27.
11:7. h. Joab did, h. peo., h. war
12:18. h. then will he vex himself
1 K. 3: 7. I know not h. to go out
12:6. h. do you advise that I ans.
14:19.h. Jerob. warred, h. reigned
18:13.h. I hid hund.of L.'s proph.
20:7. see h. man seeketh mischief
2 K. 5: 7. h. he seeketh a quarrel
10:4. two k-s stood not, h. sh. we
17:28. taught h. they sho. fear L.
18: 24. h. wilt turn aw.? Is. 36:9.
19:25. h. I have done it, Is. 37:26.
20: 3. h. I have walked, Is. 38:3.
2 Ch. 20: 11. h. they reward us
33: 19. h. G. was entreated of him
Ne.2:17.ye see h. Jerus. lieth waste
Es. 2: 11. to know h. Esther did
8: 6. h. can I endure to see evil
Jb. 9: 2. h. a man be just with G.
22:13. sayest, h. doth God know?
26:2. h. helped him with-t power!
h.savest arm hath no strength!
14. h. little portion heard of him
Ps. 11: 1. h. say to my soul, Flee
44: 2. h. didst drive heathen, h.
66:3. say unto G. h. terrible thou
73:11.h. G. know? | 89:47.h.short
84: 1. h. amiable thy tabernacles
104: 24. h. manifold thy works
119: 97. O h. love I thy law, it is
103. h. sweet are thy words
159.Consider h.I love thy precepts
132:2. h. he sware unto the Lord
139:17. h. preci. are thy thoughts
Pr. 15: 23. word in season, h. good
30: 13. a genera. O h. lofty their
Ec. 10: 15. not h. to go to the city
11: 5. knowest not h. bones grow
Can. 4: 10. h. fair is thy love, 7:6.
5:3. my coat. h. shall I put it on?
7:1. h. beautiful thy feet, O dau.
Is. 14: 12. h. art fallen, O Lucifer
20:6. say, and h. shall we escape?
48: 11. h. my name be polluted?
50:4. h. to speak a word in season
52:7.h.beautiful are feet, Ro.10:15
Je. 2: 23. h. say, I not polluted?
3:19. h. shall I put thee am. chil.
5:7. h. shall I pardon | 8:8. h. do
ye say?48:14. [ask h.thou doest
9: 19. h. are we spoiled? | 15:5. to

Je.47:7.h.can it be quiet, seeing L
50: 23. h. is the hammer cut?
La. 1: 1. h. doth city sit solitary
Eze. 16: 30. h. weak is thy heart
33: 10. if we pine, h. sho. we live
Ho. 11:8. h. sh. I give thee up? (3)
Jo. 1: 18. h. do the beasts groan?
Ob. 5. if thieves, h. art cut off
Zph. 2: 15. h. is become desolat.
Hag. 2: 3. h. do you see it now?
Zch. 9: 17. h. great is his goodness
Mat. 6:23. h. great is that darkness
7: 4. h. wilt thou say to thy bro.
11.h.to give good gifts, Lu.11:13.
10: 19. take no thought h. ye sh.
speak,Lu.12:11.[Mk.3:6.-11:18.
12: 14. h. they might destr. him,
26.h.sh. kingd. stand? Lu.11:18.
34. h. can ye, evil, speak good
16: 11. h. is it ye do not underst.
18: 12. h.think ye? If a man have
an hundred sheep
21:20. h. soon is fig tree withered
22:12.h. camest in hither not hav.
45. h. is he his son? Lu. 20: 44.
23:33. h. can ye escape damnation
26:54. h. sh. Scriptures be fulfilled
Mk. 2: 16. h. eateth with sinners?
26. h. went into ho. of G., Lu.6:4.
4: 27. seed grow, he kn-h not h.
40. h. is it that ye have no faith?
10:23.h.hardly they th.have riches
14: 1. sought h. might take him
11.sought h. betray him,Lu.22:4.
Lu. 1: 34. h. shall this be, seeing
2: 49. h. is it that ye sought me?
8:18.h. ye hear | 10:26. h. readest
12:50. h. am I straitened till it be
56. h. is it ye do not discern time
16: 2. h. is it I hear this of thee?
24:6.remem. h. he spake unto you
35. h. he was known of them in
Jn. 3: 4. h. born when he is old?
9.h.can these be? | 5:44.h.believe
5: 47. h. believe my words?
6:52. h. can this man give his fl.?
7: 15. h. kn-h this man letters?
9: 10. h. were thy eyes opened?
26. h. opened eyes? | 11: 36. h.
14: 5. h. know way? [loved him
22. h. wilt manifest to us?
Ac. 4:21. h. they might punish th.
5: 9. h. is it ye agreed to tempt?
7:25. h. God would deliver them
8:31. h. can I, except man guide?
9: 27. told, h. he had seen the L.
10:38. h. G. anointed Jes. of Naz.
11:13.shewed h. he had seen angel
14: 27. h. he opened door of faith
15: 36. let us go, see h. they do
20:20. h. kept back noth. profita.
35. h. so labouring, ye ought to
Ro. 3: 6. h. shall G. judge world?
6: 2. h. we th. are dead to sin live
7: 18. h. to perform what is good
8: 32. h. shall he not freely give
10:14.h.call? h. believe? h. hear?
11: 2. h. he maketh intercession
33.h.unsearchable his judgments
1 Co.3:10. take heed h. he buildeth
7:32. unmarried careth h. he may
33. careth h. he may please wife
34.careth h.she may please husb.
14:7. h. shall it be known what is
piped or harped?
9. h. be known what is spoken?
15: 12. h. say some is no resurr.
35. say, h. are dead raised up?
2 Co.7:15. h. with fear and trembl.
8:2.h.that in a great trial of afflic.
13: 5. kn. ye not h. C. is in you?
Ga. 4:9. h. turn to weak elements?
6: 11. ye see h. large a letter I
Ep. 6:21. that ye may know h. I do
Ph. 2:23. soon as I see h. it will go
4:12.I know h. to be abased, h. to
Col. 4: 6. know h. ye ought to ans.

1 Th. 1:9. h. ye turned to G. fr. idols
2: 10. h. holily we behaved ours.
11. h. we exhorted | 4: 1. h. ye
4:4. h. to possess his vessel [ought
2 Th. 3:7. h. ye ought to follow us
1 Ti. 3:5. if man know not h. to rule
his ho. h. take care of ch. of G.
15. h. thou oughtest to behave
He. 2:3. h. sh. we escape if we neglect
7:4. consider h. great this man was
Ja. 2:24. ye see h. that by works a
3: 5. h. great a matter a little fire
2 Pe. 2:9. L. kn-h h. to deliv. godly
1 Jn. 3:17. h. dwelleth love of G. in
4: 20. h. can he love G. not seen?
Jude 5. h. that L. having saved peo.
Re. 2: 2. h. canst not bear th. evil
3:3. Remember h. thou hast recei-d
See LONG, MANY, MUCH, OFT.

HOWBEIT. [Jac.
Ju. 4: 17. h. Sisera fled to tent of
11: 28. h. the king of Ammonites
16:22. h. hair of his head began to
18: 29. h. name of city was Laish
21: 18. h. may not give th. wives
Ru. 3: 12. h. is a kinsman nearer
1 S. 8: 9. h. yet protest solemnly
2 S. 2: 23. h. Asahel refused
12: 14. h. by deed given occasion
13: 14. h. he would not hearken
25. h. he would not go [24.
23: 19. h. not first three, 1 Ch. 11:
1 K. 2: 15. h. kingdom is turned
10: 7. h. I believed not, 2 Ch. 9: 6.
11:13. h. I will not rend kingd., 34.
22. h. let me go in any wise
2 K. 3: 25. h. slingers smote it
8: 10. h. L. shewed me, he sh. die
10: 29. h. fr. sins of Jerob. Jehu
12: 13. h. not made for ho. bowls
14:4. h. high places were not taken
away, 15: 35. 2 Ch. 20: 33.
17: 29. h. every nation made gods
40. h. they did not hearken, but
22: 7. h. there was no reckoning
1 Ch. 28: 4. h. G. of Isr. chose me
2 Ch. 18: 34. h. king of Isr. stayed
24: 5. h. Levites hastened it not
27: 2. h. he entered not temp. of L.
32: 31. h. in business of ambassa.
Ne. 9: 33. h. thou art just in all
13: 2. h. our God turned the curse
Jb. 30: 24. h. not stretch out hand
Is. 10: 7. h. he meaneth not so
Je. 44: 4. h. I sent you all my serv-ts
Mat. 17: 21. h. this kind not out but
Mk. 5:19. h. Jesus suffered him not
7:7. h. in vain do they worship me
Jn. 6: 23. h. there came boats fr.
7: 13. h. no man spake openly of
27. h. we know this man whence
11: 13. if he sleep, do well, h. Jes.
16: 13. h. when he Spirit of truth
Ac. 4: 4. h. many who heard word
7: 48. h. Most High dwelleth not
14: 20. h. he rose came into city
17: 34. h. certain clave unto him
27: 26. h. we be cast upon island
28: 6. h. when he sho. have swol.
1 Co. 2: 6. h. we speak wisdom am.
8: 7. h. not in ev. man that knowl.
14: 2. h. he speaketh mysteries
20. h. in malice be children, in
15: 46. h. not first wh. is spiritual
2 Co. 11: 21. h. any is bold, I am also
Ga. 4: 8. h. when ye knew not G.
1 Ti. 1: 16. h. I obtained mercy
He. 3: 16. h. not all th. came out

HOWL, ED. [of E.
Is. 13: 6. h. ye, day of L. at hand
14: 31. h. O gate [15: 2. Moab h.
3.-16: 7. [inhabi. of isle
23: 1. h. ships of Tarsh., 14. | 6. h.
52: 5. make them h. | 65: 14. h.
for vexation [34. h. sheph-ds
Je. 4: 8. lament and h., 48: 20. | 25:
47: 2. all inhabi. of land shall h.
Je. 48: 31. will I h. for Moab, cry
39. They shall h., How [h. for her
49: 3. h., O Heshbon | 51:8. Babylon,
Eze. 21: 12. Cry and h., son of man
30: 2. h. ye, Woe worth the day
Ho. 7: 14. they h-d upon their beds
Jo. 1: 5. h., drinkers | 11. h., vine-
13. h., ministers of altar [dressers
Mi. 1: 8. I will wail and h., go naked
Zph. 1: 11. h., inhabitants of Mak-h
Zch. 11: 2. h., fir tree; h., O ye oaks
Ja. 5: 1. ye rich men, weep and h.

HOWLING, S. [ness
De. 32: 10. found him in h. wilder-
Is. 15: 8. h. unto Eglaim, h. unto
Je. 25: 36. a h. of principal of flocks
Am. 8: 3. songs of temple sh. be h-s
Zph. 1: 10. be a h. from second gate
Zch. 11: 3. There is h. of shepherds

HOWSOEVER. [3: 7.
Ju. 19: 20. h., 2 S. 18: 22, 23., Zph.

HUGE. [h. host
2 Ch. 16: 8. Ethiopians, Lubim, a

HUK'KOK. [H.
Jos. 19: 34. coast goeth thence to

HU'KOK = HEL'KATH.
1 Ch. 6:75. Unto sons of Gershom, H.

HUL. See ARAM. [Person.]

HUL'DAH the prophetess.
2 K. 22: 14. Hilkiah went unto H. -,

HUMBLE. [Adj.] [2 Ch. 34: 22.
Jb. 22: 29. be sh. save the h. person
Ps. 9: 12. forgetteth not cry of h.
10: 12. Arise, O L., forget not the h.
17. L., hast heard desire of h.
34: 2. h. shall hear and be glad
69: 32. h. sh. see this and be glad
Pr. 16: 19 Better be of a h. spirit
29:23. honour shall uphold the h.
Is. 57: 15. with him of h. spirit, to
revive spirit of h. and [5: 5.
Ja. 4: 6. giveth grace to h., 1 Pe.

HUMBLE. [Verb.] [thys.?
Ex. 10: 3. How long refuse to h.
De. 8: 2. to h. and prove thee, 16.
Ju. 19:24. h. ye them, do with them
2 Ch. 7: 14. my peo. sh. h. thems.
34:27. Bec. didst h. thyself bef. G.
Pr. 6: 3. h. thyself, and make sure
Je. 13: 18. Say unto the king, h.
yourselves [23: 12.
Mat. 18: 4. Whoso. shall h. hims.,
2 Co. 12: 21. my God will h. me
Ja. 4: 10. h. yours. in sight of L.
1 Pe. 5: 6. h. yours. under hand of

HUMBLED. [G.
Le. 26: 41. if uncirc-d hearts be h.
De. 8: 3. he h. suff-d thee to hun.
21:14. not sell, bec. h. her, 22: 29.
22: 24. hath h. his neighb.'s wife
2 K. 22:19. bec. hast h. thys. bef. L.
2 Ch. 12:6. princes and k. h. thems.
7. L. saw that they h. themselves
12. he h. himself, wrath turned
30: 11. divers of Asher h. thems.
32:26. Hez. h. hims. for pride of his
33: 12. Manas. h. himself greatly
19. set up images bef. he was h.
23. Amon h. not hims. bef. L. as
Manasseh his father h. himself
36:12. Zed. h. not hims. bef. Jere.
Ps. 35:13. I h. my soul with fasting
Is. 2: 11. lofty looks of man be h.
5:15. mighty be h. eyes of lofty be
10:33. the haughty shall be h. [h.
Je. 44: 10. not h. to this day [is h.
La. 3: 20. soul hath in rememb. and
Eze. 22: 10. in thee have h. her
11. ano. in thee hath h. his sister
Da. 5: 22. hast not h. thine heart
Ph. 2:8. he h. hims. became obedi.

HUMBLEDST, ETH.
1 K. 21: 29. how Ahab h-h? bec. he
h-h himself
2 Ch. 34: 27. bec. thou h-t thyself
Ps. 10: 10. croucheth and h-h hims.
113: 6. h-h hims. to behold things
Is. 2: 9. mean man boweth, great h-h
Lu. 14: 11. h-h hims. be exalted,

HUMBLENESS. [18: 14.
Col. 3: 12. put on kindn., h. of mind

HUMBLY.
2 S. 16: 4. I h. beseech I may find
Mi. 6:8. and to walk h. with thy G.

HUMILIATION.
Ac. 8:33. In his h. judgm. was tak.

HUMILITY.
Pr. 15: 33. bef. honour is h., 18: 12.
22:4. By h. are riches and honour
Ac. 20: 19 Serving L. with h. of mind
Col. 2: 18. Let no man beguile in h.
23. wisdom in will worship and h.
1 Pe. 5: 5. be clothed with h.

HUM'TAH.
Jos. 15: 54. were H. and Kirjath-ar.

HUNDRED.
Ge. 11: 10. Shem was h. years old
17: 17. sh. child be born to him a
h. years old? 21: 5. Ro. 4: 19.
33: 19. Jacob bought for a h. pieces,
Jos. 24: 32. [11.-38: 9, 11.
Ex. 27: 9. hangings h. cubits long,
18. length of court be h. cubits
38: 27. h. sockets of h. talents, 25.
Le. 26: 8. five sh. chase h. and a h.
De. 22: 19. amerce him in h. shekels
Ju. 7: 19. So Gideon and the h. men
20: 10. take ten of a h. a h. of a
35. Isr. destr-d of 25,000 and a h.
1 S. 18: 25. h. foreskins, 2 S. 3: 14.
25: 18. a h. clusters, 2 S. 16: 1.
2 S. 8:4. for h. chariots, 1 Ch. 18: 4.
1 K. 4:23. provision for day h. sheep
7: 2. house of forest a h. cubits
18:4. Ob. took h. proph. and hid, 13.
2 K. 4:43. sho. I set this bef. h. men?
23:33. Pha. put land to a tribute of
a h. talents, 2 Ch. 36: 3.
1 Ch. 12: 14. one of least over a h.
25. chil. of Simeon 7,000 one h.
21: 3. make peo. h. times so many
2 Ch. 3: 16. Sol. made a h. pomegr.
4: 8. he made a h. basins of gold
25: 6. He hired men for h. talents
9. what shall we do for h. talents
27: 5. gave Jotham a h. talents
29: 32. congr. brought a h. rams
Ezr. 2: 69. gave h. priests' garm.
6: 17. at dedication a h. bullocks
7:22. done unto a h. tal-s of sil., h.
measures of wheat, h. baths
8:26. silver a h. talents, of gold a h.
Pr. 17: 10. than h. stripes into fool
Ec. 6: 3. If a man beget a h. children
8: 12. Tho. sinner do evil h. times
Is. 65: 20. child shall die h. yrs. old,
sinner h. years old be accursed
Je. 52: 23. all pomegranates were h.
Eze. 40: 19. measured a h. cubits
23. fr. gate to gate a h. cubits, 27.
47. court h. cubits long, h. broad
41: 13. the house a h. cubits long
14. place tow. east. a h. cubits
15. the galleries a h. cubits
42:8. bef. temple were h. cubits, 2.
Am. 5: 3. city th. went out by a
thous. sh. leave a h., which went
by a h. sh. leave ten [Lu. 15: 4.
Mat. 18: 12. if a man have h. sheep,
28. one who owed him a h. pence
Mk. 4:8. brought forth, some a h.,
Lu. 16:6. said, h. measures of oil [20.
7. much owest thou? A h. meas.
Jn. 19: 39. myrrh aloes h. weight

HUNDRED and five, ten.
Ge. 5:6. Seth lived h. a. f. yrs., begat
50: 22. Jo. lived h. a. t. yrs., 26.
Jos. 24: 29. Joshua died a h. a. t.
years old, Ju. 2: 8. [males
Ezr. 8: 12. with Johanan h. a. t.

HUNDRED and twelve.
1 Ch. 15: 10. of sons of Uzziel, h. a. t.
Ezr. 2: 18. chil. of Jorah, h. a. t.
Ne. 7: 24. The chil. of Hariph, h. a. t.

HUNDRED and nineteen.
Ge. 11:25. Nahor lived after he begat Terah **h. a. n.** years.

HUNDRED and twenty.
Ge. 6:3. his days sh. be **h.a.t.** yrs.
Nu. 7:86. gold of spoons **h.a.t.** shek.
De. 31:2. I am a **h. a. t.** years old
34:7. Mo. **h.a.t.** yrs. old wh. died
1 K. 10:10. she gave king **h. a. t.** talents of gold, 2 Ch. 9:9.
1 Ch. 15:5. Uriel and breth. **h.a.t.**
2 Ch. 3:4. height of porch **h. a. t.** [cubits
5:12. **h. a. t.** priests
Da. 6:1. over king. **h.a.t.** princes
Ac. 1:15. names were about **h.a.t.**

HUNDRED twenty and two, three, or eight.
Nu. 33:39. Aaron 123 yrs. wh. died
Ezr. 2:21 chil. of Beth-le. went up out of captiv. 123, Ne. 7:32.
23. men of Anathoth 128, Ne. 7:27.
27. men of Michmash, 122, Ne. 7:31.
41. the chil. of Asaph 128
Ne. 11:14. their brethren 128

HUNDRED seven and twenty.
Ge. 23:1. Sarah **h. s. a. t.** old died
Es. 1:1. Ahasuerus reigned over **h. s. a. t.** provinces, 8:9.–9:30.

HUNDRED thirty. [son
Ge. 5:3. Adam lived **h.t.** y-rs, begat
47:9. years of pilgrimage **h. t.**
Nu. 7:13. weight **h.t.** shek., 19, 25.
85. each charger **h. t.** shekels
1 Ch. 15:7. Joel and breth. **h.** and **t.**
2 Ch. 24:15. Jehoi. **h. t.** yrs. old

HUNDRED thirty and three, seven, eight, or nine.
Ge. 25:17. life of Ishm 137 years
Ex. 6:16. years of Levi were 137
18. years of life of Kohath, 133
20 the years of Amram, 137
Ezr. 2:42. chil. of Shobai in all, 139
Ne. 7:45. chil. of Shobai of Ater, 138

HUNDRED and forty, forty four, seven, or eight.
Ge. 47:28. whole age of Jac. 147 yrs.
Ne. 7:44. chil. of Asaph, 148
Jb. 42:16. Aft. this lived Job 140 yrs.
Re. 21:17. the wall 144 cubits

HUNDRED and fifty, fifty three, or six.
Ge. 7:24. waters 150 days, 8:3.
1 K. 10:29. chariot out of E., horse for 150 shekels, 2 Ch. 1:17.
1 Ch. 8:40. sons and sons' sons, 150
Ezr. 2:30. chil. of Magbish, 156
8:3. were reckoned of males 150
Ne. 5:17. at my table 150 Jews
Jn. 21:11. net full of fishes, 153

HUNDRED threescore, or threescore and fifteen.
Ge. 25:7. Ab.'s life was **h.t.a.f.** yrs.
Ezr. 8:10. with him **h. t.** males

HUNDRED sixty two.
Ge. 5:18. Jared lived 162 yrs., begat E.

HUNDRED seventy two.
Ne. 11:19. porters and breth. 172

HUNDRED fourscore, or fourscore and eight.
Ge. 35:28. days of Isaac **h. f.** yrs.
Ne. 7:26. men of Beth-le. **h.f.a.e.**
Es. 1:4. Ahas. feast for **h. f.** days

HUNDRED eighty two.
Ge. 5:28. Lamech lived 182 begat

HUNDRED eighty seven.
Ge. 5:25. Methu. lived 187 begat

See THOUSAND.

Two HUNDRED.
Ge. 11:23. begat Nahor **t. h.** years
32:14. **t. h.** she goats, **t. h.** ewes
Jos. 7:21. Achan saw **t.h.** shekels
Ju. 17:4. mother took **t.h.** shekels
1 S. 18:27. Da. slew of Philis. **t.h.**
25:13. **t. h.** abode, 30:10, 21.
18. Abig. took **t. h.** loaves, **t. h.**
2 S. 14:26. weighed hair **t.h.** shekels
2 S. 15:11. with Abs. **t. h.** men
16:1. Ziba bro-t Da. **t. h.** loaves
1 K. 7:20. pomegranates were **t. h.**
10:16. made **t. h.** targets, 2 Ch. 9:15.
1 Ch. 12:32. heads of them were **t.h.**
15:8. Shemaiah and his breth. **t.h.**
2 Ch. 29:32. burnt off-gs **t.h.** lambs
Ezr. 2:65. **t. h.** singing men
6:17. at dedication **t. h.** rams
8:4. wi. Elihoenai **t. h.** males
Can. 8:12. that keep fruit **t. h.**
Eze. 45:15. one lamb out of **t. h.**
Mk. 6:37. **t.h.** dwt. of bread, Jn. 6:7.
Jn. 21:8. as it were **t. h.** cubits [h.
Ac. 23:23. **t.h.** soldiers, spearmen **t.**

Two HUNDRED five, seven, nine, twelve or eighteen.
Ge. 11:19. Peleg lived **t.h.n.** years
21. Reub. lived **t.h.s.** y-rs begat
32. days of Terah were **t.h.f.** y-rs
1 Ch. 9:22. porters were **t. h. t.**
Ezr. 8:9. with Obad. **t. h. e.** males

Two HUNDRED twenty, twenty three or thirty two.
1 K. 20:15. princes of provinces 232
1 Ch. 15:6. sons of Merari 220
Ezr. 2:28. of Beth-el and Ai 223
8:20. service of Levites 220 Nethin.

Two HUNDRED forty two, forty five or fifty.
Ex. 30:23. of cinnamon 250 (2)
Nu. 16:2. 250 princes of assembly
17. bring bef. Lord 250 censers
35. consumed 250 men, 26:10.
2 Ch. 8:10. 250 that bare rule
Ezr. 2:66. mules 245, Ne. 7:68.
Ne. 7:67. 245 singing men, women
11:13. chief of fathers, 242
Eze. 48:17. suburbs tow. north 250

Two HUNDRED threescore and sixteen.
Ac. 27:37. in ship **t.h.t.a.s.** souls

Two HUNDRED fourscore and four or eight. [a.e.
1 Ch. 25:7. cunning in songs **t. h.f.**
Ne. 11:18. Levites in city **t.h.f.a.f.**

Three HUNDRED.
Ge. 5:22. walked with God **t.h.** y-rs
6:15. length of ark be **t. h.** cubits
45:22. gave Benj **t.h.** pieces of silv.
Ju. 7:6. that lapped were **t.h.** men
8. he retained those **t. h.** men
8:4. **t.h.** men with him faint [y-rs
11:26. Isr. by coast of Arnon **t. h.**
15:4. Samson caught **t. h.** foxes
2 S. 21:16. spear weighed **t.h.** shek.
23:18. Abishai lifted up his spear ag. **t.h.** and slew, 1 Ch. 11:11, 20.
1 K. 10:17. he made **t. h.** shields
11:3. Sol. had **t. h.** concubines
2 K. 18:14. to Hez. **t. h.** talents
2 Ch. 9:16. **t.h.** shekels of gold went
14:9. ag. Asa with **t. h.** chariots
35:8. gave unto priests **t.h.** oxen
Ezr. 8:5. wi. Shechaniah **t.h.** males
Es. 9:15. Jews slew **t.h.** men at Shu.
Jn. 12:5. sold for **t.h.** pence, Mk. 14:5.

Three HUNDRED eighteen, twenty, twenty three or eight.
Ge. 14:14. Ab. with 318 servants
Ezr. 2:17. chil. of Bezai 323, Ne. 7:23.
32. chil. of Harim, 320, Ne. 7:35.
Ne. 7:22. chil. of Hashum, 328

Three HUNDRED forty five, fifty, or sixtyfive.
Ge. 5:23. Enoch's days 365 years
9:28. Noah after flood 350 years
Ezr. 2:34. chil. of Jericho 345, Ne. 7:36.

Three HUNDRED and three score.
2 S. 2:31. of Israel **t. h. a. t.** died

Three HUNDRED seventy two, ninety, or ninety two.
Ezr. 2:4. chil. of Shephatiah, 372, Ne. [7:9.
58. chil. of Sol.'s servants, 392
Eze. 4:5. number of days, 390, 9.

Four HUNDRED.
Ge. 15:13. afflict **f.h.** y-rs, Ac. 7:6.
23:15. land worth **f.h.** shekels, 16.
32:6. Esau with **f. h.** men, 33:1.
Ju. 21:12. found **f. h.** virgins
1 S. 22:2. with Da. **f.h.**, 25:13.–30:10.
30:17. **f.h.** yo. men upon camels
1 K. 7:42. **f.h.** pomegr., 2 Ch 4:13.
18:19. prophets of groves **f. h.**
22:6. Ahab gathered of prophets about **f. h.**, 2 Ch. 18:5.
2 K. 14:13. Jehoash brake wall of Jerus. **f.h.** cubits, 2 Ch. 25:23.
Ezr. 6:17. at dedication **f. h.** lambs
Ac. 5:36. to whom about **f.h.** joined

Four HUNDRED and three, ten, twenty or thirty.
Ge. 11:13. Arphaxad lived 403 years
15. Salah aft. begat Eber 403 y-rs
17. Eber lived 430 y-rs and begat
Ex. 12:40. in Egypt 430 years, 41.
1 K. 9:28. they fetched gold, 420 tal.
Ezr. 1:10. basins of a second sort 410
Ga. 3:17. law which was 430 y-rs aft.

Four HUNDRED thirty five, fifty, or fifty four.
1 K. 18:19. prophets of Baal 450, 22.
2 Ch. 8:18. Ophir and took 450
Ezr. 2:15. children of Adin 454
67. their camels 435, Ne. 7:69.
Ac. 13:20. judges about 450 years

Four HUNDRED threescore and eight.
Ne. 11:6. all sons of Perez **f.h.t.a.e.**

Four HUNDRED eightieth
1 K. 6:1. in 480th y-r Sol. began to

Five HUNDRED.
Ge. 5:32. Noah **f. h.** y-rs old begat
11:11. Shem lived after **f. h.** years
Ex. 30:23. myrrh **f. h.** shekels
24. of cassia **f. h.** shekels after
Nu. 31:28. one soul of **f. h.** for L.
1 Ch. 4:42. **f. h.** men to mount
2 Ch. 35:9. offerings **f. h.** oxen
Es. 9:6. Jews slew **f. h.** men, 12.
Jb. 1:3. **f. h.** yoke of oxen, **f. h.**
Eze. 42:16. **f.h.** reeds, 17, 18, 19, 20.
45:2. shall be for sanctuary **f. h.** in length, with **f.h.** in breadth
Lu. 7:41. the one owed **f. h.** pence
1 Co. 15:6. seen of above **f.h.** breth.

Five HUNDRED and thirty, fifty, or ninety five.
Ge. 5:30. begat Noah 595 years
1 K. 9:23. 550 bare rule over people
Ne. 7:70. gave 530 priests' garments

Six HUNDRED. [11.
Ge. 7:6. Noah **s.h.** y-rs old wh. flood,
Ex. 14:7. Pha. took **s.h.** chariots to
Ju. 3:31. Shamgar slew **s. h.**
18:11. Danites sent **s. h.**, 16, 17.
20:47. **s.h.** Benj-s fled unto Rim.
1 S. 13:15. numbered peo. **s.h.**, 14:2.
17:7. Goliath's spear's head weighed **s. h.** shekels [27:2.–30:9.
23:13. Da. and his men about **s.h.**,
2 S. 15:18. Gittites were **s.h.** men
1 K. 10:16. Sol. made targets, **s. h.** shek. of gold to one, 2 Ch. 9:15.
29. chariot for **s.h.** shek., 2 Ch. 1: [17.
1 Ch. 21:25. Ornan **s.h.** shekels
2 Ch. 3:8. ho. with gold to **s.h.** talents
29:33. consecr. things **s. h.** oxen

Six HUNDRED twenty one, three, or eight.
Ezr. 2:11. children of Bebai, 623
26. chil. of Ramah 621, Ne. 7:30.
Ne. 7:16. chil. of Bebai, 628

Six HUNDRED forty two, or eight.
Ezr. 2:10. children of Bani, 642
Ne. 7:15. children of Binnui, 648
62. the children of Nekoda, 642

Six HUNDRED and fifty two, five, or sixty six.
Ezr. 2:13. chil. of Adonikam, 666

Ezr. 2 : 60. children of Nekoda, 652
8:26. weighed to hand 650 talents
Ne. 7 : 10. children of Arah, 652
20. children of Adin, 655

Six HUNDRED threescore and six, seven or fifteen

Nu. 31:37. trib. of sheep **s.h.t.a.f.**
1 K. 10 : 14. gold to Sol. in year **s. h. t. a.** s-x talents, 2 Ch. 9:13.
Ne. 7 : 18. chil. of Adonikam, **s. h. t. a.** s-n
Re. 13:18. his number is **s.h.t.a.s.**

Six HUNDRED ninety.

1 Ch.9:6. Jeuel and breth. were 690

Seven HUNDRED.

Ju. 20 : 15. **s. h.** chosen men, 16.
2 S. 8 : 4. Da. took **s. h.** horsemen
10 : 18. slew men of **s. h.** chariots
1 K. 11 : 3. Sol. had **s. h.** wives
2 K 3:26. k. of Moab took **s.h.** men
2 Ch.15:11.offered unto L.**s.h.**oxen

Seven HUNDRED twenty one, five or thirty.

Ex. 38 : 24. 730 shekels aft. shekel
Ezr. 2 : 33. chil. of Lod, Ono, 725
Ne. 7 : 37. chil. of Lod, Hadid, 721

Seven HUNDRED thirty six, forty three or five.

Ezr. 2 : 25. chil. of Kirj.; 743, Ne.
66. horses 736, Ne. 7 : 68. [7 : 29.
Je. 52 : 30. took cap. of Jews 745

Seven HUNDRED and threescore. [14.

Ezr. 2 : 9. of Zaccai **s.h.a.t.**,Ne. 7:

Seven HUNDRED seventy-five, seven or eighty two.

Ge.5:26.Methu. lived 782 y-rs. begat
31. days of Lamech 777 years
Ezr. 2 : 5. the children of Arah, 775

Eight HUNDRED. [y-rs

Ge. 5 : 4. after begat Seth lived 800
19.aft.begat Enoch lived 800 y-rs
2 S. 23 : 8. he lifted spear ag. 800
2 Ch.13:3.set in array **e.h.** thous-d

Eight HUNDRED seven, fifteen, twenty two or thirty.

Ge. 5 : 7. aft. begat Enos 807 years
10. aft. he begat Cainan 815 y-rs
16. after he begat Jared 830 y-rs
Ne. 11 : 12. that did work were 822

Eight HUNDRED thirty two, forty, forty five, or ninety five.

Ge. 5 : 13. after begat Mahal. 840 y.
17. all days of Mahalaleel 895 y-rs
Ne. 7 : 13. chil. of Zattu were 845
Je. 52 : 29. Neb. carried captive 832

Nine HUNDRED, five, ten or twelve.

Ge. 5:8. days of Seth were 912 y-rs
11. all days of Enos 905 years
14. all days of Cainan 910 years
Ju.4:3.Jabin had **n.h.** chariots,13.

Nine HUNDRED twenty eight, thirty or forty five.

Ge. 5 : 5. days Adam lived 930 y-rs
Ezr. 2 : 8. chil. of Zattu, 945
Ne. 11 : 8. after him Gabbai, 928

Nine HUNDRED fifty or fifty six.

Ge. 9:29. all the days of Noah were 950 years [generations 956
1 Ch. 9 : 9. brethren according to

Nine HUNDRED sixty two, nine or seventy three.

Ge. 5 : 20. days of Jared 962 years
27. days of Methuselah 969 years
Ezr. 2:36. chil. of Jedaiah 973, Ne.
See THOUSAND. [7:39.

Eleven HUNDRED.

Ju.16:5.will give **e.h.** pieces of silv.
17:2.**e. h.** shekels th.were taken,3.

Twelve HUNDRED.

2 Ch. 12 : 3. With **t. h.** chariots

HUNDREDS.

Ex. 18:21. rulers of **h.**, 25,De.1:15.
1 S 29 . 2.lords of Philistines passed on by **h.** and by thousands
2 S. 18 : 4. all people came out by **h.**
2 K. 11 : 4. Jehoiada fetched rulers over **h.** and made a covenant
19. rulers over **h.** brought king from house of L , 2 Ch. 23 : 20.
Mk. 6 : 40. sat down in ranks by **h.**
See **CAPTAINS** with **hundreds.**
See **CAPTAINS** with **thousands** and **hundreds.**

HUNDREDFOLD. [h.

Ge. 26 : 12. Isaac received that year
2 S. 24 : 3. Lord add unto people **h.**
Mat. 13 :8.brought forth fruit, some an **h.**, some, 23. Lu. 8 : 8.
19 : 29. every one for my name's sake,sh. receive a **h.**, Mk.10:30.

HUNDREDTH.

Ge. 7:11.In six **h.**year of Noah's life
8.13.In six **h.** and first year,waters
Ne. 5 : 11. Restore **h.** part of money

HUNGER. [Noun.] [h.

Ex. 16 : 3. to kill this assembly with
De. 28 :48. shalt serve enemies in **h.**
32 . 24. They shall be burnt wi. **h.**
Ne. 9 : 15. gavest bread from heaven
Ps. 34 : 10. lions do suffer **h.** [for **h.**
Pr. 19 : 15. an idle soul sh. suffer **h.**
Je 38 : 9. he is like to die for **h.** [h.
42 : 14. shall see no war nor have
La 2 : 19. faint for **h.** in every street
4 : 9. better than they slain with **h.**
Eze.34 :29 no more consumed wi. **h.**
Lu. 15 : 17. and I perish with **h.**
2 Co. 11 : 27. I have been in **h.** and
Re. 6 : 8. power given to kill wi **h.**

HUNGER. [Verb.]

De. 8 : 3. he suffered thee to **h.** and
Is. 49 : 10. They shall not **h.** nor
Mat. 5 : 6. Blessed are they that **h.** after, Lu. 6 : 21. [h.
Lu. 6:25. Woe unto you full, ye sh.
Jn. 6 : 35. cometh to me never **h.**
Ro. 12 : 20. if thine enemy **h.** feed
1 Co. 4 : 11. we both **h.** and thirst
11 : 34. if **h.** let him eat at home
Re. 7 : 16. They shall **h.** no more

HUNGERBITTEN.

Jb. 18 : 12. His strength shall be **h.**

HUNGERED.

Mat. 4 : 2. was afterw. a **h.**, Lu.4:2.
12 : 1. his disciples were a **h.** and
3.what Da. did when **h.**,Mk.2:25.
21:18. returned into the city he **h.**
25:35. I was a **h.** ye gave me meat
37.L.when saw we thee an **h.**,44.
42. I was a **h.** ye gave me no
Lu. 6 : 3. what David did when a **h.**

HUNGRY.

1 S. 2 : 5. they that were **h.** ceased
2 S. 17 : 29. The people is **h.** weary
2 K. 7 : 12. They know th. we be **h.**
Jb. 5:5.Whose harvest **h.** eateth up
22:7. hast withholden bread fr. **h.**
24 : 10. they take sheaf fr. the **h.**
Ps. 50 : 12 if **h.** I would not tell
107:5. **h.** and thirsty, soul fainted
9. he filleth **h.** soul with goodn.
36. there he maketh **h.** to dwell
146:7.L. who giveth food to the **h.**
Pr. 6 : 30. if he steal when he is **h.**
25 : 21. If enemy be **h.** give him
27:7. to **h.** soul bitter thi. is sweet
Is. 8 : 21. pass thro. it, hardly bestead **h.**when **h.**sh.fret thems.
9 : 20. snatch on right ha., be **h.**
29 : 8. be as when **h.** man dream.
32 : 6. to make empty soul of **h.**
44:12. he is **h.** and strength faileth
58:7. Is it not to deal bread to **h.**?
10 if thou draw out thy soul to **h.**
65 : 13. my serv-s sh. eat, ye be **h.**
Eze. 18:7. given his bread to **h.**,16.
Mk. 11:12. from Bethany he was **h.**
Lu. 1 : 53. filled **h.** wi. good things
Ac. 10 : 10. Peter became very **h.**
1 Co. 11:21. one is **h.** ano. drunken
Ph 4:12. I know how to be full and

HUNT. [h.

Ge. 27 : † 3. go **h.** me some venison
5. Esau went to **h.** venison
1 S. 26:20. one doth **h.** a partridge
Jb. 38 : 39. Wilt **h.** prey for lion?
Ps. 140 : 11. evil sh. **h.** violent man
Pr. 6 : 26. adulteress will **h.** for life
Je. 16:16. sh. **h.** them fr. every mt.
La. 4 : 18. **h.** our steps we can-t go
Eze. 13:18. Will ye **h.** souls of peo.?
20. pillows wherew. ye **h.** souls
Mi. 7:2. they **h.** every man his bro

HUNTED, EST, ETH.

Ge. 27 : † 33. that hath **h.** venison?
Eze.13:21. no more in hand to be **h.**
Le. 17 : 13. which **h-h** any beast
1 S. 24 : 11. yet thou **h-t** my soul
Jb. 10 : 16. **h-t** me as a fierce lion

HUNTER, S.

Ge. 10 : 9. a mighty **h.** bef. L., it is said, as Nimrod mighty **h.**
25 : 27. Esau was a cunning **h.**
Pr. 6 : 5. Deliver as a roe from **h.**
Je. 16:16. aft. will I send for many

HUNTING. [h-s

Ge. 27 : 30. Esau came in from **h.**
Pr. 12:27. roasteth not wh. he took

HUP'HAM, ITES. [in h.

Nu. 26 : 39. of H. the family of H-s

HUP'PAH.

1 Ch. 24 : 13. The thirteenth to H.

HUP'PIM. [7:12.

Ge. 46 : 21. sons of Benj H., 1 Ch.
1 Ch. 7 : 15. to wife sister of H.

HUR.

Ex.17:10.Aaron, H. went up to top
12. Aaron and H. stayed hands
24:14. Aaron and H. are with you
31 : 2. Bezaleel, son of Uri, son of H., 35 : 30.-38 : 22. 2 Ch. 1 : 5.
Nu. 31 8. slew Evi, Rekem, Zur, H. Reba, 5 kings, Jos. 13 : 21.
1 K. 4 : 8. son of H. in mt. Ephr.
1 Ch. 2 : 19. Ephratah, wh. bare H.
20.H.begat | 4:1.sons of Jud., H.
50. the sons of Caleb son of H.
4 : 4. these are the sons of H.
Ne.3:9.Rephaiah son of H. repaired

HU'RAI. See HID'DAI.

HU'RAM.

1 Ch. 8 : 5. sons of Bela, H.

HU'RAM.=HI'RAM.

2 Ch. 2:3. Sol. to H. k. of Tyre, 11.
12. H. said, Blessed be the L., 13.
4 : 11. H finished the work, 16.
8 : 18. H. sent ships | 2 -9:10, 21.
See HIROM.

HU'RI.

1 Ch.5:14. chil. of Abihail son of H.

HURL, ETH, ING.

Nu. 35:20. if **h.** at him that he die
1 Ch. 12 : 2. use right hand and left in **h-g** stones
Jb. 27 : 21. as a storm **h-h** him out

HURT. [Noun.]

Ge. 4 : 23. slain a yo. man to my **h.**
26 : 29. a covenant, that thou wilt do us no **h.** [h.
31 : 29. power of my ha. to do you
Jos.24:20 If forsake, will do you **h.**
1 S. 20 : 21. is peace to thee, no **h.**
24 : 9. Behold, Da. seeketh thy **h.**
2 S. 18 : 32. that rise to do **h.** be as
2 K.14:10.why shouldest thou meddle to thy **h.**, 2 Ch. 25 : 19.
Ezr. 4:22. why damage to **h.** of k-s?
Es. 9:2. on such as sought their **h.**
Ps. 15 : 4. sweareth to his **h.** [70:2.
35:4. confusion that devise my **h.**,
26. be asham. that rejoi. at my **h.**
38:12. seek my **h.** speak mischiev.
41 : 7. ag. me do they devise my **h.**
71:13. wi. reproach th. seek my **h.**
24.bro-t to shame th. seek my **h.**

Ec. 5 : 13. riches kept to their **h.**
8 : 9. ruleth over ano. to own **h.**
Je. 6 : 14. **h.** of peo. slightly, 8:11.
7 : 6. nei. walk aft. gods to your **h.**
8 : 21. For **h.** of my peo. am I **h.**
10 : 19. Woe is me for my **h.**
24 : 9. deliver to be remov. for **h.**
25 : 6. provoke me not, I do no **h.**
7. might provoke me to own **h.**
38 : 4. seeketh not welfare of this peo., but **h.** ⌈have done no **h.**
Da. 3 : 25. they have no **h.** | 6:22. I
6 : 23. no **h.** was found upon him
Ac. 27:10. this voyage will be wi. **h.**

HURT. [Verb, active.] ⌈me
Ge. 31 : 7. God suff-d him not to **h.**
Ex. 21:22. If **h.** woman with child
35. if one man's ox **h.** another's
Nu. 16 : 15. nei. have I **h.** one of
1 S. 25:7. thy shepherds, we **h.** not
Jb. 35 : 8. Thy wickedn. may **h.** a man ⌈ters
Ps. 105 : 18. Whose feet **h.** wi. fet-
Is. 11 : 9. They shall not **h.** in all my holy mountain, 65: 25.
27 : 3. lest any **h.** it, I will keep it
Da 6:22. that lions have not **h.** me
Mk. 16 : 18. deadly thing, it sh. not **h.** ⌈not
Lu. 4 : 35. devil came out, **h.** him
10:19. noth. by any means **h.** you
Ac. 18 : 10. no man sh. set on thee
Re. 6 : 6. see thou **h.** not oil ⌊to **h.**
7 : 2. given to **h.** earth and sea
3. Saying **h.** not earth, nei. sea
9 : 4. sho. not **h.** grass of earth
10. their power was to **h.** men
19. heads, and with them do **h.**
11 : 5. if any **h.** th., fire proceedeth

HURT. [Passive.]
Ex.22: 10. If beast **h.** no man seeing
14. if be **h.** and die the owner
1 S. 25 : 15. men good and we not **h.**
Ec. 10 : 9. removeth shall be **h.**⌈**h.**
Je. 8 : 21. For **h.** of my people am I
Re. 2:11. shall not be **h.** of sec. death

HURTFUL.
Ezr. 4 : 15. that this city is **h.** to k.
Ps. 144:10. deliv-h Da. fr. **h.** sword
1 Ti. 6 : 9. will be rich fall into **h.**

HURTING. ⌊lusts
1 S. 25 : 34. Lord kept me fr. **h.** thee

HUSBAND.
Ge. 20 : †3. for she is married to a **h.**
Ex. 4 : 25. a bloody **h.** art thou, 26.
21 : 22. woman's **h.** lay upon him
Le. 19:20. lieth with wom betrothed to **h.**, De. 22 : 23. ⌈Eze. 44 : 25.
21 : 3. defiled sister who had no **h.**
Nu. 30 : 6. if a **h.** when she vowed
De. 22 : 22. with wom. married to **h.**
24 : 3. if latter **h.** hate her or die
4. former **h.** may not take her
25 : 5. duty of a **h.**'s bro. unto her
28 : 56. her eye sh. be evil toward **h.**
Ju. 20 : 4. **h.** of woman slain, ans.
Ru. 1 : 3. Elim., Naomi's **h.** died
12. too old to have a **h.** if (2)
Je. 6 : 11. **h.** with wife be taken
31 : 32. altho. I was a **h.** unto th.
Jo. 1: 8. sackcl. for **h.** of her youth
Mat. 1 : 16. beg-t Jo-eph **h.** of Mary
Lu. 2 : 36. lived with **h.** 7 years
Jn. 4:17. I have no **h.** hast well said, I have no **h.** ⌈fr. **h.**, 3.
Ro. 7 : 2. if **h.** be dead, she is loosed
1 Co. 7 : 3. Let **h.** render unto wife due benevol. also wife unto **h.**
4. **h.** hath not power of own body
11. let not **h.** put away his wife
13. hath a **h.** that believeth not
14. unbeli-g **h.** is sanctifi. by wife, unbeli-g wife is sanctifi. by **h.**
2 Cor. 11 : 2. I espoused you to, **h.**
Ga. 4 : 27. more chil. than she who
Ep. 5 : 23. **h.** is head of wife ⌊a **h.**
1 Ti.3:2. bishop **h.** of 1 wife, Tit.1:6.

Her HUSBAND, 'S.
Ge. 3:6. Eve did eat gave unto **h.h.**
16:3. Sarai gave Hagar to **h.h.** Abr.
Le. 21:7. nor wom, put away fr. **h.h.**
Nu. 5 : 13. if hid from eyes of **h.h.**
27. if done trespass against **h.h.**
29. goeth to ano. instead of **h.h.**
30 : 7. **h. h.** heard it, and held his peace, 11, 14.
8. if **h. h.** disallow her on day
10. if she vowed in **h. h.'s** house
12. if **h.h.** made them void
13. **h. h.** may establish it or
De. 21 : 13. go in unto her, be **h.h.**
25 : 5. **h.h.'s** bro. go in unto her
11. wife near to deliver **h. h.**
Ju. 13 : 6. Then woman told **h. h.**
9. Manoah **h. h.** not with her
10. made haste, and shewed **h. h.**
19 : 3. **h. h.** went aft. her to speak
Ru. 1 : 5. Naomi left of **h. h.**
9. find rest each in hou. of **h. h.**
2 : 1. Naomi had kinsman of **h. h.**
1 S. 1: 8. Elkanah **h. h.** to her, 23.
22. said unto **h. h.** I will not go
2 : 19. came with **h. h.** to offer
4 : 19. heard th. fa. and **h. h.** dead
21. bec. of | 25: 19. told not **h. h.**
2 S. 3 : 15. Ishbo. took her fr. **h. h.**
16. **h. h.** went with her weeping
11 : 26. wife of Uriah heard **h. h.** was dead, mourned for **h. h.**
2 K. 4 : 9. said unto **h. h.** Behold I
14. hath no child, **h. h.** is old
22. called unto **h. h.**, Send me one
Pr.12:4. virtuous wife crown to **h.h.**
31 : 11. heart of **h. h.** doth trust
23. **h. h.** is known in the gates
28. **h. h.** riseth up, praiseth her
Je. 3 : 20. as wife departeth fr. **h. h.**
Eze. 16:32. strangers instead of **h.h.**
45. that loatheth **h. h.** and chil.
Ho. 2 : 2. not my wife, nei I **h. h.**
Mat. 1: 19. Joseph **h. h.** being just
Mk. 10 : 12. if wom. put away **h. h.**
Lu. 16: 18. marrieth her put fr. **h.h.**
Ac. 5 : 10. buried her by **h. h.**
Ro. 7 : 2. is bound by law to **h. h.**
3. if **h. h.** be dead, she is free
1 Co.7: 2. ev. woman have **h.** own **h.**
3. likewise the wife unto **h. h.**
10. Let not wife depart from **h. h.**
11. unmar. or be reconciled to **h.h.**
34. careth how may please **h. h.**
1 Co. 7: 39. bound long as **h.h.** liveth
Ep. 5: 33. wife see she reverence **h.h.**
Re. 21: 2. as bride adorned for **h. h.**

Mine, or my HUSBAND.
Ge. 29 : 32. now **m. h.** will love me
34. Now will **m. h.** be joined unto me ⌈**m. h.** ?
30 : 15. Is it small matt. hast taken
18. I have given maiden to **m. h.**
20. now will **m. h.** dw. with me
De 25: 7. **m. h.** bro. refus-th to raise
2 S. 14 : 5. **m-e h.** is dead, 2 K. 4: 1.
7. leave to **m. h.** nei. name ⌈**h.**
Ho. 2 : 7. will go return to **m.** first
†16. in th. day shalt call me **m.h.**

Thy HUSBAND.
Ge. 3 : 16. thy desire sh. be to **t. h.**
Nu. 5 : 19. ano. instead of **t. h.** 20.
Ju. 14 : 15. unto Sam.'s w., Entice
Ru. 2 : 11. since death of **t.h.** ⌊**t.h.**
2 K. 4 : 26. Is it well with **t. h.** ?
Is. 54 : 5. thy Maker is **t. h.** the L.
Jn. 4 : 16. call **t. h.** | 18 he not **t. h.**
Ac. 5 : 9. th. have buried **t. h.**
1 Co. 7 : 16. wh-ther shalt save **t. h.**

HUSBANDS. ⌈**h.**
Ru. 1 : 11. sons, they may be your
13. would ye stay fr. having **h.** ?
Es. 1 : 17. they sh. despise their **h.**
20. wives shall give to **h.** honour
Je. 29: 6. give your daughters to **h.**
Eze. 16 : 45. which loathed **h.** and
Jn. 4 : 18. thou hast had five **h.** he

1 Co. 14 : 35. let th. ask **h.** at home
Ep. 5:22. Wives, submit yours. unto your **h.**, 24. Col. 3:18. 1 Pe 3:1.
25 **h.**, love your wives, Col. 3:19.
1 Ti. 3 : 12. deacons be **h.** of 1 wife
Tit. 2 : 4. young women to love **h.**
5. to be obedient to own **h.**
1 Pe. 3 : 7. ye **h.** dwell with th. acc. to knowledge

HUSBANDMAN.
Ge. 9 : 20. Noah began to be **a b.**
Je. 51 : 23. will I break in pieces **h.**
Am. 5: 16. shall call **h.** to mourning
Zch. 13: 5. I am no prophet, I am **h.**
Jn. 15 : 1. I true vine, Fa. is the **h.**
2 Ti. 2 : 6. **h.** that labour-h must be
Ja. 5 : 7. **h.** waiteth for preci. fruit

HUSBANDMEN. ⌈52:16.
2 K. 25: 12. left of poor to be **h.**, Je.
2 Ch. 26 : 10. Uzziah had **h.**
Je. 31 : 24. shall dwell in Judah, **h.**
Jo. 1 : 11. be ashamed, O ye **h.** howl
Mat. 21: 33. he let it out to **h.**, Mk. 12:1. Lu 20:9. ⌈12:2. Lu. 20:10.
34. sent his servants to **h.**, 35. Mk.
38. when **h.** saw the son, Mk. 12: 7. Lu. 20 : 14. ⌈those **h.**
40. cometh what will he do unto
41. let viney. unto other **h.** ⌈20: 10.
Mk. 12:2. receive fr. **h.** of fruit, Lu.
9. he will destroy the **h.**, Lu. 20 : ⌊16.

HUSBANDRY.
2 Ch. 26 : 10. Uzziah loved **h.**
Jb. 1 : †3. Job had a very great **h.**
1 Co. 3:9. ye are God's **h.** ye are G.'s

HU'SHAH.
1 Ch. 4 : 4. Ezer the father of H.

HU'SHAI.
2 S. 15 : 37. So H. David's friend came
16 : 17. said to H., Is this thy kind-
18. H. said unto Absalom ⌊ness
17:6 when H. was come to Absalom
7. H. said, The counsel is not good
8. said H., thou knowest thy fath.
15. said H. unto Zadok and Abiath.
1 K. 4 : 16. Baanah son of H in Asher
See **Hushai the ARCHITE.**

HU'SHAM. ⌈Ch. 1:45,46.
Ge. 36 : 34. H. reigned | 35. died, 1

HU'SHATHITE.
2 S. 21 : 18. Sibbechai, the H. slew Saph, 1 Ch. 11: 29. 20: 4. 27: 11.
23: 27. Nebunnai the H.

HU'SHIM. ⌈†42.
Ge. 46 : 23. sons of Dan, H., Nu. 26:
1 Ch. 7 : 12. Shuppim, Huppim, H.
8 : 8. H. and Baara his wives | 11.

HUSK, S.
Nu. 6 : 4. kernels even to the **h.**
2 K. 4:42. bro-t full ears of corn in **h.**
Lu. 15: 16. fain filled his belly with

HUZ. ⌊**h-s**
Ge. 22 : 21. H. firstborn, Buz his

HUZ'ZAB. ⌊ho.
Ne. 2 : 7. H. shall be led away cap-

HYMENE'US. ⌊tive
1 Ti. 1 : 20. of wh. is H. and Alex.
2 Ti. 2 : 17. of wh. is H. and Phile-

HYMN, S. ⌊tus
Mat. 26: 30. had sung a **h.**, Mk. 14: 26.
Ep. 5: 19. Speaking in psalms and **h-s**
Col. 3: 16. admonishing in psalms and

HYPOCRISY, IES. ⌊**h-s**
Is. 32 : 6. iniquity, to practise **h.**
Mat. 23 : 28. within ye are full of **h.**
Mk. 12 : 15. knowing their **h.** said
Lu. 12: 1. leaven of Phari-s which is **h.**
1 Ti. 4: 2. Speak-g lies in **h.** conscien.
Ja. 3: 17. wisdom from ab. is wit-t **h.**
1 Pe. 2: 1. laying aside all malice **h-s**

HYPOCRITE.
Jb. 8: 13. the **h.**'s hope shall perish
13: 16. a **h.** shall not come bef. him
17: 8. innocent shall stir him ag. **h.**
20 : 5. joy of **h.** is but for moment
27 : 8. what is the hope of the **h.** ?
34: 30. That **h.** reign not, lest peo.

Pr. 11: 9. A h. with mouth destroy
Is. 9: 17. for every one is a h.
Mat. 7: 5. Thou h. first cast out beam
Lu. 6: 42. h. cast beam out of eye
13: 15. h. doth not each loose ox?

HYPOCRITES.

Jb. 15: 34. congr. of h. be desolate
36: 13. h. in heart heap up wrath
Is. 33: 14. fearfulness surprised h.
Mat. 6: 2. not sound trumpet as h.
5. prayest, thou shalt not be as h.
16. when ye fast, be not as h.
15: 7. h. well did Esaias prophesy,
Mk. 7: 6. [of sky, Lu. 12: 56.
16: 3. O ye h. ye can discern face
22: 18. Why tempt ye me, ye h.
23: 13. woe unto you, scribes and
Phari-s, h., 14, 15, 23, 25, 27, 29.
Lu. 11: 44.
24: 51. appoint portion with h.

HYPOCRITICAL.

Ps. 35: 16. With h. mockers in feasts
Is. 10: 6. I will send him ag. h. nation

HYSSOP.

Ex. 12: 22. take bunch of h. dip it
Le. 14: 4. take scarlet and h., 6, 49, 51.
52. sh. cleanse the house with h.
Nu. 19: 6. sh. cast h. into burning
18. a clean person sh. take h. dip it
1 K. 4: 33. cedar tree even unto h.
Ps. 51: 7. Purge me with h. and I
Jn. 19: 29. filled sponge put it upon h.
He. 9: 19. blo. with h. and sprinkled
people

I.

Ge. 6: 17. I do bring flood upon earth
9: 9. I, behold I, establish my cov.
34: 30. I shall be destr-d, I and my h.
37: 10. sh. I and breth. come to bow?
30. child is not, whither sh. I go?
39: 9. There is none greater than I
Ex. 3: 11. Who I, that I go to Phar.?
14. I AM THAT I AM [wicked
9: 27. L. righteous I and my people
14: 17. behold I will harden hearts
18: 6. I thy father in law Jethro am
31: 6. I have given with him Aho.
Le. 26: 28. even I will chastise you
Nu. 3: 12. I have taken, Le. 18: 6.
De. 7: 17. nations more than I, how
32: 39. I, even I, am he, is no God
Jos. 14: 7. Forty y-rs old I when Mo.
Ju. 5: 3. I will sing to Lord G. of Isr.
7. until I Deb. arose, that I arose
7: 18. When I blow, I and all
11: 37. bewail my virginity, I and
12: 2. I and my peo. were at strife wi.
20: 4. into Gibeah, I and concu. [I
1 S. 24: 17. Thou more righte. than
2 S. 3: 28. I and my kingd. guiltless
13: 13. I, whi. cause my shame to go?
1 K. 1: 21. I and son Sol. be counted
18: 22. I remain proph., 19: 10, 14.
1 Ch. 29: 14. who am I, 2 Ch. 2: 6.
2 Ch. 32: 13. what I and fa-s have done
Ezr. 7: 21. I, even I Artaxerxes
Ne. 5: 15. so did not I, bec. of fear
Es. 4: 16. I and maidens will fast
Jb. 1: 15. I only am escaped, 16, 17, 19.
15: 6. own mouth condemneth, not I
34: 33. whe. refuse or choose, not I
Ps. 61: 2. rock that is higher than I
142: 6. persecutors stronger than I
Ec. 2: 25. who hasten more than I?
Can. 2: 1. I am the rose of Sharon
6: 3. I am my beloved's, 7: 10.
8: 10. I am a wall [me, He. 2: 13.
Is. 8: 18. I and chil. L. hath given
41: 4. I the Lord the first, I am he,
48: 11, 12. [God, 43: 5.
10. I am with thee, for I am thy
44: 6. I am the first, I am the last,
48: 12. Re. 1: 17. [clare it?
7. who as I shall call, and shall de-
45: 12. I have made the earth
Is. 46: 4. to your old age I am he (2)
9. I am God, there is none else
48: 15. I have spoken, I called
16. fr. time, there am I, Mat. 18: 20.
49: 5. sh. I be glorious in the eyes
51: 12. I, even I am he, 52: 6.
52: 6. behold, it is I
65: 5. I am holier than thou
Je. 20: 7. I was deceived, thou art
23: 39. I will utterly forget you
Eze. 5: 8. I, even I, am ag. thee
6: 3. I will bring a sword upon you
34: 11. I will search sheep and
20. I will judge betw. fat cattle
44: 28. I am their inherit. I am
Da. 8: 15. I Dan. had seen vision
Ho. 5: 14. I, even I, will tear, I
Hag. 1: 13. I am with you, saith L.
Zch. 1: 15. I was but little displeased
Mal. 1: 13. I accept at your hands?
Mat. 3: 11. mightier than I, Mk. 1: 7.
14: 27. it is I, Mk. 6: 50. Jn. 6: 20.
16: 13. Whom do men say I am?
18: 20. there am I in midst of them
24: 5. many sh. come saying, I am
C., Lu. 21: 8.
26: 22. began to say, L. is it I?
Mk. 14: 29. all offended, yet not I
Lu. 2: 48. fa. and I sought thee
11: 19. if I by Beel. cast out devils
20. if I with finger of G. cast
22: 27. I am among you as he th.
24: 39. it is I myself, handle me
Jn. 1: 20. I am not the Christ, 3: 28.
33. I knew him not
4: 26. I that speak am he [sent
8: 16. I am not alone, but I and Fa.
23. I am from above, I am not of
28. sh. know I am he, I do noth.
58. before Abraham was, I am
10: 30. I and Fa. are one [15: 5.
38. Fa. in me, I in him, 17: 21.-
12: 32. I, if I be lifted up, will draw
13: 14. if I your L. have washed
14: 20. I in my Fa. | 15: 4. I in you
28. I go to Fa. greater than I
17: 23. I in them, 26 | 25. I have
18: 35. ans-d, Am I a Jew? [known
Ac. 11: 17. I that I co. withstand G.
22: 28. I obtained this freedom
Ro. 7: 17. is no more I, but sin, 20.
1 Co. 1: 12. I am of Paul, I of, 3: 4
2: 1. I breth. when I came to you
3: 1. I, breth. could not speak as
7: 7. I would all men were as I
8. if they abide even as I
10. yet not I, but Lord
9: 6. or I only and Barnabas
26. I so run, so fight I, not as
11: 1. followers of me, as I of C.
15: 10. grace of G. I am what I am
11. whether it were I or they
16: 10. he worketh work of C. as I
2 Co. 11: 22. they Heb.? so am I, 23.
29. who is offended, I burn not
Ga. 2: 19. I thro. law am dead to
20. I live, yet not I, but C. liveth
4: 12. Breth. be as I am, for I am
5: 11. if I yet preach circumcision
6: 14. that I should glory in cross
Ep. 1: 15. aft. I heard of your faith
4: 1. I prisoner of Lord beseech
1 Pe. 1: 16. be ye holy, for I am holy
2 Jn. 1. whom I love in the truth
Re. 1: 8. I am Alpha and Omega
3: 19. As many as I love, I rebuke
21. as I overcame | 21: 2. I saw, 22: 8.
22: 9. I am thy fellowservant
16. I am root and offspring of Da-
See **I AM**, or **AM I.** [vid

IB'HAR.

2 S. 5: 15. Da.'s son I., 1 Ch. 3: 6. - 14: 5.

IB'LEAM.

Jos. 17: 11. Manas. had I. | Ju. 1: 27.
2 K. 9: 27 going up to Gur. by I.

IBNEI'AH.

1 Ch. 9: 8. I. son of Jeroham

IBNI'JAH.

1 Ch. 9: 8. Reuel, the son of I.

IB'RI.

1 Ch. 24: 27. sons of Merari, I.

IB'ZAN.

Ju. 12: 8. I. judged Isr. | 10. I. died

ICE.

Jb. 6: 16. are blackish by reason of i.
38: 29. Out of whose womb came i.?
Ps. 147: 17. casteth i. like morsels

ICH'ABOD.

1 S. 4: 21. she named the child I.
14: 3. son of Ahitub, I. brother

ICO'NIUM.

Ac. 13: 51. Paul came unto I., 14: 21.
14: 1. in I they went into t. synag.
19. came certain Jews from I.
16: 2. well reported by breth. at I.
2 Ti. 3: 11. afflictions at I.

ID'ALAH.

Jos. 19: 15. I. and Beth-l-m 12 cities

ID'BASH.

1 Ch. 4: 3. these of fa. of Etam; I.

ID'DO.

1 K. 4: 14. Ahinadab son of I. had
1 Ch. 6: 21. Joash his son, I. his son
27: 21. tribe of Manas. I was ruler
2 Ch. 9: 29. writ. in visions of I. the
seer, 12: 15 - 13: 22. [1: 1, 7.
Ezr. 5: 1. Zech. son of I. proph., Zch.
6: 14. prophesying of Zech. son of I.
8: 17. I sent them to I. [16.
Ne. 12: 4. I went up with Zerub.,

IDLE. [cry

Ex. 5: 8. they be i. therefore they
17. he said, Ye are i. ye are i.
Pr. 19: 15. i. soul sh. suffer hunger
Mat. 12: 36. ev. i. word men sh. speak
20: 3. standing i. in marketpl., 6.
Lu. 24: 11. words seemed as i. tales
1 Ti. 5: 13. learn to be i. and not only i.

IDLENESS.

Pr. 31: 27. She eateth not br. of i.
Ec. 10: 18. thro. i. the house droppeth
Eze. 16: 49. abundance of i. in her

IDOL. [Adj.]

Zch. 11: 17. Woe to i. shepherd th.

IDOL. [Noun.]

1 K. 15: 13. made i. in grove, 2 Ch.
2 Ch. 33: 7. set i. in ho. of G. [15: 16.
15. he took i. out of ho. of Lord
Is. 48: 5. lest say Mine i. done them
66: 3. incense as if he blessed an i.
Je. 22: 28. Is this Coniah a brok. i.
Ac. 7: 41. offered sacrifice unto the i.
1 Co. 8: 4. i. is noth. in world, 10: 19.
7. some with conscience of the i.

IDOLS.

Le. 19: 4. Turn ye not unto i.
26: 1. Ye shall make you no i.
30. carcasses upon carcasses of i.
De. 29: 17. ye have seen their i.
1 S. 31: 9. publish it in ho. of their i.
1 K. 15: 12. Asa removed i. his fa
21: 26. Ahab did abomi. in foll. i.
2 K. 17: 12. served i., 2 Ch. 24: 18.
21: 11. hath made Jud. sin with i.
21. Amon served i. his fa. served
23: 24. i. that were spied in land
1 Ch. 10: 9. carry tidings to their i.
16: 26. all gods of the peo. are i.
2 Ch. 15: 8. Asa put abomi. i. out of
34: 7. Josiah cut down all i. in la.
Ps. 96: 5. all gods of nations are i.
97: 7. Confounded that boast of i.
106: 36. they serve their i. that
38. whom they sacrificed to i.
115: 4. i. are silver and gold, 135: 15.
Is. 2: 8. Their land is full of i.
18. i. he shall utterly abolish
20. shall cast away his i., 31: 7.
10: 10. my ha. found kingd-s of i.
11. unto Sama. and i. so to Jerus.
19: 1. i. of E. shall be moved [and i.
3. shall seek to i. and charmers
45: 16. makers of i. go to confusion
46: 1. their i. were on the beasts

Is.57:5. Inflaming yourselves with i.
Je. 50: 2. her i. are confounded, her
38. and they are mad upon their i.
Eze. 6: 4. cast slain bef. i., 5, 13.
6. your i. may be brok. and cease
9. eyes wh. go a whoring after i.
13. did offer sweet savour to i.
8:10. I saw all i. of Isr. pourtrayed
14: 3. set up their i. in heart, 4, 7.
5. estranged from me through i.
6. Repent, and turn from your i.
16: 36. with all i. of thy abomi.
18:6. nei. lifted eyes to i. of Isr., 15.
12. oppr-d poor, lifted eyes to i.
20: 7. defile not with i. of Egypt
8. nei. did they forsake the i. of E.
16. heart aft. i. | 24. eyes aft. i.
31. ye pollute yours. with i. even
unto this day, 22:4.-23:7, 30, 37.
39. pollute my name no more wi. i.
22: 3. city maketh i. ag. herself
23: 39. had slain their chil. to i.
49. ye shall bear sins of your i.
30: 13. I will destroy i. and cause
33:25. ye lift up your eyes tow. i.
36: 18. i. whw. they polluted it
25. fr. i. will cleanse you, 37: 23.
44: 10. went astray fr. after i.
12. miniet-d to them bef. their i.
Ho. 4: 17. Ephraim is joined to i.
8:4. of their silv. and gold made i.
13: 2. made i. acc. to underst-g
14: 8. What have I to do with i.?
Mi. 1: 7. all i. will I lay desolate
Ha. 2:18. trusteth to make dumb i.
Zph.1:†3. will consume i. with wick.
Zch.10:2. the i. have spoken vanity
13: 2. I will cut off names of i.
Ac. 15:20. abstain from pollu. of i.
29. from meats off-d to i., 21:25.
17: † 16. when saw city full of i.
Ro. 2: 22. thou that abhorrest i.
1 Co. 8: 1. touching things off-d to
i., 4, 10.-10:19, 28. Re.2:14, 20.
12: 2. Gentiles carried to dumb i.
2 Co.6:16. agreement tem. of G. wi. i.
1 Th. 1: 9. how ye turned from i.
1 Jn. 5: 21. chil. keep yours. fr. i.
Re. 9:20. not worship i. of gold, sil.

IDOLATER, S. [i-s

1 Co.5:10. Yet not with covetous or
11. if any called a brother be an i.
6: 9. i-s not inherit kingd. of God
10: 7. Nei. be ye i-s as were some
Ep.5:5. no man i. hath any inheri.
Re. 21: 8. i-s have part in lake
22: 15. without are murderers i-s

IDOLATROUS.

2 K. 23: 5. put down i. priests

IDOLATRY, IES. [i.

1 S.15:23. stubbornness as iniq. and
Ac. 17: 16. city wholly given to i.
1 Co. 10: 14. beloved, flee from i.
Ga. 5: 20. works of the flesh are i.
Col.3:5. Mortify covetousn. wh. is i.
1 Pe. 4:3. walked in abominable i-s

IDUME'A.

Is. 34: 5. my sword on I., 6.
Eze. 35: 15. all I. shall be desolate
36: 5. have I spoken against all I.
Mk. 3: 8. mult. followed him fr. I.

IF.

Ge.25:22. i. it be so, why am I thus
31:8. i. he said | 34:15. i. ye will be
43:11. i. it must be so, take of best
Jos. 14: 12. i. so be L. be with me
1 S. 14: 9. i. they say to us, Tarry
20:7. i. he say thus, it is well, 2 S.
15: 26. [i. they kill us
2 K. 7: 4. i. we say, i. we sit here,
10:6. i. ye be mine, i. will hearken
Jb. 9: 29. i. I be wicked, 10: 15.
24: 25. i. it be not so [be iniquity
Ps. 7:3. i. I have done this, i. there
Je. 27:18. i. they prophets, i. word
51: 8. balm, i. so be may be heal.
Da. 3: 17. i. it be so, our G. is able
Da.4:27. i. it may be a lengthening of
Ho. 8: 7. i. so be it yield, strangers
Mat. 4:3. i. thou be the son of God,
27: 40. Lu. 4:3. [unto thee
14: 28. i. it be thou, bid me come
27: 43. let him deliver, i. he will
Mk. 1:40. i. wilt, canst make me cl.
11: 32. i. we shall say of men
Lu. 23:35. i. he be C., 39. Jn.10:24.
Jn. 1: 25. i. thou be not Elias
15:18. i. world hate you, 1 Jn.3:13.
19: 12. i. thou let this man go
Ac. 5: 39. i. it be of God ye cannot
1 Co. 15:19. i. in this life only hope
Ga. 4: 7. i. a son, then heir of God
Ph. 2:1. i. any consolation, i. any
He. 3:†11. i. ent. into rest, 4: 3, 5.
1 Jn. 2: 19. i. they had been of us

IF not.

Ge. 18: 21. i. n. I will know
24:49. if deal kindly; i. n. tell me
Ex. 32:32. i. n. blot me, I pray, out
Ju. 9:15. i. n. let fire come out, 20.
1 S.2:16. i. n. I will take it by force
6: 9. i. n. shall know it is not his
2 S. 13: 26. i. n. let Amnon go
17: 6. after his say.? i. n. speak
2 K. 2: 10. i. n. it shall not be so
Jb. 9: 24. i. n. where, who is he?
33: 33. i. n. hearken unto me
Da. 3: 18. i. n. be it known, O k.
Zch. 11:12. my price; i. n. forbear
Lu. 10:6. i. n. it shall turn to you
13: 9. i. n. aft. that cut it down

IF now.

Ge. 18:3. i. n. I have found favour
24: 42. O God, i. n. thou prosper
49. i. n. will deal kindly with me
33: 10. i. n. I found grace in thy
sight, 47:29. Ex.34:9. Ju. 6:17.
1 Co. 4:7. i. n. thou didst receive it
See **If it WERE.**

I'GAL.

Nu. 13:3. I. son of Joseph, 2 S. 23:

IGDALI'AH. [36.

Je. 35: 4. son of I. a man of God

IG'EAL.

1 Ch. 3: 22. sons of Shemaiah, I.

IGNOMINY.

Pr. 18: 3. cometh with i. reproach

IGNORANCE.

Le. 4: 2. if a soul shall sin thro. i.,
5: 15. Nu. 15: 24, 27, 28, 29.
13. whole cong. of Israel sin thro. i.
22. ruler done somewhat thro. i.
27. if any of people sin through i.
Nu. 15: 25. forgiven, for it is i.
Ac. 3:17. I wot th. thro. i. ye did it
17: 30. times of i. God winked at
Ep.4:18. being alienated thro. the i.
1 Pe. 1:14. acc. to former lusts in i.
2:15. may put to silence i. of fool-

IGNORANT. [ish

Ps. 73: 22. So foolish was I and i.
Is. 56: 10. all i. are all dumb dogs
63: 16. our fa. tho. Ab. be i. of us
Ac.4.13. perceived they were i. men
Ro. 1: 13. not have you i. breth., 1
Co.10:1.-12:1. 2 Co.1:8. 1 Th.4:13
10:3. being i. of God's righteousn.
11:25. th. ye be i. of this mystery
1 Co. 14: 38. if any i. let him be i.
2 Co. 2:11. not i. of Satan's devices
He. 5: 2. have compassion on i.
2 Pe. 3: 5. this they willingly i. of
8. beloved, be not i. of this thing

IGNORANTLY.

Nu.15:28. atone for soul that sinn. i.
De. 19: 4. whoso killeth neighb. i.
Ac. 17: 23. Whom ye i. worship
1 Ti. 1:13. bec. I did it i. in unbel.

I'IM.

Nu. 33:45. departed fr. I. | Jos. 15:

I'JE-AB'ARIM. [29.

Nu. 21:11. they pitched in I., 33:44.

I'JON. [Ch. 16: 4.

1 K. 15: 20. Ben-hadad smote I., 2
2 K. 15: 29. Tiglath-pileser took I.

IK'KESH.

2 S. 23: 26. capt. was Ira, son of I.
the Tekoite, 1 Ch. 11:28.-27:9.

I'LAI.

1 Ch. 11: 29. valiant men were, I.

ILL.

Ge.41:3. kine i. favoured, 4, 19, 20, 21.
43: 6. Whf. dealt ye so i. with me
De. 15: 21. any i. blemish not offer
Jb. 20: 26. it shall go i. with him
Ps. 106: 32. it went i. with Moses
Is.3:11. Woe unto wicked, it sh. be i.
Je. 40: 4. if seem i. to come with me
Jo 2: 20. his i. savour sh. come up
Mi. 3:4. they behaved themselves i.
Ro. 13: 10. Love worketh no i. to

ILLUMINATED.

He.10:32. i. ye endured a great fight

ILLYR'ICUM.

Ro. 15: 19. from Jerus. unto I. I

IMAGE. [preached

Ge. 1: 26. man in our i., 27.-9: 6.
5: 3. Adam begat son in his i. (2)
Le. 26: 1. nei. rear standing i., De.
1 S. 19: 13. Michal took i. [16: 22.
16. behold was an i. in the bed
2 K. 3: 2. Jehoram put away the i.
10: 27. brake down the i. of Baal
2 Ch.33:7. set carved i. in ho. of G.
Jb. 4: 16. an i. was bef. mine eyes
Ps. 39: † 6. man walketh in an i.
73: 20. awakest, despise their i.
Eze. 8: 3. there was seat of the i., 5.
Da. 2: 31. great i. stood bef. thee
35. stone smote i. became mt., 34.
3: 1. Neb. king made an i. of gold
2. come to dedication of i., 3.
5. and worship golden i., 7, 10, 15.
12. nor worship golden i., 14, 18.
Ho. 3: 4. Israel abide without i.
Mat.22:20. Whose is this i.? Mk.12:
16. Lu. 20: 24. [Jupiter
Ac. 19: 35. of i. wh. fell down from
Ro. 1:23. changed glo. of G. into i.
8: 29. conformed to i. of his Son
11:4. not bowed knee to i. of Baal
1 Co. 11: 7. as he is i. and glo. of G.
15: 49. have borne i. of earthy
2 Co. 3: 18. changed into same i.
4:4. of C. who is i. of G., Col.1:15.
Col. 3:10. aft. i. of him th. created
He. 1: 3. express i. of his person
10: 1. not the very i. of things
Re. 13:14. sho. make an i. to beast
15. to give life unto i. of beast
14: 9. If any worship beast and i.
11. have no rest, who worsh. his i.
15:2. victory over beast and his i.
16:2. sore fell upon them worsh-d i.
19: 20. deceived them worsh-d i.
20:4. had not worsh-d beast nor i.
See GRAVEN.

Molten IMAGE.

De. 9: 12. have made them a m. i.
Ju. 17: 3. silver to make a m. i.
Ps. 106:19. made calf worsh-d m. i.
Je. 10:14. m. i. is falsehood, 51:17.
Ha. 2:18. What profiteth the m. i.
See **MOLTEN image, s.**

IMAGE work.

2 Ch. 3: 10. two cherubim of i. w.

IMAGES.

Ge. 31:19. Rachel stolen fa.'s i., 34.
35. Laban searched found not i.
Ex.23:24. thou shalt break down i.,
34: 13. De. 7: 5. Nu. 33: 52.
Le. 26: 30. I will cut down your i.
1 S.6:5. ye shall make i. of emerods
11. laid i. of emerods upon cart
2 S. 5:21. left i. David burned them
1 K. 14: 9. molten i. to provoke me
23. build them high pla. i. groves
2 K.10:26. bro-t i. out of ho. of Baal
11: 18. i. brake they, 18:4.-23:14.
17: 10. set up i. | 16. made molten
23: 24. Josiah put away i. [i.

2 Ch. 14: 3. Asa broke down i., 5.
23: 17. Jehoi. brake i. | 31: 1. Hez.
28: 2. Ahaz made i. for Baalim
33: 22. Amon sacr-d unto carved i.
34: 3. Josiah cut down carved i., 4.
Is. 17: 8. sh. not look to groves or i.
27: 9. groves and i. not stand up
30: 22. shall defile ornament of i.
41: 29. their molten i. are wind
Je. 43: 13. break i. of Beth-shem.
50: 2. her i. are broken in pieces
Eze. 6: 4. and your i. sh. be broken
6. that your i. may be cut down
7: 20. they made i. of abomina.
16: 17. gold, and madest i. of men
21: 21. k. of Bab. consulted wi. i.
23: 14. i. of Chald-s pourtrayed
30: 13. cause i. to cease out of Noph
Ho. 10: 1. they have made goodly i.
2. shall break altars, spoil i.
13: 2. have made molten i. of sil.
Am. 5: 26. borne tabern. of your i.
Mi. 5: 13. standing i. will I cut off
See GRAVEN.

IMAGERY.

Eze. 8: 12. ev. man in chamber of his i.

IMAGINATION.

Ge. 6: 5. every i. of his heart evil
8: 21. the i. of man's heart is evil
De. 29: 19. tho. I walk in i. of heart
31: 21. for I know their i.
1 Ch. 29: 18. keep this in i. of heart
Je. 23: 17. every one walketh aft. i.
Lu. 1: 51. scattered the proud in i.
See HEART—EVIL Heart.

IMAGINATIONS.

1 Ch. 28: 9. L. understands all the i.
Ps. 81: † 12. up unto hardness of i.
Pr. 6: 18. that deviseth wicked i.
La. 3: 60. seen all their i. ag. me
61. hast heard all their i. ag. me
Ro. 1: 21. but became vain in their i.
2 Co. 10: 5. Casting down i. th. exalt ag. G.

IMAGINE.

Jb. 6: 26. Do ye i. to reprove words?
21: 27. the devices ye wrongfully i.
Ps. 2: 1. why people i. vain thing?
38: 12. they i. deceits all day long
62: 3. How long will ye i. mischief?
140: 2. Which i. misch. in heart
Pr. 12: 20. Deceit in them th. i. evil
Ho. 7: 15. do they i. mischief ag. me
Na. 1: 9. What do ye i. ag. the L.?
Zch. 7: 10. let none i. evil ag., 8: 17.
Ac. 4: 25. why did peo. i. vain thi.?

IMAGINED, ETH.

Ge. 11: 6. noth. restrained, wh. they i-d
Ps. 10: 2. taken in devices they i-d
21: 11. they i-d mischievous device
Na. 1: 11. is one that i-h evil ag. L.

IM'LA = IM'LAH.

1 K. 22: 8. M. son of I., 9. 2 Ch. 18: 7, 8.

IMMAN'UEL.

Is. 7: 14. son, and call his name I.
8: 8. shall fill thy land, O I.
See EMMANUEL.

IMMEDIATELY.

Mat. 4: 22. they i. left ship foll-d
8: 3. i. his leprosy was cleans., Mk. 1: 42. Lu. 5: 13.
20: 34. i. received sight, Mk. 10: 52. Lu. 18: 43.
24: 29. i. after the tribulation
26: 74. i. the cock crew, Lu. 22: 60. Jn. 18: 27.
Mk. 1: 12. i. Spirit driveth him into wilderness
28. i. his fame spread abroad
31. and i. the fever left her
2: 8. i. when Jesus perceived
12. i. he arose, Lu. 5: 25. Ac. 9: 34.
4: 5. i. it sprang up because
15. Satan cometh i. taketh word
16. i. receive it with gladness
17. affliction ariseth, i. offended
29. i. he putteth in sickle
5: 2. i. met him out of tombs
30. Jesus i. knowing in himself
6: 27. i. king sent executioner
Mk. 6: 50. i. he talked with them
14: 43. i. while he spake
Lu. 1: 64. his mouth was opened i.
4: 39. i. she arose and ministered
5: 25. i. he rose up before them
6: 49. i. it fell | 8: 44. i. issue staunched
8: 47. she was healed i.
12: 36. may open unto him i.
13: 13. i. she was made straight
19: 11. that kingd. of G. i. appear
Jn. 5: 9. i. man was made whole
6: 21. i. ship was at the land
13: 30. received sop went i. out
21: 3. they entered into ship i.
Ac. 3: 7. i. his feet and ankle bones
9: 18. i. there fell fr. his eyes, as it
34. Eneas arose i. | 10: 33. I sent i.
11: 11. i. were three men come
12: 23. i. angel of Lord smote him
13: 11. i. fell on him a mist
16: 10. i. we endeavoured to go
26. i. all the doors were opened
17: 10. breth. i. sent aw. Paul, 14.
21: 32. Who i. took sold-s and ran
Ga. 1: 16. i. I conferred not with fle.
Re. 4: 2. and i. I was in the Spirit

IM'MER.

1 Ch. 9: 12. Meshellimith son of I.
24: 14. sixteenth lot to I.
Ezr. 2: 37. children of I. 1052
59. I. could not shew fa.'s house
10: 20. sons of | Ne. 3: 29. repaired I.
Ne. 7: 40, 61. = 11: 13. Je. 20: 1.

IMMORTAL.

1 Ti. 1: 17. unto the King eternal, i.

IMMORTALITY.

Ro. 2: 7. to them who seek for i.
1 Co. 15: 53. mortal must put on i.
54. when mortal have put on i.
1 Ti. 6: 16. Who only hath i., dwell-g
2 Ti. 1: 10. who brought i. to light

IMMUTABILITY.

He. 6: 17. i. of his counsel

IMMUTABLE.

He. 6: 18. That by two i. things

IM'NA.

1 Ch. 7: 35. sons of his bro. Helem, I.

IM'NAH = JIM'NAH.

2 Ch. 31: 14. Kore son of I. the Lev.

IMPART, ED.

Jb. 39: 17. nor i-d to her underst-g
Lu. 3: 11. two coats, let him i. to him
Ro. 1: 11. may i. some spiritual gift
1 Th. 2: 8. willing to have i-d our souls

IMPEDIMENT.

Mk. 7: 32. one that had i. in speech

IMPENITENT.

Ro. 2: 5. aft. thy i. heart treasurest

IMPERIOUS.

Eze. 16: 30. work of an i. woman

IMPLACABLE.

Ro. 1: 31. without nat-l affection, i.

IMPLEAD.

Ac. 19: 38. the law is open, let them i.

IMPORTUNITY.

Lu. 11: 8. bec. of his i. he will rise

IMPOSE, ED.

Ezr. 7: 24. not be lawful to i. toll
He. 9: 10. stood in carnal ordin-s i-d

IMPOSSIBLE.

Mat. 17: 20. nothing be i. unto you
19: 26. With men is i., Mk. 10: 27. Lu. 18: 27.
Lu. 1: 37. For with God nothing shall be i., 18: 27.
17: 1. It is i. but offences come
He. 6: 4. it is i. for those enlight-d
18. in which it was i. for G. to lie
11: 6. without faith i. to please G.

IMPOTENT.

Jn. 5: 3. lay a great mult. of i. folk
7. The i. man ans-d him, Sir
Ac. 4: 9. good deed done to i. man
14: 8. man at Lystra i. in his feet

IMPOVERISH, ED.

Ju. 6: 6. Isr. was greatly i. because
Ps. 106: † 43. were i. for their iniq.
Is. 40: 20. he so i. chooseth a tree
Je. 5: 17. shall i. thy fenced cities
Mal. 1: 4. Edom saith, We are i. but

IMPRISONED.

Ac. 22: 19. know I i. and beat them

IMPRISONMENT, S.

Ezr. 7: 26. unto death, banishm., or i.
2 Co. 6: 5. approving ours. in i-s
He. 11: 36. had trial of mockings, i.

IMPUDENT.

Pr. 7: 13. with i. face she said unto him
Eze. 2: 4. For they are i. children
3: 7. ho. of Isr. i. and hardhearted

IMPUTE, ED.

Le. 7: 18. nei. sh. it be i-d unto him
17: 4. bl. sh. be i-d unto that man
1 S. 22: 15. let not king i. anything
2 S. 19: 19. Let not my lord i. iniq.
Ro. 4: 8. to whom L. will not i. sin
11. that righteousn. be i-d unto
22. it was i. to him for righteousn.,
23. Ja. 2: 23. Ga. 3: † 6.
24. to whom it be i. if we believe
5: 13. sin is not i. when is no law

IMPUTETH, ING.

Ps. 32: 2. unto whom L. i-h not iniq.
Ha. 1: 11. i-g his power unto his god
Ro. 4: 6. unto whom G. i-h righte-n.
2 Co. 5: 19. not i-g trespasses unto

IM'RAH.

1 Ch. 7: 36. sons of Zophah, I.

IM'RI.

1 Ch. 9: 4. son of I., Ne. 3: 2.

IN.

Ge. 7: 16. and the Lord shut him i.
Jn. 14: 10. I am i. the Fa., 11: 20.
See HIM, WE, THEE, THEM, US, YOU.

INASMUCH.

De. 19: 6. i. as he hated him not
Ru. 3: 10. i. as foll-dst not yo. men
Mat. 25: 40. i. as ye done it unto one
45. i. as ye did it not to one of

INCENSE.

Ex. 30: 8. shall burn a perpetual i.
9. Ye shall offer no strange i.
37: 29. made pure i. of spices
40: 5. shalt set altar of gold for i.
Le. 10: 1. Nadab took censer, put i.
16: 13. he shall put i. upon fire
Nu. 7: 14. golden spoon full of i.,
20, 26, 32, 38, 44, 50, 56, 62, 68,
74, 80, 86.
16: 7. put i. in them bef. L., 17, 18.
35. consumed 250 men th. off-d i.
40. not seed of Aaron to offer i.
46. Moses said unto Aa., put on i.
47. he put on i. made atonem.
De. 33: 10. they sh. put i. bef. thee
2 Ch. 30: 14. altars of i. took they
34: 25. forsaken me, and burned i.
Ps. 66: 15. I will offer i. of rams
141: 2. Let my prayer be set as i.
Is. 1: 13. i. is an abomina. unto me
43: 23. I not wearied thee with i.
60: 6. shall bring i. shew praises
65: 3. burneth i. upon altars of
66: 3. burneth i. as if bless-d idol
Je. 6: 20. what purp. i. fr. Sheba?
11: 12. cry unto gods to wh. offer i.
17. anger, in off-g i. unto Baal
17: 26. and i. bringing sac. of praise
32: 29. upon roofs they have off-d i.
41: 5. offerings and i. in hand
48: 35. that burneth i. to his gods
Eze. 8: 11. thick cloud of i. went
16: 18. hast set mine oil and i. bef
23: 41. thou hast set mine i. and
Mal. 1: 11. in ev. place i. be off-d
Lu. 1: 10. praying at time of i.
Re. 5: † 8. golden vials full of i.
8: 3. was given unto him much i.
4. smoke of thy i. ascended bef. G.
See ALTAR, BURN, BURNED, BURNETH, BURNING, BURNT.

Sweet INCENSE.

Ex. 25: 6. spices for s. i., 35: 8, 28.
Nu. 4: 16. 35: 15.
31: 11. oil and s. i. for holy place,

Ex. 39 : 38. oil and s. i. unto Moses
Le. 16 : 12. Aaron's hands full of s.i.

INCENSED.

Is.41:11. all i. ag. thee be ashamed
45:24. all i. ag. him sh. be asham.

INCLINE.

Jos.24:23. i. your heart unto the L.
1 K.8:58.i. our hea. to keep his law
Ps. 78 : 1. i. your ears to words of
119 : 36. i. my heart unto testimo.
141:4. i. not my heart to any evil
See EAR.

INCLINED.

Ju. 9 : 3. their hearts i. to Abim.
Ps. 40 : 1. L. i. unto me, and, 116:2.
119 : 112. i. mine heart to perform
Pr. 5 : 13. nor i. mine ear to them
Je. 7 : 24. nor i. ear, 26.-11:8.-17:
23.-34 : 14. [35 : 15.-44 : 5.
25:4. but ye have not i. your ear,

INCLINETH.

Pr. 2 : 18. her house i. unto death

INCLOSE.

Can. 8 : 9. if she be a door, we will

INCLOSED. [i. her

Ex. 39:6. onyx stone i. in gold, 13.
Ju. 20 : 43. Israel i. the Benjamites
Ps. 17 : 10. They are i. in their own
22 : 16. assembly of wicked i. me
Can. 4 : 12. A garden i. is my sister
La. 3 : 9. He hath i. my ways with
Lu. 5 : 6. i. great multitu. of fishes

INCLOSINGS. [13.

Ex. 28 : 20. stones in gold in i., 39:

INCONTINENCY.

1 Co. 7:5. tempt you not for your i.

INCONTINENT.

2 Ti. 3:3. without affection, i. fierce

INCORRUPTIBLE. [an i.

1 Co. 9 : 25. a corruptible crown ; we
15 : 52. the dead shall be raised i.
1 Pe.1: 4. To an inheritance i. in hea.
23. born not of corruptible seed,
See UNCORRUPTIBLE. [but i.

INCORRUPTION. [in i.

1 Co. 15:42. sown in corrupt. raised
50. nei. doth corruption inherit i.
53. this corruptible must put on i.
54. corruptible sh. have put on i.

INCREASE. [Noun]

Ge. 47 : 24. in the i. ye sh. give 5th
Le. 19 : 25. that it may yield i.
25 : 7. for cattle sh. i. be meat, 12.
20. not sow nor gather in our i.
36. Take no usury of him or i.
37. not usury, lend victuals for i.
26 : 4. the land shall yield her i.
20. your land sh. not yield her i.
Nu. 18 : 30. i. of threshingfloor
32:14. in fa.'s stead i. of sinf. men
De. 7 : 13. bless i. of thy kine, 28:4.
14 : 22. shalt tithe i. of thy seed
28. shall bring forth all tithe of
i. same year, 26:12. 2 Ch. 31:5.
16:15. G. sh. bless thee in all thy i.
28:18. Cursed be i. of thy kine, 51.
32 : 13. might eat i. of fields
22. consume earth with her i.
Ju. 6 : 4. destroyed i. of earth
1 S. 2 : 33. i. of thy house sh. die
2 Ch. 32 : 28. Storehouses for i. of
Ne.9:37. yieldeth much i. unto kings
Jb. 20:28. i. of his house sh. depart
31 : 12. fire would root out mine i.
Ps 67 : 6. earth shall yield her i.
78 : 46. gave their i. unto caterpil.
85:12. and our land sh. yield her i.
107 : 37. vineyards which yield i.
Pr. 3 : 9. firstfruits of thine i.
14:4. much i. is by strength of ox
18 : 20. with i. of his lips be filled
Ec. 5 : 10. shall not be satisfi. wi. i.
Is. 9:7. Of i. of his governm. no end
30 : 23. bread of the i. of earth
Je. 2:3. Israel was holiness unto the
Lord, and first-fruits of his i.
Eze.18:8. nor hath taken any i., 17.
Eze.18:13. given upon usury, tak. i.,
34:27. earth sh. yield her i. [22:12.
36 : 30. multiply fruit and i.
48 : 18. i. shall be food unto them
Zch. 8 : 12. ground shall give her i.
1 Co. 3:6. I planted, God gave i., 7.
Ep. 4 : 16. i. of body to edifying
Col. 2 : 19. body increaseth with i.
of God

INCREASE. [Verb.]

Le. 25 : 16. by years shalt i. price
De. 6 : 3. O Isr., that ye i. mightily
7 : 22. not at once, lest beasts i.
Ju. 9 : 29. i. thy army, come out
1 Ch. 27:23. would i. Isr. like stars
Ezr.10:10. strange wives to i. tresp.
Jb. 8:7. thy lat. end sho. greatly i.
Ps. 44 : 12. dost not i. thy wealth
62 : 10. if riches i. set not your
71 : 21. Thou shalt i. my greatn.
73:12. prosp. in world, i. in riches
115 : 14. Lord shall i. you more
Pr. 1 : 5. wise man i. learning, 9:9.
13:11. that gath-h by labour sh. i.
22:16. oppresseth poor to i. riches
28:28. when they perish, righte. i.
Ec. 5 : 11. goods i. increased th. eat
6 : 11. many things that i. vanity
Is. 29 : 19. meek shall i. their joy
57 : 9. and didst i. thy perfumes
Je. 23 : 3. folds be fruitful and i.
Eze. 5:16. I will i. famine upon you
36:11. man and beast ; they sh. i.
29. I will i. it, lay no famine
37. I will i. them with men like
Da. 11 : 39. whom ye sh. i. wi. glory
Ho. 4:10. commit whoredom, not i.
Zch. 10 : 8. sh. i. as have increased
Lu. 17 : 5. said Lord, i. our faith
Jn. 3 : 30. He must i. I must decr.
2 Co. 9 : 10. i. fruits of righteousn.
1 Th. 3 : 12. L. make you i. in love
4 : 10. that ye i. more and more
2 Ti. 2:16. will i. unto more ungod-

INCREASED. [liness

Ge. 7:17. waters i. and bare ark, 18.
30 : 30. little thou hadst, it is i.
43. Jacob i. | Ex. 1 : 7. Israel i.
Ex. 23:30. until thou be i. and inh.
1 S. 14 : 19. the noise in the host i.
2 S. 15:12. peo. i. with Abs. [18:34.
1 K. 22:35. battle i. that day, 2 Ch.
1 Ch. 4 : 38. house of fa-s i. greatly
5:23. they i. fr. Bashan unto Baal-h
Ezr. 9 : 6. iniq. are i. over our head
Jb. 1 : 10. his substance is i. in la.
Ps. 3 : 1. how i. that trouble me
4:7. in time their corn and wine i.
49 : 16. when glory of his hou. is i.
105 : 24. he i. his people greatly
Pr. 9 : 11. years of thy life sh. be i.
Ec. 2 : 9. I i. more than all bef. me
5 : 11. goods increase, i. that eat
Is. 9:3. multip-d nation, not i. joy
26 : 15. thou hast i. nation, O L.
51 : 2. I blessed and i. him
Je. 3 : 16. when ye be multipl-d i.
5 : 6. and their backslidings are i.
15:8. widows are i. above the sand
29:6. Take wives, that ye may be i.
30 : 14. wounded thee, bec. sins i.,
La. 2:5. hath i. in dau. of Jud [15.
Eze. 16 : 7. hast i. and waxen great
26. hast i. whoredoms, 23 : 14.
28 : 5. by gr. wisdom hast i. riches
41:7. breadth of ho. upw. and so i.
Da. 12 : 4. knowledge shall be i.
Ho. 4 : 7. as were i. so they sinned
10 : 1. acc. to fruit, he i. altars
Zch. 10 : 8. sh. increase, as have i.
Mk. 4:8. fruit, th. sprang up and i.
Lu. 2 : 52. Jesus i. in wisdom and
Ac. 6 : 7. And the word of God i.
9 : 22. Saul i. the more in strength
16:5. churches i. in number daily
2 Co. 10 : 15. hope when faith is i.
Re. 3 : 17. sayest, I am rich, and i.

INCREASEST.

Jb. 10 : 17. i. indignation upon me

INCREASETH.

Jb.10:16. afflic. i. | 12:23. i. nations
Ps. 74 : 23. the tumult of those i.
Pr. 11 : 24. that scatt-h, and yet i.
16:21. sweetness of lips i. learning
23:28. She i. the transgressors am.
24 : 5. a man of knowl. i. strength
28 : 8. by unjust gain i. substance
29:16. wicked are multiplied, trans-
gression i.
Ec. 1 : 18. i. knowledge, i. sorrow
Is.40:29. have no might, he i. stren.
Ho. 12 : 1. daily i. lies and desola.
Ha. 2 : 6. Woe to him i. th. not his
Col.2:19. body i. with increase of G.

INCREASING.

Col. 1:10. i. in the knowledge of G.

INCREDIBLE.

Ac. 26:8. Why i. G. sho. raise dead?

INCURABLE.

2 Ch. 21 : 18. L. smote him with i.
Jb. 34 : 6. my wound is i. [disease
Je. 15 : 18. why is my wound i.
30 : 12. bruise is i. | 15. sorrow i.
Mi.1:9. her wound i. it is come unto

INDEBTED.

Lu. 11 : 4. forgive ev. one i. to us

INDEED.

Ge. 17 : 19. Sarah shall bear son i.
20 : 12. yet i. she is my sister, she
37 : 8. shalt thou i. reign over us
10. shall I, moth. breth. i. come
40 : 15. i. I was stolen away
Ex. 19:5. if obey my voice i., 23:22.
Le. 10 : 18. ye sho. i. have eaten it
Nu. 12:2. L. i. spoken only by Mo.?
21 : 2. if wilt i. deliver this people
22:37. am I not able i. to promote
De. 2 : 15. i. hand of L. was ag. th.
21 : 16. which is i. the firstborn
Jos. 7 : 20. i. I have sinned ag. L.
1 S. 1 : 11. if wilt i. look on afflic.
1 K. 8:27. God i. on earth, 2 Ch. 6:
2 K.14:10. hast i. smitten Edom [18.
1 Ch. 4 : 10. O wouldest bless me i.
21 : 17. it is I th. have done evil i.
Jb. 19 : 4. be it i. that I have erred
Ps. 58:1. do ye i. speak righteousn.
Is. 6 : 9. hear ye i. see ye i. but
Je. 22 : 4. if ye do this thing i. then
Mat. 3:11. I i. baptize, Mk. 1:8. Lu.
Mk.11:32. that he a prophet i. [3:16.
Lu. 23:41. i. justly | 24:34. risen i.
Jn. 1 : 47. Behold Israelite i.
4:42. that this is i. the Christ, the
6 : 55. flesh meat i. blood drink i.
7:26. Do rulers know i. this is C.?
8 : 31. then are ye my disciples i.
36. If Son make free, ye free i.
Ac. 4 : 16. for i. a notable miracle
Ro. 8 : 7. to law, nei. i. can be
14 : 20. all things i. are pure, but
2 Co. 11 : 1. i. bear with me
Ph. 1:15. Some i. preach C. of envy
3 : 1. to me i. is not grievous
Col. 2:23. wh. things i. have a shew
1 Th.4 : 10. i. ye do it toward breth.
1 Ti.5:3. Honour widows are wid. i.
5. she that is a widow i., 16.
1 Pe.2:4. disallowed i. of men, chosen
of God

INDIA.

Es.1:1. Ahas-s reigned fr. I. unto, 8:9.

INDIGNATION.

De. 29: 28. i. and cast th. into ano.
2 K. 3 : 27. was great i. ag. Israel
Ne. 4 : 1. Sanballat took great i.
Es. 5 : 9. Haman was full of i. ag.
Jb. 5 : 2. i. slayeth the silly one
10 : 17. increasest thine i. upon me
Ps. 69 : 24. Pour out i. upon them
78 : 49. he cast upon th. wrath, i.
102:10. Bec. of thine i. and wrath
Is. 10 : 5. staff in hand is mine i.
25. For yet a little i. sh. cease

Is.13:5. weapons of his i., Je. 50:25.
26: 20. hide until i. be overpast
30: 27. his lips are full of i. his
30. with the i. of his anger, and
34:2. i. of Lord is upon all nations
66:14. i. sh. be known tow. enem.
Je. 10: 10. nations not abide his i.
15: 17. thou hast filled me with i.
La. 2: 6. hath despised in i. the k.
Eze. 21: 31. will pour i. upon thee
22:24. not rained upon in day of i.
31. I poured out mine i. on them
Da. 8: 19. what sh. be in end of i.
11: 30. have i. ag. holy covenant
36. prosper till i. be accompl-d
Mi. 7: 9. I will bear i. of the Lord
Na. 1: 6. Who stand before his i.?
Ha. 3: 12. didst march thro. la. in i.
Zph. 3: 8. kingds. to pour mine i.
Zch. 1: 12. hast had i. 70 years
Mal. 1: 4. people ag. whom L. hath i.
Mat. 20: 24. moved with i. ag. two
26:8. they had i. saying, Mk. 14:4.
Lu. 13: 14. ruler answ-d with i.
Ac. 5: 17. they were filled with i.
Ro. 2: 8. unto them that obey unrighteousness, i. and wrath
2 Co. 7: 11. yea what i.! what fear
He. 10: 27. looking for of fiery i.
Re. 14:10. poured into cup of his i.

INDITING.

Ps. 45: 1. My heart is i. a good

INDUSTRIOUS.

1 K. 11:28. seeing young man was i.

INEXCUSABLE.

Ro. 2:1. Theref. thou art i. O man

INFALLIBLE.

Ac. 1: 3. shewed hims. by i. proofs

INFAMOUS.

Eze. 22: 5. sh. mock thee wh. art i.

INFAMY.

Pr. 25: 10. thine i. turn not away
Eze. 36: 3. ye are i. of the people

INFANT, S.

1 S. 15: 3. slay man, woman, i.
Jb. 3:16. as i-s wh. never saw light
Is. 65: 20. be no more i. of days
Ho. 13: 16. i-s be dashed in pieces
Lu. 18: 15. they bro-t i-s unto him

INFERIOR.

Jb. 12: 3. I am not i. to you, 13: 2.
Da. 2: 39. shall arise ano. kingd. i.
2 Co. 12: 13. ye i. to other churches
He. 2: † 7. him little i. to angels

INFIDEL.

2 Co. 6: 15. that believeth with an i.
1 Ti. 5: 8. and is worse than an i.

INFINITE.

Jb. 22: 5. are not thine iniquities i.?
Ps. 147: 5. his understanding is i.
Na. 2: †9. Take the spoil of i. store
3: 9. Egypt her strength, it was i.

INFIRMITIES.

Mat. 8:17. Himself took our i. and
Lu. 5: 15. came to be healed of i.
7: 21. he cured many of i., 8: 2.
Ro. 8: 26. Spi. also helpeth our i.
15:1. strong ought to bear i. of w-k
2 Co. 11: 30. which concern mine i.
12:5. I glory not, but in mine i., 9.
10. I take pleasure in mine i.
1 Ti. 5: 23. use a little wine for i.
He. 4:15. touched with feeling of i.

INFIRMITY.

Le. 12: 2. days of separa. for her i.
Ps. 77: 10. I said, This is mine i.
Pr. 18: 14. The spirit will sustain his
Lu. 13: 11. woman which had i. [i.
12. thou art loosed fr. thine i.
Jn. 5: 5. wh. had an i. 38 years
Ro. 6: 19. bec. of i. of your flesh
Ga. 4: 13. how thro. i. I preached
He. 5: 2. he also compassed with i.
7: 28. high priests which have i.

INFLAME, ING.

Is. 5: 11. continue till wine i. them
57: 5. i-g yourselves with idols

INFLAMMATION.

Le. 13: 28. it is an i. of burning
De. 28: 22. L. sh. smite thee with i.

INFLICTED.

2 Co. 2: 6. punishment which was i.

INFLUENCES.

Jb. 38: 31. Canst bind i. of Pleiades?

INFOLDING.

Eze. 1: 4. fire i. itself, a brightness

INFORM, ED.

De. 17: 10. acc. to all they i. thee
Da. 9: 22. i-d, and talked with me
Ac. 21:21. are i-d thou teachest, 24.
24: 1. i-d gov-r ag. Paul, 25:2, 15.

INGATHERING.

Ex. 23: 16. least of i. in end of y-r

INGRAFTED.

See Engrafted.

INHABIT.

Nu. 35:34. defile not land ye sh. i.
Pr. 10:30. wicked shall not i. earth
Is. 42: 11. villages Kedar doth i.
65:21. shall build houses and i. th.
22. shall not build, and ano. i.
Je. 17:6. shall i. the parched places
48: 18. dau., that dost i. Dibon
Eze. 33: 24. i. those wastes of Isr.
Am. 9:14. shall build cities and i. th.
Zph. 1: 13. sh. build houses, not i.

INHABITANT.

Jb. 28: 4. flood break-th out fr. i.
Is. 5:9. many houses fair without i.
6:11. Until cities be wasted with-t i.
9: 9. Ephr. and i. of Samaria shall
12:6. Cry out, thou i. of Zion [kn.
20: 6. i. of this isle sh. say in day
24:17. snare upon thee, O i. of ea.
33: 24. i. shall not say, I am sick
Je. 2:15. his cities burned with-t i.
4: 7. cities be laid waste with-t i.,
9: 11.-26: 9.-33: 10.-34: 22.
10:17. Gather wares, O i. of fortr.
21: 13. i. of valley | 22:23. of Leb.
44: 22. la. is a curse with-t an i.
46:19. waste and desolate, with-t i.,
51: 29, 37.
48: 19. O i. of Aroer | 43. O i. of Moab
51: 35. shall the i. of Zion say
Am. 1: 5. I will cut off i. fr. Aven
8. I will cut off i. from Ashdod
Mi. 1: 11. i. of Saphir, i. of Zaanan
12. i. of Maroth waited carefully
13. O i. of Lachish, bind chariot
15. heir to thee, O i. of Mareshah
Zph. 2: 5. I will destroy, be no i.
3: 6. cities destr-d, so is none i.

INHABITANTS.

Ge. 19: 25. overthrew all i. of cities
Ex. 15: 14. hold of i. of Palestina
15. i. of Canaan shall melt away
Le. 18:25. land vomiteth out her i.
25: 10. sh. proclaim liberty unto all
Nu 13:32. la. that eateth up t. i. [i.
De. 13: 13. withdrawn i. of city
15. shalt surely smite i. of city
Jos. 2: 24. i. of country do faint
11: 19. made peace, save i. of Gib.
17:12. not drive out i., Ju. 1:19, 27.
Ju. 2: 2. no league with i.
5: 7. i. of the villages ceased, 11.
23. curse ye bitterly i. thereof
10: 18. over all i. of Gilead, 11: 8.
21:9. none of i. of Jabesh-g. there
10. go smite i. of Jabesh-gilead
Ru. 4: 4. saying, Buy it bef. the i.
1 K. 17: 1. Elijah was of i. of Gil.
2 K. 19: 26. i. were of small power,
Is. 37: 27. [27, 28.
22:16. evil upon i., 19. 2 Ch. 34:24,
1 Ch. 9: 2. first i. th. dwelt in their
2 Ch. 20:23. stood ag. i. of mt. Seir
Jb. 26: 5. are formed from under i.
Ps. 33:8. all i. of world stand in awe
14. he looketh upon all i. of earth
49: 1. give ear, all ye i. of world
75:3. earth and all i. are dissolved
Is. 10: 13. put down i. like a man

Is. 18: 3. All ye i. of the world, see ye
23: 2. Be still, ye i. of the isle, 6.
24: 1. and scattereth abroad the i.
5. The earth is defiled under the i.
6 the i. of the earth are burned
26: 9. i. of world learn righte-n.
18. nei. have i. of world fallen
21. L. cometh to punish the i.
38: 11. man no more wi. i. of world
40: 22. the i. are as grasshoppers
42: 10. i. sing to Lord a new song
11. let the i. of the rock sing
49: 19. land too narrow by the i.
Je. 13: 13. will fill i. with drunkenn.
19: 12. thus will I do to the i.
21:6. I will smite the i. of this city
23: 14. as Sodom, and i. thereof as
25:29. a sword upon i., 9.-50: 35.
26: 15. sh. bring innoc. blood upon i.
49: 8. dwell deep, i. of Dedan, 30.
50: 34. L. will disquiet i. of Bab.
51: 35. my blood upon i. of Chal-a
La. 4: 12. i. of world not believed
Eze. 27: 35. i. of isles sh. be aston-d
29: 6. i. of E. shall know I am L.
Da. 4: 35. i. of earth are as nothing
Ho. 10: 5. i. of Sama. sh. fear bec. of
Mi. 6: 12. the i. have spoken lies
16. that I sho. make i. a hissing
Zph. 2: 5. Woe unto i. of sea coast
Zch. 8:20. sh. come i. of many cit.
21. i. of one city shall go to ano.
Re. 17: 2. i. of earth made drunk
See Jerusalem.

INHABITANTS of the land

Ge. 34:30. me to stink am. i. o. l.
Ex. 23:31. I will deliv. i. o. l. into
34: 12. lest thou a cov. with i. o. l.,
Nu. 14: 14. will tell it to i. o. l. [15.
32: 17. dwell in cities bec. of i. o. l.
33: 52. sh. drive out i. o. l., 55. 2
Jos. 2: 9. all the i. o. l. faint [Ch. 20: 7.
7: 9. all the i. o. l. shall hear of it
9: 24. to destroy all i. o. l. bef. you
Ju. 2: 2. make no league with i. o. l.
1 S. 27: 8. those were of old i. o. l.
1 Ch. 22: 18. given i. o. l. into my ha.
Ne. 9: 24. subduedst bef. them i. o. l.
Je. 1: 14. an evil shall break on i. o. l.
6: 12. stretch out my ha. upon i. o. l.
10: 18. I will fling out i. o. l. at once
47: 2. and the i. o. l. shall howl
Ho. 4: 1. L. hath controv. with i. o. l.
Jo. 2: 1. let all the i. o. l. tremble
Zch. 11: 6. I will no more pity i. o. l.

INHABITED. [la. i.

Ex. 16: 35. eat manna until came to
Le. 16: 22. goat bear iniq. to la. not i.
2 S. 24: †6. to nether land newly i.
Is. 13: 20. it shall never be i. nor
44: 26. to Jerus. Thou shalt be i.
45: 18. formed earth to be i.
54: 3. make desolate cities to be i.
Je. 6: 8. lest I make thee land not i.
17: 6. sh. inhabit in a land not i.
22: 6. will make thee cities not i.
46: 26. it shall be i. as in days of old
50: 13. sh. not be i. | 39. no more i.
Eze. 12: 20 cities i. sh. be laid waste
26: 20. sh. set, that thou be not i.
29: 11. neither sh. it be i. 40 years
36: 10. cities sh. be i. wastes builded
38: 12. upon desolate places now i.
Zch. 2: 4. Jerusalem be i. as towns
9: 5. and Ashkelon sh. not be i.
12: 6. Jerusalem shall be i. again
14: 10. lifted up, and i. in her place
11. but Jerus. shall be safely i.

INHABITERS. [12.

Re. 8: 13. Woe, woe, to i. of earth, 12:

INHABITEST, ETH, ING.

Jb. 15: 28. in houses which no man
Ps. 22: 3. that i-t praises of Isr. [i-h
74: 14. to people i-g wilderness
Is. 57: 15. lofty One that i-h eternity

INHERIT.

Ge. 15: 8. sh. I know that I sh. i. it?

Ex. 32 : 13. they shall **i.** it for ever
Nu. 18 : 24. given it to Lev. to **i.**
26:55.acc. to tribes they sh. **i.**,33:54.
32 : 19. not **i.** on yonder side Jor.
De. 1:38. he shall cause Isr. to **i.** it
12:10.which the L.giveth you to **i.**
21: 16. maketh his sons to **i.** what
31 : 7. shall cause them to **i.** it
Jos. 17 : 14. but one portion to **i.**
Ju.11:2.shalt not **i.** in our fa.'s ho.
1 S. 2 : 8. them **i.** throne of glory
Ps. 25 : 13. his seed shall **i.** earth
37 : 9. wait on Lord shall **i.** earth
11. meek shall **i.** earth, Mat. 5:5.
22. blessed of him sh. **i.** the earth
69:36. seed of his servants sh. **i.** it
82:8.O G. thou shalt **i.** all nations
Pr. 3 : 35. The wise shall **i.** glory
8:21. who love me to **i.** substance
11:29.troubleth own house, **i.**wind
14 : 18. simple **i.** folly, prudent
Is. 49 : 8. to **i.** desolate heritages
54 : 3. thy seed sh. **i.** the Gentiles
57 : 13. shall **i.** my holy mountain
65 : 9. and mine elect shall **i.** it
Je. 8 : 10. fields to them that sh. **i.**
12: 14. I caused my peo. Isr. to **i.**
49:1. why doth their king **i.** Gad?
Eze. 7 : † 24. shall **i.** holy places
47 : 14. ye shall **i.** it, one as ano.
Zch. 2 : 12. the L. shall **i.** Judah
Mat. 19 : 29. shall **i.** everlasting life
25:34. Come, **i.** kingdom prepared
Mk. 10:17. **i.** eternal life. Lu.10:25.
-18 : 18. [kingdom of God
1 Co. 6 : 9. unrighteous not **i.** the
10. nei. extortioners **i.**, Ga. 5:21.
15:50.flesh and bl.cannot **i.** kingd.
of G. nor corrup. **i.** incorrup.
He. 6 : 12. thro. faith **i.** promises
1 Pe. 3:9. that ye sho. **i.** a blessing
Re. 21 : 7. overcometh shall **i.** all

INHERIT land.

Ge. 15 : 7. to give thee this **l.** to **i.**
28:4. mayest **i. l.** wherein stranger
Ex. 23 : 30. thou incr-d and **i. l.**
Le 20 : 24. ye shall **i.** their land
Nu. 34:13. This is the **l.** ye shall **i.**
De. 2:31. th. thou mayest **i.** his **l.**
16:20.**i.** the **l.** L. giveth thee,19:3.
Ps. 37 : 29. righteous shall **i.** the **l.**
34. he sh. exalt thee to **i.** the **l.**
Is. 60:21. they sh. **i.** the **l.** for ever
Eze.47:13.whereby ye shall **i.** the **l.**

INHERITANCE, S.

Ge. 31 : 14. Is there any **i.** for us?
48:6.aft. name of breth. in their **i.**
Ex. 15 : 17. plant them in thine **i.**
Le. 25 : 46. take them as **i.** for ever
Nu. 16 : 14. or given us **i.** of fields
18 : 20. have no **i.** for I am thy **i.**
26:54. give more **i.** — less **i.**,33:54.
27:8.sh. cause **i.** to pass unto dau.
9. **i.** unto breth. | 10. unto fa.'s
11. his **i.** unto kinsman [breth
32 : 19. our **i.** on this side, 32.-34:
34:18. to divide the land by **i.** [15.
36 : 3. be put to **i.** of the tribe, 4.
9. Nei. **i.** remove from one tribe
De. 4 : 20. a people of **i.** as ye are
9 : 26. destroy not **i.** | 29. thy **i.**
18 : 2. L. is their **i.**, Jos. 13 : 33.
32 : 8. Most High divid. to na-s **i.**
9. Jacob is the lot of his **i.**
33 : 4. even **i.** of cong. of Jacob
Jos. 13:14. sacri. of L. their **i.**,18:7.
14:2. By lot was their **i.**, Ps.78:55.
14. Hebron became **i.** of Caleb
17:6.dau-s of Manasseh had **i.** am.
19 : 51. these the **i**-s Josh. divided
24:28. ev. man unto his **i.**, Ju.2:6.
Ju.21:17.**i.** for th. escaped [-21:24.
Ru. 4 : 6. can-t redeem lest I mar **i.**
1 S. 10 : 1. thee captain over his **i.**
26 : 19. from abiding in **i.** of Lord
2 S. 14 : 16. would destroy me and
my son together out of **i.** of God
2 S. 20 : 1. neither **i.** in son of Jesse,
1 K. 12 : 16.
21:3. that ye may bless **i.** of Lord
1 K. 8 : 51. thy people and **i.**, 53.
21:3. **i.** of my fathers unto thee,4.
2 K. 21 : 14. forsake remnant of **i.**
1 Ch. 16:18. Canaan, lot of your **i.**
Ne. 11:20. in cities, every one in **i.**
Jb. 31 : 2. what **i.** of the Almighty
Ps. 16:5. Lord is portion of mine **i.**
28:9.bless thine **i.** | 33:12.chos.for
37:18. their **i.** sh. be for ever [**i.**
47 : 4. He sh. choose our **i.** for us
68 : 9. thou didst confirm thine **i.**
74:2. thine **i.** thou hast redeemed
78 : 62. and was wroth with his **i.**
71. bro-t him to feed Isr. his **i.**
79:1.heathen are come into thine **i.**
94:14. neither will he forsake his **i.**
105:11. Canaan, the lot of your **i.**
106:5.th.I may glory with thine **i.**
40. that he abhorred his own **i.**
Pr. 13 : 22. A good man leaveth **i.**
17:2.have part of the **i.** am. breth.
19 : 14. House, riches are **i.** of fa-s
20:21. An **i.** may be gotten hastily
Ec. 7 : 11. Wisd. is good with an **i.**
Is. 19:25. Blessed be Israel mine **i.**
47 : 6. I have polluted mine **i.**
63 : 17. serv-ts' sake, tribes of **i.**
Je. 10:16. Isr. is rod of his **i.**,51:19.
16 : 18. filled **i.** with carcasses
32 : 8. for right of **i.** is thine
La. 5:2. Our **i.** is turned to strang.
Eze. 22 : 16. **i.** in sight of heathen
36 : 12. possess thee, be their **i.**
44 : 28. unto them for **i.** I their **i.**
46:16. the **i.** shall be his son's, 17.
18. not of peo.'s **i.** by oppression
47:22.they sh. have **i.** am. you,23.
Mat. 21 : 38. let us seize on his **i.**
Mk. 12:7. **i.** sh. be ours, Lu.20:14.
Lu. 12:13. that he divide **i.** wi. me
Ac. 20 : 32 to **i.** am. all sanctified
26 : 18. and **i.** am.them sanctified
Ga. 3 : 18. if the **i.** be of the law
Ep. 1 : 11. we have obtained an **i.**
14. which is the earnest of our **i.**
18.the riches of the glory of his **i.**
5:5.hath any **i.** in the kingd. of C.
Col. 1 : 12. partakers of **i.** of saints
3 : 24. ye sh. receive reward of **i.**
He. 1:4. hath by **i.** obtained name
9:15. receive promise of eternal **i.**
1 Pe. 1:4. begotten to an **i.** incorr.

For INHERITANCE.

Ex. 34 : 9. and take us **f.** thine **i.**
Nu. 18:21. tenth in Isr. **f.** an **i.**,26.
26:53. the land shall be divided **f.**
an **i.**, 33 : 54.-34:2.-36:2. De.4:
21,38.-15:4.-19:10. Jos. 13:6,7,
32.-14:1.-19:49, 51. Eze. 45:1.-
47 : 22.-48 : 29.
De. 20 : 16. the Lord doth give thee
f. an **i.**,21:23.-24:4.-25:19.-26:
1. Jos. 11:23.-13:6.-14:13. 1 K.
8 : 36. 2 Ch. 6 : 27. Je. 3 : 18.
1 Ch.28:8.**f.** an **i.** for chil.,Ezr.9:12.
Ps. 2:8. give thee the heathen **f. i.**
Eze. 33 : 24. la. is given us **f.** an **i.**
44:28. it shall be to them **f.** an **i.**
47:14. this land unto you **f.** an **i.**
He. 11:8. sho. after receive **f.** an **i.**

No or none INHERITANCE.

Nu. 18:20. thou shalt have **n.i.**,23,
24.-26: 62. De. 10:9.-12:12.-14:
27, 29.-18:1, 2. Jos. 13:14, 33.-
14 : 3.
2 Ch.10:16. **n.i.** in the son of Jesse
Ac. 7 : 5. he gave him **n-e i.** in it

INHERITED.

Nu. 32 : 18. not return until Isr. **i.**
Jos. 14:1. chil. of Isr. **i.** in Canaan
Ps. 105:44. they **i.** labour of people
Je. 16 : 19. our fathers have **i.** lies
Eze. 33:24. Ab. was one, he **i.** land
He. 12 : 17. would have **i.** blessing

INHERITETH.

Nu.35:8. to his inheriting wh. he **i.**

INHERITOR.

Is. 65:9. out of Judah an **i.** of mts

INIQUITY.

Ge. 15 : 16. **i.** of Amorites not full
19 : 15. lest consumed in **i.** of city
44 : 16. G. hath found **i.** of serv-s
Ex. 20 : 5. visiting **i.** of fa-s upon
chil., 34 : 7. Nu. 14:18. De. 5:9.
34:7.forgiving **i.**transgr-n, Nu. 14:
9. go am. us, pardon our **i.** [18.
Le. 18 : 25. theref. I do visit the **i.**
Nu. 5 : 15. bringing **i.** to remembr.
31. sh. the man be guiltless fr. **i.**
14 : 19. Pardon **i.** of this people
23:21.He hath not beheld **i.**in Jac.
De. 19 : 15. not rise ag. man for **i.**
32 : 4. a God of truth without **i.**
Jos. 22 : 17. Is **i.** of Peor too little
1 S. 3 : 13. judge for **i.** he knoweth
14. **i.** of Eli's ho. not be purged
15 : 23. and stubbornness is as **i.**
20:8. if be in me **i.** slay me
25:24. upon me let **i.** be, 2 S. 14:9.
2 S. 14 : 32. if be **i.** in me kill me
19 : 19. Let not impute **i.** unto me
24:10.take aw.**i.**of serv., 1 Ch.21:8.
2 Ch. 19 : 7. is no **i.** with Lord
Jb. 4 : 8. that plow **i.** reap same
5 : 16. hath hope, **i.** stop-h mouth
6 : 29. I pray you, let it not be **i.**
30. Is there **i.** in my tongue?
11:6. less than thine **i.** deserveth
14. If **i.** in thy hand, put it aw.
15:5. thy mouth uttereth thine **i.**
16. filthy is man wh. drinketh **i.**
22:23.put aw.**i.**far from thy tabern
31:11. **i.** to be punished by judges,
33 : 9. nei. is there **i.** in me [28.
34 : 32. if I have done **i.** will no
36:10. com-h they return from **i.**
21.regard not **i.** this hast chosen
23. who say, hast wrought **i.**?
Ps. 7:3. if there be **i.** in my hands
14. Behold, he travaileth with **i.**
10 : † 7. under his tongue is **i.**
32:2.unto whom L.imputeth not **i.**
5. thou forgavest **i.** of my sin
36 : 3. words of his mouth are **i.**
39:11. When dost correct man for **i.**
41:6. his heart gathereth **i.** to its.
49:5. when **i.** of my heels compass
51 : 5. Behold I was shapen in **i.**
53:1. Corrupt, and done abomi. **i.**
55 : 3. they cast **i.** upon me, and
56:7. Shall they escape by **i.**? cast
66 : 18. If I regard **i.** in my heart
85 : 2. hast forgiven **i.** of thy peo.
94:20. throne of **i.** have fellowship
107:42. all **i.** shall stop her mouth
109:14. Let **i.** of fa.'s be rememb-d
119:3. They do no **i.** walk in ways
133. let not any **i.**have dominion
125:3. lest put their hands unto **i.**
Pr. 16 : 6. By truth **i.** is purged
19: 28. mouth of wick. devour-h **i.**
22 : 8. soweth **i.** shall reap vanity
Ec. 3: 16. place of right-ss. **i.** there
Is. 1 : 4. a people laden with **i.**
13. it is **i.** even solemn meeting
5:18. Woe unto them that draw **i.**
6 : 7. thine **i.** is taken away, and
14 : 21. Prepare for **i.** of their fa-s
22:14. this **i.**not be purged fr. you
27 : 9. By this **i.** of Jac. be purged
29 : 20. th. watch for **i.** are cut off
30 : 13. this **i.** be to you as breach
40:2.cry unto her, her **i.** is pard-d
53 : 6. laid on him the **i.** of us all
57:17. For **i.** of covetousn. I wroth
59:3. your fingers are defiled wi. **i.**
4. bring forth **i.** | 6. works of **i.**
7. their thoughts thoughts of **i.**
64 : 9. nei. remember **i.** forever
Je. 2 : 5. What **i.** fa-s found in me?

Je. 2:22. thine i. is marked bef. me
3:13. Only acknowl. thine i. [cov-d
13: 22. greatn. of i. thy skirts dis.
14: 20. acknowledge i. of our fa-s
16:10. what is our i. | 17. i. hid fr.
30:14 mult. of thine i., 15. Ho. 9:7.
32: 18. recompensest i. of fathers
50: 20. the i. of Isr. be sought for
51: 6. be not cut off in her i. [i.
La. 2: 14. have not discovered thine
4: 6. For punishm. of i. of people
22. punishm. of i. accompl-d, he
will visit thine i., O daughter
Eze. 4: 4. lay i. of Israel upon it
7: 13. nei. strengthen himself in i.
9: 9. i. of house of Israel is great
16:49. this the i. of thy sister Sod.
18: 8. hath withdrawn hand fr. i.
17. he sh. not die for i. of father
30. Repent, so i. not be your ruin
21:23. call to remembr. your i., 24.
25. i. shall have end, 29.-35: 5.
28: 15. wast perfect, till i. found
18. defiled sanct-s by i. of traffic
44: 12 caused Israel to fall into i.
Da. 9: 24. to make reconcili. for i.
Ho. 7: 1. i. of Ephr. was discov-d
10:9. ag. chil. of i. | 13. ye reaped i.
12: 8. they shall find no i. in me
11. is there i. in Gilead?
13: 12. i. of Ephraim is bound up
14: 1. thou hast fallen by thine i.
2. Take aw. i. rec. us graciously
Mi. 2: 1. Woe that devise i. on beds
3: 10. They build up Jerus. wi. i.
7:18. Who G. like thee, pardon-h i.?
Ha. 1:3. Why dost thou shew me i.?
13. of purer eyes, not look on i.
2:12. Woe to him establi-h city by
Zph. 3: 5. L., he will not do i. [i.
13. remnant of Isr. sh. not do i.
Zch. 3: 4. caused i. to pass fr. thee
9. remove i. of land in one day
Mal. 2: 6. i. was not found in his
lips, did turn many aw. from i.
Mat. 13:41. sh. gather th. wh. do i.
23: 28. ye are full of hypoc. and i.
24: 12. bec. i. shall abound, love
Ac. 1: 18. purchased a field with i.
8: 23. perc. thou art in bond of i.
Ro. 6: 19. members serv-s to i. unto
1 Co. 13: 6. rejoiceth not in i. [i.
2 Th. 2: 7. mystery of i. doth work
2 Ti. 2: 19. nameth C., depart fr. i.
Tit. 2: 14. might redeem us from i.
He 1: 9. thou hast hated i. [i.
Ja. 3: 6. tongue is a fire, world of
See BEAR, COMMIT, COMMITTED.

His INIQUITY.

Nu. 15: 31. h. i. shall be upon him
Jos. 22: 20. perished not alone in h.i.
Jb. 20: 27. heavens sh. reveal h.i.
21: 19. G. layeth up h. i. for chil.
Ps. 36: 2. until h. i. be found to be
hateful [10.-7: 16.-18: 26.
Je. 31: 30. die for h. i., Eze. 3: 18,
Eze. 14:7. stumbling bl. of h. i., 4.
18: 18. he sh. die in h. i., 33:8, 9.
33: 6. he is taken away in h.i. [i.
2 Pe. 2: 16. Balaam rebuked for h.

Mine INIQUITY.

Ge. 4: † 13. m. i. is greater than
1 S. 20: 1. what is m. i. my sin?
2 S. 22:24. I kept fr. m.i., Ps. 18:23.
Jb. 7: 21. why dost not take m.i.?
10: 6 thou inquirest after m. i.
14. wilt not acquit me from m.i.
14:17. In a bag, thou sewest up m.i.
31:33. by hiding m.i. in my bosom
Ps. 25:11. pardon m.i., for it is gr.
31: 10. strength faileth bec. of m.
32: 5. m. i. have I not hid [i.
38: 18. For I will declare m. i., I
51: 2. Wash me thoroughly fr. m.

Their INIQUITY. [i.

Le. 26: 39. shall pine away in t. i.
40. If they confess t. i. and
Le. 26:41. accept punishm. of t.i., 43.
Ne. 4: 5. and cover not t. i., let
Ps. 69: 27. Add iniquity unto t. i.
78:38. forgave t.i. | 89:32. visit t.i.
94: 23. shall bring upon them t.i.
106: 43. were brought low for t. i.
Is. 13: 11. will punish wick. for t.i.
26: 21. to punish inhabit-s for t.i.
33: 24. peo. shall be forgiven t. i.
Je. 14: 10. will now remember t. i.
16: 17. nei. is t. i. hidden from
18. I will recompense t. i. [sin
18: 23. forgive not t. i. nor blot
25: 12. will punish nation for t. i.
31: 34. for I will forgive t. i.
33: 8. I will cleanse from all t. i.
36: 3. th. I may forgive t. i. [t.i.
31. I will punish his servants for
Eze. 4: 5. laid upon thee y-rs of t.i.
17. consume away for t. i.
7: 19. stumbl. block of t. i., 14:3.
14: 10. shall bear punishm. of t.i.
29: 16. bringeth t. i. to remembr.
39: 23. Isr. into captivity for t. i.
Ho. 4: 8. set their heart on t. i. [i.
5: 5. shall Isr. and Ephr. fall in t.
9: 9. he will remember t. i., he

Work INIQUITY.

Ps. 141:4. works with men th. w.i.
Is. 31: 2. ag. help of them w. i.
32:6. heart w.i. to practise hypoc
Ho. 6: 8. Gilead city of them w. i.
Mat. 7: 23. depart, ye that w. i.

Workers of INIQUITY.

Jb. 31:3. a punishm. to w. o. i.
34: 8. in company with w. o. i.
22. where w. o. i. may hide
Ps. 5: 5. thou hatest all w. o. i.
6:8. Depart all ye w.o.i., Lu. 13:27.
14:4. all w. o. i. no knowl.? 53:4.
28: 3. Draw me not with w. o. i.
36:12. There are the w.o.i. fallen
37: 1. nei. be envious ag. w. o. i.
59: 2. Deliver me from the w.o.i.
64: 2. fr. insurrection of w. o. i.
92: 7. when all w. o. i. flourish
9. all w. o. i. shall be scattered
94: 4. all w. o. i. boast thems.
16. who stand for me ag. w.o.i.?
125: 5. lead forth with w. o. i.
141: 9. Keep me fr. gins of w.o.i.
Pr. 10: 29. destruction to w. o. i.,

INIQUITIES. [21: 15.

Le. 16: 21. confess over goat all i.
26:39. in i. of fathers sh. they pine
Ezr. 9:6. i. increased over our head
7. for our i. have we been deliv-d
13. hast punished us less than i.
Ne 9: 2. Isr. confessed i. of fathers
Jb. 13: 23. How many are mine i.
26. makest me possess i. of youth
22:5. thy wickedn. great, i. infinite
Ps. 38: 4. i. are gone over my head
40: 12. mine i. taken hold upon me
51: 9. Hide thy face. blot out all i.
64:6. search out i. | 65:3. i. prevail
79: 8. remem. not ag. us former i.
90: 8. hast set our i. before thee
103: 3. Who forgiveth all thine i.
10. nor rewarded us acc. to our i.
130:3. If L. sho. mark i. who stand?
8. shall redeem Isr. fr. all his i.
Pr. 5: 22. His own i. sh. take wick.
Is. 43: 24. wearied me wi. thine i.
53: 5. he was bruised for our i.
59: 12. as for our i. we know them
64:6. our i. like wind have tak. us
7. hast consumed us bec. of i.
Je. 11: 10. back to i. of forefathers
14: 7. though our i. testify ag. us
La. 4: 13. For i. of priests th. shed bl.
Eze. 28: 18. by mult. of i. defiled
Da 4: 27. break off thine i. by [i.
9: 13. that we might turn fr. our
16. for our sins, and i. of fathers
Mi. 7: 19. he will subdue our i. [i.
Ac. 3: 26. in turning ev. one fr. his
Ro. 4: 7. Blessed whose i. forgiven
Re. 18: 5. G. hath rememb-d her i.

Their INIQUITIES. [t.i.

Le. 16: 22. goat bear upon him all
Ps. 107:17. Fools bec. of t. i.
Is. 53: 11. justify many, he sh. bear
Je. 33:8. I will pardon all t. i. [t.i.
La. 5: 7. fa-s sinned, we borne t. i.
Eze. 32:27. t. i. be upon their bones
43: 10. may be ashamed of t. i.
He. 8: 12. t. i. I remember no more,
10: 17.

Your INIQUITIES.

Nu. 14: 34. 40 years bear y. i.
Is. 50: 1. for y. i. have sold yours.
59: 2. y. i. separated betw. you and
65: 7. y. i. I will recompense [G.
Je. 5: 25. y. i. have turned aw. these
Eze. 24: 23. sh. pine away for y. i.
36: 31. sh. loathe yourselves for y.i.
33. sh. have cleansed you fr. y. i.
Am. 3: 2. I will punish you for all

INJURED. [y. i.

Ga. 4: 12. ye have not i. me at all

INJURIOUS.

1 Ti. 1: 13. bef. a persecutor and i.

INJUSTICE.

Jb. 16: 17. Not for i. in my hands

INK. [book

Je. 36: 18. I wrote them with i. in
2 Co. 3: 3. not with i. but the Spirit
2 Jn. 12. not write with i., 3 Jn. 13.

INKHORN.

Eze. 9: 2. writer's i. by his side, 3, 11.

INN.

Ge. 42: 27. his ass provender in i.
43: 21. came to i. we opened sacks
Ex. 4: 24. in the i. the L. met him
Lu. 2: 7. was no room for th. in i.
10: 34. bro-t him to an i. took care

INNER. [of

1 K. 6: 27. cherubim in the i. house
1 Ch. 28: 11. patterns of i. parlours
Es. 4: 11. unto king into i. court
5: 1. Esther stood in the i. court
Eze. 10: 3. cloud filled the i. court
42: 15. end of measuring i. house
46: 1. gate of i. court be shut days
Ac. 16: 24. thrust th. into i. prison
Ep. 3: 16. strengthened with might
See CHAMBER. [in i. man

INNERMOST. [22.

Pr. 18: 8. i. parts of the belly, 26:

INNOCENCY.

Ge. 20: 5. in i. have I done this
Ps. 26: 6. will wash my hands in i.
73: 13. in vain washed hands in i.
Da. 6: 22. bef. him i. found in me
Ho. 8: 5. how long ere attain to i.?

INNOCENT. [Adj.]

Jb. 4: 7. who ever perished being i.?
9: 28. know thou wilt not hold me i.
33: 9. I am i. nei. is iniq. in me
Ps. 19:13. I sh be i. fr. great transgr-n
Pr. 6: 29. toucheth her shall not be i.
28: 20 haste to be rich sh. not be i.
Je. 2: 35. sayest, Because I am i.
Mat. 27: 24. I am i. of bl. of this
See Innocent BLOOD.

INNOCENT, S.

Ex. 23: 7. i. and righte. slay not
De. 27: 25. tak-h reward to slay i.
1 S. 14: †41. Saul said, Shew the i.
Jb. 9:23. he will laugh at trial of i.
17: 8. i. shall stir up ag. hypoc.
22: 19. the i. laugh them to scorn
30. He sh. deliver island of the i.
27: 17. the i. sh. divide the silver
Ps. 10: 8. in secret doth murder i.
15: 5. nor taketh reward ag. the i.
Pr. 1: 11. let us lurk privily for the i.
Je. 2: 34. is found blood of poor i-s
19: 4. filled place with blood of i-s

INNUMERABLE.

Jb. 21: 33. after him, as are i. bef.
Ps. 40: 12. i. evils compassed me
104: 25. sea, are things creeping i.

Je. 46 : 23. more than grasshop-s i.
Lu. 12 : 1. an i. multitude gathered
He. 11 : 12. as sand by sea shore i.
12 : 22. to an i. company of angels

INORDINATE.

Eze. 23 : 11. she corrupt in i. love
Col. 3 : 5. mortify fornic., i.affection

INQUIRE. [i.

Ge. 24 : 57. We will call damsel, and
25 : 22. Rebekah went to i. of L.
Ex. 18 : 15. come to me to i. of G.
De. 12:30. thou i. not aft. their gods
13 : 14. shalt i. and make search
17:9. shalt come unto judge and i.
Ju. 4 : 20. when any doth i. of thee
1 S. 9:9. when a man went to i. of G.
17 : 56. i. whose son stripling is
22 : 15. Did I then begin to i. of G.?
28 : 7. Seek me a wom., th. I may i.
1 K. 22 : 5. Jehosh. said, i. at word
of L. to day, 2 Ch. 18 : 4. [6.
7. none,that we may i.of, 2 Ch.18:
8. by wh. may i. of L., 2 Ch. 18: 7.
2 K. 1 : 2. go,i. of Baal-zeb.,3,6, 16.
16. no G. in Isr. to i. of his word
3 : 11. is not here a proph. to i. by?
8 : 8. go meet the man, i. of L.
16 : 15. brazen altar for me to i. by
22 : 13. i. of L. for me, 2 Ch. 34: 21.
18. king sent you to i.,2 Ch. 34:26.
1 Ch. 10:13. familiar spirit, to i. of it
18:10.Tou to Da. to i. of his welfare
21 : 30. David not go bef. it to i.
2 Ch. 32 : 31. to i. of the wonder th.
Ezr. 7: 14. are sent to i. conc-g Jud.
Jb. 8 : 8. For i. I pray of former age
Ps. 27: 4. L. and to i. in his temple
Ec. 7 : 10. dost not i. wisely conc.
Is. 21 : 12. if ye will i. i. ye [this
Je. 21 : 2. i. I pray of Lord for us
37: 7. king that sent you to i. of me
Eze. 14 : 7. cometh to prophet to i.
20 : 1. elders came to i. of Lord
3. saith L. are ye come to i. of me?
Mat. 10 : 11. i. who in it is worthy
Lu. 22 : 23. to i. among themselves,
Jn. 16 : 19. [ful how to i.
Ac. 9:11. i. for Saul | 25: †20. doubt-
19: 39. if ye i. conc-g other matters
23:15. as tho. would i. someth., 20.
2 Co. 8 : 23. Wheth. any i. of Titus

INQUIRED.

De. 17 : 4. heard of it, i. diligently
Ju. 6 : 29. when they i. they said
8 : 14. a man of Succoth and i.
20 : 27. chil. of Israel i. of the L.
1 S. 10 : 22. they i. of the L. further
22 : 10. he i. of the L. for him, 13.
23 : 2. Da. i. of L.,4.-30 : 8. 2 S. 2:
1.-5:19,23.-21:1. 1 Ch. 14: 10,14.
28 : 6. when Saul i. L. answ. not
2 S. 11 : 3. David i. after the wom.
16: 23. as if had i. at oracle of G.
1 Ch. 10 : 14. Saul i. not of the L.
13 : 3. i. not at ark in days of Saul
Ps. 78 : 34. they i. early after God
Eze. 14 : 3. should I be i. of at all
20:3. As I live, I will not be i. of,31.
31. sh. I be i. of by you, O Isr.?
36 : 37. I will yet for this be i. of
Da. 1 : 20. in all king i. of them
Zph. 1 : 6. that have not i. for the L.
Mat. 2 : 7. Herod i. of wise men, 16.
Jn. 4 : 52. i. hour began to amend
2 Co. 8 : 23. or our brethren be i. of
1 Pe. 1 : 10. of wh. salv. prophets i.

INQUIREST. [iniq.

Jb. 10 : 6. That thou i. after my

INQUIRY.

Pr. 20 : 25. after vows to make i.
Ac. 10:17. made i.for Simon's house

INQUISITION.

De. 19 : 18. judges make diligent i.
Es. 2 : 23. i. was made of matter
Ps. 9 : 12. When he maketh i. for bl.

INSCRIPTION. [this i.

Ac. 17 : 23. I found an altar with

INSIDE. [wood

1 K. 6 : 15. covered walls on i. with

INSPIRATION.

Jb 32 : 8. i. of Al. giveth underst-g
2 Ti. 3 : 16. All Scripture is given by

INSTANT, LY. [i. of G.

Is. 29 : 5. it sh. be at an i. suddenly
30 : 13. breaking cometh at an i.
Je. 18 : 7. At what i. I speak, 9.
Lu. 2 : 38. she coming in that i.
7: 4. they besought him i-y saying
23 : 23. were i. with loud voices
Ac. 12 : †5. i. prayer made of ch.
26 : 7. our 12 tribes i-y serving G.
Ro. 12 : 12. continuing i. in prayer
2 Ti. 4 : 2. Preach, be i. in season,

INSTRUCT. [out of

De. 4 : 36. that he might i. thee
Ne. 9 : 20. gavest thy Spirit to i. th.
Jb. 40 : 2. he th. contendeth i. him?
Ps. 16 : 7. my reins i. me in night
32 : 8. I will i. thee in the way [i.
Can. 8 : 2. into mo.'s house who will
Is. 28 : 26. G. doth i. to discretion
Da. 11 : 33. that unders. sh. i. many
1 Co. 2:16. of L. that he may i. him

INSTRUCTED. [vants

Ge. 14 : †14. Abr. armed his i. ser-
De. 32 : 10. L. led him, he i. him
2 K. 12 : 2. Jehoiada priest i. him
1 Ch. 15 : 22. Chenaniah i. ab. song
25 : 7. were i. in the songs of L.
2 Ch. 3 : 3. Sol. was i. for building
Jb. 4 : 3. Behold thou hast i. many
Ps. 2 : 10. be i. judges of earth
Pr. 5 : 13. mine ear to them i. me
21 : 11. wise is i. he rec-h knowl.
Is. 8 : 11. L. spake thus and i. me
40 : 14. i. and taught him path
Je. 6:8. Be i. Jerus.,lest soul depart
31 : 19. I was i. I smote thigh
Mat. 13 : 52. every scribe who is i.
14 : 8. she, being bef. i. of her mo.
Lu. 1 : 4. of things thou hast been i.
Ac. 18 : 25. man was i. in way of L.
Ro. 2 : 18. knowest will, being i.
Ph. 4 : 12. in all things I am i.

INSTRUCTING.

2 Ti. 2 : 25. i. those that oppose

INSTRUCTION.

Jb. 33 : 16. openeth ears,sealeth i.
Ps. 50 : 17. Seeing thou hatest i.
Pr. 1 : 2. To know wisdom and i.
3. To receive the i. of wisdom
7. fools despise wisd. and i., 15: 5.
8. My son, hear i. of thy fa., 4: 1.
4 : 13. Take hold of i. keep her
5 : 12. Say, How have I hated i.
23. He shall die without i. and
6 : 23. reproofs of i. are way of life
8 : 10. Receive my i. | 33. hear i.
9 : 9. give i. to wise he be wiser
10 : 17. in way of life th. keepeth i.
12 : 1. Whoso loveth i. lov-h knowl.
13 : 1. wise son heareth fa.'s i.
18. shame to him refuseth i.
15 : 32. refuseth i. despiseth soul
33. fear of Lord is i. of wisdom
16 : 22. but the i. of fools is folly
19 : 20. Hear counsel, receive i.
27. Cease to hear i. caus-h to err
23 : 12. Apply thy heart to i.
23. Buy truth, i. and underst-g
24 : 32. I looked upon it rec-d i.
Je. 17 : 23. not hear, nor receive i.
32 : 33. not hearkened to rec. i.
35 : 13. Will ye not receive i. to
Eze. 5 : 15. it sh. be reproach, an i.
Zph. 3 : 7. Surely thou wilt rec. i.
2 Ti. 3 : 16. Scripture is profit.,for i.

INSTRUCTOR, S.

Ge. 4 : 22. Tubal-cain, an i. of ev.
Ro. 2 : 20. An i. of the foolish [C.
1 Co. 4 : 15. tho. have 10,000 i-s in

INSTRUMENT.

Nu. 35 : 16. if smite with i. of iron
Ps. 33 : 2. with i. of 10 strings, 92:3.
Ps. 71:†22. praise with i. of psaltery
144 : 9. will sing a new song on i.
Is. 28:27. fitches not threshed wi. i.
41 : 15. a new sharp threshing i.
54 : 16. bringeth forth i. for work
Eze. 33 : 32. song of one can play

INSTRUMENTS. [on i.

Ge. 49 : 5. i. of cruelty in habita-s
Ex. 25 : 9. pattern of all the i.
Nu. 3 : 8. shall keep all i. of tab.
4 : 12. sh. take i. of ministry, 26,32.
7 : 1. sanctified i. | 31 : 6. holy i.
1 S. 8 : 12. i. of war, i. of chariots
18 : 6. to meet Saul wi. i. of music
2 S. 6 : 5. played on all manner of i.
24:22.threshing i.oth.i.,1Ch.21:23.
1 K 19 : 21. boiled flesh with i.
1 Ch. 9 : 29. to oversee i. of sanc.
12 : 37. i. of war for battle, 33.
16 : 42. make sound wi. musical i.
23 : 5. i. wh. I made said Da.
28 : 14. i. of all manner of service,
2 Ch. 29 : 27. i. ordained by Da., 26.
30 : 21. singing with loud i.
Ne. 12 : 36. with musical i. of Da.
Ps. 7 : 13. prepared the i. of death
68 : 25. players on i. followed aft.
87 : 7. players on i. shall be there
150 : 4. praise him with stringed i.
Ec. 2 : 8. musical i. of all sorts
Is. 22 : †24. hang upon him all i.
32 : 7. i. of churl are evil
38 : 20. sing my songs to stringed i.
Je. 46 : †19. make thee i. of captiv.
Eze. 12 : †3. prepare i. for remov-g
16:†39. take i.of thy ornam.,23:†26.
40 : 42. i. whw. slew burnt off-g
Da. 6 : 18. nei. i. of music brought
Am. 1:3.threshed Gil. with i. of iron
6 : 5. invent to thems. i. of music.
Ha. 3 : 19. singer on my stringed i.
Zch. 11 : 15. take i. of foolish shep.
Ro. 6 : 13. Nei. members i. of un-
righte. members as i. of right.

INSURRECTION.

Ezr. 4 : 19. this city hath made i.
Ps. 64 : 2. i. of workers of iniquity
Mk. 15 : 7. bound with th. made i.
committed murder in i.
Ac. 18 : 12. Jews made i. one accord

INTEGRITY.

Ge. 20 : 5. in i. of heart done this
6. I know thou didst this in i. of
1 K. 9 : 4. as David walked in i.
Jb. 2 : 3. still he holdeth fast his i.
9. Dost thou still retain thine i.?
27 : 5. will not remove my i. fr. me
31 : 6. that God may know my i.
Ps. 7 : 8. acco. to i. that is in me
25 : 21. Let i. uprightness preserve
26 : 1. I walked in my i.
11. as for me I will walk in i.
41 : 12. thou upholdest me in my i.
78 : 72. fed them acc. to i. of heart
Pr. 11 : 3. i. of upright shall guide
19 : 1. Better is poor walketh in i.
20 : 7. just man walketh in his i.

INTELLIGENCE.

Da. 11:30. i. with them forsake cov.

INTEND, ED, EST.

Ex. 2 : 14. i-t thou to kill me as
Jos. 22 : 33. did not i. to go ag. th.
2 Ch. 28 : 13. ye i. to add to our sins
Ps. 21 : 11. they i-d evil against thee
Ac. 5 : 28. ye i. to bring man's bl.
35. i. to do touching these men

INTENDING.

Lu. 14 : 28. which of you i. to build
Ac.12:4.i. after Easter to bring him
†20. Herod i.war with th. of Tyre
20 : 13. there i. to take in Paul

INTENT, S.

2 S. 17 : 14. to the i. L. bring evil
2 K. 10 : 19. to i. he might destroy
2 Ch. 16 : 1. to i. he let none go
Je. 30:24. till performed i-s of heart
Eze. 40 : 4. to the i. I might shew

Da. 4 : 17. to i. living may know
Jn. 11 : 15. not there to i. ye belie.
13:28.for what i.he spake unto him
Ac. 9 : 21. came hither for that i.
10:29. what i. ye have sent for me
1 Co. 10 : 6. to i. we not lust after
Ep. 3:10. To i. that unto principal-s
He. 4 : 12. discerner of i-s of heart

INTERCESSION.

Is. 53 : 12. made i. for transgressors
Je. 7 : 16. nei. lift cry, nor make i.
27 : 18. let them now make i. to L.
36 : 25. Elnathan had made i.
Ro. 8 : 26. Spirit maketh i., 27, 34.
11 : 2. he maketh i. to G. ag. Isr.
1 Ti. 2 : 1. that i-s be made for all
He. 7 : 25. he ever liveth to make i.

INTERCESSOR.

Is. 59 : 16. he wondered was no i.

INTERMEDDLE, ETH.

Pr. 14 : 10. stranger not i. with joy
18 : 1. seeketh i-h with all wisdom

INTERMISSION.

La.3:49. eye ceaseth not with. any i.

INTERPRET. [15.

Ge. 41 : 8. none co. i. th. unto Pha.,
12. accord. to his dream he did i.
1 Co. 12 : 30. do all i. ?
14 : 5. except he i. [one i.
13. pray that he may i. | 27. let

INTERPRETATION, S.

Ge. 40 : 5. acc. to i. of dreams, 41:11.
8. Do not i-s belong to God ?
12.Joseph said, This is the i. of it,
18. Da. 4 : 24.-5 : 26.
16. baker saw that i. was good
Ju. 7 : 15. when Gideon heard i.
Pr. 1 : 6. To underst. proverb and i.
Ec. 8 : 1. who knoweth i. of thing
Da. 2 : 4. we will shew i., 7 : 16.
45. dream is certain, i. sure
4:19. and the i. be to thy enemies
5:12. will shew i. | 15. not shew i.
16. heard thou canst make i-s
7 : 16. he made me to know the i.
Jn. 1 : 42. Cephas, wh. by i. A stone
9 : 7. pool of Siloam, is by i. Sent
Ac. 9 : 36. Tabitha, by i. Dorcas
13: 8. Elymas sorcerer, name by i.
1 Co. 12 : 10. to ano. i. of tongues
14 : 26. every one of you hath an i.
He. 7:2. by i. King of righteousness
2 Pe. 1 : 20. no prophecy of private

INTERPRETED. [i.

Ge.40:22.as Joseph had i.,41:12,13.
Ezr. 4 : 7. i. in the Syrian tongue
Mat. 1 : 23. being i. is, God with us
Mk. 5 : 41. is, being i. Damsel arise
15: 22. is, being i. place of skull
34. i. My God, my God, why
Jn. 1 : 38. i. master | 41. i. the Ch.
Ac. 4 : 36. is. i. son of consolation

INTERPRETER, S.

Ge. 40 : 8. dreamed, and is no i.
42: 23. Joseph spake to them by i.
2 Ch. 32 : † 31. in the business of i.
Jb. 33:23. be an i. one amo. a thous.
Is. 43 : † 27. thy i-s have transgr-d
1 Co.14:28. if be no i. let him keep

INTERPRETING.

Da. 5:12. i. of dreams found in Dan.

INTREAT. See ENTREAT

INTRUDING.

Col. 2 : 18. i. into things not seen

INVADE, ED.

1 S. 23:27. Philis. have i-d the land
27 : 8. Da. and men i-d Geshurites
30:1. the Amalekites i-d the south
2 K. 13 : 20. a band of Moabites i-d
2 Ch. 20: 10. wouldest not let Isr i.
28 : 18. Philistines had i-d cities
Ha. 3: 16. will i. them with troops

INVASION.

1 S. 30: 14. We made i. on south

INVENT, ED. [men

2 Ch. 26:15. engines i-d by cunning
Am. 6 : 5. i. instruments of music

INVENTIONS.

Ps. 99 : 8. tookest vengeance of i.
106 : 29. provoked to anger with i.
39. went whoring with own i.
Pr. 8:12. find out knowl. of witty i.
Ec. 7 : 29. have sought out many i.

INVENTORS.

Ro. 1 : 30. i. of evil things, disobe.

INVISIBLE.

Ro. 1 : 20. i. things are clearly seen
Col. 1 : 15. is image of i. God [i.
16. in heav. and earth, visible and
1 Ti. 1 : 17. to King immortal, i.
He. 11 : 27. as seeing him who is i.

INVITED.

1 S. 9 : 24. I have i. the people
2 S. 13:23. Absal. i. all king's sons
Es. 5 : 12. tomorrow am I i. to her

INWARD.

Ge. 41 : † 21. had come to i. parts
Le. 13 : 55. sha. burn it, it is fret i.
1 K. 7 : 25. all hinder parts were i.
17 : † 21. child's soul into i. parts
2 Ch. 3 : 13. and their faces were i.
Jb. 19: 19. my i. friends abhor-d me
38 : 36. hath put wisd. in i. parts
Ps. 5 : 9. their i. part is wickedness
49 : 11. i. thought is, their houses
51 : 6. desirest truth in i. parts
62 : † 4. they curse in their i. parts
64: 6. i. thought of ev. one is deep
Pr. 20 : 27. all i. parts of belly
30. so do stripes i. parts of belly
Is. 16 : 11. my i. parts sound for
Je. 31 : 33. put my law in i. parts
Mk. 6 : † 19 Herodias had i. grudge
Lu. 11 : 39. i. part full of ravening
Ro. 7:22. in law of God after i. man
2 Co.4:16. i. man is renewed day by
7 : 15. his i. affection is abundant

INWARDLY.

Ps. 62:4.bless with mouth, curse i.
Mat. 7 : 15. i. are ravening wolves
Ro. 2 : 29. he a Jew who is one i.

INWARDS.

Ex. 29 : 13. fat that covereth i.,22.
Le. 3 : 3, 9, 14.-4 : 8.-7:.3-9:19.
17. thou shalt wash the i., Le. 1 :
9, 13.-9 : 14.
Le. 4 : 11. his i. and dung burn
8:16. fat on i. Mo. burnt on alt., 25.
21. he washed the i. with water

IPHEDEI'AH.

1 Ch.8:25.I.Penuel sons of Shashak

IR[1] **or IRI.**[2] [| 12. I.[1]

1 Ch. 7 : 7. sons of Bela ; Ezbon, I.[2]

I'RA.

2 S. 20 : 26.I. a chief ruler about Da.
23 :26. one of thirty; I., 1 Ch.11:28.
38. of thirty; I.Ithrite,1 Ch.11:40.
1 Ch. 27:9.sixth capt.was I., Tekoite

I'RAD. [gat

Ge. 4 : 18.unto Enoch born I.; I. be-

I'RAM. See MAGDIEL.

I'RI. See IR.

IRI'JAH. [14.

Je. 37 : 13. a captain, I., took Jer-h.

IR-NA'HASH. [I.

1 Ch. 4 : 12. Tehinnah the father of

I'RON. [Place.]

Jos. 19 : 38. fenced cities are I. and

IRON. [Adj.]

De. 4 : 20. L. bro-t you out of i. furnace, 1 K. 8 : 51. Je. 11 : 4.
27 : 5. shalt not lift any i. tool
Jos.17:18. tho. they have i. chariots
Jb. 19: 24. were graven with i. pen
20 : 24. shall flee from i. weapon
Is. 48 : 4. thy neck is an i. sinew
Je. 1:18. made thee this day i. pillar
11 : 4. out of E. from i. furnace
Eze. 4 : 3. take unto thee an i. pan
Da. 7 : 7. it had great i. teeth, it
Ac. 12: 10. came to i. gate that

IRON, S.

Nu. 35 : 16. smite with instru. of i.
De. 3 : 11. Og's bedstead was of i.
De. 8 : 9. a land whose stones are i.
28 : 23. earth under thee shall be i.
48. put yoke of i. on, Je. 28 : 14.
Jos. 8 : 31. over wh. no man lifted i.
17:16. have chariots of i., Ju. 1:19.
Ju. 4 : 3. had 900 chariots of i., 13.
1 S. 17 : 7. spear's head weighed 600
shek. of i. [of i., 1 Ch. 20: 3.
2 S. 12 : 31. harrows of i. and axes
23 : 7. man must be fenced with i.
1 K. 6 : 7. nor any tool of i. heard
22: 11. Zed made horns of i., 2 Ch.
2 K. 6 : 6. the i. did swim [18: 10.
1 Ch. 22: 3. Da. prepared i. in abun.
29:2.prepared i. for things of i., 7.
Jb. 28 : 2. i. is taken out of earth
40 : 18 behemoth's bones like i.
41:7. Canst fill skin with barbed i-s
27. He esteemeth i. as straw
Ps. 2 : 9 break them with rod of i.
105 : 18. hurt, he was laid in i.
107: 10. bound in i. | 16. bars of i.
149: 8. nobles with fetters of i.
Pr. 27 : 17. i. sharpeneth i. so man
Ec. 10 : 10. if the i. be blunt, and
Is. 10 : 34. cut down forest with i.
45 : 2. I will cut asunder bars of i.
60:17.for i. bring silv. for stones i.
Je. 15: 12. shall i. break northern i.
17:1. sin of Jud. writ. with pen of i.
28 : 13. shalt make yokes of i.
Eze. 4 : 3. take i. pan, for wall of i.
27: 12. Tarshish thy merch. with i.
19. Dan. occupied with bright i.
Da. 2:33. legs i. feet part i.,34,41,42.
35. was i. and clay broken
40.4th kingd. shall be strong as i.
43. sawest i. mixed with clay
7: 19. beast, whose teeth were of i.
Am. 1 : 3. threshed Gilead with i.
Mi. 4 : 13. I will make thy horn i.
1 Ti. 4 : 2. conscience seared with i.
Re. 2:27. with rod of i., 12:5.-19:15.
9 : 9. as it were breastplates of i.
See BRASS.

IR'PEEL.

Jos. 18 : 27. inheri. of Benj. I. and

IR-SHE'MESH.

Jos. 19 : 41. coast of their inheri. I.

I'RU.

1 Ch. 4 : 15. sons of Caleb I. Naam

IS.

Jb. 11:6. are double to that which i.
Lu. 10 : 22. who son i., who Fa. i.
Jn. 1 : 47. Israelite, in whom i. no
3:6. born of flesh i. flesh, of Sp. i.
13. Son of man wh. i. in heaven
29. He that hath bride i. brideg
4 : 23. hour cometh, and now i.
7:27. no man know h whence he i.
8 : 47. i. of G. | 18:37. i. of truth
9 : 29. know not whence he i., 30.
Ac. 4 : 24. made sea, and all that i.
17 : 19. what new doctrine i.
Eph. 5 : 17. what the will of L is
2 Th. 2 : 4 ab. all i. called G., or i.
worshipped, shewing he i. G.
1 Ti. 4 : 8. promise of life th. now i.
He. 11: 6. beli. he i., and i. reward-
1 Jn. 3 : 2. sh. see him as he i. [er
3. as he i. pure
4. sin i. transgression of law
Re. 1:4. i., was, i. to come, 8.-4:8.
17:8. beast that was, i. not, yet i.
10. one i. other i. not yet come
See BETTER, CHRIST, CLEAN, DEAD, EPHRAIM, FOOL, GOOD, LORD, NOTHING, ONE, PERFECT, POOR, RIGHT, THIS.

IS it.

Ge. 19 : 20. city i. i. not little one?
32 : 29. Whf. i. i. askest my name
42 : 14. That i. i. I spake unto you
49 : 28. this i. i. their fa-s spake
Ex. 2 : 18. How i. i. are come so
20. why i. i. ye have left man ?
5:22. whf. i. i. that thou hast sent

Ex.32:18. nei. i.i. voice of them cry
33 : 16. i. i. not thou goest wi. us?
De. 3 : 11. i.i. not in Rabbath?
30: 11. com-t, neither i. i. far off
13. neither i. i. beyond the sea
Ju. 14 : 15. take that we have, i. i.
1 S. 9 : 20. i. i. not on thee ⌊not?
10 : 1. i. i. not bec. L. anointed
12: 17. i. i. not wheat harvest?
2 K. 1: 3. i. i. not bec. no G.
4: 26. i.i. well with thee, i.i. well
9: 17. say, i. i. peace, 18, 19, 22.
20: 19. i. i. not good, if peace be
1 Ch. 21: 17. i. i. not I that com-d
Jb. 10:3. i. i. good unto thee, 18:9.
15: 23. for br. saying, Where i. i.
22: 3. i. i. any pleasure to Alm.
Pr 15: 23. a word, how good i. i.!
Is. 7: 13. i. i. small thing to weary
29: 17. i. i. not yet very little while
36: 7. i. i. not he whose high pla.
58: 5. i. i. such a fast I chosen?
7. i. i. not to deal thy bread to?
Je. 10: 5. nei. i. i. in th. to do g-d
La. 1:12. i. i. noth. to you, all ye?
Da. 3: 14. i. i. true, O Shadrach?
Am. 2: 11. i. i. not thus, O Israel?
Mi. 1: 5. transgr. of Jac., i. i. not
3: 1. i. i. to know judgm.? ⌊Sama.
Ha. 2:13. i. i. not of the L. of hosts
Hag. 2: 3. i. i. not as nothing?
Zch. 5: 6. What i. i.? Mat. 26: 62.
Mk. 14: 60. Ac. 10: 4.-21: 22.
2 Co. 12: 13. Ep. 4: 9. ⌈profit
Mal. 1:8. i. i. not evil | 3:14. what
Mat. 12: 10. i. i. lawful to heal on,
Mk. 3: 4. Lu. 6: 9.-14: 3.
16: 11. How i. i. ye do not understand, Mk.8:21. ⌈wife,Mk.10:2.
19: 3. i. i. lawful to put away his
20:15. i. i. lawf. to do what I will
22: 17. i. i. lawful to give tribute to Cesar? Mk.12:14. Lu. 20:22.
26:22. Lord, i. i. I? 25. Mk. 14:19.
62. what i. i. these witness, Mk.
Mk. 2: 9. i. i. easier to say ⌊14:60.
16. How i. i. he eateth wi. publi.
4: 40. How i. i. ye have no faith?
9: 21. How long i. i. since this
10:24. hard i. i. for them trust in
11: 17. i. i. not written, Jn. 10:34.
Lu. 2: 49. How i. i. ye sought me
12: 56. how i. i. ye do not discern
16:2. How i. i. I hear this of thee?
22: 64. who i. i. that smote thee?
Jn. 4:9. How i. i. being Jew askest
14: 22. how i. i. wilt manifest
Ac. 5: 9. How i. i. ye have agreed
22:25. i. i. lawful to scourge Rom.?
1 Co. 6: 5. i. i. so, is not a wise man
9: 11. i. i. great matter if we reap
10: 16. i. i. not communion of bl.
12: 15. i. i. not of the body, 16.
14: 26. How i. i. ev. one hath ps.
1 Pe. 2:20. what glory i. i. if, when
1 Jn. 4: 3. even now i. i. in world

It IS. ⌈to do

Ge. 31: 29. i. i. in power of my ha.
41: 16. Jo. ans-d, i. i. not in me
Nu. 13: 18. see the land what i. i.
De. 31: 8. he i. i. doth go bef. thee
1 S. 3: 18. i. i. the L., let him do
2 S. 13: 35. so i. i., Jb. 5: 27. Lu.
21: 1. i. i. for Saul and ⌊12: 54.
2 K. 10:15. thine heart right as my heart? i. i.
1 Ch. 6:10. he i. i. executed priest's
21:17. I i.i. that have sinned ⌊offi.
2 Ch. 5: 9. there i. i. unto this day
Jb. 26: 3. declared thing as i. i.
Ps. 39:4. meas. of my days what i.i.
Je. 30: 7. i. i. time of Jac.'s trouble
La. 3: 22. i. i. of Lord's mercies
Eze. 21: 27. come whose right i. i.
Mat. 6: 10. Thy will in earth, as i. i. in heaven ⌈6: 20.
14: 27. i. i. I, be not afraid, Jn.

Mat.16:7. i.i. bec. no bread, Mk.8:16.
Jn. 1: 27. He i. i. who coming aft.
7: 22. not because i. i. of Moses
13:26. He i. i. to whom I give a sop
14:21. hath com-ts, he i. i. loveth
Ac. 12: 15. said, i. i. his angel ⌈i.i.
1 Co. 3: 13. try work, of what sort
11:14. have long hair i. i. a shame
15. if a wom. have long hair i.i. a glory
2 Co. 5: 13. i. i. to God, or if we be
Ga. 4: 29. so i. i. now ⌊sober (2,
Col. 1: 6. as i. i. in all the world
2 Th. 3: 1. glorified, i. i. with you
See BEHOLD, BETTER, GOOD, WRITTEN.

IS not ⌈n., 32.

Ge. 37:30. child i. n. | 42:13. one i.
42: 36. Joseph i. n., Simeon i. n.
44: 5. i. n. this it in which my L.
Ex. 4: 14. i. n. Aaron thy bro.?
14: 12. i. n. this word we did tell
Nu. 12: 7. My serv. Moses i. n. so
16: 40. i. n. of seed of Aaron
23:19. God i. n. a man he sho. lie
De. 11: 10. the land i. n. as Egypt
29: 15. that i. n. here this day
31: 17. God i. n. among us
32: 6. i. n. he Fa. that bo-t thee?
31. their rock i. n. as our rock
34. i. n. this laid up in store?
Ju. 4: 14. i. n. L. gone bef. thee?
19: 12. a city that i. n. of Israel
1 S. 15: 29. i. n. a man he repent
20: 37. i. n. arrow beyond thee?
21: 11. i. n. this Da. king? 29:3,5.
2 S. 11: 3. i. n. this Bath-sheba
14:19. i. n. ha. of Joab with thee
20: 21. Joab said, matter i. n. so
23:17. i. n. this blood of the men
1 K. 8: 41. stranger i. n. of Isr., 2 Ch. 6: 32.
2 K. 6: 19. This i. n. the way
32. i. n. sound of master's feet
1 Ch. 22: 18. i. n. Lord with you
2 Ch. 25: 7. Lord i. n. with Israel
Es. 4: 16. i. n. acc. to the law
Jb. 4: 6. i. n. this thy fear, thy
6: 13. i. n. my help in me
9: 32. he i. n. a man as I am
21: 16. their good i. n. in hand
22: 5. i. n. thy wickedness great
12. i. n. God in height of heav.?
23:8. I go forward, he i. n. there
27:19. rich openeth eyes, he i. n.
Pr. 7: 19. goodman i. n. at home
23:5. Wilt set eyes upon that i. n.
7. but his heart i. n. with thee
Ec. 9: 11. race i. n. to the swift
Is. 10: 9. i. n. Calno, i. n. Sama.
17:14. before the morning he i. n.
55:2. spend money for that i.n.br.
Je. 5: 13. word i. n. in prophets
8:19. i. n. L. in Zion, i. n. her K.
10:16. portion of Jac. i.n. like, 51:19.
23. way of man i. n. in himself
23:29. i. n. my word like as a fire
38: 5. king i. n. he that can do
49: 10. Esau i. n.
51: 9. she i. n. healed
Eze. 18: 25. way of L. i. n. equal, i. n. my way? 29.-33: 17, 20.
Da. 2:11. gods, dwelling i.n. with fl.
30. secret i. n. revealed to me
4: 30. i. n. this great Babylon
Ho. 2: 2. for she i. n. my wife
Mi. 2: 10. Arise, this i. n. your rest
3: 11. i. n. the Lord among us
Ha. 2: 4. his soul i. n. upright
Zch. 3: 2. i. n. this a brand plucked
Mat.13:55. i. n. this carpenter's son
20:23. i. n. mine to give, Mk.10:40.
22:32. God i. n. the God of the dead, Mk. 12: 27. Lu. 20: 38.
24:6. but the end i. n. yet, Lu.21:9.
28:6. He i. n. here, risen, Lu.24:6.
Lu. 6: 40. disciple i. n. ab. master
22: 27. i. n. he sitteth at meat

Jn. 3: 18. belie-th i. n. condemned
5: 31. my witness i. n. true
9: 16. This man i. n. of God
11:4. This sickn. i. n. unto death
14:24. word y. hear i. n. mine, 7:16.
18: 36. My kingd. i. n. of world
Ro. 2: 28. i. n. a Jew outwardly
29. whose praise i. n. of men
3: 29. i. n. he also of the Gentiles
8: 24. hope th. is seen i. n. hope
14: 17. kingd. of God i. n. meat
23. whatso. i. n. of faith is sin
1 Co. 4:20. kingd. of God i. n. word
6: 13. body i. n. for fornication
7: 15. sister i. n. under bondage
11: 8. man i. n. of the woman
20. this i. n. to eat L.'s supper
12:14. the body i. n. one member
13: 4. charity, i. n. puffed up
15: 39. All flesh i. n. same flesh
58. labour i. n. in vain in L.
Ga. 1: 7. Which i. n. another, but
11. gospel by me i. n. after man
3: 12. And the law i. n. of faith
20. i. n. a mediator of one
6: 7. God i. n. mocked ⌈griev.
Ph. 3: 1. To write same to me i. n.
He. 6: 10. God i. n. unrighteous
2 Pe. 3: 9. The Lord i. n. slack
1 Jn. 1:8. the truth i. n. in us, 2:4.
1: 10. his word i. n. in us
2: 15. love of the Fa. i. n. in him
16. i. n. of Fa. ⌈G., 4: 3, 6.
3:10. doeth not righte-n., i. n. of
5: 16. sin which i. n. unto death
Re. 17: 8. beast, was, and i. n., 11.

It IS not.

Ge. 2: 18. i. i. n. good, Pr. 18: 5.-25:27.-28:21. Ho.8:6. Mat. 19:10.
31: 5. i. i. n. toward me as before
41:16. i. i. n. in me, God sh. give
Ex. 8:26. said, i. i. n. meet so to do
De. 32: 47. i. i. n. a vain thing
1 S. 6: 9. i.i.n. his hand that smote
20: 2. Jona. said, i. i. n. so
Ezr.5:16. building, yet i.i.n. finished
Jb. 9: 35. but i. i. n. so with me
28:14. depth, saith i. i. n. in me (2)
35:15. bec. i.i.n. so, he hath visited
Pr. 31:4. i. i. n. for kings, O Lem.
Je. 5: 12. belied L. said i. i. n. he
10: 23. i. i. n. in man to direct
Eze. 11: 3. which say, i. i. n. near
Mat. 10: 20. i. i. n. ye that speak
13:11. to you given, to them i.i.n.
14: 4. i. i. n. lawf. to have her, 27:6. Mk.6:18. ⌈dren's, Mk.7:27.
15: 26. i. i. n. meet to take chil-
18:14. i. i. n. the will of your Fa.
Ac. 1: 7. i. i. n. for you to know
6: 2. i. i. n. reason we sho. leave
22:22. i. i. n. fit that he sho. live
25:16. i. i. n. manner of Romans
Ro. 9: 16. i. i. n. of him th. willeth
2 Co.12:1. i. i. n. expedient to glory

IS there.

Ge. 31: 14. i. t. yet any portion or
De. 3: 24. what G. i. t. in heaven
4: 7. what nation i. t. so great, 8.
5: 26. who i. t. that hath heard
20: 5. What man i. t. built, 7, 8.
32:28. nei. i. t. underst-g in them
Ju. 4: 20. i. t. any man here
14: 3. i. t. never a woman among
21:5. Who i.t. am. tribes of Isr., 8.
1 S. 2: 2. nei. i. t. any rock like
17: 29. i. t. not cause? ⌈Is.44:8.
2 S. 7: 22. nei. i. t. any G. besides,
9: 1. i. t. any left of Saul's ho., 3.
1 K. 22: 7. i. t. not here a prophet besides? 2 K. 3:11. 2 Ch. 18:6.
2 Ch. 20: 6. in thy hand i. t. not
33:23. Who i.t. of his peo.? Ezr.1:3.
Ne. 6: 11. who i. t. being as I am
Jb.6:30. i.t. iniq. in my tongue, 33:9.
15: 11. i. t. any secret with thee?
Ps. 30: 9. What profit i. t. in my

Pr. 17 : 16. i. t. a price in a fool
Ec. 1 : 10. i. t. whereof it may be
5 : 11. what good i. t. to owners
Is. 2 : 7. nei. i. t. end of treasures,
nei. i. t. end of chariots
44 : 19. nei. i. t. knowledge to say
20. i. t. not a lie in my right ha.?
Je. 8 : 22. i. t. no balm in Gilead?
32 : 27. i. t. any thing too hard for
37 : 17. i. t. any word fr. L. ⌊me
Ho. 12 : 11. i. t. iniquity in Gilead
Am. 6 : 10. i. t. yet any with thee
Mat. 7 : 9. what man i. t. if his son
Ac. 4 : 12. nei. i. t. salva. in any
Ro.3:1. what profit i. t. of circum.?
9 : 14. i. t. unrightn. with God?

There IS.

Le. 14 : 35. t. i. as it were a plague
Nu. 11:6. t. i. noth. besides manna
De. 32 : 39. and t. i. no god wi. me
Ju. 19 : 19. Yet t. i. both straw and
21 : 19. t. i. feast of L. in Shiloh
1 S. 14 : 6. t. i. no restraint to L.
17 : 46. know t. i. a God in Israel
20:3. t. i. but a step betw. me and
21. come, for t. i. peace to thee
1 K. 5 : 4. t. i. nei. adversary nor
8:23. t. i. no God like thee in heav-
en, 2 Ch. 6 : 14. ⌈2 Ch. 6 : 36.
46. t. i. no man that sinneth not,
14 : 2. t. i. Ahijah the proph. who
1 K. 22 : 8. t. i. one man, Micaiah
2 K. 5:8. he sh. know t. i. a proph.
Ezr. 10:2.t.i. hope in Isr.,Jb.11:18.
Es. 3 : 8. t. i. a people scattered
Jb. 19:29. may know t. i. a judgm.
22 : 29. shalt say, t. i. lifting up
32 : 8. But t. i. a spirit in man
Ps. 14 : 1. said, t. i. no God, 53 : 1.
19:11. keeping them t. i. gr. rew.
34 : 9. t. i. no want to them that
46 : 4. t. i. a river whose streams
58:11. t. i. a reward for righteous
68 : 27. t. i. little Benj. wi. ruler
146 : 3. in man, in whom t. i. no
Pr. 11 : 24. t. i. that scattereth
13:7. t. i. that maketh hims. rich
14 : 9. am. righteous t. i. favour
12. t. i. a way seemeth right, 16:
23. in all labour t. i. profit ⌊25.
23 : 18. t. i. an end ⌈12, 13, 14.
30:11. t. i. a genera. that curseth,
Ec. 3:1. To ev. thing t. i. a season
7:15. t. i. a just man, t. i. a wick.
8 : 4. word of king, t. i. power
16. t. i. day nor night seeth sleep
9 : 2. t. i. one event | 4. t. i. hope
Is. 43 : 11. besides me t. i. no Sav.
44 : 6. besides me t. i. no God, 8.-
45 : 5. ⌈Chal.
47 : 1. t. i. no throne, O dau. of
48 : 22. t. i. no peace to wicked,
57:21. Je. 6:14. ⌈i. no beauty
50 : 2. bec. t. i. no water | 53:2. t.
57 : 10. saidst not, t. i. no hope,
Je. 2 : 25.-18:12. ⌈he said, t. i.
Je. 31:17. t. i. hope in end | 37:17.
Eze. 22:25. t. i. a conspiracy of her
32 : 24. t. i. Elam | 29. t. i. Edom
34:5. scattered, bec. t. i. no shep.
Da.2:28. t. i. a G. revealeth secrets
5 : 11. t. i. a man in thy kingd. in
Ho. 4 : 1. bec. t. i. no truth nor
Na. 3:19. t. i. no healing of bruise
Mat. 22 : 23. Saddu. say, t. i. no
resurrec-n, Mk.12:18.1 Co.15:12.
Mk. 10 : 18. t. i. none good but one
Lu. 14 : 22. and yet t. i. room
15 : 10 t. i. joy in
Jn. 8:44. bec. t. i. no truth in him
11 : 10. bec. t. i. no light in him
1 Co. 3 : 3. t. i. among you envying
5:1. it is reported t. i. fornication
8 : 6. but to us t. i. but one God
15:44. t. i. a natural body, t. i. a
Ga. 5 : 23. against such t. i. no law
Col. 3:25. t. i. no respect of persons
1 Jn. 4:18. t. i. no fear in love, but
5 : 16. t. i. a sin unto death, I do
17. and t. i. a sin not unto death
See NONE, ONE.

There IS not. ⌈sight of

Ge. 47 : 18. t. i. n. aught left in
2 S. 13 : 30. k.'s sons, t. i. n. one
1 K. 5 : 6. t. i. n. among us that
2 K.1:3.bec. t.i.n. a God in Isr., 6
19 : 3. t. i. n. strength to bri. forth
Jb. 41 : 33. upon earth t. i. n. his
Ec. 4 : 8. is one, and t. i. n. second
Can. 6 : 6. t. i. n. one barren am.
Lu. 7:28. t. i. n. a greater prophet
1 Co. 6 : 5. t. i. n. a wise man am.
8 : 7. t. i. n. in every man knowl.

ISAAC.

Ge.17:19.shalt call his name I.,21:3.
21. my cov. will I establ. with I.
21 : 4. Ab. circumcised his son I.
10. not be heir with my son, I.
12.God said,in I. shall thy seed be
called, Ro. 9 : 7. He. 11 : 18.
22:2. Take son I. | 9. Ab. bound I.
24:4. wife for I. | 14. appoin. for I.
63. I. went out to meditate in
67.I. was comforted aft. mother's
25 : 5. Ab. gave all he had unto I.
9. sons I. and Ishm. buried Ab.
11. G. blessed I. | 19. gene-s of I.
20. I. 40 years old took Rebekah
21. I entreated L. for his wife
26. I. 60 years old she bare Esau
28. I. loved Esau bec. of venison
26:1. I. went to Abimelech king of
8. I. was sporting with Rebekah
12. I. sowed received hun. fold
18. I. digged again the wells
19. I. serv-s digged found well,25.
35. grief of mind to I. and Rebek.
27 : 1. when I. was old — eyes dim
30. I. an end of blessing Jacob
28:1. I. called Jac., blessed him,6.
5. I. sent Jac. away, he went to
31:42. exc. fear of I. been with me
53. Jac. sware by fear of father I.
35:27.Jac.came to I. | 29.I.gave up
46 : 1. sacri-s to G. of I. ⌊ghost
48 : 15. G. bef. whom I. did walk
16. let name of I. be on them
49:31. buried I. | 50:24. sware to I.
Ex.2:24.G.rememb-d cov. with Ab.,
with I., Le. 26 : 42.-2 K. 13:23.
3:6. the God of I., 15, 16.-4:5. Ge.
28:13.-32:9. 1 K.18:36.1 Ch.29:
18. 2 Ch. 30:6. Mat. 22:32. Mk.
12:26. Lu. 20:37. Ac. 3:13.-7:32.
6 : 3. I appeared unto Abraham I.
32 : 13. Rememb. Ab. I., De. 9 : 27.
Jos. 24 : 3. I gave him I.
4. I gave unto I. Jac. and Esau
1 Ch. 1 : 28. sons of Ab. I., 34.
16:16. his oath unto I., Ps. 105 : 9.
Je. 33 : 26. his seed over seed of I.
Am.7:9.high places of I. be desolate
16.drop not thy word ag. ho. of I.
Mat. 1 : 2. Ab. begat I. and I. begat
Jacob, Lu. 3 : 34. Ac. 7 : 8.
8:11. sit down with I. in kingdom
Lu.13:28.when see I. in kingd.of G.
Ro. 9 : 10. Rebekah conceived by I.
Ga. 4:28. we, as I. was, are of prom.
He. 11 : 9. dwelling in tab. with I.
17. By faith Ab. offered I.,Ja.2:21.
20. by faith I. blessed Jac. Esau

ISA'IAH, or ESA'IAS.

2 K.19:2.sent Eliakim to I., Is.37:2.
19 : 20. I. sent to Hez., Is. 37 : 21.
20:1 Hez.sick, unto death. I. came
to him and said,14.Is.38:1.-39:3
11. I. cried unto L., 2 Ch. 32 : 20.
2 Ch. 26:22. acts did I. write, 32:32.
Is. 1 : 1. The vision of I., 2 : 1.-13:1.
2 Ch. 32 : 32.
7 : 3. said L. unto I., 20. 2.-38 : 4.
20 : 3. as I. hath walked naked
Mat. 3:3. spoken by the prophet E.,
4 : 14.-8 : 17.-12 : 17.-13:14. Lu.
3 : 4. Jn. 1 : 23.-12 : 38.
15:7. E. prophesy of you, Mk. 7:6.
Lu. 4:17. to him book of prophet E.
Jn. 12 : 39. bec. that E. said again
41. said E. when he saw his glory
Ac. 8 : 28. the eunuch read E., 30.
28:25. Well spake Holy Ghost by E.
Ro. 9 : 27. E. crieth conc. Israel
29. as E. said bef., Except the L.
10 : 16. E. saith, who hath believ.,
20. E. is very bold ⌊Jn. 12 : 38.
15:12.E.saith,sh. be a root of Jesse

IS'CAH.

Ge. 11 : 29. Haran the father of I.

ISCARIOT. See JUDAS.

ISH'BAH.

1 Ch. 4 : 17. the father of Eshtemoa

ISH'BAK.

Ge.25:2. Keturah bare I.,1 Ch.1:32.

ISH'BI-BE'NOB.

2 S. 21 : 16. I. was of sons of giants

ISH'-BO'SHETH.

2 S. 2 : 8. Abner set I. over Gilead
10. I. was 40 years old, 12, 15.
3 : 8. Abner wroth for words of I.
14. David sent messengers to I.
15. I. took her from husband, 7.
4 : 5. to ho. of I. who lay on bed
8. brought head of I. unto Da.
12. they took head of I. buried it
See ESH-BAAL.

I'SHI.

1 Ch. 2 : 31. sons of Appaim, I.
4:20. sons of I., 42.-5:24. Ho. 2:16.

ISHI'AH.

1 Ch. 7 : 3. sons of Izrahiah, I.

ISHI'JAH.

Ezr. 10:31. taken stra. wives I. Mal-

ISH'MA. ⌊chiah

1 Ch. 4 : 3. these of fa. of Etam, I.

ISH'MAEL.

Ge.16:11. shalt call his name I., 15.
16. Ab. 86 y-rs old Hagar bare I.
17:18.O that I. might live bef.thee
20. as for I. I have heard thee
25.I. 13 y-rs old when circ.,23,26.
25:9.Isaac and I. buried Abraham
12. gene. of I.,13,16.1 Ch.1:29,31.
17. these are the years of I. 137
28 : 9. went Esau unto I., 36 : 3.
2 K.25:23.I. came to Ged., Je.40:8.
25. I. came and ten, Je. 41 : 1.
1 Ch. 1:28. sons of Ab. Isaac and I.
8 : 38. Bocheru and I. sons, 9 : 44.
2 Ch. 19 : 11. Zebadiah son of I.
23 : 1. Jehoiada took I. into cov.
Ezr.10:22.I. Elasah, had stra.wives
Je. 40 : 14. king hath sent I.
15. I will slay I. | 16. falsely of I.
41 : 2. I. smote Gedaliah
3. I. slew all Jews, 7, 8, 9.
6. I. went forth to meet them
10. I. carried away captive people
11. evil I. had done | 13,14,16,18.
12. Johanan went to fight with I.
15. but I. escaped from Johanan

ISH'MAELITE, S.

Ge. 37 : 25. a company of I-s came
27. let us sell him to I-s | 28.
39 : 1. Potiphar bought him of I-s
Ju. 8 : 24. had earrings, bec. I-s
1 Ch. 2 : 17. fa. of Amasa Jether I.
27 : 30. Over camels was Obil I.
Ps. 83 : 5. Edomites and I-s confed.

ISHMAI'AH.

1 Ch. 27 : 19. of Zebulon, I. ruler

ISH'MERAI.

1 Ch.8:18. I. Jezliah sons of Elpaal

I'SHOD.

1 Ch. 7 : 18. Hammoleketh bare I.

ISH'PAN.

1 Ch.8:22. I. and Heber were heads

ISH'-TOB.

2 S.10:6. hired of I. 12,000 men | 8.

ISH'UAH or IS'UAH.

Ge. 46:17. sons of Asher, 1 Ch.7:30.

ISH'UAI. See JESUI.

ISHU'I. [-10:†2.

1 S. 14:49. sons of Saul, 1 Ch. 8:†33.

ISLAND.

Jb. 22:30. sh. deliver i. of innocent
Is. 34:14. sh meet wild beasts of i.
Ac. 27:16. under a certain i. Clauda
26. we must be cast on certain i.
28 : 1. knew i. was called Melita
7. possessions of chief man of i.
9. had diseases in i. were healed
Re. 6 : 14. ev. i. was moved out of
16 : 20. every i. fled away [place

ISLANDS.

Is. 11:11. rec. his peo. fr. i. of the sea
13:22. beasts of i. sh. cry in houses
41 : 1. Keep silence before me O i.
42 : 12. declare Lord's praise in i.
15. I will make the rivers i. and
59 : 18. to i. he will repay recomp.
Je. 50:39. beasts of i. sh. dwell there

ISLE.

Is. 20 : 6. inhabitants of the i. say
23:2. Be still, ye inhabitants of the
6. howl, inhabitants of the i. [i.
Ac. 13:6. gone thro. i. unto Paphos
28 : 11. ship wh. wintered in the i.
Re. 1:9. I John was in the i. Patmos

ISLES.

Ge. 10:5. were i. of the Gent. divided
Es. 10 : 1. Ahas. laid tribute upon i.
Ps. 72 : 10. kings of i. bring presents
97 : 1. let mult. of the i. be glad
Is. 24:15. glorify ye the L. in the i.
40 : 15. taketh up i. as little thing
41 : 5. The i. saw it and feared
42 : 4. the i. shall wait for his law
10. i. and inhabit. sing his praise
49 : 1. Listen, O i. unto me, and
51 : 5. i. sh. wait upon me, 60 : 9.
66 : 19. i. afar not heard my fame
Je. 2 : 10. pass over i. of Chittim
25:22. kings of i. drink after them
31 : 10. declare it in i. afar [fall?
Eze. 26 : 15. sh. not i. shake at thy
18. i. trembled, i. sh. be troubled
27:3. merchant of peo. for many i.
6. ivory, bro-t out of i. of Chit.
7. blue and purple fr. i. of Elisha
15. many i. were merchandise
35. inhabit. of i. shall be astonish.
39 : 6. that dwell carelessly in i.
Da. 11:18. he sh. turn his face to i.
Zph. 2:11. sh. worship him, all the i.

ISMACHI'AH.

2 Ch. 31:13. Eliel and I. were over-

ISMAI'AH. [seers

1 Ch. 12:4. I. the Gibeonite mighty

IS'PAH.

1 Ch. 8 : 16. I. Joha sons of Beriah

IS'RAEL.

Ge. 32:28. name no more Jac. but I.
35:10. I. be thy name, 1 K. 18 : 31.
47 : 27. I. dwelt in the land of E.
29. time nigh I. must die
31. I. bowed upon bed's head
48:20. In thee shall I. bless, saying
49 : 24. thence is stone of I.
50 : 2. physicians embalmed I.
Ex. 4:22. I. my son | 17:11. I. prevail.
5 : 2. I obey his voice to let I. go
14 : 5. have let I. go from serving
25. Let us flee fr. I. for L. fighteth
30. L. saved I. that day fr. Egyp.
32 : 13. Remember Ab. and I. thy
Le. 24:10. son and man of I. strove
Nu. 10 : 29. L. spoken good conc. I.
36. Return unto many thous. of I.
20:14. saith thy bro. I. Let us pass
21 : 2. I vowed a vow unto Lord
17. I. sang song, Spring, O well
23:7. Balak, saying. Come defy I.
23. said of I. What God wrought
24 : 17. Sceptre shall rise out of I.
18. and I. shall do valiantly
25:8. Phinehas went aft. man of I.
De. 25 : 6. name be not put out of I.
De. 33:10. shall teach I. thy law, Jac.
28. I. then shall dwell in safety
Jos. 7:8. when I. turned bef. enem.
11. I. sinned | 16. brought I.
11:16. Joshua took mountain of I.
22:22. G. knoweth and I sh. know
24:31. I. served L. all days of Josh.
Ju. 1:28. to pass when I. was strong
2:22. That I may prove I., 3 : 1, 4.
5 : 9. My heart toward gov-s of I.
6 : 6. I. was greatly impoverished
14. save I., 15, 36, 37. | 7:2. I. vaunt
10 : 9. I. was sore distressed
16. was grieved for misery of I.
11 : 13. bec. I. took away my land
20 : 35. Lord smote Benj. before I.
1 S. 4 : 2. I. smitten, 10. | 17. I. fled
9 : 20. on whom is desire of I.
13 : 4. heard I. was had in abom.
15 : 29. strength of I. will not lie
17:45. the God of the armies of I.
2 S. 1 : 19. The beauty of I. is slain
5:2. that broughtest in I., 1 Ch. 11:2.
7 : 23. what one nation is like I.
11 : 11. ark, and I. abide in tents
19 : 8. I. fled ev. man to his tent
21:17. that quench not light of I.
23 : 1. sweet psalmist of I. said
1 K. 4 : 20. and I. many as the sand
25. I. dwelt safely, Je. 23 : 6.
9 : 7. I. sh. be a proverb am. peo.
11:25. abhorred I. | 12:19. I. rebell.
14 : 15. Lord shall smite I.
18 : 17. Art thou he troubleth I.?
2 K. 5:12. better than all waters of I.
10 : 32. L. began to cut I. short
14 : 12. was put to worse before I.
27. not blot out name of I.
17 : 6. carried I. away, 23.-23 : 27.
34. Jacob, whom he named I.
1 Ch. 11 : 10. word of the L. conc. I.
21 : 5. I. were a thousand thous.
29:18. God of I., 1 K. 18:36. 2 Ch. 6:
16.-30 : 6. Je. 31 : 1.
2 Ch. 9 : 8. bec. thy God loved I.
Ezr. 2 : 59. whether of I., Ne. 7:61.
3 : 11. his mercy endureth tow. I.
10:10. stra. wives to incr. trespass
Ps. 14:7. I. shall be glad, 53:6. [of I.
22:23. glorify him all ye seed of I.
25 : 22. Redeem I. O G. out of all
68 : 26. Bless ye L. fr. fount. of I.
78 : 59. G. heard, he abhorred I.
71. to feed I. his inheritance
80 : 1. Give ear, O Shepherd of I.
81 : 11. I. would none of me
13. O that my peo. I. had walked
83:4. I. may be no more in remem.
114:2. Jud. his sanct. I. his domin.
121:4. keepeth I. sh. neith. slumber
125:5. peace sh. be upon I., 128:6.
130 : 7. Let I. hope in L., 131 : 3.
8. shall redeem I. from iniquities
135:4. Lord hath chosen I. for his
136:11. bro-t I. out from am. them
14. made I. pass thro. midst of it
147 : 2. he gathereth outcasts of I.
149 : 2. Let I. rejoice in him that
Can. 3 : 7. men, of the valiant of I.
Is. 1 : 3. but I. doth not know
11:12. assemble outcasts of I., 56:8.
14 : 1. For L. will yet choose I.
19 : 24. shall I. be 3d with Egypt
25. Blessed be I. mine inheritance
27 : 6. I. shall blossom and bud
41 : 8. But thou I. art my servant
42 : 24. Who gave I. to robbers?
43:28. I have giv. I. to reproaches
44:5. surname hims. by name of I.
45 : 4. For I. mine elect, I
17. I shall be saved in Lord with
25. In Lord seed of I. be justified
48 : 1. are called by name of I.
49:5. Tho. I. be not gathered, I sh.
6. to restore preserved of I.
56:8. wh. gathereth outcasts of I.
63:16. tho. I. acknowledge us not
Je. 2 : 3. I. was holiness unto Lord
14. Is I. a serv.? | 3:23. salv. of I.
10 : 16. I. rod of his inheri., 51:19.
14 : 8. O L. hope of I. Sav., 17:13.
48 : 27. For was not I. a derision
49 : 1. Hath I. no sons? no heir?
2. I. shall be heir unto his heirs
50 : 17. I. is a scattered sheep
19. I will bring I. to his habita.
20. iniquity of I. be sought for
51 : 5. I. not been forsaken of God
La. 2 : 5. L. hath swallowed up I.
Eze. 11:10. judge you in bor. of I., 11.
13. wilt thou make full end of I.
37:28. know I the Lord do sanctify
44 : 10. when I. went astray [I.
Ho. 4 : 15. Tho. thou I. play harlot
16. I. slideth back as a heifer
5:3. I. not hid fr. me, I. defiled, 6:10.
5. pride of I. doth test., I. fall, 7:10.
8 : 2. I. sh cry unto me, My God
3. I. hath cast off that is good
8. I. is swall-d | 9 : 7. I. sh. know
14. I. hath forgotten his Maker
9:10. I found I. like grapes in wil.
10:1. I. is an empty vine | 8. sin of I.
6. I. be asha. of his own counsel
11:1. when I. a child, I loved him
8. how shall I deliver thee, I.!
12 : 12. I. kept sheep for a wife
Jo. 3 : 2. plead for my heritage I.
Am. 3 : 14. visit transgr-s of I.
7 : 11. I. be led captive, 17.
Mi. 1 : 15. Adullam the glory of I.
5:1. they sh. smite judge of I. [of I.
Mat. 10:23. not have gone ov. cities
Lu 1 : 54. hath holpen his serv. I.
2:25. waiting for consolation of I.
24 : 21. wh. sho. have redeemed I.
Jn. 3 : 10. Art thou a master of I.
Ac. 28 : 20. hope of I. I am bound
Ro. 9 : 27. Esaias crieth conc. I. (2)
31. I. which foll. law of righte.
10 : 19. I say, did not I. know?
11 : 7. I. hath not obtained what
1 Co. 10:18. Behold I. aft. the flesh
Ga. 6 : 16. peace upon I. of God
Ph. 3 : 5. of stock of I. of tribe of

Against IS'RAEL.

Nu. 21:1. Arad **a.** I. | 23. Sihon **a.** I.
23 : 23. nei. any divination **a.** I.
25 : 3. anger of the L. was kindled
a. I., 32 : 13. Ju. 2:14, 20.-3:8.-
10:7. 2 S. 24:1. 2 K. 13:3. Ps. 78:21.
Jos. 8 : 14. kings of Ca. **a.** I., 11:5.
24 : 9. Balak king of Moab **a.** I. [I
Ju. 3:12. Eglon **a.** I. | 6:2. Midian **a.**
11: 4. chil. of Ammon **a.** I., 5, 20
25. Balak, did he strive **a.** I.?
1 S. 4 : 2. Philis. put thems. **a.** I.,
7 : 7, 10.-31 : 1. 1 Ch. 10 : 1.
1 K. 20:26. Ben-hadad **a.** I., 2 K. 6:8.
2 K. 1 : 1. Then Moab rebelled **a.** I.
3 : 27. was great indignation **a.** I.
17 : 13. Yet the Lord testified **a.** I.
1 Ch. 21:1. And Satan stood up **a.** I.
2 Ch. 11 : 1. Rehob. went out **a.** I.
Je. 36:2. write words I have spo. **a.** I.
Am. 7:16. sayest, Prophesy not **a.** I.
Ro. 11:2. maketh intercession **a.** I.

All IS'RAEL. [**a.** I

Ex. 18 : 25. chose able men out of
Nu. 16:34. **a.** I. fled at cry of them
De. 13 : 11. **a.** I. shall fear, 21 : 21.
Jos. 7 : 25. **a.** I. stoned Achan
Ju. 8 : 27. **a.** I. went a whoring [I.
1 S. 2: 22. all th. his sons did to **a.**
3: 20. **a.** I. knew Sam. was proph.
4 : 1. word of Sam. came to **a.** I.
11:2. lay it for a reproach upon **a.** I
18: 16. **a.** I. and Jud. loved David
28 : 3. **a.** I. had lamented Samuel
2 S. 3: 12. to bring **a.** I. unto thee
37. **a.** I. underst-d it was not of Da.
12:12. I will do this thing bef. **a.** I.
14:25. in **a.** I. none so prais. as Abs.
16 : 21. **a.** I. hear thou art abhor.

2 S.17:10. a. I. kn. thy fa. is a mighty
18: 17. a. I. fled ev. one to tent
19:11. speech of a. I. is come to k.
1 K. 1: 20. eyes of a. I. upon thee
2:15. knowest a. I. set faces on me
3:28. a. I. heard of judgm. of Sol.
8: 62. king and a. I. offered sacri.
12:18. a. I. stoned Adoram he died
14: 13. a. I. shall mourn for him
18: 19. gather a. I unto Carmel
22:17. I saw a. I. scatt., 2 Ch. 18:16.
1 Ch. 11: 4. a. I. went to Jerus.
13:8. David and a. I. played bef. G.
15:28. a. I. brought up the ark
17: 6. wheresoever I walked with a. I.
29: 23. a. I. obeyed Solomon
2 Ch. 12: 1. a. I. forsook law of L.
13:4. said, Hear me, Jerob., and a. I.
15. G. smote Jeroboam and a. I.
28: 23. they were the ruin of a. I.
29:24. atonement for a. I., Ezr. 6:17.
31: 1. a. I. brake images [7: 73.
Ezr. 2: 70. a. I. dwelt in cities, Ne.
10: 5. made a. I. swear to do this
Ne. 12: 47. a. I. gave the portions
Da. 9:7. confusion of faces unto a. I.
11. a. I. have transgr. thy law
Mal. 4:4. Remem. law of Mo. for a. I.
Ro. 9: 6. not a. I. which are of I.
11: 26. so a. I. shall be saved.

Camp of IS'RAEL. [I.

Ex. 14:19. Angel wh. went bef. c. o.
20. a cloud bet. Egyp-s and c. o. I
Jos. 6: 18. lest make c. o. I. curse
23. they left them without c. o. I.
2 S. 1: 3. out of c. o. I. escaped
2 K. 3: 24. when came to c. o. I.
See CHILDREN, CONGREGATION, DAUGHTERS, ELDERS.

For IS'RAEL.

Ex. 18: 1. all G. had done f. I., 8.
Jos. 24:31. Ju. 2:7, 10. 1 K. 8:66.
Jos. 10: 14. Lord fought f. I., 42.
Ju. 6: 4. left no sustenance f. I.
1 S. 7: 9. Sam. cried unto L. f. I.
30: 25. Da. made it an ordin. f. I.
2 K. 14: 26. was not any helper f. I.
1 Ch. 6:49. make atonement f. I. as Moses coun-d, 22: 1. Ne. 10: 33.
Ps. 81: 4. this was statute f. I. law
Is. 46:13. salv. in Zion f. I. my glory
Zch. 12: 1. burden of word of L. f. I.
Ro. 10: 1. my prayer to G. f. I. is (2)

From IS'RAEL. [13.

Ex. 12: 15. be cut off f. I., Nu. 19:
Nu. 25: 4. that anger be turned f. I.
De. 17:12. evil f. I., 22:22. Ju. 20:13.
Ju. 21: 6. is one tribe cut off f. I.
1 S. 4: 21. glory is depar. f. I., 22.
7: 14. cities taken f. I. restored
17: 26. that taketh reproach f. I.
2 S. 24: 25. plague was stayed f. I.
Ne. 13: 3. separated f. I. the mult.
Is. 9: 14. L. will cut off f. I. head
Ho. 8: 6. For f. I. was it workman
See GOD, HOUSE.

See **HOLY one of Israel.**

In IS'RAEL.

Ge. 34: 7. had wrought folly i. I., De. 22:21. Jos. 7:15. Ju. 20:6, 10.
49:7. divide Jac., scatter them i. I.
Le. 20:2. strangers sojourn i. I., 22: 18. Eze. 14: 7. [-26: 2.
Nu. 1: 3. able to go to war i. I., 45.
16. heads of thousands i. I., 10:4.
8: 13. I hallowed all firstborn i. I.
18: 14. devoted i. I. sh. be thine
21. given tenth i. I. for inheri.
23: 21. nei. seen perverseness i. I.
De. 17:4. abom. wrought i. I., 22:21.
25: 7. unto brother a name i. I.
10. his name be called i. I., The ho.
34:10. not a proph. i. I. like Moses
Jos. 6: 25. Rahab dwelleth i. I. bec.
Ju. 5: 7. ceased i. I. until I Deborah arose a mother i. I.
Ju. 5:8. was a spear am. 40,000 i. I.?
11:39. custom i. I. to lament Jeph.
17:6. no king i. I., 18:1.-19:1.-21:25.
18: 19. priest unto family i. I.
21: 3. one tribe lacking i. I. (2)
Ru. 4: 7. manner in former times i. I. this was a testimony i. I.
14. name may be famous i. I.
1 S. 3: 11. I will do a thing i. I.
9:9. i. I. wh. man went to inquire
11: 13. wrought salv. i. I., 14: 45.
17: 25. make fa.'s house free i. I.
46. earth may know is a G. i. I.
18: 18. what is my fa.'s family i. I.
26:15. Abner, who is like thee i. I.?
2 S. 3: 38. a great man fallen i. I.
5: 2. broughtest i. I., 1 Ch. 11: 2.
13:12. no such thi ought to be i. I.
13. shalt be as one of fools i. I.
19: 22. any be put to death i. I.?
20: 19. I am peaceable i. I. thou seekest to destroy mother i. I.
21: 4. neither for us kill man i. I.
1 K. 14: 10. I will cut off him that is left i. I., 21: 21. 2 K. 9: 8.
18: 36. be known, thou art G. i. I.
19: 18. I have left me 7,000 i. I.
2 K. 1:3. bec. is not a God i. I., 6, 16.
5: 8. he shall kn. is a prophet i. I.
15. is no G. in the earth but i. I.
6:12. prophet i. I. telleth k. of Isr.
1 Ch. 12: 40. for there was joy i. I.
2 Ch. 7:18. not fail thee a ruler i. I.
24: 16. bec. he had done good i. I.
34: 21. inquire for them left i. I.
33. Josiah made all i. I. serve L.
35: 18. no passover like that i. I.
25. singing men made ordin. i. I.
Ezr. 10: 2. there is hope i. I. conc.
Ps. 76: 1. his name is great i. I.
78: 5. and he appointed law i. I.
Is. 8:18. for signs and wonders i. I.
44: 23. L. hath glorified hims. i. I.
Je. 29: 23. committed villany i. I.
32: 20. set signs and wonders i. I.
Eze. 12:23. it as a proverb i. I., 18:3.
39: 7. know I am Holy One i. I.
11. unto Gog a place of graves i. I.
44:28. sh. give them no poss-n i. I.
29. dedicated thing i. I. theirs
45: 8. In the land be his poss. i. I.
16. this oblation for prince i. I.
Ho. 13:1. Ephr. exalted himself i. I.
Mi. 5: 2. out of thee, ruler i. I.
Mal. 2: 11. abom. is committed i. I.
Mat. 8: 10. so gr. faith, not i. I., Lu.
9:33. It was never so seen i. I. [7:9.
Lu. 2: 34. for fall and rising i. I.
4: 25. many widows i. I. | 27. lepers i. I.
See KING, KINGS.

Land of IS'RAEL.

1 S. 13: 19. no smith in all l. o. I.
2 K. 5: 2. little maid out of l. o. I.
6: 23. bands of Syria no more into l. o. I. [in l. o. I.
1 Ch. 13: 2. let us send unto breth.
22:2. to gather the strangers in the l. o. I., 2 Ch. 2: 17.-30:25. [I.
2 Ch. 34:7. cut down idols thro. l. o.
Eze. 7: 2. saith Lord to l. o. I.
11: 17. I will give you the l. o. I.
12: 19. saith Lord of the l. o. I.
13: 9. nei. sh. enter l. o. I., 20:38.
20: 42. bring you into l. o. I., 37:12.
21:2. prophesy against the l. o. I.
25: 3. saidst, Aha, ag. the l. o. I.
6. rejoicedst with despite ag. l. o. I.
27:17. Jud. and l. o. I. thy merch.
38: 18. when Gog come ag. l. o. I.
19. be great shaking in l. o. I.
40: 2. in visions bro-t into l. o. I.
Mat. 2: 20. go into l. o. I. they dead
21. took child came into l. o. I.

Made IS'RAEL sin.

1 K. 14: 16. Jeroboam m. I. to s., 15:26, 30, 34.-16:19, 26.-22:52.
16:2. Baasha m. peo. I. to s., 13.
1 K. 21:22. Ahab provoked L., m. I. s.
2 K. 3:3. Jeroboam son of Nebat, who m. I. to s., 10:29, 31.-13: 2, 6, 11.-14:24.-15:9, 18, 24, 28.-23:15.

Men of IS'RAEL. [I.

Jos. 10:24. Jos. called for all m. o.
Ju 20:11. m. o. I. gathered ag. city
20. m. o. I. went | 22. encouraged
36. m. o. I. gave place to Benj.
1 S. 14: 24. m. o. I. were distressed
31: 1. m. o. I. fled from Philis.
2 S. 2:17. Abner beaten and m. o. I.
15: 13. hearts of m. o. I. aft. Abs.
16: 18. whom the m. o. I. choose
19:43. of Jud. fiercer than of m. o. I.
23: 9. m. o. I. were gone away
Ps. 78: 31. smote chosen m. o. I.
Is. 41: 14. Fear not, ye m. o. I.
Ac. 2:22. m. o. I. hear these words
3: 12. Ye m. o. I why marvel?
5: 35. Ye m. o. I. take heed to
13: 16. m. o. I. give audience
21: 28. Jews crying out, m. o. I. [help

O IS'RAEL.

Ex. 32: 4. These be thy gods, O I.
Nu. 24:5. goodly thy tab., O I. [12.
De. 4:1. hearken, O I., 27:9. Is. 48:
5:1. Hear, O I., 6:3, 4.-9:1.-20:3. Ps. 50:7.-81: 8. Is. 44:1. Mk. 12:29.
33: 29. Happy art thou, O I. [O. I.
Jos. 7: 13. accursed thing in thee,
2 S. 20: 1. said, ev. man to his tents, O I., 1 K. 12: 16. 2 Ch. 10: 16.
1 K. 12: 28. behold thy gods, O I.
Ps. 115:9. O I., trust thou in the L.
Is. 40: 27. Why speakest thou, O I.
43: 1. O I. fear not, Je. 30:10. | 46: 22. been weary of me, O I. [27.
44:21. Remem. these, O I. (2), 49:3.
Je. 4: 1. if return, O I., Ho. 14: 1.
Eze. 13: 4. O I. thy proph. are like
Ho. 9: 1. Rejoice not, O I. for joy
10:9. O I. thou hast sinned fr. days
13:9. O I. thou hast destro-d thyself
Am. 4: 12. prepare to meet thy G.,
Zph. 3:14. shout, O I., be glad [O I.

Over IS'RAEL.

Ju. 9: 22. Abimelech reigned o. I.
14: 4. Philis. had dominion o. I.
1 S. 8: 1. made his sons judges o. I.
13: 1. had reigned 2 y-rs o. I. [I.
15: 26. rejected thee fr. being k. o.
2 S. 2: 10. Ish-bosheth Saul's son reigned o. I. [6:21. 1 Ch. 11:3.
3: 10. David o. I., 5: 2, 3, 12, 17.-
7: 26. L. of hosts is the God o. I.
1 K. 1:34. Sol. o. I. | 11:37. Jeroboam
14: 14. L. shall raise up k. o. I.
15: 25. Nadab o. I. | 16: 8. Elah
16: 16. Omri o. I. | 29. Ahab
22: 51. Ahaziah reigned o. I.
2 K. 3: 1. Jehoram o. I.
9: 3. Jehu, o. I., 6, 12.-10: 36.
13:1. Jehoahaz o. I. | 10. Jehoash
15: 8. Zechariah o. I. | 17. Menahem
23. Pekahiah o. I. | 17:1. Hoshea
1 Ch. 26:29. for outw-d business o. I.
29: 30. times th. went o. I. writ.
Ps. 68:34. G., his excellency is o. I.
Ec. 1: 12. I preacher was k. o. I.

IS'RAEL with people.

Nu. 21:6. much p. of I. died by serp.
De. 21: 8. Be merciful to thy p. I.
26: 15. Look down bless thy p. I.
Jos. 8: 33. should bless the p. of I.
Ju. 11:23. drave Amorites bef. p. I.
1 S. 2: 29. offerings of I. my p. [I.
9:16. anoint Saul capt. over my p.
27: 12. p. I. utterly to abhor him
2 S. 3:18. by Da. will save my p. I.
5:2. to feed p. I., 7: 7. 1 Ch. 11:2.
12. exalted kingd. for p. I.'s sake
7:10. a place for my p. I., 1 Ch. 17:9.
24. confirmed to thyself thy p. I.
1 K. 6:13. will not forsake p. I. [24.
8:33. when p. I. be smit., 2 Ch. 6: 38. what prayer by thy p. I.

1 K. 8:43. fear thee, as do thy p. I.
56. L. hath given rest to p. I. [I.
1 Ch. 14:2. lifted up, bec. of his p.
17:7. ruler over p. I., 2 Ch. 6:5.
21. what one nation is like p. I.
22. p. I. didst thou make thine
2 Ch. 7:10. goodn. shewed I. his p.
31:8. they blessed L. and his p. I.
35:3. serve now G. and his p. I.
Ezr. 7:13. of p. of I. minded to go up
9:1. p. of I. not separated thems.
Ps. 135:12. a heritage unto I. his p.
Is. 10:22. tho. thy p. I. be as sand
Je. 7:12. for wickedn. of my p. I.
12:14. caused my p. I. to inherit
23:13. caused my p. I. to err
30:3. captivity of my p. I., Am. 9:14.
Eze. 25:14. veng. upon Edom by my
36:8. yield fruit to my p. I. [p. I.
12. cause p. I. to walk upon you
38:14. when p. I. dwelleth safely
16. shalt come up ag. my p. I.
Da. 9:20. confessing sin of my p. I.
Am. 7:15. L. said, prophesy unto p. I.
8:2. end is come upon my p. I.
Mat. 2:6. a Gov. that sh. rule my p. I.
Lu. 2:32. the glory of thy p. I. [Jes.
Ac. 4:27. p. of I. were gathered ag-t
13:17. G. of p. I. chose our fath-s
See **PEOPLE** with **Israel.**

Princes of IS'RAEL.

Nu. 1:44. p. o. I. being 12 men
7:2. p. o. I. offered at setting up of tabernacle, 84.
1 Ch. 22:17. Da. com-d p. o. I. to help
23:2. Da. assembled p. o. I., 28:1.
2 Ch. 12:6. p. o. I. humbled thems.
21:4. Jehoram slew of p. o. I.
Eze. 19:1. lamentation for p. o. I
21:12. sword sh. be upon all p. o. I.
22:6. p. o. I. in thee to shed blood
45:9. Let it suffice you, O p. o. I.

To or unto IS'RAEL.

Ge. 46:2. G. spake u. I. in visions
49:2. hearken u. I. your father
Ex 18:9. goodness L. hath done t. I.
Jos. 11:23. for inheritance u. I., 21:43.
23:1. Lord had given rest u. I. fr.
Ju. 8:35. goodness shewed u. I.
1 S. 15:2. what Amalek did t. I.
2 S. 3:19. all that seemed good t. I.
1 K. 11:25. Rezon adversary t. I.
1 Ch. 16:17. confirmed the same t. I. for an everl. cov., Ps. 105:10.
21:3. why cause of trespass t. I.?
22:9. I will give quietness t. I.
2 Ch. 2:4. ordinance for ever t. I.
Ezr. 7:11. Ezr. scribe of statutes t. I.
Ne. 8:1. law, Lord had com-d t. I.
Ps. 73:1. Truly God is good t. I.
135:12. a heritage u. I., 136:22.
147:19. L. sheweth judgments u. I.
Is. 11:16. as it was t. I. in the day
Je. 2:31. I been a wilderness u. I.
31:9. I am a father t. I. Ephr. is
Ho. 14:5. I will be as the dew u. I.
Mi 3:8. power to declare t. I. his sin
Mal. 1:1. burden of the Lord t. I.
Lu. 1:80. day of his shewing u. I.
Jn. 1:31. sho. be made manifest t. I.
Ac. 1:6. wilt restore kingd. t. I.?
5:31. exalted to give repentance t. I.
13:23. raised u. I. a Saviour
Ro. 10:21. t. I. he saith, All day long
11:25. blindness is happened t. I.

Tribes of IS'RAEL.

Ge. 49:16. shall judge as one of t. o. I.
28. All these are the twelve t. o. I.
Ex. 24:4. 12 pillars acc. to 12 t. o. I.
Nu. 31:4. 1000 thro-t t. o. I. to war
36:3. if married to any of t. o. I.
9. ev. one of t. o. I. keep to his own
De. 29:21. separate out of t. o. I.
33:5. when the t. o. I. were gathered
Jos. 3:12. take 12 men out of t. o. I.
4:5. stones acc. unto number of t.
7:16. Josh. brought I. by t. [o. I., 8.
Jos. 12:7. land Josh. gave unto t. o.
19:51. heads of t. o. I. divided [I.
22:14. princes through t. o. I. sent
24:1. Josh. gathered t. o. I. to Shech.
Ju. 18:1. of Dan not among t. o. I.
20:2. chief of t. o. I. presented bef. G.
10. ten men of a hund. out of t. o. I
21:5. Who am. t. o. I. came not up, 8.
15. Lord made breach in t. o. I.
1 S. 2:28. choose him out of t. o. I.?
9:21. I am of smallest of t. o. I.
10:20. Sam. caused t. o. I. to come
15:17. wast made head of t. o. I.?
2 S. 5:1. came all t. o. I. to David
7:7. spake I a word with t. o. I.?
15:2. Thy serv. is of one of t. o. I.
10. Absalom sent spies thro. t. o. I
19:9. people at strife thro. t. o. I.
24:2. go thro. t. o. I. and number
1 K. 8:16. chose no city out of t. o. I. to build house in, 2 Ch. 6:5.
11:32. chosen Jerus. out of t. o. I., 14:21. 2 K. 21:7. 2 Ch. 12:13.-33:7. [I.
2 Ch. 11:16. after them out of t. o.
Ezr. 6:17. off-d 12 goats acc. to t. o. I.
Ps. 78:55. t. o. I. dwell in tents
Eze. 37:19. take t. o. I. put with Jud.
47:13. acc. to the 12 t. o. I., 21, 22.
48:19. serve city out of t. o. I.
31. gates be aft. names of t. o. I.
Ho. 5:9. am. t. o. I. I made known
Zch. 9:1. eyes of t. o. I. be tow. L.
Mat. 19:28. judging 12 t. o. I., Lu. 22:30. [o. I
Re. 21:12. gates with names of 12 t.

With IS'RAEL.

Ex. 17:8. Amalek fought w. I.
34:27. I made a cov. w. thee and I.
De. 18:1. Levites no inherit. w. I.
33:21. Gad executed judgm-s w. I.
Jos. 9:2. k-s of Canaan fought w. I.
10:1. inhabi. of Gibeon peace w. I.
1 S. 13:5. Philis. gathered to fight w. I., 28:1. 2 S. 21:15.
2 S. 10:19. Syrians made peace w. I.
2 K. 17:18. Lord very angry w. I.
2 Ch. 25:7. for Lord is not w. I.
Mi. 6:2. for the Lord will plead w. I.

IS'RAELITE.

Nu. 25:14. I. that was slain, Zimri
2 S. 17:25. Amasa son of Ithra an I.
Jn. 1:47. Behold an I. indeed
Ro. 11:1. I also am an I. of seed

IS'RAELITES.

Ex. 9:7. not one of cattle of I. dead
Le. 23:42. I. born sh. dwell in booths
Jos. 3:17. I. passed over on dry gr.
13:6. only divide it by lot unto I. for
Ju. 20:21. Benj-s destroyed of I.
1 S. 2:14. priests' serv-ts did unto I.
13:20. I. to Philis. to sharpen axe
14:21. Hebr. turned to be with I.
25:1. all the I. lamented Samuel
29:1. I. pitched by a fountain in
2 S. 4:1. I. troubl. at Abner's death
2 K. 3:24. I. smote Moabites
7:13. they are as all multi. of I.
1 Ch. 9:2. first inhabi. were the I.
Ro. 9:4. are I. to whom pertaineth
2 Co. 11:22. Are they I.? so am I

IS'RAELITISH.

Le. 24:10. the son of an I. woman
11. I. woman's son blasphemed

IS'SACHAR.

Ge. 30:18. Leah called his name I.
35:23. Leah's son I. | 46:13. sons of
49:14. I. is strong ass [I., 1 Ch. 7:1.
Ex. 1:3. Israel's sons, I., 1 Ch. 2:1.
Nu. 1:8. princes of I., 2:5.-7:18.
De. 27:12. I shall stand to bless
33:18. Rejoice, I. in thy tents
Jos. 17:10. they met together in I.
11. Manasseh had in I. and Asher
Ju. 5:15. princes of I. with Debo.
10:1. Tola of I. arose to defend
1 K. 4:17. Jehosh. an officer in I.
1 K. 15:27. Abijah of the house of I.
1 Ch. 12:40. they nigh unto I. bro-t
26:5. I. 7th son of Obed-edom [br.
27:18. captain of I. Omri the son
2 Ch. 30:18. many of I. not cleansed
Eze. 48:25. by border of Sim., I. a
26. by the border of I. Zebulun
33. south side, one gate of I. one

Tribe of IS'SACHAR.

Nu. 1:29. were numbered of t. o. I.
2:5. pitch next Jud. shall be t. o. I.
10:15. over t. o. I. was Nethaneel
13:7. of t. o. I. to spy land, Igal
34:26. prince of the t. o. I. Paltiel
Jos. 19:23. inheritance of t. o. I.
21:6 Gershon had by lot out of t. o. I., 28. 1 Ch. 6:62, 72.
Re. 7:7. of t. o. I. sealed 12,000.

ISSH'IAH.

1 Ch. 21:24. the first was I., 25.

ISSUE, S.

Ge 48:6. i. which thou begettest
Le. 12:7. i. of her blood, 15:25. Mat. 9:20. Mk. 5:25. Lu. 8:43, 44.
15:2. any man hath a running i., 3, 4, 6, 7, 8, 9, 11, 12, 13, 15, 32.-22:4. Nu. 5:2. [30.
19. if woman have an i., 25, 26, 28,
2 S. 3:29. fr. ho. of Joab, one an i.
Ps 68:20. unto G. belong i-s fr. death
Pr. 4:23. heart, for out of it i-s of life
Is. 22:24. sh. hang upon him the i.
Eze. 23:20. i. is like the i. of horses
Mat. 22:25. having no i. left wife

ISSUE. [Verb.]

2 K. 20:18. thy sons that i., Is. 39:7.
Eze. 47:8. these waters i. tow. east

ISSUED.

Jos 8:22. other i. out of the city
Jb. 38:8. as if it i. out of the womb
Eze. 47:1. waters i. fr. threshold
12. bec. waters i. out of sanct-y
Da. 7:10. fiery stream i. and came
Re. 9:17. out of mouths i. fire, 18.

IS'UAH. See ISHUAH.

IS'UI. See JESUI.

IT.

Pr. 4:23. Keep heart, for out of i.
Is. 6:13. in i. sh. be a tenth, and i.
7:7. saith L., i. shall not stand
11:10. to i. shall Gentiles seek
30:21. This is the way, walk in i.
51:9. Art thou i. cut Rahab?
10. Art thou i. hath dried sea?
See BETTER, GOOD, WRITTEN.

ITSELF.

Ge. 1:11. tree, whose seed is in i., 12.
Le. 7:24. beast that dieth of i. not eat, 17:15.-22:8. De. 14:21.
18:25. land i. vomiteth out inhabi.
25:11. groweth of i., Is 37:30.
1 K. 7:34. undersetters of base i.
Jb. 10:22. as darkness i. [to i.
Ps. 41:6. his heart gathereth iniq.
68:8. even Sinai i. was moved
Pr. 18:2. heart may discover i.
23:31. wine, when it moveth i.
27:16. ointment wh. bewrayeth i.
25. the tender grass sheweth i.
Is. 10:15. Sh. axe boast i. ag. him heweth, as if rod shake i. (4)
55:2. soul delight i. in fatness
60:20. nei. thy moon withdraw i.
Je. 31:24 dwell in Jud i. husbandm.
Eze. 1:4. a fire unfolding i. [44:31.
4:14. not eaten what dieth of i.,
17:14. that it might not lift i. up
29:15 nei. exalt i. above nations
Da. 7:5. raised up i. on one side
Mat. 6:34. thought for things of i.
12:25. Ev. kingdom divided ag. i. is bro-t, Mk. 3:24, 25. Lu. 11:17.
Jn. 15:4. branch can-t bear fruit of
20:7. wrapped in place by i. [i.
21:25. world i. not contain books
Ro. 8:16. Spirit i. beareth witness
21. creature i. shall be delivered

Ro. 8 : 26. Spirit i. maketh intercession for us with groanings
14 : 14. there is nothing uncl. of i.
1 Co.11:14.Doth not nature i. teach [you
13:4. charity vaunteth not i.
5. charity not behave i. unseemly
2 Co.10:5.ev. thing that exalteth i.
Ep. 4 : 16. edifying of i. in love
He 9 : 24. C. is ent-d into heaven i.
3 Jn.12.hath good report of truth i.

ITAL'IAN.

Ac. 10:1. a centurion of the I. band

IT'ALY.

Ac.18:2.certain Jew lately come fr.I.
27:1. determined th. we sail into I.
He. 13 : 24. they of I. salute you

ITCH.

De. 28: 27. L. will smite thee with i.

ITCHING.

2 Ti. 4: 3. heap teachers hav-g i. ears

ITH'AI = IT'TAI. [I.

1 Ch. 11: 31. valiant men of armies,

ITH'AMAR.

Ex. 6: 23. Aaron's sons, Eleazar and I., 28 : 1. Le. 10 : 6, 12, 16. Nu. 3 : 2.-4 : 33 -26 : 60. 1 Ch. 6 : 3.-24 : 1.
38 : 21. as counted by hand of I.
Nu. 3: 4. I. ministered, 1 Ch. 24 : 2.
4: 28. charge und. hand of I., 7 : 8.
1 Ch. 24 : 3. Ahimelech of sons of I.
4. eight chief men am. sons of I.,
6. one taken for I. [5.
Ezr. 8 : 2. sons of I. Dan. went up

ITH'IEL.

Ne. 11: 7. sons of I., son of Jesaiah
Pr. 30: 1. men spake unto I., even I.

ITH'MAH. [Moabite

1 Ch. 11: 46. valiant men I. the

ITH'NAN.

Jos. 15 : 23. cities of Jud., Hazor I.

ITH'RA = JETHER.

2 S. 17 : 25. Amasa son of I. Israelite, 1 K. 2 : 5, 32. 1 Ch. 2 : 17.

ITH'RAN. [1 : 41.

Ge. 36 : 26. chil. of Dishon, I., 1 Ch.
1 Ch. 7: 37. sons of Zophah; Suah, I.

ITH'REAM. [Ch.3:3.

2 S. 3: 5. I. by Eglah, Da's wife, 1

ITH'RITE, S. [11 : 40.

2 S. 23: 38. Ira I., Gareb I., 1 Ch.
1 Ch.2:53.families of Kirjath-je., I-s

IT'TAH-KA'ZIN.

Jos. 19 : 13. along on the east to I.

IT'TAI = ITH'AI.

2 S. 15: 19. said K. to I., Gittite, Whf. goest | 19, 21, 22.-18 : 2, 5, 12.-23 : 29.

ITURE'A.

Lu. 3 : 1. Philip, tetrarch of I.

I'VAH = A'VA.

2 K. 18 : 34. Where gods of Hena and I.? | 2 K. 17 : † 24.
19 : 13. Where king of I.? Is.37:13.

IVORY. [9 : 17.

1 K. 10: 18. made throne of i., 2 Ch.
22. bringing gold, i., 2 Ch. 9 : 21.
22: 39. i. house wh. Ahab made
Ps. 45 : 8. out of the i. palaces
•Can. 5 : 14. his belly is as bright i.
7 : 4. Thy neck is as a tower of i.
Eze. 27 : 6. made thy benches of i.
15. brought for present horns of i.
Am. 3 : 15. houses of i. shall perish
6 : 4. lie upon beds of i. and stretch
Re. 18 : 12. no man buyeth vessels [of i.

IZ'EHAR = IZ'HAR.

Ex. 6 : 18. sons of Kohath, I., Nu. 3 : 19.-16: 1. 1 Ch. 6 : 2, 18, 38. -23 : 12. [18.
21. sons of I., Korah, 1 Ch. 23 :

IZ'EHARITES.

Nu. 3 : 27. of Kohath fam. of I.

IZ'HARITES. [23,29.

1 Ch. 24 : 22. Of I. Shelomoth—26 :

IZ'RAHIAH. [I.

1 Ch. 7 : 3. sons of Uzzi; I. sons of

IZ'RAHITE. [the I.

1 Ch. 27 : 8. fifth capt. Shamhuth

IZ'RI = ZE'RI. [3.

1 Ch. 25 : 11. fourth lot came for I.

J.

JA'AKAN. [J.

De. 10 : 6. from Beeroth of chil. of

JAAK'OBAH.

1 Ch. 4 : 36. J. and Ziza were princes

JAA'LA = JAA'LAH.

Eze. 2: 56. chil of J.Neth., Ne. 7: 58.

JAA'LAM.

Ge. 36 : 5. Aholibamah bare J. [35.
14. duke Jeush, duke J., 1 Ch. 1:

JA'ANAI. [Bashan

1 Ch. 5 : 12. J. Shaphat dwelt in

JA'ARE-OR'EGIM.

2 S. 21: 19. Elhanan, son of J. slew

JA'ASAU. [bro. of

Ezr. 10 : 37. of sons of Bani, Uel, J.

JAA'SIEL. [ner

1 Ch. 27 : 21. of Benj. J. son of Ab-

JAAZANI'AH.

2 K. 25 : 23 J. came to Gedaliah
Je. 35 : 3. J. of the Rechabites
Eze. 8 : 11. J. stood with his censer
11 : 1. J. and Pelatiah princes of

JA'AZER = JAZER. [35.

Nu. 21 : 32. sent to spy out J. | 32:

JAAZI'AH.

1 Ch. 24 : 26 sons of J.; Beno, 27.

JAA'ZIEL.

1 Ch.15:18.breth. of second deg., J.,

JA'BAL. [† 20.

Ge.4:20.J.father of such as in tents

JAB'BOK.

Ge. 32:22. Jacob passed over J. [22.
Nu.21:24.fr.Arnon untoJ.,Ju.11:13,
De. 2 : 37. camest not unto river J.
3 : 16. I gave Gad border unto J.
Jos. 12 : 2. Sihon ruled to river J.

JA'BESH. [Person, place.]

1 S. 11 : 1. men of J. said Make | 3.
5. told Saul tidings of men of J.
9. shewed to the men of J., 10.
31 : 12. to J. burned body of Saul
13.buried bones at J., 1 Ch.10:12.
2 K. 15 : 10. the son of J. conspired
13. the son of J. began to reign
14. smote Shallum the son of J.

JA'BESH-GIL'EAD.

Ju. 21 : 8. came none from J., 9.
10. Go and smite inhabitants of J.
12. found 400 young virgins of J.
14. gave Benj. wives of wom. of J.
1 S.11: 1.Nahash encamped ag. J.,9.
31 : 11. inhabit-s of J. heard what Philis. had done, 1 Ch. 10 : 11.
2 S. 2 : 4. men of J. buried Saul | 5.
21: 12. bones of Saul from men of J.

JA'BEZ. [Person, place.]

1 Ch. 2 : 55. scribes who dwelt at J.
4 : 9. J. more honorable than
10. J. called on G. of Isr., saying

JA'BIN.

Jos.11:1. when J. k. of Hazor heard
Ju. 4 : 2. sold them into hand of J.
17.was peace bet. J. and Heber,7.
23. God subdued that day, J.
24. hand of Isr. prevailed ag. J.
Ps. 83 : 9. Do unto them as unto J.

JAB'NEEL.

Jos. 15 : 11. border unto J., 19 : 33.

JAB'NEH.

2 Ch. 26 : 6. brake down wall of J.

JA'CHAN.

1 Ch. 5 : 13. breth. were Jorai, J.

JA'CHIN, ITES.

Ge.46:10.sons of Simeon,J.,Ex.6:15.
Nu. 26 : 12. of J. family of J-s
1 K.7:21. called pillar J., 2 Ch.3:17.
1 Ch.9:10.priests, J.,24:17.Ne.11:10.

JACINTH.

Re. 9 : 17. having breastplates of j.
Re. 21 : 20. 11th a j.; 12th amethyst

JA'COB.

Ge. 25 : 26. was called J. | 27. J. was a plain man [Esau pottage
29. J. sod pottage | 34. J. gave
27 : 19. J. said unto fa. I am Esau
22. voice is J. | 30. J. was gone
36. Is not he rightly named J.
41. Esau hated J. | 46. J. a wife
28 : 5. Isaac sent J. | 7. J. obeyed
16. J. awaked | 20. J. vowed
29:10. J. saw Rachel dau. of Laban
20. J. served 7 years for Rachel
28. J did so, fulfilled her week
30:1.Ra. saw she bare J.no child'n
16. J. came out of field in eve.
37. J. took rods of green poplar
42. feeble Laban's, stronger J.'s
31 :1. J. taken all was our father's
20. J. stole unawares to Laban
45. speak not J. good or bad
53. J. sware by fear of his father
32 : 3. J. sent before him to Esau
4. J. saith thus | 7. J. afraid
18 shalt say,They be thy serv.J.'s
24.J.alone, there wrestled [35:10.
28. name no more J. but Israel,
30 J. called place Peniel
33 : 1. J. looked, and Esau came
17. J. to Succoth | 18. to Shalem
34 :5. J. held his peace until they
7. sons of J. 34:25.-35:26.-49:1,2. 1 K. 18:31. Ps. 77:15. [Beth el
35:6. J. to Luz | 15. J. called place
37 : 2. These are generations of J.
34 J. rent his clothes, put sackcl.
45 : 26. J.'s heart fainted, for he
46 : 6. J. and all his came into E., Jos. 24 : 4. 1 S. 12: 8 Ac. 7:15.
26. all that came with J. were 66
47:10. J.blessed Pha. | 28.age of J.
49:24. hands of mighty G of J.
Ex. 2:24. his cov. with J., Le.26:42.
3.6. the God of J., 15, 16.-4:5 2 S. 23:1. Ps. 20 : 1 -46:7, 11.-75:9 - 76:6.-81:1,4.-84:8.-94:7.-114:7. 132 : 2, 5.-146 : 5. Is. 2 : 3. Mi. 4: 2. Mat. 22:32. Mk. 12:26. Lu.20: 37. Ac. 3 : 13 -7 : 32, 46.
Nu. 23 : 7 curse me J. defy Israel
10. Who can count dust of J.
23. is no enchantment ag. J. it be said of J., What hath God
24:17. shall come a Star out of J.
19. Out of J. he that have domin.
De. 32:9. J. is lot of his inheritance
33:10. They sh. teach J. thy judg.
28. fount. of J. upon land of corn
Jos 24:32. ground J. bought of
1 Ch. 16 13. Isr. his serv. ye chil. of J his chosen, Ps. 105 : 6.
Ps. 14:7. J. shall rejoice, 53 : 6
22:23. all ye seed of J. glorify him
44:4.O God,com. deliverances for J.
47:4. of J. whom he loved, Na.2:2
78:21. a fire was kindled against J.
71. he brought him to feed J.
79 : 7. for they have devoured J.
85 : 1. hast bro-t back captiv. of J.
87:2.Zion more than dwellings of J.
105:23.J. sojourned in land of Ham
135 : 4. Lord hath chosen J. [G.
Is. 10:21. remn. of J. shall ret. unto
14 : 1. Lord will have mercy on J.
17:4. glory of J. shall be made thin
27:6. that come of J. to take root
9. By this iniq. of J. be purged
29 : 23. sh. sanctify Holy One of J
41 : 8. J. whom I have chosen
14. Fear not, thou worm J. and
42 : 24. Who gave J. for a spoil?
43: 28. I have given J. to the curse
44 : 5. another shall call himself J.
23. L. hath redeemed J., Je.31:11.
45:4. For J. sake, I called thee
48:20.L. hath redeemed his serv.J.
49 : 5. that formed me to bring J

Is.49:6. serv. to raise up tribes of J.
26. the Mighty One of J., 60: 16.
58: 14. feed with heritage of J.
66: 9. I will bring a seed out of J.
Je. 10:16. The portion of J., 51:19.
25. for they have eaten up J.
30: 7. it is the time of J.'s trouble
10. fear thou not, O my serv. J.
18. again captiv. of J., Eze. 39:25.
31:7. Sing with gladness for J. ⌈J.
33:26. Then will I cast away seed of
46: 27. J. shall return to be in rest
La. 1: 17. L. hath com. concern. J.
2: 2. swallowed inhabitants of J.
3. he burned against J. like fire
Ho. 10: 11. J. shall break his clods
12: 2. I will punish J. | 12. J. fled
Am. 6: 8. I abhor excellency of J.
7: 2. by whom shall J. arise? 5.
8: 7. L. hath sworn by excel. of J.
Ob. 10. For violence against bro. J.
Mi. 1: 5. for transgr. of J. is this
3: 1. I said, Hear, O heads of J.
5: 8. remn. of J. sh. be am. Gent.
Mal. 1: 2. was not Esau J. brother? yet I loved J.
3:6. ye sons of J. are not consumed
Mat. 1: 2. Isaac begat J., Lu. 3:34.
15. Matthan begat J., 16. ⌊Ac. 7:8.
8: 11. sh. sit down with Ab. and J.
Lu. 13:28. when ye see J. in kingd.
Jn. 4: 6. Now J.'s well was there
12. Art thou greater than fa. J.
Ac. 7: 14. Joseph called his fa. J.
Ro. 9: 13. J. have I loved, Esau
11: 26. turn ungodliness from J.
He. 11: 9. dwelling in taber. wi. J.
20. Isaac blessed J. | 21. J. blessed
See **HOUSE of Jacob.**

In JA'COB.

Ge. 49: 7. I will divide them i. J.
Nu. 23: 21. not beheld iniq. i. J.
Ps. 59: 13. know God ruleth i. J.
78: 5. he establish. a testim. i. J.
99: 4. thou executest judgm. i. J.
Is. 59: 20. that turn fr. transg. i. J.

O JA'COB. ⌈J.!

Nu. 24: 5. How goodly thy tents, O
Ps. 24: 6. that seek thy face, O J.
Is. 40: 27. sayest, O J. my way is
43: 1. that created thee, O J. ⌊hid?
22. not called upon thee O J.
44: 1. Yet hear O J. ⌈27, 28.
2. Fear not, O J., Je. 30:10.–46:
21. remem. these, O J. my serv.
48: 12. Hearken, O J.
Mi. 2: 12. I will assemble, O J. all

To or unto JA'COB.

Ge. 31:24. not t. J. good or bad, 29.
35: 9. God appeared u. J. and bl.
50:24. land he sware to give t. J., Ex. 6:8.–33: 1. Nu. 32: 11. De. 1:8.–6:10.–29:13.–30: 20.–34: 4. Eze. 28: 25.–37: 25.
1 Ch. 16: 17. hath confirmed same t. J. for a law, Ps. 105: 10.
Ps. 147:19. he shewed his word u. J.
Is. 9:8. the Lord sent a word u. J.
Mi. 3:8 to declare u. J. his transg.
7: 20. wilt perform truth t. J. and ⌊sons of J.

JA'DA.

1 Ch. 2: 28. sons of Onan, J. | 32.

JA'DAU.

Ezr. 10: 43. Of sons of Nebo; J.

JAD'DUA.

Ne. 10: 21. chief of peo.; Zadok, J.,
12: 11. Jona. begat J. ⌊Ne. 12:22.

JA'DON.

Ne. 3: 7. and next repaired J.

JA'EL. ⌈18.

Ju. 4: 17. Sisera fled to tent of J.,
21. J. took a nail of the tent and
22. J. came out to meet Barak
5: 6. in days of J. the highways
24. blessed above women shall J.

JA'GUR.

Jos. 15: 21. utterm. cities Eder, J.

JAH.

Ps. 68: 4. extol him by his name J.

JA'HATH.

1 Ch. 4: 2. begat J. J. begat | 6:20, 43.–23:10.–24:22. ⌈34:12.
23: 11. and J. was the chief, 2 Ch.

JA'HAZ, JAHA'ZA, JAHA'ZAH, JAH'ZAH.

Nu. 21:23. Sihon gath. peo. fought at J-z, De. 2: 32. Ju. 11: 20.
Jos. 13: 18. cities in the plains J-a
21: 36. J-h given to the Levites
1 Ch. 6: 78. J-h with her suburbs
Is. 15: 4. voice be heard unto J-z
Je. 48:21. judgm. is come upon J-h
34. unto J-z uttered their voice

JAHAZI'AH.

Ezr. 10: 15. Jona. and J. were em- ⌊ployed

JAHA'ZIEL.

1 Ch. 12:4. come to Da. at Ziklag J.
16: 6. Banaiah and J. the priests
23: 19. son of Hebron J., 24: 23.
2 Ch. 20: 14. upon J. Spi. of L. |

JAH'DAI. ⌊Ezr. 8:5.

1 Ch. 2: 47. sons of J. Regem and

JAH'DIEL.

1 Ch. 5: 24. and J. mighty men of ⌊valour

JAH'DO.

1 Ch. 5: 14. Jeshishai son of J.

JAH'LEEL, ITES.

Ge. 46: 14. sons of Zebulon J.
Nu. 26: 26. of J. family of J-s

JAH'MAI. See TOLA.

JAH'ZEEL, ITES.

Ge. 46:24. sons of Naph. J. Shillem
Nu. 26: 48. of J. the fam. of J-s

JAH'ZERAH.

1 Ch. 9: 12. Adiel son of J. son of

JAH'ZIEL = JAH'ZEEL.

1 Ch. 7: 13. sons of Naphtali; J.

JAI'LER.

Ac. 16:23. charging J. to keep them

JA'IR.

Nu. 32: 41. J. took towns, De. 3:14.
Jos. 13: 30. 1 K. 4: 13 1 Ch. 2:23.
Ju. 10: 3. J. judged Israel 22 years
5. J. died | 1 Ch. 2: 22. begat J.
1 Ch. 20: 5. son of J. slew Lahmi
Es. 2: 5. Mordecai the son of J.

JA'IRITE.

2 S. 20: 26. Ira J. was chief ruler

JA'IRUS. ⌈41.

Mk. 5: 22. J. ruler of syna., Lu. 8:

JA'KAN = A'KAN.

1 Ch. 1:42. sons of Ezer; Zavan, J.

JA'KEH. See AGUR.

JA'KIM. ⌈12.

1 Ch. 8: 19. J. Zichri heads of | 24:

JA'LON.

1 Ch. 4: 17. sons of Ezr., Epher, J.

JAM'BRES.

2 Ti. 3: 8. Jannes and J. withstood

JAMES. ⌈1: 19.

Mat. 4: 21. saw two breth. J., Mk.
10:2. J. son of Zebe., Mk. 3:17. ⌈13.
3. J. son of Alpheus, Mk 3:18. Ac. 1:
13:55. his breth. J. and Joses, Mk. 6:3
17:1. Jesus taketh Pe. J. and Jn., Mk. 5: 37.–9:2.–14:33. Lu. 8:51.
27: 56. Mary mother of J. and Joses, Mk. 15:40–16:1. Lu. 24:10.
Mk. 10: 41. much displeased wi. J.
13: 3. Pe., J. and John asked him
Lu. 5: 10. J. was aston. at fishes
Ac. 1:13. where abode both Peter, J.
12: 2. Herod killed J. bro. of John
17. Peter said, shew these to J.
15: 13. J. ans., Hearken unto me
21: 18. Paul went with us unto J.
1 Co. 15:7. after that was seen of J.
Ga. 1: 19. I saw none, save J. the
2: 9. J. perceived grace given me
12. bef. certain came fr. J. did eat
Ja. 1: 1. J. a serv. of G. and L. J.

JA'MIN, ITES. ⌈Ch. 4:24

Ge. 46: 10. sons of Sim.; J., Ex. 6: 15. 1
Nu. 26: 12. of J. fam. of J-s
Ne. 8: 7. J. caused the peo. | 1 Ch.

JAM'LECH. ⌊2: 27.

1 Ch. 4:34. their geneal-y Meshobab,

JANGLING. ⌊J.

1 Ti. 1: 6. turned aside to vain J.

JAN'NA.

Lu. 3: 24. Melchi who was son of J.

JAN'NES. See JAM'BRES.

JA'NOAH = JA'NOHAH.

Jos. 16:6. passed by on east to J., 7.
2 K. 15: 29. J. Kadesh and Hazor

JA'NUM = JA'NUS. ⌈J.

Jos. 15: 53†. in the mts. Eshean and

JA'PHETH.

Ge. 5: 32. Shem, Ham, J. sons of, 6:10.–7:13.–9:18.–10:1. 1 Ch. 1:4.
9: 23. Shem and J. took a garm.
27. God shall enlarge J. he shall
10: 2. sons of J., 1 Ch. 1: 5.
21. Shem, brother of J., the elder

JAPHI'A. [Person, Place.]

Jos. 10:3. sent unto J. k. of Lachish
19: 12. border goeth up into J.
2 S. 5: 15. born J., 1 Ch. 3:7.–14:6.

JAPH'LET.

1 Ch. 7: 32. begat J. | 33. sons of J.

JAPH'LETI.

Jos. 16: 3. westward to coast of J.

JA'PHO = JOP'PA.

Jos. 19: 46. with the border bef. J.

JA'RAH = JEHO'ADAH.

1 Ch. 9: 42. Ahaz begat J.; J. begat

JA'REB.

Ho. 5: 13. Ephraim, sent to king J.
10: 6. carried for a present to k. J.

JA'RED. = JE'RED.

Ge. 5:15. Mahaleel begat J., Lu. 3:37.
20. all days of J. 962 y-rs | 16, 18,

JARESI'AH. ⌊19.

1 Ch. 8: 27. J. Eliab heads of fa-s

JAR'HA.

1 Ch. 2:34. Egypt-n whose name J. |

JA'RIB. ⌊35.

1 Ch. 4: 24. Ezr. 8: 16.–10: 18.

JAR'MUTH. ⌈12:11.

Jos. 10: 3. Piram k. of J. | 5, 23.–
15: 35. in the valley J., 21: 29.
Ne. 11: 29. some of chil. of Jud. at

JARO'AH. ⌊J.

1 Ch. 5: 14. son of Huri, son of J.

JA'SHEN = HA'SHEM.

2 S. 23:32. of sons of J. Jona., 2 Ch.

JA'SHER. ⌊11:†34.

Jos. 10: 13. in book of J., 2 S. 1:18.

JASHO'BEAM.

1 Ch. 11:11. chief of capts., 12:6.–27:2.

JA'SHUB, ITES.

Nu. 26: 24. of J. family of J-s
1 Ch. 7:1. sons of Issa. J., Ezr. 10:29.

JASH'UBI-LE'HEM.

1 Ch. 4: 22. domin. in Moab and J.

JA'SIEL.

1 Ch. 11: 47. Obed. J. valiant men

JA'SON.

Ac. 17:5. Jews assaulted house of J.
6. drew J. | 7. J. hath received
9. they had taken security of J.
Ro. 16: 21. Lucius, J. salute you

JASPER.

Ex. 28: 20. fourth row a j., 39: 13.
Eze. 28:13. diamond and j. thy cov-C
Re. 4: 3. he to look upon like a j.
21: 11. her light was like to a j.
18. building of wall of city was of j.
19. the first foundation was j.

JATH'NIEL.

1 Ch. 26:2. sons of Meshelemiah, J.

JAT'TIR.

Jos. 15:48. in mts. Shamir J., 21:14.
1 S. 30:27. pres. to them in J., 1 Ch.

JA'VAN. ⌊6: 57.

Ge. 10:2. sons of Japheth; J., 1 Ch. 1:
4. sons of J. Elisha, 1 Ch. 1:7. ⌊5.
Is. 66: 19. send those escape to J.
Eze. 27: 13. J. and Tubal merch., 19

JAVELIN.

Nu. 25: 7. Phinehas took a j.

1 S. 18: 10. j. in Saul's hand, 19: 9.
11. Saul cast the j., 20: 33.
19: 10. he smote j. into the wall

JAW, S.

Ju. 15: 16. With j. of ass slain 1000
19. clave hollow place in j.
Jb. 29: 17. brake j-s of wicked
41: 2. bore his j. with a thorn?
Ps. 22: 15. tongue cleaveth to my j-s
Is. 30: 28. bridle in j-s of the people
Eze. 29: 4. put hooks in thy j., 38: 4.
Ho. 11: 4. take off yoke on their j-s

JAW teeth.

Pr. 30: 14. j. t. as knives to devour

JAWBONE.

Ju. 15: 15. Samson found a new j.
16. with j. of ass have I slain
17. he cast away j. out of hand

JA'ZER = JA'AZER.

Nu. 32: 1. saw J. was for cattle, 3.
Jos. 13: 25. coast is J., 21: 39. 1 Ch.
1 Ch. 26: 31. men of valor at J. [6: 81.
Is. 16: 8. they are come even unto J.
9. bewail with weeping of J., Je.

JA'ZIZ. [48: 32.

1 Ch. 27: 31. over the flocks was J.

JEALOUS.

Ex. 20: 5. I thy G. am a j. G., 34: 14.
De. 4: 24.-5: 9.-6: 15. Jos. 24: 19.
Nu 5: 14. j. of his wife, 30.
1 K. 19: 10. I have been j. for L., 14.
Eze. 39: 25. j. for my holy name
Jo. 2: 18. Then will the Lord be j.
Na. 1: 2. God is j. Lord revengeth
Zch. 1: 14. am j. for Jerus. | 8: 2. j. for
2 Co. 11: 2. I am j. over you [Zion

JEALOUSY, IES.

Nu. 5: 14. spirit of j. upon him, 30.
15. for it is an offering of j., 18.
25. priest sh. take j. offering from
29. is law of j-s when a wife
25: 11. consumed not Isr. in my j.
De. 29: 20. j. shall smoke ag. that man
32: 16. They provoked him to j., 1
K. 14: 22. [move them to j.
21. have moved me to j. I will
Ps. 78: 58. they moved him to j.
79: 5. How long, L., thy j. burn
Pr. 6: 34. For j. is the rage of man
27: †4. who is able to stand bef. j.?
Can. 8: 6. j. is cruel as the grave
Is. 42: 13. he shall stir up j. like
Eze. 8: 3. where seat of image of j.
5. at gate of altar this image of j.
16: 38. give thee bl. in fury and j.
42. my j. shall depart from thee
23: 25. I will set my j. against thee
36: 5. in j. have I spok., 6.-38: 19.
Zph. 1: 18. land devoured by j., 3: 8.
Zch. 1: 14. jealous for Zion wi. j., 8: 2.
Ro. 10: 19. will provoke you to j. by
11: 11. salv to Gent., to provoke to j.
1 Co. 10: 22. provoke Lord to j.?
2 Co. 11: 2. jealous ov. you wi godly j.

JE'ARIM.

Jos. 15: 10. border along mt. J.

JEAT'ERAI.

1 Ch. 6: 21. of Gershom J. his son

JEBERECHI'AH.

Is. 8: 2. witnesses Zch son of J.

JE'BUS, JEBU'SI.

Jos. 18: 16. to the side of J., 28.
Ju. 19: 10. over ag. J., 11. | 1 Ch. 11:

JEB'USITE. [4, 5.

Ge. 10: 16. Canaan begat J., 1 Ch. 1: 14
Ex. 33: 2. will drive out J., 34: 11.
Jos. 9: 1. the J., 11: 3.-15: 8. 1 Ch. 1: 14.
2 S. 24: 16. angel by threshing-pla.
of Araunah J., 18. 1 Ch. 21: 15,
28. 2 Ch. 3: 1.
Zch. 9: 7. and Ekron as a J.

JEB'USITES.

Ge. 15: 21. the J., Ex. 3: 8, 17.-13: 5.
-23: 23. De. 7: 1.-20: 17. Jos. 3:
10.-12: 8.-24: 11. Ju. 3: 5. 1 K.
9: 20. 2 Ch. 8: 7. Ezr. 9: 1 Ne 9: 8.
Nu. 13: 29. J. dwell in mountains
Jos. 15: 63. J. dwell with children of
Jud., 2 S. 5: 6. 1 Ch. 11: 4.
Ju. 1: 21. drive J. th. inhab. Jerus.
19: 11. into this city of J. and dw.
2 S. 5: 8. whoso smiteth J., 1 Ch. 11: 6.

JECAMI'AH.

1 Ch. 3: 18. sons of Jeconiah, J.

JECOLI'AH = JEZ'OLIAH.

2 K. 15: 2. mother's name J., 2 Ch.

JECONI'AH, [26: 3.

JECHONI'AS.

1 Ch. 3: 16. sons of Jehoiakim; J.
17. sons of J. Assir, Mat. 1: 12.
Je. 24: 1. had carried away captive
J., 27: 20.-29: 2. Es. 2: 6.
28: 4. I will bri. again to this pl. J.
Mat. 1: 11. Josias begat J-s
See CONIAH, JEHOIAKIM.

JEDA'IAH.

1 Ch 4: 37. son of Allon, son of J.
9: 10. of priests, J. and, Ne. 11: 10.
24: 7. second lot came to J.
Ezr. 2: 36. priests, chil. of J., Ne. 7: 39.
Ne. 3: 10. next repaired J.
12: 6. J. chief, 7, 19, 21. Zch. 6: 10, 14.

JEDI'AEL.

1 Ch. 7: 6. sons of Benj.; J.
10. sons of J., 11.
11: 45 valiant men, J. and, 26: 6.

JEDI'DAH.

2 K. 22: 1. Josiah's mo.'s name J.

JEDIDI'AH.

2 S. 12: 25. L. called Solomon, J.

JED'UTHUN.

1 Ch. 9: 16. son of J., 16: 38. 2 Ch. 29:
14. Ne. 11: 17. [5: 12.-35: 15.
16: 41. Heman, J., 42.-25: 1, 6. 2 Ch.
25: 3. J. prophesied with harp

JE'EZER, ITES.

Nu. 26: 30. of J family of J-s

JE'GAR-SAHADU'THA.

Ge. 31: 47. Laban called it J.

JEHA'LELEEL.

1 Ch. 4: 16. sons of J. Ziph, Ziphah

JEHAL'ELEL.

2 Ch. 29: 12. Lev. Azariah son of J.

JEHDEI'AH.

1 Ch. 27: 30. over asses was J. | 24: 20.

JEHEZ'EKEL.

1 Ch. 24: 16. twentieth lot to J.

JEHEZ'KEL = EZEKIEL.

JEHI'AH. [of ark

1 Ch. 15: 24. Obed-e. J. doorkeepers

JEHI'EL = JEHI'ELI.

1 Ch. 9: 35. dwelt fa. of Gibeon J.
11: 44. Shama. J. valiant men |
15: 18, 20.-16: 5.-23: 8.-26: 21, 22.
23: 8. the sons of-J., 2 Ch. 21: 2.
-29: 14. Ezr. 8: 9.-10: 2, 21, 26.
29: 8. by J. Gershonite
2 Ch. 31: 13. J. Azaziah overseers
35: 8. Zch. J rulers of hou. of G.
Ez. 8: 9. Obadiah the son of J.

JEHIZKI'AH.

2 Ch. 28: 12. J. and Amasa stood

JEHO'ADAH. [ag.

1 Ch. 8: 36. Ahaz begat J., J. begat

JEHOAD'DAN. [25: 1.

2 K. 14: 2. mother's name J. | 2 Ch.

JEHO'AHAZ.

2 K. 10: 35. J. son of Jehu reigned,
13: 1.-14: 8. 2 Ch. 25: 17.
13: 1. J. son of Jehu began to reign
4. J. besought L. | 7, 8, 22. [17.
10. Jehoash son of J., 25.-14: 1, 8,
23: 30. took J. anointed him, 2 Ch.
31. J. 23 y-rs old, 2 Ch. 36: 2. [36: 1.
34. Pharaoh-necho took J. away,
2 Ch. 36: 4. [†15.
1 Ch. 3: †12. J. his son Jotham his
2 Ch. 21: 17. Jehoram never a son
left save J., 2 Ch. 22: †6.
25: 17. Joash son of J., 23, 25. 2
K. 13: 9. See

JEHO'ASH = JO'ASH.

2 K. 11: 21. J. 7 y-rs old began to
12: 2. J. did right [reign, 12: 1.
2 K. 12: 4. J. said to priests | 6, 7, 19.
18. J. sent all hallowed things
20. serv. slew J. in hou. of Millo
13: 10. J. began to reign | 25.
14: 8. Amazi. sent messen-s to J.
15. rest of acts of J. | 9, 11, 13, 17.
16. J. slept with fathers

JEHO'HANAN.

1 Ch. 26: 3. J. 6th son
2 Ch. 17: 15. J. capt., 28: 1.
Ezr. 10: 28. J. priest, Ne. 12: 13, 42.

JEHOI'ACHIN.

2 K. 24: 6. J. reigned, 2 Ch. 36: 8.
8. J. began to reign, 2 Ch. 36: 9.
12. J. k. of Jud. to k. of Bab.
15. carried J. to Bab. | Es. 2: †6.
25: 27. lift up head of J., Je. 52: 31.
Eze. 1: 2. fifth year of J.'s captiv.

JEHOI'ADA.

2 S. 8: 18. Benaiah the son of J., 20:
23.-23: 20, 22. 1 K. 1: 8, 26, 36,
38, 44.-2: 25, 29, 34, 35, 46.-4:
4. 1 Ch 11: 22, 24.-18: 17.-27:
5, 34.
23: 20. J. son of valiant, 1 Ch. 11: 22.
2 K. 11: 4. 7th y-r J. sent | 9, 15.
17. J. made cov., 2 Ch. 23: 16.
12: 2. J. priest instructed him
9. J. took chest bored hole | 7.
1 Ch. 12: 27. J. leader of Aaronites
27: 34. was J. a counsellor [him
2 Ch. 22: 11. Jehoshab. w. of J. hid
23: 1. J. strengthened hims. | 8, 9, 11.
14. J. priest bro-t capts | 16, 18.
24: 2. right all the days of J.
6. called for J. chief | 3, 12, 14. [20.
15. J. waxed old | 17. death of J. |
17. after death of J. came princes
22. Joash remem-d not kindn J.
25. blood of sons of J. the priest
Ne. 3: 6. the old gate repaired J.
Je. 29: 26. priest instead of J.

JEHOI'AKIM.

2 K. 23: 34. turned name to J., 2 Ch
35. J. gave gold to Pha. [36: 4.
36. J. 25 y-rs old began, 2 Ch. 36: 5.
24: 1. J. became his serv. 3 y-rs, 19.
Je 1: 3. It came in the days of J.
22: 18. saith Lord concerning J.
24: 1. Jeconiah son of J., 22: 24.-
27: 20.-28: 4.-37: 1. 1 Ch. 3: 16.
25: 1. in the 4th year of J., 36: 1.-
45: 1.-46: 2.
26: 21. J. the king, 1, 22, 23.-27: 1.
22. J. sent men aft. Urij. into E
35: 1. word to Jere. in days of J.
36: 9. in 5th y-r of J. | 29, 32.
28. roll J. king hath burned
30. saith L. of J. king of Judah
37: 1. Coniah son of J.
52: 2. Zed. did evil as J. had done
Da. 1: 2. L. gave J. into his hand |
See JOSIAH. [1.

JEHOI'ARIB.

1 Ch. 9: 10. of the priests J. | 24: 7.

JEHON'ADAB.

2 K. 10: 15. he lighted on J. the son
23. J. went into house of Baal
See JONADAB.

JEHON'ATHAN.

1 Ch. 27: 25. over storehouses was J.
2 Ch. 17: 8. sent Levites J. | Ne. 12: 18.

JEHO'RAM = JO'RAM.

1 K. 22: 50. J. son of Jehosh., 2 K.
1: 17.-8: 16. 2 Ch. 21: 1, 3, 4, 5.
2 K. 3: 1. J. son of Ahab, 1: 17.-8:
16, 25, 28. 2 Ch. 22: 5.
6. J. numbered all Israel
8: 21. So J. went over to Zair
25. Ahaziah son of J., 29. 1 Ch.
3: 11. 2 Ch. 22: 1, 6.
9: †15. J. was returned to be healed
24. Jehu drew bow smote J.
2 Ch. 17: 8. sent Elishama and J.
21: 9. J. smote the Edomites
16. Lord stirred against J. the
Philistines

2 Ch.22:5.with J. to war ag. Hazael
7. Ahaziah with J. against Jehu
11. J. dau. of Joram, 2 K. 11:2.

JEHOSHAB'EATH = JEHOSH'EBA.

2 K. 11:2. J. hid Joash, 2 Ch.22:11.

JEHOSH'APHAT.

2 S. 8 : 16. J. was recorder, 20:24. 1 K. 4 : 3. 1 Ch. 18 : 15.
1 K. 4:17. J. son of Pharuah ; in Issachar [Ch. 17 : 1.
15:24. J. the son of Asa reigned, 2
22 : 2. J. came down to Ahab
4. J. Wilt go with me, 2 Ch.18:3.
5. J. said, Inquire. 2 Ch. 18: 4.
7.J.said, Is not proph.,2 Ch.18:6.
8. unto J. There is one,2 Ch.18:7.
10. Ahab and J. sat each on his throne, 2 Ch. 18:9. [Ch.18:17.
18. unto J. Did I not tell thee, 2
29. J. to Ramoth-gil., 2 Ch. 18:28.
32. J. cried out, 2 Ch. 18 : 31.
41. J. son of Asa began to reign, 15 : 24. 1 Ch. 3:10. 2 Ch. 17:1.-20: 31.
44. J. made peace | 45, 48, 51.
49. let servants go, J. would not
50. J. slept with fa-s, 2 Ch. 21 : 1.
2 K. 3 : 11. J. said, Is there not a prophet | 7. [7, 12.
14. that I regard presence of J.,
9 : 2. look out Jehu son of J., 14.
1 Ch. 15 : 24. J. blew with trumpet
2 Ch. 17 : 3. Lord was with J. bec.
10. that they made no war ag. J.
12. J. waxed great exceedingly
18:1. J. had riches, honour, 17 : 5.
19 : 4. J. dwelt at Jerusalem
20 : 1. ag. J. to battle | 2, 15, 18, 20, 25, 30, 31, 34.
3. J. set himself to seek Lord
27. returned, and J. in forefront
35. J. join with Ahaziah king of
37. Eliezer prophesied against J.
21 : 1. J. slept with his fathers
12. not walked in ways of J.
22 : 9. said they, he is son of J.
Jo.3:2. bring them unto valley of J.
12. heathen to valley of J.
See JEHORAM, JOSAPHAT [22:†11

JEHOSH'EBA. 2 K.11:2 2 Ch.

JEHOSH'UA. See JOSHUA.

JEHOSH'UAH.

1 Ch. 7 : 27. Non his son, J. his son

JEHO'VAH.

Ex. 6 : 3. by name J. I not known
Ps. 83 : 18. thou whose name is J.
Is. 12 : 2. Lord J. is my strength
26 : 4. in Lord J. is everl. strength
Je. 16 : †.21. J. is his name, 33 : † 2. Jon. 1 : † 9.

JEHO'VAH-JI'REH.

Ge. 22 : 14. Ab. called the place J.

JEHO'VAH-NIS'SI.

Ex. 17:15. Moses called the altar J.

JEHO'VAH-SHA'LOM.

Ju. 6:24. Gideon called the altar J.

JEHO'VAH-SHAM'MAH.

Eze.48:†35. name of city shall be J.

JEHO'VAH-TSID'KENU.

Je. 23 :†6. this his name, J., 33:†16.

JEHOZ'ABAD.

2 K.12:21.J. his serv. smote Joash, 1 Ch. 26 : 4. 2 Ch. 17 : 18.-24 : 26.

JEHOZ'ADAK.

1 Ch. 6 : 14. Seraiah begat J. | 15. See JOSEDECH, JOZADAK.

JE'HU.

1 K. 16 : 1. word came to J. son of Hanani, 7, 12. 2 Ch. 20 : 34.
19 : 16. J. shalt thou anoint king
17. sh. J. slay : escapeth sw. of J.
2 K. 9 : 2. look out J. | 13. J. king
14. J. conspired ag. Joram [J.
17. watchman spied company of
20. driving is like driving of J.
2 K.9:24.J. drew a bow with full str.
27. J. said, Smite | 30, 31.-10:13.
10:11. J. slew all of house of Ahab
18. J. shall serve Baal much
2 K.10:28.J. destr-d Baal out of Isr
29. J. depar. not fr. sins of Jerob
31. J. took no heed to walk in law
34. rest of acts of J. | 35,36 [of G.
12 : 1. in 7th year of J. Jehoahaz
15 : 12. the word he spake unto J.
1 Ch. 2 : 38. Obed begat J. J. begat
4:35.J.son of Josibiah | 12:3.J. son
2 Ch. 19 : 2. J. to meet Jehosh.
20 : 34. written in the book of J.
22 : 7. went with Joram ag. J. | 9.
8.J. executing judgm. upon Ahab
Ho. 1 : 4. blood of Jezreel upon J. See JEHOAHAZ.

JEHUB'BAH. See SHAMER.

JEHU'CAL = JU'CAL.

Je. 37:3. Zed. sent J. to Jere., 38:1.

JE'HUD.

Jos. 19 : 45. coast of inheri. was J.

JEHU'DI. [ruch

Je. 36 : 14. princes sent J. unto Ba-
21. J. read roll in ears of k., 23.

JEHUDI'JAH.

1 Ch. 4 : 18. his wife J. bare Jered,

JE'HUSH. [†19.

1 Ch. 8 : 39. sons of Eshek ; J. sec

JEI'EL. [son

1 Ch.5:7.were the chief J. and Zech.
15:21.J.Azaziah with harps | 16:5.
2 Ch. 26:11. num. of account by J. | 20:14.-29:13.-35:9. Ezr. 8:13.

JEKAB'ZEEL. [10:43.

Ne. 11 : 25. chil. of Jud. dwelt at J.

JEKAME'AM.

1 Ch. 23:19. sons of Hebron, J., 24:

JEKAMI'AH. [23.

1 Ch. 2:41. Shallum begat J. J. beg.

JEKU'THIEL.

1 Ch. 4 : 18. wife Jekudijah bare J.

JEMI'MA.

Jb. 42 : 14. called name of 1st J.

JEMI'NI.

1 S. 9 : † 1. Kish son of a man of J.

JE'MUEL = NEMU'EL.

Ge. 46:10.† sons of Simeon ; J., Ex. 6 : 15. Nu. 26:12.† 1 Ch. 4:24.†

JEOPARDED.

Ju.5:18. th. j. their lives unto death

JEOPARDY.

2 S. 23:17. in j. of lives, 1 Ch.11:19
1 Ch.12:19.fall to Saul,to j. of heads
Lu. 8:23. ship filled, they were in j.
1 Co. 15 : 30. why stand we in j. ev.

JEPH'THAH. [hour

Ju. 11 : 1. J. was a mighty man of valour, Gilead begat J. | 2.
3. J. fled fr. breth. | 5, 6, 7, 8.
9.J. said, If ye bri. me home | 10.
11. J. uttered all his words bef. L.
28. k. heark. not unto words of J.
29. Spirit on J. | 30. J. vowed
40. yearly to lament dau. of J.
12 : 2. J. said, I and my peo. | 1.
4. Then J. fought with Ephraim
7.J. judged Isr.6 y-rs, then died J.
1 S.12:11. L. sent J. and deliv-d you
He. 11 : 32. time fail me to tell of J.

JEPHUN'NEH.

Nu. 13 : 6. Judah, Caleb son of J., 14 : 6, 30. 38.-26:65.-31:12.-34: 19. De. 1:36. Jos. 14:6, 13, 14.-15 : 13.-21:12. 1 Ch. 4:15.-6:56.
1 Ch. 7 : 38. the sons of Jether ; J.

JE'RAH. [29.

Ge. 10:26. Joktan begat J., 1 Ch. 1:

JERAH'MEEL, ITES.

1 S. 30:2.9 were in cities of J-s | 27:
1 Ch. 2 : 9. sons of Hezron ; J. [10.
25. sons of J., 27, 33, 42 | 26.
24 : 29. son of Kish was J.
Je.36:26.king com.J.to take Baruch

JERED = JARED.

1 Ch. 4:18. Jehudijah bare J. | 1:2.

JEREMA'I. See ZABAD.

JEREMI'AH, JEREMI'AS, JERE'MY.

2 K. 23 : 31. dau. of J. of Libnah, 24 : 18. Je. 52 : 1.
1 Ch.5:24.J. a mighty man, 12:4,10,
2 Ch.35:25.J. lamented Josiah [13.
36 : 12. Zed. humbled not bef. J.
21. To fulfil word of Lord by the mouth of J., 22, Ezr. 1 : 1.
Ne. 10 : 2. J. sealed the covenant
12 : 1. J. went up with Zerubbabel
12. of J. Hananiah was priest
34. J. and Shemaiah went after
Je. 1 : 1. words of J. son of Hilkiah
7:1.word th.came to J.,11:1.-14:1.-18:1.-21:1.-25:1, 2,13 -29:30.-30 :1.-32:1,6, 26.-33:1,19.-34:1, 8,12.-35:1,12.-36:1, 27.-37:3, 6.-39:15.-40 :1.-42:7.-43:8 -44:1.-46:1, 13.-47:1.-49:24. Da 9 :2.
18 : 18. let us devise devices ag. J.
19 : 14. Then came J. from Tophet
20 : 2. Pashur smote J. and put
24 : 3. said L. What seest thou J.?
25 : 13. wh. J. proph-d ag. nation
26:9. peo. were gath-d ag. J. [7.+
24. hand of Ahikam with J. [15.†
28:5.J.said unto proph. Hananiah,
10. took yoke from J.'s neck
29 : 1. letter J. sent [Anathoth?
27. why hast not reproved J. of
32 : 2. J. was shut up in prison
34 : 6. J. spake all these of Zed.
35 : 3. took Jaazaniah son of J.
36 : 4. Baruch wrote fr. mouth of
19.said, Hide, thou and J. [J.,32.
26. L. hid Baruch and J. proph.
37:4. J. in and out am. the people
14. Irijah took J. to princes
15. princes were wroth with J.
16.When J. was ent. into dungeon
21. commit J. into prison, 38:28.
38 : 6. cast J. into dungeon, 7. +
13. drew up J. with cords out of
16. Zed. k. sware secretly unto J.
39 : 11. Neb. gave charge conc-g J.
14. took J. out out of pris., 38:10,
40 : 6. went J. unto Gedaliah [13.
43 : 2. J. Thou speakest falsely
44 : 15. in Pathros answered J.
51:60. J. wrote in book all the evil
64. Thus far are the words of J.
52 : 1. Hamutal daughter of J.
Mat. 2 : 17. was spoke by J-y, 27:9.
16 : 14. others say thou art J-s or

JEREMOTH = JERIMOTH

1 Ch. 8 : 14. J. heads of fa-s | 23 : 23.
Ezr. 10 : 26. taken strange wives, J.,

JEREMY. See JEREMIAH. [27.

JERI'AH = JERI'JAH.

1 Ch. 23:19. sons of Hebron, J., 24:

JERI'BAI. [23.

1 Ch.11:46. valiant men were Eliel,

JER'ICHO. [J.

Nu. 22:1. on this side Jordan by J., 26 : 3, 63.-31:12.-33:48, 50.-34: 15.-35 : 1.-36 : 13. Jos. 13 : 32.-16 : 1.-20: 8. 1 Ch. 6 : 78.
De. 32 : 49. Nebo over ag. J. | 34:1.
34 : 3. J. city of palm, 2 Ch. 28:15.
Jos. 2 : 1. saying, Go view la. J. +
2. king of J., 3.-6 : 2.-8 : 2.-10:28, 30.-12 : 9.
3 : 16. peo. passed over against J.
4 : 13. plains of J., 5:10. 2 K. 25:5. Je. 39 : 5.-52 : 8.
6 : 1. J. was straitly shut up
25. messen. sent to spy out J.
2. I have giv. into thine hand J.
26. Cursed that buildeth city J.
7 : 2. Joshua sent men from J.
24 : 11. ye came men of J. fought
2 S. 10:5. king said, Tarry at J. till your beards be grown, 1 Ch.19:
1 K. 16 : 34. did Hiel build J. [5.
2 K. 2 : 4. L. hath sent me to J. +
5. sons of prophets at J.

Ezr. 2 : 34. chil. of J. Ne. 7 : 36.
Ne. 3 : 2. next builded men of J.
Mat.20:29. as they departed fr. J. a gr. | Mk. 10:46.Lu. 18:35.-19:1.
Lu.10:30.cert. man went down to J.
He. 11 : 30. By faith walls of J. fell

JER'IEL. See TOLA.

JERI'JAH = JERI'AH.

1 Ch. 26:31. am. Hebronites J. chief

JER'IMOTH = JER'EMOTH.

1 Ch.7:7. J. and Iri, mighty men 8. 12 : 5. over the 30, J. | 24 : 30.-27: 19. 2 Ch. 11 : 18.-31 : 13.

JE'RIOTH.

1 Ch. 2 : 18. Caleb begat chil. of J.

JEROBO'AM.

1 K. 11 : 28. J. was a mighty man
40. Sol sought to kill J. J. fled
12:2. J. dwelt in E. | 20. was come
25. J. built Shechem and dwelt
32.J. ordained a feast in 8th mon.
13:1. J. stood by altar to burn inc.
33. J. returned not fr. evil way
34. this became sin unto h. of J.
14 : 1. Abijah son of J. fell sick
6. said, Come in, thou wife of J.
10. I will bring evil upon h. of J.
11. that dieth of J. sh. dogs eat
13. he only of J. come to grave
16. bec. of the sins of J., 15 : 30.
19. rest of acts of J.
20. J. slept with his fathers
30. was war bet. Rehob. and J.
15 : 7. war bet. J., 2 Ch. 13 : 2.
15 : 29. Baasha left not to J. any
34. walked in way of J., 16:2, 19, 26, 31.-22:52. 2 K. 13:6.-14:24.-17 : 22.
2 K. 13 : 13. J. sat upon his throne
14 : 27. L. saved Isr. by hand of J.
17 : 21. J. drave Israel from the L.
1 Ch.5:17. genealogies in days of J.
2 Ch. 10 : 2. J. returned out of E.
11 : 14. J. had cast off Levites
12 : 15. wars betw. Rehob. and J.
13 : 8. golden calves wh. J. made
15. God smote J. and all Israel
20.Neither did J.recover strength
Ho. 1:1. in the days of J., Am. 1:1.
Am. 7 : 9. rise against house of J.
11. thus Amos saith, J. shall die

JEROBO'AM with Nebat.

1 K. 11:26. J. son of N. lifted hand
12:2.J. son of N. heard, 2 Ch.10:2.
15. which Lord spake unto J. son of N., 2 Ch. 10 : 15.
15 : 1. in 18th year of J. son of N.
16 : 3. thy house like h. of J. son of N., 21 : 22. 2 K. 9 : 9.
26. walked in way of J. son of N. and his sin, 31.-22:52. 2 K. 3:3.
2 K.3:3. sins of J. son of N., 10:29, 31.-13:2,11.-14 :24.-15:9,18,24, 23:15.high pla.J.son of N.made 28.
2 Ch. 13 : 6. J. son of N. rebelled

JER'OHAM.

1 S. 1 : 1. son of J., 1 Ch. 6:27, 34.-8:27.-9:8, 12.-12:7.-27:22.2 Ch. 23 : 1. Ne. 11 : 12.

JERUB'BAAL.

Ju. 6 : 32. that day he called him J.
7 : 1. Then J. (who is Gideon) rose
8 : 29. J. dwelt in his own house
35. Nei. shewed kindn. to h. of J.
9:2. that all of sons J. reign | 5,24.
5. Abimelech slew sons of J., 1.
16. if ye dealt well with J.
19. If dealt sincerely with J.
28. is not he the son of J.?
57. curse of Jotham son of J.
1 S.12:11. L. sent J. and deliv-d you
2 S. 11 : †21. Who smote son of J.

JERUB'BESHETH.

2 S. 11:21. smote son of J., Ju.6:†32.

JER'UEL.

2 Ch.20:16. bef. the wilderness of J.

JERU'SALEM.

Jos. 10 : 1. Adoni-zedek king of J., 3, 5, 23.-12 : 10. [19 : 10.
18 : 28. Jebusi, wh. is J., 15:8. Ju.
Ju. 1 : 21. Jebusites that inhabited J., Jos. 15 : 63. 2 S. 5 : 6.
1 S.17:54. bro-t Goliath's head to J.
2 S. 5 : 6. Da. and men went to J.
8:7. Da. bro-t shields of gold to J.
12:31.Da.and people retur. unto J.
14:23. Joab bro-t Abs. to J.,15:37.
15 : 8. If L. bring me again to J.
29. they carried ark of God to J.
19 : 19. day my lord went out of J.
24 : 8. came to J. at end of 9 mo-s
16.angel stretched out hand upon J. to destroy it, 1 Ch. 21:15,16.
1 K. 3 : 1. end of building wall of J., 2 K. 14:13.-25:10.2 Ch.25:23.+ Ne. 1 : 3.-2 : 13.-4:7.-12:27. Je. 39 : 8.-52 : 14.
9 : 15. wall of J., Ne. 1 : 3.
10 : 2. came to J. with great train
11 : 13. for J.'s sake.2 Ch. 6 : 6.
15 : 4. to set up son and establ. J.
2 K. 18 : 35. that L. sho. deliver J. out of mine hand, Is. 36 : 20.
19 : 10. J. not be deliv-d into hand
31. out of J. sh. go forth a remnant, and they, Is. 37 : 32. [J.
21:12. I am bring-g such evil upon
13. I will wipe J. as a man a dish
16. shed bl.till he had filled J.,24:
23:27. I will cast off J. chosen [4.
24 : 14. he carried away all J.
25 : 9. Nebuz. burnt houses of J.
1 Ch. 15:3. Da. gath-d all Isr. to J.
21 : 15. God sent angel unto J. to
2 Ch. 11 : 14. came to J. to sacrifice
12 : 7. my wrath not upon J.
20 : 28. came to J. with psalteries
24 : 9. proclam. that J., Ezr. 10:7.
18. wrath upon J., 29 : 8.-32:25.
28 : 10. to keep under chil. of J.
24. altars in every corner of J.
29 : 8. wrath of Lord upon J.
32 : 19. they spake ag. God of J.
23. brought gifts unto L. of J.
34: 3. Josiah began to purge J., 5.
Ezr. 3 : 1. gath-d as one to J., 9 : 9.
7 : 14 sent to inquire conc. J.
19. those deliver thou bef. G. of J.
Ne. 2 : 11. came to J., 7 : 6.-13 : 7.
13.walls of J.,4:7.-12:27.Je.52:14.
17. J. lieth waste, gates burnt
4 : 22. Let ev. one lodge within J.
7 : 2. gave my bro. charge over J.
12 : 43. joy of J. was heard afar
13:20 merchants lodged without J.
Ps. 51:18. build thou the walls of J.
79 : 1. heathen laid J. on heaps
3. blood have they shed round J.
122 : 3. J. is builded as a city com-
6. Pray for the peace of J. [pact
125 : 2. As the mountains round J.
128 : 5. shalt see the good of J.
137 : 6. if I prefer not J. above my
7. remem. Edom in the day of J.
147 : 2. The Lord doth build up J.
Can. 6 : 4. comely, O my love. as J.
Is. 1 : 1. vision he saw conc. J., 2:1.
3 : 8. J. is ruined | 10 : 11. do to J.
4 : 4. L. sh. have purged bl. of J.
10:12. L. performed his work upon
22 : 10. numbered houses of J. [J.
31 : 5. so will the L. defend J.
33 : 20. J. a quiet habitation
40 : 2. Speak ye comfortably to J.
41:27. to J. one that bri. good tid.
44 : 26. to J. Thou shalt be inhab.
28. saying to J. Thou shalt be built [hath redeemed J.
52:9.sing ye waste places of J. Lord
62 : 1. for J.'s sake I will not rest
7. give him no rest till he make
64:10. J. a desolation [J. a praise
65 : 18. I create J. a rejoicing

Is. 66 : 10. Rejoice ye with J. be glad
Je.1:3.unto the carrying away of J.
2 : 2. Go, cry in the ears of J.
3 : 17. shall call J. throne of Lord
Je.5:1.Run ye through streets of J.
6 : 1. gather you to flee out of J.
7 : 34. streets of J., 11:6,13.-14:16.-33 : 10.-44 : 6, 9, 17, 21.
8 : 5. Why is peo. of J. slid. back
9 : 11. I will make J. heaps, and
11 : 6. Proclaim these words in J.
13 : 9. I will mar great pride of J.
14 : 2. the cry of J. is gone up
17:26. sh. come from pla. about J.
19 : 7. make void counsel of J.
13. houses of J. be as Tophet
23 :14. in prophets of J. a horrible
26 : 18. J. become heaps, Mi. 3:12.
32:2. king of Bab.'s army besieged J., 37 : 5. Da. 1 : 1.
33 : 13. about J. shall flocks
16. days J. shall dwell safely
35 : 11. to J. for fear of Chaldeans
38:28. until day that J. was taken
39 : 8. Chaldeans break walls of J.
44:2. seen evil I have bro-t upon J.
6. mine anger was kindled in J.
13. as I have punished J.
21. incense burned in streets of J.
51 : 50. let J. come into your mind
La. 1 : 7. J. rememb-d in affliction
8 J. hath grievously sinned
17. J. is as a menstruous woman
2 : 10 virgins of J. hang heads
Eze 4 : 7. face toward siege of J.
5 : 5. This is J | 9 : 4. Go thro. J
16 : 2. cause J. to know her abom.
17 : 12. king of Bab. is come to J.
21 : 2. Son of man set face tow. J.
20. that sword may come in J.
22. At his right divination for J.
22 : 19. I will gather you into J.
33 : 21. one escaped out of J. came
36 : 38. as flock of J. in her feasts
Da.1:1 came Neb.unto J. besieged it
6 : 10. his windows open toward J.
9 : 2. 70 years a desolation of J.
12. not been done, as upon J.
25. going of com-t to build J.
Jo. 3 : 1. when I bri. captive of J.
6. children of J. have ye sold
17. J. be holy | 20. J. sh. dwell
Ob. 11. foreigners cast lots upon J.
Mi. 1 : 5. are they not J.?
3 : 10. build up J. with iniquity
Zch. 1 : 14. jealous for J.
Zph. 1 : 12. search J. with candles
Zch.1:12. how long not mercy on J.
16 am ret-d to J. with mercies
17. L. shall yet choose J., 2 : 12.
19. horns which have scattered J.
2:2. Whither thou? To measure J.
4. J. shall be inhabited as towns
3 : 2. Lord that hath chosen J.
7 : 7. when J. was in prosperity
8:3 I will dwell in the midst of J.
4. old men, wom. dw. in streets of
15. thought to do well unto J. [J.
12 : 2. I will make J. cup of tremb.
3. make J. a burdensome stone
14 : 11. J. shall be safely inhabited
17. unto J. to worship the king
Mal. 3 : 4. offering of J. pleasant
Mat 2 : 1. wise men fr. east to J.
3. he was troubled and all J.
3 : 5. then went out to him J., Mk. 1 : 5. [J.
5:35. nei. swear by J. | 21:10. into
16 : 21. how he must go unto J.
Mk. 11:11. Jes. entered J. and tem.
Lu. 2 : 22. parents bro-t him to J.
45. turned back to J. seeking him
6:17. mult. out of J. came to hear
9 : 53. his face was as though to J.
13 : 33. a prophet perish out of J.
19:11.spake parable, bec.nigh to J.
21:20.when ye sh. see J compassed

Lu. 21:24. J. sh. be trodden of Gent.
24:52.retur. to J.with great joy [J.
Jn. 12:12. heard Jes. was coming to
Ac. 5 : 28. filled J. with your doctrine
9:2.might bri. them bound unto J.
26. when Saul was come to J.
20:22. I go bound in spirit unto J.
21 : 31. that all J. was in uproar
22 : 5. unto J. to be punished
18. get thee quickly out of J.
25 : 20. whe. he would go to J.?
Ro. 15:31. that my service for J. be
1 Co. 16 : 3. your liberality unto J.
Ga. 4 : 25. Agar answereth to J.
26. But J. which is above is free
He 12: 22. unto the heavenly J.
Re.3:12. new J.,21:2. | 21:10.holy J.
See DWELL with Jerusalem and DWELLETH, ING, DWELT.

Against JERU'SALEM.

Ju.1:8. Judah had fought a. J. and
1 K. 14 : 25. Shishak came a. J., 2 Ch. 12 : 9. [Ch. 32 : 2.
2 K. 18 : 17. Sennacherib a. J., 2
24: 10. k. of Bab. a. J., 25 : 1. Je. 34 : 1, 7.-39 : 1.-52:4. Eze. 24:2.
Ezr. 4 : 8. Rehum, wrote a. J.
Ne.4:8. they conspired to fight a.J.
Je. 4 : 16. publish a. J.
6 : 6. cast a mount a. J.
Eze.26:2. that Tyrus hath said a.J.
Zch. 12 : 9. nations th. come a. J., 14 : 12, 16.
14:2. I will gather all nations a.J.

At JERU'SALEM.

Jos. 15 : 63. Jebusites dwelt a. J.
2 S 11:1.Da. tarried a.J., 1 Ch.20:1.
16 : 3. Behold he abideth a. J.
20 : 3. Da. came to his house a. J.
1 K. 12 : 27. do sacrifice in ho. of L. a. J., 2 Ch. 9 : 25. Is. 27 : 13.
1 Ch. 9 : 34. fathers dwelt a. J., 38.
2 Ch. 3 : 1. Sol. began to build the house of L. a. J., Ezr 1:2.-5:2.
Ezr 6:12.to destr. this h. of G. a.J.
Ne.2:12. put in my heart to do a.J.
6 : 7. prophets to preach a. J.
11 : 2. willingly offer. to dwell a.J.
13 : 6. all this time was not I a. J.
Ps 68:29.Because of thy temple a.J.
135: 21. be L. who dwelleth a. J.
Is. 30 : 19. people shall dwell a. J.
Je. 35 : 11. let us to J. dwell a. J.
Zch. 14 : 14. Judah shall fight a. J.
Lu.9:31. he should accomplish a.J.
23:7. Herod himself was also a. J.
24: 47. preached, beginning a. J.
Jn. 4 : 21. nor a. J. worship the Fa.
45. having seen all he did a. J.
Ac. 1 : 19. known to dwellers a J.
8:1.gr.persecution ag. church a.J.
9 : 13. evil done to saints a. J.
18: 27. th. dwell a. J. have fulfil.
20 : 16. be a. J. day of Pentecost
21 : 11. So sh. Jews a. J. bind man
13. to die a. J. for name of Jesus
25 : 24. have dealt with me a. J.
26 : 4. am. mine own nation a. J.
20. first to them of Damas. a. J.
Ro.15:26. contrib. for poor saints a.
See DAUGHTER, DAUGHTERS. [J.

From JERUSALEM.

1 K. 2:41. th. Shimei had gone f.J.
2 K. 12 : 18. Hazael went away f. J.
24 : 15. carried f. J. to Bab., Es. 2:6.Je.24:1.-27:20.-29:1.-52:29.
Is. 2 : 3. word of L. f. J., Mi. 4 : 2.
3 : 1. L. doth take f. J. the stay
Da. 9 : 16. fury be turned f. J.
Jo. 3:16. L. utter voice f. J., Am.1:2.
Zch. 9 : 10. cut off horse f. J. [2.
14:8. living waters sh. go out f. J.
Mat. 4:25. mult. followed him f. J., Mk. 3 : 8. Lu. 6 : 17.
Lu. 10 : 30. A man went down f. J.
24 : 13. was f. J. sixty furlongs
Ac. 1 : 4. should not depart f. J.
8 : 26. way down f. J. unto Gaza
11:27. prophets f. J. unto Antioch
12:25. Barna. and Saul retu-d f.J.
28 : 17. was I deliv-d prisoner f. J.
Ro.15:19.f. J. unto Illyr.I preached

In JERUSALEM.

Ju. 1 : 21. Jebusites with Benj. i. J.
2 S. 19 : 33. feed thee with me i. J.
1 K. 2 : 36. Build thee a house i. J.
10: 27. silver i. J. as stones, 2 Ch. 9 : 27. [15 : 4.
11 : 36. light always bef. me i. J.,
2 K.18:22.worship bef.this alt. i. J.
21:4.i. J. put my name, 2 Ch.33:4.
22 : 14. Huldah dwelt i. J. in college
1 Ch.8:28. dwelt i. J., 32.-9:3.
23 : 25. may dwell i. J. forever
2 Ch. 2:7. cunning men th. are i. J.
30:14. They took away altars i. J.
26. there was great joy i. J. (2)
33:4.i.J.shall my name be for ever
7. i. J. wh. I have chosen bef. all
Ezr. 1 : 3. house of the Lord which is i. J., 5:16.-7 : 16, 17.
7:15.G.of Isr.,whose habita. is i.J.
27. beautify h. of L. which i. J.
9 : 9. to give us a wall i. J.
Ne. 2 : 20. ye have no right i. J.
11:1. bring one of ten to dwell i.J.
Ps.102:21. do declare his praise i.J.
Ec. 1 : 1. Preacher king i. J., 12.
16. been before me i. J., 2 : 7, 9.
Is. 4 : 3. remain-h i. J. called holy
24 : 23. when Lord shall reign i. J.
28:14. scornful men that rule i. J.
31 : 9. fire is in Z. his furnace i. J.
65 : 19. I will rejoice i. J. and joy
66 : 13. ye shall be comforted i. J.
Je. 4 : 5. publish i. J. and say
15 : 4. that wh. Manasseh did i. J.
Eze. 4 : 16. break staff of bread i. J.
12:10.burden concern-h prince i.J.
Jo. 2 : 32. i. J. shall be deliverance
Zch.12:6.be inhab. in her place i.J.
11. shall be great mourning i. J.
14 : 21. ev. pot i. J. be HOLINESS
Mal.2:11. an abom. is commit. i. J.
Lu. 2 : 25. a man i. J. Simeon
38. looked for redemption i. J.
43. child Jes. tarried behind i. J.
13 : 4. sinners above all dwelt i. J.
24 : 18. Art thou a stranger i. J.?
49. tarry ye i. J. until endued
Jn. 4 : 20. i. J. is place to worship
Ac.1:8. witnesses unto me i. J., 10: 39.
6 : 7. disciples multiplied i. J. [39.
9:21. them called on his name i.J.
11:22. ears of church wh. was i.J.
23 : 11. hast testified of me i. J.
26:10. Which thing I also did i. J.

Inhabitants of JERUSALEM.

2 Ch. 20 : 15. ye i.o.J. be not afraid
32:22. Thus the Lord saved i.o.J.
33.i.o.J.did him honour at death
34:32. i. o. J. did acc. to covenant
Ezr. 4:6. accusation against i. o. J.
Is. 5 : 3. i. o. J. judge bet. me and
8 : 14. for gin and snare to i. o. J.
22 : 21. he sh. be a father to i.o.J
Je. 8 : 1. bones of i. o. J. out of
11 : 9. conspiracy among i. o. J.
13:13. all i.o.J. with drunkenness
17 : 25. i. o. J. sh. remain for ever
35 : 13. Go tell Judah and i. o. J.
17. upon i. o. J., 36 : 31.-42 : 18. Zph. 1 : 4.
Eze.11:15.to whom i.o.J. have said
15:6. so will I give i. o. J. for fuel
Zch.12:5. i.o.J. sh. be my strength
7. glory of i.o.J. do not magnify
8. Lord shall defend the i. o. J.
10.pour upon i.o.J.Spirit of grace
13 : 1. fountain opened to i. o. J

O JERUSALEM.

2 Ch.20:17.salv. of L. with you O J.
Ps.116:19.pay my vows in midst O J.
122: 2. stand within thy gates, O J.
137 : 5. If I forget, O J.
147 : 12. Praise L. O J. [tidings
Is. 40 : 9. O J. that bringest good
51:17.stand,O J. | 52:2.and sit O J.
52:1. put on beauti.garments, O J.
62:6.watchm-n upon thy walls,O J.
Je. 4 : 14. O J. wash thy heart fr.
6 : 8. Be thou instructed, O J. lest
7 : 29. Cut off thine hair, O J.
13:27. O J. wilt not be made clean
15 : 5. who pity upon thee, O J.
Mat. 23 : 37. O J. J. thou that killest the prophets, Lu. 13 : 34.

Up to JERU'SALEM.

2 S.19:34 I sho. go u.with king t.J.
1 K.12:28. much for you to go u.t.
2 K. 12:17. set face to go u.t.J. [J.
16 : 5. Rezin came u. t. J. to war
Ezr. 1 : 3. let him go u. t. J., 7 : 13.
Mat. 20:18. we go u.t.J. Son of man betrayed, Mk. 10:33. Lu.18:31.
Mk. 10 : 32. were in the way u.t.J.
Lu. 2:42. u.t.J. after the custom of
19:28. he went before, u. t. J. Jn. 2 : 13.-5 : 1. Mat. 20 : 17.
Ac. 11 : 2. Peter was come u. t. J.
15 : 2. sho. go u. t. J. to apostles
21:4.said, he sho. not go u.t.J.,12.
24: 11.since I went u.t.J. to worsh.
25 : 9. Wilt go u. t. J. be judged
Ga.1:17. Nei. went I u.t.J. to apos.
18. I went u. t. J. to see Peter
2 : 1. I went u.t.J. with Barnabas

JERU'SHA = JERU'SHAH

2 K. 15:33. Jotham's moth.'s name J., 2 Ch. 27 : 1.

JESA'IAH.

1 Ch.3:21. sons of Hananiah, J.,Ne. [11:7.

JESHAI'AH.

1 Ch. 25 : 3. sons of Jeduthun, Zeri and J. | 15.-26:25. Ezr. 8:7, 19.

JESH'ANAH.

2 Ch. 13 : 19. Abijah took J. with [towns

JESHAR'ELAH.

1 Ch. 25:14. seventh lot came to J., [2.]

JESHEB'EAB.

1Ch.24:13. came forth 14th lot to J.

JE'SHER. See SHOBAB.

JESH'IMON.

Nu. 21 : 20. looketh tow. J., 23 : 28.
1 S.23:19. Hachilah so. of J.,24.-26: 1, 3.

JESHISH'AI. See JAHDO.

JESHOHAI'AH.

1 Ch. 4 : 36. J. and Asaiah princes

JESH'UA = JESH'UAH.

1 Ch.24:11.9th lot to J. | 2 Ch.31:15.
Ezr. 2 : 6. of chil. of J., Ne. 7 : 11.
36 ho. of J., Ne.7:39 | 40.Ne.7:43.
8:33.Ne. 3:19.-8:7.-9:4,5.-10:9.-12: 8, 24.
See JOSHUA, KADMIEL.

JESH'UA. [Place.] [J.

Ne. 11 : 26. of chil. of Jud. dwelt at

JESH'URUN = JES'URUN.

De. 32 : 15. J. waxed fat and kicked
33:5.king in J.when Isr. was gath.
26. is none like to the God of J.

JES'IAH.

1 Ch. 12:6.J.Joezer at Ziklag, 23:20.

JESIM'IEL.

1 Ch. 4 : 36. Adiel and J. princes

JES'SE.

Ru. 4 : 17. Obed. fa. of J., Mat. 1:5.
22. Obed begat J. and J., 1 Ch. 2 : 12. Mat. 1 : 5, 6. Lu. 3 : 32.
1 S. 16:1. I will send thee to J. the
5. sanctified J. and sons
10. J made 7 of his sons pass
11.unto J. Are here all thy chil.?
18. seen a son of J. th. is cunning
19. Saul sent messengers unto J.
17: 12. name J. and had 8 sons
58. I am son of thy servant J.
20 : 27. Whf. cometh not son of J.

1 S.20:30. thou hast chosen son of J.
31. as long as son of J. liveth
22:7. will son of J. give you fields
8. my son league with son of J.
9. Doeg said, I saw the son of J.
25:10. and who is the son of J.?
2 S. 20:1. nei. have we inheri. in son of J., 1 K.12:16. 2 Ch.10:16.
1 Ch. 10:14. kingd. unto son of J., 29:26.
12:18. on thy side are we, son of J.
Ps. 72:20. prayers of son of J. ended
Is.11:1. come a rod out of stem of J.
10. sh. be a root of J., Ro. 15:12.
Ac. 13:22. found David son of J.

JESTING.

Ep. 5:4. nor j. not convenient

JES'UI, ITES.

Ge. 46:17. sons of Asher, J., 1 Ch. 7:30.
Nu. 26:44. of Jesui, family of J-s

JES'URUN = JESH'URUN.

Is. 44:2. Fear not J. wh. I chosen

JE'SUS.

Mat. 1:21. shalt call his name J. for he sh. save, 25. Lu. 1:31.-2:21.
2:1. J. was born in Beth-lehem
3:15. J. said unto him, Suffer it
16. J. when bapt., Lu. 3:21.
4:1. J. was led of Spirit into wild.
17. Fr. that time J. began to prea.
18. J. walking by sea of Galilee
7:28. when J. had ended sayings
8:3. J. put forth hand and touched
10. J. heard it, he marvelled
14. when J. was come into Pe.'s ho
29. What to do with thee, J. thou Son, Mk. 1:24.-5:7. Lu. 4:34.-8:28.
34. whole city came out to meet J.
9:2. J. seeing their faith, Mk. 2:5.
10. J. sat at meat, Mk.2:15. Lu.7:37.
22. J. turned | 27. J. departed
30. J. straitly charged, saying, See
10:5. These 12 J. sent forth
12:25. J. knew their thoughts, 9:4. Mk. 2:8. Lu. 5:22.-9:47.
13:34. these spake J. unto mult.
53. J. had finished parables
14:1. Herod heard of the fame of J.
12. disciples went and told J.
22. J. constrained disciples to
29. Peter walked on water to J.
15:1. came to J. scribes and
30. cast them down at J.'s feet
16:21. began J. to shew unto disci.
17:1. J. taketh Pe. Ja. and, Mk.9:2.
4. unto J., L. it is good, Mk. 9:5.
8. saw no man save J. only, Mk. 9:8. Lu. 9:36.
18. J. rebuked devil he departed, Lu. 9:42.
25. when come, J. prevented him
18:2. J. called a lit. child unto him
20:30. blind heard J. passed by
34. J. had compassion on them
21:11. This is J. the prophet of Naz
22:18. J. perceived their wickedness
41. Phari. gathered J. asked
23:1. spake J. unto mult. and
26:4. take J. by subtilty kill him
19. disciples did as J. had appoin.
26. J. took bread and blessed it, Mk. 14:22.
50. and laid hands on J., Mk. 14:53.
59. false witness ag. J., Mk.14:55.
69. Thou also wast with J., 71. Mk. 14:67.
75. Peter remem. the words of J.
27:1. took counsel against J.
26. had scourged J., Mk. 15:15.
37. written, THIS IS J. THE KING OF THE JEWS, Jn. 19:19.
46. J. cried with loud, Mk. 15:37.
55. followed J. from Galilee
57. Joseph, who was J.'s disciple
28:5. I know ye seek J., Mk. 16:6.
9. J. met them | 18. J. spake unto
Mk. 1:9. J. came from Nazareth
45. J. could no more enter city
3:7. J. withdrew with disciples
5:6. when he saw J. afar off
13. J. gave them leave
19. J. suffered him not
20. great things J. had done, Lu. 8:39.
30. J. knowing virtue had gone out
9:4. Elias and Moses talking with J.
10:21. J. beholding, loved him
47. J have mercy, Lu.17:13.-18:38.
11:11. J. entered into Jerusalem
12:34. J. saw he ans-d discreetly
14:22. J. took bread and blessed
15:1. bound J. and carried him
16:9. Now when J. had risen early
Lu. 2:43. child J. tarried in Jerus.
52. J. incr-d in stature and wisd.
3:23. J. began to be about 30 y-rs of
5:19. let him down before J.
6:11. communed what do to J.
10:21. In that hour J. rejoiced
39. who sat at J.'s feet and heard
13:14. bec. J. healed on Sabbath
19:3. Zaccheus sought to see J.
22:47. Judas drew near unto J.
63. men that held J. mocked
23:26. might bear the cross after J.
24:15. J. drew near went with them
36. J. stood in midst of them
Jn. 1:29. John seeth J. coming
42. and he brought him to J.
45. J. of Nazareth son of Joseph
2:2. J. was called to marriage
11. This beginn. of miracles did J.
3:2. came to J. by night, 7:50.-19:39.
4:2. Tho. J. baptized not
6. J. wearied with his journey
53. hour J. said unto him
54. the second miracle J. did
5:15. J. wh. had made him whole
6:11. J. took the loaves and
14. seen miracle J. did
19. J. walking on sea, Mat. 14:25.
42. Is not this J. son of Joseph
64. J. knew from beginning who
7:16. J. ans-d, My doctrine is not
37. J. cried, saying, If any man
39. bec. J. was not yet glorified
50. he that came to J. by night
8:6. J. stooped and with finger
9. J. alone, and woman standing
59. J. hid hims. went out of tem.
9:1. J. saw a man was blind
11. A man, called J. made clay
10:23. J. walked in tem. Sol.'s porch
11:5. Now J. loved Martha
13. J. spake of his death | 35. J. wept
45. seen things J. did
12:3. anointed feet of J. wiped
9. came not for J.'s sake only
11. many of Jews believed on J.
16. when J. was glorif. rememb-d
12:21. Sir, we would see J. | they
22. Andrew and Philip tell J.
13:1. J. knew his hour was come
21. J. had thus said he was troubl.
23. leaning on J. bosom one whom J. loved, 20:2.-21:7, 20.
16:19. J. knew they were desirous
18:2. J. ofttimes resorted thither
4. J. knowing all that sho. come
7. Whom seek ye? they said, J.
22. one of the officers struck J.
19:1. Pilate took J. and scourged
5. came J. wearing crown of
25. stood by cross of J. his mother
28. J. knowing all things accompl.
40. took body of J. | 42. laid J.
20:2. other disciple wh. J. loved
14. she knew not it was J., 21:4.
24. Thom. not with them when J.
26. came J. doors being shut
30. many other signs did J.
31. believe J. is C., 1 Jn. 5:1, 5.
21:1. J. shewed hims. again to, 14.
4. morn. come J. stood on shore
Jn. 21:25. many other acts J. did
Ac. 1:1. of all that J. began to do
11. this J. wh. is taken up fr. you
16. Judas, guide to them took J.
2:22. J. of Naz. a man approved
2:32. this J. hath God raised up, 3:26.-5:30.-13:33.
3:13. G. of Ab. hath glorified his Son J.
4:2. preaching thro. J. resurrection
13. knowl. that they had been with J.
18. com-d not to teach in name of J.
27. of a truth ag. holy child J.
30. by name of holy child J.
5:40. not speak in name of J.
6:14. this J. sh. destroy this place
7:55. saw J. on right hand of G.
8:35. Philip preached unto him J.
9:5. I am J. thou persec-t, 22:8.-26:15.
17. J. th. appeared to thee
27. prea. at Damas in name of J.
10:38. how God anointed J. with
13:23. God raised a Saviour J.
17:7. there is another king, one J.
18. he preached J. and resurrec.
19:13. adjure you by J. wh. Paul
15. J. I know, but who are ye?
25:19. had questions of one J.
26:9. contrary to name of J.
28:23. persuading conc. J. law and
Ro. 3:26. of him wh. believeth in J.
8:11. Spirit of him th. raised up J.
1 Co.12:3. no man by Spi. calleth J.
2 Co. 4:5. your servants for J. sake
10. that life of J. be manifest
11. delivered to death for J. sake
14. who raised J. raised us by J.
11:4. for if he preach another J.
Ep.4:21. taught as the truth is in J.
Ph.2:10. at name of J. ev. knee bow
1 Th. 1:10. even J. who delivered us
4:14. that sleep in J. will G. bri.
He.2:9. J. who was made lower than
4:14. great high priest J., 6:20.
7:22. much was J. made surety
10:19. into holiest by blood of J.
12:2. Looking unto J. the author
24. to J. mediator of new cov.
13:12. J. suff-d without the gate
1 Jn. 4:15. Whoso. confess J. is Son
5:5. that believeth J. is son of G.
Re.14:12. they th. keep the faith of J.
17:6. drunk. with bl. of martyrs of J.
19:10. testimo. of J. is spirit of
20:4. beheaded for witness of J.
22:16. I J. have sent mine angel to

See **Jesus** with **CHRIST.**

JESUS with **Lord.**

Lu. 24:3. found not body of L. J.
Ac. 1:21. time L. J. went in and out
2:36. God made both L. and C.
4:33. witness of resurrection of L.J.
7:59. L. J. receive my spirit
8:16. baptized in name of L. J.
9:17. L. even J. appeared unto
29. spake boldly in name of L. J.
11:20. to Grecians, preaching L. J.
16:31. Believe on the L. J. Christ
19:10. in Asia heard word of L. J.
17. name of L. J. was magnified
20:24. ministry received of L. J.
35. to remem. words of L. J.
28:31. concerning L. J., Ro. 1:3.
Ro.4:24. raised our L. J., 2 Co.4:14.
10:9. confess with mouth L. J.
1 Co. 5:5. be saved in day of L. J.
1 Co.11:23. L.J. night he was betray.
12:3. no man can say that J. is L.
2 Co. 1:14. are ours in day of L. J.
4:10. bearing about dying of L. J.
Ga. 6:17. in my body marks of L. J.
Ep.1:15. your faith in L. J., Phm.5.
1 Th. 2:15. killed L.J. and prophets
4:1. we exhort you by the L. J.
2. what com-ts we gave by L. J.
2 Th. 1:7. when L. J. sh. be reveal.
He.13:20. brought fr. dead our L. J.

2 Pe. 1 : 2. thro. knowl. of J. our L.
Re.22:20. quickly, even so, come L.J.
See **Lord Jesus CHRIST.**
See GRACE, NAME.

JESUS said.

Mat. 4:7. J. s. unto him, It is writt.
8 : 10. J. s. I have not found so
13. J. s. unto centu. Go thy way
22. J. s. let dead bury, Lu. 9 : 60.
9:2.J. s. unto sick of palsy, Son be
6. J. s. Arise take up thy bed,
Mk. 2: 11. Lu. 5 : 24. Jn. 5 : 8.
15. J. s. Can chil. of, Mk. 2 : 19.
13:57. J. s. proph. is not, Mk. 6:4.
14 : 16. J. s. They need not depart
15:16.J.s. Are ye without underst.
32. J. s. I have compassion on
16 : 6. J. s. Take heed and beware
24. J. s. If any man come after
17:17.J.s.O perverse gene.,Lu.9:41.
20. J. s. Bec. of your unbelief
22. J. s. Son of man be betrayed
19 : 14. J. s. Suffer little chil. and
18. Which ? J. s. Do no murder
21. J. s. If thou wilt be perfect
23.s.J. a rich man hardly, Lu.18:
28.J.s. ye wh. have foll-d me [24.
21 : 21. J. s. If ye have faith [6:9.
24.J.s.I will ask you 1 thing,Lu.
22 : 37. J.s. Thou shalt love the L.
24 : 2. J. s. See ye not all these
26:34.J.s.this night bef. cock, Mk.
50.J.s. Friend, whf. come [14:72.
52.s. J. Put up thy sw.,Jn.18:11.
55. s. J. to mult. Are ye come as
ag. thief, Mk. 14:48. Lu.22:52.
27 : 11. J.s. unto him, Thou sayest
28 : 10. s. J. Be not afraid, go
Mk. 1 : 17. J. s. Come ye after me
7:27. J. s. Let chil. first be [possi.
9 : 23. J.s. If canst beli.,all things
39. J. s. Forbid him not [19.
10:18. J. s. Why callest me,Lu.18:
29. J. s. There is no man left h.
38. J. s. Ye know not wh. ye ask
39. J. s. Ye sh. drink of the cup
51. J. s. What wilt I should do
52. J. s. Go thy way thy faith
11 : 14. J. s. No man eat fruit of
12 : 24. J. s. Do ye not err
35. J. s. While he taught in tem.
13:2.J. s. Seest these gr. buildings
14:6. J. s. Let her alone, Jn. 12:7.
18. J. s. One of you shall betray
22. J. s. Take eat, this is my
62.J.s. ye sh. see Son sitting [33.
Lu.4:8.J.s.Get thee behind, Mk. 8:
5 : 10. J. s. unto Simon, Fear not
6 : 3. J. s. Have ye not read so
7 : 22. J. s. Go tell John what
40.J. s. Simon, I have somewhat
8 : 45. J. s. Who touched me
9 : 50. J. s. he not ag. us is for us
62. J. s. No man having put ha.
10 :21. J. s. I thank thee O Father
30. J. s. A cert. man went down
37. s. J. Go do thou likewise
41. J. s. Martha, thou careful
13 : 2. J. s. Suppose ye these Gali.
12. J. s. Woman thou art loosed
17:17. J. s. Were not ten cleansed
18: 22. J. s. Yet lackest 1 thing
42. J. s. Receive thy sight
19 : 9. J. s. This day is salvation
20:8.J.s. Nei. tell I you,Mk.11:33.
34. J. s. chil. of this world marry
22 : 48. J. s. Judas betrayest with
51. J. s. Suffer ye thus far [kiss?
23 : 34. J. s. Father forgive them
43. J. s. To day be in paradise
Jn. 1:48.J.s.Bef. Philip called thee
50. J. s. Bec. I said I saw these
2 : 19. J. s. Destroy this tem. and
22. disciples believed and J. s.
3 : 3. J. s. Except a man be born
10. J. s. Art thou a master
4 : 10. J. s. If knewest gift of G.
Jn.4:13.J.s.Whoso. drink-h of wat.
48. J. s. Except ye see signs
5 : 19. J. s. Son can do nothing of
6 : 10. J. s. Make men sit down
26. J. s. Ye seek me not because
29. J. s. This is the work of God
32. J. s. Mo. gave not that bread
35. J. s. I am the bread of life
43. J. s. Murmur not am. yours.
53. J. s. Except ye eat the flesh
67. J. s. Will ye also go away
7 : 6. J. s. My time is not come
33.J.s.Yet a little while,Jn.13:33.
8:11. J. s. Nei. do I condemn thee
14. J. s. Though I bear record
21. J. s. I go my way and ye
28. J. s. When ye have lifted Son
31. J. s. If ye contin. in my word
42. J. s. If G. were your father
58. Before Abraham was, I am
9 : 37. J. s. Thou hast both seen
39. J.s. For judgment I am come
41. J. s. If ye were blind
10 : 7. J. s. I am door of sheep
11:4.J.s. This sickn. not unto dea.
14. J. s. plainly Laz. is dead
25. J. s. I am the resurrection
39. J. s. Take ye away the stone
41. J. s. Fa. I thank thee hast
12 : 30. J. s. This voice came not
44. J. s. He that believ-h on me
13 : 7. J. s. What I do know-t not
21. J. s. one of you shall betray
29. J.s. Buy things we have need
31. J. s. Now is Son glorified
14 : 23. J. s. If any man love me
16 : 19. J. s. Do ye inquire among
20:21. J. s. Peace be unto you, 19.
21 : 23. J. s. not He shall not die

JESUS saith.

Mat. 8:4. J. s. Tell no man,Mk.5:43.
7. J. s. I will come heal him
20.J. s. foxes have holes,Lu.9:58.
9 : 28. J. s. Believe ye I am able
13 : 51. J. s. Have ye underst. all
15 : 34. J. s. How many loaves
17 : 26. J. s. Then are chil. free
18 : 22. J. s. I say until 70 times 7
21 : 16. J. s. have ye read, Out of
31. J. s. publicans and harlots go
42. J.s. Did ye never read
26 : 31. s. J. All be offend., Mk.
14 : 27.
64.J.s. unto priest Thou hast said
Mk. 11: 22. J. s. Have faith in God
Jn. 1 : 47. J. s. Behold an Israelite
2:4. J. s. Wom. what have I to do
4 : 7. J. s. Give me to drink
34. J. s. My meat is to do the will
50. J. s. Go; thy son liveth, 53.
8 : 39. J. s. If ye were Ab.'s chil.
11 : 23. J. s. Thy bro. shall rise
44. J. s. Loose him let him go
13 : 10. J. s. th. is washed needeth
14 : 6. J. s. I am the way, truth
9. J. s. Have I been so long wi.
18 : 5. J. s. I am he and Judas
19 : 14. J. s. Behold your king!
20 : 15. J. s. Wom. why weepest
16.J.s. Mary; she turned [me
29. J. s. Thomas bec. hast seen
21:5. J. s. Chil. have ye any meat
10. J. s. Bring of fish caught
15. J. s. to Pe., Lovest thou me?
22. J. s. If I will, he tarry

JE'SUS went.

Mat. 4 : 23. J. w. about Galilee
teaching, 9 : 35.
12 : 1. J. w. on Sab. through corn
14 : 14. J. w. and saw a gr. mult.
25. J. w. unto them on the sea
15 : 21. J. w. thence into coast of
21 : 12. J. w. into tem. and cast,
Mk. 11 : 15.
Jn. 2 : 13. J. w. up to Jerus., 5 : 1.
6 : 1. J. w. over sea | 3. into mt.
7:14.J.w. up into tem. and taught
Jn.8:1. J. w. unto the mt. of Olives

JE'SUS = JOSH'UA.

Ex.17:† 9.Moses said unto J. choose
Ac. 7:45. with J. unto possession of
He. 4:8. if J. given them rest [Gent.

JE'SUS. [A disciple.]

Col. 4 : 11. J. who is called Justus

JE'THER.

Jn. 8 : 20. to J. Up and slay | Ex.
4 : † 18. 1 Ch. 4: 17.-7 : 38.
See ITHRA.

JETH'ETH.

Ge. 36 : 40. duke J., 1 Ch. 1 : 51.

JETH'LAH.

Jos. 19 : 42. coast of their inheri. J.

JE'THRO = REUEL.

Ex. 3:1. Mo. kept flock of J., 2:†18.
4:18. Moses returned to J. his fa.
18 : 1. J. heard of all G. had done
5. J. with sons and wife unto Mo.
6. I thy fa.-in-l. J. am come
9.J.rejoiced for goodn. to Isr.,10.
12. J. took burnt offering for G.

JE'TUR.

Ge. 25 : 15. sons of Ishm. J. | 1 Ch.
1 : 31.-5 : 19.

JE'UEL. See ZERAH.

JE'USH.

Ge. 36 : 5. Aholibamah bare J., 14,
18. 1 Ch. 1 : 35.
1 Ch. 7 : 10. sons of Bilhan; J. |
23: 10, 11. 2 Ch. 11: 19.

JE'UZ. See SHAHARAIM.

JEW.

Es. 2 : 5. a certain J. Mordecai
3 : 4. he told them he was a J.
6:10. do so to Mordecai the J., 2:5.
-5 : 13.-8 : 7.-9 : 29, 31.-10 : 3.
Je. 34 : 9. none serve hims. of a J.
Zch. 8:23. take hold of skirt of a J.
Jn. 4 : 9. How is it thou a J. askest
18:35. Pilate ans., Am I a J.? [drink?
Ac. 10 : 28. it is unlawful for a J.
13 : 6. they found a sorcerer, a J.
18:2. Paul found a J. named Aquila
24. a J. named Apollos
19 : 14. Sceva a J. [22 : 3.
19:34. Alex. a J. | 21:39. Paul a J.,
Ro. 1 : 16. to the J. first, 2 : 9, 10.
2: 17. thou a J. and resteth in law
28. not a J. | 29. he J. who is one
3:1. What advantage hath the J.?
10:12. is no difference betw. J. and
Greek, Ga. 3 : 28. Col. 3 : 11.
1 Co. 9:20. unto J. I became as a J.
Ga.2:14.If thou a J. livest as Gent.

JEWS.

2 K. 16:6. Rezin drave J. fr. Elath
18 : 26. in the J.s' language, 28. 2
Ch. 32:18.Ne.13:24.Is.36:11,13.
Ezr. 4 : 12. J. are come unto Jerus.
5:5. elders of J., 6:7, 8, 14. Lu. 7:3.
Ne. 1 : 2. asked conc. J. that escap.
2:16.nei. had I told it to J. [ble J.?
4 : 2. Sanbal., What do these fee-
5 : 8. redeemed brethren the J.
17. there were at my table 150 J.
6 : 6. thou and J. think to rebel
13 : 23. I saw J. th. married wives
Es.8:10.unto Haman the J.s' enemy
4 : 3. was great mourning am. J.
14. sh. deliverance arise unto J.
6 : 13. If Mordecai be of seed of J.
8:3. Haman had devised against J.
7. Haman laid his hand upon J.
8. Write ye for J. in king's name
16. J. had light and gladness, 17.
17. fear of the J. fell upon them
9 : 2. J. gathered in their cities
3. officers of the king helped J.
5. J. smote all their enemies
6. in Shushan J. slew 500 men
22. J. rested from their enemies
28. days of Purim not fail am. J.
10 : 3. Mordecai was great am. J.
Je. 38 : 19. said, I am afraid of J.
52:28. away captive 3023 of J., 30.

Da. 3: 8. Chaldeans accused the J.
Mat.28:15.saying is reported am. J.
Jn. 2: 6. manner of purifying of J.
13.J.'s passover,5:1.-6:4 Jn.11:55.
3:25. bet. John's disciples and J.
4: 9. J. no dealings with Samari.
22. salv. is of J. | 5: 1. feast of J.
5: 16. did J. persecute Jesus
18. J.sought the more to kill him
6: 41. J. murmured at him
52. J. strove among themselves
7: 13. no man spake for fear of J.
8:31.said Jesus to J. wh. believed
9: 18. J. not believe he been blind
22. spake parents bec. feared J.
10: 19. was division again am. J.
31. J. took up stones again
11:8.J.of late sought to stone thee
19. many of J. came to Martha
33. Jesus saw her and J. weeping
12:11.many of J.believed on Jesus
18:20.taught in tem.,whi.J. resort
36. I sho. not be delivered to J.
19: 12. J. cried, If let this man
38. secretly, for fear of J., 20:19.
19: 40. as manner of J. is to bury
Ac. 9: 22. confounded J. at Damas.
11: 19. preaching unto J. only
12: 3. Herod saw it pleased the J.
13: 43. many of J. followed Paul
50. J. stirred up devout women
14: 2. unbel-g J. stirred up Gent.
4. part held with J., part with
16: 3. bec. of J. in those parts
20. These men J. trouble our city
17: 5. J. wh. believed not, moved
18: 19. he reasoned with J.
28. he mightily convinced the J.
19: 10. J. and Greeks heard word
13. certain vagabond J. exorcists
20: 3. J. laid wait for him, 19.
21:11. sh.J.at Jerus. bind the man
20. many thous. of J. wh. believe
23: 12. certain J. banded together
27. This man was taken of the J.
24:18.J. fr. Asia found me purified
25: 8. Nei. against the law of J.
10. to J. have done no wrong
26:2. I am accused of J., 7.-22:30.
Ro. 3: 29. Is he God of J. only?
1 Co. 1: 23. Christ, to J. a stumbli.
9:20. to J. I became as a Jew that
I might gain J. [40 stripes
2 Co. 11 :24. of J. 5 times received
Ga. 1: 13. in the J.s' religion, 14.
2: 13. other J. dissembled wi. him
14. as Gentiles, not as do J.
15. We who are J. by nature [J.
1 Th. 2:14. as they have suffered of
Re.2:9. say they are J. and are not,
See GENTILES. [3: 9.

All the JEWS.

Es. 3:6. sought to destroy a. J., 13.
4:13. more than a. J. | 16. gather
9:20. sent letters unto a.J. [a.J.
Je. 32:12. bef. a. J. in court of pris.
40: 11. when a. J. in Moab heard
12. a. J. returned out of all pla.
15.a.J. wh. are gath-d unto thee
41:3. Ishmael slew a. J. with him
44: 1. word conc. a. J. in Egypt
Mk. 7: 3. a. J. except they wash
Ac. 18: 2. com-d a. J. to depart fr.
19:17. was known to a. J. at Eph.
21:21.teachest a.J. to forsake Mo.
22: 12. had a good report of a. J.
24:5. a mover of sedition am. a. J.
26: 4. my life at Jerus. know a. J.

KING of the Jews.

Mat. 2: 2. Where he born K. o. J.?
27: 11. gov. asked Jesus, Art thou
K.o.J.? Mk.15:2. Lu. 23:3. Jn.
18: 33. [19: 3.
29. Hail, K. o. J. Mk. 15: 18. Jn.
37. his accusation,THIS IS JESUS,
THE KING OF THE JEWS.Mk.
15: 26. Lu. 23: 38. Jn. 19: 19.
Mk.15:9.Pilate ans.,Will ye th. I release unto you K.o.J.?Jn.18:39.
12. do unto him ye call K. o. J.
Lu. 23: 37. if K. o. J. save thyself
Jn.19:21. priests said, Write not K.
o. J., he said, I am K. o. J.

JEWEL.

Pr. 11: 22. As j. in swine's snout
20:15.lips of knowl.are precious j.
Eze.16:12.I put a j.on thy forehead

JEWELS.

Ge. 24: 53. serv. brought forth j.
Ex. 3: 22. shall borrow j. of gold,
11: 2.-12: 35. [Nu. 31: 50.
35: 22. they brought all j. of gold,
Nu. 31: 51. took gold, even all j.
1 S. 6: 8. j. of gold in a coffer, 15.
2 Ch. 20: 25. riches and precious j.
32:27. treasuries for all pleasant j.
Jb. 28: 17. exchange of it not for j.
Can. 1: 10. cheeks are comely wi. j.
7: 1. joints of thy thighs like j.
Is. 61: 10. as bride adorneth wi. j.
Eze. 16:17. hast taken j. of my gold
39. they sh.take thy fair j.,23:26.
Ho. 2: 13. decked herself with j.
Mal.3:17. mine, when I make up j.

JEW'ESS. [Jered

1 Ch. 4: † 18. his wife the J. bare
Ac. 16: 1. Timotheus was son of a J.
24: 24. Felix' wife Drusilla was J.

JEW'ISH. [bles

Tit. 1: 14. not giving heed to J. fa-

JEW'RY.

Da. 5: 13. whom fa. bro-t out of J.
Lu. 23: 5. stirreth peo. teaching
throughout J. [Jews
Jn. 7: 1. Jesus not walk in J. bec.

JEZANI'AH.

Je.40:8. J. came to Gedeliah | 42:1:
See JAAZINIAH.

JEZ'EBEL.

1 K. 16: 31. Ahaz took to wife J.
18:4. when J. cut off the prophets
13. what I did when J.slew proph.
19. proph. of Baal eat at J.'s table
19: 1. Ahab told J. all Elijah had
2. J. sent messenger unto Elijah
21: 5. J. his wife came to him, 7.
11. elders did as J. sent [14.
15. J. heard Naboth was stoned,
23.dogs shall eat J.,2 K. 9: 10, 36.
25. none like Ahab, wh. J.stirred
2 K. 9: 7. avenge at hand of J.
22. whoredoms of thy mother J.
37. carcass of J. be as dung, (2)
Re. 2: 20. sufferest that woman J.

JE'ZER, ITES. [13.

Ge.46:24.sons of Naph., J. 1 Ch. 7:
Nu. 26: 49. of J. the family of J-s

JEZI'AH. [miah, J.

Ezr. 10: 25. taken stra. wives; Ra-

JEZI'EL.

1 Ch. 12: 3. J. Pelet sons of Azma.

JEZLI'AH. See ISHMERAI.

JEZO'AR.

1 Ch. 4: 7. sons of Helah Zereth, J.

JEZRAHI'AH.

Ne. 12: 42. sung with J. overseer

JEZ'REEL. [Person and Place.]

Jos. 15: 56. in mts. J. [Jos. 17: 16.
Ju. 6: 33. pitched in valley of J.,
1 S. 25: 43. David took Ahin. of J.
29:1.Isr. pitched by fountain in J.
11. Philistines went up to J.
2 S. 2: 9. Ish-bosheth king over J.
4:4. tidings came of Saul out of J.
1 K. 4: 12. by Zartanah beneath J.
18: 45. and Ahab rode to J.
46. Elijah ran before Ahab to J.
21:1. Naboth had a vineyard in J.
23. dogs eat Jezebel by wall of J.,
2 K. 9:10, 36. [15. 2 Ch. 22: 6.
2 K.8: 29.Joram went back to J.,9:
9: 16. Jehu rode in chariot to J.
17. watchman on tower in J.
37. carcass in portion of J.
2 K.10:1.Jehu sent unto rul-s of J.
6. come to me to J. to morrow
7. sent heads of king's sons to J.
11. slew all of ho. of Ahab in J.
1 Ch. 4: 3. were of fa. of Etam, J.
Ho. 1:4. Call his name J., for I, (2)
5. I will break bow of Israel in J.
11. for great shall be day of J.
2: 22. wine and oil shall hear J.

JEZ'REELITE. See NABOTH.

JEZ'REELITESS.

1 S. 27: 3. wives, Ahinoam the J.,
30: 5. 2 S. 2: 2.-3: 2. 1 Ch. 3: 1.

JIB'SAM. See TOLA.

JID'LAPH. See MILCAH.

JIMNA, JIM'NAH, NITES.

Nu. 26: 44. chil. of Asher, of J.
fam. of J-s | Ge. 46: 17. 1 Ch.
7: 30.

JIPH'TAH.

Jos. 15:43. cities of Jud.; J. Nezib

JIPH'THAH-EL.

Jos.19:14. are in the valley of J.,27.

JO'AB. [2: 16.

2 S. 2:18. sons of Zeruiah, J., 1 Ch.
22.how hold up my face to J. thy
24. J. Abishai pursued Abner
3: 22. J. came fr. pursuing a troop
27. J. took him aside to speak
29. bl. of Abner rest on J., 1 K.2:
30.J.and Abishai slew Abner [33.
8: 16. J. was over the host, 20:23.
1 Ch. 11: 6.-18: 15.-27: 34.
10:14.J.return-d fr.chil.of Ammon
11: 7. Da. demanded how J. did
11. Isr. in tents, and my lord J.
14. David wrote a letter to J.
12: 26. J. fought against Rabbah
14: 1. J. perceived the k.'s heart
3. J. put words in widow's mouth
19. Is not hand of J. with thee
23. J. arose — brought Abs. to
29. Abs. sent for J. | 30.J.'s field
17: 25. Amasa captain instead
18:2. 3d part of peo. under of J.+
16. J. held back the people
21. said J. to Cushi tell king
19: 5. J. came unto h. of k. | 1,13.
20: 7. went out J.'s men+
9.J. killed Amasa | 17. Art thou J.
24:2.k. said to J. capt.+1 Ch.21:2.
4. king's words prevailed ag. J.
and captains, 1 Ch. 21: 4.
1 K. 1:7. Adonijah confer. wi. J.+
2:5. thou kno-t what J. did to me
28. J. fled to taber. caught horns
11: 15. J. give to bury slain+
16. six months did J. remain
1 Ch. 2: 54. Ataroth, house of J.+
4: 14. Seraiah begat J. [18: 15.
11: 6. J. went first up, was chief+
19:8. when Da. heard he sent J.+
20: 1. J. led army, smote Rabbah
21:6. k.'s word was abom. to J.+
26: 28. all that J. had dedicated
Ezr. 2: 6. of chil. of J., Ne. 7: 11.
8: 9. Of sons of J. Obadiah went

JO'AH. [3.

2 K. 18:18. J. son of Asaph, Is. 36:
26. said J., Speak I pray,Is.36:11.
37. came J. to Hez., Is. 36: 22.
1 Ch. 6:21. J. son of Zimmah | 26:4.
2 Ch. 34: 8. sent J. son of Joahaz,

JO'AHAZ. See JOAH. [29:12.

JOAN'NA.

Lu. 3: 27. Juda, was the son of J.
8: 3. J. wife of Chuza, Herod's
24: 10. it was Mary Mag. and J.

JO'ASH. [30.

Ju. 6: 11. that pertaineth unto J. |
31. J. said Will ye plead for Baal?
7: 14. sword of Gideon son of J.,
6: 29.-8: 13, 29, 32.
1 K. 22:26. 2 K. 11: 2.-13: 1, 9, 10,
12, 14, 25.-14: 1, 3, 17, 23, 27.
2 Ch. 18: 25.-22: 11.-24: 1.-26,
17, 18, 21, 23, 25.

1 K. 22:26. J. king's son, 2 Ch. 18:25.
2 K. 11: 2. stole J., 2 Ch. 22: 11.
13: 9. J. son of Jehoahaz reigned
13. J. was buried with kings of Israel, 14: 16.
14. J. king of Isr. wept over Elisha
25. J. beat Ben-hadad 3 times
14: 1. Ama. son of J. k. of Judah
23. Jerob. son of J., 27. Ho. 1:1.
1 Ch. 3: 11. J. his son. ⌊Am. 1:1.
4: 22. men of Chozeba and J.
7: 8. sons of Becher; Zemira J.
12: 3. J. the son of Shemaiah
27: 28. over cellars of oil was J.
2 Ch. 24: 2. J. did right in sight
4. J. minded to repair h., 2 K. 12:
22. J. rememb-d not kindn. ⌊4, 7.
24. they executed judgm. ag. J.

JO'ATHAM = JO'THAM.

Mat. 1: 9. Ozias begat J. J. begat

JOB. ⌈Ch. 7: † 1.

Ge. 46: 13. sons of Issachar; J., 1
Jb. 1: 1. a man in Uz name was J.
5. J. sent and sanctified sons
8. Hast consid. my serv. J.? 2: 3.
9. Doth J. fear God for nought?
20. J. arose rent his mantle
22. In all this J. sinned not, 2: 10.
2: 7. Sat. smote J. with sore boils
10. In all this did not J. sin
11. when J.'s three friends heard
3: 1. J. cursed his day and
6: 1. J. answ-d and said, 9: 1.-12: 1.-16: 1.-19: 1.-21: 1.-23: 1.-26: 1.-40: 3.-42: 1.
27: 1. J. continu. his parable, 29: 1.
31: 40. The words of J. are ended
32: 1. these 3 ceased to answer J.
2. ag. J. was Elihu's wrath kindl.
3. found no ans. yet condem-d J.
12. none of you that convinced J.
33: 31. Mark well, O J. hearken
34: 5. for J. had said I am righte.
34: 7. What man is like J. who drinketh scorning?
35. J. hath spok. without knowl.
36. that J. be tried unto the end
35: 16. J. open his mouth in vain
38: 1. Then the L. ans-d J., 40: 1.
42: 7. ye not spoken as J. hath, 8.
8. take 7 bullocks to my serv. J.
9. the Lord also accepted J.
10. Lord gave J. twice as much
12. Lord blessed latter end of J.
15. no women so fair as dau-s of J.
16. After this J. lived 140 years
17. J. died, old and full of days
Eze. 14: 14. tho. Dan. and J. in it, 20.
Ja. 5: 11. heard of patience of J.

JO'BAB. ⌈1: 23.

Ge. 10: 29. J., sons of Joktan, 1 Ch.
36: 33. J. reigned, 1 Ch. 1: 44.
34. J. died, 1 Ch. 1:45. | Jos. 11: 1. 1 Ch. 8: 9.

JOCH'EBED.

Ex. 6: 20. took J. to wife, Nu. 26: 59.

JO'ED. See PEDAIAH.

JO'EL.

1 S. 8: 2. Samuel's firstborn was J.
1 Ch. 4: 35. of family of Simeon, J.
5: 4. of Reubenites, sons of J., 8.
12. of Gadites, J. chief ⌈15: 17.
6: 33. Heman, a singer, son of J.,
36. Elkanah the son of J.
7: 3. sons of Izrahiah; Michael, J.
11: 38. J. and Mibhar valiant men
15: 7. sons of Gershom, J. chief
11. David called for J. the Levite
23: 8. sons of Laadan, chief J.
26: 22. sons of Jehieli; J.
27: 20. of tribe of Manas. J. capt.
2 Ch. 29: 12. J. son of Aza-h, 1 Ch. 6: 36. ⌈wives
Ezr. 10: 43. J. and Benaiah strange
Ne. 11: 9. J. was overseer
Jo. 1: 1. word to J. son of Pethuel
Ac. 2: 16. spoken by prophet J.

See SHAUL, VASHNI.

JOE'LAH.

1 Ch. 12: 7. and J. sons of Jeroham

JOE'ZER. See JESIAH.

JOG'BEHAH,

Nu 32: 35. chil. of Gad built J. |

JOG'LI. ⌊Ezr. 8: 11.

Nu. 34: 22. prince of tribe of Dan,

JO'HA. ⌊son of J.

1 Ch. 11: 45. and J. valiant men |

JOHA'NAN. ⌊8: 16.

2 K. 25: 23. to Gedaliah J. son of Careah, Je. 40: 8, 13, 15, 16.-41: 11, 13, 14, 16.-42: 1, 8.-43: 2, 4, 5.
1 Ch. 3: 15. sons of Josiah, J.
24. sons of Elioenai; J. ⌈12.
6: 9. begat J. | J. begat, 2 Ch. 28:
12: 4. over the 30 J. | Ne. 6: 18.
Ezr. 8: 12. J. son of Hakkatan
10: 6. Ezra into chamber of J.
Ne. 12: 22. J. recorded chief | 23.
Je. 41: 11. when J. heard of evil
43: 4. J. obeyed not voice of L.

JOHN. [Apostle.]

Mat. 4: 21. James and J. the sons of Zebedee, 10: 2. Mk. 1: 19.-3: 17.
Lu. 22: 8. Jes. sent Pe. and J. to
Ac. 3: 1. Pe. and J. went into tem.
3. seeing Pe. and J. about to go
4. Pe. and J. said, Look on us, 11.
11. as lame man held Pe. and J.
4: 13. saw boldness of Pe. and J.
8: 14. sent to Samaria Pe. and J.
12: 2. Herod killed Ja. bro. of J.
Ga. 2: 9. Cephas and J. who seemed to be pillars ⌈J.
Re 1: 1. signified it by his angel to
4. J. to the 7 churches in Asia
9. I J. who also am your brother
21: 2. I J. saw holy city new Jerus.
See JAMES.

JOHN. [Baptist.]

Mat. 3: 4. J. had raiment, Mk. 1: 6.
14. Jes. to be baptized, J. forbade
4: 12. J. cast into pris., Mk. 1: 14.
9: 14. came disciples of J., Mk. 2: 18. Lu. 5: 33 -7: 18.-11: 1. Jn. 3: 25.
11: 2. J. had heard of C., Lu. 7: 19.
4. shew J. these thi., Lu. 7: 22.
7. Jesus began to say concerning J., Lu. 7: 24. ⌈16: 16.
13. law prophesied until J., Lu.
18. J. came neither eating nor
14: 10. Herod beheaded J., Mk. 6:
16. Lu. 9: 9. ⌈11: 32. Lu. 20: 6.
21: 26. all hold J. a prophet, Mk.
32. J. came in way of righteousn.
Mk. 6: 18. J. had said unto Herod, It is not lawful, Mat. 14: 4.
20. Herod feared J. ⌈J., 60.
Lu. 1: 13. thou shalt call his name
3: 2. word of G. unto J. son of
15. all mused in hearts of J.
9: 7. that J. was risen from dead
11: 1. teach us to pray as J. his
Jn. 1: 6. a man sent fr. G., was J.
15. J. bare witness of him
19. this is the record of J., 32.
29. next day J. seeth Jes. coming
40. one of the 2 wh. heard J. speak
3: 24. J. was not yet cast into pris.
25. question betw. J.'s disci. and
27. J. ans-d A man can rec. noth.
4: 1. Jes. made more disci. than J.
5: 33. Ye sent to J. he bare witu.
36. greater witn. than that of J.
10: 41. J. did no miracle; but (2)
Ac. 18: 24. When J. had first preach.
25. And as J. fulfilled his course
See BAPTISM, BAPTIST, BAPTIZE, ED, ING.

JOHN. [Surnamed Mark.]

Ac. 12: 12. Pe. came to house of J.
25. took J. whose surname Mark
13: 5. they had J. to their minis.
13. J. departing, returned to Jerus.

Ac. 15: 37. Barnabas determ. to take

JOHN. ⌊J.

Ac. 4: 6. J. and Alex. gathered tog.

JOI'ADA.

Ne. 12: 10. begat J. | 11. J. begat
22. J. and Jona. chief | 13: 28.

JOI'AKIM.

Ne. 12: 10. begat J. J. begat
12. in days of J. were priests | 26.

JOI'ARIB.

Ezr. 8: 16. fr. Jarib. J. men of understanding ⌈11: 10.
Ne. 12: 6. J. up with Zerub. | 19.

JOIN.

Ex. 1: 10. lest they j. unto our ene.
2 Ch. 20: 35. Jehosh. j. wi. Ahaziah
Ezr. 9: 14. j. in affinity with peo.
Pr. 11: 21. hand j. in hand, 16: 5.
Is. 5: 8. woe unto them j. hou. to
9: 11. L. shall j. his enemies tog.
56: 6. sons of stranger th. j. thems.
Je. 50: 5. let us j. ours. to the L.
Eze. 37: 17. j. them one to another
Da. 11: 6. shall j. in end of years
Ac. 5: 13. durst no man j. himself
8: 29. Go j. thyself to this chariot
9: 26. Saul assayed to j. disciples

JOINED.

Ge. 14: 3. All these kings were j.
8. they j. battle in the vale of Sid.
29: 34. this time husb. be j. unto me
1 K. 28: 7. j. at the two edges (2)
Nu. 18: 2. breth. of Levi. be j., 4.
1 S. 4: 2. j. battle, Isr. was smitten
1 K. 7: 32. axletrees of wheels j.
20: 29. in 7th day battle was j.
2 Ch. 18: 1. Jehosh. j. affinity with
20: 36. he j. with Ahaziah, 37.
Ezr. 4: 12. set walls, j. foundation
Ne. 4: 6. all the wall was j. togeth.
Es. 9: 27. all that j. sho. keep Purim
Jb. 3: 6. not be j. unto days of yr.
41: 17. Leviathan's scales are j.
23. flakes of his flesh are j. toge.
Ps. 83: 8. Assur also is j. with th.
Ec. 9: 4. to him j. to living is hope
Is. 13: 15. j. unto them sh. fall by
14: 1. strangers sh. be j. wi. them
20. shalt not be j. in burial
56: 3. Nei. let him j. to L. speak
Eze. 1: 9. Their wings were j., 11.
46: 22. courts j. of 40 cubits long
Ho. 4: 17. Ephraim is j. to idols
Zch. 2: 11. many nations be j. to L.
Mat. 19: 6. what G. hath j., Mk. 10: 9.
Lu. 15: 15. j. himself to a citizen
Ac. 5: 36. about 400 j. themselves
18: 7. house j. hard to synagogue
1 Co. 1: 10. ye be perfectly j. in
6: 16. he j. to a harlot is one body
17. he j. unto the L. is one spirit
Ep. 4: 16. whole body fitly j. toge.
5: 31. and sh. be j. unto his wife
See BAAL-PEOR.

JOINING, S. ⌈j-s

1 Ch. 22: 3. Da. prepared iron for
2 Ch. 3: 12. j. to wing of cherub'

JOINT. ⌈of j.

Ge. 32: 25. Jacob's thigh was out
Ps. 22: 14. all my bones are out of j.
Pr. 25: 19. confid. like foot out of j.
Ep. 4: 16. which every j. supplieth
See Joint HEIRS.

JOINTS.

1 K. 22: 34. smote king of Isr. betw. j. of harness, 2 Ch. 18: 33.
Can. 7: 1. j. of thighs like jewels
Da. 5: 6. j. of his loins loosed
Col. 2: 19. all body by j. knit toge
He. 4: 12. dividing asunder of j. and

JOK'DEAM. ⌈Jud.

Jos. 15: 56. J., Zanoah of inher. of

JO'KIM. See SHELAH.

JOK'MEAM.

1 Ch. 6: 68. gave also J. wi. suburbs

JOK'NEAM.

Jos. 12: 22. king of J. of Carmel

Jos.19:11. river bef. J. | 21:34. 1 K.
JOK'SHAN. [4:12.
Ge.25:2. Keturah bare J., 1 Ch. 1:
3.J. begat Sheba, 1 Ch. 1:32.[32.
JOK'TAN.
Ge. 10:25, 26, 29. 1 Ch. 1:19, 20, 23.
JOK'THEEL.
2 K. 14: 7. called it J. | Jos. 15:38.
JO'NA, JO'NAS.
Jn. 1: 42. thou art Simon son of J.
21:15. Simon son of J-s lovest, 16,
See BAR-JONA. [17.
JON'ADAB. [35.
2 S. 13: 3. J., a subtle man | 5,32,
Je. 35: 6. J. our fa. com-d us, 14.
8. we obeyed voice of J.,10,16,18.
19. J. not want a man to stand
See JEHONADAB.
JO'NAH, JO'NAS.
2 K. 14: 25. word he spake by J.
Jon. 1: 1. word of L. unto J., 3: 1.
1: 3. J rose to flee unto Tarshish
7. cast lots, the lot fell upon J.
15. they cast J. into the sea
17. J. was in belly of fish 3 days
2:1. J. prayed | 10. vomited out J.
3:3. J. to Nin. | 4: 1. displeased J.
4:6. made gourd to come over J.
8. sun beat upon head of J.
9. G. said to J. Doest well angry
Mat. 12: 39. no sign but sign of
prophet J-s, 16:4. Lu. 11:29,30.
40. as J-s was in whale's belly
41. repented at preaching of J-s
JO'NAN. See ELIAKIM.
JO'NAS. See JONA, JONAH.
JON'ATHAN.
Ju. 18: 30. J. and sons were priests
1 S.13:2.1000 men with J. in Gibeah
3. J. smote garrison of Philistines
22. with Saul and J. were swords
14: 1. J. said unto young man, 6.
3. people knew not J. was gone
13. J climbed up upon his hands
27.J.heard not his fa.charged peo.
29. J. said, My fa. hath troubled
39. though in J. he sh. surely die
40. I and J. will be on other side
42. J. was tak. | 44. shalt die, J.
45. peo. rescued J. he died not
18: 1. soul of J. was knit with Da.
3. J. and Da. made a covenant
4. J. stripped himself of robe
19:1. Saul spake to J. to kill Da.+
2. J. delighted much in David
4. J. spake good of Da. unto Saul
20:1. Da. said bef. J. What have
3. Let not J. know lest grieved
13. L. do so, and more to J. [3.
16.J.made cov. with h. of Da.,18:
30.Saul's anger was kindled ag. J.
33. J. knew it determ. to slay Da.
34. J. arose in fierce anger
37. J. cried after lad, 38.
39. J. and David knew
23: 16. J. went to David
31: 2. Philis. slew J., 1 Ch. 10: 2.
2 S. 1:4. Saul and J. his son dead, 5.
17. lamentation over Saul and J.
22. bow of J. turned not back
23. Saul and J. lovely in lives
25. O J. slain in high places
26. I am distressed for thee, J.
4: 4. J. had a son lame, 9: 3.
9: 1. shew kindness for J.'s sake
7. shew thee kindn. for J. sake
15:27.J. son of Abia., 36. 1 K.1:42,
17:17. J. stayed by En-rogel [43.
21: 7. spared Mephib. son of J.
12. Da. took bones of J., 13, 14.
21. J. slew him, 1 Ch. 20: 7.
23: 32. of Jashen, J. valiant man
1 Ch. 2: 32. the sons of Jada, J.
33. sons of J. Peleth and Zaza
8: 34. son of J. Merib-baal, 9: 40.
11: 34. sons of Hashem; J. Ahiam
27: 32. J. was a counsellor

Ezr. 8: 6. Ebed the son of J.
10: 15. Only J. Jehaziah employed
Ne.12:11. begat J. | 14. of Melicu J.
35. Zechariah son of J.
Je. 37:15. Jere. in prison in h. of J.
20. not return to h. of J., 38: 26.
40: 8. J. came to Gedaliah to Miz-
See DAVID, SAUL. [pah
JOP'PA = JA'PHO.
2 Ch. 2: 16. in floats by sea to J.,
Ezr. 3: 7.
Jon. 1: 3. Jonah went down to J.
Ac. 9: 36. was at J. Tabitha
38. as Lydda was nigh to J.
42. it was known throughout J.
43. Pe. tarried many days in J.
10:5. send men to J., 8, 32.-11:13.
23. breth. from J. accomp. him
11: 5. I was in city of J. praying
JO'RA, JO'RAH.
See HARIPH.
JO'RAI. See JACHAN.
JO'RAM = JEHO'RAM.
2 S. 8: 10. Toi sent J. his son unto
David, 1 Ch.18:†10. [Jehosh.
2 K. 8: 16. J. of Ahab; J. son of
23. rest of the acts of J.
28. wounded J | 29. J. to Jezreel
9:14. Jehu conspired ag. J., 15, 16.
17. J. said, Take an horseman
and send | 21, 22, 23, 29.
11: 2. daughter of J. took Joash
1 Ch. 3: 11. J. his son, Ahaziah his
1 Ch. 26: 25. J over treasures
2 Ch.22:7.destruc. of Ahaziah by J.
Mat. 1: 8. Josaphat begat J. and J.
JOR'DAN.
Ge. 13:11. Lot chose plain of J., 10.
Nu.26:3.plains of Moab by J.,63.-31:
12.-33: 48,50.-35: 1.-36: 13.
34:12. border shall go down to J.,
Jos. 13: 27.-18: 12.-22: 25.
Jos. 3:1. to J. he and chil. of Isr.+
8. water of J. stand still in J.
11. ark passeth bef. you into J.
15. J. overfloweth all his banks
17. stood firm in midst of J., 4:10.
4: 3. Take twelve stones out of J.
7. waters of J. cut off bef. ark
8. twelve stones out of J., 3, 9, 20.
17. com. priests, Come out of J.
23. Lord dried up waters of J.
22: 25. L. hath made J. a border
28: 4. an inheri. for tribes from J.
Ju 3: 28. fords of J., 7: 24.-12: 5.
8: 4. Gid. came to J. passed over
12: 6. slew him at passages of J.
2 S. 19: 15. the king came to J.
20: 2. clave unto k. fr. J. to Jerus.
1 K. 2: 8. Shimei came to me at J.
7: 46. In plain of J. did king cast
them in clay, 2 Ch. 4: 17.
17: 3. Elijah by Cherith bef. J., 5.
2 K.2:6.tarry, L. hath sent me to J.
7. two stood by J. | 13. Elisha
5: 10. Go and wash in J. 7 times
14. Naaman dipped himself in J.
6: 2. Let us go to J. take a beam
7:15.they went aft. Syrians unto J.
Jb. 40: 23. that he can draw up J.
Ps.42:6. I will remember thee fr. J.
114: 3. fled, J. was driven back, 5.
Je. 12: 5. how do in swelling of J.?
49: 19. from swelling of J., 50:44.
Eze.47:18.meas. fr land of Isr. by J.
Zch 11: 3. pride of J is spoiled
Mat.3:5. all region about J., Lu.3:3.
6. baptized in J., Mk. 1: 5, 9.
13. cometh Jes from Galilee to J.
Mk 10:1.coasts of Judea by side of J.
Lu.4:1 Jes.full of H. G. ret-d fr. J.
Beyond JOR'DAN.
Ge. 50: 10. the floor of Atad **b.** J.
11 called Abel-mizraim, is **b.** J.
De. 3: 25. see the good land **b.** J.
Jos 9: 10. to k.'s of Amorites **b.** J.
13:8.inheri. Moses gave **b.** J.,18:7.

Ju. 5: 17. Gilead abode **b.** J. [15.
Is. 9: 1. land of Napht. **b.** J., Mat 4:
Mat.4:25.mult. from **b.** J., Mk.3:8.
19: 1. into coasts of Judea **b.** J.
Jn. 1: 28. done in Bethabara **b.** J.
3: 26. he with thee **b.** J. baptizeth
10: 40. and went again **b.** J.
On the other side JORDAN
De. 11:30. Ebal, are they not **o.-**J.
Jos.2:10. two kings that were **o.-**J.
7:7. content and dwelt **o.-**J.
12:1. Gad, and half tribe **o.-**J., 13:
27, 32.-14: 3.-17: 5.-22: 4.
20: 8. **o.-**J. Bezer, Ramoth, cities
22: 4. land Moses gave you **o.-**J.
24: 8. Amorites who dwelt **o.-**J.
Ju. 7:25. heads of Oreb, Zeeb, **o.-**J.
10:8 Israel **o.-**J oppressed by Amo
1 S. 31: 7. they **o.-**J. forsook cities
1 Ch. 6: 78. to chil. of Merari cities
12: 37. **o.-**J. 120,000 men [**o.-**J.
On this side JOR'DAN.
Nu.32:19. our inheri is fallen **o.-**J.,
32.-34: 15. Jos. 1:14, 15.-22:7.
35:14. give 3 cities **o.-**J., De. 4:41.
De. 1: 5. **o.-**J. Mo. began to declare
3: 8. we took land **o.-**J. fr. Arnon
4: 41. Mo. severed 3 cities **o.-**J.
47. Amorites wh. were **o.-**J., 3:8.
Jos.9:1.kings **o.-**J. gath-d ag. Josh,
1 Ch.26:30.1700 officers **o.-**J. [12:7.
Over JOR'DAN.
Ge. 32: 10. with staff I passed **o.** J.
Nu. 32: 5. bring us not **o.** J. [**o.** J.
21. if ye will go all of you armed
32. we will pass **o.** J. armed, 29.
33: 51. When ye are passed **o.** J.,
35: 10. De. 12: 10.-27: 2, 4, 12.
De. 2: 29. until I pass **o.** J. [-31:2
3: 27. shalt not go **o.** J., 4: 21, 22.
4: 22. must die, I must not go **o.** J.
9:1. Thou art to pass **o.** J., 11:31.
31: 13. land ye go **o.** J. to possess,
30: 18.-32: 47.
Jos. 1: 2. go **o.** this J. thou and all
11. within 3 days ye pass **o.** J.
3: 17. were passed clean **o.** J., 4:1.
4: 22. Isr. came **o.** J. on dry land
7:7. brought people **o.** J. to deliv.
24: 11. ye went **o.** J. unto Jericho
Ju. 10: 9. Ammon passed **o.** J.
1 S. 13: 7. of Hebrews went **o.** J.
2 S. 2: 29. Abner and men **o.** J.
17:22. David and peo. passed **o.** J.
24. Abs and all Isr. passed **o.** J.
19:15. conduct king **o.** J., 17, 31, 36.
1 Ch.12:15. as they that passed **o.** J.
19:17. Da. passed **o.** J. ag. Syrians
JO'RIM. See MATTHAT.
JOR'KOAM. [of J.
1 Ch. 2:44. Shema begat Raham fa.
JOS'ABAD.
1 Ch. 12: 4. among mighty men J.
JOS'APHAT.
Mat. 1: 8. Asa begat J. J. begat
JO'SE. See ELIEZER.
JOS'EDECH = JOZ'ADAK.
See JOSHUA.
JO'SEPH.
Ge. 30: 24. she called his name J.
33: 2. Jacob put J. hindermost
35: 24. sons of Jacob 12; sons of
Rachel, J. Benj., 46: 19. 1 Ch.
2: 2. [report
37: 2. J. bro-t unto fa. their evil
3. Isr. loved J. more than all
5. J. dreamed | 28. breth. sold J.
31. took J.'s coat killed a kid
33. J. is without doubt rent in
39: 1. J. was bro-t down to E.+
2. the Lord was with J., 21.
5.L. blessed Egyp.'s h. for J.'s sake
6. J. was a goodly person and
7. wife cast her eyes upon J.
20. J.'s master put him in prison
40:3. prison where J. was bound +
9. chief butler told dream to J.

Ge. 40:23. did not butler remem. J.
41 : 14. bro-t J. out of dungeon +
15. Pha said to J. I have dreamed
42. Pha. put his ring upon J.'s ha.
45. J.'s name Zaphnath-paaneah
46. J. 30 years old when bef. Pha.
49. J. gath-d corn as sand of sea
50. unto J. were born two sons
55. Go unto J. what he saith do
42 : 3. J.'s 10 breth. went to buy +
6. J. was governor of the land
8. J. knew breth. | 36. J. is not
43 : 16. when J. saw Benj. with +
17. the man did as J. bade
30. J. made haste, his bowels
44 : 4. J. said to steward follow +
45 : 1. J. could not refrain +
3. I am J., 4. | 9. saith thy son J.
26. told him J. is yet alive, 28.
46 : 4. J. sh. put ha. upon thine
29. J. went to meet his fa. ⌊eyes
47 : 1. J. came told Pharaoh +
12. J. nourished his fa. and his
15. all the Egyptians came unto J.
20. J. bought all the land of E.
29. die, and he called his son J.
48 : 1. told J. thy father is sick —
2. thy son J. cometh unto thee
9. J. said unto fa. They my sons
12. J. bro-t them from bet. knees
15. Jacob blessed J. and said
49:22. J. is a fruitful bough even a
50 : 1. J. fell upon his fa.'s face +
7. J. went to bury his father
15. J. will peradventure hate us
16. they sent a messenger unto J.
17. J. wept when they spake
22. J. lived an hund. and 10 y-rs,
24. J. said unto breth. I die ⌊26.
25. J. took oath of chil. of Israel
Ex. 1 : 5. J. was in E. already +
Ex. 1:3. king knew not J., Ac. 7:18.
13 : 19. Moses took the bones of J.
Nu. 26 : 28. sons of J., 37.–33 : 1.
27 : 1. Manas. son of J., 32 : 33.–36:
12. Jos. 17 : 1, 2.
De. 27:12. upon Gerizim to bless, J.
33:13. of J. he said, Blessed of L.
16. blessing upon J., Ge. 49 : 26.
Jos. 24 : 32. bones of J. buried they
1 Ch 5:2. but the birthright was J.'s
Ps 77 : 15. hast redeemed sons of J.
78 : 67. he refused the tabern. of J.
80 : 1. that leadest J like a flock
81 : 5. ord. in J. for a testimony
105 : 17. even J. who was sold for
Eze. 37:16. J. the stick of Ephr., 19.
47 : 13. J. shall have two portions
48 : 32. one gate of J. one of Benj.
Am. 5 : 15. L. will be gracious to J.
6:6. are not grieved for afflic. of J.
Jn. 4 : 5. ground Jacob gave to J.
Ac. 7 : 9. patriarchs sold J. into E.
13. sec. time J. was made known
14. Then J. called his father Jac.
He. 11 : 21. Jacob blessed sons of J.
22. J. made mention of Israel's

JO'SEPH with children.

Nu. 1 : 10. Of c. of J. of Ephr., 32.
34 : 23. princes of c. of J. Hanniel
Jos. 14 : 4. c. of J. two tribes, 16:4.
16 : 1. lot of c. of J. fell fr. Jordan
17:14. c. of J. spake unto Josh., 16.
1 Ch. 7 : 29. In these dwelt c. of J.
See **HOUSE of Joseph.**

JOSEPH with tribe.

Nu. 13:11. of t. of J. namely of Ma-
36:5. t. of sons of J. said well ⌊nas.
Re. 7 : 8. t. of J. were sealed 12,000

JO'SEPH. [Husband of Mary.]

Mat. 1:16. Jac. begat J. husb. of M.
18. mother M. was espoused to J.
19. J. her husb. being a just man
20. J. fear not to take Mary
24. J. did as angel had bidden
2 : 13. angel appeared to J., 19.
Lu. 1 : 27. name was J. of h. of Da.
Lu. 2:4. J. also went up to be taxed
16. shepherds found Mary, J. and
33. J. and his mother marvelled
43. J. and his mother knew not
3 : 23. being, as was supposed, son
of J. ⌈–6 : 42.
4:22. Is not this J.'s son? Jn. 1:45.

JO'SEPH. [Name of divers men.]

Nu. 13:7. of Issachar, Igal son of J.
1 Ch. 25 : 2. of sons of Asaph ; J., 9.
Ezr. 10 : 42. Shallum, J. stra. wives
Ne. 12 : 14. of Sheb. J. was a priest
Mat. 27:57. J. of Arimathea, 59. Mk.
15 : 43, 45. Lu. 23:50. Jn. 19:38.
Lu. 3:24. who was son of J., 26, 30.
Ac. 1 : 23. J. called Barsabas

JO'SES. ⌈Mk. 6 : 3.

Mat. 13 : 55. breth. James and J.,
27 : 56. moth. of J., Mk. 15:40, 47.
Ac. 4 : 36. J. surnamed Barnabas

JO'SHAH.

1 Ch. 4 : 34. J. Meshobab, princes

JOSH'APHAT.

1 Ch. 11:43. valiant, J. the Mithnite

JOSH'AVIAH. See ELNAAM.

JOSHBEK'ASHAH. ⌈24.

1 Ch. 25:4. the sons of Heman ; J. |

JO'SHEB-BAS'SEBET. ⌈3.

2 S. 23:†8. J. Tachmonite head of the

JOSH'UA, = JEHOSH'UA, JESH'UA, HOSHE'A and OSHE'A. ⌈Amalek

Ex. 17 : 9. Mo. said unto J., fight
13. J. discomfited Amalek ⌈J.
14. and rehearse it in the ears of
24 : 13. Moses and his minister J.
32 : 17. when J. heard noise of peo.
33 : 11. J. departed not out of tab.
Nu. 13 : 8. Of tribe of Ephraim, O.
16. Moses called O, Jehoshua
14:6. J. of them th. searched land
30. save Caleb and J., 38.–26:65.–
27 : 18. Take thee J. ⌊32 : 12.
22. he set J. before Eleazar
32 : 12. Caleb J. wholly foll-d L.
34:17. J. sh. divide la., Jos. 14:1.–
De. 1 : 38. J. sh. go in, 31:3. ⌊19:51.
3:28. charge J. encourage, 31:7, 23.
31 : 3. J. he shall go before thee
32 : 44. H. son of Nun † J.
34 : 9. J. was full of wisdom
Jos. 1 : 1. Lord spake unto J.
10. J. com-d the officers
2 : 1. J. sent two men spy land +
23. came to J. told him all
3 : 1. J. rose early in morn. +
5. J. said, Sanctify yourselves
7. L. said unto J., 5:9.–6:2.–7:10.
–8 : 18.–10 : 8.–20 : 1.
4 : 4. J. called the twelve men +
8. chil. of Isr. did as J. comman.
9. J. set up 12 stones in Jordan
14. that day L. magnified J.
5 : 3. J. made him sharp knives +
7. their chil. J. circumc., 2, 3, 4.
14. J. fell on his face to the earth
15. J. did so ⌈with J.
6 : 22. J. called priests | 27. L.
7 : 2. J. sent from Jericho to Ai +
6. J. rent clothes
8 : 3. J. chose 30,000 mighty +
16. and they pursued after J.
30. J. built an altar
35. which J. read not bef. cong.
9 : 3. what J. had done to Ai +
10 : 1. had heard how J. tak. Ai
12. spake J., Sun, stand still
42. their land did J. take, 11 : 23.
11 : 7. J. came and all peo. of war
9. J. did unto them as L. bade
13 : 1. J. was old and stricken
14 : 13. J. blessed Caleb and gave
17 : 17. J. spake unto house of J.
18: 10. J. cast lots for them bef. L.
19 : 49. Israel gave an inheri. to J.
22 : 6. J. blessed Reubenites and
24 : 1. J. gathered tribes of Israel
Jos. 24:25. J. made a cov. wi. the peo.
26. J. wrote these in book of law
29. J. serv. of L. died, Ju. 2 : 8.
31. Isr. served L. days of J. and
elders overlived J., Ju. 2 : 7.
Ju. 1 : 1. after death of J. it came
2 : 23. nei. deliv-d he into ha. of J.
1 K. 16 : 34. spake by J. son of Nun
Ne. 8:17. since days of Je. son of Nun

JOSH'UA = JESH'UA.

Ezr. 2 :2†. Je. came up with Zerubbabel, 4 : 3. Ne. 7 : 7.–12 : 1, 7.
3 : 2. stood up Je. son of Jozadak,
8, 9.–5 : 2.–10 : 18. Ne. 12 : 26.
Ne. 12 : 10. Je. begat Joiakim, 26.
Hag. 1 : 1. Jo. son of Josedech, 12,
14.–2 : 2, 4. Zch. 6 : 11. ⌈priest
Zch. 3 : 1. he shewed me Jo. high-
3. Jo. was clothed wi. filthy garm.
9. stone that I have laid bef. Jo.
6 : 11. crowns, set them upon Jo.

JOSH'UA.

1 S. 6 : 14. cart into field of J., 18.
2 K. 23 : 8. entering in of gate of J.

JOSI'AH, JOSI'AS.

1 K. 13 : 2. a child shall be born, J.
2 K. 21:24. made J. king, 2 Ch. 33:
25 | 26. ⌈2 Ch. 34 : 1.
22 : 1. J. 8 yrs. old began to reign,
23:16. J. he spied the sepulchres +
19. did J. take, 24. 2 Ch. 34 : 33.
29. J. went ag. Pha., 2 Ch. 35:20.
30. Jehoahaz son of J., 2 Ch. 36:1.
1 Ch. 3:15. sons of J. were Johanan
2 Ch. 35:1. J. kept passover unto +
18. nor kings such passo. as J.
19. In the 18th yr. of J. was this
passo., 2 K. 22 : 3.–23 : 23.
23. archers shot at king J. and
24. Jud. and Jerus. mourned J.
25. Jeremiah lamented for J. men
spake of J. ⌈3 : 6.
Je. 1 : 2. word of L. in days of J. +
3. Zedekiah son of J., 37 : 1.
22 : 11. Shallum son of J. king
18. Jehoiakim son of J., 1 : 3.–25 :
1.–26 : 1.–27 : 1.–35 : 1.–36 : 1.
–45: 1.–46: 2. 2 K. 23: 34. ⌈of J.
Zph. 1 : 1. word unto Zeph. in days
Zch. 6 : 10. go into the house of J.
Mat. 1: 10. begat J-s | 11. J-s begat

JOSIBI'AH. See JEHU.

JOSIPHI'AH. ⌈of J.

Ezr. 8 : 10. sons of Shelomith son

JOT. ⌈wise pass

Mat. 5 : 18. one j. or tittle in no

JOT'BAH.

2 K. 21:19. daughter of Haruz of J.

JOT'BATH, JOT'BATHAH.

Nu. 33:33. pitched at J. | 34. De. 10:7.

JO'THAM = JOA'THAM.

Ju. 9:5. J. son of Jerub. escap., 21.
57. upon them came the curse of J.
2 K. 15:5. J. judged peo., 2 Ch. 26:21.
7. J. reigned 32, 2 Ch. 26:23.–27:1.
36. rest of acts of J., 2 Ch. 27 : 7.
38. J. slept wi. fa-s, 2 Ch. 27 : 9.
16 : 1. Ahaz son of J., Is. 7 : 1.
1 Ch. 2 : 47. the sons of Jahdai, J.
3 : 12. Azariah his son, J. his son
5 : 17. were reck. by genealogies in
days of J.
2 Ch. 27 : 6. J. became mighty ⌈1.
Is. 1:1. days of J. Ahaz, Ho. 1:1. Mi. 1:

JOURNEY.

Ge. 24 : 21. L. made his j. prosper-
29 : 1. Jacob went on his j. ⌊ous
31 : 23. pursued him 7 days' j.
33 : 12. Let us take our j.
46 : 1. Israel took his j.
Ex. 13 : 20. took their j. from Succoth, De. 2 : 1.–10 : 6.
16 : 1. Israelites took j. from Elim
Nu. 9 : 10. be in j. yet keep passo.
13. is not in a j. forbeareth passo.
10 : 13. they first took their j. acc.

Nu. 33 : 12. took their j. out of wil.
De. 1 : 2. are 11 days' j. from Horeb
7. take your j., 40.-2 : 24.
10. 11. Arise, take thy j. bef. peo.
Jos. 9 : 11. Take victuals for your j.
13. old, by very long j. [honour
Ju. 4 : 9. j. thou takest is not for
1 S. 15 : 18. Lord sent thee on a j.
2 S. 11 : 10. Camest not fr. thy j.?
1 K. 18 : 27. or he is in a j.
19 : 7. the j. is too great for thee
2 K. 3 : 9. a compass of 7 days' j.
2 Ch. 1: 13. Sol. came fr. j. to high pl.
Ne. 2 : 6. how long shall thy j. be?
Pr. 7 : 19. goodman gone long j.
Mat. 10 : 10. Nor scrip for your j.
25 : 15. straightway took his j.
Mk. 6 : 8. nothing for j., Lu. 9 : 3.
13 : 34. is as man taking a far j.
Lu. 11 : 6. friend in his j. is come
15 : 13. took his j. into far country
Jn. 4 : 6. Jesus wearied with his j.
Ac. 10 : 9. as they went on their j.
22 : 6. as I made my j. and was
Ro. 1 : 10. I might have prosp. j.
15 : 24. I trust to see you in my j.
1 Co. 16: 6. ye may bring me on my j.
Ti. 3 : 13. Zenas and Apollos on j.
3 Jn. 6. whom if bring forw. on j.

Day's JOURNEY.

Nu. 11 : 31. the quails fall a d.'s j.
1 K. 19: 4. went d.'s j. into wildern.
Jon. 3: 4. began to enter city d.'s j.
Lu. 2 : 44. a d.'s j. am. acquaint.
Ac. 1: 12. fr. Jerus. a sabbath d.'s j.

Three days' JOURNEY.

Ge. 30 : 36. t. d. j. betw. hims. and
Ex. 3: 18. t. d. j. into wildern. [Jac.
5 : 3.-8 : 27. Nu. 10 : 33.-33 : 8.
Jon. 3 : 3. exc-g great city of t. d. j.

JOURNEYS.

Ge. 13 : 3. Abram went on his j.
Ex. 17: 1. j. acc. to the command-t
40: 36. they went on in j., Nu. 10: 12.
38. cloud upon tabern. thro. all j.
Nu. 10 : 6. shall blow alarm for j.
33: 1. the j. of Isr. with armies, 2.

JOURNEYED.

Ge. 11 : 2. as j. they found a plain
12: 9. Ab. j. going tow. south, 20: 1.
13: 11. Lot j. east | 33: 17. Jac. j. to
35 : 5. Isr. j. toward Beth-el [Suc.
16. j. fr. Beth-el | 21. j. to tower
Ex. 12: 37. j. fr. Rameses to Succoth
17 : 1. j. from wilderness of Sin
40 : † 36. cloud was tak. up, Isr. j.
37. cloud not up, j. not, Nu. 9: 21.
Nu. 9 : 17. after that Israel j., 18.
19. kept charge of L., and j. not
20. at com-t of the L. they j., 23.
11 : 35. peo. j. from Kibroth-Hat.
12 : 15. j. not till Miriam was bro-t
20: 22. whole cong. j. from Kadesh
21 : 4. they j. from mount Hor
11. and they j. from Oboth
33 : 22. and they j. from Rissah
De. 10 : 7. they j. unto Gudgodah
Jos. 9: 17. chil. of Isr. j. came unto
Ju. 17 : 8. to ho. of Micah as he j.
Lu. 10 : 33. cert. Samaritan as he j.
Ac. 9 : 3. Saul j. came near Damas.
7. men j. with him stood, 26: 13.

JOURNEYING, S.

Ge. 12 : † 9. Abram in j. toward
Nu. 10 : 2. make trumpets for j.
28. were j-s of Israel's armies
29. We are j. unto place L. said
Lu. 13 : 22. as he was j. tow. Jerus.
2 Co. 11: 26. In j. often, in perils of

JOY. [Noun.] [with j.

1 S. 18 : 6. came out to meet Saul
1 Ch. 12: 40. for there was j. in Isr.
15 : 16. singers, lifting voice wi. j.
25. went to bri. ark of cov. with j.
29 : 17. seen with j. the peo. offer
2 Ch. 20: 27. to go to Jerus. with j.
Ezr. 3 : 13. not discern shout of j.
Ezr. 6: 16. dedica. of house of G. wi. j.
22. kept feast seven days with j.
Ne. 8 : 10. j. of L. is your strength
12 : 43. j. of Jerus. was heard afar
† 44. for the j. of Judah and Lev.
Es. 8 : 16. Jews had light, j. and
9 : 22. mo. turned fr. sorrow to j.
make days of feasting and j.
Jb. 8 : 19. this is the j. of his way
† 21. fill thy lips with shout. for j.
20 : 5. j. of hypocrite but for mom.
29: 13. widow's heart to sing for j.
33 : 26. he will see his face with j.
41 : 22. sorrow is turned into j.
Ps. 16 : 11. in thy pres. is fuln. of j.
27 : 6. offer in tab-s sacrifices of j.
30 : 5. but j. cometh in morning
42 : 4. I went with the voice of j.
43 : 4. will go unto G. my exc-g j.
48 : 2. j. of earth is mount Zion
51: 12. Restore unto me j. of salva.
65 : † 12. little hills girded with j.
67 : 4. let the nations sing for j.
105 : 43. brought forth peo. with j.
126 : 5. sow in tears sh. reap in j.
137: 6. if prefer not Jerus. ab. my j.
Pr. 12: 20. to counsellors of peace j.
14 : 10. not intermeddle wi. his j.
15 : 21. Folly j. to him destitute of
23. man hath j. by ans. of mou.
17 : 21. father of a fool hath no j.
21 : 15. j. to the just to do judgm.
23 : 24. begett-h wise child have j.
Ec. 2: 10. I withheld not heart fr. j.
26. God giveth him wisdom, j.
5: 20. G. answ-h him in j. of heart
9 : 7. Go thy way, eat br. with j.
Is. 9 : 3. not incr-d j. acc. to j.
17. L. have no j. in their y-g men
12 : 3. with j. shall ye draw water
16 : 10. j. taken out of plentif. field
24 : 8. j. of harp | 11. j. is dark-d
29 : 19. meek sh. increase j. in L.
32 : 13. houses of j. | 14. j. of asses
35 : 2. rejoice wi. j. and singing
10. with everlasting j. upon their
heads, 51 : 11. [out with j.
52: 9. Break forth into j. | 55: 12. go
60 : 15. I will make thee a joy of
61 : 3. give oil of j. for mourning
7. everl. j. shall be unto them
65 : 14. my servants sh. sing for j.
18. behold, I create her peo. a j.
66 : 5. but he sh. appear to your j.
10. rejoice for j. with her, all ye
Je. 15 : 16. word was j. of my heart
31: 13. I will turn mourning into j.
33 : 9. it sh. be to me a name of j.
11. shall be heard voice of j. [j.
48 : 27. since spakest, skippedst for
33. j. is taken fr. plentiful field
49 : 25. city of praise, of my j.
La. 2 : 15. city, j. of whole earth
5 : 15. The j. of our heart is ceased
Eze. 24 : 25. take j. of their glory
36 : 5. with the j. of all their heart
Ho. 9 : 1. Rejoice not, O Israel for j.
Jo. 1 : 12. j. is withered aw. fr. men
Zph. 3 : 17. rejoice over thee with j.
Mat. 13 : 20. with j. receiv-h it, Lu.
44. for j. selleth all he hath [8: 13.
25 : 21. enter into j. of thy L., 23.
Lu. 1 : 44. leaped in my womb for j.
6: 23. Rejoice in th. day, leap for j.
10 : 17. the 70 returned with j.
15 : 7. j. be in heav. over one sinn.
10. is j. in presence of angels
24 : 41. they yet believed not for j.
Jn. 3 : 29. this my j. is fulfilled
15 : 11. that my j. remain in you,
and your j. might be full
16 : 20. sorrow be turned into j.
21. for j. that a man is born into
22. your j. no man taketh fr. you
24. receive, that your j. be full
17: 13. have my j. fufill-d in thems.
Ac. 2: 28. full of j. with thy counten.
Ac. 13: 52. disciples filled with j. and
20: 24. might finish my course wi. j.
Ro. 14 : 17. kingdom of God is j.
15 : 13. God fill you with all j. in
32. may come unto you with j. by
2 Co. 1: 24. we are helpers of your j.
2 : 3. that my j. is the j. of you all
7 : 13. more joyed we for j. of Tit.
8 : 2. abund. of their j. abounded
Ga. 5 : 22. fruit of Spirit is love, j.
Ph. 1 : 4. making request with j.
25. abide for your j. of faith
2 : 2. Fulfil ye my j. | 4 : 1. my j.
1 Th. 1: 6. received the word with j.
2 : 19. what is our j. | 20. ye our j.
3 : 9. j. whw. we j. before God
2 Ti. 1: 4. th. I may be filled with j.
Phm. 20. let me have j. of thee
He. 12 : 2. who for j. set bef. him
13 : 17. do it with j. not wi. grief
Ja. 1 : 2. count it j. when ye fall
4 : 9. j. be turned into heaviness
1 Pe. 1 : 8. ye rej. with j. unspeaka.
4 : 13. ye be glad with exc-g j.
1 Jn. 1: 4. j. may be full, 2 Jn. 12.
3 Jn. 4. I no greater j. than to hear
Jude 24. you faultless with exc-g j.

See GLADNESS.

Great JOY.

1 K. 1 : 40. peo. rejoiced with g. j.
1 Ch. 29: 9. David rejoiced with g. j.
2 Ch. 30 : 26. was g. j. in Jerus.
Ne. 12: 43. G. made rejoice with g. j.
Mat. 2: 10. saw star, rej-d with g. j.
28 : 8. went fr. sepulc. with g. j.
Lu. 2 : 10. good tidings of g. j.
24: 52. returned to Jerus. with g. j.
Ac. 8 : 8. there was g. j. in th. city
15 : 3. caused g. j. to all brethren
Phm. 7. we have g. j. in thy love

Shout, or shouted for JOY.

Ezr. 3 : 12. many s-d aloud f. j.
Jb. 38 : 7. all sons of God s-d f. j.
Ps. 5 : 11. let them s. f. j., 35 : 27.
32 : 11. s. f. j. all ye upright
65 : 13. valleys s. f. j. they sing
132: 9. let thy saints s. f. j., 16.

JOY, ED, ING.

Ps. 21: 1. king sh. j. in thy strength
Is. 9 : 3. j. before thee acc. to joy
65: 19. I will rej. and j. in my peo.
Ha. 3 : 18. I will j. in G. of salva.
Zph. 3 : 17. he will j. over thee
Ro. 5 : 11. but we also j. in G. [Tit.
2 Co. 7 : 13. more j-d we for joy of
Ph. 2 : 17. I j. and rej. with you all
18. For the same cause do ye j.
Col. 2: 5. am I with you in spirit j-g
1 Th. 3 : 9. joy whw. we j. for you

JOYFUL.

1 K. 8 : 66. went unto their tents j.
Ezr. 6 : 22. Lord hath made them j.
Es. 5 : 9. Haman went that day j.
Jb. 3: 7. let no j. voice come therein
Ps. 5: 11. love thy name be j. in thee
35 : 9. my soul shall be j. in Lord
63 : 5. shall praise thee with j. lips
66 : 1. Make a j. noise unto God
81: 1. make j. noise unto G. of Jac.
89: 15. Blessed peo. that kn. j. sound
95 : 1. make j. noise to rock of our
salvation
2. a j. noise unto him with psalms,
98 : 4.-100 : 1.
96 : 12. Let the field be j. and
98 : 6. make a j. noise before Lord
8. let hills be j. together bef. L.
113 : 9. barren to be a j. mother
149 : 2. let chil. of Zion be j. in k.
5. Let the saints be j. in glory
Ec. 7 : 14. In day of prosperity be j.
Is. 49 : 13. O heav., be j. O earth
56: 7. make them j. in ho. of prayer
61 : 10. my soul sh. be j. in my G.
2 Co. 7 : 4. exc-g j. in all our tribu-

JOYFULLY. [lation

Ec. 9 : 9. Live j. wi. wife thou lovest

Lu. 19 : 6. Zaccheus rec-d him j.
He. 10 : 34 ye took j. spoiling of

JOYFULNESS.

De. 28 : 47. servedst not L. with j.
Col. 1 : 11. to longsuffering with j.

JOYOUS.

Is. 22 : 2. art full of stirs, a j. city
23 : 7. Is this your j. city, whose
32 : 13. houses of joy in J. city
He. 12:11. no chastening seemeth j.

JOZ'ABAD.

2 Ch.31:13.J.overseers | 1 Ch.12:20.
35 : 9. J. chief of Lev. | Ezr. 8:33.-
10 : 22, 23. Ne. 11 : 16.
Ne.8:7. J. caused people to underst.

JOZ'ACHAR=ZA'BAD.

2 K. 12 : 21. J. son of Shimeath, 2
Ch. 24 : † 26.

JOZ'ADAK. See JOSHUA.

JU'BAL.

Ge.4:21.J. was fa. of such as handle

JUBILEE.

Le. 25 : 9. cause trumpet of j. to
10. it shall be a j. unto you, 12.
11. A j. sh. that fiftieth year be
13. In the year of j. ye sh. return
15.aft the j. shalt buy of neighb.
28. a field go out in y-r of j., 27 :
30. house not go out in j. [21, 24.
31. sh. go out in y-r of j., 33, 54.
40. serve thee unto y-r of j., 50.
52. if remain few years unto j.
27:17. If he sanctify field fr. j., 18.
23. estimation unto y-r of j., 18.
Nu. 36 : 4. when j. then inheritance

JU'CAL. See JEHUCAL.

JU'DA, JU'DAH, JU'DAS.

Ge. 29 : 35. she called his name J.
35 : 23. sons of Leah ; J. Issachar
38:1. J. went down fr. his breth.+
15. J. thought Tamar a harlot
26. J. acknowledged the signet
44:14 J.and breth.came to Josh. +
46:12. sons of J., Nu. 26:19. 1 Ch.
2 : 3.-4 : 1. [seph
28. Jac. sent J. bef. him unto Jo-
49:8.J.thou art he whom thy breth
9.J. is a lion's whelp, he couched
10. sceptre shall not depart fr. J.
Ex. 1 : 2. sons of Isr.; J., 1 Ch. 2:1.
Nu. 1:7. Of J.; Nahshon son of Am.
2 : 3. camp of J. sh. pitch on east
9 All numbered in camp of J.
De. 27 : 12. J. shall stand to bless
33 : 7. is blessing of J. voice of J.
Jos.7:17. Josh. brought family of J.
18 : 5. J. shall abide in their coast
Ju.1:2.L.said,J.sh go up first,—20:
16. wilderness of J. [18.
19. L. with J | 10 : 9 fight ag. J.
Ru.4:12. whom Tamar bare unto J.
1 S. 23:23. search thro. thous. of J.
2 S. 3 : 8. ag. J. do shew kindness
5:5. Da. reigned over J. seven y-rs
11 : 11. Isr. and J. abide in tents
19 : 15. J. to Gilgal to meet king
24 : 1. said, Go number Isr. and J.
1 K. 2:32. Amasa captain of host of
4:20.J.and Israel were many as [J.
25. J. Isr. dwelt safely under Sol.
13:1. came a man of God out of J.
to Bethel, 2 K. 23 : 17.
14 : 22. J. did evil in sight of L.
15:1. Abijam over J. | 9. Asa ov. J.
17.Baasha went ag. J., 2 Ch.16:1.
22:41.Jehosh. began to reign ov. J.
2 K. 8 : 19. L. would not destroy J.
20. revolted fr. J., 22. 2 Ch. 21 :
9 : 29. began to reign ov. J. [8, 10.
14:10.fall, thou and J., 2 Ch.25:19.
12. J. put to worse, 2 Ch. 25 : 22.
22.restored Elath to J..2 Ch.26:2.
15 : 37. Lord began to send ag. J.
17:13. L. testified ag. Israel and J.
19. J. kept not com-ts of Lord
21 : 11. Manas. made J. sin, 16. 2
12. such evil upon J. [Ch. 33:9.
2 K.23:26. anger ag. J., 2 Ch.25:10.
27. I will remove J. out of sight
24 : 2. Lord sent Chaldees ag. J.
3.at com-t of L.came this upon J.
25:21.J. was carried aw.,1 Ch.6:15.
1 Ch. 5 : 2. J. prevailed ab. breth.
27 : 18. Of J. Elihu was ruler
28 : 4. hath chosen J. to be ruler
2 Ch. 13:13. were bef. J. and behind
16. chil. of Israel fled before J.
14:4.Asa commanded J. to seek L.
17:6. Jehosh. took groves out of J.
20 : 4. J. gathered themselves +
17. see salv. of L. with you, O J.
21:11.compelled J.to commit forni.
13. hast made J. go a whoring
24:18. wrath came upon J., 28:9.-
29 : 8.-32 : 25. [made J. naked
28 : 19. the Lord brought J. low,
29:21.lambs for a sin offering for J.
30 : 25. all the cong. of J. rejoiced
33:16. Manas. com-d J. to serve L.
34 : 3. Josiah began to purge J., 5.
Ezr.7:14.art sent to i quire conc. J.
Ne. 2 : 5. wouldest send me unto J.
7. convey me till I come into J.
6 : 17. nobles of J. sent letters unto
12 : 44. J. rejoiced for the priests
13:17.I contended with nobles of J.
Ps. 60 : 7. J. is my lawgiver, 108 : 8.
114 : 2. J. was his sanctuary, Isr.
Is. 1:1. vision he saw, conc. J., 2:1.
3:1. Lord doth take fr. J. stay and
8.J. is fallen | 7:6. Let us go ag.J.
7 : 17. day Ephr. departed from J.
8:8. shall pass thro. J. shall overfl.
9 : 21. they together sh. be ag. J.
11:12. he sh. gather dispersed of J.
13. Ephr. shall not envy J. and
J. not vex Ephraim
22 : 8. he discovered covering of J.
48 : 1. are come out of wat. of J.
65 : 9. out of J. an inheritor
Je. 2:28. acc. to cities are thy gods,
O J., 11 : 13. [8, 10, 11.
3:7. her sister J. saw it, feared not,
9 : 26. J. and Edom are uncircum.
13 : 9. will I mar the pride of J.
19. J. shall be carried away cap.
14 : 2. J. mourneth, gates languish
19. Hast thou utterly rejected J.
17 : 1. sin of J. is writt. with iron
19 : 7. I will void the counsel of J.
23 : 6. J. shall be saved, 33 : 16.
32 : 35. do this to cause J. to sin
33 : 7. cause captivity of J. to ret.
36 : 2. words I have spoken ag. J.
39 : 6. k. of Bab. slew nobles of J.
42 : 15. hear word, ye remu. of J.
44 : 7. cut off man, wom. out of J.
26. not in mouth of any of J.
50 : 20. sins of J. sh. not be found
51 : 5. J. not been forsaken of G.
52:27. J. was carried aw., La. 1:3.
Eze. 8 : 1. elders of J. sat before me
21:20. that the sword may come to
27:17.J.and Isr. thy merchants [J.
37:16. write upon it For J. and Isr.
19. put them with stick of J.
48:7.border of Reub. portion for J.
31. one gate of Reuben, one of J.
Da.2:25. man of captives of J.,5:13.
Ho. 4:15. tho. Isr. harlot, let not J.
5 : 5. J. sh. fall | 13. J. saw wound
6:4. O J. what sh. I do unto thee?
11.O J. he hath set harv. for thee
10 : 11. J. shall plough Jacob shall
11 : 12. But J. yet ruleth with God
12 : 2. L. hath controversy with J.
Jo. 3 : 18. all rivers of J. flow wi. w.
20. but J. shall dwell for ever
Am. 2 : 4. For 3 transgressions of J.
5. I will send a fire upon J. it
Mi. 1:5. what are high places of J
9. her wound it is come unto J.
5:2. tho. little am. thousands of J.
Na. 1 : 15. O J. keep thy sol. feasts
Zph. 1 : 4. out mine hand upon J.
Zch. 1 : 19. horns wh. scatt-d J.,21.
2 : 12. L. sh. inherit J. his portion
9 : 13. When I have bent J. for me
11:14.brotherh'd bet J. and Israel
12 : 7. shall save tents of J. first
14 : 14. J. also shall fight at Jerus
Mal. 2:11. J. dealt treacherously (2)
3 : 4. sh. offering of J. be pleasant
Mat.1:2.Jac.begat J-s | 3. J-s begat
Lu. 3:33. Phares was son of J-a [J-a
He. 7 : 14. evident our Lord spr. of
See BENJAMIN, BETHLEHEM, CHILDREN, CITIES, DAUGHTER, DAUGHTERS, HOUSE.

All JU'DAH.

1 S. 18:16 a. Isr. and J. loved Da.
2 S. 5 : 5. Da. 33 years over a. J.
2 Ch. 15 : 15. a. J. rejoiced at oath
20 : 13. a. J. stood before the Lord
15. and he said, Hearken ye a. J.
32 : 33. a. J. did honour Hezekiah
35 : 24. a. J. mourned for Josiah
Ne.13:12. Then brought a. J. tithe
Je. 20 : 4. I will give a. J. to king
44 : 11. set my face to cut off a. J.

In JU'DAH.

1 S. 23 : 3. we be afraid here i. J.
1 K. 12:32. like unto the feast i. J.
2 K.24:20. thro. anger of L. it came
to pass i. J., Je. 52 : 3.
2 Ch. 2 : 7. cunning men with me i.
12 : 12. i. J. things went well [J.
17:9. they taught i. J. had book of
28 : 6. Pekah slew i. J. 120,000
30 : 12. i. J. hand of God was to
25. all that dwelt i. J. rejoiced
34 : 21. inquire for them left i. J.
Ezr. 5 : 1. prophesied to Jews i. J.
9 : 9. mercy to give us a wall i. J.
Ne.6:7. saying, There is a king i. J.
18. many i. J. sworn unto him
13 : 15. i. J. some treading winepr.
Ps. 76 : 1. i. J. is God known
Je. 4:5. Declare ye i. J. publi.,5:20.
22 : 30. ruling any more i. J.
Zch. 9 : 7. he shall be as a gov. i. J.
14 : 21. every pot i. J. be holiness

See KING, S of Judah.

Land of JU'DAH.

De. 34:2. L. shewed him all l. o. J.
Ru. 1 : 7. to return unto l. o. J.
1 S. 22 : 5. get thee into the l. o. J.
2 K. 23:24. abomina. spied in l.o.J.
25:22. peo. that remained in l.o.J.
2 Ch. 17:2. set garrisons in l. o. J.
Is. 19 : 17. l. o. J. be terror unto E.
26 : 1. this song be sung in l. o. J.
Je. 31 : 23. use this speech in l.o.J.
39:10. who had nothing in l. o. J.
44 : 9. have committed in l. o. J.
14. they sho. return into l. o. J.
Am.7:12. O seer, flee into the l.o.J.
Zch. 1 : 21. lifted horn over l. o. J.
Mat. 2 : 6. Bethlehem, in the l.o. J.

Men of JU'DAH.

Ju. 15 : 10. m. o. J. said, Why are
ye against us?
2 S. 2 : 4. m.o. J. anointed Da. k.
19 : 14. bowed heart of all m.o.J.
43. words of m. o. J. fiercer
20:2. m.o.J. clave unto their king
4. Assemble m.o.J.within 3 days
24 : 9. m. o. J. were 500,000
2 Ch.13:15.Then m.o.J. gave shout
Ezr. 10 : 9. all m. o. J. gathered
Is. 5 : 3. m.o.J. judge bet. me and
7. m. o. J. his pleasant plant
Je. 4:4. Circumcise hearts, ye m.o.
11:9. A conspiracy am. m.o.J. [J.
35:13.m.o.J.Will ye not rec.instr.
36 : 31. bring upon m. o. J. evil
43 : 9. hide th. in sight of m.o.J
44 : 27. m.o.J. shall be consumed
Da. 9 : 7. confusion belongeth to
m. o. J.

See PRINCES of Judah.

Tribe of JU'DAH, JU'DA.
Ex. 31:2. Bezaleel of t.o.J., 35:30.-
Nu.1:27.numbered of t.o.J. [38:22.
7: 12. Nahshon, prince of t. o. J.
13:6. Of t.o.J. Caleb to spy, 34:19.
Jos.7: 1. Achan of t. o. J. took ac-
16. t. o. J. was taken, 18. [cursed
15: 1. This was lot of t. o. J., 20.
21:4.Lev.out of t.o.J.,9.1 Ch.6:65.
1 K.12:20. t.o.J. only followed Da.
2 K. 17: 18. none left but t. o. J.
Ps. 78: 68. But he chose the t.o.J.
Re. 5: 5. Lion of t. o. J-a prevailed
7:5. Of t. o. J-a were sealed 12,000

JU'DA, JU'DAH.
Ezr.3:9.sons of J-h,2:†40. Ne.7:†43.
10:23.of the Lev.;J-h | Ne.12:8,36.
Ne. 11:9. J-h was second over city
Lu. 3:26. which was son of J-a, 30.

JU'DAS, JUDE.
Mat. 13:55.his brethren James, and
Joses, Simon, and J., Mk. 6:3.
Lu. 6: 16. J. bro. of James, Ac.1:13.
Jn. 14:22. J. saith, not Iscar., how
Ac. 5:37. After this man rose up J.
9: 11. enquire in h. of J. for Saul
15: 22. J. surnamed Barsabas, 27.
32. J. and Silas exhorted breth.
Jude 1.J-e serv. of C. bro. of James

JU'DAS, JU'DAS Iscariot.
Mat. 10: 4. J. I. who betrayed, Mk.
3:19. Lu. 6:16. Jn. 6:71.-12:4.-
13: 2. [14: 10.
26:14. J. I. unto chief priests, Mk.
47. J. one of 12 came, and great
mult., Mk.14:43. Lu. 22:47. Jn.
18: 3, 5.
27:3. Then J. repented himself and
Lu. 22: 3. entered Satan into J. I.
48. Jes. said, J. betrayest thou
Jn. 13: 26. he gave the sop to J. I.
29. thought because J. had bag
18: 2. J. wh. betrayed knew place
5. J. stood with them | 3.
Ac. 1: 16. Da. spake before conc. J.
25. from wh. J. by transgr. fell

JUDE'A.
Ezr.5:8. we went into province of J.
Mat. 24: 16. let them wh. be in J.
flee, Mk. 13: 14. Lu. 21: 21.
Jn. 4: 3. left J. departed into Gali.
7: 3. Depart and go into J., 11: 7.
Ac. 1: 8. in all J. ye sh. be witnes.
2: 14. Ye men of J. be this known
9: 31. churches had rest thro-t J.
10:37.word wh. was publi. thro. J.
12:19. went down fr. J. [of J.
28: 21. neith. received letters out
Ro. 15: 31. that do not believe in J.
2 Co. 1:16. bro-t on my way tow. J.
1 Th.2:14.churches wh. in J. are in

JUDGE. [Noun.] [C.
Ge. 18: 25. Shall not J. do right
19: 9. this fellow will needs be a j.
Ex. 2: 14. Who made thee a j. over
us? Ac. 7: 27, 35. [those days
De. 17: 9. come unto j. sh. be in
12. th. will not hearken unto j.
25: 2. j. sh. cause him to lie down
Ju. 2: 18. the L. was with the j.
19.the j.was dead, they corrupted
11: 27. the L. the J. be j. this day
1 S. 2: 25. if sin, j. sh. judge him
24: 15. The L. thf. be j. between
2 S 15: 4. O that I were made j.
Jb.9:15. make supplication to my j.
23: 7. delivered for ever fr. my j.
31: 28. iniq. to be punished by j.
Ps. 7: † 11. God is a righteous j.
50:6. heavens declare, for God is j.
68: 5. j. of widows | 75: 7. G. is j.
94: 2. thou J. of the earth, render
Is. 3: 2. doth take from Jerus. j.
33: 22. L. is our j. L. our lawgiv.
Am. 2:3. I will cut off j. from midst
Mi. 5: 1. shall smite the j. of Isr.
7:3. and the j. asketh for a reward
Mat. 5: 25. adversary deliver thee
to j. j. deliver thee, Lu. 12: 58.
Lu. 12:14. who made me a j. ov. you
18:2. was in city a j. feared not G.
6. Hear what the unjust j. saith
Ac. 10:42. of G. j. of quick and dead
18: 15. I will be no j. of such mat.
24: 10. many years a j. of this na.
2 Ti. 4: 8. L. righte. j. sh. give me
He 12: 23. are come to G. the J.
Ja. 4: 11. not doer of law, but a j.
5: 9. J. standeth bef. the door

JUDGES.
Ex.21:6.mas.shall bring him unto j.
22. shall pay as j. determine
22: 8. master sh. be bro-t unto j.
9. cause of both sh. come bef. j.
† 28. Thou shalt not revile the j.
Nu. 25: 5. Moses said unto j. Slay
De. 1: 16. I charged your j. at
16: 18. j. shalt make in thy gates
19:17.both stand bef. priests and j.
18. j. sh. make diligent inquisi.
21: 2. thy elders and j. sh. come
25: 1. come that j. may judge th.
32: 31. even our enemies being j.
Jos. 8: 33. j. stood on this side
23: 2. Josh. called for j., 24: 1.
Ju. 2: 16. the Lord raised up j., 18.
17.would not hearken unto their j
Ru. 1: 1. when j. ruled famine was
1 S. 8: 1. made sons j. over Isr., 2.
2 S. 7: 11. I com-d j. to be ov. peo.
2 K. 23: 22. from days of the j.
1 Ch. 17:6. spake I to any of j., 10.
23: 4. and 6000 officers and j.
26: 29. Chenaniah and sons for j.
2 Ch. 1: 2. Then Sol. spake to j.
19: 5. he set j. | 6. said to the j.
Ezr. 7: 25. set j. may judge people
10: 14. with them the j. of ev. city
Jb. 9: 24. he covereth faces of j.
12: 17. and he maketh the j. fools
31: 11. iniq. to be punished by j.
Ps. 2: 10. be instructed ye j. of
109: † 31. to save him fr. j. of soul
141: 6. When j. are overthrown
148:11. princes, and all j. of earth
Pr. 8:16. By me princes rule, and j.
Is. 1: 26. I will restore thy j.
40: 23. he maketh j. as vanity
Da.3:2. Neb. sent to gather the j., 3.
9:12. his words ag. our j. [j.
Ho. 7: 7. they have devoured their
13: 10. where are thy j. of whom
Zph. 3: 3. her j. evening wolves
Mat.12:27. sh. be your j., Lu.11:19.
Ac. 13:20. aft. that he gave them j.
Ja. 2: 4. become j. of evil thoughts

JUDGE. [Verb.]
[Applied to GOD and CHRIST.]
Ge. 16: 5. j. between me and thee,
1 S. 24: 12, 15. [us
31:53. G. of their father j. betwixt
Ex.5:21.The L.look upon you and j.
De. 32: 36. L. shall j. his peo., Ps.
50: 4.-135: 14. He. 10: 30.
1 S. 2: 10. L. shall j. ends of earth
24:†15.Lord j. me out of thy hand
1 K.8:32.j.thy servants, 2 Ch. 6:23.
1 Ch. 16:33. cometh to j. the earth,
Ps. 96: 13.-98: 9. [them?
2 Ch. 20: 12. O our God, wilt not j.
Jb.22:13.can he j. thro. dark cloud?
Ps. 7: 8. Lord shall j. people. 50:4.
9: 8. he sh. j. the world in righteousn.,96:10,13.-98:9.Ac.17:31.
10: 18. j. the fatherless and poor,
82: † 3. Is. 11: 4.
26: 1. j. me, O L., 7: 8.-35:24.-43:
1.-54: 1. La. 3: 59.
82: 8. Arise, O God, j. the earth
110:6. He shall j. am. the heathen
Ec. 3:17. God shall j. the righteous
Is. 2: 4. he shall j. among nations
3: 13. L. standeth to j. the people
11: 3. not j. aft. sight of his eyes
Is. 51: 5. mine arm shall j. the peo
Eze. 7: 3. will j. thee acc. to ways
34: 17. I j. bet. cattle and cattle
Jo. 3: 12. will I sit to j. heathen
Mi. 4: 3. he shall j. am. many peo.
Jn. 5: 30. as I hear I j. my judgm.
8: 15. I j. no man | 16. yet if I j.
26. things to say and j. of you
12:47. I j. him not, I came not to j.
Ro. 2: 16. G. sh. j. secrets of men
3: 6. how shall God j. world?
2 Ti. 4: 1. j. quick and dead, 1 Pe.
He. 13: 4. adulterers G. will j. [4:5.
Re. 6: 10. dost thou j. and avenge
19: 11. in righteousness he doth j.
See **I will JUDGE.**

JUDGE.
[Applied to MAN, or other things.]
Ge. 31: 37. may j. betwixt us both
49: 16. Dan shall j. his people as
Ex. 18: 13. Moses sat to j. the peo.
16. I j. between one and another
22. every small matter they sh. j.
Le. 19: 15. in righteousn. shalt j.
neighb., De. 1: 16.-16: 18.
Nu.35:24. congr. j. betw. the slayer
De. 25: 1. that judges may j. them
1 S. 2: 25. if sin, judge sh. j. him
8: 5. make us a king to j. us, 6, 20.
1 K. 3: 9. underst-g heart to j. who
able to j. great peo., 2 Ch.1:10.
7: 7. porch for throne where he j.
2 Ch. 1: 11. mayest j. my people
19: 6. ye j. not for man, but Lord
Ezr. 7:25. set judges may j. all peo.
Ps. 58: 1. do ye j. uprightly, O ye
72:2.He shall j. peo. with righte-n.
4. He shall j.poor of peo ,Pr.31:9.
82: 2. How long will ye j. unjustly
Is. 1:17. j. fatherl. plead for widow
23. they j. not fatherless, Je.5:28.
5: 3. j. betw. me and vineyard
Je. 21: † 12. j. judgment, Zch. 7:†9.
-8: † 16. [of man? 22: 2.
Eze. 20: 4. Wilt thou j. them, son
23: 24. they sh. j. thee, 45.-24:14.
36. Son of man, wilt j. Aholah
44: 24. they shall j. it acc. to my
Ob. 21. saviours come to j. mount
Mi. 3: 11. heads j. for reward
Zch. 3: 7. thou shalt j. my house
Mat.7:1. j. not th. ye be not judged
2. what judgm. ye j., Lu. 6: 37
Lu. 12: 57. why j. not what is right
Jn. 7: 24. j. not acc. to appear. j.
righteous judgment
Jn. 7: 51. Doth our law j. man bef.
8:15.Ye j.aft. the flesh I j. no [him
12: 48. word I have spoken sh. j.
12:47. believe not I j. him not, (2)
18: 31. j. him acc. to your law
Ac. 4:19. j. ye | 13:46. j. yourselves
unworthy [the law?
23: 3. sittest thou to j. me after
Ro. 2: 27. if it fulfil law, j. thee
14:†1. not to j. doubtful thoughts
3. j. him eateth | 10. why j. bro.
13. Let us not j.one another, but
j. this rather [before time
1 Co.4:3.I j.not myself | 5. j. noth.
5:12.what I to j. them without,do
not ye j. them that are within?
6: 2. not know saints sh. j. world?
3. Know ye not we sh. j. angels?
4. set them to j. least esteemed
5. sh. be able to j. betw. breth.
10: 15. j. ye what I say
11: 13. j. in yours.; is it comely
11: 31. For if we would j. ours.
14: 29. let prophets speak, other j.
2 Co. 5: 14. because we thus j.
Col.2:16.Let no man j. you in meat
Ja. 4: 11. but if thou j. the law

I will JUDGE.
1 S. 3:13. I w. j. his house for ever
Ps. 75: 2. I w. j. uprightly [33:20.
Eze. 7:3. j. acc. to thy ways, 7:27.-

Eze.11:10. I w.j. you in Israel, 11.
16:38.I w.j.thee as women th.br.
18: 30. I w.j. you, O ho. of Isr.
21:30.I w.j.thee where thou wast
34: 20. I w. j. between fat cattle,
Will I JUDGE. ⌊22.
Ge. 15: 14. nation w. I j., Ac. 7:7.
Lu. 19:22. Out of own mou. w. I j.
JUDGED. ⌊thee
Ge. 30: 6. G. hath j. me and heard
Ex.18:26. rulers j. the people, every
small matter they j. ⌈j. Isr.
Ju. 3: 10. Othniel j. | 4: 4. Deborah
10: 2. Tola j. | 3. Jair j.
12: 7. Jephthah j. | 8. Ibzan j., 9.
11. Elon j., 13. | 14. Abdon j.
15:20.Samson j.Isr. 20 yrs., 16:31.
Ru. 1: † 1. when judges j. was fam.
1 S. 4: 18. Eli j. Israel 40 years
7: 6. Samuel j. Israel, 15, 16, 17.
2 S. 18: † 19. L. j. him fr. enemies
1 K. 3: 28. heard judgm. king j.
2 K. 23:22. fr. days of judges th. j.
Ps. 9: 19. let heathen be j. in thy
37: 33. not condemn him when j.
109: 7. be j. let him be condem-d
Je. 22: 16. He j. the cause of poor
Eze. 16: 38. women shed bl. are j.
52. Thou who hast j. thy sisters
28: 23. wounded shall be j. in her
35:11. known, when I have j. thee
36: 19. acc. to doings I j. them
Da. 9: 12. ag. judges j. us ⌈Lu.6:37.
Mat.7:1.th.ye be not j. | 2.sh.be j.,
Lu. 7:43. said, Thou hast rightly j.
Jn. 16: 11. prince of world is j.
Ac. 16: 15. If j. me to be faithful
24: 6. would have j. acc. to law
25: 9. there be j. of these thi., 20.
10. stand, where I ought to be j.
26: 6. am j. for hope of promise
Ro. 2: 12. be j. by law, Ja. 2: 12.
3: 4. mightest overcome when j.
7. why yet am I j. as a sinner?
1 Co. 2: 15. yet he is j. of no man
4:3. small thing that I be j. of you
5: 3. I have j. already, as present
6: 2. if the world sh. be j. by you
10:29. why is my liberty j. of ano.
11:31.if judge ours.we sho.not be j.
32. when j. we are chast-d of L.
14: 24. convinced, he is j. of all
He. 11: 11. bec. she j. him faithful
1 Pe. 4: 6. might be j. acc. to men
Re.11:18. dead, that they sho. be j.
16: 5. art righto. bec. hast j. thus
19: 2. he hath j. the great whore
20: 12. dead j. out of those things
13. were j.ev.man acc.to his works
JUDGEST. ⌈thou j.
Ps. 51: 4. mightest be clear when
Je. 11:20. L. of hosts, j. righteously
Ro. 2: 1. whoso. thou art that j.
3. O man, that j. them which do
14:4. Who thou j.ano.man's serv.?
Ja. 4: 12. who art thou j. another?
JUDGETH.
Jb. 21:22. he j. those th. were high
36: 31. For by them j. he the peo.
Ps. 7: 11. God j. the righteous
58: 11. he is a G. that j. in earth
82: 1. in congr., he j. among gods
Pr. 29: 14. k. that faithfully j. poor
Jn. 5: 22. For the Fa. j. no man
8:50. one that j. | 12:48. that j. him
1 Co. 2: 15. that is spiritual j. all
4: 4. he that j. me is the Lord
5:13. them that are without, G. j.
Ja. 4: 11. j. bro., j. law ⌈sons j.
1 Pe. 1: 17. without respect of per-
2: 23. committed hims. to him that
Re. 18: 8. strong is L. th. j. her ⌊j.
JUDGING.
Ge. 30: † 6. Rachel called name, j.
2 K. 15:5. j. the people, 2 Ch. 26:21.
Ps. 9: 4. satest in throne j. right
Is 16: 5. shall sit j. seeking judgm.

Mat. 19: 28. j. 12 tribes, Lu. 22:30.
JUDGMENT. ⌈j.
Ge. 30: † 21. Leah called her name
Ex. 12: 12. ag. gods I will exec. j.
21: 31. acc. to this j. be it done
23: 2. to decline, to wrest j., 6.
28: 15. make the breastplate of j.
29. names in breastplate of j., 30.
Nu.27:11. to Isr. statute of j., 35:29.
21. after j. of Urim bef. L. ⌈G.'s
De. 1: 17. not afraid of man, j. is
10: 18. doth execute j. of fatherl.
16: 18. sh. judge peo. with just j.
19. not wrest j. | 17: 11. acc. to j.
17: 9. shew thee sentence of j.
24: 17. not pervert j. of stranger
25: 1. controversy, they come unto j.
27: 19. Cursed he perverteth j.
32: 4. for all his ways are j.
41. If mine hand take hold on j.
Jos. 20: 6. stand bef. congr. for j.
Ju. 4: 5. Isr. came up to Deb. for j.
1 S. 8: 3. his sons perverted j.
2 S. 8: 15. executed j., 1 Ch. 18:14.
15: 2. any came to k. for j., 6. ⌈j.
1 K.3: 11. asked underst-g to discern
28. all Isr. heard of j. k. judged
7: 7. porch of j. | 20:40. So thy j.
2 K. 25: 6. took k. and gave j. ⌊be
2 Ch. 19: 8. chief of fathers for j.
20: 9. evil upon us as sword, j.
22:8. Jehu executing j. upon Ahab
24: 24. they executed j. ag. Joash
Ezr.7:26. let j. be executed upon him
Es. 1: 13. tow. all knew law and j.
Jb. 8: 3. Doth God pervert j.? ⌈j.
9: 19. if I speak of j. | 19: 7. is no
19: 29. ye may know there is a j.
32: 9. neither do aged underst. j.
34: 4. Let us choose to us j. know
12. nei. will the Alm. pervert j.
35: 14. yet j. is before him, trust
36: 17. hast fulfilled j. of wicked,
j. and justice take hold
Ps. 7: 6. awake for me to the j.
9: 7. prepared his throne for j.
8. shall minister j. to the people
16. L. known by j. he executeth
33: 5. He loveth j., 37: 28. ⌈day
37: 6. bring forth thy j. as noon-
30. and his tongue talketh of j.
72: 2. he sh. judge thy poor wi. j.
76:8. didst cause j. heard fr. heaven
9. When God arose to j. to save
89: 14. Justice j. are habita., 97:2.
94:15. j. sh. return unto righteousn.
99: 4. king's strength loveth j.,
thou executest j. in Jac. ⌈O L.
101: 1. I will sing of mercy and j.,
103:6. L. exec-h j. for oppr-d, 146:
106: 3. Blessed they th. keep j. ⌊7.
30. Then Phinehas executed j.
111: 7. works of his hands are j.
112: † 5. guide his affairs with j.
119: 66. Teach me good j. knowl.
121. I have done j. and justice
149. O L., quicken me acc. to j.
122: 5. there are set thrones of j.
149: 9. To execute upon th. the j.
Pr. 1: 3. to rec. instruction of j.
2: 8. He keepeth the paths of j.
9. Then shalt thou understand j.
8: 20. I lead in the paths of j.
13:23. that is destr-d for want of j.
17:23. gift to pervert the ways of j.
19: 28. ungodly witn. scorneth j.
20:8. k. that sitteth in throne of j.
28: 5. Evil men understand not j.
29: 4. king by j. establisheth land
26. every man's j. cometh fr. L.
31: 5. and pervert j. of afflicted
Ec. 3: 16. saw under sun pla. of j.
5:8. If seest violent perverting of j.
8: 5. wise man discerneth time j.
6. to ev. purpose is time and j.
Is. 1: 17. seek j. | 21. was full of j.
27. Zion sh. be redeemed with j.

Is. 4: 4. purged Jerus. by spirit of j.
5: 7. looked for j. | 16:5. seeking j.
9: 7. and to establish it with j.
10: 2. To turn aside needy from j.
16: 3. execute j., Je. 21: 12.–22:3.
Eze. 18: 8.–45:9. Zch. 7:9.–8:16.
28:6. spirit of j. | 17. lay j. to line
30: 18. mercy, for L. is a God of j.
32: 16. j. shall dwell in wildern.
33: 5. L. hath filled Zion with j.
34: 5. upon peo. of my curse to j.
40: 14. taught him in path of j.?
41: 1. let us come near tog. to j.
42: 1. sh. bring forth j. to Gent.
3. he sh. bring forth j. unto truth
4. not fail, till he set j. in earth
53: 8. taken fr. prison and fr. j.
56: 1. Keep ye j. and, Ho. 12: 6.
59:8. there is no j. in their goings
9. Therefore is j. far from us
11. we look for j. but is none
14. j. is turned away backward
15. displeased him there was no j.
61: 8. I the L. love j. I hate robb.
Je. 5: 1. if any that executeth j.
4. know not j. of their God, 8:7.
5. have known j. of their God
7: 5. if ye thoroughly execute j.
9:24. wh. exercise j. and righteousn.
10: 24. correct me, but with j.
21: 12. Execute j. in the morning
23:5. Branch shall execute j., 33:15.
26: † 11. j. of death is for this man
39:5. Riblah, where he gave j., 52:9.
48: 21. j. is come upon country
47. Thus far is j. of Moab ⌈cup
49: 12. whose j. not to drink of
51: 9. her j. reacheth unto heav.
Eze. 23: 10. had executed j. upon
24. I will set j. before them ⌊her
Da. 4: 37. all whose ways are j.
7: 10. j. was set | 26. j. shall sit
22. j. was given to saints of Most
Ho.5:1. give ear, j. is tow. you ⌊High
10:4. thus j. springeth as hemlock
Am. 5: 7. turn j. into wormwood
15. love the good, and establish j.
24. But let j. run down as waters
6: 12. ye have turned j. into gall
Mi. 3: 1. Is it not to know j. | 8. I
am full of j. ⌈cute j. for me
9. that abhor j. | 7: 9. and exe-
Ha. 1: 4. j. doth never go forth
7. their j. shall proceed of thems.
12. hast ordained them for j.
Zph. 2: 3. ye which wrought his j.
3: 5. every morn. bring j. to light
Mal. 2: 17. say, Where is G. of j.?
Mat. 5:21. sh. be in danger of j., 22.
7: 2. with what j. ye judge, ye
12: 18. he shall shew j. to Gent.
20. till he send j. unto victory
23: 23. and have omitted j. mercy
Lu.10:14 more tolera. for Tyre at j.
11:42. pass over j. and love of God
Jn.5:22. hath committ-d all j. to Son
27. given him authority to execute
7: 24. but judge righteous j. ⌊j.
9: 39. For j. I am come into world
12: 31. Now is the j. of this world
16:8. he will reprove world of j., 11.
Ac. 8:33. in humil-n his j. was tak.
24: 25. as he reasoned of j. Felix
25: 15. Jews desiring j. ag. him
† 21. Paul appealed unto j. of
Ro. 1: † 28. over to a mind void of j.
32. Who knowing the j. of God
2: 2. sure j. of G. is acc. to truth
3. thinkest thou escape j. of G.?
5. revelation of righte. j. of God
3: † 19. world subject to j. of God
5: 16. j. was by one to condemna.
18. j. came upon all to condemna.
1 Co. 1: 10. joined in the same j.
4: 3. that I be judged of man's j.
11: † 29. eateth drinketh j. to hims.
† 34. that ye come not toge. to j.

2 Th. 1: 5. token of righte. j. of G.
1 Ti. 5: 24. Some sins going bef. to j.
2 Ti. 3: † 8. men of no j. conc. faith
Tit. 1: † 16. good work void of j.
He. 6: 2. Of doctrine of eternal j.
9: 27. once to die but aft. this the j.
10: 27. fearful looking for of j.
Ja. 2: 13. sh. have j. without mercy,
and mercy rejoiceth against j.
3: † 1. knowing we rec. greater j.
1 Pe. 4: 17. j. must begin at ho. of G.
2 Pe. 2: 3. whose j. lingereth not ⌋
4. reserved unto j. ⌈ecute j.
Jude 6. to j. of gr. day | 15. To ex-
Re. 14: 7. the hour of his j. is come
17: 1. shew thee j. of great whore
18: 10. in one hour is thy j. come
20: 4. and j. was given unto them
See BEAR, DAY.

Do JUDGMENT.

Ge. 18: 19. to d. justice and j., 1
K. 10: 9. Pr. 21: 3. Je. 22: 15.
1 K. 3: 28. wisdom of God to d. j.
2 Ch. 9: 8. set over them to d. j.
Pr. 21: 7. bec. they refuse to d. j.
15. It is joy to the just to d. j. ⌈52.
Je. 51: 47. I will d. j. upon images,
Eze. 18: † 5. if a man d. j., 33: † 14.

JUDGMENT with hall.

Jn. 18: 28. they led Jesus unto h.
of j., they went not into j. h.
33. Pilate entered into j. h. again
19: 9. into j. h., saith unto Jesus
Ac. 23: 35. kept in Herod's j. h.

In JUDGMENT.

Le. 19: 15. no unrighteousn. i. j., 35.
Nu. 35: 12. stand bef. congr. i. j.
De. 1: 17. not respect persons i. j.
17: 8. If arise matter too hard for
Ju. 5: 10. ye that sit i. j. ⌊thee i. j.
2 Ch. 19: 6. L., who is with you i. j.
Jb. 9: 32. we sho. come toge. i. j.
37: 23. excellent in power and i. j.
Ps. 1: 5. ungodly sh. not stand i. j.
25: 9. meek will he guide i. j.
Pr. 16: 10. transgresseth not i. j.
18: 5. to overthr. righte. i. j. ⌈i. j.
24: 23. not to have respect of pers.
Is. 5: 16. L. of hosts be exalted i. j.
28: 6. sitteth i. j. | 7. stumble i. j.
32: 1. Behold princes sh. rule i. j.
† 7. speaketh ag. poor i. j. ⌈i. j.
54: 17. tongue th. sh. rise ag. thee
Je. 4: 2. L. liveth in right-n. and i. j.
49: † 19. who will convent me i. j.?
Eze. 44: 24. in controversy stand i. j.
Ho. 2: 19. betroth thee to me i. j.
5: 11. Ephraim is broken i. j. ⌈j.
Mal. 3: 5. will come near to you i.
Mat. 12: 41. men of Nin. rise i. j.
42. queen of south rise i. j., Lu.
Ph. 1: 9. may abound i. j. ⌊11: 31, 32.

Into JUDGMENT.

Jb. 14: 3. bringest me i. j. with thee
22: 4. will he enter with thee i. j.
34: 23. that he enter i. j. with G.
Ps. 143: 2. enter not i. j. with serv.
Ec. 11: 9. God will bring thee i. j.
12: 14. G. shall bring ev. work i. j.
Is. 3: 14. L. enter i. j. with ancients

My JUDGMENT. ⌈34: 5.

Jb. 27: 2. who taken away m. j.,
29: 14. m. j. was as a robe and a
40: 8. Wilt thou disannul m. j.?
Ps. 9: † 4. For thou hast made m. j.
35: 23. Stir thys., awake to m. j.
Is. 40: 27. m. j. is passed over fr. G.
49: 4. surely m. j. is with Lord
51: 4. make m. j. to rest for a light
Eze. 39: 21. heathen shall see m. j.
Jn. 5: 30. m. j. is just | 8: 16. is true
1 Co. 7: 25. yet I give m. j.
40. happier if she abide, in m. j.

JUDGMENT seat, s. ⌈13.

Mat. 27: 19. was set on j. s., Jn. 19:
Ac. 18: 12. Jews bro-t him to j. s.
16. he drave them from the j. s.
Ac. 18: 17. beat Sosthenes bef. j. s.
25: 6. sitting on j. s. com-d Paul
10. I stand at Cesar's j. s. | 17. I
sat on j. s. ⌈Christ, 2 Co. 5: 10.
Ro. 14: 10. stand before j. s. of
Ja. 2: 6. rich men draw you bef. j.

JUDGMENTS. ⌊s-s

Ex. 6: 6. redeem you wi. gr. j., 7: 4.
21: 1. these are j. thou shalt set bef.
24: 3. Moses told the people all j.
Nu. 33: 4. upon gods L. executed j.
35: 24. shall judge acc. to these j.
36: 13. These are j. L. commanded
De. 7: 12. if ye hearken to these j.
33: 10. They sh. teach Jacob thy j.
21. he executed j. of L. with Isr.
2 S. 22: 23. his j. were before me,
Ps. 18: 22. ⌈mouth, Ps. 105: 5.
1 Ch. 16: 12. Remember j. of his
14. his j. in all earth, Ps. 105: 7.
Ne. 9: 29. but sinned against thy j.
Ps. 10: 5. thy j. are far out of sight
19: 9. the j. of the Lord are true
36: 6. thy j. are a great deep; O L.
48: 11. let Judah be glad of thy j.
72: 1. Give the king thy j. O God
97: 8. Jud. rejoiced, bec. of thy j.
119: 7. have learned thy righte. j.
13. I decl-d all the j. of thy mouth
20. longing it hath unto thy j.
30. thy j. have I laid before me
39. Turn reproach, thy j. are good
43. I have hoped in thy j.
52. I rememb-d thy j. of old ⌈164.
62. thanks, bec. of thy righte. j.,
75. I know, O L., thy j. are right
102. I have not departed fr. thy j.
106. sworn I wi. keep thy righte. j.
108. teach me thy j. | 120. afr. of
137. and upright are thy j. ⌊thy j.
156. quicken me acc. to thy j.
160. ev. one of thy righte. j. en-
175. and let thy j. help me ⌊dureth
147: 20. his j. they not known th.
Pr. 19: 29. j. prepared for scorners
Is. 26: 8. in way of thy j. we waited
9. when thy j. are in earth
Je. 4: † 12. will I utter j. ag. them
12: 1. let me talk wi. thee of thy j.
Eze. 5: 7. nei. done acc. to j. of nat-s
8. execute j. in midst, 10, 15. – 11: 9.
7: † 27. with their j. will I judge
16: 41. execute j. in sight of wom.
23: 24. judge thee acc. to their j.
25: 11. will execute j. upon Moab
28: 26. exec-d j. upon all th. despise
30: 14. I will execute j. in No
19. Thus will I execute j. in E.
34: 16. I will feed th. with j. ⌈j.
Da. 9: 5. sinned by depart-g fr. thy
Ho. 6: 5. thy j. are as the light
Zph. 3: 15. L. taken away thy j.
Ro. 11: 33. how unsearchable his j.
1 Co. 6: 4. j. of things of this life
Re. 15: 4. thy j. are made manifest
16: 7. righteous are thy j., 19: 2.

My JUDGMENTS.

Le. 18: 4. Ye shall do m. j. I am L.
5. ye shall keep m. j., 25: 18.
26: 15. if your soul abhor m. j.
43. even bec. they despised m. j.
1 Ch. 28: 7. if constant to do m. j.
Ps. 89: 30. if chil. walk not in m. j.
Je. 1: 16. will utter m. j. ag. them
Eze. 5: 6. she changed m. j. into
7. nei. have kept m. j. ⌊wick.
14: 21. I send m. 4 sore j. upon
36: 27. ye shall keep m. j. ⌊Jerus.
44: 24. shall judge it acc to m. j.

Statutes with JUDGMENTS.

Le. 18: 5. keep my s. and j., 26. –
20: 22. – 25: 18. De. 7: 11. – 11:
1. – 26: 16, 17. – 30: 16. 1 K. 2: 3.
– 8: 58. – 9: 4. – 11: 33.
19: 37. observe all my s. and j.,
De. 11: 32. – 12: 1. 2 Ch. 7: 17.
26: 46. are s. and j. L. made, De. 4: 45.
De. 4: 1. hearken to s. and j., 5: 1.
5. I taught you s. and j. | 8. hath
s. and j. so righte. ⌈Ezr. 7: 10.
14. com-d to teach s. and j., 6: 1.
5: 31. speak s. and j. thou teach
6: 20. asketh, What mean s. and j.
8: 11. forget L. in not keep. s. and
j., Ne. 1: 7. ⌈cute my j.
1 K. 6: 12. walk in my s. and exe-
1 Ch. 22: 13. if heed to fulfil s. and j.
2 Ch. 19: 10. shall come betw. s. and j.
Ne. 9: 13. gavest them right s. and j.
10: 29. curse, to do all his s. and j.
Ps. 147: 19. sheweth his s. and j.
Eze. 5: 6. they refused my j. and s.
11: 12. not walked in my s., nei.
exec-d my j., 5: 7. – 20: 13, 16, 21.
18: 9. walked in my s. and j., 17.
– 20: 19. – 36: 27. – 37: 24.
20: 11. I gave them my s., and
shewed my j. ⌈serve their j.
18. not in s. of fathers, nei. ob-
24. not exec-d my j., despised s.
25. gave them s. not good, and j.
Mal. 4: 4. Remem. law of Mo. with

JU'DITH. ⌊s. and j.

Ge. 26: 34. Esau 40 years old took

JUICE. ⌊wife J.

Can. 8: 2. wine of j. of my pomegr.

JU'LIA.

Ro. 16: 15. Salute J. and Nereus

JU'LIUS.

Ac. 27: 1. deliv-d Paul unto J., 3.

JUMPING.

Na. 3: 2. noise of the j. chariots

JU'NIA.

Ro. 16: 7. Salute Andron. J. my kins.

JUNIPER.

1 K. 19: 4. Elijah sat und. j. tree, 5.
Jb. 30: 4. cut up j. roots for meat
Ps. 120: 4. arrows with coals of j.

JU'PITER.

Ac. 14: 12. they called Barnabas, J
13. priests of J. brought garlands
19: 35. image which fell from J.

JURISDICTION.

1 K. 8: † 37. besiege in land of j.
Lu. 23: 7. knew he belonged unto
Herod's j.

JUSHAB'-HESED.

1 Ch. 3: 20. sons of Zeruh. J. Obed

JUST.

Ge. 6: 9. Noah was a j. man, and
Le. 19: 36. j. balances, j. weights,
j. ephah, j. hin, De. 25: 15. Eze.
45: 10.
De. 16: 18. judge peo. with j. judgm.
20. that is j. shalt thou follow
32: 4. a God without iniq. j. and
2 S. 23: 3. that ruleth must be j.
Ne. 9: 33. j. in all is bro-t upon us
Jb. 4: 17. man be more j. than G.?
9: 2. how sho. man be j. with G.?
12: 4. j. man is laughed to scorn
27: 17. but the j. shall put it on
33: 12. Behold, in this art not j.
Ps. 7: 9. wickedn. end, establ. j.
37: 12. wicked plotteth ag. the j.
Pr. 3: 33. blesseth habita. of the j.
4: 18. path of j. as shining light
9: 9. teach a j. man and he will incr.
10: 6. Blessings upon head of j.
7. The memory of the j. is blessed
20. tongue of j. is as choice silver
31. mouth of j. bringeth wisdom
11: 1. but j. weight is his delight
9. thro. knowl. j. be delivered
12: 13. j. sh. come out of trouble
21. shall no evil happen to j. ⌈j.
13: 22. wealth of sinner laid up for
16: 11. j. weight and bal. are L.'s
17: 15. condemneth j. is abomi.
26. to punish the j. is not good
18: 17. first in own cause seemeth j.
20: 7. j. man walketh in integrity
21: 15. joy to the j. to do judgm.
24: 16. a j. man falleth seven times

Pr. 29:10. hate upright, j. seek soul
27. An unjust man is aboml. to j.
Ec. 7 : 15. a j. man that perisheth
20. not j. man that sinneth not
8:14. j. men unto whom it happ-h
Is. 26:7. way of j. is uprightn., dost weigh path of j.
29 : 21. turn aside j. for nought
45 : 21. a j. God, and a Saviour
49 : † 24. captivity of the j. deliv-d
La. 4 : 13. have shed blood of the j.
Eze. 18 : 5. man be j. and do right
9. he is j. he shall surely live
Ho. 14 : 9. ways of L. j. walk in th.
Am. 5 : 12. they afflict the j. they
Ha. 2 : 4. the j. shall live by faith, Ro. 1 : 17. Ga. 3 : 11. He. 10:38.
Zph. 3 : 5. j. Lord is in the midst
Zch. 9 : 9. he is j. having salvation
Mat. 1 : 19. Joseph being a j. man
5 : 45. sendeth rain on j. and unj.
13 : 49. sever wicked from the j.
27:19. noth. to do with th. j. man
24. innocent of blood of j. person
Mk. 6: 20. knowing he was a j. man
Lu. 1 : 17. disobedient to wisd. of j.
2 : 25. Simeon was j. and devout
14 : 14. recomp-d at resurr. of j.
15 : 7. over 90 and nine j. persons
20 : 20. spies sho. feign thems. j.
23:50. Joseph was a good man and [j.
Jn. 5:30. and my judgment is j.
Ac. 3 : 14. denied Holy One and the [J.
10 : 22. Cornelius a j. man
24:15. sh. be resurr. of j. and unj.
Ro. 2 : 13. not hearers of law are j.
3:8. damnation is j. | 26. might be [j.
7 : 12. the com-t holy, j.
Ph. 4:8. whatso. things are j. [is j.
Col. 4 : 1. give servants that which
Tit. 1 : 8. a bishop must be j. holy
He. 2 : 2. received a j. recompence
12 : 23. spirits of j. men made perf.
Ja. 5 : 6. Ye have killed the j.
1 Pe. 3 : 18. C. suffered, j. for unj.
2 Pe. 2 : 7. delivered j. Lot, vexed
1 Jn. 1:9. if is j. to forgive our sins
Re. 15 : 3. j. and true are thy ways

Most JUST.

Jb. 34:17. wilt condemn him is m. j.

JUST One.

[J. O.
Ac. 7 : 52. shewed bef. of coming of
22 : 14. know his will, and see that [J. O.

JUSTICE.

Ge. 18 : 19. keep way of L. to do j.
De. 16 : † 20. what is j. thou follow
33:21. he executed j. of L. [14.
2 S. 8 : 15. Da. executed j., 1 Ch. 18:
15 : 4. made judge, I would do j.
Jb. 8 : 3. doth Almighty pervert j.?
31 : † 6. weigh me in balance of j.
36 : 17. and j. take hold on thee
37 : 23. is excellent in plenty of j.
Ps. 82 : 3. do j. to afflicted and
89:14. j. and judgment are habita.
119:121. I have done judgm. and j.
Pr. 1 : 3. To receive instruction of j.
8 : 15. By me princes decree j. [j.
Ec. 5 : 8. If thou seest perverting of
Is. 9:7. to establ. his throne with j.
56 : 1. and do j. for my salvation
58 : 2. they ask of me ordinances of [j.
59 : 4. None calleth for j.
9. nei. doth j. overtake us [fallen
14. j. standeth afar off, truth is
Je. 23 : 5. sh. execute judgm. and j.
31 : 23. L. bless thee, habita. of j.
50 : 7. sinned ag. L. habita. of j.
Eze. 45 : 9. O princes, execute j.
See Do JUDGMENT.

JUSTIFICATION.

Ro. 4 : 25. C. raised again for our j.
5:16. free gift of many offences to j.
18. free gift upon all men to j.

JUSTIFIED.

Jb. 11:2. sho. man full of talk be j.?
13:18. Behold, I know I shall be j.
Jb. 25 : 4. How can man be j. wi. G.
32:2. bec. he j. hims. rather than G.
Ps. 51 : 4. be j. when thou speakest
143 : 2. in thy sight no man be j.
Is. 43:9. they be j. | 26. thou mayest
45 : 25. In L. all seed of Isr. be j.
Je. 3 : 11. backsliding Isr. j. herself
Eze. 16 : 51. j. sisters in abomi., 52.
Da. 8 : † 14. sanctuary be j.
Mat. 11 : 19. wisdom is j. of her children, Lu. 7 : 35.
12 : 37. by thy words shalt be j.
Lu. 7 : 29. and publicans j. God
18:14. this man went down j. rather
Ac. 13 : 39. all that believe are j. could not be j. by the law
Ro. 2 : 13. doers of law shall be j.
3 : 4. mightest be j. in sayings
20. no flesh be j. in his sight
24. Being j. freely by his grace, Tit. 3 : 7. [2 : 16.-3 : 24.
28. a man is j. by faith, 5 : 1. Ga.
4 : 2. if Ab. were j. by works [G.
5:1. j. by faith we have peace with
9. j. by his bl. we shall be saved
8 : 30. and whom he j. he glorified
1 Co. 4 : 4. yet am I not hereby j.
6 : 11. ye are j. in name of L. J.
Ga. 2:16. man not j. by works, 3 : 11.
17. if we seek to be j. by Christ
5 : 4. whoso. j. by law. ye are fallen
1 Ti. 3 : 16. G. in flesh, j. in Spirit
Ja. 2 : 21. Was not Ab. j. by works
24. see how by works man is j.
25. was not Rahab j. by works?

JUSTIFIER.

Ro. 3 : 26. j. of him who believeth

JUSTIFIETH.

Pr. 17 : 15. that j. wicked is abomi.
Is. 50 : 8. He is near that j.
Ro. 4:5. believ-h on him j. ungodly
8:33. God's elect? It is God that j.

JUSTIFY, ING.

Ex. 23 : 7. I will not j. the wicked
De. 25 : 1. they shall j. the righte.
1 K. 8 : 32. j-g righteous, 2 Ch. 6:23.
Jb. 9 : 20. If j. myself, own mouth
27 : 5. G. forbid I should j. you
33 : 32. speak, I desire to j. thee
Is. 5 : 23. j. wicked for reward
53 : 11. my righte. serv. j. many
Lu. 10 : 29. he willing to j. himself
16:15. Ye are th. j. yours bef. men
Ro. 3 : 30. shall j. circumc. by faith
Ga. 3 : 8. foreseeing God would j. [heathen

JUSTLE.

Na. 2:4. chariots shall j. one ag. ano.

JUSTLY.

[j.
Mi. 6 : 8. what L. require but to do
Lu. 23 : 41. j. for we receive reward
1 Th. 2 : 10. holily, j. we behaved

JUS'TUS.

[named J.
Ac. 1 : 23. Joseph, who was sur-
18 : 7. into a man's ho. named J.
Col. 4 : 11. Jesus, who is called J.

JUT'TAH.

[21 : 16.
Jos. 15 : 55. in the mts. Carmel, J.,

K.

KAB'ZEEL.

Jos. 15:21. coast of Edom southw. K.
2 S. 23:20. valiant man of K., 1 Ch. [11:22.

KA'DESH.

Ge. 14 : 7. to Enmishpat wh. is K.
16:14. Beer-la. betw. K. and Bered
20:1. Ab. dwelt betw. K. and Shur
Nu. 13 : 26. wildern. of Paran to K.
20 : 1. peo. abode in K., Ju. 11:16,
20 : 16. behold, we are in K. [17.
22. Isr. journeyed fr. K., 33 : 37.
27 : 14. me at water of Meribah in K., De. 32:51. Eze. 47:19.-48:28.
33:36. in wildern. of Zin, wh. is K.
De. 1 : 46. ye abode in K. many
Ps. 29 : 8. L. shaketh wildern. of K.

KA'DESH-BARNE'A.

Nu. 32 : 8. I sent them fr. K. to see land, De. 9 : 23 Jos. 14 : 7.
34:4. the going sh. be fr. so. to K., De. 1 : 2, 19.-2 : 14. Jos. 15 : 3.
Jos. 10 : 41. smote them fr. K. unto Gaza [thee in K.
14 : 6. what L. said, conc. me and

KAD'MIEL.

Ezr. 2 : 40. chil. of Jeshua, K., 3:9.
Ne. 7:43.-9:4, 5.-10:9.-12:8, 24.

KAD'MONITES.

Ge. 15:19. the land of K. to thy seed

KAIN = KEN'ITE.

Nu. 24: † 22. K. shall be wasted until

KAL'LAI. See SALLAI.

KA'NAH.

Jos. 16:8. unto river K., 17:9.-19:28.

KARE'AH = CARE'AH.

See JOHANAN.

KAR'KAA.

Jos. 15:13. fetched a compass to K.

KAR'KOR.

[K.
Ju. 8 : 10. Zeba, Zalmunna were in

KAR'NAIM. See ASHTEROTH

KAR'TAH.

[am, K.
Jos. 21 : 34. unto the Levites, Jokne-

KAR'TAN.

[suburbs
Jos. 21 : 32. unto the Levites, K. with

KAT'TATH. See NAHALLAL.

KE'DAR.

[1 : 29.
Ge. 25:13. sons of Ishm., K., 1 Ch.
Ps. 120:5. Woe I dwell in tents of K.
Can. 1:5. but comely as tents of K.
Is. 21:16. all glory of K. shall fail, 17.
42 : 11. villages K. doth inhabit
60 : 7. flocks of K. shall be gath-d
Je. 2:10. send unto K. and consider
49 : 28. Concerning K. go up to K.
Eze. 27 : 21. all princes of K. occup.

KED'EMAH.

[Ch. 1:31.
Ge. 25 : 15. Joshua, Naphish, K., 1

KED'EMOTH.

De. 2 : 26. sent messen. out of K.
Jos. 13 : 18. Mo. gave Reub. K., 21: 37. 1 Ch. 6 : 79.

KE'DESH.

Jos. 13 : 22. Josh. smote k. of K. | 15 : 23.-19 : 37.-20 : 7.-21 : 32.
Ju. 4 : 9. Deb. went with Barak to K. | 10, 11. 2 K. 15 : 29. 1 Ch. 6 : 72, 76.

KE'DESH-NAPH'TALI.

Ju. 4:6. Deb. called Barak out of K.

KEEP.

Ge. 2:15. L. put him in Eden to k. it
3 : 24. sword turned ev. way to k.
18:19. they shall k. way of the L.
28:15. I am with thee to k. thee. 20.
30 : 31. I will again k. thy flock
33 : 9. bro. k. that thou hast unto
41:35. let them k. food in the cities
Ex. 6 : 5. whom E-ns k. in bondage
12:6. k. it until 14th day of month
14. k. it a feast to L. thro-t your genera., 23:15.-34:18. Le. 23:41.
25. ye shall k. this service, 13:5.
47. the congr. of Isr. shall k. it
13 : 10. k. this ordin. in his season
20:8. Remember sabbath day to k. it, 31 : 13, 14, 16. De. 5 : 12, 15.
22:7. If man deliv. money to k., 10.
23 : 7. k. thee far fr. false matter
14. Three times k. a feast unto me
20. I send an Angel to k. thee
Le. 6 : 2. and lie in that which was delivered him to k., 4.
18 : 4. Ye shall k. my ordinances, 30.-22 : 9. Eze. 11 : 20.
19 : 3. shall k. my sabbaths, 30.-26 : 2. Is. 56 : 4.
23:39. k. feast 7 days, 2 Ch. 30:13.
25 : 2. then sh. land k. a sabbath
18. ye sh. k. my judgments and do
Nu. 3:8. they sh. k. all instruments
6 : 24. Lord bless thee and k. thee
9:3. in 14th day at even ye sh. k. it

Nu.9:11. day of sec. month sh. k. it
18:7. and sons k.priest's office
29 : 12. k. a feast unto L. 7 days
36:7.shall k.hims.to the inheri.,9.
De.4 : 6. k. thf. and do them, 5:1.-
9. k. thy soul diligently ⌊26:16.
7:8. bec. L. loved you, wo. k. oath
12.if ye k. them, L. shall k. cov.
16 : 10. k. feast of weeks unto L.
15. shalt k. solemn feast unto L.
17:19. learn to k. all words of law
23: 9. k. thee fr. ev. wicked thing
23.That out of thy lips thou shalt
29:9.k. thf. words of this cov. ⌊k.
Jos. 6 : 18. k. from accursed thing
10 : 18. set men by cave, to k. th.
23:6.to k. all written in law of Mo.
Ju. 2 : 22. whe. will k. way of L.
Ru. 2:21. k. fast by my young men
1 S. 2 : 9. will k. feet of his saints
7:1. Eleazar his son, to k. the ark
2 S. 15:16. k. left ten concubines to
k. house, 16 : 21.-20 : 3.
18 : 18. no son to k. my name [16.
1 K.8:25. k. with serv. Da., 2 Ch.6:
20:39. bro-t man and said, k. this
2 K.11:6.sh.ye k. watch of house,7.
1 Ch. 4 : 10. wouldest k. me fr. evil
12 : 33. 50,000 could k. rank, 38.
22 : 12. mayest k. the law of Lord
29 : 18. k. this for ever in heart
2 Ch. 22 : 9. no power to k. kingd.
23:6. peo. shall k. watch of the L.
28:10.to k. under the chil. of Jud.
30 : 3. could not k. it at that time
23. took counsel to k. seven days
Ezr. 8:29. k. them till ye weigh th.
Ne.12:27. k. dedication with gladn.
13 : 22. that Levites sho. k. gates
Es. 3 : 8. nei. k. they king's laws
9 : 21. should k. 14th day of Adar
27. would k. two days of Purim
Jb. 14 : 13. O wouldest k. me secret
20:13. tho. k. it still within mouth
Ps. 12:7. shalt k. them, O L.,31:20.
17:8. k. me as the apple of the eye
19 : 13. k. fr. presumptuous sins
25 : 20. O k. my soul, and deliver
31:20. k. them secretly in pavilion
34 : 13. k. thy tongue from evil
37:34.k.his way | 39:1.k. my mou.
89:28. My mercy will I k. for him
91:11. his angels charge to k. thee
103:9.nei. will he k. anger for ever
105 : 45. they might k. his laws
106:3. Blessed they that k. judgm.
113 : 9. barren woman to k. house
119 : 2. Blessed th. k. his testimo.
4.hast com-d us to k. thy precepts
17.may live and k. thy word,101.
33.Teach me, I sh. k. it unto end
34. Give underst-g, I sh. k. law,
57.said, I would k. thy words⌊44.
63.companion of th. k. precepts
69. I will k. thy precepts, 134.
88.I will k. testimo.of thy mouth
100. I underst. bec. I k. precepts
106. I will k. thy rights. judgm-s
129.wonderful, thf. my soul k.th.
136. eyes, bec. they k. not law
146. save me, I sh. k. thy testim.
127:1. except the Lord k. the city
140: 4. k. me fr. hands of wicked
141 : 3. O L. k. door of my lips
9. k. me fr. snares they have laid
Pr. 2:11. understanding sh. k. thee
20.mayest k.paths of righteousn.
3 : 21. My son, k. sound wisdom
26. Lord shall k. thy foot from
4 : 6. love wisdom, she sh. k. thee
13. k. instruction, let her not go
21. k. my sayings in thy heart
23.k. thy heart with all diligence
5 : 2. that thy lips may k. knowl.
6 : 22. when sleepest it sh. k. thee
24. To k. thee fr. the evil woman
7:1. My son, k. my words, lay up
Pr.7:5.may k.thee fr. strange wom.
8 : 32. blessed they th. k. my ways
22:5. he that doth k. his soul shall
18. it is pleasant if thou k. them
24:†19. k. not company wi. wick.
28 : 4. such as k. the law contend
Ec. 3 : 6. time to k. and to cast aw.
5:1. k. thy foot when goest to hou.
Can. 8:12. that k. the fruit thereof
Is. 26 : 3. wilt k. him in perf. peace
27:3. I the L. do k. it, I will k. it
42 : 6. I L. called thee, I will k.
43:6. k. not back | 56:1.k. judgm.
Je. 3 : 5. will he k. anger to end?
12. I will not k. anger for ever
31 : 10. k. him as shep. his flock
42 : 4. I will k. noth. back fr. you
Eze.20:19. k. my judgments, 36:27.
43:11. th. they may k. whole form
Ho. 12: 6. k. mercy and judgment
Mi. 6:†16. doth k. statutes of Omri
7 : 5. k. the doors of thy mouth
Na.1:15. k. feasts | 2:1.k.munition
Zch. 3 : 7. shalt k. my courts
13 : 5. man taught me to k. cattle
14 : 16. k. feast of tabern., 18, 19.
Mal.2:7. priest's lips sho. k. knowl.
Mk. 7 : 9. may k. your tradition
Lu.4:10. his angels charge to k. thee
8 : 15. having heard the word k. it
11:28.blessed th. hear word and k.
19 : 43. enemies sh. k. thee [52.
Jn.8:51.k. my say. never see death,
55. I know him, and k. his say.
12:25. hateth life in world sh. k.it
14:23. If love me will k. my words
15:20.if kept my say. will k.yours.
17 : 11. k. thro. thine own name
15. I pray thou k. them fr. evil
Ac. 5 : 3. to k. back part of price
10 : 28. for man a Jew to k. comp.
12 : 4. deliv-d him to soldiers to k.
15 : 5. command them to k. law
24. be circumcised, and k. law
29. from which, if ye k. yours.
16 : 4. deliv-d them decrees to k.
23. charging jailer to k. safely
18:21. I must k. this feast in Jerus.
21 : 25. k. fr. things off-d to idols
24 : 23. com-d centurion to k. Paul
Ro. 2 : 25. circ. profiteth, if k. law
26. if circ. k. righte-n. of law
1 Co. 5:8. k. feast | 11.not k. comp.
7 : 37. decreed he will k. his virgin
9:27. I k. under my body and bri.
11:2. that ye k. the ordinances, as
15 : 2. if ye k. in memory what I
2 Co. 11 : 9. and so will I k. myself
Ga. 6 : 13. nei. circumcised k. law
Ep.4:3. to k. the unity of the Spirit
Ph. 4:7. peace of G. shall k. hearts
2 Th.3:3. establ. and k. you fr. evil
1 Ti. 5 : 22. of sins, k. thyself pure
6:20. k. that committ. to thy trust
2 Ti.1:12. able to k. th. I committ.
14. thing committed to thee k.
Ja. 1 : 27. to k. himself unspotted
2 : 10. whoso. shall k. whole law
1 Jn. 5 : 21. k. yours. from idols
Jude 21. k. yours. in the love of G.
24. unto him that is able to k. you
Re. 1 : 3. Blessed they k. those
3 : 10. I will k. thee fr. temptation
22 : 9. who k. sayings of this book

KEEP alive.

Ge. 6:19. into ark to k. them a.,20.
7:3. to k. seed a. upon all the earth
Nu. 31 : 18. women, chil. k. a. for
2 S. 8 : 2. measured wi. line to k.a.
Ps. 22 : 29. none can k. a. his soul
33 : 19. to k. them a. in famine
41 : 2. L. will preserve and k. him

KEEP charge. ⌊a.

Le. 8 : 35. and k. the c. of the L., 1
K. 2 : 3. 2 Ch. 13 : 11.
Nu. 1 : 53. Levites k. c. of tabern.,
18 : 3, 4.-31 : 30. 1 Ch. 23 : 32.
Nu 3:7. they shall k. his c., 8:26.-
18 : 3. De. 11 : 1. [of Israel
8. they shall k. the c. of children
32.k.c. of sanct., 18:5.1 Ch.23:32.
Eze.44:16. to minister and k. my c.
Zch. 3:7. if thou wilt k. my c. then

KEEP commandment, s.

Ex. 16:28. How long refuse to k. c-s
20:6. shewing mercy to them that
k. my c-s, De.5:10.-7:9.Da.9:4.
Le. 22 : 31. Thf. shall ye k. my c-s
and do th., De.4:40.-6:17.-7:11.
26:3. If ye k. my c-s, De. 11 : 22.-
19 : 9.-28 : 9.-30 : 10. 1 K. 3:14.
De. 4 : 2. th. ye may k. c-s of Lord
5 : 29. O th. they would k. my c-s
8:2. know whe. wouldest k. his c-s
6. thou shalt k. the c-s, 11:1, 8.-
13 : 4, 18. [c-s, 27 : 1.-30 : 16.
10:13. the Lord requires thee to k.
26 : 17. hast avouched L. to k. c-s
18. L. avouched that thou k. c.
28:45.hearkenedst not to k. his c-s
Jos. 22 : 5. take heed to k. his c-s
1 K. 2:3. keep charge of L. to k. c-s
6 : 12. k. my c-s, 2 K. 17 : 13. Pr.
4:4.-7:2. [hearts to k. his c-s
8 : 58. That he may incline our
61. Let heart be perfect to k. c-s
9 : 6. if not k. c-s I cut off Israel
11 : 38. if thou wilt k. my c-s, Ne.
1:9. Jn. 15:10. [c-s, 2 Ch.34:31.
2 K. 23 : 3. made a covenant to k.
1 Ch. 28 : 8. k. all the c-s of the L.
29 : 19. Sol. perfect heart to k. c-s
Ps. 78 : 7. not forget but k. his c-s
119:60. I delayed not to k. thy c-s
115. Depart evil doers, I will k. c-s
Pr. 3 : 1. let thy heart k. my c-s
6 : 20. My son, k. thy father's c.
Ec. 8:2. I counsel thee to k. k.'s c.
12:13. Fear G. and k. his c-s [k. c-s
Mat. 19 : 17. if will enter into life,
Jn. 14 : 15. If ye love me, k. my c-s
1 Ti. 6 : 14. k. this c. without spot
1 Jn. 2:3. we know him if we k. c-s
3:22. we receive, bec. we k. his c-s
5:2. when we love G. and k. his c-s
3. this is love of G. that we k. c-s
Re. 12:17. war with seed wh. k. c-s
14 : 12. are they wh. k. c-s of God
See Keep, eth, ing, or kept

COVENANT.

KEEP passover. [L.(2)

Ex. 12 : 48. a stranger will k. p. to
Nu. 9 : 2. Let chil. of Israel k. p. in
its season, 4. De.16:1. 2 K.23:21.
6. could not k.p. | 10. shall k.p.
12. all ordinances of p. they sh k.
13. forbear-h to k.p. th. soul cut
14. if a stranger will k. p. ⌊off
2 Ch.30:1. come to k.p. unto G., 5.
2. taken counsel, to k. p. in
35:16. service was prepared to k.p.
18. nei. did k-s of Isr. k. such a p.
Mat.26:18. I will k.p. at thy house

KEEP silence.

Ju.3:19. said k. s. and all went out
Ps. 35 : 22. shall k. not s., 83 : 1.
50 : 3. O Lord come and not k. s.
Ec. 3 : 7. time to k. s. time to spe.
Is. 41 : 1. k. s. before me, O islands
62 : 6. mention of L. k. not s.
65 : 6. behold, I will not k. s.
La. 2 : 10. elders of dau. of Zi. k. s.
Am. 5 : 13. the prudent shall k. s.
Ha. 2 : 20. L. in tem. let earth k.s.
1 Co. 14:28. let him k. s. in church
34. Let women k. s. in churches

KEEP statutes.

Ex. 15:26. if thou wilt k. all his s.,
De. 30 : 10. 1 K. 9 : 4.-11 : 38.
Le. 18 : 5. you shall k. my s., 26.-
19 : 19.-20:8, 22. De. 11:1. Eze.
44 : 24.
De. 4 : 40. Thou shalt k. s., 26:16.
6 : 2. mightest fear L. to k. his s.

De. 26:17. hast avouched L. to k. s.
28: 45. hearkenedst not to k. s.
1 K. 11:33. not walked to k. my s.
Ps.119:5. th. my ways were directed
8. I will k. thy s., 145. [to k.s.
Eze. 18:21. if wicked turn and k.s.

KEEPER.

Ge. 4: 2. Abel was k. of sheep
9. Am I my brother's k.?
39: 21. Jo. favour in sight of k.
22. k. of prison committed to Jo.
23. k. of prison looked not to any
1 S. 17: 20. Da. left sheep with k.
22. David left his carriage in k.
28: 2. I will make thee k. of mine
head for ever [Ch. 34: 22.
2 K. 22: 14. k. of the wardrobe, 2
Ne. 2: 8. Asaph k. of king's forest
3: 29. Shemaiah k. of east gate
Es. 2: 3. Hege k. of women, 8, 15.
Jb. 27: 18. booth that k. maketh
Ps. 121:5. L. is thy k. L. thy shade
Can. 1: 6. made me k. of viney-s
Je. 35: 4. Maaseiah k. of the door
Ac. 16: 27. k. of prison awaking
36. k. of prison told this to Paul
19:†35. city of Ephesians is temple

KEEPERS. [k.

2 K. 11:5. a 3d part be k. of watch
1 Ch. 9: 19. k. of gates of tabern.
Ec. 12: 3. when k. of ho. tremble
Can. 5: 7. k. took away my vail
8: 11. Sol. let out vineyard to k.
Je. 4: 17. As k. of the field ag. her
Eze. 40: 45. k. of charge of house,
46.-44: 8, 14. [did shake
Mat. 28: 4. for fear of him the k.
Ac. 5:23. the k. standing bef. doors
12:6. k. kept prison | 19. exam-d k.
Tit. 2: 5. chaste, k. at home, good
See **DOORKEEPER, S,** and
Keeper, s, of DOOR.

KEEPEST.

1 K. 8: 23. who k. cov. and mercy
with serv-s, 2 Ch.6:14. Ne.9:32.
Ac. 21: 24. walkest orderly and k.

KEEPETH. [the law

Ex. 21: 18. die not, but k. his bed
De. 7:9. faithful G. wh. k. cov., Ne.
1 S. 16: 11. he k. the sheep [1:5.
Jb. 33:18. k. back his soul from pit
Ps. 34: 20. He k. all his bones
121:3. k. thee will not slumber, 4.
146: 6. God, wh. k. truth for ever
Pr. 2: 8. He k. the paths of judgm.
10: 17. in way of life that k. instr.
13: 3. k. mouth k. his life, 21:23.
6. Righte-n. k. him upright [16.
16:17. k. his way preserv-h soul, 19:
19:8. k. underst-g shall find good
24:12. k. thy soul, doth not he kn.
27: 18. k. fig tree shall eat fruit
28: 7. Whoso k. law is a wise son
29:3. th. k. company with harlots
11. wise man k. it in till afterw.
18. that k. the law, happy is he
Ec. 8: 5. k. com-ts sh. feel no evil
Is. 26:2. nation k. truth may enter
56:2. k. sab. from polluting it, k.
hand from doing evil, 6.
Je. 48:10. cursed that k. back swo.
La. 3: 28. sitteth alone k. silence
Ha. 2: 5. proud, nei. k. at home
Lu. 11: 21. strong man armed k.
Jn.7:19. none of you k. law [palace
9: 16. not of G. bec. k. not sab.
14: 21. hath com-ts and k. them
24. loveth me not, k. not sayings
1 Jn. 2: 4. I know him, and k. not
5. k. word, in him is love, 3: 24.
5: 18. is begott. of God k. himself
Re. 2:26. overcometh and k. works
16: 15. Blessed he k. his garments
22: 7. blessed is he k. the sayings

KEEPING.

Ex.34:7. L. k. mercy for thousands
Nu. 3: 28. k. charge of sanct., 38.
De. 8: 11. in not k. his commands
1 S. 25: 16. were with th. k. sheep
1 Ch. 12: † 36. of Asher k. rank
Ne. 12: 25. were porters k. ward
Ps. 19:11. in k. of them gr. reward
Pr. 4:†23. Keep thy heart above all
Eze. 17: 14. by k. of his cov. [k.
Da. 9: 4. O L. great God, k. cov.
Lu. 2: 8. were shepherds k. watch
1 Co. 7: 19. but k. com-ts of God
He. 4: † 9. remaineth a k. of sab.
1 Pe. 4:19. commit k. of their souls

KEHEL'ATHAH.

Nu.33:22. pitched in K. | 23. went fr.

KEI'LAH. See GARMITE.

KEI'LAH. [Place.]

Jos. 15:44. K. Achzib, cities of Jud.
1 S. 23: 1. Philis. fight ag. K. +
4. go to K. | 5. Da. saved K.
6. when Abiathar fled to K.
10. Saul seek-h to come to K. [12.
11. Will men of K. deliv. me into,
13. Da. was escaped out of K.
Ne. 3: 17. ruler of K. repaired, 18.

KELAI'AH = KEL'ITA.

Ezr. 10: 23. taken stra. wives, K. |
Ezr. 8: 7.-10: 10.

KEM'UEL.

Ge.22:21. K. fa. of Aram [Nu. 34:24.
1 Ch. 27: 17. of Levites son of K. |

KE'NAN = CAI'NAN.

1 Ch. 1: 2. Sheth, Enosh, K. | Ge.

KE'NATH. [5: † 9.

Nu.32:42. Nobah took K., 1 Ch.2:23.

KE'NAZ. [1: 36.

Ge. 36:11. sons of Eliphaz K., 1 Ch.
15. duke K., 42. 1 Ch.1:53 [1 Ch.
See OTHNIEL. [4: 15.

KEN'EZITE.

Jos. 14: 6. Caleb son of the K., 14.

KEN'ITE.

Nu. 24: 22. K. shall be wasted, Ju.
See HEBER. [1: 16.

KEN'ITES.

Ge. 15:19. Unto thy seed I given K.
Nu.24:21. Balaam looked on K. [K.
Ju. 4: 11. Heber severed hims. fr.
1 S. 15: 6. Saul said unto K. depart
27:10. road to-day? ag. south of K.
30: 29. to them in cities of K.
1 Ch. 2: 55. K. th. came of Hemath

KEN'IZZITES. [the K.

Ge. 15: 19. Unto Ab.'s seed given

KEPT.

Ge. 26:5. Abr. k. my charge [them
29: 9. Rachel with sheep, she k.
39:9. nor hath he k. back any thi.
42: 16. ye shall be k. in prison
Ex. 3: 1. Mo. k. flock of Jethro
16: 23. to be k. till the morning
32. manna k. for genera., 33, 34.
21: 29. if owner not k. him in, 36.
Nu. 5: 13. it be k. close, and she be
defiled [we k. back
9: 5. they k. passo. | 7. whf. are
19. Isr. k. charge of the L., 23.
17: 10. Aa.'s rod to be k. for tok.
19: 9. water of separation k. for
24: 11. L. k. thee back fr. honour
31: 47. which k. charge of tab.
De. 32: 10. k. as apple of his eye
33: 9. observed word, k. covenant
Jos. 5: 10. Isr. k. passover in Gilg.
14: 10. L. that k. me alive 45 y-rs
22: 2. Ye have k. all Moses com-d
3. have k. the charge of com-t
Ru. 2: 23. k. by maidens of Boaz
1 S. 9: 24. it hath been k. for thee
13:13. hast not k. com-t of L., 14.
17:34. said, Thy serv. k. fa.'s sheep
21: 4. have k. thems. fr. wom., 5.
25:21. Surely in vain have I k. all th.
33. blessed thou who hast k. me
34. L. God hath k. me fr. evil, 39.
26: 15. whf. hast not k. lord k.?
16. bec. ye have not k. your master
2 S. 13: 34. yo. man that k. watch
2 S. 22:22. I have k. the ways of the
Lord, Ps. 18:21. [Ps. 18:23.
24. I have k. myself from iniq.,
44. k. me to be head of heathen
1 K. 2: 43. Why hast not k. oath
of L.? [kindness
3: 6. hast k. for him this great
8: 24. hast k. with Da. that thou
promisedst, 2 Ch. 6: 15.
11: 10. Sol. k. not that L. com-d
11. thou hast not k. my covenant
34. bec. Da. k. my com-ts, 14: 8.
13: 21. man of God not k. com-t
14:27. guard wh. k. door, 2 Ch.12:10.
20:†7. I k. not back silver fr. him
2 K. 9:14. Joram had k. Ra.-gilead
12:9. priests th. k. door put therein
17: 19. Judah k. not com-ts
18: 6. Hez. k. the com-ts of the L.
1 Ch. 10:13. word of L. Saul k. not
12: 1. while David k. himself close
29. had k. ward of house of Saul
2 Ch. 7: 8. Sol. k. feast 7 days
9. k. dedicat. of altar seven days
30: 21. k. feast of unl. bread, Ezr.
23. k. 7 days with gladn. [6: 22.
34:9. Levites that k. doors gath-d
21. bec. fa-s have not k. word
35: 1. and Israel k. passo., 17, 19.
18. no passo. like that k. in Isr.
36:21. long as she lay desol. k. sab.
Ezr. 3: 4. They k. feast of tabern.
6: 16. k. dedication of this house
19. chil. of captivity k. passover
Ne. 1: 7. We have not k. com-ts
8: 18. they k. the feast seven days
9: 34. nor our fathers k. thy law
11: 19. their breth. that k. gates
12:45. singers and porters k. ward
Es. 2: 14. which k. concubines
21. wh. k. door [should be k.
9: 28. that these days of Purim
Jb. 23: 11. his ways have I k.
28: 21. k. close fr. fowls of the air
Ps. 17: 4. I have k. me fr. paths of
30: 3. hast k. me alive [destroyer
42: 4. multitude that k. holy day
78: 10. they k. not cov. of God
56. they k. not his testimonies
99: 7. they k. his testimonies and
119:22. I have k. thy testimo., 167.
55. I have k. thy law
56. I k. precepts, 168. [not word
67. have I k. thy word | 158. k.
Ec. 2: 10. eyes desired, I k. not fr.
5: 13. riches k. for owners to hurt
Can. 1: 6. own viney. have I not k.
Is.30:29. as when a solemnity is k.
Je. 16: 11. fathers not k. my law
35: 18. k. Jonadab's precepts
Eze. 5: 7. nei. k. my judgm., 20:21.
18: 9. k. judgm. | 19. k. statutes
44:8. not k. charge of holy things
15. k. charge of sanct., 48: 11.
Da. 5:19. whom he wo., he k. alive
7: 28. k. matter in my heart
Ho. 12:12. served for wife, k. sheep
Am.1:11. Edom k. his wrath for ev.
2: 4. Jud. hath not k. his com-ts
Mi. 6: 16. statutes of Omri are k.
Mal. 2: 9. ye not k. my ways, 3: 7.
3: 14. what profit th. we k. ordin.
Mat. 8: 33. they that k. swine fled
13:35. utter things been k. secret
14: 6. Herod's birthday was k.
19:20. I k. fr. my youth, Lu. 18:21.
Mk. 4: 22. nei. any thing k. secret
9:10. k. that saying, Lu. 9:36. [51.
Lu. 2: 19. Mary k. things in heart,
8: 29. k. bound with chains [kin
19: 20. pound, I have k. in nap-
Jn. 2: 10. hast k. good wine until
12: 7. ag. day of my burying hat
she k. this
15: 10. as I have k. fa.'s com-ts
20. if they have k. my sayings
17:6. thine, and have k. thy word

Jn.17:12. those thou gav-t I have k.
18: 16. spake to her that k. door
17. saith damsel that k. the door
Ac. 5: 2. k. back part of price
7: 53. received law have not k. it
9: 33. Eneas had k. his bed 8 y-rs
12:5. Pe. k. in prison | 6. k. prison
20: 20. I k. back noth. profitable
22:20. k. raiment of them slew him
23: 35. com-d him to be k., 25:21.
25:4. Festus ans-d that Paul be k.
27: 43. centu. k. them fr. purpose
28:16. Paul with soldier th. k. him
Ro. 16: 25. mystery k. secret since
2 Co. 11: 9. I k. fr. being burdens.
32. gov. k. city with garrison
Ga. 3: 23. we were k. under law
2 Ti. 4: 7. my course, I k. the faith
He.11:28. Thro. faith Mo. k. passo.
Ja. 5: 4. the hire k. back by fraud
1 Pe.1:5. Who are k. by power of G.
2 Pe. 3:7. by same word k. in store
Jude 6. which k. not first estate
Re. 3: 8. hast k. my word and not
10. Bec. hast k. word of my pa-
KEPT silence. [tience
Jb. 29: 21. men k.s. at my counsel
31: 34. did I fear that I k. s.
Ps. 32:3. k. s. my bones waxed old
50: 21. hast thou done, and I k.s.
Ac. 15: 12. Then all multitude k.s.
22:2. spake Hebrew, they k. more
KERCHIEFS. [s.
Eze.13:8. make k. upon head of ev.
21. Your k. also will I tear, and
KE'REN-HAP'PUCH.
Jb. 42: 14. he called name of 3d K.
KE'RIOTH, or KIR'IOTH.
Jos.15:25. K. inheri. of Jud. [taken
Je. 48: 24. judgm. upon K. | 41. K.
Am. 2: 2. fire shall devour palaces
KERNELS. [of K.
Nu. 6: 4. eat nothing from the k.
KE'ROS.
Eze. 2: 44. the chil. of K., Ne. 7:47.
KETTLE.
1 S. 2: 14. priest's serv. struck into
KETU'RAH. [k.
Ge. 25:1. Ab. took a wife named K.
4. were chil. of K., 1 Ch. 1:32,33.
KEY, S.
Ju.3:25. they took a k. and opened
Is.22:22. k. of hou. of Da. lay upon
Mat. 16: 19. give k-s of kingdom
Lu. 11: 52. taken aw. k. of knowl.
Re. 1: 18. k-s of hell and of death
3: 7. he that hath k. of David [1.
9:1. to him k. of bottomless pit, 20:
KEZI'A.
Jb. 42: 14. the name of the 2d K.
KE'ZIZ.
Jos. 18: 21. and the valley of K.
KIB'ROTH-HATTA'AVAH.
Nu. 11: 35. journeyed fr. K. | 34.-
33: 16, 17.
De. 9: 22. at K. ye provoked Lord
KIB'ZAIM. [suburbs
Jos. 21: 22. gave them K. with her
KICK, ED.
De. 32:15. Jeshurun waxed fat k-d
1 S. 2: 29. Whf. k. ye at my sacri.
Ac.9:5. hard to k. ag. pricks, 26:14.
KID.
Ge.37:31. Joseph's breth killed a k.
38: 17. will send thee k. fr. flock
20. Judah sent k. by friend, 23.
Ex. 23: 19. shalt not seethe k. in
moth.'s milk, 34:26. De. 14:21.
Le. 4:23. bring his offering a d., 28.
-9: 3. Eze. 43: 22.-45: 23.
5: 6. bring a k. for a sin offering
23: 19. ye sh. sacrifice one k., Nu.
7: 16, 22, 28, 34, 40, 46, 52, 58,
64, 70, 76, 82.-15: 24.-28:15,30.
-29:5,11, 16, 19, 25. Eze.45:†15.
Nu. 15: 11. thus be done for a k.

Ju. 6: 19. Gideon made ready a k.
13:15. until we have made ready a
19. So Manoah took a k. with [k.
14: 6. Samson rent lion as a k.
15: 1. Samson visited wife with k.
1 S. 16: 20. Jesse took ass and k.
Is. 11: 6. leopard lie down with k.
Lu. 15: 29. thou never gavest me a
KIDS. [k.
Ge. 27: 9. fetch me thence two k.
16. she put skins of k. upon ha.
Le. 16: 5. he shall take two k. [12
Nu. 7: 87. k. of goats for sin off-g
1 S. 10: 3. one carrying three k.
1 K. 20: 27. like 2 little flocks of k.
2 Ch.35:7. Josiah gave k. for off-gs
Can. 1:8. feed thy k. beside shep-s'
KIDNEYS. [tents
Ex. 29: 13. thou shalt take two k.
and burn, 22. Le. 3: 4, 10, 15.-
4: 9.-7: 4.-8: 16, 25.
Le.9:10. k. he burnt upon altars, 19.
De. 32:14. fat of k. of wheat [rams
Is. 34: 6. sword of L. fat with d. of
KID'RON = CE'DRON.
1 K. 2: 37. passed over brook K.
15: 13. burnt it by brook K., 2 K.
23: 4, 6, 2 Ch. 15: 16.
2 K. 23:12. king cast into brook K.
See **Brook, CE'DRON.**
KIKAJON. [ov. Jon.
Jon. 4:†6. G. prepared a k. to come
KILL.
Ge 4: 15. lest finding Cain k. him
12: 12. will k. me, but save thee
26: 7. lest men of the place should
k. me [thee
27: 42. comfort purposing to k.
37:21. Reub. said, Let us not k. him
43:†16. Bring these men home, k.
Ex. 1: 16. if a son, then k. him
2:14. intendest to k. me? Ac.7:28.
4:24. L. met and sought to k. him
12: 6. cong. of Isr. shall k. it, 21.
16: 3. to k. assembly with hunger
17:3. to k. us and chil. with thirst
20: 13. Thou shalt not k., De. 5:
17. Mat. 5: 21. Ro. 13: 9.
22: 1. if man steal an ox and k.
24. I will k. you wi. sword [4:4.
29:11. k. bullock bef. L., Le.1:5.-
20. k. the ram, and take of bl.
Le.1:11. k. it on side of alt., 16:15.
3: 2. k. it at door of the tabern.
8. he shall k. it bef. tabern., 13.
4:24. k. it in place where they k.
33. d. burnt off-g, 7: 2. 14: 19.
14: 13. he shall k. sin off-g, 16:11.
25. k. lamb of trespass offering
50. he shall k. the one of the birds
20:4. seed unto Molech, and k. not
16. thou shalt k. wom. and beast
22:28. cow or ewe, ye sh. not k. it
Nu. 11: 15. if deal thus, k. me
14: 15. if k. all this people as one
16:13. bro-t us to k. us in wildern.
22:29. sword, now would I k. thee
31: 17. k. ev. male am. little k.
woman hath known man
35: 27. revenger of blood k. slayer
De. 4: 42. who sho. k. his neighb.
12:15. thou mayest k. and eat flesh
21. then shalt k. of thy herd
13:9. But thou shalt surely k. him
16: † 5. not k. passo. within gates
32: 39. I k. and I make alive, I
Ju.9:†24. strengthened hands to k.
13: 23. If L. were pleased to k. us
15: 13. surely we will not k. thee
16: 2. when day, we shall k. him
20: 31. began to k. as at other, 39.
1 S. 16: 2. if Saul hear will k. me
17: 9. if he be able to k. me then
19:1. his serv-ts, that they k. Da.
2. Saul my fa. seeketh to k. thee
17. why should I k. thee
24: 10. some bade me k. thee

1 S.30:15. Swear thou wilt nei. k. me
2 S. 13: 28. Smite Amnon, then k.
14: 7. that we may k. him, for life
32. if any iniquity, let him k. me
21: 4. nei. for us thou k. any man
1 K. 11:40. Sol. sought to k. Jerob.
12: 27. h. me, and go to Rehob.
2 K. 5: 7. Am I a God, to k. and
7: 4. if k. us, we shall but die
11: 15. followeth her k. wi. sword
2 Ch. 35: 6. k. passover, sanctify
Es. 3:13. letters by posts to k. Jews
7: † 4. sold, that they should k.
Ec. 3: 3. A time to k. time to heal
Is. 14:30. will k. thy root with fam.
29: 1. year, let them k. sacrifices
Eze. 34: 3. ye k. them that are fed
Mat 5:21. who shall k. be in danger
10: 28. fear not them which k. the
body, Lu. 12: 4. [9: 31.-10:34.
17:23 and they shall k. him, Mk.
21:38. this is the heir, come let us
h. him, Mk. 12: 7. Lu. 20: 14.
23: 34. some of them ye shall k.
24: 9. shall deliv. you and k. you
26:4 take Jes. by subtilty k. him
Mk. 3: 4. lawful to save life, or k.?
10:19. Do not k., Lu. 18:20. Ja.2:11.
Lu.13:31. depart, Herod will k. thee
15: 23. bring fatted calf k. it
22:2. priests sought how to k. him
Jn. 5:18. Jews sought to k. him, 7:1.
7: 19. Why go ye about to k. me
20. who goeth about to k. thee?
25. this he whom they seek to k.?
8: 22. said, Will he h. himself?
37. ye seek to k. me, 40.
10:10. thief cometh to steal and k.
Ac. 7: 28. k. me as thou didst E-n?
9: 23. counsel to k. Paul, 26: 21.
24. watched gates day to k. him
10: 13. Rise, Peter, k. and eat
21: 31. they went about to k. him
23: 15. we are ready to k. him
25:3. laying wait in way to k. him
27:42. counsel was to k. prisoners
Ja. 2:11. if commit not adul. yet k.
4: 2. ye k. and desire to have
Re. 2: 23. And I will k. her chil.
6: 4. that they should k. one ano.
8. power was given them to k.
9: 5. given that they sho. not k.
them [them
11: 7. beast shall overcome and k.
KILLED.
Ge. 31: † 54. Then Jacob k. beasts
37: 31. took Jo.'s coat, k. a kid
Ex. 21: 29. ox hath k. a man or
Le. 4: 15. bullock sh. be k. bef. L.
6: 25. in place where burntoff-g is
k. sh. sin off-g be k. before Lord
8:19. ram be k. | 14:5. one of birds
14: 6. dip in bl. of bird k. [be k.
Nu. 16: 41. Ye have k. peo. of L.
31: 19. whoso. hath k. any person
1 S. 24:11. cut off skirt, k. thee not
25: 11. take my flesh I have k.
28: 24. and woman hasted k. calf
2 S. 12: 9. thou hast k. Uriah
21:17. Abishai smote Philis. and k.
1 K.16:7. like Jerob. bec. he k. him
10. Zimri smote Ela. k. him
21: 19. Hast k. and taken poss-n?
2 K. 15: 25. Pekah k. Pekahiah
1 Ch. 19: 18. David k. Shophach
2 Ch.18:2. Ahab k. sheep and oxen
25: 3. he slew those that k. king
29: 22. So they k. the bullocks
24. priests k. them and
30:15. k. passo., 35:1, 11. Ezr.6:20.
Ps. 44: 22. are we k. all day long
Pr. 9: 2. She hath k. her beasts
La. 2: 21. hast k. and not pitied
Mat. 16:21. be k. and raised again,
Mk. 8:31.-9:31. [Mk. 12: 5.
21: 35. beat one, and k. another,
22: 4. my oxen and fatlings are k.

Mat.23:31.chil. of them th.k.proph.
Mk. 6:19. and Herodias would have
k. him [viney., Lu. 20 : 15.
12 : 8. k. and cast him out of
14:12. 1st day when they k. passo.
Lu. 11 : 47. your fathers k. th., 48.
12 : 5. aft. k. hath power to cast
15 : 27. fa. hath k. fatted calf, 30.
22 : 7. day when passo. must be k.
Ac. 3 : 15. k. the Prince of life
12 : 2. he k. James brother of Jn.
16:27.drew sw.would have k. hims
23:12.nor drink till had k.Paul,21
27. This man sho. have been k.
Ro. 8 : 36. we are k. all day long
11:3.L. they have k. thy prophets
2 Co. 6 : 9. as chastened and not k.
1 Th. 2 : 15. Who k. the Lord Jes.
Ja. 5 : 6. condemned and k. just
Re. 6 : 11. breth who sho. be k. as
9 : 18. By these 3d part of men k.
20. wh. were not k. by plagues
11:5.if any hurt him he must be k.
13:10. killeth with sw. must be k.
15. not worship beast, sho. be k.

KILLEDST, EST.

Ex. 2 : 14. to kill me, as k-dst E-n
1 S. 24 : 18. as thou k-dst me not
Mat.23:37.k-est prophets,Lu.13:34.

KILLETH.

Le. 17 : 3. who k. an ox, goat (2)
24 : 17. that k. any man surely be
put to death, 21. Nu. 35 : 30.
18. k. a beast, make it good, 21.
Nu. 35 : 11. flee, who k. person unawares, 15. De. 19:4.Jos.20:3,9.
1 S. 2 : 6. L. k. and maketh alive
17:25.who k. him, k. enrich,26,27.
Jb. 5 : 2. wrath k. foolish man
24 : 14. The murderer k. the poor
Pr. 21 : 25. desire of slothful k.
Is. 66 : 3. k. ox, as if slew man
Jn. 16:2. k. you, think he doeth G.
2 Co. 3 : 6. letter k. spirit giv. life
Re. 13 : 10. k. with sword must be

KILLING. [killed

Ge. 48 : † 16. men home, kill a k.
Ju. 9 : 24. aided in k. his brethren
2 Ch.30:17. had charge of k. passo.
Ps.42:†10. As with a k. mine enem.
Pr. 9 : † 2. wisd hath killed her k.
Is. 22 : 13. slaying oxen, k. sheep
Ho. 4 : 2. by swearing, lying, k.
Mk.12:5.beating some, and k. some

KIN.

Le. 18:6. none approach near of k.
20 : 19. he uncovereth his near k.
21:2. for his k. he may be defiled
25 : 25. if his k. redeem it, 49.
Ru. 2 : 20. The man is near of k.
2 S. 19 : 42. king is near of k. to us
Mk. 6:4. prophet is not, but am. his

KI'NAH. [k.

Jos. 15:22. K. Dimonah, utt-t cities

KIND. [Adj.]

2 Ch.10:7.If thou be k. to this peo
Lu. 6 : 35. God is k. to unthankful
1 Co. 13 : 4. Charity suffereth and is
Ep. 4 : 32. be k. one to another [k.

KIND. [Noun.]

Ge. 1 : 11. yielding fruit aft. his k.
12. herb yielding seed aft. his k.
21. waters brought forth after k.
every fowl after his k.
24. earth, and beast aft. their k.
25. God made beast after his k.
6 : 20. fowls after their k. cattle
aft. k. creeping thing after k.
7:14. cattle, and fowl, aft. their k.
Le. 11 : 14. in abom. hawk aft. his
k., 15, 16, 19. De. 14:13, 14,15.
29. mouse, and tortoise after k.
19 : 19. not gender with diverse k.
1 Ch. 28 : 14. instruments of ev. k.
Ne. 13 : 20. sellers of all k. of ware
Ec. 2 : 5. I planted trees of all k.
Eze. 27:12. mult. of all k. of riches

Mat. 13 : 47. gathered of every k.
17 : 21. k. goeth not out, Mk.9:29.
1 Co. 15 : 39. one k. of flesh of men
Ja. 1: 18. that we be a k. of firstfr.
3 : 7. ev. k. of beasts and birds

KINDS.

Ge. 8 : 19. creepeth after their k.
2 Ch. 16:14. with divers k. of spices
Je. 15 : 3. appoint over them k.
Eze. 47 : 10. fish acc. to their k.
Da. 3 : 5. all k. of music, 7, 10, 15
1 Co. 12 : 10. divers k. of tongues
14 : 10. are so many k. of voices

KINDLE.

Pr. 26 : 21. conten. man to k. strife
Is. 9 : 18. it shall k. in the thickets
10 : 16. k. a burning like the fire
30 : 33. breath of the L. doth k. it
43 : 2. nei. sh. flame k. upon thee
Je. 33 : 18. never want a man to k.
Ob. 18. flame shall k. in them
See **Kindle, ed, eth, FIRE.**

KINDLED.

Ge. 39:19. Potiphar's wrath was k.
Le. 10 : 6. bewail burning Lord k.
Nu. 11 : 33. the wrath of the Lord
was k., De. 11:17. 2 K.22:13,17.
Ps. 106 : 40. [18: 8.
2 S. 22 : 9. coals were k. by it, Ps.
Jb. 19:11. k. his wrath ag. me [(2)
32:2. Then was k. wrath of Elihu
3. ag. his friends was wrath k., 5.
42 : 7. My wrath is k. against thee
Ps. 2 : 12. wrath is k. but a little
124:3.when their wrath is k. ag.us
Is. 50 : 11. in sparks ye have k.
Je. 44:6. wrath k. in cities of Jud.
Eze. 20:48. that I the L. have k. it
Ho. 11 : 8. my repentings are k.
Lu. 12:49. what if it be already k.?
See **ANGER kindled.**

KINDLETH.

Jb. 41 : 21. His breath k. coals
Is. 44 : 15. he k. it, baketh bread
Ja. 3 : 5. great matter little fire k.!

KINDLY. [29.

Ge. 24 : 29. if deal k. with me, 47 :
34:3.Shechem spake k. unto dam-
50:21.Jo. spake k. unto breth.[sel
Jos. 2 : 14. that we will deal k.
Ru. 1: 8. the Lord deal k. with you
1 S. 20 : 8. deal k. with thy serv.
2 K. 25:28. k. to Jehoi-n,Je.52:32.
Ro. 12 : 10. Be k. affectioned one

KINDNESS. [shew

Ge. 20 : 13. This is k. thou shalt
21:23. acc. to k. I have done thee
24 : 12. O Lord, shew k. unto Ab.
14. shewed k. unto my master
39 : † 21. L. extended k. to Joseph
40 : 14. think on me, and shew k.
Jos. 2:12. swear, since I shewed k.
ye will shew k. unto father's
Ju. 8 : 35. nei. k. to ho. of Jerub.
Ru.2:20. not left off his k. to living
3:10. shewed more k. in latter end
1 S.15:6. ye shewed k. to Isr. when
20 : 14. shalt shew me k. of Lord
15. not cut off thy k. fr. my hou.
2 S. 2 : 5. ye have shewed this k.
6. now Lord shew k. to you, I
also will requite you this k.
3:8.ag.Judah shew k. to h.of Saul
9 : 1. shew him k. for Jona.'s
3. that I may shew k. of God
7. I will surely shew thee k. for
10 : 2. I will shew k. unto Hanun
as his fa. shewed k.,1 Ch.19:2.
16:17. Is this thy k. to thy friend?
1 K. 2 : 7. k. unto sons of Barzillai
3 : 6. kept for David this great k.
2 Ch. 24:22. Joash remem-d not k.
Ne. 9 : 17. thou art a God of gr. k.
Es. 2 : 9. maiden obtained k. [all
† 17. she obtained k. more than
Ps. 31 : 21. shewed marvellous k.
117 : 2. For his merciful k. is great

Ps.119:76. mercif. k. be my comfort
141 : 5. righteous smite, it be a k.
Pr. 19 : 22. desire of a man is his k.
31 : 26. in her tongue is law of k.
Is. 54 : 8. with overl. k. will I have
10. my k. sh. not depart [mercy
57 : † 1. men of k. taken away
Je. 2 : 2. I remem. k. of thy youth
Ho 6:†4.your k. as a morning cloud
Jo. 2 : 13. he is of great k.,Jon.4:2.
Ac. 28:2. peo. shewed us no little k.
2 Co. 6 : 6. by pureness, by k.
Ep. 2 : 7. in his k. tow. us thro. C.
Col. 3 : 12. put on k. humbleness of
1 Ti. 5:†4. learn to shew k. at home
Tit. 3:4. aft. k. of God our Saviour
2 Pe. 1 : 7. to godlin. brotherly k.
See LOVINGKINDNESS, ES.

KINDRED. [7:3.

Ge. 12:1. Get thee from thy k., Ac.
24 : 4. go to k. take a wife, 38, 40.
7. L. who took me from my k.
41. when comest to my k. if
31 : 3. Return to thy k., 13. 32:9.
43 : 7. man asked us of our k.
Nu. 10 : 30. I will depart to k.
Jos. 6 : 23. they bro-t out all her k.
Ru. 2 : 3. Boaz was of k. of, 3 : 2.
1 Ch. 12 : 29. the k. of Saul 3000
Es. 2:10. shewed not peo. or k., 20.
8: 6. how see destruction of my k.
Jb. 32 : 2. Elihu of the k. of Ram
Eze. 11 : 15. men of k. said, Get far
Lu. 1 : 61. none of thy k. called by
Ac. 4 : 6. as were of k. of high pr
7:13. Joseph's k. was made known
14. called Jac. to him and his k.
19. dealt subtilely with our k.
1 Ti. 5 : † 8. provide not for his k.
Re. 5 : 9. redeemed us out of ev. k.
14 : 6. the everlasting gospel to
preach to every k.

KINDREDS.

1 Ch. 16:28. Give unto the L. ye k.,
Ps. 96 : 7. [worship bef. thee
Ps. 22 : 27. all k. of nations shall
Ac. 3 : 25. k. of earth be blessed
Re. 1 : 7. all k. of earth shall wail
7 : 9. mult. of all k. bef. throne
11 : 9. of k. see dead bodies 3 days
13 : 7. power given him over all k.

KINE.

Ge. 32 : 15. for k., present to Esau
41: 2. came 7 well favoured k., 18.
3. seven other k. came, 4, 19, 20.
26. seven good k. are 7 years
27. seven thin k. are 7 years
De. 7 : 13. bless incr. of thy k.
28:4. Blessed sh. be incr. of thy k.
18. cursed sh. be incr. of thy k.
51. shall not leave incr. of thy k.
32 : 14. Butter of k. milk of sheep
1 S. 6 : 7. take 2 milch k. tie k.
10. took 2 k. | 12. k. took the
14. clave the wood, offered the k.
2 S. 17 : 29. cheese of k. for David
Am. 4 : 1. Hear word, k. of Bashan

KING.

Ge. 14 : 1. in days of k. of Shinar
and Tidal k. of nations
18. Melchizedek k., He. 7 : 1.
36:31. kings in Edom, bef. reigned
any k. over Isr., 1 Ch. 1: 43.
Ex. 1 : 8. there arose up a new k.
over Egypt, Ac. 7 : 18. [21:22.
Nu. 20:17. will go by k.'s highway,
23 : 21. shout of a k. among them
24 : 7. his k. be higher than Agag
De. 17 : 14. I will set a k. over me
15. shalt set him k. over thee
28 : 36. L. bring thy k. unto na.
33 : 5. he was k. in Jeshurun
Ju. 8:18. each resembled chil. of k.
9:8. trees went to anoint a k., 15.
17 : 6. in those days no k. in Isr.,
ev. man, 18 : 1.-19 : 1.-21 : 25.
1 S. 2 : 10. L. give strength unto k.

1 S. 8:5. now make us a **k.** to judge
6. Give us a **k.** to judge us ⌊us
9. shew the manner of a **k.**, 11.
10. unto peo. th. asked for a **k.**
18. ye sh. cry out bec. of your **k.**
19. will have a **k.** | 22. make **k.**
20. that our **k.** may judge us
10 : 19. Nay, but set a **k.** over us
24. people shouted, and said, God save the **k.**, 2 S. 16:16. 1 K. 1: 39. 2 K. 11 : 12. 2 Ch. 23 : 11.
11 : 15. made Saul **k.** over Gilgal
12 : 1. I have made a **k.** over you
2. behold, the **k.** walketh bef. you
12. said, Nay, a **k.** sh. reign over us, when L. was your **k.**
13. behold the **k.** ye have chosen
17. wickedn. great in asking a **k.**
19. added this evil, to ask us a **k.**
25. ye sh. be consumed, and **k.**
15 : 1. L. sent me to anoint thee **k.**
23. rejected thee fr. being **k.**, 26.
16 : 1. provided me **k.** am. his sons
19 : 4. Let not **k.** sin ag. serv. Da.
21 : 2. **k.** com-d in a business
8. **k.**'s business required haste
20 : 5. not fail to sit wi. **k.** at meat
22 : 15. let not **k.** impute unto serv.
23 : 17. thou shalt be **k.** over Isr.
24 : 20. I know thou shalt be **k.**
25 : 36. Nabal held feast like a **k.**
26 : 14. Who thou that criest to **k.**
29 : 8. ag. enemies of my lord **k.**
2 S. 2 : 9. he made Ish-bosheth **k.**
3 : 36 what **k.** did, pleased people
37. was not of **k.** to slay Abner
5 : 12. Lord had established him **k.**
11 : 8. followed him meat from **k.**
12 : 7. saith L., I anointed thee **k.**
30. he took their **k.**'s crown
13 : 13. I pray thee, speak unto **k.**
14 : 9. **k.** and throne be guiltless
17. as an angel of G. so is my lord **k.**, 19 : 27. ⌈to **k.**, 6.
15 : 2. that had a controversy, came
3. none deputed of **k.** to hear thee
19. abide with **k.** thou art stran.
21. in what place my lord **k.**
16 : 9. Why this dead dog curse **k.**?
17 : 2. I will smite the **k.** only ⌈**k.**
18 : 13. there is no matter hid fr.
21. tell **k.** what thou hast seen
19 : 9. **k.** saved us out of ha. ene.
11. speech of all Isr. is come to **k.**
19. that **k.** take it to his heart
20. go to meet my lord the **k.**
22. I know that I am this day **k.**
28. What right I to cry to the **k.**?
42. Bec. **k.** is near of kin to us
43. said, We have ten parts in **k.**
22 : 51. He is tower of salva. for **k.**
24 : 23. Araunah as a **k.** give to **k.**
1 K. 1 : 5. Adonijah said, I will be **k.**
35. Sol. shall be **k.** in my stead
47. **k.** bowed hims. upon the bed
2 : 18. will speak for thee unto **k.**
38. as **k.** hath said, servant do
3 : 7. made serv. **k.** instead of Da.
22. thus women spake before **k.**
28. Isr. heard judgm. **k.** judged
8 : 62. **k.** and Isr. offered sacr., 63.
10 : 3. was not any thing hid fr. **k.**
11 : 26. Jerob. lifted hand ag. **k.**, 27.
37. thou shalt be **k.** over Israel
12 : 1. all Isr. to make him **k.**, 2 Ch.
20. made him **k.** over Isr. ⌊10 : 1.
14 : 2. Ahijah, told me I sh. be **k.**
14. L. sh. raise up **k.** over Israel
28. when **k.** went into hou. of L.
16 : 16. Zimri hath slain the **k.**
20 : 38. waited for the **k.** by the way
39. as **k.** passed he cried unto **k.**
21 : 10. didst blaspheme G. and **k.**
22 : 8. Let not **k.** say so, 2 Ch. 18 : 7.
13. words of the prophets declare good unto **k.**, 2 Ch. 18 : 12.
47. no **k.** in Edom, a deputy **k.**

2 K. 1 : 6. Go turn again unto **k.**
11. O man of G., **k.** said, Come, 9.
15. he arose and went unto **k.**
4 : 13. wouldest be spoken for to **k.**?
7 : 2. lord on whose ha. **k.** leaned
8 : 3. went to cry unto **k.** for her
13. L. shewed thou shalt be **k.**
20. Edom, made a **k.**, 2 Ch. 21 : 8.
9 : 3. I anointed thee **k.** over Isr., 6.
10 : 5. we will not make any **k.**
11 : 8. with **k.** as he goeth, 2 Ch. 23 : 7.
17. Jehoiada made cov. betw. L. and **k.** betw. **k.** and people.
14 : 5. had slain the **k.**, 2 Ch. 25 : 3.
21 : 23. slew **k.** in his own house
22 : 9. brought the **k.** word, 20. 2 Ch. 34 : 16, 28. ⌈2 Ch. 34 : 18.
10. Shaphan read it before the **k.**,
23 : 25. like him was no **k.** bef. him
25 : 6. they took the **k.**, Je. 52 : 9.
1 Ch. 4 : 23. they dwelt with the **k.**
24 : 6. Shemaiah wrote them bef. **k.**
28 . 4. to be **k.** over Israel forever
29 : 20. worshipped L. and **k.** ⌈9 : 8.
2 Ch. 2 : 11. he hath made thee **k.**,
10 : 15. **k.** hearkened not unto peo.
11 : 22. he thought to make him **k.**
23 : 7. sh. compass **k.** round about
24 : 21. stoned him at com-d of **k.**
25 : 16. Art thou of **k.**'s counsel?
Ezr. 4 : 12. Be it known unto **k.**,
6 : 10. pray for life of **k.** ⌊13.-5 : 8.
7 : 26. who will not do law of **k.**
27. put in **k.**'s heart to beautify
8 : 22. to require of **k.** soldiers
Ne. 1 : 11. For I was **k.**'s cupbearer
2 : 19. will ye rebel ag. the **k.**?
6 : 6. be their **k.** acc. to these words
7. to preach, There is a **k.** in Jud.
13 : 26. am. many nations no **k.** like him, God made him **k.**
Es. 2 : 15. go in unto the **k.**, 4 : 8, 16.
6 : 6. **k.** delighteth to honour, 7.
7 : 8. word went out of **k.** mouth
9. Mord., had spok. good for **k.**
9 : 25. But when Esther came bef. **k.**
Jb. 15 : 24. prevail, as a **k.** ready
18 : 14. bring him to **k.** of terrors
29 : 25. I sat chief, dwelt as a **k.**
34 : 18. say to **k.**, Thou art wick.?
41 : 34. he is **k.** over chil. of pride
Ps. 2 : 6. I set my K. upon holy hill
5 : 2. hearken, my K. and G., 84 : 3.
10 : 16. Lord is K. forever, 29 : 10.
18 : 50. Great deliv. giveth he to **k.**
20 : 9. let **k.** hear us when we call
21 : 1. **k.** shall joy in thy strength,
7. **k.** trusteth in the L. ⌊O L.
24 : 7. K. of glory sh. come in, 9.
8. Who is K. of glory? L. strong
10. L., he is K. of glory ⌈host
33 : 16. no **k.** saved by mult. of
44 : 4. my K. O G., com-d deliver-s
45 : 1. things I made touching K.
5. arrows sharp in heart of K.'s
11. K. greatly desire thy beauty
13. K.'s dau. all glorious within
14. She sh. be bro-t to K. in raim-t
15. shall enter into K.'s palace
47 : 6. sing to our K. | 7. G. is K.
61 : 6. Thou wilt prolong **k.**'s life
63 : 11. the **k.** shall rejoice in God
68 : 24. seen goings of my G., my K.
72 : 1. Give **k.** thy judgments, O G.
74 : 12. God is my K. of old
89 : 18. Holy One of Isr. is our K.
98 : 6. a joyful noise bef. L. the K.
99 : 4. **k.**'s strength loveth judgm.
105 : 20. The **k.** sent and loosed him
149 : 2. chil. of Zion be joyf. in K.
Pr. 14 : 28. In mult. of peo. **k.**'s hon.
35. **k.**'s favour is tow. wise servt.
16 : 10. divine sentence in lips of **k.**
14. wrath of **k.** as messen. of dea.
15. in light of **k.**'s counten. is life
19 : 12. **k.**'s wrath as roar. of lion
20 : 2. fear of **k.** is as roar. of lion

Pr. 20 : 8. **k.** th. sitteth on throne of **j.**
26. A wise **k.** scattereth wicked
20 : 28. Mercy and truth preserve **k.**
21 : 1. **k.**'s heart is in hand of L.
22 : 11. for grace of lips, **k.** be friend
24 : 21. My son, fear L., and **k.**
25 : 5. Take wicked fr. before **k.**
6. Put not thyself in presence of **k.**
29 : 4. **k.** by judgment establ. land
14. **k.** that faithf-y judgeth poor
30 : 27. locusts have no **k.** yet go
31. **k.** ag. whom is no rising up
Ec. 2 : 12. what can man do after **k.**
4 : 13. wise child than foolish **k.**
5 : 9. **k.** himself is served by field
8 : 2. I counsel thee to keep **k.**'s commandment
4. Where word of **k.** is power
10 : 16. Woe to thee, O land, when thy **k.** is a child ⌈nobles
17. Blessed when thy **k.** is son of
20. Curse not the **k.**, in thought
Can. 1 : 4. **k.** bro-t me into chamb.
12. While the **k.** sitt-h at his table
3 : 11. behold **k.** Sol. wi. the crown
7 : 5. the **k.** is held in the galleries
Is. 6 : 5. mine eyes have seen the **k.**
7 : 6. let us set a **k.** in midst of it
8 : 21. curse their **k.** and their God
19 : 4. fierce **k.** sh. rule over them
23 : 15. acc. to the days of one **k.**
30 : 33. yea, for **k.** it is prepared
32 : 1. K. shall reign in righte-sn.
33 : 17. sh. see the K. in his beauty
22. L. is our K. he will save us
41 : 21. bring your reasons, saith K.
43 : 15. I am Creator of Isr., your K.
57 : 9. wentest to **k.** with ointm.
Je. 4 : 9. heart of the **k.** sh. perish
8 : 19. L. in Zion? is not her **k.** in
10 : 10. L. is an everl. K. ⌊her?
13 : 18. say to **k.** and queen, Humble
23 : 5. a K. shall reign and prosper
29 : 16. saith L., of **k.** that sitteth
36 : 16. We will surely tell **k.**
20. went in to the **k.** into court
21. Jehudi read it in ears of **k.**
37 : 20. hear now, O my lord the **k.**
38 : 5. **k.** is not he can do any thi.
25. what said unto **k.** **k.** unto thee
46 : 18. As I live, saith K. whose name is the L., 48 : 15.-51 : 57.
49 : 1. why doth **k.** inherit Gad
3. their **k.** shall go into captiv.
38. I will destroy **k.** and princes
52 : 8. pursued aft. **k.** | 9. took **k.**
La. 2 : 6. L. despised **k.** and priest
9. **k.** and princes are am. Gent.
Eze. 7 : 27. **k.** mourn, and princes
17 : 12. hath taken **k.** and princes
13. taken of **k.** seed and made cov.
16. where **k.** that made him **k.**
26 : 7. I will bring a **k.** of kings
37 : 22. one **k.** sh. be **k.** to all, 24.
24. Da. my serv. sh. be **k.** ov. them
Da. 1 : 19. the **k.** communed wi. them
20. **k.** enquired, he found th. better
2 : 2. came and stood bef. **k.**, 1 : 19.
10. is no **k.** asked such things at
11. none that can shew it bef. **k.**
12. for this cause **k.** was angry
24. bring me bef. **k.** I will shew **k.**
3 : 13. brought these men bef. **k.**
4 : 24. decree wh. is come upon **k.**
31. While word was in **k.**'s mouth
37. I praise, honour **k.** of heav.
5 : 5. **k.** saw part of hand th. wrote
6 : 2. the **k.** sho. have no damage
6. princes assembled to the **k.**
8 : 23. a **k.** of fierce countenance
11 : 3. mighty **k.** sh. stand to rule
5. **k.** of south, 6, 9, 11, 14, 25, 40.
7. **k.** of the north, 8, 11, 13, 15, 40.
36. **k.** shall do acc. to his will
Ho. 3 : 4. Isr. shall abide without **k.**
5. Isr. shall seek L., and Da. **k.**
5 : 13. Ephr. sent to **k.** Jareb, 10 : 6.

Ho. 7:3. make k. glad with wickedn.
5. our k. princes made him sick
8: 10. burden of the k. of princes
10: 3. We no k. what sho. k. do?
7. her k. is cut off, as the foam
11:5. Assyrian shall be his k. bec.
13:10. I will be thy k. Give me k.
11. I gave thee k. in mine anger
Am. 1: 15. k. shall go into captiv.
7: 1. latter growth aft. k.'s mow-
13. it is k. chapel, k. court [ings
Mi. 2: 13. k. shall pass bef. them
4: 9. why cry? is no k. in thee?
Zch. 9: 5. k. shall perish fr. Gaza
9. behold thy K. cometh unto
thee, Mat. 21:5. [hand of his k.
11:6. will deliver every one into the
14: 9. L. shall be K. over all earth
16. ev. one go up to worship K., 17.
Mat. 2:9. had heard k. they departed
14: 9. the k. was sorry, Mk. 6:26.
18:23. likened unto certain k., 22:2.
22:7. when k. heard, he was wroth
11. when k. came to see guests
13. said k. to servant, Bind him
25:34. sh. K. say, Come ye blessed
40. K. shall ans., Inasmuch as
Mk. 6:22. k. said unto damsel, Ask
25. she came with haste unto k.
27. k. sent an executioner [k.
Lu. 14: 31. what k. to war ag. ano.
19:38. Blessed be K. com-h in name
23: 2. that he himself is C., a k.
Jn. 6:15. by force to make him a k.
12:15. behold thy K. com-h on ass's
18: 37. Pilate said, Art thou a k.?
19:12. whoso. maketh himself a k.
14. Pilate saith, Behold your K.
15. Shall I crucify your K.? (2)
Ac. 7:18. k. arose, who knew not Jo.
12: 20. nourished by k.'s country
13:21. afterward they desired a k.
17: 7. there is another k., one Jes.
25:14. decla-d Paul's cause unto k.
26: 26. k. knoweth of these things
30. k. rose up and the governor
2 Co. 11:32. gov. under Aretas the k.
1 Ti. 1:17. Now unto the K. eternal
6: 15 who is K. of kings, and L.
He. 7:2. K. of righte-sn. K. of Salem
11: 23. not afraid of k.'s com-t [K.
27. Moses not fearing wrath of k.
1 Pe. 2:13. whe. to the k. as supreme
17. Honour all. Fear G. Honour k.
Re. 9: 11. they had a k. over them
15: 3. just thy ways, K. of saints
17:14. L. of lords, K. of kings, 19:16.
Ge. 14:2+.-20:2.-39:20. Nu. 20:14.-
21:1. Jos. 10:3+.-11:1, 10.-12:4+.
Ju. 3:8, 10.-4:2+.-11:12+. 1 S. 12:
14.-15:8+.-17:25, 56.-18:6+.-20:
24+.-22: 11+.-28: 20.-24:8.-26:
15+.-27:2.-28:13. 2 S. 3:3+.-4:8.
-5: 2+.-7: 1+.-8:3+.-9:2+.-10:
1, 5, 6.-11: 9+.-13: 4+.-14: 1+.-
15: 2+.-16: 2+.-17:16.-18:2+.-
19: 1+.-20: 3+.-21: 2+.-24: 2+.
1 K. 1:2+.-2:17+.-3: 4+.-4: 1+.
-5: 1+.-6: 2.-7: 13+.-8: 1+.-9: 1
+.-10: 6+.-11: 1+.-12: 1+.-13:
4+.-14:25+.-15:1.-16: 18+.-19:
15, 16.-20: 9.-21: 13.-22: 6+. 2 K.
3:6+.-5:8.-6:28+.-7:9+.8: 4+.-
9: 13+.-10: 6+.-11:2+.-12:6+.-
13: 16.-14:14+.-15:5, 25.-16:8+.
17:21.-18:9+.-19: 1+.-21: 24.-22:
3.-23: 1+.-24: 13, 15, 17.-25:2+.
1 Ch. 3: 2.-9: 18.-11: 2+.-14:2.-
18:3, 5, 9.-19:1+.-21:3+.23: 1+.-
25:2, 5, 6.-26:30, 32.-27: 1+.-28:
1.-29:6+. 2 Ch. 1:9+.-4:17.-7:4.-
8:10+.-9:9+.-10:2+.-11:22-12:
6+.-13:1.-15:16.-16:2, 4, 6.-17:19.
-19: 2, 11.-20:15.-22:1, 11.-23:3+.
-24:6+.-26:1+.-27:5.-28: 7, 16.-
29:15+.-30: 2+.-31:3, 13.-33: 25.
-34:19+.-35: 7+.-36: 1+. Ezr. 1:
7.-4:2+.-5:6+.-6: 1+.-7:6+. 8: 1
+.-Ne. 2: 1+.-3:15.-5: 4.-11:23,
24.-13:3. Es. 1:2+.-2: 1+.-3: 1+.
4:2+.-5: 1+.-6: 1+.-7: 1+.-8: 1
+.9: 1+.-10: 1, 2, 3. Is. 36: 1+. Je.
21: 1.-22: 6.-25: 26.-26: 10+.-27:
3.-29: 2, 16.-34: 8.-36: 22+ -37: 1
+. :4+.-39: 4.-40: 14.-41: 1+.
-48, 38-51: 59.-52: 5+. Da. 1:3+.
2: 2+.-3: 1+.-4: 1+.-5: 1+.-6: 2
+.-8: 1+.-9: 1+.-11: 7, 8. Ho. 5:
13.-10: 6. Am. 2: 1. Jon. 3: 6, 7.
Zph. 1:8. Hag. 1:1. Zch. 7:1. Mat.
2:1, 3.-22:13.-25:40. Ac. 12: 1, 20.
-25: 13, 24.-26: 2, 7, 27. 2 Co.
11: 32.

KING of Amorites.

See SIHON.

KING of Assyria. [land

2 K. 15: 19. Pul k. o. A. came ag.
20. exacted money to give k. o. A.
16: 8. sent it for present to k. o. A.
9. k. o. A. hearkened unto him
18. fr. house of L. for k. o. A.
17:4. no present to the k. o. A., (2)
6. yr. of Hoshea, k. o. A. took Sama.
18: 11. k. o. A. did carry Isr. to A.
19. saith great king, k. o. A.
23. give pledges to k. o. A., Is. 36:8.
33. deliv-d out of ha. of k. o. A.,
20: 6. 2 Ch. 32: 11. [Is. 37: 33.
19:32. saith L. concerning k. o. A.,
2 Ch. 32:7. be not afraid for k. o. A.
33:11. k. o. A. wh. took Manasseh
Ezr. 6: 22. turned heart of k. o. A.
Is. 7:17. L. bring upon thee k. o. A.
20. shave by k. o. A. head and hair
10: 12. stout heart of k. o. A. [E-ns
20: 4. So shall k. o. A. lead away
6. be delivered from k. o. A. [10.
36:15. not into hand of k. o. A., 37:
Je. 50:17. first k. o. A. devoured him
18. punish Bab-n as I punished k.
See Kings of ASSYRIA. [o. A.
See HOSHEA, PUL, SARGON, SEN-
NACHERIB, SHALMANEZER,
TIGLATH-PILESER.
See BASHAN, King of BAB-
YLON, DAVID with king.

KING of Egypt. [com.

Ex. 1: 17. midwives not as h. o. E.
2: 23. in time k. o. E. died
3:19. am sure k. o. E. not let you go
6: 13. them a charge unto k. o. E.
2 K. 24: 7. k. o. E. came not again
2 Ch. 12: 2. k. o. E. came ag. Jerus.
36:3. k. o. E. put him down at Je-
4. k. o. E. made Eliakim k. [rus.
Is. 36:6. so k. o. E. to all that trust
See PHARAOH.
See GREAT king, s, and
HOUSE with king.

KING of Israel.

1 S. 24: 14. After whom is k. o. I.
26: 20. k. o. I. is come to seek flea
2 S. 6: 20. How glorious was k. o. I.
1 K. 20:31. let us go out to k. o. I.
22:30. k. o. I. disguised, 2 Ch. 18:29.
31. Fight only with k. o. I.
32. Surely it is k. o. I., 2 Ch. 18:31.
33. perceived it was not k. o. I.
34. smote k. o. I. betw., 2 Ch. 18:33.
2 K. 3:10. k. o. I. said Alas! that L.
6: 11. shew which is for k. o. I.
12. Elisha telleth k. o. I. | 21.
16: 7. me out of hand of k. o. I.
2 Ch. 18:30. Fight only with k. o. I.
32. perceived it was not k. o. I. [11.
35:3. Sol. k. o. I. did build, Ezr. 5:
Ne. 13: 26. Did not Solo. k. o. I. sin
Is. 44: 6. saith Lord, K. o. I.
Ho. 10: 15. shall the k. o. I. be cut
Zph. 3: 15. K. o. I. in midst of thee
Mat. 27: 42. If he be K. o. I. let him
descend, Mk. 15:32. [Is K. o. I.
Jn. 1: 49. art K. o. I. [12:13. Blessed
See AHAB, AHAZ, BAASHA, HO-
SHEA, JEROBOAM, PEKAH,
SAUL, SOLOMON.
See King of the JEWS.

KING of Judah.

2 K. 8: 16. Jehosh-t being k. o. J.
22: 16. book k. o. J. read, 2 Ch.
34: 24. [quire
18. k. o. J. which sent you to in-
2 Ch. 34: 26. k. o. J. who sent you
35:21. What to do wi. thee, k. o. J.
Je. 21:11. house of k. o. J., 27:18, 21.
34: 4. hear word of L. k. o. J.
37:7. say to k. o. J. who sent you
38:22. women left in k. o. J.'s house
See AHAZIAH, AMAZIAH, ASA,
AZARIAH, HEZEKIAH, JECO-
NIAH, JEHOASH, JEHOIACHIN,
JEHOIAKIM, JEHORAM, JE-
HOSHAPHAT, JOASH, JOSIAH,
JOTHAM, MANASSEH, REHO-
BOAM, UZZIAH, ZEDEKIAH.

KING of Moab.

Nu. 22: 10. Balak k. o. M. sent me
23: 7. Balak k. o. M. brought me
Jos. 24:9. k. o. M. warred ag. Isr.
Ju. 3:14. Isr. served Eglon k. o. M.?
11: 17. Isr. sent to the k. o. M.
25. thou bet-r than Balak k. o. M.
1 S. 12:19. sold into hand of k. o. M.
22: 3. said unto k. o. M. Let my fa.
4. David brought fa. to k. o. M.
2 K. 3:4. Mesha k. o. M. sheepmas r
5. k. o. M. rebelled ag. Israel, 7.
26. when k. o. M. saw battle sore
Je. 27: 3. send bonds to k. o. M.
See BALAK, EGLON.

O KING. [k.

Ju. 3: 19. secret errand unto thee O
1 S. 17: 55. Abn. said, O k. I can-t
23: 20. now, O k. come down [tell
26: 17. my lord, O k., 2 S. 14: 9,
22.-16:4.-19: 26. 1 K. 1:13, 20,
24.-20:4. 2 K. 6:12, 26.-8: 5.
2 S. 14: 4. woman said, Help, O k.
15: 34. say, I will be thy serv., O
2 Ch. 25:7. O k. let not army go [k.
Ps. 145: 1. I will extol thee, O K.
Je. 10: 7. Who not fear thee, O K.
Da. 2: 4. O k. live for ever, 3: 9.-
5:10.-6:21. [sawest image
29. As for thee, O k. | 31. O k.,
37. Thou O k. art a king of kings
for God hath [cree
3: 10. Thou O k. hast made a de-
12. these O k. have not regarded
17. he will deliver us, O k.
18. be it known unto thee, O k.
24. True, O k. | 4:22. thou, O k.
4: 24. This is the interpret. O k.
27. O k. let thy counsel be
31. O k. Neb. to thee it is spoken
5: 18. O thou k. God gave thy fa.
6: 7. petition save of thee, O k., 12.
8. Now, O k. establish the decree
13. regardeth not thee O k.
15. know, O k. law of Medes
22. O k. have I done no hurt
Ac. 25: 26. specially bef. thee O k.
26: 13. midday, O k. I saw in light
19. O k. I was not disobedient

KING, S of Persia. [us

Ezr. 4: 3. as Cyrus, k. o. P. com-d
5. till reign of Darius k. o. P.
9: 9. mercy in sight of k-s o. P.,
Da. 10:13. I remained wi. k-s o. P.
See ARTAXERXES, CYRUS.

KING of Syria.

1 K. 20: 20. Benhadad k. o. S. esca.
22. k. o. S. will come up ag. thee
23. servs. of k. o. S. said, Their gods
22:3. take not out of ha. of k. o. S.
31. k. o. S. com-d, 2 Ch. 18: 30.
2 K. 5: 1. Naaman capt. of host of
5. k. o. S. said, Go to [k. o. S.
6: 8. Then k. o. S. warred ag. Isr.
8:7. k. o. S. sick | 9. sent me to thee
13:4. bec. k. o. S. oppressed them

2 K.11:7.k.o.S.had destroyed them
16 : 1. me out of hand of k. o. S.
2 Ch.16 : 7. Bec. hast relied on k.
o S. host of k. o. S. is escaped
2 Ch. 28 : 5. him into ha. of k.o.S.
See BENHADAD, HAZAEL, RE-
KING of Tyre. [ZIN.
1 K.9:11.Hiram k. o. T. furnished
See HIRAM and HURAM [Sol.
KINGS. [17.
Ge. 14:5. Chedor. and k. wi. him,
9. Arioch king of El. 4 k. wi. five
17 : 6. k. shall come out of thee,
16.-35 : 11. [1 Ch. 1 : 43.
36:31.these are k.reigned in Edom,
Nu. 31 : 8. they slew k. of Midian
De. 3:8. two k. 21.-4:47. Jos.2:10.-
21. L. hath done unto 2 k. [9:10.
7 : 24. sh. deliver k. into thy ha.
Jos.9:1.all the k. on this side Jord.
10 : 5. five k. of Amorites gathered
16. five k. fled and hid, 17.
22. bring out five k., 23.
24. put feet upon necks of k.
40.So Joshua smote k.,42.-11:17.
11 : 2. to k. on north of mount-s
5. when all these k. were met
12. all cities of those k. did Josh.
18.Josh. made war with those k.
12 : 1. these are k. of land, 7.
24. all these k. thirty and one
Ju. 1: 7. seventy k. thumbs cut off
5: 3. Hear, O k. | 19. k. fought
8 : 5. Zebah and Zalmun. k.,12,26.
1 S. 14:47. Saul fought ag. k. of Zo-
2 S. 10:19. k. that were servs. [bah
11 : 1. k. go to battle, 1 Ch. 20 : 1.
1 K. 3: 13. not be any am. k. like
thee, 10:23. 2 Ch. 1 : 12.-9 : 22.
4 : 24. Sol. over all k. on this side
10:15. of k. of Arabia, 2 Ch. 9:14.
29.so all k. of Hittites, 2 Ch.1:17.
20 : 1. Benhadad and 32 k., 16.
12.Benha. and k. drank in pavil.
24. Take the k. away every man
2 K. 3: 10. hath called three k., 13.
21. heard k. were come to light
23. blood, the k. are surely slain
7 : 6. hired ag. us k. of Hittites
10 : 4. two k. stood not bef. him
11 : 19. sat on throne of k.
25:28.set throne above throne of k.
1 Ch. 16:21. he reproved k.,Ps. 105:
19: 9. k. were by themselves [14.
2 Ch. 1 : 12. such as none of k. had
9 : 23. k. sought Sol., 1 K. 4 : 34.
26. he reigned over all the k.
21 : 20. not in sepul-s of k., 24:25.
24 : 16. buried am. the k. in city
26 : 23. field of burial belong. to k.
Ezr. 4: 13. endamage revenue of k.
15. this city been hurtful unto k.
19. city made insurrec. ag. k.
20. been mighty k. over Jerus.
22. why damage to hurt of k.
6 : 12. G. destroy k. that alter ho.
7:12.Artaxer.king of k. unto Ezr.
9 : 7. our k. been deliv.,Ne. 9 : 24.
Ne. 9:32. trouble little upon our k.
34. Nei. have our k. kept thy law
37. much increase unto k. thou
Jb. 3:14. had I been at rest with k.
12 : 18. He looseth the bond of k.
36 : 7. with k. are they on throne
Ps. 2: 2. k. of earth set thems.,Ac.
10. Be wise, O ye k. [4:26.
45:9.k.'s dau-s am.thy honourable
48 : 4. lo, the k. were assembled
68 : 12. k. of armies did flee apace
14. When Alm. scattered k. in it
29.sh. k. bring presents unto thee
72 : 11. all k. shall fall before him
76 : 12. is terrible to k. of earth
89 : 27. make him higher than k.
102 : 15. k. of the earth sh. fear
105 : 30. frogs in chambers of k.
110 : 5. strike thro. k. in day of
Ps. 119 : 46. speak of testimonies bef.
135:10. smote nations, slew k. [k.
136:17.him wh. smote great k.,18.
138:4.All k. sh. praise thee,148:11.
144 : 10. he giveth salva. unto k.
149 : 8. To bind their k. wi. chains
Pr. 8 : 15. By me k. reign, princes
16:12. abom. for k. to com-t wick.
13.righteous lips are delight of k.
22:29.man diligent sh.stand bef.k.
25 : 2. honour of k. to search mat.
3. heart of k. is unsearchable
30 : 28. the spider is in k.'s palaces
31 : 3. nor to that wh. destroy. k.
4.It is not for k. O Lem. to drink
Ec. 2 : 8. peculiar treasure of k.
Is. 7 : 16. land forsaken of both k.
10 : 8. Are not my princes k.?
14 : 9. hath raised all k. of nations
18. All k. of nations lie in glory
19 : 11. I am the son of ancient k.
24 : 21. L. shall punish k. of earth
41:2. Who made him ruler over k.
45 : 1. I will loose the loins of k.
49 : 7. k. sh.arise, princes worship
23. k. sh. be thy nursing fathers
52 : 15. k. sh. shut their mouths
60 : 3. k. to brightn. of thy rising
10. k. shall minister unto thee
11. that their k. may be brought
16. shalt suck breast of k.
62 : 2. all k. shall see thy glory
Je. 2 : 26. k. and princes ashamed
13:13.k. th. sit upon Da.'s throne
17 : 25. into gates of this city, k.
22:4. k. sitting upon throne of Da.
25:18. I made Judah and k. drink
20. all k. of Uz, all k. of Philis.
22. k. of the isles, Ps. 72 : 10.
24. k. of Arabia [the north
25. the k. of Zimri | 26. all k. of
32 : 32. me to anger, they, their k.
34 : 5. with burnings of former k.
44:9.wickedness of the k. of Jud.
17. as we, our k. to burn inc.
21.your k.and princes burnt inc.
46 : 25. I will punish their k. and
50:41. many k. shall be raised up
51:11.L.raised spirit of k.of Medes
28. nations with k. of Medes
52 : 32. above throne of k. wi. him
La. 4 : 12. k. wo. not have believed
Eze. 26 : 7. a king of k. from north
27:33. didst enrich k. of the earth
27 : 35. k. be sore afraid, 32 : 10.
28 : 17. I will lay thee before k.
32 : 29. There is Edom, her k. and
43 : 7. k. shall no more defile my
9. carcasses of k. far from me, 7.
Da. 2 : 21. removeth k. sett-h up k.
37. Thou O king, art a king of k.
44. in days of these k. G. set up
47.Of a truth, your G.is a L.of k.
7 : 17. four gr. beasts are four k.
24.ten horns are 10 k.subdue 3 k.
9 : 6. spake in thy name to our k.
8. to our k.princes confu. of face
11:2. up 3 k. | 27. both k.'s hearts
Ho. 7 : 7. are hot, all their k. are
8:4. have set up k. but not by me
Ha. 1 : 10. they shall scoff at k.
Mat. 10 : 18. ye shall be bro-t bef.
k., Mk. 13 : 9. Lu. 21 : 12.
11:8.wear soft clothing in k. hou-s
17:25.of whom do k. take custom?
Lu. 10 : 24. k. have desired to see
22:25.k. of Gent. exercise lordship
Ac. 4 : 26. k. of earth stood up
9 : 15. vessel to bear my name before k.
1 Co. 4 : 8. ye have reigned as k.
1 Ti. 2 : 2. prayers be made for k.
6 : 15. King of k. L. of lords, Re.
17 : 14 -19:16. [of k.
He. 7:1. Ab. returned fr. slaughter
Re. 1:5. Jes. Christ prince of the k.
6. us k. and priests unto G.,5:10.
Re.6 : 15. k. of the earth hid in dens
10 : 11. Thou must proph-y bef. k.
16:12. way of k. might be prepar.
14. spirits which go forth unto k.
17:2.with wh. k. committed forni.
10. are k. 5 are fallen, and one
12. ten k. wh. receive pow. as k.
18. gr. city wh. reigneth over k.
18 : 3. k. have committed fornica.
9. k. of earth shall bewail her-
19 : 18. That ye may eat flesh of k.
19. k. gathered to make war ag.
21 : 24. k. of earth do bring glory
KINGS of the Amorites.
De. 4 : 47. two k. o. A., 31:4. Jos.
2 : 10.-9 : 10.-24 : 12.
Jos. 5 : 1. when all k. o. A. heard
10 : 5. five k.o. A. gathered toge.,
KINGS of Israel. [6.
1 K. 14:19. written in the book of
the Chronicles of the k. o. I.,
15 : 31.-16:5, 14, 20, 27.-22 : 39.
2 K. 1 : 18.-10 : 34.-13 : 8, 12.-
14 : 15, 28.-15:11, 15, 21, 26, 31.
16:33.Ahab provoked L. more than
all k. o. I.
20:31. that k.o.I. are merciful k.
2 K. 8 : 18. Jehoram in way of k.o.
I., 2 Ch. 21:6, 13. [I., 14 : 16.
13:13. Joash was buried with k. o.
14 : 29. Jerob. slept with k. o. I.,
16:3.Ahaz walked in way of k.o.I.
2 Ch. 28 : 2. [k. o. I.
17 : 2. Hoshea did evil, but not as
8. Israel in statutes of k. o. I.
23:19. Josiah took away houses k.
o. I. made [k. o. I.
22. not such passover in days of
1 Ch. 9 : 1. were written in the book
of k. o. I. and Judah, 2 Ch.
16 : 11.-24 : 27.-25 : 26.-27 : 7.-
28:26.-32 : 32.-33 : 18.
2 Ch. 20 : 34. Jehu who is mentioned
in book of k.o.I.,35:27.-36 : 8.
28:27.Ahaz not brought into sepul.
of k. o. I. [passover
35 : 18. neither did k. o. I. keep
Mi. 1:14.Achzib sh. be a lie to k.o.
KINGS of Judah. [I.
1 S. 27 : 6. Ziklag unto k. o. J.
1 K. 14 : 29. acts of Rehoboam in
book of Chronicles of k. o. J.,
15:7, 23.-22:45. 2 K. 8 : 23.-15:
6, 36.-16 : 19.-20 : 20.-21 : 17,
25.-23 : 28.-24 : 5.
2 K.12:18. thi gs k.o.J. dedicated
19. written in book of Chronicles
of k.o.J., 14:18. 2 Ch. 25 :26.-
28 : 26.-32 : 32.-35:27.-36:8.
18 : 5. none like him of all k.o.J.
23:5.put down priests k.o.J. ord-d
11. took horses k. o. J. given to
12.down altars k.o.J. made [sun
22. not such a passover in all days
of k. o. J.
2 Ch. 34:11. houses k.o.J.destroyed
Is. 1:1. Isaiah in days of k. o. J.
Je. 1:18. made iron pillar ag.k.o.J.
8 : 1. bring out bones of k. o. J.
17:19.gate, whereby k. o.J. come
20. Hear word of L. k.o.J., 19:3.
19 : 4. to gods k.o.J. have not kn.
13. houses of k. o. J. be defiled
20 : 5. treasures of k.o.J. I give to
33 : 4. conc. houses of k.o.J. down
44:9.forgotten wickedn. of k.o.J.?
Ho. 1 : 1. word of L. unto Hosea in
days of k. o. J., Mi. 1 : 1.
See PERSIA.
Written in book of the
KINGS.
1 Ch.9:1. genealogies of Isr. w.-k.
2 Ch. 24 : 27. they are w. in story of
b.-k. [k. of Per.
Es. 10 : 2. w. i. b. of Chronicles of
KINGDOM.
Ex. 19:6. be unto me a k. of priests

Nu. 32: 33. Moses gave unto Gad,
k. of Sihon and k. of Og, De.
3: 10, 13. Jos. 13:12, 21, 27, 30.
De.3:4. took the k. of Og in Bashan
1 S. 10: 16. matter of k. told not
25. Samuel told manner of k.
11:14. renew k. | 14:47. Saul took
15: 28. rent k. of Isr., 28:17 [k.
18: 8. what can he have but k.?
2 S. 3:10. To translate k. from Saul
16:3. Isr. shall restore me k. of fa.
8. delivered k. into hand of Abs.
1 K. 2: 15. knowest k. was mine
22. ask for him k. he my brother
10:20. not like in any k., 2 Ch. 9:19.
11:11. I will rend k. fr. thee, 31, 35.
13. I will not rend aw. all k., 34.
12:21. k. again to Rehob., 2 Ch. 11:1.
26. shall k. return to ho. of Da.
14: 8. I rent k. from ho. of David
18:10. no k. my lord hath not sent
21:7. Dost govern the k. of Israel?
2 K. 14:5. soon as k. was confirmed
15: 19. to confirm k. in his hand
1 Ch. 10: 14. turned k. unto Da.,
12: 23. [Ps. 105:13.
16: 20. from one k. to ano. people,
29: 11. all is thine, thine is the k.
O Lord, Ps. 22: 28. Mat. 6: 13.
2 Ch. 11:17. strength-d k. of Judah
13:5. gave k. over Isr. to Da. forev.
2 Ch. 13:8. to withstand k. of the L.
14: 5. the k. was quiet bef. him
21: 3. the k. gave he to Jehoram
4. Jehoram was risen up to the k.
22:9. Ahaziah no power to keep k.
29: 21. for a sin offering for the k.
32: 15. no god of any k. was able
36: 20. until reign of k. of Persia
Ne. 9:35. not served thee in their k.
Es. 1:14. princes wh. sat first in k.
3:6. thro-t whole k. of Ahas., 9:30.
4:14. art come to k. for such time
5:3. be given to half of k., 6.–7:2.
Ps. 22:28. For the k. is L.'s, Ob. 21.
Is. 17:3. cease from k. of Damascus
19: 2. they shall fight, k. against
k., Mat. 24:7. Mk. 13:8. Lu. 21:10.
34:12. shall call nobles to k. [8.
60:12. k. th. will not serve, Je. 27:
Je. 18:7. I speak conc. a k. to destr.
9. conc. a k. to build and to plant
La. 2: 2. he hath polluted the k.
Eze. 16: 13. didst prosper into a k.
17: 14. That the k. might be base
29: 14. they sh. be there a base k.
Da. 2:37. God hath given thee a k.
39. sh. arise another k. 3d k. of
40. fourth k. be strong as iron
41. the k. shall be divided
42. k. shall be partly strong and
44. in their days sh. God set up k.
4:17. the Most High ruleth in the
k. of men. 25, 32.–5: 21.
29. walked in palace of k. of Bab.
30. built for house of k.
31. the k. is departed from thee
5: 7. be third ruler in k., 16, 29.
18. G. gave Neb. thy father a k.
31. Darius took the k.
6: 1. pleased Darius to set over k.
4. no fault ag. Daniel conc. k.
7:14. was given dominion and the k.
18. saints shall take k. possess k.
22. time that saints posses-d k.
23. fourth beast sh. be 4th k. [k-s
24. the 10 horns of this k. are 10
27. whose k. is an everlasting k.
8: 23. in latter time of their k.
10:13. prince of k. of Persia withst.
11:20. raiser of taxes in the k. [me
21. not give honour of the k.
Ho. 1: 4. cause to cease k. of Israel
Am. 9: 8. eyes of L. upon sinful k.
Ob. 21. the k. shall be the Lord's
Mi. 4: 8. k. come to dau. of Jerus.
Mat. 4:23. gospel of k., 9:35.–24:14.
Mat. 8:12. chil. of k. shall be cast out
12: 25. Ev. k. divided ag. itself is
bro-t to deso., Mk. 3:24. Lu. 11:17
13: 19. heareth word of the k.
38. good seed are chil. of the k.
43. shall shine as sun in k. of Fa.
25:34. inherit k. prepared for you
26:29. until I drink it new in Fa.'s
Mk. 11:10. Blessed be k. of Da. [k.
Lu. 12:32. Fa.'s pleasure to give k.
19:12. nobleman went to receive k.
15. returned, having received k.
22: 29. I appoint unto you a k. as
Ac. 1: 6. wilt restore k. to Israel?
1 Co. 15:24. he sh. have deliv-d up k.
Col. 1:13. hath translated us into k.
He. 12: 28. k. that can-t be moved
Ja. 2: 5. heirs of k. he promised
2 Pe. 1:11. an entrance into everl. k.
Re. 1: 9. companion in k. of Jesus
17:12. ten k-s wh. have rec-d no k.
17. and give their k. unto beast
See ESTABLISH, ED, THRONE.

KINGDOM of God.

Mat. 6: 33. But seek ye first the k.
o. G., Lu. 12:31. [10:9, 11.–11:20.
12: 28. k. o. G. is come unto, Lu.
19:24. than for a rich man to enter
into k. o. G., Mk. 10: 23, 24, 25.
Lu. 18: 24, 25.
21:31. harlots go into k. o. G. bef.
43. k. o. G. shall be taken fr. you
Mk. 1: 14. preaching k. o. G., Ac. 8:
12.–20: 25.–28: 31.
15. k. o. G. is at hand, repent
4: 11. mystery of k. o. G., Lu. 8:10.
26. So is k. o. G. as if man cast
30. shall lik. k. o. G.? Lu. 13:18, 20.
9: 1. till have seen k. o. G. come
47. better to enter k. o. G. with one
10:14. children, for of such is k. o.
G., Lu. 18:16. [o. G., Lu. 18:17.
15. Whoso. shall not receive k.
24. how hard for th. trust in riches to enter k. o. G., 25. Lu. 18:25.
12:34. Thou art not far fr. k. o. G.
14:25. day I drink it new in k. o. G.
15:43. waited for k. o. G., Lu. 23:51.
Lu. 4: 43. I must preach k. o. G.
6:20. poor, for yours is the k. o. G.
7: 28. least in k. o. G. greater than
8:1. preach-g glad tidings of k. o. G.
9: 2. sent to preach k. o. G., 60.
11. and spake unto them of k. o. G.
27. not taste death, till see k. o. G.
62. No man look-g back, fit for k.
13: 28. see all prophets in k. o. G.
29. shall sit down in k. o. G.
14:15. Blessed he eat br. in k. o. G.
16: 16. since time k. o. G. is prea.
17: 20. when k. o. G. should come
20. k. o. G. cometh not wi. observ.
21. behold k. o. G. within you
18: 29. left wife, chil. for k. o. G.
19:11. thought k. o. G. sho. appear
21: 31. know ye k. o. G. is nigh
22: 16. till it be fulfilled in k. o. G.
18. I will not drink until k. o. G.
Jn. 3:3. Exc. born again, can-t see k.
5. he cannot enter into k. o. G.
Ac. 1:3. things pertaining to k. o. G.,
8: 12.–19: 8. [ter k. o. G.
14: 22. thro. much tribulation en-
28: 23. expounded, testf-d k. o. G.
Ro. 14:17. For k. o. G. is not meat
1 Co. 4: 20. k. o. G. is not in word
6: 9. unrighte. not inherit k. o. G.
10. nor extortioners inherit k. o.
G., Ga. 5: 21. Ep. 5: 5.
15:50. flesh cannot inherit k. o. G.
Col. 4: 11. my fellow workers unto
the k. o. G.
2 Th. 1: 5. counted worthy k. o. G.
Re. 12:10. now is come k. o. our G.

KINGDOM of Heaven.

Mat. 3: 2. Repent, for k. o. h. is at
hand, 4: 17.–10: 7.
Mat. 5: 3. are poor in spirit, theirs is
k. o. h., 10.
19. called least in k. o. h. [L. great
in k. o. h. [18: 3. 19: 23.
20. in no case enter into [k. o. h.
7: 21. not that saith L. enter k. o.
8:11. sit with Ab. in k. o. h. [h.
11:11. least in k. o. h. greater than
12. k. o. h. suff-h violence, violent
13: 11. know mysteries of k. o. h.
24. The k. o. h. is like, 31, 33, 44,
45, 47, 52.–18: 23.–20: 1.–22: 2.–
25: 1, 14
16: 19. unto thee keys of k. o. h.
18: 1. Who greatest in k. o. h., 4.
19: 12. for the k. o. h.'s sake
14. for of such is the k. o. h.
23: 13. ye shut up k. o. h. ag. men

His KINGDOM.

Ge. 10: 10. begin-g of h. k. Babel
Nu. 24: 7. h. k. shall be exalted
De. 17:18. sitt. upon throne of h. k.
20. may prolong his days in h. k.
2 S. 5: 12. he had exalted h. k.
1 Ch. 11: 10. strengthened in h. k.
14: 2. h. k. was lifted up on high
2 Ch. 1: 1. Sol. strength-d in h. k.
2:1. to build a house for h. k., 12.
33:13. bro-t him to Jerus. into h. k.
36: 22. Cyrus made proclamation
thro-t h. k., Ezr. 1: 1. [k.
Es. 1:2. Ahas. sat upon throne of h.
4. shewed riches of h. glorious k.
2: 3. appoi. officers in all of h. k.
Ps. 103:19. and h. k. ruleth over all
145: 12. glorious majesty of h. k.
Ec. 4: 14. he that is born in h. k.
Is. 9: 7. upon h. k. to order and
Da. 4: 3. God, h. k. an everl. k.
34. h. k. from gene., 6:26.–7:14.
11: 4. h. k. shall be plucked up
9. k. of south sh. come into h. k.
17. strength of h. whole k. [18.
Mat. 12:26. how h. k. stand, Lu. 11:
13:41. gather out of h. k. all things
16:28. Son of man coming in h. k.
Lu. 1: 33. of h. k. sh. be no end
1 Th. 2: 12. called you unto h. k.
2 Ti. 4: 1. who shall judge at h. k.
18. preserve me unto h. heav-y k.
Re. 16: 10. h. k. was full of darkn.

My KINGDOM. [sin

Ge. 20: 9. brought on m. k. great
2 S. 3:28. I and m. k. are guiltless
1 Ch. 17:14. will settle him in m. k.
Da. 4:18. wise men of m. k. not able
36. for glory of m. k. in m. k.
6:26. in m. k. men tremble [m. k.
Mk. 6: 23. will give it unto half of
Lu. 22:30. eat at my table in m. k.
Jn. 18: 36. m. k. not of this world

Thy KINGDOM. [(2)

1 S. 13: 14. t. k. shall not continue
Es. 3: 8. among peo. in all t. k.
Ps. 45: 6. sceptre of t. k., He. 1:8.
145: 11. sh. speak of glory of t. k.
13. t. k. is an everl. kingd. thy
Da. 4: 26. t. k. sh. be sure to thee
5: 11. There is a man in t. k.
26. G. hath numbered t. k. and
28. t. k. is divided to the Medes
Mat. 6: 10. t. k. come, Lu. 11: 2.
20: 21. other on thy left in t. k.
Lu. 23: 42. rememb. me when into

KINGDOMS. [t. k.

De. 3:21. so sh. L. do unto all the k.
28: 25. be removed into all k. of
Jos. 11: 10. Hazor head of all k.
1 S. 10: 18. I deliv-d you out of k.
1 K. 4:21. Sol. reigned over all k. fr.
2 K. 19: 15. G. of all k., Is. 37: 16.
19. that k. may know, Is. 37: 20.
1 Ch. 29: 30. times over all k.
2 Ch. 12: 8. know service of k.
17: 10. fear of L. upon k., 20: 29.
20: 6. thou rulest over all the k.
36:23. all k. L. given me, Ezr. 1:2

Ne. 9 : 22. thou gavest them k.
Ps. 46:6. raged, the k. were moved
68 : 32. Sing unto G. k. of earth
79 : 6. wrath on k. have not called
102 : 22. k. are gath-d to serve L.
135 : 11. smote all k. of Canaan
Is. 10 : 10. hand found k. of idols
13 : 4. noise of the k. of nations
19. Bab. the glory of k., 47 : 5.
14 : 16. this the man did shake k.
23 : 11. shook k. | 37 : 16. G. of k.
17. commit fornic. with all k.
Je. 1 : 10. over k. I have set thee
15. call all fam. of k. of north
10 : 7. in all k. none like thee
15 : 4. remov. into all k., 24:9-34:
25:26. k. of world shall drink ⌊17.
28:8. prophets proph-d ag. great k.
29 : 18. make them terror to all k.
34 : 1. all k. fought ag. Jerusalem
49 : 28. Conc. Kedar k. of Hazor
51 : 20. with thee will I destroy k.
27. call ag. her the k. of Ararat
Eze. 29 : 15. It shall be basest of k.
37 : 22. nei. be divided into two k.
Da. 2 : 44. sh. consume all these k.
7:23. shall be diverse from all k.
8 : 22. four k. sh. stand out of na.
Am. 6:2. they better than these k.?
Na. 3 : 5. will shew k. thy shame
Zph. 3:8. that I may assemble the k.
Hag. 2 : 22. I will overthr. throne of
k. destr. strength of k. ⌈4 : 5.
Mat. 4 : 8. sheweth him all k., Lu.
He. 11 : 33. thro. faith subdued k.
Re. 11:15. k. of world are k. of our

KINGLY. ⌊Lord

Da. 5 : 20. deposed from k. throne

KINSFOLK, S.

1 K. 16:11. left none of Baasha's k-s
2 K. 10 : 11. Jehu slew Ahab's k-s
Jb. 19 : 14. My k. have failed me
Lu. 2:44. sought Jesus am. their k.
21:16. ye shall be betrayed by k-s

KINSMAN.

Nu. 5 : 8. if man have no k. to
27 : 11. give his inheri. unto k.
De. 25:†5. husb.'s next k. sh. go in
†7. if man like his next k. wife
Ru. 2 : 1. Naomi had a k. Boaz
3 : 9. art a near k. | 12. k. nearer
13. if he perf. part of a k. well, if
not, I will do part of a k.
4 : 1. behold k. of wh. Boaz spake
3. said unto k. Naomi, that is come
6. k. said, I cannot redeem it
8. the k. said unto Boaz, Buy it
14. not left thee without a k.
Jn. 18 : 26. his k. whose ear Pet. cut
Ro. 16 : 11. Salute Herodion my k.

KINSMEN.

Ru. 2:20. man is one of our next k.
1 Ch. 15 : † 5. Uriel and his k. 220
Ps. 38 : 11. lovers and k. stood afar
Mk. 3 :†21. when k. heard, went to
Lu. 14 : 12. call not friends, nei. k.
Ac. 10 : 24. Cornelius had called k.
Ro. 9 : 3. accursed, for my k. acc.
16:7. Salute my k. | 21. k. salute

KINSWOMAN. ⌊you

Le. 18:12. she is my father's near k.
13. she is thy mother's near k.
Pr. 7 : 4. call understanding thy k.

KINSWOMEN.

Le. 18: 17. for they are her near k.

KIR.

2 K. 16 : 9. carried peo. captive to K.
Is. 15 : 1. K. is laid waste ⌈shield
22:6. Elam bare quiver, K. uncov-d
Am. 1: 5. Syrians into captiv. to K.
9 : 7. I not bro-t Assyrians fr. K.?

KIR-HAR'ASETH, KIR-HA'RESH, KIR-HAR'E-SETH, KIR-HE'RES.

2 K. 3 : 25. only in K. left th. stones
Is. 16 : 7. for founda. of K. mourn
11. inw. parts shall sound for K.

Je. 48 : 31. heart mourn for men of
K. ⌈ 36.

KIRIATHA'IM. ⌈K.

Ge. 14 : 5. smote Emims in Shaveh
Je. 48:1. saith L., K. is confounded
23. Judgment is come upon K.
Eze. 25: 9. glory of the country, K.

KIR'IOTH. See KERIOTH.

KIR'JATH. See GIBEATH.

KIRJATHA'IM.

Nu. 32 : 37. built Heshbon and K.
Jos. 13:19. gave unto Reub. K. | 1 Ch.

KIR'JATH-AR'BA. ⌊6:76.

Ge. 23:2. Sarah died in K. the same
is Hebron in Canaan, Jos. 14:15.
-15 : † 13,-54.-20 : 7. Ju. 1 : 10.
Ne. 11:25. Some of Jud. dwelt at K.

KIR'JATH-A'RIM.

Ezr. 2:25. chil. of K. 743, Ne. 7:†29.

KIR'JATH-BA'AL. ⌈14.

Jos. 15:60. K. is Kirjath-jearim, 18:

KIR'JATH-HU'ZOTH.

Nu. 22 : 39. Balaam Balak unto K.

KIR'JATH-JE'ARIM.

Jos. 9 : 17. K. a city of the Hivites
made peace | 18 : 15. Ne. 7 : 29.
15:9. was to Baalah, wh. is K., 60.
18:14. K. a city of Jud., 1 Ch. 13 : 6.
Ju. 18 : 12. pitched in K. in Judah
1 S. 7:1. men of K. fetched the ark
1 S. 7 :2. while ark abode in K. | 6:21.
1 Ch. 13 : 5. Isr. to bring ark from K.
2 Ch. 1 :4. ark had David bro-t fr. K.
Je. 26 : 20. Urijah son of Shemaiah
[Person.] ⌊of K.
1 Ch. 2 : 50. Shobal father of K., 52.
53. families of K.; Ithrites, Pu-

KIRJATH-SAN'NAH. ⌊hites

Jos. 15 : 49. in mts., K. wh. is Debir

KIR'JATH-SE'PHER.

Jos. 15:15. name of Debir K., Ju. 1:11.
16. he that smiteth K., Ju. 1 : 12.

KISH = CIS. ⌈K.

1 S. 9 : 1. man of Benj-n, name was
3. asses of K. were lost. K. said
10:11. What is come unto son of K.?
21. Saul, the son of K., 14 : 51. 1
Ch. 8 . 33.-9 : 39.-12 : 1 -26 : 28.
2 S. 21 : 14. buried Saul in sepulchre
1 Ch. 9 : 36. Jehiel; son K., 8 :30⌊of K.
23 : 21. of Mahli; K. |22. sons of K.
24 : 29. Concerning K. (2) ⌊took
2 Ch. 29 :12. of Merari; K. son of Ab-
Es. 2 : 5. son of K. a Benjamite ⌊di

KISH'I or KUSHA'IAH.

1 Ch. 6 :44. †Ethan son of K., 15:17.†

KISH'ION[1] or KI'SH'ON.[2]

Jos. 19:20. border tow. K.[1] | 21:28. K.[2]

KI'SHON, KI'SON. [River.]

Ju. 4 : 7. I will draw to K. Sisera
13. Sisera gath-d chariots unto K.
5:21. river of K. swept th. away, (2)
1 K. 18: 40. Elijah bro-t them to K.
Ps. 83:9. as to Jabin at brook of K.

KISS, ES.

Pr. 27 : 6. k-s of an enemy deceitf.
Can. 1 : 2. Let him k. me with k-s
Lu. 7:45. Thou gavest me no k., but
22:48. betrayest Son of man wi. k.?
Ro. 16:16. Salute wi. holy k. ⌈13:12.
1 Co. 16:20. Greet wi. holy k., 2 Co.
1 Th. 5:26. Greet breth. wi. holy k.
1 Pe. 5:14. Greet with a k. of charity

KISS. [Verb.]

Ge. 27 : 26. Come k. me, my son
31:28. not suffered me to k. my sons
41 : † 40. at thy word my peo. k.
2 S. 20 : 9. took Amasa by beard to
1 K. 19:20. Let me k. my father ⌊k.
Ps. 2 : 12. k. Son, lest he be angry
Pr. 24 : 26. Ev. man sh. k. his lips
Can. 1 : 2. Let him k. me wi. kisses
8:1. I would k. thee, not be despised
Ho. 13 : 2. that sacrifice k. calves
Mat. 26 : 48. sign, saying, Whomso.
I k. same is he, Mk. 14 : 44.
Lu. 7:45. ha. not ceased to k. my feet

Lu. 22:47. Judas drew near unto Jes

KISSED. ⌊to k.

Ge. 27 : 27. Jacob came and k. him
29 : 11. Jacob k. Rachel and wept
13. Laban k. Jac. | 33:4. Esau k.
31:55. Laban k. his sons and dau-s
45 : 15. Joseph k. all his brethren
48 : 10. Jacob k. Joseph's sons
50:1. Jo. fell upon fa.'s face k. him
Ex. 4: 27. Aaron met Moses k. him
18 : 7. Moses met fa. in law k. him
Ru 1 : 9. Naomi k. her dau-s in law
14. Orpah k. her mother in law
1 S. 10:1. Samuel poured oil k. Saul
20 : 41. Jonathan and David k.
2 S. 14 : 33. and king k. Absalom
15: 5. Abs. k. any man came nigh
19 : 39. king k. Barzillai, blessed
1 K. 19:18. mouth wh. hath not k.
Jb. 31:27. or my mouth k. ha. ⌊him
Ps. 85:10. righteousn. and peace k.
Pr. 7 : 13. she caught him and k.
Eze. 3 : † 13. wings of creatures k.
Mat. 26 : 49. Hail, Master, and k.
him, Mk. 14 : 45. ⌈anointed th.
Lu. 7 : 38. Mary k. his feet and
15 : 20. fa. fell on his neck k. him
Ac. 20:37. fell on Paul's neck k. him

KITE.

Le. 11 : 14. the k. uncl., De. 14 : 13.

KITH'LISH.

Jos. 15 : 40. Lahman K. inheri. of

KIT'RON. ⌈K.

Ju. 1 : 30. Nei. drive out inhab. of

KIT'TIM = CHITTIM. ⌈7.

Ge. 10:4. sons of Javan K. | 1 Ch. 1:

KNEAD, ED.

Ge. 18 : 6. k. it, and make cakes
1 S. 28 : 24. woman took flour k-d it
2 S. 13 : 8. Tamar took flour k-d
Je. 7 : 18. women k. their dough
Ho. 7 : 4. baker k-d the dough until

KNEADINGTROUGHS.

Ex. 8 : 3. frogs sh. come into thy k.
12:34. their k. bound up in clothes

KNEE.

Ge. 41 : 43. they cried, Bow the k.
Is. 45 : 23. unto me every k. shall
bow, Ro. 14:11. Ph. 2:10. ⌈15:19.
Mat. 27:29. bowed k. bef. him, Mk.
Ro. 11:4. have not bowed k. to Baal

KNEES.

Ge. 30 : 3. Bilhah bear upon my k.
48:12. Jo. brought them fr. betw. k.
50:23. chil. brought up on Jo-s k.
De. 28:35. L. shall smite thee in k.
Ju. 7 : 5. boweth upon k. to drink,
16:19. Samson sleep upon her k. ⌊6.
1 K. 8:54. arose fr. kneeling on his k.
18 : 42. Elij. put face betw. his k.
19 : 18. k. have not bowed to Baal
2 K. 1 : 13. third capt. fell on his k.
4: 20. sat on mother's k. till noon
2 Ch. 6:13. Sol. kneeled upon his k.
Ezr. 9: 5. I fell upon k. and spread
Jb. 3 : 12. Why did k. prevent me?
4 : 4. hast strengthened feeble k.
Ps. 109 : 24. k. weak thro. fasting
Is. 35 : 3. and confirm feeble k.
66 : 12. suck, be dandled on her k.
Eze. 7 : 17. k. sh. be weak as wat.,
47 : 4. waters were to the k. ⌊21:7.
Da. 5 : 6. k. smote one ag. another
6 : 10. kneeled upon his k. 3 times
10 : 10. a hand set me upon my k.
Na. 2 : 10. she empty, and k. smite
Mk. 15 : 19. bowing k. worshipped
Lu. 5:8. Peter fell at Jesus' k. ⌈Fa.
Ep. 3 : 14. For this I bow k. unto
He. 12:12. hands th. hang feeble k.

KNEEL, ED.

Ge. 24:11. made his camels k. down
2 Ch. 6 : 13. Sol. k-d upon his knees
Ps. 95:6. let us k. bef. L. our Maker
Da. 6 : 10. Dan. k-d 3 times a day
Lu. 22 : 41. Jesus k-d and prayed
Ac. 7 : 60. Ste. k-d and cried with

Ac.9:40.Pe.k-d prayed | 20:36.Paul
21: 5. we k-d down on shore and

KNEELING.

1 K. 8: 54. Solomon rose up fr. k.
Mat. 17: 14. a man k. to him
Mk. 1: 40. came a leper k.

KNEW.

Ge. 4: 1. Adam k. Eve his wife, 25.
17. Cain k. wife she conceived
38: 26. Judah k. her no more
Ju. 11: 39. Jeph.'s dau. k. no man
19: 25. k. and abused her all night
1 S. 1: 19. Elkanah k. Hannah
1 K. 1: 4. fair, but king k. her not
Mat. 1: 25. Joseph k. her not, till

KNEW. ⌈naked

Ge. 3: 7. Adam and Eve k. they
8: 11. Noah k. waters were abated
9: 24. Noah k. what son had done
37: 33. Jac. k. it, said, my son's
38:9. Onan k. seed sho. not be his
42: 7. Joseph saw k. his breth., 8.
Nu. 24:16. k. knowl. of Most High
De. 9:24. rebellious fr. day I k. you
33: 9. nor k. his own children
34: 10. prophet L. k. face to face
Ju. 3: 2. such as bef. k. nothing
13: 21. Manoah k. he was angel
18: 3. they k. voice of young man
1 S. 3:20. Isr. k. Sam. was prophet
10: 11. when all that k. him saw
18: 28. Saul k. L. was with David
20: 9. if I k. would not tell thee
33. Jona.k. it was determ-d by S.
39.only Da. and Jona. k. matter
22: 15. servant k. nothing of this
17.slay priests bec.k.when he fled
22. Da. said to Abiathar, I k. it
23: 9. David k. Saul practised ag.
26: 12. no man saw it nor k. it
17. Saul k. David's voice, and
2 S. 11: 16. he k. valiant men were
1 K. 18: 7. Obadiah k. Elijah, and
2 Ch 33: 13. Manasseh k. L. was G.
Es. 1: 13. wise men wh.k.times (so
was k.'s manner to all th.k.law)
Jb. 23:3. O th. I k. where find him
Is. 48: 4. I k. thou art obstinate
7.lest thou say, Behold I k. them
8. I k. thou wo. deal treach-ly
Je. 1: 5. Bef. I formed, I k. thee
32: 8. I k. this was word of L.
41:4. slain Gedaliah, no man k. it
44: 15. men k. wives burnt inc.
Eze. 10: 20. I k. they were cheru.
19: 7. he k. their desolate palaces
Da. 5: 21. till he k. most high ruled
6: 10. Dan. k. writing was signed
Jon.1:10.k.he fled fr.presence of L.
4: 2. I k. thou art gracious God
Zch. 11: 11. k. it was word of L.
Mat. 7: 23. profess I never k. you
12: 15. when Jes. k. he withdrew
25. Jesus k. thoughts, Lu. 6: 8.
25: 24. I k. thou art a hard man
27:18. he k. for envy they had delivered, Mk. 15: 10. ⌈him
Mk. 1: 34. not to speak bec. they k.
6: 33.many k.him and ran thither
38.when k.they say,Five and two
54.out of ship, straightw. k. him
8:17. Jes. k. he saith, Why reason
12:12. k. he had spok. parable ag.
15:45. when he k. it he gave body
Lu. 4: 41. they k. th. he was Christ
7:37. when she k. Jes. sat at meat
9:11. peo. when k. it followed him
12: 47. servant wh. k. lord's will
18: 34. nei. k. they things spoken
23:7. k. he belonged unto Herod's
24: 31. eyes opened, they k. him
Jn. 2: 9. serv-ts k. whence it was
24. not commit hims.bec.he k.all
25. he k. what was in man ⌊men
4:1. When L. k. how Phari. heard
53. father k. it was at same hour
5: 6. Jesus k. he had been long in

Jn.6:6. for he k. what he would do
61. Jes. k. disciples murmured
64. Jesus k. from beginning who
11: 42. I k. thou hearest me alw.
57. if any man k. where he were
12:9. Much peo. of Jews k.he was
13: 1. Jesus k. his hour was come
11. he k. who should betray him
28. no man at table k. for what
16: 19. Jes. k. they were desirous
18: 2. Judas k. the place ⌊to ask
Ac. 3: 10. k. it was he sat for alms
9:30. when breth. k. they brought
12:14. when Rhoda k. Pet.'s voice
16: 3. they k. his fa. was a Greek
19: 34. when they k. he was Jew
22:29. afraid aft. k. he was a Rom.
26: 5. Which k. me fr. beginning
28: 1. k. island was called Melita
Ro. 1: 21. Bec. when they k. God
1 Co.2:8.none of princes of world k.
2 Co.5:21. him to be sin, who k.no
12:2. I k. a man in Christ, 3. ⌊sin
Col. 1: 6. since ye k. grace of God
2: 1. I wo. you k. what conflict
Jude 5.in rememb., tho. ye k. this
Re. 19:12. name written no man k.

KNEW not. ⌈n.

Ge. 28: 16. L. is in this pl., I k. it
31:32.Jac.k.n. Rachel had stolen
38: 16. Judah k. n. she was dau.
39: 6. he k. n. aught he had ⌈n.
42:8. Jo. knew breth. they k. him
23. they k. n. Joseph underst.
Ex.1:8. king wh.k. n. Jo., Ac.7:18.
Nu. 22:34. I k. n. thou in the way
De. 8: 16. manna thy fathers k. n.
29:26.gods thy fathers k.n.,32:17.
Ju. 2: 10. gene. which k. n. Lord
13:16. Manoah k. n. he was angel
14: 4. his father k. n. it was of L.
20: 34. Benj. k. n. evil was near
1 S. 2: 12. sons of Eli k. n. the L.
14: 3. people k. n.Jona. was gone
20: 39. the lad k. n. any thing
2 S. 3: 26. aft. Abner, Da. k. it n.
11:20. k. ye n. they would shoot?
15:11.went in simplicity, and k.n.
18:29. tumult, I k.n. what it was
22: 44. peo. I k. n. shall serve me
2 K.4:39.gourds for they k.them n.
Ne. 2: 16. rulers k. n. whi. I went
Jb. 2: 12. Job's friends k. him n.
29: 16. cause I k. n. I searched
42: 3. things I k. n. too wonderf.
Ps. 35:11. to my charge thi. I k.n.
15 gathered ag.me,and I k. it n.
73:†22. So foolish was I, and k.n.
Pr. 23: † 35. beaten me, I k. it n.
24: 12. if sayest, we k. it n. ⌈n.
Is.42:16. bring blind by way th. k.
25. hath set him on fire, he k.n.
55: 5. and nations that k. n. thee
Je. 2: 8. that handle law k. me n.
11: 19. I k. n. they had devised
44: 3. other gods whom they k.n.
Da. 11:38. god whom his fa-s k.n.
Ho. 8: 4. made princes I k. it n.
11: 3. they k. n. that I healed th.
Zch. 7: 14. am. nations they k. n.
Mat.17:12. Elias is come, k. him n.
24: 39. k. n. till flood came ⌈it
Lu. 2: 43. Jo. and mother k. n. of
12:48.k.n. and did commit things
Jn. 1: 10. the world k. him n.
31. And I k. him n., 33. ⌈was
2: 9. governor k. n. whence it
20: 9. as yet they k. n. Scriptures
14. k. n. that it was Jes., 21: 4.
Ac.13:27.they, bec. they k. him n.
19: 32. more part k. n. whf. came
27: 39. when day, they k. n. land
1 Co. 1: 21. world by wisd. k. n. G.
Ga. 4: 8. then when ye k. n. G., ye
1 Jn. 3: 1. knoweth us not, bec. k.

KNEWEST. ⌊him n.

De. 8:3. fed with manna thou k. not

Ru. 2:11. art come unto peo. k. not
Ne. 9: 10. k. they dealt proudly ag.
Ps. 142:3. thou k. my path in way
Is. 48: 8. heardest not, thou k. not
Da. 5: 22. not humbled heart, thou
k. all this ⌈Lu. 19: 22.
Mat.25:26. thou k. I reaped where,
Lu. 19: 44. k. not time of visitation
Jn. 4: 10. if thou k. gift of God

KNIFE. ⌈10.

Ge. 22: 6. Abr. took k. in his hand,
Ex. 4: † 25. Zipporah took sharp k.
Ju. 19: 29. took k. laid hold concu.
Pr. 23: 2. put k. to thy throat, if
Eze. 5: 1. take thee a sharp k.
2. and smite about it with a k.

KNIT.

Ju. 20: 11. Isr. were k. toge. as one
1 S.18:1.soul of Jona.was k. to Da.
1 Ch.12:17.my heart sh. be k. unto
Ac. 10: 11. I saw a sheet k. at ⌊you
Col. 2: 2. hearts being k. together
19. body k. tog. increaseth with

KNIVES.

Jos. 5: 2. Make sharp k. circumcise
3. Josh. made sharp k. circum-d
1 K. 18: 28. they cut thems.with k.
Ezr.1:9. nine and 20 k. Cyrus bro-t
Pr.30:14.teeth as k. to devour poor
Eze. 21: † 21. king of Bab. made

KNOCK, ED. ⌊bright k.

Mat.7:7.k. it sh. be opened, Lu.11:
Lu.13:25. ye begin to k. at door ⌊9.
Ac. 12: 13. as Peter k-d at the door
Re.3:20. I stand at the door and k.

KNOCKETH, ING.

Can.5:2.voice of my beloved th.k-h
Mat. 7: 8. to him that k-h shall be
opened, Lu. 11: 10. ⌈open
Lu. 12: 36. when he k-h they may
Ac. 12: 16. Peter continued k-g and

KNOP, S.

Ex. 25: 31. his k-s and his flowers,
34, 36.-37: 17. ⌈37: 19.
33.with k.and flower in 1 branch,
36. k-s branches of same, 37: 17,
1 K. 6: 18. carved with k-s ⌊20, 22.
7: 24. k-s compassing it, k-s cast
Am. 9: † 1. Smite the k. of the door
Zph. 2:†14. bittern sh. lodge in k-s

KNOW. ⌊of it

Ge. 3: 5. G. doth k. your eyes sh.
22.as one of us,to k.good and evil
15:13.k.thy seed sh. be a stranger
18: 21. I will go and see, I will k.
20:7. if restore her not, k.thou die
37:32.k.now whe. it thy son's coat
Ex. 18: 16. I make th. k. statutes
33:12. not let me k. wh. wilt send
36: 1. k. how to work all manner
Nu. 14: 31. shall k. land ye despis.
De. 4:39. k. this day consider, 11:2.
7: 9. k. the Lord he is God
8: 2. to k. what was in thy heart
3. k. man not live by br. only (2)
13: 3. to k. whe. ye love the Lord
Jos. 4: 22. ye shall let your chil. k.
22: 22. L. knoweth, Isr. shall k.
Ju. 3: 4. to k. whe. would hearken
Ru. 3: 11. city of my peo. doth k.
14.she rose bef. one could k.ano.
18. Sit still, my dau.,till thou k.
1 S.14:38.k.and see wherein this sin
17: 47. assembly shall k. the L.
20:3.he saith, Let not Jona.k.this
21: 2. Let no man k. of business
24: 11. k. and see is no evil in me
25: 17. k. and consider what thou
28: 1. Achish said unto David, k.
2. shalt k. what thy serv. can do
2 S.3:25.k. thy going out, to k. all
7: 21. done these to make serv. k.
14:20. to k. all things in the earth
19: 20. serv. doth k. I have sinn.
1 K. 8: 38. k. ev. man plague, 2 Ch.
2 K.5:8. k. is prophet in Isr. ⌊6:29.
7: 12. They k. that we be hungry

2 K.10:10.k.there shall fall nothing
1 Ch.12: 32. k.wh. Isr. ought to do
28: 9. my son, k. thou G. of thy
2 Ch. 18: 5. Ought ye to k. L. gave
Ezr. 4: 15. k. this is rebellious city
7:25.all such as k.laws of thy God
Es.2:11.Mord.to k. how Esther did
4: 5. to k. what it was, and why
11. peo. k. whoso. come unto k.
Jb. 5: 24. k. thy tabern. in peace
25. shalt k. thy seed sh. be great
27. and k. thou it for thy good
7: 10. nei. place k. him any more
8: 9. we of yesterday, k. nothing
11:6.k.G. exacteth less than thine
8.deeper than hell,what canst k.?
13: 23. make me to k. my transgr.
19: 6. k. G. hath overthrown me
21: 19. G. rewardeth, he sh. k. it
22: 13. sayest, How doth God k.?
23:5. I wo. k.words he would ans.
24:1. do they that k. him not see?
17.if one k. them, they in terrors
34: 4. let us k. what is good
37: 15. k. when G. disposed them
16. Dost k. balancing of clouds
38: 12. dayspring to k. his place
20. shouldest k. paths to house
Ps. 4: 3. k. L. hath set apart godly
9: 10. that k. thy name put trust
36: 10. lovingk. unto them k. thee
39: 4. L., make me to k. mine end
46: 10. k. that I am G., I will be
51: 6. in hid. part make me to k.
59: 13. let them k. God ruleth
73: 11. How doth God k.?
16. I thought to k. this
87:4. mention Bab. to them k. me
89: 15. Blessed that k. sound
103: 16. place shall k. it no more
139:23. k. my heart, k. my tho-ts
142: 4. was no man that wo. k. me
143:8.cause me k.way I sho. walk
Pr. 1: 2. To k. wisdom and instruc.
4: 1. Hear, attend to k. underst-g
10:32. lips of righte. k. what is ac.
27:23.diligent to k. state of flocks
29: 7. wick. regardeth not to k. it
Ec. 1: 17. gave my heart to k. wisd.
7: 25. I applied heart to k. wisd.
8:16. applied my heart to k. wisd.
17. tho. wise man think to k. it
9: 5. living k. they sh. die [judg.
11: 9. k. G. will bring thee into
Is. 7: 16. bef. child k. to refuse evil
9: 9. peo. shall k. even Ephraim
19:12.let them k.what L.purposed
21. Egyptians shall k. Lord
41: 20. That they may see and k.
22.th.we may k. latter end of th.
49: 26. all flesh shall k. I am Sav.
50: 4. k. how to speak in season
52: 6. my peo. shall k. my name
58: 2. they delight to k. my ways
60: 16. shalt k. I L. am Saviour
Je.2:19.k.it is evil thing to forsake
23. k. what thou hast done
5: 1. see now and k. and seek
6:18. k.O cong., what is am. them
9: 6. thro. deceit refuse to k. me
15:15.k. for thy sake I have suff-d
16: 21. will cause them to k. my
ha., they sh. k. my name is L.
17: 9. heart deceitful, who k. it?
22: 16. was not this to k. me?
24: 7. give them a heart to k. me
29:16. k. thus saith L. of the king
31:34. no more saying, k. the L.for
they shall all k. me, He. 8: 11.
36: 19. let no man k. where ye be
38: 24. Let no man k. of words
40: 15. slay Ishm., no man sh. k.
44: 28. Jud. shall k. whose words
Eze.2:5.k.there been proph-t,33:33.
5: 13. shall k. I L. hath spoken
16: 2. Jerus. to k. her abomination, 20: 4.-22: † 2.

Eze.17:24.trees shall k.that I the L.
20: † 11. made to k. my judgm-ts
25:14. they shall k. my vengeance
28: 19. k. thee sh. be astonished
34: 30. shall k. I am with them
36: 36. shall k. I the L. build the
37: 28. heathen shall k., 39: 23.
Da. 2:3. spirit troubled to k. dream
9. I sh. k. that ye can shew me
21. givest knowl. to them who k.
4: 25. till k. Most High ruleth, 32.
6:15. k.,O king, that law of Medes
7: 16. made me k. interpretation
19. I would k. truth of 4th beast
8: 19. make thee k. what shall be
9: 25. k. and understand, that fr.
11:32.peo.that k. G. sh. be strong
Ho. 2: 20. thou shalt k. the Lord
9: 7. recompense; Isr. shall k. it
13: 4. thou shalt k. no G. but me
5. I did k. thee in wilderness
14: 9. prudent, he shall k. them
Mi. 3: 1. Is it not to k. judgment?
Zch.2:11.shalt k. Lord sent me,4:9.
Mat. 2: 4. ye shall k. I sent this
6: 3. not left hand k. what right
7: 11. if ye k. how to give good
gifts, Lu. 11:13. [7: 24.-9: 30.
9:30. see no man k. it, Mk. 5:43.-
13: 11. it is given unto you to k.,
Mk.4:11.Lu.8:10. [29.Lu 21:20.
24: 33. k. desolat. is near, Mk.13:
43. k. this, if goodman, Lu.12:39.
Jn. 4: 42. we k. this is the Christ
7: 17. if do his will k. of doctrine
26. Do the rulers k. indeed
51. judge bef.it k. what he doeth?
10: 4. sheep follow, k. his voice
14. good sheph. I k. my sheep
13: 7. thou shalt k. hereafter
13: 35. By this k. ye are my disci.
18:21. ask th. they k. what I said
Ac. 1: 7. not for you to k. times or
2: 36. let all house of Isr. k. as-
22:14. k. his will and see Just One
19. k. I imprisoned them believ.
24: 22. I will k. the uttermost of
26: 4. My life fr. youth k. all Jews
Ro. 7: 1. I speak to th. k. the law
10: 19. but I say, Did not Isr. k.
1 Co.2:14. nei. can he k. them, bec.
4: 19. and will k. not the speech
8: 2. kn-h noth. as he ought to k.
11:3. I wo. have you k. head is C.
Ep.3:19.and to k. the love of Christ
1 Th. 2: 1. breth. k. our entrance
3: 3. yours. k. we are appointed
5. for this I sent to k. your faith
4:4. sho. k. how to poss. his vessel
5: 2. yours. k. that day of Lord
12. to k. th. who labour am. you
2 Th. 3: 7. yours. k. how ye ought
1 Ti. 4: 3. of them which k. truth
2 Ti. 3: 1. This k. that in last days
Tit.1:16.profess that they k. G.but
Ja. 2: 20. wilt thou k. O vain man
5:20.Let him k. he wh. converteth
Jude 10.but what they k.naturally
Re. 2:23. churches shall k. I am he
3: 9. make them to k. I loved thee
See CERTAIN, CERTAINLY, CERTAINTY.

I KNOW.

Ge. 12:11. I k. thou art fair woman
15: 8. sh. I k. I shall inherit it?
18: 19. I k. he will com. his chil.
20:6.I k. thou didst this in integr.
22: 12. I k. that thou fearest God
24:14. shall I k. thou hast shewed
42:33. sh. I k. ye are true men, 34.
48:19. said, I k. it, my son, I k. it
Ex. 3: 7. L. said, I k. their sorrow
4: 14. Aa. I k. he can speak well
9: 30. I k. ye will not yet fear L.
18:11.I k. L. greater than all gods
33:12. said, I k. thee by name, 17.
De. 3: 19. I k. ye have much cattle

De. 31: 21. I k. their imagination
27. I k. thy rebellion, thy stiff
29. I k. after my death ye will
Jos. 2: 9. I k. L. hath given you
Ju. 6: 37. sh. I k. thou wilt save
17: 13. k. I L. will do me good
1 S.17:28.I k.thy pride and naughti
20: 30. do not I k. chosen son of
22: 3. till I k. what God will do
24: 20. I k. thou shalt be king
29:9.I k.thou art good in my sight
2 S. 19: 22. do not I k. I am king
1 K.17:24.I k. thou art man of God
2 K. 2:3. I k. it, hold your peace, 5.
5: 15. I k. is no God in earth, but
8: 12. I k. evil thou wilt do unto
19: 27. I k. thy abode, Is. 37: 28.
1 Ch. 29: 17. I k. thou triest heart
2 Ch.2:8.I k. thy serv-s can skill to
25: 16. I k. G. hath determined
Jb. 9: 2. I k. it is so of a truth
28. I k. wilt not hold me innoc.
10: 13. I k. that this is with thee
13: 2. What ye know, same do I k.
18. I k. that I shall be justified
19: 25. I k. my Redeemer liveth
21: 27. I k. your thoughts and
30: 23. I k. thou wilt bring me to
42:2. I k. thou canst do ev. thing
Ps. 20: 6. I k. L. saveth anointed
41: 11. I k. thou favourest me
50: 11. I k. all the fowls of mts.
56: 9. this I k. for God is for me
119:75. I k. O L. thy judgm. right
135: 5. I k. the Lord is great
140:12.I k. L. will maintain cause
Ec. 3: 12. I k. is no good in them
14. I k. that whatso. God doeth
8:12. I k. it shall be well with th.
Is. 47:8. nei. shall I k. loss of chil.
50: 7. I k. I shall not be ashamed
66:18.I k.their works and thought
Je. 10: 23. I k. way of man is not
11: 18. L. given me knowl. I k. it
29: 11. I k. thoughts that I think
23. I k. am a witness, saith Lord
48: 30. I k. his wrath, saith Lord
Eze. 11: 5. I k. things that come
Da. 2:9. tell me dream, and I sh. k.
4: 9. I k. spirit of the holy gods is
Ho. 5: 3. I k. Ephraim, and Israel
13: 5. I did k. thee in wilderness
Am. 5: 12. I k. your transgr-ns
Jon. 1:12. I k. for my sake tempest
Mat. 28: 5. I k. ye seek Jesus
Mk. 1: 24. I k. thee, Lu. 4: 34.
Lu. 1: 18. Whereby shall I k. this
Jn. 4: 25. I k. that Messias cometh
5: 32. I k. witness he witnesseth
42. I k. you | 7: 29. I k. him for
8: 14. I k. whence I came
37. I k. ye are Abraham's seed
55.I k. him | 9:25. one thing I k.
10:15. as Fa. knoweth me, I k. Fa.
27. I k. my sheep, 14. [God
11: 22. I k. that what wilt ask of
24. Martha said, I k. he sh. rise
12: 50. I k. his com-t is life everl.
13: 18. I k. whom I have chosen
Ac. 12: 11. I k. of a surety L. sent
19: 15. Jes. I k. Paul I k. but
20: 25. I k. ye sh. see my face no
29. I k. this, after my departing
24:10. I k. thou hast been a judge
22. I will k. uttermost of matter
26: 3. bec. I k. thee to be expert
27. Agrippa, I k. thou believest
Ro. 7:18. I k. in me dw-th no good
14: 14. I k. and am persuaded
1 Co. 4: 4. I k. nothing by myself
19. I will k. not the speech
13:12.I k. in part, then sh. I k. as
2 Co. 9: 2. I k. forwardn. of your
Ph. 1: 19. I k. this sh. turn to salv.
25. I k. I shall abide with you all
2:19 comfort, when I k. your est.
4: 12. I k. how to be abased, I k.

2 Ti. 1 : 12. I k. whom I have believ.
1 Jn. 2 : 4. he that saith I k. him
Re. 2 : 2. I k. thy works, 9, 13, 19.-
3 : 1, 8, 15. [who say
2 : 9. I k. the blasphemy of them,

KNOW that I am the Lord.

Ex. 6 : 7. ye shall k. I a. L., 16:12.
1 K. 20:28. Eze. 6:7, 13.-7:4, 9.-
11:10, 12.-12:20.-13:9, 14, 21, 23.
-14 : 8.-15:7.-20:38, 42, 44.-23:
49.-24:24.-25:5.-35:9.-36 : 11.-
37 : 6, 13. Jo. 3 : 17.
7 : 5. the Egyptians shall k. I a.
L., 14 : 4, 18. Eze. 29 : 6.
17. thou shalt k. I a. L., 1 K.
20:13. Is. 49:23. Eze. 16:62.-22:
16.-25 : 7.-35 : 4, 12.
8 : 22. end thou mayest k. I a. L.
10 : 2. that ye may k. I a. L., 31 :
13. Eze. 20 : 20.
29 : 46. they shall k. I a. L., Eze.
6:10, 14.-7:27.-12:15, 16.-24:27.
-25:11, 17.-26:6.-28 : 22, 23, 24,
26.-29:9, 16, 21.-30:8, 19, 25, 26.-
32:15.-33:29.-34:27.-35:15.-36:
38.-38 : 23.-39 : 6, 28.
De. 29 : 6. ye might k. I a. L.
Je. 24 : 7. I will give them a heart
to k. I a. L. [k. I a. L., 26.
Eze. 20:12. sabbaths th. they might
36 : 23. the heathen shall k. I a.
L., 39 : 7. [I a. L.
39 : 22. house of Israel shall k. t.

May, or mayest KNOW.

Ge. 19 : 5. bring out that we m. k.
them [14.
Ex. 8:10. m-t k. is none like G., 9:
9:29. m-t k. that earth is the L.'s
11:7. m.k. L. doth put difference
33 : 5. I m.k. what to do to thee
13. shew way, that I m. k. thee
Le. 23 : 43. That generations m. k.
Nu. 22 : 19. I m. k. what L. say
Jos. 3 : 4. m. k. way ye should go
7. m.k. that as I was with Moses
Ju. 18:5. m.k. whe. our way prosp.
19:22. Bring forth man th. we m.k.
Ru. 4 : 4. then tell me, that I m.k.
1 S. 17 : 46. earth m. k. is a G. in
Isr., 1 K. 8 : 43, 60. 2 K. 19:19.
2 S. 24 : 2. m.k. number of people,
1 Ch. 21 : 2.
1 K. 18:37. people m.k. thou art G.
2 Ch. 6 : 33. people m.k. thy name,
and m.k. this hou. is called by
12 : 8. that they m. k. my service
Jb. 19:29. m. k. there is judgment
31: 6. that G. m. k. my integrity
37:7. that all men m. k. his work
Ps. 9:20. m.k. thems. to be but men
39 : 4. that I m.k. how frail I am
83 : 18. m. k. thou art Most High
109 : 27. m. k. this is thy hand
119:125. that I m.k. thy testimo.
Is. 5: 19. draw nigh th. we m.k. it
7 : 15. he m. k. to refuse the evil
37 : 20. all m. k. thou art the L.
41 : 23. that we m. k. ye are gods
26. hath declared, that we m. k.
43 : 10. ye m. k. and believe me
45 : 3. m. k. that I am G. of Isr.
6. m. k. from rising of the sun
Je. 6 : 27. m-t k. and try their way
44:29. m.k. my words shall stand
Eze. 21 : 5. m. k. I have drawn sw.
38 : 16. that heathen m. k. me
Da. 4:17. to intent that living m.k.
Jon. 1:7. us cast lots, that we m.k.
Mi. 6 : 5. ye m. k. righte-n. of L.
Mat. 9 : 6. m.k. Son of man power
to forgive, Mk. 2 : 10. Lu. 5:24.
Jn. 10 : 38. ye m. k. Fa. is in me
14:31. world m.k. I love Fa., 17:23.
19 : 4. m. k. I find no fault in
Ac. 17 : 19. m. we k. new doctr. is?
21 : 24. all m. k. those are noth.
Ep. 1 : 18. m. k. hope of calling
Ph. 3 : 10. I m. k. him, and power
Col. 4 : 6. m.k. how to answer man
1 Ti. 3:15. m.k. how ought. to beh.
1 Jn. 5:13. m.k. ye have etern. life
20. ye m. k. him that is true

Might, or mightest KNOW.

De. 4:35. that thou m-est k. L. is G.
Jos. 4:24. all people m.k. ha. of L.
Ju. 3:2. Isr. m.k. to teach th. war
2 Ch. 32:31. m.k. all was in his heart
Ps. 78:6. genera. to come m.k. them
Da. 2:30. m-est k. thoughts of thy
heart [had
Lu. 19:15. m.k. how much ev. man
Jn. 17:3. m.k. thee the only true G.
Ac. 22:24. m.k. wbf. cried so ag. him
1 Co. 2:12. m.k. things giv. us of G.
2 Co. 2:4. m.k. love I have unto you
9. that I m.k. proof of you, whe.
Ep. 6 : 22. that ye m.k. our affairs
Col. 4:8. that he m. k. your estate

KNOW not, or not KNOW.

Ge. 4:9. Where is Abel? said, I k.n.
27 : 2. I k.n. the day of my death
Ex. 5 : 2 I k. n. Lord, nei. will let
10 : 26. k. n. with what serve L.
De. 22 : 2. if k. him n. bring it
1 S. 3 : 7. Sam. did n. yet k. Lord
25:11. bread, give unto men I k.n.
1 K. 3 : 7. I k. n. how to go out or
18:12. Spi. carry thee whi. I k.n.
2 K. 17:26. they k. n. manner of G.
Ezr. 7:25. teach ye them that k.n.
Ne. 4 : 11. They shall n. k. nor see
Jb. 9:5. removeth mts. and th. k.n.
21. Though perf. yet n.k. my soul
15 : 9. What knowest th. we k. n.?
24 : 13. they k. n. ways thereof
16. dig in dark, they k. n. light
32 : 22. I k.n. to give flatt-g titles
36 : 26. God great, we k. him n.
Ps. 71 : 15. for I k. n. the numbers
82 : 5. They k. n. nei. understand
94 : 10. teacheth man, sh. he n.k.
101 : 4. I will n. k. wick. person
Pr. 4 : 19. k. n. at what stumble
5:6. ways moveable, thou canst n.
24 : 12. doth n. he k. it [k.
25: 8. lest k. n. what to do in end
29 : 7. wicked regardeth n. to k.
30 : 18. are four things wh. I k.n.
Ec. 9 : 5. the dead k. n. any thing
Can. 1 : 8. if thou k. n. O fairest
Is. 1 : 3. Israel doth n. k. nor con-
44 : 8. I k. n. any [sider
9. they see not nor k.n., Da. 5: 23.
47 : 11. n. k. whence it ariseth
48 : 6. hidden things, didst n. k.
59 : 8. way of peace they k. n. (2)
Je. 5 : 4. they k. n. way of Lord
8 : 7. my people k. n. judgments
9 : 3. they k.n. me, saith the Lord
10:25. fury upon heath. k. thee n.
14:18. into a land they k.n., 22:28.
Eze. 38 : 14. shalt thou n. k. it?
Ho. 2:8. she did n.k. I gave her corn
Am. 3 : 10. they k.n. to do right
Mi. 4:12. they k. n. thoughts of L.
Mat. 25:12. Verily I say unto you, I k.
you n. [thou sayest, Lu. 22:60.
26 : 70. Peter said, I k. n. what
74. began to swear, saying, I k.
n. the man, 72. Mk. 14 : 68, 71.
Lu. 1 : 34. said Mary, How shall this
be, seeing I k. n. a man
13:25. I k. n. whence you are, 27.
22:57. saying, Woman, I k. him n.
23 : 34. they k.n. what they do
24:16. eyes holden, sho. n. k. him
Jn. 8:55. if say, I k. him n. I sho lie
9 : 12. blind man said, I k. n., 25.
21. who opened his eyes, we k.n.
29. fellow, we k. n. whence he is
10:5. they k. n. voice of strangers
14 : 5. Lord, we k. n. whi. goest
15:21. they k.n. him sent me [13.
20 : 2. we k.n. where they laid him,
Ac. 21:34. when could n.k. certainty
Ro. 8 : 26. we k. n. what pray for
10:19. Did n. Israel k. [other
1 Co. 1 : 16. I k.n. whe. I baptized
2:2. I determined n. to k. any thi.
14 : 11. if I k. n. meaning of voice
2 Co. 13 : 5. k. ye n. J. C. is in you
1 Th. 4 : 5. Gentiles which k. n. G.
2 Th. 1:8. veng. on them k.n. God
1 Ti. 3 : 5. if k. n. how to rule hou.
Jude 10. speak evil of things th. k.n
Re. 3:3. shalt n.k. hour I will come

See **Ye KNOW not.**

We KNOW, or KNOW we.

Ge. 29 : 5. know Laban? w. k. him
2 Ch. 20 : 12. nei. k.w. what to do
Jb. 8:9. but of yesterday and k. noth.
36 : 26. G. is great, w. k. him not
Is. 59 : 12. our iniquities, w. k. th.
Ho. 8:2. Isr. cry, My God, w.k. thee
Mat. 22:16. w.k. thou art true, and
teachest, Mk. 12:14. Lu. 20:21.
Jn. 3 : 2. w. k. thou art a teacher
11. Verily, we speak that w. do k.
4 : 22. w.k. what we worship; for
42. k. this is indeed the Christ
6 : 42. Jes. whose father w. k.
7 : 27. w.k. whence this man is
8 : 52. Now w.k. thou hast a devil
9 : 20. w.k. that this is our son
24. w. k. this man is a sinner
29. w. k. G. spake unto Moses
31. w. k. G. heareth not sinners
14 : 5. L. w. k. not whither thou
goest, how can w. k. the way
21:24. w. k. his testimony is true
Ac. 28:22. w.k. it is spoken against
Ro. 3 : 19. w. k. things law saith
7:14. For w.k. the law is spiritual
8 : 22. w.k. creation groaneth
28. w. k. all thi. work for good
1 Co. 8 : 1. w.k. we all have knowl.
4. w. k. that an idol is nothing
13 : 9. w.k. in part, and prophesy
2 Co. 5 : 1. w. k. if earthly house
16. k. w. no man after the flesh,
yet now k. w. him no more
1 Ti. 1 : 8. w. k. the law is good
He. 10 : 30. w. k. him said, Veng.
1 Jn. 2 : 3. hereby w. k. w.k. him
5. hereby k. w. we are in him
18. w. k. that it is the last time
3 : 2. w. k. that when he appear
14. w.k. we have passed fr. death
19. w. k. th. we are of the truth
24. w. k. that he abideth in us
4:6. k.w. spirit of truth and error
13. k. w. that we dwell in him
5 : 2. By this w.k. we love chil. of
15. if w. k. he heareth us, w.k.
we have the petitions that
18. w. k. whoso. is born of God
19. w. k. that we are of God
20. w. k. the Son of G. is come,
that w. may k. him is true

We shall, or would KNOW.

De. 18:21. How s.w.k. word wh. L.
1 S. 6 : 9. s.w.k. it is not his hand
Ho. 6 : 3. Then s.w.k. if we follow
Ac. 17:20. w.w.k. what things mean

Ye KNOW, or KNOW ye.

Ge. 29 : 5. k. y. Laban, son of Na.?
31 : 6. y.k. wi. my power I served
44 : 27. y. k. my wife bare 2 sons
Ex. 23:9. y.k. the heart of a stranger
De. 29 : 16. y. k. how we dwelt in la.
Jos. 23:14. and y.k. in all your hearts
Ju. 18:14. y.k. is in hou. an ephod
1 K. 22 : 3. k. y. Ramoth is ours?
2 K. 9:11. y.k. man and his commu.
Jb. 13 : 2. What k. y. same I know
Ps. 100 : 3. k. y. that L. he is God
Is. 51 : 7. y. that k. righteousness
Je. 26:15. k.y. if ye put me to death
48 : 17. all y. that k. his name
Mat. 7 : 11. If y. being evil k. how to
give good gifts, Lu. 11 : 13.

Mat. 20:25. y.k. princes of the Gentiles, Mk.10:42. [28. Lu. 21:30.
24:32. y.k. summer nigh, Mk. 13:
25 : 13. Watch, for y. k. neith. day
26 : 2. y. k. aft. two days is feast
Lu. 21:31. k.y.kingd. of God is nigh
Jn. 7:28. y. both k. me, and whence
8:19. y. nei. k. me nor my Father
11 : 49. y. k. nothing at all
13: 12. k. y. what I have done
17. if y. k. these things, happy
14:4. whither I go y. k. way y.k.
7. from henceforth y. k. him, 17.
15 : 18. y. k. that it hated me bef.
Ac. 2 : 22. man approved, as y. k.
3:16. man strong wh. y. see and k.
10 : 28. y. k. it is unlawf for Jew
37. y. k. which was published
15 : 7. y. k. that a good while ago
19:25. y.k.th.by this craft we have
20:18. y.k. fr. 1st day that I came
34. y. k. these hands ministered
1 Co. 12 : 2. y. k. ye were Gentiles
15: 58. y. k. labour is not in vain
16 : 15. y. k. house of Stephanas
2 Co. 8: 9. y. k. grace of our Lord
Ga. 3: 7. k.y. they wh. are of faith
4:13. y.k. how through infirmities
Ep. 5 : 5. y.k. th. no whoremonger
Ph. 2 : 22. y. k. the proof of him
4:15. y.Phil-ns k.also in beginning
1 Th. 1: 5. y. k. manner of men we
2:2. shamefully entreated, as y.k.
5. nei.used flattering words, as y.
11. y. k. how we exhorted [k.
3 : 4. as it came to pass, and y. k.
4 : 2. y.k. com-ts we gave by Lord
2 Th. 2 : 6. y. k. what withholdeth
He. 12 : 17. y. k. when he wo. have
inherited [is set at
13:23. k.y. that our bro. Timothy
1 Pe.1:18. y.k. ye were not redeem.
2 Pe.1:12.in rememb. tho.y.k.them
3:17. seeing y.k. these things bef.
1 Jn. 2 : 20. y. k. all things
21. because y. k. it [ev. one
29. if y.k. he is righte. y.k. that
3:5.y.k.he was manifested to take
15. y. k. no murderer hath eter.
4 : 2. Hereby k.y. the Spirit of G.
3 Jn. 12. y. k. our record is true

Ye KNOW not, or KNOW ye not.

2 S. 3 : 38. k. y. n. is a prince fallen
2 Ch. 32 : 13. k. y. n. what I have
Jb. 21 : 29. do y.n.k. their tokens
Is.43:19.spring forth, sh. y.n.k. it
Je. 7 : 9. walk after gods y. k. n.
16:13. into land y.k.n. [mean
Eze.17:12. k.y.n.what these things
Mat. 20:22. Jesus said, y.k.n. what
ye ask, Mk. 10 : 38.
24 : 42. y.k. n.what hour your L.
Mk. 4 : 13. said, k. y. n. parable?
10 : 38. y. k. n. what ye ask
12:24. err, bec. y.k. n. Scriptures
13 : 33. watch, y. k. n. time, 35.
Lu. 9 : 55. y. k. n. spirit ye are of
Jn.1:26.one am. you, whom y.k.n.
4 : 22. Ye worship y. k. n. what
32. I have meat y. k. n. of
7 : 28. sent me is true, wh. y.k.n.
8 : 19. y. neither k. me nor Fa.
9 : 30. that y. k. n. whence he is
Ro. 6 : 3. k. y. n. that so many as
were baptized
16. k.y.n. to wh. ye yield serv-ts
7:1. k.y.n. breth. I speak [15,19.
1 Co. 3 : 16. k. y. n. ye are tem., 6:
5: 6. k.y.n. a little leaven leav-th
6 : 2. Do y. n. k. saints shall judge
3. k. y. n. we sh. judge angels?
9. k. y. n. unright. not inherit
16. k. y. n. he joined to a harlot
9:13. Do y. n. k. they wh. minister
24. k. y. n. that they which run
a race, run all

2 Co. 13 : 5. k.y.n. that Jesus is in
Ja. 4:4. k.y.n. friendship of world
14. y. k. n. what be on morrow
1 Jn.2:21. not written, bec. y.k.n.

Ye shall KNOW. [truth

Ex.16:6. at even, y.s.k. L. brought
Nu.14:34.y.s.k.my breach of prom.
16 : 28. y.s.k. L. sent me, Zch. 2:
9.–6 : 15.
Jos.3:10.y.s.k. living G. is am.you
Eze. 14 : 23. y. s. k. I have not done
without cause all I have
17: 21. y.s.k. I L. spoken, 37 : 14.
22:22. y.s.k. I the L. have poured
Jo.2:27.y.s.k. I am in midst of Isr.
Mat.7:16. y.s.k. them by fruits,20.
Jn. 8 : 28. s. y. k. that I am he
32. y.s.k. truth, truth sh. make
14 : 20. y.s.k. I am in my Father
2 Co.13:6.y.s.k. we not reprobates

KNOWEST.

Ge. 30 : 26. k. service I have done
29. k. how I have served thee
47 : 6. if k. any man of activity
Ex. 10 : 7. k. not E. is destroyed
32 : 22. k. peo. are set on mischief
Nu. 10:31. k. how we are to encamp
11: 16. thou k. to be elders of peo.
20 : 14. k. travail hath befallen
De. 7 : 15. the diseases of Egypt
which thou k.
9 : 2. children of Anakim, thou k.
20:20. k. they be not trees for meat
28 : 33. nation thou k. not sh. eat
Jos. 14 : 6. k. thing the Lord said
Ju. 15:11. k. not Philis. are rulers
1 S. 28 : 9. thou k. what Saul hath
done [dead
2 S. 1:5. How k. Saul and Jona. be
2 : 26. k. not it will be bitterness
3 : 25. Thou k. Abner son of Ner
7 : 20. k. thy serv., 1 Ch. 17 : 18.
17 : 8. said Hushai, thou k. thy fa.
1 K. 1 : 18. the king, thou k. it not
2: 5. thou k. what Joab did to me
9. k. what oughtest to do unto him
15. k. that kingdom was mine
44. k. wickedn. thou didst to Da.
5 : 3. Thou k. how Da. could not
6. k. there is not am. us that can
8 : 39. whose heart thou k. thou
only k. 2 Ch. 6:30 [master, 5.
2 K. 2 : 3. k. thou L. will take thy
4 : 1. k. thy servant did fear Lord
Jb. 10 : 7. Thou k. I am not wicked
15 : 9. What k. that we know not
20:4. k. thou not this of old, since
34: 33. speak what thou k. [if k.
38:5. Who laid measures of earth
18. breadth declare, if k. it all
21. k.it, bec. thou wast then born
33. k. thou ordinances of heaven
39:1. k. when goats bring forth, 2.
Ps. 40 : 9. O L. thou k., Je. 15 : 15.
69:5. O God, thou k., my foolishn.
139 : 2. Thou k. my downsitting
4. lo, O Lord, thou k. it altoge.
Pr. 27 : 1. k. not what day may bri.
Ec. 11 : 2. k. not what evil shall be
5. As thou k. not way of Spirit,
so k. not works of God
6. thou k. not whe. shall prosper
Is. 55 : 5. call a nation thou k. not
Je. 5 : 15. nation whose lang. k. not
12 : 3. But thou, O Lord, k. me
15: 14. into land thou k. not,17.4.
17:16.nor desired woef.day,thou k.
18: 23. k. their counsel to slay me
33:3. will shew things thou k. not
Eze. 37: 3 I ans-d, O L. thou k.
Da. 10 : 20. k. whf. I come unto thee
Zch. 4 : 5. k. not what these be, 13.
Mat. 15:12. k. Phari. were offended
Mk.10:19.Thou k. com-ts,Lu 18:20.
Lu. 22 : 34. thrice deny thou k. me
Jn. 1:48. Nath. said, Whence k. me
3:10. master, and k. not these thi.

Jn. 13:7. What I do,thou k.not now
16:30. sure thou k. all thi., 21:17.
19 : 10. k. not I power to crucify
21:15. L. thou k. I love thee, 16,17.
Ac. 1 : 24. k. hearts of all men
25 : 10. done no wrong, as thou k.
Ro. 2 : 18. k. his will and approvest
1 Co. 7 : 16. what k. O wife, O man?
2 Ti. 1 : 15. k. all in Asia be turned
18. how he ministered, thou k.
Re. 3 : 17. k. not thou art wretched
7:14. I said unto him, Sir, thou k.

KNOWETH. [tender

Ge. 33 : 13. My lord k. chil. are
Le. 5 : 3. k. of it, he be guilty, 4.
De. 2 : 7. he k. thy walking thro.
34 : 6. no man k. of Moses' sepul.
Jos. 22 : 22. L. God of gods, he k.
1 S. 3:13. Eli's house for iniq. he k.
20 : 3. Thy fa. k. I found grace
23:17. that also Saul my father k.
2 S. 14 : 22. serv k. I found grace
17:10. all Isr. k. thy fa. is mighty
Jb. 11:11. he k. vain men, he seeth
15:23. be k. day of darkn. is ready
23 : 10. he k. the way that I take
28 : 7. There is a path no fowl k.
23. God underst-h and k. place
34:25. k. their works and overturn.
Ps. 1 : 6. L. k. way of righteous
37:18. Lord k. days of the upright
44 : 21. he k. secrets of the heart
74:9. nei. any am. us k. how long
94 : 11. L. k. thoughts of man are
103:14. he k. our frame, rememb-h
104:19. the sun k. his going down
138 : 6. but proud he k. afar off
139:14. that my soul k. right well
Pr. 9 : 13. foolish woman k. noth.
14: 10. heart k. his own bitterness
Ec. 6 : 8. poor, that k. to walk bef.
7:22. own heart k. thou hast cursed
9:1. no man k. either love or hatr.
Is. 1:3. ox k. his owner, the ass his
Je.8:7. stork k. her appointed times
9:24. he understandeth and k. me
Da. 2 : 22. he k. what is in darkness
Na.1:7. L. k. them th. trust in him
Zph. 3 : 5. but unjust k. no shame
Mat. 6 : 8. Fa. k. things ye need
32. k. ye have need of all, Lu.12:30.
11:27. no man k. Son but Fa. nor
any k. Fa. save, Lu 10 : 22.
24 : 36. day k. no man, Mk. 13:32.
Lu. 16 : 15. but God k. your hearts
Jn. 7 : 15. How k. this man letters
27. C. cometh, no man k. whence
10:15. Fa. k. me | 14:17. nei. k. him
19:35. and he k. that he saith true
Ac.15:8. God wh. k. hearts bare wit.
26 : 26. king k. of these bef. whom
Ro. 8 : 27. k. what is mind of Spirit
1 Co. 2 : 11. what man k. things of
man, so things of G k. no man
8 : 2. if think he k. be k. nothing
2 Co. 11 : 11. bec. I love you not?
31. God k. I lie not [God k.
12 : 2. I cannot tell, God k., 3.
2 Ti. 2 : 19. Lord k. them are his
Ja.4:17. him that k. to do good and
2 Pe. 2 : 9. k. how to deliver godly
1 Jn. 3:20. k. all things | 4:6. that
4:7. he that loveth k. God [k. G.
Re. 2:17. new name wh. no man k.
12 : 12. he k. he hath but a short

KNOWETH not. [time

1 K. 1 : 11. and Da. our lord k. it n.
Jb.12:9. Who k.n. L. wrought this?
14 : 21. sons to honour, he k. it n.
18:21. place of him that k.n. God
28: 13. man k.n. the price of
35 : 15. visited in anger, yet k. n.
Ps. 39:6. k.n. who sh. gather them
92:6. a brutish man k.n. nei. fool
Pr. 7 : 23. k. n. it is for his life
9 : 18. he k. n. the dead are there
Ec. 8 : 7. k. n. that which shall be

Ec. 9 : 12. man also **k. n.** his time
10 : 15. he **k. n.** how to go to city
Ho. 7 : 9. gray hairs, yet he **k. n.**
Mk. 4 : 27. seed grow he **k. n.** how
Jn. 7:49. people, who **k. n.** the law
12:35. walketh in darkn. **k.n.** whi.
he goeth, 1 Jn. 2 : 11. ⌈doeth
15 : 15. servant **k.n.** what his lord
Ac. 19:35. man **k. n.** that Ephes-ns
1 Jn.3:1.therefore the world **k.** us **n.**
4 : 8. he that loveth not **k.n.** God

Who KNOWETH.

Es.4:14.**w.k.**whe. art come to king.
Jb. 12 : 3. **w. k.** not such things
Ps.90:11.**w.k.** power of thine anger
Pr. 24 : 22. **w.k.** ruin of both?
Ec. 2 : 19. **w.k.** whe. he be wise or
3:21.**w.k.** spirit of man that goeth
6 : 12. **w. k.** what is good for man
8 : 1. **w.k.** interpretation of thing?
Is. 29 : 15. Who seeth us, **w.k.** us?
Jo. 2 : 14. **w. k.** if he will repent

KNOWING.

Ge. 3 : 5. as gods, **k.** good and evil
43 : † 7. **k.** he would say, Bring
1 K. 2 : 32. slew them, Da. not **k.**
2 Ch. 2:†12. wise son, **k.** prudence
Mat.9:4.Jes.**k.** thoughts, Lu.11:17.
22 : 29. Ye err, not **k.** Scriptures
Mk. 5 : 30. Jes. **k.** in hims. virtue
33.wom. **k.** what was done in her
6 : 20. feared John, **k.** he was just
12 : 15. he **k.** their hypocrisy, said
Lu. 8 : 53. **k.** that she was dead
9 : 33. one for Elias, not **k.** what
Jn. 13:3. Jesus **k.** Fa. had given all
18:4. Jesus **k.** all that should come
19 : 28. Jesus **k.** all were accompl.
21:12. none durst ask, **k.** it was L.
Ac. 2 : 30. **k.** that God had sworn
5 : 7. wife not **k.** what was done
18 : 25. **k.** only baptism of John
20 : 22. not **k.** things sh. befall me
Ro. 1 : 32. Who **k.** judgm. of God
2 : 4. not **k.** goodness of G. leadeth
5 : 3. **k.** tribulation worketh pati.
6 : 6. **k.** this, our old man is cruci.
9. **k.** C. being raised from dead
13 : 11. **k.** the time, it is high time
2 Co 1 : 7. **k.** as ye are partakers of
4 : 14. **k.** that he wh. raised L. J.
5 : 6. **k.** whilst at home in body
11. **k.** the terror of the Lord, we
Ga. 2 : 16. **k.** a man is not justified
Ep. 6 : 8. **k.** whatso. good any doeth
9. **k.** master is in heav., Col. 4:1.
Ph. 1 : 17. **k.** I am set for defence
Col. 3 : 24. **k.** of L. ye rec. reward
1 Th. 1:4. **k.** beloved, your election
1 Ti. 1:9. **k.** this, law is for lawless
6:4.is proud,**k.**nothing, but doting
2 Ti. 2:23.questions, **k.** they gender
3 : 14. **k.** of wh. thou learned th.
Tit. 3 : 11. **k.** such, is subverted
Phm. 21. **k.** thou wilt do more
He. 10 : 34. **k.** ye have in heaven a
11 : 8. he went out, not **k.** whither
Ja. 1 : 3. **k.** this, trying of faith
3 : 1. **k.** we shall rec. greater con-
1 Pe. 3 : 9. **k.** ye are called ⌊dem.
5 : 9. **k.** same afflic. are accompl-d
2 Pe.1:14. **k.** shortly I must put off
20. **k.** that no prophecy of Scrip.
3 : 3. **k.** there shall come scoffers

KNOWLEDGE.

Ge. 2 : 9. tree of **k.** of good and, 17.
Ex. 31 : 3. filled Bezal. in **k.**, 35:31.
Le. 4 : 23. if sin come to his **k.**, 28.
Nu. 24 : 16. knew **k.** of Most High
Ru. 2 : 10. shouldest take **k.** of me
19. blessed he did take **k.** of thee
1 S. 2 : 3. the Lord is a God of **k.**
23 : 23. take **k.** of all lurking pla.
1 K. 9 : 27. Hiram sent shipmen had
k. of sea, 2 Ch. 8 : 18.
2 Ch. 1:10. Give me **k.** that ⌈ed
11. hast asked **k.** | 12.**k.**is grant-

Ne. 10 : 28. having **k.** separated
Jb. 15 : 2. wise man utter vain **k.**?
21:14. we desire not **k.** of thy ways
22. Shall any teach God **k.**
33 : 3. my lips sh. utter **k.** clearly
34 : 2. give ear ye that have **k.**
36 : 3. I will fetch my **k.** from afar
4. he that is perfect in **k.**, 37:16.
Ps. 19:2. night unto night sheweth
73:11. is there **k.** in Most High ⌊**k.**
94 : 10. he that teacheth man **k.**
119 : 66. Teach me judgm. and **k.**
139 : 6. Such **k.** is too wonderful
144:3.what is man,takest **k.** of him
Pr. 1 : 4. to give young man **k.**
7. fear of Lord is beginning of **k.**
22.fools hate **k.** | 2:3. if criest aft
29. that they hated **k.** ⌊**k.**
2 : 6. out of his mouth cometh **k.**
10. when **k.** is pleasant unto soul
3 : 20. By his **k.** depths are broken
5:2. and that thy lips may keep **k.**
8 : 9. are right to them th. find **k.**
10. **k.** rather than choice gold
12. and find out **k.** of inventions
9 : 10. **k.** of the Holy is underst-g
10:14.Wise men lay up **k.** but fool-
11:9. thro.**k.**just be delivered ⌊ish
12 : 1. loveth instruction loveth **k.**
23. A prudent man concealeth **k.**
13:16.prudent man dealeth with **k.**
14 : 6. **k.** is easy to him underst-h
7. perceivest not in him lips of **k.**
18. prudent are crowned with **k.**
15:2.tongue of wise useth **k.** aright
7. lips of wise disperse **k.** ⌈**k.**
14. heart hath underst-g seeketh
17 : 27. hath **k.** spareth his words
18:15. heart of prudent getteth **k.**
ear of the wise seeketh **k.**
19:25. reprove, he will underst. **k.**
27. Cease to err from words of **k.**
20 : 15. lips of **k.** precious jewel
21:11.wise is instructed,he rec-h **k.**
22 : 12. eyes of Lord preserve **k.**
17. apply thine heart unto my **k.**
20. written excellent things in **k.**
23 : 12. apply ears to words of **k.**
24:4. by **k.** sh. chambers be filled
5. man of **k.** increaseth strength
14.so **k.** of wisd. be unto thy soul
28:2. by man of **k.** state prolong-d
30 : 3. nor have the **k.** of holy
Ec. 1:16. my heart experience of **k.**
18. increaseth **k.** incr-h sorrow
2 : 21. a man whose labour is in **k.**
26. God giveth man **k.** and joy
7 : 12. the excellency of **k.** is life
9:10. nor **k.** in the grave, whither
12 : 9. preacher taught people **k.**
Is. 8 : 4. bef. child have **k.** to cry
11 : 2. spirit of **k.** and of fear of L.
28 : 9. Whom shall he teach **k.**?
32 : 4. heart of rash understand **k.**
33:6.wisd.and **k.** shall be stability
40 : 14. who taught him judgm. **k.**
44:19.nei.is there **k.** nor underst-g
44:25. and maketh their **k.** foolish
47:10. Thy **k.** hath perverted thee
53:11.by **k.**my righte. serv. justify
Je. 3 : 15. pastors feed you with **k.**
10:14.Ev. man is brutish in his **k.**,
11:18. L. given me **k.** of it ⌊51:17.
Da. 1 : 4. children cunning in **k.**
17. God gave **k.** | 2:21. giveth **k.**
5 : 12. excell. spirit and **k.** in Dan.
12:4. many run, **k.** shall be incr-d
Ho. 4 : 6. peo. destroyed for lack of
k., rejected **k.** I will reject thee
Ha. 2 : 14. earth filled wi. **k.** of L.
Mal. 2 : 7. priest's lips sho. keep **k.**
Mat. 14 : 35. men had **k.** of him
Lu. 1 : 77. To give **k.** of salva. by
11 : 52. ye have taken away key of
Ac. 4:13. they took **k.** of them ⌊**k.**
17:13. **k.** word of G. was preached
24 : 8. mayest take **k.** of these thi.

Ac.24:22.more perfect **k.** of th. way
Ro. 1 : 28. not like to retain G. in **k.**
2 : 20. which hast form of **k.**
3 : 20. for by law is the **k.** of sin
10 : 2. a zeal, but not acc. to **k.**
15 : 14. that ye are filled wi. all **k.**
1 Co. 1 : 5. are enriched in all **k.**
8 : 1. we all have **k.** **k.** puffeth up
7. there is not in ev. man hath **k.**
10.if see thee wh. hast **k.** at meat
11.thro.thy **k.** weak broth. per-h
12 : 8. to ano. the word of **k.** by
13 : 2. though I understand all **k.**
8. whe. be **k.** it sh. vanish away
14 : 6. exc. I speak by revela. or **k.**
2 Co.2:14.manifest savour of his **k.**
4 : 6. light of **k.** of the glory of G.
6:6.By pureness, by **k.**by longsuff.
8:7. as ye abound in faith, and **k.**
11:6. rude in speech, yet not in **k.**
Ep. 1 : 17. give wisd. in **k.** of him
3 : 4. read, ye may underst. my **k.**
19. love of C. which passeth **k.**
4:13.in unity of faith and **k.**of Son
Ph. 1 : 9. th. love abound more in **k.**
3:8. all things but loss for **k.** of C.
Col. 1:9. be filled with **k.** of his will
2 : 3. In whom are hid treas. of **k.**
3 : 10. on new man renewed in **k.**
1 Ti. 2 : 4. all to come to **k.** of truth
2 Ti. 3 : 7. never able to come to **k.**
He. 10 : 26. if we sin after rec. **k.**
Ja. 3 : 13. Who is endued with **k.**?
1 Pe. 3:7. husbands dwell acc. to **k.**
2 Pe. 1: 3. thro. **k.** of him called us
5. add to virtue **k.** to **k.** tem-
8.nor unfruitf. in **k.**of L. ⌊per.,6.
3 : 18. grow in **k.** of our L. Jesus

KNOWLEDGE of GOD.

Pr. 2 : 5. Then shalt find **k. o.** G.
Ho. 4 : 1. is no **k.o.G.** in the land
6:6.desired **k.o.**G.more than off-gs
Ro. 11 : 33. the riches of **k. o.** G.
1 Co. 15 : 34. some have not **k.o.G.**
2 Co.10:5. exalteth itself ag.**k.o.G.**
Col. 1 : 10. increasing in **k. o.** G.
2 Pe. 1 : 2. peace thro. the **k. o.** G.

KNOWLEDGE of the Lord.

2 Ch. 30 : 22. taught good **k. o.** L.
Is. 11 : 9. earth be full of **k. o.** L.
2 Pe. 2 : 20. escaped pollu. thro. **k.**

No KNOWLEDGE. ⌊o.L.

De.1:39. chil. in that day had **n.k.**
Ps.14:4.workers of iniq. **n.k.**, 53:4.
Is.5:13. into captiv. bec. have **n.k.**
45 : 20. **n. k.** that set up images
58 : 3. afflicted soul, takest **n. k.**
Je. 4 : 22. to do good, have **n. k.**

Without KNOWLEDGE.

Nu. 15:24.committed **w.k.**of cong.
Jb. 34 : 35. Job hath spoken **w. k.**
35 : 16. he multiplieth words **w.k.**
36:12.sh.perish by sword,die **w.k.**
38 : 2. darkeneth counsel **w. k.**
42 : 3. Who hideth counsel **w. k.**
Pr. 19 : 2. not good soul be **w. k.**

KNOWN.

Ex. 2 : 14. Surely this thing is **k.**
21 : 36. if **k.** that ox used to push
33 : 16. wherein shall it be **k.** here
Le. 4 : 14. When the sin sinned is **k.**
5:1.witness wheth. he hath **k.** of it
Nu 31 : 17. kill ev. woman **k.** man
De. 1:13. take wise men, and **k.**, 15.
21 : 1. it be not **k.** who slain him
Jos. 24 : 31. wh. had **k.** works of L.
Ju.21:12. virgins th. had **k.** no man
1 S. 6 : 3. be **k.** to you why his ha.
1 K. 18 : 36. let it be **k.** thou art G.
Ezr. 4:12. Be it **k.** unto ki., 13.-5:8.
Ne. 4 : 15. heard it was **k.** unto us
Es. 2 : 22. thing was **k.** to Mordecai
Ps. 9 : 16. L. is **k.** by the judgment
31 : 7. **k.** my soul in adversities
48 : 3. God is **k.** in her palaces for
67 : 2. thy way be **k.** upon earth
69 : 19. Thou hast **k.** my reproach

Ps.76:1. In Judah is G. k. his name
78: 3. sayings of old: we have k.
79: 10. let him be k. am. heathen
88: 12. thy wonders be k. in dark?
91: 14. on high, bec.k. my name
119: 79. have k. thy testimonies
152. I have k. of old thou founded
139: 1. O Lord, thou hast k. me
Pr. 10:9. pervert. his ways sh. be k.
12:16. A fool's wrath is presently k.
20: 11. a child is k. by his doings
31: 23. Her husband is k. in gates
Ec. 5: 3. fool's voice is k. by words
6: 10. and it is k. that it is man
Is. 12: 5. this is k. in all the earth
19: 21. the L. shall be k. to Egypt
61:9. their seed sh. be k. am. Gent.
66:14. hand of L. be k. tow. serv-s
Je. 5: 5. they have k. way of L.
28: 9. then shall profit be k.
Eze. 36: 32. saith Lord, be it k. unto you, Ac. 4: 10.-13:38.-28:28.
38:23. I will be k. in eyes of na-s
Da. 3:18. be it k. unto thee, O king
4: 26. aft. have k. heavens do rule
Am. 3: 2. You only have I k. of
Zch. 14: 7. day shall be k. to Lord
Mat. 12: 7. if k. what this meant
33. tree is k. by fruit, Lu. 6: 44.
24: 43. if goodman had k., Lu. 12: 39.
Lu.7:39. if prophet, wo. have k.
19: 42. If hadst k. in this thy day
24: 35. was k. in breaking of br.
Jn. 7: 4. he seeketh to be k. openly
8: 19. if ye had k. me, ye should have k. my Father also, 14: 7.
10: 14. I kn. my sheep, and am k.
17: 7. they have k. | 8. k. surely
25. I have k. thee, these have k.
18: 15. that disciple which was k. unto high priest, 16. [Jerus.
Ac. 1: 19. k. unto all dwellers at
2:14. be this k. unto you, hearken
9: 24. laying wait was k. of Saul
42. it was k. throughout all Joppa
15:18. k. unto G. are all his works
19: 17. this was k. to all the Jews
22:30. wo. have k. certainty, 23:28.
Ro. 1: 19. which may be k. of God
11: 34. For who hath k. the mind of the Lord, 1 Co. 2: 16.
1 Co. 2: 8. for had they k. it
8: 3. same is k. of him
13: 12. then shall I k., as I am k.
14: 7. how be k. what is piped
9. how be k. what is spoken?
2 Co. 3: 2. are our epistle k. and
5: 16. tho. have k. C. after flesh
6: 9. As unknown and yet well k.
Ga. 4:9. aft. have k. G. or k. of G.
Ep. 3: 10. might be k. by church
Ph. 4: 5. moderation k. unto all
2 Ti. 3: 10. hast fully k. my doctr.
15. fr. child hast k. holy Scriptu.
4: 17. preaching might be fully k.
1 Jn. 2: 13. bec. ye have k. him, 14.
4: 16. we have k. the love G. hath
2 Jn. 1. all that have k. the truth

Made or **madest KNOWN.**

Ge. 45: 1. Joseph m. himself k. unto his brethren
Ne. 9: 14. m-t k. thy holy sabbath
Ps. 98: 2. L. hath m. k. his salva.
103: 7. m. k. his ways unto Mo.
Pr. 14:33. in midst of fools is m.k.
22: 19. I have m. k. to thee this
Eze.20:5. m. myself k. unto th., 9.
Da. 2: 15. Arioch m. thing k. to
17. Daniel m. thing k. to Hana.
23. m. k. unto me what we desired m.k. unto us k.'s matter
† 28. God hath m. k. to king, 45.
Ho. 5: 9. have I m. k. that sh. be
Lu. 2: 15. wh. Lord m. k. unto us
17. they m. k. abroad saying
Jn. 15:15. all I heard, I have m.k.
Ac. 2: 28. m. k. to me ways of life
Ac.7:13. Jo. was m.k. to breth. and Jo.'s kindred m. k. unto Pha.
Ro. 16: 26. m. k. to all nations
Ep.1:9. Having m. k. unto us mys.
3: 3. how by revela. he m.k. unto
5. in other ages was not m. k.
Ph. 4: 6. requests be m.k. unto G.
2 Pe. 1: 16. we m. k. coming of L.

Make, eth, ing, KNOWN.

Nu. 12: 6. will m. myself k. unto
1 S. 28: 15. m. k. unto me what I shall do [105: 1.
1 Ch. 16: 8. m. k. his deeds, Ps.
17: 19. in m-g k. these gr. things
Ps. 78: 5. that they m. them k.
89: 1. will I m. k. thy faithfuln.
106: 8. m. k. his mighty power
145:12. To m. k. his mighty acts
Pr. 1: 23. I will m. k. my words
Is. 38:19. fa. to chil. m.k. thy tru.
64: 2. m. thy name k. to advers.
Eze. 35:11. m. myself k. am. them
39: 7. m. my holy name k. in Isr.
Da.2:5. m.k. unto me the dream, 9.
25. man that will m.k. unto king
26. Art thou able to m.k. dream?
28. Lord m-h k. to the king, 29.
30. sh. m. k. the interpretation,
4: 6, 7, 18.-5: 8, 15, 16, 17.
Ha. 3: 2. in midst of years m. k.
Mat.12:16. sho. not m.k., Mk.3:12.
Ro. 9:22. willing to m. his pow. k.
9: 23. m. k. riches of his glory
Ep. 6: 19. m. k. mystery of gospel
21. Tychicus shall m. k. to you
Col.1:27. To wh. G. will m. k. rich.
4: 9. They shall m. k. unto you

Neither, nor, or **not KNOWN.**

Ge. 19: 8. have 2 dau-s have n. k. man, Nu. 31:18, 35. Ju. 21: 12.
24: 16. n-er had any man k. her
41:21. n. be k. they had eaten th.
31. plenty shall n. be k. in land
Ex. 6:3. by my name JEHOVAH was I n. k. [k., 31: 13.
De. 11: 2. with chil. which have n.
28. gods ye have n. k., 13:2, 6, 13.
21:1. be n. k. who hath slain him
28: 36. nei. thou n-r fa-s k., 64.
Ju. 3:1. had n. k. wars of Canaan
16: 9. brake withs. So strength n.
Ru. 3: 3. make n. thyself k. [k.
14. Let it n. be k. woman came
2 S. 17: 19. and the thing was n.k.
1 K.14:2. n. k. to be wife of Jerob.
Ps. 18: 43. peo. I have n. k. shall
77: 19. and thy footsteps are n.k.
79: 6. upon heath. have n.k. thee
95: 10. n. k. my ways, He. 3: 10.
147: 20. thy judgments, they n.k.
Ec. 6: 5. he hath not seen sun, n-r k. any thing [n. k.?
Is. 40: 21. Have ye n.k.? | 28. Hast
42: 16. lead in paths they n. k.
44:18. They have n.k. ner underst.
45: 4. tho. thou hast n.k. me, 5.
Je. 4: 22. my peo. foolish, n.k. me
9: 16. they n-r fa-s have k., 19:4.
La. 4: 8. they are n. k. in streets
Eze. 32:9. countries thou hast n.k.
Da. 2: 5. if n. make k. dream, 9.
4: 7. did n. make k. interp-n, 5:8.
Ho. 5: 4. they have n. k. the L.
Na. 3: 17. their place is n. k.
Mat. 10: 26. is nothing hid shall n. be k., Lu.8:17.-12:2. [3:12.
12: 16. sho. n. make him k., Mk.
Lu.24:18. a stranger, and hast n.k.
Jn. 8: 55. Yet ye have n. k. him
14:9. yet hast thou n.k. me, Philip
16: 3. because they have n.k. Fa.
17:25. O Fa. world hath n.k. thee
Ro. 3: 17. way of peace have n. k.
7: 7. I had n. k. sin but by law (2)
Ep. 3: 5. in other ages n. made k.
2 Pe.2:21. better n.k. way of righte.
1 Jn. 3: 6. sinner not seen n-er k.
Re. 2:24. n. k. the depths of Satan

KO'A. [thee

Eze. 23: 23. Shoa, K. sh. come ag.

KO'HATH.

Ge. 46: 11. sons of Levi; Gershon, K., Ex. 6:16. Nu.3:17. 1 Ch. 6: 1, 16.-23: 6.
Ex. 6: 18. the sons of K., Nu.3:19, 27, 29.-16:1. Jos. 21:5. 1 Ch. 6: 2, 18, 22, 61, 66, 70.-15:5.-23:12.
18. years of life of K. 133
Nu. 3:27. of K. fam. of Amramites
4: 2. Take sum of sons of K.
4. service of sons of K., 15.-7: 9.
16: 1. Izhar son of K., 1 Ch. 6:38.
1 Ch. 15: 5. sons of K. Uriel chief

KO'HATHITES.

Nu. 3:27. the K., 30.-26:57. Jos.21: 10. 1 Ch.6:33.-9:32. 2 Ch 20:19.
4: 18. cut not off family of K.
34. numbered sons of K., 37.
10: 21. K. bearing the sanctuary
Jos. 21:4. lot out for K., 1 Ch.6:54.
2 Ch. 29: 12. sons of K. sanctified
34: 12. sons of K. to set work for- [ward

KOLAI'AH.

Ne.11:7. K. son of Pedaiah, Je.29:20.

KO'RAH = CORE.

Ge. 36: 5. Aholibamah bare K.
16. duke K., 18. [Nu. 16: 1.
Ex.6:21. sons of Izhar; K. Nepheg,
24. sons of K. Assir, 1 Ch. 6: 37.
Nu. 16: 6. Take censers, K. and +
19. K. gath-d all congr. ag. them
24. get you up fr. tabernacle of K.
40. that he be not as K. and his
49. that died about matter of K.
26: 9. strove in company of K.
10. swallowed them up with K.
11. notwithst. chil. of K. died not
27:3. our fa. not in company of K.
1 Ch. 1: 35. sons of Esau; Jaalam and K. [Aminadab
2: 43. son of Hebron, K. | 6:22. of
9: 19. son of K. over the work
Jude 11. perished in gainsaying of [K.

KO'RAHITE, S.

1 Ch.9:19. the K-s were ov. the work
31. the firstb. of Shallum the K.

KO'RATHITES.

Nu. 26: 58. the family of the K.

KO'RE.

1 Ch.9:19. Shallum son of K. | 26:1.
19. porters am. sons of K. | 2 Ch. [31:14.

KOR'HITES.

Ex.6:24. families of K. | 1 Ch.12:6.-[26:1.
2 Ch. 20: 19. chil. of K.

KOZ.

Ezr. 2: 61. chil. of K., Ne. 7: 63.
Ne. 3:4. son of Urijah, son of K., 21.

KUSHA'IAH = KI'SHI.

1 Ch.15:17. appoin-d Ethan son of K.

L.

LA'ADAH. See MARESHAH.

LA'ADAN.

1 Ch.7:26. L. his son, Ammihud his
23: 8. sons of L. chief | 7, 9.-26:21.

LA'BAN. [Person.] [20.

Ge.24:29. Rebekah had a bro. L., 25:
27: 43. flee thou to L. my brother
28: 2. take a wife of dau-s of L.
5. Jacob, to Padan Aram unto L.
29: 5. Know ye L. son of Nahor +
10. when Jac. saw the dau. of L.
24. L. gave Leah Zilpah, 46: 18.
29. L. gave Rachel Bilhah, 46:25.
30:25. Jac. said unto L. Send me +
36. Jacob fed rest of L.'s flocks
42. feebler were L's stronger Jac.'s
31:2. Jac. beheld counten. of L +
12. seen all L. doeth unto thee
20. Jac. stole unawares to L., 22.
24. G. came to L. in dream

Ge.31:34. L. searched all the tent, but
36. Jacob wroth, chode with L.
55. L. kissed his sons and dau-s
32:4. I have sojourned with L. until

LA'BAN. [Place.]

De 1: 1. spake betw. Paran and L.

LABOUR. [Noun.]

Ge. 31: 42. G. seen l. of my hands
35: 16. Rachel travailed had hard
De. 26:7. L. looked on our l. [l., 17.
Ne. 5: 13. G. shake ev. man fr. l.
Jb. 5:†7 man is born to l. as sparks
39: 11. wilt thou leave l. to him?
16. her l. is in vain without fear
Ps. 78: † 16. it was l. in mine eyes
78: 46 he gave their l. unto locust
90: 10. is their strength l. and sorr.
104: 23. man goeth to his l. till
105: 44. inherited l. of people
107: 12. bro-t down heart with l.
109: 11. let the stranger spoil his l.
128: 2. shalt eat l. of thy hands
Pr. 10: 16. l. of righteous tendeth
13: 11. gathereth by l. sh. increase
14: 23. In all l. there is profit, but
Ec. 1: 3. What profit of all his l.
8. All things full of l. man can-
2: 10. rejoiced in all my l. (2) [not
11. I looked on the l. I had
18. I hated all my l. I had taken
19. sh. he have rule over all my l.
20. cause heart to despair of l.
21. is a man whose l. is in wisd.
22. what hath man of all his l.
24. enjoy good in l., 3: 13.–5: 18.
4:8 yet there is no end of all his l.
9. have a good reward for their l.
5:15. noth of l. he may carry aw.
19. rejoice in l. this is gift of God
6:7. All l. of man is for his mouth
8: 15 sh. abide with him of his l.
9:9. portion in thy l. under the sun
10: 15. l. of foolish wearieth every
Is. 45: 14. l. of E. shall come unto
55: 2. whf. spend your l. for that
Je. 3: 24. shame devoured l. of
20:18. Whf. I out of womb to see l.
Eze. 23: 29. sh. take away all thy l.
29: 20. given him land of E. for his l.
Ha. 3: 17. though l. of olive fail
Hag. 1: 11. drought upon all the l.
Jn. 4: 38. reap that whereon no l.
Ro. 16:6 Mary, who bestowed much
1 Co. 3:8. man receive acc. to l. [l.
15: 58. know your l. is not in vain
Ga. 4: 11. lest I bestowed l. in vain
Ph. 1:22. if in flesh, this fruit of my
2:25. Epaph. my companion in l. [l.
1 Th. 1:3. Rememb-g your l. of love
2:9. For ye remember, breth. our l.
3:5. tempted you, our l. be in vain
2 Th. 3: 8. wrought with l. night
He. 6: 10. not forget your l. of love
Re. 2:2. I know thy l. and patience

LABOURS.

Ex. 23: 16. firstfruits of thy l. (2)
De. 28: 33. thy l. shall nation eat
Pr. 5: 10. l. be in hou. of stranger
Is. 58:3. in fast ye exact all your l.
Je. 20: 5. I will deliver all their l.
Ho. 12:8. in my l. shall find no iniq.
Hag. 2: 17. I smote you in all l. of
Jn. 4: 38. ye are ent-d into their l.
2 Co. 6: 5. in tumults, l. watchings
10: 15. not boasting of oth. men's l.
11: 23. in l. more abund. in stripes
Re. 14: 13. may rest from their l.

LABOUR. [Verb.]

Ex. 5: 9. more work, that they l.
20: 9. Six days shalt l., De. 5: 13.
Jos. 7: 3. make not all people to l.
24: 13. land, for which ye did not l.
Ne. 4: 22. a guard, and l. on day
Jb. 9: 29. wicked, why l. I in vain?
Ps. 127: 1. Except L. build l. in vain
144: 14. That oxen be strong to l.
Pr. 21: 25. his hands refuse to l.
Pr. 23: 4. l. not to be rich, cease
Ec. 4: 8. nor saith, For wh. do I l.
8: 17. tho. a man l. to seek it out
Is. 22:4. I will weep, l. not to comf.
65: 23. They shall not l. in vain
Je. 51: 58. people shall l. in vain
La. 5: 5. under persecution we l.
Mi. 4: 10. l. to bring forth, O Zion
Ha. 2: 13. that people l. in the fire
Mat. 11: 28. Come all ye that l.
Jn. 6: 27. l. not for meat perisheth
Ro. 16: 12. Tryphosa who l. in L.
1 Co. 4: 12. l. with our own hands
2 Co. 5: 9. we l. to be accepted
Ep. 4: 28. rather l. with his hands
Col. 1: 29. Whereunto I l. striving
1 Th. 5: 12. them wh. l. am. you
1 Ti. 4: 10. we both l. suffer repro.
5:17. especially they th. l. in word
He. 4:11. Let us l. to enter into that

LABOURED. [rest

Ne 4: 21. So we l. in the work
Jb. 20:18. wh. he l. for, sh. restore
Ec. 2: 11. on labour I had l. to do
19. rule over labour I have l.
21. to a man that hath not l.
22. of vexation wherein he hath l.
5: 16. what profit that l. for wind?
Is. 47: 12. sorceries wherein hast l.
15. to thee with wh. thou hast l.
49: 4. I said, I have l. in vain
62: 8. drink, for wh. thou hast l.
Da. 6: 14. king l. to deliver Dan.
Jon. 4: 10. gourd for which not l.
Jn. 4: 38. other men l. ye are ent-d
Ro. 16: 12. Persis, who l. much in
1 Co. 15: 10. I l. more abundantly
Ph. 2: 16. I have not l. in vain
4: 3. that l. with me in gospel
Re. 2: 3. hast for my name's sake l.

LABOURER, S.

Mat. 9: 37. harvest plenteous, but
l-s few, Lu. 10:2.
38. pray the Lord that he will
send l-s, Lu. 10: 2.
20: 1. went out early to hire l-s
2. when he had agreed with l-s
8. saith, Call the l-s and give
Lu. 10: 7. l. is worthy of his hire
1 Co. 3: 9. we are l-s toge. with G.
1 Ti. 5: 18. l. is worthy of reward
Ja. 5: 4. hire of the l-s that reaped

LABOURETH.

Pr. 16: 26. He that l. l. for himself
Ec. 3: 9. what profit in that he l.?
1 Co. 16: 16. submit unto ev. one l.
2 Ti. 2: 6. husbandman that l.

LABOURING.

Ec. 5: 12. sleep of l. man sweet
Ac. 20:35. so l. ye ought to support
Col. 4:12. always l. for you in prayer
1 Th. 2: 9. l. night and day

LACE.

Ex. 28: 28. bind breastplate with l.
37. thou shalt put it on a blue l.
39: 31. they tied it to a l. of blue

LA'CHISH. [unto L.

Jos. 10:31. Jos. passed from Libnah
32. Lord delivered L. to Israel
33. Horam came to help L. [lon
34. from L. Josh. passed unto Eg-
12: 11. king of L. one, 10:3, 5, 23.
15:39. had L., 2 Ch. 11:9. Ne. 11:30.
2 K. 14: 19. Amaziah fled to L., 2
Ch. 25: 27.
18: 14. Hez. sent to king to L.
17. k. of Assyria sent Rabshakeh
from L. with host, Is. 36: 2.
19:8. was departed fr. L., Is. 37:8.
2 Ch. 11: 9. Rehoboam built L.
32: 9. laid siege against L.
Je. 34: 7 k. of Bab. fought ag. L.
Mi. 1: 13. O inhabitant of L. bind

LACK. [Noun.]

Ge. 18:28. wilt destroy for l. of five?
Ex. 16:18. that gath-d little had no
l., 2 Co. 8: 15.
Jb. 4: 11. old lion perisheth for l.
of prey
38:41. young wander for l. of meat
Ho. 4:6. peo. destr-d for l. of knowl.
Ph. 2:30. life to supply l. of service
1 Th. 4: 12. may have l. of nothing

LACK. [Verb.]

Ge. 18: 28. if shall l. five of fifty
De. 8: 9. shalt not l. anything
Ps. 34: 10. young lions do l. and
Pr. 28: 27. giveth to poor not l.
Ec. 9: 8. let head l. no ointment
Mat. 19:20. have kept, what l. I yet
Ja. 1: 5. If any of you l. wisd. let

LACKED.

De. 2: 7. L. with thee hast l. noth
2 S. 2: 30. l. of David's serv. 19.
17: 22. l. not one of th. not gone
1 K. 4:27. provided victual, l. nothing
11: 22. what hast thou l. with me?
Ne. 9:21. didst sustain they l. noth.
Lu. 8: 6. withered, it l. moisture
22: 35. without purse, l. ye any
Ac. 4:34. Nei. any am. them that l.
1 Co. 12:24. honour to that which l.
Ph. 4: 10. careful, but l. opportu.

LACKEST, ETH.

Nu. 31: 49. l-h not one man of us
2 S. 3: 29. not fail one l-h bread
Pr. 6: 32. adultery, l-h underst-g
12:9. honoureth hims. and l-h br.
Mk. 10:21. One thing l-t, Lu. 18:22.
2 Pe. 1: 9. l-h these things is blind

LACKING.

Le. 2: 13. nei. suffer salt to be l.
22: 23. not offer lamb hath thi. l.
Ju. 21:3. sho. be one tribe l. in Isr.
1 S. 30: 19. was nothing l. to them
Je. 23: 4. fear no more, nor be l.
1 Co. 16: 17. that l. they supplied
2 Co. 11: 9. was l. breth. supplied
1 Th. 3: 10. might perfect what is l.

LAD, S.

Ge. 21:12. not be grievous bec. of l.
17. God heard the voice of l.
18. lift up l. | 19. gave l. drink
20. God was with the l, he grew
22: 5. I and the l. will go yonder
12. Lay not thine hand upon l.
37: 2. l. was with sons of Bilhah
43: 8. Send the l. with me and we
44: 22. l. cannot leave his father
30. the l. be not with us; his life
is bound up in l.'s life, 31, 34.
32. serv. became surety for l.
33. abide instead of l. let l. go
48: 16. The Angel bless the l-s
Ju. 16: 26. Samson said to the l.
1 S. 20: 21. Behold I will send a l.
35. Jona. with Da. and little l.
36. Jona. said to l. Run, as l. ran
37. Jonathan cried after the l., 38.
39. the l. knew not anything
40. gave his artillery unto his l.
41. soon as l. was gone Da. rose
2 S. 17: 18. l. saw them told Abs.
2 K. 4: 19. said to l. Carry him to
Jn. 6: 9. a l. hath 5 loaves [moth.

LADDER.

Ge. 28: 12. Jac. dreamed a l. set up

LADE, ED.

Ge. 42:26. l-d asses with corn, 44:13.
45: 17. l. your beasts go unto Ca.
Le. 22:† 16. l. thems. with iniquity
1 K. 12: 11. fa. did l. you wi. yoke
Ne. 4:17. that l-d wrought in work
Lu. 11: 46. ye l. men with grievous
Ac. 28:10. they l-d us with such thi.

LADEN.

Ge. 45:23. ten asses l. with good thi.
1 S. 16: 20. Jesse took an ass l.
Is. 1: 4. a people l. with iniquity
Mat. 11:28. Come, all ye are heavy l.
2 Ti. 3: 6. silly women, l. with sins

LADETH, ING.

Ne. 13: 15. some on sab. l-g asses
Ha. 2: 6. Woe to him that l-h hims.

LADING. [Noun.]
Ac. 27: 10. damage not only of l.
LADY, IES.
Ju. 5: 29. wise l-s answered her
Es.1:18. sh. l-s of Persia and Media
Is. 47: 5. no more be l. of kingd-s
7. saidst, I shall be a l. forever
2 Jn. 1. the elder to the elect l.
5. I beseech l. we love one ano.
LA'EL.
Nu. 3: 24. Eliasaph son of L.
LA'HAD.
1 Ch. 4:2. Jahath begat Ahumai, L.
LAHAI'ROI. [25:11.
Ge. 24: 62. Isaac fr. way of well L.,
LAH'MAM. See KITHLISH.
LAH'MI.
1 Ch. 20: 5. Elhanan slew L. bro. of
LAID.
Ge. 9: 23. l. it upon both shoulders
15: 10. Ab. l. each piece one ag.
22: 6. took wood l. it upon Isaac
9. Ab. built altar and l. wood
30: 41. Jacob l. rods bef. cattle
38: 19. she l. by her vail from her
48:14. l. it upou Ephr.'s head, 17.
Ex. 2: 3. she l. it in flags by river
5:9. Let more work be l. upon men
19:7. l. bef. their faces these words
21:30. give whatso. is l. upon him
Nu. 16: 18. ev. man l. incense [(2)
De. 26:6. E-ns l. upon us hard bond
29:22. sicknesses wh. L. l. upon it
Jos. 2: 6. stalks she had l. in order
7: 23. they l. them out bef. Lord
10:27.l. gr. stones in cave's mouth
Ju. 9:24. their bl. be l. upon Abim.
48. bough, l. it on his shoulder
Ru.3:15. six meas-s of barley and l.
4: 16. child and l. it in bosom
1 S. 6: 11. they l. ark upon cart
19: 13. took image l. it in bed
25: 18. figs and l. them on asses
2 S. 18: 17. l. a great heap of stones
1 K.3:20.son and l. it in her bosom,
l. her dead child in my bosom
8: 31. oath be l. upon him, 2 Ch.
13: 29. l. carcass upon ass [6: 22.
30. l. carcass in own grave
15: 27. Isr. l. siege to Gibbethon
17: 19. he l. him on his own bed
18: 33. l. bullock on the wood
2 K. 4: 21. she l. him on the bed
31. l. staff upon face of child
32. child dead, l. upon bed
5: 23. l. them upon 2 of serv-ts
9: 25. L. l. this burden upon him
12: 11. l. it out to carpenters
12. all that was l. out for house
20: 7. they took and l. it on boil
2 Ch.6:22. If man sin and oath be l.
16: 14. l. Asa in bed which was
24: 9. Moses l. on Israel in wilder.
27. greatn. of burdens l. upon him
31: 6. tithes and l. them by heaps
32: 9. hims. l. siege ag. Lachish
Ezr.3:11.shouted bec.founda. was l.
5: 8. timber is l. in walls
Ne. 3: 3. who l. beams thereof, 6.
13: 5. where they l. meat off-gs
Es.10:1. Ahas. l. tribute upon land
Jb. 6: 2. my calamity l. in balances
18: 10. snare is l. for him in gro
38: 5. Who hath l. the measures
6. or who l. the corner stone
Ps. 21: 5. majesty hast l. upon him
31: 4. Pull me out of net l. for me
35: 11. l. to my charge things I
49: 14. Like sheep are l. in grave
62: 9. to be l. in balance, vanity
79:1. they have l. Jerus. on heaps
88:6. Thou hast l. me in lowest pit
89: 19. l. help upon one mighty
105:18. feet hurt, he was l. in iron
119: 30. judgm. have I l. bef. me
110. wick. have l. a snare, 141:9.
137: † 2. they that l. on us heaps
Ps.139:5. hast l. thine ha. upon me
142: 3. privily l. a snare for me
Is. 6: 7. he l. it upon my mouth
42:25. yet l. it not to heart, 57:11.
47:6. hast very heavily l. thy yoke
51: 23. hast l. thy body as ground
53: 6. L. l. on him iniq. of us all
Je. 50:24. I have l. a snare for thee
Eze. 4:5. l. upon thee years of iniq.
11: 7. Your slain which ye have l.
32: 19. be thou l. wi. uncirc-d, 32.
27. l. swords under their heads
29. l. by them slain by sword
33: 29. have l. land most desolate
35:12. saying, They are l. desolate
40: 42. l. instruments whw. they
slew burnt offering [den
Da. 6: 17. stone l. upon mouth of
Ho. 11: 4. and I l. meat unto them
Jo. 1:17. the garners are l. desolate
Am. 2: 8. upon clothes l. to pledge
Ob. 7. have l. a wound under thee
Jon. 3: 6. he l. his robe from him
Mi. 5: 1. he hath l. siege ag. us
Ha. 2: 19. it is l. over with gold
Hag. 2: 15. from bef. a stone was l.
Zch. 3:9. behold the stone I have l.
7:14.they l. pleasant land desolate
Mat.3:10.axe is l. unto root,Lu.3:9.
8: 14. wife's mother l. and sick
27: 60. l. it in his own new tomb
Mk. 6: 29. corpse and l. it in tomb
56. they l. sick in the streets
7:30. daughter l. upon bed
15:46.l. him in a sepul., Ac.13:29.
47. Mary beheld where he was l.
16:6. behold pl. where they l. him
Lu. 2: 7. firstb. l. him in manger
16: 20. Lazarus was l. at his gate
23:53.never man bef. was l.,Jn.19:
55. beheld how body was l. [41.
24: 12. linen clothes l. by thems.
Jn. 11: 34. Where have ye l. him?
41. place where dead was l.
13: 4. l. aside garments, and took
19:42. There l. they Jesus
20:2.know not where th. l. him,13.
15. tell me where hast l. him
21: 9. fish l. thereon and bread
Ac. 3: 2. they l. at gate of temple
4:37.l. money at apostles' feet,5:2.
5: 15. l. them on beds and
7:16. into Sychem, and l. in sepul.
9: 37. they l. her in upper cham.
13:36.David was l. unto his fathers
16: 23. l. many stripes upon them
23:29.noth.l. to his charge worthy
25: 7. l. complaints co. not prove
16. cone-g the crime l. ag. him
28: 3. Pe. had l. sticks upou fire
1 Co. 9: 16. necessity is l. upon me
2 Ti.4:16.I pray it be not l. to their
See FOUNDATION. [charge
LAID down. [came
Jos. 2: 8. bef. they were l. d. she
4: 8. carried them and l. them d.
Ru. 3:7. Ruth uncov-d his feet l.d.
1 S. 3: 2. Eli was l. d. | 3. Sam. l.d.
2 S. 13: 8. Amnon was l. d.
1 K. 19: 6. Elijah did eat l. him d.
21: 4. Ahab came and l. him d.
Ps. 3:5. I l. me d. and slept, I awa.
Is. 14: 8. Since art l. d. no feller
Lu.19:22. taking up that I l. not d.
Ac. 4: 35. l. them d. at apos. feet
7: 58. witnesses l. d. their clothes
Ro.16:4. Who for my life l.d. necks
1 Jn. 3: 16. bec. he l. d. life for us
LAID hand.
Ex. 24:11. upon nobles he l. not h.
2 S. 13:19. Tamar l. h. on her head
Es. 8: 7. he l. his h. upon the Jews
9: 10. on spoil l. not h., 15.
Jb. 29: 9. princes l. h. on mouth
Ps. 139:5. hast l. thine h. upon me
Eze. 39: 21. h. I have l. upon them
Re.1:17. he l. his right h. upon me
LAID hands.
Le. 8: 14. Aa. and sons l. h., 18, 22
Nu. 27: 23. Moses l. his h. upon
Joshua, De. 34:9. [2 Ch. 23:15.
2 K. 11: 16. and they l. h. on her,
2 Ch.29:23.they l.h. upon he goats
Ob. 13. nor l. h. on substance
Mat.18:28. l. h. took him by throat
19:15.he l. h. on them and depar.
26:50.they l.h. on Jes., Mk 14:46.
Mk. 6:5. he l. h. upon few sick folk
Lu. 4: 40. he l. his h. on every one
13: 13. l. his h. on her, she was
made straight [44.-8: 20.
Jn. 7:30. but no man l. h. on him,
Ac. 4: 3. l. h. on the apostles, 5: 18.
6:6. prayed, they l. h. on deacons
8:17.Then l. they their h. on them
13: 3. they l. h. on Paul and Bar.
19:6.when Paul had l. his h. upon
21: 27. stirred peo., l. h. on Paul
28:8. Paul l. h. on Publius' father
LAID hold.
Ge.19:16. men l.h. upon Lot's hand
Ju.19:29. took knife l. h. on concu.
1 S. 15: 27. Saul l. h. upon Sam.'s
2 Ch. 7:22. l. h. on oth. gods [skirt
Jb.18:†20. went bef. l. h. on horror
Mat. 14:3. Herod had l.h. on John,
Mk. 6: 17. [Jes., Mk. 14: 51.
26:55. l. no h. on me | 57. l.h. on
Lu. 23: 26. they l. h. upon Simon
Re. 20: 2. he l. h. on the dragon
LAID up.
Ge. 39:16. she l.u. his garm. by her
41: 48. Joseph l. u. food in cities
Ex. 16:24. they l. it u. till morning
34. Aaron l. u. pot of manna
Nu. 17: 7. Moses l. u. rods bef. L
De. 32: 34. Is not this l. u. in store
1 S. 10: 25. Samuel l. it u. bef. L.
21: 12. David l. u. words in heart
2 K. 20:17. which thy fathers l. u.
Ezr.6:1. treasures were l.u. in Bab.
Jb.23:†12. I have l.u. words of his
Ps.31:19.l.u. for them th. fear thee
Pr. 13:22. wealth of sinners is l. u.
Can.7:13. fruits I have l.u. for thee
Is. 10: 28.l. u. his carriages
15:7.that l.u. sh. they carry away
23: 18. her hire shall not be l. u.
39:6.wh.fathers l. u. be carried to
Je. 36: 20. they l.u. roll in chamb.
Lu. 1: 66. all l. them u. in hearts
12:19. thou hast much goods l. u.
19:20. thy pound I have kept l.u.
Col. 1: 5. hope wh. is l. u. for you
2 Ti. 4: 8. is l. u. for me a crown
LAID wait.
Ju. 9: 34. they l. w. ag. Shechem
43. l. w. in field and looked
16:2.they l.w.all night for Samson
1 S. 15: 2 Amalek l. w. for him in
5. Saul came and l. w. in valley
Jb. 31:9. if I l. w. at neighb.'s door
La. 4: 19. l. w. for us in wilder.
Ac. 20:3. Jews l. w. for him, 23:30.
LAID waste.
Nu.21:30. l. them w. unto Nophah
Ps. 79: 7. l. w. his dwellingplace
Is. 15:1. Kir l. w. | 23:1. Tyre l w.
23:14.ye ships, your strength l.w.
37: 18. kings of Assy. l. w. na-s
64: 11. our pleasant things l. w.
Je. 4: 7. thy cities shall be l. w.,
Eze. 6: 6.-12: 20.-19: 7.-29: 12.
27: 17. whf. this city be l. w.?
Eze. 26:2. I be replen-d she is l. w.
Jo. 1: 7. l. my vine w. barked my
Am. 7:9. sanctuaries of Isr. be l.w.
Na. 3: 7. say, Nineveh is l. w.
Mal. 1: 3. I l. his heritage w. for
LAIDEST. [loins
Ps. 66: 11. l. affliction upon our
Lu. 19: 21. takest up that l. not
LAIN. [down
Ge. 26: 10. have l. with thy wife

Nu. 5: 19. If no man l. with thee
20. man l. with thee beside thy
Ju. 21: 11. destroy woman hath l.
Jb. 3: 13. now should I have l. still
Ps.68:13. though ye have l. am pots
Je. 3:2. where hast not been l. with
Jn. 11: 17. had l. in grave 4 days
20: 12. where body of Jes. had l.

LA'ISH. [Person, Place.]
Ju. 18: 7. five men came to L.
14. went to spy country of L.,27.
29. name of city was L. at first
1 S. 25: 44. Michal given to Phalti
son of L. [the son of L.
2 S.3:15. Ish-bosheth took her from
Is. 10:30. Cause thy voice be heard
to L. O Anathoth

LAKE. [ret
Lu. 5:1. Jes. stood by l. of Gennesa-
2. saw two ships standing by l.
8: 22. let us go unto other side of
23. came storm of wind on l. [l.
33.herd ran violently down into l.
Re. 19: 20. both cast into l. of fire
20: 10. devil was cast into l. of fire
14. death and hell into l. of fire
15. not in book of life, cast into l.
21:8. murderers part in l. burneth

LA'KUM. [L.
Jos. 19:33.coast was fr. Nekeb unto

LAMA. See **ELI lama.**

LAMB.
Ge. 22: 7. where is l. for a off-g?
8. My son, God will provide a l.
Ex.12:3. sh. take every man a l., 21.
4. household be too little for L.
5. Your l. sh. be without blemish
13:13. an ass redeem wi. l., 34:20.
29: 39. one l. offer in morn. other
l. at evening, 41. Nu. 28: 4.
40. with l. a tenth deal of flour,
Nu. 28: 21, 29.-29: 4, 10, 15.
Le. 3:7. If he offer a l., 4: 32.-5:6.-
22: 23.-23: 12.
4: 35. shall take fat, as fat of l.
5: 7. if not able to bring a l., 12:8.
9:3. Take a l. of first year without
blemish, 12: 6.-14:10. Nu.6:12.
-7:15, 21, 27, 33, 39, 45, 51, 57,
63, 69, 75, 81.
14: 12. priest sh. take l. and offer
13. slay l., 25. | 24. l. of tresp.-
17:3.killeth an ox, or a l. [off-g,21.
23: 12. offer a l. without blemish
Nu 6:14. he l. of 1st year for burnt
off-g, ewe l. of 1st year for a sin
15:5. with sacr. for one l. [offering
11. done for one l., 28: 7, 13, 14.
Eze. 46: 15.
1 S. 7: 9. Samuel off-d a sucking l.
17: 34. lion and bear and took a l.
2 S.12:3. noth. save one little ewe l.
4. took the poor man's l.
6. he shall restore the l. fourfold
Is. 11: 6. wolf shall dwell with l.
16:1.Send ye the l. to ruler of land
53:7.as l. to the slaughter,Je.11:19.
65: 25. wolf and l. shall feed toge.
66: 3. sacrifi-h l. as if cut off dog's
Eze. 45: 15. one l. out of flock for a
46: 13. a l. of 1st year prepare, 15.
Ho. 4: 16. L. will feed them as l.
Jn. 1: 29. Behold the L. of God, 36.
Ac. 8: 32. like l. dumb bef. shearer
1 Pe.1:19. as of a l. without blemish
Re. 5: 6. in midst of elders L. slain
8. four beasts fell down before L.
12. Worthy is the L. th. was slain
13. honour, glory, be unto L. for
6: 1. when L. opened one of seals
16. hide us from wrath of the L.
7: 9. great mult. stood bef. the L.
10. Salvation to our G. and the L.
14. made white in blood of the L.
17.L.sh.feed and lead unto fount-s
12:11.overcame him by blood of L.
13: 8. L. slain fr. founda. of world
Re. 13:11. he had 2 horns like l. and
14:1. lo, a L. stood on Mount Sion
4.these are they that follow the L.
10. tormented in presence of L.
15: 3. song of Moses and of the L.
17: 14. war with L. L. overcome
19:7. for marriage of the L. is come
9. that are called unto the marriage supper of the L.
21:9.will shew thee bride, L.'s wife
14. names of 12 apostles of L.
22. God Alm. and L. are temple
23. and the L. is light thereof
27. written in the L.'s book of life
22:1.out of throne of God and L.,3.

LAMBS.
Ge. 30:40. Jacob did separate l. [32.
33:†19. bought for 100 l., Jos.24:†
Nu. 7:17. five l. of 1st year, 23, 29,
35, 41, 47, 53, 59, 65, 71, 77, 83.
87. l. of the first year, twelve
88. l. of 1st year, sixty [29, 32.
29: 13. fourteen l., 17, 20, 23, 26,
29: 18. drink offerings for l. and
rams, 21, 24, 27, 30, 33.
De. 32: 14. with fat of l. and rams
1 S. 15: 9. Saul spared best of l.
2 K. 3: 4. Moab rendered 100,000 l.
1 Ch.29:21. off-d unto L.a thous. l.
2 Ch. 29: 22. priests killed l.
32. number of burnt off-gs 200 l.
35: 7. Josiah gave to the people l.
Ezr. 6: 17. two hund. rams, 400 l.
7: 17. mayest buy speedily l., 6:9.
8:35. seventy-seven l., 12 he goats
Ps. 37:20. wick. shall be as fat of l.
114:4. little hills skipped like l., 6.
Pr. 27: 26. l. are for thy clothing
Is. 1: 11. delight not in blood of l.
5: 17. sh. l. feed aft. their manner
34: 6. sword of l. with blood of l.
40: 11. sh. gather l. with his arm
Je. 51: 40. them like l. to slaughter
Eze. 27:21. occupied with thee in l.
39: 18. ye shall drink blood of l.
46: 4. prince sh. off. unto L. 6 l.
5. meat off-g for l. as able to give,
6. in new moons 6 l. [7, 11.
Am. 6: 4. eat the l. out of the flock
Lu. 10:3. send you as l. am. wolves
Jn. 21: 15. Jesus saith, Feed my l.

Seven LAMBS.
Ge.21:28.Ab. set s. ewe l. by thems.
29. What mean these s. ewe l. set
30.these s. ewe l. thou shalt take
Le. 23:18. offer with the bread s. l.
Nu. 28:11. sh. offer s. l. of 1st year,
19, 27.-29:2, 8, 36. [29: 4, 10.
21. a tenth deal thro-t s. l., 29.-
2 Ch.29:21.brought s. l. for sin off.

Two LAMBS. [3.
Ex. 29: 38. t. l. of first year, Nu. 28:
Le. 14: 10. on eighth day take t. l.
23: 19. then ye shall sacrifice t. l.
20. wave off-g before L. with t. l.
Nu.28:9.on sabbath t. l. of 1st year

LAME.
Le. 21: 18. a l. man not approach
De. 15: 21. if l. shalt not sacrifice it
2 S. 4: 4. Jona. had a son l., 9:3, 13.
5: 6. Exc. take away blind and l.
8. Whoso. smiteth l. and blind
19: 26. ride, bec. thy servant is l.
Jb. 29: 15. eyes to blind, feet to l.
Pr. 26: 7. legs of l. are not equal
Is. 33:23. prey divided, l. take prey
35: 6. shall l. man leap as a hart
Je. 31:8. bring with th. blind and l.
Mal. 1: 8. if ye offer l. for sacrifice
13. ye brought that torn and l.
Mat. 11:5. l. walk, 15:31.-21:14.Lu.
15: 30. those l., blind [7: 22.
Lu. 14: 13. call the poor, the l. and
Ac.3:2.a certain man, l. from womb
11. And as the l. man held Peter
8: 7. many l. were healed [way
He.12:13.lest l. be turned out of the

LA'MECH or **LE'MECH.**
Ge. 4: 18.† Methusael begat L., 5:
19. L. took 2 wives, 23(2) [25,† 26
24. If Cain sevenfold, L. 70 and s.
5: 28.L., 30, 31. 1 Ch.1:3. Lu.3:36.

LAMENT.
Ju. 11:40. dau-s of Isr. yearly to l.
69: † 20. I looked for some to l.
Is. 3: 26. her gates shall l. and
19: 8. fishers shall mourn and l.
32: 12. They shall l. for the teats
Je. 4: 8. For this l. and howl, for
16: 5. neither go to l. them, 6.
22: 18. They shall not l. for him
34: 5. will l. thee, saying, Ah, L.
49: 3. ye daughters of Rabbah, l.
La. 2: 8. he made the wall to l.
Eze. 27: 32. they sh. l. over Tyrus
32: 16. dau-s of nations sh. l. her
Jo. 1: 8. l. like virgin with sackcl.
13. Gird yourselves, l. ye priests
Mi. 2: 4. l. with a doleful lamenta.
Jn. 16: 20. ye shall weep and l.
Re. 18: 9. kings of earth sh. l. Bab.

LAMENTABLE.
Da. 6: 20. king cried with l. voice

LAMENTATION, S.
Ge. 50: 10. mourned with a sore l.
2 S. 1: 17. Da. lamented with this l.
2 Ch. 35:25. singers spake of Josiah
in l-s, they are written in l-s
Ps. 78: 64. their widows made no l.
Je. 6: 26. in ashes make bitter l.
7: 29. take up a l. on high places
9: 10. habitations of wildern. a l.
20. teach ev. one her neighb. l.
31: 15. in Ramah l., Mat. 2: 18.
48: 38. There shall be l. generally
La. 2: 5. Lord hath increased l.
Eze. 2: 10. was written therein l-s
19: 1. take thou up l. for princes
14. This is a l. and sh. be for a l.
26: 17. up a l. for Tyrus, 27:2, 32.
28: 12. l. upon the king of Tyrus
32: 2. take up l. for Pharaoh, 16.
Am. 5:1. a l. ag. you, O hou. of Isr.
16. call such as are skilful of l.
8: 10. turn all your songs into l.
Mi. 2: 4. lament with a doleful l.
Ac. 8:2. made great l. over Stephen

LAMENTED.
1 S.6:19.people l.bec.L.had smitten
7: 2. all house of Isr. l. after Lord
25: 1. all Israelites l. Sam., 28: 3.
2 S. 1: 17. David l. over Saul
3: 33. king l. over Abner and said
2 Ch. 35: 25. Jeremiah l. for Josiah
Je.16:4.sh. die and not be l., 25:33.
Mat.11:17.we mourned ye have not l
Lu. 23: 27. a great company l. Jes.

LAMP.
Ge. 15: 17. a burning l. that passed
Ex 27: 20. cause l. to burn always
1 S. 3: 3. ere l. went out, Samuel
2 S.21:†17. quench not the l. of Isr.
22: 29. thou art my l. O Lord
1 K. 11: † 36. David may have a l.
15:4. for Da.'s sake G. gave him l.
Jb. 12: 5. is as a l. despised [17.†
18: † 6. wick. man's l. put out, 21:
29: † 3. l. shined upon my head
Ps. 18: † 28. thou wilt light my l.
119:105. Thy word is a l. unto feet
132: 17. ordained a l. for anointed
Pr. 6: 23. For commandment is a l.
13: 9. l. of wicked be put out
20:20. curseth fa. his l. be put out
† 27. spirit of man is l. of the L.
Is.62:1.salvation as l. that burneth
Re.8:10. star burning as it were a l.

LAMPS.
Ex. 25: 37. they shall light l., 40:4.
30: 7. when dresseth l. burn inc.
8. when Aaron lighteth l. at even
35: 14. his l. with oil for light
39: 37. they brought l. to Moses
40:25. lighted l. bef. L., Nu. 8:2, 3.

Le. 24 : 2. l. to burn continually, 2
4. order the l. [Ch. 18 : 11.
Nu. 4 : 9. and cover his l.
Ju. 7:16. put l. within pitchers
20. held the l. in their left hand
1 K. 7:49. l. of gold, 2 Ch. 4 : 20, 21.
1 Ch. 28 : 15. for their l. of gold
2 Ch.29:7.they shut doors put out l.
Jb. 41 : 19. Out of mouth burning l.
Eze. 1:13. was like appearance of l.
Da. 10 : 6. his eyes as l. of fire
Mat. 25 : 1. ten virgins which took
7. virgins arose trimmed l. [l.,3,4.
8. Give us oil, our l. are gone out

Seven LAMPS.

Ex. 25 : 27. thou shalt make s. l.
37 : 23. made his s. l. of pure gold
Nu. 8 : 2. s. l. shall give light (2)
Zch. 4 : 2. a candlestick and s. l. (2)
Re. 4 : 5. were s. l. of fire burning

LANCE.

Je. 50:42. that hold the l. are cruel

LANCETS.

1 K. 18 : 28. cut themselves with l.

LAND.

Ge. 2:12. the gold of that l. is good
10 : 11. Out of l. went Asshur [3.
12:1. Get into l. I will shew, Ac. 7:
13:6. l. was not able to bear them
9. Is not the whole l. before thee
17. Arise, walk through the l.
17:8. will give thee and seed the l.,
13 : 15.-28 : 13.-35 : 12.
20 : 15. Behold, my l. is bef. thee
22 : 2. get thee into l. of Moriah
23 : 15. l. is worth 400 shekels
24:37. Canaanite, in whose l. I dwell
26 : 12. Isaac sowed in that l. and
34 : 10. the l. shall be before you
42:9. to see nakedness of the l., 12.
45 : 18. ye shall eat fat of the l.
47:6. in best of l. make fa. dwell, 11.
47:20. bought l. so l. became Pha.'s
22. l. of priests bought he not
49 : 15. the l. th. it was pleasant
50 : 24. l. wh. he sware, Ex. 6 : 8.-
33:1.-De. 6:10, 23.-31:20.-34:4.
Ju. 2 : 1.
Ex. 3 : 8. l. flowing with milk and
honey, 17.-13:5.-33: 3. | Le. 20:
24. Nu. 14 : 8.-16 : 13, 14. De. 6 :
3.-11:9.-26:9, 15.-27:3.-31 : 20.
Jos. 5 : 6. Je. 11 : 5.-32:22. Eze.
8 : 24. l. corrupted by flies [20 : 6.
10 : 15. so l. was darkened, 12.
12 : 25. be come to l., Le. 19 : 23.-
23 : 10.-25:2. Nu. 15 : 2, 18. De.
17 : 14.-18 : 9.-26 : 1.
20 : 12. days may be long upon l.
Le. 16 : 22. goat bear iniq-s into a l.
18 : 25. the l. is defiled, theref. 27.
28. l. spue not you out, 20 : 22.
19:29. l. become full of wickedness
25:2. shall l. keep a sab., + 26 : 34.
6. sabbath of the l. be meats
23. l. sh. not be sold, l. is mine
26:4. l. sh. yield her incr., + 25:19.
34. sh. l. rest and enjoy sabbaths
38. l. of enemies shall eat you
42. and I will remember the l.
43. The l. shall be left of them
27:†16. l. of a homer be valued
Nu. 13:16. Moses sent to spy out l. +
18. see the l. what it is, 19, 20.
32. l. is a l. eateth up inhab-ts
14:6. th. searched l. rent clothes +
23. they shall not see the l. I
24. Caleb will I bring into the l.
20 : 24. he shall not enter into l.
21:26. taken all his l. out of hand
34. into thy hand his l., De. 3 : 2.
27:12. Get thee into mt. and see l.
32:4. country L. smote l. for cattle
35:33. blood defileth l. and l.
De. 1 : 21. L. hath set l. before thee
36. to him will I give the l.
2:20. accounted l. of giants, 3 : 13.
De. 8 : 8. a l. of wheat and vines
9. + l. wherein bread, l. wh. stones
9 : 28. not able to bri. them into l.
10 : 7. a l. of rivers of waters
11 : 12. A l. Lord thy G. careth for
17. the l. yield not her fruit
15:11. poor sh. never cease out of l.
19:1. l. the L. thy G. giveth, 27:2.
29:23. whole l. brimstone and salt
28. cast them into another l. as
30:18. sh. not prolong day upon l.
32 : 43. will be merciful unto his l.
52. shalt see the l. but not go in
33 : 13. Blessed of the L. be his l.
34 : 1. Lord shewed him all the l.
Jos. 2 : 1. saying, Go view the l.
9. hath given you the l., 21 : 43.
5 : 6. L. sware he not shew the l.
11. did eat of old corn of the l.
11 : 16. Joshua took all that l., 23.
14 : 15. the l. had rest from war
15:19. given me south l., Ju. 1:15.
18 : 1. l. was subdued bef. them +
22 : 4. get you into the l. +
24:13. l. for which ye did not labour
Ju. 3:11. l. had rest 40 years, 5 : 31.
30. l. had rest fourscore years
11 : 12. come to fight me in my l.
18 : 30. until day of captivity of l.
1 S. 14 : 29. My father troubled l.
21:11. Is not this David king of l.?
27 : 9. Da. smote l. left nei man
2 S. 3 : 12. saying, Whose is the l.?
9 : 7. I will restore l. of Saul [25.
21:14. God was entreated for l., 24:
1 K. 9 : 13. called them l. of Cabul
11 : 18. victuals, and gave him l.
2 K. 2 : 21. not any more barren l.
8 : 3. to cry unto king for her l.
6. since the day that she left the l.
17 : 26. manner of God of l., 27.
18:32. l. of corn and wine, Is. 36:17.
33. Hath any of the gods of the
nations deliv-d his l., Is. 36 : 18.
21 : 8. move any more out of l., 2
Ch. 33:8. [out of his l.
24:7. the king of E. came no more
25 : 12. left of poor of l., Je. 52 : 16.
1 Ch. 4 : 40. l. was wide, and quiet
7 : 21. who were born in that l.
2 Ch. 6 : 37. if pray in l. of captiv.
38. if return in l. of captivity
7 : 20. pluck them out of my l.
14 : 7. walls, while l. is before us
34 : 8. when he had purged the l.
36 : 3. condemned l. in 100 tal.
Ezr. 9:12. may eat good of l., Is. 1:19.
Ne. 4 : 4. a prey in l. of captivity
5 : 16. nei. brought we any l.
9 : 36. the l., we are servants in it
Jb. 31 : 38. If my l. cry against me
37:13. whe. for correction, or his l.
39 : 6. barren l. his dwellings
42 : 15. in all l. no women so fair
Ps. 10:16. heath. are perish. out of l.
42:6. remember thee fr. l. of Jordan
52 : 5. root thee out of l. of living
80 : 9. deep root, it filled l.
101 : 6. Mine eyes upon faithf. of l.
8. I will destroy wicked of l.
105 : 16. called for famine upon l.
30. The l. brought forth frogs
106 : 24. they despised pleasant l.
38. l. was polluted with blood
107 : 34. fruitful l. into barrenness
143:6. thirsts aft. thee as thirsty l.
10. lead me into l. of uprightness
Pr. 12 : 11. tilleth his l. shall be
satisfied, 28 : 19. [princes
28:2. For transgression of a l. many
29 : 4. The king establisheth l.
31:23. husb. sitteth am. elders of l.
Ec. 10 : 16. Woe, O l. when k. is child
17. Blessed, O l. when k. is son
Is. 5 : 30. look unto l. behold sorr.
7:16. l. thou abhorrest be forsaken
24. l. shall become briers
Is. 9:1. l. of Zeb., l. of Napt., Mat. 4:15.
19. thro. wrath of L. l. darkened
13 : 5. come to destroy whole l.
14 : 25. break Assyrian in my l.
16:4. oppressors consumed out of l.
18 : 1. Woe to the l. shadowing
2. whose l. rivers spoiled, 7.
19 : 24. blessing in midst of l.
21:1. cometh fr. desert, terrible l.
23 : 1. fr. l. of Chittim is revealed
24 : 3. l. shall be utterly emptied
11. the mirth of the l. is gone
13. thus shall be in midst of l.
30 : 6. into l. of trouble anguish
32 : 2. of a great rock in a weary l.
13. Upon l. of my people thorns
33 : 17. behold l. is very far off
34 : 9. l. become burning pitch
35 : 7. thirsty l. springs of water
49 : 12. these from the l. of Sinim
19. l. of destruction too narrow
53 : 8. cut off out of l. of living
Je. 1 : 18. iron pillar ag. whole l.
2 : 2. after me, in a l. not sown
6. led us thro. a l. of deserts (2)
7. he ent-d, ye defiled l., 3 : 9.
15. young lions made his l. waste
3 : 1. l. be greatly polluted (2)
18. out of l. of north to l.
19. How give thee a pleasant l.?
4 : 20. the whole l. is spoiled
5:19. serve in a l. th. is not yours
6:8. lest make thee l. not inhab-d
8 : 16. whole l. trembled at sound
9:12. l. perisheth and is burned
19. bec. we have forsaken the l.
10 : 17. gather thy wares out of l.
11 : 19. cut him off fr. l. of living
12:4. How long shall the l. mourn
12. fr. one end of l. to the other
15. bring ev. man to his l. [22:28.
14:18. a l. they know not, 16 : 13.-
15 : 7. I will fan th. in gates of l.
16 : 15. from l. of north, 31 : 16.
18. bec. they had defiled my l.
17:6. inhabit wildern. into a salt l.
22 : 27. to l. they desire to return
23 : 10. the l. mourneth, Jo. 1 : 10
15. is profaneness forth into l.
25:13. bring upon that l. my words
27 : 7. till very time of his l. come
30:10. save fr. l. of captiv-y, 46:27.
33 : 11. cause to ret. captivity of l.
40:4. behold, all the l. is bef. thee
7. children and poor of l.
46 : 12. and thy cry hath filled l.
16. l. of our nativity, Eze. 23 : 15.
50:18. will punish k. of Bab. and l.
38. for it is the l. of graven images
51 : 2. fanners shall empty her l.
29. l. shall tremble and sorrow
51:43. dry l. wherein no man dw-th
47. whole l. be confounded
52. thro. l. wounded sh. groan
Eze. 7 : 2. end is come upon the l.
23. l. is full of bloody crimes
8 : 17. have filled l. with violence
9 : 9. l. is full of blood, and city
14 : 13. when the l. sinneth ag. me
15. noisome beasts to pass thro. l.
17. sword upon l. | 19. pestilence
17:5. He took also of seed of l. and
13. he hath taken mighty of l.
21 : 19. both sh. come out of one l.
32. thy blood be in l., 32 : 6.
22:24. Thou art l. is not cleansed
30. stand in gap before me for l.
27:29. fr. ships they sh. stand upon
30:12. sell l., I make l. waste l. [l.
32:4. will I leave thee upon the l.
33 : 2. When I bring sword upon l.
3. If seeth sword come upon l.
24. l. is given us for inheritance
36 : 13. Thou l. devourest up men
38 : 8. in latter y-rs come into l.
9. be like a cloud to cover l., 16.
11. up to l. of unwalled villages

Eze.38:16. I will bring thee ag. my l.
39 : 12. that they may cleanse l.
14. passing thro. l. to bury, 15.
16. Thus shall they cleanse the l.
45 : 4. holy portion of l. for priests
47 : 15. this shall be border of l.
Da. 8 : 9. toward the pleasant l.
11: 16. sh. stand in glorious l., 41.
Ho. 1 : 11. sh. come up out of the l.
4:3. Theref. shall the l. mourn [l.
Jo. 1:6. nation is come up upon my
2 : 3. l. is as the garden of Eden
18. will L. be jealous for his l.
21. O l. be glad | 3:2. parted my l.
Am.5:2 she is forsaken upon her l.
7:10. l. not able to bear his words
8 : 4. to make poor of the l. to fail
8. Shall not l. tremble for this?
9 : 5. Lord G. is he toucheth the l.
Jon.1:13. rowed hard to bring it to l.
Ha 1:6. march thro. breadth of l.
3 : 12. march thro. the l. in indig.
Zph. 1 : 2. I consume all thi. off l.
18. l. be devoured by jealousy
3:19. I will get them fame in ev. l.
Zch. 2 : 6 flee fr. l. of the north
3 : 9. I will remove iniq. of that l.
9 : 16. crown as an ensign upon his
12 : 12. l. sh. mourn [l., 11 : 6.
13 : 2. uncl spirit to pass out of l.
8. in all l. two parts be cut off
14 : 10. l. sh. be turned as a plain
Mal. 3 : 12. ye sh. be delightsome l.
Mat. 9:26. fame went into all that l.
10 : 15. more toler. for l. of Sodom,
23:15. ye compass sea and l. [11:24.
27:45. darkness over all l., Mk. 15:
Mk. 4:1. mult. by the sea on l. [33.
6 : 47. ship in sea, he on the l.
Lu. 4 : 25. famine thro-t all the l.
5 : 3. thrust out a little from l.
11. brought their ships to l.
8 : 27. when he went forth to l.
14 : 35. nei. fit for l. nor dunghill
15 : 14. arose a great famine in l.
Jn. 3 : 22. came Jes. into l. of Judea
6 : 21. immediately ship was at l.
21 : 8. not far fr. l. | 9. come to l.
11. Peter drew the net to l. full
Ac. 4 : 37. Barna. having l. sold it
5 : 3. back part of price of l.
8. Tell me whe. ye sold the l. so
7 : 3. come into l. wh. I sh. shew
27 : 39. when day, knew not the l.
43. cast thems. into sea, and get
44. they escaped all safe to l. to [l.
See BENJAMIN, CHALDEANS, CANAAN, DARKNESS, DESERT, DESOLATE, DESOLATION, DIVIDE, DIVIDED.

Dry LAND.

Ge. 1 : 9. G. said, let d. l. appear
10. and God called d. l. earth
7 : 22. of all that was in d. l. died
Ex. 4 : 9. pour water upon d. l. waters become blood upon d. l.
14 : 21. Lord made the sea d. l.
29. Israel walked on d. l.
15:19. Israel went on d. l., Ne.9:11.
Jos.4:18. priests' feet lifted unto d.l.
22. Isr. came over Jordan on d.l.
Ps. 63 : 1. longeth for thee in d. l.
66 : 6. He turned the sea into d. l.
68 : 6. rebellious dwell in a d. l.
95 : 5. and his hands formed d. l.
Is 41:18. make d. l. springs of wat.
Je. 50:12. hinderm. of nations be d.
51 : 43. Her cities are a d. l. [l.
Ho. 2 : 3. lest I set her as a d. l.
Jon. 1:9. G. who made sea and d.l.
2:10. vomited out Jon. upon d. l.
Hag. 2 : 6. I will shake sea and d.l.
He.11:29. passed Red sea as by d.l.
See DWELT, EGYPT, GOOD.

In the LAND.

Ge. 13 : . Canaanites dwelt i. t. l.
26 : 22. we shall be fruitful i. t. l.
Ge.41:31. plenty not be known i.t.l.
42: 34 and ye shall traffick i. t. l.
47 : 4. to sojourn i. t. l. are we
Ex. 8 : 25 sacri. to your God i. t. l.
9 : 5. L. shall do this thing i. t. l.
12 : 19. whether he be born i. t. l.
48. be as one is born i. t. l.
14 : 3. They are entangled i. t. l.
Le. 26 : 6. I will give peace i. t. l.
De. 4 : 14. that ye do them i. t. l.
25. sh. have remain. long i. t. l.
5 : 16. it go well with thee i. t. l.
11:9. prolong days i.t.l., 21.–25:15.
25 : 19. G. given thee rest i. t. l.
28:8. bless thee i. t. l., 11.–30:16.
31 : 13. as long as ye live i. t. l.
Jos.1:14. sh. remain i.t.l. Mo. gave
Ju. 18:7. was no magistrate i. t. l.
1 S. 28 : 23. if he i. t. l. I search
2 S. 15 : 4. th. I were judge i. t. l.
1 K. 8 : 37. If famine i. t. l., 2 Ch.6:
47. i. t. l. whi. carried cap. [28.
2 Ch. 6:31. fear thee so long as they live i. t. l., 1 K. 8: 40.
19 : 5. Jebosh. set judges i. t. l.
32:31. wonder that was done i.t.l.
Ps. 35 : 20. deceitful matter i. t. l.
74 : 8. burned synag-s of G. i.t.l.
88: 12. thy righte. i.t.l. of forgetf.
105:23. Jac. sojourned i.t.l. of Ham
27. wonders i.t.l. of Ham, 106:22.
Is. 7 : 22. honey ev. one eat i. t. l.
26:10. i.t.l. of uprightness he will
Je. 3 : 16. when ye be incr-d i. t. l.
5:30. horrible thing commit. i.t.l.
12:5. if i.t.l. of peace they wearied
33:15. execute righteousness i.t.l.
35 : 7. live many days i. t. l.
Eze. 7:7. O thou that dwellest i.t.l.
20 : 40. shall all i. t. l. serve me
37:22. make them one nation i.t.l.
Ho. 4 : 1. bec. is no truth i. t. l.
13 : 5. i. t. l. of great drought
Zch. 11 : 16. raise shepherd i. t. l.
13 : 8. i. all t. l. two parts cut off
Lu. 21 : 23. be great distress i. t. l.
He. 11 : 9. By faith sojourned i.t.l.
See INHABITANT, S, INHERIT, INHERITANCE, ISRAEL, JUDAH, LARGE, MOAB.

LAND of the living.

Jb. 28 : 13. nei. is it found in l.–
Ps.27:13. goodness of the Lord in l.–
52 : 5. root thee out of l.–
116 : 9. I will walk bef. L. in l.–
142 : 5. thou art my portion in l.–
Is 38:11. I shall not see the L. in l.–
53 : 8. he was cut off out of l.–
Je. 11 : 19. let us cut him off fr. l.–
Eze. 26 : 20. I shall set glory in l.–
32 : 23. all slain wh. caused terror in l.–, 24, 25, 26, 27, 32.

Our LAND.

Ge.47:19. buy us and o.l. for bread
Ps. 85 : 12. o. l. shall yield incr. [l.
Can. 2:12. voice of turtle heard in o.
Mi. 5:5. Assyr. shall come into o.l.
6. deliver us when cometh into o.

Own LAND. [l.

Ex. 18 : 27. Jethro went into his o. l., Nu.10:30. [my o.l., 2 Ch.9:5.
1 K. 10 : 6. true report I heard in
2 K.8:27. fr. him and return to o.l.
17 : 23. Isr. carried aw. out of o.l.
18:32. take you to a land like your o. l., Is. 36 : 17. [9, 28.
19:7. he sh. return to o.l., Da. 11:
2 Ch. 9 : 12. went away to her o. l.
32:21. returned wi. shame to o. l.
Is. 13 : 14. flee every one into o. l.
14 : 1. Isr., and set them in o. l.
37: 7. fall by the sword in his o. l.
Je. 23 : 8. dwell in o. l., 27 : 11.
37 : 7. return into o. l., 42 : 12.
50 : 16. flee every one to o. l.
Eze. 34:13. I will bring them into o. l., 36 : 24.–37 : 14, 21.–39 : 28.
Eze. 36:17. when Isr. dwelt in o. l.
Da.11:19. turn face tow. fort of o.l.
Am. 7 : 11. Isr. captive out of o. l.
See PEOPLE, POSSESS, ED, POSSESSION, STRANGER, S.

Strange LAND. [3.

Ex.2:22. been a stranger in s.l., 18:
Ps.137:4. sing Lord's song in a s.l.?
Ac.7:6. his seed sho. sojourn in s.l.

Their LAND.

Le. 20:24. said, Ye shall inherit t.l.
Nu.18:20. Aa. had no inherit. in t.l.
De. 2 : 5. not give you of t. l., 9.
4 : 38. and give thee t. l., Ju. 6:9.
12:29. succeedest and dwellest in t.
29:3. we took t.l., Jos. 10 : 42. [l.
28. L. rooted them out of t. l.
1 K. 8 : 48. pray unto thee tow. t. l.
2 Ch. 6 : 28. besiege in cities of t. l.
7 : 14. forgive sin heal t. l. [t. l.
Ps. 105 : 32. he gave flaming fire in
35. eat up all herbs in t. l.
36. He smote firstborn in t. l.
135:12. gave t. l. for heritage, 136:
Is. 2 : 7. t. l. is full of silver [21.
8. t. l. also is full of idols
34:7. t. l. shall be soaked with bl.
36:20. have deliv-d t. l. out of my
Je 12:14. will pluck them out of t.l.
16 : 15. I will bring them into t. l.
51 : 5. tho. t. l. was filled with sin
Eze. 34 : 27. they sh. be safe in t.l.
39 : 26. they dwelt safely in t. l.
Jo. 3 : 19. shed inno. blood in t. l.
Am.9:15. I will plant them upon t.l.

This LAND.

Ge. 12 : 7. Unto thy seed will give t. l., 15:18.–24:7.–48:4. Ex.32:13.
15 : 7. to give thee t. l. to inherit
24:5. not willing to follow unto t.l.
26 : 3. Sojourn in t. l. and I will
28 : 15. bring thee again into t. l.
31 : 13. get thee out from t. l. and
50:24. G. will bring you out of t. l.
Nu. 14:3. wh. L. bro-t us unto t.l.
8. he will bring us into t. l.
32:5. let t. l. be given unto serv-ts
34 : 2. t. l. sh. fall to you, 13. Jos.
De. 4 : 22. I must die in t. l. [13:2.
26 : 9. he given us t. l., Jos. 1:13.
29:24. Wh. hath L. done thus unto t. l.? 27. 1 K. 9:8 2 Ch.7:21.
34 : 4. t. l. I sware unto Abraham
Ju. 2:2. no league wi. inhab. of t.l.
2 K.18:25. Go up ag. t.l., Is. 36:10.
2 Ch. 20:7. drive out inhab. of t. l.
30 : 9. shall come again into t. l.
Je.13:13. inhab. of t.l. with drunken
14 : 15. Sword sh. not be in t. l.
16 : 3. fa-s that begat them in t. l.
6. great and small sh. dip in t. l.
13. I will cast you out of t. l.
22 : 12. he shall see t. l. no more
24:6. will bring them again to t.l.
8. residue of Jerusalem in t. l.
25 : 9. I will bring them ag. t. l.
26 : 20. who prophesied ag. t. l.
32 : 15. houses poss-d again in t. l.
22. given t. l. which thou didst
41. I will plant them in t. l.
43. fields sh. be bought in t. l.
36 : 29. the king shall destroy t. l.
37 : 19. not come ag. you nor t. l.
42 : 10. If ye will abide in t. l. I
13. We will not dwell in t. l.
45 : 4. I will pluck up t. whole l.
Ac. 7 : 4. he removed him into t. l.

Thy LAND.

Ex. 23 : 10. six years shalt sow t. l.
19. of firstfruits of t. l., 34 : 26.
26. nothing cast young in t. l.
33. they shall not dwell in t. l.
34 : 24. nei. any man desire t. l.
Le. 25 : 7. for beasts that are in t. l.
Nu. 21 : 22. Israel said, Let me pass thro. t.l., De.2:27. Ju.11:17,19.
De. 7 : 13. bless fruit of t. l., 30 : 9.

De. 15 : 7. within any gates in t. l.
19 : 2. cities in midst of t. l.
21 : 23. that t. l. be not defiled
24:14. the strangers that are in t.l.
26 : 2. fruit wh. thou bring of t. l.
28 : 12. rain to t. l. in season
18. Cursed be fruit of t. l., 33, 42.
24. make rain of t. l. powder
52. besiege thee thro-t all t. l.
2 S. 7 : 23. do great things for t. l.
24 : 13. shall famine come in t. l.
1 K. 8 : 36. give rain upon t. l.
Ps. 85:1. been favourable unto t. l.
Is. 8 : 8. wings fill breadth of t. l.
14 : 20. thou hast destroyed t. l.
23 : 10. Pass thro. t. l. as a river
60 : 18. Violence no more in t. l.
62:4. nei. t. l. be termed Desolate ; t. l. shall be married ⌈t. l.
Eze. 32: 8. I will set darkness upon
Am. 7 : 17. t. l. shall be divided
Mi. 5 : 11. will cut off cities of t. l.
Na. 3 : 13. gates of t. l. be set open

Your LAND. ⌈y. l.
Ge. 47 : 23. I have bought you and
Le. 19:9. reap harvest of y. l., 23:22.
22 : 24. any off-g thereof in y. l.
25 : 9. trumpet sound thro-t y. l.
45. children they begat in y. l.
26 : 5. sh. eat, and dwell in y. l.
6. nei. shall sword go thro. y. l.
20. y. l. not yield her increase
Nu. 10 : 9. if you go to war in y. l.
22 : 13. Get into y. l.
34: 12. this sh. be y. l. with coasts
De. 11 : 14. give you rain of y. l.
1 S. 6:5. lighten his hand fr. off y.l.
Je. 5:19. served strange gods in y.l.
27 : 10. to remove you far fr. y. l.
44 : 22. theref. is y. l. a desolation

LANDS.
Ge. 10 : 5. isles of Gent. divi-d in l.
31. after their tongues in their l.
41 : 54. dearth was in all l., 57.
47:18. not aught left but bodies, l.
22. whf. they sold not their l.
Le. 26 : 36. in l. of their enem., 39.
Ju. 11 : 13. restore those l. again peaceably
2 K. 19 : 11. what kings of Assyria have done to all l., Is. 37 : 11.
17 destr-d nations and their l.
1 Ch. 14 : 17. fame of Da. into all l.
2 Ch. 9 : 28. bro-t Sol. horses out of ⌊all l.
13:9. aft. manner of other l.
17 : 10. fear fell upon all l. round
32 : 13. done unto peo. of other l.
17. gods of other l. not deliv-d
Ezr. 9:1. I not separated fr. peo. of l.
2. mingled with peo. of those l., 11.
7. deliv-d into ha. of kings of l.
Ne. 5:3. We have mortgaged our l., 4.
5. other men have our l. and
11. Restore, I pray you, their l.
9 : 30. into hand of people of l.
10:28. had separated fr. people of l.
Ps. 49 : 11. call l. aft. own names
66:1. a joyful noise all ye l., 100:1.
105 : 44. gave them l. of heathen
106 : 27. to scatter them in the l.
107:3. gathered them out of the l.
Is. 33: 20. Who am. gods of these l.
Je. 13 : 15. brought up Isr. from l.
27 : 6. given l. into ha. of Nebu.
Eze. 20:6. which is glory of all l., 15.
39:27. gath-d them out of enem. l.
Mat. 19:29. forsaken houses, l., Mk. ⌊10:29.
Mk. 10:30. rec. hundredfold, l.
Ac. 4 : 34. as were possessors of l.

LANDED, ING.
Ac. 18 : 22. when had l-d at Cesarea
21 : 3. sailed into Syr. l-d at Tyre
28 : 12. l-g at Syracuse we tarried

LANDMARK, S.
De. 19:14. shalt not remove neighb.'s l., Pr. 22 : 28.–23 : 10. ⌈l.
27 : 17. Cursed removeth neighb.'s
Jb. 24 : 2. Some remove l-s and

LANES.
Lu. 14:21. Go quickly into l. of city

LANGUAGE, S.
Ge. 11 : 1. whole earth was of one l.
6. people one, they have all one l.
7. go, and confound their l., 9.
2 K. 18 : 26. in Syrian l., Is. 36:11.
28. cried in Jews' l., Is. 36 : 13.
Ne. 13:24. chil. not speak in Jews' l. but acc. to l. of peo. ⌈3:12.–8:9.
Es. 1:22. to ev. people after their l.,
Ps. 19 : 3. no l. where voice is not
81 : 5. heard a l. I understood not
114:1. fr. people of strange l. ⌈naan
Is. 19 : 18. five cities speak l. of Ca-
Je. 5 : 15. whose l. thou kno-t not
Eze 3 : 5. to people of hard l., 6.
Da. 3 : 4. To you, O people and l-s
7. all l-s worshipped the image
29. ev. l. that speaketh amiss
4 : 1. Neb. unto all people and l-s
5 : 19. all l-s trembled before him
6 : 25. Darius wrote unto all l-s
7:14. all peo. and l-s sh. serve him
Zph. 3 : 9. will turn to peo. pure l.
Zch. 8:23. ten men out of all l-s shall
Ac. 2:6. ev. man heard th. in his own ⌊l.

LANGUISH, ED.
Is. 16:8. For the fields of Heshbon l.
19 : 8. that spread nets shall l.
24 : 4. haughty people of earth l.
Je. 14 : 2. gates of Judah l.
La. 2:8. rampart and wall l-d togeth.
Ho. 4 : 3. every one therein shall l.

LANGUISHETH.
Is. 24 : 4. world l. and fadeth away
7. the vine l. | 33 : 9. earth l.
Je. 15:9. She th. hath borne seven l.
Jo. 1 : 10. the oil l. | 12. fig tree l.
Na. 1 : 4. Bashan l. flower of Leb. l.

LANGUISHING.
Ps. 41 : 3. L. will strengthen him upon bed of l.

LANTERNS.
Jn. 18 : 3. Judas cometh with l.

LAODICE'A, ANS. ⌈L.
Col. 2:1. conflict I have for them at
4 : 13. hath a zeal for them in L.
15. salute breth. which are in L.
16. that it be read in ch. of L-s, likewise read epistle from L.
Re. 1 : 11. unto 7 churches — unto L., 3 : † 14.
Re. 3 : 14. to angel of church of L-s

LAP. [Noun.]
2 K. 4:39. gathered gourds, his l. full
Ne. 5 : 13. I shook my l. and said
Pr. 16:33. The lot is cast into the l.

LAP'IDOTH.
Ju. 4 : 4. Deborah wife of L. judged

LAPPED, PETH.
Ju. 7 : 5. that l-h of water as a dog
6. the number that l-d were 300
7. said, By them th. l-d will I save ⌊you

LAPWING.
Le. 11 : 19. l. and bat, De. 14 : 18.

LARGE.
Ge. 34:21. land, behold is l. enough
Ex. 3 : 8. into a good and l. land
Ju. 18:10. ye shall come into a l. land
Ne. 4 : 19. The work is great and l.
7:4. city l. and great, but peo. few
9 : 35. not served thee in l. land
Ps. 119:†45. I will walk at l. ⌈and l.
Is. 31: 33. Tophet, he made deep
Eze. 23 : 32. sister's cup deep and l.
Mat. 28 : 12. l. money unto soldiers
Re. 21 : 16. length as l. as breadth
See CHAMBERS, COUNTRY, LETTER, PASTURES, PLACE, ROOM.

LARGENESS.
1 K. 4 : 29. God gave Sol. l. of heart

LASCIVIOUSNESS.
Mk. 7:22. out of the heart proceed l.
2 Co. 12 : 21. not repented of the l.
Ga. 5:19. works of flesh manifest, l.
Ep. 4 : 19. hath given thems. to l.
1 Pe. 4 : 3. when we walked in l.
Jude 4. turning grace of G. into l.

LASE'A.
Ac. 27 : 8. nigh was the city of L.

LA'SHA. ⌈unto L.
Ge. 10 : 19. fr. Sidon as thou goest

King of LASHA'RON.
Jos. 12: 18. king of Aphek, k. o. L.

LAST.
Ge. 49 : 19. Gad sh. overcome at l.
2 S. 19:11. Why l. to bring king, 12.
1 Ch. 29 : 29. acts of Da. first and l.
2 Ch. 9 : 29. acts of Sol. first and l.
12 : 15. acts of Rehoboam
16 : 11. of Asa first and l. ⌈and l.
20 : 34. acts of Jehoshaphat first
25:26. acts of Amaziah first and l.
26 : 22. acts of Uzziah first and l.
28 : 26. acts of Ahaz first and l.
35 : 27. Josiah's deeds first and l.
Ezr. 8 : 13. of l. sons of Adonikam
Ne. 8 : 18. from first day unto l.
Pr. 5: 11. and thou mourn at the l.
23:32. at the l. it biteth like serpent
Is. 41 : 4. I the Lord, the first, and with the l., 44: 6.–48:12. Re. 1: 11, 17.–2 : 8.–22 : 13. ⌈bones
Je. 50 : 17. at l. Neb hath broken
Da. 4:8. at l. Dan. came in before me
8 : 3. one higher, and came up l.
Am. 9 : 1. I will slay l. of them
Mat. 19:30. many that are first shall be l. and l. first, 20 : 16. Mk. 10 : 31. Lu. 13 : 30. ⌈first
20 : 8. beginning from the l. unto
12. l. have wrought but one hour
14. give unto l. as unto thee
21: 37. l. of all sent son, Mk. 12:6.
22:27. l. of all the woman died also, Mk. 12: 22. Lu. 20: 32.
26 : 60. at l. came 2 false witnesses
Mk. 9 : 35. if desire to be first, be l.
Jn. 8 : 9. at the eldest even unto l.
1 Co. 4 : 9. set forth us apostles l.
15 : 8. l. of all he was seen of me
45. l. Adam a quickening spirit
Ph. 4 : 10. at l. your care of me

LAST day, days.
Ge. 49:1. sh. befall you in the l. d-s
Is. 2 : 2. come to pass in l. d-s, Mi. 4 : 1. Ac. 2 : 17. ⌈d., 40, 44, 54.
Jn. 6:39. should raise it up at the l.
7 : 37. In l. d., great day of feast
11: 24. I know he shall rise at l. d.
12 : 48. same sh. judge him in l. d.
2 Ti. 3:1. in l. d-s perilous times shall
He. 1:2. spoken in l. d-s by his Son
Ja. 5 : 3. heaped treasure for l. d-s
2 Pe. 3:3. sh. come in l. d-s scoffers
See Last END, TIME, S.
See ENEMY, ERROR, MITE, PLAGUES, STATE, TRUMP, WORDS, WORKS

LASTED, ING.
De. 33:15. precious things of l-g hills
Ju. 14 : 17. she wept while feast l-d

LATCHET. ⌈broken
Is. 5 : 27. nor the l. of their shoes be
Mk. 1 :7. l. of whose shoes, Lu. 3:16. ⌊Jn. 1:27.
See SHOELATCHET.

LATE. ⌈sit up l.
Ps. 127 : 2. it is in vain for you to
Mi. 2:8. of l. my peo. is risen as an
Jn. 11:8. Jews of l. sought to stone

LATELY.
Ac. 18:2. Aquila l. come from Italy

LATIN.
Lu. 23:38. in Heb. and L., Jn. 19:20.

LATTER.
Ex. 4: 8. will believe voice of l. sign
De. 24 : 3. if l. husband hate her
Jb. 19:25. Redeemer stand at l. day
Eze. 38 : 8. in l. years shalt come
Da. 8 : 23. in l. time of their kingd.
Am. 7 : 1. in begin-g of l. growth
Hag. 2 : 9. glory of l. house greater

1 Ti. 4 : 1. in l.times some sh. depart
See DAYS, END, FORMER, RAIN.

LATTICE. [thro. l.
Ju. 5 : 28. mother of Sisera cried
2 K. 1 : 2. Ahaziah fell thro. the l.
Can. 2 : 9. shewing himself thro. l.

LAUD.
Ro. 15 : 11. Praise the L. and l. him

LAUGH.
Ge. 18 : 13. Wherefore did Sarah l.
15. said, Nay, but thou didst l.
21:6. God made me to l. all will l.
Jb. 5 : 22. At famine thou shalt l.
9:23. he will l. at trial of innocent
22 : 19. innocent l. them to scorn
Ps. 2 : 4. sitteth in heavens shall l.
22 : 7. that see me l. me to scorn
37 : 13. Lord shall l. at him for
52:6. righteous also shall l. at him
59 : 8. thou, O L. shalt l. at them
80:6. our enemies l. among thems.
Pr. 1 : 26. I will l. at your calamity
29:9. whe. rage or l. there is no rest
Ec. 3 : 4. A time to weep, time to l.
Lu. 6 : 21 ye that weep, ye shall l.
25. Woe unto you that l. now, ye

LAUGHED. [l.
Ge.17:17. Abraham l. | 18:12. Sarah
18:15. Sarah denied, saying, I l. not
2 K. 19 : 21. dau. of Zion l., Is. 37 :
2 Ch. 30 : 10. l. them to scorn [22.
Ne. 2 : 19. they l. us to scorn and
Jb. 12:4. upright man is l. to scorn
29 : 24. If I l. they believed not
Eze.23:32. thou shalt be l. to scorn
Mat. 9:24. and they l. him to scorn,
Mk. 5 : 40. Lu. 8 : 53.

LAUGHETH, ING. [l-g
Jb.8:21. Till he fill thy mouth with
41 : 29. he l-h at shaking of spear

LAUGHTER. [l.
Ps. 126 : 2. was our mouth filled wi.
Pr. 14 : 13. in l. heart is sorrowful
Ec. 2 : 2. I said of l. It is mad, and
7 : 3. Sorrow is better than l.
6. as crackling of thorns so l. of
10 : 19. a feast is made for l. [fool
Ja. 4:9. your l. be turned to mourn-

LAUNCH, ED. [ing
Lu.5:4. unto Simon, l. out into deep
8:22. let us go over, they l-d forth
Ac. 21 : 1. after we had l-d, 27:2, 4.

LAVER, S.
Ex. 30 : 18. also make a l. of brass
28. l. and foot, 31 : 9.—35 : 16.—39:
38 : 8. he made l. of brass [39.
40:7. shalt set l. | 30. he set the l.
11. shalt anoint the l., Le. 8 : 11.
1 K. 7:30. und. l. were undersetters
38. made he ten l-s of brass, one
l. 40 baths, every l. 4 cubits
40. Hiram made the l-s
43. ten l-s on bases, 2 Ch. 4:6, 14.
2 K. 16 : 17. King Ahaz removed l.

LAVISH.
Is. 46 : 6. they l. gold out of bag

LAW.
Ge. 47:26. Joseph made it a l. over
Ex. 12 : 49. One l. to homeborn and
stranger, Le.24:22 Nu.15:16, 29.
13 : 9. l. shall be in thy mouth
24 : 12. I will give thee a l. and
Le. 7 : 7. there is one l. for them
14 : 2. This sh. be l. of the leper
Nu. 19 : 2. This is ordin. of l., 31:21.
De. 17:11. Acc. to sentence of the l.
33:2. fr. his right ha. went fiery l.
4. Moses commanded us a l. even
Jos. 1:7. obs. to do acc. to all the l.
8:32. upon stones a copy of l. of Mo.
34. afterw. he read words of the l.
22 : 5. take heed to the l., 2 K. 17 :
13, 37.—21 : 8.
2 K.17:34. nei. do after l. and com-ts
23 : 24. might perform words of l.
25. acc. to all the l. of Moses
1 Ch. 16:17. confirmed to Jac. for l.
1 Ch.22:12. mayest keep the l. of G.
2 Ch.14:4. com-d Judah to do the l.
19:10. betw. l. and commandment
30 : 16. in place acc. to l. of Moses
31:21. Hez. did in ev. work, and in
33:8. heed to do acc. to whole l. [l.
34 : 19. when Josiah heard the l.
Ezr. 7 : 6. he was a ready scribe in
the l., 12, 21.
14. inquire acc. to l. of thy God
26. will not do l. of G. and l. of
10 : 3. let it be done acc. to the l.
Ne. 8 : 2. Ezra the priest bro-t the l.
7. Lev. caused peo. to underst. l.
9. people wept when heard the l.
13. were gath-d to underst. the l.
10:28. separated thems. to l. of God
29. into an oath to walk in G.'s l.
12:44. gather portions of l. for Lev.
13 : 3. had heard l. they separated
Es. 1 : 8 drinking was acc. to l.
13. all that knew l. and judgm.
15. What shall we do unto queen
Vashti according to l. ?
4:11. l. of his to put him to death
16. go in, which is not acc. to l.
Jb.22:22. Receive l. from his mouth
Ps. 1 : 2. in his l. he meditates day
37 : 31. l. of his God is in his heart
78 : 5. for he appointed a l. in Isr.
10. they refused to walk in his l.
81 : 4. this was a l. of God of Jac.
94:20. frameth mischief by a l.
105:10. confirmed unto Jac. for a l.
119:72. l. of thy mouth better than
Pr. 1 : 8. forsake not l. of moth., 6:
6:23. com-t is lamp, l. is light [20.
13 : 14. l. of wise is fount. of life
28:4. that forsake l. praise wicked
such as keep l. contend with
7. Whoso keepeth l. is a wise son
9. turns his ear from hearing the l
29 : 18. keepeth the l. happy is he
31:5. Lest they drink and forget l.
26. in her tongue is l. of kindness
Is. 1 : 10. give ear unto l. of our G.
2 : 3. out of Zion sh. go l., Mi. 4:2.
8:16. seal l. | 20. To l. and testim.
42 : 4. the isles shall wait for his l.
21. The Lord will magnify the l.
24. nei. were they obedient unto l.
51 : 4. for a l. shall proceed fr. me
Je. 2:8. that handle l. knew me not
18:18. l. shall not perish from priest
32:11. evidence was sealed acc. to l.
44:23. not obeyed, nor walked in l.
La. 2:9. l. is no more, prophets find
Eze. 7 : 26. l. shall perish fr. priests
Da. 6 : 5. except conc. l. of his God
8. l. of Medes and Persians
12. true acc. to l. of the Medes, 15.
Ho. 4:6. hast forgotten l. of thy G.
Ha. 1 : 4. Therefore the l. is slacked
Zph. 3 : 4. priests done violence to l.
Hag. 2 : 11. Ask now priests conc. l.
Zch. 7 : 12. lest they sho. hear the l.
Mal. 2 : 6. l. of truth in his mouth
7. they sho. seek l. at his mouth
8. ye caused many to stumble at l.
9. but have been partial in the l.
4 : 4. Remember l. of Moses my
Mat 5 : 17. Think not I am come to
destroy l.
18. one tittle in no wise pass fr. l.
40. if any man will sue thee at l.
11:13. prophets and the l. prophesied until John, Lu. 16 : 16.
12 : 5. have ye not read in l. how
22 : 36. wh. is great com-t in l. [l.
40. On these 2 com-ts hang all the
23:23. omitted weightier matters of
Lu. 2:22. purif-n acc. to l. of Mo. [l.
27. to do after custom of l.
5 : 17. were doctors of l. sitting by
16 : 17. than for tittle of l. to fail
Jn.1:17. l. was given by Moses but
45. of wh. Moses in l. did write
Jn.7:19. Did not Moses give you the
l. yet none of you keepeth l.
23. that l. of Moses not be broken
49. peo. who knoweth not l. cursed
51. Doth l. judge man bef. it hear
8 : 5. Now Moses in l. com-d us
17. in your l. th. testimony of two
10:34 Is it in your l. Ye are gods?
12 : 34. We heard out of l. that C.
15:25. be fulfilled what is writ. in l.
18:31. judge him acc. to l. [to die
19 : 7. We a l. by our l. he ought
Ac.5:34. Gamaliel, a doctor of the l.
6:13. to speak blasph-s words ag. l.
7 : 53. have received l. by angels
13:15. aft. reading of l. and prophets
39. ye not be justified by l. of Mo.
15:5. to command to keep l. of Mo.
24. must be circum-d and keep l.
18:13. to worship God contrary to l.
15. if question of your l. look to
19:38. l. is open | 21:20. zealous of l.
21 : 24. that thou keepest l.
28. This is the man teacheth ag. l.
22 : 3. taught acc. to manner of l.
12. Ananias devout man acc. to l.
23 : 3. to judge me aft. l., com-st
me to be smit. contrary to l. ?
29. accused of quest-s of their l.
24:6. would have judged acc. to our
25 : 8. ag. the l. of the Jews [l.
28:23. persuading them out of the l.
Ro. 2 : 12. sinned in l. judged by l.
13. not hearers of l. just bef. God
14. Gentiles wh. have not l. do
things contained in l. having
not l. are a l. unto themselves
15. shew work of l. written in
17. called a Jew, and restest in l.
18. being instructed out of the l.
20. hast form of truth in the l.
23. makest thy boast of l., thro.
breaking l. dishon-st God?
25. circumc. profiteth if thou
keep l. but if breaker of l.
26. if uncirc. keep right-sn. of l.
27. sh not uncirc. if it fulfil l.
judge thee, who transgr. l.
3:19. we know what things l. saith
20. by deeds of l. no flesh be justified, for by l. is knowl. of sin,
28. Ga. 2 : 16. [by l.
21. righteousn. of G. is witnessed
27. By what l. excluded ? by l. of
31. make void the l. ? we estab. l.
4 : 13. promise was not thro. l.
14. if they wh. are of l. be heirs
15. l. worketh wrath, where no l.
16 not to that only wh. is of l.
5 : 13. until l. sin was in world, sin
not imputed where no l.
20. l. entered, that offence abound
7 : 1. I speak to them th. know l.
l. dominion over man as long
2. wom. bound by l. to husb.; if
he dead, she is loosed from l., 3
4. ye are dead to l. by Christ
5. motions of sins were by l.
6. now we are delivered from l.
7. Is l. sin ? I had not known sin
but by l. not kn. lust, except l.
8. without the l. sin was dead
12. the l. is holy, and com-nt
14. the l. is spiritual | 16. the l. is
good, 1 Ti. 1:8. [l. of God
21. I find them a l. | 22. I delight in
23. I see ano. l. warring ag. l. of
my mind, bringing me into captiv. to l. of sin [flesh l. of sin
7 : 25. with mind I serve l. of G.,
8:2. l. of life made me free fr l. sin
3. what l. could not do
4 righteousn. of l. be fulfilled
7. carnal mind not subject to l.
9 : 4. to wh. pertain-h giving of l.
31. Isr. followed l. of righteousn.
32. they sought it by works of l.

Ro.10:4.Christ is the end of the l. for
5. describes righteousn. wh. is of
13: 8. loveth ano., fulfilled l. [l.
10. love is the fulfilling of the l.
1 Co. 6: 1. Dare any of you go to l.
6. brother goeth to l. with bro.
7. bec. ye go to l. one with ano.
7:39. wife is bound by l. as long as
9: 8. or saith not l. the same [l.
14: 34. und. obedience, as saith l.
15:56. and strength of sin is the l.
Ga. 2:16. not justified by works of l.
19. I thro' the l. am dead to the l.
21. if righteousn. come by l. then
3: 2. Received ye spirit by the l.?
5. miracles, doeth he it by the l.?
10. many as are of works of l.
11. that no man is justified by l.
12. l. is not of faith, but the man
13. C. redeemed us fr. curse of l.
17. cov. in C., l. cannot disannul
18. if the inheritance be of the l.
19. Wheref. then serveth the l.?
21. Is the l. ag. promises? if l.
given, righteousn. been by l.
24. the l. was our schoolmaster to
4: 21. Tell me, do ye not hear l.?
5: 3. he is a debtor to do whole l.
4. whoso. are justified by the l.
14. all l. is fulfilled in one word
23. temperance, ag. such is no l.
6: 2. Bear ye, and so fulfil l. of C.
13. thems. keep l. but desire
Ep. 2: 15. abolished in his flesh l.
Ph. 3: 5. touching the l. a Pharisee
6. touching righteousn. in the l.
9. not mine own righte-n. of l.
1 Ti. 1: 7. Desiring to be teachers of
9. l. is not for a righte. man [l.
Tit. 3: 9. avoid contentions about l.
He. 7: 5. to take tithes acc. to the l.
11. under it peo. received l. [l.
12. made of necessity a change of
16. not aft. l. of a carnal com-nt
19. the l. made nothing perfect
28. l. maketh men high priests,
word of oath since l. maketh
8:4. priests offer gifts acc. to l. [Son
9: 19. Moses had spoken ac. to l.
22. all things by l. purged with
10: 1. l. a shadow of good things
8. which are offered by the l.
28. He that despised Moses' l. died
Ja. 1: 25. looketh into perfect l. of
2:8. If ye fulfil royal l. ye do well
9. convinced of l. as transgressors
10. For whoso. sh. keep whole l.
11. if kill, thou art transg-r of l.
12. sh. be judged by l. of liberty
4:11. speaketh evil of l. judgeth l.
1 Jn. 3: 4. whoso. committeth sin
transgresseth l. for sin is transgression of l.

See **BOOK of the Law, DAUGHTER, FATHER, SON, MOTHER in law.**

LAW of the Lord.

2 K.10:31. no heed to walk in l.o.L.
1 Ch. 16: 40. acc. fall written in l.o.
L., 2 Ch. 31: 3.-35: 26.
2 Ch. 12:1. Rehob. forsook l. o. L.
31: 4. that they might be encouraged in l. o. L. [to l. o. L.
35:26. Josiah's goodness according
Ezr. 7:10. prepared heart to seek l.
Ps.1:2. his delight is in l.o.L. [o.L.
19:7. l. o. L. is perfect, converting
119:1. Blessed who walk in l.o.L.
Is. 5:24. they have cast aw. l. o. L.
30:9. chil. that will not hear l.o.L.
Je. 8:8. How say, l. o. L. is with us
Am. 2:4. bec. have despised l. o. L.
Lu. 2:39. performed acc. to l. o. L., [24.

My LAW.

Ex.16:4. whe. they will walk in m. l.
2 Ch. 6: 16. thy chil. walk in m. l.
Ps.78:1. O my peo., to m. l. incline
Ps. 89: 30. If his chil. forsake m. l.
Pr. 3: 1. My son, forget not m. l.
4: 2. forsake not m. l.
7: 2. keep m. l.
Is. 51:7. peo. in whose heart is m. l.
Je.6:19. have not heark-d unto m. l.
9:13. Bec. they have forsaken m. l.
16:11. forsaken me, not kept m. l.
26:4. not hearken to walk in m. l.
31: 33. m. l. in their inward parts
44: 10. feared nor walked in m. l.
Eze. 22: 26. priests violated m. l.
Ho. 8: 1. they trespassed ag. m. l.
12. written to him things of m. l.

This LAW.

Le. 14: 2. t. shall be the l. of leper
Nu. 5:30. sh. execute upon her t. l.
19:2. t. is ordinance of the l., 31:21.
De. 1: 5. began Mo. to declare t. l.
4: 8. all t. l. which I set bef. you
17:18. sh. write him a copy of t. l.
31:9. Moses wrote t. l. | 11. read t. l.

See **All WORDS of this law.**

This is the LAW.

Le. 6: 9. -l. of burnt offering, 7:37.
14. -l. of meat off-g | 25. sin off.
7:1. -l. of trespass off-g, it is holy
11. -l. of sacrifice of peace off-gs
11: 46. -l. of beasts and of fowl
12:7. -l. of her hath borne male
and [54, 57.
13:59. -l. of plague of lepr., 14:32,
15: 32. -l. of him hath an issue
Nu. 5:29. -l. of jealousies, when wife
6:13. -l. of Nazarite, when days, 21.
19:14. -l. when a man dieth in tent
De. 4: 44. -l. Moses set before Isr.
Eze. 43: 12. -l. of house upon top
Mat. 7:12. for -l. and the prophets

Thy LAW.

De. 33:10. They shall teach Isr. t. l.
Ne. 9: 26. cast t. l. behind backs
29. mightest bring them unto t. l.
34. nei. our k-s princes kept t. l.
Ps. 40: 8. t. l. is within my heart
94: 12. teachest him out of t. l.
119:18. wondrous things out of t. l.
29. grant me t. l. graciously
34. Give underst-g, I sh. keep t. l.
44. So sh. I keep t. l. continually
51. have I not declined from t. l.
53. of wicked that forsake t. l.
55. rememb-d thy name, kept t.
61. but I have not forgott. t. l. [l.
70. heart fat, but I delight in t. l.
77. for t. l. is my delight, 92, 174.
85. digged pits, wh. are not aft. t. l.
97. how I love t. l.
109. do I not forget t. l., 153.
113. t. l. I love, 163.
126. made void t. l.
136. waters run down, bec. they
keep not t. l. [t. l.
142. t. l. is truth | 150. are far fr.
165. Gr. peace they who love t. l.
Je. 32: 23. they nei. walked in t. l.
Da. 9: 11. Isr. have transg-d t. l.

Under the LAW.

Ro. 3: 19. it saith to them u. t. l.
6: 14. for ye are not u. t. l. but
15. shall we sin bec. not u. t. l.
1 Co 9: 20. to them u. t. l. as u. t.
l. th. I might gain them u. t. l.
21. not with-t law, but u. t. l. to C.
Ga. 3: 23. we were kept u. t. l.
4: 4. sent his Son made u. t. l.
5. To redeem them that were u. t. l.
21. ye that desire to be u. t. l.
5:18. if led by Spi., are not u. t. l.

Without LAW. [w. l.

2 Ch. 15: 3. a long season, Isr. been
Ro. 2: 12. sinned w. l. perish w. l.
3: 21. righteousn. of G. w. l. is
7: 8. w. l. sin was dead
9. I was alive w. l. once
1 Co. 9: 21. that are w. l. as w. l.
being not w. l. to G.

Written in the LAW.

1 K. 2: 3. as it is w. i. l. of Moses,
2 Ch. 23:18.-25:4.-31:3. Ezr. 3:
2. Ne. 10:34, 36. Da. 9: 13. Lu.
2: 23.
Ne. 8: 14. found w. i. l. that Isr.
Da. 9:11. oath that is w. i. l. of Mo.
Lu.10:26. What is w. i. l. how readest
24:44. all must be fulfilled, w. i. l.
Ac. 24:14. believ-g all things w. i. l.
1 Co. 9: 9. it is w. i. l., 14: 21.

See **LAW of the Lord.**

LAWS.

Ge.26:5. Ab. kept my statutes and l.
Ex. 16: 28. How long refuse ye to
keep my l.?
18: 16. make them know l. of God
20. shalt teach them ordin. and l.
Le. 26: 46. These are l. L. made
Ezr. 7:25. such as know l. of thy G.
Ne. 9: 13. thou gavest them true l.
14. com-dst them statutes and l.
Es. 1: 19. written am. l. of Persians
3:8. their l. diverse from all people,
neither keep they king's l.?
Ps. 105: 45. they might keep his l.
Is. 24: 5. bec. have transg-d the l.
Eze. 43: 11. shew them all the l.
44: 5. hear the l. | 24. keep my l.
Da. 7: 25. to change times and l.
9:10. Nei. obeyed to walk in his l.
He. 8: 10. put my l. into their mind
10: 16. put my l. into their hearts

LAWFUL.

Ezr. 7: 24. not be l. to impose toll
Is. 49: 24. l. captive be delivered?
Eze. 18:5. do that which is l. 21, 27.-
33: 14, 19. [33: 16.
19 son hath done that which is l.,
Mat. 12:2. do what is not l., Mk. 2:
24. Lu. 6: 2. [2: 26. Lu. 6: 4.
4. was not l. for him to eat, Mk.
10. Is it l. to heal on the sabbath
day? 12. Mk. 3:4. Lu. 6:9.-14:3.
14: 4. It is not l. for thee to have
her, Mk. 6:18. [wife? Mk.10:2.
19: 3. Is it l. for man to put away
20:15. Is it not l. to do what I will
22: 17. Is it l. to give tribute to
Cesar or not? Mk. 12: 14. Lu
20: 22.
27:6. not l. to put them in treasury
Jn. 5: 10. not l. to carry thy bed
18: 31. not l. to put man to death
Ac. 16:21. customs which are not l.
19:39. determined in a l. assembly
22: 25. is it l. to scourge Roman?
1 Co. 6: 12. All things are l. unto
me, l. for me, 10: 23.
2 Co. 12: 4. not l. for a man to utter

LAWFULLY.

1 Ti. 1: 8. law good, if man use it l.
2 Ti. 2:5. not crowned, exc. strive l.

LAWGIVER.

Ge. 49:10. nor l. from betw. his feet
Nu. 21:18. digged by direction of l.
De. 33: 21. in a portion of l.
Ps. 60: 7. Judah is my l., 108: 8.
Is. 33:22. L. is our l. and our king
Ja. 4:12. one l. who is able to save

LAWLESS.

1 Ti. 1: 9. law is for l. disobedient

LAWYER, S.

Mat.22:35. a l. asked him, Lu. 10:25.
Lu. 7: 30. l-s rejected counsel of G.
11: 45. then ans-d one of l-s
46. Woe unto you also ye l-s, 52
14: 3. Jesus ans-g spake unto l-s
Tit. 3: 13. Bring Zenas the l. and [Apollos

LAY.

Ex. 5: 8. tale of bricks; ye shall l.
16: 13. dew l. round host, 14.
14. there l. a small round thing
21: 22. husband will l. upon him
22:25. nei. shalt l. upon him usury
Le. 1: 7. l. the wood upon the fire
8. priests sh. l. parts in order, 12.

Le. 2 : 15. thou shalt l. frankincense
6 : 12. l. the burnt off-g in order
Nu. 12:11. my L. l. not sin upon us
De. 7 : 15. l. them upon them hate
11:25. l. fear of you upon la. ⌊thee
21: 8. l. not innoc. blood unto Isr.
Jos. 2:†1. Rahab's hou. and l. there
8 : 2. l. thee an ambush for city
15 : 46. that l. near Ashdod
Ju. 4 : 22. into tent, Sisera l. dead
6 : 20. flesh and cakes l. upon rock
7:12. l. in valley like grasshoppers
13. smote it that tent l. along
14:17. told her bec. she l. sore upon
16:3. Samson l. till midnight ⌊him
Ru. 3 : 8. a woman l. at his feet, 14.
1 S. 3 : 15. Sam. l. till morning
6 : 8. take ark and l. it upon cart
11 : 2. l. it for reproach upon Isr.
25 : †25. not my lord l. it to heart
26 : 5. Saul l. in the trench, 7.
2 S. 4:5. who l. on a bed at noon, 7.
12 : 3. ewe lamb l. in his bosom
16. Da. l. all night upon earth, 13:
19:32. while k. l. at Mahanaim ⌊31.
1 K. 7 : 3. beams l. on 45 pillars
13 : 31. l. my bones beside his
18 : 23. l. it on wood put no fire
19 : 5. he l. and slept und. juniper
21 : 27. Ahab fasted l. in sackcloth
2 K. 4 : 11. turned into chamb. and
29. l. staff upon face of child ⌊l.
34. he went up l. upon child
9 : 16. to Jezreel, Joram l. there
10 : 8. l. ye them in two heaps at
2 Ch. 36 : 21. long as she l. desolate
Es. 4 : 3. many l. in sackcloth
Jb. 29:19. dew l. all night upon my
34:23. not l. upon man more than
Ps. 7 : 5. l. mine honour in dust
38:12. seek my life, l. snares for me
84 : 3. where she may l. her young
Ec. 7 : 2. living will l. it to heart
Is. 5 : 8. Woe to them that l. field to
10:†6, charge to l. them a treading
13:9. to l. land desola., Eze. 33:28.
11. I will l. low haughtiness of
22 : 22. key of house of Da. l. upon
his shoulder
25 : 12. fortress shall he l. low
28 : 16. will l. in Zion tried stone
17. Judgment will I l. to the line
29 : 3. l. siege ag. thee with a mt.
21. l. snare for him reproveth
30:32. staff wh. Lord sh. l. upon him
34 : 15. sh. great owl l. and hatch
35 : 7. habita. of dragons, each l.
38 : 21. a lump of figs and l. it
47 : 7. didst not l. things to heart
54:11. l. thy stones wi. fair colours
Je. 6 : 21. I will l. stumblingblocks
before people, Eze. 3 : 20.
Eze. 4 : 1. take tile, l. it bef. thee
2. l. siege, 3. | 8. l. bands upon thee
4. l. iniquity of Israel upon it
6:5. l. dead carcasses of chil. of Isr.
25:14. l. my veng. upon Edom, 17.
26:12. l. thy stones and thy timber
28 : 17. I will l. thee before kings
32: 5. I will l. thy flesh upon mts.
36 : 29. I will l. no fam. upon you
34. land tilled, whereas it l. desol.
37 : 6. I will l. sinews upon you
42:13. L. most holy thi., 14.—44:19.
Jon. 1 : 5. he l. and was asleep
14. l. not upon us innocent blood
Mi. 1 : 7. idols will I l. desolate
Mal. 2:2. if ye will not l. it to heart,
curse upon you; bec. ye do not
l. it to heart ⌈Lu. 9 : 58.
Mat. 8:20. not where to l. his head
23 : 4. l. them on men's shoulders
28 : 6. see the place where L. l.
Mk. 1:30. mother l. sick, Mat. 8:14,
2 : 4. bed wherein sick of palsy l.
15 : 7. Barab. l. bound with them
Lu. 5 : 18. to bri. him in and l. him
Lu. 5:25. took up whereon he l. and
8:42. only dau. l. a dying ⌊depar.
19 : 44. shall l. thee with ground
Ju. 5 : 3. In these l. impotent folk
11 : 38. cave, and stone l. upon it
Ac. 7 : 60. Lord l. not this sin to
15 : 28. to l. no greater burden
27 : 20. no small tempest l. on us
28 : 8. father of Publius l. sick
Ro. 8 : 33. l. anything to G.'s elect
9 : 33. I l. in Zion stumblingstone
1 Co. 16:2. ev. one l. by him in store
He. 12 : 1. let us l. aside ev. weight
Ja. 1:21. Whf. l. apart all filthiness
1 Pe. 2:6. I l. in Zion a chief corner
See FOUNDATION, s. ⌊stone

LAY down.

Ge. 19:4. bef. they l. d. men of Sodom
33. Lot perceived not she l. d., 35.
28: 11. Jacob l. d. in that place to
Nu. 24 : 9. he l. d. as lion ⌊sleep
Ju. 5:27. he l. d. at her feet, he fell
Ru. 3 : 4. uncover his feet and l. d.
1 S. 3 : 5. Samuel went and l. d., 9.
19 : 24. Saul l. d. naked all day
2 S. 13 : 5. Jonadab said, l. thee d.
6. Amnon l. d. made hims. sick
1 K. 14 : †20. Jerob. l. d. with fa-s
Jb. 17:3. l. d. now, put me in surety
Ps. 4 : 8. I will l. me d. in peace
104 : 22. young lions l. d. in dens
Eze. 19:2. mother l. d. among lions
Am. 2:8. l. thems. d. upon clothes
Mat. 9:†36. they were tired and l. d.
Jn. 10:15. I l. d. life for my sheep, 17.
18. I l. it d. of mys. power to l. d.
13 : 37. l. d. life for thy sake, 38.
15 : 13. l. d. his life for his friends
1 Jn. 3 : 16. ought to l. d. lives for

LAY hand. ⌊breth.

Ge. 22 : 12. l. not thy h. upon lad
37:22. Shed no bl. l. no h. upon Jo.
Ex. 7:4. may l. my h. upon Egypt
Le. 3:2. l. his h. upon head of off-g, 8.
13. l. h. upon head of goat, 4:24.
4:4. shall l. h. upon bullock's head
29. he shall l. his h. upon sin
offering, 33.
Nu. 27:18. L. said, l. h. upon Josh.
Ju. 18 : 19. l. h. upon thy mouth
Es. 2 : 21. sought to l. h. on king
9 : 2. l. h. on such as sought hurt
Jb. 9 : 33. any daysman to l. his h.
21:5. l. your h. upon your mouth
40:4. I will l. my h. upon my mouth
41:8. l. h. upon him, remem. battle
Pr. 30:32. if thought evil l. h upon
Is. 11:14. l. h. upon Edom ⌊mouth
Mi. 7:16. shall l. their h. upon mouth,
Mat. 9:18. come l. thy h. upon her

LAY hands. ⌈goat

Le. 16:21. Aa. shall l. both h. upon
24 : 14. all l. h. upon head
Nu. 8:12. l. h. upon bullocks, Le. 4:15.
Ne. 13:21. if do so again, I will l. h.
Es. 3 : 6. he thought scorn to l. h.
on Mord. alone ⌈him, Lu. 20:19.
Mat. 21:46. they sought to l. h. on
Mk. 5 : 23. come l. thy h. on her
16 : 18. l. h. on sick, they recover
Lu. 21 : 12. they shall l. h. on you
Ac. 8 : 19. on whomsoever I l. h.
1 Ti. 5:22. l. h. suddenly on no man

LAY hold.

De. 21:19. shall his fa. l. h. on him
22: 28. l. h. on her and lie wi. her
2 S. 2 : 21. l. h. on one of o. men
1 K. 13:4. hand, saying, l. h. on him
Pr. 3:18. life to them l. h. upon her
Ec. 2 : 3. I sought to l. h. on folly
Is. 5 : 29. sh. roar, and l. h. of prey
Je. 6:23. sh. l. h. on bow and spear
Zch. 14:13. ev. one l. h. on neighb.
Mat. 12 : 11. will he not l. h. on it
Mk. 3 : 21. friends went out to l. h.
12 : 12. sought to l. h. on him, but
1 Ti. 6 : 12. l. h. on eternal life, 19.
He. 6: 18. to l. h. upon hope bef. us

LAY up.

Ge. 41 : 35. l. u. corn under Pha.
Ex. 16: 23. l. u. manna until morn.
33. l. u. a pot of manna to be kept
Nu. 17 : 4. sh. l. them u. in taber.
19:9. l. them u. without the camp
De. 11 : 18. l. u. my words in heart
14:28. shall l. it u. within thy gates
Jb. 22 : 22. l. u. his words in heart
24. Then shalt l. u. gold as dust
Pr. 7 : 1. l. u. my commandments
10 : 14. Wise men l. u. knowledge
Mat. 6:19. l. not u. treasures upon
20. l. u. treasures in heav. ⌊earth
2 Co. 12 : 14. chil. not to l. u. for pa-

LAY wait. ⌊rents

Ezr. 8:31. deliv-d us fr. such as l. in w
Ps. 71 : 10. that l. w. for my soul
Pr. 1 : 11. let us l. w. for blood
18. they l. w. for their own blood
24 : 15. l. not w. ag. the righteous
Je. 5:26. l. w. as he that sett. snares

LAY waste. ⌈37:26.

2 K. 19:25. shouldest be to l. w., Is.
Is. 5 : 6. I will l. it w. it shall
Eze. 35 : 4. I will l. thy cities w.

LAY with. ⌈35.

Ge. 19: 33. firstborn l. w. father, 34,
30 : 16. Jac. l. w. Leah th. night
34 : 2. Shechem l. w. Dinah and
35 : 22. Reuben l. w. Bilhah
De. 22 : 22. man that l. w. woman
25. man only that l. w. her die
29. man that l. w. her give fifty
1 S. 2 : 22. heard they l. w. women
2 S. 11 : 4. and he l. w. her, 12: 24.
13 : 14. forced Tamar l. w. her
Eze. 23 : 8. in her youth l. w. her

LAYEST.

Nu. 11:11. l. burden of peo. upon me
1 S. 28:9. whf. l. a snare for my life?

LAYETH.

Jb. 21:19. God l. up his iniq. for chil.
24:12. yet God l. not folly to them
41:26. sword of him that l. at him
Ps. 33:7. l. up depth in storehouses
104:3. he l. beams of his chambers
Pr. 2 : 7. He l. up wisdom for right-
13:16. but a fool l. open folly ⌊eous
26:24. and l. up deceit within him
31:19. She l. her hands to the spin-
Is. 26:5. lofty city he l. low (2) ⌊dle
56:2. blessed man that l. hold on it
57 : 1. righte. perish, no man l. it
Je. 9:8. in heart he l. wait ⌊to heart
12 : 11. l. it to heart ⌈earth
Zch. 12 : 1. L. l. foundations of
Lu. 12:21. So is he that l. up treasure
15:5. found, he l. it on his shoulders

LAYING.

Nu. 35 : 20. hurl at him by l. of wait
22. upon him with-t l. of wait
Ps 64:5. they commune of l. snares
Mk. 7 : 8. for l. aside the com-t
Lu. 11 : 54. l. wait for him, and
Ac. 8 : 18. l. on of apostles' hands
9:24. l. await was known of Saul
23: 16. kinsmen heard of l. in wait
25:3. l. wait in the way to kill him
1 Ti. 4:14. with l. on of the hands of
6:19. l. up in store a good founda.
He. 6 : 1. not l. again foundation of
2. baptisms, and of l. on of hands
1 Pe. 2 : 1. l. aside all malice, guile

LAZ'ARUS.

Lu. 16:20. a certain beggar named L.
23. L. in Ab.'s bosom | 24. send L.
25. L. received evil things, but
Jn. 11: 2. whose bro. L. was sick, 1.
5. Jesus loved L. | 11. L. sleepeth
14. said Jes. plainly, L. is dead
43. he cried, L. come forth
12 : 2. L. one of them at table, 1.
9. came that they might see L.
10. th. they might put L. to death
17. when he called L. out of grave

LEAD. [Noun.]
Ex. 15:10. they sank as l. in waters
Nu. 31 : 22. l. that may abide fire
Jb. 19 : 24. graven with iron and l.
Je. 6 : 29. l. is consumed of the fire
Eze. 22 : 18. they are l. in furnace
20. as they gather l. so will I gather you in anger
27 : 12. tin, l. Tarshish traded
Zch. 5:7. was lifted up a talent of l.
8. he cast weight of l. upon mouth

LEAD. [Verb.]
Ge. 33:14. I will l. on softly as cattle
Ex. 13 : 21. pillar of cloud to l. th.
32 : 34. l. the people to the place
Nu. 27 : 17. wh. may l. them out
De. 4:27. whi. L. shall l. you, 28:37.
20 : 9. make captains to l. people
32 : 12. So the L. alone did l. him
1S. 30: 22. they may l. them away
Ne. 9 : 19. pillar of cloud to l. them
Ps. 5:8. l. me, O L. in thy righteousness [plain path
25 : 5. l. me in truth | 27: 11. l. in
31:3. for thy name's sake l. me [me
43 : 3. light and truth, let them l.
60:9. who l. me into Edom? 108:10.
61 : 2. l. me to rock higher then I
125 : 5. l. th. with workers of iniq.
139:10. there sh. thine hand l. me
24. l. me in the way everlasting
143:10. l. me into land of uprightn.
Pr. 6 : 22. When goest it sh. l. thee
8 : 20. I l. in way of righteousness
Can. 8:2. I wo. l. thee unto mo.'s ho.
Is. 3 : 12. that l. cause thee to err
11 : 6. a little child shall l. them
20 : 4. king of Assyria l. Egyp-s
40:11. sh. gently l. those with young
42:16. will l. them in paths not kn.
49 : 10. th. hath mercy sh. l. them
57 : 18. I will l. him, and restore
63 : 14. so didst thou l. thy people
Je. 31 : 9. with supplica-s will I l.
32 : 5. he sh. l. Zedekiah to Bab.
Na. 2 : 7. her maids l. Huzzab, as with voice of doves [Lu. 11 : 4.
Mat. 6:13. l. us not into temptation,
15 : 14. if blind l. blind, Lu. 6 : 39.
Mk. 13:11. sh. l. you and deliver up
14 : 44. take him l. him aw. safely
Lu. 13 : 15. ox, l. him to watering
Ac. 13 : 11. seeking some to l. him
1 Co. 9:5. we not power to l. sister?
1 Ti. 2 : 2. l. a quiet life in godlin.
He. 8 : 9. to l. them out of Egypt
Re. 7:17. Lamb sh. feed and l. them
See **Lead CAPTIVE.**

LEADER, S.
1 Ch. 12:27. Jehoiada l. of Aaronites
13 : 1. David consulted with ev. l.
2 Ch. 32: 21. an angel wh. cut off l-s
Is. 9:16. l-s of peo. cause them to err
14 : † 9. stirreth up all l-s of earth
55 : 4. given him a l. to people
Eze. 4 : † 2. set chief l-s against it
Mat. 15:14. they be blind l-s of blind

LEADEST.
Ps. 80 : 1. that l. Joseph like flock

LEADETH.
1 S. 13:17. to way that l. to Ophrah
Jb. 12 : 17. He l. counsellors away
19. He l. princes away spoiled
† 23. enlargeth nations and l. in
Ps. 23 : 2. l. me beside still waters
3. he l. me in paths of righte-n.
Pr. 16: 29. l. him into way not good
Is. 48 : 17. I am L. which l. thee
Mat. 7:13. wide is way l. to destruc.
14. narrow is way l. unto life
Mk. 9 : 2. Jesus l. them into mt.
Jn. 10 : 3. calleth his sheep and l.
Ac. 12 : 10. iron gate th. l. into city
Ro. 2:4. goodness of G. l. to repen.
Re. 13: 10. that l. shall go into captivity

LEAF.
Ge. 8 : 11. in her mouth an olive l.
Le. 26 : 36. sound of a shaken l. sh.
Jb. 13:25. wilt thou break a l. driven
Ps. 1 : 3. his l. also shall not wither
Is. 1: 30. be as oak, whose l. fadeth
34 : 4. their host fall as a l.
64 : 6. we all do fade as a l.
Je. 8:13. no grapes, the l. shall fade
17 : 8. her l. shall be green, and
Eze. 47:12. l. not fade, l. for medicine

LEAGUE.
Jos. 9 : 6. make a l. with us, 11.
7. how sh. we make l. with you
15. Joshua made a l. with the, 16.
Ju. 2 : 2. make no l. with inhabit-s
1 S. 22 : 8. son made a l. with Da.
2 S. 3 : 12. Make thy l. with me
13. I will make a l. with thee
21. they may make l. with thee
5 : 3. David made a l. with them
1 K. 5 : 12. Hiram and Sol. made l.
15 : 19. is a l. between me and thee
2 Ch. 16: 3. break thy l. wi. Baasha
Jb. 5 : 23. shalt be in l. with stones
Eze. 30 : 5. men of la. in l. sh. fall
Da. 11 : 23. aft. l. he sh. work deceitfully

LE'AH.
Ge. 29:16. name of the elder was L.
17. L. was tender eyed, but Rachel
23. Laban brought L. to Jac. | 24.
25. in morning behold it was L.
30. he loved Rachel more than L.
31. when Lord saw L. was hated
32. L. bare son, 30 : 17, 19.
30:9. L. had left bearing + [46:18.
10. Zilpah L.'s maid, 12.-35 : 26.-
13. L. said, Happy am I, for dau-s
16. Jac. out of field, L. met him
31 : 4. Jac. called L. to his flock+
33:2. Jac. put L. and chil. after, 7.
34 : 1. Dinah dau. of L. went out
35 : 23. sons of L. Reuben, 46 : 15.
49:31. buried Ab. there I buried L.
Ru. 4 : 11. make this wom. like L.

LEAN. [Adj.]
Nu. 13 : 20. the land, whe. fat or l.
2 S. 13 : 4. why being king's son l.
Is. 17 : 4. fatness of his flesh wax l.
Eze. 34 : 20. betw. fat cattle and l.
Zph. 2 : † 11. Lord make l. the gods

LEAN. [Verb.]
Ju. 16:26. that I may l. upon pillars
2 K. 18:21. on which if a man l. go into hand, Is. 36: 6. [not stand
Jb. 8 : 15. l. upon his house, but it
Pr. 3 : 5. l. not to own underst-g
Mi. 3:11. yet will they l. upon the L.

LEANED.
Ju. 16 : † 29. pillars on which he l.
2 S. 1:6. Saul l. upon his spear, [17.
2 K. 7:2. lord, on whose hand king l.
2 Ch. 32 : † 8. l. upon words of Hez.
Eze. 29:7. l. upon thee thou breakest
Am. 5:19. l. hand on wall, a serpent
Jn. 21: 20. who also l. on his breast

LEANETH, ING. [of
Nu. 21:†15. stream l-h upon border
2 S. 3:29. not fail one l-h upon staff
2 K. 5 : 18. l-h in house of Rimmon
Can. 8 : 5. cometh l-g upon beloved
Jn. 13 : 23. was l-g on Jesus' bosom
He. 11:21. Jacob l-g upon top of staff

LEANFLESHED.
Ge. 41:3. kine came out of river l., 19.
4. l. eat up 7 fat kine, 20.

LEANNESS.
Jb. 16 : 8. my l. rising up in me
Ps. 106: 15. gave request but sent l.
Is. 10 : 16. L. send am. fat ones l.
24:16. I said, My l. my l. woe unto
Mi. 6 : † 10. measure of l. abomin.

LEAP.
Ge. 31: 12. rams which l. upon cattle
Le. 11 : 21. have legs to l. withal
De. 33 : 22. Dan, shall l. fr. Bashan
Jb. 41: 19. and sparks of the fire l. out
Ps. 68 : 16. why l. ye, ye high hills
Is. 35 : 6. sh. lame man l. as a hart
Jo. 2 : 5. like chariots shall they l.
Zph. 1:9. sh. punish those that l. on
Lu. 6 : 23. rejoice ye, and l. for joy

LEAPED.
Ge. 31 : 10. rams wh. l. upon cattle
2 S. 22:30. I l. over a wall, Ps. 18:29.
1 K. 18 : 26. they l. upon the altar
Lu. 1 : 41. babe l. in her womb, 44.
Ac. 14 : 10. and he l. and walked
19 : 16. in wh. evil spirit was, l. on them

LEAPING.
2 S. 6 : 16. Michal saw David l.
Can. 2:8. he cometh l. upon the mts.
Ac. 3 : 8. and he l. up, and walked

LEARN.
De. 4:10. may l. to fear me, 14 : 23.
5 : 1. that ye may l., and do them
17:19. he sh. read, th. he may l. to fear
18:9. not l. to do after abominations
31:12. may hear, l. and fear the L.
13. chil. may l. to fear the Lord
Ps. 119 :71. I might l. statutes, 73.
Pr. 22 : 25. lest thou l. his ways
Is. 1:17. l. to do well, seek judgm.
2:4. nei. l. war any more, Mi. 4:3.
26:9. inhabit-s shall l. righteousn.
10. will not wicked l. righteousn.
29 : 24. that murmured l. doctrine
Je. 10 : 2. l. not way of heathen
12:16. if diligently l. ways of people
Mat. 9 : 13. go l. what that meaneth
11:29. l. of me, for I am meek and
24:33. l. parable of fig tree, Mk. 13:
1 Co. 4 : 6. l. in us not to think [28.
14 : 31. prophesy one by one, that all l. and be comforted
35. if l. any thing, let them ask
Ga. 3 : 2. this would I l., recei-d ye
1 Ti. 1:20. l. not to blaspheme [Spirit
2 : 11. let the women l. in silence
5 : 4. l. first to shew piety at home
13. and withal they l. to be idle
Tit. 3:14. l. to maintain good works
Re. 14:3. no man could l. that song

LEARNED.
Ge. 30 : 27. I have l. by experience
Ps. 106:35. am. heathen, and l. works
119:7. when I sh. have l. thy judgm.
Pr. 30 : 3. I neither l. wisdom, nor
Is. 29 : 11. deliver to one that is l.
12. to him not l. saith, I am not l.
50 : 4. God given me tongue of l.
wakeneth ear to hear as l.
Eze. 19 : 3. it l. to catch the prey, 6.
Jn. 6:45. ev. man that hath l. of Fa.
7:15. kno-th letters, having never l.
Ac. 7: 22. Moses l. in all wisd. of E.
Ro. 16:17. contrary to doctrine ye l.
Ep. 4 : 20. ye have not so l. Christ
Ph. 4 : 9. those things ye have l. do
11. l. in every state to be content
Col. 1 : 7. as ye l. of Epaphras our
2 Ti. 3 : 14. continue in things hast l. knowing of wh. hast l. th.
He. 5 : 8. a son, yet l. he obedience

LEARNING. [Noun, Part.]
Pr. 1 : 5. wise man will increase l.
9:9. just man, he will increase in l.
16 : 21. sweetness of lips incr-th l.
23. heart of wise addeth l. to lips
Da. 1 : 4. might teach l. of Chald-s
17. God gave them skill in all l.
Ac. 26 : 24. l. doth make thee mad
Ro. 15 : 4. things written for our l.
2 Ti. 3 : 7. ever l. and never able to

LEASING.
Ps. 4:2. how long will ye seek aft. l.?
5:6. shalt destroy them th. speak l.

LEAST.
Ge. 32 : 10. not worthy l. of mercies
Nu. 11:32. gath-d l. gath-d 10 homers
Ju. 6 : 15. I am l. in father's house
1 S. 9 : 21. my family, the l. of all
2 K. 18:24. one capt. of l. of servants
1 Ch. 12:14. one of l. was over hund.
Je. 49 : 20. l. of flock draw, 50 : 45.
Am. 9:9. not l. grain fall upon earth

Mat. 2:6. art not the l. am. princes
5 : 19. break one of these l. com-ts,
sh. be called the l. in kingdom
11 : 11. John Bap., he l. in kingd.,
is greater than he, Lu. 7 : 28.
13 : 32. which is the l. of all seeds
25 : 40. as ye have done it to l., 45.
Lu. 9 : 48. he that is l. among you
12 : 26. if not able to do that is l.
16 : 10. faithful in l. unjust in l.
1 Co. 6:4. judge who are l. esteemed
15 : 9. I am the l. of the apostles
Ep. 3 : 8. am less than l. of saints

At, or at the LEAST. [days
Ge. 24:55. damsel with us, a. t. l. 10
Ju. 3:2. a. t. l. as bef. knew noth.
1 S. 21:4. if kept a. l. from women
Lu. 19 : 42. known a. l. in thy day
Ac. 5:15.a.t.l.shadow of Pe. passing
See GREATEST with least.

LEATHER, LEATHERN.
2 K. 1:8. hairy man, wi. girdle of l-r
Mat. 3:4. John had l-n girdle about

LEAVE. [Noun.] [loins
Nu. 22:13. L. refuseth to give me l.
1 S. 20 : 6. David asked l. of me, 28.
Ne. 13 : 6. obtained I l. of the king
Mk. 5:13. Jesus gave them l. [body
Jn. 19 : 38. Pilate gave l. to take
Ac. 18:18. Paul took his l. of breth.
21 : 6. had taken l. one of another
2 Co. 2 : 13. taking l. I went into

LEAVE. [Verb.] [Mace.
Ge.2:24.l.fa. and moth. cleave unto
wife,Mat.19:5.Mk.10:7.Ep.5:31.
33 : 15. let me l. wi. thee some folk
42:33. l. one of your brethren here
44 : 22. lad can-t l. his fa., if he l.
Ex. 16 : 19. Let no man l. manna
23:†5. cease to l. busin., shalt l. it
11. what they l. beasts shall eat
Le. 7 : 15. not l. peace off-g, 22 : 30.
16:23. sh. put off garments l. them
19:10. shalt l. them for poor, 23:22.
Nu. 9 : 12. l. none of the passover
10 : 31. said, l. us not, I pray thee
32 : 15. will again l. them in wil.
De 28:51. shall not l. thee corn, or
54. remnant of chil. he shall l.
Jos. 4 : 3. l. them in lodging place
Ju. 9 : 9. said, Sho. I l. my fatness
13. vine said, Should I l. my wine
Ru. 1:16. Entreat me not to l. thee
2 : 16. l. them that she may glean
1 S. 9 : 5. father l. caring for asses
14:36. let us not l. a man of them
25 : 22. if I l. of all pertain to him
S. 14 : 7. not l. to hush. a name
1 K. 8 : 57. let him not l. us nor
2 K. 4 : 43. shall eat and l. thereof
1 : 7. Nei. did he l. but 50 horsem.
1 Ch. 28 : 8. possess land, and l. it
Ezr. 9 : 8. l. us a remnant to escape
12. l. it for inheritance to chil.
Ne. 4:†2. Jews,will they l. to thems.
5 : 10. let us l. off this usury [it?
6 : 3. why work cease whilst I l.
10 : 31. that we would l. 7th year
Jb. 39 : 11. wilt l. labour to him?
Ps. 16:10. not l. my soul in hell,Ac.
17:14. l. substance to babes [2:27.
27:9. my help, l. me not, 119 : 121.
37:33. L. will not l. him in his ha.
49 : 10. die and l. wealth to others
141:8.O G.,l.not my soul destitute
Pr. 2:13. who l. paths of uprightn.
17 : 14. l. off contention, before it
Ec. 2 : 18. I sho. l. it unto man aft.
21. yet sh. he l. it for his portion
10:4.if ruler ag. thee, l.not thy pla.
Is. 10 : 3. and where l. your glory?
65 : 15. sh. l. your name for curse
Je. 9 : 2. I might l. my peo., and go
14:9. L., called by thy na., l. us not
17:11.riches,he sh.l. them in midst
18 : 14. will a man l. snow of Leb.
44 : 7. and suckling, to l. you none
Je.48:28. l. cities, and dwell in rock
49 : 9. not l. gleaning grapes?
11. l. fatherl. chil., I will preserve
Eze. 16 : 39. l. thee naked, 23 : 29.
39:2. will l. but sixth part of thee
Da. 4:15. l. stump of his root, 23,26.
Ho. 12:14. sh. l. his blood upon him
Jo. 2:14.will return, and l. blessing
Am. 5:3. shall l. hundr. l.ten to Isr.
7. ye, who l. off righteousn. in
Ob. 5. grapegath-s, not l. grapes?
Mal.4:1.l.them nei.root nor branch
Mat. 5 : 24. l. thy gift before altar
18 : 12. not l. 90 and 9, Lu. 15 : 4.
Mat. 19:5. cause a man l., Mk. 10:7.
23:23. not l. other undone, Lu. 11:
Mk.12:19. l.wife, and l. no chil. [42.
Lu. 19 : 44. not l. in thee one stone
Jn. 14 : 27. my peace I l. with you
16:28. I l. the world and go to Fa.
32.ye shall l. me alone, yet not al.
Ac. 6 : 2. not reason we sh. l. word
1 Co. 7 : 13. let her not l. him
He. 13 : 5. I will never l. thee nor
Re. 11:2. court l. out, measure not

I will, or will I LEAVE.
1 K. 19:†18. yet I w. l. 7,000 in Isr.
Jb. 9 : 27. I w. l. off my heaviness
10:1. I w. l. complaint upon mys.
Eze. 6:8. yet I w. l. a remnant
12:16. I w. l. a few men fr. sword
22 : 20. I w. l. you and melt you
29:5. I w.l. thee thrown into wil.
32 : 4. then I w. l. thee upon land
Zph. 3:12. I w. l. in thee poor peop.

I will not LEAVE. [done
Ge. 28 : 15. I -l. thee until I have
2 K.2:2. as L. liveth, I -l. thee,4:30.
4. as thy soul liveth, I -l. thee, 6.
Je.30:11.I -l. thee unpunish.,46:28.
Jn. 14 : 18. I -l. you comfortless, I

LEAVED. [gates
Is. 45 : 1. open bef. him the two l.

LEAVEN.
Ex. 12 : 15. put away l. 7 days, 19.
13:7. nei. be l. seen in thy quarters
34 : 25. not offer blood with l.
Le. 2:11. no meat off-g made with l.
6 : 17. it shall not be baken with l.
10 : 12. eat meat off g without l.
23 : 17. of fine flour, baken with l.
Am. 4 : 5. offer thanksgiving with l.
Mat. 13 : 33. kingdom of heaven is
like l., Lu. 13 : 21.
16 : 6. beware of l. of Phari. and
Sadducees,11. Mk.8:15. Lu.12:1.
12. not beware of l. bread
1 Co.5:6.little l.leaveneth whole,Ga.
7. purge out the old l. [5 : 9.
8. let us keep feast, not wi. old l.

LEAVENED. [19.
Ex. 12 : 15. whoso. eateth l. bread,
20. eat noth. l. in all habitat-s
34. peo. took dough bef. was l.,39.
13:3. shall no l. bread be eaten, 7.
Ho.7:4.hath kneaded dough until l.
Mat.13:33.till whole wasl.,Lu.13:21.
See Leavened BREAD.

LEAVENETH.
1 Co. 5:6. little leaven l. whole, Ga.

LEAVES. [5 : 9.
Ge. 3 : 7. sewed fig l. made aprons
Is. 6 : 13. as oak, when cast their l.
Je. 36 : 23. Jehudi read 3 or 4 l.
Eze. 17:9. it shall wither in all the l.
Da. 4 : 12. The l. thereof fair, 21.
14. Hew tree shake off his l.
Mat. 21:19. nothing thereon but l.,
Mk. 11 : 13. [Mk. 13 : 28.
24:32. his branch putteth forth l.,
Re. 22 : 2. l. for healing of nations

LEAVES with door, s.
1 K. 6 : † 32. l. of d-s of olive trees
34. two l. of one d. were folding
Eze. 41 : 24 d-s had two l. apiece

LEAVETH.
Jb. 39 : 14. ostrich l. eggs in earth
Pr. 13 : 22. good man l. inheritance
28:3. sweeping rain wh. l. no food
Zch.11:17. Woe to sheph. l. the flock
Mat. 4 : 11. then the devil l. him
Jn. 10 : 12. the hireling l. the sheep

LEAVING.
Mat. 4 : 13. Jesus l. Naz., dwelt in
Lu. 10:30. l. him half dead [Capern.
Ro. 1 : 27. l. natural use of woman
He. 6 : 1. l. the doctrine of Christ
1 Pe. 2:21. C. suffered, l. an example

LEB'ANA = LEB'ANAH.
Ezr. 2:45. the chil. of L., Ne. 7 : 48.

LEB'ANON.
De. 1 : 7. into L. | 11 : 24. Jos. 1 : 4.-
9 : 1.-11 : 17.-12 : 7.-13 : 5, 6.
3 : 25. see that goodly m-t and L.
Ju. 3 : 3. Hivites dwelt in m-t L.
1 K. 4 : 33. from cedar tree in L.
5:9. sh. bring them fr. L. unto sea
14. he sent 10,000 a month to L.
7 : 2. house of the forest of L., 10 :
17, 21. 2 Ch. 9 : 16, 20.
9 : 19. to build in L., 2 Ch. 8 : 6.
2 K. 14:9. thistle in L. sent to cedar
in L., 2 Ch. 25 : 18. [37 : 24.
19 : 23. am come to sides of L., Is.
2 Ch. 2 : 8. to cut timber in L., 16.
Ezr. 3:7. money to bri. cedars fr. L.
Ps. 29 : 6. L.-like a young unicorn
72:16. the fruit shall shake like L.
92:12. he sh. grow like cedar in L.
Can. 3 : 9. chariot of the wood of L.
4 : 8. Come from L. my spouse
11. garments is like smell of L.
15. a well, and streams from L.
5 : 15. his countenance is as L.
7 : 4. thy nose is as tower of L.
Is. 10 : 34. L. sh. fall by a mighty
29 : 17. L. into a fruitful field
33 : 9. L. is ashamed and hewn
35 : 2. glory of L. shall be given
40 : 16. L. is not sufficient to burn
60 : 13. glory of L. sh. come unto
Je. 18 : 14. leave snow of L.? [thee
22:6. thou art unto me head of L.
20. go up to L. and cry, lift | 23.
Ez.17:3.great eagle came up unto L.
27 : 5. have taken cedars from L.
31 : 15. I caused L. to mourn him
16. trees of Eden, choice of L.
Ho. 14 : 5. cast forth his roots as L.
6. sh. be as olive-tree, smell as L.
7. scent thereof be as wine of L.
Na. 1 : 4. flower of L. languisheth
Ha. 2 : 17. violence of L. shall cover
Zch. 10: 10. br. them into land of L.
11 : 1. open thy doors, O L.
See CEDAR, CEDARS.

LEB'AOTH. [him
Jos. 15 : 32. inheri. of Jud. L. Shil-

LEB'BEUS. [deus
Mat. 10:3. L. whose surname Thad-

LEBO'NAH.
Ju. 21 : 19. place on the south of L.

LE'CAH.
1 Ch. 4 : 21. Er the father of L.

LED.
Ge. 14:†14. l. forth trained servants
24 : 27. being in way, Lord l. me
48. L.,wh. had l. me in right way
47:†17. Joseph l. them with bread
Ex.3:1.Mo. l. flock to back of desert
13:17. G. l. not thro. la. of Philis.
18. God l. them thro. wilderness
15 : 13. in mercy hast l. forth peo.
De. 8 : 2. way L. l. thee 40 years
15.who l. thee thro. great wilder.
29 : 5. I have l. you 40 y-rs in wil.
32:10. he l. him about, instructed
Jos. 24:3. I l. him thro. all Canaan
2 K. 6 : 19. Elisha l. them to Sama.
1 Ch. 20 : 1. Joab l. forth the power
of the army [his people
2 Ch. 25 : 11. and Amaziah l. forth
Ps. 78 : 14. in day he l. with cloud
53. l. them safely, so feared not

Ps.106:9. he l. them thro. depths as thro. wilder. 136 : 16. Is. 63:13.
107:7. he l. them by the right way
Pr. 4 : 11. I l. thee in right paths
Is. 9: 16. they l. of them are destr.
48:21. thirst. not when they l. th.
55 : 12. ye sh. be l. forth wi. peace
63 : 12. l. them by hand of Moses
Je. 2 : 6. where is L. l. us through wilderness
17. forsaken God, when he l. thee
23 : 8. L. liveth which l. ho. of Isr
La.3:2. he hath l. me into darkness
Eze. 17 : 12. l. them wi. him to Bab.
39:28. caused to be l. into captiv.
47 : 2. l. me about unto outw. gate
Am. 2 : 10. I l. you 40 years thro.
Mat. 4:1. Jesus l. of Spirit, Lu. 4:1.
26 : 57. they l. him to Caiaphas, Mk. 14 : 53. Lu.22:54. Jn 18:13.
Mk. 8 : 23. took blind man l. him
Lu. 4 : 29. l. Jes. unto brow of hill
22 : 66. l. him into their counsel
23 : 1. mult. l. him unto Pilate
26. l. him aw. laid hold of Simon
32. two malefactors l. with him
24 : 50 l. them out far as Bethany
Jn. 18 : 28. th. l. Jes. unto the hall
19 : 16. took Jes. and l. him away
Ac. 8 : 32. l. as sheep to slaughter
9 : 8. l. Saul to Damascus, 22 : 11.
21:37. Paul was to be l. into castle
Ro. 8 : 14. as are l. by Spirit of God
1 Co. 12 : 2. unto idols, as ye were l.
Ga. 5 : 18. if ye be l. by the Spirit
2 Ti. 3 :6. l. away with divers lusts
2 Pe. 3:17. lest ye being l. aw. with

See Led **CAPTIVE.**

LEDDEST.

2 S. 5:2. that l. out Isr., 1 Ch. 11:2.
Ne 9 : 12. l. them by cloudy pillar
Ps. 77 : 20. l. thy people like flock
Ac 21 : 38. l. into wilderness, 4,000

LEDGES.

1 K. 7 : 28. borders were betw. l.
29. upon the l. there was a base
35. l. and borders were of same
36. on plates of l. graved cheru- [bim

LEEKS.

Nu. 11 : 5. we remem. l. and onions

LEES.

Is. 25 : 6. a feast of wine on the l.
Jer. 48 : 11. Moab hath settled on l.
Zeph. 1:12. punish men settled on l.

LEFT. [Adj.]

1 K. 7 : 21. he set l. pillar, name Boaz
2 K. 11:11. guard stood to l. corner
2 Ch. 4 : 8. ten tables, five on the l.
Re. 10:2. he set l. foot on the earth

See Left **HAND.**

See Left **SIDE.**

LEFT. [Verb.]

Ge. 18: 33. had l. communing with [Ab.
24 : 27. not l. destitute my master
29 : 35. and Leah l. bearing, 30 :9.
32: 8. other company which is l.
39: 6. l. all he had in Jo.'s hand
12. l. his garm. in her, 13, 15, 18.
41:49. gath-d corn till he l. numb.
44 : 12. at eldest, l. at youngest
47:18. not aught l. but our bodies
50 : 8. little ones l. they in Goshen
Ex 2 : 10. why ye have l. the man ?
9 : 21. l. his servants in the field
10 : 12. eat ev. herb, all hail l., 15.
26. shall not a hoof be l. behind
16 : 20. some l. of it until morning
34 : 25. nor passo. be l. unto morn.
Le. 2 : 10. which is l. of meat offer.
10 : 12. Aa.'s sons th. were l., 16.
26 : 36. upon them l. alive of you
39. they l. of you sh. pine away
43. the land shall be l. of them
Nu. 21 : 35. was none l. him alive
26 : 65. was not l. a man of them, Jos. 8 : 17. Jn. 4: 16. Ho. 9 :12.
De. 2 : 34. we l. none to remain, 3 : 3. Jos. 10 : 33, 37, 39, 40.- 11 : 8, 11, 14.
4 : 27. ye shall be l. few in numb., 28 : 62. Is. 24 : 6. Je. 42 : 2.
7:20. until they th. are l. be destr.
28 : 55. hath nothi. l. him in siege
32 : 36. there is none shut up or l.
Jos. 6 : 23. l. them with-t the camp
8 : 17. l. city open, pursued Isr.
11 : 15. he l. nothing undone of all
22. was none of the Anakim l.
22 : 3. Ye have not l. your breth.
Ju. 2 : 21. of nations wh. Joshua l.
23. Lord l. those nations, 3 : 1.
4 : 16. host fell, not a man l.
6 : 4. l. no sustenance for Israel
8 : 10. 15,000 men were l. of host
9 : 5 Jotham youngest son was l.
Ru. 1 : 3 she was l. and 2 sons, 5.
18. then she l. speaking to her
2:11. how thou hast l. fa. and mo.
14. Ru did eat was sufficed, and l.
4 : 14. L. not l. thee this day
1 S. 2 : 36. ev. one l. in thy house
5 : 4. only stump of Dagon was l.
9 : 24. that which is l. set bef. thee
10 : 2. thy fa. hath l. care of asses
11 : 11. so that two not l. togeth.
17 : 20. David l. sheep with keeper
22. David l. his carriage in ha. of
28. with wh. hast thou l. sheep
25:34. not been l. any that pisseth
27 : 9. David l. nei. man nor wom.
30 : 9. at Besor those l. beh. stayed
13. l. me because I fell sick
2 S. 5:21. there they l. their images
9 : 1. is any l. of house of Saul?
13:30. the king's sons, is not one l.
14: 7. quench my coal which is l.
15 : 16. l. ten concu., 16:21.-20 : 3.
17:12. sh. not be l. so much as one
1 K. 7:47. Sol. l. vessels unweighed
9:20. all peo. th. were l., 2 Ch. 8:7.
21. children were l., 2 Ch. 8 : 8.
14 : 10. cut off him that is l. in Isr., 21 : 21. 2 K. 9 : 8.
15:18. silv. and gold l. in treasures
29. l. not Jerob. any th. breathed
16 : 11. he l. Baasha not one that
17 : 17. was no breath l. in him
19:3. l. his servants | 10. I only l.
18 I have l. me 7,000 | 20. l. oxen
20:30. wall fell upon 27,000 men l.
2 K 3:25. only in Kir-har. l. stones
4 : 44. did eat and l. thereof [l.
7 : 7. they l. tents | 13. all that are
8 : 6. since the day she l. the land
10: 11. Jehu slew all, until l. none
14. neither l. he any of men
21. so there was not a man l.
14 : 26. was not any l. nor helper
17 : 16. they l. com-ts of the Lord
18. none l. but tribe of Judah
19:4. prayer for remnant l., Is.37:4.
20 : 17. nothing sh. be l., Is. 39:6.
25 : 11. rest of people l. in city
12. l. of poor, Je. 39 : 10.-52 : 16.
22. whom Neb. king of Bab. had l.
1 Ch. 6 : 61. sons of Kohath l.
13 : 2. send unto brethren are l.
14: 12. when they had l. gods
16 : 37. l. there bef ark of the cov.
2 Ch. 8 : 7. As for all l. of Hittites
8. But of their chil. l. in land
11 : 14. Levites l. their suburbs
12 : 5. I l. you in hand of Shishak
21 : 17. was never a son l. him
24 : 18. they l. the house of the L.
25. they l. Joash in great diseases
25 : 12. other 10,000 l. alive
28:14. armed men l. cap and spoil
31:10. we enough to eat, l. plenty
32 : 31. God l. him to try him
34:21. Inquire for them l. in Isr.
Ne. 1 : 2. I asked conc. Jews had l.
3. remnant l. are in great afflict.
6:1. wall th. there was no breach l.
Jb. 20 : 21. none of his meat be l.
26. go ill with him l. in his tab.
Ps. 106 : 11. was not one of them l.
Pr. 29 : 15. child l. to hims. bring-h
Is. 1 : 8. Zion is l. as a cottage in
9. exc. L. had l. remn., Ro. 9:29.
4 : 3. he l. in Zion be called holy
7 : 22. honey ev. one eat that is l.
10 : 14. as one gath. eggs th. are l.
11 : 11. recover remnant of peo. l.
16. a highway for remnant l.
17: 6. gleaning grapes shall be l.
9. uppermost branch they l.
18:6. They sh. be l. tog. unto fowls
24 : 12. in the city is l. desolation
29 : 10. habita. l. like a wilderness
30 : 17. till ye be l. as a beacon
32 : 14. mult. of the city sh. be l.
Je. 12: 7. I l. my heritage
21 : 7. l. in city from pestil. [Bab.
27 : 18. that vessels l. go not to
31 : 2. peo. which are l. of sword
34:7. ag. all cities of Judah, l. [ho.
38 : 22. women l. in king of Jud.'s
40 : 6 among people l. in the land
11. king of Bab. l. remn. of Jud.
43 : 6. ev. person Neb-n capt. l.
49 : 25. how is city of praise not l.
50 : 26. destroy her, let noth. be l.
Eze. 9 : 8. slaying th. and I was l.
14 : 22. shall be l. a remnant
23 : 8. nor l. her whoredo. from E.
24 : 21. dau-s ye have l. fall by sw.
31:12. strangers cut him off l. him
36:36. heathen that are l. ab. you
39 : 28. l. none of them any more
41 : 9. that l. was place of chamb.
11. doors of chambers tow. pla. l.
48 : 15. 5,000 that are l. in breadth
Da. 2 : 44. kingd. not be l. to other
10:17. nei. is there breath l. in me
Jo. 1 : 4. That palmerworm hath l. locust eaten; that locust hath l.
Hag. 2 : 3. who is l. that saw this house in her glory?
Zch. 13:8. the third part shall be l.
14 : 6. ev. one that is l. of nations
Mat. 4:20. l. their nets | 22. l. ships
8:15. he touched, and fever l. her, Mk. 1 : 31. Lu. 4:39. [Mk.8:8.
15 : 37. took up of meat that was l.
16:4. he l. them, 21:17. Mk. 8 :13.
22 : 22. l. went the way, Mk.12:12.
25. l. wife unto bro., Mk. 12 : 20.
23 : 38. your house is l. desolate
24:2. not be l. one stone upon ano., Mk. 13:2. Lu.21:6. [34,35,36.
40. one taken, other l., 41. Lu. 17:
26 : 44. Jesus l. them. and prayed
Mk. 1 : 20. l. father Zeb. in ship
10 : 28. we have l. all and followed
29. no man l. house, Lu.10:28,29.
12:22. seven had her, l. no seed, 21.
13:34. l. his house and gave author
14 : 52. l. linen cloth and fled
Lu. 4 : 39. rebuked fever and it l.
5 : 4. when he had l. speaking
28. he l. all, and followed him
10 : 40. sister l. me to serve alone
20 : 31. l. no children and died
Jn. 4 : 3. l. Judea depar. into Gali.
28. woman then l. her waterpot
52. at 7th hour the fever l. him
Ac. 2:31. his soul was not l. in hell
14:17. l. not hims. without witness
18 : 19. came to Eph. and l. them
21 : 3. l. Cyprus on the left hand
32 saw capt. l. beating of Paul
23:32. l. horsemen to go with him
24:27. Felix l. Paul bound, 25:14.
1 Th. 3 : 1. good to be l. at Athens
2 Ti. 4 : 13. cloak that I l. at Troas
20. Trophimus have I l. sick at
Tit. 1 : 5. for this l. I thee at Crete
He. 2 : 8. l. nothing that is not put
4:1. fear, lest a promise being l. us

Jude 6. angels which l. own habit-n
Re. 2 : 4. bec. thou hast l. first love
See **Left ALONE.**
LEFT off.
Ge. 11:8. they l.o. to build the city
17:22. God l. o. talking with him
Ru. 2 : 20. hath not l. o. his kindn.
1 K. 15 : 21. Baasha l. o. building,
Jb. 32:15. l.o. speaking [2 Ch.16:5.
Ps. 36 : 3. he hath l. o. to be wise
Je. 38 : 27. l. o. speaking with him
44 : 18. since we l.o. to burn ince.
Ho. 4 : 10. l.o. to take heed to Lord
LEFTEST. [mies
Ne. 9 : 28. l. them in hand of ene-
LEFTHANDED. [l.
Ju. 3:15. Ehud, a Benjamite, a man
20 : 16. there were 700 chosen men
LEG, LEGS. [l.
Ex. 12 : 9. roast with fire head, l-s
29:17. wash his l-s, Le. 1:9,13 -8:21.
Le. 4 : 11. l-s, inwards burn [-9 : 14.
11:21. have l-s above feet, these eat
De. 28:35. he shall smite thee in l-s
1 S. 17:6. greaves of brass upon l-s
Ps. 147 : 10. not pleasure in l-s of man
Pr. 26 : 7. l-s of lame are not equal
Can. 5:15. l-s as pillars of marble
Is. 3:20. I will take ornaments of l-s
47 : 2. make bare l., uncover thigh
Da. 2:33. His l-s of iron, his feet [l-s
Am. 3: 12. out of mouth of lion two
Jn. 19 : 31. besought l-s be broken
32. soldiers brake l-s of the 1st [l-s
33. saw he was dead, brake not his
LEGION, S.
Mat. 26 : 53. give me more than twelve l-s
Mk. 5 : 9. My name is L., Lu. 8:30.
15. possessed with devil, had the l.
LE'HABIM. [l : 11.
Ge. 10:13. Mizraim begat L., 1 Ch.
LE'HI. [L.
Ju. 15:9. Philistines spread thems. in
LEISURE.
Mk. 6 : 31. they had no l. to eat
LE'MECH. See LAMECH.
LEM'UEL.
Pr. 31 : 1. words of king L.
4. not for kings, O L., to drink wine
LEND.
Ex. 22 : 25. If thou l. money to any
Le. 25 : 37. not l. him thy victuals
De. 15: 6. shalt l. unto many na.
8. shalt l. him sufficient for need
23 : 19. not l. upon usury to bro.
20. unto stranger mayest l. upon
24 : 10. when dost l. bro. [usury
11. man to whom thou dost l.
28:12. shalt l. unto many nations
44. He l. to thee, thou not l. him
Lu. 6:34. if ye l. them of wh. hope to rec. what thank have ye?
sinners also l. sinners
35. love enemies, do good and l.
11:5 say, Friend, l. me three loaves
LENDER.
Pr. 22 : 7. borrower is servant to l.
Is. 24 : 2. as wi. l. so with borrower
LENDETH.
De. 15 : 2. Every creditor that l. aught unto neighbour
Ps. 37 :26. he is ever merciful and l.
112:5. good man sheweth favour l.
Pr 19:17. pity upon poor l. unto L.
22: † 7. borrower is servant to l.
LENDING. [ha.
De. 15: †2. Ev. master of the l. of his
LENGTH.
Ge. 13: 17 walk thro. land in l. of it
Eze. 31 : 7. fair in l. of his branches
40 : 18. side of gates over against l.
20. measured l. of gate [10,13.
45 :1. l. be 25,000 reeds, 3, 5.-48:9,
2. Sanctuary be 500 reeds in l.
7. l. be over ag. 1 of the portions
48 : 8. l. be as one of other parts
Eze. 48 : 18. residue in l. be 10,000
Zch. 2 :2. Jerus-m, to see what is l.
Ep. 3 : 18. l. and depth ; love of Ch.
Re. 21 : 16. l. and height equal (2)
At LENGTH. [lngk-s
Ps. 36 : † 10. draw out a. l. thy lov-
Pr. 29 :21. serv-t become his son a.l.
Ro. 1 :10. if a. l. prosperous journey
LENGTH with cubit, s.
Ge. 6 : 15. l. of ark shall be 300 c-s
Ex. 25 : 10. ark ; two c-s and half shall be l., 17.-37 : 1, 6. [37 : 10.
23. table, two c-s shall be the l.,
26 : 2. l. of one curtain shall be 28 c-s, 8, 13.-36 : 9, 15.
16. Ten c-s be l. of a board, 36:21.
27 : 11. in l. be hangings of 100 c-s
18. The l. of court shall be 100 c-s, 1 K. 7 : 2. Eze. 41 : 15.-42 : 2.
30 : 2. altar ; a c. be the l., 37 : 25.
38 : 1. altar ; five c-s the l., five c-s
18. and twenty c-s was the l., 1 K. 6 : 3, 20. 2 Ch. 4 : 1. [4 c-s the
De. 3 :11. bedstead ; nine c-s the l.,
Ju. 3 : 16. Ehud made dagger of c. l.
1 K. 6 :2. hou., the l. 60 c-s, 2Ch.3:3.
7 : 6. l. was fifty c-s, Eze. 40 : 21, 25, 36.-42 : 7, 8. [base
27. bases of brass; four c-s l. of oue
2 Ch. 3 :4 l. acc-g to breadth, 20c-s, 8.
Eze. 40 : 11. l. of gate, thirteen c-s
49. l. of porch was twenty c-s | 41:4.
41 : 2. l. was forty c-s, breadth 20 c-s
12. wall, l. 90 c-s | 22. altar, l. 2 c-s
Zch. 5 : 2. flying roll ; l. 20 c-s [(2)
See **DAYS, SPAN.**
LENGTHEN, ED.
De. 25 : 15. that thy days may be l-d
1 K. 3 :14. walk as Da. I l. thy days
Is. 54:2. l. thy cords, strengthen thy
LENGTHENING.
Da. 4 : 27. a l. of thy tranquillity
LENT.
Ex. 12:36. l. them as they required
De. 23 : 19. thing l. upon usury
1 S. 1:28. I l. him to L., he sh. be l.
2 : 20. loan which is l. to the L.
Je. 15 : 10. I have not l. on usury nor have men l. me.
LENTILES.
Ge. 25 : 34. Jacob gave Esau of l.
2 S. 17 : 28. Barzillai bro-t l. to Da.
23 : 11. a piece of ground full of l.
Eze. 4 : 9. Take thou also wheat, l.
LEOPARD, S.
Can. 4 : 8. look fr. mountains of l-s
Is. 11 : 6. l. shall lie down with kid
Je. 5 : 6. l. shall watch over cities
13 : 23. can l. change his spots?
Da. 7 : 6. and lo, another like a l.
Ho. 13 : 7. I will be to them as a l.
Ha. 1:8. their horses swifter than l-s
Re. 13 : 2. beast was like unto l.
LEPER, S.
Le. 13:45. l. in whom the plague is
14:2. this shall be the law of the l.
3. if leprosy be healed in the l.
22 : 4. man of seed of Aa. is a l.
Nu. 5 : 2. they put out of camp l.
2 S. 3: 29. fr. hou. of Joab, one a l.
2 K. 5 : 1. a mighty man but a l.
11. I thought, He will recover the
27. went from his presence a l. [l.
7:8. when l-s came to utterm. part
15:5. Azariah l. unto day of death
2 Ch. 26 : 21. Uzziah king was l.
23. buried him, for said, He is a l.
Mat. 8:2. there came a l., Mk. 1:40.
10 : 8. heal the sick, cleanse l-s
11:5. the l-s are cleansed, Lu.7:22.
26 6. in house of Simon l., Mk.14:3.
Lu. 4:27. many l-s in Isr. in time of
17:12. met him ten men that were
LEPROSY. [l-s
Le. 13:2. in the skin like plague of l.
3. plague of l., 8, 11, 15, 25, 27, 30, 42, 49.
Le. 13:9. when plague of l. is in man
12. if a l. break | 13. if l. covered
43. as the l. appeareth in the skin
47. garment th. plague of l. is in
51. plague is fretting l., 52.-14:44.
59. law of plag. of l., 14:54, 55, 57.
14 : 3. if plague of l. be healed [l.
7. sprinkle him to be cleansed fr.
32. law of him in wh. plague of l.
34. put plague of l. in a house
De. 24 : 8. take heed in plague of l.
2 K. 5:3. would recover of his l., 7.
6. mayest recover him of his l.
27. l. of Naaman cleave unto thee
2 Ch. 26 : 19. l. rose in his forehead
Mat. 8 : 3. immediately his l. was cleansed, Mk. 1 : 42. Lu. 5 : 13.
Lu. 5:12. a man full of l. besought
LEPROUS. [him
Ex. 4 : 6. his hand was l. as snow
Le. 13:44. he is a l. man, he is uncl.
Nu. 12 : 2. Miriam became l. (2)
2 K. 7 : 3. were 4 l. men at the gate
2 Ch. 26:20. Uzziah was l. in forehead
LE'SHEM.
Jos. 19:47. Dan went to fight ag. L.
LESS.
Ge. 32 : † 10. am l. than least of all
Ex. 16 : 17. some more, some l.
30 : 15. rich not give more, poor not l. than half shek. [or more
Nu. 22 : 18. bey. word of L. to do l.
26:54. to few give l. inheri., 33:54.
1 S. 22 : 15. knew noth. l. or more
25:36. Abigail told noth. l. or more
Ezr. 9 : 13. punished us l. than iniq.
Jb. 11:6. God exacteth l. than iniq.
Pr. 17 : 7. l. do lying lips a prince
19 : 10. much l. for a serv. to rule
Is. 40 : 17. all nations l. than noth.
Mk. 4 : 31. sown is l. than all seeds
15 : 40. Mary mother of Ja. the l.
1 Co. 8 : † 8. if eat not, have we l.
12 : 23. members we think l. hono.
2 Co. 12 : 15. more I love, l. am lov.
Ep. 3 : 8. am l. than least of saints
Ph. 2 : 28. that I be l. sorrowful
He. 7 : 7. the l. is blessed of better
See **How MUCH less.**
LESSER.
Ge. 1 : 16. l. light to rule the night
Is. 7 : 25. for treading of l. cattle
Eze. 16:†46. thy sister l. than thou
43:14. from the l. settle to greater
LEST.
Ge. 3:3. nei. shall touch it l. ye die, Le. 10 : 6, 7, 9. Nu. 18 : 32.
11 : 4. l. we be scattered abroad
14 : 23. l. say, I made Ab. rich
19:15. l. thou be consumed in iniq.
19. l. evil take me, and I die, 26:9.
32 : 11. l. he smite me [20 : 5, 6, 7.
38 : 11. l. he die, as his breth., De.
23. Let her take it, l. we be asha.
45 : 11. l. thou come to poverty
Ex. 5 : 3. l. he fall upon us with
13:17. l. peo. repent in war [pestil.
19 : 21. l. they break thro. unto L.
22. sanctify, l. the L. break forth
20 : 19. let not G. speak, l. we die
33 : 3. not go, l. I consume thee
Nu. 4:20. not go in, l. they die, 18:22.
De. 11 : 17. l. ye perish quickly
24 : 15. l. he cry ag. thee unto L.
25 : 3. l. if he sho. exceed and beat
Jos. 9 : 20. let them live, l. wrath
24:27. witness, l. ye deny your G.
Ju. 7 : 2. l. Israel vaunt against me
1 S. 20:3. not know, l. he be grieved
2 S. 12 : 28. l. I take the city
Jb. 36 : 18. l. he take thee wi. stroke
42 : 8. l. I deal after your folly
Ps. 2:12. kiss the Son l. he be angry
13 : 3. l. I sleep the sleep of death
50:22. consider this, l. I tear you
91:12. l. thou dash thy foot, Mat. 4 : 6. Lu. 4 : 11.

Ps. 106 : 23. Moses stood in the breach, l. he destroy them
140 : 8. grant not, l. exalt thems.
143:7.l.I be like them th. go down
Pr. 9 : 8. not scorner, l. he hate
20:13. love not sleep, l. to poverty
22: 25. l. thou learn his ways
24:18. l. L. see it, and it displease
25:8. l. thou know not what to do
10. l. he put thee to shame
17. l. he be weary of thee, and
26:4. ans. not a fool, l. be like him
30:6. not to his words, l. he reprov.
9. l. I be full and deny thee, or l. I be poor [28 : 27.
Is. 6 : 10. l. they see with eyes, Ac.
27:3. l. any hurt it, I will keep it
28:22.l.your bands be made strong
48:5.l.say, mine idol hath done, 7.
Je. 1 : 17. l. I confound thee [12.
4 : 4. l. my fury come like fire, 21 :
6 : 8. l. my soul depart from thee
37:20. not to return, l. I die there
Ho. 2:3. l. I strip her naked, and
Am. 5 : 6. seek L., l. he break out
Zch. 7 : 12. as adamant, l. hear law
Mal. 4 : 6. l. I smite earth wi. curse
Mat. 17 : 27. l. we should offend
25:9. l. not enough for us and you
Mk. 13 : 5. l. any man deceive you
36.l.coming, he find you sleeping
14 : 38. l. ye enter into temptation
Lu. 8 : 12. l. believe and be saved
21 : 34. l. your hearts overcharged
Jn.5:14.sin no more, l.a worse thing
18 : 28. went out l. sho. be defiled
Ac. 5 : 39. l. found to fight ag. G.
13 : 40. beware, l. that come
Ro. 11:21. heed, l. he spare not
1 Co. 9 : 12. l. we hinder the gospel
10:12. standeth take heed l. he fall
2 Co. 2 : 11. l. Satan get advantage
12 : 7. l. I be exalted above meas.
13:10. l. bring pres. I use sharpn.
Ga. 2 : 2. l. I should run in vain
6 : 1. consid-g, l. thou be tempted
Ep. 2 : 9. not of works, l. any boast
Ph. 2:27.l. I sho. have sorrow upon
Col. 2 : 4. l. any man beguile you
3:21.provoke not chil.,l.discourag.
1 Ti.3:6. l. being lifted up wi. pride
He. 2 : 1. l. we sho. let them slip
3 : 12. l. be in any an evil heart
13. l. any of you be hardened
4 : 1. l. a promise being left
11. l. any fall after same example
12:3. l. ye be weary in your minds
13. l. lame be turned out of way
15. l. any man fail of grace of God
Ja. 5 : 9. grudge not, l. condemned
12. l. ye fall into condemnation
2 Pe. 3:17. beware, l. being led aw.
Re. 16 : 15. garments, l. he walk [naked

LET.

Ge. 24 : 55. l. damsel abide with
60. l. thy seed possess gate
Ex. 3:19. king of E. will not l. you go, 4:21.-7 : 14. 8 : 21, 32.-9 : 7, 17, 35.-10: 20, 27.-11 : 10.
20. after that he will l. you go
5 : 1. l. my peo. go, 6 : 11.-7 : 16.-8:1, 20.-9 : 1, 13.-10 : 3.
4. why do ye l. people fr. works ?
8 : 28. I will l. you go, 9:28.-13:17.
29. l. not Pha. deal deceitfully
9:8.l.Mo.sprinkle it toward heaven
12 : 10. sh. l. nothing of it remain
14 : 5. why have we l. Israel go
18 : 27. Moses l. fa. in law depart
19 : 24. l. not priests break thro.
20 : 19. l. not G. speak with us
21 : 8. shall he l. her be redeemed
26. l. him go free for his eye, 27.
23 : 11. 7th year l. it rest [send
33:12. hast not l. me know wh.wilt
Le. 18 : 21. not l. seed pass thro. fire
19 : 19. not l. cattle gender with a
De. 2:30. Sihon would not l. us pass
15 : 12. thou shalt l. him go free
13. shalt not l. him go aw. empty
Jos. 10 : 28. he l. none remain, 30.
24 : 28. so Joshua l. people depart
Ju. 1 : 25. they l. the man go and
2 : 6. when Josh. had l. people go
1 S. 18 : 2. l. him go no more home
21 : 13. l. spittle fall upon beard
2 S. 11 : 12. tomorr. l. thee depart
13 : 6. l. Tamar my sister come
27. he l. all king's sons go
1 K. 18 : 40. l. none of them escape
2 Ch.16:1.l. none go out or come in
20 : 10. wouldest not l. Isr. invade
Es. 5 : 12. queen l. no man come in
9 : 13. l. it be granted to Jews
Jb. 27:6. righte-ss. I will not l.it go
Ps. 69 : 6. l. not those th. wait be asha. l. not those seek thee be
109:6. l. Satan stand at right ha.
119:10.l.me not wander fr. com-ts
Can. 3:4. I held him, not let him go
Is. 43 : 13. and who shall l. it ?
Je. 27 : 11. those will I l. remain
Eze. 39 : 7. not l. pollute my name
Mat. 7:4. l. me pull mote, Lu. 6 : 42.
8 : 22. l. dead bury dead, Lu. 9:60.
13 : 30. l. both grow together
27 : 49. said l. be, l. us see
Mk. 7 : 27. l. chil. first be filled
11 : 6. Jes. com-d, they l. them go
Lu. 9 : 61. l. me first go bid them
22 : 68. ye not ans. nor l. me go
Jn. 11 : 44. loose and l. him go
18 : 8. ye seek me l. these go
19 : 12. If thou l. this man go
Ac. 2 : 29. l. me freely speak
27 : 15. ship, we l. her drive
32. cut ropes, l. her fall
Ro. 1:13. come unto you, but was l.
2 Th. 2 : 7. who now letteth, will l.
He. 2:1. lest at any time we l. them [slip

See **Let ALONE.**

LET down.

Ge. 24 : 14. l. d. thy pitcher, 18, 46.
Ex.17:11.when l. d. hands, Amalek
Jos.2:15. then Rahab l. them d., 18.
1 S. 19 : 12. Michal l. David d. thro.
2 K. 13 : 21. when the man was l. d.
Je. 38:6. they l. d. Jere. with cords
11. l. the rags d. by cords
Eze. 1:24. they l. d. their wings, 25.
Mk. 2:4. they l. d. bed wherein sick of palsy lay, Lu. 5 : 19.
Lu.5:4.l.d. your nets for a draught
5. at thy word I will l. d. the net
Ac. 9:25. and l. him d. in a basket,
2 Co. 11 : 33. [l. d. boat
10:11. sheet l. d. to earth | 27:30.
11: 5. sheet l. d. by 4 corners

LET loose.

Ge. 49 : 21. Naphtali is a hind l. l.
Le. 14 : 7. l. living bird l. into field
Jb. 6 : 9. th. he would l. l. his ha.
30 : 11. they have l. l. the bridle

LET out. [keepers

Can. 8 : 11. he l. o. viney. unto
Mat. 21 : 33. viney. and l. it o. to husbandmen, 41. Mk. 12:1. Lu. [20 : 9.

LETTED.

Nu. 22.:† 16. be not thou l. from [coming

LETTER.

2 S. 11 : 14. Da. wrote l. to Joab, 15.
2 K. 5 : 5. send l. unto king of Isr.
6. when l. is come unto thee (2)
7. when king had read l.
10 : 2. soon as l. cometh to thee
6. he wrote l. the 2d time
7. came to pass when l. came
19 : 14. Hez. received l., Is. 37:14.
Ezr. 4 : 7. l. was written in Syrian
8. Rehum wrote l. ag. Jerus., 11.
18. l. sent us hath been read
23. when copy of k. Artax. l. was [read
5 : 5. returned answer by l.
7 : 11. this is copy of l., 5 : 6, 7.
Ne. 2 : 8. a l. to Asaph keeper of
6 : 5. sent to me with an open l.
Es. 9 : 26. for all words of this l.
29. to confirm this l. of Purim
Je. 29 : 1. words of l. Jere. sent
29.Zephaniah priest read this l. in
Ac.23:25.Claudius wrote l. to Felix
34. when governor had read l.
Ro. 2:27. who by l. dost transgress
29. circumc. of heart, not in l.
7:6. serve, not in oldness of the l.
2 Co. 3 : 6. ministers not of l. but
7 : 8. tho. made you sorry with l.
Ga. 6 : 11. ye see how large a l. I
2 Th. 2: 2. be not soon shaken by l.
He. 13 : 22. I have writ. l. unto you

LETTERS.

1 K. 21 : 8. Jezebel wrote l. in, 9.
11. as it was written in the l.
2 K. 10 : 1. Jehu wrote l. to Sama.
20 : 12. k. of Bab. sent l., Is. 39:1.
2 Ch. 30 : 1. Hez. wrote l. to Ephr.
6. posts went with l. from king
32:17.Sennach.wrote l.to rail on G.
Ne. 2:7. let l. be giv. me to gov-s, 9.
6 : 17. sent l. unto Tobiah, l. came
19.Tobiah sent l.to put me in fear
Es.1:22. Ahas. sent l. into provinces
3 : 13. l. were sent by posts, 8 : 10.
8:5. to reverse l. devised by Haman
9 : 20. Mordecai sent l. to Jews, 30.
25. com-d by l.th.his wick.device
Je. 29 : 25. hast sent l. in thy name
Lu. 23:38. was written in l. of Heb.
Jn. 7 : 15. how knoweth this man l.
Ac. 9:2. desired of him l. to Damas.
15 : 23. apostles wrote l. by them
22:5.fr whom I rec-d l.unto breth.
28 : 21. nei. rec-d l. out of Judea
1 Co. 16 : 3. sh. approve by your l.
2 Co. 3 : 1. Nor need we l. of commendation
10 : 9. not as if I wo. terrify by l.
10. his l. weighty and powerful
11. in word, by l. when absent

LETTEST, ETH, ING.

Ex. 8:29. deceitf-y in not l-g peo. go
2 K. 10 : 24. l-h him go, his life be for his [mouth
Jb. 15 : 13. l-t such words out of
41:1.tongue wi.cord thou l-t down
Pr.17:14. strife as when l-h out wat.
Lu. 2 : 29. now l-t thy serv. depart
2 Th. 2 : 7. he that now l-h will let

LETU'SHIM.

Ge.25:3.sons of Dedan, L., Leummim

LEUM'MIM. See LETUSHIM.

LEVI.

Ge. 29 : 34. was his name called L.
34 : 25. two of sons of Jac. L., 30.
46 : 11. the sons of L., Ex. 6 : 16.-32 : 26. Nu. 3 : 17.-4 : 2.-16 : 10.
De. 31 : 9. 1 Ch. 6 : 16.-23:6, 24.-24 : 20. Ne. 12 : 23.
49: 5. Simeon, L. are brethren, 35:23. Ex. 1 : 2. 1 Ch. 2 : 1. [L.
Ex.2:1. man of h. of L. took dau. of
6 : 16. years of the life of L. 137
19. these are families of L.
32 : 28. children of L. did acc.
Nu. 16 : 1. son of L., 1 Ch. 6:38, 43, 47. Ezr. 8 : 18. [of L., 8.
7. take too much upon you, sons
17:3. Aaron's name upon rod of L.
18 : 21. given chil. of L. all 10th
26 : 59. Amram's wife, dau. of L.
De. 10 : 9, L. no part with breth.
21 : 5. priests sons of L. sh. come
27 : 12. upon Gerizim to bless, L.
33:8. of L. said, Let thy Thummim
1 K. 12 : 31. made priests not of L.
1 Ch. 9 : 18. in companies of chil
12 : 26. Of chil. of L. 4,600 [of L
21 : 6. L. Benj. counted he not
Ezr. 8 : 15. found none of sons of L
Eze. 40 : 46. of Zadok am. sons of L
48 : 31. one gate of Jud., one of L

Mal. 2 : 4. my cov. might be with L.
8. ye have corrupted cov. of L.
3 : 3. he sh. purify the sons of L.
Mk. 2 : 14. L. the son of Alpheus
Lu. 3 : 24. Matthat, son of L., 29.
5 : 27. publican named L. sitting
29. L. made him a great feast
He. 7 : 9. L. who received tithes, 5.
See **HOUSE of Levi.**

Tribe of LEVI.

Nu. 1:49. shalt not number **t. o. L.**
3 : 6. bring the **t. o. L.** near and
18:2. **t. o. L.** bring, that they may
De. 10 : 8. Lord separated **t. o. L.**
18 : 1. **t. o. L.** shall have no part
with Israel, Jos. 13 : 14, 33.
1 Ch. 23: 14. were named of **t. o. L.**
Re. 7:7. of **t.o.L.** were sealed 12,000

LEVIATHAN.

Jb. 3 : † 8. are ready to raise up a **l.**
41 : 1. canst draw out **l.** with hook?
Ps. 74:14. thou breakest heads of **l.**
104 : 26. **l.** thou hast made to play
Is. 27 : 1. shall punish **l.** even **l.**

LEVITE.

Ex. 4 : 14. is not Aa. L. thy bro.?
De. 12 : 12. rejoice bef. Lord, and L.,
18.–16 : 11, 14.–26 : 11, 13.
14 : 29. L. sh. come and eat, 26:12.
18 : 6. if a L. come from thy gates
Ju.17:7. young man out of Beth-le.
10. So the L. went in [a L., 9.
11. L. content to dwell with man
12. Micah consecrated the L.
13. seeing I have L. to my priest
18:3. knew voice of yo. man L., 15.
19:1. certain L. sojourning on mt.
20:4. L. said, I came into Gibeah
2 Ch. 20 : 14. upon Jahaziel the L.
came the Spirit
31 : 12. Cononiah the L. over the
dedicated things [ings
14. Kore L. over free will offer-
Ezr. 10 : 15. Shabbethai L. helped
Lu. 10: 32. a L. came and looked on
Ac. 4:36. Barnabas a L. having land

LEVITES.

Ex. 6 : 25. heads of fathers of L.
38 : 21. counted for service of L.
Le. 25 : 32. cities of L. may redeem
33. cities of L. their possession
Nu. 1:47. L. were not numb-d, 2:33.
50. shalt appoint L. over taberu.
51. the L. shall take it down
53. L. shall pitch round about
2 : 17. set forward with camp of L.
3 : 9. shalt give L. unto Aa., 8 : 19.
12. I have tak. L. L. sh be mine
20. These the fam. of L., 26 : 57,
58. 1 Ch. 6 : 19. 2 Ch. 35 : 5.
32. shall be chief over chief of L.
39. all numbered of L., 4 : 46.
41. take L. for me, 45.–8 : 14, 18.
46. more than L. | 49. redeemed
4 : 18. not cut off from L. [of L.
7 : 5. shalt give wagons unto L.
6. Moses gave oxen unto L.
8 : 6. take L. from Isr. and cleanse
9. bring L. before the taberu., 10.
11. Aaron shall offer L. bef. Lord
12. L. shall lay hands upon heads
13. shalt set L. before Aaron
15. after that shall L. go in, 22.
21. and L. were purified | 20.
24. is it that belongeth unto L.
26. thus shalt thou do to the L.
18 : 6. taken L. to do service, 23.
24. the tithes I have given to L.
26. speak unto L.
30. It shall be counted unto L.
31:30. all manner of beasts unto L.
35 : 2. that they give unto L. cities.
4, 6, 7, 8. Jos. 21 : 3. 1 Ch. 6:64.
De. 18 : 7. minister, as breth. L. do
27 : 14. L. shall speak and say
31 : 25. that Moses commanded L.
Jos.14:3. unto L. gave none inheri., 4
Jos. 18 : 7. L. have no part am. you
21 : 4. chil. of Aaron wh. were L.
20. families of L., 27, 40 | 34.
41. all cities of L. were 48
1 S. 6 : 15. L. took down ark of Lord
2 S. 15 : 24. Zadok and L. with him
1 Ch. 6: 48. L. were appointed unto
all | 9 : 14, 26, 31, 33, 34.
15 : 15. chil. of L. bare the ark
16. Da. spake to chief of L., 17,
22.–23 : 26.–26 : 17.–27 : 17.
26. G. helped L. that bare ark, 27.
16 : 4. certain of L. to minister
23:3. L. numbered fr. age of 30 | 27.
24 : 6. one of L. wrote them bef. the
30. These were sons of L. [king
26:17. eastw. were 6 L. | 20.–27:17.
2 Ch. 5 : 4. and the L. took up ark
12. L. wh. were singers stood, 7:6.
8 : 14. L. to their charges
11:14. the L. left their suburbs and
13 : 9. have ye not cast out the L.
10. L. went upon business | 17:8.
19 : 11. L. shall be officers bef. you
20 : 19. L. stood up to praise Lord
23 : 2. gathered L. out of all cities
7. L. shall compass the king | 6.
8. So. L. did acc. to all com-d
24 : 5. howbeit L. hastened it not
6. why hast not required of L.
11. chest was brought by L.
29 : 5. ye L. sanctify now yours.
12. L. arose | 16. L. took it to
25. set L. in house of the Lord
26. L. with instruments of Da.
30. com-d L. to sing praise
34. L. did help them; L. upright
30 : 16. blood they received of L.
17. L. had charge of the killing
22. spake comfortably unto L.
31 : 17. L. from 20 years old and
upward, 1 Ch. 23 : 27. Ezr. 3:8.
19. by genealogies among L.
34 : 9. L. that kept the doors | 12.
13. of L. were scribes, officers
35:3. Josiah said unto L. wh. taught
9. chief of L. gave unto L. 500
11. L. flayed offerings [oxen
14. L. prepared for themselves, 15.
Ezr. 2:40. L. chil. of Jeshua | 3:9, 10.
6 : 18. set L. in courses
8 : 20. for service of L. | 33.–10:23.
Ne. 3 : 17. aft. him repaired the L.
7 : 1. singers, L. appointed | 43.
8 : 7. L. caused people to underst.
9. L. that taught the people
11. the L. stilled the people
9 : 4. stood upon stairs of L.
5. L. said, Stand and bless Lord
10 : 37. tithes unto L. | 9.
38. with L. when L. take tithes
11 : 16. chief of L. had oversight |
18. all the L. in holy city 284 [15.
22. overseer of L. was Uzzi
36. of L. were divisions in Judah
12 : 8. L. Jeshua and | 22.
24. chief of L. to give thanks
27. at dedication they sought L.
47. sanctif-d holy things unto L.
13 : 5. com-d to be given to L. | 13.
10. portions of L. not been given
for the L. were fled
22. com-d L. sho. cleanse thems.
29. have defiled priesthood of L.
Je. 33:22. multiply L. that minister
Eze. 44 : 10. L. gone shall bear iniq.
45 : 5. 25,000 of length sh. L. have
48 : 11. went not astray when L.
12. most holy by border of L. | 22.

Priests with LEVITES.

De. 17:9. shalt come unto **p.** L. and
18. out of what is bef. **p.** the L.
18 : 1. The **p.** the L. have no part
24:8. to do all **p.** and L. shall teach
27:9. the **p.** the L. spake unto Isr.
Jos. 3: 3. see **p.** and L. bearing ark
8 : 33. the **p.** the L. wh. bare ark
1 K. 8 : 4. these did **p.** and L. bring,
2 Ch. 5 : 5.
1 Ch.9:2. first inhab. were the **p.** L.
13 : 2. let us send to the **p.** and L.
15 : 11. Da. called for the **p.** and L.
14. So **p.** and L. sanctified thems.
23:2. gath-d princes with **p.** and L.
24:6. chief of fa-s of **p.** and L., 31.
28 : 13. courses of **p.** and L., 21. 2
Ch. 31 : 2.
2 Ch.8:15. unto **p.** and L. conc. any
11 : 13. **p.** and L. resorted to him
13 : 9. not cast out **p.** and L.
19 : 8. Jehosh-t set of L. and of **p.**
23:4. **p.** and L. be porters of doors
6. **p.** and they that minister of L.
18. by the hand of the **p.** the L.
24 : 5. gathered **p.** and L., 29 : 4.
29:34. **p.** and L. were more upright
30:15. **p.** and L. were ashamed [day
21. L. and **p.** praised Lord day by
25. all cong-n with the **p.** and L.
27. then **p.** and L. blessed people
31 : 4. give portion of **p.** and L.
9. Hez. questioned with **p.** and L.
34:30. **p.** L. and peo. went [and L.
35 : 8. princes gave willingly to **p.**
10. **p.** stood in places and L.
18. **p.** and L. kept passover
Ezr. 1 : 5. rose up **p.** and L. [7:73.
2:70. **p.** and L. dwelt in cities, Ne.
3 : 8. **p.** L. and all out of captivity
12. many of **p.** and L. wept
6 : 16. **p.** and L. kept dedication
18. **p.** in divisions, L. in courses
20. **p.** and L. were purifi., Ne. 12:30.
7 : 7. went up of **p.** L. and singers
13. all **p.** and L. go with thee
24. certify touching any **p.** and L.
8:30. So took **p.** and L. the weight
9:1. **p.** and L. not separated thems.
10 : 5. Ezra made **p.** and L. swear
Ne. 8:13. on 2d day gath-d **p.** and L.
9 : 38. L. and **p.** seal unto it
10:28. rest of peo. **p.** and L., 11:3, 20.
34. we cast lots am. **p.** and L.
12:1. **p.** and L. went up with Zeruh.
44. Judah rejoiced for **p.** and L.
13:30. appointed wards of **p.** and L.
Is. 66:21. take of them for **p.** and L.
Je. 33:18. **p.** and L. not want a man to
21. with the L. the **p.** my ministers
Eze. 43 : 19. give to **p.** L. a young
44 : 15. **p.** and L. that kept charge
48:13. over ag. border of **p.** and L.
Jn. 1:19. Jews sent **p.** and L. to ask
[him

LEVITICAL.

He. 7 : 11. if perfection by L. priest-
[hood

LEVY. [Noun.]

1 K. 5 : 13. Sol. raised **l.** of 300,000
14. Adoniram was over the **l.**, 1
K. 4 : † 6.
9 : 15. reason of the **l.** Sol. raised

LEVY. [Verb.]

Nu. 31 : 28. **l.** a tribute unto the L.
1 K. 9 : 21. upon those did Sol. **l.**
[tribute

LEWD.

Eze. 16 : 27. ashamed of thy **l.** way
23 : 44. went in, as unto **l.** women
Ac. 17 : 5. **l.** fellows of baser sort

LEWDLY.

Eze. 22 : 11. hath **l.** defiled his dau.

LEWDNESS.

Ju. 20 : 6. committed **l.** in Israel
Je. 11:15. she wrought **l.** wi. many
13 : 27. seen **l.** of thy whoredom
Eze. 16:43. shalt not commit this **l.**
58. hast borne thy **l.** and abomi.
22 : 9. in midst of thee commit **l.**
† 11. by **l.** hath defiled dau. in law
23:21. to remembr. **l.** of thy youth
27. will I make thy **l.** cease, 48.
29. sh. be discov-d, both thy **l.** and
35. therefore bear thou thy **l.** and
49. they shall recompense your **l.**
24 : 13. in thy filthiness is **l.** bec. I
Ho. 2:10. now will I discover her **l.**

Ho. 6 : 9. priests murder, commit l.
Ac. 18:14. if a matter of wrong or l.

LIAR.

Jb. 24 : 25. who will make me a l.?
Pr. 17 : 4. l. giveth ear to naughty
19 : 22. poor man is better than l.
30 : 6. lest thou be found a l.
Je. 15:18. wilt thou be unto me as a
Jn. 8 : 44. he is a l. and fa. of it [l.
55. if say, I know him not, sh. be l.
Ro. 3 : 4. let G. be true, ev. man l.
1 Jn. 1:10. not sinned, make him l.
2:4. keepeth not com-ts is l., 4:20.
22. Who a l. but he denieth Jes.
5:10. believeth not G. made him a l.

LIARS.

De. 33 : 29. thine enem. be found l.
Ps. 116:11. said in haste, All men l
Is. 44 : 25. frustrateth tokens of l.
Je. 50 : 36. A sword is upon the l.
1 Ti. 1:10. law is made for l.
Tit. 1:12. The Cretians are always l.
Re. 2 : 2. tried and found them l.
21: 8. all l. shall have part in lake

LIBERAL.

Pr. 11: 25. l. soul shall be made fat
Is. 32 : 5. vile shall not be called l.
8. l. deviseth l. things, and by l.
2 Co. 9 : 13. for your l. distribution

LIBERALITY.

1 Co. 16:3. bring your l. unto Jerus.
2 Co. 8 : 2. abounded unto riches of

LIBERALLY. [l.

De. 15:14. thou shalt furnish him l.
Ja. 1 : 5. G. who giveth to all men l.

LIBERTINES.

Ac. 6 : 9. called synagogue of the L.

LIBERTY.

Le. 25:10. proclaim l. thro. all the la.
Ps. 119 : 45. and I will walk at l.
Is. 61 : 1. to proclaim l. to captives
Je. 34:8. made a cov. to proclaim l.
15. done right in proclaiming l.
16. servant whom he had set at l.
17. not heark-d unto me in pro-
cl-g l. I proclaim a l. for you
Eze. 46 : 17. be his to the year of l.
Lu. 4 : 18. to set at l. them bruised
Ac. 24:23. Paul, and let him have l.
26 : 32. might have been set at l.
27 : 3. gave L. to go to his friends
Ro. 8 : 21. bondage into glorious l.
1 Co. 7 : 39. she is at l. to marry
8:9. take heed lest this l. of yours
10:29. why is my l. judged of ano.
2 Co. 3:17. where Spirit of L. is, is l.
Ga. 2 : 4. came privily to spy our l.
5 : 1. Stand fast in l. wh. Christ
13. been called unto l. use not l.
He. 10 : † 19. l. to enter the holiest
13:23. Timothy is set at l.
Ja. 1:25. whoso looketh into law of l.
2 : 12. shall be judged by law of l.
1 Pe. 2 : 16. not using l. for a cloak
2 Pe. 2:19. While promise th. l. they

LIB'NAH.

Nu. 33 : 20. pitched in L.
21. removed from L.
Jos. 10 : 29. Jos. fo ght against L.
31. And Joshua passed from L.
32. according to all done to L.
12 : 15. The king of L. one
21:13. L. to Lev., 15:42. 1 Ch. 6:57.
2 K. 8: 22. L. revolted, 2 Ch. 21:10.
19 : 8. found king of Assyria warring against L., Is. 37 : 8.
23 : 31. name was Hamutal, dau.
of Jeremiah of L., 24:18. Je. 52:1.

LIB'NI, LIB'NITES.

Ex. 6 : 17. sons of Gershon, L., Nu.
3 : 18. 1 Ch. 6:17, 20, 29.–23:†7.
–26 : † 21. [–26 : 58.
Nu. 3:21. Of Gershon family of L-s,

LIB'YA.

Eze. 30 : 5. L. shall fall by sword
38 : 5. Persia, Ethiopia, L.
Ac. 2:10. in parts of L. about Cyrene

LIB'YANS.

Je. 46 : 9. L. th. handled the shield
Da. 11 : 43. L. shall be at his steps

LICE. [17.

Ex. 8:16. dust became l. thro. all E.,
18. magicians did so to bring l.
so were l. upon man and
Ps. 105 : 31. came l. in their coasts

LICENSE. [l.

Ac. 21:40. when he had given Paul
25: 16. bef. accused have l. to ans.

LICK.

Nu. 22:4. sh. this company l. up all
1 K. 21 : 19. shall dogs l. thy blood
Ps. 72 : 9. his enemies shall l. dust
Is. 49 : 23. sh. l. up dust of thy feet
Mi. 7 : 17. shall l. dust like serpent

LICKED, ETH.

Nu. 22 : 4. lick up as ox l-h grass
1 K. 18:38. fire l-d up wat. in trench
21:19. where dogs l-d bl. of Naboth
22 : 38. the dogs l-d up his blood
Lu. 16 : 21. dogs came and l-d his

LID. [sores

2 K. 12 : 9. bored a hole in l. of it

LIE. [Noun.]

Ps. 62:9. men of high degree are a l.
119 : 69. proud forged a l. ag. me
Is. 44:20. is not l. in my right ha.?
Je. 27 : 10. they prophesy a l. unto
you, 14, 15, 16.–29 : † 9, 21.
28 : 15. makest people trust in a l.
29:31. he caused you to trust in l.
37 : † 14. said Jeremiah, It is a l.
Eze. 21:29. they divine a l. unto thee
Mi. 1 : 14. houses of Achzib be a l.
Zch. 10 : 2. diviners have seen a l.
Jn. 8 : 44. When he speaketh a l.
Ro. 1:25. changed truth of G. into l.
3 : 7. abounded thro. my l. unto
2 Th. 2:11. that they sho. believe a l.
1 Jn. 2 : 21. know no l. is of truth
27. teach. you of all, and is no l.
Re. 21: 27. nei. whatso. maketh a l.
22 : 15. without are whoso. mak. l.

LIES.

Ju. 16:10. thou hast told me l., 13.
Jb. 11:3. thy l. make men hold peace
13:4. ye are forgers of l. physicians
Ps. 40 : 4. such as turn aside to l.
58:3. wicked go astray, speaking l.
62 : 4. delight in l. curse inwardly
63:11. mouth speaketh l. be stopp.
101 : 7. telleth l. not tarry in my
Pr. 6:19. L. hates witn. speaketh l.
14 : 5. a false witness will utter l.
25. a deceitful witness speaketh l.
19:5. th. speaketh l. sh. not escape
9. he that speaketh l. sh. perish
21 : † 28. a witness of l. sh. perish
29 : 12. If a ruler hearken to l. his
30: 8. Remove fr. me vanity and l.
Is. 9 : 15. prophet that teacheth l.
16 : 6. the pride of Moab, but his l.
28 : 15. we have made l. our refuge
17. shall sweep away refuge of l.
59 : 3. your lips have spoken l.
4. they trust in vanity, speak l.
Je. 9:3. bend tongues like bow for l.
5. taught their tongue to speak l.
14:14. proph. prophesy l., 23:25, 26.
16 : 19. fathers have inherited l.
20 : 6. to whom hast prophesied l.
23:14. commit adultery, walk in l.
32. cause people to err by their l.
48 : 30. his l. shall not so effect it
Eze. 13 : 8. ye spoken vanity seen l.
9. hand be upon prophets divine l.
19. to my people th. hear your l.
22. with l. ye made righte. sad
22:28. divining l. unto them, saying
24:12. hath wearied herself with l.
Da. 11: 27. sh. speak l. at one table
Ho. 7 : 3. make princes glad with l.
13. tho. redeemed, yet spoken l.
10 : 13. ye have eaten fruit of l.
11:12. Ephr. compasseth me wi. l.
Ho. 12:1. he daily increaseth l. and
Am. 2:4. their l. caused them to err
Mi. 6:12. inhabitants have spoken l.
Na. 3 : 1. Woe to city it is full of l.
Ha. 2 : 18. image and teacher of l.
Zph. 3 : 13. Israel sh. not speak l.
Zch. 13:3. speakest l. in name of L.
1 Ti. 4 : 2. Speaking l. in hypocrisy

LIE, LIED, LIETH.

[To speak falsely.]

Ge. 21: † 23. if thou shalt l. unto me
Le. 6 : 2. If a soul l. unto his neighb.
3. found lost, and l-h conc-g it
19 : 11. Ye shall not steal nor l.
Nu. 23 : 19. G. not a man th. he l.
1 S. 15 : 29. Strength of Isr. not l.
1 K. 13 : 18. said I am prophet as
thou art, but he l-d unto him
2 K. 4 : 16. do not l. unto handm.
Jb. 6 : 28. is evident unto you if I l.
34 : 6. Should I l. against my right
Ps. 78 : 36. they l-d unto him with
89 : 35. sworn I will not l. unto Da.
Pr. 14 : 5. faithf. witness will not l.
Is. 57 : 11. of wh. afraid, th. thou l-d
63:8. my people, chil. that will not l.
Mi. 2 : 11. If a man do l.
Ha. 2 : 3. it shall speak and not l.
Ac. 5 : 3. why Sat. filled heart to l.?
4. hast not l-d unto men but G.
Ro. 9 : 1. I say truth in C. I l. not,
1 Ti. 2 : 7. [I l. not
2 Co. 11 : 31. Fa. of our L. knoweth
Ga. 1 : 20. I wrote, behold I l. not
Col. 3 : 9. l. not one to ano. seeing
ye have put off [He. 6 : 18.
Tit. 1 : 2. G. that can-t l. promised,
Ja. 3 : 14. l. not against truth
1 Jn. 1 : 6. we l. and do not the truth
Re. 3 : 9. say they are Jews, but do l.

LIE.

Ge. 39 : 10. heark-d not to l. by her
47 : 30. I will l. with my fathers
Ex. 23:11. let ground l. still [south
Nu. 10:5. camps th. l. on east | 6. l. on
De. 29:20. curses in book l. upon him
Jos. 8 : 9. went to l. in ambush, 12.
Ju. 19 : 20. let thy wants l. upon me
Ru. 3:4. mark place where he shall l.
2 S. 11: 13. went out to l. on his bed
1 K. 1:2. and let her l. in thy bosom
Ps. 57 : 4. I l. am. them are on fire
88 : 5. like slain th. l. in the grave
Ec. 4 : 11. if two l. toge. have heat
Can. 1 : 13. he sh. l. all night betwixt
Is. 13 : 21. wild beasts shall l. there
14 : 18. kings of nations l. in glory
51 : 20. sons l. at head of streets
La. 2:21. young and old l. on ground
Eze. 4 : 4. l. upon thy left side
6. l. right side, | 9. shalt l. 390 days
31 : 18. shalt l. in midst of uncirc.
32 : 21. they l. uncirc., slain, 30.
27. they shall not l. with mighty
28. l. wi. slain | 29. l. wi. uncirc.
34 : 14. there shall l. in a good fold
Jo. 1 : 13. l. all night in sackcloth
Am. 6 : 4. that l. upon beds of ivory,
and stretch [saith unto him
Jn. 5 : 6. when Jesus saw him l. he
20 : 6. Peter seeth linen clothes l.

LIE down. [20 : 16.

Le. 18:23. bef. beast. to l. d. thereto,
26:6. ye shall l. d. none sh. make
you afraid, Jb. 11:19. [eat prey
Nu. 23 : 24. Isr. not l. d. until he
De. 25 : 2. judge cause him to l. d.
31:†16. shalt l. d. with thy fathers
Ru. 3 : 7. Boaz went to l. d. at heap
13. Tarry l. d. until morning
1 S. 3 : 5. I called not, l. d. again, 6, 9.
2 S. 11 : 13. went to l. d. on his bed
Jb. 7 : 4. When I l. d. I say, When
20 : 11. sh. l. d. with him in dust
21 : 26. They sh. l. d. alike in dust
27 : 19. rich man shall l. d. but not
38 : † 37. cause to l. d. bottles of

Ps. 23 : 2. me l. d. in green pastures
Pr.3:24.shalt l.d. and sleep be sweet
Is. 11: 6. leopard sh. l. d. with kid
7. their young shall l.d.together
14 : 30. needy shall l. d. in safety
17 : 2. be for flocks which sh. l. d.
27 : 10. there sh.calf feed and l. d.
43 : 17. army and power l.d. toge
50 : 11. ye shall l. d. in sorrow
65 : 10. be a place for herds to l.d.
Je. 3 : 25. We l.d. in our shame and
33:12.sheph. causing flocks to l. d.
50: † 6. forgotten their place to l. d.
Eze. 34 : 15. will cause them to l. d.
Ho. 2: 18. make them to l. d. safely
Zph. 2 : 7. shall l. d. in evening
14.flocks l. d. | 15. beasts to l.d.
3 : 13.remnant of Israel shall l. d.

LIE in wait.

Ex. 21 : 13. if a man l. not l. w. but
De. 19 : 11. if hate neigh. and l.i.w.
Jos. 8 : 4. ye shall l. i. w. ag. city
Ju. 9 : 32. up by night, and l. i. w.
21 : 20. Go and l. i.w. in vineyards
1 S. 22 : 8.stirred serv.to l.i.w.,13.
Jb. 38 : 40. abide in covert to l.i. w.
Ps. 59 : 3. they l. i. w. for my soul
Pr. 12 : 6. words of wick. to l. i. w.
Ho. 7 : 6. like oven, while l. i. w.
Mi. 7 : 2. they all l. i. w. for blood
Ac. 23 : 21. l. i. w. for him more
than 40 men
Ep. 4:14. they l. i. w. to deceive me

LIE waste.

Is. 33 : 8. highways l. w. [l. w.
34 : 10. genera. to genera. it shall
Hag. 1: 4. and this house l. w.

LIE with. [him

Ge. 19 : 32. drink wine, we will l.w.
34. and go thou in, and l.w.him
30 : 15. he shall l. w. thee to night
39 : 7. l. w. me, 12. 2 S. 13 : 11.
14. came in unto me to l. w. me
Ex. 22 : 16. if a man l. w. a maid
Le. 15 : 18. wom.w.wh. man shall l.
24. if any man l. w. her at all
18 : 20. not l. carnally w. neigh.'s
22. shalt not l.w. mankind [wife
23. Nei.shalt thou l.w. any beast
20 : 12. if man l. w. dau. in law
13. if a man l. w. mankind
15. if a man l. w. beast
18.if man l.w.woman hav-g sick-
20. if l. w. uncle's wife [ness
Nu. 5 : 13. if a man l. w. her, and
De. 22 : 23. man find and l. w. her
25. if man force and l. w. her
28. If find damsel and l. w. her
28:30. betroth a wife, ano. l. w. her
2 S. 11 : 11. go to l. w. my wife?
12 : 11. he shall l. w. thy wives
13 : 11. Come, l. w. me my sister

LIEN. See **LAIN.**

LIERS

in wait or ambush.

Jos. 8 : 13. l. i. w. on west of city
14. he wist not there were l. i. a.
Ju. 9: 25. men of Shechem set l. i.w.
16:12. were l.i.w.abiding in cham.
20:29. Isr. set l. i. w. about Gibeah
33. l.i.w.came | 37.l.i.w. hasted
36. they trusted in l.i.w. [l.w.
38. sign betw. men of Isr. and l.
Je.51:†12.prepare l.i.w.ag.Babylon

LIEST.

Ge. 28 : 13. land whereon thou l.
De.6:7.when l.down and risest,11:19
Jos. 7:10. up whf. l. upon thy face?
Pr.3 : 24. When l.down not be afraid

LIETH.

Ge.4:7. if doest not well sin l. at door
49:25.blessings of deep that l.und.
Le. 14 : 47. l. in house shall wash
15 : 4. bed whereon he l.is unc.,24.
20. that she l. upon is uncl., 26.
24.whereon he l.shall be uncl.,33.
26 : 34. as long as it l.desolate, 35.
Le. 26 : 43. the land enjoy sabbaths,
while she l. desolate
Nu. 21: 15. l. upon border of Moab
Jos. 15 : 8. l. bef. valley of Hinnom,
17:7. coast l. bef. Shechem [18:16.
18 : 13. hill that l. on south side
14. hill that l.bef. Beth-horon
Ju. 1 : 16. wh. l. in south of Arad
16 : 5. see wh-n his gr. strength l.
6.Tell wh-n thy gr.strength l.,15.
18 : 28. valley that l. by Beth-re.
2 S. 2 : 24. l. bef. Giah, by way of
24 : 5. l. in midst of river [26, 27.
Ne. 3 : 25. tower wh.l.out fr. kings,
Jb. 40 : 21. He l. under shady trees
Ps. 41 : 8. he l. he sh. rise no more
88 : 7. Thy wrath l. hard upon me
Pr. 23 : 34. he th.l.upon top of mast
Eze. 9 : 2. way wh. l. toward north
29 : 3. l. in midst of rivers [bosom
Mi. 7 : 5. Keep mouth fr.her l.in thy
Mat.8 : 6. my servant l. at home sick
Mk. 5 : 23. dau. l. at point of death
Ac. 14 : 6. unto region wh. l. round
27 : 12. l. toward southwest
Ro. 12 : 18. as much as l. in you
1 Jn. 5 : 19. world l. in wickedness
Re. 21 : 16. the city l. foursquare

LIETH down.

Ru.3:4. when he l.d. mark the place
Jb.14:12.man l.d. and riseth not till
Pr. 23 : 34. that l. d. in midst of sea

LIETH in wait.

Ps. 10 : 9. l. i.w. as a lion l.i.w. to
Pr. 7 : 12. she l.i.w. at ev. corner
23:28. she also l. i. w. as for prey

LIETH waste.

Ne.2:3.my fathers' sepulchres l. w.
17. said I, Ye see how Jerus. l.w.

LIETH with.

Ex. 22:19.whoso l.w. beast, surely
put to death
Le. 15 : 33. l. w. her th. is unclean
19 : 20. l. carnally w. bondmaid
20:11. man that l. w. father's wife
13. lie with mankind as he l. w.
a woman [wife
De. 27:20. Cursed that l.w. father's
21. l. w. beast | 22. l. w. sister
23. Cursed th. l. w. moth. in law

LIEUTENANTS.

Ezr. 8:36. king's commission unto l.
Es. 3 : 12. Haman com-d king's l.
8 : 9. Mordecai had com-d to the l.
9 : 3. all rulers and l. helped Jews

LIFE.

Ge.1:20.moving creature th. hath l.
30. to every thing wherein is l.
2:7. God breathed the breath of l.
9. tree of l. in the garden, 3 : 22.
3 : 24. cherubim to keep tree of l.
6:17.destroy all wh-n is l.,7:15,22
7 : 11. In 600th year of Noah's l.
9:4. flesh wi. l. not eat, Le. 17 : 14.
5. of man will I require l. of man
18:10. return acc. to time of l., 14.
23 : 1. were years of l. of Sarah
25 : 7. years of Abraham's l.
17. Ishmael's l. [go, 16.
42 : 15. By l. of Pha., ye shall not
44 : 30. his l. bound up in lad's l.
45:5. G. did send me to preserve l.
47:9. not attained unto l.of my fa-s
Ex. 6 : 16. years of l. of Levi 137
18. years of l. of Kohath
20. l. of Amram [18. De. 19 : 21.
21 : 23. shall give l. for l., Le. 24:†
Le. 17 : 11. l. of flesh is in blood
24:†17. he that smiteth l. of man,
De. 19 : † 6, 11. [of murd-r
Nu. 35 : 31. take no satisf-n for l.
De. 12:23. blood is the l. not eat l.
20 : 19. tree of the field is man's l.
24:6. he taketh man's l. to pledge
30:15. set bef. thee l., 19. Je. 21:8.
32:47. not vain thing, bec. your l.
Jos. 2 : 14. ans-d, Our l. for yours
1 S. 25:29. bound up in bundle of l.
2 S. 14 : 7. l. of brother wh. be slew,
† 14. G. hath not taken aw. his l.
15:21. in death or l. there will I be
20:†3. shut up in widowhood of l.
1 K.1:12.save own l.and l.of thy son
3 : 11. nor asked l. of thine enemies, neither long l., 2 Ch. 1 : 11.
2 K. 4 : 16. acc. to time of l. shalt
embrace son, 17.
7:7. left camp, and fled for their l.
Ezr. 6 : 10. may pray for l. of king
Es. 8 : 11. Jews to stand for their l.
Jb. 3 : 20. why l. given to bitter in
10 : 12. hast granted me l. and
12 :†10. in whose hand is l. of ev.
24 : 22. and no man is sure of l.
31 : 39. or owners to lose their l.
33 : 4. breath of Alm. given me l.
36:6. He preserveth not l. of wick.
14. their l. is among the unclean
38:†39. wilt fill l. of young lions?
Ps. 16 : 11. wilt shew me path of l.
21:4. asked l. of thee, thou gavest
30 : 5. in his favor is l. weeping
34:12. What man is he desireth l.?
36 : 9. with thee is fountain of l.
61 : 6. Thou wilt prolong king's l.
63 : 3. lovingkindn. better than l.
66 : 9. God, wh. holdeth soul in l.
78 : 50. gave their l. to pestilence
91:16.Wi. long l.will I satisfy him
133 : 3. blessing, even l. for everm.
Pr. 1 : 19. taketh away l. of owners
2 : 19. I nei.take hold of paths of l.
3:2. long l. and peace sh. they add
18. She is a tree of l. to them that
22.So shall they be l.unto thy soul
4:22.are l. unto those that find th.
23. Keep heart, out of it issues of
5 : 6. Lest ponder path of l. [l.
6 : 23. reproofs are the way of l.
26.adulteress hunt for precious l.
8 : 35. whoso findeth me findeth l.
10:11. mouth of righte. a well of l.
17. in way of l. th. keep-h instr-n
11 : 30. fruit of righte. is tree of l.
12:10. righte. regard-h l. of beast
28. In way of righteousness is l.
13:8. ransom of man's l. are riches
12. desire cometh, it is tree of l.
14. law of wise is fountain of l.
14 : 27. fear of L. is fountain of l.
30. sound heart is l. of the flesh
15 : 4. wholesome tongue is tree of
24. way of l. is above to wise [l.
31. heareth reproof of l. abideth
16 : 15. In king's countenance is l.
22. Underst-g is wellspring of l.
18:21. Death l. in power of tongue
21:21. followeth mercy, findeth l.
22:4.By humility are riches,l. [ens
27:†27. goat's milk for l. for maid-
31 : 12. will do him good all her l.
Ec.2:3.good they sho. do all their l.
17. I hated l. | 7:12.wisd.giveth l.
9:†9. enjoy l. wi. wife thou lovest
Is. 38 : 16. in all these things is l.
20. we will sing songs all our l.
57 : 10. hast found l. of thy hand
Je. 8:3. death chosen rather than l.
21:7. that seek their l., 34 : 20, 21.
8. I set before you way of l. [l.
49:37. be dismayed bef. them seek
La. 2:19.lift up thy hands for the l.
Eze. 1:†20. l. in wheels,†21.-10:†17.
7:† 13. their l. was yet am. living
13 : 22. not return by promising l.
33 : 15. If wicked in statutes of l.
Da. 7:†12. a prolonging in l. given
Jon. 1 : 14. not perish for man's l.
Mal. 2 : 5. My cov-t with him of l.
Mat.2:20.dead wh. sought child's l.
3 : † 8. fruit meet for amend-t of l.
6:25. Take no thought for your l.,
Lu. 12 : 22. [Mk. 9 : 43.
18:8.to enter into l.halt or maimed,

Mat.18:9.enter l.with 1 eye,Mk.9:45
19:17. if enter into l. keep com-ts
Mk.8:4.lawful to save l. or kill, Lu.
Lu. 1:75. in holiness all our l. [6:9.
12:15. l. consisteth not in abund.
23. l. more than meat, body than
Jn.1:4. In him was l.and l.was light
3:36. believeth not Son, not see l.
5:26. as Fa. hath l. in himself, so
given Son to have l. in hims.
29. done good, to resurrec. of l.
40. will not come to me that
might have l., 10 : 10.
6 : 33. giveth l. unto world
35. I am bread of l., 48.
51. wh. I will give for l. of world
53. drink his blood, no l. in you
63. words I speak to you, are l.
8:12. but shall have the light of l.
11:25. I am resurrec. and l., 14:6.
20 : 31. believing ye might have l.
Ac. 2:28. made kn. to me ways of l.
3:15. killed the Prince of l. whom
17: 25. seeing he giveth to all l.
26:4. manner of l. from my youth
27:22. sha. be no loss of any man's
Ro.5:17. sh. reign in l. by J. C. [l.
18. upon all unto justifica-n of l.
6:4. we sho. walk in newness of l.
8 : 2. law of Spirit of l. in C. J.
6. to be spiritually minded is l.
10. Spirit is l. bec. of righte-n.
38. persuaded nei. death nor l.
11:15. receiving them be l. fr. dead
1 Co. 3:22. l. or death, all are yours
14 : 7. things without l. .giving
2 Co. 1:8. we despaired of l. [sound
2:16. to other savour of l. unto l.
3:6. letter killeth, Spirit giveth l.
4:10. that l. of J. be manifested, 11.
12. death worketh in us, l. in you
5 : 4. mortality be swall-d up of l.
Ga. 2 : 20. l. I now live in flesh
3:21. law wh. could have given l.
Ep. 4:18. being alienated fr. l. of G.
Ph. 1 : 20. whe. it be by l. or death
2:16. Holding forth word of l. that
Col. 3: 3. your l. is hid with Christ
4. When Christ our l. sh. appear
1 Ti.2:2. we may lead a peaceable l.
4:8.having promise of l. th. now is
2 Ti. 1:1. acc. to promise of l. in C.
10. brought l. to light by gospel
3:10. hast known my manner of l.
He.7:3.nei.beginning, nor end of l.
16. made aft. power of endless l.
Ja. 1: 12. he sh. receive crown of l.
4 : 14. what is your l.? a vapour
1 Pe. 3 : 7. being heirs of grace of l.
10. will love l. and see good days
4 : 3.time past of our l.may suffice
2 Pe. 1:3. given all pertain-g unto l.
1 Jn. 1:1. hands handled word of l.
2. For the l. was manifested, and
2: 16. pride of l. is not of the Fa.
5: 12.He th. hath the Son hath l.
th. hath not Son hath not l.
16. give l. for them that sin not
Re. 2 : 7. will I give to eat tree of l.
10. I will give thee a crown of l.
8 : 9. third part that had l. died
11:11. Spirit of l. from God entered
13:15. power to give l. unto beast
21 : 6. give unto him athirst of wa.
22:1. pure river of wat. of l. [of l.
2. tree of l. bare 12 manner of
14. may have right to tree of l.
17. let him take water of l. freely
† 19. G. take part out of tree of l.

All the days of his LIFE.

De. 17 : 19. shall read therein a.-l.
Jos. 4 : 14. they feared him a.-l.
1 K. 15 : 5. turned not aside a.-l.
6. And there was war a.-l.
2 K. 25: 29. eat bread bef. him a.-l.
Ec. 5 : 18. enjoy the good of all his
labour a.-l.

See **All the DAYS, BOOK of life, ETERNAL life, EVERLASTING Life.**

His LIFE. [life

Ge.44:30. h. l. is bound up in lad's
Ex. 21:30. give for ransom of h. l.
Ju. 9:17. my fa.adventured h.l.far
16 : 30. more than he slew in h. l.
1 S. 19: 5. did put h. l. in his hand
23:15. Saul was come to seek h. l.
1 K.2:23. if not spoken word ag.h.l.
19 : 3. saw that, he went for h. l.
†4. Elijah sat down,requested h.l.
20 : 39. thy life be for h. l., 42.
2 K. 10 : 24. h. l. be for life of him
Ne. 6 : 11. into temple to save h. l.
Es. 7 : 7. to make request for h. l.
Jb. 2 : 4. all man hath give for h. l.
6. he is in thy hand, but save h.l.
33:18. h. l. from perishing by sw.
20. So h. l. abhorreth bread [ers
22. h. l. draw-h near to destroy-
28. h. l. shall see the light
Ps. 49:†18. in h. l. blessed his soul
Pr. 7:23. knoweth not it is for h.l.
13:3. keepeth mouth, keepeth h.l.
Ec 8:12. rejoice and do good in h.l.
7:15. is wicked man prolongeth h.l.
Is.15:4. Moab, h. l. sh. be grievous
Je. 21 : 9. h. l. shall be unto him a
prey, 38 : 2.
44 : 30. into ha. of them seek h. l.
Eze. 3:18. nor speakest to save h.l.
7:13.nei.strengthen in iniq.of h.l.
32: 10. tremble, ev. man for h. l.
Am. 2:†14.nei. mighty deliver h. l.
Mat. 10:39. findeth h. l. sh. lose it;
that loseth h. l., 16 : 25. Mk.
8:35. Lu. 9:24.-17:33. Jn. 12:25.
20:28.h.l.a ransom for, Mk.10:45.
Lu. 14 : 26. and hate not h. own l.
Jn. 10:11. good sheph. giveth h. l.
15 : 13. lay down h. l. for friends
Ac. 8 : 33. h. l. is taken fr. earth
20:10. Trouble not, h. l. is in him
Ro. 5 : 10. much more be saved by
Ph. 2:30. not regarding h. l. [h.l.
1 Jn. 3 : 16. love of G. bec. he laid
down h. l.

Mine own or my LIFE.

Ge. 19 : 19. mercy in saving m. l.
27 : 46. weary of m. l. what good
shall m. l. do me?
32 : 30. m. l. is preserved
47:9. few and evil the days of m.l.
48 : 15. G. wh. fed me all m. l.
Nu. 23:†10. m.l. die death of righ-s
Ju. 12 : 3. m. l. in my ha-s, 1 S.
28 : 21. [or fa.'s family
1 S. 18 : 18. Da. said, What is m. l.
20 : 1. sin, that he seeketh m. l.?
22:23. seeketh m. l. seek. thy life
26 : 24. that m. l. be much set by
28 : 9. whf. layest snare for m. l.
2 S. 1 : 9. m. l. is yet whole in me
16: 11. my son seeketh m.l. [o. l.
18 : 13. wrought falsehood ag. m.
19 : † 34. how many days of m. l.
1 K. 19:4. enough, take away m.l.
10. they seek m. l., 14. Ro. 11:3.
2 K. 1:13. let m. l. be precious, 14.
Es. 7 : 3. let m. l. be given me at
Jb. 6:11. that I sho. prolong m. l.
7:7. O remember m. l. is but wind
15. soul choos-h death than m.l.
9:21.perfect, yet I wo.despise m.l.
10: 1. My soul is weary of m. l.
13:14. whf. put m.l.in my hands?
Ps. 7 : 5. let him tread down m. l.
23 : 6. follow me all days of m. l.
26 : 9. gath. not m. l. with bloody
27:1. L. is strength of m. l. [men
4. in house of L. all days of m.l.
31 : 10. m. l. is spent with grief
13. devised to take away m. l.
38:12.th.seek after m. l. lay snares
42: 8. prayer to the God of m. l.

Ps.64:1. preserve m. l. from fear of
88:3.m.l.draweth nigh unto grave
143 : 3.smitten m. l. to ground
Is. 38 : 12. cut off like weaver m. l.
La. 3: 53. cut off m. l. in dungeon
58. L., thou hast redeemed m. l.
Jon. 2:6. bro't m. l. fr. corruption
4 : 3. O. L., take, I beseech, m. l.
Jn. 10:15. lay down m. l. for sheep
17. Fa. loveth, bec. I lay do.m.l.
13:37. lay down m. l. for thy sake
Ac. 20 : 24. nor count I m. l. dear
Ro. 16:4. for m. l. laid down necks

This LIFE.

Ps. 17:14. have their portion in t.l.
Ec. 6:12. kno-h what is good in t.l.
9 : 9. this is thy portion in t. l.
Lu. 8 : 14. choked wi. cares of t. l.
21:34. overcharged with cares of t.
Ac. 5 : 20. speak words of t. l. [l.
1 Co.6:3.things th. pertain to t.l.,4.
15 : 19. if in t. l. only have hope
2 Ti. 2:4. entang-h with affairs of t.
1 Jn. 5 : 11. t. l. is in his Son [l.

Thy LIFE.

Ge. 19:17. Escape for t. l. look not
47 : † 8. how many days of t. l.
Ex. 4 : 19. are dead wh. sought t.l.
De. 28 : 66. t. l. sh. hang in doubt,
shalt have no assur. of t. l.
30:20. he is t. l. length of thy days
Ju.18:25.on thee, and thou lose t. l.
Ru. 4 : 15. sh. be a restorer of t. l.
1 S. 19:11. If save not t. l. to night
26:24.t. l. was much set by, so my
2 S.4:8.head of ene. that sought t.l.
19 : 5. thy servants saved t. l.
1 K. 19 : 2. if I make not t. l. as life
20 : 31. go, peradv. he will save t.l.
39. if missing t. l. be for his, 42.
Ps. 103:4. redeemeth t. l. fr. destru.
Pr. 4:10. years of t. l. be many, 9:11.
13. let her not go, for she is t. l.
9:11. years of t. l. shall be incre-d
Is. 43 : 4. will I give people for t. l.
Je. 4 : 30. lovers, they will seek t.l.
11 : 21. th. seek t. l., 22:25.-38:16.
39 : 18. t. l. sh. be a prey, 45 : 5.
Lu. 16 : 25. in t. l. receivedst good
Jn.13:38.lay down t. l. for my sake?

LIFE time.

Le. 18 : 8. besides other in her l. t.
See LIFETIME.

To or unto LIFE.

2 K.8:1. son he restored t.l., 5. [l.
Pr.10:16.labour of righte.tendeth t.
11:19. as righteousn. tendeth t. l.
19:23. fear of the L. tendeth t. l.
Mat. 7 : 14. narrow is the way that
leadeth u. l. [l., 1 Jn. 3 : 14.
Jn. 5:24. but is passed fr. death u.
Ac. 11:18. granted repentance u. l.
Ro. 7:10. the com-nt ordained t. l.
He. 11 : 35. rec-d their dead raised

LIFETIME. [t. l.

2 S. 18 : 18. Abs. in his l. had taken
Lu. 16 : 25. in l. receivedst thy good
He.2:15.all their l. subject to bond.

LIFT.

Ge.21:18.l. up the lad and hold him
Ex. 14 : 16. But l. thou up thy rod
20 : 25. if thou l. up a tool upon it
Nu. 6 : 26. Lord l. up his counten.
16 : 3. whf. then l. ye up yours.?
23 : 24. l. up hims. as a young lion
De. 22: 4. help him to l. them up
27: 5. not l. up iron tool, Jos.8:31.
Ru. 3 : † 4. l. clothes on his feet
2 K. 19 : 4. l. thy prayer, Is. 37 : 4.
1 Ch. 25 : 5. were to l. up the horn
Ezr. 1 : † 4. let the men l. him up
9:6. I blush to l. up my face to G.
Jb. 5 : † 7. burning coal l. up to fly
10 : 15. will I not l. up my head
11 : 15. shalt l. up thy face, 22:26.
Ps. 4 : 6. l. up light of thy counten.
7:6.O L. in thine anger, l. up thys.

Ps. 24 : 9. l. heads O ye gates, l. ye
everl. doors, 7. [86:4.-143:8.
25:1. Unto thee, O L. I l. my soul,
28:9.feed them, l. them up for ever
74 : 3. l. feet unto perpetual deso.
75:4. to wicked, l. not up horn, 5.
93 : 3. the floods l. up their waves
94 : 2. l. up thyself, judge of earth
Ec. 4 : 10. If fall, one will l. fellow
Is. 2 : 4. nation sh. not l. up sword
ag. nation, nei. learn, Mi. 4 : 3.
5 : 26. he will l. ensign to nations
10:15. as if staff should l. up itself
24. shall l. up his staff ag. thee
26. sh. l. it up after manner of E.
13 : 2. l. ye up a banner upon mt.
33:10. now will I rise, now l. mys.
59: 19. Lord shall l. up a standard
62 : 10. l. up a standard, Je. 50:†2.
Je.7:16. nei. l. prayer for th., 11:14.
51: 14. shall l. up a shout ag. thee
La. 3 : 41. Let us l. up our heart
Eze. 11 ; 22. did cherubim l. wings
17:14. that it might not l. itself up
26 : 8. sh. l. up buckler ag. thee
Ho. 4 : † 8. they l. up soul to iniq.
Mat.12:11. not l. it out on Sabbath?
Lu. 13 : 11. could in no wise l. hers.
Ja.4:10.humble yours. he sh. l. you
See **Lift** or **lifted up EYES.**
See HEAD, HEADS.

LIFT, LIFTED hand, s.

Ge. 14 : 22. l-d up mine h. unto L.
41 : 44. without thee no man l. h.
Ex. 6:†8. land conc. wh. I did l. h.
Le. 9:22. Aaron l-d up h. tow. peo.
Nu. 20:11. Mo. l-d up h. and smote
De. 32 : 40. I l. up my h. and say
2 S.20:21.Sheba hath l-d up h.ag.k.
1 K.11:26.Jere.l-d up h.ag.king,27.
Jb.31:21.If I have l-d h. ag.fatherl.
Ps. 10: 12. l. up thine h. forget not
28 : 2. when I l. h-s tow. oracle
63 : 4. I will l. h-s in thy name
106 : 26. he l-d up h. ag. them
119 : 48. h-s will I l. unto com-ts
134:2. l. up your h-s in sanctuary
Is. 26 : 11. when thy h. is l-d up
49 : 22. will l. up mine h. to Gent.
La. 2 : 19. l. up thy h-s toward him
Eze. 20 : 5. I l-d up h. to seed, 6.
15. l-d up mine h. in wil., 23.
28.I l-d h.to give land,42.-47:14.
36 : 7. saith L. I have l-d up h.
44 : 12. have I l-d up h. ag. them
Mi. 5:9. h. be l-d upon adversaries
Ha. 3 : 10. deep l-d his h-s on high
Lu. 24:50. l-d h-s and blessed them
He. 12:12. Whf. l. up h-s that hang
Re. 10 : 5. angel l-d h. to heaven

LIFT, LIFTED voice, s.

Ge. 21:16. Hagar l. up v. and wept
27:38. Esau l-d v. and wept [wept
29 : 11. Jac. kissed Ra. l-d v. and
39 : 15. he heard I l-d my v., 18.
Nu. 14 : 1. congregation l-d up v.
Ju.2:4. peo.l-d v.wept,21:2.1 S.11:4.
9 : 7. Jotham l-d v. said, Hearken
Ru.1:9.Orpah, Ruth l-d v.wept,14.
1 S. 24 : 16. Saul l-d v. and wept
30:4. Da. and peo. l-d v., 2 S. 3:32.
2 S. 13 : 36. king's sons l-d their v.
2 Ch. 5 : 13. as singers l-d up v.
Jb. 2:12. they l-d their v. and wept
38:34. Canst l. up thy v. to clouds
Ps. 93 : 3. floods have l-d their v.
Is. 10 : 30. l. up thy v. O daughter
24 : 14. shall l. up v. shall sing
40 : 9. l. up thy v. with strength
42 : 2. he shall not cry, nor l. v.
11. let wil. and cities l. their v.
52 : 8. thy watchmen shall l. up v.
58:1.cry, l. up thy v. like trumpet
Je. 22 : 20. l. up thy v. in Bashan
Eze. 21:22. to l. up v. wi. shouting
Lu. 11 : 27. a certain woman l-d v.
17 : 13. ten lepers l-d their v-s

Ac. 2 : 14. Pe. standing with 11 l-d
4:24.l-d up their v. to God [his v.
14 : 11. l-d their v-s in speech
22 : 22. l-d v-s and said, Away

LIFTED, LIFT [past tense]

Ge. 7 : 17. ark was l. ab. the earth
29 : † 1. then Jacob l. up his feet
37 : 28. they l. Joseph out of pit
40 : 20. Pha. l. up head of butler
Ex. 7 : 20. he l. rod, smote waters
Jos. 4 : 18. of priests' feet were l.
2 S.22:49.thou hast l.me up on high
23 : 8. he l. spear against 800
18. he l. spear ag. 300, 1 Ch.11:11.
2 K. 9 : 32. l. his face to windows
1 Ch.14:2. his kingd. was l. on high
Jb. 6 : † 2. calamity l. in balances
31 : 29. or l. mys. when evil found
Ps. 24 : 4. not l. soul unto vanity
24 : 7. be ye l. ye everl. doors, 9.
30 : 1. thou hast l. me up, 102:10.
41:9. l. his heel ag. me, Jn. 13:18.
74 : 5. l. up axes upon thick trees
Pr. 26:†7. legs of the lame are l. up
30:13. their eyelids are l. up
Is. 2:12 day of L. upon ev. one l. up
13. cedars th. are l. | 14.mts.l.up
6:1. L. sitting upon a throne l. up
30 : † 25. be upon ev. l. hill rivers
Je. 51 : 9. her judgm. l. up to skies
52:31.l.head of Jehoi-n k.of Judah
Eze. 1 : 19. creatures l. up fr. earth
20. wheels were l. up, 21.-10 : 17.
3 : 14. spirit l. and took me away
10 : 15. cherubim were l. up
16. cherubim l. wings, 19.-11:22.
Da.5:23.hast l. up thyself ag. the L.
7 : 4. first beast was l. up fr. earth
Ha. 2 : 4. soul l. up is not upright
Zch. 1 : 21. l. up horn over Judah
5 : 7. was l. up a talent of lead
9. l. up ephah betw. earth and
9 : 16. as stones of a crown, l. up
14:10. land sh. be l. up and inhab.
Mal. 2 : † 9. ye l. up face ag. my law
Mk. 1 : 31. by hand lifted her up,
9 : 27. Jes. l. him up [Ac. 9 : 41.
Jn. 3:14. as Moses l. up serpent, so
must Son of man be l. up
8 : 7. he l. up himself and said
10. When Jesus had l. himself
28.when ye have l. up Son of man
12:32. I, if I be l. up will draw all
34. Son of man must be l. up
Ac.3:7. took him by hand and l. up
1 Ti. 3 : 6. lest l. with pride he fall
See HEAD, HEADS.
See **His and Thine HEART.**

LIFTER.

Ps. 3:3. my glory, l. up of mine head

LIFTEST.

Jb.30:22. Thou l. me up to the wind
Ps. 9 : 13. l. me fr. gates of death
18 : 48. l. above those rise ag. me
Pr. 2 : 3. l. thy voice for underst-g

LIFTETH. [to it

De. 24:†15. poor, and l. his soul un-
1 S.2:7.L. bringeth low, and l. up,8.
2 Ch. 25 : 19. heart l. thee to boast
Jb.39:18. What time ostrich l. hers.
Ps. 107 : 25. wind which l. waves
113 : 7. l. needy out of dunghill
147:6.The Lord l. up the meek, he
Is. 18 : 3. see ye when he l. ensign
Je. 51 : 3. l. hims. in his brigandine
Na. 3 : 3. horseman l. bright sword

LIFTING.

Ju. 15 :† 17. place, l. up of jawbone
1 Ch. 11:20. Abishai chief, for l. up
15:16. by l. up voice wi. joy [spear
2 Ch. 32 : † 26. humbled for l. up of
his heart
Ne. 8 : 6. Amen, with l. up hands
Jb. 22 : 29. say, There is l. up [ing
Ps.141:2.l. up of my hands as even-
Pr. 30: 32. foolishly in l. up thyself
Is. 9:18. mount like l. up of smoke

Is.33:3.at l. of thys. nations scatt-d
Eze. 24:†25. take fr. them l. of soul
1 Ti.2:8. men pray l. up holy hands

LIGHT. [Adj.]

Ge. 44 : 3. soon as morning was l.
Ju. 19: 26. fell at door till it was l.
Ps. 139 : 11. even night shall be l.
Mi.2:1.morning is l. they practice it
Zch.14:7. at evening time it sh. be l.

LIGHT. [Adj.]

Nu. 21 : 5. soul loatheth l. bread
Ju. 9 : 4. Abim. hired l. persons
2 S. 2 : 18. Asahel was l. of foot
Zph. 3 : 4. prophets l. and treach-s
Mat. 11 : 30. yoke easy, burden l.
2 Co. 4: 17. our l. affliction worketh

LIGHT thing. [son

1 S.18:23. seemeth it l. t. to be k.'s
1 K. 16 : 31. as if been l. t. for him
2 K. 3:18. is but l. t. in sight of L.
20 : 10. It is l. t. for shadow to go
Is. 49: 6. l. t. thou shouldest be my
servant [abom.
Eze. 8 : 17. Is it l. t. they commit

LIGHT. [Adverb.]

De.27:16. Cursed th. setteth l.by fa.
Eze. 22 : 7. they set l. by fa. and
Mat. 22 : 5. But they made l. of it

LIGHT. [Noun.]

Ge. 1 : 3. Let there be l. there was l.
4. God saw the l. | 5. God called
the l. Day [the night
16. greater l. the lesser l. to rule
Ex. 10 : 23. Isr. had l. in dwellings
14 : 20. the pillar gave l. by night
25 : 6. offering oil for l.,27: 20.-35:
8, 14, 28.-39 : 37. Le. 24: 2.
Nu. 4 : 9. cover candlestick of l.
16. pertaineth oil for the l.
1 S. 29 : 10. soon as have l. depart
2 S. 21 : 17. quench not the l. of Isr.
23 : 4. he shall be as l. of morning
1 K. 7 : 4. l. ag. l. in three ranks, 5.
11 : 36. that David may have a l.
2 K. 8 : 19. prom. him a l., 2 Ch.21:7.
Ne. 8 : † 3. Ezra read from the l. till
9 : 19. pillar of fire to shew th. l.
Es. 8 : 16. Jews had l. gladn. and joy
Jb. 3 : 4. nei. let the l. shine upon it
9. let it look for l. but have none
16. as infants which never saw l.
20. is l. giv. to him in misery, 23.
4:†18. his angels in whom he put l.
10 : 22. where l. is as darkness
12:22.bring-th to l.shadow of death
25. grope in the dark without l.
18 : 5. l. of wicked shall be put out
6.l. sh. be dark in his tabernacle
22 : 28. l. shall shine on thy ways
24 : 13. of those that rebel ag. the l.
14. murderer rising with l.killeth
16. daytime, they know not the l.
25 : 3. upon wh. doth not l. arise?
28 : 11. thing hid bringeth he to l.
31 : † 26. if I beheld l. when shined
33 : 28. and his life shall see the l.
30. enlightened with l. of living
36 : 30. he spreadeth his l. upon it
32. With clouds he covereth l.
37 : † 3. he directeth his l. to ends of
† 11. he scattereth cloud of his l.
15. caused l. of his cloud to shine
21. see not bright l. in clouds
38 : 15. fr. wicked l. is withholden
19. Where way where l. dwelleth?
24. By what way is the l. parted?
41:18. By his neesings l. doth shine
Ps. 4 : 6. lift up l. of thy counten.
27 : 1. L. is my l. and my salvation
36 : 9. in thy l. shall we see l. [l.
37 : 6. bring forth thy righte-n. as
38 : 10. l. of mine eyes is gone
49 : 19. he go, they sh. never see l.
74:16. hast prepared l. and the sun
78 : 14. all night with a l. of fire
97 : 11. l. is sown for the righteous
104 : 2. coverest thyself with l. as

Ps. 118:27. L. wh. hath shewed us l.
119:105 thy word is a l. to my paths
130. entrance of thy words giv-h l.
139: 12. darkn. and l. alike to thee
148: 3. praise him, all ye stars of l.
Pr. 4: 18. path of just as shining l.
6: 23. com-t is a lamp, law is l.
13: 9. l. of righteous rejoiceth, but
15: 30. l. of eyes rejoiceth heart
21: † 4. and l. of the wicked is sin
Ec. 11: 7. Truly the l. is sweet and
12: 2. While sun or l. be not dark-d
Is. 5: 20. put darku. for l. and l. for
30. l. is darkened in the heavens
8: 20. is beo. there is no l. in them
9: 2. have seen a great l., upon
them hath l. shined [a fire
10: 17. the l. of Israel shall be for
13: 10. moon shall not cause her l.
to shine, Mat. 24: 29. Mk. 13: 24.
30: 26. l. of moon sh. be as l. of
sun, l. of sun as l. of 7 days
49: 6. a l. to the Gentiles, 42: 6.
Lu. 2: 32. Ac. 13: 47.
51: 4. my judgment to rest for a l.
59: 9. we wait for l. but obscurity
60: 19. L. be to thee an overl. l., 20.
Je. 4: 23. heavens, and they had no l.
13: 16. while ye look for l. he turn-h
25: 10. I will take l. of the candle
31: 35. L. giveth sun for l. by day,
moon and stars for l. by night
Eze. 32: † 8. l. of l. I will make dark
Da. 2: 22. the l. dwelleth with him
5: 11. l. and underst. in Dan., 14.
Ho. 6: 5. thy judgments as l. that
Mi. 7: 8. the L. sh. be a l. unto me
9. Lord will bring forth to l.
Hab. 3: 4. his brightness was as l.
11. at l. of thine arrows they went
Zph. 3: 5. morning bring judgm. to l.
Zch. 14: 6. in that day l. not clear
Mat. 4: 16. to them sat in death l.
5: 14. Ye are l. of world | 15. it
16. Let your l. so shine [giveth l.
6: 22. l. of body is eye, if eye single
body full of l., Lu. 11: 34, 36.
17: 2. his raiment white as l.
Lu. 2: 32. a l. to lighten the Gentiles
8: 16. which enter may see l., 11: 33.
Jn. 1: 4. and life was the l. of men
7. came to bear witn. of that l., 8.
9. true l. which lighteth ev. man
3: 19. condemna. th. l. is come into
20. doeth evil hateth l.
21. he th. doeth truth cometh to l.
5: 35. He a burning and shining l.,
ye willing to rejoice in his l.
8: 12. I am l. of the world, followeth me have l. of life, 9: 5.
11: 9. stumbleth not, bec. seeth l.
10. stumbleth, bec. is no l. in him
12: 35. little while is l. with you
36. While ye have l. believe in l.
46. I am come a l. into the world
Ac. 9: 3. shined about him l. fr. heav.
12: 7. a l. shined in the prison
13: 47. set thee to be a l. to Gent.
16: 29. called for a l. and sprang
22: 6. shone great l. about me
9. they wi. me saw indeed the l.
11. could not see for glory of l.
26: 13. midday, I saw in way a l.
23. sho. shew. l. to peo. and Gen.
Ro. 2: 19. a l. of them are in darkn.
13: 12. let us put on armour of l.
1 Co. 4: 5. bring to l. hidden things
2 Co. 4: 4. lest l. of gospel shine
6. com. l. to shine out of darkn.
11: 14. Satan into an angel of l.
Ep. 5: 13. all things reproved manifest
by l. whatso. make manif. is l.
Col. 1: 12. inherita. of saints in l.
1 Ti. 6: 16. in l. no man can approa.
2 Ti. 1: 10. life and immortality to l.
1 Pe. 2: 9. you into his marvell. l.
2 Pe. 1: 19. as to l. shining in dark pla.
1 Jn. 1: 5. God is l., in him no darkn.
Re. 18: 23. l. of candle shine no more
21: 11. her l. like stone most prec-s
23. and the Lamb is the l. thereof
22: 5. need no l. of sun, L. giveth l.
See **CHILDREN of light.**
See COUNTENANCE, DARKNESS.

Give, eth LIGHT.

Ge. 1: 15. let them be to g. l. upon
17. God set stars to g. l. [earth
Ex. 13: 21. pillar of fire to g. them l.
25: 37. lamps may g. l. over against
it, Nu. 8: 2. [l., 2 Ch. 21: 7.
2 K. 8: 19. he promised to g. him a
Ne. 9: 12. to g. l. in way they sho. go
Ps. 105: 39. fire to g. l. in night
Is. 13: 10. stars of heaven not g. l.
42: 6. I will g. thee for a l. to Gentiles, 49: 6. [thee, Eze. 32: 7.
60: 19. nei. shall the moon g. l. to
Mat. 5: 15. g. l. to all in house, Lu.
11: 36. [darkness
Lu. 1: 79. g. l. to them that sit in
2 Co. 4: 6. to g. l. of knowl. of G.
Ep. 5: 14. awake, Ch. shall g. the l.

In the LIGHT.

Ps. 56: 13. I may walk i. l. of living
Is. 2: 5. let us walk i. l. of the L.
50: 11. walk i. l. of your fire
Jn. 12: 36. while have life believe i. l.
1 Jn. 1: 7. if we walk i. l. as he is i. l.
2: 9. that saith he is i. l. and hateth
10. loveth brother, abideth i. l.
Re. 21: 24. nations saved, sh. walk i. l.

Morning LIGHT. [l.

1 S. 14: 36. let us spoil them until m.
25: 22. pertain to him by m. l., 34.
36. Abigail told noth. until m. l.
2 S. 17: 22. passed over Jor. by m. l.
2 K. 7: 9. said, if we tarry until m. l.

Thy LIGHT.

Ps. 36: 9. in t. l. shall we see light
43: 3. O send out t. l. and thy truth
Is. 58: 8. t. l. breaks forth as morning
10. Then shall t. l. rise in obscurity
60: 1. Arise, shine, for t. l. is come
3. Gentiles shall come to t. l.
19. sun sh. be no more t. l. by day
20. Lord sh. be t. everlasting l.

LIGHTS.

Ge. 1: 14. Let there be l. in firmament
15. let them be for l. in firmament
16. God made two great l.
1 K. 6: 4. windows of narrow l.
Ps. 136: 7. To him th. made great l.
Eze. 32: 8. bright l. will I make dark
Lu. 12: 35. loins be girded, l. burn
Ac. 20: 8. many l. in upper chamber
Ph. 2: 15. ye shine as l. in the world
Ja. 1: 17. cometh fr. Father of l.

LIGHT, ED, EST, ETH.

[To set on fire or illuminate.]

Ex. 25: 37. they sh. l. lamps, 40: 4.
30: 8. when Aa. l-h lamps at even
40: 25. he l-d lamps bef. L., Nu. 8: 3.
Nu. 8: 2. say unto Aa. when l-t lamps
Ps. 18: 28. thou wilt l. my candle
Mat. 5: 15. Nei. do men l. candle
Lu. 8: 16. when l-d candle, 11: 33.
15: 8. doth not l. candle, and sweep
Jn. 1: 9. true l. wh. l-h every man

LIGHT, ED, ETH.

[Verb intransitive.] [camel

Ge. 24: 64. saw Isaac, she l-d off
28: 11. Jac. l-d upon certain place
De. 19: 5. head slippeth from helve
and l-h [Ju. 1: 14.
Jos. 15: 18. Achsah l-d off her ass,
Ju. 4: 15. Sisera l-d off his chariot
Ru. 2: 3. hap to l. on part of field
belonging unto Boaz
1 S. 25: 23. Abigail l-d off the ass
2 S. 17: 12. we will l. upon him as dew
2 K. 5: 21. Naaman l-d fr. chariot
10: 15. Jehu l-d on Jehonadab
Is. 9: 8. word to Jac. it l. upon Isr.
Re. 7: 16. nei. shall sun l. on them

LIGHTEN, ED, ETH.

[To illuminate.]

2 S. 22: 29. Lord will l. my darkness
Ezr. 9: 8. that G. may l. our eyes
Ps. 13: 3. l. mine eyes, lest I sleep
34: 5. looked to him and were l-d
77: 18. the lightnings l-d the world
Pr. 29: 13. Lord l-h both their eyes
Lu. 2: 32. A light to l. the Gentiles
17: 24. lightning that l-h out of one
Re. 18: 1. earth was l-d with his glory
21: 23. the glory of God did l. it
See ENLIGHTENED.

LIGHTEN, ED.

1 S. 6: 5. peradv. will l. his hand
Jon. 1: 5. cast wares into sea, to l.
Ac. 27: 18. next day they l-d ship, 38.

LIGHTER.

1 K. 12: 4. Make yoke l., 9, 10. 2 Ch.
Ps. 62: 9. they l. than vanity [10: 10.
Is. 49: † 6. thou l. than to be servant
Eze. 8: † 17. l. than to commit abom.

LIGHTING. [arm

Is. 30: 30. shall shew l. down of his
Mat. 3: 16. like dove and l. upon him

LIGHTLY.

Ge. 26: 10. l. have lain with thy wife
Is. 9: 1. at first he l. afflicted land
Je. 4: 24. and all the hills moved l.
Mk. 9: 39. miracle. can l. speak evil of
See ESTEEMED. [me

LIGHTNESS.

Je. 3: 9. thro. l. of her whoredoms
23: 32. cause peo. to err by their l.
2 Co. 1: 17. thus minded, did I use l.?

LIGHTNING.

2 S. 22: 15 sent l. and discomfited
Jb. 28: 26. when he made a way for
the l. of thunder, 38: 25.
37: 3. directeth his l. unto ends of
Ps. 144: 6. Cast forth l. scatter them
Eze. 1: 13. out of fire went forth l.
14. living creatures ran as the l.
Da. 10: 6. face as appearance of l.
Na. 3: † 3. lifted up l. of the spear
Zch. 9: 14. his arrow shall go as l.
Mat. 24: 27. as l. out of east, Lu. 17:
28: 3. His countenance like l. [24.
Lu. 10: 18. I beheld Sat. as l. fall

LIGHTNINGS.

Ex. 19: 16. thunders, l. upon mount
20: 18. all the people saw the l.
Jb. 38: 35. Canst thou send l.
Ps. 18: 14. shot out l. discomfited th.
77: 18. l. lighted the world. 97: 4.
78: † 48. he gave their flocks to l.
135: 7. he maketh l. for the rain
Je. 10: 13. maketh l. wi. rain, 51: 16.
Na. 2: 4. chariots shall run like l.
Zch. 10: † 1. so the L. shall make l.
Re. 4: 5. out of throne proceeded l.
8: 5. were thunderings, and l., 11: 19.
16: 18. were l. and a great earthq.

LIGNALOES.

Nu. 24: 6. trees of l. L. hath planted

LIGURE.

Ex. 28: 19. the third row a l., 39: 12.

LIKE. [Adj.]

Ge. 13: 10. Sodom was l. land of E.
Ex. 15: 11. Who is l. unto thee? De.
33: 29. 1 K. 8: 23. 2 Ch. 6: 14.
Ps. 35: 10. - 71: 19.
16: 31. manna l. coriander seed
24: 17. glory of L. l. devouring fire
30: 32. nei. make ointment l. that
33. compoundeth any thing l. it
34. of each be a l. weight [38.
34: 1. two tables l. first, 4. De. 10: 1, 3.
Nu. 23: 10 let my last end be l. his
De. 4: 32. thing been heard l. it
7: 26. lest be a cursed thing l. it
17: 14. king l. all nations, 1 S. 8: 5, 20.
18: 15. Prophet of thy breth. l. me,
Ac. 3: 22. - 7: 37. [unto thee
18. raise Prophet from breth. l.
Jos. 10: 14. no day l. that bef. or
Ju. 13: 6. his counten. l. angel of

Ru. 2:13. I be not l. one of handm.
4:11.make woman l. Rachel l.Leah
1 S. 2 : 2. nei. any rock l. our God
26:15.valiant, who is l. thee in Isr.
2 S 7 : 23. what one nation in earth
is l. peo. Isr.? ⌈ari-e l. thee, 13.
1 K. 3 : 12. none l. thee bef. nei.
10:20. not l. made in any kingdom
16 : 3. l. house of Jerob., 7.-21:22.
2 K. 9 : 9.
22:13.word l. word of, 2 Ch. 18:12.
2 K. 3 : 2. not l. his fa. l. his mother
5: 14. his flesh came l. flesh of lit.
9 : 9. l. the house of Baasha son
14:3.yet not l. Da., 16:2.2 Ch.28:1.
17:15. charged they not do l. them
18 : 32. land l. your own, Is.33:17.
23:25. l. him no k., 18:5. Ne.13:26.
2 Ch. 1:12. nei. any after have the l.
30 : 7. be not l. fa-s and breth.
26. since Sol. not the l. in Jerus.
33 : 2. l. abominations of heathen
35 : 18. no passover l. that in Isr.
Jb.5:26. to grave l. as shock of corn
14 : 2. he cometh forth l. a flower
36 : 22. God, who teacheth l. him?
40 : 9. hast thou an arm l. God
41 : 33. Upon earth is not his l.
42 : 8. ye not spoken right l. Job
Ps. 28:1. I become l. th. go into pit
78 : 57. they dealt unfaithf. l. fas.
89:8. strong L. l. thee, 113:5.Mi.7:
102:6. I am l. pelican, l. owl ⌊18.
103 : 13. l. as a fa. pitieth his chil.
113:5.Who is l. unto the L. our G.
115:8. make them are l. them,135:
126 : 1. we l. them th. dream ⌊18.
143:7. lest I be l. them go into pit
Pr. 26 : 4. Answer not fool lest be l.
him ⌈l. a pome.
Can. 4:3. thy lips l. scarlet, temples
7 : 4. eyes | 5. head, hair l.
Is. 1 : 9. been l. Gomorrah, Ro. 9:29.
11 : 16. be a highway, l. as to Isr.
14: 10. art thou become l. unto us
14. I will be l. the Most High. ⌊l.
46:5.To wh. compare th. we may be
63 : 2. l. him treadeth in winefat
Je. 5 : 19. l. as ye have forsak. me
10:16. portion of Jac not l., 51:19.
11:19. l. a lamb bro-t to slaughter
23 : 29. is not my word l. fire l. a
26:6. make this house l. Shiloh, 9.
29 : 22. make thee l. Zedekiah l.
38 : 9. he is l. to die with hunger
49:19. who is l. me, who appoint?
Eze. 5 : 9. I will not do any more l.
12:11.l. as I have done, so be unto
18:10. doeth l. to any of these ⌊th.
31:2. Whom l. in thy greatness? 18.
8.not tree l. him in beauty (3)⌈l.
45:25. in 7th month sh. he do thee
Da. 3:25. form of 4th is l. Son of G.
5 : 21. his heart l. beasts, l. oxen
7 : 13. one l. the Son of man came
Ho. 4 : 9. shall be l. people l. priest
5:10.princes l.them th. remove the
Jo. 2 : 2. not been ever l. nei. sh. be
Am. 6 : 5. instruments of music l.
Jon. 1 : 4. ship was l. to be ⌊David
Mi. 7 : 18. Who is a G. l. unto the
Zch. 1 : 6. l. as L. thought to do
Mat. 6 : 8. Be not ye l. unto them
29. was not arrayed l., Lu. 12:27.
11:16. l. chil. in market, Lu. 7: 32.
12 : 13. restored whole l. as other
22:39 second is l.unto it,Mk.12:31.
Lu.6:47. I will shew wh. he is l., 48.
7 : 31. and to what are they l. ⌈l.?
13 : 18. Unto what is kingd. of God
Jn.8:55. I shall be a liar l.unto you
9 : 9. other- said, He is l. him
Ac. 3:22. Prophet l. unto me, 7:37.
17:29.not to think Godhead l. gold
Ro. 6 : 4. l. as C. was raised fr. dead
Ph. 3 : 21. l. unto his glorious body
He. 4:15. in all points tempted l. as
He. 7 : 3. made l. unto Son of God
1 Jn. 3 : 2. he appear, we be l. him
Re. 1 : 13. one l. Son of man, 14:14.
13 : 4. Who is l. unto the beast
See ADDER, APPLES, ARMY, ASHES, BALL, BARS, BEAM, BEARS, BLIND, BRANCH, BRETHREN, BRIMSTONE, BURNING, CEDAR, S, CHAFF, CHARIOTS, CHEESE, CHILDREN, CITY, COLT, CRANE, CRIMSON, CRYSTAL, CURTAIN, DOG, DOVE, S, DUNG, DUST, FAITH, FEAST, FEET, FIELD, FIGURE, FIRE, FLOCK, S, FLOOD, FROGS, GAIN, GARDEN, GARMENT, GIANT, GIFT GLASS, GOBLET, GAIN, GRASS, HAND, HARP, HEARTH, HEATH, HEATHEN, HEIFER, HORSES, HOST, HOUSE, HOUSEHOLDER, JASPER, JEWELS, JOB [person], KING, LEAVEN, LEOPARD, LIGHTNING, LILIES, LION, MAN, MANNER, MEN, MERCHANT, MILLSTONE, MOSES, MOTH, MOUNTAINS, NAME, NET.

None LIKE.

Ex.8:10.is n.l. the L. our God,9:14.
De. 33:26. 2 S. 7:22. 1 Ch.17:20.
9 : 24. n. l. the hail
11 : 6. n. l. cry of Egypt
1 S. 10 : 24. n. l. Saul am. people
21:9. Da. said, There is n. l. that
1 K. 3:12. was n. l. Sol. | 21:25. n.
2 K. 18 : 5.was n. l. Hez. ⌊l. Ahab
Jb. 1:8. there is n. l. him in earth,
2 : 3. ⌈Je. 10:6, 7.
Ps. 86 : 8. Am. gods n. l. unto thee,
Is. 46 : 9. am God, there is n. l. me.
Je. 30 : 7. that day is great, n. l. it
Da. 1:19. am. all was found n.l. Dan.
See OCCUPATION, OIL, OVERTHROW, OX, PALM, PASSIONS, PILLARS, POISON, PORTIONS, PRINCES, RAIN, RAZOR, RIVER, ROD, ROE, S, SEA, SEPULCHRES, SHADOW, SHEEP, SLAIN, SPRING, STARS.

Such LIKE. ⌈s. l.

Eze. 18 : 14. cousid-h, and doeth not
Mk.7:8. many s. l. things ye do,13.
Ga. 5 : 21. drunkenness, and s. l.
See SWORD, THINGS, THREAD, TOOTH, TOWER, TREASURE, TREE, VANITY, VESSEL, WATER, WAVE, WAX, WEAVER, WHEAT, WHEEL, WILDERNESS, WIND.

LIKE wise. ⌈what

Mat. 21 : 24. I in l. w. will tell by
See LIKEWISE, WOMAN, WOMEN, WOOL, WORDS.

LIKE, ED.

De. 25:7. if man l. not to take her,8.
1 Ch. 28 : 4. he l-d me to make me
king over all Israel ⌈knowledge
Ro. 1 : 28. did not l. to retain God in

LIKEMINDED.

Ro. 15 : 5. God grant you to be l. ⌈l.
Ph. 2 : 2. ye be l. | 20.I have no man

LIKEN, ED. ⌈L.?

Ps. 89 : 6. who can be l-d unto the
Is. 40 : 18. To whom l. G. ? 25.-46:5.
Je. 6 :2. I l-d dau. of Zion to a comely
La. 2:13. what sh. I l. to thee, Jerus.?
Mat. 7 :24.I will l. him unto wise m.
26. shall be l-d unto a foolish man
11 : 16.l. this generation? Lu.7:31.
13 : 24. kingdom of heaven is l-d
unto a, 18:23.-25:1. ⌈Lu. 13:20.
Mk. 4 . 30. Whereunto we l. kingd.,

LIKENESS. ⌈l., 5:1.

Ge. 1 : 26. Let us make man aft. our
5 : 3. Adam begat son in his own l.
Ex. 20 : 4. not make l. of any thing
De. 4 : 16. lest make l. of male or
female, 17, 18, 23, 25.-5 : 8.
Ps. 17 : † 12. l. of him is as a lion
17:15.satisfi., when awake wi. thy l.
Is. 13 : † 4. l. of great people gath-d
40 : 18. what l. compare to him ?
Eze. 1:5. l. of 4 living creatures,13.
10. As for l. of their faces, 10:22.
16. they four had one l., 10: 10.
22. l. of firmament as crystal
26. l. of throne l. of man, 10 : 1.
28. was l. of the glory of the L.
8 : 2. a l. as appearance of fire
10 : 21. l. of the hands of a man
19 : † 10. moth. like a vine in thy l.
Ac. 14 : 11. gods come in l. of men
Ro. 6:5. if planted in l. of his death,
shall be in l. of his resurr-n
8:3. his Son in the l. of sinful flesh
Ph. 2 : 7. was made in the l. of men

LIKETH, ING.

De.23:16.dwell where it l-h him best
Es. 8 : 8. write ye for Jews as it l-h
Jb. 39 : 4. young ones are in good l-g
Da. 1 : 10. why see your faces worse
Am. 4:5. for this l-h you, O Isr. ⌊l-g

LIKEWISE.

Ex. 22 : 30. l. do with thine oxen
Le. 7 : 1. l. this is law of tresp. off-g
De. 12 : 30. serve their gods, I do l.
15 : 17. unto maidserv. shalt do l.
22 : 3. of brother's lost goods do l.
Ju.7:5.l. ev.one th. boweth to drink
17. Look on me, and do l.
1 S.19:21. messengers, prophesied l.
31 : 5. fell l. upon his sword, died
2 S. 17 : 5. let us hear l. what he
1 K. 11 : 8. l. did he for all his wives
1 Ch. 19 : 15. l. fled before Abishai
23 : 30. to praise morning l. at ev.
Ne. 5 : 10. I l. might exact money
Es. 4 : 16. I and maidens will fast l.
Ps. 49 : 10. l. fool and brutish pers.
52 : 5. God shall l. destroy thee
Ec. 7 : 22. thou l. cursed others
Na. 1 : 12. tho. they quiet l. many
Mat. 17:12. l. sh. Son of man suffer
18:35. So l. shall my heavenly Fa.
20 : 5. he went ab. 6th hour, did l.
10. l. received ev. man a penny
21 : 30. came to second and said l.
36. other serv-ts, did unto them l.
22:26. l. the second and third died,
Mk. 12 : 21. ⌈Lu. 21 : 31.
24:33.so l. when ye see these things,
25 : 17. l. he that rec-d 2 talents
26:35. l. also said all his disciples,
Mk. 14 : 31. ⌈Mk. 15 : 31.
27 : 41. l. the chief priests mocked,
Mk. 4 : 16. these are they l. wh. are
Lu. 2 : 38. she gave thanks l. to L.
3:11. let him do l. | 5: 33. l. disciples of the Phari. ⌈and do l.
6 : 31. do ye to them l. | 10 : 37. go
10 : 32. l. a Levite when he was
13 : 3. ye shall all l. perish, 5.
14 : 33. l. who forsaketh not all
15 : 7. l. joy sh. be in heaven, 10.
16 : 25. l. Laz. received evil things
17 : 10. l. when ye have done all
28. l. as in the days of Lot
31. let him l. not turn back
22 : 20. l. also the cup aft. supper
36. l. his scrip and he th. hath
Jn.5:19,what he doeth, doeth Son l.
6 : 11. l. of the fishes as much
21 : 13. giveth bread and fish l.
Ac. 3 : 24. prophets have l. foretold
Ro. 1 : 27. l. men leaving nat-l use
6 : 11. l. reckon yours. dead to sin
8:26. l. Spirit helpeth our infirmi.
16 : 5. l. greet church in house
1 Co. 7 : 3. l. the wife to husband
4. l. the husband hath not
22. l. also he that is called
14 : 9. l. exc. ye utter words easy
Ga. 2 : 13. other Jews dissembled l.

Col. 4 : 16. l. read epistle fr. Laodi-a
1 Ti. 3 : 8. l. must deacons be grave
5 : 25. l. good works of some are
Tit. 2 : 3. The aged women l.
6. young men l. exhort to be sob.
He. 2 : 14. he l. took part of same
Ja. 2 : 25. l. was not Rahab justif.
1 Pe. 3 : 1. l. wives be in subjection
7. l. ye husbands dwell with
4 : 1. arm yours. l. wi. same mind
5 : 5. l. ye younger submit yours.
Jude 8. l. these filthy dreamers
Re. 8 : 12. day shone not, night l.

LIK'HI. See SHECHEM.

LILIES.

1 K.7:26.with flowers of l., 2 Ch.4:5.
Can.2:16. beloved feedeth am. l.,6:3.
4:5. like two young roes am. the l.
5 : 13. lips like l. dropping myrrh
7:2. thy belly like wheat set wi. l.
Mat.6:28.consid. the l. how, Lu. 12 : [27.

LILY.

Can. 2:1. I am rose, and l. of vallies
2. As l. am. thorns, so is my love
Ho. 14:5. Israel shall grow as the l.

LILY flower or work.

1 K.7:19. the chapiters were of l. w.
22. upon top of pillars was l. w.
2 Ch. 4 : † 5. work of it like l. f.

LIME.

Is. 33:12. peo. be as burnings of l.
Am. 2 : 1. bones of k. of Edom to l.

LIMIT, ED, ETH.

Ps. 78 : 41. they l-d Holy One of Isr.
Eze. 43 : 12. l. shall be most holy
He. 4 : 7. Again, he l-d a certain day

LINE, S.

Jos.2:18. l. of scarlet thread in win.
21. she bound scarlet l. in window
2 S. 8 : 2. measured Moab wi. a l.,
2 l-s to put to death, 1 l. to keep
1 K. 7:15. and a l. of twelve cubits
23. a l. of 30 cubits, 2 Ch. 4 : 2.
2 K.21:13. over Jerus. l. of Samaria
Jb. 38 : 5. stretched l. upon earth?
Ps. 16 : 6. l-s fallen in pleas. places
19 : 4. Their l. is gone thro. earth
78 : 55. divided them inheri. by l.
Is.18:†2.nation of l. l. and treading
28 : 10. l. upon l., l. upon l., 13.
17. Judgment will I lay to the l.
34 : 11. upon it the l. of confusion
17. hath divided it unto th. by l.
44 : 13. he marketh it out with a l.
Je. 31 : 39. measuring l. go forth
La. 2 : 8. L. hath stretched out l.
Eze. 40 : 3. man that had l. of flax
47 : 3. man th. had l. went eastw.
Am. 7 : 17. thy la. be divided by l.
Zch.1:16.a l. stretched upon Jerus.
2 : 1. man with measuring l.
2 Co 10:16.not boast in ano.man's l.

LINEAGE.

Lu. 2 : 4. bec. he was of l. of David

LINEN. [Adj.]

Ex. 28 : 42. make them l. breeches
Le. 6:10. l. garm. l. breeches, 16:4.
13:47.woollen or l. garm.,48,52,59.
16 : 23. Aaron put off l. garments
32. l. clothes and l. garments,
Eze. 44 : 17, 18.
1 S. 2 : 18. Samuel with l. ephod
22 : 18. slew 85 did wear l. ephod
2 S. 6 : 14. Da. girded with l. ephod
1 K. 10 : 28. Sol. had l. yarn, merchants rec-d l. yarn, 2 Ch.1:16.
Je. 13 : 1. get thee l. girdle [19:40.
Mat. 27 : 59. wrapped in l. cloth, Jn.
Mk. 14 : 51. l. cloth about his body
52. left l. cloth, fled naked [6.
Lu.24:12.Pe.beheld l. clothes,Jn.20:
Jn. 20 : 5. John saw the l. clothes

LINEN. [Noun.]

Le. 19 : 19. nor garment of l. and wooll. upon thee, De. 22 : 11.
1 Ch. 15 : 27. Da. had ephod of l.
2 Ch. 5 : 12. arrayed in white l.
Mk. 15:46. wrapped in l., Lu.23:53.
Re. 15 : 6. seven angels in white l.
See CLOTHED, FINE.

LINGERED, ETH.

Ge. 19 : 16. Lot l-d men laid hold
43:10.exc. we had l-d had returned
2 Pe. 2:3. judgm. of a long time l-h

LINTEL, S. [not

Ex. 12 : 22. strike l. and two posts
23.seeth blood upon l.he will pass
1 K.6:31. l. and posts were 5th part
Am. 9 : 1. Smite l. that posts shake
Zph. 2 : 14. bittern lodge in upper l-s

LI'NUS.

2 Ti.4:21. greeteth thee, Pudens, L.

LION.

Ge. 49 : 9. Judah couched as a l.
Nu. 24 : 9. Isr. lay down as a l. (2,
De. 33 : 20. Gad dwelleth as a l.
Ju. 14 : 8. turned to see carcass of l.
honey in carcass of l., 9.
18. what is stronger than a l.?
1 S. 17 : 34. came l. and took a lamb
37. delivered me out of paw of l.
2 S. 17 : 10. heart is as heart of l.
23:20. slew a l. in pit, 1 Ch. 11 : 22.
1 K. 13 : 24. l. met him by way and slew him, l. stood by carcass
25. men saw l. by carcass, 24, 28.
26. Lord hath deliv-d him unto l.
20:36. l. sh. slay thee; a l. found and slew him
Jb. 4 : 10. roaring of l. voice of l.
10:16. Thou huntest me as fierce l.
28 : 8. nor the fierce l. passed by it
38:39. Wilt thou hunt prey for l.?
Ps. 7:2. Lest he tear my soul like l.
10 : 9. lieth in wait secretly as l.
17: 12. Like a l. greedy of his prey
22:13. gaped upon me as roaring l.
21. Save me from the l.'s mouth
91:13.Thou shalt tread upon the l.
Pr 19:12. k.'s wrath as roaring of l.
20 : 2. fear of a k. as roaring of l.
22 : 13. slothful saith, There is a l.
26 : 13. l. in the way, l. in street
28 : 1. righteous are bold as a l.
15. As roaring l. so wicked ruler
30 : 30. A l. strongest am. beasts
Ec. 9 : 4. living dog than dead l.
Is. 5:29. Their roaring sh. be like l.
11:7. l. sh. eat straw like ox,65:25.
21 : 8. he cried, A l. My lord
29 : † 1. woe to the l. of God, city
35:9. No l. shall be there, nor rav.
38:13. as a l. so break all my bones
Je. 2 : 30. devoured prophets like l.
4 : 7. l. is come up fr. his thicket
5 : 6. l. out of forest sh. slay them
12 : 8. Mine heritage unto me as l.
25:38. forsaken his covert as l.
49:19.he sh. come up like l., 50:44.
La. 3 : 10. he was unto me as a l.
Eze. 1 : 10. face of a l. on right side
10 : 14. third was the face of a l.
22 : 25. conspiracy like roaring l.
Da. 7 : 4. first like a l. had wings
Ho. 5:14. I will be unto Ephr. as l.
11: 10. he shall roar like a l. when
13 : 7. unto them as l. | 8. devour as l. [a great l.
Jo. 1 : 6. teeth of a l. cheek teeth of
Am. 3:4. Will l. roar hath no prey?
8. l. hath roared, who not fear?
12. taketh out of mouth of l.
5 : 19. As if a man did flee from l.
Mi. 5 : 8. remnant of Jac. be as l.
Na.2:12. l. tear in pieces for whelps
2 Ti.4:17. deliv-d out of mouth of l.
1 Pe. 5 : 8. devil as roaring l. walk-h
Re. 4 : 7. first beast was like a l.
5 : 5. the l. of the tribe of Judah
10:3. loud voice as when l. roareth
13 : 2. his mouth as mouth of a l.
See BEAR, DEN.

Old LION.

Ge. 49 : 9. as o. l. who rouse him
Jb. 4 : 11. o. l. perisheth for lack
Is. 30:6. whence come yo. and o.l.?
Na.2:11. where lion, the o.l.walked

LION'S whelp, whelps.

Ge. 49 : 9. Judah is l.w. from prey
De. 33 : 22. Dan is l. w. he sh. leap
Jb. 4 : 11. stout l. w-s are scattered
28 : 8. l. w-s have not trodden it
Je. 51 : 38. they shall yell as l. w-s

Young LION.

Nu. 23: 24. sh. lift up hims. as y. l.
Ju. 14 : 5. a y. l. roared ag. him
Ps. 17 : 12. as it a y. l. lurking in
91:13. y. l. thou trample und. feet
Is. 11 : 6. calf and y. l. lie together
31:4. Like y. l. roaring on his prey
Eze.19:3. became a y.l. and learned,
5. took ano. made him a y. l. [6.
32:2. Thou art like y. l. of nations
41:19.face of y.l. toward palm tree
Ho. 5 : 14. I will be as y. l. to hou.
Am. 3 : 4. will a y. l. cry out of den
Mi. 5 : 8. as a y.l. am. flocks of she.

LIONS.

2 S.1:23.Saul, Jona.stronger than l.
1 K. 7 : 29. on borders l. beneath l.
36. he graved cherubim, l. and
10:19. two l. stood beside the stays,
2 Ch. 9 : 18. [side, 2 Ch. 9 : 19.
20. twelve l. stood on the one
2 K. 17 : 25. Lord sent l. am. them
26. he hath sent l. among them
1 Ch. 12 : 8. faces like faces of l.
Ps. 22: 21. save me from l.'s mouth
35 : 17. L. rescue my darling fr. l.
57:4. My soul is among l. I lie am.
Is. 15 : 9. l. upon him that escapeth
Je. 50 : 17. l. have driven Isr. away
51:38. They shall roar toge. like l.
Eze. 19 : 2. lioness, she lay am. l.
6. he went up and down am. l.
Da. 6 : 24. l. had mastery of them
27. delivered Dan. fr. power of l.
Na. 2 : 11. Where is dwelling of l.?
Zph. 3:3. princes are roaring l.
He.11:33.faith stopped mouths of l.
Re. 9 : 8. their teeth as teeth of l.
17. heads of horses as heads of l.
See DEN.

Young LIONS.

Jb. 4 : 10. teeth of y. l. are broken
38 : 39. wilt fill appetite of y. l.?
Ps. 34 : 10. y. l. do lack and suffer
58 : 6. break out gr. teeth of y. l.
104 : 21. y. l. roar after their prey
Is. 5 : 29. they shall roar like y. l.
Je. 2 : 15. y. l. roared upon him
Eze.19:2. nourished whelps am.y.l.
38:13. with y. l. sh. say unto thee
Na. 2 : 11. where feeding place of y.
13. sword sh. devour thy y.l. [l.?
Zch. 11 : 3. a voice of roaring of y.l.

LIONESS, ESSES.

Eze. 19:2. What is thy mother? a l.
Na. 2 : 12. lion strangled for his l-s

LIONLIKE.

2 S.23:20.slew 2 l.men of,1 Ch.11:22.

LIP.

Ge. 11 : † 1. whole earth of one l.
22:†17. as the sand upon the sea l.
Le. 13 : 45. sh. put cov-g upon l.
Ju. 7:†22. host fled to l. of Abel-m.
1 K. 9:†26. Ezion-g. on l. of Red sea
2 K. 2 : † 13. stood by l. of Jordan
Jb. 12 : † 20. removeth l. of faithful
Ps.22:7. they shoot out the l.shake
Pr. 12 : 19. l. of truth be establ-d
17:†7. A l. of excellency
Eze. 3:† 5. sent to a peo. deep of l., 6.
36 : † 3. made to come upon l.
Mi. 3: † 7. they shall cover upper l.

LIPS.

Ex. 6 : 12. who am of uncirc-d l., 30.
Nu. 30:6. aught out of her l., 8, 12.
1 S. 1 : 13. spake in her heart, only her l. moved [l., Is. 36:†5.
2 K. 18 : † 20. they are but words of

Ps. 12 : 2. with flattering l. speak
3. L. sh. cut off all flattering l.
4. l. our own, who lord over us?
17 : 1. prayer not out of feigned l.
31:18. Let lying l. be put to silence
59:7. behold, swords are in their l.
12. For words of l. let th. be taken
63 : 5. praise thee with joyful l.
120 : 2. Deliver my soul fr. lying l.
140:3. adders' poison und. their l.
9. let mischief of own l. cover th.
Pr. 4 : 24. perverse l. put from thee
5:3. l. of strange woman drop as a
7 : 21. with flatt-g of l. forced him
10 : † 8. a fool of l. shall fall
13. l. of him hath understanding
18. hideth hatred wi. lying l. is fool
21. l. of righteous feed many
32. l. of righteous know what is
acceptable [to the Lord
12:22. Lying l. are an abomination
14 : 3. l. of wise sh. preserve them
7. perceiv. not in him l. of knowl.
23. talk of l. tendeth to penury
15 : 7. l. of wise disperse knowl.
16 : 10. divine sentence is in l. of
13. Righte. l. are delight of kings
21. sweetness of l. increaseth
learning [false l.
17 : 4. wicked doer giveth heed to
7. less do lying l. become prince
18:6. fool's l. enter into contention
20 : 15. l. of knowledge are a jewel
24 : 2. and their l. talk of mischief
26:23. Burning l. are like potsherd
Ec. 10 : 12. l. of fool swallow hims.
Can. 5 : 13. his l. like lilies
.9. l. of those asleep to speak
Is. 6 : 5. I am a man of uncl. l. I
dwell in midst of peo. of uncl. l.
28:11. with stammering l. speak
29 : 13. peo. with l. do honour me
57 : 19. I create the fruit of the l.
59 : 3. your l. have spoken lies
La. 3 : 62. l. of those rose ag. me
Eze. 24 : 22. ye shall not cover l.
36 : 3. ye are taken in l. of talkers
Da. 12 : † 5. this side of l. of river
Ho. 14:2. render the calves of our l.
Mi. 3:7. they shall all cover their l.
Mal. 2:7. priest's l. sho. keep knowl.
Mat. 15 : 8. honoureth me with l.,
Mk. 7 : 6.
Ro. 3:13. poison of asps under their l.
1 Co. 14 : 21. wi. other l. will I speak
He. 13 : 15. fruit of l. giving thanks

His LIPS.

Le. 5 : 4. with h. l. to do evil
Jb. 2 : 10. did not Job sin with h. l.
11 : 5. G. wo. open h. l. ag. thee
23 : 12. Nei. gone fr. com. of h. l.
Ps. 21:2. not withhol. request of h. l.
106: 33. unadvisedly with h. l.
Pr. 10 : 19. refraineth h. l. is wise
12: 13. snared by transgr. of h. l.
13 : 3. ope. wide h. l. have destruc.
16:23. wise addeth learning to h. l.
27. in h. l. there is burning fire
30. moving h. l. he bringeth evil
17 : 28. shutteth h. l. is a man of
18 : 7. h. l. are snare of his soul
20. with increase of h. l. be filled
19: 1. than he th. is perverse in h. l.
20:19. him th. flattereth with h. l.
22 : 11. for grace of h. l. the king
24:26. kiss h. l. th. giv-h right ans.
26:24. hateth dissembleth wi. h. l.
Can. 5 : 13. h. l. like lilies dropping
Is. 11 : 4. breath of h. l. slay wick.
30 : 27. h. l. are full of indignation
Mal. 2: 6. iniq. not found in h. l.
1 Pe. 3 : 10. h. l. they speak no guile

My LIPS.

Jb. 13:6. hearken to pleading of m. l.
16 : 5. m. l. sho. assuage your grief
27 : 4. m. l. sh. not speak wickedn.
32 : 20. I will open m. l. and ans.
Jb. 33:3. and m. l. shall utter knowl.
Ps. 16 : 4. nor take names into m. l.
40 : 9. lo, I have not refrained m. l.
51 : 15. O Lord, open thou m. l.
63 : 3. m. l. shall praise thee
66:14. I will pay vows m. l. uttered
71 : 23. m. l. shall greatly rejoice
89:34. nor alt. that gone out of m. l.
119:13. m. l. I declared thy judgm.
171. m. l. shall utter thy praise
141 : 3. O Lord, keep door of m. l.
Pr. 8 : 6. opening of m. l. right thi.
7. wickedness an aboml. to m. l.
Je. 17 : 16. out of m. l. was right
Da. 10:16. one like men touched m. l.
Ha. 3 : 16. m. l. quivered at voice

Thine own or thy LIPS.

De. 23 : 23. that out of t. l. perform
2 K. 19:28. my bridle in t. l., Is. 37:29.
Jb. 8 : 21. fill t. l. with rejoicing
15 : 6. t. o. l. testify against thee
Ps. 17: 4. by word of t. l. I kept me
34 : 13. keep t. l. fr. speaking guile
45 : 2. grace is poured into t. l.
Pr. 5 : 2. that t. l. keep knowledge
22 : 18. they shall be fitted in t. l.
23 : 16. rejoi. when t. l. speak right
24 : 28. deceive not with t. l.
27:2. let ano. praise thee, not t. o. l.
Can. 4 : 3. t. l. like thread of scarlet
11. t. l. O spouse, as honeycomb
Is. 6 : 7. Lo, this hath touched t. l.
Eze. 24:17. cover not t. l. eat not br.

LIQUOR, S.

Ex. 22 : 29. not delay to offer thy l-s
Nu. 6 : 3. nei. drink any l. of grapes
Can. 7:2. goblet, which wanteth not l.

LISTED, ETH.

Ma. 17 : 12. done unto Elias whatsoever they l-d, Mk. 9 : 13.
Jn. 3 : 8. wind bloweth where it l-h
Ja. 3 : 4. the ships, whithersoever
the governor l-h

LISTEN.

Is. 49 : 1. l. O isles, unto me hearken

LITTERS. [l.

Is. 66 : 20. sh. bring your breth. in

LITTLE. [bef.

Ge. 30 : 30. it was but l. thou hadst
43 : 2. Go buy us a l. food, 44 : 25.
11. carry l. balm, l. honey [lamb
Ex. 12 : 4. if household too l. for
16 : 18. he that gathered l. had no
lack, 2 Co. 8:15. [ont, De. 7: 22.
23: 30. by l. and l. I will drive them
De. 28 : 38. much out, gather l. in
Jos. 19 : 47. coast of Dan too l.
22 : 17 Is iniq. of Peor too l. for us?
Ru. 2 : 7. she tarried a l. in house
1 S. 14 : 29. I tasted a l. of honey, 43.
15 : 17. when wast l. in own sight.
22 : † 15. knew noth. of this l. or
2 S. 12 : 8. if that had been too l. I
16 : 1. when Da. was l. past top of
1 K. 8 : 64. brazen altar was too l.
2 K. 10 : 18. Ahab served Baal, a l.
Ne. 9 : 32. let not trouble seem l.
Jb. 4 : 12. and my ear received a l.
10 : 20. that I may take comfort a l.
36 : 2. suffer me a l. I will shew
Ps. 2 : 12. wrath is kindled but a l.
8 : 5. l. lower than angels, He. 2: 7.
37 : 16. l. th. a righteous man hath
42 : † 6. remem. thee from l. hill
68 : 27. There is l. Benjamin, with
114:4. l. hills skipped like lambs, 6.
Pr. 6 : 10. a l. sleep, l. slumber, a
l. folding, 24 : 33.
10: 20. heart of the wicked is l. worth
15 : 16. Better is l. with fear of L.
16 : 8. Better is l. with righteousn.
30 : 24. four things l. upon earth
Ec. 5: 12. sweet, whe. we eat l. or much
12 : † 4. fail because they grind l.
Can. 3 : 4. but a l. I passed fr. them
Is. 28 : 10. here a l. there a l., 13.
Je. 30:† 18. city be built upon l. hill
Eze. 31 : 4. sent l. rivers unto trees
Ho. 8 : 10. sorrow a l. for burden
Mi. 5 : 2. tho. l. among thousands
Hag. 1 : 6. sown much, bring in l.
9. looked for much, lo, it came to l.
Zch. 1 : 15. I was but l. displeased
Mat. 15:34. seven, and a few l. fishes
26 : 39. went a l. further, Mark 1:
19.-14 : 35. [of death
Mk. 5 : 23. My l. daughter at point
14 : 70. a l. after, they th. stood by
Lu. 5 : 3. thrust out l. fr. land [l.
7:47. to wh. l. forgiven ; same loveth
19 : 17. been faithful in very l.
Jn. 6 : 7. that ev. one may take a l.
Ac. 20 : 12. were not a l. comforted
27:28. when they had gone l. furth.
2 Co. 8:15. that gath-d l. had no lack
11 : 1. could bear with me a l.
16. that I may boast myself a l.
Ep. 3 : † 3. as I wrote a l. before
1 Ti. 4:8. bodily exercise profiteth l.
He. 2 : 9. made l. lower than angels
Ja. 3 : 5. tongue l. member, a l. fire
2 Pe. 2 : † 18. were for a l. escaped
See BOOK, CAKE, CHAMBER, S, CHILD, CHILDREN, CITY, CLOUD, COAT, FAITH, FINGER, FLOCK, S, FOLLY, FOXES, HELP, HILLS, HORN, HOUSE, KINDNESS, LAMB, LEAVEN, MAID, OIL, ONE, ONES, OWL, PORTION, REVIVING, SANCTUARY, SEASON, SHIP, S, SISTER, SPACE, STATURE, STRENGTH, THING, TIME, WATER, WAY, WHILE, WINE, WRATH.

LIVE. [Adj.]

Ex. 21 : 35. they shall sell the l. ox
Is. 6 : 6. a seraphim having l. coal
See GOAT. [in hand

LIVE. [Verb.]

Ge. 3 : 22. take of tree of life, l. for
ever [thee
12 : 13. my soul shall l. because of
17 : 18. Ishm. might l. bef. thee!
19 : 20. me escape, my soul sh. l.
20 : 7. pray for thee, thou shalt l.
27 : 40. by sword shalt thou l.
31 : 32. with whomso. findest thy
gods, him not l.
42 : 18. Joseph said, This do, and l.
45 : 3. doth my father yet l.?
Ex. 1 : 16. if a dau. then she shall l.
22 : 18. shalt not suffer witch to l.
33 : 20. shall no man see me and l.
Le. 18 : 5. if a man do he shall l.
Ne. 9 : 29. Eze. 20 : 11, 13, 21.
Nu. 21:8. looketh upon serp. shall l.
24 : 23. who l. when G. doeth this?
De. 4 : 10. fear me all days they l.
33. ever peo. hear as thou and l.
42. that fleeing he might l.
8 : 3. by ev. word of the L. doth
12:1. all the days that ye l. [man l.
19:5. unto one of these cities and l.
31 : 13. fear Lord as long as ye l.,
1 K. 8 : 40.
33 : 6. let Reuben l. and not die
Jos. 6 : 17. only Rahab harlot sh. l.
9 : 15. made league to let them l.
20. will let them l. lest wrath, 21
1 S. 10 : † 24. said, Let the king l.,
2 S. 16:† 16. 1 K. 1:† 25. 2 K. 11:†
12. 2 Ch. 23 : † 11.
20 : 14. while I l. shew me kindn.
2 S. 19 : 34. How long have I to l.
1 K. 20 : 32. I pray thee let me l.
2 K. 4 : 7. l. thou and thy children
7:4. if they save us alive, we sh. l.
2 Ch. 6 : 31. in thy ways long as l.
Jb. 7:† 8. I can l. no longer
10 : † 1. soul is cut off while I l.
14:14. If a man die, sh. he l. again
21 : 7. Whf. do the wicked l. old?
Ps. 22:26. your heart shall l. for ever

Ps. 49:9. still l. and not see corrup.
63 : 4. will I bless thee while I l.
69 : 32. hearts shall l. that seek G.
72: 15. shall l., to him be giv. gold
118 : 17. I shall not die but l.
119 : 144. give underst-g I shall l.
175. Let my soul l. it shall praise
146 : 2. While I l. will I praise L.
Pr. 4:4. keep my com-ts and l., 7:2.
9 : 6. Forsake the foolish, and l.
15:27. he that hateth gifts shall l.
Ec. 6 : 3. if l. many years, 6.–11 : 8.
9:3. madness in heart while they l.
9. l. joyfully wi. wife thou lovest
Is. 26:19. Thy dead men shall l. toge.
38:16. by these men l. make me l.
55 : 3. hear, and your soul shall l.
Je. 21 : 9. falleth to Chaldeans shall
l., 27 : 12, 17.–38 : 2, 17.
38: 20. Obey, and thy soul shall l.
La. 4:20. Under his shadow we shall l
Eze. 3 : 21. he shall surely l., 18: 9,
17, 19, 21, 28.–33 : 13, 15, 16.
16 : 6. I said unto thee when thou
wast in thy blood, l. (2)
18 : 19. kept my statutes shall l.,
21, 22.–20 : 11, 25. [33:11.
23. that the wicked return and l.,
24. righte. turneth aw. shall he l.
32. wheref. turn yourselves and l.
33:10. If sins upon us, how sho. we l.
12. nei. shall righto. be able to l.
19. If do that is right, he shall l.
37:3. Son of man, can th. bones l.?
5. breath to enter ye sh. l., 6, 14.
47:9. ev. thing l. whi. river com-h
Ho. 6 : 2. will revive us, we shall l.
Am. 5:4. Seek me, and ye shall l., 6.
Jon. 4:3. is better to die, than to l., 8.
Ha. 2 : 4. the just shall l. by his
faith, Ro. 1:17. Ga. 3:11. He. 10:38.
Zch. 10 : 9. they shall l. with chil.
Mat. 9 : 18. she shall l., Mk. 5 : 23.
Lu. 7 : 25. they which l. delicately
10:28. this do, thou shalt l.
20:38. not G. of dead, all l. unto him
Jn. 5 : 25. dead hear voice and l.
6 : 57. I l. by Father, so he that
eateth me, even shall l. by me
11:25. tho. were dead, yet he shall l.
14 : 19. because I l. ye shall l. also
Ac. 17 : 28. in him we l. and move
22:22. it is not fit that he should l.
Ro. 6 : 2. dead to sin, l. longer th-n?
8. we believe we shall l. with him
8 : 12. debtors, not to l. after flesh
13. if l. aft. flesh ye sh. die, if thro.
spirit mortify body ye shall l.
10:5. doeth these l. by th., Ga. 3:12.
12 : 18. if possible, l. peaceably
14:8. whe. we l. we l. unto the L.;
whe. we l. or die, we are Lord's
1 Co. 9 : 13. l. of things of temple
14. preach gospel, sho. l. of gos.
2 Co. 4:11. wh. l. are deliv d unto dea.
6 : 9. as dying, and behold we l.
7:3. in hearts to die and l. with you
13 : 4. we shall l. with him by G.
11. be of one mind, l. in peace
Ga. 2 : 14. compellest Gent. to l. as
19. that I might l. unto G. [Jews
20. I l. yet not I, but C. in me,
life I now l. in flesh I l. by faith
5:25. If we l. in Spirit, let us walk
Ph. 1 : 21. For to me to l. is Christ
22. if I l. in the flesh, this is fruit
1 Th. 3 : 8. we l. if ye stand fast in
5:10. died, that we sho. l. with him
2 Ti. 2 : 11. we sh. also l. with him
3:12. all th. will l. godly shall suffer
Tit. 2:12. teaching we sho. l. soberly
He. 12:9. in subjec. unto Fa. and l.
13: 18. in all willing to l. honestly
Ja. 4 : 15. If the L. will we shall l.
1 Pe. 2:24. that we l. unto righte-n.
4:2. th. he no longer l. in the flesh
6. l. acc. to God in the Spirit
2 Pe. 2 : 6. unto those th. l. ungodly
18. escaped from them l. in error
1 Jn. 4:9. sent Son, that we might l.
Re. 13:14. beast had wound and did
See **Live for EVER.** [l.

As I LIVE.

Nu. 14 : 21. As truly a. I l. earth
shall be filled, 28. [33.–116 : 2.
Jb. 27 : 6. so long a. I l., Ps. 104 :
Je. 46 : 18. a. I l. saith the king
See **Saith the LORD.**

May, or mayest LIVE.

Ge. 42:2. that we m. l., 43:8.–47:19.
Le. 25 : 35. relieve that he m. l.
36. take no usury, that bro. m. l.
Nu. 4: 19. do unto them they m. l.
De. 4:1. teach to do them th. ye m.
l., 5 : 33.–8 : 1.–30 : 6, 16.
16 : 20. is just follow, that m-t l.
30:19. choose life, th. thy seed m. l.
2 S. 12:22. gracious, that child m. l.
2 K. 18:32. land of br that you m. l.
Ne. 5:2. corn, that we m. eat and l.
Es. 4 : 11. hold sceptre, th. he m. l.
Ps. 119:17. bountifully, that I m. l.
77. let mercies come, that I m. l.
116. Uphold me that I m. l.
Je. 35 : 7. that ye m. l. many days
Eze. 37:9. upon slain, that they m. l.
Am. 5 : 14. Seek good th. ye m. l.
Ep. 6 : 3. m. l. long on the earth

Not LIVE.

Ex. 19:13. that touch mt. shall n. l.
22 : 18. shalt n. suffer witch to l.
De. 8 : 3. man doth n. l. by bread
only, but by, Mat. 4:4. Lu 4:4.
2 S. 1 : 10. I was sure he could n. l.
2 K. 10 : 19. whoso. wanting he n. l.
20 : 1. Set thine house in order,
thou shalt n. l., Is. 38 : 1.
Jb. 7 : 16. I would n. l. always
Ps. 55 : 23. wicked n. l. half da,s
Is. 26 : 14. dead, they shall n. l.
Eze. 13 : 19. to save souls sho. n. l.
18 : 13. shall he live? shall n. l.
20:25. Judg-ts whereby th. sh. n. l.
Zch. 13:3. unto him, Thou shalt n. l.
Lu. 12:†29. l. n. in careful suspense
Ac. 7:19. cast out chil. th. they n. l.
25 : 24 he ought n. to l. longer
28 : 4. vengeance suffereth n. to l.
2 Co. 5:15. they sho n. l. unto thems.

LIVED.

Ge. 25 : 6. from Isaac while he l.
7. years of Ab.'s life which he l.
47 : 28. Jacob l. in Egypt 17 years
50:22. Joseph l. a hund. and 10 y-rs
Nu. 14 : 38. Josh. and Caleb l. still
21: 9. beheld serpent of brass he l.
De. 5 : 26. heard voice of G. and l.
2 S. 19 : 6. if Abs. l. and we died
1 K. 12 : 6. old men th. stood bef.
Sol. while he l., 2 Ch. 10 : 6.
2 K. 14 : 17. Amaziah l. aft. death
of Jehoash 15 y-rs, 2 Ch. 25:25.
Jb. 42:16. Aft. this l. Job 140 years
Ps. 49 : 18. while l. he blessed soul
Eze. 37 : 10. breath came, they l.
Lu. 2 : 36. l. with a husb. 7 years
Ac. 23 : 1. I have l. in good consci.
26:5. after our religion I l. a Phari-
Col. 3 : 7. when ye l. in them [see
Ja. 5 : 5. Ye have l. in pleasure
Re. 18:7. how much she hath glori-
fied herself and l. deliciously, 9.
20 : 4. they l. and reigned with C.
5. rest l. not again until 1000 y-rs
See BEGAT, HUNDRED, YEARS.

LIVELY.

[are l.
Ex. 1 : 19. Because Hebrew women
Ps. 38 : 19. But mine enemies are l.
Ac. 7 :38. who received the l. oracles
1 Pe. 1 :3. begotten us unto a l. hope
2 : 5. Ye, as l. stones, are built up

LIVER.

[his l.
Pr. 7 : 23. Till a dart strike through
La. 2 : 11. my l. is poured upon earth
Eze. 21:21 he consulted, he looked in
See CAUL. [the l.

LIVES.

Ge. 9 : 5. blood of your l. I require
45 : 7. your l. by a great deliver.
47 : 25. Thou hast saved our l. let
Ex. 1 : 14. l. bitter with bondage
Jos. 2 : 13. deliver our l. fr. death
9 : 24. were sore afraid of our l.
Ju. 5 : 18. peo. that jeoparded l.
18:25. lose thy life wi. l. of househ.
2 S. 1 : 23. Saul and Jonathan were
lovely and pleasant in their l.
19 : 5. saved l. of thy sons, wives
23:17. in jeopardy of l., 1 Ch. 11:19.
Es. 9:16. other Jews stood for their l.
Pr. 1 : 18. lurk privily for own l.
Je. 19 : 7. wh. seek their l., 46 : 26.
9. seek their l. sh. straiten them
48:6. save your l. be like the heath
La. 5: 9. We gat br. with peril of l.
Da. 7 : 12. l. prolonged for a season
Lu. 9: 56. Son not come to destr. l.
Ac. 15: 26. men th. hazarded their l.
27:10. voyage be with damage of l.
1 Jn. 3: 16. lay down l. for breth.
Re. 12 : 11. loved not their l. unto

LIVEST.

[death
De. 12:19. forsake not Lev. long as l.
Ga. 2 : 14. if a Jew l. after manner
Re. 3:1. a name thou l. and art dead

LIVETH.

Ge. 9 : 3. Ev. thing that l. be meat
16 : † 14. the well of him that l.
De. 5 : 24. G. talk with man, he l.
1 S. 1:28. long as he l. be lent to L.
20 : 31. long as son of Jesse l. upon
25 : 6. say to him l. in prosperity
2 S. 2:27. As G. l. unless thou spok.
15 : 21. as my lord king l. [18:46.
22:47. L. l. blessed be my rock, Ps.
1 K. 3 : 23. This is my son that l.
17 : 12. As the L. thy G. l., 18 : 10.
23. Elijah said. See thy son l.
Jb. 19 : 25. I know my Redeemer l.
27:2. As G. l. who hath tak. judgm.
Ps. 89:48. What man l. not see death
Je. 4 : 2. shalt swear, L. l. in truth
5 : 2. say, L. l. they swear falsely
12 : 16. to swear, The L. l. as they
16 : 14. The Lord l., 15.–23 : 7, 8.
44:26. in Egypt. saying, The Lord l.
Eze. 47:9. ev. thing that l. and moveth
Ho. 4 : 15. nor swear, The Lord l.
Am. 8 : 14. Thy God, O Dan, l. and
The manner of Beer-sheba l.
Jn. 4:50. Go thy way, son l., 51, 53.
11 : 26. whosoever l. and believeth
Ro. 6:10. in that he l. he l. unto G.
7:1. law over man as long as he l., 2
3. if while husb. l. she be married
14:7. For none l. or dieth to hims.
1 Co. 7:39. wife bound long as husb.
2 Co. 13 : 4. l. by power of God [l.
Ga. 2 : 20. I live, but C. l. in me
1 Ti. 5 : 6. l. in pleasure dead while
He. 7: 8. witnessed th. he l. [she l.
25. he ever l. to make intercession
9 : 17. no strength while testa. l.
Re. 1 : 18. I am he that l. and was
See **For EVER.** [dead

As the Lord LIVETH.

Ju. 8:19. a. L. l. if ye have saved th.
Ru. 3:13. de part of kinsman, a. L. l.
1 S. 14: 39. a. L. l. tho' it be in Jona.
45. a. L. l., 19 : 6.–20 : 21.–25:26.–
26:10, 16.–28:10.–29:6. 2 S. 4:9.
–12: 5.–14:11 1 K. 1:29.–2:24.–
22 : 14. 2 K. 5 : 20. 2 Ch. 18:13.
Je. 38 : 16.
20:3. a. L. l. is but a step betw. me
25:34. a. L. of Isr. l. who kept me
2 S. 15 : 21. a. L. l. and the king l.
1 K. 17: 1. a. L. God of Isr. l., 18:15
12. a. L. thy God l., 18:10. [4:30.
2 K. 2:2. a. L. l. and thy soul, 4, 6.
3 : 14. a. L. of hosts l. bef., 5 : 16.

As thy soul LIVETH.
1 S.1:26.**a.t.s.l.** I am a woman who
17:55. Abner said, **a.t.s.l.** O king
20:3. **a.t.s.l.** is but step betw. me
25:26. **a.t.s.l.** seeing L. withhold.
2 S.11:11. **a.t.s.l.** I will not do this
14:19. **a. t. s. l.** none can turn to
2 K.2:2.**a.t.s.l.** I will not leave thee,
so they went, 4, 6.-4:30.

LIVING. [Adj., Part.]
Ge. 1:28. dominion over ev. **l.** thing
2:7. and man became a **l.** soul
6:19. of **l.** thing of all flesh, two
7:4. ev. **l.** substance I will destroy
23. ev. **l.** substance was destr-d
8:1. G. rememb-d every **l.** thing
17. bring forth every **l.** thing
21. not smite any more thing **l.**
26:† 19. found well of **l.** water
Le. 11:10. **l.** thing wh. is in water
13:† 10. if a quickening of **l.** flesh
20:25. abominable by **l.** thing
Nu. 19:†17. for uncl. **l.** waters given
2 S. 20:3. shut up **l.** in widowh-d
1 K. 3:22. the **l.** is my son, 23.
25. Divide the **l.** child in two
26. whose the **l.** child, give her **l.**
27. king said, Give her the **l.** child
Jb. 12:10. is soul of every **l.** thing
Ps.38:†19. enem. being **l.** are strong
58:9. sh. take them away both **l.**
143:2. shall no man **l.** be justified
145:16. thou satisfiest ev. **l.** thing
Ec. 9:4. **l.** dog better than dead lion
Can. 4:15. a well of **l.** water, streams
Is. 19:†10. make ponds of **l.** things
Je.2:13. fountain of **l.** waters, 17:13.
La. 3:39. Whf. a **l.** man complain?
Da. 2:30. wisd. I have more than **l.**
Zch. 14:8. **l.** waters out fr. Jerus.
Jn. 4:10. have given thee **l.** water
11. whence hast thou **l.** water?
6:51. I am the **l.** bread wh. came
57. As the **l.** Father hath sent me
7:38. out of belly rivers of **l.** water
Ro. 12:1. bodies a **l.** sacrifice [soul
1 Co. 15:45. Adam was made a **l.**
Col. 2:20. **l.** in world, are ye subject
Tit. 3:3. **l.** in malice, envy, hating
He. 10:20. enter by new and **l.** way
1 Pe. 2:4. coming as unto a **l.** stone
Re.7:17.Lamb lead unto **l.** fountains
16:3. every **l.** soul died in the sea
See BIRD, CREATURE, S, GOD.

LIVING. [Noun.]
Is. 57:†10. hast found **l.** of thy ha.
Mk.12:44.cast in all her **l.**, Lu.21:4.
Lu. 8:43. spent all her **l.** upon
15:12. he divided unto them his **l.**
13. wasted subst. with riotous **l.**,

All or the LIVING. [30.
Ge.3:20.name Eve, bec. moth.of **a.l.**
Nu. 16:48. stood betw. dead and **t.l.**
Ru. 2:20. not left off kindn. to **t. l.**
Jb. 28:21. is hid from eyes of **a. l.**
30:23. house appointed for **a. l.**
33:30.enlightened with light of **t.l.**
Ps. 56:13.may walk in light of **t. l.**
69:28. blotted out of book of **t. l.**
Ec. 4:2. dead more than **t. l.**
15. I considered all **t. l.** under
6:8. knoweth to walk before **t. l.**
7:2. **t. l.** will lay it to his heart
9:4. to all **t. l.** there is hope
5. **t. l.** know they shall die
Is. 4:3. written am. **t. l.** in Jerus.
8:19. seek unto God for **t. l.**
38:19. **t. l.** he sh. praise thee as I
Eze.7:†13. tho. his life be am. **t. l.**
Da. 4:7. to intent **t. l.** may know
Mat. 22:32. God is not G. of dead
but of **t. l.** Mk. 12:27. Lu. 20:38.
Lu.24:5. Why seek ye **t. l.** am. dead?
Ro.14:9.be L. both of **t.** dead and **l.**
See **LAND of the Living.**

LIZARD.
Le. 11:30.**l.** snail, and mole unclean

LO.
Ge. 18:10. **l.** Sarah shall have a son
29:7. **l.** it is yet high day, water
50:5. **l.** I die | Ex. 19:9. **l.** I come
Nu. 14:40. **l.** we be here, and will
24:11. **l.** L. kept thee from honour
1 S.14:43. taste honey, **l.** I must die
2 S. 24:17. **l.** I have sinned
Jb. 9:19. if speak of strength, **l.** he
Ps. 37:36. and **l.** he was not [it at
40:7. **l.** I come | 132:6. **l.** we heard
52:7. **l.** man that made not God his
73:27. **l.** they far fr. thee sh. perish
92:9. for **l.** thine enemies perish (2)
139:4. **l.** thou knowest it altog.
Ec. 7:29. **l.** this only have I found
Can. 2:11. **l.** the winter is past
Is. 25:9. **l.** this is our G., we waited
Je. 4:23. **l.** it was without form
25. I beheld, and **l.** was no man
8:8. **l.** in vain made he it [city
25:29. **l.** I begin to bring evil on
Eze. 17:18. **l.** he had given his hand
30:9. **l.** it cometh | 33:33. **l.** it will
Ho. 9:6. for **l.** they are gone [come
Am. 4:2. **l.** the days shall come
Hag. 1:9. for much, **l.** it came to lit.
Mat. 2:9. **l.** star went before them
3:16. **l.** heavens were opened
24:23. **l.** here is Christ, Mk. 13:21.
25:25. **l.** thou hast t at is thine
28:7. **l.** I have told you
20. **l.** I am with you alway
Mk. 10:28. **l.** we left all, Lu. 18:28.
Lu. 1:44. For **l.** as soon as voice
13:16. bound, **l.** these 18 years
17:21. **l.** here! or **l.** there!
23:15. **l.** nothing worthy of death
Ac. 13:46. **l.** we turn to Gentiles
He. 10:7. **l.** I come to do thy will,
Re. 5:6. **l.** in midst of throne [9.
14:1. looked and **l.** a lamb

LOADEN, LOADETH.
Ps. 68:19. daily **l-h** us with benefits
144:†14. oxen may be **l-n** with flesh
Is. 46:1. your carriages were heavy

LOAF. [l-n
Ex. 29:23. one **l.** of bread, one cake
1 Ch. 16:3. Da. dealt to ev. one a **l.**
Mk.8:14. nei. had more than one **l.**
See **Loaf of BREAD.**

LO-AMMI.
Ho. 1:9. said G. Call his name L.

LOAN.
De. 24:† 10. **l.** of any thing to bro.
1 S. 2:20. **l.** which is lent to the L.

LOATHE, LOATHED.
Ex. 7:18. E-ns sh. **l.** to drink of river
Jb. 7:16. I **l.** it, I would not live
Je. 14:19. hath thy soul **l-d** Zion?
Eze. 6:9. shall **l.** thems. for evils
16:45. thy sisters **l-d** husbands
20:43 sh. **l.** yours. for evils, 36:31.
Zch. 11:8. my soul **l-d** them, their

LOATHETH, ING.
Nu. 21:5. our soul **l-h** this light br.
Pr. 27:7. full soul **l-h** a honeycomb.
Eze. 16:5. cast out to **l-g** of person
16:45. **l-h** her husband and chil.

LOATHSOME.
Nu. 11:20. month, until **l.** unto you
Jb. 7:5. my skin is become **l.**
Ps. 38:7. loins filled with **l.** disease
Pr. 13:5. a wicked man is **l.**

LOAVES.
Le. 23:17. shall bring two wave **l.**
1 S. 17:17. take ten **l.** run to camp
25:18. Abigail took 200 **l.**
1 K. 14:3. take ten **l.** and cracknels
2 K. 4:42. brought man of G. 20 **l.**
Mat. 14:17. We have here but 5 **l.**
19. and he took the five **l.**, Mk. 6:
38, 41. Lu. 9:13, 16. [6:38.-8:5
15:34. How many **l.** have ye? Mk.
36. he took the seven **l.**, Mk. 8:6.
16:9. neither remember the five
l. of the 5,000, Mk. 8:19.
Mat.16:10. Nei. the 7 L of the 4,000
Mk. 6:44. did eat of **l.** were 5,000
52. considered not miracle of **l.**
Lu. 11:5. say, Friend, lend me 3 **l.**
Jn. 6:9. lad who hath 5 barley **l.**
11. Jesus took **l.** and distributed
13. fragments of 5 barley **l.**
26. because ye did eat of the **l.**
See **Loaves of BREAD.**

LOCK.
Can. 5:5. myrrh upon handles of **l.**
Eze. 8:3. took me by **l.** of head

LOCKS.
Nu. 6:5. let **l.** of his head grow
Ju. 16:13. If thou weavest the 7 **l.**
19. she caused him to shave 7 **l.**
Ne. 3:3. set up doors, **l.**, 6, 13, 14, 15.
Can. 4:1. doves' eyes within thy **l.**
3. piece of pomegr. within thy **l.**
5:2. my **l.** with drops of the night
11. his **l.** are bushy, and black
6:7. are thy temples within thy **l.**
Is. 47:2. uncover thy **l.** make bare
Eze. 44:20. nor suffer **l.** to grow long
See BARS.

LOCKED.
Ju. 3:23. Ehud shut doors **l.** them
24. doors of the parlor were **l.**

LOCUST. [E.
Ex. 10:19. remained not one **l.** in all
Le. 11:22. **l.** af. his kind, bald **l.** eat
De. 28:38. seed; **l.** shall consume it
42. thy trees shall **l.** consume
1 K. 8:37. if in land **l.**, 2 Ch. 6:28.
Ps. 78:46. gave labour unto **l.**
109:23. tossed up and down as **l.**
Jo.1:4. hath **l.** eaten, that wh. **l.** left
2:25. restore years **l.** hath eaten

LOCUSTS.
Ex. 10:4. to morrow I will bring **l.**
12. Stretch hand over Eg-t for **l.**
13. morning, east wind bro-t **l.**
14. **l.** went over all Eg.; bef no such
19. west wind took away the **l.** [l.
2 Ch. 6:28. If in the land blasting **l.**
7:13. if I command **l.** to devour
Ps. 105:34. He spake, and **l.** came
Pr. 30:27. The **l.** have no king, yet
Is. 33:4. as running to and fro of **l.**
Na. 3:15. make thyself many as **l.**
17. Thy crowned are as the **l.**
Mat. 3:4. his meat was **l.**, Mk. 1:6.
Re. 9:3. came out of the smoke **l.**
7. **l.** like horses prepared unto

LOD. [battle
1 Ch. 8:12. Shamed built Ono, L.
Ezr. 2:33. chil. of L.; Ono, Ne.7:37.
Ne. 11:35. L., O., valley of craftsmen

LO-DE'BAR. See AMMIEL.

LODGE. [Noun.]
Is. 1:8. Zion is left as a **l.** in garden

LODGE. [Verb.]
Ge. 24:23. is there room for us to **l.**
25. provender, and room to **l.** in
Nu. 22:8. said, **l.** here this night
Jos. 4:3. in place where ye shall **l.**
Ju. 19:9. **l.** here, th. heart be merry
11 into city of Jebusites and **l.**
13. to **l.** in Gibeah, 15.-20:4.
20. said, only **l.** not in the street
Ru. 1:16. where lodgest I will **l.**
2 S. 17:8. fa. will not **l.** with peo.
16. **l.** not this night in plains of
Ne.4:22. Let ev. one **l.** within Jerus.
13:21. Why **l.** ye about wall?
Jb. 17:† 2. eye **l.** in their provoca.?
24:7. naked to **l.** with-t clothing
31:32. stranger did not **l.** in street
Ps. 25:†13. his soul sh. **l.** in goodn.
91:† 1. shall **l.** under shadow of
Can.7:11.beloved, let us **l.** in villages
Is. 21:13. in Arabia shall ye **l.**
65:4. **l.** in monuments, and eat
Je. 4:14. How long vain thoughts **l.**
Zph. 2:14. beasts sh. **l.** in lintels
Mat. 13:32. so birds of air come and
l. in branches thereof, Mk. 4:32.

Lu. 9: 12. and l. and get victuals
Ac. 21: 16. Mnason with whom we

LODGED. [sho. l.

Ge. 32: 13. Jac. l. there that night
21. hims l. that night in company
Jos.2:1.spies into harlot's ho.,and l.
3:1. to Jord., he and all Isr., and l.
4:8. carried them where they l.
6:11. they came unto camp, and l.
8:9. Joshua l. that night am. peo.
Ju. 18: 2. house of Micah, they l.
19: 4. did eat and drink, and l.
7. urged, th-f. he l. there again
1 K. 19: 9. came into cave and l.
1 Ch. 9: 27. l. round house of God
Ne.13:20.merchants l.with-t Jerus.
Is. 1:21. righte-ss. l. in it, but now
Mat. 21: 17. into Bethany and l.
Lu.13:19. fowls of air l. in branches
Ac. 10:18. whe. Simon were l. there
23. called he them in, and l. th.
32. he is l. in house of one Simon
28: 7. Publius l. us three days
1 Ti. 5: 10. if she have l. strangers

LODGEST, ETH.

Ru. 1: 16. Where l-t I will lodge
Ac. 10: 6. He l-h with one Simon

LODGING, S.

Ju. 19: 15. no man took them to l.
2 K. 19: 23. enter into l-s of borders
Is. 10: 29. taken their l. at Geba
Ac. 28: 23. came many into his l.
Phm. 22. withal prepare me a l.

LODGING place.

Jos. 4: 3. stones leave them in l. p.
Je. 9:2. that I had in wildern. l. p.

LOFT.

1 K. 17: 19. he carried him into a l.
Ac. 20: 9. Eutychus fell fr. third l.

LOFTILY.

Ps. 73: 8. corrupt, they speak l.

LOFTINESS.

Is. 2: 17. l. of man shall be bowed
Je. 48:29. heard pride of Moab, his l.

LOFTY. [eyes l.

Ps. 131: 1. heart not haughty, nor
Pr. 30: 13. O how l. are their eyes!
Is. 2:11. l. looks be humbled, 5:15.
12. day of L. be upon ev. one is l.
26: 5. the l. city he layeth low to
57:7. Upon l. mt. hast set thy bed
15. thus saith high and l. One

LOG.

Le. 14: 10. shall take l. of oil, 12, 24.
15. shall take some of l. of oil
21. if poor, then take a l. of oil

LOINS. [thy l.

Ge. 35: 11. kings sh. come out of
37: 34. Jac. put sackcloth upon l.
46: 26. wh. came of his l., Ex. 1: 5.
Ex: 12: 11. eat it with l. girded
28: 42. breeches from l. unto thighs
De. 33: 11. smite thr. the l. of them
2 S. 20: 8. sword fastened upon l.
1 K. 2: 5. blood in girdle about l.
8: 19. son shall come forth of thy
l., 2 Ch. 6: 9. [2 Ch. 10: 10.
12:10. thicker than my father's l.,
18: 46. Elijah girded up l. and ran
20:31. let us put sackcloth on our l.
32. they girded sackclo. on their l.
2 K. 1: 8. girdle of leather about
his l., Mat 3: 4. Mk. 1: 6.
4: 29. Gird up thy l., 9: 1. Jb. 38:
3.-40: 7. Je. 1: 17.
Ne. 4: † 18. each his sword on his l.
Jb. 12: 18. he girdeth l. of kings
31: 20. if his l. have not blessed me
40: 16. his strength is in his l.
Ps. 38: 7. my l. are filled wi. disease
66:11. laidest affliction upon our l.
69: 23. make l. continually shake
Pr. 30: † 31. a horse girt in the l.
31: 17. girdeth her l. with strength
Is. 5: 27. nei. girdle of l. be loosed
11: 5. righte-n. be girdle of his l.
20: 2. loose the sackcloth fr. thy l.
Is. 21: 3. are my l. filled with pain
32: 11. gird sackcloth upon your l.
45: 1. I will loose l. of kings [2, 4.
Je. 13: 1. linen girdle upon thy l.,
11. As girdle cleaveth to l.
30:6. see ev. man with hands on l.
48: 37 upon l. shall be sackcloth
Eze. 1: 27. fr. appearance of his l.
8: 2. fr. l. downward fire, fr. l. upw.
9: † 2. writer's inkhorn upon l.
21: 6. sigh with breaking of thy l.
23: 15. with girdles upon their l.
29: 7. madest their l. to be at stand
44: 18. linen breeches upon their l.
47: 4. the waters were to the l.
Da. 5: 6. loints of l. were loosed
10:5. l. were girded with fine gold
Am.8:10. bring sackcl upon your l.
Na. 2: 1. make thy l. strong
10. much pain is in all l.
Lu. 12: 35. Let your l. be girded
Ac. 2:30. of his l. he would raise C.
Ep. 6: 14. l. girt about with truth
He. 7: 5. tho. came out of l. of Ab.
10. he was yet in the l. of his fa.
1 Pe. 1: 13. gird up l. of your mind

LO'IS.

2 Ti. 1: 5. which dwelt first in thy
grandmother L.

LONG. [Adj. Adv.]

Ge. 48: 15. G. fed me all my life l.
Ex. 19: 13. trumpet sounded l., 19.
20: 12. that thy days may be l.
Nu. 9: 19. cloud tarried l. upon tab.
De. 1: 6 l. enough in mount, 2: 3.
4: 25. have remained l. in land
14: 24. if way be too l. for thee
19: 6. overtake him bec. way is l.
28: 59. plagues and of l. continu.
Jos. 6: 5. when they make a l. blast
2 S.3: 1. was l. war betw. ho. of Saul
2 Ch. 3: † 15. his pillars 35 cubits l.
Ps. 95: 10. forty years l. was I griev.
120: 6. l. with him hateth peace
129: 3. plough made l. furrows
143: 3. those th. have been l. dead
Pr. 23: 30. they th. tarry l. at wine
25: 15. By l. forbearing is a prince
Ec. 12: 5. man goeth to his l. home
Is. 65: 22. my elect sh. l. enjoy work
Je. 29: 28. This captivity, l. is build
La. 2: 20. women eat chil. of span l.
Eze. 17: 3. a great eagle l. winged
31: 5. his branches became l. bec.
44: 20. nor suffer locks to grow l.
45: 6. possession 25,000 reeds l.
Dan. 10: 1. time appointed was l.
Ho. 13: 13. not stay l. in the place of
Mat. 23: 14. for pretence make l.
prayers, Mk. 12: 40. Lu. 20:47.
Mk. 12: 38. go in l. clothing, Lu.
16: 5. in a l. white garment [20:46.
Lu. 18: 7. tho. he bear l. with them
Ac. 20: 9. as Paul was l. preaching
11. talked l. while till day
27: 14. not l. after arose a tempest
21. aft. l. abstinence, Paul stood
1 Co. 13: 4. Charity suffereth l.
Ep. 6: 3. That thou mayest live l.
1 Ti. 3: 15. if I tarry l. that thou
Ja. 5: 7. the husbandman hath l.
See AGO. [patience

As LONG as.

Le 18: 19. a. l. a. she is put apart
26:34. enjoy sab. a. l. a. it lieth, 35.
Nu. 9: 18. a. l. a. the cloud abode
De. 12: 19. forsake. not Lev. a. l. a.
31: 13. fear Lord a. l. a. you live
1 S. 1: 28. lent to L. a. l. a. liveth
20: 31. a. l. a. son of Jesse liveth
25: 15. a. l. a. we were conversant
2 Ch. 26: 5. a. l. a. he sought the L.
36:21. a. l. a. desolate she kept sab.
Ps. 72: 5. fear a. l. a. sun endure
17. name be continu. a. l. a. sun
104: 33. sing unto L. a. l. a. I live
116: 2. call upon him a. l. a. I live
Eze. [illegible] 11. a. l. a. they, as broad
Mat. [illegible]: 15. a. l. a. bridegroom is
with them, Mk. 2: 19
Jn. 9: 5. a. l. a. I am in the world
Ro. 7: 1. over man a. l. a. liveth
1 Co. 7: 39. wife bound a. l. a.
husband liveth
Ga. 4: 1. heir a. l. a. he is a child
1 Pe. 3: 6. dau-s a. l. a. ye do well
2 Pe. 1: 13. a. l. a. I am in this tab.

LONG, with cubit, s.

Ex. 27: 1. altar 5 c. l.
9. hangings 100 c. l., 11.
Eze. 40: 5. reed 6 c. l. | 29. it was
30. arches 25 c. l. [50 c. l.
33. court was 50 c. l., [100 c. l.
42. tables c. and half l. | 47. court
41: 13. measured house, 100 c. l.
43: 16. altar shall be 12 c. l.
43: 17. settle shall be 14 c. l.
See CUBITS, DAY, HOUR, JOURNEY, LIFE, SEASON.

How LONG.

Ex. 10: 3. h. l. refuse to humble?
7. h. l. this man be snare unto us?
16: 28. h. l. refuse to keep com-ts
Nu. 14: 11. h. l. will peo. provoke?
h. l. ere they believe me?
27. h. l. sh. I bear with evil cong.?
Jos. 18: 3. h. l. slack to possess la.?
1 S. 1: 14. h. l. thou be drunken?
16: 1. h. l. wilt mourn for Saul?
2 S. 19: 34 h. l. have I to live?
1 K. 18: 21. h. l. halt ye betw. two?
Ne. 2: 6. k. said, h. l. journey be?
Jb. 7: 19. h. l. not depart from me?
8:2. h. l. wilt speak? h. l. sh. words
be like strong wind?
18: 2. h. l. ere make end of words?
19: 2. h. l. will ye vex my soul?
Ps. 4: 2. h. l. turn my glory into
shame? h. l. love vanity? [h. l.
6: 3. My soul is vexed; thou, O L.
13: 1. h. l. forget me, O L.?
2. h. l. shall I take counsel in
soul? h. l. ene. exalted over me?
35: 17. L. h. l. wilt thou look on?
62:3. h. l. will ye imagine mischief?
74: 9. nor is any that knoweth h. l.
10. h. l. sh. adversary reproach?
79: 5. h. l. be angry for ever? 80: 4.
82: 2. h. l. wilt judge unjustly?
89: 46. h. l. L. wilt hide thyself?
90: 13. Return, O Lord, h. l.? [(2)
94: 3. L. h. l. sh. wicked triumph?
4. h. l. sh. they utter hard things?
Pr. 1: 22. h. l. simple ones?
6: 9. h. l. wilt sleep, O sluggard?
Is. 6: 11. Then said I, Lord, h. l.?
Je. 4: 14. h. l. shall vain thoughts?
21. h. l. shall I see standard?
12: 4. h. l. shall land mourn?
23:26. h. l. shall this be in prophets?
47: 5. h. l. wilt cut thyself?
6. O sword of L. h. l. ere quiet?
Da. 8: 13. h. l. be vision of sacrifi.
12:6. h. l. to end of these wonders?
Ho. 8: 5. h. l. ere attain innocen.?
Ha. 1:2. h. l. I cry, thou not hear?
2: 6. increaseth that not his! h. l.?
Zch 1: 12. h. l. not mercy on Jer.
Mat. 17: 17. h. l. shall I be with
you? h. l. suffer? Mk. 9: 19.
Lu. 9: 41. [unto him?
Mk. 9: 21. h. l. since this came
Jn. 10: 24. h. l. make us doubt?
Re. 6: 10. h. l. O L. holy and true?

So LONG.

Ju.5:28. Why chariot s. l. in coming?
1 S. 29: 8. in servant s. l. as I have
2 K. 9: 22. s. l. as the whoredoms of
2 Ch. 6: 31. fear thee s. l. as live
Es. 5: 13. s. l. as I see Mordecai
Jb. 27: 6. reproach s. l. as I live
Ps. 72: 7. peace s. l. as moon endu.
Lu. 1: 21. marvelled he tarried s. l.
Ro. 7: 2. to hush. s. l. as he liveth

He. 4 : 7. to day after s. l. a time
See **Long TIME.**

LONG winged. See WINGED.

Jb. 3 : 21. l. for death, it cometh not
6 : 8. O that G. grant me that I l. for
Ro. 1 : 11. For I l. to see you
2 Co. 9 : 14. prayer which l. after you
Ph. 1 : 8. how greatly I l. after you

LONGED, EDST.

Ge. 31 : 30. sore l-t aft. fa.'s house
2 S. 13 : 39 Da. l. to go unto Abs.
23:15. Da. l. O that one, 1 Ch. 11:17.
Ps. 119 : 40. I have l. aft. precepts
131. I l. for thy commandments
174. I have l. for thy salvation
Ph. 2 : 26. For he l. after you all
4:1. breth. dearly belov. and l. for

LONGER.

Ex. 2 : 3. when could no l. hide him
9 : 28. let you go, ye sh. stay no l.
Ju. 2 : 14. co. not l. stand bef. enem.
2 S. 20 : 5. he tarried l. than set time
2 K. 6 : 33. sho. I wait for L. any l.?
Jb. 7:†8. eyes upon me, I can live no l.
11 : 9. measure is l. than the earth
Je. 44 : 22. that L. could no l. bear
Lu. 16 : 2. mayest be no l. steward
Ac. 18 : 20. desired him to tarry l.
25 : 24. he ought not to live any l.
Ro. 6 : 2. dead to sin, how live any l.
Ga. 3 : 25. no l. under schoolmaster
1 Th. 3 : 1. when no l. forbear, 5.
1 Ti. 5 : 23. Drink no l. water, but
1 Pe. 4 : 2. no l. live rest of time
Re. 10 : 6. there should be time no [l.

LONGETH.

Ge. 34 : 8. Shechem l. for your dau.
De. 12 : 20. thy soul l. to eat flesh
Ps. 63 : 1. flesh l. for thee in dry la.
84:2. My soul l. for courts of Lord

LONGING. [them

De. 28 : 32. eyes sh. fail with l. for
Ps. 107 : 9. he satisfieth the l. soul
119 : 20. My soul breaketh for l.

LONGSUFFERING.

Ex. 34 : 6. Lord gracious, l., Nu. 14:
18. Ps. 86 : 15. 2 Pe. 3 : 9.
Je. 15 : 15. take me not aw. in thy l.
Ro. 2 : 4. despisest riches of his l.
9:22. endured with much l. vessels
2 Co. 6 : 6. by knowledge, by l., by
Ga. 5 : 22. fruit of Spirit is love, l.
Ep. 4 : 2. with l. forbearing one ano.
Col. 1 : 11. strengthened to all l.
3 : 12. Put on, as elect of God, l.
1 Ti. 1 : 16. in me C. might shew l.
2 Ti. 3 : 10. hast fully known my l.
4:2. exhort with all l. and doctrine
1 Pe. 3 : 20. when l. of G. waited in
2 Pe. 3 : 15. l. of our L. is salvation

LOOK, S.

Ps. 18 : 27. wilt bring down high l-s
101 : 5. a high l. I will not suffer
Pr. 6 : 17. Lord hateth a proud l.
21:4. high l. and proud heart is sin
Is. 2:11. lofty l-s of man be humbl.
10: 12. punish glory of his high l-s
Eze. 2 : 6. nor dismayed at l-s, 3: 9.
Da. 7 : 20. whose l. was more stout

LOOK. [Verb.]

Ge. 13:14. l. fr. place where thou art
15 : 5. l. toward heaven, tell stars
19 : 17. for thy life. l. not behind
40 : 7. Whf. l. ye so sadly to day?
41 : 33. Pha. l. out man discreet
Ex. 10 : 10. l. to it; evil is bef. you
25 : 20. faces shall l. one to ano.
40. l. that thou make aft. pattern
Le. 13 : 39. priests shall l. if spots
53. priest shall l. and behold the plague, 56.-14 : 3, 37, 39, 44.
De. 9 : 27. l. not unto stubbornness
28 : 32. thine eyes shall l. and fail
1 S. 16 : 12. David goodly to l. to
17 : 18. l. how thy brethren fare
1 K. 18 : 43. Go up now, l. tow. sea
2 K. 3 : 14. I would not l. tow. thee
2 K. 6 : 32. l. when messenger cometh
9 : 2. l. out there Jehu, and go in
10 : 3. l. out best of master's sons
23. l. there be none of servants
14 : 8. let us l. one ano. in face
1 Ch. 12 : 17. God of our fa-s l. thereon
Jb. 3 : 9. let it l. for light, have none
5 : † 1. to which of saints wilt l.?
20 : 21. shall no man l. for his goods
21 : †5. l. unto me and be astonished
33 : † 27. He shall l. upon men and
35 : 5. l. unto heavens and see, and
Ps. 5 : 3. prayer unto thee, and l. up
40 : 12. iniq-s so not able to l. up
123 : 2. as serv-s l. to their masters
145 : † 15. eyes of all l. unto thee
Pr. 4 : 25. Let thine eyes l. right on
27 : 23. and l. well to thy herds
Ec. 12 : 3. that l. out at the windows
Can. 4 : 8. l. from top of Amana
Is. 5 : 30. if one l. unto the land
8 : 17. wait upon L. I will l. for him
21. shall curse king and l. upw.
22. they shall l. unto earth, and
17 : 7. shall a man l. to his Maker
8. he shall not l. to the altars
22 : 4. l. away from me I will weep
8. didst l. in that day to armour
31 : 1. l. not unto Holy One of Isr.
42 : 18. Hear ye deaf, l. ye blind
45 : 22. l. unto me and be saved
51 : 1. l. unto rock whence hewn
2. l. unto Ab. your fa, and Sarah
56 : 11. they all l. to their own way
59 : 11. we l. for judgm. but none
66 : 2. this man will I l. that is poor
Je. 13 : 16. and while ye l. for light
39 : 12. Take and l. well to him
40 : 4. come, I will l. well unto thee
46 : 5. mighty are fled, l. not back
47 : 3. fathers sh. not l. back to chil.
Eze. 23 : 15. all of th. princes to l. to
29 : 16. iniq. to rememb. when they l.
43 : 17. his stairs shall l. tow. east
Ho. 3 : 1. who l. to other gods, and
Jon. 2 : 4. I will l. tow. holy temple
Mi. 7 : 7. Theref. I will l. unto the L.
Na. 2 : 8. stand, but none sh. l. back
Mat. 11 : 3. or do we l. for another?
Lu. 7 : 19, 20. [made him l. up
Mk. 8 : 25. put hands upon eyes,
Lu. 21 : 28. things begin, then l. up
Jn. 7 : 52. l. for out of Galilee no
Ac. 6 : 3. l. ye out 7 men of honest
18 : 15. if question of words, l. ye to it
1 Co. 16 : 11. I l. for him wi. breth.
2 Co. 3 : 13. Isr. not steadf-y l. to end
4 : 18. While we l. at things seen
Ph. 3 : 20. whence we l. for Saviour
He. 9 : 28. to th. l. for him appear
1 Pe. 1 : 12. angels desire to l. into
2 Pe. 3 : 13. we l. for new heavens
14. seeing ye l. for such be dilig.
2 Jn. 8. l. to yours. th. we lose not
Re. 5 : 3. no man able to l. thereon
4. worthy to read the book nei. l.

LOOK down.

De. 26 : 15. l. d. from thy holy habita.
Ps. 80 : 14. l. d. and visit this vine
85 : 11. righto-n. l. d. from heaven
Is. 63 : 15. l. d. from heaven
La. 3 : 50. Till L. l. d. from heaven

LOOK on, or upon.

Ge. 9 : 16. bow in cloud, I will l. u. it
12 : 11. art a fair woman to l. u.
24 : 16. Rebekah fair to l. u., 26:7.
42 : 1. Why do ye l. one u. ano.?
Ex. 3 : 6. Moses afraid to l. u. God
5 : 21. Lord l. u. you and judge
39 : 43. Moses did l. u. all work
Le. 13 : 3. priests sh. l. o. plague, 21,
25, 26, 31, 32, 34, 43, 50.-14:48.
3. priest shall l. o. him, 5, 6, 27, 36.
Nu. 15 : 39. fringe, th. ye may l. u. it
Ju. 7 : 17. Gideon said, l. o. me,
1 S. 1 : 11. if wilt l. o. the affliction
16 : 7. l. not o. his countenance
2 S. 9 : 8. l. u. such a dead dog as I am
11 : 2. woman very beautif. to l. u.
16 : 12. may be L. l. o. mine afflic.
2 Ch. 24 : 22. Lord l. u. it and require
Es. 1 : 11. Vashti was fair to l. o.
Jb. 6 : 28. Now be content, l. u. me
40 : 12. l. o. every one that is proud
Ps. 22 : 17. bones stare and l. u. me
25 : 18. l. u. mine affliction and
35 : 17. L. how long wilt l. o.?
84 : 9. l. u. face of thine Anointed
119 : 132. l. u. me, be merciful
142 : †4. l. o. the right hand and see
Pr. 4 : 25. Let thine eyes l. right o.
23 : 31. l. not u. wine when it is red
Can. 1 : 6. l. not u. me, I am black
6 : 13. return, th. we may l. u. thee
Is. 14 : 16. shall narrowly l. u. thee
33 : 20. l. u. Zion | 51 : 6. l. u. earth
66 : 24. go l. u. carcasses of the men
Mi. 4 : 11. and let our eye l. u. Zion
Na. 3 : 7. that l. u. thee, shall flee
Ha. 1 : 13. eyes than to l. o. iniq.
2 : 15. mayest l. o. their nakedn.
Zch. 12 : 10. sh. l. u. me they pierced
Lu. 9 : 38. master, l. u. my son
Jn. 4 : 35. Lift eyes, and l. o. fields
19 : 37. shall l. u. him they pierced
Ac. 3 : 4. Pe. John said, l. o. us, 12.
2 Co. 10 : 7. l. o. things after outward
Ph. 2 : 4. l. not ev. man o. his own
Re. 4 : 3. was to l. u. like jasper

LOOKED.

Ge. 6 : 12. God l. upon earth and it
8 : 13. Noah l. and behold ground
18 : 2. l. and lo 3 men stood
16. men rose and l. tow. Sodom,
19 : 26. wife l. back [19 : 28.
22 : 13. Ab. l. and behold ram
26 : 8. Abimelech l. out at window
29 : 2. Jacob l. and behold well
32. Lord hath l. upon my afflic.
39 : 23. keeper of pris. l. not to any
40 : 6. Joseph l. upon th. were sad
Ex. 2 : 11. Moses l. on their burdens
12. he l. this way and that way
25. God l. upon chil. of Israel
3 : 2. l. behold bush burned
4 : 31. l. upon their afflic., De. 26:7.
14 : 24. Lord l. unto host of Eg-ns
16 : 10. that they l. tow-d wilderness
33 : 8. peo. l. after Moses until gone
Nu. 12 : 10. Aaron l. upon Miriam
16 : 42. that they l. toward tabern.
17 : 9. l. and took ev. man his rod
24 : 20. he l. on Amalek, he took
21. l. on Kenites, took parable
Jos. 8 : 20. men of Ai l. behind them
Ju. 5 : 28. mother of Sisera l. out at
6 : 14. Lord l. upon him, said, Go
9 : 43. l. behold people were come
13 : 19. Manoah and wife l. on, 20.
20 : 40. Benjamites l. behind them
1 S. 6 : 19. bec. they had l. into ark
9 : 16. I have l. upon my people
14 : 16. the watchmen of Saul l.
16 : 6. were come, he l. on Eliab
17 : 42. Philis. l. about, saw David
24 : 8. Saul l. behind him, 2 S. 1:7.
2 S. 2 : 20. Abner l. behind him
6 : 16. Michal l. through a window
22 : 42. they l. but was none to save
24 : 20. Araunah l. saw k., 1 Ch. 21:21
1 K. 18 : 43. Elijah's serv. went and l.
19 : 6. l. and behold a cake
2 K. 2 : 24. Elisha turned and l.
6 : 30. people l. he had sackcloth
9 : 30. Jezebel l. out at a window
32. l. out to him 2 or 3 eunuchs
11 : 14. she l. k. stood by pillar, 2 Ch.
14 : 11. l. one ano. in face [23:13.
2 Ch. 13 : 14. Jud. l. back, the battle
20 : 24. l. unto mult. and behold
26 : 20. l. upon him, he was leprous
Es. 2 : 15. favour of all who l. upon
Jb. 6 : 19. The troops of Tema l. [her
Ps. 14 : 2. L. l. to see if any underst.

Ps.34:5.l.unto him, were lightened
53:2. G. l. down upon chil. of men
102: 19. he hath l. down fr. sanct.
109:25. when l. shaked their heads
Can. 1:6. bec. sun hath l. upon me
Is. 5: 2. l. that it sho. bring grapes
7. he l. for judgm. behold oppr.
22: 11. ye have not l. unto maker
64: 3. terrible things we l. not for
Je. 8: 15. We l. for peace, 14: 19.
La. 2: 16. this is day that we l. for
Eze. 10: 11. whi. head l. they foil-d
16:†4. not washed I l. upon thee, 8.
21: 21. consulted he l. in liver
46:19. chambers wh. l. tow. north
Da. 1:13. let our counten. be l. upon
Ob. 12. not l. on day of brother
13. shouldest not have l. on affile.
Hag. 1: 9. Ye l. for much and lo
Mk. 3:5. l. round about, 5:32.-10:23.
34. he l. round on them, 11: 11.
6; 41. he l. up to heaven, blessed
8: 24. he l. said, I see men as trees
33. when he had l. on his disciples
9: 8. when they had l. about
14: 67. she l. upon him and said
16: 4. when l. saw stone rolled
Lu. 1: 25. l. on me, to take reproach
2: 38. to all that l. for redemption
10: 32. a Lev. came and l. on him
19: 5. when J. came he l. and saw
21:1. He l. up and saw rich casting
22: 56. earnestly l. upon him
61. L. turned and l. upon Peter
Jn. 13: 22. disciples l. onoon ano.
20: 11. she stooped and l. into sep.
Ac. 1: 10. l. steadfastly tow. heaven
7: 55. l. up steadf. into heaven
10: 4. had l. on him he was afraid
28:6. aft. they had l. a great while
He. 11: 10. l. for acity hath founda.
1 Jn. 1: 1. we have l. upon, declare

LOOKED with eyes. ⌊we
Ge.28:1. Jacob lifted up his e. and l.
37:25. they lifted up their e. and l.
Jos. 5: 13. 2 S. 13: 34.-18: 24.
Da. 10:5. Then I lifted up mine e. l.
Zch. 2:1. Zech. lifted e. and l., 5:9.-

I LOOKED. [6: 1.
Ge. 16: 13. Have I here l. aft. him
De. 9: 16. I l. and ye had sinned
1 S. 9: 16. I have l. upon my people
Ne. 4: 14. I l. and rose up and said
Jb. 30: 26. When I l. for good evil
Ps. 69: 20. I l. for some to take pity
142: 4. I l. on my right hand
Pr. 7: 6. I l. through my casement
24: 32. I l. upon it and rec-d instr.
Ec. 2: 11. I l. on all the works that
Is. 5: 4. I l. it sho. bri. forth grapes
63: 5. I l. there was none to help
Eze.1:4. I l. and behold, 2:9.-8:7.-10:
1, 9.-44: 4.
16: 8. I passed by thee and l. upon
Da. 12: 5. Then I Dan. l. there stood
Zch. 4: 2. I l. behold candlestick
Ac. 22: 13. same hour I l. upon him
Re. 4: 1. I l. and behold a door was
opened, 6: 8.-14: 1, 14.-15: 5.

LOOKEST.
Jb.13:27. l. narrowly unto my paths
Ha.1:13. why l. upon th. deal treach-

LOOKETH. ⌊er-sly?
Le.13:12. if leprosy whereso. priest l.
Nu.21:8. he l. upon serp. he shall live
20. Pisgah, which l. tow., 23: 28.
Jos. 15: 2. fr. bay th. l. southward
1 S. 13: 18. border th. l. to Zeboim
16: 7. man l. on outward appear.
Jb. 7: 2. as hireling l. for reward
28: 24. he l. to ends of the earth
33:27. He l. upon men, if any say I
Ps. 33: 13. the Lord l. from heaven
14. he l. upon all inhabi. of world
104: 32. He l. on earth it trembled
Pr. 14: 15. prudent l. well to goings
31: 27. She l. well to her househ.

Can. 2: 9. he l. forth at window
6: 10. Who she l. forth as morn.?
7: 4. tower which l. tow. Damas.
Is. 28: 4. when he that l. upon it
Eze. 8: 3. door that l. tow. north
11: 1. gate which l. eastw., 40: 6,
22.-43: 1.-44: 1.-46: 1, 12.-47: 2.
40: 20. gate of court that l. tow.
Mat. 5: 28. l. on woman to lust
24:50. when l. not for him, Lu. 12:
Ja. 1:25. whoso l. into perf. law ⌊46.

LOOKING.
Jos. 15: 7. northw. l. toward Gilgal
1 K. 7:25. three oxen l. tow. north
1 Ch. 15: 29. Michal l. out at window
2 Ch. 4: 4. three oxen l. tow. south
Is. 38: 14. eyes fail with l. upward
Mat. 14: 19. l. up to heaven, he
blessed, Mk. 6: 41. Lu. 9: 16.
Mk.7:34. and l. up to heav., he sighed
10:27. Jes. l. upon th. saith, With
15: 40. women l. on afar off ⌊men
Lu. 6: 10. l. round about them all
9:62. and l. back, is fit for kingd.
21: 26. hearts failing them for l.
Jn. 1: 36. John l. upon Jesus saith
20: 5. l. in, saw linen cloths lying
Ac. 6:15. l. steadfastly on him, saw
23: 21. l. for a promise from thee
Tit. 2: 13. l. for that blessed hope
He. 10:27. fearful l. for of judgment
12: 2. l. unto Jesus the author and
15. l. diligently, lest any fail of
2 Pe. 3:12. l. for the coming of God
Jude 21. l. for the mercy of our L.

LOOKINGGLASS, ES.
Ex. 38: 8. of l-s of women assemb-g
Jb. 37:18. spread sky as a molten l.

LOOPS.
Ex. 26: 4. shalt make l. of blue, 5.
5. l. make, 10. | 11. taches in l.
36:11. l. of blue | 12. fifty l. made

LOOSE. [Adj.] ⌊he, 17.
Da. 3: 25. lo I see 4 men l. walking
See LET loose.

LOOSE. [Verb.]
De. 25: 9. l. his shoe off his foot
Jos. 5: 15. l. thy shoe off thy foot
Jb. 38: 31. Canst l. bands of Orion
Ps. 102: 20. l. those appointed to
Is.20:2. l. sackcloth fr. loins ⌊death
45: 1. I will l. the loins of kings
52:2. O Jerus., l. thyself fr. bands
58:6. to l. the bands of wickedness
Je. 40: 4. Behold I l. thee this day
Mat. 16:19. whatso. thou l. on earth
sh. be loosed in heaven, 18: 18.
21: 2. ass and colt, l. and bring
them, Mk. 11: 2, 4. Lu. 19: 30.
Lu. 13: 15. on sab. l. his ox or ass
19:31. if ask, Why do ye l. him? 33.
Jn. 11: 44. Jesus said, l. him, and
Ac. 13:25. shoes, I am not worthy to
24: 26. money given, that he l. ⌊l.
Re. 5: 2. who is worthy to l. seals
5. hath prevailed to l. the 7 seals
9: 14. l. four angels bound in

LOOSED. ⌊Euphra.
Ex.28:28. breastplate be not l., 39: 21.
De. 25:10. him that hath his shoe l.
Ju. 15: 14. his bands l. off his ha.
Jb. 30: 11. Because he l. my cord
39: 5. who hath l. bands of ass?
Ps. 105:20. The king sent and l. him
116: 16. thou hast l. my bands
Ec. 12: 6. Or ever silver cord be l.
Is. 5: 27. nor girdle of loins be l.
33:23. Thy tacklings are l. they co.
51: 14. exile hasteneth that he be l.
Je. 6:†8. lest my soul be l. fr. thee
Eze. 23:†17. and her mind was l. fr.
them ⌈were l.
Da.5:6. so that the joints of his loins
Mat. 18:27. compassion, and l. him
Mk.7:35. his tongue was l., Lu.1:64.
Lu. 13: 12. art l. from thy infirmity
16. ought not this dau. to be l.

Ac. 2[:24. h]aving l. pains of death
13: 13. when Paul l. from Paphos
16: 26. every one's bands were l.
22: 30. he l. him from his bands
27: 21. not have l. fr. Crete ⌈sail
40. l. rudder bands, hoised main-
Ro. 7: 2. if husb. be dead, she is l.
1 Co. 7: 27. Art thou l. from wife?
Re. 9: 15. the four angels were l.
20:3. after that he must be l. a lit-

LOOSETH. ⌊tle, 7.
2 S. 22: † 23. God he l. my way
Jb. 12: 18. He l. the bond of kings
†21. he l. the girdle of the strong
Ps. 146: 7. the L. l. the prisoners

LOOSING.
Mk. 11: 5. What do you l. the colt?
Lu. 19: 33. as they were l. the colt
Ac. 16: 11. l. from Troas we came
27: 13. l. thence sailed close by

LOP. ⌊Crete
Is.10:33. the Lord shall l. the bough

LORD. ⌈L.?
Ge. 18: 14. Is any thing too hard for
30. let not the L. be angry
24: 40. L. bef. whom I walk will
26: 28. We saw L. was with thee
28:21. then shall the L. be my God
39: 2. L. was with Joseph, 21, 23.
Ex. 5:2. who is L. I sho. obey him?
8: 24. L. did so, and came flies
9:27. L. is righteous and I wicked,
2 Ch. 12: 6. ⌈10: 26, 28.
29. earth is the L., Ps. 24: 1. 1 Co.
10: 10. the L. be so with you, as I
13: 8. that which L. did unto me
12. firstling of beast, males be L.'s
14:14. The L. sh. fight for you, 25.
15: 18. The L. shall reign for ever
30: 37. it shall be holy for the L.
32: 26. Who is on the L.'s side
34:14. for L. whose name is jealous
Le. 8: 16. food of offering, fat is L.'s
16:8. cast one lot for L., 25:4.-27:2.
Nu. 14:14. heard thou L. art among
peo., thou L. seen face to face
42. Go not up; L. is not am. you
43. theref. L. will not be with you
18:6. are given as a gift for the L.
22: 19. may kn. what L. will say
23: 15. while I meet the L. yonder
26. All L. speaketh must I do
24: 11. L. kept thee from honour
31: 50. brought an oblation for L.
32: 12. followed the L., De. 1: 36.
De. 1:37. L. was angry with me, 4: 21.
3: 21. so L. do unto all kingdoms
4:35. know L. he is G., 39. 1 K. 18:
5: 5. I stood betw. L. and you ⌊39.
6: 12. beware lest thou forget L.
7: 7. L. did not set love upon you
8. bec. L. loved you L. bro-t you
10: 14. heaven of heavens is L.'s
17. L. of lords a great G. mighty
29:2. seen all that L. did in Egypt
4. L. hath not g[iven] you heart to
24. Wh. hath L. done thus unto
land? 1 K. 9: 8. 2 Ch. 7: 21.
31: 4. L. sh. do unto th. as did to
8. L. he it is doth go bef. thee ⌊Og
32: 6. Do ye thus requite the L.
12. So L. alone did lead them
27. L. hath not done all this
30. except L. had shut them up
33: 29. happy, O peo., saved by L.
Jos. 2: 12. swear unto me by the L.,
1 S. 24: 21. ⌈over, 13.
3: 11. even L. of all earth passeth
6: 27. So the L. was with Joshua
10: 25. thus sh. L. do to enemies
14: 12. if L. be with me, then
Ju. 1: 19. the L. was with Judah
22. L. was with house of Joseph
2: 10. generation wh. knew not L.
4: 14. Is not L. gone before thee?
6: 13. If L. be with us, why is this
11: 31. cometh to meet me be L.'s

Ju.17:13.know I L. will do me good
Ru. 1: 17. L do so to me and more,
1 S. 20 : 13. [17. 2 Th. 3 : 16.
2:4. The L. be with you, 2 Ch. 20:
1 S. 2 : 2. There is none holy as L.
8. pillars of the earth are L.'s
3 : 18. It is L.let him do what seemeth, 2 S. 10 : 12. 1 Ch. 19:13. Jn.
21 : 7.
19. Samuel grew, L. was wi. him,
18:12, 14. 2 K. 18:7. 1 Ch. 9:20.
12 : 16. great thing wh. L. will do
14 : 6. may be L. will work for us
17 : 37. the L. be with thee, 20 : 13.
1 Ch. 22 : 11, 16. [me, 42.
20 : 23. the L. be between thee and
2 S. 7:24. L. art their G., 1 Ch.17:22.
22 : 19. L. was my stay, Ps. 18:18.
32.who is G.save the L., Ps.18:31.
1 K. 1 : 37. As L. hath been with k.
11 : 6. went not fully after the L.
18 : 21. if L. be God, follow him
19 : 11. the L. was not in the wind
2 K. 6 : 27. If the L. do not help
33. sh. I wait for L. any longer?
10 : 16. Come see my zeal for L.
18:25. Am I now come without the
L., Is. 36:10. [48:1.-145:3.
1 Ch. 16 : 25. For great is the L., Ps.
31. let men say, The L. reigneth
17 : 26. now L. thou art G. and
21 : 24. not take that which for L.
2 Ch.19:6. judge not for man, but L.
11. the L. shall be with the good
33:13. Manasseh knew L. was God
Ne. 9 : 6. thou art L. alone, Is. 37:20.
Ps. 4 : 3. L. hath set apart godly
16 : 8. have set L. alway bef. me
33:12. Blessed nation, whose G. is L.
20. Our soul waiteth for the L.
35 : 10. L. who is like unto thee?
45 : 11. he is thy L. worship him
66:18. If I regard iniq., L. not hear
86 : 5. thou L. art good, ready to
17. bec. thou L. hast holpen me
89:8. who strong L. like unto thee?
92:8. thou L. art most high, 97 : 9.
93 : 4. The L. on high is mightier
94 : 7. say, The L. shall not see [G.
100 : 3. Know ye that the L. be is
109:21. do thou for me, O L., 140:7.
27. know thou L. hast done it
116:5. gracious is L. and righteous
118:13. L. helped me | 18.chastened
23. this is L.'s doing, Mat. 21:42.
27. G. is L. which hath shewed
124 : 1. if it had not been the L., 2.
130 : 3. if thou L. sho. mark iniq-s
132 : 5. until I find place for L.
144 : 3. L. what is man, that
Pr. 24 : 18. lest L. see and it disple.
30 : 9. lest I say, Who is the L.?
Is. 6:11. Then said I, L. how long?
10 : 20. shall stay upon the L.
19 : 21. L. sh. be known to Egypt
25 : 9. this is L.; we have waited
33 : 21. L. a place of broad rivers
42:24. did not L. ag. whom we sinn.
44 : 5. One sh. say, I am the L.'s
23. sing, O heav. L. hath done it
52 : 12. the L. will go before you
60:19. L. sh. be an everl. light, 20.
Je. 2 : 6. where L. that bro-t us, 8.
5:10. her battlements, they not L.'s
8 : 19. is not the L. in Zion? is not
16 : 21. shall know my name is L.
21 : 2. if so be L. will deal with us
23:6. called, THE L. OUR RIGHT-
EOUSNESS, 33 : 16.
31 : 34. saying, Know L., He. 8:11.
50 : 7. L. the hope of their fathers
51 : 50. remember the L. afar off
La. 1 : 5. L. hath afflicted her +
2 : 22. in day of L.'s anger none
3 : 31. L. will not cast off for ever
50. till L. look down, and behold
Eze. 35 : 10. whereas L. was there

Da. 2 : 47. your God is L. of kings
9 : 14. hath L. watched upon evil
17. face to shine for L.'s sake [L.
Ho. 2 : 20. and thou shalt know the
5 : 4. they have not known the L.
6 : 3 if we follow on to know the L.
11 : 10. they shall walk after the L.
12 : 14. his reproach sh. L return
Jo. 2 : 21. fear not, L. do gr. things
3 : 16. L. be the hope of his people
Am. 3:6. evil in city, L. not done it?
5 : 14. so the L. shall be with you
7 : 15. L. took me as I followed
Ob. 21. kingdom shall be the L.'s
Mi 2 : 13. L. on the head of them
3 : 11. lean upon L. and say, Is not
4 : 7. L. shall reign over them [L.
6:7. Will L. be pleased with thous.
8. what L. require of thee?
Zph. 1 : 5. swear by L. and Malch
6. those that have not sought L.
12. say, The L. will not do good
Zch. 9 : 1. when eyes of man betow.
14. L. sh. be seen over them [L.
10 : 1. L. shall make light clouds
14 : 3. then shall the L. fight ag.
9. in that day sh. there be one L.
Mat. 7 : 21. not every one that saith
L. L. sh. enter, 22. Lu. 13 : 25.
8 : 2. L. if thou wilt, thou canst,
Lu. 5 : 12. [Yea, L., 13 : 51.
25. L. save us | 9 : 28. they said,
9:38. Pray L. of harvest, Lu. 10:2.
11:25. O Fa., L. of heaven, Lu.10:21.
12 : 8. Son of man is L. of Sabbath
14:30. L. save me | 15:25. L. help me
15 : 27. she said, Truth, L.
16 : 22. Be it far from thee L.
21 : 3. ye sh. say, L. hath need of
them, Mk. 11 : 3. Lu. 19:31, 34.
22 : 43. How then doth David call
him L.? 45. Mk.12:37. Lu.20:44.
24 : 42. kn. not hour L. will come
25:21. enter thou into joy of thy L.
37. L. when saw we thee a hungered? 44. [L. lay
26 : 22. L. is it I? | 28:6. where the
Mk. 2 : 28. is L. of sabbath, Lu. 6:5.
5 : 19. how great things L. done
9 : 24. L. I believe, help thou, Jn.
9 : 38.-11 : 27. [Mat. 20 : 33.
10:51. L. that I may receive sight,
13 : 20. exc. L. had shortened days
16 : 20. L. working with them
Lu. 1 : 17. ready a people for L.
25. L. dealt with me, to take
46. My soul doth magnify L.
2 : 11. Saviour, which is C. the L.
29. L. now lettest servant depart
6:46. why call me L. L. and do not
9:57. said L. I will follow thee, 61.
11:1. L. teach us to pray, as John
17 : 5. said unto L. Incr. our faith
37. they said unto him, Where L.?
22 : 61. L. looked upon Peter
23 : 42. L. remember me when thou
24 : 34. The L. is risen indeed
Jn. 6 : 68. L. to whom shall we go
8 : 11. she said, No man, L.
9 : 36. Who is he, L. that I might
11 : 21. L. if thou hadst been here
34. they said, L. come and see
13 : 13. Ye call me master and L.
25. He saith, L. who is it?
20 : 25. said, We have seen the L.
20 : 2. taken L. out of the sepul.
21 : 7. unto Peter, It is the L.
12. none ask, knowing it was L.
21. L. what shall this man do?
Ac. 2 : 25. I foresaw L. before face
36. ye crucified, both L. and C.
4:24. L. thou art G. | 29. L. behold
their threatening [22:8.-26:15.
9 : 5. he said, Who art thou, L.?
6. L. what wilt thou have me do?
10. Behold, I am here, L.
27. had seen the L. in the way

Ac. 10 : 4. and said, What is it L.?
14. Peter said, Not so L., 11 : 8.
36. Jesus Christ, he is L. of all
17 : 24. he is L. of heav. and earth
20 : 19. Serving L. with humility
22 : 10. I said, What shall I do L.
Ro. 9 : 28. short work will L. make
29. Except L. of Sabaoth had
10 : 12. same L. over all is rich
16. L. who hath believed report?
12:11 Not slothful, serving the L.
14 : 8. live or die we are the L.'s
9. be L. of dead and living
1 Co. 2 : 8. not crucified L. of glory
3 : 5. as L. gave to every man
20. L. knoweth thoughts of wise
4 : 4. he that judgeth me is L.
5. judge nothing until L. come
19. will come if L. will, Ja. 4 : 15.
6 : 13. body for L. and L. for body
14. God hath raised up the L.
7:10. I command, yet not I but L.
32. how he may please the L.
11 : 20. is not to eat L.'s supper
29. not discerning the L.'s body
12:5. administrations, but same L.
15 : 47. sec. man is L. from heav.
16: 7. awhile with you if L. permit
2 Co. 5 : 8. to be present with the L.
11 : 17. I speak it not after the L.
12:8. For this I besought L. thrice
Ga. 4 : 1. a servant tho. be L. of all
Ep. 4 : 5. One L. one faith, one bapt.
5 : 29. even as the L. the church
Ph. 2 : 11. tongue confess J. C. is L.
4 : 5. moderation, L. is at hand
Col. 3 : 20. is well pleasing unto L.
1 Th.4:16. L. sh. descend fr. heaven
17. so shall we ever be with L.
5 : 27. I charge you by the L.
2 Th. 3 : 5. L. direct your hearts
1 Ti. 6 : 15. King of k-s L. of Lords
2 Ti. 1 : 18. L. grant he may find
2 : 19. L. knoweth them are his
22. with them that call on L.
3 : 11. out of all L. delivered me
4 : 8. L. sh. give me at that day
17. Notwithst-g L. stood wi. me
He. 1 : 10. Thou L. in beginn. laid
2 : 3. began to be spoken by L.
7 : 14. our L. sprang out of Juda
8 : 11. Know L. for all shall know
12 : 6. whom L. loveth he chast-h
14. without which no man see L.
Ja. 1 : 12. crown L. hath promised
4 : 15. ought to say if the L. will
5 : 15. L. shall raise the sick up
2 Pe. 2 : 1. denying L. bought them
3 : 8. day is with L. as thousand
Jude 5. how L. having saved peo.
9. Michael said, L. rebuke thee
14. L. cometh with 10,000 saints
Re. 1 : 10. in the Spirit on L.'s day
11 : 8. where L. was crucified
15. are become kingd-s of our L.
17 : 14. for he is L. of lords, 19:16.
See ACTS, AH.

Against the LORD.

Ex. 10:16. I have sinned **a.** L. your
God, Jos. 7 : 20. 2 S. 12 : 13.
16 : 7. that he heareth your murmurings **a.** L., 8. [-31 : 16.
Le. 5 : 19. trespassed **a.** L., Nu. 5:6.
6 : 2. if soul commit tresp. **a.** L.
Nu. 14:9. rebel not **a.** L., Jos.22:19.
16:11. are gathered together **a.** L.,
27 : 3. Ps. 2 : 2. Ac. 4 : 26. [L.
21:7. sinned, for we have spoken **a.**
26 : 9. of Korah, when strove **a.** L.
32:23. sinned **a.** L., Je.40:3.-44:23.
De. 1:41. have sinned **a.** L., 1 S. 7 :
6. Je. 3 : 14. [24.-31 : 27.
9:7. ye have been rebellious **a.** L.,
13 : 5. hath spoken revolt **a.** L.
Jos.22:16. might rebel this day **a.** L.
18. seeing ye rebel this day **a.** L.
22. or if in transgression **a.** L.

Jos.22:29. G. forbid we rebel a. L. [L.
31. not committed this trespass a.
1 S.2:25. if man sin a. L. who entreat
12: 23. sin a. L. in ceasing to pray
14: 33. people sin a. L. in that
34. slay them here, sin not a. L.
2 K. 17: 7. Israel had sinned a. L.
9. secretly things not right a. L.
1 Ch. 10:13. transgr-n committed a.
2 Ch. 12: 2. had transgr-d a. L. [L.
19:10. that they trespass not a. L.
28: 13. we have offended alr. a. L.
19. Ahaz transgressed sore a. L.
22. did he trespass yet more a. L.
Ps. 2: 2. rulers take counsel a. L.
Pr. 19: 3. his heart fretteth a. L.
21: 30. there is no wisdom a. L.
Is. 3: 8. bec. their doings are a. L.
32:6. work iniq. to utter error a. L.
59:13. transgr-g and lying a. L. [32.
Je. 28:16. taught rebellion a. L., 29:
48: 26. magnified hims. a. L., 42.
50: 7. bec. they have sinned a. L.
14. Bab. she hath sinned a. L., 29.
24. hast striven a. L., Zph. 1: 17.
Da. 5: 23. hast lifted up thys. a. L.
Ho. 5: 7. dealt treacherously a. L.
Na. 1: 9. What do ye imagine a. L.
11. is one that imagineth evil a. L.

Altar of the LORD. [L.

Le. 17:6. sprinkle blood upon a. o.
Jos. 9: 27. a. o. L., 1 K. 8: 22, 54.-
18: 30. 2 K. 23: 9. 2 Ch. 6: 12.-
8: 12.-15: 8.-29: 19, 21.-33:16.
Mal. 2: 13.

See ALTAR, ANGEL.

See **ANGER of the Lord, ANGER kindled.**

See ANOINTED, APPEARED.

Ark of the LORD. [o.L.

Jos. 6:6. bear 7 trumpets before a.
7. a. o. L. followed, 11, 12, 13.
1 S. 4: 6.-5: 3, 4.-6: 1, 2, 8, 11,
15, 18, 19, 21.-7: 1.
2 S. 6:9. How sh. a. o. L. come to
me | 10, 11, 13, 15, 16, 17. 1 K.
8:1, 4. 1 Ch. 16: 4, 39.-28: 18.
2 Ch. 8: 11.

See ARK, ARM.

See **As the Lord LIVETH.**

Before the LORD.

Ge. 10: 9. was mighty hunter b. L.
13:10. wat-d, b. L. destroyed Sod.
13. men of Sod. were sinners b. L.
18: 22. Ab. stood yet b. L., 19:27.
27:7. may eat and bless thee b. L.
Ex. 6: 12. Moses spake b. L., 30.
16: 9. congr-n, Come near b. L.
33. lay it up b. L. to be kept, 1
S. 10: 25.
23: 17. times in year males appear
b. L., 34:24. De.16:16. 1 S.1:22.
27:21. order the lamps b. L., 40:25.
28: 12. bear names b. L. [31: 54.
29. memorial b. L., 30: 16. Nu.
30. Aa.'s heart when goeth b. L.
38. they be accepted b. L. [4: 4.
29:11. kill bullock b. L., Le.1: 5.-
23. wafer out of basket b. L.
24. for wave off-g b. L., 26.
25. for a sweet savour b. L.
42. door of tab. b. L., Le.1:3.-4:4.
30: 8. perpetual incense b. L.
34: 34. Mo. went in b. L. to speak
Le. 1:11. kill on side of altar, b. L.
3: 1. offer without blemish b. L.
7. lamb, sh. he offer it b. L., 12.
4: 6. priest shall sprinkle seven
times b. L., 17.-14: 16, 18. [L.
7. put blood upon horns of alt. b.
9: 5. all congregation stood b. L.
24. came a fire out from b. L. and
10: 1. offered strange fire b. L.,
Nu. 3: 4.-26: 61. [Nu.3:4.
2. fire devoured, they died b. L.,
16: 1. they offered b. L. and died
Nu. 5:16. shall set her b. L., 18, 30.
Nu.10:9. ye sh. be remembered b. L.
16:7. put incense in them b. L., 17.
16. thou and all company b. L.
18: 19. cov-t of salt for ever b. L.
25: 4. hang them up b. L. ag. sun
27: 5. Mo. bro-t their cause b. L.
De. 9: 18. I fell down b. L. 40 days
12: 18. thou must eat them b. L.
18:7. breth. which stand there b. L.
19:17. controversy is, sh. stand b.
Jos. 6:26. Cursed be man b. L. [L.
Ju. 11:11. uttered his words b. L. in
18: 6. b. L. is way wherein ye go
20:26. people sat b. L., 2 S. 7: 18.
1 S. 1:15. poured out my soul b. L.
2: 17. sin of men very great b. L.
12: 3. witness against me b. L.
7. I may reason with you b. L.
21: 7. was that day detained b. L.
26:19. if men, cursed be they b. L.
2 S. 6: 21. b. L. which chose me
21: 9. hanged them in hill b. L.
2 K. 19:14. Hez. spread it b. L., Is.37:
1 Ch. 22:18. land subdued b. L. [14.
29:22. did drink b. L. with gladn.
2 Ch. 19:2. wrath upon thee fr. b. L.
20: 13. all Judah stood b. L.
27:6. Jotham prepared ways b. L.
Jb. 1:6. when sons of God came b. L.
Ps. 95: 6. let us kneel b. L.
96:13. b. L. he com. to judge, 98:9.
109:15. Let th. be b. L. continually
116: 9. I will walk b. L. in land of
Pr. 15: 11. Hell and destruc. b. L.
Is. 23:18. for them that dwell b. L.
Je. 36:7. present supplications b. L.
Eze. 44:3. sit in it to eat bread b. L.
46: 3. worsh. at door of gate b. L.
9. come b. L. in sol. feasts b. L.
Da. 9: 13. made we not prayer b. L.
Mi. 6: 6. Whw. shall I come b. L.
Zch. 2:13. Be silent, O all flesh, b. L.
6:5. spirits wh. go fr. standing b. L.
7: 2. and their men to pray b. L.,
8: 21, 22. [L.
Ma. 3: 14. we walked mournfully b.
2 Ti. 2:14. charging them b. L. [L.
2 Pe. 2:11. no railing accusation b.

See **BEFORE the Lord, REJOICE before the Lord.**

See BLESS, BLESSED, BLESSING, BURDEN, BURNT, CALLED, CAST, CHARGE, CHOOSE, CHOSEN, COMMANDED, COMMANDMENT, CONGREGATION, COUNSEL, COURTS.

Covenant of the LORD.

Nu. 14: 44. ark of c. o. L. departed
1 K. 8:21. whn. is c. o. L., 2 Ch.6: 11.

See COVENANT, CRIED, DAY, EARS, END, ENEMIES, EYE, S, FACE, FEAR, ED, FEAST, FIRE.

From the LORD.

Ge. 4: 1. I have gotten a man f. L.
19: 24. the L. rained fire f. L. [L.
24: 50. said The thing proceedeth f.
Nu. 11: 31. went forth a wind f. L
16: 35. there came out a fire f. L.
46. is wrath gone out f. L. [19:9.
1 S. 16: 14. evil spirit f. L. troubled,
26: 12. a deep sleep f. L. was fallen
1 K. 2:15. my bro.'s, it was his f. L.
33. shall be peace for ever f. L.
Ps. 24:5. shall receive blessing f. L.
109:20. reward of mine adversaries
121:2. My help cometh f. L. [f. L.
Pr. 16: 1. answer of tongue is f. L.
19: 14. and a prudent wife is f. L.
29:26. man's judgment cometh f. L.
Is. 29:15. to hide their counsel f. L.
40: 27. sayest, My way hid f. L.
Je. 7: 1. word that came to Jeremiah
f. L., 11: 1.-18: 1.-21: 1.-26: 1.-
27: 1.-30: 1.-32: 1.-34: 1, 8, 12.-
35: 1.-36: 1.-40: 1. [f. L
17: 5. cursed whose heart departeth
37: 17. k. asked, is any word f. L.
Je. 49: 14. I have heard a rumour f. L
La. 2: 9. prophets no vision f. L.
3:18. My strength is perished f. L.
Eze. 11: 15. Jerus. said, get ye f. L.
33: 30. hear what is the word f. L.
Ho. 1:2. whoredom, departing f. L.
Ob. 1. we have heard rumour f. L.
Mi. 1: 12. but evil came down f. L.
5:7. remnant shall be as a dew f. L.
Zph. 1: 6. them th. are turned f. L.
Zch. 14: 13. tumult f. L. am. them
Lu. 1: 45. which were told her f. L.
2 Co. 5:6. in body we are absent f. L.

See **Lord** with **GIVE, Lord had, hath GIVEN, GLORY of the Lord.**

LORD God. [G.

Ge. 3:8. Adam and wife hid from L.
9: 26. Blessed be L. G. of Shem
15:2. Ab. said, L. G what wilt give
8. L. G., whereby know I inherit
24: 27. Blessed be the L. G. of Ab.
28: 13. I am L. G. of Abraham
Ex. 34:6. The L., the L. G. merciful
Jos. 7: 7. Joshua said, Alas, O L. G.
22: 22. L. G. of gods, L G. of gods
Ju. 6:22. Gideon said, Alas, O L. G.
16: 28. O L. G., remember me once
1 S. 6:20. who stand bef. holy L. G.?
2 S. 7: 18. Who am I, O L. G., what
19. a small thing O L. G. is this
the manner of man, O. L. G.?
20. L. G., knowest thy servant
22. Whf. thou art great, O. L. G.
25. now O L. G. the word, 28.
29. thou O L. G. hast spoken
1 K. 1: 36. L. G. of my lord king
18:37. thou art L. G., 2 K. 19: 19.
2 K. 2:14. Where is L. G. of Elijah?
1 Ch. 17:17. man of high deg., O L. G.
29: 1. palace not for man but L G.
2 Ch. 26: 18. nei. for thine honour
32:16. spake more ag. L. G. [fr. L. G.
Ne. 1: 5. I beseech thee O L. G.
9: 7. L. G. didst choose Abram
Ezr. 10: 11. confession unto L. G.
Ps. 31:5. hast redeemed me, O L. G.
68:18. L. G. might dwell am. them
71: 5. thou art my hope, O L. G.
16. go in strength of L. G.
73: 28. put my trust in L. G.
84:11. For L. G. is a sun and shield
85:8. I will hear what L. G. speak
88: 1. L. G. of my salv. I cried
94: 1. O. L. G. to whom vengeance
Is. 50: 7. the L. G. will help me, 9.
56:8. L. G. wh. gather-h outcasts
61: 11. L. G. will cause righte-sn.
65: 15. for L. G. shall slay thee
Je. 44: 26. saying, the L. G. liveth
Eze. 5:11. as I live, saith L. G., 14:16.
13:9. know I am L. G., 23:49.-24:24.
37:3. I ans-d, O. L. G., thou knowest
Da. 9: 3. I set my face unto L. G.
Am. 3: 7. L. G. revealeth his secret
8. L. G. spoken, who can prophesy?
6: 8. L. G. hath sworn by himself
7: 1. hath L. G. shewed, 4.-8: 1.
Mi. 1:2. let L. G. be witness ag. you
Ha. 3: 19. L. G. is my strength [G.
Zph. 1: 7. Hold peace in pres. of L.
Zch 9:14. L. G. shall blow trumpet
Lu. 1:32. L. G. give unto him throne
1 Pe. 3: 15. sanctify L. G. in hearts
Jude 4. denying the only L. G.
Re. 4:8. Holy, holy, L. G. Almighty,
11: 17.-16: 7. [G. Almighty
15:3. marvellous are thy works, L.
18: 8. strong is L. G. who judgeth
19: 6. L. G. omnipotent reigneth
21:22. L. G. and Lamb are temple
22: 5. L. G. giveth them light
6. L. G. of holy proph. sent angel

See **Saith the LORD.**

LORD God of fathers.

Ex. 3: 18. L. hath sent me | 2 Ch.
4:5. may believe that the L. [28:9.

De. 1 : 21. possess it as L.- said
4 : 1. land which L.- giveth, 12 : 1.
6 : 3. as L.- hath promised, 27 : 3.
12 : 1. land which L.-, Jos. 18 : 3.
26 : 7. we cried unto L.- 2 Ch. 20 : 6.
29 : 25. forsaken covenant of L.-
Ju. 2 : 12. forsook L.-, 2 K. 21 : 22.
1 Ch. 29 : 20. L. G. o. their f., 2 Ch.
7 : 22.-11 : 16.-13 : 18.-14 : 4.-15 :
12.-19 : 4.-24 : 18, 24.-28 : 6.-30 :
7, 22.-34 : 33.-36 : 15.
2 Ch. 13 : 12. fight ye not ag. L.-
21 : 10. bec. he had forsaken L.-
24 : 18. they left house of L.-
28 : 25. provoked to anger L.-
30 : 19. prepared to seek the L.-
Ezr. 7 : 27. Blessed be L.-
8 : 28. freewill offering unto L.-
10 : 11. confession unto L.-

LORD God of hosts.

1 K. 19 : 10. very jealous for L.-, 14.
1 S. 17 : 45. name of L.-, 2 S. 6 : 2.
2 S. 5 : 10. the L.- was with him
Ps. 59 : 5. O L.- awake to visit heathen
69 : 6. that wait on thee, O L.-
84 : 8. L.- hear my prayer
89 : 8. O L.- who is a strong L.-
Is. 10 : 23. L.- shall make a consump.
22 : 5. perplexity by L.- [| 28 : 22.
12. that day did L.- call to weeping
Je. 15 : 16. called by thy name O L.-
46 : 10. day of L.- L.- hath a sacrif.
50 : 25. this the work of L.-
Ho. 12 : 5. Even L.- is his memorial
Am. 4 : 13. The L.- is his name
5 : 14. the L.- shall be with you
15. L.- will be gracious
9 : 5. L.- is he toucheth the land

See GOD of Hosts
LORD of hosts, and,
Saith the LORD God of hosts. [s. L.-

Is. 3 : 15. mean ye to beat my peo.
10 : 24. s. L.- O my peo. be not afraid
22 : 14. iniq-y not purged till, s. L.-
15. s. L.- Go unto this treasurer
Je. 2 : 19. my fear is not in thee s. L.-
5 : 14. s. L.- Bec. ye speak this
35 : 17. s. L.- I will bri. upon Jud. evil
38 : 17. s. L.- If wilt go unto princes
44 : 7. s. L.- Whf. commit gr. evil?
49 : 5. I will bri. fear upon thee s. L.-
50 : 31. I am ag. thee, proud, s. L.-
Am. 3 : 13. testify in h. of Jac. s. L.-
5 : 16. L.- s. Wailing sh. be in streets
6 : 8. s. L.- I abhor excel-y of Jac.
14. I will raise ag. you a nat. s. L.-

LORD God of Israel.

Ex. 32 : 27. the L. G. o. I., Jos. 9 :
18, 19.-10 : 40, 42.-13 : 14.-14 :
14.-24 : 2.-Ju. 4 : 6.-5 : 3, 5.-
11 : 21, 23.-21 : 3. 1 S. 2 : 30.-
14 : 41.-20 : 12.-23 : 10.-25 : 32,
34. 1 K. 1 : 30. 1 Ch. 23 : 25.-
24 : 19. Is. 24 : 15.
34 : 23. thrice in y-r appear bef. L.-
Jos. 7 : 19. glory to L.-, 1 S. 6 : 5.
13 : 33. L.- was their inheritance
22 : 24. What have ye to do wi. L.-
24 : 23. incline your heart unto L.-
Ru. 2 : 12. reward given thee of L.-
1 K. 1 : 48. Blessed be the L.-, 8 : 15.
1 Ch. 16 : 36.-29 : 10. Ps. 41 :
13.-72 : 18.-106 : 48. Lu. 1 : 68.
14 : 13. some good toward the L.-
17 : 1. Elijah said, As L.- liveth
2 Ch. 15 : 13. would not seek the L.-
Ezr. 6 : 21. were come to seek L.-
Je. 28 : 2. Thus speaketh the L.-, 29 :
25.-30 : 2. Hag. 1 : 2. Zch. 6 :
12.-7 : 9.

See GOD of Israel, and Saith the LORD God of Israel.

Jos. 7 : 13. s. L.- There is an accursed
24 : 2. s. L.- Your fa-s dwelt on
Ju. 6 : 8. s. L.- I bro-t you from E.
2 S. 12 : 7. s. L.- I anointed thee k.
over Israel, 2 K. 9 : 6. [out
1 K. 11 : 31. s. L.- I will rend kingd.
14 : 7. s. L.- as I exalted thee am.
17 : 14. s. L.- meal shall not waste
2 K. 19 : 20. s. L.- That hast prayed
21 : 12. s. L.- I am bringing evil upon
22 : 15. s. L.- Tell man sent you to
me, 2 Ch. 34 : 23.
18. s. L.- Bec. thine heart was
tender, 2 Ch. 34 : 26. [L.-
Is. 17 : 6. gleaning grapes be left, s.

LORD his God.

Ex. 32 : 11. Moses besought L. h. G.
Le. 4 : 22. ag. com-ts of the L. h. G.
Nu. 23 : 21. the L. h. G. is with him
De. 17 : 19. may learn to fear L. h. G.
18 : 7. minister in name of L. h. G.
1 S. 30 : 6. David encouraged hims.
in L. h. G. [G.
1 K. 5 : 3. house unto name of L. h.
11 : 4. not perf. with L. h. G., 15 : 3.
15 : 4. L. h. G. give him lamp
2 K. 5 : 11. on name of L. h. G.
16 : 2. not right in sight of L. h. G.
2 Ch. 1 : 1. L. h. G. was with him
14 : 2. right in eyes of L. h. G.
11. Asa cried unto the L. h. G.
15 : 9. when saw L. h. G. with him
26 : 16. Uzziah transgr-d ag. L. h. G.
27 : 6. Jotham prepared his ways
bef. L. h. G. [hands of
28 : 5. L. h. G. delivered Ahaz into
31 : 20. Hez. wrought right bef. L.
h. G. [sought L. h. G.
33 : 12. Manasseh in affliction be-
34 : 8. Josiah sent to repair house
of the L. h. G. [12.
36 : 5. Jehoi. evil in sight of L. h. G.,
23. L. h. G. be with him, and let
Ezr. 7 : 6. hand of L. h. G. upon him
Ps. 146 : 5. whose hope is in L. h. G.
Jon. 2 : 1. Jon. prayed unto L. h. G.
Mi. 5 : 4. majesty of name of L. h. G.

LORD my God.

Nu. 22 : 18. bey. word of L. m. G.
De. 4 : 5. as L. m. G. com-d me
18 : 16. not hear voice of L. m. G.
26 : 14. heark-d to voice of L. m. G.
Jos. 14 : 8. wholly foll-d L. m. G., 9.
2 S. 24 : 24. burnt off-gs unto L. m. G.
1 K. 3 : 7. O L. m. G., 8 : 28.-17 : 20, 21.
1 Ch. 21 : 17. 2 Ch. 6 : 19. Ps. 7 :
1, 3.-13 : 3.-30 : 2, 12.-35 : 24.-38 :
15.-40 : 5.-86 : 12.-109 : 26. Jon.
2 : 6. Ha. 1 : 12.
5 : 4. L. m. G. hath given me rest
5. build a house unto name of L.
m. G., 1 Ch. 22 : 7. 2 Ch. 2 : 4.
Ezr. 7 : 28. as hand of L. m. G. upon
9 : 5. I spread ha. unto L. m. G. [me
Ps. 18 : 28. L. m. G. will enlighten
Je. 31 : 18. turn me, thou L. m. G.
Da. 9 : 4. I prayed unto L. m. G.
20. present. supplic. bef. L. m. G.
Zch. 11 : 4. saith L. m. G., feed flock
14 : 5. the L. m. G. shall come

LORD our God.

Ex. 3 : 18. sacrifice to L. G., 5 : 3.-8 :
27.-10 : 25. [Ps. 113 : 5.
8 : 10. there is none like to L. o. G.,
10 : 26. must take to serve L. o. G.
De. 1 : 6. L. o. G. spake in Horeb
19. thro. wilderness as L. o. G.
commanded us, 41.-6 : 20.
20. which L. o. G. doth give un-
unto us, 25.-2 : 29.
2 : 33. L. o. G. deliv-d him, 3 : 3.
36. L. o. G. delivered all unto us
37. whatso. L. o. G. forbade us
4 : 7. so nigh to them as L. o. G.
5 : 2. L. o. G. made a covenant
24. L. o. G. shewed us his glory
25. if we hear voice of L. o. G.
27. go hear all L. o. G. shall say
6 : 4. L. o. G. is one L., Mk. 12 : 29.
6 : 20. wh. L. o. G. hath com-d you
De. 6 : 24. to fear L. o. G. | 25. to do
before L. o. G. [L. o. G.
29 : 15. that standeth this day bef.
29. secret things unto L. o. G.
Jos. 18 : 6. lots for you bef. L. o. G.
22 : 19. besides altar of L. o. G., 29.
24 : 17. L. o. G. brought us up out of
24. The L. o. G. will we serve
Ju. 11 : 24. whomso. L. o. G. drive out
1 S. 7 : 8. Cease not to cry unto L. o. G.
1 K. 8 : 57. L. o. G. be with us, as
59. let my words be nigh L. o. G.
65. unto river of E. bef. L. o. G.
2 K. 18 : 22. say, We trust L. o. G.
19 : 19. O L. o. G. save thou us out
1 Ch. 13 : 2. be of L. o. G. let us send
15 : 13. L. o. G. made breach upon us
16 : 14. He is L. o. G., Ps. 105 : 7.
29 : 16. O L. o. G., 2 Ch. 14 : 11. Ps.
99 : 8.-106 : 47. Is. 26 : 13.-37 : 20.
Je. 14 : 22. Da. 9 : 15.
2 Ch. 13 : 11. keep charge of L. o. G.
14 : 7. because we sought L. o. G.
19 : 7. is no iniquity with L. o. G.
29 : 6. was evil in eyes of L. o. G.
32 : 8. with us is L. o. G. to help
11. L. o. G. shall deliver us out
Ezr. 9 : 8. grace shewed fr. L. o. G.
Ne. 10 : 34. burn upon alt. of L. o. G.
Ps. 20 : 7. rememb. name of L. o. G.
90 : 17. let beauty of L. o. G. be upon
94 : 23. L. o. G. shall cut them off
99 : 5. Exalt L. o. G. he is holy, 9.
8. Thou ans-dst them O L. o. G.
105 : 7. He is the L. o. G. his
122 : 9. Because of house of L. o. G.
123 : 2. eyes wait upon L. o. G.
Je. 3 : 22. thee, for thou art L. o. G.
23. in L. o. G. is salva. of Israel
25. we have sinned ag. L. o. G. (2)
5 : 19. Whf. doth L. o. G. these
24. Let us now fear the L. o. G.
8 : 14 L. o. G. put us to silence
16 : 10. committed ag. L. our G.
26 : 16. spoken in name of L. o. G.
31 : 6. let us go to Zion unto L. o. G.
37 : 3. Pray now to L. o. G., 42 : 20.
42 : 6. will obey voice of L. o. G.
43 : 2. L. o. G. hath not sent thee
50 : 28. to declare veng. of L. o. G.
51 : 10. let us declare work of L. o. G.
Da. 9 : 9. To L. o. G. belong mercies
10. Nei. obeyed voice of L. o. G.
13. not our prayer before L. o. G.
14. for the L. o. G. is righteous
Mi. 4 : 5. walk in name of L. o. G.
7 : 17. shall be afraid of L. o. G.
Ac. 2 : 39. many as L. o. G. call
Re. 19 : 1. honour, and power unto L.

LORD their God. [o. G.

Ex. 10 : 7. may serve L. t. G., 2 Ch.
34 : 33. Je. 30 : 9.
29 : 46. shall know I am L. t. G.,
Eze. 28 : 26.-34 : 30.-39 : 22, 28.
Le. 26 : 44. break covenant, I am L.
t. G., Zch. 10 : 6. [12 : 9. Je. 3 : 21.
Ju. 3 : 7. forgat L. t. G., 8 : 34. 1 S.
1 K. 9 : 9. forsook L. t. G., Je. 22 : 9.
2 K. 17 : 7. Isr. had sinned ag. L. t. G.
9. things were not right ag. L. t. G.
14. fathers, not believe in L. t. G.
16. left all the com-ts of L. t. G.
19. kept not com-ts of L. t. G.
18 : 12. obeyed not L. t. G., Je. 7 : 28.
2 Ch. 31 : 6. consecrated unto L. t. G.
33 : 17. did sacrifice unto L. t. G.
Ne. 9 : 3. law of L. t. G., worship (2)
4. cried wi. loud voice unto L. t. G.
Je. 43 : 1. end of speaking words of L.
t. G. for wh. L. t. G. sent him
50 : 4. shall seek L. t. G., Ho. 3 : 5.
Ho. 1 : 7. save them by L. t. G.
7 : 10. do not return to L. t. G.
Zph. 2 : 7. the L. t. G. sh. visit them
Hag. 1 : 12. people obeyed L. t. G.
Zch. 9 : 16. L. t. G. shall save them
Lu. 1 : 16. many sh. he turn to L. t. G.

LORD thy God.

Ge. 27:20. Bec. L.t.G. bro-t it to me
Ex. 20:2. I am L. t. G., De. 5:6. Ps. 81:10. Is. 51:15. Ho. 12:9.-13:4.
5. I the L.t.G. am a jealous God, De. 5:9.-6:15.
De. 1:31. how L. t. G. bare thee
2:7. L. t. G. been with thee
4:24. L. t. G. is a consuming fire
31. L. t. G. is a merciful God
5:15. remem. L. t. G. bro-t thee out, 6:10, 12.-7:19.-11:29.
7:9. Know that L. t. G. he is G.
21. L. t. G. is among you, 23:14.
8:5. as son, so L.t.G. chest-h thee
9:3. Understand L. t. G. is he
11:1. shalt love L. t. G., 30:16, 20. Mat. 22:37. Mk. 12:30. Lu. 10:
12:31. not do so unto L.t.G. [27.
18:15. L. t. G. will raise up Proph.
20:1. L.t.G. is with thee, Jos. 1:9.
23:14. L. t. G. walketh in camp
26:5. shalt say bef. L. t. G., 13.
28:8. L. t. G. set thee on high
58. fear this glorious and fearful name THE LORD THY GOD.
30:7. L. t. G. will put all curses
31:3. L. t. G. he will go bef. thee
Jos. 1:17. only L. t. G. be with thee
1 S. 12:19. Pray for serv. unto L.t.G.
25:29. bundle of life with L. t. G.
2 S. 14:11. let king remem. L.t.G.
17. tbf. L. t. G. will be wi. thee
24:3. L. t. G. add unto people
23. said, The L. t. G. accept thee
1 K. 13:6. Entreat face of L. t. G.
17:12. As the L. t. G. liveth I have not a cake, 18:10.
Is. 41:13. L. t. G. will hold thy ha.
43:3. I am L.t.G. Holy One of Isr.
55:5. run unto thee, bec. of L.t.G.
Je. 40:2. L. t. G. hath pronounced
42:2. pray for us unto L. t. G.
3. That L. t. G. may shew us way
Mi. 7:10. said, Where is L. t. G.?
Zph. 3:17. L. t. G. is mighty
Mat. 4:7. not tempt L.t.G., Lu. 4:12.
10. shalt worship L. t. G., Lu. 4:8.

LORD your God.

Ex. 8:28. may sacrifice to L. y. G.
10:17. entreat the L. y. G.
Le. 19:2. be holy, for I L. y. G. am
De. 1:10. L. y. G. multiplied you
30. L. y. G. fight for you, 3:22.
32. did not believe L. y. G. [3.
3:21. all L.y.G hath done, Jos. 23:
4:4. cleave unto L. y. G., Jos. 23:8.
6:16. Ye shall not tempt L. y. G.
9:16. ye had sinned ag. L. y. G.
10:17. the L. y. G. is God of gods
11:2. not seen chastis-m. of L.y.G.
25. L. y. G. shall lay fear of you
12:4. sh. not do so unto L. y. G.
13:3. L. y. G. proveth you to kn.
4. ye shall walk after L. y. G.
14:1. Ye are children of L. y. G.
20:4. L. y. G. goeth with you
18. so should ye sin ag. L. y. G.
Jos. 2:11. L. y. G. is God in heav.
4:23. L.y.G. dried wat. of Jordan
23:3. L.y.G. is he fought for you, 10.
5. L. y. G. shall expel them
1 S. 12:12. when L. y. G. was your k.
14. shall continue foll-g L. y. G.
1 K. 8:61. heart be perf. with L.y.G.
2 K. 17:39. the L. y. G. ye sh. fear
1 Ch. 22:18. Is not L. y. G. with you?
2 Ch. 20:20. Believe in the L. y. G.
28:10. are there not sins ag. L.y.G.
30:9. L. y. G. is gracious
Ne. 8:9. This day holy unto L. y. G.
Ps. 76:11. Vow and pay unto L.y.G.
Je. 42:20. when ye sent me unto L. y. G. [raise up, 7:37.
Ac. 3:22. a prophet shall L. y. G.

See **I am LORD your God, HAND of the Lord.**

LORD of hosts.

1 S. 1:3. to sacrifice unto L.-
11. O L.-, Ps. 59:5.-84:1, 3, 12.
2 S. 7:27. Is. 37:16. Je. 11:20.-20:12. Zch. 1:12.
4:4. ark of covenant of L.-
17:45. I come in the name of the L.-
2 S. 6:2. called by name of L.-,
18. Da. blessed peo. in name of L.
7:26. The L. is God over Israel
1 K. 18:15. as L.- liveth, 2 K. 3:14.
2 K. 19:31. the zeal of the L.- shall do this, Is. 9:7.-37:32.
1 Ch. 11:9. greater, for L.- with him
17:24. L.- G. of Israel, 2 S. 7:26.
Ps. 24:10. L.- is king of glory
46:7. The L.- is with us, 11.
48:8. I have seen in city of L.-
Is. 1:9. Except the L.- left remu.
2:12. day of L.- be upon proud
3:1. L.- doth take from Jerus.
5:7. vineyard of L.- is Israel
9. said L.- many houses desolate
16. L.- shall be exalted in
24. they have cast aw. law of L.-
6:3. said, Holy, holy, holy is L.-
5. mine eyes have seen the L.-
8:13. Sanctify the L.- himself
18. for signs in Israel from L.-
9:13. neither do seek L.- [ened
19. Thro. wrath of L.- land dark-
10:16. L.- shall send leanness
26. L.- shall stir up scourge
33. L.- shall lop the bough
13:4. L.- mustereth the battle
13. earth remove in wrath of L.-
14:24. L.- hath sworn [23:9.
27. L.- hath purposed, 19:12.-
18:7. place of name of L.-
19:16. bec. of shaking of ha. of L.-
17. counsel of L.- | 20. witness of
18. sh. 5 cities swear to L.- [L.-
25. Whom L.- shall bless
21:10. which I have heard of L.-
22:14. it was revealed by L.-
24:23. when L. shall reign in Zion
25:6. in this mt. L.- make a feast
28:5. L.- be for crown of glory
29:6. visited of L.- with thunder
31:4. L.- shall come down
31:5. so will L.- defend Jerusalem
39:5. Hear the word of the L.-
47:4. L.- is his name, 48:2.-51:15.-54:5. Je. 10:16.-31:35.-32:18.-50:34.-51:19.
Je. 6:6. hath L.- said, Hew down
11:17. L.- that planted thee
23:36. perverted words of the L.-
27:18. make intercession to L.-
28:2. Thus speaketh L.-, 29:25
Hag. 1:2. Zch. 6:12.-7:9.
33:11. shall say, Praise the L.-
46:18. King, whose name is the L.-, 48:15.-51:57.
51:5. Isr. not been forsaken of L.-
14. L.- hath sworn, I will fill
Ha. 2:13. is it not of L.- th. people
Zph. 2:10. against people of L.-
Hag. 1:14. did work in house of L.-
Zch. 1:6. Like as L.- thought to do unto us [4:9.-6:15.
2:9. shall know L.- sent me, 11.-
7:3. speak unto priests in h. of L.-
4. word of L.- unto me, 8:1, 18.
12. came great wrath from L.-
8:3. be called mountain of L.-
21. let us go to pray, and seek L.-
22. many people shall seek L.-
9:15. L.- shall defend them
10:3. L.- hath visited his flock
12:5. shall be my strength in L.-
14:16. to worship King, L.-, 17.
21. every pot holiness unto L.-
Mal. 2:7. he is the messenger of L.-
12. cut off him offereth unto L.-
3:14. walked mournfully bef. L.-

See **LORD God of hosts.**

Saith the LORD of hosts.

Is. 1:24. s. L.- Ah I will ease me
14:22. I will rise ag. them s. L.-
23. with besom of destruc. s. L.-
17:3. sh. be as glory of Isr. s. L.-
19:4. fierce k. shall rule them s. L.-
22:25. sh. nail fastened be removed
45:13. not for price nor reward s. L.
Je. 8:3. death sh. be chosen s. L.
30:8. s. L.- I will break his yoke
46:25. L.- s. I will punish, No
49:26. young men shall fall s. L.-
Na. 2:13. I am ag. thee, s. L.-, 3:5.
Hag. 1:9. Why? s. L.- mine ho. waste
2:4. I am with you, s. L.-
7. will fill hou. with glory, s. L.-
8. gold is mine s. L.- [s. L.- (2)
9. glory of latter sh. be greater
23. S. L.- will I take thee O Zeruh.
I have chosen thee s. L.-
Zch. 1:16. my h. shall be built s. L.-
3:9. I will engrave gravings s. L.-
10. s. L.- sh. ye call eve. man his
4:6. but my Spirit s. L.- [neig-hb.
5:4. I will bring curse forth s. L.-
7:13. cried I wo. not hear s. L.-
8:11. I will not be unto peo. s. L.-
13:2. s. L.- I will cut off names of idols [s. L.-
7. Awake O sword of my sheph.
Mal. 1:6. if master, where my fear s. L.- unto you, O priests [L.-9.
8. will he accept thy person? s.
10. I no pleasure in you s. L.-
11. my name be gr. am. heathen s.
13. ye have snuffed at it s. L.- [L.-
14. I am great King s. L.- [s. L.-
2:2. If ye will not lay it to heart
4. ye sh. know I sent com-t s. L.-
8. ye corrupted cov. of Levi, s. L.-
16. covereth violence with garment s. L.- [come s. L.-
3:1. Beloved, my messenger shall
5. I will be swift witness ag. s. L.-
7. Return unto me and I s. L.-
10. prove me now s. L.- [s. L.-
11. nei sh your vine cast fruit
12. ye sh. be delightsome la. s. L.-
17. And they shall be mine s. L.-
4:1. day shall burn them up s. L.-
3. ye sh. tread down wicked s. L.-

Thus saith the LORD of hosts.

1 S. 15:2. t. s. L.- I remember which that Amalek did to Israel
2 S. 7:8. t. s. L.- I took thee fr. sheepcote, 1 Ch. 17:7. [last
Is. 44:6. t. s. L.- I am the first and
Je. 6:9. t. s. L.- They sh. glean Isr.
7:3. t. s. L.- Amend your ways
21. t. s. L.- Put your burnt off-gs
9:7. t. s. L.- I will melt them
15. t. s. L. Behold, I will feed th.
17. t. s. L.- Consider ye and call
11:22. t. s. L.- I will punish them
16:9. t. s. L.- I will cause to cease
19:3. t. s. L.- I will bring evil, 15.
11. t. s. L.- will I break people
23:15. t. s. L.- will feed proph. with wormwood [prophets
16. t. s. L.- Hearken not unto
25:8. t. s. L.- Bec. ye not heard words
27. t. s. L.- Drink and be drunken, 28.
32. t. s. L.- evil sh. go fr. nation to
26:18. t. s. L.- Zion sh. be ploughed
27:4. command them to say unto masters, t. s. L.-
21. t. s. L.- vessels that remain shall be carried to Bab., 19.
28:14. t. s. L.- I have put yoke
29:4. t. s. L.- unto captives, Build
8. t. s. L.- Let not proph. deceive
17. t. s. L.- I will send sword, fam.
21. t. s. L.- I will deliv. into hand
31:23. t. s. L.- they sh. use this speech in land of Judah

Je. 32: 14. t. s. L.- Take these wid-s
15. t. s. L.- Houses, fields, be p[illegible]-d
33: 12. t. s. L.- in this pla. be hab[illegible].
35: 13. t. s. L.- tell men of Ju[illegible]
18. t. s. L.- Bec. obeyed com-t of
Jonadab [a man before me
19. t. s. L.- Jonadab sh. not want
39: 16. t. s. L.- I will bring upon city
42: 15. t. s. L.- If set faces to enter E.
18. t. s. L.- As mine anger been
43: 10. t. s. L.- I will take Neb.
44: 2. t. s. L.- ye seen evil upon Jerus
11. t. s. L.- will set face ag. you
25. t. s. L.- ye and wives spoken
48: 1. t. s. L.- Woe unto Nebo
49: 7. t. s. L.- Is wisd. no more in
Teman? [Elam
35. t. s. L.-, will break the bow of
50: 18. t. s. L.- I will punish k. of
33. t. s. L.- Isr. were oppressed
51: 33. t. s. L.- Dau. of Bab. is like
58. t. s. L.- walls of Bab. be broken
Hag. 1: 5. t. s. L.- Consider your
ways, 7. [tle while
2: 6. t. s. L.- Yet once, it is a lit-
11. t. s. L.- ask priest conc. law
Zch. 1: 3. t. s. L.- Turn ye unto me, 4.
14. t. s. L.- I jealous for Zion, 8: 2.
17. t. s. L.- My cities shall be spread
2: 8. t. s. L.- After glory sent me
3: 7. t. s. L.- If wilt walk in my
8: 4. t. s. L.- sh. old men dw. in Jerus.
6. t. s. L.- If marvellous in eyes.(2)
7. t. s. L.- I will save my people
9. t. s. L.- Let hands be strong
14. t. s. L.- As I thought to punish
19. t. s. L.- The fast shall be joy
20. t. s. L.- It sh. come to pass
23. t. s. L.- In those days ten men
Mal. 1: 4. t. s. L.- They sh. build,
I will throw down

See **LORD God of hosts.**

See **HOUSE** with **Lord.**

I the LORD.

Le. 19: 2. for I t. L. your G. am
holy, 20: 26.-21: 8. [-22: 9, 16.
21: 15. I t. L. do sanctify him, 23.
Nu. 12: 5. I t. L. make mys. known
14: 35. I L. have said it, Eze. 21: 17.
35: 34. I t. L. dwell am. chil. of Isr.
Is. 27: 3. I t. L. do keep it, I will
41: 4. I t. L. the first, wi. the last
17. needy seek, I t. L. will hear
42: 6. I t. L. have called thee in
45: 3. I t. L. call thee by thy name
7. I t. L. do all these things
8. I t. L. have created it
19. I t. L. speak righteousness
21. told it, have not I t. Lord
60: 16. that I t. L. am thy Saviour
22. I t. L. will hasten it in time
61: 8. For I t. L. love judgment
Je. 17: 10. I t. L. search the heart
Eze. 5: 13. I t. L. have spoken it,
15, 17.-17: 21.-21: 32.-22: 14.-
24: 14.-26: 14.-30: 12.
14: 4. I t. L. will answer him, 7.
9. I t. L. have deceived proph.
17: 24. I t. L. have bro-t down (2)
20: 48. that I t. L. have kindled it
21: 5. that I t. L. drawn my sword
22: 22. I t. L. poured out my fury
34: 24. I t. L. will be their G.
30. know I t. L. am with them
36: 36. that I t. L. do build, (2)
37: 14. I t. L. have performed it
28. I t. L. do sanctify Israel

I am the LORD. [Ur

Ge. 15: 7. I a. t. L. bro-t thee out of
Ex. 6: 2. I a. t. L., 6, 8, 29.-12: 12.-
Le. 18: 5, 6, 21.-19: 12, 14, 16,
18, 28, 30, 32, 37.-21: 12.-22:
2, 3, 8, 30, 31, 33.-26: 2, 45.
Nu. 3: 13, 41, 45. Is. 43: 11, 15.
20: 2 I a. t. L. brought thee out
Le. 11: 45. I a. t. L th. bringeth you
20: 8. I a. t. L. wh. sanctify you
Le. 22: 32. I a. t. L. which hallow you
Is. 42: 8. a. t. L. that is my name
44: 24. I a. t. L. maketh all things
45: 5. I a. t. L. is none else, 6, 18.
Je. 9: 24. glory he knoweth I a. t. L.
32: 27. I a. t. L. God of all flesh
Eze. 12: 25. I a. t. L. I will speak
Mal. 3: 6. For I a. t. L I change not
See **KNOW I am the Lord.**

I am the LORD your God.

Ex. 6: 7. shall know I a. L. y. G.,
16: 12. De. 29: 6. Jo. 3: 17.
Le. 11: 44. I a. t. L. y. G., 18: 2, 4,
30.-19: 3, 4, 10, 25, 31, 34, 36.
-20: 7, 24.-23: 22, 43.-24: 22.-
25: 17, 38, 55.-26: 1, 13. Nu.
10: 10.-15: 41. Ju 6: 10. Eze.
20: 5, 7, 19, 20. Jo. 2: 27.
See **JESUS** with **Lord.**

In the LORD.

Ge. 15: 6. he believed i. t. L. and
Jos. 22: 25. ye have no part i. t. L., 27.
1 S. 2: 1. My heart rejoic-h i. t. L. (2)
Ps. 31: 24. all ye that hope i. t. L.
32: 11. Be glad and rejoice i. t. L.
34: 2. My soul make boast i. t. L.
35: 9. my soul be joyful i. t. L.
37: 4. Delight thyself i. t. L., Is. 58: 14
7. Rest i. t. L. wait patiently
56: 10. i. t. L. will I praise word
64: 10. righteous i. t. L., 104: 34.
112: 7. heart fixed trusting i. t. L.
Is. 26: 4. i. t. L. Jehovah is everl.
29: 19. meek increase joy i. t. L.
45: 17. Isr. shall be saved i. t. L
24. i. t. L. have I righteousness
25. i. t. L. seed of Isr. be justified
Je. 3: 23. i. t. L. is salva. of Israel
Zph. 3: 2. she trusted not i. t. L.
Zch. 12: 5. Jerus. be my strength i.
Ac. 9: 42. many believed i. t. L. [t. L.
14: 3. abode, speaking boldly i. t. L.
Ro. 16: 2. That ye receive her i. t. L.
8. Great Amplias my belov. i. t. L.
11. household of Narcissus i. t. L.
12. Persis, who laboured i. t. L.
13. Salute Rufus, chosen i. t. L.
22. I Tertius salute you i. t. L.
1 Co. 1: 31. glorieth, let him glory
i. t. L., 2 Co. 10: 17. [i. t. L.
4: 17. faithful i. t. L. | 7: 22. called
7: 39. be married only i. t. L. [t. L.
9: 1. apostle, are ye not my work i.
2. seal of apostleship i. t. L. [L.
11: 11. nei. woman with-t man i. t.
15: 58. labour not in vain i. t. L.
16: 19. Priscilla salute you i. t. L.
Ep. 2: 21. unto holy temple i. t. L.
4: 17. I testify i. t. L. th. ye walk
5: 8. now are ye light i. t. L.
6: 1. Chil. obey parents i. t. L.
10. my brethren be strong i. t. L.
21. a faithful minister i. t. L.
Ph. 1: 14. breth. i. t. L. confident
2: 24. I trust i. t. L. I come shortly
29. Receive him therefore i. t. L.
4: 1. stand fast i. t. L., 1 Th. 3: 8.
2. be of the same mind i. t. L.
10. But I rejoiced i. t. L. greatly
Col. 3: 18. submit to hus-h-s i. t. L.
4: 7. Tychicus fellow serv. i. t. L.
17. ministry hast received i. t. L.
1 Th. 5: 12. know them over you i. t.
2 Th. 3: 4. have confidence i. t. L. [L.
Phm. 16. both in flesh and i. t. L.
20. joy of thee i. t. L. refresh my
bowels i. t. L.
Re. 14: 13. Blessed are dead die i. t. L.
See REJOICE, TRUST.

See **KNOWLEDGE of the Lord.**

LORD is.

Ge. 28: 16. Surely L. i. in this place
Ex. 9: 27. the L. i. righteous, I
wicked, 2 Ch. 12: 6.
15: 2. the L. i. my strength and
song.
Ex. 15: 3. L. i. man of war, L. i. his
18: 11. I know L. i. greater than
Nu. 14: 9. L. i. with us, fear not
18. L. i. longsuffering, Na. 1: 3.
42. Go not up, L. i. not am. you
16: 3. holy, and L. i. am. them
De. 10: 9. the L. i. his inheritance
18: 2. the L. i. their inheritance
Jos. 22: 34. witness, that L. i. God,
De. 4: 5, 39. Ps. 100: 3. [1: 28.
Ju. 6: 12. The L. i. with thee, Lu.
1 S. 2: 3. L. i. a God of knowledge
16: 18. L. i. with David, 2 S. 7: 3.
28: 16. the L. i. departed fr. thee
2 S 22: 2. L. i. my rock, Ps. 18: 2.
1 K. 8: 60. may know L. i. God
20: 28. The L. i. the God of the hills
2 Ch. 13: 10. as for us, L. i. God
15: 2. L. i. with you while ye wi.
Ps. 9: 16. L. i. known by judgm.
10: 16. L. i. king for ever
11: 4. The L. i. in his holy temple
14: 6. poor, bec. L. i. his refuge
16: 5. L. i. portion of mine inheri.
23: 1. The L. i. my shepherd, I
27: 1. The L. i. my light and my
salva., L. i. the strength of my
28: 7. L. i. my strength, 118: 14.
8. The L. i. their strength. and he
34: 8. O taste and see, L. i. good
47: 2. the L. most high i. terrible
54: 4. L. i. with them th. uphold
89: 18. L. i. our defence and king
92: 15. To shew that L. i. upright
93: 1. L. i. clothed with strength
94: 22. L. i. my defence and rock
95: 3. the L. i. a great God, 96: 4.-
99: 2.-135: 5.-147: 5.
100: 5. the L. i. good, 25: 8.-34: 8.-
135: 3.-145: 9. Je. 33: 11. La. 3:
25. Na. 1: 7.
103: 8. L. i. merciful and gracious,
111: 4.-145: 8.
113: 4. The L. i. high ab. nations
118: 6. L. i. on my side, not fear
121: 5. L. i. thy keeper, L. i. thy
125: 2. L. i. round about his peo.
129: 4. L. i. righteous, 145: 17. La.
1: 18. Da. 9: 14. [upon him
145: 18. L. i. nigh unto all th. call
Pr. 15: 29. L. i. far from wicked
22: 2. L. i. the maker of them all
Is. 30: 18. L. i. a God of judgment
33: 5. The L. i. exalted
22. L. i. our judge [righteousn.
42: 21. L. i. well pleased for his
Je. 10: 10. the L. i. the true God
17: 7. whose hope the L. i.
20: 11. L. i. with me as mighty one
La. 3: 24. L. i. my portion
Eze. 48: 35. name of city, The
L. i. there
Am. 5: 8. The L. i. his name, 9: 6.
Ha. 2: 20. L. i. in his holy temple
Zph. 3: 5. just L. i. in the midst, 15.
Zch. 10: 5. fight, bec. L. i. with them
13: 9. shall say, The L. i. my God
Lu. 24: 34. The L. i. risen indeed
2 Co. 3: 17. Now L. i. that Spirit
Ph 4: 5. moderation, L. i. at hand
1 Th. 4: 6. the L. i. the avenger
2 Th 3: 3. but the L. i. faithful
He. 13: 6 The L. i. my helper
Ja 5: 11. L. i. very pitiful and
1 Pe. 2: 3. tasted that L. i. gracious
2 Pe. 3: 9. The L. i. not slack conc.
See JUDGMENT, S, JUSTICE,
KINGDOM

See **LAW of the Lord, and As the Lord LIVETH.**

See LONGSUFFERING, MADE
[Lord as agent], MAJESTY,
MERCIES, MERCY, MIND, MIN-
ISTER, MOUNT, MOUNTAIN.

Mouth of the LORD.

Le. 24: 12. expound unto them acc. to
m. o. L. | Nu. 3: 16. 1 S. 12: 14.

De. 8 : 3. proceedeth out of **m.o.L.**
Jos. 9: 14. asked not counsel at **m.**
1 K.13:21. disobeyed **m.o.L.** [o.L.
2 Ch. 36: 12. speaking from **m.o.L.**
Is. 1 : 20. **m. o. L.** hath spoken it,
40 : 5.-58 : 14. Je. 9:12. Mi. 4:4.
62:2. new name **m. o. L.** sh. name
Je. 23: 16. speak not out of **m.o.L.**

My LORD.

Ex. 4 : 10. O **m. L.** I am not eloq.
13. O **m. L.** send by hand of wh.
34: 9. let **m. L.** go among us
Nu. 14: 17. power of **m. L.** be great
Ju. 6 : 13. O **m. L.** if L. be with us
15. O **m. L.** whw. I save Isr. ?
13: 8. O **m. L.** let man of G. come
Ps.16:2.said unto L. Thou art **m.L.**
35:23. Stir up thyself my G. **m.L.**
110 : 1. L. said unto **m. L.**, Mat.
22:44. Mk. 12:36. Lu.20:42. Ac.
2 : 34. [gotten
Is.49:14. Zion said, **m. L.** hath for-
Lu.1:43. mother of **m.L.** sho. come
Jn. 20 : 13. have taken away **m. L.**
28. Thomas ans-d **m. L.** and my
Ph. 3 : 8. knowl. of C. Jesus **m. L.**

See **Lord**,
[as applied to angel or man].

Name of the LORD, or
LORD'S name.

Ge. 12 : 8. Abram called upon the
n. o. L., 13 : 4.-21 : 33.
16:13. she called **n.o.L.** that spake
26: 25. Isaac called upon **n. o. L.**
Ex. 20:7. Thou shalt not take **n.o.**
L. in vain, De. 5 : 11.
33: 19. I will proclaim **n. o. L.**
34: 5. Lord proclaimed **n. o. L.**
Le.24:11.son blasphemed **n.o.L.**,16
De. 18 : 5. to minister in **n.o.L.**, 7.
22. prophet speaketh in **n. o. L.**
21:5.God chosen to bless in **n.o.L.**
28: 10. thou art called by **n. o. L.**
32 : 3. Bec. I will publish **n. o. L.**
Jos. 9 : 9. are come bec. of **n. o. L.**
1 S.20:42. we have sworn in **n.o.L.**
1 K. 3 : 2. no house built to the **n.**
o. L., 5:3, 5.-8:17,20. 1 Ch. 22:
7, 19. 2 Ch. 2 : 1, 4.-6: 10.
10: 1. of Sheba heard conc. **n.o.L.**
18: 32. Elij. built altar in **n. o. L.**
22 : 16. tell me nothing but is true
in **n.o.L.**, 2 Ch. 18:15. [o. L.
2 K. 2:24. Elisha cursed them in **n.**
1 Ch. 16: 2. blessed peo. in **n. o. L.**
21:19. which he spake in **n. o. L.**,
2 Ch. 33 : 18. [Ps. 113 : 2.
Jb. 1 : 21. blessed be the **n. o. L.**,
Ps. 7:17. will sing praises to **n.o.L.**
20 : 7. we will remember **n. o. L.**
102:15. heathen shall fear **n. o. L.**
21. To declare **n. o. L.** in Zion
113 : 1. praise the **n.o.L.**, 135 : 1.-
148 : 5, 13. Jo. 2 : 26. [praised
3. fr. rising of sun L.'s **n.** to be
116: 4. called I upon **n. o. L.** [12.
118:10. in **n.o.L.** destroy them, 11,
26. Blessed be he that cometh in
n. o. L., Mat. 21:9.-23:39. Mk.
11 : 9, 10. Lu. 13:35.-19:38. Jn.
122 : 4. thanks unto **n.o.L.** [12:13.
124:8. Our help is in **n.o.L.** [o.L.
129 : 8. nei. say, we bless you in **n.**
Pr. 18: 10. **n.o.L.** is a strong tower
Is. 24:15. glorify the **n.o.L.** in isles
30:27. the **n.o.L.** cometh from far
48 : 1. which swear by **n.o.L.** and
50:10. let him trust in **n.o.L.** and
56 : 6. to love the **n.o.L.** to be his
59: 19. shall they fear **n. o. L.**
60:9. to bring their gold unto **n. o.**
Je.3:17. nations gath-d to **n.o.L.** [L.
11:21. Prophesy not in the **n.o.L.**
26: 9. Why prophesied in **n. o. L.**
16. spoken to us in **n.o.L.**, 44:16.
20. Urijah prophesied in **n. o. L.**
Am. 6: 10. not mention of **n. o. L.**

Mi. 4 : 5. we will walk in **n. o. L.**
5 : 4. feed in majesty of **n. o. L.**
Zph. 3 : 12. they sh. trust in **n.o.L.**
Zch. 13: 3. speakest lies in **n. o. L.**
Ac. 9 : 29. spake boldly in **n. o. L.**
10 : 48. to be baptized in **n. o. L.**,
8 : 16.-19 : 5.
15 : 26. hazarded lives for **n. o. L.**
19 : 13. to call over them **n. o. L.**
17. **n. o. L.** Jesus was magnified
21:13. am ready to die for **n. o. L.**
22:16. wash sins, calling on **n.o.L.**
1 Co. 6 : 11. are justified in **n. o. L.**
Col. 3 : 17. do all in **n. o. L.** Jesus
2 Th. 1 : 12. **n. o. L.** Jes. be glorified
3:6. we command you in **n.o.L.** J.
Ja. 5 : 10. have spoken in **n. o. L.**
14. anointing him in the **n. o. L.**

See **CALL on the name.**
See **LORD of hosts.**

O LORD.

Ge. 49 : 18. waited for thy salv., O L.
Ex. 15 : 11. Who is like thee, O L.
Nu. 10 : 36. Return O L., Ps. 6 : 4.
De.26: 10. Wh. thou, O L. hast given
Jos. 7 : 8. O L. Israel turneth
Ju. 5 : 31. let enemies perish, O L.
2 S. 15 : 31. O L. turn counsel of
22 : 29. thou art my lamp, O L.
23:17. Be it far from me, O L. [11.
24:10. O L. take away iniq-y, Ps. 25:
1 K. 19:4. O L. take my life, Jon.4:3.
2 K. 20 : 3. O L. remember how I
walked, Ps. 106 : 4. Is. 38 : 3.
1 Ch. 17 : 20. O L none like thee
29 : 11. Thine O L. is the greatness,
thine, O L. [L. thou art
2 Ch. 14 : 11. help us O L. our G. **o.**
Ne. 1 : 11. O L. let thine ear be
Ps. 3 : 3. thou O L. a shield, 59:11.
7. Arise O L. ; save me O L.
5 : 8. Lead me, O L. [long?
6 : 2. O L. heal me | 3. O L. how
7:6. Arise, O L., 9:19.-10:12.-17:13.
8. judge O L. acco. to my righte-n.
26 : 1. [praise thee, O L.
8 : 1. O L. our L., 9. | 9 : 1. I will
9 : 13. have mercy upon me, O L.
31: 9.-86: 3.-123 : 3.
10 : 1. Why standest afar off ?
12 : 7. Thou shalt keep them, O L.
13 : 1. How long forget me, O L.
17 : 1. O L. attend unto my cry
18 : 1. O L. my strength, 19 : 14.
22 : 19. be not far, O L., 35 : 22.
27 : 7. Hear, O L., 30:10.-39 : 12.-
69 : 16.-86 : 6.-102 : 1.-119 :
145.-140 : 6.
30 : 1. I will extol thee, O L.
31 : 14. I trusted in thee, O L.
38 : 22. Make haste to help, O L. 40:
13.-70 : 1, 5. [O L.
40 : 9. I ha. not refrained my lips,
44 : 23. why sleepest thou, O L. ?
54 : 6. I will praise, O L., 57 : 9.
86 : 8. am. gods none like thee, O L.
11. Teach me thy way, O L., 25:4.-
27 : 11.
115 : 1. O L. not unto us, but
119 : 151. Thou art near, O L. thy
143 : 1. Hear my prayer, O L., 7. Is.
37 : 17. Dan. 9 : 19. [will
Is. 25 : 1. O L. thou art my God, I
63 : 16. thou, O L. art our Fa. 64:8.
Je. 10 : 6. O L. thou art great
11 : 5. answered I, So be it, O L.
12 : 3. but thou, O L. knowest me
14 : 9. O L. art in the midst of us
17 : 13. O L. the hope of Israel
14. Heal me, O L. and I shall be
20 : 7. O L. thou hast deceived me
La. 1 : 9. O L. behold my affliction
11. see, O L. I am vile, 2 : 20.
5 : 19. Thou, O L. remainest forever
21. Turn us unto thee, O L. we
Da. 9 : 4. O L. the dreadful God
Jon. 1 : 14. We beseech thee, O L.

Ha. 1 : 2. O L. how long shall I cry?
12. O L. thou ordained them
3 : 2. O L. revive thy work [31.
Mat. 15:22. O L. thou Son of, 20 : 30,
Lu. 5 : 8. for I am a sinful man, O L.
Re. 4 : 11. Thou art worthy, O L.
6: 10. How long, O L. holy and true?
15 : 4. Who shall not fear thee, O L.
16 : 5. O L. which art, and wast

See **LORD God.**
See OATH, OBLATIONS.

Of the LORD.

Jos.11:20. was **o. L.** to harden hearts
1 S. 1 : 20. I have asked him **o. L.**
2 S. 6 : 9. David was afraid **o. L.**
12:25. name Jedidiah because **o. L.**
† Jedidiah, Beloved **o. L.** [o.L.
2 K. 3 : 11. a proph. we may inquire
6 : 33. Behold, this evil is **o.L.** [L.
20 : 9. This sign shalt thou have **o.**
2 Ch. 20 : 4. Jud. to ask help **o. L.**
Ps. 21 : 4. One thing I desired **o. L.**
37 : 39. salv. of righteous is **o. L.**
91 : 2. say **o. L.** He is my refuge
Pr. 12 : 2. obtaineth favour **o. L.**,
16 : 33. disposing is **o. L.** [18 : 22.
20 : 24. Man's goings are **o. L.**
21 : 31. battle ; but safety is **o. L.**
22 : 14. abhorred **o. L.** shall fall
Is. 49 : 7. bec. **o. L.** that is faithful
54:13. thy chil. shall be taught **o.L**
Je. 23:9. am like drunken bec **o. L.**
La. 3 : 22. **o. L.**'s mercies we not
Jon.2:9. Salvation is **o.L.** [consum.
Ha. 2 : 13. it is not **o. L.** that people
Zch. 10 : 1. ask ye **o. L.** rain
1 Co. 7 : 25. obtained mercy **o. L.**
11 : 23. I have received **o. L.**
32 we are chastened **o. L.** [o. L.
2 Cor. 2 : 12. door opened unto me
Ep. 6 : 8. same sh. he receive **o. L.**
Col. 3 : 24. that **o. L.** ye rec. reward
2 Th. 2 : 13. brethren beloved **o. L.**
2 Ti. 1 : 18. grant he find mercy **o.L.**
Ja. 1 : 7. receive anything **o. L.**

See BLESSED, INQUIRE, ED.

Offering, s, of the LORD.

Ex. 30 : 13. half shekel, the **o. o. L.**
35 : 5. an **o. o. L.** gold and silver
Le. 21 : 6. for **o. o. L.** made by fire
Nu. 9 : 7. whf. we not offer **o. o. L.**
13. He brought not **o. o. L.**
1 S. 2 : 17. men abhorred **o. o. L.**

See **Heave OFFERING.**
See **PEOPLE of the Lord.**
See **PRAISE the Lord.**
See PRAISE, PRAISES, PRESENCE, PRIESTS.

Prophet, s, of the LORD.

1 S. 3 : 20. Samuel to be a **p. o. L.**
1 K. 18 : 4. Jezebel cut off **p-s o. L.**
13. Jezebel slew the **p-s o. L.**
22. I only remain a **p. o. L.**
22 : 7. is not here a **p. o. L.** to inquire of him ? 2 K. 3 : 11. 2 Ch.
18 : 6. [was Oded
2 Ch. 28 : 9. a **p. o. L.** there, name

See REBUKING, REDEEMED.
See **REJOICE in the Lord.**
See SABAOTH, SABBATH, S.

LORD said. [| 9:15.

Ge. 4 : 6. L. s. unto Cain, why wroth?
6 : 3. L. s. My spirit sh. not always
7:1. L. s. unto Noah, Come into ark
8 : 21. L. s. I will not curse
11 : 6. L. s. Behold people is one
12 : 1. L. s. unto Ab. Get thee out
18 : 26. L. s., If I find in Sodom
Ex. 4 : 4. the L. s. unto Moses, 19,
21.-6 : 1.-7 : 1, 14.-8 : 16, 20.-
9 : 1, 8, 13, 22.-10 : 1, 12, 21.-
11 : 1, 9.-14 : 15, 26.-16 : 4, 28.-
17 : 5, 14.-19 : 9, 10, 21, 23,
24.-20 : 22.-24 : 12.-30 : 34.-32:
7, 9, 33.-33 : 17.-34 : 1, 27.-
Le. 16 : 2. Nu. 3 : 40.-7 : 11.-
11 : 16, 23.-12 : 14.-14 : 11.-

15 : 35.-17 : 10.-21 : 8, 34.-25 :
4.-27 : 12, 18. De. 31 : 14, 16.
Jos. 11 : 23.
Ex. 7 : 13. he hearkened not as the
L. s., 22.-8 : 15, 19.-De. 9 : 3.-
Ju. 2 : 15.-6 : 27. ⌈morrow
16 : 23. This is that which L. s. to
24 : 3. Moses told them all the L. s.
7. All L. s. we will, Nu. 32 : 31.
Nu. 10 : 29. unto place of which L. s.
14 : 20. L. s. I have pardoned
16 : 40. as the L. s. to him by Moses
26 : 65. L. had s. They shall die
32 : 31. As the L. s. will we do
De 1 : 42. the L. s. unto me, 2 : 9,
31.-3 : 2. 26.-9 : 12.-10 : 1, 11.-
18 : 17.-31 : 2.-Je. 1 : 7, 9, 12,
14.-3 : 6, 11.-11 : 6, 9.-13 : 6.-
14 : 11, 14.-15 : 1.-24 : 3.-Am.
7 : 8, 15.-8 : 2.-Zch. 11 : 13, 15.
31 : 3. as L. hath s., Jos. 14 : 12.
Jo. 2 : 32.
Jos. 3 : 7. the L. s. unto Joshua, 5 :
2, 9.-6 : 2.-7 : 10.-8 : 1, 18.-10 :
8.-11 : 6.-13 : 1.
14 : 6. Thou knowest thing L. s.
Ju. 6 : 23. L. s. Peace be unto
7 : 2. L. s. unto Gideon, 4, 5, 7.
9. L. s. unto Gid., Arise, for I
10 : 11. L. s. unto Isr. Did I not deliv.
20 : 18. L. s. Jud. shall go up first
1 S. 3 : 11. L. s. to Sam. I will do a
17. what thing L. s. unto thee?
15 : 16. tell thee what L. s. to me
24 : 4. day of which L. s. unto thee
2 S. 16 : 10. L. s. unto him, Curse Dav.
1 K. 8 : 12. L. s. he would dw., 2 Ch. 6 : 1.
11 : 2. nations cone-g which L. s.
14 : 5. L. s. unto Ahijah
22 : 17. L. s. these have no master,
2 Ch. 18 : 16.
20. L. s. Who. sh. persuade Ahab?
2 K. 14 : 27. L. s. not he would blot
17 : 12. L. had s. Ye shall not do
21 : 4. of which L. s., 7. 2 Ch. 33 : 4.
24 : 13. Sol. made in temple as L. s.
2 Ch. 23 : 3. as L. s. of sons of Da.
Ps. 2 : 7. L. hath s. Thou art my Son
110 : 1. L. s. unto my L., Mat. 22 :
44. Mk. 12 : 36. Lu. 20 : 42.-
Ac. 2 : 34.
Isa. 7 : 3. Then s. the L., 8 : 3. Eze.
44 : 2. Ho. 3 : 1. Jon. 4 : 10.
18 : 4. For L. s. I will take my rest
21 : 16. hath L. s. unto me, Je. 4 : 27.
29 : 13. L. s. as this people draw
Je. 42 : 19. L. s. O remnant of Jud.
Eze. 21 : 17. cause fury, I L. have s. it
23 : 36. L. s. Son of man wilt judge
Ac. 9 : 10. to him s. the L., Ananias

Saith the LORD.

Nu. 24 : 13. what t. L. s., that will
I speak, 1 K. 22 : 14. ⌈me
1 S. 2 : 30. now t. L. s., Be it far fr.
2 K. 9 : 26. seen bl. of Naboth, - L.
20 : 17. shall be carried unto Bab.
- L., Is. 39 : 6. ⌈Ch. 34 : 27.
22 : 19. I have heard thee, - L., 2
Is. 1 : 11. To what purpose sacrif. - L.
18. let us reason together, - L.
3 : 16. t. L. s. Bec. daus. of Zion
haughty
28 : 16. - L. I lay in Zion a stone
30 : 1. Woe to rebellious chil. - L.
15. - L. In returning ye be saved
33 : 10. will I rise - L., Ps. 12 : 5.
41 : 14. fear not thou worm Jacob
- L., Je. 30 : 3.-46 : 28.
21. Produce your cause, - L.
43 : 10. Ye are my witnesses, - L., 12.
48 : 22. no peace - L. unto wicked
49 : 5. - L. Tho. Isr. be not gath-d
18. As I live - L., Je. 22 : 24. Eze.
5 : 11.-14 : 16, 18, 20.-16 : 48.-17 :
16, 19.-18 : 3.-20 : 3, 31. 33.-33 :
11, 27.-34 : 8.-35 : 6, 11. Zph. 2 : 9.
Ro. 14 : 11.
Is. 54 : 1. more than chil. of wife - L.
8. In a little wrath I hid - L. ⌈L.
10. nei. cov-t of peace be remov. -
17. their right-su. is of me - L.
55 : 8. nei. your ways my ways - L.
56 : 8. t. L. s. Yet will I gath. others
57 : 19. Peace to him far off - L.
59 : 20. Redeemer sh. come to Zion -
21. this is my cov-t - L. (2) ⌊L.
65 : 7. I will recomp. your iniq-s - L.,
Je. 51 : 24. Eze. 11 : 21.-16 : 43.-
18 : 30.-22 : 31.-24 : 14. He. 10 : 30.
25. sh. not hurt in my mt. - L.
66 : 2. things mine hand made - L.
9. not cause to bring forth? - L.
20. sh. bring breth. for an off-g - L.
21. I will take them for priests - L.
Je. 1 : 8. I am wi. thee, - L., 19.-15 :
20.-30 : 11.-42 : 11.-46 : 28. Hag.
1 : 13. ⌈L.
2 : 3. evil shall come upon them, -
12. Be aston-d O heavens, - L. ⌈L.
22. tho. wash thee with nitre, -
29. ye have transgr-d ag. me, - L.
3 : 1. thou hast played harlot, - L.
10. Judah not turned with heart
but feignedly, - L. ⌈L., 14.
12. Return thou backsli. Isr. -
13. Only acknowledge thine iniquity, - L. ⌈- L., 5 : 11.
20. ye have dealt treach-y wi. me,
4 : 1. If thou wilt return O Isr. - L.
9. - L. that heart of king sh. perish
17. she hath been rebellious ag.
me, - L. ⌈- L., 29.-9 : 9.
5 : 9. Shall I not visit for these,
15. I will bring a nation upon you,
- L. ⌈end, 46 : 26.
18. - L. I will not make a full
22. Fear ye not me? - L. ⌈-49 : 16.
6 : 15. shall be cast down, - L., 8 : 12.
7 : 11. Behold I have seen it, - L.
13. bec. ye have done these works,
19. Do they provoke me, - L. ⌊- L.
30. chil. of Judah done evil, - L.
32. - L. no more be called Tophet,
19 : 6. ⌈of k-s
8 : 1. - L. they sh. bring out bones
13. I will surely consume th., - L.
17. serpents shall bite you, - L.
9 : 3. they know not me, - L., 6.
13. - L. Bec. have forsak. my law
24. in these things I delight, - L.
25. - L. I will punish, 27 : 8.
12 : 17. I will pluck up nation - L.
13 : 25. This is thy lot, - L.
15 : 3. appoint ov. them 4 kinds, - L.
6. Thou hast forsaken me, - L.
16 : 5. taken my peace fr. peo. - L.
11. Bec. fathers forsaken me, - L.
16. I will send for fishers, - L.
18 : 6. I do with you as potter? - L.
21 : 10. I have set face against city,
- L. ⌈51 : 25. Eze. 13 : 8.
13. I am ag. thee O inhab. - L.,
22 : 5. If not hear - L. h. be desol.
16. was not this to know me? - L.
23 : 1. Woe be unto the pastors, - L.
2. - L. Ye scattered my flock | 4.
5. - L. will raise unto Da. a Branch
11. in my ho. found their wickedness - L. ⌈visita., - L., 48 : 44.
12. will bring upon them y-r of
23. Am I a God at hand, - L.
24. Can any hide himself, - L. Do
not I fill heav. and earth? - L.
28. What is chaff to the wheat? - L.
29. Is not my word like a fire? - L.
30. I am ag. the prophets, - L., 31,
33. I will forsake you, - L. ⌊32.
25 : 7. Ye have not hearkened, -
L., 27 : 19. ⌈- L.
31. he will give wicked to sword,
27 : 15. I have not sent th., - L., 29 : 9.
11. thoughts I think tow. you, - L.
29 : 14. I will be found of you, - L. (2)
23. I know, and am witness, - L.
Je. 30 : 3. I will bring again captivity
- L., 32 : 44.-33 : 11.-49 : 6, 39
Am. 1 : 5, 15.-5 : 27.
17. I will heal thee, - L. ⌈L.
21. he shall approach unto me -
31 : 1. - L. will I be G. of Israel
14. my peo. sh. be satisfied, - L.
16. thy work sh. be rewarded, - L.
17. is hope in thine end, - L. ⌈- L.
20. I will have mercy upon him,
27. - L. I will sow house of Isr.
28. will I watch ov. them to build,
31. - L. I will make new cov. ⌊- L.
32. altho. I was a husb. unto th.
33. - L. I will put my law in ⌊- L.
34. sh. all know me fr. least unto,
36. If ordinances depart, - L. ⌊- L.
37. I will cast off seed of Isr. - L.
38. - L. the city shall be built
32 : 5. sh. lead Zede. to Bab. - L.
33 : 13. under hands of him telleth
them, - L. ⌈Isr.
14. - L. I will perform good unto
34 : 17. I proclaim a liberty, - L.
35 : 13. Will ye not rec. instruc. - L.
39 : 17. I will deliver thee, - L., 18.
18. bec. hast put trust in me, - L.
42 : 11. Be not afraid of k. - L. ⌈- L.
44 : 29. this sh. be a sign unto you,
45 : 5. I will bri. evil upon all, - L.
46 : 5. Whf. turned back and, - L.
23. sh. cut down her forest, - L.
26. be inhabited as of old, - L.
48 : 12. - L. I will send wanderers
25. horn of Moab is cut off, - L.,
| 35, 38, 47.
30. I know his wrath, - L. ⌈- L.
43. Fear, pit, snare upon thee,
49 : 2. - L. I will cause an alarm (2)
13. - L. Bozrah sh. become desola.
30. Flee, dwell deep, O Hazor, - L.
31. get you unto wealthy nation,
- L. ⌈37. Eze. 11 : 8.
32. I will bring their calamity - L.,
50 : 4. Isr. sh. come and Jud. going
weeping, - L. + ⌈- L.
30. her men of war sh. be cut off,
35. sword is upon Chaldeans, - L.
51 : 26. desolate for ever, - L. +
Eze. 5 : 8. - L. G.: I even I am ag.
thee, 13 : 8.-38 : 3.-39 : 1.
11. - L. Bec. thou hast defiled my
sanctuary ⌈- L., 25.
12 : 28. word spoken shall be done
13 : 6. saying - L. and L. not sent
16. there is no peace - L. ⌊them, 7.
14 : 11. that I may be their G. - L.
14. Noah, Daniel, Job, they should
deliver but own souls, - L., 16.
23. not done without cause, - L.
16 : 8. I ent-d into cov. with, - L. +
14. comeliness put upon thee - L.
19. sweet savour: thus it was - L. G.
23. woe, woe unto thee, - L. G.
30. How weak is thine heart - L.
48. Sodom thy sister not done as
thou, - L. ⌈founded - L.
63. thou remember and be con-
18 : 3. - L. ye sh. not have occasion
9. he is just, he shall live, - L.
23. Have I pleasure that wicked
die? - L., 32.-33 : 11.
30. I will judge ev. one acc. to his
ways, - L. G. ⌈| 40.
20 : 36. will I plead with you - L.
21 : 7. be brought to pass, - L. G.
13. if sword contemn rod? - L.
22 : 12. gained by extortion - L. G.
25 : 14. sh. know my vengeance, - L.
26 : 21. tho. sought for yet shalt
never be found, - L. ⌈- L.
28 : 10. shalt die deaths of uncirc.
29 : 20. bec. they wrought for me - L.
31 : 18. This is Pha. and all his mult.,
- L. G., 32 : 16, 31, 32. ⌈land - L.
32 : 8. will set darkness upon thy
14. their rivers to run like oil, - L.

Eze. 34 : 8. - L. bec. my flock became
15. I will feed my flock, - L. ⌊prey
30. sh. know they are my peo., - L.
31. ye are men I am your God, - L.
35 : 6. - L. G. I will prepare blood
36 : 23. sh. know I am L. - L. G.
32. not for your sakes, - L. G.
37 : 5. - L. G. unto these bones
38 : 21. ev. man's sword ag. bro., - L.
39 : 5. I have spoken it, - L. G., 23 :
34.-26 : 5, 14.-28 : 10.
8. and it is done, - L. G.
13. with men of war, - L. G.
43 : 27. I will accept you, - L. G.
44 : 12. lifted hand ag. them - L. G.
27. he sh. offer for sin off-g - L. G.
45 : 9. exactions from my peo. - L. G.
15. reconciliation for them, - L. G.
47 : 23. give stranger inher., - L. G.
Ho. 2 : 13. she went aft. lovers, - L.
16. at that day shalt call me Ishi,
21. - L. I will hear the heavens ⌊- L
11 : 11. tremble as bird out of E., - L.
Jo. 2 : 12. - L. turn to me wi. all heart
Am. 1 : 8. Philis. shall perish, - L. G.
2 : 3. I will slay princes, - L.
11. Is it not thus, O Israel ? - L.
3 : 10. they know not to do right, - L.
15. gr. houses shall have an end, - L
4 : 5. this liketh you, - L. G. ⌈G., 3.
7 : 6. L. repented ; It sh. not be, - L.
8 : 3. songs of temp. be howlings, - L.
11. - L. I will send fam. not of br.
9 : 7. Are ye not as Ethiopians, - L.
8. I will not destroy h. of Jac., - L.
12. called by my name, - L. ⌈take
13. - L. that ploughmen sh. over-
Ob. 4. Tho. exalt thys. I will bri., - L.
8. sh. I not, - L. destroy the wise
Mi. 4 : 6. - L. will I assemble her
6 : 1. Hear ye what L. s., Arise
Zph. 1 : 3. will cut off man fr. land, - L.
10. - L. shall be noise of a cry from
3 : 8. wait ye upon me, - L., until
20. I will make you a praise, - L.
Hag. 2 : 4. be strong all ye peo., - L.
14. So is peo. and na. bef. me, - L.
17. I smote yet ye turned not, - L.
23. - L. I will make thee a signet
Zch. 1 : 4. they did not hear, - L.
2 : 5. I, - L., will be glory in her
6. flee fr. land of north, - L. (2)
10. I will dwell in thee, - L.
8 : 17. all these things I hate, - L.
11 : 6. I will no more pity inhab. - L.
12 : 2. I will make Jerus. a cup of
4. - L. I will smite every horse
Mal. 1 : 2. I have loved you, - L. (2)
13. sho. I accept this at your
hand ? - L.
2 : 16. - L. be hateth putting away
3 : 13. your words stout ag. me, - L.
Ac. 7 : 49. Heaven is my throne, - L.
15 : 17. - L. who doeth all these
Ro. 12 : 19. Vengeance is mine, - L.
1 Co. 14 : 21. will they not hear me, - L
2 Co. 6 : 17. come out be separate, - L.
18. ye sh. be my sons and dau-s, - L.
He. 8 : 8. - L. I will make new cov.
9. I regarded them not, - L. ⌈10 : 16.
10. cov. I will make with Isr., - L.,
Re. 1 : 8. am beginn. and ending - L.

See As I LIVE, LORD God.
See LORD God of hosts.
See LORD God of Israel.

Thus saith the LORD.

Ex. 4 : 22. t. s. L. Israel is my son
7 : 17. t. s. L. shalt kn. I am L. ⌈9 : 1.
8 : 1. t. s. L. Let my peo. go, 20.-5 : 1-
11 : 4. t. s. L. About midnight I
1 S. 2 : 27. t. s. L. did I appear unto
2 S. 7 : 5. t. s. L. Shalt build me hou.
12 : 11. t. s. L. I will raise up evil
24 : 12. t. s. L. I offer thee 3 things
1 K. 12 : 24. t. s. L. ye sh. not go up
13 : 2. t. s. L. a child sh. be born
21. t. s. L. as thou hast disobeyed
1 K. 20 : 13. t. s. L. Hast seen this mult.
14. t. s. L. Even by the young men
28. t. s. L. Bec. Syrians have said
42. t. s. L. Bec. hast let go man
21 : 19. t. s. L. Hast thou killed ⌈10.
22 : 11. t. s. L. push Syrians, 2 Ch. 18 :
2 K. 1 : 4. t. s. L. shalt not come fr. bed
6. t. s. L. Is it bec. is not a G. in
16. t. s. L. as thou hast messengers
2 : 21. t. s. L. I have healed waters
3 : 16. t. s. L. Make valley full | 17.
4 : 43. t. s. L. They shall eat
9 : 3. t. s. L. I anointed thee k., 12.
19 : 6. t. s. L. Be not afraid, 2 Ch. 20 :
15. Is. 37 : 6. ⌈into city, Is. 37 : 33.
32. t. s. L. k. of Assyr. not come
20 : 1. t. s. L. Set h. in order, Is. 38 : 1.
5. t. s. L. I seen thy tears, Is. 38 : 5.
22 : 16. t. s. L. I will bring evil upon
pla., 2 Ch. 34 : 24. ⌈build me hou.
1 Ch. 17 : 4. t. s. L. Thou shalt not
21 : 10. t. s. L. I offer 3 things | 11.
2 Ch. 11 : 4. t. s. L. Ye sh. not go up
12 : 5. t. s. L. ye have forsaken me
21 : 12. t. s. L. G. Bec. hast not walked
Is. 7 : 7. t. s. L. G. It sh. not stand
29 : 22. t. s. L. Jac. not be asham.
43 : 1. t. s. L. Fear not I redeemed,
14. t. s. L. For your sake I ⌊44 : 2.
16. t. s. L. They sh. lie down toge.
44 : 6. t. s. L. I am the first and
24. t. s. L. I am L. th. maketh
45 : 1. t. s. L. I will loose loins of k-s
11. t. s. L. Ask me conc. my sons
14. t. s. L. labour of E. be thine
18. t. s. L. I am the L. and there
48 : 17. t. s. L. I am L. teacheth thee
49 : 7. t. s. L. Kings shall see
8. t. s. L. In an acceptable time
22. t. s. L. I will lift ha. to Gent.
25. t. s. L. captives sh. be taken
50 : 1. t. s. L. Where bill of divorc-t
52 : 3. t. s. L. sold yours. for nought
4. t. s. L. My people went into E.
56 : 1. t. s. L. Keep ye judg-t and
4. t. s. L. unto eunuchs give pla.
65 : 8. t. s. L. As new wine in cluster
13. t. s. L. my serv-s sh. eat but ye
66 : 1. t. s. L. The heav. is my throne
12. t. s. L. I will extend peace
Je. 4 : 3. t. s. L. Break fallow ground
6 : 16. t. s. L. Stand ye in the way
21. t. s. L. I will lay stumblingbl-ks
22. t. s. L. a peo. cometh fr. north
7 : 20. t. s. L. G. mine anger shall
8 : 4. t. s. L. Sh. they fall not arise?
9 : 22. t. s. L. carcasses shall fall
23. t. s. L. Let not wise glory
10 : 2. t. s. L. Learn not way of heath.
18. t. s. L. I will sling out inhab-ts
11 : 3. t. s. L. Cursed be man | 11,
21.-17 : 5. ⌈of their land
12 : 14. t. s. L. I will pluck th. out
13 : 1. t. s. L. get girdle | 9, 13. ⌈ | 15.
14 : 10. t. s. L. they loved to wander
15 : 2. t. s. L. Such as are for death
19. t. s. L. If thou return
16 : 3. t. s. L. They sh. die of | 5.
17 : 19. t. s. L. Go stand in gate
21. t. s. L. Take heed to yours.
18 : 11. t. s. L. I frame evil ag. | 13.
19 : 1. t. s. L. get potter's bottle
20 : 4. t. s. L. I will make thee a
terror to thyself and to
21 : 8. t. s. L., I set bef. you life and
22 : 1. t. s. L. Go to house of king
of Jud. | 3. 6, 11, 18, 30.
23 : 38. t. s. L. Bec. ye say this word
24 : 8. t. s. L. I will give Zede. k.
26 : 2. t. s. L. stand in court | 4.
27 : 2. t. s. L. make thee bonds
16. t. s. L. Heark. not to prophets
28 : 11. t. s. L. will I break yoke
of Neb-r | 13, 16. ⌈32.
29 : 10. t. s. L. after 70 y-rs | 31,
30 : 5. t. s. L. We heard voice of
trembling
Je. 30 : 12. t. s. L. Thy bruise is incura.
18. t. s. L. I will bri. again captiv.
31 : 2. t. s. L. people found grace | 16.
7. t. s. L. sing with gladness
15. t. s. L. a voi. heard in Ramah
37. t. s. L. If heav. can be meas-d
32 : 3. t. s. L. I will give city, 28. | 42.
33 : 2. t. s. L. The L. his name
20. t. s. L. If break covenant of
day, 25. | 10, 17.
34 : 2. t. s. L. speak to Zede. | 4, 17.
36 : 29. t. s. L. hast burned roll, 30.
37 : 9. t. s. L. Deceive not yours.
38 : 2. t. s. L. If go unto princes | 3.
44 : 30. t. s. L. I will give Pha. into
45 : 2. t. s. L. didst say, Woe me
47 : 2. t. s. L. waters rise out of
48 : 40. t. s. L. he sh. fly as eagle
49 : 1. t. s. L. Hath Isr. no sons ? | 12.
28. t. s. L. go up to Kedar
51 : 1. t. s. L. I will raise ag. Bab. | 36.
Eze. 2 : 4. t. s. L. shalt say unto them,
3 : 11. t. s. L. whe. will hear ⌊t. s. L.
27. t. s. L. He th. heareth let him
5 : 5. t. s. L. This is Jerus. ; I have,
8. t. s. L. even I am ag. thee ⌊ | 7.
6 : 3. t. s. L. I will bring sword
11. t. s. L. Smite with hand, stamp
11 : 7. t. s. L. your slain, 5, 16. ⌈peo.
17. t. s. L. I will gather you fr.
12 : 10. t. s. L. This burden concern-h
19. t. s. L. They sh. eat with caref.
23. t. s. L. will make proverb cease
28. t. s. L. shall none of words be
prolonged ⌈prophets
13 : 3. t. s. L. Woe unto foolish
8. t. s. L. Bec. ye spoken vanity
13. t. s. L. I will rend it
18. t. s. L. Woe to women that sew
20. t. s. L. I am ag. your pillows
14 : 21. t. s. L. I send 4, sore judgt-s
15 : 6. t. s. L. As the vine am. trees
16 : 3. t. s. L. Thy birth is of Can.
36. t. s. L. Bec. thy filthiness was
59. t. s. L. I will deal wi. thee as
17 : 3. t. s. L. A great eagle with gr.
9. t. s. L. sh. it prosper ? ⌊wings
19. t. s. L. surely mine oath
22. t. s. L. I will take of highest bra.
20 : 3. t. s. L. Are ye come to inqui.
5. t. s. L. In the day I chose Isr.
27. t. s. L. your fa-s blasph-d me
30. t. s. L. Are ye polluted | 39, 47.
21 : 3. t. s. L. I am ag. thee, 26 : 3, 7.
-28 : 22.-29 : 3.-30 : 22.-35 : 3.-38 :
3.-39 . 1. ⌈24, 28.
9. t. s. L. A sword is sharpened |
26. t. s. L. Remove the diadem
22 : 3. t. s. L. The city sheddeth blood
19. t. s. L. Bec. ye are dross | 28.
23 : 22. t. s. L. will raise lovers ag. thee
32. t. s. L. drink of sister's cup | 28.
35. t. s. L. Bec. hast forgot me | 46.
24 : 3. t. s. L. Set on pot, pour wat.
6. t. s. L. Woe to bloody city, 9 | 21.
25 : 3. t. s. L. Bec. saidst Aha ag.
6. t. s. L. Bec. clapped hands | 8,
13, 16.
26 : 15. t. s. L. sh. not isles shake | 19.
27 : 3. t. s. L. O Tyrus hast said
28 : 2. t. s. L. Because heart is
lifted, 6.-31 : 10.
12. t. s. L. sealest sum, 25. ⌈19.
29 : 13. t. s. L. At end of 40 y-rs | 8,
30 : 2. t. s. L. Howl ye, Woe the day
13. t. s. L. I will dest-y idols | 6, 10.
31 : 15. t. s. L. he went down to grave
32 : 3. t. s. L. will spread my net | 11.
33 : 25. t. s. L. Ye eat with blood | 27.
34 : 2. t. s. L. Woe to shepherds feed
10. t. s. L. I am ag. the sheph-s
11. t. s. L. I will search my sheep
17. t. s. L I judge betw. cattle, 20.
35 : 14. t. s. L. When earth rejoiceth
36 : 2. t. s. L. Bec. enemy said, Aha
4. t. s. L. surely in fire of my
jealousy, 5, 6.

Eze. 36 : 22. t.s.L. not this for your
sakes | 7, 13, 33.
37. t. s. L. I will be inquired of
37 : 5. t. s. L. I will cause breath
9. t. s. L. Come from 4 winds, O
breath [seph | 12.
19. t. s. L. I will take stick of Jo-
21.t.s.L.I will take Isr. fr. heath.
38:14. t. s. L. when my peo. dw-h
17. t. s. L. Art thou he [safely
39 : 17. t. s. L. Speak unto ev. fowl
25. t.s.L. bri. again captiv.of Jac.
43:18. t.s.L. These the ordinances
44:6.t.s.L.O Isr. let it suffice, 45:9.
45:18. t. s. L. take bullock | 9. [16.
46:1.t.s.L. gate tow. east be shut |
47 : 13. t. s. L. This sh. be border
Am. 1:3.t.s.L.For 3 transgressions,
6, 9, 11, 13.–2:1, 4, 6.
3:11. t.s.L. G. an adversary sh. be
3:12.t.s.L.As sheph. taketh of lion
5:3.t.s.L.city th.went out by thous
4. t. s. L. Seek ye me, ye sh. live
7:17. t.s.L. Thy wife sh. be harlot
Mi. 2 : 3. t. s. L. ag. family I devise
3:5. t. s. L. Night sh. be unto you
Na. 1:12.t.s.L.Tho. quiet and many
Zch. 1 : 16. t. s. L. I am returned to
Jerus. with mercies, 8 : 3.
11:4. t.s.L. Feed flock of slaughter
See SALVATION, SANCTUARY.
See **Lord SAVED, SAW** with
Lord, SAYING.

LORD with **seek.**

De. 4 : 29. if thence thou shalt s. L.
1 Ch. 16 : 10. heart rejoice, that s.
L., Ps. 105 : 3. [105 : 4.
11. s. the L. and his strength, Ps.
22:19.set heart to s.L., 2 Ch.11:16.
2 Ch. 12 : 14. prepared not to s. L.
14:4. And com-d Judah to s. L.God
15 : 12. entered into a cov. to s. L.
13. whoso. would not s. L.
20 : 3. Jehosh-t set hims. to s. L.
4. out of cities of Jud.came to s.L.
Ps. 22:26. sh. praise L. that s. him
34:10.that s.L. shall not want any
Pr. 28:5. they that s. L. understand
all things [Ho. 7 : 10.
Is. 9 : 13. nei. do they s. L., 31 : 1.
51:1. Hearken to me, ye that s. L.
55:6. s. L. while he may be found
Je. 50 : 4. they sh. go and s. the L.
Ho. 3 : 5. shall return and s. the L.
5 : 6. sh. go with herds to s. the L.
10 : 12. for it is time to s. the L.
Am. 5:6. s. the L. and ye shall live
Zph. 2 : 3. s. ye the L. all ye meek
Zch. 8 : 21. Let us go to s. the L.
22. people shall come to s. the L.
Mal. 3:1. L. ye s. sh. suddenly come
Ac.15:17.th. residue might s.the L.
17 : 27. should s. the L. if haply

LORD with **sent.**

Ge. 3 : 23. L. s. him from garden
19 : 13. the L. s. us to destroy it
Ex.4:28.words of L.who had s. him
7:16.L. God of Hebrews s. me unto
9: 23. and L. s. thunder and hail
upon Egypt, 1 S. 12 : 18.
Nu. 16 : 28. ye shall know L. s. me
29. if die common death, L. not s.
20 : 16. when we cried, L. s. angel
21 : 6. L. s. fiery serpents am. peo.
De. 9:23. L.sent you fr.Kadesh-bar.
34 : 11. in wonders L. s. him to do
Ju. 6:8. that L. s. prophet unto Isr.
1 S. 12 : 8. then the L. s. Moses
11. L. s. Jerub. | 18.L.s. thunder
15 : 1. L. s. me to anoint thee king
18. the L. s. thee on a journey
20. I have gone way L. s. me
20 : 22. the L. hath s. thee away
2 S. 12 : 1. L. s. Nathan unto David
24:15. L. s. pestilence upon Israel,
1 Ch. 21 : 14. [to Beth-el
2 K. 2:2. Tarry, for L. hath sent me
2 K.2:4.L.s.me to Jeri. | 6. to Jord.
17 : 25. thf. L. s. lions am. them
24:2. L. s. ag. him bands of Chald.
2 Ch. 32:21. L.s. angel, who cut off
Is. 9:8. the L. s. a word into Jacob
Je. 19 : 14. L. s. him to prophesy
25 : 4. And L. hath s. unto you all
17. nations to whom L. had s.me
26:12.L.s.me to prophesy ag.ho.,15
28 : 9. be known L. truly s. him.
15. Hear Hananiah, L. not s.thee
Eze. 13:6. and the L. hath not s.th.
Jon. 1:4. the L. s. out a great wind
Hag. 1:12. obeyed, as L. had s. him
Zch. 1:10. whom L. hath s. to walk
2:9. know L. s. me, 11.–4:9.–6:15.
7 : 12. lest hear words L. hath s.
Ac. 9:17. Saul, L. Jesus hath s. me
12:11. know I L. hath s. his angel

Servant, s of the LORD, or
LORD'S servant.

De. 34:5.Moses s.o.L. died in Moab
Jos.1:1.after death of Moses s.o.L.
13. which Moses s. o. L. commanded, 8:31, 33.–11:12.–22:2,
5. 2 K. 18 : 12.
15.which Moses s. o. L. gave you,
12:6.–13:8.–18:7.–22:4.
12:6. them did Moses s.o.L. smite
14 : 7. Moses s.o.L. sent me [2:8.
24 : 29. Joshua s. o. L. died, Ju.
2 K. 9 : 7. avenge blood of s-s o. L.
10:23. see there be none of s-s o.L.
2 Ch. 1:3. tab. Moses s. o. L. made
24:6. acc. to com-t of Moses s.o.L.
Ps. 113:1. Praise L., O ye s-s o. L.,
134:1.Bless L., ye s-s o. L. [135:1.
Is. 42 : 19.who is blind as L.'s s.?
54 : 17. is heritage of s-s o. L.
2 Ti. 2 : 24. s. o. L. must not strive

Serve the LORD.

Ex.10:7. men go,th.they may s.t.L.
8.Pha. said, Go s.t.L.your G., 11,
24.–12 : 31.
26. thereof must we take to s. t. L.
know not with what s. t. L.
23 : 25. ye shall s. t. L. your God
De. 10 : 12. to s. t. L. thy God
Jos. 24 : 14. theref. fear and s. t. L.
15. if seem evil unto you to s. t.L.
18. theref. will we s. t. L., 21, 24.
19. Josh. said, Ye cannot s. t. L.
1 S. 12 : 20. s. t. L. with all heart
2 S. 15 : 8. then will I s. t. L. [3.
2 Ch.30:8. but yield, and s. t. L.,35:
33 : 16. com. Judah to s.t.L.,34:33.
Ps. 2 : 11. s. t. L. with fear and
100 : 2. s. t. L. with gladn. come
102 : 22. kingd-s gath-d to s. t. L.
Col.3:24. rec. reward, for ye s.t.L.C.
See **SHEWED.** [Lord as agent.]

Sight of the LORD.

Gen. 38 : 7. Er.was wicked in s.o.L.
Le. 10 : 19. been accepted in s. o. L.
De. 6 : 18. do good in s. o.L., 12 : 28.
9 : 18. doing wickedly in s. o. L.
12 : 25. do what is right in s. o. L.
21 : 9. 2 K. 12 : 2.–14 : 3.–15 :
3, 24.–18 : 3.–22 : 2. 2 Ch. 20 :
32.–24 : 2.–25 : 2.–26 : 4.–27 :
2.–29 : 2.–34 : 2.
1 S. 12 : 17. wickedn. great ye done
in s. o. L., 1 K. 21 : 25. 2 K.
21 : 6. [s. o. L.
2 K. 3 : 18. is but a light thing in
16 : 2. did not what was right in s.
o. L., 2 Ch. 28 : 1.
Ps. 116 : 15. Precious in s. o. L. is
death of his saints [s. o. L.
Mal. 2 : 17. say, doeth evil, is good in
Lu. 1 : 15. be great in s. o. L.
2 Co. 8:21.not only in s. o. L. but of
Ja. 4 : 10. Humble yours. in s. o. L.
See **EVIL in sight of L.**
See **SMITE.** [Lord as agent.]

LORD with **spake.**

Ge.16:13. name of L. that s.unto her
Ex. 6 : 10. And the L.s. unto Moses,
saying, 28, 29.–7 : 19.–8 : 5.–
13 : 1.–14 : 1.–16 : 11.–25 : 1.–
30 : 11, 17, 22.–31 : 1, 12.–33 :
11.–40 : 1. Le. 4 : 1.–5 : 14.–6 :
8, 19, 24.–7 : 22, 28.–8 : 1.–12 :
1.–14 : 1.–16 : 1.–17 : 1.–18 : 1.–
19 : 1.–20 : 1.–21 : 16.–22 : 1, 17,
26.–23 : 1, 9, 23, 26, 33.–24 : 1,
13.–25 : 1.–27 : 1. Nu. 3 : 5, 11,
14, 44.–4 : 21.–5 : 1, 5, 11.–6 : 1,
22.–7 : 4.–8 : 1, 5, 23.–9 : 9.–10 :
1.–13 : 1.–15 : 1, 17, 37.–16 : 23,
36, 44.–17 : 1.–18 : 25.–20 : 7.–
25 : 10, 16.–26 : 1, 52.–27 : 6.–
28 : 1.–31 : 1, 25.–33 : 50.–34 : 1,
16.–35 : 9.
13. L. s. unto Moses and Aaron, 7:
8.–12 : 1.–Le. 11 : 1.–13 : 1.–14
33.–15 : 1.–Nu. 2 : 1.–4 . 1, 17.–
12 : 4.–14 : 26.–16 : 20.–19 : 1.–
20 : 12, 23. [I will
Le. 10 : 3. This is it that the L. s.,
Nu. 3 : 1. day L. s. with Moses, 9 : 1.
5 : 4. as L. s. unto Moses
21 : 16. well whereof L. s. to Moses
De. 2 : 1. L. s. unto me, 2, 17.–9 : 13.
4 : 12. L. s. to you out of fire
15. no similitude in day L. s.
5:22. These words L.s. unto assem.
9 : 10. written all words L. s.
10 : 4. the ten com-ts which L. s.
Jos. 14 : 10. since L. s. this word to
12. This mountain whereof L. s.
1 S. 16:4. Sam. did that which L. s.
1 K. 2 : 4. L. continue word wh. he s.
27. fulfil word of L. which he s.
5 : 5. as L. s. unto David my fa.
8 : 20. L. hath performed word he
s., 2 K. 10 : 10.
12 : 15. perform his saying the L.
s. 2 Ch. 10 : 15.
13 : 26. according to word of L. he
s., 14 : 18.–16 : 12, 34.–17 : 16.–
22 : 38. 2 K. 10 : 10.–24 : 2.
15 : 29. acc. to saying of L. which
he s. by Ahijah, 2 K. 10 : 17.
21:23. And of Jezebel also s. the L.
2 K. 21 : 10. L. s. by ser-ts prophets
1 Ch. 21:9. L. s. unto Gad, Da.'s seer
2 Ch.33:10. L.s.to Manasseh and his
Is. 7 : 10. the L. s. again unto Ahaz
8 : 5. L. s. unto me again, saying
11. For L. s. to me wi. strong hand
20 : 2. same time s. L. by Isaiah
Je. 30 : 4. these are the words L. s.
50 : 1. word that L. s. ag. Babylon
51 : 12. L. hath done that wh. he s.
Jon. 2 : 10. the L. s. unto the fish
Ac.18:9.s.the L. to Paul in the night
See **SPAKE.**
[Referring to God or Lord.]
See **SPEAKETH,** and
Word of the LORD.

Spirit of the LORD.

Ju. 3 : 10. S.o.L. came upon Othniel
6 : 34. S. o. L. came upon Gideon
11 : 29. S. o. L. came upon Jepthah
13:25.S.o.L. began to move Sams.,
14 : 6, 19.–15 : 14.
1 S. 10 : 6. S. o. L. upon Saul
16 : 13. S. o. L. upon David
16 : 14. S. o. L. departed from Saul
2 S. 23 : 2. S. o. L. spake by me
1 K. 18 : 12. S.o.L. shall carry thee
22 : 24. Which way went S. o. L.
from me? 2 Ch. 18 : 23.
2 K. 2:16. lest S.o.L. hath taken him
2 Ch. 20 : 14. upon Jahaziel S. o. L.
Is. 11 : 2. S. o. L. sh. rest upon him
40 : 7. S. o. L. bloweth upon it
13. who hath directed S. o. L.
59 : 19. S. o. L. shall lift standard
61 : 1. S. o. L. is upon me, Lu. 4:18.
63 : 14. S. o. L. caused him to rest
Eze. 11 : 5. S. o. L. fell upon me
37 : 1. carried me out in S. o. L.

Mi. 2: 7. O Jac. is S. o. L. straitened
8: 8. I am full of power by S. o. L.
Ac. 5:9. How agreed to tempt S. o.L.
8:39. the S.o.L.caught away Philip
2 Co. 3: 17. S. o. L. is liberty
18. to glory, even as by S. o. L.
See **SPIRIT of God.**

LORD with spoken.

Ge. 12: 4. Abram departed as the L.
had s.,21: 1.-24: 51. Ex. 9: 12,
35. De. 6: 19.
Ex.4:30. Moses spake words L.had s.
19: 8. All that L. hath s. will we do
34: 32. gave in com-t all L. had s.
Le. 10: 11. teach statutes L. s.
Nu. 1: 48. L. had s. to Moses,15:22.
10: 29. L. hath s. good conc. Isr.
12: 2. Hath L. s. only by Moses?
23:17.Balak said, What hath L. s.?
De. 18: 21. word L. hath not s., 22.
Jos. 21:45.failed not aught L.had s.
1 S. 25: 30. L. shall have done the
good he hath s.
2 S. 3: 18. do it, for the L. hath s.
7:29.continue,for thou, O L.hast s.
1 K. 13: 3. is the sign L. hath s.
14: 11. for the L. hath s. it, Is. 1:
2.-21: 17.-22: 25.-24: 3.-25:
8. Joel 3: 8. Ob. 18. [18: 27.
22: 28. L. hath not s. by me, 2 Ch.
2 Ch. 18: 22. L. hath s. evil ag. thee
27. Micaiah said, hath not L. s.
by me [Job
Jb. 42: 7. after the L. had s. unto
Ps. 50: 1. L. hath s., and called
Is.16:13. L. hath s. conc. Moab | 14.
31: 4. thus hath L. s. unto me
38: 7. L. will do thing he hath s.
Je.13:15. be not proud, for L. hath s.
23: 35. sh. say, What hath L. s.,37.
27: 13. as the L. hath s. ag. nation
48: 8. be destroyed, as L. hath s.
Eze. 5: 13. I the L. have s. it, 15,
17.-17: 21, 24.-21: 32.-22: 14.-
24: 14.-26: 14.-30: 12.-34: 24.-
36: 36.-37: 14. [not s.
22: 28. thus saith L., when L. hath
23:34. I have s. it, saith the L.,26:
5.-28: 10.-39: 5. [s. it
Jo. 3: 8. sell to Sabeans, for L. hath
Am. 3: 1. Hear word L. hath s.
8. L. hath s. who but prophesy?
Mat. 1: 22. which was s. of L., 2:15.
Mk. 16: 19. after L. s. unto them
Ac. 9: 27. seen L. and that he s.
He. 2: 3. first began to be s. by L.
See **LORD God, I the LORD, Mouth of the LORD.**
See TABERNACLE, TABLE.

Temple of the LORD.

1 S. 1: 9. Eli sat by a post of t. o. L.
3: 3. ere lamp went out in t. o. L.
2 K. 11: 13. she came into t. o. L.
18: 16. cut gold fr. doors of t. o. L.
23: 4. bring out of t. o. L. vessels
24: 13. vessels Sol. made in t. o. L.
2 Ch. 26:16. Uzziah went into t. o. L.
27: 2. Jotham ent. not into t. o. L.
29: 16. took aw. uncleann. in t.o.L.
Ezr. 3: 6. founda. of t. o. L. not yet
10. laid founda. of t. o. L., Hag.
2: 18. [are these (3)
Je. 7: 4. The t. o. L. The t. o. L.
24: 1. baskets of figs set bef. t. o. L.
Eze. 8: 16. at door of t. o. L. 25
men, with back toward t. o. L.
Hag. 2. 15. bef. stone was laid in t.o.L.
Zch. 6: 12. shall build t. o. L., 13, 15.
14. crown for memorial in t. o. L.
Lu. 1: 9. Zach. went into t. o. L.
See TENTS, TESTIMONY, THINGS, THOUGHTS, THRONE.

To or unto the LORD.

Ge. 8: 20. Noah builded altar u. L.
12:7. Ab. built altar u. L., 8.-
14: 22. I have lifted hands t. L.
Ge. 18:27. tak. on me to speak t.L.,31.
Ex. 5: 17. let us do sacri. t.L., 8:8, 29.
10:9. must hold a feast u.L., 12:14.
-32: 5. Le. 23:39, 41. Nu. 29:12.
13: 12. shall set apart u. L. all
15: 1. sing u. L., 21. Ju. 5:3. 1 Ch.
16: 23. Ps. 13: 6.-30:4.-68:32.-
95: 1.-96:1, 2.-98:1, 5.-104:33.-
147: 7.-149: 1. Is. 12: 5.-42: 10.
Je. 20: 13.
16:25. to day a sab. u.L., 35:2. Le.
22: 20. sacrificeth save u.L. [25:2.
30:10. it is most holy u. L., 31:15.
Le. 28:20.-27: 21, 30, 32. Nu. 6:
8. Ezr. 8: 28. [Ac. 8: 24.
Nu. 21:7. said, pray u. L., Je.29:7.
29:39. things sh. do u. L. in feasts
De. 12:31. shalt not do so u. L. thy
Ju.11:35. opened my mouth u.L.,36.
17:3. I wholly dedicated silver u.L.
21: 8. that came not up t. L.
1 S. 1: 28. I have lent him t. L.
10. Hannah prayed u. L. and
8: 6. Samuel prayed u. L.
12: 17. I will call u. L.
14: 6. is no restraint t. L. to save
2 S. 21: 6. hang them up u. L.
1 K. 2:27. Abiat. fr. being priest u.L.
2 K. 4:33. Elisha prayed u. L.,6:18.
18:6. Hezekiah clave t.L. and kept
20:2. Hez. turned face prayed u.L.,
2 Ch. 32: 24. Is. 37: 15.-38: 2.
23: 23. this passover holden t. L.
1 Ch. 11:18. but poured it out t. L.
16:8. Give thanks u. L., 41. Ps. 92:
1.-105: 1.-106: 1.-107: 1.-118: 1.-
136: 1, 3.
-29: 22. anointed him u. L. chief
2 Ch. 13:11. they burn t. L. morning
24: 9. to bring t. L. the collection
30: 8. yield yours. u. L. and serve
Ps. 3: 8. Salvation belongeth u. L.
18:41. they cried u. L. he ans-d not
30:8. u. L. I made supplica., 142:1.
89:6. who be compared u. L. (2)
116: 12. What shall I render u. L.
140:6. I said t. L. Thou art my God
Pr. 3:32. abomination t. L., 11:1, 20.
-12: 22.-15: 8, 9, 26.-16: 5.-17:
15.-20: 10, 23.
16: 3. Commit thy works u. L.
19:17. pity upon poor lendeth u. L.
Is. 19: 21. shall vow a vow u. L.
22. they shall return even t. L.
23: 18. shall be holiness t. L., Je.
2: 3. Zch. 14: 20.
37:15. Hez. prayed u. t. L., 38: 2.
2 K. 20: 2. 2 Ch. 32: 24.
55: 13. shall be t. L. for a name
56:3. that hath joined hims. t.L.,6.
58:5. this an acceptable day t. L.?
Je. 32: 16. Jeremiah prayed u. L.
50: 5. Come, let us join ours. t. L.
Ho. 4: 10. left off to take heed t. L.
Jon. 4:2. Jonah prayed u. L. [(2)
Mi. 4:13. I will consecrate gain u.L.
7:7. thf. I will look u. L. [L.
Zch. 14:7. day, wh. shall be known t.
Mat. 5:33. perform u. L. thine oaths
Lu. 2: 22. to present him t. L.
23. Ev. male be called holy t. L.
Ac. 5:14. believers more added t. L.
11:23. exhorted they wo. cleave u.
13: 2. As they ministered u.L. [L.
14:23. they commended them t.L.
16: 15. If judged me faithful t. L.
Ro. 14: 6. regardeth it u. L. eateth
u. L. [die u. L.
8. whe. we live, we live u. L., we
2 Co. 8:5. first gave their selves t.L.
Ep. 5: 10. what is acceptable u. L.
22. submit as u. L., 6:7. Col. 3:23.
See CRIED, CRY, GIVE, RETURN.
See **TURN to the Lord.**
See TREASURE, S, TRIBES, TRUTH
See **TRUST, Put TRUST.**
See **TRUST in the LORD.**

Voice of the LORD, or LORD'S voice.

De. 30: 8. and obey v.o.L., Je. 26:
13.-38: 20.
Jos. 5: 6 because they obeyed not
the v.o.L., 1 S. 28: 18. 1 K. 20:
36. Je. 3: 25.-7: 28.-42: 13, 21.
-43: 4, 7.-44: 23. Da. 9: 10.
1 S. 15:19. Wh. didst not obey v.o.L.
20. Yea I have obeyed v. o. L.
22. sacrif. as in obeying v. o. L.?
Ps. 29: 3. v. o. L. is upon waters
4. The v.o.L. is powerful, full, 5
7. v. o. L. divideth flames of fire
8. The v. o. L. shaketh wildern.
9. The v.o.L. maketh hinds calve
106: 25. heark-d not unto v. o. L.
Is. 6: 8. I heard the v.o. L. saying
30. 31. thro. v.o.L. Assyr-s beaten
66:6. v.o.L. that rendereth recomp.
Je. 42: 6. we will obey v. o. L. (2)
Mi. 6: 9. L.'s v. crieth unto city
Hag. 1: 12. remnant obeyed v.o.L.
Zch. 6: 15. if diligently obey v.o.L.
Ac. 7: 31. v. o. L. came unto Moses

Way of the LORD.

Ge. 18:19. com. househ. to keep w.o.
Ju. 2: 22. whe. will keep w.o.L. [L.
2 K. 21: 22. Amon walked not in
w. o. L.
Pr. 10:29. w. o. L. is strength to upri.
Is. 40: 3. Prepare ye w.o.L, make,
Mat. 3: 3. Mk. 1: 3. Lu. 3: 4.
Je. 5: 4. they know not w. o. L.
5. great men, for they have known
w. o. L. [-33: 17, 20.
Eze. 18:25. w.o.L. is not equal, 29.
Ju. 1: 23. Make straight w. o. L.
Ac. 18: 25. Apollos instructed in w.

Ways of the LORD. [o.L.

2 S. 22:22. I kept w.o.L., Ps. 18:21.
2 Ch. 17: 6. Jehosh. lifted up in w.
Ps. 138:5. shall sing in w.o.L. [o.L.
Ho. 14: 9. for the w.o.L. are right
Ac. 13:10. to pervert right w.o. L.
See WATCH, WHIRLWIND.

Word of the LORD.

Ex. 9: 20. He th. feared w. o. L.
21. that regarded not w.o.L. left
Nu. 3: 16. according to the w.o.L.,
51.-4: 45.-36: 5. De. 34: 5. Jos. 8:
27.-19: 50.-22: 9. 1 K. 12: 24.-13:
26.-14: 18.-16: 12, 34.-17: 5, 16.
-22: 38. 2 K. 1: 17.-4: 44.-7: 16.-
9: 26.-14: 25.-23: 16.-24: 2. 1 Ch.
11: 3, 10.-12: 23.-15: 15. 2 Ch. 35:
6. Je. 13: 2.-32: 8. Jon. 3: 3.
15: 31. he hath despised w. o. L.
22:18. I can-t go beyond w. o. L.
De. 5:5. time to shew you w. o. L.
1 S. 3: 1. w.o.L. was precious [Sam.
7. nei. w. o. L. yet revealed unto
21. to Sam. in Shiloh by w. o. L.
15:23. bec. hast rejected w.o.L.,26.
2 S. 7:4. w.o.L. came unto Nathan
22: 31. w.o.L. is tried, Ps. 18: 30.
1 K. 2:27. fulfil w. o. L., 2 Ch. 36:21.
12: 24. They hearkened to w.o.L.
and retur., 2 Ch. 11: 4. Je. 37: 2.
13: 1. a man of God by w. o. L.
2. he cried ag. altar in w. o. L.
5. sign man of G. given by w.o.L.
9. so was charged me by w. o. L.
17. said by w.o.L. Thou sh. eat no
18. angel spake by w.o.L. Bring
20. w. o. L. came unto prophet
26. man disobed-t unto w. o. L.
32. saying he cried by w. o. L.
14: 18. buried him acc. to w. o. L.
17:24. w.o.L. in my mouth is truth
20:35. prophet said in w.o.L. Smite
22:5. Enquire at w.o.L., 2 Ch. 18:4.
2 K. 3: 12. Jehoshaphat said, w.o.
L. is with him [was w. o. L.
9: 36. This is w.o.L. | 15:12. This
10:10. unto earth noth. of w. o. L.
20:19. said, Good is w.o.L., Is. 39:8.

1 Ch. 10:13. committed ag. w.o.L.
2 Ch.30:12.com-t of king by w.o.L.
34:21. fathers not kept w. o. L.
36:22.that w.o.L.be accomp., Ezr. [1:1.
Ps. 33: 4. w. o. L. is right
6. By w.o.L. were heavens made
105:19. the w.o.L. tried him
Is. 2: 3. w.o.L.from Jerus. Mi. 4:2.
28:13. w.o.L.was precept on prec.
Je. 2: 31. O genera. see ye w. o. L.
6:10. w.o.L. unto them reproach,
8: 9. they rejected w.o.L. [20: 8.
17: 15. say, Where is the w. o. L.
25: 3. unto this day w.o.L. come
27:18. if the w.o.L. be with them
32:8.Then I knew this was w.o.L.
Ho. 1: 2. The beginning of the w. o. L. by Hosea, 1. [w. o. L.
Am. 8: 12.sh. run to and fro to seek
Zph. 2: 5. the w. o. L. is ag-t you
Zch.4:6.This is w.o.L. unto Zerub.
9: 1. The burden of the w. o. L. in Hadrach, 12: 1. Mal. 1:1. [o.L.
11:11.poor of flock knew it was w.
Lu. 22: 61. Peter rememb-d w.o.L.
Ac.8:25.when had preached w.o.L.
11: 16.Then remembered I w.o.L.
13: 48. glad, and glorified w.o.L.
49. w. o. L. was published thro-t
15: 35.Paul, B.preaching w. o. L.
36. go where we preached w.o.L.
16:32.they spake unto him w.o.L.
19. 10. all in Asia heard w. o. L.J.
1Th.1:8.fr.you sounded out w.o.L.
4: 15. we say unto you by w. o. L.
2 Th. 3: 1.w. o. L. have free course
1 Pe. 1.25.w.o. L. endureth for ev.

See **WORD of Lord came.**
See **WORD of God,**
HEAR word of the Lord.
See **LORD** with **spake.**

Words of the LORD.

1 S. 15:1.hearken thou unto w.o.L.
2 Ch. 11:4.they obeyed the w. o. L.
29:15. came by w. o. L. to cleanse
Je. 36: 6. go, read w. o. L. in ears of the people in L-'s house, 8.
11.when Micaiah heard all w.o.L.
37: 2. nei. hearken unto w. o. L.

See **WORDS of the Lord.**
See **WORDS of God.**

Work of the LORD.

Ex. 34:10. all peo. shall see w.o.L.
Is. 5: 12. they regard not w. o. L.
Je. 48:10. doeth w.o.L. deceitfully
50: 25. for this is the w. o. L.
51: 10. declare in Zion the w.o.L.
1 Co. 15: 58. abounding in w. o. L.
16: 10. he worketh w. o. L. as I

Works of the LORD.

Jos. 24: 31. had known all w. o. L.
Ju. 2: 7. had seen all great w.o.L.
Ps. 28: 5. they regard not w. o. L.
46: 8. Come, behold the w. o. L.
77: 11. I will remember w. o. L.
107:24. These see the w. o.L. and
111: 2. The w. o. L. are great
118: 17. I shall declare w. o. L.

See **WORK, S of God.**

Wrath of the LORD, or **LORD'S wrath.**

Nu.11:33.ere chewed w.o.L.kindled
De.11:17. L.'s w. be kindled ag.you
2 K. 22:13.great is w.o.L.,2 Ch.34: [21.
2 Ch. 12:12. w.o.L. turned fr.
29:8. the w.o.L. was upon Judah
32:26.w.o.L. came not upon them
36: 16. until w.o.L. arose ag. peo.
Ps. 106: 40. was w. o. L. kindled
Is.9:19.Thro. w.o.L.land darkened
13: 13. earth remove in w. o. L.
Je. 50:13. of w.o.L. not be inhabit.
Eze.7:19. gold not be able to deliver in day of w. o. L., Zph 1: 18.

See **WRATH of God.**

LORD. [As applied to angel.]

Ge. 19: 18. Lot said, Oh not so,my l.
Jos. 5: 14.What saith l. unto serv.?
Ju. 6: 13. O my l. if L. be with us
Da. 10: 16. O my l. my sorrows [l.
17.can serv. of my l. talk with my
19. I said, Let my l. speak.
12: 8. O my l. what sh. be the end?
Zch. 1: 9. O my l. what these? 4 4.-
4: 5. I said No, my l., 13. [6 4.

LORD. [As applied to man.]

Ge. 18: 12. I am old, my l. being old
23: 11. my l. hear me | 15 My l.
24 18.Drink, my l. and she [heark.
27:29.be l.over thy breth. [thy l.
37. Isaac ans-d I have made him
31: 35. Let it not displease my l.
32: 4. Thus speak unto my l. Esau
5. tell my l. th. I may find grace
18. a present sent unto my l. Esau
33: 8. find grace in sight of my l., 47: 25. [came home
39: 16. laid up garm. until his l.
40: 1. offended their l., k.'s of E.
7. with him in ward of l.'s house
42: 10. my l. to buy food are we
30 man who is l. of land, 33.
44: 5. in which my l. drinketh?+
8. sho. we steal out of l.'s house
9. we will be my l.'s bondmen
24. we told him words of my l.
45: 8. made me l. of all his house
9. God hath made me l. of all E.
47: 18. not hide it from my l. how nothing left in sight of my l.
Ex. 32: 22. anger of my l. wax hot
Nu. 11: 28. My l. Moses forbid th.
12: 11. My l. lay not sin upon us
32: 25. do as my l. com-th, 27.
36: 2. Lord com-d my l. to give la.
Ju. 3: 25. their l. was fallen dead
4: 18. Turn in my l. turn in to me
19: 26. woman fell where her l. was
27. her l. rose up in morning
Ru. 2: 13. favour in thy sight, my l.
1 S. 1: 15. my l. I am of sorrowful
26. O my l. I am woman
22: 12. he ans-d, Here I am my l.
24: 8. cried aft. Saul, saying, My l.
10. put forth my hand ag. my l.
25: 24. my l. upon me let this iniq.
25. Let not my l. regard this man
26. evil to my l. be as Nabal
27. young men that follow my l.
29. soul of my l. be bound in the
31. L. shall have dealt with my l.
26: 15. whf. not kept thy l. king?
17. It is my voice, my l., O k.
18. Whf. doth my l. pursue serv.?
29: 8. not fight ag. enemies of my l.
2 S 1: 10. brought them unto my l.
3: 21. will gather all Isr. to my l.
9: 11. Acc. to all my l.com-d [l., 13.
11: 9. Uriah slept with serv-s of his
13: 32. Let not my l. suppose they
14: 9. my l. the iniquity be on me
12. let handm. speak unto my l.
17. as angel of G. so is my l.
19. from aught my l. hath spoken
20. my l. is wise acc. to wisdom of
16: 9. Why dead dog curse my l.?
18: 31. Cushi said, Tidings, my l.
19: 19. Let not my l. impute iniq. day my l. went out of Jerus.
20. I am come first to meet my l.
30. my l. is come again in peace
35. serv. be a burden unto my l.
37. let him go over with my l.
20: 6. take thou thy l.'s servants
24: 3. th. eyes of my l. may see why my l. delight, 1 Ch. 21: 3.
22. Let my l. offer what seemeth
1 K. 1: 2. that my l. may get heat
27. Is this thing done by my l.
36. L. God of my l. king say so
37. As L. been with my l. king
2: 38. as my l. hath said, will I do
3: 17. O my l. I and woman dwell
26. O my l. give her living child
1 K.11:23. who fled fr. his l. Hadad-e
18: 7. Art thou that my l. Elijah?
13. Was it told my l. what I did?
14. tell thy l. Behold Elijah is
20: 4. My l. I am thine, and all I
9. Tell my l. all thou didst send
2 K.2:19. situation pleasant as my l.
4: 16. my l. do not lie to handm.
28. Did I desire a son of my l.?
5: 3. Wo. God my l. wi. prophet
4. One went in and told his l.
6: 12.one of serv-s said, None, my l.
26. wom. cried, Help my l. O k.
7:2. l. on whose hand k. leaned, 17.
8: 5. My l. this is the woman [l.?
12. Hazael said, Why weepeth my
9: 11. Jehu came to serv-s. of l.
18: 23. I pray give pledges to my l.
2 Ch. 2: 14. cunning men of my l.
Ezr. 10: 3. acc. to counsel of my l.
Ps. 12: 4. lips own, who l. over us?
Is. 21: 8. My l. I stand upon watch-
22:18. shame of l.'s house [tower
Jer.22:18.Ah l., or ah his glory, 34:5.
37: 20. hear now, I pray, my l.
38: 9. My l. these men done evil
Da. 1:10. said unto Dan., I fear my l.
2:10.is no l.that asked such things
4: 19. My l. the dream be to them
24. decree wh. is come upon my l.
Mat. 10: 24. nor is servant above l.
25. enough that serv. be as his l.
18: 26. l. have patience with me
31. told their l. all th. was done
20: 8. l. of vineyard, 21: 40. Mk. 12: 9. Lu. 20: 13, 15.
24:46. l. find so doing, Lu.12:36, 43.
48.My l.delayeth his coming, Lu. 12: 45. [19.-Lu. 12: 46.
50. l. of that serv. shall come, 25:
25: 11. saying l. l. open unto us
18.th. received one, hid l.'s money
21. l. said, enter into joy of thy l.
26. l. ans-d, Thou wicked serv. of thy l., 23. [their l.
Lu. 12: 36. like men that wait for
42. l. shall make ruler of his
46. l. of servant come in a day
47. Knew l.'s will, prepared not
13: 8. l. let it alone this year
14: 21. serv. showed l. these thing
22. l. it is done as thou com-d
16: 3. my l. taketh aw. stewardsh.
5. How much owest unto my l.?
8. l. commended unjust steward
19: 16. l. thy pound gained ten +
Jn. 15: 15. knoweth not his l.doeth
20. serv. not greater than l., 13:16
Ac. 25: 26. no thing to write unto
Ga. 4: 1. servant, tho. l. of all [l.
1 Pet.3:6. Sarah obeyed Ab. calling [him l.

LORDS.

Ge. 19: 2. Behold now my l. turn in
Nu. 21: 28. consumed l. of high pla.
De. 10: 17. is Lord of l., 1 Ti. 6: 15. Re. 17: 14. [3. 1 S.6: 16, 18.
Jos. 13: 3. five l. of Philis., Ju. 3:
Ju. 16: 5. l. of Philis. came, 8, 18.
23. l. of Philis. gathered, 27.
30. the house fell upon the l.
1 S. 5: 8. gathered l. of Philis., 11.
6: 4. one plague on you and l.
12. l. of Philis. went after them
16. when 5 l. of Philis. seen it, 18.
7: 7. l. of the Philis. went ag. Isr.
29: 2. the l. passed on by hundreds
6. nevertheless l. favour thee not
7. return, th. thou displease not l.
1 Ch. 12:19. l. of Philis.sent him aw.
Ezr. 8: 25. weighed off-gs l. off-d
Is.16: 8. l. of heathen broken plants
26: 13. other l. had domin. over us
Je. 2: 31. whf. say peo. We are l.?
Eze. 23: 23. great l. and renowned
Da. 4: 36. my l. sought unto me
5: 1. great feast to thous. of his l.
9. his l. were astonished

Da. 5:10. by words of king and his l.
23. thou and l. have drunk wine
6: 17. king with own signet of l.
Mk. 6: 21. Herod made supper to l.
1 Co. 8: 5. gods many, and l. many
1 Pe.5:3.Nei.as l.over God's heritage
LORDLY.
Ju. 5: 25. brought butter in l. dish
LORDSHIP. [25.
Mk. 10: 42. Gent. exercise l., Lu. 22:
LO-RU'HAMAH.
Ho. 1: 6. G. said, Call her name L.
8. when she had weaned L.
LOSE, LOSETH.
Ju.18: 25. upon thee, and l. thy life
1 K. 18:5. th. we l. not all the beasts
Jb. 31: 39. or caused owners l. life
Pr. 23: 8. and l. thy sweet words
Ec. 3: 6. time to get, a time to l.
Mat.10:39. he findeth his life shall l.
it, that l-th life for my sake, 16:
25. Mk. 8: 35. Lu. 9: 24.
42. he shall in no wise l. his reward, Mk. 9: 41.
16: 26. and l. his own soul, Mk. 8:
36. Lu. 9: 25. [piece
Lu. 15: 4. if he l. sheep | 8. if she l.
17: 33. whoso. l. life shall preserve
Jn. 6:39. Fa.'s will I l. nothing [it
12: 25. that loveth his life sh. l. it
2 Jn. 8. look we l. not those things
LOSS. [Noun.]
Ge. 31: 39. that torn, I bear l. of it
Ex. 21: 19. shall pay for l. of time
Is. 47: 8. nei. shall know l. of chil.
9. in day l. of chil. and widowh.
Ac. 27: 21. gained this harm and l.
22. sh. be no l. of any man's life
1 Co. 3: 15. if work burned, suffer l.
Ph. 3: 7. I counted l. for C.
8. yea, I count all things but l.
for C., for wh. I suff-d l. of all
LOST. [Actively.]
De. 22: 3. thing of thy bro.'s he l.
1 K. 20: 25. army like that thou l.
Is. 49: 20. after thou hast l. other
21. seeing I have l. my children
Mat. 5: 13. if salt l. savour, Mk. 9:
50. Lu. 14: 34. [had l.
Lu. 15: 9. I have found the piece I
Jn. 18: 9. Of th. gavest me, I l. none
LOST. [Passively.]
Ex. 22: 9. any l. thing, De. 22: 3.
Le. 6: 3. Or found that wh. was l.
4. shall restore l. thing be found
Nu. 6: 12. days before shall be l.
1 S. 9: 3. the asses of Kish were l.
20. asses that were l. are found
Ps. 119: 176. I astray like l. sheep
Je. 50: 6. My people been l. sheep
Eze. 19: 5. saw that her hope was l.
34: 4. nor ye sought that was l.
16. I will seek that which was l.
37: 11. they say, our hope is l.
Mat. 10: 6. go rather to l. sheep
15: 24. not sent but unto l. sheep
18: 11. Son is come to save l., Lu.
Lu. 15: 4. go aft. that is l. [19: 10.
6. have found my sheep was l.
24. my son was l. | 32. bro. was l.
Jn. 6:12. fragments that noth. be l.
17: 12. none is l. but son of perdi.
2 Co. 4:3. gospel hid, to them are l.
LOT. [Person.]
Ge. 11: 27. Haran begat L.
31. Zerah took L. [5.-13: 1.
12: 4. Ab. departed, L. with him,
13: 5. L. had flocks tents + [L.
7. strife betw. herdmen of Ab. and
8. unto L. Let there be no strife
11. L. chose plain of Jordan
12. L. dwelt in cities of plain
14: 12. took L. and his goods | 16.
19: 1. L. sat in the gate of Sodom
10. men pulled L. into house
15. the angels hastened L.
18. L. said, O not so my Lord
Ge.19: 23. sun risen wh. L. ent-d Zoar
29. G. sent L. out of overthrow
30. L. went up out of Zoar
36. both dau-s of L. with child
De.2:9. given Ar unto chil. of L., 19.
Ps. 83: 8. have holpen chil. of L.
Lu.17:28. as it was in the days of L.
29. day L. went out of Sodom
32. Remember L.'s wife
2 Pe. 2:7. deliv-d just L. vexed with
LOT.
Le.16:8. one l. for L. other for, 9, 10.
Nu. 26:55. land shall be divid. by l.
56. Acc. to the l. sh. be possess-n
33: 54. he sh. divide land by l. for
inheri., 36: 2. Jos. 13: 6.-19: 51.
Eze. 45: 1.-47: 22.-48: 29.
34: 13. land ye shall inherit by l.
36: 3. be taken fr. l. of our inheri.
De. 32: 9. Jacob is l. of his inheri.
Jos. 14: 2. By l. was their inheri.
15: 1. was the l. of Jud. [Manas., 2.
16: 1. l. of Joseph | 17: 1. l. for
17: 14. Why given me but one l.?
17. thou shalt not have one l. only
18: 11. l. of tribe of Benj. came
19: 1. second l. came to Simeon
10. third l. came for Zebulon
17. fourth l. came to Issachar
24. fifth l. for Asher | 32. sixth l.
40. seventh l. for Dan [to Naph.
21: 4. l. for families of Kohathites,
5, 20. 1Ch. 6: 54, 61. [unto Lev.
6. Gershon had by l. | 8. by l.
10. theirs was the first l.
40. by their l. twelve cities
23: 4. have divided unto you by l.
Ju. 1: 3. Come into my l. to fight
Can-s, I will go into thy l.
20: 9. we will go up by l. ag. it
1 S.14: 41. Saul said, Give a perfect l.
1 Ch. 6: 63. sons of Merari by l., 65.
16: 18. Unto thee Canaan the l. of
your inheritance, Ps 105: 11.
24: 5. Thus were they divided by l.
7. first l. came to Jehoiarib, sec.
8. The third to Harim, fourth to
9. fifth to Malchijah, sixth to M.
10. seventh to Hakkoz, eighth to
11. ninth to Jeshuah, 10th to S. [A.
12. eleventh to Eliashib, twelfth
13. 13th to Huppah, 14th to Jesh.
14 15th to Bilgah, 16th to Immer
15. 17th to Hazir, 18th to Aphses
16. 19th to Pethahiah, 20th to J.
17. one and 20th to Jachin, two
and 20th to Ga. [four and 20th
18. three and 20th to Delaiah,
25: 9 first l. for Asaph, second to
10. third to Zaccur | 11. fourth to
12. fifth to Nethaniah | 13. 6th to
14. seventh to Jesharelah | 15. 8th
16. ninth to Mattaniah | 17. tenth
18. 11th to Azareel | 19. 12th to H.
20. 13th to Shubael | 21. 14th to
22. 15th to Jeremoth | 23. 16th to
24. 17th to Joshbek-h | 25. 18th to
26. 19th to Mallothi | 27. 20th to
28. The one and 20th to Hothir
29. two and 20th to G. [and 20th
30. three and 20th to | 31. four
26: 14. l. eastward fell; l. northw.
Es. 3: 7. cast l. bef. Haman, 9: 24.
Ps. 16: 5. thou maintainest my l.
125: 3. not rest upon l. of righte.
Pr. 1: 14. Cast in thy l. among us
16:33. l. is cast into lap [cease
18: 18. l. causeth contentions to
Is. 17: 14. is l. of them th. rob us
34: 17. he hath cast l. for them
57:6. smooth stones of stream thy l.
Je. 13: 25. This is thy l. from me
Eze. 24: 6. let no l. fall upon it
Da. 12: 13. in thy l. at end of days
Jon. 1: 7. the l. fell upon Jonah
Mi. 2:5. none that cast a cord by l.
Lu. 1: 9. his l. was to burn incense
Ac. 1: 26. the l. fell upon Matthias
8: 21. Thou nei. part nor l. in this
13: 19. he divided their land by l.
LOTS.
Mat. 27: 35. parted his garments,
casting l. (2), Mk. 15: 24. [Mat-s
Ac. 1: 26. gave their l.; lot fell upon
See **CAST lots.**
LO'TAN. [38.
Ge. 36: 20. sons of Seir; L., 1 Ch. 1:
22. chil. of L., 1Ch. 1: 39. | 29. duke L.
LOTHE, ING. See LOATHE,
LOUD, LOUDER. [ING.
Ex. 19: 16. trumpet exceed-g l. [l-r
19. voice of trumpet waxed l-r and
2 Ch. 30: 21. singing with l. instru.
Ezr. 3: 13. people shouted with l.
Ne. 12: 42. singers sang l. [shout
Es. 4: 1. Mord. cried with a l. cry
Ps. 33: 3. play skilfully with a l. noise
98: 4. make a l. noise and rejoice
150: 5. Praise him upon l. cymbals
Pr. 7: 11. She is l. and stubborn
Re. 14: 18. angel cried with a l. cry
See **Loud VOICE, S.**
LOVE, S. [Noun.] [her
Ge. 29: 20. few days for l. he had to
1 S. 20: † 17. to swear by his l. tow.
2 S. 1: 26. passing the l. of women
13: 15. hatred was greater than l.
Pr. 5: 19. be ravished with her l.
7: 18. Come let us take our fill of l.;
let us solace ours. with l-s [sins
10: 12. stirreth strifes, l. covereth
15: 17. a dinner of herbs where l. is
17: 9. covereth transgr-n seeketh l.
27: 5. rebuke better than secret l.
Ec. 9: 1. no man knoweth l. or hatr.
6. their l. and hatred is perished
Can. 2: 4. banner over me was l.
5. comfort me, I am sick of l., 5: 8.
3: 10. midst being paved with l.
7: 6. art thou, O l. for delights!
12. there will I give thee my l-s
8: 6. l. is strong as death, jealousy
7. Many waters can-t quench l. if
man give his substance for l.
Je. 2: 2. the l. of thy espousals
33. Why trimmest way to seek l.?
12: † 7. given l. of my soul to ene.
31: 3. loved thee with an everl. l.
Eze. 16: 8. thy time was time of l.
23: 11. corrupt in her inordinate l.
17. the Bab-s to her into bed of l.
33: 31. with mouth shew much l.
† 32. thou art a song of l-s
Da. 1: 9. bro-t Dan. into tender l.
Ho. 3: 1. acc. to l. of L. toward Isr.
11: 4. I drew them wi. bands of l.
Mat. 24: 12. l. of many wax cold
Jn. 13: 35. if ye have l. one to ano.
15: 13. Greater l. no man than th. s
17: 26. l. whw. hast loved me
Ro. 8: 35. Who separate fr. l. of C.?
12: 9. Let l. be without dissimula.
10. affectioned with brotherly l.
13: 10. l. worketh no ill, l. is fulfill-g
15: 30. I beseech for l. of Spirit
2 Co. 2: 4. may kn. l. I have unto you
8. wo. confirm your l. tow. him
5: 14. l. of Christ constraineth us
6: 6. by Holy Gh., by l. unfeigned
8: 8. prove sincerity of your l.
24. to churches proof of your l.
13: 11. God of l. sh. be with you
Ga. 5: 6. faith wh. worketh by l.
13. brethren by l. serve one ano.
22. fruit of the Spirit is l. joy
Ep. 1: 15. heard of your l. to saints
3: 19. to know the l. of C. passeth
6: 23. and l. with faith. from God
Ph. 1: 9. pray, your l. may abound
17. other of l. doth preach Christ
2: 1. if there be any comfort of l.
2. likeminded, having same l.
Col. 1: 4. l. which ye have to all saints
8. Who declared to us your l.

1 Th. 1:3. rememb-g your labour of
3:12.abound in l. one tow. ano. [l.
4:9. touching brotherly l. ye need
5: 8. breastplate of faith and l.
2 Th. 2: 10. rec-d not l. of truth
1 Ti. 1:14. abundant wi. faith and l.
6: 10. l. of money is root of evil
11. follow after righteousness, l.
2 Ti. 1: 7. not spirit of fear, but l.
Phm. 9. for l-s sake I beseech thee
He. 6: 10. to forget your work of l.
10: 24. provoke unto l. and good
13: 1. let brotherly l. continue
1 Pe. 1:22. unfeigned l. of brethren
1 Jn. 2: 15. l. of Fa. is not in him
3: 1. behold what manner of l. Fa.
4: 7. let us love one ano. l. is of G.
8. G. is l. | 10. Herein is l. not
that we loved G. [God is l.
16. known the l. God hath to us,
17. Herein is our l. made perfect
18. no fear in l. perfect l. casteth
2 Jn.6.is l.that we walk after com-ts
Jude 2. peace and l. be multiplied

LOVE of God.

Lu.11:42.ye pass judgm. and l.o.G.
Jn. 5:42. ye have not l.o.G. in you
Ro. 5:5. l.o.G. is shed in our hearts
8: 39. to separate us from l. o. G.
2 Co. 13: 14. l.o.G. be with you all
2 Th. 3: 5. direct hearts into l.o.G.
Tit. 3:4. after the l. o. G. appeared
1 Jn. 2: 5. in him l. o. G. perfected
3: 16. Hereby perceive we l. o. G.
17. how dwelleth l. o. G. in him
4:9. In this was manifested l.o. G.
5: 3. is l.o.G. that we keep com-ts
Jude 21. Keep yours. in the l.o.G.

His LOVE.

De.7:7.L.did not set h. l. upon you
Ps. 91: 14. Bec. hath set h.l. upon
Is.63:9.in h.l.and pity redeemed [me
Zph. 3: 17. he will rest in h. l.
Jn. 15:10. kept com-ts abide in h.l.
Ro. 5: 8. God commended h. l. to-
ward us [loved us
Ep. 2: 4. G. for h. great l. wh w he
1 Jn. 4: 12. if love one another h.
l. is perfected

In LOVE.

1 K. 11:2. Sol. clave unto these i.l.
Is. 38: 17. i. l. to my soul deliv-d it
1 Co.4:21.unto you with rod, or i.l.
2 Co. 8: 7. as ye abound i. l. to us
Ep.1:4. without blame bef. him i.l.
3: 17. rooted and grounded i. l.
4: 2. forbearing one another i. l.
15. but speaking the truth i. l.
16. to edifying of itself i. l.
5:2.walk i. l. as Ch. hath loved us
Col. 2:2. hearts comforted, knit i.l.
1 Th. 3: 12. L. make you incr. i. l.
5:13. esteem highly i. l. for work's
2 Ti.1:13.i. faith and l. in Ch. Jesus
1 Jn. 4:16. dwelleth i. l. dw-h in G.
18. no fear i. l. that feareth not
made perfect i. l. [and l.
2 Jn.3. Jesus the Son of Fa. i. truth

My LOVE. [saries

Ps. 109:4. For m. l. they are adver-
5. rewarded me hatred for m. l.
Can. 1:9. compared, O m. l. to hors.
15. behold thou art fair, m. l.,4: 1.
2:2. as lily, so is m. l. am dang-s
7. nor awake m. l. till he please,
3:5.-8:4. [fair m. l.
10. Rise up m. l., 13. | 4:7. art all
5: 2. Open to me m. l. my dove
6: 4. beautiful, O m. l. as Tirzah
Jn. 15: 9. continue ye in m. l. [l.
10. if keep com-ts sh. abide in m.
1 Co. 16:24. m.l. be with you all in

Thy LOVE. [C. J.

2 S.1:26. t. l. was wonderful, passing
Can.1:2.t. l. better than wine,4:10.
4. remember t. l. more than wine
4: 10. How fair is t. l. my sister

Phm. 5. Hearing of t. l. and faith
7. we have great joy in t. l.
Re. 2:4. bec. thou hast left t. first l.

LOVE. [Verb.]

Le. 19: 18. l. neighb. as thyself, 34.
Mat. 19: 19.-22: 39. Mk. 12:31.
De. 6: 5. shalt l. the Lord thy God
with all thy heart, 10:12.-11:1,
13, 22.-19: 9.-30:6. Mat. 22:37.
Mk. 12: 30, 33. Lu. 10: 27.
7:9. cov. with them l. him. Da.9:4.
13. he will l. thee, bless thee
10: 15. a delight in thy fa.'s to l.
19. l. stranger, ye were strangers
13: 3. to know whether ye l. L.
30:16.in th.I command thee to l.L.
20. That thou mayest l. the L.
Jos.22:5.take heed to l.the L.,23:11.
Ju. 5:31. them th. l. him be as sun
1 S 18: 22. king's servants l. thee
2 Ch.19:2.thou l. them that hate L.?
Ne. 1:5. keepeth mercy for th. l.him
Ps. 4:2. how long will ye l. vanity?
5:11. let. th. l. thy name be joyful
18:1. will l. thee, O L. my strength
31: 23. O l. the Lord, all ye saints
40:16.let such as l.thy salva.,70:4.
69: 36. that l. his name sh. dwell
97:10.Ye that l. the Lord hate evil
119: 132. those that l. thy name
165.Gr. peace they who l. thy law
122:6. they sh. prosper that l. thee
145:20. L. preserveth them l. him
Pr.1:22. How long will ye l. simplic.
4:6. l. wisdom, she shall keep thee
8:36. all they that hate me,l.death
9:8.rebuke wise man he will l.thee
16:13. kings l. him speaketh right
18:21. that l. it shall eat the fruit
Ec. 3: 8. time to l. a time to hate
Can. 1: 3. thf. do the virgins l. thee
4. more than wine, upright l.thee
Is. 56: 6. to serve and l. name of l.
61:8. I the Lord l. judgm., I hate
66:10. be glad with Jerus. th. l. her
Je. 5: 31. my people l. to have it so
Ho. 3: 1. l. a woman belov., l. wine
4: 18. her rulers with shame do l.
9: 15. drive out, I will l. them no
14:4. I will l. them freely [more
Am.4:†5. publish free off-gs, so ye l.
5:15. Hate the evil and l. the good
Mi. 3:2. Who hate good and l. evil
6:8. to l. mercy and walk humbly
Zch. 8:17. l. no false oath | 19. l. the
Mat.5:43. said, l.thy neighb. [truth
44. l. your enemies, Lu. 6:27, 35.
46. if l. them l. you, Lu. 6: 32.
6:5. they l. to pray, in synagogues
24. hate one l. other, Lu. 16: 13.
23:6. l. uppermost rooms at feasts
Mk. 12:38. l. to go in long clothing
Lu. 7: 42. which will l. him most?
11:43.l.greetings in markets,20:46.
Jn.14:21. I will l. him and manifest
23. if man l. me, Fa. will l. him
15:19. if of world, world l. his own
Ro. 8:28. all for good, to th. l. God
13: 9. thou shalt l. thy neighbour
as thyself, Ga. 5: 14. Ja. 2: 8.
1 Co. 2:9. prepared for them l. him
8:3. if any man l. G. same is known
Ep. 5:25 Husbands l. your wives as
C. loved ch., 28, 33. Col. 3: 19.
6: 24. Grace be with all l. our L.
2 Ti. 4:8. them that l. his appearing
Tit. 2:4. teach yo. wom. to l. husb.
3:15. Greet them l. us in the faith
Ja. 1:12. promised to th. l. him,2:5.
1 Pe. 1: 8. having not seen ye l.
2: 17. Honour all men, l. brother-
3:8. l. as brethren [hood
10. he that will l. life [l. world
1 Jn. 2: 15, l. not world,if any man
3:14. fr. death unto life, bec. we l.
4:19. l. him, bec. he first loved us
20. how l. God whom not seen?

1 Jn.4:21.who loveth God,l.his bro.
5:2. we l. chil. of God, when we l.

I LOVE. [G.

Ge. 27:4. savoury meat, such as I l.
Ex. 21: 5. if serv. say, I l. master
Ju. 16:15. How say, I l. thee when
2 S. 13: 4. I l. Tamar Abs.'s sister
Ps. 116: 1. I l. Lord, bec. he heard
119: 97. O how I l. thy law
113. thy law do I l., 163.
119. therefore I l. thy testimonies
127. I l. thy com-ts above gold
159. Consid. how I l. thy precepts
167. thy testimonies I l.exceed-ly
Pr. 8: 17. I l. them that l. me
Is. 61: 8. I the L. l. judgment
Jn. 14:31. world may know I l. Fa.
21: 15. knowest I l. thee, 16, 17.
2 Co. 12:15. more I l. you, less I be
1 Jn. 4: 20. if a man say, I l. God
2 Jn. 1. I l. in the truth, 3 Jn. 1.
Re. 3:19. As many as I l. I rebuke

LOVE me.

Ge. 29:32. now my husb. will l. m.
Ex. 20: 6. shewing mercy unto them
l. m., De. 5:10. [herit subst.
Pr.8:21.cause those that l.m.to in-
Jn.8:42.If G.your Fa. you wo. l.m.
10: 17. thf. doth my Fa. l. m.
14:15. If ye l. m., keep my com-ts
23. l. m., he will keep my words

LOVE not. [poverty

Pr. 20: 13. l. n. sleep, lest come to
1 Co. 16: 22. If any man l. n. L. J.
2 Co. 11: 11. because I l. you n.?
1 Jn. 2: 15. l. n. the world
3:18.let us n. l.in word nei.tongue

LOVE one another.

Jn. 13:34. as I loved you l. o. a.(2)
15: 12. com-t That ye l. o. a., 17.
Ro. 13:8.Owe nothing, but to l.o.a.
1 Th. 4:9. are taught of G. to l.o.a.
1 Pe. 1: 22. see ye l.o.a. with pure
1 Jn. 3:11. heard fr. beginning that
ye l. o. a., 4: 7, 11. 2 Jn. 5.
23.l.o.a.as he gave us command-t
4: 12. If we l. o. a. God dwelleth

LOVED.

Ge. 24:67. Isaac took Rebek., l. her
25:28. Isaac l. Esau, Rebek. l. Ja.
27: 14. mother made as his fa l.
29: 18. Jacob l. Rachel more than
34:3. Shechem l. Dinah [Leah, 30.
37:3. Isr. l. Joseph more than all,
De. 4:37. bec. he l. thy fathers [4.
7: 8. bec. Lord l. you, 23:5.-33:3.
Ju. 16:4. Samson l. wom. in Sorek
1 S. 1: 5. Elkanah l. Hannah
16:21. Saul l. Da. [soul, 3.-20: 17.
18:1. Jonathan l. Dav. as his own
16. Israel and Judah l. David
20. Michal, Saul's dau., l. Da.,28.
2 S. 12: 24. name Sol.; Lord l. him
13:1. Amnon l. Tamar [her
15. hatred greater than love he l.
1 K.3:3. Sol.l.L.walking in statutes
10: 9. bec. L l. Isr., 2 Ch. 9: 8.
11:1. Sol. l. many strange women
2 Ch. 2:11. L. l. his peo., Is. 48:14.
11: 21. Rehob. l. Maachah ab. all
26: 10. Uzziah, he l. husbandry
Es. 2: 17. king l. Esther above all
Jb. 19:19. whom I l. are turned ag.
Ps. 47: 4. excellency of Jac. he l.
78:68. chose mount Zion wh. he l.
109: 17. As he l. cursing, so let it
Isa. 38: † 17. hast l. me fr. the pit
Je. 8: 2. host of heav. they have l.
14:10. Thus have they l. to wander
Eze. 16: 37. gather all thou hast l.
Ho. 9:1. thou hast l. a reward upon
10. abomin-s were acc. as they l.
11: 1. When Isr. a child, I l. him
Mal. 1: 2. Wherein hast thou l. us?
2:11. profaned holiness of L. he l.
Mk. 10: 21. Jesus beholding, l. him
Lu. 7:47. forgiven, for she l. much

Jn. 3: 16. God so l. the world
19. l. darkness rather than light
11:5. Jes. l. Martha and her sister
36. said, Behold how he l. him
12: 43. they l. praise of men more
13:1. having l. his own, he l. them unto the end [-21: 7, 20.
23. disciple Jesus l., 19:26.-20:2.
14:21. loveth me sh. be l. of my Fa.
28. if ye l. me, ye would rejoice
15: 9. As Fa. l. me, so I l. you
16:27. Fa. loveth you, bec. ye l. me
17: 23. hast l. th., as thou l. me
26. love whw. thou hast l. me
Ro. 8:37. conquerors thro. him th. l.
2 Co. 12:15. more I love, less I be l.
Ga. 2: 20. who l. me, and gave
Ep. 2: 4. great love whw. he l. us
5: 2. As C. l. us | 25. C. l. church
2 Th. 2: 16. God our Fa. hath l. us
2 Ti. 4: 10. Demas having l. world
He. 1: 9. thou hast l. righteousn.
2 Pe. 2:15. Balaam l. wages of unri.
1 Jn. 4:10. not that we l. God, but that he l. us [first l. us
11. if God so l. us | 19. bec. he
Re. 1:5. Unto him l. and washed us
12: 11. they l. not lives to death

I have or have I LOVED.

Ps. 26: 8. I h. l. habita. of thy ho.
119:47. commands which I h. l., 48.
Is. 43: 4. I h. l. thee, therefore will
Je. 2: 25. I h. l. strangers, aft. th.
31: 3. I h. l. with everlasting love
Mal. 1:2. I h. l. you, Yet ye say [12.
Jn. 13: 34. as I h. l. you, ye also, 15:
15:9. As Fa. loved me, so I l. you
Ro. 9: 13. Jacob h. I l. but Esau
Re. 3:9. make them kn. I h. l. thee

LOVEDST.

Is. 57: 8. thou l. their bed where
Jn. 17:24. thou l. me bef foundation

LOVELY.

2 S. 1: 23. Saul and Jona. were l.
Can. 5:16. he is altogether l. O daugh.
Eze. 33: 32. art as a very l. song
Ph. 4: 8. whatsoever things are l.

LOVER.

1 K. 5: 1. Hiram was l. of David
Ps. 88:18. l. and friend hast put far
Tit. 1: 8. l. of hospitality, as l. of

LOVERS. [good men

Ps. 38: 11. my l. stand aloof fr. my
Je. 3:1. played harlot with many l.
4: 30. thy l. will despise thee
22:20. cry, for thy l. are destroyed
22. thy l. shall go into captivity
30: 14. thy l. have forgotten thee
La. 1:2. am. her l. none to comfort
19. called for l. they deceived
Eze. 16: 33. givest gifts to thy l.
36. nakedness discovered with
37. I will gather thy l. [thy l.
23: 5. Aholah doted on her l.
23: 9. I deliv-d her into hand of l.
22. I will raise up thy l. ag. thee
Ho. 2: 5. I will go after my l.
7. shall follow her l. [of l.
10. discover her lewdness in sight
12. rewards my l. have given me
13. went aft. her l. and forgat me
8:9. Ephr. hath hired l. [selves
2 Ti. 3: 2. men be l. of their own
4. l. of pleasures more than l. of

LOVEST. [God

Ge. 22: 2. take son Isaac thou l.
Ju. 14: 16. dost hate, and l. me not
2 S. 19:6. that thou l. thine enemies
Ps. 45: 7. Thou l. righteousness
52:3. Thou l. evil more than good
4. Thou l. all devouring words
Ec. 9:9. Live joyfully with wife thou
Jn. 11: 3. whom thou l. is sick [l.
21: 15. Simon, l. thou me? 16, 17.

LOVETH.

Ge. 27:9. meat for fa., such as he l.
44:20. little, and his father l. him
De. 10: 18. Lord l. the stranger in
15:16. I will not go bec. he l. thee
Ru. 4: 15. dau. in law who l. thee
Ps. 11: 5 and him that l. violence
7. righte. Lord l. righte-n., 33:5.
34: 12. what man l. many days?
37: 28. Lord l. judgment, 99: 4.
87:2. L. l. gates of Zion more than
119:140. word is pure, thy serv. l.
146: 8. L. l. the righteous [recteth
Pr. 3: 12. For whom Lord l. he cor-
12:1. Whoso. l. instruc-n, l. knowl.
13:24. he th. l. him, chasten-h him
15: 9. l. him that foll-h righte-sn.
12. scorner l. not one reproveth
17: 17. a friend l. at all times
19. l. transgression that l. strife
19: 8. getteth wisdom l. own soul
21:17. l. pleasure, he that l. wine
22:11 He that l. pureness of heart
29:3. Whoso. l. wisdom rejoiceth fa.
Ec. 5: 10. l. silver, that l. abund.
Can. 1: 7. O thou whom my soul l.
3:1. on bed I sought him wh. soul l.
2. I will seek him wh. my soul l.
3. Saw ye him whom my soul l.
4. I found him whom my soul l.
Is. 1:23. ev. one l. gifts and follow-h
Ho. 10:11. Ephr. as heifer l. to tread
12: 7. merchant he l. to oppress
Mat. 10:37. that l. father or mother, he th. l. son or dau. more than
Lu. 7: 5. For he l. our nation
47. little forgiven same l. little
Jn. 3: 35. The Father l. Son, 5: 20.
12:25. He that l. his life sh. lose it
14: 21. hath my comt-s, he it is l. me, l. me be loved of my Fa.
24. l. me not, keepeth not sayings
16: 27. the Father himself l. you
Ro. 13: 8. l. ano. hath fulfill. law
2 Co. 9: 7. for G. l. a cheerful giver
Ep. 5: 28. that l. his wife l. hims.
He. 12:6. wh. Lord l. he chasteneth
1 Jn. 2: 10. He that l. his brother
3:10. l. not bro. is not of G. [8, 20.
14. l. not bro. abideth in death, 4:
4: 7. every one l. is born of God
21. he who l. G. love brother also
5:1. l. him th. begat, l. him begotten
3 Jn. 9. Diotrephes l. preeminence
Re. 22: 15. whoso. l. and mak. a lie

LOVING.

2 S. 19: † 6. by l. thine enemies
Pr. 5: 19. Let her be as the l. hind
22: 1. l. favour rather than silver
Is. 56:10. lying down, l. to slumber

LOVINGKINDNESS, ES.

Ps. 17: 7. Shew marvellous l., 92:2.
25: 6. Remember L. thy l-s
26: 3. thy l. is before mine eyes
36: 7. How excellent is thy l.
10. O continue thy l. unto them
40: 10. I have not concealed thy l.
11. let l. continually preserve me
42: 8. Lord will command his l.
48: 9. We have thought of thy l.
51:1. have mercy upon me acc. to l.
63: 3. thy l. is better than life
69: 16. Hear me, thy l. is good
88: 11. thy l. be declared in grave?
89:33. my l. will I not take fr. him
49. where are thy former l-s?
92: 2. To shew l. in the morning
103: 4. who crowneth thee with l.
107: 43. shall understand l. of L.
119: 88. Quicken me after l., 159.
149. Hear my voice acc. to l.
138: 2. will praise thy name for l.
143: 8. Cause me to hear thy l. in
Is. 63: 7. will mention the l-s of L. acc. to multitude of his l-s
Je. 9: 24. Lord which exercise l.
16: 5. taken aw. my peace, even l.
31: 3. with l. have I drawn thee
32: 18. shewest l. unto thousands
Ho. 2:19. betroth thee unto me in l.

LOW.

De. 28: 43. shalt come down very l.
Ju. 1:†9. Canaanites in l. countries
1 S. 2: 7. L. bringeth l. and lifteth
1 Ch. 27: 28. syc. trees in l. plains
2 Ch. 9: 27. syc. trees in l. plains
26: 10. much cattle in l. country
28: 18. invaded cities of l. country
Jb. 5:11. To set on high those be l.
22:†29. save him that hath l. eyes
40: 12. look on proud bring him l.
Ps. 49:2. Both high and l. rich and
62: 9. men of l. degree are vanity
136: 23. rememb-d us in l. estate
Pr. 29:23. A man's pride bring him l.
Ec. 10: 6. the rich sit in l. place
12: 4. sound of the grinding is l.
Is. 2:17. haughtiness of men bro-t l.
13: 11. I will lay l. haughtiness
25:12. the high fort shall he lay l.
26: 5. the lofty city he layeth it l.
29: 4. thy speech be l. out of dust
32: 19. city sh. be l. in a l. place
40:4. ev. mt. and hill sh. be made l.
La. 3:55. I called out of l. dungeon
Eze. 17: 6. spreading vine of l. stat.
24. know I have exalted l. tree
21: 26. exalt him that is l. abase
26: 20. set thee in l. parts of earth
29: † 14. shall be there a l. kingd.
Lu. 1: 48. l. estate of his handmaid
52. exalted them of l. degree
Ro. 12:16. condescend to men of l. est
Ja. 1: 9. brother of l. degree rejoice
10. the rich in that he is made l.

See **BROUGHT low.**

LOWER. [make ark

Ge. 6: 16. with l. 2d and 3d stories
Le. 13: 20. if rising l. than the skin, 26.
21. if it be no l. than the skin
14: 37. in sight are l. than wall
Ne. 4:13. I set in l. places the people
Jb. 12: † 3. I fall not l. than you
Ps. 8: 5. hast made him a little l. than the angels, He. 2: 7, 9.
63: 9. into l. parts of earth
Pr. 25:7. be put l. in pres. of prince
Is. 22: 9. gath-d waters of l. pool
44: 23. shout ye l. parts of earth
Eze. 40: 18. was the l. pavement
19. meas-d fr. forefront of l. gate
42: 5. than the l. and middlemost
43: 14. fr. bottom even to l. settle
Ep. 4: 9. descended 1st into l. parts

LOWERING or LOWRING.

Mat. 16: 3. It will be foul weather to day; for the sky is red and l.

LOWEST.

De. 32: 22. shall burn unto l. hell
1 K. 12: 31. made priests of l. of people, 13: 33. 2 K. 17: 32.
Ps. 86: 13. delivered soul fr. l. hell
88: 6. Thou hast laid me in l. pit
139:15. wrought in l. parts of earth
Eze. 41: 7. increased fr. l. chamber
42: 6. was straitened more than l.
Lu. 14:9. wi. shame to take l. room
10. go and sit down in l. room

LOWETH, ING.

1 S. 6: 12. the kine went along l-g
15:14. What meaneth l-g of oxen?
Jb. 6: 5. l-h the ox over his fodder?

LOWLINESS.

Ep. 4: 2. that ye walk with all l.
Ph. 2:3. in l. of mind let each esteem

LOWLY.

Ps. 138: 6. hath he respect unto l.
Pr. 3:34. but he giveth grace unto l.
11: 2. but with l. is wisdom
16:19. to be of humble spirit with l.
Zch. 9: 9. l. and riding upon an ass
Mat. 11: 29. for I am meek and l.

LU'BIM, S. [16:8.

2 Ch. 12: 3. out of E. L-s Sukkiim
Na. 3: 9. Put and L. thy helpers

LU'CAS=LUKE.

Phm. 24. Demas, L. my fellow lab-s

LU'CIFER.
Is. 14 : 12. How art thou fallen, O L.
LU'CIUS.
Ac. 13 : 1. teachers Barnabas, L.
Ro. 16 : 21. L. Sosipater salute you
LUCRE.
1 S. 8 : 3. Sam.'s sons turned after l.
1 Ti. 3 : 3. not greedy of filthy l., 8.
Tit.1:7.a bishop not given to filthy l.
11. teaching thi. not for filthy l.'s
1 Pe. 5:2. feed flock not for filthy l.
LUD. [17.
Ge. 10:22. chil. of Shem ; L., 1 Ch.1:
Is.66:19.nations,Pul.L. | Eze.27:10.
LU'DIM.
Ge. 10:13. Mizraim begat L.,1 Ch.1:
LU'HITH. [11.
Is. 15:5. mounting up of L.,Je.48:5.
LUKE = LU'CAS.
Col. 4: 14. L. the beloved physician
2 Ti.4 : 11. only L. is with me, bring
LUKEWARM. [Mk.
Re. 3 : 16. then because thou art l.
LUMP, S. [raisins
1 S. 25 : † 18. Abigail took 100 l-s
2 K.20:7. Take a l. of figs, Is.38:21.
Ro. 9 : 21. of same l. one vessel to
11 : 16. if firstfruit holy l. is holy
1 Co. 5: 6. leaveneth the l., Ga.5:9.
7. purge out, that ye be a new l.
LUNATIC.
Mat. 4 : 24. which were l. he healed
17 : 15. have mercy on my son, he
LURK, LURKING. [is l.
1 S. 23 : 23.knowl. of all l-g places
Ps.10:8. He sitteth in the l-g places
17:12. young lion l-g in secret pla.
Pr. 1:11. let us l. privily for inuoc.
18. l. privily for their own lives
LUST. [Noun.]
Ex. 15 : 9. my l. shall be satisfied
Nu. 11: † 4. the mixed multitude lusted a l. [of l.
†34. he called the place the graves
33 : † 16. pitched at the grave of l.
Ps. 78 : 18. asking meat for their l.
30. were not estranged fr. their l.
81 : 12. I gave them unto hearts l.
Ro.1:27. burned in their l. one tow.
7 : 7. I had not known l. exc. law
Ga.5:16.ye shall not fulfil l. of flesh
1 Th.4:5. Not in l. of concupiscence
Ja. 1:14. when drawn of his own l.
15.when l. hath conceived, it bri.
2 Pe.1:4 corruption in world thro.l.
2 : 10. after flesh in l. of uncleann.
1 Jn. 2 : 16. l. of flesh, l. of eye
17. world passeth aw. and the l.
LUSTS. [word
Mk. 4 : 19. l. of other things choke
Jn. 8 : 44. l. of father ye will do
Ro. 1:24. up to uncleanness thro. l.
6 : 12. ye should obey it in l.
13 : 14. no provision to fulfil l. [l.
Ga. 5:24. are C.'s crucified flesh wi.
Ep. 2 : 3. conversation in l. of flesh
4 : 22. corrupt acc. to deceitful l.
1 Ti. 6 : 9. rich fall into hurtful l.
2 Ti.2:22.Flee youthful l.but follow
3:6.silly women led aw. with divers
4:3. after own l. heap teachers [l.
Tit. 2 : 12. that denying worldly l.
3 : 3. disobedient, serving divers l.
Ja. 4 : 1. come they even of l. ? [l.
3.ask th.ye may consume it upon
1 Pe. 1:14. not fashioning acc. to l.
2 : 11. you abstain from fleshly l.
4 : 2. no longer live to l. of men
3. we walked in lasciviousness, l.
2 Pe. 2 : 18. allure thro. l. of flesh
3 : 3. shall come scoffers, walking after their own l.
Jude 16. complainers, walking after
18. walk after own ungodly l. [l.
LUST, LUSTED.
Nu.11:34. buried the people that l-d
Ps.106:14.l-d exceedingly in wilder.
Pr. 6 : 25. l. not after her beauty
Mat.5:28.looketh on wom. to l. aft.
1 Co.10:6. we sho. not l. after evil as
Ja.4:2.Ye l. and have not | they l-d
Re. 18 : 14. fruits thy soul l-d after
LUSTETH, LUSTING.
Nu.11:4. mixed multitude fell a l-g
De. 12 : 15. what thy soul l-h after,
20, 21.-14 : 26. [and Spirit
Ga.5:17.the flesh l-h ag. the Spirit,
Ja. 4 : 5. spirit in us l-h to envy
LUSTY.
Ju. 3 : 29. slew 10,000 men, all l.
LUZ.
Gen. 28 : 19. city called L. at first,
Ju. 1 : 23, 26.
35 : 6. Jacob came to L. [L.
48:3. G. Alm. appeared unto me at
Jos.16:2.goeth fr.Bethel to L.,18:13.
LYCAO'NIA. See MYRA. [of L.
Ac. 14 : 6. Lystra and Derbe, cities
11. lifted up voices in speech of L.
LY'CIA. See MYRA.
LYD'DA.
Ac. 9 : 32. Peter came to saints at L.
35. all at L. turned to the Lord
38. as L. was nigh to Joppa
LYD'IA. [Person.] [ed
Ac. 16:14. L. whose heart Lord open-
40. they entered into house of L.
LYD'IA, LYD'IANS.
Je. 46 : 9. L-s that handle the bow
Eze. 30 : 5. L-a shall fall by sword
LYING. [Speaking falsely.]
Ps. 52:3. lovest l. rather than righte.
59 : 12. cursing and l. they speak
119 : 29. Remove from me way of l.
163. I hate and abhor l. but thy
Pr. 13 : 5. A righteous man hateth l.
20 : † 17. Bread of l. is sweet to
Is. 59 : 13. In transg-g and l. ag. L.
Eze. 13:19. by your l. to my people
Ho. 4:2. By swearing, l. and killing
Ep. 4 : 25. putting away l. speak
See Lying TONGUE.
See CHILDREN, DIVINATION, LIPS, SPIRIT, VANITIES, WONDERS AND SIGNS, WORDS.
LYING. [Posture.] [by it
Ge. 29 : 2. were 3 flocks of sheep l.
Ex. 23 : 5. ass of him hateth thee, l.
De. 21 : 1. if one be slain, l. in field
Ps. 139 : 3. compassest my l. down
Is. 56 : 10. l. down, loving to slumb.
Mat.9:2. man sick of palsy, l. on bed
Mk. 5 : 40. in where the damsel was l.
Lu. 2 : 12. find babe l. in manger, 16.
Jn. 13 : 25. He l. on Jesus' breast
20 : 5. he saw the linen clothes l.
7. napkin not l. with the linen
LYING in wait. [city
Jos. 8 : † 13. l. i. w. on west side of
Ju. 9 : 35. Abim. rose from l. i. w.
16 : 9. men l. i. w. in the chamb.
La. 3 : 10. unto me as a bear, l. i. w.
Ac.20:19. befell me by l.i.w.of Jews
23 : 16. Paul's sister's son heard of their l. i. w.
LYING with.
Ge. 34 : 7. folly in l. w. Jacob's dau.
Nu. 31 : 17. kill every woman hath known man by l. w. him
18. all th. not known man by l.w. him keep for yours., Ju. 21 : 12.
35. women not known man by l. w. him [w. a woman
De. 22 : 22. if a man be found l.
Ju. 21 : † 11. that knoweth l. w.man
LYSA'NIAS.
Lu. 3 : 1. L. tetrarch of Abilene
LYS'IAS=CLAU'DIUS.
Ac. 23 : 26. L. unto excellent Felix
24 : 7. chief captain L. came | 22.
LYS'TRA.
Ac. 14 : 6. ware of it,and fled unto L.
8. a man at L. impotent in feet
21. taught many returned to L.
Ac. 16: 1. Paul to L. | 2. breth. at L.
2 Ti.3 : 11. Persecutions at L.

M.

MA'ACAH, MA'ACHAH.
[Person and Place.]
Ge.22:24.Nahor's concubine bare M.
2 S.3:3.M.mother of Abs., 1 Ch.3:2.
10 : 6. hired of king M. 1000 men
8.Syrians of Zoba and M.by thems
1 K. 2 : 39. unto Achish son of M.
15 : 2. M. mother of Abijam, dau. of Abish., 10. 2 Ch. 11 : 22.
13. M. his mother, her he remov.
1 Ch. 2 : 48. M. Caleb's concubine
7 : 15. Shuppim, sis. name was M.
16. M. wife of Machir bare Peresh
8 : 29. wife's name was M., 9 : 35.
11:43. Hanan son of M. was valiant
19 : 7. king of M. and people came
27 : 16. Shephatiah son of M.
2 Ch. 11 : 20. after that he took M.
21. Rehob. loved M. above all
MAACH'ATHI.
De. 3 : 14. unto coasts of M.
MAACH'ATHITE, S.
Jos. 12 : 5. reigned unto border of M-s, 13 : 11.
13 : 13. Isr. expelled not M. (2)
2 S. 23 : 34. son of M., 2 K. 25:23.Je.
1 Ch.4:19.fa.of Eshtemoa, M. [40:8.
MAA'DAI.
Ezr. 10: 34. Of the sons of Bani ; M.
MAADI'AH = MOADI'AH.
Ne. 12 : 5. th. went up with Zeruh.
MAA'I. [M., 17.
Ne. 12:36. his breth. Milalai and M.
MAAL'EH-ACRAB'BIM.
Jos. 15:3. border went to M., Ju. 1:
MA'ARATH. [†36.
Jos.15:59.And M.6 cities wi.villages
MAASEI'AH.
1 Ch.15:18.of sec.degree Benaiah M.
20. M. Benaiah | Ezr.10:18,21,22,
30. Ne. 3: 23.-8:4, 7.-12: 41, 42.
2 Ch.23:1. M. son of Adaiah
26:11.M.ruler | 28:7.Zichri slew M.
34 : 8. M. governor of the city
Ne. 10: 25. Rehum M. sealed cov-t
11 : 5. M. son of Barak, -.
Je.21:1.Zeph. son of M.,29:25.-37:3.
29 : 21. saith L. of Zedekiah son of
32:12.Neraiah son of M.,51:59. [M.
35 : 4. above chamber of M. son of
MAASI'AI.
1 Ch. 9:12. of the priests, M. son of
MA'ATH.
Lu. 3:26. Nagge, wh. was son of M.
MA'AZ.
1 Ch.2:27. the sons of Ram were M
MAAZI'AH. [M.
1 Ch. 24:18. the four and 20th lot to
Ne.10:8.M.Bilgai ; these were priests
MABNAD'EBAI.
Ezr. 10:†40. Of the sons of Bani ; M.
MACEDO'NIA, AN.
Ac. 16:9. saying, Come over into M.
10. to go into M., 20:1, 3. 2 Co. 1:
16. -2 : 13. 1 Ti. 1: 3.
12. which is chief city of M.
18:5.Silas and Tim. were come fr.M.
19:21. when passed thro. M., 1 Co.
22. sent unto M. two of th. [16:5.
29. Gaius and Aristar. men of M.
27 : 2. Aristarchus a M-n with us
Ro. 15 : 26. it hath pleased th. of M.
2 Co. 7 : 5. we were come into M.
8:1. grace of G. on churches of M
9 : 2. I boast of you to them of M.
4.if they of M. find you unprepa.
11 : 9. brethren wh. came from M.
Ph. 4 : 15. when I departed from M.
1 Th. 1 : 7. ensamples to all in M.
8. sounded out word, not only in
4 : 10. toward all breth. in M. [M

MACH'BANAI.
1 Ch. 12 : 13. of the Gadites M. the
MACH'BENAH. ⌊11th
1 Ch. 2:49. She bare Sheva fa. of M.
MA'CHI. ⌈M.
Nu. 13:15. tribe of Gad, Geuel son of
MA'CHIR, ITES.
Ge. 50: 23. M. the son of Manasseh,
Nu. 32 : 39. Jos. 13 : 31.
Nu. 26 : 29. of M. the family of M-s
29. M. begat Gilead, 27 : 1.-36 : 1.
Jos. 17: 1. 1 Ch. 2:23.-7:14, 17.
32 : 40. Mo. gave Gilead unto M.,
Jos.17:3.Zeloph. son of M. ⌊De.3:15.
Ju. 5:14. out of M. came governors
2 S.9:4. M. son of Ammiel, 5.-17:27.
1 Ch. 7 : 15. M. took to wife
16. Maachah wife of M. bare son
MACHNADE'BAI.
Ezr. 10 : 40. of the sons of Bani, M.
MACHPE'LAH.
Ge. 23:9.may give me cave of M., 17.
19.Ab.buried Sarah in cave of M.
25 : 9. sons buried Abraham in M.
49:30. bury me in field of M., 50:13.
MAD.
De.28:34. **m.** for sight of thine eyes
1 S. 21 : 13. David feigned hims. **m.**
14. Achish said, Ye see man is **m.**
2 K.9:11.whf. this **m.** fellow to thee
Ps. 102 : 8. they that are **m.** ag. me
Ec. 2 : 2. I said of laughter, It is **m.**
7 : 7. oppression maketh wise man
Is. 44 : 25. maketh diviners **m.**⌊**m.**
59 : † 15. from evil is counted **m.**
Je.25:16. sh. drink, and be **m.** ⌈on
29:26. ev. man **m.**,put him in pris-
50:38.they are **m.** upon their idols
51 : 7. of her wine, nations are **m.**
Ho. 9 : 7. the spiritual man is **m.**
Jn. 10: 20. is **m.** why hear ye him?
Ac. 12: 15. to Rhoda, Thou art **m.**
26 : 11. being exceedingly **m.** ag.
24. much learning make thee **m.**
25. I am not **m.** most noble Fes.
1 Co. 14:23. will they not say ye are
MAD man. See MADMAN.⌊**m.**
MAD'AI. See MESHECH.
MADE. ⌈**m.**?
Ge. 3 : 7. sewed fig leaves, **m.** aprons
31:46. they took stones **m.** a heap
42:7 Jo.**m.** hims. strange unto th.
Ex. 2:14. Who **m.** thee prince over
us? Ac. 7 : 27. ⌈mouth?
4:11. L. said, Who hath **m.** man's
9:20.**m.** his servants and cattle flee
32 : 4. aft. he **m.** it a molten calf
25. Aaron had **m.** them naked
31. **m.** them gods of gold, Ho.8:4.
36 : 4. came ev. man fr. his work
they **m.** | 37:1.+38 : 1+39 : 1.
+Le. 2 : 7.
39:42. chil. of Isr. **m.** all the work
Nu.20:5.whf. **m.** us come from E.?
De. 9 : 21. I took calf he had **m.**
Jos. 8 : 15. Isr. **m.** as if were beaten
9 : 4. **m.** as if they ambassadors
14:8 **m.** heart of people melt ⌈**m.**
22 : 28. pattern of altar our fathers
Ju. 2 : 1. I **m.** you go up out of E.
16 : 19. she **m.** Samson sleep upon
25. Samson **m.** Philis. sport, 27.
18 : 24. Ye have taken gods I **m.**
1 S. 3 : 13. his sons **m.** thems. vile
8 : 1. Samuel **m.** his sons judges
12:1.I have **m.** king ov. you,11:15.
15 : 33. sword **m.** women childless
27 : 10. Whither have ye **m.** road
2 S.3:6. Abner **m.** hims. strong for
13:6. Amnon lay do. **m.** hims. sick
1 K. 12 : 32. sacrifi-g unto calves he
15 : 12. removed idols fa-s **m.** ⌊**m.**
13.she had **m.** an idol,2 Ch.15:16.
20:34.streets as my fa.**m.** in Sama.
2 K. 11 : 12. they **m.** him king
16 : 11. as Ahaz sent, Urijah **m.** it
17:32. **m.** of lowest of them priests
1 Ch.19:6. saw they had **m.** thems.
26:10.his fa. **m.** him chief ⌊odious
2 Ch. 28 : 19. Ahab **m.** Jud. naked
33:7.set idol he had **m.** in ho.of G.
34 : 33. Josiah **m.** all to serve L.
Ezr. 5 : 14. Sheshbazzar he **m.** gov.
Ne. 4 : 9. we **m.** our prayer unto G.
8:4.Ezra stood upon pulpit they **m.**
Es. 2 : 17. Ahasuerus **m.** her queen
9:17.they **m.** it day of feasting,18.
Ps. 7:15. is fallen into pit he **m.** (2)
9 : 15. are sunk into pit they **m.**
30 : 8. unto L. I **m.** supplication
45 : 8. whereby they **m.** thee glad
52 : 7. man that **m.** not G. his
Ec.2:4.I **m.** me great works ⌊streng.
5. I **m.** gardens | 6. I **m.** pools of
Can.1:6.**m.** me keeper of vineyards
3 : 10. He **m.** the pillars of silver
6:12. my soul **m.** me like chariots
Is. 2 : 8. wh. own fingers have **m.**
20. **m.** each one for hims. ⌈ble?
14:16.this the man **m.** earth trem-
17:8.nei. respect th. his fingers **m.**
28 : 15. we have **m.** lies our refuge
25. When he hath **m.** plain the
face ⌈me not
29 : 16. say of him **m.** it, He **m.**
31:7.your hands have **m.** for a sin
40 : † 14. who **m.** him understand
59:†2. your sins **m.** him hide face
8. **m.** crooked paths ⌈heavens
Je. 10 : 11. gods that have not **m.**
12: 10 **m.** my portion a wildern.
18: 4. vessel he **m.** was marred (2)
37:15.they had **m.** that the prison
41:9. which Asa the k. **m.** for fear
51:34.Neb. **m.** me an empty vessel
Eze. 13 : 5. nei. **m.** hedge for house
22. ye **m.** heart of righteous sad
17:16.king dwelleth th. **m.** him k.
20:28. they **m.** their sweet savour
21:24. **m.** your iniq. to be remem.
27:11. have **m.** thy beauty perfect
31:4. waters **m.** him great ⌈gicians
Da. 5: 11. thy fa. **m.** master of ma-
9:13. **m.** we not our prayer bef. L.
Ho. 2 : † 8. silver whw. **m.** Baal
7 : 5. princes **m.** him sick wi. wine
8: 6. workman **m.** it, it is not God
Am. 5: 26 god wh. ye **m.** to yours.
Zch.7:†11.they **m.** their ears heavy
12. **m.** their hearts as adamant
Mat. 9:22. Daughter, thy faith hath
m. thee whole, Mk. 5 : 34.-10:
52. Lu. 8 : 48.-17 : 19. ⌈effect
15:6. have **m.** com-t of G. of none
21:13. ho. of prayer, ye have **m.** it
den of, Mk. 11 : 17. Lu. 19 : 46.
22:5. they **m.** light of it and went
25 : 16. **m.** them other 5 talents
Lu. 12: 14. Man, who **m.** me judge
Jn.5:15.Jes.wh. had **m.** him whole
19 : 23. took his garm. **m.** 4 parts
Ac. 3 : 12. power we **m.** man walk
16. his name **m.** this man strong
7:43. figures ye **m.** to worship th.
8: 3. Saul, he **m.** havoc of church
23:13. than 40 who **m.** conspiracy
27 : 40. hoised sail, **m.** tow. shore
Ro. 8 : 2. **m.** free from law of sin
1 Ti.1:19. conc. faith **m.** shipwreck
He. 7 : 19. law **m.** nothing perfect
1 Jn.5:10. hath **m.** G. a liar ⌈of L.
Re. 7 : 14. **m.** them white in blood
14:8.she **m.** nations drink of wine
See AFRAID, COVENANT, DESO-
LATE, END, FEAST, FIRE.
MADE.
[God, Lord, or Christ as agent.]
Ge. 1:7. G. **m.** firmament ⌈136:5,7.
16. **m.** 2 gr. lights, **m.** stars, Ps.
25. God **m.** the beast of the earth
31.God saw ev.thing **m.** was good
2:2.G. rested fr.work he had **m.**,3.
4.God **m.** the earth and heavens,
Ex. 20 : 11.-31: 17. 2 Ch. 2 : 12.
Ps. 115 : 15.-146: 6. Is. 45 : 18.
Je. 10 : 12.-51: 15. Ac. 14 : 15.
Ge. 2 : 9. **m.** to grow every tree
22. **m.** he a woman ⌈9 : 6.
5:1. in likeness of God **m.** he him,
6:6. repented the L. he **m.** man, 7.
7:4.destroy living subst.I have **m.**
8 : 1. G. **m.** wind to pass ov. earth
17:5. fa. of nations have I **m.** thee,
Ro. 4 : 17.
21 : 6. G. hath **m.** me to laugh
24: 21. L. **m.** his journey prosper.
26:22.L. hath **m.** room for us ⌊ous
39:3. **m.** all Jo. did to prosper, 23.
41 : 51. G. **m.** me forget all toil
45: 8. G. hath **m.** me a fa. to Pha.
9.God hath **m.** me lord of all E.
Ex. 1 : 21.he **m.** midwives houses
7 : 1. I have **m.** thee god to Pha.
14:21.L.**m.** sea dry land, Ps.78:13.
15:17.plant thee in pl.thou hast **m.**
Le.23:43. I **m.** Isr. dwell in booths
26 : 13. and I have **m.** you go up-
Nu. 32:13. he **m.** th. wander ⌊right
De. 2: 30. L. **m.** his heart obstinate
4:36. Out of heav. he **m.** thee hear
10:22.L. hath **m.** thee as the stars
11 : 4. how he **m.** Red sea overflow
26 : 19. ab. all nations he hath **m.**
32:6. hath he not **m.** thee ⌈honey
13. He **m.** him ride, **m.** him suck
15. forsook God which **m.** him
Jos.22:25. the L. **m.** Jordan border
Ju. 5 : 13. **m.** him have dominion
21: 15. L. had **m.** breach in tribes
1 S.12:8 **m.** them dwell in this pla.
15:35.L. repented he **m.** Saul king
2 S. 6 : 8. bec. the Lord had **m.** a
breach upon,1 Ch.13:11.-15:13.
7:9.I **m.** thee gr. name, 1 Ch.17:8.
22 : 12. he **m.** darkness pavilions
36. gentleness **m.** me great, Ps.
1 K.2:24. hath **m.** me a ho. ⌊18:35.
3: 7. thou hast **m.** thy serv. king
9:3. I heard supplication thou **m.**
10 : 9. L. loved Isr. thf. **m.** thee
king, 14:7.-16 : 2. 2 Ch. 1 : 11.-
9 : 8. Ne. 13 : 26.
2 K. 19 : 15. O God, thou hast **m.**
heav. and earth, Ps. 115 : 15.
Is. 37: 16. Je. 32:17.-51:15. Ac.
4 : 24.
1 Ch. 16 : 26. but the Lord **m.** the
heavens, Ne. 9: 6. Ps. 33:6.-96:
5.-121: 2.-124 : 8.-134 : 3.
2 Ch. 20:27. L. had **m.** them rejoice
26:5.sought the Lord, God **m.** him
to prosper ⌈ful, Ne. 12 : 43.
Ezr. 6 : 22. Lord had **m.** them joy-
Jb.1:10.hast thou **m.** hedge ab.him
10 : 8. Thy hands have **m.** me
9. thou hast **m.** me as the clay
16: 7. he hath **m.** me weary, thou
17:6.He hath **m.** me a byword ⌊(2)
28:26. When he **m.** decree for rain
31 : 15. Did not he that **m.** me in
33 : 4. The Spirit of God **m.** me
38:9. When I **m.** cloud thy garm.
40:15.behemoth wh.I **m.** with thee
19.that **m.** him can make his sw.
Ps.8:5.**m.** him little lower than ang.
18 : 11. He **m.** darkness his secret
43. hast **m.** me head of heathen
21:6. hast **m.** him most blessed for
30 : 1. hast not **m.** my foes rejoice
7. hast **m.** my mountain stand
39 : 5. **m.** my days as handbreadth
46 :8.what desolations he hath **m.**
60 : 2. hast **m.** earth to tremble
3. hast **m.** us drink wine of aston.
74:17.hast **m.** summer and winter
78 : 13. he **m.** waters stand as heap
50. He **m.** a way to his anger
52. **m.** peo. go forth like sheep
55. He **m.** Israel dwell in tents
86:9. nations hast **m.** sh. worship
88:8. hast **m.** me an abomination

Ps.89:42.hast **m.** his enem. to rejoice
43. not **m.** him stand in battle
44. hast **m.** his glory to cease
47. wh-f. hast **m.** men in vain?
91:9. Bec. hast **m.** L. thy habitation
92:4. thou L. hast **m.** me glad thro.
95:5. The sea is his and he **m.** it
100:3. is God; it is he that **m.** us
104:24. in wisd m hast **m.** them all
26. leviathan, wh. hast **m.** to play
105:24. **m.** th. stronger than enem.
28. sent darkn. and **m.** it dark
106:46. He **m.** them to be pitied
111:4. **m.** his works to be rememb-d
118:24. This is the day L. hath **m.**
119:73. Thy hands have **m.** me
98. hast **m.** me wiser than enem.
136:5. by wisd. **m.** heavens, Ac.
14. **m.** Isr. pass thro. midst ⌊14:15.
148:6. he hath **m.** a decree which
149:2. Let Isr. rejoice in him **m.** him
Pr. 8:26. as yet had not **m.** earth
16:4. L. **m.** all things for hims.
20:12. L. hath **m.** even both of them
Ec. 3:11. hath **m.** ev. thing beautiful
7:13. straight wh. he **m.** crooked
29. that God hath **m.** man upright
Is. 16:10. I have **m.** shouting cease
21:2. sighing have I **m.** to cease
25:2. hast **m.** of city a heap
26:14. **m.** their memory to perish
27:11. **m.** them will not have mercy
30:33. hath **m.** Tophet deep
43:7. yea, I have **m.** him, 46:4.
44:2. saith the L. that **m.** thee
45:12. I have **m.** the earth, Je. 27:5.
49:2. **m.** my mouth like sword
51:10. hath **m.** the depths of the sea
53:9. **m.** his grave with wicked
12. **m.** intercession for transgr-rs
57:16. fail and souls wh. I have **m.**
63:17. O L. why hast **m.** us to err
66:2. all these hath mine hand **m.**
Je. 1:18. I **m.** thee defenced city
8:8. certainly in vain **m.** he it
14:22. thou hast **m.** all these thi.
29:26. L. **m.** thee priest instead of
32:20. who hast **m.** thee a name
38:16. As Lord liveth, that **m.** us
49:10. But I have **m.** Esau bare
La. 1:13. hath **m.** me desolate, 3:11.
14. he hath **m.** my strength to fall
2:8. he **m.** the rampart to lament
3:4. My flesh and skin hath he **m.**
7. hath **m.** my chain heavy ⌊old
9. **m.** my paths crooked ⌈wood
15. **m.** me drunken with worm-
45 thou hast **m.** us as offscouring
Eze. 3:8. I have **m.** thy face strong, 9.
17. I have **m.** thee a watchman
13:22. sad, whom I have not **m.** sad
17:24. I have **m.** dry tree flourish
22:4. thf. have I **m.** thee a reproach
29:3. river, I have **m.** it for myself,
31:9. I **m.** him fair by branches ⌊9.
16. I **m.** nations shake at sound
Am. 4:10. I **m.** stink of camps come
Ob. 2. I have **m.** thee small am.
Jon. 1:9. I fear G. who hath **m.** sea
Zph. 3:6. I **m.** their streets waste
Zch. 9:13. **m.** thee as sword of mighty
10:3. **m.** th. as goodly horse in battle
Mal. 2:9. have I **m.** you contemptible
Mat. 19:4. he **m.** them male and
female, Mk. 10:6 ⌈wh. is without
Lu. 11:40. did not he th. **m.** that
24:28. **m.** as tho. he wo. have gone
Jn. 1:3. without him not any thi. **m.**
2:15. had **m.** scourge of sm. cords
4:1. Jesus **m.** more disciples
46. **m.** water wine ⌈Take
5:11. He th. **m.** me whole said,
7:23. bec. I have **m.** a man whole
9:6. he **m.** clay of spittle, 11, 14.
19:7. bec. he **m.** himself Son of G.
Ac. 2:36. G. hath **m.** that same Jes.
7:10. he **m.** him gov. over Egypt
50. Hath not my hand **m.** all
14:15. turn unto G. wh. **m.** heaven
15:7. ye know G. **m.** choice am. us
17:24. G. that **m.** the world and all
26. **m.** of one blood all nations
20:28. H. G. hath **m.** you overseers
1 Co. 1:20. **m.** foolish the wisdom of
2 Co. 3:6. hath **m.** us able ministers
5:21. hath **m.** him to be sin for us
Gal. 5:1. whw. Christ hath **m.** us free
Ep. 1:6. he hath **m.** us accepted
2:6. God hath **m.** us sit in heavenly
14. our peace who **m.** both one
Phm. 2:7. **m.** hims. of no reputation
Col. 1:12. **m.** us meet to be partak.
2:15. he **m.** a shew of them openly
He. 1:2. by whom he **m.** the worlds
6:13. when G. **m.** promise to Ab.
Re. 1:6. hath **m.** us kings and priests
5:10. hast **m.** us unto our G. kings
14:7. worship him that **m.** heaven

MADE haste.

Ge. 24:46. Rebekah **m. h.** and let
down her pitcher ⌈Moses **m. h.**
43:30. Joseph **m. h.** | Ex. 34:8.
Ju. 13:10. Manoah's wife **m. h.**
1 S. 23:26. Da. **m. h.** | 25:18. Abigail
2 S. 4:4. Mephibosheth's nurse **m. h.**
Ps. 119:60. I **m. h.**, and delayed not
Lu. 19:6. Zaccheus **m. h.**, and came

I have, or have I MADE.

Ge. 14:23. lest say, I **h. m.** Ab. rich
27:37. Behold, I **h. m.** him thy lord
1 K. 8:59. whw. I **h. m.** supplication
1 Ch 29:19. for wh. I **h. m.** provision
Ezr. 6:11. I Darius **h. m.** decree, 12.
Jb. 17:13. I **h. m.** my bed in darkn.
31:24. if I **h. m.** gold my hope
39:6. Whose house I **h. m.** wilder.
Ps. 45:1. speak of things I **h. m.**
Pr. 20:9. Who say, **h. m.** heart clean
Da. 3:15. worship image I **h. m.**
Ac. 1:1. treatise **h.** I **m.** O Theoph.
1 Co. 9:19. **h.** I **m.** myself servant unto all

See Made ISRAEL sin, KING, Made or madest KNOWN.

MADE manifest. ⌈m.

Lu. 8:17. nothing secret not be **m.**
Jn. 1:31. that he should be **m. m.**
3:21. to light, that deeds be **m. m.**
9:3. works of G. should be **m. m.**
Ro. 10:20. I was **m. m.** unto them
16:26. Mystery now is **m. m.** ⌈m.
1 Co. 3:13. Every man's work be **m.**
11:19. th. they approved be **m. m.**
14:25. secrets of his heart **m. m.**
2 Co. 4:10. life of Jes. be **m. m.**, 11.
5:11. we are **m. m.** unto God ⌈m.
11:6. we have been thoroughly **m.**
Ep. 5:13. are **m. m.** by the light
Col. 1:26. is **m. m.** to his saints
2 Ti. 1:10. **m. m.** by appearing of C.
He. 9:8. way into holiest not **m. m.**
1 Jn. 2:19. out, that they be **m. m.**
Re. 15:4. thy judgments are **m. m.**

MADE peace.

Jos. 9:15. And Joshua **m. p.** 10:1, 4.
11:19. not a city that **m. p.** with Isr.
2 S. 10:19. kings were smitten, they
m. p. with Israel, 1 Ch. 19:19.
1 K. 22:44. Jehosh. **m. p.** with Isr.

MADE ready.

Ge. 43:25. they **m. r.** the present
46:29. Joseph **m. r.** his chariot to
Ex. 14:6. Pharaoh **m. r.** his chariot
Ju. 6:19. Gideon went and **m. r.** kid
13:15. until we have **m. r.** a kid
1 K. 6:7. **m. r.** bef. it was brought
2 K. 9:21. Joram's chariot was **m. r.**
1 Ch. 28:2. had **m. r.** for building
2 Ch. 35:14. afterward they **m. r.**
Ps. 7:12. bent his bow and **m.** it **r.**
Ho. 7:6. they have **m. r.** their heart
Mat. 26:19. disciples **m. r.** passover, Mk. 14:16. Lu. 22:13.
Ac. 10:10. while they **m. r.** Peter
fell into a trance ⌈r. to our
2 Co. 10:16. not boast of things **m.**
Re. 19:7. his wife hath **m.** hers. **r.**

See SPEED, SUPPLICATION, VOID.

Thou hast or Hast thou MADE.

Ex. 29:36. when **t. h. m.** atonement
Jos. 2:17. oath **t. h. m.** us swear, 20.
1 Ch. 22:8. saying **t. h. m.** great wars
Is. 43:24. **t. h. m.** me serve with sins
Je. 2:28. where are gods **t. h. m.**
Eze. 16:24. **t. h. m.** thee a high place
25. **t. h. m.** thy beauty abhorred
22:4. hast defiled in idols **t. h. m.**
13. dishonest gain which **t. h. m.**
Da. 3:10. **t.** O king **h. m.** a decree
Mat. 20:12. hour, and **t. h. m.** equal
Ro. 9:20. say, Why **h. t. m.** me thus

MADE. [Passively.]

Ge. 49:24. his hands were **m.** strong
Le. 22:5. whereby he be **m.** uncl.
Nu. 4:26. sh. bear all is **m.** for th.
6:4. eat noth. is **m.** of vine tree
1 S. 15:17. wast thou not **m.** head
1 K. 8:38. supplication be **m.**, 2
Ch. 6:29. ⌈7:15.
2 Ch. 6:40. prayer **m.** in this pla.,
25:16. Art thou **m.** of k.'s counsel
Ezr. 5:17. be search **m.** in king's ho.
6:1. search was **m.** in ho. of rolls
11. let his house be **m.** a dunghill
Es. 5:14. Let a gallows be **m.** of 50
Jb. 7:3. I am **m.** to possess months
15:7. wast thou **m.** bef. the hills?
41:33. not his like, who is **m.**
without fear ⌈m. rich
Ps. 49:16. Be not afraid when one is
72:15. prayer **m.** for him contin.
139:14. I am fearfully **m.** ⌈m.
15. substance not hid when I was
Pr. 11:25. liberal soul sh. be **m.** fat
13:4. soul of diligent sh. be **m.** fat
15:19. way of righteous is **m.** plain
21:11. simple is **m.** wise
28:25. putteth trust in L. be **m.** fat
Ec. 1:15. crooked can-t be **m.** strai-t
7:3. by sadness heart is **m.** better
10:19. feast is **m.** for laughter
Is. 2:17. haughtiness be **m.** low
28:22. not mockers lest bands be
m. strong ⌈ness
34:6. word of L. is **m.** fat with fat-
40:4. Every hill shall be **m.** low
51:12. wh. shall be **m.** as grass
66:8. shall earth be **m.** to bring
forth in one day? ⌈m. clean?
Je. 13:27. Jerus.! wilt thou not be
19:11. vessel that can-t be **m.** whole
20:8. word of L. was **m.** a reproach
Da. 5:21. heart was **m.** like beasts
12:10. Many sh. be **m.** white and
Mat. 4:3. command stones be **m.** br.
9:16. rent is **m.** worse, Mk. 2:21.
14:36. **m.** perfectly whole, 9:22.
15:28. Mk. 6:56. Lu. 8:50. Jn. 5:
18:25. sold and payment **m.** ⌊4, 9.
23:15. when **m.** ye make him two-
25:6. midnight was a cry **m.** ⌊fold
27:24. th. rather a tumult was **m.**
64. Command sepulc. be **m.** sure
Mk. 2:27. sabbath was **m.** for man
14:4. Why this waste of ointm. **m.**
Lu. 2:2. taxing first **m.** when Cy.
3:5. crooked sh. be **m.** straight, 13:
4:3. command stone be **m.** br. ⌊13.
8:50. believe she sh. be **m.** whole
14:12. lest a recompense be **m.**
23:12. Pil. and Herod **m.** friends
Jn. 1:3. All things were **m.** by him,
with-t him not any thi. **m.** th.
10. world was **m.** by him ⌊was **m.**
14. Word was **m.** flesh, and dwelt
2:9. tasted water that was **m.** wine
5:4. stepped in was **m.** whole, 9.
6. Wilt be **m.** whole? | 14. art
8:33. Ye sh. be **m.** free ⌊**m.** whole

Jn. 9:39. wh. see might be **m.** blind
17:23. that they may be **m.** perfect
Ac 4:9. what means he is **m.** whole
35. distribution was **m.** unto every man [17:24
7:48. not in temp-s **m.** with hands,
12:5. prayer was **m.** for Peter
13:32. promise which was **m.** unto our fathers, 26:6. Ro. 15:8.
14:5. when there was an assault **m.**
16:13. prayer was wont to be **m.**
19:26. they be no gods wh. are **m.**
21:40. when there was **m.** gr. silence
Ro. 1:3. Jes. who was **m.** of seed of
20. understood by things are **m.**
2:25. thy circumc. is **m.** uncire.
5:19. many **m.** sinners, many **m.**
6:18. Being **m.** free from sin, 22.
7:13. Was good, **m.** death unto me?
8:20. creature was **m.** subject to
9:†22. vessels of wrath **m.** [mor.
29. we had been **m.** like unto Go-
10:10. with mouth confession is **m.**
11:9. Let their table be **m.** a snare
14:21. whereby thy bro. is **m.** weak
15:27. if Gent. been **m.** partakers
1 Co. 1:17. lest cross be **m.** of none
30. who of G. is **m.** unto us wisd.
4:9. we are **m.** spectacle unto world
13. we are **m.** as filth of world
7:21. thou mayest be **m.** free
9:22. I am **m.** all things to all men
12:13. **m.** to drink into one Spirit
15:22. so in Ch. sh. all be **m.** alive
45. The first man Adam was **m.** a living soul, last Adam was **m.**
2 Co. 2:2. same wh. is **m.** sorry, 7:9.
3:10. that which was **m.** glorious
5:1. a house not **m.** with hands
21. might be **m.** righte-n. of God
12:9. my strength is **m.** perfect in
Ga. 3:3. are ye now **m.** perfect by
13. Ch., being **m.** a curse for us
16. to Ab. and seed were promises
19. to whom promise was **m.** [m.
4:4. sent Son, **m.** of a woman, **m.**
Ep. 2:11. circumc. in flesh **m.** by ha.
13. far off, are **m.** nigh by blood of
3:7. I was **m.** a minister, Col. 1:23,
Ph. 2:7. **m.** in likeness of men [25.
3:10. being **m.** conformable unto
Col. 1:20. having **m.** peace thro.
23. I Paul am **m.** minister, 25. [bl
2:11. circumc. **m.** without hands
1 Ti. 1:9. law is not **m.** for a righte.
2:1. giving of thanks be **m.** for all
Tit. 3:7. justified, we sho. be **m.** heirs
He. 1:4. **m.** so much better than ang.
2:17. it behoved him to be **m.** like
3:14. **m.** partakers of Ch. [high pr.
5:5. Ch. glorified not hims. to be **m.**
9. **m.** perfect, he became Author
6:4. were **m.** partakers of Holy G.
20. Jesus **m.** an high priest for ev.
7:3. **m.** like unto the Son of God
12. is **m.** of necessity a change
16. **m.** not after law of a carnal
20. not with-t an oath **m.** priest
21. those priests **m.** with-t oath
22. Jes. was **m.** surety of a better
9:2. was tabernacle **m.** wh-in was
11. tabernacle not **m.** with hands
24. into holy places **m.** wi. hands
10:3. remembr. **m.** of sins ev. year
13. till his enemies be **m.** footstool
33. whilst ye were **m.** gazingstock
11:3. not **m.** of things wh appear
34. out of weakness were **m.** stro.
40. without us sho. not be **m.** perf.
12:23. spirits of just men **m.** perf.
27. shaken, as of thi. that are **m.**
Ja. 1:10. rich, in that he is **m.** low
2:22. by works was faith **m.** perf.
3:9. **m.** after similitude of G. [ner
1 Pe. 2:7. same is **m.** head of cor-
2 Pe. 2:12. these **m.** to be destroyed
Re. 8:11. waters, bec. were **m.** bitter
R17:2. been **m.** drunk wi. her fornic.
18:15. merchants were **m.** rich by
19. in one hour is she **m.** desolate

MADEST. [ion

Ps. 8:6. Thou **m.** him to have domin-
80:15. visit branch that thou **m.** strong [strong
17. son of man, whom thou **m.**
Eze. 16:17. and **m.** images of men
29:7. **m.** all their loins to be at a
Jon. 4:10. neither **m.** it grow [stand
Ac. 21:38. Egyp-n which **m.** uproar
He. 2:7. **m.** him a little lower than

MA'DIAN. [angels

Ac. 7:29. a stranger in land of M.

MADMAN or MAD man.

1 S. 21:15. bro-t this fellow to play **m.**
Pr. 26:18. **m. m.** who casteth fireb-ds

MADMAN'NAH. [31.

Jos. 15:31. cities Ziklag, M., Is. 10:†
1 Ch. 2:49 she bare Shaaph fa. of M.

MADMEN. [ye

1 S. 21:15. Have I need of **m.** that

MADMEN. [Place.]

Je. 48:2. O M. sword sh. pursue you

MADME'NAH.

Is. 10:31. M. is removed

MADNESS. [m.

De. 28:28. Lord sh. smite thee with
2 K. 9:†20. Jehu, he driveth in **m.**
Ec. 1:17. I gave heart to know **m.**
2:12. I turned myself to behold **m.**
7:25. wickedness of folly, and **m.**
9:3. **m.** is in heart, while they live
10:13. this talk is mischievous **m.**
Zch. 12:4. will smite horse and rider
Lu. 6:11. were filled wi **m.** [wi. m.
2 Pe. 2:16. dumb ass forbad **m.** of

MA'DON. [proph.

Jos. 11:1. sent to Jobab king of M.,

MAG'BISH. [12:19.

Ezr. 2:30. children of M. 156

MAG'DALA. [of M.

Mat. 15:39. Jesus came into coasts

MAGDALE'NE. See MARY.

MAG'DIEL. [Ch. 1:54.

Ge. 36:43. Duke M., duke Iram, 1

MAGICIAN.

Da. 2:10. that asked such at any **m.**

MAGICIANS.

Ge. 41:8. Pha. called for **m.** of E.
24. I told this unto **m.** but none
Ex. 7:11. **m.** of E. did so with enchantm-s, 22.-8:7, 18. [finger
8:19. **m.** said unto Pha., This is
9:11. **m.** could not stand bef. Mo.
Da. 1:20. ten times better than **m.**
2:2. king com-ded to call the **m.**
27. secret cannot **m.** shew [known
4:7. came in **m.** but did not make
9. O Belteshazzar master of **m.**
5:11. whom thy fa. made master

MAGISTRATE. [of m.

Ju. 18:7. was no **m.** in the land
Lu. 12:58. when thou goest to **m.**

MAGISTRATES.

Ezr. 7:25. Ezr. set **m.** and judges
Lu. 12:11. bring you unto **m.** [m.
Ac. 16:20. brought Paul and Silas to
22. **m.** commanded to beat them
35. **m.** sent the sergeants. 36.
38. sergeants told these unto **m.**
Tit. 3:1. put them in mind to obey

MAGNIFICAL. [m.

1 Ch. 22:5. the house must be **m.**

MAGNIFICENCE.

Ac. 19:27. her **m.** sho. be destroyed

MAGNIFIED.

Ge. 19:19. thou hast **m.** thy mercy
Jos. 4:14. L. **m.** Josh. in sight of Is.
2 S. 7:26. And let thy name be **m.** forever, 1 Ch. 17:24. [2 Ch. 1:1.
1 Ch. 29:25. the Lord **m.** Solomon,
2 Ch. 32:23. Hezekiah was **m.** in
Ps. 35:27. say, Let the L. be **m.** [4.
40:16. say contin., L. be **m.**, 70:
41:†9. Mine own friend **m.** ag. me
Ps. 126:†2. L. hath **m.** to do wi. them
138:2. thou hast **m.** thy word ab.
Je. 3:†16. nei. it be **m.** any more
48:26. he **m.** himself against the L., 42. Eze. 35:†13. Da 8:11.
La. 1:9. the enemy hath **m.** hims.
Ob. 1:†12. nei. have **m.** thy mouth
Zph. 2:8. **m.** themselves ag. border
10. **m.** thems. against peo. of L.
Mal. 1:5. Lord will be **m.** from Isr.
Ac. 5:13. but the people **m.** them
19:17. name of Lord Jes. was **m.**
2 Co. 10:†15. that we be **m.** in you
Ph. 1:20. Christ be **m.** in my body

MAGNIFY. [m. thee

Jos. 3:7. This day will I begin to
Jb 7:17. What is man thou **m.** him
19:5. If ye will **m.** yours. ag. me
36:24 Rememb. thou **m.** his work
Ps. 34:3. O **m.** the Lord with me
35:26. with shame that **m.** thems.
38:16. my foot slipp. they **m.** thems
55:12. did **m.** himself against me
69:30. will **m.** him with thanks-g-g
Is. 10:15. Sh. saw **m.** ag. him shak-
42:21. he will **m.** the law [eth it
Eze. 38:23. Thus will I **m.** myself
Da. 8:25. shall **m.** hims. in heart
11:36. king shall **m.** himself ab.
37. he shall **m.** himself above all
Zch. 12:7. **m.** not thems. ag. Judah
Lu. 1:46. My soul doth **m.** the L.
Ac. 10:46. heard him speak and **m.**
Ro. 11:13. I **m.** mine office [God

MA'GOG. [5.

Ge. 10:2. son of Japheth, M., 1 Ch. 1:
Eze. 38:2. set thy face ag land of M.
39:6. I will send a fire on M.
Re. 20:8. gather Gog and M. to battle

MA'GOR-MIS'SABIB.

Je. 20:3. not called thy name Pashur

MAG'PIASH. [but M.

Ne. 10:20. chief of people M.

MA'HALAH.

1 Ch. 7:18. sis. Hammoleketh bare M.

MAHAL'ALEEL.

Ge. 5:12. Cainan lived 70 y-rs begat
15. M. begat Jared, 16. [M. | 13.
17. all days of M. were 895 years
1 Ch. 1:2. Kenan, M. Jared
Ne. 11:4. son of M. chil. of Perez
See MALELEEL.

MA'HALATH.

Ge. 28:9. Esau took M. | 2 Ch. 11:18.

MA'HALI = MAH'LI.

Ex. 6:19 sons of Merari, M.

MAHANA'IM. [ts.

Ge 32:2 Jac. called place M. | Can. 6:
Jos 13:26. from M. unto border, 30.
21:38. out of Gad to Levites, M., 1 Ch. 6:80.
2 S. 2:8. brought Ish bosheth to M.
12. went out from M. to Gibeon
29. Abner and his men came to M.
17:24. Da. came to M., 27. [at M.
19:32. Barzillai provided susten
1 K. 2:8. cursed me when I went to
4:14. Ahinadab had M. [M.
1 Ch. 6:80. M. with her suburbs

MA'HANEH-DAN.

Ju. 18:12. they called the name M.

MAHAR'AI.

2 S. 23:28. M. the Netophathite, 27:13. 1 Ch. 11:30.

MA'HATH.

1 Ch. 6:35. M. son of Amasai, 2 Ch. 29:12. [seers
2 Ch. 31:13. M. and Benaiah, over-

MA'HAVITE.

1 Ch. 11:46. valiant men, Eliel, M.

MAHA'ZIOTH.

1 Ch. 25:4. M. son of Heman
30. three and 20th lot to M.

MA'HER-SHAL'AL-HASH'-BAZ.

Is. 8:1. write in roll concerning M.
3. said the Lord, Call his name M

MAH'LAH.
Nu. 26:33. dau-s of Zelophehad, M., 27 : 1.-36 : 11. Jos. 17 : 3.

MAH'LI, ITES.
Ex. 6 : 19. sons of Merari M. and Mushi, Nu. 3: 20. 1 Ch. 6 : 19, 29.-23:21.-24:26, 28. Ezr. 8:18.
Nu. 3 : 33. family of M-s, 26 : 58.
1 Ch. 6:47. M. son of Mushi, 23 : 23.

MAH'LON. [-24 : 30.
Ru. 1 : 2. his sons, M. and Chilion
5. M. and Chilion died also both
4:9. I have bought all th. was M.'s
10. Ruth wife of M. have I pur- [chased

MA'HOL.
1 K. 4 : 31. wiser than sons of M.

MAID.
Ge. 16 : 2. go in unto m. Hagar, 3.
6. Behold, thy m. is in thy hand
8. Hagar, Sarai's m. whence cam-
29:24. Zilpah his m. unto Leah [est
29. gave Bilhah to be Rachel's m.
30:3. my m. Bilhah go in unto her
7. Rachel's m. conceived [to wife
9. took Zilpah her m. gave Jac.
10. Leah's m. bare Jacob son, 12.
Ex. 2 : 5. ark, she sent m. to fetch
8. m. called the child's mother
21:20, if man smite his m. wi. rod
26. or eye of m. that it perish
22 : 16. if entice m. not betrothed
Le. 25:6. sab. shall be meat for thy m
De. 22:14. I found her not a m., 17.
2 K. 5:2. brought captive a little m.
4. thus said the m. that is of Isr.
Es. 2 : 7. m. was fair and beautiful
12. when ev. m.'s turn was come
Jb. 31:1. why sho. I think upon m.
Pr. 30 : 19. way of a man with m.
Is. 24:2. as with m. so with mistress
Je. 2:32. Can a m. forget ornam-s?
51: 22. wilt break yo. man and m.
Am. 2:7. man and fa. in unto same m.
Mat. 9:24. Give place, m. is not dead
25. and the m. arose [69. Lu. 22:56.
26 : 71. ano. m. saw him, Mk. 14:
Lu. 8 : 54. called, saying, m. arise

MAID child. See CHILD.

MAIDS.
Ezr. 2:65. Besides their serv-s and m.
Es. 2:9. her and m. unto best place
Jb. 19:15. my m. count me stranger
La. 5 : 11. They ravished the m.
Eze. 9 : 6. Slay both m. and chil.
Na. 2 : 7. m. sh. lead her with voice
Zch. 9 : 17 cheerful, and new wine the m. [high priest
Mk 14 : 66. cometh one of m. of

MAIDEN.
Ge. 30:18. given my m. to my husb.
Ju. 19 : 24. here is my dau. a m.
2 Ch. 36:17. no compassion upon m.
Es. 2:13. came ev m. unto king, 4, 9.
Ps. 123:2. eyes of m. unto mistress
Lu. 8 : 51. father and mother of m.

MAIDENS.
Ex. 2 : 5. her m. walked by river
Ru. 2 : 8. abide here fast by my m.
22. good that thou go with his m.
23. she kept fast by m. of Boaz
3 : 2. with whose m. thou wast?
1 S. 9 : 11 m. going to draw water
Es. 2:8. many m. gath-d unto Shu-
9. he gave her 7 m. meet for her
4 : 16. I and my m. will fast
Jb. 41 : 5. wilt bind him for m.?
Ps. 78:63. m. not given to marriage
148: 12. y-g men and m. praise L.
Pr. 9:3. She hath sent forth her m.
27:27. for maintenance for thy m.
31 : 15. she giveth a portion to m.
Ec. 2 : 7. I got me servants and m.
Eze. 44 : 22. shall take m. of Israel
Lu. 12 : 45. shall begin to beat m.

MAIDSERVANT.
Ex. 11:5. even unto firstborn of m.
20 : 10. m. sh. do no work, De. 5:14.
Ex. 20:17. sh. not covet neighb.'s m.
21 : 7. if man sell dau. to be a m.
27. if he smite out his m.'s tooth
32. If an ox push a m. he shall
De. 5 : 14. that thy m. rest as thou
21. nei. desire neighb.'s m. [14.
12:18. eat them, thou and m., 16:11,
15:17. unto thy m. shalt do likew.
Ju. 9 : 18. Abim. son of m. king
Jb. 31 : 13. if I did despise cause of
Je. 34:9. let his m. go free, 10. [m.

MAIDSERVANTS.
Ge. 12 : 16. Abram had m., 24 : 35.
20:17. healed Abim.'s wife and m.
30:43. Jacob had much cattle, m.
31 : 33. Laban entered 2 m.' tents
De. 12 : 12. shall rejoice, ye and m.
1 S. 8 : 16. he shall take your m.
2 S. 6:22. of m. shall I be in honour
2 K. 5:26. Is it a time to receive m.
Ne. 7 : 67. Besides their manserv-s [and m.

MAIL.
1 S. 17 : 5. was armed with m., 38.

MAIMED. [offer
Le. 22 : 22. Blind or m. ye sh. not
Mat. 15 : 30. those that were m.
31. wondered when saw m. whole
18:8. to enter into life m., Mk. 9:43.
Lu. 14 : 13. makest a feast call m.
21. bring in hither the poor and [m.

MAINSAIL.
Ac. 27 : 40. they hoised up the m.

MAINTAIN, ED, EST.
1 K. 8 : 45. hear their prayer, m. their cause, 49, 59. 2 Ch. 6:35, 39.
1 Ch. 26:27. dedicate to m. ho. of L.
Jb. 13:15. I will m. mine own ways
Ps. 9:4. For thou hast m-d my right
16 : 5. L. my portion, m-t my lot
140:12. L. will m. cause of afflict.
Tit. 3 : 8. careful to m. good works
14. learn to m. good works for [uses

MAINTENANCE.
Ezr. 4:14. bec. we have m. fr. king
Pr. 27 : 27. for m. of thy maidens

MAJESTY.
1 Ch. 29:11. Thine, O Lord, is the m.
25. bestowed upon him royal m.
Es. 1 : 4. shewed honour of his m.
Jb. 37 : 22. with God is terrible m.
40 : 10. Deck thyself now with m.
Ps. 21 : 5. m. hast laid upon him
29 : 4. voice of Lord is full of m.
45 : 3. with thy glory and m.
4. in thy m. ride prosperously
93 : 1. Lord, he is clothed with m.
96:6. honour and m. are bef. him
104 : 1. thou art clothed with m.
145: 5. speak of honour of thy m.
12. to make known m. of his kingd
Is. 2 : 10. for glory of his m., 19, 21.
24:14. they shall sing for m. of L.
26 : 10. will not behold m. of L.
Eze 7:20. ornament he set it in m.
Da. 4:30. built for honour of my m.
36. excellent m. added unto me
5:18. God gave Neb. thy father m.
19. for the m. all peo. trembled
Mi. 5 : 4. feed in m. of name of L.
He. 1 : 3. on right hand of m., 8:1.
2 Pe. 1 : 16. eyewitnesses of his m.
Jude 25. To only wise G. be glory [and m.

MA'KAZ.
1 K. 4 : 9. The son of Dekar in M.

MAKE.
Ge. 1:26. God said, Let us m. man
2 : 18. I will m. him a help meet
3 : 6. tree desired to m. one wise
21. m. coats of skins
6 : 14. m. thee an ark [us a name
11:3. let us m. brick | 4. let us m.
12:2. I will m. of thee a great nation, 21:13, 18.-46:3. Ex. 32:10.
13 : 16. I will m. thy seed as dust
17:6. I will m. thee fruitful, 48:4.
20. I will m. Ishm. fruitful (2)
19:32. let us m. fa. drink wine, 34.
Ge. 26:4. I will m. thy seed as stars
27:4. Isaac said, m. savoury meat
28 : 3. G. Alm. m. thee fruitful
32 : 12. I will m. thy seed as sand
34:9. m. ye marriages with us and
30. ye m. me to stink am. inhab.
35: 1. go to Beth-el and m. an alt.
3. I will m. there an altar unto G.
47:6. in best of la. m. thy fa. dwell
48 : 20. God m. thee as Ephr. and
Ex. 5:5. ye m. them rest fr. burdens
16. no straw, say, m. brick, 7, 8.
12 : 4. sh. m. your count for lamb
20 : 4. shalt not m. unto thee any graven image, Le. 26:1. De. 5:8.
23. Ye shall not m. gods of silver
24. An altar of earth shalt thou m.
25. if wilt m. me altar of stones
22 : 3. m. full restitution, 5, 6, 12.
23:27. I will m. enem. turn backs
33. lest they m. thee sin ag. me
25 : 8. m. me a sanctuary +
9. so sh. ye m. it, 27:8. [44. He. 8:5.
40. m. them aft. pattern, Ac. 7:
26 : 1. m. taber. with 10 curt. +
28:2. m. holy garments for Aa., 4.
4. these are garments they sh. m.
6. they shall m. ephod of gold +
40. for Aaron's sons shalt m. coats
42. shalt m. them linen breeches
30 : 1. m. altar of shittim wood +
25. shalt m. it an oil of holy oint.
32 nei. sh. ye m. any like it, 37, 38.
31 : 6. m. all I commanded, 35:10.
32: 1. m. us gods to go, 23. Ac. 7:40.
10. I will m. of thee a gr. nation
33:19. I will m. my goodness pass
34 : 16. m. thy sons go a whoring
17. not m. molten gods, Le. 19:4.
36:6. man nor woman m. any more
Le. 5:16. he sh. m. amends for harm
11: 43. not m. yourselves abominable, 20 : 25. [for dead
19:28. not m. any cuttings in flesh
21 : 5. shall not m. baldness, De. [14:1.
26 : 9. I will m. you fruitful
19. I will m. your heaven as iron
22. beasts, wh. shall m. you few
27 : 2. When a man m. a singular [vow
Nu. 5 : 21. L. m. thee a curse
22. m. belly swell, thigh to rot, 21.
6:7. sh. not m. hims. uncl. for fa.
25. The Lord m. his face to shine
8:7. wash, and so m. thems. clean
14:4. Let us m. a captain and ret.
12. I will m. of thee greater nation than, De. 9 : 14. [over us
16 : 13. exc. m. thyself a prince
30. if the Lord m. a new thing
38. let them m. them broad plates
17 : 5. I will m. to cease murmur-[ings
21:8. m. thee a fiery serpent
30: 8. sh. m. her vow of none effect
31 : 23. ye shall m. it go thro. fire
De. 1:11. L. m. you a thous. times
13. I will m. them rulers ov. you
4:10. I will m. th. hear my words
16. lest ye m. graven image, 23, 25.
7: 3. Nei. m. marriages with them
8 : 3. m. thee know man doth not live by bread only
19:18. shall m. diligent inquisition
20:11. if it m. thee answer of peace
21; 14. not m. merchandise of her
16. not m. son of beloved firstborn
22:8. shalt m. battlement for roof
26:19. to m. thee high ab. nations
28 : 11. L. shall m. thee plenteous,
13. L. shall m. thee head [30:9.
24. L. sh. m. rain of land powder
59. L. will m. thy plagues wonderf.
32:26. m. remembr. of them cease
39. I kill, I m. alive, I wound
42. will m. mine arrows drunk
Jos. 1:8. shalt m. thy way prosperous
5 : 2. m. thee sharp knives
6 : 5. when they m. a long blast

Jos.6:18.lest ye m.yours. accursed, and m. camp of Israel a curse
7:19. and m. confession unto him.
Ezr. 10 : 11. [chil cease
22 : 25. so shall your chil. m. our
23:12. sh. m. marriages with them
Ju. 16:25. that he may m. us sport
Ru. 4:11. L. m. woman like Rachel
1 S. 1 : 6. provoked to m. her fret
2 : 8. to m. them inherit glory
24. ye m. L.'s people transgress
29. to m. yours. fat with off-gs
6 : 5. ye sh. m. images of emerods
7.m.a new cart | 8:5.m.us a king
8 : 22. Hearken, m. them a king
12:22.it hath pleased L.to m. you his people, 1 Ch. 17 : 22.
25:28. L. will m. my lord a house
28:2.I will m. thee keeper of mine
29 : 4. m. this fellow return
2 S. 7 : 11. he will m. thee a house
23. God, to m. him a name
11:25. m. thy battle strong ag.city
13 : 5. and m. thyself sick
15 : 20. should I m. thee go up and down with us?
23:5. though he m. it not to grow
1 K. 1 : 37. m. his throne greater
47. God m. name of Sol. better
2 : 42. Did I not m. thee to swear
8 : 29. prayer wh. thy serv. shall m. tow. this place, 2 Ch. 6:21.
11 : 34. I will m. him prince all
12 : 4. m. heavy yoke thy fa. put upon us lighter,9,10.2 Ch.10:10
16 : 3. I will m. thy house like ho. of Jerob., 21 : 22. 2 K. 9 : 9.
17 : 13. m. for thee and thy son
19 : 2. if m. not thy life as life
2 K. 3:16. m. valley full of ditches
4 : 10. Let us m. a little chamber
5 : 7. Am I G. to kill, to m. alive?
6 : 2. let us m. a place, where
7 : 2. if L. would m. windows, 19.
9:2. m. him rise, anoint him king
10 : 5. we will not m. any king
18 : 31. m. an agreement with me, Is. 36 : 16. [move more
21 : 8. nei. will I m. feet of Israel
23:10. that no man m. son or dau. pass thro. fire, Eze. 20 : 31.
1 Ch. 11 : 10. all Israel to m. him king, 12 : 31, 38. [ness
17:21. to m. thee a name of great-
21 : 3. L. m. his people 100 times
28 : 4. be liked me to m. me king
29 : 12. L. in thine hand to m. gr.
2 Ch. 7 : 20. will m. it a proverb
11:22. he thought to m. him king
25:8. God shall m. thee fall before
Ezr. 6 : 8. I m. a decree, 7 : 13, 21.
Ne. 2 : 4. For what dost m. request
8. timber to m. beams for palace
8 : 12. peo. went to m. great mirth
15. fetch branches to m. booths
Es. 1 : 20. king's decree he shall m.
7 : 7. Haman stood to m. request
9 : 22. m. them days of feasting
Jb. 5 : 18. and his hands m. whole
8 : 6. m. habitation prosperous
9:30. if I m. hands never so clean
11 : 3. thy lies m. men hold peace?
19:3. that ye m. yours. strange to
24:25.who will m.me a liar? [me
31:15.th.made me in womb m.him
34 : 29. who then can m. trouble?
35:9. they m. the oppressed to cry
39:27.Doth eagle m. nest on high?
40:19. can m. his sw. to approach
41 : 6. companions m. banquet of
Ps. 5:8. m. thy way straight [him?
† 10. m. them guilty, O God, let
6:6. all night m. I my bed to swim
20 : †3. L. m. fat thy burnt sacri.
21 : 9. Thou shalt m. them as oven
12.shalt m. them turn their back
22 : 9. thou didst m.me hope when

Ps.25:†14.will m. them kn. his cov.
31:16. m. thy face shine,119:135.
34 : 2. My soul shall m. boast in L.
39:8.m.me not reproach of foolish
40 : 17 m. no tarrying, 70 : 5.
41:3.wilt m. all his bed in sickness
45:16.chil.thou mayest m. princes
17. I will m. thy name rememb.
46 : 4. shall m. glad the city of God
51:8.m. me to hear joy and [61:†4.
57 : 1. wings will I m. my refuge,
66:2.m.his praise glorious [heard
8. m. voice of his praise to be
83 : 2. lo, thine enemies m. tumult
11. m. their nobles like Oreb and
13. O God, m. them like a wheel
84:6. valley of Baca, m. it a well
89:27. I will m. him my firstborn
29. His seed will I m. to endure
90 : 15. m. us glad,acc. to the days
110 : 1. until I m. thine enemies footstool, Mat. 22 : 44. Mk. 12 : 36. Lu. 20 : 43. Ac. 2 : 35. He. 1 : 13. [135 : 18.
115:8. that m. them are like them,
119 : 35. m. me go in path of com.
132:17.will I m.horn of David bud
137 : † 7. m.bare to the foundation
139:8. if I m. my bed in hell, thou
Pr. 6 : 3. go and m. sure thy friend
14:9. Fools m. mock at sin [quiry
20 : 25. a snare after vows to m. in-
22 : 21. m. thee know certainty
24. m. no friendship with angry
23 : 5. for riches m. thems. wings
24 : 27. m. it fit for thys. in field
27 : 11. My son,m. my heart glad
30: 26. m. they houses in the rocks
Ec. 7 : 13. who can m. that straight
16.nei.m.thyself over wise [gold
Can. 1 : 11. will m. thee borders of
Is. 1 : 15. when ye m. many prayers
16. Wash you, m. you clean
3 : 7. m. me not a ruler of the peo.
6 : 10. m. heart of this people fat
7:6. and let us m. a breach therein
†11.m.thy petition deep, or in the
10 : 23. Lord sh.m. a consumption
11 : 3. m. him of quick underst·ng
15. sh. m. men go over dryshod
13:12.I will m. a man more precio.
16:3. m. thy shadow as the night
19 : 10. all that m. sluices for fish
23:16. m.sweet melody, sing songs
25 : 6. Lord m. unto all peo. a feast
29 : 21. m. a man offender for word
32 : 6. to m. empty soul of hungry
38 : 16. wilt recover me, m. me live
40 : 3. m. straight in desert a highway, Mat. 3 : 3. Mk. 1 : 3. Lu.
41:15. m. a new sharp instru. [3:4.
18. I will m. the wildern. a pool
42 : 15. I will m. the rivers islands
16. I will m. darkness light bef.
21. he will m. the law honourable
43 : 19. I m. a way in wilderness
44 : 9. m. graven image are vanity
45 : 2. m. crooked places straight
† 13.I will m.straight all his ways
46:5. To whom will ye m. me equal
47 : 2. m. bare leg, uncover thigh
48 : 15. sh. m. his way prosperous
49 : 11. will m. all my mts. a way
50 : 2. I m. the rivers a wilderness
51:4.I will m. my judgment to rest
52 : 5. they th. rule, m. them howl
53:10. shalt m. his soul an offering
54 : 12. will m. windows of agates
56 : 7. will m. them joyful in my house of prayer
57:4.ag. whom m. ye wide mouth?
58 : 4. to m. your voice heard
11. Lord shall m. fat thy bones
60 : 13. m. place of my feet glori.
15. I will m. thee eternal excel-
17. will m. thy officers peace [cy
62 : 7. till he m. Jerusalem a praise

Is.63:6.m. them drunk in my fury
12. to m. hims. an everl. name
14. to m. thyself a glorious name
66:22. as new earth which I will m.
Je. 4 : 30. in vain shalt m. thys. fair
5 : 14. m. words in thy mouth fire
6:26. m. thee mourning as for son
9:11.I will m.Jerusalem heaps and
13 : 16. and m. it gross darkness
15 : 14. m. thee to pass into land
20. I will m. thee a fenced wall
16 : 6. nei.sh.m.thems.bald for th.
20. Sh. a man m. gods unto hims.
18 : 4. good to the potter to m. it
19:7.I will m. void counsel of Jud.
12. I will m. this city as Tophet
20:4. I will m.thee a terror to thys.
22 : 6. I will m. thee a wilderness
23:16. prophets, they m. you vain
26:6.will m. this house like Shiloh
27 : 2. m. thee bonds and yokes
25 : 9. m. them an astonishm., 18.
28 : 13. thou sh. m. yokes of iron
29 : 17. I will m. them like vile figs
22. Lord m. thee like Zedekiah
31:21.Set waymarks m.high heaps
34 : 17. I will m. you be removed
44 : 19. m. cakes to worship her?
48:26. m. him drunken, he magni.
49:15.will m.thee small am.heath.
51 : 25. I will m. thee a burnt mt.
36.m.springs dry | 39.m. drunk.
57. I will m. drunk her princes
La. 3 : † 21. This I m. return to my
Eze. 4 : 9. m. bread thereof [heart
7 : 23. m. a chain [erb
14:8.I will m.him a sign and prov-
16 : 42. I will m. my fury to rest
17 : 17. m. for him in the war
18 : 31. and m. you a new heart
21 : 10. should we then m. mirth?
†27 Perverted,perverted will m.it
22 30.sought man sho.m.up hedge
24 : 17. m. no mourning for dead
25 : 5. I will m. Rabbah a stable
26: 4. m. her like top of a rock,14.
21. I will m. thee a terror, thou
32 : 7. I will m. the stars dark, 8.
34 : 26. I will m. them a blessing?
37:19. m.them one stick, sh. be one
22. I will m. them one nation in
44 : 14. I will m. them keepers of
Da. 4 : 25.sh.m.thee to eat grass,32.
11 : 35. shall fall to m. them white
44. go utterly to m. aw. many
Ho. 2:3. lest I m.her as a wilderness
6. m. a wall that she not find path
12. I will m. them a forest
18. I will m.them lie down safely
7:3. They m. king glad with wick-
10 : 11. I will m. Ephr. ride [edu.
11:8. how shall m.thee as Admah?
12 : 9.I will m. thee dwell in taber.
Jo. 2:19. no more m.you a reproach
Am. 8 : 4. to m. poor of land fail
10.I will m. it as mourning of son
9 : 14. they shall m. gardens [err
Mi. 3 : 5. prophets that m. my peo.
4:7.will m. her th. halted a remn.
13. I will m. thine horn iron, (2)
6:13. I will m. thee sick in smiting
Na. 1 : 14. I will m. thy grave for
2 : 1. m. thy loins strong, fortify
3 : 6. I will cast filth, m. thee vile
15. m.thys.many,as cankerworm or locust [plain
Ha. 2 : 2. Write vision, and m. it
18. trusteth to m. dumb idols
3:19. he will m. my feet like hinds'
Zph. 1:18. shall m. speedy riddance
3 : 20. for I will m. you a name
Hag. 2:23. I will m. thee as a signet
Zch. 10:1. L. shall m. bright clouds
12:2. will m. Jerus. cup of trembl.
3. m. Jerus. a burdensome stone
Mal. 2 : 15. did not he m. one? [els
3:17. in day when I m. up my jew-

Mat. 1 : 19. not willing to **m.** her a public example [Mk. 1:17.
4 : 19. I will **m.** you fishers of men,
5 : 36. canst not **m.** one hair white
8 : 2. leper said, L. thou canst **m.** me clean, Mk. 1 : 40. Lu. 5 : 12.
12:33. **m.** tree good, **m.** tree corrupt
17 : 4. Pe. said, Lord, let us **m.** 3 taberu., Mk. 9 : 5. Lu. 9 : 33.
23 : 14. for pretence **m.** long prayers, Mk. 12 : 40. Lu. 20 : 47.
15. to **m.** one proselyte, and when
25. ye **m.** clean outside of the cup, Lu. 11 : 39.
24 : 47. **m.** him ruler over all, Lu. 12 : 42, 44. [many
25 : 21. I will **m.** thee ruler over
27 : 65. **m.** it as sure as ye can
Mk. 5:39. Why **m.** this ado and weep?
Lu. 5 : 33. Why do disciples of John **m.** prayers [ber fast.
34. Can ye **m.** chil. of bridechamber
11 : 40. did he not **m.** that within
14 : 18. all began to **m.** excuse
15 : 19. **m.** me as one of thy hired
16 : 9. **m.** friends of mammon of
Jn. 1:23. **m.** straight the way of L.
2:16. **m.** not my Fa.'s house ho. of
6 : 10. **m.** the men sit down
15. by force to **m.** him a king
8:32. and the truth sh. **m.** you free
36. If the Son **m.** you free, ye sh.
10:24. How long **m.** us to doubt?
14:23. will **m.** our abode with him
Ac. 2:28. **m.** me full of joy with thy
7 : 40. **m.** us gods to go before us
44. shall **m.** it acc. to fashion
9:34. Pe. said, arise and **m.** thy bed
22 : 1. hear ye defence I now **m.**
26 : 16. to **m.** thee a minister and
24. learning doth **m.** thee mad
Ro. 3:3. **m.** faith of G. without eff.
31. Do we then **m.** void the law
9:21. to **m.** one vessel unto honour
28. short work will the Lord **m.**
13 : 14. **m.** not provision for flesh
14:4. God is able to **m.** him stand
19. follow things **m.** for peace
15:26. to **m.** a contribution [harlot
1 Co. 6 : 15. **m.** them members of
8:13. if meat **m.** my bro. to offend
9 : 18. may **m.** gospel of C. with-t
10:13. **m.** a way to escape [charge
2 Co. 2:2. if I **m.** you sorry, who glad?
9 : 5. **m.** up beforeh. your bounty
8. God is able to **m.** grace abound
12:17. Did I **m.** gain of you by any
Ga. 2:18. I **m.** myself a transgressor
3:17. **m.** the promise of none effect
6 : 12. as desire to **m.** a fair shew
Ep. 2:15. to **m.** of twain 1 new man
1 Th. 3:12. L. **m.** you to incr. in love
2 Th. 3:9. to **m.** ours. an ensample
2 Ti. 3:15. **m.** thee wise unto salva.
4:5. **m.** full proof of thy ministry
He. 2:10. to **m.** captain of their salva.
17. to **m.** reconciliation for sins
8 : 5. **m.** all things acc. to pattern
9 : 9. could not **m.** him perfect
10:1. **m.** comers thereunto perfect
12 : 13. **m.** straight paths for feet
13:21. **m.** you perf. in ev. good work
Pe. 5:10. God of grace **m.** you perfect
2 Pe. 1:8. **m.** you th. ye nei. be barren
10. **m.** your calling and elec. sure
1 Jn. 1 : 10. we **m.** him a liar
Re. 3 : 9. I will **m.** th. worship bef.
12. I will **m.** a pillar in the temple
10 : 9. it shall **m.** thy belly bitter
13 : 14. sho. **m.** an image to beast
21:5. Behold, I **m.** all things new
See AFRAID, ARK, ATONEMENT, COVENANT, DECREE, DESOLATE, DESOLATION, END, FEAST, FIRE, GOOD.

MAKE haste.

De. 20 : † 3. fear not do not **m.** h.
De. 32 : 35. things that come **m. h.**
Ju. 9 : 48. said, **m. h.** and do as I
1 S. 9 : 12. he is before you, **m. h.** now
1 Ch. 12: †8. roes upon mts. to **m. h.**
2 Ch. 35:21. God com-d me to **m. h.**
Es. 5:5. Cause Haman to **m. h.**, 6:10.
Jb. 20:2. to answer, for this I **m. h.**
Ps. 38 : 22. **m. h.** to help me, O L., my salva., 40 : 13.–70:1.–71:12.
70 : 5. am poor needy, **m. h.**, 141:1.
Pr. 1:16. **m. h.** to shed bl., Is. 59:7.
Can. 8 : 14. **m. h.**, my beloved
Is. 28:16. believeth shall not **m. h.**
49 : 17. Thy children shall **m. h.**
Je. 9:18. let them **m. h.**, take wailing
Na. 2 : 5. they shall **m. h.** to wall
Lu. 19:5. he said, Zaccheus, **m. h.**
Ac. 22:18. **m. h.** and get thee quickly out of Jerusalem
See IMAGE, INTERCESSION, KING.
See **KNOW, Make KNOWN.**

MAKE manifest. [heart

1 Co. 4 : 5. will **m. m.** counsels of
2 Co. 2 : 14. **m. m.** the savour of knowledge [light
Ep. 5 : 13. whatso. doth **m. m.** is
Col. 4:4. may **m.** it **m.** as I ought
See MENTION, MERRY, NATION, NOISE, OFFERING, PEACE.

MAKE ready.

Ge. 18:6. **m. r.** 3 measures of meal
43:16. **m. r.**, for these men sh. dine
2 K. 9 : 21. Joram said, **m. r.** and
Ps. 11 : 2. they **m. r.** their arrow
21 : 12. when shalt **m. r.** arrows
Eze. 7 : 14. blown trumpet to **m. r.**
Mk. 14:15. **m. r.** for us, Lu. 22:12.
Lu. 1:17. to **m. r.** a people prepared
9:52. village of Samaritans to **m.**
17 : 8. **m. r.**, whw. I may sup [r.
Ac. 23 : 23. **m. r.** 200 soldiers to go to Cesarea
See RECONCILIATION, SEARCH.

MAKE speed.

1 S. 20:38. he cried, **m. s.**, haste, stay
2 S. 15 : 14. **m. s.** to depart, lest he
Is. 5 : 19. that say, Let him **m. s.**
See **Make SUPPLICATION.**
See UNDERSTAND [verb], WAR.

MAKE waste.

Le. 26 : 31. I will **m.** your cities **w.**
Is. 42 : 15. I will **m. w.** mountains
Eze. 5:14. I will **m.** Jerus. **w.** [30:12.
29:10. I will **m.** Egypt utterly **w.**,

MAKEBATES. [†3.

2 Ti. 3:†3. trucebreakers, **m.**, Tit. 2:

MAKER, S. [M.?

Jb. 4:17. man be more pure than his
32:22. my M. will soon take me aw.
35:10. saith, Where is God my M.?
36 : 3. ascribe right-n to my M.
Ps. 95 : 6. kneel bef. L. our M. [M.
Pr. 14 : 31. oppr-h poor, reproach-h
17:5. mocketh poor reproach-th M.
22:2. rich and poor, L. is **m.** of all
Is. 1:31. and the **m.** of it as a spark
17:7. that day a man look to his M.
22:11. ye have not looked unto the
33 : † 22. L. is our statute **m.** [m.
45:9. Woe unto him striveth wi. M.
11. saith Holy One of Isr. his M.
16. confusion that are **m**-s of idols
51 : 13. forgettest the Lord thy M.
54 : 5. thy M. is thy husband, and
Je. 33:2. Thus saith the L. the **m.**
Ho. 8:14. Isr. hath forgotten his M.
Ha. 2 : 18. What profiteth image **m.** hath graven, **m.** trusteth [G.
He. 11:10. whose builder and **m.** is

MAKEST.

Ju. 18:3. what **m.** thou in this place?
Jb. 13:26. **m.** me possess iniquities
22 : 3. is it gain to him that thou **m.** thy ways perfect?
Ps. 4 : 8. **m.** me to dwell in safety
39 : 11. **m.** his beauty to consume
44 : 10. Thou **m.** us to turn back fr.
Ps. 44:13. **m.** us reproach to neigh-s
14. **m.** us a byword am. heathen
65:8. **m.** the outgoings of morning
10. **m.** the earth soft with showers
80 : 6. **m.** us strife unto neigh-s
104:20. **m.** darkness, and it is night
144:3. man, th. thou **m.** account of
Can. 1:7. where **m.** thy flock to rest
Is. 45:9. sh. clay say, What **m.** thou?
Je. 22:23. that **m.** thy nest in cedars
28:15. **m.** this peo. to trust in a lie
Eze. 16:31. **m.** thy high pla. in street
Ha. 1 : 14. **m.** men as fishes of sea
2:15. thy bottle, and **m.** him drunk.
Lu. 14:12. When thou **m.** a dinner
13. when **m.** feast, call poor [self?
Jn. 8:53. proph. dead, whom **m.** thy-
10:33. bec. being man **m.** thys. God
Ro. 2:17. Jew, and **m.** thy boast of
23. Thou that **m.** boast of law [G.

MAKETH.

Ex. 4:11. who **m.** the dumb, or deaf
Le. 7:7. priest that **m.** atonem., 14:11.
17 : 11. blood **m.** the atonement
De. 18:10. **m.** son to pass thro. fire
20:20. city that **m.** war with thee
21:16. when he **m.** his sons inherit
24:7. **m.** merchandise of him, or
27:15. Cursed that **m.** graven image
18. Cursed that **m.** blind wander
29:12. oath which L. **m.** with thee
1 S. 2 : 6. L. killeth and **m.** alive
7. The L. **m.** poor, and **m.** rich
2 S. 22:33. God **m.** my way perfect, Ps. 18 : 32. [feet, Ps. 18 : 33.
22 : 34. He **m.** my feet like hinds'
Jb. 5:18. he **m.** sore, and bindeth up
9 : 9. Lord **m.** Arcturus, Orion
12 : 17. he **m.** the judges fools
25. he **m.** to stagger like drunken
15 : 27. he **m.** collops of fat on his
23:16. God **m.** my heart soft, and
25 : 2. **m.** peace in his high places
27:18. as booth that the keeper **m.**
35:11. who **m.** us wiser than fowls
36:27. he **m.** small the drops of wat.
41:31. He **m.** deep to boil like pot
32. He **m.** a path to shine aft. him
Ps. 9:12. he **m.** inquisition for blood
23 : 2. He **m.** to lie down in green
29:6. He **m.** them to skip like a calf
9. voice of L. **m.** hinds to calve
33 : 10. **m.** devices of peo. of none
40:4. Blessed that **m.** L. his trust
46:9. He **m.** wars to cease unto the
104 : 3. who **m.** clouds his chariot
4. **m.** his angels spirits, He. 1 : 7.
15. wine that **m.** glad the heart
107:†25. **m.** stormy wind to stand
29. He **m.** the storm a calm
36. there he **m.** hungry to dwell
41. **m.** him families like a flock
113 : 9. **m.** barren woman to keep
135 : 7. he **m.** lightnings for rain
147:8. **m.** grass to grow upon mts.
14. He **m.** peace in thy borders
Pr. 10:1. wise son **m.** a glad fa., 15:
4. hand of diligent **m.** rich [20.
22. blessing of the L. it **m.** rich
12 : 4. she that **m.** ashamed is as rottenness in his bones
25. Heaviness in heart **m.** it stoop a good word **m.** it glad
13 : 7. **m.** himself rich, yet hath noth., is that **m.** hims. poor, yet hath great riches [sick
12. Hope deferred **m.** the heart
15:13. A merry heart **m.** a cheerful
30. a good report **m.** bones fat
16 : 7. he **m.** his enemies to be at peace [mouth
† 23. heart of wise **m.** wise his
18 : 16. man's gift **m.** room for him
19 : 4. wealth **m.** many friends, but
28 : 20. that **m.** haste to be rich
31 : 22. **m.** hers. coverings of tapes.
24. She **m.** fine linen and selleth

Ec. 3:11. no man find out work G. **m.**
7:7. oppression **m.** wise man mad
8:1. wisdom **m.** his face to shine
11:5. works of God, who **m.** all
Is 24:1. the Lord **m.** earth empty, (2)
27:9. **m.** stones of altar as chalk
40:23. he **m.** the judges as vanity
43:16. L. which **m.** a way in sea
44:15. he **m.** a god, and worshippeth it, 13, 17.-46:6.
24. I am the L. that **m.** all things
25. I am L. **m.** diviners mad
55:10. earth, and **m.** it bring forth
59:15. he that departeth from evil **m.** himself a prey
Je. 4:19. my heart **m.** noise in me
10:13. he **m.** lightnings, 51:16.
17:5. Cursed that **m.** flesh his arm
21:2. for Neb. **m.** war against us
29:26. that **m.** himself a proph., 27.
48:28. like dove that **m.** her nest
Eze. 22:3. **m.** idols against herself
Da. 6:13. **m.** petition 3 times a day
11:31. abomi. that **m.** desolate, 12:
Am. 4:13. **m.** morning darkn. [11.
5:8. Seek him that **m.** 7 stars
Na. 1:4. He rebuketh sea, **m.** it dry
Mat. 5:45. he **m.** his sun rise on evil
Mk. 7:37. he **m.** both deaf to hear
Lu. 5:36. both the new **m.** rent
Jn. 19:12. whoso. **m.** himself a king
Ac. 9:34. Jes. Christ **m.** thee whole
Ro. 5:5. hope **m.** not ashamed, bec.
8:26. Spirit **m.** intercession, 27, 34.
11:2. he **m.** intercession to G.
1 Co. 4:7. who **m.** thee to differ
2 Co. 2:2. who is he that **m.** me glad
14. **m.** manifest savour of his knowledge [no matter to me
Ga. 2:6. whatso. they were it **m.**
Ep. 4:16. **m.** increase of the body
He. 7:28. the law **m.** men high pri., word of the oath **m.** the Son
Re. 13:13. he **m.** fire come down
21:27. nei. whatso. **m.** a lie, 22:15.

MAK'HELOTH. [M.
Nu. 33:25. pitched in M. 26. from

MAKING. [Noun and part.]
Ex. 5:14. Whf. have ye not fulfilled your task in **m.** brick
2 Ch. 30:22. **m.** confession to the L.
Ps. 19:7. of L. is sure, **m.** wise simp.
Ec. 12:12. of **m.** many books is no
Is. 3:16. **m.** tinkling with their feet
Je. 20:15. tidings **m.** him very glad
Eze. 27:16. mult. of wares of thy **m.**,
Ho. 10:4. falsely in **m.** cov-t [18.
Am. 8:5. **m.** ephah small, and shek.
Mi. 6:13. **m.** thee desolate bec. of
Mk. 7:13. **m.** word of G. of none
Jn. 5:18. **m.** himself equal with G.
Ro 1:10. **m.** request if by any means
2 Co. 6:10. poor, yet **m.** many rich
Ep. 2:15. so **m.** peace, Col. 1:† 20.
5:19. **m.** melody in your heart to
Ph. 1:4. in prayer for you **m.** request
2 Pe. 2:6. **m.** them an ensample
Jude 22. compassion **m.** a difference
See MENTION, MERRY, NOISE, SUPPLICATION, WAR.

MAKKE'DAH.
Jos. 10:10. Smote them unto M.
16. hid thems. in cave at M., 17.
21. people returned to camp at M.
28. That day Joshua took M. (2)
12:16. The king of M. one [| 29.
15:41. and M., 16 cities with villages

MAK'TESH.
Zph. 1:11. Howl ye inhabit-s of M.

MAL'ACHI.
Mal. 1:1. word of L. to Israel by M.

MAL'CHAM.
1 Ch. 8:9. he begat of Hodesh, M.
Zph. 1:5. that swear by L. and M.

MALCHI'AH = MALCHI'-JAH.
Ezr. 10:25. of sons of Parosh, M.
Ezr. 10:31. of the sons of Harim, M.
Ne. 3:14. M. repaired dung gate
31. after him repaired M.
8:4. and on his left hand, M.
10:3. those that sealed, Amariah, M.
11:12. Pashur son of M., Je. 38:1.
Je. 38:6. cast him into dungeon of M.

MAL'DHIEL, ITES.
Ge. 46:17. sons of Beriah, M., 1 Ch. 7:
Nu. 26:45. of M. family of M-s [31.

MALCHI'JAH = MALCHI'AH.
1 Ch. 9:12. Pashur son of M.
24:9. The 5th lot to M.
Ezr. 10:25. of sons of Parosh, M.
Ne. 3:11. M. son of Harim.
12:42 M. stood to give thanks

MALCHI'RAM.
1 Ch. 3:18. sons of Jeconiah, M.

MALCHI-SHU'A. [10:2.
1 Ch. 8:33. Saul begat M., 9:39.

MAL'CHUS.
Jn. 18:10. servant's name was M.

MALE. [34:15, 22, 24.
Ge. 17:23. every **m.** circumcised,
Ex 12:5. for passover a **m.** of first year
Le. 1:3. a **m.** without blemish, 10.-4:23.-22:19. [thereo
7:6. Every **m.** am priests shall eat
27:3. thy estimation sh. be of the **m.**, 5, 6, 7. [20 years
Nu. 1:2. every **m.** by their polls fro
20. every **m.** from 20 years old
3:15. every **m.** from a month old
31:17. kill ev. **m.** am. little ones
De. 20:13. thou shalt smite ev. **m.**
Ju. 21:11. ye shall destroy ev. **m.**
12. by lying with any **m.** [16.
1 K. 11:15. smitten ev **m.** in Edom,
Je. 30:† 6. see if a **m.** doth travail
Eze. 16:† 17. madest images of **m.**
Mal. 1:14. which hath in his flock a
See CHILDREN, FEMALE. [**m.**

MALES.
Ge. 34:25. Sim. and Levi slew all **m.**
Ex. 12:48. let all his **m.** be circum.
13:12. **m.** shall be the L.'s, 34:19
15. I sacri. to L. all being **m.**, 12.
23:17. Three times in year **m.** sh. appear bef. L. G., De. 16:16.
Le 6:18. **m.** of Aa. sh. eat of it, 29.
Nu. 3:22. acc. to **m.** fr. month old upw., 28, 34, 39.-26:62. [43.
40. number of all firstborn of **m.**,
31:7. ag. Midianites, and slew **m.**
De. 15:19. firstling **m.** sanctify unto
Jos. 5:4. **m.** th. came out of E. died
2 Ch. 31:16. genealogy of **m.**, Ezr. 8:
19. portions to **m.** am. priests [3.
Ezr. 8:4. Elioenai with him 200 **m.**
5. son of Jahaziel with him 300 **m.**
6. Ebed, with him 50 **m.**
7. Jehaiah and with him 70 **m.**
8. Zebadiah and fourscore **m.**
9. Obadiah and with him 218 **m.**
10. son of Josiphiah and 160 **m.**
11. Zechariah, with him 28 **m.**
12. Johanan with him 110 **m.**
13. Jeiel, Shemaiah, with th. 60 **m.**
14. Uthai, Zabbud with th. 70 **m.**

MALEFACTOR, S.
Lu. 23:32. were two **m-s** with him
33. there crucified him, and **m-s**
39. one of the **m-s** railed on him
Jn. 18:30. If he were not a **m.** we

MALELE'EL.
Ge. 5:† 12. Cainan begat M, Lu 3:37.

MALICE.
1 Co. 5:8. not with leaven of **m.**
14:20. howbeit in **m.** be ye children
Ep. 4:31. away fr. you with all **m.**
Col. 3:8. now put off all these, **m.**
Tit. 3:3. sometimes living in **m.** and
1 Pe. 2:1. laying aside all **m.** guile

MALICIOUS.
3 Jn. 10. prating ag. us wi. **m.** words

MALICIOUSNESS.
Ro. 1:29. being filled with all **m.**
1 Pe. 2:16. not liberty for cloak of **m.**

MALIGNITY.
Ro. 1:29. full of murder, debate, **m.**

MAL'LOTHI.
1 Ch. 25:4. sons of Heman, M.
26. the 19th lot to M.

MALLOWS.
Jb. 30:4. Who cut up **m.** for meat

MAL'LUCH.
1 Ch. 6:44. son of Abdi, son of M.
Ezr. 10:29. of Bani, M. | 32. of Harim, M.
Ne. 10:4. sealed were M., 27. [rim, M.
12:2. M. went up with Zerub-l

MAM'MON. [Lu. 16:13.
Mat. 6:24. Can-t serve G. and **m.**,
Lu. 16:9. make friends of **m.** of
11. not faithful in unrighte-s **m.**

MAM'RE. [Person, place.]
Ge. 13:18. in the plain of M., 14:13.
14:24. Eshcol, M. let take portion
18:1. L. appeared to Ab. in M.
23:17. Machpelah before M., 19.-25:9.-49:30.-50:13.
35:27. Jacob came to Isaac to M.

MAN.
Ge. 1:26. God said, Let us make **m.** in our image, 27.-9:6.
2:7. L. G. formed **m.** of the dust
18. is not good **m.** sho. be alone
25. both naked, **m.** and his wife
3:12. **m.** said, The wom. thou gav.
22. the **m.** is become as one of us
6:3. Spirit not alw. strive with **m.**
6. it repent-d L. he had made **m.**
7. will destroy **m.** whom I crea.
8:21. not curse gro-d for **m.**'s sake
9:6. **m.**'s blood, by **m.** shall his blood be shed [**m.** Nu 31:35.
19:8. two dau-s wh. have not known
20:3. thou art but a dead **m.**
7. restore the **m.** his wife, he
24:21. **m.** wondering at her +
29. Laban ran out to **m.** to well
65. What **m.** is this walketh [**m.**
29:19. than I sho. give her to ano.
37:15. **m.** asked, What seekest thou
38:25. By the **m.** am I with child
41:11. each **m.** acc. to his dream, 12.
43:3. **m.** did solemnly protest, +
13. arise, go again to the **m.**
44:17. **m.** in whose hand cup is
Ex. 2:20. why is it ye left the **m.**?
21. Moses content to dwell wi. **m.**
4:11. Who hath made **m.**'s mouth?
30:32. Upon **m.**'s flesh shall it not be poured [of Egypt, 23.
32:1. the **m.** that brought us out
Le. 17:4. blood sh. be imputed unto that **m.** that **m.** be cut off
Nu. 5:15. **m.** bring his wife to priest
9:13. But the **m.** that is clean, and
12:3. the **m.** Moses was very meek
15:35. The **m.** shall be put to death, De. 22:25. [be holy
16:7. **m.** whom the L. doth choose,
17:5. **m.**'s rod wh. I choose sh. bloss
19:20. **m.** that shall be unclean [15.
24:3. **m.** whose eyes are open said,
25:8. Phinehas went aft. **m.** of Isr.
De. 4:32 since day G. created **m.**
5:24. God doth talk with **m.**
8:3. know **m.** doth not live by bread only, but, Mat. 4:4. Lu. 4:4.
20:5. What **m.** th. hath built a ho.
6. what **m.** is he hath planted vineyard [wife
7. what **m.** that hath betrothed
8. What **m.** is there is fearful and
20:19. tree of the field is **m.**'s life
28:54. the **m.** that is tender am. you
Jos. 7:14. sh. come **m.** by **m.**, 17, 18.
Ju. 1:25. they let go the **m.** and all
4:22. I will shew **m.** thou seekest
8:21. as **m.** is, so is his strength
9:9. by me they honour G. and **m.**,

Ju.9:13.wine wh.cheereth G.and m.
10:18. What m. will fight Ammon?
13:10. m. hath appeared th. came
11. Art thou m.spak.unto wom.?
16:7. weak, and as ano. m., 11,17.
19:7.when the m. rose to depart+
22. Bring forth the m. that came
28. m. took her upon an ass
21:22. reserved not to each m.wife
Ru. 1: 2. m. was Elimelech, 2: 19.
2: 20. m. is near of kin unto us
3: 18. m. will not be in rest until
1 S. 2: 33. m. whom I not cut off
4:14. m. came hastily, told Eli,16.
9:6.a m. of G.,and honourable m.
7. if we go, what bring the m.?
17. Behold m. whom I spake of
10:22. if m. sho. yet come thither
16: 7. Lord seeth not as m.
17: 26. What be done to m. that
killeth this Philistine
24. men of Isr. when saw m. fled
21:14. Lo, ye see m. is mad [25,27.
2 S.12:5.Da.'s anger kindled ag. m.
said, m. who did this shall die
7. said to David, Thou art the m.
16:7.come out, thou bloody m., 8.
17: 3. m. thou seekest is as if returned [told him
18: 11. Joab said unto the m. that
26.watchman saw ano. m.runn-g
21: 5. m. that consumed us, and
22: 26. with upright m.wilt shew
49. hast deliv-d from violent m.
23:1.m.who was raised up on high
7. m. that shall touch them
1 K. 20: 20. slew every one his m.
2 K. 5: 26. m. turned to meet thee
6:19. bring you to m. ye seek
9: 11. Ye know the m. and
15:20. exacted of each m. 50 shek.
22: 15. Tell the m. that sent you,
2 Ch. 34:23. [were 38,000
1 Ch. 23: 3. the Levites m. by m.
29: 1. palace is not for m. but L.
2 Ch. 14:11. not m. prevail ag.thee
19: 6. ye judge not for m. but L.
Es. 6:6.What be done unto m., 7,9.
7: †6. the m. is this wick. Haman
Jb. 4:17. m. be more just than G.?
5:7. Yet m. is born to trouble, as
7:1.Is not an appointed time for m.
17.What is m.th. thou shouldest
magnify him? 15: 14. Ps. 8: 4.
9:2.how should m.be just with G.?
10: 4. seest thou as m. seeth?
5. thy days as days of m.? years
as m.'s days? [m. be born
11:12. vain m. would be wise, tho.
14: 1. m. that is born of a woman
10. m. dieth, m. giveth up ghost
12. So m. lieth down, riseth not
15:7. Art thou first m. was born?
14. What is m. that he be clean?
16. How much more filthy is m.?
20:4. since m. was plac. upon earth
21: 4. is my complaint to m.?
22: † 8. m. of arm dwelt in it [G.?
25: 4. How can m. be justif. with
6. How much less m. that is a
worm, and son of m.
28:13.m.knoweth not price thereof
28. unto m. he said, fear of L.
32:8.is a spirit in m. inspiration of
13.G.thrusteth him down,not m.
33:12.I ans., G. is greater than m.
14.G. speaketh, m. perceiv-h not
17. he may withdraw m. fr. purpose, and hide pride from m.
23.to shew unto m. his uprightn.
26. render unto m. his righte-n.
29. things worketh G.oft.with m.
34: 7. What m. is like Job, who
14. If he set his heart upon m. if
15. m. shall turn ag. unto dust
23. For he will not lay upon m.
more than right

Ps. 8: 4. What is m. that thou art
mindful of him? 144:3. He. 2:6.
9: 19. O Lord let not m. prevail
10: 18. that m. no more oppress
12:1. Help L. for godly m.ceaseth
25:12. What m. is he feareth L.?
34:12.What m. is he desireth life?
37: 7. bec. of m. who bringeth
wicked devices to pass
39:11. When thou dost correct m.
49:12.m.in honour abideth not,20
56: 1. m. would swallow me up
11. not be afraid what m. can do
68: † 18. received gifts in the m.
78:25. m. did eat angels' food, he
80:17. thy hand be upon m.of thy
89:48.What m.is he liveth,and not
90:3. Thou turnest m. to destruc.
94:10. teacheth m. sh. not he kn.?
103:15.As for m. days are as grass
104: 23. m. goeth unto his work
118: 6. will not fear what m. can
do, He. 13: 6.
8. than to put confidence in m.
120: † 7. I am a m. of peace, they
144:4.m. is like to vanity,his days
Pr. 2: 12. m. that speaketh froward
3:4. good underst-g in sight of m.
6: 11. want as armed m., 24: 34.
16: 1. preparations of heart in m.
20:24. m.'s goings are of the Lord,
how can a m.
25. It is snare to m. who devoureth that is holy [the way
21: 16. m. that wandereth out of
28.m.th.heareth speaketh const-y
26:19.m.that deceiveth neighbour
27: 2. Let another m. praise thee
Ec. 1: 8. things full of labour, m.
cannot utter it [king? 18.
2: 12. what can m. do cometh af.
22. what hath m. of his labour?
6: 10. and it is known th. it is m.
11.what is m. better? [m.
12. who knoweth what is good for
7: 29. G. hath made m. upright
9: 12. m. knoweth not his time
12: 5. bec. m. goeth to long home
Is.2:22.Cease from m.whose breath
6: 11. Until houses be without m.
38: 11. I shall behold m. no more
40:†13. or being m. of his counsel
45:12. I have made and created m.
46:11.m.th. executeth my counsel
Je. 3:1.If she become another m.'s
10: 23. not in m. to direct his
La. 3: 1. I m. that seen affliction
Eze.4:15. cow's dung for m.'s dung
9: 3. m. clothed wi. linen, 11.-10:
2, 6. Da. 12: 6, 7.
43:6. m. stood by me
47:3. when the m. that had line went
18: 8. judgment betw. m. and m.
Da.4:16.Let heart be changed fr.m.
9:21. m. Gabriel whom I had seen
10: 19. said, O m. greatly beloved
Ho. 11:9. for I am God, and not m.
Am.4:13.declareth unto m.what is
Mi. 5: 7. tarrieth not for m. [good
6: 8. shewed thee, O m. what is
9. m. of wisd. shall see thy name
Ha. 1: 13. the wicked devoureth m.
Zph. 1: 3. I will cut off m. fr. land
Zch.1:10.m.th.stood among myrtle
6: 12. m. whose name is Branch
13:5. m. taught me to keep cattle
7.awake, ag. m. that is my fellow
Mal. 2: 12. L. will cut off m. doeth
Mat. 7: 9. what m. is there of you,
if son ask bread,12:11. Lu.15:4.
15:18.fr. the heart, they defile m.,
11,20. Mk. 7:15,18,20,23. [10:9.
19:6. let not m. put asunder, Mk.
26: 72. I do not know the m., 74.
Mk. 2:27. sabbath was made for m.
not m. for sabbath
3:3. m. stand forth, 5. Lu. 6:8, 10.

Mk. 5: 8. Come out of m., Lu.8:29.
11: 2. colt, whereon never m. sat,
Lu. 19: 30. [devout
Lu. 2: 25. same m. was just and
52. in favour with God and m.
5: 20. m. thy sins are forgiven
8:33. went devils out of m., 35, 38.
12: 14. m. who made me a judge
18:2.feared not G.nei.regarded m.
4. fear not God, nor regard m.
22:58.Pe. said,m. I am not [sayest
60. Pe. said, m. I know not what
23: 6. whether m. was a Galilean
53. never m. was laid, Jn. 19:41.
Jn. 2: 25. he knew what in m.
4: 50. m. believed word Jes. said
5:9.imme.m.was made whole | 15.
12. What m. is that which said
34. I rec-d not testimony fr. m.
7:46. Never m. spake like this m.
9: 30. m.ans-d,Why herein is [did
15:24. works which none other m.
19: 5. Pilate said, Behold the m.
Ac. 4: 9. deed done to impotent m.
14. beholding m. wh. was healed
22. m. was about forty years old
8:31.How, exc. some m. guide me?
34. of himself, or some other m.?
11:12. we entered into m.'s house
17:29. stone graven by m.'s device
19: 16. m. in whom evil spirit was
35. what m. th. knoweth not how
21: 9. same m. had 4 dau-s [city
11. bind m. owneth this girdle
23: 30. how Jews laid wait for m.
25:17.com-d the m. to be brought
22. Agrippa said,I would hear m.
Ro.2:1. thou art inexcusable, O m.
3. thinkest, O m. that judgest
4:8. m. unto wh. L. imputeth not
7: 3. If married to another m. (2)
22. in law of God after inward m.
24.O wretched m. that I am, who
9:20. O m. who thou that repliest
10:5.the m.who doeth these things
shall live by them, Ga. 3: 12.
10. with the heart m. believeth
14:4. Who thou judgest m.'s serv.
15:20. lest I build upon ano. m.'s
1 Co.2:4. not enticing words of m.'s
wisdom, 13. [m.?
11. what m. knoweth things of
14. natural m. receiveth not
4: 3. judged of m.'s judgment
7:16. how knowest,O m.whe.thou
10:13. tempta. as is common to m.
29. why my liberty judged of ano.
11:3.head of woman is the m.[m.'s
8.m.is not of the woman,but (2)
9. Nei.was m.created for wom.(2)
11. nei. is m. without the woman,
nei. woman with-t m. in the L.
12. even so is m. by woman [m.
15:21. since by m. came death, by
35. some m. will say, How dead
45. first m. Adam was made a
47. first m. is of earth, earthy;
second m. is the L. from heav.
2 Co. 4:16. tho. outward m. perish,
yet inward m. is renewed [m.
Ga. 1:1. apostle, not of men, nei.by
11. gospel I preached is not aft.
Ep. 2: 15. of twain one new m. [m.
3: 16. by his Spirit in inner m.
4: 24. that ye put on the new m.
Col. 3: 10. have put on the new m.
1 Th. 4:8. despiseth not m.but God
1 Ti. 2:5. betw. G. and men, m.C.J.
12. not to usurp authority ov.m.
Tit. 3:4.love of G. our Savi. tow.m.
He 3:4. ev. ho. is built by some m.
8:2. taber. L. pitched, and not m.
Ja.1:8. doubleminded m.is unstable
2: 20. know, O vain m. that faith
1 Pe.3:4.the hidden m. of the heart
2 Pe.2:16.ass speaking wi.m.'s voice
See **ANOTHER** man.

A MAN.

Ge.2:5. was not a m. to till ground
24. Thf. shall a m. leave his fa. and Mat.19:5.Mk.10:7.Ep.5:31.
4: 1. I have gotten a m. from L.
23. slain a m. to my wounding
11:†3. a m. said to his neighbour
13: 16. if a m. can number dust
19:31.not a m. to come in unto us
20:3.thou a dead m. she is a m.'s
25: 27. Esau a m. of field ⌊wife
32:24. there wrestled a m. wi.him
41:33. let Pha. look out a m. wise
38. a m. in wh. Spirit of God is
44:15. wot ye a m. as I can divine
49: 6. in anger they slew a m.
Ex. 2: † 14. Who made thee a m.
18:†16.I judge betw. a m. and his
21:7. If a m. sell his daughter +
22:1. if a m. sh. steal an ox or +
33:11.as a m.speaketh unto friend
Le.5:3.If he touch unclean. of a m.
6: 3. in these a m. doeth sinning
13: 9. When leprosy is in a m.
18: 5. if a m. do he shall live in them, Ne.9:29. Eze.20:11,13,21.
20: 12. If a m. lie with his dau.+
24:10.and a m. of Isr. strove toge.
20.hath caused a blemish in a m.
27:14.when a m.sanctify ho.,16,22
28. no thing a m. shall devote
31. if a m. redeem his tithes
Nu. 1: 4. shall be a m. of ev. tribe
13:2. of ev. tribe sh. ye send a m.
15:32. found a m. gathered sticks
19:14.law when a m. dieth in tent
23: 19. God is not a m. that he should lie, 1 S. 15: 29.
26: 64. was not a m. of them
65. was not left a m. save Caleb
27:16. set a m. over the congrega.
18. Josh. a m. in wh.Spirit ⌈son
De. 1: 31. L. bare thee, as a m. his
3: 11. breadth, aft. cubit of a m.
8:5. that as a m. chast-th his son
15: 12. if bro. a Heb. m. be sold
19:15. One witn. not rise ag. a m.
21:15.If a m.,+22:23.+ | 24:1.+
Jos.3:12. of every tribe a m.,4:2,4.
5:13. a m. over ag. him wi. sword
8: 17. was not a m. left in Ai
10:8.not a m.of th.stand bef.thee
14. the L. hearkened unto a m.
14:15. which Arba was a great m.
21:44.stood not a m.of their enem.
Ju.1:24.spies saw a m. come out of
3:29. escaped not a m., 1 S.30:17.
4: 16. and there was not a m. left
7: 13. was a m. th. told a dream
14. sword of Gideon a m. of Isr.
10: 1. Tola a m. of Issachar
16: 19. she called a m.
Ru. 4: 7. a m. plucked off his shoe
1 S.9:16.send thee a m.out of Benj.
11:13.sh. not a m. be put to death
13:14.Lord hath sought him a m.
14:36. let us not leave a m. of th.
39.not a m.am.people ans-d him
16:16.a m. who is cunning player
17.Provide me a m.can play well
17: 8. choose you a m. for you
10. give me a m. that we fight
24: 19. If a m. find enemy will he
25:2. a m. in Maon whose poss-ns
17. a m. cannot speak to him
29. a m. is risen to pursue thee
2 S. 1: 2. a m. came out of camp
3: 34. as a m. falleth bef. wicked
38. Abner a great m. is fallen
16:23.as if a m. inquired at oracle
18:†20.shalt not be a m.of tidings
24. behold a m. running alone
20: 1. happ-d to be a m. of Belial
1 K. 2: 2. and shew thyself a m.
4. not fail thee a m. on throne, 8: 25.–9: 5. 2 Ch. 6: 16.–7: 18.
7: 14. fa.a m. of Tyre, 2 Ch. 2:14.
1 K.20:39. a m.turned aside, bro-t a m. ⌈struction
42. a m. wh. I appointed to de-
2 K. 1: 6. came a m. to meet us
4: 42. a m. from Baal-shalisha
6: 32. king sent a m. before him
10:21. not a m. left that came not
13:21. as they were burying a m.
18:21.on wh. if a m. lean,Is.36:6.
1 Ch. 22: 9. son sh. be a m. of rest
2 Ch.6:22.If a m. sin ag.neighbour
Ne. 2: 10. a m. seek welfare of Isr.
6: 11. Should such a m. as I flee
Jb. 2: 4. all a m. hath will he give
3: 23. Why is light given to a m.
4: 17. a m. more pure than Ma-
9:32. he is not a m. as I am ⌊ker?
11:2. a m. full of talk be justified
12: 14. he shutteth up a m.
14:14.If a m. die sh. he live again
16: 21. might plead for a m. with G.as a m.pleadeth for neighb.
22:2.Can a m.be profitable unto G
34:9.said,It profiteth a m.nothing
29. whether ag. a nation or a m.
35:8.Thy wickedn. may hurt a m.
37:20. if a m. speak he be swall-d
Ps. 38: 14. I as a m. heareth not
55:13.it was thou a m.mine equal
62: 3. imagine mischief ag. a m.?
74: 5. a m. was famous acc. as he
88: 4. I as a m. hath no strength
105:17. He sent a m. before them
147:10.not pleasure in legs of a m.
Pr. 3: 30. Strive not with a m.
6: 34. jealousy is the rage of a m.
12:2.a m. of wicked devices,14:17.
3.a m.uot to be estab.by wickedn
8.a m. sh. be commended acc.to
13: 2. a m. sh. eat goodly fruit of
8. ransom of m.'s life are riches
14:12. There is a way which seem-eth right unto a m., 16: 25.
15: 23. a m. hath joy by ans. of
16: 2. All ways of a m. clean in
7. when a m.'s ways please the L.
9. a m.'s heart deviseth his way
18:1.Thro. desire a m. hav-g sepa.
19:19.a m.of gr.wrath suffer pun-t
22. desire of a m. is his kindness
20:3.honour for a m.to cease fr.str
24. how a m. underst. own way?
23:2. if a m. given to appetite
26: † 10. a great m. grieveth all
21. so a contentious m. to kindle
27:8.so is a m. wandereth fr.place
21.furnace, so a m. to his praise
28:12. when wick. rise a m.is hid.
23.rebuketh a m. sh. find favour
29:†1. a m. of reproofs be destroy.
† 4. a m. of oblations overthr-th
20.Seest a m.that is hasty ⌈bour
Ec. 1: 3. What profit a m. of la-
2:21.a m. whose labour is in wisd. yet to a m. hath not labour
24. nothing better for a m.,8:15.
26.G. giveth to a m. that is good
4: 4. for this a m. is envied of his
6:2.a m.to wh.G.hath given riches
12.who can tell a m. what sh. be
7:5. for a m. to hear song of fools
8:17.a m.can-t find out work done
10:14. a m. can-t tell what sh. be
11:8. if a m. live many years and
Can. 8: 7. if a m. would give all
Is. 3: 6. a m. sh. take hold of bro.
6:5.bec. I am a m. of unclean lips
13:12.I will make a m.more prec.
17:7. shall a m. look to his Maker
28:20.than a m. can stretch hims.
29: 21. a m. an offender for word
32:2. a m. shall be a hiding place
44:15. shall it be for a m. to burn
47:3. I will not meet thee as a m.
53:3. He is a m. of sorrows ⌈soul?
58: 5. a day for a m. to afflict his
66: 3. killeth ox, is as if slew a m.
Je. 4: 29. not a m. dwell therein
5: 1. if we can find a m. ⌈neighb.
7: 5. judgm. between a m. and
14: 9. Why be as a m. astonied?
15:10.hast borne me a m. of strife
16: 20. Shall a m. make gods unto
18:14. Will a m. leave snow of Leb.
22:30. a m. that shall not prosper
29:32. not have a m. to dwell am.
30: 6. see whe. a m. doth travail
31:22. A woman sh. compass a m.
33:17.David shall never want a m.
18. Nei. shall priests want a m.
35:19. Jonadab sh. not want a m.
La. 3: 26. is good for a m. to hope
27. good for a m. he bear yoke
36. To subvert a m. in his cause
39. complain, a m. for punishm.
Eze.22:30.I sought for a m.⌊of sins
28:2. thou art a m. and not G., 9.
33: 2. if people of land take a m.
39:15. when any seeth a m.'s bone
40:3. was a m. whose appearance
Da. 2: 10. not a m. that can shew
25.I have found a m. of captives
5:11.is a m.in thy kingdom in wh.
7: 4. stand as a m. and a m.'s
9: † 23. art a m. of desires ⌊heart
10:11.O Dan.a m. greatly beloved
Ho. 6: 9. as robbers wait for a m.
9:12.that there sh.not be a m.left
11: 4. with cords of a m. ⌈maid
Am. 2: 7. a m. and fa. in unto one
5: 19. As if a m. did flee fr. lion
Mi. 2: 2. oppress a m. and his ho.,
11. If a m. walking in spirit ⌊(2)
7: 6. a m.'s enemies are the men of his own house, Mat. 10: 36.
Mal. 3:17. as a m. spareth own son
Mat. 8:9. a m. und. authority, Lu. 9: 9. a m. named Matthew ⌊7:8.
10: 35. to set a m. at variance
11:8. a m. in soft raim., Lu. 7:25.
12:10. a m. which had hand with-ered,Mk.3:1.Lu.6:6.⌈than sheep
12. How much is a m. better
43. uncl. spirit is gone out of a m., Lu. 11: 24.
13:24.a m. which sowed good seed
31. which a m. took and sowed
44. wh. when a m. hath found
15:11. out of mouth defileth a m.
20. to eat with unwash. hands defileth not a m. ⌈8: 36.
16: 26. what is a m. profited, Mk.
18:12. if a m. have 100 sheep
19: 3. Is it lawful for a m. to put away wife, Mk. 10: 2. ⌈ding
22:11.saw a m. had not on a wed-
24. If a m. die having no chil.
25:14.as a m.travelling, Mk.13:34.
26:18. he said, Go into the city, to such a m., Mk.14:13.Lu.22:10.
27: 32. found a m. of Cyrene
Mk. 1: 23. a m. with unclean spirit
4: 26. as if a m. should cast seed
5:2. out of tombs a m. with nuel.
6: 20. knowing he was a jnst m.
7: 11. If a m. say to fa. Corban
15. noth. without a m. can defile
8:4.whence can a m. satisfy these
12: 19. If a m.'s brother die
13:34.Son of man is as a m.taking
14: 13. meet you a m. bearing pitcher ⌈m.?
Lu. 1: 34. How, seeing I know not a
2: 25. was a m. in Jerus. Simeon
4:33. a m. who had spirit of devil
5: 8. for I am a sinful m. O Lord
18. brought a m. with palsy
8: 41. came a m. named Jairus
9: 25. what is a m. advantaged
38.a m. of company cried Master
12: 15. a m.'s life consisteth not
13:19.which a m. cast into garden
19: 2. a m. named Zaccheus
7. to be guest with a m. a sinner

Lu. 23 : 50. was a m. named Joseph
Jn. 1 : 6. There was a m. sent fr. G.
30. After me a m. who is preferred
3 : 1. was a m. of the Pharisees
3. Except a m. be born again, 5.
4. How a m. be born when old?
27. a m. can receive nothing, exc.
4 : 29. see a m. which told me all
6 : 50. a m. may eat and not die
7 : 22. sabbath day circumc. a m.
23. angry, bec. I made a m. whole
8:40. a m. that hath told you truth
51. If a m. keep my saying, 52.
9 : 11. a m. called Jes. made clay
16. How can a m. do such mira-
10:33. a m. makest thyself G. ⌊cles
11:10. if a m. walk in night stumbl.
14:23. If a m. love me, he will keep
15 : 6. If a m. abide not in me
13. that a m. lay down his life
16 : 21. for joy that a m. is born
Ac. 2:22. Jesus a m. approved of G.
6 : 5. Stephen a m. full of faith
8:27. behold a m. of Ethiopia ⌈12.
9 : 12. a m. named Ananias, 22 :
10 : 26. stand up, I also am a m.
28. unlawful, for a m. is a Jew
30. a m. stood bef. me in bright
13:7. Sergius Paulus, a prudent m.
21. Saul a m. of tribe of Benj.
22. David, a m. after mine heart
41. not believe, tho. a m. declare
16 : 9. stood a m. of Macedonia
21 : 39. I am a m. a Jew, 22 : 3.
22 : 25. scourge a m. is a Roman
Ro. 2: 21. preachest a m. not steal
22. a m. sho. not commit adultery
3 : 5. I speak as a m.
28. a m. justified by faith ⌈liveth
7:1. law dominion over a m. ⌊long as
8:24. what a m. seeth why hope for
1 Co. 4:1. Let a m. so account of us
2. required, a m. be found faithful
6 : 18. Every sin a m. doeth is
7:1 good for a m. not to touch wom
26. it is good for a m. so to be
9 : 8. Say I these things as a m. or
11:7. a m. ought not to cover his
14. if a m. have long hair ⌊head
28. But let a m. examine hims.
13 : 11. became a m. I put away
2 Co. 2 : 6. Sufficient to such a m.
is punishment
8:12. according to that a m. hath
11:20. if a m. bring you into bondage, if a m. devour you (5)
12:2. I knew a m. in C. caught, 3.
4. is not lawful for a m. to utter
Ga. 2:16. a m. is not justi by works
6 : 1. if a m. be overtak. in fault
3. if a m. think hims. something
7. whatso. a m. soweth sh. he reap
Ph. 2 : 8. found in fashion as a m.
1 Ti. 1 : 8. good, if a m. use it lawf.
3:1. If a m desire office of bishop
5. if a m. kn. not how to rule ho.
2 Ti. 2:5. if a m. strive for master-
21. If a m. thf. purge hims. ⌊ies
Tit. 3:10. a m. a heretic reject ⌈ring
Ja. 2 : 2. if come a m. with a gold
14. though a m. say he hath faith
18. a m. may say, Thou hast faith
24. how by works a m. is justifi.
5:17. Elias was a m. subject to like
1 Pe. 2 : 19. if a m. for conscience
2 Pe. 2:19. of wh. a m. is overcome
1 Jn. 4:20. if a m. say, I love God
Re. 4 : 7. beast had a face as a m.
9 : 5. scorpion, when he striketh a

A certain MAN. ⌊m.

Ge. 37:15. a c. m. found him, and
Ju. 13:2. there was a c. m. of Zorah
Ru. 1:1. a c. m. of Bethlehem-jud.
1 S. 1 : 1. c. m. of Ramathaim-zo.
21 : 7. a c. m. of serv-s of Saul
2 S. 18:10. a c. m. saw it, told Joab
1 K. 20:35. c. m. of sons of prophets
1 K. 22 : 34. a c. m. drew bow at
venture, 2 Ch. 18 : 33.
Da. 10: 5. a c. m. clothed in linen
Mat. 17:14. a c. m. kneeling to him
21:28. a c. m. had 2 sons, Lu. 15:11.
Mk. 12:1. a c. m. planted vineyard
Lu. 8 : 27. met him a c. m. wh. had
9 : 57. c. m. said, L. I will ⌊devil
10:30. a c. m. went down fr. Jerus.
12:16. The ground of a c. rich m.
13:6. a c. m. had a fig tree planted
14:2. a c. m. wh. had the dropsy
16. a c. m. made a great supper
16:1. a c. m. which had a steward
18:35. a c. blind m. sat by the way
20:9. a c. m. planted a vineyard,
Jn. 5:5. a c. m. wh. had an infirmity
11 : 1. a c. m. sick, named Lazar.
Ac. 3 : 2. a c. m. lame from womb
5:1. a c. m. named Ananias, sold
8 : 9. a c. m. who used sorcery
9:33. found a c. m. named Eneas
10:1. There was a c. m. Cornelius
14:8. sat a c. m. at Lystra, impotent
18 : 7. into a c. m.'s house named
19 : 24. a c. m. Demetrius ⌊Justus
25:14. is a c. m. left in bonds by

Any MAN. ⌊Felix

Ge. 24:16. nei. had a. m. known her
Ex. 24 : 14 if a. m. have matters
34 : 3. neither let a. m. be seen
throughout mount
24. nei. shall a. m. desire thy la.
Le. 1:2 If a. m. bring off-g unto L.
7:8. th. offereth a. m.'s burnt off-g
15:2. When a. m. a running issue
16. if a. m.'s seed of copula. go
24. if a. m. lie with her at all, he
24 : 17. killeth a. m. sh. be put to
27:9. all a. m. giveth unto L. ⌊dea.
Nu. 5:10. whatso. a. m. giveth priest
12. if a. m.'s wife go aside, and
6 : 9. if a. m. die suddenly by him
9 : 10. If a. m. sh. be unclean ⌈13.
19:11. toucheth dead body of a. m.,
21:9. if a serpent had bitten a. m.
De. 19:11. if a. m. hate his neighb.
16. If false witness rise ag. a. m.
22 : 8. blood upon thy ho. if a. m.
13. If a. m. take wife and go ⌊fall
23:10. be a. m. am. you is not clean
Jos. 1:5. not a. m. be able to stand
2:11. nei. courage in a. m. ⌈here?
Ju. 4:20. if a. m. enquire, Is a. m.
18 : 7. no business with a. m., 28.
1 S. 2:13. when a. m. off-d sacrifice
16. If a. m. said, not fail to burn
12 : 4. nei. taken aught at a. m.'s
14 : 52. Saul saw a. strong m. ⌊ha.
2 S. 15:2. a. m. that had controversy
5. it was so, th. when a. m. came
19:22. shall a. m. be put to death
21 : 4. nei. for us shalt kill a. m.
1 K. 8:31. If a. m. trespass ag. neigh.
38. supplication by a. m., 2 Ch. 6:
2 K. 4:29. meet a. m. salute not ⌊29.
12:4. all the money th. cometh into
a. m.'s heart to bring
2 Ch. 6 : 5. nei. chose I a. m. ruler
Ne. 2:12. nei. told I a. m. what G. put
Jb. 32:21. not accept a. m.'s person
Pr. 30:2 am more brutish than a. m.
Is. 52: 14. more marred than a. m.
Je. 44:26. my name no more in mouth
of a. m. of Judah ⌈mark
Eze. 9:6. not near a. m. upon wh.
Da. 6:7. sh. ask petition of a. m., 12.
Mat. 5 : 40. if a. m. sue thee at law
11:27. nei. knoweth a. m. the Fa.
12 : 19. nei. shall a. m. hear his
voice in the streets ⌈Lu. 9:23.
16:24. If a. m. will come after me,
21:3. if a. m. say aught unto you,
say, L. hath need, Mk. 11 : 3.
Lu. 19 : 31. ⌈m.
22:16. true, nei. carest thou for a.
46. nei. durst a. m. from that day
Mat. 24:23. if a. m. say, Lo, Mk. 13:21.
Mk. 1:44. say noth. to a. m. but go
4 : 23. If a. m. hath ears to hear,
7:16. Re. 13 : 9.
5:4. neither could a. m. tame him
9:30. would not a. m. sho. know it
35. If a. m. desire to be first, same
11:16. not suffer a. m. sho. carry
13:5. Take heed, lest a. m. deceive
16:8. nei. said any thing to a. m.
Lu. 14:8. When bid. of a. m. to a wed.
26. If a. m. come to me, and hate
19:8. if taken any thing fr. a. m.
20:28. If a. m.'s bro. die, hav-g wife
Jn. 4:33. Hath a. m. bro-t him aught
6:46. Not that a. m. hath seen Fa.
51. If a. m. eat of this bread he sh.
7:17. If a. m. do his will he sh. know
37. If a. m. thirst, let him come
51. Doth our law judge a. m. bef.
8 : 33. never in bondage to a. m.
9 : 22. if a. m. did confess Christ
31. if a. m. be a worshipper of G.
32. that a. m. opened eyes of blind
10 : 9. by me, if a. m. enter in, be
28. nei. shall a. m. pluck th. out
11:9. If a. m. walk in the day, he
57. if a. m. knew where he were
12:26. If a. m. serve me, let him foll.
47. if a. m. hear my words
16:30. needest not a. m. ask ⌈death
18 : 31. not lawful to put a. m. to
Ac. 10 : 28. not call a. m. common
47. can a. m. forbid water. these
19 : 38. if have a matter ag. a. m.
24 : 12. me disputing with a. m.
25:16. of Romans to deliver a. m.
27:22. be no loss of a. m.'s life ⌈C.
Ro. 8:9. if a. m. have not Spirit of
1 Co. 3 : 12. if a. m. build on this
14. If a. m.'s work abide ⌊founda.
15. if a. m.'s work burned
17. If a. m. defile the temple of G.
18. If a. m. seemeth to be wise
5:11. if a. m. a bro. be a fornicat.
7:18. is a. m. called, being circum.
36. if a. m. think he behaveth
8 : 2. if a. m. think he knoweth
3. if a. m. love God | 11:34. if a.
m. hunger let him ⌈knowledge
10. if a. m. see thee which hast
9:15. that a. m. make my glorying
10 : 28. if a. m. say, This is offered
11 : 16. if a. m. seem contentious
14:27. If a. m. speak in unknown
37. If a. m. think hims. prophet,
38. if a. m. be ignorant, let him
16:22. if a. m. love not the L. Jes.
2 Co. 5 : 17. if a. m. be in C. he is a
10:7. If a. m. trust that he is C.'s
12:6. lest a. m. think of me above
Ga. 1 : 9. If a. m. preach other gos.
Ep. 2 : 9. of works, lest a. m. boast
6:8. good thing a. m. doeth ⌈wh-f
Ph. 3:4. If a. m. thinketh he hath
Col. 2:4. lest a. m. beguile you wi.
8. Beware lest a. m. spoil you
3 : 13. if a. m. hath a quarrel ag.
1 Th. 5:15. that none render evil for
evil to a. m. ⌈for nought
2 Th. 3 : 8. Nei. did eat a. m.'s br.
14. if a. m. obey not our word
1 Ti. 5 : 16. If a. m. have widows
6 : 3. if a. m. teach otherwise
He. 4:11. lest a. m. fall after same
10:38. if a. m. draw back, my soul
12:15. lest a. m. fail of grace of G.
Ja. 1 : 13. nei. tempteth he a. m.
26. If a. m. seem to be religious
3 : 2. if a. m. offend not in word
1 Pe. 4:11. If a. m. speak, let him sp.
16. yet if a. m. suffer as Christian
1 Jn. 2:1. if a. m. sin, we have an
15. if a. m. love world, the love
27. ye need not a. m. teach you
5 : 16. If a. m. see his brother sin
Re. 3 : 20. if a. m. hear my voice

Re.11:5.if a.m.will hurt them, fire
14 : 9. If a. m. worship the beast
22:18. If a. m. add to these things
19. if a. m. take away fr. words
See BLESSED, CHIEF.

MAN child. [12.
Ge. 17:10. Every m. c. be circum-d,
14. uncirc-d m.c. shall be cut off
Le. 12:2.If woman have borne m.c.
1 S.1:11.if give unto handmaidm.c.
Jb. 3 : 3. wherein it was said, There
is a m. c. conceived, Je. 20:15.
Is. 66:7. delivered of m. c.,Re.12:5.
Re. 12:13. persecuted wom.brought
See CURSED, EACH. [forth m. c.

Every MAN.
Ge. 7 : 21. all flesh died and e. m.
9 : 5. of e. m. brother require life
16:12.ha. ag. e.m. and e.m.'s ha.
42 : 25. to restore e. m.'s money
35. e. m.'s money in sack, 43:21.
44 : 11. took down e. m. his sack
13. laded e. m. his ass, and ret.
45:1. Jo. cried, Cause e. m. to go
47:20. Egyp-s sold e. m. his field
Ex. 1 : 1. e. m. and his household
7:12. they cast down e. m. his rod
11 : 2. let e. m. borrow of neighb.
12 : 3. shall take e. m. a lamb
4. e. m. according to his eating,
16 : 16.-18 : 21. [that only
16. save that wh. e. m. must eat,
16 : 29. abide ye e. m. in his place
25 : 2. of e. m. giveth willingly
30:12. e. m. a ransom for his soul
32:27. put e. m. a sword by side,
slay e.m. his bro.,e.m.neigh.
33 : 8. stood e. m. at his tent door
10.worshipped e.m. in tent door
36 : 4. came e. m. from his work
38 : 26. A bekah for e. m. [fa.
Le. 19:3. fear e. m. his mother and
25 : 10. sh. return e. m. unto his
family (2), 13. [2, 17.
Nu. 1:52. e. m. by his standard, 2 :
5 : 10. e. m.'s hallowed things his
7 : 5. to e. m. acc. to his service
16:17.take e.m.his censer,and put
18.they took e.m.his censer and
17:2. write thou e.m. name upon
9. they took e. m. his rod [rod
31:50.for L.what e.m.hath gotten
53.had taken spoil e.m.for hims.
32:18.Isr.inherited e. m.his inher.
27. pass over e. m. armed, 29.
De. 1:16. judge right-ly betw. e.m.
3:20.return e.m.unto his possess.
12:8. not do e. m.whatso. right in
16:17. e.m.give as able [own eyes
24:16. e. m. shall die for his own
sin, 2 K. 14 : 6. 2 Ch. 25 : 4.
Jos.4:5.take up e.m.of you a stone
6:5. ascend e. m. straight bef.,20.
11:14.e.m.they smote with sword
24:28. e. m. unto his inheri., Ju.
Ju. 5 : 30. to e. m. a damsel [2 : 6.
7 : 7. go e. m. unto his place, 8.
16. put trumpet in e. m.'s hand
22.Lord set e.m.'s sword against
his fellow, 1 S. 14 : 20.
8:24.would give e.m.his earrings,
9 : 49. cut e. m. his bough [25.
17 : 6. e. m. did right in his eyes,
21 : 25. [dau-s of Shiloh
21:21. catch you e. m. his wife of
24. e.m. to his tribe, e.m.to his
1 S. 4 : 10. fled e. m. into his tent
8:22. Sam. said, Go e. m. into city
14:34.Bring hither e.m.his ox (2)
25:10. break away e. m. fr.master
13. Gird you on e. m. his sword
26 : 23. the Lord render to e. m.
his righteousness, 2 Ch. 6 : 30.
30 : 6. grieved e. m. for his sons
22. save to e. m. his wife and
2 S. 13:9. went out e. m. from him
29. e. m. gat him upon his mule
2 S.15:4.that e.m.wh.hath any suit
30. covered e. m. his head
19 : 8. Isr. had fled e. m. to tent
20:1. Sheba said e. m. to his tents
1 K. 4 : 25. safely e. m. under vine
8 : 38. know e. m. plague of heart
39. give e. m. acc. to his ways,
Jb. 34:11. Je. 17:10. [Ch.9:24.
10 : 25. bro-t e. m. his present, 2
12 : 24. not go up, return e. m. to
his ho., 22 : 17, 36. 2 Ch. 11 : 4.
20:24.Take kings e.m.out of place
2 K. 6 : 2. Let us take e. m. a beam
11:8. e. m. with weapons in hand
12 : 4. the money e. man is set at
14 : 12. Judah fled e. m. to tents
18 : 31. eat ye e. m. of own vine
Ne.5:13.So God shake out e. m. fr.
Es. 1:8. do acc. to e. m.'s pleasure
22.e.m. sho. bear rule in his ho.
Jb. 21:33. e.m. shall draw att. him
36:25. e. m. may see it; man may
37:7. He sealeth up hand of e. m.
Ps.39:5.e.m.at his best state is, 11.
6. e. m. walketh in a vain show
62:12. to thee, O L., thou renderest
to e. m. acc. to work, Pr.24:12.
Pr. 19 : 6. e. m. is a friend to him
giveth gifts [right ans.
24:26.e. m. sh. kiss lips th. giveth
29 : 26. e. m.'s judgment from L.
Ec. 5:19 e. m. to wh. G. hath given
Is. 9:20. eat e. m. flesh of own arm
13 : 7. Thf. e.m.'s heart shall melt
14.shall e.m.turn to his own peo.
31:7.day e. m. shall cast aw.idols
Je. 10 : 14. e. m. is brutish, 51:17.
12 : 15. e. m. to his heritage [den
23:36.e. m.'s word sh. be his bur-
26 : 3. turn e. m. from evil way,
35 : 15.-36 : 3.
29 : 26. for e. m. that is mad
30:6. see e.m.with hands on loins
31 : 34. teach no more e. m. his
neighbour, He. 8 : 11.
34:15. in proclaiming liberty e.m.
to neighbour, 17.
37 : 10. sho. rise up e. m. in tent
51 : 45. deliver ye e. m. his soul
Eze. 8:11. with e. m. censer in ha.
12. e. m. in chambers of imagery
9 : 1. e. m. with his weapon, 2.
20 : 7. Cast away e. m. abomina.
8. did not e. m. cast aw. abomi.
32 : 10. e. m. shall tremble for life
46:18.not scattered e.m.fr.posses.
Da. 3 : 10. e. m. that sh. hear sound
6:12. e. m. that shall ask petition
Jon. 1:5. mariners cried e. m. to his
Mi. 4 : 4. e. m. under his vine [god
7 : 2. they hunt e. m. his brother
Hag. 1:9. ye run e.m. unto own ho.
Zch. 3 : 10. call e. m. his neighb.
8 : 4. e. m. with his staff in hand
16. speak e. m. truth, Ep. 4 : 25.
Mal. 2:10.treach-ly e.m.ag.brother
Mat. 16 : 27. Son of man sh. reward
e. m. acc., Ro. 2 : 6. Re. 22 : 12.
20:9. received e. m. a penny, 10.
25 : 15. to e. m. acc. to his ability
Mk. 8 : 25. he saw e. m. clearly
13:34. and gave to e. m. his work
15:24. casting lots what e.m.take
Lu. 6:30. Give to e. m. that asketh
16 : 16. and e. m. presseth into it
19:15. how much e.m.had gained
Jn. 1:9. light, which lighteth e. m.
2:10. e. m. at beginning doth set
6:45. e.m. that hath heard of Fa.
16 : 32. ye shall be scattered e. m.
Ac.2:6.bec.e. m. heard them speak
8. how hear we e. m. in our own
45.to all, as e.m. had need, 4:35.
11:29.e.m.determ-d to send relief
Ro.2:10.peace to e.m.worketh good
3: 4. let G. be true, but e. m. liar
12 : 3. as God dealt to e. m. faith
Ro.14:5.Let.e.m.be fully persuaded
1 Co. 3:5. as L. gave to e. m.,7:17.
13. e.m.'s work shall be manifest
4 : 5. then e. m. have praise of G.
7 : 2. let e. m. have his own wife
7. But e. m. his proper gift of G.
20. Let e. m. abide in calling,24.
8:7. not in e. m. that knowledge
10:24. let e. m. seek ano.'s wealth
11 : 3. know head of e. m. is Ch.
12:7. Spirit given to e.m.to profit
15 : 23. but e. m. in his order, C.
2 Co. 4:2. ours. to e.m.'s conscience
Ga.5:3.I testify to e. m.is circumc.
6 : 4. let e. m. prove own work
5 e. m. shall bear own burden
Ph. 2:4. Look not e. m.on his own
Col. 1:28. teaching e. m. in all wisdom to present e. m. perf. in C.
4 : 6. how ye ought to ans. e. m.
He.2:9.should taste death for e. m.
Ja. 1:14.But e.m. is tempted,when
19. let e. m. be swift to hear
1 Pe.1:17.judgeth acc.to e.m.work
3 : 15. to give ans. to e. m. asketh
4 : 10. As e.m. hath rec-d gift [rea.
1 Jn. 3:3.e.m. that hath this hope
Re.20:13.judged e.m. acc.to works
22 : 18. I testify to e. m. heareth
See EVIL man, FOOLISH.

MAN of God.
De. 33:1. Moses m. o. G., Jos. 14 :
6. 1 Ch. 23:14. 2 Ch. 30:16. Ezr.
3:2. [unto me
Ju. 13 : 6. saying, m. o. G. came
8. let m.o.G. come again unto us
1 S. 2:27. came a m. o. G. unto Eli
9:6. there is in this city a m. o. G.
7. not a present to bring m.o.G.
8.will I give to m.o.G. to tell us
1 K. 12:22. to Shemaiah the m.o.G.
13:1. came a m. o. G. out of Jud.
26. m. o. G.who was disobedient
17:18.What I with thee,O m.o.G.?
24. I know thou art a m. o. G.
20:28. came a m. o. G. and spake
2 K. 1:9. Thou m. o. G. king hath
said, Come down, 11. [ious
13. O m.o.G., let my life be prec-
4 : 7. she came and told m. o. G.
9. I perceive this is m. o. G.
16. m. o. G., do not lie unto
22.I may run to m.o.G. [handm.
25.she came unto the m.o.G.,27.
40. O m. o. G., is death in pot
42. brought m. o. G. bread [o.G.
5 : 14. dipped, acc. to saying of m.
20. serv.of Elisha, m. o. G., 8:4.
6:10. place which m.o.G.told him
15. servant of m. o. G. was risen
7:2. a lord answered m. o. G., 19.
17. people trode upon him as m.
o. G. had said, 18.
8 : 2. did aft. saying of m. o. G.
7. m. o. G. is come | 11. wept
8. Take present meet m. o. G.
13:19. m.o. G. was wroth wi. him
23:16. acc. to word which m.o.G.
17. It is the sepulchre of m.o.G.
2 Ch. 8 : 14. David the m.o.G., Ne.
12 : 24, 36.
25 : 7. came m. o. G. to Amaziah
9. m. o. G. answered, L. is able
Je. 35 : 4. son of Igdaliah m. o. G.
1 Ti. 6:11. O m.o.G. flee these thi.
2 Ti.3:17. that m.o.G.may be perf.
See GOOD man, MADMAN.

Like MAN.
Ju.16:17.weak and l. any other m.
Jb. 12 : 25. to stagger l. a drunken
m., Ps. 107 : 27.
38:3. Gird up loins l. a m., 40 : 7.
Is.10:13.put down inhab. l.val. m.
Je. 23 : 9. I am l. a m. whom wine
50 : 42. array l. a m. to battle
Mat.13:52.l.a m. householder,20:1.
Lu.6:48.l. a m. wh.built house, 49.

Jn.7:46. Nev. man spake l. this m.
Ro. 1 : 23. made l. corruptible m.
Ja. 1 : 23. l. m. beholding his face

Mighty MAN. [m.

Ru. 2 : 1. Naomi had kinsman a m.
1 S. 9 : 1. Kish a Benjamite, m. m.
16 : 18. David m. m. man of war,
2 S. 17 : 10. [the
1 Ch. 12 : 4. Ismaiah a m. m. am.
2 Ch.28:7. Zichri, m.m. slew Maas.
Jb. 22 : 8. m.m. he had the earth
Ps.33:16.m.m.not deliv-d by stren
52:1.Why boastest in mischief,m.
78:65. L. awaked like m.m. [m.
127:4.As arrows in hand of m.m.
Is. 3 : 2. L. doth take away m. m.
5:15.the m. m. shall be humbled
31:8.sh.fall with sw. not of m.m.
42 : 13. L. shall go forth as m.m.
Je. 9:23. nei. let the m.m.glory in
14 : 9. shouldst be as a m.m. that
cannot save [m. stumbled
46 : 6. nor m. m. escape | 12. m.
50 : 9. arrows as of m. expert m.
Zph. 1: 14. m.m.shall cry bitterly
Zch.9:13.made thee as sw. of m.m.
10 : 7. they of Ephr. be like m. m.
See **Mighty man of VALOUR.**

No MAN.

Ge. 31 : 50. n. m. is with us, see
41:44. without thee n.m.lift hand
45 : 1. stood n. m. while Jo. made
Ex. 2 : 12. he saw there was n. m.
16:19.Let n.m.leave of it till morn
29. let n. m. go out on 7th day
22:10.driven away, n.m. seeing it
33:4. n.m. did put on ornaments
20. shall n. m. see me and live
34:3.n.m.shall come up with thee
Le. 16:17. shall be n.m. in tabern.
21 : 21. n.m. that hath a blemish
27 : 26. n.m. sh. sanctify it, it is
Nu.5:19.If n.m. hath lain wi. thee
De. 7:24. n.m. able to stand,11:25.
24:6. n. m. take nether millstone
28:26. n.m. shall fray them away
29. n. m. shall save thee, 68.
34 : 6. n.m. knoweth of his sepul.
Jos. 8 : 31. over wh. n.m. lift iron
23:9. n.m. been able to stand bef.
Ju. 11 : 39. Jephthah's daughter
knew n. m. [house, 18.
19 : 15. n. m. took them into
21:12.virgins th. had known n.m.
1 S. 2 : 9. by strength n.m. prevail
11 : 3. if there be n.m. to save us
14:26.n.m.put hand to his mouth
17:32. Let n. m.'s heart fail [thee
21 : 1. Why alone and n. m. with
2. Let n. m. know of business
26 : 12. and n.m. saw nor knew it
2 S. 15:3. n.m. deputed of the king
1 K. 8 : 46. is n. m. sinneth not, 2
2 K.7:5.n.m.in camp,10. [Ch.6:36.
23:10.n.m.make son to pass thro.
18. let n. m. move his bones
1 Ch. 16 : 21. suffered n. m. to do
them wrong, Ps. 105 : 14.
Es. 5: 12. queen did let n.m. come
in with king
8 : 8. writing may n. m. reverse
9 : 2. n. m. could withstand Jews
Jb.11:3. n.m. make thee ashamed?
15:28.houses wh.n.m. inhabiteth
20:21.shall n.m.look for his goods
24:22. and n.m. is sure of his life
38 : 26. to rain where n.m. is (2)
Ps. 22 : 6. I am a worm and n. m.
142:4. there was n.m., Is. 41:28.-
59 : 16. Je. 4 : 25. [justified
143 : 2. in thy sight shall n.m. be
Pr. 1:24. hand, and n.m. regarded
28 : 1. wicked fleeth when n. m.
17. to the pit, let n.m. stay him
Ec. 3 : 11. n.m. can find out work
8 : 8. n.m. hath power over spirit
Ec.9:1.n.m.knoweth love or hatred
15.n. m. rememb-d th. poor man
Is. 9 : 19. n.m. shall spare his bro.
13 : 14. as sheep n. m. taketh up
24 : 10. ev. house is shut that n.
m. may come in
33 : 8. he regardeth n. m.
50:2.when I came was there n.m.
57: 1. n.m. layeth it to heart, Je.
60:15.n.m.went thro. thee [12:11.
Je. 2 : 6. land where n. m. dwelt
8:6.n.m. repented of his wickedn.
22:30.n.m. of his seed sh. prosper
30:17. is Zion whom n.m. seeketh
36:19. let n.m. know where ye be
38 : 24. Let n. m. know of words
40 : 15. slay Ishm. n. m. know it
41 : 4. slain Gedal. n. m. knew it
44: 2. n. m. dwelleth th-n, 51:43.
49:18. n.m. shall abide there, 33.
-50 : 40. [it unto them
La. 4 : 4. ask bread n.m. breaketh
Eze.14:15.that n.m.may pass thro.
44:2.n.m. shall enter by this gate
Ho. 4:4. let n.m. strive or reprove
Na. 3 : 18. scattered, n.m. gath-h
Zph. 3 : 6. so that there is n. m.
Zch.1:21. n.m. did lift up his head
7: 14. n.m. passed thro. nor retur.
Mat. 6 : 24. n. m. can serve two
masters, Lu. 16 : 13.
8 : 4. tell n. m., 16 : 20. Mk. 7:36.
Lu. 5 : 14.-9 : 21.
28.fierce,so that n.m.might pass
9:16. n.m. putteth new cloth unto
old garm., Mk. 2:21.Lu.5:36.
30. charged, See that n.m. know
it, Mk. 5 : 43.-7 : 24.-8: 30.-9:9.
11 : 27. n. m. knoweth Son but
Father,Lu.10:22. [only,Mk.9:8.
17 : 8. they saw n. m. save Jesus
9. Tell vision to n. m. until Son
20 : 7. Bec. n. m. hath hired us
22:46. n.m. was able to ans. him
23:9. call n.m. father upon earth
24 : 4. Take heed n.m. deceive
36. hour know. n.m., Mk.13:32.
Mk. 2 : 22. n. m. putteth new wine
3 : 27. n.m. can enter into strong
5:3. n.m. could bind him [man's
37.suff-d n.m.to follow, Lu.8:51.
9 : 39. n. m. wh. shall do miracle
10 : 29. n.m. that hath left house,
Lu. 18 : 29. [after
11:14. n.m. eat fruit of thee here-
12:14. know thou carest for n.m.
34. n.m. durst ask him question
Lu. 3 : 14. Do violence to n. m.
10 : 4. salute n. m. by the way
5:39.n.m. having drunk old wine
8:16. n.m. lighteth candle,11:33.
51. suffered n.m. to go in, save
9 : 36. told n. m. in those days
62. n. m. having put his hand
15:16. husks, n.m. gave unto him
Jn. 1:18. n.m. seen G., 1 Jn. 4:12.
3 : 2. n. m. can do these miracles
13. n. m. hath ascended up to
32. n.m. receiveth his testimony
4 : 27. n. m. said, What seekest
5:22. Father judgeth n. m.
6 : 44. n. m. can come to me, except
the Father draw him, 65.
7:4.n.m. doeth anything in secret
13. n. m. spake openly of him
27. n. m. knoweth whence he is
30. n.m. laid hands on him, 44.
-8 : 20. [demned thee?
8 : 10. Woman, hath n. m. con-
11. She said, n. m. Lord [n.m.
15.ye Judge aft. the flesh, I judge
9 : 4. night when n. m. can work
10 : 18. n. m. taketh it from me
29. n.m. is able to pluck th. out
13:28.n.m.at the table knew why
14:6.n.m.cometh unto the Fa.but
15:13.Greater love hath n.m.than
Jn.16:22. and your joy n.m.taketh
Ac. 1 : 20. let n. m. dwell therein
4 : 17. that they speak to n. m.
5 : 13. of the rest durst n.m. join
23.we found n.m. within [hims.
9:7. hearing voice, seeing n.m., 8
... n.m. sh. set on thee to hurt
20 : 33. I coveted n. m.'s silver
23 : 22. See thou tell n. m. [them
25 : 11. n. m. may deliv. me unto
28:31. preaching n.m. forbidding
Ro.12:17. Recompense to n.m. evil
13: 8. Owe n.m. anything, but to
14:7.and n.m.dieth to hims.[love
13.that n.m. put a stumblingbl.
1 Co.2:11. things of G. kno-th n.m.
15. he himself is judged of n. m.
3 : 11. other founda. can n.m. lay
18. Let n.m. deceive himself.21.
10:24. Let n.m. seek his own, but
12 : 3. n. m. speaking by Spirit
14 : 2. n. m. understandeth him
16 : 11. Let n. m. despise him
2 Co.5:16.henceforth know we n.m.
7 : 2. we have wronged n. m. (2)
8 : 20. that n. m. shall blame us
11 : 9. I was chargeable to n. m.
10.n.m.sh.stop me of this boast-
16. Let n.m. think me a fool [ing
Ga.2:6. G. accepteth n.m.'s person
3 : 11. n. m. is justified by law
15. n.m. disannulleth or addeth
6 : 17. let n. m. trouble me
Ep. 5 : 6. Let n. m. deceive you, 2
Th. 2 : 3. [own flesh
29. For n. m. ever yet hated his
Ph. 2:20. I have n. m. likeminded
Col. 2 : 16. Let n. m. judge you in
18. Let n.m. beguile you of your
1 Th. 3:3. That n. m. be moved by
4:6.That n.m. go beyond his bro.
6 : 16. whom n. m. hath seen
1 Ti. 4 : 12. Let n. m. despise thy
youth, Tit. 2 : 15.
5:22. Lay hands suddenly on n.m.
2 Ti. 2: 4. n.m. that warreth entan-
4 : 16. n.m. stood with me [gleth
Tit. 3 : 2. To speak evil of n. m.
He. 5 : 4. n.m. taketh this honour
to himself [ance
7:13. of which n. m. gave attend-
12: 14. with-t which n. m. see L.
Ja.1:13.Let n.m.say when tempted
3 : 8. the tongue can n. m. tame
1 Jn. 3 : 7. chil. let n. m. deceive
4:12.n.m.hath seen G.at any time
Re.2:17.name which n.m.knoweth
3 : 7. shutteth and n.m. openeth
8. open door n. m. can shut it
11. that n. m. take thy crown
5:3. n.m.was able to open book,4.
7 : 9. which n. m. could number
13:17. th. n. m. might buy or sell
14: 3. n.m. could learn that song
15:8. n.m. was able to enter temp.
18 : 11. n.m.buyeth merchandise
19:12.had a name that n.m.knew
See NOBLEMAN.

Of MAN.

Ge.9:5.at hand o.m. will I require
life o. m. [Nu. 18 : 15.
Ex. 13 : 13. all the firstborn o. m.,
De. 1:17. not be afraid of face o.m.
2 S.7:19. is this manner o.m.O L.?
24:14. into hand o.m.,1 Ch.21:13.
2 K.1:7.What manner o.m.was he
6:10.no man there, nei.voice o.m.
1 Ch.17:17.estate o.m.of high degr.
Jb.10:5.Are thy days as days o.m.
14:19. thou destroyest hope o.m.
34 : 11. work o. m. sh. he render
21. his eyes are upon ways o. m.
Ps.60:11. vain is help o.m.,108:12.
76:10. wrath o.m. sh. praise thee
Pr.3:4.good underst. in sight o.m.
5:21.ways o.m.are before L. [life
†26.woman o. a m. will hunt for

Pr. 8: 4. my voice is to sons o. m.
18:14. spirit o.m. will sustain his
19:3. foolishness o. m. perverteth
11. The discretion o.m. deferreth
22. desire o. m. is his kindness
21: 2. Ev. way o. m. right in own
8. way o.m. froward and strange
27:19. heart o. m. answ-h to man
29: 25. fear o. m. bringeth snare
30:2. have not the underst-g o. m.
19. the way o. a m. with a maid
Ec.3:21. Who knoweth spirit o. m.
6: 7. All labour o.m. is for mouth
8:6. misery o.m. is great upon him
12:13. this is the whole duty o.m.
Is. 22: † 17. with captivity o. a m.
44:13. he maketh it after figure o.
m. acc. to beauty o. a m. [m.
51:12. that thou sho. be afraid o. a
Je. 10:23. way o.m. is not in hims.
La.3:35. To turn aside right o.a m.
Eze. 1: 5. likeness o. a m., 26.
10. had face o. a m., 10: 14.
10: 21. likeness of hands o. a m.
29:11. No foot o.m. sh. pass thro. it
32:13. nei. shall foot o.m. trouble
Da. 8:15. as appear. o. a m., 10:18.
Zch.9:1. when eyes o. a m. tow. L.
12: 1. who formeth spirit o. m.
Mat. 8:27. What manner o.m. this
th. winds obey him? Mk. 4:41.
Lu. 8: 25. [wife
19: 10. If case o. m. be so with
Mk. 5:8. Come out o. m., Lu. 8:29.
Jn. 1: 13. nor of the will o.m. but
2: 25. needed not any testify o.m.
Ac. 12:22. voice of a god, not o.m.
Ro. 2: 9. soul o. m. th. doeth evil
4:6. describeth blessedn. o. the m.
1 Co. 2: 4. enticing words o. m.'s
9. nei. ent-d heart o. m. [wisd.
11. what man knoweth things o.
a m. save spirit o.m. in him
4:3. judged of you, or o.m. judgm.
11:7. woman is the glory o. the m.
8. the woman is o. the m., 12.
Ga. 1: 12 I nei. received it o. m.
Ja. 1: 20. wrath o.m. worketh not
24. forgetteth what manner o.m.
1 Pe. 1: 24. glory o.m. as flower of
2:13. to ev. ordinance o.m. [m.
2 Pe.1:21. not in old time by will o.
Re. 13:18. it is the number o. a m.
21:17. acc. to the measure o. a m.

Old MAN.

Ge. 25: 8. Abraham died an o. m.
43:27. the o. m. is he alive? [m.
44:20. said, We have a father, an o.
Le.19:32. shalt honour face of o.m.
Ju. 19: 16. came an o.m. fr. work
17. the o. m. said, 20.
22. spake to the o.m. [house, 32.
1 S.2:31. sh. not be an o.m. in thy
4: 18. Eli an o. m. [Saul
17: 12. Jesse an o. m. in days of
28: 14. an o. m. cometh up
2 Ch.36:17. no compassion on o.m.
Is. 65: 20. an infant nor o. m.
Lu. 1: 18. I am an o. m. my wife
Ro. 6: 6. our o. m. is crucified
Ep. 4: 22. put off the o. m. corrupt
Col. 3:9. ye have put off the o. m.

One MAN.

Ge. 42: 11. We all o. m.'s sons, 13.
Ex.16:22. gath-d 2 homers for o.m.
21:35. if o.m.'s ox hurt another's
Nu. 14: 15. if kill this peo. as o.m.
16: 22. o.m. sin, thou be wroth?
31: 49. lacked not o. m. of us
Jos. 23: 10. o.m. sh. chase thous.
Ju. 6: 16. smite Midianites as o.m.
18: 19. priest to house of o. m.
20: 1. congr. was gath-d as o. m.
8. all the people arose as o. m.
1 S. 2: 25. If o.m. sin ag. another
11: † 7. people came out as o. m.
2 S. 19: 14. even as heart of o. m.
1 K. 22: 8. There is yet o. m. Micaiah, 2 Ch. 18: 7. [Ne. 8: 1.
Ezr.3:1. gathered together as o.m.,
Jb.13:9. as o. m. mocketh another
Ec. 7:28. o. m. among a thousand
8: 9. wherein o. m. ruleth ano.
Is. 4: 1. seven wom. hold of o. m.
Eze. 9: 2. o. m. clothed wi. linen
Jn. 11:50. o.m. die for peo., 18:14.
Ro. 5: 12. as by o. m. sin entered
15. by grace, which is by o.m. Jes
17. if by o. m.'s offence death
19. as by o. m.'s disobedience
14:5. o.m. esteemeth one day abo.
1 Ti. 5:9. having been wife of o.m.

Poor MAN. [cause

Ex.23: 3. Nei countenance p. m. in
De. 15:7. If p.m. harden not heart
24:12. if p.m. sleep not wi. pledge
1 S.18:23. k.'s son, seeing I am p.m.
2 S. 12:3. p. m. had nothing, save
4. took the p.m.'s ewe lamb [one
Ps. 34: 6. This p.m. cried, and L.
109:16. persecuted p. and needy m.
Pr. 19: 22. p.m. is better than liar
21:17. loveth pleasure sh. be p.m.
28:3. a p.m. that oppresseth poor
29:13. the p. and deceitful m. meet
Ec. 9: 15. was found in it a p. wise
m. no man rememb-d th. p.m.
16. the p.m.'s wisdom is despised
Ja. 2:2. come in a p.m. in vile rai-

Rich MAN. [ment

2 S. 12: 2. r. m. had many flocks
4. came a traveller unto the r.m.
Jb. 27: 19. r.m. shall lie down but
Pr. 10:15. the r. m.'s wealth is his
strong city, 18: 11.
28: 11. r. m. wise in own conceit
Je. 9: 23. not r. m. glory in riches
Mat. 19:23. r.m. hardly ent. kingd.
24. easier for r m. to ent. kingd.
of G., Mk. 10: 25. Lu. 18: 25.
27: 57. came a r.m. of Arimathea
Lu. 12: 16. ground of a r.m. bro-t
16:1. certain r. m. had a steward
19. a r.m. was clothed in purple
21. crumbs from r. m.'s table
22. r. m. died and was buried
Ja. 1:11. so shall the r.m. fade aw.

Righteous MAN.

Ps.37:16. little a r.m. hath is better
Pr. 10: 11. mouth of r.m. is a well
12:10. r.m. regardeth life of beast
13:5. r.m. hateth lying, but wicked
21: 12. r. m. considereth house
25:26. r.m. falling down bef. wicked
Is. 41: 2. who raised r. m. fr. east
Eze. 3: 20. when r. m. doth turn,
21. if thou warn the r.m. [18:26.
Mat. 10: 41. receiveth a r. m. in
name of r.m. sh. receive r.m.'s
Lu. 23:47. Certainly this was r.m.
Ro. 5: 7. scarcely for r.m. will one
1 Ti.1:9. law not made for r.m. [die
Ja. 5: 16. fervent prayer of a r.m.
2 Pe. 2: 8. that r. m. dwelling am.

Son of MAN. [them

Nu.23:19. nei. s.o.m. that he repent
Jb. 25: 6. s.o.m. which is a worm
35:8. righteousn. may profit s.o.m
Ps. 8:4. s. o. m. that thou visitest
him, He. 2: 6. [strong
80:17. s.o.m. whom thou madest
144: 3. or s.o.m. that thou makest account of him
146: 3. put not trust in s. o. m.
Is. 51:12. be not afraid of s. o. m.
56: 2. blessed is the s. o. m. that
Je. 49: 18. nei. shall s.o. m. dwell
in it, 33.-50: 40. [thereby
51: 43. nei. doth any s.o.m. pass
Eze.2:1. s.o.m. stand upon thy feet
3. s. o. m. I send thee to Israel
6. s. o. m. be not afraid of them
8. thou s.o. m. hear what I say
3: 1. s.o.m. eat that thou findest
Eze. 3:3. s. o. m. cause belly to eat
4. s. o. m. go get thee to Israel
10. s. o. m. w-ds I speak receive
17. s.o.m. I made thee watchman
25. O s.o.m. they sh. put bands
4:1. s.o.m. take a tile before thee
16. s.o.m. I will break staff of br.
5: 1. s. o. m. take sharp knife
6:2. s.o.m. prophesy ag. mts., 36:1.
7:2. thou s.o.m. thus saith L. G.
8: 5. s. o. m. lift eyes tow. north
6. s. o. m. seest what they do?
8. s.o.m. dig now in wall
12. s.o.m. seen what ancients do?
15. hast seen this, O s.o.m.? 17.
11:2. s.o.m. these are men devise
4. prophesy ag. them, O s. o.m.
15. s.o.m. thy brethren are they
12:2. s.o.m. dwellest in rebellious
3. s.o.m. prepare thee stuff [ho.
9. s. o. m. hath not Israel said
18. s.o.m. eat br. with quaking
22. s.o. m. what is that proverb
27. s. o. m. they of Israel say
13:2. s.o.m. prophesy ag. prophets
17. s.o.m. set thy face ag. thy peo.
14: 3. s.o.m. these have set idols
13. s.o.m. when the land sinneth
15:2 s.o.m. what is vine tree more
16:2. s.o.m. cause Jerus. to know
17: 2. s. o. m. put forth a riddle
20:3. s.o.m. speak unto elders of
4. s.o.m. wilt thou judge them?
27. s.o.m. speak unto ho. of Isr.
46. s. o. m. prophesy ag. forest
21:2. s. o.m. prophesy ag. Israel
6. sigh thou s.o.m. wi. bitterness
9. s.o.m. prophesy, A sword, 28.
12. howl s.o.m. it sh. be on peo.
14. s.o.m. prophesy smite hands
19. s. o. m. appoint thee 2 ways
28. s.o.m. prophesy, Thus saith
L. conc-g Ammonites, 25: 2.
22:2. s.o.m. wilt thou judge city?
18. s.o.m. house of Isr. is dross
24. s.o.m. say unto her, Thou
23:2. s.o.m. there were two wom.
36. s.o.m. wilt thou judge Aholah
24: 2. s.o. m. write name of day
16. s.o.m. I take away the desire
25. s. o. m. sh. it not be in day
26: 2. s. o. m. because Tyrus said
27: 2. s.o. m. take up a lamentation, 28: 12. [of Tyrus
28: 2. s.o.m. say unto the prince
21. s. o. m. prophesy ag. Zidon
29: 2. s. o. m. prophesy ag. Pha.
18. s.o.m. Neb-r caused his army
30: 2. s. o. m. prophesy
21. s.o.m. I have broken arm of
31:2. s.o.m. speak unto Pha. [Pha.
32:2. s.o.m. take up lamentation
18. s. o. m. wail for mult. of E.
33: 2. s.o.m. speak to chil. of thy
7. s.o.m. I have set thee watchm.
10. O s. o. m. speak unto Israel
12. s.o.m. say unto chil. of Israel
24. s.o.m. they th. inhabit wastes
30. s.o.m. thy peo. are talking ag.
34:2. s.o.m. prophesy ag. sheph.
35: 2. s. o. m. prophesy ag. Seir
36: 17. s.o.m. when Israel dwelt
37:3. s.o.m. can these bones live?
9. prophesy, s.o.m. say to wind,
11. s. o. m. these bones are hou.
16. s. o. m. take thee one stick
38: 2. s.o.m. set face against Gog
prophesy ag. him, 14.-39: 1.
39:17. s.o.m. thus saith L., 43:18.
40: 4. s. o. m. behold and hear
43: 7. s.o.m. place of my throne
10. s.o.m. shew the house to Isr.
44: 5. s.o.m. mark well, behold
47: 6. s. o. m. hast seen this?
Da. 7:13. one like the S.o.m. came
with clouds, Re. 1: 13.-14: 14.
8:17. Underst. O s.o.m. for at time

Mat. 8 : 20. S.o.m. hath not where
to lay his head, Lu. 9 : 58.
9 : 6. know S.o.m. hath power to
forgive, Mk. 2 : 10. Lu. 5 : 24.
10 : 23. not gone over, till the S.o.
m. be come [Lu. 7 : 34.
11 : 19. The S. o. m. came eating,
12:8. S.o.m. is L. of sabbath, Mk.
2 : 28. Lu. 6 : 5. [Lu. 12 : 10.
32. whoso. speaketh ag. S.o.m.
40. shall S. o. m. be three days
13:37. soweth good seed is S.o.m.
41. S. o. m. shall send angels
16: 13. say that I the S.o.m. am ?
27.S.o.m.sh.come in glory of Fa.
28. see S.o.m. coming in kingd.
17 : 9. until the S. o. m. be risen
again, Mk. 9 : 9. [8: 31.
12. shall also S.o.m. suffer, Mk.
22. the S.o.m. shall be betrayed,
20 : 18.-26:2, 45. Mk.14:41. Lu.
9 : 44. [is lost
18 : 11. S. o. m. come to save that
19 : 28. S. o. m. sit in throne of
20 : 28. S. o. m. came not to be
ministered unto, Mk. 10 : 45.
24 : 27. so shall the coming of the
S. o. m. be, 37, 39. Lu. 17 : 26.
30. shall see S. o. m. coming,
Mk. 13 : 26. Lu. 21 : 27.
44. hour ye think not S. o. m.
cometh, 25 : 13. Lu. 12 : 40.
25:31. When S.o.m. shall come in
26:24. The S.o.m. goeth, Mk. 14 :
21. Lu. 22 : 22. [62. Lu. 22 : 69.
64. see S. o. m. sitting, Mk. 14 :
Mk. 8 : 38. of him shall the S.o.m.
be ashamed, Lu.9:26. [Lu.18:31:
9 : 12. how it is written of S.o.m.,
31. the S. o. m. is delivered, 10 :
33. Lu. 24 : 7. [a journey
13 : 34. S.o.m. is as a man taking
Lu. 6:22. reproach for S. o.m.sake
9 : 22. The S.o.m. must suffer, 26.
56.S.o.m. is not come to destroy
11 : 30. so shall S.o.m. be, 17: 24.
12:8. him shall the S.o.m.confess
17 : 22. see one of days of S. o. m.
30. day when S.o.m. is revealed
18:8. S.o.m. cometh shall he find
19 : 10. S.o.m. is come to save lost
21:36.worthy to stand bef. S.o.m.
22 : 48. betrayest S.o.m. wi. kiss?
Jn. 1 : 51. descending upon S. o.m.
3 : 13. S. o. m. which is in heaven
14. so must S. o. m. be lifted up
5:27. authority, bec. he is S o.m.
6 : 27. S.o.m. shall give unto you
53. Except ye eat flesh of S.o.m.
62. if ye see S. o. m. ascend [m.
8 : 28. when ye have lifted up S. o.
12 : 23. that S. o. m. be glorified
34. S. o. m. must be lifted up,
who is this S. o. m.? [glorified
13 : 31. Jesus said, Now is S.o.m.
Ac. 7:56. I see S.o.m. standing on
right hand
See STATURE, STRONG.

That MAN.

Le. 17 : 9. even t. m. shall be cut off
20:3. set my face ag. t.m., 5. Eze.
Nu. 9 : 13. t. m. bear sin [14 : 8.
De. 17:5. stone t.m. or woman, 12.
22 : 18. elders shall take t.m. and
25:9.So shall it be done unto t.m.
29:20. jealousy sh. smoke ag. t.m.
Jos.22:20.t. m. perisheth not alone
Jb. 1 : 1. t.m. was perfect upright
Ps. 37 : 37. end of t. m. is peace
40:4.Blessed is t.m.who maketh L.
87 : 5. This and t. m. born in her
Pr.28:21.for bread t.m.will transgr.
Je. 20 : 16. let t. m. be as cities L.
23:34. I will punish t.m. [11:26.
Mat. 12 : 45. last state of t.m.. Lu.
18:7.woe to t.m. by whom offence
26: 24. woe to t.m. by wh. Son of
man is betrayed, Mk. 14 : 21.
Lu. 22 : 22.
Mat.26:24.good for t.m. if not born
27:19.Have noth. to do with t. just
Ac.17:31.t.m. wh.he ordained [m.
Ro. 14:20. evil for t.m. who eateth
2 Th. 2 : 3. t. m. of sin be revealed
3:14. note t.m. have no company
Ja. 1:7. let not t.m. think he shall

This MAN. [receive

Ge. 24 : 58.Wilt thou go with t.m.?
26:11.He th.toucheth t. m.or wife
Ex. 10:7. How long t.m.be a snare
De.22:16.I gave my dau. unto t.m.
Ju.19:23. t.m. is come into my ho.
24.unto t.m. do not so vile thing
1 S.1:3.t.m.went yearly to worship
10 : 27. How shall t. m. save us?
17:25. Have you seen t.m.is come
25:25.Let not my lord regard t.m.
1 K.20:7. how t.m. seeketh misch.
39. bro-t man said, Keep t. m.
2 K.5:7. t.m. send to recov. a man
Ne. 1 : 11. mercy in sight of t. m.
Es. 9 : 4. t.m. Mord. waxed greater
Jb. 1 : 3. t.m. was greatest of men
Ps.52:7.t.m.made not G. his stren.
87 : 4. t.m. was born there, 5, 6.
Is.14:16.t.the m.made earth tremb.
66 : 2. to t. m. will I look [idol?
Je. 22: 28. Is t.m. Coniah a broken
30.saith L. Write ye t.m.childless
26: 11. t. m. is worthy to die, 16.
38 : 4. let t. m. be put to death, t.
m. seeketh not welfare of peo.
Da. 8 : 16. make t. m. understand
Jon.1:14. let us not perish for t.m.
Mi. 5 : 5. t. m. shall be the peace
Mat.8:9.I say to t. m. Go, he goeth
9 : 3. scribes said t. m. blasphemeth, Mk. 2:7. [dom? 56.Mk.6:2.
13: 54. whence had t.m. this wis-
27 : 47. said t.m. calleth for Elias
Mk. 14:71. I know not t.m. [God
15 : 39. Truly t.m. was the Son of
Lu. 7:39. t.m. if he were a prophet
14 : 9. and say, Give t. m. place
30. saying, t. m. began to build
15 : 2. t. m. receiveth sinners and
18 : 14. t. m. went down justified
19 : 14. not have t. m. to reign
22 : 56. said, t. m. was with him
23 : 4. I find no fault in t. m., 14.
18. Away with t. m. release
41.t.m.hath done nothing amiss
52. t. m. unto Pilate and begged
Jn. 6 : 52. How can t. m. give us
his flesh to eat?
7 : 15. how knoweth t. m. letters
27. we know t. m. whence he is
31. miracles t. m. hath done
9:2. who did sin, t.m. or parents
3. neither hath t.m. sinned, nor
16. t.m. is not of G. keepeth not
24. we know t. m. is a sinner
33. If t.m. were not of G. he cn.
10:41. all that John spake of t.m.
11 : 37. Could not t. m. wh. opened
eyes of blind, have caused that
t. m. should not have died?
47. t. m. doeth many miracles
18:17. Art not thou of t.m.'s disci.?
29. What accusation ag. t. m.?
40. Not t. m. but Barabbas, now
19 : 12. If let t. m. go, not Cesar's
21:21. saith, and what sh. t.m.do
Ac. 1 : 18. t. m. purchased a field
3 : 12. had made t.m. to walk, 16.
4 : 10. by him t. m. stand whole
5:28. to bring t.m.'s blood upon us
37. After t. m. rose up Judas
6 : 13. t.m. ceaseth not blasphem.
8 : 10. t. m. is great power of God
9 : 13. I heard of t.m. how much
evil he hath done
13:23.Of t. m.'s seed G.raised Jes.
38.thro.t.m.is preached forgiven.
Ac.18:25.t.m. was instructed in L
21:28.t. is the m. teacheth ag.law
22 : 26. t. m. is a Roman
23 : 9. We find no evil in t. m.
23:27. t.m. was taken of the Jews
24:5. found t.m. a pestilent fellow
25 : 5. accuse t.m. if there be any
24.ye see t.m. about whom Jews
26:31. t.m. doeth noth. worthy of
32. t. m. might have been set at
28 : 4. No doubt t.m. is murderer
He. 3 : 3.t.m. was counted worthy
7 : 4. consider how great t.m. was
24. t.m. bec. he continueth ever
8 : 3. that t. m. have also to offer
10 : 12. t. m. after he had offered
Ja. 1 : 25. t. m. shall be blessed in
26. deceiveth, t. m.'s religion is
See UNDERSTANDING. [vain

MAN of war, s.

Ex. 15 : 3. the Lord is a m. o. w.
Jos. 17 : 1. Machir was a m. o. w.
1 S. 16 : 18. David a m. o. w.,2 S.
17 : 8. 1 Ch. 28 : 3. [his youth
17 : 33. Goliath was a m. o.w. fr.
1 Ch. 18 : † 10. Hadarezer m.o.w-s
Is. 3:2. L. doth take aw. m. o. w.
42:13. stir jealousy like a m.o.w.

Wicked MAN.

De.25:2. if w. m. worthy to be beat-
Jb.15:20. The w.m. travaileth [en
20:29.the portion of a w.m.,27:13.
Ps. 109:6. Set thou w.m. over him
Pr.6:12.w.m.walketh with froward
9:7. rebuketh w.m. getteth a blot
11:7.When w.m. dieth,his expec.
13 : 5. a w. m. is loathsome
17:23 A w.m. taketh a gift out of
21:29.w.m.hard-th face [dwell-g
24: 15. Lay not wait, O w. m. ag.
Ec. 7:15. w.m.th. prolongeth days
Eze. 3 : 18. w. m. shall die in iniq.
18:24. doeth that wh. w.m.doeth
27. when w.m. turneth fr.wick.
33: 8. when I say, O w. m. thou
shalt die, that w. m. shall die

Wise MAN.

Ge. 41:33. look out m. discreet and
1 K. 2 : 9. Solomon was w. m. [w.
1 Ch. 27:32. Jonathan was a w.m.
Jb. 15:2. a w.m. utter vain knowl.
17 : 10. I cannot find one w. m.
34:34.let a w.m.hearken unto me
Pr. 1 : 5. w.m. will hear and incr.
9:8.rebuke w.m. he will love thee
9. give instruction to a w. m. he
14:16.A w.m. departeth from evil
16 : 14. a w.m. will pacify the k.
17:10. reproof ent-h into a w. m.
21 : 22. A w. m. scaleth the city
26 : 12. Seest m.w. in his conceit
29:9.If w.m.contendeth wi.foolish
11.w.m.keepeth it in till afterw.
Ec. 2 : 14. w. m.'s eyes are in his
16. And how dieth the w. m.?
19. whe. he shall be w. m. or a?
7 : 7. oppr-n maketh w. m. mad
8:1. Who is as w. m. and kno-th
5. w. m.'s heart discerneth time
17. tho. a w.m. think to know it
9 : 15. was found in it poor w. m.
10:2. w. m.'s heart is at right ha.
12. The words of w. m.'s mouth
Je.9:12. Who is w.m.may underst.?
23. Let not w. m. glory in wisd.
Mat.7:24.will liken him unto w.m.
1 Co. 6 : 5. is not a w. m. am. you
Ja. 3 : 13. Who is a w. m. endued

MAN with woman. [m.

Ge.2:23.w.bec.she was taken out of
3:12. m. said, The w. thou gavest
20:3. dead m., for w. thou hast is
Ex. 35:29. m. and w. whose heart
36:6. Let nei.m.nor w.make work
Le. 13:29. If a m.or w.have plague
38. If m. or w. have in the skin
15:18.w. with whom the m.sh.lie

Le. 15 : 33. hath issue, of m. and w.
20:18. If m. lie with w. having her
27. A m. or w. that hath a spirit
Nu. 5:6. When m. or w. commit sin
6:2. When m. or w. shall separate
31:17. kill w. that hath known m.,
Ju. 21 : 11. [wickedn.
De. 17 : 2. m. or w. that wrought
5. bring forth m. or w., and stone
22:5. w. not wear that pertain. to
m. nei. m. put on w.'s garm.
22. If a m. be found lying with a
w., m. that lay wi. w., and w.
29:18. Lest be among you m. or w.
Jos. 6:21. destroyed both m. and w.
1 S. 15 : 3. but slay both m. and w.
27:9. Da. left nei. m. nor w. alive, 11.
1 Ch. 16:3. dealt to m. and w. loaf
2 Ch. 15:13. not seek L., m. or w. die
Es. 4:11. whe. m. or w. come unto k.
Je. 44:7. to cut off m., w., ch. [w.
51:22. I will break in pieces m. and
1 Co. 7:1. good for m. not to touch
11:3. head of the w. is the m. [w.
7. w. is the glory of the m. [m.
8. m. is not of the w.; but w. of
12. as w. is of m., so is m. by w.
1 Ti 2:12. w. usurp authority ov. m.
5 : 16. If any m. or w. have widows
See **Born of a WOMAN.**
See **WOMAN** with **man.**

Young MAN.

Ge. 4 : 23. slain a y. m. to my hurt
18:7. Abraham gave it unto y. m.
34:19. y. m. deferred not to do thi.
41 : 12. with us a y. m. a Hebrew
Ex. 33:11. Joshu. a y. m. departed
Nu. 11:27. ran y. m. told Moses [not
De. 32:25. destroy y. m. and virgin
Ju. 8:14. caught a y. m. of Succoth
9:54. Abimelech called hastily unto
y. m. his y. m. thrust him thro.
17:7. was a y. m. of Beth-le., 11.
12. the y. m. became his priest
18:3. knew voice of the y. m., 15.
19:19. bread for y. m. wh. is with
1 S. 9 : 2. Saul was a choice y. m.
14:1. Jonathan said unto y. m., 6.
17 : 58. Whose son art thou, y. m.?
20:22. if I say thus unto the y. m.
30 : 13. he said, I am y. m. of E.
2 S. 1:5. Da. said unto y. m., 6, 13.
13:34. y. m. that kept watch lifted
14 : 21. go bring y. m. Abs. again
18:5. Deal gently with the y. m., 12.
29. Is the y. m. Absalom safe? 32.
32. enem. of lord be as that y. m.
1 K. 11 : 28. Solomon seeing y. m.
2 K. 6:17. Lord opened eyes of y. m.
9:4. so the y. m. went to Ramoth
1 Ch. 12:28. Zadok, a y. m. mighty
2 Ch. 36:17. no compassion upon y.
m. or maiden [way
Ps. 119 : 9. Whw. y. m. cleanse his
Pr. 1 : 4. to y. m. knowledge and
7:7. a y. m. void of understanding
Ec. 11:9. Rejoice, O y. m. in youth
Is. 62:5. as y. m. marrieth a virgin
Je. 51:22. break the y. m. and maid
Zch. 2 : 4. Run, speak to this y. m.
Mat. 19 : 20. y. m. said, All these
have I kept, 22. [y. m.
Mk. 14 : 51. followed him a certain
16:5. a y. m. sitting on right side
Lu. 7:14. y. m. I say unto thee, Arise
Ac. 7:58. laid clothes at a y. m.'s feet
20:9. sat in a window a y. m. named
12. they brought the y. m. alive
23:17. Bring y. m. unto capt., 18.
22 captain then let the y. m. de-

MANACLES. [part

Je. 40:†1. Jeremiah being bound in

MAN'AEN. [m.

Ac. 13 : 1. M. bro-t up with Herod

MAN'AHATH. [1 : 40.

Ge. 36:23. chil. of Shobal, M., 1 Ch.
1 Ch. 8:6. they removed them to M.

MANA'HETHITES.

1 Ch. 2 : 52. and half of the M., 54.

MANAS'SEH. [48 : 14.

Ge. 41 : 51. Jo. called firstborn M.,
48 : 5. thy two sons M. and Ephr.
are mine, 1.-46:20. Nu. 26:28.
13. M. in left hand toward Isr.
17. from Ephraim's head to M.
20. God make thee as Ephr. and
M. he set Ephraim before M.
50:23. Machir son of M., Nu. 26:29.
-32:39, 40. Jos. 13:31.-17 : 1, 3.
1 Ch. 7 : 17. [2 : 20.-10 : 23.
Nu. 1:10. of M. Gamaliel was prince,
7 : 54. Gamaliel prince of M. off-d
26 : 34. families of M., 27 : 1. [4:13.
32:41. Jair son of M., De. 3:14. 1 K.
36 : 12. married into family of M.
De. 33 : 17. are the thousands of M.
34 : 2. land of M. unto utmost sea
Jos. 14:4. of Jo. two tribes, M. Ephr.
16:4. M. and Ephr. took their inher.,
17:2. these the male chil. of M. [9.
3. Zeloph. son of M. had no sons
5. fell ten portions to M. besides
6. dau-s of M. had inheritance
7. coast of M. was from Asher
8. M. had land of Tappuah (2) [10.
9. cities of Ephr. am. cities of M.,
11. M. had in Issachar, Beth-sh.
12. M. co. not drive out, Ju. 1:27.
17. Joseph spake even to M.
Ju. 6 : 15. my family is poor in M.
35. sent messengers thro. all M.
7:23. out of M. and pursued aft. M.
11 : 29. Jephthah passed over M.
18 : 30. son of Gershom, son of M.
2 K. 20:21. M. reigned, 2 Ch. 32:33.
21:1. M. was 12 years old when he
began, 2 Ch. 33: 1.
9. M. seduced them to do more evil
11. Bec. M. hath done abomi.
16. M. shed innocent blood, till he
17. rest of acts of M., 2 Ch. 33:18.
18. M. slept with fathers, 2 Ch. 33:
20. Amon did evil as M. did [20.
23 : 12. altars M. made Josiah beat
26. provocations M. had provoked
24:3. for sins of M. this upon Jud.
1 Ch. 3:13. Ahaz his son, M. his son
7 : 14. The sons of M. Ashriel
29. by the borders of the chil. of M.
9 : 3. in Jerus. dwelt of chil. of M.
12 : 19. fell some of M. to David
20. there fell to him of M. (2) [Asa
2 Ch. 15 : 9. strangers of M. fell to
30 : 1. Hez. wrote to Ephr. and M.
10. thro. country of Ephr. and M.
11. divers of M. humbled thems.
18. many of M. not cleansed
31:1. Isr. cut down the groves in M.
33:9. M. made Jud. and Jerus. err
10. L. spake to M. he not hearken
11. captains took M. am. thorns
13. then M. knew Lord was G. [M.
23. Amon humbled not hims., as
34 : 6. so did Josiah in cities of M.
9. money they had gathered fr. M.
Ezr. 10:30. M. had strange wives, 33.
Ps. 60 : 7. Gilead, M. is mine, 108:8.
80 : 2. bef. M. stir up thy strength
Is. 9:21. M. shall eat Ephr., Ephr. M.
Je. 15 : 4. removed. because of M.
Eze. 48 : 4. a portion for M., 5.
See MANASSES.

Tribe of MANAS'SEH.

Nu. 1 : 35. of the t. o. M., 32,200.
2:20. by Ephr. shall be the t. o. M.
13 : 11. of the t. o. M. Gaddi
32:33. to half t. o. M. kingd. of Og.
34 : 14. half t. o. M. have received
23. prince for t. o. M. Hanniel
Jos. 1:12. to half t. o. M. spake Josh.
4:12. half t. o. M. passed over armed
13 : 7. to 9 tribes and half t. o. M.
29. Moses gave inheri. to half t.
o. M. this was possess. of half
t. o. M., 22 : 7. Nu. 32:33.-De.
3 : 13.-29 : 8. Jos. 12 : 6.-18 : 7.
Jos. 17 : 1. was also a lot for t. o. M.
20:8. Golan out of t. o. M., 21:27.
21 : 5. out of half t. o. M. cities, 6,
25. 1 Ch. 6 : 61, 62.
22 : 9. the half t. o. M. returned
10. half t. o. M. built altar, 11.
21. half t. o. M ans-d. The L. G.
1 Ch. 5 : 18. Reuben, Gad, and half
t. o. M. valiant, Jos. 22 : 13, 15.
23. half t. o. M. dwelt in land
26. bro-t half t. o. M. unto Halah
6 : 70 of half t. o. M. to Lev., 71.
12:31. half t. o. M. 18,000 to make
David king, 37. [27 : 20, 21.
26:32. rulers over Gad half t. o. M.,

MANAS'SES.

Mat. 1:10. Ezekias begat M., M. begat
Re. 7 : 6. of tribe of M. sealed 12,000

MANAS'SITES.

De. 4:43. Golan in Bashan of the M.
Ju. 12:4. Among Ephraimites and M.
2 K. 10 : 33. and the M. from Aroer

MANDRAKES.

Ge. 30 : 14. Reuben found m. (2)
15. wouldest take my son's m. he
shall lie with thee for son's m.
16. I hired thee with my son's m.
Can. 7 : 13. m. give a smell, and

MANEH. [m.

Eze. 45 : 12. fifteen shekels be your

MANGER.

Lu. 2 : 7. she laid him in a m. [m.
12. Ye shall find babe lying in a
16. they found babe lying in a m.

MANIFEST. [Adj.]

Ac. 4:16. miracle was m. to all [m.
Ro. 1:19. what may be kno. of G. is
1 Co. 15:27. it is m. he is expected
Ga. 5:19. works of the flesh are m.
Ph. 1:13 my bonds in Christ are m.
2 Th. 1:5. a m. token of judgm. of
1 Ti. 3 : 16. God was m. in the flesh
5:25. works of some are m. before
2 Ti. 3 : 9. their folly shall be m.
He. 4:13. is no creature th. is not m.
1 Pe. 1:20. was m. in these last times
1 Jn. 3:10. In this the chil. of G. are
See MADE. MAKE. [m.

MANIFEST. [Verb.]

Ec. 3 : 18. that God might m. them
Jn. 14:21. love him, and m. myself
22. m. thyself unto us, and not
unto world?

MANIFESTATION.

Ro. 8 : 19. for m. of sons of God
1 Co. 12 : 7. m. of Spirit is given to
2 Co. 4:2. by m. of the truth [man

MANIFESTED. [m.

Mk. 4:22. noth hid which sh. not be
Jn. 2:11. did Jesus, and m. his glory
17:6. I have m. thy name unto men
Ro. 3:21. righteousness of G. is m.
1 Ti. 3:†16. God was m. in the flesh
Tit. 1 : 3. hath in due time m. word
1 Jn. 1 : 2. life was m. we seen it
3 : 5. was m. to take aw. our sins
8. for this was the Son of God m.
4:9. In this was m. the love of God

MANIFESTLY.

2 Co 3:3. m. declared to be epistle

MANIFOLD.

Ne. 9 : 19. in m. mercies forsookest
not in wilderness [iours
27. acc. to m. mercies gavest sav-
Ps. 104 : 24. how m. are thy works
Am. 5:12. I know your m. transg-us
Lu. 18:30. who not receive m. more
Ep. 3:10. be known m. wisd. of God
1 Pe. 1:6. heaviness, thro. m. tempta.
4 : 10. stewards of m. grace of G.

MANKIND. [wom.

Le. 18 : 22. not lie with m. as with
20:13. if man lie with m. as wom.
Jb. 12:10. in hand, breath of all m.
1 Co. 6:9. abusers of thems. with m.

1 Ti.1:10. law for them defile wi.m.
Ja. 3:7. and hath been tamed of m.

MANNA.

Ex. 16: 15. they said, It is m., 31.
33. take a pot and put a homer
full of m. therein
35. Israel did eat m. forty years
Nu.11:6. is nothing besides this m.
7. the m. was as coriander seed
9. when dew fell the m. fell on it
De. 8: 3. he fed thee with m., 16.
Ne. 9: 20. Ps. 78: 24. [more
Jos. 5: 12. m. ceased, had m. no
Jn.6:31. Our fathers did eat m..49.
58.not as your fathers did eat m.
He.9:4. was golden pot that had m.
Re.2:17. will I give to eat of hidden [m.

MANNER.

Ge. 25:23. two m. of peo. separated
Ex. 12: 16. no m. of work be done
22: 9. or for any m. of lost thing
Le. 5: 10. burnt offering according
to m., Nu. 9: 14.-29: 6.
7: 23. shall eat no m. of fat of ox
26. ye shall eat no m. of blood,
27.-17:10, 14. [m. of creeping
11: 44. nei. defile yours. with any
20: 25. abomi. by any m. of living
23: 31. ye shall do no m. of work
24:22.have one m.of law,Nu.15:16.
Nu. 5:13.nei. she be taken with m.
15:24.drink offering acc. to the m.
28: 18. do no m. of servile work
De.4:15.ye saw no m. of similitude
15: 2. this is of m. release
27: 21. lieth with any m. of beast
Ju. 6:†26. built altar in orderly m.
8:18.What m. of men they ye slew
13:†12.What sh.be m. of the child
Ru. 4: 7. was m. in former time
1 S. 8: 9. shew them m. of k., 11.
10:25. Sam. told peo. m. of kingd.
21: 5. bread is in a m. common
27: 11. so will be his m. all the
2 S. 7: 19. is this the m. of man
1 K. 18:28. cut thems. aft. their m.
2 K.1:7. What m. of man who told
11:14.k. stood by pillar, as m.was
17: 26. know not m. of G. of land
27. teach them m. of G. of land
1 Ch.24:19. their m. under Aa. [ing
2 Ch.2:14.to grave any m. of grav-
30:16. stood in place aft. their m.
Ne.8:18. assembly acc. unto the m.
Es. 1: 13. was king's m. toward all
2: 12. Acc. to the m. of women
Is. 5: 17. lambs feed after their m.
Je 22: 21. been thy m. fr. youth
Da. 6: 23. no m. of hurt upon him
Am. 8: 14. m. of Beer-sheba liveth
Mat. 8: 27.What m. of man is this
that winds, Mk. 4:41. Lu. 8:25.
Mk. 13: 1. see what m. of stones
Lu. 1: 29. what m. of salutation
66. What m. of child sh. this be?
7: 39. what m. of woman [ye are
9: 55. know not what m. of spirit
24:17.what m. of communications
Jn. 7:36. What m. of saying is this
19:40.as m. of the Jews is to bury
Ac.17:2. Paul, as his m. was, went
20:18.Ye know aft. what m.I have
22: 3. taught acc. to perfect m. of
25:16.It is not m. of Romans [law
20.doubted of such m. of quest-s
26:4. My m. of life from my youth
2 Co.7:9. made sorry after godly m.
1 Th.1:5. know what m. of men we
9. what m. of entering in we had
2 Ti. 3: 10. hast known my m. of
He.10:25. as the m. of some is [life
Ja.1:24. forgetteth what m. of man
1 Pe. 1: 11. what m. of time Spirit
2 Pe.3:11. what m.of persons ought
1 Jn. 3: 1. behold what m. of love
Re. 11: 5. must in this m. be killed
22: 2. wh. bare 12 m. of fruits

After the MANNER.

Ge.18:11.with Sarah a. m. of wom.
19:31. to come in unto us a.m. of
Ex.21:9.with her a.m.of dau-s [all
Nu. 29:18. acc. to number, a.m.+
Jos.6:15.compassed city a.same m.
Ju. 18: 7. careless, a.m. of Zidoni-
1 S.17:30.he spake a.same m. [ans
2 K. 17: 33. a.m. of the nations, 2
Ch. 13: 9. [before oracle
2 Ch. 4: 20. lamps they burn a.m.
Ne. 6: 4. I ans-d them a. same m.
Jb. 31: † 33. If I covered my trans-
gressions a. m. of men
Is.10:24.a.m.of Egypt,26.Am.4:10.
Je. 30: 18. palace sh. remain a.m.
Eze.20:30. polluted a.m. of fathers
23: 15. a. m. of the Babylonians
45. a. m. of adulteresses, a. m.
of women that shed blood
Jn. 2:6. a. m. of purifying of Jews
Ac.15:1. circumcised a.m.of Moses
Ro. 6: 19. I speak a. m. of men, 1
Co. 15: 32. Ga. 3: 15. [cup
1 Co.11:25. a. same m. he took the
Ga.2:14. Jew, livest a. m. of Gent.
See FORMER.

After this MANNER.

Ge.18:25.far from thee to do a.t.m.
39:19.a.t.m.did thy servant to me
45:23.to his father he sent a.t.m.
Nu.28:24. a.t.m. offer daily,15:13.
1 S. 17: 27. ans. a.t.m. So sh. it be
2 S.17:6.Ahithophel spoken a.t.m.
1 K. 7: 37. a. t. m. made 10 bases
Ezr. 5: 4. said a. t. m. What are
Je.13:9.a.t.m.will I mar the pride
Mat. 6: 9. a.t.m. pray ye, Our Fa.
Ac. 15: 23. letters a.t.m., 23: 25.
1 Co. 7: 7. one a.t.m. another aft.
1 Pe.3:5. a.t.m. in old time, wom- [en

All MANNER.

Ge.40:17.a.m.of bakemeats for Pha
Ex. 1: 14. bitter in a.m. of service
22: 9. For a. m. of trespass, whe.
31:3. in a.m. of workmanship, 5.-
35: 29, 31, 35.-36: 1. 1 Ch. 22:
15.-28: 21.-29: 5.
Le. 11:27. upon paws among a. m.
of beasts, Nu. 31: 30.
14:54. law for a. m. of the plague
19: 23. a.m. of trees, Ne. 10: 37.
2 S.6:5.played on a.m. of lustrum.
1 Ch.6:48.a.m.of service,2 Ch.34:13
12:37. a.m. of instruments of war
18: 10. a. m. of vessels of gold
23:29.for a.m.of measure and size
28: 14. instruments for a. m. of
29:2. a.m. of preci. stones [jewels
2 Ch. 32: 27. treasuries for a.m. of
28. stalls for a. m. of beasts
Ne.13:15. figs and a.m. of burdens
16.men which bro-t a.m.of ware
Ps. 107:18. abhorreth a.m.of meat
144: 13. garners affording a.m. of
Can.7:13.a.m.of pleas.fruits [store
Mat.4:23. healing a.m.of sickn.,10:
5: 11. a. m. of evil ag. you [1.
12:31.a.m. of sin be forgiven men
Lu. 11: 42. ye tithe a.m. of herbs
Ac. 10: 12. wherein a. m. of four
footed beasts [cence
Ro. 7: 8. in me a. m. of concupis-
1 Pe.1:15.holy in a.m. of conversa.
Re. 18: 12. a.m. vessels of ivory (2)
21:19.with a.m.of precious stones

Like MANNER.

Ex. 7: 11. in l.m. with enchant-ts
23: 11. In l. m.deal wi.thy viney.
De. 22: 3. In l. m. do with his ass
Ju. 11: 17. in l. m. they sent unto
1 S.19:24.prophesied bef. Sam. in l.
Ne 6:5.Sanballat sent in l. m. [m.
Is. 51:6. dwell there sh. die in l.m.
Mk. 13: 29. ye in l. m. when ye see
Lu. 6: 23. in l.m. did their fathers
20:31. third took her, in l.m. 7th
Ac. 1: 11. come in l. m. as ye seen
1 Ti.2:9.In l.m. that women adorn
Jude 7. in l. m. giving thems. to
fornication

On this MANNER.

Ge.32:19.o.t.m.ye speak unto Esau
1 S. 18: 24. o. t. m. spake David
2 S. 14: 3. spake o.t.m. unto him
15: 6. o.t.m. did Abs. to all Isr.
1 K.7:28. work of bases o.t.m. [19.
22: 20. one said o.t.m., 2 Ch. 18:
2 Ch. 32: 15. persuade you o.t.m.

MANNERS.

Le. 20:23. not walk in m.of nations
2 K.17:34. they do after former m.
Eze. 11:12. done aft. m. of heathen
Ac. 13: 18. forty years suff-d their
1 Co. 15: 33. corrupt good m. [m.
He. 1: 1. God in divers m. spake

MANO'AH.

Ju.13:2. a man whose name was M.
8. then M. entreated the Lord
9. God hearkened to voice of M.
11. M. went after wife and came
12. M. said, Now let thy words
16. M. knew not that he was angel of the Lord, 13, 15, 17, 21.
19. M. took a kid and offered it
20. M. and his wife looked on it
21. M. knew he was angel of Lord
22.M.said unto his wife, We shall
16:31. Samson in burying-pl.of M.

MANSERVANT, S.

Ex. 20:10. not do work, thy m.,De.
5: 14. [m., De. 5: 21.
17. sh. not covet thy neighbour's
21: 27. if he smite out m.'s tooth
32. If ox shall push m. he shall
De.12:18. must eat th.thou and m.
16:11.rejoice, thou and thy m.,14.
Ne.7:67. Besides their m-s they had
Jb.31:13.if I did despise cause of m.
Je. 34:9.ev. man let his m. go free,

MANSIONS.

Jn. 14: 2. In Father's house many [10.

MANSLAYER, S.

Nu. 35: 6. six cities appoint for m. [m.
12.that m. die not until he stand
1 Ti.1:9. that law was made for m-s

MANTLE, S.

Ju.4:18.Jael covered Sisera with m.
1 S. 15: 27. upon skirt of his m.
28:14.old man, and covered wi.m.
1 K. 19: 13. Elijah wrapped face in
19. cast his m. upon Elisha [m.
2 K. 2:8. Elijah took m. and smote
13. Elisha took Elijah's m., 14.
Ezr 9:3.heard this,I rent my m.,5.
Jb.1:20. Job arose and rent his m.
2: 12. they rent every one his m.
Ps. 109: 29. confusion as with a m.
Is. 3: 22. I will take away the m-s
Da. 3:†21. men were bound in their [m-s

MANY.

Ex. 19:21. they gaze and m. perish
23: 2. to decline after m.
Nu. 10: 36. Return, O L. unto m.
thousands of Israel
13: 18. see whe. they be few or m.
26: 54. To m. give more inherit.
35:8.that have m.cities,sh.give m
Ju. 9: 40. m. were overthrown
16:24. destroyer wh. slew m. of us
2 S. 24:†14. for his mercies are m.
1 K.4:20. Jud.and Israel m.as sand
7:47.unweighed, bec. exceed-g m.
18: 25. dress it first, for ye are m.
2 K. 9:22.her witchcrafts so m. [few
2 Ch.14:11. noth. to help wi. m. or
30: 17. m. in congr. not sanctified
18. m. of Ephraim not cleansed
32: 23. m. brought gifts unto L.
Ezr.10:13. we m.th. have transgr-d
Ne.6:18.m.in Jud. sworn to Tobiah
7: 2. he feared God above m.
Es. 4:3. m. lay in sackcloth [m.
Jb.4:3.Behold, thou hast instructed

Jb.11:19.m.sh.make suit unto thee
Ps. 3:1. m.they that rise up ag. me
2. be m. that say of my soul,4:6.
25:19.mine enem.they are m.,56:2
31:13. I have heard slander of m.
37:16.better than riches of m.wick
40:3.m.shall see it, fear, and trust
5.m. O L. are thy wonderf.works
55: 18. for there were m. with me
71: 7. I am as a wonder unto m.
Pr. 7: 26. she hath cast down m.
10:21.The lips of righteous feed m.
19:6. m.will entreat favour, 29:26.
28: 2 For the transgression of a
land m. are the princes thereof
27. hideth eyes have m. a curse
Ec.11:8. days of darkn. shall be m.
Is.8:15. m. am. them will stumble
31:1. trust in chariots bec. are m.
52: 14. m. were astonied at thee
53: 11. by knowl. shall justify m.
12. he bare the sin of m. and
66: 16. slain of the L. shall be m.
Je.11:15.she wrought lewdness with
20:10.I heard defaming of m.⌊m.
42: 2. for we are left but few of m.
46:16. He made m. to fall, one fell
Eze. 33: 24. we are m. land giv. us
37:2. were very m. in open valley
Da. 8: 25. by peace sh. destroy m.
9: 27. confirm covenant with m.
11:14. shall m. stand up ag. king
18.face unto isles,and sh.take m.
26. m. shall fall down slain ⌈m.
33. that understand sh. instruct
34. m. shall cleave with flatteries
39.he sh.cause th.to rule over m.
44. and utterly to make away m.
12:2.m.th. sleep in dust sh.awake
4. m. shall run to and fro
Na.1:12. Tho. they be quiet and m.
3:15. thyself m.as cankerworm (2)
Zch. 8: 20. come inhab. of m. cities
Mal. 2: 6. did turn m. fr. iniquity
8. have caused m. to stumble
Mat. 7: 13. m. there be that go in
22. m. will say in that day, L.L.
8:11.m.sh. come fr. east and west
16. m. that were poss-d, Ac. 8:7.
13:58. not m. mighty works there
19:30. m. that are first, Mk.10:31.
20:16. for m. be called, but,22:14.
28. life ransom for m., Mk.10:45.
24:5. sh. m. come in my name deceive m., Mk. 13:6. Lu. 21:8.
10. And then sh. m. be offended
12. the love of m. shall wax cold
26:28.blood shed for m.,Mk.14:24.
27:53. of saints appeared unto m.
Mk.2:15.disciples for there were m.
5:9. Legion, we are m., Lu. 8:30.
6:2. m. hearing him were aston-d
13. anointed with oil m. sick
31.m.coming going | 33.m.knew
9: 26. m. said, He is dead ⌊him
10:48.m.charged, he sho. hold his
11: 8. m. spread their garments
12: 41. m. rich cast in much
13: 6. m. sh. come in my name
Lu. 1:1. as m. have taken in hand
14. m. shall rejoice at his birth
16.m.shall he turn to the L. ⌈Isr.
2: 34. this child for rising of m. in
4: 25. m. widows | 27. m. lepers
41. devils also came out of m.
7: 21. he cured m. of infirmities
47. Her sins are m. are forgiven
13: 24. m. will seek to enter in
14:16.made great supper, bade m.
Jn. 6: 9. what are they am. so m.?
60. m. of his disciples said, 66.
10: 20. m. said, He hath a devil
41. and m. resorted unto him
11:55. m. went up to Jerus.
21:11.for all so m. net not broke
Ac. 9:13. I heard by m. of this man
10:27. found m. were come togeth.
Ac. 14:21. had taught m. they ret-d
19:19. m. bro-t books and burned
26: 10. m. of saints did I shut up
28: 23. came m. into his lodging
Ro. 5: 15. if thro. offence of one m. dead, grace abounded unto m.
19. For as m. were made sinners, shall m. be made righteous
12:5. So we, m., are one body in C.
16: 2. she been succourer of m.
1 Co.1:26.not m. wise, not m. mighty
8:5. as there be gods m. lords m.
10: 5. with m. G. not well pleased
17. we being m. are one bread
33. profit of m. th. they be saved
11:30.For this m.are weak m.sleep
12: 14. body not one member, m.
2 Co. 1: 11. thanks be given by m.
2: 6. punishment inflicted of m.
17. we are not as m. wh. corrupt
4:15. thro. thanksg. of m.redound
6:10. as poor, yet making m. rich
9: 2. your zeal hath provoked m.
11:18. Seeing m. glory in the flesh
12:21.I sh.bewail m.which sinned
Ga. 1: 14. profited above m. ⌈m.
3:16. saith not, And to seeds, as of
Ph.1:14.m. breth. waxing confident
3:18. m. walk of whom I told ⌈m.
He. 9:28. C.was off-d to bear sins of
11:12. sprang of one so m.as stars
12: 15. thereby m. be defiled
2 Pe. 2:2. m.sh.follow pernici.ways
See ADVERSARIES, AFFLICTIONS, ALTARS, ANTICHRISTS.

As MANY as.

Ex. 35: 22. a. m. a. were willing
Ju. 3:1. a. m. a. had not kn. wars
2 S. 2: 23. a. m. a. came to place
2 Ch. 29: 31. a. m. a. of free heart
Mat. 14: 36. a. m. a. touched, Mk.
22: 9. a. m. a. ye find bid ⌊6: 56.
10. gathered a. m.a. they found
Mk. 3: 10. touch him a. m. a. had
Lu. 11:8. will give a.m.a. ⌊plagues
Jn. 1: 12. a. m a. received him
17: 2. give eternal life to a. m. a.
Ac. 2: 39. even a. m. a. L. sh. call
3: 24. a. m. a. have spoken have
4:6. a. m. a. of kindr. of high pr.
34.a.m.a. were possessed of land
5:11.fear came upon a.m a. heard
36. and a. m. a. obeyed him,37.
10: 45. a. m. a. came with Peter
13:48. a.m.a.were ordained to life
Ro.2:12.a.m.a. have sinned with-t law, a. m. a. sinned in law
8:14. a. m. a. are led by Spi. of G.
Ga. 3: 10. a. m. a. are of the works
27. a. m. a. have been baptized
6:12.a.m.a.desire to make a shew
16. a. m.a. walk acc. to this rule
Ph. 3: 15. a. m. a. be perfect
Col. 2: 1. a. m. a. not seen my face
1 Ti.6:1.a. m. servants a. un. yoke
Re. 2: 24. a. m. a. have not doct.
3: 19. a. m. a. I love I rebuke
13:15.a.m.a.would not wors.beast
18:17. a. m. a. trade by sea stood
See BACKSLIDING, BELIEVED, CHARIOTS, CHILDREN, COLOURS, COUNTRIES, DAYS, DISCIPLES, EVILS, FATHERS, FEW, FRIENDS, GATHERED, GENERATIONS.

How MANY.

1 K. 22: 16. h. m. times sh. I adjure thee, tell true? 2 Ch.18:15.
Jb.13:23. h.m. are mine iniquities?
Ps.119:84.h.m. are days of serv-s?
Mat. 15: 34. h. m. loaves have ye?
Mk. 6: 38.-8: 5. ⌈Mk.8:19,20.
16: 9. h. m. baskets ye took up?
Mk.15:4.h. m. things they witness
Lu.15:17.h.m. hired serv-s.of fa.'s
2 Ti. 1:18. in h.m. things he ministered unto me at Ephesus
See JEWS, MASTERS, NATIONS, OTHERS, PEOPLE, S, PERSECUTORS, PRIESTS, PROPHETS, SIGHS, SLAIN, SONS, SORROWS, THINGS, TIME, TIMES, WATERS, WIVES, WORDS, WORKS, YEARS.

MA'OCH. ⌈M.

1 S. 27:2. passed unto Achish son of

MA'ON. [Person. Place.]

Jos. 15: 55. in the mts. M. Carmel
1 S. 23: 24. men in wildern. of M., 25.
25: 2. there was a man in M.
1 Ch. 2:45. Son of Shammai was M.

MA'ONITES.

Ju. 10: 12. the M. did oppress you

MAR, MARRED.

Le. 19: 27. nei. m. corners of beard
Ru. 4:6. lest I m. mine inheritance
1 S. 6: 5. your mice th. m. the land
2 S. 20:†15. m. to throw down wall
2 K. 3:19. m. ev. good piece of land
Jb. 30: 13. They m. my path
Is. 52: 14. his visage was so m-d
Je. 13:7. the girdle was m-d ⌊more
9. will I m. the pride of Judah
18: 4. vessel was m-d in hand of
Na.2:2.and m-d their vine branches
Mk.2:22.and the bottles will be m-d

MA'RA.

Ru. 1: 20. Ruth said, call me M.

MA'RAH. ⌈of M.

Ex. 15: 23. co. not drink of waters
Nu. 33:8. three days, and pitched in
9. removed fr. M. unto Elim ⌊M.

MAR'ALAH. ⌈M.

Jos. 19: 11. border went up toward

MARAN ATHA.

1 Co.16:22.let him be Anathema M.

MARBLE. ⌈dance

1 Ch. 29: 2. prepared m. in abun-
Es. 1: 6. pillars of m. pavement of
Can. 5:15. legs as pillars of m. ⌊m.
Re. 18:12.vessels of m. no man buy-

MARCH. ⌊eth

Ps. 68:7. when didst m. thro. wilder.
Is. 27:†4. briars, I wo. m. ag. them
Je. 46:22. sh. m. with army ⌈ways
Jo. 2: 7. shall m. every one on his
Ha. 1: 6. which sh. m. thro. land
3:12. Thou didst m. thro. the land

MARCHED, EDST, ING.

Ex.14:10.Egyptians m-d after them
Ju. 5: 4. thou m-t earth trembled
2 K. 9: † 20. m-g is like driving of

MAR'CUS. ⌊Jehu

Col.4:10.M.sister's son to Barnabas
Phm. 24.M.saluteth you, 1 Pe.5:13.

MARE'SHAH. [Person.]

1 Ch. 2:42. sons of M. fa. of Hebron
4: 21. Laadah the father of M.

MARE'SHAH. [Place.]

Jos.15:44.M.nine cities with villages
2 Ch. 11: 8. Rehoboam built M. ⌈10.
14: 9. Zerah wi. host came unto M.,
20: 37. Eliezer son of Dodavah of M.
Mi. 1: 15. Bring an heir unto thee, O

MARINERS. ⌊M.

Eze.27:8.inhabit-ts of Zidon thy m.
9. ships of the sea with their m.
27. thy m. shall fall into the seas
29. m. shall come down fr. ships
Jon. 1: 5. Then the m. were afraid

MARISHES. See MARSHES.

MARK. [Person.]

Ac. 12: 12. John, whose surname was M., 25.-15: 37.
15:39. Barnabas took M. and sailed,
2 Ti. 4: 11. take M. and bring him

MARK, S. [Noun.]

Ge. 4: 5. Lord set a m. upon Cain
Le. 19: 28. not print m-s upon you
1 S. 20:20. as though I shot at a m.
21:†13. made m-s on doors of gate
Jb. 7: 20. why hast set me as a m. against thee? 16:12. La. 3:12.
Eze.9:4.set a m.upon men that sigh

Eze. 9 : 6. come not near any man on whom is the **m.**
Ga. 6 : 17. I bear in body **m**-s of L.
Ph. 3 : 14. I press toward the **m.**
Re. 13:16. caused all to receive a **m.**
17. none buy, save he that had **m.**
14:9. If any receive **m.** in forehead
11. no rest, whoso receiv-h his **m.**
15:2. victory over his image, and **m.**
16:2. sore upon men had **m.** of beast
19 : 20. deceived them received **m.**
20:4. nei. received his **m.** lived with [C.

MARK. [Verb.]

Ru. 3 : 4. thou shalt **m.** the place
2 S. 13:28. **m.** when Amnon's heart
1 K. 20:7. **m.** how man seek misch
22. **m.** and see what thou doest
Jb. 18 : 2. **m.** and we will speak
21:5. **m.** me and be astonished, and
33 : 31 **m.** well, O Job, hearken
39 : 1. canst **m.** when hinds calve?
Ps. 37 : 37. **m.** the perfect man, his
48 : 13. **m.** ye well her bulwarks
56:6. **m.** my steps, when they wait
130:3. If thou shouldest **m.** iniq-s
Eze 44:5. **m.** well, **m.** the entering
Ro. 16:17. **m.** th. who cause divisions
Ph. 3 : 17. **m.** them who walk so

MARKED.

1 S. 1:12. prayed, Eli **m.** her mouth
Jb. 22 : 15. Hast **m.** way wh. wicked
24:16. wh. they had **m.** in daytime
Je. 2 : 22. thine iniq. is **m.** bef. me
23 : 18. who hath **m.** his word
Lu. 14:7. **m.** how they chose rooms

MARKEST, ETH.

Jb. 10:14. If I sin, thou **m**-t and wilt
33:11. in stocks, he **m**-h my paths
Is. 44 : 13. the carpenter **m**-h it out

MARKET, S. [19, 25.

Eze. 27 : 13. traded in thy **m.**, 17,
Mat. 11:16. like chil. sitting in **m** s
23 : 7. love greetings in the **m** s, Lu. 11:43.-20:46.
Mk. 7:4. when they come from **m.**
Jn. 5:2. pool at Jerus. by sheep **m.**
Ac. 17:17. he disputed in the **m.** daily

MARKETPLACE, S.

Mat. 20:3. others standing idle in **m.**
Mk. 12 : 38. love salutations in **m**-s
Lu. 7 : 32. like chil. sitting in **m.**
Ac. 16 : 19. drew them into the **m.**

MA'ROTH. [for good

Mi. 1 : 12. inhabitant of M. waited

MARRED. See MAR.

MARRIAGE, S.

Ge. 34 : 9. make ye **m**-s with us [ish
Ex. 21 : 10. her duty of **m.** not dimin-
De. 7 : 3. Nei. make **m**-s with them
Jos. 23: 12. if ye make **m**-s with them
Ps. 78:63. maidens not given to **m.**
Mat. 22:2. king who made a **m.** for
4. come unto the **m.** [son
9. all ye find, bid to the **m.**
30. in the resurrection not given in **m.** but, Mk. 12:25. Lu. 20:35.
24:38. given in **m.** until day th. Noe
25:10. th were ready went in to **m.**
Lu. 17:27. they were given in **m.**, 20:
Jn. 2:1. there was a **m.** in Cana [34.
2. Jesus was called to the **m.**
1 Co. 7 : 38. giveth her in **m.** doeth well, giveth not in **m.** better
He. 13 : 4. **m.** is honourable in all
Re. 19 : 7. **m.** of the Lamb is come
9. called to the **m.** supper of Lamb

MARRIED.

Ge. 19 : 14. Lot spake unto sons in law which **m.** his daughters
20:†3. woman is **m.** to a husband
Ex. 21:3. if **m.** wife sh. go with him
Le. 22: 12. If **m.** to a stranger, she
Nu. 12:1. Ethiopian wom. he had **m.**
36 : 3. **m.** to sons of other tribes
11. **m.** unto fa.'s bro-s' sons, 12.
De. 22 : 22. If lying with woman **m.**
24 : 1. taken a wife and **m.** her
1 Ch. 2 : 21. **m.** when 60 years old
2 Ch. 13 : 21. Abijah **m.** 14 wives
Ne. 13:23. had **m.** wives of Ashdod
Pr. 30 : 23. odious when she is **m.**
Is. 54:1. more chil. of desolate than
62:4. thy land shall be **m.** [of **m.**
Je. 3 : 14. Turn, I am **m.** unto you
Mal. 2 : 11. **m.** dau. of strange god
Mat. 22 : 25. first when he had **m.**
Mk. 6 : 17. Philip's wife he had **m.**
10:12. **m.** to ano. committ-h adult.
Lu. 14: 20. I have **m.** a wife, can-t
17:27. They did eat, they **m.** wives
Ro. 7 : 3. if husb. liveth she be **m.**
4. dead, that ye be **m.** to ano.
1 Co. 7:10. unto the **m.** I command
33. he that is **m.** careth for world
34. she that is **m.** careth for
39. to be **m.** to wh. she will, only

MARRIETH. [in L.

Is. 62:5. as young man **m.** a virgin
Mat. 19:9. whoso **m.** her put away, doth commit, Lu. 16 : 18.

MARROW.

Jb. 21:24. his bones moistened wi. **m.**
Ps. 63:5. My soul satisfied as wi. **m.**
66:†15. I will offer sacrifices of **m.**
Pr. 3:8. health and **m.** to thy bones
Is. 25:6. a feast of things full of **m.**
He. 4:12. to dividing of joints and **m.**

MARRY, ING. [her

Ge. 38 : 8. unto bro-s wife, and **m.**
Nu. 36:6 **m.** to wh. think best, only
• to family of fa.'s tribe **m.**
De. 25: 5. wife of dead shal not **m.**
Ne. 13:27. evil in **m**-g strange wives
Is. 62: 5. so shall thy sons **m.** thee
Mat. 5 : 32. **m.** her divorced commit. adultery, 19 : 9. Mk. 10:11.
19 : 10. If so, it is not good to **m.**
22:24. his brother shall **m.** his wife
30. in resurrection they nei. **m.** nor, Mk. 12: 25. Lu. 20:34, 35.
24:38. **m**-g and giving in marriage
1 Co. 7 : 9. if cannot contain, let th. **m.** better to **m.** than to burn
28. if thou **m.** if virgin **m.**
36. he sinneth not: let them **m.**
1 Ti. 4 : 3. Forbidding to **m.** and
5:11. begun to wax wanton, will **m.**
14. that the younger women **m.**

Chief MARSHAL. [c.m.

Ge. 37 : † 36. sold Jo. unto Potiphar
2 K. 25:†8. Neb-n **c. m.** of king of Bab., Je. 39:†9.-52:†12. [c.m.
Da. 2 : † 14. Daniel ans-d Arioch the

MARS' hill. [h.,†19.

Ac. 17:22. Paul stood in midst of M.

MARSE'NA. See MEMUCAN

MARSHES = MARISHES.

Eze. 47 : 11. **m.** shall not be healed

MART.

Is. 23 : 3. Tyre, she is **m.** of nations

MAR'THA.

Lu. 10 : 38. a woman named M.
40. M. was cumbered about much
41. M. M. thou art careful
Jn. 11 : 1. town of Mary and sis. M.
5. Jesus loved M. Mary and
19. many of Jews came to M. | 20.
21. said M. L if thou hadst been
30 Jes. in pla. where M. met [| 24.
39. M. saith, L. by this time he
12:2. made him supper, M. served

MARTYR, S.

Ac. 22:20. blood of thy **m.** Stephen
Re. 2:13. Antipas was my faithful **m**
17:6. woman drunken wi. blood of

MARVEL, S. [Noun.] [**m.**

Ex. 34:10. I will do **m**-s such as not
2 Co. 11:14. no **m.** for Satan is transf.

MARVEL. [Verb.]

Ec. 5:8. If seest, **m.** not at the matter
Mk. 5 : 20. and all men did **m.**
Jn. 3:7. **m.** not that I said, Ye must
5:20. greater works, th. ye may **m.**
28. **m.** not at this, hour is coming
Jn. 7:21. done one work, and ye **m.**
Ac. 3 : 12 men of Isr. why **m.** ye
Ga. 1:6. I **m.** ye are so soon remov.
1 Jn. 3:13. **m.** not if world hate you
Re. 17:7. angel said, Wh. didst **m.**

MARVELLED.

Ge. 43 : 33. men **m.** one at another
Ps. 48:5. They saw it, and so they **m.**
Mat. 8:10. When Jesus heard he **m.**
27. men **m.** saying, What man
9 : 8. **m.** and glorified God, 33.
21 : 20. disciples saw it, they **m.**
22:22. they **m.** at him, Mk. 12:17. Lu. 20 : 26. [15 : 5, 44.
27: 14. that the governor **m.**, Mk.
Mk. 6 : 6. **m.** bec. of their unbelief
Lu. 1 : 21. people **m.** that he tarried
63. His name is John. And they
2 : 33. Joseph and mother **m.** [**m.**
7:9. When Jesus heard these he **m.**
11 : 38. when Phari. saw it he **m.**
Jn. 4:27. **m.** he talked with woman
7: 15. Jews **m.** How knoweth this man letters [Galileans?
Ac. 2 : 7. **m.** saying, Are not these
4:13 **m.** and took knowledge of th.

MARVELLOUS.

2 S. 13:†2. was **m.** in eyes of Amnon
Jb. 5 : 9. who doeth **m.** things
10 : 16. thou shewest thyself **m.**
Ps. 17:7. Shew thy **m.** lovingkindn.
31:21. shewed me his **m.** kindness
78:12. **m.** things did he in sight of
98:1. L. for he hath done **m.** things
118 : 23. Lord's doing, it is **m.** in our eyes, Mat. 21:42. Mk. 12:11.
Da. 11:36. sh. speak **m.** things ag. G.
Mi. 7 : 15. will I shew **m.** things
Zch. 8 : 6. If **m.** sho. it be in mine
Jn. 9:30. herein is **m.** thing [eyes?
1 Pe. 2:9. out of darkn. into **m.** light
Re. 15:1. sign in heav. great and **m.**

MARVELLOUS work, s.

1 Ch. 16:12. Remember his **m. w**-s,
24. Declare his **m. w**-s [Ps. 105:5.
Ps. 9:1. I will shew forth thy **m. w**-s
139 : 14. **m.** are thy **w**-s, Re. 15:3.
Is. 29:14. I will proceed to do **m. w.**

MARVELLOUSLY.

2 Ch. 26 : 15. he was **m.** helped till
Jb. 37:5. G. thundereth **m.** with his
Ha. 1:5. Behold, regard, wonder **m.**

MA'RY. [Mother of our Lord.]

Mat. 1:16. Joseph the husband of M.
18. M. was espoused to Joseph
20. fear not to take unto thee M.
2:11. they saw young child with M.
13:55. is not his mother M.? Mk. 6:
Lu. 1 : 27. virgin's name was M. [3.
30. fear not, M. | 56. M. abode
34. said M. How shall this be
38. M. said, Behold the handmaid
39. And M. arose in those days
41. Elis. heard salutation of M.
46. M. said, My soul doth magni.
2 : 5. Joseph to be taxed with M.
16. shepherds found M. and babe
19. M. kept all these in her heart
34. Simeon said unto M. Behold
Ac. 1 : 14. continued in prayer with

MA'RY. [M.

Mat. 27 : 56. M. mother of James, 61.-28:1. Mk. 15 : 40, 47.-16 : 1. Lu. 24 : 10.
Lu. 10: 39. she had sister called M.
42. M. hath chosen that good part
Jn. 11:1. town of M. | 20. M. sat still
2. M. that anointed Lord
19. Jews came to Martha and M.
28. she called M. her sis. secretly
31. Jews when they saw M.
32. when M. was come where Jes.
45. many of Jews wh. came to M.
12 : 3. M. took pound of ointment
19 : 25. M. wife of Cleophas stood
20 : 11. M. stood without at sepul
16. Jesus saith unto her, M. she

Ac. 12 : 12. Peter came to house of M.
Ro. 16 : 6. Greet M., who bestowed

MA'RY Magdale'ne.

Mat. 27 : 56. many women, amo. wh. was M. M., Mk. 15:40. Jn. 19:25.
61 M M. sitting over ag. sepulchre
28 : 1. came M. M. to see sepulchre, Mk. 15 : 47. Jn. 20 : 1.
Mk. 16 : 1. M. M. and Mary mother of James bought spices, Lu. 24:10.
9. he appeared first to M. M., out of whom he cast 7 devils, Lu. 8:2.
Jn. 20:18. M. M. told the disciples

MAS'CHIL.

MASH. See MESHECH, UZ.

MA'SHAL. See MISHAL.

MASONS.

2 S. 5:11. Hiram sent to David m., 1 Ch. 14 : 1. [6. Ezr. 3 : 7.
2 K. 12 : 12. gave money to m., 22:
1 Ch. 22:2. he set m. to hew stones
†15. in abundance m. carpenters
2 Ch. 24:12. hired m. to repair hou.

MAS'REKAH.

Ge. 36:36. Samlah of M., 1 Ch. 1:47.

MAS'SA. See MISHMA.

MAS'SAH.

Ex. 17: 7. Moses called the place M
De. 6:16. ye tempted him in M., 9:22
33:8. whom thou didst prove at M.

MAST, S. [m.

Pr. 23 : 34. as he that lieth on top of
Is. 30 : †17. left as a m. upon mt.
33:23. co. not strengthen their m.
Eze. 27:5. cedars from Leb. to make

MASTER. [m-s

Ge. 39:20. Jo.'s m. put him in pris.
Ex. 21 : 4. wife and chil. sh. be her
8. if she please not her m. [m.'s
32. shall give to m. 30 shekels
22 : 8. m. of ho. be bro-t to judge
De. 15:†2. Ev. m. of lending his ha.
Ju. 19:22. spake to m. of the house
23. m. of house went out unto th.
1 S. 25:14. Da. sent to salute our m.
17. evil is determined ag. our m.
26:16. you have not kept your m.
2 S. 2 : 7. for your m. Saul is dead
1 K. 22: 17. Lord said, These have no m., 2 Ch. 18:16. [borrowed
2 K. 6 : 5. cried, Alas m. for it was
22. may eat, drink, and go to m.
23. they went to their m. [you
10:2. seeing your m.'s sons are wi.
3. Look out best of your m.'s sons
6. take heads of your m.'s sons
19:6. Thus say to your m., Is. 37:6.
1 Ch. 15:27. Chenaniah, m. of song
Ec. 10:†11. m. of tongue no better
Is. 24 : 2. as with serv. so with m.
50:†8. who is the m. of my cause
Da. 1:3. k. spake unto m. of eunuchs
4 : 9. m. of magicians, 5 : 11.
Mal. 1: 6. if I a m. where my fear?
2 : 12. the Lord will cut off the m.
Mat. 8 : 19. m. I will follow thee
9:11. Why eateth your m. wi. sin-
10:25. If called m. Beelzebub [ners
12 : 38. m. we would see a sign fr.
17:24. Doth not your m. pay trib.?
19:16. m. what sh. I do? Lu 18.18.
22 : 16. m. we know that thou art true, Mk. 12 : 14. Lu. 20 : 21.
24. m. Mo. said, Mk. 12:19. Lu. 20:28
36. m. wh. is great command-t
23 : 8. one is your m. even C., 10.
26 : 18. m. saith, My time is at ha.
25. Judas said, m. is it I ?
49. Hail m. and kissed, Mk. 14:45.
Mk. 4 : 38. m. carest not we perish
5 : 35. why troublest thou the m.
9:5. m. it is good to be here, Lu. 9:33.
17. m. I have brought my son
38. m. we saw one casting, Lu. 9:
49. [Lu. 10 : 25.
10 : 17. Good m. what shall I do?
20. m. all these have I observed

Mk. 10:35. m. we would thou sho. do
11 : 21. m. behold fig tree [for us
12:32. Well m. thou hast spok. truth
13:1. m. see what manner of stones
35. ye know not when m. cometh
14 : 14. m. saith, Where is guest-chamber, Lu. 22:11. [sh. we do?
Lu. 3 : 12. publicans said, m. what
5:5. Simon said, m. we have toiled
7 : 40. he saith, m. say on
8 : 24. saying, m., m. we perish
8 : 45. Peter said, m. mult throng
49. Thy dau. dead, trouble not m.
9 : 38. m. look upon my son
11:45. m. thou reproachest us also
12 : 13. m. speak to my brother
13 : 25. When m. of house is risen
17 : 13. m. have mercy on us
19 : 39. m. rebuke thy disciples
21 : 39. m. thou hast well said
21:7. m. when sh. these things be
Jn. 1 : 38. m. where dwellest thou?
3:10. Art thou a m. in Israel, and
4 : 31. discip. prayed him m. eat
8 : 4 m. this woman was taken
9 : 2. m. who did sin, this man or
11 : 8. m. the Jews of late sought
28. The m. is come and calleth
13:13. Ye call me m. and say well
14. If I your m. washed your feet
20:16. Rabboni, which is to say m.
Ac. 27:11. centurion believed the m.
Ep. 6:9. our m. is in heav., Col. 4:1.
2 Ti. 2:21. vessel meet for m.'s use

His MASTER.

Ge. 24:9. hand under thigh of h. m.
10. took ten camels of h. m., for goods of h. m. in his hand
39:2. Joseph was in house of h. m.
3. h. m. saw L. was with him
7. h. m.'s wife cast her eyes upon
8. said unto h. m.'s wife, Behold
19. when h. m. heard his wife
Ex. 21 : 4. If h. m. have given wife
6. h. m. shall bore his ear thro.
De. 23:15. shalt not deliver unto h. m. serv. escaped from h. m.
Ju. 19 : 11. servant said unto h. m.
12. h. m. said, We will not turn
1 S. 20:38. arrows and came to h. m.
25:10. serv-s break ev. one fr. h. m.
29 : 4. reconcile him s. unto h. m.
2 K. 5: 1. Naaman great with h. m.
25. Gehazi stood before h. m.
6 : 32. is not sound of h. m.'s feet
8:14. Hazael came to h. m. [m.
9:31. Had Zimri peace, who slew h.
19 : 4. h. m. hath sent, Is. 37 : 4.
1 Ch. 12:19. He will fall to h. m. Saul
Jb. 3:19. servant is free from h. m.
Pr. 27: 18. he th waiteth on h. m.
30:10. Accuse not serv. unto h. m.
Is. 1 : 3. ass knoweth h. m.'s crib
24 : 2. as with serv. so with h. m.
Mal. 1 : 6. servant honoureth h. m.
Mat. 10 : 24. disci. not above h. m.,
25. that disci be as h. m. [Lu. 6:40
Lu. 6:40 one perfect sh. be as h. m.
Ro. 14:4. to h. own m. he standeth

My MASTER.

Ge. 24: 12. O G. of m. m. Ab. shew kindness unto m. m., 27. 42, 48.
14. hast shewed kindn. unto m.
35. Lord hath blessed m. m. [m.
36. m. m.'s wife bare son to m.
37 m. m. made me swear [m.
39. said unto m. m. Peradven.
44. L. appointed for m. m.'s son
48. blessed L. G. of m. m. Ab. (2)
49. if you will deal truly wi. m. m.
54. said, Send me unto m. m., 56.
65. servant said, It is m. m. [me
39: 8. m. m. wotteth not what wi.
Ex. 21: 5. if serv. say, I love m. m.
1 S. 24 : 6. the Lord forbid that I sho. do this thing unto m. m.
30:13. m. m. left me bec. I fell sick

1 S. 30:15. nor deliver me into hands of m. m. [Rimmon
2 K. 5 : 18. m. m. goeth into ho. of
20. m. m. hath spared Naaman
22. m. m. hath sent me, saying
6:15. Alas, m. m. how shall we do?
10 : 9 I conspired ag. m. m. ; and
18:24. How turn aw. capt. of least of m. m.'s serv-s, Is. 36 : 9.
27. m. m. sent me to thy master? Is. 36 : 12. [m.
Is. 36: 8. give pledges, I pray to m.

Thy MASTER. [wife

Ge. 24 : 51. let her be t. m.'s son's
1 S. 29 : 10. rise with t. m.'s serv-s
2 S. 9 : 9. I gave t. m.'s son all that
10. that t. m.'s son may have food
12 : 8. I gave thee t. m.'s house, t. m.'s wives [m.'s son
16 : 3. the king said, Where is t.
2 K. 2:3 L. will take t. m. to day, 5.
16. let them go and seek t. m.
9 : 7. shalt smite ho. of Ahab t. m.

MASTERS.

Ps. 123 : 2. as eyes of servants unto m.
Pr. 25:13. refresheth soul of his m.
Ec. 12:11. fastened by m. of assem.
Je. 27:4. command th. to say unto
Am. 4:1. say to m. let us drink [m.
Zph. 1 : 9. fill m.'s houses wi. vio.
Mat. 6 : 24. No man can serve two m., Lu. 16 : 13. [table
15 : 27. dogs eat crumbs from m.'s
23 : 10. Nei. be ye called m. one is
Ac. 16 : 16. bro-t her m. much gain
19. m. saw hope of gains gone
Ep. 6:5. Servants, be obedient to m., Col. 3:22. Tit. 2: 9 1 Pe. 2 : 18.
9. ye m. do same things, Col. 4:1.
1 Ti. 6:1. count their m. worthy of
2. believing m. let th. not despi.
Ja. 3 : 1 brethren, be not many m.

MASTERBUILDER.

1 Co. 3:10 as wise m. I laid founda.

MASTERY, IES. [m.

Ex. 32 : 18. voice of them shout for
Da. 6 : 24. lions had m. of them
1 Co. 9:25. that striveth for the m.
2 Ti. 2:5. if a man also strive for m-s

MATE. [m.

Is. 34:15. vultures ev. one wi h her
16. not one fail, none want m.

MATHU'SALA.

Lu. 3 : 37. Lamech, son of M. | Ge. 5 : †21.

MA'TRED.

Ge. 36:39. M. dau. of Mezahab. 1 Ch. 1 : 50.

MA'TRI.

1 S. 10 : 21. family of M. was taken

MATRIX. [15.

Ex. 13:12. unto L. all that open m.
34: 19. All th. openeth m. is mine
Nu. 3:12. firstborn that open the m.
18:15. ev. thing openeth m. is thine

MAT'TAN.

2 K. 11:18. slew M priest of, 2 Ch 23:
Je. 38 : 1 Shephatiah son of M. [17.

MAT'TANAH.

Nu. 21:18. fr. wilderness to M. | 19.

MATTANI'AH.

2 K. 24 : 17 made M. king in his stead, 1 Ch. 1:†16. 2 Ch. 36:†10.
1 Ch. 9 : 15. M., son of Micah, Ne. 11 : 17, 22. [M.
25 : 4. sons of Heman, Bukkiah,
16. the 9th lot came to M.
2 Ch. 20:14. son of M. a Levite, 29:13.
Ezr. 10:26. of Elam, M. | 27. of Zattu,
30. of Pahath, M. | 37. of Bani, M.
Ne. 12:8. M. wh. was over thanksgiv-
25. M. Akkub were porters [ing
35. M. son of Michaiah [of M.
13 : 13. Hanan, son of Zaccur, son

MAT'TATHA.

Lu. 3 : 31. Menan was the son of M.

MAT'TATHAH.

Ezr. 10:33. Of sons of Hashum, M

MATTATHI'AS.
Lu. 3: 25. Joseph son of M., 26.
MATTENA'I. [| 37.
Ezr. 10: 33. Of sons of Hashum, M.,
Ne. 12: 19. priests of Joiarib, M.
MATTER.
Ge.24:9.sware to him conc.that m.
30:15. Is it a small m. thou taken
Ex. 5:†13. fulfil m. of a day in day
18:16.have m.they come unto me
22. ev. great m. shall bring unto
thee,ev.small m.they sh.judge
26. but ev. small m. they judged
23:7.Keep thee far from a false m.
Nu. 16:49. died about m. of Korah
25:18.in m.of Peor,in m. of Cozbi
31:16. commit tresp. in m.of Peor
De. 17: 8. If arise a m. too hard
19:15. mouth of 3 witn-s m.be est.
24:†1. found m. of nakedn. in her
Ju. 19:†24. do not m. of this folly
Ru. 3: 18. until know how m. fall
1 S. 10: 16. of m. of kingd. told not
20:23. m. thou and I have spok.of
39.only Jona.and David knew m.
2 S. 1: 4. How went the m.?
18: 13. there is no m. hid fr. king
20:18. ended m. | 21. m. is not so
1 K. 8: 59. all times as m. require
15:5. save only in the m. of Uriah
1 Ch. 26:32. ev. m. pertaining to G.
27: 1. that served king in any m.
2 Ch. 8: 15. not fr. command in any
19:†6. who is with you in m. [m.
24: 5. hasten m., they hast-d not
Ezr. 3:†4. as m. of the day required
5: 5. till m. came to Darius (2)
10: 16. sat down to examine m.
Ne. 6: 13. have m. for evil report
Es. 2: 23. when inquisition of m.
Jb.19:28. root of m. is found in me
32:8. will answer, I am full of m.
Ps. 45: 1. heart inditing good m.
64: 5. encourage thems. in evil m.
Pr.11:13.faithful concealeth the m.
16: 20. that handleth a m. wisely
17:9. repeateth m. separ-h friends
18:13. answ-h m. bef. he heareth
25:2.honour of kings to search m.
Ec. 5: 8. marvel not at the m.
10: 20. th. hath wings sh. tell m.
12:13.Let us hear conclusion of m.
Je. 7: † 22. conc-g m. of offerings
38: 27. the m. was not perceived
52: † 34. m. of the day in his day
Eze.9:11.had inkhorn, reported m.
16:20. thy whoredoms a small m.?
Da. 2: 10. not a man shew k.'s m.
23. hast made known king's m.
7:28. the end of the m. I kept m.
9:23. understand the m. consider
Mk. 1: 45. to blaze abroad the m.
10: 10. his disciples asked of same
Ac.11:4.Peter rehearsed the m.[m.
15: 6. elders came to consider m.
18:14. said, If it were m. of wrong
19: 38. if Demetrius have a m. ag.
24: 22. I will know utterm. of m.
1 Co. 6:1. dare having m. go to law?
2 Co. 9:5. ready as a m. of bounty
Ga. 2: 6. whatso., it maketh no m.
1 Th.4:6.no man defraud in any m.
Ja. 3: 5. how gr. a m. a little fire
This MATTER. [t.m.
De. 3:26. L. said, speak no more of
22:26.slayeth neighbour so is t.m.
1 S. 30:24. who will heark. in t.m.?
2 S. 19: 42. whf. angry for t. m.?
Ezr.5:5.returned answer conc.t.m.
17. send his pleasure conc. t. m.
10:4.for t. m.belongeth unto thee
9. people trembling bec. of t. m.
14. wrath of our God for t. m.
15.Jonathan, Asahel, about t.m.
Es. 9: 26. they had seen conc. t.m.
Da. 1: 14. Melzar consented in t.m.
3:16.not careful to answer in t.m.
Da.4:17.t.m.by decree of watchers
Ac. 8:21. nei. part nor lot in t. m.
17:32.We will hear thee again of t.
2 Co.7:11.yours. clear in t.m.[m.
MATTERS. [come
Ex. 24: 14. if any have m. let him
De. 16:†19. a gift perverteth m. of
17: 8. if arise m. of controversy
1 S.16:18.son of Jesse prudent in m.
2 S. 11: 19. made end of telling m.
15:3.See thy m.are good and right
19: 29. Why speakest of thy m.?
1 Ch. 25:†5. king's seer in m. of G.
2 Ch.19:11.Amariah over you in m.
of L. Zebadiah for king's m.
Ne. 6:†19. uttered my m.to Tobiah
11:24. Pethahiah in m. conc. peo.
Es. 3: 4. whe. Mordecai's m. stand
9: 31. the m. of the fastings, 32.
Jb. 33:13. giveth not account of his
Ps. 35:20. devise deceitful m. [m.
65:†3. m. of iniq-s prevail ag. me
131:1.nor exercise myself in gr.m.
Pr. 22:†12. overthr-h m. of transg.
29: † 20. seest man hasty in m.?
Da. 1:20. in m.of wisdom he found
7:1.he wrote dream,told sum of m.
Mat. 23: 23. omitted weightier m.
Ac. 18:15.I be no judge of such m.
19:39. if ye inquire conc. other m.
25:20. there be judged of these m.
1 Co. 6:2. ye unworthy to judge m.
1 Pe. 4: 15. as a busybody in men's
MAT'THAN. [m.
Mat. 1: 15. begat M. M. beg. Jacob
MAT'THAT.
Lu. 3: 24. Jorim was son of M., 29.
MAT'THEW. [and
Mat. 9: 9. saw a man named m.
10:3.Thomas and M. the publican,
Mk. 3: 18. Lu. 6: 15. Ac. 1:13.
MATTHI'AS. [M.
Ac.1:23.Joseph called Barsabas,and
26.lot fell on M.he was numbered
MATTITHI'AH.
1 Ch. 9: 31. M. one of the Levites
15: 18. M. and Eliph-h porters, 21.
16: 5. next to him M. and Eliab
25: 3. Of sons of Jeduthun, M.
21. The 14th lot came to m.
Ezr. 10: 43. Of sons of Nebo, M.
Ne. 8: 4. besides Ezra stood M.
MATTOCK, S.
1 S. 13: 20. to sharpen axe and m.
13: 21. they had a file for m-s
2 Ch. 34:6. did Josiah wi.their m-s
Is.7:25. on all hills digged with m.
MAUL, S. [m-s
2 Ch. 34: † 6. did Josiah with their
Pr. 25:18. beareth false witness, is a
MAW. [m.
De. 18: 3. to priest two cheeks and
MAY. [m.
2 S. 15:20. seeing I go whither I m.
Mat. 9: 21. If I m. but touch garm.
26:42. if this cup m. not pass aw.
He. 7: 9. as I m. so say, Levi paid
MAY be.
Ge.16:2. it m.b. I may obtain chil.
21: 30. they m. b. witn. I digged
Ex.13:9.L.'s law m.b. in thy mou.
20:20.his fear m. b. bef. your face
26:11. couple tent th. it m. b. one
Le. 11: 34. meat wh. m. b. eaten
21: 3. for sister he m. b. defiled
23: 21. m. b. a holy convocation
Nu. 10: 10. m. b. for a memorial
32:32. that possession m. b. ours
De.29: 13. he m. b. unto thee a G
31:26.that it m.b.a witness against
Jos. 22:27.th. it m.b.witness betw.
1 S. 14: 6. it m. b. L. will work
18: 21. she m. b. snare to him (2)
2 S. 14:15. it m. b. king will perf.
16:12. m. b. L. will look on afflic.
2 K. 19:4.m.b. L.will hear,Is.37:4.
1 Ch. 17: 27. it m. b. before thee
Ezr. 9: 12. that ye m. b. strong
Jb. 1:5. m. b. my sons have sinned
Ps. 59:13. wrath th. they m. not b.
83:4.Isr. m.b. no more in remem.
144:12. that sons m. b. as plants
13. that our garners m. b. full
14. that our oxen m. b. strong to
Pr. 22:19. th. thy trust m. b. in L.
Ec. 1: 10. m. b. said, this is new
Is. 30: 8. m. b. for time to come
18. waiteth th. he m. b.gracious
46: 5. liken that we m. b. like
60:21.that I m.b. glorified [mem.
Je. 11:19. name m. b. no more re-
36:3.m. b. house of Jud.will hear
7.m.b.they will present supplic.
51: 8. if so be she m. b. healed
La. 3: 29. if so be there m. b. hope
Eze. 12:3.it m.b.they will consider
14:11. that they m. b. my people
Da. 4: 27. it m. b. lengthening of
Ho. 8: 4. that they m. b. cut off
Am. 5:15. m. b. L. will be gracious
Zph. 2: 3. m. b. ye be hid in day
Mat. 5:45. th. ye m. b. chil. of Fa.
6:4. that thine alms m.b.in secret
Lu. 20:13.m.b. they will reverence
14. kill, that inheri-e m. b. ours
Jn. 12: 36. th ye m.b. chil.of light
14: 3. that where I am, ye m. b.
17:11. that they m. b. one, 21,26.
26. that the love m. b. in them
Ro. 1: † 20. m. b. without excuse
1 Co. 3: 18. that he m. b. wise
5: 7. that ye m. b. a new lump
7:34. that she m. b. holy in body
14:10. are, it m.b.,so many voices
15: 28. that God m. b. all in all
16:6. m.b. I will winter with you
10. m. b. with you without fear
2 Co. 4:7. excellency of power m.b.
8: 11. m. b. a performance out of
14. your abund. m. b. a supply
9: 3. as I said, ye m. b. ready
Ph. 2: 15. That ye m. b. blameless
19. that I m. b. of good comfort
28. th. I m. b. the less sorrowful
1 Ti. 5:7. that they m. b.blameless
2 Ti. 3:17. man of God,m.b.perfect
Tit. 1:13. they m. b. sound in faith
Ja. 1: 4. that ye m. b. perfect and
See KNOWN, WELL.
MAYEST.
Ge. 28: 3. that thou m. be a mult.
Nu. 10:31. m. be to us inst. of eyes
De. 26: 19. thou m. be a holy peo.
Ne. 6: 6. th. thou m. be their king
Jb. 40: 8. that thou m. be justified
Ps. 130: 4. that thou m. be feared
Is.23:16.that thou m.be rememb-d
49:6.that thou m.be my salvation
Je. 4: 14. that thou m. be saved
30: 13. that thou m. be bound up
Lu. 16: 2. m. be no longer steward
Ac. 8:37. If believest wi. heart thou
1 Co. 7: 21. m. be made free [m.
MAZ'ZAROTH.
Jb. 38: 32. canst thou bring forth
ME. [M. in
Ge.22:†1.Behold m.,†7,†11.Is.65:1.
41: 10. in ward m. and baker
42:36.m. have ye bereaved of chil.
Ex. 9:14. none like m. in all earth
1 S. 2:29. honourest sons above m.
1 K. 1:26. but m., even m. thy serv.
Ps. 118: 13. hast thrust sore at m.
Is. 57: 8. discov. thys. to ano. than
Je.17:18.let not m.be dismayed[m.
50:44.who like m.,who appoint m.
Hos.13:4.know no G. but m. [time?
Mat.10:37.loveth fa. more than m.
26:11. m. ye have not always,Mk.
14:7. Jn. 12:8. [made a man
Jn. 7:23. are ye angry at m. bec. I
16: 3. not known the Fa. nor m.
See ADVANTAGETH,ASKEST, BE-
GUILED, BELIEVE, ED, CALL-

EST, DELIVER, ED, DESPIS-
ETH, FOLLOW, ED, GLORIFY,
HATED, ETH, KNOW, KNOWN,
LOVEST, PERSECUTEST, RE-
CEIVETH, 'REJECTED, RE-
STORED, SENT, SMITEST.

About ME.

De. 17 : 14. like the nations **a. m.**
Jb. 10 : † 8. hands took pains **a.m.**
29 : 5. when my chil. were **a. m.**
Ps. 3:†3. O Lord, art a shield **a.m.**
88:17.they came round **a.m.**daily
139:11. night shall be light **a. m.**
Jon. 2 : 6. earth with bars **a. m.**
Ac. 22 : 6. shone a great light **a.m.**,

After ME. ⌊26 : 13.

1 S.14:12.arm-r bearer, Come **a.m.**
24 : 21. not cut off my seed **a. m.**
Ec. 2 : 18. man that shall be **a. m.**
Is. 43 : 10. neither shall be **a. m.**
Mat. 10:38. taketh not his cross and
followeth **a. m.**, Lu. 14 : 27.
Ro. 10:20. unto th. asked not **a.m.**
See COME, COMETH, COMING,
FOLLOW, PURSUED, REIGN,
WENTEST.

Against ME.

Ge.42:36. all these things are **a.m.**
50 : 20. you, ye thought evil **a. m.**
Ju.6:39. Let not anger be hot **a.m.**
Ru.1:13. hand of L. gone out **a.m.**
† 16. be not **a. m.** to leave thee
1 S.26:19.if L.stirred thee up **a.m.**
2 S. 24 : 17. let thy hand be **a. m.**
2 K. 5 : 7. seeketh quarrel **a. m.**
Jb. 10:17. renewest witnesses **a.m.**
13: 26. writest bitter things **a. m.**
16:8.wrinkles, wh. is witness **a.m.**
30:21. thou opposest thyself **a.m.**
33: 10. he findeth occasions **a. m.**
Ps. 41 : 7. **a. m.** do devise my hurt,
whisper **a. m.** ⌈sworn **a. m.**
102: 8. they are mad **a. m.** are
Mal. 3 : 13. your words stout **a. m.**
Mat. 12 : 30. that is not with me is
a. m., Lu. 11: 23.
Jn. 13 : 18. lifted up his heel **a. m.**
19:11.couldest have no power **a.m.**
Ac. 24 : 19. object, if had aught
a. m.
See ABIDE, AROSE, CONSPIRED,
CRIED, CRY, GATHERED, IMAG-
INE, IMAGINATION, MOUTH,
MURMUR[verb], PLEAD, REBEL,
REBELLED, REVIVE, RISE,
RISEN, ROSE, SIN, SINNED,
SINNETH, SINNING, SPEAK,
SPOKEN, TESTIFY, TRANS-
GRESS, ED, TRESPASS [Noun],
TRESPASSED, TURNED, VAUNT,
WAR, WITNESS, WRITEST.

Before ME. ⌈m.

Ge. 6: 13. end of all flesh is come **b.**
7:1. thee have I seen righte. **b.m.**
27 : † 20. bec. God bro-t it **b. m.**
40 : 9. In my dream, a vine **b. m.**
Ex.20:3. no other gods **b. m.**,De 5:
Nu.22:32. way is perverse **b.m.** ⌊7.
1 S.9:19.go up **b.m.** unto high pla.
2 S. 22 : 23. his judgments were **b.**
m., Ps. 18 : 22.-119 : 30.
1 K. 8 : 25. as thou hast walked **b.**
m., 2 Ch. 6 : 16. ⌈m.
11 : 36. David may have a light **b.**
21: 29. how Ahab humbleth **b.m.**
2 K. 22 : 19. wept **b.m.**, 2 Ch.34:27.
Ezr. 4 : 18. letter plainly read **b.m.**
Ne. 5 : 15. former governors **b. m.**
Es. 7: 8. Will he force queen **b.m.**?
Ps. 39 : 1. keep my mouth, while
wicked **b. m.**
51 : 3. my sin is ever **b. m.**
89:36. throne endure as sun **b.m.**
Ec. 1:16. all that been **b.m.**, 2:7,9.
Can. 8 : 12. my vineyard is **b. m.**
Is.41:1.Keep silence **b.m.** O islands
Je.28:8.prophets th.have been **b.m.**
Je.32:30.Israel have done evil **b.m.**
33:18.Nei.want a man **b.m.**,35:19.
34:15.ye had made a coven-t **b.m.**
Jon. 1 : 2. wickedness is come **b. m.**
Ha. 1:3. spoiling and violence **b.m.**
Hag. 2 : 14. So is this people **b. m.**
Jn. 1 : 15. is preferred **b. m.**; for
he was **b. m.**, 27, 30 (2).⌈**b. m.**
Ac. 25 : 9. be judged of these things
Ro. 16 : 7. who were in Christ **b. m.**
See **BEFORE** me.
See APPEAR, CAME, CONTINUAL-
LY, FAIL, FORMED, GO, MARK-
ED, PREPAREST, REMAIN, SAT,
SET, SLAY, STAND, STEPPETH,
STOOD, WALK, WAY, WRITTEN.

Behind ME.

See GET, HEARD, TURN.

Beside or Besides ME.

1 K. 3:20.she took my son fr. **b. m.**
Is.43:11.**b. m.** no Saviour,Ho 13:4.
44 :6. **b-s m.** no God, 8.-45:5,6,21.
47:8.I am,and none else **b-s m.**,10.

Between or Betwixt ME.

Ge. 9 : 12. covenant I make **b. m.**
and you, 13,15,17.-17:2,7,10,11,
28:15.what th.**b-t m.**and thee ⌊b-t
31 : 51. pillar cast **b-t m.** and thee
1 S. 14:42. Cast lots **b-t m.** and Jon.
20 : 23. Lord be **b. m.** and thee, 42.
1 K. 15 : 19. There is a league **b. m.**
and thee, and b,. 2 Ch. 16 : 3.
See JUDGE [Verb], LOTS, SIGN
[Noun], STEP, STRIFE, WALL,
WATCH, WITNESS [Noun].

By ME.

Ge.48:7.Rachel died **b.m.**in Canaan
Ex. 33 : 21. there is a place **b. m.**
Ezr. 4 : † 19. **b. m.** a decree is set,
6 : † 8. Da. 3 : † 29. ⌈was **b. m.**
Ne. 4: 18. he that sounded trumpet
Is.54:15. shall gather but not **b.m.**
Ho 8 : 4. set up k-s, but not **b.m.**
Jn. 6 : 57. eateth me shall live **b.m.**
10:9. door, **b.m.** if any man enter
14 : 6. no man unto Fa. but **b.m.**
2 Co. 2 : 2. same is made sorry **b.m.**
See BORNE, GOETH, HONOUR
[Verb], MULTIPLIED, PASS,
PREACHED, PREACHING, PROF-
ITED, REIGN, RULE, SPAKE,
SPOKEN, STAND, STOOD.
WROUGHT.

Concerning ME.

Jos. 14:6. L. said unto Moses **c.m.**
1 K. 2 : 4. word L. spake **c.m.** ⌈18.
22:8.doth not prophesy good **c. m.**
Eze. 14:7. to proph. to inquire **c.m.**
Lu. 22:37. things **c.m.** have an end
24 : 44. written in psalms **c. m.**
Ac. 22:18. not rec. thy testimony **c.**
See CONCERN, ETH. ⌊**m.**
See **FOLLOW, ED** me.

For ME.

Ge. 23 : 8. entreat **f. m.**, Ex. 8: 28.
27:36. hast reserved blessing **f.m.**
30 : 31. if wilt do this **f. m.**
50 : 5. in grave I digged **f. m.**
Nu. 3 : 41. take Levites **f. m.**
11 : 14. bec. it is too heavy **f. m.**
22 : 6. they are too mighty **f. m.**
De. 31 : 19. song be witness **f. m.**
Jos. 24 : 15. as **f.m.** and my ho. we
Ju. 7:2. people are too many **f. m.**
11 : 37. Let this thi. be done **f.m.**
14:2. now get her **f. m.** to wife, 3.
19 : 19. is bread and wine **f. m.**
1 S. 12:23. as **f. m.**, 1 Ch. 22:7.-28:
2.-29: 17. Jb. 21:4. Ps. 5:7.-17:
15.-35: 13.-41:12.-55:16.-69:13.
Is. 59: 21. Je. 17:16.-26:14.-40:
10. Eze. 9 : 10. Da. 2: 30.-7:28.-
10 : 17.
22:8. none of you th. is sorry **f.m.**
27:1.noth. better **f.m.** than escape
2 S. 3 : 39. be too hard **f. m.**
7 : 5. Shalt thou build house **f.m.**
14 : 32. good **f. m.** to have been
15:34. mayest **f.m.** defeat counsel
1 K 13:6. pray **f. m.** that my hand
2 K.4:24. slack not thy riding **f.m.**
16 : 15. the brazen altar be **f. m.**
Ps. 3: 3. thou, O L. art shield **f.m.**
56 : 9. this I know, for G. is **f. m.**
61 : 3. hast been shelter **f.m.** ⌈m.
94 : 16. Who rise up **f.m.**, stand **f.**
119:71.good **f.m.**I have been afflic.
131 : 1. or in things too high **f.m.**
Is. 44 : 7. who set it in order **f. m.**?
65:1. sought of th. asked not **f.m.**
Zch. 9 : 13. have bent Judah **f. m.**
2 Ti. 4 : 8. laid up **f. m.** a crown
See ABIDE, ANSWER, AWAKE,
BETTER, CONVENIENT, DIG-
GED, DO, DRESS, EXECUTE,
GAVE, GIVE, GIVETH, HARD,
HID, INQUIRE, LAID, LAWFUL,
NURSE [Verb], PAINFUL, PER-
FORMETH, PRAY, PRAYING,
PREPARED, READY, SEARCH,
SENT, SNARE, S, STRAIT [Adj.],
STRIVE, STRONG, UNDERTAKE,
VALIANT, WAIT, WAITED,
WEEP, WROUGHT.

From ME.

Ge. 39 : 9. nei. kept any thing **f.m.**
44 : 28. one went **f. m.** he is torn
45 : 1. Cause ev. man to go **f. m.**
Ex. 10 : 28. Get thee **f. m.** ⌈3:17.
Jos.7:19. tell, hide it not **f. m.**,1 S.
Ju.16:17. my strength will go **f.m.**
2 S. 13:9. said, Have out all men **f.**
17.Put this woman out **f.m.** ⌊**m.**
1 K. 12 : 24. return, for this is **f.m.**
22:24.went Spirit of L. **f.m.**,2 Ch.
2 K.4:27.L.hath hid it **f.m.** ⌊18:23.
18 : 14. have offended, return **f.m.**
Ne. 13 : 28. thf. I chased him **f. m.**
Ps. 13 : 1. how long hide face **f. m.**
18 : 22. did not put statutes **f. m.**
38:10.light of mine eyes, gone **f.m.**
88 : 14. L. why hidest face **f. m.**?
102:2. Hide not thy face **f.m.**,143:
119 : 19. hide not com-ts **f. m.** ⌊7.
Is. 22 : 4. Look away **f. m.** ⌈**f. m.**
Je. 13 : 25. portion of thy measures
51 : 53. **f. m.** shall spoilers come
Eze. 3:17. give warning **f. m.**,33:7.
14 : 5. they are all estranged **f.m.**
11. Jud. go no more astray **f. m.**
44 : 10. Isr. went astray **f.m.**, 15.
Ho.11:7. peo. bent to backsl-g **f.m.**
14 : 8. **f. m.** is thy fruit found
See **FAR from me, They
FLED, Not HID, TAKE
away, TOOK away.
TURN, TURNED away.**
See DEPART, ED, DRIVEN, GONE,
HID, HIDE, PASS, PROCEED,
REMOVE, ED, SEPARATE, ETH,
STEAL, TAKE, ETH, TURN,
WITHHELD, WITHHOLD.

In ME.

Ge. 41 : 16. answered, It is not **i.m.**
2 S. 1: 9. my life is yet whole **i. m.**
Jb. 6 : 13. Is not my help **i. m.**?
19:28.root of matter is found **i.m.**
23 : 6. he would put strength **i.m.**
27 : 3. while my breath is **i. m.**
28 : 14. depth saith, It is not **i.m.**
Ps. 7:8. acc. to mine integrity **i.m.**
38:2. thine arrows stick fast **i. m.**
42 : 4. I pour out my soul **i. m.**
5. why art thou disquieted **i. m.**
139:24. if be any wicked way **i.m.**
Can. 5:†4. bowels were moved **i.m.**
Is. 27 : 4. fury is not **i. m.**
La. 3: 20. My soul is humbled **i.m.**
Da.10:8.remained no strength **i.m.**,
Ho. 13 : 9. **i. m.** is thy help ⌊17.
Mat. 18: 6. little ones wh. believe **i.**
m., Mk. 9 : 42.

Jn.11:25.believeth i.m.shall live,26
14: 20. you i. m. and I in you
30.prince cometh, and hath noth.
15: 4. Every branch i. m. [i. m.
16. 33. i. m. ye might have peace
17: 21. thou Fa. art i. m. and I
23. I in them, and thou i. m.
Ac. 26: 18. sanctified by faith i.m.
28: 18. was no cause of death i.m.
Ro. 1:15. as much as i.m. is, I am
7: 18. i. m. dwelleth no good thi
2 Co. 11: 10. As truth of C. is i.m.
Ga. 2: 8. mighty i. m. tow. Gent.
Ph. 1:30. conflict ye saw i.m. hear
to be i. m.
1 Ti. 1:16. that i. m. C. might shew
See Was FOUND, Put TRUST.
See ABIDE, ACCOMPLISHED, BELIEVE, DELIGHTED, DWELLETH, FOUND, GLORIFIED, INIQUITY, LIVETH, OFFENDED, TRUST [Verb], REVEAL, SEEN, SPEAKING, WORKETH, WORKING, WROUGHT.

Of ME.

2 Ch. 11:4. this thing is done o.m.
Ps. 60: 8. triumph thou bec. o. m.
81:11.and Israel would none o.m.
Is. 44: 21. shalt not be forgot. o.m.
45:†24. he sh. say o. m. In the L.
54:17. and their righteousn. o. m.
Je.10:20. chil. are gone forth o. m.
Lu. 8: 46. virtue is gone out o. m.
Ac.1:4.promise ye have heard o.m.
Ph. 4: 10. your care o. m. [oner
2 Ti. 1:8. testimony o. m. his pris-
13.words which hast heard o.m.
See ACCEPT, ASHAMED, ASK, ASKEST, BECAUSE, CALL, COMPASSION, COUNSEL [Noun], DESPAIR, END, EVIL, FOLLOWERS, HEARD, INQUIRE, KNOWLEDGE, LEARN, PREACHED, REMEMBRANCE, SALUTATION, SAY, SEEN, SPEAK, SPOKEN, TELL, TESTIFIED, TESTIFY, THINK, TRUST, WEARY, WITNESS [Noun], WORTHY, WRITTEN, WROTE.

On ME, or upon ME.

Ge. 18: 27 I have taken u. m. to
speak unto L., 31.
27:13. u.m. be thy curse, my son
31: 35. custom of women is u. m.
Ju.19:20. let all thy wants lie u.m.
1 S. 13: 12. Philis. will come u.m.
1 K. 2:15. Isr. set their faces o.m.
1 Ch. 21: 17. let thy hand be o.m.
Ezr.7:28.hand of L.u.m., Ne.2:8,18.
Jb. 3: 25. which I greatly feared is
4:14.fear came u.m. [come u.m.
7: 8. thine eyes are u.m. and I
10: 16. thyself marvellous u. m.
16:14. he runneth u.m. like giant
Ps. 32:4. night thy ha.heavy u.m.
56: 12. Thy vows are u. m. I will
91:14. Bec. hath set his love u.m.
Is. 61:1. Spirit of L. u.m.,Lu.4:18.
Je.15:†16. thy name is called u.m.
Eze. 11: 5. Spirit of L. fell u. m.
Zch. 6: 8. cried he u.m. and spake
Jn.16:9. bec. they believe not o.m.
17:20.wh. shall believe o.m. thro.
Ac 8: 24. none of these come u.m.
Ph. 2: 27. G. had mercy o.m. also
See His HAND, HAND of the Lord, LAID hand, Hast LAID, LOOK on, Have MERCY.
See BELIEVETH, BRING, BROUGHT, CALL, CALLED, CAST, COME, COMETH, FALL, FELL, INIQUITY, LAID, LOOKED, PITY [Noun], REST [Verb], THINK, THINKETH, WAIT, WAITED, WROUGHT.

Over ME.

De. 17:14. say, I will set king o.m.
Ps. 19: 13. not have dominion o.
m., 119: 133. [m.
60: †8. Philistia, triumph thou o.
See BANNER, EXALTED, GLORY [Verb], GOETH, GONE, PASSED, TRIUMPH, WATCH.

To or unto ME.

Ge. 4: 10. bro.'s blood crieth u.m.
15: 3. t.m. thou hast giv. no seed
29:25. What this hast done u.m.?
31: 9. G. hath given them t. m.
40:14.shew kindness, I pray,u.m.
46: 31. fa.'s house are come u.m.
Ex. 3: 9. cry of Isr. is come u. m.
4: 25. bloody husb. art thou t.m.
14:15.Wh. criest thou u. m. [m.
18: 16. have matter, they come u.
19: 5. be peculiar treasure u. m.
6. be u. m. a kingdom of priests
22: 23. they cry at all u. m., 27.
29.firstborn shalt thou give u.m.
31. ye shall be holy men u. m.
32:26.L.'s side, let him come u.m.
Le. 25: 55. u. m. Isr. are servants
De. 18: 15. of brethren like u. m.,
Ac. 3: 22.—7: 37.
Ju. 11: 7. why are ye come u. m.
17: 10. be u. m. a fa. and priest
1 S. 16: 3. anoint u.m. him I name
2 S. 1:26. pleasant hast been u.m.
15: 4. ev. man might come u. m.
1 K.2:5.know-t what Joab did t.m.
22:14. what Lord saith u.m. that
2 K. 10: 6. come t. m. to Jezreel
1 Ch. 13: 12. how bring ark t. m.?
2 Ch.18:17.not prophesy good u.m.
Ezr. 9: 4. were assembled u.m. ev.
one that trembled at [u. m.
Jb. 3: 25. I was afraid of, is come
7: 3. wearisome nights are t. m.
13:20.Only do not two things u.m
29: 21. u. m. men gave ear
Ps. 16: 6. lines are fallen u. m. in
17:6. O G. incline ear u.m.,31:2.—
28: 1. be not silent t. m. [102: 2.
56: 4. not fear what flesh do u.m.
11. not afraid what man do u.m.,
81:8. if wilt hearken u.m. [118:6.
89: 26. cry u. m. Thou art my fa.
139: 17. precious thy thoughts u.
141:1.Lord, make haste u.m. [m.
Pr. 1: 33. whoso hearkeneth u.m.
24: 29. do as he hath done t. m.
Can. 1: 13. myrrh is well beloved
u. m., 14. [m.
Is. 1: 13. incense is abomination, u.
14. new moons, a trouble u. m.
29: 2. shall be u. m. as Ariel
45: 23. u. m. every knee sh. bow
50:8.adversary, let him come t.m.
54: 9. is as waters of Noah u. m.
65: 5. not near t.m. I am holier
Je. 11:11. tho. cry u.m. I not hear
12:8.Mine heritage is u.m.as lion,
13:11. might be u.m. for peo. [9.
15:16. thy word was u.m. the joy
18. wilt thou be u. m. as liar?
23: 14. are all u. m. as Sodom
32:31. city been t. m. provocation
33: 9. shall be t.m. a name of joy
La. 1: 21. they shall be like u. m.
22.do unto th. as hast done u.m.
Eze.22:18. Isr.is t.m. become dross
23: 38. this they have done u. m.
44: 13. to do office of priest u. m.
15. near t.m. to minister u. m.
Ho.2:19. will betroth thee u.m.,20.
23. I will sow her u. m. in earth
3: 2. So I bought her t. m. for 15
4: 6. thou shalt be no priest t.m.
7: 14. not cried u. m. with heart
8: 2. Israel shall cry u. m. My G.
Am.9:7.Are ye not as Ethio-s u.m.
Mi.5:2.out of thee shall come u.m.
7: 8. L. shall be a light u. m.

Zch. 1: 3. Turn ye u. m. saith L
Mat. 11: 28. Come u. m. ye that
25:36. prison, ye came u. m. [m.
45. not to these, ye did it not t.
Lu.1:38. u.m. acc. to thy word [37.
Jn.6:35.cometh t.m. never hunger,
44. No man come t. m. exc., 65.
7:37. If thirst, let him come u. m.
12: 32. I will draw all men u. m.
Ac. 2: 28. made kno. t.m. ways of
9:15.he is chosen vessel u.m. [life
Ro. 7:13. is good made death u.m.
12:3. grace given u.m., 1 Co.3:10.
1 Co.14:11. he be a barbarian u.m.
2 Co. 11.9. which was lacking t.m.
Ga. 2: 6. it maketh no matter t.m.
Ep. 3: 8. u. m. who am less than
Ph. 1:21. For t. m. to live is Christ
3: 1. t. m. indeed is not grievous
Col.4:11.have been a comfort u.m.
2 Ti. 4: 8. crown not t. m. only
Phm.16. bro. belov. specially t. m.
He.13:6.not fear what man do u.m.
See ASCRIBED, BELONGETH, BORNE, BRING, BROUGHT, CALLETH, CAME, COME, COMEST, COMETH, COMMITTED, DECLARE, DELIVERED, DID, DO, DONE, EXTENDED, FAST, FEAST [Noun], GAIN, GIVEN, HAPPENETH. HEARKENED, INCLINED, LAWFUL, LOOK, MERCIFUL, OPENED, OWEST, PRESENT [Verb], PROFITABLE, RETURN, RETURNED, REVEALED, SAID, SAIDST, SANCTIFY, SAY, SAYEST, SEND, SENT, SOUGHT, SPAKE, SPEAKEST, SPEAKING, SWEAR, TAKE, TURN, TURNED, WITNESSES, WOE.

Toward ME.

Ge. 31: 5. countenance not t. m.
Ps. 86: 13. great is thy mercy t.m.
116: 12. for all his benefits t. m.
Can. 7:10.beloved's, his desire t.m.
Is. 29:13. their fear t. m. is taught
63:15.thy bowels and mercies t.m.
Da. 4: 2. God hath wrought t. m.
2 Co. 7:7. your fervent mind t. m.
Ph. 2:30. your lack of service t. m.

Under ME.

2 S.22:37. enlarged my steps u.m.,
Ps. 18: 36. [18: 39.
40. thou hast subdued u.m., Ps.
48.bringeth peo. u.m., Ps.18:47.
Ne. 2: 14. for beast that was u. m.
Ps. 144:2. subdueth my peo. u.m.
Mat. 8: 9. soldiers u.m., Lu. 7: 8.

With ME.

Ge. 12: 13. that it be well w. m.
28: 20. if G. be w.m., Jos 14:12.
30: 29. knowest how cattle w. m.
31: 5. God of my fa. been w. m.
32. discern what is thine w. m.
39:7. and she said, Lie w. m., 12,
14. 2 S. 13: 11. [be not w.m.
43: 8. send lad w. m. | 44:34. lad
Ex. 17: 2. Why chide ye w. m.
20:23. Ye sh. not make w.m. gods
33:15.If thy presence go not w.m.
Le. 26: † 21. all adventures w. m.
Nu. 11: 15. if thou deal thus w.m.
De.32:34.this laid up in store w.m.
39. and there is no G. w. m.
Jos. 8: 5. I and peo. that are w. m.
Ju. 4: 8. If thou wilt go w. m.
7: 18. I and all that are w. m.
11: 12. What thou to do w. m.?
16:15.when thy heart is not w.m.
17: 2. the silver is w. m.
10. dwell w. m. [go w. m.
Ru.1:8. as ye dealt w.m. | 11.why
1 S. 9: 19. ye shall eat w.m. to day
17: 9. if he be able to fight w. m.
22:23. w.m. shalt be in safeguard
24: 18. thou hast dealt well w.m.

1 S. 28:19. to mo rrow thou be w.m.
2 S. 19:25. Wut. wentest not w.m
33. will feed thee w.m. in Jerus.
23:5. w. m. an everl. covenant
1 Ch. 4:10. that thine ha. be w.m.
2 Ch. 2:3. deal w.m. | 7.are w. m.
35:21. meddling with G. who is w.
Jb.9:35. but it is not so w.m. [m.
23:† 10. he knoweth way w. m.
28:14. sea saith, It is not w. m.
29:5. when Almighty was w. m.
Ps.7:4.peace w.m. | 23:4.art w.m.
42:8. in night his song be w. m.
50:5. that have made cov. w. m.
† 11. wild beasts of field w. m.
55:18. for there were many w.m.
101:6. that they may dwell w.m.
119:98. com-ts are ever w. m.
Pr. 8:18. Riches and honour are w.
Can.4:8.Come w.m.from Leb. [m.
Is. 27:5. he sh. make peace w. m.
50:8. who will contend w. m.
63:3. of people was none w. m.
Je. 20:11. L. w. m. as a mighty
23:14. do w. m. as seemeth good
Da. 10:21. none holdeth w. m.
Ho. 2:7. then it was better w. m.
Jo. 3:4. what ye to do w. m.?
Mal.2:6. he walked w. m. in peace
Mat. 12:30. He that is not w. m.,
gath-h not w. m., Lu. 11:23.
18:26. L. have patience w.m., 29.
20:13. agree w. m. for a penny
26:38. Tarry here, watch w. m.,
Lu. 11:7. my chil. w.m. in bed [40.
15:6. Rejoice w. m., 9. Ph. 2:18.
31. Son, thou art ever w. m.
22:21. hand of him w.m. on table
22:28. Ye have continued w. m.
23:43. shalt be w. m. in paradise
Jn. 8:29. he that sent me is w. m.
13:8. wash thee not, no part w.m.
18. He that eateth bread w. m.
15:27. been w. m. fr. beginning
16:32. not alone, bec. Fa. w. m.
17:24. that they be w. m. where
Ac. 20:34. ministered to th. w.m.
22:9. they w. m. saw light, 11.
Ro.7:21.evil is present w.m.
15:30.strive w.m.in your prayers
1 Co.4:3. w.m. it is very sm. thing
15:10. grace of G. that was w.m.
16:4.that I go,they shall go w.m.
2 Co. 1:17. w. m. sho. be yea, yea
Ph. 1:†7. partakers w. m. of grace
2:22. served w. m. in gospel
23. soon as I see how it go w.m.
4:3. women, who laboured w. m.
15. no ch. communicated w. m.
2 Ti. 4:11.only Luke w. m [w.m.
16. none stood w. m.| 17. L.stood
Phm.13.would have retained w.m.
Re. 3:4. shall walk w. m. in white
20. sup with him, and he w. m.
21. grant to sit w. m. in throne
See WITH me.

Within ME.

Jb. 6:4. arrows of Almighty w. m.
19:27. tho. reins consumed w.m.
32:18. spirit w. m. constraineth
Ps. 39:3. My heart was hot w. m.
42:6, my soul is cast down w. m.
11. why disquieted w. m.? 43:5.
51:10. renew a right spirit w. m.
94:19. in mult. of thoughts w. m.
103:1. all that is w. m. bless his
142:3.spir. was overwhelmed w.m.
143:4.my heart w.m.is desolate(2)
Is. 26:9. with spirit w. m. I seek
Je. 23:9.Mine heart w.m.is broken
La. 1:20.heart is turned w. m., Ho.
See WITHIN me.[11:8.

Without ME.

Is. 10:4. w. m. they sh. bow down
Jn. 15:5.for w. m. ye can do noth-
MEADOW, S. [ing
Ge. 41:2.came seven kine, fed in m.

Ju.20:33.came out of m-s of Gibeah

ME'AH.

Ne. 3:1.even unto tower of M.,12:39.

MEAL.

Nu. 5:15. of an ephah of barley m.
2 K. 4:41. bring m. cast it into pot
1 Ch.12:40.that were nigh bro-t m.
Is. 47:2. Take millstones grind m.
Ho. 8:7. the bud shall yield no m.
See BARREL, MEASURES.

MEALTIME.

Ru. 2:14. At m. come thou and eat

MEAN. [Adjective.]

Pr.22:29.shall not stand bef.m.men
Is. 2:9. m. man boweth down
5:15. m. man shall be bro-t down
31:8. sw. not of a m. man devour
Ac. 21:39. am citizen of no m. city
Ro. 12:†16.condescend to m. things

MEAN time.

Lu. 12:1.m.t.when were multitude

MEAN while.

1 K. 18:45. m.w. heaven was black
Jn. 4:31. in m.w.disci. prayed him
Ro. 2:15. thoughts m. w. accusing

MEAN. [Verb.]

Ge. 21:29.What m. these 7 lambs?
Ex. 12:26. What m. ye by service?
De. 6:20. What m. testimonies?
Jos. 4:6.What m. ye by stones? 21.
Is.3:15.What m. that ye beat peo.?
Eze.17:12. Know ye what these m.?
18:2.What m. that ye use proverb?
Mk. 9:10. what rising fr. dead m.
Ac. 10:17. doubted what vision m.
17:20. we wo. know what these m.
21:13. What m. ye to weep and
2 Co. 8:13. I m. not other men be

MEANEST. [eased

Ge. 33:8. what m. thou by drove
2 S. 16:2. What m. by these? Eze.
Jon.1:6.What m., O sleeper [37:18.

MEANETH.

De. 29:24.what m. this gr. anger?
1 S. 4:6. What m. this shout? 14.
15:14.What m. then this bleating
Is. 10:7. howbeit he m. not so, nor
Mat. 9:13. go, learn what that m.
12:7. if ye had kn. what this m.
Ac.2:12. saying 1 to ano.,What m.?

MEANING. [Noun and Part.]

Da. 8:15. I Dan. had sought for m.
Ac 27:2.m. to sail by coasts of Asia
1 Co. 14:11. if I kn. not m. of voice

MEANS. [14:18.

Ex. 34:7. by no m. clear guilty,Nu.
Le. 25:† 54. if not redeemed by m.
Ju. 5:22.broken by m. of prancings
16:5. by what m. we may prevail
2 S. 14:14. yet doth he devise m.th.
his banished [m., 2 Ch. 1:17.
1 K.10:29.did bring th. out by their
20:39. if by any m.be be missing
Ezr. 4:16. by this m. thou no por.
Ps. 49:7. none by any m. redeem
Pr. 6:26. by m. of whorish woman
Je. 5:31. priests bear rule by their
Mal. 1:9.this been by your m. [m.
Mat. 5:26.Thou by no m. come out
Lu. 5:18. sought m. to bring him
8:36. by what m. he th.was poss-d
10:19.nothing by any m.hurt you
Jn. 9:21. by what m. he now seeth
Ac. 4:9. by what m. he is whole
18:21. I must by all m. keep feast
27:12. if by any m. they attain
Ro. 1:10. if by any m. a journey
11:14. by any m. I may provoke
1 Co. 8:9. lest by any m. liberty
9:22. might by all m. save some
27.lest by any m.when I preached
2 Co. 1:11. by m. of many, thanks
4:†8. yet not altogeth. without m.
11:3. lest by any m.as the serpent
Ga.2:2.lest by any m.I run in vain
Ph. 3:11. if by any m. I attain
1 Th. 3:5. lest by some m. tempter

2 Th. 2:3. deceive you by any m.
3:16. G. give you peace by all m.
He. 9:15. that by m. of death they
Re.13:14.deceiv-h by m. of miracles

MEANT.

Ge. 50:20. but God m. it unto good
Lu. 15:26. asked what these th. m.
18:36.mult.pass.,asked what it m.

MEA'RAH. [ans

Jos. 13:4. M. th. is beside Sidoni-

MEASURE. [Noun.]

Ex.26:2.curtains sh.have one m.,8.
Le. 19:35. do no unright-n. in m.
De. 25:15. just m. shalt thou have
Jos. 3:4. about 2,000 cubits by m.
1 K. 6:25. cubits one m. [-46:22.
7:37. bases had one m., Eze 40:10.
2 K. 7:1. a m. of fine flour, 16, 18.
1 Ch. 11:† 23.slew E-n, a man of m.
20:† 6. at Gath a man of m.
23:29. all manner of m. and [m.
2 Ch. 3:3. length by cubits aft. 1st
Ne. 3:† 11. Malchijah repaired m.
Jb. 11:9. m. is longer than earth
28:25. he weigheth waters by m.
Ps. 39:4. to know m. of my days
80:5.givest tears to drink in gr m.
Is. 5:14. hell opened without m.
27:8. In m. when it shooteth forth
40:12. compreh-d the dust in a m.
Je 30:11. correct thee in m.,46:28.
51:13. and m. of thy covetousness
Eze.4:11.shalt drink wat. by m.,16.
40:21. arches aft. m. of gate, 22.
41:17.wall within and with-t by m.
45:3. of this m. shalt measure
11. Ephah and bath be of one m.
Mi. 6:10. scant m. is abominable
Mat. 7:2. with what m. ye mete, it
sh., Mk. 4:24. Lu. 6:38.
23:32. Fill ye up m. of your fa-s
Mk. 6:51. were amazed beyond m.
7:37. beyond m. astonished,10:26.
Lu. 6:38. good m. pressed down
Jn. 3:34. G. giveth not Spi. by m.
Ro. 12:3. dealt to ev. man the m.
2 Co. 1:8.we were pressed out of m.
10:13. not boast of things with-t
our m. but. acc. to m., 14. 15.
11:23. in stripes above m. in pris.
12:7. lest I sho be exalted ab. m.
Ga. 1:13. beyond m. I persecuted
Ep. 4:7. acc to m. of gift of C.
13. unto m. of stature of C.
16. working in m. of every part
Re. 6:6. A m. of wheat for a penny
21:17. acc. to the m. of a man

MEASURES.

Ge. 18:6. Make ready 3 m. of meal
De. 25:14. shalt not have divers m.
Ru. 3:17. these 6 m.gave he me,15.
1 S. 25:18. five m. of parched corn
1 K. 4:22. Sol.'s provision for day
30 m. of flour, 60 m. of meal
5:11. Sol. gave Hiram 20,000 m.of
wheat, 20 m. of, 2 Ch. 2:10.
7:9. acc. to m. of hewed stones,11.
18:32.as wo.contain two m.of seed
2 K.7:1, 16. two m.barley for shekel
2 Ch. 27:5. gave 10,000 m. of wheat
Ezr. 7:22. done to a 100 m.of wheat
Jb. 38:5.Who hath laid m. thereof
Pr. 20:10. divers m. are abominati.
Je. 13:25. this is portion of thy m.
Eze. 40:24 arches acc. to m., 29
28.measured gate acc. to these m.,
43:13. m. of altar [32, 35
48:16 are m. of profane place
30. on north side 4,500 m.
33. at south side 4,500 m.
35 It was round about 18,000 m.
Hag. 2:16. to a heap of 20 m. there
were but ten [Lu. 13:21.
Mat 13:33. hid in three m. of meal,
Lu. 16:6. said, An hundred m. of oil
7. owest? he said, An hund. m.
See BARLEY. [of wheat

MEASURE. [Verb.]

Nu.35:5. ye shall **m.**fr.without city
De. 21 : 2. they shall **m.** unto cities
Is.65:7.**m.** former work into bosom
Eze. 43 : 10. let them **m.** pattern
45 : 3. of this meas. shalt **m.** length
Zch. 2:2.To **m.** Jerus.to see what is
Re. 11 : 1. Rise and **m.** temple of G.
2. the court without **m.** not
21:15. he had a golden reed to **m.**

MEASURED. ⌊city

Ru. 3:15. **m.** six measures of barley
2 S. 8:2. **m.** with a line, wi. 2 lines
1 K.17:†21. **m.** hims. on child ⌊**m.**
Jb. 7:†4. when sh. evening be **m.**?
Is. 40 :12.Who **m.** waters in hand?
Je. 31 : 37. If heaven ab. can be **m.**
33:22. sand of the sea can-t be **m.**
Eze. 40 : 5. he **m.** the building
6. **m.** threshold | 8. porch, 9.
11. he **m.** entry | 13. gate, 20, 32.
23. **m.** from gate to gate, 27.
24. **m.** posts, 48.–41 : 1, 3.
47. So he **m.** court 100 cubits
41 : 5. **m.** the wall | 13. **m.** house
15. he **m.** the length of building
42:16. **m.** east side, 15. | 17. north
18. he **m.** south side | 19. west
47 : 3. he **m.** a thous. cubits, 4, 5.
Ho. 1:10.as sand of sea wh. can-t be
Ha.3:6. He stood and **m.** earth ⌊**m.**
Mat. 7 : 2. ye mete it shall be **m.** to
you again, Mk. 4:24. Lu. 6:38.
Re.21:16.he **m.** city | 17.he **m.**wall

MEASURING.

Je. 31:39. **m.** line sh. go forth upon
Eze. 40 : 3. man with a **m.** reed, 5.
42 : 15. he had made an end of **m.**
16. measured with **m.** reed, 17,18,
Zch. 2:1. man with **m.** line ⌊19.
2 Co.10:12.they **m.**thems.by thems.

MEAT.

Ge. 1: 29. to you it shall be for **m.**
30.I have given every herb for **m.**
9:3. Every moving thing sh.be **m.**
24 : 33. there was set **m.** bef. him
27 : 4. make me savoury **m.** such
as I love, 7, 9, 14, 17. ⌈bro-t it
31. Esau made savoury **m.** and
45:23. bread and **m.** for his father
Le. 11 : 34. all **m.** wh. may be eaten
22:11.born in his ho. eat of his **m.**
13.she shall eat of her father's **m.**
25:6. sabbath of land sh. be **m.**,7.
Nu. 28 : 24. **m.** of sacr. made by fire
De. 2 : 6. Ye shall buy **m.** of them
28. shalt sell me **m.** for money
20 : 20. destroy trees not for **m.**
28:†30. not use it as a common **m.**
Ju.1:7.kings gathered their **m.**und.
14:14. Out of eater came forth **m.**
1 S. 20 : 5. sit with k. at **m.**, 24, 27.
34. Jona. did eat no **m.** sec. day
2 S. 3:35.peo.to cause Da. to eat **m.**
11 : 8. foll-d him a mess of **m.** fr
12:3. it did eat of his own **m.** ⌊k.
13 : 5. let Tamar dress the **m.** in
1 K.10:5. **m.** of his table, 2 Ch.9:4.
19:8. in strength of the **m.** 40 days
1 Ch.12:40.that were nigh bro-t **m.**
Ezr. 3 : 7. they gave **m.** and drink
Jb.3:†24.sighing cometh bef.my **m.**
6 : 7. are as my sorrowful **m.**
12:11. Doth not mouth taste his **m.**
20 : 14. **m.** in his bowels is turned
21. shall none of his **m.** be left
30:4.cut juniper roots for their **m.**
33:20.his soul abhorreth dainty **m.**
34 : 3. words, as mouth tasteth **m.**
36:31. he giveth **m.** in abundance
38:41. they wander for lack of **m.**
Ps.42:3.My tears have been my **m.**
44:11. hast given us like sheep for
59:14.Let them wander for **m.**⌊**m.**
69:21.They gave me gall for my **m.**
74:14. gavest him to be **m.** to peo.
78 : 18. tempted God by asking **m.**
Ps 78:25.he sent them **m.**to the full
30. while **m.** was yet in mouths
104:21. young lions seek **m.** fr. G.
27. mayest give them **m.** in due
season, Mat. 24 : 45. Lu. 12: 42.
107:18.Their soul abhorreth all **m.**
111:5. given **m.** unto them th. fear
145 : 15. givest them **m.** in season
Pr. 6 : 8. the ant provideth her **m.**
23:3. his dainties, are deceitful **m.**
30:22.fool when he is filled with **m.**
25. they prepare **m.** in summer
31:15. she giveth **m.** to household
Is. 9:†5. wi. burning and **m.** of fire
62 : 8. no more give corn to be **m.**
65:25. dust sh. be the serpent's **m.**
La.1:11.given pleasant things for **m**
19. elders died while sought **m.**
4 : 10. sodden chil., they were **m.**
Eze. 4 : 10. thy **m.** sh. be by weight
16:19. My **m.**wh. I gave thee,thou
25:†7. deliver thee for **m.**to heath.
29 : 5. thee for **m.**to beasts, 34:5,8.
34 : 10. that they may not be **m.**
47:12.grow trees for **m.**fruit for **m**
Da.1:8.not defile hims. with k.'s **m.**
10.hath appointed your **m.**,5,13,
4 : 12. in it was **m.** for all, 21. ⌊15.
11 : 26. feed of his **m.** sh. destroy
Ho.11:4. I laid **m.** unto them ⌊him
Jo. 1 : 16. Is not **m.** cut off before
Ha. 1 : 16. bec. their **m.** plenteous
3 : 17. altho. fields sh. yield no **m.**
Hag. 2 : 12. if one touch **m.** it holy
Mal.1:12.say,his **m.**is contemptible
3:10.Bring tithes, that may be **m.**
Mat. 3 : 4. his **m.** was locusts and
6:25. life more than **m.**? Lu.12:23.
9:10. Jesus sat at **m.** in house, 26:
7. Mk. 2:15.–14:3.–16:14. Lu.7:
36, 37, 49.–11:37.–14:15.–24:30.
10:10.workman is worthy of his **m.**
14:9. that sat with him at **m.** ⌈8:8.
15: 37. took up of broken **m.**, Mk.
25 : 35. hungered, ye gave me **m.**
42. hungered, ye gave me no **m.**
Lu. 3 : 11. that hath **m.** let him do
8:55.he commanded to give her **m.**
9:13. except we buy **m.** for people
12:37. make them to sit do. to **m.**
14 : 10. in pres. of them sit at **m.**
17:7.say unto serv. sit down to **m.**
22:27. greater, he th. sitteth at **m.**
24 : 41. Have ye any **m.**? Jn. 21:5.
Jn. 4 : 8. disci. were gone to buy **m.**
32. I have **m.** to eat ye kn. not of
34.my **m.** is to do the will of him
6 : 27. Labour not for **m.** wh. perisheth,but for **m.** wh.endureth
55. For my flesh is **m.** indeed,my
Ac.2:46.did eat their **m.**with gladn.
9:19.received **m.**he was strength-d
16: 34. the jailer set **m.** before th.
27:33. Paul besought them to take
36. they took some **m.** ⌊**m.**, 34.
Ro. 14:15. if bro. be grieved wi. thy
m.Destroy not him wi. thy **m.**
17. For kingdom of God is not **m.**
20.For **m.** destroy not work of G.
1 Co.3:2. fed you with milk, not **m.**
8:8. **m.** commendeth us not to G.
10. if see thee at **m.** in idol's tem.
13. if **m.** make my bro. to offend
10:3. did eat same spirit-l **m.** ⌈**m.**
Col. 2:16. Let no man judge you in
He.5:12.need of milk,not strong **m.**
14.strong **m.** belong.to th.of age
12 : 16. for morsel of **m.** sold his
See FOWLS. ⌊birthright
See Meat **OFFERING, S.**

MEATS.

Pr. 23 : 6. nei. desire his dainty **m.**
Mk.7:19. into draught, purging **m.**
Ac. 15 : 29. abstain fr. **m.** offered to
Ro.14:†23. putteth difference in **m.**
1 Co.6:13.**m.** for belly, belly for **m.**
1 Ti.4:3. to abstain fr. **m.** God hath
He. 9 : 10. stood only in **m.** drink
13:9.established with grace,not **m.**

MEBUN'NAI. ⌈11:†29

2 S.23:27. one of Da.'s 30, M., 1 Ch.

MECH'ERATHITE. ⌈M

1 Ch.11:36.sons of Hashem,Hepher,

MEDAD. See ELDAD.

ME'DAN.

Ge.25:2.Keturah bare M.,1 Ch.1:32

MEDDLE.

De.2:5.**m.** not with them of mt. Seir
19. **m.** not with chil. of Ammon
2 K. 14 : 10. why **m.** to thy hurt? 2
Ch. 25 : 19. ⌈flattereth
Pr. 20 : 19. **m.** not with him that
24:21.**m.**not wi.th.given to change

MEDDLED, ETH, ING.

2 Ch. 35:21. forbear fr. **m-g** with G.
Pr.17:14.leave contention bef. it be
20:3.but ev.fool will be **m-g** ⌊**m-d**
26:17. **m-h** with strife not belong-

MEDE. ⌊ing

Da.11:1.in 1st year of Darius the M.

MEDES.

2 K.17:6.placed in cities of M.,18:11.
Ezr. 6:2. in province of the M.a roll
Es. 1 : 19. laws of Persians and M.
Is.13:17. I will stir up M., Je.51:11.
Je. 25:25. I made kings of M. drink
51 : 28. Prepare ag. her kings of M.
Da. 5:28. kingd. given to M. and P.
6:8. acc. to law of M. and P.,12,15.
9 : 1. Darius of the seed of the M.
Ac. 2 : 9. Parthians and M. we hear

MED'EBAH. ⌈M.

Nu.21:30.Nophah wh.reacheth unto
Jos. 13: 9. all the plain of M., 16.
1 Ch.19:7. came and pitched bef.M.
Is. 15 : 2. Moab shall howl over M.

ME'DIA.

Es. 1 : 3. all power of Persia and M.
14. princes of Persia and M.saw k.
18. ladies of Persia and M. sh.say
unto princes ⌈and Persia
10 : 2. writ. in book of kings of M.
Is. 21 : 2. O M. all sighing ceaseth
Da.8:20. horns are k-s of M. and Per-

ME'DIAN. ⌊sia

Da. 5 : 31. Darius the M. took kingd.

MEDIATOR.

Ga.3:19.by angels in the hand of **m.**
20. a **m.** is not a **m.** of one, but
1 Ti.2:5. but one **m.** betw. God and
He. 8 : 6. he is **m.** of a better cov-t
9 : 15. he is **m.** of the new testam.
12 : 24. Jesus the **m.** of new cov-t

MEDICINE, S. ⌈22.

Pr.3:†8.It sh.be **m.**to thy navel, 4:†
17 : 22. merry heart doeth like **m.**
20:†30. blueness of a wound is **m.**
Je. 30:13. thou hast no healing **m-s**
46:11. in vain shalt use many **m-s**
Eze. 47: 12. the leaf shall be for **m.**

MEDITATE, ETH.

Ge. 24 : 63. Isaac went out to **m.**
Jos.1:8.thou shalt **m.**day and night
Ju. 5:† 10. **m.** ye on white asses
1 K.18:†17.Cry aloud:either he **m-h**
Ps. 1: 2. in his law doth he **m.** day
2:†1. why do peo. **m.** vain thing?
63:6. **m.** on thee in night watches
77 : 12. I will **m.** of all thy work
119 : 15. I will **m.** in thy precepts,
23. did **m.** in thy statutes ⌊78.
48. and I will **m.** in thy statutes
148. that I might **m.** in thy word
143 : 5. I **m.** on all thy works, I
Is.33:18.Thine heart shall **m.**terror
Lu. 21 : 14. not **m.** bef. what ye ans.
1 Ti. 4 : 15. **m.** upon these things

MEDITATION. ⌈**m.**

1 S. 1 : † 16. out of abundance of my
Ps. 5 : 1. Give ear, consider my **m.**
19 : 14. let **m.** of heart be accepta.
49:3. **m.** of my heart be of under-g
90:†9. we spend our years as a **m.**
104:34.My **m.**of him shall be sweet

Ps.119:97. love thy law, it is my **m.**
99. for thy testimonies are my **m.**

MEEK.

Nu. 12 : 3. man Moses was very **m.**
Ps. 22 : 26. **m.** sh. eat and be satis.
25 : 9. **m.** will he guide in judgm.
37 : 11. the **m.** inherit the earth
69:†32. **m.** sh. see this and be glad
76:9. God arose to save all the **m.**
147:6. The Lord lifteth up the **m.**
149:4. will beautify the **m.** [**m.**
Is. 11:4. reprove wi. equity, for the
29 : 19. **m.** shall increase joy in L.
61:1. preach good tidings unto **m.**
Am. 2:7. that turn aside way of **m.**
Zph. 2 : 3. Seek ye the L. all ye **m.**
Mat. 5 : 5. Blessed are the **m.** for
11 : 29. for I am **m.** and lowly in
21:5. thy king cometh unto thee **m.**
1 Pe. 3 : 4. ornament of a **m.** spirit

MEEKNESS. [me

Ps. 18:†35. with thy **m.** multiplied
45:4. ride prosperously, bec. of **m.**
Zph. 2:3. seek **m.**: may be ye be hid
1 Co. 4:21. sh. I come in spirit of **m.**
2 Co. 10 : 1. I beseech by **m.** of C.
Ga. 5 : 23. fruit of the Spirit is **m.**
6 : 1. restore such in spirit of **m.**
Ep. 4 : 2. With all lowliness and **m.**
Col. 3 : 12. Put on **m.** longsuffering
1 Ti. 6 : 11. follow after faith, **m.**
2 Ti. 2 : 25. In **m.** instructing those
Tit. 3 : 2. shewing all **m.** unto all
Ja. 1 : 21. receive with **m.** the word
3:13. let him shew works with **m.**
1 Pe. 3:15. give a reason of hope wi.

MEET, EST. [Adj.] [**m.**

Ge. 2 : 18. I will make a help **m.**
20. not found a help **m.** for Adam
Ex. 8 : 26. Moses said, It is not **m.**
De. 3 : 18. all that are **m.** for war
Ju. 5 : 30. **m.** for necks of th. [sons
2 K. 10:3. look out **m**-t of master's
Ezr. 4:14. not **m.** to see k.'s dishon.
Es. 2:9. **m.** to be given her out of k.'s
3: † 8. it is not **m.** for king's profit
Jb. 34:31. it is **m.** to be said to God
Pr. 11:24. withhold-h more than **m.**
Je. 26:14. do wi. me as seemeth **m.**
27:5. given earth to wh. seemed **m.**
Eze. 15 : 4. Is it **m.** for any work?
5. whole, it was **m.** for no work
Mat. 3 : 8. bring forth fruits **m.** for
repent., Lu. 3:†8. [bread, Mk. 7:27
15 : 26. not **m.** to take children's
Lu. 15 : 32. **m.** we sho. make merry
Ac. 26:20. works **m.** for repentance
Ro. 1:27. th. recompence wh. was **m.**
1 Co. 15 : 9. not **m.** to be an apost.
16 : 4. if it be **m.** that I go also
Ph. 1 : 7. is **m.** for me to think this
Col. 1:12. made us **m.** to be partakers
2 Th. 1:3. thank G. for you, as is **m.**
2 Ti. 2:21. vessel **m.** for master's use
He. 6:7. herbs **m.** for them by whom
12:†10. chastened us as seemed **m.**
2 Pe. 1:13. I think it **m.** to stir you

MEET. [Verb.] [up

Ge. 14:17. king of Sodom to **m.** him
18:2. Abraham saw, ran to **m.** th.
19:1. Lot seeing, rose to **m.** them
24:17. servant ran to **m.** Rebekah
65. What man walketh to **m.** us?
29 : 13. Laban ran to **m.** Jacob
30:16. Leah went out to **m.** Jacob
32:6. Esau cometh to **m.** thee, 33:4.
46 : 29. Joseph went up to **m.** Isr.
Ex. 4:14. Aaron cometh to **m.** thee
27. Go into wildern. to **m.** Moses
18: 7. Moses went to **m.** fa. in law
19: 17. bro-t people to **m.** with G.
23 : 4. If **m.** enemy's ox astray
25 : 22. there I will **m.** and commune with thee, 29: 42, 43.-30:
6, 36. Nu. 17 : 4. [Balaam
Nu. 22 : 36. Balak went out to **m.**
23:3. aerad. L. will come to **m.** me
Nu. 23:15. Stand here, while I **m.** L.
31:13. to **m.** them with-t camp [**m.**
Jos. 2:16. Rahab said, lest pursuers
9 : 11. Take victuals, go to **m.** th.
Ju. 4:18. went out to **m.** Sisera, 22.
6 : 35. they came up to **m.** Gideon
11: 31. whatever cometh to **m.** me
34. his dau. came to **m.** him [him
19 : 3. fa. of damsel rejoiced to **m.**
Ru. 2 : 22. that they **m.** thee not in
1 S. 10 : 3. shall **m.** thee three men
5. shalt **m.** company of prophets
13 : 10. Saul went to **m.** Samuel
15: 12. Sam. rose early to **m.** Saul
17:48. Philis. drew nigh to **m.** David
18:6. the women came to **m.** Saul
25 : 32. L. sent thee to **m.** me, 34.
30 : 21. men went to **m.** David (2)
2 S. 6 : 20. Michal came to **m.** Da.
10:5. Da. sent to **m.** men, 1 Ch. 19:
15:32. Hushai came to **m.** him [5.
19:15. Judah to Gilgal to **m.** king
16. Shimei came to **m.** k. David, 20.
24. Mephibosheth came to **m.** k-g,
1 K. 2:8. Shimei came to **m.** me [25.
19. Sol. rose up to **m.** Bath-sheba
18 : 16. Obadiah went to **m.** Ahab,
Ahab went to **m.** Elijah
21 : 18. go down to **m.** Ahab
2 K. 1:3. go to **m.** messengers of k.
6. there came a man to **m.** us
7. What man came to **m.** you?
2 : 15. sons of proph. to **m.** Elisha
4:26. Run now, to **m.** her, and say
29. if **m.** any man salute him not
31. he went again to **m.** him
5:21. lighted fr. chariot to **m.** him,
8 : 8. go **m.** the man of God [26.
9. So Hazael went to **m.** him
9:17. Take horseman, send to **m.** th.
18. went one horseback to **m.** him
10:15. Jonadab coming to **m.** him
16 : 10. Ahaz went to **m.** the king
1 Ch. 12:17. Da. went out to **m.** them
2 Ch. 15:2. And he went to **m.** Asa
19:2. Jehu the seer went to **m.** him
Ne. 6 : 2. let us **m.** in the plain, 10.
Jb. 5:14. They **m.** darkn. in daytime
39 : 21. horse goeth on to **m.** men
Pr. 7 : 15. Thf. came I to **m.** thee
17 : 12. Let a bear robbed **m.** man
22:2. The rich and poor **m.** togeth.
29: 13. poor and deceitful man **m.**
Is. 7: 3. Go forth to **m.** Ahaz, thou
14 : 9. Hell is moved to **m.** thee at
34:14. wild beasts of desert sh. **m.**
47: 3. I will not **m.** thee as a man
53:†6. made iniq-s of all **m.** on him
Je. 41 : 6. Ishmael went to **m.** th.
51:31. one post sh. run to **m.** ano.
Ho. 13:8. will **m.** th. as bear bereav.
Am. 4 : 12. prepare to **m.** thy God
Zch. 2:3. ano. angel to **m.** him [Jes.
Mat. 8 : 34. whole city came to **m.**
25:1. went forth to **m.** bridegroom
6. bridegr. cometh, go to **m.** him
Mk. 14:13. **m.** you a man, Lu. 22:10.
Lu. 14:31. with ten thous. to **m.** him
Jn. 12:13. peo. went forth to **m.** him
Ac. 28:15. came to **m.** us far as Appii Forum [Lord
1 Th. 4:17. in the clouds to **m.** the

MEETEST, ETH.

Ge. 32 : 17. When Esau **m**-h thee
Nu. 35 : 19. slay murderer when he
m-h him, 21. [eth
Is. 64: 5. thou **m**-t him that rejoic-

MEETING. [ments

Nu. 24 : † 1. not to **m.** of enchant-
Ju. 14 : † 5. lion roared in **m.** him
1 S. 16:†4. elders trembled at his **m.**
21 : 1. afraid at **m.** of David
Is. 1:13. it is iniquity, the solemn **m.**

MEGID'DO.

Jos. 12 : 21. the king of M. one
17 : 11. M. and towns, 1 Ch. 7 : 29.
Ju. 1:27. Canaanites wo. dwell in M.
Ju. 5:19. k-s fought by waters of **M.**
1 K. 4 : 12. to Baana pertained M.
9 : 15. Sol. raised levy to build M.
2 K. 9 : 27. Ahaziah fled to M. and
died there, 2 Ch. 22 : † 9.
23 : 29. Josiah was slain at M., 30.
2 Ch. 35 : 22.

MEGID'DON.

Zch. 12 : 11. as the mourning in M.

MEHET'ABEEL.

Ne. 6 : 10. son of Delaiah, son of M.

MEHET'ABEL.

Ge. 36 : 39. Hadar, wife's name M., 1

MEHI'DA. [Ch. 1:50.

Ezr. 2 : 52. children of M., Ne. 7 : 54.

ME'HIR. See SHUAH.

MEHOL'ATHITE. [M.

1 S. 18 : 19. Merab given unto Adriel
2 S. 21:8. sons bro-t up for Adriel M.

MEHU'JAEL.

Ge. 4 : 18. Irad begat M. M. begat

MEHU'MAN. [lains

Es. 1:10. com-d M. Zethar, chamber-

MEHU'NIM, S.

2 Ch. 26 : 7. G. helped him ag. the M.
Ezr. 2:50. the Nethinim; chil of M.

ME-JAR'KON.

Jos. 19:46. M. and Rakkon wi. border

MEK'ONAH.

Ne. 11: 28. at M. and villages thereof

MELATI'AH.

Ne. 3:7. next unto them repaired M.

MEL'CHI.

Lu. 3 : 24. Levi, which was son of M.

MELCHI'AH.

1 Ch. 6 : 40. son of M., Je. 21 : 1.

MELCHI-SHU'A.

1 S. 14 : 49. sons of Saul, M., 31 : 2.

MELCHIZ'EDEK.

Ge. 14:18. M. brought bread and wine
Ps. 110: 4. thou art a priest for ever
after order of M., He. 5 : 6, 10.-
6 : 20.-7 : 17, 21.
He. 7 : 1. M. king, priest of God
10. in loins of fa. when M. met him
11. a priest after the order of M.
15. after the similitude of M.

MEL'COM = MIL'COM.

Je. 49:†1. why doth M. inherit Gad [

MELE'A. [†3.

Lu. 3:31. was son of M. son of Menan

ME'LECH. See MICAH.

MEL'ICU = MAL'LUCH.

Ne. 12:14. priests of M. Jonathan, 2.†

MEL'ITA.

Ac. 28 : 1. they knew island was M.

MELODY.

Is. 23:16. make sweet **m.** sing songs
51:3. joy sh. be found, voice of **m.**
Am. 5: 23. will not hear **m.** of viols
Ep. 5 : 19. making **m.** in your heart

MELONS.

Nu. 11:5. we remember the **m.** and

MELT.

Ex. 15:15. inhab. of Canaan shall **m.**
De. 20:†8. lest his breth.'s heart **m.**
Jos. 2:†9. inhab. **m.** bec. of you, †24.
11. as we heard hearts did **m.**
14 : 8. my breth. made people **m.**
2 S. 17 : 10. as heart of lion, sh. **m.**
Ps. 39:†11. makest his beauty to **m.**
58:7. Let them **m.** away as waters
112: 10. he sh. gnash and **m.** aw.
Is. 13 : 7. every heart sh. **m.**, Eze.
19 : 1. heart of E. sh. **m.** [21 : 7.
Je. 9 : 7. Behold, I will **m.** th. [you
Eze. 22:20. iron to **m.** so will I **m.**
Am. 9:5. L. toucheth land, it sh. **m.**
13. all the hills shall **m.**, Na. 1:5.
2 Pe. 3 : 10. elements shall **m.** with

MELTED. [heat, 12.

Ex. 16:21. when sun waxed hot it **m.**
De. 1:†28. breth. have **m.** our heart
Jos. 5 : 1. heard, their heart **m.**
7 : 5. hearts of the people **m.**
Ju. 5 : 5. mountains **m.** before L.
15:†14. bands were **m.** off his hands

1 S. 14: 16. the multitude m. away
2 K.22:†9. servants have m.money
2 Ch. 34 : † 17. they m. the money found [my bowels
Ps. 22 : 14. heart is m. in midst of
46 : 6. uttered his voice, earth m.
97:5. hills m. like wax at presence
107:26.their soul m.bec.of trouble
Is. 34 : 3. mts. be m. with blood
64:†7.hast m. us bec. of our iniq-s
Je. 49:†23. Hamath, Arpad, are m.
Eze. 22:21. ye shall be m. in midst
22. As silver is m. in the furnace

MELTETH.

Jb.6:†14.him th. m. pity be shewed
Ps. 58:8. As a snail which m.let th.
68 : 2. As wax m. let wicked perish
119 : 28. my soul m. for heaviness
147:18. He sendeth word m. them
Is. 40 : 19. the workman m. image
Je. 6 : 29. the founder m. in vain
Na. 2 : 10. the heart of Nineveh m.

MELTING.

Is. 31 : † 8. young men be for m.
64 : 2. as when m. fire burneth

MEL'ZAR.

Da. 1 : 11. Then said Daniel to M.
16. Thus M. took away portion

MEMBER.

De. 23 : 1. hath his privy m. cut off
1 Co.12:14.body not one m.but ma-
19. if all one m.where body ? [ny
26. whether one m. suffer all suffer, or one m. be honoured
Ja. 3:5. so the tongue is a little m.

MEMBERS.

Jb. 17 : 7. all my m. are as shadow
Ps. 139 : 16 in thy book all my m.
Mat.5:29.th. 1 of thy m. perish, 30.
Ro. 6:13. Nei. yield your m. instru.
19. yielded your m. serv-s to sin
7:5. the motions of sins in our m.
23. I see ano. law in my m. warring; to law of sin, in my m.
12 : 4. we have many m. in 1 body, and all m. not same office
5. we are ev. one m. one of ano.
1 Co.6:15. your bodies are m. of C.?
sh. I then take m. of C.? [body
12 : 12. body many m. all m. one
18. hath G. set m. in the body
20. now are they many m. yet
22 much more m.wh.seem feeble,
25. m. sho. have same care [23.
26. one mem. suffer, all m. suffer
27. ye are body of C.,m.in partic.
Ep. 4 : 25. we are m. one of another
5 : 30. we are m. of his body, of his
Col. 3 : 5. Mortify your m. on earth
Ja. 3 : 6. so is tongue among our m.
4:1. your lusts th. war in your m.

MEMORIAL. [tions

Ex. 3:15. is my m. unto all genera-
12:14.this day be unto you for m.
13: 9. be for a m. betw. thine eyes
17:14.Write this for a m.in a book
28:12. for stones of m. unto Israel
29. a m. bef. L. continually,39:7.
30 : 16. atonement money for m.
Le. 2:2. priest shall burn the m. of it, 9 : 16.-5 : 12.-6:15. Nu. 5:26.
23 : 24. a m. of blowing trumpets, Nu. 10 : 10. [bread for a m.
24 : 7. put pure frankincense on
Nu. 5 : 15. an off-g of m. of iniq-y
18. put off-g of m. in her hands
16: 40. brazen censers to be a m.
31 : 54. took gold of capt-s for m.
Jos. 4 : 7. these stones sh. be for m.
Ne. 2 : 20. you have no m. in Jerus
Es. 9:28. nor the m. of them perish
Ps. 9 : 6. their m. is perished [12.
30 : † 4. at m. of his holiness, 97:†
135 : 13. thy m. thro-t all generat.
Is.66:†3.maketh m. as if he blessed
Ho. 12 : 5. L. of hosts, L. is his m.
14:†7. the m. as the wine of Leb.

Zch. 6 : 14. crowns be for a m. [14:9.
Mat.26:13. told for a m. of her, Mk.
Ac.10:4. alms are come up for a m.

MEMORY.

Ps. 109:15. may cut off m. of them
145:7.shall utter m. of thy goodn.
Pr. 10 : 7. The m. of just is blessed
Ec. 9 : 5. m. of them is forgotten
Is. 26 : 14. made their m. perish
1 Co. 15 : 2. if ye keep in m. what I

MEM'PHIS. [preach

Ho. 9 : 6. E. shall gather them, M.

MEMU'CAN. [bury

Es. 1 : 14. Marsena and M. 7 princes
16. M. answ-d before the king
21.king did acc. to the word of M.

MEN. [L.

Ge.4:26.then began m.to call upon
6 : 1. when m. began to multiply
18 : 2. lo, three m. stood by him
19 : 4. m. of city, m. of Sodom+
5. Where are m. came in to thee
8.only unto these m. do nothing
11.smote m.at door with blindn.
32 : 28. power with God and m.
34 : 21. These m. are peaceable
22. only herein will m. consent
39 : 14. she called unto m. of house
42:11. one man's sons ; we true m.,
43:16.bring these m. home (2) [31.
44:4. Jo. said, Up, follow after m.
46:32.m.are shepherds, their trade
Ex. 5:9. Let more work be laid upon
10:11. ye th. are m. serve L. [m.
18 : 21. able m.such as fear G.,25.
Nu. 1: 17. Moses and Aa. took m.
44. princes of Isr. bring 12 m.
9:6.certain m.defiled by dead body
11 : 16. gather 70 m. of elders, 24.
13 : 2. Send m. search la., 14 : 36.
14:37. m. th. did bring evil report
16:2.250 princes m. of renown, 35.
29. If there m.die death of all m.
22:9. God said,What m.are these?
20. If the m. call thee rise and go
35. said unto Balaam,Go with m.
25:5. Slay ye every one his m. th.
26 : 10. time fire devoured 250 m.
31:42.Mo.divided fr.m.that warred
32:11.none of m.th.came out of E.
De. 1 : 22. said,We will send m. bef.
23. I took 12 m. of you [us
19 : 17. m. betw. whom is controversy sh. stand bef. L., 25:1, 11.
22 : 21. m. of city shall stone her
32:26.make rememb. cease am. m.
33 : 6. Reu. live, let not m. be few
Jos. 2 : 2. came two m. in to night
3. Bring forth m.+, 1 S. 11 : 12.
3:12. take ye 12 m.of tribes,4:2,4.
6 : 9. armed m. went bef. priests
7 : 5. m. of Ai smote about 36 m.
9 : 14. and m. took of victuals
18:4.Give out fr.among you 3 m.+
Ju. 6 : 27. Gideon took 10 m. of his serv-s bec. he feared m. of city
8:8. m. of Penuel answ-d as m. of
14.elders of Succoth threesc.17m.
15. bread unto thy m. weary ?
9:18. Abim. k. over m. of Shech.+
9:54.th. m. say.A wom. slew him
14 : 19. Samson slew thirty m.
16:9. m. lying in wait in chamber
18:2. sent 5 m. fr. coasts, 7, 14, 17.
19 : 22. m. of city beset the house
20:5. m. of Gibeah rose ag. me +
10.we will take 10 m. of 100
13. deliver us m. of Belial [39.
31. began to kill ab. 30 m.of Isr.,
Ru. 4 : 2. Boaz took 10 m. of elders
1 S. 2 : 17. m. abhorred off-g of L.!
26. was in favor with L. and m.
†33.incr.of thine house sh.die,m.
5 : 9. he smote the m. of the city
12.m. that died not were smitten
6 : 10. m. did so ; took two milch
10:3. shall meet thee 3 m. [kine+

1 S. 11:12. m. th.we may put to de.
14 : 8. we will pass unto these m.
14. slaughter Jona. made 20 m.
17:12.man went am.m.for old man
26. Da. spake to m. by him, 28.
23 : 3. Da.'s m. said unto him +
24 : 2. Saul went to seek Da. and
9.Whf.hearest m.'s words [m.+
25:11. give bread unto m. I know
15.m.were very good unto us[not
28:1. shalt go to bat. thou and m.
29:2. David and his m. passed on,
30 : 1.+2 S. 2 : 3.+5 : 6, 21.-16:
13.-19: 41.-21 : 17.
2 S.2:30.lacked of Da.'s serv-s 19 m.
31.Abner's m. 300 threescore m.
3:20.Abner came to Da.with 20 m.
39. m. sons of Zeruiah too hard
10:5. m. were ashamed,1 Ch.19:5.
12.let us play the m.for peo.[23.
11:17.m. of city fought with Joab,
15 : 1. Abs. prepared 50 m. to run
18:28. m. that lifted hand ag. king
19:28. were but dead m. bef. king
20 : 7. went out aft. him Joab's m.
21 : 6. 7 m. of his sons, we will hang them [m. of
12. Da. took bones of Jona. from
23 : 3. ruleth over m. must be just
1 K. 1 : 5. Adonijah 50 m.
10:8.Happy m.hear wisd.,2 Ch.9:7.
11:18. They took m. out of Paran,
13 : 2. m.'s bones sh. be burnt [24.
25. m. passed by and saw carcass
20 : 17. are m. come out of Sama.
33. the m. did diligently observe
21:11.m.of city did as Jezebel had
2 K.2:7.fifty m.of sons of prophets,
19. m. of city unto Elisha [16,17.
4 : 40. poured out for m. to eat
5 : 24. he let the m. go and
7 : 3. there were 4 leprous m. [m.
10 : 14. they slew at pit two and 40
24. Jehu appointed fourscore m.
11:9.took ev.man his m.,2Ch.23:8.
12:15. they reckoned not with m.
15 : 25. Pekah slew 50 m. of Gil-s
17:24. k.of Assyr. brot. m. fr.Bab.
30. m. of Bab. made Succoth-be., m. of Cuth, Nergal, m. of
18:27. sent me to the m.? Is.36:12.
20 : 14. him, What said these m., Is. 39 : 3. [chre of
23 : 17. m. of city told, It is sepul-
20. Josiah burned m.'s bones
25:19.took 5 m.in king's presence, threescore m. of la., Je. 52 : 25.
23. when m. heard that k., 24.
25. Ishm. and 10 m., Je. 41 : 1, 2.
1 Ch.4:12.m.of Rechah | 22.of Cho-
5:18. m.able to bear buckler [zeba
9:13 Very able m. for service,26:8.
12 : 32. m. wh. had underst-g of
16:31. let m. say, L. reigns [times
2 Ch. 6 : 18. will God dwell with m.?
28:15.m.expressed by name,31:19.
34 12. m. did the work faithfully
Ezr. 1 : 4. let m. of his pla. help him
4 : 21. Give com-t these m. cease
6 : 8. expenses be given these m.
Ne.2:12.I arose in night and few m.
3:2.m.of Jericho | 22. m. of plain
4 : 23. nor m. of the guard
5 : 5. other m. have our lands and
7 : 26. m. of Beth-lehem+ [33:15.
Jb. 4 : 13. deep sleep faileth on m.,
11:3. thy lies make m.hold peace?
19:† 19. m. of my secret abhorred
22 : 29. When m. are cast do. [me
24 : 12. m. groan from out of city
27:23. m. sh. clap hands at him
28 : 4. they are gone aw. from m.
29:21. Unto me m. gave ear, 30:5.
31 : 31. if m. of my taber. said not
36:24. magnify work wh. m. behold
37:21. now m. see not bright light
24. m. do therefore fear him

Ps. 9: 20 may know thems. but m.
17:14. Fr. m. which are thy hand,
fr. m. of the world wh. have
29:†10.m.of blood hate the upright
49: 18. m. will praise thee when
62:9.m.of low degree are vanity (2)
68: 18. hast received gifts for m.
72: 17. m. shall be blessed in him
73:5 are not in trouble as other m.
nei. plagued like other m. [m.
78:60.Shiloh the tent he placed am.
83:18. m. may know thou over all
105:12.when but few m.in number
107:8. O that m. would praise the
Lord, 15, 21, 31. [counsel
119:†24. testimonies are m. of my
124: 2. on our side, when m. rose
141: 4. with m. that work iniq-y
145:6. m. shall speak of the might
Pr.6:30.m. do not despise a thief, if
8: 4. to you, O m. I call
16:6.m.depart from evil [goodness
20: 6. Most m.procl. each his own
23:28. increaseth transgr-s am. m.
25: 1. wh. m. of Heze. copied out
27. so for m. to search own glory
28: 28. When wicked rise, m. hide
30:14. to devour needy fr. am. m.
Ec. 2: 8. I gat me m. singers and
3: 14. G. doeth it that m. sho. fear
7: 19. more than 10 mighty m. in
Can. 3: 7. threesc. valiant m. [city
Is.3:25.Thy m.sh.fall by the sword
6: 12. the L. have removed m. far
7: 13. sm. thing for you to weary
24. with bows sh. m. come [m.?
29: 19. poor among m. sh. rejoice
31:3. Egyptians are m. and not G.
38:16.O L.,by these things m. live
43: 4. thf. I will give m. for thee
45: 24. even to him shall m. come
46: 8. Remember, shew yours. m.
60:11. m. may bring to thee forces
61: 6. m. shall call you ministers
64:4. m. have not heard, nor perc.
Je. 5: 26. set a trap, they catch m.
6:23.horses in array,as m. for war
9: 10. nei. can m. hear the cattle
15:10. nor m. lent to me on usury
18:21. let their m. be put to death
26: 22. Jehoi-m sent m. unto E.
32:20. set signs in E. am.other m.
34: 18. give thee m. that transgr.
38: 9. m. have done evil to Jerem.
10. take 30 m. with thee, 11.
40:8 came to Gedaliah they and m.
41: 1. ten m. unto Gedaliah | 2.
5. came fr. Samaria fourscore m.
8. ten m. that said, Slay us not
15. Ishmael escaped with 8 m.
44:19.did we pour offerings without
47: 2. then the m. shall cry [m.?
49:15. will make thee despised am.
28. Arise ye, spoil m. of east [m.
51:14.I will fill thee with m.as wl.
52: 25. took 7 m. near the king
La. 2: 15. that m. call perfection
Eze. 8: 11. stood before them 70 m.
16. betw. porch and altar 25 m.
9: 2. six m. from way of gate
11:1. behold at door of gate 25 m.
2. are m. that devise mischief
15. thy breth. m. of thy kindred
12:16. I will leave few m. fr. sword
14:3.these m. set up idols in heart
14. though these m. Noah, Dan.,
15: 3. will m. take a pin [16, 18.
22:9. In thee are m. carry tales to
23:40.ye sent for m.to come fr.far
25:4.I will deliver thee to m.of,10.
26: 10. as m. enter city wh-n a
30: 5. m. of land that is in league
34: 31. ye, my flock, are m. I G.
35: 8. I will fill his mts. with slain
36:10. I will multiply m., 37. [m.
Da.3:12.these m. not regarded thee
22. fire slew m. took up Shadr.

Da. 3: 25. I see 4 m. walking in fire
23. these 3 m. Shadrach, Meshach and, 24. [power
27. m. upon whose bodies fire no
4: 25. drive thee from m., 32, 33.
6:5.said m., We shall not find occa.
26. that m. fear bef. G. of Dan.
Ho.6:7. But they like m. transgr-d
13:2.Let m.th.sacrifice kiss calves
Am. 6: 9. if remain 10 m. in house
Ob. 7. m. at peace deceived thee
Mi. 2: 8. m. averse from war
5: 5. raise ag. him 8 principal m.
7: 6. enemies are m. of own house
Ha. 1: 14. makest m. as the fishes
Zph. 1: 17. will bring distress upon
m.,sh. walk like blind m. [m.
Hag.1:11. I, called for drought upon
Zch. 3: 8. they are m. wondered at
7: 2. sent their m. to pray bef. L.
8:23.ten m.take hold of him a Jew
11:6. I will deliver the m. ev. one
Mat. 5:16. Let your light shine bef.
19.sh.teach m.so, shall be [m.
6: 1. do not your alms before m.
14. if ye forgive m. tresp-s, 15.
16. may appear unto m. to fast
18, appear not unto m. to fast
7:12.whatsoever ye would that m.
should do to you, Lu. 6: 31.
8: 27. But the m. marvelled
9: 8. given such power unto m.
10:32.confess me bef. m., Lu.12:8.
33. whoso. shall deny me before
m., Lu. 12: 9. [unto m.
12: 31. All manner of sin forgiven
36. ev. idle word m. shall speak
41. m. of Nin. sh. rise, Lu.11:32.
13:25.while m. slept, enemy came
14:35. when m. had knowledge of
him . [8: 27.
16:13.Whom do m. say I am? Mk.
19: 26. With m. it is impossible,
Mk. 10:27. Lu. 18:27. [ders
23: 4. lay burdens on m.'s shoul-
13. shut kingd. of heaven ag. m.
28. ye appear righteous to m.
Mk. 6: 12. preached m.sho. repent
8: 24. I see m. as trees walking
Lu.1:25.take away reproach am.m.
2: 14. peace, good will toward m.
5:10. hencef. thou shalt catch m.
6: 22. Blessed ye when m. hate
38. running over shall m. give
7:31. liken m. of this generation
9:56.not come to destroy m.'s lives
11:31. rise up wi. m. of this gener.
44.m.th. walk ov. them not aware
46. ye lade m. with burdens
12: 36. like unto m. wait for lord
48. to whom m. committed much
14: 35. nei. fit for la., m.cast it out
16:15.ye wh. justify yours. bef. m.
17: 12. met him 10 m., lepers
18:1.that m. ought always to pray
18: 11. I am not as other m. are
21:26.m.'s hearts failing th.for fear
22:63.m.that held Jes.mocked him
Jn. 3: 19. m. loved darkness rather
4: 28. woman saith to m. Come
5:41. I receive not honour fr. m.
6: 10. Make the m. sit down [cles
14.those m. when had seen mira-
17:6.I manif-d thy name unto m.
Ac. 1: 21. m. wh. have companied
2:13.These m. are full of new wine
4:12.none other name given am.m.
13. perc-d they were ignorant m.
16. What shall we do to these m.
5: 4. hast not lied unto m. but G.
25.m.ye put in prison are in tem.
Ac.5:29. to obey G. rather than m.
35. intend to do, touching these
38. I say,Refrain fr.these m. [m.
6: 11. they suborned m. wh. said
9:7. m. with him stood speechless
10:5. send m. to Joppa, 11:13.

Ac.10:17.m.sent fr.Cornel.made in-
19. Behold 3 m. seek thee [quiry
21. Peter went down to m. sent
11: 3. wentest in to m. uncircum.
11. behold 3 m. already come
20. some were m. of Cyprus
14: 15. We are m. of like passions
15:1.certain m.wh. came fr. Judea
26. m. that hazarded their lives
16:17. These m. servants of G.
20. These m. Jews do trouble [go
35.sent serjeants, saying, Let m.
17: 25. Nei. worshipped with m.'s
34.certain m. clave unto [hands
18:13.This fellow persuadeth m.to
19: 7. all the m. were about 12
37. ye have bro-t hither these m.
20: 30. of yourselves sh. m. arise
21:23.We have 4 m. th. have a vow
26. Paul took m.and ent.into tem
23: 21. lay in wait more than 40 m.
24: 16. void of offence toward G.
and toward m. [m.
25: 23. Bernice entered with prin.
Ro. 1: 27. m. with m. working
which is unseemly [low estate
12: 16. but condescend to m. of
1 Co. 1:25. foolishn. of G. wiser than
3: 3. carnal and walk as m. [m.
21. thf. let no man glory in m.
4: 9. a spectacle to angels and m.
14:2.speaketh not unto m. but G.
3. speaketh unto m. to edification
20. but in understanding be m.
21.with m. of other tongues [m.
2 Co. 5: 11. terror of L. we persuade
8:13.I mean not other m.be eased
Ga. 1:10. do I now persuade m.? or
seek to please m.?
Ep. 4: 8. he led captivity captive,
and gave gifts unto m.
5: 28. So ought m. to love wives
6: 7. as to L. not to m., Col. 3: 23.
1 Th. 2: 4. speak not as pleasing m.
1 Ti.2:5. mediator betw. G. and m.
8. I will that m. pray ev. where
5: 24. Some m.'s sins are open
6:9. lusts wh. drown m. in perdi-n
2 Ti.3:2. m. sh. be lovers of thems.
8. m. of corrupt minds [m.
Tit. 3: 8. These are profitable unto
He.6:16. m. verily swear by greater
7:8. here m. th. die receive tithes
28. law maketh m. high priests
9: 17. of force after m. are dead
27. appointed unto m. once to die
12:23.spirits of just m. made perf.
Ja. 3: 9. therewith curse we m.
1 Pe.4:6. judged acc. to m. in flesh
15. busybody in other m.'s mat-
2 Pe.1:21.holy m. of G. spake. [ters
Jude 16.m.'s persons in admiration
Re.8:11.many m. died of the waters
9:4.only those m.wh.have not seal
6. m. seek death and sh. not find
10. power to hurt m. 5 mos. [m.
14:4. These were redeemed fr. am.
16: 2. fell grievous sore upon m.
8. power to scorch m. with fire,9.
18. such as not since m. were
21. fell upon m. great hail
21:3. tabernacle of God is with m.
See AGED, AMONG, ARMED, BLIND, BLOODY, BRETHREN, CERTAIN, CHIEF, CHILDREN, CHOSEN, CUNNING, DEAD, DEVOUR, ED, EST, DEVOUT, EVIL, FEW, GOOD, GREAT, HUNDRED, HONOURABLE, ISRAEL, JUDAH.

All MEN.

Ge. 17:27. a.m. of his ho. circumc
Ex.4:19.a. the m. dead wh. sought
Nu 12:3. Mo. was meek above a.m.
14:22.a.those m.wh.seen my glory
16:29. die common death of a. m.
De. 4: 3. a. m. that foll-d Baal-P.

De.21:21.a.m.ofcityshall stonehim
Jos. 8:25. fell that day a.m. of Ai
10 : 2. a. the m. were mighty
Ju. 9:2. Speak in ears of a. m. of+
1 S. 11 : 15. a. m. of Israel, 14 : 22.
-17 : 19, 24. ⌈with him
2 S. 1:11. Da. rent clothes and a.m.
13:9. Amnon said, Have out a.m.
17 : 12. of a. m. not one left
19:42. a.m. of Jud. ans-d men of
1 K.4:31. Sol. was wiser than a.m.
Ezr.10:17. a.m.th.taken stra.wives
Jb.1:3.this man greatest of a.m. of
37:7.that a.m.may know his work
Ps. 64 : 9. a. m. shall fear
89 : 47. whf. made a. m. in vain?
116:11. I said in haste, a. m. liars
Ec. 7 : 2. that is the end of a. m.
Je.41:12. Took a.m. to fight Ishm.
42: 17. a. the m. that set faces
Eze. 38:20. a.m. upon face of earth
Ob. 7. a.m. of confederacy bro-t
Zch. 8:10. I set a.m. ag.his neighb.
Mat 10:22. ye sh. be hated of a.m.,
Mk. 13 : 13. Lu. 21 : 17.
19 : 11. a. m. cannot receive this
saying, save they to whom
26:33. Tho. a. m. shall be offended
Mk. 1 : 37. said a.m. seek for thee
5 : 20. And a.m. did marvel ⌈et
11:32.a.m.counted John a proph-
Lu.3:15.a.m.mused in hearts of Jn.
6 : 26. Woe when a. m. speak well
13:4. sinners above a. m.in Jerus.
Jn. 1 : 7. that a. m. might believe
2 : 24. because he knew a. m.
3 : 26. the same baptizeth, and a.
m. come to him
5:23.That a.m should honour Son
11 :48. let alone, a. m. will believe
12:32. if lifted up, will draw a.m.
13:35. By this a.m. know ye disci.
Ac. 1 : 24. knowest hearts of a. m.
2 : 45. parted goods to a. m.
4 : 21. a. m. glorified G. for what
17:30.now comm-th a.m.to repent
31. given assurance unto a. m.
19 : 7. a. the m.were about twelve
19. burned their books bef a.m.
20:26. I am pure fr blood of a.m.
21 : 28. teacheth a. m. ag. people
22:15.shalt be his witn.unto a.m.
26:24.Fes. said,King Ag.and a.m.
Ro. 5 : 12. death passed upon a.m.
18. judgm. came upon a. m. to
condemn., free gift upon a.m.
12:17. things honest in sight of a.
18. live peaceably wi. a.m. ⌊m.
16:19. your obedi. is come unto a.
1 Co.7:7. would a.m.were as I ⌊m.
9:19 For tho. I be free from a.m.
22. I am made all things to a.m.
10 :33. as I please a. m. in all thi.
15:19. we of a. m. most miserable
2 Co. 3 : 2. our epistle read of a.m.
9 : 13. liberal distribu. unto a m.
Ga. 6:10 let us do good unto a.m.
Ep 3:9.a.m. see what is fellowship
Ph.4:5. Let moderation be kn. unto
1 Th.2:15.contrary to a.m. ⌊a.m.
3:12. to abound in love tow a.m.
5 : 14. be patient toward a.m.
15. follow that is good to a.m.
2 Th. 3:2. for a.m. have not faith
1 Ti.2:1. giving of thanks for a.m.
4.Who will have a.m to be saved
4:10. God, who is Saviour of a.m.
2 Ti.2:24.be gentle unto a.m. ⌈m.
3:9.their folly be manifest unto a.
4:16. no man wi me, a.m.forsook
Tit. 2:11. grace of G. appeared to a.
3:2.shewing meekn. unto a.m.⌊m.
He. 12:14. Follow peace with a.m.
Ja. 1 : 5. ask of G. giveth to a. m.
1 Pe.2:17. Honour a.m.Love broth.
3 Jn. 12. hath good report of a.m.
Re.19:18.flesh of a.m.both free and

Like MEN.

1 S.4:9.quit yours. l.m.,1 Co.16:13.
Ps.73:5.nei. are plagued l.other m.
82 : 7. gods, but ye shall die l. m.
Ho. 6 : 7. they l.m. have transgr-d
Lu.12:36.l.m. that wait for L.⌊cov.
See MADMEN, MIGHT.

Mighty MEN.

Ge. 6 : 4. m.m. which were of old
Ex.15:15.m.m. of Moab trembling
Jos.6:2.I have given thee the m.m.
8 : 3. Joshua chose 30,000 m. m.
10 : 2. all m. of Gibeon were m.
1 S. 2 : 4. bows of m. m. broken
2 S. 10 : 7. David sent Joab and all
host of m. m., 20:7.1 Ch.19:8.
16:6.m.m.were on his right hand
17:8. and his m. that they be m.
23 : 8. names of m.m. David had
9.Eleazar one of the three m.m.
16. three m. m. brake host, 17.
22.Benaiah had name am.3 m.m.
1 K. 1 : 8. m. m. not with Adonijah
10. m. m. he called not
2 K.15:20.exacted of m.m.of wealth
1 Ch. 11 : 10. These are chief of m.
12:1. they were am. m.m. ⌊m.,11.
28 : 1. with m. m. unto Jerus.
29:24. m.m. submitted unto Sol.
2 Ch. 25 : 6. Amaz. hired 100,000 m.
26 : 12. chief of fa-s of m.m. ⌊m.
32:3. Hez. took counsel wi. m.m.
Jb.34:24. sh. break in pieces m.m.
Ec.7:19. wisdom more than ten m.
Can. 4:4. all shields of m.m. ⌊m.
Is.21:17. m.m. of Kedar sh. be diminished ⌈m. m.,
Je. 5:16. open sepulchre they are all
26:21.Jehoiakim king with m.m.
41 : 16. recovered m. m. of war
46 : 9. let m.m. come
48 : 14. We are m. m.
48:41. hearts of m.m. of Moab, as
49:22. heart of m.m. of Edom sh.
50:36. a sword is upon her m.m.
51 : 30. m. m. of Bab. forborne to
56. her m. m. are taken ⌊fight
57. I will make drunk her m.m.
La.1:15.L. hath trodden my m.m.
Eze. 39:20. at my table with m.m.
Da.3:20.com-d m.m. to bind Shad.
Ho 10 : 13. trust in mult. of m. m.
Jo. 2 : 7. run like m. m. and climb
3 : 9. Prepare war, wake up m.m.
Ob.9. thy m.m. O Teman, shall be
Na. 2 : 3. shield of his m. m. is red
Zch. 10 : 5. be as m. m. that tread
Re. 6 : 15. m. m. hide in dens ⌈m.
19:18.That ye may eat flesh of m.
See Mighty men of
VALOUR.

Of MEN.

Ge. 6:2. sons of G. saw dau-s o.m.
4. sons of G. in unto dau-s o. m.
39 : 11. none o.m. of house within
Le. 27 : 29. none devoted o. m.
Nu. 14:38. o. m. wh. went to search
16 : 14. wilt put out eyes o. m.
18:15. o.m. or beasts, be thine
31:11.took all prey both o.m. and
32:11.none o.m.th.came out of E.
De. 1 : 35. not one o. m. sh. see land
Ju. 8 : 18. What manner o. m. they
1 S.1:†11.unto handm.a seed o.m.
10 : 26. with him a band o. m.
2 S.7:14 ch.sten him wi. rod o.m.
2 K. 6 : 20. L. open eyes o. these m.
10 : 24. If any o m. whom I bro-t
13:21. they spied a band o.m.
23:14.their places with bones o.m.
1 Ch. 11:19. I drink bl. o. these m.?
12 : † 23. numbers o. m. armed
2 Ch. 22 : 1. band o. m. slain oldest
26:11.Uzziah had host o.fight-g m.
Jb. 7 : 20. O Preserver o. m. ? ⌈m.
31:†33. If I covered aft. manner o.
32 : 5. no ans. in mouth o. 3 m.

Jb. 33 : 16. he openeth ears o. m.
Ps. 17 : 4. Concerning works o. m.
22 : 6. I am a reproach o. m.
Is.2:11. haughtiness o.m.be bowed
17. haughtin. o.m. be made low
29:13.their fear is by precept o.m.
44: 11. workmen, they are o. m.
51 : 7. fear ye not reproach o. m.
53 : 3. He is despis. rejected o. m.
Je. 9 : 22. carcasses o. m.,Is.66 24.
33 : 5. to fill wi. dead bodies o. m.
38 : 16. into ha. o. m. seek thy life
Eze.16:17. and madest images o.m.
24 : 17. eat not bread o. m., 22.
26:17. was inhab-d o. seafaring co.
27 : 13. they traded persons o. m.
36:12. shalt no more bereave o.m.
38.cities be filled wi. flocks o.m.
Da. 2: 43. sh. mingle wi. seed o.m.
4 : 17. know Most High ruleth in
kingd. o. m., 25, 32.-5 : 21.
17. setteth over it basest o. m.
Mi. 2 : 12. by mult. o.m., Zch.2:4.
Mat.4:19.you fishers o.m.,Mk.1:17
5:13.to be trodden under foot o.m.
6:2. may have glory o.m. | 5.seen
o. m., 23 : 5. ⌈ouchs o. m.
10 : 17. beware o. m. | 19: 12. eu-
15 : 9. for doctrines, commandm-ts
o. m., Mk.7:7. ⌈m., Mk.8:33.
16: 23. but the things that be o.
17: 22. betrayed into hands o.m.,
Mk. 9:31. Lu. 9:44.-24:7. ⌈m.
21: 25. Jn.'s baptism fr. heav or o.
26. If we say o. m., Mk. 11: 30,
32. Lu. 20:4, 6. ⌈Mk. 12:14.
22:16.regardest not persons o.m.,
23:7. love to be called o.m. Rabbi
Mk.7:8. ye hold the tradition o.m.
21. out of heart o. m. proceed
Lu. 14 : 24. none o.m.wh. were bid.
Jn. 1 : 4. the life was light o. m.
12 : 43. they loved the praise o.m.
18 : 3. Judas having a band o. m.
Ac. 5:36.wh. a number o. m. joined
38. if work be o. m. it will come
14:11.gods are come in liken.o.m.
15:17. residue o.m. might seek G.
17:12. women, and o.m. not a few
26 of one blood nations o. m.
Ro.1:18. ag.all unrighteousn. o.m.
2 : 16. when G. judge secrets o.m.
29. whose praise is not o.m. but
6 : 19. I speak after manner o. m.
14:18.serveth C. is approved o.m.
1 Co. 2: 5. not stand in wisd. o.m.
4:6.learn in us not to think o.m.
7 : 23. be not servants o. m.
13:1 Tho.I speak wi.tongues o.m.
15:32.If aft. manner o.m.I fought
39. one kind of flesh o. m. ⌈m.
2 Co. 8 : 21. honest things in sight o.
Ga. 1 : 1. Paul an apostle, not o. m.
3 : 15. I speak after manner o. m.
Ep. 4 : 14. doctrine, by sleight o.m.
Ph. 2 : 7. made in the likeness o.m.
Col. 2 : 8. vain deceit, after tradition
22. after doctrines o. m. ⌊o. m.
1 Th.1:5.what manner o.m.we were
2:6.Nor o.m. sought we glory ⌈m.
13. ye received it not as word o.
1 Ti. 5 : 22. partaker o. m.'s sins
6 : 5. disputings o. m. ⌈truth
Tit.1:14. com-ts o. m. that turn fr.
1 Pe. 2 : 4. disallowed indeed o. m.
15. silence ignora. o. foolish m.
4 : 2. no longer live to lusts o. m.
1 Jn. 5 : 9. If we receive witn. o. m.
Re 9 : 7. faces were as faces o. m.
15.to slay the third part o m.,18.
20. rest o. m. not killed
13:13. fire come do. in sight o.m.
18 : 13. merchandise of souls o.m.
See CHILDREN of men.
See HANDS, NAMES, NUMBER.

Old MEN.

1 K.12:6.Rehob. consulted wi. o.m.

1 K. 12: 8. forsook counsel of **o. m.**, 13. 2 Ch. 10: 6, 8, 13.
Ps.148: 12. **o.m.** and chil. praise L.
Pr. 17: 6. chil. the crown of **o. m.**
20: 29. beauty of **o. m.** gray head
Je. 31: 13. rejoice in dance, young
Jo.1:2.hear this ye **o.m.** [m.and o
2: 28. **o. m.** shall dream dreams, Ac. 2: 17. [streets
Zch. 8: 4. **o.m.** and wom. dwell in

Rich MEN.

Mi. 6: 12. **r. m.** full of violence
Lu.21:1.**r. m.** casting into treasury
Ja. 2: 6. Do not **r. m.** oppress you
5: 1. Go to now, ye **r. m.** weep
Re. 6: 15. great men, **r. m.** hid

Righteous MEN.

Pr.28:12.When **r.m.**rejoice is glory
Eze.23:45.**r.m.** they shall judge th.
Mat.13:17.many **r.m.** desired to see

Seven MEN. [liv-d

2 S. 21:6. Let **s. m.** of his sons be de-
Pr.26:16. **s.m.**that can render rea-
Je. 52:25. took **s.m.**near king [son
Ac. 6: 3. look out **s.m.** of honest re-
See **SINGING men.** [port

Sons of MEN.

Ps.4:2. O ye **s.o.m.** how long,58:1.
31:19.th. trust in thee bef.**s.o.m.**
33: 13. L. beholdeth all **s.o.m.**
57:4. I lie among the **s.o.m.** [acts
145: 12. to make kn. to **s.o.m.** his
Pr. 8: 31. my delights with **s.o.m.**
Ec.1:13. travail G. given to **s.o.m.**
2:3. see what was good for **s.o.m.**
8. I gat me delights of **s. o. m.**
3: 10. travail G. given to **s. o. m.**
18. I said conc. estate of **s. o.m.**
19. which befalleth **s. o. m.**
8:11.heart of **s.o.m.**is set to do evil
9: 3. heart of **s. o. m.** full of evil
12. so are the **s. o. m.** snared in
Is.52:14.his form more than **s.o.m**
Je. 32: 19. thine eyes upon **s. o.m.**
Da. 5: 21. he was driven fr. **s.o.m.**
10: 16. like similitude of **s. o. m.**
Jo. 1: 12. joy is withered fr. **s.o.m.**
Mi.5:7.nor waiteth for **s.o.m.** [m.
Mk. 3:28. all sins forgiven unto **s.o.**
Ep. 3: 5. Which in other ages was not made known unto **s. o. m.**
See STATURE, STRONG, THOUSAND.

Two MEN.

Ex. 2: 13. **t. m.** of Hebrews strove
Nu. 11: 26. remained **t. m.** in camp
Jos. 2: 1. he sent **t. m.** to spy, 6:22.
4. Rahab hid the **t. m.**
23. the **t. m.**returned [sepulchre
1 S. 10: 2. find **t. m.** by Rachel's
28:8. Saul went and **t.m.**with him
2 S. 4: 2. Saul's son had **t.m.** cap-
12: 1. were **t.m.** in one city [tains
23:20. slew **t.** lionlike **m.** of Moab, 1 Ch. 11: 22. [teous
1 K. 2: 32. fell upon **t.m.**more righ-
21: 10. set **t. m.** bef. Naboth, 13.
Mat. 9: 27. **t.** blind **m.** followed him
20: 30. **t.** blind **m.** sitting by way
Lu. 9: 30. talked with him **t.m.**, 32.
17: 34. that night **t.m.** in one bed
36. **t. m.** in field, one be taken
18:10. **t.m.** went up to the temple
24:4. **t.m.** stood by them in shining garments, Ac. 1:10. [true
Jn. 8: 17. the testimony of **t.m.** is
Ac.9:38. they sent **t.m.** unto Peter
See UNDERSTANDING, UNGODLY, VALIANT, VALOUR.

MEN of war. [w.

Nu. 31: 21. Eleazar said unto **m.o.**
28.levy tribute unto L of **m.o.w.**
32. prey wh. **m.o.w.** caught was
49.servants taken sum of **m.o.w**
53. For **m.o.w.** had taken spoils
De. 2: 14. until all **m. o. w.** were wasted, 16. Jos. 5: 4, 6.

Jos. 6: 3. compass city, ye **m.o.w.**
10:24.unto capt-s of **m.o.w.**Come
Ju. 20: 17. all these were **m. o.w.**
1 S.18:5. Saul set him over **m.o.w.**
1 K. 9:22. were **m.o.w.**, 2 Ch. 8:9.
2 K. 25:4. and all the **m.o.w.** fled, Je. 52: 7. [w., Je. 52: 25.
19. took an officer set over **m. o.**
1 Ch. 12: 8. of Gadites **m. o. w.**
38. All these **m.o.w.** to Hebron
2 Ch. 13: 3. set battle with **m.o.w.**
17: 13. **m. o. w.** were in Jerus.
Je. 38: 4. he weakeneth **m. o. w.**
39: 4. Zed. saw **m.o.w.** they fled
41: 3. slew **m.o.w.** [and women
16. Johanan took the **m. o. w.**
49: 26. **m.o.w.** be cut off, 50: 30.
51: 32. **m. o. w.** are affrighted
Eze. 27:10. They of Phut thy **m.o.**
27. all thy **m.o.w.** shall fall [w.
39: 20. at my table with **m. o. w.**
Jo.2:7. sh. climb wall like **m.o.w.**
3: 9. let all **m. o. w.** draw near
Lu. 23:11. Herod with his **m.o.w.**

MEN with wicked. [set

Ge. 13: 13. **m.** of Sodom were **w.**
Nu. 16:26. depart fr. tents of **w. m.**
1 S. 30: 22. Then ans-d all **w. m.**
2 S.3:34. as man falleth bef. **w.m.**
4:11. when **w. m.** slain righteous
Jb. 22: 15. marked old way **w. m.**
34:8.walketh with **w.m.** [trodden
26. he striketh them as **w.m.** in
36. bec. of his answers for **w.m.**
Ec. 8:14. **w.m.** to whom it happ-h
Je. 5: 26. am. my people are **w.m.**
Mat.21:41.miserably destroy **w.m.**
2 Th. 3: 2. may be deliv-d from **w.**

Wise MEN. [m.

Ge. 41: 8. Pharaoh called for all **w. m.**, Ex. 7: 11.
Ex. 36: 4. **w.m.** that wrought work
De. 1: 13. Take **w. m.** [m.
15. I took chief of your tribes,**w.**
Es.1:13.**w.m.** that knew the times
6: 13. Then said Haman's **w. m.**
Jb. 15: 18. Wh. **w.m.** have told fr.
34:2. Hear my words, O ye **w. m.**
Ps. 49:10. he seeth that **w. m.** die
Pr. 10: 14. **w.m.** lay up knowledge
13:20. walketh with **w.m.** be wise
29:8. but **w. m.** turn away wrath
Ec. 9: 17. words of **w.m.** are heard
Is. 19: 12. where are thy **w. m.**
29:14. wisdom of **w.m.** sh. perish
44: 25. turneth **w. m.** backward
Je. 8: 9. The **w. m.** are ashamed
10: 7. am. all **w. m.** of nations
50:35.sword upon Bab. and **w.m.**
51:57. will make drunk. her **w.m.**
Eze. 27: 8. **w. m.** O Tyrus, pilots
9. **w.m.** thereof were thy calkers
Da.2:12. destroy **w. m.** of Bab., 24.
13. decree th. **w.m.** be slain [(2)
14. gone forth to slay **w. m.**
18. not perish with rest of **w.m.**
48.made Dan. ruler over **w.m.**(2)
27. cannot **w.m.** shew unto king
4: 6. decree to bring in **w.m.**, 18.
5:7. Belshaz. spake to **w.m.**,8,15.
Ob. 8. destroy **w. m.** out of Edom
Mat.2:1. came **w.m.** from the east
7. Herod, when had called **w.m.**
16. saw he was mocked of **w.m.**
23:34.Whf. I send unto you **w.m.**
1 Co.1:26.not many **w.m.**not noble
10:15.I speak as to **w.m.** judge ye

MEN with women. [lets

Ex.35:22.**m.**and **w.** brought brace-
De.2:34. destroyed **m.w.** and little ones, Jos. 8: 25. [w.
Ju. 9: 49. died about thous. **m.** and
51.thither fled all the **m.**and **w.**
16: 27. house full of **m.** and **w.** upon roof about 3,000 **m. w.**
2 S. 6: 19. he dealt to the **w.** as **m.**
Ne.8:2. bro-t law bef. **m.** and **w.**,3.

Je. 44: 20. Jere. said to **m.** and **w.**
Ac.5:14.were added to L.**m.**and **w.**
8: 3. Saul haling **m.** and **w.** committed them [and **w.**
12. they were baptized, both **m.**
9:2.**m.**or **w.**he might bring bound
22:4.deliv-g into prisons **m.**and **w**
See **Men, women, and CHILDREN.**

Ye MEN.

Ju.9:7. Hearken, **y.m.** of Shechem
Jb.34:10.Hearken, **y.m.**of underst.
Ac. 1: 11. **y. m.** of Galilee [of Isr.
2:14. **y. m.** of Judea | 5:35. **y. m.**
13: 15. **y. m.** and breth. if ye have
17: 22. **y. m.** of Athens
19:35. **y. m.** of Ephesus,what man

Young MEN.

Ge. 14: 24. which **y. m.** have eaten
22:3.Ab.took two of his **y.m.**,5,19.
Ex. 24: 5. Moses sent **y. m.** which
Nu. 11: 28. Josh. one of the **y. m.**
Jos. 6: 23. **y. m.** that were spies
Ju. 14: 10. so used **y. m.** to do
Ru.2:9.have I not charged **y.m.**,15.
21. Thou sh. keep by my **y. m.**
3:10. as thou followedst not **y.m.**
1 S. 2: 17. sin of the **y.m.** very gr.
8: 16. he will take goodliest **y. m.**
21:4.if the **y.m.** kept from women
5. vessels of the **y. m.** are holy
25: 5. Da. sent 10 **y.m.**, 9, 12, 14.
8. Ask thy **y. m.** they will shew
25. handmaid saw not the **y. m.**
27.let blessings be giv.unto **y.m.**
26: 22. let one of **y.m.** come over
30: 17. 400 **y.m.** rode upon camels
2 S. 1: 15. David called one of **y.m.**
2: 14. Let the **y. m.** play bef. us
21. lay hold on one of **y. m.**
4:12. Da. comm-ed **y.m.** they slew
13: 32. not suppose slain all **y.m.**
16: 2. and summer fruit for **y.m.**
18:15.ten **y.m.**bare Joab's armour
1 K.12:8.Rehoboam consulted with **y. m.**, 10. [2 Ch. 10: 8, 10, 14.
14. spake aft. counsel of **y. m.**,
20:14.by **y.m.** of princes,15,17,19.
2 K. 4: 22. Send one of the **y. m.**
5:22.be come two **y.m.**of prophets
8: 12. their **y.m.** wilt thou slay
1 Ch.19:†10.Joab chose out of **y.m.**
2 Ch. 36: 17. who slew their **y. m.**
Jb. 1:19. it fell upon **y. m.** they are
29: 8. **y.m.** saw me and hid [dead
Ps.78:63. fire consumed their **y.m.**
148: 12. praise L. **y. m.** maidens
Pr. 20:29. glory of **y.m.** is strength
Is. 9: 17. L. no joy in their **y. m.**
13:18.Their bows shall dash **y.m.**
23:4.neither do I nourish up **y.m.**
31: 8. **y. m.** shall be discomfited
40: 30. the **y. m.** sh. utterly fall
42: † 22. spoiled in snaring **y. m.**
Je. 6: 11. fury upon assembly of **y.**
9:21.to cut off **y.m.** fr.streets [m.
11: 22. **y. m.** shall die by sword
15: 8. I bro-t ag. mother of **y. m.**
18: 21. let their **y. m.** be slain
31:13. **y.m.** and old rejoice [ter
48:15.chosen **y.m.** gone to slaugh-
49:26. her **y.m.** sh. fall in streets,
51:3.spare ye not her **y.m.** [50:30.
La. 1: 15. assembly to crush **y.m.**
18. **y. m.** are gone into captivity
2:21. my **y.m.** are fallen by sword
5:13. They took the **y.m.** to grind
14. **y.m.** have ceased from music
Eze. 23:6. all desirable **y.m.**,12,23.
30: 17. **y. m.** of Aven shall fall
Jo. 2:28. **y.m.** sh. see visions,Ac 2:
Am. 2: 11. **y. m.** for Nazarites [17.
4: 10. your **y. m.** have I slain
8: 13. your **y. m.** shall faint
Zch.9:17. corn make **y.m.** cheerful
Mk. 14: 51. **y.m.** laid hold on him
Ac. 5:6. **y.m.** arose, wound him up

Ac. 5 : 10. y. m. came, found her d.
Tit. 2 : 6. y. m. exhort to be soberm.
1 Jn. 2 : 13. I write unto you, y. m., 14.

MENA'HEM. [8 : † 4.
2 K. 15 : 14. M. smote Shallum, Ho.
16. M. smote Tiphsah | 17, 19.
20. M. exacted the money of Isr.
21. acts of M. are they not | 22, 23.

ME'NAN. See MELEA.

MEND, ING. [the L.
2 Ch. 24 : 12. brass to m. house of
Mat. 4 : 21. with Zebedee m-g nets,

ME'NE. [Mk. 1 : 19.
Da. 5 : 25. M., M. God hath number-

ME'NI. Is. 65 : † 11. [ed, 26.

MENPLEASERS.
Ep. 6 : 6. not as m., Col. 3 : 22.

MENSERVANTS.
Ge. 12 : 16. Abram had m. maidserv.
20 : 14. Abimelech gave m. unto Ab.
24 : 35. God given my master m.
30 : 43. Jacob had m. camels, 32 : 5.
Ex. 21 : 7. she sh. not go out as m.
De. 12 : 12. rejoice bef. L., ye and m.
1 S. 8 : 16. king will take your m.
2 K. 5 : 26. is it a time to receive m.?
Lu. 12 : 45. shall begin to beat the m.

MENSTEALERS.
1 Ti. 1 : 10. the law is made for m.

MENSTRUOUS.
Is. 30 : 22. cast them aw. as m. cloth
La. 1 : 17. Jerus. is as a m. woman
Eze. 18 : 6. nei. come near m. woman

MENTION. [Noun.]
Ge. 40 : 14. make m. of me unto Pha.
Ex. 23 : 13. make no m. of other
gods, Jos. 23 : 7. [of G.
1 S. 4 : 18. when he made m. of ark
Jb. 28 : 18. No m. be made of coral
Ps. 71 : 16. make m. of thy righte-n.
87 : 4. I will make m. of Rahab
Is. 12 : 4. make m. his name is ex-
19 : 17. maketh m. be afraid [alted
26 : 13. will make m. of thy name
48 : 1. make m. of the God of Isr.
49 : 1. hath made m. of my name
62 : 6. ye that make m. of the Lord
Je. 4 : 16. Make ye m. to nations
20 : 9. I will not make m. of him
Am. 6 : 10. we may not make m. of L.
Ro. 1 : 9. I make m. of you in prayers
Ep. 1 : 16. making m. of you in my
prayers, 1 Th. 1 : 2. Phm. 4 [of you
Ph. 1 : 3. I thank God upon ev. m.
He. 11 : 22. made m. of departing of

MENTION. [Verb.] [Isr.
Is. 63 : 7. I will m. lovingkindnesses
Je. 23 : 36. burden of L. m. no more

MENTIONED.
Jos. 21 : 9. these cities, which are m.
1 Ch. 4 : 38. These m., were princes
2 Ch. 20 : 34. Jehu is m. in book of k.
Eze. 16 : 56. sister Sodom was not m.
18 : 22. his transgr-s shall not be m.
24. his righteousn. shall not be m.
33 : 16. none of his sins shall be m.

MENU'CHA, CHITES.
1 Ch. 2 : † 52. Haroeh and half of M-s
Je. 51 : † 59. Seraiah was prince of M.

MENU'CHAH.
Ju. 20 : † 43. trode them down fr. M.

MEON'ENIM. [M.
Ju. 9 : † 37. company come by plain of

MEONO'THAI.
1 Ch. 4 : 14. And M. begat Ophrah

MEPH'AATH. [M.
Jos. 13 : 18. cities in plain, Kedemoth,
21 : 37. M. wi. suburbs, 1 Ch. 6 : 79.
Je. 48 : 21. judgment is come upon m.

MEPHIB'OSHETH. [34.
2 S. 4 : 4. Jona. a son, M., 1 Ch. 8 : †
9 : 6. when M. was come unto Da.
10. M. eat bread at my table, 11.
12. M. had a yo. son Micha. (2)
13. So M. dwelt in Jerusalem
16 : 1. Ziba the serv. of m. met him
4. thine all pertained unto m.
2 S. 19 : 24. M. son of Saul came down
25. whf. wentest not with me M.?
30. M. said, Let him take all
21 : 7. king spared M. son of Jona.
8. king took Armoni and M.

ME'RAB. [17.
1 S. 14 : 49. Saul's eldest dau. M., 18 :
18 : 19. when M. sho. been given to

MERAI'AH. [Da.
Ne. 12 : 12. were priests, of Seraiah, M.

MERA'IOTH.
1 Ch. 6 : 6. Zerahiah begat M.
7. M. begat Amariah | 52. M. son
9 : 11. of Zadok, son of M., Ne. 11 : 11.
Ezr. 7 : 3. son of Azariah son of M.
Ne. 12 : 15. were priests, of M. Helkai,

MER'ARI, ITES. [† 3.
Ge. 46 : 11. sons of Levi, Gershon,
Kohath, M., Ex. 6 : 16. Nu. 3 : 17.
1 Ch. 6 : 1, 16.–23 : 6.
Ex. 6 : 19. sons of M. Mahali, Mushi,
Nu. 3 : 20. 1 Ch. 6 : 19, 29, 47.–
23 : 21.–24 : 26. [45.
Nu. 3 : 33. families of M., 35.–4 : 33,
36. under charge of sons of M.
4 : 29. number sons of M., 42.
7 : 8. oxen given unto sons of M.
10 : 17. sons of M. set forward bear-
26 : 57. M. of family of M-s [ing
Jos. 21 : 7. chil. of M. had 12 cities,
1 Ch. 6 : 63, 77.
1 Ch. 6 : 44. sons of M. stood [M.
9 : 14. of Lev., Shemaiah of sons of
15 : 6. Of sons of M. Asaiah
17. Levites appointed of sons of M.
24 : 27. sons of M. by Jaaziah
26 : 10. Hosah of chil. of M. had sons
19. porters among the sons of M.
2 Ch. 29 : 12. of sons of M. Kish
34 : 12. overseers were sons of M.
Ezr. 8 : 19. Jeshaiah of the sons of M.

MERATHA'IM.
Je. 50 : 21. Go up against land of M.

MERCHANDISE.
De. 21 : 14. shalt not make m. of her
24 : 7. stealing breth-n, maketh m.
Pr. 3 : 14. m. of it better than m. of
31 : 18. perceiveth her m. is good
Is. 23 : 18. her m. shall be holiness
45 : 14. m. of Ethiopia shall come
Je. 14 : † 18. priests make m. ag. land
Eze. 26 : 12. make a prey of thy m.
27 : 9. ships in thee to occupy m.
15. many isles were the m. of thy
hands, 24, 27, 33.
34. thy m. and all thy company
28 : 16. By thy m. they have filled
Mat. 22 : 5. one to farm, ano. to m.
Jn. 2 : 16. my Fa.'s house a h. of m.
2 Pe. 2 : 3. with words make m. of you
Re. 18 : 11. no man buyeth their m.
12. The m. of gold, and silver.

MERCHANT. [and
Ge. 23 : 16. current money with m.
Pr. 31 : 24. delivereth girdles unto m.
Can. 3 : 6. perfumed wi. powders of
Is. 23 : 11. com-t ag. m. city [m.
Eze. 27 : 3. art m. of peo. for isles
12. Tarshish thy m. | 16. Syria
18. Damascus thy m. | 20. Dedan
Ho. 12 : 7. he a m., balances of deceit
Zph. 1 : 11. all m. peo. are cut down

MERCHANTS.
1 K. 10 : 15. traffic of spice m. [1 : 16.
28. king's m. received yarn, 2 Ch.
2 Ch. 9 : 14. besides that m. brought
Ne. 3 : 32. the goldsmiths and m., 31.
13 : 20. m. lodged without Jerus.
Jb. 41 : 6. sh. they part him am. m.?
Pr. 31 : 14. she is like the m.'s ships
Is. 23 : 2. m. of Zidon replenished
8. city whose m. are princes
47 : 15. even thy m. they sh. wander
Eze. 17 : 4. he set it in a city of m.
27 : 13. Javan, Tubal, Meshech, m.
15. Dedan | 17. Judah, Isr. m. [23.
21. were thy m. | 22. m. of Sheba,
Eze. 27 : 24. These thy m. in all sorts
36. m. shall hiss at thee
38 : 13. m. of Tarshish [stars
Na. 3 : 16. multiplied thy m. ab.
Re. 18 : 3. m. are waxen rich, 15.
11. m. of earth shall weep ov. her
23. thy m. were the great men of

MERCHANTMAN. [earth
Is. 23 : † 11. L. given com-t cone-g m.
Mat. 13 : 45. like m. seeking pearls

MERCHANTMEN.
Ge. 37 : 28. passed by Midianites m.
1 K. 10 : 15. besides that he had of m.

MERCIES.
Ge. 32 : 10. not worthy of least of thy
2 S. 24 : 14. his m. are gr., 1 Ch. 21 :
2 Ch. 6 : 42. remember m. of Da. [13.
Ne. 9 : 31. m.' sake didst not consume
19. in thy m. forsookest th. not
27. acc. to thy m. gavest saviours
28. didst deliver acc. to thy m.
31. for thy m. not consume them
Ps. 6 : 4. save for thy m. sake, 31 : 16.
44 : 26. redeem us for thy m. sake
51 : 1. acc. to mult. of m. blot
69 : 16. ac. to mult. of thy tender m.
89 : 1. I will sing of m. of L. [m.
106 : 7. rememb-d not mult. of thy
45. repented acc. to mult. of m.
119 : 41. Let thy m. come unto me
Is. 54 : 7. with gr. m. will I gath. thee
55 : 3. sure m. of David, Ac. 13 : 34.
63 : 7. he bestowed acc. to his m.
15. where is thy m. toward me?
Je. 16 : 5. have taken my m. fr. peo.
42 : 12. I will shew m. unto you [ed
La. 3 : 22. of L.'s m. we not consum-
32. compassion acc. to mult. of m.
Da. 2 : 18. desire m. conc. secret
9 : 9. To L. our G. belong m. [m.
18. not for our righte-n., but thy
Ho. 2 : 19. I will betroth thee in m.
Zch. 1 : 16. am retur. to Jerus. wi. m.
Ro. 12 : 1. beseech you by m. of G.
2 Co. 1 : 3. Fa. of m. and God of all
Ph. 2 : 1. If there be any bowels of m.
Col. 3 : 12. put on bowels of m. kind.

Tender MERCIES.
Ps. 25 : 6. Remember thy t. m., 51 : 1.
40 : 11. Withhold not thy t. m.
69 : 16. turn unto me acc. to t. m.
77 : 9. hath he in anger shut t. m.
79 : 8. let thy t. m. prevent us
103 : 4. crowneth thee with t. m.
119 : 77. Let thy t. m. come unto me
156. Great are thy t. m. O Lord
145 : 9. his t. m. are over all his
Pr. 12 : 10. t. m. of wicked are cruel

MERCIFUL.
Ge. 19 : 16. Lord being m. unto Lot
Ex. 34 : 6. proclaimed Lord God m.
De. 21 : 8. Be m. O L., to thy peo.
32 : 43. and will be m. unto his land
2 S. 22 : 26. with m. wilt shew thyself m. with upright, Ps. 18 : 25.
1 K. 20 : 31. heard kings of Isr. are m.
2 Ch. 30 : 9. L. G. is gracious and m.
Ne. 9 : 17. art G. ready to pardon, m.
Ps. 26 : 11. redeem me, and be m.
unto me, 41 : 4, 10.–56 : 1.–57 : 1.–
86 : 3.–119 : 58, 132. [lendeth
37 : 26. righteous is ever m. and
59 : 5. be not m. to any transgr-s
67 : 1. G. be m. unto us, and bless us
103 : 8. Lord is m. and gracious
117 : 2. m. kindness is great [comf.
119 : 76. Let m. kindness be my
145 : † 17. L. is m. in all his works
Pr. 11 : 17. m. man doeth good to his
Is. 57 : 1. m. men are taken away
Je. 3 : 12. Return, I am m. saith L.
Jo. 2 : 13. he is gracious and m.
Mi. 7 : † 2. The m. man is perished
Jon. 4 : 2. I knew thou art a m. God
Mat. 5 : 7. Blessed are the m. they sh.
Lu. 6 : 36. Be m. as your Fa. is m.
18 : 13. God be m. to me a sinner

He. 2 : 17. might be a **m.** high priest
8 : 12. I **m.** to their unighteousn-s
See **Merciful GOD.**

MERCU'RIUS. Ac. 14 : 12.

MERCY. [of **m.**
Ge. 24:27. not left desti. my master
43 : 14. God give you **m.** bef. man
Ex. 34 : 7. **m.** for thous., Da. 9 : 4.
Nu. 14 : 18. the Lord is of great **m.**
forgiving, Ps. 103 : 11.-145 : 8.
De.7:9.who keepeth cov.and **m.**,12.
2 S. 7 : 15. my **m.** shall not depart
fr. him, 1 Ch. 17:13. Ps. 89 : 24.
15 : 20. **m.** and truth be with thee
1 K. 8 : 23. keepest covenant and **m.**
with thy servants,Ne.1:5.-9:32.
1 Ch. 16 : 34. his **m.** endureth for
ever,41.2 Ch.5:13.-7:3,6.-20:21.
Ezr. 3 : 11. Ps. 106 : 1.-107 : 1.-
118:1†.-136 : 1. + Je. 33 : 11.
Ezr.7:28.hath extended **m.** unto me
9 : 9. **m.** unto us in sight of kings
Ne. 1 : 11. grant him **m.** in sight of
Jb. 37 : 13. for correction or for **m.**
Ps. 21 : 7. thro. **m.** of Most High
23 : 6. goodness **m.** sh. follow me
25:10. All paths of L. are **m.** [him
32 : 10. trusteth in L. **m.** compass
33 : † 5. earth is full of **m.** of L.
18 eye of L. upon th. hope in **m.**
52:8. I trust in **m.** of God for ever
57 : 3. God shall send forth his **m.**
59:10 God of my **m.** prevent me,17.
61 : 7. O prepare **m.** and truth
62 : 12. unto thee, belongeth **m.**
66 : 20. hath not turned **m.** fr. me
77:8. Is his **m.** clean gone for ev.?
85 : 10. **m.** and truth are met tog.
86:5.art plenteous in **m.**,15.-103:8.
89 : 2 I said, **m.** shall be built up
14. **m.** truth sh. go bef. thy face
28. My **m.** will I keep for him
98:3. rememb-d his **m.** tow. Israel
100 : 5. L. is good, his **m.** is everl.
101:1.I will sing of **m.** and judgm
103:17. **m.** of the L. is from everl.
109 : 12. Let be none to extend **m.**
130:7. with Lord is **m.** [unto him
144:†2.L.is my **m.** and fortress[**m.**
147 : 11. pleasure in those hope in
Pr. 3 : 3. Let not **m.** forsake thee
14:21.he that hath **m.** on the poor
22. **m.** sh. be to them devise good
31. honour-h G. hath **m.** on poor
16 : 6. By **m.** iniquity is purged
20 : 28. **m.** and truth preserve k.,
throne upholden by **m.**,Is.16:5.
21 : 21. foll-h after **m.** findeth life
Is. 49 : 10. hath **m.** shall lead them
54:10.saith L.that hath **m.** on thee
60 : 10. in favour I had **m.** on thee
Ho. 1 : † 6. not having obtained **m.**
2:†1.to breth.,having obtained **m.**
4:1 bec. there is no **m.** in the land
6:†4.your **m.** is as morning cloud
6. I desired **m.** and not sacrifice
10:12. reap in **m.** [12:6. keep **m.**
14:3. in thee fatherless findeth **m.**
Jon. 2:8.they forsake their own **m.**
Mi.6:8. to do justly,and to love **m.**
7 : 18. because he delighteth in **m.**
20. thou wilt perform **m.** to Ab.
Ha. 3 : 2. L., in wrath remember **m.**
Mat. 5 : 7. merciful shall obtain **m.**
23 : 23. omitted judgment and **m.**
Lu. 1 : 50 his **m.** is on th. fear him
54.holpen Isr.in remem.of his **m.**
72. To perform the **m.** promised
78.remission thro.tender **m.** of G.
Ro. 9 : 23.his glory on vessels of **m.**
11 : 30. obtained **m.** thro. unbelief
31. thro. your **m.** may obtain **m.**
15:9.Gent. might glorify G. for **m.**
1 Co. 7 : 25. as one th. obtained **m.**
2 Co. 4 : 1. as we have received **m.**
Ga. 6:16. peace be on them, and **m.**
Ep. 2 4. G. who is rich in **m.**, hath
Ph.2:27.nigh unto death,G.had **m.**
1 Ti. 1 : 2. **m.** and peace from God
our Fa., 2 Ti.1:2. Tit.1:4.2 Jn.3.
13.obtained **m.** bec.I did it ignor.
16. for this cause I obtained **m.**
2 Ti. 1 : 16. L. give **m.** unto house
of Onesiphorus
18. that he may find **m.** of the L.
Tit. 3 : 5. acc. to his **m.** he saved us
He. 4 : 16. that we may obtain **m.**
10:28. despised law died with-t **m.**
Ja. 2 : 13. judgm. without **m.** that
sheweth no **m.** and **m.** rejoi-th
3:17.wisdom fr.above is full of **m.**
5:11. L. is pitiful, and of tender **m.**
1 Pe. 1 : 3. acc. to his abundant **m.**
2:10. had not obtained **m.** but now
have obtained **m.** [love
Jude 2. **m.** unto you, peace and
21. looking for the **m.** of L. J.

Have MERCY.
Ps. 4 : 1. **h. m.** upon me, 6:2.-9:13.
-25 : 16.-27 : 7.-30:10.-31:9.-51:
1.-86:16. [Zion
102 : 13. Thou shalt **h. m.** upon
123 : 2. until he **h. m.** upon us, 3.
Pr.28:13.forsaketh sins shall **h.m.**
Is. 9 : 17. nei. **h. m.** on fatherless
14 : 1. Lord will **h. m.** on Jacob
27:11.that made th.will not **h. m.**
30:18.that he may **h.m.** upon you
49:13.God will **h.m.** upon afflicted
54 : 8. with everl-g kindness will I
h. m. [will **h.m.** upon him
55 : 7. wicked return unto L., he
Je. 6 : 23. they are cruel **h.** no **m.**
13:14.nor **h. m.** but destroy them,
21:7. [ingplaces
30 : 18. I will **h. m.** on his dwell-
31 : 20. I will surely **h. m.** upon
him, 33 : 26. Eze. 39 : 25. Ho. 1:
7.-2 : 23.
42 : 12. that he may **h.m.** upon you
Ho. 1 : 6. no more **h. m.** upon Isr.,
Zch.1:12. how long not **h. m.** [2:4.
10 : 6. for I **h. m.** upon them
Mat. 9 : 13. I will **h. m.** not sacrifice, 12 : 7. [us, 20 : 30, 31.
27.Thou Son of David, **h. m.** on
15 : 22. **h.m.** on me O L., Mk. 10:
47, 48. Lu. 18 : 38, 39.
17 : 15. Lord, **h. m.** on my son
Lu. 16:24. father Ab., **h. m.** on me
17:13. Jesus, Master, **h. m.** on us
Ro. 9 : 15. I will **h. m.** on whom I
will **h. m.**, 18. [**m.** upon all
11:32. in unbelief, th. he might **h.**

MERCY seat.
Ex. 25 : 17. make a **m. s.** of gold
18. make cherub. in ends of **m.**
s., 19.-37 : 7, 8. [9 : 5.
20. cherubim covering **m. s.**, He.
21. put **m. s.** above upon ark
22. I will commune with thee
from above **m. s.**, Le. 16 : 2.
Nu. 7 : 89. [40:20.
26 : 34. shalt put **m. s.** upon ark,
30:6. put it bef. **m. s.** that is over
31 : 7. and make **m. s.** thereupon
35:12.make ark with the **m.s.** and
37 : 6. made **m. s.** of pure gold
9. cov-d with their wings **m. s.**
39:35. bro-t unto Mo. **m.s.** [**m.s.**
Le. 16 : 2. come not within vail bef.
13. cloud may cover **m. s.**
14. sprinkle blood upon **m.s.** eastward, 15. (2)
1 Ch.28:11.gave Sol.pattern of **m.s.**

MERCY
with shew, ed, est, eth, ing.
Ge.39:21.L.wi Joseph, s-d him **m.**
Ex. 20 : 6. s-g **m.** unto thousands of
them love me, De. 5 : 10. [s. **m.**
33:19. will shew **m.** on whom I will
De.7:2. make no covenant,nor s.**m.**
13 : 17. that Lord may s. thee **m.**
Ju.1:24.s.us city,we will s.thee **m.**
2 S. 22 : 51. s-h **m.** to his anointed,
unto Da.and his seed, Ps.18:50.
1 K. 3:6.Sol.said,Thou hast s-d unto David, my father, great **m.**,
2 Ch. 1 : 8. [servants
2 Ch. 6 : 14. and s-t **m.** unto thy
Ps. 37 : 21. righteous s-h **m.** and
85:7. s. us thy **m.** O L., and grant
109:16. he rememb-d not to s. **m.**
Is. 47 : 6. thou didst s. them no **m.**
Je. 50:42. cruel, and will not s. **m.**
Da. 4 : 27. break off sins, by s-g **m.**
Zch.7:9.Execute true judgm-t.s.**m.**
Lu. 1 : 58. L. s-d great **m.** upon her
10:37.said, He that s-d **m.** on him
Ro. 9 : 16. but of G. that s-h **m.**
12 : 8. s-h **m.** with cheerfulness
Ja. 2 : 13. without **m.** that hath s-d

Thy MERCY. [no **m.**
Ge. 19 : 19. magnified **t.m.** unto me
Ex. 15:13. in **t. m.** hast led people
Nu.14:19.acc unto greatn. of **t. m.**
Ne. 13 : 22. Spare me acc. to **t. m.**
Ps 5:7.thy house,in multi. of **t. m.**
13 : 5. I have trusted in **t. m.** my
25 : 7. acc. to **t. m.** remember me
31:7.I will rejoice in **t.m.** for thou
33:22.Let **t.m.** O Lord, be upon us
36 : 5. **t. m.** O Lord, is in heavens
57:10 **t. m.** is great unto heavens
59 : 16. I will sing aloud of **t. m.**
69 : 13 in multi. of **t. m.** hear me
85 : 7. Shew us **t. m.** O Lord
86:13.For great is **t.m.** toward me
90:14.O satisfy us early with **t. m.**
94 : 18. **t. m.** O Lord, held me up
108 : 4. **t. m.** is great ab. heavens
109 : 21. **t. m.** is good, deliver me
26. O L., save me acc. to **t. m.**
115 : 1. for **t. m.** and truth's sake
119:64.earth,O L., is full of **t. m.**
124 Deal with servants acc-g to **t.**
138:8. **t.m.** endureth for ever [**m.**
143:12.of **t.m.** cut off mine enemies

ME'RED.
1 Ch. 4 : 17. sons of Ezra, M. | 18.

MER'EMOTH.
Ezr. 8 : 33. vessels weighed by M.
10 : 36. Of the sons of Bani, M.
Ne.3:4.next unto th.repaired M.,21.
10:5.that sealed were, M
12 : 3. Levites that went up with
Zerubbabel M.

ME'RES.
Es. 1 : 14. M. and Shethar princes of

MER'IBAH. [Persia
Ex. 17 : 7. he called the place M
Nu. 20 : 13. water of M., 27:14. [S.
24. rebelled at wat. of M., De.33 :
Ps.81:7. proved thee at waters of M.
Eze. 47 : † 19. from Tamar to waters
of M.

MER'IBAH-KA'DESH.
De.32:51. trespassed at waters of M.
Eze. 48 :†28. fr. Tamar unto waters

MERIB'-BAAL. [of M.
1 Ch. 8 : 34. son of Jonathan M. M.
begat Micah, 9 : 40. 2 S. 9 : † 6.

MERO'DACH.
Je. 50:2. Babylon taken, M. is brok.

MERO'DACH-BAL'ADAN
Is.39:1.M.sent letters and a present
to Hezekiah. 2 K. 20 : † 12.

ME'ROM.
Jos. 11:5. pitched at waters of M..7.

MERON'OTHITE. [M.
1 Ch. 27:30. over asses Jehdiah the
Ne. 3:7. next unto him repaired Ja-

ME'ROZ. [don M.
Ju. 5 : 23. curse ye M said angel

MERRILY.
Es. 5 : 14. go thou in **m.** with king

MERRY.
Ge. 43:34. they drank and were **m.**
Ju. 9 : 27. trode grapes, made **m.**
16 : 25. **m.** they said, Call Samson
19 : 6. tarry all night, and be **m.**

Ju.19:9.lodge here.that heart be m.
22. as were making hearts m.
Ru.3:7. Boaz and his heart was m.
1 S.25:36.Nabal's heart was m. [m.
2 S. 13 : 28. when Amnon's heart is
1 K.4:20.Judah and Isr.making m.
21:7.eat, and let thine heart be m.
2 Ch. 7:10. sent the people away m.
Es. 1 : 10. heart of the king was m.
Pr.15:13. m. heart maketh cheerful
15. he of m. heart hath a feast
17 : 22. m. heart doeth good like
Ec. 8:15. noth. better than to be m.
9:7. drink thy wine with m. heart
10:19.wine maketh m. but money
Je 30:19.voice of them th. make m.
31 : 4. dances of them th. make m.
Lu. 12: 19 take ease, eat and be m.
15: 23. let us eat and be m., 24.
29. nev. kid th I might make m.
32. was meet we should make m.
Ja. 5: 13. Is any m.? let him sing
Re.11:10.shall rejoice and make m.

MERRYHEARTED.

Is. 24 : 7. vine languish-h, m. sigh

ME'SECH = ME'SHECH.

Ps. 120: 5. woe th. I sojourn in M.

ME'SHA. [Country.]

Ge. 10 : 30. dwelling was fr. M. unto

ME'SHA. [Person.]

2 K. 3:4. M. king was a sheepmaster
1 Ch. 2 : 42. sons of Caleb, M. | 8:9.

ME'SHACH. See SHADRACH.

ME'SHECH = ME'SECH.

Ge. 10 : 2. sons of Japheth, Gomer,
Madai, Tubal, M., 1 Ch. 1 : 5.
1 Ch.1:17. sons of Shem ; M ,†Mash
Eze 27 :13.Tubal and M.,merchants
32:26.is M. Tubal, and mult.[39:1.
38:2. chief prince of M. Tubal, 3.-

MESHELEMI'AH.

1 Ch.9:21.son of M.was porter, 26:1,
26:2.sons of M. Zechariah, 9. [†14.

MESHEZ'ABEEL.

Ne. 3: 4. son of M., 11 : 24.
10 : 21. The chief of the people, M.

MESHIL'LEMITH.

1 Ch. 9 : 12. son of M. son of Immer

MESHIL'LEMOTH.

2 Ch. 28 : 12. Berechiah son of M.
Ne. 11 : 13. son of M. son of Immer

MESHO'BAB. See JOSHAH.

MESHUL'LAM.

2 K. 22 : 3. Shaphan son of M.
1 Ch.3:19.sons of Zerub.,M. | 5:13.-
6:† 12. Zadok begat M. [8:17.
9: 7. son of M., 11, 12. 2 Ch.34:12.
Ne. 11 : 7.-11 : 11. [M.
Ezr. 8 : 16. I sent for Zechariah and
10 : 15. M. and Shabbethai helped
29. of the sons of Bani,M.Malluch
Ne 3: 4. next repaired M., 6, 30.
6:18. Johanan had tak. dau. of M.
8 : 4. beside Ezr. stood Zech., M. |
10: 20. chief of peo was M. [10:7.
12: 13. priests of Ezra, M., 16.
25. M., Talmon, were porters | 33.

MESHUL'LEMETH.

2 K. 21: 19. Amon's mother's name

MES'OBAITE. [was M.

1 Ch. 11:47. valiant men, Jasiel the

MESOPOTA'MIA. [M.

Ge 24:10. Eliezer went to M. city of
De. 23 : 4. they hired Balaam of M.
Ju.3:8.Chushan-rishathaim k.of M.
8 : 10. L. delivered king of M. into
1 Ch.19:6. to hire chariots out of M.
Ac. 2 : 9. the dwellers in M. we hear
7 : 2. G. of glory appeared to Ab. in

MESS, MESSES. [M.

Ge.43:34. Joseph sent m-s unto th.
Benj.'s m. five times so much
2 S. 11 : 8. followed Uriah m. fr. k.

MESSAGE.

Ju.3:20. I have a m.fr.G.unto thee
1 K.20:12. Benhadad had heard m.
Pr. 26: 6. that sendeth a m. by fool

Hag. 1:13. spake Haggai in L.'s m.
Lu. 19:14. citizens sent m. aft. him
1 Jn. 1:5. This is m. we have heard,

MESSENGER. [3:11.

Ge. 50: 16. they sent a m. unto Jo.
Ju. 2 : † 1. m. of L. came fr. Gilgal
1 S. 4 : 17. m. said, Israel is fled
23 : 27. came a m. unto Saul [25.
2 S.11:19. charged m. saying,22,23,
15 : 13. came m. to David
1 K. 19 : 2. Then Jezebel sent m.
unto Elijah [2 Ch. 18 : 12.
22 : 13. m. went to call Micaiah,
2 K. 5 : 10. sent m. saying, Go wash
6 : 32 ere the m. came to him,
when m.cometh, shut door,33.
9 : 18. The m. came but not again
10 : 8. came m. saying, They have
Jb. 1:14. there came a m. unto Job
33:23.If there be m.an interpreter
Pr. 13:17. A wicked m. falleth into
17:11.cruel m. sh. be sent ag.him
25:13.so is faithful m. to them th.
Is. 42 : 19. Who is blind as my m.
Je. 51 : 31. one m. run to meet ano.
Eze. 23:40. unto wh. a m. was sent
Hag.1:13. spake Haggai, Lord's m.
Mal. 2 : 7. he is m. of L. of hosts
3:1. I will send my m. even m. of
cov.,Mat.11:10.Mk.1:2.Lu.7:27.
2 Co. 12 : 7. m. of Sat. to buffet me
Ph. 2 : 25. my companion, your m.

MESSENGERS.

Ge. 32:3. Jacob sent m. to Esau, 6.
Nu. 20:14. Moses sent m. from Kadesh, De. 2 : 26. [Ju. 11 : 19.
21: 21. Israel sent m. unto Sihon,
22 : 5. Balak sent m. unto Balaam
24 : 12. Spake I not also to thy m.
Jos. 6: 17. Rahab hid the m., 25.
7:22. Josh. sent m. unto Achan's
Ju. 6: 35. Gideon sent m. [tent
7:24.Gideon sent m. saying, Come
9 : 31. Zebul sent m. unto Abim.
11:12. Jephthah sent m. unto k.,
13. answ-d m. Bec. Isr. took [14.
17.Isr.sent m.unto king of Edom
1 S. 6 : 21. sent m. to inhabitants
11:3. may send m. unto coasts, 7.
11 : 4. came m. to Gibeah of Saul
9. they said unto m. Thus say (2)
16:19.Saul sent m.unto Jesse [21.
19:11. sent m. unto Da., 14,15.20,
25:14.Da. sent m. to salute master
42. Abigail went after m. of Da.
2 S.2:5.David sent m. unto Jabesh
3 : 12. Abner sent m. to David
14. David sent m. to Ish-bosheth
26. Joab sent m. after Abner [1.
5:11.Hiram sent m.to Da.,1 Ch.14:
11:4.David sent m. to Bath-sheba
12:27. Joab sent m. to David
1 K. 20 : 2. Benhadad sent m. to A-
5.m.came again and said [hab,9.
2 K. 1 : 3. go meet m. of Ahaziah
5. when m. turned back, he said
16.m.to inquire of Baal-zebub,2.
7 : 15. m. ret-d and told the king
14:8. Amaziah sent m. to Jehoash
16:7. Ahaz sent m. to Tiglath-pil.
17 : 4. Hoshea had sent m. to So
19 : 9. Sennacherib sent m. unto
Hez., 14. Is. 37 : 9, 14. [the L.
23. by thy m. hast reproached
1 Ch. 19: 2. Da. sent m. to comfort
16. sent m. drew forth Syrians
2 Ch. 36:15. L. sent to them by m.
16. they mocked the m. of God
Ne. 6 : 3. m. saying, I am doing gr.
Pr.16:14. wrath of k as m.of death
Is.14:32. What answer m.of nation
18 : 2. Go ye swift m. to nation
33:† 7. their m. sh. cry [peeled
37:14.Hez. received letter from m.
44 : 26. performeth counsel of m.
57 : 9. didst send thy m. afar off
Je. 27 : 3. send by hand of the m.

Eze. 23 : 16. sent m. into Chaldea
30 : 9. sh. m. go from me in ships
Na. 2 : 13. thy m. be no more heard
Lu.7:24. when m. of Jn. were gone
9 : 52. And sent m. before his face
2 Co. 8 : 23. are m. of the churches
Ja. 2:25. when Rahab had rec-d m.

MESSIAH = MESSIAS.

Da. 9 : 25. fr. com-t to build Jerus.
unto M-h Prince, be 7 weeks
26. after 62 weeks M-h be cut off
Jn. 1 : 41. We have found M-s wh. is
4:25.saith, I know M-s cometh [C.

MET.

Ge. 32 : 1. angels of God m. him
33:8. What meanest by drove I m.
Ex. 3 : 18. G. of Hebrews m. wi. us,
4:24.L.m. sought to kill him [5:3
27. Aaron m. Moses in mount
5 : 20. they m. Moses and Aaron
Nu. 23 : 4. God m. Balaam, 16.
De.23:4. they m. you not, Ne.13:2.
25 : 18. Amalek m. thee by way
Jos.11:5. when these kings were m.
17:10. they m. in Asher on north
1 S. 10:10. a company of proph. m.
25 : 20. Abigail m. David [Saul
2 S. 2: 13. m. by pool of Gibeon
16 : 1. Ziba m. David with asses
18: 9. Absalom m. servants of Da.
1 K. 13:24. when gone, lion m. him
18 : 7. Elijah m. Obad., knew him
2 K.9:21. Joram, Ahaziah m. Jehu
10:13. Jehu m. breth. of Ahaziah
Jb. 4: † 14. Fear m. me that made
my bones shake
Ps. 85 : 10. mercy and truth are m.
Pr. 7 : 10. there m. him a woman
Je. 41 : 6. as he m. them he said
Am. 5:19. fr. lion, and bear m. him
Mat. 8 : 28. m. him two possessed
with devils, Mk. 5 : 2. Lu. 8:27.
28:9.Jes. m. them, saying,All hail
Mk.11:4. place where two ways m.
Lu.9:37. much peo. m. him, Jn.12:
17:12. m. him ten men lepers [18.
Jn.4:51. his servs. m. him and told
11:20.Martha went and m.him, 30.
Ac. 10 : 25. Cornelius m. him [us
16:16. certain damsel possessed m.
17:17. disputed with them m. him
20:14.when he m. with us at Assos
27 : 41. a place where two seas m.
He.7:1.who m.Abraham returning
10. when Melchisedec m. him

METE, ED.

Ex. 16: 18. did m. it with a homer
Ps. 60 : 6. I will m. out valley of
Succoth, 108 : 7. [trodden, 7.
Is. 18 : 2. Go to a nation m-d out,
40:12. m-d out heaven with a span
Mat.7:2. with what measure ye m.
it shall be, Mk. 4: 24. Lu. 6:38.

METEYARD. [m.

Le. 19:35. Ye sh. do no unright-ss in

ME'THEG-AM'MAH.

2 S. 8 : 1. David took M. fr. Phils.

METHEINKETH.

2 S. 18 : 27. m. running of foremost

METHU'SAEL.

See MEHUJAEL.

METHU'SELAH.

Ge. 5 : 21. And Enoch begat M., 22.
25. M. lived, begat Lamech, 26.
27. all days of M. were 969 years
1 Ch. 1 : 3. Henoch, M., Lamech
See MATHUSALA.

MEU'NIM. [M.

Ne. 7 : 52. The porters, the chil of

MEZ'AHAB. See MATRED.

MI'AMIN. [M.

Ezr.10:25. sons of Parosh ; Ramiah,
Ne. 12 : 5. went up with Zerub-l, M.

MIB'HAR. See HAGGERI.

MIB'SAM. [Ch 1:29.

Ge. 25 : 13. sons of Ishmael ; M , 1
1 Ch 4:25.M.his son, Mishma his son

MIB'ZAR. See TEMAN.

MI'CAH.

Ju. 17:1. a man of mount Ephr. M.
4. house of M., 8 -18:2,3,13,15,18,
5. M. had a house of gods [22.
9. M. said, Whence comest thou
12. M. consecrated the Levite [10.
13. said M., know I L. will do me
18:4. Thus dealeth M. with me
23. said unto M. What aileth thee
26. When M. saw they too strong
27. they took things M. had made
31. they set up M.'s graven image
1 Ch. 5: 5. M. his son, Reaia his
8: 34. Merib-baal begat M., 9: 40.
35. sons of M., Pithon, Melech, 9:41
2 Ch. 34: 20. son of M., 2 K. 22:†12.
Je. 26: 18 M. the Morashite prophesied in days of Hezekiah, Mi. 1:1.
See MICHA, MICHAH.

MICA'IAH.

1 K. 22: 8. There is yet one man M.,
13. 2 Ch. 18: 7, 12. [2 Ch. 18:8.
9. king said, Hasten hither M.,
14 M. said, 25, 28. 2 Ch. 18: 13, 24, 27
15. M., shall we go ag-t Ramoth-gil., 2 Ch. 18: 14. [2 Ch. 18:23.
24. Zedekiah smote M. on cheek,
26. Take M. unto Amon, 2 Ch. 18: [25.

MICE.

1 S. 6: 4. five golden m. acc., 11, 18.
5. shall make images of your m.

MI'CHA[1] or MI'CAH.[2]

2 S. 9: 12. Mephibosheth had son, M.[1]
Ne. 10: 11. that sealed; M.[1], Rehob
1 Ch. 9: 15. Mattaniah, son of M.[2],

MI'CHAEL. [Ne. 11: 17, 22.

Nu. 13: 13. M., 1 Ch. 5: 14.-6: 40.-7: 3.-8: 16.-27: 18. 2 Ch. 21: 2. Ezr. 8: 8.
1 Ch. 5: 13. brethren were M. Zia
7: 3. sons of .., M., 8: 16. 2 Ch. 21: 2.
12: 20. fell to Dav. of Manas-h. M.
Da. 10: 13. M., one of chil. of princes
21. none holdeth with me but M.
12: 1. shall M. stand up for people
Jude 9. M., archangel, contending
Re. 12: 7. M. fought ag-t the dragon

MI'CHAH[1] or MI'CAH.[2] [(2)

1 Ch. 23: 20. of Uzziel; M.[2], 24: 24. M.[1],
24: 25. brother of M.[1] was Isshiah

MICHA'IAH.

2 K. 22: 12. Achbor the son of M.
2 Ch. 13: 2. Abijah, mother's name was M., 11: †20. 1 K. 15: †2.
17: 7. Jehosh-t sent M. to teach
Ne. 12: 35. trumpets, son of M., 41.
Je. 36: 11. M. heard what Baruch, 13.

MI'CHAL. [David, 28.

1 S. 18: 20. M., Saul's dau-r, loved
27. Saul gave him M. | 14: 49.
19: 11. M. David's wife told him
12. M. let David through window
13. M. took image laid it in bed
17. Saul said unto M. Why hast (2)
25: 44. M. David's wife to Phalti
2 S. 3: 13. exc. thou first bring M.
14. deliver me my wife M. whom
6: 16 M. looked thro. window saw king Da. dancing, 1 Ch. 15: 29.
20. M. dau. of Saul came out to
21. Da. said unto M. It was bef. L.
23. M. had no child to her death
21: 8. king took five sons of M.

MICH'MASH=MICH'MAS.

1 S. 13: 2. with Saul in M. 2000 m.
5. Philis. pitched in M., 11, 16.
23. Philis. went out to passage of
14: 5. forefront of one over ag M. [M.
31. smote Philis. fr. M. to Aijalon
Ezr. 2: 27. The men of M-s, Ne. 7: 31.
Ne. 11: 31. chil. of Benj. dwelt at M.
Is. 10: 28. at M. laid up his carriages

MICH'METHAH.

Jos. 16: 6. border went out to M.
17: 7. coast was from Asher to M.

MICH'RI. [M.

1 Ch. 9: 8. the son of Uzzi, the son of

MIDDAY.

1 K. 18: 29. m. was past, Elijah said
Ne. 8: 3. read from morning to m.
Ac. 26: 13. At m. O king, I saw a light

MID'DIN.

Jos. 15: 61. In the wildern. M. and

MIDDLE. [Secacah

Jos. 12: 2. and from m. of river
Ju. 7: 19. in beginning of m. watch
9: 37. come people by m. of land
16: 29. took hold of two m. pillars
1 S. 25: 29. as out of m. of a sling
2 S. 10: 4. cut off garments in m.
1 K. 6: 6. the m. was 6 cubits broad
8: 64. hallow m. court, 2 Ch. 7: 7.
2 K. 20: 4. afore Isaiah had gone into m. court word of L. came
Je. 39: 3. princes sat in the m. gate
Eze. 1: 16. a wheel in m. of wheel
Ep. 2: 14. broken down the m. wall
See BAR.

MIDDLEMOST. [ing, 6.

Eze. 42: 5. higher than m. of build-

MID'IAN. [Person.]

Ge. 25: 2. Keturah bare M., 1 Ch. 1: 32.
4. sons of M. Ephah, Epher, 1 Ch.

MID'IAN. [Place.] [1: 33.

Ge. 36: 35. Hadad smote M., 1 Ch. 1: 46
Ex. 2: 15. Moses dwelt in land of M.
16. priest of M. had 7 dau-s | 3: 1.
4: 19. L. said unto Mo. in M. Go
18: 1. Jethro priest of M. heard all
Nu. 22: 4. said unto elders of M., 7.
25: 15. Cozbi dau. of chief h. in M.,
31: 3. let them avenge L. of M. [18.
8. slew kings of M. beside the rest
9. Isr. took women of M. captives
Jos. 13: 21. Sihon, k. of Amorites, wh. Moses smote with princes of M.
Ju. 6: 1. the Lord delivered them into hand of M., 2.-7: 15.-8: 3.
7: 8. the host of M. was beneath
13. a cake tumbled into host of M.
14. into his hand God deliv-d M.
25. men of Ephraim pursued M.
8: 5. Zeba and Zalmunna kings of
22. delivered us fr. M., 9: 17. [M., 12.
26. purple raiment on kings of M.
28. was M. subdued before Israel
1 K. 11: 18. Edomites arose out of M.
Is. 9: 4. broken yoke as in day of M.
10: 26. acc. to the slaughter of M.
60: 6. dromedaries of M. sh. cover
Ha. 3: 7. curtains of M. did tremble

MID'IANITE. [law

Nu. 10: 29. Raguel M. Mo.'s fa. in

MID'IANITES.

Ge. 37: 28. passed by M. merchantmen
36. M. sold him into Egypt to
Nu. 25: 17. L. spake saying, vex M.
31: 2. avenge Israel of the M., 3, 7.
Ju. 6: 3. M. came up against them
7. Israel cried because of M., 2, 6.
11. wheat to hide it from M. [14.
13. L. deliv-d us into hand of M.,
16. shalt smite M. as one man
33. all the M. were gath-d together
7: 1. M. were on north side of them
2. to give M. into their hands, 7.
12. the M. lay along in the valley
23. Israel pursued after the M., 24.
25. they took two princes of M.
8: 1. when wentest to fight wi. M.
Ps. 83: 9. do unto them as unto M.

MID'IANITISH. [14.

Nu. 25: 6. Zimri bro-t a M. woman,
15. name of M. woman Cozbi

MIDNIGHT. [E.

Ex. 11: 4. About m. will I go into
12: 29. at m. L. smote firstborn
Ju. 16: 3. Samson lay till m. (2)
Ru. 3: 8. at m. man was afraid [son
1 K. 3: 20. she arose at m. took my
Jb. 34: 20. peo sh. be troubled at m.
Ps. 119: 62. At m. I will give thanks
Mat. 25: 6. at m. there was a cry
Mk. 13: 35. whe. come at even, or m.
Lu. 11: 5. go at m. and say, lend me
Ac. 16: 25. at m. Paul prayed [m.
20: 7. Paul continued speech until
27: 27. about m. shipmen deemed

MIDST.

Ex. 14: 16. shall go on dry ground thro. m. of sea, Nu. 33: 8. Ne. 9: 11. Ps. 136: 14. [of thee
23: 25. I will take sickness from m.
27: 5. net may be to m. of altar
De. 4: 11. mt. burnt unto m. of heav.
34. take a nation from m. of ano.
13: 5. put evil away fr. m. of thee
18: 15. G. will raise a Prophet fr. m.
1 K. 8: 51. fr. m. of furnace of iron
2 Ch. 32: 4. brook thro. m. of land
Can. 3: 10. the m. paved with love
Is. 4: 4. purged blood fr. m. of Jerus.
30: 28. breath reach to m. of neck
58: 9. take from m. of thee yoke
Je. 30: 21. gov. proceed fr. m. of th.
48: 45. flame from m. of Sihon
Eze. 9: 4. Go through m. of city
11: 23. glory of L. from m. of city
14: 8. cut him off fr. m. of peo., 9.
† 16. tho. three were in m. of it
15: 4. m. of it is burnt, Is it meet
28: 16. m. of thee with violence
18. I will bring fire fr. m. of thee
41: 7. fr. lowest to highest by m.
Da. 3: 26. came forth of m. of fire
Am. 2: 3. I will cut off judge fr. m.
Mk. 7: 31. through m. of the coasts
Lu. 4: 30. he passing thro. m. of th.
17: 11. he passed thro. m. of Sama.
Jn. 7: 14. about the m. of the feast
8: 59. going thro. the m. of them
Re. 8: 13. angel flying thro. m. of

In the MIDST. [heav.

Ge. 1: 6. firmament i. m. of heaven
2: 9. tree of life i. m. of garden, 3: 3.
15: 10. Ab. divided them i. m.
48: 16. into a mult. i. m. of earth
Ex. 3: 20. wonders I will do i. m.
8: 22. I am the Lord i. m. of earth
14: 27. overthrow E-ns i. m. of sea
29. upon dry la. i. m. of sea, 15: 19.
33: 3. I will not go up i. m. of thee
34: 12. it be for snare i. m. of thee
Le. 16: 16. i. m. of their uncleanness
Nu 2: 17. tabernacle i. m. of camp
5: 3. defile not camp i. m. I dwell
35: 5. city sh. be i. m., Eze. 48: 15.
De. 11: 3. acts he did i. m. of E.
6. swallowed up i. m. of Israel
19: 2. separate 3 cities i. m. of la.
23: 14. G. walketh i. m. of camp
32: 51. ye sanctified me not i. m.
Jos. 3: 17. firm i. m. of Jord., 4: 10.
4: 9. set 12 stones i. m. of Jordan
7: 13. is an accursed thing i. m. of
21. they are hid i. m. of my tent
1 S. 16: 13. anointed him i. m. of
2 S. 18: 14. he alive i. m. of oak
23: 12. he stood i. m. of ground
20. slew a lion i. m. of a pit in
1 K. 3: 8. thy serv. is i. m. of thy peo
† 28. wisdom of G. i. m. of him
2 K. 6: 20. they were i. m. of Samaria
1 Ch 19: 4. cut off garments i. m.
Ne. 4: 11. nei. see, till we come i. m.
Jb. 1: † 6. Satan came also i. m.
20: † 13. keep sin i. m. of palate [in.
21: 21. num. of his months cut off, i.
Ps. 22: 14. melted i. m. of my bowels
22. i. m. of congr. praise, He. 2: 12.
40: † 8. law is i. m. of my bowels
46: 5. G. is i. m. of her, she sh. not
55: 10. mischief i. m. | 11. Wickedn.
74: 4. enemies roar i. m. of congr.
12. working salva. i. m. of earth
78: 28. he let it fall i. m. of camp
102: 24. take me not i. m. of days
110: 2. rule thou i. m. of thine enemies
116: 19. pay vows i. m. of thee [mies
138: 7. Tho. I walk i. m. of trouble
Pr. 4: 21. keep them i. m. of heart

Pr.5:14.was in all evil i.m.of congr.
8:20.I lead i.m.of paths of judgm.
14: 33. that i. m. of fools is folly
23: 34. th. lieth down i.m. of sea
30: 19. way of a ship i. m. of sea
Is. 5: 2. I built tower i. m. of it
6: 5. I dwell i. m. of a people of
12. great forsaking i. m. of land
7: 6. set king i. m. of it [9.
12:6.Holy One i.m.of thee,Ho.11:
16: 3. as night i. m. of noonday
19:14.mingled perverse spirit i.m.
24. even a blessing i. m. of land
24:13. thus it sh. be i. m. of land
41:18. open fountains i.m. of thee
66: 17. i. m. eating swine's flesh
Je. 6: 6. she is oppression i. m. of
9: 6. habitation is i.m. of deceit
14:9. thou, O Lord, art i.m. of us
17:11. leave them i.m. of his days
37:12. separate hims. i.m. of peo.
51: 1. i.m. of them th. rise up ag.
La. 4: 13. shed blood of just i. m.
Eze. 5: 2. burn third part i. m. of
5. I have set it i. m. of nations
8. execute judgm. i. m. of thee
6: 7. slain fall i. m. of you, 11: 7.
17: 16. i.m. of Babylon he sh. die
22:3.The city sheddeth blood i.m.,
21. ye sh. be melted i. m. [24:7.
22.As silver is melted i. m.of fur.
25.have made many widows i.m.
27. Her princes i. m. like wolves
23: 39. thus done i. m. of my ho.
26:5. spreading of nets i.m. of sea
28: 22. O Zidon, I will be glori. i.
36:23. ye have profaned i.m. [m.
37: 26. will set my sanctuary i.m.
28. when my sanct. i.m. of them
43: 7. I will dwell i.m. of Isr., 9.
46:10. prince i. m. sh. go in [fire
Da. 3: 25. four men walking i.m.of
9: 27. i. m. of the week, oblation
Ho. 5:4. spirit of whoredoms i. m.
Jo. 2: 27. know I am i. m. of Isr.
Am. 7: 10. conspired i. m. of Isr.
Mi. 5:7. remnant be i.m. of peo., 8.
6:14.thy casting down sh. be i.m.
Na. 3:13. thy peo. i. m. are women
Ha. 3: 2. i. m. of the years revive
Zph.2:14.flocks shall lie i.m.of her
3: 5. just Lord is i. m. thereof
12. leave i.m. of thee a poor peo.
15. the Lord is i. m. of thee, 17.
Zch. 2: 5. I be glory i. m. of her
10. I will dwell i. m. of thee, 11.
5:4.curse sh.remain i.m. of his ho.
7. woman that sit. i.m. of ephah
8: 3. will dwell i.m. of Jerus., 8.
14:4. mount of Olives cleave i.m.
Mat. 10: 16. as sheep i.m. of wolves
14: 24. ship was i. m. of the sea,
Mk. 6: 47. [Mk. 9: 36.
18:2. set a little child i.m.of them,
20. are gathered, there am I i.m.
Mk. 14: 60. high priest stood i. m.
Lu.2:46.him sitting i.m. of doctors
4: 35. devil had thrown him i.m.
5:19.let him down i. m. bef. Jesus
6:8.Rise, and stand forth i.m. and
21: 21. let them i. m. of it depart
22: 55. kindled fire i. m. of hall
23: 45. vail of temp. was rent i.m.
24:36.Jes. stood i.m.,Jn.20:19,26.
Jn. 8: 3. when had set her i.m., 9.
19:18.on either side one, Jes. i.m.
Ac.1:15. Pe. stood up i.m. of disci.
18. Judas falling burst asund. i.
2: 22. God did by him i. m. [m.
4: 7. had set them i. m. asked
17:22.Paul stood up i.m. of Mars'
27: 21. Paul stood forth i.m. [hill
Ph.2:15.blameless i.m.of a crooked
Re. 1: 13. i.m. of candlesticks, 2:1.
2:7.wh. is i.m. of paradise of God
4: 6. i. m. of throne four beasts
5:6.lo,i.m.of throne a Lamb,7:17.

Re.6:6. heard voice i.m. of 4 beasts
22: 2. i.m. of street of it was tree

Into the MIDST. [E.

Ex. 11: 4. midnight will I go i.m. of
14: 22. Israel went i. m. of sea
24:18.Moses went i.m.of the cloud
33: 5. I will come i. m. of thee
Nu. 16:47. Aa. ran i. m. of congr-n
De.13:16. gather spoil i.m. of street
Jos. 4: 5. Pass over i.m. of Jordan
8:13. Joshua went i. m. of valley
1 S. 11: 11. they came i.m. of host
2 S. 4: 6. they came i. m. of house
1 K.20:39. serv. went i.m.of battle
22: 35. blood ran i. m. of chariot
Es. 4:1. Mordecai went i.m. of city
Ps.46:2.tho.mts. carried i.m.of sea
57: 6. i. m. they are fallen
Je.21:4.assemble them i.m. of city
51: 63. cast it i. m. of Euphrates
Eze. 5: 4. cast them i. m. of fire
22: 19. gather you i. m. of Jerus.
20. gather silver i. m. of furnace
27:27.i.m. of seas, in day of thy
Da.3:6.be cast i.m. of furnace [11.
Zch. 5:8. he cast it i. m. of ephah,

Out of the MIDST.

Ge. 19:29. Lot o.-m. of overthrow
Ex. 3: 2. angel o.-m. of a bush
4. G. called o.-m. of bush, 24:16.
De. 4:12. Lord spake unto you o.-m. of the fire, 15, 33, 36.-5: 4, 22, 23, 24, 26.-9: 10.-10. 4.
34. to take him a nation o.-m. of another [stones, 8.
Jos. 4: 3. Take o.-m. of Jordan 12
18. priests o.-m. of Jordan
7:23. they took them o.-m.of tent
Is. 24:18.that cometh o.-m. of pit
52: 11. Depart, go o.-m. of her,
Je. 50: 8.-51: 6, 45.
Eze. 1: 4. o.-m. as colour of amber, o.-m. of fire [tures
5. Also o.-m. likeness of 4 crea-
11:7.will bring you o.-m. of it,9.
29: 4. bring thee o.-m. of rivers
32:21. speak to him o.-m. of hell
Am. 6: 4. eat calves o.-m. of stall
Mi. 5:10. I will cut off horses o.-m.
13.will I cut off thy images o.-m.
14. I will pluck up thy groves o.-m. of thee [joice in thy
Zph. 3: 11. take o.-m. them re-

MIDWIFE. [Fear not

Ge. 35: 17. m. said unto Rachel,
38:28. m. bound upon his hand a
Ex. 1: 16. When ye do office of m.

MIDWIVES. [18.

Ex. 1: 15. k. of E. spake to Heb. m.,
17.m.feared God,and did not,21.
18. king of Egypt called for m.
19. are delivered ere the m. come
20. th-f. God dealt well with m.

MIG'DAL-EL. See HOREM.

MIG'DAL-GAD.

Jos.15:37.cities of chil. of Judah, M.

MIG'DOL. [Nu. 33:7.

Ex. 14:2. encamp betw. M. and sea,
Je. 44:1. couc. Jews wh. dwell at M.
46:14. Declare in E. publish in M.

MIGHT. [Noun.]

Ge. 49: 3. Reuben, thou art my m.
Nu.14:13.broughtest peo.in thy m.
De. 3: 24. can do acc. to thy m.
6:5. shalt love G. with all thy m.
8:17. m. of hand gotten me wealth
28:32. sh. be no m. in thine hand
Ju. 5: 31. as sun goeth in his m.
6: 14. L. said, Go in this thy m.
16:30. Samson bowed with his m.
2 S. 6: 14. Da. danced with his m.
1 K. 15: 23. acts of Asa and his m.
16: 5. Baasha, what he did, his m.
27. Omri, what he did, his m.
22:45. Jehosh-t and m. he shewed
2 K. 10: 34. acts of Jehu and his m.
13: 8. acts of Jehoahaz and his m.

2 K. 13: 12. acts of Joash and his m.
14: 15. Jehoash his m., [his m.
14: 28. Jerob. his m. [20:20. Hez.
23:25.Josiah turned to L. with m.
24:16.all the men of m.,1 Ch.7:2,5.
1 Ch. 12:8. men of m. unto David
29:2. prepared for ho. with my m.
12.in thine hand is m., 2 Ch.20:6.
30. of Da., with his reign and m.
2 Ch. 20:12. we no m. ag. company
Es. 10: 2. Ahasuerus, acts of his m.
Ps. 76: 5. none of men of m. found
89:†13.Thou hast an arm with m.
145:6. sh. speak of m. of thy acts
Pr. 24:†5. knowl. strengtheneth m.
Ec.9:10.hand findeth, do it with m.
Is. 3: † 25. thy m. shall fall in war
11:2.sh.rest upon him spirit of m.
33: 13. ye near, acknowl. my m.
40: 26. calleth them by greatness of his m. [creaseth
29. to them have no m. he in-
Je. 9: 23. nei. mighty man glory in
10:6. thy name is great in m. [m.
16: 21. cause th. to know my m.
49:35.I will break chief of their m.
51: 30. their m. hath failed, they
Eze. 32: 29. princes wh. with their m. are laid by slain
32: 30. are ashamed of their m.
Da.2:20.G. for wisd. and m. are his
23. O G., who hast given me m.
3:†4.he cried with m.,4:†14.-5:†7.
4: 30. built by m. of my power
Mi.3:8.I am full of judgm-t and m.
7:16. nations be confounded at m.
Zch. 4: 6. Not by m. nor by power
Ep. 1: † 19. of the m. of his power
21. Far above all m. power [11.
3:16. strengthened with m.,Col.1:
6:10.be strong in L.,and in his m.
2 Pe.2:11.angels wh. greater in m.
Re.7:12.glory and m.be unto our G.

MIGHT or MIGHTEST be.

Ge. 30:34.it m. b. acc. to thy word
Ex. 36: 18. tent, that it m. b. one
39: 21. m. b. above curious girdle
Le. 26: 45. that I m. b. their God
De. 5: 29. fear me,that it m.b. well
1 S. 18: 27. m.b. king's son in law
1 K. 8: 16. that my name m.b. put
2 K. 7:2.windows, m. this thing b.
15:19. that his hand m. b.wi.him
2 Ch. 6: 5. my name m.b. there,6.
36:22.th.word of L. m.b. accompl.
Ps. 51: 4. th. thou m-st b. justified
78: 8. m. not b. as their fathers
Je. 13: 11. m. b. unto me a people
44: 8. that ye m. b. a curse and
Eze. 17: 8. th. it m. b. goodly vine
36: 3. that ye m. b. a possession
Ho. 6: † 5. judgm-s m. b. as light
Mal. 2: 4. my cov. m. b. with Levi
Mk. 5:18. m. b. with him, Lu.8:38.
Lu. 8: 9. What m. this parable b.?
Jn. 15:11. that your joy m. b. full
19:31. the bodies m. b. taken aw.
Ro. 4: 11. m. b. fa. of them believe
16. of faith, th. it m. b. by grace
14: 9. m. b. Lord of dead and liv.
2 Th. 3: 8. m. not b. chargeable
Phm. 8. though I m. b. much bold
He. 2:17.m.b. merciful high priest
12: 10. that we m. b. partakers
1 Pe. 1:21. that your hope m. b. in
See FULFILLED, KNOW. [God.

MIGHTIER. [we

Ge. 26: 16. thou art much m. than
Ex.1:9. chil. of Isr. are m. than we
Nu. 14: 12. greater nation and m.,
De. 4: 38.-7: 1.-9: 1, 14.-11:23.
Ps.93:4. L. is m. than many waters
Ec. 6:10. nei. contend with him m.
Mat. 3:11. he that cometh after me is m. than I, Mk. 1: 7. Lu. 3:16.

MIGHTIES.

1 Ch. 11:12. Eleazar one of the 3 m.

1 Ch. 11 : 34. Benaiah name am. the
[8 m.

MIGHTIEST.

1 Ch. 11 : 19. These things did these
[8 m.

MIGHTILY.

De. 6 : 3. do it, that ye may incr. m.
Ju. 4 : 3. Jabin m. oppressed Israel
14:6. spirit m. upon Samson, 15:14.
1 S. 14 : † 48. Saul wrought m.
Is. 10:† 34. and Lebanon sh. fall m.
42 : † 13. L. shall behave hims. m.
Je. 25 : 30. L. shall m. roar upon
Jon. 3 : 8. let man and beast cry m.
Na. 2:1. fortify thy power m. [Jews
Ac. 18 : 28. For he m. convinced the
19 : 20. So m. grew the word of God
Col. 1:29. which worketh in me m.
Re. 18:2. he cried m. saying, Babylon

MIGHTY.

Ge. 10 : 9. He was m. hunter bef. L.
18:18. Ab. shall become m. nation
23:6. Hear us, thou art a m. prince
Ex. 1 : 7. chil. of Isr. waxed m., 20.
9:28. be no more m. thunderings
10:19. Lord turned a m. west wind
15 : 10. sank as lead in m. waters
Le. 19:15. nor honour person of m.
Nu. 22 : 6. curse peo., they too m.
De. 4 : 37. out with m. power, 9:29.
7:23. destroy th. with m. destruc.
26:5. became there a gr. nation, m.
Ju. 5 : 13. have dominion over m.
23. came not to help of L. ag. m.
1 S. 4 : 8. out of hand of m. gods
2 S. 1:19. how are m. fallen! 25, 27.
21. shield of the m. is cast away
22. fr. blood of slain, fr. fat of m.
2 K. 24:15. m. of land carried captiv.
1 Ch. 1 : 10. Nimrod m. upon earth
12 : 28. Zadok m. [Abijah m.
27 : 6. Benaiah m. | 2 Ch. 13 : 21.
2 Ch. 26:13. made war with m. power
27 : 6. So Jotham became m. bec.
Ezr. 4:20. been m. kings over Jerus.
7:28. mercy unto me bef. m. princes
Ne. 3:16. Neh. unto house of the m.
9:11. threwest stone in m. waters
Jb. 5 : 15. he saveth poor fr. the m.
6 : 23. Redeem me fr. hand of m.?
9 : 4. He is wise in heart, and m.
12 : 19. and he overthroweth m.
21. He weakeneth strength of m.
21:7. Wherefore are the wicked m.
24:22. He draweth m. with power
34:20. the m. shall be taken away
35:9. they cry out by reason of m.
41:25. raiseth hims., m. are afraid
Ps. 24 : 8. L. m. Lord m. in battle
29:1. Give unto L., O ye m. glory
45 : 3. Gird thy sword, O most M.
59 : 3. lo, m. are gathered ag. me
68 : 33. send out voice, a m. voice
69:4. mine enemies wrongf. are m.
74 : 15. thou driest up m. rivers
82 : 1. G. standeth in congr. of m.
89 : 6. who am. sons of m. likened
13. Thou hast a m. arm [unto L.?
19. I have laid help upon one m.
50. in my bosom reproach of m.
93:4. L. is mightier than m. waves
103:† 20. Bless the L., ye angels m.
106 : 8. make his m. power known
112 : 2. His seed be m. upon earth
120 : 4. Sharp arrows of m. [kings
135:10. smote gr. nations, slew m.
Pr. 16 : 32. slow to anger better than
18 : 18. lot parteth betw. m. [m.
21:22. wise man scaleth city of m.
23:11. their Redeem. is m. sh. plead
Is. 3 : 25. thy m. shall fall in war
5:22. Woe unto th. m. to drink wine
11:15. with m. wind shake his ha.
17 : 12. like rushing of m. waters
22 : 17. carry thee with m. captiv.
28:2. L. hath a m. and strong one
43 : 16. a path in the m. waters
49:24. Shall prey be taken fr. m.?
25. captives of the m. taken away
Is. 63 : 1. in righteousn., m. to save
Je. 5 : 15. is m. and ancient nation
32:19. Great in counsel. m. in work
33 : 3. I will shew thee m. things
Eze. 17 : 13. hath taken m. of land
17. Nei. sh. Pha. with his m. army
32:12. By swords of m. will I make
21. strong am. m. shall speak to
27. shall not lie with m. fallen
38:15. shalt come with a m. army
39:18. Ye shall eat the flesh of m.
Da. 4 : 3. how m. his wonders!
8:24. his power shall be m. but not
11 : 3. a m. king shall stand up
25. sh. be stirred up with m. army
Am. 2:14. nei. shall m. deliver hims.
2 : 16. he courageous am. m. shall
5 : 12. I know your m. sins [flee
24. righteousness as a m. stream
Jon. 1 : 4. was a m. tempest in sea
Zph. 3:17. L. in midst of thee is m.
Zch. 11:2. Howl, bec. m. are spoiled
Lu. 1:49. is m. hath done gr. things
52. He hath put down the m. fr.
9 : 43. amazed at m. power of God
15 : 14. arose a m. famine in land
19:37. praised God for the m. works
24 : 19. was a prophet m. in deed
Ac. 2 : 2. as of a rushing m. wind
7 : 22. Moses was m. in words and
18:24. Apollos was m. in Scriptures
Ro. 15 : 19. obedient thro. m. signs
1 Co. 1 : 26. not many m. not many
27. chosen weak, to confound m.
2 Co. 10 : 4. weapons of warfare m.
12 : 12. in wonders, and m. deeds
13 : 3. is not weak, but m. in you
Ga. 2 : 8. same m. in me tow. Gent.
Ep. 1 : 19. working of his m. power
2 Th. 1:7. be revealed with m. angels
Re. 6:13. she is shaken of m. wind
10 : 1. I saw ano. m. angel, 18:21.
16:18. so m. an earthquake [ings
18:10. m. city | 19:6. m. thunder-
See ACTS, GOD, HAND, MAN, MEN.

MIGHTY one, ones.

Ge. 10:8. Nimrod began to be a m. o.
Ex. 15:† 11. Who like thee amo. m.
Ju. 5:22. by prancing of m. o-s [o-s?
Is. 1:24. saith L. of hosts, m. o. of
Isr., 30 : 29.—49 : 26.—60 : 16.
10:34. Lebanon shall fall by m. o.
13 : 3. I have called my m. o-s
28:2. Lord hath a m. and strong o.
Je. 20:11. Lord is with me as a m. o.
46 : 5. m. o-s are beaten [m. o.
Eze. 31:11. deliv-d him into hand of
Jo. 3 : 11. cause thy m. o-s to come
See Mighty WORKS.

MIG'RON. [M.

1 S. 14:2. utterm. part of Gibeah in
Is. 10 : 28. to Aiath, he is passed to

MIJ'AMIN. [M.

1 Ch. 24 : 9. the 6th lot came to M.
Ne. 10 : 7. those that sealed were M.

MIK'LOTH.

1 Ch. 8 : 32. M. begat Shimeah, 9:38.
9 : 37. sons of Jehiel, M. [ruler
27 : 4. of his course was M. also

MIKNEI'AH.

See OBED-EDOM.

MILALA'I. See MAAI.

MIL'CAH.

Ge. 11 : 29. M. daughter of Haran
22 : 20. M. bare chil. unto Nahor
23. Pildash, Jidlaph M. did bear to
24 : 15. Bethuel son of M., 24, 47.
Nu. 26:33. Zelophehad's dau.'s name
was M., 27:1.—36:11.—Jos. 17 : 3.

MILCH. [colts

Ge. 32 : 15. Thirty m. camels with
1 S. 6 : 7. cart, take two m. kine, 10.

MIL'COM=MEL'COM.

1 K. 11:5. Sol. went after M. abomin.
33. worshipped M. god of Ammon
2 K. 23:13. which Sol. builded for M.
Zph. 1 : † 5. that swear by M.

MILDEW.

De. 28:22. L. sh. smite thee with m.
1 K. 8:37. if blasting, m., 2 Ch. 6:28.
Am. 4:9. smitten you with m., Hag.
[2 : 17.

MILE, S.

Mat. 5:41. sh. compel thee to go m.
Jn. 11 : † 18. Bethany nigh Jerusalem about two m-s [lem

MILE'TUM.

2 Ti. 4 : 20. Trophimus I left at M.
[sick

MILE'TUS.

Ac. 20 : 15. next day we came to M.
17. fr. M. he sent to Ephesus to
[elders

MILK. [Noun.]

Ge. 18 : 8. Ab. took butter and m.
49:12. his teeth be white with m.
Ex. 23:19. sh. not seethe kid in his
mother's m., 34:26. De. 14:21.
De. 32 : 14. Butter of kine and m. of
Ju. 4 : 19. Jael opened bottle of m.
5:25. He asked water, she gave m.
Jb. 10:10. not poured me out as m.?
21 : 24. His breasts are full of m.
Pr. 27:27. thou shalt have goat's m.
30:33. churning of m. bring. butter
Can. 4:11. honey m. und. thy tongue
5 : 1. I have drunk wine with m.
12. His eyes washed with m.
Is. 7:22. for abund. of m. they sh. give
28:9. that are weaned from the m.
55 : 1. come, buy wine and m.
60 : 16. shalt suck the m. of Gent.
La. 4 : 7. Nazarites whiter than m.
Eze. 25:4. sh. eat thy fruit, drink m.
Jo. 3 : 18. the hills sh. flow with m.
1 Co. 3 : 2. I have fed you with m.
9 : 7. who feed. flock, eateth not of
He. 5:12. as have need of m.? [m.?
13. ev. one that useth m. is babe
1 Pe. 2: 2. As newborn babes, desire
See FLOWETH, FLOWING. [m.

MILK. [Verb.]

Is. 66 : 11. may m. out and be de-
[lighted

MILKPAILS.

Jb. 21:† 24. His m. are full of milk

MILL, S.

Ex. 11 : 5. maidserv. behind the m.
Nu. 11:8. peo. ground manna in m-s
Mat. 24:41. Two women be grinding
[at m.

MILLET.

Eze. 4 : 9. Take m. and make bread

MILLIONS.

Ge. 24:60. be thou mother of thous.
[of m.

MIL'LO.

Ju. 9 : 6. all house of M. gathered
20. let fire devour house of M.
2 S. 5:9. built round fr. m., 1 Ch. 11:8.
1 K. 9 : 15. of the levy to build M.
24. did Solomon build M., 11:27.
2 K. 12 : 20. slew Joash in ho. of M.
2 Ch. 32:5. repaired M. in city of Da.

MILLSTONE, S.

De. 24 : 6. No man take the m. to
pledge [m., 2 S. 11 : 21.
Ju. 9 : 53. a woman cast a piece of
Jb. 41 : 24. heart hard as nether m.
Is. 47 : 2. Take m-s and grind meal
Je. 25:10. will take aw. sound of m-s
Mat. 18:6. better a m. were hanged
about neck, Mk. 9:42. Lu. 17:2.
Re. 18:21. angel took stone like m.
22. sound of m. be heard no more

MINCING.

Is. 3:16. walking and m. as they go

MIND. [Noun.]

Ge. 26: 35. a grief of m. unto Isaac
Le. 24:12. m. of L. might be shewed
De. 18 : 6. come wi. desire of his m.
28 : 65. L. give thee sorrow of m.
30: 1. call them to m. am. nations
1 Ch. 28 : 9. serve him with willing
Ne 4:6. peo. had a m. to work [m.
Jb. 23:13. he is of one m. who turn
Ps. 31:12. am as dead man out of m.
Pr. 21:27. bringeth it wi. wicked m.
29 : 11. A fool uttereth all his m.
Is. 26:3. whose m. is stayed on thee

Is. 46:8. bring it to m. O transgr-rs
65:17.former sh. not come into m.
Je.3:16. ark of cov. not come to m.
22: † 27. to land they lift their m.
44: 21. came it not into his m.?
Da.5:20.when his m. was hardened
Ha. 1: 11. then shall his m. change
Mk. 5: 15. in right m.. Lu. 8: 35.
14: 72. Pe. called to m. words of
Lu.1:29. Mary cast in her m. [Jes.
12: 29. nei. be ye of doubtful m.
Ac.2:†6. mult. were troubled in m.
12:†20. Herod bore a hostile m.ag.
17:11.word with all readiness of m.
20: 19. Serving L. with humility of
Ro.1:28. up to a reprobate m. [m.
7: 25. with m. I serve law of God
8: 7. carnal m. is enmity ag. God
27. knoweth what is m. of Spirit
11: 34. who hath known m. of L.?
12:16. be of the same m. one tow.
14:5.fully persuaded in his own m.
15: 6. with one m. glorify God
15. putting you in m. because of
1 Co. 1: 10. ye be joined in same m.
2: 16. who hath known m. of L.
But we have the m. of Christ
2 Co.8:12.if willing m.it is accepted
13: 11. brethren be of one m., Ph.
1: 27.-2: 2. [and m.
Ep.2:3. fulfilling the desires of flesh
4: 17. Gent. walk in vanity of m.
Ph. 2: 3. in lowliness of m. let each
5. Let this m. be in you,was in C.
4: 2. be of the same m. in the L.
Col.2:18.puffed up by his fleshly m.
3:†2. Set your m. on things above
12.Put on kindn.,humblen.of m.
2 Th.2: 2. be not soon shaken in m.
2 Ti.1:7.given us spirit of sound m.
Tit.1:15. m. and conscience defiled
3:1. Put them in m. to be subject
He.8:10. put my laws into their m.
12:† 17. no way to change his m.
1 Pe. 3: 8. be ye all of one m.
4:1. arm yours. with the same m.
5:2. not for lucre, but of ready m.
Re.17:9. is m. which hath wisdom
13. These have one m. and shall
See ALIENATED. [give

Mine own or my MIND.

Nu. 16: 28. I have not done them
of m. o. m. [m. o. m.
24:13. I cannot do good or bad of
1 S. 2: 35. acc. to that is in m. m.
1 Ch. 22: 7. in m. m. to build ho.
Is. 21: † 4. m. m. wandered [peo.
Je. 15: 1. m. m. could not be tow.
19: 5. nei. came it into m. m.,32:
La.3:21.This I recall to m.m. [35.
Ro. 7: 23. law warring ag. law of m.

Thy MIND. [m.

1 S. 9: 20. set not t.m. on the asses
20: † 4. say what is t.m. I will do
Jb. 34:33. Should it be acc. to t.m.
Eze. 38: 10. things come into t.m.
Da. 2: 29. thoughts came into t.m.
Mat.22:37.shalt love L. thy G. with
all t.m., Mk. 12: 30. Lu.10:27.
Phm. 14. without t. m. would I do

Your MIND. [noth.

Ge. 23: 8. If it be y.m. I sho. bury
Je.51:50. let Jerus. come into y.m.
Eze. 11: 5. I know things come into
20:32.wh.cometh into y.m.[y.m.
Ro.12:2. transf-d by renewing of y.
2 Co.7:7.y. fervent m. tow.me [m.
8: 19. declaration of y. ready m.
9: 2. I know forwardn. of y. m.
Ep. 4: 23. renewed in spirit of y.m.
Col. 1: 21. were enemies in y. m.
3: † 2. Set y. m. on things above
1 Pe.1:13. gird up the loins of y.m.

MINDS.

Ju. 19: 30. consider, speak your m.
2 S. 17: 8. be chafed in their m.
2 K. 9: 15. If your m. let none go
Eze. 24: 25. whereupon they set m.
36: 5. with despiteful m. to cast
Ac. 14: 2. their m. evil affected
28:6.changed m. said he was a god
2 Co.3:14. but their m.were blinded
4: 4. god of this world blinded m.
11:3.so your m. sho. be corrupted
Ph. 4: 7. peace of G. keep your m.
1 Ti. 6: 5. men of corrupt m., 2 Ti.
3: 8. [write them
He. 10: 16. and in their m. will I
12: 3. lest ye be faint in your m.
2 Pe. 3:1. I stir up your pure m. by

MIND. [Verb]

Ro. 8: 5. after flesh, m. thi. of flesh
12: 16. m. not high things, but
Ph. 3: 16. let us m. the same thing
19. many who m. earthly things

MINDED.

Ru.1:18.she was steadfastly m.to go
2 Ch. 24: 4. Joash was m. to repair
Ezr. 7: 13. are m. of own free will
Mat.1:19.Jo. was m. to put her aw.
Ac. 27: 39. were m. to thrust ship
Ro.8:6. to be carnally m. is death,
to be spiritually m. is life
2 Co. 1: 15. I was m. to come [ness
17.when thus m. did I use light-
Ga. 5: 10. you be no otherwise m.
Ph. 3: 15. as many as be perfect, be
thus m.if ye be otherwise m.G.
See DOUBLEMINDED, FEEBLE-MINDED, HIGHMINDED, LIKE-MINDED, SOBERMINDED.

MINDFUL.

1 Ch. 16: 15. Be ye m. of his cov-t
Ne. 9: 17. fa-s not m. of wonders
Ps. 8:4. What is man, that thou art
m. of him, He. 2: 6. [covenant
111: 5. he will ever be m. of his
115:12.the Lord hath been m.of us
Is. 17: 10. not been m. of the rock
2 Ti. 1: 4. being m. of thy tears
He. 11: 15. if been m. of country
2 Pe. 3: 2. that ye be m. of words

MINDING.

Ac.20:13. Paul m. hims.to go afoot
Ro.8:†6.m. of flesh, m.of spirit,†7.

MINE. [Noun.]

Jb. 28: † 1. surely is a m. for silver

MINE.

Ge. 31:43. all that thou seest is m.
48:5. are m. as Reuben sh. be m.
Ex. 13: 2. all firstborn, of man and
beast, it is m., 34:19. Nu.3:13.
19: 5. the earth is m., Ps. 50: 12.
Le. 20: 26. ye sho. be m., Is. 43: 1.
25: 23. land is m. ye are strangers
Nu.3:12. Lev. shall be m.,45.-8:14.
8: 17. firstborn of Israel are m.
2 S. 14: 30. Joab's field is near m.
1 K.2:15.knowest kingdom was m.
3:26.Let it be neither m. nor thine
20:3.Thy silver, gold, wives,are m.
2 K.10:6.If ye will be m.and heark.
Jb.41:11.whatso. under heav. is m.
Ps. 18: 23. I kept from m. iniquity
50:10. ev. beast of the forest is m.
11. wild beasts of field m. [108:8.
60:7.Gilead is m. Manasseh is m.,
Pr. 8: 14. Counsel is m. and wisd.
Can. 2: 16. My beloved is m., 6: 3.
8:12.vineyard, wh. is m. is bef.me
Je.44:28. whose words stand, m. or
Eze 16:8. sware, thou becamest m.
18:4.all souls are m.; as the soul of
the father, so soul of son is m.
23: 4. and they were m.
5.played harlot when she was m.
29: 9. The river is m. I made it
35: 10. two countries shall be m.
Hag. 2: 8. silver is m. gold is m.
Mal. 3: 17. they sh. be m. saith L.
Mat.7:24. heareth sayings of m.,26.
20: 23. to sit on my right hand is
not m. to give, Mk. 10: 40.
Lu.11:6.friend of m. in his journey
Jn. 2: 4. m. hour is not yet come
7:16.Jes.said,My doctrine is not m
10:14.sheep, and am known of m.
14:24. word wh. ye hear is not m.
16:14.he sd. receive of m.and shew
15.All things Father hath are m.
17: 10. all m. thine, thine are m.
Ro. 12: 19. Vengeance is m. I will
Ph.1:4. in ev. prayer of m. making

MINGLE.

Is. 5: 22. men to m. strong drink
9 :† 11. Lord shall m. his enemies
19:†2. I will m. Egyp-ns with E-s
Da. 2:43. shall m. with seed of men

MINGLED.

Ex. 9: 24. was fire m. with the hail
Le. 19:19. not sow field wi. m. seed
Ezr. 9: 2. holy seed m. with people
Jb. 24:†6. reap every one m. corn
Ps.102:9.m. my drink with weeping
106: 35. were m. among heathen
Pr. 9: 2. she hath m. her wine
5. drink of wine wh. I have m.
Is. 19: 14. Lord m. perverse spirit
Je. 25: 20. cup to all m. peo., 24.
50: 37.A sword upon chariots and
all the m. peo., Eze. 30: 5.
Mat. 27: 34. gave him vinegar m.
Mk. 15: 23. gave him wine m. with
Lu.13:1.whose blood Pilate had m.
Re. 8:7. hail and fire m. with blood
15: 2. as a sea of glass m.with fire

MINI'AMIN. [M.

2 Ch. 31: 15. next him were Eden,
Ne. 12:17. chief of fa-s of M. | †5,41.

MINISH, ED. [task

Ex. 5: 19. Ye sh. not m. aught of
Ps. 107: 39. Again they are m-d

MINISTER. [Noun.]

Ex. 24: 13. Moses and his m. Josh.
Jos.1:1.spake unto Josh.Moses' m.
2 K.6:†15. m. of Elisha [Mk.10:43.
Mat. 20: 26. let him be your m.,
Lu. 4: 20. gave book again to m.
Ac. 13: 5. had John to their m.
26: 16. to make thee m. and witn.
Ro. 13: 4. is m. of G. to thee
15: 8. Christ was a m. of circumc.
16. I sho. be m. of Jes. to Gent.
Ga. 2: 17. is Christ the m. of sin?
Ep. 3: 7. Whereof I was made a m.,
Col. 1: 23, 25. [L., Col. 4: 7.
6: 21. Tychicus, a faithful m. of
Col. 1: 7. Epaphras a faithful m.
1 Th. 3: 2. Timothy bro. and m. of
1 Ti. 4: 6. thou shalt be a good m.
He. 8: 2. A m. of the sanctuary

MINISTER. [Verb.]

Ex. 28: 1. m. unto me in priest's
office, 3, 4, 41.-29: 1, 4.-30:30.-
31:10.-35:19.-39:41.-40: 13, 15.
Je. 33: 22. Eze. 43: 19.
35. it shall be upon Aaron to m.
43.unto altar to m.,29:30.-30:20.
29: 44. I will sanctify Aa. to m.
39:26. round hem of robe to m. in
41. garms. to m. in priest's office
Le. 7: 35. he presented them to m.
16: 32. consecrate to m., Nu. 3:3.
Nu. 1: 50. they shall m. unto it
3: 6. that they may m. unto him
31. vessels wh. they m., 4:9,12,
8:26. sh. m. with their breth. [14.
16:9.before congr.to m. unto them
18:2. joined unto thee and m. (2)
De.10:8.tribe of Levi to m.unto him
17: 12. priest that standeth to m.
18: 5. to m. in name of L., 7.
21:5. God hath chosen them to m.
1 S. 2: 11. the child did m. unto L.
1 K. 8: 11. priests could not stand
to m. bec. of cloud, 2 Ch.5:14.
1 Ch.15:2. chosen to m. before him
16: 4. Levites to m. before ark
37. Asaph and breth. to m. bef.
23: 13. to m. and give thanks, 2
26:12. to m. in ho. of L. [Ch.31:2.

2 Ch. 8 : 14. to praise and **m.** before priests [Aaron
13 : 10. priests wh. **m.** are sons of
23:6. save they that **m.** of Levites
24:14.for h.of L.even vessels to **m.**
29:11.chosen you th.ye **m.**unto L.
Ne. 10:36. unto priests that **m.**, 39.
Ps. 9 : 8. shall **m.** Judgment to peo.
Is. 60 : 7. rams of Nebaioth sh. **m.**
10. their kings sh. **m.** unto thee
Je. 33: 22. multiply Levites that **m.**
Eze. 40 : 46. near to **m.**, 44 : 15, 16.
42:14. lay garms. wherein they **m.**
44:11. shall stand bef. them to **m.**
17.no wool upon th.while they **m.**
27. goeth into sanctuary to **m.**
45:4. wh. come near to **m.** unto L.
Mat.20:28. not to be ministered unto, but to **m.**, Mk. 10 : 45.
25 : 44. when saw we thee naked, or sick, and did not **m.** unto thee
Ac. 24 : 23. sh. forbid none of his acquaintance to **m.** unto him
Ro.15:25.I go to **m.** unto the saints
27. duty is to **m.** in carnal things
1 Co.9:13.wh. **m.**about holy things
2 Co. 9 : 10. both **m.** bread for food
Ep. 4 : 29. **m.** grace unto hearers
1 Ti.1:4.which **m.** questions rather
He. 1 : 14. to **m.** to heirs of salva.
6:10. minist-d to saints and do **m.**
1 Pe. 1:12. but unto us they did **m.**
4 : 10. so **m.** the same one to ano.
11.if any man **m.** let him do it as

MINISTERS.

1 K.10:5.attendance of **m.**,2 Ch.9:4.
Ezr. 7 : 24. not lawful to impose toll upon **m.** of house
8 : 17. should bring unto us **m.**
Ps. 103 : 21. ye **m.** of his that do
104 : 4. **m.** a flaming fire, He. 1:7.
Is.61:6. sh. call you **m.** of our God
Je.33:21.my cov.be broken with **m.**
Eze.44:11. shall be **m.** in my sanct.
45:4. holy portion for **m.** of sanct.
5. **m.** of house have for thems.
46 : 24. **m.** of house shall boil sac.
Jo. 1 : 9. the Lord's **m.** mourn
13. howl ye **m.** of the altar
2:17.Let **m.** of L.weep betw.porch
Lu. 1 : 2. from beginn. were **m.** of
Ro.13:6. they are G.'s **m.** attending
1 Co. 3 : 5. **m.** by whom ye believed
4 : 1. so account of us as **m.** of C.
2 Co. 3 : 6. who made us able **m.**
6:4. approving ours. as **m.** of God
11:15. if his **m.** be transformed as **m.** of righteousness [more
23. Are they **m.** of Christ? I am

MINISTERED.

Nu. 3 : 4. Eleazar **m.**, De. 10 : 6.
1 S. 2 : 18. Samuel **m.** bef. L., 3: 1.
2 S. 13 : 17. Amnon called serv. that
1 K.1:4.Abishag **m.**to Da.,15. [**m.**
19 : 21. went after Elijah, and **m.**
2 K. 25 : 14. they took aw. pots, and vessels whw. they **m.**,Je.52:18.
1 Ch. 6:32. **m.** bef. dwellingplace of
28:1. **m.** unto king by course [tab.
2 Ch.22:8.found that **m.**to Ahaziah
Es. 2 : 2. king's serv-s that **m.**, 6:3.
Eze. 44 : 12. they **m.** bef. their idols
19.sh.put off garms.whw.they **m.**
Da. 7 : 10. thousands **m.** unto him
Mat.4:11. angels came and **m.** unto him,Mk.1:13.[Mk.1:31.Lu.4:39.
8 : 15. she rose and **m.** unto them
20:28.not to be **m.** unto,Mk.10:45.
Mk. 15 : 41. Who also **m.** unto him
Lu. 8 : 3. **m.** unto him of substance
Ac. 13 : 2. as they **m.** and fasted
19 : 22. sent into Macedonia two that **m.** [necessities
20 : 34. hands have **m.** unto my
2 Co. 3 : 3. epistle of C. **m.** by us
Ph. 2 : 25. he that **m.** to my wants
Col. 2 : 19. having nourishment **m.**

1 Ti. 3:†13. **m.** office of deacon [me
2 Ti. 1:18. many things he **m.** unto
Phm. 13. thy stead he might have
He.6:10. ye have **m.** to saints [**m.**
2 Pe. 1:11. an entrance be **m.** unto

MINISTERETH. [you

2 Co. 9 : 10. he th. **m.** seed to sower
Ga. 3 : 5. that **m.** to you the Spirit

MINISTERING. [N. and P.]

1 Ch. 9: 28. had charge of **m.** vessels
Eze.44:11.**m.**to the house [Jes. **m.**
Mat. 27 : 55. many women followed
Ro. 12:7. ministry let us wait on **m.**
15 : 16. That I **m.** the gospel
2 Co. 8:4. take upon us **m.**to saints
9:1.for as touching **m.**to the saints
He.1:14. Are they not all **m.** spirits
10:11. ev. priest standeth daily **m.**

MINISTRATION. [ended

Lu. 1 : 23. soon as days of **m.** were
Ac.6:1.widows neglected in daily **m.**
2 Co. 3 : 7. if **m.** of death glorious
8. **m.** of the Spirit be glorious? 9.
9:13. by the experiment of this **m.**

MINISTRY, IES.

Nu. 4 : 12. sh. take all instru. of **m.**
47. that came to do service of **m.**
2 Ch. 7 : 6. Da. praised by their **m.**
Ho.12:10. used similitudes by **m.** of
Ac. 1 : 17. had obtained part of **m.**
25.That may take part of this **m.**
6 : 4. we will give ourselves to **m.**
12:25. when had fulfilled their **m.**
20:24.so that I might finish my **m.**
21:19.things G.wrought by his **m.**
Ro. 12 : 7. Or **m.** let us wait on our
1 Co. 12: † 5. are differences of **m**-s
16 : 15. addicted to **m.** of saints
2 Co. 4 : 1. seeing we have this **m.**
5:18. given us **m.** of reconciliation
6 : 3. no offence, that **m.** be not
Ep. 4 : 12. for work of **m.** [blamed
Col. 4:17.Take heed to the **m.** thou
1 Ti. 1:12.putting me into **m.** [**m.**
2 Ti. 4 : 5. make full proof of thy
11. he is profitable to me for **m.**
He. 8 : 6. obtained more excell-t **m.**
9:21.he sprinkled vessels of the **m.**

MIN'NI.

Je. 51:27. call ag. her kingd-s of M.

MIN'NITH. [to M.

Ju. 11 : 33. smote th. till thou come
Eze. 27:17. traded wheat of M. and

MINSTREL, S. [Pannag

2 K.3:15.but now bring me a **m.**(2)
Mat. 9:23. when Jesus saw the **m**-s

MINT.

Mat. 23:23. ye pay tithe of **m.**anise
Lu. 11:42.ye tithe **m.**and all herbs

MIPH'KAD. [M.

Ne. 3 : 31. of merchants ov. ag. gate

MIRACLE.

Ex. 7 : 9. Pha. saying, Shew a **m.**
2 Ch. 32 : † 24. wrought **m.** for him
Mk. 6:52. consid-d not **m.** of loaves
9:39. wh. shall do **m.** in my name
Lu. 23 : 8. hoped to have seen **m.**
Jn. 4 : 54. this is sec. **m.** Jesus did
6 : 14. they had seen **m.** Jesus did
10 : 41. many said, Jn. did no **m.**
12:18. heard he had done this **m.**
Ac. 4 : 16. a notable **m.** been done
22. on whom this **m.**was shewed

MIRACLES.

Nu. 14 : 22. seen **m.** I have done
De. 11:3.chil.,th. have not seen **m.**
29:3.thine eyes have seen great **m.**
Ju. 6 : 13. where his **m.**our fa-s told
Jn.2:11.This beginn. of **m.** did Jes
23. man believed, when saw **m.**
3 : 2. no man do these **m.** exc. G.
6 : 2. mult. foll-d, bec. they saw **m.**
26. seek me, not bec. ye saw **m.**
7:31.will he do more **m.** than this
9:16.How can a sinner do such **m.**?
11 : 47. this man doeth many **m.**
12:37.tho. he had done so many **m.**

Ac.2:22. A man approved of God by
6 : 8. Stephen did great **m.** [**m.**
8 : 6. hearing and seeing the **m.**
13. wondered, beholding the **m.**
15 : 12. declaring **m.** God wrought
19 : 11. God wrought special **m.** by the hands of Paul [**m.**
1 Co. 12 : 10. To another working of
28. teachers, after that **m.** gifts of
29. are all workers of **m.**?
Ga. 3:5. th. worketh **m.** doeth be it
He. 2:4. God bearing witu. with **m.**
Re. 13 : 14. deceiveth them by **m.**
16:14. spirits of devils working **m.**
19 : 20. false prophet that wrought

MIRE. [**m.**

2 S. 22:43. I did stamp them as **m.** of street, Is. 10 : 6. Mi. 7 : 10.
Jb. 8:11.Can rush grow with-t **m.**?
30:19.He hath cast me into the **m.**
38 : † 38. dust is turned into **m.**
41:30.he spreadeth things upon **m.**
Ps. 69 : 2. I sink in deep **m.** where
14. Deliver me out of the **m.** let
Is. 57:20. whose waters cast up **m.**
Je. 38 : 6. in dungeon no water, but
22. thy feet are sunk in **m.** [**m.**
Zch. 9 : 3. fine gold as **m.** of streets
10:5.wh.tread their enemies in **m.**
2 Pe. 2 : 22. sow to her wallowing in

MIR'IAM. [**m.**

Ex. 15:20. M. took a timbrel in ha.
21. M. answered, Sing ye to L.
Nu. 12 : 1. M. spake against Moses
4. L. spake suddenly unto M., 5.
10. M. became leprous white
15. M. was shut out seven days
20 : 1. desert of Zin, M. died there
26 : 59. she bare unto Amram, M., 1 Ch. 6 : 3. [unto M.
De. 24 : 9. remember what God did
1 Ch. 4 : 17. she bare M., Shammai
Mi. 6 : 4. I sent bef. thee Moses, M.

MIR'MA.

1 Ch.8:10.Shachia, M.These his sons

MIRTH. [with **m.**

Ge. 31 : 27. I might have sent thee
Ne. 8:12. peo. went to make gr. **m.**
Jb. 21:†13. spend their days in **m.**
Ps. 137 : 3. wasted us desired **m.**
Pr. 14 : 13. end of **m.** is heaviness
Ec. 2 : 1. I will prove thee with **m.**
2. I said of **m.**, What doeth it?
7:4. heart of fools is in hou. of **m.**
8 : 15. then I commended **m.** bec.
Is. 24 : 8. **m.** of tabrets, joy of harp
11. **m.** of land is gone [ceaseth
Je. 7 : 34. I will cause to cease the voice of **m.** from Judah and Jerusalem,16:9.-25:10.Ho.2:11.
Eze. 21 : 10. furbished, should we

MIRY. [make **m.**?

Ps. 40 : 2. bro-t me out of **m.** clay
Eze. 47:11. **m.** places not be healed
Da. 2 : 41. iron mixed with **m.** clay

MISCARRYING.

Ho. 9 : 14. give them a **m.** womb

MISCHIEF, S.

Ge. 42 : 4. Lest some **m.** befall him
38.if **m.**befall him by way, 44:29.
Ex. 21 : 22. fruit depart, yet no **m.**,
32:12.For **m.**did bring th.out [23.
22. knowest people are set on **m.**
De. 32 : 23.I will heap **m**-s upon th.
1 S. 23 : 9. knew Saul practised **m.**
2 S. 16 : 8. thou art taken in thy **m.**
1 K. 11 : 25. besides **m.** Hadad did
20:7. see how this man seeketh **m.**
2 K. 7:9. if we tarry, **m.** will befall
Ne. 6 : 2. thought to do me **m.**
Es. 8 : 3. to put away **m.** of Haman
Jb.15:35.They conceive **m.** and bri.
Ps.7:14.he conceived **m.** bro-t forth
16. His **m.** sh. return upon head
10 : 7. under his tongue is **m.** and
14. thou beholdest **m.** and spite
26: 10. In whose hands is **m.** their

Ps. 28 : 3. speak peace, m. in hearts
36 : 4. wick. deviseth m. upon bed
52:1. Why boastest in m. O man?
2. Thy tongue deviseth m-s like
55 : 10. m. and sorrow in midst
62:3.How long will ye imagine m.
94:20. which frameth m. by a law
119:150. nigh that follow after m.
140 : 2. Wh. imagine m-s in heart
9. let m. of own lips cover them
Pr. 4 : 16. sleep not, except done m.
6 : 14. he deviseth m. continually
18. feet swift in running to m.
10:23.It is sport to a fool to do m.
11:27.seeketh m.it sh.come to him
12:21. wicked sh. be filled with m.
13:17.wick.messenger fall. into m.
17:20. hath perverse tongue falleth
24:2.their lips talk of m. [into m.
16. wicked sh. fall into m.,28:14.
Is. 47 : 11. m. shall fall upon thee
59:4. trust in vanity, conceive m.
Eze. 7 : 26. m. shall come upon m.
11 : 2. these the men devise m.
Da. 11:27.king's hearts be to do m.
Ho. 7 : 15. do imagine m. ag. me.
Mi.7:†3. great man uttereth the m.
Ac.13:10.O full of all m.thou child

MISCHIEVOUS.

Ps. 21:11. they imagined m. device
38:12. th. seek my hurt, speak m.
Pr. 24 : 8. be called a m. person
Ec. 10 : 13. his talk is m. madness
Eze. 38 : † 10. conceive m. purpose
Mi. 7:3. gr. man uttereth m. desire

MISERABLE.

Jb. 16 : 2. Job said, m. comforters
1 Co. 15 : 19. we of all men most m.
Re. 3 : 17. knowest not thou art m.

MISERABLY.

Mat. 21 : 41. will m. destroy wicked

MISERY, IES.

[men
Ju. 10:16.was grieved for m.of Isr.
Jb. 3:20.Wh. light to him is in m.?
11:16.Bec.thou shalt forget thy m.
Pr. 31 : 7. remem. his m. no more
Ec. 8 : 6. the m. of a man is great
La.1:7.Jerus. rememb-d in her m-s
3 : 19. Rememb-g mine afflic. m.
Ro. 3 : 16. Destruc. m.in their ways
Ja. 5:1 howl for your m-s that sh.

MIS'GAB.

Je. 48 : 1. M. is confounded and

MISH'AEL.

Ex.6:22. sons of Uzziel, M. Elzaphan
Zithri.
Le. 10:4. And Moses called M.
Ne.8:4.on Ezra's left hand stood M.
Da. 1 : 6. of the chil. of Judah, M.
7. gave unto M.name of Meshach
11. prince of eunuchs set Melzar
19.was found none like M. [ov.M.
2:17.Dan.made thing known to M.

MI'SHAL = MA'SHAL.

Jos. 21:30. out of tribe of Asher.M.

MI'SHAM.

1 Ch.8:12.sons of Elpaal,M.Shamed

MI'SHEAL = MI'SHAL.

Jos.19:26. border was Amad and M.

MISH'MA.

[1 : 30.
Ge. 25 : 14. sons of Ishm. M., 1 Ch.
1 Ch. 4 : 25. M son | 26. sons of M.

MISHMAN'NAH.

1 Ch.12:10.men of war,M.the fourth

MISH'RAITES.

[the M.
1 Ch. 2 : 53. families of Kirjath-je.,

MIS'PERETH = MIZ'PAR.

Ezr. 2 : 2†. Which came with Zerubbabel, M. Rehum, Ne. 7 : 7.

MIS'REPHOTH = MA'IM.

Jos.11:8. Isr. chased them unto M.,

MISS, ED, ING.

[13:6.
Ju.20:16.at hair breadth and not m.
1 S. 20 : 6. if thy fa. at all m. me
18. shalt be m-d† thy seat m-d
25:7.neither was there aught m-g
15. nei. m-d any thing as long as
1 S. 25 : 21. noth. m-d pertained to
1 K.20:39.if he be m-g then thy life

MIST.

Ge. 2 : 6. went up a m. from earth
Ac. 13 : 11. there fell on him a m.
2 Pe.2:17. to whom m. of darkn. is

MISTRESS.

[reserved
Ge. 16:4. Sarah her m.was despised
8. I flee from my m. Sarai
9. angel said, Return to thy m.
1 K. 17 : 17. son of the m. fell sick
2 K.5:3.said unto her m.,Would G.
Ps. 123 : 2. as eyes of maiden to m.
Pr. 30 : 23. that is heir to her m.
Is. 24 : 2. as with maid so with m.
Na. 3 : 4. m. of witchcrafts, that

MISUSED.

2 Ch. 36 : 16. they m. his prophets

MITE, S.

[2.
Mk. 12 : 42. threw in 2 m-s, Lu. 21 :
Lu.12:59.till hast paid very last m.

MITH'CAH.

Nu. 33 : 28. and pitched in M., 29.

MITH'NITE. See JOSHAPHAT.

MITH'REDATH.

Ezr. 1:8.did Cyrus bring by ha. of M.
4 : 7. days of Artaxerxes wrote M.

MITRE.

[-39 : 28.
Ex. 28:4. they shall make a m., 39.
37. a blue lace upon the m., 28 :
37.-39 : 31.
29:6. shalt put m. upon his head
Le. 8 : 9. put holy crown upon m.
16 : 4. with linen m. be attired
Zch. 3 : 5. a fair m. on his head (2)

MITYLE'NE.

Ac. 20 : 14. took Paul in came to M.

MIXED.

Ex. 12 : 38. a m. multitude went up
Nu. 11 : 4. m. multi. fell a lusting
Ne. 13 : 3. separated from Israel m.
Pr. 23:30. go to seek m. wine [mult.
Is. 1 : 22. thy wine m. with water
Da. 2:41. sawest iron m.wi.clay,43.
Ho. 7 : 8. Ephr. m. himself am. peo.
He. 4 : 2. not being m. with faith

MIXTURE.

Ex. 8 : † 21. m. of noisome beasts
12:†38. a great m. went wi. them
Ps 75 : 8. is a cup, it is full of m.
Can.7:†2.goblet wh. wanteth not m.
Jn.19:39. Nicodemus, and bro-t m.
Re. 14 : 10. poured out without m.

MI'ZAR.

Ps.42:6.I will remember thee fr m.

MIZ'PAH.

Ge. 31 : 49. name of heap was M.
1 K. 15 : 22. Asa built Geba of Benj.
and M., 2 Ch. 16 : 6.
2 K. 25 : 23. came to Gedaliah to M.
even Ishmael, Je. 41 : 1.
25. Ishm. smote Chaldees at M.
Ne. 3 : 7. men of Gibeon and M.
15. Shallum ruler of M. | 19.Ezer
Je. 40 : 6. Jere. went to M., 8, 15.
10. behold, I will dwell at M.
12. unto M. and gather wine and
41 : 3. Ishmael slew all Jews at M.
6. Ishmael went forth from M.
14.Ishm.carried cap.from M. [M.
16. Johanan took peo. recov-d fr.
Ho. 5:1. ye have been a snare on M.

MIZ'PAR. See MISPERETH.

MIZ'PEH.

Jos.11:3.und.Hermon in land of M.
8. unto valley of M. eastward
15 : 38. Dilean M. cities of Judah
18:26. M. Chephirah cities of Benj.
Ju. 10 : 17. Israel encamped in M.
11 : 11. Jeph. uttered words in M.
29. Jeph. passed over M. M., 34.
20 : 1. Isr. was gathered in M., 3.
21:1. men of Isr. had sworn in M.
5. came not to M. shall die, 8.
1 S. 7 : 5. Gather all Israel to M.
6. Samuel judged Isr. in M., 16.
11. men of Isr. went out of M.
1 S. 7:12. Sam. took stone set it btw.
10:17.Samuel called peo. to M. [M.
22 : 3. David went to M. of Moab

MIZ'RAIM.

Ge.10:6.sons of Ham, Cush, M., 1 Ch.
13.M.begat Ludim, 1 Ch. 1:11. [1:8.

MIZ'ZAH. See REUEL.

MNA'SON.

Ac. 21 : 16. bro-t M. an old disciple

MO'AB.

Ge. 19 : 37. firstb. bare son, name M.
36:35. Hadad smote Midian in M.,
1 Ch. 1 : 46. [men of M.
Ex. 15 : 15. trembl. take hold upon
Nu. 21 : 11. wilderness of M. [8.
13. border of M., 15.-33:44.Is.15:
21: 20. country of M., Ru. 1:6, 22.
-2: 6.-4 : 3. 1 Ch. 8 : 8.
28. it hath consumed Ar of M.
29. Woe to thee, M., Je. 48 : 46.
22 : 3. M. was sore afraid, and M.
4. M. said to elders of Midian | 7.
36. to meet him unto a city of M.
24 : 17. shall smite corners of M.
31 : 12. bro-t spoil to camp at M.
De. 1 : 5. in land of M. began Moses
2 : 18. art to pass thro. coast of M.
29:1.make cov.with Isr.in la. of M.
32 : 49. mount wh. is in land of M.
34 : 5. Moses died in land of M.
6. buried Moses in a valley in M.
Ju. 3 : 29. they slew of M. 10,000
30. M. was subdued under Israel
10 : 6. Israel served the gods of M.
11 : 15. Israel took not land of M.
18. compassed land of M.
Ru. 1 : 2. Elimelech came into M.
4. sons took wives of wom. of M.
1 S. 14 : 47. Saul fought against M.
22 : 3. David went to Mizpeh of M.
2 S. 8 : 2. David smote M. and
23 : 20. slew 2 lionlike men of M.
1 K.11:7. Chemosh the abom. of M.
2 K. 1 : 1. M. rebelled against Israel
3:7.wilt go with me ag. M. | 10,13.
23.kings slain, thf. M.to the spoil
1 Ch. 4 : 22. Saraph had dominion
18 : 2. David smote M. [in M.
11. silver, gold, he brought fr. M.
2 Ch. 20 : 1. M. came ag. Jehosh-t
10. how children of M. reward us
22. ambushment ag. chil. of M. |
Ne. 13 : 23. married wives of M. | 23.
Ps. 60 : 8. M. is my washpot, 108:9.
83 : 6. M. is confederate ag. thee
Is. 11 : 14. shall lay hand upon M.
15 : 1. burden of M. Ar of M. Kir
of M. laid waste, 16: 13. Je. 48:
1. Eze. 25 : 8. Am. 2 : 2.
2. M. shall howl over Nebo
4. armed soldiers of M. sh. cry
5. my heart shall cry out for M.
16 : 4. Let outcasts dwell with thee
6.heard pride of M.,Je.48:29. [M.
11. my bowels like harp for M.
13. word L. hath spoken conc. M.
14.glory of M.shall be contemned
25 : 10. M. shall be trodden down
Je. 9 : 26. I will punish E. Jud. M.
25:21. I made M. drink of the cup
40:11. all the Jews returned fr. M.
48 : 2. be no more praise of M. | 4.
9.give wings to M. that it may flee
11.M. hath been at ease fr. youth
13.M.sh. be ashamed of Chemosh
15.M. is spoiled, 18. | 18.calam.of
20.tell in Arnon M. is spoiled [M.
24. judgm. is come upon cities of
25. The horn of M. is cut off [M.
26. M. shall wallow in his vomit
28.O ye in M.leave the cities | 31.
33. joy and gladn. is taken fr. M.
38. upon housetops of M. | 35,36.
39. how hath M. turned the back
40. wings over M. | 41, 43, 44, 45.
47. will bring again captiv. of M.
Eze. 25: 9. will open side of M. | 11

Am. 2 : 1. for 3 transgr-ns of M. I
will not turn away punishment
2. will send a fire upon M.
Zph.2:9.Surely M. shall be as Sodom
See DAUGHTERS,KING,PRINCES,
PLAIN, S.

MO'ABITE.

De.23:3. a M. shall not enter congr.
to 10th generation, Ne. 13 : 1.
1 Ch. 11 : 46. valiant man, Ithmah

MO'ABITES. [the M.

Ge. 19 : 37. same is fa. of the M.
Nu. 22:4. Balak was king of the M.
De. 2 : 9. Lord said, Distress not M.
11. the M. call them Emim
29. As the M. wh. dwell in Ar, did
Ju. 3 : 28. Lord hath delivered M. to
2 S. 8 : 2. M. became David's serv-s
and brought gifts, 1 Ch. 18 : 2.
1 K. 11 : 1. Sol. loved women of M.
33. wersh-d Chemosh god of M.
2 K. 3 : 18. he will deliver M. into
21. when M. heard kings were come
22. the M. saw water red as blood
24. the Israelites smote the M.
13 : 20. bands of M. invaded land
24 : 2. L. sent ag. him bands of M.
Ezr.9:1. acc. to abominations of M.

MOABI'TESS. [M.

Ru. 1:22. Naomi ret-d and Ruth the
2 : 2. Ruth M. said Let me now go
21. Ruth M. said, He said unto me
4:5. must buy field of Ruth the M.
10. Ruth the M. have I purchased
2 Ch. 24 : 26. the son of Shimrith a

MOABI'TISH. [M.

Ru.2:6.and said, It is the M. damsel

MOADI'AH. See MAADIAH.

MOCK. [Noun.]

Pr. 14 : 9. Fools make a m. at sin

MOCK. [Verb.]

Ge.39:14.bro-t Hebrew to m. us,17.
1 S. 31 :† 4. lest uncirc-d thrust me
thro. and m. me, 1 Ch. 10 :† 4.
Jb. 13 : 9. as one mocketh, ye so m.
21 : 3. after I have spoken, m. on
Pr. 1: 26. I will m. when your fear
Je. 9:†5. will m. ev. one neighbour
38: 19. lest deliver me, and m. me
La. 1 : 7. did m. at her sabbaths
Eze.22:5.m. thee who art infamous
Mat.20:19.deliver to Gent.to m. him
Mk. 10 : 34. sh. m. him and scourge
Lu.14:29. lest they begin to m. him

MOCKED.

Ge.19:14. he seemed as one that m.
Nu.22:29.Because thou hast m. me
Ju. 16:10. Thou hast m. me,13,15.
1 K. 18: 27. at noon, Elijah m. th.
2 K.2:23.little chil.of city m.Elisha
2 Ch.30:10.laughed to scorn and m.
36:16. they m. messengers of God
Ne. 4 : 1. Sanballat m. the Jews
Jb. 12 : 4. I am as one m. of neighb.
Mat. 2 : 16. Herod saw he was m.
27 : 29. they bowed knee and m.,
31. Mk. 15 : 20. [entreated
Lu. 18 : 32. sh. be m. and spitefully
22:63. men that held Jes. m. him
23:11. Herod m. him | 36. soldiers
Ac.17:32.heard of resurr-n,some m.
Ga.6:7.Be not deceived,G. is not m.

MOCKER, S. [me?

Jb. 17 : 2. Are there not m-s with
Ps. 35 : 16. With hypocritical m-s
Pr.20:1. Wine is a m. stronk drink
Is.28:22. not m-s lest bands strong
Je. 15 : 17. I sat not in assembly of
Jude 18.be m-s in latter time-[m-s

MOCKEST, ETH.

Jb.11:3.when m-t sh. no man make
thee ashamed?
13:9. as one m-h do ye mock him?
39 : 22. He m-h at fear, is not affrighted [Maker
Pr. 17 : 5. m-h poor reproacheth
30:17.eye that m-h at his fa.eagles
Je. 20 : 7. I a derision, ev. one m-h

MOCKING. [Part.] [me

Ge. 21:9. saw the son of Hagar m.
Mat. 27 : 41. priests m., Mk. 15:31.
Ac.2:13. others m. said, These men

MOCKING, S.

Eze. 22 : 4. I made thee a m. to all
He. 11 : 36. had trial of cruel m-s

MODERATE. [m.

1 Co.10:†13.no tempta.but such as is

MODERATELY.

Jo. 2 : 23. given you former rain m.

MODERATING.

Ep. 6 : † 9. masters m. threatening

MODERATION. [to all

Ph. 4 : 5.Let your m. be known un-

MODEST.

1 Ti.2:9.women adorn in m.apparel
3 : † 2. A bishop must be sober, m.

MOIST.

Nu. 6:3. nor shall he eat m. grapes
Ju. 15 : † 15. m. jawbone
16 : † 7. If bind me with 7 m. withs
Ps. 66:†12. bro-test us unto m. pla.

MOISTENED. [row

Jb. 21 : 24. bones are m. with mar-
Is. 43:†24. hast m. me with sacrif.

MOISTENING.

Pr. 3:†8. It sh. be m. to thy bones

MOISTURE.

De.34:†7.nor m. abated [drought
Ps. 32 : 4. my m. is turned into
Lu. 8 : 6. withered bec. lacked m.

MOL'ADAH. [M.

Jos. 15 : 26. cities of Jud. Shema,
19 : 2. in their inherit. Sheba, M.
1 Ch.4:28.they dwelt at M.,Ne.11:26

MOLE, S.

Le. 11 : 30. snail, and m. are uncl.
Is.2:20.sh.cast idols to m-s and bats

MO'LECH. [to M.

Le. 18: 21. not let seed pass thro. fire
20:2.giveth of seed unto M. be put
to death, 3, 4. Je. 32 : 35.
1 K. 11:7. Sol. built high pla.for M.
2 K.23:10. make son pass thro. to M.

MO'LID.

1 Ch. 2: 29. she bare him Ahban and

MOLLIFIED. [M.

Is. 1: 6. nor m. with ointment

MO'LOCH.

Am.5:26.borne tabernacle of M , Ac.

MOLTEN. [7:43.

Ex. 32 : 4. fashioned it aft. he had
made m. calf, 8. De. 9 : 12, 16.
Ne. 9 : 18. Ps. 106 : 19. [19 : 4.
34:17. shalt make no m. gods, Le.
1 K. 7:16. two chapiters of m.brass
23. he made a m. sea, 2 Ch. 4: 2.
30. und. laver were undersetters
33. their spokes were all m. [m.
Jb. 28 : 2. brass is m. out of stone
37 : 18. sky as a m. lookingglass
Eze. 24 : 11. filthiness of it be m.
Mi. 1 : 4. mts. shall be m. und. him
Na. 2 : † 6. palace of Nineveh sh. be

MOLTEN image, s. [m.

Ju. 17 : 4. the founder made a m. i.
18:14.Do ye know is in houses m.i.
17. the 5 men came and took ter-
raphim and m. i., 18. [i.-s Ye
Is. 42 : 17. ashamed that say to m.
48 : 5. my m.i. hath com-d th. [i.
Na.1:14. out of ho. will I cut off m.
Ha. 2 : 18. what profiteth m. i.
See Molten IMAGE, IMAGES.

MOMENT.

Ex. 33: 5. into midst of thee in a m.
Nu.16:21. consume them in m.,45.
Ezr. 9 :† 8. a m. grace been shewed
Jb. 7: 18. shouldest try him ev. m.
20 : 5. joy of hypocrite but for m.
21 : 13. in a m. go down to grave
34:20. In a m. shall they die [m.
Ps. 30 : 5. his anger endureth but a
73:19.wicked into desola.as in a m.
Pr.12:19.lying tongue is but for m.
Is. 26 : 20. hide as for a little m.
27 : 3. I the L. will water it ev. m.
47:9. two things sh. come in a m.
54:7 For a small m. have I forsak.
8. I hid my face fr. thee for a m.
Je. 4 : 20. and my curtains in a m.
La. 4 : 6. Sodom overthrown in a m.
Eze. 26:16. tremble at ev. m.,32:10.
Lu. 4 : 5. shewed kingd-s of world in
1 Co.15:52.all be changed in m.[m
2 Co.4:17. our affliction, but for m.

MONEY.

Ge. 23 : 9. as much m. as it is worth
13. I will give thee m. for field
16. 400 shekels silver, current m.
31:15.hath quite devoured our m.
42: 25. Joseph comm-ed to restore
ev. man's m., 35. [is restored
27. he espied his m. | 28. My m.
43:12. take double m. in hand, 15.
18. afraid, Bec. of m. returned
21. our m. in full weight
22. other m. we have brought (2)
23. fear not, I had your m.
44:1. put ev. man's m. in his sack's
mouth, 2, 8.-43: 21. [in Egypt
47:14. Joseph gathered all the m.
15.m. faileth | 18.our m. is spent
16. give cattle if m. fail
Ex. 21 : 11. she sh. go out with-t m.
21. he is his m. | 35. divide m.
30. if he laid on him a sum of m.
34. give m. unto owner of them
22:7.if unto his neighb. m. to keep
17.pay m. acc.to dowry of virgin
25. if lend m. to any of my peo.
30 : 16. take atonement m. of Isr.
Le. 25 : 37. Thou shalt not give m.
upon usury, De. 23 : 19.
27 : 15. add 5th part of m., 19.
18. priest sh. reckon to him m.
Nu. 3: 48. give m. unto Aaron, 51.
49. Moses took redemption m.
50.of firstborn of Isr. took he m.
18 : 16. redeem for m. of 5 shekels
De. 2 : 6. buy meat, wat. for m., 28.
14:25. turn it into m. | 26. bestow
m.or whatso.soul lusteth [m.
21 : 14. shalt not sell her at all for
Ju. 5 : 19. they took no gain of m.
16 : 18. lords bro-t m. to Delilah
17 : 4. restored m. unto his moth.
1 K. 21: 2. I will give worth of it in
6. Give me viney.for m.,15. [m.
2 K. 5 : 26. Is it a time to receive m.
12: 4. All the m. of dedicated thi.
7. now receive no more m., 8.
10. they saw was much m. in
chest, and told m. that was
found, 9. 2 Ch. 24 : 5, 11, 14.-
34 : 9, 14, 17. [was
16. The trespass m. and sin m.
15:20.Menahem exacted m. of Isr.
22 : 7. no reckoning made of m.
23:35. Jehoiakim gave m. to Pha.
Ezr. 3:7. gave m. unto masons and
7 : 17. buy speedily with m. rams
Ne.5:4.We have borrowed m.for k.
10. I and serv-s exact of th. m.
11. also 100th part of m. restore
Es. 4 : 7. m. Haman had promised
Jb.31:39.If I eaten fruits with-t m.
Ps. 15 : 5. putteth not m. to usury
Pr.7:20.He hath taken a bag of m.
Ec. 7 : 12. wisd. and m. is a defence
10:19 m. answer-h all things [m.
Is 43:24. bought no sweet cane wi.
52:3.ye sh. be redeemed with-t m.
55 : 1. he that hath no m. come,
buy without m. [not bread
2. Wh. spend ye m. for that is
Je. 32 : 9. I weighed him the m., 10.
25. Buy thee the field for m.
44. Men shall buy fields for m.
La. 5: 4. drunken our water for m.
Mi.3:11. the prophets divine for m.
Mat. 25 : 18. in earth, hid lord's m.

Mat. 25 :27. oughtest to have put my m. to exchangers, Lu. 19:15,23
28: 12. gave large m. unto soldiers
15. took m., did as taught ⌈9 : 3.
Mk. 6 : 8. take no m. in purse, Lu.
12 : 41. peo. cast m. into treasury
14 : 11. promised him m., Lu. 22:5.
Ac. 4 :37. m., laid it at apostles' feet
8:18. Simon offered th. m. ⌈thee (2)
20. Peter said, Thy m. perish wi.
24 : 26. He hoped m. given of Paul
1 Ti. 6 : 10. love of m. root of all evil
See BOUGHT, PIECE, TRIBUTE.

MONEY with changers.

Mat. 21 : 12. Jesus overthrew tables of m. c. and seats of them that sold doves, Mk. 11 : 15. ⌈of m.
Jn. 2 : 14. Jesus found in temple c.
15. he poured out the c.' m. and

MONSTER, S.

Is. 34:†14. night m. sh. rest there
La. 4 : 3. sea m-s draw out breast

MONTH. ⌈m.

Ge. 29 : 14. Jac. abode with Laban a
Ex. 13 : 4. came ye out in m. Abib
23 : 15. keep the feast in m. Abib
34:18. in m. Abib thou camest out from E., De. 16 : 1. Jos. 5 : 10.
Le. 27:6. if it be fr. m. old to 5 years
Nu. 3 : 15. number ev. male fr. m. old, 22, 28, 34, 39, 40. 43.–26:62.
9:22. m. or y-r that cloud tarried
11 : 20. eat flesh, a whole m., 21.
18 : 16. from m. old shalt redeem
28 : 14. burnt off-g of ev. m., 29:6.
De. 16: 1. Observe m. Abib and (2)
21 : 13. remain in house a full m.
1 S. 20:27. 2d day of m. David's place
1 K. 4 : 7. each his m. made pro-
5:14. a m. were in Lebanon ⌊vis.,27
12:33. in m. which he had devised
2 K. 15 : 13. reigned a full m. ⌈m.
1 Ch. 27: 1. came in went out m. by
2 Ch. 29 :17. 8th day of m. to porch
Es. 8 : 9. 3d m. that is m. Sivan
9: 15. Jews gathered in m. Adar, 17, 19, 21. ⌈row to joy
22. m. which was turned fr. sor-
Je. 2:24. in her m. they sh. find her
Ho. 5:7. now shall a m. devour them
Am. 8 : † 5. When will m. be gone
Zch. 1:7. 11th m. wh. is m. Sebat
11:8. shepherds I cut off in one m.
Re. 9:15. prepared for a day and m.
22 : 2. yielded her fruit every m.
See BUL, CHISLEU, DAY, ELUL, ETHANIM, NISAN, TEBETH, ZIF.

First MONTH.

Ge 8:13. in f. m. the first day of m.
Ex. 12:2. sh. be the f. m. of the year
40:2. f. m. sh. thou set up tab., 17.
Nu. 9 : 1. wildern. of Sinai in f. m.
20 : 1. into desert of Zin in f. m.
28:16. 14th day of f. m. is passover, Ex. 12: 18. Le. 23:5. 2 Ch. 35:1. Ezr. 6:19. Eze. 45:21. ⌈of f. m.
33:3. fr. Rameses in f. m. 15th day
Jos. 4 : 19. people came up out of Jordan 10th day of f. m.
1 Ch. 12 : 15. over Jordan in f. m.
27 : 2. course for the f. m., 3.
2 Ch. 29:3. f. m. opened doors of ho.
17. f. m. to sanctify, f. m. made end
Ezr. 7 : 9. f. m. began to go to Bab.
8 : 31. f. m. to go unto Jerusalem
10 : 17. stra. wives by 1st day of f.
Es. 3:7. f. m. that is m. Nisan ⌊m.
12. scribes called on 13th day of f.
Eze. 30:20. came to pass in f. m. ⌊m.
45:18. In f. m. in first day, 29:17.
Da. 10:4. f. m. as I was beside river
Jo. 2:23. the latter rain in the f. m.

Second MONTH. ⌈up

Ge. 7 : 11. In s. m. fountains broken
8:14. in s. m. was earth dried ⌈m.
Ex. 16:1. unto wildern. of Sin on s.
Nu. 1 : 1. on s. m. take sum of congregation, 18. ⌈2, 13, 15.
9 : 11. s. m. keep passo., 2 Ch. 30 :
10:11. on s. m. cloud was taken up
1 K. 6 : 1. s. m. Sol. began to build, 2 Ch. 3 : 2. ⌈was Dodai
1 Ch. 27 : 4. over the course of s. m.
Ezr. 3 : 8. in s. m. began Zeruh. to appoint

Third MONTH.

Ex. 19:1. in t. m. came into wildern.
1 Ch. 27 : 5. capt. for t. m. Benaiah
2 Ch. 15:10. gath-d at Jerus. in t. m.
31:7. in t. m. began to lay founda.
Es. 8:9. scribes were called in t. m.
Eze. 31 : 1. in t. m. word of L. unto

Fourth MONTH. ⌊Eze.

2 K. 25 : 3. in f. m. famine prevailed
1 Ch. 27:7. capt. for f. m. was Asahel
Je. 39 : 2. f. m. city was broken up
52 : 6. in f. m. famine sore in city
Eze. 1:1. in f. m. Ezekiel saw visions
Zch. 8 : 19. The fast of f. m. be joy

Fifth MONTH.

Nu. 33:38. Aa. died 1st day of f. m.
2 K. 25:8. f. m. came Nebuz., Je. 52:
1 Ch. 27 : 8. capt. for f. m. ⌊12.
Ezr. 7 : 8 Ezra to Jerus. in f. m., 9.
Je. 1 : 3. Jerus. captive in the f. m.
28:1. f. m. Hananiah spake unto me
Eze 20:1. f. m. the elders sat bef. me
Zch. 7:3. Should I weep in the f. m.
5. ye fasted and mourned in f. m.
8:19. fast of f. m. be joy and gladn.

Sixth MONTH.

1 Ch. 27:9. sixth capt. for s. m. Ira
Eze. 8 : 1. in s. m. elders of Jud. sat
Hag. 1:1. s. m. word of Lord by Hag
15. in s. m. did work in h. of L.
Lu. 1 : 26. in s. m. Gabriel was sent
36. is s. m. with her that was bar-

Seventh MONTH. ⌊ren

Ge. 8:4 ark rested in s. m. upon mts.
Le. 16:29. in s. m. afflict your souls, 23 : 27.–25 : 9. Nu. 29 : 7.
23 : 24. in s. m. sh. ye have a sab.
39. 15th day of s. m., 34. Nu. 29:12.
41. ye shall celebrate it in s. m.
Nu. 29:1. in s. m. a convocation, 12.
1 K. 8:2. assembled at feast of s. m.
2 K. 25 : 25. in s. m. Ishmael smote Gedaliah, the Jews, Je. 41 : 1.
1 Ch. 27:10. 7th capt. for s. m. Helez
2 Ch. 7:10. s. m. Sol. sent them aw.
31: 7. they finished heaps in s. m.
Ezr. 3 : 1. when s. m. was, Ne. 7:73.
6. from first day of s. m. to offer
Ne. 8:2. first day of s. m. Ezra read
14. dw. in booths in feasts of s. m.
Je. 28 : 17. Hananiah died in s. m.
Eze. 45:25. s. m. shall he do the like
Hag. 2: 1. s. m. word came to Hag.
Zch. 7:5. when ye mourned in s. m.
8 : 19. fast of s. m. be to Jud. joy

Eighth MONTH. See EIGHTH.

Ninth MONTH. ⌈ezer

1 Ch. 27: 12. ninth capt for n. m. Abi-
Ezr. 10:9. n. m. people sat trembling
Je. 36:9. in n. m. proclaimed a fast
22. k. sat in winter ho. in n. m.
Hag. 2 : 10. n. m. came word of L.
18. fr. n. m. consider it ⌊by Hag.
Zch. 7 : 1. word came unto Zech. in

Tenth MONTH. ⌊n. m.

Ge. 8:5. waters decreased until t. m.
2 K. 25:1. to pass in t. m. that Neb.
1 Ch. 27:13. 10th capt. for t. m. Maharai ⌈examine
Ezr. 10 : 16. sat down in t. m. to
Es. 2:16. Es. taken unto k. in t. m.
Je. 39:1. t. m. Neb. ag. Jerus., 52:4.
Eze. 24 : 1. t. m. word of L., 29 : 1.
33:21. t. m. one th. escaped told me
Zch. 8 : 19. fast of t. m. be to Jud.

Eleventh MONTH.

De. 1:3. in e. m. Mo. spake unto Isr.
1 Ch. 27:14. capt. for e. m. Benaiah
Zch. 1:7. e. m. came word unto Zech.

Twelfth MONTH.

2 K. 25 : 27. on 27th day of t. m.
1 Ch. 27:15. the 12th capt. for t. m.
Es. 3:7. cast lots bef. Haman t. m.
13. 13th day of t. m., 8: 12.–9: 1.
Je. 52 : 31. in t. m. Evil-merodach
Eze. 32:1. t. m. word of L. came un-

This MONTH. ⌊to me

Ex. 12:2. t. m. be beginn. of months
3. t. m. take every man a lamb
13:5. keep this service in t. m., Nu. 9 : 3.–28 : 17. ⌈a convoca.
Nu. 29:7. have on 10th day of t. m.
Ne. 9:1. t. m. Isr. assembled wi. fast-

MONTHS. ⌊ing

Nu. 10:10. in beginnings of m. blow
28 : 11. in beginnings of m. offer a
14. this is burnt offering thro. m.
Ju. 11:37. let me alone two m., 38.
39. at end of two m. she returned
19 : 2. his concu. with her fa. 4 m.
20:47. in rock Rimmon 4 m. ⌈m.
1 S. 6 : 1. ark in country of Philis. 7
27:7. Da. with Philis. y-r and 4 m.
2 S. 24 : 8. to Jerus. at end of 9 m.
1 K. 5:14. two m. they were at home
11 : 16. six m. Joab remained in Edom ⌈12 m.
Es. 2 : 12 maids turned aft. she been
1 Ch 27:1. mo. by mo. thro m. of y-r
Jb. 3:6. not come into numb. of m.
7: 3. made to possess m. of vanity
14 : 5. number of his m. with thee
21 : 21. number of his m. is cut off
29 : 2. O that I were as in m. past
39 : 2. Canst thou number the m.
Is. 47:†13. that give knowl. conc. m.
Eze. 39 : 12. seven m. be burying of
14. aft. 7 m. sh. they search ⌊Gog
47 : 12. bring new fruit acc. to m.
Da. 4:29. end of 12 m. Neb. walked
Lu. 1:24. Elisa. conceiv. and hid 5 m.
Jn. 4 : 35. yet 4 m. then harvest
Ga. 4 : 10. Ye observe days and m.
Re. 9:5. sho. be tormented 5 m., 10.

Three MONTHS.

Ge. 38:24. t. m. after it was told ⌈m.
Ex. 2:2. goodly child, she hid him t.
2 S. 6:11. ark of L. in house of Obed-edom, t. m., 1 Ch. 13 : 14.
24 : 13. wilt thou flee t. m. before thine enemies, while, 1 Ch. 21:12.
2 K. 23 : 31. Jehoahaz, reigned t. m. in Jerus., 2 Ch. 36:2 ⌈Ch. 36:9.
24 : 8. Jehoiachin reigned t. m.. 2
Am. 4 : 7. were yet t. m. to harvest
Lu. 1:56. abode with her about t. m.
Ac. 7:20. Moses was nourished t. m.
19 : 8. Paul spake boldly t. m.
20 : 3. Paul abode in Greece t. m.
He. 11 : 23. Moses was hid t. m.

Six MONTHS.

2 S. 2:11. David was king in Hebron 7 years, s. m., 5 : 5. 1 Ch. 3 : 4.
1 K. 11 : 16. s. m. Joab remain. in
2 K. 15:8. Zach. reigned s. m. ⌊Edom
Es. 2 : 12. s. m. wi. oil of myrrh, s. m. wi. sweet odours for purify-g
Lu. 4:25. when heaven was shut up 3 years and s. m., Ja. 5 : 17.
Ac. 18:11. Paul at Corinth a year s.
See FORTY and two. ⌊m.

MONTHLY.

Is. 47:13. Let the m. prognosticators

MONUMENTS.

Is. 65:4. people which lodge in the m

MOON, S. ⌈m. †m-s

De. 33 : 14. precious things by the
Jos. 10 : 12. stand, m. in Ajalon, 13.
Ju. 8:† 21. took ornaments like m.
Jb. 25:5. Behold m. it shineth not
31:26. or m. walking in brightness
Ps. 8 : 3. When I consider the m.
72 : 7. peace long as m. endureth
89 : 37. be establ-d for ever as m.
104:19. appointeth m. for seasons

Is.3:18.their round tires like the m.
13:10. m. not cause light to shine,
Eze. 32:7. Mat. 24:29.Mk.13:24.
24: 23. the m. sh. be confounded
60: 19. neither shall m. give light
20. neither m. withdraw herself
Jo.2:31. m. into blood, Ac.2:20.Re.
Re.8:12.3d part of m.smitten [6:12.
12: 1. the m. under her feet
See STARS, SUN.

New MOON, S. [24.
1 S. 20: 5. to morrow is n. m., 18,
2 K. 4: 23. it is nei. n.m. nor sab.
1 Ch. 23: 31. to offer burnt sacrifices
in n.m-s, 2 Ch. 2:4.-8:13.-31:
3. Ezr. 3:5. Ne. 10:33. Eze.46:3.
Ps.81:3. Blow up trumpet in n.m.
Pr. 7:†20. will come home at n.m.
Is. 1:13. n.m-s I cannot away with
14. your n. m-s my soul hateth
66: 23. from one n.m. to another
Eze.45:17. drink offerings in n.m-s
46: 1. in n. m. it shall be opened
6. in n.m. offer a young bullock
Ho. 2:11. cause to cease her n.m-s
Am. 8: 5. When will n.m. be gone?
Col.2:16.no man judge you of n.m.

MO'RASTHITE. See MICAH.

MOR'DECAI. [7.
Ezr.2:2.M. came with Zerub-l,Ne.7:
Es. 2: 5. Jew, whose name was M.
7.whom M.took for own dau. | 10.
11. M. walked ev. day bef. court
19.M. sat in king's gate,21.| | 15.
20. as M. charged; Es. did com-t
22. thing was known to M.| of M.
3:3.k.'s servants said unto M.Why
4.Haman to see whe. M.'s matters
5. Haman saw M. bowed not
6.they had shewed him peo.of M.
4:1. M. rent his clothes, and put
4. she sent raiment to clothe M.
5.to M.to know what it was | 6,7.
9.Hatach told Es.words of M.[13.
10. Es. gave him com-t to M. | 12,
15.Es.bade ih. return M.this ans.
17. So M. went his way and did
5:9.when Haman saw M.that he(2)
13.long as I see M.at k.'s gate,6:12
14. gallows, th. M. be hanged [4.
6: 2. M. had told of Bigthana | 6:
3. what honour been done to M.
10. make haste, do even so to M.
11. arrayed M. and bro-t him on
13.if M.be of the seed of the Jews
7:9.gallows Haman made for M.,10.
8: 1. M. came before the king
2. king took his ring gave it unto
M.Es.set M. over ho. of Haman
7. king said to M. Behold I have
9. acc. to all M. com-d unto Jews
15. M. went out in royal apparel
9:3. bec. fear of M. fell upon them
4. M. was great in k.'s house (2),
20. M. wrote these, 23, 29. [10:2.
31. acc. as M. had enjoined them
10: 3. M. was next unto Ahasue-

MORE. [rus
Ge.29:30.Jac. loved Rachel m.than
36: 7. riches m. than that they
37:3. Isr. loved Jo. m. than all, 4.
5.breth. hated him yet the m., 8.
9. I have dreamed a dream m.
Ex. 1: 9. chil. of Israel m. than we
12. m. afflicted the m.they grew
5:9.Let m. work be laid upon men
9:34.Pha.sinned yet m.and hard-d
11:1.bring one plague m.upon Pha
16:17. gathered some m. some less
30: 15. rich not give m. nor poor
Le. 6: 5. sh. add fifth part m. [less
11:42.whatso. hath m. feet am.all
13:5.shut him up 7 days m.,33,54.
26:18. punish you 7 times m., 21.
Nu.3:46.firstborn are m. than Lev.
22:15. sent princes m. honourable
18.bey.word of L. to do less or m.

Nu.22:19.kn.what L say unto me m
26:54.to many give the m., 33:54.
De.1:11.L.make you thous.times m
7:7.not set love upon you, bec.m.
17. if say,nations m. than I,20:1.
19: 9. shalt thou add 3 cities m.
Jos. 10: 11. m. wh. died with hail
Ju. 2:19. they corrupted thems. m.
16:30. m. than they he slew in life
18: 24. Ye gone, what have I m.?
Ru. 1: 17. Ru. said, L. do so to me
and m., 1 S. 14: 44. 2 S. 3: 35.
-19: 13.
3: 10. m. kindn. in the latter end
1 S. 3: 17. G. do so to thee and m.
18: 8. what have m. but kingd.?
20:13.L.do so and much m.to Jona
22:15. serv. knew noth. less or m.
24:17.Thou art m.righteous than I
25:22.so and m. do G. unto enem.
36. she told him noth. less or m.
2 S. 3: 9. so do G. to Abner, and m.
5: 13. David took him m. concub.
6:22.I will yet be m.vile than thus
7:20.what can David say m.,1 Ch.
18:8.wood devoured m.than[17:18
19: 43. we have m. right in David
1 K. 2: 23. God do so, m. also, 20:
10. 2 K. 6: 31. [to anger
16:33. Ahab did m. to provoke G.
19:2. So let gods do to me,and m.
2 K. 4: 6. There is not a vessel m.
6: 16. they with us are m. than
they that be with them, 2 Ch.
32: 7. [do m. evil
21: 9. Manasseh seduced them to
1 Ch.21:3.L. make peo.so many m.
24: 4. were m. chief men found
2 Ch. 10: 11. I will put m. to yoke
20:25.found m. spoil than they co.
25: 9. Lord is able to give thee m.
28:13.intend to add m. to our sins
22. Ahaz did trespass yet m. ag.
29:34.the Levites were m. upright
32: 16. his serv-s spake m. ag. L.
33:23.Amon trespassed m.and m.
Ezr. 7: 20. whatso. m. be needful
Ne. 13: 18. yet ye bring m. wrath
Es.2:17.Es.obtained favour m.than
4:13.not thou escape m.than Jews
6:6.To wh.delight to do honour m.
Jb.3:21.dig for it m.than hid treas.
23:12. his words m. than my food
34:19. nor regardeth rich m. than
23. not lay upon man m. than
35:2.My righteousn.is m.than G.'s
11. who teach-h m. than beasts
42:12.blessed latter end of Job m.
Ps. 4: 7. m. than when their corn
19: 10. m. to be desired than gold
40:5.thy thoughts m. than can be
12.iniquities are m.than the hairs
52:3.thou lovest evil m. than good
69:4.th.hate me are m. than hairs
71:14.I will praise thee m. and m.
73:7. have m. than heart co. wish
78:17. they sinned yet m. ag. him
87:2.gates of Zion m. than all dw.
115:14.L. increase you m. and m.
119: 99. I have m. understanding
100. I underst. m. than ancients
130:6.m. than they that watch for
Pr. 3: 15. wisdom is m. precious
4:18.that shineth m.and m. unto
11:24.withholdeth m.than is meet
17:10.A reproof ent-h m. into wise
26: 12. is m. hope of a fool, 29:20.
Ec. 2: 9. I increased m. than all
16. no rememb. of wise m. than
25. who hasten m. than I? [fool
4:2.praise dead m. than the living
5: 1. be m. ready to hear than to
6: 8. hath wise m. than fool [10
7:19. Wisd.strength-h wise m.than
9:17. words of wise heard m. than
Can.1:4.we will remem. thy love m.
5:9.What is thy beloved m.than,9.

Is.5:4.What been done m.to viney.
9: 1. did m. grievously afflict her
15: 9. I will bring m. upon Dimon
52: 14. visage so marred m. than
54: 1. m. chil. of desolate than
Je. 3: 11. Israel justified herself m.
46: 23. are m. than grasshoppers
Eze.5:6. changed my judgments m.
7. be multiplied m. than nations
15:2.What is vine m.than any tree
16:47.thou wast corrupted m.than
they, 51, 52.-23:11. [m. than
Da. 2: 30. not for any wisd. I have
3:19. sho. heat furnace 7 times m.
11:8.sh.continue m. years than k.
Ho.6:6.knowl. of G. m. than burnt
13:2.now they sin m.and m.[off-g
Jon.1:†11. m.and m. tempestuous
Ha.1:13. devoureth man m. righte.
2: † 16. filled m. with shame [evil
Mat.5:37. m. than these cometh of
47. what do ye m. than others?
6: 25. Is not the life m., Lu.12:23.
10: 31. of m. value than, Lu.12:7.
37. that loveth fa. or mother m.
11:9. m. than a prophet, Lu.7:26.
12: 45. taketh 7 spirits m. wicked
13: 12. he sh. have m. abundance
18:13. he rejoiceth m. of th. sheep
16. take with thee one or two m.
20: 10. supposed sho. received m.
31. cried the m. Have mercy,27:
23. Mk. 10:48.-15:14. Lu. 18:39.
21: 36. other serv-s m. than first
23: 15. twofold m. child of hell
26:53. give me m. than 12 legions
Mk. 4: 24. unto you th. hear m. be
7:36. m. he charged th. so the m.
12:33.is m.than whole burnt off-gs
43. widow cast in m., Lu. 21: 3.
14: 5. might have been sold for m.
Lu. 10: 35. what thou spendest m. I
12: 48. of him they will ask m.
18:30. sh. not receive manifold m.
Jn. 4:41. many m. believed, bec. of
5: 18. Jews sought the m. to kill
7: 31. do m. miracles than these?
12:43.they loved praise of men m.
15:2.th.it may bring forth m.fruit
21: 15. Simon, lovest me m. than
Ac.4:19. hearken unto you m.than
5:14. believers were the m. added
9:22.Saul incr-d the m.in strength
19: 32. the m. part knew not why
20:35. It is m. blessed to give than
23: 13. m. than 40 conspired, 21.
27:11.believed master m.than Pa.
Ro. 1: 25. served creature m. than
3: 7. if truth hath m. abounded
8: 37. we are m. than conquerors
1 Co. 8:†8.nei.if eat,have we the m.
9: 19. serv., that I might gain the
14:18. I speak wi. tongues m.[m.
2 Co. 7: 7. so I rejoiced the m.
13. exceedingly the m. joyed we
10:8.tho.I sho.boast somewhat m.
11:23. am m.; in prisons m.freq.
Ga. 4: 27. desolate many m. chil.
Ph.1:9.abound m.and m., 1 Th.4:
3:4.if he trust in flesh, I m. [1,10
2 Ti 3:4. lovers of pleasure m.than
Phm. 21. wilt do m. than I say
11: 32. what shall I say m.
12:26.once m.I shake not earth,27.
Ja. 4: 6. he giveth m. grace
2 Pe. 1:19. we have a m. sure word
Re. 2: 19. last to be m. than first
9:12.there come two woes m.here-
See ABUNDANTLY. [after

Any MORE.
Ge. 8: 12. dove returned not a. m.
21. not curse ground a. m.,9:11.
17:5.Nei.thy name a.m.be Abram
35: 10. not be called a. m. Jacob
Ex.8:29.let not Pha. deal deceitfully
9: 29. nei. be a. m. hail [a. m.
11:6. nor shall cry be like it a.m.

Ex 36:6. man nor wom. make **a. m.**
Le. 27: 20. not be redeemed **a. m.**
Nu. 18: 5. no wrath **a. m.** upon Isr.
De. 5: 25. if hear voice of L. **a. m.**
18: 16. nei. let me see fire **a. m.**
Jos.5:12.nei. had Isr. manna **a.m.**
7:12. nei. will I be with you **a.m.**
Ru. 1: 11. **a.m.** sons in my womb?
1 S. 27: 1. despair to seek me **a.m.**
2 S. 7: 10. of wickedn. afflict **a. m.**
10: 19. feared to help Ammon **a. m.**, 1 Ch. 19: 19. ⌈matters
19:29. Why speakest **a. m.** of thy
2 K. 21: 8. nei. make Isr. move **a. m.** out of land, 2 Ch. 33:8. †9.
Jb. 7:10.nei. place know him **a.m.**,
34:31.I will not offend **a.m.**⌊20:9.
Ec. 9: 5. nei. **a. m.** a reward ⌈**m.**?
Is. 1: 5. Why sho. ye be stricken **a.**
2:4. nei. learn war **a. m.**, Mi. 4:3.
30:20.not teachers be remov.**a.m.**
62:4.nei. **a.m.** be termed desolate
Je. 3:16. nei. sh. that be done **a.m.**
17. n.walk **a. m.** after imaginat.
10: 20. there is none to stretch my tent **a. m.** ⌈name
20: 9. I will not speak **a.m.** in his
22: 11. He shall not return **a. m.**
30. no man prosper, ruling **a.m.**
31:12. they shall not sorrow **a.m.**
40. sh. not be thrown down **a.m.**
34:10.not serve thems. of th. **a.m.**
Eze. 5:9. I will not do **a. m.** the like
12: 28. none of my words be prolonged **a. m.**
16: 41. shalt give no hire **a. m.**
63. mayest never open mouth **a.**
21:5.my sw. not return **a.m.** ⌊**m.**
23:27. shalt not remember E. **a.m**
24:13. not from thy filthin. **a. m.**
27: 36. terror, and never be **a.m.**,
29:15.nei.exalt itself **a. m.** ⌊28:19.
32:13.n.trouble them **a.m.**, 37:23.
39:28. I have left none of th.**a.m.**
29. Nei.will I hide my face **a.m.**
Ho.14: 3. nei. say **a.m.** to the work
8.What I to do **a. m.** with idols?
Jo.3:17.no strangers thro.her **a.m.**
Am. 7: 8. not pass by th.**a.m.**,8:2.
13.prophesy not **a. m.** at Beth-el
Zph. 3: 15. shalt not see evil **a. m.**
Mat. 22:46. nor durst any ask **a.m.**
Mk 9:8.saw no man **a.m.**save Jesus
Lu. 20: 36. Nei. can they die **a.m.**
22:16. I will not eat **a. m.** thereof
Ro: 14: 13. Let us not judge **a. m.**
He.12:19. word not be spoken **a.m.**
Re.12:8.nei.their place found **a.m.**
18: 11. no man buyeth her merch.
22.No craftsm.found **a.m.** ⌊**a.m.**
21:4. nei.sh.be **a.m.** pain

How much MORE.

De. 31:27. **h. m. m.** aft. my death?
1 S. 14: 30. **h. m. m.** if peo. eaten
23:3.**h. m.m.** if we come to Keil.
2 S. 4: 11. **h. m. m.** when wicked
16: 11. **h. m. m.** may Benjamite
Jb. 15: 16. **h. m. m.** filthy is man?
Pr. 15: 11. **h. m. m.** then hearts of
19: 7. **h.m.m.** friends go fr. him?
21:27. **h. m. m.** with wick. mind
Eze. 14: 21. **h. m. m.** when sore
Mat. 7: 11. **h.m. m.** your heavenly Fa.give good things? Lu.11:13.
10: 25. **h. m. m.** call them of his household ⌈than
Lu. 12: 24. **h. m. m.** are ye better
28. **h. m. m.** will clothe you
Ro. 11: 12. **h. m. m.** their fulness
24. **h. m. m.** natural branches?
1 Co. 6:3. **h.m.m.**th. that pertain
Phm.16.a bro. to me, **h.m.m.**unto

Much MORE. ⌊thee?

Ex.36:5. peo. bring **m.m.**than eno.
Pr.11:31.**m.m.**the wicked and sin.
Is. 56: 12. as this day, and **m. m.**
Mat. 6:30. not **m. m.** clothe you?
Mat 10:25.**m.m.** call th.of househ.
Mk.7:36.so **m.m.**they published it
Lu.5:15.so **m.m.**went fame of him
7:26. I say, **m.m.**than a prophet
18: 39. but he cried so **m.** the **m.**
Ro. 5: 9. **m.m.** being now justified
10.**m.m.** being reconciled,we sh.
15.**m.m.** the grace of G. and gift
17. **m. m.** they which receive abundance ⌈**m. m.**
20.where sin abounded, grace did
1 Co.12:22.Nay **m. m.** those mem-
2Co.3:9.**m.m.**ministration of ⌊bers
11. **m. m.**wh.remaineth is glori.
8:22. we have proved **m. m.** dilig.
Ph. 1: 14. are **m. m.** bold to speak
2: 12. now **m. m.** in my absence
He.10:25.**m.m.**as ye see day appro.
12:25. **m. m.** shall not we escape
1 Pe.1:7.**m.m.**precious than of gold

No MORE. ⌈flood

Ge. 9: 15. waters **n. m.** become
32: 28. Thy name be called **n. m.**
38:26.Judah knew her **n.m.** ⌊Jac.
44: 23. my face **n. m.**, Ex. 10: 28.
Ex. 5: 7. sh. **n. m.** give peo. straw
10: 29. I will see thy face **n. m.**
14: 13. ye sh. see them **n. m.** for
Le. 17: 7. sh.**n.m.**offer unto devils
Nu. 8: 25. fr. age of 50 serve **n. m.**
De.3:26.speak **n.m.** unto me of this
5: 22. L. spake, and added **n. m.**
10: 16. and be **n. m.** stiffnecked
13:11.do **n. m.** such wickedn., 17:
17:16. return **n.m.**that way ⌊13.
28: 68. Thou shalt see it **n.m.** ⌈in
31:2. I can **n. m.** go out and come
Jos. 23:13.God will **n.m.** drive out
Ju. 8:28.lifted up their heads **n.m.**
10:13.whf. I will deliver you **n.m.**
1 S.1:18.her countenance **n.m.**sad
2: 3. talk **n. m.** so exc. proudly
7:13. came **n.m.** into coast of Isr.
15:35.Sam. came **n. m.** to see Saul
18:2. let him go **n.m.**home to fa.'s
26:21.return, I will **n.m.** do harm
27: 4. he sought **n. m.** for him
28:15.ans-th me **n.m.**by prophets
2 S. 2: 28. pursued after Isr. **n.m.**
7: 10. I will plant Isr., that they may move **n. m.**, 1 Ch. 17: 9.
21:17.Thou shalt go **n. m.** out to battle ⌈9: 4.
1 K. 10:5. **n. m.** spirit in her, 2 Ch.
2 K. 2: 12. Elisha saw Elijah **n.m.**
6:23.bands of Syria came **n.m.**into
9:35.found **n.m.**of her than skull
1 Ch. 23: 26. **n. m.** carry tabern.
Ne. 2:17.th.we be **n.m.** a reproach
13:21. they came **n.m.**on sab. ⌈k.
Es. 1: 19. Vashti came **n. m.** bef.
2:14.she came **n.m.**in to the king
Jb. 7: 7. mine eyes **n. m.** see good
8. eye shall see me **n. m.**, 20: 9.
9. to grave shall come up **n. m.**
10.He shall return **n.m.**to house
14:12. man riseth not, till heavens be **n. m.** ⌈bered
24: 20. he shall be **n. m.** remem-
32:15.amazed,they ans-d **n. m.**,16.
34:32.if done iniq-y,I will do **n.m.**
41:8.remember the battle,do **n.m.**
Ps.10:18.th.man may **n.m.**oppress
39:13.bef.I go hence,and be **n. m.**
41:8.he lieth,he shall rise up **n.m.**
74: 9. there is **n. m.** any prophet
77:7. Will he be favourable **n. m.**
83:4.name of Isr. **n.m.** in remem.
88: 5. slain, thou rememb-t **n. m.**
103:16.the place sh.know it **n. m.**
104:35.let wicked be **n.m.** ⌈**n.m.**
Pr.10:25.As whirlwind, so is wicked
31:7. remember his misery **n. m.**
Ec. 4:13.king,**n.m.** be admonished
Is. 1:13. Bring **n.m.**vain oblations
10:20. shall **n. m.** stay upon him
19:7. be driven away, and be **n.m.**
Is. 23: 10. there is **n. m.** strength
12. shalt **n. m.** rejoice O virgin
26:21. earth shall **n. m.** cover her
30:19. thou sh. weep **n. m.** ⌊slain
38: 11. I shall behold man **n. m.**
32:5.vile person be **n.m.**called lib.
47:1. shalt **n. m.** be called tender
5.shalt **n.m.**be called the lady of
51: 22. thou shalt **n. m.** drink it
52:1.**n.m.**come into thee uncirc-d
60:18.violence **n.m.**be heard in la.
19. sun shall be **n. m.** thy light
20. Thy sun shall **n. m.** go down
62: 4. **n. m.** be termed Forsaken
8. I will **n. m.** give thy corn to
65:19.weeping shall be **n.m.**heard
20.Sh.be **n.m.** an infant of ⌈thee
Je. 2: 31. We will come **n. m.** unto
3:16.shall say **n.m.**The ark of cov.
7:32. **n. m.** be called Tophet,19:6.
11:19. name may be **n.m.**rememb.
16:14. be **n.m.**said, L.liveth, 23:7.
22:10.return **n.m.** nor see country
12. die and see this land **n. m.**
23: 4. fear **n. m.** nor be dismayed
36.burden of L.ye mention **n. m.**
25:27. rise **n. m.** bec. of the sword
31:34. sh. teach **n. m.** ev. man his neighb.,I will remem.sin **n.m.**
33:24. they sho. be **n. m.** a nation
42:18. ye shall see this place **n.m.**
44:26. my name be **n.m.** in Egypt
49: 7. Is wisdom **n. m.** in Teman?
50: 39. it shall **n. m.** be inhabited
La. 2: 9. law is **n. m.**, her prophets
4:22.will **n.m.**carry thee into cap.
Eze.12:24.be **n. m.** any vain vision
25. my word shall be **n. m.** pro-
13: 15. the wall is **n.m.** ⌊longed
21. they sh. be **n.m.**in your hand
23. Thf. ye shall see **n.m.** vanity
14:11.that Isr. may go **n.m.**astray
16: 42. I will be **n. m.** angry
19:9.his voice sho. be **n.m.** heard
20:39. pollute my holy name **n.m.**
21:13. shall be **n. m.** saith L., 27.
32.thou shalt be **n.m.**rememb-d.
24:27. shalt speak, be **n. m.** dumb
26:14. be **n.m.**built | 21. be **n.m.**
28:24. **n. m.** a pricking brier unto
29:15. **n.m.** rule over nations ⌊Isr.
16. sh.be **n.m.** confidence of Isr.
30:13. sh. be **n. m.** a prince of E.
34:22. sh. be **n. m.** a prey, 28, 29.
36: 14. shalt devour men **n. m.**
37:22. they sh. be **n. m.** 2 nations
43:7. my name sh. Isr. **n. m.**defile
45:8. my princes sh. **n. m.**oppress
Ho. 1: 6. I will **n. m.** have mercy
2: 16. shalt call me **n. m.** Baali
17. they shall **n.m.**be rememb-d
9: 15. I will love th. **n.m.** ⌈proach
Jo. 2:19. will **n. m.** make you a re-
Am. 5: 2. virgin, she shall **n.m.**rise
9: 15. **n. m.** be pulled out of land
Mi. 5: 12. have **n. m.** soothsayers
13. **n. m.** worship work of hands
Na. 1: 12. I will afflict thee **n. m.**
14. th.**n.m.** of thy name be sown
15. wicked shall **n. m.** pass thro.
2: 13. messengers **n. m.** be heard
Zph. 3: 11. shalt **n. m.** be haughty
Zch. 11: 6. I will **n. m.** pity inhabi.
13: 2. shall **n. m.** be rememb-d
14:11. be **n. m.** utter destruction
21.be **n.m.**Canaanite in ho.of L.
Mat.19:6. are **n.m.** twain,Mk.10:8.
Mk.7:12. ye suffer him **n. m.** to do
9:25. come out of him, enter **n.m.**
14: 25. I will drink **n. m.** of fruit
Lu. 3: 13. Exact **n. m.** than what
9:13.We have **n.m.**but five loaves
12: 4. aft. that have **n. m.** can do
Jn. 5: 14. whole, sin **n. m.**, 8: 11.
6:66. many walked **n.m.**with him
11: 54. **n. m.** openly among Jews
14:19. while, world seeth me **n. m.**

Jn.15:4.**n.m.** can ye,exc. ye abide
16:10. to Fa., and ye see me **n. m.**
21. she rememb-th **n.m.** anguish
25.when I **n.m.**speak in parables
17:11. I am **n. m.** in the world
Ac. 8:39. eunuch saw him **n. m.**
13:34.**n.m.**to return to corruption
20:25. ye sh. see my face **n.m.**, 38.
Ro.6:9.dieth **n.m.**death hath**n.m.**
7:17.is **n.m.**I th. do it,but sin,20.
11:6.is it **n.m.**of works: otherwise
grace is **n. m.** grace (4) ⌈**n.m.**
2 Co. 5:16.henceforth know we him
Ga. 3:18. if of law,**n.m.** of promise
4:7. art **n.m.**a servant, but a son
Ep. 2:19. ye are **n. m.** strangers
4:14. we be **n. m.** children tossed
28. Let him that stole steal **n.m.**
He. 8:12. their iniquities will I remember **n. m.**, 10:17.
10:2. **n. m.** conscience of sins
18.is **n.m.**offering for sin,26.⌈out
Re. 3:12. Him overcometh go **n.m.**
7:16. hunger **n.m.** nei. thirst any
18:14. shalt find them **n. m.**, 21.
22. musicians be heard **n. m.**,23.
20:3. sho. deceive nations **n. m.**
21:1. **n. m.** sea | 4. **n. m.** death
22:3. And there sh. be **n. m.** curse

MO'REH.

Ge.12:6.Ab. passed unto plain of **M.**
De. 11:30. ag.Gilgal, beside plains of
Ju. 7:1. by hill of **M.** in valley ⌊**M.**

MOREOVER.

2 S.12:8.I would **m.**have given thee
Ezr. 6:8. **m.** I make a decree what
Ps. 19:11. **m.** by th. is serv.warned
105:16.**m.**he called a famine ⌈wise
Ec. 12:9. **m.** bec. the preacher was
Is. 39:8. **m.** there sh. be peace ⌈ca.
Eze.16:29. hast **m.** multiplied forni-
Zch.5:6.**m.**this is their resemblance
Lu. 16:21. **m.** dogs came and licked
Ac.2:26.**m.**my flesh sh.rest in hope
Ro. 8:30.**m.**wh. he did predestinate
1Co.4:2.**m.**it is required in stewards
He. 11:36. of mockings, **m.**of bonds

MOR'ESHETH-GATH.

Mi. 1:14. shalt thou give presents to

MORI'AH. ⌊**M.**

Ge.22:2.get thee into land of **M.**⌈**M.**
2 Ch.3:1.ho.of L.in Jerus.at mount

MORNING. ⌈Lot

Ge. 19:15. **m.** arose, angel hasten.
24:54. Ab. and serv-ts rose in **m.**
26:31. they rose betimes in the **m.**
29:25. in **m.** behold it was Leah
32:†24. until ascending of the **m.**
40:6. Joseph came into them in **m.**
41:8. in **m.** his spirit was troubled
44:3. **m.** was light, men were sent
49:27. in **m.** he shall devour prey
Ex. 7:15. Get thee unto Pha. in **m.**
10:13. in **m.**east wind bro-t locusts
14:27. sea retu-d to strength in **m.**
16:7 in **m.** ye sh. see glory of L.
8. shall give you in **m.** bread, 12.
13. in **m.** dew lay round host
29:39. one lamb offer in **m.**, Nu.
41. acc. to meat off-g of **m.** ⌊28:4.
34:2. be ready in **m.** come in **m.**
25. nei. passover be left unto **m.**
Le.6:9.burning upon altar unto **m.**
20. offer half in **m.** and half at
9:17. besides the burnt sacr. of the **m.**, Nu. 28:23. 2 K. 16:15.
Nu. 9:21. cloud taken up in **m.**
22:21. Balaam rose in the **m.**, 13.
28:8. as meat off-g of **m.**, 2 K.3:20.
De. 16:7. turn in **m.** go unto tents
28:67. In **m.** Wo. God it were even
Ju. 6:31. be put to death whilst **m.**
16:2. In the **m.** when it is day,we
19:27. her lord rose in **m.** opened
20.19. chil. of Israel rose up in **m.**
Ru. 2:7. contin-d fr. **m.** until noon
3:13. it sh. be in **m.** that if

1 S.19:11.unto Da.to slay him in **m.**
20:35. in **m.** Jona. went into field
2 S. 2:27. in **m.** people had gone up
11:14. in **m.** David wrote a letter
13:†4. Why art thou lean **m.**by **m.**?
23:4. he shall be as **m.** when sun riseth, a **m.** without clouds
24:11. when David was up in **m.**
15. fr. **m.** even to time appointed
1 K. 3:21. I had consid-d it in **m.**
18:26. on Baal fr. **m.** until noon
2 K. 10:9. in **m.** that he went out
Ne. 4:21. So we laboured : half held spears fr. **m.** till stars appeared
8:3. read from **m.** until midday
Jb. 3:†9. nei.let it see eyelids of **m.**
7:21. thou shalt seek me in **m.**but
11:17. shine forth, and be as **m.**
24:17. **m.** is as shadow of death
38:12. Hast thou commanded **m.**
41:18. his eyes like eyelids of **m.**
Ps. 5:3. My voice shalt thou hear in **m.** O L.: in **m.** will I direct
30:5. weeping for a night, joy in **m.**
46:†5 God shall help her when **m.**
49:14. dominion over them in **m.**
59:16.will sing of thy mercy in **m.**
88:13. in **m.**sh.my prayer prevent
90:5. in the **m.** they are like grass
6. In the **m.** it flourisheth and
92:2. lovingkindness in **m.**,143:8
110:3.holiness fr.womb of **m.** ⌈**m.**
119:147. I prevented dawning of
130:6. than they th. watch for **m.**
139:9. If I take the wings of **m.**
Ec.10:16. and princes eat in the **m.**
11:6. In **m.** sow thy seed, in ev-g
Can.6:10.Who is she looketh as **m.**
Is. 8:†20. it is bec.is no **m.** in them
14:12. O Lucifer, son of the **m.**
17:11. in **m.** make seed flourish
14.behold,bef.**m.**he is not ⌈com-h
21:12. The watchman said, The **m.**
28:19. by **m.** shall it pass over
47:†11. shalt not know **m.** thereof
50:4. he wakeneth **m.** by **m.** be
58:8. thy light break forth as **m.**
Je. 5:8. were as fed horses in **m.**
20:16. let him hear the cry in **m.**
21:12.Execute judgment in the **m.**
Eze. 7:7. The **m.** is come unto thee
10. the **m.** is gone forth, rod hath
12:8. in the **m.** came word of L.
24:18. I spake unto people in **m.**
I did in **m.** as commanded ⌈**m.**
33:22. until he came to me in the
Ho.6:3.his going forth is as the **m.**
7:6. in **m.** it burneth as a fire
10:15.in **m.** king of Isr. be cut off
Jo. 2:2. as **m.** spread upon mts.
Am.4:13. th maketh the **m.** darkn.
5:8. shadow of death into the **m.**
Jon. 4:7. a worm when the **m.**rose
Mi. 2:1. **m.** is light they practise it
Mat. 16:3. say in **m.** It will be foul
21:18. in **m.** as he retur-d into city
27:1. **m.** was come, elders took
Mk. 1:35. in **m.** rising up a gr.while
11:20. in **m.** as they passed by
13:35.at the cockcrowing,or in **m.**
15:1. straightw. in **m.** chief priest
Jn. 21:4. **m.** was come Jes. stood on
See **Morning CLOUD.**

Early in the MORNING.

Ge. 19:27. Abraham gat up **e. i. m.**, 21:14.-22:3.
20:8. Abimelech rose **e. i. m.**
28:18.Jacob rose up **e.i.m.**and set
31:55. Laban rose **e. i. m.** kissed
Ex. 8:20 L. said, Rise **e.i.m.**,9:13.
24:4. Moses rose **e. i. m.** built an altar, 34:4.
Nu.14:40. And they rose **e.i.m.**,Ju. 9:33. 1 S. 1:19.-29:11. 2 K. 3:22.-19:35. 2 Ch.20:20. Is.37:36.
Jos. 3:1. Joshua rose **e. i. m.**, 6:12.-7:16.-8:10.

Ju. 6:28. the men of the city rose **e.**
38 Gideon rose **e. i. m.** ⌊**i. m.**
19:5 Levite **e. i. m.**, 8. ⌈David
1 S. 15:12.Sam.rose **e. i. m.** ⌈17:20.
29:10. rise **e. i. m.** and depart
Jb. 1:5. Job rose **e. i. m.** and off-d
Pr. 27:14. blesseth friend, rising **e. i. m.**, a curse to him ⌊**m.**
Is. 5:11. Woe unto them, rise **e. i.**
37:36. arose **e. i. m.** they were all dead corpses
Da. 6:19. Darius rose very **e. i. m.**
Mat. 20:1. **e. i. m.** to hire lab-rs
Mk. 16:2. **e. i. m.** came unto sepulchre, Lu. 24:1. ⌈Jn. 8:2.
Lu. 21:38. the people came **e. i. m.**,
Ac.5:21.entered into temple **e.i.m.**
See **EVENING** with **Morning.**

Every MORNING.

Ex. 16:21. gathered manna **e. m.**
30:7. sh. burn sweet incense **e.m.**
36:3. brought free offerings **e. m.**
Le. 6:12. sh. burn wood on it **e. m.**
1 Ch. 9:27. opening **e.m.**pertained
23:30. to stand **e. m.** to thank L.
2 Ch.13:11.they burn unto L. **e.m.**
Jb. 7:18. shouldest visit him **e. m.**
Ps.73:14. I have been chast-d **e.m.**
Is. 33:2. O L., be our arm **e. m.**
La. 3:23. L.'s mercies new **e. m.**
Eze. 46:13. prepare a lamb **e. m.**
14. meat off. **e. m.** | 15.burnt off.
Am. 4:4. bring your sacrifices **e.m.**
Zph.3:5.**e.m.**doth he bring judgm.
See **Morning LIGHT, STAR.**

Till or until the MORNING.

Ex. 12:10. let nothing of it remain **u. m.**, 16:19.-23:18.-29:34. Le. 7:15. Nu. 9:12. ⌈door **u. m.**
22.none of you shall go out at the
16:20. some of them left of it **u.m.**
23. lay up to be kept **u. m.**, 24.
Le. 19:13. wages not abide **u. m.**
Nu.9:15.as appearance of fire **u. m.**
De.16:4.nei. any flesh remain **u.m.**
Ju. 19:25. they abused her **u. m.**
Ru.3:13.lie down **u.m.** | 14. she lay
1 S. 3:15. Samuel lay **u. m.** ⌊**u. m.**
19:2. take heed to thys. **u. m.** ⌈**m.**
2 K. 10:8. heads of k-s in 2 heaps **u.**
Pr. 7:18. take our fill of love **u. m.**
Is. 38:13. I reckoned **t. m.** that as
See **Morning WATCH.** ⌊lion

MORROW. ⌊**m.**

Ge. 30:†33. my righteousness ans. to
Ex. 8:10. To **m.**, he said, Be it acc.
23.to **m.**shall this sign be, the L.
29. flies may depart fr.Pha. to **m.**
9:5. To **m.** L. shall do this thing
6. Lord did that thing on **m.**
18. to **m.** I will cause rain
10:4. to **m.** I will bring locusts
13:†14. asketh thee to **m.**, De. 6:†20. Jos. 4:†6. ⌈sabbath
16:23. To **m.** is the rest of the holy
17:9. to **m.** I will stand upon hill
18:13. on **m.** Mo. sat to judge peo.
19:10.sanctify th.to day and to **m.**
32:5. To **m.** is feast to the L. ⌈5:4.
6. rose early on **m.**, Ju. 21:4. 1 S.
30 on **m.**Mo.said unto people,Ye
Le. 7:16. on **m.** shall be eaten, 19:6.
22:30. leave none of it until **m.**
23:11. on **m.** after sabbath priest
15. ye sh. count fr.**m.**aft.sab.,16.
Nu. 11:18. Sanctify yourselves ag. to **m.** ye shall eat, Jos. 7:13.
14:25. To **m.** get you into wildern.
16:5. to **m.** L. will shew who his
7. put incense before L. to **m.**
16. be thou and all bef. L. to **m.**
41. on **m.** the congre. murmured
17:8. on **m.** Moses went into tab.
22:41. on **m.** Balak took Balaam
33:3.on **m.**aft.passover chil.of Isr.
Jos. 3:5. to **m.** L. will do wonders
4:†21. When chil.ask fathers to **m.**

Jos.5:11. eat of old corn on m.after
5:12. manna ceased on the m.after
11:6. to m. I deliver up all slain
22:18. to m. be wroth with congr.
†24. to m. your chil. speak unto
Ju.9:42. on m.peo. told Abim. ⌊our
19:9. to m. get early on your way
20:28. Go up to m. I will deliver
1 S. 9:16. To m. I will send a man
19. to m. I will let thee go
11:9. To m. by time sun be hot
10. to m. we will come out unto
you ⌈panics
11. on m. Saul put peo.in 3 com-
18:10. on m. evil spirit came upon
19:11. to m. thou be slain ⌊Saul
20:5. to m. is the new moon, 18.
12. sounded my fa. about to m.
27. on m. David's place was empty
28:19. to m. sha. thou be with me
30:†17. smote unto evening of m.
31:8. on m. when Philis. came to
strip slain, 1 Ch. 10:8. ⌈to m.
1 K. 19:2. as life of one of them by
20:6. I send servts. unto thee to m.
2 K. 6:28. we will eat my son to m.
7:1. To m. a measure of flour be
8:15. on m. took thick cloth ⌊sold
10:6. come to me to Jezreel to m.
1 Ch. 29:21, off-d burnt off-s on m.
2 Ch. 20:16. To m. go ag. them, 17.
Es. 2:14. on m. she ret-d into house
5:8. I will do to m. as the king said
12. to m. am I invited unto her,
9:13. do to m. acc. unto decree ⌊14.
Pr. 3:28. say not to m. I will give
27:1. Boast not thyself of to m.
Is. 22:13. for to m. we die, 1 Co.
56:12. to m. be as this day ⌊15:32.
Je. 20:3. on m. Pashur bro-t Jere.
Zph. 3:3. gnaw not bones till m.
Mat. 6:30. and to m. is cast into
the oven, Lu. 12:28.
34. Take no thought for m. for
m. sh. take thought for itself
Mk. 11:12. on m. when were come
Lu. 10:35. on m. when he departed
13:32. I do cures to day to m.
33. I must walk to-day and to-m.
Ac. 4:5. came to pass on m. rulers
10:9. on m. as they went on journ.
23. on the m. Peter went away
24. m. aft. they ent-d into Cesarea
20:7. Paul ready to depart on m.
22:30. on m. bec. he wo have known
23:15. bring him down to m., 20.
32. on m. they left horsemen
25:17. on m. I sat on judgm. seat
22. To m. thou shalt hear him
23. on m. when Agrippa was come
Ja. 4:13. To day or to m. we will go
14. ye know not what be on m.

MORSEL, S.

Ju. 19:5. Comfort heart with m. of
Ru. 2:14. dip thy m. in vinegar
2 S. 12:†3. it did eat of his own m.
Jb. 31:17. or eaten my m. alone
Ps. 147:17. casteth forth ice like m-s
Pr. 17:1. Better is a dry m. and
23:8. m. hast eaten shalt vomit
Jn. 13†:26. he to whom I sh. give m.
He. 12:16. who for one m. sold birth-
See BREAD. ⌊right

MORTAL.

2 Ch. 14:†11. let not m. man prevail
Jb. 4:17. m. man be more just than
Ro. 6:12. not sin reign in m. body
8:11. shall quicken your m. bodies
1 Co. 15:53. this m. must put on
immortality, 54.
2 Co. 4:11. life of Jes. in our m. flesh

MORTALITY.

2 Co. 5:4. m. be swallowed up of life

MORTALLY.

De. 19:11. and smite his neighbor m.

MORTAR = MORTER.

Ge. 11:3. and slime had they for m.
Ex. 1:14. they made th. serve in m.
Le. 14:42. take m. and plaster house
45. shall break down m. of ho.
Is. 41:25. he upon princes as m.
Eze. 13:10. daubed it with untem-
pered m., 11, 14, 15.–22:28.
Na. 3:14. go into clay, and tread m.

MORTAR

Nu. 11:8. in mills, or beat it in m.
Pr. 27:22. Tho. thou bray a fool in

MORTGAGED. ⌊m.

Ne. 5:3. said, We have m. our lands

MORTIFY. ⌈live

Ro. 8:13. if m. deeds of body ye sh.
Col. 3:5. m. your members which

MOSE'RA. ⌈to M.

De. 10:6. took journey from Beeroth

MOSE'ROTH.

Nu. 33:30. they encamped at M., 31.

MOSES. ⌈M.

Ex. 2:10. Pha.'s dau. called his name
14. M. feared and said, this thing
15. Pha. sought to slay M. but M
17. M. stood and helped th. ⌊fled
3:3. M. said, I will turn and see
4. Lord called unto him, M. M.
6. M. hid his face, he was afraid
11. M. said unto God, Who am I?
14. said unto M. I AM | 13.
4:1. M. ans-d, they will not believe
3. M. fled from before serpent
4. L. said unto M. Put forth thine
hand, 19, 21.–6:1.–7:1, 14.
10. M. said, I am not eloquent
14. L.'s anger was kindled ag. M.
27. go into wilderness to meet M.
5:22. M. returned unto the Lord
6:10. Lord spake unto M., 28.–7:19.
–13:1–14:1.–16:11.–25:1.–30:11,
17, 22.–31:1, 12.–33:11.–40:1.
Le. 4:1.–5:14.–6:1, 8, 19, 24.–7:
22, 28.–8:1.–12:1.–14:1.–16:1.–
17:1.–18:1.–19:1.–20:1.–21:16.–
22:1, 17, 26.–23:1, 9, 23, 26, 33.–24:
1, 13.–25:1.–27:1. Nu. 3:5, 11, 14,
44.–4:21.–5:1, 5, 11.–6:1, 23.–7:
4.–8:1, 5, 23.–9:9.–10:1.–13:1.–
15:1, 17, 37.–16:23, 36, 44.–17:1.–
18:25.–20:7.–25:10, 16.–26:1,
52.–27:6.–28:1.–31:1, 25.–33:
50.–34:1, 16.–35:1, 9. De. 32:48.
8:9. M. said unto Pha. Glory ov. me
13. according to word of M., 31.–
9:12, 35.–12:35.
9:8. let M. sprinkle it ⌈fore M.
11. magicians could not stand be-
10:9. M. said, We will go with
22. M. stretched hand tow. heaven
24. Pha. said unto M. Go serve L.
11:3. man M. was very gr. in land
12:21. M. called for elders | 35.
13:3. M. said unto peo. Remember
19. M. took bones of Joseph wi.
14:11. they said unto M., 20:19.
31. people believed L. and M.
15:1. sang M. and the chil. of Isr.
22. So M. brought Isr. fr. Red Sea
24. people murmured ag. M., 17:3.
16:8. M. said, This shall be +
20. they hearkened not unto M.
25. M. said, Eat that to day
34. as Lord commanded M., 39:
1, 5, 7, 21, 26, 29, 31.–40:19, 21,
23, 25, 27, 29, 32. Le. 8:4, 9,
13, 17, 21, 29.–9:10.–16:34.–24:
23. Nu. 1:19.–2:33.–3:51.–4:49.
–8:3, 22.–15:36.–26:4.–27:11.–
31:7, 31, 41, 47.–36:10. De. 34:
9. Jos. 11:15, 20.–14:2, 5.
17:2. people did chide with M. +
4. M. cried unto Lord | 6. M. did
so, Nu. 17:11. ⌈altar
12. M.'s hands heavy | 15 M. built
18:1. M.'s fa. in law, 2, 5, 6, 8, 12, 14, 17.
13. M. sat to judge the people
25. M. chose able men out of Isr.
26. hard cases they bro-t unto M.
Ex. 19:3. M. went up unto God + ⌈L.
8. M. returned words of peo. unto
20. L. called M up to m-t Sinai
20:21. M. drew near thick darkness
24:2. M. alone sh. come near L. +
4. M. wrote all words of the Lord
8. M. took blood sprinkled it
18. M. went into midst of cloud,
M. was in the mount 40 days
31:18. gave unto M. two tables of
32:1. as for M. we wot not what
become, 23. Ac. 7:40.
11. M. besought the Lord his God
19. M.'s anger waxed hot ⌈+
25. when M. saw peo. were naked
33:7. M. took tabern. and pitched
9. the Lord talked with M. ⌈+
34:4. M. went up unto mount Sinai
35. M. put the veil upon his face
35:1. M. gathered all congrega-
tion of Israel | 4, 20, 29, 30.
36:2. M. called Bezaleel and | 3, 5, 6.
38:21. counted acc to com-t of M.
22. all that L. commanded M., 39:
32, 42.–40:16. Nu. 1:54.–2:34.
–8:20.–9:5.–29:40. ⌈(2)
39:43. M. did look upon all work
40:18. M. reared up the tabern. | 33
35. M. not able to enter tent
Le. 1:1. Lord called unto M.
7:38. which L. com-d M. in mount
8:4. M. did as L. commanded +
9:6. M. said, This is thing which L.
10:4 M. called Mishael +
16. M. sought the goat of ⌈of
23:44. M. declared unto Isr. feasts
24:11. brought blasphemer unto M.
Nu. 1:1. L. spake unto M. in wil. | 48.
3:16. M. numbered them acc. +,
5:4. as L. spake unto M. so ⌊4:49.
7:1. day M. had fully set up
8:4. pattern wh. Lord shewed M.
10:29. M. said to Hobab, We are
11:2. peo. cried unto M. and M.
10. M. heard people weep ⌊prayed
29. M. said, Enviest for my sake?
12:2. Hath L. indeed only by M.
3. M. was very meek above all men
7. M. is not so, who is faithful in
8. whf. not afraid to speak ag. M.?
13. M. cried unto the Lord
13:3. M. by com-t of L. sent men
16. men M. sent to spy, 14:36.
14:41. Whf. do ye now transgress
44. M. departed not out of camp
16:4. M. heard he fell upon face +
8. M. said to Korah, Hear | 12.
17:7. M. laid up rods before L. +
20:3. the people chode with M. +
21:5. peo. spake ag. God and M. +
9. M. made a serpent of brass and
32. M. sent to spy out Jaazer ⌈M.
25:6. Midianitish wom. in sight of
26:63. that were numbered by M.
27:5. M. bro-t their cause bef. L. +
31:6. M. sent them to the war +
14. M. was wroth with officers
32:6. M. spake unto chil. of Gad +
33:2. M. wrote their goings out by
36:1. came near spake before M.
De 1:1. words that M. spake +
4:44. law M. set before Isr. +
5:1. M. called all Israel and
27:1. M. with elders of Israel | 9.
11. M. charged people same day
31:9. M. wrote this law and deliv-d
22. M. wrote this song, and taught
33:1. M. the man of God blessed Isr.
34:1. M. went up fr. plains of Moab
5. M. servant of Lord died there
7. M. 120 years old when he died
8. children of Israel wept for M.
10. not a prophet like unto M.
12. wh. M. shewed in sight of Isr.
Jos. 1:1. after death of M. +
2. saying, M. my serv. is dead | 3.
5. as with M. so I with thee, 3:7.

Jos.1:17.as we hearkened unto M.so
4: 14. feared Joshua, as feared M.
8: 31. law of M., 23: 6. 2 K. 14:6.-
23:25. 2 Ch.30:16. Ezr. 7:6. Ne.
8:1. Da. 9:11. Mal. 4:4. Lu.2:22.
-24:44. Jn.7: 23. Ac. 13:39.-15:
5.-28: 23. 1 Co. 9: 9.
18:8. M. gave them bey. Jordan +
14:6.knowest thing L. said unto M.
10. since L. spake word unto M.
11. as strong as in day M. sent me
1K.8:9.two tables wh.M.,2 Ch.5:10.
53. by hand of M. thy serv., 56.
1Ch. 21: 29. tabern. which M. made
in wilderness, 2 Ch. 1: 3.
22: 13. judgments L. charged M.
23: 14. conc. M. the man of God
15. sons of M. Gershom and
26: 24. son of M. ruler of treasures
2 Ch. 24: 9. collection M. laid upon
34: 14. law given by M., Ne. 10:29.
Ps. 103: 7. made kn. ways unto M.
105:26.He sent M. his serv.and Aa.
106: 16. They envied M. in camp
23. had not M. stood in breach
32.it went ill wi.M. for their sakes
Is.63:11. rememb-d M. and his peo.
12. That led them by hand of M.
Je. 15:1.Tho.M. and Sam. stood bef.
Mal. 4: 4. Remember law of M.[me
Mat. 17: 3. appeared M. and Elias
talking, Mk. 9: 4. Lu. 9: 30.
4. one tabernacle for M., Mk. 9:5.
19:7.Why did M. command to give
8. M. suff-d you to put aw. wives
22: 24. M. said, If a man die
23: 2. Pharisees sit in M.'s seat
Mk. 10: 3. What did M. command
12:19.M. wrote, If a man's brother
die, Lu. 20: 28.
Lu.16:29. they have M. and proph.
31. if they hear not M.and proph.
20:37.th.dead are raised,M.shewed
24:27. beginning at M. and proph.
Jn. 3: 14. as M. lifted up serpent in
5: 45. one accuseth you, even M.
46. had ye believed M. ye had
6: 32. M. gave you not that bread
7: 22. not bec. it is of M., but fa-s
9:28. thou art his disci. we are M.'s
29. We know God spake unto M.
Ac. 3: 22. M. truly said unto fa-s
6:11. speak blasphem. words ag.M.
14. change customs M. delivered
7: 20. in which time M. was born
22. M. was learned in all wisdom
29. Then fled M. at this saying
31. When M. saw he wondered
32. M. trembled and durst not
35. This M. whom they refused
37. This is that M. said unto Isr.
15:1.be circumc-d aft.manner of M.
21. M. hath in every city them
21: 21. teachest Jews to forsake M.
26:22. things M. did say sho. come
28:23. out of law of M. and proph.
Ro. 5: 14. death from Adam to M.
10:5. M. describeth right-su.of law
19.M.saith, I will provoke to jeal.
1 Co.10:2. baptized unto M.in cloud
2 Co. 3: 7. co. not behold face of M.
13. not as M. who put a vail over
15. when M. is read, vail is on
2 Ti. 3: 8. as Jannes withstood M.
He. 3: 2. M. faithful in all house,5.
3. worthy of more glory than M.
16. not all that came out of E.by
7:14. wh tribe M. spake noth. [M.
8: 5. as M. was admonished of G.
9: 19. M. had spoken ev. precept
11: 23. By faith M was hid 3 mos.
24. M. refused to be called son of
12: 21. M. said, I exceedingly fear
Jude 9. disputed about body of M.
Re. 15: 3. they sing the song of M.
See AARON, BOOK, COMMANDED,
JETHRO, LAW.

See **Written in the LAW, LORD said, Servant of the LORD.**

MOST.

Pr.20:6. m. men proclaim goodness
Mat.11:20.wh-n m.of mighty works
Lu. 7: 42. which will love him m.?
43. he to whom he forgave m.
Ac. 20: 38. Sorrowing m. of all for
1 Co. 14: 27. be by two, or at m. by [three

MOTE.

Mat. 7: 3. why beholdest m. in thy
brother's eye, but, Lu. 6: 41.
4. Let me pull m. of thine eye
5. then shalt thou see to cast out
m. out of bro.'s eye, Lu. 6: 42.

MOTH.

Jb. 4:19. which are crushed bef.m.
27: 18. He buildeth house as a m.
Ps. 39: 11. beauty consume like m.
Is. 50: 9. m. sh. eat them up, 51:8.
Ho.5: 12. will I be unto Ephr.as m.
Mat.6:19.where m.and rust corrupt
20.m. nor rust doth corrupt, Lu. [12:33.

MOTHEATEN.

Jb. 13: 28. consumeth as garm. m.
Ja. 5: 2. riches corrupted, garments [m.

MOTHER.

Ge. 2: 24. Thf. shall a man leave fa.
and m. and cleave unto wife,
Mat. 19: 5. Mk. 10: 7. Ep. 5:31.
3: 20. bec. she was m. of all living
17: 16. she shall be a m. of nations
20: 12. is dau. of my fa. not of m.
24:28. told them of her m's. house
53. he gave to her m. prec. things
55. her m. said, Let damsel
60.be m.of thous.of millions [m.
28: 5. Laban, broth. of Reb. Jac.'s
32:11. lest he smite m. with chil.
Ex. 2: 8. maid called child's m.
Le.19: 3. sh.fear ev.man his m.and
20: 14. to take a wife and her m.is
Nu.26:59. whom her m.bare to Levi
De. 21: 13. bewail her m. a month
18. if son will not obey his m.
Jos. 2: 13. save alive my fa. and m.
Ju.5: 7. until I Deb.arose m.in Isr.
28.m. of Sisera looked out at win.
14: 16. I not told it to fa. nor m.
Ru.1:8.return each to her m.'s hou.
2: 11. hast left thy father and m.
1 S. 22: 3. Let my fa. and m. come
2 S. 17:25. sis. to Zeruiah,Joab's m.
20:19. seekest to destroy m. in Isr.
1 K. 1: 11. Bathsheba m. of Sol.
2: 19. caused a seat for king's m.
3:27. Give her child, she is the m.
11:26.whose m.'s name was Zeru-h
19: 20. Let me kiss my fa. and m.
2 K. 4: 30. m. of child said, As L.
11: 1. m. of Ahaziah saw son,2 Ch.
24: 15. carried aw. k.'s m. [22:10.
1 Ch. 2:26. She was the m. of Onam
2 Ch. 15: 16. he removed m. of Asa
Ps. 113: 9. be joyful m. of chil.
Pr. 28:24. Whoso robbeth fa. or m.
30: 11. a generation not bless m.
Can. 6: 9. she is only one of her m.
Is.50:1.Where bill of m.'s divorc-t?
Je. 15: 8. ag. m. of the young men
50:12.Your m.shall be confounded
Eze. 16: 44. As is the m. so is dau.
45. your m. was a Hittite, fa., 3.
21: † 21. king stood at m. of way
22:7. They set light by fa. and m.
23:2. two women, dau-s of one m.
Ho. 2: 2. Plead with your m. for
5. their m. hath played harlot
10: 14. m. was dashed in pieces
Mi.7: 6. daughter riseth up against
her m. Mat. 10: 35. Lu.12: 53.
Zch. 13: 3. father and m. shall
thrust him through (2)
Mat. 8: 14. saw Peter's wife's m.
sick, Mk. 1:30. Lu. 4: 38. [than
10: 37. He th. loveth fa. m. more

Mat.12:50. same is sis. and m., Mk.
14:8.being instruc.of her m. [3:35.
11. bro-t it to her m., Mk.6:28.
15:6. honour not his father or m.
19: 12. are some eunuchs so born
from m.'s womb
29.forsaken m.or wife, Mk.10:29.
20: 20. came m. of Zebedee's chil.
27:56.Mary m.of James,Mk.15:40.
Mk.6: 24. unto m. What sh. I ask?
7: 10. Moses said, Honour fa. and
m.? 10:19. Lu. 18:20. Ep. 6: 2.
15: 47. Mary the m. of Joses, 16:1.
Lu. 24: 10. [come to me?
Lu. 1: 43. m. of my Lord should
12:53. son ag. fa. m.ag.the daugh.
Jn.2:1.m.of Jesus there,3. Ac.1:14.
6: 42. Jes. whose fa. m. we know
Ac.12:12. to ho. of Mary,m.of John
Ga. 4: 26. Jerusalem m. of us all
Re. 17: 5.m. of harlots and abomi-
See FATHER. [nations.

His MOTHER.

Ge. 21: 21. h. m. took him a wife
24:67. Isaac bro t Rebekah into h.
m. Sarah's tent, and was comforted after h. m.'s death
27:11. Jac.said to h.m. Esau is an
13. h.m. said, Upon me be curse
14.Jacob brot.them to h.m.[bro.
29:10. Rachel dau. of Lab.,h.m.'s
30: 14. bro. mandrakes unto h.m.
43:29. he saw bro.Benj.h.m.'s son
44: 20. he alone is left of h. m.
Ex. 23:19. not seethe kid in h. m.'s
milk, 34: 26. De. 14: 21. [see her
Le. 20: 17. sh. take h.m.'s dau.and
24:11. h.m.'s name was Shelomith
Nu. 12: 12. cometh out of h. m.'s
womb. [m.
De. 27: 22. lieth with daughter of h.
Ju. 9: 1. Abim.unto h. m.'s breth.
3. h. m.'s brethren spake of him
17: 2. he said unto h. m.
3. he restored to h. m., 4.
1 S. 2: 19. h. m. made a little coat
1 K.1: 6. h. m. bare him after Abs.
2: 22. Solomon said unto h. m.
14: 21. h. m.'s name Naamah, 31.
2 Ch. 12: 13. [Maachah
15: 2. Jeroboam, h. m.'s name
13.h.m. removed fr. being queen
17:23.Elijah deliv-d him unto h.m
22: 42. h.m.'s name Azubah, 2 Ch.
52.walked in way of h.m. [20:31.
2 K.4:19. to lad Carry him to h. m.
20. and brought him to h. m.
8: 26. h. m.'s name was,12: 1.-14:
2.-15:2,33.-18:2.-21: 1, 19.-22:
1.-23:31,36.-24:8,18.-2 Ch. 13:
2.-22:2.-24: 1.-25: 1.-26: 3.-27:
1.-29: 1.-Je. 52: 1. [and h. m.
24: 12. k. of Jud. to k. of Bab. h
1 Ch. 4: 9. h. m. called name Jabes
2 Ch. 22: 3.h.m. was his counsellor
Ps.35:14. that mourneth for h. m.
109:14. not sin of h. m. be blotted
131:2. child th. is weaned of h. m.
Pr.10:1. foolish son heavin.of h.m.
15: 20. foolish despiseth h. m.
29:15. child left bring. h.m.to sha.
30: 17. despiseth to obey h. m.
31: 1. prophecy h. m. taught him
Ec.5:15.came forth of h.m.'s womb
Can.3:11. crown whw. h. m.crown
Is. 66: 13. As one h. m. comfort-h
Mat. 1:18. when h. m.was espoused
2:11. saw yo.child with Mary h.m.
13. take yo.child h.m.and flee, 12,
14, 20, 21. [31.Lu.8:19.
12:46.h.m. stood without, Mk. 3:
13: 55. is not h. m. called Mary?
Lu. 1: 15. he sh. be filled with H. G.
from h. m's. womb
60. h. m. said,he sh.be called Jn.
2: 33.Joseph and h. m. marvelled
34. said unto Mary,h.m., Behold

Lu.2:43.Jo.and h.m.knew not of it
48. h.m. said,Son,why hast thou
51. but h. m. kept these sayings
7:12. only son of h.m. she a widow
15. he delivered him to h. m.
Jn.2:5.h.m.said unto serv.Whatso.
12. to Capernaum, he and h. m.
3:4.second time into h.m.'s womb?
19: 25. h. m. stood by the cross
26. Jes. saw, he saith unto h. m.
Ac. 3:2. lame fr.h.m.'s womb, 14:8.
Ro. 16: 13. Salute Rufus and h. m.

MOTHER in law. ⌈l.

De.27:23. Cursed th.lieth with m.i.
Ru. 1: 14. Orpah kissed her m. i. l.
2: 11. hast done unto m. i. l. ⌈19.
18.m. i.l. saw what she gleaned,
23. Ruth dwelt with her m. i. l.
3:1.Naomi, her m. i. l. said, dau.
6. to all her m. i. l. bade her
16.came to m.i.l.,said,Who thou
17. Go not empty unto thy m.i.l.
Mi. 7: 6. daughter in law riseth up
ag. m. i. l., Mat. 10: 35. Lu.

My MOTHER. ⌊12:53.

Ge. 20:12. she is not dau. of m. m.
Ju. 8:19. breth. even sons of m.m.
16: 17.Nazarite fr.m.m.'s womb
1 K.2:20. king said, Ask on, m.m.
Jb.1:21.Naked out of m.m.'swomb
3:10.it shut not up m. m.'s womb
17:14.said to worm, Thou m. m.
31:18.guided her fr.m.m.'s womb
Ps.22:9.when upon m.m.'s breasts
10. art my God fr. m. m.'s belly
51:5. in sin did m.m. conceive me
69:8.I an alien unto m. m.'s chil.
71:6.took me out of m.m.'sbowels
139:13. cov. me in m. m.'s womb
Pr. 4: 3. beloved in sight of m. m.
Can.1:6.m.m.'s chil. angry wi. me
3:4.I bro-t him into m.m.'s house
8: 1. bro.sucked breasts of m. m.
2.wo.bring thee into m. m.'s ho.
Is. 49: 1. from bowels of m. m. he
Je. 15: 10. Woe is me, m. m. thou
20: 14. let not day m. m. bare me
17.th. m.m. have been my grave
Mat. 12: 48. Jesus said, Who is m.
m.? Mk. 3: 33.
49. Behold, m m., Mk. 3: 34.
Lu.8: 21. m. m. and breth. ⌈womb
Ga. 1: 15. separated me fr. m. m.'s

Thine own or thy MOTHER.

Ge.27:29.let t.m.'s sons bow to thee
28: 2. go to Bethuel t. m.'s father
37: 10. Sh.I and t.m. bow to thee?
Le. 18: 7.nakedn.of t.m.not uncov.
9. not uncover dau.of t.m. ⌈19.
13. not uncover sister of t.m., 20:
De. 13: 6. son of t. m. entice thee
1 S.15:33. so shall t. m. be childless
20:30.confusion of t. m.'s nakedn.
2 K.9:22.whoredoms of t. m. many
Ps. 50: 20. slanderest t. o. m.'s son
Pr. 1: 8. not law of t. m., 6: 20.
23: 22. despise not t. m. when old
Can.8:5. there t.m. bro-t thee forth
Je. 22: 26. t. m. that bare thee
Eze. 16: 3. fa. Amorite,t.m. Hittite
45. Thou art t. m.'s dau. that
19: 2. What is t. m.? A lioness
10. t. m. like a vine in thy blood
Ho. 4: 5. and I will destroy t. m.
Mat. 12: 47. one said unto him, Behold t.m., Mk. 3: 32. Lu.8:20.
Jn. 19: 27.
2 Ti.1: 5. wh. dwelt in t. m. Eunice

MOTHERS.

Is. 49:23. queens be thy nursing m.
Je. 16: 3. saith L. conc. their m.
La. 2: 12. say to m., Where is corn?
soul poured into m.' bosom
5: 3. fatherless, our m. as widows
Mk. 10:30. hundredfold, sisters, m.
1 Ti. 1: 9. law for murderers of m.
1 Ti. 5:2. entreat the elder women as

MOTIONS. ⌊m.

Ro.7:5.m. of sins did work in mem-

MOULDY. ⌊bers

Jos. 9: 5. bread was dry and m., 12.

MOUNT, S. [Noun.] ⌈m.

Ge. 31: 54. Jacob offered sacr. upon
Ex. 18: 5. he encamped at m. of G.
19: 2. there Isr. camped before m.
12. toucheth m. be put to death
13. soundeth,they sh.come to m.
14.Moses went down from the m.,
32:15.-34:29. ⌈15.
16.a thick cloud upon the m.,24:
17. stood at nether part of m.
23.charged, set bounds about m.
24:17. devouring fire on top of m.
32:1.Mo.delayed to come out of m.
19. Moses brake th. beneath m.
34:3.nei.let any man be seen thro-t
m. nei. let flocks feed bef. m.
Nu. 10: 33. departed from m. of L.
De. 1: 7.Turn, go to m. of Amorites
9:15. I came fr. m., and m. burn-
21. brook out of the m. ⌊ed,10:5.
Jos. 15:11. borders along m.Baalah
16:1. fr. Jericho thro-t m. Bethel
Ju. 3: 27. Isr. went with him fr.m.
2 S. 15: 30. David went up by m.
32. m. where he worshipped God
1 K. 19: 8. to Horeb, the m. of God
11. Go and stand upon m. bef. L.
2 K.23:13. right of m. of corruption
Ne.8:15.Go unto m. fetch olive bra.
Is. 10: 32. m. of dau. of.Zion, 16:1.
14: 13. will sit upon m. of congr.
27:13.shall worship in the holy m.
He.12:18.unto m.might be touched

In, or into the MOUNT.

Ge.22:14.i. m. of L. it shall be seen
54. they tarried all night i. m.
Ex. 4: 27. he met him i. m. of God
19: 12. Take heed ye go not up i-o
m., De. 5:5. ⌈De. 10: 1, 3.
24:12. said to Moses, Come i-o m.,
13.Moses went i-o m.of G.,15,18.
18. Moses was i. m. forty days
and forty nights,De.9:9.-10:10.
25:40. after pattern shewed thee i.
m., 26: 30.-27: 8. He. 8: 5.
De. 1: 6. dwelt long enough i. m.
5: 4. L. talked face to face i. m.,
22.-9:10.-10:4.
32:50.die i.m.as Aaron died ⌈Heres
Ju.1:35.Amorites would dwell i.m.
12: 15. buried in m. of Amalek-s
2 K.23:16.Josiah spied sepul-s i.m.
Is. 27: 13. worship L. i. holy m.
2 Pe.1:18.when with him i. holy m.
See ABARIM, CARMEL, EBAL,
EPHRAIM, ESAU, GERIZIM,
GILBOA, GILEAD, HALAK, HE-
RES, HERMON, HOR, LEBA-
NON, MORIAH, NAPHTALI,
NEBO, OLIVES, OLIVET,
PARAN, PERAZIM, SEIR, SE-
PHAR, SHAPHER, SINAI,
SION, TABOR, ZALMON, ZION.

MOUNT, S.

Is. 29:3.lay siege ag.thee with a m.
Je. 6: 6. Hew trees cast a m. ag.
Jerus., Eze. 4:2.-21:22.-26:8.⌈it
32:24.m-s are come unto city take
33:4. houses thrown down by m-s
Eze.17:17.for him,by casting up m-s
Da. 11: 15. king shall cast up a m.

MOUNT, ED. [Verb.] ⌈ens

Jb.20:6.Tho. excellency m. to heav-
39:27. Doth eagle m. at thy com.?
Ps. 107: 26. They m. up to heaven
Is. 9:18. they shall m. up as smoke
40:31. they shall m.up with wings
Je. 51:53.Tho.Bab. m.up to heaven
Eze.10:16.cherubim lift to m.up,19
19.cherubim lifted wings m-d up

MOUNTAIN. ⌈m.

Ge.14:10.they that remained fled to
Ge.19:17.escape to the m. lest thou
19. I cannot escape to m. lest
Ex. 3: 1. came to m. of G. Horeb
12.fr.E.,sh. serve G. upon this m.
19:3. L. called unto him out of m.
20: 18. all people saw m. smoking
Nu. 14: 40. gat them into top of m.
De. 1: 19. by way of m. of Amorites
20. come unto m. of Amorites,44.
2: 3. Ye compassed this m. long
3: 25. let me see that goodly m.
4:11.the m. burned with fire,5:23.
33: 19. shall call peo. unto m.
34:1. Mo. went up fr. plains of m.
Jos. 2:16. Get ye to the m. and hide
11:16. Joshua took m. of Isr. ⌊thine
14: 12. Now give me this m.
17: 18. the m. shall be thine
18: 16. border came to end of m.
Ju. 1: 19. drave out inhabit-ts of m.
1 S. 17: 3. Philis. stood on m. on 1
side, Isr. stood on m. on other
23:26.Saul went on this side of m.
and David on that side of m.
2 K.2:16.Spirit cast him on some m.
6:17.m.was full of horses ⌈nought
Jb. 14: 18. m. falling cometh to
Ps. 11: 1. flee as a bird to your m.?
30:7. hast made my m. stand stro.
78:54.m.his right hand purchased
Can. 4:6.will get me to m. of myrrh
Is. 2:2.m. of L.'s house established,
Mi. 4: 1. ⌈L., Mi. 4: 2.
3. let us go up to the m. of the
30: 17. left as beacon on top of m.
29. goeth with pipe to m. of L.
40:4. ev. m. be made low, Lu. 3: 5.
Je.16:16.sh.hunt them from ev. m.
17: 3. O my m. in field, I will give
26: 18. and the m. of ho. as high
places of forest, Mi.3:12. ⌈holin.
31: 23. O hab-n of justice, m. of
50:6. peo. have gone fr. m. to hill
51: 25. O destroying m. saith L.,
I will make thee a burnt m.
La. 5: 18. dim, bec. of m. of Zion
Eze.11:23.glory of L.stood upon m.
28:16.will cast thee out of m.of G.
43:12.limit be holy upon top of m.
†15. Hariel, the m. of God, shall
Da. 2:35.stone became gr. m. ⌈han.
45. stone cut out of m. with-t
Mi. 7:12. come to thee fr. m. to m.
Hag. 1: 8. go up to m. bring wood
Zch. 4:7.Who art thou, O great m.
8: 3. be called m. of L., holy m.
14:4. half of m. shall remove tow.
Mat. 8: 1. When he was come fr. m.
17:9. as they came fr. m., Mk.9:9.
20. if have faith, sh. say unto this
m. Remove, 21:21. Mk. 11: 23.
28:16. went into a m. where Jesus
Lu.8:32. many swine feeding on m.
He. 12: 20. if a beast touch the m.
Re. 6: 14. ev. m. island were remov.
8:8. as it were a great m. burning

High MOUNTAIN.

Is.13:2.Lift ye a banner upon h.m.
30:25. sh. be upon ev. h.m. rivers
40:9. O Zion, get thee into h. m.
57:7. Upon h. m. hast set thy bed
Je. 3: 6. Isr. is gone upon ev. h. m.
Eze. 17:22. will plant it upon h. m.
40:2. he set me upon a very h. m.
Mat.4:8.devil taketh him up into an
exceeding h. m., Lu. 4: 5.
17:1.Jes.taketh Peter,James,John
into an h. m., Mk. 9: 2.
Re. 21:10. carried me in spirit to h.
See HOLY mountain. ⌊m.

In or into MOUNTAIN. ⌈m.

Ge.19:30.Lot went fr. Zoar, dwelt i.
Ex.15:17.plant them i. m. of inher.
Nu. 13:17. Moses said, Go up i-o m.
De. 1: 24. turned and went i-o m.
Jos. 20: 7. Kirjath-arba i. m. of
Ju. 1:9. Canaanites that dwell i.m.

Ju.1:34.Amor.forced chil.of Dan i-o
8:37. trumpet i. m. of Ephr. [m.
1 S. 23 : 14. David i. a m. of Ziph
2 Ch. 2 : 2. told 80.000 to hew i. m.
Ps. 48 : 1. G. to be praised i. m. of
his holiness [plant it
Eze. 17 : 23. i. m. of Israel will I
Am. 4 : 1. ye kine, i. m. of Samaria
6:1.Woe to th.trust i. m. of Sama.
Mat. 5:1. and seeing the multitudes,
he went up i-o a m., 14:23.-15:
29. Mk. 3 : 13.-6 : 46. Lu. 6:12.-
9:28. Jn. 6:3, 15.

In or into this MOUNTAIN.

De. 32 : 49.Get thee i-o t.m.Abarim
Is.25:6.i. t. m. shall L. make feast
7. destroy i.t.m. face of covering
10. i. t. m. shall hand of L. rest
Jn. 4 : 20. fa-e worshipped i. t. m.
21. nei. i. t. m. nor Jerus. wor- [ship Fa.

MOUNTAINS.

Ge. 7 : 20. and the m. were covered
8 : 4. ark rested upon m.of Ararat
5. in 10th month tops of m. seen
Nu. 33 : 48. departed fr. m. of Abar.
De. 12:2.destr. places upon high m.
Jos. 11 : 21. cut off Anakim fr. m.
18 : 12. border was thro. m. westw.
Ju. 5 : 5. m. melted from before L.
11:37.I go up and do. upon m.[m.
38. bewailed her virginity upon
2 S. 1 : 21. m. of Gilboa, let no dew
1 K. 19 : 11. a strong wind rent m.
1 Ch.12:8.swift as roes upon the m.
2 Ch.18:16.see all Isr.scattered upon
Jb. 9 : 5. Which removeth m. [m.
28:9. overturneth m. by the roots
40 : 20. Surely m. bring him food
Ps. 36 : 6. Thy righte-n. like gr. m.
46 : 2. tho. m. be carried into sea
3.though m.shake with.swelling
65 : 6. by strength setteth fast m.
72:3.m.shall bring peace to people
76:4.Thou art more glori. than m.
83:14. as flames setteth m. on fire
90 : 2. Bef. m. were brought forth
104 : 6. the waters stood above m.
8. They go up by m. down by
114 : 4. m. skipped like rams, 6.
125:2. As the m. are round Jerus.
133:3. as dew descended upon m.
144 : 5. touch m. they sh. smoke
147:8.maketh grass grow upon m.
148 : 9. m.and all hills praise L.
Pr. 8 : 25. Before m. were settled
Can. 2 : 8. cometh leaping upon m.
17.be thou like a roe upon m., 8:
4:8. look fr.Amana and m. of [14.
Is. 2:14. day of L. be upon high m.
14:25.upon my m. tread him und.
18 : 3. lifteth up an ensign on m.
34 : 3. m. be melted with their bl.
40 : 12. who weighed m. in scales
41 : 15. thou shalt thresh the m.
42:15.I will make waste m. [49:13.
44 ; 23. break into singing, ye m.,
49 : 11. I will make my m. a way
52:7. How beautiful upon m., Na.
54 : 10. For m. shall depart [1:15.
55:12. m. shall break into singing
64:1.m. might flow at thy pres-e,3.
65:7.have burned incense upon m.
9. out of Jud. inheritor of my m.
Je. 4 : 24. I beheld m. they trembl.
9 : 10. For m. will I take weeping
13 : 16. feet stumble upon dark m.
17:26. come fr. m. bringing off-gs
31:5.plant vines upon m.of Sama.
46 : 18. as Tabor am. m. so sh. ye
50:6. have turned them a.w.on m.
La. 4 : 19. pursued us upon m.
Eze. 6 : 2. set thy face tow.m.of Isr.
3. Ye m. of Isr., hear word of L.
7:16. they sh. be on m. like doves
18:6. hath not eaten upon m., 15.
11.eaten upon m.and defiled [m.
19:9. voice no more be heard upon
Eze. 22 : 9. in thee they eat upon m.
31 : 12. upon m. branches fallen
32:5. I will lay thy flesh upon m.
33:28. m. of Isr. shall be desolate
34:6. My sheep wandered thro m.
13. will feed th. upon m. of Isr.,
35:8.will fill m. with his slain [14.
12. hast spoken against m.of Isr.
36 : 1. prophesy unto m. of Isr.,
and say, Ye m. of Isr., hear
word of L., 4. [branches
8.ye,O m. of Isr.ye sh.shoot forth
37 : 22. one nation upon m. of Isr.
38:8. is gathered out ag. m. of Isr.
20. the m. shall be thrown down
21.call sword ag.him thro.my m.
39:2.will bri. thee upon m. of Isr.
4.Thou shalt fall upon m. of Isr.
17. a great sacrif. upon m.of Isr.
Jo. 2:2.as morning spread upon m.
3 : 18. m. sh. drop down new wine
Am.1:†13. bec. they divided the m.
3 : 9. Assemble upon m. of Sama.
4 : 13. formeth m. L. is his name
9 : 13. m. shall drop sweet wine
Mi.1:4.m.sh. be molten under him
6 : 1. Arise, contend thou bef. m.
2. Hear, O m. L.'s controversy
Na. 1 : 5. The m. quake at him
3:18.thy peo.is scattered upon m.
Ha. 3 : 6. everl. m. were scattered
10. m. saw thee, and trembled
Hag.1:11.for a drought upon the m.
Zch. 6 : 1. chariots between 2 m. of
Mal. 1 : 3. and laid Esau's m. waste
Mat. 18:12. goeth into m.and seek.
24:16. let th.in Judea flee into m.
1 Co. 13:2. so that I co. remove m.
Re. 16 : 20. the m. were not found
17 : 9. seven heads are seven m.

In the MOUNTAINS.

Ex. 32:12. bring out to slay them i.
Nu.13:29.Amorites dwell i. m. [m.
33 : 47. pitched i. m. of Abarim
De.2:37.camest not unto cities i.m.
Jos. 10 : 6. kings i. m. are gathered
11 : 3. to the Jebusite i. m. [sion
12 : 8. i. m. Jos. gave for a posses-
15 : 48. i. m. Shamir and Jattir
Ju.6:2.Israel made them dens i. m.
1 S.26:20.doth hunt partridge i.m.
1 K. 5 : 15. 80,000 hewers i. m.
2 Ch. 21:11. made high places i.m.
26 : 10. Uzziah had vine dressers i.
27 : 4. built cities i. m. of Jud.[m.
Ps. 87:1. His founda. is i. holy m.
Is.13:4. noise of multitude i.m.like
Mk.5:5. night and day he was i.m.
He.11:38.wandered in deserts and i.

Of the Mountains. [m.

Ge.8:5. tops o. m. seen in 10th mo.
22 : 2. offer him upon one o.m. I
Nu. 23 : 7. Balak bro-t me out o.m.
De 32:22. set on fire founda-s o.m.
33: 15. chief things o. ancient m.
Jos. 11 : 2. to kings on north o.m.
Ju. 9 : 25. liers in wait in top o. m.
36.come people down fr.top o.m.
seest shadow o. m. as if men
2 K.19:23. to height o.m.,Is.37:24
Jb. 24 : 8. wet with showers o. m.
39 : 8. range o. m. in his pasture
Ps.50:11. I know all the fowls o.m.
72:16.handful of corn upon top o.
Pr. 27:25. herbs o.m. are gath.[m.
Is. 2 : 2. shall be established in the
top o. m., Mi. 4 : 1. [o. m.
17: 13. shall be chased as the chaff
18 : 6. shall be left to fowls o. m.
42:11. let them shout fr. top o.m.
Je. 3 : 23. hoped for fr. mult. o.m.
32:44.take witnesses in cities o.m.
33:13.in cities o.m. sh. flocks pass
Eze.6:13.slain shall be in tops o.m.
7: 7. not the sounding again o.m.
Ho. 4 : 13. sacrifice upon tops o. m.
Jo. 2 : 5. of chariots on tops o. m.
Jon. 2 : 6. I went to bottom o. m.
Zch.14:5. ye sh. flee to valley o.m.
Re. 6:15. hid thems. in rocks o.m.

To or unto the MOUNTAINS.

Is. 22 : 5. it is a day of crying t.m.
Eze. 6 : 3. Thus saith L. t.m., 36:4.
32 : 6. water with thy blood t. m.
36:1.son of man,prophesy u.m.,6.
Ho. 10 : 8. shall say t. m. Cover us
Mk. 5 : 11. nigh u. m. herd of swine
13: 14. that be in Judea flee t.m.,
Lu. 21: 21. [on us, Re. 6: 16.
Lu. 23 : 30. begin to say t. m. Fall

MOUNTING. [Noun.]

Is. 15:5. by m. up of Luhith sh. go

MOURN.

Ge. 23 : 2. Ab. came to m. for Sarah
1 S. 16 : 1. How long wilt thou m.
2 S.3:31.and m.bef. Abner [for Saul
1 K. 13:29. old prophet came to m.
14 : 13. all Israel shall m. for him
Ne. 8 : 9. day is holy unto L. m. not
Jb.2:11. appointment to m.wi. him
5:11. that those wh. m. be exalted
14:22. his soul within him sh. m.
Ps.55:2. I m. in my complaint, and
Pr. 5 : 11. And thou m. at the last
29 : 2. wicked bear rule, people m.
Ec. 3 : 4. a time to m. time to dance
Is.3:26.her gates sh. lament and m.
16: 7. for Kir-hareseth shall ye m.
19:8.fishers sh.m. | 38:14.I did m.
59: 11. we m. sore like doves [m.
61 : 2. sent me to comfort all that
3. to appoint unto them m.in Zi.
66:10. rejoice all ye th. m. for her
Je.4:28. For this shall earth m. and
12 : 4. How long shall the land m.
48:31. sh. m. for men of Kir-heres
La. 1 : 4. ways of Zion do m. bec.
Eze. 7 : 12. let not the seller m.
27.king shall m.prince be clothed
24:16.nei. shalt thou m. nor weep
23.ye sh. pine away and m. [him
31 : 15. I caused Lebanon to m. for
Ho. 4 : 3. Theref. shall the land m.
10 : 5. people sh. m. over Samaria
Jo. 1 : 9. priests, L.'s ministers m.
Am. 1 : 2. habita-s of shepherds sh.
8 : 8. and every one m., 9 : 5. [m.
Zch. 12 : 10. shall m. for him as one
12. land sh. m. ev. family apart
Mat. 5 : 4. Blessed are they that m.
9 : 15. chil. of bridechamber m.?
24 : 30. shall all tribes of earth m.
Lu. 6 : 25. that laugh, for ye sh. m.
Ja. 4 : 9. Be afflicted, and m. and
Re.18:11. merchants shall weep and

MOURNED. [m.

Ge. 37 : 34. Jacob m. for his son
50 : 3. Egyptians m. for Jacob, 10.
Ex. 33 : 4. people heard these evil
tidings, they m., Nu. 14 : 39.
Nu. 20:29. congregation m. for Aa-
1 S.15:35. Samuel m. for Saul [ron
2 S.1:12.they m. for Saul and Jona.
11 : 26. Bath-sheba m. for Uriah
13 : 37. David m. for his son Abs.
14:2.as one that had long time m.
1 K.13:30. they m. over man of God
14:18.all Israel m. for Jerob.'s son
1 Ch.7:22. Ephraim their father m.
2 Ch. 35: 24. all Jud. m. for Josiah
Ezr. 10 : 6. he m. for transgression
Ne. 1 : 4. I sat and m. certain days
Zch. 7 : 5. When ye m. did ye fast
Mat. 11 : 17. We have m. unto you
ye have not lamented, Lu.7:32.
Mk.16:10. she told them as they m.
1 Co. 5 : 2. puffed up, and have not

MOURNER, S. [m.

2 S. 14 : 2. feign thyself to be a m.
Jb. 29:25. one that comforteth m-s
Ec. 12:5. m-s go about streets [m-s
Is. 57 : 18. comforts unto him and
Ho.9:4.sacrifices be as bread of m-s

MOURNETH.
2 S. 19 : 1. king **m.** for Absalom
Ps.35:14.as one that **m.** for mother
88 : 9. Mine eye **m.** by affliction
Is. 24 : 4. The earth **m.** and fadeth,
7. The new wine **m.** ⌊33 : 9.
Je. 12 : 11. my vineyard desolate **m.**
14 : 2. Judah **m.** gates languish
23 : 10. bec. of swearing land **m.**
Jo.1:10. land **m.** for corn is wasted
Zch. 12 : 10. as one that **m.** for first-
MOURNFULLY. ⌊born
Mal. 3 : 14. what profit we walked
MOURNING. [Noun.] ⌊m.
Ge. 27:41. days of **m.** for my father
50:4.when days of his **m.**were past
10. he mourning a **m.** for his father Jacob 7 days ⌈grievous **m.**
11. Canaanites saw **m.** This is a
De. 26:14. have not eaten in my **m.**
34: 8. so the days of **m.** for Moses
2 S. 11 : 27. **m.** was past David sent
19:2. the victory that day into **m.**
Es. 4 : 3. was great **m.** among Jews
9 : 22. turned fr. **m.** into good day
Jb. 3 : 8. who are ready to raise **m.**
30 : 31. My harp is turned to **m.**
Ps.30:11.turned my **m.** into dancing
Ec. 7 : 2. better to go to house of **m.**
4. heart of wise is in house of **m.**
Is. 22 : 12. that day did L. call to **m.**
51 : 11. sorrow and **m.** sh. flee aw.
60:20. days of thy **m.** shall be end-
61 : 3. to give oil of joy for **m.** ⌊ed
Je. 6 : 26. make thee **m.** as for only
16 : 5. enter not into ho. of **m.** ⌊son
7. Nei. sh. men tear thems. in **m.**
31:13. I will turn their **m.** into joy
La. 2 : 5. in daughter of Judah **m.**
5 : 15. our dance is turned into **m.**
Eze.2:10. lamentations, **m.** and woe
24 : 17. make no **m.** for the dead
31 : 15. I caused a **m.** I covered
Jo. 2 : 12. turn ye to me with **m.**
Am.5:16. sh. call husbandm. to **m.**
8 : 10. I will turn your feasts into **m.** make it as **m.** of only son
Mi. 1 : 8. I will make a **m.** as owls
11. came not in **m.** of Beth-ezel
Zch.12:11.**m.** in Jerus. as **m.** of Had.
Mat. 2 : 18. was heard gr. **m.** Rachel
2 Co. 7 : 7. when he told us your **m.**
Ja. 4 : 9. laughter be turned into **m.**
Re. 18 : 8. in one day death and **m.**
MOURNING. [Part.]
Ge. 37 : 35. down to grave unto my
2 S.14:2.put on **m.** apparel ⌊son **m.**
Es. 6 : 12. Haman hasted to ho **m.**
Jb. 30 : 28. I went **m.** without sun
Ps.38:6.I go **m.** all day long ⌈43:2.
42: 9.why go **m.** bec. of oppression,
Je.9:17.Consider, call for **m.** women
Eze. 7 : 16. all of them **m.** for iniq-s
Da. 10 : 2. I Daniel was **m.** 3 weeks
MOUSE. ⌈uncl.
Le. 11 : 29. weasel and **m.** shall be
Is.66:17.eating the abomi-n and **m.**
MOUTH.
Ge. 8 : 11. in her **m.** an olive leaf
24:57.call damsel, inquire at her **m.**
29:2. gr. stone was upon well's **m.**
3. rolled stone from well's **m.**, 10.
34:†26. slew Hamor wi. **m.** of sw.
42:27. his money was in his sack's **m.**, 43 : 12, 21.—44 : 1, 2, 8.
43:†7. we told acc. to **m.** of words
45:†21. wagons, acc. to **m.** of Pha.
Ex.4:11. Who hath made man's **m.**
16.he shall be to thee inst. of **m.**
Nu.4:†27.At **m.** of Aaron be service
12:8.Wi. him will I speak **m.** to **m.**
35:30.Whoso killeth any person, be put to death by **m.** of witnesses, De. 17 : 6.—19 : 15. ⌈one **m.**
Jos. 9 : †2. they gathered toge. with
10:18.gr. stones upon **m.** of cave, 27.
1 S.1:12.prayed, Eli marked her **m.**
2 S. 17: 19. covering over well's **m.**
1 K. 7 : 31. **m.** of it within chapiter
19:18. **m.** wh. hath not kissed Baal
22 : 13. prophets declare good unto king with one **m.**, 2 Ch. 18:†12.
22. I will be lying spirit in **m.** of prophets, 23. 2 Ch. 18 : 21, 22.
2 K.10:†21.full, they stood **m.** to **m.**
21:†16. filled Jerus. from **m.** to **m.**
2Ch.18:†12.decl. good to k. with 1 **m.**
Ezr.9:†11.abom. filled land fr. **m.** to
Jb. 5:16. iniq. stoppeth her **m.** ⌊**m.**
12:11.Doth not **m.** taste meat? 34:
32 : 5. no ans. in **m.** of these ⌊3.
†19. my belly as wine hath no **m.**
34:†27.Doth eagle mount by thy **m.**
Ps. 8 : 2. Out of **m.** of babes, Mat.
22:21.Save me fr. lion's **m.** ⌊21:16.
32: 9. **m.** must be held in with bit
37:30. **m.** of right. speaketh wisd.
38 : 14. in whose **m.** no reproofs
63: 11. **m.** that speaketh lies shall
69:15.let not pit shut **m.** upon me
107:42.all iniquity sh. stop her **m.**
109:2.**m.** of wicked, **m.** of deceitful
126:2.was our **m.** filled with laugh-
141:7.Our bones at grave's **m.** ⌊ter
144:8. Whose **m.** speak. vanity, 11.
Pr. 4 : 24. Put away a froward **m.**
5 : 3. her **m.** is smoother than oil
6:12. walketh with frow **m.**, 10:32.
8:13. froward **m.** do I hate ⌈11.
10:6. violence cover-h **m.** of wick.,
14. **m.** of foolish is near destruc.
31. **m.** of just bringeth wisdom
11:11.city overthr. by **m.** of wick.
12 : 6. **m.** of upright shall deliver
14 : 3. In **m.** of foolish is a rod of
15:2. **m.** of fools poureth foolishn.
14. **m.** of fools feed. on foolishn.
28. **m.** of wicked poureth evil
18 : 4. words of **m.** as deep waters
7. A fool's **m.** is his destruction
19:28. the **m.** of wicked devoureth
22:14. The **m.** of a strange woman
26 : 7. so parable in **m.** of fools, 9.
28. flattering **m.** worketh ruin
30 : 20. she eateth, wipeth her **m.**
Is. 9:12. shall devour Isr. with open
17. every **m.** speaketh folly ⌊**m.**
19:7. paper reeds by **m.** of brooks
57 : 4. ag. whom make wide **m.**?
59:21.my Spi. not depart out of **m.**
Je. 32 : 4. with him **m.** to **m.**, 34:3.
36:4.from **m.** of Jerem., 27, 32.—45:1
44 : 17. what thing out of our **m.**
26. no more named in **m.** of man
48 : 28. nest inside of hole's **m.**
La. 3 : 38. Out of **m.** of Most High
Da. 3 : 26. near to **m.** of furnace
6 : 17. stone laid upon **m.** of den
7 : 5. it had three ribs in **m.** of it
8. a **m.** speaking great things, 20.
Ho.2:17.names of Baalim out of **m.**
Am. 3 : 12. As shepherd tak-h out of
Na. 3 : 12. fall into **m.** of eater ⌊**m.**
Zch. 5 : 8. weight of lead upon **m.**
Mat. 12 : 34. of abundance of heart **m.** speaketh, Lu. 6 : 45. ⌈17.
15: 11. goeth into **m.** defileth not,
18. things out of **m.** come fr. heart
18:16. in **m.** of two or 3 witnesses, 2 Co. 13 : 1. ⌈perfected
21 : 16. Out of **m.** of babes hast
Lu. 1 : 70. spake by **m.** of prophets
21:15.I will give you **m.** and wisd.
Ac. 1 : 16. Holy Ghost spake by **m.** of David, 4 : 25. ⌈prophets, 21.
3 : 18. God shewed by **m.** of his
15 : 27. shall tell you same by **m.**
23 : 2. com-d to smite him on **m.**
Ro.3:14.Whose **m.** is full of cursing
19. that every **m.** may be stopped
10:10. with **m.** confession is made
15: 6. may with one **m.** glorify G.
1 Co. 9 : 9. not muzzle **m.** of ox
2 Ti. 4 : 17. deliv-d out of **m.** of lion
Ja. 3:10. Out of same **m.** proceed-h
2 Jn.†12.speak **m.** to **m.**, 3 Jn.†14.
Re. 13 : 5. **m.** speaking blasphemies
16 : 13. spirits out of **m.** of dragon
His MOUTH.
Ge. 25:†28. for venison was in **h.m.**
Ex. 4 : 15. I will be with **h. m.**
Nu. 30 : 2. proceedeth out of **h.m.**
1 S.14:26. no man put ha. to **h.m.**,
17:35.I deliv-d it out of **h.m.** ⌊27.
2 S.17:†5.let us hear what in **h.m.**
18:25. If alone, is tidings in **h.m.**
22:9.fire out out of **h.m.** devoured, Ps. 18 : 8. ⌈Da., 2 Ch. 6 : 4.
1 K. 8 : 15. spake with **h. m.** unto
2 K.4:34.put **h.m.** upon **h.m.** ⌈m.
1 Ch.16:12.Remem judgments of **h.**
Jb.15:30. by breath of **h.m.** be sh.
20:12.Tho. wickedness sweet in **h.**
13.tho. keep it within **h.m.** ⌊m.
22:22. Receive the law from **h.m.**
37:2. sound th. goeth out of **h.m.**
40:23. draw up Jordan into **h.m.**
41:19. Out of **h.m.** burning lamps
21. a flame goeth out of **h. m.**
Ps. 10 : 7. **h. m.** is full of cursing
33:6.host made by breath of **h.m.**
105:5.Remem. judgments of **h.m.**
Pr. 2 : 6. out of **h. m.** knowledge
11:9.hypocrite with **h.m.** destroy-h
13:2.sh. eat good by fruit of **h.m.**
3. keepeth **h. m.** keepeth his life
15 : 23. hath joy by ans. of **h. m.**
16 : 10. **h. m.** transgresseth not
23. heart of wise teacheth **h. m.**
26. for **h. m.** craveth it of him
18:6. and **h.m.** calleth for strokes
19:24. not bring it to **h.m.**, 26:15.
20 : 17. **h.m.** be filled with gravel
21:23. keepeth **h.m.** keepeth soul
Ec. 6 : 7. labour of man is for **h.m.**
10 : † 13. end of **h. m.** is madness
Can.1:2. Let him kiss me wi. **h.m.**
5 : 16. **h. m.** is most sweet, this
Is. 11:4. smite the earth with **h.m.**
53: 9. nei. was any deceit in **h.m.**
Je.9:8.speak-h peaceably with **h.m.**
51:44. out of **h.m.** that he swall-d
La.1:†18. I have rebelled ag. **h.m.**
3:29. he putteth **h.m.** in the dust
Zch. 9: 7. will take bl. out of **h.m.**
Mal. 2 : 6. law of truth was in **h.m.**
7. should seek law at **h.m.** ⌈m.
Lu.11:54.catch somewhat out of **h.**
22 : 71. have heard of **h.** own **m.**
Jn.19:29.sponge and put it to **h.m.**
Ac.22:14.shouldest hear voice of **h.**
2 Th. 2 : 8. consume with **h.m.** ⌊**m.**
1 Pe.2:22. nei. guile found in **h.m.**
Re.1:16. out of **h.m.** went a sharp sword, 19 : 15, 21. ⌈m. water
12 : 15. the serpent cast out of **h.**
16.flood dragon cast out of **h.m.**
13 : 2. **h.m.** was as mouth of lion
See FRUIT.
See Mouth of the LORD.
Mine own or my MOUTH.
Ge.45:12. it is **m.m.** that speaketh
1 S. 2 : 1. **m. m.** is enlarged over
Jb. 7 : 11. I will not refrain **m. m.**
9 : 20. **m. o. m.** sh. condemn me
16 : 5. strengthen you with **m.m.**
19:16. entreated serv. with **m.m.**
23:4.wo. fill **m.m.** with arguments
31:27.or **m.m.** hath kissed my ha.
30. Nei. suffered **m. m.** to sin
33: 2. tongue hath spok. in **m.m.**
40: 4. I will lay hand upon **m.m.**
Ps.17:3. **m.m.** shall not transgress
34 : 1. his praise shall be in **m.m.**
39: 1. will keep **m.m.** with bridle
40:3.hath put a new song in **m.m.**
49 : 3. **m.m.** shall speak of wisd.
51:15.**m.m.** sh. shew forth praise
63 : 5. **m. m.** shall praise thee
66 : 14. **m.m.** hath spoken, when
17. I cried unto him with **m.m.**

Ps.71:8.Let **m.m.** be filled wi.praise
15.**m.m.**sh. shew forth righte-n.
89:1.wi.**m.m.** make known faithf.
109:30.I will praise L. with **m.m.**
119:108. Accept offerings of **m.m.**
141:3. Set a watch, O L.bef.**m.m.**
145: 21. **m. m.** speak praise of L.
Pr. 8: 7. **m. m.** shall speak truth
Is.6:7. he laid the coal upon **m.m.**
30: 2. have not asked at **m. m.**
34: 16. **m.m.** it hath commanded
48: 3. former things out of **m.m.**
49:2.made **m. m.** like a sharp sw.
Je. 1: 9. put forth touched **m. m.**
15: 19. saith L., shalt be as **m.m.**
36: 6. roll hast written fr. **m. m.**
Eze.3:3. it was in **m.m.** like honey
4:14. nei.abomina.flesh into **m.m.**
Da. 10: 3. flesh nor wine in **m. m.**
Ac.11:8. at any time entered **m.m.**
Re.2:16. fight with sword of **m.m.**
3:16.I will spue thee out of **m.m.**
10: 10. book was in **m.m.** sweet

MOUTH with open.

Nu.16:30. L. make new thing,earth
Jos. 10: 22. **o.m.** of the cave⌊**o.m.**
Jb.35:16. doth Job **o.**his **m.**in vain
Ps.78:2.I will **o.**my **m.** in a parable
81: 10. **o.** thy **m.** wide,I will fill it
Pr. 31: 8. **o.** thy **m.** for the dumb
9. **o.** thy **m.** judge righteously
Is. 9:12. sh. devour Isr. with **o.m.**
Eze. 2: 8. **o.** thy **m.** and eat that I
3:27.when I speak I will **o.**thy **m.**
16: 63. never **o.** thy **m.** any more
21:22. appoint capt-s to **o.** the **m.**
Mat. 13:35. I will **o.m.** in parables
Ac. 18: 14. Paul was about to **o. m.**
2 Co. 6: 11. our **m.** is **o.** unto you
Ep. 6: 19. may **o.** my **m.** boldly

MOUTH with opened.⌈bl.

Ge.4:11.earth **o.m.**to receive bro.'s
Nu. 16: 32. earth **o.** her **m.** ewallowed them up, 26:10. De. 11:6.
22:28. L. **o.m.** of the ass, she said
Ju.11:35.have **o.**my **m.**unto L.,36.
36. if hast **o.** thy **m.** unto L.
Jb. 3: 1. **o.** Job his **m.** and cursed
29: 23. **o.m.** wide ag. me, Ps. 35:
33:2.Behold, I have **o.** my **m.**⌊21.
Ps.39:9.I was dumb, I **o.**not my **m.**
109:2.**m.** of deceitful are **o.** ag.me
119:131.I **o.**my **m.**and panted,for
Is.5:14.hell hath **o.**her **m.**without
10:14.was none th. **o.m.**or peeped
53:7. oppressed, yet **o.** not his **m.**
Eze. 3:2. I **o.** my **m.** he caused ⌈22.
24:27.**m.** be **o.** to him escap-d, 33:
Da. 10: 16. I **o.** my **m.** and spake
Mat.5:2.he **o.**his **m.**and taught th.
17: 27. hast **o.** his **m.** shalt find
Lu.1:64.his **m.** was **o.** immediately
Ac. 8:32. like lamb dumb, **o.**not his
35.Philip **o.m.** | 10:34.Peter⌊**m.**
2 Co. 6:11. O Cor. our **m.**is **o.**unto
Re.12:16.earth **o.m.** helped woman
13: 6. he **o.** his **m.** in blasphemy

MOUTH with openeth, ing.

Ps. 38: 13. dumb that **o-h** not **m.**
Pr.24:7.fool **o-h** not his **m.** in gate
31:26. She **o.** her **m.** with wisdom
Is. 53: 7. as sheep, so **o.** not his **m.**
Eze. 29:21. will give thee **o-g** of **m.**

MOUTH with roof.

Jb. 29:10. tongue cleaved to **r.**of **m.**
Ps. 137: 6. let my tongue cleave to **r.** of my **m.** ⌈best wine
Can. 7: 9. the **r.** of thy **m.** like the
La. 4: 4. tongue of child cleaveth to **r.** of **m.** ⌈to **r.** of **m.**
Eze. 3: 26. make thy tongue cleave
Ho. 8: † 1. trumpet to **r.** of thy **m.**

Their MOUTH. ⌈tried

De. 21: † 5.by **t. m.** every controv. be
Ju. 7: 6. lapped, putting their hand to **t. m.** ⌈**t. m.**
Ne. 9:20. withheldest not manna fr.
Jb. 5: 15. saveth poor from **t. m.**
16: 10. gaped upon me with **t. m.**
29: 9. princes laid hand on **t. m.**
Ps. 5: 9. is no faithfuln. in **t. m.**
17: 10. with **t. m.** speak proudly
49: † 13. posterity delight in **t. m.**
58:6. Break teeth, O God, in **t.m.**
59: 7. they belch out with **t. m.**
12. For the sin of **t.m.** and words
62: 4. bless with **t. m.** curse in-
73:9.set **t.m.** ag. heavens ⌊wardly
78: 36. did flatter him with **t. m.**
149:6.high praises of G.be in **t.m.**
Is. 29:13. peo. draw near with **t. m.**
Je. 7: 28. truth is cut off fr. **t. m.**
12: 2. thou art near in **t.m.** far fr.
La. 2: 16. enemies have open. **t.m.**
Eze. 33: 31. with **t. m.** shew love
34:10. will deliv. my flock fr. **t.m.**
Mi. 6: 12. tongue is deceitf. in **t.m.**
7:16.lay their ha. upon **t.m.** ⌈**m.**
Zph.3:13. nei. deceitful tongue in t.
Zch.14:12. tongue consume in **t.m.**
Mat. 15: 8. draweth nigh with **t.m.**
Re. 9: 19. power is in **t.m.** and tails
11: 5. fire proceedeth out of **t. m.**
14. 5. in **t.m.** was found no guile

Thine own or thy MOUTH.

Ex. 4: 12. I will be with **t. m.**, 15.
13: 9. that L.'s law be in **t. m.**
23:13. no mention of gods out of **t.**
De.23:23.th.promised wi.**t.m.** ⌊**m.**
Jos.1:8. law not depart out of **t.m.**
Ju.9:38. said Zebul, Where is **t.m.**
11:36. proceeded out of **t.m.** ⌈32.
18:19. lay hand upon **t.m.**, Pr.30:
2 S. 1: 16. **t. m.** testified ag. thee
1 K. 8: 24. spakest with **t.m.**, 2 Ch.
Jb.8:21. **t. m.** with laughing ⌊6:15.
15:5. **t.m.** uttereth thine iniquity
6. **t. o. m.** condemneth thee
33:†6. Behold, I am acc. to **t. m.**
39:†27. Doth eagle mount by **t.m.**
Ps. 50:16. shouldest take my cov. in
19.Thou givest **t.m.**to evil ⌊**t.m.**
103: 5. satisfieth **t. m.** with good
119:13.declared judgments of **t.m.**
72.The law of **t.m.** is better than
88. sh. I keep testimony of **t. m.**
Pr.27:2. let ano. praise, not **t.o.m.**
Ec. 5: 2. Be not rash with **t. m.** to
6. Suffer not **t.m.** to cause to sin
Eze.16:56. Sodom not mentioned by **t. m.** ⌈in thy bosom
Mi.7:5 keep doors of **t.m.** from her
Lu. 19: 22. out of **t. o. m.** will I
Ro. 10: 9. if confess with **t.m.** L.J.
Re.10:9. be in **t.m.** sweet as honey

MOUTH with word, s.

Ex. 4: 15. shalt put **w-s** in his **m.**
Nu.22:38. **w.** G. putteth in my **m.**, shall I speak, 23: 12. ⌈16.
23:5. L. put a **w.** in Balaam's **m.**,
De. 8:3. by ev. **w.** out of **m.** of God doth man live, Mat. 4: 4. ⌈**m.**
18: 18. and will put my **w-s** in his
30: 14. **w.** is nigh thee, in thy **m.** and in thy heart, Ro. 10: 8.
32:1.hear, O earth, **w-s** of my **m.**
2 S.14:3.Joab put **w-s**in her **m.**,19.
1 K. 17: 24. **w.** of L. in thy **m.** is
22:13. **w.** of prophets declare good to k. wi. one **m.**, 2 Ch. 18: 12.
2 Ch. 35: 22. hearkened not unto **w-s** from **m.** of G. ⌈1: 1.
36:21. **w.** by **m.** of Jere., 22. Ezr.
Ezr. 8: † 17. I put **w-s** in their **m.**
Es.7:8. as **w.** went out of king's **m.**
Jb.8:2.**w-s**of thy **m.** be like winds?
15:13.lettest such **w-s** go out of **m.**
23: 12. I esteemed **w-s** of his **m.** more than my food ⌈acceptable
Ps. 19: 14. Let **w-s** of my **m.** be
36: 3. **w-s** of his **m.** are iniquity
54:2.give ear to the **w-s** of my **m.**,
78: 1. Pr. 7: 24. ⌈than butter
55:21. The **w-s** of his **m.** smoother
Ps. 119: 43. take not **w.** of truth out of my **m.** ⌈**m.**
103. **w-s** sweeter than honey to
138: 4. praise when they hear **w-s** of thy **m.** ⌈**m.**, 5: 7.
Pr. 4: 5. nei. decline fr. **w-s** of thy
6:2 snared with **w-s** of **m.** ⌈**m.**
7: 24. O chil. attend to **w-s** of my
8:8.all **w-s** of my **m.** are in right.
18:4. **w-s** of man's **m.** are as deep
Ec.10:12. **w-s** of wise man's **m.** gra-
13. **w-s** of his **m.** foolishn. ⌊cious
Is. 45: 23. **w.** is gone out of my **m.**
51:16.put my **w-s** in thy **m.**,Je.1:9
55:11.So **w.**be goeth out of my **m.**
59: 21. **w-s** I have put in thy **m.**
Je.5:14.make my **w-s** in thy **m.**fire
9: 20. let ear rec. **w.** of **m.**, 10: 1
36: 17. How didst thou write these **w-s** at his **m.** ⌈15: 7.
18. **w-s** unto me with his **m.**,Ac.
Eze. 3: 17. hear **w.** at my **m.**,33:7.
Da.4:31. While **w.** was in king's **m.**
Ho.6:5.slain them by **w-s** of my **m.**
Zch. 8:9. hear **w-s** by **m.** of proph-s
Lu.4:22. gracious **w-s** out of his **m.**
Ac.15:7.Gent.by my **m.**should hear **w.** of gospel ⌈swelling **w-s**
Jude 16. their **m.** speaketh great

Your MOUTH.

Nu. 32: 24. proceeded out of **y. m.**
1 S.2:3. not arrogancy out of **y.m.**
Jb. 21:5. lay your hand upon **y.m.**
Eze.35:13.with **y.m.** ye have boast-
Jo. 1:5. wine is cut off fr. **y.m.** ⌊ed
Ep. 4: 29. let no corrupt communi. proceed out of **y.m.**, Col. 3: 8.

MOUTHS.

De. 31: 19. song, put it in their **m.**
21. not forgott. out of **m.** of seed
1 S. 13: † 21. they had file with **m.**
Ps. 22: 13. gaped upon me with **m.**
78: 30. while meat was in their **m.**
115:5. have **m.** speak not, 135:16.
135:17.nei. breath in their **m.**⌈**m.**
Is. 41:† 15 threshing instru.having
52: 15. kings sh. shut **m.** at him
Je. 44:25. Ye spoken with your **m.**
La. 3: 46. enemies opened their **m.**
Eze.39:†11.sh.stop **m.**of passengers
Da. 6: 22. God hath shut lions' **m.**
Mi. 3: 5. putteth not into their **m.**
Tit.1:11.Whose **m.**must be stopped
He. 11: 33. who stopped **m.** of lions
Ja. 3: 3. we put bits in horses' **m.**
Re. 9: 17. out of **m.** issued fire, 18.

MOVE. ⌈man

Ex. 11: 7. not a dog **m.** tongue ag.
Le. 11: 10. of all that **m.** in waters
De. 23:25. not **m.** sickle unto neighbour's standing corn
32: 21. I will **m.** them to jealousy
Ju. 13: 25. Spirit of L. began to **m.**
2 S.7:10.may **m.** no more, 2 K. 21:
2 K. 5:†11. he will **m.** his hand ⌊8.
23: 18. let no man **m.** his bones
Je. 10:4. fasten with nails it **m.** not
Am. 9: † 9. cause to **m.** ho. of Isr.
Mi. 7:17. sh. **m.** out of their holes
Mat.23:4.they thems.will not **m.**th.
Ac. 17: 28. For in him we live, **m.**
20:24. none of these things **m.** me

MOVEABLE.

Pr. 5:6. her ways are **m.** canst not

MOVED. ⌊know

Ge.1:2.Spirit of God **m.**upon waters
7:21. flesh died th. **m.** upon earth
De. 32: 21. have **m.** me to jealousy
Jos. 10: 21. none **m.** tongue ag. Isr.
15:18.**m.**him to ask field, Ju.1:14.
Ru. 1: 19. city was **m.** about them
1 S. 1: 13. she spake, only lips **m.**
2 S. 18: 33. the king was much **m.**
22:8.the foundations of heaven **m.**
24: 1. he **m.** David against them
1 Ch. 16: 30. world sh. be stable, th. it be not **m.**, Ps. 93: 1.-96: 10.

1 Ch.17:9. sh. dwell, be m. no more
2 Ch.18:31. God m. them to depart
Ezr. 4 : 15. m. sedition of old time
Es. 5 : 9. Haman saw Mord. m. not
Jb. 37 : 1. At this my heart is m.
41:23. The flakes of his flesh, they cannot be m. [30:6.-62:2, 6.
Ps. 10 : 6. I shall not be m., 16:8.-
13 : 4. they rejoice when I am m.
15:5. doeth these sh. never be m.
17:†5.that my footsteps be not m.
18 : 7. foundations of the hills m.
21:7.king trusteth in L.,not be m.
46:5.she sh.unt be m.G.shall help
6. heathen raged,kingd-s were m.
55:22.never suffer righte-s to be m.
66:9. suff-th not our feet to be m.
68 : 8. Sinai was m. at pres. of G.
78 : 58. they m. him to jealousy
82:†5. foundations of earth are m.
99:1. L. reigneth, let earth be m.
112:6. he shall not be m. for ever
121:3. not suffer thy foot to be m.
Pr. 12 : 3. root of righte. not be m.
Can.5:4.my bowels were m.for him
Is. 6 : 4. posts of the door m.
7 : 2. heart was m. as trees are m.
10 : 14. was none that m. the wing
14:9.Hell fr.beneath is m.for thee
19:1. idols of Egypt shall be m. at
24:19. earth is brok.down,and m.
40:20.image that sh.not be m.,41:[7.
Je. 4 : 24. all the hills m. lightly
25:16. they shall drink, and be m.
46 : 7. waters are m. as rivers, 8.
49 : 21. The earth is m. at noise of
50:46.at taking of Bab. earth is m.
Da. 8 : 7. he was m. with choler
10:†10. wh. m. me upon my knees
11:11.king shall be m.with choler
Mat. 9:36. was m. with compassion, 14:14.-18:27. Mk. 1 : 41.-6:34.
20:24. m.with indigna-n ag.breth.
21 : 10. all the city was m. saying
Mk.15:11.chief priests m. peo. [m.
Ac. 2 : 25. on my right ha., I not be
7:9. patriarchs, m.with envy, sold
17:5. But Jews m.with envy, took
21:30. city was m. and people ran
Col. 1:23.not m.from hope of gosp.
1 Th. 3 : 3. no man be m. by afflict.
He. 11 : 7. Noah m.with fear, prep-d
12 : 28. kingd. which cannot be m.
2 Pe. 1 : 21. spake as m. by H. Gh.
Re. 6 : 14. every mt. and island m.

MOVEDST. [cause

Jb. 2 : 3. tho. m.me ag. him with-t
Je. 48 : †27. since spakest, thou m.

MOVER.

Ac.24:5.this fellow a m. of sedition

MOVETH.

Ge. 1 : 21. G.created ev. creature m.
28. domin. over every thing that m. upon earth
9:2.fear of you sh. be on all th. m.
Le.11:46.law of every creat.that m.
20 : † 25. abominable by any thing that m. [a cedar
Jb. 40:17.Behemoth m. his tail like
Ps. 69 : 34. let ev. thing m. praise
Pr.23:31.not upon wine when it m.
Eze. 47 : 9. m. whi. rivers come

MOVING. [Noun. Part.]

Ge. 1 : 20. bring forth m. creatures
9 : 3. Ev. m. thing shall be meat
Jb.16:5.m. of my lips assuage grief
Pr. 16 : 30. m. lips, he bring-h evil
Ha.1:†14.makest men as m. things
Jn. 5 : 3. waiting for m. of water

MOWER.

Ps.129:7.Wh-w. m.filleth not hand

MOWINGS.

Am.7:1.latter growth aft. king's m.

MOWN.

Ps. 72 : 6. like rain upon m. grass

MO'ZA. [bare M.

1 Ch. 2 : 46. Ephah, Caleb's concu.
1 Ch. 8 : 36. and Zimri begat M., 9 :
37. M. begat Binea, 9 : 43. [42.

MO'ZAH.

Jos. 18:26. cities of tribe of Benj. M.

MUCH. [than we

Ge. 26 : 16. thou art m. mightier
Ex. 12 : 42. night to be m. observed
16:18. th. gathered m., 2 Co. 8:15.
Le.13:7.if scab spread m., 22,27,35.
Nu.21:4. of peo. was m.discouraged
De. 28 : 38. m. seed into field
Ru.1:13.It grieveth me m. for your
1 S. 14 : 30. a m. greater slaughter
18 : 30. so his name was m. set by
19 : 2. Jona. delighted m. in Da.
26:24. as thy life was m. set by, so let my life be m. set by [m.
1 K.4:29.Sol.had underst.exceeding
2 K. 10:18.Jehu shall serve him m.
2 Ch.27:3.on wall of Ophel built m.
33 : 6. Manasseh wrought m. evil
Ne. 9 : 37. m. increased unto kings
Jb. 5:†25. know thy seed sh. be m.
31 : 25. mine hand had gotten m.
Ps. 19:†13. innocent fr. m. transgr
129 : †1. m. have they afflicted me
Pr. 17 : 7. m. less do lying lips
19 : 10. m. less serv-t to have rule
Ec. 5 : 12. whe. he eat little or m.
7 : 16. Be not righteous over m.
17. Be not over m. wicked nei.
Eze. 23 : 32. cup, it containeth m.
33 : 31. with mouth shew m. love
Mi. 6 : † 16. doth m. keep statutes
Hag. 1 : 6. Ye have sown m.
9. ye looked for m. [they ?
Mat.6:26.Are ye not m. better than
26:9. might have been sold for m.
Mk. 1 : 45. began to publish it m.
5:10. besought him m. not to send
12:41.many th.were rich cast in m.
Lu. 1:†28. thou that art m. graced
7 : 47. forgiven, for she loved m.
12:48.unto wh.m.given,of him m. required, to wh. committed m.
16:10. faithful in m.unjust in m.
Jn.14:30.I will not talk m.with you
Ac. 18 : 27. who helped them m.
26:24.Festus said,m.learning doth
Ro. 3 : 2. m. every way [in L.
16 : 12. Persis, which laboured m.
1 Co. 16 : 19. Salute you m.in the L.
2 Co. 2 : 4. out of m. afflic. I wrote
He. 12:9. m. rather be in subject-n
25.m.more sh.not we escape [m.
Ja. 5 : 16. prayer of righte. availeth
Re. 5:4. I wept m. bec. no man was

As MUCH. [found

Ge. 23:9. give it for a. m. money as
43 : 34. mess was five times a. m.
44:1.Fill sacks with food a.m.[22.
Ex.16:5. twice a.m.as they gather,
Le.7:10.Aa.'s sons one a.m.as ano.
1 S. 2:16. take a. m. as soul desir.
2 Ch. 2:16. cut wood a. m. as thou
Jb.42:10.L. gave Job twice a.m.as
Ps. 119 : 14. a. m. as in all riches
Lu. 6:34. sinners lend, to rec. a.m.
Jn. 6 : 11. of fishes a.m.as they wo.
Ro. 1 : 15. a. m. as in me is, I am
12 : 18. a. m. as lieth in you, live
See CATTLE, EARTH, FRUIT, GAIN, GOOD.

How MUCH. [Wash

2 K.5:13.h.m.rather when he saith,
Ezr.7:22.without prescribing h.m.
Pr. 16 : 16. h.m. better to get wisd.
Can. 4:10. h. m. better is thy love
Mat. 12:12.h.m.is man better than
Lu. 16 : 5. h. m. owest my lord ? 7.
19 : 15. h. m. every man gained
Ac. 9 : 13. h.m.evil done thy saints
He. 8 : 6. by h. m. he is mediator
10 : 29. of h. m. sorer punishment
Re. 18 : 7. h. m. hath glorified her-[self

How MUCH less.

1 K. 8 : 27. heaven cannot contain thee, h. m. l. this house, 2 Ch. 6 : 18.
2 Ch. 32:15. h. m. l. shall G.deliver
Jb. 4 : 19. h. m. l. in th. dwell in
9:14. h. m. l. shall I answer him
25 : 6. h. m. l. man that is worm
34 : 19. h. m. l. to him accepteth not the persons [the work
Eze. 15 : 5. h. m. l. it be meet for
See MORE, PEOPLE, RICHES.

So MUCH.

Ge. 34:12. ask me never s.m.dowry
Ex. 14:28.remained not s.m.as one
30:23. sweet cinnamon half s. m.
Le.14:21.if poor and can-t get s.m.
De. 2 : 5. not s. m. as footbreadth
2 S.14:25.none s.m.praised as Abs.
17 : 12. not be left s. m. as one
2 Ch.20:25.spoil, it was s.m.[mou.
Pr. 19 : 24. not s. m. as bring it to
25:16. eat s. m. as is sufficient for
Je. 2:36.Why gaddest thou s. m.to
Mal. 3:13. we spoken s. m. ag.thee?
Mat.15:33.Whence have s.m.bread?
Mk. 2:2. no not s.m.as about door
3:20. could not s. m. as eat, 6:31.
Lu. 6 : 3. Have ye not read s.m. as
18:13.not lift up s. m.as his eyes
Ac. 5 : 8. if ye sold it for s. m. she said, Yea, for s. m. [set foot
7:5. no inheritance, not s. m. as to
19:2. not s.m. as heard whe.H.G.
1 Co. 5 : 1. not s. m.as named am.
2 Co.9:†5. bounty been s.m.spoken
He. 1 : 4. s. m. better than angels
7:22. by s. m. Jesus made surety
10 : 25. s. m. more as ye see day
12:20.if s. m. as a beast touch mt.
Re. 18 : 7. s. m. torment give her
See SOAP, SORROW, WICKEDNESS

Too MUCH. [t. m.

Ex. 36 : 7. stuff was sufficient, and
Nu. 16:3.Ye take t. m. upon you,7.
Jos. 19 : 9. part of Judah was t. m.
1 K. 12 : 28. t. m. to go to Jerus.
Es. 1 : 18. Thus sh. arise t. m. con-[tempt

Very MUCH.

Ge. 41 : 49. Jos. gath-d corn, v. m.
Ex. 12:38.v.m.cattle went up with
Jos. 13:1.v.m. land to be possessed
22:8. v. m. cattle,v.m.raim.[gold
1 K.10:2.queen of Sheba with v.m.
2 K. 21 : 16. shed innoc.blood v. m.
1 Ch.18:8.from Chun Da.v.m.brass
2 Ch. 14 : 13. carried aw. v.m. spoil
32:29. given him substance v. m.
36 : 14. priests and people trans-grossed v. m.
Ps. 119 : 107. I am afflicted v. m.
Je. 40 : 12. gathered summer fruits, [v. m.

MUFFLERS.

Is. 3 : 19. I will take away the m.

MULBERRY trees.

2 S.5 : 23. but come upon them over ag. m. t., 1 Ch. 14 : 14 [14:15.
24. sound in tops of m. t., 1 Ch.
Ps.84:†6. passing thro. valley of m.

MULCT. [Noun.] [t.

2 K.23:†33.Pha. set a m.upon land

MULCTED. [talents

2 Ch. 36 : † 3. king m. land in 100
Am. 2:†8. wine of such as have m.

MULE.

2 S. 13:29. ev. man gat upon his m.
18:9. Absalom rode upon a m. (2)
1 K. 1 : 33. Sol. upon my m., 38:44.
Ps. 32:9. Be not as the horse or m.
Zch. 14:15. so shall be plague of m.

MULES.

Ge.36:24.Anah found m.in wildern.
1 K.4:†28.they bro-t barley for m.
10:25. brought m. rate, 2 Ch.9:24.
18 : 5. find grass to save m. alive
2 K. 5:17. to serv-t two m. burden
1 Ch. 12 : 40. brought bread on m.
Ezr. 2 : 66. m. were 245, Ne. 7 : 68.
Es. 8:10.letters by riders on m.,14.

Is.66:20.bring breth. upon m. ⌈m.
Eze. 27 : 14. Togarmah traded with

MULTIPLIED. ⌈20.

Ge.47:27. Isr. grew and m.,Ex. 1:7,
Ex. 1 : 12. more afflicted, they m.
11 : 9. th. my wonders be m. in E.
De. 1 : 10. L. your G. hath m. you
8 : 13. thy gold is m. and all is m.
11 : 21. That your days be m. in la.
Jos.24 . 3. I m. his seed, gave Isaac
Ju. 16 : †24. who m. our slain
1 S. 1 : †12. as she m. to pray, Eli
2 S.22:†36.thy gentleness m.me,Ps.
1 Ch.5: 9.cattle were m. ⌊18 : †35.
23 : †17. sons of Rehabiah were m.
2 Ch. 33 : †23. Amon m. trespass
Ne.6:†17. nobles m. letters unto To.
Jb.27 : 14. If chil. be m. it is for sw.
35 : 6. if thy transgressions be m.
Ps.16 : 4. their sorrows shall be m.
38 : 19. they that hate me are m.
107:38. He blesseth, so they are m.
Pr. 9 : 11. by me thy days sh. be m.
29 : 16. When wicked are m. trans-
Is. 9 : 3. Thou hast m. nation ⌊gr-n
59 : 12. For our transg-ns are m.
Je.3:16.when ye be m. they sha. say
46:†16. He m. the faller, one fell
Eze.5:7. ye m. more than nations
11:6. Ye have m. slain in this city
16 : 25. m. thy whoredoms, 23 : 19.
29. m. fornication | 51. m.abom.
21:15.that heart faint, ruins be m.
31 : 5. his boughs were m. ⌈me
35 : 13. ye have m. your words ag.
Da.4:1. Peace be m. unto you, 6:25.
1 Pe. 1 : 2. 2 Pe. 1 : 2. Jude 2.
Ho.2:8.did not know I m.her silver
8 : 14. Jud. hath m. fenced cities
12 : 10. I have m.visions, and used
Na. 3 : 16. hast m. thy merchants
Ac. 6:1. number of disci. was m., 7.
7 : 17. people grew and m. in E.
9 : 31. walking in fear of L. were m.
12 : 24. the word of G. grew and m.

MULTIPLIEDEST, ETH.

Ne. 9 : 23. chil. m-t thou as stars
Jb. 9 : 17. he m-h my wounds
34:37. he m-h his words against G.
35 : 16. m-h words without knowl.
Ec. 10 : †14. a fool also m-h words

MULTIPLY.

Ge. 1 : 22. be fruitful and m.,28.–
8 : 17.–9 : 7.–35 : 11. ⌈ception
3:16.I will m. thy sorrow and con-
6 : 1. men began to m. on earth
16:10.I will m.Hagar's seed,17:20.
17 : 2. will m. thee exceed., 48 : 4.
22 : 17. I will m. thy seed, 26:4, 24.
28 : 3. God Al. bless and m. thee
Ex.1:10. let us deal wisely, lest they
7:3.I will m.my signs in E. ⌊m.
23 : 29. lest beast of field m. ag. thee
30:†15.rich sh. not m. half shekel
32 : 13. I will m. your seed, Le. 26:
9. De. 7 : 13.–13 : 17.–28:63.–30:5.
Le. 11 : † 42. whatso. doth m. feet
Nu. 26:†54. m. his inheri.,33 : † 54.
De.8:1. may m. and go in, 30 : † 16.
13. when thy flocks and herds m.
17:16.the king shall not m. horses
17. Nei. shall he m.wives nor silv.
2 S. 14 : † 11. revenger do not m.
1 Ch.4:27. neither did all family m.
23 : † 11. Jeush Beriah not m. sons
Jb. 29:18. I sh. m. my days as sand
Is. 1 : † 15. when ye m. prayer, I
55 : † 7. God, he will m. to pardon
Je. 30 : 19. I will m. them not few
33:22.so will I m. the seed of David
Eze. 16:7. I have caused thee to m.
36 : 10. I will m. men upon you
11. I will m. upon you man and
30. I will m. fruit of tree ⌊beast
37 : 26. I will place and m. them
Am. 4:4. at Gilgal m. transgression
2 Co. 9 : 10. and m. your seed sown

MULTIPLYING.

Ge.22:17. m. I will multiply, He. 6 :

MULTITUDE. ⌊14.

Ge. 16 : 10. it sh. not numbered for
m., 32 : 12. 1 K. 3 : 8. 2 Ch. 5:6.
17:†4.shall be fath.of m. of nations
28 : 3. G. make thee a m. of people
30:30.it is now increased unto a m.
48 : 4. make of thee a m. of peo.,16,
Ex. 12 : 38. a mixed m. went ⌊19.
23 : 2. not follow a m. to do evil
Le.25:16.acc. to m.of years increase
Nu. 11 : 4. mixed m. fell a lusting
De. 1:10. ye are this day as stars for
m., 10 : 22.–28 : 62. He. 11:12.
Jos. 11:4. as sand upon sea shore for
m., Ju. 7 : 12. 1 S. 13 : 5. 2 S.
17:11. 1 K.4:20. ⌈and his m.
Ju.4:7. I will draw unto thee Sisera
6 : 5. as grasshoppers for m., 7:12.
1 S. 14 : 16. behold, m. melted aw.
2 S.6:19.he dealt am. whole m.of Isr.
1 K.7:†47. unweighed for exc-g m.
8 : 5. oxen co. not be told for m.
2 K.7:13. are as all m. th. are left
19 : 23. With m. of chariots I am
come up to Leb.,Is.37:24.
25 : 11. with remnant of m. did
Neb-n carry away, Je. 52 : 15.
1 Ch. 12 : †29. m. of them had kept
ward ⌈m.,Is.29:5.
2 Ch. 1 : 9. over a peo. like dust for
11†:23. Rehob. desired m. of wives
14 : 11. in thy name we go ag. m.
20 : 24. the m. were dead bodies
30 : 18.m. had not cleansed thems.
32 : 7. be not afraid of the m. ⌈m.
Ne. 13:3. separated from Isr. mixed
† 22. spare me, acc. to m. of mercy
Es. 5 : 11. Haman told of m.of his
10:3.Mord.accepted of m. of breth.
Jb. 4 : †14. m. of my bones to shake
11:2. Sho. m. of words be answ-d ?
32 : 7. m. of years sho. teach wisd.
33 : 19. m. of his bones with pain
35 : 9. By m. of oppres. they made
39:7.He scorneth the m.of the city
Ps.5:10.cast th. out in m. of transg.
33:16. no king saved by m. of host
42 : 4. I had gone with m. to ho. of
49 : 6. boast in m. of riches⌊G. (2)
68 : 30. Rebuke the m. of bulls
74 : 19. deliver me not unto m. of
94:19.in m.of my thoughts ⌊wick.
97 : 1. let m. of isles be glad th-of
109 : 30. I will praise him am. m.
Pr. 10 : 19. In m. of words wanteth
11 : 14. in m. of counsellors, 24 : 6.
14:28.In m.of peo.is king's honour
15 : 22. in m. of counsellors establ.
20 : 15. is gold, and a m. of rubies
Ec. 5 : 3. dream thro. m. of busin.,
fool's voice by m. of words
7. in m. of dreams divers vanities
Is. 1:11. To what purpose m. of sac-
5:13.m. dried up with thirst ⌊rifi.
14. their m. and pomp into hell
13 : 4. noise of a m. in mountains
17 : 12. Woe to m. of many people
29 : 7. m. of all nations that fight
8. so m. of nations that fight Zion
31:†4.when m.of sheph-s is ag.him
32 : 14. m. of city shall be left
47 : 9. upon thee for m.of sorceries
12. Stand now wi. m. of sorceries
13. wearied in m. of thy counsels
60:6. m. of camels shall cover thee
63 : 7. m. of his loving kindnesses
† 15. m. of thy bowels, are they
Je.3:23. in vain salva. fr. m. of mts.
10 : 13. is a m. of waters, 51 : 16.
12 : 6. have called a m. aft. thee
30:14.wounded thee for m. of iniq.
46:25. I will punish the m. of No,
Eze. 30 : 15.
49 : 32. the m. of cattle a spoil
51:42.she is cov-d with m.of waves
La. 1 : 5. for m. of her transgr-ns
3 : 32. compassion according to m.
of his mercies ⌈14.
Eze. 7 : 12. wrath is upon all m., 11,
13. vision is touching whole m.
14 : 4. ans. acc. to m. of his idols
23 : 42. voice of m. being at ease
27 : 12. by m. of riches, 18, 33.
16. m. of thy wares, 18.–28 : 16.
28 : 18. defiled sanc. by m.of iniq-s
30 : 4. they sh. take her m., 29:19.
31 : 2. speak unto Pha. and M.
5. branches bec. of m. of waters
9.made him fair by m.of branches
18. Pha. and all his m., 32 : 32.
32:16. Egypt and m., 12,18.–30:10.
24. Elam and m. | 26. Tubal and
25. in midst of slain with her m.
31. Pha. be comforted, all his m.
39 : 11. bury Gog, and his m., †14.
†16. name of city sh. be the m.
Da. 10 : 6. his words like voice of m.
11 : 10. sh. assemble a m. of forces
12. taken aw. m. heart be lifted
13. king shall set forth a m.
Ho. 9 : 7. the m. of thine iniquity
10:1. acc. to m. of fruit inc-d altars
13. didst trust in m. of mighty
Mi. 2 : 12. great noise by m. of men
Na. 3 : 3. there is a m. of slain
4. bec. of the m. of whoredoms
Zch. 2:4. Jerus. as towns for the m.
8:†4. with his staff for m. of days
Mat.13:2.whole m.on shore,Mk.4:1.
34.Spake Jesus unto the m. ⌈36.
36.Jes.sent m.away, 15:39. Mk.4:
14 : 5. he feared the m., 21 : 46.
15. send the m. away, Lu. 9 : 12.
19. com-d m. to sit down, 15 : 35.
15 : 10. he called the m., Ac. 6 : 2.
31. Insomuch the m. wondered
32. compassion on m., Mk. 8 : 2.
36. disci. gave to the m.,Lu.9:16.
17:14. When they were come to m.
20 : 31. the m.rebuked them ⌈et
21:11.m.sd. This is Jes. the proph-
22 : 33. when m. heard this
27:20. persuaded m. they sho. ask
24. Pilate washed hands bef. m.
Mk. 2:13. all m. resorted unto him
3 : 9. ship wait because of the m.
20. m. cometh together again
32. m. sat about him
Mk. 5:31. seest m. thronging, Lu.8:
7 : 33. took him aside fr. m. ⌊45.
9 : 17. one of the m. ans-d, Master
15:8.m.crying aloud began ⌈ing
Lu.1:10.whole m.of peo. were pray-
2:13. was with angel a m. of host
3:7. said to m.,O gener-n of vipers
5:19. because of m.upon housetop
6:19.whole m.sought to touch him
8 : 37. whole m. besought him to
12:1.gath-d innumerable m.⌊depa.
18:36. hearing m. pass by, asked
19 : 37. whole m. of disciples began to rejoice, 23 : 1. ⌈Master
39. Pharisees among m. said,
22 : 6. betray him in absence of m.
47. while he spake, behold a m.
23:1.whole m. led him unto Pilate
Jn. 5 : 13. a m. being in that place
21 : 6. not draw it for m. of fishes
Ac.2:6.m.came together ⌈heart
4 : 32. m. that believed were of one
5 : 16. came m. out of the cities
6 : 5. saying pleased whole m.
14 : 4. m. of the city was divided,
15 : 12. all m. kept silence ⌊23:7.
30.when had gathered m. togeth.
16 : 22. the m. rose up ag. them
19 : 9. spake evil before the m.
33. drew Alexander out of m.
21:22. m. must needs come togeth.
34. some cried one thing am. m.
36. m. of people followed after
24 : 18. nei. with m. nor tumult

Ac 25:24. about wh. all m. of Jews
Eph. 4. † 8. he led a m. of captives
Ja. 5 : 20. sh. hide m. of sins [sins
1 Pe. 4 : 8. charity shall cover m. of
See GREAT, MERCIES, MERCY.

MULTITUDES.

Eze. 32:20. draw her and all her m.
Jo.3:14. m. m. in valley of decision
Mat. 5:1. seeing m. he went into mt.
9 : 8. when m. saw they marvelled
33. dumb spake, m. marvelled
36. when he saw m. he was moved
11 : 7. Jesus began to say unto m.
14 : 22. while he sent m. away, 23.
21 : 9. m. cried, saying, Hosanna
Ac.5:14. m. were added both of men
13 : 45. Jews saw m. they wi. envy
Re.17:15. waters are m. and nations
See GREAT Multitude, s.

MUNITION, S. [m.

Is.29:7. all that fight ag. her and her
33:16. his defence be m-s of rocks
Da.11:†15. king take city of m-s
†38. he will honour the G. of m-s
† 39. do in the fortresses of m-s
Na. 2 : 1. keep m. watch the way

MUP'PIM. [21 : † 39.

Ge.46:21. sons of Benj. Rosh. M., Nu.

MURDER, S. [Noun.] [7:21.

Mat. 15 : 19. out of heart m-s, Mk.
19 : 18. Thou shalt do no m. [m.
Mk. 15:7. Barabbas, who committed
Lu. 23:19. for m. cast into pris., 25.
Ro. 1 : 29. full of envy, m. debate
Ga. 5 : 21 works of the flesh, m-s
Re 9:21. nei. repented of their m-s.

MURDER. [Verb.]

Ps. 10 : 8. in secret doth m. innoc.
94 : 6. slay widow and m. fatherl.
Je. 7 : 9. Will ye steal, m. and com.
Ho. 6 : 9. so priests m. in the way

MURDERER.

Nu. 35 : 16. if he smite he is a m.,
m. be put to death, 17, 18, 21.
19. revenger of blood slay m., 21.
30. m. sh. be put to death by witn.
31. take no satisfac. for life of m.
2 K. 6 : 32. See how this son of m.
Jb. 24 : 14. m. rising with the light
Ho. 9:13. Ephr. bring his chil. to m.
Jn. 8 : 44. He was a m. fr. beginn.
Ac. 3 : 14. ye desired a m. to be
28 : 4. No doubt this man is a m.
1 Pe. 4 : 15. let none suffer as m.
1 Jn. 3 : 15. hateth his bro. is a m.,
ye know no m. hath etern. life

MURDERERS.

2 K. 14 : 6. child. of m. he slew not
Is. 1 : 21. righteousn. in it, now m.
Je. 4 : 31. soul wearied, bec. of m.
Mat. 22 : 7. he destroyed those m.
Ac. 7 : 52. of whom ye been the m.
21 : 38. leddest out 4,000 men m.
1 Ti. 1 : 9. law made for m. of fa-s
Re.21:8. m. their part in lake [m.
22 : 15. without are whoremongers,

MURMUR.

Ex. 16 : 7. what are we, that ye m.
8. L. heareth murmurings ye m.
Nu. 14:27. I have heard wh. they m.
36 spies made the congr-n to m.
16:11. what is Aaron, th. ye m. ag.
17 : 5. whereby they m. ag. you
La. 3 : † 39. Wht. doth a man m. ?
Jn. 6 : 43. Jesus said, m. not am.
1 Co. 10 : 10. Nei. m. as some of them

MURMURED. [17:3.

Ex. 15 : 24 people m. ag. Moses,
16 : 2. whole congr. of Isr. m. ag.
Mo. and Aa., Nu. 14:2.-16:41.
Nu. 14 : 29. fr. 20 years old, wh. m.
De. 1 : 27. And ye m. in your tents
Jos. 9:18. all congr. m. ag princes
Ps 106 : 25. believed not, m. in tents
Is. 29 : 24. that m. sh. learn doctr.
Mat. 20 : 11. when rec-d penny, they
Mk. 14:5. they m. against her [m.
Lu. 5 : 30. Scribes and Pharisees m.
15:2. m. saying, This man receiveth
19:7. m. he was guest to Zaccheus
Jn. 6 : 41. the Jews m. at him, bec.
61. he knew his disciples m. at it
7:32. Phari. heard that people m.
1 Co. 10:10. Nei. murmur as some m.

MURMURERS.

Jude 16. These are m. complainers

MURMURING, S.

Ex. 16 : 7. he heareth your m-s, 8,
9, 12. Nu. 14 : 27. [the L.
8. your m-s are not ag-t us, but
Nu. 17 : 5. make cease m-s of Isr.
10. shalt take their m-s from me
Jn. 7 : 12. was much m. am. people
Ac. 6 : 1. a m. of Grecians ag. Hebr.
Ph. 2:14. Do all things without m-s

MURRAIN.

Ex. 9:3. shall be a very grievous m.
Ps. 78 : † 50. gave their beasts to m.

MUSE, ED.

Ps.143:5. I m. on work of thy hands
Lu. 3 : 15. all m-d in hearts of John

MU'SHI, ITES. See MAHLI.

MUSIC. [low

Ec 12 : 4. daughters of m. be bro-t
La.3 :63. I am their m. Render unto
5 : 14. ceased the young men fr. m.
Da. 3 : 5. time ye hear cornet and all
kinds of m., fall down, 7, 10, 15.
Lu. 15 : 25. his elder son, heard m.
See INSTRUMENTS.

MUSICAL.

See Musical INSTRUMENTS

MUSICIAN, S.

Ps. 4.* To the chief M., * of Ps. 6:9:
11:12:13:14:18:19:20:21:22:31:36:
39:40:41:42:44:45:46:47:49:51:52:
53:54:55:56:57:58:59:60:61:62:64:
65:66:67:68:69:70:75:76:77:80:81:
84:85:88:109:139:140. [more
Re. 18 : 22. voice of m-s be heard no

MUSING.

Ps. 39 : 3. while I was m. fire burned

MUST. [country

Ge. 29 : 26. It m. not be so in our
30 : 16. thou m. come in unto me
43 : 11. If it m. be so now do this
Le. 11 : 32. it m. be put in water
23:6. seven days ye m. eat unleav.
Nu. 6 : 21. m. do aft. law of separa.
20 : 10. m. we fetch water out of
23 : 12. m. I not take heed [rock
26. All L. speaketh th. I m. do
De. 1 : 22. by what way we m. go
4:22. I m. die in this la., I m. not go
12:18. thou m. eat them bef. the L.
31:14. days approach thou m. die
Jos. 3 : 4. may know way ye m. go
Ju. 13 : 16. thou m. offer it unto L.
21 : 17. m. be inheritance for them
1 S.14:43. but taste little, lo I m. die
2 S. 23 : 3. ruleth men m. be just
7. touch them m. be fenced with
1 K. 18 : 27. he m. be awaked [iron
Mat.16:21. how he m. go unto Jerus.
17:10. Elias m. 1st come, Mk.9:11.
24 : 6. m. come to pass, Lu. 21 : 9.
26 : 54. fulfilled, th. thus it m. be
Mk. 2 : 22. but new wine m. be put
into new, Lu. 5:38. [among all
13:10. gospel m. first be published
Lu. 2 : 49. I m. be about my Fa.'s
4:43. I m. preach kingdom of God
13 : 33. I m. walk to day and to
19:5. Zaccheus, to day I m. abide
22 : 7. when passover m. be killed
37. things m. be accompl., 24:44.
23:17. he m. release one unto them
24 : 7. Son of man m. be deliv. into
Jn.3:7. Ye m. be born again [12:34.
14. so m. Son of man be lifted, Jn.
30. He m. increase, but I m. decr.
4 : 24. m. worship him in spirit
9 : 4. I m. work the works of him
10:16. other sheep, them I m. bri.
20 : 9. knew not he m. rise again
Ac. 1 : 22. m. one be ord. to be a witn.
3:21. Whom the heaven m. receive
4 : 12. whereby we m. be saved
9 : 6. be told thee what thou m. do
14:22. we m. thro. much tribulation
15 : 24. ye m. be circumcised
18:21. I m. by all means keep this
19 : 21. I m. also see Rome [feast
23:11. m. thou bear witn. at Rome
27:24. thou m. be bro-t bef. Cæsar
26. we m. be cast on cert. island
1 Co. 11 : 19. m. be heresies am. you
15:25. he m. reign till he hath put
53. this corruptible m. put on
2 Co.5:10. we m. all appear bef judg.
1 Ti. 3 : 2. bishop m. be blamel., Tit.
7. m. have a good report [1:7.
8. Likewise m. deacons be grave
2 Ti.2:6. husbandman m. be 1st par-
24. serv. of L. m. not strive [taker
Tit. 1:11. Whose mouths m. be stop.
He.4:6. remaineth th. some m. enter
9 : 16. m. be the death of testator
11 : 6, cometh to God, m. believe
13:17. as they th. m. give account
Re. 1 : 1. things wh. m. shortly come
4 : 1. shew thee things wh. m. be
10:11. Thou m. prophesy again bef.
11 : 5. if any hurt he m. be killed
13 : 10. m. be killed with sword
17 : 10. m. continue a short space
20 : 3. m. be loosed a little season
22:6. things wh. m. shortly be done
See Must DO, Must NEEDS.
See SUFFER, SUFFERED.

MUSTARD. See GRAIN.

MUSTERED, ETH. [25.

2 K. 25:19. scribe which m-d, Je.52:
Is. 13 : 4. Lord m-h host of battle

MUTTER, ED.

Is. 8:19. wizards that peep, and m.
16:†7. for Kirhareseth shall ye m.
59 : 3. tongue hath m-d perverse-

MUTUAL. [ness

Ro. 1 : 12. comforted by the m. faith

MUZZLE. [Noun.] [m.

Ps. 39:†1. will keep my mouth with

MUZZLE. [Verb.]

De. 25: 4. Thou shalt not m. the ox
when he treadeth out the corn,
1 Co. 9 : 9. 1 Ti. 5 : 18.

MY'RA.

Ac. 27 : 5. to M. a city of Lycia

MYRRH. [m.

Ge. 37:25. Ishmaelites came bearing
43:11. carry man present, m. nuts
Ex 30 : 23. of pure m. 500 shekels
Es. 2 : 12. six months wi. oil of m.
Ps. 45 : 8. thy garments smell of m.
Pr. 7 : 17. perfumed my bed wi. m.
Can.1:13. bundle of m. is my belov-
3:6. perfumed wi. m. frankinc. [ed
4:6. I will get me to mount. of m.
14. m. and aloes wi. chief spices
5 : 1. gathered my m. with spice
5. my hands dropped with m.
fingers with sweet m.
13. lips like lilies, dropping sweet
smelling m.
Mat. 2 : 11. presented gold and m.
Mk. 15 : 23. wine mingled with m.
Jn. 19 : 39. mixture of m. and aloes

MYRTLE.

Ne. 8 : 15. Go fetch m. branches
Is.41:19. I will plant in wildern. m.
55:13. instead of brier the m. tree
Zch.1:8. he stood am. m trees, 10, 11.

MYSELF.

Ge. 3: 10. I was afraid, and hid m.
22 : 16. By m. have sworn, I will
bless, Is. 45:23. Je.22:5.-49:13.
Ex. 19 : 4. I brought you unto m.
Nu. 8: 17. I sanctified them for m.
12:6. I the L. will make m. known
De. 1:9. not able to bear you m., 12.
Ju. 16 : 20. I will go and shake m.
Ru. 4 : 6. I cannot redeem it for m.

1 S. 13 : 12. I forced m. and offered
20:5.let me go, that I may hide m.
25: 33. kept me from avenging m.
2 S. 18 : 2. I will go with you m.
22 : 24. I have kept m. from iniq.
1 K.18:15. I will shew m. unto him
22:30.will disguise m., 2 Ch.18:29.
2 K. 5 : 18. I bow m. in h. of Rimm.
2 Ch. 7 : 12. chosen this place to m.
Ne. 5 : 7. I consulted with m. and
Es.5:12. let no man with k. but m.
6 : 6. do honour more than to m.
Jb.6:10.would harden m. in sorrow
7:20. that I am burden to m.
9: 20. If I justify m. mine own
27. If I say I will comfort m.
30. If I wash m. with snow water
10:1. leave my complaint upon m.
13: 20. then not hide m. fr. thee
19:4.if I erred, mine error with m.
27. whom I shall see for m. and
31 : 17. or eaten morsel m. alone
29. or if I lift m. when evil found
42:6. Whf. I abhor m. and repent
Ps. 35:14. I behaved m. as tho. he
57 : 8. I m. awake early, 108 : 2.
101 : 2. I will behave m. wisely in
109 : 4. but I give m. unto prayer
119:16. will delight m. in statutes
47. will delight m. in thy com-ts
52.rememb-d judgm.comforted m
131:1.nei.exercise m.in gr.matters
2. I have quieted m. as child
Ec.2:3. sought to give m.unto wine
19. labour wh-n I shewed m.wise
Is. 33:10. saith L. now will I lift m.
43 : 21. this peo. I formed for m.
44 : 24. spreadeth the earth by m.
Je. 8 : 18. I would comfort m. ag.
21:5. I m. will fight ag. you [m.
Eze. 14 : 7. I L. will answer him by
20:5. in day I made m. known, 9.
29:3. river, I have made it for m.
35: 11. I will make m. known am.
38 : 23. will I magnify m. sanctify
Da. 10 : 3. nei. did I anoint m.[m.
Mi. 6 : 6. bow m. before high God
Ha. 3 : 16. heard, I trembled in m.
Zch.7:3.separat. m. as I have done
Lu. 7 : 7. nei. thought I m. worthy
24 : 39. that it is I m. handle me
Jn. 5 : 31. If I bear witness of m.
7:17. sh. know whe. I speak of m.
28. I am not come of m. but he
8:14.Tho.bear record of m.my rec.
18. I am one bear witness of m.
28. ye sh. know I do noth. of m.
42. nei. came I of m. he sent me
54. If I honour m. my honour is
10 : 18. but I lay it down of m.
12 : 49. I have not spoken of m.
14:3.I will come, rec. you unto m.
10. words I speak, I speak not of
21.I will manifest m. to him[m.
17:19.for their sakes I sanctify m.
Ac. 7 : † 37. a prophet as I m. [man
10:26.saying, Stand up, I m. am a
20:24.nei. count life dear unto m.
24:10. I do cheerfully ans. for m.
16. do I exercise m. to have
25 : 22. I would hear the man m.
26 : 9. I verily thought with m. I
Ro. 9 : 3. I could wish m. accursed
11 : 4. reserved to m. 7,000 men
15 : 14. m. am persuaded of you
16 : 2. succourer of many, and m.
1 Co. 4 : 4. I know nothing by m.
6. I have in figure transf-d to m.
7 : 7. I would all were as I m.
9 : 19. made m. servant unto all
27. lest I m. sho. be a castaway
2 Co. 10 : 1. I Paul m. beseech you
11 : 7. an offence in abasing m.?
9. kept m. from being burdensome unto you [m.
16. receive me, that I may boast
12 : 5. of m. I will not glory but
2 Co.12:13.I m.was not burdensome
Ga. 2 : 18. I make m. a transgr-r
Ph. 2 : 24. that I m. shall come
3:13.count not m.to have appreh.
Phm. 17. receive Onesimus as m.

MYS'IA.

Ac. 16 : 7. aft. they were come to M.
8. passing by M. came to Troas

MYSTERIES.

Mat.13:11.given to you to know m.
of kingdom, to them not, Lu. 8:
1 Co.4:1.stewards of m. of God [10.
13: 2. and tho. I understand all m.
14:2. in the Spirit he speaketh m.

MYSTERY.

Mk.4:11. Unto you to know the m.
Ro. 11 : 25. that ye be igno. of this
16:25.acc. to revelation of m. [m.
1 Co. 2 : 7. speak wisd. of G. in m.
15 : 51. I shew you m. We sh. not
Ep. 1 : 9. made known to us m.
3 : 3. how made known to me m.
4. my knowl. in the m. of Christ
9. see what is fellowship of m.
5:32. This is great m. but I speak
6 : 19. boldly, to make known m.
of gospel, Col. 1 : 26, 27.-4:3.
Col. 2 : 2. to acknowl-t of m. of G.
2 Th. 2 : 7. m. of iniq. doth work
1 Ti. 3 : 9. holding m. of faith in
16. great is m. of godliness
Re. 1 : 20. The m. of the seven stars
10:7.the m.of God sho.be finished
17 : 5. M. BABYLON THE GREAT
7. I will tell m. of the woman

N.

NA'AM. See IRU.

NA'AMAH. [Person.]

Ge.4:22. sister of Tubal-cain was N.
1 K. 14 : 21. Rehoboam's mother's
name was N., an Ammonitess,
31. 2 Ch. 12 : 13.

NA'AMAH. [Place.]

Jos. 15 : 41. and N.; 16 cities with

NA'AMAN. [villages

Ge.46:21.sons of Benj.; N. and Rosh
Nu.26:40. son of Bela, N., 1 Ch.8:4.
2 K. 5 : 1. N. captain was a leper
2. little maid waited on N.'s wife
6. I have sent N. to thee
9. So N. came with his horses and
11. N. was wroth and went away
17. N. said, Sh. be given thy serv-
20.my master hath spared N.[ant
21. Gehazi followed after N.
23. N. said, Be content, take two
27.leprosy of N. sh. cleave to thee
1 Ch.8:7. N. and Ahiah he removed
Lu. 4 : 27. none cleansed, saving N.

NA'AMATHITE.

See ZOPHAR.

NA'AMITES.

Nu.26:40. Naaman, the family of N.

NA'ARAH. [Ashur

1 Ch. 4 : 5. Helah and N. wives of
6. N. bare him Ahuzam and

NA'ARAI=PA'ARAI.

1 Ch. 11 : 37.† valiant men, were N.

NA'ARAN=NA'ARATH.

Jos. 16 : 7. border went down to N-h
1 Ch.7:28.† possessions,eastward N-n

NAASH'ON=NAAS'ON.

Ex.6:23. Aa. took Elisheba sis. of N.
Mat. 1 : 4. Aminadab begat N. N.
begat Salmon, Lu. 3 : 32.
See NAHSHON.

NA'BAL.

1 S. 25 : 3. name of the man was N.
4.N.did shear his sheep | 5.go to N
9. spake to N. | 10. N. answered
14. Abigail N.'s wife, 27 : 3.-30:5.
19. She told not N. | 2 S. 2:2.-3:3.
25. N. his name, folly is with him
26. th. seek evil be as N. | 34, 36.
1 S. 25 : 37. when wine gone out of N
38. Lord smote N. that he died
39.L.hath returned wickedn.of N.

NA'BOTH.

1 K.21:1. N.Jezreelite had vineyard
2. Ahab spake unto N. | 3. +
4.Ahab displeased bec.of word N.
6. Bec. I spake unto N. the Jez.
7. give the viney. of N. Jezreelite
8. sent letters unto elders with N.
9. set N. on high, 12. [(2)
13. men of Belial witnessed ag N.,
14. saying, N. is stoned and dead
15.Arise, take viney.of N.Jez.,16.
16.when Ahab heard N. was dead
18. Ahab is in the vineyard of N.
19. place where dogs licked bl. of
2 K. 9 : 21. in portion of N. Jez. [N.
25. cast him in the field of N.Jez.
26.I have seen yesterday bl.of N.

NA'CHON=CHI'DON.

2 S. 6 : 6. to N.'s threshingfloor, 1
Ch. 13 : † 9.

NA'CHOR. See NAHOR.

NA'DAB. [9.

Ex. 24 : 1. Come up, N. and Abihu,
Nu. 3 : 4. N. and Abihu died bef. L.,
26:61. 1 Ch. 24:2. [15:25,27,31
1 K.14:20. N. son of Jerob. reigned,
1 Ch. 2 : 28. N. son of Shammai
30. the sons of N. Seled, Appaim
8 : 30. Baal and N. sons of Gibeon,
9 : 36.

NAG'GE.

Lu. 3 : 25. Esli, which was son of N.

NAHAL'AL.

Jos. 21 : 35. unto chil. of Merari N.

NAHA'LIEL.

Nu.21:19.Isr. journeyed fr.N.to Ba-

NAHAL'LAL. [moth

Jos. 19 : 15. Kattath, N. inheri. of

NA'HALOL. [Zebulon

Ju. 1 : 30. Neither did Zebulon drive
out inhabitants of N.

NA'HAM. See GARMITE.

NAHAM'ANI. [bel

Ne.7:7. N. who came with Zerubba-

NAHAR'AI=NAHA'RI.

2 S. 23 : 37. N. armourbearer, 1 Ch.

NA'HASH. [11: 39.

1 S. 11 : 1. N. ag. Jabesh, 2.-12: 12.
2 S. 10 : 2. I will shew kindness unto
son of N., 1 Ch. 19 : 2.
17:25.went in to Abigail dau. of N.
27. Shobi son of N. brought beds
1 Ch. 4 : † 12. The city of N.
19: 1. N. king of Ammon died

NA'HATH. [Ch.1:37.

Ge. 36 : 13. sons of Reuel, N., 17. 1
1 Ch. 6 : 26. sons of Elkanah, N.
2 Ch.31:13.N. and Asahel overseers

NAH'BI.

Nu.13:14. N. son of Vophsi Mo.sent

NA'HOR or NA'CHOR.

Ge. 11 : 22. Serug begat N., 23.
29. N.'s wife Milcah
24. N. lived 29 years, begat Terah, 25. 1 Ch. 1 : 26. Lu. 3 : 34.
26. Terah begat Abram, N. and,
27. Jos. 24 : 2.
22:20. Milcah, she hath borne chil-
to thy bro. N., 23.-24:15,24,47.
24:10.Ab.'s serv. went to city of N.
31:53.G.of Ab.and N.judge bet-t us

NAH'SHON=NAASH'ON.

Nu. 1 : 7. prince was N., 2:3. | 10:14.
7 : 12. that offered 1st day was N.
17. off-g of N. son of Amminadab
Ru 4 : 20. Amminadab begat N. N.
begat Salmon, 1 Ch. 2 : 10, 11.

NA'HUM. [N.

Na. 1 : 1. The book of the vision of

NAIL.

Ju. 4 : 21. Jael took n. smote n.
22. Sisera lay dead, n. in temples
5 : 26. She put her hand to n.
Ezr. 9 : 8. us a n. in his holy place

Is. 22 : 23. I will fasten him as a n.
25. shall n. fastened be removed
Zch.10:4.of him came n. battle bow

NAILS.

Le. 1 : † 15. pinch off head with n.
De.21:12.she sh.shave head,pare n.
1 Ch. 22 : 3. iron in abnud. for n.
2 Ch. 3 : 9. weight of n. 50 shekels
Ec.12:11.n.fastened by the masters
Is. 41 : 7. fastened idol wi. n., Je.10:
Da.4:33. his n. like birds' claws ⌊4.
7 : 19. 4th beast, n. were of brass
Jn.20:25. my finger into print of n.

NAILING.

Col. 2 : 14. he took it, n. it to his ⌊cross

NAIN.

Lu. 7: 11. Jesus went into a city N.

NA'IOTH.

1 S. 19 : 18. Samuel and David dwelt
at N., 19, 22. ⌈fled from N.
23. Saul went to N. | 20:1. David

NAKED.

Ge. 2: 25. were n. and not ashamed
3:7. they knew they were n.,10,11.
Ex.32:25.Moses saw people were n.,
for Aaron had made them n.
Le. 20 : † 18. made n. her fountain
1 S.19 : 24. Saul lay down n. all day
2 Ch.28:15. with spoil clothed all n.
19. Ahaz made Judah n. and
Jb. 1: 21. n. came I out of mother's
womb, n. shall I return ⌈ing
22:6. hast stripped the n. of cloth-
24:7.cause n. to lodge without, 10.
26 : 6. Hell is n. before him and
Pr. 29:†18. Where no vision, peo. is
Ec.5:15.n.shall he return ⌊made n.
Is. 22 : † 6. Kir made n. the shield
58: 7. when thou seest the n. that
Je. 48 : † 6. be like a n. tree in wil.
51: † 58. walls of Bab. be made n.
La. 4 : 21. thou shalt make thys. n.
Eze. 16 : 7. thou wast n. and bare
22. when wast n. and polluted
39. sh. leave thee n. and bare,23:
18: 7. if he covered the n.,16.⌊29.
Ho. 2 : 3. lest I strip her n. and set
Am.2:16.courageous sh.flee away n.
Mi. 1: 8. I will wail, go stripped n.
11. Pass ye, having thy shame n.
5 : † 6. waste with her n. swords
Ha.3:9.Thy bow was made quite n.
Mat.25:36.n. ye clothed me not,43.
38. When saw we thee n. and,44.
Mk.14:51.linen cloth about n. body
52. he left linen cloth and fled n.
Jn. 21 : 7. Simon Peter was n. and
Ac. 19 : 16. fled out of that house n.
1 Co.4:11. unto present hour we are
2Co.5:3. we sh. not be found n.⌊n.
He.4:13. all things are n. unto him
Ja.2:15. If a brother or sister be n.
Re. 3 : 17. miserable, poor, and n.
16 : 15. keepeth garm. lest walk n.
17:16. shall make her desolate and ⌊n.

NAKEDNESS.

Ge. 9 : 22. Ham saw n.of his father
23.covered n. saw not father's n.
42:9. to see the n. of the land, 12.
Ex. 20:26. thy n. be not discovered
28 : 42. breeches to cover their n.
Le. 18 : 6. None sh.uncover their n.
7. The n. of father or mother, 8,
11, 15.-20 : 11. ⌈son's dau.
9. The n. of thy sister | 10. n. of
11. n. of father's wife's daughter,
shalt not uncover her n.
12. n. of fa.'s sister | 13.mother's
sister, 20 : 19. ⌈dau. in law
14. n. of fa.'s brother | 15. n. of
16. n. of bro.'s wife, it is bro.'s n.
17. n. of a woman and her dau.
19.n.of a woman put apart,20:18.
20:17. see sister's n.she see his n.
20. uncovered his uncle's n.
21. hath uncovered brother's n.
De.23:†14. that he see no n. in thee

De. 24 : † 1. if found matter of n. in
28:48. shalt serve enem. in n.⌊her
1 S. 20:30. confusion of mother's n.
Is. 20:†4. uncovered to the n. of E.
47 : 3. Thy n. shall be uncovered
La. 1 : 8. bec. they have seen her n.
Eze. 16 : 8. I covered thy n. ⌈23:18.
36. n. discovered thro. whored-s,
16:37. will discover thy n. unto th.
22:10.In thee they discov-d fa.'s n.
23 : 10. discovered her n. and slew
29.n.of thy whored. be discovered
Ho. 2 : 9. wool and flax to cover n.
Na. 3: 5. I will shew nations thy n.
Ha. 2 : 15. mayest look on their n.
Ro. 8 : 35. shall n. separate us fr.
2 Co. 11 : 27. in fastings, cold and n.
Re.3:18.shame of thy n. not appear

NAME.

Ge.2:11.n.of first was Pison | 13,14.
4:19.wives n. of 1 Adah, n. of oth.
21. his brother's n. was Jubal
10 : 25. n. of 1 Peleg, bro.'s n., 1
11:4.let us make us a n. ⌊Ch.1:19.
29.n.of Ab.'s wife Sarai; n.of Na-
16:1.handmaid whose n. w. Hagar
17:15.n. Sarai but Sarah her n. be
22:24.concubine whose n.Reumah
25 : 1. Ab. took wife n. Keturah
26 : 33. n. of city Beer-sheba
29 : 16. n. of elder, Leah, n. of
36:32.n.of city,35,39. Ju.1:17.-18:
29. 1 K.16:24. 1 Ch.1:43,46,50.
39. wife's n., Nu. 26 : 59. 1 S. 14:
50. 1 Ch. 1 : 50.-2:26,29.-8:29.-
9 : 35. Ru. 1 : 2. 1 S. 25:3. Eze.
39 : 16.
38 : 1. Adullamite whose n. Hirah
2. whose n. was Shuah, 6. ⌈fa-s
48 : 16. my name on th. and n. of
Ex.1:15.midwives, n.of 1,n.of other
18 : 3. sons, n. of 1 Gershon | 4.
23: 13. no mention of n. of other
gods, Jos. 23 : 7.
34:14.the Lord, whose n.is Jealous
Le. 18 : 21. nei. shalt profane n. of
thy God, 19 : 12.-21:6.-22:2,32.
Nu. 11 : 26. n. of one Eldad, n. of
17 : 2. write ev. man's n. upon rod
3.write Aaron's name upon rod of
25 : 14. n. of the Israelite slain
15. n. of Midianitish wom. slain
26 : 46. n. of dau. of Asher, Sarah
27:4.Why n.of our fa. be done aw.
De.7:24. shall destroy their n. from
9 : 14. blot out their n. from und.
22:14.bring up an evil n.upon her
19. he bro-t evil n. upon virgin
25 : 6. firstb. succeed in n. of bro.
7. to raise up to bro. a n. in Isr.
26 : 19. to make the high in n.
28 : 58. mayest fear this glorious
n. THE LORD THY GOD
Jos. 14 : 15. n. of Hebron, Ju.1:10.
15 : 15. n. of Debir was, Ju. 1 : 11.
Ju. 13 : 2. man whose n. Manoah
16:4. woman whose n. was Delilah
17 : 1. man whose n. was Micah
Ru. 1 : 2. n. of man was Elimelech
4. n. of one Orpah, n. of other
2:19. man's n. is Boaz
4:5. to raise up n. of the dead, 10.
17. her neighbours gave it a n.
1 S. 8 : 2. n. of his firsth. Joel, n. of
9:1. a man of Benj. whose n. Kish
2. he had a son whose n. was Saul
14 : 4. n. of one Bozez, n. of other
49. n. of firstb. Merab, and n. of
50. n. of captain of host ⌈n.
17:12. Da. son of Ephrathite whose
25 : 3. n. of the man was Nabal
9. spake to Nabal in n. of David
2 S. 3 : 7. Saul had concu. n. Rizpah
4:2. capts.; n. of one ; n. of other
7: 9. made thee a n. like n. of gr.
men, 1 Ch. 17 : 8. ⌈Ch. 17 : 21.
23. redeemed to make him n., 1

2 S. 8:13. David gat him a n. when
9: 2. serv. whose n. was Ziba | 12.
13:1.sister,whose n.was Tamar | 3.
14:7. not leave to my husb. n. nor
27.one dau. whose n. was Tamar
16 : 5. a man whose n. Shimei
17:25.Amasa a man's son whose n.
20 : 1. man of Belial whose n.
23 : 18. Abishai had n. am. three
22. Benaiah, had n. among 3
mighty men, 1 Ch. 11 : 20, 24.
1 K. 1 : 47. God make n. of Sol. better than thy n. and throne
14 : 21. choose to put his n. there,
2 Ch. 12 : 13. ⌈gods, 25, 26.
18 : 24. call ye on the n. of your
21 : 8. Jezebel wrote in Ahab's n.
2 K. 14: 27. not blot out n. of Isr.
1 Ch. 4 : 3. n. of sister, 7 : 15.
2 Ch. 28 : 9. prophet whose n. Oded
Ezr.5:1. prophesied in n.of G.of Isr.
14. one whose n.was Sheshbazzar
Ne. 9 : 7. gavest him n. of Abraham
10. So didst thou get thee a n.
Es. 2 : 5. a Jew whose n. Mordecai
22. Esther certified the king in
Mordecai's n. ⌈10.-3 : 12.
8:8.Write ye for Jews in king's n.,
Jb. 18 : 17. he sh. have no n. in st.
30 : † 8. were chil. of men of no n.
Ps. 9:5. hast put out their n. for ev.
20 : 1. n. of God of Jacob defend
5. in n. of G. will set up banners
44:20. If we have forgott. n. of G.
69 : 30. I will praise the n. of God
83:4.n.of Isr. be no more in remem.
18. whose n. is JEHOVAH
99 : 3. Let them praise thy great n.
109:13. let their n. be blotted out
113 : 3. L.'s n. is to be praised
Pr. 10 : 7. n. of the wicked sh. rot
18 : 10. n. of Lord is strong tower
22:1.A good n.is rather to be chos.
30 : 9. lest I take n. of G. in vain
Ec. 7 : 1. A good n. better than prec.
Is. 14 : 22. will cut off from Bab. n.
55:13. it shall be to the L. for a n.
56 : 5. I will give a n. an everl. n.
57:15. n. is holy | 62:2. by new n.
63:12. to make himself an everl. n.
14. to make thyself a glorious n.
65 : 15. sh. leave your n. for curse
L. sh. call serv-s by another n.
66:22.sh. your seed and n. remain
Je. 13 :11. be unto me for a n., 33:9.
32 : 20. made thee a n., Da. 9:†15.
37 : 13. captain whose n. Irijah
46:18. As I live, saith King, whose
n. is L. of hosts, 48:15.-51:57.
Eze.22:†5.thee wh.art polluted of n.
23:†10.she became a n. am.women
24 : 2. Son of man, write n. of day
48:35. n. of city be,The L. is there
Da. 1 : 7. unto Dan. n. of Belteshazzar, 2 : 26.-4 : 8, 19.-10 : 1.
2 : 20. Blessed be the n. of God
4: 8. Da. came, acc. to n. of my god
Ho.2:17.no more be rememb-d by n.
Am. 5 : 27. n. is The God of hosts
Mi. 4 : 5. walk ev. one in n. of his
god, we in the n. of our G. ⌈rim
Zph. 1:4. I will cut off n. of Chema-
3 : 20. I will make you a n.
Zch.6:12. man whose n. is BRANCH
Mat. 10:41.prophet in n. of prophet,
righte. man in n. of righteous
42. of water only in n.of disci.
28 : 19.baptizing them in n. of Fa.
Lu. 1 : 5. her n. was Elizabeth
27. to a man whose n.was Joseph
63.he wrote, saying,His n.is John
2 : 25. man in Jerus. n. Simeon
6:22. shall cast out your n. as evil
24 : 18. whose n. was Cleopas
Jn. 1 : 6. man from G., n. was John
3:18. not believed in n. of only be-
5: 43. I am come in Fa.'s n. ⌊gott

Jn.10:25.works I do in my Fa.'s **n.**
18:10. servant's **n.** was Malchus
Ac.2:38. be baptized in **n.** of J. C.
3:6. In **n.** of Jesus Christ, rise up
4:7. By what **n.** have ye done this?
12. is none other **n.** under heaven
17. speak to no man in this **n.**, 18.
30. wonders be done by **n.** of Jes.
5:28. sho. not teach in this **n.**, 40.
40. sh. not speak in **n.** of Jesus
7:58. at yo. man's feet, **n.** was Saul
8:12. preaching, conc. **n.** of Jesus
9:27. preached boldly in **n.** of Jes., ⌊29.
13:6. Jew whose **n.** Bar-jesus
16:18. I com-d in **n.** of Jes. come out
26:9. to do contrary to **n.** of Jesus
28:7. whose **n.** was Publius
1 Co.1:13. baptized in **n.** of Paul?
5:4. In **n.** of our L., Ep. 5:20.
Ep.1:21. far above every **n.** that
Ph.2:9. given him **n.** above ev. **n.**
10. at **n.** of Jes. ev. knee sho. bow
2 Ti.2:19. that nameth **n.** of Christ
He.1:4. obtained a more excel. **n.**
1 Pe.4:14. if reproach for **n.** of C.
1 Jn.3:23. we sho. believe on **n.** of Son, J. C., 5:13. ⌈knoweth
Re.2:17. a **n.** written, wh. no man
3:1. thou hast a **n.** that thou livest
12. will write upon him **n.** of G. (3)
9:11. whose **n.** in Heb. is Abaddon
13:1. upon heads **n.** of blasphemy
14:1. his Fa.'s **n.** in their foreheads
16:9. men blasphemed the **n.** of G.
17:5. upon forehead **n.**, MYSTERY
19:12. a **n.** no man knew but hims.
16. on his thigh a **n.** written, KING OF KINGS.
See BLASPHEME, ED.

By NAME, or by the NAME.

Ex.6:3. I appeared **b. t. n.** of G. Almighty ⌈17.
33:12. hast said, I know thee **b. n.**,
Nu.4:32. **b. n.** reckon instruments
Jos.21:9. gave cities mentioned **b. n.**
1 S.17:23. Philistine, Goliath **b. n.**
2 S.20:21. Sheba, son of Bichri **b. n.**
1 K.13:2. child be born, Josiah **b. n.**
1 Ch.4:41. these writt. **b. n.** smote
2 Ch.28:15. men expressed **b. n.**, took the captives, 31:19.
Is.44:5. shall call hims. **b. t. n.** of Jacob surname himself **b. t. n.** of Israel, 48:1. ⌈**b. n.**
Mat.27:32. man of Cyrene, Simon
Mk.5:22. of synag. Jairus **b. n.**
Jn.10:3. he calleth his sheep **b. n.**
Ac.4:10. **b. t. n.** of Jesus this man is
30. wonders **b. t. n.** of holy child
1 Co.1:10. I beseech you **b. t. n.** of L.
3 Jn.14. friends salute. Greet friends ⌊**b. n.**
See CALL, EXPRESSED.

NAME with called. ⌈**n.**

Ge.2:19. whatso. Adam **c.** that was
3:20. Adam **c.** his wife's **n.** Eve
4:17. **c. n.** of city aft. **n.** of son
5:2. created th. **c.** their **n.** Adam
11:9. Thf. is **n.** of it **c.** Babel
12:8. builded altar, **c.** upon **n.** of L., 13:4.–21:33.–26:25.
16:15. Abram **c.** his son's **n.** Ishmael
19:22. **n.** of city was **c.** Zoar
25:26. his **n.** was **c.** Jacob ⌈30.
28:19. he **c. n.** of place Beth-el; but **n.** was **c.** Luz, Ju. 1:23.
29:34. therf. was his **n. c.** Levi
30:21. dau. and **c.** her **n.** Dinah
31:48. Thf. was **n.** of it **c.** Galeed
32:28. Thy **n.** sh. be **c.** no more Jacob but Israel, 35:10. (4)
33:17. **n.** of place is **c.** Succoth
35:8. **n.** of it was **c.** Allon-bachuth
38:29. thf. his **n.** was **c.** Pharez ⌊30.
41:45. Pha. **c.** Joseph's **n.** Zaphnath-
52. **n.** of second **c.** he Ephraim
48:6. sh. be **c.** after **n.** of brethren
50:11. **n.** of it was **c.** Abel-mizraim

Ex.15:23. thf. **n.** was **c.** Marah
31:2. have **c.** by **n.** Bezaleel, 35:30.
Nu.32:42. **c.** it Nobah after own **n.**
De.3:14. **c.** them after his own **n.**
28:10. sh. see thou art **c.** by **n.** of L.
Jos.5:9. **n.** of place is **c.** Gilgal
7:26. **n.** of place was **c.** The valley
19:47. **c.** Leshem Dan after **n.** of fa.
Jos.21:†9. cities wh. are here **c.** by **n.**
Ju.1:17. **n.** of city was **c.** Hormah
8:31. son whose **n.** he **c.** Abimelech
2 S.6:2. ark whose **n.** is **c.** by **n.** of L., 1 Ch. 13:6. ⌈my **n.**
12:28. take city and it be **c.** after
18:18. Abs. **c.** pillar after own **n.**
1 K.8:43. that peo. may know house is **c.** by thy **n.**, 2 Ch. 6:33. ⌈mer
16:24. **c. n.** of city after **n.** of Shemer
18:26. **c.** on **n.** of Baal, O Baal
1 Ch.22:9. his **n.** sh. be **c.** Solomon
2 Ch.20:26. **n.** of place was **c.** Berachah
Ezr.2:61. **c.** after their **n.**, Ne. 7:63.
Es.2:14. unto k. exc. she were **c.** by
9:26. **c.** days Purim aft. **n.** Pur ⌊**n.**
Ps.79:6. kingd-s th. not **c.** upon thy
116:4. Then **c.** I. upon **n.** of L. ⌊**n.**
Is.48:1. O house of Jac. **c.** by **n.** of
Je.11:16. L. **c.** thy **n.** A olive tree ⌊Isr.
20:3. L. hath not **c.** thy **n.** Pashur
Je.23:6. This is **n.** he shall be **c.**
33:16. **n.** wherewith she sh. be **c.**
Da.10:1. Daniel, **n. c.** Belteshazzar
Lu.1:59. **c.** him Zach. after **n.** of fa.
61. none of kindred **c.** by this **n.**
Ac.9:21. destroyed th. **c.** on this **n.**
Ja.2:7. blaspheme **n.** by wh. ye are **c.**
Re.19:13. his **n.** is **c.** Word of God
See CALL, CALLETH.

Called by my NAME.

2 Ch.7:14. If my peo. wh. are **c.-n.**
Is.43:7. bring, every one **c.-n.**
65:1. behold, to nation not **c.-n.**
Je.7:10. this house **c.-n.**, 11, 14, 30.–32:34.–34:15.
25:29. I bring evil on city **c.-n.**
Am.9:12. remnant of heath. **c.-n.**

Called by thy NAME.

1 K.8:43. house **c. b. t. n.**, 2 Ch. 6: ⌊33.
Is.4:1. only let us be **c. b. t. n.**
43:1. I have **c.** thee **b. t. n.**, 45:4.
63:19. they were not **c. b. t. n.**
Je.14:9. O Lord, we are **c. b. t. n.**
15:16. for I am **c. b. t. n.** O L.
Da.9:18. behold the city **c. b. t. n.**
19. for city and peo. are **c. b. t. n.**

Called his NAME. ⌈5:3.

Ge.4:25. **c. h. n.** Seth: For God,
26. to Seth a son; **c. h. n.** Enos
5:29. Lamech **c. h. n.** Noah ⌈ab.
19:37. firstb. bare son **c. h. n.** Mo-
38. younger bare son **c. h. n.** Ben- ⌊ammi
25:25. first, they **c. h. n.** Esau
29:32. **c. h. n.** Reuben | 33. Simeon
35. she **c. h. n.** Judah ⌈30:6. Dan
30:8. **c. h. n.** Naphtali | 11. Gad
13. **c. h. n.** Asher | 18. Issachar
20. **c. h. n.** Zebulun | 24. Joseph
35:10. God **c. h. n.** Israel (4)
18. she **c. h. n.** Ben-oni, but his father **c.** him Benj. ⌈Onan
38:3. son; Judah **c. h. n.** Er | 4.
5. Judah **c. h. n.** Shelah
Ex.2:10. **c. h. n.** Moses | 22. Gershom
Ju.13:24. woman **c. h. n.** Samson
Ru.4:17. neighbours **c. h. n.** Obed
1 S.1:20. Hannah **c. h. n.** Samuel
2 S.12:24. David **c. h. n.** Solomon
25. Nathan **c. h. n.** Jedediah
1 Ch.4:9. mother **c. h. n.** Jabez
7:16. Maachah **c. h. n.** Peresh
23. Ephraim **c. h. n.** Beriah
Mat.1:25. Joseph **c. h. n.** JESUS, 21. Lu. 1:31.–2:21.

Called the NAME. ⌈of

Ge.4:17. Cain **c. n.** of city after **n.**
16:13. she **c. n.** of L., Thou G. seest
21:3. Ab. **c. n.** of his son, Isaac

Ge.22:14. **c. n.** of pla. Jehovah-jireh
26:20. Isaac **c. n.** of the well Esek, 21, 22. ⌈35:15.
28:19. Jac. **c. n.** of place Beth-el,
32:2. Jac. **c. n.** of pla. Mahanaim
30. Jacob **c. n.** of place Peniel
41:51. Joseph **c. n.** of firstb. Manasseh
Ex.16:31. Israel **c. n.** Manna
17:7. Mo. **c. n.** of place Massah
15. Mo. **c. n.** of alt. JEHOVAH-nissi
Nu.11:3. Mo. **c. n.** of pla. Taberah
34. Mo. **c. n.** of place Kibroth-hatt.
21:3. he **c. n.** of place Hormah
Ju.1:26. he **c. n.** of city Luz (2)
2:5. Isr. **c. n.** of place Bochim
15:19. Samson **c. n.** En-hakkoro
18:29. they **c. n.** of city Dan
1 S.7:12. **c. n.** of stone Eben-ezer
2 S.5:20. Da. **c. n.** of pla. Baal-perazim, 1 Ch. 14:11. ⌈1 Ch. 13:11.
6:8. Da. **c. n.** of place Perez-uzzah,
1 K.7:21. he **c. n.** of right pillar Jachin (2), 2 Ch. 3:17.
16:24. **c. n.** of city after **n.** of Shemer, Samaria
Jb.42:14. he **c. n.** of 1st Jemima (3)

His NAME.

Ex.3:13. What is **h. n.**? Pr. 30:4.
15:3. the L. is **h. n.**, Je. 33:2. Am. 5:8.–9:6. ⌈De. 5:11.
20:7. that taketh **h. n.** in vain,
28:21. every stone with **h. n.**, 39:14.
De.6:13. shalt swear by **h. n.**, 10:20.
10:8. to bless in **h. n.**, 1 Ch. 23:13.
12:5. Lord shall choose to put **h. n.** there, 21.–14:23.–16:6, 11.–26:2. 1 K. 14:21. 2 Ch. 12:13.
11. cause **h. n.** to dwell there, Ezr. 6:12. ⌈there
14:24. L. shall choose to set **h. n.**
25:6. **h. n.** be not put out of Isr.
29:20. L. shall blot out **h. n.** from
Ju.13:6. neither told me **h. n.**
Ru.2:1. **h. n.** was Boaz ⌈in Israel
4:14. that **h. n.** may be famous
1 S.1:1. a man **h. n.** Elkanah
18:30. **h. n.** was much set by
21:7. **h. n.** was Doeg, chief ⌈**n.**
25:25. as **h. n.**, so is he, Nabal is **h.**
2 S.4:4. **h. n.** was Mephibosheth
2 K.24:17. made Mattaniah king, changed **h. n.**, 23:34. 2 Ch. 36:4.
1 Ch.16:8. Give thanks unto L., call upon **h. n.**, Ps. 105:1. Is. 12:4. ⌈Ps. 29:2.–96:8.
29. Give the glory due unto **h. n.**,
2 Ch.26:8. to Uzziah: and **h. n.** spread, 15.
Ps.34:3. let us exalt **h. n.**, 66:2.
41:5. When die and **h. n.** perish?
68:4. rideth upon heavens by **h. n.** ⌊JAH
69:36. love **h. n.** sh. dwell
72:17. **h. n.** sh. endure for ever (2)
19. blessed be **h.** glorious **n.** for ⌊ever
76:1. **h. n.** is great in Israel
96:2. Sing unto L. bless **h. n.**, 100:4.
99:6. Sam. among them call upon ⌊**h. n.**
111:9. and reverend is **h. n.**
135:3. sing praises unto **h. n.** for it
148:13. praise **h. n.** for **h. n.** is excel.
149:3. Let th. praise **h. n.** in dance
Pr.21:24. haughty scorner is **h. n.**
30:4. what **h. n.**? and his son's **n.**
Ec.6:4. **h. n.** be cov-d with darkn.
Is.7:14. shall call **h. n.** Immanuel
8:3. Call **h. n.** Maher-shalal—
12:4. make mention **h. n.** is exalt.
47:4. the Lord of hosts is **h. n.**, 48:2.–51:15.–54:5. Je. 10:16.–31:35.–32:18.–50:34.–51:19.
48:19. **h. n.** not have been cut off
Je.11:19. **h. n.** be no more remem.
20:9. I not speak more in **h. n.**
48:17. know **h. n.** say, How is staff
Am.4:13. L., the G. of hosts is **h. n.**
Zch.10:12. walk up and do. in **h. n.**
14:9. in that day one L. **h. n.** one

Mal. 3 : 16. that thought upon h. n.
Mat. 1 : 23. sh. call h. n. Emmanuel
12 : 21. in h.n. shall Gentiles trust
Mk. 6 : 14. h. n. was spread abroad
Lu. 1 : 63. saying, h. n. is John, 13.
24 : 47. remission of sins preached
Jn.1:12.th.believe on h.n. ⌊in h.n.
2:23. many believed in h. n. when
5 : 43. if ano. come in h. own n.
20:31.ye might have life thro. h.n.
Ac. 3: 16. h. n. thro. faith in h.n.
5 : 41. worthy to suffer for h. n.
10:43. thro. h. n. remission of sins
13 : 8. Elymas sorcerer, so is h. n.
15:14. to take out a peo. for h. n.
Ro. 1 : 5. faith am. nations for h. n.
He. 6 : 10. love ye shewed tow. h.n.
13:15.praise,giving thanks to h.n.
Re. 3 : 5. not blot out h. n. but will
confess h. n. ⌊Death
6:8. and h.n. that sat on him was
9 : 11. in the Greek h. n. Apollyon.
13:17.had number of h.n.,15:2.⌈n.
14:11.whoso. receiveth mark of h.
22 : 4. h. n. shall be in their fore-
See CALL, HOLY. ⌊heads
See **Name of the LORD, His MOTHER.**

Mine own or my NAME.

Ge.32:29.Whf. dost ask after m. n.
48:16.let m.n. be named on them
Ex. 3 : 15. this is m. n. for ever and
9:16.m. n. may be declared ⌈come
20:24. where I record m. n. I will
23:21. provoke not,m.n.is in him
Le. 19 : 12. not swear by m. n.
20:3.Molech,to profane m.holy n.
Nu. 6 : 27. put m. n. upon Isr. ⌈20
De. 18 : 19.wh. he sh.speak in m.n.,
Ju. 13 : 18.Why askest after m. n.?
1 S. 24 : 21. wilt not destroy m. n.
25: 5. to Nabal, greet him in m.n.
2 S. 7 : 13. sh. build a ho. for m.n.
1 K. 5: 5.-8:18, 19. 1 Ch. 22:10.
18:18. I have no son to keep m.n.
1 K. 8 : 16. that m. n. might be
therein, 29.-9 : 3.-11 : 36. 2 K.
21 : 4, 7.-23 : 27. 2 Ch. 6:5, 6.-7:
16.-33 : 4, 7. ⌈n.
9:7. house I have hallowed for m.
1 Ch. 22 : 8. sh. not build a house
unto m. n., 28 : 3. ⌈for m. n.
2 Ch. 6 : 8. in heart to build a ho.
9. Sol. sh. build house for m. n.
7 : 20. ho. I sanctified for m. n.
Ne.1:9. chosen to set m.n.,Je.7:12.
Ps. 89 : 24. in m. n. horn be exalt.
91 : 14. bec. he hath known m. n.
Is. 29: 23. they shall sanctify m.n.
41 : 25. fr. rising of sun call upon
42:8. I am L. that is m.n. ⌊m.n.
48:11. how sho. m.n. be polluted?
49:1. hath made mention of m. n.
52: 6. my people shall know m.n.
Je. 14 : 14. lies in m.n., 15.-23: 25.
16:21. shall know that m.n. is L.
23: 27. cause my peo. to forget m.
n. as fa-s forgotten m. n.
27:15. prophesy a lie in m.n., 29:
34:16.ye polluted m. n. ⌊9, 21, 23.
44 : 26. sworn by m. n., m.n. no
more named ⌈n.
Eze. 36 : 23. I will sanctify m. great
Mal.1:6.O priests, th. despise m.n.
11. m.n.shall be great am.Gent.
in ev. place incense be to m.n.
14.m.n. is dreadful am. heathen
2 : 2. to give glory unto m. n.
5. and was afraid before m. n.
4:2.unto you th. fear m.n. sh.sun
Mat. 18:5. whoso. receive a child in
m. n., Mk. 9 : 37. Lu. 9 : 48.
20. two or three are gathered together in m. n.
24 : 5. many shall come in m. n.
and deceive, Mk. 13 : 6. Lu.21:8.
Mk. 5 : 9. he ans-d, m.n. is Legion
Mk.9:39. shall do a miracle in m.n.
41. cup of wat. to drink in m.n.
16:17. In m.n. sh. cast out devils
Jn.14:13. whatso. ye sh. ask in m.
n.,14.-15:16.-16:23,24, 26. ⌈n.
26. Comforter he will send in m.
Ac.9:15.chosen vessel to bear m.n.
Ro. 9 : 17. that m. n. be declared
1 Co. 1 : 15. I baptized in m. o. n.
Re. 2 : 13. thou holdest fast m. n.
3:8. hast kept my word, not denied
12. I will write m. new n. ⌊m.n.
See CALL.

NAME'S sake. ⌈s.

1 S. 12 : 22. not forsake people for n.
1 K.8:41.a stranger out of far country for thy n. s., 2 Ch. 6 : 32.
Ps. 23:3. he leadeth me for his n.s.
25 : 11. For thy n. s. pardon mine
31 : 3. for thy n. s. lead me ⌊iniq.
79 : 9. purge our sins for thy n. s.
106 : 8. he saved them for his n.s.
109:21.do thou for me for thy n.s.
143 : 11. Quicken me for thy n. s.
Is. 48 : 9. For my n. s. defer anger
66 : 5. cast you out for my n. s.
Je. 14 : 7. O L. do it for thy n. s.
21. Do not abhor us for thy n.s.
Eze. 20 : 9. I wrought for my n. s.
that it, 14, 22, 44.-36 : 22.
Mat. 10 : 22. ye sh. be hated for my
n. s., 24:9. Mk.13:13. Lu.21:17.
19:29. forsaken lands for my n. s.
sh. receive, Mk.10:29.Lu.18:20.
Lu.21:12.bro-t bef. rulers for my n.
Jn.15:21.do unto you for my n.s.⌊s.
Ac.9:16. he must suffer for my n.s.
1 Jn.2:12. sins forgiven for his n. s.
3 Jn.7.for his n.s. they went forth
Re. 2 : 3. for my n.s. hast laboured

Thine own or thy NAME.

Ge. 12 : 2. I will make t. n. great
17:5. t.n. Abram, but t.n. sh. be
Abraham ⌈29. Ju. 13 : 17.
32:27.said unto him, What is t.n.?
35:10.t.n.is Jacob but Israel shall
be t. n., (4) 1 K. 18 : 31.
Ex.5:23.to Pharaoh to speak in t.n.
Jos. 7 : 9. what do unto t. great n.?
2 S. 7 : 26. let t.n. be magnified
22:50. I will sing praise unto t.n.,
Ps.9:2.-18:49.-61:8.-66:4.-92:1.
1 K. 1 : 47. name of Solomon better
than t. n. ⌈Ch. 6 : 24, 26.
8 : 33. turn and confess t.n., 35. 2
42. they shall hear of t. great n.
43. that all peo. may know t. n.
44. house I built for t. n., 48. 2
Ch. 6 : 34, 38. ⌈for ever
1 Ch. 17 : 24. t. n. may be magnified
29 : 13. we praise t. n., Ps. 44 : 8.
2 Ch. 6 : 20. that wouldest put t. n.
14 : 11. in t. n. we go ag. multitude
20 : 8. have built sanct. for t. n.
9. for t. n. is in this house
Ne. 1 : 11. who desire to fear t. n.
9 : 5. blessed be t. glorious n.
Ps. 5 : 11. let th. love t.n. be joyful
8 : 1. how excellent is t. n., 9.
9 : 10. that know t. n. will trust
22:22. I will declare t.n., He.2:12.
44 : 5. thro. t.n. will we tread th.
8. and praise t. n. forever
45:17.I will make t.n. to be remem.
48 : 10. Acc. to t. n. so thy praise
52 : 9. I will wait on t. n.
54 : 1. Save me by t. n.
6. I will praise t. n. O Lord
61 : 5. heritage of those fear t. n.
63 : 4. I will lift my hands in t. n.
74 : 7. defiled dwellingpl. of t. n.
10. enemy blaspheme t.n. for ever
21. let poor and needy praise t.n.
75:1.that t.n. is near, works decla.
79:9.Help us, O G. for glory of t.n.
80 : 18. we will call upon t. n.
83 : 16. that they may seek t. n.
Ps.86:9.All nat-s sh.glorify t.n.,12.
11. unite my heart to fear t. n.
89:12.Hermon sh.rejoice in t.n.,16
99:3. let them praise t. terrible n.
115:1. not unto us, but unto t. n.
119: 55. I rememb-d t. n. in night
132. usest to do unto those love t.
135 : 13. t. n. O L. endureth ⌊n.
138 : 2. will praise t.n. for lovingkindn. magnified word ab. t.n.
139 : 20. enemies take t.n. in vain
140 : 13. sh. give thanks unto t.n.
142:7. prison, th. I may praise t.n.
145:1. I will bless t.n. for ever, 21.
2. will praise t.n. for ever, Is.25:
Can. 1: 3. t. n. is as ointment ⌊1.
Is.26:8. desire of our soul is to t.n.
13. will make mention of t. n.
63:16. O Lord, t. n. is from everl.
64 : 2. make t. n. kno. to adversa-
7. is none that call upon t.n. ⌊ries
Je.10:6.t.n. is great in might ⌈rus.
29:25. sent letters in t.n. unto Je
La.3:55. upon t. n. out of dungeon
Da. 9 : 6. prophets spake in t. n.
Mi. 6 : 9. man of wisdom sh. see t.n.
Na. 1 : 14. no more of t.n. be sown
Mal.1:6. Wherein despised t.n.? (2)
Mat.6:9.Hallowed be t.n., Lu.11:2.
7 : 22. in t. n. cast out devils
Mk. 5 : 9. he asked him, What is t.
n.? Lu. 8 : 30. ⌈Lu. 9 : 49.
9 : 38. casting out devils in t. n.,
Lu. 10: 17. devils subject thro. t.n.
Jn. 12 : 28. Father, glorify t. n.
17: 6. I have manifested t. n., 26.
11. Father, keep thro. t.o.n.,12.
Ro.15:9.I will confess,and sing unto
t. n. ⌈that fear t. n.
Re. 11 : 18. give reward unto them
15:4.Who not fear and glorify t.n.
See CALL.
See **NAME** with **called.**

NAMES.

Ge.2:20. Adam gave n. to all cattle
25 : 13. n. of sons of Ishm., (2) 16.
26:18.their n. after n. his fa. called
36: 10. These are n. of Esau's sons
40. n. of dukes came of Esau (2)
46 : 8. n. of chil. of Isr., Ex. 1 : 1.
Ex. 6 : 16. are n. sons of Levi
28 : 9. grave on them n. of chil. of
Isr., 11, 21.-39 : 6, 14. ⌈other
10. six n. on one stone, 6 n. on
12. Aaron sh. bear n. bef. L., 29.
Nu. 1: 2. sum of cong-n by house of
fathers with number of their n.
by their poll, 18, 20, 22, 24, 26,
28, 30, 32, 34, 36, 38, 40, 42. 1
Ch. 23 : 24. ⌈you
5. n. of men that shall stand with
17. Aa. took men expressed by n.
3:2. These are n. of sons of Aa., 3
17. These were sons of Levi by
their n., Ex. 6 : 16. ⌈Ch. 6:17
18. are n. of sons of Gershom, 1
40. take number of n. of Levites
43. all firstb. males by numb. of n.
13 : 4. heads of Israel their n.
16. n. of men Moses sent to spy
26 : 33. n. of daughters of Zelophehad, 27 : 1. Jos. 17 : 3. ⌈tribes
55. land sh. be divided acc. to n. of
32:38. Nebo, Baal-meon (n. changed)
34 : 17. n. of men divide land
19. n. of princes are these
1 S. 14 : 49. n. of Saul's two dau-s
17:13. n. of Jesse's 3 sons that went
2 S. 5:14. n. of those born unto Da.
23 : 8. n. of mighty men Da. had
1 K. 4 : 8. Sol. had 12 officers; these
their n. ⌈were princes
1 Ch. 4 : 38. These mentioned by n.
6 : 65. cities called by their n.
8:38. Azel had 6 sons whose n., 9:
14 : 4. are n. of David's chil. ⌊44.
23:24. Number of n. by their polls

Ezr.5:4. What n. of men made this building [write n.
10. We asked n. that we might
8 : 13. sons of Adonikam whose n.
10:16.all of them by n.were separa.
Ps. 16 : 4. nor take n. into my lips
49:11. they call lands after own n.
147 : 4. the stars by n., Is. 40 : 26.
Eze. 23 : 4. n. of them were Aholah
48 : 1. these are n. of tribes [tribes
31. gates of city be after n. of
Ho.2:17. will take aw. n. of Baalim
Zch. 13 : 2. cut off n. of the idols
Mat. 10 : 2. n. of 12 disciples are
Lu. 10 : 20. your n. written in heav.
Ac.1:15. number of the n. were 120
18 : 15. if question of n. look to it
Ph. 4 : 3. whose n. in book of life
Re.3:4. thou hast a few n. in Sardis
11:†13.were slain n.of of men 7,000
13 : † 1. upon heads n. of blasphe.
8. whose n. are not in book,17:8.
17:3. wom. full of n. of blasphemy
21 : 12. n. written, n. of 12 tribes
14. in them n. of twelve apostles

NAME. [Verb.] [n.
1 S. 16 : 3. anoint unto me him wh. I
28:8. bring him up whom I sh. n.
Is. 62 : 2. which mouth of L. sh. n.

NAMED. [n.
Ge.23:16. Ab. weighed silver he had
27:36. Is not he rightly n. Jacob?
48:16. let my name be n. on them
Jos. 2 : 1. harlot's house n. Rahab
1 S. 4 : 21. she n. the child Ichabod
17:4. went a champion n. Goliath
22 : 20. son of Ahim. n. Abiathar
2 K. 17 : 34. Jacob whom he n. Isr.
1 Ch. 23:14. Moses' sons were n. of the tribe of Levi
Ec. 6 : 10. hath been is n. already
Is. 61:6. ye shall be n. Priests of L.
Je. 44 : 26. my name no more be n.
Da. 5: 12. whom k. n. Belteshazzar
Am. 6 : 1. are n. chief of nations
Mi. 2 : 7. O thou that art n. of Jac.
Mat. 9 : 9. n. Matthew | 27 : 57. Jo-
Mk. 14 : 32. n. Gethsemane [seph
15:7. n. Barabbas | Lu.1:5. Zacha-
Lu.1:26.unto city n. Nazareth [rias
2 : 21. Jesus was so n. of angel
5 : 27. saw a publican n. Levi
6 : 13. chose 12 wh. he n. apostles
14. Simon (whom he n. Peter)
8: 41. n. Jairus | 10:38. n. Martha
16 : 20. n. Lazarus | Jn. 11 : 1.
19 : 2. n. Zaccheus | 23:50. Joseph
Jn. 3 : 1. n. Nicodemus | 11:49. Ca-
Ac. 5 : 1. n. Ananias [iaphas
34. n. Gamaliel | 9 : 10. Ananias,
9 : 33. n. Eneas sick of [12.
36. disci. n. Tabitha | 11 : 28. n. Agabus, 21 : 10. [theus
12 : 13. n. Rhoda | 16: 1. n. Timo-
16:14. n. Lydia | 17:34.n.Damaris
18 : 2. n. Aquila | 7. Justus
24. n. Apollos | 19:24. Demetrius
20 : 9. young man n. Eutychus
24 : 1. n. Tertullus | 27 : 1. Julius
Ro. 15 : 20. not where Christ was n.
1 Co.5:1. fornica. not n. am. Gent.
Ep. 1 : 21. ab. every name th. is n.
3:15.family in heav.and earth is n.
5:3.covetousn.let it not be once n.

NAMELY.
De. 4 : 43. n. Bezer in the wildern.
13 : 7. n. of the gods of the people
Ju. 3 : 3. n. five lords of the Philis.
1 Ch. 6 : 57. gave cities n. Hebron
9:23. n. house of taberu. [Jeshua
Ezr. 10 : 18. stra. wives n. of sons of
Ec. 5 : 13. sore evil, n. riches kept
Is.7:20.with razor, n. by Assyr. [n.
Je. 26 : 22. Jehoi-m sent men into E.
Mk. 12 : 31. sec. is like, n. love thy

NAMETH. [neighb.
2 Ti.2:19.Let ev. one n. name of C.

NAOMI. [3.
Ru.1:2. Elimelech, name of wife N.,
8. N. said unto her 2 dau-s | 11.
19. Is this N.? | 20.Call me not N.
21.why call me N.seeing the L.,22.
2 : 1. N. had a kinsman Boaz
2. Ruth said to N. | 6, 20,21.-3:1.
4 : 3. N. that is come out of Moab
5. what day buyest field of N.
9. I have bought all at ha. of N.
14. women said unto N. Blessed |
17. There is a son born to N. [16.

NA'PHISH. See KEDEMAH.

NAPH'TALI.
Ge. 30 : 8. Rachel called his name N.
35 : 25. sons of Bilhah, Dan, N.
46:24. sons of N., Nu. 1:42.-26:48.
1 Ch. 7 : 13. [gives goodly
49 : 21. N. is a hind let loose, he
Ex. 1 : 4. sons of Israel ; N. Gad
Nu. 1 : 15. of N. Ahira was prince,
42.-2 : 29.-7 : 78. [50.
26 : 48. of N. after their families,
De.27:13. upon Ebal to curse ; Dan,
33 : 23. he said, O N. satisfied [N.
34 : 2. Lord shewed Moses all N.
Jos. 19 : 32. sixth lot came out to N.
20: 7. Kedesh in Galilee, in m-t N.
Ju. 1 : 33. nei. N. drive out inhab-ts
4 : 10. Barak called N. to Kedesh
5 : 18. and N. jeoparded their lives
6:35. Gid. sent messengers unto N.
7:23.Isr. gathered thems. out of N.
1 K. 4 : 15. Ahimaaz officer in N.
15 : 20. Ben-hadad smote N.
2 K. 15 : 29. N. captive to Assyria
1 Ch.2:2. sons of Israel, N. and Gad
12 : 34. And of 1,000 N. captains
40. N. brought bread on asses
27: 19. captain of N. was Jerimoth
2 Ch. 16 : 4. smote store cities of N.
34 : 6. Josiah in N. brake altars
Ps. 68 : 27. princes of Zebulun, N.
Is. 9 : 1. he lightly afflicted la. of N.
Eze. 48:3. by Asher a portion for N.
4. border of N. portion for Manas.
34.one gate of Asher, 1 gate of N.
See KEDESH-NAPHTALI, NEPHTHALIM.

Tribe of NAPH'TALI.
Nu. 1 : 43. numb-d of t.o.N. 53,400
2 : 29. Then t. o. N. and captain
10 : 27. over host of t. o. N. Ahira
13 : 14. of t. o. N. Nahbi Mo. sent
34 : 28. prince of t. o. N. Pedahel
Jos. 19 : 39. inheritance of t. o. N.
21: 32. cities out of t. o. N., 1 Ch.
6 : 62, 76. [t. o. N.
1 K. 7 : 14. Hiram a widow's son of
See NEPHTHALIM.

NAPH'TUHIM. [11.
Ge. 10:13. Mizraim begat N., 1 Ch.1:

NAPKIN.
Lu. 19 : 20. pound I have kept in n.
Jn. 11 : 44. his face bound with n.
20 : 7. n. that was about his head

NARCIS'SUS. [of N.
Ro. 16 : 11. greet them of household

NARD.
Mk. 14 : † 3. having a box of pure n.

NARROW, ER.
Nu.22:26.angel of L.stood in n.way
Jos.17:15. if mount Ephr. be too n.
1 K. 6 : 4. made windows of n. lights
Pr. 23 : 27. strange woman is n. pit
24:†10.If thou faint, strength is n.
Is. 28 : 20. covering n-r than that he can wrap himself in it
49:19.land of thy destruc.be too n.
Mat. 7 : 14. n. is way leadeth unto

NARROWED. [life
1 K.6:6.in wall of hou.made n.rests

NARROWING, S.
1 K. 6 : † 6. in wall of ho. he made n.

NARROWLY. [paths
Jb. 13 : 27. lookest n. unto all my
Is. 14 : 16. shall n. look upon thee

NA'THAN. [5.-14:4.
2 S. 5 : 14. son of David, N., 1 Ch. 3:
7 : 2. N. prophet, 1 Ch. 17 : 1.
3. N. said to king, Go do all
4. word of L. came unto N.
17. so did N. speak unto David
12 : 1. Lord sent N., 25.
5. Da. said to N. As Lord liveth
7.N. said to Da.Thou art the man
13. Da. said to N., I have sinned
15.N.departed unto his house | 25
23 : 36. Igal son of N. one of Da.'s
1 K.1:8.N.proph.and mighty men+
10. N. prophet be called not [came
22. while she talked with Da., N.
23. told king, Behold N. prophet
24. N. said, My lord O king | 31.
32. Call N. the prophet, 38, 44.
34. let N. anoint him king, 45.
4:5. Azariah son of N. over officers
1 Ch. 2 : 36. Attai begat N. N. begat
11:38. Joel brother of N. a valiant
17 : 2. N. said, Do all that is in
3. same night word of G. came to
15. acc. to vision did N. speak [N.
29 : 29. David's acts in book of N.
2 Ch. 9 : 29. acts of Sol. in book of N.
29 : 25. acc. to com-t of N. prophet
Ezr. 8 : 16. I sent fr. Ahava for N.
10:39. Shelemiah, N. strange wives
Zch. 12 : 12. family of N. apart
Lu. 3 : 31. Mattatha, wh. was son of

NATHAN'AEL. [N.
Jn. 1:45. Philip findeth N. and saith
46. N. said, Can any good thing
47. Jesus saw N. coming to him
48. N. saith unto him, Whence
49. N. answered, Rabbi, thou art
21:2.were come Thomas N. of Cana

NA'THAN-ME'LECH.
2 K. 23:11.chamber of N. the cham-

NATION. [berlain
Ge. 15:14. n. they serve will I judge
20:4. L., wilt thou slay righte. n.?
21 : 13. of bondwom. will make n.
35 : 11. n. and k. sh. come of thee
Ex. 9 : 24. in all E., since it a n.
19:6. ye sh. be a holy n., 1 Pe. 2:9.
21:8. to sell her unto a strange n.
33 : 13. consider this n. is thy peo.
34 : 10. not been done in any n.
Le.18:26.nei.any of your n.commit
20 : 23. not walk in manners of n.
Nu. 14 : 12. of thee a gr. n., De.9:14.
De. 4 : 7.what n. is there so great, 8.
34. hath G. assayed to take n. fr. midst of ano. n.
28:33. fruit of thy land sh. a n.eat
36.L.sh. bring thee and k.unto n.
49. L. sh. bring a n. ag. thee (2)
50. A n. of fierce countenance
32:21.I will provoke them to anger with foolish n., Ro. 10 : 19.
28. are n. void of counsel [17:21.
2 S. 7 : 23. what n. like thy, 1 Ch.
1 K. 18:10. no n. whi. my lord hath not sent, took an oath of th.n.
2 K.17:29. ev.n. made gods of own
1 Ch. 16 : 20. they went fr. n. to n.
2 Ch. 15 :6. n. was destroyed of n.
32 : 15. no god of any n. was able
Jb. 34 : 29. be done ag. n. or man
Ps.33:12. Blessed is n.whose G.is L.
43 : 1. O God plead ag. ungodly n.
83:4.let us cut them off fr. being n.
105:13. went from one n. to anot.
106:5. may rejoice in gladu. of thy
147:20.not dealt so with any n. [n.
Pr. 14:34. Righteousn. exalteth a n.
Is. 1 : 4. Ah, sinful n. a people laden with iniq-y [n., Mic. 4 : 3.
2 : 4. n. shall not lift up sword ag.
9 : 3. Thou hast multiplied n. [n.
10:6. I will send him ag. hypocrit-l
14:32. What ans. messengers of n.?
18:2.Go,ye swift messengers,to a n. peeled, a n. meted out, 7.

Is. 26:2. Open that righte. n. enter
15. hast increased the n. O L. (2)
49:7. L. to him whom n. abhorreth
51:4. Hearken unto me, O my n.
55:5. shalt call a n. thou kno. not
58:2. a n. that did righteousn. [ish
60:12. n. will not serve thee sh. per-
22. small one sh. become strong n.
65:1. a n. not called by my name
66:8. shall a n. be born at once?
Je. 2:11. Hath a n. changed gods?
5:9. avenged on such n., 29.-9:9.
15. I will bring a n. upon you, O
Isr., a mighty n., ancient n.
7:28. a n. that obeyeth not the L.
12:17. I will utterly destroy th. n.
18:7. conc. a n. to pluck it up, 9.
8. If n. ag. whom I pronounced
25:12. punish that n. for iniq., 27:8.
32. evil shall go forth fr. n. to n.
27:8. n. wh. will not serve Neb., 13.
31:36. Isr. sh. cease fr. being n.
33:24. should be no more a n.
48:2. cut off Moab from being a n.
49:31. get you up unto wealthy n.
36. shall be no n. whither Elam
50:3. out of north a n. against her
La. 4:17. we have watched for a n.
Eze. 2:3. thee to Isr., rebellious n.
37:22. I will make them one n.
Da. 3:29. n. which speak amiss
8:22. four kingd. stand out of n.
12:1. trouble, as never since a n.
Jo. 1:6. n. is come upon my land
Am. 6:14. I will raise ag. you a n.
Mi. 4:7. I will make her a strong n.
Ha. 1:6. Chaldeans, that bitter n.
Zph. 2:1. gather, O n. not desired
5. Woe unto n. of Cherethites
Hag. 2:14. so is this n. before me
Mal. 3:9. whole n. have robbed me
Mat. 21:43. kingdom of God given to
a n. [8. Lu. 21:10.
24:7. n. shall rise ag. n., Mk. 13:
Mk. 7:26. a Syrophenician by n.
Lu. 7:5. For he loveth our n. and
23:2. this fellow perverting the n.
Jn. 11:48. Romans sh. take our n.
50. one die, that n. perish not
51. prophesied Jesus sho. die for
52. And not for that n. only [n.
18:35. Thine own n. hath delivered
thee unto me [n.
Ac. 2:5. devout men out of every
7:7. n. to wh. they be in bondage
10:22. of good report am. all the n.
28. unlawf. to come unto 1 of ano.
35. in ev. n. he that feareth [n.
24:2. worthy deeds are done unto n.
10. hast been judge unto this n.
17. I came to bring alms to my n.
26:4. my life at first am. own n.
28:19. not aught to accuse my n.
Ga. 1:14. profited ab. equals in own
Ph. 2:15. in midst of perverse n. [n.
Re. 5:9. redeemed us out of ev. n.
14:6. gospel to preach to ev. n. and
See **GREAT nation**, s. [kingd.

NATIONS. [20, 31.

Ge. 10:5. after families, in their n.,
32. by these were the n. divided
14:1. Tidal k. of n. made war, 9.
17:4. shalt be a father of many n.,
5. Ro. 4:17, 18. [48:19.
6. I will make n. of thee, 35:11-
16. Sarah, she sh. be mother of n.
25:16. twelve princes acc. to the n.
23. L. said, Two n. in thy womb
27:9. let n. bow down to thee
Ex. 34:24. I will cast out the n. bef.
thee, De. 4:38.-7:22.-8:20.
Le. 18:24. in these, n. are defiled
28. as it spued out n. before you
Nu. 14:15. n. have heard of thy fame
23:9. sh. not be reckoned am. n.
24:8. Israel shall eat up the n.
20. Amalek was the first of the n.
De. 2:25. put fear of thee upon n.
4:6. your wisdom in sight of n.
27. L. scatter you am. n., Ne. 1:8.
7:1. L. hath cast out many n.
7. n. greater and mightier, 17, 22.
9:1. to possess n. greater than thyself, 11:23. Ne. 9:22.
4. for wickedn. of n. did L. drive
them out, 5. [30.
12:2. places wh-n n. served gods,
29. when God shall cut off the n.,
19:1. 2 K. 21:9. [28:12.
15:6. thou shalt lend unto many n.,
18:9. abom. of those n., 1 K. 14:24.
28:1. the L. will set thee ab. all n.
29:16. how we came thro. the n.
32:8. Most High divided to the n.
43. Rejoice, O ye n. with his peo.
Ju. 2:23. Thf. Lord left those n., 21.
1 S. 27:8. n. were of old the inhab-s
2 S. 7:23. thou redeemedst from n.
1 K. 11:2. n. conc. which L. said
2 K. 17:26. The n. wh. thou removed
33. served gods aft. manner of n.
18:33. Hath any of the gods of the
n. delivered, 19:12. 2 Ch. 32:
13, 14. Is. 36:18.-37:12.
19:17. k-s of Assyr. destroyed n.
21:9. more evil than did the n.
1 Ch. 16:31. say among n. The L.
reigneth [ple
17:21. driving out n. bef. thy peo-
2 Ch. 13:9. priests aft. manner of n.
Ezr. 4:10. n. whom great Asnapper
Ne. 13:26. am. many n. no k. like
Jb. 12:23. He increaseth n. enlarg-
Ps. 9:20. that n. may know [eth n.
22:27. all the n. sh. worship thee
28. t. Lord is governor am. the n.
47:3. sh. subdue n. und. our feet
57:9. I will sing unto thee am. n.,
66:7. his eyes behold n. [108:3.
67:4. let the n. be glad and sing (2)
96:5. all the gods of n. are idols
106:27. To overthr. their seed am. n.
34. They did not destroy the n.
Pr. 24:24. peo. curse, n. sh. abhor him
Is. 2:4. shall judge among n.
5:26. will lift up an ensign to n.
9:1. bey. Jordan, in Galilee of n.
10:7. it is in his heart to cut off n.
11:12. he shall set up ensign for n.
13:4. noise of kingdoms of n. gath-d
14:6. he that ruled the n. in anger
9. raised up all kings of the n.
12. which didst weaken the n.
18. All kings of the n. lie in glory
17:12. and to the rushing of n., 13.
23:3. Sihor, she is a mart of n.
25:3. city of terrible n. shall fear
33:3. at thy lifting n. were scatt.
34:1. Come, ye n. to hear, Je. 31:10.
40:15. n. are as a drop of bucket
41:2. gave the n. bef. him, 45:1.
45:20. ye that are escaped of n.
52:15. So shall he sprinkle many n.
55:5. n. that knew not thee, shall
60:12. those n. sh. be wasted [run
64:2. n. may tremble at thy pres.
66:19. send those th. escape unto n.
Je. 1:5. ord. thee a prophet unto n.
10. have this day set thee over n.
3:19. heritage of the hosts of n.
4:2. n. sh. bless themselves in him
16. make ye mention to n. publish
6:18. hear ye n. and know, 31:10.
10:7. Who not fear thee, O K. of n.?
am. wise men of n. none like
10. n. not be able to abide indign.
22:8. many n. sh. pass by this city
25:14. n. sh. servo thems. of th., 27:7.
31. L. hath controversy with n.
27:7. many n. sh. serve thems. of him
11. n. th. bring neck under yoke
31:7. saith L., shout am. chief of n.
46:12. n. have heard of thy shame
50:2. Declare am. n. Bab. is taken
Je. 50:12. hindermost of n. be a wil.
23. Bab. become desolation am. n.
46. the cry is heard among the n.
51:7. n. have drunk. of her wine,
therefore the n. are mad
20. with thee will I break n.
27. prepare the n. ag. her (2) 28.
41. Bab. is an astonishment am. n.
44. n. sh. not flow tog-r any more
La. 1:1. city that was great am. the n.
Eze. 5:5. Jerus.; I set in midst of n.
6. wickedness, more than the n., 7.
7. ye multiplied more than the n.
14. thee a reproach am. the n., 15.
6:8. remnant shall escape am. n.
9. th. escape sh. remem. me am. n.
12:15. When I scatter them am. n.
19:4. The n. also heard of him. he
8. n. set ag. him on ev. side [n.
25:10. Ammonites not remem-d am.
26:3. cause many n. to come ag. thee
5. it shall become spoil to n.
28:7. I will bring upon thee, terrible
of n., 30:11.-31:12.-32:12.
29:12. I will scatter E-s am. n., 30:23
15. they sh. no more rule over n.
31:16. I made n. shake at his fall
32:2. Thou art like a lion of the n.
9. bring thy destruction am. n.
16. dau-s of n. shall lament her, 18.
35:10. These two n. sh. be mine
36:13. hast bereaved thy n., 14, 15.
37:22. they shall be no more two n.
38:8. it is bro-t forth out of n., 12.
23. I will be known in eyes of n.
39:27. am sanctified in sight of n.
Da. 3:4. To you it is com-ded O n.
Ho. 8:10. tho. have hired am. n.
9:17. they sh. be wanderers am. n.
Jo. 3:2. they have scattered am. n.
Am. 6:1. Woe to them chief of n.
Mi. 4:2. many n. sh. say, let us go
3. he sh. rebuke strong n. afar off
11. many n. are gathered ag. thee
7:16. the n. shall see, be confounded
Na. 3:4. selleth n. thro. whoredoms
5. I will show the n. thy nakedn.
Ha. 1:17. shall not spare to slay n.
2:8. Bec. thou hast spoiled many n.
3:6. he beheld, drove asunder n.
Zph. 2:14. sh. lie down in her beasts
3:6. I have cut off the n. [of n.
8. my determination to gather n.
Zch. 2:8. unto n. wh. spoiled you
11. many n. shall be joined to L.
8:22. strong n. sh. come to seek L.
23. out of all languages of the n.
14:3. sh. the Lord fight ag. those n.
Lu. 12:30. these do n. seek after
21:25. upon earth distress of n.
Ac. 13:19. had destr. 7 n. in Chanaan
Ro. 4:17. made thee fa. of many n., 18.
Re. 2:26. will I give power ov. n.
10:11. thou must prophesy bef. n.
11:9. n. shall see their dead bodies
18. n. were angry, thy wrath is
16:19. cities of the n. fell [come
17:15. waters thou sawest are n. and
19:15. with sword he sh. smite n.
20:3. th. he deceive n. no more, 8.
21:24. n. which are saved sh. walk
26. sh. bring honour of n. into it
22:2. leaves were for healing of n.

All NATIONS. [to a. n.

De. 4:19. which L. hath divided un-
26:19. make high ab. a. n., 28:1.
28:37. byword am. a. n., 2 Ch. 7:20.
29:24. a. n. sh. say, Whf. hath L.
2 S. 8:11. gold of a. n. Da. subdued
1 K. 4:31. his fame was in a. n.
1 Ch. 14:17. fear of Da. upon a. n.
16:24. Declare marvellous works
among a. n. [n.
2 Ch. 32:23. magnified in sight of a.
Ps. 67:2. saving health am. a. n.
72:11. kings, a. n. shall serve him
17. a. n. shall call him blessed

Ps. 82:8. O G., thou sh. inherit a. n.
86 : 9. a. n. sh. come and worship
113 : 4. L. is high above a. n. glory
117 : 1. praise the Lord, a. ye n.
118:10. a. n. compassed me about
Is. 2 : 2. a. n. shall flow unto it
25:7. he will destroy vail ov. a. n.
34 : 2. indigna. of L. is upon a. n.
40:17. a.n. bef. him are as nothing
66 : 18. I will gather a. n., Jo. 3 : 2.
20. they shall bring your brethren out of a. n. ⌈14.
Je. 27:7. a.n. shall serve him, Da. 7:
28:11. yoke of Neb. fr. neck of a.n.
44 5. remnant returned fr. a. n.
Da. 4 : 1. Neb. the king unto a. n.
5 : 19. a. n. trembled before him
6 : 25. k. Darius wrote unto a. n.
Am. 9 : 9. I will sift ho. of Isr. am. a.
Ha. 2 : 5. gath-th unto him a.n. ⌊n.
Hag. 2:7. I will shake a. n., and desire of a. n. shall come ⌈rus.
Zch. 14:2. I will gather a. n. ag. Je-
19. punishm. of a. n. that come
not to keep feast of taborn.
Mal. 3:12. a. n. sh. call you blessed
Mat. 24 : 9. hated of a. n. for sake
14. this gospel of kingdom shall
be preached unto a. n., Mk.
13: 10. Lu. 24 : 47. Ro. 16 : 26.
25 : 32. bef. him be gathered a. n.
28 : 19. Go teach a. n., baptizing
Mk. 11:17. called of a. n. ho. of prayer
Lu. 21 : 24. led captive into a. n.
Ac. 14 : 16. suffered a. n. to walk
17 : 26. made of one blood a. n.
Ro. 1 : 5. obed. to the faith am. a.n.
16:26. made kno. to a. n. for obed.
Ga. 3:8. In thee sh. a. n. be blessed
Re. 7:9. a mult. of a. n. bef. throne
12:5. who was to rule a. n. with rod
13:7. power was given him ov. a.n.
14:8. made a. n. drink of wine, 18:3.
15 : 4. a. n. sh. come and worship
18:23. by thy sorceries a. n. deceived

All the NATIONS.

Ge. 18:18. a.t.n. of earth be blessed,
22 : 18.-26 : 4. ⌈on earth
De. 14: 2. chosen thee above a. t. n.
17 : 14. set a king over me, as a. t.
n., 1 S. 8 : 5, 20. ⌈a.t.n.
30 : 1. shalt call them to mind am.
3. L. will gather thee fr. a. t. n.
Ps. 9:17. into hell, a. t. n. that for-
Is. 14:26. hand upon a. t. n. ⌊get G.
29:7. mult. of a. t. n. that fight, 8.
37:18. laid waste a. t. n. and coun-
43 : 9. Let a. t. n. be gath-d ⌊tries
52:10. bare his arm in eyes of a.t.n.
61 : 11. cause praise before a. t. n.
Je. 3 : 17. a. t. n. shall be gathered
25 : 13. Jere. prophesied ag. a. t.n.
15. cause a. t. n. to drink it, 17.
26: 6. make city a curse to a.t.n.
29:14. I will gather you fr. a.t.n.
18. reproach among a.t.n., 44:8.
33:9. name of honour bef. a. t. n.
36:2. words spoken against a. t. n.
46 : 28. make a full end of a. t. n.
Zch. 7:14. scattered them am. a.t.n.
12:9. destroy a.t.n. come ag. Jerus.
14 : 16. left of a. t. n. came ag.
See **In the SIGHT.** ⌊Jerus.

These NATIONS.

De. 7: 17. if say, t. n. more than I
9 : 4. for wickedn. of t. n. L., 5.
11: 23. will L. drive out all t. n.
12: 30. How did t. n. serve gods
18 : 14. t. n. heark-ed to observers
20 : 15. do unto cities not of t. n.
28 : 65. am. t. n. shalt find no ease
29 : 18. lest any serve gods of t. n.
31 : 3. Lord will destroy t.n. ⌈t.n.
Jos. 23 : 3. seen what L. done unto
4. I have divided unto you by lot
7. that ye come not am. t. n. ⌊t. n.
12. if cleave unto remnant of t. n.
Jos. 23:13. G. no more drive out t. n.
Ju. 3 : 1. t. n. L. left to prove Isr.
2 K. 17:41. t. n. feared L. and served
1 Ch. 18:11. gold fr. all t. n. ⌊images
Je. 9:26. all t. n. are uncircumcised
25 : 9. bring them against t. n.
11. t. n. shalt serve king of Bab.
28 : 14. yoke of iron upon neck of

NATIVE. ⌊t. n.

Je. 22 : 10. no more see his n. coun-

NATIVITY. ⌊try

Ge. 11 : 28. Haran died in land of n.
Ru. 2 : 11. hast left land of thy n.
Je. 46 : 16. let us go to la. of our n.
Eze. 16 : 3. thy n. is of land of Ca.
4. as for thy n. in day wast born
21 : 30. will judge thee in land of n.
23 : 15. Chaldea, land of their n.

NATURAL.

De. 34 : 7. nor his n. force abated
Ro. 1 : 26. women did change n. use
27. men leaving n. use of woman
31. with-t n. affection, 2 Ti. 3 : 3 ⌈24.
11 : 21. G. spared not n. branches,
1 Co. 2 : 14. n. man receiveth not Sp.
15 : 44. sown a n. body. There is n.
46. that wh. is n. was first ⌊body
Ja. 1 : 23. man beholding his n. face
3 † : 15. this wisdom is n. devilish
2 Pe. 2:12. these as n. brute beasts

NATURALLY.

Ph. 2:20. will n. care for your state
Jude 10. know n. as brute beasts

NATURE.

Ro. 1:26. did change into that ag. n.
2 : 14. do by n. things in the law
27. sh. uncirc-n by n. judge thee?
11 : 24. olive tree, wh. is wild by n.
and wert graffed contrary to n.
1 Co. 11:14. Doth not n. teach you?
Ga. 2 : 15. Jews by n., not sinners
4:8. them, which by n. are no gods
Ep. 2 : 3. were by n. chil. of wrath
He. 2 : 16. he took not n. of angels
Ja. 3 : 6. setteth on fire course of n.
† 7. n. of beasts hath been tamed
by n. of men ⌈vine n.
2 Pe. 1 : 4. might be partakers of di-

NAUGHT. ⌈n.

2 K. 2:19. city pleasant, but water is
Pr. 20:14. It is n. it is n. saith buyer
See NOUGHT.

NAUGHTINESS.

1 S. 17 : 28. I know thy pride and n.
Pr. 11 : 6. transg-rs taken in own n.
Ja. 1:21. filthin. and superfluity of n.

NAUGHTY.

De. 13 : † 13. Certain men n. men
Pr. 6 : 12. A n. person walketh with
17 : 4. liar giveth ear to n. tongue
Je. 24:2. the basket had very n. figs

NA'UM.

Lu. 3 : 25. Amos, wh. was son of N.

NAVEL.

Ju. 9 : † 37. come by n. of the land
Jb. 40 : 16. his force is in n. of belly
Pr. 3 : 8. It shall be health to thy n.
Can. 7:2. Thy n. is like a goblet ⌈cut
Eze. 16:4. when born, thy n. was not

NAVES.

1 K. 7:33. n. and spokes were molten

NAVY.

1 K. 9: 26. Solo. made a n. of ships
27. Hiram sent in the n.
10 : 11. n. of Hiram brought gold
22. Sol. had at sea n. of Tarshish

NAY.

Ge. 18 : 15. n. but thou didst laugh
1 K. 2 : 17. Speak, he will not say n.
20. say me not n., I will not say n.
Mat. 5 : 37. let your communication
be Yea, yea, n. n., Ja. 5 : 12.
13:29. n. lest while ye gather tares
Lu. 12 : 51. I tell you n. but
13:3. I tell you n. exc. ye repent, 5.
16 : 30. and he said, n. father Ab.
Jn. 7 : 12. n. he deceiveth the peo.
Ac. 16 : 37. n. verily, let them come
Ro. 3 : 27. by law of works? n. but
7 : 7. n. I had not known sin
8 : 37. n. in all we are more than
9:20. n. but O man, who art thou
1 Co. 6:8. n. ye do wrong and ⌈bers
12 : 22. n. much more those mem.
2 Co. 1: 17. with me be yea, yea, n.n.
18. our word was not yea and n.
19. Jesus C. was not yea and n.

NAZARENE', S.

Mat. 2 : 23. He shall be called a N.
Ac. 24:5. a ringleader of sect of N.

NAZ'ARETH. ⌈2 : 4.

Mat. 2 : 23. Joseph dwelt in N., Lu.
4 : 13. Leaving N. dwelt at Jerus.
21 : 11. This is Jesus of N., Mk. 1:
24.-10 : 47. Lu. 4 : 34.-18 : 37.-
24 : 19. ⌈Mk. 14 : 67.
26:71. This fellow with Jesus of N.,
Mk. 16:6. affrighted, ye seek Jes. of N.
Lu. 1 : 26. Gabriel was sent unto N.
2:39. returned to their own city, N.
51. Jesus came to N. and, 4 : 16.
Jn. 1:45. Jes. of N., 18 : 5, 7.-19 : 19.
Ac. 2 : 22.-4 : 10.-6 : 14.-22:8.
46. Can any good come out of N.?
Ac. 3 : 6. In name of Jes. of N. rise
10:38. how G. anointed Jesus of N.
26:9. contrary to name of Jes. of N.

NAZ'ARITE, S.

Nu. 6 : 2. a vow of a N. to separate
13. this is the law of the N., 21.
18. the N. shall shave the head ⌈N.
19. shall put them upon hands of
20. aft. that N. may drink wine
Ju. 13 : 5. the child shall be a N.
unto God, 7.-16 : 17.
La. 4 : 7. Her N-s purer than snow
Am. 2 : 11. I raised yo. men for N-s
12. ye gave the N-s wine to drink

NE'AH.

See REMMON-METHOAR.

NEAP'OLIS.

Ac. 16 : 11. next day we came to N.

NEAR.

Ge. 19:20. this city is n. to flee unto
27 : 22. Jacob went n. unto Isaac
25. Bring it n., he brought it n.
29: 10. Jac. went n., rolled stone
45 : 10. thou shalt be n. unto me
48:10. bro-t them n. and kissed, 13.
Ex. 13:17. not land of Philis., altho.
Le. 18:6. not approach n. of kin ⌊n.
12. she thy fa.'s n. kinswoman
13. she thy mother's n. kinsw., 17.
20 : 19. he uncovereth his n. kin
21 : 2. for kin n., he may be defiled
Nu. 3 : 6. Bring the tribe of Levi n.
5 : 16. bring her n., set her bef. L.
16 : 9. to bring you n. to hims., 10.
17:13. Whoso cometh n. the tabern.
26:3. in plains of Moab, n. Jericho,
31:12.-33:48, 50.-35 : 1.-36 : 13.
De. 5:27. Go n., hear all G. shall say
16:21. not plant grove of trees n. alt.
25:11. wife n. to deliver husb. ⌈13.
Jos. 15 : 46. th. lay n. Ashdod | 18:
Ju. 18 : 22. men n. Micah's house
20:34. they knew not evil was n. th.
Ru. 2:20. The man is n. of kin unto us
3:9. thou art n. kinsman, 12. ⌈liv-d
1 S. 4:19. Phinehas' wife n. to be de-
2 S. 14: 30. Joab's field n. mine
19:42. Bec. king is n. of kin to us
1 K. 8 : 46. enemy far or n., 2 Ch.
6: 36. ⌈my house
21 : 2. vineyard, bec. it is n. unto
2 Ch. 21:16. Arabians n. Ethiopians
Jb. 41 : 16. One is so n. ano. no air
Ps. 22:11. trouble n. | 75:1. name n.
119 : 151. Thou art n., O Lord, thy
com-ts ⌈unto him
148 : 14. horn of Isr. a people n.
Pr. 7:8. thro. the street, n. her corner
10 : 14. mouth of foolish is n. destruction

Pr.27:10. better is a neighb. th. is **n.**
Is. 33 : 13. ye that are **n.** acknowl.
45 : 21. Tell ye, and bring them **n.**
46: 13. I bring **n.** my righteousness
50 : 8. He is **n.** that justifieth me
51 : 5. My righte-n. is **n.** my salva.
55 : 6. call upon L. while he is **n.**
56 : 1. my salvation is **n.** to come
57: 19. Peace be to him is **n.** saith L.
Je.12:2. thou art **n.** in their mouth
25:26. all kings far and **n.** sh. drink
48:24. upon cities of Moab, far and
52 : 25. men **n.** king's person ⌊n.
La. 4 : 18. our end is **n.** our days
Eze.6:12. that is **n.** shall fall by sw.
7 : 7. day of trouble is **n.**, 30 : 3.–
Jo. 3 : 14. ⌈houses
11: 3. It is not **n.**, let us build
22:5. those th. be **n.** sh. mock thee
Da. 7 : 13. bro-t him **n.** before him
9:7. confusion unto Isr. that are **n.**
Ob. 15. day of Lord is **n.**, Zph. 1 : 14.
Mat. 24 : 33. know it is **n.** at doors
Mk.13:28. ye know th. summer is **n.**
Jn.3:23. baptizing in Enon **n.** Salim
4:5. **n.** to parcel of ground Jo. gave
11 : 54. unto country **n.** wildern.
Ac.10:24. Cornelius called **n.** friends
See **CAME, COME near.**
See **DRAW, DREW, GO near.**

NEARER.

Ru. 3:12. there is kinsman **n.** than I
Ro. 13 : 11. our salva. **n.** than when

NEARI'AH.

1 Ch. 3 : 22. sons of Shemaiah, N.
23. sons of N. Elioenai and Hez.

NEB'AI. ⌈sealed

Ne. 10 : 19. Hariph, Anathoth, N.

NEBA'IOTH = NEBA'JOTH.

Ge.25:13. son of Ishm., N., 1 Ch. 1:29.
28 : 9. Mahalath sis. of N. his wife
36 : 3. And Bashemath sister of N.
Is. 60 : 7. rams of N. shall minister

NEBAL'LAT.

Ne. 11 : 34. chil. of Benj. dwelt at N.

NE'BAT. See JEROBOAM.

NE'BO.

Nu. 32 : 3. N. is a land for cattle
38. children of Reuben built N.
33 : 47. pitched in mts. before N.
De.32:49. Get thee unto m-t N., 34:1.
1 Ch. 5 : 8. Bela dwelt even unto N.
Ezr. 2 : 29. the children of N., 10:43.
Ne. 7 : 33 men of the other N. 52
Is. 15 : 2. Moab shall howl over N.
46 : 1. Bel boweth N. stoopeth
Je. 48 : 1. Woe unto N. it is spoiled
22. judgment is come upon N.

NEBUCHADNEZ'ZAR = NEBUCHADREZ'ZAR.

2 K. 24 : 1. in his days N. came up ag. Jerusalem, 10, 11.–25 : 1, 8. 2 Ch. 36:6. Je.39:1. Da.1:1.–5:2.
25 : 22. as for people whom N. had left ⌈N., Je. 29 : 1.
1 Ch. 6 : 15. carried away Judah by
2 Ch 36:7. N. carried vessels to Bab., Ezr.1:7.–5:14.–6:5. Je 28:3. ⌈13.
10. N. bro-t Jehoiachin to Bab. |
Ezr. 2 : 1. chil. N. had carried unto Babylon, Ne. 7 : 6. Es. 2 : 6. ⌈N.
5 : 12. God gave them into hand of
Je.27:6. given lands into hand of N.
8. kingdom wh. will not serve N.
20. vessels which N. took not
28 : 11. so will I break yoke of N.
14. that they may serve N. king
29 : 3. wh. Zedekiah sent unto N.
21. I will deliver into hand of N.
32:28. give this city into ha. of N.
39 : 5. brought Zedekiah up to N.
Da. 1 : 18. brought 4 chil. before N.
2 : 1. in sec. year N. dreamed, 4:18.
28. G. maketh known to N. what
46. N. fell upon his face ⌊sh. be
Da.3:1. N. made image of gold, 3, 5.
9. said, O king N. live forever
13. N. com-ded to bring Shadrach,
19. N. was full of fury ⌊14, 16.
24. N. was astonied and rose
26. N. came to mouth of furnace, 28
4:28. All this came upon king N., 33.
31. fell voice from heaven O N.
34. at end I N. lift up mine eyes
37. I king N. extol K. of heaven
5:11. wh. N. made master of magic.
18. most high G. gave N. kingd.

NEBUCHADREZ'ZAR.

Je. 21: 2. N. maketh war ag. us | 7.
22 : 25. Jehoiakim into hand of N.
24:1. N. carried captive Jeconiah
25:1. N. k. of Bab., 9.–29:21.–32:1.
34:1. N. fought ag. Jerusalem, 35: 11.–39 : 1.–52 : 4. ⌈Jere.
39 : 11. N. gave charge concerning
43 : 10. I will take N. and | 44 : 30.
46:2. N. smote army of Pha. | 13, 26.
49 : 28. N. shall smite Kedar
30. N. hath taken counsel ag. you
50 : 17. N. hath broken his bones
51:34. N. hath devoured me | 52:12.
52:28. peo. N. carried captive, 29, 30.
Eze. 26:7. I will bri. upon Tyrus N.
29:18. N. caused his army to serve
19. I will give E. unto N., 30: 10.

NEBUSHAS'BAN.

Je. 39 : 13. N. and all princes sent

NEBUZAR'-ADAN.

2 K. 25 : 8. N. capt. of guard came unto Jerusalem
11. people left did N. carry away, 20. Je.39:9.–52:15, 26, 30. ⌈52:16.
Je. 39 : 10. N. left of poor and gave,
11. Neb. gave charge cone-g Jere. to N. | 13.–40: 1.–41:10.–43:6.–

NECESSARY. ⌊52:12.

Jb. 23 : 12. his words more than my **n.** food ⌈spoken to you
Ac. 13 : 46. **n.** the word first be
15 : 28. no burden than these **n.**
28:10. laded us with things **n.** ⌊thi.
1 Co.12:22. members wh. seem to be more feeble are **n.**
2 Co. 9 : 5. I thought it **n.** to exhort
Ph. 2 : 25. I supposed it **n.** to send Epaphroditus
Tit. 3 : 14. good works for **n.** uses
He. 9: 23. **n.** patterns sho. be puri-

NECESSITY, IES. ⌊fied

Lu. 23:17. of **n.** he must release one
Ac. 20 : 34. these hands have ministered unto my **n-s**
Ro.12:13. Distributing to **n.** of saints
1 Co. 7 : 37. having no **n.** and
9 : 16. for **n.** is laid upon me, woe
2 Co. 6 : 4. as ministers of G. in **n-s**
9:7. give, not grudgingly, or of **n.**
12 : 10. I take pleasure in **n-s** in
Ph. 4 : 16. ye sent again unto my **n.**
Phm. 14. not be as it were of **n.** but
He. 7 : 12. of **n.** change of the law
8:3. of **n.** this man have somewhat
9:16. must of **n.** be death of testator

NE'CHO. ⌈fight

2 Ch. 35 : 20. N. king of E. came to
22. Josiah heark-d not unto words
36:4. N. carried Je-haz to E. ⌊of N.

NECK. ⌈n.

Ge. 27:16. skins upon smooth of his
40. shalt break yoke off thy **n.**
33:4. Esau fell on his **n.** and kissed
41 : 42. Pha. put gold chain about Jo.'s **n.**, Eze.16:11. Da.5:7, 16, 29
45: 14. Joseph fell upon Benj 's **n.**
46:29. he fell on Jac.'s **n.** wept (2)
49 : 8. thy ha. be in **n.** of enemies
Ex. 13: 13. if not redeem, break his
23:†27. enemies turn **n.** ⌊n., 34:20.
Le. 5 : 8. wring off his head from **n.**
De. 21 : 4. strike off the heifer's **n.**
28:48. put yoke of iron upon thy **n.**
31 : 27. For I know thy stiff **n.**
1 S. 4 : 18. his **n.** brake, he died
2 Ch. 29:†6. our fa-s have given the
36:13. Zedekiah stiffened his **n.** ⌊n.
Ne. 9 : 29. hardened their **n.** wo. not
Jb.15:26. He runneth even on his **n.**
16:12. he hath taken me by the **n.**
39:19. clothed his **n.** wi. thunder?
41:22. In his **n.** remaineth strength
Ps. 75 : 5. speak not with a stiff **n.**
Pr. 1 : 9. shall be chains ab. thy **n.**
3 : 3. bind them about thy **n.**, 6:21.
22. sh. be life and grace to thy **n.**
Can.1:10. thy **n.** is comely wi. gold
4:4. Thy **n.** is like the tower of Da.
9. ravished wi. one chain of thy **n.**
7 : 4. Thy **n.** is a tower of ivory
Is. 8 : 8. he sh. reach even to the **n.**
10:27. his yoke sh. be taken fr. thy
30:28. sh. reach to midst of **n.** ⌊n.
48:4. thy **n.** is an iron sinew ⌈n.
52:2. loose thyself fr. bands of thy
66 : 3. as if he cut off a dog's **n.**
Je.2:†27. hinder part of **n.** unto me
17 : 23. obeyed not, made **n.** stiff
27:2. Make yokes, put th. upon **n.**
8. not put **n.** under yoke of k., 11.
28:10. took yoke fr. Jere.'s **n.**, 12.
14. I put a yoke upon **n.** of nations
30 : 8. I will break yoke fr. thy **n.**
48 : † 39. Moab hath turned the **n.**
La. 1:14. transgr-ns are upon my **n.**
Ho.10:11. I passed over upon her **n.**
Ha. 3 : 13. discovering founda. to **n.**
Mat.18:6. better that millstone were about **n.**, Mk. 9 : 42. Lu. 17: 2.
Lu. 15 : 20. his father fell on his **n.**
Ac. 15:10. put yoke upon **n.** of disci.
20 : 37. they fell on Paul's **n.** and
See HARDEN, ED, ETH. ⌊kissed

NECKS. ⌈n.

Jos.7:†8. when Israel turneth their
10 : 24. put feet upon **n.** of kings
Ju. 5 : 30. **n.** of them th. take spoil
8:21. ornaments on camel's **n.**, 26.
2 S. 22 : 41. **n.** of enemies, Ps. 18:40.
Ne. 3: 5. nobles put not **n.** to work
Is.3:16. walk wi. stretched forth **n.**
Je.27:12. Bring your **n.** under yoke
La.5:5. Our **n.** are und. persecution
Eze.21:29. bri. thee upon **n.** of slain
Mi. 2: 3. ye sh. not remove your **n.**
Ro. 16 : 4. who laid down own **n.**

NECROMANCER. ⌈a n.

De.18:11. shall not be found am. you

NEDABI'AH.

1 Ch. 3 : 18. sons of Jeconiah, N.

NEED. [Noun.] ⌈n.

De. 15 : 8. lend him sufficient for his
1 S. 21 : 15. Have I **n.** of madmen
Ezr.6:9. th. they have **n.** of be giv-
Pr.31:11. sh. have no **n.** of spoil ⌊en
Mat. 3:14. I have **n.** to be baptized
6 : 8. your Father knoweth what things ye have **n.** of bef., 32. Lu. 12 : 30.
21 : 3. L. hath **n.** of them, he will send them, Mk.11:3. Lu.19:31, 34
26: 65. what further **n.** of witnesses? Mk. 14 : 63. Lu. 22 : 71. ⌈n.
Mk.2:25. what Da. did when he had
Lu.9:11. healed th. had **n.** of healing
Jn.13:29. Buy things we have **n.** of
Ac.2:45. as every man had **n.**, 4:35.
Ro. 16 : 2. assist in what she hath **n.**
1 Co.7:36. if **n.** so require, let him do
12:21. unto ha. I have no **n.** of thee
24. our comely parts have no **n.**
Ph. 4 : 12. I know how to suffer **n.**
19. my G. shall supply all your **n.**
1 Th. 5 : 1. of times no **n.** th. I write
He.4:16. grace to help in time of **n.**
5 : 12. ye have **n.** one teach you, and are such as have **n.** of milk
7: 11. what **n.** that ano. priest rise
10 : 36. For ye have **n.** of patience
1 Pe. 1 : 6. if **n.** be ye are in heavin.
1 Jn.3:17. goods, and see bro. have **n.**

Re. 3 : 17. I rich, have n. of nothing
21 : 23. city no n. of sun or moon
NEED. [Verb.]
2 Ch.2:16.cut wood as thou shalt n.
20:17.Ye sh. not n. to fight in bat.
Mat.9:12.they th.be whole n. not a
physician, Mk. 2 : 17. Lu. 5:31.
14:16. They n. not depart, give ye
Lu. 15 : 7.persons wh. n. no repent.
2 Co. 3 : 1. or n. we epistles of com-
mendation
1 Th. 1 : 8. so that we n. not speak
4:9.brotherly love n.not th.I write
1 Jn.2:27. ye n. not any man teach
Re. 22 : 5. they n. no candle, nor
NEEDED, EST. [man
Jn.2:25.he n-d not th.any testify of
16 : 30. n-t not th. any ask thee
Ac.17:25. as tho. he n-d any thing
NEEDETH.
Ge. 33 : 15. Jacob said, What n. it
Lu. 11 : 8. will give him as he n.
Jn. 13 : 10. n. not save to wash feet
Ep.4:28.have to give to him that n.
2 Ti.2:15. that n. not to be asham.
He. 7 : 27. who n. not daily to offer
NEEDFUL. [of G.
Ezr. 7 : 20. shall be n. for the house
Lu. 10 : 42. one thing is n. and Mary
Ac.15:5. was n. to circumcise them
Ph.1:24.to abide in flesh is more n.
Ja.2:16. things wh. are n. for body
Jude 3. it was n. for me to write
NEEDLE. [unto you
Mat. 19 : 24. easier for camel to go
thro. eye of n., Mk. 10:25. Lu.
NEEDLEWORK. [18:25.
Ex.26:36. make a hanging wrought
with n., 27 : 16.-36 : 37.-38:18.
28:39. make the girdle of n.,39:29.
Ju.5:30.prey of divers colours of n.
Ps.45:14. she be bro-t in raim.of n.
NEEDS. [judge
Ge. 19 : 9. This fellow will n. be a
31:30. though thou wouldest n. be
Must NEEDS. [gone
Ge. 17 : 13. be m. n. be circumcised
24:5. m. I n. bring thy son again
unto the land?
2 S. 14 : 14. we m.n. die, and are as
water spilt on ground [not go
Je. 10: 5. m.n. be borne bec. can-
Mat. 18 : 7. m. n. be offences come
Mk. 13 : 7. for such things m. n. be
Lu.14:18.bought ground,I m.n.go
Jn. 4 : 4. he m.n. go thro. Samaria
Ac. 1: 16. Scripture m.n. been ful-
17:3.Christ m.n.have suff-d [filled
21 : 22. the multitude m. n. come
Ro. 13 : 5. ye m. n. be subject
1 Co.5:10.m. ye n. go out of world
2 Co. 11 : 30. If I m.n. glory, I will
NEEDY. [glory
De 15: 11. open thy hand to the n.
24:14.hired serv.that is poor and n
Jb. 24 : 4. They turn n. out of way
14. murderer killeth poor and n.
Ps. 9 : 18. n. not always be forgott.
12:5.for sigh-g of n.will I arise [13.
35:10. deliverest poor and n., 72:4,
37 : 14. bent bow to cast down n.
40 : 17. I am poor and n. make no
tarrying, 70 : 5.-86 : 1.-109: 22.
72:12. he shall deliver the n.,82:4.
13. He shall spare the poor and
n. and sh.save souls of the n.
74:21. let poor and n. praise name
82: 3. do justice to afflicted and n.
4. Deliver the poor and n. rid fr.
109:16.persecuted the poor and n.
113:7. he lifteth n. out of dunghill
Pr. 30:14. devour n. fr. among men
31 : 9. plead cause of poor and n.
20.she reacheth forth hands to n.
Is.10 : 2. To turn aside n. fr. judgm.
14: 30. n. shall lie down in safety
25 : 4. been a strength to the n. in

Is.26:6.steps of n. sh.tread it down
32 : 7. when the n. speaketh right
41:17.when poor and n.seek water
Je. 5 : 28. right of n. do not judge
22:16. judged cause of poor and n.
Eze. 16:49. nei. strengthen hands of
18 : 12. oppressed poor and n. [n.
22 : 29.peo. have vexed poor and n.
Am.4:1. kine of Bashan, wh. crush
8 : 4. O ye that swallow up n. [n.
6. may buy n. for pair of shoes
NEESINGS.
Jb.41:18.By his n. light doth shine
NEGLECT, ED, ING.
Mat.18:17.if he n. to hear th.tell it
to church, if he n. to hear ch.
Ac.6:1.widows were n-d in ministra
Col.2:23.n-g the body not in honour
1 Ti. 4 : 14. n. not gift in thee
He.2:3.How escape,if n.so gr.salva.
NEGLIGENT. [L.
2 Ch. 29 : 11. My sons, be not n. for
2 Pe. 1 : 12. not n. to put you in re.
NEHEL'AMITE. [mem.
Je. 29: 24. Shemaiah the N., 31, 32.
NEHEMI'AH. [7:7.
Ezr. 2 : 2. N. came with Zerubb.,Ne.
Ne.1:1.words of N.son of Hachaliah
3 : 16. N. son of Azbuk repaired
8 : 9. N. wh. is the Tirshatha, 10:1.
12:47. Israel in days of N. gave,26.
NE'HUM = RE'HUM.
Ne. 7 : 7. came with Zerub. N., Ezr.
NEHUSH'TA. [2:†2.
2 K.24:8. Jehoiachin's moth. name
NEHUSH'TAN. [N.
2 K. 18 : 4. he called brazen serpent
NE'IEL. [N.
Jos. 19 : 27. border reacheth to N.
NEIGHBOUR. [Adj.]
Je. 49 : 18. in overthrow of Sodom,
Gomorrah and n. cities, 50:40.
NEIGHBOUR. [Noun.][2.
Ex.3:22.ev.woman borrow of n.,11:
1 S. 15: 28. given it to a n. of thine
Pr. 27:10. better is a n. that is near
Je. 6 : 21. n. and friends shall perish
9 : 20. and teach every one her n.
Lu.10:36. n. to him fell am.thieves
His NEIGHBOUR.
Ex.12:4.let him and h.n.take lamb
21 : 14. if a man upon h.n. to slay
†18. if one smite h.n. and he die
22 : 7. If deliver unto h.n. money
8. whether he have put hands
unto h. n.'s goods, 11.
9. sh. pay double unto h.n. [ass
10. If man deliver unto h. n. an
14. if borrow of h. n. and it be
32:27.go,slay ev. man h.n. [hurt
Le 6:2. lie unto or deceived h.n.
20 : 10. committeth adultery with
h. n.'s wife, be put to death,
De. 22 : 24. [n.
24 : 19. if man cause blemish in h.
De. 4 : 42. which sho. kill h.n. unawares, 19 : 4, 5. Jos. 20 : 5.
15 : 2. creditor that lendeth aught
unto h. n. not exact of h. n.
19 : 11. if hate h.n. and lie in wait
22:26. riseth ag. h.n. and slayeth
27: 17. removeth h.n.'s landmark
24.Cursed be he th. smiteth h.n.
Ru.4:7. plucked off shoe, gave h.n.
1 K. 8 : 31. If man trespass ag. h.n.
20 : 35. man said unto h.n. Smite
2 Ch.6:22. If any man sin ag. h.n.
Jb.12:4. am as one mocked of h.n.
16:21. as a man pleadeth for h.n.
Ps.12:2. speak vanity each wi.h.n.
15:3. nor doeth evil to h.n. taketh
101:5. Whoso privily sland-h h.n.
Pr.6:29.that goeth in to h.n.'s wife
11 : 9. hypocrite destroyeth h. n.
12. void of wisdom despiseth h.
n., 14 : 21. [than h. n.
12 : 26. righteous is more excellent

Pr. 14 : 20 poor is hated of h. n.
16:29. A violent man enticeth h.n.
18:17. h.n. cometh searcheth him
19 : 4. poor is separated from h.n.
21 : 10. h.n. findeth no favour
25:18.beareth false witness ag.h.n
26 : 19. So is man deceiveth h. n.
29:5. flattereth h.n. spread-h net
Ec.4:4. for this man is envied of h.
Is. 3 : 5. be oppressed by h. n. [n.
19:2. shall fight every one ag.h.n.
41: 6. They helped every one h.n.
Je. 5 : 8. neighed after h. n.'s wife
7:5. judgment betw. man and h.n.
9:4.Take ye heed every one of h.n.
5. they will deceive ev. one h. n.
8. peaceably to h. n. wi. mouth
22:8.sh.say ev. man to h.n.,28:35.
13. h. n.'s service with-t wages
23 : 27. dreams they tell to h. n.
30. steal words ev. one fr. h. n.
31:34.teach no more every man h.
n., He. 8 : 11. [n., 17.
34:15. in proclaiming liberty to h.
Eze.18:6.nei. defiled h.n.'s wife,15.
11.hath defiled h.n.'s wife,22:11.
-33 : 26. [h. n. drink
Ha.2:15. Woe unto him that giveth
Zch.3:10. shall call every man h.n.
8 : 10. I set all, ev. one ag. h. n.
16. speak ev. man truth to h. n.
17. let none imagine evil ag.h.n.
11:6.deliv.ev.one into h.n.'s hand
14:13.hold ev.one on hand of h.n.
Mk. 12 : 33. to love h.n. as himself
Ac. 7 : 27. he that did h.n. wrong
Ro.13:10.love worketh no ill to h.n.
15 : 2. let every one please h. n.
Ep.4:25.every man truth with h.n.
My NEIGHBOUR.
Jb.31:9. If I laid wait at m.n.'s door
Lu.10:29.said unto Jesus, Who is m.
Thy NEIGHBOUR. [n.?
Ex. 20 : 16. shalt not bear false witness ag. t. n., De. 5:20. [21. (3)
17. not covet t. n.'s house, De. 5 :
22:26. if thou take t. n.'s raiment
Le. 18:20. not lie carnally wi. t.n.'s
19:13.shalt not defraud t.n. [wife
15. in right-n. judge t. n. [t. n.
16. nei. shalt stand ag. blood of
17. shalt in any wise rebuke t.n.
18. shalt love t. n. as thyself
25 : 14. if buyest aught of t. n.,15.
De. 5:21. shalt not desire t.n.'s wife
19:14. not remove t.n.'s landmark
23 : 24. when into t. n.'s vineyard
25. corn of t. n. mayest pluck
1 S. 28 : 17. given kingdom to t. n.
2 S.12:11.wives, and give th.to t.n.
Pr. 3:28. Say not unto t. n.,Go,and
29. Devise not evil against t. n.
24 : 28. Be not witness against t. n.
25:8. when t.n. put thee to shame
9. Debate thy cause with t. n.
17.Withdraw foot fr.t.n.'s house
Mat. 5:43. thou shalt love t. n., 19:
19.-22:39. Mk. 12:31. Lu. 10:27.
Ro. 13 : 9. Ga. 5 : 14. Ja 2 : 8.
NEIGHBOURS.
Jos. 9 : 16. heard they were their n.
Ru. 4 : 17. women her n. gave name
2 K.4:3.borrow vessels of all thy n.,
Ps. 28:3.who speak peace to their n.
31:11. I was a reproach am. my n.
44 : 13. makest us a reproach to n.
79 : 4. We are a reproach to our n.
12. render unto our n. sevenfold
80:6.makest us a strife unto our n.
89 : 41. he is a reproach to his n.
Je. 12:14. saith L. ag. all my evil n.
29:23.adultery with their n.'wives
49:10. his seed is spoiled and his n.
Eze.16:26.fornication with E., thy n
22:12.hast gained of n.by extortion
23:5.doted on Assyrians her n.,12.
Lu. 1 : 58. her n. heard how Lord

Lu. 14:12. mak. upper, call not rich
15:6. calleth together his n., 9. [n.
Jn. 9 : 8. n. wh. had seen him blind

NEIGHED.

Je.5:8. ev. one n. after neigh.'s wife

NEIGHING, S.

Je.8:16.tremble at n.of strong ones
13:27. I have seen thine adulteries

NEITHER. [and n-s

Ge. 3 : 3. the tree, n. sh. ye touch it
1 K.22:31.fight n.with small nor gr.
Mat.21:27.n. tell I by what author-
Mk. 5 : 4. n. co. any man tame [ity
13 : 19. unto this time n. shall be
16:8. n. said anything to any man
Lu. 1 : 15. drink n. wine nor strong
15:29.n.transgressed I at any time
Ac. 24 : 12. n. raising up the people
Ja. 1 : 13. n. tempteth he any man
17. n. shadow of turning

NE'KEB. See LAKUM.

NEKO'DA. [50, 62.

Ezr. 2 : 48. the chil. of N. 60. Ne. 7 :

NEMU'EL. See JEMUEL.

NEMU'ELITES. [of N.

Nu. 26 : 12. of Nemuel the family

NE'PHEG.

Ex. 6 : 21. sons of Izhar: Korah, N.
2 S. 5 : 15. Sons born to David : N.
1 Ch. 3:7. born unto Da. Nogah, N.,

NEPHEW, S. [14 : 6.

Jb. 18:19. shall nei. have son nor n.
Is. 14 : 22. I will cut off son and n.
Ju.12:14.Abdon had 40 sons 30 n-s
1 Ti. 5 : 4. if any widow have chil. or

NE'PHISH. [n-s

1 Ch.5:19. made war with N. Nodab

NEPHISH'ESIM. [7:52.

Ezr.2:†50 Nethinim: chil of N., Ne.

NEPH'THALIM.

Mat.4:13.borders of Zebulon and N.
15. land of N. by way of the sea

NEPH'TOAH.

Jos. 15 : 9. fountain of water of N.,

NEPHU'SIM. [18 : 15.

Ezr. 2:50. Nethinim : chil.of N.,Ne.

NEP'THALIM. [7:†52.

Ge. 30 : † 8. she called his name N.
Re. 7 : 6. Of tribe of N. were sealed

NER. [12,000

1 Ch. 8 : 33. N. begat Kish, 9:36, 39.

Abner son of NER.

1 S. 14 : 50. capt. was A.-N. Saul's
26 : 5. where Saul lay and A.-N.
14. David cried to peo. and A.-N.
2 S.2:8.A.-N. took Ishbosheth | 12.
3 : 23. A.-N. came to the king
25.knowest A.-N.came to deceive
28.Da.said,I am guiltless for bl. of
37.not of king to slay A.-N.[A.-N
1 K. 2 : 5. what Joab did unto A.-N.
32. slew A.-N. capt. and Amasa
1 Ch.26:28. all that A.-N. had ded-
See ABNER. [icated

NE'REUS.

Ro.16:15.Salute Julia, N. and sister

NER'GAL.

2 K.17:30. men of Cuth made N. god

NER'GAL-SHARE'ZER.

Je. 39:3. all princes came, N.and,13.

NE'RI.

Lu. 3 : 27. which was the son of N.

NERI'AH.

Je. 32:12. Baruch son of N., 16.-36:
4, 8, 14, 32.-43 : 3, 6.-45 : 1. [N.
51:59. Jere.com-ded Seraiah son of
See BARUCH.

NEST, NESTS.

Ge. 6 : † 14. n-s shalt make in ark
Nu. 24 : 21. puttest thy n. in a rock
De. 22 : 6. If a bird's n. be bef. thee
32:11.As an eagle stirreth up her n.
Jb.29:18.I sh die in my n.[on high?
39:27. eagle at thy com-d make n.
Ps. 84 : 3. swallow hath found a n.
104 : 17.Where the birds make n-s
Pr. 27 : 8. that wandereth fr. her n.
Is. 10:14. found as n. riches of peo.
16 : 2. as wandering bird out of n.
34:15.There sh. great owl make n.
Je. 22 : 23. makest thy n. in cedars
48:28. dove maketh her n. in holes
49 : 16. tho. make n. high as eagle
Eze. 31 : 6. fowls of beav. made n-s
Ob. 4. tho. thou set n. am. stars
Ha. 2 : 9. that he may set n. on high
Mat. 8:20. birds of the air have n-s,

NET. [Lu. 9 : 58.

Ex. 27 : 4. upon n. make 4 rings, 5.
Jb. 18 : 8. cast into a n. by his own
19 6.G.compassed me with n. [feet
Ps.9:15. in n. they hid, is their foot
10:9.when he draweth him into n.
25:15. sh. pluck my feet out of n.,
35:7.have hid for me their n.[31:4.
8.let his n.th.he hid catch hims.
57:6.They prepared n.fer my steps
66 : 11. Thou broughtest us into n.
140 : 5. they spread n. by wayside
Pr. 1 : 17. Surely in vain n. is spread
12:12. wick. desireth n. of evil [n.
29:5. man th. flattereth spreadeth
Ec. 9 : 12. as fishes taken in evil n.
Is. 51 : 20. sons lie, as bull in a n.
La. 1 : 13. he spread n. for my feet
Eze. 12:13.My n.will I spread,17:20.
19 : 8. nations sh. spread their n.
32 : 3. I will spread my n. ov. thee
Ho. 5 : 1. ye a n. spread upon Tabor
7:12.I will spread my n.upon them
Mi. 7 : 2. hunt ev. man his bro. with
Ha.1:15.they catch them in n. [n.
16.they sacrifice unto their n.and
17. Shall they empty their n.?
Mat.4:18. casting n. into sea,Mk.1:
13:47.kingd. of heaven like n. [16.
Lu. 5:5. at thy word I will let do.n.
6. mult. of fishes, their n. brake
Jn. 21 : 6. Cast the n. on right side
8. came in a ship, dragging the n.
11. drew n. to land, yet not n.

NETS. [broken

1 K. 7 : 17. n. of checker work [n.
Ps. 141:10. Let wicked fall into own
Ec. 7 : 26. woman whose heart is n.
Is. 19:8. that spread n. sh. languish
Eze. 26 : 5. spreading of n. in sea
14. place to spread n.upon,47:10.
Mat. 4:21. saw Ja. and Jn. mending
n., Mk. 1:19.Lu.5:2. [Mat.4:20.
Mk. 1:18.they forsook n. and foll-d,
Lu.5:4.let down your n.for draught

NETHAN'EEL.

Nu.1:8.N.the son of Zuar was prince,
2:5.-7 : 18, 23.-10 : 15.
1 Ch. 2 : 14. N. 4th son of Jesse
15:24.N.blew with trumpets [vites
24 : 6. son of N. scribe, one of Le-
26 : 4. sons of Obed-edom, Joah, N.
2 Ch. 17:7. Jehosh. sent N. to teach
35:9.N.gave unto Lev.for passover
Ezr. 10 : 22 Ishm., N. strange wives
Ne.12:21. in days of Joiakim N. was
36. N. with musical instruments

NETHAN'IAH.

2 K. 25 : 23. Ishmael son of N., 25.-
Je.40:8, 14, 15.-41 : 1, 2, 6, 7, 9,
11, 12, 15, 16, 18. [and N.
1 Ch. 25 : 2. sons of Asaph, Joseph
12. fifth lot came forth to N. he
2 Ch.17:8. Levites to teach, even N.
Je. 36: 14. princes sent the son of N.

NETHER.

Ex.19:17. stood at n. part of mount
De. 24 : 6. No man take n. millstone
Jos.15:19. he gave her upper springs
and n. springs, Ju. 1 : 15.
2 S. 24 : † 6. to n. land newly inhab.
1 K. 9 : 17. Sol. built Gezer Beth-
horon the n.,1 Ch.7:24. [stone
Jb. 41 : 24. heart hard as n. mill-

NETHER parts of earth.

Eze.31: 14. are deliv-d unto death to
16. sh. be comforted in n.- [n.-
Eze.31 : 18. sh. be bro-t down to n.-
32 : 18. cast them down unto n.-
24. Elam gone down into the n.-

NETHERMOST.

1 K. 6 : 6. The n. chamber 5 cubits

NETHINIM. [broad

1 Ch. 9 : 2. first inhabitants were N.
Ezr. 2 : 43. N. went up with Zerub.
58. all the N. were 392, Ne. 7 : 60.
70.N.dwelt in their cities,Ne.7:73.
7 : 7. some of N. went to Jerus. [N.
24. not lawful to impose toll upon
8:17.what to say unto breth. the N.
20. the N. whom David appointed
Ne. 3 : 26. N. dwelt in Ophel,-11 : 21.
31. repaired unto place of thy N.
7 : 46. The N.: the children of Ziba
10 : 28. N. had separated from peo.
11:3. in Judah dwelt priests and N.
21. Ziha and Gispa were over N.

NETO'PHAH.

Ezr. 2: 22. chil. of N. fifty and six
Ne. 7 : 26. men of Bethlehem and N.

NETOPH'ATHI. [188

Ne. 12:28. gathered themselves from
villages of N.

NETOPH'ATHITE, S.

2 S.23:28.Mahari the N.,1 Ch.11:30.
29. Heleb a N. was one of the 30,
1 Ch. 11:30. [meth the N.came
2 K. 25 : 23. Seraiah son of Tanhu-
1 Ch. 2 : 54. sons of Salma, the N-s
9 : 16. dwelt in villages of the N-s
27 : 13. capt. for 10th month Maharai the N. [the N.
15. capt. for 12th month Heldai
Je. 40 : 8. the sons of Ephai the N.

NETTLES.

Jb.30:7. under n. they were gath-d
Pr. 24 : 31. n. had covered the face
Is. 34 : 13. n. brambles in fortresses
Ho.9:6.n.sh.possess pleasant places
Zph.2:9.Moab sh. be breeding of n.

NETWORK, S.

Ex.27:4. a grate of n. of brass,38:4.
1 K. 7 : 18. two rows upon n., 20,42.
41.the two n-s upon the chapiters
42. 400 pomegranates for two n-s
Is 3:†18.L. will take away their n-s
19:9.that weave n-s be confounded
Je.52 : 22. with n. on the chapiters
23. pomegranates upon n. were

NEVER. [100

Ge.41:19.kine,such as I n.saw in E.
Le. 6 : 13. fire on altar sh. n. go out
Nu. 19:2. heifer, upon wh. n. yoke
De.15:11.poor sh.n. cease out of la.
Ju. 2 : 1. I will n. break my cov-t
14:3. Is n. a woman am. my peo.?
16 : 7. with 7 green withs n. dried
11.If with ropes n. were occupied
2 S.12:10.the sword sh.n.depart fr.
2 Ch. 18 : 7. he n. prophesieth good
21: 17. there was n. a son left him
Jb.3:16. as infants wh. n. saw light
9:30.if make my hands n. so clean
21:25.ano. n. eateth with pleasure
Ps. 10 : 6. I shall n. be in adversity
11. hideth face, he will n. see it
15:5.doeth these shall n.be moved
30 : 6. I said, I shall n. be moved
31:1.I trust, let me n. be ashamed
49 : 19. they shall n. see light
55:22.n. suffer righte. to be moved
58 : 5. charming n. so wisely
71:1.let me n. be put to confusion
119:93.I will n.forget thy precepts
Pr.10:30.righte. shall n. be remov.
27:20.Hell and destruction n. full,
so eyes of a man n. satisfied
30:15.three things that are n.satis.
Is. 13 : 20. Babylon n. be inhabited
14 : 20. seed of evil doers sh. n. be
25:2.it shall n.be built [renowned
56:11.dogs wh. can n.have enough
62:6.that shall n. hold their peace
63:19. thou n. barest rule over th.

Je.20:11.confusion sh.n. be forgott.
23:17. David shall n. want a man
Eze.16:63. n. open thy mouth more
26:21. Tyrus sh. n. be found again
27:36. n. shall be any more,28:19.
Da. 2:44. kingdom n. be destroyed
12:1. be trouble. such as n. was
Jo.2:26.peo.shall n.be ashamed,27.
Am.8:7.I will n. forget their works
14.they shall fall and n.rise again
Ha.1:4.judgment doth n. go forth
Mat. 7:23. I will profess I n. knew
9:33.It was n. so seen in Isr. [yon
21:16. Have ye n. read, Out of
mouth of babes, 42. Mk. 2:25.
26:33.Pe.said,will I n. be offended
27:14. he ans-d him to n. a word
Mk.2:12.We n.saw it on this fashion
3:29. ag. H. G. hath n. forgiven.
9:43. fire n. sh. be quenched, 45.
11:2.whereon n.man sat,Lu.19:30.
14:21. good if he had n. been born
Lu. 15:29. thou n. gavest me a kid
23:29.Blessed are wombs th.n.bare
53. wherein n. man bef. was laid,
Jn. 19:41. [give, sh. n. thirst
Jn.4:14. whoso. drinketh of water I
6:35.cometh to me shall n.hunger,
believeth on me shall n. thirst
7:15. How knoweth this man letters having n. learned?
46. n. man spake like this man
8:33.we were n. in bondage to any
51. he shall n. see death, 52.—10:
28.—11:26. [wash my feet
13:8. Peter saith, Thou shalt n.
Ac.10:14. n. eaten anythi. common
14:8. cripple, who had n. walked
1 Co. 13:8. Charity n. faileth, but
2 Ti. 3:7. n. able to come to knowl.
He.10:1.n. wi. sacrifices make perf.
11.sacrifices wh.n.take away sins
13:5. I will n. leave thee, nor
2 Pe. 1:10. do these ye shall n. fall
See So MUCH.

NEVERTHELESS.

Ex. 32:34. n. in day when I visit
Le. 11:4. n. these not eat, De. 14:7.
36.n.a fountain or pit sh.be clean
Nu. 13:28. n. the people be strong
14:44. n. ark of cov. departed not
18:15. n. firstborn of man redeem
24:22. n. the Kenite sh. be wasted
31:23. n. it sh. be purified with
De. 23:5. n. L. would not hearken
Jos. 13:13. n. Israel expelled not
14:8.n.my breth. that went wi. me
Ju.1:33.n.inhab-s of Beth-shemesh
2:16. n. L. raised up judges [Sam.
1 S. 8:19. n. peo. refused to obey
15:35. n. Sam. mourned for Saul
20:26. n. Saul spake not that day
29:6. n. the lords favour thee not
2 S.5:7.n. Da. took the strong hold
17:18. n. a lad saw and told Abs.
23:16.n.he would not drink thereof
1 K.8:19.n.thou shalt not build ho.
15:4. n. for Da.'s sake did L. give
14. n. Asa's heart was perfect
23. n. in old age he was diseased
22:43.n. high places were not tak.
2 K. 2:10. n. if see me when taken
8:3.n.he cleaved unto sins of Jerob
13:6. n. departed not from sins of
23:9. n. priests came not [Jerob.
1 Ch. 11:5. n. David took castle
21:4. n. the king's word prevailed
2 Ch.12:8. n. they sh. be his serv-s
15:17.n. the heart of Asa was perf.
19:3. n. are good things in thee
30:11. n. divers of Asher humbled
33:17.n. the people did sacrifice in
35:22. n. Josiah would not turn
Ne. 4:9. n. we made our prayer
9:26.n. were disobed. and rebelled
31. n. thou didst not consume
13:26.n.him did outland-h women
Es.5:10. n. Haman refrained hims.
Ps. 31:22. n. heardest my supplica.
49:12. n. man being in honour
73:23. n. I am contin-y with thee
78:36. n. they did flatter him
89:33.n. my lovingkindn. not take
106:8. n. saved for his name's
44.n. he regarded their afflictions
Pr. 19:21. n. counsel of L. stand
Ec.9:16. n. the poor man's wisdom
is despised [as was
Is. 9:1. n. dimness sh. not be such
Je.5:18. n. I will not make full end
26:24.n. hand of Ahikam wi.Jere.
28:7.n.hear thou this word I speak
36:25.n. Elnathan made intercess.
Eze.3:21. n. if warn righteous man
16:60. n. I will remember my cov.
20:17. n. mine eye spared them
22. n. I withdrew my hand, and
33:9. n. if thou warn the wicked
Da.4:15. n. leave stump of his roots
Jon. 1:13. n. the men rowed hard
Mat.14:9. n. for the oath's sake, he
26:39.n. not as I will, but as thou
64.n. ye shall see the Son of man
Mk. 14:36. n. not what I will, Lu.
22:42. [down net
Lu. 5:5. n. at thy word I will let
13:33. n. I must walk to day, and
18:8. n. when Son of man cometh
shall he find [go unto him
Jn. 11:15. Lazarus dead, n. let us
12:42.n. am. rulers many believed
16:7. n. I tell you truth, it is expedient [with-t witness
Ac. 14:17. n. he left not himself
27:11. n. the centurion believed
Ro. 5:14. n. death reigned fr.Adam
15:15.n. I have writt. more boldly
1 Co.7:2.n. to avoid fornicat. [flesh
28.n. such sh. have trouble in the
37. n. he that standeth steadfast
9:12. n. we not used this power
11:11.n. nei. is man with-t woman
2 Co. 3:16. n. when it turn to L.
7:6. n. G. that comforteth those
12:16.n.being crafty, I caught you
Ga.2:20. n. I live, yet not I, but C.
4:30. n. what saith Scripture,Cast
Ep. 5:33. n. let ev. one so love wife
Ph. 1:24. n. to abide in the flesh is
3:16. n. whereto we have attained
2 Ti. 1:12. n. I am not ashamed
2:19.n. founda. of G. standeth sure
He. 12:11. n. it yieldeth peaceable
2 Pe.3:13. n. we look for new heav.
Re.2:4.n. I have somewhat ag.thee

NEW.

Ex 1:8.arose a n. king over E. [26.
Le.23:16. a n. meat offering,Nu.28:
26:10.bring forth old,bec.of the n.
Nu. 16:30. if the L. make n. thing
De. 20:5. hath built n. house,22:8.
24:5. n. wife, he sh. not go to war
32:17.sacrificed unto devils,n.gods
Ju. 5:8. They chose n. gods [11,12.
15:13. bound him wi. n. cords, 16:
1 S. 6:7. make n. cart, and take
2 S. 6:3. ark upon n. cart, 1 Ch.13:
21:16. girdled with n. sword [7.
1 K.11:29.Jerob. with a n.garment
30.Ahijah caught the n. garment
2 K.2:20. Bring a n. cruse, put salt
2 Ch.20:5. Jehosh-t in the n. court
Ezr. 6:4. and a row of n. timber
Ec. 1:9. is no n. thing und.the sun
10. Is anything whereof may be
said, this is n.? [n. and old
Can. 7:13. are all pleasant fruits,
Is.41:15.make a n.threshing instru.
42:9. n. things do I declare, 48:6.
43:19.I will do a n. thing, make a
62:2. shalt be called by n. name
65:17. I create n. heavens and a
n. earth, 66:22. [house, 36:10.
Je. 26:10. the n. gate of the Lord's
Je. 31:22. L. hath created n. thing
La. 3:23. Lord's mercies are n.
every morning [26.
Eze.11:19. I will put a n. spirit,36:
18:31.make you n. heart, n.spirit
47:12.wh.shall bring forth n. fruit
Mat.9:16. No man putteth n. cloth
unto old, Mk. 2:21. Lu. 5:36.
17. they put n. wine into n. bottles, both, Mk. 2:22. Lu. 5:38.
13:52. bringeth out of his treasure
things n. and old [Mk. 14:25.
26:29.until I drink it n. with you,
27:60. Joseph laid body in n.tomb
Mk.16:17.sh. speak with n.tongues
Jn.19:41.A n. sepul. wherein never
Ac.17:21. tell or hear some n. thing
1 Co.5:7. that ye may be a n. lump
2 Co.5:17. all things are become n.
Ep. 2:15. of twain, one n. man
4:24. ye put on n. man, Col. 3:10.
He. 10:20. By a n. and living way
2 Pe.3:13.look for n.heavens and n.
Re. 2:17. n. name writt. no man
3:12.n. Jerusalem, 21:2. [knoweth
3:12. I will write my n. name
21:1.I saw n. heaven and n. earth
5. Behold I make all things n.
See BOTTLES, COMMANDMENT,
COVENANT, CREATURE, DOCTRINE, MOON, S, SONG, TESTAMENT, WINE.

NEWBORN. [milk

1 Pe. 2:2. As n. babes desire the

NEWLY. [n. up

De.32:17. sacrificed to gods th.came
Ju. 7:19. they had but n. set watch
2 S. 24:†6. to the land n. inhabited
1 Ti. 3:†6. not one n. come to faith

NEWNESS.

Ro. 6:4. we should walk in n.of life
7:6. th. we sho. serve in n.of spirit

NEWS.

Pr. 25:25. is good n. fr. far country

NEXT.

Ge. 17:21. Sarah shall bear n. year
Ex.12:4.let his neighb. n.take lamb
Nu.2:5.th. pitch n.unto him be Is-
11:32. stood all n. day [sachar
27:11 inheri. unto his kinsman n.
De. 21:3. city n. unto slain man
6. elders of city n. slain man
25:†5.her n. kinsman sh. take her
Ru. 2:20. is one of our n. kinsmen
1 S.17:13.Eliab the firstborn and n.
23:17. I shall be n. unto thee
30:17.smote unto evening of n.day
2 K.6:29. I said n.day,Give thy son
1 Ch. 5:12. Joel chief, Shaphan n.
16:5. n. to him, 2 Ch. 17:15,16,18.
—31:12, 15.
2 Ch. 28:7. Elkanah was n. to king
Ne.3:2.n. unto him builded man of
4. n. unto them repaired, 5, 7, 8,
9, 10, 12, 17, 19. [was Carshena
13:13. n. was Hanan | Es.1:14. n.
Es. 10:3. Mordecai was n. to king
Jon.4:7 a worm n.day smote gourd
Mat. 27:62. n. day that followed
Mk. 1:38. Let us go into n. towns
Jn.1:29.n.day Jn.seeth Jes.coming
Ac.7:26.n.day Moses shewed hims.
13:42.words be preached n.sab.,44
16:11. n. day we came to Neapolis
21:26.Paul, n.day purifying hims.
27:18. n. day they lightened ship
28:13. n. day we came to Puteoli
See Next DAY.

NEZI'AH.

Ezr. 2:54. The chil. of N., Ne.7:56.

NE'ZIB. See JIPHTAH.

NIB'HAZ. [tak

2 K. 17:31. Avites made N.and Tar-

NIB'SHAN. [of Salt

Jos. 15:62. In wildern. N. and city

NIC'ANOR. [N.

Ac. 6:5. chose Stephen, Philip and

NICODE'MUS.
Jn. 3 : 1. N. a ruler of the Jews, 4, 9.
7:50. N. came to Jes. by night, 19:39.

NICOLA'ITANS.
Re. 2 : 6. hatest the deeds of the N.
15. that hold the doctrine of the ⌊N.

NIC'OLAS.
Ac. 6 : 5. N. a proselyte of Antioch

NICOP'OLIS.
Tit. 3 : 12. diligent to come unto me ⌊to N.

NI'GER.
Ac. 13 : 1. Simeon who was called N.

NIGH.
Le. 21:3. a virgin that is n. unto him
25 : 49. any n. of kin may redeem
Nu. 24:17. I sh. behold him, but not ⌊n.
De. 1 : 7. all places n. ther-to
4:7. what nation, who hath G. so n.
13:7. entice thee to gods of peo. n.
22 : 2. if bro. be not n. unto thee
30 : 14. word is n. thee, Ro. 10 : 8.
2 S. 11:20. Whf. approached so n.? 21
1 K. 8 : 59. let my words be n. L.
1 Ch. 12:40. they n. brought bread
Ps. 34:18. L. is n. them of brok. heart
85:9. his salva. is n. them that fear
145 : 18. L. is n. unto all that call
Jo. 2 : 1. day of the L. is n. at hand
Mat. 24 : 32. that summer is n., Lu.
Mk. 5:11. n. unto mts. gr. herd ⌊21:30.
21. he was n. unto the sea
13 : 29. that it is n. even at doors
Lu. 19:11. because he was n. to Jerus.
21 : 20. know that desolation is n.
28. your redemption draweth n.
31. know that kingd. of G. is n.
Jn. 6 : 4. passo., feast of Jews was n.
19. see Jes. drawing n. unto ship
23. n. place where they did eat
11:18. Bethany was n. unto Jerus.
55. Jews passover was n. at hand
19 : 20. crucified, was n. unto city
42. for sepulchre was n. at hand
Ac. 9 : 38. Lydda was n. unto Joppa
27 : 8. n. whereunto was Lasea
Ep. 2 : 13. ye are made n. by blood
17. preached peace to them were n
Ph. 2:27. was sick, n. unto death, 30.
He. 6:8. is rejected, is n. unto cursing
See **CAME, COME, COMETH, DRAW. DREW nigh.**

NIGHT.
Ge. 1 : 5. and the darkness he called ⌈n.
14. lights, to divide the day fr. n.
16. he made lesser light to rule n.
19:2. tarry all n., Nu. 22:8, 19. Ju. 19 : 6, 9. ⌈this n.?
5. Where are men came in to thee
33. made him drink that n., 34, 35.
24: 54. tarried all n., 28:11.–31:54.
–32 : 13, 21, 22. ⌈n.
26:24. L. appeared unto Isaac same
30 : 15. Rachel said, He shall lie with thee to n., 16. ⌈41 : 11.
40 : 5. dreamed each man in 1 n.,
49:27. at n. he sh. divide the spoil
Ex. 12 : 8. eat the flesh that n. roast
12. I will pass thro. Egypt this n.
42. a n. to be much observed (2)
14:20. one came not near other all
21. strong east wind all th. n. ⌊n.
Le. 6 : 9. burning upon altar all n.
20. half in morning, half at n.
19:13. wages not abide wi. thee all n
Nu. 11 : 32. people stood all that n.
14:1. peo. wept that n. murmured
22:20. God came unto Balaam at n.
De. 16 : 4. neither sh. any of flesh thou sacrificedst remain all n.
21:23. His body not all n. upon tree
Jos. 2 : 2. came men in hither to n.
8:13. Josh. went that n. into valley
10 : 9. Josh. went fr. Gilgal all n.
Ju. 6 : 25. to pass same n. that L. said, 7 : 9. 2 S. 7 : 4. 1 Ch. 17 : 3.
40. G. did so that n. for it was dry
16 : 2. laid wait all n. quiet all n.
Jn. 19 : 10. man would not tarry th.
13. to lodge all n. in Gibeah ⌊n.
25. and abused her all n. until
Ru. 1:12. if I sho. have husband to n.
3: 2. Boaz winnoweth barley to n.
13. Tarry this n. and it shall be
1 S. 14 : 34. ev. man his ox that n.
15 : 11. Sam. cried unto L. all n.
16. tell what L. said to me this n.
19:10. David fled and escaped th. n.
11. If thou save not thy life to n.
28: 25. Saul rose went aw. that n.
31 : 12. men of Jabesh went all n.
2 S. 2:29. Abner and men walked all
32. Joab and men went all n. ⌊n.
4:7. gat them away thro. plain all n.
12 : 16. David all n. upon earth
17:1. I will pursue after Da. this n.
19:7. not tarry one wi. thee this n.
2 K. 19:35. that n. angel of L. smote
2 Ch. 1:7. n. did G. appear unto Sol.
35 : 14. busied in offering until n.
Es. 6 : 1. that n. could not k. sleep
Jb. 3:3. n. perish in wh. it was said
6. As for that n. let darkness seize
7. let that n. be solitary
7: 4. When arise, and n. be gone?
29:19. dew all n. upon my branch
30:†3. famine dark as n. ⌈cut off
36 : 20. Desire not n. when peo. are
Ps. 6 : 6. all n. make I my bed swim
19:2. n. unto n. sheweth knowledge
30:5. weeping may endure for a n.
59:†15. if not satisfi. will stay all n.
78 : 14. he led th. all n. with light
92:2. to shew thy faithfulness ev. n.
104 : 20. makest darkness, it is n.
139:11. n. shall be light about me
Pr. 7:9. passing in the black dark n.
31:15. She riseth while it is yet n.
Can. 1:13. lie all n. betw. my breasts
5:2. my locks with drops of the n.
Is. 5:11. until n. till wine inflame th.
16 : 3. make thy shadow as the n.
21 : 4. n. of my pleasure into fear
†8. I am set in my ward every n.
11. Watchman, what of the n.? (2)
12. morning cometh, also the n.
Je. 14:8. turneth aside to tarry for n.
Da. 5 : 30. that n. Belshazzar slain
6 : 18. king passed the n. fasting
Ho. 7 : 6. their baker sleepeth all n.
Jo. 1 : 13. lie all n. in sackcloth ⌈n.
Am. 5 : 8. maketh the day dark with
Jon. 4:10. up in a n. perished in a n.
Mi. 3 : 6. Thf. n. shall be unto you
Mat. 14:25. in 4th watch of n. Jesus went to them on sea, Mk. 6 : 48.
26 : 31. All ye shall be offended because of me this n., Mk. 14:27.
34. this n. thou shalt deny me
Lu. 5 : 5. we have toiled all n. and
6:12. he continued all n. in prayer
12:20. this n. thy soul be required
17:34. that n. two sh. be in one bed
21 : 37. at n. he abode in mount
Jn. 9 : 4. n. when no man can work
13 : 30. he went out and it was n.
21:3. that n. they caught nothing
Ac. 12:6. same n. Peter was sleeping
16:33. he took th. same hour of n.
23:11. n. following L. stood by him
23. ready soldiers at 3d hour of n.
27:23. stood by me this n. the angel
27. when the 14th n. was come
Ro. 13 : 12. The n. is far spent, day is
1 Co. 11 : 23. same n. in wh. he was
1 Th. 5 : 5. we are not of n. ⌊betray.
Re. 21:25. shall be no n. there, 22:5.

By NIGHT. ⌈b. n.
Ge. 14 : 15. ag. them, he and serv-s
20:3. to Abimelech in dream b. n.
31 : 24. to Laban in dream b. n.
39. wh. e. stolen by day, or b. n. ⌈n.
40. drought consumed me, frost b.
Ex. 12 : 31. he called for Moses b. n.
13:21. Lord went before them b. n. in a pillar of fire, 22.–14:20.–40:
38. Nu. 14 : 14. Ne. 9 : 12, 19.
Nu. 9 : 16. appearance of fire b. n.
21. cloud taken up by day or b. n.
De. 1 : 33. in fire b. n. to shew way
16:1. G. brought you out of E. b. n.
23:10 uncleann. that chanceth b. n.
Jos. 8:3. Joshua sent them aw. b. n.
Ju. 6 : 27. it was that he did it b. n.
9 : 32. up b. n. thou and peo. | 34.
20 : 5. beset the house about b. n.
1 S. 14:36. go after Philistines b. n.
26:7. David came to the people b. n.
28 : 8. Saul came to woman b. n.
2 S. 21 : 10. nor beasts of field b. n.
1 K. 3 : 5. L. appeared to Sol. b. n., 2 Ch. 7 : 12. ⌈city
2 K. 6:14. came b. n. and compassed
8 : 21. rose b. n. and smote Edomites, 2 Ch. 21 : 9. ⌈Je. 52 : 7.
25:4. all the men of war fled b. n.,
Ps. 91 : 5. shalt not be afraid b. n.
121 : 6. nor moon smite thee b. n.
134 : 1. b. n. stand in house of L.
136:9. moon and stars to rule b. n.,
Je. 31 : 35. ⌈b. n.
Pr. 31:18. her candle goeth not out
Can. 3:1. b. n. on my bed I sought
Is. 4 : 5. the shining of a fire b. n.
Je. 6 : 5. b. n. and destroy palaces
39 : 4. they went out of city b. n.
49 : 9. if thieves b. n. will destroy
Ob. 5. if robbers b. n. wo. they not
Zch. 1 : 8. I saw b. n. behold a man
Mat. 2:14. took child and moth. b. n.
27: 64. lest disci. come b. n., 28:13.
Lu. 2 : 8. watch ov. their flock b. n.
Jn. 3 : 2. Nicodemus came to Jesus b. n., 7 : 50.–19 : 39. ⌈doors
Ac. 5:19. angel b. n. opened prison
9:25. took Paul b. n. let him down
17:10. sent aw. Paul and Silas b. n.
23:31. bro-t Paul b. n. to Antipatris

NIGHT with day.
Nu. 9:21. by d. or n. they journeyed
1 S. 28:20. eaten no br. all d. nor n.
1 K. 8 : 59. let my words be nigh unto L. d. and n. ⌈d. and n.
1 Ch. 9 : 33. singers were employed
1 Th. 5:2. d. of Lord cometh as thief in the n. ⌈for ever
Re. 20: 10. be tormented d. and n.
See **DAY with night.**

In the NIGHT. ⌈n.
Ex. 12:30. Pha. and servants rose i.
Nu. 11 : 9. dew fell upon camp i. n.
1 K. 3 : 19. woman's child died i. n.
2 K. 7 : 12. king arose i. n. ⌈up i. n.
Ne. 2 : 12. I arose i. n. | 15. I went
4 : 22. i. n. may be a guard to us
6 : 10. i. n. will come to slay thee
9 : 12. and i. n. by pillar of fire
Jb. 5 : 14. grope in noonday as i. n.
24 : 14. i. n. murderer is as a thief
27 : 20. tempest stealeth him i. n.
30:17. My bones pierced in me i. n.
34 : 25. he overturneth them i. n.
35:10. God, who giveth songs i. n.?
Ps. 16 : 7. my reins instruct me i. n.
17:3. thou hast visited me i. n. and
22 : 2. I cry i. n. season, and am
42: 8. i. n. his song sh. be with me
77: 2. my sore ran i. n. ceased not
6. I call to remem. my song i. n.
90: 4. thous. years but as watch i.
105:39. a fire to give light i. n. ⌊n.
119 : 55. rememb-d thy name i. n.
Ec. 2 : 23. heart taketh not rest i. n.
Can. 3:8. his sword, bec. of fear i. n.
Is. 15 : 1. i. n. Ar and Kir is laid
26:9. have I desired thee i. n. ⌊waste
30 : 29. Ye sh. have a song as i. n.
59:10. we stumble at noonday as i.
Je. 36 : 30. sh. be cast out i. n. ⌊n.
La. 1 : 2. she weepeth sore i. n.
2 : 19. O dau. of Zion, cry out i. n.
Ho. 4 : 5. the prophet shall fall i. n.

Jn.11:10. if walk i.n. he stumbleth
1 Th. 5 : 7. they that sleep, sleep i. n. ; drunken are drunken i. n.
See LODGE, LODGED.
See VISION, S with night.

NIGHT watches.

Ps.63:6. I meditate on thee in n.w.
119 : 148. Mine eyes prevent n. w.

NIGHTS. [12.

Ge. 7 : 4. cause it rain 40 days 40 n.,
Ex. 24 : 18. in mount 40 days 40 n.,
34:28. De. 9:9, 11, 18, 25.-10:10.
1 S. 30:12. nor drunk water 3 days and 3 n. [and 40 n.
1 K. 19 : 8. strength of meat 40 days
Jb. 2 : 13. with him upon ground seven days and seven n.
7:3. wearisome n. are appointed [n.
Is. 21 : 8. I am set in my ward whole
Jon.1:17. Jonah in fish 3 n., Mat.4:2
Mat. 4 : 2. when fasted 40 days 40 n.

NIGHTHAWK. [15.

Le.11:16. n. ye shall not eat, De. 14 :

NIM'RAH. [cattle

Nu. 32 : 3. N., Shebam a land for
† 36. children of Gad built N.

NIM'RIM.

Is.15:6. waters of N. be desol., Je.48:

NIM'ROD. [34.

Ge. 10: 8. Cush begat N., 1 Ch. 1:10.
9. as N. mighty hunter bef. Lord
Mi. 5 : 6. they shall waste land of N.

NIM'SHI. [anoint

1 K. 19 : 16. Jehu son of N. thou
2 K. 9 : 2. Jehu son of N., 14, 20. 2

NINE. [Ch. 23 : 7.

Nu. 29 :26. on fifth day n. bullocks
De. 3 : 11. Og's bedstead n. cubits
Jos.15:44. n. cities with villages, 54.
21 : 16. n. cities out of two tribes
Lu. 17:17. ten cleansed, where are n.?
See HUNDRED, MONTHS, PARTS, TRIBES, YEARS.
See NINE and thirtieth year

NINETEEN.

Jos. 19 : 38. n. cities with villages
See MEN.

NINETEENTH.

See LOT, YEAR.

NINETY. [cubits

Eze. 41 : 12. length of building, n.
See Ninety YEARS.

NINETY five or six.

Ezr. 2 : 20. children of Gibbar n. f.
Ne. 7 : 25. children of Gibeon n. f.
Je. 52 : 23. were n. s. pomegranates
See RAMS.

NINETY eight or nine.

Ezr.2:16. chil. of Ater n. e., Ne.7:21.
Mat. 18 : 12. doth he not leave the n. n., and seeketh that, 13. Lu.
See YEARS. [15 : 4, 7.

NIN'EVEH.

Ge.10:11. Ashur went and builded N.
12. Resen betw. N. and Calah [37.
2K.19:36. Sennach. dwelt at N., Is.37:
Jon. 1 : 2. go to N., 3 : 2.
4 : 11. should not I spare N.?
3 : 3. N. was an exceeding gr. city
4. in 40 days N. be overthrown
5. people of N. believed God
6. word came unto king of N.
7. be proclaimed thro. N. [pool
Na.1:1. burden of N. | 2:8. N. like a
3:7. N. is waste, who bemoan her?
Zph. 2 : 13. he will make N. a desola.
Mat. 12 : 41. men of N. shall rise in judgm. and condemn, Lu.11:32.

NIN'EVITES.

Lu. 11 : 30. Jonas was a sign unto N.

NINTH. [Gad

1 Ch. 12 : 12. Elzabad n. captain of
Re. 21 : 20. n. foundation was topaz
See DAY, HOUR, LOT, MONTH, YEAR.

NISAN. [month N.

Ne. 2 : 1. month N. | Esth. 3:7. first

NIS'ROCH.

2 K. 19 : 37. house of N. his god, Is. 37 : 38.

NITRE.

Pr.25:20. as vinegar upon n. so is he
Je.2:22. tho. thou wash thee with n.

NO. [Adj.]

See ANSWER, BLEMISH, BLOOD, BODY, BREAD, BREASTS, BREATH, BURNING, BUSINESS, CANDLE, CASE, CHANGES, CHASTENING, CHILD, CHILDREN, CITY, CLOAK, COMFORTER, COMPANY, CONFIDENCE, CORRECTION, COVENANT, CUSTOM, DARKNESS, DAUGHTER, DAY, DEAD, DELIGHT, DELIVERER, DEW, DIFFERENCE, DWELLING, EASE, END, ESCAPE, EVIL, EYE, FAITH, FAT, FAULT, FEAR, FIRE, FLESH, FORM, FOUNDATION, FURTHER, GIFT, GOD, GODS, GOOD, GRAVES, GREATER, GUILE, HAIR, HAIRS, HAND, HARM, HEALING, HEART, HERD, HEIR, HELP, HELPER, HOPE, HURT, HUSBAND, IDOLS, ILL, INCENSE, INHERITANCE, INIQUITY, INTERCESSOR, INTERPRETER, JOY, JUDGE, JUDGMENT, KING, KINGDOM, KINSMAN, KNOWLEDGE, LACK, LAW, LEAVEN, LIFE, LIGHT, MAGISTRATE, MAN, MANNER, MEANS, MERCY, MIGHT, MISCHIEF, MONEY, NAME, NEED, NIGHT, OATH, OFFENCE, OIL, ONE, OPENING, OPPRESSOR, OTHER, PART, PASSOVER, PASTURE, PEACE, PEOPLE, PITY, PLACE, PLAGUE, PLEASURE, POOR, PORTION, POWER, PRIEST, PROPHECY, PROPHET, RAZOR, REMEDY, REMISSION, REMNANT, REPENTANCE, REPORT, REPUTATION, REST, RESURRECTION, RULER, SATISFACTION, SAVIOUR, SEED, SHAME, SHEPHERD, SIMILITUDE, SIN, SON, SONS, SORROW, SOUNDNESS, SPIES, SPOT, STRANGER, STRAW, STRENGTH, STRIFE, SWARMS, TARRYING, TEMPTATION, TEMPLE, THING, THOUGHT, TRANSGRESSION, TRUST, TRUTH, UNDERSTANDING, UNRIGHTEOUSNESS, USURY, VALUE, VARIABLENESS, VINEGAR, VISION, WAGES, WALL, WANT, WAR, WATER, WEAPON, WIDOW, WICKEDNESS, WISDOM, WITNESS, WORK, WRATH, WRONG.

NO. [Adverb.]

Ex. 3 : 19. will not let you go, n.
16:4. whe. in my law or n., De. 8:2.
Ju. 4 : 20. Is any man here, say n.
15 : 13. n., but we will bind thee
1 S. 1 : 15. n. I am of sorrowful
10:14. when saw they were n. where
20 : 15. n. not when L. hath cut off
1 K.3:22. said n. the dead is thy son
Jb. 23:6. n. but he wo. put strength
36 : 19. n. not gold, nor the forces
Ps.14:3. doeth good, n. not one, 53:3.
Ec. 10 : 20. n. not in thy thought
Is. 30:16. n. we will flee upon horses
Je. 2 : 25. n. for I loved strangers
42:14. n. but we will go into E. [n.
Am. 6:10. any with thee? he sh. say
Hag. 2 : 12. priests answered n.
Zch. 4 : 5. these be, I said, n., 13.
Mat.8:10. so great faith, n., Lu. 7:9.
24:21. to this time n., nor ever sh.
36. n. not the angels, but my Fa.
Mk. 2:2. no room, n. not about door
5 : 3. bind him, n. not with chains
Lu.20:22. tribute unto Cesar, or n.?
23 : 15. n. nor yet Herod, for I sent
Jn. 1:21. Art thou prophet? said n.
9:25. Whe. sinner or n. I know not
21 : 5. have ye meat? they ans-d n.
Ac. 7 : 5. n. not so as to set his foot
Ro. 3 : 9. we better than they ? n.
10. is none righte. n. not one, 12.
1 Co. 5 : 11. with such n. not to eat
6:5. n. not one that be able to judge
Ga. 2 : 5. subjection, n. not an hour
See No MORE, In no WISE.

NO. [Place.] [15,16.

Je.46:25. I will punish N., Eze.30:14,
Na.3:8. † Art thou better than populous N.?

NOADI'AH.

Ezr. 8:33. N. son of Binnui, a Levite
Ne. 6 : 14. My G. think on prophet-

NO'AH=NO'E. [ess N.

Ge.5:29. † Lamech called his name N.
30. Lamech aft. he begat N. [6:10.
32. N. was 500 y-rs old, N. begat,
6:8. N. found grace in eyes of Lord
9. These are the generations of N., 9 : 19.-10 : 1, 32. 1 Ch. 1 : 4.
9. N. just man, walked with God
13. G. said unto N. The end of all
22. did N. acc. to all G. com-ded, 7:5.
7 : 1. L. said unto N. Come into ark
6. N. was 600 y-rs old | 7, 9, 11, 13,
7 : 23. N. only remained alive [15.
8 : 1. God remembered N. and ev.
6. N. opened window of ark +
20. N. builded an altar unto L.
9 : 1. God blessed N. and sons +
24. N. awoke from his wine, 28.
29. days of N. 950 years; he died
Is. 54:9. this is as waters of N. [20.
Eze.14:14. tho. these 3, N., Dan., Job,
Mat.24:37. in days of N-e, Lu. 17:26.
38. until N-e ent-d ark, Lu. 17:27.
Lu. 3 : 36. Shem was son of N-e
He. 11 : 7. By faith N. being warned
1 Pe. 3 : 20. God waited in days of N.
2 Pe. 2 : 5. God spared not the old world, but saved N.

NO'AH. [Woman.]

Nu. 26 : 33. daus. of Zelophehad N. Tirzah, 27 : 1.-36:11. Jos. 17:3.

NOB.

1 S.21:1. David came to N. to Ahim.
22 : 9. I saw son of Jesse coming to
11. k. sent to call priests in N. [N.
19. Doeg smote N. city of priests
Ne. 11 : 32. chil. of Benj. dwelt at N.
Is. 10 : 32. as yet sh. he remain at N.

NO'BAH.

Nu. 32:42. N. went and took Kenath
Ju. 8:11. dwelt in tents on east of N.

NOBLE.

Ezr. 4 : 10. whom n. Asnapper bro-t
Es. 6 : 9. one of k.'s most n. princes
Je. 2 : 21. I planted thee a n. vine
Ac. 17 : 11. Bereans more n. than
24:3. We accept most n. Felix, 26:25.
1 Co. 1 : 26. not many n. are called

NOBLES. [band

Ex. 24 : 11. upon n. of Isr. laid not
Nu. 21 : 18. n. of people digged it
Ju.5:13. dominion over the n. [11.
1 K. 21:8. Jezebel sent letters to n.,
2 Ch. 23 : 20. Jehoiada took the n.
Ne.2:16. nor had I told it to the n.
3 : 5. n. put not necks to the work
4 : 14. said unto n., Be not, 19.
5 : 7. I rebuked the n. and rulers
6:17. n. of Judah sent letters unto
7 : 5. into mine heart to gather n.
10:29. They clave to breth. their n.
13 : 17. I contended with n. of Jud.
Es. 1 : 3. Media, the n. and princes
Jb. 29 : 10. The n. held their peace
Ps. 83 : 11. Make their n. like Oreb
149 : 8. To bind their n. wi. fetters
Pr. 8 : 16. By me princes rule, and n.

Ec. 10 : 17. when thy k. is son of n.
Is. 13 : 2. may go into gates of n.
34 : 12. They shall call n. to kingd.
43 : 14. have brought down all n.
Je. 14 : 3. the n. sent their little ones
27 : 20. Neb. carried captive n.
30 : 21. their n. shall be of thems.
39:6. king slew all the n. of Judah
Jon. 3:7. by decree of k. and his n.
Na.3:18. thy n. sh. dwell in the dust

NOBLEMAN.

Lu. 19 : 12. n. went into far coun- try
Jn.4:46. cert. n. whose son was sick
49. cert. n. saith, Come ere child die

NOD.

Ge. 4 : 16. Cain dwelt in land of N.

NO'DAB. See NEPHISH.

NO'E. See NOAH.

NO'GAH. See NEPHEG.

NO'HAH. See RAPHA.

NOISE.

Ex.20:18. peo. heard n. of trumpets
32 : 17. is a n. of war in camp
18. the n. of them that sing I hear
Jos. 6 : 10. not shout nor make n.
Ju. 5 : 11. delivered fr. n. of archers
1 S. 4 : 6. What meaneth the n.? 14.
14:19. n. in host of Philis. increas- ed
1 K.1:41. Wherefore is this n. of city?
45. This is n. that ye have heard
18:†41. is a n. of abundance of rain
2 K.7:6. n. of chariots, n. of horses
11:13. heard n. of guard, 2 Ch.23:12.
1 Ch.15:28. making n. wi. psalteries
Ezr. 3 : 13. not discern n., of joy fr. n. of weeping
Jb. 36:29. can any understand n. of his tabern.?
33. n. thereof sheweth conc. it
37:2. Hear attentively n. of his voi.
Ps.33:3. play skilfully with loud n.
40:†2. brought me out of pit of n.
42 : 7. Deep calleth at n. of water- spouts
55 : 2. I mourn, make a n.
59:6. they make a n. like dog, 14.
65:7. stilleth n. of seas, n. of waves
66:1. Make a joyful n. unto God, all ye, 81:1.-95:1,2.-98:4, 6.-100:1.
93:4. L. mightier than n. of waters
Is. 9 : 5. battle is with confused n.
13:4. The n. of a multitude in mts., a tumultuous n. of nations
14:11. n. of thy viols is bro-t down
17 : 12. make a n. like n. of seas
24:8. n. of them th. rejoice endeth
18. he who fleeth from n. of fear
: 5. bring down n. of strangers
: 6. be visited of L. with gr. n.
: 4. nor abase hims. for n. of th.
:3. At n. of tumult the peo. fled
:†5. n. of sea sh. be turned tow.
66 : 6. A voice of n. from the city
Je. 4 : 19. heart maketh a n. in me
29. city sh. flee for n. of horsemen
10 : 22. the n. of the bruit is come
11:16. with the n. of a great tumult
25:31. A n. to ends of the earth
46:17. Pha. king of Egypt is but a n.
47:3. n. of stamping of his horses
49:21. earth is moved at n. of their fall, n. was heard in Red sea
50:46. At n. of taking of Babylon
51:55. a n. of their voice is uttered
La.2:7. enemy made n. in ho. of L.
Eze.1:24. I heard n. of their wings, like n. of great waters, 43 : 2.
3:13. n. of wheels, n. of gr. rushing
19:7. land desolate by n. of roaring
26:10. thy walls sh. shake at the n.
13. cause n. of my songs to cease
37 : 7. as I prophesied, was a n.
Jo.2:5. Like n. of chariots, n. of fire
Am.5:23. Take fr. me n. of thy songs
Mi.2:12. they shall make a great n.
Na.3:2. n. of a whip, n. of wheels
Zph. 1: 10. n. of cry from fish gate
Zch. 9 : 15. sh. drink and make a n.
Mat. 9 : 23. saw people making a n.
2 Pe. 3 : 10. heavens shall pass with great n.
Re. 6 : 1. I heard as it were n. of thunder

NOISED.

Jos. 6 : 27. Joshua, his fame was n.
Mk. 2 : 1. n. that he was in the ho.
Lu. 1 : 65. all these sayings were n.
Ac. 2 : 6. when this was n. abroad

NOISOME.

Ex. 8:†21. will send a mixture of n. beasts
Jb. 31†:40. n. weeds inst. of barley
Ps.91:3. shall deliver fr. n. pestilence
Eze. 14 : 21. when I send n. beast
Re.16:2. fell a n. and grievous sore

NON. See NUN.

NONE.

Ge. 23 : 6. n. sh. withhold fr. thee sepul.
28:17. n. other but the house of G.
Ex. 12 : 22. n. of you shall go out
15:26. put n. of diseases upon thee
16:26. on 7th day, in it shall be n.
27. to gather, and they found n.
23:15. n. sh. appear empty, 34:20.
Le. 18 : 6. n. shall approach to kin
21 : 1. n. be defiled for dead
22 : 30. n. of it until morrow, Nu. 9:12.
25 : 26. if man have n. to redeem
26:6. n. shall make you afraid
17. sh. flee when n. pursueth, 36, 37.
27 : 29. n. devoted sh. be redeemed
Nu. 7 : 9. to sons of Kohath gave n.
32:11. n. that came out of E. sh. see
De. 2 : 34. we destroyed left n. to remain, 3:3. Jos.8:22.-10:28,30, 33, 37, 39, 40.-11 : 8.
5 : 7. have n. other gods bef. me, Ex.20:3.
7:15. put n. of diseases of E. on you
28:31. thy sheep and n. to rescue
66. shalt have n. assurance of life
Jos. 6:1. n. went out of Jericho, n.
9:23. n. be freed fr. being bondmen
10:21. n. moved his tongue ag. Isr.
11 : 13. Isr. burned n. save Hazor
Ju.19:28. Up be doing, But n. ans-d
21 : 8. n. to camp from Jabesh, 9.
1 S. 2 : 2. is n. holy as the Lord
3:19. let n. of his words fall to gro.
14 : 24. So n. of people tasted food
2 S. 14 : 19. n. can turn to right ha.
15 : †3. n. will hear thee fr. king
18 : 12. that n. touch young man
1 K. 10 : 21. n. of silver, 2 Ch. 9:20.
15:22. proclamation, n. exempted
2 K. 5 : 16. As L. liveth, I will rec. n.
6 : 12. n. but Elisha telleth king
9 : 10. shall be n. to bury Jezebel
15. let n. go forth out of city, 10:25.
10:11. until Jehu left Ahab n.
19. prophets, let n. be wanting
23. look there be n. of serv-s of G.
1 Ch.15:2. n. ought to carry ark but
2 Ch. 1:12. honour, as n. of k-s had
9:11. n. such seen bef. in la. of Jud.
20. vessels of gold; n. of silver
16 : 1. n. go out or come in to Asa
20 : 6. n. is able to withstand thee
24. dead bodies fallen, n. escaped
23:19. n. unclean sho. enter in
Ezr. 8 : 15. I found n. of sons of Levi
Ne. 4 : 23. n. of us put off clothes
Es. 1 : 8. drinking, n. did compel
4:2. n. enter king's gate in sackcl.
Jb. 2 : 13. n. spake a word unto him
3:9. let it look for light but have n.
11:19. and n. shall make thee afraid
18:15. tabernacle, bec. it is n. of his
20 : 21. shall n. of his meat be left
29 : 12. deliv-d him had n. to help
35 : 10. But n. saith, Where is God
12. they cry, but n. giveth answ.
41:10. n. so fierce th. dare stir him
Ps.10:15. his wickedness till find n.
22 : 29. n. can keep alive his soul
25:3. n. that wait on thee be asham.
34: 22. n. th. trust in him be deso.
37 : 31. n. of his steps shall slide
49 : 7. n. can redeem his brother
Ps. 50 : 22. tear you, and be n. to deliver
69 : 20. looked for comforters, but found n.
25. and let n. dwell in their tents
76 : 5. n. of men of might found their hands
81 : 11. Isr. would n. of me
109:12. Let be n. to extend mercy
Pr. 1 : 25. ye wo. n. of my reproof
30. they would n. of my counsel
2 : 19. n. that go unto her return
3 : 31. and choose n. of his ways
Can. 4:2. and n. is barren am. them
Is 1:31. shall burn and n. sh. quench
5 : 27. n. sh. be weary, n. slumber
29. carry it safe, n. sh. deliver it
14 : 6. is persecuted, n. hindereth
31. n. shall be alone in his times
17:2. n. make them afraid, Zph. 3:13.
22 : 22. n. shall shut, n. open
34 : 10. n. sh. pass thro. it for ever
12. call nobles but n. sh. be there
16. n. shall want her mate
42 : 22. n. delivereth, n. saith, Re- store
44 : 19. n. considereth in his heart
47:8. I am, and n. else besides, 10.
10. n. seeth me | 15. n. save thee
57 : 1. n. considering righte-s is taken
59 : 4. n. calleth for justice
66:4. when I called, n. did answer
Je. 4 : 4. n. can quench it, 21 : 12.
7 : 33. beasts, n. shall fray them
9:10. burned, so th. n. can pass, 12.
22. fall as dung, n. shall gather
13 : 19. cities be shut, n. sh. open
14 : 16. cast out, n. to bury them
23:14. n. doth return fr. wickedness
30:10. n. sh. make him afraid, 46:27.
34:9. n. sho. serve himself of them
10. n. sho. serve thems. of them
35:14. unto this day they drink n.
36:30. n. to sit upon throne of Da.
42 : 17. n. shall remain or escape
44:14. n. sh. return, but such as, 7.
48 : 33. n. sh. tread with shouting
49:5. n. gather him that wandereth
50 : 3. land desolate, n. sh. dwell
9. arrows, n. shall return in vain
20. iniquity sought, and sh. be n.
29. camp against it, let n. escape
32. proud sh. fall, n. sh. raise him
51 : 62. n. shall remain, Eze. 7:11.
La. 1 : 2. hath n. to comfort her, 17.
4. bec. n. come to solemn feasts
7. her peo. fell, n. did help her
Eze. 7 : 14. n. goeth to the battle
25. seek peace, and shall be n. ed
12 : 28. n. of my words be prolong-
16 : 34. n. to commit whoredoms
18 : 7. hath spoiled n. by violence
22:30. I sought for a man, found n.
31 : 14. th. n. of trees exalt thems.
33 : 16. n. of his sins be mentioned
28. mts. desolate, that n. sh. pass
34 : 6. n. did search after them
28. and n. shall make them afraid, 39 : 26. Mi. 4 : 4. Na. 2 : 11.
39 : 28. have left n. of them there
Da.1:19. n. found like Daniel among
4 : 35. n. say unto him, What doest
6 : 4. co. find n. occasion nor fault
8:27. at vision, but n. understood it
11 : 16. n. shall stand before him
45. come to his end, n. shall help
12:10. n. of wicked sh. understand
Ho.2:10. n. sh. deliver her out, 5:14.
11 : 7. n. at all would exalt him
Jo.2:27. I am L. your G., and n. else
Am. 5 : 6. n. to quench it in Beth-el
Mi. 2 : 5. n. that shall cast a cord
3 : 11. n. evil can come upon us
5:8. he teareth, and n. can deliver
Na. 2 : 8. but n. shall look back
Zph.3:6. streets waste th. n. passeth
Zch. 7 : 10. let n. imagine evil, 8 : 17.
Mal. 2 : 15. n. deal treach-y ag. wife
Mat. 12 : 43. unclean spirit seeking rest findeth n., Lu. 11 : 24.

Mat. 26 : 60. witnesses came, found n., Mk. 14 : 55. [n.
Lu. 3 : 11. impart to him that hath
4:26. unto n. of them was Elias sent
27. n. was cleansed save Naaman
13:6. sought fruit and found n., 7.
14 : 24. n. shall taste of my supper
18:19. n. good, save one, that is G.
34. they understood n. of these
Jn. 7:19. n. of you keepeth the law
8 : 10. Jes. saw n. but the woman
15 : 24. if not done works n. other
16:5. n. of you asketh me, Whither
17:12. n. is lost but son of perdition
18 : 9. of them gavest me, I lost n.
21 : 12. n. of discip. durst ask him
Ac. 3 : 6. Silver and gold have I n.
7 : 5. he gave him n. inheritance
8 : 16. he was fallen upon n. of th.
24. Pray n. of these things come
11:19. preaching word to n. but Jews
18 : 17. Gallio cared for n. of these
20 : 24. n. of these things move me
24:23. forbid n. of his acquaintance
25 : 11. if n. of these they accuse
18. they bro-t n. accusation [say
26 : 22. n. other than prophets did
26. n. of these things are hidden
Ro. 8 : 9. if not Spirit, he is n. of his
14:7. n. liveth, and n. dieth to hims.
1 Co. 1:14. I thank G. I baptized n.
2 : 8. n. of princes of world knew
7:29. have wives be as they had n.
9 : 15. I have used n. of these thi.
10 : 32. Give n. offence to the Jews
14 : 10. n. is without signification
2 Co. 1:13. we write n. other things
Ga. 1:19. other of apostles saw I n.
5 : 10. that ye will be n. otherwise
1 Th. 5 : 15. See that n. render evil
1 Ti. 5 : 14. n. occasion to adversary
1 Pe. 4:15. let n. suffer as murderer
Re. 2 : 10. Fear n. of these things
24. I will put upon you n. other
See EFFECT, LIKE. [burden

There is NONE. [than I
Ge. 39 : 9. t. i. n. greater in this ho.
41:15. t. i. n. that can interpret it
39. t. i. n. so discreet as thou art
De. 4 : 35. the Lord is God, t. i. n. else, 39. 1 K. 8 : 60. Is. 45 : 5, 6, 14, 18, 22,-46 : 9. Mk. 12 : 32.
32:36. t. i. n. shut up or left
Ru. 4:4. t. i. n. to redeem it besides
1 S. 2 : 2. t. i. n. holy as the L.: t. i. n. besides [that is sorry
22 : 8. t. i. n. sheweth me, t. i. n.
1 Ch. 29:15. days are as a shadow t. i. n. abiding
Jb. 10 : 7. t. i. n. that can deliver, Ps. 7 : 2.-71 : 11.
Ps. 14:1. corrupt, t. i. n. that doeth good, 3.-53 : 1, 3. Ro. 3 : 12.
22:11. trouble near, t. i. n. to help
73 : 25. t. i. n. upon earth I desire besides [t. i. n.
Is. 41:17. when the needy seek water,
26. t. i. n. sheweth, t. i. n. that
43:13. t. i. n. can deliver out of my
51:18. t. i. n. to guide her am. sons
59 : 11. we look for judgm., t. i. n.
64:7. t. i. n. calleth on thy name
Je. 10:20. t. i. n. to stretch my tent
30 : 13. t. i. n. to plead thy cause
La. 1 : 21. t. i. n. to comfort me
5 : 8. t. i. n. that doth deliver us
Da. 2 : 11. t. i. n. other can show it
10 : 21. t. i. n. holdeth with me in
Ho. 7:7. t. i. n. that calleth unto me
Am. 5:2. forsaken, t. i. n. to raise her
Ob. 7. t. i. n. understanding in him
Mi. 7:2. t. i. n. upright among men
Na. 2 : 9. t. i. n. end of the glory
3 : 3. t. i. n. end of their corpses
Zph. 2:15. said, I am, t. i. n. besides
3 : 6. that t. i. n. inhabit. [warm
Hag. 1 : 6. ye clothe you, but t. i. n.

Mat. 19 : 17. t. i. n. good but one, that is God, Mk. 10:18. Lu. 18:19.
Mk. 12:31. t. i. n. other com-t greater
32. One G.; t. i. n. other, 1 Co. 8:4.
Lu. 1 : 61. t. i. n. of thy kindr. called
Ac. 4 : 12. t. i. n. other name under
Ro. 3:10. t. i. n. righteous, not one
11. t. i. n. understandeth, t. i. n. seeketh God [bling
1 Jn. 2:10. t. i. n. occasion of stum-

There was NONE. [within
Ge. 39:11. t. w. n. of men of house
41:8. t. w. n. could interpret them
24. t. w. n. could declare it to me
Nu. 21:35. until t. w. n. alive [save
De. 22 : 27. damsel cried, t. w. n. to
Jos. 11 : 22. t. w. n. of Anakim left
2 S. 14 : 6. t. w. n. to part th. [Abs.
25. t. w. n. so much praised as
22 : 42. t. w. n. to save, Ps. 18:41.
1 K. 12 : 20. t. w. n. followed house of Da. but Judah, 2 K. 17 : 18.
Jb. 32:12. t. w. n. th. convinced Job
Ps. 69 : 20. to have pity, but t. w. n.
79:3. shed blood, t. w. n. to bury th.
107 : 12. fell down, t. w. n. to help
139 : 16. when as yet t. w. n. of th.
Is. 10 : 14. t. w. n. moved the wing
50:2. when I called, t. w. n. to ans.
63 : 3. of people t. w. n. with me
5. I looked, t. w. n. to help; I wondered t. w. n. to uphold
Da. 8 : 7. t. w. n. could deliver ram
Jn. 6 : 22. saw t. w. n. other boat

NOON. [n.
Ge. 43 : 16. these sh. dine with me at
25. present ag. Joseph came at n.
Ju. 19:8. they tarried until after n.
2 S. 4:5. Ish-bosheth, on a bed at n.
1 K. 18 : 26. called on Baal until n.
27. at n. Elijah mocked them [n.
20:16. numbered, they went out at
2 K. 4:20. he sat on her knees till n.
Ps. 55 : 17. at n. will I pray and
Can. 1 : 7. makest flock to rest at n.
Je. 6 : 4. arise, let us go up at n.
Am. 8:9. cause sun to go down at n.
Ac. 22 : 6. about n. shone gr. light

NOONDAY. [round me
De. 28 : 29. thou shalt grope at n.
Jb. 5 : 14. grope in n. as in night
11:17. thine age be clearer than n.
Ps. 37:6. sh. bring forth judgm as n.
91 : 6. destruc. that wasteth at n.
Is. 16:3. as the night, in midst of n.
58 : 10. thy darkness shall be as n.
59:10. we stumble at n. as in night
Je. 15 : 8. I brought a spoiler at n.
Zph. 2 : 4. shall drive out Ashdod at

NOONTIDE. [n.
Je. 20 : 16. let him hear shouting at

NOPH. [n.
Is. 19 : 13. princes of n. are deceived
Je. 2:16. chil. of n. have brok. crown
44:1. conc. all Jews wh. dwell at N.
46:14. Declare in E., publish in N.
19. for N. shall be waste [N.
Eze. 30:13. cause images to cease out
16. N. shall have distresses daily

NO'PHAH.
Nu. 21 : 30. laid them waste unto N.

NORTH. [Adj.] [corner
Ex. 26 : 35. side of tabern. tow. n.
Nu. 34:7. this sh. be your n. border, 9.
Jos. 15:5. Jud.'s border in n. quarter
18:19. border at n. bay of salt sea
Je. 23 : 8. Isr. out of n. country, 31:
46:10. L. a sacrif. in n. country [8.
50:9. ag. Babylon nations fr. n. coun
Eze. 38 : 6. Togarmah of n. quarters
39:2. cause thee to come fr. n. parts
48:1. From the n. end to the coast
See North SIDE, WIND.

NORTH. [Noun.] [n.
Ge. 28 : 14. thou shalt spread to the
Jos. 8 : 13. host th. was on n. of city
11:2. kings on the n. of mountains

Jos. 15:6. passed by n. of Beth-arabah
17 : 10. they met in Asher on n.
18:5. Joseph abide in coasts on n.
16. valley of giants on n.
1 K. 7 : 25. a molten sea upon 12 oxen, 3 looking tow. n., 2 Ch. 4:4.
1 Ch. 9 : 24. porters were tow. the n.
Jb. 26 : 7. He stretcheth out the n.
37:9. and cold cometh out of the n.
22. Fair weather cometh out of n.
Ps. 48:2. Beautif. is Zion on sides of
89 : 12. n. and south thou crea. [n.
Ec. 1 : 6. wind turneth unto the n.
11:3. if the tree fall toward the n.
Is. 14:13. I will sit in sides of the n.
43 : 6. I will say to the n. Give up
Je. 1:13. the pot's face is tow. the n.
14. Out of n. an evil break, 4:6.-
15. families of kingd-s of n. [46:20.
3:12. proclaim these words tow. n.
18. shall come together out of n.
6:1. for evil appeareth out of the n.
25 : 9. I will take all families of n.
26. all kings of the n. far and near
46: 6. sh. stumble and fall tow. n.
24. she sh. be deliv-d to peo. of n.
47 : 2. waters rise up out of the n.
50:3. out of the n. cometh a nation
Eze. 1 : 4. whirlwind came out of n.
8 : 3. gate th. looketh toward n., 9 : 2.-40 : 23, 35, 40.-44:4.-46:9.
5. I lifted mine eyes toward the n.
14. tow. the n. sat women weeping
20 : 47. all faces from south to n.
21 : 4. all flesh from south to n.
32 : 30. There be the princes of n.
38:15. come fr. thy place out of n.
40:20. court looked toward n. [46.
44. having prospect toward n.,
41:11. one door was tow. n., 42: 4.
42 : 1. court and building tow. n.
4. doors tow. n. | 11. chambers, 13.
46 : 19. chambers looked tow. n.
48: 10. for priests be oblation tow. n.
17. suburbs of city sh. be tow. n.
Da. 11 : 6. shall come to king of n.
7. into fortress of king of the n.
8. continue more years than king
11. shall fight with k. of n. [of n.
13. the king of the n. shall return
15. king of n. sh. cast up mount, 40.
44. tidings out of n. sh. trouble
Zph. 2 : 13. will stretch hand ag. n.
Zch. 6:6. black horses into n. coun.
8. quieted my spirit in n. country
14:4. mountain sh. remove tow. n.
Re. 21:13. on the n. were three gates

From the NORTH.
Ps. 107:3 gathered f. t. n. and south, Is. 49 : 12. Je. 16 : 15.-23 : 8.
Is. 14: 31. shall come f. t. n. a smoke
41:25. I raised up one f. t. n. he sh.
Je. 4 : 6. I will bring evil f. t. n., 6 : 22.-10 : 22 -50 : 9, 41.-51 : 48.
13:20. behold them th. come f. t. n.
Eze. 26 : 7. I will bring a king of kings f. t. n.
Am. 8:12. shall wander f. t. n. to east
Zch. 2:6. and flee f. the land of t. n.
Lu. 13:29. come f. t. n. and sit down

NORTHERN.
Je. 15 : 12. break n. iron, and steel
Jo. 2:20. I will remove the n. army

NORTHWARD. [27.
Ge. 13:14. look n. and eastw., De. 3:
Ex. 40 : 22. tabern. n. without vail
Le. 1 : 11. kill it on side of altar n.
Nu. 3 : 35. pitch on side of tab. n.
De. 2 : 3. ye compassed mt., turn n.
Jos. 13 : 3. borders went n., 15:7, 8, 11.-17 : 10.-18 : 18, 19. [thah
Ju. 12 : 1. went n. said unto Jeph-
1 S. 14 : 5. front of one rock was n.
1 Ch. 26:14. Zechariah's lot came n.
17. n. were four Levites a day
Eze. 8 : 5. n. was image of jealousy
40: 19. 100 cubits eastward and n.

Eze.47 : 2. he bro-t me out of gate **n.**
17. Damascus and north **n.**, 48: 1.
48: 31. three gates **n.** one of Reuben
Da. 8 : 4. saw ram pushing **n.**

NORTHWEST.

Ac. 27 : 12. Crete, lieth tow. **n.** and

NOSE, NOSES.

Le. 21: 18. hath flat **n.** sh. not offer
De. 33 : † 10. put incense at thy **n.**
2 K. 19 : 28. hook in thy **n.**, Is. 37: 29.
Jb. 40 : 24. his **n.** pierceth snares
41: 2. Canst put a hook into his **n.**
Ps. 115: 6. **n**-s have they, smell not
Pr. 30: 33. wringing of the **n.** bring-
eth blood ⌈Lebanon
Can. 7 : 4. thy **n.** is as the tower of
8. smell of thy **n.** like apples
Is. 65: 5. These are smoke in my **n.**
Eze. 8: 17. put the branch to their **n.**
23 : 25. shall take thy **n.** and ears
39 : 11. it shall stop **n**-s of passen-

NOSE jewels. ⌊gers

Is. 3: 21. L. will take away. rings and

NOSTRILS. ⌊n. j.

Ge. 2 : 7. G. breathed into man's **n.**
7 : 22. All in whose **n.** was breath
Ex. 15 : 8. with blast of thy **n.** ⌊died
Nu. 11 : 20. eat till it come out at **n.**
2 S. 22: 9. smoke of his **n.**, Ps. 18: 8.
16. of breath of his **n.**, Ps. 18: 15.
Jb. 4: 9. by breath of his **n.** consum.
27 : 3. the spirit of G. is in my **n.**
39: 20. the glory of his **n.** is terrible
41 : 20. Out of his **n.** goeth smoke
Is. 2: 22. man, whose breath is in **n.**
La. 4 : 20. breath of our **n.** taken
Am. 4 : 10. stink of camps into **n.**

NOT.

Ge. 19 : 18. Lot said, Oh **n.** so my L.
29 : 26. **n.** be so done in our coun.
48 : 18. **n.** so my fa. this is firstb.
Ex. 10: 11. **n.** so, go ye that are men
17 : 7. Is the Lord am. us or **n.**?
Ju. 2 : 17. but they did **n.** so ⌈n. so
14: 15. Is it **n.** so? | 1 S. 20: 2. it is
2 S. 20 : 21. matter is **n.** so ⌈G.
23: 5. Altho. my house be **n.** so with
2 K. 2 : 10. but if **n.** it sh. **n.** be so
Jb. 9 : 35. but it is **n.** so with me
24 : 25. if **n.** so, who make me liar
35 : 15. bec. it is **n.** so he visited
Ps. 115 : 1. **n.** unto us, O L. **n.** unto
Je. 31: 15. bec. they were **n.**, Mat. 2:
48 : 30. it sh. **n.** be so, his lies ⌊18.
Am. 7 : 3. it shall **n.** be, saith Lord
Mat. 16 : 22. L. this **n.** be unto thee
19 : 8. from beginning it was **n.** so
20: 26. it shall **n.** be so among you,
Mk. 10 : 43. ⌈to me
25: 45. did it **n.** to one of these, **n.**
26 : 39. **n.** as I will but, Mk. 14: 36.
Lu. 22 : 26. But ye shall **n.** be so
58. Pe. said, Man, I am **n.** ⌈have
Jn. 14 : 2. if it were **n.** so, I would
Ac. 10 : 14. Pe. said, **n.** so, L., 11: 8.
13 : 25. think I am? I am **n.** he
Ro. 5 : 3. **n.** only so, we glory, 11.
2 Co. 8: 5. **n.** acc. to that he hath **n.**
Ph. 2: 27. **n.** on him only but on me
2 Ti. 4: 8. **n.** to me only but unto th.
Ja. 3 : 10. things ought **n.** so to be
4 : 2. Ye lust and have **n.**
Re. 19 : 10. See thou do it **n.**, 22: 9.
See ABLE, AFRAID, ALLOW,
ANSWERED, ASHAMED, BE-
LIEVE, ED, COME, CONFOUND-
ED, DARE, DEPARTED, DE-
STROY, DIE, EAT, ENTER,
FAINT, FEAR, FEW, FIND,
FORSAKEN, GIVE, GIVEN,
GIVETH, GOOD, HEAR, HEARK-
EN, HID, IS, KNEW, KNOW,
KNOWETH, KNOWING, KNOWN,
LEAVE, LIVE, LOVE, OBEY,
OBEYED, ONE, PASS, RETURN,
SEE, SEEK, SLEEP, SPEAK,
TAUGHT, WILL, WOULD, EST.

NOTABLE. ⌈eyes

Da. 8 : 5. goat had a **n.** horn betw.
8. for it came up four **n.** ones, tow.
Mat. 27: 16. had then a **n.** prisoner
Ac. 2: 20. bef. that **n.** day of L. come
4: 16. a **n.** miracle hath been done

NOTE. [Noun.]

Ro. 16: 7. who are of **n.** am. apostles

NOTE, NOTED.

Is. 30 : 8. Now go, **n.** it in a book
Da. 10 : 21. that is **n**-d in Scripture
of truth ⌈company
2 Th. 3 : 14. **n.** that man, have no

NOTHING. ⌈them

Ge. 11 : 6. **n.** will be restrained fr.
19 : 8. only unto these men do **n.**
26: 29. done unto thee **n.** but good
40 : 15. have I done **n.** to put me
Ex. 9: 4. **n.** die that is chil.'s of Isr.
12: 10. let **n.** of it remain until morn.
20. Ye shall eat **n.** leavened in
16 : 18. had **n.** over, 2 Co. 8 : 15.
22: 3. if have **n.** he be sold for theft
23 : 26. shall **n.** cast their young
Nu. 6: 4. eat **n.** that is made of vine
16 : 26. touch **n.** of theirs, lest ye
22 : 16. Let **n.** hinder from coming
De. 2 : 7. hast lacked **n.**, Ne. 9 : 21.
20 : 16. thou shalt save alive **n.**
22: 26. unto damsel thou shalt do **n.**
28 : 55. hath **n.** left him in siege
Jos. 11 : 15. Joshua left **n.** undone
Ju. 2: †19. let **n.** fall of own doings
3 : 2. at least such as bef. knew **n.**
14 : 6. rent him and had **n.** in ha.
1 S. 3 : 18. Sam. told, and hid **n.**
20 : 2. my fa. will do **n.** but shew
22: 15. thy serv. knew **n.** of all this
25 : 21. that **n.** was missed, 30: 19.
36. she told him **n.** less or more
2 S. 12: 3. poor man had **n.** save lamb
24: 24. not offer of that cost me **n.**
1 K. 4 : 27. victuals, they lacked **n.**
8 : 9. There was **n.** in the ark save
10: 21. silver was **n.** accounted of in
11 : 22. he ans-d **n.**, Lu. 22: 35. ⌈15.
22: 16. tell me **n.** but truth, 2 Ch. 18:
2 K. 10 : 10. fall **n.** to earth of word
20 : 13. **n.** in house he shewed not
17. **n.** shall be left, Is. 39 : 2, 6.
2 Ch. 9: 2. **n.** hid from Solomon which
he told her not ⌈ing
Ezr. 4: 3. **n.** to do with us in build-
Ne. 5 : 8. they found **n.** to answer
12. We will restore, and require **n.**
8: 10. portions for wh. **n.** is prepared
9: 21. sustained, so that they lacked
Es. 2 : 15. Esther required **n.** ⌊n.
5 : 13. Yet all this availeth me **n.**
6 : 10. let **n.** fail of all hast spoken
Jb. 6 : 18. they go to **n.** and perish
21. For ye are **n.**
8 : 9. we are of yesterday, know **n.**
24 : 25. make my speech **n.** worth
26: 7. he hangeth the earth upon **n.**
34 : 9. said, It profiteth a man **n.**
that he delight hims. with God
Ps. 17 : 3. hast tried me and find **n.**
39: 5. mine age is as **n.** before thee
49: 17. dieth, he shall carry **n.** aw.
119: 165. love thy law, **n.** sh. offend
Pr. 9: 13. foolish woman knoweth **n.**
10 : 2. Treasures of wickedn. profit
13 : 4. desireth, hath **n.**, 20: 4. ⌊n.
7. maketh hims. rich, yet hath **n.**
22: 27. If thou hast **n.** to pay ⌈to it
Ec. 3: 14. God doeth, **n.** can be put
5 : 15. he sh. take **n.** of his labour
6: 2. that he wanteth **n.** for his soul
7: 14. that man sho. find **n.** aft. him
Is. 34: 12. all her princes shall be **n.**
40 : 17. nations bef. him are as **n.**
counted less than **n.**, 41 : 29.
23. bringeth princes to **n.**, 41 : 11,
43: †10. bef. me was **n.** formed ⌊12.
Je. 10: 24. anger, lest bring me to **n.**
32 : 23. done **n.** of all thou com-st
Je. 38: 14. I will ask, hide **n.** from me
39: 10. of poor which had **n.** in Jud.
42: 4. I will keep **n.** back from you
50: 26. destroy, let **n.** of her be left
La. 1 : 12. Is it **n.** to you, all ye ⌈n.
Eze. 13 : 3. prophets that have seen
Da. 4: 35. all inhab-s of earth as **n.**
9: †26. Messiah be cut off, sh. have
Jo. 2 : 3. **n.** shall escape them ⌊n.
Am. 3: 4. yo. lion cry if he taken **n.**?
5. taken up snare, and taken **n.**
7. Surely Lord God will do **n.**
Hag. 2: 3. is it in comparison as **n.**?
Zch. 8: † 10. hire of man became **n.**
Mat. 15: 32. they have **n.** to eat,
Mk. 6: 36.—8: 1, 2. ⌈you, Lu. 1: 37.
17: 20. **n.** shall be impossible unto
21 : 19. **n.** thereon but leaves, Mk.
26: 62. Answerest thou **n.**? ⌊11: 13.
27 : 12. he answered **n.**, Mk. 14:
60, 61.—15 : 3, 4, 5. Lu. 23 : 9.
19. Have **n.** to do with just man
24. Pilate saw he co. prevail **n.**
Mk. 1 : 44. See thou say **n.** to any
5 : 26. spent all, was **n.** bettered
6: 8. sho. take **n.** for journey, Lu. 9: 3.
9: 29. come forth by **n.** but prayer
Lu. 4 : 2. in those days he did eat **n.**
5: 5. all night and tak. **n.**, Jn. 21: 3.
7 : 42. had **n.** to pay, he forgave
8 : 17. **n.** secret that shall not be
10: 19. **n.** sh. by any means hurt you
11 : 6. I have **n.** to set before him
23 : 15. **n.** worthy of death is done
unto him, Ac. 23 : 29.—25 : 25.—
26 : 31. ⌈n.
35. lacked ye anything? They say
41. this man hath done **n.** amiss
Jn. 3: 27. man can receive **n.** except
4: 11. Sir, thou hast **n.** to draw with
5: 19. Son can do **n.** of himself, 30.
6 : 12. gather, that **n.** be lost
39. of all given me I sho. lose **n.**
63. Spirit quickeneth, the flesh
profiteth **n.** ⌈myself
7: 26. they say **n.** | 8: 28. I do **n.** of
9 : 33. If not of God, he could do **n.**
11 : 49. Ye know **n.** at all ⌈n.?
12 : 19. Perceive ye how ye prevail
14 : 30. prince of world hath **n.** in
15: 5. without me ye can do **n.** ⌊me
16: 23. in that day ye sh. ask me **n.**
24. Hitherto asked **n.** in my name
18 : 20. in secret have I said **n.**
21 : 3. that night they caught **n.**
Ac. 4 : 14. they could say **n.** ag. it
21. finding **n.** how might punish
10: 20. go, doubting **n.**, 11: 12. ⌊th.
11: 8. **n.** common or uncl. hath at
19 : 36. ye ought to do **n.** rashly
20 : 20. I kept back **n.** profitable
21 : 24. all may know those are **n.**
23 : 14. eat **n.** until we slain Paul
27: 33. ye fasting, having taken **n.**
28: 17. I have committed **n.** ag. peo.
1 Co. 1 : 19. bring to **n.** underst-g of
4 : 4. I know **n.** by myself
5. judge **n.** before the time
8 : 2. knoweth **n.** yet as he ought
9: 16. tho. I preach, I **n.** to glory of
13: 2. not charity, I am **n.**, 2 Co. 12:
3. not charity, it profiteth **n.** ⌊11.
2 Co. 6: 10. having **n.** yet possessing
8 : 15. gathered much had **n.** over
13 : 8. we can do **n.** ag. the truth
Ga. 2 : 6. conference added **n.** to me
4: 1. heir when child, differeth **n.** fr.
5 : 2. C. shall profit you **n.** ⌊serv.
Ph. 2: 3. Let **n.** be done thro. strife
1 Ti. 4 : 4. creature good, **n.** to be re-
5: 21. doing **n.** by partiality ⌊fused
6: 4. He is proud, knowing **n.** ⌈out
7. we bro-t **n.** and can carry **n.**
Tit. 3 : 13. th. **n.** be wanting ⌈do **n.**
Phm. 14. without thy mind wo. I
He. 2: 8. he left **n.** th. is not put und.
7: 14. Mo. spake **n.** conc-g priesth.

He. 7 : 19. For law made n. perfect
Ja. 1 : 4. be perfect, wanting n. [ing
6. let him ask in faith, n. waver-
3 Jn.7.went, taking n. of the Gent.
For NOTHING. [f. n.
Ex.21:2.7th yr. he shall go out free
Is. 44:10. an image profitable f. n.
Je. 13 : 7. girdle profitable f. n., 10.
Mat. 5:13. unsavoury salt good f.n.
Lu. 6 : 35. do good lend, hoping f.n.
Ph.4:6.be careful f.n.but by prayer
In NOTHING. [n. else
Ac. 17 : 21. Athenians spent time i.
2 Co. 7:9. receive damage by us i.n.
12 : 11. i. n. am I behind chiefest,
though I be n. [be ashamed
Ph. 1 : 20. my hope, that i. n. I sh.
28. i. n. terrified by your adver-
Is NOTHING. [saries
Nu. 11 : 6. i. n. besides this manna
Ju. 7:14. i. n. save sword of Gideon
1 S. 27 : 1. i. n. better than I escape
1 K. 18 : 43. he said, There i. n.
2 K. 20 : 15. there i. n. among my
treas., Is. 39 : 4. [with many
2 Ch.14:11. it i. n.with thee to help
Ne. 2 : 2. this i. n. else but sorrow
Es. 6 : 3. There i. n. done for him
Ps. 19 : 6. i. n. hid from the heat
Pr. 8:8. there i. n. froward in them
Ec.2:24. i.n. better for a man,3:22.
5:14. begetteth son, i.n. in his ha.
Je. 32 : 17. i. n. too hard for thee
Mat. 10 : 26. i. n. covered sh. not be
revealed, Mk. 4 : 22. Lu. 12 : 2.
23 : 16. swear by temple, it i. n.
18. Whoso. swear by altar, it i. n.
Mk.7:15. i. n. from without defileth
Jn. 8:54. honour mys., honour i. n.
Ro. 14 : 14. i. n. unclean of itself
1 Co. 7:19. Circ-n i. n. uncirc-n i.n.
8 : 4. we know that an idol i. n.
Ga. 6 : 3. he i. n. he deceiveth hims.
Tit. 1: 15. to them defiled i. n. pure
Of NOTHING. [work
Is. 41:24. Behold, ye are o.n. your
1 Th. 4 : 12. ye may have lack o. n.
Re.3:17. I am rich, have need o. n.
NOTICE.
2 S. 3 : 36. took n. of it, and it
2 Co. 9:5. bounty whereof ye had n.
NOTWITHSTANDING.
Ex. 16 : 20. n. they hearkened not
unto Moses, 1 S.2:25. 2 K.17:14.
21:21. n. if he continue day or two
De. 1 : 26. n. ye would not go up
1 K. 11:12. n. in thy days I will not
Je. 35:14. n. I have spok. unto you
Mat. 2 : 22. n. being warned of God
11:11. n. he that is least in kingd.
17 : 27. n. lest we should offend
Lu. 10:11. n. be sure kingd. is come
20.n.in this rejoice not th.spirits
Ph. 1 : 18. n. whether in pretence or
4 : 14. n. ye have well done
1 Ti. 2 : 15. n. she shall be saved
in childbearing
2 Ti. 4 : 17. n. L. stood wi. me [ful
Ja.2:26.n. ye give not things need-
Re. 2 : 20. n. I have few things ag.
NOUGHT. [thee
Ge.29:15.shouldest serve me for n.?
De. 13:17. cleave n. of cursed thing
15:9. poor bro., thou givest him n.
28:63.L. rejoice to bring you to n.
Ne. 4 : 15. G. brought counsel to n.
Jb. 1 : 9. Doth Job fear God for n.?
8 : 22. place of wicked come to n.
14 : 18. mt. falling cometh to n.
22 : 6. taken pledge fr. bro. for n.
Ps. 33:10. L. bringeth counsel to n.
44:2.thou sellest thy people for n.
Pr. 1:25. have set at n. my counsel
Is. 8:10.Take counsel, it come to n.
29:20.terrible one is brought to n.
21. turn aside just for thing of n.
41:12.they shall be as a thing of n.
Is.41:24.ye are of noth.,your work of
49:4. spent my strength for n. [n.
52:3.Ye have sold yourselves for n.
5. my people is taken away for n.
Je. 14 : 14. false vision, a thing of n.
Am.5:5. and Beth-el sh. come to n.
6:13. ye wh. rejoice in thing of n.
Mal. 1 : 10. Who wo. shut doors for
n.? nei.kindle fire on alt.for n.
Mk.9:12.must be set at n.,Lu.23:11.
Ac. 4 : 11. This is stone set at n.
5 : 36. all scattered and bro-t to n.
38. if of men, it will come to n.
19:27.craft in danger to be set at n.
Ro. 14 : 10. why set at n. thy bro.?
1 Co. 1:28. to bring to n. things th.
2:6. wisdom of world cometh to n.
2 Th. 3 : 8. Nei. any man's br. for n.
Re.18:17.hour so gr. riches come to
NOURISH. [n.
Ge.45:11. there will I n. thee,50:21.
Is.7:21.that man shall n.young cow
23:4.nor do I n.up young men nor
44 : 14. an ash, the rain doth n. it
NOURISHED.
Ge. 47:12. Joseph n. his father and
2 S.12:3.lamb wh.he bought and n.
Is. 1:2. I have n. and bro-t up chil.
Eze. 19 : 2. n. her whelps am. lions
Ac.7:20.n. in father's house 3 mo-s
21. Pha.'s dau. n. him for her son
12:20. their country was n. by k.'s
1 Ti. 4 : 6. n. up in words of faith
Ja. 5 : 5. n. your hearts as in day of
Re. 12 : 14. n. for a time, times, and
NOURISHER, S. [age
Ru. 4 : 15. He shall be n. of thy old
2 K. 10:†1. Jehu sent to the n-s of
Ahab's childr. [and queens
Is. 49 : † 23. kings shall be thy n-s
Je. 46 : † 25. I will punish n. of No
NOURISHETH, ING.
Da.1:5. n-g them to stand bef.king
Na. 3 : †8. thou better than n-g No?
Ep.5:29.n-h his flesh, as L. the ch.
NOURISHMENT.
Col. 2 : 19. body by joints having n.
NOVICE. [pride
1 Ti. 3:6. not a n. lest lifted up with
NOW.
See BEHOLD, HEAR, IF.
NOWADAYS. [away
1 S. 25 : 10. many serv-s n. break
NUMBER, S. [Noun.]
Ge.34:30.few in n. they sh. slay me
41:49. much, for it was without n.
Ex. 12 : 4. lamb acc. to n. of souls
16:16.manna, acc. to n. of persons
30 : 12. chil. of Israel aft. their n.
Le. 25 : 15. n. of yrs. aft. jubilee, n.
of years of fruits, 16, 50, 52.
26:22.beasts,sh.make you few in n.
Nu. 3:22. n. of males from a month
old, 28, 34, 40, 43.
48. odd n. of them is to be redeemed unto Aaron
14 : 29. whole n. from 20 years old
15 : 12. Acc. to n. ye sh. prepare,
do to ev. one acc. to their n.
23:10.Who can count the n. of Isr.
29 : 18. offerings shall be acc. to
their n., 21, 24, 27, 30, 33, 37.
31:36.half of their portion was in n.
De 4:27. few in n. am. heathen, 28:
7:7. more in n. than any peo. [62.
25:2.cause him to be beaten by n.
32:8. bounds acc. to the n. of Isr.
Jos. 4 : 5. ev. man a stone, acc. unto
Ju.6:5. camels with-t n.,7:12. [n. 8.
7 : 6. n. of them lapped were 300
21:23.acc-g to n.of them th.danced
1 S. 6 : 4. n. of the lords of Philis.
18. to n. of all cities of Philis.
27 : † 7. n. of days David dwelt in
2 S. 2 : 15. went over by n. twelve
21 : 20. fingers and toes 24 in n.
24 : 2. that I may know n. of peo.
2 S. 24:9. Joab gave sum of n. of the
people, 1 Ch.21:2, 5. [acc. to n.
1 K. 18 : 31. Elijah took 12 stones,
1 Ch. 7 : 2. whose n. in days of Da.
9.n. of them after genealogy, 40.
11 : 11. n. of mighty men Da. had
12:23.these are the n-s of the bands
16:†19.,but men of n. even a few
22 : 16. of gold and silver, is no n.
23:3.n.by their polls, man by man
24. counted by n. of names
† 27. Levites n. from twenty
31. offer on the set feasts by n.
25 : 1. and the n. of workmen
7. the n. instructed in the songs
27:1. their n., to wit, the chief fa-s
23. Da.took not the n.of them,20.
2 Ch.12.3.people with-t n.that came
17 : 14. these are the n-s of them
26:11.acc.to the n.of their account
12. whole n. of chief of fathers
29:32.the n. of the burnt offerings
30:24. great n. of priests sanctified
35:7.all present to the n. of 30,000
Ezr.1:9. this is the n. of the vessels
2 : 2. n. of men of Isr., Ne. 7 : 7.
3:4.offered daily burnt off-gs by n.
6 : 17. he goats, acc. to n. of tribes
8 : 34. By n. and weight of ev. one
Es.9:11.n.of those slain in Shushan
Jb. 1 : 5. Job offered acc. to n. of all
5 : 9. marvellous things without
n., 9 : 10. [pressor
15 : 20. n. of years is hidden to op-
16:†22. when years of n. are come,
25:3. Is there any n. of his armies
31 : 37. wo. declare n. of my steps
34:24. in pieces mighty men with-t
36: 26. nei n. of y-rs searched [n.
Ps. 71 : 15. I know not n-s thereof
105:12. When but a few men in n.
34.caterpillars,and that with-t n.
139 : 18. are more in n. than sand
147:4.He telleth the n.of the stars
†5. of his understanding is no n.
Ec. 2 : † 3. n. of days of their life,
5 : † 18.-6 : † 12. [without n.
Can. 6 : 8. are queens and virgins
Is.10:†19. rest of the trees sh. be n.
21:17. residue of n. of archers [n.
40 : 26. bringeth out their host by
65 : 11. furnish drink off-g unto n.
Je.2:28. as n. of cities are thy gods
11:13.to n.of thy cities,n.of streets
44:28.a small n. that escape sword
Eze.5:3.Thou shalt take a few in n.
12 : † 16. leave men in n. fr. sword
43 : † 10. let th. measure n. [y-rs
Da. 9:2. I understood by books n. of
Ho.1:10.n. of Isr. as sand,Ro.9:27.
Jo.1:6. nation is come up with-t n.
Na. 3 : 3. there is gr. n. of carcasses
Mk. 10 : 46. disci. and gr. n. of peo.
Lu. 22:3. Judas, of n. of the twelve
Jn. 6 : 10. men in n. 5,000, Ac. 4:4.
Ac. 5 : 36. to Theudas a n. of men
6:1. n. of disci. was multiplied, 7.
11:21.a gr. n. believed and turned
16:5.churches were increased in n.
2 Co. 10 : 12. dare not make ourselves of the n. [into the n.
1 Ti. 5 : 9. Let not a widow be taken
Re.5:11. n. was 10,000 times 10,000
7: 4. n. of them which were sealed
9 : 16. n. of the army of horsemen
13:17.n. of his name | 18.count n.
18. it is n. of a man, his n.is 666
15 : 2. had victory over n. of beast
20 : 8. n. of Gog is as sand of sea
See **DAYS, Thy DAYS.**
See MONTHS, NAMES.
NUMBER. [Verb.]
Ge. 13:16. if a man can n. the dust
15:5.tell stars,if be able to n.them
Le. 15 : 13. he shall n. 7 days for
28. she shall n. 7 days [cleansing
23:16. aft. 7th sab. shall n. 50 days

Le. 25 : 8. shalt n. 7 sabb-s of years
Nu. 1 : 3. Aaron n. them by armies
49. thou shalt not n. tribe of Levi
3:15. n. chil. of Levi fr. month old
40. n. all firstborn of males of Isr.
4:23. until 50 years old n. them, 30.
29. sons of Merari thou shalt n.
37. Moses and Aaron did n., 41.
De. 16:9. Seven weeks n. begin to n.
1 S. 14 : 17. n. and see who is gone
2 S. 24 : 1. Go n. Israel and Judah
2. Go n. the people, 4. 1 Ch. 21:2.
1 K. 20 : 25. n. army like army lost
1 Ch. 21:1. provoked David to n. Isr.
27 : 24. Joab began to n. finished
Jb. 38 : 37. Who can n. clouds ⌊not
39 : 2. Canst thou n. the months
Ps. 90:12. So teach us to n. our days
Is. 65:12. will I n. you to the sword
Re. 7:9. multitude no man could n.

NUMBERED.

Ge. 13:16. then shall thy seed be n.
16:10. sh. not be n. for mult, 32:12.
Ex. 30:13. among them th. are n., 14.
38:25. that were n. of congr-n, 26.
Nu. 1:19. he n. them in the wildern.
21. Those that were n. of them,
23, 25, 27, 29, 31, 33, 35, 37, 39,
41, 43, 44, 46.–2 : 4, 13, 15, 19,
21, 23, 26, 28, 30.–3 : 22, 34, 43.
–4 : 36, 40, 44, 48.–26 : 7, 18, 22,
25, 27, 34, 37, 41, 43, 47, 50, 62.
47. Levites were not n., 2 : 33.
2:9. all that were n. in camp of Jud.
16. n. of Reuben | 24. n. of Ephr.
31. n. of Dan | 3:16. Mo. n. them,
3:39. n. of Levites were 22,000 ⌊42.
4:34. n. of sons of Kohathites, 37.
38. were n. of Gershonites, 41.
42. were n. of sons of Merari, 45.
45. whom Mo. and Aaron n., 46.
7:2. princes over them that were n.
14:29. fell in wilder all that were n.
26:51. These were n. of chil. of Isr.
54. inher. given acc. to those n.
57. n. of Levites | 63. Moses n.
Jos. 8:10. Joshua rose early n. peo.
Ju. 20:15. chil. of Benjamin were n.
17. Isr. besides Benjamin were n.
21:9. peo. were n. and behold none
1 S. 11:8. Saul n. them in Bezek, 13:15
14 : 17. when they had n. behold
15:4. Saul n. peo. in Telaim ⌊Jona.
2 S. 18 : 1. David n. the people ⌈peo.
24:10. Da.'s heart smote after he n.
1 K. 3 : 8. people that cannot be n.
8 : 5. oxen c'd not be n., 2 Ch. 5:6.
20 : 15. n. princes of provinces
26. Benhadad n. the Syrians
27. Israel were n. and like 2 flocks
2 K. 3 : 6. king Jehoram n. all Isr.
1 Ch. 21:17. I com-d people to be n.
23:3. Levites were n. fr. 30 years, 27.
2 Ch. 2:17. Solomon n. all strangers
25:5. he n. them from 20 years old
Ezr. 1 : 8. Cyrus n. the vessels to
Ps. 40 : 5. are more than can be n.
Ec. 1:15. that is wanting can-t be n.
Is. 22 : 10. have n. houses of Jerus.
53 : 12. he was n. with transgressors, Mk. 15:28. ⌈cannot be n.
Je. 33 : 22. as the host of heaven,
Da. 5:26. God hath n. thy kingdom
Ho. 1 : 10. as sand, wh. cannot be n.
Mat. 10:30. hairs of head all n., Lu.
Ac. 1 : 17. he was n. with us ⌊12:7.
26. Matthias was n. with 11 apos-

NUMBEREST. ⌊tles

Ex. 30:12. give ev. man ransom when
thou n. th. no plague when n.
Jb. 14: 16. For now thou n. my steps

NUMBERING. ⌈left n.

Ge. 41 : 49. gathered corn until he
2 Ch. 2 : 17. after the n. wh w. David

NUN=NON. ⌈7 : †27.

Nu. 13:8. Oshea son of N., 16. 1 Ch.
See **JOSHUA.**

NURSE. [Noun.] ⌈n.

Ge. 24:59. they sent away Rebek. and
35 : 8. Deborah, Rebekah's n. died
Ex. 2 : 7. Shall I call a n. of Hebrew
Ru. 4:16. Naomi took child, became n
2 S. 4 : 4. his n. took him and fled
2 K. 11:2. hid him and n., 2 Ch. 22:
Ac. 13 :† 18. as n. beareth child ⌊11.
1 Th 2:7. as n. cherisheth her child

NURSE, ED, ING.

Ex. 2 : 7. that she may n. the child
9. Take this child, n. it for me,
woman took child, and n-d it
Nu. 11:12. Carry them as n-g father
Is. 49 : 23. kings be n-g fathers,
queens n-g mothers
60:4. dau-s shall be n-d at thy side

NURTURE.

Ep. 6 : 4. bring them up in n. of L.

NUTS.

Ge. 43:11. carry present, n. almonds
Can. 6 : 11. I went into garden of n.

NYM'PHAS. ⌈house

Col. 4 : 15. Salute N. and ch. in his

O.

See **O GOD, O ISRAEL, O JACOB, O JERUSALEM,** OH.

OAK.

Ge. 35:4. Jacob hid the gods under o.
8. Deborah was buried under an o.
Jos. 24:26. and set it up under an o.
Ju. 6:11. angel of L. sat under o., 19.
9:†6. made Abimele. k. by the o.
2 S. 18:9. Abs.'s mule went under o.
10. Absalom hanged in an o.
14. Abs. alive in midst of the o.
1 K. 13:14. found man of G. und. an o
1 Ch. 10:12. buried und. o. in Jabesh
Is. 1 : 30. be as o. whose leaf fadeth
6:13. teil tree, or o. whose substance
44:14. he taketh o. to make a god
Eze. 6:13. their idols under ev. thick

OAKS. ⌊o.

Is. 1:29. ashamed of the o. ye desired
2 : 13. day of L. upon o. of Bashan
57 :† 5. inflaming yours. among o.
Eze. 27:6. Of o. of Bashan made oars
Ho. 4 : 13. burn incense under o.
Am. 2 : 9. Amorite was strong as o.
Zch. 11 : 2. howl, O ye o. of Bashan

OAR, OARS.

Is. 33:21. shall go no galley with o-s
Eze. 27 : 6. Of oaks of Bashan made
29. that handle the o. shall cry ⌊o-s

OATH, OATHS. ⌈41.

Ge. 24:8. shalt be clear from my o.,
26 : 3. I will perform the o. which
I sware unto Abraham, De. 7:8.
Ps. 105 : 9. Jer. 11 : 5. ⌈and thee
28. Let there be an o. betwixt us
50:25. Jo. took an o. of chil. of Isr.
Ex. 22 : 11. o. of L. shall be betw. us
Le. 5:4. man sh. pronounce wi. an o.
Nu. 5:19. priest sh. charge her by o.
21. L. make thee an o. among peo.
30 : 2. If man swear o. to bind soul,
13. ev. binding o. afflict soul ⌊10.
De. 29: 12. o. Lord maketh with thee
14. nei. with you only make o.
Jos. 2:17. We blameless of thine o., 20
9:20. lest wrath be on us, bec. of o.
Ju. 21:5. Israel had make a great o.
1 S. 14:26. peo. feared the o., 28. ⌈28.
27. Saul charged them with t. o.,
2 S. 21:7. spared Mephib-h, bec. of o.
1 K. 2:43. Why hast not kept o. of L.?
8:31. o. be laid upon him, and o.
come bef. thine altar, 2 Ch. 6:
18:10. he took an o. of kingd. ⌊22.
2 K. 11:4. Jehoiada took o. of them
1 Ch. 16:16. mindful of o. unto Isaac
2 Ch. 15 : 15. all Jud. rejoiced at o.
Ne. 5 : 12. Neh. took o. of priests
10 : 29. an o. to walk in G.'s law
Ec. 8 : 2. in regard of o. of God
9:2. sweareth, as he th. feareth o.
Eze. 16 : 59. hast despised o., 17:18,
17:13. hath taken an o. of him ⌊19.
16. king, whose o. he despised ⌈o-s
21:23. divination to th. have sworn
Da. 9:11. o. written in law of Moses
Ha. 3 : 9. bow naked acc. to o-s
Zch. 8:17. love no false o. this I hate
Mat. 5:33. perform unto L. thine o-s
14 : 7. he promised with o. to give
9. for the o.'s sake, Mk. 6 : 26.
26 : 72. again he denied with an o.
Lu. 1 : 73. o. he sware to our father
Ac. 2 : 30. God had sworn with an o.
23:†12. bound wi. o. of execration
21. have bound thems. wi. an o.
He. 6 : 16. o. for confirmation is an
17. God confirmed it by an o.
7:20. not with-t o. made priest, 21.
28. o. which was since the law
Ja. 5 : 12. swear not by any other o.

OBADI'AH. ⌈L.

1 K. 18 : 3. Ahab called O., O. feared
4. O. took 100 prophets and hid
5. Ahab said unto O., Go into land
6. O. went another way by hims.
7. as O. was in the way, Elijah met
16. So O. went to meet Ahab, and
1 Ch. 8 : 21. sons of O. ⌈Azel, 9 : 44.
7:3. son of Izraiah, O. | 8:38. son of
9:16. O. the son of Shemaiah ⌈sec.
12 : 9. of Gadites men of might, O.
27 : 19. Ishmaiah son of O.
2 Ch. 17 : 7. he sent to O. to teach
34:12. overseers were Jahath and O.
Ezr. 8 : 9. O. son of Jehiel went up
Ne. 10:5. O. sealed | 12:25. O. porter
Ob. 1. vision of O., Thus saith L.

OBADI'AHU.

1 K. 18 : † 3. and Ahab called O.

O'BAL.

Ge. 10:28. Joktan begat O. Abimael

O'BED.

Ru. 4 : 17. they called his name O.
21. Boaz begat O., 1 Ch. 2:12. Mat.
1 : 5. ⌈begat
1 Ch. 2 : 37. Ephlal begat O. | 38. O.
11 : 47. valiant men were; O.
26 : 7. sons of Shemaiah, Othni, O.
2 Ch. 23: 1. Azariah son of O. into cov.
Lu. 3:32. Jesse, which was son of O.

O'BED-E'DOM.

2 S. 6:10. David carried ark into ho.
of O., 11. 1 Ch. 13 : 13, 14. ⌈14.
11. L. blessed ho. of O., 12. 1 Ch. 13:
12. David bro-t ark fr. house of
O. into city of Da., 1 Ch. 15:25.
1 Ch. 15:18. porters Mikneiah, O. ⌉
21. the singers, Mikneiah, O. ⌊24.
16 : 5. O. and Jeiel with psalteries
38. O. with breth., O. Hosah, port-
26:4. sons of O. for service, 8. ⌊ers
15. lot southw. fell to O. and sons
2 Ch. 25:24. Joash took vessels found

OBEDIENCE. ⌊with O.

2 S. 22:†45. Strangers sh. yield feigned
o. unto me, Ps. 18:†44–66:†3.
Ps 81 : † 15. haters of Lord should
have yielded feigned o.
Is. 11:†14. chil. of Ammon their o.
Ro. 1 : 5. for o. to faith am. nations
5:19. by o. of one sh. many be made
6:16. death, or of o. unto righte-n.
16:19. your o. is come abroad unto
26. known to all for o. of faith
1 Co. 14:34. women are to be under o.
2 Co. 7 : 15. he rememb-h o. of you
10:5. bringing ev. thought to o. of
6. when your o. is fulfilled ⌊C.
Phm. 21. Having confidence in thy o.
He. 5:8. learned o. by things suff-d
1 Pe. 1 : 2. sanctification of spirit to

OBEDIENT. ⌊o.

Ex. 24:7. Lord hath said, we will do,
and be o. ⌈Isr. be o.
Nu. 27 : 20. honour upon him, that

De. 4 : 30. if turn to L. and be o.
8 : 20. perish, bec. ye would not be
2 S. 22 : 45. Strangers shall be o. [o.
Pr. 25 : 12. wise reprover upon o. ear
Is. 1 : 19. if o. ye sh. eat good of land
42 : 24. nei. were they o. unto his law
Ac. 6 : 7. priests were o. to the faith
Ro. 15 : 18. to make Gent. o. by word
2 Co. 2 : 9. might know whe. ye be o.
Ep. 6 : 5. Servants, be o., Tit. 2 : 9.
Ph. 2 : 8. Ch. became o. unto death
Tit. 2 : 5. yo. women to be o. to husb.
1 Pe. 1 : 14. As o. chil. be ye holy

OBEISANCE. [my
Ge. 37 : 7. your sheaves made o. to
9. sun, moon, 11 stars made o. to
43 : 28. they made o. to Joseph [me
Ex. 18 : 7. Moses did o. to fa.inlaw
2 S. 1 : 2. Amalekite did o. to David
14 : 4. woman of Tekoah did o. to k.
15 : 5. when any man came to do o.
16 : †4. Ziba said, I do o. that I
1 K. 1 : 16. Bath-sheba did o. to Da.
2 Ch. 24 : 17. princes of Judah made

OBEY. [o. to k.
Ge. 27 : 8. my son, o. my voice, 13, 43.
Ex. 5 : 2. Who is L., that I sho. o. him?
19 : 5. if ye will o. my voice indeed
23 : 21. o. his voice, De. 13 : 4.-27 : 10.
-30 : 2, 8. 1 S. 12 : 14. [will be
22. if shalt indeed o. his voice I
De. 11 : 27. A blessing, if ye o. Lord
30 : 20. that thou mayest o. his voice
Jos. 24 : 24. Lord's voice will we o.
1 S. 8 : †9. Now o. unto their voice
19. peo. refused to o. voice of Sam.
15 : 22. to o. is better than sacrifice
Ne. 9 : 17. refused to o. nei. mindful
Jb. 36 : 11. If they o. and serve him
Ps. 18 : 44. As soon as they hear, sh. o.
Pr. 30 : 17. that despiseth to o. moth.
Is. 11 : 14. chil. of Ammon sh. o. th.
Je. 7 : 23. o. my voice, and I will be
your God, and ye sh., 11 : 4, 7.
26 : 13. amend your ways, and o.
voice of L., 38 : 20. Zch. 6 : 15.
35 : 14. Rechabites o. father's com-ts
42 : 6. we will o. voice of Lord, th.
it be well with us when we o.
Da. 7 : 27. all dominions shall o. him
Mat. 8 : 27. What manner of man is
this, that winds and sea o. him?
Mk. 4 : 41. Lu. 8 : 25.
Mk. 1 : 27. even unclean spirits o. him
Lu. 17 : 6. Be thou plucked up, it sh. o.
Ac. 5 : 29. ought to o. G. rather than
32. G. hath given to them that o.
Ro. 2 : 8. unto them th. o. unright-n.
6 : 12. that ye sho. o. it in the lusts
16. yield yours. servants to o., his
serv-ts ye are to wh. ye o. [20.
Ep. 6 : 1. Chil., o. your parents, Col. 3 :
Col. 3 : 22. Servants, o. your masters
Tit. 3 : 1. in mind to o. magistrates
He. 5 : 9. salvation to all that o. him
13 : 17. o. them that have the rule
Ja. 3 : 3. put bits, that they may o.

Not OBEY, OBEY not.
De. 11 : 28. a curse, if ye will n. o.
the commandments of Lord
your God, 28 : 62. 1 S. 12 : 15. Jb.
36 : 12. Je. 12 : 17.-18 : 10. [20.
21 : 18. wh. will n. o. voice of his fa.,
1 S. 15 : 19. Wh. didst thou n. o.?
Je. 42 : 13. if say, We will n. o. L.
Da. 9 : 11. they might n. o. thy voice
Ac. 7 : 39. whom our fathers wo. n. o.
Ro. 2 : 8. contentious, do n. o. truth
Ga. 3 : 1. who bewitched you, that ye
sho. n. o. ? 5 : 7. [n. gospel
2 Th. 1 : 8. taking veng. on them o.
3 : 14. if any man o. n. our word
1 Pe. 3 : 1. if any o. n. the word
4 : 17. what end of them o. n. gospel?

OBEYED.
Ge. 22 : 18. blessed, bec. hast o., 26 : 5.
28 : 7. Jacob o. his father and moth.
Jos. 22 : 2. have o. my voice in all
1 S. 15 : 20. Saul said, I have o. voice
24. bec. I feared peo., and o. voice
28 : 21. handmaid hath o. thy voice
1 Ch. 29 : 23. all Israel o. Solomon
2 Ch. 11 : 4. they o. the words of L.
Je. 34 : 10. they o. and let them go
35 : 8. we o. voice of Jonadab, 10.
18. Bec. ye o. com-t of your fath.
Da. 9 : 10. Nei. have we o. voice of L.
Hag. 1 : 12. people o. voice of Lord
Ac. 5 : 36. many as o. Theudas, 37.
Ro. 6 : 17. o. fr. heart that doctrine
Ph. 2 : 12. o. not in my pres. only
He. 11 : 8. by faith Abraham o. and
1 Pe. 3 : 6. Sarah o. Abraham, calling

Not OBEYED.
Jos. 5 : 6. consumed, bec. they o. n.
Ju. 2 : 2. ye n. o. my voice, 6 : 10.
1 K. 20 : 36. hast n. o. voice of Lord
2 K. 18 : 12. Bec. they o. n. voice of L.
Pr. 5 : 13. n. o. voice of my teachers
Je. 3 : 13. ye have n. o. my voice, 25.
-42 : 21.-43 : 4, 7.-44 : 23.
9 : 13. they have n. o. my voice, 11 :
8.-17 : 23.-32 : 23.-40 : 3. Da. 9 : 10,
Zph. 3 : 2. She o. n. the voice [14.
Ro. 10 : 16. have n. all o. the gospel
11 : †30. in times past have n. o. God

OBEYEDST.
1 S. 28 : 18. Bec. o. not the voice of L.
Je. 22 : 21. that thou o. not my voice

OBEYETH. [derst-g
Pr. 15 : † 32. o. reproof getteth un-
Is. 50 : 10. who o. voice of servant?
Je. 7 : 28. This a nation o. not Lord
11 : 3. Cursed be man that o. not

OBEYING. [so
Ju. 2 : 17. fathers o. L.; they did not
1 S. 15 : 22. in sacri., as in o. voi. of L.
1 Pe. 1 : 22. purified your souls in o.

O'BIL. [truth
1 Ch. 27 : 30. over camels was O. the

OBJECT. [Ishm.
Ac. 24 : 19. and o. if they had aught

OBLATION. [ag. me
Le. 2 : 4. o. of meat off-g, 5, 7, 13.
12. As for o. of firstfruits, ye sh.
3 : 1. if his o. be sacrifice of peace
7 : 14. sh. offer one out of whole o.
29. He sh. bring his o. unto Lord
22 : 18. offer his o. for all his vows
Nu. 18 : 9. ev. o. of theirs be holy
31 : 50. We have brought an o. for L.
Is. 19 : 21. Eg-s shall do o. unto L.
40 : 20. impoverished he hath no o.
66 : 3. offereth o. as if swine's flesh
Je. 14 : 12. offer o. I will not accept
Eze. 44 : 30. every o. sh. be priest's
45 : 1. when divide land, offer o.
6. o. of holy portion, 7.-48 : 18.
13. o. ye shall offer, 48 : 9, 20, 21.
16. give this o. for prince in Isr.
48 : 10. for priests sh. be holy o. | 12.
Da. 2 : 46. should offer an o. to Dan.
9 : 21. about the time of evening o.
27. shall cause sacr. and o. to cease

OBLATIONS. [o.
Le 7 : 38. he commanded Isr. to offer
2 Ch. 31 : 14. to distribute the o. of L.
Pr. 29 : † 4. man of o. overthrow-h
Is. 1 : 13. Bring no more vain o. [it
Eze. 20 : 40. I will require firstfr. of o.
44 : 30. ev. sort of o. sh. be priest's

O'BOTH. [33 : 43.
Nu. 21 : 10. chil. of Isr. pitched in O.,
11. journeyed from O., 33 : 44.

OBSCURE. [darkn.
Pr. 20 : 20. his lamp be put out in o.
22 † : 29. sh. not stand before o. men

OBSCURITY. [of o.
Is. 29 : 18. eyes of blind sh. see out
58 : 10. then sh. thy light rise in o.
59 : 9. we wait for light, but behold

OBSERVATION, S. [o.
Ex. 12 : †42. It is a night of o-s unto L.
Ne. 13 : † 14. my deeds done for o-s
Mal. 3 : †14. what profit we kept o.?
Lu. 17 : 20. kingdom of God not with

OBSERVE. [o.
Ex. 12 : 17. ye shall o. feast of unleav-d
bread, 24. De. 16 : 1. [of weeks
31 : 16. o. sabbath | 34 : 22. o. feast
34 : 11. o. that I command this
day, De. 12 : 28.-24 : 8. [times
Le. 19 : 26. nei. use enchant-s nor o.
37. o. all my statutes, 2 Ch. 7 : 17.
Ne. 1 : 5. Ps. 105 : 45. Eze. 37 : 24
Nu. 28 : 2. my sacrifice shall ye o.
De. 12 : 32. What I command, o. to do
16 : 13. o. feast of tabernacles
28 : 1. to o. and do all his com-ts
Jos. 1 : 8. mayest o. and do acc. to all
Ju. 13 : 14. All that I com-d let her o.
1 K. 20 : 33. men did diligently o.
Ps. 5 : † 8. those wh. o. me, 27 ; † 11.
54 : †5. reward evil unto those o. me
71 : †10. that o. my soul take counsel
107 : 43. Whoso is wise, and will o.
119 : 34. I sh. o. it wi. whole heart
Pr. 23 : 26. let thine eyes o. my ways
Je. 8 : 7. crane and swallow o. time
Eze. 20 : 18. nei. o. their judgments
Ho. 13 : 7. as leopard will I o. them
Jo. 2 : 8. th. o. lying vanities, forsake
Mat. 23 : 3. All they bid you o. that o.
28 : 20. Teaching th. to o. all things
Ac. 16 : 21. customs not lawful to o.
21 : 25. that Gentiles o. no such thing
Ga. 4 : 10. Ye o. days, and months
1 Ti. 5 : 21. o. these things without
preferring

See **Observe** with **DO.**

OBSERVED.
Ge. 37 : 11. his father o. the saying
Ex. 12 : 42. It is a night to be much o.
Nu. 15 : 22. erred, and not o. com-ts
De. 33 : 9. Levi o. thy word, kept
2 S. 11 : 16. when Joab o. city [law
2 K. 10 : † 31. Jehu o. not to walk in
21 : 6. Manasseh o. times, 2 Ch. 33 :
Ho. 14 : 8. I heard him, o. him [6.
Mk. 6 : 20. Herod feared Jn., o. him
10 : 20. all these have I o. from my

OBSERVER, S. [youth
De. 18 : 10. sh. not be found an o. of
times [o-s of times
De. 18 : 14. nations hearkened unto
Ps. 56 : †2. mine o-s wo. swallow me
59 : †10. me see my desire upon my

OBSERVEST, ETH. [o-s
Jb. 13 † : 27. thou o-t all my paths
Ec. 11 : 4. He th. o-h wind not sow
Is. 42 : 20. Seeing many things, but
thou o-t not [it unto L.
Ro. 14 : †6. He th. o-h. day, regardeth

OBSTINACY.
La. 3 : †65. Give them o. of heart

OBSTINATE.
De. 2 : 30. Lord made his heart o.
Is. 48 : 4. Bec. I knew thou art o.

OBTAIN. [her
Ge. 16 : 2. may be I may o. chil. by
Le. 25 : † 47. if his hand o. riches
1 Ch. 29 : †14. that we sho. o. strength
Pr. 8 : 35. shall o. favour of the L.
Is. 35 : 10. they shall o. joy, 51 : 11.
Da. 11 : 21. o. the kingd. by flatteries
Lu. 20 : 35. worthy to o. that world
Ro. 11 : 31. thro. mercy may o. mercy
1 Co. 9 : 24. So run that ye may o.
25. do it to o. corruptible crown
1 Th. 5 : 9. but to o. salvation by C.
2 Ti. 2 : 10. may o. salvation in C.
He. 4 : 16. that we may o. mercy
11 : 35. might o. a better resurrec-
Ja. 4 : 2. ye kill and cannot o. [tion

See **Obtain, ed FAVOUR.**

OBTAINED.
2 Ch. 2 : † 6. hath o. strength to
Ne. 13 : 6. I o. leave of king [build
Es. 2 : 9. Es. o. kindness | 17. grace
Ho. 1 : † 6. Call name, Not o. mercy
2 : 23. her, that had not o. mercy

Ac. 1 : 17. had o. part of ministry
22:28. With a gr. sum o. I freedom
26:22. Having o. help of G. I contin.
27 : 13. supposing they o. purpose
Ro. 11 : 7. Isr. hath not o. what he
seeketh, election hath o. it
30. ye o. mercy thro. their unbelief
1 Co. 7:25. as one th. hath o. mercy
Ep. 1 : 11. In wh. we o. inheritance
1 Ti. 1 : 13. I o. mercy, bec. I did it,
He. 1:4. o. a more excell. name ⌊16.
6 : 15. endured, he o. promises
8 : 6. o. a more excel. ministry
9:12. having o. eternal redemption
11:2. the elders o. a good report, 39.
4. Abel o. witness he was righte.
33. o. promises, stopped mouths
of lions ⌈now have o.
1 Pe. 2:10. which had not o. mercy,
2 Pe. 1:1. o. like precious faith wi. us

OBTAINETH.

See **Obtaineth FAVOUR.**

OBTAINING. ⌈Jes. C.
2 Th. 2 : 14. to o. of glory of our L.

OCCASION, S. ⌈us
Ge. 43 : 18. that he may seek o. ag.
De. 22 : 14. And give o-s of speech
against wife, 17. ⌈10 : 7.
Ju. 9 : 33. do as shalt find o., 1 S.
14:4. Samson sought o. ag. Philis.
2 S. 12:14. given great o. to enemies
Ezr. 7 : 20. shalt have o. to bestow
Jb. 33 : 10. he findeth o-s ag. me
Je. 2:24. in her o. who can turn her
Eze. 18:3. not have o. to use proverb
Da. 6:4. sought o. co. find none o., 5.
Ro. 7:8. sin taking o. by com-t, 11.
14 : 13. put not o. to fall in bro.'s
2 Co. 5 : 12. we give you o. to glory
8 : 8. I speak by o. of forwardness
11 : 12. cut off o. fr. them desire o.
Ga. 5 : 13. use not liberty for o.
1 Ti. 5:14. younger wom. give none o.
1 Jn. 2 : 10. none o. of stumbling in

OCCASIONED. ⌊him
1 S. 22 : 22. I have o. the death of
all the persons of thy father's

OCCUPATION. ⌈Jon. 1:8.
Ge. 46 : 33. What is your o. ? 47 : 3.
Ac. 18:3. by o. they were tentmakers
19:25. with the workmen of like o.

OCCUPIED, ETH.
Ex. 38:24. gold th. was o-d for work
Ju. 16:11. If bind with ropes nev. o-d
Eze. 27:16. Syria o-d | 19. Dan ⌈fairs
21. Arabia o-d | 22. Sheba o-d in
1 Co. 14:16. o-h room of unlearned
He. 13 : 9. meats not profited them

OCCUPIERS. ⌊th. o-d
Eze. 27 : 27. o. of merchandise sh.

OCCUPY. ⌊fall
Eze. 27:9. mariners to o. merchandi.
Lu. 19 : 13. he said, o. till I come

OCCURRENT. ⌈o.
1 K. 5 : 4. is nei. adversary nor evil

OC'RAN.
Nu. 1:13. Pagiel the son of O., 2:27.-7:

ODD. ⌊72, 77.-10:26.
Nu. 3:48. o. number to be redeemed

O'DED. ⌈of O.
2 Ch. 15 : 1. Spirit upon Azariah son
8. when Asa heard prophesy of O.
28: 9. prophet was there, called O.

ODIOUS. ⌈o.
1 Ch. 19:6 Ammonites made thems.
Pr. 30:23. For an o. woman married

ODOUR. ⌈ment
Jn. 12:3. hou. filled with o. of oint.
Ph. 4 : 18. an o. of sweet smell, a

ODOURS. ⌈o.
Le. 26:31. not smell savour of sweet
2 Ch. 16 : 14. Asa in bed of sweet o.
Es. 2 : 12. six months with sweet o.
Je. 34:5. shall they burn o. for thee
Da. 2 : 46. offer sweet o. unto Dan.
Re. 5 : 8. and golden vials full of o.
18:13. no man buyeth their o. and

OFF. See **BREAK Off, CUT Off, Off THEE.**

OFFENCE, S. ⌈my lord
1 S. 25 : 31. this sh. be no o. unto
Ec. 10:4. yielding pacifieth great o-s
Is. 8 : 14. rock of o. to both houses
Ho. 5 : 15. till they acknowledge o.
of Israel ⌈unto me
Mat. 16 : 23. Satan, thou art an o.
18 : 7. Woe bec. of o-s! for it must
needs be o-s come ; but woe to
man by wh. o. cometh, Lu. 17:1.
Ac. 24 : 16. a conscience void of o.
Ro. 4:25. Who was deliv-d for our o-s
5 : 15. not as the o. so free gift, if
through o. of one many, 18.
16. but the free gift is of many o-s
17. if by one man's o. death
reigned ⌈abound
20. law entered that o. might
9 : 33. I lay in Sion a rock of o. ⌈o.
14:20. evil for man who eateth wi.
16:17. mark them which cause o-s
1 Co. 10 : 32. Give none o., 2 Co. 6:3.
2 Co. 11 : 7. Have I commit. an o. in
Ga. 5 : 11. then is o. of cross ceased
Ph. 1 : 10. without o. till day of C.
1 Pe. 2 : 8. rock of o. to them wh.

OFFEND. ⌊stumble
Jb. 34 : 31. I will not o. any more
Ps. 73 : 15. I should o. ag. thy chil.
119:165. love thy law, nothing sh. o.
Je. 2:3. all that devour him shall o.
50 : 7. adversaries said, We o. not
Ho. 4:15. Tho. Isr. harlot let not Jud.
Ha. 1:11. he sh. pass over and o. ⌊o.
Mat. 5 : 29. if thy right eye o. thee
30. if thy right hand o. thee, 18 :
8, 9. Mk. 9 : 43, 45, 47. ⌈that o.
13:41. they shall gather all things
17 : 27. lest we o. them, go to sea
18 : 6. whoso. shall o. one of these
little ones, Mk. 9 : 42. Lu. 17:2.
Mk. 9:†43. if thine hand cause to o.
47. if thine eye cause thee to o.
Jn. 6 : 61. said, Doth this o. you?
1 Co. 8 : 13. if meat make bro. o. I
will eat no meat lest bro. o.
Ja. 2 : 10. yet o. in one point he is
guilty of all ⌈any o. not
3 : 2. in many things we o. all. If

OFFENDED.
Ge. 20 : 9. what have I o., Je. 37:18.
40:1. butler and baker had o. lord
2 K. 18 : 14. Hez. saying, I have o.
2 Ch. 28:13. we have o. ag. the Lord
Ezr. 10 :† 13. for we have greatly o.
Pr. 18 : 19. A brother o. is harder
Eze. 25 : 12. Edom hath greatly o.
Ho. 13:1. when Ephraim o. in Baal,
he died ⌈o., Lu. 7 : 23.
Mat. 11 : 6. blessed is he who not be
13: 21. persecution ariseth, by and
by he is o., Mk. 4 : 17. ⌈6 : 3.
57. And they were o. in him, Mk.
15: 12. Pharisees were o. aft. they
24:10. shall many be o. and betray
Mat. 26:31. All ye shall be o. because
of me this night, Mk. 14 : 27.
33. Tho. all men shall be o. yet
will I never be o., Mk. 14 : 29.
Jn. 16 : 1. spoken, that ye not be o.
Ac. 25 : 8. nor ag. Cesar have I o.
Ro. 14:21. whereby thy brother is o.
2 Co. 11 : 29. who is o. and I burn

OFFENDER, S. ⌊not?
1 K. 1 : 21. I and son be counted o-s
Is. 29 : 21. make man o. for word
Ac. 25 : 11. if I be an o. or commit-

OFFER. ted
Ex. 22 : 29. not delay to o. the first
of the fruits, Le. 2:12. Nu. 18:12.
29:36. shalt o. every day a bullock
38. shalt o. upon altar two lambs
39. one lamb o. in morn., other
lamb at even, 41. Nu. 28 : 4, 8.
35:24. Every one that did o. silver
Le. 1 : 3. o. a male without blemish,
3 : 6.-22 : 19, 20, 22, 24.
2:13. with all thine offerings o. salt
3 : 1. he sh. o. it without blemish,
6.-9:2.-19:5.-23:12. Eze. 43:23.
3 : 12. goat he sh. o. before L., 14.
4:14. o. a young bullock, Nu. 15:24.
6:14. sons of Aaron shall o. it, 22.-
14 : 19.-15 : 15, 30. Nu. 6 : 11.
7 : 3. he shall o. of it all the fat
12. If he o. it for thanksg-g, 22:29.
38. Israel to o. their oblations unto the Lord, 22 : 18. 2 Ch. 35:12.
9 : 2. Take calf with-t blemish o. it
12:7. o. it before L. make atonem.
14 : 30. he sh. o. one of turtledoves
17:4. unto taberu. to o. an offering
9. bringeth it not unto door to o.
19:6. It sh. be eaten same day ye o.
21: 6. bread of their G. they do o.
21. hath blemish not come to o., 17
22 : 15. not profane things they o.
18. Whatso. he th. will o. oblation
23. mayest o. for freewill offering
25. Nei. from stranger's hand o.
Nu. 7:18. prince did o., 24, 30. | 36.
9:7. whf. kept that we may not o.?
15 : 7. o. third part of hin of wine
18 : 12. firstfruits wh. they sh. o.
28 : 2. to o. in their season, 3, 4, 8.
21. tenth deal o. for every lamb
24. ye shall o. daily the meat
29:†39. These ye sh. o. unto Lord
De. 12 : 14. place L. choose, there o.
Ju. 3:18. made an end to o. present
1 S. 2 : 28. did I choose him my
priest to o. upon altar ⌈21 : 10.
2 S. 24 : 12. I o. thee 3 things, 1 Ch.
22. let k. o. what seemeth good
1 K. 13 †1 Jerob. stood by altar to o.
2. upon thee sh. o. priests of high
places ⌈willingly, 17.
1 Ch. 29 : 14. should be able to o. so
2 Ch. 24:14. were made vessels to o.
28:†25. made high places to o. inc.
29:21. commanded sons of Aa. to o.
35:12. might give ac. to families to o.
Ezr. 7 : 17. buy speedily lamb to o.
Ps. 16:4. off-gs of blood will I not o.
50 : 14. o. unto God thanksgiving
51 : 19. o. bullocks upon thine alt.
72 : 10. k-s of Sheba and Seba o.
Eze. 6 : 13. they did o. to idols ⌊gifts
20 : 31. when ye o. your gifts
43:22. sec. day shall o. kid of goats
44:7. when ye o. my bread, the fat
15. o. unto me the fat and blood
45 : 1. ye shall o. an oblation unto
L., 13, 14.-48:8, 9, 20. ⌈to Dan.
Da. 2 : 46. that they o. oblation un-
Hag. 2 : 14. that they o. is unclean
Mal. 1:7. Ye o. polluted bread upon
8. if ye o. blind, if ye o. lame is
it not evil? o. unto thy gov-r
Mat. 5 : 24. then come o. thy gift
8 : 4. o. the gift Moses commanded, Mk. 1 : 44. Lu. 5 : 14.
Lu. 6 : 29. smiteth on one cheek, o.
also other ⌈pion
11 : 12. if ask egg, will he o. scor-
1 Ti. 3 : † 3. not ready to o. wrong
He. 5:1. th. he may o. both gifts and
3. he ought for hims. to o. for sins
8 : 3. high priest is ordained to o.
this man have somewhat to o.
4. are priests that o. acc. to law
9:25. Nor yet that he sho. o. himself
Re. 8 : 3. he should o. it with prayers of all saints
See INCENSE, OFFERING, S, SACRIFICE, SACRIFICES.

OFFERED.
Le. 9 : 15. slew goat, o. it for sin
10 : 1. Nadab, Abihu o. strange
fire, 16 : 1. Nu. 3 : 4.-26 : 61.
Nu. 7:2. princes o. for dedication, 10.
12. he that o. first was Nahshon

Nu. 7 : 42. prince of childreu o., 48, 54, 60, 66, 72, 78. ⌈39.
16:35. 250 men that o. incense,38,
22:40. Balak o. oxen, 23:2,4,14,30.
31 : 52. gold they o. unto L. ⌈9.
Ju. 5: 2. people willingly o. thems.
6 : 28. bullock was o. upon altar
13 : 19. Manoah took kid and o. it
1 S. 1: 4. the time that Elkanah o.
2:13. any o. the priest's serv.came
1 K. 8 : 62. Sol. and all Israel o., 63.
12:32. Jeroboam o. unto calves,33.
22:43. people o. yet in high places
2 K. 16 : 12. Ahaz approached altar and o. ⌈rams
1 Ch. 15 : 26. they o. 7 bullocks 7
29 : 6. captains with the rulers o.
9. rejoiced that they o. willingly
17. mine heart I have willingly o.
2 Ch. 7: 4. king and all peo. o., 5†.
15 : 11. Asa o. unto L. of spoil
17:16. Amaziah willingly o. hims.
30 :† 24. Hez. o. to cong. 1000 bullocks ⌈bullocks
35 : † 7. Josiah o. to peo. 33,000
Ezr. 1 : 6. all that was willingly o.
2:68. some of fa-s o. freely for hou.
6 : 17. o. at dedication of this hou.
7:15. counsellors freely o. unto G.
8:25. the king and all Israel had o.
10 : 19. o. a ram for their trespass
Ne.11:2. willingly o. thems. to dwell
12:43. that day they o. great sacrifi.
Is.66:3. oblation, as if o. swine's bl.
Eze. 22:†26. Her priests o. violence
48 : 12. land that is o. be holy
Da.11:18. reproa. o. by him to cease
Mat. 2 :† 11. they o. unto him gifts
Ac. 8 : 18. Simon o. them money
15:29. from meats o. to idols,21:25.
17 : † 31. whereof he hath o. faith
1 Co. 8 : 1. things o. unto idols, 4,7, 10.-10 : 19, 28. ⌈your faith
Ph. 2 : 17. if I be o. upon service of
2 Ti. 4 : 6. I am now ready to be o.
He.5:7. when he had o. up prayers
7:27. did once, when he o. himself
9 : 7. not without blood, wh. he o.
9. were o. gifts | 14. o. hims. to G.
28. C. was once o. to bear sins
10 : 1. which they o. year by year
2. not have ceased to be o.
8. which are o. by the law ⌈Isaac
11 : 17. Abraham when tried, o.
Ja. 2 : 21. Ab. justified when he o.
See INCENSE, OFFERING, S, SACRIFICE, SACRIFICES.

OFFERETH, ING.

Le. 6 : 26. priest th. o-h it sh. eat it
7 : 16. be eaten same day he o-h
18. nei. be imputed unto him o-h
21 : 8. he o-h the bread of thy God
2 Ch 8:13. o-g acc. to com-t of Moses
29:29. made end of o-g king bowed
30 : 22. eat 7 days o-g peace off-gs
Ezr.7:16. priests o-g willingly for ho
Ps.50:23. Whoso o-h praise glorif-h
Is.66:3. o-h oblation as if swine's bl.
Je. 11 : 17. provoke in o-g unto Baal
48 : 35. him th. o-h in high places
Lu. 23 : 36. to him and o-g vinegar
He.10:11. ev. priest o-g same sacrif.
See Offer burnt OFFERING.

OFFERING. [Noun.]

Ge. 4 : 3. Cain brought an o. unto L.
4. L. had respect unto Abel and o.
5. unto Cain and his o. had not
Ex. 25 : 2. bring me an o.; of every man take my o. ⌈5 (2)
3. this is the o. ye shall take, 35 :
30 : 13. half shekel sh. be o. of Lord
14. 20 yrs. and above sh. give o. ⌊15.
35 : 22. ev. man offered o. of gold, 21. -38 : 24. Nu. 31 : 52. Ezr. 8 : 25.
24. every one that did offer o. of silver, brought L.'s o., 38 : 29.
29. chil. of Isr. brought willing o.
Ex. 36 : 3. received of Mo. all o., 6.
Le. 1 : 2. ye shall bring o. of cattle
3. If his o. be a burnt sacrifice
10. if his o. be of the flocks
14. if o. be of fowl he sh. bring o.
2 : 1. his o. sh. be of fine flour ⌈8.
3:2. hand upon the head of his o.,
7. If he offer lamb for o., 14 : 12. Nu. 6 : 14. ⌈28.
12. And if his o. be a goat, 4 : 23,
6 : 20. This is o. of Aaron and sons
7 : 13. offer for his o. leavened br.
16. if o. be a vow or voluntary o.
9 : 7. offer an o. for the people
17 : 4. o. unto the L. before whom
22:12. not eat of o. of holy things
24. nei. make any o. of bruised or
23 : 14. until day ye have bro-t o.
27 : 9. if a beast men bring an o.
Nu. 5 : 9. o. of all the holy things
15. o. of jealousy, o. of memorial,
26. take handful of o. ⌊18, 25.
6 : 21. law of Nazarite and his o.
7 : 3. they brought o. before the L.
10. princes off-d o. before altar
11. shall offer o. each prince
13. his o. was one silver charger, 19, 25, 31, 37, 43, 49, 55, 61, 67, 73, 79.
8:11. offer Levites for o., 13, 15,21.
9 : 7. that we may not offer an o.
15 : 4. that off-h o. unto L. bring
14. if stranger will offer an o. ⌊o.
13. o. of L. in appointed season
16:15. Mo. said, Respect not their o.
1 S. 2 : 29. Whf. kick ye at mine o.?
3:14. shall not be purged with o.
26 : 19. If L. have stirred thee up ag. me, let him accept an o.
1 K. 18 : 29. prophesied until o. of evening sacrifice, 36. ⌈Ps.96:8.
1 Ch. 16:29. bring an o. and come,
Ne.10:39. Isr. shall bring o. of corn
Is. 43 : 23. not caused thee to serve
53 : 10 make his soul an o. ⌊wi. o.
66 : 20. sh. bring your breth. for o.
Eze. 20 : 28. provocation of their o.
40 : 43. upon tables was flesh of o.
48:8. o. ye sh. offer of 25,000 reeds
Zph. 3 : 10. daughter of my dispersed shall bring mine o.
Mal. 1 : 10. nei. will I accept an o.
11. incense be off-d and pure o.
13. lame, sick, ye brought an o.
2 : 12. cut off him off-h o. unto L.
13. he regardeth not o. any more
3 : 3. offer unto Lord an o. in righ-
4. o. of Jerus. be pleasant ⌊te-u.
Ac. 21:26. o. be off-d for every one
Ro.15:16. o. up of Gent. be accepta.
Ep. 5 : 2. an o. and a sacrifice to G.
He. 10 : 5. Sacrifice and o. thou wouldest not, but, 8. Ps. 40 : 6.
10. thro. the o. of the body of Jes.
14. by one o. he perfected for ever
18. where remission is, is no more

Burnt OFFERING. ⌊o.

Ge. 22 : 3. Ab. clave wood for b. o.,6.
7. where is the lamb for b. o.?
8. G. will provide a lamb for b.o.
13. for a b. o. instead of Isaac
Ex. 18 : 12. Jethro took b. o. for God
29:18. ram is a b. o. unto the Lord
Le.1:4. put hand upon head of b. o.
6. he shall slay the b. o. and cut
4:29. slay sin offering in place of b. o., 33.-6 : 25.-7 : 2.-14 : 13.
5 : 7. and the other pigeon for a b. o., 10 : 19.-12 : 8.-14 : 22, 31.
6 : 9. This is law of b. o., 7:37. ⌈o.
10. ashes fire consumed with b.
12. priest shall lay b.o. in order
7:8. priest shall have skin of b. o.
9:2. ram for a b. o., 16:3, 5.-23:18.
3. and lamb for b. o., 12:6.-23:12.
12. Aaron slew b. o. and, 13.
14 : 19. afterw. priest sh. kill b. o.
Nu. 7 : 15. one lamb of the 1st year for b. o., 21, 27, 33, 39, 51, 57, 63, 69, 75, 81. Eze. 45 : 15.
87. All the oxen for b. o. were 12
15 : 3. When ye make unto L. b. o.
5. 4th part of hin of wine wi. b.o.
8. preparest bullock for b. o.
23:3. Stand by thy b. o. I will go,15.
27. Balak stood by his b. o.
28:10. This is the b. o. of ev sabbath
13. for a b. o. of a sweet savour
14. this is the b. o. of ev. month
29:6. beside meat off. and daily b.o.
Jos.22:26. to build altar not for b.o.
Ju. 13:23. would not have rec. b.o.
1 S. 13 : 9. Saul said, Bring b. o. to
2 K. 16 : 13. the king burnt his b.o.
15. Upon the gr. altar burn b.o.(3)
2 Ch.7:1. fire came and consum. b.o.
29 : 24. b. o. be made for all Israel
28. all this until b. o. was finish.
32. all these for a b.o. to L. | 35.
Ps.40:6. b.o. hast thou not required
51 : 16. thou delightest not in b.o.
19. be pleased wi. b.o. whole b.o.
Is. 40 : 16. nor the beasts for a b.o.
61:8. I the L. hate robbery for b.o.
Eze.40:38. gates where they washed
39. tables to slay b. o., 42. ⌊b. o.
42. instruments whw. slew b. o.
44 : 11. they shall slay the b. o.
45 : 17. princes shall prepare b. o.
23. seven days he sh. prepare b.o.
25. sh. he do the like unto b. o.
46:2. priest sh. prepare prince's b.o.
12. prince sh. prepare voluntary b.
13. shalt daily prepare a b. o. ⌊o.
See ALTAR.

Continual burnt OFFERING.

Ex. 29 : 42. a c. b. o., Nu. 28 : 3, 6, 10, 15, 23, 24, 31.-29 : 11, 16, 19, 22, 25, 28, 31, 34, 38. Ezr. 3 : 5 Ne. 10 : 33. Eze. 46 : 15.

Offer, ed, eth, or ing burnt OFFERING, S.

Ge. 8 : 20. Noah o-d b. o-s on altar
22 : 2. Take Isaac, o. him for b. o.
Ex. 24:5. he sent yo. man wh. o-d b.
32 : 6. rose early, o-d b.o-s ⌊o-s
40 : 29. Moses o-d upon altar b. o.
Le. 5:10. he shall o. the 2d for b.o.
7:8. priest th. o-h any man's b. o. sh. have skin of b. o. he o-d
9:7. Go unto altar o. thy b. o., 15 : 15, 30. Nu. 6 : 16.-15 : 24. ⌈ner
16. he o-d. b. o. acc. to the man-
22. Aaron came from o-g b. o.
10:19. this day o-d b. o. bef. Lord
14:20. priest sh. o. b. o. upon altar
15:15. priest sh. o. one for sin off-g, other for b.o., Nu. 6:11.-8 : 12.
16:24. Aa. shall come and o.b.o.(2)
17:8. Whatso. man of Isr. o-h b.o.
22:18. which they will o. for b.o.
23:12. shall o. lamb for b.o., Nu.6: 18. with head 7 lambs for b.o. ⌊14.
37. to o. a b. o. upon his day
Nu.28:11. in beginn. of months o.b.
23. shall o. there beside b. o. ⌊o.
27. ye shall o. b. o. for sweet savour unto L., 29:2, 8, 13, 36.
De. 12 : 13. o. not b. o-s in every place ⌈o-s, 27.
14. in place L. choose o. thy b.
27 : 6. o. b. o-s unto the Lord, 2 K. 10:24. 1 Ch. 16:40. 2 Ch. 23:18.- 35:16. Ezr. 3 : 6.
Jos. 8 : 31. they o-d b. o-s unto L., Ju. 20 : 26.-21:4. 1 S. 6 : 15 Ezr. 3 : 3. ⌈meat
22 : 23. or if to o. thereon b. o. or
Ju. 11 : 31. I will o. it up for a b. o.
13:16. if thou o.b.o. o. it unto Lord
20 : 26. people wept and o-d b. o-s
21:4. people built altar o-d b. o-s
1 S. 6 : 14. they o-d kine for b. o.

1 S.6:15.men of Beth-sh. o-d b.o-s
1:9.Sam.o-d sucking lamb for b.o.
10. as Sam. was o-g b. o. Philis.
10 : 8. come unto thee to o. b. o-s
13:10. made end of o-g, b. o., 9. 2
K. 10 : 25. 2 S. 6 : 18. 1 Ch. 16:2.
12. I forced myself and o-d b.o-s
2 S. 6 : 17. David o-d b. o-s, 24 : 25.
1 Ch.21:26. [nothing,1 Ch.21:24
24:24. nei. will I o. b. o-s that cost
25. David built altar o-d b. o-s
1 K.3:4.a thousand b.o-s did Sol.o.
15. Solomon stood and o-d b.o-s,
2 Ch. 1 : 6. [b. o-s, 2 Ch. 7 : 7.
8:64. middle of court, Solomon o-d
9:25. times a year did Sol. o.b.o-s
2 K. 3:27. king o-d his son for b.o.
5:17. will hencef. o. nei. b. o. nor
10:25. Jehu made end of o-g b. o.
1 Ch.29 : 21. they o-d b.o-s unto L.
2 Ch. 8 : 12. Sol. o-d b. o-s on altar
24:14. they o-d b. o-s continually
29:7.fathers have not o-d b. o-s in
27. Hez-h commanded to o. b. o.
35:14. sons of Aa. busied in o-g b.
16.So service was to o.b.o-s [o-s
Ezr. 3 : 2. builded altar to o. b. o-s
3. o-d b. o-s morn. and even., 4.
8 : 35. o-d b. o-s unto G. of Israel
Jb. 1 : 5. o-d b. o-s acc. to number
42:8. go to Job o. for yours. a b.o.
Je. 14 : 12. o. b. o. I will not accept
33 : 18. not want man to o. b. o-s
Eze. 43 : 18. ordinances to o. b. o-s
24. they sh. offer for b.o. unto L.
46:4. b. o. prince shall o. in sab.
Am.5:22.Tho.ye o. b. o-s I will not
See DRINK, FREEWILL. [accept
See **Made by FIRE.**

Heave OFFERING.

Ex. 29 : 27. sanctify the shoulder of
h.o., 28.Le.7:32.Nu.18:11. [29.
Le. 7:14. if he offer for h. o., Nu.18:
Nu. 5 : † 9. every h. o. shall be his
15 : 19. offer up a h. o., 20, 21. [L.
21.of first of dough give h.o.unto
18 : 24. tithes they offer as h. o.,
26, 27, 28.
28. give Lord's h. o. unto Aaron
29.Out of your gifts sh.offer h. o.
31:29.give it unto Eleazar for h.o.
41. tribute which was L.'s h. o.
31:†52.gold of h.o.was 16,750 shek
De.12:17. not eat within gates h.o.,

Jealousy OFFERING. [11.

Nu. 5 : 25. j. o. out of woman's
hands, 15 : 18.

Lord's OFFERING.

Ex. 35 : 21. they bro-t L. o. to work
See **Offering, s of the LORD,**
and Made by FIRE.

Meat OFFERING.

Ex.29:41. acc. to m.o.of the morn.
30 : 9. shall offer no m. o. thereon
40 : 29. upon altar of burnt off-g
offered m. o.
Le. 2 : 1. when any will offer a m.
o., 4, 5, 6, 7, 8, 9, 13, 14.
3. remnant of m. o. shall be Aaron's, 10.-5 : 13. Nu. 18 : 9.
11. No m.o. be made with leaven
6:14. this is law of m.o. | 15,20,21,
23.-7 : 9, 10, 37.-9 : 17.-10 : 12.
14 : 10. deals of flour for a m. o.,
23 : 13. Nu. 15 : 4, 9.-28:20, 28.-
29 : 9. 1 Ch. 23 : 29. [23 : 18, 37.
20. priest shall offer m. o. | 31.-
23 : 16. ye sh. offer a new m. o.
Nu.4:16. to Eleazar the daily m.o.
6 : 17. priest shall offer his m. o.
7 : 13. mingled with oil for m. o.,
19, 25, 31, 37, 43,49,55,61,67,73,
79.-8 : 8.-28 : 5, 12, 13, 20, 26.
Le. 9:4. 1 Ch. 23 : 29.
15 : 6. for m.o. two tenth deals of
flour, 28 : 5, 9, 12.
24. sh. offer bullock with m. o.

Nu.28:8.as m.o.of morning offer it
26. when bring new m.o.unto L.
31. beside his m.o., 29 : 6, 11, 16.
19, 21, 22, 25, 28, 31, 34, 38.
29 : 18. m.o. shall be acc. to number, 24, 27, 30, 33, 37.
Jos. 22 : 23. if altar to offer m. o.
Ju.6:†18. depart not until bri.m.o.
13:19.Manoah took kid with m.o.
23. not have received m.o.at our
2 K. 3: 20. when m.o. was offered
16:13.he burnt his m.o. and pour.
15.evening m.o.— their m.o.(3)
1 Ch. 21 : 23. wheat for m.o. I give
Ezr. 7 : 17. mayest buy lambs wi.m.
Ne. 10 : 33. for continual m. o. [o.
13 : 9. bro-t I m. o. frankincense
Is. 57 : 6. hast thou offered a m.o.
Eze. 42:13. there sh. they lay m.o.
44:29.They sh.eat m.o.and sin off.
45 : 15. one lamb for a m. o. and
17. he shall prepare m. o., 24.
25. shall do the like acc. to m.o.
46:5. m.o. be an ephah for a ram
7. m. o. and ephah for bullock,
14.m.o. every morning | 20. [11.
15.Thus shall they prepare m.o.
Jo. 1 : 9. m.o. and drink off-g is cut
13. the m. o. is withholden [off
2:14.leave a blessing, even a m.o.

Peace OFFERING.

Le. 3 : 1. if a sacrifice of p. o. he sh.
offer it, 3, 6, 9.-19 : 5.

Sin OFFERING.

Ex. 29:14. the flesh of bullock shalt
thou burn, it is a s. o., 36. Le.
4 : 21, 24.-5 : 9, 12.-8 : 2, 14.-
16 : 6. Nu. 8 : 12.
30 : 10. atonement wi. blood of the
s. o. of atonements, Le. 9 : 7.
Nu. 18 : 22.-29 : 11. Eze. 45 : 17.
Le. 4 : 3. yo. bullock without blemish for s. o.,4.-16:3,27.Nu.8:8.
25. the priest shall take of the
blood of s. o., 5 : 9. Eze. 45:19.
29. hand upon head of s. o. slay
s. o. in place of burnt off-g,33.
32. if a lamb for s. o., Nu. 6 : 14.
5 : 6. he shall bring a lamb or a kid
of goats for a s. o., 9:3,15.-16:
5, 6, 9, 15, 27.-23:19. Nu. 6:11,
16.-7:16, 22, 28, 87.-15:24, 27.-
28:15, 22.-29:5, 11, 16, 22. 2 Ch.
29:21, 23. Ezr. 6:17. Eze. 45:23.
8. priest shall offer that for s. o.
11. bring fine flour for a s. o., 12.
6 : 17. as is s. o. and as trespass
offering, 7:7.-14:13,19.Nu.18:9
25. This is law of the s. o., 7 : 37.
30. no s. o. whereof blood is bro-t
9:2.Take thee young calf for s.o.,8.
7.Mo.said unto Aa. Offer thy s. o.
22. Aa. came down fr. off-g s. o.
10 : 16. Moses sought goat of s. o.
17.Whf. have ye not eaten s.o. in
19. this day have off-d their s. o.
12:6. she shall bring a turtledove
for a s. o., 8.-5 : 7.-14 : 22,31.-
15 : 15, 30. Nu. 6 : 11.
16 : 25. fat of s. o. shall he burn
upon altar [norance
Nu. 15 : 25. s. o. bef. L. for their ig-
2 Ch. 29:24. s.o. be made for all Isr.
Ezr. 8:35.offered 12 he goats for s. o.
Ps.40:6. s.o. hast thou not required
Eze.40:39.two tables to slay s.o., 42:
43:19. give bullock for s.o.21. [13.
22. sec. day offer kid for s. o.
25. prepare ev. day a goat for s. o.
44:27.sanctuary,he shall offer s.o.
29. They shall eat the s. o.
46 : 20. place where priests shall
boil trespass offering and s. o
See **GOATS.**

Trespass OFFERING.

Le. 5 : 6. sh. bring his t. o. unto L
15. ram without blem. for t. o.

Le. 5 : 16. make atonem. with ram
of t. o., 18, 19.-6:6.-19 : 21, 22.
6: 5. he sh. give it, in day of t. o.
7 : 1. this the law of t. o., 37. [| 5.
2 where kill burnt off-g slay t.o.
14:12. he lamb for t. o., 21, 24,25.
Nu. 6 : 12. [7 : 7. Nu. 18 : 9.
13. t. o. ; it is most holy, 6 : 17.-
14. sh. take blood of t. o., 17, 28.
1 S.6:3.in any wise return him t.o.
4. What shall be the t. o. ? 8, 17.
Eze. 40 : 39, two tables to slay t.o.,
44:29. eat the t.o. and ev. [42:13.
46:20. where priests shall boil t.o.
See **Sin OFFERING.**

Wave OFFERING.

Ex. 29 : 24. wave them for a w. o.,
26. Le. 7 : 30.-8 : 27, 29.-9 : 21.-
10:15 -14:12,24.-23:20.Nu.6:20.
27. shalt sanctify breast of w. o.
Le.23:15. ye brought sheaf of w.o.
Nu. 8:†8. Aa. shall offer Levites for

Wood OFFERING. [w.o.

Ne. 10 : 34. cast lots for the w. o.
13:31. for w.o. at times appointed

OFFERINGS.

Ex. 36:3. Bro-t yet unto him free o.
Le. 2 : 13. with all thy o. offer salt
1 S. 2 : 29. fat with chiefest of all o.
2 S. 1:21. let there be no fields of o.
2 K. 16:15.Upon altar burn drink o.
2 Ch. 31 : 12. peo. brought in o., 10.
35:13.other holy o. sod they in pots
Ne. 10 : 37. should bring the first-
fruits of o.,12:44.-13:5. [thy o.
Ps. 20 : 3. the Lord remember all
Je. 41: 5. with o. and inc. in hands
Eze. 20 : 40. there will I require o.
Ho.8:13. sacrificed flesh for mine o.
Am. 5 : 25. Have ye off-d o. 40 y-rs?
Mal. 3 : 8. Wherein robbed thee? in
tithes o. [to o.
Lu. 21 : 4. of abundance cast in un-
Ac 24 : 17. I came to bring alms o.

Burnt OFFERINGS.

Ex.10:25.give us sacrifices and b.o.
20:24. shalt sacrifice thereon b.o.
Nu. 10 : 10. blow over your b. o.
29:39.These sh.ye do for your b.o.
De. 12:6. bring your b.o., 11, 14,27.
Jos.22:27. do service of L. with b.o.
28.altar fa-s made not for b.o.,29.
1 S. 15 : 22. Hath L. as great delight in b. o. as obeying
1 K. 8 : 64. alt. too little to rec. b.o.
1 Ch. 21 : 23. I give oxen for b. o.
2 Ch. 2 : 4. I build a house for b.o.
7:7. altar not able to receive b.o.,
1 K. 8 : 64. [bro-t b. o.
29 : 31. many as were of free heart
32. number of b. o. cong-n bro-t
34. priest could not slay all b. o.
35. the b. o. were in abundance
30 : 15. Levites brought in b. o.
31 : 2. Hez. appointed for b. o.
3. appointed k.'s portion for b.o.
35 : 12. they removed b. o.
Ezr.6:9. they have need of for b.o.
Ps.50:8. I not reprove for thy b.o.
66 : 13. into thy house with b. o.
Is. 1 : 11. I am full of the b. o. [o.
43: 23. not bro-t small cattle of b.
56: 7. their b. o. shall be accepted
Je.6:20.your b.o. are not acceptab.
7:21. Put your b.o. unto sacrifices
22. to your fathers conc-g b. o.
17: 26. from south, bringing b. o.
19:5. burn sons for b.o. unto Baal
Eze.43:27. sh. make b.o.upon altar
45 : 17. princes' part to give b. o.
Ho. 6 : 6. knowledge of G. than b.o.
Mi. 6 : 6. I come bef. him with b.o.
Mk. 12 : 33. love neighb. than b. o.
He. 10 : 6. In b.o.for sin no pleasure
8. Sacrifice, offering and b. o.
See DRINK, FREEWILL.
See **Made by FIRE.**

Heave OFFERINGS.
Nu.18:8. given charge of mine h.o.
19. all the h.o. chil. of Isr. offer
De. 12:6. thither ye sh. bring h.o.
See Offering, s of the LORD.

Meat OFFERINGS.
Nu.29:39. These ye shall do for m.o.
Jos. 22:29. to build altar for m. o.
1 K. 8:64. Sol. offered m.o., altar
too little to rec. m.o., 2 Ch.7:7.
Ezr. 7:17. buy lambs with m. o.
Ne.13:5. chamb. where they laid m.o.
Je. 17:26. fr. Judah to bring m. o.
33:18. not want man to kindle m.o.
Eze.45:17. prince's part to give m.o.
Am. 5:22. offer m. o. I not accept

Passover OFFERINGS.
2 Ch.35:8. gave priests for p.o., 7, 9.

Peace OFFERINGS.
Ex.20:24. sacrifice thereon thy p.o.
24:5. sacrificed p.o. of oxen unto L.
29:28. it is heave offering of p. o.
32:6. peo. brought p. o. and sat
Le.4:10. taken from bullock of p.o.
26. shall burn as fat of p. o., 31,
35.–6:12.
7:11 this is law of sacrifice of p.
o., 13, 29, 37.
14. b ood of p. o., 33. 2 K. 16:13
15. p. o. sh. be eaten same day
29. he that off-h sacrifice of p. o.
32. give unto priest of p. o., 34.
33. He that offer-h blood of p. o.
9:4. bullock and ram for p.o., 18.
22. Aaron came fr. offering p. o.
10:14. given out of sacrifice of p.o.
17:5. offer them for p. o., 23:19.
19:5. if ye offer a sacrifice of p.o.,
22:21, Nu. 15:8. [for p. o.
Nu. 6:14. lamb for p.o. | 17. a ram
18. fire wh. is under sacr. of p.o.
7:17. for sacrifice of p. o. 2 oxen
5 lambs, 23, 29, 35, 41.–29:39.
10:10. blow over sacrifice of p.o.
De. 27:7. offer p. o. and eat there
Jos. 8:31. Joshua sacrificed p. o.
22:23. if offer p. o. let L. require it
27. might do service of L. wi. p.o.
Ju. 20:26. all Isr. offered p.o., 21:4.
1 S. 10:8. I will offer p. o., 11:15.
13:9. Saul said, Bring hither p.o.
2 S. 6:17. David offered p. o., 18.–
24:25. 1 Ch. 16:1, 2.–21:26.
1 K. 3:15. Solomon offered p.o., 8:
63, 64. [fered p. o., 2 Ch. 7:7.
9:25. thrice in a year Solomon of-
2 K.16:13. king sprinkled the blood
of p. o. [of p. o.
2 Ch. 29:35. burnt off-gs with fat
31:2. Hez. appointed priests for p.
33:16. Manasseh offered p. o. [o.
Pr.7:14. she said to him, I have p.o.
Eze. 43:27. p. o. and I will accept
45:15. p.o. to make reconciliation,
46:2. priest prepare p. o. [17.
12. prince prepare voluntary p.o.
Am.5:22. not regard p.o. of fat thi.

Sin OFFERINGS.
Ne. 10:33. s.o. to make atonement

Thank OFFERINGS.
2 Ch.29:31. come near and bring t.o.
33:16. repaired altar, sacrificed t.o.
Eze.43:†27. sh. make your t. o. [†17.
46:†15. t. o. to make reconcil-n,
Am. 5:†22. nei. will regard the t.o.

Wave OFFERINGS.
Nu. 18:11. w. o. I have given unto

Wine OFFERINGS. [thee
Ho. 9:4. They sh. not offer w.o. to

OFFICE, S. [L.
Ge. 41:13. me he restored to o., him
Ex. 1:16. When ye do o. of midwife
Nu. 3:†36. o. of the sons of Merari
4:16. o. of Eleazar the son
1 S. 2:36. Put me into 1 of priest's o-s
2 K. 11:†18. priests appointed o-s
1 Ch. 6:32. they waited on their o.
1 Ch. 9:22. Da. ordain in their set o.
26. four porters in their set o., 31.
23:28. o. was to wait on sons of Aa.
24:3. Da. distributed acc. to o-s
2 Ch. 7:6. priests waited on their o-s
23:18. Jehoi. appointed o-s of hou.
24:11. chest brought unto k.'s o.
31:15. set o. to give to breth. by
18. in their set o. they sanctified
Ne.13:13. their o. was to distribute
14. wipe not out my good deeds
for o-s [Ac. 1:†20.
Ps. 109:8. let another take his o.,
Eze. 44:13. not near to do o. of pri.
Da.11:†7. one sh. stand up in his o.
Ro. 11:13. apos. I magnify mine o.
12:4. all members have not same o.
1 Ti. 3:1. If desire o. of bishop
10. let them use o. of deacon, 13.
He.7:5. who receive o. of priesthood

Priest's OFFICE.
Ex. 28:1. that he may minister unto me in the p. o., 3, 4, 41.–
29:1, 44.–30:30.–35:19.–40:13,
15. Le. 7:35.–16:32. Nu. 3:3.
29:9. p. o. shall be theirs for
statute [41.
31:10. to minister in the p.o., 39:
Nu. 3:4. Ithamar ministered in the
p. o., 1 Ch. 24:2. [their p. o.
3:10. Aaron and sons shall wait on
18:7. thou and thy sons keep p.o.
De.10:6. Eleazar ministered in p.o.
1 Ch. 6:10. Azariah executed p.o.
2 Ch. 11:14. off fr. executing p.o.
Lu. 1:8. while Zacharias executed

OFFICER. [p. o.
Ge. 37:36. Potiphar o. of Pha., 39:1.
Ju. 9:28. is not Zebul his o.?
1 K. 4:†2. Azariah the chief o.
5. Zabud was the principal o.
19. Geber was the only o. in land
22:9. Ahab called o. said, Hasten
2 K. 8:6. k. appointed o. to restore
23:†11. chamber of Nathan-mel. o.
25:19. Nebuz-n took an o. of city
2 Ch. 24:11. o. came, emptied chest
Mat. 5:25. judge deliver thee to o.
and o. cast thee into, Lu.12:58.

OFFICERS. [o.
Ge. 40:2. Pha. was wroth with two
7. Joseph asked Pha.'s o. Whf.
41:34. let Pha. appoint o. over land
Ex. 5:15. o. of Israel cried unto
Pharaoh, 6, 10, 14, 19. [evil case
19. o. did see that they were in
Nu. 11:16. Gather the o., De.31:28.
31:14. Moses was wroth with o.
48. o. wh. were over thousands
De.1:15. I made them o. am. [make
16:18. Judges and o. shalt thou
20:5. o. sh. speak unto peo., 8, 9.
Jos. 3:2. o. went thro. host, 1:10.
8:33. o. and their judges stood
23:2. Josh. called for Isr. and o.,
24:1. De. 29:10. [to his o.
1 S. 8:15. take vineyards and give
1 K. 4:5. Azariah over the o.
7. Sol. had 12 o. over all Isr., 27.
28. unto place where o. were
5:16. Besides chief of Sol.'s o., 9:23.
2 K. 11:15. Jehoiada com-ded o.
18. appointed o. over the house,
2 Ch. 23:18. [his o.
24:12. Jehoiachin went out with
15. o. and mighty men carried he
1 Ch. 23:4. six thous. were o. judges
26:29. Chenaniah and sons for o.
and judges, 30.–27:1.–28:1.
2 Ch. 8:10. Solomon's o. 250 that
18:8. king called for one of o.
19:11. Levites shall be o., 34:13.
Es. 1:8. had appointed to all o., 2:3.
9:3. o. of the king helped Jews
Is. 60:17. I will make thine o. peace
Je. 29:26. sho. be o. in hou. of L.
Jn.7:32. priests sent o. to take him
Jn.7:45. Then came o. to chief priests
46. o. answ-d, Never man spake
18:3. Judas having received o.
12. Then o. took Jesus and bound
22. one of the o. struck Jesus
18. the serv-s and o. stood there
19:6. chief priests thereof and o.
Ac. 5:22. o. found th. not in prison
26. went capt. with o. and bro-t

OFFSCOURING. [them
La. 3:45. Thou hast made us as o.
1 Co. 4:13. are the o. of all things

OFFSPRING.
Jb.5:25. thy o. as the grass of earth
21:8. o. is established bef. eyes
27:14. o. not be satisfied with br.
31:8. yea, let my o. be rooted out
Is. 22:24. sh. hang upon him the o.
44:3. pour blessing upon thine o.
48:19. o. of thy bowels like gravel
61:9. o. shall be known am. peo.
65:23. seed of the blessed, and o.
Ac.17:28. For we are also his o., 29.
Re. 22:16. I am the root and o. of

OFT. [Da.
2 K. 4:8. as o. as he passed by
Jb.21:17. How o. is candle of wick.
put out, how o. cometh destruc.
Ps. 78:40. How o. did provoke him
Mat. 9:14. Why do Pharis. fast o.?
18:21. how o. sh. bro. sin ag. me?
Mk. 7:3. exc. they wash o. eat not
Ac.26:11. I punished them o. in ev.
1 Co.11:25. this do as o. as ye drink
2 Co.11:23. in prisons, in deaths o.
2 Ti. 1:16. for he o. refreshed me
He.6:7. drinketh rain th. cometh o.

OFTEN, OFTENER.
Pr. 29:1. He th. being o. reproved
Mal. 3:16. that feared L. spake o.
Mat. 23:37. how o. would I have
gathered thy chil., Lu. 13:34.
Mk.5:4. been o. bound with fetters
Lu.5:33. Why do disci. of Jn. fast o.?
Ac. 24:26. Felix sent for him o-r
1 Co.11:26. as o. as ye eat this bread
2 Co. 11:26. In journeyings o. in
27. I have been in watchings o. (2)
Ph. 3:18. of wh. I have told you o.
1 Ti. 5:23. little wine for o. infirmi.
He. 9:25. Nor that he offer hims. o.
26. then he must o. have suffered
Re. 11:6. to smite earth as o. as

OFTENTIMES. [o.
Jb. 33:29. these things worketh G.
Ec. 7:22. o. thine heart knoweth
Lu. 8:29. for o. it had caught him
Ro. 1:13. o. I purposed to come
15:†22. I have been o. hindered
2 Co.8:22. brother o. proved dilig-t
He. 10:11. offering o. same sacrifices

OFTTIMES.
Mat. 17:15. son; o. he falleth into
fire, o. into water, Mk. 9:22.
Jn. 18:2. Jesus o. resorted thither

OG.
De. 31:4. unto them, as to Sihon
and O.
Jos. 2:10. heard what you did to O.
13:31. cities of O. pertaining to
1 K. 4:19. Geber was in country of
See BASHAN, SIHON. [O.

O'HAD. [6:15.
Ge. 46:10. sons of Simeon; O., Ex.

O'HEL.
1 Ch. 3:20. sons of Zerubbabel; O.

OIL. [35:14.
Ge. 28:18. Jac. poured o. upon stone,
Ex. 25:6. take of them o. for light,
35:8, 14, 28–39:37. Nu. 4:16.
29:2. cakes tempered with o., 40.
30:25. make it an o. of holy ointm.
Le. 2:1. meat offering unto Lord, he
shall pour o. upon it, 2, 6, 15.
4. cakes of fine flour mingled with
o., 5, 7.–14:10, 21.–23:13. Nu.6:
15.–7:13, 19, 25, 31, 37, 43, 49,

55, 61, 67, 73, 79.–8 : 8.–28:13.–
29 : 3, 9, 14. ⌈it, 6 : 21.
Le. 2 : 15. meat offering put **o.** upon
16. priest shall burn part of **o.**
5 : 11. he shall put no **o.** upon it,
Nu. 5 : 15. ⌈o., 9 : 4.–14 : 10.
7 : 10. meat offering mingled with
12. cakes mingled wi. **o.**, Nu. 6:15.
14 : 16. priest dip right finger in **o.**
17. rest of the **o.** that is in his
hand, 18, 26, 27, 28, 29. ⌈ter
Nu. 4:9. **o.** vessels whw. they minis-
11 : 8. taste as taste of fresh **o.**
15 : 4. with fourth part of hin of **o.**
6. with third part of hin of **o.**, 9.
28 : 12. **o.** for bullock, **o.** for ram
De. 28:40. olive trees, but not anoint
with **o.**, 2 S. 14 : 2. Mi. 6 : 15.
32 : 13. suck **o.** out of flinty rock
33:24. Let Asher dip his foot in **o.**
1 S. 10 : 1. Samuel took a vial of **o.**
16:1. fill thy horn with **o.** and go,
1 K. 1:39. Zadok took horn of **o.** ⌊13.
5:11. gave Hiram 20 measures of **o.**
6:†23. two cherubim of trees of **o.**
17 : 12. a little **o.** in a cruse ⌈16.
14. nei. shall the cruse of **o.** fail,
2 K. 4 : 2. nothing in house save **o.**
6. not a vessel. And the **o.** stayed
7. Go sell the **o.** and pay thy debt
9 : 1. take this box of **o.** go to, 3.
6. he poured the **o.** on his head
1 Ch. 27 : 28. over cellars of **o.** Joash
Ezr. 3 : 7. gave **o.** unto th. of Zidon
Es. 2:12. six mos. with **o.** of myrrh
Jb. 24 : 11. make **o.** within walls
29 : 6. rock poured me rivers of **o.**
Ps. 23:5. anointest my head with **o.**
55 : 21. words were softer than **o.**
104 : 15. **o.** to make face to shine
109:18. come like **o.** into his bones
141 : 5. be a kindness, an excell. **o.**
Pr. 5:3. her mouth smoother than **o.**
21 : 20. **o.** in dwelling of wise ⌈o.
Is. 1 : † 6. wounds, nei. mollified wi.
5 : † 1. in the horn of the son of **o.**
61 : 3. give **o.** of joy for mourning
Je. 41 : 8. we have treasures of **o.**
Eze. 16 : 9. I anointed thee with **o.**
13. didst eat flour, **o.**, 19. ⌈41.
18. set mine **o.** and incense, 23 :
27 : 17. Judah traded in honey, **o.**
32 : 14. cause rivers to run like **o.**
45 : 14. ordinance of **o.** bath of **o.**
24. a hin of **o.** for an ephah, 25.–
46 : 5, 7, 11, 14, 15. ⌈br. and **o.**
Ho. 2 : 5. my lovers th. give me my
12 : 1. and **o.** is carried into Egypt
Mi. 6 : 7. pleased wi. 10,000 rivers of
Zch. 4 : 12. empty the golden **o.** ⌊o.?
† 14. two sons of **o.** stand by L.
Mat. 25 : 3. the foolish took no **o.**
4. wise took **o.** | 8. Give us of **o.**
Lu. 7:46. head wi. **o.** didst not anoint
16 : 6. An hundred measures of **o.**
See ANOINT, ANOINTED, ANOINTING, BEATEN, HOLY, LOG.

OIL olive.

Ex. 27:20. pure **o. o.** beaten for light
30 : 24. take thou of **o. o.** a hin
Le. 24:2. bring unto thee pure **o. o.**
De. 8:8. land of **o. o.** and, 2 K. 18 :
⌊32.

OIL tree.

Is. 41:19. I will plant in wildern. **o. t.**

Wine with OIL.

Nu. 18 : 12. best of **o.** and **w.** offer
De. 7:13. L. will bless thy **w.** and **o.**
11:14. mayest gather thy **w.** and **o.**
12 : 17. not eat tithe of thy **w.** and
o., 14:23. Ne. 13:5, 12. ⌈Ch. 31:5.
18:4. the firstfruits of **w.** and **o.**, 2
28 : 51. sh. not leave thee **w.** or **o.**
1 Ch. 9 : 29. to oversee **w.** and **o.**
12:40. they bro-t **w.** and **o.** ⌈o., 15.
2 Ch. 2 : 10. 20,000 baths of **w.** and
11:11. Rehoboam put in **o.** and **w.**
2 Ch. 32:28. storehouses for **w.** and
Ezr. 6:9. give **w.** and **o.** acc. to ap. ⌊o.
7:22. to 100 baths of **w.**, 100 of **o.**
Ne. 5:11. Restore **w.** and **o.** ye exact
10:37. bring firstfruits of **w.** and **o.**
39. off-g of corn, new **w.** and **o.** ⌈12.
13:5. tithes of corn, new **w.** and **o.**,
Pr. 21 : 17. loveth **w.** and **o.** sh. not
Je. 31:12. shall flow to L. for **w.** and
40 : 10. gather ye **w.** and **o.** ⌊o.
Ho. 2:8. not know I gave **w.** and **o.**
22. sh. hear corn, **w.** and the **o.**
Jo. 1:10. **w.** is dried, **o.** languisheth
2:24. fats overflow with **w.**, **o.**, 19.
Hag. 1:11. drought on new **w.** and **o.**
2 : 12. If touch **w.** or **o.** sh. it be
Lu. 10:34. pouring in **o.** and **w.** ⌊holy
Re. 6:6. see thou hurt not **w.** and **o.**
18:13. no man buyeth their **w.** and
⌊o.

OILED.

Ex. 29 : 23. one cake of **o.** bread, Le.
⌊8 : 26.

OILY.

1 K. 6:†23. made 2 cherubim of **o.** tree

OINTMENT, S.

⌈pound
Ex. 30:25. oil of holy **o.** an **o.** com-
2 K. 20 : 13. Hezekiah shewed them
house of precious **o.**, Is. 39 : 2.
1 Ch. 9 : 30. made the **o.** of spices
Jb. 41 : 31. sea to boil like pot of **o.**
Ps. 133 : 2. It is like the precious **o.**
Pr. 27 : 9. **o.** perfume rejoice heart
16. **o.** of his right ha. bewrayeth
Ec. 7 : 1. good name better than **o.**
9 : 8. and let thy head lack no **o.**
10 : 1. Dead flies cause **o.** to stink
Can. 1 : 3. Because of thy good **o-s**
thy name is as **o.** poured forth
4 : 10. smell of thine **o-s** is better
Is. 1:6. nei. bound, nor mollified wi. **o.**
57 : 9. wentest to king with **o.**
Am. 6:6. anoint thems. with chief **o-s**
Mat. 26:7. a box of precious **o.**, Mk.
14 : 3. Lu. 7 : 37. ⌈Jn. 12 : 5.
9. this **o.** might have been sold,
12. she hath poured **o.** on my body
Mk. 14 : 4. Why this waste of **o.**?
Lu. 7 : 38. anointed feet with **o.**, 46.
23 : 56. they prepared spices, **o-s**
Jn. 11 : 2. Mary anointed L. with **o.**
12:3. Mary took pound of **o.**, house
was filled with odour of **o.**
Re. 18 : 13. no man buyeth their **o-s**

OLD.

⌈Shem
Ge. 5 : 32. Noah 500 years **o.** begat
7 : 6. Noah 600 yrs. **o.** when flood
11:10. Shem 100 yrs. **o.** and begat
12:4. Ab. 75 yrs. **o.** when from Haran
15 : 9. Take a heifer of 3 years **o.**
16:16. Abram was 86 y-rs **o.** when
Hagar bare Ishmael ⌈to Ab.
17:1. was 99 y-rs **o.** L. appeared un-
12. is 8 days **o.** sh. be circumc. ⌈o.
17. a child born unto him 100 y-rs
24. Ab. 99 y-rs **o.** when circumc.
25. Ishmael 13 y-rs **o.** when circ.
18:11. Now Ab. and Sarah were **o.**
12 after I am **o.** my lord being **o.**
13. surety bear child, who am **o.**?
19:4. compass. house, **o.** and young
31. Our fa. is **o.** | 24:1. Ab. was **o.**
21:4. Ab. circumc. Isaac 8 days **o.**
5. Ab. 100 y-rs **o.** when Isaac born
23:1. Sarah was 127 years **o.** ⌈Reb.
25: 20. Isaac 40 y-rs old when took
26. Isaac 60 y-rs **o.** when she bare
26:34. Esau 40 years **o.** took Judith
27:1. when Isaac was **o.**, 2.–35:29.
37:2. Joseph 17 y-rs **o.** feeding flock
47:8. Pha. said unto Jac., How **o.**?
49:9. coucheth as **o.** lion, who sh.
50 : 26. Jo. died, 110 y-rs **o.** ⌊rouse
Ex. 7:7. Moses 80 y-rs **o.** Aa. 83 y-rs
o. when they spake unto Pha.
10 : 9. We will go with yo-g and **o.**
30:14. every one numbered from 20
years **o.** and above, 38:26. Nu.
1 : 3, 18.–14:29.–26:2, 4.–32 : 11.
1 Ch. 23 : 27. 2 Ch. 25:5.–31:17.
Ezr. 3 : 8.
Le. 13:11. It is an **o.** leprosy in skin
25:22. eat **o.** fruit | 26:10. **o.** store
27:3. male fr. 20 y-rs **o.** unto 60 y-rs
5. if it be from 5 unto 20 y-rs **o.**
6. if from a month **o.** unto 5 y-rs
7. if it be fr. 60 y-rs **o.** or ab. ⌊o.
Nu. 3 : 15. ev. male, fr. a month **o.**
number, 22, 28, 34, 39, 40, 43.
4:3. From 30 years **o.** until 50 am.
sons of Levi, 23, 30. 1 Ch. 23:3.
8 : 24. Levites from 25 y-rs **o.** and
18 : 16. fr. month **o.** shalt redeem
26:62. numbered 23,000 fr. mouth
33:39. Aaron 123 years old died ⌊o.
De. 28:50. not regard person of the **o.**
31 : 2. Moses said, I am 120 y-rs **o.**
34 : 7. Moses 120 years **o.** died
Jos. 5 : 11. they did eat **o.** corn, 12.
6:21. utterly destroyed young and **o**
9:4. took **o.** sacks | 5. **o.** shoes on, 13.
13:1. Joshua was **o.** in y-rs, 23:1, 2.
14 : 7. Forty y-rs **o.** was I, when Mo.
10. I am this day 85 y-rs **o.** ⌈2:8.
24:29. Joshua died, 110 y-rs **o.**, Ju.
Ru. 1 : 12. I am too **o.** to have husb.
1 S. 2 : 22. Now Eli was very **o.** and
4:15. Eli was 90 and eight years **o.**
8 : 1. when Sam. was **o.**, 5.–12: 2.
2 S. 2 : 10. Saul's son was 40 y-rs **o.**
4 : 4. Mephibosheth lame, 5 y-rs **o.**
5:4. David 30 y-rs **o.** began to reign
19:32. Barzillai was 80 y-rs **o.**, 35.
1 K. 1:1. David was **o.**, 15. 1 Ch. 23:1.
11 : 4. Sol. was **o.** his wives turned
13:11. **o.** prophet in Beth-el, 25, 29.
2 K. 4:14. no child, and her husb. is **o.**
1 Ch. 2:21. Hezron married 60 y-rs **o.**
27:23. took not number fr. 20 y-rs **o.**
2 Ch. 31:16. males from three y-rs **o.**
Es. 3:13. to destroy Jews, yo. and **o.**
Jb. 21 : 7. Whf. wicked, become **o.**
22:15. **o.** way wh. wicked have trod.
32 : 6. I am young, ye are very **o.**
42 : 17. Job died being **o.** and full
Ps. 37:25. I have been yo. now am **o.**
71 : 18. now when I am **o.** O God
Pr. 22 : 6. **o.** he will not depart
23 : 10. Remove not **o.** landmark
22. despise not thy moth. when **o.**
Ec. 4:13. wise child than an **o.** king
Can. 7:13. pleasant fruits new and **o.**
Is. 15 : 5. heifer 3 y-rs **o.**, Je. 48 : 34.
23 : † 18. her merchandise shall be
for **o.** clothing
20:4. captives, young and **o.** naked
58:12. build **o.** waste places, 61 : 4.
65 : 20. child shall die 100 y-rs **o.**
but sinner 100 y-rs **o.** accursed
Je. 6:16. see and ask for the **o.** paths
38 : 11. took **o.** clouts, **o.** rags, 12.
51 : 22. break in pieces yo. and **o.**
La. 2 : 21. yo. and **o.** lie on ground
3 : 4. My flesh hath he made **o.**
Eze. 9 : 6. Slay utterly **o.** and young
23:43. her that was **o.** in adulteries
25 : 15. to destroy it for **o.** hatred
36 : 11. settle you aft. **o.** estates ⌈o.
Da. 5:31. Darius took kingd. 62 y-rs
Mi. 6:6. bef. him with calves y-r **o.**
Mat. 2 : 16. Herod slew children
from 2 years **o.** ⌈unto **o.**
9 : 16. No man putteth new cloth
17. Nei. do put new wine into **o.**
bottles, Mk. 2:21, 22. Lu. 5:36, 37.
13 : 52. treasure things new and **o.**
Lu. 2 : 42. Jesus 12 y-rs **o.** went to
5:39. he saith, the **o.** wine is better
9:8. one of the **o.** prophets is risen
Jn. 3:4. How man be born when **o.**?
8:57. Thou art not yet fifty years **o.**
21:18. when **o.** ano. shall lead thee
Ac. 4 : 22. man was ab. 40 years **o.**
7 : 23. when Moses was 40 years **o.**
21:16. bro-t Mnason, an **o.** disciple
Ro. 4:19. Ab. went about 100 y-rs **o.**

1 Co. 5 : 7. Purge out the o. leaven
8. keep feast, not with o. leaven
2 Co. 3 : 14. in reading of o. testam.
5 : 17. o. things are past away, all
1 Ti.4:7. refuse o. wives' fables [o.
5:9.widow not be taken und.60 y-rs
He.8:13. A new cov-t, he made first
o.wh.wax o. is ready to vanish
2 Pe.1:9.was purged from his o.sins
2 : 5. if God spared not o. world
1 Jn.2:7.o.com-t is word fr.beginn.
Re. 12:9. th. o. serpent, called devil
20 : 2. laid hold on th. o. serpent

OLD age. [o. a.
Ge. 15 : 15. shalt be buried in good
21:2.Sarah bare Ab. son of o.a., 7.
25:8. Abraham died in a good o.a.
37:3. Joseph son of his o. a.,44:20.
Ju. 8 : 32. Gideon died in good o. a.
Ru.4:15.be nourisher in thine o.a.
1 K. 15:23. Asa in o.a.was diseased
1 Ch.29:28.David died in good o. a.
Jb.30:2.in whom o. a. was perished
Ps. 71 : 9. Cast me not off in o. a.
92:14. sh. bring forth fruit in o.a.
Is. 46:4. even to your o. a. I am he
Lu.1:36.Elis. conceived son in o.a.

Days of OLD; See **Of OLD.**
See **Old GATE, Old LION, Old MAN, Old MEN.**

Of OLD.
Ge. 6 : 4. were o. o. men of renown
De. 32:7. Remember the days o. o.
1 S. 27:8. nations were o. o.inhab-s
1 Ch.4:40. they of Ham dwelt o.o.
Ne.12:46. o.o. were chief of singers
Jb. 20 : 4. Knowest not this o. o.
Ps.25:6.thy tender mercies evero.o.
44:1. work thou didst in times o.o.
55 : 19. even he that abideth o. o.
68 : 33. heavens which were o. o.
74 : 2. thy cong-n purchased o. o.
12. God is my king o.o. working
77 : 5.I have considered days o.o.
11. I will remem. wonders o. o.
78:2.I will utter dark sayings o.o.
93 : 2. Thy throne is establ-d o.o.
102 : 25. o. o. hast laid founda.[o.
119 : 52. I rememb-d judgments o.
152. thy testimo. I have kno.o.o.
143 : 5. I remember the days o. o.,
Is. 63 : 11. [works o. o.
Pr. 8 : 22. L. possessed me bef. his
Is.25:1. counsels o.o.are faithfuln.
30 : 33. Tophet is ordained o. o.
43:18.nei. consider the things o.o.
46:9.Remember former things o.o.
51:9.Awake, as in generations o.o.
57:11. have not I held peace o.o.?
63 : 9. carried them all days o. o.
Je. 28 : 8. prophets bef. thee o. o.
31 : 3. Lord appeared o. o. to me
46 : 26. inhabited as in days o. o.
La.1:7.things she had in days o. o.
2:17.word he had comm-d in days o.o.
3 : 6. me in dark pla. as dead o. o.
5:21. O L., renew our days as o.o.
Eze. 26 : 20. thee in pla. desolate o.
35 : † 5. hast had hatred o. o. [o.
Am. 9 : 11. build it as in days o. o.
Mi. 5:2. whose goings been fr. o. o.
7 : 14. in Bashan, as in days o. o.
20. sworn unto fa-s fr. days o. o.
Na. 2 : 8. Nineveh is o. o. like pool
Mal. 3 : 4. pleasant as in days o. o.
2 Pe. 3:5. by G. heavens were o. o.
Jude 4.o.o. ordained to condemna.
See **TIME, WAX, ED, ETH.**

OLDNESS. [ter
Ro. 7 : 6. sho. not serve in o. of let-

OLIVE, S. [Adj., Noun.]
Ge. 8 : 11. in her mouth was o. leaf
De. 28 : 40. thine o. shall cast fruit
Ju. 15 : 5. foxes burnt viney-ds and
Ne.8:15. Go, fetch o. branches [o-s
Jb. 15 : 33. he sh. cast flower as o.
Ps.128:3. thy children like o. plants
Mi.6:15. tread o-s but sh. not anoi.
Ha. 3:17. Altho. labour of o. sh.fail
Zch.4:12.What these 2 o. branches?
Ja.3:12.Can fig tree bear o. berries?
See **OIL olive.**

OLIVE tree.
De. 24 : 20. When beatest thine o.t.
Ju. 9 : 8. they said unto o. t., Reign
9.o. t.said, Sho.I leave my fatn.?
1 K. 6 : 23. made 2 cherubim of o. t.
31. two doors were of o. t., 32.
33. made for door posts of o. t.
Ps.52:8.like green o. t. in ho. of G.
Is.17:6.as shaking of an o. t.,24:13.
Je. 11 : 16. thy name A green o. t.
Ho. 14 : 6. his beauty be as o. t.
Hag. 2 : 19. o. t. not brought forth
Ro.11:17.if thou a wild o.t. graffed
in and partakest of fatn. of o.t.
24. cut out of the o. t. wh. is wild
and graffed into a good o. t.

OLIVE trees. [o. t.
Ex. 23:†11. thus shalt thou do with
De. 6 : 11. o.t.wh. thou plantest not
8:†8. land of vines and o. t., of oil
28:40.Thou shalt have o.t.,but not
1 Ch. 27 : 28. over o. t. Baal-hanan
Am.4:9.o.t. increased, palmerworm
Zch. 4 : 3. two o. t. upon right and
Re.11:4.These the two o.t.standing

Mount of OLIVES. [m. o. O
2 K. 13 : † 23. high places on right of
Zch. 14 : 4. his feet sh. stand upon
m. o. O., the m. o. O. shall
Mat. 21:1. they were come to m. o.
O., Lu. 19 : 29. [Mk. 13 : 3.
24:3. and as he sat upon m. o. O.,
26 : 30. sung hymn, they went out
into m. o. O., Mk. 14 : 26.
Lu. 22 : 39. Went as he was wont to
the m. o. O.
19 : 37.at descent of m. o. O.
21:37.at night he abode in m.o. O.
Jn. 8 : 1. Jesus went unto m. o. O.

OL'IVET. [m-t O.
2 S. 15 : 30. Da. went by ascent to
Ac. 1 : 12. returned fr. m-t called O.

OLIVEYARD, S. [o.
Ex. 23 : 11. thou shalt do with thy
Jos. 24 : 13. of vineyards and o-s ye
planted not, do ye eat, Ne. 9:25.
1 S. 8 : 14. king shall take your o-s
2 K.5:26.time to rec. money and o-s
Ne. 5 : 11. Restore to them their o-s

OLYM'PAS.
Ro.16:15. salute Julia, O. and saints

O'MAR. See TEMAN.

OMEGA. See ALPHA.

O'MER, S.
Ex.16:22.twice as much bread, 2 o-s
33. an o. full of manna, 16,18,32.
36. an o. is 10th part of an ephah

OMITTED. [law
Mat. 23 : 23. o. weightier matters of

OMNIPOTENT.
Re. 19 : 6. Alleluia, for Lord God o.

OM'RI. [reigneth
1 K. 16 : 16. all Israel made O. king
17. O. went up from Gibbethon
21. half followed O. | 22. peo. fol-
23.began O.to reign,29. [lowed O.
25. O. wrought evil [fas.
27. acts of O. | 28. O. slept with
30.Ahab son of O.did evil in sight
2 K. 8 : 26.Athaliah daughter of O.,
2 Ch. 22 : 2. [son of Imri
1 Ch. 7 : 8. O. son of Becher | 9:4. O.
27 : 18. O. son of Michael, ruler of
Mi. 6 : 16. the statutes of O.are kept

ON. [50.-46 : 20.
Ge. 41 : 45. Poti-pherah priest of O.,
Nu.16:1. O. son of Peleth took men

O'NAM.
Ge. 36 : 23. children of Shobal, She-
pho and O., 1 Ch. 1 : 40. [of O.
1 Ch. 2 : 26. Atarah was the mother
28. sons of O. Shamai and Jada

O'NAN.
Ge.38:4. son and called his name O.
8. Judah said unto O., Go in
9. O. knew seed should not be his
46 : 12. sons of Jud., Er, O. Er and
O. died in Canaan, Nu. 26 : 19.

ONCE. [1 Ch. 2 : 3.
Ge. 18 : 32. I will speak but this o.
Ex.10:17.forgive my sins only this o.
30 : 10. Aa. shall make atonem. o.
a year, Le. 16 : 34. He. 9 : 7, 12.
Nu.13:30.Let us go at o.and possess
De. 7 : 22. not consume them at o.
Jos. 6 : 3. go round city o., 11, 14.
Ju. 6 : 39. I will speak but this o.
prove but this o. [me this o.
16:18.Come up o. | 28. strengthen
1 S. 26 : 8. let me smite him at o.
1 K. 10 : 22. o. in 3 years came navy
of Tarshish, 2 Ch.9:21. [o. thi.
2 K 4:†35. Elijah walked o. hither,
6 : 10. saved hims. not o. or twice
Ne.5:18.o. in ten days store of wine
13:20. lodged without Jerus. o. or
Jb. 33 : 14. G. speaketh o. yea twice
40 : 5. o. have I spoken, but I will
Ps. 62:11. God hath spoken o. twice
74:6.break down carved work at o.
76:7.who stand when o.art angry?
89:35.o.have I sworn by my holin.
Pr. 28 : 18. perverse shall fall at o.
Is. 42 : 14. I will devour at o. [o.?
66 : 8. or shall a nation be born at
Je. 10 : 18. sling out inhab-ts at o.
13:27.be clean? when shall it o.be?
16:21. this o. cause them to know
Hag. 2 : 6. Yet o.it is a little while, I
will shake heavens, He. 12 : 26.
Lu. 13:25.When o. master of house
23 : 18. they cried all at o. saying
Ro. 6 : 10. died, he died unto sin o.
7:9. I was alive without the law o.
1 Co.15:6.seen of ab.500 breth. at o.
2 Co.11:25. thrice beaten, o. stoned
Ga.1:23.preach-h faith he o.destroy.
Ep. 5 : 3. fornica., not be o. named
Ph. 4:16. ye sent o. and again to my
1 Th.2:18.wo.have come unto you o.
He.6:4.those who were o.enlight-ed
7:27.this he did o.when off-d hims.
9:26.o.in end of world he appeared
27.is appointed unto men o.to die
28.Ch.was o. offered to bear sins,
10:2.worshippers o. purged [10:10.
12:27. word,Yet o.more, signifieth
1 Pe. 3 : 18. Ch. suffered o. for sins
20. o. longsuffering of God waited
Jude 3. contend for faith o. deliv-d
5. in rememb.,tho.ye o.knew this

ONE.
Ge. 2 : 24. and they shall be o. flesh,
Mat.19:5,6.-Mk.10:8.1 Co.6:16.
10:25. name of o. Peleg, 1 Ch.1:19.
14 : 13. o. had escaped, Eze. 33:21.
15 : 3. o. born in my house is heir
27:38. Hast but o. blessing, fa. ?
34:14. not give sister to o. uncirc.
38:28. she travailed o. put out ha.
42:13. youngest wi. fa. o.is not,32.
16 Send o. of you, let him fetch
44 : 28. And the o. went out fr. me
48 : 1. o. told Joseph | 2. told Jac.
Ex. 10:5.th. o. cannot see the earth
11 : 1. will bring o. plague more
12:46. in o. house shall it be eaten
49. o. law shall be to homeborn,
and stranger, Le. 24 : 22. Nu.
15 : 16, 29.
26 : 2. every curtain shall have o.
measure, 8.-36 : 9, 15. [13.
6. and it shall be o. tabernacle,36:
11. couple tent th. it be o., 36:18.
29 : 23. o. loaf, o. cake, o. wafer
Le. 5 : 4. guilty in o. of these, 5, 13.
7 : 14. sh. offer o. out of oblation
16 : 27. sh. o. carry with-t camp
16 : 29. o. of own country, 17 : 15.

Le.26:26.ten wom.bake br.in o.oven
Nu. 10 : 4. if blow with o. trumpet
16 : 15. I have not taken o. ass fr.
17 : 3. o. rod for the head of house
19 : 3. o. sh. slay her bef. his face
36 : 8. be wife unto o.of the family
De. 1 : 23. I took 12 men, o. of tribe
4:42.fleeing untoo.of cities,19:5,11.
19 : 15. o. witness not rise ag. man
21 : 1. If o. be found slain in land
25:11. men strive and wife of o.
32:30. How sho. o. chase a thous.?
Jos.10:42.these Josh.took at o.time
12:9.of Jericho o.k. of Ai o. ⌈o.+
10. k. of Jerus. o. k. of Hebron,
17:14. Why given me but o. lot and
17. shalt not have o. lot only ⌊o.
Ju. 4:†16. there was not unto o.left
6 : 31. bec. o. cast down his altar
9 : 2. Whe.is better, that o. reign
16:†7.sh.I be weak, and as o. man
20:31. highways of wh. o. goeth to
21:8. What o. is there of the tribes
1 S. 6 : 4. o. plague was on you all
and your lords ⌈lon o.
17. for Ashdod o. Gaza o. Ashke-
11 : 7. came out with o. consent
14:28. then, ans-d o. of the people
18:21.son in law in o. of the twain
19 : 22. o. said they be at Naioth
26:15.o.of the peo. to destroy king
2 S. 7 : 23. what o. nation like thy
3:29.not fail fr.ho.of Joab o.a leper
4 : 10. o. told me Saul is dead
8 : 2. with o. full line to keep alive
11 : 3. o. said, Is this Bath-sheba
15 : 31. o. told Da. Ahithophel is
19 : 7. will not tarry o. with thee
23 : 8. slew at o. time, 1 Ch. 11:11.
15. O that o. wo. give me to drink
water of Bethle., 1 Ch. 11 : 17.
1 K.1:48. me o. to sit on my throne
2 : 16. I ask o. petition of thee
6:25.cherubim of o.measure,o.size
8:56. not failed o. word of promise
11 : 13. o. tribe to thy son, 32, 36.
12:30.peo. went to worship bef. o.
22 : 13. prophets declare good unto
k. with o. mouth, 2 Ch. 18 : 12.
38. o. washed chariot in pool
2 K.4:39.o.went out to gather herbs
5 : 4. o. told his lord, Thus said
6 : 3. o. said, Be content ⌊maid
9:18. o. on horseback to meet him
17 : 27. carry thither o. of priests
28. o. of priests dwelt in Bethel
18:24. turn face of o. capt., Is.36:9.
1 Ch. 10 : 13. counsel of o. had fame
12:14. o. of least was over a hund.
2 Ch.32:12.Ye sh.worship bef.o.alt.
Ne. 1 : 2. Hanani, o. of my breth.
11 : 1. o. of ten to dwell in Jerus.
Jb. 1 : 1. o. that feared G., 8.–2 : 3.
6:26. speeches of o. desperate is as
9:3. can-t answer him o. of thous.
† 33. nei. is o. that should argue
23 : 13. in o. mind, who turn him?
24:17.if o.know they are in terrors
33 : 23. if interpreter o. am. thous.
41:32. o. wo. think the deep hoary
Ps. 22:†20.Deliv. my only o. fr.dog
35:†17. rescue my only o. fr. lions
49:16. Be not afraid when o.is rich
72 : † 15. o. sh. give him of gold of
82 : 7. shall fall like o. of princes
86:†2. I am o. wh. thou favourest
89:19. laid help upon o. is mighty
137 : 3. Sing us o. of songs of Zion
Pr. 1 : 14. let us all have o. purse
15 : 12. loveth not o. th. reproveth
19 : 25. o. that hath underst-g.
26 : 17. like o. taketh dog by ears
Ec.2:14. I perceived o.event happ-h
3 : 19. yea, they have all o. breath
20. All go unto o. place, all are of
4:9. Two better than o. ⌊dust, 6:6.
10. if they fall, o. lift his fellow

Ec.4:11.how can o. be warm alone?
12. if o. prevail against him, two
5 : 18. comely for o. to eat and dri.
7:27. counting o. by o. to find out
9:18. o. sinner destr-th much good
12:11.words,given from o.shepherd
Can. 4 : 9. ravished my heart, my
spouse, with o. of thy eyes,
with o. chain ⌈o.
6:9.my undefiled is but o.the only
Is. 5 : 10. ten acres sh. yield o. bath
14:32. What sh.o.answer messeng.
19:18. o. be called, The city of de-
23:15.acc.to days of o. king ⌊struc.
27:12.ye shall be gathered o.by o.
30 : 17. o. thousand shall flee at
rebuke of o. ⌈mt.
29. when o. goeth with pipe into
34 : 16. no o. of these shall fail
41:25. I have raised up o. fr.north
27. I will give Jerus.o.bring. good
44 : 5. o. shall say I am the Lord's
45:24.o.say, In L. have I righte-n.
65 : 8. o. saith, Destroy it not
Je. 9 : 8. o. speaketh peaceably with
10 : 3. o. cutteth tree out of forest
Eze. 1 : 16. they four had o. likeness
28. I heard a voice of o.th. spake
19:3. she bro-t up o. of her whelps
21:19.twain sh.come out of o.land
22:11. o. committed abomi-n with
23:13. I saw they took both o.way
33 : 24. saying Abraham was o.
32. as a lovely song of o. ⌈24.
34:23. I will set up o. shepherd, 37:
37:17. they sh. become o. in thine
hand ⌈be o.
19. make them o. stick they sh.
22. make th. o. nation, o.king sh.
46:12. o. sh. open gate, o. sh.shut
Da. 2 : 9. is but o. decree for you
7:13. o. like son of man, 10:16, 18.
9:27. confirm covenant for o. week
11 : 7. of her roots shall o. stand
10. o. shall certainly overflow
27. they sh. speak lies at o. table
12 : 6. o. said to the man in linen
Ho. 1 : 11. Isr. sh. appoint o. head
Am. 3 : 5. sh. o. take up snare fr.
4 : 8. cities wandered unto o. city
6:9. if remain ten men in o. house
12. will o. plough there wi. oxen?
Mi. 2 : 4. sh. o. take parable ag. you
Zph. 3 : 9. serve L. with o. consent
Hag. 2 : 12. If o. bear holy flesh in
13. if o. unclean touch ⌊skirt
16. when o. came to pressfat (2)
Zch. 3:9. upon o. stone sh.be 7 eyes
11 : 8. cut off 3 shepherds in o. mo.
13:6.o.sh.say What these wounds?
14:9. sh. be o. L., and his name o.
Mal. 2 : 3. o. sh. take you with dung
15. did not he make o.? whf. o.?
16.o.covereth violence with garm
Mat. 3 : 3. voice of o. crying in wilder., Mk. 1:3. Lu. 3:4. Jn. 1:23.
5:18. o. jot, or o. title sh. not pass
19. Whoso. break o. of these least
29. o. of thy members perish, 30.
36. canst not make o. hair white
6 : 27. Wh. of you can add o.cubit
29. was not arrayed like o. of
these, Lu.12:27. ⌈have o.sheep?
12 : 11. What man among you sh.
22. unto him o.possessed wi.devil
47.o.said,Behold thy mother and
16:14. Elias, or o. of the prophets,
Mk. 6 : 15.–8 : 28. Lu. 9 : 8, 19.
17:4. three tabernacles, o. for thee,
o. for Moses, and o. for Elias,
Mk. 9 : 5. Lu. 9 : 33. ⌈more
18 : 16. if not hear, take o. or two
24. o. was bro-t wh. owed 10,000
19 : 17. none good but o., Mk. 10 :
18. Lu. 18 : 19.
23 : 4. will not move them with o.
of their fingers, Lu. 11 : 46.

Mat.23:8.o.is your Master,even Ch.,
9.o.is your Father in heaven ⌊10.
25 : 18. he th. had received o., 24.
40. as ye done it unto o. of least
45. as ye did it not to o. of least
26:21. I say unto you, o.of you sh.
betray me, Mk. 14:18. Jn.13:21.
Mk.7:32.unto him o. that was deaf
8 : 14. nei. had more than o. loaf
9 : 37.Whoso. sh. receive o. of such
38. o. casting out devils, Lu.9:49.
10 : 17. came o. running and
11:29. I will ask of you o. question
12 : 6. Having o. son, he sent him
14:19. began to say o.by o., Is it I?
15 : 6. he released o., Lu. 23 : 17.
36. o. ran and filled a sponge
Lu.3:16. o. mightier than I cometh
8:42.o. only daughter, she a dying
49. o. from ruler of synagogue's
12 : 52. sh. be five in o. house ⌊ho.
13:23. said, o. L. are there few sav.
15:7. joy in heaven ov.o.sinner, 10.
16 : 17. than o. title of law to fail
30. if o. went from the dead, 31.
17 : 22. to see o. of days of the Son
22:36. let him sell garment, buy o.
23 : 17. must release o., Jn. 18:39.
Jn. 1 : 26. there standeth o. am.you
40. o. of the two wh. heard John
6:22. none other boat, save that o.
70. o. of you is a devil
7:21.I have done o.work, ye marvel
8 : 9. went out o. by o. beginning
18. I am o. bear witness of mys.
41. We have o. Father, even God
9:32. opened eyes of o. born blind
10:16. shall be o. fold, o. shepherd
30. I and my Father are o.
11:52. sho. gather in o. chil. of God
12:48.he hath o. that judgeth him
17:11. may be o. as we are, 21, 22.
23. be made perfect in o. ⌈25.
18:17. Art thou not o. of disciples?
19:18.on either side o.Jes.in midst
Ac.1:22.o.be ordained to be witness
4:32.were of o.heart and of o.soul
5 : 25. came o. and told them, the
34.stood up o. in council, Gamal.
9 : 11. go and inquire for o. Saul
10:2. devout man o. th. feared G.,
28.for Jew to come unto o.of ⌊22.
13 : 25. cometh o. aft. me, whose
17 : 7. there is ano. king, o. Jesus
26. G. hath made of o. blood all
18:7. Justus o. th. worshipped G.
24:21. Except it be for this o.voice
25 : 19. had questions of o. Jesus
28:25. aft. Paul had spok. o. word
Ro. 5 : 7. for a righte. man will o. die
15.For if through the offence of o.
16. not as by o. th. sinned, for
judgm. was by o. to condem.
17. if death reigned by o. much
more life by o.J.C. ⌈ousn.of o.
18. by offence of o. so by righte-
19.obedience of o.many be righte.
9:10.when Rebek. conceived by o.
1 Co.3:4.while o. saith, I am of Paul
8. planteth and watereth are o.
5:1. fornica., that o. have fa.'s wife
8:4. there is none other God but o.
6. to us is but o. God, and o. L.
9:24. all run, but o. receiveth prize
10:17.we many are o. br. o. body
12:13.by o. Spirit baptized into o.
14:24.come in o. th. believeth not,
or o. unlearned, he is judged
27. and let o. interpret
31. ye may all prophesy o. by o.
15:8. as of o. born out of due time
2 Co. 5 : 14. if o. died for all, then
11 : 2. I espoused you to o. husb.
24. received I 40 stripes save o.
13:11. be of good comfort, be of o.
mind, and G. of love sh. be with
you, Ph.2:2. 1 Pe.3:8. Re.17:13.

Ga. 3 : 16. saith, as of o. And to thy
28. ye are all o. in Christ ⌊seed
5:14. the law is fulfilled in o. word
Ep.1:10. might gather in o. all thi.
2 : 14. who hath made both o.
15. to make of twain o. new man
18. we both have access by o. Spi.
4 : 4. as ye are called in o. hope
5. o. faith, o. Lord, o. baptism
6. o. God and Father of all
Ph. 1 : 27. that stand fast with o.
spirit, with o. mind ⌈Tit. 1 : 6.
1 Ti. 3 : 2. the husband of o. wife.
4. bishop, o. th. ruleth own house
3:12. deacons be husb-ds of o. wife
Tit.1:12. o. of thems., prophet, said
He. 2 : 6. o. in a cert. place testifieth
11. th. are sanctified are all of o.
5 : 12. ye have need o. teach you
10:12. aft he had off-d o. sacrifice
14. by o. offering he perfected
11 : 12. sprang even of o. so many
12 : 16. for o. morsel of meat sold
13:14. here no city, but we seek o.
Ja. 2 : 10. offend in o. point, he is
16. o. of you say, Depart, be warmed
5 : 19. if any err, and o. convert
1 Jn. 5 : 7. these three are o. ⌊him
8. these agree in o. ⌈throne
Re. 4 : 2. in heaven o. sat on the
9:12. o. woe is past, there come two
13:3. I saw o. of his heads wounded
14:14. upon clouds o. sat like Son
18:17. For in o. hour so great riches is come to nought
21 : 21. every gate was of o. pearl
See ACCORD.

ONE another. ⌈rose

Ex. 10 : 23. They saw not o. a. nei.
Le. 25 : 14. sh. not oppress o.a., 17.
1 S.14:16. went on beating down o.
18 : 7. women ans-d o. a. as ⌊a.
20:41. David and Jona. kissed o.a.
1 K.6:27. their wings touched o.a.
2 K. 3 : 23. kings have smitten o.a.
14 : 8. saying, Come let us look o.
a. in the face, 11. 2 Ch.25:17,21.
2 Ch. 20 : † 22. Ammon, Moab smote
o. a. ⌈o. a.
Eze. 3 : 13. creatures that touched
Mat 24: 10. many shall betray o.a.
Jn. 13:14. ought to wash o.a.'s feet
Ac. 19 : 38. let them implead o. a.
Ro. 2 : 15. accusing or else excus. o.
12:10. in honour preferring o.a. ⌊a.
14 : 13. Let us not judge o. a.
15 : 7. receive ye o. a. as Ch. also
14. able to admonish o. a., Col.
Ga. 5 : 13. by love serve o.a. ⌊3:16.
15. if ye bite and devour o. a.
26. provoking o.a. envying o.a.
6 : 2. Bear ye o. a.'s burdens
Ep. 4 : 2. forbearing o.a., Col. 3:13.
32. forgiving o. a., Col. 3 : 13.
1 Th. 4 : 18. comfort o.a. with these
Tit. 3 : 3. hateful and hating o. a.
He. 3 : 13. exhort o. a. daily, 10:25.
10 : 24. let us consider o. a. to
Re. 6 : 4. that they should kill o.a.
See GREET.

See LOVE one another.

ONE Joined with another.

Ge. 11:3. said o. to a., Go to, let us
15 : 10. laid each piece o. ag. a.
26 : 31. and sware o. to a.
31 : 49. L. watch between me and
thee when we absent o. fr. a.
37:19. said o. to a. Behold dreamer
42 : 1. Why do ye look o. upon a.
21. said o. to a. We are guilty
28. o. to a. What is this G. hath
43 : 33. marvelled o. at a. ⌊done?
Ex. 16 : 15. said o. to a. It is manna
18 : 16. I judge between o. and a.
21: 18. if o. smite a. with stone or
35. if o. man's ox hurt a.'s ⌈9.
25:20. faces shall look o. to a., 37:
Ex.26:3. five curtains sh. be coupled
o. to a. (2), 36 : 10, 12, 13. ⌈a.
5. that loops may take hold o. of
17. two tenons set o. ag. a., 36:22.
Le. 7 : 10. sons of Aa. have o. much
18:† 18. not take o. wife to a. ⌊as a.
19 : 11. nei. lie o. to a., Col. 3 : 9.
25 : 46. not rule o. over a. with
rigour
26 : 37. sh. fall o. upon a.
Nu.14:4. said o. to a. make captain
36 : 9. nei. remove fr. o. tribe to a.
De. 21 : 15. wives o. beloved, a. hated
25 : 11. When men strive o. with a.
Ju.6:29. said o. to a. Who hath done
Ru 3:14. rose up bef. o. c'd know a.
1 S. 2 : 25 If o. man sin against a.
10:3. o. carrying 3 kids, a. 3 loaves
of bread, a. a bottle
10 : 11. said o. to a. What is this
20 : 41. wept o. with a. until Da.
21 : 11. did they not sing o. to a.
of David in dances, 29 : 5.
2 S.11:25. devour-h o. as well as a.
1 K.22:20. o. said on this manner, a.
2 K. 7 : 3. said o. to a. Why sit we
6. said o. to a. Lo the king of Isr.
9. said o. to a. We do not well
10 : 21. from o. end to a., 21 : 16.
Ezr. 9 : 11. ⌈105 : 13.
1 Ch. 16 : 20. fr. o. nation to a., Ps.
17 : 5. from o. tabernacle to a.
24 : 5. by lot o. sort with a.
26 : 12. chief men, wards o. ag. a.
2 Ch.18:19. o. after this manner, a.
20 : 23. Every o. helped destroy a.
Ne. 4 : 19. upon wall o. far from a.
Es. 1 : 7. vessels diverse o. fr. a. ⌈22.
9 : 19. of sending portions o. to a.,
Jb. 13 : 9. as o. mocketh a. do ye
mock? ⌈dieth
21: 25. o. dieth in full strength a.
41 : 16. o. is so near to a. that
17. scales are joined o. to a. ⌈a.
Ps.75:7. putteth down o. setteth up
Ec. 1 : 4. o. generation passeth, a.
8 : 9. o. ruleth over a. to his hurt
Is. 3 : 5. be oppressed every o. by a.
6 : 3. o. cried unto a. Holy, holy
13 : 8. they sh. be amazed o. at a.
66 : † 17. purify thems. o. after a.
Je.13:14. I will dash them o. ag.a.
25:26. all kings of north o. with a.
46:16. many to fall, o. fell upon a.
51:31. o. post shall run to meet a.
46. rumour shall come o. year
and in a. year ⌈11.
Eze.1:9. wings were joined o. to a.,
4:8. sh. not turn from o. side to a.
17. may be astonied o. with a.
22 : 11. o. committed abomination
with neighb.'s wife, a. defiled
daughter in law
24: 23. ye sh. mourn o. toward a.
33:30. speak o. to a. Come I pray
37:17. And join them o. to a. into o.
40 : 49. o. on this a. on that side
41 : 6. side chambers 3, o. over a.
11. o. door toward north, a. tow.
47 : 14. sh. inherit o. as well as a.
Da.2:43. they sh. not cleave o. to a.
5 : 6. king's knees smote o. ag. a.
7 : 3. four beasts diverse o. from a.
Jo. 2 : 8. Neither shall o. thrust a.
Na.2:4. chariots sh. jostle o. ag. a.
Zch. 8 : 21. of o. city sh. go to a.
11 : 9. rest eat, every o. flesh of a.
Mal. 3 : 16. spake often o. to a.
Mat. 21 : 35. beat o. and killed a.
Mk. 12 : 5. Lu. 20 : 11.
22:5. o. to his farm a. to merchandise, Lu. 14 : 19.
24:2. shall not be left o. stone upon
a., Mk. 13 : 2. Lu. 19: 44.–21:6.
25:15. unto o. 5 talents to a. two (2)
32. shall separate them o. fr. a.
27:38. o. on the right, a. on the left
Mk. 4 : 41. said o. to a. What manner of man, Lu. 8 : 25.
9 : 10. questioning o. with a.
50. have peace o. with a.
Lu. 2 : 15. shepherds said o. to a.
6 : 11. communed o. with a. what
7 : 8. I say unto o. Go, to a. Come
7 : 32. like children calling o. to a.
12 : 1. people trode o. upon a.
24: 17. ye have o. to a. as ye walk
32. said o. to a. Did not our hearts
Jn. 4 : 33. disci. o. to a. Hath any
37. o. soweth a. reapeth ⌊man
5 : 44. wh. receive honour o. of a.
13 : 22. disciples looked o. on a.
35. disciples if have love o. to a.
Ac. 2 : 7. marvelled, saying o. to a.
12. saying o. to a. What meanu.
7 : 26. why do wrong o. to a.? ⌊eth
19:32. some cried o. thing some a.,
21:6. taken our leave o. of a. ⌊21:34.
Ro. 1 : 27. burned in lust o. tow. a.
9:21. o. vessel unto honour a. unto
12 : 5. members o. of a., Ep. 4:25.
10. Be kindly affectioned o. to a.
16. same mind o. tow. a., 15 : 5.
14 : 2. o. believeth he may eat all
things, a. weak eateth herbs
5. o. man esteemeth o. day above
a. : a. esteemeth ev. day alike
19. o. may edify a., 1 Th. 5 : 11.
1 Co.3:4. o. saith, I am of Paul ; a.
4 : 6. no o. be puffed up, o. ag. a.
6 : 7. brother go to law o. with a.
7 : 7. o. after this manner a. after
11:21. o. is hungry a. is drunken
33. come to eat tarry o. for a.
12:8. to o. given word of wisd. to a.
25. members have care o. for a.
Ga. 5 : 15. ye be not consumed o.
Ep. 4 : 32. be ye kind o. to a. ⌊of a.
5 : 21. submitting yours. o. to a.
1 Th.3:12. abound in love o. tow. a.
1 Ti.5:21. without preferring o. bef.
6 : † 5. Gallings o. of a. ⌊a.
Ja. 4 : 11. Speak not evil o. of a.
5 : 9. Grudge not o. ag. a. breth.
16. Confess your faults o. to a.
and pray o. for a. ⌈a.
1 Pe. 3 : 8. having compassion o. of
4 : 9. Use hospitality o. to a.
10. gift, minister same o. to a.
5 : 5. yea all be subject o. to a.
1 Jn.1:7. have fellowship o. with a.
Re. 11 : 10. he sh. send gifts o. to a.
See **ANOTHER** with **one.**

As ONE.

Ge. 3: 22. man is become a.o. of us
19:14. he seemed a.o. that mocked
49:16. Dan sh. judge a.o. of tribes
Ex. 12 : 48. circumc. he sh. be a.o.
born in land, Le. 19 : 34.–24:22.
Nu. 12 : 12. Let her not be a.o. dead
Jos.10:2. Gibeon a.o. of royal cities
Ju. 17:11. yo. man a. o. of his sons
1 S.17:36. Philistine be a.o. of them
26:20. a. o. doth hunt a partridge
2 S. 6 : 20. a. o. of vain fellows
9: 11. at my table a.o. of k.'s sons
13 : 13. be a. o. of fools in Israel
14 : 13. k. speaketh a. o. is faulty
17:12. sh. not be left so much a.o.
2 K. 6 : 5. a. o. was felling a beam
2 Ch.5:13. trumpeters, singers a.o.
Ezr.3:† 9. sons of Jud. a.o. set forw.
Jb. 2:10. a.o. of the foolish women
12:4. I am a.o. mocked of neighb.
19:11. he counteth me a.o. of enem.
Ps. 35 : 14. a. o. that mourneth for
78:65. L. awaked a.o. out of sleep
89 : 10. broken Rahab a.o. slain
119:162. a.o. that findeth gr. spoil
Pr.6:11. a.o. that travaileth, 24:34.
17:14. strife is a. o. letteth out wat.
Can. 1:7. why sho. I be a.o. turneth
8 : 10. I was in his eyes a. o. that
Is. 10:14. a. o. that gathereth eggs

Is. 29:4. thy voice a. o. hath a spirit
66:13. a.o. his mother comforteth
Je.19:11.a.o. breaketh potter's ves.
Eze. 40 : 40. a. o. goeth up to north
42 : 9. a. o. goeth from outer court
12. a. o. entereth into doors
48 : 1. a. o. goeth to Hamath
Zch. 12 : 10. mourn a. o. in bitterness for firstborn ⌈Mk. 1 : 22.
Mat. 7 : 29. a. o. having authority,
Mk. 6 : 15. or a. o. of the prophets
9 : 26. he was a. o. dead ⌈serv-s
Lu. 15 : 19. make me a. o. of thy
23:14.this man a.o.th. perverteth
1 Co.7:25.a.o. that obtained mercy
9 : 26. not a. o. that beateth air
1 Ti.3:†3. Not quarrel a.o. in wine
See BODY, DAY, EVERY, GATE, GOD, HEART, HOLY, HOUR, HUNDRED.

Is ONE. ⌈26.
Ge. 11 : 6. peo. i. o. | 41 : 25. dream,
Ex. 2:6. This i. o. of Hebrews' chil.
De.6:4.L. our God i.o.L.,Mk.12:29.
Ru.2:20. Boaz i. o. of our kinsman
Mat. 12 : 6. i.o. greater than temple
Mk. 14 : 20. it i. o. of the twelve
Ro. 2 : 28. not Jew that i.o. outw-y
29. he a Jew who i. o. inwardly
3 : 30. it i. o. God who sh. justify
1 Co.6:17.joined unto L. i. o.spirit
12 : 12. For as body i. o. and
15:40. glory of celestial i. o. ⌈i.o.
Ga. 3 : 20. not mediator of one, God
Col. 4 : 9. Onesimus, who i. o. of
See JUST one. ⌊you,12.

Little ONE.
Ge. 19 : 20. It is a l.o. is it not l. o.
44: 20. we have l. o. his bro. dead
Is.60:22.A l.o. sh. become a thous.
See Little ONES, One MAN, MIGHTY one, ones.

Not ONE.
Ge. 24 : 41. if they give n. thee o.
Ex. 8 : 31. remained n. o., 10 : 19.
9 : 6. of cattle of Isr. died n.o., 7.
12: 30. not a ho. where n. o. dead
De.1:35. n.o. of these see that land
2 : 36. n. o. city too strong for us
2 S. 13 : 30. is n. o. of them left
17 : 13. until be n. o. small stone
1 K.16:11. left him n.o. th. pisseth
Jb. 14 : 4. clean out of uncl., n. o.
31:15.did n.o. fashion us in womb
41:9. sh. n.o.be cast down at sight
Ps. 14 : 3. filthy, there is none that doeth good, n.o., 53:3.Ro.3:12.
106:37.n.o.feeble person am. them
Is. 40 : 26. he is strong, n.o.faileth
Ro. 3:10. is none righteous, no n.o.
1 Co. 6 : 5. no n. o. able to judge
12 : 14. the body is n. o. member

ONE with other, s. ⌈lah
Ge.4:19.name of o. Adah, of o. Zil-
13:11. they separated o. fr. the o.
47:21. fr. the o. end of Egypt to o.
Ex. 1 : 15. name of o. Shiphrah, of
14:20.o.came not near o. ⌊o.Puah
17 : 12. stayed Moses' hands o. on o. side, and the o. on o. side
18 : 3. name of o. Gershom, of o.
25 : 12. two rings in o. side 2 in o.
26 : 26. five bars for o. side of tabern. 5 for o., 36:31. ⌈on o. end
37 : 8. o. cherub. on this side ano.
Le. 5 : 7. pigeons, o. for sin off-g, o. for, 12:8. Nu. 6:11.-8:12. ⌈goat
16:8. o. lot for Lord, o. for scape-
Nu.11:26. name of o. Eldad, the o.
28:4. o. lamb in morn. o. at even
De.4:32. fr. o. side of heav. unto o.
13 : 7. fr. o. end of earth unto o.,
28 : 64. ⌈pillar and o.
Ju. 16 : 29. Samson took hold of o.
20 : 31. o. goeth to house of G. o. to Gibeah ⌈of o. Ruth
Ru. 1:4. name of the o. was Orpah,
1 S. 1 : 2. name of o. Hannah, of o.
2 S. 2 : 13. o. on the o. side, the o. on the o. side, Da.12:5.Zph.4:3.
4 : 2. name of o. Baanah, of the o.
12:1. two men, o. rich, the o.poor
1 K.3:23. o. saith, This my son, o.
25.give half to o.half to o. ⌊saith
6 : 27. wing of o. touched o. wall, wing of o. touched o. wall
12 : 29. set o. in Bethel, o. in Dan
20 : 29. pitched o. ag. o. 7 days
2 Ch. 9 : 19. twelve lions on o. side and on o. ⌈with o. held
Ne. 4 : 17. with o. hand wrought,
Ec.3:19. as o. dieth, so dieth the o.
7:14.G. hath set o. over ag. the o.
Je.12:12.o. end of land to o., 25:33.
24:2.o. basket had good figs,o.had
36 : 16. were afraid both o. and o.
Eze. 1 : 23. wings straight o. tow. o.
13:10 o. built wall o. daubed with
21:16. Go thee o. way or o.
Da.8:3. o. horn was higher than o.
Zch. 11 : 7. o. Beauty, the o. Bands
Mat. 6 : 24. he will hate the o. and love the o. or hold to the o. and despise the o., Lu. 16 : 13.
20:21. my sons may sit, o. on thy right, o. on left, Mk. 10 : 37.
24 : 31. gather fr. o. end of heaven to the o. ⌈17 : 34, 35, 36.
40. o. taken, the o. left, 41. Lu.
Mk. 15 : 27. two thieves, o. on his right, o. on his left, Lu. 23:33.
Lu.6:29.if smite on o.cheek,offer o.
7 : 41. o. owed 500 pence o. fifty
17 : 24. lightning out of o. part, shineth unto the o.
18 : 10. o. a Phari. o. a publican
Jn.20:12. o. angel at the head,o.at
Ac. 15 : 39. departed asunder o.fr.o.
23:6. o. part Sadducees, o. Phari.
1 Co. 7 : 5. Defraud ye not o. the o.
2 Co.2:16. to o. savour of life, to o.
Ga. 4 : 22. o. by bondmaid, o. by a
5 : 17. these are contrary, o. to o.
Ph. 1 : 16. o. preach C. of conten. ;
Re.17:10.o. is, o. is not yet ⌊the o.
See One PEOPLE.

Such a ONE.
Ge. 41:38. Can we find s.a.o.as this
Ru. 4 : 1. Ho, s. a. o. turn aside
Jb.14:3.dost open eyes upon s.a.o.
Ps. 50:21. that I was s.a.o.as thys.
68:21.hairy scalp of s.a.o.as goeth
1 Co.5:5.to deliver s.a.o. unto Sat.
11. with s. a. o. no not to eat
2 Co. 2 : 7. s. a. o. be swallowed up with sorrow
10 : 11. Let s. a. o. think this
12:2. s.a.o. caught up to 3d heav.
5. of s.a.o. will I glory, yet not
Ga. 6 : 1. restore s.a.o. in meekness
Phm. 9. being s. a. o. as Paul the

ONE of them. ⌊aged
Ge. 42 : 27. as o. - opened his sack
Ex. 14:28. remained not so much as
Nu.16:15.nei.have I hurt o. -⌊o. -
De. 25 : 5. if o. - die, and have no child ⌈me
Ju.11:35.thou art o. - that trouble
1 S.17:36.this Philis.shall be as o. -
2 S. 13 : 30. king's sons not o. - left
17:22.lacked not o. - not over Jor.
20:19.I am o. - that are peaceable
24:12. 3 things, choose o. -, 1 Ch. 21 : 10. ⌈o. - escape
1 K.18:40. prophets of Baal, let not
19 : 2. if I make not thy life as the life of o.-
22:13.thy word be like word of o.-
1Ch.21:10.I offer 3 things choose o.-
Ps. 34 : 20. bones, not o.- is broken
53:3. Every o.- is gone back, none
58 : 8. As a snail let ev. o.- pass
64 : 6. thought of ev. o.- is deep
84:7. every o.- in Zion appeareth
Ps.106:11.enemies,was not o. - left
Pr.22:26.Be not o.- th.strike hands
Ec.10:15.of foolish wearieth ev.o. -
Je. 15 : 10. ev. o. - doth curse me
30:16.every o. - sh. go into captiv.
Eze.11:5.I know the things, ev.o. -
Da. 7 : 16. I came near o. - th.stood
8 : 9. out of o. - a little horn
Ob. 11. cast lots, thou wast as o. -
Mat. 10 : 29. two sparrows, and o. - shall not fall, Lu. 12 : 6.
18 : 12. have sheep, o. - be gone astray, Lu. 15 : 4.
20:13.he ans-d o.- and said,Friend
22:35. o. - wh. was a lawyer asked
26 : 51. o. - with Jesus drew his sword and, Mk.14:47. Lu.22:50.
73. thou art o. -, Mk. 14 : 69, 70.
Lu. 14 : 15. o. - that sat at meat
24:18.o. - Cleopas ans-g said unto
17 : 15. o. - when he was healed
Jn. 6 : 7. ev. o. - may take a little
7:50. to Jesus by night, being o. -
11:49.o. - Caiaphas said, Ye know
12:2.Lazarus o. - that sat at table
Ac. 7 : 24. seeing o. - suffer wrong
11:28.stood up o. - named Agabus

There is ONE.
Le. 7 : 7. trespass off-g t. i. o. law,
Ju. 21 : 6. t.i.o. tribe cut off fr. Isr.
Es. 4 : 11. t. i. o. law to put him to death except to whom king
Ec. 4 : 8. t.i.o. alone, not a second
9 : 2. t.i.o. event to righteous and
3. evil, that t.i.o. event unto all
Da. 2 : 9. if ye will not, t.i.o. decree
Na. 1 : 11. t. i. o. come out of thee
Mk.12:32. t.i.o. God, 1 Ti. 2:5. Ja. 2 : 19. ⌈even Mo.
Jn. 5: 45. t.i.o. that accuseth you,
8:50. t.i.o. that seeketh and judg.
1 Co. 15 : 39. t.i.o. kind of flesh of
41. t.i.o. glory of sun, ano.⌊men
Ja.4:12. t.i.o. lawgiver,able to save
See One THING.

Wicked ONE. ⌈eth
Mat.13:19. cometh w. o.and catch-
38.tares are chil. of the w.o. ⌈14.
1 Jn. 2 : 13. ye have overcome w.o.,
3:12.Not as Cain, who was of w.o.
5:18. that w.o. toucheth him not
See One YEAR, YOUNG one.

ONES. ⌈o.
Ps. 83: 3. consulted ag. thy hidden
Is. 13 : 3. I have com-ded my sanctified o. called my mighty o.
Da. 8 : 8. came up four notable o.
11 : 17. and upright o. with him
Zch. 4 : 14. These are the 2 anointed

Little ONES. ⌊o.
Ge. 34 : 29. all l. o. took they capt.
43 : 8. live, we, thou, and our l.o.
45 : 19. take wagons out of Egypt for your l. o. ⌈for l. o.
46:5. carried their l.o. | 47:24.food
47:†12. wi. bread acc. to their l.o.
50:8.only l.o. left they in Goshen
21. I will nourish you and l. o.
Ex. 10 : 10. let you go and l.o., 24.
Nu. 14 : 31. your l. o. will I bring
31 : 9. took women captives and l.
17. kill every male am. l. o. ⌊o.
32:16. build cities for our l.o., 24.
17.our l.o. sh. dwell in cities,26.
De. 1 : 39. your l. o. sh. go in thith.
2 : 34. we destroyed wom. and l.o.
20 : 14. the women and l. o. take
29:11. Your l.o. wives and ⌈3 : 19.
Jos. 1 : 14. Your l.o. sh. remain,De.
8:35.Josh.read bef. wom. and l.o.
Ju. 18 : 21. they put l.o. bef. them
2 S. 15 : 22. Ittai passed and all l.o.
2 Ch. 20 : 13. Judah bef. L. and l.o.
31 : 18. genealogy of all their l. o.
Ezr. 8 : 21. a right way for our l.o.
Es. 8 : 11. to cause to perish l. o.
Jb.21:11. They send forth their l.o.

Ps.137:9.dasheth thy l.o. ag.stones
Je. 14 : 3. nobles sent l. o. to pit
48 : 4. her l. o. have caused a cry
Zch. 13 : 7. turn my hand upon l.o.
Mat.10:42.to drink unto one of l.o.
18:6. offend one of l. o., Mk. 9:42.
10.that ye despise not one of l.o.
14. that one of these l. o. perish
Lu. 17:2. than that he offend one of
See **MIGHTY one**, s. ⌊l.o.
Strong ONES.
Ps. 10 : 10. poor may fall by s. o.
Je. 8 : 16. at neighing of his s. o.
See **YOUNG ones.**
ONES'IMUS.
Col. 4 : 9. O. a faithful beloved bro.
Phm. 10. I beseech thee for my son
ONESIPH'ORUS. ⌊O.
2 Ti. 1 : 16. L. give mercy unto ho.
4:19.Salute household of O. ⌊of O.
ONLY. ⌈ually
Ge.6:5. thoughts are o. evil contin-
7:23. Noah o. remained alive, and
19:8.o.unto these men do nothing
22:2. Take now thine o. son Isaac
12. not withheld thine o. son,16.
24: 8. o. bring not my son thither
27: 13. o. obey my voice, fetch th.
34:22. o. herein will the men consent unto us, 23.
41 : 40. o. in the throne will I be
greater than thou ⌈he not, 26.
47:22.o.the land of priests bought
Ex. 8:9. may remain in river o.,11.
28. o. you shall not go far away
10 : 17. Now forgive my sin o. this
once th. he take this death o.
24. o. let your flocks be stayed
12:16.eat,th.o.may be done of you
21 : 19. o. he sh. pay for his time
22 : 20. sacrificeth save unto L. o.
27. covering, o. it is his raiment
Le. 21: 23. o. he sh. not go in unto
27 : 26. o. firstling of beasts ⌊vail
Nu. 1 : 49. o. shalt not number Levi
12 : 2. Hath L. o. spoken by Mo.?
14 : 9. rebel not ye ag. the Lord o.
18: 3. o. sh. not come nigh vessels
20 : 19. o. go on my feet, De. 2:28.
22 : 35. o. the word I shall speak
31 : 22. o. the gold and the silver
36:6. o. marry family of fa.'s tribe
De. 4 : 9. o. take heed to thyself
12. no similitude, o. ye heard
8:3. man doth not live by bread o.
10:15.o. L. had delight in thy fa-s
12:16. o. not eat blood, 23.-15:23.
22 : 25. man o. that lay with her
28:13. o. not be beneath ⌊shall die
29. thou shalt be o.oppressed,33.
29:14. nei. with you o. do I make
Jos.1:7. o. be thou strong,18. ⌊cov.
17. o. L. thy God be with thee
6 : 15. o. th. day compassed city 7
17. o. Rahab shall live ⌊times
11 : 13. Isr. burned none, Hazor o.
17 : 17. shalt not have one lot o.
Ju. 3 :2. o. know to teach th. war
6 : 37. if dew be on the fleece o.
39. not be dry o. upon fleece, 40.
10 : 15. deliver us o. we pray thee
11 : 34. and she was his o. child
16:28. strengthen me, o. this once
19 : 20. said, o. lodge not in street
1 S.1:13.Hannah o. moved her lips
23.o. the Lord establish his word
5 : 4. o. stump of Dagon was left
7:3. serve him o., 4. Mat. 4:10.Lu.
12 : 24. o. fear the Lord, and ⌊4:8.
18 : 17. o. be thou valiant for me
20 : 14. not o. while I live, shew me
39.o.Jona. and Da. knew ⌊kindu.
2 S. 13 : 32. said, o. Amnon is dead,
17 : 2. I will smite the king o. ⌊33.
20 : 21. deliver him o. I will depart
23:10.returned o. to spoil ⌈pla., 3.
1 K. 3 : 2. o. peo. sacrificed in high

I K.4:19. Geber o.officer in the land
7:†25. o. if thy chil. take heed ⌈o.
12: 20. none followed Da. but Jud.
14 : 8. Da. did that o. wh. was right
13. he o. of Jerob. come to grave
15:5.o. in matter of Uriah ⌈life,14.
19 : 10. I o. am left, they seek my
22:31. fight not, save o. with king
2 K. 10 : 23. worshippers of Baal o.
17:18.none left but tribe of Jud.o.
19:19.thou art L. thou o.,Is.37:20.
1 Ch. 22 : 12. o. the L. give wisdom
2 Ch. 2 : 6. save o. to burn sacrifice
6 : 30. thou o. knowest hearts of
children of men, 1 K. 8 : 39.
33 : 17. sacrifice unto Lord God o.
Es. 1 : 16. not done wrong to king o.
Jb.1:12.o.upon hims. put not hand
15. I o. am escaped to, 16, 17,19.
2 :†6. he is in thine hand, o. save
13 : 20. o. do not two thi. unto me
34:29.whether ag.nation or man o.
Ps. 4 : 8. L. o. makest me dwell in
35 :† 17. rescue my o. one fr. lions
51 : 4. Ag. thee o. have I sinned
62 : † 1. o. my soul silent upon G.
2. He o. is my rock my salv., 6.
4. o. consult to cast him down
5. My soul, wait thou o. upon G.
71:16.mention thy right-n.thine o.
72:18. G. of Isr. o. doth wondrous
91:8. o. with thine eyes behold ⌈er
Pr.4:3. o. beloved in sight of moth-
5:17.Let them be o.thine own,and
11 : 23. desire of righte. is o. good
13:10. o. by pride cometh conten-n
14 : 23. talk tendeth o. to penury
17:11.evil man seeketh o.rebellion
21 : 5. o. to plenteousn. o. to want
Ec.7:29.this o.have I found,that G.
Can.6:9. is the o. one of her moth.
Is.4:1.o. let us be called by thy na.
26:13. o. make mention of thy na.
28 : 19. vexation o. to underst. re-
Je.3:13.o.acknowl.thine iniq. ⌊port
6 : 26. as for an o. son, Am. 8 : 10.
32:30.o. done evil, o.provoked me
Eze. 7 : 5. an o. evil is come
14:16. they o. sh. be delivered, 18.
44:20. they sh. o. poll their heads
Am.3:2. You o. have I known of all
Mat. 5 : 47. if salute breth. o. what
8:8. said, Lord, speak the word o.
10:42. cup of cold wat. o. in name
12:4.not lawful to eat,o.for priests
14:36. they might o. touch hem
17 : 8. no man, save Jes. o.,Mk.9:8.
21:19. found nothing but leaves o.
21. sh. not o. do this wh. is done
24:36.not the angels,but my Fa.o.
Mk. 2 : 7. who forgive, but God o.?
5:36.Jes. saith, o. believe,Lu.8:50.
6:8.noth.for journey,save a staff o.
Lu.7:12.dead man, o.son of mother
8:42.one o. dau. | 9:38.my o.child
24 : 18. Art thou o. stranger in Je-
Jn.5:18.not o.bec.broken sab.⌊rus.
44. seek not honour from God o.
11:52.that Jes.die,not for nation o.
12:9. came not for Jes. sake o.but
13 : 9. Lord, not my feet o. but
17:3. might know thee, o. true G.
Ac. 8 : 16. o. they were baptized ⌈o.
11:19. preaching to none but Jews
18:25. Apollos taught, knowing o.
19:27.not o. our craft is in danger
21:13.ready not to be bound o.but
25.o. keep thems. fr. things off-d
26 : 29. I would to G. not o. thou
27 : 10. not o. of lading and ship
Ro. 1 : 32. not o. do same, but have
3 : 29. Is he God of Jews o.? ⌊pleas.
4:9.blessedn. upon circumc.o.? 12.
16. not to that o. which is of law
5:3. not o. so,11. | 8:23.not o.they
9:10. n. o. this, but when Rebecca
24.whom he called,not of Jews o.

Ro.13:5.be subject, not o.for wrath
16:4.unto wh. not o.I give thanks
27.To God o. wise be glory, 1 Ti.
1 : 17. Jude 25. ⌈and Barna.
1 Co. 7 : 39. o. in the L. | 9 : 6. I o.
14:36.came word of God fr. you o.
15:19.If in this life o.we have hope
2 Co.7:7. comforted not by his com-
8 : 10. begun not o. to do ⌊ing o.
19. thro-t churches and not that
21.not o.in sight of Lord but ⌊o.
Ga.1:23.heard o.he who persecuted
2 : 10. o. that we remember poor
3 : 2. This o. would I learn of you
4 : 18. not o. when I am present
5:13.o.use not liberty for occasion
6:12.o.lest they suffer persecution
Ep. 1 : 21. ev. name not o. in world
Ph. 1 : 27. o. let your conversa. be
29. not o. to believe but suffer
2:12. obeyed,not in my presence o.
27. mercy not on him o. but me
4:15. no ch. communica. but ye o.
Col. 4 : 11. o. my fellow workers ⌈o.
1 Th. 1: 5. gospel came not in word
2 : 8. to you not gospel of God o.
2 Th. 2 : 7. o. he who now letteth
1 Ti. 5 : 13. not o. idle, but tattlers
6 : 15. is blessed and o. Potentate
16. Who o. hath immortality
2 Ti. 4 : 8. not to me o. but unto all
11. o. Luke is with me
He. 9 : 10. which stood o. in meats
12 : 26. I shake not earth o. but
Ja. 1 : 22. be doers, not hearers o.
2:24. justif. by works, not faith o.
1 Pe.2:18.not o. to good and gentle
1 Jn.2:2. not for ours o. but sins of
5:6.not by water o.but wat.and bl.
2 Jn. 1. whom I love, and not I o.
Jude 4.denying the o.Lord God and
Re. 9 : 4. o. those wh. have not seal
15 : 4. Who not fear thee? thou o.
See BEGOTTEN. ⌊art holy
ONIONS. ⌈lic
Nu. 11 : 5. we remember o. and gar-
O'NO. ⌈Ne. 11 : 35.
1 Ch. 8 : 12. O. and Lod with towns,
Ezr. 2 : 33. chil. of Lod, O., Ne.7:37.
Ne. 6 : 2. villages in plain of O.
ONWARD.
Ex. 40 : 36. when cloud was up, Isr.
ONYCHA. ⌊went o.
Ex. 30 : 34. Take thee spices, o. and
ONYX.
Ex. 28:20. 4th row an o., 39 : 13. ⌈o.
Jb. 28:16. wisd. can-t be valued wi.
Eze. 28 : 13. topaz and o. thy cov-
See STONES. ⌊ering
OPEN. [Adj.] ⌈mament
Ge. 1 : 20. fowl th. may fly in o. fir-
38:14.Tamar sat in o.place by way
Nu. 19 : 15. every o. vessel is uncl.
Jos. 8 : 17. left Ai o. and pursued
1 S.3:1. word of Lord precious, was
no o. vision ⌈flowers, 29,32,35.
1 K. 6 : 18. cedar carved with o.
Ne.6:5.Sanballat with o.letter sent
Jb. 34: 26. as wick. men in o. sight
Ps. 5 : 9. their throat is an o. sepul-
chre, Ro. 3 : 13. ⌈o. places
Pr. 8 : † 26. not made earth nor the
13:16.fool layeth o. his folly ⌈love
27 : 5. o. rebuke better than secret
Is.24:18. windows fr. on high are o.
Je. 5:16. quiver is o. sepulchre ⌈14.
32:11.both what was sealed and o.,
19.thine eyes o.upon ways of men
Eze. 37: 2. many bones in o. valley
Da.6:10.his windows o. in chamber
Jn. 1 : 51. ye shall see heaven o.
Ac. 16 : 27. prison doors o. drew sw.
19: 38. law is o. there are deputies
2 Co.3:18. we wi. o. face beholding
1 Ti. 5 : 24. Some men's sins are o.
He. 6 : 6. they put him to o. shame
Re. 3 : 8. I have set bef. thee o.door

Re. 10 : 2. had in hand a little book
See EARS, EYES. [o., 8.
See **Open FIELD, FIELDS, GATES, MOUTH** with **open.**

OPEN. [Verb.]

Ex. 21 : 33. if a man shall o. a pit
Nu.8:16 instead of such as o.womb
De.15:8.o. hand wide unto him, 11.
20:11.if make ans.and o.unto thee
28:12.L. o. unto thee his treasure
Ps. 22: † 7. All that see me o. lip
49:4.I will o.my dark saying upon
Can. 5 : 2. o. to me, my sis. my love
5. I rose up to o. to my beloved
9:†12.see whe. the tender grape o.
Is.22:22.o. none shut, shut none o.
28:24. doth he o. clods of ground?
41:18.I will o.rivers in high places
45:8.let earth o. bring forth salva.
Je.13:19. cities sh. be shut, shall o.
50:26. o. her storehouses, cast her
Eze. 25 : 9. I will o. side of Moab fr.
37:12. I will o. your graves [cities
46 : 12. one shall o. gate tow. east
Am. 8: † 5. sab. that we o. wheat
Mal. 3: 10. if I will not o. windows
Mat. 25 : 11. saying Lord, Lord, o. to us, Lu. 13: 25. [may o.
Lu. 12 : 36. when he knocketh they
Jn.1:51. sh. see heaven o., Ac.7:56.
Col.4:3.God wo.o.door of utterance
Re. 3 : 20. hear voice and o. door
5 : 9. thou art worthy to o. seals
See BOOK, DOOR, DOORS, EYES, GATES, LIPS, WINDOW.
See **MOUTH** with **open.**

OPENED.

Ge.41:56. Joseph o. all storehouses
42:27.one o.his sack, 43:21.-44:11.
Ex. 2 : 6. had o. ark she saw child
Ju. 4 : 19. she o. a bottle of milk
2 S. 7:†27. O L. hast o. ear of serv.
2 K. 13 : 17. he o. window eastward
15:16.they o.not thf. he smote th.
Ne.13:19.gates not be o.till aft.sab.
Jb.29:†19.my root was o. by waters
32:†19. belly as wine wh. is not o.
38: 17. gates of death been o. unto
Ps. 22:†13. o. mouths ag. me [thee
66 : † 14. pay vows my lips have o.
105:41. He o. rock, waters gushed
106:17. earth o. swallowed Dathan
Can. 5 : 6. I o. to my beloved, but
Is. 14 : 17. o. not house of prisoners
Je.1:†14. out of north an evil be o.
20:12.unto thee have I o.my cause
50 : 25. Lord hath o. his armoury
Eze. 1 : 1. heavens were o., Mat. 3: 16. Mk. 1:10. Lu.3:21. Ac.7:56.
16: 25. hast o. thy feet to ev. one
37:13. when I have o. your graves
44 : 2. gate not be o. no man enter
46 : 1. on sabbath it sh. be o. [Da.
Zch. 13 : 1. fountain be o. to ho. of
Mat. 2 : 11. when had o. treasures
7:7. knock, it shall be o. to you, 8. Lu. 11 : 9, 10. [arose
27: 52. graves were o. many bodies
Mk. 7 : 34. saith Ephphatha, Be o.
Lu.24:32.while he o.to us Scriptures
45.Then o.he their understand-g
Ac. 5 : 23. had o. we found no man
10 : 11. Peter saw heaven o. and a
16: 14. Lydia, whose heart L-d o.
He. 4:13. all things are o. unto him
Re. 6 : 1. I saw Lamb o. one of seals
3. o. second | 5. third | 7. fourth
9. o. fifth | 12. sixth | 8:1.seventh
9 : 2. he o. the bottomless pit, and
11:19.tem. of God was o. in heaven
15: 5. tabern. of testimony was o.
19 : 11. I saw heaven o. and white
20:12.dead bef. God, books were o.
See BOOK, S, DOOR, S, EAR, S, EYES, GATE, GATES, MOUTHS.
See **MOUTH** with **opened.**
See WINDOW, WINDOWS, WOMB.

OPENEST.

Ps. 104 : 28. thou o. hand, are filled with good [satisfiest
145 : 16. Thou o. thine hand and

OPENETH. [is not

Jb. 27:19. rich man o. his eyes, and
36:10. He o. their ear to discipline
146 : 8. L. o. the eyes of the blind
Pr. 13 : 3. he that o. wide his lips
Jn.10:3.To him the porter o., sheep
Re. 3 : 7. he that o. and no man shutteth, shutteth and no man
See EARS, MATRIX, WOMB. [o.
See **MOUTH** with **openeth.**

OPENING. [Part.]

Is. 42:20. o. ears but he heareth not
Ac.17:3.o.and alleging Christ must

OPENING, S. [†29,†32.

1 K.6:†18.carved with o-s of flowers,
1 Ch. 9 : 27. o. of house of G. [o.
Jb. 12:14. shutteth up a man, be no
Pr. 1 : 21. in o-s of gates wisdom
8 : 6. the o.of my lips sh. be right
Is. 61 : 1. proclaim the o. of prison
Eze. 29 : 21. I will give thee o. of

OPENLY. [mouth

Ge.38:21. harlot th. was o. by way
2 S. 6 : † 20. vain fellow o. uncover-
Ps.98:2.righte-n. he o. shewed [eth
Mat. 6 : 4. Fa. shall reward o., 6:18.
Mk. 8 : 32. he spake that saying o.
Jn. 7 : 4. he seeketh to be known o.
10. then went he to feast, not o.
13. no man spake of him o. [11:45.
11:54. Jes. walked no more o., Mk.
18 : 20. Jesus ans-d, I spake o. to
Ac. 10 : 40. Him God shewed o.
16 : 37. They have beaten us o.
Col.2:15. he made a shew of them o.

OPERATION, S.

Ps. 28:5. regard not o. of his hands
Is. 5 : 12. nei. consider o. of his ha.
Col. 2 : 12. risen thro. faith of o. of
1 Co. 12:6. are diversities of o-s [G.

O'PHEL.

2 Ch.27:3.Jotham built on wall of O.
33:14. Manasseh compassed ab-t O.
Ne.3:26.Nethinim in O., 11 : 21. [O.
27. Tekoites repaired unto wall of

O'PHIR. [Person, Place.] [23.

Ge. 10:29. Joktan begat O., 1 Ch. 1:
1 K.9:28.they came to O and fetched thence gold, 2 Ch. 8 : 18.-9 : 10.
10:11.brought from O. almug trees
22 : 48. ships to go to O. for gold
1 Ch.29:4.3,000 talents of gold of O.
Jb.22:24.shalt lay up the gold of O.
28:16. can-t be valued with gold of
Ps. 45 : 9. queen in gold of O. [O.
Is. 13 : 12. more preci. than wedge

OPH'NI. [of O.

Jos. 18 : 24. cities of Benj. O.

OPH'RAH. [Person, Place.]

Jos. 18 : 23. cities of Benj. Parah O.
Ju. 6 : 11. sat under oak in O.
24. unto this day altar is in O.
8 : 27. Gideon put ephod in O.
32. Gideon was buried in O. [O.
9:5.Abim. went unto fa.'s house at
1 S. 13 : 17. way that leadeth to O.
1 Ch. 4 : 14. Meonothai begat O.

OPINION, S. [o-s?

1 K. 18 : 21. How long halt bet. two
Jb.32:6.durst not shew you mine o.
10. I also will shew you mine o.,

OPPORTUNITY. [17.

Le. 16: † 21. scapegoat by man of o.
Mat. 26 : 16. he sought o. to betray him, Lu. 22 : 6. [good unto all
Ga. 6 : 10. as we have o. let us do
Ph. 4 : 10. careful, but we lacked o.
He.11:15.might have had o.to retur.

OPPOSE, ED, EST, ETH.

Jb.30:21.with strong hand o-t thys.
Ac. 18 : 6. they o-d themselves and blasphemed [hims.
2 Th. 2 : 4. Who o-h and exalteth

2 Ti. 2:25. instructing those that o.

OPPOSITION, S. [eas

Ha. 1 : † 9. o. of faces towa d the
1 Ti. 6 : 20. avoiding o-s of science

OPPRESS.

Ex. 3 : 9. whw. Egyptians o. them
22:21.nei.vex nor o. stranger, 23: 9.
Le. 19 : †33. if stranger, not o. him
25:14. ye shall not o. one ano., 17.
De. 23 : 16. shalt not o. servant
24 : 14. shalt not o. a hired servant
Ju. 10 : 12. Moabites did o. you
Jb.10:3.Is it good thou shouldest o.?
Ps 10:18. that man may no more o.
17:9. hide me from wicked that o.
119 : 122. let not proud o. me [me
Pr. 22 : 22. nor o. the afflicted in
Is. 49:26.will feed them that o.thee
Je. 7 : 6. If yo o. not stranger and
30:20. I will punish all that o. th.
Eze. 45 : 8. princes shall no more o.
Ho. 12:7. merchant, he loveth to o.
Am. 4 : 1. kine of Bashan o. poor
Mi. 2 : 2. they o. a man and his hou.
Zch. 7 : 10. o. not the widow nor [o.
Mal. 3:5. swift witness ag. those th.
1 Th. 4 : † 6. no man o. his brother
Ja. 2: 6. Do not rich men o. you

OPPRESSED.

De. 28:29. thou shalt be only o., 33.
Ju. 2:18. by reason of them that o.
4:3. Jabin o. Isr. | 10:8. Philis. o.
6:9.I deliv-d you out of hand of all o. you, 1 S. 10 : 18. [whom I o.
1 S. 12 : 3. whose ox have I taken?
4. hast not defrauded, nor o. us
2 K. 13:4. bec. king of Syria o.them
22. Hazael king of Syria o. Israel
2 Ch. 16 : 10. Asa o. some of people
Jb. 20:19. Bec. he hath o. the poor
35 : 9. they made the o. to cry
Ps. 9 : 9. L. will be a refuge for o.
10 : 18. judge the fatherless and o.,
103 : 6.-146 : 7. [ashamed
74 : 21. O let not the o. return
106 : 42. Their enemies o. them
Ec. 4 : 1. the tears of such as were o.
Is.1:17. Learn to do well, relieve o.
3 : 5. people shall be o. ev. one
23 : 12. O thou, o. virgin, dau. of
38 : 14. O Lord, I am o. undertake
52 : 4. Assyrian o. without cause
53 : 7. He was o. and afflicted, yet
58 : 6. the fast to let o. go free
Je. 50:32. Israel and Judah were o.
Eze. 18 : 7. hath not o. any, but, 16.
12. Hath o. the poor and needy
18. his father, bec. he cruelly o.
22 : 29. they have o. the stranger
Ho.5:11. Ephraim is o. and broken
Am. 3:9. behold the o. in the midst
Ac. 7 : 24. Moses avenged him o.
10 : 38. Jesus healed all o. of devil

OPPRESSETH.

Nu. 10 : 9. if to war ag. enemy o.
Jb. 40:†23. Behemoth o. river [you
Ps. 56 : 1. he fighting daily o. me
Pr.14:31.He that o. the poor, 22:16.
28 : 3. a poor man that o. the poor

OPPRESSING. [sword

Je. 46 : 16. Arise, let us go from o.
50 : 16. for fear of o. sword, they
Zph. 3 : 1. Woe to o. city, obeyed

OPPRESSION. [not

Ex. 3:9. I have seen o. wh-w. Eg-ns
De. 26 : 7. Lord looked on our o.
2 K. 13 : 4. Lord saw the o. of Israel
Jb.36:15.he openeth their ears in o.
Ps. 12 : 5. For o. of poor will I arise
42 : 9. because of the o. of the enemy, 43:2.-55:3.[Trust not in o.
44 : 24. forgettest our o. | 62 : 10.
73 : 8. speak wickedly conc. o.
107 : 39. are brought low thro. o.
119:134. Deliver me from o.of man
Ec. 5 : 8. If thou seest the o. of poor
7 : 7. o. maketh a wise man mad

Is.5:7.behold o. | 30:12. trust in o.
30:†20. tho. L. give you wat. of o.
54 : 14. thou shalt be far from o.
59 : 13. speaking o. and revolt
Je. 6 : 6. she is wholly o. in midst
22: 17. thine eyes and heart for o.
Eze.22:7. dealt by o. with stranger
29. people of land have used o.
46:18.prince not take inherit.by o.

OPPRESSIONS.

Jb. 35 : 9. By reason of mult. of o.
Ec. 4 : 1. I considered the o. done
Is. 33 : 15. that despiseth gain of o.
Am. 3 : †9. behold the o. in midst

OPPRESSOR. [o.

Es.3:†10. king gave ring unto Jews'
Jb. 3 : 18. they hear not voice of o.
15:20. number of y-rs is hidd. to o.
Ps. 72 : 4. shall break in pieces o.
Pr. 8:31. Envy not o. choose [an o.
28:16. prince th.wanteth underst-g
Is. 9 : 4. hast broken rod of his o.
14 : 4. How hath the o. ceased!
51 : 13. feared bec. of fury of o.
Je. 21:12. deliver him that is spoiled out of hand of o., 22 : 3.
25 : 38. bec. of the fierceness of o.
Zch.9:8. no o. shall pass thro. them
10:4. out of him came ev.o.togeth.

OPPRESSORS.

Jb. 27 : 13. this is heritage of o.
Ps. 54 : 3. and o. seek after my soul
119 : 121. leave me not to mine o.
Ec. 4 : 1. on side of o. was power
Is. 3:12. chil. are their o.wom. rule
14 : 2. they shall rule over their o.
16 : 4. o. are consumed out of land
19 : 20. shall cry to Lord bec. of o.

ORACLE, S. [of God

2 S. 16 : 23. as if one inquired at o.
1 K. 6:5.ag. wall of o. made chamb.
16. he built them for it, for o.
19. o. he prepared in the house
20. o. in forefront was 20 cubits
21. chains of gold before o.
22. altar by o. overlaid with gold
23. within o. made 2 cherubim
31. for entering of o. made doors
7:49. before the o., 8:8. 2 Ch. 3:16.
8:6. priests bro-t ark into o. [5:9.
2 Ch. 4:20. burn bef. o. of pure gold
5:7. o. of house in most holy place
Ps.28:2.when I lift hands tow. holy
Ac.7:38.who received lively o-s [o.
Ro. 3 : 2. were committed o-s of G.
He. 5 : 12. first princip. of o-s of G.
1 Pe. 4 : 11. let him speak as o-s of

ORATION. [God

Ac. 12:21. upon set day Herod made

ORATOR. [o.

Is.3:3. L. fr. Judah the eloquent o.
Ac. 24:1.certain o. named Tertullus

ORCHARD, S.

Ec. 2 : 5. I made me gardens o-s
Can. 4 : 13. Thy plants are an o. of

ORDAIN.

1 Ch. 9 : 22. Sam. did o. in set office
17 : 9. I will o. a place for my peo.
Is. 26:12. L., thou wilt o. peace for
1 Co. 7 : 17. so o. I in churches [us
Tit.1:5.that thou shouldest o.elders

ORDAINED.

Nu. 28:6. offering th. was o. in Sinai
1 K. 12 : 32. Jeroboam o. feast, 33.
2 K. 23:5. put down idola. priests o.
2 Ch.11: 15. Jeroboam o. priests for
23:18.to offer off-gs, as o.by David
29:27.the instruments o. by David
Es. 9 : 27. Jews o. feasts of Purim
Ps.8:2. Out of mouth of babes hast
3.moon and stars thou hast o. [o.
81 : 5. o. in Joseph for testimony
132: 17. I have o. a lamp for mine
Is. 30 : 33. Tophet is o. of old
Je. 1 : 5. I o. thee to be a prophet
Da.2:24.king o. to destroy wise men
Ha.1:12. O Lord, thou hast o.them
Mk. 3 : 14. Jes. o. 12 to be with him
Jn.15:16: I o. ye should bring fruit
Ac. 1 : 22. one o. to be witness with us of resurrection
10:42.o. of G. to be judge of quick
13 : 48. as were o. to eternal life
14:23.when they had o.them elders
16:4. decrees that were o. of apos.
17 : 31. judge world by man he o.
Ro. 7 : 10. com-t which was o. to life
13:1. powers that be are o. of God
1 Co.2:7.hidden wisdom wh. God o.
9:14. Lord o. that they wh.preach
Ga. 3 : 19. the law was o. by angels
Ep. 2 : 10. good works, which G. o.
1 Ti. 2 : 7. I am o. apostle to Gent.
He. 5 : 1. ev. high priest is o., 8 : 3.
9:6.when these things were thus o.
Jude 4. of old o. to this condemna- [tion

ORDAINETH.

Ps. 7 : 13. he o. his arrows ag. perse- [cutors

ORDER. [Noun.]

Ju. 17 :† 10. thee an o. of garments
2 K. 23:4. com-ded priests of sec. o.
1 Ch.6:32.they waited acc. to o.[o.
15:13. we sought him not aft. due
23:31. o. commanded them bef. L.
25 : 2. acc. to the o. of David, 6. 2 Ch. 8 : 14. [out any o.
Jb. 10 : 22. a land of darkness, with-
Ps. 110:4. priest aft. o. of Melchizedek, He.5:6,10.-6:20.-7:11,17,21
Ac. 11 : 4. Peter expounded it by o.
1 Co.16:1.I have giv. o. to churches
Col. 2 : 5. joying beholding your o.
He. 7 : 11. not be called aft.o. of Aa- [ron

In ORDER.

Ge. 22 : 9. Abraham laid wood i. o.
Ex.26:17.Two tenons sh. be set i.o.
39:37.with the lamps to be set i.o.
40:4.thou shalt set i.o. the things that are to be set i.o., Le. 1: 7, 8, 12.-6: 12.-24:8. [Lord
23. he set bread i.o. upon it bef.
Jos. 2 : 6. stalks of flax she laid i.o.
2 S. 17 : 23. Ahith. put house i. o.
1 K. 18:33. Elijah put wood i.o. [1.
2 K. 20 : 1. Set thine ho. i.o., Is. 38:
2 Ch.13:11. shewbread set they i.o.
29:35. service of ho. of L. set i. o.
Jb. 33 : 5. set words i. o. before me
Ps. 40 : 5. can-t be reckoned up i.o.
50: 21. will set i.o. bef. thine eyes
Ec. 12:9. Preacher set i.o. proverbs
Is. 44:7. who set it i.o. before me?
Eze. 41 : 6. side chambers 30 i. o.
Lu. 1 : 1. in hand to set forth i.o., 3.
8. Zach. served bef. God i. his o.
Ac.18:23.he went over Phrygia, i.o.
1 Co. 11 : 34. rest will I set i.o.when
14 : 40. Let all things be done i.o.
15:23. every man sh. rise i. his o.
Tit.1:5. I left thee to set i.o.things

ORDER. [Verb.] [3, 4.

Ex. 27:21. Aaron shall o. it, Le.24:
Ju.13:12. How shall we o.the child
1 K. 20 : 14. Who shall o. the battle
Jb. 23 : 4. I would o. my cause bef.
37:19.we can-t o. our speech [him
Ps.40:†5. thy thoughts none can o.
78:† 19. Can God o. table in wild.?
119 : 133. o. my steps in thy word
Is. 9 : 7. upon his kingdom to o. it
Je. 46 : 3. o. ye buckler and shield

ORDERED, ETH.

Ju. 6 : 26. build altar in o-d place
2 S. 23 : 5. everl. covenant o-d and
Jb. 13 : 18. I have o-d my cause, I
32 : † 14. not o-d his words ag. me
Ps.37:23. steps of good man are o-d
50:23.who o-h his conversa.aright
Pr. 4 : † 26. let ways be o-d aright
Ro.13:†1. powers th. be are o.of G.

ORDERING, S. [of o.

1 Ch. 9:†32. Kohathites over bread
24:19. these were their o-s in their service under Aaron

ORDERLY.

Ju. 6 : † 26. build alt. in o. manner
Ac. 21 : 24. walkest o. keepest law

ORDINANCE.

Ex. 12 : 14. keep feast of passover, for an o. for ever, 24, 43.-13:16.
15 : 25. he made a statute and o.
Le. 5 : † 10. offer acc. to o., 9 : † 16.
18:30.sh.keep mine o., 22:9. [35:13
Nu. 9: 14. acc. to o. of passo., 2 Ch
10: 8. be to you for an o. for ever
15 : 15. One o. shall be for you in
† 24. shall offer acc. to o.
18:8.to sons by o.for ev., 2 Ch.2:4.
19 : 2. o. of law L. com-ded, 31:21.
Jos.24:25. set th. an o. in Shechem
Ju. 11 : †39. And it was an o. in Isr.
1 S. 30:25. he made it an o. for ever
1 K. 6 : † 38. house finished with o.
2 Ch. 35 : 25. made them o. in Isr.
Ezr. 3 : 10. after the o. of David
Ne. 11 : † 23. sure o. be for singers
Ps. 99:7. they kept o. he gave them
Is. 24 : 5. transgr-d law, changed o.
58 : 2. forsook not o. of their God
Eze.40:†45. priests that keep the o.
44 : † 8. have set keepers of my o.
45 : 14. Conc. o. of oil, bath of oil
46: 14. an offering by perpetual o.
48:†11. priests wh.have kept my o.
Zch. 3 : † 7. if thou wilt keep my o.
Mal.3:14.what profit that we kept o.
Ro. 13 : 2. resisteth, resisteth o. of G.
1 Pe. 2 : 13. Submit to ev. o. of man

ORDINANCES.

Ex. 18 : 20. teach them o. and laws
Le. 18:3. nei.shall ye walk in their o.
4. ye shall keep o., 30.-22:9. 2 Ch. 33:8. Eze. 11:20.-43:11. 1 Co. 11:2.
Nu. 9 : 12. acc. to o. of passover, 14.
1 K. 6 : † 38. finished house with o.
2 K. 17:34. nei. do they aft. their o.
37. o. he wrote for you, observe
Ne. 10 : 32. made o. to charge ours
Jb. 38 : 33. Knowest thou the o. of heaven? Je. 31 : 35.-33 : 25.
Ps. 119:91. continue acc. to thine o.
Is. 58 : 2. ask of me o. of justice
Je.10 :† 3. o. of the peo. are vanity
31:36.If those o. depart fr. bef me
Eze.43:18. These are o. of the altar
44:5.conc. o. of the house of the L.
Mal. 3 : 7. ye are gone fr. mine o.
Lu. 1 : 6. walking in com-ts and o.
Ep. 2 : 15. law of com-ts in o. [of L.
Col. 2:14. Blotting out handwriting
20.why are ye subject to o.? [of o.
He. 9 : 1. first cov-t had o. of divine
10. stood in carnal o. imposed

ORDINARY. [food

Eze. 16 : 27. I diminished thine o.
Ac.19:†39.determined in o.assembl.

O'REB.

Ju. 7 : 25. slew princes of Midian, Zeeb, O., 8 : 3.
Ps. 83 : 11. nobles like O. and Zeeb
Is.10:26.slaughter at the rock of O.

O'REN. See OZEM.

ORGAN, S. [dle o.

Ge. 4 : 21. Jubal, fa. of such as han-
Jb.21:12. rejoice at the sound of o.
30 : 31. my o. turned into voice of
Ps. 150 : 4. praise him with the o-s

ORI'ON.

Jb.9:9. maketh O. Pleiades, Am.5:8.
38 : 31. canst loose bands of O.?

ORNAMENT.

Pr.1:9.be o. of grace unto thy head
4 : 9. She sh. give to thine head o.
25 : 12. as an o. of fine gold, so is
Is. 30 : 22. defile o. of molten imag.
49:18. shalt clothe thee as with o.
Eze. 7 : 20. beauty of his o. he set it
16 : †7. art come to o. of ornam-ts
†39. take instruments of thine o.
Da. 11 :† 16. sh. stand in land of o.
† 41. he sh. enter into land of o.

1 Pe. 3 : 4. o. of meek, quiet spirit
ORNAMENTS.
Ex.33:4. no man put on him his o.
5.now put off thy o.from thee,6.
Ju.8:21. Gideon took o. on camels'
26. golden earrings; besides o.
2 S. 1 : 24. weep ov.Saul, who put o.
Is.3:18. take aw. tinkling o. ab.feet
†19.chains, bracelets, spangled o.
20.bonnets, and the o.of the legs
61:10. as bridegr. decketh with o.
Je. 2 : 32. Can maid forget her o.
4 : 30. tho. deckest with o. of gold
Eze. 16 : 7. art come to excellent o.
11.decked thee wi. o. put bracel.
23:40.for wh. thou deckest with o.
OR'NAN. [of O.
2 S.24:†16. angel by threshingplace
1 Ch. 21 : 15. threshingfloor of O.,
18, 28. 2 Ch. 3 : 1.
20. O. turned, and saw the angel
22.Da.said to O.Grant me | 21,23.
24.Da. said to O. Nay ; I will buy
25. Da. gave O. for place 600 she-
OR'PAH. [kels
Ru. 1: 4. name of one was O. other
14. O. kissed Naomi, but Ruth
ORPHANS.
La. 5 : 3. We are o. our mothers as
Jn. 14 : † 18. I will not leave you o.
O'SEE. See HOSEA.
OSHE'A. See JOSHUA.
OSPRAY, OSSIFRAGE.
Le. 11 : 13. eagle, o. and o. not eat,
De. 14 : 12.
OSTRICH, ES. [o-s
Jb. 30 : † 29. I am companion to
39 : 13. Gavest thou wings unto o.
Is. 13:†21. and o. shall dwell there
34 : † 13. it shall be a court for o-s
43:†20.beast sh.honour me and o-s
La. 4 : 3. become cruel, like o-s
OTHER.
Ge. 8:10. Noah stayed o. 7 days,12.
20 : 16. cov-g of eyes unto all o.
28:17. is none o. but house of God
29:27. serve with me o. 7 years,30.
31:50.if shalt take o.wives besides
32 : 8. o. company left sh. escape
41 : 3. seven o. kine came up, 19.
43:14. may send away your o.bro.
22. o. money have we bro-t down
Ex.4:7. was turned again as o.flesh
18:7.asked each o. of welfare[28:8.
29 : 41. o. lamb offer at even, Nu.
30:32. not make any o. like th. oil
Le. 6 : 11. he shall put on o. garments, Eze. 42:14.-44:19. [use
7 : 24. fat may be used in any o.
14 : 42. take o. stones, o. mortar
18 : 18. Nei. take a wife besides o.
20:24.I separated you fr.o.peo.,26.
Nu. 10 : 21. o. did set up tabernacle
32 : 38. gave o. names to the cities
36:3. if married to any of o. tribes
De. 28 : 36. shalt serve o. gods, 64.
29:26. went and served o. gods
Jos. 11 : 19. o. cities they took
Ju. 13: 10. man that came o. day
16 : 17. weak and like any o. man
1 S. 21 : 9. take it, there is no o.
2 S.13:16.this evil is greater than o.
1 K. 9 : 6. if ye go and serve o. gods
2 Ch. 30 : 23. to keep o. seven days
32:22. Lord saved Hez. from all o.
Ne. 4 : 16. o. half held both spears
5 : 5. o. men have our lands and
Jb.8:12. flag withereth bef. o. herb
24 : 24. taken out of way, as all o.
Ps. 73 : 5. wicked not in trouble as
o.men, neither plagued like o.
85:10.right-n. peace kissed each o.
Ec. 6:5. this hath more rest than o.
Is. 26 : 13. o. lords had dominion
49 : 20. chil. aft. thou hast lost o.
Da. 2 : 11. none o. can shew it bef.
7:20. of 10 horns and o. wh. came
Ho. 13 : 10. where is any o. to save
Mat. 4 : 21. going he saw o. 2 breth.
5 : 39. on right cheek, turn the o.
12:13. restored whole as o., Mk. 3:
5. Lu. 6 : 10. [its, Lu. 11 : 26.
45. then he taketh seven o. spir-
13:8. o. fell into good ground,Mk.
4 : 8. Lu. 8 : 8. [more, 22 : 4.
21 : 36. Again he sent o. servants
41.hisvineyard unto o.husbandm
23:23. not leave o. undone, Lu.11:
25:11. afterw. came o. virgins [42.
16. made them o. five talents,20.
17. he also gained o. two, 22. [1.
27:61. Mary Mag. and o. Mary,28:
Mk. 12 : 31. none o. com-t is greater
32. one God, and there is none o.
Lu.10:1. Lord appointed o. seventy
14 : 32. while o. is yet gr. way off
18 : 11. thank thee, I am not as o.
14. justified rather than o. [men
23: 40. the o. answ-g rebuked him
Jn. 4 : 38. o. men laboured and ye
10:1. climbeth up some o. way
16. o. sheep I have, not of this
15:24.If not done works none o.did
19 : 18. crucified him and two o.
32.brake legs of o.wh. was crucif.
20:25.o.disci.said,We have seen L.
30. many o. signs did Jesus
Ac. 2 : 4. to speak with o. tongues
40. wi. many o. words did testify
4:12. Nei. is there salvation in any
o. none o. name under heaven
8 : 34. of hims. or of some o. man
15 : 2. Barnabas and o. of them
17 : 9.security of Jason and o. [o.
18. said, What will babbler say?
Ro. 1 : 13. even as am. o. Gentiles
8 : 39. nor any o. creature be able
13 : 9. if be any o. com-t, it is
1 Co.1:16. know not I bapt-d any o.
3 : 11. o. foundation no man lay
10:29. not thine own, but of the o.
11:21. eating ev. one taketh bef.o.
14 : 17. but the o. is not edified
21. men of o. tongues and o. lips
29. Let prophets speak, o. judge
15:37. chance of wheat, or o. grain
2 Co. 8:13. not that o. men be eased
10 : 15. Not boasting of o. men's
11:8.I robbed o.churches [labours
12:13. were inferior to o. churches
13 : 2. I write to them and to all o.
Ga. 2:13. o. Jews dissembled likew.
Ep. 3 : 5. which in o. ages was
4:17. ye walk not as o. Gent. walk
Ph. 1 : 13. palace, and all o. places
17. the o. preach Christ of love
2:3. let each esteem o. better than
3:4. If any o. think.he might trust
4 : 3. Clement and o. my fellow
2 Th. 1 : 3. charity toward each o.
1 Ti. 1 : 3. they teach no o. doctrine
5 : 22. partaker of o. men's sins
Ja. 5 : 12. nei. swear by any o. oath
1 Pe. 4 : 15. busybody in men's mat.
2 Pe. 3 : 16. wrest, as o. Scriptures
Re. 2 : 24. upon you none o. burden
8 : 13. by reason of the o. voices.
See APOSTLES, BOAT, CITIES, DISCIPLE, S, GOD, GODS, SIDE, THING, S, TIMES.
See ONE with other.
OTHERS.
Jb. 8 : 19. out of earth shall o. grow
31 : 10. let O. bow down upon her
34 : 24. he sh. set o. in their stead
26.He striketh them in sight of o.
Ps. 49 : 10. leave their wealth to o.
Pr. 5 : 9. Lest give honour unto o.
Ec. 7 : 22. thou likewise hast cursed
Is. 56 : 8. will I gather o. to him [o.
Je.6:12.their houses be turned to o.
8:10.I will give their wives unto o.
Eze. 13 : 6. have made o. to hope
10. o. daubed it with untempered
Eze.14:†6.Repent,and turn o.fr.idols
Da 7 : 19. fourth beast diverse fr. o.
11 : 4. kingd. be plucked up for o.
Mat. 5:47.what do ye more than o.?
15:30. having lame, blind, many o.
16 : 14. o. say, that thou art Jeremias, or, Mk. 6 : 15.-8 : 28. Lu.
9 : 8, 19.
20:3. o. standing idle in market[8.
21:8.o. cut down branches, Mk.11:
26 : 67. o. smote him with palms
27:42.He saved o.himself he can-t,
Mk. 15:31. Lu. 23:35. [many o.
Mk. 12 : 5. and him they killed, and
9. give vineyard to o., Lu. 20:16.
Lu. 5:29. and o. that sat down with
8:3. many o. wh. ministered unto
10. but to o. in parables [him
11:16.o.tempting him sought sign
18:9.thems. righte.and despised o.
Jn. 7 : 12. a good man, o. said Nay
41. o. said, This is the Christ
9 : 9. o. said, He is like him [such
16. o. said, How can a man do
10:21. o. said, These are not words
12:29. o. said, angel spake to him
18:34. or did o. tell it thee of me?
Ac. 2:13. o. said, These men are full
15:35. Paul preaching, with many
17 : 34. Damaris and o. with [o.
28:9. o. wh. had diseases came [o.
1 Co. 9 : 2. If I be not apostle unto
12.If o.be partakers of power[o.
27. lest when I have preached to
10:29.Conscience, not thine, but of
14 : 19. that I might teach o. [o.
2 Co.3:1.need we,as some o. epistles
8 : 8. by the forwardness of o. [of
Ep. 2 : 3. were child. of wrath, as o.
Ph. 1:†13. my bonds manifest to all
2:4. every man on things of o. [o.
1 Th. 2 : 6. nor yet of o. sought we
4:13. that ye sorrow not, as o.wh.
5 : 6. let us not sleep as do o. [fear
1 Ti. 5 : 20. sin rebuke, that o. may
2 Ti. 2 : 2. shall be able to teach o.
He. 9 : 25. ev. year with blood of o.
11 : 35. o. were tortured
36. o. had trial of cruel mockings
Jude 23. o. save with fear, pulling
OTHERWISE. [falseh.
2 S. 18 : 13. o. I sho. have wrought
1 K. 1 : 21. o. I and Sol. be counted
2 Ch. 30 : 18. they eat passover o.
Ps.38:16.Hear me,lest o.they rejoice
Mat.6:1.o.have no reward of Father
Lu. 5 : 36. if o. both new mak-h rent
Ro. 11 : 6. not of works, o. grace no
grace; no more of grace, o.
22. tow. thee goodn. o. be cut off
2 Co.11:16.if o. yet as a fool receive
Ga. 5:10. that ye be none o. minded
Ph. 3 : 15. if ye be o. minded
1 Ti. 5 : 25. that are o. can-t be hid
6 : 3. If any teach o. and consent
He.9:17.o. it is of no strength at all
OTH'NI. [Raphael
1 Ch. 26 : 7. sons of Shemaiah, O.
OTHNI'EL. [1 : 13.
Jos.15:17.O. son of Kenaz took, Ju.
Ju. 3:9. L. raised a deliv-r, O.son of
11. O. son of Kenaz died [Kenaz
1 Ch. 4 : 13. sons of Kenaz, O. (2)
27 : 15. 12th captain was Heldai of
OUCHES. [O.
Ex. 28 : 11. set the stones in o. of
gold, 39 : 6, 13.
13. shalt make o. of gold, 39 : 16.
14.and fasten wreathen chains to
the o., 39 : 18.
25. fasten in the two o.
OUGHT (Noun). See AUGHT.
OUGHT. [Verb.]
Ge. 20 : 9. that o. not be done, 34:7.
Le. 4 : 2, 27. [done in Isr.
2 S. 13 : 12. no such thing o. to be
1 Ch. 12:32. know what Isr. o.to do

1 Ch. 15: 2. None o. to carry ark but
2 Ch. 13: 5. o. ye not to know L. gave
Ne. 5: 9. o. ye not to walk in fear
Ps. 76: 11. unto him who o. be feared
Mat. 23: 23. these o. ye to have done, Lu. 11: 42.
Mk. 13: 14. desolation where it o. not
Lu. 12: 12. teach what ye o. to say
13: 14. are six days men o. to work
16. o. not this woman to be loosed
18: 1. that men o. always to pray
24: 26. o. not C. to have suffered?
Jn. 4: 20. where men o. to worship
13: 14. o. to wash one ano.'s feet
19: 7. and by our law he o. to die
Ac. 5: 29. We o. to obey God rather
17: 29. we o. not to think Godhead
19: 36. ye o. to be quiet, and
20: 35. ye o. to support the weak
21: 21. that they o. not to circumc.
24: 19. Who o. to have been here
25: 10. where I o. to be judged
24. that he o. not to live longer
26: 9. th. I o. to do many things contrary to Jesus ⌈as we o.
Ro. 8: 26. kn. not what to pray for
12: 3. of hims. more highly than he
15: 1. o. to bear infirmities of ⌊o.
1 Co. 8: 2. knoweth noth. as he o.
11: 7. man o. not to cover his head
10. woman o. to have power on
2 Co. 2: 3. sorrow fr. wh. I o. to rejoi.
7. ye o. rather to forgive him
12: 11. for I o. to have been commended of you ⌈parents
14. children o. not to lay up for
Ep. 5: 28. So o. men to love wives
6: 20. speak boldly, as I o., Col 4: 4.
Col. 4: 6. know how ye o. to answer
1 Th. 4: 1. of us how ye o. to walk
2 Th. 3: 7. know how ye o. to follow
1 Ti. 5: 13. speaking things o. not
Tit. 1: 11. teaching things o. not
He. 2: 1. we o. to give more heed
5: 3. he o. for peo., to offer for sins
12. for time ye o. to be teachers
Ja. 3: 10. these things o. not so to
4: 15. ye o. to say, If L. will ⌊be
2 Pe. 3: 11. what persons o. ye to be
1 Jn. 2: 6. o. to walk as he walked
3: 16. o. to lay down our lives for
4: 11. we o. also to love one ano.
3 Jn. 8. We thf. o. to receive such

OUGHTEST.

1 K. 2: 9. knowest what thou o. to do
Mat. 25: 27. o. to have put my money
Ac. 10: 6. he shall tell what o. to do
1 Ti. 3: 15. how thou o. to behave

OUR.

See BRETHREN, BROTHER, CATTLE, CHILDREN, ENEMIES, EYES, FATHER, S, GOD, HAND, S, HEART, S, LAND, LORD, SIN, S, SOUL, WILL, WORK.

OURS.

Ge. 26: 20. saying, The water is o.
31: 16. taken fr. our fa. that is o.
34: 23. sh. not every beast be o.?
Nu. 32: 32. on this side Jord. be o.
1 K. 22: 3. know that Ramoth is o.
Eze. 36: 2. ancient high places are o.
Mk. 12: 7. and inheritance shall be o., Lu. 20: 14. ⌈theirs and o.
1 Co. 1: 2. all that call upon Jesus,
2 Co. 1: 14. As ye are o. in day of L.
Tit. 3: 14. let o. learn to maintain
1 Jn. 2: 2. not for o. only, but sins of

OURSELVES.

Ge. 37: 10. Shall we bow down o.?
44: 16. said, How sh. we clear o.?
Nu. 32: 17. we o. will go armed
De. 2: 35. cattle for a prey unto o., 3: 7.
1 S. 14: 8. will discover o. unto
Ezr. 4: 3. we o. will build unto Lord
8: 21. that we afflict o. before God
Ne. 10: 32. to charge o. yearly wi. 3d.
Jb. 34: 4. know am. o. what is good
Ps. 83: 12. take to o. houses of God
100: 3. he that made us, and not o.
Pr. 7: 18. let us solace o. wi. loves
Is. 28: 15. und. falsehood have hid o.
56: 12. will fill o. with stro. drink
Je. 50: 5. let us join o. to Lord
Lu. 22: 71. we o. have heard, Jn. 4: 42.
Ac. 6: 4. we will give o. to prayer
23: 14. have bound o. und. curse
Ro. 8: 23. not only they but o. also, even we o. groan within o.
15: 1. we ought not to please o.
1 Co. 11: 31. if we would judge o.
2 Co. 1: 4. whw. o. are comforted
9. that we should not trust in o.
3: 1. Do we begin to commend o.
5. Not that we are sufficient of o. to think anything as of o.
4: 2. commending o. to every man's
5. we preach not o. but C. J., and o. your servants for Jes.' sake
5: 12. we commend not o. again
13. whether we be besides o. it is
6: 4. approving o. as ministers
7: 1. let us cleanse o. fr. all filthiness
10: 12. compare o. with some that
14. we stretch not o. beyond measure
12: 19. think ye we excuse o. ⌊sure
Ga. 2: 17. we o. are found sinners
1 Th. 2: 10. how unblam-y behaved
2 Th. 1: 4. we o. glory in you ⌊o.
3: 7. we behaved not o. disorderly
9. but to make o. an ensample
Tit. 3: 3. we o. were foolish ⌈of o.
He. 10: 25. Not forsaking assembling
1 Jn. 1: 8. we deceive o., truth is

OUT. ⌊not in us

Ge. 2: 9. o. of ground made God to

OUTCAST. ⌊grow

Je. 30: 17. bec. they called thee an o.

OUTCASTS. ⌈56: 8.

Ps. 147: 2. gathered o. of Israel, Is.
Is. 11: 12. shall assemble o. of Isr.
16: 3. hide o. | 4. Let my o. dwell
27: 13. o. in Egypt shall worship
49: 36. o. of Elam shall not come

OUTER. See DARKNESS. ⌈way

Eze. 47: 2. he led me unto o. gate by
See Outer = Utter COURT.

OUTGOINGS.

Jos. 17: 9. o. of it were at sea, 19: 29.
18. and the o. of it shall be thine
18: 19. o. of border were at north
19: 14. o. are in valley of Jiphthahel
22. the o. of border at Jordan, 33.
Ps. 65: 8. thou makest o. of morn-

OUTLANDISH. ⌊ing

Ne. 13: 26. o. women caused Sol. to

OUTLIVED. ⌊sin

Ju. 2: 7. the elders that o. Joshua

OUTMOST. ⌈beav.

De. 30: 4. If driven into o. parts of
2 S. 20: †15. the bank stood ag. o. wall
Is. 17: 6. four or five in the o.
See UTMOST ⌊branches

OUTPLACES. ⌈o.

Jb. 5: † 10. sendeth waters upon the

OUTRAGEOUS.

Pr. 27: 4. Wrath is cruel, anger is o.

OUTRUN.

Jn. 20: 4. other disciple did o. Peter

OUTSIDE. ⌈men

Ju. 7: 11. Gideon went to o. of armed
17. when I come to o. of camp
19. they came unto o. of camp
1 K. 7: 9. so on o. tow. great court
Eze. 40: 5. a wall on o. of house
Mat. 23: 25. clean o. of cup, Lu. 11:
26. that o. of them be clean ⌊39.

OUTSPREAD. ⌈o.

Is. 18: †2. Go, messengers to a nation
†7. bro-t unto Lord a people o.

OUTSTRETCHED. ⌈arm

De. 26: 8. L. brought us out with o.
Je. 21: 5. I will fight you with o. ha.
27: 5. I made earth by my o. arm

OUTWARD.

Nu. 35: 4. reach o. 1000 cubits
1 S. 16: 7. looketh on o. appearance
1 Ch. 26: 29. Chenaniah for o. busi.
Ne. 11: 16. chief of Lev. for o. business
Es. 6: 4. Haman into o. court ⌊ness
Eze. 40: 17. bro-t me into o. court
44: 1. gate of o. sanc., 40: 20, 34.
Mat. 23: 27. wh. appear beautiful o.
Lu. 17: †20. kingd. of G. not wi. o.
Ro. 2: 28. circumc. which is o. ⌊shew
2 Co. 4: 16. tho. our o. man perish
10: † 1. in o. appearance am base
7. Do ye look on things aft. o. app.
1 Pe. 3: 3. not that o. adorning

OUTWARDLY.

Mat. 23: 28. ye o. appear righteous
Ro. 2: 28. he is not a Jew wh. is one

OUTWENT. ⌊o.

Mk. 6: 33. many ran afoot and o.

OVEN, S. ⌊them

Ex. 8: 3. frogs sh. come into thine o-s
Le. 2: 4. offering baken in o., 7: 9.
11: 35. unclean, whe. o. or ranges
26: 26. women bake your br. in 1 o.
Ps. 21: 9. make them as a fiery o.
La. 5: 10. Our skin black like an o.
Ho. 7: 4. adulterers, as an o. heated
6. made ready their heart like o.
7. are all hot as an o. have devour.
Mal. 4: 1. the day cometh that shall burn as an o. ⌈o., Lu. 12: 28.
Mat. 6: 30. to morrow is cast into

OVER. [Prep.] ⌈(5) 28.

Ge. 1: 26. dominion o. fish, o. cattle,
9: 14. when I bring cloud o. earth
27: 29. be lord o. thy brethren, let
41: 33. o. the land of Egypt, 34.-42: 6.-47: 26. Ex. 10: 13, 21. Ac. 7: 11.
40. Thou shalt be o. my house
47: 6. make them rulers o. my cattle
Ex. 8: 5. o. streams, o. rivers, o...
14: 7. chariots, captains o. ev. one
30: 6. mercy seat o. the testimony
37: 9. with wings o. mercy seat ⌈50.
Le. 14: 5. killed o. running water, 6,
Nu. 3: 49. o., above them redeemed
5: 30. be be jealous o. his wife ⌈(2)
10: 10. with trumpets o. offerings
27: 16. Let L. set a man o. cong-n
De. 28: 23. heaven o. thy head brass
Ju. 5: 13. o. the nobles, o. mighty
9: 9. promoted o. the trees? 11, 13
10: 18. he sh. be head o. all of Gil.
Ru. 2: 5. his servant o. the reapers
1 S. 17: 50. Dav. prevailed o. Philist-e
2 S. 1: 17. lamented o. Saul, o. J., 24.
24. Ye dau-s of Israel weep o. Saul
2: 9. Ish-bosheth, k. o. Gilead, o.
20: 23. Benaiah was o. Cherethites
1 K. 4: 5. Azariah o. the officers
5: 7. a wise son o. this gr-t people
14. Adoniram o. levy, 4: 6.-12: 18.
16. Solo-n's officers o. work (2) 9: 23.
2 K. 5: 11. strike his hand o. place
8: 20. Edom a king o. themselves
10: 22. said unto him o. the vestry
25: 19. an officer o. the men of war
1 Ch. 29: 3. gold o. and above all
Ezr. 9: 6. iniquities o. our head
Jb. 14: 16. dost watch o. my sin?
41: 34. is king o. children of pride
Ps. 145: 9. mercies o. all his works
Je. 1: 10. set thee o. nations and o
Da. 6: 3. thought to set him o. realm
Mi. 3: 6. day shall be dark o. them
Mat. 25: 21. make thee ruler o. many,
Lu. 2: 8. keeping watch o. flock ⌊23.
15: 7. joy o. sinner that repent-h,
Jn. 6: 1. Jes went o. sea, 17. ⌊(2) 10.
Ac. 7: 10. made him governor o. Eg
20: 28. o. wh. Holy Gh. hath made
Ro. 7: 1. law hath dominion o. man
9: 21. Hath not potter power o. clay
1 Co. 7: 37. hath power o. own will
1 Ti. 2: 12. nor usurp authority o.
He. 2: 7. o. works of thy hands ⌊man

1 Pe. 3 : 12. eyes of Lord o. righteous
Re. 2:26. give power o. nations, 13:7.
6 : 8. power o. fourth part of earth
11 : 6. power o. waters to turn them
14 : 18. angel wh. had power o. fire
15 : 2. victory o. beast, o. image(4)
16 : 9. hath power o. these plagues
17:18. city which reigneth o. kings
See ALL [Noun], BROOK, BUSINESS, CAME, CAPTAIN,S, CITY, IES, COME, GO, GONE, HER, HIM, HOST, HOUSE, HOUSEHOLD, ISRAEL, JORDAN, ME, PASS, PASSED, PEOPLE, REIGN, RULE, SET, SPREAD, STOOD, TABERNACLE, THEE, THEM, US, WALL, WENT, YOU.

OVER. [Adv.] [garm-t
Ge. 25 : 25. red, all over like hairy
32 : 23. Jacob sent o. that he had
Ex. 16 : 18. he that gathered much had nothing o. [morning
23. remaineth o. lay up until the
Nu. 32 : 7 discourage from going o.
De. 9 : 3. God goeth o. before thee
2 S. 19 : 18. carry o. king's househ-d
Ne. 2 : 7. that they may convey me o.
Ps. 23 : 5. table, my cup runneth o.
27 : 12. Deliver me not o. unto ene.
65 : 13. valleys covered o. with corn
78 : 50. their life o. to pestilence
62. gave his people o. unto sword
118 : 18. not given me o. unto death
Pr. 24 : 31. all grown o. with thorns
Can. 2 : 11. winter is past, rain is o.
Is. 31 : 5. passing o., he will preserve
40 : 19. spreadeth it o. with gold [it
Ha. 2 : 19. it is laid o. with gold
Mk. 15 : 26. written o., THE KING
Lu. 6 : 38. good measure, running o.
Jn. 6 : 13. fragments wh. remained o.
Ac. 7 : 16. carried o. into Sychem
16 : 9. Come o. into M-a and help us
21 : 2. ship sailing o. unto Phenicia
Ep. 4 : 19. given o. unto lascivious-
See Over AGAINST. [ness

OVER much, OVERMUCH.
Ec. 7 : 16. Be not righteous o. m.
17. Be not o. m. wicked, neither
2 Co. 2 : 7. swallowed up with o. sor-

OVER wise. [row
See Over WISE.

OVERCAME.
Ac. 19 : 16. man in wh. evil spirit was, leaped on them, and o.
Re. 3 : 21. as I also o. and am set
12 : 11. they o. him by bl. of Lamb

OVERCHARGE, ED.
Lu. 21 : 34. lest your hearts be o-d
2 Co. 2 : 5. that I may not o. you all

OVERCOME.
Ge. 49 : 19. troop shall o. him, but he shall o. at last [ing o.
Ex. 32 : 18. of them that cry for be-
Nu. 13 : 30. we are able to o. it
22 : 11. peradv. I be able to o. them
2 K. 16 : 5. Ahaz could not o. him
Can. 6 : 5. Turn away eyes, they o. me
Is. 28 : 1. head of them o. with wine
Je. 23 : 9. man whom wine hath o.
Lu. 11 : 22. when a stronger o. him
Jn. 16 : 33. cheer, I have o. world
Ro. 3 : 4. o. when thou art judged
12 : 21. Be not o. of evil, but o. evil
Ep. 6 : † 13. having o. all to stand
2 Pe. 2 : 19. of whom a man is o.
20. if are again entangled and o.
1 Jn. 2 : 13. ye have o. wick. one, 14.
4 : 4. Ye are of God and have o. th.
Re. 11 : 7. beast sh o. the witnesses
13 : 7. to make war wi. saints, and
17 : 14. and Lamb shall o. them [o.

OVERCOMETH.
1 Jn. 5 : 4. is born of God, o. world, this is victory that o. world
5 Who is he that o. world, but
Re. 2 : 7. To him o. will give of tree
Re. 2 : 11. He that o. shall not be hurt
17. To him o. will I give to eat
26. to him th. o. will I give power
3 : 5. He th. o. be clothed in white
12. Him that o. will I make pillar
21. To him o. will I grant to sit
21 : 7. He that o. shall inherit all

OVERDRIVE.
Ge. 33 : 13. if men o. all flock die

OVERFLOW. [o.
De. 11 : 4. made water of Red sea to
Ps. 69 : 2. I am where floods o. me
15. Let not water floods o. me, nei.
Is. 8 : 8. he shall pass thro. Judah, o.
10 : 22. consumption decreed sh. o.
28 : 17. waters sh. o. hiding place
43 : 2. rivers they shall not o. thee
Je. 47 : 2. waters of north sh. o. [40.
Da. 11 : 10. one sh. certainly o., 26.
Jo. 2 : 24. fats sh. o. with wine, 3 : 13.

OVERFLOWED, EST.
2 Ch. 32 : †4. the brook o-d the land
Jb. 14 : †19. o-t the things wh. grow
Ps. 78 : 20. smote rock, streams o-d
2 Pe. 3 : 6. world being o-d with water

OVERFLOWETH.
Jos. 3 : 15. in harvest Jord. o-h banks

OVERFLOWING.
Jb. 28 : 11. He bindeth floods fr. o.
38 : 25. a watercourse for o. [an o.
Pr. 27 : † 4. Wrath is cruelty, anger
Is. 28 : 2. flood of mighty waters o.
15. when o. scourge sh. pass, 18.
30 : 28. his breath as an o. stream
Je. 47 : 2. out of north be o. flood
Eze. 13 : 11. sh. be an o. shower, 13.
38 : 22. I will rain upon him o. rain
Ha. 3 : 10. o. of water passed by

OVERFLOWN.
1 Ch. 12 : 15. over Jordan when o.
Jb. 22 : 16. whose foundation was o.
Da. 11 : 22. with flood shall be o.

OVERLAID.
Ex. 26 : 32. of shittim wood o. wi. gold
36 : 36. o. wi. gold, 2 Ch. 3 : 5, 7, 8, 9.
37 : 4. staves, o. them wi. gold, 15, 28.
38 : 6. o. staves with brass, 2, 28.
1 K. 3 : 19. child died bec. she o. it
Can. 5 : 14. belly is as bright ivory o.

OVERLAY.
1 Ch. 29 : 4. silver to o. walls of hou.
See BRASS, GOLD.

OVERLAYING.
Ex. 38 : 17. o. of chapiters of silver
19. o. of chapiters fillets of silver

OVERLIVED.
Jos. 24 : 31. elders that o. Joshua

OVERMUCH.
See OVER much.

OVERPASS, OVERPAST.
Ps. 57 : 1. until calamities be o-t
Is. 26 : 20. hide until indigna. be o-t
Je. 5 : 28. they o-s deeds of wicked

OVERPLUS.
Le. 25 : 27. let him restore the o.

OVERRAN.
2 S. 18 : 23. Ahimaaz o. Cushi

OVERREACH.
1 Th. 4 : †6. That no man o. his bro.

OVERRULING.
1 Pe. 5 : †3. Nei. as o. God's heritage

OVERRUNNING.
Na. 1 : 8. with o. flood make an end

OVERSEE.
1 Ch. 9 : 29. appointed to o. vessels
15 : †21. with harps on eighth to o.
23 : † 4. 24,000 were to o. the work
2 Ch. 2 : 2. three thous six hun. to o.

OVERSEER, S. [th.
Ge. 39 : 4. him o. ov. his house, 5.
41 : † 34. let Pharaoh appoint o-s
2 Ch. 2 : 18. Solomon set 3,600 o-s
31 : 13. were o-s under Cononiah
34 : 12. o-s of all that wrought, 13.
17. money into hands of o-s
Ne. 11 : 9. Joel was o. | 14. Zabdiel
22. o. of Levites was Uzzi
Ne. 12 : 42. singers with Jezrahiah o.
Pr. 6 : 7. ant having no guide o. or
Ac. 20 : 28. Holy Ghost made you o-s

OVERSHADOW, ED.
Mat. 17 : 5. a bright cloud o-d them, Mk. 9 : 7. Lu. 9 : 34. [o. thee
Lu. 1 : 35. power of the Highest sh.
Ac. 5 : 15. th. shadow of Pe. might

OVERSIGHT. [o. them
Ge. 43 : 12. peradvent. it was an o.
Nu. 3 : 32. o. of them keep charge
4 : 16. the o. of all their tabernacle
2 K. 12 : 11. them that had o. of house of L., 22 : 5, 9. 2 Ch. 34 : 10.
1 Ch. 9 : 23. o. of the gates of house
Ne. 11 : 16. o. of outward business
13 : 4. o. of chamber of house of G
1 Pe. 5 : 2. taking o. not by constraint

OVERSPREAD, ING.
Ge. 9 : 19. of them was the earth o.
Da. 9 : 27. for o-g of abominations

OVERTAKE. [say
Ge. 44 : 4. Up. when dost o. them,
Ex. 15 : 9. I will pursue, I will o.
De. 19 : 6. Lest avenger o. slayer
28 : 2. all these blessings sh. o. thee
15. all these curses sh. o. thee, 45.
Jos. 2 : 5. pursue, for ye sh. o. them
1 S. 30 : 8. shall I o.? thou shalt o.
2 S. 15 : 14. lest Absal. o. us suddenly
Is. 59 : 9. neither doth justice o. us
Je. 42 : 16. sword ye feared shall o
Ho. 2 : 7. she shall not o. her lovers
10 : 9. battle in Gibeah did not o. th.
Am. 9 : 10. The evil shall not o. us
13. ploughman shall o. reaper
Zch. 1 : †6. words, did they not o. fa-s
1 Th. 5 : 4. day o. you as a thief

OVERTAKEN, ETH.
1 Ch 21 : 12 or 3 months while sword of enemies o-h [and o-n
Ps. 18 : 37. I have pursued enem.
Ga. 6 : 1. if a man be o-n in fault

OVERTHREW.
Ge. 19 : 25. God o. these cities, 29.
Ex. 14 : 27. L. o. Eg-ns, Ps. 136 : 15.
De. 29 : 23. which L. o. in his anger
Is. 13 : 19. Babylon sh. be, as when God o. Sodom, Je. 50 : 40. Am. 4 : 11
Je. 20 : 16. man be as cities L. o.
Mat. 21 : 12. Jesus o. tables of the money changers. Mk. 11 : 15. Jn. 2 : 15.

OVERTHROW. [Noun.]
Ge. 19 : 29. G. sent Lot out of the o.
De. 29 : 23. like o. of Sodom, Je. 49 : 18.
Is. 1 : †7. land deso. as o. of strangers
2 Pe. 2 . 6. condemned cities with o.

OVERTHROW. [Verb.]
Ge. 19 : 21. I will not o. this city
Ex. 23 : 34. sh. lt utterly o. their gods
De. 12 : 3. ye shall o. their altars
2 S. 10 : 3. hath not David sent to o.
11 : 25. make battle strong, o. it
1 Ch. 19 : 3. Da. hath sent to o. land
Ps. 106 : 26. to o. them in wilderness
27. To o. their seed am. nations
140 : 4. purposed to o. my goings
11. evil hunt violent man to o.
Pr. 18 : 5. not good to o. righteous
Hag. 2 : 22. I will o. throne of kingdoms, I will o. chariots
Ac. 5 : 39. if of God, ye cannot o. it
2 Ti. 2 : 18. and o. the faith of some

OVERTHROWETH.
Jb. 12 : 19. leadeth princes, o. mighty
Pr. 13 : 6. wickedness o. the sinner
21 : 12. God o. the wicked for their
22 : 12. he o. words of transgressor
29 : 4. he th. receiveth gifts o. land

OVERTHROWING
Is. 13 : †19. beauty of Bab. as o. of Sod.

OVERTHROWN. [om
Ex 15 : 7. hast o. them rose ag. thee
Ju. 9 : 40. many were o. and wounded
2 S. 17 : 9. when some of them be o.
2 Ch. 14 : 13. the Ethiopians were o.

Jb. 19:6. Know now God hath o. me
Ps. 141:6. When their judges are o.
Pr. 11:11. city is o. by wicked
12:7. wicked are o. | 14:11. house
of wicked o. [by strangers
Is. 1:7. your land is desolate as o.
Je. 18:23. let them be o. bef. thee
La. 4:6. Sodom, o. as in a moment
Da. 11:41. many countries sh. be o.
Am. 4:11. I have o. some of you
Jo. 3:4. Yet 40 days Nineveh be o.
1 Co. 10:5. they were o. in wilder- [ness

OVERTOOK.

Ge. 31:23. o. Jacob in m-t Gilead
25. Laban o. Jac. | 44:6. steward o.
Ex. 14:9. Eg-ns o. them encamping
Ju. 18:22. Micah o. chil. of Dan
20:42. battle o. the men of Benj.
2 K. 25:5. army of Chaldees o. Zedekiah in plains, Je. 39:5.-52:8.
La. 1:3. all her persecutors o. her

OVERTURN, ED, ETH.

Ju. 7:13. smote the tent and o-d it
Jb. 9:5. which o-h mountains
12:15. sendeth waters, they o. earth
28:9. he o-h mountains by roots
34:25. knoweth works, and o-h th.
Eze. 21:27. I will o. o. o. it, until

OVERWHELM, ED.

Jb. 6:27. ye o. fatherless, dig a pit
Ps. 55:5. and horror hath o-d me
61:2. heart o-d lead me to rock
77:3. spirit was o-d, 142:3.-143:4.
78:53. but sea o-d their enemies
124:4. Then the waters had o-d us

OWE, ED. [talents

Mat. 18:24. one o-d him 10,000
28. one which o-d him 100 pence
Lu. 7:41. one o-d 500 pence, other
Ro. 13:8. o. no man anything, but

OWEST, ETH. [o-t

Mat. 18:28. saying, Pay me that thou
Lu. 16:5. How much o-t thou, 7.
Phm. 18. If wronged, or o-h aught
19. thou o-t unto me thine own [self

OWL, OWLS.

Le. 11:17. shall not be eaten; little o. great o., 16. De. 14:15, 16(2).
Jb. 30:29. I am a companion to o-s
Ps. 102:6. I am like an o. of desert
Is. 13:21. o-s shall dwell there, satyrs, 34:11, 13, 15. Je. 50:39.
43:20. dragons, o-s sh. honour me
Mi. 1:8. I will make a mourning as
See **SCREECH owl.** [the o-s

OWN. [o-s

Ge. 1:27. created man in o. image
5:3. Adam begat a son in o. liken.
15:4. sh. come of thine o. bowels
47:24. four parts be your o. for seed
Ex. 21:36. dead shall be his o.
22:5. of best of o. field make restitu
Le. 7:30. o. hands sh. bring off-g
14:15, into palm of o. left hand, 26.
18:10. theirs is thine o. nakedness
26. nei. any of your o. nation, nor
25:5. wh. groweth of its o. accord
41. shall return unto his o. fami y
Nu. 1:52. ev. man by his o. camp,
his o. standard [mind, 24:13.
16:28. not done them of mine o.
38. censers of sinners ag. o. souls
32:42. after his o. name, De. 3:14.
36:9. keep hims. to o. inheritance
De. 23:24. eat grapes at o. pleasure
24:13. he may sleep in his o. raiment
16. ev. man shall be put to death
for o. sin, 2 K. 14:6. 2 Ch. 25:4.
28:53. shalt eat fruit of o. body
33:9. nor knew he his o. children
Jos. 7:11. have put it am. o. stuff
Ju. 2:19. ceased not from o. doings
7:2. Mine o. hand hath saved me
1 S. 2:20. they went unto o. home
15:17. When wast little in o. sight
25:26. from avenging with o. hand
2 S. 6:22. I will be base in o. sight
2 S. 7:10. may dwell in pla. of their
12:3. did eat of his o. meat [o.
20. then he came to his o. house
17:11. go to battle in o. person
1 K. 2:23. spoken word ag. o. life
37. thy blood sh. be upon o. head
11:22. seekest to go to o. country
13:30. laid carcass in his o. grave
17:19. Elijah laid him upon o. bed
2 K. 17:29. every nation made gods
of their o. [given thee
1 Ch. 29:14. of thine o. have we
16. store we prepared, all thine o.
Jb. 20:7. shall perish like o. dung
Ps. 12:4. our lips our o. who is lord
67:6. God, our o. G. shall bless
78:29. he gave them their o. desire
81:12. them up unto o. hearts' lust
94:23. sh. bring upon them o. iniq.
and cut off in o. wickedness
Pr. 5:17. let them be only thy o.
Is. 37:35. to save it for mine o. sake,
43:25.-48:11. [nor o.
58:13. not finding thine o. pleas.
Eze. 29:3. said, My river is mine o.
Ho. 7:2. o. doings have beset them
Jon. 2:8. they forsake their o. mercy
Mat. 20:15. what I will with mine o.
Lu. 16:12. who give that is your o.
19:23. might have required mine
o. with usury, Mat. 29:27.
Jn. 1:11. came unto his o. his o.
received him not
8:44. a lie, he speaketh of his o.
10:12. whose o. the sheep are not
13:1. having loved his o. in world
15:19. world would love his o.
16:32. scattered ev. man to his o.
Ac. 3:12. as tho. by our o. power
4:32. nei. said any aught was his o.
5:4. was it not thine o.? was it not
in thine o. power [o. blood
20:28. which he purchased with his
Ro. 4:19. consid-d not his o. body
8:32. He that spared not his o. Son
14:4. to his o. master he standeth
1 Co. 6:19. ye are not your o. for
7:2. let every man have his o. wife
10:24. Let no man seek his o. but
29. conscience, not thine o. but
13:5. charity seeketh not her o.
Ph. 2:21. all seek their o. things
1 Ti. 5:8. if any provide not for his
o. and especially for o. house
Tit. 1:12. a prophet of their o. said
He. 9:12. by his o. blood he ent-d
Re. 1:5. washed us in his o. blood
See COUNSEL, COUNTRY, EYES, **HEAD, HEART, HOUSE, LAND, LIFE, PEOPLE, PLACE, RIGHTEOUSNESS.**

OWN self, selves. [o.s.

Ex. 32:13. to wh. swarest by thine
Jn. 5:30. I can of o. s. do noth. [s.
17:5. glorify thou me with thine o.
Ac. 20:30. of your o. s-s sh. men rise
1 Co. 4:3. I judge not mine o. s.
2 Co. 8:5. but first gave their o. s-s
to the Lord [not your o. s-s
13:5. prove your o. s-s. Know ye
2 Ti. 3:2. men be lovers of o. s-s
Phm. 19. owest unto me thine o. s.
Ja. 1:22. hearers, deceiving o. s-s
1 Pe. 2:24. Who his o. s. bare our
See SOUL, WAY, WAYS, WILL. [sins

OWNER.

Ex. 21:28. o. of the ox sh. be quit
29. if been testified to o. o. sh. die
34. o. of the pit sh. make it good
36. his o. hath not kept him in
22:11. o. of it shall accept thereof
12. he sh. make restitution unto o
14. o. not being with it
15. if o. be with it not make it good
1 K. 16:24. Shemer, o. of the hill
Is. 1:3. ox knoweth his o. [ship
Ac. 27:11. centurion believed o. of

OWNERS.

Jb. 31:39. or caused o. to lose lives
Pr. 1:19. wh. taketh away life of o.
3:†27. Withhold not good fr. the o.
Ec. 5:11. what good is there to o.
13. A sore evil, riches kept for o.
Lu. 19:33. o. said, Why loose colt?

OWNETH.

Le. 14:35. th. o. house sh. tell priest
Ac. 21:11. sh. bind man o. this girdle

OX.

Ex. 20:17. not covet o., De. 5:21.
21:28. if o. gore a man, be stoned,
29. If o. wont to push, 36. [29, 32.
32. If o. push a manservant or
33. if an o. or ass fall into pit
35. if one man's o. hurt another
22:1. If a man steal an o. or sheep
4. whe. o. or ass, be shall restore
9. For all trespass whe. for an o.
10. If man deliver an o. to keep
23:4. If meet enemy's o. astray
12. that thine o. and ass may rest
34:19. firstling of o. or sheep mine
Le. 7:23. eat no fat of o. or sheep
17:3. What man killeth o. or lamb
Nu. 7:3. for each of princes an o.
22:4. as the o. licketh up grass
De. 5:14. o. sh. do no work on sab.
14:4. o. sheep, goat, ye may eat
5. ye sh. eat goat and wild o.
18:3. priest's due, whe. o. or sheep
22:1. not see brother's o. go astray
4. shalt not see brother's o. fall
10. not plough with an o. and ass
25:4. not muzzle the o. treadeth
out corn, 1 Co. 9:9. 1 Ti. 5:18.
28:31. Thine o. shall be slain
Jos. 6:21. destroyed o. and sheep
Ju. 6:4. left sheep nor o. for Israel
1 S. 12:3. Whose o. or ass have I tak.
14:34. Bring ev. man o. and sheep
15:3. slay man, woman, o. sheep, 15.
Ne. 5:18. for me daily 1 o. 6 sheep
Jb. 6:5. loweth o. over his fodder?
24:3. take widow's o. for pledge
40:15. behemoth eateth grass as o.
Ps. 69:31. sh. please L. better than o.
106:20. glory into similitude of o.
Pr. 7:22. goeth aft. her as o. to slau.
14:4. increase is by strength of o.
15:17. better than a stalled o., and
Is. 1:3. o. knoweth his owner, ass
11:7. lion shall eat straw like o.
32:20. that send forth feet of o.
66:3. killeth o., as if he slew man
Je. 11:19. I was like a lamb or an o.
Eze. 1:10. they four had face of an o.
Lu. 13:15. doth not each loose o. on
14:5. o. or ass fallen into pit [sab.

OXEN.

Ge. 12:16. Abram had sheep, and o.
20:14. Abime gave Ab. sheep and o.
21:27. Ab. gave Abim. sheep and o.
32:5. Jacob said, I have o. [o.
34:28. sons of Jac. took Shechem's
Ex. 9:3. hand of Lord upon o.
20:24. thou shalt sacrifice thine o.
22:1. he sh. restore 5 o. for one ox
30. shalt do with thine o. and sheep
24:5. peace off-gs of o. unto Lord
Nu. 7:3. princes brought twelve o.
7. four o. unto sons of Gershom
8. eight o. unto sons of Merari
17. sacrifice of peace off-gs of two
o. five rams, 23, 29, 35, 41, 47, 53, 59, 65, 71, 77, 83.
22:40. Balak offered o. and sheep
23:1. prepare me here 7 o. 7 rams
De. 14:26. bestow money for o. or
sheep [and sheep
Jos. 7:24. Josh. took Achan, his o.
1 S. 11:7. Saul hewed a yoke of o.
in pieces, so be done unto his o.
14:14. wh. yoke of o. might plough
32. peo. took sheep and o. slew th.
15:9. spared Agag and best of o., 21.

1 S.15:14. Wh. meaneth lowing of o.
15. spared best of sheep and o.
22:19. Doeg smote o. and sheep
27:9. David took away sheep, and o.
2 S. 6:6. Uzza took hold of ark, for o. shook it, 1 Ch. 13:9.
13. David sacrificed o. and fatlings
24:22. here be o. for burnt sacrifi.
24. Da bought threshingfl. and o.
1 K. 1:9. Adonijah slew sheep and o., 19, 25.
4:23. Sol.'s daily provision, 10 fat o. 20 o., 100 sheep
7:25. twelve o. 3 looking toward north, 3 toward west, 3 toward south, 3 toward east, 2 Ch. 4:4.
44. one sea, 12 o. under it, 2 K. 16:17. 2 Ch. 4:3, 15. [5:6.
8:5. sacrificing sheep and o., 2 Ch.
63. Sol. offered a sacrifice of 22,000 o., 120,000 sheep, 2 Ch.7:5.
19:19. Elisha with 12 yoke of o.
20. Elisha left o. ran after Elijah
21. took a yoke of o. and slew th.
2 K.5:26. time to receive sh-p and o.
1 Ch. 12:40. brought bread on o.
21:23. give thee o. for burnt off-gs
2 Ch. 15:11. offered of spoil 700 o.
18:2. Ahab killed sh-p and o. [sh-p
29:33. consecr-d things 600 o. 3,000
31:6. bro-t in tithes of o. sheep
35:8. gave for passover 300 o., 12.
Jb.1:3. his substance 500 yoke of o.
14. o. ploughing, asses feeding
42:12. L. gave him 1,000 yoke of o.
Ps.8:7. him to have dominion ov. o.
144:14. That our o. may be strong
Pr. 14:4. Where no o. crib is clean
Is. 7:25. be for sending forth of o.
22:13. joy and gladness, slaying o.
30:24. o. shall eat clean provender
Je.51:23. I will break husbandman and his o. [32, 33.-5:21.
Da.4:25. make thee eat grass as o.,
Am. 6:12. one plough there with o.
Mat.22:4. my o. and fatlings killed
Lu. 14:19. bought 5 yoke of o. [o.
Jn. 2:14. in temple those th. sold
15. he drove all out, sheep and o.
Ac. 14:13. priest of Jupiter bro-t o.
1 Co.9:9. Doth God take care for o.

OXGOAD. [o.

Ju. 3:31. Shamgar slew 600 with

O'ZEM.

1 Ch. 2:15. O. was 6th son of Jesse
25. sons of Jerahmeel, Oren and

OZI'AS. [O.

Mat.1:8. Joram begat O. | 9. O. begat

OZ'NI, OZ'NITES.

Ge. 46:† 16. sons of Gad O.
Nu. 26:16. of O. the family of O.

P.

PA'ARAI = NA'ARAI.

2 S. 23:35. one of the thirty P. the Arbite

PACES. [oxen

2 S. 6:13. gone six p. he sacrificed

PACIFY, IED, IETH. [p-d

Es.7:10. hanged Haman k.'s wrath
Pr.16:14. a wise man will p. wrath
21:14. A gift in secret p-h anger
Ec.10:4. yielding p-h great offences
Eze.16:63. when I am p-d tow. thee

PA'DAN. [died

Ge. 48:7. when I came fr. P. Rachel

PA'DAN-A'RAM. [of P.

Ge. 25:20. Rebek. dau. of Bethuel
28:2. go to P. to hou. of Bethuel
5. Jacob went to P. unto Laban
6. Isaac sent Jacob away to P.
7. Jac. obeyed fa., was gone to P.
31:18. away what he had gott. in P.
33:18. he came fr. P. pitched tent
35:9. G. to Jac. when he came fr. P.

Ge.35:26. sons born to him in P., 46:

PADDLE. [15.

De. 23:13. have a p. upon thy wea-

PA'DON. [pon

Ezr. 2:44. children of P., Ne. 7:47.

PA'GIEL. [7:72.

Nu. 1:13. P. son of Ocran, prince,
2:27. capt. of chil. of Asher P., 10:
7:77. this the offering of P. [26.

PA'HATH-MO'AB.

Ezr. 2:6. chil. of P. 2,812, Ne.7:11.
8:4. Of sons of P., 10:30.
Ne.3:11. Hashub, son of P. repaired
10:14. The chief of peo. Parosh, P.

PA'I = PA'U. [39.

1 Ch. 1:50. his city was P., Ge. 36:

PAID. [them

Ezr. 4:20. toll and custom was p.
Pr. 7:14. this day have I p. vows
Jon. 1:3. so he p. fare and went
Mat.5:26. not come out till hast p. uttermost farth., Lu. 12:59.
He. 7:9. Levi p. tithes in Abraham

PAIN.

Jb. 14:22. But his flesh sh. have p.
15:20. wicked man travaileth wi. p.
33:19. He is chastened with p. [p.
Ps. 25:18. Look upon mine afflic.,
29:† 9. maketh hinds to be in p.
48:6. p. as a woman in travail, Is. 13:8.-26:17. Je.6:24.-22:23 Mk. 13:† 8. [me
139:† 24. see if be any way of p. in
Is. 21:3. are my loins filled with p.
26:18. We have been wi. child, in p.
66:7. bef. p. came, she was deliv-d
Je.12:13. put thems. to p. not prof-
15:18. Why is my p. perpetual [it
30:23. with p. upon head of wicked
51:8. Babylon, take balm for her p.
Eze. 30:4. great p. in Ethiopia, 9.
16. Sin shall have great p. No sh.
Mi.4:10. Be in p. to bri. forth, O Zi-
Na.2:10. much p. is in all loins [on
Ro. 8:22. creation travaileth in p.
Re.16:10. th. gnawed tongues for p.
21:4. nei. shall there be any more
See PANGS. [p.

PAINS.

1 S. 4:19. for her p. came upon her
Ps. 116:3. p. of hell gat hold upon
Mk.13:† 8. these are p. of woman in
Ac. 2:24. having loosed p. of death
Re. 16:11. blasphemed, bec. of their

PAINED. [p.

Ps.55:4. My heart is sore p. within
Is. 23:5. sorely p. at report of Tyre
Je. 4:19. I am p. at very heart
Lu. 12:† 50. how am I p. till it be
Jo. 2:6. people shall be much p.
Re. 12:2. travailing, and p. to be

PAINFUL. [deliv.

Ps. 73:16. to know this, was too p.

PAINFULNESS. [for me

2 Co. 11:27. In weariness and p. in

PAINTED, PAINTEDST.

2 K 9:30. Jezebel p-d her face, and
Je. 22:14. and p-d with vermilion
Eze. 23:40. thou p-t thy eyes, and

PAINTING. [p.

2 K. 9:† 30. Jezebel put her eyes in
Je. 4:30. tho. rentest thy face with

PAIR. [p.

Lu. 2:24. to offer p. of turtledoves
Re. 6:5. he had a p. of balances

PALACE.

1 K. 16:18. Zimri burnt k.'s p. [p.
21:1. Naboth had viney. hard by
2 K. 15:25. smote Pekahiah in p.
20:18. be eunuchs in p. of k. of
1 Ch.29:1. p. is not for man, but L
19. Sol. a perfect heart to build p.
2 Ch. 9:11. made terraces to k.'s p.
Ezr. 4:14. have maintenance fr. p.
6:2. found at Achmetha, in p. a roll
Ne. 2:8. timber for gates of p.
7:2. ruler of p. charge over Jerus.

Es. 1:2. Shushan the p., 5.-2:3, 5, 8. -3:15.-8:14.-9:6, 11, 12. Ne.1:1. Da. 8:2.
2:3. gather all virgins unto p.
7:8. king retu-d out of p. garden
9:12. Jews destroyed 500 men in p.
Ps. 45:15. sh. enter into king's p.
69:† 25. Let their p. be desolate
144:12. after the similitude of a p.
Can.8:9. build upon her p. of silver
Is.25:2. p. of strangers to be no city
Je.30:18. p. sh. remain aft. manner
Da. 1:4. ability to stand in k.'s p.
4:4. I was flourishing in my p.
29. Neb. walked in p. of kingd.
5:5. wrote upon plaster of king's p.
6:18. k. went to p. passed night
11:45. shall plant his p. betw. seas
Am. 4:3. ye shall cast them into p.
Na. 2:6. and p. shall be dissolved
Mat. 26:58. Peter followed Jesus afar off unto high priest's p., 3, 69. Mk. 14:54, 66. Jn. 18:15.
Lu. 11:21. strong man keepeth p.
Ph.1:13. my bonds manifest in all p.

PALACES. [p.

2 Ch. 17:† 12. Jehosh-t built in Jud.
36:19. burnt all the p. with fire
Ps. 45:8. of myrrh, out of ivory p.
48:3. G is known in p. for refuge
13. bulwarks, consider her p.
78:69. he built sanct. like high p.
122:7. prosperity within thy p.
Pr. 30:28. spider is in kings' p.
Is.13:22. dragons sh. cry in thy p.
23:13. they raised up the p. thereof
32:14. Bec. p. shall be forsaken
34:13. thorns sh. come up in her p.
Je. 6:5. Arise, let us destroy her p.
9:21. death is entered into our p.
17:27. fire sh. devour p. of Jerus.
49:27. sh. consume p. of Benhadad
La. 2:5. hath swallowed her p.
Eze. 19:7. knew their desolate p.
25:4. they sh. set their p. in thee
Am. 3:9. Publish in p. at Ashdod, in p. of Egypt [p.
10. who store up robbery in their
11. thy p. shall be spoiled [p.
6:8. I abhor Jacob and I hate his
Mi.5:5. when he sh. tread in our p.
See DEVOUR. [then

PA'LAL.

Ne. 3:25. P. son of Uzai over

PALATE.

Jb. 6:† 30. cannot my p. discern
12:† 11. Doth not p. taste his meat
31:† 30. Nei. suffered my p. to sin
33:† 2. tongue hath spok. in my p.
34:† 3. as the p. tasteth meat
Pr. 5:† 3. her p. smoother than oil
24:† 13. honeycomb sweet upon p.
Can. 2:† 3. his fruit sweet to my
5:† 16. His p. is most sweet [p.

PALE.

Is. 29:22. nei. shall his face wax p.
Re. 6:8. a p. horse, his name was

PALENESS. [Death

Je.30:6. and all faces turned into p.

PALESTI'NA.

Ex. 15:14. sorrow on men of P.
Is.14:29. Rejoice not, thou whole P.
31. cry, O city, thou P. art dissolv-

PAL'ESTINE. [ed

Jo. 3:4. What with me, all coasts

PAL'LU, ITES. [of P.

Ex.6:14. sons of Reuben P., 1 Ch.5:3.
Nu. 26:5. of P. the family of P-s.
8. And the sons of P. Eliab

PALM branches.

Ne 8:15. Go unto mount fetch p.b.

PALM, S of hand, s. [26

Le.14:15. pour it into p. o. left h.,
1 S. 5:4. p-s o. his h-s were cut off
2 K. 9:35. skull and p-s o. her h-s
Is.48:† 13. p. o. my h. spread heavens
49:16. graven thee upon p-s o. h-s

Da.10:10.set me upon p-s o.my h-s
Ha. 2:†9. be delivered fr. p. o. h.
Mat. 26:67. spit in his face, others smote with p-s o. their h-s, Mk. 14:65. [his h.
Jn.18:22. struck Jes. with p. o.

PALM tree.

Ju. 4:5. dwelt under p. t. of Deb.
Ps.92:12.righteous flourish like p.t.
Can. 7:7. thy stature is like p. t.
8. I said, I will go up to the p.t.
Je. 10:5. They are upright as p.t.
Eze. 41:18. p. t. was betw. cherub
19. face of a man was tow. p. t.
Jo. 1:12. p. t. apple tree are with-

PALM trees.

Ex.15:27.to Elim where were 70 [out
Le.23:40.take you branches of p.t.
De.34:3. L. shewed him city of p.t.
Ju. 1:16. Kenite out of city of p.t.
3:13. Moab possessed city of p. t.
1 K. 6:29. he carved with carved figures of p. t., 32, 35.-7:36. 2 Ch.3:5. Eze. 40:16. [city of p.t.
2 Ch. 28:15. and brought them to
Eze. 40:22. p.t.were aft.measure of
26.had p.t. one on this side gate
31.p.t.were upon the posts,34,37.
41:18.was made with p.t.,20,25,26.

PALMCRIST.

Jon.4:†6.L.prepared a p.to come up

PALMERWORM.

Jo.1:4.what p.left locust hath eaten
2:25. restore years p. hath eaten
Am. 4:9. fig trees the p. devoured

PALMS in hands.

Re.7:9.with white robes and p.in h.

PALSY, IES. [he

Mat. 4:24. those that had the p. healed, 9:2. Mk. 2:3,4. Lu.5:18.
8:6. serv. lieth at home sick of p.
9:2.Jesus said unto sick of p., thy sins, Mk.2:5,9. [Arise, Lu.5:24.
Mk. 2:10. Jes. saith unto sick of p.
Ac. 8:7. many with p-s were healed
9:33.Eneas, who was sick of the p.

PAL'TI.

Nu. 13:9. Of tribe of Benjamin P.

PAL'TIEL. [char P.

Nu. 34:26. prince of tribe of Issa-

PAL'TITE. See HELEZ.

PAMPHYL'IA.

Ac. 2:10. Phrygia and P. in Egypt
13:13.Paul fr.Paphos to Perga in P
15:38. John departed fr.them fr.P.
14:24. passed, they came to P.
27:5. had sailed over sea of P.

PAN, PANS.

Ex.27:3. make p-s to receive ashes
Le. 2:5. if meat off-g baken in a p.
6:21. In a p. it shall be made with
7:9.all dressed in p. be priest's[oil
Nu. 11:8. they baked manna in p-s
1 S. 2:14. servant stuck it into p.
2 S. 13:9. Tamar took p. poured
1 Ch.9:31.things made in p-s,23:29.
2 Ch.35:13.offerings sod they in p-s
Eze. 4:3. take unto thee an iron p.

PANGS.

2 S. 22:†5. p. of death compassed
Is. 13:8. p. shall take hold of them
21:3.p. have taken hold upon me, as p. of a woman [her p. so we
26:17. as a woman crieth out in
Je. 22:23. gracious thou when p.
48:41. heart of wom. in p., 49:22.
50:43. p. as of a woman, Mi. 4:9.

PANNAG. See MINNITH.

PANT, ED, ETH.

Ps. 38:10. My heart p-h, strength
42:1. As hart p-h so p-h my soul
119:131. I opened mouth and p-d
Ec. 1:†5. the sun p-h to his place
Is. 21:4. at the vision my heart p-d
Am. 2:7. that p. after dust of earth

PAPER.

Is. 19:7. the p. reeds shall wither
2 Jn.12.I wo. not write with p.and

PA'PHOS. [ink

Ac. 13:6. had gone thro. isle to P.
13. when Paul loosed from P.

PAPS. [youth

Eze. 23:21. lewdness for p. of thy
Lu. 11:27. Blessed are p. thou hast
23:29. Blessed are p. never gave
Re. 1:13. girt p. with golden gir-

PARABLE. [dle

Nu. 23:7. Balaam took up p. and said, Balak, 24:3, 15, 20, 21, 23.
18. took up his p. Rise up, Balak
Jb.27:1. Job continued his p.,29:1.
Ps. 49:4. I will incline ear to a p.
78:2. I will open my mouth in p.
Pr. 26:7. p. in mouth of fools, 9.
Eze. 17:2. speak a p. unto Israel
24:3.utter p. unto rebellious hou.
Mi. 2:4 one sh. take up p. ag. you
Ha. 2:6. Sh. not all take p. ag. him
Mat. 13:18. Hear ye p. of the sower
24. Another p. put he forth, 31, 33.-21:33. [Mk. 4:34.
34. without a p. spake he not,
36. Declare unto us the p. of the tares, 15:15.
24:32. learn a p. of the fig tree, Mk. 13:28. Lu. 21:29. [8:9.
Mk. 4:10. asked him of p.,7:17.Lu.
13. he said, Know ye not this p.?
12:12. spoken p. ag. th., Lu.20:19.
Lu. 5:36. he spake a p. unto them
6:39.-8:4.-12:16.-13:6.-14:7.-15:3.-18:1, 9.-19:11.-20:9, 19.-21:29. Jn. 10:6.
8:11. Now the p. is this, The seed
12:41. Lord, speakest thou this p.
unto us, or to all?
Jn.16:†29.now speakest thou no p.

PARABLES. [p.

Eze. 20:49. say, Doth he not speak
Mat. 13:3. he spake many things unto them in p.,13,34,53.-22:1. Mk. 3:23.-4:2, 13, 33.-12:1.
10. Why speakest thou in p.
35. I will open my mouth in p.
21:45.when Pharisees heard his p.
Mk.4:11.these things are done in p.
13. how then will ye know all p.
Lu.8:10.but others in p.that seeing
Jn.16:†25.I sh.no more speak in p.

PARADISE. [in p.

Lu. 23:43. To day shalt be with me
2 Co. 12:4. was caught up into p.
Re. 2:7. in midst of the p. of God

PA'RAH. See OPHRAH.

PARAMOURS. [p.

Eze. 23:20.she doted upon their

PA'RAN.

Ge. 14:†6. Seir unto plain of P.
21:21. in wilderness of P., Nu. 10:12.-12:16.-13:3, 26. 1 S. 25:1.
De. 1:1. over ag. Red Sea betw. P.
33:2.Lord shined forth from m-t P.
1 K. 11:18. Hadad arose came to P
Ha. 3:3. Holy One came fr. P. [(2)

PAR'BAR.

1 Ch. 26:18. porters at causeway at

PARCEL. [P.

Ge. 33:19. Jacob bought a p. of a field, Jos. 24:32. Jn. 4:5.
Ru. 4:3. Naomi selleth a p. of land
1 Ch.11:13.p. of ground full of bar-

PARCHED. [ley, 14.

Is. 35:7. p. ground become a pool
Je. 17:6. he shall inhabit p. places
See CORN.

PARCHMENTS. [the p.

2 Ti. 4:13. bring books, especially

PARDON. [gr-ns

Ex. 23:21. will not p. your trans-
34:9. p. our iniquity, Nu. 14:19.
1 S. 15:25. I pray thee p. my sin
2 K.5:18.In this the L. p. thy serv.
24:4.innoc.blood, L. would not p.
2 Ch. 30:18. The good L. p. ev. one
Ne 9:17. thou art a G. ready to p.
Jb.7:21. why not p. my transgr-n?
Ps. 25:11. for name's sake p. iniq.
Is. 55:7. return unto L. he abun-
Je. 5:1. and I will p. it [dantly p.
7. How shall I p. thee for this?
33:8. I will p. all their iniquities
50:20. I will p. whom I reserve
Ho. 1:†6. I sho. altogether p. them

PARDONED, ETH.

Nu.14:20.L. I have p-d acc.to word
Is.40:2. tell her her iniquity is p-d
La. 3:42.We rebelled, thou not p-d
Mi. 7:18. Who a G. like unto thee

PARDONS. [that p-h

Ne. 9:†17. thou art a God of p.

PARE. [nails

De. 21:12. shall shave head p. her

PARENTS.

Mat. 10:21. children shall rise up ag. their p., Mk. 13:12. [Jesus
Lu. 2:27. when p. brought in child
41. his p. went to Jerus. ev. year
8:56. her p. were astonished, but
18:29. is no man that hath left p.
21:16. ye shall be betrayed by p.
Jn. 9:2. who did sin, man or p.? 3,
22.These words spake p.,18,20,23
Ro. 1:30. disobed-t to p., 2 Ti. 3:2.
2 Co.12:14.chil. not to lay up for p.
Ep. 6:1. obey your p., Col. 3:20.
1 Ti. 5:4. learn to requite their p.
He. 11:23. Moses was hid of his p.

PARLOUR, S.

Ju. 3:20. Eglon was sitting in p.
23. Ehud shut doors of p., 24,25.
1 S. 9:22. Sam. bro-t them into p.
1 Ch.28:11. David gave Sol. pattern

PARMASH'TA. [of p-s

Es. 9:9. slew sons of Haman, P.

PAR'MENAS. [and

Ac. 6:5. chose Timon, P.and Nicolas

PAR'NACH. [P.

Nu. 34:25. prince Elizaphan son of

PA'ROSH = PHA'ROSH.

Ezr. 2:3. chil. of P. 2172, Ne. 7:8
10:25. of sons of P. Ramiah
Ne.3:25. aft. him Pedaiah son of P.
10:14. chief of the people, P.

PARSHAN'DATHA.

Es. 9:7. slew sons of Haman, P.

PART.

Ex.19:17. stood at nether p. of m-t
29:26. take breast, it sh. be thy p.
Le.2:16. p. of beaten corn, p.of oil
7:33. right shoulder for his p.
8:29. breast of consecra. Moses' p.
11:37. if any p. of carcass fall, 38.
13:41.hair fallen fr. p. of his head
27:16. sanctify unto L. p. of field
Nu. 18:20. neither shalt thou have any p. among them, De. 10:9.-12:12.-14:27, 29.-18:1. Jos. 14:4.-18:7.
I am thy p. and inheritance
29. L. of all, even hallowed p.
De.33:21.provided first p. for hims.
Jos. 15:13. unto Caleb he gave a p.
19:9. p. of Judah was too much
22:25. ye have no p. in the L.,27.
Ru. 2:3. her hap was to light on a p. of field [kinsman
3:13. if he perform unto thee p. of
1 S. 5:†4. only fishy p. to Dagon
23:20. our p. sh. be to deliv. him
30:24.as his p. th. goeth to battle, so his p. th. tarrieth by stuff
2 S. 20:1. We have no p. in David
2 K. 18:23.if able on thy p. to set riders, Is. 36:8. [Ch. 34:†22.
22:†14. dwelt in the second p., 2
1 Ch. 12:29. p. kept house of Saul
2 Ch. 29:16. priests into inner p.
Ne.5:11. Restore 100th p. of money
7:†70.p.of fa-s gave unto the work
Jb. 32:17. I will answer my p. will
Ps. 16:†5. Lord is portion of my p.

Ps.51:6. in hidden **p.** know wisdom
118:7. Lord taketh my **p.** with th.
Pr. 1: † 7. fear of L. is principal **p.**
8 : 26. nor highest **p.** of the dust
31. Rejoicing in habitable **p.** of
17:2.have **p.** of inheri. am. breth.
Is. 44 : 16. burneth **p.** in the fire,
with **p.** he eateth flesh, 19.
Eze.4:11. shalt drink sixth **p.**of hin
39 : 2. leave but sixth **p.** of thee
45 : 13. sixth **p.** of an ephah of a
17. princes' **p.** to give offerings
46 : 14. the sixth **p.** of an ephah
Da. 2:33. his feet **p.** of iron, and **p.**
of clay, 41, 42. [wrote, 24.
5 : 5. the king saw **p.** of hand that
11 : 31. arms shall stand on his **p.**
12 : † 7. be for a time and a **p.**
Am. 7 : 4. devoured deep, did eat **p.**
Mk. 9 : 40. he not ag. us is on our **p.**
Lu.10:42 Mary hath chosen good **p.**
11 : 36. full of light no **p.** dark
17 : 24. lightning lighteneth 1 **p.**
shineth unto other **p.** under
Jn. 13 : 8. wash thee not hast no **p.**
19:23.four parts, to ev.soldier a **p.**
Ac. 1 : 17. obtained **p.** of ministry
25.Th he may take **p.**of ministry
5:2.Ananias kept back **p.** of price,
brought certain **p.** and laid, 3.
8:21. Thou hast neither **p.** nor lot
14 : 4. **p.** held with Jews, **p.** with
16 : 12. city of that **p.** of Macedo-
19:32. more **p.** knew,not whf. [nia
23 : 6. the one **p.** were Sadducees
9. scribes of the Pharis. **p.** arose
27 : 12. more **p.** advised to depart
1 Co.12:24.honour to **p.** wh. lacked
15 : 6. of whom greater **p.** remain
16 : 17. what lacking on your **p.**
2 Co.6:15. what **p.** he th. believeth
Ep. 4 : 16. in the measure of ev. **p.**
Col.2:†16.**p.**of holydayor new moon
Tit. 2 : 8. that he of the contrary **p.**
He.2:14. hims. took **p.** of the same
1 Pe. 4 : 14. on their **p.** he is evil
spoken of, on your **p.** glorified
Re. 20: 6. hath **p.** in 1st resurrec-n
21:8. all liars shall have **p.** in lake
22: 19. God shall take away his **p.**
See HINDER, INWARD, UTMOST,
UTTERMOST.

In PART. [ed
Ro.11:25. blindness **i. p.**is happen-
1 Co. 13 : 9. we know **i. p.** and we
prophesy **i. p.** [done aw.
10. then that wh. is **i. p.** shall be
12. I know **i. p.** then sh. I know
2 Co. 1:14. ye acknowledged us **i.p.**
2:5.it hath not grieved me but **i.p.**

Third PART.
Nu. 15 : 6. flour mingled with **t. p.**
of hin of oil, 28 : 14. Eze. 46:14.
7. offer **t. p.** of hin of wine
2 S. 18 : 2. David sent a **t.p.** of peo.
2 K.11:5 **t. p.** that enter on sab., 6.
2 Ch. 23 : 4. a **t. p.** shall be porters
Ne. 10 : 32. charge ours. with **t. p.**
Eze. 5: 2. burn with fire a **t. p.**
smite a **t. p.** with a knife : a **t.**
p. scatter in the wind, 12.
Zch. 13 : 8. the **t. p.** shall be left
9. I will bring **t. p.** through fire
Re. 8 : 7. **t.p.** of trees was burnt up
8. **t. p.** of the sea became blood
9. **t. p.** of the creatures died, **t.**
p. of ships were destroyed
10. it fell upon **t. p.** of the rivers
11.**t.p.**of waters became wormw.
12. **t. p.** of sun, moon, was smitten, the day shone not for **t.p.**
9:15. prepared to slay **t.p.** of men
18. by these was **t. p.** killed
12 : 4. his tail drew **t. p.** of stars

Fourth PART.
Ex. 29 : 40. flour with **f.p.** of a hin
of oil, Nu. 15 : 4.-28 : 5.
Ex. 29 : 40. **f. p.** of a hin of wine,
Le. 23 : 13. Nu. 15 : 5.-28 : 7, 14.
Nu.23:10.Who can count **f.p.**of Isr.
1 S. 9 : 8. I have **f. p.** of a shekel
1 K. 6 : 33. posts of olive tree **f. p.**
2 K.6:25.**f.p.**of a cab of doves'dung
Ne. 9 : 3. read one **f. p.** ano. **f. p.**
Re. 6 : 8. power given over **f. p.**

Fifth PART.
Ge. 41 : 34. take up **f. p.** of Egypt
47:24. sh. give **f. p.** unto Pha.,26.
Le. 5 : 16. shall add **f. p.**, 6 : 5.-22:
14.-27:13, 15, 19, 27,31.Nu.5:7.
1 K.6:31. lintel and posts were **f.p.**

Tenth PART.
Ex. 16 : 36. homer is **t. p.** of ephah
Le. 5 : 11. shall bring **t. p.** of an
ephah of flour, 6 : 20. Nu. 28:5.
Nu. 5 : 15. **t. p.** of ephah of barley
18:26. offer even **t. p.** of the tithe
Eze. 45 : 11. bath may contain **t.p.**
14. ye shall offer **t. p.** of a bath
He.7:2.To whom Ab. gave a **t. p.**,4.
Re. 11 : 13. the **t. p.** of the city fell

PARTS.
Ge. 47 : 24. four **p.** shall be own
Le. 1 : 8. Aaron's sons sh. lay the **p.**
22: 23. any thing lacking in his **p.**
Nu. 31 : 27. divide prey into two **p.**
De. 19 : 3. divide coasts into 3 **p.** [**p.**
30 : 4. If any driven unto outmost
Jos.18:5. sh. divide it into 7 **p.**,6,9.
1 S. 5 : 9. emerods in their secret **p.**
2 S. 19 : 43. We have ten **p.** in king
1 K. 6 : 38. house finished thro-t **p.**
16:21.Isr. were divided into two **p.**
2 K. 11 : 7. two **p.** keep watch about
Ne.4:†13.fr. lower **p.** of place [king
11 : 1. nine **p.** in other cities
Jb. 26 : 14. these are **p.** of his ways
41 : 12. I will not conceal his **p.**
136 : 13. divided Red Sea into **p.**
15.curiously wrought in lowest **p.**
Pr. 18 : 8. go in to innerm. **p.**, 26:22.
Is.3:17. L. will discover their secret
Je.34:18. passed between **p.**,19. [**p.**
Eze. 26: 20. set thee in the low **p.**of
37:11. are cut off for our **p.**[earth
38:15.fr.place out of north **p.**,39:2
48 : 8. offering as one of other **p.**
Zch. 13 : 8. two **p.** sh. be cut off and
Mat. 2 : 22. aside into **p.** of Galilee
Mk. 8 : 10. into **p.** of Dalmanutha
Jn. 19 : 23. his garm. and made 4 **p.**
Ac. 2 : 10. in the **p.** of Libya about
20 : 2. gone over those **p.** he came
Ro.15:23. no more place in those **p.**
1 Co.12:23 uncomely **p.** have more
24. our comely **p.** have no need
Re. 16 : 19. great city into three **p.**
See BACK, HINDER, INWARD,
LOWER,NETHER,UTTERMOST.

PART. [Verb.]
Le.2:6. Thou shalt **p.** meat offering
Ru.1:17. if aught but death **p.** thee
1 S.30:24.they sh. **p.** alike [and me
2 S.14:6. was none to **p.** th.[chants
Jb.41:6. shall they **p.** him am.mer-
Ps.22:18.They **p.** my garments am.

PARTAKER.
Ps. 50 : 18. been **p.** with adulterers
1 Co.9:10.he sho. be **p.** of his hope
23. that I might be **p.** with you
10:30.if I by grace be **p.** why am I
1 Ti.5:22.nei.**p.** of other men's sins
2 Ti. 1 : 8. be thou **p.** of afflictions
2:6.husbandman be 1st **p.**of fruits
1 Pe. 5 : 1. who am a **p.** of glory
2 Jn. 11. biddeth G. speed, is **p.** of

PARTAKERS.[his evil
Mat.23:30. would not been **p.**in bl.
Ro. 15: 27. if Gentiles been made **p.**
of spiritual things, their duty
1 Co. 9 : 12. If others be **p.** of power
13. wait at altar, are **p.** wi. altar
10: 17. we are all **p.** of that bread
18.are not they wh. eat **p.** of alt.
1 Co. 10 : 21. cannot be **p.** of L.'s
table, and of the table of devils
2 Co. 1 : 7. as ye are **p.** of sufferings
Ep. 3 : 6. **p.** of his promise in Christ
5:7. Be not ye therefore **p.** with th.
Ph. 1 : 7. ye all are **p.** of my grace
Col. 1 : 12. made us meet to be **p.** of
1 Ti. 6 : 2. bec. are **p.** of the benefit
He.2:14. as chil. are **p.** of flesh and
3 :1. breth **p.** of heavenly calling
14. we are made **p.** of Christ, if
6: 4. were made **p.** of Holy Ghost
12:8. chastisement, wh-f all are **p.**
10. that we be **p.** of his holiness
1 Pe.4:13.as ye are **p.**of Ch.'s suff-gs
2 Pe.1:4.th.ye be **p.**of divine nature
Re. 18 : 4. that ye be not **p.** of her

PARTAKEST.
Ro. 11:17. and with them **p.** of root

PARTED.
Ge.2:10.river was **p.**into four heads
2 K. 2 : 11. chariot **p.** them asunder
14. waters **p.** hither and thither
Jb. 38:24. By what way is light **p.**?
Jo. 3 : 2. scattered, and **p.** my land
Mat. 27 : 35. they **p.** his garments,
Mk. 15:24. Lu. 23:34. Jn. 19:24.
Lu.24:51.while he blessed th.,was **p**
Ac. 2 : 45. **p.** them to all, as each

PARTETH.
Le.11:3.Whatsoever **p.**hoof,De.14:6.
Pr. 18 : 18. the lot **p.** between migh-

PAR'THIANS. [ty
Ac. 2 : 9. **P.** we hear them speak

PARTIAL.
Mal. 2 : 9 but have been **p.** in law
Ja. 2:4. Are ye not then **p.** in yours.

PARTIALITY. [by **p.**
1 Ti.5:21.observe these, doing noth.
Ja. 3 : 17. without **p.** and hypocrisy

PARTICULAR, LY.
Ac.21:19.Paul declared **p-y** what G.
1 Co.12:27.of Christ, members in **p.**
Ep. 5 : 33. ev. one in **p.** so love wife
He. 9 : 5. wh. we cannot now speak

PARTIES. [**p-y**
Ex.22:9.both **p.**sh.come bef. judges

PARTING. [way
Eze. 21 : 21. king stood at **p.** of the

PARTITION. [gold
1 K. 6 : 21. he made **p.** by chains of
Ep. 2 : 14. broken middle wall of **p.**

PARTLY. [broken
Da. 2 : 42. kingd. be **p.** strong, **p.**
1 Co. 11: 18. divisions, I **p.** believe it
He.10:33.**p.**whilst ye were a gazingstock, **p.** whilst companions

PARTNER, S. [hateth
Pr. 29 : 24. Whoso is **p.** with thief
Lu. 5 : 7. beckoned unto **p-s** to help
10. James, John **p-s** with Simon
2 Co. 8 : 23. Titus, he is my **p.** and
Phm. 17. If count me a **p.** receive

PARTRIDGE. [him
1 S.26:20.as when one doth hunt **p.**
Je. 17 : 11. as **p.** sitteth on eggs

PAR'UAH.
1 K. 4 : 17. Jehoshaphat son of **P.**

PARVA'IM.
2 Ch. 3 : 6. the gold was gold of **P.**

PA'SACH.
1 Ch. 7 : 33. the sons of Japhlet, **P.**

PAS-DAM'MIM.
1 Ch. 11 : 13. Eleazar with Da. at **P.**

PASE'AH=PHASE'AH.
1 Ch. 4 : 12. And Eshton begat **P.**
Ezr. 2 : 49. children of **P.** [gate
Ne. 3:6. Jehoiada son of **P.** repaired

PASH'UR. [11:12.
1 Ch. 9:12. **P.** son of Malchijah, Ne.
Ezr. 2 : 38. the children of **P.**, 10:22.
Ne. 7 : 41. [captivity
Ne. 10:3. **P.** sealed | Je. 20:6. **P.** into
Je. 20 : 1. **P.** smote Jeremiah, 2.
3. L. called not thy name **P.** but
21 : 1. when king Zedekiah sent **P.**
38:1. Gedaliah son of **P.** and **P.** son

PASS.

Ge. 18 : 5. after that ye shall **p.** on
32:†23. caused th. to **p.** over brook
41:32. G. will shortly bring it to **p.**
Ex. 33:19. I will make my goodn-s **p.**
Nu. 27:7. inherita. **p.** unto them, 8.
34 : 4. your borders shall **p.** to Zin
— shall **p.** on to Azmon
Jos. 1:14. ye sh. **p.** bef. breth. armed
6:7. he said unto people, **p.** on, and
1 S. 9 : 27. Bid servants **p.** on bef. us
16:8. made Abinadab **p.** bef. Sam.
10. Jesse made 7 of his sons **p.**
Ezr. 1:†1. Cyrus caused a voice to **p.**
Ne. 2 : 14. no place for beast to **p.**
Jb. 6 : 15. as a stream they **p.** away
11:16. remember it as waters th. **p.**
34:20. peo. be troubled, and **p.** aw.
36:†12. if obey not they sh. **p.** away
Ps. 58 : 8. as snail let them **p.** away
73 : † 7. they **p.** thoughts of heart
119:†37. make to **p.** mine eyes from
Pr. 16:30. he bringeth evil to **p.** [12.
22:3. simple **p.** on are punished, 27:
Is. 2 : † 18. idols sh. utterly **p.** away
30:32. where grounded staff sh. **p.**
31 : † 9. his rock shall **p.** away
33 : 21. nei. gallant ship shall **p.**
37:26. now have I brought it to **p.**
Je. 8 : 13. things given sh. **p.** away
15 : 14. make thee **p.** with enemies
33 : 13. flocks sh. **p.** under hands
51:43. nei. doth any son of man **p.**
Eze. 5: 1. razor to **p.** upon thine head
20:37. will cause you to **p.** und. rod
32:19. Wh. dost thou **p.** in beauty?
Am. 6 : 2. **p.** ye unto Calne hand see
Mi. 1 : 11 **p.** ye away, inhabitant
2:13. their king shall **p.** before th.
Zph. 2:2. Bef. decree bri. forth, day **p.**
Zch. 3:4. have caused thy iniq. to **p.**
Mat. 5 : 18. heaven and earth sh. **p.**
one tittle not **p.**, Lu. 16: 17. [35.
26:39. let cup **p.** from me, Mk. 14 :
Lu. 16:26. which wo. **p.** to you can-t;
nei. can they **p.** to us fr. you
19 : 4. for he was to **p.** that way
Ac. 18 : 27. when was disposed to **p.**
1 Co. 7:36. if she **p.** flower of her age
15 : 54. then sh. be brought to **p.**
Ja. 1 : 10. as grass he shall **p.** away
1 Pe. 1:17. **p.** time of your sojourn-g
2 Pe. 3 : 10. heavens shall **p.** away

PASS by.

Ex. 33 : 22. cover thee while I **p. b.**
De. 2 : 30. Sihon would not let us **p.**
b. him, Nu. 20: 18. [mah to **p. b.**
1 S. 16 : 9. Then Jesse made Sham-
Ps. 80 : 12. all that **p. b.** do pluck
89:41. All that **p. b.** way spoil him
Je. 22:8. nations shall **p. b.** this city
La. 1 : 12. all ye that **p. b.**, behold
2 : 15. All that **p. b.** clap hands at
Eze. 5 : 14. in sight of all that **p. b.**
37 : 2. caused me to **p. b.** them
46:21. caused me to **p. b.** 4 corners
Am. 7 : 8. I will not **p. b.** them, 8:2.
Mi. 2:8. pull off garm. of them **p. b.**
Mat. 8:28. th. no man might **p. b.**
Lu. 18:36. hearing multitude **p. b.**
2 Co. 1:16. to **p. b.** you into Macedonia

Came to PASS. [-**p.**

Jos. 21:45. failed not any thing; all
1 S. 10:9. all those signs -**p.** that day
Is. 48 : 3. I did them suddenly; they

It came to PASS. [-**p.**

Ge. 7:10. -**p.** after — days, 8:6. De.
9:11. Jos. 3:2.-9:16. 1 S. 25:38.
1 K. 18 : 1. Je. 13 : 6. Eze. 3:16.
Lu. 2 : 46.-9 : 18, 28. Ac. 28 : 17.
8:13. -**p.** in — year, De. 1 : 3. 2 S.
11:1. 1 K. 6:1.-14:25.-22:2. 2 K.
18 : 1, 9.-22 : 3.-25 : 1, 27. 2 Ch.
12 : 2. Ne. 1 : 1. Is. 36 : 1. Je.
28 : 1. -36 : 1, 9.-52 : 4, 31. Eze.
1 : 1.-8 : 1.-20:-29 : 17.-30 : 20.-
31 : 1.-32 : 1.-33 : 21. Zch. 7 : 1.
Ge. 12:14. **p.** wh. Abraham was come.
11. | 37 : 23. Joseph | Jos. 4:18.
priests, 1 K. 8 : 10. 2 Ch. 5 : 11.
| Ru. 1:19. Naomi and Ruth |
1 S. 16:6. they, 2 K. 6:20. | 2 S.
15 : 32. David, 17 : 27. | 16 : 16.
Hushai | 19 : 25. Mephibosheth
| 2 Ch. 25 : 14. Amaziah | Lu.
18 : 35. Jesus, 19 : 29.
14 : 1. -**p.** in days of, Es. 1 : 1. Is.
7 : 1. Ac. 11 : 28.
19 : 34. -**p.** on the morrow, Ex.
18 : 13.-32 : 30. Nu. 17 : 8.-22 :
41. Ju. 9 : 42.-21 : 4. 1 S. 18 : 10.
-20 : 27.-31 : 8. 2 K. 8 : 15. 1
Ch. 10 : 8. Je. 20 : 3. Ac. 4 : 5.
21:22. -**p.** at that time, 31:10.-38:
1, 27.-39:5, 11. Jos. 2:5.-6:16.-
10:27.-23:1. 1 S. 3:2. 1 K. 11:29.
-15 : 36, 44. Ne. 4 : 16. Lu. 9 :51.
22 : 1. -**p.** after these things, 20.-
39 : 7.-40 : 1.-48 : 1. Jos. 24 : 29.
1 K. 17 : 7.-21 : 1.
24 : 52. -**p.** when servants heard |
29:13. Laban | 39:15. he, 18. |
19. master | De. 5:23. Ye | Jos.
10 : 1. Adoni-zedek | 11 : 1. Ja-
bin | 1 K. 5 : 7 Hiram | 12 : 2.
Jeroboam, 13 : 4. 2 Ch. 10 : 2.
| 1 K. 12 : 20. Israel | 15 : 21.
Baasha | 20 : 12. Benhadad | 21:
15. Jezebel | 16. Ahab, 27. | 2 K.
6:30. king, 22:11. 2 Ch. 34:19. |
2 K. 19 : 1. Hezekiah Is. 37 : 1.
| Ne. 1 : 4. I heard | 4 : 15. ene-
mies, 6 : 1, 16. | 13 : 3. they, Je.
36 : 16. | Lu. 1 : 41, Elizabeth
25:11. -**p.** after death of, Ju. 1 : 1.
-2 : 19.-8 : 33. 2 S. 1 : 1.
26:32. -**p.** same day Isaac's servants
came [2 S. 11 : 2.
29 : 23. -**p.** in evening, Ex. 16 : 13.
25. -**p.** in the morning, 41:8. Ex.
14 : 24. 1 S. 20 : 35.-25 : 37. 2 S.
11 : 14. 2 K. 3 : 20.-10 : 9.
34 : 25. -**p.** on 3d day, 40 : 20. Ex.
19: 16. 1 S. 30 : 1. 1 K. 3 : 18. Es.
5 : 1. [Ju. 11 : 39.
38 : 24. -**p.** about 3 months aft. |
39:10. -**p.** as she spoke | Ex. 16:10.
Aaron | Jos. 1 : 1. Lord | 6 : 8.
Joshua | Ju. 2 : 4. Angel of L.
| 2 K. 7 : 18. man of God | Es.
3 : 4. they | Lu. 11 : 27. Jesus
41 : 1. -**p.** at end of — years, 2 S.
15 : 7. 1 K. 2: 39.-9 : 10. 2 K.
8 : 3. 2 Ch. 24 : 23.
Ex. 2:11. -**p.** in those days, 1 S. 28:
1. 2 S. 1 : 2. Mk. 1:9. Lu. 2: 1.-6:
12.-20: 1. Ac. 9:37. [4. 2 Ch. 21: 19.
23. -**p.** in process of time, Ju. 11:
6 : 28. -**p.** on — day, 16:22, 27. Le.
9 : 1. Nu. 7: 1.-10: 11. Ju. 14: 15.-
19 : 5. 1 S. 14 : 1. 2 S. 12: 18. Je.
41: 4. Lu. 1: 59.-5: 17.-7: 11.-8:22.
12:29. -**p.** that at midnight, Ru. 3:8.
41. -**p.** at end of 430 yrs. selfsame
day -**p.**, 51. [34 : 29.
17 : 11. -**p.** when Moses, 33:8, 9.-
40 : 17. -**p.** in — month, 2 K. 25:
25. Ne. 1 : 1. Je. 41 : 1.
Nu. 16 : 31 -**p.** as he made an end,
Ge. 27:30. De. 31:24. Ju. 15:17.
1 S. 13:10.-18: 1.-24:16. 2 S. 13:
36. 2 K. 10:25. Je. 26:8.-43: 1.
De. 2 : 16. So -**p.** 1 S. 13 : 22. 2 K.
15 : 12. Es. 2 : 8. Ac. 27 : 44.
Jos. 3 : 14. -**p.** when people, 4 : 1,
11.-6 : 20. Je. 41 : 13. Lu. 5 : 1.
5 : 1. -**p.** when kings, 9 : 1.
8 : 14. -**p.** when king, 2 S. 7 : 1. 2
K. 5 : 7. 1 Ch. 17 : 1. [1 : 28.
17 : 13. -**p.** when Isr. strong, Ju.
Ju. 6 : 25. -**p.** same night, 7 : 9.
2 S. 7 : 4. -**p.** th. night, 2 K. 19 : 35.
1 Ch. 17 : 3.
13 : 30. For -**p.**, 15 : 1. 1 K. 11 : 4,
15. 2 K. 3 : 5. Ne. 2 : 1.-4 : 1, 7.
-6 : 1.-7 : 1. Je. 35 : 11.
1 S. 1 : 20. -**p.** when time was come
16 : 23. -**p.** when evil spirit fr. G.
2 S. 2 : 1. -**p.** after this, 8 : 1.-10:1.
-13:1.-15 : 1.-21 : 18. 2 K. 6:24.
1 Ch. 18:1.-19:1.-20:4. 2 Ch. 20:1.
1 K. 18:1. -**p.** at noon Elijah [-24:4.
22 : 32. -**p.** when captains saw Jehoshaphat, 33. 2 Ch. 18 : 31, 32.
Is. 48 : 5. before -**p.** I shewed thee
1 Th. 3 : 4. tribulation even as -**p.**

Come to PASS.

Ge. 24 : 14. let it -**p.** that damsel
Ex. 1 : 10. -**p.** they join our enemies
De. 24 : 1. -**p.** wife find no favour
29 : 19. -**p.** when he heareth curse
2 S. 17:9. -**p.** when some be overthr.
Da. 2:45. known to king what sh. -**p.**
Re. 1: 1. wh. must shortly -**p.**, 22:6.

It shall come to PASS.

Ge. 4 : 14. -**p.** every one sh. slay me
9 : 14. -**p.** when I bring cloud over
12:12. -**p.** when Eg-ns see thee they
24 : 43. -**p.** when virgin cometh
27:40. -**p.** when thou have domin.
44 : 31. -**p.** when seeth lad is not
46:33. -**p.** when Pha. sh. call you
47:24. -**p.** ye sh. give 5th unto Pha.
Ex. 3 : 21. -**p.** ye sh. not go empty
12 : 25. -**p.** when ye come to land
26. -**p.** when chil. say, What mean
ye by this service? [pare
16:5. -**p.** on 6th day they sh. pre-
22 : 27. -**p.** when he crieth I will
33:22. -**p.** while my glory passeth
Nu. 5 : 27. -**p.** if she be defiled
21 : 8. -**p.** every one that is bitten
33:55. -**p.** those be pricks in your
56 -**p.** I sh. do as I thought [eyes
De. 11: 29. -**p.** when L. hath bro-t
28 : 63. -**p.** as L. rejoiced over you
30 : 1. -**p.** when blessing and curse
31:21. -**p.** when evils and troubles
Jos. 3 : 13. -**p.** as soon as feet of
6 : 5. -**p.** when make long blast
8 : 5. -**p.** when they come ag. us
23 : 15. -**p.** as all good things
1 S. 2 : 36. -**p.** ev. one sh. crouch
10 : 5. -**p.** thou meet a company
16 : 16. -**p.** when evil spirit fr. G.
23:23. -**p.** I will search him thro-t
25:30. -**p.** when L. done to my lord
1 K. 1:21. -**p.** when k. sleep with fa-s
19:17. -**p.** him escapeth Jehu slay
1 Ch. 17:11. -**p.** when days be expir.
Is. 3 : 24. -**p.** instead of sweet smell
4 : 3. -**p.** he th. is left in Zion sh.
7:18. -**p.** L. sh. hiss for fly, 21, 23.
22. -**p.** he shall eat butter
8:21. -**p.** they sh. curse king and G.
10 : 12. -**p.** I will punish | 20, 27.
11 : 11. -**p.** in that day, 14 : 3.-22:
20.-23:15.-24:21.-27:12, 13. Je.
4:9.-30:8. Eze. 39:11 -47:22, 23.
Ho. 2 : 21. Mi. 5 : 10. Zph. 1:10.
Zch. 12 : 9.-13 : 4.-14 : 6, 13.
16 : 12. -**p.** when Moab is weary
17:4. -**p.** glory of Jac. sh. be thin
22 : 7. -**p.** thy choicest valleys
23 : 17. -**p.** after 70 years, Je. 25: 12.
24 : 18. -**p.** he who fleeth sh. fall
65: 24. -**p.** bef. they call I answer
66:23. -**p.** fr. one new moon to ano.
Je. 3:16. -**p.** when ye be multiplied
| 5: 19.-12:15, 16.-15:2.-16:10.
-27:8.-31:28.-42:16. Eze. 38:10.
-44 : 17. Zch. 8: 20.-14 : 16.
42 : 4. -**p.** whatso. L. shall answer
49: 39. -**p.** in the latter days I
Eze. 38: 18. -**p.** when Gog came ag.
47 : 9. -**p.** ev. thing sh. live [Isr.
10. -**p.** fishers sh. stand upon it
Ho. 1 : 10. -**p.** in place it was said
Ye are not my peo., Ro. 9 : 26.
Jo. 2 : 28. -**p.** I will pour my Spirit
3:18. -**p.** mts. shall drop new wine

Am. 6 : 9. -p. if remain ten men
Na. 3 : 7. -p. all look upon thee flee
Zph.1:8. -p. in day of L.'s sacrifice
12. -p. I will search Jerus. with
Zch. 8 : 13. -p. as ye were a curse
23. -p. that 10 men sh. take hold
13 : 3. -p. when any sh. prophesy
4. -p. prophets shall be ashamed
14 : 6. -p. light not be clear nor
7. -p. at evening time be light
13. -p. that a tumult from Lord

See COME to pass.

Cannot or not PASS.

Nu. 20 : 17. we will n.p. thro. fields
18. Edom said, shalt n. p. by me
De. 24:†5. When man tak. new wife
shall n. any thing p. on him
Es.9:†27.n.p. th. they keep 2 days
†28.these days of Purim sho.n.p.
Jb. 14:5. appointed bounds he c.p.
19 : 8. fenced my way that I c. p.
Ps. 104 : 9. a bound they may n.p.
148 : 6. a decree, which shall n. p.
Pr.8:29. th. waters n. p. his com-t
Je. 5 : 22. by a decree, that it c. p.
Da. 7 : 14. dominion that shall n.p.
Mat. 24 : 34. This generation shall
n. p. away, till, Mk. 13 : 30.
Lu. 21 : 32.
35. earth shall p. but my word
shall n. p.,Mk.13:31.Lu.21:33.
26:42. if this cup may n. p. fr. me

PASS not.

Ge. 18:3. p.n. away from thy serv.
2 K. 6 : 9. Beware p.n.such a place
Es. 1:†19. am. laws th.it p.n. away
Pr. 4 : 15. Avoid it, p. n. by it
Am. 5 : 5. p. n. to Beer-sheba: for

PASS over.

Ge.8:1.God made wind to p.o.earth
31:52.th. I will not p.o. this heap
32 : 16. p.o. bef. me and put space
† 23. caused them to p. o. brook
33:14.Let my lord p.o.bef.servant
Ex. 12 : 13. when I see blood, I will
p. o. you, 23. [all th. open
13 : † 12. cause to p. o. unto Lord
15: 16. still as stone, till peo. p. o.
Nu. 8 : † 7. cause a razor to p. o.
32:27.thy servants will p.o.,29,32.
30. if not p. o. with you armed
De. 2 : 18. p. o. thro. Ar this day
24. p.o. Arnon | 29.until I shall
p. o. Jordan [brethren
3:18.ye shall p.o. armed bef.your
6 : † 1. do th. in land whi. ye p. o.
9:1. p.o. Jordan this day, 11:31.-
27:2. Jos. 1 : 11.-3 : 6, 14.-4 : 5.
Jos. 22 : 19. then p. o. unto land
Ju. 3 : 28. suffer not a man to p. o.
19:12. said, We will p.o.to Gibeah
1 S. 14 : 8. we will p. o. to these
20 : † 36. shot arrow to p. o. him
2 S. 15 : 22. Da. said to Ittai, p. o.
17:16. lodge not, speedily p.o.,21.
Ps.104:9. bound, they may not p.o.
141:†10.Let wick.fall,whilst I p.o.
Pr. 19 : 11. glory to p.o. transgr-n
Is. 23 : 2. merchants that p. o. sea
6. p. o. to Tarshish, howl ye
12. arise, p. o. to Chittim
28 : 19. by morning shall it p. o.
31:9.he sh. p.o. to his strong hold
35:8. way of holin. unclean not p.
47:2.uncover thigh, p.o.rivers [o.
51 : 10. way for ransomed to p.
Je. 2 : 10. For p. o. isles of Chittim
5 : 22. roar, yet can they not p.o.
Eze. 47 : 5. river that I co. not p.o.
Da. 4 : 16. let 7 times p. o. him, 25.
11:†20. causeth an exactor to p.o.
40. king of the north shall p. o.
Ha. 1:11. mind change, he sh. p.o.
Mk.4:35. Let us p.o. unto oth. side
Lu.11:42.p.o.judgm.and love of G.

PASS through.

Ge.30:32.I will p.t. thy flock to day
Ex.12:12. I will p.t. Eg. this night
23. Lord will p. t. to smite Eg-ns
Le. 18 : 21. not let any of thy seed
p.t.the fire,De.18:10.2 K.17:17.
Nu.20:17. Let us p. t. thy country
21:22. Let me p.t. thy land, De.2:
27. Ju. 11 : 17, 19. [Ju. 11: 20.
23. Sihon not suffer Isr. to p. t.,
De. 2 : 4. Ye are to p. t. Edom
28. only I will p. t. on my feet
Jos. 1 : 11. p. t. host and command
2 S. 12 : 31. made th. p.t. brickkiln
1 K. 18 : 6. divided land to p. t. it
2 K. 16 : 3. to p.t. the fire, 21:6.-23:
10. 2 Ch. 33 : 6. Je. 32: 35. Eze.
16:21.-20:26,31.-23:27. [136:14.
Ps. 78 : 13. caused them to p.t.sea,
Is.8:8.he sh.p.t. Judah,and go ov.
21 shall p. t. it hardly bestead
21: 1. As whirlwinds in south p.t.
23:10.p.t. thy land as a river [18.
28:15. overflowing scourge sh.p.t.,
34: 10. none shall p. t. it for ever
Je.9:10.burned,so th. none can p.t.
La. 3 : 44. th. our prayers not p. t.
4:21. the cup shall p.t. unto thee
Eze.5:17. and blood shall p. t. thee
14 : 15. If I cause beasts p.t. land
th. no man may p. t., 29: 11.-
39:15. passengers that p.t. [33:28.
Da. 11 : 10. shall p. t. and overflow
Jo. 3 : 17. no stranger shall p. t. her
Am.5:17. I will p. t. thee, saith L.
Na. 1 : 12. be cut down, when he p.
15. wicked no more p. t. thee [t.
Zch. 9 : 8. no oppressor shall p. t.
10 : 11. p. t. the sea wi. affliction
1 Co.16:5. when I shall p.t.Maced.

PASSAGE, S.

Nu.20:21.Edom refused to give Isr. [p.
Jos.22:11. an altar at the p. of Isr.
Ju. 12 : 6. slew him at p-s of Jordan
1 S.13:23.Philistines went out to p.
14 : 4. betw. p-s were sharp rocks
Is. 10 : 29. They are gone over p.
Je. 22 : 20. lift voice, cry from p-s
51:32.to shew Bab.p-s are stopped

PASSED.

Ge. 15 : 17. a lamp that p. between
Nu.20:17. until we have p. borders
Jos. 3 : 4. ye have not p. this way
6 : 8. the 7 priests p. on before
10:29.Josh. p.fr. Makkedah,31,34.
15:3. the border p. to Zin, 4, 6, 7,
10, 11.-18 : 18, 19. [we p.
24:17.among all people thro. whom
Ju. 3 : 26. Ehud escaped and p. bey.
1 S. 15 : 12. Saul is gone and p. on
29 : 2. lords of Philistines p. on
2 S. 15 : 18. David's servants p. on
2 K. 4 : 8. that Elisha p. to Shunem
31. Gehazi p. on before them
2 Ch.9:22. Sol. p. all kings in wisd.
Es. 4 : † 17. So Mordecai p. and did
Jb. 4 : 15. a spirit p. before my face
9 : 26. my days are p. away, as the
15:19. no stranger p. among them
Ps. 18 : 12. At brightness, clouds p.
37:36. Yet he p. away, he was not
81 : † 6. his hands p. away fr. pots
90:†4.1000 y-rs as yesterd.when p.
9. our days are p. in thy wrath
Can. 3 : 4. a little that I p. fr. them
Is.10:28.to Aiath,he is p.to Migron
41 : 3. pursued and p. safely
Je.11:15. holy flesh is p. from thee
34 : 18. p. between the parts, 19
46 : 17. he hath p. time appointed
Da. 3 : 27. nor smell of fire p. on th.
6 : 18. king p. the night fasting
Na.1:†12.and he should have p.aw.
3 : 19. hath not thy wickedness p.
continually ? [man
Mat. 9 : 9. as Jes. p. forth he saw a
Mk. 6 : 35. now the time is far p.
Jn. 5:24. but is p. from death unto
life, 1 Jn. 3 : 14.
Ro. 5 : 12. so death p. upon all men
for all have sinned
2 Co. 5 : 17. old things are p. away
He.4:14.high priest is p. into heav.
Re.21:1.and first earth were p.away
4. the former things are p. away

PASSED by.

Ge. 37 : 28. there p. b. Midianites
Ex. 34 : 6. Lord p. b. before him
De. 2 : 8. when we p. b. we p. b.
way of wilderness
29:16.thro. nations which ye p.b.
Jos. 16 : 6. border p. b. on the east
1 K. 13 : 25. men p. b. and saw lion
19:11. Lord p.b. | 19. Elijah p.b.
20:39.as king p.b.he cried unto k.
2 K.4:8. oft as he p.b.he turned in
6 : 30. king p. b. upon the wall
14 : 9. p.b. wild beast,2 Ch. 25:18.
Jb.28:8. nor hath fierce lion p.b.it
Ps. 48:4. lo, the kings p.b.together
Eze. 16 : 6. I p.b. and saw thee, 8.
15.fornicat.on every one p.b.,25.
36:34. desolate in sight of all p.b.
Ha. 3 : 10. overfl-g of waters p. b.
Mat. 20 : 30. heard that Jes. p. b.
27:39. they that p.b. reviled him,
Mk. 15 : 29.
Mk. 2 : 24. as he p. b. he saw Levi
6 : 48. he would have p. b. them
11 : 20. as they p. b. saw fig tree
15:21.compel one Simon who p.b.
Lu. 10 : 31. p. b. on other side, 32.
Jn. 8 : 59. thro. midst of th. so p.b.
9:1.as Jes. p.b. he saw man blind
Ac. 17 : 23. as I p. b. and beheld

PASSED over.

Ge. 31:21. Jacob p. o. river, 32:22.
32:10.with staff I p.o. this Jordan
31. as he p. o. Penuel sun rose
33 : 3. p. o. bef. them and bowed
Ex. 12 : 27. who p.o. houses of Isr.
Nu. 33 : 51. When ye are p. o. Jordan into Canaan, De. 27 : 3.
Jos. 2 : 23. men p.o. came to Josh.
3:1.came to Jordan bef. they p.o.
3 : 16. they p. o. right ag. Jericho
17. Israelites p.o.on dry ground
4:1. when all people were clean p.
o., 11, 23.-5 : 1. [p. o., 7.
10. peo. hasted and p.o. | 11.ark
12.Reubenites,Gadites p.o.armed
13. about 40,000 p. o. into battle
Ju. 8 : 4. Gideon p.o. and 300 men
10:9. chil. of Ammon p.o. Jordan
11: 29. Jephthah p.o. to fight, 32.
12:3. p.o. ag. the chil. of Ammon
1 S.14:23. battle p. o. to Beth-aven
27 : 2. David p. o. with 600 unto
Achish, 2 S. 10:17.-17:22.1 Ch.
19 : 17. [dan
2 S. 2 : 29. Abner and men p.o. Jor-
15 : 22. Ittai p. o. | 23. king p. o.
17 : 24. Absalom p. o. Jordan
24:5. Joab and capt-s p.o. Jordan
Is. 40 : 27. my judgm. is p.o. fr. G.
Eze.47:5. river that co. not be p.o.
Ho.10:11. I p.o.upon her fair neck
Jon. 2 : 3. all thy waves p. o. me
Mat. 9 : 1. went into ship and p. o.
Mk.5:21.when Jes. was p.o.by ship
6:53. p.o. into land of Gennesaret

PASSED through.

Ge.12:6. Abram p.t.land to Sichem
Nu. 14 : 7. land we p. t. to search
33 : 8. they p. t. midst of sea into
Jos.18:9.men p.t. land described it
1 S. 9 : 4. Saul p.t. mount Ephraim
2 Ch. 30 : 10. posts p. t. country of
Je. 2 : 6. land no man p. t. [Ephr.
Mi.2:13. breaker is come, they p.t.
Zch.7:14. la. desolate, no man p.t.
Mk. 9 : 30. they departed p.t. Gall.
Lu.17:11. he p.t. midst of Samaria
19 : 1. Jes. ent-d and p. t. Jericho
Ac. 9 : 32. as Peter p. t.all quarters
12 : 10. they p. t. one street

Ac.14:24. aft. they had p.t. Pisidia
15 : 3. they p. t. Phenice and Sa.
17 : 1. when had p. t. Amphipolis
19:1.Paul having p. t. upp. coasts
21. when had p. t. Macedonia
1 Co. 10 : 1. our fathers p. t. sea
He. 11 : 29. By faith they p. t. Red

PASSEDST. [sea
Ju.12:1. Whf. p. to fight ag. Ammon?

PASSENGERS.
Pr. 9 : 15. she standeth to call p.
Eze.39:11. the valley of p.; it shall
stop noses of the p. [main
14.to bury with p. those that re-
15. when p. see a man's bone

PASSEST. [thou p.
De. 3 : 21. unto all kingdoms whi.
30:18.upon land whi. thou p. over
2 S. 15 : 33. If p. on, be a burden
1 K. 2 : 37. day thou p. over Kidron
Is. 43 : 2. When p. thro. waters I

PASSETH. [14.
Ex. 30:13. ev. one that p.am. them,
33:22.cover thee,while my glory p.
Le. 27:32. whatso. p. under the rod
Jos. 3 : 11. even L. p. over bef. you
16 : 2. lot p. unto borders, 19 : 13.
1 K. 9 : 8. at this house ev. one p.
by it shall hiss, 2 Ch. 7 : 21.
2 K. 4 : 9. holy man of God, wh. p.
12:4. money of ev. one p. account
Jb. 9 : 11. he p. but I perceive not
14:20.prevailest ag.him, and he p.
30 : 15. my welfare p. as a cloud
37:21.wind p. and cleanseth them
Ps. 8 : 8. over whatso. p. thro. seas
78 : 39. are a wind that p. away
103 : 16. the wind p. over it, and
144: 4. his days as shadow that p.
Pr. 10 : 25. As whirlw. p. so wicked
26:17.He that p. by and meddleth
Ec. 1 : 4. One generat. p. away, and
Is. 29 : 5. terrible be as chaff th. p.
Je.9:12. wild'ness that none p.thro.
18 : 24. as stubble that p. away
18:16.that p.shall be aston-d,19:8.
Eze. 35 : 7. I will cut off him p. out
Da. 6 : † 8. law of Medes wh. p. not
Ho.13:3. be as early dew that p.aw.
Mi.7:18.G. that p. by transgression
Zph. 2 : 15. that p. by her shall hiss
3:6. streets waste, that none p. by
Zch. 9:8. encamp, bec. of him th.p.
Lu. 18 : 37. they told him Jes. p. by
1 Co. 7: 31. fashion of this world p.
away, 1 Jn. 2 : 17. [knowledge
Ep. 3 : 19. love of Christ which p.
Ph. 4 : 7. peace which p. underst-g
He.7:†24.hath priesthood wh.p.not

PASSING. [lebem
Ju. 19 : 18. We are p. from Beth-
2 S. 1 : 26. love p. love of women
15:24. had done p. out of the city
2 K. 6 : 26. as king of Israel was p.
Ne. 6 : † 17. letters p. to Tobiah
Ps.84:6. p. thro. the valley of Baca
Pr. 7: 8. p. thro. street near corner
Is. 30:†32. And in ev. p. of the rod
31 : 5. p. over preserve Jerusalem
Eze. 39 : 14. p. thro. land to bury
Lu.4:30. he p. thro. midst of, went
Ac. 5 : 15. the shadow of Peter p.by
8: 40. Philip p. through, preached
16 : 8. they p. by Mysia, came to
27 : 8. hardly p. Crete we came to

PASSION.
Ac. 1:3. shewed hims. alive after p.

PASSIONS. [p.
Ac. 14 : 15. We also are men of like
Ro.7:†5.p.of sin did work in memb.
Ja. 5: 17. Elias subject to like p. as

PASSOVER, S.
Ex.12:11. it is Lord's p. eat it girded, 27. Le. 23 : 5. Nu. 28 : 16.
21. kill the p. | 43. This is ordi-
nance of the p. [Jos. 5 : 10.
Nu. 9 : 5. they kept the p. at even,
Nu.33:3.on morrow of p., Jos. 5:11.
De. 16 : 2. sacrifice p. unto Lord, 6.
5. not sacrifice p. within gates
2 K. 23 : 22. not such p. fr. days of
23. p. was holden to L. [judges
2 Ch. 30 : 15. Then they killed p. in
second month, 35:1,6,11.Ezr. 6:
20. Mk. 14 : 12. Lu.22:7.[of p-s
17. Levites had charge of killing
18.did eat p.otherw.than written
35:1. Josiah kept a p. unto L., 17,
19. Ezr. 6 : 19. [ings, 8, 9.
7.Josiah gave all for the p. offer-
8. unto priests for p. offerings, 9.
13. they roasted p. with fire, acc.
16.service prepared to keep p.[(2)
18.was no p.like that kept in Isr.
Eze. 45 : 21. shall have p. of 7 days
Mat.26:17. Where wilt that we prepare p.? Mk. 14:12, 14. Lu. 22:
8, 11.
19. And the disciples made ready
the p., Mk. 14 : 16. Lu. 22 : 13.
Lu. 22 : 1. feast drew nigh called p.
7. when the p. must be killed
15. I have desired to eat this p.
Jn.2:13.Jews' p.was at hand,11:55.
23. when he was in Jerus. at p.
11:55. many went to Jerus. bef.p.
12 : 1. Jesus came six days bef. p.
18 : 28. that they might eat the p.
39.sho.release unto you one at p.
19:14. it was the preparation of p.
1 Co.5:7. Christ our p. is sacrificed
He.11:28. Through faith he kept p.
See FEAST, KEEP.

PAST. [11:27.
Ge. 50 : 4. days of mourning p., 2 S.
Ex. 21:29. if ox push in time p.,36.
Nu. 21 : 22. until we be p. borders
De. 2 : 10. Emim dwelt in times p.
4 : 32. ask now of days wh. are p.
42. hated neighbour not in times
p., 19 : 4, 6. [death is p.
1 S. 15 : 32. Agag said, bitterness of
19:7.in his presence as in times p.
2 S. 3 : 17. sought for Da. in time p.
5:2.in time p.when Saul was king
over us, 1 Ch. 11 : 2. [the hill
16 : 1. David was a little p. top of
1 K. 18 : 29. when midday was p.
1 Ch.9:20.Phinehas ruler in time p.
Jb. 9 : 10. doeth thi. p. finding out
14 : 13. keep me, until wrath be p.
17:11.My days are p.,my purposes
29 : 2. that I were as in months p.
Ps. 90 : 4. years as yesterd. when p.
Ec.3:15. requireth that which is p.
Can. 2 : 11. For lo the winter is p.
Je.8:20. The harvest is p. the sum.
Mat. 14 : 15. time is now p. send th.
Mk. 16 : 1. when sab. was p. Mary
Lu. 9 : 36. voice p. Jes. was alone
Ac. 12 : 10. when p. 1st and 2d ward
14:16. in times p. suffered nations
27 : 9. fast was already p. Paul
Ro.3:25. remission of sins th.are p.
11:30.in times p.have not believed
33. his ways are p. finding out
2 Co. 5 : 17. old things p. away ; all
Ga. 1 : 13. my conversa. in time p.
23. he wh. persecuted in times p.
5:21. as I have told you in time p.
Ep. 2 : 2. wh-n in time p. ye walked
3. had our conversa. in times p.
11. ye being in time p. Gentiles
4:19. Who being p.feeling havegiv.
2 Ti. 2:18.saying resurrection is p.
Phm. 11. in time p. unprofitable
He. 1: 1. spake in time p. unto fa-s
11:11.strength to conceive,when p.
1 Pe. 2 : 10. in time p. were not peo.
4:3. time p. of our life may suffice
1 Jn. 2 : 8. because darkness is p.
Re. 9 : 12. One woe is p. | 11:14.sec.

PASTE. [woe is p.
2 S.13:†8.Tamar took p. kneaded it

PASTOR.
Je. 17 : 16. I not hastened fr. being

PASTORS. [a p.
Je. 2 : 8. p. also transgressed ag. me
3 : 15. I will give p. acc. to mine
10 : 21. For p. are become brutish
12:10.p.have destroyed my viney.
22:22. wind shall eat up all thy p.
23:1.Woe unto p.th. destroy sheep
2.saith Lord ag. p. that feed peo.
Ep.4:11.he gave some p.and teach-

PASTURE. [ers
Ge. 47 : 4. thy servants have no p.
1 Ch. 4:39. they went to seek p. for
40. found fat p. | 41. bec. was p.
Jb. 39 : 8. range of mts. is his p.
Ps.74:1.anger smoke ag.sheep of p.
79 : 13. we sheep of p. give thanks
95 : 7. we are peo. of his p., 100:3.
Is. 32 : 14. joy of asses, p. of flocks
Je.23:1. that scatter sheep of my p.
25 : 36. Lord hath spoiled their p.
La.1:6. like harts th. find no p.[p.
Eze. 34 : 14. feed them in good p.fat
18. sm. thing to have eaten good
31. ye flock of my p. are men [p.
Ho. 13 : 6. Acc. to their p. so filled
Jo. 1 : 18. beasts groan, bec. no p.
Jn.10:9. sh. go in and out and find

PASTURES. [p.
1 K.4:23.Sol. had 20 oxen out of p.
Ps. 23 : 2. maketh me lie in green p.
65 : 12.drop upon p. of wilderness
13. p. are clothed with flocks
Is.30:23.cattle shall feed in large p.
49:9.their p. sh. be in high places
Je. 9:†10. p. of wildern. will I take
Eze. 34 : 18. ye tread down your p.
45 : 15. one lamb out of flock of p.
Jo. 1 : 19. fire hath devoured p., 20.
2 : 22. p. of wilderness do spring

PAT'ARA.
Ac. 21:1. from Rhodes we came un-

PATE. [to P.
Ps. 7 : 16. his dealing upon own p.

PATH. [in p.
Ge. 49 : 17. Dan a serpent, an adder
Nu. 22 : 24. angel of L. stood in p.
Jb. 28 : 7. is a p. no fowl knoweth
30:13. They mar my p.set forward
41:32. maketh p. to shine aft.him
Ps. 16 : 11. wilt shew me p. of life
27: 11. Teach me, lead me in plain
77:19.thy p.is in great waters [p.
78 :† 50. weighed a p. to his anger
119:35. Make me to go in p. of thy
105.Thy word a light unto my p.
139 : 3. Thou compassest my p.
142:3. overwhelmed, thou knewest
Pr. 1 : 15. refrain foot fr. p. [my p.
2 : 9. shalt understand ev. good p.
4 : 14. Enter not into p. of wicked
18. p. of just is as shining light
26. Ponder the p. of thy feet,and
5 : 6. Lest thou ponder p. of life
Is. 26 : 7. dost weigh p. of the just
30 : 11. out of way, turn out of p.
40:14. taught him in p. of judgm.
43:16.maketh a p. in mighty wat.
Jo. 2 : 8. shall walk every one in his

PATHS. [p.
Ju.5:†6. walkers of p. walked thro.
† 20. stars in their p. fought Sis.
Jb.6:18. p. of their way are turned
8:13.So are p. of all that forget G.
13:27.lookest narrowly unto my p.
19 : 8. hath set darkness in my p.
24:13. neither abide they in the p.
33:11.feet in stocks,marketh my p.
38 : 20. shouldest keep p. of house
Ps. 8 : 8. passeth through p. of seas
17:4.I have kept fr.p. of destroyer
5. Hold up my goings in thy p.
23:3. leadeth me in p. of righte-n.
25 : 4. O Lord, teach me thy p.
10. All p. of the Lord are mercy
65 : 11. and thy p. drop fatness

Pr. 2 : 8. He keepeth p. of judgment
13. Who leave p. of uprightness
15. and they froward in their p.
18. her p. incline unto the dead
19. nei. take hold of the p. of life
20. mayest keep p. of righteous
3:6.acknowl. him he sh. direct thy
17. all her p. are peace ⌊p.
4 : 11. I have led thee in right p.
7 : 25. go not astray in her p.
8 : 2. She standeth in places of p.
20. I lead in p. of judgment ⌈4:2.
Is. 2 : 3. we will walk in his p., Mi.
3 : 12. they destroy way of thy p.
42 : 16. lead them in p. not known
58:12.be called, The restorer of p.
59 : 7. wasting, destruc. in their p.
8. they have made crooked p.⌈p.
Je. 6 : 16. Stand in way, ask for old
18 : 15. fr. ancient p. to walk in p.
La. 3 : 9. hath made my p. crooked
Ho. 2 : 6. a wall, she sh. not find p.
Mat.3:3. make his p. straight, Mk.
1 : 3. Lu. 3 : 4. ⌈feet
He.12:13.make straight p. for your

PATH'ROS. ⌈P.
Is. 11:11. to recover his people from
Je.44:1.word to Jere. conc. Jews in
15. all peo. that dwelt in P. ⌊P.
Eze.29:14.cause them return into P.
30 : 14. will make P. desolate

PATHRU'SIM.
Ge. 10 : 14. Mizraim begat P., 1 Ch.

PATHWAY. [1 : 12.
Pr. 12 : 28. in p. thereof is no death

PATIENCE. ⌈29.
Mat. 18 : 26. Lord have p. with me,
Lu. 8 : 15. bring forth fruit with p.
21:19. In p. possess ye your souls
Ro.5:3. that tribulation worketh p.
4. p. experience, experience hope
8 : 25. we see not, then wi. p. wait
15:4. we thro. p. might have hope
5.G. of p. grant you to be likemi.
2 Co.6:4.ministers of G.in much p.
12 : 12. signs am. you in all p.
Col. 1 11. strengthened unto all p.
1 Th.1:3.Rememb-g your p.of hope
2 Th. 1 : 4. So we glory for your p.
3:†5. L. direct your hearts into p.
1 Ti.6:11. follow aft. love, p. ⌊of C.
2 Ti. 3 : 10. hast fully known my p.
Tit. 2 : 2 aged be sound in faith, p.
He. 6:12. thro. p. inherit promises
10:36. ye have need of p. that aft.
12 : 1. let us run with p. the race
Ja. 1: 3. trying of faith worketh p.
4. let p. have her perfect work
5:7.the husbandman hath long p.
10. example of p. | 11. p. of Job
2 Pe.1:6.add to temperance p.to p.
Re. 1 : 9. your companion in p. of
2 : 2. I know thy p., 19. ⌊Jesus
3. and hast borne and hast p.
3:10.Bec. hast kept word of my p.
13 : 10. Here is p. of saints, 14:12.

PATIENT. ⌈proud
Ec. 7 : 8. p. in spirit is better than
Ro. 2 : 7. by p. continuance in well
12 : 12. in hope, p. in tribulation.
1 Th. 5 : 14. breth. be p. toward all
2 Th. 3 : 5. into p. waiting for C.
1 Ti. 3 : 3. not greedy of lucre, but
p., 2 Ti. 2 : 24. ⌈also p.
Ja. 5 : 7. be p. brethren | 8. Be ye

PATIENTLY.
Ps. 37 : 7. Rest in the Lord, wait p.
40 : 1. I waited p. for the Lord
Ac. 26 : 3. I beseech thee hear me p.
He. 6 : 15. after he had p. endured
1 Pe. 2 : 20. if buffeted take it p.;
but if ye do well and suffer,
take it p.

PAT'MOS.
Re. 1 : 9. I was in the isle called P.

PATRIARCH, S.
Ac. 2 : 29. let me speak of p. David
Ac. 7 : 8. Jacob begat the twelve p-s
9. p-s moved with envy sold Jo.
He. 7 : 4. to whom p. Ab.paid tithes

PATRIMONY.
De. 18 : 8. besides that cometh from
sale of his p.

PAT'ROBAS.
Ro. 16 : 14. Salute P. Hermes and

PATTERN, S. ⌈ments
Ex. 25 : 9. after the p. of all instru-
40. make them after their p.
Nu. 8 : 4. candlestick was after p.
Jos. 22 : 28. Behold the p. of altar
2 K. 16 : 10. Ahaz sent p. of altar
1 Ch.28:11.David gave Sol.p.,12,18,
Eze.43:10. let them measure p. ⌊19.
1 Ti. 1 : 16. in me C. might shew p.
Tit. 2:7. shewing thyself p. of good
He. 8 : 5. acc. to p. I shewed thee
9 : 23. necessary that p-s of things

PA'U. See PAI.

PAUL.
Ac. 13 : 9. Then Saul, called P. filled
13.when P. and his loosed fr. Pa-
16.Then P.said, Men of Isr.⌊phos
43. many proselytes followed P.
46. P. and Barnabas waxed bold
50. Jews raised persecution ag.P.
14:9. a cripple heard P. speak ⌈voi.
11. saw what P. had done lifted
12. called P. Mercurius, he was
14.Barna. and P.rent clothes and
19. having stoned P. drew him
15:2.P. and Barna. had dissension
12. all mult. gave audience to P.
22. to Antioch with P. and,25,35.
38. P. tho-t not good to take him
40. P. chose Silas and departed
16 : 3. Him would P. have to go wi.
9. vision appeared to P. in night
14. Lydia attended unto the
things spoken of P. ⌈grieved
17. damsel foll-d P. | 18. P being
19. caught P. and Silas and drew
25. P. and Silas prayed, and sang
28. P. cried, Do thyself no harm
29. sprang in, fell down before P.
36.keeper of prison told P.⌈openly
37. P. said, They have beaten us
17 : 2. P. as his manner was, went
4.some consorted wi. P.and Silas
10.breth.sent away P.by night,14
13. word preached of P. at Berea
15. they brought P. unto Athens
16. while P. waited at Athens
22. P. stood in midst of Mar's hill
18:1.P. fr.Athens came to Corinth
5. P. was pressed in spirit
9. Lord spake to P. in the night
12. Jews made insurrec-n ag. P.
14.P. about to open mouth Gallio
18. P. tarried a good while
19 : 1. P. came to Ephesus | 4, 6.
11. God wrought miracles by P.
13.adjure by Jes.wh.P.preacheth
15. P. I know; but who are ye?
21. P. purposed to go to Jerus.
26. this P. hath persuaded and
29. P.'s companions | 30.-21 : 8.
20 : 1. P. departed for Macedonia
7. P. preached unto them
9.as P.was long preaching,Eutyc.
10. P. went, and embracing him
13. intending to take in P.
16.P. had determ. to sail by Eph.
37. all wept, and fell on P.'s neck
21 : 4. who said to P. thro. Spirit
11. Agabus took P.'s girdle and
13.P.ans-d What mean ye to weep
18.day foll-g P.went in unto Jam.
26. P. purifying hims. entered |
30. they drew P. out of tem. ⌊29.
32. saw soldiers, they left beating
37. P. was led into castle ⌊P.
39. P. said, I am Jew of Tarsus
40. P. stood on the stairs ⌈a Rom.
22:25.P. said, Is it lawf. to scourge
Ac. 22 : 28. P. said, I was free born
30. bro-t P. and set him bef.them
23 : 1. P. beholding council said
3. P. said, God shall smite thee
5. said P., I wist not he high pr.
6.P. perceived 1 part were Saddu.
10. lest P. been pulled in pieces
11. L. said, Be of good cheer P.
12. not eat till they killed P., 14.
16. when P.'s sister's son heard
17. P. called one of centurions
18.P. prayed me to bring yo.man
20.wouldest bring P. into council
24. beasts th. they may set P. on
31. soldiers bro-t P. to Antipatris
24 : 1. who informed gov-r ag. P.
10. P. after gov-r had beckoned
23. he com-ded centurion to keep
24.Felix sent for P. and heard ⌊P.
26.th.money sho. been given him
27. Felix left P. bound ⌊of P.
25:2. chief of Jews informed ag. P.
4. Festus ans-d that P. be kept
6. he com-ded P. to be brought
7. laid grievous complaints ag.P.
10. said P. I stand at Cesar's | 9.
14. Festus declared P.'s cause
19.Jes.wh. P. affirmed to be alive
21. when P. had appealed
23. at Festus' com-t P. was bro-t
26 : 1. Agrippa said unto P. (2)
24. said, P. thou art beside thys.
28. Agrippa said unto P. Almost
29. P. said, I would to God
27 : 1. deliv-d P. unto one Julius
3.Julius courteously entreated P.
9. fast was past P. admonished
11. believed owner more than P.
21.P.said,ye sho. have hearkened
24. angel saying, Fear not P.
31. P. said, Except these abide in
33. P. besought all to take meat
43. centurion, willing to save P.
28:3. when P. had gathered sticks
8.to wh.P. entered in and prayed
15. when P. saw he thanked God
16.P.was suff-d to dwell by hims.
17. aft. 3 days P. called chief of
25.aft. P.had spok. 1 word ⌊Jews
30.P.dwelt 2 y-rs in his own hou.
Ro. 1 : 1. P. a serv. of J. C., Ph. 1:1.
1 Co.1:1. P. called to be an apostle,
2 Co. 1 : 1. Ga. 1 : 1. 1 Ti. 1:1. 2
Ti. 1 : 1. Tit. 1 : 1.
12. ev. one saith, I am of P.,3:4.
13. was P. crucified for you? (2)
3 : 5. Who then is P. who Apollos
22. Whether P. or Apollos, or
16:21. the salutation of me P.with
own hand, Col. 4:18. 2 Th.3:17.
2 Co.10:1. Now I P. beseech you by
Ga. 5 : 2. I P. say if ye be circumc.
Ep. 3 : 1. I P. the prisoner of J. C.,
Phm. 1, 9. ⌈minister
Col. 1 : 23. whereof I P. am made a
1 Th.1:1.P.and Tim.unto church of
2:18.unto you even I P. but Satan
Phm. 9. being such as P. the aged
2 Pe.3:15. as our beloved brother P.

PAU'LUS. ⌈P.
Ac.13:7. a Jew with deputy Sergius

PAVED.
Ex. 24 : 10. under his feet a p. work
Can. 3 : 10. midst being p. with love

PAVEMENT.
2 K.16:17. put sea upon p.of stones
2 Ch. 7 : 3. all Israel bowed upon p.
Es. 1 : 6. beds were upon p. of red
Eze.40:17.chambers and p.for court
30 chambers upon the p. ⌈p.
18. p. by side of gates, was lower
42 : 3. over against p. was gallery
Jn. 19:13. Pilate sat in pla. called P.

PAVILION, S.
2 S. 22:12.made darkness p-s about
him, Ps. 18 : 11. ⌈ing in p-s 16.
1 K.20:12. Benhadad and k-s drink-

Ps. 27:5. he shall hide me in his p.
81 : 20. shalt keep them in a p.
Je.43 : 10. Neb. spread his royal p.

PAW, S. ⌈uncl.

Le. 11 : 27. whatso. goeth upon p-s
1 S. 17 : 37. L. deliv-d me out of p.

PAWETH. ⌊of lion

Jb.39:21. the horse p. in the valley

PAY, PAYETH.

Ex. 21 : 19. only p. for loss of time
22. he sh. p. as judges determine
36. shall surely p. ox for ox
22:7.if thief be found, p. double,9.
17. p. acc. to dowry of virgins
Nu. 20 : 19. if I drink water will p.
De.23:21. vow, shall not slack to p.
2 S. 15 : 7. let me go p. my vow
1 K. 20 : 39. else shalt p. a talent
2 K. 4 : 7. Go sell oil, p. thy debt
2 Ch.8:8.did Sol. make to p.tribute
27:5. So much did chil. of Am. p.
Ezr. 4 : 13. then will not p. toll
Es. 3 : 9. I will p. 10,000 talents,4:
Jb. 22 : 27. shalt p. thy vows ⌊7.
Ps. 22:25. I will p. my vows, 66:13.
-116 : 14, 18.
37 : 21. wicked borroweth p-h not
50 : 14. p. vows unto Most High
76 : 11. Vow and p. unto the Lord
Pr. 19 : 17. given will he p. again
22 : 27. If hast nothing to p. why
Ec. 5 : 4. defer not to p. it, p. that
5. not vow, than vow and not p.
Jon. 2 : 9. will p. that I have vowed
Mat. 17 :24. your master p. tribute?
18 : 25. had not to p. he forgave
him, Lu. 7 : 42. ⌈thou owest
26. I will p. all, 29. | 28. p. that
30. into prison till he p. debt
34. till he should p. all was due
23 : 23. ye p. tithe of mint, anise
Ro.13:6.for this cause p. ye tribute

PAYED. See PAID.

PAYMENT.

Mat. 18 : 25. all to be sold, and p.

PEACE. [Interj.] ⌊made

Mk.4:39. said to the sea, P. be still

PEACE.

Ge.29:†6.he said, Is there p.to him
37:†14. Go see the p. of thy breth.
41:16.G.sh. give Pha. answer of p.
43:† 27. he asked of p. Is there p.
to your father ⌈their p.
Ex. 18:†7. they asked each other of
Le.26:6. I will give p. in land,none
Nu. 6 : 26. L. lift counten. give p.
25:12.I give him my cov-t of p.⌈p.
De. 2:26. unto Sihon with words of
20:10. when nigh city proclaim p.
11. if it make thee answer of p.
12. if it will make no p. wi. thee
23:6. Thou shalt not seek their p.
29:19.I shall have p. tho.I walk in
Ju.4:17. p. betw. Jabin and Heber
6:†24. called altar, The L. send p.
18:†15.they asked the Levite of p.
21 :† 13. to proclaim p. unto them
1 S.7:14.p. betw. Isr. and Amorites
10:†4. they will ask of thee p. and
17:†22.David asked his breth.of p.
20:7.if say, It is well, serv.have p.
21. come, there is p. to thee
25:†5.ask Nabal, of p. in my name
2 S.8:†10.unto Da. to ask him of p.
11:†7. Da. demanded of p. of Joab
18 :† 29. the king said, Is there p.
1 K.2:33. upon his throne sh. be p.
4 : 24. Solomon had p. on all sides
5:12.p. betw. Hiram and Solomon
20:18.come for p. take them alive
2 K. 4 :† 23. she said, It shall be p.
5 : † 21. Naaman said, Is there p.
9:17. say, Is it p. Jehu? 18. ⌈22.
19.What hast thou to do with p.
22.What p.so long as witchcrafts
31.Had Zimri p. who slew master
10 : † 13. to p. of children of king
2 K.20:19.if p. in my days? Is.39:8.
1 Ch.22:9. I will give p. unto Israel
2 Ch. 15 : 5. in those times no p. to
Ezr.4:17.ans.unto Rehum, p. ⌊him
5:7.thus; Unto Darius king, all p.
7: 12. unto Ezra, priest, perfect p.
9: 12. nor seek their p. or wealth
Es. 2.†11. Mord. to know p. of Es.
9 : 30. sent letters wi. words of p.
10 : 3. Mordecai speaking p. to all
Jb. 5:23. beasts sh. be at p.wi.thee
21 : †9. houses are p. from fear
22 : 21. Acquaint thyself be at p.
25:2.maketh p.in high places ⌈me
Ps. 7:4. If I evil unto him at p.wi.
28:3.which spake p. to neighbours
29:11.L. will bless his peo. with p.
34:14. do good, seek p., 1 Pe.3:11.
35 : 20. speak not p. but devise
37 : 11. meek delight thems. in p.
37. end of the upright man is p.
38:†3. nei. any p. in my bones
41 : †9. man of my p. lifted heel
55:20.his hands ag.such as be at p.
72:3.The mountains shall bring p.
7. p. so long as moon endureth
85:8.he will speak p. unto his peo.
10.righteousn. and p.have kissed
119 : 165. Great p. they which love
120:6. long dwelt with him hateth
7. I am for p. they for war ⌊p.
122 : 6. Pray for p. of Jerusalem
125: 5. but p. shall be upon Israel
128: 6. thou shalt see p. upon Isr.
147 : 14. He maketh p. in thy bor-
Pr.3:17.wisdom's paths are p. ⌊ders
12 : 20. to counsellors of p. is joy
16 : 7. maketh his enemies be at p.
Ec. 3 : 8. a time of war, a time of p.
Can. 8 : † 10. I as one that found p.
Is. 9 : 6. mighty G. The Prince of P.
7. Of increase of his p. be no end
26 : 12. Lord, thou wilt ordain p.
27 : 5. p. with me he sh. make p.
32:17.work of righte-n. shall be p.
33:7.ambassadors of p. shall weep
38 : 17. for p. I had gr. bitterness
45 : 7. I make p. and create evil
48 : 18. had thy p. been as a river
22. is no p. unto wicked, 57 : 21.
52:7. that publisheth p., Na. 1:15.
53 : 5. chastisement of our p. was
54:10.nei. cov-t of my p.be remov.
13. great sh. be p. of thy children
55:12. ye shall be led forth with p.
57:2. He shall enter into p. ⌈near
19. p. p. to him far off and him
59 : 8. way of p. they know not
60:17. I will make thine officers p.
66 : 12. I will extend p. to her like
Je. 4 : 10. Ye shall have p. ⌊river
6: 14. saying, p.p. when there is
no p., 8 : 11. ⌈came, 14 : 19.
8 : 15. We looked for p. no good
12 : 5. if in land of p. wearied thee
12.sword devour,no flesh have p.
14 :13.but I will give you assured p.
15 :† 5. who sh. go to ask of thy p.
16 : 5. I have taken my p. fr. peo.
20 : † 10. every man of p. watched
28:9. prophet wh. prophesied of p.
29:7. seek p. of city whi. I caused
11. I think tow. you thoughts of
30:5. a voice of fear, not of p. ⌊p.
33 :6. reveal unto them abun.of p.
38:†4.man seeketh not p.of hispeo.
† 22.men of thy p. have prevailed
La. 3 : 17. removed my soul from p.
Eze. 7 : 25. sh. seek p. sh. be none
13:10. saying p. was no p., 16.
34:25. will make cov-t of p.,37:26.
Da.8:25. by p. he sh. destroy many
Ob.7. men at p. deceived thee
Mi.3 : 5. bite with teeth and cry p.
5:5.this man sh.be p.when Assyr.
Na.1:†12.If they wo.have been at p.
Hag.2:9. in this place I will give p.
Zch.6:13. counsel of p. betw. them
8:10. nei. was there any p. to him
† 12. seed shall be of p. the vine
16.execute judgm.of truth and p.
19. theref. love the truth and p.
9.10.he sh. speak p. unto heathen
Mal.2:5.My cov. was with him of p.
Mat. 10 : 13. if house worthy, let p.
come; if not, let your p. ret.
34. Think not I am come to send
Mk.9:50. have p. one with ano. ⌊p.
Lu. 1 : 79. to guide into way of p.
2 : 14. on earth p. good will tow.
10:6. if son of p. there, p. sh. rest
12 : 51. that I am come to give p.
14:32. he desireth conditions of p.
19 : 38. p. in heaven, glory in
42. things wh. belong to thy p.
Jn. 14 : 27. p. I leave, my p. I give
16:33. th. in me ye might have p.
Ac. 10 : 36. preaching p. by Jes. ⌈p.
12:20. made Blastus friend, desired
Ro.1:7. Grace and p. from God our
Father, 1 Co. 1:3. 2 Co. 1:2.Ga.
1 : 3. Ep. 1:2. Ph. 1:2. Col. 1:2.
1 Th. 1 : 1. 2 Th. 1:2. 1 Ti. 1:2.
2 Ti. 1 : 2. Tit. 1:4. Phm. 3. 2
Jn. 3. ⌈good
2 : 10. p. to ev. man that worketh
3 : 17. way of p. have not known
5:1. justified,we have p. with God
8:6. to be spiritually minded is p.
10 : 15. that preach gospel of p.
14 : 17. kingdom of God is joy p.
19. follow things th. make for p.
15: 13. fill you with all joy and p.
1 Co. 7 : 15. G. hath called us to p.
14:33. author of p. as in churches
Ga.5:22. fruit of the Spirit is joy,p.
Ep.2:14.he is our p. | 15.making p.
17. C. came and preached p.
4 : 3. unity of Spirit in bond of p.
6 : 15. preparation of gospel of p.
Ph.4:7. p. of God passeth underst-g
3 : 15. let p. of God rule in hearts
1 Th.5:3. For when they sh. say, p.
13. be at p. among yourselves
2 Th.3:16.Now L. of p. give you p.
2 Ti.2:22.follow p. wi. all, He.12:14.
He. 7 : 2. king of Salem, king of p.
11 : 31. Rahab received spies in p.
Ja. 3 : 18. sown in p. of th. make p.
Re. 1 : 4. p. from him that is, was
6:4. power given him to take p. fr.

PEACE be. ⌊earth

Ge. 43 : 23. he said, p. b. to you
Ju. 6 : 23. Lord said, p. b. to thee
19:20. old man said, p. b. wi. thee
1 S. 25 : 6. p. b. to thee, p. b. to
house, p. b. to all ⌈thee
2 S. 18:†28. Ahimaaz said, p. b. to
1 Ch.12:18. p.b. unto thee, p.b. to
Ps. 122 : 7. p. b. within thy walls
8. I will say, p. b. within thee
Da. 4 : 1. p. be multiplied unto you,
6:25. 1 Pe. 1:2. 2 Pe.1:2. Jude 2.
10 : 19. p. b. unto thee, be strong
Lu. 10:5. first say, p. b. to this ho.
24 : 36. he saith, p. b. unto you,
Jn. 20 : 19, 21, 26. ⌈Isr. of God
Ga.6:16.p.b.on them, and mercy on
Ep. 6 : 23. p. b. to breth., and love
1 Pe. 5 : 14. p. b. with you all in C.
3 Jn. 14. p. b. to thee. Our friends

God of PEACE.

Ro. 15 : 33. G. o. p. be with you all
16 : 20. G. o. p. shall bruise Satan
2 Co. 13 : 11. G. o. p. shall be with
you, Ph. 4 : 9. ⌈wholly
1 Th. 5 : 23. G. o. p. sanctify you
He. 13:20. G.o.p. make you perfect
See **HELD, HOLD peace.**

In PEACE.

Ge. 15 : 15. shalt go to thy fa-s i. p.
26 : 29. we have sent thee aw. i. p.
31. they departed from Isaac i.p.
28 : 21. I come to fa.'s house i. p.

Ge. 44 : 17. get you up i.p. unto fa.
Ex. 18:23. peo. go to their place i.p.
Jos. 10 : 21. came to Joshua, i. p.
Ju. 8 : 9. When I come again i. p.
11:31. when I return i. p. whatev.
1 S. 25:35. Go up i. p. to thine hou.
2 S. 3 : 21. Abner went i. p., 22.
23. Abner is gone i. p. [sons
15:27. return into city i.p. and two
17 : 3. all the people shall be i. p.
19 : 24. until the day he came i. p.
30. as the king is come again i.p.
1 K. 2 : 5. Joab shed bl. of war i. p.
6. let not head go to grave i. p.
22 : 17. return every man i. p., 2
Ch. 18 : 16. [Ch. 18 : 26.
27. in prison until I come i. p., 2
28. If thou return i.p., 2 Ch. 18:27.
2 K. 22 : 20. shalt be gathered into
thy grave i. p., 2 Ch. 34 : 28.
2Ch.19:1. Jehoshaphat returned i.p
Ezr. 4 :† 7. in days of Artax. wrote i.
Jb. 5 : 24. tabernacle sh. be i.p. [p.
Ps. 4 : 8. I will lay me down i. p.
55 : 18. hath deliv-d my soul i. p.
Pr. 18 : † 13. feareth com-t be i. p.
Is. 26:3. wilt keep him i. perfect p.
41:†3. he pursued, and passed i.p.
Je. 29 : 7. i. p. shall ye have peace
34 : 5. thou shalt die i. p. they
43:12. he sh. go forth thence i. p.
Mal. 2 : 6. he walked with me i. p.
Lu.2:29. lettest servant depart i.p.
11 : 21. palace, his goods are i. p.
1 Co. 16:11. conduct him forth i.p.
2 Co. 13 : 11. be perfect, live i. p.
Ja. 2 : 16. Depart i. p. be warmed
3:18. fruit of righte-n. is sown i.p.
2 Pe. 3:14. that ye be found of him
See **GO in peace.** [i. p.
See **MADE peace, Peace OFFERING, S.**

PEACEABLE.

Ge. 34:21. These men are p. with us
2 S. 20 : 19. I am one of them are p.
1 Ch. 4 : 40. land was wide, and p.
22 : † 9. for his name shall be P.
Is. 32:18. peo. dwell in a p. habitat.
Je. 25 : 37. p. habitations are cut
Da. 11:† 24. sh. enter into p. places
1 Ti. 2 : 2. lead a quiet and p. life
He. 12 : 11. it yieldeth the p. fruit of
Ja. 3: 17. wisdom is pure, p. gentle

PEACEABLY. [him

Ge. 37 : 4. could not speak p. unto
Ju. 11 : 13. restore those lands p.
21 : 13. sent some to call p. unto
1 S. 16 : 4. Comest thou p. ? [Benj.
5. he said, p., 1 K. 2:13. [speak p.
2 S. 3:† 27. Joab took Abner aside to
1 Ch. 12:17. If ye become p. unto me
Je. 9 : 8. one speaketh p. to neighb
Da. 11 : 21. he shall enter p., 24.
Ro. 12:18. if possible, live p. with all

PEACEMAKERS.

Mat. 5 : 9. Blessed are p. for they

PEACOCKS. [9 : 21.

1 K. 10:22. navy, bringing p., 2 Ch.
Jb. 39:13. gavest goodly wings unto

PEARL. [p.?

Mat. 13:46. found one p. of gr. price
Re. 21:21. every gate was of one p.

PEARLS. [or p.

Jb. 28:18. No mention made of coral
Mat. 7 : 6. nei. cast ye p. bef. swine
13 : 45. merchantman seeking p.
1 Ti. 2:9. not wi. p. or costly array
Re. 17:4. woman was decked with p.
18 : 12. no man buyeth merchandise of p. and silk, 16.
21 : 21. twelve gates were twelve p.

PECULIAR. [me

Ex. 19:5. ye sh. be p. treasure unto
De. 14 : 2. to be a p. people unto
himself, 26 : 18. 1 Pe. 2 : 9.
Ps. 135 : 4. Lord hath chosen Israel
for his p. treasure

Ec. 2 : 8. I gath-d p. treasure of k-s
Tit. 2 : 14. purify unto hims. p. people

PED'AHEL.

Nu. 34:28. prince of chil. of Naphtali,

PED'AHZUR. [P.

Nu. 1 : 10. Gamaliel son of P., 2:20.
-7 : 54, 59.-10 : 23.

PEDA'IAH.

2 K. 23 : 36. Zebudah the dau. of P.
1 Ch. 3 : 18. sons of Jeconiah, P.
19. sons of P. were Zerub., 27:20.
Ne. 3 : 25. Aft. him P. son of Parosh
8 : 4. on his left hand stood P.
11 : 7. the son of Joed, son of P.
13 : 13. and of the Levites, P.

PEDIGREE, S.

Nu. 1 : 18. they declared their p-s
Ezr. 2 : † 59. could not shew p., Ne.
7 : † 61. [mother, p.
He. 7 : † 3. without father, without
† 6. he whose p. is not counted

PEELED.

Is. 18 : 2. nation scattered and p., 7.
Eze. 29 : 18. every shoulder was p.

PEEP, PEEPED. [mutter

Isa. 8 : 19. to wizards that p. and
10 : 14. that opened mouth or p-d
29:† 4. thy speech sh. p. out of dust

PE'KAH.

2 K. 15 : 25. P. conspired ag., 27, 31.
29. In days of P. came Tiglath-
30. Hoshea made conspiracy ag. P.
32. P. son of Remaliah, k. of Isr.
37. send ag. Judah P., 16 : 1, 5.
2 Ch. 28 : 6. P. slew in Jud. 120,000.
Is. 7:1. Rezin and P. went tow. Jerus.

PEK'AHIAH.

2 K. 15 : 22. P. his son reigned, 23.
26. acts of P., written in book

PE'KOD.

Je. 50 : 21. Go up ag. inhab-s of P.
Eze. 23 : 23. All Chaldeans, P. and

PELAI'AH. [Shoa

1 Ch. 3 : 24. sons of Elioenai, P.
Ne. 8:7. P. caused peo. to understand
10 : 10. those that sealed were, P.

PELALI'AH.

Ne. 11 : 12. son of P. son of Amzi

PELATI'AH. [Judah

1 Ch. 3 : 21. son of Hananiah, P. of
4:42. of Simeon, having for capt. P.
Ne. 10 : 22. P. Hanan sealed cov-t
Eze. 11 : 1. P. son of Benaiah, 13.

PE'LEG. [1 : 19.

Ge. 10:25. name of one was P., 1 Ch.
11:16. Eber lived 34 y-rs and begat
18. Peleg begat Reu, 19. [P., 17.
1 Ch. 1:25. Sons of Joktan, P., Reu.

PE'LET. See EPHAH, JEZIEL.

PE'LETH, ITES.

Nu. 16 : 1. On, son of P. took men
2 S. 8:18. And Benaiah was over the
P-s, 20 : 23. 1 Ch. 18 : 17.
15:18. all the P-s passed on bef. king
20 : 7. went out aft. Sheba the P-s
1 K. 1:38. P-s caused Sol. to ride, 44.
1 Ch. 2:33. sons of Jonathan P. Zaza

PELICAN. [14 : 17.

Le. 11 : 18. swan and p. uncl., De.
Ps. 102 : 6. I am like p. of wilder.
Is. 34 : † 11. p. sh. possess it, Zph.

PEL'ONITE. [2 : † 14.

1 Ch. 11:27. valiant, Helez the P. | 36
27 : 10. capt. for 7th month Helez

PELU'SIUM=SIN. [the P.

PEN.

Ju. 5 : 14. they that handle the p.
Jb. 19:24. were graven with iron p.
Ps. 45 : 1. my tongue is p. of writer
Is. 8 : 1. write in it with a man's p.
Je. 8 : 8. p. of scribes is in vain [on
17 : 1. sin of Jud. writt. with p. of Ir.
3 Jn. 13. I will not with p. write thee

PENCE.

Mat. 18 : 28. wh. owed him a 100 p.
Mk. 14 : 5. might been sold for more
than 300 p., Jn. 12 : 5.

Lu. 7:41. one owed 500 p. other fifty
10:35. on morrow he took out two

PENI'EL=PENU'EL. [p.

Ge. 32:30. Jacob called the place P.

PENIN'NAH.

1 S. 1:2. P. had chil. Hannah had no
4. gave to P. and dau-s portions

PENKNIFE.

Je. 36:23. Jehudi cut roll with a p.

PENNY. [a p.

Mat. 20:2. agreed with labourers for
9. they received every man a p., 10
13. didst thou not agree for a p.
22:19. they brought unto him a p.
Mk. 12 : 15. bring me p., Lu. 20 : 24.
Re. 6 : 6. A measure of wheat for p.,
3 measures of barley for a p.

PENNYWORTH.

Mk. 6 : 37. buy 200 p. of bread
Jn. 6 : 7. 200 p. is not sufficient

PENTECOST.

Ac. 2 : 1. When day of P. was come
20:16. he hasted to Jerus. day of P.
1 Co. 16:8. I will tarry at Eph. until P

PENU'EL. (Person.) [Ezer

1 Ch. 4 : 4. P. father of Gedor and
8 : 25. Iphedeiah, P. sons of Sha-

PENU'EL=PENI'EL. [shak

Ge. 32 : 31. as Jacob passed over P.
Ju. 8 : 8. Gideon went up to P., 9.
17. he beat down the tower of P.
1 K. 12 : 25. Then Jerob. built P.

PENURY. [p.

Pr. 14:23. talk of the lips tendeth to
Lu. 21:4. she of her p. hath cast in

PEOPLE. [all

Ge. 27 : 29. Let p. serve thee
48 : 19. he shall become a p. great
Ex. 6:7. I will take you for a p., De.
4 : 20. 2 S. 7 : 24. Je. 13 : 11.
33:3. stiffnecked p., 5.-34:9. De. 9:6.
Le. 20:24. I separated you fr. other p.
17. cut off in sight of their p. [26.
Nu. 21 : 29. undone, O p. of Chem.
22:5. is a p. come out fr. Egypt, 11.
25 : 15. head over a p. in Midian
De. 4 : 6. nation is as a wise p.
20. unto him a p. of inheritance
33. Did ever p. hear voice of God
7:6. L. hath chosen thee special p.
7. not choose bec. more than any
20 : 1. a p. more be not afraid [p.
16. of the cities of these p.
28 : 32. sons be given unto ano. p.
29:13. estab. thee for p. unto hims-f
32 : 21. move th. with those not p.
33 : 29. who is like unto thee, O p.
Ju. 9:37. Gaal said, See, there come p.
14:17. she told riddle to her p. [27.
18:10. ye sh. come unto a p. secure,
Ru. 1:15. sis. gone back unto her p.
2 : 11. unto a p. thou knowest not
1 S. 2 : 24. ye make L.'s p. transgr.
5:10. brought ark, to slay us and p.
11. that it slay us not, and our p.
13 : 5. p. as the sand on sea shore
2 S. 7:23. God went to redeem for p.
24. p. Israel to be a p. for ever
10 : 12. let us play men for our p.
18 : 8. wood devoured more p. than
19 : 3. as p. ashamed steal away
22 : 28. afflicted p. thou wilt save,
Ps. 18 : 27. [me, Ps. 18: 43.
44. a p. I knew not shall serve
1 K. 22 : 28. Hearken, O p. ev. one
2 K. 4 : 13. I dwell am. mine own p.
11:17. shalt be L.'s p., 2 Ch. 23:16.
1 Ch. 16 : 20. went fr. 1 kingdom to
ano. p., Ps. 105:13. [our p.
19 : 13. let us behave valiantly for
2 Ch. 1 : 9. hast made me king ov. p.
32:17. As gods not deliv-d their p.
so G. of Hez. not deliver his p.
Es. 1:22. he sent letters to every p.,
3 : 12.-8 : 9. Ne. 13 : 24.
2 : 10. Esther had not shewed her p.
3:8. There is a certain p. scattered

Es. 4 : 8. go in before him for her **p.**
Jb. 36 : 20. when **p.** are cut off in
Ps. 22:31. unto a **p.** that sh. be born
62 : 8. ye **p.** pour out your hearts
66 : 8. O bless our God, ye **p.**
89 : 50. I bear reproach of mighty
95 : 10. It is a **p.** that do err ⌊p.
114 : 1. went out fr. **p.** of strange
144:15. Happy is that **p.** yea happy
Pr. 14:34. sin is a reproach to any **p.**
28 : 15. so wicked ruler ov. poor **p.**
30 : 25. ants are a **p.** not strong
Can. 6 : † 12. on chariots of willing
Is. 1 : 4. a **p.** laden with iniquity ⌊p.
10. give ear unto law, **p.** of Gomor.
7 : 8. Ephr. be broken, be not a **p.**
8 : 9. Associate yours. O ye **p.**
19. sho. not a **p.** seek their God
18:2. to a **p.** terrible fr. beginning
7. a **p.** scattered and peeled
25:3. the strong **p.** sh. glorify thee
27:11. it is a **p.** of no understanding
30 : 6. to a **p.** that sh. not profit
9. write, this is rebellious **p.**, 65:2.
33:19. a **p.** of deeper speech
34 : 1. and hearken ye **p.**, 49 : 1.
43 : 4. I will give **p.** for thy life
8. Bring forth blind **p.** have eyes
44 : 7. since I appointed ancient **p.**
65:2. my hands unto rebellious **p.**
3. A **p.** that provoketh me ⌈joy
18. I create Jerus. and her **p.** a
Je. 6:22. **p.** cometh fr. north, 50:41.
13 : 11. be unto me for a **p.** ⌈a p.
48:42. Moab be destroyed fr. being
La. 1 : 1. solitary th. was full of **p.**
7. her **p.** fell into hand of enemy
Eze. 3 : 5. not sent to a **p.** of strange
27 : 33. filledst many **p.** enrich k-s
Da. 2:44. kingd. not be left to other
3:4. herald cried O **p.** nations ⌊p.
29. I make a decree, That ev. **p.**
11:23. become strong with small **p.**
Ho. 4 : 9. shall be like **p.** like priest
9:1. Rejoice not, O Isr. as other **p.**
Jo. 2 : 5. as strong **p.** set in battle
Jon. 1:8. Tell us, of what **p.** art thou
Mi. 4 : 1. exalted, **p.** sh. flow unto it
Zph. 1:11. merchant **p.** are cut down
3 : 12. an afflicted and poor **p.**
Zch. 8:20. sh. come **p.** and inhab-ts
Lu. 1 : 17. ready a **p.** prepared for L.
Ac. 15 : 14. to take out of them a **p.**
28 : 2. barbarous **p.** shewed kindn.
Ro. 10:19. provoke by th. are no **p.**
21. my hands unto gainsaying **p.**
He. 8 : 10. shall be to me a **p.** ⌈a p.
1 Pe. 2:10. **p.** of G. in time past not
Re. 5 : 9. redeemed us out of ev. **p.**
14:6. gospel to preach to every **p.**

All PEOPLE.

Ex. 19 : 5. ye shall be a peculiar
treasure above **a. p.** ⌈a. p.
De. 7: 6. G. hath chosen thee above
7. for ye were the fewest of **a. p.**
14. Thou be blessed above **a. p.**
10 : 15. he chose you above **a. p.**
28:10. **a. p.** of earth shall see that
64. L. sh. scatter thee am. **a. p.**
1 K. 4:34. came of **a. p.** to hear Sol.
8 : 43. **a. p.** may know thy name,
2 Ch. 6 : 33. ⌈am. a. p.
9:7. shall be a proverb and byword
2 Ch. 18:27. said, Hearken **a.** ye **p.**
Ezr. 6:12. and G. destroy **a. p.** that sh.
Es. 3 : 8. their laws diverse fr. **a. p.**
14. writing published unto **a. p.**,
9 : 2. fear fell upon **a. p.** ⌊8 : 13.
Ps. 47:1. O clap your hands, **a.** ye **p.**
49 : 1. Hear this **a.** ye **p.** give ear
96:3. Declare his wonders am. **a. p.**
99 : 2. Lord is high above **a. p.**
117:1. O praise L. **a.** ye **p.** for his
kindness, 148 : 11. Ro. 15 : 11.
Is. 25 : 6. L. make unto **a. p.** a feast
7. face of covering cast over **a. p.**
56 : 7. house of prayer for **a. p.**
La. 1 : 11. **a.** her **p.** sigh, seek bread
18. hear, **a. p.** behold, Mi. 1 : 2.
Da. 4 : 1. Neb-r unto **a. p.** nations
5 : 19. **a. p.** feared before him
6:25. k-g Darius wrote unto **a. p.**
7 : 14. that **a. p.** should serve him
Mi. 4 : 5. **a. p.** will walk in name
Ha. 2:5. heapeth unto him **a. p.** ⌈p.
Zph. 3:20. make you a praise am. **a.**
Zch. 12:3. burdensome stone for **a.**
Mat. 4 : 24. unto him **a.** sick **p.** ⌊p.
Lu. 2 : 10. tidings of joy for **a. p.**
31. prepared before face of **a. p.**
Ro. 15 : 11. and laud him **a.** ye **p.**

All the PEOPLE. ⌈Lot's

Ge. 19:4. **a. t. p.** of Sodom compass.
35:6. Jac. came to Luz, and **a. t. p.**
42 : 6. Joseph sold to **a. t. p.** of E.
Ex. 11: 8. Get thee out, and **a. t. p.**
18 : 14. **a. t. p.** stand by thee
21. provide out of **a. t. p.** able
19 : 8. **a. t. p.** ans-d together, 24:3.
11. L. come in sight of **a. t. p.**
16. **a. t. p.** in the m-t trembled
20 : 18. **a. t. p.** saw lightnings
23:27. will destroy **a. t. p.**, Jos. 24:
24:3. **a. t. p.** ans-d with 1 voice ⌊18.
32:3. **a. t. p.** brake off gold earrings
33 : 8. **a. t. p.** rose and stood, 10.
10. **a. t. p.** saw cloudy pillar (2)
16. So we be separated fr. **a. t. p.**
34 : 10. **a. t. p.** sh. see work of L.
Le. 9 : 23. glory of L. unto **a. t. p.**
24. when **a. t. p.** saw they shouted
10 : 3. bef. **a. t. p.** I will be glorifi.
6. lest wrath come upon **a. t. p.**
16:33. sh. make atonem. for **a. t. p.**
Nu. 11:29. that **a. t.** L.'s **p.** prophets
13:32. **a. t. p.** men of great stature
15:26. seeing **a. t. p.** were in ignor.
De. 7:16. thou shalt consume **a. t. p.**
19. so shall L. do unto **a. t. p.**
13 : 9. the hand of **a. t. p.**, 17 : 7.
17 : 13. **a. t. p.** shall hear and fear
20 : 11. **a. t. p.** shall be tributaries
27:15. **a. t. p.** shall say, Amen, 16,
17, 18, 19, 20, 21, 22, 23, 24, 25, 26.
Jos. 3:17. until **a. t. p.** were passed
ov., 4:1, 11. 2 S. 15:23, 24.–19:39.
4 : 24. that **a. t. p.** might know
5 : 4. **a. t. p.** were circum., 5, 8.
6. forty y-rs in wilderness till **a.**
t. p. ⌈not a. t. p. go up (2)
6 : 5. **a. t. p.** shall shout | 7: 3. Let
8 : 1. take **a. t. p.** of war, go up to
Ai, 3, 5, 11.–10 : 7, 21.–11 : 7.
16. **a. t. p.** in Ai were called
24:2. Josh. said unto **a. t. p.** | 17.
18. Lord drave bef. us **a. t. p.**
Ju. 4 : 13. Sisera gathered **a. t. p.**
7 : 1. Gideon and **a. t. p.** rose
7. L. unto Gideon let **a. t. p.** go
9:34. Abim. and **a. t. p.** | 44, 48, 49.
16 : 30. house fell upon **a. t. p.**
20 : 8. **a. t. p.** arose as one man.
Ru. 4:9. Boaz unto elders and **a. t. p.**
11. **a. t. p.** and elders said, We
1 S. 10 : 24. none like him among **a.**
t. p. And **a. t. p.** shouted (3)
25. Sam. sent **a. t. p.** away
11:4. **a. t. p.** wept | 15. **a. t. p.** went
to Gilgal ⌈unto Sam.
12:18. **a. t. p.** feared | 19. **a. t. p.** said
13:7. **a. t. p.** trembling, 14:15, 34, 39.
14 : 20. Saul and **a. t. p.** assembled
15 : 8. Saul utterly destr. **a. t. p.**
18 : 5. accepted in sight of **a. t. p.**
23 : 8. Saul called **a. t. p.** to war
30 : 6. soul of **a. t. p.** was grieved
2 S. 2 : 28. **a. t. p.** stood still ⌈34.
3:32. at grave of Abner, **a. t. p.** wept,
35. **a. t. p.** to cause David
36. **a. t. p.** took notice of it
37. **a. t. p.** understood that day
6:2. Da. went with **a. t. p.** to Baale
19. So **a. t. p.** departed (2) ⌈ | 31.
12:29. Da. gath-d **a. t. p.** and fought
2 S. 15 : 17. k. went and **a. t. p.** after
30. **a. t. p.** weeping as they went
16 : 6. **a. t. p.** on Da.'s right and
14. king and **a. t. p.** refreshed
15. Absalom and **a. t. p.** to Jerus.
17 : 2. **a. t. p.** with him shall flee
3. I will bring back **a. t. p.** so **a.**
t. p. shall be in peace
16. k. be swallowed up and **a. t. p.**
22. Da. and **a. t. p.** passed ov. Jord.
18 : 4. **a. t. p.** came out by hund-s
19 : 2. into mourning unto **a. t. p.**
8. **a. t. p.** came before king (2)
9. **a. t. p.** at strife thro-t Israel
40. **a. t. p.** conducted the king
20 : 12. man saw **a. t. p.** stood still
15. **a. t. p.** battered the wall | 13.
22. woman went unto **a. t. p.** ⌈40.
1 K. 1 : 39. **a. t. p.** said God save k. |
8 : 53. didst separate from **a. t. p.**
60. **a. t. p.** may know L. is God
9: 20. **a. t. p.** left of Amorites, Hittites ⌈2 Ch. 10 : 12.
12:12. Jerob. and **a. t. p.** to Rehob.,
18:24. **a. t. p.** said, It is well spok.
30. Elijah said unto **a. t. p.** (2)
39. **a. t. p.** fell on their faces
20 : 8. **a. t. p.** said Hearken not
10. if dust of Sama. suffice for **a.**
15. he numbered **a. t. p.** ⌊t. p.
2 K. 10:9. said to **a. t. p.**, Ye be righte-
18. Jehu gathered **a. t. p.** ⌊ous
14 : 21. **a. t. p.** took Azariah
23:2. k. into ho. of L. and **a. t. p.**,
2 Ch. 34 : 30. ⌈enant
3. and **a. t. p.** stood to the cov-
21. com-ded **a. t. p.** keep passover
25 : 26. **a. t. p.** came to Egypt
1 Ch. 13 : 4. right in eyes of **a. t. p.**
16:36. **a. t. p.** said, Amen, Ne. 8:6.
43. **a. t. p.** every man to house
28 : 21. **a. t. p.** will be at thy com-t
2 Ch. 7 : 4. **a. t. p.** offered sacrifices
5. **a. t. p.** dedicated house of G.
23 : 5. **a. t. p.** be in courts of ✝
24 : 10. princes and **a. t. p.** rejoiced
26 : 1. **a. t. p.** made Uzziah king
29 : 36. Hez. rejoiced and **a. t. p.**
32 : 13. unto **a. t. p.** of other lands
35:13. divided them among **a. t. p.**
Ezr. 3 : 11. **a. t. p.** shouted bec.
7:25. judges wh. may judge **a. t. p.**
10 : 9. **a. t. p.** sat in the street
Ne. 8 : 1. **a. t. p.** gath-d into street
5. opened book in sight of **a. t. p.**;
for he was above **a. t. p.** (3)
9. unto **a. t. p.** This day holy (2)
11. So Levites stilled **a. t. p.**
12. **a. t. p.** went their way to eat
13. chief of fathers of **a. t. p.**
Es. 1 : 5. k. made feast unto **a. t. p.**
16. queen done wrong to **a. t. p.**
Ps. 67 : 3. O G. let **a. t. p.** praise, 5.
97 : 6. **a. t. p.** see his glory
99 : 2. L. is high above **a. t. p.**
106 : 48. let **a. t. p.** say Amen
Ec. 4 : 16. There is no end of **a. t. p.**
Is. 9:9. **a. t. p.** sh. know, even Ephr.
Je. 19:14. Jere. said to **a. t. p.**, 25:1,
2.–26 : 7, 8, 12.–38:1.–43:1.–44:
20, 24.
25 : 20. **a. t.** mingled **p.**, 24.–50:37
Eze. 30 : 5.
26:9. **a. t. p.** were gathered ag. Jeremiah
11. spake priests unto **a. t. p.**, 16.
18. Micah spake to **a. t. p.**
28:1. in presence of **a. t. p.**, 5, 7, 11.
29 : 1. **a. t. p.** Neb-r carried away
16. of **a. t. p.** dwelleth in this city
25. letters unto **a. t. p.** in Jerus.
34 : 1. **a. t. p.** fought ag. Jerus.
8. Zed. made cov-t with **a. t. p.**, 10.
19. eunuchs, priests, **a. t. p.** of la.
36 : 9. fast to **a. t. p.** in Jerus. (2)
38 : 4. weakeneth hands of **a. t. p.**
41 : 13. when **a. t. p.** saw Johanan
14. **a. t. p.** Ishm. had carried aw.

Je.42:1. a.t.p. from the least came,
43:4. a. t. p. obeyed not the L.⌊8.
44:15. a.t.p. in E. ans-d Jere. (2)
Eze.31:12.a.t.p.gone fr.his shadow
Da. 3:7. when a. t. p. heard
Zch.11:10. break cov-t with a.t.p.
12:2. Jerus. a cup of trembling unto a. t. p. ⌈it
3. tho.a.t.p. be gathered against
6. governors shall devour a. t. p.
14:12.plague whw. L.smite a.t.p.
Mal.2:9. made you base bef.a.t.p.
Mat. 12:23. a. t. p. were amazed,
Mk. 9:15.-11:18. ⌈on us and
27:25. ans-d a.t.p. His blood be
Lu. 3:21. when a.t.p. were baptiz.
7:29. a.t.p. th. heard justified G.
8:47.declared unto him bef.a.t.p.
13:17. a.t.p. rejoiced for glorious
18:43. a.t.p. gave praise unto G.
19:48. a.t. p. were very attentive
20:6. say, Of men, a.t.p.stone us
45. then in audience of a. t. p.
21:38. a.t.p. came early in morn.
23:48. a.t. p. smote their breasts
24:19.prophet bef. God and a.t.p.
Jn. 8:2. a. t. p. came unto him
Ac.2:47. having favour with a.t.p.
3:9. a. t. p. saw him walking
11. a.t.p. ran togeth. wondering
4:10. Be it known to a.t.p. of Isr.
10:41. Not to a.t.p. but witnesses
13:24.baptism of repent. to a.t.p.
21:27. stirred up a. t. p. and
He. 9:19. Moses spoken ev. precept to a. t. p. sprinkled a. t. p.

Among the PEOPLE.

Le.18:29. shall be cut off from a.p.
Nu. 5:27. woman be a curse a. p.
16:47. plague was begun a. p.
21:6. L. sent fiery serpents a. p.
De. 2:16. men of war dead fr. a.p.
Jos.8:9. Josh. lodged th. night a.p.
Ju. 1:16. chil. of Kenite dwelt a.p.
5:9. gov-rs offered thems. a. p.
13. dominion over nobles a. p.
1S.4:17. gr. slaughter am.a.p.⌈any
10:23. Saul a.p. was higher than
14:34. Disperse yours. a. p. ⌈p.
31:9.publish in ho. of idols and a.
2 S. 17:9. slaughter a.p. follow Abs.
1 K. 14:7. Jerob. I exalted fr. a.p.
21:9. set Naboth on high a.p., 12.
1 Ch. 16:8. make known his deeds a.p., Ps.9:11.-105:1. Is. 12:4.
Ne. 10:34. we cast the lots a. p.
Es. 3:8. is a peo. scattered a. p.
Ps. 44:14. makest us byword a. p.
45:12. rich a. p. entreat favour
57:9. praise thee, O L. a.p.,108:3.
77:14. hast declared strength a.p.
94:8. Understand ye brutish a. p.
105:1. make known his deeds a.p.
Is. 61:9. offspring known a. p.
Je.37:4.Jere.came in went out a.p.
39:14. so he dwelt a. p., 40:5, 6.
40:5. go dwell with him a.p., 6.
Eze.28:19. All that know thee a.p.
Da.11:33.they th. understand a.p.
Ho. 7:8. Ephr. mixed hims. a. p.
Jo.2:17. whf. should they say a.p.
Zch.10:9. And I will sow them a.p.
Mat. 4:23. all disease a. p., 9:35.
26:5. feast day, lest be an uproar a. p., Mk. 14:2. ⌈p.
Jn. 7:12. was much murmuring a.
43. was a division a. p. bec.
Ac. 3:23. be destroyed from a. p.
4:17. th. it spread no further a.p.
5:12. many wonders a. p., 6:8.
34. Gamaliel in reputation a. p.
6:8. Stephen did miracles a. p.
14:14.Barna. and Paul ran in a.p.
2 Pe. 2:1. were false prophets a. p.

Before the PEOPLE.

Ge. 23:12. Ab. bowed b.p. of land
Ex. 13:22. nor pillar of fire fr. b.p.
Ex.17:5.L.said to Moses,Go on b.p.
Jos.3:6.Take ark pass over b.p.(2),
8:10. Joshua went b.p. to Ai ⌊14.
1 S.18:13.he went out came in b.p.
2 K.15:10.Shallum smote him b.p.
Mk. 8:6. disci. did set loaves b. p.
Lu.20:26.not hold of his words b.p.
See COMMON, DAUGHTER, EARS, ELDERS, FOOLISH.

PEOPLE of God.

Ju. 20:2. in assembly of the p.o.G.
2 S.14:13. thought such ag. p.o.G.
Ps. 47:9. even p.o.G. of Abraham
He. 4:9. remaineth a rest to p.o.G.
11:25. suffer affliction with p.o.G.
1 Pe. 2:10. not a peo. but now p.o.
See GREAT people. ⌊G.

His PEOPLE.

Ge. 17:14. shall be cut off from h. p., Ex. 30:33, 38.-31:14. Le. 7:20, 21, 25, 27.-17:4, 9.-19:8.-23:29. Nu. 9:13.-15:30.
25:8. Ab. was gathered to h. p.
17.Ishm. was gathered unto h.p.
26:11. Abim. charged all h.p.
35:29.Isaac was gathered unto h.p
49:16. Dan shall judge h. p., 33.
Ex.1:9. new k.over E. said to h. p.
22. Pharaoh charged all h. p.
8:29. flies may depart fr. h.p.,31.
14:6. Pha. made ready took h.p.
17:13.discomfited Amalek and h.p
18:1. done for Moses and Isr. h.p.
32:14.L.repented of evil unto h.p.
Le. 17:10. that soul I will cut off from h. p., 20:3, 6.-23:30.
21:1.none defiled for dead am. h.p.
4. being a chief man among h.p.
15. Nei. shall profane his seed among h. p. ⌈unto h. p., 26.
Nu. 20:24. Aaron sh. be gathered
21:23.Sihon gath-d all h.p.toget., De.2:32. Ju. 11:20. ⌈rei, De.3:1.
33. Og and h. p. to battle of Ed-
34. Og, I have deliv-d into thy hand, h. p.,35. De.2:33. ⌈p.,3.
De. 3:2. I will deliver Og and all h.
32:9. For Lord's portion is h. p.
36.L. shall judge h.p., Ps. 135:14.
43. Rejoice, O nations, with h.p. he will be merciful unto h. p.
50. Aaron was gath-d unto h. p.
33:7. L. and bring Jud. unto h.p.
Jos. 8:1. given thee Ai, k. and h.p.
14. ag. Israel k. of Ai and h. p.
10:33.Josh.smote Horam and h.p.
Ju. 11:21. deliv-d Sihon and h.p.
23.dispossessed Amorites bef.h.p
Ru.1:6.how the L. had visited h.p.
1 S. 12:22. L. will not forsake h.p. pleased L. to make you h. p.
13:14. to be captain over h. p.
15:1. to anoint thee k. over h. p.
27:12.made h.p. Israel abhor him
2 S. 8:15. David executed justice unto all h. p., 1 Ch. 18:14.⌈p.
1 K.20:42.thy people shall go for h.
1 Ch.21:3. Joab answ-d L. make h. p. 100 times more ⌈h. p.
22:18. land subdued bef. Lord and
23:25. God given rest unto h. p.
2 Ch. 2:11. Bec. Lord loved h. p.
13:17.Abijah and h.p. slew of Isr.
20:25. Jehosh-t and h. p. came
21:19. h. p. made no burning for Jehoram ⌈valley of
25:11. Amaziah led forth h. p. to
31:10. the Lord hath blessed h.p.
32:14.Who co. deliver h.p.?15,17.
33:10.L. spake to Manas. and h.p.
36:15. he had compassion on h.p.
16. wrath of L. arose ag. h. p.
23. Who among you of all h. p. go up, Ezr. 1:3.
Es. 10:3. Mordecai seeking the wealth of h. p.
Jb. 18:19. not have son am. h. p.
Ps.14:7.back captivity of h.p.,53:6.
29:11. L. will give strength unto h.p.,bless h.p.wi.peace,68:35.
50:4. call, th. he may Judge h.p.
73:10. Theref. h.p. return hither
78:20. can he provide flesh for h.
62.He gave h.p. unto sword⌊p.?
71. bro-t him to feed Jacob h.p.
85:8.he will speak peace unto h.p.
94:14. L. will not cast off h. p.
100:3. we are h. p. and the sheep
105:24. increased h. p. greatly
43. bro-t forth h.p. with joy ⌈p.
25. turned their heart to hate h.
106:40. wrath of L. kindled ag. h. p. that, Is. 5:25. ⌈works
111:6. shewed h. p. power of his
9. He sent redemption unto h.p.
113:8.set him with princes of h.p.
116:14. in presence of all h.p.,18.
125:2. so is L. round about h. p.
136:16. who led h.p. thro. wilder.
148:14. he exalteth horn of h. p.
149:4. L. taketh pleasure in h. p.
Is. 3:14. with the ancients of h.p.
7:2. his moved, and heart of h.p.
11:11. recover remnant of h. p.
16. highway for remnant of h.p.
14:32. poor of h. p. sh. trust in
25:8. rebuke of h. p. sh. he take
28:5. diadem unto residue of h.p.
30:26. bindeth up breach of h.p.
49:13.G.hath comforted h.p.,52:9.
51:22. G. pleadeth cause of h. p.
56:3.L. hath separated me fr. h.p.
63:11.remembered Moses and h.p.
Je.22:4.enter this hou. he and h.p.
25:19.Pha.his princes and all h.p.
27:12. and serve him and h. p.
49:1. why h. p. dwell in cities?
50:16. sh. return ev. one to h. p.
Eze. 18:18. did not good am. h. p.
30:11.He and h.p. sh. be brought
Da. 11:15. neither h.chosen p. nei.
Jo. 2:18. then will Lord pity h. p.
19.L. will ans. and say unto h.p.
3:16. L. will be the hope of h. p.
Mi. 6:2. L. a controversy wi. h. p.
Zch. 9:16. save th. as flock of h. p.
Mat. 1:21. Jesus, he shall save h.p.
Lu. 1:68. he hath redeemed h. p.
77. knowl. of salvation unto h.p.
7:16. that God hath visited h. p.
Ro.11:1. Hath God cast away h.p.?
2. God hath not cast away h. p.
15:10. Rejoice ye Gentiles wi. h.p.
He. 10:30. The Lord sh. judge h.p.
Re. 21:3. sh. be h. p. God their G.
See HOLY people.

PEOPLE with Israel.

2 S. 7:11. Judges over my p. I., 1 Ch. 17:10.
18:7. When p. of I. were slain
19:40. conducted king bef. p. of I.
24:4. Joab came to number p. I.
1 K. 8:16. I chose David over p. I. (2) 2 Ch. 6:6. ⌈2 Ch. 6:21.
30. supplication of thy p. I., 52.
33. When thy p. I. be smitten, 2 Ch. 6:24. ⌈6:25, 27.
34. forgive sin of p. I., 36. 2 Ch.
41. stranger not of p. I., 2 Ch. 6:
59. maintain cause of p. I. ⌊32.
14:7. I made thee prince ov. p. I.,
16:2. hast made my p.I. sin ⌊16:2.
21. Then were p. I. divided
2 Ch. 6:33. fear thee as doth p. I.
2 Ch. 20:7. drive out bef. thy p. I.
Ezr. 2:2. number of men of p. I., Ne. 7:7. ⌈signs, 1 K. 8:16.
Je. 32:21. bro-t forth p. I. with
Eze. 14:9. will destroy him fr. p. I.
39:7. name in midst of p. I.
Am. 7:8. a plumbline in midst of p.
Ac. 4:10. Be it known to p. I. ⌊I.
13:24.preached repentance to p.I.
See ISRAEL with people.

PEOPLE of the land, s.
Ge.23:7. Ab. bowed to **p. o. l.**, 12.
13. Ab. spake in audience of **p.o.l.**
42:6. Joseph sold to all **p. o. l.**
Ex. 5:5. **p. o. l.** are many
Le. 4:†27. if **p. o. l.** sin thro' igno.
20:2. **p. o. l.** shall stone him
4. if **p.o.l.** hide their eyes fr. him
Nu. 14:9. neither fear ye **p. o. l.**
2 K. 11:14. all **p. o. l.** rejoiced and blew, 20. 2 Ch. 23:13, 21.
18. **p.o.l.** went into house of Baal
19. took **p.o.l.** came to k.'s house
15:5. Jotham judged **p. o. l.**, 2 Ch. [26:21.
16:15. burnt off-g of **p.o.l.**
21:24. **p. o. l.** slew all th. conspired ag. Amon, and **p. o. l.** made Josiah king, 2 Ch. 33:25.
23:30. **p. o. l.** took Jehoahaz his son, 2 Ch. 36:1.
35. silver and gold of **p. o. l.**
25:3. no bread for **p.o.l.**, Je. 52:6.
19. Nebu. took him that mustered **p. o. l.** and sixty men of **p. o. l.**, Je. 52:25. [o. l.
1 Ch. 5:25. went after the gods of **p.**
2 Ch. 23:20. he took gov-s and **p.o.l.**
Ezr. 4:4. **p. o. l.** weakened hands of
9:1. Isr. not separated fr. **p.o.l**-s (2)
2. mingled with **p. o. l**-s
10:2. taken wives of the **p. o. l.**
11. separate yours. from **p. o. l.**
Ne. 9:10. wonders on all **p. o. l.**
24. gave **p. o. l.** into hands
10:28. th. had separated fr. **p.o.l**-s
30. not give dau-s unto **p. o. l.**
31. if the **p. o. l.** bring ware, or
Je. 1:18. an iron pillar ag. **p. o. l.**
34:19. all **p. o. l.** which passed
37:2. **p. o. l.** did not hearken [l.
44:21. did not L. remember **p. o.**
Eze. 7:27. hands of **p. o. l.** be troubl.
12:19. say unto **p. o. l.**, saith L.
22:29. **p. o. l.** have used oppression
33:2. if **p.o. l.** take a watchman
39:13. all **p. o. l.** shall bury them
45:16. All **p.o.l.** shall give oblation
22. prince prepare for **p. o. l.**
46:3. **p. o. l.** shall worship at gate
9. when **p. o. l.** come in sol. feasts
Da. 9:6. which spake to **p.o. l.**
Hag. 2:4. be strong, all ye **p. o. l.**
Zch. 7:5. Speak unto all **p. o. l.**

PEOPLE of the Lord.
Ju.5:11. sh. **p.o. L.** go down to gates
2 S. 1:12. they mourned for **p. o. L.**
6:21. me ruler over **p. o. L.**
2 K.9:6. anointed thee k. over **p.o.L.**
Eze. 36:20. These are **p. o. L.**
Zph. 2:10. magnified ag. **p. o. L.**

PEOPLE with many.
Ex. 5:5 **p.** of the land now are **m.**
De. 2:21. a **p.** great and **m.** and tall
Ju. 7:2. The **p.** are too **m.** for me
4. unto Gid: The **p.** are yet too **m.**
1 S. 6:19. L. had smitten **m.** of **p.**
2 S. 1:4. and **m.** of the **p.** are fallen
Ezr. 10:13. **p. m.** and time of rain
Es. 8:17. **m. p.** of land became Jews
Is.2:3. **m. p.** shall go and say, Come
4. he sh. judge and rebuke **m.p.**
10:†13. I put down inhab-s like **m.**
17:12. Woe to mult. of **m. p.** [p.
Eze. 3:6. not to **m. p.** of stra. speech
17:9. without **m. p.** to pluck it
27:33. out of seas filledst **m. p.**
32:3. my net wi. company of **m.p.**
9. I will vex hearts of **m. p.**
10. make **m. p.** amazed at thee
38:6. thou and **m. p.** wi. thee, 9, 15.
8. land th. is gath-d out of **m.p.**
22. will rain upon **m. p.** wi. him
Mi.4:3. he shall judge among **m. p.**
13. beat in pieces **m. p.** [**m.p.**, 8.
5:7. remnant of Jac. in midst of
Ha.2:10. shame by cutting off **m. p.**
Zch. 8:22. **m. p.** shall seek the L.
Jn. 7:31. **m.** of **p.** believed on him

Much PEOPLE.
Ge. 50:20. G. meant it to save **m.p.**
Nu.20:20. Edom ag. him with **m. p.**
Jos.11:4. they went with **m. p.** even
2 S.13:34. there came **m. p.** by way
2 Ch. 30:13. assembled at Jerus. **m.**
32:4. there was gath-d **m. p.** [p.
Ps. 35:18 praise thee am. **m. p.**
Eze. 17:15. give him horses **m. p.**
Mk. 5:21. **m. p.** gathered unto him
24. Jesus went, **m. p.** foll-d him
6:34. Jesus saw **m. p.** was moved
Lu. 7:11. disci. with him and **m.p.**
12. **m. p.** of city was with her
8:4. when **m. p.** were gathered
9:37. come from hill **m. p.** met
Jn. 12:9. **m. p.** of Jews knew he was there [trees
12. **m. p.** took branches of palm
Ac. 5:37. drew **m. p.** after him
11:24. **m. p.** added unto the L.
26. assembled and taught **m. p.**
18:10. for I have **m. p.** in this city
19:26. Paul hath turned aw. **m.p.**
Re. 19:1. I heard a voice of **m. p.**
See MULTITUDE.

My PEOPLE. [I it
Ge. 23:11. in presence of **m. p.** give
41:40. unto thy word **m.p.** be ruled
49:29. I am to be gath-d unto **m.p.**
Ex. 3:7. affliction of **m. p.**, Ac. 7:34.
10. mayest bring forth **m.p.**, 7:4
5:1. Let **m. p.** go, 7:16.-8:1, 20.-9:1, 13.-10:3.
8:8. take frogs fr. me and **m. p.**
21. if wilt not let **m. p.** go, 10:4.
22. I sever land in wh. **m.p.** are, 23
9:17. exaltest thyself ag. **m. p.**
27. I and **m. p.** are wicked
12:31. get you forth fr. am. **m. p.**
22:25. If lend money to **m. p.**
Le. 26:12. ye shall be **m. p.**, Je. 11:4.-30:22. [**m. p.**
Nu. 24:14. now behold I go unto
Ju. 12:2. I and **m. p.** at gr. strife
14:3. never a woman am. **m. p.**?
16. a riddle unto chil. of **m. p.**
Ru. 1:16. thy people shall be **m. p.**
3:11. all city of **m. p.** doth know
1 S. 9:16. shalt anoint him over **m. p.** that he may save **m. p.**; for I looked upon **m. p.**
17. man I speak of reign ov. **m.p.**
2 S. 3:18. By Da. I will save **m. p.**
7:8. I took thee to be ruler over **m. p.**, 2 Ch. 6:5. [**m. p.**
22:44. delivered me fr. strivings of
1 K. 22:4. I am as thou, **m. p.** as thy peo., horses as thy horses, 2 K. 3:7. 2 Ch. 18:3.
2 K. 20:5. tell Hez., capt. of **m. p.**
1 Ch. 17:6. I com-ded to feed **m.p.**
28:2. Da. said, Hear me, **m. p.**
29:14. what **m.p.** to be able to offer
2 Ch. 1:11. that thou judge **m. p.**
6:5. Since day I bro-t **m. p.** out
7:13. if I send pestilence am. **m. p.**
14. If **m. p.** shall humble thems.
Es. 7:3. let **m. p.** be given me at
4. we are sold, I and **m. p.**
8:6. to see evil sh. come unto **m. p.**
Ps.14:4. eat up **m. p.** as bread, 53:4.
50:7. Hear, O **m. p.** I will speak and testify, 81:8. Is. 51:4.
59:11. Slay them not, lest **m. p.** forget, scatter
68:22. I will bring **m. p.** fr Bashan
78:1. Give ear, O **m. p.** to my law
81:11. **m. p.** would not hearken
13. O that **m. p.** had hearkened
144:2. who subdued **m. p.** und. me
Is. 1:3. **m. p.** doth not consider
3:12. As for **m. p.** chil. are their oppressors, O **m. p.** they
15. What mean that ye beat **m.p.**
5:13. **m. p.** are gone into captivity
Is.10:2. take right fr. poor of **m. p.**
24. **m. p.** that dwellest in Zion
19:25. Blessed be Egypt, **m. p.** and
26:20. **m. p.** enter thy chambers
32:13. Upon land of **m. p.** thorns
18. **m. p.** sh. dwell in a peaceable
40:1. Comfort ye, comfort ye **m.p.**
43:20. give drink to **m.p.** my chosen
47:6. I was wroth with **m. p.** [p.
51:16. say unto Zion, Thou art **m.**
52:4. **m. p.** went down into Egypt
5. **m. p.** is taken aw. for nought
6. Thf. **m. p.** shall know my name
53:8. for transg-n of **m. p.** stricken
57:14. stumblingbl. out of way of
58:1. shew **m. p.** transgr-n [**m.p.**
63:8. Surely they are **m. p.** chil.
65:10. Sharon a fold for **m. p.** [p.
19. I will rej. in Jerus., joy in **m.**
22. as a tree, are days of **m. p.**
Je. 2:11. **m. p.** changed their glory
13. **m. p.** have committed 2 evils
31. why say **m. p.**, We are lords
32. **m. p.** have forgott. me, 18:15.
4:22. **m.p.** is foolish, have not kno.
5:26. am. **m. p.** are wicked men
31. **m. p.** love to have it so, what
6:27. thee for a fortress am. **m.p.**
7:23. Obey my voice, ye sh. be **m. p.**
8:7. **m. p.** know not judgm. of L.
9:2. th. I might leave **m. p.** and go
12:16. if diligently learn ways of **m.p.** as they taught **m.p.** to (3)
15:7. I will destroy **m. p.** [**m. p.**
23:2. saith L. ag. pastors th. feed
22. if had caused **m. p.** to hear
27. cause **m.p.** to forget my name
32. cause **m. p.** to err by lies
24:7. they shall be **m. p.**, 31:1, 33.-32:38. Eze. 11:20.-36:28.-37:23, 27. Zch. 8:8. [do for **m. p.**
29:32. nei. behold good that I will
31:14. **m. p.** shall be satisfied with
33:24. they have despised **m. p.**
50:6. **m. p.** hath been lost sheep
51:45. **m. p.** go ye out of midst of her, Re. 18:4. [p. and
La. 3:14. I was a derision to all **m.**
Eze. 13:9. not in assembly of **m. p.**
10. have seduced **m.p.** | 18. hunts souls of **m. p.** [lying to **m. p.**
19. ye pollute me among **m. p.** by
21. I will deliver **m. p.** out of, 23.
14:8. cut him off fr. midst of **m.p.**
11. th. they be **m. p.** I their G.
21:12. terrors sh. be upon **m. p.**
34:30. even house of Isr. are **m.p.**
37:12. Behold, O **m. p.** I will open your graves, 13.
38:16. thou shalt come ag. **m. p.**
44:23. sh. teach **m. p.** difference
45:8. princes no more oppress **m.p.**
9. take your exactions from **m. p.**
46:18. that **m. p.** be not scattered
Ho.1:9. said G., Ye are not **m.p.**, 10.
2:†1. say unto your breth., **m. p.**
23. say to them were not **m. p.**
4:6. **m.p.** are destroyed for lack
8. They eat up the sin of **m. p.**
12. **m. p.** ask counsel at stocks
6:11. I returned captiv. of **m. p.**
11:7. **m. p.** are bent to backsliding
Jo. 2:26. **m. p.** never be asham., 27.
3:2. will plead with th. for **m. p.**
3. they have cast lots for **m. p.**
Am. 9:10. sinners of **m. p.** shall die
Ob. 13. not entered gate of **m. p.**
Mi.1:9. be is come unto gate of **m.p.**
2:4. hath changed portion of **m.p.**
8. **m. p.** is risen up as an enemy
9. women of **m. p.** ye cast out
3:3. who also eat flesh of **m. p.**
5. prophets that make **m. p.** err
6:3. O **m. p.** what have I done, 5.
16. ye sh. bear reproach of **m. p.**
Zph. 2:8. they reproached **m. p.**
9. residue of **m. p.** sh. spoil them

Zch. 2 : 11. many nations be **m. p.**
8:7. I will save **m. p.** fr. east coun-
13:9. I will say, It is **m. p.** ⌊try
Ac. 7 : 34. have seen afflic. of **m.p.**
Ro. 9 : 25. I will call them **m. p.**
which were not **m. p.**
26. where it was said, Ye are not
m. p.; there sh. they be called
2 Co.6:16.their G. they sh. be.**m.p.**
Re. 18 : 4. Come out of her **m. p.**
See **DAUGHTER of my people.**
See NUMBER, NUMBERED.

Of, of a or of the PEOPLE.

Ge. 17 : 16. kings **o. p.** shall be of
Sarah ⌈24:7. Ne. 13:1. Lu. 7:1.
23:13. in the audience **o.t.p.**, Ex.
25 : 23. two manner **o. p.** ⌈wi. wife
26 : 10. one **o.t.p.**might have lain
29:1. Jac. into land **o.t.p.** of east
49 : 10. unto him gathering **o.t.p.**
Ex.4:30.Aa.did signs in sight **o.t.p.**
5 : 6. Pha. commanded taskmasters
o. t. p., 10.
16 : 27. went out some **o. t. p.**
19:8.Mo. returned words **o.t.p.**,9.
32 : 17. Joshua heard noise **o.t.p.**
28. fell **o. t. p.** about 3,000 men
Le. 4 : 3. sin according to sin **o.t.p.**
9 : 7. and offer the offering **o.t.p.**,
16 : 24. Ezr. 7 : 16. ⌈**t.p.**wi.thee
Nu. 11 : 17. they sh. bear burden **o.**
21:4.soul **o.t.p.**much discouraged
18. nobles **o. t. p.** digged well
22 : 3. Moab sore afraid **o. t. p.**
41. see utmost part **o. t. p.**
25 : 4.Take heads **o.t.p.** and hang
26:4. Take sum **o.t.p.** fr. 20 years
De. 6:14. gods **o.t.p.**, 13:7.Ju.2:12.
1 Ch. 16:26. 2 Ch. 25:15.-32:19.
32 : 8. he set the bounds **o. t. p.**
33:5. heads **o.t.p.** were gath-d,21.
Jos. 1 : 10. Josh. com-ded officers **o.**
4 : 2. Take 12 men out **o.t.p.**⌊**t. p.**
11. ark ov. in presence **o. t. p.**
7 : 4. up to Ai **o. t. p.** about 3000
Ju. 7 : 3. returned **o. t. p.** 22,000
18:20. priest went in midst **o.t.p.**
20:31. Benj. began to smite **o.t.p.**
1 S. 6 : 19. smote **o. t. p.** 50,070 (3)
8 : 7. Hearken unto voice **o. t. p.**
9:2.higher than any **o.t.p.**,10:23.
12. sacrifice **o. t. p.** to day
13: 22. nei. sword in hand **o. t. p.**
14 : 24. none **o. t. p.** tasted food
28.one **o.t.p.**said,Thy fa.charged
26 : 15. one **o.t.p.** to destroy king
2 S. 1 : 4. many **o.t.p.** fallen, 11:17.
18 : 2. Da. sent 3d part **o. t. p.**
24:15. died **o.t.p.** 70,000 ⌈13 : 33.
1 K. 12 : 31. priests of lowest **o.t.p.**,
16 : 21. half **o. t. p.** foll-d Tibni
2 K. 11 : 13. when Athaliah heard
noise **o. t. p.** ⌈**t. p.**
12:8.priests to receive no money **o.**
13 : 7. nei. leave **o. t. p.** to Jeho-z
22:4. keepers have gath-d **o. t. p.**
23 : 6. powder upon graves **o. t.p.**
1 Ch. 16 : 28. kindreds **o. t. p.**, Ps.
96 : 7. ⌈**o. t. p.**
2 Ch. 16 : 10. Asa oppressed some
23 : 12. noise **o. t. p.** running
20. he took the governors **o.t.p.**
30 : 18. mult. **o. t. p.** not cleansed
35 : 12. acc. to families **o. t. p.**
Ezr. 2 : 70. some **o. t. p.** dwelt in
their cities, Ne. 7 : 73.
3 : 3. bec. **o.t.p.** of those countries
13. noise of weeping **o. t. p.**
4 : 4. weakened the hands **o. t. p.**
9 : 11. filthiness **o. t. p.** of lands
Ne. 5 : 1. gr. cry **o. t. p.** and wives
9 : 30. gavest into hands **o.t. p.** of
12 : 38. half **o. t. p.** upon the wall
Es. 8 : 11. perish the power **o. t. p.**
Jb.12:24. taketh heart of chief **o.t.**
17 : 6. me a byword **o. t. p.** ⌊**p.**

Ps. 3 : 6. I will not be afraid of 10
thousands **o. p.** ⌈ings **o. t. p.**
18: 43. hast deliv-d me from striv-
22 : 6. I am despised **o. t. p.**
33 : 10. devices **o. t. p.** of none ef-
65 : 7. stilleth tumult **o. t. p.** ⌊feet
68 : 30. Rebuke the calves **o. t. p.**
72:4. he sh. judge the poor **o.t.p.**
89:19. exalted one chos. out **o. t.p.**
105 : 44. inherited labour **o. t. p.**
107:32. exalt him in cong-n **o.t.p.**
Pr.14:28.In mult. **o.p.** is k.'s honour, in want **o. p.** destruc. of
Is. 6 : 5. I dwell in midst **o. a p.** of
10:13.I have removed bounds **o.t.**
14. as a nest the riches **o.t.p.**⌊**p.**
11 : 10. stand for ensign **o. t. p.**
18:7.**o.a.p.** peeled, **o.a p.** terrible
30:5.ashamed **o.a p.** co. not profit
28. bridle in the jaws **o. t. p.**
42:6. give thee for a cov-t **o. t. p.**
51:4.my judgment for light **o.t.p.**
62 : 10. prepare ye way **o. t. p.**
63 : 3. **o. t. p.** was none with me
Je. 10 : 3. customs **o.t. p.** are vain
17:19. Go stand in the gate **o.t.p.**
19 : 1. take of the ancients **o. t. p.**
26 : 24. not into the hand **o. t. p.**
39 : 8. Chaldeans burned houses **o.**
10.Neb-n left of poor **o.t.p.**⌊**t.p.**
46 : 24. into hand **o. t. p.** of north
52 : 15. Neb-n carried poor **o.t.p.**
La. 3 : 45. us refuse in midst **o.t.p.**
Eze.20:35. bring into wilder. **o.t.p.**
23 : 24. they sh. come ag. thee with
assembly **o. t. p.** ⌈**t. p.**
26:2. she broken that was gates **o.**
27 : 3. Tyrus a merchant **o. t. p.**
36 : 3. ye are an infamy **o. t. p.**
15.nei.shalt bear reproach **o.t.p.**
46: 18. prince not take **o.t.p.**'s in-
24. boil sacrifice **o. t. p.** ⌊heri.
Zch. 12 :4. I will smite ev. horse **o.**
Mat.2:4.gath-d scribes **o.t.p.**⌊**t.p.**
4:25.gr.multitudes **o.p.**,Lu.6:17.-
Mk.14:2.lest be uproar **o.t.p.**⌊12:1.
Lu.23:27.followed gr.company **o.p.**
Jn. 7 : 31. many **o. t. p.** believed
40. many **o.t.p.** said, Of a truth
11 : 42. bec. **o. t. p.** that stand by
Ac. 4 : 21. they let th. go bec. **o.t.p.**
12 : 11. fr. all the expectat. **o.t.p.**
21:35. for violence **o.t.p.** ⌈**t. p.**
He. 2:17. make reconcil. for sins **o.**
7 : 5. a com-t to take tithes **o.t.p.**
9 : 7. offered for errors **o. t. p.** ⌈ies
Re. 11 : 9. they **o.t.p.** see dead bod-
See ASSEMBLY, CHIEF, EARS, ELDERS, GODS, HEART. S, MIDST, MULTITUDE, NUMBER, PRINCE, S, REMNANT, RESIDUE, REST, RULER, S, THOUSANDS.

One PEOPLE. ⌈other

Ge.25:23. **o.p.** sh. be stronger than
34:16. with you, and become **o. p.**
22. consent to dwell wi. us, to be

Own PEOPLE. ⌊**o.p.**

Ex. 5: 16. the fault is in thine **o.p.**
Le.21:14.sh.take a virgin of his **o.p.**
1 Ch.17:21.G.redeem to be his **o.p.**
2 Ch. 25: 15. could not deliver **o.p.**
Ps. 45: 10. O dau. forget thine **o.p.**
78 : 52. made his **o. p.** to go forth
Is. 13: 14. ev. man turn to his **o.p.**
Je.46:16.Arise, let us go to our **o.p.**

The PEOPLE.

Ge. 11 : 6. L. said, Behold **t.p.**is one
14:16. Ab. brought back **t. p.**
32 : 7. Jacob divided **t.p.**with him
41:55. **t.p.** cried to Pha. for bread
47 : 21. as for **t. p.** he removed
Ex. 1 : 20. **t. p.** multiplied, waxed
3:12.When hast bro-t **t.p.**out of E.
4 : 21. he shall not let **t. p.** go
31. And **t. p.** believed
5:4. Whf. do ye let **t.p.** fr. works?

Ex. 5:5.sh. no more give **t. p.** straw
12. **t. p.** were scattered thro-t E.
7 : 14. refuseth to let **t. p.** go
8 : 8. take frogs, I let **t. p.** go
29. deceitfully in not letting **t.p.**
go, 32.-9 : 7. ⌈of E-ns, 12 : 36.
11 : 3. L. gave **t.p.** favour in sight
12:27. **t.p.** bowed head and worsh.
33. E-ns were urgent upon **t. p.**
34.**t.p.** took dough bef. leavened
13:17.when Pha. had let **t.p.**go(2)
18. God led **t. p.** thro. wilderness
14:5. told king of E. **t.p.** had fled
31. **t. p.** believed L. and Mo. ⌊(2)
15 : 13. in mercy hast led **t. p.**
14. **t. p.** shall hear and be afraid
16. till **t. p.** pass over ⌈drink
24. **t. p.** murmured What sh. we
16 : 4. **t.p.** sh. gather rate ev. day
30. So **t. p.** rested 7th day
17: 1. was no water for **t. p.** ⌈3.
2.**t.p.** did chide with Mo.,Nu.20:
3. **t.p.** thirsted, **t. p.** murmured
6. come water that **t. p.** drink
18:10. Blessed be G. who deliv-d **t.**
13. Moses sat to judge **t. p.** ⌊**p.**
15.Bec.**t.p.**come to inquire of G.
19. Be thou for **t. p.** to Godward
22.let th. judge **t.p.**all seasons,26.
25. made them heads over **t. p.**
19:9. I in cloud th. **t. p.** may hear
17. Mo. bro-t **t. p.** to meet God
21. Go down, charge **t. p.**
23. **t. p.** cannot come up to Sinai
24. let not **t. p.** break thro. to L.
20 18. **t. p.** saw it stood afar, 21.
24 2. nei. **t. p.** go up with him
3. Mo told **t. p.** all words of L.
8. Mo. sprinkled blood on **t. p.**
32 1. **t. p.** saw Mo. delayed (2)
6.**t.p.** sat down to eat, 1 Co.10:7.
22.knowest **t.p.** are set on misch.
25.when Mo. saw **t.p.**were naked
34. lead **t. p.** unto place I have
35. plagued **t. p.** bec. made calf
33:1.**t.p.** thou hast bro-t out of E.
4. when **t. p.** heard evil tidings
36:5. **t.p.** bring more than eno.,6.
Le.9:7. make atonement for thyself
and **t. p.**, 16 : 24. Nu. 16: 47.
15. he brought **t. p.**'s offering,
18.-16 : 15, 24. ⌈23.
22. Aa. lifted hand toward **t. p.**,
Nu. 11 : 1. **t. p.** complained, it displ.
2. **t. p.** cried unto Moses
8. **t. p.** gath-d manna, ground it
10. Then Mo. heard **t. p.** weep
21. **t. p.** are 600,000 footmen
24. Moses told **t. p.** words of L.
32. **t. p.** stood that day ⌈**t. p.**
33. wrath of L. ag. **t.p.**,L. smote
34. buried **t. p.** that lusted
35. **t. p.** journeyed fr. Kibroth-
12:15. **t.p.** journeyed not till Mir-
16. **t. p.** pitched in Paran ⌊iam
13:18.see **t.p.**whe. they be strong,
30.Caleb stilled **t.p.**bef.Moses⌊28.
31.We not able to go against **t.p.**
14:1. **t. p.** wept | 39. **t.p.**mourned
16 41. ye have killed **t. p.** of L.
20: 1. **t. p.** abode in Kadesh
3 **t. p.** chode with Moses, saying
21: 5. **t. p.** spake against Moses
6 fiery serpents, they bit **t. p.**
7. Moses prayed for **t. p.** (2)
16. Gather **t. p.** I will give water
22 12. shalt not curse **t. p.**
23 9. lo, **t. p.** shall dwell alone
24. **t. p.** shall rise as great lion
25:1.**t.p.**began to commit whored.
2. **t. p.** did bow down to gods (2)
33 : 14. was no water for **t. p.**
De. 1 : 28. **t. p.** is greater than we
2 : 4. command thou **t. p.**
4:10.Gather **t.p.**I will make,31:12.
16 : 18. judge **t. p.** with just
17:16.nor cause **t. p.** return to E.

18:3. sh. be priests due from t.p.
9. make captain to lead t. p.
1. com-ded t. p. keep com-ts
9. this day thou art become t. p.
11. Moses charged t. p. same day
12. upon m-t Gerizim to bless t.p.
33:3. The lord loved t. p.
17. sh. push t.p. to ends of earth
19. They shall call t. p. unto mt.
Jos. 1:10. officers commanded t. p.
14. t. p. removed fr. tents to pass over Jordan and the priests bearing ark before t. p.
16. t.p.passed ov.right ag.Jericho
4:10. t. p. hasted and passed over
19. t. p. came up out of Jordan
6:10. Josh. com-ded t.p.not shout
20. t. p. shouted when priests
8:13.Josh. set t. p. on west of city
20. t. p. that fled to wilderness
10: 13. sun stood till t.p. avenged
24:16.t.p.ans-d Joshua, God forbid
21. t.p.said, we will serve L., 24.
25.Joshua made a cov-t with t.p.
28. So Joshua let t. p. depart
Ju.2:4. when Angel spake t.p.wept
6. when Joshua had let t. p. go
7.t.p.served L.all days of Joshua
3:18.Ehud sent away t.p. th.bare
5: 2. t. p. willingly offered thems.
7:5. Gideon bro-t t.p. to the water
8. t.p. took victuals in hands
9:32. up thou and t. p. lie in wait in the field, 33, 34, 35.
36. when Gaal saw t. p. he said
42. t. p. went out into the field
45. Abim. slew t. p. in the city
10:18.t.p.said,What manwill fight
11:11. t.p.made Jephthah captain
16:24.t.p.saw Samson they praised
18:7. five men to Laish saw t. p.
20:10.ten to fetch victuals for t.p.
31. chil. of Benj. went ag. t. p.
21:2. t.p. came to the house of G.
4. t. p. rose early and built altar
15. t. p. repented them for Benj.
1 S.2: 13. priests' custom with t.p.
4:3. t. p. were come into the camp
4.t.p. sent to Shiloh to bring ark
6:6. did E-ns not let t. p. go
8: 19. t. p. refused to obey Sam.
9:13. t.p. not eat until Sam. come
24. Sam. said I have invited t.p.
10:11. t.p. said, Is Saul am. proph-
17. Sam. called t.p. unto L. [ets?
25.Sam.told t.p.manner of kingd.
11: 5. Saul said, What aileth t. p.
7. fear of the Lord fell on t. p.
11.put t.p.in companies,Ju.9:43.
12.t.p. said unto Sam. Who is he
13: 4. t. p. were called to Gilgal
6. t. p. distressed, t. p. did hide
8.t.p.were scattered from Saul,11.
15. Saul numbered t. p., 15 : 4.
16.t.p.with Saul and Jona.abode
14:2.t.p. with Saul were about 600
3. t. p. knew not Jona. was gone
24. Saul adjured t. p. saying
26. t. p. feared the oath (2)
28.Thy fa.charged t.p.with oath,
28. And t. p. were faint, 31. [27.
30. if haply t. p. had eaten freely
32. t. p. flew upon the spoil (2)
33. Behold t. p. sin ag. the Lord
40. t.p. said unto Saul, Do what
41. Saul,Jona.taken, t.p.escaped
45. t.p. said, Shall Jona. die? (2)
15:9.t.p.spared best of sheep,15:21
24. Saul said, I feared t. p. [30.
17: 27. t. p. ans-d, So be done to,
26: 5. t. p. pitched round about
30:4. David and t.p. wept [Saul,7.
6. t. p. spake of stoning David
21. 200 men went to meet t.p.(2)
2 S.1:4.ans-d t. p. are fled fr. battle
2:26. how long ere bid t.p. return
27. in the morn. t. p. had gone

2 S.6:18. Da. blessed t.p.in name of
10:13. Joab drew nigh and t.p.[L.
11:7.David demanded how t.p.did
14:15.bec.t.p.have made me afraid
15 : 12. t. p. inc-d continually with Absalom [p.
17:8. [illegible] will not lodge with t.
29. honey &c. David and t. p.(2)
18:3.t.p. ans-d David. Thou shalt
6. t. p. went ag. Israel [not go
16.t.p. returned fr. pursuing (2)
19: 3. t.p. got by stealth into city
22:48. is G. bringeth t.p. und. me
23:10. t.p.returned after David to
23:11. t.p. fled from Philis. [spoil
24: 16. L. to angel th. destroyed t. p. It is enough, 17.[Ch. 21: 2.
21. th.plague be stayed fr. t.p.,1
1 K. 1:40. t.p.piped with pipes and
3:2. t.p. sacrificed in high pla.[(2)
5: 16. 3,300 which ruled over t. p.
8 : 66. Sol. sent t. p. away (2) [p.
9: 23. 550 officers bare rule over t.
12 : 5. said, Depart, and t. p.depa.
13. Rehoboam ans-d t.p.roughly
16. t. p. answered, What portion we in David? 2 Ch. 10 : 16.
30. t. p. went to worship bef. calf
16:15.t.p.encamped ag.Gibbethon
21.t.p. divided into two parts (2)
22. t.p.th.followed Omri prevailed against t. p. that
18:21.t.p. ans-d Elijah not a word
22: 43. t. p. burnt incense in high places, 2 K. 12 : 3.-14: 4.-15:4, 35. 2 Ch. 33:17.[t.p. to eat,43.
2 K. 4:41. Elisha said, Pour out for
6 : 30. t. p. looked, he had sackcl.
7: 16. t.p. spoiled tents of Syrians
17.t.p.trode upon him in gate,20.
8:21. t.p. fled into their tents
11: 17. Jehoi-a made cov-t between L. and t. p. that they be L.'s p.
16:9.carried t.p.of Damas.cap.[(3)
18: 36. But t. p. held their peace
22:13.inquire of L. for me and t.p.
25: 22. as for t. p. th. remained in
1 Ch.11:13.t.p.fled bef.Philis.[Jud
16: 2. Da. blessed t. p. in name of
19 : 14. t.p. drew nigh unto battle
20:3.Da.cut t.p.wi.saws,2 S.12:31.
29 : 9. Then t. p. rejoiced for they off-d willingly [t. p. a-work
2 Ch. 2 : 18. 3,600 overseers to keep
7 : 10. he sent t. p. away glad
8 : 10. 250 th. bear rule over t. p.
10 : 5. Come again, t. p. departed
10. Thus answer t. p. that spake
12 : 3. t. p. were without number
14 : 13. Asa and t. p. pursued th.
17: 9. thro-t cities and taught t.p.
18 : 2. Ahab killed sheep for t. p.
19:4.went thro. t.p.fr. Beer-sheba
20:21. had consulted with t. p. he
33. t. p. had not prepared hearts unto Lord, 30 : 3.
24: 20. priest wh. stood above t.p.
27 : 2. And t. p. did corruptly
30: 20. L. heark-d and healed t.p.
27. Then the priests blessed t. p.
31: 4. com-ded t.p. to give portion of Levites [off-gs
10. Since t. p. began to bring
32:8.t.p.rested upon words of Hez.
35:5. divisions of your breth. t. p.
36: 14. t. p. transg-d very much
Ezr.3:1.t.p. gath-d as one to Jerus.
13. t. p. not discern shout of joy
5: 12. Neb-r who carried t.p. into
8:15.I viewed t.p. and found[Bab
36.furthered t.p.and house of G.
9: 14. Should we join with t. p. of these abominations?
10: 1. t.p. wept very sore, Ne.8:9.
Ne. 4: 6. t. p. had a mind to work
13. I set t. p. aft. families with
5:13. t. p. did acc. to this promise

Ne. 5: 15. serv-s bare rule over t. p.
7 : 4. city large but t. p. few [t.p.
5. G. put into my heart to gather
8: 7. caused t. p. to understand
9.Levites that taught t.p. [law(2)
16. So t. p. made thems. booths
11:2.t.p. blessed all off-d willingly
24. at k.'s hand in matters conc.
12: 30. priests purified t. p. [t. p.
Es. 3: 6. shewed him t. p. of Mord.
11.t.p. to do with th. as seemeth
4: 11. t. p. of k.'s provinces know
Jb. 12 : 2. No doubt but ye are t.p.
34:20.t.p. be troubled at midnight
30.reign not lest t.p. be ensnared
36 : 31. by them judgeth he t. p.
Ps. 2:1.Why do t.p. imagine a vain thing? Ac. 4: 25.
7: 8. L. sh. judge t. p., 67 : 4.-96: 10. Is. 3 : 13.-51 : 5. [under me
18 : 47. It is God subdueth t. p.
33 : 12. Blessed are t. p. he hath
44 : 2. how thou didst afflict t. p.
45 : 5. arrows, whereby t. p. fall
17. sh. t. p. praise thee for ever
47:3. He sh. subdue t. p. under us
56:7. in anger cast down t.p. O G.
67:3. Let t. p. praise thee, O G.,5.
68: 30. scatter t. p. delight in war
87 : 6. when writeth up t. p.
89 : 15. Blessed is t. p. that know
95 : 7. we are t. p. of his pasture
96: 13. he sh. judge t. p. wi. truth
98:9. he sh. judge t. p. wi. equity
99:1. L. reigneth, let t. p. tremble
102: 18. t. p. created sh. praise L.
22.When t.p. gath-d to serve L.
105: 40. t.p. asked, he bro-t quails
149:7. execute punish-ts upon t.p.
Pr. 11 : 14. no counsel is, t. p. fall
26. t. p. shall curse him, 24 : 24.
29 : 2. righteous in authority t. p. rejoice: t. p. mourn [ish
18. Where is no vision, t. p. per-
Is. 8 : 5. t. p. shall be oppressed
9 : 2. t. p. that walked in darkness
13. t. p. turneth not unto him
19. t. p. shall be as fuel [smiteth
10 : 6. ag. t. p. of my wrath give
14 : 2. And t. p. shall take them
6. He smote t. p. in wrath
24 : 2. as with t. p. so with priest
4.t.haughty p. of earth languish
26 : 11. ashamed for envy at t. p.
30 : 19. t. p. shall dwell in Zion
33 : 3. At the tumult t. p. fled
12. t. p. be as burnings of lime
24. t. p. shall be forgiven iniq-y
34:5.my sword sh. come upon t.p.
40 : 7. surely t. p. is grass
41: 1. let t. p. renew their strength
43 : 9. and let t. p. be assembled
51:7.t.p. in whose heart is my law
60 : 2. gross darkness cover t. p.
62 : 10. lift up standard for t. p.
63 : 6. I will tread t. p. in anger
18. t. p. of thy holin. possessed
Je.14:16. t.p. to wh. they prophesy
21 : 7. I will deliver t. p.
23 : 34. t. p. that say, The burden
31: 2. t. p. wh. were left of sword
48:46.Woe,t.p. of Chemosh perish
51: 58. t. p. shall labour in vain
52:28.This is t.p.Neb-r carried aw.
Eze. 11: 17. will gather you fr. t.p.
20:34. you out fr. t. p., 41.-34:13.
24 : 19. t. p. said, Wilt tell us
25 : 7. I will cut thee off fr. t. p.
26:20. down with t. p. of old time
28: 25 Isr. from t. p. am. whom
29 : 13. Eg-s from t. p. whi. scat-d
33 : 6. sw. come, t. p. not warned
31. unto thee as t. p. cometh
38: 12. t. p. gath-d out of nations
39:4. Thou shalt fall, and t. p.[p.
27. When I have bro-t th.from t.
42:14.those things wh. are for t.p.

Eze.44:11.sh. slay sacrifice for t.p.
Da. 9: 26. t. p. of the prince that
11: 32. t. p. that know their God
Ho.4:14.t.p.that doth not underst.
10: 5. t. p. shall mourn over it
10. t. p. sh. be gathered ag. them
Jo. 2: 6. t. p. shall be much pained
16. Gather t. p. sanctify cong-n
Am. 1: 5. t. p. of Syria into captiv.
3:6.trumpet blown, t.p.not afraid
Jon. 3: 5. t. p. of Nineveh believed
Ha. 2: 13. t. p. sh. labour in fire,
t. p. shall weary for vanity
Hag. 1. 12. t. p. did fear bef. the L.
Mal.1:4.t.p.ag.whom L.hath indign
Mat.4:16. t. p. that sat in darkness
7:28. t. p. astonished at his doctr.
9: 23. and t. p. making noise
25.t.p.were put forth he took her
14:13. when t. p. heard, Lu. 9:11.
21: 26. if we shall say, Of men, we
fear t. p., Mk. 11:32. [parting
Mk. 6: 33. And t. p. saw them de-
45. while he sent away t. p.
7:17.entered into house from t. p.
8:6. he com-ded t.p.to sit down (2)
34. he had called t. p., 7: 14.
9: 25. Jes. saw t. p. running, Ac.
10:1. t. p. resort unto him [21: 30.
12:12. sought him but feared t.p.,
Lu. 20: 19.-22: 2. Ac. 5: 26.
41. beheld how t. p. cast money
15: 11. chief priests moved t. p.
15. Pilate willing to content t.p.
Lu. 1: 21. t. p. waited for Zacharias
3:10. t. p. asked, What shall we do?
15. as t. p. were in expectation
4: 42. t. p. sought him
5: 1. t. p. pressed [5: 25.
3. he taught t. p., 20: 1. Ac. 4:2.
8: 40. t. p. gladly received him
42. t. p. thronged him as he went
9:11. t. p. when knew it, foll-d him
18. Whom say t. p. that I am?
11:14. dumb spake t. p. wondered
29. when t. p. were gath-d thick
23: 5. He stirreth up t. p.
13. Pilate called together t. p.
14. this man as one perverteth t.
35. and t. p. stood beholding [p.
Jn 6:22.when t.p. saw was no boat
24. when t. p. saw Jes. not there
7:12. said Nay; he deceiveth t. p.
20. t. p. ans-d, Thou hast a devil!
32. Phari. heard t. p. murmured
11:50. that one die for t. p., 18:14.
12: 17. t. p. with him bare record
18. For this cause t. p. met him
29. t. p. said, it thundered
34. t. p. ans-d, We have heard
Ac. 5: 13. t. p. magnified them [p.
25. men in prison are teaching t.
6: 12. they stirred up t. p., 17: 13.
7: 17. t. p. multiplied in Egypt
8: 6. t. p. with accord gave heed
9. bewitched t. p. of Samaria
12: 22. t. p. saying It is voice of G.
13: 15. if ye bare word from t. p.
17. G. exalted t. p. wherein E.
14:11.t.p. saw what Paul had done
13. priest of Jupiter would have
done sacrifice with t. p.
18. scarce restrained t. p. [Paul
19. persuaded t. p. and stoned
17:8. they troubled t. p. and rulers
19: 35. town clerk appeased t. p.
21:28. This is man teacheth ag.t.p.
30. city was moved, t.p. ran tog-r
24:12.found me nei.raising up t.p.
26: 17. Delivering thee from t. p.
28:17.I committ-d nothing ag.t.p.
1 Co. 10: 7. t. p. sat to eat and [27.
He. 5: 3. as for t. p. so for hims., 7:
7: 11. under it t. p. received law
Jude 5. how that L. having saved t.

This PEOPLE. [p.

Ex. 3: 21. I will give t. p. favour
Ex. 5: 22. whf. evil entreated t. p.?
23. Pha. hath done evil to t. p.
17: 4. What shall I do unto t. p.?
18: 18. wear away, thou and t. p.
23. all t. p. sh. go to their place in
32: 9. L. said, I have seen t. p.,
De. 9: 13.
21. What did t. p. unto thee
31. t. p. have sinned a great sin
33: 12. thou sayest, Bring up t. p.
Nu.11:11.burden of all t.p.upon me
12 Have I conceived all t. p.?
13. whence flesh to give unto t.p.
14. I am not able to bear all t. p.
14:11. How long t. p. provoke me?
13. broughtest up t. p. in might
14. they heard thou art am. t. p.
15. if thou kill t. p. as one man
16. not able to bring t. p. into la.
19. Pardon t. p. as thou hast forgiven t. p. [t. p.
21: 2. If thou wilt indeed deliver
22: 6. I pray thee, curse t. p., 17.
24:14. what t.p. sh. do to thy peo.
32: 15. ye shall destroy all t. p.
De. 3: 28. Josh. sh. go over bef. t. p.
5: 28. I have heard voice of t. p.
9:27.look not unto stubbornness of
31:7. thou must go with t. p. [t.p.
16. t. p. will go whoring aft. gods
Jos. 1: 2. go over Jord. and all t. p.
6. unto t. p. divide the land
7: 7. whf. hast bro-t t. p. over Jor.
Ju.2:20.Bec. t. p. have transgressed
9:29.would t. p. were und. my ha.
38. is not t. the p. thou despised?
20: 16. amo. t. p. 700 lefthanded
1 S. 2: 23. your evil doings by t. p.
2 S. 16: 18 whom L. and t.p. choose
1 K. 12: 6. that I may ans. t. p., 9
2 Ch. 10: 6, 9. [p. this day
7. If thou wilt be a serv. unto t.
10. Thus speak unto t. p.
27. If t. p. do sacrifice at Jerus.,
heart of t. p. sh. turn to Rehob
14:2. told me I sho. be king ov. t.p.
18: 37. O L., that t. p. may know
2 K. 6:18. smite t. p. with blindness
2 Ch. 1:10. I may go out and in bef.
10: 7. If thou kind to t. p. [t. p.
Ne. 5:18. bondage heavy upon t. p.
19. acc. to all I have done for t.p.
Is. 6: 9. go tell t. p. Hear ye
10. Make the heart of t. p. fat,
Mat. 13: 15. Ac. 28: 26, 27.
8:6.t.p. refuseth waters of Shiloah
11. I sho. not walk in way of t. p.
12. t. p. shall say, A confederacy
9: 16. leaders of t. p. cause to err
23: 13. t. p. was not till Assyr.
28: 11. with ano. tongue to t. p.
14. hear, ye scornful, th.rule t.p.
29:13. t. p. draw near with mouth
14. a marvellous work am. t. p.
42:22. t. is a p. robbed and spoiled
43:21. t. p. have I formed for mys.
Je. 4:10. hast greatly deceived t. p.
11. At that time he said to t. p.
5: 14. my words fire, t. p. wood
23. t. p. hath a revolting heart
6: 19. I will bring evil upon t. p.
21. lay stumblingblocks bef. t. p.
7: 16. Thf. pray not thou for t. p.
neither, 11: 14.-14: 11.
33. carcasses of t.p. meat for fowls
8: 5. Why is t. p. slidden back?
9:15. I will feed t. p. wi. wormwood
13:10. t. evil p. who refuse to hear
14:10. Thus saith the L. unto t.p.
15:1. my mind co. not be tow. t. p.
20. thee unto t. p. a brazen wall
16:5. I have tak. my peace fr. t. p.
10. shalt show t. p. these words
19: 11. Even so will I break t. p.
21:8. unto t. p. say, Thus saith L.
23: 32. they shall not profit t. p.
33. and when t. p. shall ask thee
Je.27:16.I spake to priest and t. p.
28: 15. makest t. p. to trust in lie
29:32. not a man to dwell am. t.p.
32:42. bro-t this gr. evil upon t.p.
33: 24. not what t. p. have spoken
35: 16. t. p. have not hearkened
36: 7. great is anger ag. t. p. [p.?
37: 18. What have I offended ag. t.
38: 4. seeketh not welfare of t. p.
Mi. 2: 11. he sh. be prophet of t.p.
Hag. 1: 2. t. p. say, The time is not
2:14. Haggai said, So is t.p.bef. me
Zch.5:†3.ev.one of t.p. that stealeth
8: 6. in eyes of remna.' of t. p.
11. I not be to t. p. as in former
12. I will cause t. p. to possess
Mat. 15: 8. t. p. draweth nigh with
Mk. 7:6. t. p. honoureth me wi. lips
Lu. 9:13. exc. we buy meat for t.p.
21: 23. shall be wrath upon t. p.
Jn. 7:49. t. p. knoweth not the law
Ac.13:17.God of t. p. chose our fa-s
1 Co. 14:21. wi. other lips speak to t.

Thy PEOPLE. [p.

Ex. 5: 23. nei. hast delivered t. p.
8: 3. frogs upon t. p., 4.
9. when shall I entreat for t. p.
11. frogs shall depart from t. p.
21. send swarms of flies upon t.p.
9:14. I will send plagues upon t.p.
15. I may smite t. p. with pestil.
15:16.still, till t. p. pass ov. [23:5.
22: 28. nor curse ruler of t. p.,Ac.
23: 11. th. poor of t. p. may eat
32: 7. t. p. corrupted, De. 9: 12.
11. why wrath wax hot ag. t. p.
12. L. repent of this evil ag. t. p.
33: 13. consider this nation is t. p.
16. I and t. p. have found grace
34: 10. I make a cov-t bef. all t. p.
Le. 19:16. not as talebearer am. t.p.
18. any grudge ag. chil. of t. p.
Nu. 5:21.make thee a curse am. t.p.
24:14. what this peo. shall do t.p.
27:13. shalt be gathered unto t. p.,
31: 2. De. 32: 50.
De. 9: 26. destroy not t. p. [1: 10.
29. they are t. p. and inheri., Ne.
Ju. 5:14. aft. thee Benj. among t.p.
Ru. 1: 10. we will return unto t. p.
16. t. p. shall be my people
2 S. 7: 23. what nation like t. p.? t.
p. which thou redeemest from
Egypt, 1 Ch. 17: 21.
1 K. 3: 8. thy serv. in midst of t. p.
9. heart to judge t. p., 2 Ch. 1:10.
8: 44. If t. p. go out to battle
50. forgive t. p. that have sinned,
2 Ch. 6: 34, 39. [for his people
51. they be t. p. | 20: 42. t. p.
22: 4. I am as thou art, my people
as t. p., 2 K. 3: 7. [t. p.
1 Ch. 21: 17. let not thy hand be on
29: 17. I have seen with joy t. p.
18. keep this in thoughts of t. p.
2 Ch.21:14.with plague will L. smite
t. p., childr., wives [on t. p.
Ne. 9: 32. let not trouble seem little
Ps. 3:8. L. thy blessing is upon t.p.
28:9. Save t. p. and bless, Je. 31:7.
44:12.Thou sellest t. p. for nought
60:3. hast shewed t. p. hard things
68:7. when thou wentest bef. t. p.
72:2. sh. judge t. p. with right-ss.
77: 15. Thou hast redeemed t. p.
20. Thou leddest t. p. as flock by
79:13. we t.p. will give thee thanks
80:4.long angry ag. prayer of t.p.?
83:3. taken crafty counsel ag. t. p.
85: 2. hast forgiven iniq-y of t. p.
6. revive us, that t. p. rejoice
94: 5. They break in pieces t. p.
106:4. favour thou bearest to t. p.
110:3. t. p. shall be willing in day
Is. 2: 6. Thf. hast forsaken t. p.
7: 17. L. sh. bring upon t.p. days
14:20. hast destroyed la. and t. p.

Is. 60:21. t.p. shall be all righteous
63 : 14. so didst thou lead t. p.
64 : 9. Be not wroth; we are t. p.
Je. 22:2. Hear, thou and t. p. [t. p.
27 : 13. Why will ye die, thou and
Eze. 3:11. get thee unto t. p. speak
13:17. set thy face ag. dau-s of t.p.
26 : 11. he shall slay t. p. wi. sword
33 : 2. speak to chil. of t. p., 12.
17. t. p. say, way of L. not equal
30. chil. of t. p. still are talking
37 : 18. when chil. of t. p. speak
Da. 9:15. L. that bro-t t. p. out of E.
16. t. p. are become reproach
19. t. p. are called by thy name
24. 70 weeks determined upon t.p.
10 : 14. what shall befall t. p.
11 : 14. robbers of t. p. shall exalt
12 : 1. Michael, who standeth for t.
p. at that time t. p. be deliv.
Ho. 4 : 4 t. p. as they that strive
10 : 14. sh. tumult arise am. t. p.
Jo. 2:17. Spare t. p. | Mi. 7:14. Feed
Na. 3 : 13. t. p. are women [t. p.
18. t. p. is scattered on mts. [t.p.
Ha. 3 : 13. thou wentest for salva. of

To or unto the PEOPLE.

Ge. 47 : 23. Joseph said u. p.
Ex. 4:16. he sh. be spokesman u.p.
5 : 10. taskmasters spake t. p.
13 : 3. Moses said u.p., 14 : 13.-19:
15.-20 : 20.-32 : 30. Nu. 31 : 3.
18 : 14. Jethro saw all he did t. p.
What is this thou doest t. p.?
19 : 10. L. said to Moses, Go u. p.
12. thou shalt set bounds u. p.
14. Moses went from mt. u. p.
Nu. 11:18. say u. p., sanctify yours.
De. 20 : 2. that priest speak u. p.
5. officers shall speak u. p., 8.
9. an end of speaking u. p.
Jos. 3 : 5. Josh. said u. p., Sanctify
4:10. com-ded Josh. to speak u. p.
6 : 7. Joshua said u. p. pass on
8. when Joshua had spoken u. p.
16. Joshua said, u. p., Shout
24 : 19. Joshua said u. p. Ye can-t
serve the Lord [nesses
22. Joshua said u. p. Ye are wit-
Ju. 8 : 5. Give loaves u. p.
1 S. 8:10. Sam. told all words u. p.
11 : 14. said Sam. t. p., Come
12 : 6. Sam. said u. p., It is the L.
20. Samuel said u. p., Fear not
14:17. said Saul u.p., Number now
26 : 7. Da. and Abishai came t. p.
14. Da. cried t. p. and to Abner
30 : 21. Da. came near t. p. saluted
2 S. 18 : 2. king said u. p. I will go
24:3. Now the L. add u. p. [wi. you
1 K. 12 : 15. the king hearkened not
u. p., 2 Ch. 10 : 15. [long halt
18:21. Elijah came u. p. said, How
22. send Elijah u. p., I only [eat
19 : 21. Elisha gave u. p. they did
2 K. 4 : 42. Give u. p. that may eat
11 : 13. Athaliah t. p., 2 Ch. 23:12.
1 Ch. 10:9. Philis. sent tidings t. p.
2 Ch. 32 : 18. in Jew's speech u.p.
35 : 7. Josiah gave t. p. lambs and
8. his princes gave willingly u.p.
Ne. 4:22. at same time said I u. p.
5 : 15. gov-rs were chargeable u. p.
Ps. 9:8. sh. minister judgment t. p.
72 : 3. mts. sh. bring peace t. p.
74 : 14. leviathan to be meat t. p.
Is. 42 : 5. he th. giveth breath u. p.
49 : 22. I will set up standard t. p.
55 : 4. given him for witness t. p.
a leader and commander t. p.
Eze. 24:18. So I spake u. p. in morning
44 : 19. when priests go forth t. p.
Da. 2 : 44. kingd. be left t. other p.
7 : 27. kingdom t. p. of saints
Jo. 3 : 8. shall sell them t. p. far off
Ha. 3:16. when he cometh up u. p.
Zph. 3:9. I will turn t. p. pure lang.
Hag. 1:13. spake Hag. L.'s message u.
Mat. 12:46. While he talked t. p. [p.
27 : 15. to release u. p. a prisoner
64. lest disci. say u. p. He is risen
Lu. 3 : 18. many thi. preached u. p.
7 : 9. Jes. said u. p. I not found
24. began to speak u.p. conc. John
12:54. said t. p., When ye see cloud
13 : 14. ruler said u. p., There are
20:9. to speak t.p. parable [6 days
23 : 4. Pilate t. p. I find no fault
Ac. 3:12. Pe. ans-d u. p. Ye men of
4 : 1. as spake u. p., priests came
5:20. speak in tem. t. p. all words
10:2. wh. gave alms t.p. and prayed
42. he com-ded us to preach u.p.
12:4. to bring Pe. forth t. p. [u.p.
13 : 31. seen of them his witnesses
17 : 5. sought to bring th. out t.p.
19:4. Jn. baptized saying u. p. [p.
19:30. Paul wo. have entered in u.
33. wo. have made defence u. p.
21 : 39. suffer me to speak u. p.
40. Paul beckoned with hand u.p.
26 : 23. suffer, and shew light u.p.

PEOPLES. [many p.

Re. 10:11. Thou must prophesy bef.
17 : 15. waters thou sawest are p.

PE'OR. [of P.

Nu. 23 : 28. bro-t Balaam unto top
25 : 18. they have beguiled you in
matter of P., 31 : 16.
Jos. 22 : 17. Is iniq-y of P. too little

PERADVENTURE.

Ge. 18:24. p. there be fifty righteous
28. p. there lack five of the fifty
29. p. there be forty | 30. thirty
31. p. twenty | 32. p. ten be found
24 : 5. p. woman not be willing, 39.
27 : 12. My father p. will feel me
31:31. p. take by force thy dau-s
32:20. p. he will accept of me [him
42 : 4. said, Lest p. mischief befall
43 : 12. again, p. it was oversight
44 : 34. lest p. evil come on my fa.
50 : 15. Joseph will p. hate us, and
Ex. 13 : 17. lest p. the people repent
32 : 30 p. I shall make atonement
Nu. 22:6. curse peo., p. I prevail, 11.
23 : 3. p. L. will come to meet me
27. p. it please God thou curse th.
Jos. 9:7. said, p. ye dwell among us
1 S. 6:5. p. he will lighten his hand
9 : 6. p. he can shew us our way
1 K. 18 : 5. p. we may find grass
27. p. he sleepeth, must be awaked
20 : 31. k., p. he will save thy life
2 K. 2 : 16. p. Spirit hath cast him
Je. 20 : 10. p. he will be enticed
Ro. 5 : 7. p. for a good man some
2 Ti. 2 : 25. p. give them repentance

PER'AZIM.

Is. 28:21. L. sh. rise up as in mt. P.

PERCEIVE.

De. 29 : 4. not given you heart to p.
Jos. 22 : 31. we p. Lord is among us
1 S. 12:17. ye may p. your wickedn.
2 S. 19 : 6. I p. if Abs. had lived
2 K. 4 : 9. I p. this is a holy man
Jb. 9 : 11. he passeth I p. him not
23 : 8. go backward I can-t p. him
Pr. 1 : 2. to p. words of underst-g
Ec. 3:22. I p. there is noth-g better
Is. 6 : 9. see ye indeed, but p. not
33 : 19. deeper speech than canst p.
Mat. 13:14. seeing, ye shall see, and
shall not p., Mk. 4:12. Ac. 28:26.
Mk. 7:18. do ye not p. whatso. ent-th
8:17. p. ye not yet, nei. underst-d?
Lu. 8 : 46. I p. virtue is gone out
Jn. 4:19. I p. that thou art prophet
12 : 19. said, p. ye prevail nothing
Ac. 8 : 23. I p. thou art in gall of
10:34. I p. G. is no respecter of per.
17:22. I p. ye are too superstitious
27:10. I p. voyage will be wi. hurt
2 Co. 7:8. I p. epistle made you sorry
1 Jn. 3 : 16. hereby p. we love of G.

PERCEIVED. [do., 35.

Ge. 19 : 33. he p. not when she lay
Ju. 6 : 22. Gideon p. he was angel
1 S. 3 : 8. Eli p. L. called the child
28 : 14. Saul p. that it was Samuel
2 S. 5 : 12. Da. p. Lord had establi-d
him k. over Isr., 1 Ch. 14 : 2.
12:19. David p. the child was dead
14:1. Joab p. k.'s heart was to Abs.
1 K. 22 : 33. when the captains p. it
was not king, 2 Ch. 18 : 32.
Ne. 6 : 12. I p. G. had not sent him
16. p. work was wrought of God.
13:10. I p. portions of Lev. not given
Es. 4 : 1. Mord. p. all that was done
Jb. 38 : 18. Hast p. breadth of earth?
Ec. 1 : 17. I p. this is vexation
2:14. I p. one event happ-th to all
Is. 64 : 4. nor p. what G. prepared
Je. 23 : 18. who hath p. his word
38 : 27. left off, matter was not p.
Mat. 16:8. when Jes. p. he said, O ye
21:45. p. he spake of th., Lu. 20:19.
22 : 18. Jes. p. their wickedness
Mk. 2 : 8. Jes. p. they reasoned am.
Lu. 1 : 22. p. he had seen a vision
5 : 22. when Jes. p. their thoughts
9 : 45. was hid, that they p. it not
20 : 23. but he p. their craftiness
Jn. 6:15. Jes. p. wo. make him a k.
Ac. 4 : 13. p. they were unlearned
23 : 6. Paul p. part were Pharisees
29. I p. to be accused of questions
Ga. 2 : 9. James p. grace given me

PERCEIVEST, ETH, ING.

Jb. 14:21. low, but he p-h it not
33 : 14. G. speaketh, man p-h it not
Pr. 14:7. p-t not in him lips of knowl.
31:18. p-h her merchandise is good
Mk. 12 : 28. p-g he had answ-d well
Lu. 6 : 41. p-t not beam in own eye
9 : 47. Jesus p-g thought of heart
Ac. 14 : 9. p-g he had faith to be

PERDITION. [healed

Jn. 17 : 12. none lost but son of p.
Ph. 1 : 28. to them evident token of
2 Th. 2:3. be revealed, son of p. [p.
1 Ti. 6 : 9. which drown men in p.
He. 10 : 39. th. who draw back unto
2 Pe. 3: 7. and p. of ungodly men [p.
Re. 17 : 8. beast sh. go into p., 11.

PE'RES.

Da. 5 : 28. P., Thy kingd. is divided

PE'RESH. [resh

1 Ch. 7:16. Maachah bare P. and She-

PE'REZ.

1 Ch. 27:3 Of chil. of P., Ne. 11 : 4.
Ne. 11 : 6. sons of P. that dwelt at

PE'REZ-UZ'ZAH. [Jerus.

2 S. 6:8. called place P., 1 Ch. 13:11.

PERFECT. [Adj.]

Ge. 6 : 9. Noah p. | 17:1. be thou p.
Le. 22: 21. freewill offering sh. be p.
De. 18 : 13. Thou shalt be p. with L.
25 : 15. have p. weight. p. measure
1 S. 14 : 41. Saul said, Give p. lot
2 S. 22 : 33. he maketh my way p.,
Ps. 18 : 32. [p. gold
2 Ch. 4:21. lamps and tongs made of
Ezr. 7 : 12. Artax. to Ezra, p. peace
Jb. 1 : 1. that man was p., 8.-2 : 3.
8 : 20. G. not cast away p. man
9:20. If say, I am p. prove perverse
21. Tho. p. yet not know my soul
22. He destroyeth p. and wicked
22:3. is it gain makest thy ways p.?
Ps. 37 : 37. Mark p. man, his end
64 : 4. may shoot in secret at p.
101 : 2. I will behave in a p. way
6. he that walketh in a p. way
119 : † 1. Blessed are p. in the way
139:22. I hate them with p. hatred
Pr. 2 : 21. the p. shall remain in it
4 : 18. path of just shineth unto p.
11: † 1. p. stone his delight [day
5. righteousness of p. sh. direct

Is. 26 : 3. wilt keep him in p. peace
Eze. 16 : 14. p. thro. my comeliness
27 : 3. hast said, I am of p. beauty
11. have made thy beauty p., 28 : 12.
28 : 15. wast p. in thy ways
Mat. 5 : 48. Be ye p. as Fa. is p.
19 : 21. If thou wilt be p. go sell
Lu. 1 : 3. having had p. underst-g
Jn. 17 : 23. may be made p. in one
Ac. 3 : 16. given him p. soundness
22 : 3. taught acc. to p. manner of
24 : 22. more p. knowl. of way⌊law
Ro. 12 : 2. what is p. will of God
1 Co. 2 : 6. wisdom am. them are p.
14 : † 20. in understanding be p.
2 Co. 12 : 9. strength p. in weakness
13 : 11. Be p. be of good comfort
Ga. 3 : 3. are ye made p. by flesh?
Ep. 4 : 13. till we come unto p. man
Ph. 3 : 12. Not as though already p.
15. as many as be p. thus minded
Col. 1 : 28. present ev. man p. in Ch.
4 : 12. may stand p. in will of God
2 Ti. 3 : 17. That man of God be p.
He. 2 : 10. make capt. of salvation p.
5 : 9. made p. he became Author
†14. meat belongeth to them p.
7 : 19. For law made nothing p. but
9 : 9. not make him did service p.
11. by greater and more p. tabern.
10 : 1. law can never make comers p.
11 : 40. without us not be made p.
12 : 23. spirits of just men made p.
13 : 21. G. make you p. in ev. good
Ja. 1 : 4. let patience have p. work,
that ye be p. and entire
17. Every good and p. gift is fr.
25. looketh into p. law of liberty
2 : 22. by works faith made p.
3 : 2. offend not in word, is p. man
1 Pe. 5 : 10. after suff-d, make you p.
1 Jn. 4 : 17. Herein is love made p.
18. but p. love casteth out fear;
He that feareth is not made p.
Re. 3 : 2. I not found thy works p.
See **Perfect HEART.**

Is PERFECT.

De. 32 : 4. is rock, his work i. p.
2 S. 22 : 31. his way i. p., Ps. 18 : 30.
Jb. 36 : 4. that i. p. in knowl., 37 : 16.
Ps. 19 : 7. law of the Lord i. p.
Is. 18 : 5. afore harvest, when bud i. p.
42 : 19. who blind as he that i. p.
Mat. 5 : 48. as Fa. in heaven i. p.
Lu. 6 : 40. ev. one i. p. be as master
1 Co. 13 : 10. when that i. p. is come

PERFECT. [Verb.] ⌈me

Ps. 138 : 8. L. will p. that concern-h
1 Th. 3 : 10. might p. that lacking in

PERFECTED. ⌊faith

2 Ch. 8 : 16. So house of G. was p.
24 : 13. and work was p. by them
Eze. 27 : 4. builders p. thy beauty
Mat. 21 : 16. of babes hast p. praise
Lu. 6 : † 40. one be p. as his master
13 : 32. third day I shall be p.
2 Ti. 3 : †17. That man of G. may be p.
He. 7 : †28. Son, who is p. for everm.
10 : 14. by one offering hath p. for ev.
1 Jn. 2 : 5. in him is love of G. p.
4 : 12. if love one ano., his love is p.

PERFECTING.

2 Co. 7 : 1. p. holiness in fear of G.
Ep. 4 : 12. For p. of the saints, for

PERFECTION, S.

2 Ch. 4 : † 21. tongs of p-s of gold
Jb. 11 : 7. canst find Almighty to p.?
15 : 29. nei. shall he prolong the p.
21 : †23. One dieth in strength of p.
28 : 3. he searcheth out all p. ⌈ty
Ps. 50 : 2. Out of Zion the p. of beau-
119 : 96. I have seen an end of p.
Is. 47 : 9. come upon thee in their p.
La. 2 : 15. city men call The p. of
Lu. 8 : 14. bring no fruit to p.⌊beauty
2 Co. 13 : 9. this we wish, your p.
He. 5 : †14. by reason of p. have senses

He. 6 : 1. let us go on unto p. ⌈hood
7 : 11. If p. were by Levit. priest-

PERFECTLY. ⌈p.

Je. 23 : 20. in latter days consider it
Mat. 14 : 36. as many as touched
were made p. whole
Ac. 18 : 26. expounded way more p.
23 : 15. ye wo. inquire more p., 20.
1 Co. 1 : 10. be p. joined together
1 Th. 5 : 2 yours. know p. that day
of Lord ⌈grace
1 Pe. 1 : † 13. hope p. to the end for

PERFECTNESS.

Col. 3 : 14. charity, wh. is bond of p.

PERFORM.

Ge. 26 : 3. I will p. oath I sware unto
Abraham, De. 9 : 5. Lu. 1 : 72.
Ex. 18 : 18. thou not able to p. it alone
Nu. 4 : 23. th. enter to p. service ⌈p.
De. 4 : 13. cov-t he comm-ded you to
23 : 23. That gone out of thy lips p.
25 : 5. p. duty of a husband's bro.
7. he not p. duty of husb.'s bro.
Ru. 3 : 13. if he p. part of kinsman
1 S. 3 : 12. that day I will p. ag. Eli
2 S. 14 : 15. king will p. the request
1 K. 6 : 12. then I will p. my word
12 : 15. that he might p. his saying,
2 Ch. 10 : 15. ⌈cov-t, 24. 2 Ch. 34 : 31
2 K. 23 : 3. to p. the words of this
Es. 5 : 8. if it please king to p. my
request let Haman come
Jb. 5 : 12. hands can-t p. enterprise
Ps. 21 : 11. device they not able to p.
61 : 8. that I may daily p. vows
119 : 106. sworn, and I will p. it
112. inclined my heart to p. stat-
Is. 9 : 7. zeal of L. will p. this ⌊utes
19 : 21. pay vow unto L. and p. it
44 : 28. Cyrus shall p. my pleasure
Je. 1 : 12. will hasten my word to p.
11 : 5. I may p. oath I have sworn
28 : 6. Lord p. words hast proph-d
29 : 10. will p. my good word, 33 : 14.
44 : 25. ye will surely p. your vows
Eze. 12 : 25. I will say word, p. it
Mi. 7 : 20. Thou wilt p. truth to Jac.
Na. 1 : 15. keep feasts, p. thy vows
Mat. 5 : 33. p. unto Lord thine oaths
Ro. 4 : 21. promised, he able to p.
7 : 8. how to p. that which is good
2 Co. 8 : 11. Now p. the doing of it
Ph. 1 : 6. he will p. it until day of J.

PERFORMANCE. ⌊C.

Lu. 1 : 45. sh. be a p. of those things
2 Co. 8 : 11. be a p. out of that ye

PERFORMED. ⌊have

1 S. 15 : 11. Saul not p. my com-ts
13. I have p. the com-t of the L.
2 S. 21 : 14. they p. all king com-ded
1 K. 8 : 20. Lord hath p. his word,
and I, 2 Ch. 6 : 10. Ne. 9 : 8. ⌈of king
Es. 1 : 15. Vashti hath not p. com-t
5 : 6. to half of kingdom be p., 7 : 2.
Ps. 65 : 1. unto thee shall vow be p.
Is. 10 : 12. when Lord hath p. work
Je. 23 : 20. till he p. thoughts, 30 : 24.
34 : 18. have not p. words of cov-t
35 : 14. words of Jonadab are p., 16.
51 : 29. ev. purpose of the L. be p.
Eze. 37 : 14. have p. it, saith L.
Lu. 1 : 20. until day things be p.
2 : 39. when they had p. all things
Ro. 15 : 28. When I have p. this, I

PERFORMETH. ⌈ise

Ne. 5 : 13. ev. man p. not this prom-
Jb. 23 : 14. he p. thing that is ap-
pointed for me ⌈for me
Ps. 57 : 2. I will cry to G. p. all things
Is. 44 : 26. p. counsel of messengers

PERFORMING.

Nu. 15 : 3. an offering in p. a vow, 8.

PERFUME, S.

Ex. 30 : 35. thou shalt make it p., 37.
Pr. 27 : 9. Ointment p. rejoice heart
Can. 5 : † 13. cheeks as towers of p-s
Is. 57 : 9. thou didst increase thy p-s

PERFUMED. ⌈myrrh

Pr. 7 : 17. I have p. my bed with
Can. 3 : 6. Who is this that cometh p.

PERFUMER.

Ex. 30 : †25. compound aft. art of p.

PER'GA. ⌈to P.

Ac. 13 : 13. Paul and company came
14. when they departed from P.
14 : 25. when had preached word in

PER'GAMOS. ⌊P.

Re. 1 : 11. send it to P. and Thyatira
2 : 12. to angel of church in P. write

PERHAPS. ⌈given

Ac. 8 : 22. if p. thy thought be for-
2 Co. 2 : 7. lest p. such be swall-d up
Phm. 15. p. he departed for season

PERI'DA = PERU'DA.

Ezr. 2 : † 55. chil. of P., Ne. 7 : † 57.

PERIL, S. ⌈lives

La. 5 : 9. gat our bread with p. of
Ro. 8 : 35. sh. famine, p. separate us
2 Co. 11 : 26. in p-s of waters, in p-s
by countrymen, in p-s in city

PERILOUS. ⌊(8)

2 Ti. 3 : 1. in the last days p. times

PERISH.

Ge. 41 : 36. land p. not thro. famine
Ex. 19 : 21. lest they gaze, and p.
21 : 26. if smite eye of maid, th. it p.
Nu. 17 : 12. we die, we p. we all p.
24 : 20. latter end that he p. for ev.
De. 11 : 17. lest ye p. quickly fr. land
26 : 5. A Syrian ready to p. my fa.
28 : 20. until thou p. quickly, 22.
Jos. 23 : 13. sh. be snares until ye p.
Ju. 5 : 31. let thine enemies p. O L.
1 S. 26 : 10. he into battle, and p.
Es. 3 : 13. cause to p. Jews, 7 : 4.
4 : 16. if I p. I p. | 8 : 11. p. all power
9 : 28. nor the memorial p. fr. seed
Jb. 3 : 3. Let the day p. I was born
4 : 9. By the blast of God they p.
20. they p. for ever, without any
6 : 18. paths go to nothing and p.
29 : 13. blessing of him ready to p.
31 : 19. If have seen any p. for want
Ps. 2 : 12. lest he be angry and ye p.
49 : 10. fool and brutish person p.
12. man is like beasts that p., 20.
68 : 2. as wax melteth, so let wicked p., 83 : 17. ⌈counten.
80 : 16. they p. at the rebuke of thy
146 : 4. very day his thoughts p.
Pr. 11 : 10. when wicked p., 28 : 28.
29 : 18. Where no vision, people p.
31 : 6. Give drink unto him ready
Ec. 5 : 14. riches p. by travail ⌊to p.
Is. 26 : 14. made their memory p.
27 : 13. wh. were ready to p. ⌈mirth
Je. 25 : † 10. will cause to p. voice of
27 : 10. drive you out, and ye p., 15.
40 : 15. that remnant in Jud. sho.
Eze. 25 : 7. I will cause thee to p. ⌊p.
Da. 2 : 18. that Dan. sho. not p. ⌈3 : 9.
Jon. 1 : 6. think upon us we p. not,
14. let us not p. for this man's life
Mat. 5 : 29. th. one of members p., 30.
8 : 25. L. save us, we p., Lu. 8 : 24.
9 : 17. wine runneth out, bottles p.
18 : 14. that one of little ones p.
Mk. 4 : 38. Master, carest not we p.
Lu. 13 : 33. th. prophet p. out of Je-
15 : 17. bread enough, and I p. ⌊rus.
Jn. 3 : 15. whoso. believeth not p., 16.
11 : 50. that whole nation p. not
Ac. 8 : 20. thy money p. with thee
13 : 41. ye despisers, wonder, and p.
1 Co. 1 : 18. preaching of the cross is
to them that p. foolishness ⌈p.
2 Co. 2 : 15. a savour of C. in them th.
4 : 16. tho. outward man p. inward
Col. 2 : 22. are to p. with the using
2 Th. 2 : 10. unright-n. in them th. p.
2 Pe. 3 : 9. not willing any sho. p.

Shall or shall not PERISH.

Le. 26 : 38. ye s. p. among heathen
Nu. 24 : 24. he also s. p. for ever

De. 4 : 26. ye s. soon utterly p., 8 : 19, 20.-30 : 18. Jos. 23 : 16.
1 S. 27 : 1. I s. one day p. by Saul
2 K. 9 : 8. whole house of Ahab s.p.
Jb. 8 : 13. hypocrite's hope s. p.
11 : † 20. flight s. p. from wicked
18 : 17. His remembra. s. p., 20:7.-
34:15. all flesh s. p. togeth. ⌊36:12.
Ps. 1 : 6. way of the ungodly s. p.
9 : 3. they s. p. at thy presence
18. expectation of poor s.n.p. ⌈p.
37:20. wicked s.p. 1 92:9. enemies s.
41 : 5. When s. he die, and name p.
73 : 27. they far from thee s. p.
102:26. They s.p. but thou endure
112 : 10. desire of the wicked s. p.
Pr. 10 : 28. expecta. of wicked s. p.,
19:9. that speaketh lies s. p. ⌊11:7.
21 : 28. A false witness s. p. but
Is. 29 : 14. wisdom of wise men s. p.
41 : 11. that strive with thee s. p.
60 : 12. kingd. not serve thee s. p.
Je. 4 : 9. the heart of the king s. p.
6:21. neighbour and his friend s.p.
10 : 11. The gods s. p., 15.-51 : 18.
18:18. land s.n.p. from the priest
25:†35. flight s.p. from shepherds
48 : 8. valley also s. p. and plain
Eze. 7 : 26. law s. p. from priest
Am. 1 : 8. remnant of Philis. s. p.
2 : 14. Thf. flight s. p. from swift
3 : 15. the houses of ivory s. p.
Zch. 9 : 5. king s. p. from Gaza
Mat. 26:52. take sword s.p. with sw.
Lu. 5 : 37. wine spilled, bottles s. p.
8 : 24. Master, master, we p.
13 : 3. exc. ye repent ye s. all p., 5.
21:18. s.n. an hair of your head p.
Jn. 10:28. s. never p. nor any pluck
Ro. 2 : 12. sinned, s. p. without law
1 Co. 8:11. s. weak brother p. for wh.
He. 1 : 11. they s. p. thou remain-t
2 Pe. 2 : 12. s. p. in own corruption

PERISHED.

Nu. 16:33. they p. from the congr-n
21 : 30. Heshbon is p. unto Dibon
Jos. 22 : 20. that man p. not alone
2 S. 1 : 27. How weapons of war p.
Jb. 4 : 7. whoever p. being innocent
30 : 2. me, in whom old age was p.
Ps. 9 : 6. their memorial is p. ⌈land
10 : 16. heathen are p. out of his
83 : 10. Sisera, Jabin, p. at Endor
119 : 92. I should have p. in afflic.
142 : † 4. refuge p. fr. me, no man
Ec. 9 : 6. their love and envy is p.
Je. 7:28. truth is p. from their mouth
48 : 36. riches he hath gott. are p.
49 : 7. is counsel p. from prudent?
La. 3:18. My strength and hope is p.
Jo. 1 : 11. bec harvest of field is p.
Jon. 4 : 10. came up and p. in night
Mi. 4:9. why cry? is counsellor p.?
7 : 2. good man is p. out of earth
Mat. 8:32. herd of swine p. in waters
Lu. 11 : 51. p. betw. altar and temp.
Ac. 5:37. he p. and many as obeyed
1 Co. 15:18. fallen asleep in C. are p.
He. 11 : 31. the harlot Rahab p. not
2 Pe. 3 : 6. world being overfl-d p.
Jude 11. p. in gainsaying of Core

PERISHETH.

Jb. 4:11. old lion p. for lack of prey
Ps. 31 : † 12. I am like a vessel th. p.
Pr. 11:7. the hope of unjust men p.
Ec. 7:15. there is a just man that p.
Is. 57 : 1. righteous p. and no man
Je. 9 : 12. land p. and is burned up
48 : 46. the people of Chemosh p.
Jn. 6:27. Labour not for meat wh. p.
Ja. 1 : 11. grace of fashion of it p.
1 Pe. 1:7. more precious than of gold

PERISHING. ⌊th. p.

Jb. 33 : 18. his life from p. by sword

PER'IZZITE.

Ge. 13:7. P. dwelled then in the land
Ex. 33 : 2. I will drive out P., 34:11.
Jos. 9 : 1. when P. and Hivite heard
11:3. Jabin sent to P. and Jebusite

PER'IZZITES.

Ge. 15 : 20. I have given unto thy seed the land of the P., Ex. 3 : 8, 17.-23 : 23. De. 7 : 1.-20 : 17.- Jos. 3:10.-12:8.-24 : 11. 1 K. 9 : 20. Ne. 9 : 8.
34 : 30. to make me to stink am. P.
Jos. 17 : 15. cut down wood in land
Ju. 1:4. L. delivered P. into, 5. ⌊of P.
3 : 5. chil. of Israel dwelt among P.
2 Ch. 8 : 7. Sol. made P. pay tribute
Ezr. 9 : 1. acc. to abominations of P.

PERJURED.

1 Ti. 1:10. law is for liars and p. per- ⌊sons

PERMISSION.

1 Co. 7 : 6. I speak this by p. not by ⌊com-t

PERMIT, TED.

Ac. 26:1. Thou art p-d to speak for
1 Co. 14:34. not p-d women to speak
16 : 7. I trust to tarry if Lord p.
He. 6 : 3. this will we do, if God p.

PERNICIOUS.

2 Pe. 2 : 2. many sh. follow their p.

PERPETUAL. ⌊ways

Ge. 9 : 12. covenant for p. generat-s
Ex. 29 : 9. priest's office for p. stat-
30 : 8. a p. incense before L. ⌊ute
31 : 16. keep sabbath for p. cov-t
Le. 3 : 17. p. statute not to eat fat
6 : 20. a p. meat offering for Aaron
24:9. off-gs of L. made by p. statute
25:34. not be sold, it is p. possess-n
Nu. 19:21. p. statute, he th. sprink-h
Ps. 9 : 6. destructions to a p. end
78 : 66. he put them to p. reproach
Je. 5 : 22. p. decree, th. it can-t pass
8:5. Why peo. slidden by p. back-
15:18. Why is my pain p. ⌊sliding?
18:16. To make their land p. hissing
23 : 40. bring upon you p. shame
49:13. the cities shall be p. wastes
50 : 5. let us join L. in p. covenant
51 : 39. may sleep a p. sleep, 57.
Eze. 25:†15. destroy it with p. hatred
35 : 5. Bec. hast had a p. hatred
46 : 14. by a p. ordinance unto L.
Ha. 3 : 6. and the p. hills did bow
Zph. 2 : 9. Moab sh. be p. desolation
See DESOLATIONS.

PERPETUALLY. ⌈7:16.

1 K. 9:3. my heart be there p., 2 Ch.
Am. 1 : 11. his anger did tear p. and

PERPLEXED.

Es. 3 : 15. the city Shushan was p.
Jo. 1 : 18. the herds of cattle are p.
Lu. 9 : 7. Herod p. bec. it was said
24 : 4. as women were p., behold 2
2 Co. 4 : 8. we p. but not in despair
Ga. 4 : † 20. I am p. for you

PERPLEXITY.

Is. 22 : 5. it is a day of p. by L. G.
Mi. 7 : 4. day cometh, now their p.
Lu. 21:25. distress of nations, with p.

PERSECUTE.

Jb. 19 : 22. why do ye p. me as God
28. Why p. him, seeing root in me
Ps. 7 : 1. save me from them p. me
5. Let the enemy p. my soul, and
10 : 2. The wicked doth p. the poor
31 : 15. deliver me fr. them p. me
35 : 3. stop the way ag. them p. me
6. let angel of the L. p. them ⌈ten
69:26. they p. him thou hast smit-
71:11. p. take him, is none to deliv.
83:15. so p. them with thy tempest
119:84. execute judgm-t on them p.
86. they p. me wrongfully ⌊me
Je. 17 : 18. Let th. be confounded p.
29:18. I will p. them wi. sword ⌊me
La. 3 : 66. p. and destroy in anger
Mat. 5:11. blessed when men p. you
44. pray for them which p. you
10 : 23. when they p. you in 1 city
23 : 34. p. them from city to city
Lu. 11:49. some they shall p., 21:12.
Jn. 5 : 16. thf. did Jews p. Jesus
15 : 20. if me, they will also p. you
Ro. 12 : 14. Bless them wh. p. you

PERSECUTED.

De. 30:7. put curses on them p. thee
Ps. 109 : 16. because he p. the poor
119:161. Princes p. me with-t cause
143:3. enemy hath p. my soul
Is. 14 : 6. he th. ruled in anger is p.
La. 3 : 43. thou hast wi. anger p. us
Mat. 5 : 10. wh. are p. for righte-n.
12. so p. they prophets bef. you
Jn. 15:20. If they p. me, will you ⌈p.
Ac. 7:52. Wh. prophets have not fa-s
22:4. I p. this way unto the death
26 : 11. I p. th. unto strange cities
1 Co. 4 : 12. being p. we suffer it
15 : 9. I p. church of G., Ga. 1 : 13.
2 Co. 4 : 9. we are p. but not forsak.
Ga. 1 : 23. wh. p. us in times past
4 : 29. he born after flesh p. him
1 Th. 2 : 15. who killed L. and p. us
Re. 12 : 13. dragon p. woman that

PERSECUTEST, ING.

Ac. 9 : 4. Saul, Saul, why p t thou me? 22 : 7.-26 : 14. ⌈8.-26 : 15.
5. I am Jesus whom thou p-t, 22:
Ph. 3:6. Concerning zeal, p-g church

PERSECUTION, S.

La. 5 : 5. Our necks are under p.
Mat. 13:21. when p. ariseth, Mk. 4:17.
Mk. 10:30. shall have lands with p-s
Ac. 8 : 1. was great p. ag. church
11:19. wh. were scattered upon p.
13:50. raised p. ag. Paul and Barna.
Ro. 8:35. shall p. separate us fr. C.?
2 Co. 12 : 10. I take pleasure in p-s
Ga. 5 : 11. why do I yet suffer p.?
6 : 12. lest they suffer p. for cross
2 Th. 1 : 4. your faith in all your p-s
2 Ti. 3:11. thou hast known my p-s at Antioch, what p-s I endured
12. all that live godly shall suffer

PERSECUTOR. ⌊p.

1 Ti. 1 : 13. Who was before a p.

PERSECUTORS. ⌈deeps

Ne. 9 : 11. p. thou threwest into
Ps. 7 : 13. he ordaineth arrows ag. p.
119:157. Many are my p. and ene-
142 : 6. deliver me from p. ⌊mies
Je. 15:15. O L. revenge me of my p.
20 : 11. thf. my p. shall stumble
La. 1 : 3. all her p. overtook her
4:19. Our p. are swifter than eagles

PERSEVERANCE.

Ep. 6 : 18. and watching with all p.

PER'SIA. ⌈of P.

2 Ch. 36 : 20. until reign of kingdom
Eze. 27:10. They of P. and Lud were
38 : 5. P. Ethiopia, Libya, with th.
Da. 10:13. prince of P. withstood me
21 days; I remained wi. k-s of P.
20. to fight with the prince of P.
11 : 2. shall stand up yet 3 kings
See KING, MEDIA. ⌊in P.

PER'SIAN.

Ne. 12 : 22. to reign of Darius the P.
Da. 6:28. in the reign of Cyrus the P.

PERSIANS. See MEDES.

PER'SIS.

Ro. 16 : 12. Salute P. wh. laboured much in the Lord

PERSON.

Ge 39:6. Joseph was goodly p. ⌈eat
Ex. 12:48. no uncircumcised p. sh.
Le. 19 : 15. nor honour p. of mighty
Nu. 5:6. any sin and that p. be guilty
19:17. unclean p. sh. take of ashes
18. clean p. shall take hyssop and
22. whatso. unclean p. toucheth
31 : 19. whosoever hath killed any p., 35 : 11, 15, 30. Jos. 20 : 3, 9.
35 : 30. one witness not testify ag. any p. to cause him to die
De. 15:22. uncl. and clean p. sh. eat
27 : 25. reward to slay innocent p.
28 : 50. not regard p. of old or y-g

1 S. 9 : 2. not a goodlier p. than he
16 : 18. son of Jesse a comely p.
2 S. 4 : 11. have slain a righteous p.
14:14. nei. doth God respect any p.
17:11. go to battle in thine own p.
Jb.22:29. he sh. save the humble p.
Ps. 15 : 4. a vile p. is contemned
49 : 10. fool and brutish p. perish
101 : 4. I will not know wicked p.
105 : 37. not feeble p. am. tribes
Pr. 6 : 12. naughty p. walks with
24 : 8. be called mischievous p.
28 : 17. violence to blood of any p.
Is. 32 : 5. vile p. no more called lib-
6. vile p. will speak villany ⌊eral
43:†4. I will give people for thy p.
Je. 43 : 6. Johanan took ev. p. left
52:25.took seven near the king's p
Eze. 16 : 5. to loathing of thy p.
33 : 6. if sword take any p. am. th.
44 : 25. priests come at no dead p.
Da. 11 : 21. shall stand up a vile p.
Mat. 22:16. regardest not p. of men,
Mk. 12 : 14. ⌈this just p.
27 : 24. I am innocent of blood of
1 Co. 5 : 13. put aw. that wicked p.
2 Co.2:10.forgave I it in the p.of C.
Ep.5:5.nor unclean p. hath inherit.
He. 1: 3. the express image of his p.
12 : 16. or profane p. as Esau, who
2 Pe.2:5.but saved Noah,the eighth

PERSONS. ⌊p.
Ge. 14 : 21. Give me p. and take the
36 : 6. all p. of his house ⌊goods
Ex. 16:16. Gather acc. to number of
Le. 27 : 2. p. shall be for the L. ⌊p.
Nu. 19:18. shall sprinkle it upon p.
31:28. both of the p. beeves, asses
30. one portion of 50, of the p. of
35. 32,000 p. in all, of women
40. And the p. were 16,000, 46.
of which L.'s tribute was 32 p.
De. 10:17. God,wh. regardeth not p.
22. fa-s went into E with 70 p.
Ju. 9 : 2. sons of Jeruh. were 70 p.
4. Ahim. hired vain and light p.
5. Ahim. slew breth. 70 p.,18. ⌈p.
20:39. Benj. began to kill of Isr. 30
1 S. 9 : 22. those hidden about 30 p.
22:18. Doeg slew on that day 85 p.
22. occasioned death of all the p.
2 K. 10 : 6. king's sons being 70 p.
7. took king's sons and slew 70 p.
Ps.26:4. I have not sat with vain p.
Pr. 12 : 11. followeth vain p., 28:19.
Je. 52 : 29. carried fr. Jerus. 832 p.
30. carried captive of Jews 745 p.
La. 4:16. respected not p. of priests
Eze. 7 : † 11. of their tumultuous p.
17 : 17. forts to cut off many p.
27 : 13. they traded the p. of men
Jon. 4:11. are more than 120,000 p.
Zph. 3 : 4. Her prophets treach-s p.
Mal. 1 : 9. will he regard your p.?
Lu. 15 : 7. than over 99 just p.
Ac. 10 : 34. G. is no respecter of p.
17:17. Paul disputed wi. devout p.
2 Co. 1 : 11. gift on us by many p.
1 Ti. 1 : 10. law is for perjured p.
2 Pe.3:11. what manner of p. ought
Jude 16.having men's p.in admira.
See ACCEPT, ED, EST, ETH.
See RESPECT. [Noun, Verb]

PERSUADE.
Ge. 9 :† 27. God shall p.Japhet, and
1 K. 22 : 20. Who sh. p. Ahab to go
21.spirit bef. L.said, I will p.him
22.Thou shalt p. him and prevail
2 Ch.32:11.Doth not Hez.p.you,15.
Is. 36 : 18. Beware, lest Hez. p. you
Mat. 28 : 14. we will p. him and secure you ⌈p. men?
2 Co.5:11. we p. men | Ga.1:10.do I
1 Jn. 3:† 19. shall p. our hearts bef.

PERSUADED. ⌊him
2 Ch. 18 : 2. Ahab p. Jehoshaphat
Pr. 25:15. By forbearing is prince p.
Mat. 27 : 20. chief priests p. multi.
Lu. 16 : 31. will not be p. if one rose
20 : 6. they be p. Jn. was prophet
Ac. 13 : 43. p. them to continue in
14 : 19. p. the people and having
18:4. Paul p. the Jews and Greeks
19:26.this Paul hath p. much peo.
21 : 14. when he would not be p.
26:26.I am p. none of these things
Ro. 4 : 21. p. what he had promised
8:38.I am p. noth. can separate us
14 : 5. Let every man be fully p.
14.I am p. there is noth. unclean
15 : 14. I myself also am p. of you
2 Ti. 1 : 5. and I am p. that in thee
12.I am p.that he is able to keep
He. 6 : 9. are p. better things of you
11:13.having seen afar off, were p.

PERSUADEST, ETH, ING.
2 K. 18 : 32. when Hezekiah p-h you
Ac. 18:13. Paul p-h men to worship
19:8. p-g things conc. kingd. of G.
26 : 28. Almost p-t me to be Chris.
28:23. p-g them conc. Jesus fr.law

PERSUASIBLE.
1 Co. 2 : † 4. preaching not with p.

PERSUASION. ⌊words
Ga. 5 : 8. This p. cometh not of him

PERTAIN. ⌈21.
Le. 7 : 20. peace offerings p.unto L.,
1 S.25:22.if I leave all that p.to him
Ro. 15 : 17. things which p. to God
1 Co. 6 : 3. things th. p. to this life
2 Pe.1:3.all things that p. unto life

PERTAINED.
Nu.31:43. half that p.unto congr-n
Jos. 24 : 33. buried in a hill that p.
Ju.6:11. an oak that p. unto Joash
1 S. 25:21. of all that p. unto Nabal
2 S. 2 : 15. which p. to Ish-bosheth
9 : 9. master's son all p. to Saul
16:4. thine are all p.unto Mephib.
1 K.4:10.to son of Hesed p. Sochoh
7:48.Sol. made vessels that p.unto
24 : 7. all that p. to king of E. ⌈p.
1 Ch. 9 : 27. opening ev. morning
2 Ch. 12:4.took cities wh. p.to Jud.
34:33. took away abom-s p. to Isr.

PERTAINETH. ⌈ing
Le. 14:32. get that wh. p. to cleans-
Nu. 4 : 16. to office of Eleazar p. oil
De. 22 : 5. woman not wear what p.
1 S. 27 : 6. Ziklag p. to kings of Jud.
2 S.6:12. of Obed-e. and all p. unto
Ro. 9 : 4. to whom p. the adoption
He. 7 : 13. he p. to another tribe

PERTAINING.
Jos. 13:31. half Gilead p. to Machir
1 Ch. 26 : 32. for ev.matter p.to God
Ac. 1 : 3. things p. to kingd. of God
Ro. 4 : 1. Ab. our fa. as p. to flesh
1 Co.6:4.of things p. to this life ⌈G.
He.2:17. High priest in things p. to
5 : 1. ordained in things p. to God
9:9. not perfect, as p. to conscien.

PERU'DA.
See PERIDA.

PERVERSE.
Nu. 22 : 32. thy way is p. before me
De. 32 : 5. they are a p. generation
1 S. 20 : 30. Thou son of p. woman
Jb. 6:30. my taste discern p. things
9:20. my mouth shall prove me p.
Pr. 4 : 24. p. lips put far from thee
8:8. nothing froward or p. in them
12 : 8. he of a p. heart be despised
14 : 2. he that is p. despiseth him
17:20.that hath a p.tongue faileth
19 : 1. than he th. is p. in his lips
23 : 33. thine heart utter p. things
28 : 6. than he that is p. in ways
18. he p. in his ways shall fall
Is. 19 : 14. L. hath mingled p. spirit
Mat.17:17.O p. generation, Lu.9:41.
Ac. 20 : 30. men speaking p. things
Ph. 2 : 15. blameless in a p. nation
1 Ti. 6 : 5. p. disputings of men of

PERVERSELY.
2 S.19 : 19. neither remember that
which thy servant did p.
1 K. 8 : 47. We have done p.
Ps. 119 : 78. they dealt p. with me

PERVERSENESS.
Nu. 23 : 21. nei. hath seen p. in Isr.
Pr. 4 : † 24. Put from thee p. of lips
11:3. p.of transgressors sh.destroy
15 : 4. p. is a breach in the spirit
Is. 19 : † 14. L. mingled spirit of p.
30 : 12. ye trust in p. and stay
59:3.your tongue hath muttered p.
Eze. 9 : 9. land full of blood, city of

PERVERT. ⌊p.
De. 16 : 19. a gift doth p. words of
24:17. Thou shalt not p. judgment
Jb. 8 : 3. Doth God p. judgment or
34 : 12. nei. will Alm. p. judgment
Pr. 17 : 23. to p. ways of judgment
31 : 5. to p. judgment of afflicted
Mi. 3 : 9. Hear this, ye th. p. equity
Ac. 13 : 10. wilt not cease to p. right
Ga. 1 : 7. would p. gospel of C.⌊ways

PERVERTED.
1 S. 8:3. Samuel's sons p. judgment
Jb. 33 : 27. I have p. what is right
Is. 47 : 10. thy wisdom, it hath p.
Je. 3 : 21. they have p. their way
23 : 36. ye have p. the words of G.
Eze. 21 : † 27. p.p.p. will I make it

PERVERTETH.
Ex. 23 : 8. the gift p. the righteous
De.27:19.Cursed be he th.p. judgm.
Pr.10:9. p. his ways shall be known
19 : 3. foolishness of a man p. way
Is. 24 : † 1. L. p. face of the earth
Lu.23:14.man as one that p. people

PERVERTING. ⌈ment
Ec. 5 : 8. if seest violent p. of judg-
Am: 8 :† 5. p. the balances of deceit
Lu. 23 : 2. found this fellow p. na-

PESTILENCE, S. ⌊tion
Ex. 5 : 3. lest he fall on us with p.
9:15.that I may smite thee with p.
Le. 26 : 25. I will send p. am. you
Nu. 14 : 12. I will smite them wi. p.
De. 28 : 21. L. shall make p. cleave
2 S. 24 : 13. there be three days' p.,
1 Ch. 21 : 12. ⌈rael, 1 Ch.21:14.
15. the Lord sent a p. upon Is-
1 K.8:37.if there be in land famine,
p., 2 Ch. 6 : 28.-7 : 13.-20 : 9.
Ps. 78 : 50. gave their life over to p.
91:3. deliver thee from noisome p.
6. Nor for p. walketh in darkness
Je. 14 : 12. I will consume them by
p., 24 : 10.-27 : 8. ⌈by p.
21 : 6. inhab-ts of this city sh. die
7. I will deliver Zedekiah from p.
9. abideth in city die by p., 38:2.
27 : 13. Why will ye die by p.? ⌈p.
28:8. prophets of old prophesied of
29 : 17. I will send upon them p.
18. I will persecute them with p.
32 : 24. city is given bec. of p., 36.
34 : 17. a liberty for you to the p.
42:17.that go to E.sh.die by p.,22.
44:13. have punished Jerus. by p.
Eze. 5 : 12. third part die with p.
17. p. and blood pass thro. thee
6:11. they sh. fall by sword,and p.
12. He that is far off sh. die by p.
7 : 15. a sword without, p. within
12 : 16. I will leave few men fr. p.
14:19. if I send a p. into that land
21. when I send p. to cut off man
28:23. I will send to her p. and bl.
33 : 27. in caves shall die of the p.
38:22. I will plead ag. him with p.
Am. 4 : 10. I have sent am. you p.
Ha. 3 : 5. Before him went the p.
Mat. 24:7. there shall be p-s,Lu.21:

PESTILENT. ⌊11.
Ac. 24:5. found this man a p.fellow

PESTLE.
Pr. 27 : 22. bray a fool with a p.

PE'TER. [house
Mat. 8:14. Jes. was come into P.'s
14:28. P. answered, 15:15.-17:4.-
19:27. Mk. 8:29. [of the ship
29. when P. was come down out
16:18. I say to thee that thou art P.
22. P. began to rebuke him, Mk. 8:
32. [me, Mk. 8:33.
23. he said to P. Get thee behind
17:24. that received tribute money
came to P. [ers
26. P. saith unto him, Of strang-
18:21. P. said, L. how oft shall my
bro. sin ag. me [Mk. 14:29.
26:33. P. said, Tho. all offended,
35. P. said, Though I should die
37. took P. and 2 sons of Zebedee, Lu. 9:28. [37.
40. P. could ye not watch, Mk. 14:
58. P. followed him to palace
69. P. sat without in palace
73. and said to P., Surely thou art
one of them, Mk. 14:70.
75. P. remembered words of Jesus
Mk. 8:29. P. answereth, Thou art C.,
Lu. 9:20. [Lu. 9:33.
9:5. P. ans-d, it is good to be here,
10:28. P. began to say, L. we have
left all, Lu. 18:28. [Master
11:21. P. calling to remem. saith,
14:54. P. followed afar off, Lu. 22:54.
66. as P. was in palace one of maids
67. P. warming hims., Jn. 18:18.
72. P. called to mind word Jesus
16:7. go tell his disciples and P.
Lu. 8:45. Who touched me? P. said
9:32. P. and they heavy with sleep
12:41. P. said, speakest this parable
22:34. I tell thee, P. the cock sh.
55. P. sat down among them
60. P. said, Man, I know not
61. L. turned and looked upon P.
62. P. went out wept bitterly
24:12. arose P. and ran unto sepul.
Jn. 1:†42. shalt be called P., A stone
44. the city of Andrew and P.
13:8. P. saith, Thou shalt nev. wash
37. P. saith, why can-t I follow
18:11. Jes. unto P. Put up sword
16. P. stood at door without (2)
17. damsel unto P. Art not thou 1
26. his kinsman, whose ear P. cut
27. P. then denied again
20:3. P. and other disci. to sepul.
4. other disciple did outrun P.
21:17. P. was grieved bec. he said
20. P. seeth disciple Jes. loved [do
21. P. saith. L. what sh. this man
Ac. 1:15. in those days P. stood up
2:14. P. standing up wi. the eleven
37. said unto P. what shall we do
38. P. said, Repent and be baptiz.
3:6. P. said, Silver and gold none
12. P. saw it he ans-d, Ye men of
4:8. P. filled with the Holy Ghost
19. P. and Jn. ans-d, Whe. it right
5:3. P. said, Ananias why [9.
8. P. ans-d, Tell me whe. ye sold,
15. at least the shadow of P. might
29. P. said, We ought to obey God
8:20. P. said, Thy money perish
9:32. P. passed thro-t all quarters
34. P. said, Jes. C. maketh whole
38. disci. had heard P. was there,
40. P. said, Tabitha, arise (2) [39.
10:9. P. went to housetop to pray
13. voice, Rise, P. kill and eat, 11:7.
14. P. said, Not so L. I have nev.
17. while P. doubted | 19, 21, 23.
25. P. coming, Cornelius met him
26. P. took him up saying, Stand,
44. while P. spake these words [34.
45. astonished, as many as wi. P.
46. ans-d P. Can any forbid wat
11:2. when P. was come to Jerus.,
12:3. he proceeded to take P. [4.
5. P. theref. was kept in prison
Ac. 12:6. P. sleeping betw. 2 soldiers
7. angel smote P. on the side | 11.
13. as P. knocked at door of gate
14. when she knew P.'s voice (2)
16. P. continued knocking [of P.
18. no small stir what was become
15:7. been much disputing P. rose
Ga. 1:18. I went to Jerus. to see P.
2:7. gospel of circumc. committed
8. wrought effectually in P. [to P.
11. when P. was come to Antioch
14. I said unto P. before them all
1 Pe. 1:1. P. an apostle of Jesus C.
See JAMES, JOHN.

Simon PETER.
Mat. 4:18. Jesus saw S. called P.
10:2. the first S. who is called P.
16:16. S. P. ans-d, Thou art the C.
Mk. 3:16. S. he surnamed P. [knees
Lu. 5:8. S. P. fell down at Jesus'
6:14. chose S. wh. he named P.
Jn. 1:40. One was Andrew S. P.'s
bro., 6:8. [shall we go
6:68. S. P. ans-d, Lord, to whom
13:6. then cometh he to S. P.
9. S. P. saith, L. not my feet only
24. S. P. beckoned that he sho. ask
36. S. P. said, L. whi. goest thou?
18:10. S. P. having sword drew it
15. S. P. foll-d Jes. and so did ano.
25. S. P. stood and warmed hims.
20:2. Then she runneth to S. P.
6. Then S. P. went into sepulchre
21:2. were together S. P. and Thos.
3. S. P. saith, I go a fishing
7. when S. P. heard it was the L.
11. S. P. drew net to land full
15. Jes. saith to S. P. Simon son
Ac. 10:5. call for one S. whose surname is P., 18, 32.-11:13.
2 Pe. 1:1. S. P. a serv. and apostle

PETHAHI'AH.
1 Ch. 24:16. the 19th lot came to P.
Ezr. 10:23. of the Levites P.
Ne. 9:5. then P. said, Stand up
11:24. And P. son of Meshezabeel

PE'THOR. [to P.
Nu. 22:5. messengers unto Balaam
De. 23:4. hired ag. thee Balaam of P.

PETHU'EL.
Jo. 1:1. word came to Joel son of P.

PETITION, S.
1 S. 1:17. God grant thee thy **p.**
27. Lord hath given me my **p.**
†28. he whom I obtained by **p.**
2:†20. L. give seed, for **p.** she asked
1 K. 2:16. I ask one **p.** deny me not
20. I desire one small **p.** of thee
Es. 5:6. What is thy **p.**? 7:2.-9:12.
7. Then Esther said, My **p.** is [**p.**
8. if it please the king to grant my
7:3. let my life be given at my **p.**
Ps. 20:5. the Lord fulfil all thy **p-s**
Is. 7:†11. ask sign, make **p.** deep
Da. 6:7. whoso. ask **p.** of any god, 12.
13. maketh his **p.** 3 times a day
1 Jn. 5:15. have the **p-s** we desired

PE'TRA.
Is. 16:†1. ruler of land from P. to

PEUL'THAI. [the 8th
1 Ch. 26:5. sons of Obed-edom, P.

PHA'LEC = PELEG.
Lu. 3:35. was son of P., Ge. 11:†16.

PHAL'LU = PAL'LU.
Ex. 46:9. sons of Reuben, P. Hezron

PHAL'TI = PHAL'TIEL.
1 S. 25:44†. Saul given Michal to P.
2 S. 3:15†. Ish-bosheth took her fr.

PHANU'EL. [P.
Lu. 2:36. Anna prophetess dau. of P.

PHA'RAOH.
Ge. 12:15. commended Sarai bef. P.
17. L. plagued P. and his house
18. P. called Ab. What is this
20. P. com-ded his men conc. Ab.
37:36. sold him unto Potiphar an
officer of P.'s, 39:1.
Ge. 40:2. P. was wroth ag. two of his
7. Jo. asked P.'s officers [(8), 13.
11. And P.'s cup was in my hand
13. P. shall lift up thine head, 19.
14. make mention of me unto P.
17. all manner of bakemeats for P.
20. P.'s birthday he made a feast
41:1. P. dreamed | 4. P. awoke, 7.
8. P. told magicians his dream (2)
9. spake chief butler unto P.
10. P. was wroth with his servants
14. P. called Joseph they bro-t him
16. God sh. give P. answer of peace
25. Jo. said unto P. dream is one
28. What G. do sheweth unto P.
32. dream was doubled unto P. [(2)
33. let P. look out a man wise
34. Let P. do this, appoint officers
35. lay up corn under hand of P.
37. thing was good in eyes of P. |
38, 39, 41, 45. [man lift hand
44. I am P., without thee sh. no
55. people cried to P. for bread (2)
42:15. By life of P. ye sh. not go
44:18. thou art even as P.
45:2. Joseph wept; hou. of P. heard
8. he hath made me a father to P.
16. it pleased P. well (2) [brethren
17. P. unto Joseph, Say to thy
21. gave wagons acc. to com-t of P.
46:5. carried Jac. in wagons P. sent
31. Joseph said, I will shew P. [pa.
33. when P. sh. say What occu-
47:1. Joseph told P. My fa. and
brethren | 2, 3, 4, 5, 7, 11, 14, 19.
8. P. said to Jac. How old art, 9.
10. Jac. blessed P. went from P.
20 Joseph bought all E. for P., 23.
22. priests had portion assigned of
24. ye sh. give 5th part unto P. [P.
25. and we will be P.'s servants
26. land of priests became not P.
50:4. speak, I pray you, in ears of P
6. P. said, Go bury thy father, 7.
Ex. 1:†11. built for P. treasure cities
22. P. charged people, Ev. son | 19.
2:5. dau. of P. to wash | 7, 8, 9, 10.
15. P. sought to slay Moses (2)
3:10. I will send thee unto P., 11.
4:21. do those wonders bef. P. | 22.
5:1. Mo. told P. Let my peo. go
2. P. said, Who is L. I sho. obey
5. P. said, The people are many
6. P. com-ded the taskmasters, 14.
10. saith P., I will not give straw
15. officers cried unto P. [| 20.
21. savour abhorred in eyes of P.
23. since I came to P. to speak
6:1. Now see what I will do to P.
11. speak unto P., 13, 27.-9:1.-
12. how sh. P. hear me? 30. [10:1.
7:1. I have made thee a god to P.
2. Aa. thy bro. shall speak unto P.
4. P. sh. not hearken unto you
7. Mo. 80 y-rs old spake unto P.
9. P. saying shew miracle, say
unto Aa., Take rod (2), 10.
11. Then P. called the sorcerers
15. Get thee unto P. in morning
20. he smote waters in sight of P.
23. P. turned went into his house
8:1. Go unto P. say, Let my peo.
8. P. called for Mo. said, Entreat
the L., 25.-9:27.-10:16:24.
9. Mo. said unto P. Glory ov. me
12. Mo. and Aa. went out from P.,
30.-9:33.-10:6, 18. [ed
15. P. saw was respite he harden-
19. magicians said unto P. This
8:20. stand before P., 9:13. [is G.
24. swarm of flies in house of P.,
25. P. said, I will let you go [31.
29. let not P. deal deceitfully
9:8. sprinkled it in sight of P., 10.
34. when P. saw thunders ceased
10:7. P.'s servants said, 9:20. [8, 28.
11. they were driven fr. P.'s pres.,

Ex.11:1.bring 1 plague more upon P
5. firstborn die fr. firstborn of P.
8. Mo. went fr. P. in great anger
9. L. said, P. shall not hearken
10.did all these wonders before P.
12:29. fr. firstborn of P. on throne
30.P. arose in night, gr. cry in E.
13:15. P. would hardly let us go.
17. when P. let people go G. led
14:3. P. say, They are entangled
4. I will be honoured upon P.,17,
5. heart of P. was turned ⌊18.
9. horses and chariots of P., 10,
23, 28.-15:4, 19.
28. waters covered host of P.
18:4. delivered me fr. P., 8, 10. ⌈E.
De.6:21. We were P.'s bondmen in
22.L.shewed wonders upon P.,Ne.
7:8. L. redeemed you from P.⌊9:10.
18. shalt remember what L. did
unto P., 11:3.-29:2.-34:11.
1 S.2:27. when in E. in P.'s house
1 K.3:1. Sol. took P.'s daughter(2)
7:8. Solomon made house for P.'s
dau., 9:24. 1 Ch. 8:11. ⌈It
9:16. P.had taken Gezer and burnt
11:1. Solomon loved dau. of P.⌈18.
19. Hadad favour in sight of P.,
20.Genubath in P.'s household(3)
21.Hadad to P. Let me depart,22.
2 K.17:7. Lord brought them from
under hand of P. ⌈Is. 36:6.
18:21. so is P. to all trust in him,
23:35. according to com-t of P.
1 Ch. 4:18. Bithiah dau. of P.
Ps.135:9.Who sent wonders upon P.
136:15. overthrew P. in Red sea
Can.1:9. to a company of horses in
P.'s chariots ⌈of wise
Is. 19:11. how say unto P. I am son
30:2. strengthen in strength of P.
3. strength of P. be your shame
Je.25:19. I made P. drink ⌈E., 7.
37:5. P.'s army was come out of
37:11. brok. for fear of P.'s army
43:9. P.'s house in Tahpanhes
46:17. P. king of E. is but a noise
25. I will punish the mult. of P.
47:1. word before P. smote Gaza
Eze.17:17. Nei. sh. P. make for him
29:2. set thy face ag. P. king of E.
3.I am ag.thee,P.king of E.,30:22.
30:21. broken arm of P., 24, 25.
31:2. Son of man speak unto P.
31:18.This is P. and his multitude
32:2. take up a lamentation for P.
31. P. sh. be comforted, 32. ⌈P.
Ac.7:10. Joseph favour in sight of
13. kindred made known unto P.
21.P.'s daughter took him up and
Ro.9:17. for Scripture saith unto P.
He.11:24.to be called son of P.'s dau
See JOSEPH, HARDEN, ED.

PHA'RAOH-HOPH'RA.

Je.44:30. will give P. into hand of

PHA'RAOH-NE'CHOH.

2 K.23:29. P. went against Assyria
33. P. put Jehoahaz in bands
34. P. made Eliakim k. ⌈unto P.
35. he taxed land to give money
Je.46:2. word to Jeremiah ag. P.

PHA'REZ=PHA'RES.

Ge.38:29. his name was called P-z
46:12. sons of Judah; P-z and Zerah, 1 Ch. 2:4.-4:1.-9:4.
12. the sons of P-z were Hezron
and Hamul, Nu. 26:20, 21. Ru.
4:18. 1 Ch. 2:5. ⌈of P-z
Ru.4:12. let thy house be like hou.
Ne.11:† 4. of the children of P-z
Mat.1:3. Judas begat P-s, Lu.3:33.

PHARISEE.

Mat.23:26. blind P. cleanse within
Lu.7:37. Jes. sat in P.'s house, 36.
11:37. a certain P. besought him
to dine, 38.-7:36, 39. ⌈publican
18:10. went to pray, one a P. other
Lu.18:11. P. stood and prayed thus
Ac.5:34. stood up one in council a
23:6. I am a P. the son of a P.⌊P.
26:5. aft. strictest sect I lived a P.
Ph.3:5.Hebrew,as touching law,a P.

PHARISEES. ⌈tism

Mat.3:7. P. and Saddu. to his bap-
5:20. exceed righteousness of P.
9:11.P.said, Why eateth your mas.
14. Why do we and the P. fast
oft? Mk.2:18. Lu.5:33.
34. P. said, He casteth out devils
by prince of devils, 12:24.
12:14. P. held counsel against him
38. P. ans-d, Master, we would
see sign, 16:1. Mk. 8:11. ⌈7:1.
15:1.came to Jes.P. of Jerus., Mk.
12. Knowest P. were offended
16:6. beware of leaven of P. and
Saddu.,11,12.Mk. 8:15.Lu.12:1.
19:3. P. came saying, Is it lawful
to put away wife, Mk. 10:2.
21:45. P. heard his parables
22:15. P. took counsel how,Mk.3:
35. one of P. a lawyer asked ⌊6.
41. While P. were gath-d together
23:2.scribes and P. sit in Mo.' seat
13. woe unto you scribes and P.
hypocrites, 14, 15, 23, 25,27,29.
Lu. 11:42, 43, 44.
27:62. priests, P. came unto Pilate
Mk.2:16. when P. saw him eat
24. P. said, why do they on sab.
that not lawful, Lu. 6:2. ⌈15:1.
7:3. P. except wash hands, 5.Mat.
8:11. P. began to question him
12:13. send P. to catch him in
Lu.5:17. were P. sitting by ⌈this
21. P. began to reason, Who is
30. scribes, P. murmured, 15:2.
6:7. scribes, P. watched him, 14:1.
7:30. P. rejected counsel of God
36. one of P. desired Jes. wo. eat
11:39.P. make clean outside of cup
53. P. began to urge him
13:31. P. saying,Get thee out ⌈man
15:2. P. murmured, saying, This
16:14. P. who were covetous, heard
17:20.demanded of P. when kingd.
19:39. P. said, Master, rebuke thy
Jn.1:24. wh. were sent were of P.
3:1. man of the P. named Nicode.
4:1. P. heard Jes. bapt-d more
7:32. P. sent officers to take him
45. came officers to the P.
47. ans-d P. Are ye also deceived?
48. Have any P. believed on him?
8:3. P. bro-t unto him a woman
13.P. said, Thou bearest record of
9:13.bro-t to P.him that was blind
15. P. asked how he rec-d sight
16. P. said, This man not of G.
40. P. said, Are we blind also?
11:46. told P. what Jes. had done
47. Then the P. gathered a council, Mat. 12:14.-22:15. Mk. 3:6.
57. Now the P. had given com-t
12:19. P. said, Perceive ye how
42. bec. of P. they did not confess
18:3. Judas having officers fr. P.
Ac.15:5. rose up certain of the P.
23:6. one part Saddu. other P., 9.
7. dissension betw. P. and Saddu.
8. Saddu. say is no resurrection,
nei. spirit; P. confess both

PHA'ROSH=PA'ROSH.

Ezr.8:3. of sons of P.; Zechariah

PHAR'PAR. See ABANA.

PHAR'ZITES.

Nu.26:20. of Pharez, family of P.

PHASE'AH=PASE'AH.

Ne.7:51. Nethinim: the chil. of P.

PHE'BE.

Ro.16:1. I commend unto you P.

PHENI'CE.

Ac.11:19. they travelled as far as P.
15:3. Paul and Bar. passed thro. P.
Ac.27:12. if by any means they
might attain to P., to winter

PHENIC'IA.

Ac.21:2.finding ship sailing unto P.

PHI'COL.

Ge.21:22. P. chief captain of his
host spake unto Ab., 32.-26:26.

PHILADEL'PHIA.

Re.1:11. write and send it unto P.
3:7. to angel of the church in P.

PHIL'EMON.

Phm.1. unto P. our dearly beloved

PHILE'TUS. See HYMENEUS.

PHIL'IP.

Mat.10:3. P. and Bartholomew,
Mk. 3:18. Lu. 6:14. Ac. 1:13.
14:3. for Herodias' sake his bro.
P.'s wife, Mk. 6:17. Lu. 3:19.
Lu.3:1.his bro.P. tetrarch of Iturea
Jn.1:43. Jesus findeth P. and saith
44. P. was of Bethsaida, the city
45.P.findeth Nathanael,and saith
46. P. saith, Come and see
48. Bef. P. called thee I saw thee
6:5. he saith unto P. Whence
7. P. ans-d, 200 pennyworth of
12:21.same came to P. and desired
22. P. telleth Andrew, Andr. told
14:8. P. saith, L. shew us the Fa.
9. hast thou not known me P.?
Ac.1:13. upper room where Pe. Ja.
Jn. Andr. P. ⌈unto P.
6:5. P.the deacon | 8:29. Spirit said
8:5. P. went to Samaria, preached
Christ ⌈spake
6. peo. gave heed to things P.
12. when they believed P. preach-
13. Simon continued with P. ⌊ing
26. angel of Lord spake unto P.
30. P. heard eunuch read Esaias
31.desired P.wo.sit with him | 34.
35. Then P. opened his mouth
37. P. said, If thou believest
38.went into water P.and eunuch
39. Spirit of the L. caught aw. P.
40. P. was found at Azotus
21:8. we entered house of P. evan-

PHILIP'PI. ⌊gelist

Mat.16:13. Jes. to coast of Cesarea
Mk.8:27. town of Cesarea P. ⌊P.
Ac.16:12. fr. Neapolis we came to P.
20:6. we sailed from P. and came
Ph.1:1. to all saints of C. at P.
1 Th.2:2. shamefully entreated at

PHILIP'PIANS. ⌊P.

Ph.4:15. Now ye P. know also

PHILIS'TIA.

Ps.60:8. P. triumph thou bec. of me
87:4. P. and Tyre, this man was
108:9.over P. will I triumph ⌊born

PHILIS'TIM.

Ge.10:14. out of whom came P.

PHILIS'TINE.

1 S.17:8. am not I a P.? ye serv-s
10. said, I defy armies of Isr., 11,
23. the P. of Gath, Goliath ⌊16.
26. Da. spake, Who is this uncircumcised P., 36. ⌈P.
32. Da. said, Thy serv. will fight
33. Thou not able to go ag. this
P. | 37, 40, 41, 42. ⌈44, 45, 48.
43. P. cursed Da. Am I a dog, |
49. David smote P. in forehead |
50, 51, 54, 55, 57.
21:9. sword of Goliath the P.whom
thou slewest is here
22:10. gave him sword of Goliath
2 S.21:17. Abishai smote the P.⌊P.

PHILIS'TINES. ⌈of P.

Ge.21:32. Abim. returned into land
34. Ab. sojourned in P.' land
26:1. Isaac went unto king of P.
14. Isaac had flocks, P. envied
15.P. stopped wells Ab. digged,18.
Ex.13:17. led them not thro. la.of P.
23:31. fr. Red sea unto sea of P.
Jos.13:2. borders of P. not conquered

1 S.15:33. Samuel hewed Agag in p.
1 K.11:30. Ahijah rent garm. in 12 p.
31. Ahijah said, Take thee ten p.
19 : 11. wind brake in p. the rocks
2 K. 2:12. Elisha rent clothes in 2 p.
5:5. Naaman took 6,000. p. of gold
6 : 25. ass's head was sold for 80 p.
of silver, cab of dung for 5 p.
11 : 18. images of Baal in p., 23:14.
2 Ch. 23:17.-31:1.-34:4. Mi.1:7.
18 : 4. brake in p. brazen serpent
2 Ch. 15: † 6. nation beaten in p. of
Jb. 16 : 12. hath shaken me in p.
40:18. His bones as str. p. of brass
41 : † 15. p. of shields are his pride
†30. Sharp p. of potsherd und. him
Ps. 7 : 2. rending in p. none deliver
50:22. consid., lest I tear you in p.
68 : 30. till submit with p. of silver
74:14 Thou brakest leviathan in p.
Can. 8 : 11. for fruit bring 1,000 p.
of silver [my peo. to p.
Is. 3 : 15. What mean th. ye beat
13:18. bows sh. dash yo. men to p.
65 : † 4. wh. eat p. of abomi. things
Je. 5 : 6. th. goeth out be torn in p.
23:29. hammer breaketh rock in p.
32 : † 9. weighed him, 10 p. of silv.
46:†5. mighty ones are broken in p.
La. 3 : 11. he hath pulled me in p.
Eze. 4 : 14. not eaten that torn in p.
9:†2. weapon of his breaking in p.
24 : 4. Gather p. thereof into pot
Da. 2 : 34. brake image in p., 45.
40. as iron breaketh in p.
3 : 29. sh. speak ag. G. be cut in p.
6:24. lions brake their bones in p.
7 : 7. beast brake in p., 19. [silv.
Ho. 3 : 2. I bought her for 15 p. of
10 : 14. mother was dashed in p.
Mi. 3 : 3. who chop my people in p.
4 : 13. shalt beat in p. many peo.
5 : 8 lion teareth in p. none can
Na. 2 : 12. lion did tear in p. enough
Zch. 11 : 12. weighed for my price 30
p. of silver, Mat. 26 : 15.
13. took 30 p. of silver, Mat. 27:6,
16. eat fat, tear claws in p. [9.
Mat. 26:15. covenanted with him for
30 p. of silver [silver
27 : 3. brought again the 30 p. of
5. cast down p. of silver hanged
himself [ver
Lu.15:8. woman having ten p. of sil-
Ac. 19:19. the price 50,000 p. of silv.
23 : 10. lest Paul be pulled in p.
27 : 44. some on broken p. of ship
See BEATEN, BREAK, BROKEN,
CUT, DASH, DASHED, SHOUL-
DERPIECES.

PIERCE. [rows
Nu. 24 : 8. he sh. p. them with ar-
2 K. 18 : 21. if lean, it will go into
his hand and p. it, Is. 36 : 6.
Lu. 2 : 35. a sword sh. p. thy soul

PIERCED. [ples
Ju. 5 : 26. when she had p. his tem-
Jb. 30 : 17. My bones are p. in me
Ps.22:16. they p. my hands and feet
Hag. 1 : † 6. to put into bag p. thro.
Zch. 12 : 10. sh. look upon me whom
they have p., Jn. 19 : 37. [side
Jn.19 : 34. one of the soldiers p. his
1 Ti.6:10. p. thems. wi. many sorrows
Re. 1 : 7. which p. him shall see him

PIERCETH, ING.
Jb.40:24. behemo-'s nose p-h snares
Is. 27 : 1. L. sh. punish p-g serpent
He. 4:12. word of G. is quick, p-g to

PIERCINGS.
Pr. 12 : 18. speaketh like p. of sword

PIETY.
1 Ti. 5 : 4. learn to shew p. at home
He. 5 : † 7. he was heard for his p.

PIGEONS. See YOUNG.

PI-HAHI'ROTH. [7, 8.
Ex. 14 : 2. encamp bef. P., 9. Nu. 33:

PI'LATE.
Mat. 27 : 2. they delivered him to
Pontius P. governor, Mk. 15 : 1.
13. P. unto Jes., Hearest not how
17. P. said, whom will ye I release,
Mk. 15 : 9. [Jesus, Mk. 15: 12.
22. P. saith, What shall I do with
24. P. saw he could prevail nothing
58. Joseph went to P. begged body
of Jesus, P. commanded body
be delivered, Mk. 15 : 43. Lu.
23 : 52. Jn. 19 : 38.
62. priests and Pharisees unto P.
65. P. said, Ye have a watch
Mk. 15 : 2. P. asked, Art thou King,
4. Lu. 23 : 3. Jn. 18 : 37.
5. So that P. marvelled, 44.
14. P. said, What evil hath he
done, Lu. 23 : 4. [released
15. P. willing to content people
Lu. 3 : 1. Pontius P. being gov-r of
13 : 1. whose blood P. had mingled
23 : 1. multitude led him to P.
6. When P. heard of Galilee he
11. Herod sent Jesus again to P.
12. same day P. and Herod friends
13. P. called priests and rulers
20. P. willing to release Jesus
24. P. gave sentence as they
Jn. 18 : 29. P. went out and said
31. said P., Take and judge him
33. Pilate entered into judgment
35. P. ans-d, Am I a Jew? [hall
38. P. saith, What is truth? [him
19 : 1. P. took Jesus and scourged
4. P. saith, Behold, I bring him
5. P. saith, Behold the man
6. P. saith, Take and crucify him
8. When P. heard, he was afraid
10. saith P., Speakest not unto me
12. P. sought to release him
13. P. heard that he bro-t Jes forth
15. P. saith Sh. I crucify your king
19. P. wrote title, put it on cross
21. said priests to P., Write not,
The King of | 22. [broken
31. Jews besought P. th. legs be
Ac. 3 : 13. denied him in pres. of P.
4 : 27. against Jesus, Herod and P.
13 : 28. desired they P. that he
should be slain [confession
1 Ti. 6 : 13. bef. P. witnessed good

PIL'DASH. See MILCAH.

PILE.
Is. 30 : 33. p. of it is fire and wood
Eze.24:9. I will make p. for fire grate

PIL'EHA.
Ne 10 : 24 chief of peo. P., Shobek

PILGRIMAGE.
Ge. 47:9. days of my p. 130 y-rs, not
attained unto life of fa-s in days
of their p. [p.
Ex. 6 : 4. to give them land of their
Ps. 119:54. songs in house of my p.

PILGRIMS.
He 11 : 13. confessed they were p.
1 Pe. 2 : 11. as p. abstain from lusts

PILLAR.
Ge. 19 : 26. she became a p. of salt
28 : 18. Jacob set it up for a p., 22.-
31 : 45.-35 : 14. [edst the p.
31:13. Beth-el, where thou anoint-
51. Behold this p.
52. and this p. be witness
35 : 20. Jacob set p. upon Rachel's
grave, that is the p.
Le. 26:†1. ye shall not rear up a p.,
De. 16 : † 22. [plain of P
Ju. 9 : 6. made Abimelech king by
20 : 40. flame arose wi. p. of smoke
2 S. 18 : 18. Absalom reared up a p.
called the p. [the left p.
1 K. 7 : 21. Sol. set up the right p.
2 K. 11 : 14. the king stood by p., 23:
3. 2 Ch. 23 : 13. [Je. 52: 21.
25 : 17. height of one p. 18 cubits,
Is. 19 : 19. and a p. at the border

Je. 1 : 18. I have made thee iron p.
Ho. 3:†4. chil. of Isr. without a p.
1 Ti. 3 : 15. p. and ground of truth
Re. 3 : 12. overcometh will I make a
See CLOUD, CLOUDY, FIRE. [p.

PILLARS.
Ex. 24 : 4. Moses built altar 12 p.
26 : 32. shalt hang vail upon 4 p.
37. make for hanging 5 p., 36: 38.
27 : 10. twenty p. books of the p.,
11.-38 : 10, 11, 12, 17, 28.
12. p. ten | 14. their p. three, 15.
-38 : 14, 15.
16. p. shall be four, 36:36.-38 : 19.
17. p. sh. be filleted with silver
38 : 17. sockets for p. of brass
40 : 18. Moses reared up his p.
Nu. 3 : 36. the p. of the tabernacle,
37. p. of the court, 4: 32. [4: 31.
De. 7 : † 5. break their p., 12 : 3.
Ju.16:25. set Samson betw. p., 26, 29.
1 S. 2 : 8. p. of the earth are L.'s
1 K. 7 : 2. upon 4 rows of cedar p. (2)
3. beams lay on 45 p. 15 in row
†5. all the p. square in prospect
6. he made a porch of p., 21.
15. he cast two p. of brass of
18. he made the p. and 2 rows
19. chapiters upon top of p., 20,
22, 41, 42. 2 Ch. 3:16.-4:12, 13.
10:12. king made of almug trees p.
2 K. 18 : 16. Hez. cut gold from p.
25 : 13. Chaldees brake in pieces p.
of brass, 16. Je. 52: 17, 20.
2 Ch. 3 : 15. two p. 35 cubits high
17. Sol. reared up p. bef. temple
4:12. 2 p. and pommels (2) [marble
Es. 1 : 6. hangings fastened to p. of
Jb. 9 : 6. p. thereof tremble, 26 : 11.
Ps. 75 : 3. I bear up the p. of it
Pr. 9 : 1. hath hewn out her 7 p.
Can. 3 : 6. cometh like p. of smoke
10. Sol. made p. thereof of silver
5:15. legs as p. of marble upon gold
Je. 27 : 19. L. of host conc-g the p.
52 : 20. The 2 p. one sea, 12 brazen
Eze. 41:†15. he meas-d walks with p.
42 : 6. had not p. as p. of court
Jo. 2 : 30. I will shew p. of smoke
Ga. 2 : 9. Jn. and Cephas seemed to
Re.10:1. feet were as p. of fire [be p.

PILLED. [rods
Ge. 30 : 37. Jac. p. white streaks in
38. he set rods he had p. bef. flocks
Le. 13 : † 40. man whose head is p.

PILLOW, S. [p-s
Ge. 28 : 11. Jacob put stones for his
18. Jac. took stone he put for p-s
1 S. 19 : 13. a p. of goats' hair, 16.
Eze. 13 : 18. Woe to women sew p-s
20. Behold, I am against your p-s
Mk. 4 : 38. Jesus in ship asleep on p.

PILOTS. [p., 27.
Eze. 27 : 8. wise men, O Tyrus, thy
28. suburbs shake at cry of thy p.
29. all the p. of the sea sh. come

PIL'TAI.
Ne. 12 : 17. priests, of Moadiah P.

PIN, PINS.
Ex. 27 : 19. make p-s of tabern. of
brass, 35 : 18.-38: 20, 31.-39:40.
Nu. 3:37. pillars, sockets, p-s, 4:32.
Ju. 16 : 14. Delilah fastened it with
p. Samson went away with p. of
Ezr. 9 : † 8. give us a p. in holy pla.
Eze. 15 : 3. take a p. of vine tree?

PINCH.
Le. 1 : † 15. sh. p. off head wi. nail

PINE. [Adj., Noun.]
Ne.8:15. fetch olive, and p. branches
Is. 41 : 19. I will set fir tree and p.
60 : 13. come unto thee p. tree and

PINE, ETH, ING. [box
Le. 26 : 39. that are left of you sh. p.
away; in iniq-s of fathers sh. p.
Is. 38:12. cut me off wi. p-g sickness
La.4:9. these p. away, stricken thro.

Eze. 24:23. ye shall p. away for your
iniquities [p. away in them
33:10. if sins be upon us, and we
Mk. 9:18. gnasheth with his teeth,
and p-h away

PINNACLE. [9.
Mat. 4:5. him on p. of temple, Lu. 4:

PI'NON. [1:52.
Ge. 36:41. names of dukes, P., 1 Ch.

PIPE, PIPES. [p.
1 S. 10:5. company of prophets with
1 K. 1:40. the people piped with p-s
Ps. 149:†3. praise, with p., 150:†4.
Is. 5:12. harp and p. are in feasts
30:29. as when one goeth with p.
Je. 48:36. sound for Moab like p-s
Eze. 28:13. workmanship of thy p-s
Zch. 4:2. seven p-s to seven lamps
12. thro. golden p-s empty thems.
1 Co. 14:7. things without life, p.

PIPED. [or harp
1 K. 1:40. people p. with pipes
Mat. 11:17. We have p. unto you,
Lu. 7:32.
1 Co. 14:7. how be known what is p.?

PIPERS.
Re. 18:22. voice of p. heard no more

PI'RAM.
Jos. 10:3. sent unto P. k. of Jarmuth

PIR'ATHON, ITE.
Ju. 12:13. Abdon a P-e judged Isr.
15. Abdon the P-e was buried in P.
2 S. 23:30. Benaiah the P-e one of
the 30, 1 Ch. 11:31.–27:14.

PIS'GAH. [of P.
Nu. 23:14. brought Balaam to top
De. 3:27. Get thee up into the top of
P., 34:1. Nu. 21:20.
4:49. sea of plain, under springs of

PISID'IA. [P.
Ac. 13:14. they came to Antioch in P.
14:24. after they had passed thro-t

PI'SON. [P.
Ge. 2:11. The name of the first is P.

PIS'PAH.
1 Ch. 7:38. sons of Jether, P., Ara

PISS.
2 K. 18:27. drink own p., Is. 36:12.

PISSETH. See WALL.

PIT, PITS.
Ge. 37:20. let us cast him into p., 22
29. Joseph was not in p., 28. [24
Ex. 21:33. if man shall open a p. (2
34. owner of p. make it good
Le. 11:36. a p. wherein is water
Nu. 16:30. down quick into p., 33.
1 S. 13:6. men of Isr. did hide in p-s
2 S. 17:9. he is now hid in some p.
18:17. cast Absalom in a great p.
23:20. slew lion in a p., 1 Ch. 11:22.
2 K. 10:14. Jehu slew them at the p.
18:†31. drink ev. one waters of his
Jb. 17:16. shall go down to p. [p.
33:18. keepeth soul fr. p., 30. [28.
24. Deliver him fr. going into p.,
Ps. 9:15. heathen are sunk into p.
28:1. become like them that go
down into p., 143:7. Pr. 1:12.
30:3. th. I sho. not go down to p.
9. What profit, when I go do. to p.?
35:7. they hid for me net in p.
40:2. bro-t me up out of horrible
55:23. them into p. of destruc. [p.
69:15. let not p. shut upon me
88:4. I am counted with th. go into
6. hast laid me in lowest p. [p.
119:85. proud digged p. for me [p-s
140:10. let them be cast into deep
Pr. 22:14. strange women a deep p.
23:27. strange woman is narrow p.
28:10. he sh. fall into his own p.
17. he shall flee to p. let no man
Is. 14:15. he brought to sides of p.
19. that go down to stones of p.
24:17. p. and snare are upon thee
18. cometh out of p., Je. 48:43, 44.
22. as prisoners are gathered in p.
Is. 30:14. to take water out of p.
38:17. deliv-d it fr. p. of corruption
18. that go down to p. can-t hope
51:14. hasteneth, th. he not die in p.
Je. 2:6. L. led us thro. land of p-s
14:3. came to p-s found no water
41:7. cast them into midst of p.
9. p. Asa made for fear of Baasha
La. 4:20. anointed of L. taken in p-s
Eze. 19:4. he taken in their p., 8.
26:20. that descend into p., 28:8.
–31:14, 16.–32:18, 24, 25, 29, 30.
32:23. Whose graves in sides of p.
Jon. 2:†6. hast bro-t my life fr. p.
Zch. 9:11. sent prisoners out of p.
Mat. 12:11. if sheep fall into a p. on
sabbath day, Lu. 14:5.
See BOTTOMLESS, DIG, DIGGED,
ETH, SALTPITS, SLIMEPITS.

PITCH. [Noun.] [p.
Ge. 6:14. pitch it within with-t with
Ex. 2:3. she daubed it with p.
Is. 34:9. streams shall be turned in-
to p. land become burning p.

PITCH. [Verb.]
Nu. 1:52. Israel shall p. by his camp
53. Levites shall p. round tabern.
2:2. ev. man p. by own standard
3. on east side sh. they of Judah p.
5. that p. next sh. be Issachar, 12.
3:23. Gershonites sh. p. westward
29. families of Kohath p. southw.
35. Merari shall p. northward
De. 1:33. search out place to p. in
Jos. 4:20. Joshua did p. 12 stones
Is. 13:20. nei. shall Arabian p. tent
Je. 6:3. shepherds sh. p. their tents

PITCHED.
Ge. 12:8. Abram p. his tent, and
13:12. Lot p. his tent toward Sodom
26:17. Isaac p. in valley, 25.
31:25. Jacob p. in mount, Laban
p. in Gilead [Shalem
33:18. Jacob p. his tent bef. city
Ex. 17:1. Israel p. in Rephidim
19:2. to desert, had p. in wildern.
33:7. Moses took tabernacle, p. it
Nu. 1:51. when tabern. is p. Levites
2:34. so they p. by their standards
9:18. at com-t of Lord they p.
12:16. peo. p. in wildern. of Paran
21:10. Israel p. in Oboth
11. p. in Ije-abarim [Arnon
12. p. in Zared | 13. p. on side of
22:1. Israel p. in plains of Moab
33:5. p. in Succoth | 6. p. in Ethan
7. and they p. before Migdol | 8, 9.
15. p. in wilderness of Sinai | 16,
18, 19, 20, 21, 22, 23, 25, 27, 28,
29, 31, 33, 36, 37, 41, 42, 43, 44,
45, 47, 48, 49.
Jos. 8:11. ambush p. on north of Ai
11:5. kings p. at waters of Merom
Ju. 4:11. Hobab p. tent unto plain
6:33. Midianites p. in Jezreel
7:1. Gid. p. beside well of Harod
11:18. Israel p. on side of Arnon
20. Sihon p. in Jabez and fought
15:9. Philistines p. in, 18:12. 1 S.
4:1.–13:5.–17:1.–28:4. 2 S.
23:13.
1 S. 4:1. Israel p. beside Eben-ezer
17:2.–28:4.–29:1.
26:3. Saul p. in Hachilah, 5.
2 S. 24:5. Joab p. in Aroer
1 Ch. 19:7. king p. before Medeba
2 S. 6:17. ark in taber. Da. had p.
17:26. Isr. and Abs. p. in Gilead
1 K. 20:27. Israel p. bef. them, 29.
2 K. 25:1. Neb. p. against it, Je. 52:4.
1 Ch. 15:1. Da. prepared place for
ark, and p. tent, 16:1. 2 Ch. 1:4.
Ezr. 8:†15. p. wo by river Ahava
He. 8:2. of true tabern. which L. p.

PITCHER, S.
Ge. 24:14. Let down p. I pray thee,
that I may drink, 17, 18, 43, 46.
Ge. 24:15. Rebekah came with her
p., 45, 16, 20.
Ju. 7:16. empty p-s lamps within p-s
19. brake p-s in their hand, 20.
Ec. 12:6. p. be broken at fountain
La. 4:2. esteemed as earthen p-s
Mk. 14:13. bearing p. of water, Lu.

PITCHING. [22:10.
Ju. 19:†9. it is the p. time of day

PI'THOM.
Ex. 1:11. treasure cities P., Raamses

PI'THON. See MICAH.

PITIED, ETH.
Ps. 103:13. as a fa. p-h his chil. so
the L. p-h them that fear him
106:46. He made them to be p-d
La. 2:2. L. hath not p-d, 17, 21.–3:43.
Eze. 16:5. None eye p-d thee, to do
24:21. I will profane what your soul

PITIFUL. [p-h
La. 4:10. p. women have sodden chil.
Ja. 5:11. ye have seen L. is very p.
1 Pe. 3:8. love as brethren, be p.

PITY. [Noun.]
De. 7:16. thine eye shall have no p.
2 S. 12:6. restore lamb, bec. he no p.
Jb. 6:14. To afflicted p. be shewed
19:21. Have p. upon me, p. O my
Ps. 69:20. looked for some to take p.
Pr. 19:17. that hath p. upon poor
Is. 13:18. no p. on fruit of womb
63:9. in his p. he redeemed them
Je. 15:5. who sh. have p. O Jerus.
21:7. he sh. not spare, nei. have p.
Eze. 5:11. nei. will I have p., 7:4, 9.
–8:18.–9:10. [have p.
9:5. let not your eye spare, neither
24:†21. I profane p. of your soul
36:21. I had p. for mine holy name
Am. 1:11. bec. Edom did cast of all p.
Jon. 4:10. hast had p. on the gourd
Mat. 18:33. even as I had p. on thee
Tit. 3:†4. p. of G. tow. man appeared

PITY. [Verb.]
De. 13:8. nei. shall thine eye p.
him, 19:13, 21. [shall not p.
25:12. cut off her hand, thine eye
Pr. 28:8. for him that will p. poor
Je. 13:14. I will not p. nor spare
Jo. 2:18. then L. will p. his people
Zch. 11:5. own shepherds p. them not
6. I will no more p. inhabitants
Mat. 16:†22. Pet. saying p. thyself L.

PLACE. [Noun.] [p.
Ge. 1:9. Let water be gath-d unto 1
13:14. Lord said, look from p.
18:24. wilt thou not spare the p.?
26. I will spare p. for their sakes
20:13. kindness thou shew at ev. p.
22:4. third day Ab. saw p. afar
29:†26. not be done so in our p.
35:7. Jacob called p. El-bethel
14. Jacob set up pillar in p., 13.
38:14. Tamar sat in an open p.
40:3. prison p. where Joseph was
50:19. Fear not, I am in p. of G,
Ex. 3:5. p. where thou standest is
holy, Jos. 5:15. Ac. 7:33. [made
15:17. plant them in p. thou hast
Le. 1:16. sh. cast it by p. of the ashes
4:24. kill it in p. where kill off-g,
29, 33.–6:25.–7:2.–14:13.
13:19. in p. of boil white rising
14:28. p. of blood of trespass off-g
42. put them in p. of those stones
Nu. 9:17. in p. where cloud abode
10:14. In first p. went standard of
13:24. p. was called brook Eschol
18:31. ye shall eat it in every p. ye
33:54. inheritance in p. where lot
De. 11:24. Every p. your feet tread
be yours, Jos. 1:3.
12:13. offer not offerings in ev. p.
21. if the p. be too far, 14:24.
16:11. p. Lord hath chosen to
Jos. 3:3. remove from p. after ark
4:9. Josh. set 12 stones in the p.

Jos. 8 : 19. ambush rose out of their
15:†46. th. lay by p. of Ashdod [p.
Ju. 6 : 26. build altar in ordered p.
11:19. through thy land into my p.
15 : 19. G. clave hollow p. in jaw
20: 36. men of Isr. gave p. to Benj-s,
Ru. 3:4. mark p. where he lieth [33.
1 S. 9 : 22. made them sit in chiefest
10 : 12. one of same p. answ-d [p.
20: 25. Da.'s p. was empty, 27. [(2)
26:5. Da. beheld p. where Saul lay,
2 S. 2 : 23. fell and died in same p.
14 : † 30. Joab's field near my p.
15:21. in what p. the king shall be
17 : 9. hid in some pit, or other p.
12. sh. come upon him in some p.
18 : 18. it is called Absalom's p.
23 : 7. shall be burned in same p.
1 K. 8:7. cherubim spread wings ov.
p. of ark, 2 Ch. 5 : 8. [Ch. 6:20.
29. thine eyes be open tow. p., 2
10:19. stays on p. of seat, 2 Ch. 9:18.
13 : 22. hast drunk water in p.
21:19. in p. where dogs licked blood
2 K. 5 : 11. strike his hand over p.
6 : 6. And he shewed him the p.
1 Ch. 21:22. grant p. of threshingfl.
25. Da. gave Ornan for p. 600 shek.
2 Ch. 30:16. priests stood in p., 35:10.
35 : 15. singers were in their p.
Ezr. 1 : 4. whoso. remaineth in p.
8 : 17. chief at p. Casiphia
Ne. 2:3. p. of my father's sepulchre
14. no p. for beast und. me to pass
4 : 20. In what p. ye hear trumpet
8 : 7. peo. stood in their p., 9 : 3.
13 : 11. I set singers and Lev. in p.
Es. 4 : 14. deliverance from ano. p.
7 : 8. king retu. into p. of banquet
Jb. 6 : 17. consumed out of their p.
8 : 17. His roots seeth p. of stones
9 : 6. shake the earth out of her p.
16:18. blood, let my cry have no p.
18 : 21. p. of them knoweth not G.
26:7. stretcheth north ov. empty p.
28 : 6. stones of it p. of sapphires
28:12. where is p. of underst-g? 20.
23. he knoweth p. thereof
34 :† 26. striketh in p. of beholders
36 : 20. when peo. are cut off in p.
38 : 10. brake up my decreed p.
19. for darkness, where is the p.
40 : 12. tread wicked in their p.
Ps. 26 : 8. p. where thine honour
12. My foot standeth in even p.
33 : 14. Fr. p. of habita. he looketh
44 : 19. broken us in p. of dragons
103: 16. p. shall know it no more
Pr. 1 : 21. in chief p. of concourse
15 : 3. eyes of Lord are in ev. p.
25 : 6. stand not in p. of gr. men
Ec. 3 : 16. the p. of judgment, p. of
righteousness
10 : 6. and the rich sit in low p.
11 : 3. in p. where tree falleth it
Is. 5 : 8. field to field, till be no p.
13 : 13. earth sh. remove out of p.
22 : 25. nail fastened in sure p.
28 : 8. so that there is no p. clean
25. the barley and rye in their p.
30 : 32. in ev. p. where staff pass
49 : 20. p. too strait for me, give p.
54 : 2. Enlarge the p. of thy tent
60 : 13. make p. of my feet glorious
66 : 1. where is the p. of my rest?
Je. 4 : 26. fruitful p. was a wildern.
7 : 12. go unto my p. in Shiloh
13 : 7. girdle from p. I had hid it
17 : 12. glorious throne is the p. of
18 : 14. waters come from ano. p.
22 : 12. sh. die in p., 38 : 9.—42:22.
29 : 14. bring you into p. whence I
Eze. 6 : 13. their slain on p. where
17 : 16. in p. where king dwelleth
21 : 30. judge thee in p. where cre-
41:9. was p. of chambers, 11. [ated
42:†9 fr. the p. was entry on east

Is. 43:7. p. of my throne shall Israel
no more defile (2)
13. this shall be higher p. of altar
21. shall burn it in appointed p.
46 : 20. this is p. where priests boil
Da. 2 :35. no p. was found for them
8 : 11. p. of sanctuary cast down
Ho. 1 : 10. in p. it was said, ye not
my people, Ro. 9 : 26. [chil.
13 : 13. in p. of breaking forth of
Jo. 3 : † 16. L. will be p. of repair
Am. 2 : † 13. press your p. as a cart
8:3. be many dead bodies in ev. p.
Na. 2:11. where is feeding p. of lions
3 : 17. their p. is not known
Zch. 10 : 10. p. shall not be found
12:6. be inhabited in her p., 14:10.
14:†5. valley of mts. to p. be sepa.
Mal. 1 : 11. incense be off-d in ev. p.
Mat. 17 : 20. Remove to yonder p.
28 : 6. see p. where Lord lay
Mk. 2:†14. sitting at p. where custom
6 : 10. In what p. ye enter house
16:6. behold p. where they laid him
Lu. 4 : 17. p. where it was written
37. fame of him went into ev. p.
10 : 1. L. sent two and two unto ev.
32. Levite at the p. passed by [p.
22 : 40. at the p. he said, Pray
Jn. 4 : 20. Jerus. p. to worship
6 : 10. was much grass in the p.
8 : 37. my word hath no p. in you
10:40. into p. where John baptized
11 : 6. abode two days in same p.
41. took away stone from the p.
48. Romans sh. take away our p.
18:2. Judas wh. betrayed knew p.
19:20. p. where Jes. was crucified, 41
Ac. 2 : 1. with one accord in one p.
4 : 31. had prayed, p. was shaken
7 : 49. or what is the p. of my rest
8 : 32. p. of Scripture he read was
12 : 17. Peter went into another p.
25 : 23. Agrippa unto p. of hearing
Ro. 15:23. no more p. in these parts
1 Co. 1 : 2. that in ev. p. call on J.C.
11 : 20. When ye come into one p.
14:23. church be come into one p.
2 Co. 2 : 14. his knowledge in ev. p.
Ga. 2 : 5. gave p. by subjection not
1 Th. 1:8. ev. p. your faith is spread
1 Ti. 2:†2. prayers for all in eminent
He. 5 : 6. as he saith in ano. p. [p.
8:7. no p. should have been sought
12:17. he found no p. of repentance
Ja. 3 : 11. at same p. sweet water
Re. 12 : 8. nei. was there p. found
14. fly into wildern. into her p.
20 : 11. was found no p. for them

A PLACE.

Ge. 28:11. lighted upon a certain p.
39:20. a p. where king's prisoners
Ex. 33 : 21. L. said, is a p. by me
Nu. 22 : 26. angel stood in a narrow
32 : 1. place was a p. for cattle [p.
De. 1 : 33. search out a p. to pitch
23:12. shalt have a p. with-t camp
Ju. 17 : 8. where he co. find a p., 9.
18:10. a p. where is no want of any
21 : 19. in a p. on north of Beth-el
1 S. 15 : 12. Saul sent him up a p.
20:41. David arose out of a p. tow.
21 : 2. appointed my serv-s to a p.
2 S. 11:16. Joab assigned Uriah to a
15: 17. k. tarried in a p. far off [p.
22 : 20. He bro-t me forth into a
large p., Ps. 18 : 19. [settled p.
1 K. 8 : 13. I built thee house in a
21. I set a p. for ark, 1 Ch. 15 : 1.
2 K. 6 : 8. In such a p. be my camp
9. Beware thou pass not such a p.
1 Ch. 14:†11. called a p. of breaches
17 : 9. I will ordain a p. for Isr.
2 Ch. 6:2. I have built a p. for thy
Jb. 28 : 1. a p. for gold they fine it
36:16. out of strait into a broad p.
Ps. 66 : 12 us out into a wealthy p.
Ps. 118 : 5. Lord set me in a large p.
132 : 5. Until I find a p. for L.
Pr. 14 : 26. chil. have a p. of refuge
Is. 4 : 6. a p. of refuge from rain
32 : 19. city sh. be low in a low p.
33 : 21. L. be a p. of broad rivers
34 : 14. find for herself a p. of rest
40:†4. crooked made a straight p.
56 : 5. and within my walls a p.
65: 10. Achor a p. for herds to lie
Eze. 25 : 5. Ammonites a crouching
26 : 5. a p. for nets, 14.—47:10. [p.
45:4. sh. be a p. for priests' houses
46:19. was a p. on two sides westw.
48 : 15. sh. be a profane p. for city
Ho. 4 : 16. L. feed th. in a large p.
9 : 13. Ephraim is in a pleasant p.
Mi. 1:†11. in mourning of a p. near
Zph. 2:15. she a p. for beasts [14:32.
Mat. 26 : 36. a p. Gethsemane, Mk.
27 : 33. that is, a p. of a skull, Mk.
15 : 22. Lu. 23 : † 33. Jn. 19 : 17.
Mk. 11 : 4. found colt in a p. where
12 : 1. digged a p. for winefat
Lu. 11:1. Jes. praying in a certain p.
Jn. 19 : 13. in a p. called Pavement
20 : 7. wrapped tog. in a p. by its.
Ac. 27 : 41. into a p. where 2 seas
He. 2 : 6. one in a cert. p. testified
4 : 4. he spake in a certain p. of
11 : 8. called into a p. be obeyed
Ja. 2 : 3. say, Sit here in a good p.
See APPOINT, CALLED, CHOOSE, CLEAN, DARK, DESERT, DRY, DWELL, DWELLINGPLACE, EMINENT, FENCED, GIVE, HIDING.

High PLACE.

Nu. 23:3. Balaam went up to a h.p.
1 S. 9 : 12. there is a sacrifice to day
in h. p., 13, 14, 19, 25. [fr. h.p.
10 : 5. shalt meet prophets coming
13. made end, Saul came to h. p.
1 K. 3:4. was great h. p., 1 Ch. 16:39.
11:7. Sol. built a h.p. for Chemosh
2 K. 23 : 15. h. p. that Jeroboam
made, Josiah brake down the
h.p. burnt the h.p. [Ch. 21:29.
2 Ch. 1:3. Solomon went to h. p., 1
13. fr. journey to h. p. at Gibeon
Ps. 9 : † 9. Lord will be a h. p. for
20 : † 1. G. of Jac. set thee on h.p.
46 :† 7. G. of Jac. is a h. p. for us
59 :† 9. for God is my h. p., 62:†2.
Is. 16 : 12. Moab is weary on h. p.
Je. 48 : † 1. h.p. is confounded and
Eze. 16: 24. h.p. in ev. street, 25, 31.
20 : 29. What is the h.p. wh-to ye

His PLACE. [go?

Ge. 18 : 33. Ab. returned unto h.p.
29 : 3. stone upon well's mouth in
31: 55. Laban unto h. p. [h. p.
Ex. 10:23. nei. rose from h.p. 3 days
16:29. abide ev. man in h. p. none
go out of h. p. [h. p.
Le. 13 : 23. But if bright spot stay in
Nu. 2 : 17. shall set forward ev. man
in h. p. by standards
24 : 25. Balaam returned to h. p.
De. 21:19. and bring him unto h.p.
Ju. 7 : 7. ev. man unto h.p., 9 : 55.
21. stood every man in h. p.
19:28. the man gat him unto h.p.
Ru. 4 : 10. name of dead be not cut
off from gate of h. p. [h. p.
1 S. 3 : 2. when Eli was laid down in
9. So Samuel lay down in h. p.
5 : 3. they set Dagon in h.p. again
11. ark go down to h. own p., 6:2.
23:22. Go see h. p. where haunt is
26 : 25. Saul returned to h. p.
29:4. Da. that he go again to h.p.
2 S. 6 : 17. they set ark of L. in h. p.
19:39. Barzillai returned unto h.p.
1 K. 8 : 6. priests brought ark unto
h. p., 2 Ch. 5 : 7. [out of h.p.
20 : 24. Take kings away, ev. man

1 Ch. 15 : 3. to bring ark unto h.p.
16: 27. strength gladness in h. p.
2 Ch. 24 : 11. carried chest to h. p.
34 : 31. king stood in h. p. and
Ezr. 1 : 4. let men of h. p. help him
2 : 68. for house of God to set it in
h. p., 5 : 15.-6 : 7. [own p.
Jb. 2 : 11. came every one from h.
7:10. neither shall h.p. know him
8 : 18. if he destroy him from h.p.
14:18. rock is removed out of h.p.
18:4. rock be removed out of h.p.
20 : 9. nei. h. p. behold him [p.
27:21. storm hurleth him out of h.
23. Men sh. hiss him out of h. p.
37:1. my heart is removed out of h.
38:12. dayspring to know h.p. [p.
Ps. 37 : 10. diligently consider h. p.
Pr. 27:8. that wandereth from h.p.
Ec. 1 : 5. the sun hasteth to h. p.
Is. 26:21. Lord cometh out of h. p. to
punish, Mi. 1:3. [nitions of rocks
33:16. h. p. of defence sh. be mu-
46 : 7. set him in h. p.: fr. h. p.
shall he not remove
Je. 4 : 7. he is gone from h. p. to
6 : 3. feed ev. one in h. p. [h. p.
Eze. 3 : 12. Blessed be glory of L. fr.
Da. 11:†7. sh. stand in h.p., †20, †21.
Zph. 2:11. worship ev. one fr. h. p.
Zch. 6: 12. sh. grow up out of h. p.
Mat. 26:52. Put up sword into h.p.
Ac. 1: 25. that he go to h. own p.
Re. 2:5. thy candlestick out of h. p.
See **HOLY, Most HOLY.**
See **NAME** with **called,** and
Called the NAME.

Of the PLACE.

Ge. 26 : 7. men o. p. asked him of
wife; lest men o. p. kill me
29:22. Laban gathered all men o.p.
Jos. 4:3. Take ye out o.p. 12 stones
Ju. 19:16. men o.p. were Benjamites
Ru. 1: 7. Naomi went forth out o.p.
1 Ch. 28 : 11. David gave Sol. pat-
tern o. p. of mercy seat
Eze. 41 : 11. breadth o. p. 5 cubits
Jo. 3:7. raise them out o.p. whither
Na. 1 : 8. make an utter end o. p.
See PREPARE, ED, RESTING, SE-
CRET [Adj.], SEPARATE, SOLI-
TARY, STEEP, TOPHET.

That PLACE.

Ge. 21:31. Ab. called t.p. Beer-sheba
28 : 11. Jac. lay down in t. p. (2)
38 : 21. Judah asked men of t. p.
De. 12 : 3. destroy them out of t. p.
17:10. sentence they of t.p. sh. shew
Ju. 15: 17. called t. p. Ramath-lehi
18 : 12. called t. p. Mahaneh-dan
1 S. 23 : 28. called t. p. Selah-ham-
mahlekoth [hazzurim
2 S. 2 : 16. t. p. was called Helkath-
Mat. 14:35. men of t. p. had knowl.
Mk. 6 : 10. till ye depart from t. p.
Jn. 5:13. a multitude being in t. p.
11:30. t.p. where Martha met him
Ac. 21 : 12. we and they of t. p.

This PLACE.

Ge. 19 : 12. sons, dau-s bring out of
13. we will destroy t. p. [t. p.
14. Lot spake, get out of t. p.
20 : 11. fear of God is not in t. p.
28:16. L. in t.p. | 17. dreadful is t.
38:21. was no harlot in t.p., 22. [p.
48:9. sons, G. hath given me in t.p.
Ex. 13: 3. Lord brought you fr. t.p.
Nu. 20: 5. to bring us unto t. evil p.
De. 1 : 31. how God bare thee until
ye came unto t. p., 9 : 7.-11 :5.
26:9. hath bro-t us into t. p. [hon
29 : 7. when ye came unto t. p. Si-
Ju. 18:3. what makest thou in t.p.
1 K. 8 : 29. hearken unto prayer toward t. p., 30, 35. 2 Ch. 6: 20,
21, 26, 40.-7:15. [ter in t. p., 16
13: 8. nei. eat bread, nor drink wa-
2 K. 18 : 25. not without L. ag. t.p.
22 :16. I will bring evil upon t.p.,
17, 19, 20. 2 Ch. 34 : 24, 25, 27,
28. Je. 19 : 3, 7. [self
2 Ch. 7:12. have chosen t.p. to my-
15. prayer made in t. p.
Jb. 18 : 21. t. the p. of him that
knoweth not God
Je. 7 : 6. shed not innocent blood in
t. p., 22 : 3. [upon t. p.
20. my fury shall be poured out
14 : 13. give assured peace in t. p.
16:2. have sons nor dau-s in t.p., 3.
9. cease out of t.p. voice of mirth
19:4. estranged t.p. filled t.p. with
6. t. p. no more be called Tophet
12. Thus will I do unto t.p., 40:2.
22:11. went forth out of t.p., 24:5.
27:22. restore them to t. p., 32:37.
28:3. bring into t.p. all vessels, 6.
4. bri. again to t.p. Jeconiah [p.
29 : 10. causing you to return to t.
33:10. heard in t.p. voice of joy, 12.
42 : 18. ye shall see t. p. no more
44 : 29. I will punish you in t. p.
51:62. L. thou hast spok. ag. t. p.
Zph. 1 : 4. remnant of Baal fr. t. p.
Hag. 2 : 9. in t. p. will I give peace
Mat. 12 : 6. in t.p. one greater than
Lu. 16 : 28. into t. p. of torment
23 : 5. beginning fr. Galilee to t. p.
Ac. 6 : 14. Jesus shall destroy t. p.
7 : 7. they shall serve me in t. p.
21 : 28. teacheth ag. law and t. p.
He. 4:5. in t. p. again, If they enter

Thy PLACE. [p.

Ge. 40:13. Pha. restore thee unto t.
Nu. 24:11. Thf. now flee thou to t.p.
2 S. 15 : 19. to t. p. abide with king
Ec. 10 : 4. if ruler ag. leave not t.p.
Eze. 12:3. remove from t. p., 38:15.

To or unto the PLACE.

Ge. 12:6. Ab. passed u.p. of Sichem
13 : 3. Abram u.p. where tent, 4.
19:27. Ab. gat t.p. where he stood
22:3. went u.p. of wh. God told, 9.
30 : 25. I may go u. mine own p.
Ex. 3:8. bri. you u. p. of Canaanite
18 : 23. people sh. go t.p. in peace
32: 34. people u. p. of wh. I spake
Nu. 10 : 29. we are journeying u. p.
14:40. go up u.p.L. hath promised
23:13. Come wi. me u. another p., 27
32 : 17. until have bro-t them u.p.
De. 2 : 37. nor u. p. of river Jabbok
Jos. 4 : 8. carried stones u.p. where
18. waters of Jordan retur-d u.p.
1 S. 14 : 46. Philis. went t. own p.
17 :† 20. Da. came t. p. of carriage
going forth t. p. of fight
20 : 19. come t.p. where didst hide
37. lad was come t. p. of arrow
2 S. 2 : 23. many as came t.p. stood
1 K. 4 : 12. u.p. beyond Jokneam |
5 : 9. by sea in floats u. p. [28.
2 K. 6 : 10. sent t.p. man of G. told
2 Ch. 25 : † 10. army go t. their p.
Ne. 1 : 9. them t. p. I have chosen
3 : 26. in Ophel u. p. over ag. wat.
31. goldsmith's son u. p. of Neth.
Es. 2:9. Esther and maids u. best p.
Ps. 104 : 8. u. p. thou hast founded
Ec. 1:7. u.p. whence the rivers come
3 : 20. All go u. one p., all, 6 : 6.
Is. 14 : 2. people bring them t. p.
18 : 7. present t. p. of name of L.
Je. 7 : 12. go u. p. in Shiloh [foil-d
Eze. 10 : 11. t. p. head looked they
Ho. 5 : 15. I will return t. my p.
Mk. 15:22. bring him u.p. Golgotha
Lu. 19 : 5. when Jesus came t. p.
23 : 33. come t. p. called Calvary
Jn. 6 : 23. nigh u.p. where did eat
See UNCLEAN, VOID.

PLACES.

Ge. 28 : 15. I will keep thee in all p.
Ge. 36:40. aft. their p. by their names
Ex. 20 : 24. p. where I record name
25 : 27. rings be for p. of staves, 26:
29.-36 : 34.-37 : 14, 27.-38 : 5.
De. 1:7. m-t of Amorites and p. nigh
12 : 2. shall utterly destroy all p.
Jos. 5:8. abode in their p. till whole
Ju. 5:11. in the p. of drawing water
19 : 13. to one of these p. to lodge
20 : 33. liers in wait came out of p.
1 S. 7 : 16. judged Isr. in those p.
23 : 23. lurking p. where he hideth
30:31. David sent presents to all p.
2 S. 7 : 7. In all p. spake I a word
22 : 46. afraid out of their close p.
2 K. 23:5. put down priests in p.ab.
14. he filled p. with bones of men
Ne. 4 : 12. Fr. p. whence ye return
13. I set the people in lower p.
and on higher p. [all p.
12 : 27. they sought Levites out of
Jb. 37 : 8. beasts remain in their p.
39 : † 6. made salt p. his dwellings
Ps. 10 : 8. He sitteth in lurking p.
16:6. lines are fallen in pleasant p.
18 : 45. afraid out of their close p.
73:18. didst set them in slippery p.
74:20. dark p. of the earth are full
103 : 22. Bless the Lord in all p.
105:41. they ran in dry p. like river
110 : 6. he sh. fill p. with the dead
141 : 6. judges overthr. in stony p.
Pr. 8 : 2. She standeth in p. of paths
† 26. not made earth nor open p.
9 : 3. she crieth upon highest p.
Is. 32 : 18. dwell in quiet resting p.
40 : 4. straight, and rough p. plain
44 : 26. I will raise up decayed p.
45:2. will make crooked p. straight
Je. 4:12. wind fr. those p. sh. come
5 : 1. seek in broad p. of Jerus.
8:3. in p. whi. I have driven, 29:14.
17 : 6. shall inhabit parched p.
26. sh. come from p. about Jerus.
23:10. pleasant p. of wil. are dried
24 : 9. a taunt and curse in all p.
29 : 14. I will gather you fr. all p.
32 : 44. in p. about Jerus., 33 : 13.
40 : 12. Jews returned out of all p.
45 : 5. thy life for a prey in all p.
La. 2 : 6. destroyed p. of assembly
3:6. He hath set me in dark p.
Eze. 34 : 12. will deliver out of all p.
13. feed them in all inhabited p.
26. p. round my hill a blessing
36 : 36. I the Lord build ruined p.
38 : 20. steep p. sh. fall and wall
45 : † 2. fifty cubits for the void p.
46 : 23. made with boiling p., 24.
47:11. miry p. shall not be healed
Da. 11:24. shall enter upon fattest p.
Ho. 9 : 6. pleasant p. for their silv.
Am. 4 : 6. want of bread in your p.
Zch. 3: 7. I will give thee p. to walk
Mat. 12 : 43. unclean spirit walketh
through dry p., Lu. 11 : 24.
13 : 5. some fell on stony p., 20.
Ac. 24:3. We accept it in all p. Felix
Ph. 1 : 13. bonds manifest in all p.
Re. 6:14. mt. island moved out of p.
See BESIEGED, DEEP, DESOLATE,
DIVERS, DWELLINGPLACES,
FENCED, HEAVENLY.

High PLACES.

Le. 26 : 30. I will destroy your h.p.
Nu. 21 : 28. consumed lords of h.p.
22 : 41. him up into h. p. of Baal
33 : 52. pluck down all their h. p.
De. 32 : 13. made him ride on h. p.
33:29. shalt tread upon their h.p.
Ju. 5 : 18. jeoparded lives in h. p.
1 S. 13 : 6. people hide in h. p. [p.
2 S. 1 : 19. beauty of Isr. slain in h.
25. Jonathan, thou wast slain in
thy h. p. [Ps. 18 : 33.
22 : 34. setteth me upon my h. p.,
1 K. 3 : 2. Only the people sacrificed
in h.p., 2 K. 17:32. 2 Ch. 33:17.

1 K.3:3.burnt incense in h.p.,22:43.
2 K. 12:3.–15:4,35.–16:4.–17:11.
12:31. Jerob. made house of h.p.
32. placed in Beth-el priests of h.
13:2. offer priests of h. p. ⌊p.
32.he cried ag.houses of the h.p.
1 K. 13:33. Jerob. made of lowest of
peo. priests of h. p.,2 K.17:32.
15:14. h.p. were not removed, 22:
43. 2 K. 12:3.–14:4.–15:4, 35.
2 K. 17:29. gods in houses of h. p.
18:4.Hez. removed h.p.,22.–23:19.
23:5.ordained to burn inc. in h.p.
8. defiled h.p. brake down h.p.,
13. 2 Ch. 31:1.–32:12. Is.36:7.
9. priests of h.p. not to alt. of L.
20 he slew all priests of h. p. ⌈p.
2 Ch. 11:15. ordained priests for h.
14:3. Asa took away the h. p., 5.
15:17. h. p. not taken away.20:33.
17:6. Jehoshaphat took away h.
21:11. Jehoram made h. p. ⌊p.
28:4. he sacrificed in the h. p.
25. in every city Ahaz made h.p.
34:3. Josiah purge Jerus. fr. h.p.
Jb. 16:† 19. my record is in h. p.
25:2. maketh peace in his h. p.
Ps. 78:58. provoked him wi. h. p.
Pr.8:2. She standeth in top of h.p.
9:14. she on seat in h. p. of city
Is. 15:2. is gone to h. p. to weep
33:† 16. He shall dwell on h. p.
41:18. I will open rivers in h. p.
49:9. pastures sh. be in all h. p.
58:14.cause thee to ride upon h.p.
Je. 3:2. Lift thine eyes unto h. p.
21. voice heard upon h.p.weep-g
4:11. dry wind in h.p. of wildern.
7:29. take up lamenta. in h. p.
12:12. spoilers are come on h. p.
14:6. wild asses did stand in h.p.
17:3. I will give thy h. p. for sin
26:18. mountain of house become
as h. p. of forest, Mi. 3:12.
48:35. him that offereth in h. p.
Eze.6:3. I will destroy your h.p.,6.
16:16. deckedst thy h.p. with col-
39.sh.break down thy h.p. ⌊ours
36:2. the ancient h. p. are ours
43:7. carcasses of kings in h. p.
Da. 7:† 18. the saints of the h. p.
Ho.10:8. h.p. of Aven be destroyed
Am. 4:13. L. treadeth upon h. p.
of the earth, Mi. 1:3. ⌈desolate
7:9. the h. p. of Isaac shall be
Mi. 1:5. what are h. p. of Judah?
Ha. 3:19. make me walk upon h.p.
Ep. 6:12. spiritual wickedness in h.
See BUILT, HOLY, SECRET. ⌊p.

Waste PLACES. ⌈eat

Is.5:17. w. p. of fat ones strangers
51:3. Lord will comfort her w.p.
52:9. sing ye w. p. of Jerusalem
58:12. they shall build the old w.

PLACE. [Verb.] ⌊p.

Ge. 33:† 15. Let me p. some of folk
Ex. 18:21. p. such to be rulers
De. 14:23. place he sh. choose to p.
his name,16:2,6,11.–26:2.⌈gines
1 K. 20:† 12. Benhadad said, p. en-
Ezr. 6:5. p. them in house of God
Is.46:13. I will p. salvation in Zion
Eze.37:14.I sh.p.you in own la.,26.
Da.11:31.they shall p. abomination
Ho.11:11.I will p. th. in their hou.
Zch. 10:6. I will bring them to p.

PLACED. ⌊them

Ge. 3:24. God p. at east of garden
47:11. Joseph p. his fa. and breth.
1 K. 12:32. Jeroboam p. in Beth-el
2 K.17:6.p. them in Halah ⌊priests
24. p. them in cities of Sama.,26.
2 Ch. 1:14. p. in chariot cities
4:8. made tables, p. them in tem.
17:2. he p. forces in fenced cities
Jb. 20:4. since man p. upon earth
Ps. 78:60. tent he had p. am. men
Can. 5:† 12. eyes of doves fitly p.
Is. 5:8. that they may be p. alone
Je. 5:22. p. sand for bound of sea
Eze. 17:5. eagle p. it by gr. waters

PLAGUE. [Noun.]

Ex.11:1.will bring one p.upon Pha.
12:13. p. sh. not be to destroy you
30:12.that there be no p.am.them
Le. 13:2. in skin of flesh like p.
3. when hair in p. turned white
(4), 13, 17, 20, 25. ⌈6.–14:48.
5. if the p.spread not in the skin,
12. cover all skin of him hath p.
27. spread much, it is the p., 22.
29. a p. upon the head or beard
30. if a man or woman hath a p.
priest shall see p., 31, 32, 50,
51, 55.–14:37. ⌈his head
44. is leprous man, his p. is in
45. leper in whom p. is shall cry,
Unclean, 46.
47. garment that the p. of leprosy is in, 49, 52, 53, 54,55,56,59.
50. shut up it hath p. 7 days, 4.
52.anything wherein the p. is,54.
53.if p.be not spread in garment,
56. if p. be somewhat dark ⌊55.
57. if in warp, it is spreading p.
58.if p. be departed, it be washed
14:34.p.of leprosy in a h.,36,39,43,
35. is as it were a p. in house ⌊44.
40. the stones in which the p. is
Nu. 8:19. that be no p. am. Israel
11:33. Lord smote people with p.
14:37. those men died by p. bef. L.
16:46. wrath is gone out, p. is begun, 47. Nu. 31:16. ⌈24:25.
48. p. was stayed, 50.–25:8. 2 S.
49. Now they that died in the p.
were, 25:9, 18. ⌈book
De. 28:61. every p. not written in
Jos. 22:17. not cleansed, altho. was
1 S. 6:4. one p. was on you all ⌊p.
2 S. 24:21. that p. be stayed, 1 Ch.
1 K. 8:37. p. or sickness ⌊21:22.
38. know every man p. of heart
2 Ch. 21:14. with p. will L. smite
Ps. 91:10. nei. any p. come nigh thy
106:29. the p. brake in upon them
30. judgment, so p. was stayed
Zch.14:12.p.the L. will smite,15,18.
Mk. 5:29. she was healed of that p.
34.go in peace,be whole of thy p.
Re. 16:21. blasphemed bec. of p. of
See LEPROSY. ⌊hail

PLAGUES. ⌈p.

Ge.12:17.L.plagued Pha. with great
Ex. 9:14. I will send all my p.
Le.26:21. bring seven times more p.
De 28:59.L. make thy p. wonderful
29:22. when they see p. of land
1 S. 4:8. that smote E-ns with p.
Jb. 10:† 17. renewest thy p. ag. me
Je. 19:8. hiss, because of the p., 49:
17.–50:13. ⌈six p.
Eze. 30:† 2. I will strike thee with
Ho. 13:14. O death I will be thy p.
Mk.8:10.touch him as many as had
Lu. 7:21. he cured many of p. ⌊p.
Re. 9:20. rest not killed by these p.
11:6. power to smite earth with p.
15:1. seven angels having 7 last p.
8. till 7 p. of 7 angels fulfilled
16:9. God, who hath power over p.
18:4. that ye receive not of her p.
8. shall her p. come in one day
21:9. seven vials full of 7 last p.
22:18. God shall add unto him the

PLAGUE. [Verb.] ⌊p.

Ps. 89:23. I will p. them th. hate

PLAGUED. ⌊him

Ge. 12:17. Lord p. Pha. and his
Ex. 32:35. Lord p. people for calf
Jos. 24:5. p. Egypt and afterw. ⌈p.
1 Ch. 21:17. not on peo. th. they be
Ps. 73:5. nei. are p. like other men
14. all day long have I been p.

PLAIN. [Adj.]

Ge. 25:27. Jacob was a p. man
Ne. 12:28. p. country round Jerus.
Ps. 27:11. lead me in a p. path
Pr. 8:9. p. to him that underst-th
15:19. way of righte. is made p.
Is. 28:25. When he made p. the face
40:4.straight, and rough places p.
Je. 48:21. judgm. upon p. country
Ha. 2:2. Write vision, make it p.
Mk. 7:35. tongue loosed, he spake

PLAIN. [Noun.] ⌊p.

Ge. 11:2. p. in the land of Shinar
12:6. Ab. passed unto p. of Moreh
13:10. Lot beheld all p. of Jordan
11. Lot chose him p. of Jordan
12. Lot dwelled in cities of the p.
18.Abram dwelt in the p., 14:13.
19:17.nei.stay thou in all p.escape
25. overthrew cities in all the p.
28. he looked tow. land of the p.
29. G. destroyed cities of the p.
De.1:1. Mo. spake unto Isr.in the p.
7. go unto the places, in the p.
2:8. thro. way of the p. from Elath
3:10. All cities of p. and Gilead
17.p.and coast unto sea of the p.
4:49.all the p. on this side Jordan
unto the sea of the p. ⌈cho
34:3. the p. of the valley of Jeri-
Jos. 3:16. came tow. sea of the p.
8:14. ag. Isr. to battle bef. the p.
11:16. Joshua took valley and p.
12:1. all p. on the east, 13:9, 16.
3. fr.p. to sea, and unto sea of p.
13:17. all her cities in the p., 21.
20:8. in wilderness upon the p.⌈p.
Ju. 4:11. pitched his tent unto the
9:6. made Abimelech king by p.
11:33. smote Ammonites unto p.
1 S. 10:3. come to the p. of Tabor
23:24. David and men were in p.
2 S.2:29. Abner walked thro. p.⌈p.
4:7. Baanah and Rechab gat thro.
5:† 20. place the p. of breaches
15:28. I will tarry in p. until I
18:23. Ahimaaz ran by way of p.
1 K. 7:46. In p. of Jordan did king
cast them, 2 Ch. 4:17. ⌈p., 25.
20:23. let us fight against them in
2 K. 14:25. coast unto sea of p.
25:4. king went tow. p., Je. 52:7.
Ne. 3:22. aft. him priests of the p.
6:2. let us meet in the p. of Ono
Je. 17:26. fr. p. bringing offerings
21:13. I am ag. thee, O rock of p.
48:8. p. shall be destroyed, as L.
Eze. 3:22. Arise, go forth in p.,23.
8:4. acc. to vision I saw in the p.
47:† 8. These waters go into p.
Da. 3:1. set image in p. of Dura
Am. 1:5. off inhab. fr. p. of Aven
Ob. 19. they of p. sh. possess Philis.
Zch. 4:7. bef. Zerub. thou become a
7:7. when men inhabited k. ⌊p.
14:10. All land be turned as a p.
Lu. 6:17. Jesus stood in the p.

PLAINS.

Ge.18:1.L.appeared in p. of Mamre
De. 11:30. dwell beside p. of Moreh
Jos. 11:2. p. south of Chinneroth
12:8. in the mts valleys,p.springs
2 S.17:16.Lodge not in p. of wilder.
1 Ch. 27:28. over trees in the low p.
2 Ch. 9:27. made cedars in low p.
26:10.Uzziah had much cattle in p.
See JERICHO.

PLAINS of Moab. ⌈33:48,49.

Nu. 22:1. Isr. pitched in p. o. M.,
26:3. Mo.spake wi. them in p.o.M.
63. who numbered Isr. in p.o.M.
31:12. camp at p.o.M. by Jordan
33:50. L. spake unto Mo. in p. o.
M., 35:1. ⌈M.
36:13. Lord commanded in p. o.
De. 34:1. Moses went from p. o. M.
unto Nebo

De 34:8. Isr. wept for Mo.in p.o.M.
PLAINLY. ⌊40 days
Ex. 21:5. if serv. p. say, I love mas.
De. 27 : 8. write this law very p.
1 S.2:27.Did I p.appear unto house
10 : 16. told us p. asses were found
2 S. 20 : † 18. p. spake in beginning
Ezr. 4 : 18. letter hath been p. read
Is. 32 : 4. stammerers to speak p.
Jn.10:24.If thou be Christ,tell us p.
11:14. Jes. said p. Lazarus is dead
16 : 25. I shall shew you p. of Fa.
29. now speakest thou p.
He. 11 : 14. that say such things de-
PLAINNESS. ⌊clare p.
Ps. 27 : † 11. lead me in way of p.
2 Co.3:12.we use great p. of speech
PLAISTER. See PLASTER.
PLAITED, ING.
1 Ti. 2 : † 9. adorn not wi. p-d hair
1 Pe. 3 : 3. adorning not be p-g of
PLANES. ⌊hair
Is. 44 : 13. fitteth the image with p.
PLANETS.
2 K.23: 5. burned incense to sun,p.
PLANKS. ⌈fir
1 K. 6 : 15. covered floor with p. of
Eze. 41 : 25. thick p. upon porch
26. upon side chambers,and thick
PLANT. [Noun.] ⌊p.
Ge. 2 : 5. Lord God made every p.
Jb. 14:9. bring forth boughs like p.
Is.5 : 7. men of Judah his pleasant
17:11. In the day thy p. grow ⌊p.
53 : 2. he sh. grow as a tender p.
Je. 2 : 21. turned into degenerate p.
Eze. 34:29. for them a p. of renown
Mat.15:13.Ev. p. my Fa. not plant-
PLANTS. ⌊ed
1 Ch. 4 : 23. those that dwell am. p.
Ps. 128:3. thy children like olive p.
144:12.That our sons may be as P.
Can. 4 : 13. Thy p. as an orchard of
Is. 16 : 8. broken down principal p.
17:10.shalt thou plant pleasant p.
Je. 48 : 32. thy p. are gone over sea
Eze. 31 : 4. rivers running ab. his p.
PLANT. [Verb.] ⌈herit.
Ex. 15:17. p. them in mt. of thy in-
De.16:21. Thou shalt not p. a grove
2 S. 7:10. I will p. them, 1 Ch.17:9.
Ec. 3 : 2. a time to p. and time to
Is. 17 : 10. thf. p. pleasant plants
41 : 19. I will p. in wildern. cedar
51 : 16. I may p. heavens and lay
65:22.they shall not p.and ano.eat
Je. 1:10. set thee to build and to p.
18 : 9. a kingdom to build and p.
24:6. I will p. and not pluck,42:10.
29 : 5. p. gardens and eat fruit, 28.
31 : 5. p. vines upon mts. of Sama.
28. I will watch over them to p.
32 : 41. I will p. them in this land
Eze. 17:22. I will p. it upon mt.,23.
36: 36. Lord p. that was desolate
Da. 11 : 45. he shall p. tabernacles
Am.9:15. I will p. them upon their
PLANTATION. ⌊land
Eze. 17:7. water it by furrows of p.
PLANTED.
Ge. 2 : 8. God p. a garden eastward
21:33.Abraham p.grove in Beer-sh
Le. 19:23. when ye sh. have p. trees
Nu. 24 : 6. as trees which Lord p.
Ps. 1:3. a tree p. by rivers, Je.17:8.
80 : 8. hast cast out heath. p. vine
92:13.those th. be p.in house of L.
94:9. He th. p. ear, sh. he not hear
104:16.cedars of Lebanon wh.he p.
Ec. 2 : 5. I p. trees of all kind ⌈p.
3:2. a time to pluck up that wh. is
Is. 5 : 2. p. it with the choicest vine
40:24. they sh. not be p. nor sown
Je. 2:21. I had p. thee a noble vine
11 : 17. Lord of hosts that p. thee
12:2. hast p. them, they taken root
45 : 4. what I have p. I will pluck
Eze. 17 : 5. p. it in a fruitful field,8.
10. being p. shall it prosper?
19:10.p.by waters she was fruitful
13. now she is p. in wilderness
Ho. 9:13. Ephr. is p. in pleas. place
Mat.15:13 plant my Fa. hath not p.
Lu. 17 : 6. and be thou p. in the sea
28. they bought,they sold,they p.
Ro. 6 : 5. if p. together in his death
1 Co.3:6. I have p. Apollos watered
See **Plant,ed VINEYARD,S.**
PLANTEDST, ETH.
Ps. 44 : 2. didst drive out heathen
and p-t them ⌈rain
Is. 44 : 14. he p-h an ash, and the
1 Co. 3 : 7. nei. is he that p-h any
thing, neither he ⌈one
8. he th. p-h he th. watereth are
See **Plant, edst, planteth.**
VINEYARD, S.
PLANTERS.
Je.31:5.p. shall plant,and eat them
PLANTING, S.
Is. 60 : 21. branch of my p. work of
61 : 3. be called the p. of the Lord
Mi.1:6.make Samaria as p-s of vine-
PLASTER. [Noun.] ⌊yard
De.27:2.plaster gt.stones with p.,4.
Is. 38 : 21. lay it for p. upon boil
Da. 5 : 5. wrote upon p. of palace
PLASTER, ED.
Le.14:42. take mortar and p. house
43. if plague come after p-d ⌈p-d
48. plague not spread after house
De.27:2.p.gr. stones with plaster,4.
PLAT.
2 K. 9:26. I will requite thee in this
p. Now cast him into the p.
PLATE, PLATES.
Ex. 28 : 36. make a p. of pure gold
39 : 3. did beat gold into thin p-s
30. p. of holy crown of gold
Le. 2 : † 5. meat offering in p., 7:†9.
8 : 9. upon his forefront golden p.
Nu.16:38.make of censers broad p-s
39. broad p-s for a cov-g of altar
1 K. 7:30. base had p-s of brass, 36.
1 Ch. 9:† 31. ov. things made on flat
23 : † 29. is baked in the flat p. ⌊p-s
Je. 10 : 9. Silver spread into p-s is
Eze. 4 : † 3. take a flat p. for a wall
PLATTED.
Mat. 27 : 29. when they had p. a
crown of thorns, Mk.15:17. Jn.
PLATTER. ⌊19 : 2.
Mat. 23 : 25. ye make clean outside
of the p. but, 26. Lu. 11 : 39.
PLAY.
Ex. 32:6. peo. rose to p., 1 Co.10:7.
De. 22 : 21. to p. whore in fa.'s hou.
1 S. 16 : 16. he sh. p. with his hand
17. Provide me man can p. well
21 : 15. this fellow to p. madman
2 S. 2 : 14. Let young men p. bef. us
6 : 21. thf. will I p. bef. the Lord
10 : 12. let us p. men for our peo.
Jb. 40 : 20. where beasts of field p.
41 : 5. Wilt p. with him as a bird?
Ps. 33 : 3. p. skilfully with a noise
104:26.leviathan thou madest to p.
Is. 11 : 8. sucking child shall p. on
Eze. 33 : 32. can p. well on instru-
PLAYED. ⌊ment
Ju. 19 : 2. his concubine p. whore
1 S. 16 : 23. David p., 18 : 10.-19 : 9.
18 : 7. women answered as they p.
26:21. I have p. the fool,and erred
2 S. 6 : 5. all Israel p., 1 Ch. 13 : 8.
2 K. 3:15. to pass when minstrel p.
Eze. 16 : 28. hast p. whore with As-
See HARLOT. ⌊syrians
PLAYER, S.
1 S. 16 : 16. a cunning p. on a harp
Ps. 68 : 25. the p-s on instruments
87 : 7. As well the singers as p-s on
PLAYETH, ING.
Le.21 : 9. by p-g whore she profaned
1 S. 16 : 18. son of Jesse cunning in
21:†14.man p-h the madman ⌊p-g
1 Ch. 15 : 29. Michal saw David p-g
Ps. 68:25. among them damsels p-g
Eze. 23 : 44. as unto a woman that
p-h the harlot ⌈streets
Zch. 8 : 5. boys and girls p-g in the
See HARLOT.
PLEA.
De. 17 : 8 matter too hard betw. p.
PLEAD. ⌊and p.
Ju. 6 : 31. Will ye p. for Baal? he
that will p.for him ⌈him,bec.he
32. saying, Let Baal p. against
Jb. 9 : 19. who set me a time to p.?
13 : 19. Who is he will p. with me?
16:21. O th. one might p. for man
19 : 5. if he p. ag. me my reproach
23 : 6. Will he p. ag. me with his
Is. 1:17. p. for the widow ⌊gr.power
3 : 13. L. standeth to p. and judge
43 : 26. let us p. toge. declare ⌊peo.
66 : 16. by fire will L. p. with all
Je. 2 : 9. I will yet p. with you, 35,
with your chil.'s chil. will p.
29. Wherefore will ye p. with me?
12:1. Righte. thou. O L. when I p.
25 : 31. Lord will p. with all flesh
50:†44. who will convent me to p.?
Eze. 17:20. I will p. with him there
20 : † 4. Wilt thou p. for them? 22:
† 2.-23 : † 36. ⌈to face
35. there will I p. with you face
36. so will I p. with you, saith L.
38:22. I will p. ag. him with pestil.
Ho. 2 : 2. p. with your mother, p.
5:†13. Ephr.sent to king th. sho.p.
Jo. 3 : 2. I will p. wi. them for peo.
Mi. 6 : 2. and the Lord will p. with
See **Plead CAUSE.** ⌊Isr.
PLEADED, ETH. ⌈cause
1 S. 25 : 39. Blessed be L. that p-d
Jb. 16:21. as a man p-h for neighb-r
Is.51:22.God, that p-h cause of peo.
59 : 4. nor any p-h for truth ⌈soul
La. 3 : 58. L. hast p-d causes of my
Eze.20:36.as I p-d with your fathers
PLEADINGS.
Jb. 13 : 6. hearken to p. of my lips
PLEASANT. ⌈is p.
Ge. 2 : 9. God made every tree that
3 : 6. was p. to the eyes, and a tree
49 : 15. Issachar saw land was p.
2 S.1:23. Saul and Jonathan were p.
26. Jona., very p. hast thou been
1 K. 20 : 6. p. they shall take away
2 K. 2:19. situation of this city is p.
2 Ch. 32 : 27. treasuries for p. jewels
Ps. 16 : 6. lines fallen in p. places
81:2. bring hither the p. harp with
106 : 24. they despised the p. land
133:1. how p. for brethren to dwell
135 : 3. sing praises,it is p., 147 : 1.
Pr. 2:10. knowl. is p. unto thy soul
5 : 19. Let her be as the p. roe
9 : 17. bread eaten in secret is p.
15 : 26. words of pure are p. words
16 : 24. p. words are as honeycomb
22 : 18. For it is p. if thou keep th.
24 : 4. chambers with all p. riches
Ec. 11 : 7. p. it is to behold the sun
Can. 1 : 16. fair, my beloved, yea p.
4 : 13. an orchard with p. fruits
16. Let my beloved eat p. fruits
7 : 6. How fair and p. thou, O love
13. at our gates are all p. fruits
Is. 2:16. day of L. upon p. pictures
5 : 7. men of Judah his p. plant
13:22. dragons sh. cry in p.palaces
17 : 10. shalt thou plant p. plants
32 : 12. they lament for p. fields
54 : 12. all thy borders of p. stones
64:11. our p. things are laid waste
Je. 3 : 19. how give thee a p. land?
12:10. made my p. portion wilder.
23 : 10. p. places of the wilderness
25 : 34. ye sh. fall like a p. vessel

Je.31:20.Is Ephraim,is he a p.child?
La. 1 : 7. rememb-d her p. things
10.spread hand upon her p.things
11. given their p. things for meat
2:4. slew all that were p. to the eye
Eze. 26:12. sh. destroy thy p.houses
33 : 32. song of one hath p. voice
Da. 8 : 9. waxed great tow. p. land
10:3. I ate no p. bread, nei. flesh in
11 : 38. honour a god wi. p. things
Ho. 9 : 6. p. places nettles possess
13. Ephr. is planted in a p. place
13 : 15. spoil treasure of p. vessels
Jo. 3: 5. into your tem. my p.things
Am. 5 : 11. ye planted p. vineyards
Mi. 2 : 9. women out from p. houses
Na. 2 : 9. glory out of p. furniture
Zch. 7 : 14. laid p. land desolate
Mal. 3 : 4. offering of Jerus. p. unto

PLEASANTNESS. ⌊L.
Pr. 3:17.Her ways are the ways of p.
15:†26. words of pure are words of

PLEASE. ⌊p.
Ex. 21 : 8. If she p. not her master
Nu.23:27. may p.G.thou curse them
1 S. 20 : 13. p. my fa. to do thee evil
2 S. 7 : 29. let it p. thee to bless
house of thy serv., 1 Ch. 17:27.
1 K. 21 : 6. if it p. I will give thee
another vineyard
2 Ch.10:7.If thou p. they thy serv-s
Ne. 2 : 5. If it p. king and thy servant found favour, 7. Es. 1 : 19.
-3:9.-5:8.-7:3.-8:5.-9:13. ⌈me
Jb. 6:9. that it wo. p. God to destroy
20:10. His chil. shall seek to p.poor
Ps. 69:31. this shall p. the L. better
Pr. 16 : 7.When a man's ways p. L.
Can. 2 : 7. nor awake my love till he
p., 3 : 5.-8 : 4.
Is.2:6.p. thems.in chil. of strangers
55:11. sh. accomplish that wh. I p.
56:4. choose the things that p. me
Jn. 8:29. I do always things p. him
Ro. 8 : 8. they in flesh can-t p. God
15 : 1. ought to bear, not p. ours.
2. Let every one p. his neighbour
1 Co.7:32. careth how he may p. L.
33. married careth how he p. wife
34. how she may p. her husband
10:33. as I p. all men in all things
Ga. 1 : 10. do I seek to p. men?
1 Th. 2:15. they p. not G., are contrary to all men
4 : 1. ought to walk and to p. God
2 Ti. 2 : 4. p. him who hath chosen
Tit. 2 : 9. p. them well in all things
He. 11:6. without faith impossible to

PLEASED. ⌊p. God
Ge.28:8.dan-s of Canaan p.not Isaac
33 : 10. seen thy face, thou wast p.
34 : 18. And their words p. Hamor
45 : 16. it p. Pharaoh well and his
Nu. 24 : 1. Balaam saw it p. Lord
De. 1 : 23. the saying p. me well
Jos. 22:30. princes heard,it p.them,
Ju. 13:23. If L. were p.to kill us ⌊33.
14:7. he talked, she p. Samson well
1 S. 12 : 22. if p. L. to make you his
18 : 20. it p. Saul Michal loved Da.
26. it p.Da.to be king's son in law
2 S. 3 : 36. whatso. king did p. peo.
7†:29. be thou p. bless hou.of serv.
17 : 4. saying p. Absalom well
19 : 6. if we had died, it had p. thee
1 K. 3 : 10. Sol.'s speech p. the Lord
9 : 1. Sol.'s desire he was p. to do
12. cities Sol. gave p. not Hiram
1 Ch. 17 : † 27. p. thee to bless house
2 Ch. 30 : 4. thing p. the king and
all cong., Ne. 2:6. Es. 1:21.-2:4.
Es. 2 : 9. the maiden p. the king
5 : 14. thing p. Haman, he caused
Ps. 40 : 13. Be p. O L., to deliver me
51:19.shalt thou be p.with sacrifi.
115 : 3. our God, he hath done
whatso. he p., 135 : 6. Jon.1:14.

Is. 53 : 10. Yet it p. L. to bruise him
Da. 6 : 1. It p. Darius to set over
Mi. 6:7. L. be p. with thous.of rams?
Mal. 1 : 8. offer it, will he be p. ?
Mat.14:6.Herodias danced bef.them,
p. Herod, Mk. 6 : 22. ⌈tude
Ac. 6 : 5. saying p. the whole multi-
12 : 3. bec. Herod saw it p. Jews
15 : 22. p. it the apostles to send
34. p. Silas to abide there
Ro. 15 : 3. even Christ p. not hims.
26.hath p. them of Macedonia,27.
1 Co. 1 : 21. it p. God by foolishness
7 : 12. she be p. to dwell with him
13. if he be p. to dwell with her
12 : 18. God set members as it p.
15 : 38. G. giveth it a body as it p.
Ga. 1 : 10. if I yet p. men, I sho. not
15. when it p. God to reveal Son
Col. 1 : 19. it p. Father that in him
He. 11 : 5. had testimony, that he p.

Well PLEASED. ⌊God
Ps. 85 : † 1. thou hast been w. p.
Is. 42:21. L. is w. p. for his righte-n
Mat. 3 : 17. beloved Son, in whom I
am w. p., 12 : 18.-17 : 5. Mk. 1:
11.-Lu. 3 : 22. 2 Pe. 1 : 17. ⌈p.
1 Co.10:5.with many of th.G.not w.
He. 13 : 16. such sacrifices God is w.

PLEASETH. ⌊p.
Ge. 16:6. said, do to her as it p. thee
20 : 15. land, dwell where it p. thee
Ju. 14 : 3. Get her, she p. me well
Es. 2 : 4. let maiden wh. p. king be
Ec. 7 : 26. whoso p. God sh. escape
8 : 3. he doeth whatsoever p. him

PLEASING.
Es. 8 : 5. and if I be p. in his eyes
Ho. 9:4. nei. sh. they be p.unto him
Col. 1:10. worthy of Lord unto all p.
1 Th. 2 : 4. we speak, not as p. men
1 Jn. 3 : 22. do things p. in his sight

Well PLEASING.
Ph. 4 : 18. a sacrifice, w. p. to God
Col.3:20.obey, this is w.p. unto L.
He. 13 : 21. working in you what is

PLEASURE. ⌊w. p.
Ge. 18:12. waxed old, sh. I have p.
De. 23 : 24. mayest eat grapes at p.?
1 Ch. 29:17. hast p. in uprightness
Ezr. 5 : 17. let k. send his p. to us
10:11. confession unto L., do his p.
Ne. 9:37. over our cattle at their p.
Es.1:8. drink acc. to every man's p.
Jb. 21:21. what p. in house aft.him?
25. ano. dieth, never eateth wi.p.
22 : 3. Is it any p. to Alm. th. thou
Ps.5:4. not a G. hath p.in wickedn.
35:27. p. in prosperity of his serv.
51:18. Do good in good p.unto Zion
102:14.serv-s take p. in her stones
103:21. Bless L. ye, that do his p.
105 : 22. To bind his princes at p.
111 : 2. sought of all them have p.
147:10.taketh not p.in legs of man
11. L. taketh p. in them fear him
149 : 4. L. taketh p. in his people
Pr. 21:17. that loveth p. sh. be poor
Ec. 2 : 1. I said, thf. enjoy p. ⌊man
5 : 4. he hath no p. in fools
12:1. shalt say, I have no p. in th.
Is. 21 : 4. night of my p. he turned
29 : † 9. take your p. and riot ⌈p.
44 : 28. Cyrus shall perform all my
46 : 10. stand, I will do all my p.
48:14. he will do his p. on Babylon
53:10. p. of L. shall prosper in his
58 : 3. day of your fast ye find p.
13. from doing thy p. on my holy
day, not finding thine own p.
Je. 2:24. she snuffeth wind at her p.
22 : 28. is he a vessel wh-n is no p.?
34:16. liberty at their p. to return
48:38. Moab like vessel wh-n no p.
Eze. 16:37. with whom hast taken p.
18 : 23. Have I any p. that wicked
die, saith Lord, 32.-33 : 11.

Ho. 8:8. Isr. as a vessel wh-n is no p.
Hag. 1:8. build house, I will take p.
Mal. 1 : 10. I have no P. in you⌊in it
Lu. 12 : 32. Father's good p. to give
Ac.24:27.Felix, to do Jews p. left P.
25 : 9. Festus to do Jews a p. said
Ro. 1 : 32. p. in them that do them
2 Co. 12 : 10. I take p. in infirmities
Ep. 1 : 5. good p. of his will, 9. ⌈p.
Ph. 2 : 13. will and to do of his good
2 Th. 1 : 11. fulfil the good p. of his
2 : 12.but had p.in unrighteousness
1 Ti. 5:6. she th. liveth in p. is dead
He. 10 : 6. in sacrifices had no p., 8.
38. my soul sh. have no p. in him
12 : 10. chastened us after own p.
Ja. 5 : 5. Ye lived in p. on earth
2 Pe. 2:13. count it p. to riot in day-
Re. 4 : 11. for thy p. they were cre-

PLEASURES. ⌊ated
Jb. 36:11.sh. spend their years in p.
Ps. 16 : 11. at thy right hand are p.
36:8. them drink of river at thy p.
Is. 5 : † 7. Judah plant of his p.
47 : 8. thou that art given to p.
Lu. 8:14. choked with p. of this life
2 Ti. 3 : 4. lovers of p. more than
Tit. 3:3. serving divers lusts and p.
He. 11 : 25. to enjoy the p. of sin

PLEDGE, S. ⌈a p.?
Ge. 38:17. Tamar said,Wilt give me
18. What p. shall I give thee?
20. Judah sent to receive his p.
Ex. 22:26. if neighb.'s raiment to p.
De. 24 : 6. No man take millstone to
p.for he taketh man's life to p.
10. not into his ho. to fetch p.,11.
12. shalt not sleep with his p.,13.
17.nor take widow's raiment to p.
1 S. 17 : 18. fare, take their p. ⌈8.
2 K. 18 : 23.give p-s to k., Is. 36:
Jb. 22 : 6. has taken a p. from bro.
24 : 3. take widow's ox for a p.
9. and they take a p. of the poor
Pr.20:16.take p.of him for a strange
woman, 27 : 13. ⌈his p., 16.
Eze. 18 : 7. hath restored to debtor
12. not restored p.; shall he live?
33 : 15. If wicked restore p. not die
Am. 2 : 8. upon clothes laid to p. by

PLEDGED. ⌊altar
Eze. 18 :† 16. son that not p. pledge

PLEI'ADES.
Jb. 9:9. Which maketh Orion and P.
38:31. bind sweet influences of P.?

PLENTEOUS.
Ge. 41 : 34. take 5th part in p. years
47. in p. years earth bro-t forth
De.28:11.L. shall make thee p.,30:9.
2 Ch. 1 : 15. Sol. made gold as p. as
Ps. 86:5. art p. in mercy unto all,15.
103 : 8. L. is gracious, p. in mercy
130 : 7. with him is p. redemption
Is. 30:23. the bread sh. be fat and p.
Ha. 1 : 16. their portion fat, meat p.
Mat. 9 : 37. the harvest truly is p.

PLENTEOUSNESS.
Ge. 41 : 53. seven years of p. ended
Pr. 21 : 5. thoughts of diligent tend

PLENTIFUL. ⌊to p.
Ps. 68 : 9. Thou didst send a p. rain
Is. 16 : 10. joy is tak. out of p. field
Je. 2:7. I bro-t you into p. country
48 : 33. gladness taken fr. p. field

PLENTIFULLY.
Jb. 26 : 3. hast p. declared thing
Ps. 31 : 23. p. rewardeth the proud
Lu. 12:16. ground of rich bro-t forth

PLENTY. ⌊p.
Ge. 27 : 28. God give thee p. of corn
41:29. come seven years of great p.
30. all p. shall be forgotten in E.
31. p. sh. not be known in land
Le. 11 : 36. a pit, wh-n p. of water
1 K. 10 : 11. bro-t p. of almug trees
2 Ch. 31 : 10. enough to eat, left p.
Jb. 22 : 25. shalt have p. of silver

Jb. 37 : 23. excellent in p. of justice
Pr. 3 : 10. thy barns be filled wi. p.
28:19. that tilleth sh. have p.of br.
Je. 44:17. then had we p. of victuals
Jo. 2:26. shall eat in p. and praise L.

PLOTTETH.

Ps. 37:12. wicked p. against the just

PLOUGH. [Noun.]

Lu. 9:62. having put his hand to p.

PLOUGH. [Verb.]

De. 22:10. not p. with an ox and ass
1 S. 14 : 14. a yoke of oxen might p.
Jb. 4:8. that p. iniquity, reap same
Pr. 20 : 4. sluggard will not p. by
Is.28:24. Doth ploughman p.all day
Ho. 10 : 11. Judah shall p. Jacob
Am. 6 : 12. will one p. with oxen?
1 Co.9:10. plougheth sho. p. in hope

PLOUGHED, ERS, ETH.

Ju. 14 : 18.If not p-d with my heifer
Ps.129 :3.The p-s p-d upon my back
Je. 26:18.Zion shall be p-d, Mi.3:12.
Ho. 10 : 13. ye have p-d wickedness
1 Co. 9 : 10. p-h sho. plough in hope

PLOUGHING. [Noun. Part.]

1 K. 19 : 19. Elijah found Elisha p.
Jb. 1:14. oxen were p. asses feeding
Pr. 21 : 4. p. of the wicked is sin
Lu. 17 : 7. you having a servant p.

PLOUGHMAN. [sow?

Is. 28:24. Doth p. plough all day to
Am. 9 : 13. p. shall overtake reaper

PLOUGHMEN. [p.

Is. 61 : 5. sons of aliens sh. be your
Je. 14 : 4. the p. were ashamed

PLOUGHSHARES.

Is. 2:4. beat swords into p., Mi.4:3.
Jo. 3 : 10. Beat your p. into swords

PLUCK.

Le. 1 : 16. shall p. away his crop
Nu. 33 : 52. p. down high places
De. 7 : † 22. God will p. off nations
23 : 25. thou mayest p. the ears
2 Ch. 7 : 20. Then will I p. them up
Jb. 24:9. p. the fatherless fr. breast
Ps. 25 : 15. sh. p. my feet out of net
52 : 5. p. thee out of dwellingplace
74 : 11. thy ha. p. it out of bosom
80 : 12. they which pass do p. her
Ec. 3 : 2. and a time to p. up what
Je. 12 : 14. p. out house of Judah
17. I will utterly p. up th. nation
18 : 7. conc. a kingdom, to p. it up
22 : 24. yet would I p. thee thence
24 : 6. will plant, not p. th., 42:10.
31 : 28. watched over th. to p. up
45 : 4. wh. I planted I will p. up
Eze. 17 : 9. with-t many peo. to p. it
23 : 34. shalt p. off own breasts
Mi. 3 : 2. who p. off skin from them
5 : 14. I will p. up thy groves out
Mat. 5 : 29. if thy right eye offend,
p. it out, 18:9. Mk. 9:47. [2:23.
12 : 1. began to p. ears of corn,Mk.
Jn.10:28.nei.p. them out of my ha.
29. no man able to p. them out
of my Father's hand

PLUCKED.

Ge. 8 : 11. an olive leaf p. off
Ex. 4 : 7. p. his hand out of bosom
De. 28 : 63. ye shall be p. from land
Jos. 4 : † 18. soles of priests' feet p.
Ru. 4 : 7. a man p. off his shoe
2 S. 23 : 21. p. spear out of Eg-n's
hand, and slew him,1 Ch 11:23.
Ezr. 9 : 3. I p. off hair of my head
Ne. 13 : 25. I cursed, p. their hair
Jb. 29 : 17. p. spoil out of his teeth
Pr. 2 : † 22. transgr-s shall be p. up
Is. 16 : † 8. her branches are p. up
50 : 6. my cheeks to th. p. off hair
Je. 6 : 29. wicked are not p. away
12 : 15. aft. I have p. them out, I
31:40. sh.not be p. up, nor thrown
Eze. 19 : 12. she was p. up in fury
Da. 7 : 4. I beheld till wings were p.
8. three of first horns p. up
Da.11:4 his kingdom shall be p. up
Am. 4 : 11. as a firebrand p. out
Zch. 3 : 2. is not this a brand p. out
Mk. 5 : 4. chains p. asunder by him
Lu. 6 : 1. disciples p. ears of corn
17 : 6. Be thou p. up by root [eyes
Ga. 4 : 15. ye wo. have p. out own
Jude 12. twice dead, p. up by roots

PLUCKETH.

Pr. 14 : 1. the foolish p. it down

PLUMBLINE.

Am. 7 : 7. L. stood on a wall made
by a p. with a p. in his hand
8. Amos, what seest? I said, A p.
I will set a p. in midst of Isr.

PLUMMET. [p.

2 K.21:13.I will stretch over Jerus.
Is. 28 : 17. I will lay righte-n. to p.
Zch. 4 : 10. sh. see p. in hand of Ze-

PLUNGE. [rub.

Jb. 9 : 31. shalt thou p. me in ditch

PLUNGINGS.

Ju. 5 : †22. horsehoofs broken by p.

POCH'ERETH.

Ezr. 2:57. chil. of P. of Zebaim, Ne.

POETS. [7 : 59.

Ac. 17:28. as certain of your p. said

POINT, S. [die

Ge. 25 : 32. Esau said, I am at p. to
Ec. 5 : 16. in all p-s he came, so go
Je. 17 : 1. written wi. p. of diamond
Mk. 5 : 23. My dau. at p. of death
Jn. 4 : 47. he was at the p. of death
He. 4 : 15. in all p-s tempted like
Ja. 2 : 10. offend in one p. is guilty

POINT, POINTED.

Nu.34:7. sh. p. out for you m-t Hor
8. ye shall p. out your border, 10.
Jb. 41 : 30. he spreadeth sharp p.
things upon the mire

POISON.

De. 32 : 24. with the p. of serpents
33. Their wine is p. of dragons
Jb.6:4.the p. drinketh up my spirit
20:16.He sh.suck p.of asps [pents
Ps. 58 : 4. Their p. is like p. of ser-
140 : 3. adders' p. is und. their lips
Je. 8:†14. hath given us p. to drink
Zch. 12 :† 2. make Jerus. a cup of p.
Ro. 3 : 13. p. of asps und. their lips
Ja. 3 : 8. their tongue full of deadly

POISONFUL. [p.

De. 29:†18. root th. beareth p. herb

POLE. [p., 9.

Nu. 21 : 8. L. said, set serpent upon

POLICY. [prosp.

Da. 8 : 25. thro. his p. cause craft to

POLISHED. [ace

Ps. 144:12. p. aft. similitude of pal-
Is. 18 : † 2. nation outspread. p., †7.
49 : 2. he hath made me a p. shaft
Da. 10 : 6. his feet like to p. brass

POLISHING.

La. 4 : 7. their p. was of sapphire

POLL, S.

Ex. 16:†16. gather homer for ev. p.
38 :† 26. A bekah for every p. that
Nu. 1 : 2. names every male by their
p-s, 18, 20, 22. 1 Ch. 23 : 3, 24.
3 : 47. take 5 shekels apiece by p.

POLL, POLLED.

2 S. 14 : 26. when he p-d his head,
(at year's end he p-d it)
Je. 9 : † 26. having corners of their
hair p-d, 25 : † 23.-49 : † 32.
Eze.44:20. they shall only p. heads
Mi. 1 : 16. and p. thee for children

POLLUTE.

Nu. 18 : 32. neither p. holy things
35 : 33. So shall ye not p. the land
Is.23:†9. Lord purposed to p. pride
Je.7:30. house by my name, to p. it
Eze.7:21.sh. p. my secret place, 22.
13 : 19. will ye p. me am. my peo.
20 : 31. ye p. yourselves with idols,
23 : 30.-36 : 18. [more, 39 : 7,
39. but p. ye my holy name no
Eze.44:7. strangers in sanct-y to p.
Da. 11 : 31. they shall p. sanctuary

POLLUTED. [p. it

Ex. 20 : 25. if lift tool upon it, hast
2 K. 23 : 16. Josiah p. alt. at Beth-el
2 Ch. 36 : 14. priests p. house of L.
Ezr. 2 : 62. were they as p., Ne.7:64.
Ps. 106 : 38. land was p. wi. blood
Is.47 : 6. I have p. mine inheritance
48 : 11. how should my name be p.
Je. 2 : 23. How say, I am not p.?
3 : 1. sh. not land be greatly p.? 2.
34 : 16. ye turned and p. my name
La. 2 : 2. he hath p. the kingdom
4 : 14. have p. thems. with blood
† 15. they cried, Depart ye p. dep.
Eze. 4:14. my soul hath not been p.
14:11.nei.be p.with transgressions
16 : 6. I saw thee p. in own bl., 22.
20 : 9. for my name's sake, that it
sho. not be p., 14, 22. [21, 24.
13. sabbaths they greatly p., 16,
26. I p. them in their own gifts
30. Are ye p. aft. your fathers?
22 : † 5. mock thee p. in name
23:17. she was p. with Babylonians
30. thou art p. with their idols
36 : 18. idols whw. they had p. it
Ho. 6 : 8. Gilead is a city that is p.
9 : 4. all that eat thereof sh. be p.
Am. 7 : 17. shalt die in a p. land
Mi. 2 : 10. this not your rest, it is p.
Zph. 3 : 1. Woe to her that is p.
4. her priests have p. sanctuary
Mal. 1 : 7. Ye offered p. bread upon
altar, and say, Wherein have we
p. thee?
12. ye say, The table of L. is p.
Ac. 21 : 28. hath p. this holy place

POLLUTING.

Is.56:2.keepeth sabbath fr. p. it, 6.

POLLUTION, S.

Eze.22:10. her that was apart for p.
Ac. 15 : 20. abstain from p-s of idols
2 Pe. 2 : 20. escaped p-s of world

POL'LUX. See CASTOR.

POMEGRANATE. [26

Ex. 28 : 34. golden bell and p., 39:
1 S. 14 : 2. Saul tarried und. p. tree
Can. 4 : 3. thy temples like p., 6 : 7.
8 : 2. cause thee to drink of my p.
Jo. 1 : 12. p. tree all trees withered
Hag. 2 : 19. p. hath not bro-t forth

POMEGRANATES.

Ex.28:33. make p. of blue, 39:24,25.
Nu. 13 : 23. brought of p. and figs
20 : 5. no place of seed, figs, or p.
De. 8 : 8. into a land of p. honey
1 K. 7 : 18. to cover the chapiters
upon top with p., 20, 42. 2 K.
25 : 17. 2 Ch. 3 : 16. Je. 52 : 22.
2 Ch. 4:13. 400 p. on the 2 wreaths;
2 rows of p. on a wreath
Can. 4 : 13. Thy plants are an orchard of p. [ded, 7 : 12.
6 : 11. I went to see whe. p. bud-
Je. 52 : 23. were 96 p. on side

POMMELS. [ters

2 Ch. 4 : 12. pillars and p. of chapi-

POMP. [hell

Is. 5 : 14. their p. sh. descend into
14 : 11. Thy p. is brought to grave
Eze. 7 : 24. make p. of strong cease
30:18. p. of her strength cease, 33:
32 : 12. they sh. spoil p. of E. [28.
Ac. 25:23. Agrippa come with great

PONDER, ED, ETH. [p.

Pr. 4 : 26. p. the path of thy feet
5 : 6. Lest thou p. the path of life
21. the Lord p-h all his goings
21 : 2. but the Lord p-h the hearts
24 : 12. doth he that p-h the heart
Lu. 2:19. Mary p-d th. in her heart

PONDS. [p., 8 : 5.

Ex. 7 : 19. stretch hand upon their
Is.19:10. brok. in purposes th. make

PON'TIUS. See PILATE. [p.

PON'TUS.
Ac. 2 : 9. dwellers in P. and Asia
18:2. Jew named Aquila born in P.
1 Pe. 1 : 1. to strangers thro-t P.
POOL, POOLS.
Ex. 7 : 19. stretch hand on their p-s
2 S. 2 : 13. one sat on one side of p.
4:12. hanged them ov. p. at Hebron
1K. 22 : 38. chariot in p. of Samaria
2 K. 18 : 17. they stood by conduit
of upper p., Is. 7:3.-36:2. [duit
20 : 20. how he made a p. and con-
Ne. 2 : 14. I went on to king's p.
3 : 15. Shallum built wall of p., 16.
Ps. 84 : 6. rain also filleth p-s
Ec. 2 : 6. I made me p-s of water to
Is. 7 : 3. conduit of upper p., 36 : 2.
14 : 23. make it for p-s of water
22 : 9. gathered waters of lower p.
11. ditch for water of old p.
35 : 7. parched ground become p.
41 : 18. I will make wilderness a p.
42 : 15. I will dry up p-s and herbs
Na. 2 : 8. Nineveh of old is like p.
Jn. 5 : 2. at Jerus. by sheep market
4. angel went down into p. [a p.
7. have no man to put me into p.
9 : 7. Go wash in p. of Siloam, 11.
See FISHPOOLS.
POOR.
Ge. 41 : 19. after them 7 p. kine
Ex. 23 : 11. that p. of peo. may eat
30 : 15. p. shall not give less than
Le. 14 : 21. if p. and cannot get
19:10. thou shalt leave them for p.
15. shalt not respect person of p.
25 : 25. If brother be p., 35, 39, 47.
De. 15 : 4. when no p. among you
11. p. sh. never cease out of land
Ru. 3 : 10. followedst not p. or rich
1 S. 2 : 7. Lord maketh p. and rich
8. He raiseth up the p., Ps. 113:7.
2 S. 12 : 1. one rich, the other p.
2 K. 25 : 12. captain of guard l-ft of
p., Je. 39 : 10.-40 : 7.-52:15, 16.
Jb. 5 : 15. he saveth p. from sword
16. p. hath hope, iniq. stoppeth
20 : 10. chil. shall seek to please p.
19. bec. he hath oppressed the p.
24 : 4. p. of the earth hide thems.
9. they take a pledge of the p.
29 : 12. Because I delivered p. [p.?
30 : 25. was not my soul grieved for
31 : 16. If I withheld p. fr. desire
19. if I seen p. without covering
34:19. nor regard-h rich more than
28. cause cry of p. to come [p.
36:15. He delivereth the p. in affliction, Ps. 72 : 12. [not perish
Ps. 9 : 18. expectation of the p. sh.
10 : 2. wicked doth persecute p.
8. his eyes are privily set ag. p.
9. he lieth in wait to catch the p.
10. p. may fall by his strong ones
14. p. committeth hims. unto thee
12 : 5. For oppression of the p. I
14 : 6. Ye shamed counsel of p.
37 : 14. bent bow to cast down p.
41 : 1. Blessed is he considereth p.
49 : 2. low and high, rich and p.
68 : 10. hast prepared of thy goodness for the p.
69 : 29. I am p. and sorrowful
33. L heareth p. and despiseth not
2 : 4. He shall judge p. of people
82 : 3. Defend the p. and fatherless
107 : 41. Yet setteth he p. on high
109:31. sh. stand at right ha. of p.
132:15. will satisfy her p. with br.
140 : 12. will maintain right of p.
Pr. 10 : 4. p. that dealeth with slack
15. destruction of p. is poverty
13 : 7. maketh hims. p. yet hath
8. p. heareth not rebuke [riches
23. Much food is in tillage of p.
14:20. The p. is hated of neighbour
21. hath mercy on p. happy he
Pr. 14:31. oppr-th p. reproa-h Maker:
honoureth him mercy on p.
17 : 5. mocketh p. reproa-h Maker
18:23. The p. useth entreaties, but
19:4. p. is separated fr. neighbour
7. all brethren of p. do hate him
21 : 13. stoppeth ears at cry of p.
22:2. The rich and p. meet togeth.
7. The rich ruleth over the p. and
16. He that oppresseth the p. to
28 : 8. gather for him will pity p.
11. p. that hath understanding
15. so wicked ruler over p. people
29 : 7. considereth cause of p., 13.
14. king th. faithfully judgeth p.
30 : 9. lest I be p. and steal, and
14. teeth as swords, to devour p.
Ec. 4 : 14. in his kingd. becometh p.
5 : 8. If seest oppression of p.
6 : 8. what hath p. that knoweth
Is. 3 : 14. spoil of p. in your houses
15. What mean ye grind faces of
10 : 2. to take the right fr. p. [p.?
30. unto Laish, O p. Anathoth
11:4. with righte-n. shall judge p.
14:30. firstborn of p. sh. feed in it
32. p. of his peo. shall trust in it
26:6. feet of the p. sh. tread it down
29:19. p. shall rejoice in Holy One
32 : 7. destroy p. with lying words
58 : 7. bring p. that are cast out
Je. 2 : 34. blood of the p. innocents
5 : 4. I said, Surely these are p.
20 : 13. he hath deliv-d soul of p.
52:15. Neb. carried certain of the p.
Eze. 16 : 49. nei. did she strengthen
18:17. taken off his hand fr. p. [p.
Am. 2 : 6. sold p. for pair of shoes
7. pant after dust on head of p.
4 : 1. oppress the p. crush needy
5 : 11. as your treading is upon p.
12. they turn aside the p. in gate
8 : 4. to make p. of land to fail
6. That we may buy p. for silver
Ha. 3:14. rejoicing was to devour p.
Zph. 3 : 12. p. shall trust in Lord
Zch. 7:10. oppress not widow nor p.
11 : 7. I will feed even you, O p.
11. p. of flock th. waited upon me
Mat. 5:3. Blessed are the p. in spirit
11 : 5. p. have the gospel, Lu. 7:22.
26 : 11. For ye have the p. always
with you, but, Mk. 14:7. Jn. 12:8.
Mk. 12 : 42. there came a certain p.
widow, Lu. 21 : 2. [Lu. 21 : 3.
43. this p. widow cast more in,
Lu. 6 : 20. Blessed be ye p.: your's
14 : 13. call the p. the maimed, 21.
Jn. 12 : 6. not that he cared for p.
Ro. 15 : 26. contribution for p. [p.
1 Co. 11:†22. shame ye them th. are
13 : 3. bestow my goods to feed p.
2 Co. 6:10. p. yet making many rich
8 : 9. for your sakes he became p.
Ga. 2 : 10. that we remember the p.
Ja 2:5. Hath not God chosen the p.
6. But ye have despised the p.
Re. 3 : 17. knowest not thou art p.
13:16. rich and p. to receive a mark
See NEEDY.
Is POOR.
Ex 22 : 25. If lend to any that i. p.
De. 24 : 15. i. p. and setteth heart
Ju. 6:15. my family i. p. in Manas.
Pr. 19:1. Better i. the p. that walk-
eth in integrity, 28 : 6. [p.
22 : 22. Rob not poor because he i.
Ec. 4:13. Better i. p. and wise child
Is. 40 :† 20. that i. p. chooseth tree
66 : 2. i. p. and of contrite heart
See Poor MAN.
To or unto the POOR. [p.
Le. 23 : 22. thou shalt leave them p.
Es. 9 : 22. days of sending gifts t. p.
Jb. 29 : 16. I was a father t. p. and
36 : 6. but he giveth right t. p. [9.
Ps. 112 : 9. hath given t. p., 2 Co. 9:
Pr. 22 : 9. giveth of his bread t. p.
28 : 27. giveth u. p. sh. not lack
31 : 20. stretcheth her hand t. p.
Is. 25 : 4. hast been a strength t. p.
Da. 4:27. shewing mercy t. p. [10:21.
Mat. 19 : 21. sell all, give t. p., Mk.
26 : 9. ointment might been sold
given t. p., Mk. 14:5. Jn. 12:5.
Lu. 4:18. to preach gospel t. p., 7:22.
18 : 22. sell all and distribute u. p.
19:8. half of my goods I give t. p.
Jn. 13:29. sho. give something t. p.
Ja. 2 : 3. say t. p. Stand thou there
Thy POOR.
Ex. 23 : 6. not rest judgment of t. p.
De. 15:7. nor shut hand fr. t. p. bro.
9. eye be evil ag. t. p. brother
11. shalt open hand wide to t. p.
Ps. 72:2. sh. judge t. p. with judgm.
74:19. forget not congr. of t. p. for
POORER, EST. [ever
Le. 27:8. if he be p-r than thy estim.
2 K. 24:14. none save p-t sort of peo.
POPLAR, S.
Ge 30:37. Jac. took rods of green p.
Ho. 4:13. they burn incense und. p-s
POPULOUS.
De. 26 : 5. became a nation great, p.
Is. 9 : † 1. afflict in Galilee p.
Na. 3:8. Art thou better than p. No?
POR'ATHA.
Es. 9 : 8. sons of Haman, P.
PORCH, PORCHES.
Ju. 3 : 23. Then Ehud went thro. p.
1 K. 6 : 3. p. bef. temple, 2 Ch. 3:4.
7 : 6. he made a p. of pillars
7. made p. for throne | 8, 9, 12,
19, 21. [of p.
1 Ch. 28:11. David gave Sol. pattern
2 Ch. 8 : 12. altar he built before p.
15 : 8. altar of Lord before p. of L.
29 : 7. have shut up doors of p. [p.
17. eighth day of month came to
Eze. 8 : 16. betw. p. and alt. 25 men
40 : 7. by p. of gate was one reed
8. He measured also the p. of
gate, 9, 15, 39, 40, 48, 49.
† 16. were narrow windows to p-s
† 21. p-s were aft. measure of gate
41 : 15. within temple and p-s [26.
25. were thick planks upon p-s |
44:3. sh. enter by way of p., 46:2, 8.
Jo. 2 : 17. weep betw. p. and altar
Mat. 26:71. when he was gone into p.
Mk. 14 : 68. went into p. cock crew
Jn. 5:2. pool Bethesda having 5 p-s
10 : 23. Jes. walked in Sol.'s p. [p.
Ac. 3:11. peo. ran together in Sol.'s
5 : 12. with one accord in Sol.'s p.
POR'CIUS FES'TUS.
Ac. 24:27. P. F. came into Felix' room
PORPHYRY. [p.
Es. 1 : † 6. beds upon pavement of
PORT.
See **DUNG port, SEA port.**
PORTER.
2 S. 18:26. watchman called unto p.
2 K. 7 : 10. lepers called unto the p.
1 Ch. 9 : 21. Zech. was p. of taberu.
2 Ch. 31 : 14. Kore the p. tow. east
Mk. 13 : 34. commanded p. to watch
Jn. 10 : 3. To him p. openeth, sheep
PORTERS. [hear
2 K. 7 : 11. called p. and they told
1 Ch. 9 : 17. the p. were Shallum,
Akkub, Talmon | 18, 22, 24, 26.
2 Ch. 34 : 13. Ezr. 10 : 24. Ne. 7:
45.-12 : 25. [p.
15 : 18. Obed-edom, and Jehiel the
16 : 38. Obed-edom, Hosah p.
42. sons of Jeduthun were p.
23:5. moreover 4,000 were p.
26:1. Cone-g divisions of p., 12, 19.
2 Ch. 8 : 14. p. by their courses at
every gate, 23 : 4, 19. Ne. 11:19.
35 : 15. the p. waited at every gate
Ezr. 7 : 7. p. up unto Jerus., 2 : 42.

Ezr.7:24.not lawf. to impose toll up-
Ne. 7:1. p. singers appointed ⌊on p.
73. p. dwelt in their cities, Ezr.2:
10:28. Levites, p. singers, and ⌊70.
39.the chambers where are the p.
12:45. p. kept ward of their God

PORTION.

Ge. 14:24. Aner, Eschol, let take p.
31 : 14. Is there yet any p. for us?
47 : 22. priest had a p. assigned,
and did eat their p. ⌈brethren
48:22. I have given thee one p. ab.
Ex. 16 : † 4. gather p. of day in day
† 15. it is a p. for they wist not
Le. 6 : 17. have given them it for p.
7:35. This is p. of anointing of Aa.
Nu. 31:30. of Isr.'s half take one p.,
47. took one p. of fifty for Lev.⌊36.
De. 21 : 17. by giving him double p.
29:†26. had not given them any p.
32 : 9. for Lord's p. is his people
33 : 21. in a p. of the lawgiver was
Jos. 17:14. Why given me but 1 p.?
19:9. Out of p. of children of Jud.
1 S. 1 : 5. unto Hannah a worthy p.
9 : 23. Sam. said, Bring p. I gave
1 K. 12 : 16. What p. have we in David, 2 Ch. 10 : 16. ⌈be upon me
2 K. 2 : 9. double p. of thy spirit
9 : 10. dogs shall eat Jezebel in p. of Jezreel, 36, 37.
21. Joram met him in p. of Naboth
25. cast him in p. of Naboth's
†26. I will requite thee in this p.
2 Ch. 28 : 21. Ahaz took a p. out of
31:3. Hezekiah appointed king's p.
4. to give the p. of the priests, 16.
Ezr. 4 : 16. have no p. on this side
Ne. 2 : 20. ye have no p. in Jerus.
11 : 23. a certain p. be for singers
12 : 47. gave porters ev. day his p.
Jb. 20:29. This is p. of wicked man
23 : † 12. than my appointed p.
24 : 18. their p. is cursed in earth
26:14. how little p. is heard, 27:13.
31 : 2. what p. of G. is fr. above?
Ps. 11 : 6. shall be p. of their cup
16 : 5. Lord is p. of mine inherit.
17:14. men wh. have p. in this life
50 : † 18. thy p. with adulterers
63 : 10. they shall be a p. for foxes
73 : 26. God is my p. for ever ⌈5.
119:57. Thou art my p. O Lord, 142:
Pr. 31 : 15. giveth p. to her maidens
Ec. 2:10. and my p. of all my labour
21. to a man sh. leave it for his p.
3 : 22. that is his p., 5:18.–9:9. ⌈p.
5:19. God given him power to take
9 : 6. nei. have they any more p.
11 : 2. Give a p. to seven, and also
Is. 17 : 14. p. of them that spoil us
53 : 12. divide him a p. with great
57 : 6. Am. smooth stones is thy p.
61 : 7. they shall rejoice in their p.
Je. 10 : 16. The p. of Jacob is not like them, 51 : 19.
12 : 10. have trodden my p. have made my p. a desolate wildern.
13 : 25. This is p. of thy measures
52 : 34. every day a p. until death
La. 3 : 24. L. is my p. saith my soul
Eze. 45 : 1. I shall offer a holy p., 4.
6. oblation of holy p., Eze. 48:18.
7. a p. be for prince on one side
48:1. to coast of Hethlon p. for Dan
2. by border of Dan p. for Asher
3. a p. for Naphtali | 4. a p. for Manasseh ⌈Reuben
5. a p. for Ephraim | 6. p. for
7. a p. for Judah | 23. Benj. shall have a p. ⌈p.
24. Simeon a p. | 25. Issachar a
26. Zebulon a p. | 27. Gad a p.
Da. 1 : 8. not defile hims. with p. of king's meat, 13, 15, 16. ⌈beasts, 23
4 : 15. and let his p. be with the
11 : 26. that feed of p. of his meat

Mi. 2 : 4. he changed p. of my peo.
Ha. 1 : 16. by them their p. is fat
Zch. 2:12. L. shall inherit Jud. his p.
Mat. 24 : 51. his p. with hypocrites
Lu. 12 : 42. their p. in due season
46. appoint his p. with unbelievers
15:12. give me the p. of goods that

PORTIONS. ⌈eat

De. 18:8. They shall have like p. to
Jos. 17 : 5. fell ten p. to Manasseh
1 S. 1 : 4. gave sons and dau-s p.
2 Ch. 31 : 19 to give p. to all males
Ne. 8:10. eat the fat send p., 12. ⌈ers
12:44. p. for priests | 47. p. of sing-
13 : 10 p. of Levites not been giv
Es. 2:†9. gave her things with her p.
9 : 19. a day of sending p. to, 22.
Eze. 47 : 13. Joseph sh. have two p.
48 : 21. over ag. p. for prince, 45:7.
29. these are their p. saith L.
Ho. 5 : 7. month devour th. with p.

PORTRAY, ED.

Eze. 4 : 1. p. upon it city of Jerus.
8 : 10. idols of Israel p-d upon wall
23:14. she saw men p-d upon wall, images of the Chaldeans p-d

POSSESS. ⌈24 : 60.

Ge. 22 : 17. thy seed shall p. gate,
Nu. 13 : 30. Let us go up and p. it, for we are able to, De. 1 : 21.
27:11. his next kinsman shall p. it
De. 1 : 39. I give it, they shall p. it
2 : 31. begin to p. th. thou inherit
11 : 23. ye shall p. greater nations, 12 : 2, 29.–18:14.–31:3 ⌈cust p.
28 : † 42. fruit of thy land shall lo-
30 : 18. over Jordan to p. it, 31:13.
33 : 23. p. thou the west and south
Jos. 24 : 4. unto Esau Seir to p. it
Ju. 11 : 23. shouldest thou p. it?
24. Wilt p. what Chemosh giv-h
14 : † 15. have ye called us to p. us
1 K. 21 : 18. he is gone to p. viney.
Jb. 7 : 3. made to p. mo-s of vanity
13:26. makest me p. iniq-s of youth
Is. 34:11. and bittern shall p. it, 17.
Eze. 7:24. they shall p. their houses
35:10. countries be mine, we will p.
36 : 12. I will cause Isr. to p. thee
Da. 7 : 18. saints shall p. kingd. ⌈p.
Ho. 9 : 6. pleasant places, nettles sh.
Am. 9 : 12. Th. they may p. Edom
Ob. 17. the house of Jac. shall p.
19. p. m-t Esau, Benj. p. Gilead
20. Isr. sh. p. that of Canaanites
Jerus. shall p. cities of south
Ha. 1 : 6. Chaldeans to p. not theirs
Zph. 2 : 9. my people shall p. them
Zch. 8 : 12. will cause remn. to p. all
Lu. 18 : 12. I give tithes of all I p.
21:19. In patience p. ye your souls
1 Th. 4:4. sho. know how to p. vessel

POSSESS with land.

Le. 20 : 24. I give you their l. to p., Nu. 33:53. De. 3:18.–5:31.–17:14.
Nu. 14 : 24. l. his seed shall p. it
De. 1 : 8. go in and p. the l., 4 : 1.–6:18.–8:1.–9:5, 23.–10:11.–11:31. Jos. 1 : 11.
2 : 24. begin to p. l. and contend
3 : 20. until they also p. the l.
4:5. l. whi. ye go to p. it, 14, 26.–5:33.–6:1.–7:1.–11:10, 11, 29.–23:20.–30 : 16.–32 : 47.
22. ye sh. go and p. that good l.
9 : 4. L. bro-t me to p. this l., 5.
6. giveth not this l. to p. for thy
11 : 8. ye may be strong and p. l.
12 : 1. l. which Lord God of thy fathers giveth thee to p., 3:18.–15 : 4.–17 : 14.–19:2, 14.–21:1.–25 : 19. ⌈to p.
28 : 21. consumed off l. thou goest
63. plucked off l. thou goest to p.
Jos. 13 : † 1. remain-h much l. to p.
18 : 3. How long slack to p. l.
23 : 5. drive them out, ye sh. p. l.

Jos. 24 : 8. that ye might p. their l.
Ju. 2 : 6. Isr. went ev. man to p. l.
18 : 9. be not slothful to p. the l.
1 Ch. 28 : 8. that ye p. this good l.
Ezr. 9 : 11. l. ye go to p. is uncl. l.
Ne. 9 : 15. that they should p. l.
23. broughtest them to p. l., 24.
Is. 14 : 2. Isr. shall p. them in l. of
21. do not rise nor p. the l. ⌊L.
57:13. putteth trust in me sh. p. l.
61 : 7. in their l. shall p. double
Je. 3:†18. l. I caused your fa-s to p.
30 : 3. to return to l. and p. it
Eze. 33:25. shed bl. shall ye p. l.? 26.
Am. 2:10. I bro-t you to p. l. of Am-

POSSESSED. ⌊orite

Nu. 21 : 24. Israel p. Sihon's land
35. they smote Og and have p. land, De. 3 : 12.–4:47. Ne. 9:22.
De. 30 : 5. thee into land thy fa-s p.
Jos. 1 : 15. until breth. have p. land
12 : 1. p. their land on other side
13:1. yet very much la. to be p. ⌈it
19:47. chil. of Dan took Leshem p.
21 : 43. they p. it and dwelt, 22 : 9.
Ju. 1 : † 19. Judah p. the mountain
3 : 13. Eglon p. city of palm trees
11 : 21. Isr. p. la. of Amorites, 22.
2 K. 17 : 24. men of Ava p. Samaria
Ps. 139 : 13. thou hast p. my reins
Pr. 8 : 22. Lord p. me in beginning
Is. 63 : 18. people of holiness p. it
Je. 32 : 15. vineyards sh. be p. again
23. they p. it, but obeyed not
Da. 7 : 22. that saints p. kingdom
Lu. 8 : 36. he that was p. was cured
Ac. 4 : 32. none said th. aught he p.
8:7. spirits out of many th. were p.
16 : 16. a damsel p. with a spirit
1 Co. 7:30. they th. buy as tho. they
See DEVIL, S. ⌊p. not

POSSESSEST, ETH, ING.

Nu. 36:8. dau. that p-h inheritance
De. 12 : † 29. thou p-t them and dwellest, 19 : † 1.
26 : 1. when into land and p-t it
Pr. 15 : † 32. obeyeth reproof p-h a heart ⌈he p-h
Lu. 12 : 15. consisteth not in things
2 Co. 6 : 10. having nothing, yet p-g

POSSESSION. ⌊all

Ge. 17:8. I will give land of Canaan for an everlasting p., 48 : 4.
23 : 4. give me a p. of a burying-place, 9, 18, 20.–49 : 30.–50 : 13.
26:14. Isaac had p. of flocks, herds
36 : 43. dukes of Edom in land of p.
47 : 11. gave them p. in land of E.
Le. 14 : 34. Canaan I give you for p.
25 : 10. ye sh. return ev. man unto his p., 13, 27, 28, 41. De. 3 : 20.
24. in la. of p. grant redemption
25. If brother sold some of his p.
33. Levites' p. go out in jubilee
34. it is their perpetual p.
45. strangers shall be your p., 46.
27 : 16. if man sanctify part of p.,
21. p. shall be the priest's ⌊22, 28.
24. return to whom p. of the land did belong ⌈a p.
Nu. 24 : 18. Edom shall be a p. Seir
26 : 56. acc. to lot shall the p. be
27 : 4. give us a p. among breth.
7. to dau-s of Zeloph. give a p.
32:5. let land be given serv-s for p.
22. this land sh. be your p. bef. L.
29. give land of Gilead for p. ⌈8.
35:2. give unto Levites of their p.,
28. slayer return into la. of his p.
De. 2:5. m-t Seir unto Esau for a p.
9. I have giv. Ar unto Lot for p.,
12. as Isr. did in land of his p. ⌊19.
11 : 6. earth swallowed all in p.
32:49. Canaan, I gave Isr. for a p.
Jos. 1 : 15. retu. unto land of p., 22:
12 : 6. Moses gave it for p. ⌊4, 9.
7. Joshua gave unto Isr. for p.

Jos. 18:29. p. of half tribe of Manas.
21.12. gave to Caleb for his p. [Isr.
41. cities of Levites within p. of
22:7. to half tribe of Manasseh a p.
19. if your p. uncl. take p. am. us
1 K. 21:15. p. of viney. of Naboth, 16.
19. hast thou killed and tak. p.?
1 Ch. 28 : 1. stewards ov. p. of king
2 Ch. 11:14. Lev. left suburbs and p.
20 : 11. to cast us out of thy p.
31:1. returned every man to his p.
Ne. 11 : 3. dwelt every one in his p.
Ps. 2 : 8. uttermost parts for thy p.
44 : 3. got not land in p. by sword
69 : 35. may dwell and have in p.
83:12. Let us take houses of G. in p.
105:† 21. made him ruler of his p.
Pr. 28:10. upright have good things
Is. 14 : 23. it a p. for bittern [in p.
Eze. 11:15. unto us is la. given in p.
25:4. thee to men of east for p., 10.
36:2. ancient high places ours in p.
3. ye be a p. unto heathen
5. appointed land into their p.
44 : 28. give them no p. in Israel,
I am their p. [7.-48: 20,21,22.
45 : 6. ye shall appoint p. of city,
8. In land shall be his p. in Israel
46 : 18. son's inheri. out of own p.,
48 : 20. with the p. of the city [16.
22. from the p. of the Levites
Ac. 5 : 1. Ananias sold a p.
7 : 5. would give it to him for a p.
45. with Jesus into p. of Gentiles
Ep. 1 : 14. until redemption of p.

POSSESSIONS. [p.

Ge. 34 : 10. dwell, trade, and get you
47 : 27. Isr. had p. and multiplied
Nu. 32:30. shall have p. among you
1 S. 25 : 2. whose p. were in Carmel
1 Ch. 7:28. their p. were Beth-el and
9 : 2. inhabitants dwelt in p.
2 Ch. 32 : 29. provided p. of flocks
Jb. 17:† 11. broken off p. of my heart
Ec. 2 : 7. I had great p. of great
Ob. 17. Jacob shall possess their p.
Mat. 19:22. he had gr. p., Mk. 10:22.
Ac. 2 : 45. sold p. and parted them
28 : 7. in same quarters p. of Pub-

POSSESSOR, S. [lius

Ge. 14:19. most high G. p. of heav.,
Ju. 18:† 7. was no p. in the land [22.
Zch. 11:5. Whose p-s slay them, and
Ac. 4 : 34. many as were p-s of lands

POSSIBLE.

Mat. 19 : 26. with God all things are
p., Mk. 10 : 27. [Mk. 13 : 22.
24 : 24. if p. shall deceive the elect,
26 : 39. if p. let this cup pass from
me, Mk. 14 : 35. [believeth
Mk. 9 : 23. all things are p. to him
14 : 36. all things are p. unto thee,
Lu. 18 : 27. [of it
Ac. 2 : 24. not p. he sho. be holden
20:16. if p. be at Jerus. day of Pente.
27 : 39. if p. to thrust in the ship
Ro. 12 : 18. if p. live peaceably
2 Co. 12:† 4. not p. for man to utter
Ga. 4 : 15. if p. ye wo. have plucked
He. 10 : 4. not p. blood of bulls take

POST, S. [sins

2 Ch. 30 : 6. So p-s went with letters
fr. king, 10. Es. 3 : 13, 15.-8: 10.
Es. 8 : 14. p-s rode on mules and
Jb. 9 : 25. my days swifter than p.
Je. 51 : 31. One p. run to meet ano.

POST.

1 S. 1 : 9. Eli sat by a p. of temple
Eze. 40:14. unto the p. of the court
16. upon each p. were palm trees
41 : † 21. p. of temple was squared
See **DOOR** with **post, s.**

POSTS. [house

De. 6 : 9. write them upon p. of thy
Ju. 16 : 3. Samson took the two p.
1 K. 6 : 33. he made p. of olive tree
7 : 5. doors and p. were square

Pr. 8 : 34. waiting at p. of my doors
Is. 57 : 8. Behind p. set up remembr.
Eze. 40:9. the p. thereof two cubits
10. p. had one measure, 41 : 1.
14. he made p. of threesc. cubits
21. p. aft. measure of first gate
24. he measured p. thereof, 29, 33.
26. palm trees upon p., 31, 34, 37.
38. chambers were by p. of gates
49. there were pillars by the p.
41 : 21. p. of temple were squared
43 : 8. setting of their p. by my p.
45 : 19. blood of off-g. put it on p.
Am. 9:1. smite lintel. that p. shake

Side POSTS. [22.

Ex. 12 : 7. strike blood upon 2 s.p.,
23. when he seeth blood on s. p.
1 K. 6 : 31. lintel and s. p. were 5th

POSTERITY. [part

Ge. 45 : 7. to preserve you a p. in
Nu. 9 : 10. if any of your p. be uncl.
1 K. 16 : 3. I will take p. of Baasha
21 : 21. I will take p. of Ahab
Ps. 49 : 13. p. approve their sayings
109 : 13. Let his p. be cut off
Da. 11 : 4. not be divided to his p.
Am. 4:2. take your p. with fishhooks

POT.

Ex. 16:33. Take a p. and put manna
Le. 6 : 28. if sodden in brazen p.
Ju. 6 : 19. Gideon put broth in a p.
1 S. 2 : 14. he struck it into the p.
2 K. 4 : 2. not thing, save p. of oil
38. set on great p. for prophets,
40. there is death in the p. [39.
41. he cast meal into the p. no
harm in the p. [ing p.
Jb. 41 : 20. smoke, as out of a seeth-
31. maketh deep to boil like p.
Pr. 17 : 3. fining p. for silver, 27:21.
Ec. 7 : 6. as thorns under a p.
Je. 1 : 13. what seest? I see seething
Eze. 24 : 3. saith L. Set on a p. [p.
6. Woe to p. whose scum is therein
Jo. 2 : † 6. all faces shall gather p.
Mi. 3 : 3. chop in pieces as for p.
Zch. 14 : 21. ev. p. in Jerus. be holi-
He. 9:4. golden p. with manna [ness
See WASHPOT, WATERPOT, S.

POTS.

Ex. 16:3. when we sat by the flesh p.
38 : 3. Bezaleel made the p. and
Le. 11:35. whe. oven, or ranges for p.
1 K. 7 : 45. p. and shovels of brass,
2 K. 25:14. 2 Ch. 4:16. [shovels
2 Ch. 4:11. Huram made the p. and
35:13. holy offerings sod they in p.
Ps. 58 : 9. Before p. can feel thorns
68 : 13. Tho. ye have lien among p.
81:6. hands were deliv-d fr. the p.
Je. 35:5. bef. Rechabites p. of wine
Mk. 7 : 4. washing of cups and p., 8.

POTENTATE. [P.

1 Ti. 6 : 15. who is blessed and only

POT'IPHAR. See PHARAOH.

POTI-PHE'RAH.

Ge. 41:45. Asenath, dau. of P., 50.-

POTSHERD. S. [46:20.

Jb. 2 : 8. took a p. to scrape himself
41:† 30. Sharp pieces of p. und. him
Ps. 22 : 15. My strength is like a p.
Pr. 26 : 23. are like a p. covered
Is. 45:9. Let the p. strive with p-s

POTTAGE.

Ge. 25 : 29. Jacob sod p. and Esau
30. Esau said, Feed me with p.
34. Jacob gave Esau bread and p.
2 K. 4 : 38. seethe p. for prophets
39. and shred them into pot of p.
40. were eating p. they cried out
Hag. 2 : 12. if one do touch bread or

POTTER, S. [p.

1 Ch. 4 : 23. these were the p-s
Ps. 2:9. dash in pieces like p.'s vessel
Is. 30 : 14. sh. break it as breaking
of p.'s vessel, Je. 19:11. Re. 2:27.
Je. 18 : 2. go down to p.'s house, 3.

Je. 18:4. vessel was marred in hands
of p., as seemed good to the p.
6. can-t I do with you as this p.
19 : 1. Go get p.'s earthen bottle
La. 4 : 2. work of hands of the p.
Zch. 11 : 13. L. said, Cast it unto p.
Mat. 27:10. gave them for p.'s field,
See CLAY. [7.

POUND, S. [shield

1 K. 10 : 17. three p-s of gold to one
Ezr. 2 : 69. gave 5,000 p-s of silver
Ne. 7:71. to treasure 2,200 p-s of silver [and gold
72. the rest gave 2,000 p-s of silver
Lu. 19:13. delivered to serv-s 10 p-s
16. second said, Lord, thy p. hath
gained ten p-s [is thy p.
18. hath gained five p-s | 20. here
24. Take from him the p. give it
to him hath 10 p-s
25. they said, L. he hath 10 p-s
Jn. 12 : 3. Mary took p. of ointment
19 : 39. aloes about 100 p. weight

POUR.

Ex. 4 : 9. p. water upon dry land
25 : † 29. shalt make bowls to p.
out of gold, 37 :† 16. Nu. 4 : † 7.
29:7 p. anointing oil upon his head
12. p. blood of bullock beside altar, Le. 4 : 7, 18, 25, 30, 34.
30 : 9. nei. shall ye p. drink-off-gs
Le. 2 : 1. p. oil upon meat off-gs, 6.
14:15. p. it into palm of left ha., 26.
18. p. it upon head to be cleansed
41. p. out dust th. they scrape off
17 : 13. he sh. p. out blood thereof
Nu. 5 : 15. p. no oil upon her off-g
24 : 7. sh. p. water out of buckets
De. 12 : 16. p. blood out, 24.-15:23.
Ju. 6 : 20. take flesh, p. out broth
1 K. 18 : 33. p. water on burnt sacr.
2 K. 4 : 4. p. oil into those vessels
41. p. out for people, th. may eat
9 : 3. p. the oil on Jehu's head
Jb. 36 : 27. they p. down rain acc.
Ps. 42 : 4. remem. I p. out my soul
62 : 8. ye people, p. out your heart
69:24. p. out indignation upon th.
79:6. p. out thy wrath upon heath.
Pr. 1 : 23. I will p. spirit unto you
Is. 44 : 3. I will p. my Spirit upon
thy seed, Jo. 2:28, 29. Ac. 2:17,
I will p. water upon thirsty [18.
45 : 8. let skies p. down righte-n.
Je. 6:† 6. p. out engines of shot ag.
6 : 11. I will p. it out upon chil.
7 : 18. to p. off-gs unto other gods
10:25. p. out thy fury upon heath.
14 : 16. I will p. their wickedness
18:21. p. out their blood by sword
44 : 17. to p. out drink off-gs unto
queen of heav., 18, 19, 25. [bef. L.
La. 2 : 19. p. out heart like water
Eze. 7 : 8. now will I p. out fury,
14 : 19.-20 : 8, 13, 21.-30 : 15.
21 : 31. I will p. out indignation,
Zph. 3 : 8.
24 : 3. set on the pot and p. water
Ho. 5 : 10. I will p. out my wrath
Mi. 1 : 6. I will p. down the stones
Zch. 12:10. I will p. upon ho. of Da.
Mal. 3 : 10. if I will not p. out bless-
Re. 16 : 1. p. vials of wrath [ing

POURED.

Ge. 28 : 18. Jacob p. oil upon stone
35 : 14. Jacob p. a drink offering
Ex. 9 : 33. rain not p. upon earth
30 : 32. Upon man's flesh not be p.
Le. 4 : 12. where ashes are p. he sh.
8:12. Moses p. oil upon Aa.'s head
15. p. bl. at bottom of alt., 9 : 9.
21:10. upon whose head oil was p.
Nu. 28 : 7. p. unto L. for drink-off-g
De. 12 : 27. blood of sacr. be p. out
Jos. 7 : † 23. p. them out bef. Lord
1 S. 1 : 15. have p. out my soul bef.
7 : 6. drew water, p. it bef. L. [L.

1 S. 10 : 1. Sam'l p. oil upon Saul's
2 S. 13:9. Tamar p. them out [head
23 : 16. David wo. not drink but p.
it unto L., 1 Ch. 11:18. [out, 5.
1 K.18:3. altar shall be rent, ashes p.
18:†28. till they p. blood upon them
2 K.3:11. p. wat. on hands of Elijah
4 : 5. vessels to her, and she p. out
40. they p. out for men to eat
9:6. Elisha p. oil on his head
16 : 13. Ahaz p. his drink offering
2 Ch. 12:7. wrath not p. upon Jerus.
34 : † 17. have p. out money
21. gr. is wrath of L., p. upon us
25. my wrath sh. be p. upon pla.
Jb. 3 : 24. my roarings are p. out
10 : 10. Hast not p. me out as milk
22:†16 flood was p. upon founda.
29 : 6. rock p. me out rivers of oil
30 : 16. now my soul is p. out
38 :† 38. When dust is p. into hard-
Ps. 22 : 14. I am p. like water [ness
45 : 2. grace is p. into thy lips, thf.
77 : 17. clouds p. out water, skies
142 : 2. I p. out my complaint [p.
Can. 1 : 3. thy name is as ointment
Is. 26 : 16. p. prayer, when chast-g
29 : 10. Lord hath p. on you sleep
32 : 15. Until the Spirit be p. on us
42 : 25. he hath p. upon him fury
53 : 12. p. out his soul unto death
57 : 6. hast p. out a drink off-ing
Je. 7 : 20. my fury be p. upon place
19 : 13. p. out drink off-gs, 32 : 29.
42 : 18. as fury been, so be p. out
44 : 6. my fury and anger was p.
19. p. drink offerings unto queen
La. 2 : 4. he p. fury like fire, 4 : 11.
11. my liver is p. on earth
12. soul p. into mothers' bosom
4 : 1. stones of sanctuary are p.
Eze. 16 : 36. thy filthiness was p. out
20 : 28. p. out their drink offerings
33. with fury p. out will I rule, 34.
22 : 22. I the Lord p. out my fury
31. Thf. I p. out mine indignation
23:8. p. their whoredom upon her
24 : 7. she p. it not upon ground
35 : † 5. thou hast p. out blood of
36 : 18. whf. I p. out my fury
39:29. I p. out my Spirit upon Isr.
Da. 9 : 11. thf. curse is p. upon us
27. that determined shall be p.
Mi. 1:4. as waters are p. do. steep pl.
Na. 1 : 6. fury is p. out like fire [out
Zph. 1 : 17. their blood shall be p.
Mat. 26:7. p. ointment on his head,
12. Mk. 14 : 3. [money
Jn. 2 : 15. he p. out the changers'
Ac. 10 : 45. on Gentiles was p. gift
Ph. 2 : † 17. if I be p. upon service
Re. 14 : 10. wine of wrath of God p.
16 : 2. p. out his vial, 3, 4, 8, 10, 12,

POUREDST. [17.

Eze. 16 : 15. p. out thy fornications

POURETH.

Jb. 12 : 21. He p. contempt upon
princes, Ps. 107 : 40. [ground
16 : 13. he p. out my gall upon the
20. mine eye p. out tears unto G.
Ps. 75 : 8. wine is red, he p. out
Pr. 15 : 2. of fools p. out foolishness
28. mouth of wicked p. out evil
Am. 5:8. p. out waters on earth, 9:6.
Jn. 13 : 5. p. water into a basin

POURING.

Le.4:†12. at p. out of ashes be burnt
Eze. 9 : 8. in thy p. fury upon Jerus.
Lu. 10 : 34. his wounds, p. in oil

POURTRAY. See PORTRAY.

POVERTY.

Ge. 45 : 11. lest thou come to p. [thou.
1 Ch. 22 † : 14. in p. I prepared for
Pr. 6 : 11. thy p. as armed man, 24:34.
10 : 15. destruction of poor is p.
11:24. withholdeth, it tendeth to p.
13 : 18. p. to him refuseth instr. [p.
20 : 13. Love not sleep, lest come to
Pr. 23 : 21. drunkard and glutton to
p. [have p. enough
28. 19. followeth vain persons, shall
22. considereth not p. shall come
30 : 8. give me nei. p. nor riches
31 : 7. Let him drink and forget p.
2 Co. 8 : 2. p. abounded unto riches
9. yo thro. his p. might be rich
Re. 2 : 9. I know thy works and p.

POWDER, S.

Ex. 32 : 20. Moses burnt calf to p.
De. 28 : 24. L. make rain of land p.
2 K. 23 : 6. stamped the grove to p.
cast p. upon graves [2 Ch 34:7.
15. he stamped the altar to p.,
Can. 3 : 6. perfumed with all the p-s
Mat 21 : 44. will grind him to p.,

POWER. [Lu. 20 : 18.

Ge. 32 : 28. as prince hast thou p.
49 : 3. of dignity, excellency of p.
Le. 26 : 19. break pride of your p.
Nu. 5:† 19. being in p. of thy hush.
22 : 38. have I p. to say any thing?
De. 3:† 18. over all th. are sons of p.
4:37. bro-t thee with his mighty p.
8 : 18. giveth thee P. to get wealth
32:36. when he seeth their p. gone
Ru. 4 : † 11. get thee p. in Ephratah
2 S. 22 : 33. G. my strength and p.
2 K. 19 : 26. inhabitants of sm. p.
1 Ch. 20 : 1. Joab led p. of the army
29:11. Thine is the p. and the glory,
Mat. 6 : 13. [2 Ch. 20 : 6.
12. in thine hand is p. and might,
2 Ch. 25 : 8. God hath p. to help
26 : 13. made war with mighty p.
32:9. Sennach. laid siege, and his p.
Ezr. 4 : 23. made them cease by p.
8:22. his p. ag. all th. forsake him
Ne. 5 : 5. nei. in our p. to redeem
Es. 1 : 3. made feast to p. of Persia
8 : 11. to cause to perish p. of peo.
9 : 1. Jews hoped to have p. over
10 : 2. acts of his p., are they not
Jb. 5 : 20. redeem from p. of sword
24:22. He draweth mighty with p.
26 : 2. hast helped him is with-t p.
12. He divided the sea with his p.
14. his p. who can understand?
36:22. G. exalteth by his p. [nor p.
41 : 12. I will not conceal his parts
Ps. 22 : 20. my darling fr. p. of dog
49:15. redeem my soul fr. p. of grave
62 : 11. p. belongeth unto G.
65 : 6. mountains girded with p.
66 : 7. He ruleth by his p. for ever
68:35. he giveth p. unto his pople
78 : 26. by p. he bro-t south wind
90 : 11. Who knoweth p. of anger?
106 : 8. his mighty p. to be known
111 : 6. shewed peo p. of his works
150:1. praise in firmament of his p.
Ec. 4 : 1. on side of oppressors p.
5 : 19. hath given him p. to eat
6 : 2. God giveth him not p. to eat
8 : 4. Where word of king is, is p.
8. no man hath p. over spirit
Is. 37 : 27. inhabitants of small p.
40 : 29. He giveth p. to the faint
43 : 17. bringeth forth army and p.
47:14. not deliver from p. of flame
Je. 10 : 12. made earth by his p., 51:
Eze. 22:6. to their p. to shed bl. [15.
30 : 6. pride of her p. sh. come do.
Da. 2 : 37. God hath given thee p.
6:27. delivered Daniel fr. p. of lions
8 : 6. ran in fury of his p.
22. but not in his p. [by his p.
24. his p. shall be mighty, but not
11 : 6. she sh. not retain p. of arm
25. sh. stir up his p. and courage
43. he sh. have p. over treasures
12 : 7. to scatter p. of holy people
Ho. 12 : 3. by strength he had p. wi.
4. he had p. over the angel [G.
13:14. ransom them fr. p. of grave
Mi. 3:8. I am full of p. by the Spirit
Ha. 1 : 11. imputing his p. unto his
2:9. be delivered fr. p. of evil [god
3 : 4. there was hiding of his p.
Zch. 4:6. Not by might, nor by my p.
9 : 4 the Lord will smite her p.
Mat. 9:6. Son of man hath p. to forgive sins, Mk. 2 : 10. Lu. 5 : 24.
8. had given such p. unto men
10:1. gave p. against unclean spirits, Mk 6 : 7. Lu. 9 : 1.
24 : 30. coming in the clouds with
p., Lu. 21 : 27.
26 : 64. sitting on right hand of p.,
Mk. 14 : 62. [heaven and
28 : 18. All p. is given unto me in
Mk. 3 : 15. have p. to heal sicknesses
9 : 1. kingdom of God come with p.
Lu. 1:35. p. of Highest overshadow
4:6. devil said, All this p. will I give
32. for his word was with p.
36. wi. p. he commandeth spirits
5 : 17. p. of the Lord was present
10:19. I give p. to tread on serpents,
and over p. of enemy [hell
12:5. fear him hath p. to cast into
20:20 deliver him unto p. of gov.
22:53. is hour. and p. of darkness
24 : 49. until ye be endued with p.
Jn. 1 : 12. gave p. to become sons
10 : 18. I p. to lay it down, and p.
17 : 2 given him p. over all flesh
19:10. I have p. to crucify thee, p.
Ac. 1 : 7. Fa. hath put in own p.
8. shall receive p. after H. Ghost
3:12. as tho. by own p. or holiness
4:7. By what p. have ye done this?
6 : 8. Stephen full of faith and p.
8 : 19. Saying, Give me also this p.
10:38. how G. anointed Jes. with p.
26:18. to turn them fr. p. of Satan
Ro. 1 : 4. declared Son of G. with p.
20. his eternal p. and Godhead
9:21. Hath not potter p. over clay?
22. if G , willing to make p. kno.
13:2. Whoso. therefore resisteth p.
3. Wilt thou not be afraid of p.?
15:13. in hope, thro p. of Holy G.
19. wond-rs, by p. of Sp. of God
16 : 25. Now to him that is of p.
1 Co. 2 : 4 in demonstration of p.
4:19 I will not know speech, but p.
5:4. with p. of our L. Jesus Christ
6 : 12. I will not be bro-t under p.
14. will raise us up by his own p.
7:4. wife and husband have not p.
37. hath p. ov. his own will [bio.
8:†9. lest this p. become stumbling-
9 : 4. Have not we p. to eat and to
5 Have we not p. to lead a wife?
6. we not p. to forbear working?
12. if others partakers of p. over
you, we have not used this p.
11 : 10. woman ought to have p.
15:24. he hath put down all p. [G.
2 Co 4:7. excellency of p. may be of
8 : 3. to their p. yea, bey. their p.
12 : 9. that p. of C. rest upon me
13 : 10. acc. to p. L. hath given me
Ep. 1 : 19. greatness of his p. toward
us, working of his mighty p.
21. Far above all principality, p.
2 : 2. to prince of p. of the air
3:7. by effectual working of his p.
20. acc. to p. that worketh in us
Ph. 3:10. know p. of his resurrection
Col. 1 : 11. acc. to his glorious p.
13. delivered us fr. p. of darkness
2 : 10. head of principality and p.
2 Th. 1:†7. revealed wi. angels of p.
9. punished from glory of his p.
11. fulfil work of faith with p.
2 : 9. working of Satan with all p.
3:9. Not because we have not p. but
1 Ti. 6 : 16. whom be honour and p.
2 Ti. 1:7. God hath given spirit of p.
3 : 5. form of godliness, denying p.
He. 1 : 3. upholding all things by p.

He.2:14.destroy him had p. of death
7:16. after the p. of an endless life
2 Pe. 1: 3. his divine p. hath giv. all
16. made known p. of our Lord
Jude 25. to our Saviour glory and p.
Re. 2: 26. to him give p. ov. nations
4:11. art worthy to receive p.,5:12.
5: 13. glory and p. be unto him
6: 4. p. was given to him that sat
8. p. given them over 4th part
7:12. p. and might be giv. unto G.
9:3. unto them p. as scorpions have
10. their p. was to hurt men [p.
19. their p. is in their mouth and
11: 3. give p. unto my witnesses
6. p. to shut heaven, p. ov. waters
12: 10. Now is p. of Christ come
13: 2. dragon gave him p., 4. [7.
5. p. given unto him to continue,
12. exerciseth p. of 1st beast, 14.
15. p. to give life unto image
14:18. angel had p. ov. fire [his p.
15: 8. temple filled with smoke fr.
16: 8. p. given him to scorch men
9. blasphemed God wh. hath p.
17: 12. receive p. as kings 1 hour
13. shall give their p. unto beast
18:†3. merchants rich thro. p. of her
19:1. glory, honour, and p. unto L.

POWER of God.

Mat. 22: 29. Ye err, not knowing
Scriptures, nor p. o. G., Mk.12:
Lu. 9:43. all amazed at p. o. G. [24.
22: 69. Son sit on right of p. o. G.
Ac. 8: 10. This man is great p. o. G.
Ro. 1: 16. the gospel is the p. o. G.
1 Co. 1: 18. unto us it is p. o. G.
24. Christ the p. o. G. and wisd.
2:5. faith not stand but by p. o. G.
2 Co. 6: 7. By the word, by p. o. G.
13:4. crucified, yet liv-h by p. o. G.
we sh. live with him by p. o. G.
2 Ti. 1: 8. be partaker of afflictions
of gospel, acc. to p. o. G.
1 Pe. 1: 5. who are kept by p. o. G.
See **GREAT power.**

In or in the POWER.

Ge. 31:29. i. t. p. of my hand to do
you hurt [rious i. p.
Ex. 15:6. Thy right hand O L. is glo-
Jb. 21: 7. why wicked mighty i. p.?
37: 23. he is excellent i. p. and in
Ps. 29: † 4. voice of Lord is i. p.
Pr. 3:27. when i. t. p. of thy hand
18: 21. Death, life i. t. p. of tongue
Is. 40: 26. that he is strong i. p.
Mi. 2: 1. is i. t. p. of their hand
Na. 1:3. L. slow to anger, great i. p.
Lu. 1: 17. bef. him i. p. of Elias [rit
4: 14. Jes. returned i. t. p. of Spi-
1 Co. 4: 20. not in word, but i. p.
15:43. sown in weakn., raised i. p.
Ep. 6:10. strong i. t. p. of his might
1 Th.1:5. gos. came in word, and i. p.
2 Pe. 2:11. angels who are greater i.

My POWER. [p.

Ge. 31: 6. with all m. p. I served
Ex. 9:16. raised thee to show m. p.
De. 8: 17. m. p. gotten this wealth
Da. 4: 30. Babylon built by m. p.
Ro. 9:17. might shew m. p. in thee
1 Co. 9: 18. that I abuse not m. p.

No POWER. [p.

Ex. 21:8. to sell her, he sh. have no
Le.26:37. sh. have n. p. bef. enemies
Jos. 8: 20. men of Ai n. p. to flee
1 S. 30: 4. peo. had n. p. to weep
2 Ch. 14:11. help with th. have n. p.
22: 9. house of Ahaziah had n. p.
Is. 50: 2. or have I n. p. to deliver?
Da. 8: 27. upon bodies fire n. p.
8:7. was n. p. in the ram to stand
Jn. 19: 11. have n. p. ag. me, exc.
Ro.13:1. there is n. P. but of G. [p.
Re.20:6. on such sec. death hath n.

Thine own or thy POWER.

De. 9: 29. broughtest out by t. p.
Jb. 1: 12. all th. he hath is in t. p.
Ps. 21: 13. so will we praise t. p.
59: 11. scatter them by t. p. O L.
16. But I will sing of t. p.
63: 2. To see t. p. and thy glory
66:3. thro. greatness of t. p. enem.
71: 18. t. p. to ev. one is to come
79: 11. acc. to greatness of t. p.
110: 3. peo. willing in day of t. p.
145: 11. they shall talk of t. p.
Na. 2: 1. fortify t. p. mightily
Ac. 5: 4. was it not in t. o. p.?

POWERS.

Mat. 24:29. p. of heaven be shaken,
Mk. 13: 25. Lu. 21:26. [thought
Lu. 12:11. bri. you unto p. take no
Ro. 8: 38. nor p. able to separate
13:1. p. that be are ordained of G.
1 Co. 12: † 29. teachers? are all p.?
Ep. 3: 10. p. in heavenly places [p.
6: 12. we wrestle ag. principalities
Col. 1: 16. p. were created by him
2: 15. spoiled p. be made a shew
Tit. 3: 1. mind to be subject to p.
He. 6: 5. p. of the world to come
1 Pe 3:22. angels p. subject unto him

POWERFUL.

Ps. 29:4. The voice of the Lord is p.
2 Co. 10: 10. for his letters are p.
He. 4: 12. word of God is quick, p.

PRACTICES. [p.

2 Pe. 2: 14. exercised with covetous

PRACTISE, ED, ETH.

1 S. 23:9. Saul secretly p-d mischief
Ps. 37:†12. The wicked p-h ag. just
141: 4. not to p. wicked works
Pr. 3:† 29. p. no evil ag. neighbour
Is. 32: 6. vile shall p. hypocrisy
Da. 8: 12. little horn p-d and prosp.
24. a king shall destroy, and p.
Mi. 2: 1. morning is light they p. it

PRÆTORIUM.

See PRETORIUM.

PRAISE. [Noun.]

Ge. 29: † 35. she called his name P.
De. 10: 21. He is thy p. and thy God
26: 19. to make thee high in p.
Ju. 5: 3. I will sing p. to the Lord
God of Isr., Ps. 7:17.-9:2.-57:7.
-61: 8.-104: 33. [thy p.
1 Ch. 16: 35. that we may glory in
2 Ch. 23: 13. as taught to sing p.
29: 30. com-ded Levites to sing p.
Ne. 9: 5. wh. is exalted above all p.
12: 46. in days of Da. songs of p.
Ps.9:14. that I may shew all thy p.
22: 25. my p. shall be of thee in
30: 12. that my glory may sing p.
33: 1. p. is comely for the upright
34: 1. his p. shall be in my mouth
35: 28. my tongue sh. speak of thy
40: 3. even p. unto our God [p.
42: 4. to ho. of G. with voice of p.
48: 10. thy p. unto ends of earth
50:23. Whoso offereth p. glorifieth
51: 15. my mouth sh. shew thy p.
65: 1. p. waiteth for thee, O God
66: 2. Sing, make his p. glorious
8. make voice of his p. be heard
71: 6. my p. be contin-y of thee
8. Let my mouth be filled with p.
79: 13. we will shew forth thy p.
98: 4. make loud noise, sing p.
100: 4. enter into his courts wi. p.
102: 21. to declare his p. in Jerus.
106: 2. who can shew all his p.?
12. Then believed they, sang his
47. and to triumph in thy p. [p.
108:1. I will sing and give p. with
109: 1. Hold not peace, O G. of my
111:10. his p. endureth for ev. [p.
119: 171. My lips shall utter p.
138: 1. bef. the gods will I sing p.
145: 21. mouth sh. speak p. of L.
147: 1. p. is comely | 7. sing p.
upon the harp [his saints
148: 14. He exalteth the p. of all
Ps.149:1. Sing his p. in congregation
Pr. 27:21. furnace, so man to his p.
Is. 42: 8. not give my p. to images
10. sing his p. from end of earth
12. declare his p. in the islands
43:21. they shall shew forth my p.
48: 9. and for my p. will I refrain
60:18. thou shalt call thy gates P.
61: 3. garment of p. for heaviness
11. L. will cause p. to spring forth
62: 7. till he make Jerusalem a p.
Je. 13: 11. might be unto me a p.
17:14. save me, O L. thou art my p.
26. bringing sacrifices of p., 33:11.
33: 9. it shall be to me a joy, a p.
48: 2. shall be no more p. of Moab
49: 25. How is city of p. not left
51:41. how is p. of earth surprised
Ha. 3: 3. earth was full of his p.
Zph. 3: 19. I will get them p. fame
20. make you a p. am. all people
Mat. 21: 16. thou hast perfected p.
Lu. 18: 43. saw it, gave p. unto G.
Jn. 9:24. Give God the p. this man
is a sinner [p. of G.
12: 43. loved p. of men more than
Ro. 2: 29. whose p. is not of men
13: 3. do good, have p. of same
1 Co. 4: 5. ev. man have p. of God
2 Co. 8:18. whose p. is in the gospel
Ep. 1: 6. predestinated to p. of glo.
12. p. of glory who trusted in C.,
Ph.1:11. by J.C. unto p. of God [14.
4: 8. if any p. think on these thi.
He. 2: 12. in church will I sing p.
13:15. By him offer a sacrifice of p.
1 Pe. 1: 7. trial of your faith unto p.
2: 14. for p. of them that do well
4:11. to whom be p. and dominion

PRAISES. [p.?

Ex. 15: 11. Who like thee, fearful in
2 S. 22: 50. I will give thanks and
sing p., Ps. 18:49.-92:1.-135:3.
2 Ch. 29:30. they sang p. with glad-
Ps. 9:11. Sing p. to L. in Zion [ness
22: 3. O thou that inhabitest p. of
27: 6. sing, yea I will sing p. unto
God, 47: 6.-68: 32.-75:9.-108:3.
47:7. sing ye p. with understanding
56:12. I will render p. unto, 144:9.
68: 4. to God, sing p. to his name
78:4. shewing to genera. p. of Lord
146: 2. I will sing p. unto my G.
147:1. good to sing p. unto our God
149:3. let them sing p. with timbrel
6. Let high p. of G. be in mouths
Is. 60: 6. shall shew forth p. of L.
63:7. mention of the p. of the Lord
Ac. 16: 25. Paul, Silas sang p. to G.
1 Pe. 2: 9. shew forth the p. of him

PRAISE. [Verb.] [p.

Ge. 49: 8. art he whom brethren sh.
Le. 19: 24. the fruit holy to p. Lord
De. 32: † 43. p. his peo. ye nations
2 S. 14:†25. not a man to p. greatly
1 Ch.23:5. instruments I made to p.
29: 13. we p. thy glorious name
2 Ch. 8: 14. Levites to p. bef. priests
20: 21. sho. p. beauty of holiness
22. they began to sing and to p.
31: 2. p. in gates of tents of Lord
Ne. 12: 24. p. and give thanks acc.
Ps. 21: 13. so will p. thy power
22: 23. Ye that fear the L. p. him
30:9. to pit, shall the dust p. thee?
42: 5. I shall yet p. him, 11.-43:5.
44: 8. In G. we boast and p. name
45: 17. thf. shall people p. thee
49:18. men will p. thee when doest
63: 3. my lips shall p. thee [well
5. my mouth shall p. thee with
67:3. Let the people p. thee, O G., 5.
69:34. Let heaven and earth p. him
71:14. I will p. thee more and more
74:21. let poor and needy p. name
76: 10. wrath of man shall p. thee
88: 10. shall the dead arise and p.

Ps. 89:5. heaven sh. p. thy wonders
99:3. Let them p. thy great name
107:32. p. him in the assembly
113:1. p. him, O serv-s of L., 135:1.
115:17. The dead p. not the Lord
119:164. Seven times a day do I p.
175. Let my soul live it sh. p. thee
138:2. I will p. thy name for thy
4. All kings of earth shall p. thee
142:7. out of prison that I may p.
145:4. One genera. sh. p. thy works
10. All thy works shall p. thee
147:12. p. Lord, Jerus. p. God, O Zi.
148:1. p. ye L. p. him in heights
2. p. him, angels, p. him ye hosts
3. p. him, sun, moon, p. ye stars
4. p. him, ye heaven of heavens
5. Let them p. name of Lord, 13.
149:3. Let them p. name in dance
150:1. p. God in his sanctuary, p.
2. p. him for mighty acts, p. him
3. p. him with trumpet, p. him
4. p. him with timbrel, p. him
5. p. him upon loud cymbals, p.
Pr. 27:2. Let another man p. thee
28:4. th. forsake law, p. the wicked
31:31. let her own works p. her
Is. 38:18. the grave cannot p. thee
19. The living he sh. p. thee, as I
Je. 31:7. p. ye and say, O L. save
Da. 2:23. I thank and p. thee, O G.
4:37. I p. and extol King of heaven
Jo. 2:26. p. the name of the Lord
Lu. 19:37. disciples began to p. G.
1 Co. 11:2. I p. you th. ye remember
17. in this I p. you not, 22. ⌊me
Re. 19:5. saying, p. our God, all

I will, or will I PRAISE.

Ge. 29:35. Leah said, w. I p. Lord
Ps. 7:17. I w. p. Lord, acc. to his
9:1. I w. p. thee, O Lord, with my
whole heart, 111:1.–138:1
22:22. in congregation w. I p. thee
28:7. with my song w. I p. him
35:18. I w. p. thee among much
people, 57:9.–108:3.–109:30.
43:4. upon harp w. I p. thee, O God
52:9. I w. p. thee forever, because
54:6. I w. p. thy name, O Lord
56:4. in God I w. p. his word, 10.
69:30. I w. p. name of God with
71:22. I w. p. thee with psaltery
86:12. I w. p. thee, O Lord my G.
109:30. I w. greatly p. the Lord
118:19. into gates, and I w. p. L.
21. I w. p. thee, thou heard me
28. Thou art my G. I w. p. thee
119:7. I w. p. thee with uprightn.
139:14. I w. p. thee, I am wonderf-y
145:2. I w. p. thy name for ever
Is. 12:1. I w. p. thee, tho. angry
25:1. I w. p. thy name, done won-

PRAISE the Lord. ⌊ders

Ju. 5:2. p. ye L. for avenging of Isr.
1 Ch. 16:4. appointed Lev. to p. L.
23:30. stand ev. morning to p. L.
25:3. prophesied wi. harp to p. L.
2 Ch. 7:6. wh. Da. had made to p. L.
20:19. Levites stood up to p. L.
21. p. L. for his mercy endureth
Ezr. 3:10. Lev. with cymbals to p. L.
Ps. 22:26. shall p. L that seek him
33:2. p. L. with harp, sing, 117:1.
102:18. people created shall p. L.
104:35. p. ye L., 105:45.–106:1, 48.–
111:1.–112:1.–113:1, 9.–115:18.–
116:19.–117:2.–135:1.–146:1, 10.
–147:1, 20.–148:1, 14.–149:1, 9.–
150:1, 6. Je. 20:13. ⌈21, 31.
107:8. Oh that men would p. L., 15,
135:3. p. L. for the Lord is good
146:2. While I live will I p. L.
147:1. p. ye L. for it is good to sing
12. p. L. O Jerus. praise God, O
148:7. p. L. fr. earth, ye dragons
Is. 12:4. p. L. call upon his name
62:9. they shall eat it, and p. L.
Je. 33:11. p. L. of hosts, L. is good
Ro. 15:11. p. L. all ye Gentiles

PRAISED.

Ju. 16:24. people p. god Dagon
2 S. 14:25. none so much p. as Abs.
22:4. L. worthy to be p., Ps. 18:3.
1 Ch. 16:25. L. is great and greatly
to be p., Ps. 48:1.–96:4.–145:3.
36. all the people p. the Lord
23:5. 4,000 were porters, and 4,000
p. Lord, 2 Ch. 7:3. Ne. 5:13.
2 Ch. 5:13. with instruments p. L.
7:6. David p. by their ministry
30:21. priests p. the L. day by day
Ezr. 3:11. great shout when p. L.
Ps. 72:15. and daily shall he be p.
78:†63. their maidens were not p.
113:3. fr. rising of sun Lord's name
is to be p. ⌈shall be p.
Pr. 31:30. woman that feareth L.
Ec. 4:2. I p. dead more than living
Can. 6:9. queens and concubines p.
Is. 64:11. where our fa-s p. thee ⌊her
Da. 4:34. I p. him th. liveth for ever
5:4. they p. the gods of gold, 23.
Lu. 1:64. Zacharias spake and p. G.

PRAISERS.

2 Ch. 20:†21. appointed p. of beauty

PRAISETH. ⌊of

Pr. 31:28. her husband he p. her

PRAISING. ⌈in p. L.

2 Ch. 5:13. one sound to be heard
23:12. Athaliah heard peo. p. king
Ezr. 3:11. sang by course in p. L.
Ps. 84:4. they will be still p. thee
Lu. 2:13. the heavenly host p. God
20. shepherds returned p. God
24:53. continually in temple p. God
Ac. 2:47. did eat with gladn. p. God
3:8. walking, leaping, and p. God,

PRANCING, S. ⌊9.

Ju. 5:22. horsehoofs broken by p-s
Na. 3:2. the noise of the p. horses

PRATING.

Pr. 10:8. but a p. fool shall fall, 10.
3 Jn. 10. p. ag. us with malicious

PRAY. ⌊words

Ge. 20:7. prophet, and sh. p. for thee
24:†63. Isaac went to p. in field
Nu. 21:7. p. L. that he take serpents
1 S. 1:†12. Hannah multiplied to p.
7:5. Sam. said, I will p. for you
12:19. p. for thy servants unto L.
23. sin in ceasing to p. for you ⌈25.
2 S. 7:27. in his heart to p., 1 Ch. 17:
1 K. 8:30. hearken thou when they
p. tow. this place, 33, 35, 42,
44, 48. 2 Ch. 6:26, 34, 38. ⌈stored
13:6. p. that my hand may be re-
2 Ch. 6:†21. supplications thy peo. p.
24. shall p. and make suppli., 32.
37. p. in land of their captivity
7:14. If my people sh. p. and seek
Ezr. 6:10. p. for the life of king
Ne. 1:6. hear the prayer which I p.
Jb. 21:15. what profit if we p.
33:26. p. unto G. he be favourable
42:8. my serv. Job shall p. for you
Ps. 5:2. my God, unto thee will I p.
55:17. morning, noon will I p.
122:6. p. for peace of Jerus. ⌈p.
Is. 16:12. sh. come to sanctuary to
45:20. p. unto a god cannot save
Je. 7:16. p. not thou for this people, 11:14.–14:11. ⌈it
29:7. peace of city, p. unto L. for
12. p. unto me, I will hearken
37:3. p. now unto L. for us, 42:2,
42:4. I will p. unto the Lord ⌊20.
Zch. 7:2. sent men to p. bef. Lord
8:21. go speedily to p. bef. L., 22.
Mat. 5:44. p. for them that despitefully use you, Lu. 6:28.–16:27.
6:5. they love to p. standing in
6. p. to thy Father wh. is in secret
7. when ye p. use not vain repeti.
9. Aft. this manner p. ye, Our Fa.
Mat. 9:38. p. L. of harvest, Lu. 10:2.
14:23. he went up into a mountain to p.: he was there alone,
Mk. 6:46. Lu. 6:12.–9:28.
19:13. that he should put his hands
on them and p.
24:20. p. your flight be not in
winter, Mk. 13:18.
26:36. Jes. saith, Sit ye here while
I go and p. yonder, Mk. 14:32.
41. Watch and p. that ye enter
not into temptation, Mk. 13:33.
–14:38. Lu. 21:36.–22:40, 46.
53. Thinkest thou I cannot p. to
my Father?
Mk. 5:17. began to p. him to depart
11:24. what ye desire when ye p.
Lu. 11:1. Lord, teach us to p. as
2. When ye p. say, Our Father
14:18. I p. have me excused, 19.
16:27. I p. fa. send him to my fa.'s
18:1. that men ought always to p.
10. Two men went into tem. to p.
Jn. 14:16. I will p. the Fa., 16:26.
17:9. I p. for th. I p. not for world
15. I p. not that thou take them
20. Nei. p. I for these alone, but
Ac. 8:22. p. G., if perhaps thought
24. Simon said, p. ye to L. for me
34. I p. of wh. speaketh prophet
10:9. Peter upon housetop to p.
24:4. I p. thou wouldst hear us
27:34. I p. you take some meat
Ro. 8:16. know not what we sho. p.
1 Co. 11:13. th. woman p. uncov-d?
14:13. let him p. that he interpret
14. if I p. in unknown tongue
15. I will p. with Spirit, p. with
2 Co. 5:20. we p. you in C.'s stead
13:7. I p. to God, ye do no evil
Ph. 1:9. this I p. that your love
Col. 1:9. we do not cease to p. for you
1 Th. 5:17. Rejoice, p. with-t ceasing
23. I p. G. your spirit be preserv
25. Brethren p. for us, 2 Th. 3:1.
He. 13:18. ⌈for you
2 Th. 1:11. Wherefore we p. always
1 Ti. 2:8. I will men p. ev. where
2 Ti. 4:16. I p. God it be not laid
Ja. 5:13. Is any afflicted? let him p?
14. p. over him | 16. p. one for ano.
1 Jn. 5:16. I do not say he shall p.
3 Jn. †2. I p. thou mayest prosper
See I pray THEE, I pray YOU.

PRAYED. ⌈ed

Ge. 20:17. Abraham p. and God heal-
Nu. 11:2. Mo. p. fire was quenched
21:7. Moses p. for peo., De. 9:26.
De. 9:20. I p. for Aaron same time
1 S. 1:10. Hannah, p. unto L., 2:1.
27. for this child I p. | 8:6. Sam-
uel p. unto the Lord ⌈6:17, 18.
2 K. 4:33. Elisha p. unto the Lord,
19:15. Hezekiah p. before the Lord,
20:2. 2 Ch. 30:18.–32:24.
20. that which thou hast p. to me,
Is. 37:15, 21.–38:2. ⌈nasseh p.
2 Ch. 32:20 Isaiah p. | 33:13. Ma-
Ezr. 10:1. Now when Ezra had p.,
Ne. 1:4.–2:4. ⌈Job p.
Jb. 42:10. L. turned captivity when
Je. 32:16. Jeremiah p.
Jon. 2:1. Jonah p., 4:2. ⌈9:4.
Da. 6:10. Daniel p. three times a day,
Mat. 26:39. Jesus fell on his face and
p., 42, 44. Mk. 14:35, 39. Lu.
22:41.
Mk. 1:35. into solitary place and p.
5:18. he possessed wi. devil p. him
Lu. 5:3. Jes p. him he wo. thrust
16. withdrew into wildern. and p.
9:29. p., his counten. was altered
18:11. Pharisee stood and p. thus
22:32. I have p. thy faith fail not
44. in agony he p. more earnestly
Jn. 4:31. his disciples p. him, eat
Ac. 1:24. disciples p. Thou Lord

Ac. 4 : 31. they p., place was shaken
6:6. when they p. they laid hands
8 : 15. Peter and John p. for them
9:40. Peter p. | 10:2. Cornelius p.,
10 : 48. they p. him to tarry [30.
13:3. they had fasted and p., 14:23.
16 : 9. p. him, Come into Macedon.
25. at midnight Paul and Silas p.
20 : 36. Paul kneeled down and p.
21 : 5. we kneeled on shore and p.
22 : 17. while I p. in the temple, 1
23:18. Paul p. me to bring yo. man
28 : 8. to wh. Paul entered and p.
Ja. 5 : 17. Elias p. it might not rain
18. he p. again, heaven gave rain

PRAYER.

2 S. 7:27. in his heart to pray this p.
1 K. 8 : 28. respect unto p. of serv.
29. mayest hearken unto the p.,
2 Ch. 6 : 19, 20. [2 Ch. 6 : 29.
38. What p. be made by any man,
45. hear thou in heaven their p.,
49. 2 Ch. 6 : 35, 39, 40. [this p.
54. Sol. made an end of praying
2 K. 19 : 4. wherefore lift up thy p.
for the remnant, Is. 37 : 4.
2 Ch. 7:15. my ears be attent unto p.
30:27. p. came to his holy dwelling
33 : 18. Manasseh's p. how God, 19.
Ne. 1 : 6. mayest hear p. of serv., 11.
4 : 9. Nevertheless we made our p.
Jb. 15 : 4. thou restrainest p. bef. G.
22:27. shalt make thy p. unto him
Ps. 65 : 2. O thou that hearest p.
72:15. p. be made for him contin-y
80 : 4. how long be angry ag. p. of
102 : 17. he will regard the p. of
destitute, not despise their p.
109 : 4. I give myself unto p. [sin
7. condemned, let his p. become
Pr. 15 : 8. p. of upright his delight
29. he heareth p. of righteous
28 : 9. his p. shall be abomination
Is. 26 : 16. a p. when thy chest-g
56:7. make them joyful in my house
of p. my ho. shall be called a
a ho. of p., Mat. 21 : 13. Mk. 11:
17. Lu. 19 : 46. [11 : 14.
Je. 7 : 16. nei. lift up my p. for them,
La. 3 : 44. that our p. sho. not pass
Da. 9 : 3. my face unto L., to seek by
13. made we not our p. bef. L. [p.
17. O God, hear p. of thy servant
Ha. 3 : 1. p. of Habakkuk prophet
Mat. 17 : 21. this kind goeth not out
but by p. and fasting, Mk. 9:29.
23 : 14. for pretense make long p.
Lu. 1 : 13. Zacharias, thy p. is heard
22:45. when Jes. rose fr. p. and was
Ac. 3 : 1. into temple at hour of p.
6 : 4. we will give ourselves to p.
10 : 31. Cornelius, thy p. is heard
12:5. p. was made without ceasing
16 : 13. where p. wont to be made
16. as we went to p. a damsel
1 Co. 7 : 5. that ye give yours. to p.
2 Co. 1 : 11. Ye helping by p. for us
9 : 14. by their p. for you, which
Ep. 6:18. praying always with all p.
Ph. 1 : 4. in ev. p. of mine for you
19. to my salvation thro. your p.
4:6. in ev. thing by p. let requests
1 Ti. 4 : 5. it is sanctified by p.
Ja. 5 : 15. p. of faith shall save sick
16. effectual p. of righteous man
† 17. he prayed in his p. that it
might not rain
1 Pe. 4 : 7. be sober, watch unto p.
See HEARD.

In PRAYER.

Ne. 11:17. began thanksgiving i. p.
Da. 9:21. while I was speaking i. P.
Mat. 21 : 22. whatever ye ask i. p.
Lu. 6:12. he continued all night i. p.
Ac. 1:14. continued wi. 1 accord i. p.
Ro. 12 : 12. continuing instant i. p.
Col. 4 : 2. Continue i. p. and watch

My PRAYER. [pure

Jb. 16 : 17. not injustice, m. p. is
Ps. 4:1. have mercy, hear m. p., 17:
1.-39 : 12.-54 : 2. [p. unto thee
5 : 3. in morning will I direct m.
6:9. Lord will receive m. p. [bosom
35 : 13. m. p. returned into own
42 : 8. m. p. unto God of my life
55 : 1. Give ear unto m. p. O God
61 : 1. O God, attend unto m. p.,
64:1.-84:8.-86:6.-102:1 -143:1.
66:19. hath attended to voice of m.
20. G. not turned away m. p. [p.
69:13. m. p. is unto thee in accepta.
88 : 2. Let m. p. come before thee
13. in morning m. p. prevent thee
141:2. Let m. p. be set before thee
5. m. p. sh. be in their calamities
La. 3:8. I cry, he shutteth out m. p.
Jon. 2:7. m. p. came into holy tem.
Ro. 10 : 1. m. p. to God for Israel is

PRAYERS.

Ps. 72 : 20. p. of David, are ended
Is. 1 : 15. when ye make many p.
Mk. 12 : 40. for pretence make long
p., Lu. 20 : 47. [and night
Lu. 2:37. Anna continued in p. day
5 : 33. Why disci. of John make p.?
Ac. 2:42. breaking of bread and in p.
10 : 4. Thy p. and alms are come
Ro. 1 : 9. I make mention of you always in my p., Ep. 1 : 16. 1 Th.
1 : 2. 2 Ti. 1 : 3. Phm. 4. [God
15:30. strive with me in your p. to
Col. 4 : 12. Epaphras labouring for
you in p. [men
1 Ti. 2 : 1. that p. be made for all
5:5. widow continueth in p. night
Phm. 22. I trust thro. your p. I sh.
He. 5 : 7. when he had offered up p.
1 Pe. 3:7. that your p. be not hinder.
12. his ears are open unto their p.
Re. 5:8. which are the p. of the saints
8 : 3. offer it with p. of saints
4. smoke with the p. of saints

PRAYEST. [6.

Mat. 6 : 5. p., be not as hypocrites,

PRAYETH.

1 K. 8 : 28. hearken to prayer thy
servant p., 2 Ch. 6 : 19, 20. [it
Is. 44:17. worshippeth and p. unto
Ac. 9 : 11. inquire for Saul, for, behold, he p. [head uncovered
1 Co. 11 : 5. woman that p. witl
14:14. my spirit p. but underst-g is

PRAYING.

1 S. 1 : 12. as Hannah continued p.
26. I am the woman that stood p.
1 K. 8:54. Solomon had made an end
of p., 2 Ch. 7 : 1. [Daniel p.
Da. 6:11. these assembled and found
9:20. while I was p. and confessing
Mk. 11:25. when ye stand p. forgive
Lu. 1:10. multitude of peo. were p.
3 : 21. Jesus p. heaven was opened
9 : 18. as he was alone p. his disci.
11 : 1. as he was p. in certain place
Ac. 11 : 5. I was in city of Joppa p.
12 : 12. many were gathered p.
1 Co. 11 : 4. p. with his head cov-d
2 Co. 8:4. p. us with much entreaty
Ep. 6 : 18. p. in Spirit for all and me
Col. 1 : 3. p. always for you [door
4 : 3. p. for us that G. would open
1 Th. 3 : 10. night and day p. to see
Jude 20. beloved p. in Holy Ghost

PREACH. [p.

Ne. 6 : 7. hast appointed prophets to
Is. 61 : 1. L. hath anointed me to p.
Jon. 3 : 2. p. unto it preaching I bid
Mat. 4:17. that time Jes. began to p.
10 : 7. p. kingdom of G. is at hand
27. what ye hear, that p. upon the
11 : 1. he departed to p. in cities
Mk. 1 : 4. John did p. the baptism
38. that I may p. there, Lu. 4:43.
3:14. might send th. to p., Lu. 9:2.
Lu. 4 : 18. to p. deliverance, 19.
9 : 60. go and p. kingdom of God
Ac. 5 : 42. ceased not to p. Jes. C.
10 : 42. com-ded us to p. unto peo.
14 : 15. p. that ye return unto G.
15 : 21. Moses hath in every city
them that p. him [in Asia
16:6. forbidden by H. G. to p. word
17 : 3. Jesus I p. unto you is C.
Ro. 10 : 8. word of faith which we p.
15. how shall they p. exc. sent?
1 Co. 1:23. But we p. Christ crucified
15 : 11. so we p. so ye believed
2 Co. 4 : 5. we p. not ours., but C. J.
Ga. 1:16. might p. him am. heathen
2:2. gospel which I p. am. Gentiles
5 : 11. breth., if I yet p. circumc-n
Ep. 3 : 8. th. I sho. p. am. Gentiles
Ph. 1 : 15. some p. Christ of envy
16. one p. C. of contention
Col. 1:†25. dispensat. given to p. word
28. whom we p. warning ev. man
2 Ti. 4 : 2. p. the word, be instant
See **GOSPEL** with **preach.**

PREACHED. [congre.

Ps. 40 : 9. I have p. righte-n. in gr.
Mk. 1:7. John p., There cometh one
39. he p. in their synagogues thro.
Galilee, Lu. 4 : 44. [word
2:2. many were gathered, he p. the
6 : 12. they p. that men repent
16 : 20. they went p. every where
Lu. 3 : 18. many other things p. he
16 : 16. the kingdom of God is p.
24 : 47. that remission of sins be p.
Ac. 3 : 20. J. Christ, wh. bef. was p.
4:2. p. thro. Jesus the resurrection
8 : 5. Philip to Samaria and p. C.
25. they p. the word of the Lord
35. Philip p. unto eunuch Jesus
40. Philip p. in all cities to Cesarea
9 : 20. Saul p. Christ in synagogue
27. Barnabas told how Saul had p.
10:37. after baptism which John p.
13:5. p. word of God in synagogues
24. When John had first p. before
38. is p. unto you, forgiven. of sins
42. might be p. the next sabbath
14:25. when had p. word in Perga
15:36. Let us visit where we have p.
17 : 13. word p. of Paul at Berea
18. bec. he p. Jesus and resurr-n
20 : 7. Paul p. ready to depart on
1 Co. 9 : 27. lest when I p. to others
15:2. if ye keep what I p. unto you
12. if Christ be p. that he rose fr.
2 Co. 1 : 19. Jes. who was p. by us
11:4. ano. Jesus wh. we have not p.
Ga. 1 : 8. other gospel than th. we p.
11. gospel p. of me is not aft. man
Ep. 2:17. p. peace unto you who afar
Ph. 1 : 18. Christ is p. and I rejoice
Col. 1 : 23. was p. to every creature
1 Ti. 3:16. p. unto Gentiles, believed
He. 4:2. word p. did not profit them
6. they to whom it was first p.
1 Pe. 3 : 19. p. unto spirits in prison
See **Gospel** with **preached.**

PREACHER. [of Da.

Ec. 1 : 1. The words of the p. son of
2. Vanity of vanities, saith p., 12:8.
12. I the p. was king over Isr.
7 : 27. this have I found, saith p.
12 : 9. bec. p. was wise, he taught
10. p. sought to find acceptable
Ro. 10 : 14. how hear without p.?
1 Ti. 2 : 7. I am ordained a p., 2 Ti.
2 Pe 2:5. Noah, a p. of right-n [1:11.

PREACHEST, ETH. [p-h

Ac. 19:13 adjure by Jes. whom Paul
Ro. 2 : 21. that p-t a man not steal
2 Co. 11 : 4. if he p-h another Jesus
Ga. 1:23. p-h faith once he destroyed

PREACHING. [Part.]

Mat. 3 : 1. came John p., Lu. 3 : 3.
Lu. 8:1. p. and shewing glad tidings
Ac. 8 : 4. went every where p. word

Ac.8:12.p.the things conc. kingd.of
10:36. p. peace by Jesus Christ [G.
11 : 19. p. word to none but Jews
20. to Grecians,p. Lord Jesus [p.
15 : 35. Paul continued in Antioch
20:9. as Paul was long p.Eutychus
25. ye, am. whom I have gone p.
28 : 31. p. the kingdom of God
See **GOSPEL with preaching.**

PREACHING, S. [thee
Jon. 3 : 2. preach the p. I bid thee
Mat. 12 : 41. repented at p. of Jonas;
a greater is here, Lu. 11 : 32.
Ro.10:†16.who hath believed our p.?
16:25.establish you acc.to p.of Jes.
1 Co. 1 : 18. p. of cross is foolishness
21. by foolishness of p. to save
2 : 4. my p. was not with enticing
15:14. if C. be not risen, our p.vain
2 Co. 1:†18. p. tow. you was not yea
2 T.4:†15.greatly withstood our p-s
17. by my p. might be known
Tit.1:3. manifested his word thro.p.

PRECEPT.
Is. 28 : 10. For p. must be upon p.
p. upon p., 13. [p. of men
29 : 13. their fear is taught by the
Mk. 10 : 5. for hardness he wrote p.
He. 9 : 19. Moses had spoken ev. p.

PRECEPTS.
Ne. 9 : 14. commandest them p. and
Ps. 119:4. com-ded us to keep thy p.
15. I will meditate in thy p., 78.
27. Make me to understand thy p.
40. I have longed after thy p.[p.
45. I seek thy p. | 87. forsook not
56. bec. I kept thy p., 100, 168.
63. companion of th keep thy p.
69. but I will keep thy p., 134.
93. I will never forget thy p.
94. save me, I have sought thy p.
104. Thro. thy p. I get underst-g
110. yet I erred not from thy p.
128. I esteem all thy p. to be right
141. small, yet do not I forget thy
159. Consider how I love thy p.
173. help me, I have chos. thy p.
Je.35:18. ye have kept Jonadab's p.
Da. 9 : 5. we rebelled from thy p.

PRECIOUS. [things
Ge. 24 : 53. to Rebekah's mother p.
De. 33 : 13. for p. things of heaven
14. p. fruits brought forth by sun
15. p. things of the lasting hills
16. for p. things of the earth
1 S. 3 : 1. word of L. p. in those days
18:†30. Da. behaved so name was p.
26 : 21. my soul p. in thine eyes
2 K. 1 : 13. let my life be p. in, 14.
20 : 13. Hezekiah shewed them p.
things, Is. 39 : 2. [stripped off
2 Ch. 20 : 25. p. jewels which they
21:3. Jehosh. gave them p. things
32 : † 23. brought p. things to Hez.
Ezr. 1:6. strengthened wi. p. things
8 : 27. vessels of copper, p. as gold
Jb. 28 : 10. eye seeth every p. thing
16. can-t be valued with p. onyx
Ps. 36 : † 7. How p. is thy lovingki.
49 : 8. redemption of their soul p.
72:14. p. their blood be in his sight
116:15. p. in sight of L. is death of
126 : 6. goeth forth bearing p. seed
133 : 2. It is like the p. ointment
139:17. How p. thy thoughts, O God
141:†5. let not p. oil break my head
Pr. 1 : 13. shall find p. substance
3:15. wisdom is more p. than rubies
6 : 26. adulteress hunt for p. life
12 : 27. substance of diligent is p.
20 : 15. lips of knowledge a p. jewel
24:4. chambers filled with p. riches
Ec. 7 : 1. A good name is better than
p. ointment
Is. 13:12. I will make a man more p.
43:4. since thou wast p. in my sight
Je. 15 : 19. if thou take p. from vile

Je.20:5. I will deliv. all the p. things
La. 4:2. The p. sons of Zion [things
Eze. 22 : 25. taken treasure and p.
27:20. Dedan merch. in p. clothes
Da. 11 : 8. carry away p. vessels
43. have power over all p. things
Zch. 14:†6. that day, light not be p.
Mat. 26 : 7. having alabaster box of
very p. ointm., Mk. 14:3. [fruit
Ja. 5:7. husbandman waiteth for p.
1 Pe. 1:7. trial of your faith more p.
19. with the p. blood of Christ [p.
2:4. living stone, chosen of G., and
7. Unto you wh. believe he is p.
2 Pe. 1:1. have obtained like p. faith
4. unto us exceeding p. promises
Re. 18:12. no man buyeth p. vessels
See **Precious STONE, S.**

PRECIOUSNESS. [lambs
Ps. 37 : † 20. enemies of L. as p. of

PREDESTINATE, ED.
Ro. 8:29. whom foreknow, he did p.
30. wh. he did p. them he called
Ep.1:5. Having p-d us unto adoption
11. being p-d acc. to purpose of

PREEMINENCE. [him
Ec. 3 : 19. a man no p. above beast
Col. 1:18. that he might have the p.
3 Jn. 9. Diotrephes, loveth to have

PREFER, RED, RING. [p.
Es. 2 : 9. he p-d her and maidens
Ps.137:6. if I p. not Jerus. above my
Da. 6:3. Daniel was p-d ab. presidents
Jn. 1:15. cometh after me is p-d, 27.
30. is p-d bef. me, for he was bef.
Ro. 12 : 10. in honour p-g one ano.
1 Ti. 5 : 21. without p-g one bef. an-

PREJUDICE. [other
1 Ti. 5:†21. observe these with-t p.

PREMEDITATE.
Mk. 13:11. nei. p. but whatso. is given

PREPARATION, S.
1 Ch. 22 : 5. I will now make p. for it
Pr. 16 : 1. p-s of heart in man fr. L.
Na. 2 : 3. torches in the day of p.
Mat. 27 : 62. next day that followed
the day of p., Mk. 15 : 42. Lu.
23 : 54. Jn. 19 : 14, 31, 42.
Ep. 6 : 15. feet shod with p. of the

PREPARE. [gospel
Ex. 15:2. I will p. him a habitation
16:5. on 6th day sh. p. that they bri.
Le. 14:†36. command they p. house
Nu. 15 : 5. for drink offering p. 4th
6. or for a ram p. for a meat off-g
12. Acc. to number that ye sh. p.
23 : 1. Balaam said, p. me 7 oxen
29. Build 7 altars, p. 7 bullocks
De. 19 : 3. thou shalt p. thee a way
Jos. 1 : 11. p. your victuals to pass
22 : 26. Let us now p. to build alt.
1 S. 7 : 3. p. your hearts unto the L.
23:22. Go, I pray you, p. his place
1 K.18:44. p. chariot, get thee down
1 Ch. 9:32. to p. shewbread ev. sab.
29:18. O L., p. their heart unto thee
2 Ch. 2 : 9. to p. timber in abnud.
31:11. p. chambers | 35:4. p. yours.
35 : 6. sanctify yours. p. brethren
Es. 5 : 8. come to banquet I shall p.
Jb. 8 : 8. p. thyself to the search of
11 : 13. If thou p. heart tow. him
27 : 16. tho. he p. raiment as clay
17. He may p. it but just sh. put
Ps. 10 : 17. Lord, thou wilt p. heart
59 : 4. p. thems. without my fault
61:7. O p. mercy and truth, which
107 : 36. may p. city for habitation
Pr. 24 : 27. p. thy work without
30 : 25. they p. meat in summer
Is. 14 : 21. p. slaughter for his chil.
21 : 5. p. the table, watch in the
40:3. crieth, p. ye way of L., Mat.
3:3. Mk. 1 : 2, 3. Lu. 1 : 76.-3:4.
-7 : 27. [image
20. seeketh workman to p. graven
57:14. say, Cast ye up, p. the way

Is.62:10. p. ye the way of the people
65:11. that p. table for that troop
Je. 6 : 4. p. ye war against her, arise
12:3. p. them for day of slaughter
22 : 7. I will p. destroyers ag. thee
46:14. say ye, Stand fast and p. thee
51 : 12. set watchmen, p. ambushes
27. p. the nations against her, 28.
Eze. 4 : 15. thou shalt p. thy bread
12 : 3. p. thee stuff for removing
35 : 6. I will p. thee to blood [pany
38:7. p. for thyself, thou and com-
43:25. p. a goat, they shall also p.
45 : 17. prince shall p. sin off-g, 23.
22. prince shall p. for hims., 46:12.
24. shall p. meat off-g, 46 : 7, 14.
46:2. priest shall p. burnt off-g, 13.
15. they shall p. the lamb and
Jo. 3:9. p. war wake up mighty men
Am. 4 : 12. p. to meet thy God
Mi. 3 : 5. they even p. war ag. him
Mal. 3 : 1. messenger shall p. way
before me, Mat. 11 : 10.
Mat. 26 : 17. Where wilt thou we p.
to eat passover? Mk. 14 : 12.
Lu. 22 : 8, 9.
Jn. 14 : 2. I go to p. a place for you
3. if I go and p. a place for you
1 Co. 14 : 8. who shall p. to battle?
Phm. 22. But p. me also a lodging

PREPARED.
Ge. 24:31. I p. the house and room
27 : 17. bread and meat she had p.
41 : † 32. for the thing is p. of God
Ex. 12 : 39. nei. had p. any victual
23 : 20. thee into place I have p.
Nu. 21 : 27. let city of Sihon be p.
23 : 4. I have p. seven altars [p.
Jos. 4 : 4. Josh. called 12 men, he
13. 40,000 p. for war, 2 Ch. 17:18.
2 S. 15 : 1. Absalom p. chariots and
1 K. 1 : 5. Adonijah p. chariots and
5:18. they p. timber to build house
6 : 19. oracle he p. in house within
2 K. 6 : 23. he p. provision and sent
1 Ch. 12:†24. 6,800 ready p. for war
39. their breth. had p. for them
15 : 1. David p. a place for the ark
of God, 3, 12. 2 Ch. 1 : 4.-3 : 1.
22 : 3. David p. iron in abundance
5. David p. abundance before his
death, 14.-29 : 2, 3, 16. [was p.
2 Ch. 8 : 16. all the work of Solomon
12 : 14. Rehoboam p. not his heart
16:14. spices p. by apothecaries' art
19 : 3. Jehosh-t p. heart to seek G.
20:33. people had not p. their heart
26 : 14. Uzziah p. shields, spears
27 : 6. Jotham p. his ways bef. L.
29 : 19. vessels Ahaz cast aw. we p.
36. rejoiced that God p. people
31 : 11. p. chambers in house of L.
35 : 10. service p. priests stood, 16.
14. the Levites p. for thems., 15.
20. when Josiah had p. temple
Ezr. 7 : 10. Ezra had p. his heart
Ne. 5:18. which was p. for me daily
8:10. them for whom nothing is p.
13 : 5. had p. for a great chamber
Es. 5 : 4. unto the banquet that I
have p., 5, 12.-6:14. [p., 7:10.
6 : 4. Mordecai on gallows Haman
Jb. 28 : 27. he p. it, searched it out
29 : 7. when I p. my seat in street
Ps. 7:13. He p. instrum-ts of death
9:7. he hath p. his throne for judgm
57 : 6. They p. a net for my steps
† 7. my heart is p. I will sing
68:10. p. of thy goodn. for the poor
74 : 16. thou hast p. light and sun
78 : † 8. genera. that p. not hearts
103 : 19. The L. hath p. his throne
Pr. 8 :† 19. by underst-g p. heavens
8 : 27. When he p. the heavens, I
19 : 29. Judgments p. for scorners
21 : 31. horse p. ag. day of battle
Is. 2:†2. mt. of L.'s house sh. be p.

Is.16:† 5. in mercy sh. throne be **p.**
30:33. Tophet of old, for king it is
64:4. nei. eye seen what he **p.** ⌊p.
Eze. 23:41. bed, and table **p.** bef. it
28:13. workmanship of pipes was **p.**
38:7. Be **p.** and prepare thyself
Da. 2:9. ye have **p.** lying words
Ho. 2:8. gold wh. they **p.** for Baal
6:3. his going forth **p.** as morning
Jon. 1:17. Lord had **p.** great fish
4:6. God **p.** a gourd | 7. a worm
8. God **p.** a vehement east wind
Na. 2:5. the defence shall be **p.**
Zph. 1:7. Lord hath **p.** a sacrifice
Mat. 20:23. it shall be given to them for whom it is **p.**, Mk. 10:40.
22:4. tell them, I have **p.** my din-
25:34. inherit the kingdom **p.** ⌊ner
41. everlasting fire **p.** for devil
Mk. 14:15. a large upper room **p.**
Lu. 1:17. ready a people **p.** for Lord
2:31. hast **p.** bef. face of all people
12:47. knew lord's will, but **p.** not
23:56. **p.** spices, and rested. 24:1.
Ro. 9:23. vessels of mercy afore **p.**
1 Co. 2:9. things G. hath **p.** for them
Ep. 2:† 10. good works God hath **p.**
2 Ti. 2:21. **p.** unto every good work
He. 10:5. but a body hast thou **p.** me
11:7. Noah **p.** an ark to the saving
16. he hath **p.** for them a city
Re. 8:6. the 7 angels **p.** to sound
9:7. locusts like horses **p.** for bat.
15. wh. were **p.** for an hour, a day
12:6. woman hath a place **p.** of G.
16:12. that way of kings may be **p.**
21:2. the holy city **p.** as a bride

PREPAREDST, EST. ⌈ing
Nu. 15:8. when **p-t** bullock for off-
Ps. 23:5. Thou **p-t** a table bef. me
65:9. thou waterest earth, **p-t** corn
80:9. thou **p-dst** room before it

PREPARETH, ING.
2 Ch. 30:19. **p-h** his heart to seek G.
Ne. 13:7. **p-g** him chamber in hou. of
Jb. 15:35. their belly **p-h** deceit ⌊G.
Ps. 147:8. who **p-h** rain for the earth
1 Pe. 3:20. days of Noah while ark

PRESBYTERY. ⌊was **p-g**
1 Ti. 4:14. with laying on hands of

PRESCRIBED, ING. ⌊p.
Ezr. 7:22. salt with-t **p-g** how much
Is. 10:1. grievousn. they have **p-d**

PRESENCE.
Ge. 3:8. hid thems. from **p.** of L.
4:16. Cain went from **p.** of the L.
27:30. scarce gone fr. **p.** of Isaac
45:3. Joseph's brethren, for they were troubled at his **p.** ⌈p.?
47:15. why should we die in thy
Ex. 10:11. driven out from Pha.'s **p.**
33:14. said, My **p.** sh. go with thee
15. If thy **p.** go not with me carry
35:20. Isr. departed fr. **p.** of Moses
Le. 22:3. soul be cut off fr. my **p.**
Nu. 20:6. Moses went from the **p.**
1 S. 18:11. Da. avoided his **p.** twice
19:7. in his **p.** as in times past
10. he slipped aw. out of Saul's **p.**
21:15. to play madman in my **p.**
2 S. 16:19. as I served in thy father's **p.** so will I be in thy **p.** ⌈battle
17:† 11. I counsel that thy **p.** go to
1 K. 1:28. she came into king's **p.**
12:2. Jeroboam fled fr. **p.** of Sol.
2 K. 3:14. I regard **p.** of Jehoshaphat
5:27. went out from his **p.** a leper
13:23. nei. cast he them fr. his **p.**
24:20. until he cast them fr. his **p.**
25:19. five of them that in king's **p.**
1 Ch. 16:27. Glory and honour in
33. sh. trees sing at **p.** of G. ⌊his **p.**
2 Ch. 9:23. king sought **p.** of Sol.
20:9. when we stand in thy **p.** ⌈p.
34:4. brake altars of Balaam in his
Ne. 2:1. I had not been sad in his **p.**
Es. 7:† 6. Haman afraid at **p.** of k.
Ne. 8:15. Mordecai went fr. **p.** of king
Jb. 1:12. Satan went fr. **p.** of L., 2:7.
23:15. I am troubled at his **p.**
Ps. 9:3. they shall perish at thy **p.**
16:11. in thy **p.** is fulness of joy ⌈p.
17:2. Let my sentence come fr. thy
31:20. shalt hide them in secret of
42:† 5. his **p.** is salvation ⌊thy **p.**
51:11. Cast me not away fr. thy **p.**
68:2. let wicked perish at **p.** of G.
8. Sinai moved at **p.** of God
95:2. come bef. his **p.** with thanksg.
97:5. hills melted at **p.** of God
100:2. come bef. his **p.** with singing
114:7. Tremble, earth, at **p.** of L.
139:7. whither sh. I flee fr. thy **p.**?
140:13. upright sh. dwell in thy **p.**
Pr. 14:7. Go fr. **p.** of a foolish man
Is. 1:7. sh. devour land in your **p.**
19:1. idols of E. be moved at his **p.**
63:9. angel of his **p.** saved them
64:1. th. mts. might flow at thy **p.**
2. nations may tremble at thy **p.**
3. mts. flowed down at thy **p.**
Je. 4:26. cities broken at **p.** of L.
5:22. will ye not tremble at my **p.**
23:39. cast you out of my **p.**, 52:3.
Eze. 38:20. men sh. shake at my **p.**
Jon. 1:3. Jon. rose to flee fr. **p.** of L.
10. men knew he fled fr. **p.** of L.
Na. 1:5. earth is burned at his **p.**
Zph. 1:7. Hold thy peace at **p.** of L.
Lu. 13:26. eaten and drunk in thy **p.**
Ac. 3:19. refreshing come fr. **p.** of L.
5:41. departed from **p.** of council
1 Co. 1:29. th. no flesh glory in his
2 Co. 10:1. who in **p.** am base ⌊p.
10. but his bodily **p.** is weak
Ph. 2:12. obeyed, not in my **p.** only
1 Th. 2:17. taken fr. you in **p.**, not
2 Th. 1:9. destruction fr. **p.** of the L.
Jude 24. present you faultless bef.

In the PRESENCE. ⌊p. of
Ge. 16:12. sh. dwell **i. p.** of breth.
23:11. **i. p.** of my people I give it
18. made sure **i. p.** of chil. of Heth
25:18. Ishmael died **i. p.** of breth.
De. 25:9. brother's wife come **i. p.**
Jos. 8:32. wrote **i. p.** of chil. of Isr.
2 S. 16:19. should I not serve **i. p.**
1 K. 8:22. Solomon stood **i. p.** of congregat., 2 Ch. 6:12. ⌈people
21:13. against Naboth, **i. p.** of the
2 K. 25:19. that were **i.** king's **p.**
1 Ch. 24:31. cast lots **i. p.** of Da.
Ps. 23:5. table **i. p.** of mine enemies
116:14. **i. p.** of all his people, 18.
Pr. 17:18. surety **i. p.** of his friend
25:6. Put not thyself **i. p.** of king
7. be put lower **i. p.** of prince
Je. 28:1. Hananiah spake **i. p.** of the princes, 5. ⌈witnesses
11. **i. p.** of people | 32:12. **i. p.** of
Da. 2:27. Daniel ans-d **i. p.** of king
Lu. 1:19. I Gabriel, stand **i. p.** of G.
14:10. shalt have worship **i. p.** of
15:10. is joy **i. p.** of angels ⌈disci.
Jn. 20:30. signs did Jesus **i. p.** of
Ac. 3:13. denied him **i. p.** of Pilate
16. given him soundn. **i. p.** of all
27:35. gave thanks to G. **i. p.** of
1 Th. 2:19. Are not ye, **i. p.** of L. J.
He. 9:24. to appear **i. p.** of God
Re. 14:10. **i. p.** of angels, **i. p.** of

PRESENT. [Adj.] ⌊Lamb
1 S. 13:15. Saul numbered peo. **p.**, 16.
21:3. give me 5 loaves, or what is **p.**
2 S. 20:4. Assemble Jud. be **p.** ⌈p.
1 K. 20:27. Isr. were numbered, and
1 Ch. 29:17. have seen thy people **p.**
2 Ch. 5:11. priests **p.** were sanctified
29:29. king and all **p.** bowed
30:21. Isr. **p.** at Jerus. kept feast
31:1. all **p.** brake images ⌈33.
34:32. caused all **p.** to stand to it,
35:7. Josiah gave for all were **p.**
17. children of Israel that were **p.**
Ezr. 8:25. king, and all **p.** offered
Es. 4:16. gather Jews **p.** in Shushan
Ps. 46:1. God is a very **p.** help in
Lu. 5:17. power of L. was **p.** to heal
13:1. there were **p.** at that season
18:30. sh. rec. more in this **p.** time
Jn. 14:25. I have spoken, being **p.**
Ac. 10:33. Now are we all **p.** bef. G.
21:18. and all the elders were **p.**
25:24. all men wh. are here **p.** with
28:2. received us bec. of **p.** rain ⌊us
Ro. 7:18. to will is **p.** with me, but
21. when I wo. do good, evil is **p.**
8:18. th. sufferings of this **p.** time
38. nor things **p.** are able to separ.
11:5. at this **p.** time, a remnant
1 Co. 3:22. things **p.** or things to
4:11. unto this **p.** hour we hunger
5:3. but **p.** in spirit, have judged as tho. I were **p.** ⌈distress
7:26. that this is good for the **p.**
15:6. greater part remain to this **p.**
2 Co. 5:8. willing to be **p.** with L.
9. labour, that whe. **p.** or absent
10:2. that I may not be bold when
11:9. when I was **p.** with you ⌊p.
13:2. I foretell, as if I were **p.**
10. I write, lest being **p.** I should
Ga. 1:4. deliver us fr. this **p.** world
4:18. and not only when I am **p.**
20. I desire to be **p.** with you
2 Ti. 4:10. having loved **p.** world
Tit. 2:12. live godly in **p.** world
He. 9:9. a figure for time then **p.**
12:11. no chastening for **p.** seemeth
2 Pe. 1:12. established in **p.** truth

PRESENT, S. [Noun.]
Ge. 32:13. took a **p.** for Esau, 18.
20. I will appease him with **p.**
21. So went the **p.** over before him
33:10. then rec. my **p.** at my hand
43:11. Isr. said, carry the man a **p.**
15. men took **p.** | 25. made ready
26. bro-t him **p.** in their hand ⌊p.
Ju. 3:15. Isr. sent **p.** unto Eglon
17. he brought **p.** unto Eglon, 18.
6:18. depart not until I bring my
1 S. 9:7. is not a **p.** for man of G. ⌊p.
10:27. they brought him no **p-s**
25:† 27. let this **p.** be for yo. men
30:26. a **p.** of spoil of the enemies
1 K. 4:21. bro-t **p-s** and served Sol.
9:16. given **p.** unto his dau. ⌈9:24.
10:25. bro-t ev. man his **p.**, 2 Ch.
15:19. I have sent thee **p.** of silver
2 K. 8:8. the king said, Take a **p.**
9. So Hazael took a **p.** ⌈Assy.
16:8. sent it for **p.** to king of
17:3. Hoshea gave Shalmaneser **p-s**
4. no **p.** to king of Assyria
18:31. agreement by **p.**, Is. 36:16.
20:12. a **p.** unto Hez., Is. 39:1.
2 Ch. 17:5. Judah brought Jehoshaphat **p-s**, 11.
32:23. many brought **p-s** to Hez.
Ps. 68:29. kings shall bring **p-s**
72:10. and the isles shall bring **p-s**
76:11. let all bring **p-s** unto him
Is. 18:7. a **p.** brought unto Lord of
Eze. 27:15. for **p.** horns of ivory
Ho. 10:6. be carried unto Assyria for a **p.** to king Jareb
Mi. 1:14. give **p-s** to Moresheth-gath

PRESENT. [Verb.]
Ex. 34:2. **p.** thyself to me in mount
Le. 14:11. **p.** man to be made clean
16:7. two goats, **p.** them before L.
27:8. shall **p.** hims. before priest
11. he shall **p.** beast before priest
Nu. 8:6. **p.** tribe of Levi bef. Aaron
De. 31:14. **p.** yours. in tabernacle
1 S. 10:19. now **p.** yours. bef. Lord
Jb. 1:6. sons of G. came to **p.** thems.
2:1. Satan came to **p.** hims. bef. L.
Lu. 2:22. they brought him to **p.** to the Lord ⌈sacrifice
Ro. 12:1. that ye **p.** your bodies a

2 Co. 4 : 14. sh. raise us up and p. us
11 : 2. that I may p. you to Christ
Ep. 5 : 27. p. it a glorious church
Col. 1:22. p. you holy, unblameable
28. p. ev. man perfect in Christ
Jude 24. is able to p. you faultless
See SUPPLICATION, S.

PRESENTED. [fa.
Ge. 46:29. Joseph p. hims. unto his
47 : 2. p. 5 of his breth. unto Pha.
Le. 2:8. when off-g is p. unto priest
7:35. in day when he p. them [18.
9:12. Aaron's sons p. unto him bl.,
13. they p. burnt off-g unto him
16:10. scapegoat sh. be p. bef. Lord
Jos. 24 : 1. p. themselves bef. God
Ju. 6:19. Gideon bro-t it out and p.
20:2. tribes of Israel p. themselves
1 S. 17:16. Goliath p. himself 40 days
2 Ch. 11 : † 13. Levites p. thems. to
Je. 38:26. I p. my supplies. bef. king
Eze. 20 : 28. p. provocation of off-g
Mat. 2 : 11. they p. unto him gifts
Ac. 9 : 41. called saints, p. her alive
23 : 33. they p. Paul bef. governor

PRESENTING.
Da. 9 : 20. p. my supplication bef.

PRESENTLY. [Lord
1 S. 2 : 16. not fail to burn fat p.
Pr. 12 : 16. fool's wrath is p. known
Mat. 21 : 19. p. the fig tree withered
26:53. p. give more than 12 legions
Ph. 2:23. Him thf. I hope to send p.

PRESERVE.
Ge. 19:32. may p. seed of our fa., 34.
45 : 5. send me bef. you to p. life
7. God sent me to p. you posterity
De. 6 : 24. that he might p. us alive
Ps. 12:7. shalt p. fr. this generation
16 : 1. p. me, O God, in thee I put
25:21. Let integrity, uprightness p.
32 : 7. shalt p. me fr. trouble [me
40 : 11. let thy lovingkindn. p. me
41 : 2. L. will p. him and keep him
61:7. and truth which may p. him
64 : 1. p. my life fr. fear of enemy
79 : 11. p. those appointed to die
86 : 2. p. my soul, for I am holy
121 : 7. L. p. thee from all evil, he
sh. p. thy soul [and coming in
8. The L. shall p. thy going out
140:1. p. me from violent man, 4.
Pr. 2 : 11. Discretion shall p. thee
4:6. Forsake her not, she sh. p. thee
14:3. lips of the wise shall p. them
20 : 28. Mercy and truth p. king
22 : 12. eyes of Lord p. knowledge
Is. 31 : 5. passing he will p. Jerus.
49 : 8. I will p. thee, and give thee
Je. 49 : 11. fatherless chil., I will p.
Ha. 3 : † 2. p. alive thy work in y-rs
Lu. 17 : 33. whoso. lose his life p. it
2 Ti 4 : 18. Lord will p. unto his king-

PRESERVED. [dom
Ge. 32 : 30. seen God, my life is p.
Jos. 24 : 17. and p. us in all the way
1 S. 30 : 23. Lord, who hath p. us
2 S. 8 : 6. L. p. David whithersoever
he went, 14. 1 Ch. 18:6, 13. [spirit
Jb. 10:12. thy visitation hath p. my
29 : 2. as in days when God p. me
Ps. 37:28. saints, they are p. for ev.
Is. 49:6. and to restore the p. of Israel
Ho. 12:13. and by prophet was he p.
Mat. 9 : 17. but they put new wine
into new bottles, and both are
p., Lu. 5 : 38. [p. blameless
1 Th. 5:23. your spirit soul and body
Jude 1. sanctified, and p. in Jesus
Christ, and called

PRESERVER.
Jb. 7:20. what shall I do unto thee,
O thou p. of men?

PRESERVEST, ETH.
Ne. 9 : 6. thou Lord p-t them all
Jb. 36:6. He p-h not life of wicked
Ps. 31:23. the Lord p-h the faithful
Ps. 36 : 6. O L. thou p-t man, beast
97 : 10. he p-h souls of his saints
116 : 6. the Lord p-h the simple, I
145:20. Lord p-h all that love him
146 : 9. The Lord p-h the strangers
Pr. 2 : 8. he p-h way of his saints
16 : 17. keepeth his way p-h soul

PRESIDENTS.
Da 6 : 2. over 3 p. Daniel was first
3. Daniel was preferred above p.
4. p. sought occasion ag. Daniel
6. these p. and prim-es assembled,

PRESS. [Noun.] [7.
Mk. 2:4. could not come nigh for the
p., Lu. 8 : 19. [his garment
5 : 27. came in p. behind, touched
30. Jesus turned about in the p.
Lu. 19 : 3. Zaccheus not see Jes. for

PRESS, PRESSES. [the p.
Pr. 3:10. thy p-s sh. burst with wine
Is. 16:10. tread no wine in their p-s
Jo. 3 : 13. p. is full, fats overflow
Hag. 2:16. draw 50 vessels out of p.
See WINEPRESS, ES.

PRESS, ED, ETH, ING.
Ge. 19 : 3. Lot p-d upon two angels
9. they p-d sore upon Lot, and
40:11. I took grapes and p-d them
Ju. 16 : 16. Delilah p-d him daily
2 S. 13 : 25. Absalom p-d him, 27.
Es. 8 : 14. posts p-d on by king's
Ps. 38: 2. thy hand p-h me sore [p-g
Je. 30 : † 13. none to plead cause for
Eze. 23 : 3. their breasts p-d [is p-d
Am. 2:13. I am p-d und. you as cart
Mk. 3:10. p-d upon him to touch him
Lu. 5:1. peo. p-d to hear word of G.
6:38. good measure, p-d down and
8:45. multitude throng and p. thee
16:16. kingdom, ev. man p-h into it
Ac. 18 : 5. Paul was p-d in spirit
2 Co. 1 : 8. we were p-d ab. measure
Ph. 3 : 14. I p. toward the mark

PRESSFAT. [sels
Hag. 2 : 16. came to p. to draw ves-

PRESUME, ED.
Nu. 14:44. they p-d to go to hill top
De. 18 : 20. prophet who p. to speak
Es. 7 : 5. th. durst p. in heart to do

PRESUMPTUOUS, LY.
Ex. 21:14. if man p-y upon neighb.
Nu. 15:30. doeth aught p-y, De. 17:
De. 1 : 43. went p-y into hill † p. [12.
17:13. people shall do no more p-y
18 : 22. prophet hath spoken it p-y
Ps. 19 : 13. Keep thy serv. fr. p. sins
2 Pe. 2 : 10. p. are they, selfwilled

PRETENCE.
Mat. 23:14. for a p. make long pray-
er, Mk. 12 : 40. [is preached
Ph. 1 : 18. whe. in p. or in truth C.

PRETORIUM. [P.
Mk. 15 : 16. led him into hall called

PREVAIL. [p.
Ge. 7 : 20. 15 cubits upw. did waters
Nu. 22 : 6. peradven. I shall p., † 11.
Ju. 16 : 5. see by what means we p.
1 S. 2:9. by strength sh. no man p.
17 : 9. if I p. ag. him, ye be serv-s
26 : 25. shalt do gr. things and p.
1 K. 22:22. Thou shalt persuade him,
and p. also, 2 Ch. 18 : 21. [thee
2 Ch. 14:11. O Lord, let not man p. ag.
Es. 6 : 13. thou shalt not p. ag. him
Jb. 15 : 24. shall p. ag. him, as a k.
18 : 9. the robber shall p. ag. him
Ps. 9 : 19. Arise, O L., let not man p.
12 : 4. With our tongue will we p.
65 : 3. Iniquities p. ag. me, as for
Pr. 6 : † 3. so shalt p. with friend
Ec. 4 : 12. if one p. against him, two
Is. 7 : 1. but could not p. ag. it
16:12. Moab shall come, but not p.
42 : 13. he shall p. ag. his enemies
47 : 12. stand now, if so be thou p.
Je. 1 : 19. they shall not p. ag. thee,
saith L., 15 : 20.-20 : 11.
Je. 5:22. waves toss, yet can they not
20:10. be enticed, and we sh. p. [p.
Da. 11 : 7. who deal ag. him and p.
Mat. 16:18. gates of hell shall not p.
27:24. Pilate saw he co. p. nothing
Jn. 12 : 19. Perceive how ye p. noth.

PREVAILED. [ing
Ge. 7 : 18. waters p. and incr-d, 19.
24. wat. p. upon earth 150 days
30 : 8. I wrestled with sister and p.
32 : 25. he saw he p. not ag. him
28. power with God and hast p.
47 : 20. bec. famine p. over them
49 : 26. blessings of thy fa. have p.
Ex. 17:11. Moses held up his ha. Isr.
p. let down hand Amalek p.
Ju. 1 : 35. hand of house of Jo. p.
3:10. Othniel's ha. p. ag. Chushan
4 : 24. chil. of Israel p. ag. Jabin
6 : 2. hand of Midian p. ag. Israel
1 S. 17:50. So David p. over Goliath
2 S. 11 : 23. Surely the men p. ag. us
24 : 4. the king's word p. against
Joab, 1 Ch 21 : 4. [p.
1 K. 16:22. people that followed Omri
2 K. 25 : 3. famine p. in the city
1 Ch. 5 : 2. Judah p. above breth.
2 Ch. 8:3. Sol. p. ag. Hamath-zobah
13:18. Judah p. bec. relied on the L.
27 : 5. Jotham p. ag. Ammonites
Ps. 13:4. Lest mine enemy say, I have
129:2. they have not p. ag. me [p.
Je. 20 : 7. thou stronger than I, and
38:22. friends have p. ag. thee [p.
La. 1 : 16. I weep bec. enemy p.
Da. 7 : 21. same horn p. ag. saints
Ho. 12 : 4. power over angel and p.
Ob. 7. men deceived thee and p.
Lu. 23 : 23. voices of chief priests p.
Ac. 19:16. man in wh. evil spi. was p.
20. mightily grew the word and p.
Re. 5 : 5. root of David hath p.
12:8. Dragon and his angels p. not

PREVAILEST, ETH.
Jb. 14:20. Thou p-t for ever ag. him
La. 1 : 13. fire into my bones, and it

PREVENT. [p-h
Jb. 3 : 12. Why did the knees p. me?
Ps. 17 : † 13. arise, O L., p. his face
59:10. God of my mercy sh. p. me
79 : 8. let thy tender mercies p. us
88:13. in morn. my prayer p. thee
95 : † 2. p. his face with thanksg-g
119:148. Mine eyes p. night watches
Am. 9 : 10. The evil shall not p. us
1 Th. 4 : 15. not p. them who are

PREVENTED. [asleep
2 S. 22:6. compassed me; the snares
of death p. me, Ps. 18 : 5.
19. They p. me in day of calamities, but the L. my stay, Ps. 18:18.
Jb. 30 : 27. days of affliction p. me
41:11. Who p. that I should repay
Ps. 119 : 147. I p. dawning of morn.
Is. 21 : 14. they p. with their bread
Mat. 17:25. Jes. p. him, saying, Simon

PREVENTEST.
Ps. 21:3. thou p. him with blessings

PREY. [Noun.]
Ge. 49:9 fr. p. my son, thou art gone
27. in morning he shall devour p.
Nu. 14 : 3. that our wives and chil.
shall be a p.? 31. De. 1:39. [of p.
23 : 24. Isr. not lie down till he eat
31 : 12. bro-t captives and p. unto
26. Take the sum of p. taken [Mo.
27. divide the p. into two parts
32. booty being rest of the p.
De. 2:35. Only cattle we took for p.,
3 : 7. Jos. 8 : 2, 27.-11:14. [col-rs
Ju. 5 : 30. divided p. a p. of divers
8 : 24. give me earrings of his p.
25. did cast earrings of his p.
2 K. 21:14. Judah shall become a p.
Ne. 4 : 4 give them for a p. in land
Es. 3 : 13. take them for a p., 8 : 11.
9:15. on p. laid not their hand, 16.

Jb.4:11. lion perisheth for lack of p.
9 : 26. as eagle that hasteth to p.
24 : 5. as wild asses rising for a p.
38:39. Wilt thou hunt p. for lion?
39 : 29. thence she seeketh the p.
Ps. 17 : 12. Like a lion greedy of p.
76:4. more excell. than mts. of p.
104 : 21. young lions roar after p.
111 : † 5. He hath given p. unto th.
124 : 6. hath not given us for a p.
Pr. 23 : 28. She lieth in wait for p.
Is. 5 : 29. roar and lay hold of p.
8:† 1. speed to spoil, he hasteneth p.
10:2. that widows may be their p.
6 p. of an hypocritical nation
31:4. young lion roaring on his p.
33 : 23. p. of a great spoil divided
42 : 22. for a p. and none deliv-h
49:24. Sh. p. be taken from mighty?
25. p. of terrible be delivered
59:15. from evil maketh hims. a p.
Je. 21 : 9. his life shall be unto him
for p., 38:2.-39:18.-45:5. ⌈for p.
Eze. 7 : 21. into hands of strangers
19 : 3. lion learned to catch p. ⌈p.
22 : 25. prophets like lion ravening
27. princes like wolves ravening p.
26:12. make p. of thy merchandise
29:19. he sh. take her spoil, and p.
34 : 8. bec. my flock became a p.
22. my flock no more be a p., 28.
36:4. to the cities that became a p.
5. minds to cast it out for a p.
38 : 12. I will go up to take a p., 13.
Da. 11:24. sh. scatter am. them the p.
Am. 3 : 4. will lion roar hath no p.?
Na. 2:12. lion filled his holes with p.
13. I will cut off thy p. fr. earth
3 : 1. bloody city, p. departeth not
Zph. 3 : 8. until day that I rise up to
See PREY. [Verb.] ⌊the p.

PREY. [Verb.]

Je. 30:16. and all that p. upon thee
will I give for a prey

PRICE, PRICES.

Le. 25 : 16. acc. to years increase p.
acc. to fewness diminish p., 50.
52. give p. of his redemption, 51.
De. 23 : 18. not bring p. of a dog
2 S. 24:24. Nay, but I will surely buy
it at a p., 1 Ch. 21 : 22, 24.
1 K. 10:28. Sol.'s merchants received
yarn at a p., 2 Ch. 1 : 16.
Jb. 28:13. Man knoweth not p., 15.
18. p. of wisdom is above rubies
Ps. 44 : 12. Thou dost not increase
wealth by p. of thy people
Pr. 17 : 16. why p. in hand of fool?
27 : 26. goats are p. of the field
31 : 10. her p. far above rubies ⌈p.
Is. 45 : 13. let go my captives not for
55:1. buy wine and milk with-t p.
Je. 15:13. subst. to spoil without p.
Da. 11 : † 39. sh. divide land for p.
La. 5:† 4. our wood cometh for p.
Zch. 11 : 12. give me my p.; they
weighed for my p. 30 pieces ⌈at
13. a goodly p. that I was prized
Mat. 13 : 46. found pearl of great p.
27 : 6. not into treasury, bec. p. of
9. took 30 pieces the p. of him ⌊bl.
Ac. 4 : 34. brought p-s of the things
5 : 2. kept back part of the p., 3.
19 : 19. counted p. of books burnt
1 Co. 6:20. are bought with p., 7:23.
1 Pe. 3 : 4. meek spirit is of great p.

PRICKED, ING.

Ps. 73 : 21. I was p-d in my reins
Eze. 28:24 sh. be no more a p-g briar
Ac. 2:37. they were p-d in their heart

PRICKS.

Nu. 33 : 55. those th. remain be p.
Ac. 9 : 5. hard to kick ag. the p., 26:

PRIDE, PRIDES. ⌊14.

Le. 26 : 19. break p. of your power
1 S. 17:28. I know thy p. and ⌈for p.
2 Ch. 32 : 26. Hezekiah humbled
Jb. 9 : † 13. helpers of p. do stoop
26:† 12. by undorst-g smiteth thro.
33:17. he may hide p. fr. man ⌊p.
35 : 12. cry bec. of p. of evil men
38 : † 11. p. of thy waves be stayed
41 : 15. His scales are his p.
34. a king over all thy chil. of p.
Ps. 10 : 2. wicked in p. persecute
4. thro. p. of counten. not seek G.
31:20. hide them fr. p. of man ⌈me
36 : 11. Let not foot of p. come ag.
59:12. let them be taken in their p.
73 : 6. p. compasseth them about
Pr. 8 : 13. p. arrogancy do I hate
11:2. When p. cometh then shame
13:10. Only by p. cometh contention
14:3. In mouth of foolish rod of p.
16 : 18. p. goeth before destruction
21:† 24. who dealeth in wrath of p.
29:23. A man's p. sh. bring him low
Is. 9 : 9. say in p. of their hearts
16 : 6. We heard of p. of Moab,
haughtiness and p., Je. 48 : 29.
23 : 9. to stain the p. of all glory
25 : 11. he sh. bring down their p.
28 : 1. Woe to the crown of p., 3.
Je. 13:9. I will mar the p. of Judah
17. my soul shall weep for your p.
49 : 16. p. of heart deceived thee
50 : † 31. I am ag. thee, O thou p.
† 32. p. shall stumble and fall
Eze. 7:10. rod blossomed, p. budded
16:49. iniq. of thy sister Sodom, p.
56. Sodom was not mentioned in
day of thy p. † p-s
30 : 6. p. of her power sh. come do.
Da. 4 : 37. those that walk in p. ⌈p.
5:20. his mind was hardened in p.
Ho. 5:5. p. of Isr. doth testify, 7:10.
Ob. 3. p. of heart deceived thee
Na. 2:† 2. Lord hath turned away p.
of Jacob and p. of Israel ⌈p.
Zph. 2 : 10. This sh. they have for
3 : 11. take them rejoice in thy p.
Zch. 9 : 6. I cut off p. of Philistines
10 : 11. p. of Assyria be bro-t down
11:3. for the p. of Jordan is spoiled
Mk. 7:22. out of heart proceedeth p.
1 Ti. 3 : 6. lest lifted up with p.
1 Jn. 2 : 16. p. of life is not of Father

PRIEST. ⌈7 : 1.

Ge. 14:18. p. of most high God, He.
41 : 45. dau. of p. of On, 50.-46:20.
Ex. 2 : 16. p. of Midian had 7 dau-s
3 : 1. Jethro p. of Midian, 18 : 1.
29:30. son p. in his stead, Le. 16:32.
31:10. Aaron the p., 35:19.-38:21.
-39 : 41. Le 1 : 7.-13:2.-21:21.-
Nu. 3:32.-4 : 28, 33.-7:8.-10:8.-
18 : 28.-33 : 38.
Le. 1 : 9. The p. shall burn it all on
the altar, 13, 15, 17.-2:2, 9, 16.
-3 : 11, 16.-4 : 10, 31, 35 -5 12.-
6 : 12, 22.-7 : 5, 31. ⌈wood
12. p. shall lay them in order on
2:8. when presented unto p., 12:6.
4 : 3. if p. that is anointed do sin
6. p. shall dip finger in bl., 17.
16. p. sh. bring of bullock's blood
20. the p. shall make an atonement for them, 26.-5 : 6, 13, 16,
18.-6:6, 7.-7:7.-12:8.-14:18, 20,
31.-15:15, 30.-16:30.-19:22. Nu.
15 : 25, 28.
25. And the p. shall take of the
blood, 30, 34.-14 :14, 25.-17 : 5,
6. Eze. 45 : 19.
5 : 8. he shall bring them unto p.
13. remnant shall be the p.'s
6:10. p. shall put on linen garment
23. offering for p. sh. be burnt ⌈34.
7 : 32. right shoulder give unto p.,
13 : 3. p. sh. look on plague, 5, 6,
7, 8, 10, 12, 17, 19, 20, 21, 25,
26, 27, 30, 31, 32.-14:3, 36, 39.
3. p. pronounce him unclean, 8,
11, 15, 20, 22, 25, 27, 30, 44.
Le. 13 : 4. the p. shall shut him up 7
days, 5, 21, 26, 31, 33, 50, 54.
6. p. sh. pronounce him clean,
13, 17, 23, 28, 34, 37.-14:7. ⌈14:2
9. shall be brought unto p., 16.-
13. Then the p. shall consider
15. the p. shall see the raw flesh
14:11. p. that maketh him clean (2)
13. off-g is p.'s, 5 : 13.-6 : 26.-7:7.
16. p. shall dip his finger in oil,
15, 17, 26, 27, 28. ⌈tell p.
35. that owneth the house shall
48. p. sh. pronounce hou. clean
21 : 9. if dau. of a p. profane hers.
22 : 10. a sojourner of p. not eat
11. if p. buy any soul with money
12. if p.'s dau. married unto stran-
13. if p.'s dau. be a widow ⌊ger
14. give 5th part unto p. wi. holy
23:10. bring sheaf of firstfruits unto
11. p. shall wave it bef. L. ⌊p.
20. shall be holy to Lord for p.
27 : 8. p. shall value him, acc. to
11. present beast before the p.
12. p. shall value it, 14, 18, 23.
21. possession of field, sh. be p.'s
Nu. 3 : 32. Eleazar, son of Aa. the
p., 4 : 16.-16 : 37, 39.-19:3, 4.-
25 : 7, 11.-26 : 1, 3, 63.-27:2, 19,
21, 22.-31 : 6, 12, 13, 21, 26, 29,
31, 41, 51, 54.-32 : 2, 28.-34:17.
Jos. 14 : 1.-17 : 4.-19:51.-21:1.-
22:13, 31, 32. 1 Ch. 15:24. ⌈9, 10.
5:8. trespass be recompensed to p.,
15. man shall bring wife unto p.
17. p. shall take holy water
18. p. set woman bef. L., 16, 19, 21.
23. p. shall write curses in book
25. p. sh. take jealousy off-g, 26.
30. p. sh. execute upon her all law
6 : 19. p. sh. take sodden shoulder
20. this is holy for the p. with
19 : 6. p. shall take cedar wood
7. p. shall wash and be unclean
De. 17:12. that will not hearken un-
18:3. p.'s due fr. the people ⌊to p.
20:2. nigh unto battle, p. sh. speak
26:3. go unto p. and say, I profess
Jos. 21:4. chil. of Aa. the p., 13, 19.
Ju. 17 : 5. one of sons became p. ⌈19.
10. be unto me fa. and p., 12.-18:
13. seeing I have a Lev. to my p.
18 : 4. Micah hired me, I am his p.
6. p. said, Go in peace
17. p. stood in entering of gate
18. said p. What do ye?
20. the p.'s heart was glad
24. ye have taken away the p., 27.
1 S. 1 : 9. Eli the p. sat upon seat
2 : 11. child ministered bef. Eli p.
13. p.'s custom with people was
14. all that the p. took for hims.
15. Give flesh to roast for the p.
28. did I choose him to be my p.?
35. I will raise me up faithful p.
14 : 3. son of Eli L.'s p. in Shiloh
19. while Saul talked unto the p.
36. said p. draw near unto God
21:1. came David to Ahim. the p., 2.
4. p. answered David, There is no
common bread, 5.
6. p. gave them hallowed bread
9. p. said, The sword of Goliath
23 : 9. Da. said to Abiathar the p.,
30:7. 1 K. 1:7, 19, 25, 42.-2:22, 26.
2 S. 15 : 27. Zadok the p., 1 K. 1 : 8,
26, 32, 34, 38, 39, 44, 45.-2 : 35.
-4 : 2. 1 Ch. 16 : 39.-24 : 6. ⌈p.
1 K. 2:27. thrust Abiathar fr. being
2 K. 11 : 9. Jehoiada the p., 12:2, 7,
9. 2 Ch. 22 : 11.-23:8, 9, 14.-24:
2, 20, 25. ⌈spears
10. to captains p. gave David's
15. p. said, Let her not be slain
18. Mattan p. of Baal, 2 Ch. 23:17.
16 : 10. Urijah the p., 11, 15, 16.
Ezr. 8 : 33. Is. 8 : 2.

2 K.22: 10. Hilkiah the p., 12, 14.-23:
24. 2 Ch. 34 : 14, 18.
12. commanded Hilkiah the p.
2 Ch. 13 : 9. the same may be a p. of
15 : 3. Israel without a teaching p.
26 : 17. Azariah the p. went in
Ezr. 2 : 63. stood up a p., Ne. 7 : 65.
7 : 11. Ezra the p., 12, 21.-10 : 10,
16. Ne. 8 : 2, 9.-12 : 26. [vites
Ne 10 : 38. the p. shall be with Le-
13 : 4. Eliashib the p. was allied
13. treasurers Shelemiah the p.
Ps. 110 : 4. Thou art a p. for ever
after order, He 5 : 6.-7 : 17, 21.
Is. 8 : 2. I took witnesses, Uriah p.
24:2. as with the people, so with p.
61 : † 10. bridegroom decketh as p.
Je.20:1. Pashur son of Immer the p.
21:1. Zeph. son of Maaseiah the p.,
29 : 25, 29.-37 : 3.-52 : 24.
29:26. made thee p. inst. of Jehoi.
La. 2 : 6. hath despised king and p.
Eze.1:3. word came unto Eze. the p.
7 : 26. law shall perish from p.
44 : 13. not near to do office of p.
21. nei. shall any p. drink wine
22. or a widow that had a p. bef.
30 give unto p. the first of dough
45:19. p. sh. take blood of sin off-g
Ho. 4:4. as they that strive with the
6. thou shalt be no p. to me [p.
9. there sh. be like people like p.
Am.7:10.p.of Bethel sent to Jerob.
Zch.6:13. he sh. be p. upon throne
Mal. 2:7. p.'s lips sho. keep knowl.
Mat. 8 : 4. tell no man, shew thyself
to p., Mk. 1 : 44. Lu. 5 :14
Lu. 1:5. certain p. named Zacharias
10:31. there came down certain p.
Ac.14:13.p.of Jupiter brought oxen
He. 7 : 3. abideth a p. continually
11. what need ano p. rise, not
called after order of Aaron?
15.aft.Melchisedec ariseth ano.p.
20. not without an oath made p.
8 : 4. if on earth, he sho. not be p.
10:11. every p.standeth daily ministering

PRIEST with chief.

2 K. 25 : 18. took Seraiah c. p., Je.
1 Ch. 27 : 5. Benaiah a c. p. [52:24.
29 : 22. anointed Zadok to be c. p.
2 Ch.19:11. Amariah c.p. is ov.you
26:20. Azariah c. p. looked, 31:10.
Ezr. 7 : 5. son of Aaron the c. p.

High PRIEST. [head

Le. 21 : 10. h. p. shall not uncover
Nu. 35 : 25. abide in city of refuge
unto death of h.p.,28.Jos.20:6.
2 K. 12 : 10. much money in chest
h.p. put it in bags,2 Ch.24:11.
22 : 4. Go to Hilkiah the h.p. that
Ne. 3 : 1. Eliashib the h. p. rose up
Zch. 3 : 1. Joshua the h. p, 8.-6:11.
Mat. 26 : 3. unto the palace of the
h. p., 58. Mk. 14 : 54.Lu.22:54.
51. one struck a servant of h. p.,
Mk. 14: 47. Lu. 22:50. Jn.18:10.
57. led him to Caiaphas the h.
p.,Jn.18:24. [thou nothing?63.
62. the h. p. said, Answerest
65. h. p. rent his clothes,Mk.14:
Mk.2:26.days of Abiathar h.p.[63.
14 : 53. led Jesus away to h. p.
60. the h. p. stood up in midst
61. h. p. asked, Art thou C.? Jn.
18 : 19. [Thou
66. one of maids of h. p. said,
Jn. 11:49. Caiaphas h.p.,51.-18:13.
18 : 15. disci. known unto h.p.,16.
22. Answerest thou the h. p. so?
Ac. 4 : 6. of kindred of h. p., 5 : 17.
5 : 21. h.p. called council togeth.
27.h.p.asked,Did not we straitly
7 : 1. said h.p. Are these things so
9:1. Saul went to h.p. and desired
22: 5. h. p. doth bear me witness

Ac.23:2. h.p. Ananias com-ded th.
4. Revilest thou God's h. p.? [p.
5. Paul said, I wist not he was h.
24 : 1. Ananias h. p. descended
25:2. Then h.p. informed ag. Paul
He. 2 : 17. might be a faithful h.p.
3:1. consider the Apostle and H.P.
4 : 14. we have great h.p.is passed
15. we have not a h.p.wh.cannot
5 : 1. ev. h. p. taken fr. am. men
5.C.glorified not hims. to be h. p.
10.Called a h.p. after order,6:20.
7:26. such a h.p. became us, who
8:1.We have such h. p. on throne
3. every h.p. is ordained to offer
9 : 7. into second went h. p. alone
11. C. being h.p. of good things
25. as h. p. entereth holy place
10:21. having h.p. over hou. of G.
13 : 11. blood into sanctuary by h.
See OFFICE, PROPHET. [p.

PRIESTS.

Ge. 47 : 22. land of p.bought he not,
p.had portion assigned of Pha.
26. except the land of the p.only
Ex. 19:6. be unto me a kingd. of p.
22. p. also sanctify thems. lest L.
Le.1:8.p.sh. lay the parts, the head
11. p. sh. sprinkle blood, 5.-3 : 2.
6: 29. males am. p. shall eat, 7 : 6.
13 : 2. unto one of Aa.'s sons the p.
16 : 33. he sh. make atonem for p.
De.19:17 shall stand before p.,21:5.
31 : 9. Moses delivered law unto p.
Jos. 3 : 17. p. that bare ark stood
firm, 13, 14, 15.-4:10,11, 16, 18.
4 : 3. where the p'. feet stood, 9.
6 : 4. p. bear 7 trumpets, 6, 8, 13.
12. p. took up ark of the Lord
Ju.18:30.he and his sons were p. to
1 S. 1 : 3. Hophni and Phinehas p.
of Lord were there [threshold
5 : 5. nei. the p. of Dagon tread on
6 : 2. Philistines called for the p.
22 : 17. king said, slay p. of Lord
18. to Doeg, fall upon p. of Lord
19. smote Nob, city of the p., 11.
21. that Saul had slain Lord's p.
2 S. 8:17. Zadok and Ahim. were p.
1 K. 8 : 3. elders and p. took ark
11. p. could minister because of
cloud, 10. 2 Ch. 5 : 14.-7 : 2.
12:31.Jeroboam made p. of lowest
of the people, 13 : 33. 2 K.17:32.
13:2. upon thee shall he offer the p.
2 K. 10 : 11. Jehu slew Ahab's p.
19. call me all Baal's p. let none
12:6. p. had not repaired breaches
8. p. consented to rec. no more,
16. sin money was the p'. [4, 5.
17 : 27. Carry thither one of the p.
23 : 4. k. com-ded p. of sec. order
5. he put down idolatrous p.
9. p. of high places not to altar
20. slew all p. of high places
1 Ch. 16:6. Benaiah and Jahaziel p.
2 Ch. 4 : 6. sea for p. to wash in
9. he made court of the p.
5:11. p. were come out of holy pla.
12.120 p.sounding with trumpets
6 : 41. let p. be clothed with salva.
8 : 14. he appointed courses of p.
11:15. ordained p. for high places
13:9. Have ye not cast out p. of L.
12. p. wi. trumpets to cry alarm
23 : 6. none into hou. of L. save p.
26:17. with him fourscore p. of L.
19. Uzziah was wroth with p.
29 : 24. p. killed goats and made
34. p. too few, could not flay all
30 : 3. p. had not sanctified thems.
16. p. sprinkled the blood, 29:22.
34:5. Josiah burnt the bones of p.
35 : 2. Josiah set the p. in charges
8.gave unto p. for passover off-gs
11. p. sprinkled blood fr. hands
Ezr. 6 : 18. they set p. in divisions

Ezr. 6:20. killed the passover for p.
7 : 16. of peo. and p. offering will-
8 : 15. I viewed peo. and p. [ingly
9:7. our p. been deliv-d into ha.of
10:18.p.th. had strange wives [k-s
Ne. 2 : 16. nor had I told it to the p.
3 : 22. after him repaired p., 28.
9:32. trouble that hath come upon
us and our p. [law
34. neither we nor p. kept thy
10:37.bri. firstfruits unto p.,36,39.
12 : 12. in days of Joiakim p. | 22.
41. And the p.; Eliakim and
13:5.where they laid offerings of p.
Ps. 78:64. Their p. fell by the sword
99 : 6. Moses and Aaron am. his p.
132 : 9. Let thy p. be clothed with
16. I will clothe her p.with salva.
Is. 37 : 2. sent elders of p. unto Is.
61 : 6. ye sh. be named p. of Lord
Je. 1 : 18. against the p. and people
2 : 8. p. said not, Where is the L.?
26. p. ashamed | 4 : 9. astonished
5 : 31. p. bear rule by their means
8 : 1. bones of p. they shall bring
13:13. I will fill p. with drunkenn.
31:14. I will satiate the souls of p.
32:32. to provoke me, they and p.
48 : 7. captivity with his p., 49 : 3.
La. 1 : 4. her p. sigh, her virgins
19. my p. gave up the ghost
4:13. iniq-s of her p.th.shed blood
16. respected not persons of p.
Eze. 22 : 26. Her p. violated my law
40:45. said, This chamber is for p.
43 : 24. p. sh. cast salt upon them
44:31. p. not eat that dead of itself
45 : 4. shall be for p., 48 : 10, 11.
46:19. holy chambers of p., 42:13.
20. place where p. shall boil off-g
Ho. 5 : 1. Hear this, O p. hearken
6:9 company of p. murder in way
10 : 5. p. that rejoiced for glory
Jo. 1:9. p. L.'s ministers mourn,13.
Mi. 3 : 11. p. teach for hire [.-2 : 17.
Zph. 1 : 4. I will cut off names of p.
3:4.her p.have polluted sanctuary
Hag. 2 : 11. Ask now p. conc. law
Zch. 7 : 3. speak unto p. Sho. I weep
Mal.1:6.unto you, O p.that despise
2 : 1. O p. this com-t is for you
Mat.12:4 not lawful to eat but only
for p., Mk. 2 : 26. Lu. 6 : 4.
5. p. in temple profane sabbath
Lu. 17 : 14. Go shew yours. unto p.
Ac. 4 : 1. The p. and captains came
6 : 7. a company of p. obedient
He. 7 : 21. p. made without an oath
23. they truly were many p. bec.
8 : 4. seeing there are p. that offer
9 : 6. p. went into first tabernacle
Re. 1 : 6. made us p. unto God, 5:10.
20 : 6. shall be p. of God and of C.

PRIESTS with chief.

2 Ch. 36:14. all c. of p.transgressed
Ezr. 8 : 24. separated 12 of c. of p.
29.weigh them before the c. of p.
10:5. Ezr. made c.p.and Isr.swear
Ne. 12 : 7. c. of p.in days of Joshua
Mat. 2 : 4. gath-d c. p. and scribes
16 : 21. suffer many things of c. p.
20:18. betrayed unto c. p., Mk.10:
21:15. c.p.saw wonderf.things[33.
23.c.p.came unto him,Mk.11:27.
45 when c.p. heard his parables
26:3. Then assembled the c.p. and
26 : 14. Judas Iscariot went unto
c.p.,Mk. 14:10.[p., Mk. 14 : 43.
47. multitude with staves fr. c.
27:1.all c.p. took counsel ag.Jesus
3. Judas bro-t 30 pieces to c.p.,6.
12. when he was accused of c.p.,
Mk. 15 : 3. Lu. 23 : 10.
20. c. p. persuaded multitude
41. c. p. mocking him, Mk.15:31.
62.c.p.and Pharisees unto Pilate
28 : 11. shewed unto c. p. all thi.

Je.36:19. Said p. unto Baruch, hide
37:14. Irijah took Jere. to p.
15. p. were wroth with Jeremiah
38:4. p. said, let man be put to dea.
17. King of Babylon's p., 18, 22.–
39:3.–41:1. Je. 39:3, 13.
25. if p. hear I talked with thee
44:17. burn incense as our p.
21. incense ye and p. burn
48:7. his p. go into captivity, 49:3.
49:38. I will destroy fr. thence p.
50:35. a sword is upon her p. and
51:57. I will make drunk her p.
La. 1:6. p. are become like harts
2:2. he hath polluted kingd. and p.
9. her kings and p. are am. Gent.
5:12. p. are hanged by their hand
Eze. 11:1. am whom I saw p. of peo.
17:12. king taken p. of Jerus.
22:27. Her p. like wolves
23:15. in dyed attire, all of th. p.
32:29. Edom and p. with might
30. p. of the north, all of them
39:18. ye sh. drink blood of the p.
45:8. my p. shall no more oppress
Da. 1:3. of king's seed and of the p.
3:2. king sent to gather the p.
3. p. governors, judges, 27.–5:7.
5:2. th. Belshazzar and p. drink, 3.
6:1. to set over kingdom 120 p., 2.
3. Daniel was preferred above p.
4. p. sought occasion ag. Daniel
6. presidents and p. assembled
8:25. sh. stand up ag. Prince of p.
9:6. prophets who spake to our p.
8. confusion of face to our p.
11:5. one of his p. shall be strong
8. carry cap. into Egypt their p.
Ho. 7:3. make p. glad with lies
5. p. have made him sick wi. wine
16. their p. shall fall by sword
8:4. they made p. I knew it not
10. sorrow for burden of king of p.
9:15. all their p. are revolters
13:10. saidst, Give me king and p.
Am. 1:15. into captivity, he and his
Mi. 3:1. hear ye p. of Israel, 9. [p.
5:†5. raise ag. him eight p. of men
Ha. 1:10. the p. shall be a scorn
Zph. 1:8. I will punish the p. and
3:3. p. within her are roaring lions
Mat. 20:25. p. of Gentiles exercise
1 Co. 2:6. nor the wisd. of p. of world
8. none of p. of this world knew

All PRINCES. [ecute
Ex. 12:†12. ag. a. p. of Egypt ex-
Nu. 31:13. a. p. of cong-n went forth
Jos. 9:19. a. p. said, We have sworn
2 K. 24:14. carried away a. p. and
1 Ch. 29:24. a. p. submitted thems.
2 Ch. 24:10. a. p. cast into chest
23. destroyed a. p. of people [p.
Ezr. 7:28. bef. a. the king's mighty
Es. 1:3. feast unto a. his p., 2:18.
16. done wrong to a. p. and peo.
3:1. set his seat above a. p. with
Ps. 83:11. a. their p. as Zeba and
Je. 26:12. Jere. spake unto a. p., 21.
34:10. when a. p. heard that ev.
one sho. let his manservant go
36:12. K.'s house; a. p. sat there,
21. Jehudi read in ears of a. p. [14
38:27. a. p. unto Jere. and asked
Eze. 26:16. a. p. of the sea came
27:21. Arabia and a. p. of Kedar
Am. 2:3. will slay a. p. with him
See **CHIEF** with prince, s.
See **Princes** of **ISRAEL.**

PRINCES of Judah or Juda
2 Ch. 24:17. p. o. J. made obeisance
Ne. 12:31. I brought up p. o. J.
Ps. 68:27. with p. o. J., and council
Je. 52:10. he slew all the p. o. J. in
Ho. 5:10. p. o. J. like them th. remove
Mat. 2:6. thou art not least am. p.

PRINCELY. [o. J-a
Ho. 12:†3. Jac. hath behaved hims. p.

PRINCESS, ES.
1 K. 11:3. Sol. had 700 wives p-s
Is. 49:†23. p-s thy nursing mothers
La. 1:1. she that was p. am. prov-

PRINCIPAL. [inces
Ex. 30:23. Take thou also p. spices
Le. 6:5. he shall restore it in the p.
Nu. 5:7. recompense his tresp. wi. p.
1 K. 4:5. Zabud was p. officer
2 K. 25:19. the p. scribe of the host,
Je. 52:25. [for Eleazar
1 Ch. 24:6. one p. household taken
31. priests p. fathers cast lots
27:†5. Benaiah was a p. officer
Ne. 11:17. Mattaniah p. to begin
Jb. 30:†15. they pursue my p. one
Pr. 1:†7. fear of the Lord is p. part
4:7. Wisdom is the p. thing, theref.
Is. 16:8. broken down p. plants
28:25. cast in p. wheat and barley
Je. 25:34. in ashes, ye p. of flock
35. nor the p. of flock escape, 36.
38:†14. took Jere. into p. entry
Eze. 47:†12. sh. bring forth p. fruit
Mi. 5:5. raise ag. him eight p. men
Ac. 25:23. p. men of city with Ag-

PRINCIPALITY, IES. [rippa
Je. 13:18. your p-s shall come down
Ro. 8:38. nor angels, p-s powers be
Ep. 1:21. Far above all p. power
3:10. p-s and powers in heavenly
6:12. we wrestle ag. p-s powers
Col. 1:16. by him created p-s powers
2:10. is head of all p. and power
15. having spoiled p-s and powers
Tit. 3:1. to be subject to p-s powers
Jude †6. angels wh. kept not their

PRINCIPLES. [p.
He. 5:12. that one teach you first p.
6:1. leaving the p. of doctrine of

PRINT [Noun.] [C.
Jb. 13:27. thou settest a p. on heels
Jn. 20:25. Except I see p. of nails,
and put my finger into p. of

PRINT, PRINTED.
Le. 19:28. not p. marks upon you
Jb. 19:23. O that my words were p-d

PRISCA=PRISCILLA.
2 Ti. 4:19. Salute P. and Aquila

PRISCIL'LA.
Ac. 18:18. with Paul P. and Aquila
See Aquila.

PRISED. See Prized.

PRISON, PRISONS.
Ge. 39:20. Potiphar put Joseph in p.
21. L. gave Joseph favour in sight
of keeper of p., 22, 23.
40:3. put butler and baker into p.
42:19. let one be bound in your p.
1 K. 22:27. Put this fellow in p., 2
Ch. 18:26. [Hoshea in p.
2 K. 17:4. king of Assyria bound
25:27. bro-t Jehoiachin out of p.
29. And changed his p. garments,
Je. 52:31, 33. [the p.
Ne. 3:25. Palal repaired by court of
12:39. they stood still in p. gate
Ps. 142:7. Bring my soul out of p. to
Ec. 4:14. out of p. cometh to reign
Is. 24:22. they shall be shut in p.
42:7. to bring out prisoners fr. p.
22. they are all hid in p. houses
53:8. He was taken fr. p. and judgm.
61:1. to proclaim opening of the p.
Je. 29:26. shouldest put him in p.
32:2. Jeremiah was shut in p., 8.
12. bef. Jews in court of the p.
33:1. word unto Jere. while in p.,
37:21.–38:6, 13, 28.–39:15. [p.
37:4. for they had not put him into
15. put him in p. in Jona.'s hou.,
39:14. they took Jere. out of p. [18.
52:11. put Zedekiah in p. till death
Mat. 4:12. th. John was cast into p.
5:25. thou be cast into p., Lu. 12:58.
11:2. Jn. heard in p. works of C.
14:3. Herod put him in p. for Hero.
Mat. 14:10. beheaded John in p., Mk
18:30. him into p. till he pay [6:27.
25:36. I was in p. and ye came
39. when saw we thee in p., 43, 44.
Mk. 1:14. after John was put in p.
6:17. Herod had bound John in p.
Lu. 3:20. he shut up John in p. [p-s
21:12. persecute you, deliv-g unto
22:33. with thee into p. and death
23:19. for murder cast into p., 25.
Jn. 3:24. John not yet cast into p.
Ac. 5:18. put apostles in common p.
19. angel by night opened p. doors
21. high priest sent to p. [23.
22. officers found them not in p.,
25. men ye put in p. are standing
8:3. haling men and women to p.
12:4. Peter in p. | 5. kept in p.
6. keepers before door kept the p.
7. behold a light shined in p. [9.
17. how Lord brought him out of
16:23. Paul, Silas were cast into p.
24. Who thrust them into inner p.
26. foundations of p. shaken
27. keeper seeing p. doors open
37. being Romans cast us into p.
40. Paul and Silas went out of p.
22:4. deliv-g unto p-s men and
26:10. many saints did I shut in p.
2 Co. 11:23. in p-s more frequent [p.
1 Pe. 3:19. preached unto spirits in
Re. 2:10. devil sh. cast some into p.
20:7. Satan shall be loosed out of

PRISON house. [his p.
Ju. 16:21. Samson did grind in p. h.
25. called for Samson out of p. h.
2 Ch. 16:10. Asa put Hanani in p. h.
Is. 42:7. bring them in darkn. out

PRISONER. [of p. h.
Ps. 79:11. Let sighing of p. come
102:20. To hear groaning of the p.
Mat. 27:15. was wont to release p.
16. had a notable p., Mk. 15:6.
Ac. 23:18. Paul p. called me
25:27. unreasonable to send a p.
28:17. was I deliv-d p. to Romans
Ep. 3:1. I Paul the p. of Jesus, 4:1.
Phm. 1, 9. [me his p.
2 Ti. 1:8. Be not thou ashamed of
See **FELLOW** prisoner, s.

PRISONERS.
Ge. 39:20. where k.'s p. were bound
22. committed to Joseph all p.
Nu. 21:1. Arad took some of Isr. p.
Jb. 3:18. There the p. rest together
Ps. 69:33. Lord despiseth not his p.
146:7. The Lord looseth the p.
Is. 10:4. they shall bow down und. p.
14:17. opened not house of his p.
20:4. Assyria shall lead Eg-ns p.
24:22. they sh. be gathered as p.
42:7. to bring out p. from prison
49:9. mayest say to p., Go forth
La. 3:34. To crush under feet p.
Zch. 9:11. I have sent forth thy p.
12. to strong hold, ye p. of hope
Ac. 16:25. sang praises, p. heard
27. supposing p. had been fled
27:1. delivered Paul and other p.
42. soldiers' counsel was to kill p.
28:16. centurion delivered p. to

PRIVATE. [capt.
2 Pe. 1:20. no prophecy of p. in-

PRIVATELY. [terpr-n
Mat. 24:3. disciples came unto Ch. p.
Mk. 6:32. Jes. went into a ship p.,
Lu. 9:10. [p., 13:3.
9:28. John and Andrew ask him
Lu. 10:23. unto disciples and said p.
Ac. 23:19. with Paul's kinsman p.
Ga. 2:2. but p. to them of reputa-

PRIVILEGE. [tion
Jn. 1:†12. as received him gave he

PRIVILY. [p.
Ju. 9:31. messengers unto Abim. p.
1 S. 24:4. David cut Saul's skirt p.
Ps. 10:8. his eyes are p. set ag. poor

Ps. 11 : 2. may **p.** shoot at upright
31:4. me out of net laid **p.**, 142 : 3.
64:5. commune of laying snares **p.**
101:5. Whoso **p**. slander-h neighb.
Pr. 1:11. let us lurk **p.** for innocent
18. they lurk **p.** for own lives [p.
Mat. 1 : 19. minded to put her away
2 : 7. Herod, when he had **p.** called
Ac. 16 : 37. do they thrust us out **p.**?
Ga. 2 : 4. who came in **p.** to spy out
2 Pe. 2:1. **p.** bring in damnable her-

PRIVY. [esies
De. 23 : 1. hath **p.** member cut off
1 K. 2 : 44. wickedn. thy heart **p.** to
Eze.21:14. sword enters **p.** chambers
Ac. 5 : 2. his wife also being **p.** to it

PRIZE. [p.
1 Co. 9 : 24. all run, but one rec-h
Ph. 3 : 14. I press tow. the mark for

PRIZED. [the p.
Zch. 11 : 13. goodly price that I was

PROCEED. [p.
Ex. 25:35. acc. to 6 branches that **p.**
Jos. 6:10. nei. word **p.** out of mouth
2 S. 7 : 12. seed which shall **p.** out
Jb. 40 : 5. but I will **p.** no further
Is. 29 : 14. I **p.** to do marvell. work
51 : 4. for a law shall **p.** from me
Je. 9:3. for they **p.** from evil to evil
30:19. out of them sh. **p.** thanksg.
21. their governor shall **p.** from
Ha. 1:7. and dignity sh. **p.** of thems.
Mat. 15 : 18. **p.** out of mouth defile
19. out of the heart **p.** murders,
Mk. 7 : 21. [munication **p.**
Ep. 4:29. Let no corrupt communi-
2 Ti. 3 : 9. they shall **p.** no further

PROCEEDED. [lips
Nu. 30 : 12. whatever **p.** out of her
32 : 24. do that which hath **p.** out
of your mouths, Ju. 11 : 36.
Jb. 36 : 1. Elihu also **p.**, Suffer me
Lu. 4 : 22. gracious words which **p.**
Jn. 8 : 42. I **p.** forth and came fr. G.
Ac. 12 : 3. he **p.** to take Peter also
Re. 4 : 5. out of throne **p.** lightn-gs
19 : 21. sword **p**. out of his mouth

PROCEEDETH.
Ge. 24 : 50. thing **p.** from the Lord
Nu. 30 : 2. acc. to all **p.** out of mou.
De. 8 : 3. by ev. word that **p.** out of
mouth of God, Mat. 4 : 4.
1 S. 24 : 13. Wickedn. **p.** fr. wicked
Ec. 10 : 5. error which **p.** from ruler
La. 3 : 38. out of Most High **p.** not
Ha. 1 : 4. wrong judgment **p.** [evil
Jn. 15 : 26. Spirit of truth **p.** fr. Fa.
Ja. 3 : 10. out of same mouth **p.**
Re. 11 : 5. fire **p.** out of their mouth

PROCEEDING.
Re.22:1. water of life **p.** out of throne

PROCESS of time.
Ge. 4 : 3. in **p.** - Cain bro-t offering
38 : 12. in **p.** - Judah's wife died
Ex. 2 : 23. in **p.** - king of E. died
Ju. 11:4. in **p.** - Ammon made war
2 Ch.21:19. in **p.** - Jehoram's bowels

PROCH'ORUS.
Ac. 6 : 5. mult. chose P. and Timon

PROCLAIM.
Ex. 33 : 19. I will **p.** name of the L.
Le. 23 : 2. feast of the Lord ye shall
p., 4, 21, 37. [peace
25 : 10. **p.** liberty | De. 20 : 10. **p.**
Ju. 7 : 3. to **p.** in ears of the people
21 : † 13. sent to **p.** peace to Benj.
Ru. 4 : † 11. **p.** thy name in Beth-le.
1 K. 21 : 9. **p.** a fast, set Naboth on
2 K. 10 : 20. Jehu said, **p.** assembly
Ne. 8 : 15. **p.** th. they fetch branches
Es. 6 : 9. **p.** before him, Thus sh. it
Pr. 20 : 6. Most **p.** own goodness
Is. 12:†4. Praise the L., **p.** his name
61 : 1. hath sent me to **p.** liberty
2. To **p.** acceptable year of Lord
Je. 3. 12. Go and **p.** these words, 11:
6.-19 : 2.
Je. 7:2. Stand in gate of Lord, and **p.**
34 : 8. made a cov-t to **p.** liberty
17. I **p.** liberty for you to sword
Jo. 3 : 9. **p.** ye this among Gentiles
Am. 4 : 5. and **p.** the free offerings

PROCLAIMED.
Ex. 34 : 5. and **p.** name of the L., 6.
36:6. caused it to be **p.** thro. camp
1 K. 21 : 12. **p.** a fast, set Naboth
2 K. 10:20. sol. assembly, they **p.** it
23:16. acc. to word wh. man of God
p. who **p.** these words, 17.
2 Ch.20:3. Jehosh-t feared and **p.** fast
Ezr. 8 : 21. I **p.** a fast at Ahava [sh.
Es. 6 : 11. Haman **p.** bef. him, Thus
Is. 62:11. L. hath **p.**, salva. cometh
Je. 36 : 9. they **p.** a fast before Lord
La. 1 : † 21. bring day thou hast **p.**
Jon. 3:5. **p.** a fast, and put on sackol.
7. caused it to be **p.** thro. Nineveh
Lu. 12 : 3. shall be **p.** upon house-

PROCLAIMETH, ING. [tops
Pr. 12:23. heart of fools **p-h** foolishn.
Je. 34:15. in **p-g** liberty ev. man, 17.
Re. 5 : 2. I saw a strong angel **p-g**

PROCLAMATION. [row
Ex. 32 : 5. Aaron made **p.**, To mor-
Ju. 4:†13. Sisera gath-d by **p.** chari-
1 K. 15 : 22. king Asa made **p.** [ots
22 : 36. went a **p.** thro-t the host
2 Ch. 24:9. Joash made **p.** thro. Jud.
30 : 5. to make **p.** thro-t all Israel
36 : 22. Cyrus made **p.**, Ezr. 1 : 1.
Ezr. 10 : 7. Ezra made **p.** thro. Jud.
Da. 5:29. Belshazzar made **p.** conc-g

PROCURE, ED, ETH. [Dan.
Pr. 11 : 27. seeketh good **p-h** favour
17:†9. covereth transgr-n **p-h** love
Je. 2 : 17. Hast thou not **p-d** this
4 : 18. thy doings have **p-d** these
26:19. Thus might we **p.** great evil
33:9. shall fear for all prosperity I

PRODUCE. [p.
Is. 41:21. **p.** your cause, saith Lord

PROFANE. [Adj.] [14.
Le. 21:7. shall not take a wife is **p.**,
Je. 23 : 11. prophets and priests **p.**
Eze. 21 : 25. thou **p.** prince of Israel
22:26. difference betw. holy and **p.**
28:16. cast thee as **p.** out of mt. of G.
42 : 20. betw. sanct-y and **p.** place
44:23. difference betw. holy and **p.**
48 : 15. shall be a **p.** place for city
1 Ti. 1 : 9. law is made for the **p.**
4 : 7. refuse **p.** old wives' fables
6:20. avoid **p.** babblings, 2 Ti. 2:16.
He. 12 : 16. Lest be any **p.** person as

PROFANE. [Verb.] [Esau
Le. 19 :† 29. Do not **p.** thy daughter
21:4. chief am. his peo. to **p.** hims.
9. dau. of priest, if she **p.** herself
12. he shall not **p.** sanctuary, 23.
15. Nei. shall he **p.** his seed am.
22 : 9. die, if they **p.** my ordinance
15. sh. not **p.** holy things of Isr.
Nu. 30 :† 2. he shall not **p.** his word
De.28:†30. plant viney. and not **p.** it
Ne.13:17. evil ye do, and **p.** sabbath
Ps. 89 : † 31. If they **p.** my statutes
Je.31:†5. the planters shall **p.** them
Eze. 23 : 39. into my sanctuary to **p.**
24 : 21. I will **p.** my sanctuary [it
Mat. 12:5. the priests **p.** the sabbath
Ac. 24 : 6. gone about to **p.** temple
See **NAME, HOLY name.**

PROFANED.
Le. 19 : 8. hath **p.** hallowed things
Ps. 55:†20. he hath **p.** his covenant
89 : 39. thou hast **p.** his crown
Is.43:28. I have **p.** princes of sanct-y
Eze. 22 : 8. hast **p.** my sab-s, 23 : 38.
†16. shalt be **p.** in sight of heath.
26. **p.** my holy things, I am **p.** am.
25:3. ag. sanctuary, when it was **p.**
36 : 20. they **p.** my holy name
21. my name wh. Isr. **p.**, 22, 23.
Mal. 1 : 12. have **p.** it, in that ye say
Mal.2:11. Jud. hath **p.** holiness of L.

PROFANENESS.
Je. 23:15. fr. prophets of Jerus. is **p.**

PROFANETH, ING.
Le. 21 : 9. **p-h** her father be burnt
Ne. 13 : 8. bring wrath by **p-g** sab.
Mal. 2 : 10. by **p-g** covenant of fa-

PROFESS. [thers
De. 26 : 3. I **p.** this day unto the L.
Mat. 7 : 23. will **p.** I never knew you
Tit.1:16. They **p.** that they know G.
3 : † 14. learn to **p.** honest trades

PROFESSED, ING.
Ro. 1 : 22. **p-g** themselves to be wise
2 Co. 9 : 13. **p-d** subject-n unto gosp.
1 Ti. 2:10. wh. becometh women **p-g**
6 : 12. hast **p-d** a good profession
21. some **p-g** have erred conc.

PROFESSION. [faith
1 Ti. 6 : 12. hast professed a good **p.**
†13. bef. Pilate witnessed good **p.**
He. 3 : 1. the High Priest of our **p.**
4:14. let us hold fast our **p.**, 10:23.

PROFIT. [Noun.]
Ge.25:32. what **p.** birthright dome
37:26. What **p.** if we slay our bro.
Es. 3 : 8. not for king's **p.** to suffer
Jb. 21 : 15. what **p.** if we pray unto
30:2. whereto strength **p.** me [him
35 : 3. what **p.** if I be cleansed fr.
Ps. 30 : 9. What **p.** is in my blood?
Pr. 14 : 23. In all labour there is **p.**
Ec. 1 : 3. What **p.** hath a man of all
his labour? 3 : 9.-5 : 16.
2 : 11. there was no **p.** under sun
5 : 9. the **p.** of the earth is for all
7 : 11. by wisdom there is **p.** to th.
Is. 30 : 5. help nor **p.** but a shame
Je. 16 : 19. have inherited things
wherein is no **p.** [ordinance?
Mal. 3 : 14. what **p.** that we kept
Ro. 3 : 1. what **p.** of circumcision?
1 Co. 7 : 35. this I speak for your **p.**
10:33. not seeking own **p.** but **p.** of
2 Ti. 2 : 14. not about words to no **p.**
He. 12 : 10. he chasteneth us for our

PROFIT. [Verb.] [p.
1 S. 12:21. after things wh. can-t **p.**
Jb. 35 : 8. thy righteousness may **p.**
Ps. 120 : † 3. what shall it **p.** thee,
false tongue [nothing
Pr. 10 : 2. Treasures of wickedn. **p.**
11:4. Riches **p.** not in day of wrath
Is.30:5. of people th. could not **p.**, 6.
44:9. delectable things shall not **p.**
47 : 12. if so be thou be able to **p.**
48:17. L. which teacheth thee to **p.**
57 : 12. works, they sh. not **p.** thee
Je. 2 : 8. after things that do not **p.**
11. changed, for that wh. doth not
7:8. in lying words that can-t **p.** [p.
12:13. thems. to pain, but sh. not **p.**
23:32. they shall not **p.** this people
Mk. 8 : 36. what **p.** if he gain world
1 Co. 12:7. is given to ev. man to **p.**
14 : 6. tongues, what sh. I **p.** you?
Ga. 5 : 2. Christ sh. **p.** you nothing
He. 4 : 2. word preached did not **p.**
Ja. 2:14. What doth it **p.** my breth.
16. if not things needful doth it **p.**

PROFITABLE.
Jb. 22 : 2. Can a man be **p.** unto
God, as **p.** to himself [rect
Ec. 10 : 10. but wisdom is **p.** to di-
Is. 44 : 10. image that is **p.** for noth.
Je. 13 : 7. girdle was **p.** for nothing
Mat. 5:29. **p.** that one of thy mem-
bers perish, 30. [unto you
Ac. 20 : 20. I kept back nothing **p.**
1 Co.6:†12. All things lawful, not **p.**
1 Ti. 4 : 8. godliness is **p.** unto all
2 Ti. 3 : 16. All Scripture is **p.**
4:11. Mark is **p.** to me for ministry
Tit. 3 : 8. These things are **p.** unto
Phm. 11. now **p.** to thee and me [men

PROFITABLY.
Ep. 4:†29. which is good to edify **p.**

PROFITED, ETH. [not
Jb.33:27. if say I sinned, and it p-d
34:9. It p-h noth. to delight in G.
Ha. 2 : 18. What p-h graven image
Mat. 15 : 5. It is a gift by whatso. thou mightest be p-d, Mk.7:11.
16:26.what is a man p-d if he gain the whole world and lose [ing
Jn.6:63.quickeneth, flesh p-h noth-
Ro. 2: 25. circumcision p-h if thou
1 Co.13:3. not charity, it p-h noth.
Ga. 1:14. I p-d in the Jews' religion
1 Ti. 4 : 8. bodily exercise p-h little
He. 13 : 9. not p-d them been occu-
PROFITING. [pied
1 Ti. 4:15. that thy p. appear to all
PROFOUND.
Ho. 5 : 2. revolters are p. to make
PROGENITORS.
Ge. 49:26. above blessings of my p.
PROGNOSTICATORS.
Is. 47 : 13. Let monthly p. stand up
PROLONG, ED, ETH, ING.
Nu. 9 : † 19. cloud p. journeyed not
Jos. 24 : † 31. Isr. served all days th. p-d after Josh., Ju. 2 : † 7.
Jb.6:11. what end, that I sho. p. life
15:29. wicked sh. not p. perfection
Ps. 61 : 6. Thou wilt p. king's life
Pr. 28 : 2. by knowl. state sh. be p-d
Ec. 7 : 15. wicked man that p-h life
Da. 7 : † 12. a p-g in life was given
Eze. 12:25. word sh. be no more p-d
28.shall none of my words be p-d
Da. 7:12.their lives were p. for time
See **Prolong, ed, eth DAYS.**
PROMISE. [Noun.] [p.
Nu.14:34.ye sh. know my breach of
1 K. 8 : 56. not failed one word of p.
2 Ch. 1 : 9. let p. unto Da. be establ.
Ne. 5 : 12. should do acc. to this p.
13. performeth not this p. be he shaken out, peo. did acc. to p.
Ps. 77 : 8. doth this p. fail everm.?
105:42. he remembered his holy p.
Lu. 24 : 49. I send p. of my Father
Ac. 1 : 4. wait for p. of the Father
2:33.received of Fa. p. of Holy Gh.
39. the p. is unto you and chil.
7 : 17. when time of p. drew nigh
13:23.acc. to p. hath raised a Sav.
32. p. made to fa-s God fulfilled
23 : 21. looking for a p. fr. thee
26 : 6. hope of p. made of G. [G
7. unto wh. p. our tribes serving
Ro. 4 : 13. p. that he shall be heir
14. p. is made of none effect
16. p. might be sure to the seed
20. He staggered not at the p.
9 : 9. this is word of p. I will come
Ga. 3 : 14. might receive p. of Spirit
17. sho. make p. of none effect
18. if be of law, it is no more of p. God gave it to Ab. by p.
19. seed shall come, to wh. p. was
22. that the p. by faith of Jes. C.
29. then are ye heirs acc. to p.
4 : 23. he of free woman was by p.
Ep. 1 : 13. sealed wi. Holy Spi. of p.
2:12. strangers fr. covenants of p.
3 : 6. Gentiles be partakers of p.
6 : 2. which is first com-t with p.
1 Ti. 4 : 8. having p. of the life now
2 Ti. 1 : 1. acc. to p. of life in C. J.
He. 4 : 1. fear, lest p. left us of ent-g
6 : 13. when God made p. to Ab.
15. after he endured obtained p.
17. willing to shew unto heirs of
9 : 15. p. of eternal life, 10 : 36. [p.
11 : 9. By faith sojourned in la. of p. heirs with him of same p.
39. these all received not p.
2 Pe.3:4. Where is p. of his coming?
9. Lord is not slack conc. his p.
13. acc. to p. we look for new
1 Jn.2:25.this is the p. he promised
See **CHILDREN of promise.**

PROMISES.
Ro. 9 : 4. to whom pertain the p.
15:8. to confirm p. made unto fa-s
2 Co.1:20. all p. of God are yea and
7 : 1. Having these p. dearly belov.
Ga. 3:16. to Abraham were p. made
21. Is the law then ag. p. of God?
He. 6:12. who thro. faith inherit p.
7 : 6. Melchis. blessed him had p.
8 : 6. cov-t establ-d upon better p.
11:13. died, not having received p.
17. he that received p. off-d son
33. who thro. faith obtained p. and [cious p.
2 Pe. 1 : 4. given us exceeding pre-
PROMISE. [Verb.]
2 Pe 2:19.while they p. them liberty
PROMISED.
Ex.12:25.will give you acc. as he p.
Nu. 14 : 40. will go unto place L. p.
De. 1 : 11. Lord bless you as he p.
6 : 3 th. ye may increase as L. p.
9 : 28. to bring them unto la. he p.
10 : 9. L. his inheritance, as he p.
12:20. L. enlarge thy border, as he
15: 6. L. blesseth thee as he p. [p.
19 : 8. give thee land he p., 27 : 3.
23 : 23. shall keep that which thou hast p. unto God
26 : 18. his peculiar peo. as he p.
Jos. 9 : 21. live, as princes had p.
22:4.given rest unto breth. as he p.
23 : 5. ye sh. possess land, as L. p.
10. God fighteth for you, as he p.
15. good things are come Lord p.
1 K. 2 : 24. made me house, as he p.
5:12. L. gave Sol. wisdom, as he p.
8:20. I sit on throne of Isr. as L. p.
56. given rest to people as he p.
9 : 5. as I p. to David thy father
2 K. 8 : 19. as he p. to give him a light, 2 Ch. 21 : 7.
1 Ch. 17 : 26. p. this goodness unto thy servant, 2 S. 7 : 28.
2 Ch. 6 : 10. set on throne as L. p.
15. hast kept that thou p. Da., 16.
Ne. 9 : 23. conc. which thou p. fa-s
Es. 4 : 7. sum Haman p. to pay
Je. 32:42. bring all good I p., 33 : 14.
Mat.14:7.Herod p. with oath to give
Mk. 14 : 11. glad, p. to give money
Lu. 1 : 72 To perform the mercy p.
22:6. he p. to betray him unto th.
Ac. 7 : 5. yet he p. to give it to him
Ro. 1 : 2. gospel which he had p.
4 : 21. what he p. able to perform
Tit.1:2.in hope of eternal life, p. bef.
He. 10 : 23. he is faithful that p. [p.
11:11.judged him faithful that had
12 : 26. hath p. saying, once more
Ja. 1:12. L. p. to them th. love, 2:5.
1 Jn.2:25. he hath p. us eternal life
PROMISEDST. [p., 25.
1 K. 8 : 24. keep with Da. that thou
Ne. 9 : 15. p. they sho. go into land
PROMISING. [life
Eze. 13:22. not fr. wicked way by p.
PROMOTE, ED.
Nu. 22 : 17. will p. thee unto great honour, 24 : 11.
37. am I not able to p. thee to
Ju. 9:9. to be p-d over trees, 11, 13.
Es. 3 : 1. Ahasuerus p. Haman
5 : 11. told wh-n king had p-d him
Pr. 4:8. Exalt her, she shall p. thee
Da. 3 : 30. king p-d Shadrach, Me-
PROMOTION. [shach
Ps. 75 : 6. p. cometh not from east
Pr. 3 : 35 shame shall be p. of fools
PRONOUNCE.
Le. 5 : 4. man shall p. with an oath
13:59. the law to p. it clean or uncl.
Ju. 12 : 6. could not frame to p. it
See PRIEST. [right
PRONOUNCED.
Ne. 6 : 12. p. this prophecy ag. me
Je. 11 : 17. L. hath p. evil ag. thee

Je. 16 : 10. p. this great evil, 19 : 15.
-35 : 17.-40 : 2. [I p. turn
18 : 8. If that nation against whom
25 : 13. word wh. I have p. ag. it
26 : 13. L. will repent of evil he p.
19. Lord repented of evil he p.
34 : 5. I have p. the word, saith L.
36 : 7. Lord hath p. ag. this peo.
18. Jere. p. all these words, 31.
PRONOUNCING. [or
Le. 5 : 4. if soul swear, p. to do evil
PROOF, S. [p-s
Ac.1:3.shewed hims. alive by many
2 Co. 2 : 9. I might know p. of you
8 : 24. shew ye to them p. of love
13:3. Since ye seek a p. of C. in me
Ph. 2 : 22. ye know p. of him
2 Ti. 4 : 5. make full p. of thy minis-
PROP. [try
1 K. 10:†12. king made of trees a p.
PROPER.
1 Ch. 29 : 3. I have of own p. good
Ac. 1 : 19. in p. tongue, Aceldama
1 Co. 7:7. ev. man hath p. gift of G.
He. 11 : 23. saw he was a p. child
PROPHECY, IES. [jah
2 Ch. 9:29. Sol.'s acts in p. of Ahi-
15 : 8 when Asa heard p. of Obed
Ne. 6:12. pronounced this p. ag. me
Pr. 30 : 1. p. man spake unto Ithiel
31:1. p. th. his mother taught him
Da. 9 : 24. seal up vision and p.
Mat. 13 : 14. is fulfilled p. of Esaias
Ro.12:6.whe. p. let us prophesy acc.
1 Co. 12 : 10. to ano. p. by same Spi.
13 : 2. though I have the gift of p.
8. but whether p-s they sh. cease
1 Ti. 1 : 18. acc. to p-s th. went bef.
4 : 14. Neglect not gift given by p.
2 Pe. 1 : 19. a more sure word of p.
20. no p. of Scripture is of private
21. p. came not in old time by
Re. 1 : 3. Blessed that hear this p.
11 : 6. rain not in days of their p.
19:10. testim. of Jes. is spirit of p.
22 : 7. blessed th. keepeth this p.
10. Seal not the p. of this book
18. that heareth p. of this book
19. if any man take from this p.
PROPHESIED.
Nu. 11 : 25. they p. did not cease
26. Eldad and Medad p. in camp
1 S. 10 : 10. Spirit came upon Saul, he p., 11.-18 : 10.-19 : 23, 24.
19 : 20. messengers of Saul p., 21.
1 K. 18 : 29. they p. until evening
22 : 10. prophets p. before them, 12. 2 Ch. 18 : 9. [to order
1 Ch. 25 : 2. sons of Asaph p. acc.
3. sons of Jeduthun p. with harp
2 Ch.18:7. he nev. p. good unto me
20 : 37. Eliezer p. ag. Jehoshaphat
Ezr. 5 : 1. prophets Haggai, Zech. p. unto Jews [by Baal
Je. 2 : 8. transgressed, prophets p.
20 : 1. Pashur heard that Jere. p.
6. die, and all to wh. thou p. lies
23:13.prophets of Sama. p. in Baal
21. I not spoken, yet they p.
25 : 13. all that Jeremiah hath p.
26 : 9. Why hast p. in name of L.?
11. he hath p. ag. this city, 20.
18. Micah p. in days of Hezekiah
20. Urijah p. against city
28 : 6. Lord perform words thou p.
8. prophets p. ag. many countries
29 : 31. Shemaiah p. unto you a lie
37:19. Where prophets wh. p. unto
Eze.11:13. when I p. Pelatiah [you
37:7. So I p. as I was commanded, and as I p., 10. [ag. them
38 : 17. who p. I would bring thee
Zch.13:4.proph-s ashamed when p.
Mat. 7:22. L. have we not p. in thy
11:13.prophets and law p. until Jn
Mk. 7:6. Well hath Esaias p. of you
Lu. 1:67. his father Zach. p. saying

Jn. 11 : 51. Caiaphas p. Jes. sho. die
Ac. 19:6. spake with tongues and p.
1 Co. 14 : 5. I would rather ye p.
1 Pe. 1 : 10. p. of grace should come
Jude 14. Enoch p. of these things

PROPHESIETH.

Je. 28 : 9. prophet wh. p. of peace
Eze. 12 : 27. he p. of times far off
Zch. 13 : 3. thrust him when he p.
1 Co. 11 : 5. p. with head uncov-d
14:3. he that p. speaketh unto men
4. he that p. edifieth the church
5. greater is he that p. than he

PROPHESY. [Verb.]

Nu. 11 : 27. Eldad and Medad do p.
1 S. 10 : 5. they shall p. | 6. thou p.
1 K. 22 : 8. he doth not p. good but
18. wo. not p. good, 2 Ch. 18 : 17.
1 Ch. 25:1. who should p. with harps
Is. 30 : 10. p. not unto us right
things, p. deceits [and priests
Je. 5 : 31. the prophets p. falsely,
11:21. saying, p. not in name of L.
14 : 14. prophets p. lies, p. false
15. prophets that p. in my name
16. people to wh. they p. be cast
19 : 14. L. sent Jere. to p. [that p.
23 : 16. Hearken not unto prophets
25. what prophets said, that p.
lies in my name, 26, 32 -27:10,
14, 15, 16.-29 : 9, 21. [earth
25 : 30. p. ag. inhabitants of the
26 : 12. L. sent me to p. ag house
32:3. Whf. dost p. I will give city?
Eze. 4 : 7. shalt p. against Jerus.
13 : 16. prophets which p. conc.
36:6. p. conc. land of Israel [Jerus.
37:4. he said, p. upon these bones
43 : † 3. to p. city be destroyed
Jo. 2 : 28. sons shall p., Ac. 2:17, 18.
Am. 2 : 12. ye commanded prophets,
saying, p. not, Mi. 2 : 6.
3 : 8. L. spoken, who can but p.?
7 : 12. unto Amos, Go unto Jud. p.
13. p. not any more at Beth-el
15. Lord said, Go p. unto Israel
16. p. not ag. Israel and house of
Mi. 2:11. I will p. unto thee of wine
Zch. 13 : 3. when any shall yet p.
Mat. 15 : 7. well did Esaias p. of you
26 : 68. p. unto us, thou Christ,
Mk. 14:65. Lu. 22:64. [wh. did p.
Ac. 21 : 9. four daughters, virgins,
Ro. 12 : 6. whe. prophecy let us p.
1 Co. 13 : 9. in part, we p. in part
14 : 1. that ye may p. | 24. if all p.
31. we may all p. one by one
39. Whf. brethren covet to p.
Re. 10:11. Thou must p. bef. nations
11 : 3. witnesses shall p. 1260 days
See **Son of MAN.**

PROPHESYING, S.

1 S. 10:13. when he made an end of p.
19 : 20. saw company of proph-s p.
Ezr. 6:14. prospered thro. p. of Hag.
1 Co. 11 : 4. p. having head covered
14 : 6. except I speak to you by p.
22. p. serveth not for them that
1 Th. 5:20. Despise not p-s, prove all

PROPHET.

Ex. 7 : 1. Aaron shall be thy p.
De. 18 : 20. p. which shall presume
22. p. spoken it presumptuously
2 S. 12:25. David sent by Nathan p.
1 K. 13:11. dwelt old p. in Beth-el, 25.
20. word of L. came unto p. | 26.
23. p. whom he had bro-t back
29. p. took carcass of man of G.,
old p. came to bury him
14 : 2. there is Ahijah the p., 18.
16:7. by p. Jehu came the word, 12.
18 : 36. Elijah p. said, God of Abr.
20 : 22. p. came to king of Israel
38. p. departed and waited for k.
2 K. 5 : 3. Would G. my lord with p.
13. if p. had bid do some great
6 : 12. Elisha the p. telleth what
2 K. 9:1. Elisha p. called one of chil.
4. yo. man p. went to Ramoth-g.
14 : 25. spake by hand of Jonah p.
19 : 2. Hez. to Isaiah p., Is 37 : 2.
20 : 1. p. Isaiah son of Amoz came
to him, 14. Is. 38 : 1.-39 : 3.
11. Isaiah p. cried unto Lord
23 : 18. with bones of p. that came
1 Ch. 29:29. acts written in book of
Nathan p., 2 Ch. 9 : 29. [Iddo
2 Ch. 13 : 22. written in story of p.
15 : 8. Asa heard prophecy of p.
21:12. a writing fr. Elijah p. [Oded
25:16. p. forbare, and said, I know
26:22 acts of Uzz. did Isa. p. write
32 : 20. p. Isaiah cried to heaven
36:12. humbled not before Jere. p.
Ezr. 5 : 1. Haggai p. prophesied
6:14. thro. prophesying of Hag. p.
Ps. 74 : 9. no more any p. am. you
Is 3 : 2. Lord doth take away p.
9 : 15. p. that teacheth lies, is tail
Je. 23:28. p. that hath a dream let
37. Thus shalt thou say to p.
25:2. Jere. p. spake unto peo., 42:4.
28 : 1. Hananiah, son of Azur p.
5. p. Jere. spake unto Hananiah
6. p. Jeremiah said, Amen [p., 15.
9. p. which prophesieth of peace
when word of p. come to pass
then p. be known
10. p. took yoke off p. Jer., 12.
11. p. Jeremiah went his way
17. Hananiah p. died same year
29 : 1. letter Jere. the p. sent | 29.
32 : 2. Jeremiah p. was shut up
34:6. Jeremiah p. spake unto king
33 : 3. all Jere. p. com-ded, 51 : 59.
26. to take Baruch. and Jere. p.
37:2. nor servants hearken unto p.
3. king sent unto Jeremiah p.
13. took Jere. p., 38 : 14.-43 : 6.
38:10. take Jere. p. out of dungeon
42 : 2. he said unto Jere. p. [ruch
45 : 1. word Jere. p. spake unto Ba-
46:13. word L. spake unto Jere. p.
Eze. 14 : 4. cometh to p. I will ans.
9. if p. be deceived when he hath
spoken I have deceived p.
10. punishment of p. shall be as
Da. 9 : † 24. to seal up vision and p.
Ho. 4 : 5. p. also shall fall with thee
9 : 7. p. is a fool | 8. p. is a snare
Am. 7 : 14. I was no p. nor p.'s son
Mi. 2 : 11. he shall be p. of people
Hag. 1:12. obeyed words of Hag. p.
Zch. 13 : 5. I am no p., a husbandm.
Mal. 4 : 5. I will send you Elijah, p.
Mat. 1 : 22. spoken by p., 2:15.-21:4.
2:5. In Bethlehem : thus writ. by p.
17. spoken by Jeremy, p., 27 : 9.
13 : 35. was spoken by the p., 27:35.
21:11. This is Jesus, p. of Naz-h [14.
24 : 15. spoken by Dan., p., Mk. 13:
Lu. 1 : 76. child be called p. of High-t
4 : 24. No p. is accepted in his own
27. many lepers in time of Eliseus,
7 : 28. not greater p. than John [p.
Jn. 7 : 40. Of a truth this is the P.
52. out of Galilee ariseth no p.
Ac. 7 : 48. not in temples made with
hands; as saith the p. [p., 30
8 : 28. in his chariot he read Esaias,
34. of whom speaketh the p. this?
13:20. he gave judges until Sam-l p.
28 : 25. spake Holy Gh. by Esaias p.
2 Pe. 2 : 16. ass forbade madness of p.
See AHIJAH, ESAIAS, GAD,
HABAKKUK, HAGGAI,
JEREMIAH, JONAS, NATHAN,
SHEMAIAH, ZECHARIAH.

A PROPHET. [a p.

Ge. 20 : 7. restore his wife; for he is
Nu. 12 : 6. If be a p. among you, I
De. 13 : 1 If arise a p. or dreamer
18 : 15 God will raise up a P. of thy
brethren, 18, Ac. 3 : 22,-7 : 37.
De. 18 : 22. When a p. speaketh in
34 : 10. not a p. in Isr. like [name
Ju. 6 : 8. Lord sent a p. unto Isr.
1 S. 3 : 20. Samuel was estab. a p.
9 : 9. he now called a p. was seer
1 K. 13 : 18. I am a p. as thou art
18 : 22. I, only remain a p. of L.
19 : 16. anoint Elisha to be a p.
20:13. there came a p. unto Ahab
2 K. 5 : 8. sh. know is a p. in Isr.
2 Ch. 25:15. L. sent a p. unto Amaz-h
Je. 1 : 5. I ordained thee a p. [27.
29:26. mad and maketh hims. a p.,
Eze. 2:5. been a p. am. them, 33:33.
14 : 7. cometh to a p. to inquire of
Ho. 12 : 13. by a p. L. brought Isr.
out of E., by a p. preserved
Mat. 10 : 41. He that receiveth a p.
in name of a p. shall receive
a p.'s reward [a p.? Lu. 7 : 26.
11 : 9. what went ye out for to see?
13 : 57. a p. is not without honour
save in own, Mk. 6:4. Jn. 4:44.
14 : 5. bec. they accounted him as
a p., 21:26. Mk. 11:32. Lu. 20:6.
21:46. multitude, took him for a p.
Mk. 6 : 15. a p. or as one of prophets
Lu 7 : 16. saying, a great p. is risen
39. This man, if he were a p. wo.
13 : 33. it can-t be that a p. perish
24:19. Jesus, who was a p. mighty
Jn. 4 : 19. I perceive thou art a p.
9 : 17. blind man said, He is a p.
Ac. 2 : 30. David a p. and knowing
21 : 10 came a certain p. Agabus
1 Co. 14 : 37. If any think to be a p.
Tit. 1 : 12. even a p. of own land

False PROPHET.

Ac. 13 : 6. a f. p. a Jew named Bar-
Re. 16:13. like frogs out of f. p. [jesus
19:20. beast taken, with him f. p.
20 : 10. devil was cast where f. p.
See **Prophet of the LORD.**

PROPHET with priest.

Is. 28:7. p. and p. erred thro. drink
Je. 6 : 13. from p. even unto p.
every one dealeth falsely, 8:10.
14:18. p. and p. go into land they
know not [nor word fr. p.
18 : 18. law shall not perish fr. p.
23 : 11. both p. and p. are profane
33. when p. or p. ask thee, 34.
La. 2 : 20. p. and p. slain in sanct.
Eze. 7:26. they seek vision of p. but
the law shall perish from p.

That PROPHET.

De. 18 : 3. not hearken unto t. p.
5. t. p. or dreamer sh. die, 18:20.
Eze. 14 : 9. I L. have deceived t. p.
Jn. 1:21. asked, Art thou t. p.? 25.
6 : 14. This is of a truth t. p. that
Ac. 3:23. soul wh. will not hear t. p.

PROPHETS. [p.

Nu. 11 : 29. that all L.'s peo. were
1 S. 10:5. thou shalt meet a company
of p. | 10. p. met him
11. prophesied among the p.
12. Is Saul also am. p.? 19 : 24.
28:6. Lord ans-d him not by p., 15.
1 K. 18 : 4. Obadiah hid 100 p. by
50 in cave [Baal 450, 22.
13. Jezebel slew p., 4. | 19. p. of
20. king of Isr. gathered p., 22:6.
25. Elijah said unto p. of Baal
40. Take the p. of Baal, let none
19:10. Israel have slain thy p. with
the sword, 14. Ne. 9 : 26.
22:22. I will be a lying spirit in p.,
23. 2 Ch. 18 : 21. [mother
2 K. 3 : 13. to p. of thy father, p. of
23:2. Josiah and p. to house of L.
1 Ch. 16 : 22. saying, do my p. no
harm, Ps. 105 : 15. [ye prosper
2 Ch. 20 : 20. believe his p. so shall
24 : 19. sent p. | 36:16. misused p.
29 : 25. commandment of L. by his
Ezr. 5 : 2. with them p. helping [p.

Ne. 6:7. hast appointed p. to preach
9:30. testifiedst by thy Spirit in p.
32. trouble that hath come on p.
Is. 29:10. p. and seers he covered
Je. 2:30. your sword devoured your
5:13. p. shall become wind [p.
13:13. I will fill p. with drunkenn.
14:13. p. say, Ye shall not see sw.
15. By sword sh. p. be consumed
23:13. seen folly in p. of Samaria
14. seen in p. a horrible thing
15. from p. is profaneness gone
21. I have not sent these p. yet
26. are p. of deceit of own heart
30. am ag. p. steal my words, 31.
26:11. spake p., This man worthy
27:9. hearken not to p., 10. [to die
15. that ye and p. might perish
18. if they be p. and word of L.
29:1. letter Jeremiah sent to p.
8. saith L., Let not p. deceive you
15. L. hath raised us p. in Bab.
32:32. they and p. provoke me
37:19. Where are now your p.
La. 2:9. her p. find no vision fr. L.
14. Thy p. have seen vain things
Eze. 13:2. prophesy ag. p. of Israel
3. saith L., Woe unto foolish p.
4. O Israel, thy p. are like foxes
9. my hand shall be upon the p.
22:25. is a conspiracy of her p. in
28. p. daubed with untemp. mortar
Ho. 6:5. I have hewed them by p.
12:10. I have spoken by p. and
Am. 2:11. I raised up of your sons
12. com-ded p. Prophesy not [p.
Mi. 3:6. sun shall go down over p.
Zch. 1:4. unto wh. former p. cried
5. the p. do they live for ever?
7:7. Lord hath cried by former p.
12. words Lord sent by former p.
13:2. I will cause p. to pass out
4. p. shall be ashamed, each of
Mat. 2:23. which was spoken by p.
5:12. persecuted p., Lu. 6:23.
17. Think not I am come to destr.
7:12. this is the law and the p. [p.
13:17. p. desired to see | Lu. 10:24.
22:40. On these hang law and p.
23:31. chil. of them who killed p.
34. I send unto you p., Lu. 11:49.
37. O Jerus. thou that killest p.
Mk. 1:2. As it is written in the p.,
Lu. 18:31.-24:25. Jn. 6:45.
Lu. 1:70. As he spake by his holy
p., 2 Pe. 3:2. [apostles
11:49. I will send them p. and
16:16. law and p. were until John
29. They have Moses and p., 31.
24:25. slow to believe what p. spok-
Jn. 1:45. him of wh. p. did write [en
8:52. Ab. and the p. are dead, 53.
Ac. 3:18. God shewed by his p., 21.
11:27. p. from Jerus. unto Antioch
13:1. in church at Antioch cert. p.
15. aft. reading of law and the p.
40. upon you wh. is spoken in p.
15:32. Judas and Silas being p.
24:14. believing all written in p.
26:22. none other than p. did say
27. Agrippa, believest thou p.?
Ro. 1:2. he promised afore by p.
3:21. witnessed by the law and p.
11:3. Lord, they have killed p.
1 Co. 12:28. secondarily p., thirdly
29. are all p.? | 14:29. Let p. speak
Ep. 2:20. upon foundation of p.
3:5. is now revealed unto his p.
4:11. he gave some p. and teachers
1 Th. 2:15. killed Lord and own p.
He. 1:1. spake unto fathers by p.
Ja. 5:10. Take p. who have spoken
1 Pe. 1:10. Of salvation p. inquired
Re. 11:10. these two p. tormented
18:20. Rejoice over her, ye holy p.
24. in her was found blood of p.
22:9. for I am of thy breth. the p.

All the PROPHETS.
1 K. 19:1. told Jezebel how slain a. p.
22:10. kings on throne, a. p.
prophesied, 12. 2 Ch. 18:9, 11.
2 K. 10:19. now call a. p. of Baal
17:13. L. testified ag. Isr. by a. p.
Mat. 11:13. a. p. prophesied until Jn.
Lu. 11:50. blood of a. p. required
13:28. when ye see a. p. in kingd.
24:27. beginning at a. p. expounded
Ac. 3:24. a. p. from Sam. foretold
10:43. To him give a. p. witness

False PROPHETS.
Mat. 7:15. Beware of f. p. in sheep's
24:11. many f. p. shall rise, 24.
Mk. 13:22. [f. p.
Lu. 6:26. for so did their fathers to
2 Pe. 2:1. there were f. p. am. them
1 Jn. 4:1. many f. p. are gone out
See **Prophets of the LORD.**

Of the PROPHETS. [5.
1 S. 10:10. company o. p. met him,
19:20. when saw company o. p.
1 K. 20:35. cert. man of sons o. p.
41. king discerned he was o. p.
22:13. words o. p. declare good
unto king, 2 Ch. 18:12.
2 K. 2:3. sons o. p. that were at
Beth-el came
5. sons o. p. came to Elisha, 6:1.
7. fifty sons o. p. went to view
15. sons o. p. said, spirit of Elij.
4:1. woman of wives of sons o. p.
38. seethe pottage for sons o. p.
5:22. two young men of sons o. p.
Ne. 6:14. My God, think of rest o. p.
Je. 23:9. bec. o. p. my bones shake
16. Hearken not unto the words
o. p., 27:14. [heart o. p.
26. How long shall this be in the
Ho. 12:10. similitudes by ministry o.
Zch. 8:9. hear by mouth o. p. [p.
Mat. 16:14. Elias or one o. p., Mk.
6:15-8:28. [Lu. 11:47.
23:29. ye build the tombs o. p.,
30. partakers in blood o. p. [filled
26:56. that Scriptures o. p. be ful-
Lu. 9:8. that one o. p. was risen, 19.
Ac. 3:25. Ye are children o. p.
7:42. as written in book o. p.
52. Which o. p. not persecuted?
13:27. they knew not voice o. p.
15:15. to this agree words o. p.
28:23. persuading them out o. p.
Ro. 16:26. manifest by Script. o. p.
1 Co. 14:32. spirits o. p. are subject to the p. [o. p.
Ep. 2:20. built upon the foundation
He. 11:32. time wo. fail to tell o. p.
Re. 16:6. they shed blood o. p.
22:6. L. God o. holy p. sent angel
See PROPHESY, IED.

PROPHETS with priests.
2 K. 10:19. p. of Baal and his p.
23:2. p. and p. and all the peo.,
Je. 13:13.-26:7, 8, 11.-29:1.-
32:32.
Je. 2:8. p. said not, Where is L.?
p. prophesied by Baal
26. p. and p. ashamed, Ne. 9:32.
4:9. p. be astonished, p. wonder
5:31. p. prophesy falsely, p. bear
8:1. bring out bones of p. and p.
La. 4:13. sins of her p. iniq-s of p.
Mi. 3:11. p. teach for hire, p. divine
for money [polluted
Zph. 3:4. p. are treacherous, p.
Zch. 7:3. speak unto p. and p.

Servants the PROPHETS.
2 K. 9:7. avenge blood of my s. t. p.
17:13. law I sent you by s. t. p.
23. as L. had said by his s. t. p.
21:10. L. spake by his s. t. p., 24:2.
Ezr. 9:11. hast com-ded by s. t. p.
Je. 7:25. I have sent you all my s.
t. p., 25:4.-29:19.-35:15.-44:4.
26:5. hearken to words of s. t. p.
Eze. 38:17. in old time by my s. t. p.
Da. 9:6. Nei. hearkened unto s. t. p.
10. laws set before us by s. t. p.
Am. 3:7. revealeth secret unto s. t.
Zch. 1:6. words I com-ded s. t. p. [p.
Re. 10:7. as he declared to s. t. p.
11:18. shouldest give reward unto
[s. t. p.

PROPHETESS.
Ex. 15:20. Miriam p. took timbrel
Ju. 4:4. Deborah a p. judged Isr.
2 K. 22:14. went to Huldah p., 2
Ch. 34:22. [Noadiah
Ne. 6:14. My God, think on the p.
Is. 8:3. I went unto p. she conceiv.
Lu. 2:36 Anna a p. of great age
Re. 2:20. Jezebel, called hers. a p.

PROPITIATION.
Ro. 3:25. Whom God set to be a p.
1 Jn. 2:2. he is p. for our sins, 4:10.

PROPORTION.
1 K. 7:36. acc. to p. of every one
Jb. 41:12. not conceal his comely p.
Ro. 12:6. let us prophesy acc. to p.

PROSELYTE, S. [of
Mat. 23:15. sea and land to make
Ac. 2:10. Jews and p-s we hear [p.
6:5. chose Nicholas p. of Antioch
13:43. Jews and religious p-s foll-d

PROSPECT. [Paul
1 K. 7:†5. posts were square in p.
Eze. 40:44. chambers whose p., 45.
46. p. to north | 42:15. p. to east,

PROSPER. [43:4.
Ge. 24:40. God send angel p. thee
42. if thou do p. my way
39:3. made all Joseph did to p., 23.
Nu. 14:41. transgress, it sh. not p.
De. 28:29. shalt not p. in thy ways
29:9. that ye may p. in all that
ye do, Jos. 1:7. 1 K. 2:3.
1 K. 22:12. Go up to Ramoth-gilead
and p. 15. 2 Ch. 18:11, 14.
1 Ch. 22:11. Now my son L. p. thee
13. shalt p. if thou takest heed
2 Ch. 13:12. fight not, ye sh. not p.
20:20. believe prophets, sh. ye p.
24:20. Why transgress, ye can-t p.?
26:5. sought L. God made him p.
Ne. 1:11. p. I pray thee thy serv.
2:20. G. of heaven, he will p. us
Jb. 12:6. tabernacles of robbers p.
Ps. 1:3. whatso. he doeth shall p.
45:†4. and in thy majesty p. thou
73:12. ungodly who p. in the world
122:6. they shall p. that love thee
Pr. 28:13. covereth sins sh. not p.
Ec. 11:6. knowest not whe. shall p.
Is. 52:†13. Behold my servant sh. p.
53:10. pleasure of L. p. in his ha.
54:17. No weapon ag. thee sh. p.
55:11. it shall p. in thing I sent
Je. 2:37. thou shalt not p. in them
5:28. Judge not cause yet p. [20:11.
10:21. pastors brutish, sh. not p.,
12:1. Wh. doth way of wicked p.
22:30. man that sh. not p. in his
days, no man of his seed sh. p.
23:5. a King shall reign and p.
32:5. tho. ye fight ye shall not p.
La. 1:5. are chief, her enemies p.
Eze. 16:†4. vine burnt, will it p.?
16:3. thou didst p. unto a kingd.
17:9. saith L. G. Shall it p.? 10.
15. Shall he p.? shall he escape?
Da. 8:†30. king made Shadrach p.
8:24. he shall destroy and p. [p.
25. thro. policy sh. cause craft to
11:27. speak lies, it sh. not p., 36.
3 Jn. 2. I wish that thou mayest p.

PROSPERED.
Ge. 24:56. seeing L. hath p. my way
Ju. 4:24. hand of Isr. p. ag. Jabin
1 S. 18:†5. and David p., †14. [p.
2 S. 11:7. David demanded how war
2 K. 18:7. Hezekiah p., 2 Ch. 31:
21.-32:30. [7. Asa p.
1 Ch. 29:23. Solomon p. | 2 Ch. 14:

Ezr. 6 : 14. p. through prophesying
of Haggai ⌈p.?
Jb. 9 : 4. who hardened ag. him and
Da. 6 : 28. So Daniel p. in reign of
8 : 12. it cast down truth and it p.
1 Co.16:2.lay by, as G. hath p.him

PROSPERETH.

Ezr. 5 : 8. this work p. in their ha.
Ps. 37:7. fret not bec.of him who p.
Pr. 17 : 8. whither. it turneth it p.
3 Ju.2.in health even as thy soul p.

PROSPERITIES.

Je. 22:†21. I spake unto thee in thy

PROSPERITY. ⌊p.

De. 23 : 6. shalt not seek their p.
1 S. 25 : 6. say to him liveth in p.
1 K. 10 : 7. thy p. exceedeth fame
Jb. 15 : 21. in p. destroyer sh. come
36:11. if sh. spend their days in p.
Ps. 30 : 6. in p. I said, I sh. never
35 : 27. L. pleasure in p. of servant
73 : 3. when I saw p. of wicked
118 : 25. O L. I beseech, send p.
122:7. walls, p. within thy palaces
Pr. 1 : 32. p. of fools destroy them
Ec. 7 : 14. In the day of p. be joyful
Je. 22 : 21. I spake unto thee in p.
33 : 9. all p. that I procure to it
La. 3 : 17. far fr. peace, I forgat p.
Da. 8 : † 25. by p. destroy many
Zch. 1 : 17. cities thro. p. be spread
7 : 7. when Jerusalem was in p.

PROSPEROUS. ⌈p.

Ge. 24:21. whe. L. made his journey
39:2. L. with Joseph, he a p. man
Jos. 1 : 8. shalt make thy way p.
Ju. 18 : 5. whe. way we go sh. be p.
Jb. 8 : 6. habitation of righte-n. p.
Is. 48 : 15. he sh. make his way p.
Zch. 8 : 12. For the seed shall be p.
Ro. 1:10. if I might have p. journey

PROSPEROUSLY.

2 Ch. 7 : 11. Solomon p. effected all
Ps. 45:4. and in thy majesty ride p.

PROSTITUTE.

Le. 19 : 29. Do not p. thy daughter

PROTECTEST. ⌈p. th.

Ps. 5 : † 11. shout for joy, bec. thou

PROTECTION.

De. 32 : 38. let them rise, be your p.

PROTEST, ED, ING.

Ge. 43 : 3. The man did solemnly p.
† 3. man p-g protested unto us
1 S. 8:9. yet p. solemnly unto them
1 K. 2 : 42. and I p-d unto thee
Je. 11 : 7. I earnestly p-d unto your
fa-s p-g saying, Obey my voice
Zch. 3 : 6. the angel of the Lord p-d
unto Joshua ⌈in Christ
1 Co. 15 : 31. I p. by your rejoicing

PROTRACT.

Ne 9 :† 30. years didst p. over them

PROUD.

Jb. 9 : 13. the p. helpers do stoop
26:12.by underst-g smiteth thro.p.
38:11. here thy p. waves be stayed
40 : 11. behold every one that is p.
12. Look on every one that is p.
Ps. 12 : 3. that speaketh p. things
31:23. plentifully reward-h p. doer
40:4. Blessed who respecteth not p.
86 : 14. the p. are risen against me
94 : 2. render a reward to the p.
101 : 5. him that hath a p. heart
119 : 21. Thou hast rebuked the p.
51. p. have had me in derision
69. p. have forged a lie against me
78. Let p. be ashamed, they dealt
85. The p. digged pits for me,not
122. let not p. oppress me ⌈of p.
123 : 4. soul filled with contempt
124 : 5. p. waters had gone ov. our
138 : 6. p. he knoweth afar off
140 : 5. p. have hid a snare for me
Pr. 6 : 17. Lord hateth a p. look
15 : 25. L. will destroy house of p.
16:5. p. in heart is abomina. to L.

38

Pr.16: 19. than to divide spoil with p.
21 : 4. high look a p. heart is sin
24. p. scorner is his name, who
dealeth in p. wrath ⌈up strife
28 : 25. He of a p. heart stirreth
Ec. 7 : 8. patient better than p. in
spirit ⌈that is p.
Is. 2 : 12. day of L. upon every one
13 : 11. cause arrogancy of p. cease
Je. 13 : 15. be not p. for Lord hath
43 : 2. all p. men ans-d Jeremiah
48 : 29. heard pride of Moab, he is
exceeding p., Is.16:6. ⌈most p.
50 : 29. she been p. | 31. O thou
32. most p. shall stumble and fall
Ha. 2 : 5. he is a p. man, neither
Mal. 3 : 15. we call the p. happy
4 : 1. all the p. shall be stubble
Lu. 1 : 51. he hath scattered the p.
Ro. 1 : 30. haters of God,p., boasters
1 Ti. 6 : 4. He is p., knowing noth.
2 Ti. 3 : 2. lovers of themselves, p.
Ja. 4 : 6. God resisteth p., 1 Pe. 5:5.

PROUDLY. ⌈them

Ex. 18 : 11. dealt p. he was above
1 S. 2 : 3. Talk no more so exc-g p.
Ne. 9:10. knewest they dealt p., 16,
Ps. 17:10. with mouth speak p. ⌊29.
31:18.wh. speak grievous things p.
Is. 3 : 5. child sh. behave hims. p.
Da. 5:†20. mind hardened to deal p.
Ob. 12. nei. shouldest have spoken

PROVE. ⌊p.

Ex. 16 : 4. I may p. them, De. 8:16.
20 : 20. God is come to p. you
De. 8 : 2. to humble, and to p. thee
33 : 8. holy one, wh. thou did'st p.
Ju. 2 : 22. That I may p. Isr., 3:1,4.
6 : 39. let me p. thee but this once
1 K. 10 : 1. she came to p. Solomon,
2 Ch. 9 : 1. ⌈me perverse
Jb. 9 : 20. if I say perfect, it sh. p.
13 : † 15. I will p. mine own ways
26 : 2. Examine me, O L. p. me
Ec. 2 : 1. I will p. thee with mirth
Da. 1 : 12. p.thy servants, I beseech
Mal. 3 : 10. Bring the tithes, p. me
Lu. 14 : 19. oxen, I go to p. them
Jn. 6 : 6. this he said to p. him
Ac. 24 : 13. Nei. can p. things, 25:7.
Ro. 12 : 2. p. what is th. good will
2 Co. 8 : 8. to p. sincerity of love
13:5. p. your own selves, know ye
Ga. 6 : 4. let ev. man p. his work
1 Th. 5 : 21. p. all things, hold fast

PROVED. ⌈Pha.

Ge. 42 : 15. ye shall be p. by life of
16. that your words may be p.
Ex. 15 : 25. and there he p. them
1 S. 17 : 39. he had not p. his sword,
David said, I have not p. them
Ps. 17 : 3. Thou hast p. my heart
66 : 10. thou, O God, hast p. us
81:7. I p. thee at waters of Meribah
95:9. When your fathers p. me and
Ec. 7:23. All this have I p. by wisd.
Da. 1 : 14. he p. them ten days
Ro. 3 : 9. we bef. p. Jews and Gent.
2 Co. 8 : 22. wh. we have p. diligent
1 Ti. 3 : 10. let these also be first p.
He. 3 : 9. your fathers p. me, and

PROVETH, ING. ⌊saw

De. 13 : 3. Lord your God p-h you
Ac. 9 : 22. Saul p-g that this is C.
Ep. 5 : 10. p-g what is acceptable

PROVENDER. ⌊unto L.

Ge. 24 : 25. We have straw and p.
32. gave straw and p. for camels
42 : 27. opened sack to give ass p.
43:24. the man gave their asses p.
Ju. 19 : 19. there is both straw and
21. he gave p. unto the asses ⌊p.
Is. 30 : 24. asses shall eat clean p.

PROVERB.

De. 28 : 37. ye shall be a p. and a
1 S. 10 : 12. it became a p. Is Saul
24 : 13. As saith p. of the ancients

1 K. 9 : 7. Israel shall be a p. and
2 Ch. 7 : 20. house will I make a p.
Ps. 69 : 11. I became a p. to them
Pr. 1 : 6. To understand a p. and
Is. 14 : 4. take up this p. ag. king
Je. 24 : 9. I will deliver th. to be p.
Eze. 12 : 22. what is that p. ye have
23. I will make p. cease, no more
use it as p., 18 : 2, 3.
14:8. I will make him a sign,and p.
Ha. 2 : 6. all take up a p. ag. him
Lu. 4 : 23. p. Physician, heal thyself
Jn. 16 : 29. speakest plainly, no p.
2 Pe. 2 : 22. it is happened acc. to p.

PROVERBS. ⌈p.

Nu. 21 : 27. Whf. they that speak in
1 K. 4 : 32. Solomon spake 3,000 p.
Pr. 1 : 1. p. of Solomon, 10 : 1.–25:1.
Ec. 12 : 9. preacher set in order p.
Eze. 16 : 44. ev. one that useth p.
Jn. 16:25. these have I spoken in p.
I shall no more speak in p.

PROVIDE.

Ge. 22 : 8. God will p. hims. a lamb
† 14. Ab. called place, L. will p.
30:30. when sh. I p. for own hou.
Ex. 18 : 21. shalt p. able men
1 S. 16 : 17. p. me a man can play
2 Ch. 2 : 7. men whom David did p.
Ps. 78 : 20. can he p. flesh for peo.?
Mat.10:9. p. neither gold nor silver
Lu. 12 : 33. p. bags wh. wax not old
Ac. 23 : 24. p. beasts to set Paul on
Ro. 12 : 17. p. things honest in sight
1 Ti. 5 : 8. if any p. not for own

PROVIDED. ⌊house

De. 33:21. be p. first part for hims.
1 S. 16 : 1. I have p. me a king
2 S. 19 : 32. p. king of sustenance
1 K. 4 : 7. p. victuals for king, 27.
2 Ch. 32 : 29. Hezekiah p. flocks
Ps. 65:9. preparest corn, when thou
hast p. for it ⌈be thou hast p.?
Lu. 12 : 20. whose shall those things
He. 11 : 40. God having p. better
things for us

PROVIDENCE. ⌈p.

Ac. 24 : 2. done to this nation by thy

PROVIDEST, ETH, ING.

Jb. 38 : 41. Who p-h for raven food
Pr. 6 : 8. p-h her meat in summer
Is. 57:†8. lovedst their bed, thou p-t
2 Co. 8 : 21. p-g for honest things

PROVINCE, S. ⌈19.

1 K. 20 : 14. princes of p-s, 15, 17,
Ezr. 4:15. this city hurtful unto p-s
6 : 2. was found in p. of Medes
7 : 16. gold thou canst find in p.
Ne. 7 : 6. chil. of that p. went up
11:3. these are chief of p., 1:3. ⌈p-s
Es. 1 : 1. Ahasuerus reigned ov. 127
3. princes of p-s being bef. hims.
16. done wrong to peo. in p-s,22.
2 : 3. let k. appoint officers in p-s
18. king made a release to p-s
3 : 8. a people scattered in all p-s
12. governors over ev. p. (2) ⌈p-s
13. Haman sent by post unto k.'s
4:3. in ev. p. there was mourning
11. people of king's p-s know
8:5. Jews wh. are in the king's p-s
9. rulers of p-s from India unto
Ethiopia 127 p-s unto every p.
11. cause to perish power of p. th.
12. Upon one day in all p-s of k.
13. com-t to be given in ev. p., 17.
9 : 2. Jews gathered thro-t the p-s
3. rulers of p-s helped the Jews
4. Mordecai's fame went thro.p-s
12. what have they done in p-s
20. Mordecai sent letters unto
Jews in p-s ⌈every p.
28. these days sho. be kept thro-t
30. he sent letters to 127 p-s
Ec. 2 : 8. I gathered treasure of p-s
5 : 8. If seest oppression in a p.
La. 1 : 1. she was princess am. p-s

Eze. 19 : 8. nations ag him fr. p-s
Da. 2 : 48. made Daniel rule ov. p
3 : 1. set up image in p. of Bab. [3.
2. k. sent to gather rulers of p-s,
12. Jews thou set over p. of Bab.
30. promoted Shadrach in the p. of Babylon, 2 : 49.
8:2. I was at Shushan in p. of Elam
11 : 24. enter fattest places of p.
Ac. 23 : 34. asked of what p. he was
25 : 1. when Festus was come into

PROVISION. [p.
Ge. 42 : 25. to give them p. for way
45 : 21. Joseph gave th. p. for way
Jos. 9 : 5. bread of their p. was dry
12. bread we took hot for our p.
1 K. 4 : 7. each his month made p.
22. Sol.'s p. for one day was 30
2 K. 6 : 23. prepared great p. for th.
1 Ch. 29 : 19. for wh. I have made p.
Ps. 132 : 15. I will bless her p.
Da. 1 : 5. king appointed daily p.
Ro. 13 : 14. make not p. for flesh

PROVOCATION, S.
1 K. 15 : 30. Jerob. made Is. sin by p.
21 : 22. p. whw. Ahab provoked
2 K. 23 : 26. bec. of p-s Manasseh pro-
Ne. 9 : 18. wrought gr. p-s, 26. [voked
Jb. 17 : 2. eye continue in their p.?
Ps. 95:8. Harden not your hearts as in p., He. 3 : 8, 15. [2 K. 19 : †3.
Is. 37 : † 3. This a day of trouble, p.,
Je. 32 : 31. this city hath been a p.
Eze. 20 : 28. presented p. of offering

PROVOKE.
Ex. 23 : 21 obey, and p. him not
Nu. 14 : 11. How long will peo. p. me?
De. 31 : 20. if ye p. and break cov-t
Jb. 12 : 6. that p. God are secure
Ps. 78 : 40. How oft did they p. him
Is. 3 : 8. doings ag. Lord to p. eyes
Lu. 11 : 53. began to p. him to speak
Ro. 11 : 14. If I may p. to emulation
He. 3 : 16. when they heard, did p.
10 : 24. p. to love and good works
See **Provoke, ed. eth, ing, to ANGER, JEALOUSY, WRATH.**

PROVOKED. [see it
Nu. 14 : 23. nei. sh. any that p. me
16 : 30 ye sh. know these p. Lord
1 S. 1 : 6. adversary p. her sore
7. so she p. her, theref. she wept
2 K. 23 : 26. Manasseh had p. him
1 Ch. 21 : 1. Satan p. Da. to number
Ezr. 5 : 12. our fathers had p. God
Ps. 78 : 56. p. the most high God
106 : 7. p. him at the sea, Red sea
29. p. him with own inventions
33. they p. spirit of Moses, 43.
1 Co. 13 : 5. charity is not easily p.
2 Co. 9 : 2. your zeal p. very many

PROVOKEDST, ETH, ING.
De. 9 : 7. Forget not how thou p-t L.
32 : 19. bec. of p-g sons and dau-rs
Ps. 78 : 17. by p-g Most High in wild.
Eze. 8 : 3. image wh. p-h to jealousy
Ga. 5 : 26. not p-g, envying one an-
See ANGER. [other

PRUDENCE.
2 Ch. 2 : 12. son endued with p. and
Pr. 8 : 12. I wisdom dwell with p.
19 : †11. p. of man deferreth anger
Ep. 1 : 8. he abounded in wisd. and

PRUDENT. [p.
1 S. 16 : 18. David p. in matters, and
Pr. 12 : 16. p. man covereth shame
23. p. man concealeth knowledge
13 : 16. Ev. p. man dealeth with knowl.
14 : 8. wisdom of p. to understand
15. p. man looketh well to going
18. p. are crowned with knowl.
15 : 5. he th. regardeth reproof is p.
16 : 21. wise in heart be called p.
18 : 15. heart of p. getteth knowl.
19 : 14. a p. wife is from the Lord
22 : 3. A p. man foreseeth evil, 27 : 12.

Is. 3 : 2. take away p. and ancient
5 : 21. Woe unto p. in their own sight
10 : 13. I have done it, for I am p.
29 : 14. understand-g of their p. men
Je. 49 : 7. is counsel perished fr. p.?
Ho. 14 : 9. who is p. and sh. know
Am. 5 : 13. the p. shall keep silence
Mat. 11 : 25. hid these things from the wise p., Lu. 10 : 21. [p. man
Ac. 13 : 7. deputy Sergius Paulus, a
1 Co. 1 : 19. to nothing underst-g of

PRUDENTLY. [p.
Is. 52 : 13. my serv. shall deal p. he

PRUNE, ED.
Le. 25 : 3. six years p. thy vineyard
4. 7th year not show field nor p.
Is. 5 : 6. it shall not be p-d nor digged

PRUNINGHOOKS.
Is. 2 : 4. they shall beat their spears into p., Mi. 4 : 3. [p.
18 : 5. he shall cut off the sprigs with
Jo. 3 : 10. beat your p. into spears

PRY.
Je. 5 : † 26. p. as fowlers lie in wait

PSALM.
1 Ch. 16 : 7. David delivered first
Ps. 81 : 2. Take a p. [this p.
98 : 5. with the voice of a p.
Mat. 26 : †30. sung a p. they went into m-t of Olives, Mk. 14 : † 26.
Ac. 13 : 33. as it is written in sec. p.
35. Whf. he saith in another p.
1 Co. 14 : 26. how is it ev. one hath

PSALMS. [p.
1 Ch. 16 : 9. sing p. unto him, Ps. 105 : 2.
Ne. 12 : †8. Lev. over p. of thanksg.
Ps. 95 : 2. make a joyful noise wi. p.
Lu. 20 : 42. David saith in book of P.
24 : 44. were written in p. conc. me
Ac. 1 : 20. it is written in book of P.
Ja. 5 : 13. Is any merry? let him sing
See HYMN, s. [p.

PSALMIST.
2 S. 23 : 1. David, sweet p. of Israel

PSALTERY, IES. [p.
1 S 10 : 5. prophets coming with a
1 Ch. 15 : 20. Aziel with p-s on Ala.
2 Ch. 20 : 28. came to Jerus. wi. p-s
Ps. 33 : 2 sing unto him wi. p., 144 : 9.
57 : 8. awake p. and harp, 108 : 2.
71 : 22. I will praise with p., 92 : 3.
81 : 2. bring pleasant harp with p.
150 : 3. praise him with p. and harp
Da. 3 : 5. when ye hear p., 7, 10, 15.
See **CYMBALS with psalteries.**
See HARPS.

PTOLEMA'IS.
Ac. 21 : 7. from Tyre we came to P.

PU'A,[1] PU'AH[2] or PHU'VAH[3]
Ge. 46 : 13. † sons of Issachar; Tola, P.,[3] and Shimron, 1 Ch. 7 : 1. †
Nu. 26 . 23. of P.,[1] family of Punites
Ju. 10 : 1. arose Tola the son of P.[2]

PU'AH. [Woman.] [rah, P.
Ex. 1 : 15. Hebrew midwives, Shiph-

*** PUBLIC = PUBLICK.**
Mat. 1 : 19. not make her a p. example

PUBLICAN, S. [47.
Mat. 5 : 46. do not the p-s the same?
9 : 10. many p-s and sinners sat with him, Mk. 2 : 15. Lu. 5 : 29.
11. Why eateth your Master with p-s and sinners, Mk. 2 : 16. Lu.
10 : 3. and Matthew the p. [5 : 30.
11 : 19. A friend of p-s and sinners, Lu. 7 : 34. [heathen and p.
18 : 17. let him be unto thee as a
21 : 31. p-s go into kingdom bef. you
32. p-s and harlots believed him
Lu. 3 : 12. came p-s to be baptized
5 : 27. he saw a p., Levi, sitting at
7 : 29. p-s justified God, baptized
15 : 1. drew near p-s to hear him
18 : 10. one a Pharisee, other a p.
11. G., I thank, I am not as this p.
Lu. 18 : 13. p. standing afar, said

Lu. 19 : 2. Zaccheus chief among

PUBLICK. See PUBLIC. [p-s

PUBLICKLY=PUBLICLY
Ac. 18 : 28. he p. convinced Jews
20 : 20. taught you p. fr. house to

PUBLISH. [ho.
De. 32 : 3. I will p. name of Lord
1 S. 31 : 9. p. it in house of idols
2 S. 1 : 20. p. it not in Askelon
Ne. 8 : 15. p. that they bring branches
Es. 1 : †22. sh. p. it acc. to language
Ps. 26 : 7. may p. with voice of
Je. 4 : 5. p. in Jerus. | 16. p. ag. Jerus.
5 : 20. Declare this, p. it in Judah
31 : 7. p. and say, O L., save people
46 : 14. p. in Migdol, p. in Noph
50 : 2. p. say Babylon is taken
Am. 3 : 9. p. in palaces of Ashdod
4 . 5. proclaim and p. free off-gs
Mk. 1 : 45. began to p. it much, 5 :

PUBLISHED. [20.
Es. 1 : 20. decree p. thro. empire, 22.
3 : 14. Haman's decree was p., 8 : 13.
Ps. 68 : 11. great was company p. it
Jon. 3 : 7. be p. through Nineveh
Mk. 7 : 36. more a gr. deal they p.
13 : 10. gospel must first be p. [it
Lu. 8 : 39. he p. thro-t whole city
Ac. 10 : 37. word ye know, wh. was p.
13 : 49. word of Lord was p. thro.

PUBLISHETH. [tion
Is. 52 : 7. that p. peace, p. salva-
Je. 4 : 15. voice p. affliction fr. mount
Na. 1 : 15. feet of him that p. peace

PUB'LIUS.
Ac. 28 : 7. chief man, name was P.
8. father of P. lay sick of fever

PU'DENS. See LINUS.

PUFF. [Noun.]
Jb. 11 : †20. hopes sh. be p. of breath

PUFFED up. [u.
Can 6 : †5. for thine eyes have p. me
1 Co. 4 : 6. no one be p. u. ag. ano.
18. some are p. u., as though I
19. not speech of them are p. u.
5 : 2. ye are p. u., and not mourned
13 : 4. charity, is not p. u. [mind
Col. 2 : 18. vainly p. u. by fleshly

PUFFETH at or up.
Ps. 10 : 5 his enemies, he p. a. them
12 : 5. in safety fr. him p. a. him
2 Co. 8 : 1. Knowledge p. u., charity

PU'HITES.
1 Ch. 2 : 53. families of Kirjath-jea.

PUL. [the P.
2 K 15 : 19. P. king came ag. Isr. (2)
1 Ch. 5 : 26. G. stirred up spirit of P.
Is. 66 : 19. send those that escape to

PULL, ED. [P.
Ge. 8 : 9. Noah p-d dove into ark
19 : 10 men p-d Lot into the house
Jos. 8 : † 6. till we have p-d them fr. city [hand in again
1 K. 13 : 4. Jerob could not p. his
Ezr. 6 : 11. let timber be p-d down
Ps. 31 : 4. p. me out of net they laid
Is. 22 : 19. fr. thy state sh. p. thee
Je. 1 : 10. set thee to p. down, 18 : 7.
12 : 3. p. them out like sheep for
24 : 6. I will not p. down, 42 : 10.
La. 3 : 11. He hath p-d me in pieces
Eze. 17 : 9. shall he not p. up roots
Am. 9 : 15. they no more be p-d up
Mi. 2 : 8. ye p. off robe wi. garment
Zch 7 : 11. they p-d away shoulder
Mat. 7 : 4. p. out mote of, Lu. 6 : 42.
Lu 12 : 18. I will p. down my barns
14 : 5. will not p. him out on sab.?
Ac. 23 : 10. lest Paul been p-d in

PULLING. [pieces
2 Co. 10 : 4. mighty to the p-g down
Jude 23. save with fear, p-g out of

PULPIT. [fire
Ne. 8 : 4. Ezra scribe stood upon a p.

PULSE.
2 S. 17 : 28. Barzillai bro-t parched p.
Da. 1 : 12. let them give p. to eat, 16

PUNISH.

Le. 26 : 18. p. you 7 times more, 24.
Pr. 17 : 26. to p. just is not good
Is. 10 : 12. p. stout heart of king
13:11. I will p. world for their evil
24:21. L.shall p. host of high ones
26:21. Lord cometh to p. inhab-ts
27 : 1. In that day L. p. leviathan
Je. 9 : 25. I will p. all circumcised
11 : 22. I will p. men of Anathoth
13: 21. What say when he shall p.
21 : 14. I will p. you acc. to doings
23 : 34. I will p. man and house
25:12. p. king of Babylon, 50 : 18.
27:8.nation and kingdom will I p.
29 : 32. I will p. Shemaiah and his
30:20. I will p. all that oppress th.
36:31. I will p. Jehoiakim and his
44:13. I will p. them in Egypt,as I
29. a sign that I will p. you in
46 : 25. I will p. multitude of No
51 : 44. I will p. Bel in Babylon
Ho. 4 : 9. I will p. them for ways
14. I will not p. your daughters
12 : 2. p. Jacob acc. to his ways
Am. 3 : 2. I will p. you for iniq-s
†14. in the day that I will p. Isr.
Zph.1:8.in the day that I p.princes
9. I will p. all those that leap on
12.I will p.men are settled on lees
Zch. 8:14. As I thought to p. when
Ac.4:21.finding nothing how might [p.

PUNISHED.

Ex. 21:20. if smite, he sh. be p., 22.
21. not be p. for he is his money
Ezr. 9 : 13. hast p. less than iniq-s
Jb. 31:11. is an iniquity to be p.,28.
Pr. 21 : 11. When the scorner is p.
22:3. simple pass on are p., 27:12.
Je. 44 : 13. as I have p. Jerusalem
50 : 18. will punish as I have p. k.
Ho.4:†14. peo. not understand be p.
Zph. 3 : 7. not cut off, howso. I p.
Zch. 10 : 3. ag. shepherds, I p. goats
Ac. 22:5. bound unto Jerus. to be p.
26:11. I p. them in ev. synagogue
Col. 2 : †23. and p-g of the body, not
2 Th. 1:9. sh. be p. with everlasting
2 Pe. 2 : 9. unto day of judgment to [be p.

PUNISHING.

Col. 2 : † 23. shew of wisd. in p. the [body

PUNISHMENT, S.

Ge. 4:13. p. greater than I can bear
19:†15. lest consumed in p. of city
Le. 26 : 41. accept p. of iniq-y, 43.
1 S. 28:10 No p. sh. happen to thee
2 K.7:†9. If we tarry, we sh. find p.
Jb.19:29. wrath bringeth p-s of sw.
21 :† 19. G. layeth p. of iniq-y for
31:3. strange p. to workers of iniq.
Ps. 69 : † 27. Add p. of iniq-y unto
149 : 7. to execute p-s upon people
Pr. 19 : 19. man of wrath suffer p.
Je. 44 : † 9. forgot p-s of your fa-s?
La. 3 : 39. a man for p. of his sins
4 : 6. p. of my people is greater
than p. of Sodom [complished
22. p. of thine iniquity is ac-
Eze. 14 : 10. they shall bear p. of
iniq-y : p. of prophets be as p.
of him seeketh unto him [is sin
Ho.12:†8.he shall have p. in whom
Am. 1 : 3. for four I will not turn a-
way p.,6, 9, 11, 13.-2 : 1, 4, 6.
Zch. 14 : 19. This sh. be p. of Egypt
Mat. 25 : 46. shall go into everl-g p.
2 Co. 2 : 6. sufficient to such is p.
He. 10 : 29. Of how much sorer p.
1 Pe. 2 : 14. sent for p. of evil doers

PU'NITES. See PUA.

PU'NON.

Nu.33:42.pitched in P. | 43.from P.

PUR.

Es. 3:7. they cast P. that is, the lot
9 : 24. Haman had cast P. [of P.
26. called days Purim, aft. name
See PURIM.

PURCHASE. [Noun.]

Ge. 49 : 32. p. of field and cave [p.
Le. 22 : † 11. if priest buy soul with
Je. 32 : 11. I took evidence of the p.
12. I gave evidence of p., 14, 16.

PURCHASE, ED.

Ge. 25 : 10. field Ab. p-d of sons of
Heth [thou hast p-d
Ex.15:16.till people pass over which
Le. 25 : 33. if a man p. of Levites
Ru. 4 : 10. Ruth I p-d to be my wife
Ps.74:2.Remember cong-n thou p-d
78 : 54. mt. his right hand had p-d
Ac. 1 : 18. this p-d a field with iniq.
8:20.thought gift of G.may be p-d
20:28. hath p-d wi. his own blood
Ep. 1 : 14. redemption of p-d poss-n
1 Ti. 3 : 13. deacon p. good degree
1 Pe. 2 : † 9. ye are a p-d people

PURE.

Ex. 25:36. beaten work of pure gold
27 : 20. bring the p. oil, Le. 24 : 2.
30 : 23. Take spikes of p. myrrh
34. L. said, Take p. frankincense
35. make it a perfume p.
31:8.p. candlestick, 39:37.Le.24:4.
Le. 24 : 6. set cakes upon p. table
7. p. frankincense upon each row
De. 32 : 14. drink p. blood of grape
2 S. 22 : 27. with the p. thou wilt
shew thyself p., Ps. 18 : 26.
1 K. 5:11. twenty measures of p. oil
2 Ch.13:11.shewbread upon p.table
Ezr. 6 : 20. priests p. killed passover
Jb. 4:17. man more p. than Maker?
8 : 6. if thou wert p. and upright
11 : 4. hast said, My doctrine is p.
16:17.not injustice,my prayer is p.
25 : 5. stars are not p. in his sight
Ps. 12 : 6. words of the Lord are p.
19 : 8. com-t of the Lord is p.
119 : 140. Thy word is very p. thf.
Pr. 15 : 26. words of p. are pleasant
20 : 9. who say, I am p. from sin?
11. whether his work be p. whe.
21 : 8. as for p. his work is right
30 : 5. Every word of God is p.
12. a generation p. in own eyes
Je. 51 : † 11. Make p. arrows
Da.7:9.hair of his head like p. wool
Mi.6:11.Shall I count them p. with
Zph. 3 : 9. turn to peo. p. language
Mal. 1 : 11. in ev. place a p. offering
Mk. 14 :† 3. alabaster box of p. nard
Ac. 20 : 26. I am p. fr. blood of all
Ro. 14 : 20. All things indeed are p.
Ph. 4 : 8. whatsoever things are p.
1 Ti. 3 : 9. of faith in a p. conscience
5:22. nei. partaker of sins, keep p.
2 Ti. 1 : 3. serve with p. conscience
Tit. 1 : 15. Unto p. all things are p.
unto them defiled nothing is p.
He. 10 : 22. and our bodies washed
with p. water [before God
Ja. 1 : 27. p. religion and undefiled
3:17. wisdom from above is first p.
2 Pe. 3 : 1. I stir up your p. minds
1 Jn. 3:3. purifieth hims. as he is p.
Re. 15 : 6. angels clothed in p. linen
22 : 1. he shewed p. river of water
See HEART, GOLD. [of life

PURELY.

Is. 1 : 25. I will p. purge thy dross

PURENESS.

Jb. 22 : 30. delivered by p. of thine [hands
Pr.22:11. He that loveth p.of heart
Is. 1 : † 25. acc. to p. purge dross
2 Co. 6:6. approving ourselves by p.

PURER.

La. 4:7. Her Nazarites p. than snow
Ha. 1 : 13. Thou art of p. eyes than

PURGE.

2 Ch. 34 : 3. Josiah began to p. Jud.
Ps. 51 : 7. p. me with hyssop, and I
65:3. our transgr-ns thou shalt p.
79 : 9. p. our sins for name's sake
Is. 1 : 25. purely p. away thy dross

Eze. 20 : 38. will p. from you rebels
43:20. thus shalt cleanse and p. it
26. Seven days shall they p. altar
Da. 11 : 35. some sh. fall to p. them
Mal. 3 : 3. p. them as gold and silv.
Mat. 3 : 12. he will thoroughly p.
his floor, Lu. 3 : 17. [leaven
1 Co. 5 : 7. p. out therefore the old
2 Ti. 2 : 21. If a man thf. p. himself
He. 9 : 14. p. conscience from dead [works

PURGED.

1 S. 3:14. Eli's house shall not be p.
2 Ch.34:8.when he had p. the land
Pr. 16 : 6. By mercy iniquity is p.
Is. 4 : 4. sh. have p. blood of Jerus.
6 : 7. thy iniq. is taken thy sin p.
22:14. this iniquity shall not be p.
27:9. By this iniquity, of Jac. be p.
Eze. 24 : 13. because I have p. thee
and thou wast not p. thou
shalt not be p. from filthiness
He. 1 : 3. when he had p. our sins
9:22.almost all things are p. by bl.
10 : 2. because worshippers once p.
2 Pe.1:9.forgotten he was p. fr. sins

PURGETH, ING. [cine

Pr.20:†30.of a wound is a p-g medi-
Mk. 7 : 19. into draught p-g meats
Jn. 15:2. branch th. beareth,he p-h [it

PURIFICATION, S.

Nu. 19 : 9. be kept, it is a p. for sin
17. of the burnt heifer of p. for sin
2 Ch. 30:19. acc. to p. of sanctuary
Ne. 12 : 45. porters kept ward of p.
Es. 2 : 3. things of their p. be given
9. gave her her things for p.
12. so were days of p-s accompl-d
Lu. 2 : 22. when days of her p. were
Ac. 21 : 26. accomplishment of days [of p.

PURIFIED.

Le. 8 : 15. p. altar poured blood
Nu. 8 : 21. the Levites were p., Ezr.
6:20. Ne. 12 : 30. [of separation
31 : 23. shall be p. with the water
2 S. 11 : 4. Bathsheba was p. from
Ps.12:6.are pure words, as silver p.
Pr. 30 :† 5. every word of God is p.
Da. 12 : 10. Many shall be p. white
Ac. 24:18. Jews found me p. [blood
He. 9:†18. nei. 1st testam. p. with-t
23. the patterns of things be p.
1 Pe. 1 : 22. Seeing ye p. your souls

PURIFIER. [of silver

Mal. 3:3. he sh. sit as refiner and p.

PURIFIETH. [not

Nu. 19 : 13. toucheth dead body p.
1 Jn. 3 : 3. hath this hope p. hims.

PURIFY.

Nu.19:12. shall p. hims. with it,19.
20 be unclean, and not p. hims.
31:19. p. yours. and your captives
20. p. all your raiment [p. thems.
Jb. 41 : 25. by reason of breakings
Is. 66:17. they p. thems. in gardens
Eze. 43 : 26. Seven days sh. p. altar
Mal. 3 : 3. he shall p. sons of Levi
Jn. 11 : 55. to Jerus. to p. thems.
Ac.21:24.take and p. thyself with th.
Tit. 2 : 14. p. to himself a peculiar
people [minded
Ja. 4 : 8. p. your hearts, double-

PURIFYING. [Noun, Part.]

Le.12:4. continue in bl. of her p.,5.
6. when days of her p. fulfilled
Nu.8:7.Sprinkle water of p. upon th
1 Ch. 23 : 28. office in p. holy things
Es. 2 : 12. things for p. of women
Jn. 2 : 6. manner of p. of the Jews
3:25.Then arose question about p.
Ac. 15 : 9. p. their hearts by faith
21 : 26. and the next day p. hims.
He.9:13.sanctifieth to p. of the flesh

PURIM. [Pur

Es. 9 : 26. called these days P. after
28. that days of P. should not fail
29. confirm sec. letter of P., 31.
32. decree of Esther confirmed P.

PURITY. [in p.
1 Ti. 4 : 12. be an example in faith,
5:2. rebuke the younger, as sisters,
PURLOINING. [wi. p.
Tit. 2 : 10. not p. shewing fidelity
PURPLE. [scarlet
Ex. 25 : 4. offering, blue, p. and
26 : 1. curtains of linen, p. scarlet
39:3. gold cut to work in p. scarlet
Nu. 4 : 13. and spread a p. cloth
Ju. 8:26. p. raiment was on the kings
2 Ch. 2:7. cunning to work in p., 14.
Es. 1 : 6. fastened with cords of p.
8:15. Mord. went with garm. of p.
Pr. 31:22. her clothing is silk and p.
Can. 3 : 10. he made covering of p.
7 : 5. hair of thine head like p.
Je. 10 : 9. blue and p. their clothing
Eze. 27:16. Syria in thy fairs with p.
Da. 5 : † 7. Whoso. shew interpretation shall be clothed with p.
Mk. 15 : 17. soldiers clothed him with p., Jn. 19 : 2.
20. mocked him, they took off p.
Lu. 16 : 19. rich man clothed in p.
Jn. 19:5. came Jes. wearing p. robe
Ac. 16:14. Lydia, a seller of p. [book
He. 9 :† 19. Moses took p. sprinkled
Re. 17 : 4. woman in p. and scarlet
18:12. no man buyeth merchandise of gold, p. silk and scarlet
16. great city, th. was clothed in p. and scarlet. See BLUE.
PURPOSE, S.
Ge. 6 : † 5. p-s of man's heart evil
Nu. 14 : † 34. know my altering of p.
Ru. 2 : 16. fall handfuls of p. for her
Ezr. 4:5. counsellors to frustrate p.
Ne. 8 : 4. a pulpit they made for p.
Jb. 17 : 11. my p-s are broken off
33 : 17. may withdraw man from p.
Pr. 15 : 22. without counsel p-s are disappointed; but in multitude
20:18. p. is established by counsel
Ec. 3 : 1. time to every p., 17.–8 : 6.
5:†8. oppression, marvel not at p.
Is. 1 : 11. To what p. your sacrifi-s
14 : 26. This is p. that is purposed
19 : 10. they shall be broken in p-s
30:7. Egyptians shall help to no p.
Je. 6:20. To what p. to me incense?
49:20. counsel of L. and p-s, 50:45.
30. Neb-r conceived p. ag. Hazor
51:29. ev. p. of Lord be performed
Eze. 38:†10. conceive a mischiev. p.
Da. 3 : † 14. Is it of p. O Shadrach
6:17. p. be not changed conc. Dan.
Mat. 26 : 8. To what p. is this waste
Ac. 11 : 23. with p. of heart cleave
26 : 16. I have appeared for this p.
27 : 13. supposing had obtained p.
43. centurion kept them from p.
Ro. 8 : 28. the called acc. to his p.
9 : 11. that p. of G. acc. to election
17. for this p. have I raised thee
Ep. 1 : 11. to p. of him who work-
3 : 11. acc. to eternal p. in C. [eth
6 : 22. I sent for same p., Col. 4:8.
2 Ti. 1:9. called us acc. to his own p.
3:10. thou hast fully known my p.
1 Jn. 3:8. For this p. Son of G. was
PURPOSE, ED. [manif
1 K. 5:5. I p. to build hou. unto L.
2 Ch. 28:10. ye p. to keep und. Jud.
32:2. Sennacherib p-d to fight ag.
Ps. 17:3. I am p-d my mouth sh. not
140:4. p-d to overthrow my goings
Is. 14 : 24. as I p-d so shall it stand
26. purpose p-d upon whole earth
27. L. hath p-d who disannul it?
19:12. what L. hath p-d upon Eg.
23 : 9. L. hath p-d to stain pride
46 : 11. I have p-d it, I will do it
Je. 4 : 28. I p-d it, will not repent
26 : 3. repent me of evil which I p.
36 : 3. will hear all evil which I p.
49:20. purposes he hath p-d, 50:45.
La. 2 : 8. Lord p-d to destroy wall
Da. 1:8. Dan. p-d not to defile hims.
Ac. 19 : 21. Paul p-d to go to Jerus.
20:3. Paul p-d to return thro. Mac.
Ro. 1 : 13. oftentimes I p-d to come
2 Co. 1 : 17. things I p. do I p. acc.
Ep. 1 : 9. his will which he hath p-d
3:11. purpose which he p-d in C. J.
PURPOSETH, ING.
Ge. 27 : 42. Esau p-g to kill thee
2 Co. 9:7 ev. man as he p-h in heart
PURSE, PURSES.
Pr. 1 : 14. Cast in, let us have one p.
Mat. 10:9. silv. nor brass in your p-s
Mk. 6 : 8. sho. take no money in p-s
Lu. 10:4. Carry neither p. nor scrip
22 : 35. I sent you with-t p. scrip
36. hath a p. let him take it and
PURSUE. [scrip
Ge. 35 : 5. did not p. sons of Jacob
Ex. 15 : 9. The enemy said, I will p.
De. 19 : 6. lest avenger p., Jos. 20:5.
28 : 22. they sh. p. thee until, 45.
Jos. 2 : 5. p. after them, overtake
8 : 16. men of Ai were called to p.
10 : 19. but p. after your enemies
1 S. 24:14. after whom dost thou p.?
25 : 29. a man is risen to p. thee
26 : 18. Whf. doth my lord p. me?
30 : 8. Shall I p. after this troop? he answered, p. [David
2 S. 17 : 1. I will arise and p. after
20 : 6. take servants, p. Sheba, 7.
24 : 13 flee while enemies p. thee?
Jb. 13:25. wilt thou p. dry stubble?
30 : 15. Terrors p. my soul as wind
Ps. 34 : 14. seek peace and p. it
Is. 5 :† 11. continue till wine p. th.
30:16. sh. they that p. you be swift
Je. 48 : 2. O Madmen; sword sh. p.
Eze. 35 : 6. and blood shall p. thee
Ho. 8 : 3. Isr. enemy shall p. him
Am. 1:11. bec. Edom did p. brother
Na. 1:8. darkness sh. p. his enemies
PURSUED.
Ge. 14 : 14. Abram p. unto Dan, 15.
31 : 23. Laban and breth. p. Jacob
36. what sin, that thou p. aft. me
Ex. 14 : 8. Pharaoh p. after Isr., 9, 23. De. 11:4. Jos. 24:6. [p., 17.
Jos. 2 : 7. p. spies | 8:16. they of Ai
Ju. 1 : 6. p. after Adoni-bezek, and
4 : 16. Barak p. after chariots, 22.
7:23. Gideon p. Midianites, 25.–8 :
20 : 45. Israel p. Benjamin [12.
1 S. 7 : 11. Israel p. Philis., 17 : 52.
23 : 25. Saul p. David
30 : 10. David p. Amalekites
2 S. 2:19. and Asahel p. after Abner
24. Joab p. Abner | 28. Joab p. Israel no more [Sheba
20:10. so Joab and Abishai p. after
22 : 38. I p. enemies, Ps. 18 : 37.
1 K. 20:20. Syrians fled, and Israel p.
2 K. 25 : 5. army of Chaldeans p. k. and overtook, Je. 39:5.–52:8.
2 Ch. 13 : 19. Abijah p. Jerob. [rar
14:13. Asa p. Ethiopians unto Ge-
Is. 41 : 3. He p. and passed safely
La. 4 : 19. they p. us upon mts.
PURSUER, S. [you
Jos. 2 : 16. Get to mt. lest p-s meet
22. until p-s returned: p-s sought
8:20. people turned back upon p-s
La. 1 : 6. gone without strength bef.
PURSUETH, ING. [p.
Le. 26:17. ye sh. flee when none p-h
36. shall fall when none p-h, 37.
Ju. 8:4. Gideon with 300 men, faint yet p-g them
5. I am p-g Zebah and Zalmunna
1 S. 23:28. Saul from p-g after David
2 S. 3 : 22. Joab came fr. p-g a troop
18:16. people returned fr. p-g Isr.
1 K. 18 : 27. your god is p-g or in a
22 : 33. they turned back from p-g Jehosh-t, 2 Ch. 18 : 32.
Pr. 11:19. p-h evil p-h it to his own
13:21. Evil p-h sinners, to righteous
19:7. he p-h them with words, yet
28:1. wicked flee when no man p-h
PURSUIT. [a p.
1 K. 18 : † 27. a god, talking, or hath
PURTENANCE.
Ex. 12 : 9. roast with fire, legs, and
PUSH. [p.
Ex. 21:29. if ox were wont to p., 36.
32. If the ox p. a manservant or
De. 33 : 17. with them shall p. peo.
1 K. 22:11. With these shalt p. Syrians, until consumed, 2 Ch. 18:10.
Jb. 30 : 12. they p. away my feet
Ps. 44 : 5. will we p. down enemies
Da. 11 : 40. sh. king of south p. at
PUSHED, ING. [him
Eze. 34 : 21. p-d diseased with horns
Da. 8:4. I saw the ram p-g westward
PUT. See PHUT.
PUT. [Verb.]
Ge. 2 : 8. there God p. the man, 15.
3 : 15. I will p. enmity betw. thee,
28:11. Jac. p. stones for pillows, 18.
30 : 40. he p. his flocks by thems.
42. cattle feeble, he p. not rods
31:34. p. images in camel-' furnitu.
32:16. p. a space betw-t drove and
33:2. p. handmaids chil. foremost
38:14. Tamar p. off widow's garm.
39:4. all he p. into Joseph's hand
40 : 15. p. me into dungeon, 39:20.
43 : 22 p. money in our sacks, 44:
50:26. Joseph was p. in a coffin [1, 2.
Ex. 3 : 5. p. shoes from off thy feet, Is. 20 : 2. Ac. 7 : 33. [bosom, 7.
4 : 6. L. said, p. now hand into thy
15. shalt p. words in his mouth
8 : 23. I will p. division betw. peo.
11 : 7. know L. doth p. difference
16 : 33 p. a homer full of manna
22 : 5 p. beast in ano. man's field
24 : 6 Mo took blood p. in basins
25:12. four rings p. in four corners, 26.–37 : 13. 38 : 7. [37 : 5.
14. thou shalt p. staves into rings,
16. p. into ark the testimony, 40:20
21. shalt p. mercy seat above ark
27 : 5. thou shalt p. it under altar
28 : 24. p. chains in rings. 25, 27.–
30. p. in breastplate Urim [39:17
29 : 3. p. them into one basket
17. p. inwards unto his pieces
30 : 6 p. it. bef. vail th. is by ark
18. p. it betw. tabern. p. water th-n
36. p. of perfume bef. testimony
31 : 6 in hearts of wise hearted I have p. wisdom, 35:34.–36:1, 2. 1 K. 10 : 24.
32:27. p. every man sword by side
33 : 5. now p. off thy ornaments
22. I will p. thee in cleft of rock
40 : 3. p. therein ark of testimony
5. p. hanging of door to tabern.
7. p. water therein, 30. Nu. 19 : 17.
18. p. in bars th-f | 19. p. covering
22. p. table in tent | 24. candlest.
26. he p. golden altar in tent
Le. 2 : 1. sh. p. frankincense, 24 : 7.
6 : 10. he sh. p. them beside altar
10 : 1. censer and p. fire th-n, Nu.
10. Ye p. diff. betw. holy and [16:7.
11:32. vessel must be p. into water
14 : 34. if I p. plague of leprosy
42. p. them in pla. of these stones
15 : 19. she sh. be p. apart 7 days
16 : 23. shall p. off linen garments
18:19. not approa. woman p. apart
19 : 14. nor p. stumblingblock bef.
20:25. p. diff. betw. clean and [blind
22:14. he shall p. fifth part unto it
26 : 8. p. 10,000 to flight, De. 32:30.
Nu. 4 : 8. p. in staves thereof
12. p. instruments in cloth of blue
5 : 17. priest sh. p. dust into water
18. p. off-g of memorial in her ha.

Nu.6:18. Nazarite sh. **p.** hair in fire
16:17. take his censer **p.** incense in
23:5. Lord **p.** a word in Balaam's mouth, 12, 16. [ark
De. 10:2. thou shalt **p.** them in the
5. I **p.** tables in the ark I made
12:5. place he sh. **p.** his name, 21.
18:18. **p.** my words in his mouth
23:24. not **p.** any grapes in vessel
Jos. 7:11. **p.** it am. their own stuff
Ju. 4:† 21. Jael **p.** nail **p.** hammer
12:3. I **p.** my life in my hands
1 S. 2:36. **p.** me into priest's offices
8:16. k. will **p.** your asses to work
17:39. And David **p.** them off him
54. **p.** Goliath's armour in tent
19:5. he did **p.** his life in his hand
2 S.3:34. nor thy feet **p.** into fetters
1 K. 2:† 5. **p.** blood of war in peace
5:3. Lord **p.** them under his feet
9:3. to **p.** my name, 11:36.–14:21.
12:29. other of calves **p.** he in Dan
18:23. on wood and **p.** no fire
22:27. saith k., **p.** fellow in prison
2 K. 18:11. king **p.** Israel in Halah
19:28. **p.** hook in nose, Is. 37:29.
21:7. in Jerus. will I **p.** my name, 2 Ch. 6:20.–12:13.–33:7.
1 Ch. 11:19. **p.** their lives in jeopardy
19:16. Syrians were **p.** to worse, 19.
21:27. angel **p.** up his sword again
27:24. nei. number **p.** in account
2 Ch. 2:14. ev. device wh. ✱ **p.** to him
6:11. in house have I **p.** ark
24. if Israel be **p.** to the worse
25:22. Jud. was **p.** to worse, 2 K. [14:12
36:3. king of Eg. **p.** him down
22. **p.** decree in writing, Ezr. 1:1.
Ezr. 2:62. **p.** fr. priesthood, Ne. 7:64.
7:27. **p.** such a thing in k.'s heart
8:† 17. I **p.** words in their mouth
Ne. 2:12. what God had **p.** in my heart to do 7:5. [the work
3:5. nobles **p.** not their necks to
4:23. ev. one **p.** th. off for washing
6:14. wo. have **p.** me in fear, 19.
Es. 9:1. decree to **p.** in execution
Jb. 17:3. **p.** me in a surety with thee
19:13. He hath **p.** my brethren far
23:6. he would **p.** strength in me
38:36. Who **p.** wisdom in inw. parts
41:2. Canst **p.** hook into his nose?
Ps. 4:7. hast **p.** gladn. in my heart
8:6. thou hast **p.** all things under his feet, 1 Co. 15:25, 27. Ep. 1:22. He. 2:8. [may know
9:20. **p.** in fear, O L., that nations
30:11. thou hast **p.** off my sackcloth
31:18. Let lying lips be **p.** to silence
40:3. **p.** new song in my mouth
56:8. **p.** my tears into thy bottle
70:2. **p.** to confusion that desire
71:1. let me never be **p.** to confus.
78:66. **p.** them to perpet. reproach
88:18. Lover and friend hast **p.** far
118:8. in L. than to **p.** confid. in man
9. in L. than to **p.** confid. in princes
Pr. 23:2. **p.** a knife to thy throat
25:7. than be **p.** lower in presence
Ec. 3:14. G. doeth noth. be **p.** to it
10:10. must **p.** to more strength
Can. 5:3. I have **p.** off my coat, how
4. beloved **p.** in his hand by door
Is. 5:20. that **p.** darkness for light
10:13. I have **p.** down inhabitants
21:† 4. my pleasure he **p.** into fear
37:† 7. I will **p.** a spirit into him
43:26. **p.** me in remembrance, let
47:11. shalt not be able to **p.** it off
51:16. I have **p.** words in thy mouth, Je. 1:9. [afflict thee
23. **p.** it into hand of them that
53:10. he hath **p.** him to grief
59:† 19. Spirit of L. **p.** him to flight
21. words I **p.** in thy mouth shall
63:11. where he th. **p.** his Holy Spi.
Je. 3:19. How shall I **p.** thee am. chil.
Je. 7:21. **p.** burnt off-gs unto sacr.
8:14. our G. hath **p.** us to silence
12:13. they have **p.** thems. to pain
31:33. **p.** my law in inward parts
32:40. I will **p.** my fear in hearts
47:6. O sword **p.** up thyself into
50:42. sh. ride ev. one **p.** in array
Eze. 8:17. they **p.** branch to nose
11:19. I will **p.** a new spirit within you, 36:26, 27.–37:14.
17:† 5. he **p.** seed in a field of seed
22:26. her priests **p.** no difference
29:4. I **p.** hooks in thy jaws, 38:4.
30:13. I will **p.** a fear in Egypt
32:† 25. her princes are **p.** by slain
37:6. **p.** breath in, ye shall live
Da. 5:19. whom he would he **p.** do.
Jo. 3:13. **p.** in sickle, harvest is ripe
Mi. 2:12. I will **p.** them as sheep of Bozrah [guide
7:5. **p.** ye not confidence in a
Hag. 1:6. earneth wages to **p.** in bag
Mat. 5:15. Nei. light candle and **p.** it under bushel, Mk. 4:21.
9:16. that wh. is **p.** in taketh from garment [bottles
17. Neither **p.** new wine into old
14:3. John and **p.** him in prison
19:6. no man **p.** asunder, Mk. 10:9.
22:34. had **p.** Sadduc. to silence
25:27. to **p.** money to exchangers
26:52. **p.** up thy sword, Jn. 18:11.
27:6. not lawf. to **p.** into treasury
Mk. 1:14. after John was **p.** in prison
2:22. new wine must be **p.**, Lu. 5: [38.
7:33. **p.** fingers into his ears
Lu. 1:52. hath **p.** down the mighty
3:† 14. **p.** no man in fear, neither
9:62. having **p.** hand to plough
Jn. 5:7. none to **p.** me into pool
12:6. Judas bare what was **p.** in
13:2. devil having **p.** into Judas
20:25. unless I **p.** finger into print
Ac. 1:7. Fa. hath **p.** in own power
4:3. they **p.** the apostles in hold
5:18. **p.** them in prison, 12:4.
25. men whom ye **p.** in prison
13:46. **p.** the word of G. from you
15:9. **p.** no difference between us
27:6. centur. found ship **p.** us th-n
Ro. 14:13. no man **p.** stumblingblock
1 Co. 15:24. shall **p.** down authority
25. till he **p.** all enemies under
27. hath **p.** all under him, 28.
2 Co. 3:13. **p.** vail over his face
5:† 19. **p.** in us word of reconcili.
8:16. God **p.** same care in Titus
Ep. 4:22. **p.** off old man, Col. 3:9.
Col. 3:8. ye also **p.** off these, anger
1 Ti. 4:6. If thou **p.** brethren in remembrance, 2 Ti. 2:14. [brance
2 Ti. 1:6. Wh. I **p.** thee in remem-
Tit. 3:1. **p.** in mind to be subject
He. 2:5. hath he not **p.** in subject.
8. nothing th. is not **p.** under him we see not yet all **p.** under
8:10. I will **p.** my laws into mind
10:16. I will **p.** my laws into hearts
Ja. 3:3. **p.** bits in horses' mouths
1 Pe. 2:15. **p.** to silence ignorance
2 Pe. 1:12. to **p.** you in remembr.
14. I must **p.** off this tabernacle
Jude 5. I will **p.** you in remembr.
Re. 11:9. not dead be **p.** in graves
17:17. God hath **p.** in their hearts

PUT away.

Ge. 35:2. **p. a.** strange gods am. you
Ex. 12:15. **p. a.** leaven out of houses
Le. 21:7. nei. take a woman **p. a.**
De. 19:13. **p. a.** guilt of blood, 21:9.
22:19. he may not **p.** her **a.**, 29.
Jos. 24:14. **p. a.** strange gods your fathers served, 23. Ju. 10:16. 1 S. 7:3, 4.
1 S. 1:14. Eli said, **p. a.** thy wine
28:3. Saul had **p. a.** wizards
2 S. 7:15. Saul whom I **p. a.** before
2 S. 12:13. said, L. hath **p. a.** thy sin
2 K. 3:2. Jehoram **p. a.** the image
23:24. abominations Josiah **p. a.**
2 Ch. 15:8. Asa **p. a.** abomi. idols
Ezr. 10:3. a covenant to **p. a.** wives
19. gave hands to **p. a.** their wives
Jb. 11:14. If iniquity be, **p.** it **a.**
22:23. **p. a.** iniquity fr. thy taber.
Ps. 18:22. I did not **p. a.** his statutes
27:9. **p.** not thy serv. **a.** in anger
88:8. hast **p. a.** mine acquaintance
Pr. 4:24. **p. a.** a froward mouth
Is. 50:1. mother's divorcem-t wh. I **p. a.**, for your transg-ns **p. a.**
Je. 3:1. If a man **p. a.** his wife
8. I had **p.** her **a.** and given bill
4:1. If thou wilt **p. a.** abominations
Eze. 43:9. let them **p. a.** whoredom
44:22. nor priest take her **p. a.**
Ho. 2:2. let her **p. a.** whoredoms
Am. 6:3. Ye that **p.** far **a.** evil day
Mat. 1:19. Joseph minded to **p.** her [a.
2:† 16. if he hate **p.** her **a.**
5:31. Whoso. shall **p. a.** his wife, 32.–19:9. Mk. 10:11. Lu. 16:18.
Mk. 10:2. Is it lawful for man to **p. a.** his wife? 4. Mat. 19:3, 7, 8.
12. if a woman sh. **p. a.** her husband
1 Co. 5:13. **p. a.** that wicked person
7:11. let not husband **p. a.** wife, 12.
13:11. man, I **p. a.** childish things
Ep. 4:31. Let evil speaking be **p. a.**
1 Ti. 1:19. wh. some having **p. a.**
He. 9:26. to **p. a.** sin by sacrifice of [hims.
See ARRAY, DEATH, EVIL.

PUT forth.

Ge. 3:22. lest he **p. f.** and take of
8:9. Noah **p. f.** hand took dove
19:10. men **p. f.** hand pulled Lot
Ex. 4:4. **p. f.** thine hand take it
De. 33:14. precious things **p. f.** by
Ju. 3:21. Ehud **p. f.** his left hand
6:21. angel **p. f.** end of the staff
14:12. I will **p. f.** a riddle, 13, 16.
15:15. Samson **p. f.** took jawbone
1 S. 14:27. Jonathan **p. f.** the rod
22:17. servants not **p. f.** to slay
24:10. not **p. f.** hand ag. Lord's
2 S. 15:5. to do Absalom obeisance, he **p. f.** his hand [**p. f.** dried
1 K. 13:4. Jerob. **p. f.** hand, ha. he
Ps. 55:20. He **p. f.** hands ag. him
125:3. lest righteous **p. f.** hands
Pr. 8:1. underst-g **p. f.** her voice?
25:6. **p.** not **f.** in presence of king
Je. 1:9. L. **p. f.** hand touched mouth
Eze. 8:3. he **p. f.** form of a hand
17:2. Son of man **p. f.** a riddle
Mat. 8:3. Jesus **p. f.** hand and touched him, Mk. 1:41. Lu. 5:13.
9:25. people were **p. f.**, he went in
13:24. Another parable **p.** he **f.**, 31. Lu. 14:7. [apostles f.
Ac. 5:34. commanded to **p.** the
9:40. Peter **p.** them **f.**, and kneeled
See **His, mine, my, their, thine, thy, HAND** and **HANDS.**

PUT on, or upon.

Ge. 24:47. I **p.** earring **u.** her face
27:15. Rebek. **p.** raiment **u.** Jac.
16. she **p.** skins of kids **u.** his ha.
29:3. **p.** stone **u.** well's mouth
28:20. bread, and raiment to **p. o.**
38:19. Tamar **p. o.** garments of
46:4. Joseph sh. **p.** hand **u.** eyes
48:18. **p.** right hand **u.** his head
Ex. 3:22. ye shall **p.** them **u.** sons
15:26. will **p.** none of diseases **u.**
26:35. **p.** table **o.** north side [thee
28:12. shalt **p.** stones **u.** ephod, 39:7. [19, 20.
23. **p.** rings **o.** breastplate, 39:16,
37. shalt **p.** it on blue lace [40:13.
41. **p.** them **u.** Aaron, 29:5, 6.
29:8. **p.** coats **u.** Aaron's sons, 9. Le. 8:13.

Ex.29:10.Aa.p.hands u.bullock,15.
12. p. it u. horns of altar, Le. 4:
7, 18, 25, 30, 34.-8:15.-9:9.-
16:18. [24.-14:14, 17, 25, 28.
20.p.it u.tip of right ear, Le.8:23,
29:30. priest, shall p. them o.
33:4. no man did p. o. ornaments
34:33. Moses p. vail o. his face, 35.
39:18. p. o. shoulderpieces of
ephod [fering
Le. 1:4. sh. p. hand u. head of of-
7. sons of Aaron p. fire u. altar
2:15 p. oil u. it | 5:11. p.no oil u.
8:7. p. u. him coat p. ephod u.
8. And he p. breastplate u. him
9.he p.mitre u.his head (2), 16:4.
27. he p. all u. Aaron's hands
9:20.they p. the fat u. the breasts
11:38. if any water be p. u. seed
13:45.shall p.covering u.upper lip
14:29 oil he shall p. u. head
16:4. he sh. p. o. holy linen coat
32. priest p. o. linen clothes
Nu. 4:7. u. table of shewbread p.
14. p. u. it all the vessels [dishes
6:19. shall p. them u. Nazarite
27.they shall p. my name u. Isr.
8:10. Israel sh. p. hands u.Levites
11:17.spirit upon thee,I p.u.them
29. L. would p. his Spirit u.them
16:46.p.o.incense, go unto cong-n
47.he p.o.incense,made atonem.
21:9. serpent of brass, p. it u.pole
De.11:29.p.blessings u.m-t Gerizim
2 S. 1:24. Saul,who p.o.ornaments
14:2. p. o. now mourning apparel
20:8. Joab's garment he had p.o.
1 K. 22:10. kings having p.o. robes
30. p. o. thy robes, 2 Ch.18:29.
2 K. 3:21. all able to p. o. armour
4:34. he p. mouth u. his mouth
11:12. king's son they p.crown u.
Es. 4:1. Mordecai p. o. sackcloth
5:1.Esther p.o. her royal apparel
Jb. 27:17. but the just shall p. it o.
29:14. I p. o. righteousness, and
Can. 5:3. coat, how shall I p. it o.?
Is.42:1.I p.Spirit u.him,Mat.12:18.
51:9. Awake, p.o.strength, 52:1.
59:17. he p.o. righteousness as a
Je. 13:1. girdle p. it o. thy loins,2.
46:4. furbish the spears, and p.o.
the brigandines
Eze. 16:14. comeliness I p. u. thee
24:17. p. o. thy shoes [44:19.
42:14. sh. p. o. other garment,
Jon. 3:5. Nineveh p. o. sackcloth
Mat. 6:25. nor what ye shall p.o.,
Lu. 12:22. [clothes
21:7. ass and colt and p. o. them
27:28. they p.o. him scarlet robe
29. platted crown of thorns, p. it
o. his head, Mk. 15:17.Jn.19:2.
31. p. his own raiment on him,
Mk. 15:20.
48. p. a sponge o.reed,Mk.15:36.
Mk. 6:9. sandals,not p.o.two coats
Lu. 15:22. p. o. him best robe (2)
Jn. 9:15. He p. clay u. mine eyes
19:19. wrote title p. it o. cross
29. p. it u. hyssop and p. to his
Ac. 15:10. to p. a yoke u. disciples
Ro. 13:12. us p. o. armour of light
14. p. ye o. Lord Jesus Christ
1 Co. 12:† 23. u. these we p.honour
15:53. this corruptible must p.o.
54. this mortal shall have p. o.
Ga. 3:27. baptized have p. o. C.
Ep. 4:24. p.o. new man, Col. 3:10.
6:11. p. o. whole armour of God
Col. 3:12. p. o. bowels of mercies
14. p.o.charity, which is bond of
Phm. 18. If he oweth thee, p. o.
mine account [den
Re. 2:24.I will p.u. you none bur-
See His, Thine HAND, S.
See GARMENT, GARMENTS.

PUT out. [hand
Ge. 38:28. she travailed, one p. o.
Ex. 17:14. p.o. remem. of Amalek
Le.6:12. fire upon altar not be p.o.
Nu. 5:2. p.o. of camp leper, 4.
3. male and female shall ye p. o.
16:14. wilt thou p. o. the eyes
De. 7:22. L. will p. o. those na-s
25:6. name be not p. o. of Israel
Ju. 16:21. p. o. Samson's eyes
2 S. 13:17. p. this woman o. fr. me
2 K. 6:7. he p. o. his hand took axe
25:7. they p.o. the eyes of Zedekiah, Je. 39:7.-52:11. [lamps
2 Ch. 29:7. also they have p.o. the
Jb.18:5. light of wicked sh. be p.o.
6. dark, and his candle be p. o.,
21:17. Pr. 13:9.-20:20.-24:20.
Ps. 9:5. hast p. o. their name
Eze. 32:7. when I p. thee o. I will
Mk. 5:40. when he had p. them all
o., Lu. 8:54. [ardship
Lu. 16:4. when I am p.o. of stew-
PUT to shame. [s.
Ju. 18:7. was none to p. them t.
Ps. 35:4. p. them t. s. seek soul
40:14.be p.t.s.wish me evil,83:17.
44:7. hast p. t. s. them hated us,
9. hast cast off, p. us t. s. [53:5.
119:31. O Lord p. me not t. s.
Pr. 25:8. when neighb. p. thee t. s.
10.Lest he th.heareth p.thee t.s.
Is.54:4.fear not, shall not be p.t.s.
Zph. 3:19.get praise where p. t.s.
He. 6:6. and p. him t. an open s.
See SYNAGOGUE, S, WARD.
See Put TRUST.
PUTE'OLI.
Ac. 28:13. we came next day to P.
PU'TIEL.
Ex. 6:25. Elea. took one of dau-s of
PUTRIFYING. [P.
Is. 1:6. wounds, bruises, p. sores
PUTTEST. [rock
Nu. 24:21. thou p. thy nest in a
De. 12:18. all p. hands unto,15:10.
2 K.18:14.that p. on me will I bear
Jb.13:27. thou p. my feet in stocks
Ps. 119:119. Thou p. away wicked
Ha. 2:15. that p. thy bottle to him
PUTTETH. [ger
Ex. 30:33. whoso. p. it upon stran-
Nu. 22:38. word G. p. in my mou.
De. 25:11. woman p. forth her ha.
27:15. image, and p. it in secret
1 K. 20:11. as he that p. off harness
Jb. 28:9. p. forth hand upon rock
33:11. He p. my feet in the stocks
Ps. 15:5. He that p. not his money
66:† 9. which p. our soul in life
75:7. G. p. down one and setteth
Pr. 26:† 8. that p. precious stone
Can.2:13. fig tree p.forth green figs
Je. 43:12. as shepherd p. on garm.
La. 3:29. He p. his mouth in dust
Eze. 14:4. p. the stumblingblock, 7.
Mi. 3:5. p. not into their mouths
Mat. 9:16. p. new cloth, Lu. 5:36.
24:32. When branch p. forth
leaves, Mk. 13:28.
Mk. 2:22. no man p. new wine into
old bottles, Lu. 5:37.
4:29. immediately he p. in sickle
Lu.8:16. No man p.candle und.bed
11:33. no man p. candle in secret
16:18.Whoso. p.away his wife and
Jn. 10:4. he p. forth his own sheep
Ro. 14:† 23. p. difference betw.meats
See Put, putteth TRUST.
PUTTING.
Ge. 21:14. bottle p. it on Hagar's
Le. 6:† 2. a trespass in p. of hand
16:21. p. upon head of goat
Ju. 7:6. lapped p. hand to mouth
Is. 58:9. p. forth of the finger and
Mal. 2:16. that he hateth p. away
Ac. 9:12. Ananias p. his hand, 17.

Ac.19:33.Alex. Jews p.him forward
Ro. 15:15. sort, as p. you in mind
Ep. 4:25. Wherefore p. away lying
Col. 2:11. in p. off body of sins
1 Th. 5:8. p. on breastplate of faith
1 Ti. 1:12. p. me into the ministry
2 Ti. 1:6. gift by p. on of my hands
1 Pe. 3:3. not of p. on of apparel
21. not p. away of filth of flesh
2 Pe. 1:13. stir you by p. in remem.
PYGARG.
De. 14:5. not eat p. and wild ox

Q.

QUAILS.
Ex. 16:13. that at even q. came up
Nu. 11:31. wind fr. Lord brought q.
32. people stood and gathered q.
Ps. 105:40. people asked, he bro-t
QUAKE, ED. [q.
Ex. 19:18. the mount q-d greatly
1 S. 14:15. host trembled, earth q-d
Jo. 2:10. earth shall q. before them
Na. 1:5. The mountains q. at him
Mat. 27:51. earth did q. rocks rent
He. 12:21. Moses said, I fear and q.
QUAKING. [Noun.]
Eze. 12:18. Son of man, eat with q.
Da. 10:7. a great q. fell upon them
QUANTITY.
Is. 22:24. upon him vessels of small
QUARREL. [Noun.] [q.
Le. 26:25. a sword shall avenge q.
2 K. 5:7. see how he seeketh a q.
Mk. 6:19. Herodias had q. ag. John
Col. 3:13. forgiving, if any have q.
QUARREL. [Verb.]
1 Ti. 3:† 3. a bishop not ready to q.
QUARRIES. [q.
Ju. 3:19. Ehud turned again fr. the
26. Ehud escaped beyond the q.
QUARTER. [Lot's
Ge. 19:4. all peo. from every q. to
Jos. 18:14. Kirjath-jearim, we-t q.
Is. 47:15. merchants wander to his
56:11. ev. one for gain fr.his q.[q.
Mk. 1:45. came to him fr. every q.
See NORTH, SOUTH, WEST.
QUARTERS. [q.
Ex 13:7. no leaven be seen in thy
De.22:12. make fringes upon four q.
1 Ch. 9:24. In four q. were porters
Je. 49:36. winds fr. 4 q. of heaven
Eze. 38:6. Togarmah of north q.
Ac.9:32.as Peter passed thro. all q.
16:3. because of Jews in those q.
28:7.in same q.possessions of Pub.
Re. 20:8. deceive nations in 4 q. of
QUAR'TUS. [earth
Ro.16:23. Q. a brother saluteth you
QUATERNIONS.
Ac. 12:4. delivered Peter to four q.
QUAVER.
Am. 6:† 5. They q. to sound of viol
QUEEN, QUEENS.
1 K.10:1.q. of Sheba heard of fame
of Sol.she came,2 Ch.9:1. [dom
4. when q. had seen Sol's wis-
10. no such spices as q. of Sheba
gave Solomon
13. Solomon gave q. of Sheba all
her desire, 2 Ch. 9:9, 12.
11:19.Pha. gave Hadad sister of q.
1 K. 15:13. Asa removed mother
Maachah fr.being q.,2 Ch.15.16.
2 K. 10:13. we go to salute chil. of
Ne. 2:6. king said, q. sitting by [q.
Es. 1:9. Vashti the q. made a feast
11. to bring the q.
12. the q. refused to come [Vashti
15. What shall we do unto the q.
16. q. not done wrong to k. only
17. deed of q. shall come abroad
18. have heard deed of the q.
2:4. maiden that pleaseth k. be q.

Es. 2 : 17. Esther q. instead of Vashti
22. Mord. told thing unto Es. the q.
4 : 4. was q. exceedingly grieved
5 : 2. when king saw Es. q. stand- ⌊ing
3. What wilt thou q. Esther?
12. q. let no man to banquet but
7 : 1. came to banquet with Es. q.
2. What is thy petition, q. Esther
3. Es. q. answ-d, If I have found
5. king said unto Es. q., 8:7.-9:12.
6. Haman afraid bef. king and q.
7. Haman make request to q.
8. Will he force q. also before me
8 : 1. house of Haman unto Es. q.
9:31. as Mord. and Es. q. enjoined
Ps. 45 : 9. did stand the q. in gold
Can. 6:8. there are threescore q-s, 9.
Is. 49:23. their q-s nursing mothers
Je. 7 : 18. cakes to the q. of heaven
13 : 18. say to king and q. Humble
29 : 2. Jeconiah the king, and q.
44 : 17. incense unto q. of heaven, 18, 19. ⌈q. of heaven
25. vowed to burn incense to the
Da. 5:10. q. came into banquethouse
Mat. 12 : 42. q. of south sh. rise up in the judgment, Lu. 11 : 31.
Ac. 8 : 27. Candace q. of Ethiopians
Re. 18 : 7. I sit a q. and am no wid- ⌊ow

QUENCH.

2 S. 14 : 7. so they shall q. my coal
21:17. that thou q. not light of Isr.
Ps. 104 : 11. the wild asses q. thirst
Can. 8:7. waters cannot q. love, nor
Is. 1 : 31. both sh. burn, none sh. q.
42 : 3. smoking flax shall he not q., Mat. 12:20. ⌈can q. it, 21:12.
Je. 4 : 4. lest fury burn that none
Am. 5 : 6. be none to q. it in Beth-el
Ep. 6 : 16. able to q. the fiery darts
1 Th. 5:19. q. not Spirit, despise not

QUENCHED. ⌈34 : 25.

Nu. 11 : 2. prayed, fire was q., 2 Ch.
2 K. 22:17. my wrath shall not be q.
Ps. 118 : 12. they are q. as thorns
Is. 34 : 10. not be q. night nor day
43 : 17. extinct, they are q. as tow.
66:24. worm not die, nei. fire be q.
Je. 7 : 20. my fury not be q., 17:27.
Eze. 20 : 47. flame sh. not be q., 48.
Mk. 9 : 43. fire that never be q., 45.
44. where the fire is not q., 46, 48.
He. 11 : 34. q. the violence of fire.

QUESTION. [Noun.]

Mat. 22 : 35. a lawyer asked him a q.
Mk. 11:29. I will ask you one q. ans.
12 : 34. no man durst ask him any q., Lu. 20 : 40.
Jn. 3 : 25. arose q. betw. disciples
Ac. 15 : 2. unto apos. about this q.
18 : 15. if it be q. of words, names
19 : 40. in danger to be called in q.
23:6. of resurr. called in q., 24:21.
1 Co. 10 : 25. asking no q. for, 27.

QUESTIONS. ⌈q.

1 K. 10 : 1. queen to prove him with
3. Sol. told her q., 2 Ch. 9 : 1, 2.
Mat. 22 : 46. nei. durst any ask more
Lu. 2 : 46. hearing and asking q. ⌊q.
Ac. 23:29. accused of q. of their law
25 : 19. had certain q. against him
20. because I doubted of such q.
26 : 3. I know thee expert in q.
1 Ti. 1 : 4. minister q. than edifying
6 : 4. doting about q. and strifes
2 Ti. 2 : 23. unlearned q. avoid, Tit. ⌊3:9.

QUESTION, ED, ING.

2 Ch. 31 : 9. Hezekiah q-d wi. priests
Mk. 1 : 27. they q-d among thems.
8 : 11. Pharisees began to q. him
9:10. q-g what rising fr. dead sho.
14. scribes q-g with them ⌊mean
16. he asked scribes, What q. ye
Lu. 23 : 9. Pilate q-d with him in ⌊many words

QUICK.

Le. 13 : 10. q. raw flesh in rising
24. q. flesh th. burneth have spot
Nu. 16 : 30. they go down q. into pit
Ps. 11:†6. Upon wicked rain q. coals
55 : 15. let them go q. into hell
124 : 3. had swallowed us up q.
Is. 11 : 3. make him of q. underst-g
Ac. 10:42. ordained to be judge of q.
2 Ti. 4 : 1. shall judge q. and dead
He. 4 : 12. word of God is q. and
1 Pe. 4 : 5. is ready to judge q. and ⌊dead

QUICKEN.

Ps. 71 : 20. Thou shalt q. me again
80:18. q. us, we will call upon thy
119 : 25. q. thou me according to thy word, 107, 154.
37. q. me in thy way
40. q. me in thy righteousn. ⌈159.
88. q. me after thy lovingkindn.,
149. q. me acc. to thy judgm., 156.
143 : 11. q. me L. for name's sake
Ro. 8 : 11. shall q. mortal bodies

QUICKENED.

Ps. 119:50. for thy word hath q. me
93. wi. precepts thou hast q. me
1 Co. 15:36. wh. thou sowest is not q.
Ep. 2 : 1. you he q. who were dead
5. q. us togeth. with C., Col. 2:13.
1 Pe. 3 : 18. to death in flesh, q. by ⌊Spi.

QUICKENETH.

Jn. 5 : 21. Father q. them, Son q.
6:63. Spirit q., flesh profiteth noth.
Ro. 4 : 17. believed G. who q. dead
2 Co. 3 : † 6. letter killeth, Spirit q.
1 Ti. 6 : 13. in sight of G. who q. all

QUICKENING.

Eze. 13:†22. fr. wicked way by q. him
1 Co. 15 : 45. last Adam a q. spirit

QUICKLY. ⌈ures

Ge. 18:6. Make ready q. three meas-
27:20. how hast found it so q. son?
Ex. 32:8. turned aside q. out of way, De. 9: 12, 16. Ju. 2 : 17. ⌈congr.
Nu. 16 : 46. put on inc. go q. unto
De. 9 : 3. so shalt destroy them q.
12. L. said, Get down q. fr. hence
11 : 17. lest ye perish q. from land
28:20. perish q. bec. of thy doings
Jos. 2 : 5. pursue q. overtake
8:19. ambush arose q. out of place
10 : 6. come to us q. and save us
23 : 16. ye shall perish q. from land
1 S. 20 : 19. thou shalt go down q.
2 S. 17 : 16. send q. and tell David
18. they went both away q.
21. said to Da. pass q. over water
2 K. 1 : 11. king said, Come down q.
2 Ch. 18 : 8. Fetch q. Micaiah son of
Ps. 94 : † 17. my soul had q. dwelt
Ec. 4 : 12. threef. cord not q. brok.
Mat. 5 : 25. Agree with adversary q.
28 : 7. go q. tell disciples he is risen
8. they departed q., Mk. 16 : 8.
Lu. 14 : 21. Go q. into the streets
16:6. sit down q. write fifty ⌈Jes.
Jn. 11 : 29. Mary arose q. came unto
13 : 27. said Jes. That thou doest ⌊do q.
Ac. 12 : 7. Arise q. Peter
22 : 18. Paul, get q. out of Jerus.,
Re. 2 : 5. repent, else I come q., 16.
3 : 11. behold, I come q., 22 : 7, 12.
11:14. behold third woe cometh q.
22:20. I come q. even so, come L. J.

QUICKSANDS.

Ac. 27 : 17. lest they fall into the q.

QUIET. ⌈q.

Ju. 16 : 2. Philis. laid wait and were
18 : 7. aft. manner of Zidonians, q.
27. unto Laish a people at q.
2 K. 11:20. city was in q., 2 Ch. 23:21.
1 Ch. 4 : 40. land was wide and q.
2 Ch. 14 : 1. In his days land was q.
5. kingdom was q. bef. him, 20:30.
Jb. 3:13. now should I have been q.
26. nei. was I q. yet trouble came
21:23. One dieth, being at ease, q.
Ps. 35 : 20. devise ag. them q. in la.
107 : 30. are glad, bec. they be q.
Pr. 1 : 33. whoso hearkeneth be q.
Ec. 9 : 17. words of wise are heard in
Is. 7 : 4. say unto him, be q. ⌊q.
14 : 7. earth is at rest, and is q.
32:18. my peo. in q. resting places
33 : 20. shall see Jerus. a q. habita.
Je. 30 : 10. Jac. sh. return and be q.
47 : 6. O sword, how long ere be q.
7. How be q. seeing L. hath given
49 : 23. sorrow on sea, cannot be q.
51 : 59. this Seraiah was q. prince
Eze. 16:42. I will be q. and no more
Am. 1:†3. for 4 transg-ns I not be q.
Na. 1 : 12. q. they sh. be cut down
Ac. 19 : 36. ye ought to be q. and do
1 Th. 4:11. And th. ye study to be q.
1 Ti. 2 : 2. th. we may lead a q. life
1 Pe. 3 : 4. ornament of a q. spirit

QUIETED, ETH. ⌈wind

Jb. 37 : 17. he q-h earth by south
Ps. 131:2. I have q-d mys. as a child
Zch. 6 : 8. q-d my spirit in north

QUIETLY. ⌊country

2 S. 3 : 27. Joab took Abner to speak
La. 3 : 26. q. wait for salva. of L. ⌊q.

QUIETNESS.

Ju. 8 : 28. country in q. 40 years
1 Ch. 22 : 9. I will give q. unto Isr.
Jb. 20:20. he sh. not feel q. in belly
34:29. giveth q. who make trouble
Ps. 23 : † 2. beside the waters of q.
Pr. 17 : 1. Better a dry morsel and q.
Ec. 4 : 6. Better is a handful with q.
Is. 30 : 15. in q. be your strength
32 : 17. effect of righteousn. q. and
Eze. 19 :† 10. mother like vine in q.
Ac. 24 : 2. by thee we enjoy great q.
2 Th. 3 : 12. we exhort that with q.

QUIT. [Adj.]

Ex. 21 : 19. he that smote him be q.
28. owner of the ox shall be q.
Jos. 2:20. we will be q. of thine oath

QUIT. [Verb.]

1 S. 4 : 9. q. yours. like men, 1 Co. ⌊16 : 13.

QUITE.

Ge. 31 : 15. q. devoured our money
Ex. 23 : 24. q. break down images
Le. 25 : † 23. land not be q. cut off
Nu. 17 : 10. q. take aw. murmurings
33 : 52. q. pluck down high places
2 S. 3 : 24. sent Abner, he is q. gone
Jb. 6 : 13. wisdom driven q. fr. me?
Ha. 3:9. Thy bow was made q. naked

QUIVER.

Ge. 27 : 3. take thy q. and thy bow
Jb. 39 : 23. q. rattleth against him
Ps. 127 : 5. man that hath q. full
Is. 22 : 6. Elam bare q. wi. chariots
49:2. polished shaft in his q. ⌊ulch.
Je. 5:16. Their q. is as an open sep-
La. 3 : 13. arrows of his q. to enter ⌊reins

QUIVERED.

Ha. 3 : 16. When I heard, my lips q.

R.

RA'AMAH.

Ge. 10 : 7. sons of Cush, R., 1 Ch. 1:9.
Eze. 27:22. merchants of Sheba and ⌊R.

RAAMI'AH.

Ne. 7 : 7. came with Zerubbabel, Nehemiah, R., Ezr. 2 : † 2.

RAAM'SES. See RAMESES.

RAB'BAH, or RAB'BATH.

De. 3:11. is it not in R-th of Ammon?
Jos. 13 : 25. coast unto Aroer bef. R.
15 : 60. and R.; two cities
2 S. 11 : 1. Joab besieged R. ⌈27.
12:26. Joab fought ag. R. took city,
29. David to R. and fought ag. it
17 : 27. Shobi of R. brought beds
1 Ch. 20 : 1. Joab smote R. and
Je. 49:2. an alarm to be heard in R.
3. cry, ye daughters of R. gird
Eze. 21:20. sword may come to R-th
25 : 5. I will make R., a stable
Am. 1 : 14. I will kindle a fire in R.

RABBI. ⌈R. R.
Mat. 23 : 7. loved to be called of men
8. be not ye called R. for one is
Jn. 1 : 38. R. where dwellest thou?
49. saith, R. thou art Son of G.
3 : 2. R. we know thou art teacher
26. R. he th. was with thee, bapt.
6:25. R. when camest thou hither?
RAB'BITH. ⌈R.
Jos. 19 : 20. their border was tow.
RAB'BONI. ⌈R.
Jn. 20 : 16. Mary turned hers. saith
RAB'-MAG. See RAB-SARIS.
RAB'-SARIS.
2 K.18:17. king of Assyr.sent Tartan
and R. to Hez. ⌈mag, 13.
Je. 39 : 3. princes came in, R. Rab-
RAB'-SHAKEH.
2 K. 18 : 17. the king of Assyria sent
R., Is. 36 : 2. ⌈Is. 36 : 4.
19. R. said, Speak now to Hez.,
26. said Eliakim unto R. Speak
27. R. said, Hath mas., Is. 36 : 12.
28. R. cried with loud, Is. 36 : 13.
37. they told him the words of R.,
Is. 36 : 22. ⌈R., Is. 37 : 4.
19 : 4. God will hear the words of
8. R. returned and found king
RA'CA.
Mat.5:22. whoso. sh. say to brother
RACE. ⌊R.
Ps. 19 : 5. as strong man to run a r.
Ec. 9 : 11. the r. is not to the swift
1 Co. 9 : 24. wh. run in a r. run all
He. 12 : 1. run with patience the r.
RA'CHAB = RA'HAB.
Mat. 1 : 5. Salmon begat Booz of R.
RA'CHAL. ⌈R.
1 S. 30 : 29. Da. sent present to th. in
RA'CHEL = RA'HEL.
Ge. 29 : 6. R. his dau. with sheep, 9.
10. when Jac. saw R. he went near
12. Jacob told R. he Rebek.'s son
16. name of the younger was R.
17. R. was beautiful and well fa-
18. Jacob loved R., 30. ⌊voured
20. Jacob served 7 y-rs for R., 25.
28. Laban gave him R. his dau.
29. Laban gave R. Bilhah, 30:7.-
31. but R. was barren ⌊46 : 25.
30 : 1. R. bare no chil. envied Leah
2. Jac.'s anger was kindled ag. R.
6. R. said, God hath judged me
8. R. said, With great wrestlings
14. R. said to Leah, Give me
15. R. said, he shall lie with thee
22. God opened R.'s womb
31 : 4. Jacob called R. and Leah
14. R. and Leah ans-d Jac. Is there
19. R. had stolen fa.'s images, 32,
33. Laban went into R.'s tent ⌊34.
33 : 1. divided chil. unto Leah and
2. Jacob put R. hindermost ⌊R.
7. Joseph and R. bowed themselves ⌈bour
35 : 16. R. travailed, had hard la-
19. R. died and was buried, 48 : 7.
20. that is pillar of R.'s grave
24. sons of R., 46 : 19, 22.
25. sons of Bilhah R.'s handmaid
Ru. 4 : 11. L. make the woman like R.
1 S. 10 : 2. find two men by R.'s sepulchre ⌈2 : 18.
Je. 31 : 15. R. weeping for chil., Mat.
RAD'DAI.
1 Ch. 2 : 14. R. fifth son of Jesse
RAFTER. [Verb.]
2 Ch. 34 : † 11. buy timber to r.
RAFTERS. ⌊house
Can. 1 : 17. beams are cedar, r. of fir
RA'GAU.
Lu. 3 : 35. Saruch was son of R.
RAGE. [Noun.]
2 K. 5 : 12. Naaman turned in a r.
19 : 27. I know thy r. against me,
28. Is. 37 : 28, 29. ⌈the seer
2 Ch. 16 : 10. Asa was in a r. with
2 Ch. 28 : 9. ye have slain them in r.
Jb. 39 : 24. swalloweth ground with r.
40 : 11. Cast abroad r. of thy wrath
Ps. 7 : 6. lift bec. of r. of enemies
Pr. 6 : 34. jealousy is r. of a man
Da. 3 : 13. Neb. commanded in his r.
Ho. 7 : 16. fall for r. of their tongue
RAGE, ED, ETH.
Ps. 2 : 1. Why do heathen r.? Ac. 4 : 25.
46 : 6. heathen r-d kingdoms were
Pr. 14 : 16. fool r-h and is confident
29 : 9. whether he r. or laugh
Je. 46 : 9. ye horses, r. ye chariots
Na. 2 : 4. chariots shall r. in streets
RAGGED.
Is. 2 : 21. go into tops of r. rocks
RAGING.
Ps. 89 : 9. Thou rulest the r. of sea
Pr. 20 : 1. mocker, strong drink is r.
Jon. 1 : 15. sea ceased from her r.
Lu. 8 : 24. he rebuked r. of water
Jude 13. r. waves of the sea foam-
RAGS. ⌊ing
Pr. 23 : 21. sh. clothe a man with r.
Is. 64 : 6. righte-n-ses are as filthy r.
Je. 38 : 11. Ebed-me. took rotten r.
12. Put r. under thine armholes
RAGU'EL. See MIDIANITE.
RA'HAB. [Person.]
Jos. 2 : 1. spies entered house of R.
3. k. of Jericho sent unto R. ⌈fa.
6 : 23. spies bro-t out R. and her
See HARLOT, RACHAB.
RA'HAB. [Place.]
Ps. 87 : 4. I will make mention of R.
89 : 10. Thou hast brok. R. in pieces
Is. 51 : 9. Art thou that cut R.?
RA'HAM. See JORKOAM.
RA'HEL. See RACHEL.
RAIL, RAILED.
1 S. 25 : 14. Nabal r-d on David's
messengers
2 Ch. 32 : 17. wrote letters to r. on L.
Mk. 15 : 29. that passed by r-d on Jes.
Lu. 23 : 39. one of malefactors r-d on
RAILER. ⌊him
1 Co. 5 : 11. keep not company with r.
RAILING, S.
1 Ti. 5 : † 14. give none occasion for r.
6 : 4. whereof cometh strife, r-s
1 Pe. 3 : 9. not rendering r. for r. but
See ACCUSATION.
RAILS. ⌈r.
1 K. 10 : † 12. k. made of almug trees
RAIMENT.
Ge. 24 : 53. serv. gave r. to Rebekah
27 : 15. Rebekah took goodly r. of
27. Isaac smelled r. and blessed
28 : 20. if the Lord will give me r.
41 : 14. Joseph shaved, changed r.
45 : 22. to each man changes of r.
to Benj. 5 changes of r. ⌈12 : 35.
Ex. 3 : 22. borrow of Egyptians r.,
21 : 10. her r. sh. he not diminish
22 : 9. any trespass for sheep, r.
26. If thou take neighb.'s r., 27.
Le. 11 : 32. when uncl. dead fall upon
Nu. 31 : 20. purify your r. ⌊r.
De. 8 : 4. Thy r. waxed not old
10 : 18. L. loveth stranger, giving r.
21 : 13. put r. of captivity from her
22 : 3. lost r. restore, and lost things
24 : 13. that he may sleep in his r.
17. shalt not take a widow's r.
Jos. 22 : 8. Return with much r. ⌈r.
Ju. 3 : 16. Ehud girded dagger und.
8 : 26. purple r. that was on kings
Ru. 3 : 3. wash thyself and put r.
1 S. 28 : 8. Saul disguised put on r.
2 K. 5 : 5. Naaman took 10 changes
7 : 8. lepers carried r. hid it ⌊of r.
2 Ch. 9 : 24. presents to Sol. gold, r.
Es. 4 : 4. queen sent r. to Mordecai
Jb. 27 : 16. tho. prepare r. as clay
Ps. 45 : 14. unto King in r. of needlew.
Is. 14 : 19. cast out as r. of slain
63 : 3. and I will stain all my r.
Eze. 16 : 13. thy r. was of fine linen
Zch. 3 : 4. clothe thee wi. change of
Mat. 3 : 4. Jn. had r. of camel's ⌊r.
6 : 25. body more than r., Lu. 12 : 23.
28. why take thought for r.?
11 : 8. clothed in soft r., Lu. 7 : 25.
17 : 2. his r. was white as light,
Mk. 9 : 3. Lu. 9 : 29. ⌈and led
27 : 31. they put his own r. on him
28 : 3. his r. was white as snow
Lu. 10 : 30. thieves stripped him of r.
23 : 34. they parted his r., Jn. 19 : 24.
Ac. 18 : 6. Paul shook his r.
22 : 20. I kept r. of them slew Ste.
1 Ti. 6 : 8. having food and r. let
Ja. 2 : 2. come poor man in vile r.
Re. 3 : 5. same be clothed in white r.
18. buy white r. that thou be
4 : 4. I saw 24 elders in white r.
RAIN. [Noun.]
Ge. 7 : 12. r. upon earth 40 days
8 : 2. r. fr. heaven was restrained
Ex. 9 : 33. the r. was not poured
34. Pha. saw r. ceased, he sinned
Le. 26 : 4. Then I will give you r. in
due season, De. 11 : 14.-28 : 12. ⌈r.
De. 11 : 11. land drinketh water of the
17. he shut up heaven that no r.,
1 K. 8 : 35. 2 Ch. 6 : 26.-7 : 13. ⌈der
28 : 24. L. make r. of thy land pow-
32 : 2. My doctrine sh. drop as r.
1 S. 12 : 17. unto L. he shall send r.
12 : 18. Lord sent thunder and r.
2 S. 1 : 21. let there be no dew nei. r.
23 : 4. by clear shining after r. ⌈27.
1 K. 8 : 36. hear and give r., 2 Ch. 6 :
17 : 1. there sh. not be dew nor r.
7. brook dried bec. been no r.
14. until day the Lord send r. ⌈r.
18 : 1. shew unto Ahab, I will send
41. is sound of abundance of r.
44. that r. stop thee not
45. was a great r. ⌈see r.
2 K. 3 : 17. ye shall not see wind, nei.
Ezr. 10 : 9. peo. trembling for gr. r.
13. and it is a time of much r.
Jb. 5 : 10. Who giveth r. upon earth
28 : 26. When he made decree for r.
29 : 23. waited for me as for the r.
36 : 27. clouds pour down r. acc.
37 : 6. to small r. and to great r.
38 : 28. Hath r. a father? who hath
Ps. 65 : † 9. hadst made it desire r.
† 10. causest r. to descend
68 : 9. O G. didst send a plentif. r.
72 : 6. He shall come down like r.
84 : 6. the r. also filleth the pools
105 : 32. He gave them hail for r.
135 : 7. he maketh lightnings for r.
147 : 8. Lord prepareth r. for earth
Pr. 25 : 14. like clouds without r.
23. north wind driveth away r.
26 : 1. As r. in harvest ⌈r.
28 : 3. oppresseth poor like sweeping
Ec. 11 : 3. If clouds be full of r.
12 : 2. nor clouds return aft. the r.
Can. 2 : 11. winter past, r. is over
Is. 4 : 6. for covert fr. storm and r.
5 : 6. clouds th. they rain no r. on
18 : † 4. like clear heat after r. ⌊it
30 : 23. Then shall he give thee r.
44 : 14. an ash, r. doth nourish it
55 : 10. as r. cometh from heaven
Je. 5 : 24. fear the L. th. giveth r.
10 : 13. lightnings with r., 51 : 16.
14 : 4. ground chapped, was no r.
22. any vanities of Gent. cause r.
Eze. 1 : 28. As bow in cloud in r.
38 : 22. I will rain overflowing r.
Ho. 6 : 3. shall come unto us as r.
Jo. 2 : 23. cause to come down r.
Am. 4 : 7. I have withholden the r.
Zch. 14 : 17. upon them sh. be no r.
18. if family of E. th. have no r.
Mat. 5 : 45. sendeth r. on just and
7 : 25. r. descended and floods, 27.
Ac. 14 : 17. did good, and gave us r.

Ac. 28 : 2. received us bec. of the r.
He. 6 : 7. earth which drinketh in r.
Ja. 5 : 18. prayed, heaven gave r.

Latter RAIN.

De. 11 : 14. will give you 1st and l. r.
Jb. 29 : 23. opened mou. as for l. r.
Pr. 16 : 15. favour as cloud of l. r.
Je. 3 : 3. hath been no l. r.
5 : 24. former and l. r. in his season
Ho. 6 : 3. he come as l. and former r.
Jo. 2 : 23. l. r. in first month
Zch. 10 : 1. Ask rain in time of l. r.
Ja. 5 : 7. receive early and l. r.

RAIN. [Verb.]

Ge. 2 : 5. L. had not caused it to r.
7 : 4. cause it to r. 40 days and 40
Ex. 9 : 18. to morrow cause it to r.
16 : 4. I will r. bread from heaven
Jb. 20 : 23. G. shall r. fury upon him
38 : 26. To cause it to r. on earth
Ps. 11 : 6. Upon wicked r. snares
Is. 5 : 6. th. they r. no rain upon it
Eze. 38 : 22. I will r. overflow-g rain
Ho. 10 : 12. till he r. righteousness
Am. 4 : 7. I caused to r. upon 1 city
Ja. 5 : 17. Elias prayed it might not r.
Re. 11 : 6. r. not in days of prophecy

RAINBOW.

Re. 4 : 3. was r. about the throne
10 : 1. I saw angel, r. upon his head

RAINED.

Ge. 19 : 24. L. r. upon Sodom and
Ex. 9 : 23. Lord r. hail upon Egypt
Ps. 78 : 24. had r. down manna, 27.
Eze. 22 : 24. art land not r. upon
Am 4 : 7. one piece was r. upon; piece whereupon it r. not, withered
Lu. 17 : 29. the same day it r. fire
Ja. 5 : 17. it r. not for 3 years 6 mos.

RAINY.

Pr. 27 : 15. a continual dropping in r. day

RAISE.

Ge. 38 : 8. marry her, and r. up seed
Ex. 23 : 1. shalt not r. false report
De. 18 : 15. L. will r. up prophet like me, 18. Ac. 3 : 22 -7 : 37. [name
25 : 7. refuseth to r. unto bro. a
Jos. 8 : 29. r. thereon heap of stones
Ru. 4 : 5. r. up name of dead, 10.
1 S. 2 : 35. I will r. faithful priest
2 S. 12 : 11. I will r. evil ag. thee
17. elders went to him to r. him
1 K. 14 : 14. Lord shall r. king in Isr.
1 Ch. 17 : 11. I will r. up thy seed
Jb. 3 : 8. ready to r. up mourning
19 : 12. His troops r. way ag. me
30 : 12. r. ag. me ways of destruo.
Ps. 41 : 10. Lord be merciful, r. me
48 : †13. bulwarks, r. up her palaces
Is. 15 : 5. shall r. cry of destruction
29 : 3. I will r. forts against thee
44 : 26. I will r. up decayed places
49 : 6. servant to r. tribes of Jacob
† 8. for a cov-t to r. up earth
58 : 12. r. foundations of generat-s
61 : 4. sh. r. up former desolations
Je. 23 : 5. r. unto David a Branch
30 : 9. Da. their king I will r. up
50 : 9. I will r. ag. Bab. assembly
32. proud sh. fall, none sh. r. him
51 : 1. r. ag. Bab. destroying wind
Eze. 23 : 22. r. thy lovers ag. thee
34 : 29. I will r. plant of renown
Ho. 6 : 2. in 3d day he will r. us
Jo. 3 : 7. I will r. them whither sold
Am. 5 : 2. virgin of Isr. none to r. her
6 : 14. I will r. a nation ag. you
9 : 11. I will r. tabernacle of Da. I will r. up his ruins [herds
Mi. 5 : 5. we shall r. ag. him 7 shep-
Ha. 1 : 3. there are that r. up strife
6. I will r. up the Chaldeans
Zch. 11 : 16. I will r. up a shepherd
Mat. 3 : 9. God able of these stones to r. up chil. unto Ab., Lu. 3 : 8.
10 : 8. cleanse lepers, r. the dead
Mat. 22 : 24. marry wife, and r. seed unto bro., Mk. 12 : 19. Lu. 20 : 28.
Jn. 2 : 19. in three days I will r. it
6 : 39. I will r. it up again at last day, 40, 44, 54. [throne
Ac. 2 : 30. he would r. Christ to sit on
26 : 8. Why incredible God r. dead?
1 Co. 6 : 14. will r. up us by power
2 Co. 4 : 14. shall r. up us by Jesus
He. 11 : 19. Accounting G. able to r.
Ja. 5 : 15. Lord shall r. him [him

RAISED.

Ex. 9 : 16. I r. thee up to shew my power, Ro. 9 : 17. [stead
Jos. 5 : 7. children whom he r. up in
7 : 26. r. over him heap of stones
Ju. 2 : 16. the Lord r. up Judges, 18.
3 : 9. Lord r. deliverer to Isr., 15.
2 S. 23 : 1. man who was r. on high
1 K. 5 : 13. Sol. r. levy of Isr., 9 : 15.
2 Ch. 32 : 5. r. it to towers, 33 : 14.
Ezr. 1 : 5. all whose spirit God r.
Jb. 14 : 12. nor be r. out of sleep
Pr. 15 : † 19. way of righte. is r. up
Can. 8 : 5. I r. thee und. apple tree
Is. 14 : 9. it r. up kings of nations
23 : 13. Assyrian r. palaces of Chal.
41 : 2. Who r. righte. man fr. east
25. I have r. up one from north
45 : 13. I have r. him in righte-n.
Je. 6 : 22. a great nation shall be r.
25 : 32. a great whirlwind sh. be r.
29 : 15. L. hath r. us prophets in Bab.
50 : 41. many kings shall be r. fr.
51 : 11. L. r. spirit of k-s of Medes
Da. 7 : 5. a bear r. up on one side
Am. 2 : 11. I r. up of your sons for prophets [habitation
Zch. 2 : 13. is r. up out of his holy
9 : 13. when I have r. thy sons, O Zi.
Mat. 1 : 24. Joseph being r. fr. sleep
11 : 5. the dead are r., Lu. 7 : 22.
16 : 21. he must be killed, and r. third day, 17 : 23. Lu. 9 : 22.
Lu. 1 : 69. hath r. horn of salvation
20 : 37. dead are r. Moses shewed
Jn. 12 : 1. Lazarus wh. he r., 9, 17.
Ac. 2 : 24. Whom God hath r. up, 32. -3 : 15, 26.-4 : 10.-5 : 30.-10 : 40.-13 : 30, 33, 34, 37.-17 : 31. Ro. 10 : 9. 1 Co. 6 : 14. 2 Co. 4 : 14. Ga. 1 : 1. Ep. 1 : 20. [r. David
12 : 7. angel r. up Peter | 13 : 22. he
18 : 23. God r. unto Israel a Savi.
50. Jews r. persecution ag. Paul
Ro. 4 : 24. believe on him th. r. Jes.
25. r. again for our justification
6 : 4. as C. was r. fr. dead by Father
9. C. r. from dead, dieth no more
7 : 4. married, to him r. fr the dead
8 : 11. if Spirit of him that r. up Jes. in you, he that r. up C. sh.
1 Co. 15 : 15 r. up C.; wh. he r. not
16. if dead rise not, is not C. r.
17. if C. not r. your faith is vain
35. say, How are dead r.? [52.
42. sown in corruption, r. in incor.,
43. it is r. in glory, r. in power
44. sown natural body, r. spiritu.
Ep. 2 : 6. hath r. us together in C.
Col. 2 : 12. operation of G. who r. him
1 Th. 1 : 10. Son, whom he r. fr. dead
2 Ti. 2 : 8. Jesus of seed of Da. was r.
He. 11 : 35. Women received dead r.
1 Pe. 1 : 21. believe in G. that r. him

RAISER.

Da. 11 : 20. sh. stand up r. of taxes
Ho. 7 : †4. r. will cease after he hath

RAISETH.

1 S. 2 : 8. r. poor out of dust, Ps. 113 : 7.
Jb. 41 : 25. he r. hims., mighty afraid
Ps. 107 : 25. For he r. stormy wind
145 : 14. he r. those he bowed, 146 : 8.
Jn. 5 : 21. as Father r. up dead
2 Co. 1 : 9. trust in God wh. r. the

RAISING. [dead

Ho. 7 : 4. baker who ceaseth from r.
Ac. 24 : 12. nei. found us r. the peo.

RAISINS. [of r.

1 S. 25 : 18. Abig. took 100 clusters
30 : 12. gave Eg-n 2 clusters of r.
2 S. 16 : 1. Ziba met David with r.
1 Ch. 12 : 40. they bro-t bunches of r.

RA'KEM. See ULAM.

RAK'KATH.

Jos. 19 : 35. cities are Ziddim, Zer, R.

RAK'KON. See ME-JARKON.

RAM. [Person.] [10.

Ru. 4 : 19. Hezron begat R., 1 Ch. 2 : 9,
1 Ch. 2 : 25. Sons of Jerahmeel, R.
27. sons of R. firstb. of Jerahmeel
Jb. 32 : 2. Elihu of kindred of R.

RAM.

Ge. 15 : 9. Take r. of three years old
22 : 13. behind him a r. caught in a
Ex. 29 : 15. take one r., 19. [20.
16. shalt slay the r., 17, 20. Le. 8 :
18. burn the whole r., Le. 8 : 21.
22. it is a r. of consecration, 27, 31. Le. 8 : 18, 22, 29.
26. take r. of Aaron's consecration
32. Aa. and sons sh. eat flesh of r.
Le. 5 : 15. r. with-t blemish, 18.-6 : 6.
16. atonement for him with r.
9 : 2 Take r. for burnt off-g, Nu. 7 : 15, 21, 27.-28 : 11.-29 : 2, 8, 36.,
4. r. for peace off-gs, 18. Nu. 6 : 17.
19 : 21. r. for trespass offering, 22.
Nu. 5 : 8. beside r. of atonement
15 : 11. Thus sh. it be done for one r.
23 : 2. on every altar a r., 4. 14, 30.
28 : 14. 3d part of hin unto a r.
20. two tenth deals for a r., 12, 28.-15 : 6.-29 : 3, 9, 14, 37.
Ezr. 10 : 19. they off-d r. for trespass
Eze. 43 : 23. r. without blemish, 25.
45 : 24. prepare an ephah for a r.,
46 : 5, 7, 11.
46 : 4. prince shall offer Lord a r.
6. in day of the new moon a r.
Da. 8 : 3. I saw a r. had 2 horns
4. I saw r. pushing westward
6. goat came to r. had 2 horns
7. I saw him come close unto the r. and he smote r. (4) [kings
20. The r. having two horns are
See BULLOCK.

RAMS. [streaked, 12.

Ge. 31 : 10. r. which leaped ring-
38. r. of thy flock have I not eat.
32 : 14. Jacob sent Esau 20 r. [18.
Ex. 29 : 1. bullock 2 r., 3. Le. 8 : 2.-23 :
Nu. 7 : 17 peace offerings, five r., 23, 29, 35, 41, 47, 53, 59, 65, 71, 77, 83.
87. for offering, bullocks, r., 88.
23 : 1. Balaam said, prepare 7 r., 29.
29 : 13. two r., 17, 20, 23, 26, 29, 32.
14. two tenth deals to each of 2 r.
27. offerings for the r. sh. be, 30, 33.
De. 32 : 14. wi. r. of breed of Bashan
1 S. 15 : 22. hearken than fat of r.
2 K. 3 : 4. Moab rendered 100,000 r.
1 Ch. 29 : 21. they sacrificed 1,000 r.
2 Ch. 13 : 9. young bullock and 7 r.
17 : 11. Arabians bro-t 7,700 r.
29 : 22. killed r. they sprinkled [r.
32. number of burnt off-gs was 100
Ezr. 6 : 9. r. for offerings of God
17. offered at dedication 200 r.
7 : 17. buy wi. this money r. lambs
8 : 35. offered 96 r. for a sin offering
Jb. 42 : 8. take 7 bullocks and 7 r.
Ps. 66 : 15. with fat of r., Is. 34 : 6.
114 : 4. The mts. skipped like r. 6.
Is. 1 : 11. I full of burnt off-gs of r.
34 : 6. sword is filled with fat of r.
60 : 7. r. of Nebaioth sh. minister
Je. 51 : 40. bring to slaughter like r.
Eze. 27 : 21. Kedar occupied in r.
34 : 17. I judge betw. r. and goats
39 : 18. ye sh. drink blood of r. [r.
Mi. 6 : 7. L. be pleased with thous. of
See BATTERING, HORNS, SKINS.
See SEVEN bullocks.

RA'MAH, RA'MA.
Jos 18: 25. R. city of tribe of Benj.
19 : 29. then coast turneth to R.
36. the fenced cities are R. and
Ju. 4 : 5. Deborah dwelt between R.
19 : 13. lodge all night in R.
1 S. 1 : 19. Elkanah to ho. in R., 2:11.
7 : 17. Samuel's return was to R.,
15 : 34.-16 : 13. [unto R.
8 : 4. all the elders came to Samuel
19:18. David fled, to Sam. to R., 19.
22. Saul went also to R., 23.
20:1. David fled fr. Naioth in R. [R.
22: 6. Saul abode under tree in R.
25: 1. Sam. was buried at R., 28:3.
1 K. 15 : 17. Baasha built R., 2 Ch.
16 : 1. [2 Ch. 16 : 5.
21. Baasha left off building of R.,
22. took stones of R., 2 Ch. 16 : 6.
2 K. 8 : 29. Joram went to be healed
of the wounds which the Syrians had given him at R., 2 Ch.
22: 6. [621, Ne. 7 : 30.
Ezr. 2 : 26. children of R. and Geba,
Ne. 11:33. the children of Benj. dwelt
Is.10:29. R. is afraid, Gibeah is [at R.
Je. 31 : 15. voice heard in R.
40 : 1. captain let him go from R.
Ho. 5 : 8. Blow ye the trumpet in R.
Mat. 2 : 18. In R. a lamentation and

RA'MATH. [weeping
Jos. 19 : 8. all villages to R. of south

RAMATHA'IM-ZO'PHIM.
1 S. 1 : 1. was a certain man of R.

RA'MATHITE. [the R.
1 Ch. 27 : 27. over vineyards Shimei

RA'MATH-LE'HI. [R.
Ju. 15 : 17. Samson called that place

RA'MATH-MIZ'PEH.
Jos.13:26. coast fr. Heshbon unto R.

RAME'SES or RAAM'SES. [R
Ge. 47:11. gave possession in land of
Ex. 1:11. treasure cities, Pithom, R.
12:37. Isr. journeyed from R., Nu.

RAMI'AH. See JEZIAH. [33:3,5

RA'MOTH. [Person.]
Ezr. 10 : 29. sons of Bani, Sheal, R.

RA'MOTH. [Place.]
De. 4:43. R. in Gilead of Gadites, city
of refuge, Jos. 20 : 8.-21 : 38.
1 S. 30 : 27. which were in south R.
1 K. 22 : 3. Know ye that R. is ours
1 Ch. 6 : 73. And R. with suburbs
80. out of tribe of Gad to Levites,

RA'MOTH-GIL'EAD. [R.
1 K. 4 : 13. son of Geber officer in R.
22 : 4. Wilt thou go with me to battle to R.? 2 Ch. 18 : 3, 5. [18:14.
6. Shall I go against R.? 15. 2 Ch.
12. Go up to R. prosper, 2 Ch. 18:11.
20. persuade Ahab to fall at R.,
2 Ch. 18 : 19. [Ch. 18 : 2, 28.
29. king of Isr. went up to R., 2
2 K. 8 : 28. Joram went ag. Hazael in
R. and, 2 Ch. 22 : 5. [to R.
9:1. Elisha said, Take box of oil, go
4. So the prophet went to R.
14. Now Joram had kept R. bec.

RAMPART.
La. 2 : 8. he made r. to lament
Na. 3 : 8. No, whose R. was the sea

RAN.
Ge. 18:2. Abraham r. to meet them
7. Ab. r. unto herd, fetched calf
24 : 17. servant r. to meet Rebekah
20. Rebekah r. unto well to draw
28. damsel r. and told her mother's
29. Laban r. out unto the man
29 : 12. Rachel r. told her father
13. Laban r. to meet Jacob and
33 : 4. Esau r., and embraced him
Ex. 9 : 23. fire r. upon the ground
Nu. 11 : 27. r. young man told Mo.
16:47. Aaron r. into congr-n [tent
Jos. 7 : 22. messengers r. unto Aa.'s
8 : 19. ambush r. into Ai, set fire
Ju. 7 : 21. all the host of Midian r.
Ju. 9 : 21. Jotham r. away, and fled
44. two companies r. upon people
13 : 10. Manoah's wife r. shewed
1 S. 3 : 5. Samuel r. unto Eli, said
4 : 12. man of Benj. r. out of army
10 : 23. they r. and fetched Saul
17 : 22. David r. saluted brethren
51. David r. stood upon Philist., 48.
20 : 36. as lad r. he shot an arrow
2 S. 18 : 21. Cushi bowed unto Joab
23. Ahimaaz r. by plain [and r.
1 K. 2 : 39. serv-s of Shimei r. away
18 : 35. water r. about the altar
46 Elijah r. bef. Ahab to Jezreel
19:20. Elisha left oxen r. aft. Elijah
22 : 35. blood r. into chariot
2 K. 23:†12. king beat down, and r.
2 Ch. 32 : 4. stopped brook that r.
Ps. 77 : 2. my sore r. in night
105:41. waters r. in the dry places
133 : 2. ointment r. do. upon beard
Je. 23 : 21. I have not sent, they r.
Eze. 1 : 14. the living creatures r.
47 : 2. r. out waters on right side
Da. 8 : 6. goat r. unto ram in fury
Mat. 8 : 32. herd of swine r. into sea,
Mk. 5 : 13. Lu. 8 : 33. [15 : 36.
27 : 48. one r. filled a sponge, Mk.
Mk. 5 : 6. he r. and worshipped him
6 : 33. many knew him, r. afoot
55. r. through that whole region
Lu. 15 : 20. father r. fell on his neck
19:4. Zaccheus r. and climbed a tree
24 : 12. Peter r. unto sepulchre
Jn. 20 : 4. So they r. both together
Ac. 3 : 11. the people r. unto them
7 : 57. they r. upon Stephen with
8 : 30. Philip r. to the chariot [in
12 : 14. knew Peter's voice, she r.
14 : 14. Paul and Barnabas r. in
21 : 30. people r. and took Paul in
32. captain took soldiers and r.
27 : 41. they r. the ship aground
Jude 11. r. greedily aft. error of Ba-

RANG. [laam
1 S. 4 : 5. shouted, so the earth r.
1 K. 1 : 45. Israel shouted, so city r.

RANGE, S.
Le. 11:35. r-s for pots'sh. be broken
2 K. 11:8. cometh within r-s be slain
15. Have her forth without the
r-s, 2 Ch. 23 : 14. [pasture
Jb. 39 : 8. r. of the mountains is his

RANGED.
1 S. 17:†2. Saul and Israel r. battle

RANGERS.
1 Ch. 12 : † 33. r. of battle 50,000

RANGING.
Pr. 28:15. as r. bear, so wicked ruler

RANK, RANKS.
Ge. 41:5. ears upon one stalk, r. good
7. thin ears devoured 7 r. ears
Ex. 13 : † 18. Isr. went by five in r.
Nu. 2 : 16. shall set forth in sec. r.
24. shall go forward in third r.
Ju. 7 : † 11. went unto outside of r-s
1 K. 7 : 4. light was against light in
three r-s, 5. [keep r.
1 Ch. 12:33. of Zebulun 50,000 could
† 36. of Asher keeping r. 40,000.
38. men of war th. could keep r.
Ps. 55:†13. thou man acc-g to my r.
Jo. 2:7. they shall not break their r-s
Mk. 6 : 40. sat down in r-s by hund.
Ga. 4 : † 25. Agar is in same r. with

RANSOM. [Noun.] [Jerus.
Ex. 21 : 30. sh. give for r. of his life
30:12. give ev. man r. for his soul
1 S. 12 :† 3. of whose hand I any r.?
Jb. 33 : 24. Deliver, I have found r.
36:18. great r. cannot deliver thee
Ps. 49 : 7. nor can give God a r.
Pr. 6 : 35. He will not regard any r.
13 : 8. r. of a man's life are riches
21 : 18. wicked be r. for righteous
Is. 43:3. I gave Egypt for thy r. [r.
Am. 5:†12. they afflict the just, take
Mat. 20 : 28. as Son of man came to
give his life a r., Mk. 10 : 45.
1 Ti. 2 : 6. Who gave hims. r. for all

RANSOM. [Verb.]
Ho. 13 : 14. I will r. them fr. grave

RANSOMED.
Is. 35 : 10. r. of the L. shall return
51 : 10. made sea a way for the r.
Je. 31 : 11. Lord redeemed Jacob and

RA'PHA=REPHA'IAH. [r.
1 S. 21:†18. Saph which was of sons
of R., 1 Ch. 20 : † 4.
1 Ch. 8 : 2. Benj. begat Nohah, R.
37. R., Azel, sons of Binea / 9:43.

RA'PHU. [R-h
Ne. 13 : 9. of Benj. Palti son of R.

RARE.
Da. 2:11. it is r. thing king requireth

RASE.
Ps. 137 : 7. r. it, r. it, to foundation

RASH.
Ec. 5 : 2. Be not r. with thy mouth
Is. 32 : 4. heart of r. sh. understand
1 Co. 13 : † 4. charity is not r. not

RASHLY. [puffed
Ac. 19 : 36. be quiet, and do nothing

RASHNESS. [r.
2 S. 6 : † 7. G. smote Uzzah for his r.

RATE. [day
Ex. 16 : 4. sh. gather certain r. ev.
1 K. 10 : 25. a r. year by y-r, 2 Ch. 9:
2 K. 25:30. a daily r. for ev. day [24.
2 Ch. 8 : 13. a certain r. every day

RATHER.
Jos. 22 : 24. if not r. done it for fear
2 K. 5 : 13. much r. when he saith
Jb. 7:15. death r. than life, Je. 8:3.
32:2. justified himself r. than God
36 : 21. hast chosen r. than afflic.
Ps. 52:3. lying r. than speak right-n.
84 : 10. had r. be a doorkeeper in
Pr. 8:10. Receive knowledge r. than
16 : 16. underst-g r. to be chosen
17 : 12. r. than a fool in his folly
22:1. A good name r. to be chosen
loving favour r. than silver
Mat. 10 : 6. go r. to lost sheep of Isr.
28. r. fear him able to destroy
18:8. r. than having two hands to
9. than having two eyes to be
25 : 9. go ye r. to them that sell
27 : 24. that r. tumult was made
Mk. 5 : 26. nothing bettered, but r.
15 : 11. that he r. release Barabbas
Lu. 10:20. r. rej. your names writt.
11 : 28. r. blessed they that hear
41. r. give alms of such things [G.
12 : 31. But r. seek ye kingdom of
51. to give peace, Nay r. division
17 : 8. will not r. say, Make ready
18 : 14. he went down justified r.
Jn. 3 : 19. men loved darkn. r. than
Ac. 5 : 29. obey God r. than men
Ro. 3 : 8. not r. let us do evil, that
8 : 34. yea, r. that is risen again
11 : 11. r. thro their fall salvation
12 : 19. r. give place unto wrath
14 : 13. not judge one ano., this r.
1 Co. 5:2. and have not r. mourned
6 : 7. Why do ye not r. take wrong
7 : 21. if be made free, use it r.
9:12. If of this power are not we r.
14 : 1. desire r. th. ye prophesy, 5.
19. had r. speak 5 words with
2 Co. 2 : 7. ought r. to forgive him
3:8. How ministration of the spirit
be r. glorious? [the body
5 : 8. willing r. to be absent from
12 : 9. I will r. glory in infirmities
Ga. 4:9. known G. or r. known of G.
Ep. 4 : 28. steal no more, r. labour
5:4. nei. jesting, r. giving of thanks
11. works of darkness r. reprove
Ph 1:12. r. unto furtherance of gos.
1 Ti. 1 : 4. questions r. than edifying
4 : 7. exercise r. unto godliness
6 : 2. r. do them service

Phm. 9. for love's sake I r. beseech
He. 11:25. Choosing r. to suffer affl.
12:9. r. be in subjection unto Fa.
13. lame turned out, r. be healed
13:19. I beseech you r. do this
2 Pe. 1:10. r. give diligence to make

RATTLETH.

Jb. 39:23. quiver r. ag. him, spear

RATTLING. [and

Na. 3:2. noise of the r. of wheels

RAVEN, S.

Ge. 8:7. Noah sent forth a r. [14.
Le. 11:15. Every r. is uncl., De. 14:
1 K. 17:4. com-ded r-s to feed thee
6. the r-s brought Elijah bread
Jb. 38:41. Who provided for r. food
Ps. 147:9. to the young r-s wh. cry
Pr. 30:17. r. of valley shall pick it
Can. 5:11. his locks black as a r.
Is. 34:11. the r. shall dwell in it
Lu. 12:24. Consider r-s they neither

RAVEN. (Verb.)

Ge. 49:27. Benjamin shall r. as a wolf
Ps. 17:†12. as lion that desireth to r.

RAVENING. [Noun, Part.]

Ps. 22:13. gaped upon me as r. lion
Eze. 22:25. like roaring lion r.
27. her princes like wolves r.
Mat. 7:15. inwardly are r. wolves
Lu. 11:39. inward part is full of r.

RAVENOUS.

Is. 35:9. nor any r. beast shall go
46:11. Calling a r. bird from east
Eze. 39:4. I will give thee unto r.

RAVIN. [Noun.] [birds

Na. 2:12. lion filled his dens with r.

RAVIN. [Verb.] See RAVEN.

RAVISHED.

Pr. 5:19. be thou r. with her love
20. why be r. wi. strange woman
Can. 4:9. Thou hast r. my heart
Is. 13:16. wives of Bab. shall be r.
La. 5:11. They r. women in Zion
Zch. 14:2. women in Jerus. shall be

RAW. [r.

Ex. 12:9. Eat not it r. nor sodden
Le. 13:10. if be quick r. flesh
14. when r. flesh appeareth, 16.
15. see r. flesh, r. flesh is uncl.
1 S. 2:15. not sodden flesh, but r.
Mat. 9:†16. No man putteth r. cloth
unto an old garment, Mk. 2:†21.

RAZOR.

Nu. 6:5. all the days no r. upon
head, Ju. 13:5.-16:17. 1 S. 1:11.
8:†7. cause r. to pass over Levites
Ps. 52:2. thy tongue like sharp r.
Is. 7:20. L. shave with a r. hired
Eze. 5:1. take thee a barber's r.

REACH. [heav.

Ge. 11:4. tower whose top r. unto
Ex. 26:28. bar r. from end to end
28:42. breeches sh. r. unto thighs
Le. 5:†7. if his hand cannot r. to a
lamb, 14:†21.
26:5. threshing sh. r. unto vintage, vintage sh. r. unto sowing
Nu. 34:11. border shall r. unto sea
Jb. 20:6. tho. head r. unto clouds
Is. 8:8. he sh. r. even to the neck
30:28. breath r. to midst of neck
Je. 48:32. plants r. to sea of Jazer
Zch. 14:5. valley sh. r. unto Azal
Jn. 20:27. r. hither thy finger, r.
2 Co. 10:13. measure to r. unto you

REACHED.

Ge. 28:12. ladder's top r. to heaven
Ru. 2:14. he r. her parched corn
Da. 4:11. tree r. unto heaven, 20.
2 Co. 10:14. as tho. we r. not unto you
Re. 18:5. Babylon's sins r. unto

REACHETH. [heav.

2 Ch. 28:9. rage that r. unto heav.
Ps. 36:5. thy faithfulness r. clouds
108:4. thy truth r. unto clouds
Pr. 31:20. she r. hands to needy
Je. 4:10. sword r. unto the soul
Je. 4:18. bitter, it r. unto thine heart
51:9. Babylon's judgm. r. heaven
Da. 4:22. thy greatness r. unto heav.

REACHING.

Ph. 3:13. r. forth unto those things

READ. [Pronounced Reed.]

De. 17:19. king shall r. all his life
31:11. r. this law bef. all Israel
Is. 29:11. r. this, I pray, 12. [r.
34:16. Seek out of book of L. and
Je. 36:6. go and r. in the roll
15. said, Sit and r. it in our ears
51:61. When to Bab. and shalt r.
Da. 5:7. Whoso. shall r. this and
shew interp-n, 15, 16. [writing
8. king's wise men could not r.
17. Let gifts be to thys. I will r.
Mat. 21:42. Did ye never r. in Scrip-
Lu. 4:16. Jes. stood up to r. [tures?
Ac. 8:30. Philip heard him r. Esaias
2 Co. 1:13. write none than what ye
Ep. 3:4. when ye r. may underst. [r.
Col. 4:16. r. epistle from Laodicea
Re. 5:4. none worthy to r. book

READ. (Pronounced Red.)

Ex. 24:7. r. in audience of people
Jos. 8:34. he r. words of law, 35.
2 K. 5:7. king of Isr. had r. letter
19:14. Hezekiah r. the letter
22:8. Shaphan r. the book of the
law, 10. 2 Ch. 34:18, 24.
16. book king of Judah hath r.
23:2. king Josiah r. in their ears
book of cov-t, 2 Ch. 34:30. [r.
2 Ch. 34:24. I will bring all curses
Ezr. 4:18. letter hath been plainly r.
23. king's letter was r. they made
Ne. 8:3. he r. before all book of the
law, 8.-13:1. [he r. the law
18. from first day unto the last
9:3. stood in their place r. in law
Es. 6:1. book of records was r.
Is. 37:14. he received letter, r. it
Je. 29:29. Zeph. priest r. letter
36:10 r. Baruch the words of Jeremiah, 13, 14, 15. [and princes
21. Jehudi r. in the ears of king
23 he r. 3 or 4 leaves, king cut it
Mat. 12:3. Have ye not r.? 5.-19:4.
-21:16.-22:31. Mk. 2:25.-12:10,
26. Lu. 6:3. [Jews
Jn. 19:20. This title r. many of the
Ac. 8:28. eunuch r. Esaias prophet
32. place of Scripture he r.
13:27. prophets are r. every sab.,
15:31. had r. they rejoiced [15:21.
23:34. when governor r. letter
2 Co. 3:2. Ye our epistle r. of all
15. when Moses is r. the vail is
Col. 4:16. when this epistle is r.
1 Th. 5:27. I charge this epistle be

READEST, ETH. [r.

Ha. 2:2. that he may run that r-h it
Mat. 24:15. (whoso r-h let him understand), Mk. 13:14.
Lu. 10:26. What is written in law,
how r-t thou? [r-t
Ac. 8:30. understandest what thou
Re. 1:3. Blessed is he that r-h and

READING. [Noun, Part.]

Ne. 8:8. caused them to underst. r.
Ec. 12:†12. much r. is a weariness
Je. 36:8. r. in the book of the Lord
51:63. when made end of r. book
Ac. 13:15. after the r. of the law
2 Co. 3:14. vail untaken in r. old
1 Ti. 4:13. give attendance to r. [test.

READINESS. [r.

Ac. 17:11. received the word with
2 Co. 8:11. as there was a r. to will
10:6. r. to revenge disobedience

READY.

Ex. 17:4. people be r. to stone me
19:11. be r. ag. the third day, 15.
34:2. be r. in morning, and come
Nu. 32:17. we will go r. armed
De. 1:41. ye were r. to go up
De. 26:5. A Syrian r. to perish my fa.
Jos. 4:†13. 40,000 r. armed passed
8:4. go not far f om city, be all r.
1 S. 25:18. took five sheep r. dressed
2 S. 15:15. thy servants are r. to do
18:22. Whf. run, hast no tidi gs r.
Ezr. 7:6. Ezra was r. scri e in law
Ne. 9:17. art a God r. to pardon
Es. 3:14. be r. ag. that day, 8:13.
Jb. 3:8. r. to raise their mourning
12:5. is r. to slip with his feet
15:23. knoweth day of darkn. is r.
24. anguish prevail as king r. to
28. houses r. to become heaps [bat.
17:1. the graves are r. for me [side
18:12. destruction sh. be r. at his
29:13. blessing of him r. to perish
32:19. my belly is r. to burst like
Ps. 38:17. For I am r. to halt
45:1. my tongue pen of a r. writer
86:5. L. art good, r. to forgive
88:15. I am r. to die from my youth
Pr. 24:11. to deliver those r. to be
slain [r. to perish
31:6. Give strong drink unto him
Ec. 5:1. be more r. to hear than
Is. 27:13. shall come, r. to perish
30:13. iniq-y as breach r. to fall
32:4. tongue of stammerers be r.
38:20. Lord was r. to save me
41:7. It is r. for the soldering
51:13. as if he were r. to destroy
Da. 3:15. Now if ye be r. to worsh.
Mat. 22:4. fatlings, all things are r.
8. The wedding is r., Lu. 14:17.
24:44. be ye also r., Lu. 12:40.
25:10. they that were r. went in
Mk. 14:38. spirit is r. but flesh
Lu. 7:2. servant sick, r. to die
22:33. Lord, I am r. to go with thee
Jn. 7:6. your time is always r.
Ac. 20:7. Paul preached r. to depart
21:13. I am r. not to be bound only
23:15. we are r. to kill him
21. are r. looking for a promise
Ro. 1:15. am r. to preach at Rome
2 Co. 8:19 declaration of r. mind
9:2. Achaia was r. a year ago
3. sent breth. that ye may be r.
5. same might be r. as bounty
12:14. 3d time I am r. to come
1 Ti. 6:†3. not be r. to quarrel, as
6:18. that ye be r. to distribute
2 Ti. 4:6. I am r. to be offered
Tit. 3:1. r. to every good work
He. 8:13. old, is r. to vanish away
1 Pe. 1:5. salvation, r. to be reveal.
3:15. be r. always to give an ans.
4:5. to him that is r. to judge quick
5:2. not for lucre, but of r. mind
Re. 3:2. things that are r. to die
12:4. woman was r. to be delivered
See MADE, MAKE.

REA'IA. See MICAH.

REAI'AH. [2:†52.

1 Ch. 4:2. R. son of Shobal, 1 Ch.
Ezr. 2:47. chil. of R., Ne. 7:50.

REALM.

2 Ch. 20:30. r. of Jehosh-t was quiet
Ezr. 7:13. they of my r. minded to
23. why be wrath ag. the r.? [go
Da. 1:20. better than all in his r.
6:3. k. thought to set him ov. r.
9:1. Darius, k. over r. of Chald.
11:2. sh. stir up all ag. r. of Grecia

REAP.

Le. 19:9. when ye r. harvest, 23:
not wholly r. corners [10, 22.
25:5. groweth of itself shalt not r.
11. in jubilee neither sow nor r.
Ru. 2:9. Let eyes be on field they r.
1 S. 8:12. set your servants to r.
2 K. 19:29. third year r., Is. 37:30.
Jb. 4:8. sow wickedness r. same
24:6. They r. every one his corn
Ps. 126:5. sow in tears r. in joy
Pr. 22:8. soweth iniquity r. vanity

Ec. 11 : 4. regardeth clouds not r.
Je. 12 : 13. They have sown wheat but shall r. thorns
Ho. 8 : 7. sown wind r. whirlwind
10:12. Sow in right-n. r. in mercy
Mi. 6 : 15. shalt sow, but not r.
Mat. 6 : 26. fowls r. not, Lu. 12 : 24.
25 : 26. I r. where I sowed not
Jn. 4 : 38. to r. whereon no labour
1 Co. 9 : 11. if we r. carnal things
2 Co. 9 : 6. soweth sparingly sh. r. sparingly, soweth bountifully r. bountifully [sh. he r.
Ga. 6 : 7. whatso. man soweth, that
8. soweth to flesh r. corruption, to Spirit, r. life everlasting
9. in due season sh. r. if faint not
Re. 14 : 15. Thrust in sickle and r. time is come for thee to r.

REAPED.

Ho. 10 : 13. wickedn. ye r. iniquity
Ja. 5 : 4. labourers, which r. your fields, cries of them are entered, (2) [was r.
Re. 14 : 16. thrust in sickle, earth

REAPER, S.

Ru. 2 : 3. Ruth gleaned after the r-s
4. Boaz said unto r-s Lord be
7. I pray, let me glean after r-s
2 K. 4 : 18. out to his fa. to r-s [the r.
Am. 9 : 13. ploughman sh. overtake
Mat. 13 : 30. say to r-s, Gather tares
39. enemy is devil, r-s are angels

REAPEST, ETH, ING. [r-t

Le. 23 : 22. not clean riddance when
1 S. 6 : 13. they of Beth-shemesh r-g
Is. 17 : 5. harvestman r-h ears
Mat. 25 : 24. Lord, thou hard man, r-g where not sown, Lu. 19 : 22.
Lu. 19 : 21. and thou r-t that thou didst not sow
Jn. 4 : 36. r-h receiveth wages, th. he that soweth and he th. r-h
37. true, One soweth another r-h

REAR, ED.

Ex. 26 : 30. r. up the tabernacle, 40: 17, 18, 33. Nu. 9 : 15.
Le. 26 : 1. nei. r. up standing image
2 S. 18 : 18. r-d for hims. a pillar
24 : 18. Go up r. an altar unto L.
1 K. 16 : 32. he r-d an altar for Baal, 2 K. 21 : 3. 2 Ch. 33 : 3. [ple
2 Ch. 3 : 17. he r-d pillars bef. tem-
Jn. 2 : 20. wilt thou r. it in 3 days

REARWARD.

Nu. 10 : 25. standard of Dan his r.
Jos. 6 : 9. r. came after the ark, 13.
1 S. 29 : 2. Da. and men passed in r.
Is. 52 : 12. G. of Isr. will be your r.
58 : 8. glory of Lord be thy r.

REASON, S.

1 K. 9 : 15. is r. of levy Sol. raised
Jb. 32 : 11. I waited, gave ear to r-s
Pr. 26 : 16. seven that render a r.
Ec. 7 : 25. I applied to search r. [r.
† 27. weighing one by one to find
Is. 41 : 21. bring your r-s saith king
Da. 4 : 36. same time my r. retur-d
Ac. 6 : 2. It is not r. we leave word
18 : 14. O Jews r. I should bear
1 Pe. 3 : 15. asketh you a r. of hope

By REASON. [ine

Ge. 41 : 31. not known b. r. of fam-
47 : 13. Canaan fainted b. r. of fam-
Ex. 2 : 23. Isr. sighed b. r. of bond-
3 : 7. cry b. r. of taskmasters [age
8 : 24. land corrupted b. r. of flies
Nu. 9 : 10. If unclean b. r. of dead
18 : 8. things given b. r. of anointing
32. shall bear no sin b. r. of it
De. 5 : 5. ye afraid b. r. of fire
Jos. 9 : 13. shoes old b. r. of journey
† 14. rec-d men b. r. of victuals
Ju. 2 : 18. b. r. of them that vexed
1 K. 14 : 4. eyes set b. r. of age
2 Ch. 5 : 14. not minis. b. r. of cloud
20 : 15. Be not afraid b. r. of mult.
2 Ch. 21 : 15. bowels fall b. r. of sickn.,
Jb. 6 : 16. blackish b. r. of ice [19.
17 : 7. Mine eye dim b. r. of sorr.
31 : 23. b. r. of his highness I not
35 : 9. b. r. of oppressions cry, cry out b. r. of mighty [darkn.
37 : 19. not order speech b. r. of
41 : 25. b. r. of breakings purify
Ps 38 : 8. roared b. r. of disquietness
44 : 16. blasphemeth b. r. of enemy
78 : 65. that shouteth b. r. of wine
88 : 9. mourneth b. r. of affliction
90 : 10. if b. r. of strength fourscore.
102 : 5. b. r. of groaning my bones
Pr. 20 : 4. not plough b. r. of cold
Is. 49 : 19. narrow, b. r. of inhab-s
Eze. 19 : 10. branches b. r. of waters
21 : 12. terrors b. r. of sword shall
26 : 10. b. r. of abundance of horses
27 : 16. Syria merchant b. r. of wares, 12. [brightness
28 : 17. Tyrus corrupted b. r. of
Da. 8 : 12. host b. r. of transgr-n
Jon. 2 : 2. I cried b. r. of affliction
Mi. 2 : 12. great noise b. r. of mult.
Jn. 6 : 18. sea arose b. r. of wind
12 : 11. b. r. of him many believed
Ro. 8 : 20. b. r. of him who subjec.
2 Co. 3 : 10. b. r. of glory excelleth
He. 5 : 3. b. r. ought offer for sins
14. who b. r. of use have senses exercised [b. r. of death
7 : 23. priests not suff-d to continue
2 Pe. 2 : 2. b. r. of wh. truth evil spoken
Re. 8 : 13. b. r. of other voices [of
9 : 2. sun darkened b. r. of smoke
18 : 19. rich b. r. of her costliness

REASON. [Verb.]

1 S. 12 : 7. may r. with you bef. L.
Jb. 9 : 14. choose words to r. wi. him
13 : 3. Surely I desire to r. with G.
15 : 3. Sho. he r. with unprofit. talk
Is. 1 : 18. Come let us r. together
Je. 12 : † 1. let me r. case with thee
Mat. 16 : 8. Jesus said, Why r. ye am. yourselves, Mk. 2 : 8.-8 : 17.
Lu. 5 : 21. scribes, Phari. began to r.
22. Jes. said, What r. ye in your

REASONABLE. [hearts

Ro 12 : 1. sacrifice your r. service

REASONABLY.

He. 5 : †2. Who can r. bear with ignor-

REASONED. [ant

Mat. 16 : 7. they r. among thems., 21 : 25. Mk. 8 : 16.-11 : 31. Lu. 20 : 5.
Mk. 2 : 8. Jesus perceived they so r.
Lu. 3 : † 15. all men r. in hearts
20 : 14. husbandmen r. am. thems.
24 : 15. while they r. Jes. drew near
Ac. 17 : 2. three sabbaths Paul r.
18 : 4. he r. in synagogue every sab.
19. Paul r. with Jews at Ephesus
24 : 25. as he r. of righteousness and
1 Co. 13 : † 11. When a child I r. as a

REASONING, S. [Noun.]

Jb. 13 : 6. Hear now my r. hearken
Lu. 9 : 46. Then arose a r. am. them
Ac. 28 : 29. Jews departed, had gr. r.
2 Co. 10 : † 5. Casting down r-s and

REASONING. [Part.]

Mk. 2 : 6. cert. scribes r. in their hearts
12 : 28. having heard them r. to- [gether

RE'BA. See HUR.

REBATEMENTS.

1 K. 6 : † 6. he made r. round about

REBEK'AH, REBEC'CA.

Ge. 22 : 23. And Bethuel begat R.
24 : 15. R. came with pitcher, 45.
29. R. had brother Laban, 28 : 5.
30. when Laban heard words of R.
51. R. is before thee, take her
53. brought jewels and gave to R.
58. called R. Wilt go with this man
59. sent away R. | 60. blessed R.
61. R. arose — servant took R.
64. R. lifted eyes and saw Isaac [20.
67. Isaac took R.; became wife, 25 :
Ge. 25 : 21. R. his wife conceived
28. but R. loved Jacob
26 : 7. lest men of place kill me for R.
8. Isaac was sporting with R. [R.
35. grief of mind unto Isaac and
27 : 5. R. heard when Isaac spake, 6.
11. Jac. said to R. Esau is a hairy
15. R. put goodly raim. upon Jac.
42. words of Esau told to R.
46. R. said, I am weary of life
29 : 12. told Rachel he was R.'s son
35 : 8. Deborah R.'s nurse died
49 : 31. they buried Isaac and R.
Ro. 9 : 10. but when R-a had conceived by Isaac, Ge. 22 : † 23.

REBEL. [Verb.]

Nu. 14 : 9. Only r. not against Lord
Jos. 1 : 18. Whoso. doth r. shall die
22 : 16. an altar that ye might r.
18. seeing that ye r. to day ag. L.
19. r. not ag. Lord, nor r. ag. us
29. God forbid we r. ag. L. [L.
1 S. 12 : 14. if ye obey and not r. ag.
15. if ye will not obey L. but r.
Ne. 2 : 19. will ye r. against king?
6 : 6. thou and Jews think to r.
Jb. 24 : 13. those that r. ag. the light
Ps. 78 : † 40. How oft did r. ag. him
Is. 1 : 20. If r. ye shall be devoured
Ho. 7 : 14. assemble for corn, and r.

REBELLED.

Ge. 14 : 4. in thirteenth year they r.
Nu. 20 : 24. ye r. at waters of Meribah, 27 : 14. De. 1 : 26, 43.-9 : 23.
1 K. 12 : 19. So Israel r. ag. the house of David, 2 Ch. 10 : 19.
2 K. 1 : 1. Moab r. ag. Israel, 3 : 5, 7.
18 : 7. Hez. r. ag. king of Assyria
24 : 1. Jehoiakim r. ag. Neb-r [3.
20. Zedekiah r., 2 Ch. 36 : 13. Je. 52 :
2 Ch. 13 : 6. Jerob. r. ag. his lord
Ne. 9 : 26. disobedient, r. ag. thee
Ps. 5 : 10. they have r. against thee
105 : 28. they r. not ag. his word
107 : 11. they r. ag. words of God
Is. 1 : 2. I nourished children they r.
63 : 10. r. and vexed Holy Spirit
La. 1 : 18 I have r. | 20. I have grievously r. [pardoned
3 : 42. we have r. thou hast not
Eze. 2 : 3. thee to a nation that r.
17 : 15. he r. in sending ambassa-
20 : 8. they r. ag. me, 13, 21. [dors
Da. 9 : 5. we have r. by departing fr
9. to G. mercy, tho. we r. [thee
Ho. 13 : 16. Samaria r. ag. her God

REBELLEST.

2 K. 18 : 20. Hezekiah on whom trust, that thou r.? Is. 36 : 5.

REBELLION. [r.

Nu. 17 : † 10. as a token ag. chil. of
De. 31 : 27. I know thy r. and stiff
Jos. 22 : 22. Isr. shall know; if in r.
1 S. 15 : 23. r. is as witchcraft
20 : † 30. Thou son of perverse r.
Ezr. 4 : 19. that r. hath been made
Ne. 9 : 17. in r. appointed a capt.
Jb. 34 : 37. addeth r. unto his sin
Pr. 17 : 11. evil man seeketh r.
Je. 28 : 16. bec. hast taught r., 29 : 32.
Eze. 2 : † 7. bear or forbear, they are

REBELLIOUS. [r.

De 9 : 7. ye have been r. ag. the Lord, 24.-31 : 27. [and r. son
21 : 18. If a man have a stubborn
20. shall say, This our son is r.
1 S. 20 : 30. Thou son of r. woman
Ezr. 4 : 12. building the r. city, 15.
Ps. 66 : 7. let not r. exalt thems.
68 : 6. the r. dwell in a dry land
18. hast received gifts for r. also
78 : 8. not be as fa-s, r. generation
Is. 1 : 23. Thy princes are r.
30 : 1. Woe to the r. children
9. this is a r. people
50 : 5. I was not r. [people
65 : 2. spread out my hands to a r.

Je. 4 : 17. she hath been r. ag. me
5 : 23. this people hath a r. heart
Eze. 2 : 3. I send thee to r. nation
5. they are a r. house, 6, 7.–3 : 9,
26, 27.–12 : 2, 3, 9, 25.
8. Be not r. like that r. house
12 : 2. dwellest in r. house [6.
17 : 12. Say to r. house, Know, 44:
24 : 3. utter parable unto r. house

REBELS. [r.

Nu 17 : 10. Aaron's rod a token ag.
20 : 10. Moses said, Hear ye r.
Je 50 : † 21. Go up ag. the land of r.
Eze. 2 : † 6. tho. r. and thorns be
20 : 38. I will purge fr. you the r.

REBUKE, REBUKES.

De. 28:20. L. shall send upon thee r.
2 K. 19 : 3. is a day of r., Is. 37 : 3.
Ps. 18 : 15. at thy r. at the blast
39 : 11. When with r-s dost correct
76 : 6. At thy r. horse into a sleep
80:16. perish at r. of thy counten.
104 : 7. At thy r. they fled, they
Pr. 13 : 1. a scorner heareth not r.
8. the poor heareth not r. [love
27:5. Open r. is better than secret
Ec. 7 : 5. better to hear r. of wise
Is. 25 : 8. r. of his peo. sh. he take
Eze. 5 : 15. judgments in furious r-s
25 : 17. vengeance with furious r-s
30 : 17. thousand flee at r. of one,
at r. of five shall ye flee
50 : 2. at my r. I dry up the sea
51 : 20. thy sons lie full of r. of G.
66 : 15. to render his r. with fire
Je. 15 : 15. for thy sake I suffered r.
Ho. 5 : 9. Ephr. desolate in day of r.
Ph. 2:15. without r. in perverse na-

REBUKE. [Verb.] [tion

Le. 19 : 17. in any wise r. neighbour
Ru. 2 : 16. that she glean, r. her not
1 Ch. 12 : 17. G. look thereon and r.
Ps. 6 : 1. O Lord r. me not, 38 : 1.
68 : 30. r. company of spearmen
Pr. 9 : 8. r. wise man, he will love
24 : 25. to them th. r. him delight
Is. 2 : 4. r. many nations, Mi. 4 : 3.
17 : 13. nations rush, God shall r.
54 : 9. I not be wroth nor r. thee
Zch. 3 : 2. L. said unto Satan, L. r.
thee, that chosen Jerus. r. thee
Mal. 3 : 11. I will r. the devourer
Mat. 16:22. Pe. began to r., Mk. 8:32.
Lu. 17 : 3. If bro. trespass, r. him
19 : 39. said, Master, r. disciples
1 Ti. 5 : 1. r. not elder, but entreat
20. Them that sin, r. bef. all, that
2 Ti. 4 : 2. r. with all longsuffering
Tit. 1:13. Whf. r. them sharply, 2:15.
Jude 9. Michael said, L. r. thee
Re. 3 : 19. As many as I love, I r.

REBUKED.

Ge. 31:42. God hath seen and r. thee
37 : 10. his father r. him, and said
Ne. 5 : 7. I r. nobles and rulers
Ps. 9 : 5. hast r. the heathen, hast
106:9. He r. the Red sea also, and
119 : 21. Thou hast r. the proud
Mat. 8 : 26. he r. the wind, Mk. 4 :
39. Lu. 8 : 24. [parted out
17 : 18. Jesus r. devil, and he de-
19 : 13. disciples r. them, Mk. 10 :
13. Lu. 18 : 15. [men
20 : 31. the multitude r. the blind
Mk. 1 : 25. he r. the devil, 9:25. Lu.
4 : 35.–9 : 42. [behind me
8 : 33. Jesus r. Peter, saying, Get
Lu. 4 : 39. he stood and r. fever
9:55. Jesus turned, r. Ja. and Jn.
18:39. that went bef. r. blind man
23 : 40. other thief answ-g r. him
He. 12 : 5. nor faint when art r.
2 Pe. 2 : 16. Balaam was r. for in-

REBUKER. [iquity

Ho. 5:2. tho. I have been a r. of all

REBUKETH.

Pr. 9 : 7. he that r. a wicked man
Pr. 28:23. He that r. sh. find favour
Am. 5 : 10. They hate him that r.
Na. 1 : 4. He r. sea, maketh it dry

REBUKING. [Noun, Part.]

2 S. 22 : 16. foundations discovered
at r. of Lord [speak
Lu. 4 : 41. he r. suffered th. not to

RECALL.

La. 3:21. This I r. to mind, thf. hope

RECEIPT.

Mat. 9 : 9. Matthew sitting at r. of
custom, Mk. 2 : 14. Lu. 5 : 27.

RECEIVE.

Ex. 29 : 25. shalt r. wave offering
Nu. 18:28. tithes ye r. of chil. of Isr.
De. 33 : 3. ev. one sh. r. thy words
1 S. 10 : 4. bread r. of their hands
2 S. 18 : 12. Tho. r. a thous. shekels
1 K. 5 : 9. shalt r. cedar and fir [G.
Jb. 2 : 10. sh. we r. good at hand of
27 : 13. they shall r. of Almighty
Ps. 6 : 9. Lord will r. my prayer
24 : 5. He shall r. blessing fr. Lord
49 : 15. God will redeem, sh. r. me
73 : 24. afterward r. me to glory
75 : 2. When I r. cong-n will judge
Pr. 2 : 1. son, if thou r. my words
10 : 8. wise in heart will r. com-ts
Is. 57 : 6. Sho. I r. comfort in these
Eze. 16:61. ashamed, when r. sisters
Da. 2 : 6. ye shall r. of me gifts
Ho. 10 : 6. Ephraim shall r. shame
Mi. 1 : 11. r. of you his standing
Zph. 3 : 7. thou wilt r. instruction
Mat. 10 : 41. shall r. a prophet's reward, r. a righte. man's reward
11 : 5. blind r. their sight, lame
14. if ye r. it, this is Elias which
18:5. whoso r. one such little child,
Mk. 9 : 37. Lu. 9 : 48. [10 : 30.
19 : 29. shall r. hundredfold, Mk.
20 : 7. whatso. is right, shall ye r.
21:22. ye ask, believing, ye shall r.
34. th. they might r. fruits of it
23 : 14. ye shall r. greater damnation, Mk. 12:40. Lu. 20:47. [8:13.
Mk. 4 : 16. r. word with gladn., Lu.
20. such as hear word and r.
10:51. L. that I r. sight, Lu. 18:41.
11 : 24. when pray, believe ye r.
12 : 2. might r. from husbandmen
Lu. 10 : 8. city ye enter, and they r.
16 : 4. may r. me into houses
9. r. you into everl-g habitations
23 : 41. we r. reward of our deeds
Jn. 5 : 43. if in own name, ye r.
44. How believe, which r. honour
7 : 23. If man on sab. r. circum-n
39. Spirit, wh. they that believe r.
14 : 3. I will come again, r. you
16:14. he sh. r. of mine, and shew
24. ask, ye shall r. that your joy
Ac. 1:8. ye sh. r. power aft. Holy Gh.
2 : 38. ye shall r. gift of Holy Gh.
3 : 21. Jes. whom heavens must r.
8 : 15. prayed, might r. Holy Gh.
19. I lay hands, may r. Holy Gh.
9 : 12. that he might r. his sight
17. that thou mightest r. sight
10 : 43. believeth, sh. r. remission
26 : 18. may r. forgiveness of sins
Ro. 5:17. wh. r. abundance of grace
13 : 2. that resist sh. r. damnation
16 : 2. That ye r. her in Lord, as
1 Co. 3 : 8. ev. man shall r. reward
14. If work abide, he r. reward
4:7. if thou didst r. it, why glory?
14 : 5. that church r. edifying
2 Co. 5 : 10. r. things done in body
6:17. touch not uncl. I will r. you
7 : 9. that ye r. damage in nothing
8 : 4. praying we would r. gift
11 : 4. or if ye r. another spirit ye
Ga. 3 : 14. might r. promise of Spirit
4 : 5. we might r. adoption of sons
Ep. 6 : 8. same shall he r. of Lord
Col. 3 : 24. shall r. reward of inheri.
Col. 3:25. he shall r. for wrong done
Phm. 15. shouldest r. him for ever
He. 7 : 5. who r. office of priesthood
8. here men that die r. tithes
9 : 15. called might r. promise, 10 :
11 : 8. sho. after r. for inheri. [36.
Ja. 1 : 7. not think he sh. r. any
12. he shall r. crown of life [tion
3 : 1. ye shall r. greater condemna-.
5 : 7. until he r. early, latter rain
1 Pe. 5 : 4. ye sh. r. crown of glory
2 Pe. 2:13. sh. r. reward of unright.
1 Jn. 3 : 22. whatso. we ask, we r.
5 : 9. If we r. witness of men, God
2 Jn. 8. that we r. a full reward
Re. 14 : 9. If any man r. his mark
17 : 12. r. power as kings one hour

RECEIVE. [Imperatively.]

Ge. 33 : 10. r. present at my hand
Jb. 22 : 22. r. law from his mouth
Pr. 4 : 10. O son, r. my sayings
8 : 10. r. my instruction, 19 : 20.
Je. 9 : 20. let your ear r. the word
Eze. 3 : 10. r. my words in heart
Ho. 14 : 2. say, r. us graciously
Mat. 19 : 12. able, let him r. it [13.
Lu. 18 : 42. saith, r. sight, Ac. 22 :
Jn. 20 : 22. saith, r. ye Holy Ghost
Ac. 7 : 59. Lord Jesus r. my spirit
Ro. 14 : 1. Him weak in faith, r. ye
15 : 7. r. one another as C. received
2 Co. 7 : 2. r. us, wronged no man
11 : 16. yet as a fool r. me, that
Ph. 2 : 29. r. him in L. with gladn.
Col. 4:10. Marcus, if he come, r. him
Phm. 12. r. him that is mine own
17. If count me a partner, r. him
Ja. 1 : 21. r. with meekness word

RECEIVE. [Infinitively.]

Ge. 4:11. earth opened to r. bro.'s bl.
38:20. to r. pledge fr. woman's ha.
Ex. 27 : 3. make pans to r. ashes
De. 9 : 9. gone up to r. tables
1 K. 8 : 64. altar too little to r. burnt
off-gs, 2 Ch. 7 : 7. [ments?
2 K. 5:26. time to r. money, to r. gar-
12 : 8. priest to r. no more money
Pr. 1 : 3. To r. instruction of wisd.
Je. 5 : 3. they refused to r. correc.
32 : 33. not hearkened to r. instruc.
Mal. 3 : 10. sh. not be room to r. it
Mat. 19 : 12. able to r. it, let him r.
Mk. 2 : 2. was no room to r. them
Lu. 6:34. of wh. hope to r. as much
19:12. nobleman went to r. kingd.
Ac. 3 : 5. expecting to r. something
16 : 21. customs not lawful to r.
18 : 27. exhorting discip. to r. him
20:35. more blessed to give than r.
3 Jn. 8. We ought to r. such
Re. 4 : 11. worthy, O L., to r. glory
5 : 12. Worthy is Lamb to r. power
13:16. causeth to r. a mark in hand

RECEIVE. [Negatively.]

Ex. 23 : † 1. shalt not r. false report
2 K. 5 : 16. Elisha said, I r. none
12 : 7. r. no more money of your
Jb. 2 : 10. sh. we r. good, not r. evil?
Je. 17 : 23. might not r. instruction
35:13. Will ye not yet r. instruction
Eze. 36 : 30. shall r. no more famine
Mat. 10:14. whoso. shall not r. you,
shake dust, Mk. 6 : 11. Lu. 9 : 5.
19 : 11. All men cannot r. saying
Mk. 10 : 15. Whoso. not r. kingdom
of God as child, Lu. 18 : 17.
Lu. 9 : 53. they did not r. him, bec.
10 : 10. r. you not, go into streets
18 : 30. Who shall not r. manifold
Jn. 3 : 11. ye r. not our witness
27. A man can r. nothing, except
5 : 34. I r. not testimony from man
41. I r. not honour from men
43. I in Fa.'s name, ye r. me not
14 : 17. Spirit, whom world can-t r.
Ac. 22 : 18. will not r. thy testimony
1 Co. 4 : 7. what thou didst not r.?

2 Co. 6 : 1. r. not grace of G. in vain
1 Ti. 5 : 19. Ag. elder r. not accusa-
Ja. 4 : 3. Ye ask and r. not, bec.⌊tion
2 Jn. 10. r. him not into your house
3 Jn. 10. nei. doth he r. brethren
Re. 18:4. that ye r. not of her plagues

RECEIVED.

Ge. 26 : 12. Isaac r. a hundredfold
Ex. 32 : 4. Aaron r. the earrings
36 : 3. they r. of Moses all offering
Nu. 12 : 14. aft. that let Miriam be r.
23 : 20. I have r. com-t to bless
34:14. two tribes r. inheritance, 15.
36 : 3. tribe whereunto are r., 4.
Jos. 9 : † 14. r. men by reason of
13 : 8. Gadites r. their inheritance
18 : 2. wh. had not r. inheritance
7. r. inheritance beyond Jordan
Ju. 13:23. not have r. burnt offering
1 S. 12 : 3. have I r. any bribe?
25 : 35. David r. of Abigail that
1 K. 10 : 28. merchants r. linen yarn
at price, 2 Ch. 1 : 16. ⌈37 : 14.
2 K. 19 : 14. Hezekiah r. letter, Is.
1 Ch. 12 : 18. Thine; David r. them
Es. 4 : 4. raiment, Mord. r. it not
Jb. 4 : 12. mine ear r. little thereof
Ps. 68 : 18. hast r. gifts for men
Pr. 24 : 32. I looked, r. instruction
Is. 40 : 2. she hath r. of L.'s hand
Je. 2 : 30. your chil. r. no correction
Eze. 18 : 17. hath not r. usury nor
Zph. 3 : 2. she r. not correction
Mat. 10 : 8. freely ye r. freely give
13 : 19. which r. seed by way side
20. r. into stony places | 22. r. am.
23. r. into good ground ⌊thorns
17 : 24. they that r. tribute money
20 : 9. they r. every man a penny,
11. had r. it they murmured ⌊10.
34. immed-ly their eyes r. sight
25 : 16. he that r. five talents, 20.
17. that r. two, 22. | 18. r. one, 24.
27. I sho. have r. mine with usury
Mk. 2 : † 14. where custom was r.
7 : 4. things which they r. to hold
10 : 52. he r. his sight, Lu. 18 : 43.
Ac. 9 : 18. ⌈r. it not
15 : 23. gave him wine with myrrh,
16 : 19. r. into heaven, Ac. 1 : 9.
Lu. 6 : 24. rich, ye r. your consola-
8 : 40. people gladly r. him ⌊tion
9 : 11. r. them and spake of kingdom
51. when time he should be r. up
10 : 38. Martha r. him into house
15 : 27. bec. he hath r. him safe
19 : 6. Zaccheus r. him joyfully
15. returned, having r. kingdom
Jn. 1 : 11. unto his own, own r. not
12. as many as r. him, gave he
16. have all we r. grace for grace
3 : 33. that hath r. testimony
4 : 45. was come Galileans r. him
6 : 21. willingly r. him into ship
9 : 11. I went washed, and r. sight
15. Phari. asked how he r. sight
18. not believed he had r. sight (2)
10 : 18. This com-t I r. of my Fa.
13:30. He, having r. sop, went out
17:8. given thy words, they r. th.
18:3. Judas having r. band of men
19:30. When Jesus had r. vinegar
Ac. 1 : 9. cloud r. him out of sight
2 : 33. having r. of Father promise
41. they th. r. word were baptized
3 : 7. feet, ankle bones r. strength
7 : 38. who r. the lively oracles to
† 45. our fa-s having r. possession
53. Who have r. law by angels
8 : 14. heard Samaria r. the word
17. laid hands, they r. Holy Gh.
9 : 19. r. meat he was strengthened
10 : 16. vessel was r. into heaven
47. which have r. Holy Ghost
11 : 1. heard Gentiles had r. word
15 : 4. they were r. of the church
16 : 24. Who having r. such charge
Ac. 17 : 7. Wh. Jason hath r.: these
11. Bereans r. word with readin.
19 : 2. Have ye r. the Holy Ghost?
20 : 24. ministry I have r. of L.
21 : 17. brethren r. us gladly
22 : 5. I r. letters unto brethren
26:10. r. authority fr. chief priests
28:2. barbarians kindled fire r. us
7. Publius r. us | 30. Paul r. all
21. we nei. r. letters out of Judea
Ro. 1 : 5. By whom we have r. grace
4 : 11. he r. sign of circumcision
5 : 11. by whom we r. atonement
8:15. ye have not r. spirit of bondage, have r. spirit of adoption
14 : 3. eateth, for God hath r. him
15 : 7. receive one ano., as Ch. r. us
1 Co. 2 : 12. we r. not spirit of world
4 : 7. why glory, as if not r. it?
11 : 23. I r. of Lord, that which
15 : 1. which ye r. | 3. which I r.
2 Co. 4:1. have r. mercy, we faint not
7 : 15. how with fear ye r. him
11 : 4. if spirit, wh. ye have not r.
24. five times r. I forty stripes
Ga. 1 : 9. ano. gospel that ye have r.
12. I r. it not of man, neither
3 : 2. r. ye Spirit by works of law?
4 : 14. r. me as an angel of God
Ph. 4 : 9. things r. and seen in me
18. † I have r. all, r. of Epaphro.
Col. 2 : 6. As ye have r. C., so walk
4 : 10. touching wh. ye r. com-ts
17. take heed to ministry thou r.
1 Th. 1 : 6. having r. word in afflic.
2:13. when ye r. word, r. it not as
4 : 1. as ye r. of us how to walk
2 Th. 2 : 10. r. not the love of truth
3 : 6. not aft. tradition he r. of us
1 Ti. 3 : 16. believed, r. into glory
4 : 3. meats God created to be r.
4. creature good, if r. with thank.
He. 2 : 2. transgr-n r. recompense
7 : 6. r. tithes of Ab. and blessed
11. under it people r. the law
10 : 26. if we sin after r. knowledge
11:11. Sarai r. strength to conceive
13. died, not having r. promises
17. th. r. promises off-d only son
19. whence he r. him in figure
31. Rahab r. spies, Ja. 2 : 25.
35. Women r. their dead raised
39. these r. not the promise, God
1 Pe. 1 : 18. r. by tradition from fa-s
4:10. As every one hath r. the gift
2 Pe. 1 : 17. he r. from God honour
1 Jn. 2 : 27. anointing ye have r.
2 Jn. 4. as we have r. command-t
Re. 2 : 27. even as I r. of my Father
3 : 3. Remember how thou hast r.
17 : 12. kings who r. no kingdom
19 : 20. had r. mark of beast
20:4. had not r. the mark, reigned

RECEIVEDST. ⌈things

Lu. 16 : 25. in lifetime r. thy good

RECEIVER. ⌈r.?

Is. 33 : 18. Where scribe? where is

RECEIVETH.

Ju. 19 : 18. no man r. me to house
Jb. 35 : 7. what r. he of thine hand?
Ps. 15 : † 3. not r. reproach ag. his
Pr. 21:11. wise instructed, r. knowl.
29 : 4. he th. r. gifts, overthroweth
Je. 7:28. nation th. r. not correction
Mal. 2 : 13. r. off-g with good will
Mat. 7:8. that asketh, r., Lu. 11:10.
10:40. He that r. you r. me, r. me
r. him sent me, Jn. 13 : 20.
41. He that r. a prophet, that r. a
13 : 20. heareth word, anon r. it
18 : 5. rec. one such child, r. me
Mk. 9 : 37. whoso receive me, r. not
me, but him sent me, Lu. 9:48.
Lu. 15 : 2. This man r. sinners
Jn. 3 : 32. no man r. his testimony
4 : 36. he that reapeth r. wages
12 : 48. he that r. not my words
1 Co. 2:14. natural man r. not things
9 : 24. run all, but one r. prize
He. 6:7. earth r. blessing from God
7 : 8. he r. tithes of wh. witnessed
9. Levi who r. tithes, paid tithes
12:6. scourgeth ev. son whom he r.
3 Jn. 9. but Diotrephes r. us not
Re. 2:17. knoweth, saving he th. r. it
14:11. whoso. r. mark of his name

RECEIVING.

2 K. 5 : 20. in not r. at his hands
Ac. 17 : 15. r. a com-nt unto Silas
Ro. 1 : 27. r. in thems. recompense
11 : 15. what shall r. of them be
Ph. 4 : 15. concerning giving and r.
He. 12 : 28. whf. we r. a kingdom
1 Pe. 1 : 9. r. the end of your faith

RE'CHAB, ITES.

2 S. 4 : 2. R. the son of Rimmon, 5.
6. R. and Baanah escaped
9. David answ'd R. as Lord liveth
2 K. 10 : 15. Jehonadab son of R.
23. son of R. went into ho. of Baal
1 Ch. 2 : 55. father of house of R.
Ne. 3 : 14. Malchiah son of R.
Je. 35:2. Go unto house of R-s, 3, 18.
5. I set bef. sons of R-s pots of
See JONADAB. ⌊wine

RE'CHAH.

1 Ch. 4 : 12. Tehinnah men of R.

RECKON.

Ge. 40 : † 13. Pharoah shall r., † 19.
Le. 25 : 50. r. with him bought him
27 : 18. priest sh. r. unto him, 23.
Nu. 4 : 32. by name r. instruments
Eze. 44 : 26. r. unto him 7 days
Mat. 18 : 24. when he began to r.
Ro. 6 : 11. r. yourselves dead to sin
8 : 18. I r. sufferings of this time
2 Co. 10 : † 2. r. of us as tho. we walk-

RECKONED. ⌊ed

Ge. 40 : † 20. he r. with the butler
Nu. 18 : 27. your heave offering r.
23:9. people not be r. am. nations
2 S. 4 : 2. Beeroth was r. to Benj.
2 K. 12 : 15. they r. not with men
1 Ch. 5 : 1. genealogy not to be r. by
7. genealogy of generations was r.
17. All these were r. by genealogies, 7 : 5, 7.-9 : 1, 22. 2 Ch. 31:
19. Ezr 2 : 62. | 8:3. Ne. 7:5, 64.
Ps. 40 : 5. thy thoughts can-t be r.
Is. 38 : 13. I r. till morning, that
Lu. 22 : 37. he was r. am. transg-rs
Ro. 4 : 4. reward is not r. of grace
9. faith was r. to Ab. for right-n.
10. How was it then r.?

RECKONETH.

Mat. 25:19. lord of those servants r.

RECKONING.

2 K. 22:7. was no r. made wi. them
1 Ch. 23:11. thf. they were in one r.

RECOMMENDED.

Ac. 14 : 26. whence they had been r.
15:40. Paul departed, being r. unto

RECOMPENSE, S.

De. 32 : 35. To me belongeth r.
Jb. 15 : 31. vanity shall be his r.
Pr. 12 : 14. r. of a man's hand sh. be
Is. 34:8. it is year of r. for controversy
35:4. God will come with a r.⌊of Zion
40 : † 10. r. for his works, 62 : † 11.
59 : 18. repay r. to his enemies, r.
†. acc. to their r-s he will repay
66 : 6. L. th. rendereth r. to enem.
Je. 51 : 6. will render unto her r.
56. L. God of r. shall surely requite
La. 3 : 64. Render unto them r. O L.
Ho. 9 : 7. days of r. are come, Isr.
Jo. 3 : 4. will ye render me a r.?
7. will return r. upon your head
Lu. 14 : 12. and a r. be made thee
Ro. 1 : 27. receiving r. of error
11 : 9. let their table be made a r.
2 Co. 6 : 13. Now for a r. in the same
He. 2 : 2. every transgression received just r. of reward

He. 10 : 35. your confidence which hath great r. of reward
11:26. had respect unto r. of reward
RECOMPENSE. [Verb.]
Nu. 5 : 7. he shall r. his trespass
8. if he have no kinsman to r.
Ru. 2 : 12. The Lord r. thy work
2 S. 19 : 36. why sho. king r. me?
Jb. 34 : 33. he r. it, whe. thou refuse
Pr. 20 : 22. Say not, I will r. evil
Is. 65 : 6. I will r. into bosom (2)
Je. 16 : 18 I will r. their iniquity
25:14. will r. acc. to deeds, Ho. 12:2.
50 : 29. r. her acc-g to her work
Eze. 7 : 3. I will r. upon thee, 8.
7 : 4. r. the ways, 9.-9 : 10.-11:21.-16:43. ⌈I will r.
17:19. mine oath and my covenant
23:49. they shall r. your lewdness
Jo. 3 : 4. if ye r. me, speedily will I
Lu. 14:14. blessed, they can-t r. thee
Ro. 12 : 17. r. no man evil for evil
2 Th. 1 : 6. to r. tribulation to them
He. 10 : 30. that hath said, I will r.
RECOMPENSED.
Nu. 5 : 8. let trespass be r. unto L.
2 S. 22 : 21. acc-g to cleanness hath r. me, 25. Ps. 18 : 20, 24.
Pr. 11 : 31. the righteous shall be r.
Je. 18:20. Shall evil be r. for good?
Eze. 22:31. their own way have I r.
Lu. 14 : 14. be r. at resurrection
Ro. 11 : 35. it shall be r. again
RECOMPENSEST, ETH.
Je. 32 : 18. r-t iniquity of fathers
Ps. 136 : † 8. happy he that r-h thee
RECOMPENSING.
2 Ch. 6 : 23. r. way upon own head
RECONCILE.
Le. 6 : 30. blood is brought to r.
1 S. 29 : 4. whw. should he r. hims.
Eze. 45 : 20. so shall ye r. the house
Ep. 2 : 16. might r. both unto God
Col. 1 : 20. to r. all things unto ⌊hims.
RECONCILED.
Mat. 5:24. first be r. to thy brother
Ro. 5 : 10. when enemies we were r.
1 Co. 7 : 11. let her be r. to husband
2 Co. 5 : 18. who hath r. us to hims.
20. in Christ's stead, be ye r.
Col. 1:21. were enemies, yet hath he ⌊r.
RECONCILIATION.
Le. 8 : 15. sanctified it to make a r.
2 Ch. 29:24. made r. with their blood
Eze. 45:15. one lamb to make r., 17.
Da. 9 : 24. to make r. for iniquity
Ro. 5 : † 11. by whom we received r.
2 Co. 5 : 18. given us ministry of r.
19. committed unto us word of r.
He. 2 : 17. to make r. for sins of ⌈r.
RECONCILING.
Le. 16 : 20. when he made an end of
Ro. 11 : 15. if casting away be r.
2 Co. 5 : 19. God was in Christ, r. ⌊world
RECORD, S.
Ezr. 4 : 15. search be made in r-s
6:2. therein was a r. written
Es. 6 : 1. he com-ded to bring r-s
Jb. 16 : 19. behold, my r. is on high
Jn. 1 : 19. this is the r. of John
32. John bare r. saying, I saw, 34
8 : 13. Thou bearest r. of thyself, thy r. is not true ⌈r. is true
14. Tho. I bear r. of myself, my
12 : 17. people with him, bare r.
19 : 35. th. saw bare r. his r. true
Ro. 10 : 2. I bear r. they have a zeal
2 Co. 1 : 23. I call God for a r. upon
8 : 3. to their power I bear r. ⌈sible
Ga. 4 : 15. I bear you r. if it possi-
Ph. 1 : 8. God is my r. how I long
Col. 4 : 13. I bear r. he hath a zeal
1 Jn. 5 : 7. are three that bear r. in
10. he believeth not r. God gave
11. this is r. God hath given us
3 Jn. 12. we bear r. our r. is true
Re. 1 : 2. who bare r. of word of G.

RECORD, ED. ⌈name
Ex. 20 : 24. places where I r. my
De. 30:19. I call heaven to r., 31:28.
1 Ch. 16 : 4. appointed Levites to r.
Ne. 12:22. Lev. were r-d chief of fa-s
Is. 8:2. took faithful witnesses to r.
Ac. 20:26. I take you to r. this day
RECORDER.
2 S. 8 : 16. Jehoshaphat was r., 20 : 24. 1 K. 4 : 3. 1 Ch. 18 : 15. ⌈22.
2 K. 18 : 18. Joah the r., Is. 36 : 3,
2 Ch. 34:8. Joah r. to repair ho. of G.
RECOUNT.
Na. 2 : 5. He shall r. his worthies
RECOVER.
Ju. 11 : 26. why did ye not r. them
1 S. 30 : 8. shalt without fail r. all
2 S. 8 : 3. r. his border at Euphrates
2 K. 1 : 2. inquire whether I shall r.
5 : 3. would r. him of his leprosy
6. sent Naaman, that thou r. him
7. doth send unto me to r. a man
11. strike his hand, and r. leper
8 : 8. Shall I r. of this disease? 9.
10. Elisha said, Thou mayest r.
14. He told me thou shouldest r.
2 Ch. 13 : 20. Nei. did Jereboam r.
14:13. th. they could not r. thems.
Ps. 39 : 13. spare me, that I may r.
Is. 11 : 11. to r. remnant of people
38 : 16. so wilt r. me make me live
21. for a plaster, and he shall r.
Ho. 2 : 9. I will r. wool and flax
Mk. 16 : 18. lay hands on sick, they
2 Ti. 2 : 26. r. thems. out of ⌊sh. r.
RECOVERED.
1 S. 30:18. Da. r. all Amal. took, 19.
22. not give aught of spoil we r.
2 K. 13 : 25. Joash r. cities of Israel
14 : 28. warred, and r. Damascus
16 : 6. Rezin k. of Syria r. Elath
20 : 7. laid it on the boil, and he r.
Is. 38 : 9. when Hez. was r., 39 : 1.
Je. 8 : 22. why is not my people r.?
41:16. Johanan took peo. he had r.
RECOVERING. ⌈blind
Lu. 4 : 18. to preach r. of sight to
RECTIFY.
Pr. 11:†5. right-n of perfect sh. r. way
RED.
Ge. 25 : 25. 1st came out r. all over
30. Feed me with that r. pottage
49:12. His eyes sh. be r. with wine
Ex. 35 : 23. found r. skins of rams
Nu. 19 : 2. bring thee a r. heifer
2 K. 3 : 22. Moabites saw water r.
Es. 1 : 6. on pavement of r., blue
Ps. 68 :†23. foot may be r. in blood
75 : 8. wine is r. full of mixture
Pr. 23:31. Look not on wine when r.
Is. 1 : 18. though your sins be r.
27:2. sing a vineyard of r. wine
63 : 2. wht. art thou r. in apparel?
Na. 2 : 3. shield of his mighty is r.
Zch. 1:8. I saw a man upon r. horse behind him were r. horses
6:2. In first chariot were r. horses
Mat. 16:2. fair weather, sky is r., 3.
Re. 6:4. went out ano. horse was r.
12:3. great r. dragon, seven heads
See Rams' SKINS.
RED sea.
Ex. 10 : 19. cast locusts into R. s.
13 : 18. God led them by the R. s.
15:4. captains are drowned in R. s.
22. Moses brought Israel fr. R. s.
23:31. will set thy bounds fr. R. s.
Nu. 14:25. got into wilderness by R. s., De. 2 : 1. Ju. 11 : 16. ⌈R. s.
21 : 4. journeyed from m-t Hor. by
14. said, What he did in R. s.
33:10. encamped by R. s., 11. ⌈R. s.
De. 1 : 1. Mo. spake unto Isr. over ag.
40. take your journey by R. s.
11 : 4. made R. s. overflow them
Jos. 2 : 10. how Lord dried up R. s.
4 : 23. as L. your God did to R. s.

Jos. 24 : 6. Eg-ns pursued unto R. s.
1 K. 9 : 26. Ezion-geber, on shore of
Ne. 9 : 9. heardest cry by R. s. ⌊R. s.
Ps. 106 : 7. provoked him at R. s.
9. He rebuked R. s., it was dried
22. done terrible things by R. s.
136:13. him who divided the R. s.
15. overthrew Pharaoh in the R. s.
Je. 49 : 21. noise was heard in R. s.
Ac. 7 : 36. shewed wonders in R. s.
He. 11 : 29. By faith passed thro. R. ⌊s.
REDDISH.
Le. 13 : 19. spot somewhat r., 24, 43.
42. a white r. sore, it is a leprosy
49. if plague be r. in garment or
14:37. if plague be with streaks, r.
REDEEM.
Ex. 6:6. I will r. you with stretched
13:13. firstling of ass shalt r., 34:20.
15. firstborn of chil. I r., 34 : 20.
Le. 25 : 25. if any of his kin to r. it
26. if he have none to r. it
29. dwellinghouse he may r. it
32. the cities may the Levites r.
† 33. if one of Levites r. them
48. sold, one of breth. may r. him
49. uncle, or any kin may r. him
27 : 13. if he will at all r. it, 27.
15. if he will r. house, 19, 20, 31.
Nu. 18 : 15. firstborn of man r.
16. from month old shalt thou r.
17. firstling of goat shalt not r.
Ru. 2 : † 20. man is one that hath right to r., 3 : † 9. ⌈I will r. it
4 : 4. if thou wilt r. it, r. it, if not
6. I can-t r. it for myself, r. thou
2 S. 7 : 23. what nation like Isr. wh. God went to r., 1 Ch. 17 : 21.
Ne. 5 : 5. nei. in our power to r. th.
Jb. 5 : 20. in famine he sh. r. thee
6 : 23. to r. me from the mighty
Ps. 25:22. r. Isr. O. G., out of troubles
26 : 11. r. me and be merciful
44 : 26. r. us for thy mercies' sake
49:7. None of them can r. his bro
15. G. will r. my soul from grave
69:18. Draw nigh unto my soul, r.
72 : 14. shall r. soul from deceit ⌊it
130 : 8. sh. r. Israel from all iniq-s
Is. 50:2. shortened th. it cannot r.?
Je. 15 : 21. I will r. thee out of hand
Ho. 13:14. I will r. them from death
Mi. 4 : 10. Lord sh. r. thee from Bab.
Ga. 4 : 5. To r. them. were und. law
Tit. 2 : 14. he might r. us fr. iniqui- ⌊ty
REDEEMED.
Ge. 48 : 16. The angel which r. me
Ex. 15 : 13. led peo. whom thou r.
21 : 8. if please not, let her be r.
Le. 19 : 20. with bondmaid not r.
25 : 30. if a house in city be not r.
31. houses of villages may be r.
48. bro. sold to stranger may be r.
54. if he be not r. then go out in
27 : 20. if sold field, it not be r.
27. unclean beast not r. be sold
28. no devoted thing sh. be r., 29.
33. tithe and change not be r.
Nu. 3 : 46. those to be r. are more than Levites, 48, 49, 51. ⌈old
18 : 16. that are to be r. fr. month
De. 7:8. hath L. r. you out of house of bondmen, 15 : 15.-24 : 18.
9:26. thy people thou hast r. thro.
13 : 5. Lord r. you out of bondage
21:8. Be merciful unto Isr. thou r.
2 S. 4 : 9. L. r. my soul, 1 K. 1 : 29.
1 Ch. 17 : 21. whom thou hast r. out of E., Ne. 1 : 10. Ps. 77 : 15.
Ne. 5 : 8. after our ability r. Jews
Ps. 31 : 5. thou hast r. me, O L. G
71:23. my soul which thou hast r.
74:2. Remember inheritance thou r.
106 : 10. he r. them from enemy
107 : 2. Let the r. of Lord say so, whom he hath r. ⌈enemies
136 : 24. And hath r. us from our

Is. 1 : 27. Zion be r. with judgment
29 : 22. saith L., who r. Abraham
35 : 9. But the r. shall walk there
43 : 1. Fear not, I have r. thee
44 : 22. return, for I have r. thee
23. the Lord hath r. Jacob, 48 :
20. Je. 31 : 11. [return
51:11. Thf. the r. of the Lord shall
52 : 3. ye sh. be r. without money
9. r. Jerusalem | 62:12. holy peo. r.
63 : 4. year of my r. is come
9. in his love and pity r. them
La. 3 : 58. L., thou hast r. my life
Ho. 7 : 13. tho. I r. them, yet they
Mi. 6 : 4. I r. thee out of the house
Zch. 10 : 8. I will hiss, I r. them
Lu. 1 : 68. visited and r. his people
24 : 21. he who should have r. Isr.
Ga. 3 : 13. Christ r. us from curse
1 Pe. 1 : 18. not r. with corruptible
Re. 5 : 9. thou hast r. us to God
14 : 3. but 144,000 which were r.
4. These were r. from among men

REDEEMEDST, ETH.

2 S. 7 : 23. which thou r-t fr. Egypt
Ps. 34 : 22. L. r-h souls of servants
103:4. Who r-h life fr. destruction

REDEEMER.

Ru. 4 : †14. not left thee with-t a r.
Jb. 19 : 25. I know that my R. liveth
Ps. 19:14. O L., my strength, my r.
78 : 35. rememb-d high God was R.
Pr. 23 : 11. their R. is mighty
Is. 41:14. thy R. the Holy One, 54: 5.
43 : 14. Thus saith Lord your R.
44 : 6. Thus saith the Lord, his R.
24. saith the Lord thy R., 48:17.-
49 : 7.-54 : 8. [his name
47 : 4. As for our R. L. of hosts is
49:26. I the Lord am thy R., 60:16.
59 : 20. R. shall come to Zion, unto
63:16. O L., art our Father, our R.
Je. 50 : 34. their R. is strong, L. of

REDEEMING. [hosts

Ru. 4: 7. manner in Israel cone-g r.
Ep. 5:16. r. the time, bec., Col. 4: 5.

REDEMPTION. [people

Ex. 8 :† 23. I will put a r. betw. my
Le. 25 : 24. ye sh. grant r. for land
†31. houses of villages r. belongeth
51. he shall give price of r., 52.
Nu. 3 : 49. Moses took r. money
Ps. 49 : 8. r. of their soul precious
111 : 9. He sent r. unto his people
130 : 7. with Lord is plenteous r.
Je. 32 : 7. the right of r. is thine, 8.
Lu. 2 : 38. looked for r. in Jerus.
21 : 28. look up, for your r. nigh
Ro. 3 : 24. justified thro. r. in Ch.
8 : 23. for adoption, r. of our body
1 Co. 1:30. Christ is made unto us r.
Ep. 1 : 7. In wh. have r., Col. 1 : 14.
14. until r. of purchased poss-n
4 : 30. are sealed unto day of r.
He. 9 : 12. obtained etern. r. for us
15. for r. of the transgressions

REDNESS. [eyes?

Pr. 23 : 29. woe? who hath r. of

REDOUND. [G.

2 Co. 4:15. grace might r. to glory of

REED.

1 K. 14:15. Lord shall smite Isr. as r.
2 K. 18 : 21. trustest upon staff of
bruised r., Is. 36:6.
Jb. 40 : 21. He lieth in covert of r.
Is. 42 : 3. A bruised r., Mat. 12 : 20.
Eze. 29 : 6. been staff of r. to Israel
40 : 3. a man with measuring r., 5,
6, 7, 8.-41 : 8.
42 : 16. He measured east side with
measuring r., 17, 18, 19.
Mat. 11 : 7. what to see? r.? Lu. 7 :
27 : 29. put a r. in right hand [24.
30. smote him with r., Mk. 15 : 19.
48. put sponge on a r., Mk. 15:36.
Re. 11 : 1. given me a r. like a rod
21 : 15. a golden r. to measure city

Re. 21 : 16. measured with r. 12,000

REEDS.

Ps. 68 . † 30. Rebuke beasts of the r.
Is. 19 : 6. r. flags shall wither, 7.
35 : 7. in habita. of dragons be r.
Je. 51 : 32. the r. they have burnt
Eze. 42 : 16. measured east side five
hundred r., 17, 18, 19, 20.
45 : 1. shall be length of 25,000 r.

REEL. [ger

Ps. 107: 27. They r. to and fro, stag-
Is. 24 : 20. earth shall r. to and fro

REELA'IAH. [R.

Ezr. 2 : 2. Which came with Zerub.

REFINE. [refined

Zch. 13 : 9. I will r. them as silver is

REFINED.

2 S. 22:†31. word of the Lord is r.,
Ps. 18:†30.-119:†140. [weight
1 Ch. 28 : 18. for altar r. gold by
29 : 4. 7,000 talents of r. silver
Is. 25 : 6. wines on the lees well r.
48 : 10. I have r. thee, not with silv.
Zch. 13 : 9. refine them, as silver is

REFINER. [r.

Mal. 3 : 2. he is like a r.'s fire, and
3. he shall sit as a r. and purifier

REFORMATION.

He. 9 : 10. on them until time of r.

REFORMED.

Le. 26 : 23. if ye will not be r. by

REFRAIN. [these

Ge. 45 : 1. Joseph could not r. hims.
Jb. 4 : † 2. who can r. from words?
7 : 11. Thf. I will not r. my mouth
Pr. 1 : 15. son, r. thy foot from path
Ec. 3 : 5. time to r. from embracing
Is. 48 : 9. for my praise I will r.
64 : 12. Wilt thou r. thyself, O L.?
Je. 31 : 16. r. voice from weeping
Ac. 5 : 38. I say, r. from these men
1 Pe. 3 : 10. let him r. tongue fr. evil

REFRAINED.

Ge. 43 : 31. Joseph r. hims. and said
Es. 5 : 10. Haman r. himself
Jb. 29 : 9. princes r. talking, laid ha.
Ps. 40 : 9. I have not r. my lips
119 : 101. I have r. feet from evil
Is. 42 : 14. I have been still and r.
Je. 14 : 10. have not r. their feet

REFRAINETH.

Pr. 10 : 19. he that r. his lips is wise

REFRESH.

1 K. 13 : 7. Come with me r. thyself
Ac. 27 : 3. suffered Paul to r. hims.
Phm. 20. brother, r. my bowels in

REFRESHED. [L.

Ex. 23 : 12. that stranger may be r.
31 : 17. seventh day rested was r.
1 S. 16 : 23. Da. played, Saul was r.
2 S. 16 : 14. David and peo. r. thems.
Jb. 32 : 20. I will speak that I be r.
Ro. 15 : 32. I may with you be r.
1 Co. 16 : 18. they r. my spirit and
2 Co. 7 : 13. Titus, his spirit was r.
2 Ti. 1 : 16. Onesiphorus often r. me
Phm. 7. bowels of saints are r. by

REFRESHETH. [thee

Pr. 25 : 13. r. soul of his masters

REFRESHING.

Is. 28 : 12. is r. yet they not hear
Ac. 3: 19. when times of r. come fr. L

REFUGE.

De. 33 : 27. eternal God is thy r.
Jos. 20: 3. sh. be your r. fr. avenger
2 S. 22 : 3. he my high tower my r.
Ps. 9 : 9. L. will be a r. for oppressed,
a r. in times of trouble
14 : 6. because the Lord is his r.
46 : 1. God is our r., 7, 11.
48 : 3. G. known for r. [r., 61 : † 4.
57: 1. shadow of thy wings make my
59:16. thou hast been my r. in day
of trouble [r. for us
62 : 7. my r. is in God | 8. God is a
71: 7. thou art my strong r., 142: 5.
91 : 2. he is my r., 9.

Ps. 94: 22. God is rock of my r. [goats
104: 18. The high hills a r. for wild
142: 4. r. failed me | 5. Thou my r.
Pr. 14 : 26. his children a place of r.
Is. 4 : 6. tabernacle for place of r.
25 : 4. to needy a r. from storm
28 : 15. we have made lies our r.
17. hail sweep away r. of lies
Je. 16 : 19. O L., my r. in affliction
He. 6 : 18. who have fled for r. to

REFUGE with city, cities.

Nu. 35: 6. sh. be six c-s for r., 13, 15.
11. appoint c-s of r., 14. Jos. 20: 2.
12. they sh. be unto you c-s for r.
25. shall restore him to c. of r.
26. without border of c. of r., 27.
28. sho. have remained in c. of r.
32. him that is fled to c. of r.
Jos. 21: 13. Hebron c. of r., 1 Ch. 6: 57.
21. Shechem c. of r. | 27. Golan
32. Hedesh c. of r. | 38. Ramoth

REFUSE. [Adj.]

1 S. 15 : 9. every thing that was r.
Je. 6 : †30. r. silver sh. men call th.
La. 3 : 45. thou hast made as r.
Am. 8 : 6. we may sell r. of wheat

REFUSE. [Verb.]

Ex. 4 : 23. if thou r. to let them go,
8 : 2.-9 : 2.-10 : 4. [thyself?
10 : 3. How long wilt r. to humble
16 : 28. r. ye to keep my com-ts
22 : 17. If her father r. to give her
Jb. 34 : 33. whe. thou r. or choose
Pr. 8:33. Hear instruction, r. it not
21 : 7. bec. they r. to do judgment
25. slothful, his hands r. to labour
Is. 1 : 20. if ye r. shall be devoured
7 : 15. he may know to r. evil, 16.
Je. 8 : 5. peo. of Jerus. r. to return
9 : 6. they r. to know me saith L.
13 : 10. This evil people r. to hear
25 : 28. if they r. to take the cup
38 : 21. if thou r. to go forth
Ac. 25 : 11. if offender, I r. not to die
1 Ti. 4 : 7. r. old wives' fables
5 : 11. but the younger widows r.
He. 12 : 25. r. not him th. speaketh

REFUSED.

Ge. 37:35. Jacob r. to be comforted
39 : 8. said, Lie with me. Joseph r.
48:19. Jacob r. to remove his hand
Nu. 20 : 21. Edom r. Israel passage
1 S. 8 : 19. people r. to obey Sam.
16:7 look not on him I have r. him
28 : 23. Saul r., I will not eat
2 S. 2 : 23. Asahel r. to turn aside
13 : 9. she poured, Amnon r. to eat
1 K. 20 : 35. man r. to smite him
21 : 15. vineyard he r. to give thee
2 K. 5 : 16. Naaman urged, but he r.
Ne. 9 : 17. our fathers r. to obey
Es. 1 : 12. queen Vashti r. to come
Jb. 6 : 7. things my soul r. to touch
Ps. 77 : 2. soul r. to be comforted
78 : 10. they r. to walk in his law
67. he r. tabernacle of Joseph
118 : 22. stone which builders r.
Pr. 1 : 24. I have called and ye r.
Is. 54 : 6. when wast r. saith God
Je. 5 : 3. they r. to receive correction, they r. to return [words
11 : 10. their fathers r. to hear my
31 : 15. Rachel r. to be comforted
50 : 33. all that took r. to let th. go
Eze. 5 : 6. they r. my judgments
Ho. 11 : 5. k., bec. they r. to return
Zch. 7 : 11. but they r. to hearken
Ac. 7 : 35. This Moses whom they r.
1 Ti. 4 : 4. and nothing to be r. if
He. 11 : 24. Moses r. to be called son
12 : 25. who r. him that spake on

REFUSEDST. [earth

Je. 3 : 3. thou r. to be ashamed

REFUSETH.

Ex. 7 : 14. Pha. r. to let people go
Nu. 22 : 13. L. r. to give me leave
14. Balaam r. to come with us

De. 25 : 7. brother r. to raise name
Pr. 10 : 17. he th. r. reproof, erreth
13 : 18. shame to him r. instruction
15:32. he that r. instruc. despiseth
Is. 8 : 6. people r. waters of Shiloah
Je. 15:18. my wound r. to be healed

REGARD. [Noun.]

Ec. 8 : 2. in r. of the oath of God
Da. 3 : † 13. have set no r. on thee
Ac. 8 : 11. to him they had r. bec.

REGARD. [Verb.]

Ge. 45:20. r. not your stuff, for Egypt
Ex. 5 : 9. let th. not r. vain words
Le. 19:31. r. not them that have familiar spirits ⌈aged
De. 28 : 50. shall not r. person of
1 S. 4 : 20. ans-d not, nei. did she r.
25:25. Let not my lord r. this man
2 S. 13 : 20. r. not this, he thy brot.
2 K. 3 : 14. that I r. Jehoshaphat
Jb. 3 : 4. that day, let not G. r. it
35 : 13. nei. will the Almighty r. it
36 : 21. Take heed, r. not iniquity
Ps. 28 : 5. they r. not works of L.
31 : 6. hated them r. lying vanities
66:18. If I r. iniquity in my heart
94 : 7. nei. shall God of Jacob r. it
102 : 17. will r. prayer of destitute
Pr. 5 : 2. thou mayest r. discretion
6 : 35. He will not r. any ransom
Is. 5 : 12. they r. not work of L.
13 : 17. Medes who will not r. silv.
18 : † 4. I will r. my set dwelling
La. 4 : 16. L. will no more r. them
Da. 11 : 37. Nei. r. God, nor r. any
Am. 5:22. nei. I r. peace off-gs ⌊god
Ha. 1 : 5. r., wonder marvellously
Mal. 1 : 9. will he r. your persons?
Lu. 18 : 4. I fear not G., nor r. man
Ro. 14 : 6. to Lord he doth not r. it

REGARDED.

Ex. 9 : 21. he r. not word of Lord
1 K. 18 : 29. nei. voice, nor any th. r.
1 Ch. 17 : 17. hast r. me as of high
Ps. 106 : 44. he r. their affliction
Pr. 1 : 24. I stretched out my hand, and no man r. ⌈not r. thee
Da. 3 : 12. these men, O king, have
Lu. 1 : 48. hath r. the low estate of his handmaid ⌈neither r. man
18 : 2. the judge feared not God,
He. 8 : 9. I r. them not, saith Lord

REGARDERS.

Ju. 9 : † 37. plain of the r. of times

REGARDEST.

2 S. 19 : 6 thou r. princes nor serv-s
Jb. 30 : 20. thou r. me not
Mat. 22:16. r. not the person of men, ⌊Mk. 12:14.

REGARDETH.

De. 10 : 17. mighty, r. not persons
Jb. 34:19. nor r. rich more than po.
39 : 7. neither r. crying of driver
Pr. 12 : 10. righteous r. life of beast
13 : 18. r. reproof sh. be honoured
15:5. he that r. reproof is prudent
29 : 7. wicked r. not cause of poor
Ec. 5 : 8. he higher than highest r.
11 : 4. r. clouds shall not reap
Is. 33:8. he despised cities, r. no man
Da. 6 : 13. Daniel r. not thee, O king
Mal. 2 : 13. he r. not the offering
Ro. 14 : 6. He that r. day, r. it unto ⌊L.

REGARDING.

Jb. 4 : 20. perish without any r. it
Ph. 2 : 30. not r. his life to supply

RE'GEM. See JAHDAI.

RE'GEM-ME'LECH.

Zch. 7 : 2. they sent Sherezer and R.

REGENERATION. ⌈r.

Mat. 19:28. which followed me in the
Tit. 3 : 5. saved us by washing of r.

REGION.

De. 3 : 4. r. of Argob kingd. of Og, 13.
1 K. 4 : 11. The son of Abinadab in all the r. of Dor
13. to him pertained r. of Argob
24. Sol. had dominion over all r.

Jo. 25 : † 22. king of r. by sea side
Mat. 3 : 5. Then went to him all r.
4:16. them which sat in r. of death
Mk. 1 : 28. his fame spread thro. r. round Galilee, Lu. 4 : 14.-7 : 17.
6 : 55. ran through that whole r.
Lu. 3 : 1. of the r. of Trachonitis
Ac. 8 : 1. scattered thro. r-s of Judea
13:49. word of L. published thro. r.
14 : 6. they fled unto r. that lieth
16 : 6. had gone thro. r. of Galatia
2 Co. 10:16. To preach in r-s beyond
11 : 10. stop me in r-s of Achaia
Ga. 1 : 21. I came into r-s of Syria

REGISTER. ⌈64.

Ezr. 2 : 62. These sought r., Ne. 7 :
Ne. 7 : 5. I found a r. of genealogy

REHABI'AH. ⌈25.

1 Ch. 23 : 17. sons of Eliezer, R., 26:
24:21. Conc. R.; sons of R. Isshiah

REHEARSE, ED.

Ex. 17 : 14. r. it in ears of Joshua
Ju. 5 : 11. r. righteous acts of Lord
1 S. 8 : 21. he r-d in ears of Lord
17 : 31. r-d David's words bef. Saul
Ac. 11 : 4. Peter r-d the matter from
14 : 27. they r-d all God had done

RE'HOB. [Person.]

2 S. 8 : 3. son of R. king of Zobah,
Ne. 10 : 11. that sealed were, R. ⌊12.

RE'HOB. [Place.]

Nu. 13:21. fr. wildern. of Zin unto R.
Jos. 19:28. border goeth out to R., 30.
21 : 31. R. wi. suburbs, 1 Ch. 6 : 75.
Ju. 1 : 31. Nei. Asher drive inhab-s of R. ⌈thems.
2 S. 10 : 8. Syrians of R. were by

REHOBO'AM=ROBO'AM.

1 K. 11 : 43. R. the son of Solomon reigned, 14:21. 2 Ch. 9:31.-12:13.
12:1. R. went to Shechem, 2 Ch. 10:1.
3. Isr. spake unto R., Thy fa. made
6. R. consulted with the old men, 2 Ch. 10 : 6. ⌈R., 2 Ch. 10:3, 12.
12. Jeroboam and people came to
17. R. reigned over them, 2 Ch. 10 : 17. ⌈10 : 18.
18. king R. sent Adoram (2) 2 Ch.
21. kingdom again to R., 2 Ch. 11: 1.
27. hearts shall turn again unto R.
14 : 25. fifth year of k. R., 2 Ch. 12: 2.
29. rest of acts of R., 2 Ch. 12 : 15.
30. war betw. R. and Jerob, 15:6.
31. R. slept with fa-s, 2 Ch. 12 : 16.
1 Ch. 3 : 10. R. was Solomon's son
2 Ch. 10:13. R. forsook counsel of old
11 : 3. speak unto R. son of Sol.
5. R. dwelt in Jerusalem
17. they made R. strong three y-rs
21. R. loved Maachah dau. of Abs.
22. R. made Abijah the chief
12:1. when R. established kingdom
5. Then came Shemaiah to R.
13 : 7. R. young tenderhearted (2)
Mat. 1 : 7. Solomon begat Ro-m (2)

REHO'BOTH. ⌈R.

Ge. 10:11. Asshur, builded Nineveh
26 : 22. Isaac called the well R.
36:37. Saul of R. reigned, 1 Ch. 1:48.

RE'HUM. ⌈12 : 3.

Ezr. 2 : 2. R. came with Zerub., Ne.
4 : 8. R. chancellor wrote ag., 9.
17. king sent an answer unto R.
23. when letter was read bef. R.
Ne. 3 : 17. repaired R. son of Bani
10 : 25. R. of chief of people sealed

RE'I. ⌈ijah

1 K. 1 : 8. Shimei, R. not with Adon-

REIGN. [Noun.]

1 Ch. 4 : 31. their cities to r. of Da.
29:30. David's acts with r. written
2 Ch. 36:20. r. of kingdom of Persia
Ezr. 4 : 5. until r. of Darius
6. in the beginning of his r., Je. 26 : 1.-28 : 1.-49 : 34.
7 : 1. r. of Artaxerxes, 8 : 1. ⌈Dari.
Ne. 12 : 22. priests recorded to r. of
Da. 6:28. Dan. prospered in r. of Da-
See YEAR with numerals. ⌊rius

REIGN. [Verb.] ⌈us?

Ge. 37 : 8. said, Shalt thou r. over
Ex. 15 : 18. Lord shall r. for ever, Ps. 146 : 10. ⌈over you
Le. 26 : 17. that hate you shall r.
De. 15 : 6. shalt r. over many nations, they shall not r. over thee
Ju. 9:2. that 70 r. over you, or that one r. over you ⌈10, 12, 14.
8. the trees said, r. thou over us,
1 S. 8:7. that I sho. not r. over th.
9. manner of king that sh. r., 11.
9:17. L. said, this sh. r. over peo.
11:12. said, Shall Saul r. over us?
12:12. Nay, a king shall r. over us
2 S. 3 : 21. r. over all th. thy heart
1 K. 1 : † 5. Adonijah said, I will r.
11. Hast heard Adonijah doth r.
13. Sol. shall r. after me, 17, 30.
24. hast said, Adonijah shall r.
2 : 15. Isr. set faces that I sho. r.
11:37. will take thee, thou shalt r.
16 : 15. Zimri did r. seven days in
2 K. 11 : 3. Athaliah did r. over
15 : 8. did Zachariah r. over Isr.
23 : 33. that Hamath might not r.
2 Ch. 1:8. made me to r. in his stead
23 : 3. he said, king's son shall r.
Jb. 34 : 30. that the hypocrite r. not
Pr. 8 : 15. By me kings r., princes
Ec. 4:14. out of prison cometh to r.
Is. 24 : 23. when L. shall r. in Zion
32 : 1. a king shall r. in righte-n.
Je. 22:15. shalt r. bec. thou closest
23 : 5. a king shall r. prosper and
33:21. that Da. not have son to r.
Mi. 4 : 7. L. shall r. over th. in Zion
Mat. 2 : 22. heard Archelaus did r.
Lu. 1:33. he shall r. over Jacob ⌈us
19:14. will not have this man r. ov.
27. enemies would not I should r.
Ro. 5 : 17. shall r. in life by Jesus Christ ⌈by J. C.
21. even so might grace r. to life
6 : 12. Let not sin r. in your bodies
15 : 12. shall rise to r. over Gent.
1 Co. 4 : 8. would to God ye did r. that we might r. ⌈all enemies
15 : 25. For he must r. till he put
2 Ti. 2 : 12. If we suffer, we shall r.
Re. 5 : 10. we also sh. r. on earth
11 : 15. he shall r. for ever and ev.
20 : 6. shall r. with him 1,000 y-rs
22:5. they shall r. for ever and ev.

Began to REIGN.

2 S. 2 : 10. Ish-bosheth b. t. r.
5 : 4. David 30 y-rs old b. t. r. ⌈13.
1 K. 14:21. Rehob. b. t. r., 2 Ch. 12:
15:25. Nadab b. t. r. | 33. Baasha
16 : 8. Elah b. t. r. | 11. Zimri
23. Omri b. t. r. | 29. Ahab
22 : 41. Jehoshaphat b. t. r., 42. 2 Ch. 20 : 31. ⌈9 : 29. 2 Ch. 22 : 2.
51. Ahaziah b. t. r., 2 K. 8 : 26.-
2 K. 3 : 1. Jehoram b. t. r., 8 : 16, 17. 2 Ch. 21 : 5, 20.
11 : 21. Jehoash b. t. r., 12 : 1.-13: 10. 2 Ch. 24 : 1. ⌈oboam
13:1. Jehoahaz b. t. r. | 14:23. Jer-
14:2. Amaziah b. t. r., 2 Ch. 25:1.
15 : 1. Azariah b. t. r., 2. 2 Ch. 26:3.
13. Shallum b. t. r.
17. Menahem b. t. r. ⌈b. t. r.
23. Pekahiah b. t. r. | 27. Pekah
32. Jotham b. t. r., 33. 2 Ch. 27:1, 8.
16 : 1. Ahaz b. t. r., 2. 2 Ch. 28:1.
17:1. Hoshea b. t. r.
18:1. Hezekiah b. t. r., 2 Ch. 29:1.
21:1. Manasseh b. t. r., 2 Ch. 33:1.
19. Amon b. t. r., 2 Ch. 33 : 21.
22 : 1. Josiah b. t. r., 2 Ch. 34 : 1.
23 : 31. Jehoahaz b. t. r., 13 : 1. 2 Ch. 36 : 2. ⌈5.
36. Jehoiakim b. t. r., 2 Ch. 36:
24 : 8. Jehoi-n b. t. r., 2 Ch. 36 : 9.

2 K. 24 : 18. Zedekiah b. t. r., 2 Ch.
36 : 11. Je. 52 : 1.
25 : 27. Evil-merodach b. t. r.
2 Ch. 13 : 1. Abijah b. t. r.

REIGNED.

Ge. 36 : 31. kings that r. in Edom
before any king r. over Israel,
32, 33. 1 Ch. 1 : 43, 44, 45.
Jos. 13 : 10. which r. in Heshbon, 21.
12. Og in Bashan which r., 12 : 5.
Ju. 4 : 2. Jabin that r. in Hazor
9 : 22. Abimelech had r. 3 years
1 S. 13 : 1. Saul r. one year, and (2)
2 S. 2 : 10. Ish-bosheth r. 2 years
5 : 4. David r. forty years over Judah
5. David r. seven years in Hebron,
thirty three in Jerusalem, 1 K.
2 : 11. 1 Ch. 3 : 4.-29 : 27.
8 : 15. David r. over Israel, 1 Ch.
18 : 14.-29 : 26. [1 Ch. 19 : 1.
10 : 1. Hanun his son r. in his stead,
16 : 8. Saul, in whose stead thou r.
1 K. 4 : 21. Solomon r. over all kingdoms, 11 : 42. 1 Ch. 29 : 28. 2 Ch.
1 : 13.-9 : 26, 30. [over Syria
11 : 24. Rezon r. in Damas. | 25. r.
43. Rehoboam r., 12 : 17.-14 : 21.
2 Ch. 9 : 31.-10 : 17.-12 : 13. [r., 20.
14 : 19. Jerob. how he warred and
31. Abijam his son r., 15 : 1, 2. 2
Ch. 12 : 16.-13 : 2. [Ch. 14 : 1.
15 : 8. Asa r. in his stead, 9, 10. 2
24. Jehoshaphat his son r., 2 Ch.
17 : 1.-20 : 31. [r., 29.
25. Nadab r., 14 : 20. | 28. Baasha
16 : 6. Elah r. | 10. Zimri r. [r.
22. Omri r., 23. | 28. Ahab his son
22 : 40. Ahaziah, Ahab's son, r., 51.
2 K. 8 : 24, 26. 2 Ch. 22 : 1, 2. [31.
42. Jehosh-t r. 25 years, 2 Ch. 20 :
50. Jehoram r., 2 K. 1 : 17.-8 : 1.-
8 : †16, 17. 2 Ch. 21 : 1, 5, 20. [r.
2 K. 8 : 27. eldest son that sho. have
8 : 15. Hazael r. | 10 : 35. Jehoahaz
36. Jehu r. | 12 : 1. Jehoash r.
12 : 21. Amaziah r., 14 : 1, 2. 2 Ch.
24 : 27.-25 : 1. [Benhadad
13 : 9. Joash r., 2 Ch. 21 : 1. | 24.
14 : 16. Jerob. r., 23. | 29. Zecha-
15 : 2. Azariah r., 2 Ch. 26 : 3. [riah
7. and Jotham r., 33. 2 Ch. 26 : 23.
-27 : 1, 8. [r., 17.
10. Shallum r., 13. | 14. Menahem
22. Pekahiah his son r., 23.
25. Pekah r., 27. [2 Ch. 28 : 1.
30. Hoshea r. | 38. Ahaz r., 16 : 2.
16 : 20. Hezekiah r., 18 : 2. 2 Ch. 28 :
27.-29 : 1. [Is. 37 : 38.
19 : 37. Esar-haddon r. in his stead,
20 : 21. Manasseh r., 21 : 1. 2 Ch. 32 :
33.-33 : 1. [33 : 20, 21.
21 : 18. Amon r. in stead, 19. 2 Ch.
26. Josiah r., 22 : 1. 2 Ch. 34 : 1.
23 : 31. Jehoahaz r., 2 Ch. 36 : 2.
36. Jehoiakim r., 2 Ch. 36 : 5.
24 : 6. Jehoiachin his son r., 8. 2
Ch. 36 : 8, 9. [37 : 1.-52 : 1.
18. Zedekiah r., 2 Ch. 36 : 11. Je.
2 Ch. 22 : 12. Athaliah r. over land
Es. 1 : 1. Ahasuerus r. from India
Je. 22 : 11. Shallum r. inst. of Josiah
52 : †1. Zed. 21 y-rs old when he r.
Ro. 5 : 14. death r. fr. Adam to Moses
17. by one man's offence death r.
21. as sin hath r. unto death so
might grace r. [out us
1 Co. 4 : 8. ye have r. as kings with-
Re. 11 : 17. hast taken power, and r.
20 : 4. r. with Christ a thousand

REIGNEST. [years

1 Ch. 29 : 12. thou r. over all, and in

REIGNETH. [you

1 S. 12 : 14. ye and king that r. ov.
2 S. 15 : 10. Absalom r. in Hebron
1 K. 1 : 18. Adonijah r.
2 K. 9 : †13. Jehu r. [-97 : 1.-99 : 1.
1 Ch. 16 : 31. The Lord r., Ps. 96 : 10.
Ps. 47 : 8. God r. over the heathen
93 : 1. L. r. is clothed with majesty
Pr. 30 : 22. a servant when he r.
Is. 52 : 7. saith unto Zion, Thy G. r.
Re. 17 : 18. r. over kings of earth
19 : 6. The Lord God omnipotent r.

REIGNING.

1 S. 16 : 1. I rejected him fr. r. ov. Isr.

REINS. [4.

Le. 15 : † 2. a running of the r., 22 : †
Jb. 16 : 13. he cleaveth my r. asun.
19 : 27. tho. my r. be consumed
Ps. 7 : 9. God trieth the heart and r.
16 : 7. my r. instruct me in night
26 : 2. Examine me, O L. try my r.
73 : 21. thus I was pricked in my r.
139 : 13. thou hast possessed my r.
Pr. 23 : 16. my r. shall rejoice when
Is. 11 : 5. faithfulness girdle of his r.
Je. 11 : 20. O Lord, th. triest the r.
12 : 2. thou art far from their r. [r.
17 : 10. I try the r. | 20 : 12. seest the
La. 3 : 13. his arrows to enter my r.
Re. 2 : 23. I am he who searcheth the

REJECT. [r.

La. 5 : † 22. wilt thou utterly r. us
Ho. 4 : 6. I will r. thee, be no priest
Mk. 6 : 26. oath's sake wo. not r. her
7 : 9. full well ye r. com-t of God
Tit. 3 : 10. after second admonition r.

REJECTED. [r. me

1 S. 8 : 7. they have not r. thee, but
10 : 19. ye have this day r. your G.
15 : 23. hast r. word of L. he hath
r. thee from being king, 26.
16 : 1. I have r. him fr. being king
2 K. 17 : 15. they r. his statutes and
20. Lord r. all the seed of Israel
Is. 53 : 3. He is despised and r. of men
Je. 2 : 37. L. hath r. thy confidence
6 : 19. r. my law | 30. L. r. them
7 : 29. Lord hath r. the generation
8 : 9. they have r. word of Lord
14 : 19. Hast thou utterly r. Judah
La. 5 : 22. thou hast utterly r. us
Ho. 4 : 6. thou hast r. knowledge
Mat. 21 : 42. stone which builders r.,
Mk. 12 : 10. Lu. 20 : 17. [Lu. 9 : 22.
Mk. 8 : 31. he shall be r. of elders,
Lu. 7 : 30. lawyers r. counsel of God
17 : 25. first be r. of this generation
Ga. 4 : 14. my temptation ye r. not
He. 6 : 8. which beareth thorns is r.
12 : 17. wo. have inherited blessing

REJECTETH. [was r.

Jn. 12 : 48. that r. me receiveth not
1 Th. 4 : † 8. that r. r. not man but

REJOICE. [God

De. 12 : 7. ye shall r. in all, 14 : 26.
16 : 14. thou shalt r. in thy feast
15. God shall bless, thou shalt r.
26 : 11. shalt r. in ev. good thing
28 : 63. Lord will r. over you, 30 : 9.
32 : 43. r. O nations, with his peo.
33 : 18. r. Zebulon, in going out
Ju. 9 : 19. r. ye in Abimelech, and
16 : 23. lords of Philis. gath-d to r.
1 S. 2 : 1. bec. I r. in thy salvation
19 : 5. thou sawest it, and didst r.
1 Ch. 16 : 10. let heart of them r.
that seek L., Ps. 105 : 3. [therein
32. let fields r. and all that is
2 Ch. 6 : 41. and let thy saints r. in
20 : 27. L. made them r., Ne. 12 : 43.
Jb. 3 : † 6. let it not r. among days
22. r. exceedingly and are glad
20 : 18. and he shall not r. therein
21 : 12. they r. at sound of organ
Ps. 2 : 11. Serve L., r. with trembling
5 : 11. let all put their trust in thee
9 : 14. I will r. in thy salvation [r.
13 : 4. those that trouble me r. [tion
5. my heart shall r. in thy salva-
14 : 7. Jacob shall r. and Israel
20 : 5. We will r. in thy salvation
21 : 1. in thy salvation shall he r.
30 : 1. hast not made my foes to r.
Ps. 33 : 21. our heart shall r. in him
35 : 9. my soul shall r. in his salva.
19. Let not enemies r. over me
24. O L. let them not r. over me
26. be ashamed that r. at mine
38 : 16. lest they r. over me [hurt
48 : 11. Let mount Zion r. let Jud.
51 : 8. bones thou hast brok. may r.
58 : 10. righte. shall r. when seeth
60 : 6. G. hath spok., I will r., 108 : 7.
63 : 7. in shadow of thy wings will I
11. the king shall r. in God [r.
65 : 8. morning and evening to r.
12. hills r. | 66 : 6. there did we r.
68 : 3. let the righteous r. yea, exceedingly r. [shall r.
4. r. before him | 71 : 23. My lips
85 : 6. revive us, th. thy peo. may r.
86 : 4. r. the soul of thy servant
89 : 12. Tabor and Hermon shall r.
16. In thy name shall they r. all
42. hast made his enemies to r.
96 : 11. Let heavens r. | 12. trees r.
97 : 1. Lord reigneth, let earth r.
98 : 4. make a loud noise, r. and
104 : 31. Lord shall r. in his works
106 : 5. that I may r. in gladness of
107 : 42. righteous sh. see it and r.
109 : 28. be ashamed, let servant r.
119 : 162. I r. at thy word, as one
149 : 2. Let Isr. r. in him that made
Pr. 2 : 14. Who r. to do evil, delight
5 : 18. r. with wife of thy youth
23 : 15. if wise, mine heart shall r.
16. my reins sh. r. when thy lips
24. father of righteous shall r.
25. she that bare thee shall r.
24 : 17. r. not when enemy faileth
27 : 9. Ointment, perfume r. heart
28 : 12. When righte. men r. is glory
29 : 2. righte. in authority, peo. r.
6. the righteous doth sing and r.
31 : 25. she shall in time to come
Ec. 3 : 12. man to r. and do good
22. man sho. r. in his works, 5 : 19.
4 : 16. that come after shall not r.
11 : 8 if man live many y-rs, and r.
9. r. O young man, in thy youth
Is. 8 : 6. r. in Rezin and Remaliah's
9 : 3. as men r. when divide spoil
13. 3. them that r. in my highness
14 : 8. yea, the fir trees r. at thee
29. r. not thou, whole Palestina
23 : 12. shalt no more r. O virgin
24 : 8. noise of them that r. endeth
29 : 19. poor shall r. in Holy One
35 : 1. desert shall r. and blossom, 2.
61 : 7. for confusion they shall r.
62 : 5. as bridegr., so G. r. over thee
65 : 13. my servants shall r. but ye
19. I will r. in Jerusal., and joy
66 : 10. r. ye with Jerusal., be glad
14. see this, your heart shall r.
Je. 31 : 13. shall virgin r. in dance,
I will make them r. fr sorrow
32 : 41. I will r. to do them good
51 : 39. that they may r. and sleep
La. 2 : 17. caused thine enemy to r.
Eze. 7 : 12. let not the buyer r. nor
35 : 15. As thou didst r. at inherit.
Ho. 9 : 1. r. not, O Israel, for joy
Am. 6 : 13. Ye which r. in nought
Mi. 7 : 8. r. not ag. me, O enemy
Zph. 3 : 11. will take them r. in thy
17. Lord will r. over thee [pride
Zch. 2 : 10. Sing r. O dau. of Zion
4 : 10. † seven eyes of Lord shall r.
9 : 9. r. greatly, O dau. of Zion
10 : 7. heart shall r. as thro. wine
Lu. 1 : 14. many sh. r. at his birth
6 : 23. r. ye in that day, and leap
10 : 20. in this r. not, rather r. bec.
15 : 6. r. for I have found sheep
9. r., I have found piece I lost
19 : 37. disciples began to r. [may r.
Jn. 4 : 36. soweth and he that reapeth
5 : 35. for season to r. in his light

Jn.14:28.If ye loved me,ye would r.
16: 20. ye shall weep, world sh. r.
22. I will see you, your heart sh.
Ac. 2: 26. thf. did my heart r. [r.
Ro. 5: 2. r. in hope of glory of G.
12:15. r. with them th. do r., weep
15: 10. he saith, r. ye Gentiles
1 Co.7:30.r.as tho. they rejoiced not
12: 26. honoured, all members r.
2 Co. 2: 3. sorrow of wh. I ought to
7: 9. I r. not ye were sorry [r.
16. I r. I have confidence in you
Ga. 4: 27. r. barren that bearest not
Ph. 1: 18. I do r. yea, and will r.
2: 16. that I may r. in day of Ch.
17. if I be offered, I joy and r.
18. For same cause do ye r.
28.when see him again, ye may r.
3:3. we worship God, and r. in Ch.
Col. 1: 24. r. in my suff-gs for you
1 Th. 5: 16. r. evermore, pray
Ja. 1: 9. Let brother of low degree r.
4: 16. now ye r. in your boastings
1 Pe. 1: 6. Wherein ye greatly r. tho.
8. r. with joy unspeakable and
4: 13. But r. as ye are partakers
Re. 11:10. that dwell upon earth sh.
12: 12. therefore r. ye heavens [r.
18: 20. r. over her, thou heaven
See **GLAD with rejoice, ed.**

REJOICE before the Lord.

Le. 23: 40. ye shall r. b. L. 7 days
De. 12:12. ye shall r. b. L. your G.
18.shall r.b.L.thy G.,16:11.-27:7.

REJOICE in the Lord.

Ps. 33: 1. r. i. L., O righte., 97: 12.
Is. 41:16. r. i. L., glory in Holy One
61: 10. I will greatly r. i. L.
Jo. 2: 23. ye children of Zion, r. i. L.
Ha. 3: 18. I will r. i. L., I will joy
Zch. 10: 7. their heart shall r. i. L.
Ph. 3: 1. Finally, brethren, r. i. L.
4: 4. r. i. L. alway, again, I say r.

REJOICED.

Ex. 18:9. Jethro r. for goodo. to Isr.
De. 28: 63. L. r. to do you good
30: 9. as he r. over thy fathers
Ju.19:3.fa. of damsel saw him, he r.
1 S. 6: 13. they of Beth-shemesh r.
11: 15. Saul and men of Israel r.
1 K. 1: 40. peo. r. so that earth rent
5: 7. Hiram r. at Solomon's words
2 K. 11: 14. the people r. when Joash
king, 20. 2 Ch. 23: 13, 21.
1 Ch. 29: 9. people r. David r.
2 Ch. 15: 15. all Judah r. at oath
24:10. all princes and all people r.
29: 36. Hezekiah r. and all people
30: 25. strangers out of Israel r.
Ne. 12: 43. offered sacrifices and r.,
the wives and children r. [vites
44. Judah r. for priests and Le-
Es. 8: 15. the city of Shushan r.
Jb. 31: 25. If I r. bec. my wealth
29. If I r. at destruction of him
Ps. 35: 15. in mine adversity they r.
97: 8. the daughters of Judah r.
119: 14. I have r. in thy testimo-s
Ec. 2: 10. heart r. in all my labour
Je. 15: 17. I r. not in the mockers
50: 11. ye r. O destroyers of mine
Eze. 25: 6. Ammonites r. ag. Israel
Ho. 10: 5. priests that r. sh. mourn
Ob. 12. nei. shouldest thou have r.
Jon. 4: † 6. Jonah r. with great joy
Mat.2:10. When saw the star, they r.
Lu. 1: 47. my spirit hath r. in God
58. Elizabeth's cousins r. with
10:21. that hour Jesus r. in spirit
13: 17. people r. for the things
Jn. 8: 56. Abraham r. to see my day
Ac. 7: 41. r. in works of own hands
15: 31. they r. for the consolation
16: 34. jailer r. believing in God
1 Co. 7: 30. rejoice, as tho. r. not
2 Co. 7: 7. told us, so I r. the more
Ph. 4: 10. I r. in the Lord greatly

2 Jn. 4. I r. greatly th. I found, 3 [Jn. 3.

REJOICEST.

Je. 11: 15. when doest evil, then thou

REJOICETH. [r.

1 S. 2: 1. Hannah said, My heart r.
Jb. 39: 21. horse r. in his strength
41: † 22. sorrow r. bef. leviathan
Ps. 16: 9. heart glad, my glory r.
19: 5. r. as a strong man to run
28: 7. theref. my heart greatly r.
Pr. 11: 10. well with righte., city r.
13: 9. The light of the righteous r.
15: 30 light of the eyes r. heart
29: 3. Whoso loveth wisdom r. fa.
Is. 5: 14. he that r. shall descend
62: 5. as bridegroom r. over bride
64: 5. Thou meetest him that r.
Eze. 35: 14. When whole earth r. I
Mat. 18: 13. he r. more of that sheep
Jn. 3: 29. friend of bridegroom r.
1 Co. 13: 6. r. not in iniq-y, but r. in
Ja. 2: 13. mercy r. ag. judgment

REJOICING.

1 K. 1: 45. and they are come up r.
2 Ch. 23: 18. burnt offerings with r.
Jb. 8: 21. Till he fill thy lips with r.
Ps. 19: 8. statutes right, r. heart
45: 15. With r. be bro-t to palace
107: 22. declare his works with r.
118: 15. voice of r. is in tabernacle
119: 111. they are r. of my heart
126: 6. doubtless come with r.
Pr. 8: 30. r. always before him
31. r. in habitable part of earth
Is. 65: 18. I create Jerusalem a r.
Je. 15: 16. thy word r. of my heart
Ha. 3: 14. r. was to devour poor
Zph. 2: 15. This is r. city that said
Lu. 15: 5. layeth it on shoulders r.
Ac. 5: 41. r. they were worthy to
8: 39. eunuch went on his way r.
Ro. 12: 12. r. in hope, patient in
1 Co. 15: 31. I protest by your r.
2 Co. 1: 12. our r. is this, testimony
14. we are your r. as ye are ours
6: 10. As sorrowful yet always r.
Ga. 6: 4. shall he have r. in himself
Ph. 1: 26. your r. be more abund.
1 Th. 2: 19. what is our crown of r.
He. 3: 6. r. of hope firm unto end
Ja. 4: 16. boastings, such r. is evil

RE'KEM. [Person, Place.]

1 Ch. 2: 43. sons of Hebron, R. | 44
See HUR, TARALAH.

RELEASE. [Noun.]

De. 15: 1. end of 7 years make a r.
2. manner of r. it is Lord's r.
9. 7th year, year of r. at hand
31: 10. solemnity of year of r.
Es. 2: 18. he made a r. to provinces

RELEASE, ED. [r. it

De. 15: 2. creditor that lendeth shall
3. that which is thine with thy
brother, thine hand shall r.
Mat. 27: 15. governor was wont to r.
prisoner, Lu. 23: 17. Jn. 18: 39.
17. Pilate said, Whom will ye that
I r., 21. Mk. 15: 9. Jn. 18: 39.
Mat.27: 26. r-d he Barabbas, scourged Jes., Mk. 15: 15. Lu. 23: 25.
Mk. 15: 6. at feast he r-d 1 prisoner
11. moved people, that he should
r. Barabbas, Lu. 23: 18.
Lu. 23:16. I will chastise, and r. him
20. Pilate, willing to r. Jes. spake
Jn. 19: 10. I have power to r. thee?
12. Pilate sought to r. him

RELIED.

2 Ch. 13: 18. bec. they r. upon L.G.
16: 7. hast r. on Syria, not r. on L.

RELIEF. [r.

Ac. 11: 29. disci. determined to send

RELIEVE, ED, ETH.

Le. 25: 35. if brother poor, r. him
Ps. 146: 9. he r-h fatherless widow
Is. 1: 17. r. oppressed, † righten
La. 1: 11. given for meat to r. soul

La. 1: 16. comforter that sho. r. is far
19. they sought meat to r. souls
1 Ti. 5: 10. if she have r-d afflicted
16. If any have widows, let them r.
them, that ch. may r. widows

RELIGION. [indeed

Ac. 26: 5. after straitest sect of our r.
Ga. 1: 13. my conversa. in Jews' r.
14. profited in Jews' r. above many
Ja. 1: 26. this man's r. is vain
27. Pure r. and undefiled before

RELIGIOUS. [God

Ac. 13: 43. r. proselytes followed Paul
Ja. 1: 26. if any among you seem r.

RELY.

2 Ch. 16: 8. bec. thou didst r. on L.

REMAIN.

Ge. 38: 11. r. widow at thy father's
Ex. 8: 9. frogs r. in river only, 11.
12: 10. let nothing r. until morning
23: 18. nei. fat of sac. r. until morn.
29: 34. if flesh of consecration r.
Le. 19: 6. if aught r. until third day
25: 28. wh. is sold shall r. in hand
27: 18. reckon acc. to years that r.
Nu. 33: 55. those ye let r. be pricks
De. 2: 34. all, we left none to r.
16: 4. nei. any flesh r. until morn.
19: 20. those which r. shall hear
21: 13. she shall r. in thine house
23. His body not r. all night upon
Jos. 1: 14. little ones shall r. [tree
2: 11. nei. r. any more courage
8: 22. they let none r., 10: 28, 30.
23: 4. I divided nations that r.
7. come not am. nations that r.
12. if ye cleave unto nations th. r.
Ju. 5: 17. why did Dan r. in ships
21: 7. for wives for them th. r., 16.
1 S. 20: 19. shalt r. by stone Ezel
1 K. 11: 16. six months did Joab r.
18: 22. I, I only r. prophet of L.
2 K. 7: 13. take five of horses th. r.
Ezr. 9: 15. for we r. yet escaped
Jb. 21: 32. yet shall he r. in tomb
27: 15. Those that r. shall be buried
37: 8. beasts go into dens and r.
Ps. 55: 7. would I r. in wilderness
Pr. 2: 21. perfect shall r. in land
21: 16. shall r. in congr-n of dead
Is. 10: 32. As yet shall he r. at Nob
32: 16. righteousn. shall r. in field
44: 13. that God may r. in house
65: 4. Which r. among the graves
66: 22. new heavens sh. r. bef. me,
so shall your name r.
Je. 8: 3. that r. of this evil family
17: 25. this city shall r. for ever
24: 8. give residue of Jerus. that r.
27: 11. those will I let r. in own la.
19. saith L., conc. vessels th. r., 21.
30: 18. palace shall r. after manner
† 23. sh. r. with pain upon head
38: 4. weakeneth men that r.
42: 17. none of them shall r., 44: 14.
-51: 62. [none to r.
44: 7. Whf. commit ye evil to leave
Eze. 7: 11. Violence risen, none sh. r.
17: 21. that r. shall be scattered
31: 13. Upon his ruin shall fowls r.
32: 4. cause fowls to r. upon Pha.
39: 14. men to bury those that r. of
Am. 6: 9. if r. ten men in one hou.
Ob. 14. those that r. in distress
Zch. 5: 4. flying roll r. in his house
12: 14. families that r. shall mourn
Lu. 10: 7. in same house r. eating
Jn. 6: 12. Gather fragments that r.
15: 11. that my joy might r. in you
16. chosen you, th. fruit should r.
19: 31. bodies sho. not r. upon cross
1 Co. 7: 11. let her r. unmarried
15: 6. of whom the greater part r.
1 Th. 4: 15. wh. r. unto coming of L.
17. we which r. sh. be caught up
He. 12: 27. can-t be shaken may r.
1 Jn. 2: 24. If th. ye heard r. in you

Re. 3:2. strengthen things which r.

REMAINDER.

[r.
Ex.26:†13.cubit on other side in the
29:34. then thou shalt burn the r.
Le. 6 : 16. the r. shall Aaron eat
7 : 16. on morrow r. shall be eaten
17. r. on 3d day shall be burnt
18:†6.none approach any that is r.
2 S. 14 : 7. leave nei. name nor r.
2 Ch. 36 : † 20. r. from sword carried
Ps. 76 : 10. r. of wrath restrain
Je. 51 : † 35. violence done to my r.

REMAINED.

Ge. 7 : 23. Noah only r. alive, and
14:10.they that r. fled to mountain
Ex. 8 : 31. removed flies, r. not one
10 : 15. r. not any green thing
19. r. not one locust in all coasts
14 : 28. r. not so much as 1 chariot
Nu. 11 : 26. r. two of men in camp
35:28. sho. have r. in city of refuge
36:12. inheritance r.in house of fa.
De. 3 : 11. Og r. of the giants
4 : 25. when have r. long in land
Jos. 10 : 20. rest wh. r. entered cities
11: 22. in Gath there r. Anakim
13 : 12. r. of remnant of giants
18 : 2. there r. of Israel 7 tribes
21 : 20. which r. of Kohathites, 26.
Ju. 7 : 3. r. with Gideon 10,000
1 S. 11 : 11. wh. r. were scattered
23 : 14. David r. in a mountain in
24:3. David and his men r. in cave
2 S. 13 : 20. Tamar r. desolate in
1 K. 22:46. Sodomites wh. r. he took
2 K. 10 : 11. Jehu slew all that r.,17.
13 : 6. r. the grove in Samaria
25:22. people that r.in Judah [ed.
1 Ch.13:14. ark r. in family of Obed-
Ec. 2 : 9. my wisdom r. with me
Je. 34 : 7. these defenced cities r.
37 : 10. there r. but wounded men
16. Jere. had r. in dungeon [13.
21. he had r. in court of pris.,38:
39:9. Neb-n carried captive people
that r. in city, 52 : 15. [that r.
41 : 10. Ishmael carried cap. them
48 : 11. theref. his taste r. in him
51 : 30. mighty men r. in holds
La. 2 : 22. in the L.'s anger none r.
Eze. 3 : 15. I r. astonished 7 days
Da. 10 : 8. r. no strength in me, 17.
13. I r. with the kings of Persia
Mat. 11 : 23. in Sod. it would have r.
14:20.they took up fragments that
r., Lu. 9 : 17. Jn. 6 : 13.
Lu. 1:22. he beckoned, r. speechless
Ac. 5:4. While it r. was it not thine
27 : 41. forepart stuck fast, and r.

REMAINEST.

La. 5:19. Thou, O Lord, r.,He.1:11.

REMAINETH.

Ge. 8 : 22. While earth r. seed time
Ex. 10 : 5. that which r. from hail
12 : 10. that wh. r. until morning
16 : 23. that which r. over lay up
26:12.remn-t that r.of curtains (2)
13. wh. r. in length of curtains
Le. 8 : 32. that r. of flesh sh. burn
10 : 12. Take meat offering that r.
16 : 16. so do for tabernacle that r.
Nu. 24 : 19. sh. destroy him that r.
Jos. 8 : 29. gr. heap of stones that r.
13:1. r. much land to be possessed
2. land that yet r. : all Geshuri
Ju. 5 : 13. him that r. have domin.'
1 S. 6 : 18. Abel, which stone r.'
16:11.Jesse said, There r.youngest
2 K. 19 : † 30. escaping of Judah th.
r. shall take root, Is. 37 : † 31.
1 Ch. 17 : 1. ark of L.r.und. curtains
Ezr. 1 : 4. whoso. r. in any place
Jb. 19 : 4. my error r. with myself
21 : 34. in your answers r. falseh.
41 : 22. In his neck r. strength
Is. 4 : 3. r. in Jerus. be called holy
Je. 38 : 2. r. in this city die by sw.
Je.47:4.fr.Tyrus every helper th. r.
Eze. 6 : 12. that r. besieged sh. die
Hag. 2 : 5. so my Spirit r. am. you
Zch. 9 : 7. that r. sh. be for our G.
Jn. 9 : 41. We see; thf. your sin r.
1 Co. 7 : 29. it r. they th. have wives
2 Co. 3 : 11. that which r. is glorious
14. until this day r. same vail
9 : 9. his righteousness r. for ever
He. 4 : 6. it r. that some must enter
9. there r. a rest to people of G.
10 : 26. r. no more sacrifi. for sins
1 Jn.3:9. not sin, his seed r. in him

REMAINING.

Nu. 9 : 22. cloud r. upon tabernacle
De. 3 : 3. until none left r. to Og
Jos. 10 : 33. he left none r., 37, 39,
40.-11 : 8. [Levites
21 : 40. were r. of the families of
2 S. 21 : 5. destroyed fr. r. in coasts
2 K. 10 : 11. Jehu left Ahab none r.
1 Ch. 9:33. who r. in chambers free
Jb. 18 : 19. nor any r. in his dwell-g
Je. 30 : † 23. r. whirlwind on wicked
Ob. 18. not any r. of house of Esau
Jn. 1 : 33. Upon whom see Spirit r.

REMALI'AH.

[R.
Is. 7:4. fear not, for anger of son of
5. son of R. taken evil counsel
9. head of Samaria is R.'s son
8 : 6. rejoice in Rezin and R.'s son

REMEDY.

2 Ch. 36 : 16. wrath arose, was no r.
Pr. 6 : 15. he be broken without r.
29:1.he be destroyed,and without r

REMEMBER.

Ge. 9 : 16. that I may r. everl. cov-t
40 : 23. did not butler r. Joseph
Ex. 13 : 3. Moses said, r. this day
20 : 8. r. sab. day to keep it holy
32 : 13. r. Ab. Isaac, and, De. 9:27.
Nu. 11 : 5. We r. fish we did eat in E.
15 : 39. r. all com-ts of Lord
40. ye may r. and do my com-ts
De. 5:15. r.thou wast servant in E.,
15 : 15.-16 : 12.-24 : 18, 22.
7 : 18. r. what Lord did unto Pha.
8 : 2. r. all the way Lord led thee
18. r. L. giveth pow. to get wealth
9 : 7. r. how thou provokedst L.
15 : 15. r. thou wast a bondman in
Egypt, 16:12.-24:18, 22. [Egypt
16 : 3. r. day thou camest out of
24 : 9. r. what L. did unto Miriam
25 : 17. r. what Amalek did unto
32 : 7. r. days of old, consider years
Jos. 1 : 13. r. word Mo. com-ded you
Ju. 9 : 2. r. I am your bone, flesh
1 S. 25 : 31. Abigail said, r. handm.
2 S. 14 : 11. let the king r. the Lord
19 : 19. nei. r. what thy serv. did
2 K. 9:25. r., when I rode, aft. Ahab
20 : 3. r. how I have walked before
thee, Is. 38 : 3. [Ps. 105 : 5.
1 Ch.16:12. r.his marvellous works,
2 Ch. 6 : 42. r. the mercies of David
Ne. 1 : 8. r. word thou com-dst Mo.
4 : 14. r. the Lord, which is great
13 : 29. r. them th. defiled priesth.
Jb. 4 : 7. r. who perished, innocent?
7:7. O r. my life is wind, eye shall
10 : 9. r. thou made me as clay
11:16. r. it as waters that pass aw.
36 : 24. r. thou magnify his work
41:8. Lay hand upon him, r. battle
Ps. 20 : 3. r. thy offerings, accept
7. we will r. name of the Lord
22 : 27. all ends of world shall r. L.
25 : 6. r. thy mercies, ever of old
7. r. not sins of my youth, r. me
74 : 2. r. cougr-n thou purchased
18. r. this, enemy reproached [eth
22. r. how foolish man reproach-
79 : 8. O r. not ag. us iniquities
89:47. r. how short my time is, why
50. r. L. reproach of thy servants
103 : 18. those that r. his com-ts
Ps. 119 : 49. r. word unto thy serv.
132 : 1. L. r. David, his afflictions
137 : 7. r. O L. children of Edom
Pr. 31 : 7. drink, r. misery no more
Ec. 5 : 20. sh. not r. days of his life
11 : 8. let him r. days of darkness
12 : 1. r. now thy Creator in days
Can. 1 : 4. we will r. thy love
Is.43:18. r. not former things? 46:9.
25. for own sake I not r. thy sins
44:21. r. these, O Jacob and Israel
46 : 8. r. this, shew yours. men [it
47 : 7. neither didst r. latter end of
54 : 4. not r. reproach of widowhood
64 : 5. meetest those that r. thee
9. neither r. iniquity for ever
Je. 3 : 16. neither shall they r. it
14:10. he will now r. their iniquity
21. r. break not thy covenant
17:2. children r. altars and groves
18 : 20. r. I stood bef. thee to speak
31 : 20. I do earnestly r. him still
44 : 21. people, did not L. r. them
51 : 50. ye that have escaped, r. L.
La. 3 : † 19. r. mine affliction and
5 : 1. r. O Lord, what is upon us,
Eze. 16 : 61. Then shalt r. thy ways,
20 : 43.-36 : 31. [founded
63. thou mayest r. and be con-
23:27. shalt not r. Egypt any more
Ho. 8 : 13. now will he r. their iniq.
9:9. he will r. iniq-y and visit sins
Mi. 6 : 5. O my peo. r. what Balak
Ha. 3 : 2. O L. in wrath r. mercy
Mal. 4 : 4. r. the law of Moses [18.
Mat. 16 : 9. nei. r. five loaves, Mk. 8 :
27:63. Sir, we r. that deceiver said
Lu. 16 : 25. r. thou in thy lifetime
17 : 32. r. Lot's wife
24 : 6. r. how he spake unto you
Jn. 15 : 20. r. word I said unto you
16:4. when time sh. come ye may r.
Ac. 20 : 31. r. that by space of 3 y-rs
35. r. words of Lord Jesus
Ga. 2 : 10. that we sho. r. the poor
Ep. 2 : 11. r. that being in time past
Col.4:18. r. my bonds. Grace [Gent.
1 Th.2:9. ye r. brethren, our labour
2 Th. 2 : 5. r. ye not I told you
2 Ti. 2 : 8. r. Jesus C. was raised
He. 13 : 3. r. them th. are in bonds
7. r. them which have the rule
Jude 17. r. words spoken of apostles
Re. 2 : 5. r. whence thou art fallen
3 : 3. r. how thou hast received

See **Remember, ed.**
COVENANT.

I REMEMBER.

Ge. 41:9. I do r. my faults this day
1 S. 15 : 2. I r. that wh. Amalek did
Jb. 21 : 6. when I r. I am afraid
Ps.42:4. When I r. these, I pour my
63:6. When I r. thee upon my bed
137 : 6. If I do not r. thee, let my
143:5. I r. the days of old, I muse
Je. 2 : 2. I r. kindness of thy youth
Ho. 7 : 2. consider not that I r. all
their wickedness

I will, or will I REMEMBER.

Ps. 42 : 6. w. I r. thee from Jordan
77 : 10. I w. r. years of right hand
11. I w. r. works of the Lord, I
w. r. thy wonders of old
Je. 31 : 34. I w. r. their sin no more,
He. 8 : 12.-10 : 17.
3 Jn. 10. I w. r. deeds which he doeth

REMEMBER me.

Ge.40:†14. r. m. and shew kindness
Ju. 16 : 28. r. m. that I be avenged
1 S. 1 : 11. look on handmaid, r. m.
Ne. 13 : 14. r. m. O G. conc., 22, 31.
Jb. 14 : 13. me a set time, and r. m.
Ps. 25 : 7. r. m. for goodness' sake
106:4. r. m. with favour thou bear.
Je. 15 : 15. L. thou knowest, r. m.
Eze. 6 : 9. escape of you shall r. m.

Zch. 10 : 9. shall r. m. in far coun.
Lu. 23 : 42. L. r. m. when comest
1 Co. 11 : 2. th. ye r. m. in all things

REMEMBERED.

Ge. 8 : 1. God r. Noah | 19 : 29. God r.
Abraham [r. dreams
30 : 22. God r. Rachel | 42 : 9. Joseph
Nu. 10 : 9. ye shall be r. before Lord
Ju. 8 : 34. chil of Israel r. not Lord
1 S. 1 : 19. and the Lord r. Hannah
2 Ch. 24 : 22. Joash r. not kindness
Es. 2 : 1. Ahasuerus r. Vashti, what
9 : 28. that days of Purim sho. be r.
Jb. 24 : 20. sinner sh. be no more r.
Ps. 45 : 17. I will make thy name r.
77 : 3. I r. God and was troubled
78 : 35. r. God was their Saviour
39. he r. that they were but flesh
42. They r. not his hand, when he
98 : 3. He r. his mercy toward Isr.
105 : 42. For he r. his holy promise
106 : 7. they r. not mult. of mercies
109 : 14. Let iniq-y of his fa-s be r.
16. Bec. he r. not to shew mercy
111 : 4. wonderful works to be r.
119 : 52. I r. thy judgments of old
55. I have r. thy name in night
136 : 23. Who r. us in our low estate
137 : 1. we wept, when we r. Zion
Ec. 9 : 15. yet no man r. poor man
Is. 23 : 16. songs, that thou be r.
57 : 11. thou hast not r. me, nor laid
63 : 11. Then he r. days of old, Mo.
65 : 17. former heavens sh. not be r.
Je. 11 : 19. his name be no more r.
La. 1 : 7. Jerus. r. in her afflictions
2 : 1. r. not his footstool in anger [13.
Eze. 3 : 20. his right-n. not be r., 33:
16 : 22. not r. days of thy youth, 43.
21 : 24. ye made your iniquity to be
32. thou shalt be no more r. [r.
25 : 10. Ammonites may not be r.
Ho. 2 : 17. no more be r., Zch. 13 : 2.
Am. 1 : 9. r. not the brotherly cov-t
Jon. 2 : 7. soul fainted, I r. the L.
Mat. 26 : 75. Peter r. words of Jes.,
Lu. 24 : 8. they r. his words [Lu. 22 : 61.
Jn. 2 : 17. disciples r. it was written
22. When he was risen, they r. [r.
12 : 16. when Jes. was glorified they
Ac. 11 : 16. Then r. I word of the L.
He. 11 : † 22. Joseph r. the departing
Re. 18 : 5. God hath r. her iniquities

REMEMBEREST, ETH.

Ps. 9 : 12. maketh inquisition, he r-h
88 : 5. slain whom thou r-t no more
103 : 14. he r-h we are but dust
Ec. 5 : † 20. he r-h days of his life
La. 1 : 9. she r-h not her last end
Mat. 5 : 23. r-t thy bro. hath aught
Jn. 16 : 21. she r-h no more anguish
2 Co. 7 : 15. r-h obedience of you all

REMEMBERING.

La. 3 : 19. r. mine affliction and
1 Th. 1 : 3. r. your work of faith

REMEMBRANCE, S.

Ex. 17 : 14. will put out r. of Amalek
Nu. 5 : 15. bringing iniquity to r.
De. 25 : 19. blot out r. of Amalek
32 : 26. wo. make r. of them cease
2 S. 18 : 18. no son to keep name in
1 K. 17 : 18. to call my sin to r. [r.
Jb. 13 : 12. Your r-s are like ashes
18 : 17. His r. sh. perish fr. earth
Ps. 6 : 5. in death is no r. of thee
30 : 4. thanks at r. of his holin., 97:
34 : 16. to cut off r. of them [12.
38 : *. psalm of Da. to bring to r.,
77 : 6. to r. my song in night [70 : *.
83 : 4. that Israel be no more in r.
102 : 12. thy r. unto all generations
112 : 6. righteous shall be in everl. r.
Ec. 1 : 11. is no r. of former things
2 : 16. no r. of wise more than fool
Is. 26 : 8. our soul is to r. of thee
43 : 26. Put me in r. let us plead
57 : 8. behind doors set up thy r.
La. 3 : 20. My soul hath them in r.
Eze. 21 : 23. he will call to r. iniquity
24. because ye are come to r.
23 : 19. to r. days of her youth, 21.
29 : 16. bringeth their iniquity to r.
Mal. 3 : 16. a book of r. was written
Mk. 11 : 21. Peter calling to r. saith
Lu. 1 : 54. he hath holpen Isr. in r.
22 : 19. this do in r. of me, 1 Co. 11:
Jn. 14 : 26 all things to your r. [24.
Ac. 10 : 31. thine alms are had in r.
1 Co. 4 : 17. Tim. bring you into r.
11 : 25. oft as ye drink it in r. of me
Ph. 1 : 3. I thank God upon every r.
1 Th. 3 : 6. th. ye have good r. of us
1 Ti. 4 : 6. If thou put brethren in r.
2 Ti. 1 : 3. r. of thee in my prayers
5. I call to r. unfeigned faith
6. I put thee in r. that thou stir
2 : 14. of these thi. put them in r.
He. 10 : 3. in sacrifices a r. of sins
32. But call to r. former days
2 Pe. 1 : 12. to put you in r., Jude 5.
13. stir you by putting you in r.
15. have these things always in r.
3 : 1. stir up your pure minds by r.
Re. 16 : 19. Babylon came in r. bef

REMEMBRANCER. [God

2 S. 8 : † 16. Jehoshaphat was r., 20 :
† 24. 1 K. 4 : † 3. 1 Ch. 18 : † 15.
Is. 62 : † 6. ye that are L.'s r. keep

RE'METH. [not

Jos. 19 : 21. border was toward R.

REMISSION.

Mat. 26 : 28. blood shed for r. of sins
Mk. 1 : 4. baptism of repentance for
r. of sins, Lu. 3 : 3. [r. of sins
Lu. 1 : 77. knowledge of salvation by
24 : 47. that r. should be preached
Ac. 2 : 38. be baptized for r. of sins
10 : 43. believeth shall receive r. of
Ro. 3 : 25. for r. of sins past [sins
He. 9 : 22. without blood is no r.
10 : 18. where r. is, is no more offer-

REMIT, TED. [ing

Jn. 20 : 23. Whoso. sins ye r. they

REM'MON. [are r-d

Jos. 19 : 7. R. 4 cities with villages

REM'MON-METHO'AR.

Jos. 19 : 13. border goeth to R. to

REMNANT. [Neah

Ge. 45 : † 7. to put for you a r. [tains
Ex. 26 : 12. r. that remain-h of cur-
Le. 2 : 3. r. of meat off-g be Aaron's
5 : 13. r. shall be priest's as offering
14 : 18. r. of the oil in priest's hand
De. 3 : 11. only Og remained of r. of
giants, Jos. 12 : 4.–13 : 12.
28 : 54. his eye evil toward r. of chil.
Jos. 23 : 12. if ye cleave unto r.
2 S. 21 : 2. Gibeonites r. of Amorites
1 K. 12 : 23. speak to r. of people
14 : 10. I will take r. of Jeroboam
22 : 46. r. of Sodomites Jehosh-t took
2 K. 19 : 4. lift up thy prayer for the
r., Is. 37 : 4. [Is 37 : 31.
30. the r. escaped shall take root,
31. out of Jerus. go a r., Is. 37 : 32.
21 : 14. forsake r. of mine inherit.
25 : 11. r. did Neb-n carry away
1 Ch. 6 : 70. r. of sons of Kohath
2 Ch. 30 : 6. will return to r. of you
34 : 9. all r. of Israel and Judah
Ezr. 3 : 8. r. of their breth. priests
9 : 8. grace from L. to leave us a r.
14. so that there should be no r.
Ne. 1 : 3. r. left of the captivity
Jb. 22 : 20. r. of them fire consumed
Is. 1 : 9. unless L. left us a small r.
7 : † 3. The r. shall return, even the
r., 10 : 20, 21, 22. [of people
11 : 11. set his hand, to recover r.
16. shall be a highway for the r.
14 : 22. I will cut off from Bab. r.
30. and he shall slay thy r. [land
15 : 9. I will bring lions on r. of
16 : 14. r. shall be very small and
Is. 17 : 3. kingd. cease fr. r. of Syria
37 : 4. lift up thy prayer for r. left
46 : 3. Hearken all th. r. of Israel
Je. 6 : 9. They shall glean r. of Isr.
11 : 23. there sh. be no r. of them
15 : 11. it shall be well with thy r.
23 : 3. I will gather r. of my floc
25 : 20. the r. of Ashdod did drink
31 : 7. O Lord, save peo., r. of Isr.
39 : 9. Neb-n carried away r. of peo.
40 : 11. king of Babylon left r.
15. and r. of Judah perish [43 : 5.
41 : 16. Johanan took r. of people,
42 : 2. pray for us even for this r.
15. hear word of L., r. of Judah
19. O r. of Judah, go not into E.
44 : 12. I will take the r. of Judah
14. So none of r. of Judah escape
28. r. shall know whose words
47 : 4. Lord will spoil r. of country
5. Ashkelon is cut off, with r.
Eze. 5 : 10. r. of thee will I scatter
6 : 8. Yet will I leave a r. that ye
11 : 13. wilt thou make end of r.?
14 : 22. therein shall be left a r.
23 : 25. thy r. shall fall by sword
25 : 16. I will destroy r. of sea coast
Jo. 2 : 32. r. whom Lord shall call
Am. 1 : 8. r. of Philist. shall perish
5 : 15. God gracious unto r. of Jo-
9 : 12. may possess r. of Edom [seph
Mi. 2 : 12. I will gather r. of Israel
4 : 7. will make her th. halted, a r.
5 : 3. r. of brethren sh. return unto
7. r. of Jacob in midst of peo. [Isr.
8. r. of Jacob shall be am. Gent.
7 : 18. transgr-n of r. of heritage
Ha. 2 : 8. r. of people spoil thee
Zph. 1 : 4. I will cut off r. of Baal
2 : 7. coast shall be for the r. of Jud.
9. r. of my people sh. possess th.
3 : 13. r. of Isr. shall not do iniq-y
Hag. 1 : 12. r. of people obeyed Lord
14. L. stirred spirit of r. of people
Zch. 8 : 6. If marvellous in eyes of r.
12. will cause r. of peo. to possess
Mat. 22 : 6. r. took serv-ts, and slew
Ro. 9 : 27. Esaias crieth, r. be saved
11 : 5. at this present time is a r.
Re. 11 : 13. the r. were affrighted
12 : 17. dragon went to war with r.
19 : 21. the r. were slain with sword

REMORSE.

Ro. 11 : † 8. God hath given spirit of r.

REMOVE. [it

Ge. 48 : 17. held father's hand to r.
Nu. 36 : 7. So shall not the inherit-
tance of Israel r., 9. [landmark
De. 19 : 14. shalt not r. thy neighb.'s
Jos. 3 : 3. ye shall r. fr. your place
Ju. 9 : 29. would I r. Abimelech
2 S. 6 : 10. David would not r. ark
2 K. 23 : 27. L. said, I will r. Judah
24 : 3. came upon Judah, to r. them
2 Ch. 33 : 8. Neither will I r. Israel
Jb. 24 : 2. Some r. the landmarks
27 : 5. I will not r. integrity fr. me
Ps. 36 : 11. let not the wicked r. me
39 : 10. r. thy stroke away from me
119 : 22. r. from me reproach and
29. r. from me the way of lying
Pr. 4 : 27. Turn not, r. foot fr. evil
5 : 8. r. thy way far from her [10.
22 : 28. r. not ancient landmark, 23:
30 : 8. r. far fr. me vanity and lies
Ec. 11 : 10. r. sorrow from thy heart
Is. 10 : † 27. burden r. fr. shoulder
13 : 13. earth sh. r. out of her place
31 : † 2. wise, and will not r. words
46 : 7. from his place sh. he not r.
Je. 4 : 1. return, then shalt not r.
27 : 10. prophesy a lie to r. you far
32 : 31. that I r. it from bef. my face
50 : 3. they shall r. man and beast
8. r. out of midst of Babylon
52 : † 18. took instrum-s to r. ashes
Eze. 12 : 3. r. by day, thou shalt r.

Eze. 21: 26. saith Lord, r. the diadem
45: 9. O princes, r. violence and
Ho. 5: 10. like them that r. bound
Jo. 2: 20. I will r. northern army
3: 6. th. ye r. them from border
Mi. 2: 3. ye shall not r. your necks
Zch. 3: 9. I will r. iniquity of land
14: 4. half the mountain shall r.
Mat. 17: 20. say, r. hence, it sh. r.
Lu. 22: 42. if willing, r. this cup fr.
1 Co. 13: 2. so I could r. mountains
Re. 2: 5. else I will r. thy candlestick

REMOVED.

Ge. 8: 13. Noah r. covering of ark
12: 8. Abram r., 13: 18. | 26: 22. Isaac
30: 35. Jacob r. he goats spotted
47: 21. Joseph r. people to cities
Ex. 8: 31. L. r. swarms of flies
14: 19. angel of God r. and went
20: 18. people saw it and r. afar
Nu. 12: 16. people r. fr. Hazeroth
21: 12. r. and pitched in Zared
13. r. and pitched on other side
33: 5. chil. of Israel r. fr. Rameses
7. they r. from Etham | 9. Marah
| 10. Elim | 11. Red sea | 14.
Alush | 16. desert of Sinai | 21.
Libnah | 24. m-t Shapher | 25.
Haradah | 26. Makheloth | 28.
Tarah | 32. Bene-jaakan | 34.
Jotbathah | 36. Ezion-gaber |
37. Kadesh | 46. Dibon-gad |
47. Almon-diblathaim
De. 28: 25. be r. into all kingdoms
Jos. 3: 1. they r. from Shittim, and
14. people r. to pass over Jordan
11: † 15. Joshua r. nothing of all
1 S. 6: 3. known why his hand is not
r. from you
18: 13. Saul r. David from him
2 S. 20: 12. he r. Amasa out of, 13.
1 K. 15: 12. Asa r. idols father made
13. Maachah he r. from being
queen, 2 Ch. 15: 16. [15: 4, 35.
14. high places were not r., 2 K.
2 K. 16: 17. Ahaz r. the laver from
17: 18. Lord r. Israel out of his
sight, 23.-23: 27. [know not
26. nations which thou hast r.
18: 4. Hezekiah r. the high places
1 Ch. 8: 6. r. them to Manahath, 7.
13: † 13. David r. not ark home
2 Ch. 35: 12. they r. burnt offerings
36: † 3. king of Egypt r. Jehoahaz
Jb. 14: 18. rock is r. out of place
18: 4. sh. rock be r. out of place?
19: 10. mine hope hath he r. like
32: † 15. r. speeches from thems.
36: 16. so would he have r. thee
Ps. 46: 2. not fear, tho. earth be r.
81: 6. I r. his shoulder fr. burden
103: 12. so far he r. our transg-ns
104: 5. earth, that it sho. not be r.
125: 1. as m-t Zion, wh. cannot be r.
Pr. 10: 30. righteous sh. never be r.
Is. 6: 12. Until L. have r. men far
10: 13. I have r. bounds of people
31. Madmenah is r. [heritance
17: † 11. harvest be r. in day of in-
22: 25. nail in sure place sh. be r.
24: 20. earth sh. be r. like cottage
26: 15. hast r. it unto ends of earth
29: 13. have r. their heart fr. me
30: 20. sh. not thy teachers be r.
33: 20. not one of stakes sh. be r.
38: 12. Mine age is r. fr. me as tent
54: 10. hills shall be r. covenant of
my peace shall not be r.
Je. 15: 4. cause to be r. into kingd-s
24: 9. I will deliver them to be r.,
29: 18.-34: 17. [she is r.
La. 1: 8. Jerusalem sinned, theref.
3: 17. hast r. my soul far fr. peace
Eze. 7: 19. their gold shall be r.
23: 46. I will give them to be r. [an
36: 17. way as uncleann-s of r. wom-
Am. 6: 7. banquet of them sh. be r.

Mi. 2: 4. how hath he r. it from me
7: 11. that day sh. decree be r. [23.
Mat. 21: 21. if say, Be thou r., Mk. 11:
Ac. 7: 4. he r. Ab. into this land
13: 22. had r. Saul, he raised Da.
Ga. 1: 6. I marvel ye are so soon r.

REMOVETH.

De. 27: 17. Cursed that r. landmark
Jb. 9: 5. Which r. the mountains
12: 20. He r. speech of the trusty
Ec. 10: 9. Whoso r. stones be hurt
Is. 27: † 8. be r. his rough wind in
Da. 2: 21. changeth seasons, he r.

REMOVING. [kings

Ge. 30: 32. r. from flock speckled
De. 28: † 25. sh. be for r. into kingd-s
Is. 14: † 6. smote people without r.
49: 21. I am a captive r. to and fro
Je. 15: † 4. I will give them for a r.,
24: † 9.-34: † 17. [r.
La. 1: † 8. thf. Jerusalem is become a
Eze. 12: 3. thf. prepare stuff for r., 4.
† 11. by r. sh. go into captivity
23: † 46. I will give them for a r.
He. 12: 27. signifieth r. of things

REM'PHAN. [god R.

Ac. 7: 43. ye took up star of your

REND.

Ex. 39: 23. that ephod should not r.
Le. 10: 6. nei. r. your clothes, lest
13: 56. priest r. plague out of garm.
1 K. 11: 11. I will r. kingdom, 12, 31.
13. I will not r. aw. all kingdom
31. I will r. the kingdom, 14: 8.
2 Ch. 34: 27. didst r. thy clothes and
Ec. 3: 7. A time to r. time to sew
Is. 64: 1. Oh that thou r. heavens
Eze. 13: 11. stormy wind sh. r. it, 13.
29: 7. thou didst r. their shoulder
Ho. 13: 8. will r. caul of their heart
Jo. 2: 13. r. your heart, not garm.
Mat. 7: 6. lest they turn and r. you
Jn. 19: 24. Let us not r. it, but cast

RENDER. [lots

Nu. 18: 9. ev. offering they r. be holy
De. 32: 41. I will r. vengeance
43. he will r. veng. to adversaries
Ju. 9: 57. evil of men of Shechem did
God r. [faithfulness
1 S. 26: 23. Lord r. to ev. man his
2 Ch. 6: 30. r. unto every man acc.
Jb. 33: 26. will r. unto man right-n.
34: 11. work of a man shall he r.
Ps. 28: 4. r. to them their desert
38: 20. They that r. evil for good
56: 12. O God, I will r. praises
79: 12. r. our neighbours sevenfold
94: 2. r. a reward to proud
116: 12. What shall I r. unto the L.
Pr. 24: 12. sh. not he r. to ev. man
acc. to works? Ro. 2: 6. [to work
29. Say not, I will r. to man acc.
26: 16. seven that can r. a reason
Is. 66: 15. L. will come, to r. anger
Je. 51: 6. he will r. unto Babylon, 24.
Ho. 14: 2. will we r. calves of lips
Zch. 9: 12. I will r. double unto thee
Mat. 21: 41. shall r. him fruits in
22: 21. r. unto Cesar things are
Cesar's, Mk. 12: 17. Lu. 20: 25.
Ro. 13: 7. r. to all their dues [lence
1 Co. 7: 3. husb. r. unto wife benevo-
1 Th. 3: 9. what thanks can we r.
5: 15. See that none r. evil for evil
See RECOMPENSE.

RENDERED. [Ahim.

Ju. 9: 56. God r. wickedness of
2 K. 3: 4. k. of Moab r. unto k. of Isr.
17: † 3. Hoshea r. Shalmaneser trib.
2 Ch. 32: 25. Hezekiah r. not acc.
Pr. 12: 14. recompense of man's
hands shall be r. unto him

RENDEREST, ETH.

Ps. 62: 12. r-t to man acc. to work
Is. 66: 6. voice of L. r-h recompense

RENDERING.

1 Pe. 3: 9. Not r. evil for evil

RENDING. [pieces

Ps. 7: 2. Lest tear my soul, r. it in

RENEW.

1 S. 11: 14. let us go to Gilgal r. kingd.
2 Ch. 24: † 4. minded to r. house of L.
Ps. 51: 10. r. right spirit within me
Is. 40: 31. wait upon L. r. strength
41: 1. let people r. their strength
La. 5: 21. O L., r. our days as of old
He. 6: 6. if they fall away, to r.
them again unto repentance

RENEWED, EST.

2 Ch. 15: 8. Asa r-d altar of the Lord
Jb. 10: 17. r-t thy witnesses ag. me
29: 20. bow was r-d in my hand
Ps. 103: 5. youth is r-d like eagle's
104: 30. thou r-t face of earth [by
2 Co. 4: 16. inward man is r-d day
Ep. 4: 23. r-d in spirit of your mind
Col. 3: 10. man wh. is r-d in knowl-

RENEWING. [edge

Ro. 12: 2. transformed by r. of mind
Tit. 3: 5. saved us by r. of Holy Ghost

RENOUNCED.

2 Co. 4: 2. have r. hidden things of

RENOWN.

Ge. 6: 4. giants, of old, men of r.
Nu. 16: 2. famous in cong-n, men of r.
Eze. 16: 14. thy r. went am. heathen
15. playedst harlot bec. of thy r.
34: 29. I will raise a plant of r.
39: 13. sh. be to them a r. saith L.
Da. 9: 15. gotten thee r. as at this

RENOWNED. [day

Nu. 1: 16. These were r. of cong.
Is. 14: 20. seed of evil doers never r.
Eze. 23: 23. captains, lords, and r.
26: 17. r. city which was strong in

RENT. [Noun.] [sea

Is. 3: 24. instead of girdle be a r.
Mat. 9: 16. r. is made worse, Mk. 2: 21.
Lu. 5: 36. then new maketh a r.

RENT. [Verb.]

Ge. 37: 33. Joseph is r. in pieces
Ex. 28: 32. ephod, that it be not r.
Jos. 9: 4. wine bottles, old and r., 13.
Ju. 14: 6. Samson r. the lion as he
would have r. a kid
1 S. 15: 27. Saul r. Sam.'s mantle
28. L. hath r. kingdom fr., 28: 17.
2 S. 13: 19. Tamar r. her garment
15: 32. Hushai with his coat r.
1 K. 1: 40. earth r. with the sound
11: 30. Ahijah r. Jerob.'s garment
13: 3. altar be r. | 5. altar was r.
14: 8. r. kingdom away from David
19: 11. strong wind r. mountains
2 K. 17: 21. he r. Isr. from David
22: 11. king heard he r. clothes
19. hast r. thy clothes, and wept
Ezr. 9: 3. heard this, I r. garment
5. having r. my garments and
Jb. 1: 20. Job arose, and r. mantle
2: 12. Job's friends r. ev. one mantle
26: 8. cloud is not r. under them
Je. 36: 24. not afraid, nor r. garm-s
Eze. 30: 16. Sin have pain, No be r.
Mat. 27: 51. vail of temple was r. and
rocks r., Mk. 15: 38. Lu. 23: 45.
Mk. 1: † 10. John saw the heavens r.
9: 26. spirit cried, and r. him sore
See Rent CLOTHES.

RENTEST. [ing

Je. 4: 30. tho. thou r. face wi. paint-

REPAID. [be r.

Pr. 13: 21. to righteous good shall

REPAIR.

2 K. 12: 5. let priests r. breaches of
house of G., 22: 5. [house?
7. Why r. ye not breaches of the
8. neither to r. breaches of house
12. and hewed stone to r. breaches,
22: 6. [L., 34: 8, 10.
2 Ch. 24: 4. minded to r. house of
24: 5. gather money to r. house
12. hired carpenters to r. house
Ezr. 9: 9. give reviving to r. house

Is. 61 : 4. they shall r. waste cities
Jo. 3 : † 16. L. will be the place of r.

REPAIRED.

Ju. 21 : 23. Benjamin r. cities, and
1 K. 11 : 27. Sol. r. breaches of city
18 : 30. Elijah r. the altar of Lord
2 K. 12:6. priests had not r. breaches
14. r. the house of the Lord
1 Ch. 11 : 8. Joab r. rest of the city
2 Ch. 26 : † 9. Uzziah r. the towers
29 : 3. Hezekiah r. doors of house
32 : 5. Hezekiah r. Millo in city of
33 : 16. Manasseh r. altar of L.
Ne. 3 : 4. next unto them r., 5, 7, 8,
10, 12, 19. [24.
16. after him r., 17, 18, 20, 22, 23,
† 26. The Nethinim in Ophel r.

REPAIRER.

Is. 58 : 12. be called r. of breach

REPAIRING.

2 Ch. 24 : 27. conc. r. of the house

REPAY.

De. 7 : 10. he will r. him to his face
Jb. 21 : 31. who r. him what done?
41 : 11. Who prevented th. I r. him?
Is. 59 : 18. acc-g to deeds he will r.
fury, to islands r. recompense
Lu. 10 : 35. when I come, I will r.
Ro. 12 : 19. Veng. is mine, I will r.
Phm. 19. I Paul have writ., I will r.

REPAYED. See REPAID. [it

REPAYETH.

De. 7 : 10. r. them that hate him

REPEATETH.

Pr. 17:9. he th. r. matter, separateth

REPENT.

Ex. 13 : 17. Lest peradv. people r.
32 : 12. Turn from wrath r. of this
Nu. 23:19. nei. son of man th. he r.
De. 32 : 36. L. r. for servants
1 S. 15 : 29. Strength of Isr. will not
r. he is not man that he r.
1 K. 8 : 47. if they r. in captivity
Jb. 42 : 6. I abhor myself, and r. in
Ps. 19:13. let it r. thee conc. servant
110:4. L. sworn, will not r., He. 7:21.
135 : 14. he will r. conc. serv-ts
Je. 4 : 28. I purposed it, will not r.
18 : 8. turn, I will r. of evil, 26:13.
10. if do evil, I will r. of good
26:3. that I may r. | 42:10. for I r.
Eze. 14 : 6. r. and turn fr. idols, 18:
24 : 14. spare, neither will I r. [30.
Jo. 2:14. Who knoweth if he will r.,
Jon. 3 : 9. [ing r., 4 : 17.
Mat. 3 : 2. John Bap. preached, say-
Mk. 1 : 15. Jesus preached, r. ye
6 : 12. they preached that men r.
Lu. 13 : 3. exc. ye r. ye sh. perish, 5.
16:30. if one went fr. dead, will r.
17 : 3. if thy brother r. forgive, 4.
Ac. 2 : 38. r. and be baptized every
3 : 19. r. ye thf. and be converted
8 : 22. r. of this thy wickedness
17 : 30. commandeth all men to r.
26 : 20. that they r. turn to God
2 Co. 7 : 8. I do not r. tho. I did r.
Re. 2:5. Remem. and r., exc. thou r.
16. r. else I will come quickly
21. I gave her space to r. of fornica.
22. except they r. of deeds
3 : 3. Rememb. how thou rec-d, r.
19. I chasten, be zealous thf. and

REPENTANCE. [r.

Ho. 13 : 14. r. be hid from mine eyes
Mat. 3:8. fruits meet for r., Lu. 3:8.
11. I baptize you unto r.
9 : 13. not to call righteous but sinners to r., Mk. 2 : 17. Lu. 5 : 32.
Mk. 1 : 4. John did preach baptism
of r., Lu. 3 : 3. Ac. 13:24.-19:4.
Lu. 15 : 7. ninety nine wh. need no r.
24 : 47. that r. be preached am. all
Ac. 5 : 31. God exalted for to give r.
11 : 18. God to Gentiles granted r.
20 : 21. testifying to the Greeks r.
26 : 20. do works meet for r.
Ro. 2 : 4. goodness of God leadeth to
11:29. gifts of G. are without r. [r.
2 Co. 7 : 9. I rejoice ye sorrowed to r.
10. godly sorrow worketh r.
2 Ti. 2 : 25. if God will give r. [r.
He. 6 : 1. not laying again founda. of
6. If fall, to renew them to r.
12 : 17. he found no place of r. tho.
2 Pe. 3 : 9. that all should come to

REPENTED. [r.

Ge. 6 : 6. it r. Lord, he made man
Ex. 32 : 14. L. r. of evil he thought, 2
S. 24:16. 1 Ch. 21:15. Je. 26:19.
Ju. 2 : 18. it r. Lord bec. of groanings
21 : 6. the children of Israel r., 15.
1 S. 15 : 35. L. r. he made Saul king
Ps. 106 : 45. L. r. acc. to mercies
Je. 8 : 6. no man r. of wickedness
20 : 16. cities L. overthrew, r. not
31 : 19. after I was turned I r.
Am. 7 : 3. The Lord r. for this, 6.
Jon. 3 : 10. God r. of the evil that
Zch. 8 : 14. to punish you, I r. not
Mat. 11 : 20. to upbraid, bec. r. not
21. wo. have r. long ago, Lu. 10:13.
12:41. men of Nineveh r. at preaching of Jonas, Lu. 11 : 32.
21 : 29. afterward he r. and went
32. when ye had seen it, r. not
27 : 3. Judas r. hims. brought silver
2 Co. 7 : 10. repentance not to be r.
12 : 21. not r. of uncleanness
Re. 2 : 21. space to repent, she r. not
9 : 20. not killed by plagues, yet r.
21. Nei. r. of their murders [not
16 : 9. blasphemed God, r. not, 11.

REPENTEST, ETH.

Ge. 6 : 7. it r-h me I made them
1 S. 15 : 11. r-h me I set up Saul
Jo. 2:13. slow to anger, and r-h him
Jon. 4 : 2. gracious God, and r-t thee
of the evil [r-h, 10.
Lu. 15 : 7. joy over one sinner that

REPENTING, S.

Je. 15 : 6. I am weary with r.
Ho. 11:8. my r-s are kindled together

REPETITIONS.

Mat. 6:7. use not vain r. as heathen

RE'PHAEL. See OTHNI.

RE'PHAH.

1 Ch. 7:25. sons of Ephr. R. Resheph

REPHAI'AH=RA'PHA.

1 Ch. 3:21. sons of R. sons of Arnan
4:42. having for their captains, R.
7 : 2. sons of Tola, Uzzi and R.
9 : 43. Binea; R. his son
Ne. 3 : 9. next unto them repaired R.

REPH'AIM.

Jos. 17:†15. land of Perizzites and R.
2 S. 5 : 18. Philis. spread in valley of
R., 22.-23:13. 1 Ch. 11:15.-14:9.
Is. 17 : 5. gathereth ears in valley of

REPH'AIMS. [R.

Ge. 14 : 5. smote R. in Ashteroth K.
15 : 20. to thy seed given land of R.

REPH'IDIM. [33 : 14.

Ex. 17 : 1. Isr. pitched in R., Nu.
8. Amalek fought with Isr. in R.
19 : 2. departed fr. R., Nu. 33 : 15.

REPLENISH, ED.

Ge. 1:28. multiply, and r. earth, 9:1.
Is. 2 : 6. bec. they be r-d from east
23 : 2. merchants have r-d Tyre
Je. 31 : 25. r-d every sorrowful soul
Eze. 26 : 2. I shall be r-d now she
27 : 25. wast r-d made glorious

REPLIEST.

Ro. 9:20. who thou that r. ag. God?

REPORT. [Noun.]

Ge. 37:2. Joseph brought their evil r.
Ex. 23 : 1. shalt not raise false r.
Nu. 13 : 32. brought evil r. of land
14 : 37. that did bring evil r. died
De. 2 : 25. who shall hear r. of thee
1 S. 2 : 24. it is no good r. I hear
1 K. 10 : 6. It was true r., 2 Ch. 9 : 5.
Ne. 6 : 13. have matter for evil r.
Pr. 15 : 30. good r. maketh fat
Is. 23 : 5. As at r. conc. Egypt, so
be pained at r. of Tyre
28:19. vexation only to underst. r.
53:1. Who hath believed our r.? to
whom? Jn. 12 : 38. Ro. 10 : 16.
Je. 50 : 43. king of Bab. heard the r.
Eze. 16 : †56. Sodom was not for a r.
Ha. 3 : † 2. I have heard thy r. and
Ac. 6 : 3. seven men of honest r.
10 : 22. Cornelius was of good r.
22:12. let Ananias having a good r.
2 Co. 6 : 8. by evil r. and good r. as
Ph. 4 : 8. whatso. things of good r.
1 Ti. 3 : 7. bishop must have good r.
He. 11 : 2. elders obtained good r.
39. these having obtained good r.
3 Jn. 12. Demetrius hath a good r.

REPORT. [Verb.]

Je. 20 : 10. r. say they, we will r. it
1 Co. 14 : 25. he will r. G. is in you

REPORTED. [mu

Ne. 6 : 6. It is r. am. heathen, Gash-
7. shall it be r. to king according
19. they r. his good deeds bef. me
Es. 1 : 17. despise husbands, when r.
Eze. 9 : 11. man wh. had inkhorn r.
Mat. 28 : 15. this saying commonly r.
Ac. 4 : 23. r. all chief priests said
16 : 2. Timotheus was well r. of
Ro. 3 : 8. as we be slanderously r.
1 Co. 5 : 1. It is r. there is fornication
1 Ti. 5 : 10. a widow, well r. of
1 Pe. 1 : 12. minister things now r.

REPOSSESS.

Ex. 15 : † 9. my hand shall r. them

REPROACH. [Noun.] [Eg.

Jos. 5 : 9. I have rolled away r. of
Ju. 5 : † 18. Zebulun exposed to r.
1 S. 17 : 26. taketh r. from Israel
Ne. 1 : 3. remnant are in great r.
4 : 4. turn their r. upon own head
5 : 9. because of r. of the heathen
Ps. 39 : 8. make me not r. of foolish
57 : 3. he shall save me from r.
69 : 7. for thy sake I have borne r.
20. r. hath broken my heart, I am
71:13. let them be covered with r.
78:66. he put them to perpetual r.
79 : 12. r. whw. they reproach thee
89 : 50. Remember r. of thy serv-ts
I bear r. of the mighty
119 : 22. Remove from me r. and
Pr. 6 : 33. his r. shall not be wiped
18 : 3. with ignominy cometh r.
19:26. son th. causeth shame and r.
22 : 10. Cast out scorner, r. cease
Is. 4 : 1. thy name to take our r.
51 : 7. fear ye not the r. of men
54 : 4. not rememb. r. of widowhood
Je. 23 : 40. I will bring an everl. r.
31 : 19. I did bear r. of my youth
51:51. confounded, bec. we heard r.
La. 3 : 30. he is filled full with r.
61. Thou hast heard their r. O L.
5:1. L. consider and behold our r.
Eze. 16 : 57. as at time of thy r.
21 : 28. conc-g r. of Ammonites
36 : 15. nei. shalt bear r. of people
30. ye rec. no more r. of famine
Da. 11 : 18. a prince sh. cause r. offered to cease, without his r.
Ho. 12 : 14. his r. sh. his L. return
Jo. 2 : 17. give not heritage to r.
Mi. 6 : 16. ye sh. bear r. of my peo.
Zph. 2 : 8. I have heard r. of Moab
3 : 18. to whom r. of it was burden
2 Co. 11 : 21. I speak as conc-g r.
1 Ti. 3:7. good report lest fall into r.
4 : 10. we both labour and suffer r.
He. 11 : 26. Esteeming r. of Christ
13 : 13. Let us go, bearing his r.

A REPROACH.

Ge. 34 : 14. do this, that were a r.
1 S. 11 : 2. lay it for a r. upon Isr.
Ne. 2 : 17. that we be no more a r.
Ps. 15 : 3. taketh not a r. ag. neighb.

Ps. 22 : 6. a r. of men, and despised
31 : 11. I was a r. among enemies
109 : 25. I became a r. unto them
Pr. 14 : 34. sin is a r. to any people
Is. 30 : 5. a people that were a r.
Je. 6 : 10. word of the Lord is a r.
20:8. word of the L. was made a r.
24 : 9. I will deliver them to be a
r., 29 : 18.–42 : 18.–44 : 8, 12.
49 : 13. Bozrah shall become a r.
Eze. 5 : 14. I will make thee a r. am.
15. Jerus. shall be a r. and taunt
22 : 4. I have made thee a r. unto
Da. 9 : 16. thy peo. are become a r.
Jo. 2 : 19. I will no more make you

My REPROACH. ⌊a r.

Ge. 30 : 23. God hath taken m. r.
1 S. 25 : 39. pleaded cause of m. r.
Jb. 19 : 5. ye plead against me m. r.
20:3. I have heard check of m. r.
Ps. 69 : 10. I wept, that was m. r.
19. Thou hast known m. r. and
119 : 39. Turn m. r. which I fear
Lu. 1 : 25. to take away m. r. am.
See NEIGHBOURS. ⌊men

REPROACHES.

Ps. 69:9. r. of them reproached thee
are upon me, Ro. 15 : 3.
Is. 43 : 28. I have given Israel to r.
2 Co. 12 : 10. I take pleasure in r.
He. 10 : 33. made gazingstock by r.

REPROACH. [Verb.]

Ru. 2 : 15. Let her glean, r. her not
2 K.19:4. whom king of Assyria sent
to r. God, 16. Is. 37 : 4, 17.
Ne. 6 : 13. that they might r. me
Jb. 27 : 6. heart not r. me long as I
Ps. 42:10. mine enemies r. me ⌊live
74 : 10. how long adversary r. me?
102 : 8. Mine enemies r. me all day
Lu. 6 : 22. men shall r. you for my

REPROACHED. ⌊sake

Le. 19 : † 20. lieth with bondmaid r.
2 S. 21:†21. when he r. Israel, Jona.
slew, 1 Ch. 20 : † 7. ⌈37 : 23.
2 K. 19 : 22. Whom hast thou r.? Is.
23. By thy messengers thou hast
r. the Lord, and, Is. 37:24. ⌈me
Jb. 19 : 3. These ten times have ye r.
Ps. 55 : 12. not an enemy that r. me
74:18. Remem., that enemy hath r.
79 : 12. whw. they r. thee, O Lord,
89:51. whw. enemies have r., O Lord
have r. footsteps of anointed
Zph. 2 : 8. whereby they r. my peo.
10. because they r. and magnified
1 Pe. 4 : 14. If ye be r. for Christ
See REPROACHES.

REPROACHEST, ETH.

Nu.15:30. doeth presumpt-ly, r-h L.
Ps. 44 : 16. voice of him that r-h
57 : † 3. he r-h him wo. swallow me
74 : 22. how foolish man r-h thee
119:42. to answer him that r-h me,
Pr. 27 : 11. ⌈Maker, 17 : 5.
Pr. 14 : 31. oppresseth poor r-h
Lu. 11 : 45. Master, thou r-t us also

REPROACHFULLY.

1 S. 6 : † 6. he had wrought r.
Jb. 16:10. smitten me upon cheek r.
1 Ti. 5 : 14. none occasion to speak r.

REPROBATE.

Je. 6 : 30. r. silver sh. men call them
Ro. 1 : 28. G. gave them to r. mind
2 Ti. 3 : 8. men r. conc. the faith
Tit. 1 : 16. to every good work r.

REPROBATES. ⌈r.

2 Co. 13 : 5. Christ is in you, exc. ye
6. ye shall know we are not r.
7. do that is honest, tho. we be as

REPROOF, S. ⌊r.

Jb. 26 : 11. are astonished at his r.
Ps. 38 : 14. In whose mouth no r-s
Pr. 1 : 23. Turn you at my r.: I will
25. But ye would none of my r.
30. they despised all my r.
5:12. say, How my heart despised r.

Pr. 6 : 23. r-s of instruction are life
10 : 17. he that refuseth r. erreth
12 : 1. he that hateth r. is brutish
13 : 18. regardeth r. be honoured
15 : 5. that regardeth r. is prudent
10. he that hateth r. shall die
31. heareth r. of life, abideth am.
32. heareth r. getteth underst-g
17 : 10. A r. ent-h more into wise
29 : † 1. man of r-s hardeneth neck
15. the rod and r. give wisdom
Ha. 2 : † 1. what answer upon my r.
2 Ti. 3 : 16. Scripture is profitable

REPROVE. ⌊for r.

2 K. 19 : 4. r. Rab-shakeh, Is. 37 : 4.
Jb. 6 : 25. what doth your arguing r.
26. Do ye imagine to r. words
13 : 10. He will r. if ye accept per-
22 : 4. Will he r. thee for fear ⌊sons
Ps. 50 : 8. I will not r. for offerings
21. I will r. thee, and set in order
141 : 5. let him r. me, it sh. be oil
Pr. 9 : 8. r. not a scorner lest he
19 : 25. r. one that hath underst-g
30 : 6. lest he r. and thou be liar
Is. 11 : 3. nei. r. after hearing of ears
4. r. with equity for the meek
Je. 2 : 19. backslidings shall r. thee
Ho. 4 : 4. let no man r. another
Mal. 2:†3. behold I will r. your seed
Jn. 16 : 8. he will r. world of sin
Ep. 5 : 11. no fellowship, rather r.
2 Ti. 4 : 2. r., rebuke, exhort with

REPROVED.

Ge. 20 : 16. thus Sarah was r.
21:25. Abraham r. Abimelech bec.
1 Ch.16:21. yea he r. kings for their
sakes, Ps. 105 : 14. ⌈hardeneth
Pr. 29 : 1. He that being often r.
Je. 29 : 27. why hast not r. Jere.?
Ha. 2:1. what I sh. answer when r.
Lu. 3 : 19. Herod being r. by John
Jn. 3 : 20. nei. to light lest deeds r.
Ep. 5 : 13. things r. are made mani-

REPROVER. ⌊fest

Pr. 25 : 12. so is a wise r. upon
Eze. 3 : 26. shalt not be to them a r.

REPROVETH. ⌈it

Jb.40:2. he that r. G. let him ans-r
Ps. 119 : † 42. so answer him r. me
Pr. 9 : 7. r. a scorner getteth shame
15 : 12. scorner loveth not one r.
Is. 29:21. lay a snare for him th. r.

REPROVING.

Eze. 3:†26. thou shalt not be man r.

REPUTATION. ⌈wisd.

Ec. 10 : 1. little folly him in r. for
Ac. 5 : 34. Gamaliel had in r. am.
Ga. 2 : 2. privately to them of r.⌊peo.
Ph. 2 : 7. But made himself of no r.
29. receive him, hold such in r.

REPUTED.

Jb.18:3. Whf. r. vile in your sight?
Da. 4 : 35. inhabitants r. as nothing

REQUEST, S.

Ju. 8 : 24. Gideon said, I desire a r.
2 S. 14 : 15. that king perform the r.
22 king hath fulfilled r. of servant
Ezr. 7 : 6. king granted all his r.
Ne.2:4. For what dost thou make r.
Es. 4 : 8 go unto king, to make r.
5 : 3. what is thy r. queen Esther?
6, 7, 8.–7 : 2.–9 : 12. ⌈my r.
7:3. my life be given, my people at
7. Haman stood to make r. for life
Jb. 6:8. O that I might have my r.!
Ps. 21 : 2. not withholden r. of lips
106:15. gave their r. sent leanness
Ro. 1 : 10. r. for prosperous journey
Ph. 1 : 4. in every prayer making r.
4:6. let your r-s be known unto G.

REQUEST. [Verb.]

1 Th 4:†1. we r. that as ye received

REQUESTED.

Ju. 8 : 26. weight of earrings he r.
1 K. 19 : 4. Elijah r. he might die
1 Ch. 4:10. God granted Jabez he r.

Ne. 13 : † 6. Neh. earnestly r. of king
Da. 1 : 8. r. of prince of eunuchs
2 : 49. Daniel r. of king, and he set

REQUIRE.

Ge 9 : 5. your blood will I r. of ev.
beast, of man will r. life of man
31 : 39. of my hand didst thou r. it
43 : 9. of my ha. shalt thou r. him
De. 10 : 12. what doth L. r.? Mi. 6:8.
18 : 19. not hearken, I will r. it
23 : 21. L. will surely r. it of thee
Jos. 22 : 23. let Lord r. it, 1 S.20:16.
2 S. 3 : 13. one thing I r. of thee
4 : 11. shall I not r. his blood at
19 : 38. whatso. thou r. will I do
1 K.8:†31. and he r. an oath of him
59. maintain cause as matter r.
1 Ch. 21 : 3. why lord r. this thing?
2 Ch. 24:22. Lord, look upon it, r. it
Ezr. 7 : 21. whatso. Ezra r. of you
8 : 22. ashamed to r. of king a band
Ne.5:12. We will r. nothing of them
Ps. 10 : 13. said, Thou wilt not r. it
Eze. 3 : 18. wicked, his blood will I
r. at thine hand, 20.–33 : 6, 8.
20:40. there will I r. your offerings
34:10. will r. my flock at their ha.
Lu. 12 : † 20. this night r. thy soul
1 Co. 1 : 22. Jews r. a sign, Greeks
7 : 36. need r. let him do what he

REQUIRED. ⌊will

Ge.42 : 22. behold, his blood is r.
Ex. 12 : 36. they lent such as they r.
1 S. 21 : 8. king's business r. haste
2 S.12:20. when he r. they set bread
1 Ch. 16 : 37. as every day's work r.
2 Ch. 8 : 14. as duty of every day r.,
Ezr. 3 : 4. ⌈bring
24:6. Why hast not r. of Levites to
Ne. 5 : 18. r. not I bread of gov-r
Es. 2 : 15. she r. nothing but what
Ps. 40 : 6. sin offering hast not r.
137:3. they th. wasted us, r. mirth
Pr. 30 : 7. Two things have I r. of
Is. 1 : 12. who r. this at your hand
Lu. 11 : 50. be r. of this genera., 51.
12:20. this night thy soul sh. be r.
48. much given, shall be much r.
19 : 23. r. mine own with usury
23 : 24. sentence it be as they r. ⌈ful
1 Co.4:2. r. in stewards man be faith-

REQUIREST, ETH, ING.

Ru. 3 : 11. I will do to thee all thou
Ec. 3 : 15. G. r-h that wh. is past ⌊r-t
Da. 2 : 11. it is a rare thing king r-h
Lu. 23 : 23. r-g he might be crucified

REQUITE, ED, ING.

Ge. 50 : 15. Joseph will r. us evil
De. 32 : 6. Do ye thus r. the Lord
Ju. 1 : 7. as I have done, G. r-d me
1 S. 25 : 21. he r-d me evil for good
2 S. 2 : 6. I will r. you this kindness
16 : 12. may be L. will r. me good
2 K. 9 26. I will r. thee in this plat
2 Ch. 6 : 23. judge serv-s by r-g wick-
Ps. 10 : 14. beholdest spite to r. it ⌊ed
41 : 10. L. raise me that I may r.
Je. 51 : 56. G. of recompenses sh. r.
1 Ti.5:4 let them learn to r. parents

REREWARD. See REARWARD

RESCUE, ED, ETH.

De. 28 : 31. shalt have none to r. th.
1 S. 14 : 45. people r-d Jonathan
30 : 18. and David r-d his two wives
Ps. 35 : 17. r. my soul fr. destruct-ns
Da. 6:27. He delivereth and r-h and
Ho. 5 : 14. I will take none sh. r. him
Ac. 23 : 27. came I with army, r-d

RESEMBLANCE. ⌊him

Zch. 5 : 6. This their r. thro. earth

RESEMBLE, ED.

Ju. 8 : 18. each one r-d chil. of king
Lu. 13 : 18. shall I r. kingdom of G.

RE'SEN.

Ge 10 : 12. R. the same is great city

RESERVE.

Ps. 79 : † 11. r. the children of death

Je. 3:5. Will he r. his anger for ever
50:20. I will pardon them wh. I r.
2 Pe. 2 : 9. r. unjust to day of judg-

RESERVED. [ment
Ge. 27 : 36. not r. blessing for me?
Nu. 18 : 9. thine of holy things r.
Ju. 21 : 22. we r. not each his wife
Ru. 2 : 18. gave mother that she r.
1 S. 9 : † 24. Behold that which is r.
2 S. 8 : 4. r. horses for 100 chariots,
1 Ch. 18 : 4. [struction
Jb. 21 : 30. wick. is r. to day of de-
38:23. I have r. ag. time of trouble
Ac. 25 : 21. Paul had appealed to be
Ro. 11 : 4. I have r. 7,000 men [r.
1 Pe. 1 : 4. inheritance r. in heaven
2 Pe. 2:4. deliv-d to be r. unto judgm
17. to whom mist of darkness is r.
3 : 7. heaven and earth r. unto fire
Jude 6. angels he hath r. in chains
13. to wh. is r. blackness of dark-

RESERVETH. [ness
Je. 5 : 24. he r. weeks of harvest
Na. 1 : 2. Lord r. wrath for enemies

RE'SHEPH. See REPHAH.

RESIDUE.
Ex. 10 : 5. locusts shall eat the r.
1 Ch. 6 : 66. r. of sons of Kohath
Ne. 11 : 20. r. of Israel were in cities
Is. 21:17. r. of archers be diminished
28 : 5. Lord be a diadem unto r.
38 : 10. I am deprived of r. of years
44 : 17. r. thereof he maketh a god
19. shall I make the r. abomina.
Je. 8 : 3. chosen, by all the r. of
15 : 9. r. will I deliver to sword
24 : 8. r. of Jerusalem that remain
27 : 19. saith, conc. r. of vessels
29 : 1. Jere. sent unto r. of elders
39:3. with all r. of princes of Bab.
41 : 10. Ishmael carried captive r.
52 : 15. r. of people that remained
Eze. 9 : 8. wilt destroy r. of Israel?
23 : 25. r. sh. be devoured by fire
34 : 18. must tread r. of pastures
36:3. possession unto r. of heathen
4. a derision to the r. of heathen
5. have I spoken ag. r. of heathen
48 : 18. r. in length ag. oblation
21. the r. shall be for the prince
Da. 7 : 7. stamped r. with feet, 19.
Jo. 1 : † 4. r. of palmerworm locusts
Zph. 2 : 9. r. of my people sh. spoil
Hag. 2 : 2. speak to Josh. and r. of
Zch. 8:11. I will not be to r. as [peo.
14 : 2. r. of people not be cut off
Mal. 2 : 15. had he r. of the Spirit
Mk. 16 : 13. they told it unto the r.
Ac. 15:17. That r. might seek the L.

RESIST.
Zch. 3 : 1. Satan at right hand to r.
Mat. 5 : 39. But I say r. not evil [r.
Lu. 21:15. adversaries not be able to
Ac. 6 : 10. were not able to r. spirit
7 : 51. ye do always r. Holy Ghost
Ro. 13 : 2. r. sh. receive damnation
2 Ti. 3 : 8. so do these r. the truth
Ja. 4 : 7. r. devil he will flee [you
5 : 6. ye killed just, he doth not r.
1 Pe. 5 : 9. Whom r. stedfast in faith

RESISTED, ETH.
Ro. 9:19. say, who hath r-d his will?
13:2. Whoso. r-h power, r-h ordin.
He. 12 : 4. ye have not r-d unto bl.
Ja. 4:6. God r-h the proud, 1 Pe. 5:5.

RESOLVED.
Lu. 16 : 4. I am r. what to do, when

RESORT. [Verb.]
Ne. 4:20. r. ye thither unto us, God
Ps. 71 : 3. wh-to I may contin-y r.
Mk. 10 : 1. the people r. unto him
Jn. 18 : 20. temple, whither Jews r.

RESORTED. [him
2 Ch. 11 : 13. priests and Lev. r. to
Mk. 2 : 13. multitude r. unto him
Jn. 10 : 41. and many r. unto him
18:2. Jesus ofttimes r. thither with
Ac. 16:13. spake unto women who r.

RESPECT. [Noun.] [thi.
Ge. 4:4. the Lord had r. unto Abel
5. unto Cain, and off-g, had not r.
Ex. 2 : 25. God had r. unto them
Le. 26 : 9. I will have r. unto you
1 K. 8 : 28. have thou r. unto prayer
of thy servant, 2 Ch. 6 : 19.
2 K. 13 : 23. Lord had r. unto them
2 Ch. 19 : 7. is no r. of persons with
G., Ro. 2 : 11. Ep. 6:9. Col. 3:25.
Ps. 74 : 20. Have r. unto covenant
119 : 6. I have r. unto thy com-ts
15. I will have r. unto thy ways
117. I will have r. unto thy stat-
138:6. hath he r. unto lowly [utes
Pr. 24 : 23. not good to have r. of
persons in judgment, 28 : 21.
Is. 17:7. eyes sh. have r. to Holy One
22:11. nor r. unto him fashioned it
2 Co. 3 : 10. had no glory in this r.
Ph. 4 : 11. Not speak in r. of want
Col. 2 : 16. judge in r. of holyday
He. 11 : 26. Moses had r. to recomp.
Ja. 2 : 1. not faith with r. of persons
3. ye have r. to him weareth gay
9. if ye have r. to persons, ye
1 Pe. 1:17. who without r. of persons

RESPECT, ED.
Le. 19:15. shalt not r. person of poor
Nu. 16 : 15. Moses said, r. not off-g
De. 1 : 17. Ye shall not r. persons in
judgment, 16 : 19. [person
2 S. 14 : 14. neither doth God r. any
Is. 17 : 8. nei. r. th. wh. fingers made
La. 4 : 16. r-d not persons of priests

RESPECTEDST, ETH.
Jb. 37 : 24. r-h not any that are wise
Ps. 40 : 4. Blessed is man th. r-h not
Is. 57 : † 9. thou r-t king [proud

RESPECTER. [pers.
Ac. 10 : 34. I perceive G. is no r. of

RESPIRATION.
Es. 4 : † 14. then sh. r. arise to Jews

RESPITE.
Ex. 8 : 15. Pha. saw there was r.
1 S. 11:3. said, Give us seven days r.

REST. [Remainder.]
Ge. 30 : 36. Jacob fed r. of flock
Ex. 28 : 10. names of the r. on stone
Le. 5 : 9. r. of blood be wrung
14:17. r. of the oil in his hand, 29.
Nu. 31 : 8. r. of them were slain
32. booty being r. of the prey
De. 3 : 13. the r. of Gilead gave I
Jos. 10 : 20. r. entered fenced cities
Ju. 7 : 6. r. bowed down to drink
8. r. of Israel unto tent, 1 S. 13:2.
1 S. 15 : 15. r. have we destroyed
2 S. 10 : 10. r. of people he delivered
to Abishai, 1 Ch. 19 : 11.
12 : 28. gather r. of peo. together
1 K. 20 : 30. the r. fled to Aphek to
2 K. 4 : 7. live and chil. of the r.
25 : 11. r. of people left in city, Je.
39 : 9.-52 : 15.
1 Ch. 11 : 8. Joab repaired r. of city
16 : 41. r. chosen to give thanks
2 Ch. 24 : 14. they bro-t r. of money
Ne. 2 : 16. nor told it to the r. that
6 : 1. r. of enemies heard I built
11:1. r. of the people also cast lots
Es. 9 : 12. what in r. of provinces?
Ps. 17 : 14. leave r. to their babes
Is. 10 : 19. r. of the trees be few [Isr.
Eze. 45 : 8. r. of land sh. they give to
48 : 23. as for r. of tribes Benj. sh.
Da. 2 : 18. Daniel not perish with r.
Zch. 11 : 9. let r. eat flesh of another
Mat. 27 : 49. r. said, let see if Elias
Lu. 12 : 26. why take thought for r.
24 : 9. told unto eleven and all r.
Ac. 2 : 37. said unto Peter and r. of
5:13. of r. durst no man join hims.
27 : 44. the r. escaped all safe
Ro. 11 : 7. election, r. were blinded
1 Co. 7 : 12. to r. speak I, not Lord
1 Co. 11 : 34. the r. will I set in order
1 Pe. 4 : 2. not live r. of his time to
Re. 2 : 24. and unto r. in Thyatira
9 : 20. r. not killed repented not
20:5. r. of the dead lived not again
till 1,000 years
See **The rest of the ACTS.**

REST of the people.
Ju. 7:6. r.- bowed upon knees to dri.
1 S. 13 : 2. r. - he sent unto tent
2 S. 10:10. r. - he deliv-d into hand
12 : 28. gather r. -, encamp ag. city
2 K. 25:11. r. - th. were left in city
Ne. 4 : 14. I said to nobles and r. -
7 : 72. r.- gave 20,000 drams of gold
10 : 28. r. - priests, Levites and
Je. 39 : 9. fell to him with the r. -

REST. [Repose.]
Ge. 8:†21. Lord smelled savour of r.
49 : 15. Issachar saw r. was good
Ex. 16 : 23. To morrow r. of sabbath
31 : 15. in seventh is sabbath of r.,
35 : 2. Le. 16:31.-23:3, 32.-25:4.
33 : 14. and I will give thee r.
Le. 25 : 5. is a year of r. unto land
Nu. 28 : † 2. offering for savour of r.
De. 3 : 20. until Lord have given r.
unto brethren, Jos. 1 : 13.
12:9. ye are not yet come to the r.
10. giveth you r. from enemies
25 : 19. when L. hath given thee r.
28 : 65. nei. sh. sole of foot have r.
Jos. 1 : 15. L. have given brethren r.
14 : 15. the land had r. from war,
Ju. 3 : 11.-5 : 31. [about
21 : 44. Lord gave them r. round
22 : 4. God hath given r.
23 : 1. Lord had given r. [years
Ju. 3 : 30. the land had r. eighty
Ru. 1 : 9. L. grant ye find r. each
3 : 1. dau. shall I seek r. for thee
18. the man will not be in r. till
2 S. 7:1. L. given him r. fr. enemies,
1 K. 5 : 4.-8 : 56. 2 Ch. 14 : 6, 7.
14 : † 17. word of king be for r.
1 Ch. 6 : 31. after that ark had r.
22 : 9. who shall be a man of r. and
I will give him r. [ev. side
18. hath he not given you r. on
23 : 25. God hath given r. to peo.
28:2. in heart to build a hou. of r.
2 Ch. 15 : 15. L. gave them r. about
20 : 30. for his God gave him r.
Ezr. 6 : † 10. may offer sacrifi-s of r.
Ne. 9 : 28. after they had r. did evil
Es. 2 : † 18. made a r. to provinces
9 : 16. Jews had r. from enemies
Jb. 3:13. slept, then had I been at r.
17. there the weary be at r.
26. I was not in safety, nei. had r.
11 : 18. shalt take thy r. in safety
17 : 16. our r. together is in dust
36:† 16. r. of thy table sho. be full
Ps. 38 : 3. nei. any r. in my bones
55 : 6. wo. I fly away and be at r.
94 : 13. give him r. from adversity
95 : 11. sho. not enter into my r.
116:7. Return unto thy r. my soul
132 : 8. Arise, O Lord, into thy r.
14. This is my r. forever, here
Pr. 29 : 17. Correct son, he give r.
Ec. 2 : 23. his heart taketh not r.
6 : 5. this hath more r. than other
Is. 11 : 10. his r. shall be glorious
14 : 3. L. sh. give r. fr. thy sorrow
7. whole earth is at r., Zch. 1:11.
18 : 4. L. said, I will take my r. [ry
28 : 12. This is r. wh w. ye cause wea-
30 : 15. In return-g and r. be saved
34 : 14. find for herself place of r.
66 : 1. where is place of my r.?
Je. 6 : 16. ye shall find r. for souls
30 : 10. Jacob shall be in r., 46 : 27.
50 : 34. that he give r. to land
Eze. 16 : † 19. bef. them for savour of
20:†41. accept with savour of r. [r.
38 : 11. I will go to them are at r.

Da. 4 : 4. I Neb-r at r. in mine house
Mi. 2 : 10. depart, this is not your r.
Zch. 9 : 1. Damascus shall be the r.
Mat. 11 : 28. Come, I will give you r.
29. ye sh. find r. unto your souls
12:43. seeking r. findeth none, Lu.
11 : 24. [14 : 41.
26 : 45. Sleep on, take your r., Mk.
Jn.11:13.he had spoken of taking r.
Ac. 7 : 49. what is place of my r.?
9 : 31. Then had the churches r.
2 Th.1:7. to you who are troubled r.
He.3:11.sh.not enter into my r.,18.
4:1. promise left us of ent-g into r.
3.we wh. believed do enter into r.
5. If they shall enter into my r.
8. For if Jesus had given them r.
9. remaineth a r. to peo. of God
10. he that is entered into his r.
11. Let us labour to ent. into that [r.

No REST.

Ge. 8 : 9. dove found n. r. for foot
Jb. 30 : 17. my sinews take n. r.
Pr. 29 : 9. rage or laugh there is n.r.
Is. 23 : 12. shalt thou have n. r.
62 : 7. give him n. r. till he establ.
Je. 45 : 3. I fainted, and find n. r.
La. 1 : 3. am. heathen findeth n. r.
2 : 18. give thyself n. r.
5 : 5. we have n. r. [bec.
2 Co. 2 : 13. I had n. r. in my spirit
7 : 5. into Macedon., our flesh n. r.
Re. 14:11. have n. r. day nor night

REST. [Verb.]

Ge. 18 : 4. wash feet r. under tree
Ex. 5 : 5. ye make them r. fr. burd.
23 : 11. seventh year shalt let it r.
12. seventh day shalt r., 34 : 21.
34 : 21. in earing time and harvest
Le. 23 : † 32. fr. even to even r. [r.
25:†2. then shall the land r.,26:34.
26:35.bec. it did not r. in sabbaths
De. 5 : 14. thy maidservant may r.
Jos. 3 : 13. soon as feet of priests r.
2 S. 3 : 29. Let it r. on head of Joab
7 : 11. caused thee to r. fr. enemies
21 : 10. nei. birds to r. on by day
2 K. 2 : 15. spirit of Elijah r. on Eli-
2 Ch. 14 : 11. we r. on thee [sha
Jb. 3 : 18. There prisoners r. toget.
14 : 6. r. till he shall accomplish
Ps. 16 : 9. my flesh sh. r. in hope,
37:7. r. in the Lord, wait [Ac.2:26.
125 : 3. rod of wicked not r. upon
Pr. 6 : 35. will r. content [righte.
Can. 1 : 7. where makest thy flock r.
Is. 7 : 19. shall r. in desol. valleys
11:2. Spirit of L. shall r. upon him
25 : 10. in this mt. hand of L. r.
28 : 12. ye may cause weary to r.
30:†32. the staff shall r. upon him
34 : 14. screech owl shall r. there
51 : 4. my judgment to r. for light
57 : 2. they shall r. in their beds
20. troubled sea, when it can-t r.
62 : 1. for Jerus.' sake I will not r.
63:14. Spirit of L. caused him to r.
Je. 31 : 2. I went to cause him to r.
47 : 6. put up into thy scabbard, r.
Eze. 5 : 13. I will cause my fury to
r. upon them, 16 : 42.-21 : 17.-
24 : 13.
44 : 30. may cause blessing to r.
Da. 12 : 13. shalt r. in thy lot
Ha.3:16. might r. in day of trouble
Zph. 3 : 17. he will r. in love, he
Mk. 6 : 31. into desert place, and r.
Lu. 10 : 6. your peace shall r. [me
2 Co. 12 : 9. power of C. may r. upon
He. 4 : 4. God did r. seventh day
Re. 4 : 8. they r. not day and night
6 : 11. they should r. for a season
14 : 13. that they may r. from la-
[bours

RESTED.

Ge. 2:2. he r. on seventh day, 3. Ex.
20 : 11.-31 : 17. [E
8:4. ark r., Ex. 10:14. locusts r. in

Ex. 16 : 30. people r. on 7th day
Nu.9:18. as cloud abode they r., 23.
10 : 12. cloud r. in wild. of Paran
36. when it r. he said, Return, O
11:25. Spirit r. upon them, 26. [L.
Jos. 11 : 23. And land r. from war
1 S. 25 : † 9. spake in Da.'s name, r.
1 K. 6 : 10. chambers r. on house
2 Ch.32:8.peo. r.upon words of Hez.
Es. 9 : 17. on 14th day r., 18.
22. wh-n Jews r. from enemies.
Jb. 30 : 27. My bowels boiled r. not
Lu. 23 : 56. they r. sabbath day

RESTEST.

Ro. 2 : 17. thou art a Jew, r. in law

RESTETH.

Jb.24:23.given in safety, wh-n he r.
Pr. 14 : 33. Wisdom r. in heart of
Ec. 7 : 9. anger r. in bosom of fools
Is. 7 : † 2. saying, Syria r. on Ephr.
1 Pe. 4 : 14. Spirit of G. r. upon you

RESTING place, s.

Nu. 10 : 33. to search out a r. p.
2 Ch. 6 : 41. arise, O L. into thy r.p.
Pr. 24 : 15. spoil not his r. p.
Is. 32 : 18. my peo. dwell in r. p-s
Je. 50 : 6. have forgotten their r. p.

RESTITUTION.

Ex. 22 : 3. make full r., 5, 6, 12.
Jb.20.18.acc. to his substance r. be
Ac. 3 : 21. until times of r. of all
[things

RESTORE.

Ge. 20 : 7. r. the man his wife, if r.
her not, thou shalt die
40:13.Pha. will r.thee unto thy pla.
42 : 25. to r. every man's money
Ex. 22 : 1. r. five oxen for an ox
4. If theft found, he sh. r.double
Le. 6 : 4. he shall r. that he took
5. he shall r. it in the principal
24 : 21. killeth beast, he sh. r. it
25 : 27. r. overplus unto whom sold
28. But if he be not able to r. it
Nu. 35 : 25. congr-n shall r. him
De. 22 : 2. things strayed shalt r.
Ju. 11 : 13. r. those lands peaceably
17 : 3. I will r. it, 1 S. 12 : 3. 1 K.
20 : 34. [of Saul
2 S. 9 : 7. I will r. thee all the land
12 : 6. he sh. r. the lamb fourfold
16:3. To day sh. house of Isr. r.me
2 K. 8 : 6. r. all that was hers, fruits
Ne. 5 : 11. r. I pray you vineyards
12 they said, we will r. them
Jb. 20 : 10. his hands shall r. goods
18. That he laboured for shall r.
Ps. 51 : 12. r. unto me joy of salva.
Pr.6:31.found, he shall r. sevenfold
Is. 1 : 26. I will r. thy judges
42 : 22. are for spoil, none saith r.
49 : 6. to r. preserved of Israel
57 : 18. I will r. comforts unto him
Je. 27:22. I will r. them to this pla.
30 : 17. I will r. health unto thee
Eze. 33 : 15. If the wicked r. pledge
Da. 9 : 25. command to r. Jerusalem
Jo. 2 : 25. I will r. you the years
Mat. 17 : 11. Elias shall r. all things
Lu. 19 : 8. taken, I r. him fourfold
Ac. 1 : 6. L. will r. kingdom to Isr.?
Ga. 6 : 1. r. such a one in meekness

RESTORED.

Ge. 20 : 14. Abimelech r. him Sarah
40 : 21. he r. chief butler unto his
41 : 13. me he r. unto mine office
42 : 28. My money is r. in my sack
De. 28 : 31. thine ass shall not be r.
Ju. 17 : 3. had r. 1,100 shekels, 4.
1 S. 7 : 14. cities taken fr. Israel r.
1 K. 13 : 6. pray my hand may be r.:
king's hand was r. [life, 5.
2 K. 8 : 1. whose son he had r. to
14 : 22. he r. Elath to Jud., 2 Ch.
25. He r. coast of Israel fr. [26:2.
2 Ch. 8 : 2. cities Huram had r. [r.
Ezr. 6 : 5. vessels bro-t unto Bab. be
Ps. 69 : 4. I r. that which I took not

Eze. 18 : 7. r. to debtor his pledge
12. violence, hath not r. pledge
Mat. 12 : 13. hand it was r. whole
like other, Mk. 3 : 5. Lu. 6 : 10.
Mk. 8 : 25. his sight was r. he saw
He.13:19. that I be r. to you sooner

RESTORER.

Ru. 4 : 15. be to thee a r. of life
Is. 58 : 12. sh. be called r. of paths

RESTORETH, ING.

Ps. 19 : † 7. law perfect, r-g the soul
23 : 3. He r-h my soul, leadeth
Mi. 2 : † 4. instead of r-g he divided
Mk. 9 : 12. Elias cometh first, r-h all

RESTRAIN.

1 S. 9 : † 17. this shall r. my people
2 K. 4 : † 24. r. not for me to ride
Jb. 15 : 8. dost thou r. wisdom [r.
Ps. 76 : 10. remainder of wrath shalt
Da. 9 : † 24. Seventy weeks to r.

RESTRAINED.[traneg.

Ge. 8 : 2. rain from heaven was r.
11 : 6. nothing will be r. fr. them
16 : 2. said, Lord r. me fr. bearing
Ex. 36 : 6. peo. were r. fr. bringing
1 S. 3 : 13. Eli's sons vile, he r. not
Is. 63 : 15. thy mercies, are they r.?
Eze. 31 : † 18. the day shall be r.
31 : 15. I r. floods and great waters
Ac.14:18. with sayings scarce r.peo.

RESTRAINEST.

Jb. 15 : 4. thou r. prayer before God

RESTRAINT, S.

Le. 23:†36. it is a day of r., De. 16:†8.
2 Ch. 7:†9. Ne. 8 : †18. Jo. 1:†14.
Ju. 18 : † 7. was no heir of r. that
might put them to shame
1 S. 14 : 6. is no r. to Lord to save
Je. 14 : † 1. word of Lord conc. r-s
17 : † 8. not be careful in year of r.

RESTS.

1 K. 6:6.he made narrowed r.round

RESURRECTION.

Mat. 22:23. Sadducees, who say is no
r. Mk. 12:18. Ac. 23:8. 1 Co.15:12.
28. in the r. whose wife she be of
the seven? Mk. 12:23. Lu.20:33.
Mat. 22 : 30. in the r. they neither
marry, nor, Lu. 20:35. [read th.
31. as touching the r. have ye not
27 : 53. out of graves after his r.
Lu. 14 : 14. be recompensed at r.
20 : 27. deny any r. | 36. chil. of r.
Jn. 5 : 29. done good unto r. of life,
done evil unto r. of damnation
11:24. my brother sh. rise in the r.
25. Jesus said, I am the r. and
Ac. 1 : 22. witness with us of his r.
2 : 31. David spake of r. of Christ
4 : 2. they preached thro. Jesus r.
33. gave witness of r. of the Lord
17 : 18. he preached Jesus and r.
32. heard of r. some mocked
23 : 6. of r. I am called in question
24 : 15. there shall be a r. of dead
21. I cried, touching r. of dead
Ro. 1 : 4. declared by r. from dead
6 : 5. we sh. be in liken. of his r.
1 Co. 15 : 13. if be no r. of dead
21. by man came the r. of dead
42. So is r. of the dead [r.
Ph. 3 : 10. I may know power of his
11. If I attain unto r. of the dead
2 Ti. 2 : 18. saying, that r. is past
He. 6 : 2. of r. fr. dead, and eternal
11 : 35. might obtain a better r.
1 Pe. 1 : 3. hope, by r. of Je-us from
3 : 21. save us, by r. of J. C. [dead
Re. 20 : 5. This is the first r. [r.
6. Blessed is he hath part in first

RETAIN.

1 Ch. 29:†14. that we sho. r. strength
Jb. 2 : 9. Dost thou still r. integrity
Pr 4 : 4. Let thine heart r. my words
11 : 16. strong men r. riches
Ec. 8 : 8. no man power to r. spirit
Da. 11:6. she sh. not r. power of arm

Jn. 20 : 23. Whosesoever sins ye r.
Ro. 1 : 28. did not like to r. God in [knowl.

RETAINED.

Ju. 7 : 8. Gideon r. those 300 men
19 : 4. the damsel's father r. him
Da. 10 : 8. and I r. no strength, 16.
Jn. 20 : 23. sins ye retain, they are r.
Phm. 13. Whom I would have r.

RETAINETH.

Pr. 3 : 18. happy is every one r. her
11 : 16. gracious woman r. honour
Mi. 7 : 18. he r. not anger for ever

RETIRE, ED.

Ju. 20 : 39. men of Isr. r-d in battle
2 S. 11 : 15. Set him in battle, and r.
20 : 22. they r-d fr. city every man
Je. 4 : 6. Set up standard tow. Zion, r.

RETURN. [Noun.]

Ge. 14 : 17. to meet Abram aft. his r.
1 S. 7 : 17. Sam.'s r. was to Ramah
2 S. 11 : † 1. at r. of year Dav. sent,
1 Ch. 20 : † 1. [will come, 26.
1 K. 20 : 22 at r. of y-r king of Syria
2 Ch. 36 : † 10. at r. of year Neb-r sent

RETURN. [Verb.]

Ge. 3 : 19. till thou r. unto ground ; dust thou art, unto dust r.
16 : 9. r. to thy mistress, submit [14.
18 : 10. I will certainly r. unto thee,
31 : 3. r. unto la. of thy kindred, 13.
32 : 9. Lord, wh. saidst unto me, r.
Ex. 4 : 18. Let me r. unto breth. in
19. L. said unto Mo., r. into Eg.
13 : 17. lest peo. repent, and r. to E.
Le. 25 : 10. shall r. unto his possession, 13, 27, 28. [family
41. and he shall r. unto his own
27 : 24. year of jubilee, field sh. r.
Nu. 8 : † 25. age of 50 r. fr. warfare
10 : 36. r. L. unto many thousands
14 : 4. Let us make capt., r. into E.
23 : 5. Lord said, r. unto Balak
32 : 22. ye shall r. and be guiltless
35 : 28. slayer shall r., Jos. 20 : 6.
De. 3 : 20. then sh. ye r. ev. man unto his possession, Jos. 1 : 15.
17 : 16. nor cause peo. r. to Egypt
20 : 5. let him r. to house, 6, 7, 8.
30 : 3. God will r. and gath. thee
8. thou shalt r. and obey the L.
Jos. 22 : 4. now r. ye unto tents
8. r. wi. much riches unto tents
Ju. 7 : 3. Whoso. is fearful, let him r.
11 : 31. when I r. fr. chil. of Ammon
Ru. 1 : 6. that she might r. fr. Moab
8. Naomi said, go r. to mother's
10. surely we will r. with thee
15. r. thou after thy sister in law
1 S. 6 : 3. in any wise r. offering, 4.
8. jewels of gold wh. ye r. him
9 : 5. Saul said, Come, let us r.
26 : 21. Then said Saul, r. my son Da.
29 : 4. said, Make this fellow r., 7.
2 S. 2 : 26. ere thou bid people r.?
3 : 16. said Abner unto him, Go, r.
10 : 5. beards be grown, r., 1 Ch. 19:
15 : 19. Wh. goest with us? r. [5.
20. I go whither I may, r. thou
34. if thou r. to the city and, 27.
19 : 14. said, r. thou and servants
24 : 13. see what answer I shall r.
1 K. 2 : 32. L. shall r. his blood, 33.
44. Lord shall r. thy wickedness
8 : 48. r. unto thee with all their soul
12 : 24. r. every man to house
26. Now shall kingdom r. to David
19 : 15. r. on thy way to wilderness
† 20. Elijah said, Go r. again
22 : 17. let r. ev. man to house in peace, 2 Ch. 11 : 4.-18 : 16. [18 : 27.
28. If thou r. at all in peace, 2 Ch.
2 K. 18 : 14. I have offended, r. fr. me
19 : 7. king of Assyria shall r. to own land, 33. Is. 37 : 7, 34.
20 : 10. let the shadow r. backward
2 Ch. 6 : 24. r. and confess thy name
38. If they r. with all their heart

2 Ch. 10 : 9. we may r. answer to peo.
18 : 26. fellow in prison until I r.
30 : 6. he will r. to you | 9. if ye r.
Ne. 2 : 6. king said, when wilt r.?
4 : 12. whence ye shall r. unto us
Es. 4 : 15. Es. bade them r. answer
9 : 25. device of Haman r. upon own
Jb. 1 : 21. naked shall I r. thither
6 : 29. r. yea, r. again, my right-n.
7 : 10. He sh. r. no more to his ho.
15 : 22. believeth not he shall r.
17 : 10. But as for you all, do ye r.
22 : 23. If thou r. to the Almighty
33 : 25. sh. r. to days of his youth
35 : † 4. I will r. words to thee [ty
36 : 10. com-doth they r. fr. iniqui-
Ps. 6 : 4. r. O L., deliver my soul
10. let mine enemies r. ashamed
7 : 7. for their sakes r. thou on high
16. mischief sh. r. upon own head
59 : 6. They r. at evening
14. and at evening let them r.
73 : 10. Theref. his people r. hither
74 : 21. let not oppressed r. ashamed
80 : 14. r. we beseech thee, O God
90 : 3. sayest, r. ye chil. of men
13. r. O Lord, how long? and
94 : 15. judgment sh. r. unto right-n
104 : 29. they die, r. to their dust
116 : 7. r. unto thy rest, O my soul
Pr. 2 : 19. None that go unto her r.
26 : 27. rolleth a stone, it will r.
Ec. 1 : 7. rivers come, thither they r.
5 : 15. naked r. to go as he came
12 : 2. nor clouds r. after the rain
7. dust shall r. to earth, and spirit r. unto God [that we
Can. 6 : 13. r. r. O Shulamite, r. r.
Is. 1 : † 27. th. r. of her be redeemed
6 : 13. yet in it a tenth shall r.
10 : 21. remnant of Jacob sh. r., 22.
21 : 12. if ye will, inquire, r. [11.
35 : 10. ransomed of L. shall r., 51:
41 : † 28. no man could r. a word
44 : 22. r. unto me, for I redeemed
63 : 17. r. for thy servant's sake
Je. 3 : 1. shall he r. unto wife again?
yet r. unto me [Isr.
12. proclaim words, r. backsliding
22. r. ye backsliding children
4 : 1. if wilt r. saith L., r. unto me
12 : 15. I will r. have compassion
15 : 19. saith L., If r. thou shalt stand bef. me : let them r. unto thee, r. not unto them [35 : 15.
18 : 11. r. ye ev. one fr. evil way,
22 : 10. r. no more to his country
23 : 14. none doth r. fr. wickedness
24 : 7. shall r. with whole heart
30 : 10. Jacob shall r. and, 46 : 27.
31 : 8. great company sh. r. thither
36 : 3. may r. ev. man fr. evil way
7. will r. every one fr. evil way
37 : 7. Pha.'s army shall r. to Eg.
Je. 44 : 14. that they r. into land of Jud. for none shall r. but, 28.
50 : 9. arrows none shall r. in vain
Eze. 16 : 55. when Sodom, Samaria r. thou and dau-s shall r. [live
18 : 23. that wicked r. fr. ways and
46 : 17. aft. it shall r. to the prince
Da. 9 : † 25. sh. street r. and be built
10 : 20. will I r. to fight Persia
11 : 9. r. into his own land, 10, 28.
13. the king of the north shall r.
29. the time appointed he sh. r.
30. thf. he sh. be grieved and r.
Ho. 2 : 7. I will r. to my first husb.
9. will r. and take my corn and
3 : 5. shall the children of Israel r.
5 : 15. I will go and r. to my place
7 : 16. They r. but not to Most High
8 : 13. they shall r. to Egypt, 9 : 3.
12 : 14. reproach sh. L. r. unto him
14 : 7. dwell under shadow shall r.
Jo. 2 : 14. Who knoweth if he will r.
3 : 4. speedily will I r. recomp., 7.

Ob. 15. thy reward sh. r. upon head
Mi. 1 : 7. sh. r. to hire of harlot
5 : 3. remnant of his breth. shall r.
Mal. 1 : 4. Edom saith, we will r. and
3 : 7. r. unto me, and I will r. unto you, saith Lord. But ye said, Wherein shall we r.? [righte.
18. sh. ye r. and discern betw.
Mat. 10 : 13. if not worthy, let peace r.
12 : 44. I will r. unto my hou., Lu.
24 : 18. Nei. let him in field, r. [11 : 24.
Lu. 8 : 39. r. to thine own house
12 : 36. he will r. from wedding
Ac. 15 : 16. Aft. this I will r. and build
18 : 21. I will r. unto you, if G. will

Not RETURN.

Nu. 32 : 18. We will n. r. unto houses
De. 28 : † 31. thy ass taken, sh. n. r.
1 S. 15 : 26. Sam. said, I will n. r.
2 S. 12 : 23. he shall n. r. to me
1 K. 13 : 16. he said, I may n. r.
Jb. 7 : † 7. eye n. r. to see good
10 : 21. go whence I sh. n. r., 16 : 22.
39 : 4. they go forth, and r. n.
Is. 45 : 23. word is gone out, sh. n. r.
55 : 11. it sh. n. r. unto me void
Je. 8 : 4. he turn away, and n. r.?
15 : 7. they r. n. fr. their ways
22 : 11. He shall n. r. thither, 27.
23 : 20. anger of L. shall n. r., 30 : 24.
Eze. 7 : 13. seller n. r. to what is sold, whole multitude shall n. r.
13 : 22. that he n. r. fr. wicked way
21 : 5. my sword n. r. into sheath
35 : 9. thy cities shall n. r. and ye
46 : 9. sh. n. r. by way he came
Ho. 7 : 10. they do n. r. to the Lord
11 : 5. he shall n. r. into Egypt
9. I will n. r. to destroy Ephraim
Mat. 2 : 12. warned they n. r. to Herod
Lu. 17 : 31. let him likewise n. r.

To RETURN. [back

Ex. 4 : 21. When goest t. r. into Eg.
Nu. 14 : 3. better for us t. r. into Eg.?
De. 17 : 16. cause peo. t. r. to Egypt
Ru. 1 : 7. t. r. unto land of Judah
16. entreat me not to leave or t. r.
1 S. 29 : 11. Da. rose early t. r. [9.
2 Ch. 10 : 6. What counsel t. r. ans.,
Ne. 9 : 17. appointed a captain t. r. to bondage [11 : 5.
Je. 5 : 3. have refused t. r., 8 : 5. Ho.
22 : 27. land they desire t. r., 44 : 14.
29 : 10. in causing you t. r. to this place, 30 : 3.-32 : 44.-33 : 7, 11, 26.
-34 : 22.-42 : 12. [16.
34 : 11. they caused servants t. r.,
37 : 20. cause me not t. r., 38 : 26.
La. 3 : † 21. I make t. r. to heart
Eze. 21 : 30. cause t. r. into sheath?
29 : 14. cause them t. r. into Pathros
47 : 6. caused me t. r. to river
Ho. 4 : † 9. I will cause t. r. doings
11 : 5. king, bec. they refused t. r.
Lu. 19 : 12. receive kingd. and t. r.
Ac. 13 : 34. no more t. r. to corrupt.
20 : 3. purposed t. r. thro. Maced.

RETURN to or unto Lord.

De. 30 : 2. shalt r. u. L., and obey
1 S. 7 : 3. If ye r. u. L. with hearts
Is. 19 : 22. shall r. t. L. he sh. heal
55 : 7. r. u. L., he will have mercy
Ho. 6 : 1. Come and let us r. u. Lord
7 : 10. they do not r. t. L. nor seek
14 : 1. O Israel, r. u. L. thy G. for

RETURNED.

Ge. 8 : 3. waters r. fr. off earth [not
9. dove r. unto him | 12. dove r.
18 : 33. Abraham r. unto his place
22 : 19. So Ab. r. unto young men
31 : 55. Laban r. unto his place
32 : 6. messengers r. to Jacob
33 : 16. So Esau r. that day
37 : 29. Reuben r. unto the pit
30. Reuben r. unto his brethren
38 : 22. And he r. to Jud. and said
42 : 24. Joseph r. again communed

Ge.43:10. we had r. this second time
18. money that was r. in our sacks
44:13. rent clothes, r. to the city
50:14. And Joseph r. into Egypt
Ex. 4:18. Moses r. to Jethro and
20. Moses r. to land of Egypt
Ex. 5:22. Moses r. unto L., 32:31.
14:27. sea r. to his strength, 28.
19:8. Moses r. words of peo. unto L.
34:31. congregation r. unto him
Le. 22:13. if she is r. unto father's
Nu. 11:† 4. the children of Israel r.
and wept, and said, De. 1:45.
14:36. r. and made cong-n mur-
16:50. Aaron r. unto Moses ⌊mur
23:6. Balaam r. unto him and, lo
24:25. Balaam rose, r. to his place
Jos.2:16. hide till pursuers be r., 22.
4:18. waters of Jordan r. unto pla.
22:9. chil. of Reuben and Gad r.
32. Phinehas and the princes r.
Ju.2:19. judge was dead they r.
5:29. yea, she r. answer to hers.
7:3. r. of peo. 22,000 fr. Gideon
15. he r. into host of Israel
8:13. Gideon r. from battle before
11:39. Gideon's dau. r. unto father
14:8. aft. time he r. to take her
21:23. the Benjamites r. unto their
Ru. 1:22. So Naomi and Ruth r.
1 S. 1:† 27. wh. I obtained sh. be r.
6:16. r. to Ekron same day
17:57. Da. r. fr. slaughter of Goliath
25:39. Lord r. wickedness of Nabal
2 S. 1:22. sword of Saul r. not empty
3:16. said Abner, Go, return, he r.
6:20. David r. to bless his househ.
16:8. Lord r. upon thee bl. of Saul
17:3. man thou seekest, is as if r.
19:15. So the king r. to Jordan
23:10. people r. after him to spoil
1 K. 13:10. r. not by way he came
33. Jeroboam r. not from evil
19:21. he r. from him took oxen
2 K. 4:35. Elisha r. and walked
5:15. he r. to man of God, he and
13:† 25. Jehoash r. and took out of
2 Ch. 19:† 4. Jehosh-t r. and went
25:10. r. home in great anger
32:21. Sennacherib r. with shame
33:† 3. he r. built high places
Ezr. 5:11. thus they r. us answer
Ne. 4:15. we r. to wall to work
9:28. yet when they r. and cried
Ps. 35:13. my prayer r. into bosom
78:34. they r. and inquired aft. G.
126:† 1. L. r. returning of Zion
Ec. 4:1. I r. and consid-d oppressions
7. I r. and saw vanity, 9:11.
Is. 38:8. So sun r. ten degrees
Je. 3:7. I said, Turn. But she r. not
14:3. they r. with vessels empty
18:† 4. r. and made it ano. vessel
40:12. all Jews r. out of all places
Eze. 1:14. living creatures ran, r.
8:17. r. to provoke me to anger
9:† 11. man with the inkhorn r.
47:7. when I had r. lo, at river
Da. 2:† 14. Dan r. with counsel and
4:34. understanding r. unto me
36. same time reason r. unto me
Ho. 6:11. I r. captivity of people
Am. 4:6. yet have ye not r. unto
me, 8, 9, 10, 11. ⌈thought
Zch. 1:6. they r. and said, as L
16. saith L. I am r. to Jerus. ⌈r.
7:14. that no man passed thro. nor
8:3. I am r. unto Zion, will dwell in
Mat. 21:18. morn. as he r. into city
Mk. 14:40. r. he found them asleep
Lu. 1:56. Mary r. to own house
2:20. shepherds r. glorifying God
39. they r. into Galilee to ⌈ried
43. as they r. the child Jes. tar-
4:1. Jesus full of Holy Ghost r. fr.
14. Jesus r. in power of Spirit
8:37. he went up into ship and r.
Lu. 8:40. when Jes. r. peo. gladly rec-d
9:10. apostles when r. told all
10:17. seventy r. again with joy
17:18. that r. to give glory to G.
19:15. when he was r. having
23:48. peo. smote breasts and r.
56. they r. and prepared spices
24:9. r. from sepulchre and told
33. same hour, and r. to Jerus.
52. worshipped r. to Jerusalem
Ac. 1:12. Then r. they unto Jerus.
5:22. officers found not, they r.
8:25. the apostles r. to Jerusalem
12:25. Barna. and Saul r. fr. Jerus.
13:13. John departing, r. to Jerus.
14:21. r. to Lystra and Iconium
21:6. we took ship: they r. home
23:32. left horsemen, r. to castle
Ga. 1:17. I r. again unto Damascus
† 18. after 3 years I r. to Jerus.
He. 11:15. opportunity to have r.
1 Pe. 2:25. now r. unto Shepherd

RETURNETH.

Ps. 146:4. breath goeth, he r. to earth
Pr. 18:† 13. r. a word bef. heareth
26:11. as a dog r. to his vomit, so
a fool r. ⌈circuits
Ec. 1:6. the wind r. according to
Is. 55:10. rain r. not thither, but
Eze. 35:7. that r. I will cut off
Zch. 9:8. encamp bec. of him that r.

RETURNING.

Ge. 8:† 3. waters returned in r.
† 7. raven went in going and r.
Ps. 126:† 1. L. returned r. of Zion
Is. 30:15. in r. and rest ye be saved
Lu. 7:10. r. found servant whole
Ac. 8:28. Was r. sitting in chariot
He. 7:1. met Abraham r. fr. slaugh-
⌊ter

RE'U.

Ge. 11:18. Peleg begat R., 19. 1 Ch.
20. And R. begat Serug, 21. ⌊1:25.

REU'BEN.

Ge. 29:32. bare a son, called name R.
30:14. R. went in days of harvest
35:22. R. went and lay with Bilhah
23. of Leah, R. Jacob's firstb., 46:
8.-49:3. Nu. 26:5. 1 Ch. 5:1.
37:21. R. heard it delivered Joseph
22. R. said unto th. Shed no blood
29. R returned unto pit, Joseph
42:22. R. answered, Spake I not
37. R. spake unto fa. Slay my sons
46:9. the sons of R., Ex. 6:14. Nu.
16:1.-32:1, 2, 37. De. 11:6. Jos 4:
12. 1 Ch. 5:3, 18. ⌈mine
48:5. as R. and Sim. they sh. be
Ex. 1:2. chil. of Isr., R Sim., 1 Ch. 2:
Nu. 1:20. chil. of R. by genera-s ⌊1.
2:10. the standard of the camp of
R., 10:18. ⌈33.
10. children of R., 32:6, 25, 29, 31,
16. all numbered of camp of R.
7:30. Elizur prince of chil. of R.
32:33. gave to chil of R., Jos. 13:23.
De. 27:13. on Ebal to curse R. Gad
33:6. Let R. live, let not be few
Jos. 15:6. stone of Bohan son of R.,
18:7. R. received inheritan. ⌊18:17.
22:13. Isr. sent unto children of R.
Ju. 5:15. for the divisions of R., 16.
Eze. 48:6. a portion for R. | 7.
31. gates of city: one gate of R.

Tribe of REU'BEN.

Nu. 1:5. of t. o. R. Elizur prince
21. of the t. o. R. were 46,500
13:4. Of t. o. R. Shammua to spy
34:14. the t. o. R. have received
inheritance, Jos. 13:15.
Jos. 20:8. out of t. o. R. Gad, Levites
had cities, 21:7, 36. 1 Ch. 6:63,
78.
Re. 7:5. Of t. o. R. were sealed 12,000

REU'BENITES.

Nu. 26:7. These are families of R.
De. 3:12. these cities gave I unto R.,
16.-29:8. Jos. 12:6.-13:8
De. 4:43. Bezer in country of R.
Jos. 1:12. Josh. spake to R., 22:1.
2 K. 10:33. Hazael smote the R.
1 Ch. 5:6. Beerah prince of R
26. Tilgath-pilneser carried R.
11:42. Adina a captain of the R.
12:37. of the R. and the Gadites
26:32. wh. Da. made rulers over R.
27:16. Eliezer was ruler of R.

REU'EL = RA'GUEL.

Ge. 36:4. Bashemath bare R., 10.
13. sons of R. Mizzah, 17. 1 Ch. 1:
Ex. 2:18. came to R. their fa. ⌊37.
1 Ch. 1:35. sons of Esau, R. Jeush
See DEUEL.

REU'MAH.

Ge. 22:24. R. bare Tebah, Thahash

REVEAL.

Ru. 4:† 4. said, I will r. in thine ear
Jb. 20:27. heaven sh. r. his iniq-y
Ps. 119:† 18. r. mine eyes that I
Je. 33:6. I will r. abun. of peace
Da. 2:47. thou couldest r. this secret
Mat. 11:27. he to whomsoever Son
will r. him, Lu. 10:22. ⌈r. his Son
Ga. 1:16. called me by his grace, to
Ph. 3:15. God sh. r. this unto you

REVEALED.

De. 29:29. things r. unto us and chil.
1 S. 3:7. nei. was word of Lord r.
21. L. r. himself to Sam. in Shiloh
9:† 15. Now L. had r. ear of Sam.
2 S. 7:27. thou hast r. to thy serv.
1 Ch. 17:† 25. hast r. ear of thy serv.
Es. 8:† 13. writing r. unto people
Ps. 98:† 2. righteousness hath he r.
Is. 22:14. r. in mine ears by Lord
23:1. fr. land of Chittim it is r.
40:5. glory of the Lord sh. be r.
53:1. to whom is arm of Lord r.?
Jn. 12:38. ⌈to be r.
56:1. and my righteousness is near
Je. 11:20. unto thee I r. my cause
Da. 2:19. was secret r. unto Daniel
30. secret is not r. to me for
10:1. a thing was r. unto Daniel
Mat. 10:26. nothing covered, that
sh. not be r., Lu. 12:2. ⌈Lu. 10:21.
11:25. hast r. them unto babes,
16:17. flesh and blood hath not r.
Lu. 2:26. it was r. unto Simeon
35. thoughts of many hearts be r.
17:30. day when Son of man r.
Ro. 1:17. therein is right-n of God r.
18. wrath of God is r. fr. heaven
8:18. glory which sh. be r. in us
1 Co 2:10. God r. them unto us by
3:13. because it shall be r. by fire
14:30. If any thing be r. to ano.
Ga. 3:23. faith which should be r.
Ep. 3:5. as now r. unto his apostles
2 Th. 1:7. when Lord Jesus sh. be
2:3. and that man of sin be r. ⌊r.
6. he might be r. in his time
8. Wicked be r. whom L. consume
1 Pe. 1:5. ready to be r. in last time
12. Unto whom it was r.
4:13. when his glory shall be r.
5:1. partaker of glory that shall be
⌊r.

REVEALER.

Da. 2:47. your God a r. of secrets

REVEALETH.

Jb. 33:† 16. he r. ears of men ⌈19.
Pr. 11:13. talebearer, r. secrets, 20:
Da. 2:22. r. deep and secret things
28. God in heaven that r. secrets
29. that r. secrets maketh known
Am 3:7. he r. secrets unto prophets

REVELATION, S.

Ro. 2:5. r. of righte. judgment of G
16:25. acc to r. of the mystery
1 Co. 1:† 7. waiting for r. of our L.
14:6. except I speak to you by r.
26. every one hath a r. hath ⌈L.
2 Co. 12:1. I will come to r-s of the
7. lest I sho. be exalted thro. r-s
Ga. 1:12. by the r. of Jesus Christ

Ga.2:2. I went up by r. and commu.
Ep. 1 : 17. may give you spirit of r.
8:3. by r. he made known unto me
1 Pe. 1 : 13. grace bro-t at r. of J.C.
Re. 1 : 1. r. of Jes. Christ, wh. God

REVELLINGS. ⌊gave
Ga. 5 : 21. works of the flesh are r.
1 Pe.4:3. when ye walked in lusts, r.

REVENGE, S.
De. 32 : 42. from beginning of r-s
Ps. 94 : † 1. O God of r-s shew thys.
Je. 20 : 10. we shall take r. on him
Eze. 25 : 15. Philis. have dealt by r.
2 Co. 7 : 11. wrought in you, what zeal, r.!

REVENGE, ED.
Je. 15 : 15. r. me of my persecutors
Eze. 25 : 12. Edom r-d hims. upon Jud.
2 Co. 10 : 6. readiness to r. disobedi-e
Eze. 25 : † 12. Edom r. himself

REVENGER, S of blood.
Nu.35: 19. r. - sh. slay murderer, 21.
24. cong. judge bet slayer and r.-
25. deliv. slayer out of hand of r.-
27. if r. - find and r. - kill slayer
2 S. 14 : 11. not suffer r-s - to destroy
Na. 1 : † 2. Lord a jealous God, and r.
Ro. 13 : 4. he is a minister of God, a r.

REVENGETH.
Na. 1 : 2. the Lord r. ; the Lord r.

REVENGING.
Ps. 79 : 10. by r. of blood of thy servants

REVENUE, S.
Ezr. 4 : 13. shalt endamage r. of kings
Pr. 8 : 19. my r. is better than silver
15 : 6. in r-s of wicked is trouble
16 : 8. than great r-s without right
Is. 23 : 3. harvest of river is her r.
Je. 12 : 13. be ashamed of your r-s

REVERENCE. [Noun.]
2 S. 9 : 6. Mephibosheth did r. to Da.
1 K. 1 : 31. Bath-sheba did r. to k.
Es. 3 : 2. Mordecai, nor did him r., 5.
Ps. 89 : 7. to be had in r. of all
He. 12 : 9. fathers, we gave them r.
28. grace we may serve God with r.
1 Pe 3 : † 15. answer of your hope wi.

REVERENCE, ED. ⌊r.
Le. 19 : 30. r. my sanctuary, 26 : 2.
Es. 3 : 2. king's servants r-d Haman
Mat. 21 : 37. sent, saying, they will r. my son, Mk. 12:6. Lu. 20:13.
Ep. 5 : 33. wife see that she r. husband

REVEREND. ⌊band
Ps. 111 : 9. holy and r. is his name

REVERSE.
Nu. 23 : 20. he hath blessed, I can-t
Es 8 : 5. to r. letters devised ⌊r. it
8. sealed with k.'s ring, no man r.
Je. 2 : † 24. in her occasion who r. it

REVILE.
Ex. 22 : 28. Thou shalt not r. gods
Mat. 5 : 11. Blessed are ye when men

REVILED. ⌊r.
Ne. 13 : † 25. I contended and r. th.
Mat. 27 : 39. that passed by r. him
Mk. 15 : 32. that were crucified r. him
Jn. 9 : 28. r. him, said, Thou his dis-
1 Co 4 : 12. being r. we bless ⌊ciple
1 Pe. 2 : 23. Who when he was r. r.

REVILERS. ⌊not
1 Co. 6 : 10. nor r. inherit kingd. of G.

REVILEST, ETH.
Ex. 21 : † 17. r-h fa. be put to death
Ac. 23 : 4. r-t thou God's high priest?

REVILINGS.
Is. 51 : 7. nei. be afraid of their r.
Zph. 2 : 8. r. of children of Ammon

REVIVE.
Ne. 4 : 2. will they r. the stones out
Ps. 85 : 6. Wilt thou not r. us again
138 : 7. thou wilt r. me, thou shalt
Is. 57 : 15. to r. spirit of the humble, and r. heart of contrite
Ho. 6 : 2. After two days will he r. us
14 : 7. they shall r. as corn, grow

Ha. 3 : 2. O Lord, r. thy work in

REVIVED.
Ge. 45 : 27. the spirit of Jacob r.
Ju. 15 : 19. spirit came again, he r.
1 K. 17 : 22. soul of child came, he r.
2 K. 13 : 21. touched bones of Elisha,
1 Ch. 11 : † 8. Joab r. city ⌊he r.
Ro. 7 : 9. when com-t came, sin r.
14 : 9. to this end Christ died, and r.
Ph. 4 : † 10. your care of me hath r.

REVIVING.
Ezr. 9 : 8. give us a little r. in, 9.

REVOLT. [Noun.]
De. 13 : † 5. prophet spoken r. ag. L.
Is. 59 : 13. speaking oppress. and r.
Je. 28 : † 16. thou hast taught r., 29 : †

REVOLT, ED. ⌊32.
2 K. 8 : 20. in his days Edom r-d, 22.
2 Ch. 21 : 8, 10. ⌈time
22. Then Libnah r-d at the same
2 Ch. 21 : 10. same time did Libnah r.
Is. 1 : 5. stricken ye will r. more
31 : 6. fr. whom Israel deeply r-d
Je. 5 : 23. this people, they are r-d

REVOLTERS.
Je. 6 : 28. are all grievous r. walking
Ho. 5 : 2. r. are profound to make
9 : 15. all their princes are r. ⌊slaugh.

REVOLTING.
Je. 5 : 23. this people hath r. heart

REVOLUTION. ⌈y-r
Ex. 34 : † 22. observe feast at r. of
1 S. 1 : † 20. the r. of days was come
2 Ch. 24 : † 23. in r. of the year Syria

REWARD. [Noun.] ⌊came
Ge. 15 : 1. Abram, I am thy great r.
Nu. 18 : 31. it is your r. for service
De. 10 : 17. God, who taketh not r.
27 : 25. Cursed that taketh r. to slay
Ru. 2 : 12. full r. be given thee of L.
2 S. 4 : 10 tho-t I wo. given him r.
19 : 36. recompense me with such r.
1 K. 13 : 7. k. said, I will give thee r.
Jb. 6 : 22. Did I say, Give a r. for me
7 : 2. as a hireling looketh for r.
Ps. 15 : 5. nor taketh r. ag. innocent
19 : 11. keeping of them is great r.
40 : 15. Let them be desolate for r.
58 : 11. there is a r. for righteous
70 : 3. Let th. be turned back for r.
91 : 8. shalt see the r. of wicked
94 : 2. render a r. to the proud
109 : 20. Let this be r. of adversaries
127 : 3. fruit of the womb is his r.
Pr. 11 : 18. soweth right-n. a sure r.
21 : 14. a r. in the bosom pacifieth
22 : † 4. the r. of humility is riches
23 : † 18. surely there is a r. and
24 : 14. hast found wisdom, then a r.
20. shall be no r. to the evil man
Ec. 4 : 9. have good r. for labour
9 : 5. nei. have they any more a r.
Is. 3 : 11. r. of his hands be given
5 : 23. Which justify wicked for r.
40 : 10. his r. is with him, 62 : 11.
45 : 13. let go my captives, not for r.
49 : † 4. and my r. is with my God
Je. 40 : 5. captain gave Jere. a r.
Eze. 16 : 34. givest r. no r. is given
Ho. 9 : 1. loved a r. upon cornfloor
Ob. 15. r. upon thine own head
Mi. 3 : 11. heads thereof judge for r.
7 : 3. prince, judge asketh for r.
Mat. 5 : 12. your r. in heav., Lu. 6 : 23.
46. if love them love you, what r.
6 : 1. otherwise ye no r. of your Fat.
2. Verily, they have their r., 5, 16.
10 : 41. shall receive prophet's r. shall receive righteous man's r.
42. in no wise lose his r., Mk. 9 : 41.
Lu. 6 : 35. your r. shall be great
23 : 41. we receive due r. of deeds
Ac. 1 : 18. a field with r. of iniquity
Ro. 4 : 4. him th. worketh is r. not
1 Co. 3 : 8. every man his own r.
14. work abide he sh. receive r.
9 : 17. if do willingly I have a r.

1 Co. 9 : 18. What is my r. then? Verily, that when I preach
Col. 2 : 18. Let no man beguile you of
3 : 24. ye shall receive the r. ⌊r.
1 Ti. 5 : 18. labourer worthy of r.
2 Pe. 2 : 13. receive r. of unright-n.
2 Jn. 8. that we receive a full r.
Jude 11. aft. error of Balaam for r.
Re. 11 : 18. thou shouldest give r.
22 : 12. I come quickly, my r. with
See RECOMPENSE. ⌊me

REWARDS.
Nu. 22 : 7. with the r. of divination
Is. 1 : 23. every one followeth r.
Da. 2 : 6. ye shall receive of me r.
5 : 17. Dan. said, give thy r. to ano.
Ho. 2 : 12. These are r. my lovers,

REWARD. [Verb.] ⌊given
De. 32 : 41. I will r. them hate me
1 S. 24 : 19. whf. Lord r. thee good
2 S. 3 : 39. L. shall r. doer of evil
2 Ch. 20 : 11. Behold, how they r. us
Ps. 54 : 5. sh. r. evil unto mine ene.
Pr. 25 : 22. heap coals, Lord shall r.
Ho. 4 : 9. I will r. their doings
Mat. 6 : 4. shall r. thee openly, 6, 18.
16 : 27. he shall r. every man acc.
2 Ti. 4 : 14. Lord r. him acc. to
Re. 18 : 6. r. her, as she rewarded

REWARDED. ⌊you
Ge. 44 : 4. Whf. have ye r. evil
1 S. 24 : 17. for thou hast r. me good, I have r. thee evil
2 S. 22 : 21. Lord r. me acc. to my righteousness, Ps. 18 : 20. ⌈r.
2 Ch. 15 : 7. be strong, your work be
Ps. 7 : 4. If I have r. evil unto him
35 : 12. r. me evil for good, 109 : 5.
103 : 10. nor r. us acc. to iniqui-s
Pr. 13 : 13. feareth the com-t be r.
Is. 3 : 9. have r. evil unto themselves
Je. 31 : 16. thy work be r. saith L.
Re. 18 : 6. reward her as she r. you

REWARDER. ⌈him
He. 11 : 6. a r. of them that seek him

REWARDETH. ⌈it
Jb. 21 : 19. he r. him he sh. know it
Ps. 31 : 23. plentifully r. the proud
137 : 8. happy he that r. thee, as
Pr. 17 : 13. whoso r. evil for good
26 : 10. r. the fool, and r. transg-rs

RE'ZEPH.
2 K. 19 : 12. nations, Gozan, R., Is.

REZI'A. ⌊37 : 12.
1 Ch. 7 : 39. sons of Ulla ; Haniel, R.

RE'ZIN.
2 K. 15 : 37. to send ag. Judah R. king of Syria, 16 : 5. Is. 7 : 1.
16 : 6. R. recovered Elath to Syria
9. the king of Assyria slew R.
Ezr. 2 : 48. children of R., Ne. 7 : 50.
Is. 7 : 4. fear not fierce anger of R.
8. the head of Damascus is R.
8 : 6. as this people rejoice in R. ⌈R.
9 : 11. L. shall set up adversaries of

RE'ZON. See ELIADAH.

RHE'GIUM. ⌈R.
Ac. 28 : 13. fetched compass came to

RHE'SA.
Lu. 3 : 27. Joanna, wh. was son of R.

RHINOCEROSES.
Is. 34 : † 7. the r. shall come down

RHO'DA.
Ac. 12 : 13. damsel came, named R.

RHODES.
Ac. 21 : 1. day following we came

RIB, S. ⌊unto R.
Ge. 2 : 21. God took one of his r-s
22. the r. God had taken fr. man
Ex. 30 : † 4. rings by two r-s of alt.
2 S. 2 : 23. Abner smote und. 5th r.
3 : 27. Joab smote Abner und. 5th r.
4 : 6. Rechab smote Ish-bo. und. 5th
20 : 10. smote Amasa und. 5th rib. ⌊r.
1 K. 6 : † 5. and he made r-s about
7 : † 3. covered with cedar upon r-s
Da. 7 : 5. beast had 3 r-s in mouth

RI'BAI.
2 S. 23 : 29. Ittai son of R., 1 Ch. 11 :
RIBBAND. ⌊31.
Nu. 15 : 38. upon fringe of borders a
RIB'LAH. ⌊r.
Nu. 34 : 11. fr. Shepham to R. ⌈at R.
2 K. 23 : 33. Pha. put him in bands
25:6. bro-t king up to k. of Bab. to
R., Je. 39 : 5.–52 : 9. ⌈52 : 26.
20. Nebuz-n bro-t them to R., Je.
21. king of Bab. slew them at R.,
Je. 39 : 6.–52 : 10, 27.
RICH.
Ge. 13:2. Abram was very r. in cattle
14:23. lest say, I have made Ab. r.
Ex. 30 : 15. r. shall not give more
Le. 25 : 47. if stranger wax r. ⌈r.
Ru. 3:10. foll-dst not yo. men poor or
1 S. 2 : 7. Lord maketh poor and r.
2 S. 12:1. two men in one city, one r.
Jb. 15:29. He shall not be r. neither
34:19. nor regardeth r. more than
Ps. 45 : 12. r. sh. entreat thy favour
49 : 2. hear this, both r. and poor
16. Be not afraid when one is r.
Pr. 10:4. hand of diligent maketh r.
22. blessing of Lord, it maketh r.
13:7. is that maketh himself r. yet
14:20. poor is hated, r. hath friends
18 : 23. the r. answereth roughly
21 : 17. that loveth wine not be r.
22 : 2. r. and poor meet together
7. The r. ruleth over the poor
16. giveth to r. sh. come to want
23 : 4. Labour not to be r. cease
28 : 6. he that is perverse, tho. r.
20. th. maketh haste to be r., 22.
Ec. 5:12. abun. of r. not suffer him
10 : 6. r. sit in low place ⌊to sleep
20. curse not r. in thy bedcham.
Is. 53 : 9. with the r. in his death
Je. 5 : 27. are great, and waxen r.
Eze. 27 : 24. in chests of r. apparel
Ho. 12 : 8. Ephraim said, Yet I am r.
Zch. 11:5. say, Blessed be L., I am r.
Mk. 12 : 41. many r. cast in much
Lu. 1 : 53. r. he hath sent empty
6:24. But woe unto you that are r.
12 : 21. he that is not r. tow. God
14 : 12. call not r. neighbours, lest
18 : 23. very sorrowful, for very r.
19:2. man Zaccheus, and he was r.
Ro. 10 : 12. same Lord is r. unto all
1 Co. 4 : 8. Now ye are full, now r.
2 Co. 6:10. poor, yet making many r.
8 : 9. tho. r. for your sakes became
poor, that ye might be r.
Ep. 2 : 4. God who is r. in mercy
1 Ti. 6 : 9. they that will be r. fall
17. Charge them th. are r. in this
18. do good, be r. in good works
Ja. 1 : 10. let the r. rejoice in that
2 : 5. God chosen poor, r. in faith ?
Re. 2 : 9. thy poverty, but thou r.
3:17. Because thou sayest, I am r.
18. to buy of me gold, mayest be r.
13:16. poor and r. to receive mark
18:3. merchants are waxed r., 15, 19.
See **Rich MAN, Rich MEN.**
RICHER.
Da. 11 : 2. the fourth shall be far r.
RICHES.
Ge. 31:16. r. God taken, that is ours
36:7. r. more than they might dw.
Jos. 22 : 8. Return with much r. to
Ru. 4 : † 11. get thee r. in Ephratah
1 S. 17 : 25. king will enrich with r.
1 K. 3:11. Bec. neither hast asked r.,
2 Ch. 1 : 11. ⌈honour, 2 Ch. 1:12.
13. I have given thee r. and
10 : 23. Solomon exceeded all kings
of earth for r., 2 Ch. 9:22. ⌈thee
1 Ch. 29 : 12. r. and honour come of
28. Da. died full of days, r. ⌈18 : 1.
2 Ch. 17:5. Jehosh. had r. in abun.,
20 : 25. found r. with dead bodies
32:27. Hez. had exceeding much r,
Es. 1 : 4. shewed r. of his kingdom
5 : 11. Haman told them of his r.
Jb. 20 : 15. He swallowed down r.
36 : 19. Will he esteem thy r.? no
Ps. 37 : 16. better than r. of wicked
39 : 6. heapeth up r. knoweth not
44:†12. sellest thy people with-t r.
49 : 6. they that boast thems. in r.
Ps. 52:7. trusted in abundance of r.
62 : 10. if r. increase, set not heart
73 : 12. ungodly prosper, incr. in r.
104:24. O L., earth is full of thy r.
112:3. Wealth r. sh. be in his hou.
119 : 14. I have rejoiced as in all r.
Pr. 3 : 16. and in her left hand r.
8 : 18. r. and honour are with me
11 : 4. r. profit not in day of wrath
16. woman honour, strong men r.
28. that trusteth in his r. sh. fall
13:7. maketh hims. poor, yet hath r.
8. ransom of man's life are r.
14 : 24. crown of wise is their r.
19 : 14. r. are inheritance of fa.'s
22:1. A good name to be chos. than
4. By the fear of the Lord are r. ⌊r.
16. oppresseth poor to increase r.
23 : 5. r. make themselves wings
24:4. chambers be filled with all r.
27 : 24. For r. are not for ever, and
30 : 8. give me nei. poverty nor r.
31:†29. Many dau-s have gotten r.
Ec. 4 : 8. nei. is eye satisfied with r.
5 : 13. r. kept for owners to hurt
14. those r. perish by evil travail
19. man to wh. G. given r., 6 : 2.
9 : 11. nor r. to men of underst-g
Is. 8 : 4. r. of Damascus be taken
10 : 14. found as nest r. of people
30 : 6. carry r. upon young asses
45 : 3. I will give thee hidden r.
61 : 6. ye shall eat r. of Gentiles
Je. 9 : 23. let not rich glory in r.
17:11. that getteth r. not by right
48:36. r. he hath gott. are perished
Eze. 26 : 12. sh. make spoil of thy r.
27 : 12. Tarshish thy merchant by
multitude of r., 18, 27, 33.
28 : 4. with underst-g hast got. r.
5. by traffic hast increased r. and
heart is lifted bec. of thy r.
Da. 11 : 2. thro. his r. sh stir up all
13. king of north sh. come with r.
24. scatter am. them prey, and r.
28. return into his land with gr. r.
Mat. 13 : 22. deceitfulness of r. choke
the word, Mk. 4 : 19. Lu. 8 : 14.
Mk. 10 : 23. hardly they th. have r.
24. them that trust in r. to enter,
Lu. 18 : 24. ⌈right-n.
Lu 16 : † 9. Make friends of r. of un-
11. who will commit the true r.?
Ro. 2 : 4. Or despisest thou the r.
9 : 23. make known r. of his glory
11 : 12. if fall of th. be r. of world,
and diminishing of th. r. of Gen.
33. O depth of r. of wisdom of G.
2 Co. 8 : 2. r. of their liberality
Ep. 1:7. redemption acc. to r. of grace
18. r. of glory of his inheritance
2 : 7. shew exceeding r. of his grace
3:8. preach unsearchable r. of Christ
16. grant you acc. to r. of glory
Ph. 4:19. acc. to his r. in glory by C.
Col. 1 : 27. what the r. of the glory
2:2. knit in love, unto all the r. of
the full assurance
1 Ti. 6:17. nor trust in uncertain r.
He. 11:26. reproach of C. greater r.
Ja. 5 : 2. Your r. are corrupted
Re. 5 : 12. Worthy is Lamb to rec. r.
18 : 17. in one hour so great r. to
RICHLY. ⌊nought
Col. 3 : 16. Let word of C. dwell r.
1 Ti. 6 : 17. living G, who giveth r.
Tit. 3 : † 6. shed on us r. thro. Jesus
RID, DETH. ⌊Christ
Ge. 37 : 22. might r. him out of hand
Ex. 6 : 6. I will r. you out of bond.
Le. 26 : 6. I will r. evil beasts out
2 S. 22 : † 33. God, he r. my way
Ps. 82 : 4. r. them out of wicked
144:7. Send thine hand, r. me, 11.
RIDDANCE.
Le. 23 : 22. not make clean r. of field
Zph. 1 : 18. sh. make speedy r. of all
RIDDEN. ⌈r.?
Nu. 22 : 30. Am not I ass, thou hast
RIDDLE.
Ju. 14 : 12. Samson said, I will put
forth r., 13, 14, 15, 16, 17, 18, 19.
Eze. 17 : 2. Son of man, put forth r.
1 Co. 13:†12. now we see in a r. then
RIDE. ⌊face
Ge. 41 : 43. made him r. in chariot
De. 32:13. made him r. on high plac.
Ju. 5 : 10. that r. on white asses
2 S. 6 : † 3. they made to r. the ark,
1 Ch. 13 : † 7. ⌈to r. on
16:2. asses are for king's household
19 : 26. will saddle ass I may r.
1 K. 1 : 33. Sol. r. upon mule, 38, 44.
2 K. 4:†24. restrain not for me to r.
10 : 16. made him to r. in chariot
13 : † 16. Make hand r. upon bow
1 Ch. 13 : † 7. ark to r. in new cart
Es. 6 : † 9. him to r. thro. the city
Jb. 30 : 22. me to r. upon the wind
Ps. 45 : 4. in majesty r. prosperously
66 : 12. men to r. over our heads
Is. 30 : 16. We will r. upon the swift
58 : 14. thee to r. upon high places
Je. 6:23. they r. upon horses, 50:42.
Ho. 10:11. Ephr. to r. Judah plough
14 : 3. we will not r. upon horses
Ha. 3 : 8. thou didst r. upon horses
Hag. 2 : 22. overthrow those that r.
RIDER, RIDERS. ⌈ward
Ge. 49 : 17. that his r. sh. fall back-
Ex. 15 : 1. horse and r. into sea, 21.
2 K. 18 : 23. if thou be able to set r-s
upon them, Is. 36 : 8. ⌈on mules
Es. 8 : 10. and he sent letters by r-s
Jb. 39:18. she scorneth horse and r.
Je. 51 21. will I break in pieces horse
and his r. chariot and r.
Hag. 2 : 22. horses and r-s come do.
Zch. 10 : 5. r-s shall be confounded
12 : 4. I will smite r. with madness
RIDETH.
Le. 15:9. saddle her. upon sh. be uncl.
De. 33 : 26. who r. upon heaven
Es. 6 : 8. horse that king r. upon
Ps. 68:4. extol him r. on heavens, 33.
Is. 19 : 1. L. r. on a swift cloud
Am. 2 : 15. nei. he that r. horse de-
RIDICULOUS. ⌊liver
Is. 33 : † 19. shalt not see peo. of r.
RIDGES. ⌊tongue
Ps. 65:10. Thou waterest r. thereof
RIDING.
Nu. 22 : 22. Balaam r. upon ass
2 K. 4 : 24. slack not thy r. for me
Je. 17 : 25. kings sh. enter r., 22 : 4.
Eze. 23:6. yo. men, horsemen r., 12.
23. great lords, all of them r.
38 : 15. thou and many people r.
Zch. 1 : 8. a man r. upon red horse
9 : 9. thy king cometh r. upon an
RIE. See RYE. ⌊ass
RIFLED.
Zch. 14 : 2. houses r. women ravish-
RIGHT. [Adj.] ⌊ed
Ge. 24 : 48. L. who led me in r. way
De. 32 : 4. God of truth, just and r.
Jos. 9 : 25. do as seemeth r. unto
1 S. 12 : 23. I will teach you r. way
2 S. 15 : 3. thy matters good and r.
1 K. 7 : 21. he set up the r. pillar
9 : † 12. cities not r. in his eyes
2 K. 10 : 15. Is thy heart r. as my
11 : 11. guard stood fr. r. corner
17:9. Isr. did secretly things not r.
Ezr. 8 : 21. to seek of him a r. way
Ne. 9 : 13. thou gavest r. judgments

Es. 8 : 5. thing seem r. before king
Jb. 6:25. How forcible are r. words!
34:23. not upon man more than r.
35 : 2. Thinkest thou this be r.
Ps. 19 : 8. statutes of Lord are r.
45 : 6. sceptre of kingd. r. sceptre
51 : 10. O God, renew a r. spirit
107 : 7. he led them forth by the r.
119 : 75. thy judgments are r. [way
128. I esteem thy precepts to be r.
Pr. 4 : 11. I led thee in r. paths
8 : 6. opening of lips be r. things
9. all r. to them th. find knowl.
12 : 5. thoughts of righteous are r.
14:12. is a way wh. seemeth r., 16:
20 : 11. whether his work be r. [25.
23 : 16. lips shall speak r. things
24 : 26. kiss his lips giveth r. ans.
Ec. 4 : 4. I considered ev. r. work
11:†6. knowest not whe-r sh. be r.
Is. 30 : 10. Prophesy not r. things
45:19. I L. declare things th. are r.
Je. 2 : 21. I planted thee a r. seed
23 : 10. course is evil, force not r.
Ho. 14 : 9. ways of the Lord are r.
Mat. 5 : 39. whoso. smite r. cheek
Mk. 5 : 15. in r. mind, Lu. 8 : 35.
Ac.4:19. Whe. it be r. in sight of G.
13 : 10. to pervert r. ways of L.
2 Pe. 2 : 15. have forsaken r. way
See **Right EAR, EYE, S.**
RIGHT foot or **feet.**
Ex. 29 : 20. put blood upon gr. toe of
their r. f. o. Le. 14: 14. 17, 25, 28.
Le. 8 : 23. put blood upon great toe
of Aaron's r. **foot**
24. upon gr. toes of their r. **feet**
Re.10:2. he set his r. **foot** upon sea
See **Right HAND, HANDS.**
Is or is not RIGHT.
Ex. 15 : 26. If thou wilt do that wh.
i. r., 1 K. 11 : 38. [12:25.-21:9.
De. 6 : 18. thou shalt do that i. r.,
12 : 8. whatsoever i. r. in own eyes
28. when doest that i. r., 13 : 18.
Ju. 14 : † 3. she i. r. in mine eyes
1 K. 11:33. not walked to do that i.
2 K.10:30. wh. i. r. in mine eyes [r.
Jb. 42:7. not spoken of me th. i. r.,
Ps. 33 : 4. word of Lord i. r. [8.
Pr. 12 : 15. way of fool i. r. in own
21:2. way of man i. r. in own eyes
8. as for pure, his work i. r.
Je. 26 : † 14. do with me as i. r. in
Eze. 18 : 5. if a man do that i. r.
19. he hath done that which i. r.,
21 : 27.-33 : 14, 16, 19. [give you
Mat. 20 : 4. whatsoever i. r. I will
7. whatsoever i. r. sh. ye receive
Lu.12:57. why judge not what i. r.?
Ac. 8 : 21. thy heart i. n. r. in sight
Ep. 6:1. obey parents in L. this i. r.
See **Right SIDE, Right SHOULDER.**
Was, or was not RIGHT.
Ju. 17 : 6. ev. man did that wh. w.
r. in own eyes, 21 : 25.
1 S.18:†20. thing w. r. in Saul's eyes
2 S. 17 : † 4. w. r. in eyes of Absalom
1 K. 14 : 8. Da. that wh. w. r., 15:5.
15 : 11. Asa did that which w. r.,
2 Ch. 14 : 2. [2 Ch. 20 : 32.
22:43. Jehoshaphat did that w. r.,
2 K. 12 : 2. Jehoash did that wh. w.
r., 2 Ch. 24 : 2. [2 Ch. 25 : 2.
14 : 3. Amaziah did that wh. w. r.,
15:3. Azariah did that which w. r.,
2 Ch. 26 : 4. [2 Ch. 27 : 2.
34. Jotham did that which w. r.,
16 : 2. Ahaz did not that wh. w. r.
18 : 3. Hezekiah did that w. r., 2
Ch. 29 : 2.-31 : 20. [Ch. 34 : 2.
22 : 2. Josiah did that wh. w. r., 2
1 Ch.13 :4. thing w. r. in eyes of peo.
2 Ch. 30 : † 4. w. r. in eyes of Hez.
Jb. 33 : 27. I perverted that w. r.
Ps. 78 : 37. their heart w. n. r.

Je. 17 : 16. that out of my lips w. r.
RIGHT. [Adverb.] [r.
Ge. 18:25. Sh. not Judge of earth do
Nu. 27 : 7. dau-s of Zeloph. speak r.
Jos. 3:16. passed over r. ag. Jericho
Ju. 12 : 6. could not pronounce it r.
Ne.9:33. thou hast done r. we wick.
Ps. 9:4. satest in the throne judging
46 : 5. God sh. help her r. early [r.
139 : 14. my soul knoweth r. well
Pr. 4 : 25. Let thine eyes look r. on
9 : 15. To call passengers who go r-
16 : 13. love him speaketh r. [on
Is.32:7. when the needy speaketh r.
Je. 34 : 15. ye had done r. in my
48:†30. on wh. he stayeth do not r.
49 : 5. ye shall be driven r. forth
Am. 3 : 10. they know not to do r.
Lu. 10 : 28. hast answ-d r. : this do
RIGHT, S. [Noun.]
De. 21 : 17. r. of firstborn is his
Ru. 2 †: 20. hath r. to redeem, 3:†9.
4 : 6. redeem thou my r. to thyself
2 S. 19 : 28. What r. I to cry to k.?
43. we more r. in David than ye
1 K. 8:†45. hear their prayer, maintain r., † 49. 2 Ch. 6 : † 35, †39.
Ne. 2 : 20. ye have no r. in Jerus.
Jb. 34 : 6. Should I lie ag. my r.?
17. Sh. he that hateth r. govern?
36 : 6. he giveth r. to the poor
Ps.9:4. thou hast maintained my r.
17 : 1. Hear the r. O L. attend to
140 : 12. L. will maintain r. of poor
Pr. 16 : 8. great revenues without r.
Is. 10 : 2. to take the r. from poor
59 : † 8. is no r. in their goings
Je. 5 : 28. r. of needy do not judge
17 : 11. getteth riches, not by r.
32 : 7. r. of redemption is thine, 8.
La. 3 : 35. To turn aside r. of man
Eze. 21 : 27. he come whose r. it is
22 : † 29. oppr-d stranger with-t r.
Da.11:†6. k.'s dau. come to make r-s
Am. 5 : 12. they turn poor from r.
Mal. 3 : 5. turn stranger from his r.
Jn. 1 : † 12. gave r. to be sons of G.
He. 13 : 10. altar, wh-f no r. to eat
Re.22:14. may have r. to tree of life
RIGHTEN.
Is.1:†17. seek judgment, r. oppressed
RIGHTEOUS.
Ge. 7:1. thee have I seen r. bef. me
18:23. thou destroy r. wi. wicked?
24. if be 50 r. wilt thou destroy,
and not spare place for 50 r.
25. be far from thee to slay r.
26. If I find fifty r. in the city, I
28. Peradv. there lack five of 50 r.
20 : 4. wilt thou slay r. nation
38:26. Jud. said, She more r. than
Ex. 23 : 7. innocent and r. slay not
8. gift perverteth the words of the
r., De. 16 : 19. [r.
Nu. 23 : 10. Let me die death of the
De. 4 : 8. what nation judgm-s so r.
25 : 1. shall justify r., 2 Ch. 6 : 23.
Ju. 5 : 11. r. acts of L., 1 S. 12 : 7.
1 S. 24 : 17. Thou more r. than I
2 S. 4 : 11. wicked slain r. person
1 K. 2 : 32. fell upon 2 men more r.
8 : 32. justifying the r. to give him
2 K. 10 : 9. Jehu said to peo. Ye be r.
Ezr. 9 : 15. L. G. of Isr. r., Ne. 9 : 8.
Jb. 4 : 7. where were r. cut off?
9 : 15. tho. I were r. wo. not ans.
10 : 15. if I be r. yet not lift head
15:14. What is man, that he be r.?
17 : 9. r. shall hold on his way
22:3. any pleas. to Almi. thou art r.
19. r. see it, are glad, Ps. 107 : 42.
23 : 7. There the r. might dispute
32 : 1. bec. he was r. in own eyes
34 : 5. Job hath said, I am r.
35 : 7. If thou r. what givest him
36 : 7. He withdraweth not his eyes
from r., Ps. 34 : 15.

Jb.40 : 8. wilt condemn me that thou
mayest be r.
Ps. 1 : 5. nor sinners in cong-n of r.
6. Lord knoweth way of the r.
5:12. thou wilt bless r. with favour
7 : 9. the r. God trieth the hearts
11. G. judgeth the r. angry with
11 : 3. what can r. do? [wicked
5. Lord trieth r. but wicked
7. the r. Lord loveth righteousn.
14 : 5. God is in generation of r.
19 : 9. judgments of L. true and r.,
119 : 7, 62, 106, 160, 164. [ag. r.
31 : 18. lips speak contemptuously
32 : 11. Be glad in the Lord, ye r.
33 : 1. Rejoice in L. O ye r., 97 : 12.
34 : 17. The r. cry, Lord heareth
19. Many are the afflictions of r.
21. that hate r. shall be desolate
35:27. glad th. favour my r. cause
37 : 17. the Lord upholdeth the r.
21. r. sheweth mercy and giveth
25. have I not seen r. forsaken
29. The r. shall inherit the land
30. mouth of r. speaketh wisdom
32. wicked watcheth r. to slay
39. salvation of r. is of the Lord
52 : 6. The r. shall see, fear, laugh
55 : 22. never suffer r. to be moved
58 : 10. r. rejoice when seeth veng.
11. Verily is a reward for the r.
64 : 10. The r. shall be glad in L.
68 : 3. let r. be glad, let th. rejoice
69 : 28. not be written with the r.
72 : 7. In his days shall r. flourish
75 : 10. horns of r. sh. be exalted
92 : 12. r. shall flourish like palm
94 : 21. they gather ag. soul of r.
97:11. Light is sown for the r. [5.
112:4. L. full of compassion, r., 116:
6. r. shall be in everl. remembr.
118 : 15. rejoicing in tabern-s of r.
20. gate, into which r. sh. enter
119 : 106. I will keep r. judgments
137. r. art thou, O Lord, Je. 12:1.
138. Thy testimonies are r. and
125 : 3. rod of wicked not rest upon
r. lest r. put forth hands
140:13. r. give thanks unto thy na.
141 : 5. Let r. smite me, it kindness
142 : 7. r. shall compass me about
145 : 17. Lord is r. in all his ways
146:8. Lord loveth the r. preserveth
Pr. 2 : 7. He layeth up wisdom for r.
20. mayest keep paths of the r.
3 : 32. but his secret is with r.
10 : 3. Lord not suffer r. to famish
16. labour of r. tendeth to life
21. the lips of the r. feed many
24. desire of r. shall be granted
25. r. is an everl-g foundation
28. hope of r. shall be gladness
30. The r. shall never be removed
32. lips of r. know what acceptab.
11 : 8. r. is deliv-d out of trouble
10. well with r. city rejoiceth
21. seed of r. shall be delivered
23. desire of the r. is only good
28. r. shall flourish as a branch
30. fruit of the r. is a tree of life
31. r. sh. be recomp-d in earth
12 : 3. root of r. sh. not be moved
5. thoughts of the r. are right
7. house of the r. shall stand
12. root of the r. yieldeth fruit
26. r. more excellent than neighb.
13 : 9. The light of the r. rejoiceth
21. to the r. good sh. be repaid
25. r. eateth to satisfying of soul
14 : 9. among r. there is favour
19. wicked bow at gates of r.
32. r. hath hope in his death
15 : 6. In house of r. is treasure
19. way of the r. is made plain
28. heart of r. studieth to answer
29. he heareth the prayer of r.
16 : 13. r. lips are delight of kings

Pr.18:5.It is not good to overthr. r.
10. r. runneth into it, is safe
21:18. wicked sh. be ransom for r.
26. r. giveth, and spareth not
23 : 24. father of r. greatly rejoice
24 : 15. lay not wait ag. dwelling of
24. saith unto wicked, Thou r.⌊r.
28 : 1. wicked flee, r. bold as lion
10. caus. r. to go astray, sh. fall
28. when wicked perish, r. incr.
29 : 2. r. in authority, peo. rejoice
6. the r. doth sing and rejoice
7. r. considereth cause of poor
16. but the r. shall see their fall
Ec. 3 : 17. God shall judge the r.
7 : 16. Be not r. over much, nei.
8 : 14. happen-h acc. to work of r.
9:1. r. and wise are in hand of God
2. one event to the r. and wicked
Is. 3 : 10. Say ye to r. it sh. be well
5:23. take away righ-n. of r.⌈the r.
24 : 16. heard songs, even glory to
26:2. Open ye, that r. nation enter
41:26. who hath declared, He is r.
53 : 11. r. servant sh. justify many
57 : 1. r. perisheth, no man layeth
to heart : r. is taken from evil
60 : 21. Thy people shall be all r.
Je. 12 : 1. r. thou, O L. when I plead
20 : 12. O L. of hosts, that triest r.
23 : 5. raise unto David r. branch
Eze. 13 : 22. with lies ye made r. sad
16 : 52. sisters more r. than thou
18 : 20. right-n. of r. be upon him
24. when r. turneth away, 33:18.
21:3. I will cut off r. and wick., 4.
33 : 12. right-n. of r. not deliver
him, nor r. be able to live
13. When I say to r. he shall live
Am. 2:6. bec. they sold r. for silver
Ha. 1 : 4. wicked compass about r.
13. wick. devoureth him more r.
Mal. 3 : 18. discern between r. and
the wicked
Mat. 9 : 13. I not come to call r. but
sinners, Mk. 2 : 17. Lu. 5 : 32.
13 : 43. shall r. shine forth as sun
23 : 28. ye outwardly appear r. but
29. ye garnish sepulchres of r.
35. upon you may come all r.
blood shed, fr. blood of r. Abel
25:37. Then shall the r. answer, L.
46. r. shall go into life eternal
Lu. 1 : 6. they were both r. bef. G.
18:9. trusted they were r. ⌈but r.
Jn. 7 : 24. Judge not acc. to appear.
17 : 25. O r. Fa. world not known
Ro. 2 : 5. revelation of r. judgment
3 : 10. There is none r. no not one
5 : 19. obedience of one, many be r.
2 Th. 1 : 5. token of r. judgm. of G.
6. r. thing with God to recomp.
2 Ti. 4 : 8. r. Judge, shall give me
He. 11 : 4. obtained witness he was r.
1 Pe. 3 : 12. eyes of L. are over r.
4 : 18. if r. scarcely saved, where
2 Pe. 2 : 8. Lot vexed his r. soul
1 Jn. 2 : 1. advocate, Jes. Ch. the r.
29. If ye know that he is r. ye
3:7. he that doeth righteousness is
r. as he is r. ⌈er's r.
12. his own works evil, his broth-
Re. 16 : 5. heard angel say, Thou r.
7. O L. r. are thy judgm-ts, 19:2.
22 : 11. that is r. let him be r. still
See **LORD is, Righteous MAN, Righteous MEN.**

RIGHTEOUSLY. ⌈31 : 9.
De. 1 : 16. hear causes, judge r., Pr.
Ps. 67 : 4. judge people r., 96 : 10.
Is. 33 : 15. walketh r. dw. on high
Je. 11 : 20. O Lord, that judgest r.
Tit. 2:12. we should live soberly, r.
1 Pe.2:23. committed to him judgeth

RIGHTEOUSNESS. ⌊r.
De. 6 : 25. it shall be our r. if we do
24:13. it sh. be r. unto thee bef. L.
De.33 : 19. shall offer sacrifices of r.
Jb. 29:14. I put on r. it clothed me
36 : 3. will ascribe r. to my Maker
Ps. 4 : 5. Offer the sacrifices of r.
11:7. righteous L. loveth r., 33 : 5.
15 : 2. worketh r. never be moved
23 : 3. he leadeth me in paths of r.
24 : 5. r. from G. of his salvation
40 : 9. I preached r. in gr. cong-n
45:4. because of, meekness, and r.
7. Thou lovest r. hatest, He. 1:9.
48 : 10. right hand, O G., full of r.
51 : 19. pleased wi. sacrifices of r.
52:3. lovest lying, than to speak r.
58 : 1. Do ye speak r. O congre-n?
72 : 2. He shall judge peo. with r.
3. mts. bring peace, hills by r.
85 : 10. r. and peace have kissed
11. r. sh. look down from heaven
13. r. go before him, set us in way
94 : 15. judgment return unto r.
96:13. he judge world with r., 98:9.
97 : 2. r. habitation of his throne
99 : 4. executest r. in Jac., 103 : 6.
106 : 3. Blessed is he that doeth r.
118 : 19. open to me the gates of r.
119:†75. thy judgments are r., †138.
144. r. of thy testimonies everl-g
172. thy commandments are r.
132 : 9. Let priests be clothed with
Pr. 2 : 9. Then shalt underst. r. ⌊r.
8 : 18. durable riches, r. with me
20. I lead in way of r. in midst
10:2. r. delivereth fr. death, 11 : 4.
11 : 5. r. of perfect shall direct way
6. r. of upright shall deliver
18. to him that soweth r. a sure
19. As r. tendeth to life so he
12 : 17. speaketh truth, sheweth r.
28. In the way of r. is life
13 : 6. r. keepeth him is upright
14 : 34. r. exalteth a nation, sin
15 : 9. loveth him th. followeth r.
16:8. Better is a little with r. than
12. throne is established by r.
31. glory, if found in way of r.
21 : 21. He that followeth r. mercy
findeth life, r. honour
Ec. 3:16. place of r. iniq-y was there
Is. 1 : 21. r. lodged in it, now mur-
26. The city of r. ⌊derers
27. her converts redeemed with r.
5 : 23. wh. take away r. of righte.
10:22. consumption overfl. with r.
11 : 4. with r. shall he judge poor
5. r. shall be girdle of his loins
16:5. seeking judgment, hasting r.
26:9. inhab-s of world will learn r.
10. yet will he not learn r.
28 : 17. r. will I lay to plummet
32 : 16. r. sh. remain in the field
17. work of r. shall be peace, effect of r. quietness assurance
33 : 5. Lord filled Zion with judgment and r.
41 : † 2. who raised up r. from east
45 : 8. let skies pour down r. and
let r. spring up together
19. I Lord speak r. I declare
24. in the Lord have I r. † in the
Lord is all r. ⌈r.
46:12. Hearken unto me, ye far from
51 : 1. Hearken ye that follow r.
7. Hearken ye that know r.
54 : 17. their r. is of me, saith L.
58 : 2. seek me as nation th. did r.
59 : 17. he put on r. as breastplate
60 : 17. officers peace, exactors r.
61 : 3. might be called trees of r.
10. he covered me with robe of r.
11. Lord will cause r. to spring
62 : 1. until the r. thereof go forth
64:5. Thou meetest him worketh r.
Je. 9 : 24. I am Lord wh. exercise r.
22 : 3. Execute ye judgment and r.
23:6. this is his name, THE LORD
OUR RIGHTEOUSNESS, 33 : 16.
Je. 33 : 15. will I cause Branch of r.
to grow, he shall execute r.
51 : 10. L. brought forth our r. ⌈20.
Eze. 14 : 14. deliver own souls by r.,
18:20. r. of righteous be upon him
33 : 12. r. of righteous not deliver
Da. 4 : 27. break off thy sins by r.
9 : 7. O L., r. belongeth unto thee
24. to bring in everlasting r. and
12 : 3. they that turn many to r. sh.
Ho. 10 : 12. till he come and rain r.
Jo. 2 : † 23. teacher of r. acc. to r.
Am. 5 : 7. who leave off r. in earth
24. let r. run down as a mighty
6 : 12. turned fruit of r. into hem-
Mi. 6 : 5. may know r. of L. ⌊lock
Zph. 2 : 3. ye meek of earth, seek r.
Mal. 4 : 2. unto you Sun of r. arise
Mat. 3 : 15. becometh us to fulfil r.
5:6. that hunger and thirst after r.
20. except r. exceed r. of scribes
6 : † 1. heed ye do not r. bef. men
21 : 32. John came in way of r.
Lu. 1 : 75. In r. bef. him all our life
Jn. 16 : 8. reprove world of sin, of r.
10. of r. bec. I go to my Father
Ac. 10 : 35. worketh r. is accepted
13 : 10. thou enemy of all r. wilt
24 : 25. he reasoned of r. judgment
Ro. 1 : 17. is the r. of God revealed
2 : 26. if uncirc-n keep r. of law
3 : 5. if our unright-n. commend r.
21. r. of G. without law ⌊of G.
22. even the r. of God by faith
4 : 6. unto whom God imputeth r.
11. circ-n, a seal of r. of faith,
that r. might be imputed
13. promise was thro. r. of faith
5:17. they wh. receive gift of r. sh.
18. so by r. of one the free gift
21. grace reign thro. r. unto life
6:13. yield members instrum. of r.
16. sin unto death, or obedi. unto
18. ye became servants of r. ⌊r.
19. yield members servants to r.
20. when servant of sin, free fr. r.
8 : 4. That r. of law be fulfilled
10. the Spirit is life because of r.
9 : 30. Gentiles followed not r. attained to r. even r. of faith
31. Israel wh. followed law of r.
not attained to law of r.
10 : 3. to establish own r. have not
submitted unto r. of God
5. Moses describeth r. of law
6. r. which is of faith speaketh
10. heart man believeth unto r.
14 : 17. kingdom not meat, but r.
1 Co. 1 : 30. made unto us wisdom, r.
15 : 34. Awake to r. and sin not
2 Co. 3 : 9. the ministration of r.
5 : 21. we might be made r. of G.
6 : 7. by armour of r. on right ha.
14. what fellowship hath r. with
9 : 10. increase fruits of your r.
11 : 15. transformed as ministers of
Ga 2 : 21. if r. by law, C. is dead ⌊r.
3 : 21. r. should have been by law
5:5. thro. Spirit wait for hope of r.
Ep. 5 : 9. fruit of Spirit is in r.
6 : 14. having on breastplate of r.
Ph. 1:11. Being filled wi. fruits of r.
3 : 6. touching r. which is in law
9. r. which is of God by faith
1 Ti. 6 : 11. follow r., 2 Ti. 2 : 22.
2 Ti.4:8. laid up for me a crown of r.
Tit. 3 : 5. Not by works of r.
He. 1 : 8. a sceptre of r. is sceptre
5 : 13. is unskilful in word of r.
7 : 2. by interpretation King of r.
11 : 7. became heir of r. by faith
33. subdued kingdoms, wrought r.
12 : 11. yield-h peaceable fruit of r.
Ja. 1 : 20. wrath worketh not r. of
3 : 18 fruit of r. is sown in peace
1 Pe. 2 : 24. dead to sin sho. live unto
2 Pe. 1 : 1. like faith thro. r. of G. ⌊r.

2 Pe. 2:5. saved Noah preacher of r.
21. better not have kno. way of r.
3:13. new earth, wh-n dwelleth r.
1 Jn. 2:29. doeth r. is born of God
3:7. he that doeth r. is righteous
10. whoso. doeth not r. not of G.
Re. 19:8. fine linen is r. of saints

For RIGHTEOUSNESS.

Ge. 15:6. believed, L. counted it, f. r., Ps. 106:31. Ro. 4:3.
Ps. 143:11. f. thy r.' sake bring
Is. 5:7. he looked f. r. but a cry
42:21. L. well pleased for r.' sake
Mat. 5:10. are persecuted f. r.' sake
Ro. 4:5. faith counted f. r., Ga. 3:6.
9. reckoned to Abraham for r.
22. imputed to him f. r., Ja. 2:23.
10:4. Christ is end of law f. r.
1 Pe. 3:14. if ye suffer f. r.' sake ye

His RIGHTEOUSNESS.

1 S. 26:23. L. render to ev. man h. r.
1 K. 8:32. acc. to h. r., 2 Ch. 6:23.
Jb. 33:26. will render man h. r.
Ps. 7:17. will praise L. acc. to h. r.
22:31. shall declare h. r. unto peo.
50:6. heavens declare h. r., 97:6.
98:2. h. r. hath he openly shewed
103:17. h. r. unto children's chil.
111:3. and h. r. endureth for ever, 112:3, 9. [h. r.
Ec. 7:15. just man that perisheth in
Is. 59:16. and h. r. sustained him
Eze. 3:20. When righteous man doth turn from h. r., 18:24, 26.–33:18.
18:22. in h. r. that he hath done
33:12. not be able to live for h. r.
13. if he trust h. own r. and commit iniq. h. r. not be rememb-d
Mi. 7:9. and I shall behold h. r.
Mat. 6:33. seek kingd. of G. h. r.
Ro. 3:25. to declare h. r. for, 26.
2 Co. 9:9. given to poor h. r. remain.

In RIGHTEOUSNESS.

Le. 19:15. i. r. shalt thou judge
1 K. 3:6. as he walked bef. thee i. r.
Ps. 9:†4. thou sattest, judging i. r.
8. he shall judge the world i. r.
17:15. I will behold thy face i. r.
65:5. By terrible things i. r. wilt
Pr. 8:8. words of my mouth i. r.
25:5. his throne be establi-d i. r.
Is. 5:16. God sh. be sanctified i. r.
32:1. a king shall reign i. r.
42:6. I L. have called thee i. r.
45:13. I have raised him i. r. and
23. word out of my mouth i. r.
48:1. mention G. of Isr., not i. r.
54:14. i. r. shalt thou be establ-ed
63:1. I speak i. r. mighty to save
Je. 4:2. swear, the L. liveth, i. r.
Ho. 2:19. I will betroth thee i. r.
10:12. Sow i. r. reap in mercy
Zch. 8:8. I will be their God i. r.
Mal. 3:3. may offer offering i. r.
Ac. 17:31. he will judge world i. r.
Ro. 9:28. he will cut it short i. r.
Ep. 4:24. after God is created i. r.
2 Ti. 3:16. Scripture for instruc. i. r.
Re. 19:11. and i. r. he doth judge

Mine own or my RIGHTEOUSNESS.

Ge. 30:33. So m. r. answer for me
De. 9:4. For m. r. Lord brought me
2 S. 22:21. Lord rewarded me acc. to m. r., 25. Ps. 18:20, 24.
Jb. 6:29. return again, m. r. is in it
27:6. m. r. I hold fast, will not let
35:2. saidst, m. r. more than G.'s
Ps. 4:1. Hear me, O God of my r.
7:8. judge me, O L., acc. to m. r.
35:†27. be glad that favour m. r.
Is. 41:10. uphold thee with m. r.
46:13. I bring near m. r.
51:5. m. r. is near, my salvation
6. m. r. shall not be abolished
8. but m. r. shall be for ever
56:1. m. r. near to be revealed

Ph. 3:9. found, not having m. o. r.

Thy RIGHTEOUSNESS.

De. 9:5. Not for t. r. or uprightn., 6.
Jb. 8:6. habita. of t. r. prosperous
35:8. t. r. may profit son of man
Ps. 5:8. Lead me, O Lord, in t. r.
31:1. deliver me in t. r., 71:2.
35:24. Judge me, O L., acc. to t. r.
28. tongue speak of t. r., 71:24.
36:6. t. r. is like great mountains
10. O continue t. r. to upright
37:6. he shall bring t. r. as light
40:10. I have not hid t. r. within
51:14. tongue shall sing of t. r.
69:27. let th. not come into t. r.
71:15. My mouth shall shew t. r.
16. I will make mention of t. r.
19. t. r. O God, is very high
72:1. give t. r. unto king's son
88:12. t. r. be known in land of
89:16. in t. r. shall be exalted
119:†7. I learned judgm-s of t. r.
40. quicken me in t. r.
123. eyes fail for word of t. r.
142. t. r. is an everl. righteousness
143:1. in faithfulness ans., in t. r.
11. for t. r.' sake bring my soul
145:7. and they shall sing of t. r.
Is. 48:18. had t. r. been as waves
57:12. I will declare t. r. and
58:8. t. r. shall go before thee
62:2. And Gentiles shall see t. r.
Da. 9:16. O Lord, acc. to all t. r.

RIGHTEOUSNESSES.

Ju. 5:†11. shall rehearse r. of the L.
1 S. 12:†7. may reason of r. of L.
Is. 33:†15. he that walketh in r.
45:†24. in the Lord have I r.
64:6. all our r. are as filthy rags
Eze. 3:†20. righte. turneth fr. his r.
33:13. all his r. not be rememb-d
Da. 9:18. not for our r. but thy mer- [cies

RIGHTLY.

Ge. 27:36. Is not he r. named Jac.?
Lu. 7:43. said, Thou hast r. judged
20:21. we know thou teachest r.
2 Ti. 2:15. r. dividing word of truth

RIGHTNESS.

Ex. 4:†4. I considered r. of work
He. 1:†8. a sceptre of r. is the sceptre

RIGOUR.

Ex. 1:13. made Isr. serve with r., [14.
Le. 25:43. not rule with r., 46, 53.

RIM'MON.

Jos. 15:32. Shilhim, Ain and R. cities
Ju. 20:45. Benjamites fled unto rock R., 47.–21:13.
2 S. 4:2. and Rechab sons of R., 5, [9.
2 K. 5:18. goeth into house of R.
1 Ch. 4:32. villages of Simeon, R.
6:77. was given unto Merari, R.
Zch. 14:10 as a plain fr. Geba unto R.

RIM'MON-PA'REZ.

Nu. 33:19. fr. Ritmah, pitched at R.

RING. [20.

Ge. 41:42. Pharaoh took off his r.
Ex. 26:24. coupled unto one r., 36:29.
Es. 3:10. k. Ahasuerus took his r.
12. sealed with king's r., 8:8, 10.
8:2. king took off r. gave Mord.
Can. 5:†12. as stone in foil of r.
Lu. 15:22. fa. said, put r. on hand
Ja. 2:2. if come in man with a r.

RINGS.

Ex. 25:12. cast 4 r. of gold, 38:5.
14. shalt put staves into the r., 15.–27:7.–37:5.–38:7.
26. make for it 4 r. of gold
26:29. make their r. of gold, 25:27.–28:23, 26, 27.–30:4.–36:34.–37:3, 13, 14.–39:16, 19, 20.
27:4. make upon net 4 brazen r.
28:28. shall bind breastplate by the r., 24.–37:27.–39:17, 21.
35:22. bro-t bracelets, r. jewels
Nu. 31:50. prey gotten of jewels, r.
Es. 1:6. hangings fastened to r.

Can. 5:14. his hands are as gold r.
Is. 3:21. will take r. and jewels
Eze. 1:18. r. so high were dreadful, their r. were full of eyes

RINGLEADER.

Ac. 24:5. r. of sect of Nazarenes

RINGSTREAKED.

Ge 30:35. removed he goats were r.
39. bef. rods, bro-t forth cattle r.
40. set faces of flocks toward r.
31:8. The r. shall be thy hire
10. rams were r. speckled, gris- [zled, 12.

RIN'NAH.

1 Ch. 4:20. sons of Shimon R. Tilon

RINSED.

Le. 6:28. pot he both scoured and r.
15:11. not r. his hands in water
12. ev. vessel of wood shall be r.

RIOT. [Noun.]

Is. 29:†9. Stay yours. wonder, take r.
Tit. 1:6. children not accused of r.
1 Pe. 4:4. that you run not to r.

RIOT. [Verb.]

2 Pe. 2:13. count it pleasure to r.

RIOTING.

Ro. 13:13. walk not in r., drunken- [ness

RIOTOUS.

Pr. 23:20. be not among r. eaters
28:7. he that is companion of r.
Lu. 15:13. wasted subst. with r. living

RIP, RIPPED.

2 K. 8:12. thou wilt r. up their wom.
15:16. all the women with child he r-d up, Ho. 13:16.
Am. 1:13. they have r-d up women

RIPE.

Ge. 40:10. brought forth r. grapes
Ex. 22:29. to offer first of r. fruits
Jo. 3:13. in sickle, harvest is r. [kle
Mk. 4:†29. fruit is r. putteth in sic-
1 Co. 14:†20. in underst-g be of r.
Re. 14:15. harvest of earth is r. [age
18. gather clusters, her grapes r.
See FIRST ripe.

RIPENING.

Is. 18:5. sour grape is r. in flower

RI'PHATH. See TOGARMAH.

RISE.

Ex. 21:19. If he r. again, walk
Nu. 24:17. Sceptre shall r. out of Isr.
De. 33:11. smite them that r. that they r. not again [the land
Jos. 18:4. they shall r. and go thro.
Ju. 8:21. said, r. and fall upon us
9:33. shalt r. early, set upon city
1 S. 22:13. he r. to lie in wait
24:7. suffered not to r. ag. Saul
2 S. 12:21. child dead, thou didst r.
18:32. that r. ag. thee be as Abs.
Jb. 30:12. Upon my right r. youth
Ps. 18:38. wounded, not able to r.
27:3. though war sho. r. ag. me
36:12. they sh. not be able to r.
119:62. At midnight I will r. to
140:10. pits, that they r. not up
Pr. 24:22. For their calamity shall r. suddenly
28:12. wicked r. man is hid., 28.
Can. 3:2. I will r. now about city
Is. 14:21. Prepare slaughter, that they do not r.
24:20. earth shall fall not r. again
26:14. deceased, they shall not r.
33:10. Now will I r. saith Lord
43:17. lie together they sh. not r.
54:17. every tongue that shall r.
58:10. thy light r. in obscurity
Je. 25:27. Drink, fall, r. no more
51:64. Babylon shall not r. fr. evil
Am. 5:2. virgin of Isr. no more r.
7:9. I will r. ag. house of Jerob.
Mat. 5:45. mak-h sun to r. on evil
20:19. third day he shall r., Mk. 9:31.–10:34. Lu. 18:33.–24:7.
24:7. For nation shall r. against nation, Mk. 13:8. Lu. 21:10.
11. false prophets sh. r., Mk. 13:22.

Mat.26:46.r.let us be going, behold
27:63. After 3 days I will r., Mk.8:
Mk. 4:27. and r. night and day [31.
10:49. Be of good comfort, r. [25.
12:23. In resurr-n, when they r.,
26. touching the dead, th. they r.
Lu.11:7. Trouble me not, I can-t r.
8. he will not r. bec. his friend
12:54. When ye see a cloud r. out
22:46. Why sleep ye? r. and pray
24:46. behoved C. to suffer and r.
Jn. 5:8. Jes. saith, r. take thy bed
11:23. Jes. saith, Thy bro. shall r.
24. Martha saith, I know he sh. r.
20:9. knew not Scrip. th. he must
Ac. 10:13. r. Peter, kill and eat [r.
26:16. r. and stand upon thy feet
23. be first th. should r. from dead
Ro. 15:12. he that shall r. to reign
1 Co. 15:15. if dead r. not, 16,29,32.
1 Th. 4:16. dead in Ch. sh. r. first
He. 7:11. what need ano. priest r.
Re. 11:1. r. and measure temple of

RISE up. [G.

Ge. 19:2. ye sh. r. u. early and go
31:35. not displease, th. I can-t r. u.
Ex. 8:20. r. u. stand bef. Pha., 9:
12:31. r. u. get forth fr. peo. [13.
Le. 19:32. r. u. bef. hoary head
Nu. 10:35. r. u. Lord, let enemies
22:20. If men come r. u. and go
23:18. r. u. Balak, hear, thou son
24. the people sh. r. u. as a lion
De. 2:13. r. u. get over brook
24. r. ye u. pass ov. river Arnon
19:11. if a man r. u. ag. neighb-r
15. One witness not r. u. ag. man
16. If false witness r. u. ag. any
28:7. L. sh. cause enemies that r. u.
29:22. generation that shall r. u.
31:16. peo. will r. u. go whoring
32:38. gods, let them r. u. and help
Jos. 8:7. Then r. u. from ambush
Ju. 20:38. make great flame r. u., 40.
1 S. 29:10. r. u. early in morning
2 K. 16:7. king of Isr. wh. r. u. ag.
Ne. 2:18. Let us r. u. and build [me
Jb. 20:27. earth shall r. u. ag. him
Ps. 3:1. many that r. u. ag. me
17:7. save from those r. u. ag. them
18:48. liftest me ab. those r. u. ag.
35:11. False witnesses did r. u.
41:8. lieth, he shall r. u. no more
44:5. them under that r. u. ag. us
59:1. defend fr. them r. u. ag. me
74:23. tumult of those th. r. u. ag.
92:11. wicked that r. u. ag. me [thee
94:16. Who will r. u. for me ag.
127:2. vain for you to r. u. early
139:21. grieved with those r. u. ag.
Ec. 10:4. If ruler r. u. ag. thee
12:4. sh. r. u. at voice of bird
Can. 2:10. My beloved said, r. u.
Is. 5:11. Woe unto th. r. u. in morn.
14:22. I will r. u. ag. them, saith
28:21. Lord r. u. as in Perazim [L.
32:9. r. u. ye women at ease
Je. 37:10. r. u. every man in tent
47:2. waters r. u. out of north
49:14. Gather, and r. u. to battle
51:1. ag. them that r. u. ag. me
La. 1:14. I am not able to r. u.
Am. 8:8. it sh. r. u. as flood, 9:5.
14. they sh. fall, and never r. u.
Ob. 1. let us r. u. against Edom
Na. 1:9. affliction not r. u. sec. time
Ha. 2:7. Sh. they not r. u. suddenly
Zph. 3:8. day I r. u. to the prey
Zch. 14:13. hand r. u. ag. neighb.
Mat. 10:21. children shall r. u. ag.
parents, Mk. 13:12. [Lu. 11:32.
12:41. men of Nineveh shall r. u.,
42. queen of south r. u., Lu. 11:31.
Mk. 3:26. if Satan r. u. ag. hims.
14:42. r. u. lo, he th. betrayeth
Lu. 5:23. Whe. is easier to say, r. u.
6:8. he said, r. u. and stand forth
Ac. 3:6. In name of Jesus r. u.
Re. 13:1. I saw beast r. u. out of

RISEN. [sea

Ge. 19:23. sun was r. when Lot
Ex. 22:3. If sun be r. upon him, bl.
Nu. 32:14. ye r. in father's stead
Ju. 9:18. ye are r. ag. my father's
Ru. 2:15. she was r. up to glean
1 S. 25:29. man r. to pursue thee
2 S. 14:7. whole family is r. up
1 K. 8:20. I am r. up in room of
David, 2 Ch. 6:10. [was r.
2 K. 6:15. servant of the man of God
2 Ch. 13:6. servant of Solomon is r.
21:4. Jehoram was r. to kingdom
Ps. 20:8. we are r. stand upright
27:12. false witn-s are r. ag-t me
54:3. strangers are r. up ag. me
86:14. O God, proud are r. ag. me
Is. 60:1. glory of L. is r. upon thee
Eze. 7:11. Violence is r. into a rod
47:5. waters were r. to swim in
Mi. 2:8. my peo. is r. as enemy [Jn.
Mat. 11:11. not r. a greater than
14:2. said, This is John Bap. he is
r. fr. dead, Mk. 6:14,16. Lu. 9:7.
17:9. Son of man be r., Mk. 9:9.
26:32. am r. I will go, Mk. 14:28.
27:64. les. disciples steal him away,
and say unto people, He is r.
28:6. not here, he is r. as he said,
Mk. 16:6,17. Lu. 24:6. [first day
Mk. 16:9. when Jesus was r., early
14. seen him aft. he was r., Jn. 21:
Lu. 7:16. a great prophet is r. [14.
9:8. th. one of old prophets r., 19.
13:25. When master of house is r.
24:34. The Lord is r. indeed
Jn. 2:22. When he was r. fr. dead
Ac. 17:3. Ch. must needs have r.
Ro. 8:34. yea rather that is r. again
1 Co. 15:13. if no resurr. Christ not r.
14. if C. be not r. preaching vain
20. But now is Christ r. fr. dead
Col. 2:12. in baptism ye are r. with
3:1. If ye be r. with Ch. seek those
Ja. 1:11. the sun is no sooner r.

RISEST. [11:19.

De. 6:7. talk of them when thou r.,

RISETH. [bour

De. 22:26. when man r. ag. neigh-
Jos. 6:26. that r. buildeth Jericho
2 S. 23:4. sh. be as light when sun r.
Jb. 9:7. commandeth sun it r. not
14:12. So man lieth down, r. not
24:22. he r. up, no man is sure
27:7. that r. ag. me, as unrighte-s
31:14. What sh l do when God r.
Pr. 24:16. just man falleth, r. up
31:15. She r. while it is yet night
Is. 47:11. not know whence it r.
Je. 46:8. Egypt r. up like a flood
Mi. 7:6. dau. r. up ag. her mother
Jn. 13:4. Jesus r. from supper, and

RISING. [Noun.]

Le. 13:2. if in skin of his flesh a r.
10. shall see if r. be white, 19,43.
28. if spot stay, it is r. of burning
14:56. this is the law for a r.
Ne. 4:21. spears from r. of morning
Pr. 30:31. king ag. whom is no r.
Is. 60:3. to the brightness of thy r.
Mk. 9:10. what r. from dead mean
Lu. 2:34. this child is set for fall and

RISING of sun. [r.

Nu. 2:3. on east side tow. r. o. s.
2 K. 10:†33. From Jordan tow. r. o.
Ps. 50:1. called earth fr. r. o. s. [s.
113:3. fr. r. o. s. L.'s name praised
Is. 41:25. fr. r. o. s. call upon my
45:6. may know from r. o. s. [name
59:19. fear his glory from r. o. s.
Mal. 1:11. from r. o. s. my name
be great among the Gentiles
Mk. 16:2. early they came unto
the sepulchre at r. o. s.

See SUNRISING.

RISING. [Part.] [times

2 Ch. 36:15. sent by messeng. r. be-
Jb. 16:8. my leanness r. in me
24:5. asses r. betimes for prey
14. murderer r. with light killeth
Pr. 27:14. blesseth friend, r. early
Je. 7:13. I spake unto you, r. early
ye heard not, 25:3.–35:14.
25. I sent my servants prophets
unto you r. early, 25:4.–26:5.–
29:19.–35:15.–44:4. [my voice
11:7. r. early, and saying, Obey
32:33. tho. I taught them, r. early
La. 3:63. sitting, r. I am their music
Mk. 1:35. r. before day, he prayed

RIS'SAH. [R.

Nu. 33:21. pitched at R. | 22. from

RITES. [it

Nu. 9:3. keep it acc. to all the r. of
Ac. 6:†14. this Jesus sh. change r.
He. 9:†10. stood in washings carnal

RITH'MAH. [r.

Nu. 33:18. pitched in R. | 19. from R.

RIVER.

Ge. 2:10. a r. went out of Eden
31:21. Jacob rose passed over r.
36:37. Rehoboth by r., 1 Ch. 1:48.
41:1. Pha. dreamed, stood by r., 17.
2. there came up out of r., 3, 18.
Ex. 1:22. Every son cast into the r.
2:5. dau. of Pha. came to wash at
4:9. water of r. become blood [r.
7:17. waters in r. turned into blood,
18. fish in r. sh. die, r. stink [20.
24. digged around r. for water
25. after Lord had smitten the r.
8:3. the r. shall bring forth frogs
9. may remain in the r. only, 11.
17:5. rod whw. smotest r., 7:25.
23:31. bounds fr. desert unto the r.
Nu. 24:6. as gardens by the r. side
De. 2:24. take journey, pass over r.
3:16. Gave fr. Gilead unto r. Arnon
Jos. 13:9. the city in the midst of
r., 16. 2 S. 24:5. [Sisera
Ju. 4:7. I will draw to r. Kishon,
5:21. r. Kishon that ancient r.
2 S. 17:13. will draw city into r.
1 K. 4:21. Solomon reigned over
from r., 24. 2 Ch. 9:26.
8:65. fr. Hamath unto r. of Egypt,
2 Ch. 7:8.
2 K. 10:33. Aroer wh. is by r. Arnon
17:6. r. Gozan, 18:11 2 Ch. 7:8.
Ezr. 4:10. rest on this side the r., 11.
16. no portion on this side the r.
5:3. Tatnai, governor on this side
the r., 6.–6:13. Ne. 3:7. [Ahava
8:15. them to r. that runneth to
21. I proclaimed fast at r. Ahava
31. we departed from r. Ahava
36. governors on this side the r.
Jb. 40:23. Behold he drinketh up r.
Ps. 36:8. drink of r. of thy pleas
46:4. a r. streams sh. make glad
65:9. enrichest it with r. of God
72:8. dominion from the r. unto
ends of earth, Zch. 9:10. [unto r.
80:11. she sent out her branches
105:41. ran in dry places like r.
Is. 8:7. upon them waters of r.
11:15. sh. shake his hand over r.
19:5. the r. shall be wasted
23:3. harvest of r. is her revenue
10. Pass through land as r. O dau.
27:12. beat off from channel of r.
48:18. then thy peace been as a r.
66:12. extend peace to her like r.
Je. 2:18. to drink waters of the r.
17:8. spreadeth her roots by r.
La. 2:18. let tears run down like r.
Eze. 29:3. said, My r. is my own, 9.
47:5. it was a r. I could not pass
9. shall live whither r. cometh
19. from the r. to the great sea
Da. 8:3. stood before the r. a ram
12:5. one on this side of r. other (2)

Da.12:6.wh.was upon waters of r.,7.
Am. 6: 14. afflict you unto the r. of
Mi. 7: 12. sh. come fr. fortress to r.
Zch. 10: 11. deeps of r. shall dry up
Mk. 1: 5. baptized in r. of Jordan
Ac. 16: 13. sabbath we by a r. side
Re. 22: 1. shewed me pure r. of wat.
2. on either side of r. tree of life
See BANK, BRINK, BEYOND, CHEBAR, EUPHRATES.

RIVERS.

Ex. 7: 19. stretch hand upon r., 8: 5.
Le. 11: 9. whatsoever hath fins in r.
10. that have not fins in r.
De. 10: 7. Jotbath, land of r. of waters
2 K. 5: 12. Are not r. of Damascus
19: 24. I have dried r., Is. 37: 25.
Jb. 20: 17. He sh. not see r. of honey
28: 10. He cutteth out r. am. rocks
29: 6. rock poured out r. of oil
Ps. 1: 3. like tree by r. of water
74: 15. driedst up mighty r.
78: 16. caused waters to run like r.
44. had turned their r. into blood
89: 25. will set his right hand in r.
107: 33. He turneth r. into wildern.
119: 136. r. of waters run down
137: 1. By r. of Babylon we wept
Pr. 5: 16. r. of waters in streets
21: 1. in hand of L. as r. of water
Ec. 1: 7. All r. run into the sea
Can. 5: 12. doves by r. of waters
Is. 7: 18. shall hiss for fly in r.
18: 1. land beyond r. of Ethiopia
2. whose land r. spoiled, 7.
19: 6. they shall turn r. far away
30: 25. upon ev. high hill r. [pla.
32: 2. man be as r. of wat. in dry
33: 21. Lord be place of broad r.
41: 18. I will open r. in high places
42: 15. I will make the r. islands
43: 2. When passest through the r.
19. I will make r. in desert, 20.
44: 27. to deep, Be dry and dry r.
47: 2. uncover thigh, pass over r.
50: 2. I make the r. a wilderness
Je. 31: 9. cause them to walk by r.
46: 7. waters are moved as r., 8. [er
La. 3: 48. eye runneth wi. r. of wat-
Eze. 6: 3. Thus saith L., to r., 36: 4.
29: 3. great dragon that lieth in r.
4. I will cause fish of thy r. to
stick, I will bring thee out of r.
5 I will leave thee, and fish of r.
10. I am against thee, and thy r.
30: 12. I will make the r. dry
31: 4. deep set him on high wi. r. (2)
12. his boughs are broken by r.
32: 2. thou camest forth with thy r.
6. and the r. shall be full of thee
14. will I cause r. to run like oil
34: 13. will feed them upon mts. by
35: 8. in all thy r. sh. fall slain [r.
36: 6. say to the hills, r. valleys
47: 9. whitherso. r. come, sh. live
Jo. 1: 20. r. of waters are dried up
3: 18. r. of Judah sh. flow wi. waters
Mi. 6: 7. ten thousands of r. of oil
Na. 1: 4. rebuketh sea, drieth r.
2: 6. gates of r. shall be opened
3: 8. populous No, situate am. r.
Hab. 3: 8. Was L. displeased ag. r.?
9. didst cleave earth with r.
Jn. 7: 38. out of belly r. of living wat.
Re. 8: 10. star fell upon 3d part of r.
16: 4. poured out his vial upon r.

RIZ'PAH.

2 S. 3: 7. Saul had concub., name R.
21: 8. David deliv-d two sons of R.
10. R. spread sackcl. upon rock
11. was told Da. what R. had done

ROAD.

1 S. 27: 10. Whither made a r. to day

ROAR. [98: 7.

1 Ch. 16: 32. Let sea r., Ps. 96: 11.–
Ps. 46: 3. not fear, though waters r.
74: 4. enemies r. in thy congre-ns
Ps. 104: 21. young lions r. aft. prey
Is. 5: 29. shall r. like young lions
30. in that day shall r. ag. them
42: 13. L. sh. r. prevail ag. enemies
59: 11. We r. all like bears, mourn
Je. 5: 22. tho. they r. yet not pass
25: 30. Lord shall r. from on high
31: 35. divideth sea, when waves r.
50: 42. their voice sh. r. like sea
51: 38. shall r. together like lions
55. her waves r. like gr. waters
Ho. 11: 10. he shall r. like a lion,
when he shall r. [Am. 1: 2.
Jo. 3: 16. Lord shall r. out of Zion,
Am. 3: 4. Will a lion r. if he no prey?

ROARED.

Ju. 14: 5. young lion r. ag. Samson
Ps. 38: 8. I have r. by reason of
Is. 51: 15. divided sea, waves r.
Je. 2: 15. young lions r. upon him
Am. 3: 8. lion r. who will not fear

ROARETH. [dereth

Jb. 37: 4. After it voice r.: he thun-
Je. 6: 23. their voice r. like sea
Re. 10: 3. angel cried, as a lion r.

ROARING. [Adj.]

Ps. 22: 13. gaped upon me as a r. lion
Pr. 28: 15. As r. lion, so wick. ruler
Is. 31: 4. as young lion r. on prey
Eze. 22: 25. conspiracy, like r. lion
Zph. 3: 3. Her princes are r. lious
Lu. 21: 25. distress, sea and waves r.
1 Pe. 5: 8. devil, as r. lion, walketh

ROARING, S.

Jb. 3: 24. my r-s are poured likewaters
4: 10. The r. of the lion broken
Ps. 22: 1. why so far from my r.?
32: 3. bones waxed old thro. my r.
Pr. 19: 12. king's wrath as r. of lion
20: 2. fear of king is as r. of lion
Is. 5: 29. Their r. shall be like a lion
30. they shall roar like r. of sea
Eze. 19: 7. land desolate by his r.
Zch. 11: 3. voice of r. of young lions

ROAST. [Noun.]

Is. 44: 16. he roasteth r. is satisfied

ROAST, ED, ETH.

Ex. 12: 8. shall eat in that night flesh
r. with fire, 9. De. 16: 7.
1 S. 2: 15. Give flesh to r. for priest
2 Ch. 35: 13. they r-d passover [took
Pr. 12: 27. slothful r-h not that he
Is. 44: 16. he r-h and is satisfied
19. I have r-d flesh, and eaten
Je. 29: 22. whom king of Bab. r-d

ROB. [in fire

Le. 19: 13. shalt not r. neighbour
26: 22. beasts, sh. r. you of chil.
1 S. 23: 1. they r. threshingfloors
Pr. 22: 22. r. not poor, because poor
Is. 10: 2. that may r. fatherless
17: 14. is lot of them that r. us
Eze. 39: 10. r. those th. robbed them
Mal. 3: 8. Will a man r. God? Yet ye

ROBBED.

Ju. 9: 25. they r. all came by them
2 S. 17: 8. chafed in minds, as bear r.
Ps. 119: 61. bands of wicked r. me
Pr. 17: 12. Let a bear r. of whelps
Is. 10: 13. I have r. their treasures
42: 22. is a people r. and spoiled
Je. 50: 37. her treasures shall be r.
Eze. 33: 15. if wicked give that he r.
39: 10. they sh. rob those r. them
Mal. 3: 8. ye have r. me, Wherein
have we r. thee? [have r. me
9. Ye are cursed wi. curse, for ye
2 Co. 11: 8. I r. other churches

ROBBER.

Jb. 5: 5. r. swalloweth their substance
18: 9. the r. shall prevail ag. him
Pr. 23: † 28. She lieth in wait as a r.
Eze. 18: 10. If he beget a son a r.
Jn. 10: 1. same is a thief and a r.
18: 40. not this man. Now Barab-

ROBBERS. [bas was r.

Jb. 12: 6. tabernacles of r. prosper
Is. 42: 24. who gave Israel to r.
Je. 7: 11. Is this house a den of r.?
Eze. 7: 22. r. sh. enter and defile it
Da. 11: 14. r. of people exalt thems.
Ho. 6: 9. troops of r. wait for man
7: 1. troop of r. spoileth without
Ob. 5. if r. by night, would they not
Jn. 10: 8. All that came bef. me r.
Ac. 19: 37. these not r. of churches
2 Co. 11: 26. in perils of waters, of r.

ROBBERY.

Ps. 62: 10. become not vain in r.
Pr. 21: 7. r. of wicked destroy them
Is. 61: 8. I hate r. for burnt offering
Eze. 22: 29. have exercised r. and
Am. 3: 10. store up r. in palaces
Na. 3: 1. city is full of lies and r.
Ph. 2: 6. thought it no r. to be equal

ROBBETH. [wi. G.

Pr. 28: 24. Whoso r. father or mother

ROBE.

Ex. 28: 4. make an ephod, and a r.
31. shalt make r. of the ephod of
blue, 39: 22. [24, 25, 26.
34. golden bell upon hem of r., 39:
29: 5. put upon Aaron r., Le. 8: 7.
39: 23. there was a hole in r.
1 S. 18: 4. Jona. stripped hims. of r.
24: 4. Da. cut off skirt of Saul's r.
11. see skirt of thy r. in my ha. I
cut off thy r. killed thee not
1 Ch. 15: 27. David clothed with r.
Jb. 1: † 20. Job arose, rent his r.
29: 14. my judgment was as a r.
Is. 22: 21. will clothe him wi. thy r.
61: 10. covered me wi. r. of right-n.
Jon. 3: 6. king laid his r. from him
Mi. 2: 8. ye pull off r. with garment
Mat. 27: 28. put on Jesus scarlet r.
31. after that, they took r. off
Lu. 15: 22. Bring forth the best r.
23: 11. arrayed him in a gorgeous r.
Jn. 19: 2. put on Jesus purple r.
5. Jesus came, wearing purple r.

ROBES.

2 S. 13: 18. with such r. were virgins
1 K. 22: 10. kings having put on r.
30. put on thy r., 2 Ch. 18: 9, 29.
Eze. 26: 16. princes sh. lay away r.
Lu. 20: 46. the scribes in long r.
Re. 6: 11. white r. were given th. [r.
7: 9. bef. Lamb, clothed with white
13. What are these in white r.?
14. they wh. have washed their r.

ROBO'AM=REHOBOAM.

ROCK. [r.

Ex. 17: 6. I will sta. bef. thee upon
33: 21. Thou shalt stand upon r.
22. I will put thee in cleft of r.
Nu. 20: 8. speak unto r. bef. eyes
10. fetch you water out of r.?
11. Moses smote the r. twice
24: 21. thou puttest thy nest in a r.
De. 8: 15. bro-t thee water out of r.
32: 4. He is the R. his work perfect
13. suck honey and oil out of r.
15. lightly esteemed R. of salva.
18. Of the R. that begat thee
30. except their R. had sold them
31. their R. is not as our r. our en.
37. Where r. in wh. they trusted?
Ju. 1: 36. to Akrabbim fr. r. upward
6: 20. lay them upon this r.
21. fire out of r. consumed flesh
26. build altar upon top of r.
7: 25. slew Oreb upon r. and Zeeb
13: 19. Manoah offered it upon r.
15: 8. Samson dwelt in top r. Etam,
13. bro-t Samson up from r. [11.
20: 45. Benjamites turned unto r.
of Rimmon, 47.–21: 13.
1 S. 2: 2. nei. is any r. like our God
14: 4. sharp r. on one side, sharp
r. on the other side
23: 25. David came down into a r.
† 28. they called it r. of divisions
2 S. 21: 10. spread sackcloth upon r.

2 S. 22 : 2. he said, Lord is my r., Ps. 18 : 2.-92 : 15. [trust
3. The God of my r. in him will I
32. who r. save G.? Ps. 18 : 31.
47. blessed be my r., exalted be G. of r. of salvation, Ps. 18 : 46.
23 : 3. God of Isr. said, R. of Israel
2 K. 14 : † 7. Amaziah took the r.
1 Ch. 11:15. capt-s went to r. to Da.
2 Ch. 25 : 12. cast them down fr. r.
Ne. 9 : 15. water out of r. for their thirst, Ps. 78 : 16.-105 : 41.
Jb. 14 : 18. r. is removed out of place
18 : 4. shall the r. be removed
19 : 24. were graven in r. for ever
24:8. embrace r. for want of shelter
28 : 9. putteth his hand upon r.
29 : 6. r. poured out rivers of oil
39 : 1. wild goats of r. bring forth?
28. she dwelleth on r. crag of r.
Ps. 19 : † 14. O Lord, my r. my
27 : 5. he sh. set me upon r., 40 : 2.
28 : 1. Unto thee will I cry, my r.
31 : 2. be thou my strong r. for [3.
3. thou art my r. my fortress, 71:
42 : 9. G. my r., Why forgotten me
61 : 2. lead me to r. higher than I
62 : 2. God only is my r., 6.
7. r. of my strength [habitation
71 : 3. †, Be thou to me for a r. of
73 : † 26. God is the r. of my heart
78 : 20. he smote r. waters gushed
35. rememb-d God was their r.
81 : 16. with honey out of the r. I
89 : 26. r. of my salvation
94 : 22. God is r. of my refuge
95 : 1. joyful noise to r. of salvation
114:8. turned r. into standing wat.
137 : † 9. dasheth little ones ag. r.
144 : † 1. Blessed be Lord of my r.
Pr. 30 : 19. way of serpent upon r.
Can. 2 : 14. dove, art in clefts of r.
Is. 2 : 10. Enter r. hide thee in dust
10 : 26. slaughter at r. of Oreb
16 : † 1. Send lamb to ruler fr. a r.
17 : 10. not mindful of r. of stren.
22 : 16. graveth a habitation in r.
26 : † 4. in the Lord is r. of ages
30 : † 29. one goeth to r. of Israel
31 : † 9. his r. shall pass for fear
32 : 2. man as shadow of great r.
42 : 11. let inhabitants of r. sing
44 : † 8. no r. I know not any [r.
48:21. caused waters to flow out of
51 : 1. look unto r. whence hewn
Je. 5 : 3. made faces harder than r.
13 : 4. hide girdle in a hole of r.
18 : 14. snow which cometh from r.
21:13. I am ag. thee, O inhab. of r.
23 : 29. hammer that breaketh r.
48 : 28. leave cities, dwell in r.
49 : 16. dwellest in clefts of r.
Eze. 24 : 7. she set it upon top of r.
8. I set her blood upon top of r.
26 : 4. make her like top of a r., 14.
Am. 6 : 12. Sh. horses run upon r.?
Ob. 3. dwellest in clefts of r.
Ha. 1 : † 12. O r. thou hast estab-d
Mat. 7 : 24. man built ho. upon r.
25. founded upon a r., Lu. 6 : 48.
16 : 18. upon this r. build church
27:60. own new tomb, he had hewn out in r., Mk. 15 : 46.
Lu. 8 : 6. some fell upon a r.
13. They on the r. are they, which
1 Co. 10:4. drank of that spiritual R. and that R. was Christ
See OFFENCE.

ROCKS.

Nu. 23 : 9. fr. top of r. I see him
1 S. 13 : 6. then people hid in r.
24 : 2. went to seek David upon r.
1 K. 19 : 11. strong wind brake the r.
Jb. 28 : 10. cutteth out rivers am. r.
30 : 6. to dwell in caves, and in r.
Ps. 78 : 15. He clave r. in wilderness
104 : 18. r. are a refuge for conies
Pr. 30 : 26. make houses in r.
Is. 2 : 19. shall go into holes of r.
21. into clefts of r. and tops of the ragged r. [r.
7:19. they shall rest in holes of the
33 : 16. defence munitions of r.
57:5. slaying the chil. under the r.
Je. 4 : 29. city shall climb upon r.
16 : 16. sh. hunt out of holes of r.
51 : 25. I will roll thee down fr. r.
Na. 1 : 6. r. thrown down by him
Mat. 27 : 51. earth quake, r. rent
Ac. 27 : 29. lest we fallen upon r.
Re. 6 : 15. hid in dens and in r.
16. and said to the r., Fall on us

ROD.

Ex. 4 : 4. it became r. in his hand 2.
17. shalt take r. in hand, 17 : 5.
20. Moses took r. of God, 17 : 9.
7 : 9. shalt say unto Aaron, Take thy r., 19.-18 : 5, 16, 17.
10. Aaron cast down r. bef. Pha.
12. cast down every man his r. (2)
15. r. wh. was turned into serpent
17. I will smite thee with r.
20. lifted r. smote waters, 14 : 16.
9:23. Mo. stretched forth r., 10:13.
21 : 20. if man smite servant with r.
Le. 27 : 32. whatso. passeth und. r.
Nu. 17 : 2. write man's name upon r.
3. one r. sh. be for head of house
5. man's r. I choose sh. blossom
6. princes gave him a r. apiece, r. of Aaron was among their rods
8. r. of Aaron budded, He. 9 : 4.
9. every man took his r., 2. | 10.
20:8. Take r. and gath. assembly, 9.
11. with his r. he smote rock
1 S. 14 : 27. Jona. put forth r., 43.
2 S. 7 : 14. I will chasten him wi. r.
Jb. 9 : 34. Let him take r. from me
21:9. neither is r. of G. upon them
Ps. 2 : 9. shalt break them with r.
23 : 4. thy r. and thy staff comfort
74:2. Remember r. of thine inherit.
89 : 32. will visit transgr-n with r.
110:2. L. shall send r. of thy stren.
125 : 3. r. of wicked not rest upon
Pr. 10:13. r. is for back of fools, 26:3.
13 : 24. spareth r. hateth his son
14 : 3. In mouth of foolish is r.
22 : 8. the r. of his anger shall fail
15. r. of correction shall drive it
23 : 13. shalt beat him with r., 14.
29 : 15. r. and reproof give wisdom
Is. 9 : 4. broken r. of oppressor
10 : 5. O Assyrian, r. of mine anger
15. as if the r. should shake itself
24. shall smite with a r. and
26. as his r. was upon sea, so
11 : 1. come a r. out of stem of Jesse
4. shall smite with r. of mouth
14 : 29. r. of him th. smote thee
28 : 27. cummin is beaten with r.
30:31. be beaten wh. smote with a r.
Je. 1 : 11. I see a r. of an almond tree
10 : 16. Isr. r. of his inheri., 51 : 19.
48:17. How is beautiful r. broken!
La. 3 : 1. have seen affliction by r.
Eze. 7 : 10. the r. hath blossomed
11. Violence is risen up into a r.
19 : 14. fire is gone out of r. of branches, hath no strong r.
20 : 37. cause you to pass und. r.
21 : 10. contemneth r. of son, 13.
Mi. 5 : 1. smite judge of Isr. with r.
6 : 9. hear ye r. who appointed it
7 : 14. Feed thy people with thy r.
Jn. 18 : † 22. struck Jesus with r.
1 Co. 4 : 21. sh. I come with a r. or
Re. 2:27. shall rule wi. r. of iron, 19:
11 : 1. given me a reed like r. [15.
12 : 5. was to rule with a r. of iron

RODS.

Ge. 30 : 37. Jacob took r. of poplar
38. set r. before the flocks, 41.
41. might conceive among r., 39.
Ex. 7 : 12. Aaron's swallowed up r.
Nu. 17 : 6. princes gave twelve r., (2)
7. Moses laid up r. bef. L., 9. [2.
Eze. 19 : 11. she had strong r. for
12. her strong r. were broken [r.
Mat. 26: † 67. others smote him with
2 Co. 11:25. Thrice was beaten wi. r.

ROD'ANIM = DODANIM.

Ge. 10: † 4. sons of Javan, R., 1 Ch. 1: [† 7.

RODE.

Ge. 24 : 61. Rebekah and damsels r.
Ju. 10 : 4. thirty sons r. on 30 colts
12 : 14. thirty nephews r. on colts
1 S. 25 : 20. Abigail r. on the ass, 42.
30 : 17. save 400 wh. r. upon camels
2 S. 13: † 29. every man r. upon mule
18 : 9. Absalom r. upon a mule
22:11. he r. upon cherub, Ps. 18:10.
1 K. 13 : 13. old prophet r. on ass
18:45. Ahab r. and went to Jezreel
2 K. 9 : 16. Jehu r. in a chariot
25. remember when I and thou r.
Ne. 2 : 12. save beast that I r. upon
Es. 8 : 14. posts that r. upon mules

RO'E = DORCAS.

ROE, S.

2 S. 2 : 18. light of foot as wild r.
1 Ch. 12 : 8. swift as r. upon mts.
Pr. 5 : 19. Let her be as pleasant r.
6 : 5. Deliver thyself as a r. from
Can. 2 : 7. I charge you by r., 3 : 5.
9. My beloved is like a r. yo. hart
17. be thou like a r. or hart, 8:14.
4 : 5. Thy breasts like 2 yo. r., 7:3.
Is. 13 : 14. it shall be as chased r.

ROEBUCK, S.

De. 12 : 15. ye may eat of the r., 22.
-14 : 5.-15 : 22. [harts and r-s
1 K. 4 : 23. a hundred sheep, besides

RO'GEL = EN-ROGEL.

ROGE'LIM.

2 S. 17 : 27. Barzillai of R. bro-t beds
19 : 31. Barzillai came down fr. R.

ROH'GAH. See SHAMER.

ROLL, S.

Ezr. 6 : 1. search made in house of r-s
2. found at Achmetha a r.
Is. 8 : 1. Take thee a great r. write
Je. 36 : 2. Take thee r. of book, 4.
6. go and read in the r. [32.
14. Take in thine hand r. (2), 28,
20. they laid the r. in chamber
21. king sent Jehudi to fetch the r
23. until all the r. was consumed
25. intercession to king that he would not burn r., 27. [r.
29. saith L. Thou hast burned this
Eze. 2 : 9. hand was sent, lo, a r.
3 : 1. eat this r. go speak unto Isr.
2. he caused me to eat that r.
3. fill thy bowels with this r.
Zch. 5 : 1. and behold, a flying r., 2.

ROLL. [Verb.]

Ge. 29 : 8. cannot, till r. stone
43: † 18. th. he may r. hims. upon us
Jos. 10 : 18. Joshua said, r. gr. stone
1 S. 14 : 33. r. a gr. stone unto me
Ps. 37: † 5. r. thy way upon the Lord, Pr. 16 : † 3. [rocks
Je. 51 : 25. I will r. thee down from
Am. 5 : † 24. let Judgment r. down
Mi. 1 : 10. in Aphrah r. in dust
Mk. 16: 3. who shall r. us aw. stone

ROLLED.

Ge. 29 : 3. r. stone fr. well's mouth
10. Jacob went near, r. stone
Jos. 5 : 9. I have r. away reproach
Jb. 30 : 14. r. themselves upon me
Ps. 22 : † 8. He r. hims. on the Lord
Is. 9:5. with noise, and garments r. in blood [Re. 6 : 14.
34 : 4. heavens shall be r. together,
La. 3 : † 16. he hath r. me in ashes
Mat. 27:60. he r. great stone to door of sepulchre, Mk. 15 : 46.
28:2. angel came and r. back stone
Mk. 16:4. they saw stone was r. aw

Lu. 24 : 2. found stone r. away

ROLLER.

Eze. 30 : 21. to put a r. to bind it

ROLLETH.

Pr. 26 : 27. r. stone it will return

ROLLING. [Adj., Noun.] [r.

Ezr. 5 : † 8. house of G. with stones of

Is. 17 : 13. nations sh. flee like r. thi.

ROMAM'TI-E'ZER.

1 Ch. 25 : 4. the sons of Heman, R.

31. four and 20th lot came to R.

ROMAN, ROMANS.

Jn. 11 : 48. R-s shall come and take

Ac. 16 : 21. not lawful for us to observe, being R-s [were R-s

37. beaten us, R-s | 38. heard they

22 : 25. is a R., 26. | 27. Tell me, art thou a R.? [R., 23 : 27.

29. after he knew that he was a

25 : 16. it is not the manner of R-s

28 : 17. prisoner into hands of R-s

ROME. [speak

Ac. 2 : 10. strangers of R. we hear

18 : 2. all Jews to depart from R.

19 : 21. I must also see R.

23 : 11. must thou bear witness at R.

28 : 14. so we went toward R.

16. we came to R. Paul dwelt

Ro. 1 : 7. To all in R. beloved of G.

15. to preach gos. to you at R.

2 Ti. 1 : 17. when he was in R. he

ROOF, S.

Ge. 19 : 8. came und. shadow of r.

Ex. 30 : † 3. overlay r. with gold

De. 22 : 8. make battlement for r.

Jos. 2 : 6. she brought them to r. hid with flax she laid upon r.

8. she came unto them upon r.

Ju. 16 : 27. upon r. were 3,000

2 S. 11 : 2. Da. walked upon r. (2)

18 : 24. watchman went up to r.

Ne. 8 : 16. peo. made booths upon r.

Je. 19 : 13. upon r-s burned incense, 32 : 29.

Eze. 40 : 13. he measured gate fr. r.

Mat. 8 : 8. not worthy thou shouldest come under my r., Lu. 7 : 6.

Mk. 2 : 4. they uncovered the r.

See **MOUTH** with roof, s.

ROOM.

Ge. 24 : 23. is r. in father's house

25. we have straw, r. to lodge in

31. I have prepared r. for camels

26 : 22. Lord hath made r. for us

De. 2 : † 12. chil. of Esau in their r.

2 S. 19 : 13. not captain in r. of Joab

1 K. 2 : 35. king put Benaiah in Joab's r. Zadok in r. of Abiathar

5 : 1. anointed him king in r. of his father, 2 K. 23 : 34. 2 Ch. 26 : 1.

5. son whom I will set in thy r.

8 : 20. I am in r. of Da., 2 Ch. 6 : 10.

19 : 16. Elisha thou anoint in thy r.

2 K. 15 : 25. Pekah reigned in his r.

Ps. 31 : 8. hast set my feet in large r.

80 : 9. Thou preparedst r. before it

Pr. 18 : 16. A man's gift maketh r.

Is. 57 : † 8. bed, thou providest r.

Mal. 3 : 10. not be r. enough to rec.

Mat. 2 : 22. reigned in r. of Herod

Mk. 2 : 2. was no r. to receive them

14 : 15. shew large upper r., Lu. 22:

Lu. 2 : 7. no r. for them in inn [12.

12 : 17. I have no r. to bestow my

14 : 8. sit not down in highest r.

9. with shame to take lowest r.

10. go and sit down in lowest r.

22. Lord, it is done, and yet is r.

Ac. 1 : 13. went up into an upper r.

24 : 27. Festus came into Felix' r.

1 Co. 14 : 16. he that occupieth the r.

ROOMS.

Ge. 6 : 14. r. shalt thou make in ark

1 K. 20 : 24. put captains in their r.

1 Ch. 4 : 41. and dwelt in their r.

Mat. 23 : 6. they love the uppermost r. at feasts, Mk. 12 : 39. Lu. 20 : 46.

Lu. 14 : 7. they chose out chief r.

ROOT. [Noun.]

De. 29 : 18. a r. that beareth gall

Ju. 5 : 14. Out of Ephraim was a r.

2 K. 19 : 30. Judah sh. again take r.

Jb. 5 : 3. I have seen foolish taking

14 : 8. Though the r. wax old [r.

19 : 28. seeing r. of the matter is

29 : 19. My r. was spread by waters

Ps. 80 : 9. didst cause vine take r. [ed

Pr. 12 : 3. r. of righteous sh. not mov-

12. r. of righteous yieldeth fruit

Is. 5 : 24. their r. sh. be rottenness

11 : 10. be a r. of Jesse, Ro. 15 : 12.

14 : 29. out of the serpent's r. a

30. I will kill thy r. with famine

27 : 6. of Jacob to take r., 37 : 31.

40 : 24. their stock sh. not take r.

53 : 2. he sh. grow up as a r. out

Je. 12 : 2. they have taken r.

Eze. 31 : 7. his r. was by great waters

Ho. 9 : 16. Ephr. smitten, r. dried

Mal. 4 : 1. it shall leave r. nor branch

Mat. 3 : 10. and now the axe is laid unto r. of trees, Lu. 3 : 9.

13 : 6. bec. had not r. they withered,

21. Mk. 4 : 6. 17. Lu. 8 : 13.

Lu. 17 : 6. Be thou plucked by r.

Ro. 11 : 16. if r. be holy so are

17. with them partakest of r.

18. bearest not r. but r. thee

1 Ti. 6 : 10. love of money is r. of

He. 12 : 15. lest any r. of bitterness

Re. 5 : 5. r. of Da. hath prevailed [vid

22 : 16. I am r. and offspring of Da-

ROOTS.

2 Ch. 7 : 20. will pluck them by r.

Jb. 8 : 17. His r. are wrapped about

13 : † 27. a print upon r. of my feet

18 : 16. His r. shall be dried up

28 : 9. overturneth the mts. by r.

30 : 4. cut up juniper r. for meat

36 : † 30. God covereth r. of sea

Is. 11 : 1. branch grow out of his r.

Je. 17 : 8. spreadeth out her r. by

Eze. 17 : 6. r. were under him [river

7. vine did bend her r. tow. him

9. shall he not pull up the r.?

Da. 4 : 15. leave stump of r., 23, 26.

7 : 8. horns plucked up by r.

Da. 11 : 7. out of branch of her r.

Ho. 14 : 5. he shall cast forth r. as

Am. 2 : 9. I destroyed his r. from

Mk. 11 : 20. fig tree dried up from r.

Jude 12. twice dead, plucked up by

ROOT. [Verb.] [r.

1 K. 14 : 15. he shall r. up Israel

Jb. 31 : 12. r. out all mine increase

Ps. 52 : 5. r. thee out of the land

Je. 1 : 10. I have set thee to r. out

Mat. 13 : 29. lest ye r. up wheat wi.

ROOTED. [them

De. 29 : 28. L. r. them out of land

Jb. 18 : 14. confidence sh. be r. out

31 : 8. let my offspring be r. out

Pr. 2 : 22. transgressors be r. out

Zph. 2 : 4. Ekron sh. be r. up [up

Mat. 15 : 13. Fa. not planted, be r.

Ep. 3 : 17. ye r. grounded in love

Col. 2 : 7. r. and built up in him

ROOTING.

Ezr. 7 : † 26. whe. unto death, or to r.

ROPES. [out

Ju. 16 : 11. If bind me with new r.,

2 S. 17 : 13. Isr. bring r. to city [12.

1 K. 20 : 31. put r. upon our heads, 32.

Ac. 27 : 32. soldiers cut r. of boat

ROSE. [Noun.]

Can. 2 : 1. I am r. of Sharon [r.

Is. 35 : 1. desert shall blossom as the

ROSE. [Verb.]

Ge. 4 : 8. Cain r. ag. Abel, slew him

18 : 16. the men r. up from thence

19 : 1. Lot r. up to meet them, and

21 : 32. Abimelech r. up, Ju. 9 : 34,

22 : 3. Ab. r. early, and went [35.

19. young men r. up and went

Ge. 25 : 34. Esau did eat, r. up, and

32 : 22. Jac. r. and took his 2 wives

31. as he passed Penuel sun r.

37 : 35. sons, dau-s r. to comfort him

43 : 15. men r. up and went to Eg.

46 : 5. Jacob r. up from Beer-sheba

Ex. 10 : 23. nei. r. any for 3 days

12 : 30. Pharaoh r. in the night

15 : 7. overthrown them r. ag. thee

24 : 13. Moses r. up and his minister

32 : 6. eat, drink, and r. to play

† 25. shame am. those that r. up

33 : 8. r. up and stood at tent door

10. all people r. and worshipped

Nu. 16 : 2. Korah r. up before Moses

25. Moses r. went unto Dathan

22 : 14. Princes of Moab r. went

24 : 25. Balaam r. up and went

25 : 7. Phinehas r. up fr. congr-n

De. 33 : 2. Lord r. up from Seir

Jos. 2 : † 11. neither r. up any courage

3 : 16. waters r. up upon a heap

Ju. 6 : 21. there r. fire out of rock

38. Gideon r. early on morrow

7 : 1. all peo. r. up early, 21 : 4.

19 : 5. he r. to depart, 7, 9, 10, 28.

20 : 5. men of Gibeah r. ag. me

33. men of Israel r. put in array

Ru. 3 : 14. she r. bef. one co. know

2 S. 18 : 31. avenged of all r. ag. thee

22 : 40. them that r. up ag. me, hast thou subdued, 49. Ps. 18 : 39.

1 K. 2 : 19. king r. up to meet her

2 K. 7 : 5. lepers r. in twilight

2 Ch. 26 : 19. leprosy r. in forehead

28 : 15. men expressed by name r.

29 : 20. Hezekiah the king r. early

Ezr. 1 : 5. then r. up chief of fathers

5 : 2. Then r. up Zerubbabel

10 : 6. Ezra r. from bef. house of G.

Ne. 3 : 1. Eliashib r. up, 4 : 14. [r. up

Ps. 124 : 2. L. on our side when men

Can. 5 : 5. I r. to open to my beloved

Je. 26 : 17. r. certain of elders

La. 3 : 62. lips of those r. against me

Da. 3 : 24. Neb-r r. up in haste

8 : 27. I r. up did king's business

Jon. 1 : 3. Jonah r. up to flee unto

Zph. 3 : 7. r. early and corrupted [r.

Mk. 10 : 50. Bartim. casting aw. garm.

Lu. 4 : 29. r. and thrust him out

5 : 25. be r. up bef. them, took

28. he left all, r. and followed

16 : 31. nor be persuaded tho. one r.

22 : 45. when he r. from prayer

24 : 33. they r. up the same hour

Jn. 11 : 31. saw Mary that she r.

Ac. 5 : 17. Then high priest r. up

36. bef. these days r. up Theudas

37. r. up Judas of Galilee

10 : 41. drink with him after be r.

14 : 20. Paul r. up came into city

15 : 5. r. up certain of Pharisees

7. Peter r. and said, Men and

16 : 22. multitude r. up ag. them

26 : 30. king r. up, and governor

Ro. 14 : 9. Christ both died and r.

1 Co. 10 : 7. did eat and r. to play

15 : 4. was buried and r. third day

12. If C. be preached that he r.

2 Co. 5 : 15. to him who died and r.

1 Th. 4 : 14. if believe Jes. died and r.

Re. 19 : 3. her smoke r. up for ever

See **MORNING**. [and ev.

ROSH. See **MUPPIM.**

ROSIN.

Eze. 27 : † 17. Judah traded in oil, r.

ROT. [22, 27.

Nu. 5 : 21. L. make thy thigh to r.,

Pr. 10 : 7. name of wicked shall r.

Is. 40 : 20. chooseth a tree will not r.

ROTTEN.

Jb. 13 : 28. And he, as a r. thing

41 : 27. esteemeth brass as r. wood

Je. 38 : 11. Ebed-melech took r. rags

12. Put r. rags under armholes

Jo. 1 : 17. seed is r. und. their clods

ROTTENNESS. [is as r.
Pr. 12 : 4. she that maketh asham.
14 : 30. envy is the r. of bones
Is. 5 : 24. so their root shall be as r.
Ho. 5 : 12. I will be to Judah as r.
Ha. 3 : 16. when I heard r. entered
ROUGH. [bones
De. 21 : 4. bri. heifer unto r. valley
Is. 27 : 8. he stayeth his r. wind in
40 : 4. r. places sh. be made plain
Je. 51 : 27. to come as r. caterpillars
Da. 8 : 21. r. goat is king of Grecia
Zeh. 13 : 4. neither wear r. garment
Lu. 3 : 5. r. ways sh. be made smooth
ROUGHLY. [30.
Ge. 42 : 7. Joseph spake r. unto th.,
1 S. 20 : 10. what if fa. answer r.?
1 K. 12 : 13. king answered people r.
and forsook old, 2 Ch. 10 : 13.
Pr. 18 : 23. the rich answereth r.
ROUND.
Ge. 19 : 4. compassed the house r.
Ex. 16 : 14. lay a small r. thing on
Jos. 7 : 9. inhabitants environ us r.
1 K. 7 : 23. molten sea was r., 2 Ch. 4:
31. mouth r. | 35. r. compass [2.
10 : 19. top of the throne was r.
Ps. 22 : 12. strong bulls beset me r.
Can. 7 : 2. Thy navel like r. goblet
Is. 3 : 18. L. will take away r. tires
Eze. 41 : † 7. broader and went r.
Lu. 19 : 43. enemies compass thee r.
ROUND about. [r. a.
Ge. 35 : 5. terror of God upon cities
Ex. 7 : 24. digged r. a. river for water
16 : 13. in morn. dew lay r. a. host
19 : 12. set bounds unto peo. r. a.
Le. 14 : 41. house to be scraped r. a.
Nu. 1 : 50. encamp r. a. tabernacle
11 : 24. Moses set elders r. a. taber.
16 : 34. all Israel, r. a. them fled
22 : 4. sh. lick up all are r. a. us
De. 6 : 14. gods of people r. a., 13 : 7.
12 : 10. giveth rest from all enemies
r. a., 25 : 19. Jos. 21 : 44. 2 Ch. 15:
21 : 2. measure cities r. a. him [15.
Jos. 6 : 3. ye sh. go r. a. city once
Ju. 19 : 22. men beset house r. a., 20 : 5
1 S. 23 : 26. Saul compassed Da. r. a.
31 : 9. Saul's head, and sent into
land of Philis. r. a., 1 Ch. 10 : 9.
2 S. 22 : 12. he made darkness pavilions r. a. him, Ps. 18 : 11. [r. a.
1 K. 4 : 24. Sol. had peace on all sides
31. his fame in all nations r. a.
18 : 35. water ran r. a. altar [sha
2 K. 6 : 17. chariots of fire r. a. Eli-
1 Ch. 9 : 27. they lodged r. a. ho. of G.
Jb. 10 : 8. hands fashioned me r. a.
16 : 13. archers compass me r. a.
19 : 12. troops encamp r. a. my taber.
22 : 10. snares are r. a. thee
37 : 12. turned r. a. by counsels
41 : 14. his teeth are terrible r. a.
Ps. 3 : 6. that set ag-t me r. a. [a.
: 6. head above mine enemies r.
: 7. angel encampeth r. a. them
: 13. derision to them r. a., 79 : 4.
: 12. Walk about Zion, go r. a. her
: 6. noise, and go r. a. city, 14.
: 11. let all r. a. bring presents
: 17. They came r. a. me daily
: 8. thy faithfulness r. a. thee
97 : 3. burneth up his enemies r. a.
125 : 2. As mts. are r. a. Jerus.
128 : 3. like olive plants r. a. table
Is. 29 : 3. I will camp ag. thee r. a.
42 : 25. hath set him on fire r. a.
49 : 18. Lift up thine eyes r. a., 60 : 4.
Je. 20 : † 3. called thy name, Fear r. a.
21 : 14. fire shall devour all r. a.
46 : 5. for fear was r. a., saith L.
50 : 29. camp ag. Babylon r. a.
51 : 2. in trouble sh. be ag. her r. a.
Eze. 10 : 12. wheels full of eyes r. a.
34 : 26. places r. a. hill a blessing
46 : 23. was a row of building r. a., (3)

Jo. 3 : 11. gather yourselves r. a.
12. will sit to judge heathen r. a.
Am. 3 : 11. An adversary r. a. land
Jon. 2 : 5. the depth closed me r. a.
Zch. 2 : 5. unto her wall of fire r. a.
Mat. 21 : 33. hedged vineyard r. a.
Mk. 3 : 34. Jes. looked r. a. on them
6 : 6. Jesus went r. a. the villages
36. into country r. a. and buy
Lu. 1 : 65. fear on all dwelt r. a.
2 : 9. glory of the Lord shone r. a.
9 : 12. that they may go into towns
r. a. and get victuals
Jn. 10 : 24. came the Jews r. a. him
Ac. 5 : 16. came mult. fr. cities r. a.
9 : 3. shined r. a. him light fr. heav.
14 : 20. disci. stood r. a. Paul rose
Ro. 15 : 19. r. a. to Illyricum, I prea.
He. 9 : 4. overlaid r. a. with gold
Re. 4 : 3. was rainbow r. a. throne
4. r. a. throne four and 20 seats
6. r. a. the throne were 4 beasts
5 : 11. angels r. a. throne, 7 : 11.
See **Round about CAMP.**
ROUND. [Verb.] [heads
Le. 19 : 27. not r. corners of your
ROUSE.
Ge. 49 : 9. an old lion who shall r. him
ROVERS.
1 Ch. 12 : 21. helped David against r.
ROW, ROWS.
Ex. 28 : 17. set in it four r-s of stones,
17. the first r., 39 : 10. [39 : 10.
18. the second r., 39 : 11.
19. the third r., 39 : 12.
20. the 4th r., 39 : 13. [upon table
Le. 24 : 6. cakes in 2 r-s six on a r.
7. pure frankincense on each r.
1 K. 6 : 36. built inner court with 3 r-s
7 : 2. four r-s of cedar pillars
3 beams on 45 pillars 15 in a r.
4. windows in 3 r-s and light
12. the great court round about
was with three r-s [Ch. 4 : 13.
18. two r-s pomegranates, 42. 2
24. knops were cast in 2 r-s
2 Ch. 4 : 3. Two r-s of oxen cast when
it was cast [r-s of stones
Ezr. 6 : 4. a r. of new timber, three
Can. 1 : 10. Thy cheeks comely with
r-s of jewels
Eze. 46 : 23. a r. of building with boiling places under the r-s
ROWED. [land
Jon. 1 : 13. men r. hard to bri. it to
Jn. 6 : 19. had r. 25 or 30 furlongs
ROWERS.
Eze. 27 : 26. r. bro-t thee into gr.
ROWING. [waters
Mk. 6 : 48. he saw them toiling in r.
ROYAL.
Ge. 49 : 20. Asher sh. yield r. dainties
Jos. 10 : 2. Gibeon one of r. cities
1 S. 27 : 5. why I dwell in r. city?
2 S. 12 : 26. Joab took the r. city
1 K. 10 : 13. Sol. gave her of r. bounty
2 K. 11 : 1. Athaliah destroyed all
seed r., 2 Ch. 22 : 10. [41 : 1.
25 : 25. Ishmael of seed r. came, Je.
1 Ch. 29 : 25. upon Sol. r. majesty
Es. 1 : 7. they gave them r. wine
9. made feast for wom. in r. house
11. to bring Vashti with crown r.
19. give her r. estate unto another
2 : 16. Esther taken into house r.
17. set crown r. upon her head
5 : 1. Esther put on her r. apparel,
and king sat upon his r. throne
in his r. house [crown r.
6 : 8. Let r. apparel be brought, and
8 : 15. Mordecai went in r. apparel
Is. 62 : 3. r. diadem in hand of God
Je. 43 : 10. sh. spread his r. pavilion
Da. 6 : 7 to establish a r. statute
Ac. 12 : 21. Herod in r. apparel, sat
Ja. 2 : 8. If ye fulfil the r. law, ye
1 Pe. 2 : 9. ye are a r. priesthood

RUBBING. [hands
Lu. 6 : 1. did eat, r. them in their
RUBBISH.
Ne. 4 : 2. will revive stones out of r.
10. decayed, and there is much r.
RUBY, RUBIES.
Ex. 28 : † 17. first row a r., 39 : † 10.
Jb. 28 : 18. price of wisdom is above
r-s, Pr. 8 : 11. [than r-s
Pr. 3 : 15. wisdom is more precious
20 : 15. gold, and multitude of r-s
31 : 10. her price is far above r-s
La. 4 : 7. Nazarites more ruddy than
Eze. 28 : † 13. r. was thy covering [r-s
RUDDER bands. [up
Ac. 27 : 40. loosed r. b., and hoised
RUDDY.
1 S. 16 : 12. David was r. and, 17 : 42.
Can. 5 : 10. My beloved white and r.
La. 4 : 7. Her Nazarites were more r.
RUDE.
2 Co. 11 : 6. though I be r. in speech
RUDIMENTS. [world
Ga. 4 : † 3. in bondage under r. of
† 9. how turn ye to beggarly r.
Col. 2 : 8. lest any spoil you after r.
20. if dead with Christ from r. of
RUE. [world
Lu. 11 : 42. ye tithe the mint, r. herbs
RU'FUS. [cross
Mk. 15 : 21. Simon fa. of R. to bear
Ro. 16 : 13. Salute R. chosen in the
RUG. [L.
Ju. 4 : † 18. Jael covered him with a
RU'HAMAH. [r.
Ho. 2 : 1. say ye to your sisters, R.
RUIN, S.
2 Ch. 28 : 23. they were the r. of him
Ps. 89 : 40. bro-t strong holds to r.
Pr. 24 : 22. who knoweth r. of both
26 : 28. flattering mouth worketh r.
Is. 3 : 6. let r. be under thy hand
23 : 13. bro-t land of Chald-s to r.
25 : 2. made of a defenced city a r.
Eze. 18 : 30. iniquity not be your r.
21 : 15. that r-s be multiplied
27 : 27. company fall in day of thy r.
31 : 13. Upon his r. shall fowls
Am. 9 : 11. that day will I raise his r-s
Lu. 6 : 49. r. of that house was great
Ac. 15 : 16. I will build again r-s
RUINED. [thereof
Is. 3 : 8. Jerusalem is r. and Judah
Eze. 36 : 35. r. cities are fenced
36. know I the Lord build r. places
RUINOUS.
2 K. 19 : 25. to lay waste fenced cities
into r. heaps, Is. 37 : 26.
Is. 17 : 1. Damascus sh. be a r. heap
RULE. [Noun.]
Ge. 1 : † 16. greater light for r. of day
1 K. 22 : 31. r. over Ahab's chariots
Es. 9 : 1. Jews had r. over them
Ps. 19 : † 4. r. is gone thro. earth
Pr. 17 : 2. A wise servant r. over son
19 : 10. serv. to have r. over princes
25 : 28. hath no r. over own spirit
29 : 2. when wicked heareth r., peo.
Ec. 2 : 19. shall be have r. over all
Is. 44 : 13 carpenter stretcheth r.
63 : 19. never barest r. over them
1 Co. 15 : 24. sh. have put down all r.
2 Co. 10 : 13. acc. to measure of r.
15. be enlarged acc. to our r.
† 16. not to boast in ano. man's r.
Ga. 6 : 16. as walk acc. to this r.
Ph. 3 : 16. let us walk by same r.
He. 13 : 7. Remember them have r.
17. Obey them that have the r. ov.
24. Salute them that have the r.
See **BARE, BEAR rule.**
RULE. [Verb.]
Ge. 1 : 16. greater light to r. the day
and lesser light to r. night
18. to r. over the day, and night
3 : 16. thy husband sh. r. over thee
4 : 7. desire, thou shalt r. over him

Le. 25 : 43. not r. wi. rigour, 46, 53.
Ju. 8 : 22. r. over us, thou and son
23. I will not r. over you, nei. shall
my son r. over you [Israel
1 Ch. 11:†2. thou shalt r. my people
Ps. 28 : † 9. r. them, and lift them
110:2. r. thou in midst of enemies
136:8. sun to r. by day, his mercy
9. moon and stars to r. by night
Pr. 8 : 16. By me princes r. and
Is. 3 : 4. babes shall r. over them
12. my people, women r. over th.
14:2. shall r. over their oppressors
19:4. a fierce king sh. r. over them
28 : 14. that r. this people in Jerus.
32 : 1. princes shall r. in judgment
40 : 10. his arm shall r. for him [k-s
41 : 2. made righteous man r. over
52:5. they that r. make them howl
Eze. 19:14. hath no strong rod to r.
20:33. with fury will I r. over you
29 : 15. sh. no more r. over nations
Da. 4 : 26. known that heavens r.
11 : 3. mighty kings that shall r.
39. sh. cause them to r. ov. many
Jo. 2 : 17. heathen sho. r. over them
Mi. 5 : † 4. sh. r. in strength of Lord
7 : † 14. r. thy people with thy rod
Zch. 6:13. he sh. r. upon his throne
Mat. 2:6. a Governor that sh. r. Isr.
Mk. 10:42. accounted to r. over Gen-
Col. 3 : 15. let peace of God r. [tiles
1 Ti. 3:5. know not how to r. house
5 : 17. elders that r. well worthy of
Re. 2 : 27. r. wi. rod of iron, 12 : 5.-

RULED. [19 : 15.

Ge. 24 : 2. his eldest servant that r.
41 : 40. at thy word my peo. be r.
Ru. 1 : 1. in days when judges r.
1 K. 5 : 16. 3,300 r. over the people
1 Ch. 26 : 6. r. thro't house of their
Ezr. 4 : 20. r. over all countries [fa.
Ps. 106:41. they that hated them r.
Is. 14:6. he that r. nations in anger
La. 5 : 8. Servants have r. over us
Eze. 34 : 4. with cruelty have ye r.
Da. 5 : 21. till he knew that God r.
11:4. nor acc. to dominion wh. he r.

RULER.

Ge. 41:43. Pha. made Joseph r. over
all E., 45 : 8. Ps. 105 : 21.
43:16. Joseph said to r. of his hou.
Ex. 22 : 28. thou shalt not curse r.
Le. 4:22. When r. hath sinned thro.
Nu. 13 : 2. every one r. am. them
Ju. 9 : 30. Zebul r. of city heard
1 S. 25:30. appointed thee r. over my
people Isr., 2 S. 6 : 21.-7 : 8. 1
Ch. 11 : 2.-17 : 7.
2 S. 7 : 8. I took thee from following
sheep to be r., 1 Ch. 17 : 7.
20:26. Ira was chief r. about David
23 : † 3. thou r. over men, ruling in
1 K. 1 : 35. I appointed Sol. to be r.
11 : 28. him r. over all the charge
2 K. 25 : 22. he made Gedaliah r.
1 Ch. 5 : 2. of Judah came chief r.
9 : 11. Azariah r. of house of God,
2 Ch. 31 : 13. [the r.
28 : 4. he hath chosen Judah to be
2 Ch. 7 : 18. not fail a man to be r.
11 : 22. made Abijah r. am. breth.
19:11. Zebadiah, r. of house of Jud.
26 : 11. by hand of Maaseiah the r.
Ne. 3 : 9. Rephaiah r. of Jerus., 12.
14. Malchiah r. of Beth-haccerem
15. r. of part of Mizpah, 19.
16. Neh. r. of half of Beth-zur
17. H. r. of half part of Keilah, 18.
7 : 2. Hananiah r. of palace
11 : 11. Seraiah r. of house of God
Ps. 68 : 27. little Benj. with their r.
105 : 20. king loosed r. of people,
Pr. 6 : 7. ant having no guide, or r.
23 : 1. When sittest to eat with r.
28 : 15. so is wicked r. over poor
29 : 12. if a r. hearken to lies, his
Pr. 29 : 26. Many seek r.'s favour,
Ec. 10 : 4. If spirit of r. rise ag. thee
5. error which proceedeth from r.
Is. 3:6. Thou hast clothing, be our r.
7. make me not r. of people
16 : 1. Send ye lamb to r. of land
Je. 51:46. violence in land, r. ag. r.
Da. 2 : 10. no r. asked such things
38. made thee r. over th. all, 48.
5 : 7. be 3d r. in kingdom, 16, 29.
Mi. 5:2. out of thee he that is to be r.
Ha. 1 : 14. things that have no r.
Mat. 9 : 18. there came a certain r.
23. when Jes. came into r.'s house
24:45. whom his Lord hath made r.,
Lu. 12 : 42. [Lu. 12 : 44.
47. sh. make him r. over his goods,
25:21. thee r. over many things, 23.
Mk. 5:25. came from r. of synagogue's
house, 36, 38. Lu. 8 : 41, 49.
Lu. 13 : 14. r. of synagogue answ-d
18 : 18. a certain r. asked, Master
Jn. 2 : 9. When r. of feast tasted
3 : 1. Nicodemus, a r. of the Jews
4 : † 46. a certain r. whose son sick
Ac. 4 : † 1. r. of the temple came
7 : 27. Who made thee a r. and, 35.
35. same did God send to be a r.
18:17. Greeks beat Sosthenes r., 8.
23:5. shalt not speak evil of the r.

RULERS.

Ge. 47 : 6. make them r. over cattle
Ex. 16 : 22. all r. of cong. told Moses
18:21. r. of thous., r. of hundreds,
34:31. Moses called r. of cong-n [25.
35 : 27. r. brought onyx stones
De. 1 : 13. I will make them r. [r.
Ju. 15 : 11. Knowest not Philis-s are
2 S. 8 : 18. Da.'s sons were chief r.
1 K. 9 : 22. were r. of his chariots
2 K. 10 : 1. wrote unto r. of Jezreel
11:4. Jehoi. set r. ov. hundreds, 19.
1 Ch. 21 : 2. David said to r. of peo.
26 : 32. whom king David made r.
27 : 31. All were r. of substance
2 Ch. 29:20. Hez. gathered r. of city
35 : 8. r. of the house of God
Ezr. 9:2. hand of r. chief in trespass
10 : 14. Let r. of cong-n stand
Ne. 2 : 16. r. knew not whi. I went
4 : 16. r. behind house of Judah
5:7. I rebuked r. and said, Ye exact
17. there were at table 150 r.
7 : 5. in my heart to gather r.
11 : 1. r. of people dwelt at Jerus.
12 : 40. So stood I, and half of r.
13 : 11. contended I with r. [8 : 9.
Es. 3:12. r. of ev. peo. of ev. province,
9 : 3. r. of provinces helped Jews
Ps. 2 : 2. r. take counsel ag. Lord
Is. 1 : 10. Hear L., ye r. of Sodom
14 : 5. Lord broken sceptre of r.
22 : 3. All thy r. are fled together
29 : 10. your r. hath he covered
49 : 7. saith Lord to servant of r.
Je. 33 : 26. not any of his seed be r.
51:23. will I break in pieces capt-s
28. prepare ag. her nations r. [r.
57. I will make drunk her r.
Eze. 23:6. her lovers, capt-ns and r.
12. captains r. clothed gorgeously
23. I will raise those r. ag. thee
Da. 3 : 2. king sent to gather all r.
3. all the r. were gathered together
7 : † 27. and all r. shall obey him
Ho. 4 : 18. her r. wi. shame do love
Mk. 5 : 22. one of r. of synagogue
13:9. be brought bef r., Lu. 21:12.
Lu. 23 : 13. Pilate when he called r.
35. r. with people derided him
24 : 20. how our r. delivered him
Jn. 7 : 26. Do r. know this is Christ?
48. Have any of the r. believed
12 : 42. many chief r. believed
Ac. 3 : 17. thro. ignorance, as did r.
4 : 5. r. and elders were gathered
8. Ye r. of peo. and elders of Isr.
Ac. 4:26. the r. were gathered ag. L.
13 : 15. r. of synag. sent unto Paul
27. r., because they knew him not
14 : 5. an assault of Jews, with r.
16:19. damsel's masters' drew unto
17 : 8. troubled people and r., 6. [r.
Ro. 13 : 3. r. not a terror to good
Ep. 6 : 12. we wrestle ag. r. of dark-

RULEST. [ness

2 Ch. 20 : 6. r. not thou over kingd-s
Ps. 89 : 9. Thou r. raging of the sea

RULETH.

2 S. 23 : 3. He that r. must be just
Ps. 59 : 13. let them know God r.
66 : 7. He r. by his power for ever
103 : 19. his kingdom r. over all
Pr. 16:32. that r. his spirit is better
22 : 7. rich r. over the poor and
Ec. 8 : 9. one man r. over another
9 : 17. cry of him that r. am. fools
Da. 4 : 17. the Most High r., 25, 32.
Ho. 11 : 12. Judah yet r. with God
Ro. 12 : 8. he that r. with diligence
1 Ti. 3 : 4. One that r. well his own

RULING, S. [house

2 S. 23 : 3. be just, r. in fear of God
Ps. 136 : † 8. The sun for r-s. by day
Je. 22 : 30. r. any more in Judah
1 Ti. 3 : 12. r. children and houses

RU'MAH. [well

2 K. 23:36. Zebudah dau. of P. of R.

RUMBLING.

Je. 47:3. at r. of his wheels, fathers

RUMOUR, S. [7.

2 K. 19 : 7. he shall hear r., Is. 37 :
Je. 49 : 14. I have heard r. fr. Lord
51:46. lest ye fear for r. in the land,
a r. shall come one year, in ano.
year shall come a r.
Eze. 7:26. mischief, r. sh. be upon r.
Ob. 1. We have heard a r. fr. Lord
Mat. 24 : 6. ye sh. hear of r-s of wars
Mk. 13 : 7. when hear of r-s of wars
Lu. 7 : 17. this r. of him went thro.

RUMP. [Judea

Ex. 29 : 22. take of ram the fat and
r., Le. 3 : 9.-7 : 3.-8 : 25.-9 : 19.

RUN.

Ge. 41:†14. Joseph r. out of dungeon
49 : 22. branches r. over the wall
Le. 15 : 3. whe. flesh r. with issue
25. if woman's issue r. bey. time
Ju. 18:25. lest angry fellows r. upon
1 S. 8 : 11. sh. r. before his chariots
17 : 17. r. to camp to thy brethren
20 : 6. that he might r. to Beth-le.
36. r. find out now the arrows
2 S. 15 : 1. Abs. prepared 50 men to
r. bef. him, 1 K. 1 : 5. [22, 23.
18 : 19. Let me r. and bear tidings,
22 : 30. by thee I have r. thro. a
troop, Ps. 18 : 29. [God
2 K. 4 : 22. that I may r. to man of
26. r. now, I pray thee, to meet her
5:20. liveth, I will r. after Naaman
2 Ch. 16 : 9. eyes of L. r. to and fro
Jb. 5 : † 14. they r. into darkness in
Ps. 19 : 5. as strong man to r. a race
58 : 7. as waters, wh. r. continually
59 : 4. They r. and prepare thems.
78 : 16. he caused waters to r. down
104:10. springs, which r. am. hills
119 : 32. I will r. way of thy com-ts
136. Rivers of waters r. down mine
Pr. 1 : 16. feet r. to evil, Is. 59 : 7.
Ec. 1 : 7. All the rivers r. into sea
Can. 1 : 4. Draw, we will r. aft. thee
Is. 33:4. as locusts shall he r. upon
40:31. they sh. r. and not be weary
55 : 5. nations shall r. unto thee
Je. 5:1. r. ye to and fro thro. streets
9 : 18. your eyes may r. with tears
12:5. If thou hast r. with footmen
13:17. mine eyes shall r. with tears,
49 : 3. lament, r. to and fro [14:17.
19. I will make him r. fr. her, 50:
51:31. One post r. to meet ano. [44.

La. 2 : 18. let tears r. like a river
Eze. 24:16. neither shall thy tears r.
32 : 14. cause rivers to r. like oil
Da. 12 : 4. many shall r. to and fro
Jo. 2 : 4. as horsemen, shall they r.
7. They shall r. like mighty men
9. They shall r. in city, r. on wall
Am. 3 : † 6. Shall trumpet be blown,
and people not r. together?
5 : 24. let judgment r. as waters
6 : 12. Sh. horses r. upon the rock?
8 : 12. shall r. to and fro to seek L.
Na. 2 : 4. they sh. r. like lightnings
Ha. 2 : 2. he may r. that readeth it
Hag. 1 : 9. ye r. ev. man unto house
Zch. 2 : 4. r. speak to young man
4:10. eyes of the Lord r. to and fro
Mat. 28 : 8. r. to bring disci. word
1 Co. 9 : 24. they which r. in a race
r. all, So r. that ye may obtain
26. I thf. so r. not as uncertainly
Ga. 2 : 2. lest I r. or had r. in vain
5:7. Ye did r. well, who did hinder
Ph. 2 : 16. that I have not r. in vain
2 Th. 3 : † 1. that word of L. may r.
He. 2 : † 1. lest we should r. out
12 : 1. let us r. with patience race
1 Pe. 4:4. that ye r. not to same ex- [cess

RUNNERS.

1 S. 22:†17. king said to r., Turn slay
1 K. 14:†27. shields unto chief of r.

RUNNEST.

Pr. 4 : 12. when r. shalt not stumble

RUNNETH.

Jb. 15:26. He r. upon him, on neck
16 : 14. he r. upon me like a giant
Ps. 23:5. anointest head, my cup r.
147:15. his word r. very swiftly [ov.
Pr. 18 : 10. righteous r. into it [48.
La. 1 : 16. mine eye r. wi. water, 3 :
Mat. 9 : 17. bottles break, wine r.
Jn. 20 : 2. she r. and cometh to Pet.
Ro. 9:16. willeth, nor of him that r.

RUNNING.

Le. 14:5. bird be killed over r. wat., [6, 50.
51. dip them in r. water, sprinkle
52. cleanse house wi. r. water [4.
15 : 2. When man hath r. issue, 22:
13. sh. bathe his flesh in r. water
Nu. 19:17. uncl. person take r. water
2 S. 18 : 24. a man r. alone, 26.
27. r. of foremost like r. of Ahi- [maaz
2 K. 5:21. Naaman saw him r.
2 Ch. 23 : 12. Athaliah heard peo. r.
Pr. 5 : 15. r. waters out of well
6 : 18. feet swift in r. to mischief
Can. 5:†5. my fingers with myrrh r.
Is. 33 : 4. as r. to and fro of locusts
Je. 18 : † 14. r. waters be forsaken?
Eze. 31 : 4. rivers r. about his plants
Mk. 9 : 15. people r. to him saluted
25. When Jesus saw the people r.
10 : 17. came one r. and kneeled
Lu. 6 : 38. good measure and r. over
Ac. 27 : 16. r. under certain island
Re. 9:9. sound of chariots r. to battle

RUSH, RUSHES.

Jb. 8 : 11. Can r. grow with-t mire?
Is. 9:14. L. will cut off branch and r.
19:15. nor any work wh. r. may do
35:7. where dragons lay be reeds, r-s

RUSH, ED, ETH.

Ju. 9 : 44. Abimelech r-d forward
20:37. liers in wait r-d upon Gibeah
Jb. 1:†17. Chaldeans r-d upon camels
Is. 17:13. nations sh. r. like many wa- [ters
Je. 8:6. as horse r-h into battle
Mk. 3 : † 10. r-d upon Jes. to touch [him
Ac. 19:29. they r-d into theatre

RUSHING.

Is. 17 : 12. Woe to multitude and r.
of nations, that make a r. like
r. of many waters [waters
13. nations sh. rush like r. of many
Je. 47 : 3. at r. of chariots fathers
Eze. 3 : 12. I heard a great r., 13.
Ac. 2:2. sound as of r. mighty wind

RUST.

Mat. 6 : 19. where moth and r. cor- [rupt, 20.
Ja. 5 : 3. r. of them sh. be a witness

RUTH.

Ru. 1 : 4. name of the other was R.
14. but R. clave unto Naomi
16. R. said, Entreat me not
2:8. said Boaz unto R., Hearest not
22. Naomi said unto R., It is good
3 : 9. Who art thou? I am R.
4:13. Boaz took R. she was his wife
Mat. 1 : 5. Boaz begat Obed of R.
See MOABITESS.

RYE.

Ex. 9 : 32. wheat and r. not smitten
Is. 28 : 25. cast in wheat, barley, r.

S.

SABACTHANI. See ELI.

SABAOTH.

Ro. 9 : 29. Except L. of S. had left [seed
Ja. 5 : 4. are entered into ears of L. [of S.

SABBATH.

Ex. 16 : 23. To morrow is the holy s.
25. to day is a s. unto the Lord
29. Lord hath given you the s.
20 : 10. seventh day is the s. of the
Lord thy God, 31 : 15.-35:2. Le.
23 : 3. De. 5 : 14. [fore, 16.
31 : 14. Ye shall keep the s. there-
Le. 16 : 31. It shall be a s. of rest
unto you, 23 : 3, 32. [wave it
23 : 11. morrow aft. s. priest shall
15. count from morrow after s.
16. after 7th s. number 50 days
24. 1st day of mo. sh. ye have s.
32. from even unto even your s.
39. on the first day shall be a s.
on the eighth a s. [bef. Lord
24:8. Every s. he shall set in order
25:2. then sh. land keep a s., 4, 6.
Nu. 28 : 10. burnt offering of ev. s.
2 K. 4 : 23. neither new moon nor s.
11 : 5. A third part of you that enter in on s., 2 Ch. 23 : 4.
7. two parts of all you that go
forth on s., 9. 2 Ch. 23 : 8.
16 : 18. covert for s. turned Ahaz
1 Ch. 9 : 32. prepare shewbread ev. s.
2 Ch. 36 : 21. desolate, she kept s.
Ne. 9 : 14. madest known holy s.
10 : 31. we would not buy it on s.
13 : 15. treading winepresses on s.
16. men of Tyre sold on the s. [s.
18. wrath upon Isr. by profaning
19. gates began to be dark bef. s.
21. came they no more on the s.
Is. 56:2. Blessed is man keepeth s., 6.
58 : 13. turn thy foot from the s.
call s. a delight [all worship
66 : 23. from one s. to another sh.
Eze. 46 : 1. on s. it sh. be opened
12. prince prepare as on s. day
Am. 8 : 5. When will s. be gone?
Mat. 12 : 2. not lawful upon s. day
28 : 1. In the end of s. came Mary
Mk. 1 : 21. straightway on s. day
2:27. The s. was made for man, not
man for s. [s., Lu. 6 : 5.
28. the Son of man is Lord of the
15 : 42. that is the day before s.
16 : 1. when s. was past, Mary Mag.
Lu. 6 : 1. on second s. after first
6. ano. s. he entered synagogue
7. whether he would heal on s. day
13:10. teaching in synagogue on s.
14. bec. Jesus healed on s. day
15. doth not each one on s. loose ox
23 : 54. preparation, and s. drew on
Jn. 5 : 18. he not only had broken s.
7 : 23. If on s. day receive circumc.
Ac. 1:12. from Jerus. s. day's journey
13 : 42. words be preached next s.
44. next s. day came whole city
16 : 13. on s. we went out of city
Ac. 18:4. reasoned in synag. ev. s. [s.
He. 4 : † 9. remaineth a keeping of a
See Sabbath DAY, DAYS.

SABBATHS.

Ex. 31 : 13. my s. ye shall keep, Le.
19 : 3, 30.-26 : 2. [plete
Le. 23 : 15. seven s. shall be com-
38. Beside the s. of the Lord, and
25 : 8. shalt number 7 s. of years
26 : 34. sh. the land rest and enjoy
her s., (2) 43. 2 Ch. 36 : 21.
35 bec. it did not rest in your s.
1 Ch. 23 : 31. offer burnt sacrifices
in s., 2 Ch. 2 : 4.-8 : 13.-31 : 3.
Ne. 10 : 33. [away with
Is. 1 : 13. new moons and s. I can-t
56 : 4. eunuchs that keep my s.
La. 1 : 7. adversaries did mock at s.
2 : 6. L. caused s. to be forgotten
Eze. 20 : 12. gave my s. to be sign
13. my s. they polluted, 16, 21, 24.
20. And hallow my s., 44 : 24.
22 : 8. hast profaned my s., 23 : 38.
26. priests have hid eyes fr. my s.
45:17. prince's part to give off-g's in
46 : 3. worship at this gate in s. [s.
Ho. 2:11. I will make to cease her s.

SABE'ANS.

Jb. 1 : 15. S. fell on the oxen of Job
Is 45 : 14. merchandise of S. to thee
Eze. 23 : 42. of common sort were S.
Jo. 3 : 8. they sh. sell them to S.

SAB'TA, SAB'TAH, SAB-TE'CHA, SABTE'CHAH.

Ge. 10:7. sons of Cush, S. and S., 1 Ch. [1:9.

SA'CAR = SHA'RAR.

1 Ch. 11 : 35. valiant, Ahiam son of
26:4 sons of Obed-edem, S. 4th [S.

SACK.

Ge. 42:25. Joseph com-ded to restore
ev. man's money into his s.,
28, 35.-43 : 21.-44 : 1. [ass
27. as one opened s. to give his
44:2. put my silv. cup in s. mouth
11. took down every man his s.
12. cup was found in Benj's s.
Le. 11 : 32. s. of uncl. be put in water

SACKS.

Ge. 42 : 25. to fill s. with corn, 44:1.
35. as they emptied s., 43 : 21.
43 : 12. money was bro-t again in
your s., 18.-44 : 8. [our s.
22. cannot tell who put money in
23. God given you treasure in s.
Jos. 9 : 4. Gibeonites took old s.

SACKBUT.

Da. 3 : 5. hear sound of s., 7, 10, 15.

SACKCLOTH, ES.

Ge. 37 : 34. Jacob put s. upon his [loins
2 S. 3 : 31. gird you with s. mourn
21 : 10. Rizpah took s. spread it
1 K. 20:31. let us put s. on loins, 32.
21 : 27. Ahab put s. and lay in s.
2 K. 6 : 30. looked, he had s. within
19 : 1. Hezekiah covered himself
with s., Is. 37 : 1. [Is. 37 : 2.
2. elders of priests covered wi. s.,
1 Ch. 21:16. elders were clothed with
Ne. 9 : 1. Isr. assembled with s-s [s.
Es. 4 : 2. none enter clothed with s.
4. clothe Mordecai, take aw. his s.
Jb. 16 : 15. I sewed s. upon my skin
Ps. 30 : 11. Thou hast put off my s.
35 : 13. they sick, my clothing was
69 : 11. I made s. my garment [s.
Is. 3 : 24. stomacher, a girding of s.
15:3. In streets gird thems. with s.
20 : 2. Go, loose s. from thy loins
22:12 did L. call to girding with s.
32:11. strip you, gird s. upon loins,
Je. 4:8.-6:26.-48:37.-49:3.
50:3. I make s. covering of heavens
La. 2 : 10. have girded thems. with
s., Eze. 7 : 18.-27 : 31. [and s.
Da. 9 : 3. to seek Lord with fasting
Jo. 1:8. Lament like a virgin with s.
13. lie all night in s. ye ministers

Am. 8: 10. will bring s. up. all loins
Jon. 3: 5. peo. of Nineveh put on s.
8. let man and beast be cov-d with
Re. 6: 12. sun became black as s. [s.
11: 3. prophesy 1200 days, clothed
See ASHES. [in s.

SACRIFICE. [Noun.]

Ge. 31: 54. Jacob off. s. up. mt. 46: 1.
Ex. 5: 17. Let us do s. to Lord, 8: 8.
12: 27, say, It is s. of L.'s passover
23: 18. not offer blood of s., 34: 25.
34: 15. one call, and thou eat of s.
25. nor s. of passover be left
Le. 3: 1. if s. be Peace off-g, 3, 6, 9.
7: 16. if s. be vow, eaten same day
17. remainder of flesh of s.
29. offereth s. of peace off-gs (2)
17: 8. whoso offereth s., and bring.
27: 11. beast of wh. do not offer s.
Nu. 15: 3. a s. in perform. vow, 8.
25. a s. made by fire unto L., 28:
6, 8, 13, 19, 24.-29: 6, 13, 36. [s.
De. 18: 3. priests' due fr. them th. off.
Jos. 22: 26. build altar, not for s.
Ju. 16: 23. to offer gr. s. unto Dagon
1 Sa. 1: 21. to offer yearly s., 2: 19.
2: 13. any off-d s., priest's servant
29. Wherefore kick ye at my s.?
3: 14. Eli's house not purged wi. s.
9: 12. s. of peo. to day in high place
13. because he doth bless the s.
15: 22. to obey is better than s.
16: 3. call Jesse to s. I will shew, 5.
20: 6. yearly s. for all family, 29.
1 K. 8: 62. k and all Isr. offered s.
12: 27. If peo. do s. at Jerusalem
2 K. 5: 17. nor offer s. un. other gods
10: 19. I have gr. s. to do to Baal
14. 4. peo. did s. on hi. pl., 2 Ch. 33:
17: 36. to him shall ye do s. [17.
2 Ch. 2: 6. save only to burn s.
7: 5. Sol. off. s. of 22,000 oxen.
12. chosen this place for ho. of s.
28: † 3. Ahaz off-d s. in the valley
29: † 11. L. hath ch. you to offer s.
Ps. 40: 6. s. thou didst not desire, 51:
50: 5. made cov. with me by s. [16.
118: 27. bind s. unto horns of alt.
Pr. 15: 8. s. of wicked is abom. 21:
21: 3. is more accept. than s. [27.
Ec. 5: 1. than to give s. of fools
Is. 19: 21. Egyptians shall do s.
34: 6. Lord hath a s. in Bozrah
57: 7. thither wentest thou to off. s.
Je. 33: 11. that bring s. of praise
18. nor want man to do s. contin.
46: 10. God hath a s. in north
Eze. 39: 17. gather to my s. a gr. s.
19. dri. blood till drunk. of my s.
44: 11. shall slay s. for peo., 40: 42.
46: 24. ministers boil s. of people
Da. 8: 11. daily s. was taken away,
9: 27.-11: 31. [daily s.
12. a host was given him against
13. How long vision of daily s.?
12: 11. from time daily s. be taken
Ho. 3: 4. Isr. shall abide without s.
6: 6. I desired mercy, and not s.
Mat. 9: 13.-12: 7.
Jon. 1: 16. men feared and off-d a s.
Zph. 1: 7. Lord hath prepared a s., 8.
Mal. 1: 8. if ye offer blind for s.
Mk. 9: 49. every s. shall be salted
Lu. 2: 24. to offer a s. acc. to law
Ac. 7: 41. they offered s. unto idol
14: 13. would have done s. wi. peo.
18: had not done s. unto them
Ro. 8: † 3. by a s. for sin condem. sin
12: 1. your bodies a liv. s. [19, 28.
1 Co. 8: 4. are off-d in s. un. idols, 10:
Ep. 5: 2. a s. to God for a sw. savour
Ph. 2: 17. if off-d up. s. of your faith
4: 18. a s. well pleasing to God
He. 7: 27. daily as those to offer s.
9: 26. to put away sin by s. of hims.
10: 5. saith, s. thou wouldest not, 8.
12. after he off-d one s. for sins
He. 10: 26. rema-th no more s. for sins
11: 4. Abel off-d more excellent s.
13: 15. By him offer s. of praise
See **BURNT Sacrifice**, s.
See EVENING. [Adj.]
See **Peace OFFERING, S.**

SACRIFICE, S. of thanksgiving.

Le. 7: 12. he shall offer with s. o. t.
13. leav-d bread with s. o. t. 22: 29.
Ps. 107: 22. sacrifice s-s o. t.
116: 17. I will offer s. o. t.
Am. 4: 5 offer s. o. t. with leaven

SACRIFICES.

Ge. 46: 1. Isr. at Beer-sheba off-d s.
Ex. 10: 25. Moses said, give us s.
18: 12. Jethro took s. for God.
Le. 10: 13. of s. of Lord made by fire
17: 5. s. they offer in open field
7. no more off. s. unto devils
Nu. 25: 2. call. peo. unto s. of gods
28: 2. my s. observe to offer
De. 12: 6. thither ye sh. bring s., 11.
27. blood of s. be poured up. altar
32: 38. Which did eat fat of s.
33: 19. there off. s. of righteousness
Jos. 13: 14. s. of L. their inheritance
22: 27. do service of L. with our s.
28. alt. not for s. but witness, 29.
1 S. 6: 15. sacrificed s. same day [ing
15: 22. hath L. delight in s. as obey-
2 S. 15: 12. fr. Gilonite while he off-d
2 K. 10: 24 went in to offer s. [s.
1 Ch. 29: 21. sacrificed s. in abund.
2 Ch. 7: 1. fire came consumed s.
4. k. and all people offered s.
29: 31. bring s. And cong. br-t s.
Ezr. 6: 3. Let place where he off-d s.
10. That they may offer s. unto G.
Ne. 12: 43. that day offered great s.
Ps. 4: 5. Offer s. of righteousness
27: 6. will I offer s. of joy
50: 8. not reprove thee for thy s.
51: 17. s. of God are a broken spirit
19. pleased with s. of righte-sness
106: 28. Baal-peor, and ate s. of de.
Pr. 17: 1. house full of s. with strife
Is. 1: 11. To what purpose mul. of s.?
29: 1. add ye year, let them kill s.
43: 23. neither honoured me wi. s.
24. neither hast filled me with s.
56: 7. their s. shall be accepted
Je. 6: 20. nor are your s. sweet
7: 21. Put burnt off-gs to your s.
22. nor com. them concerning s.
17: 26. bringing s. of praise unto
Eze. 20: 28. saw ev. hill and off-d s.
40: 41. table whereupon th. slew s.
Ho. 4: 19. sh. be ashamed, bec. of s.
8: 13. They sacrifice flesh for s.
9: 4. s. sh. be as bread of mourners
Am. 4: 4. bring your s. every morn.
5: 25. Have ye offered s.
Mk. 12: 33. to love L. is more than s.
Lu. 13: 1. blood Pilate ming-d wi. s.
Ac. 7: 42. have ye off-d s. 40 years?
1 Co. 10: 18. eat s. partakers of altar
He. 5: 1. may offer s. for sins
8: 3. high priest ordained to off. s.
9: 9. were offered gifts and s.
23. heavenly things with better s.
10: 1. never wi. s. make comers per-
3. in those s. is remembrance [fect
6. In s. for sin thou no pleasure
11. off-g same s. th. never can
13: 16. with such s. G. well pleased
1 Pe. 2: 5. priesthood, to offer spirit-l

SACRIFICE. [Verb.] [s.

Ex. 3: 18. let us go and s. to the L.,
5: 3, 8.-8: 27.-10: 25.
8: 25. go ye s. to your God, 28
26. shall we s. abom. of Egypti.?
29. in not letting people go to s.
13: 15. I s. to L. all openeth matrix
20: 24. s. thereon burnt offerings
Le 23: 19 s. one kid of goats [17: 1.
De. 15: 21. any blemish, not s. it,
De. 16: 2. Thou shalt s. passover, 6.
5. not s. passover within gates
1 S. 1: 3. Elkanah went p to s.
15: 15. peo. spared the best to s.
21. sho. have been destroyed to s.
16: 2. say, I am come to s., 5.
1 K. 3: 4. Sol. went to Gibeon to s.
12: † 32. Jerob. off-d to s. to calves
2 K. 14: 4. as yet the people did s.
on high places, 2 Ch. 33: 17.
17: 35. nor shall s. to other gods
2 Ch. 11: 16. came to Jerus. to s.
28: 23. will I s. to gods of Syria
Ezr. 4: 2. we seek your G., and do s.
Ne. 4: 2. What do Jews? will they s.?
Ps. 54: 6. I will freely s. unto thee
107: 22. s. sacrifices of thanksg.
Eze. 39: 17. gather sacr. that I s. for
Ho. 4: 13. They s. up. tops mts. [you
14. they s. with harlots
8: 13: They s. but L. accepteth not
12: 11. they s. bullocks in Gilgal
13: 2. Let men that s. kiss calves
Jon. 2: 9. I will s. wi. thanksgiving
Ha. 1: 16. Thf. they s. un. their net
Zch. 14: 21. they that s. shall seethe
Mal. 1: † 8. if ye offer the blind to s.
1 Co. 10: 20. wh. Gentiles s. to devils

SACRIFICED. [(2)

Ex. 32: 8. they made a calf and s.
De. 32: 17. s. unto devils, not to God
Jos. 8: 31. they s. peace offerings
Ju. 2: 5. they s. there unto Lord
1 S. 2: 15. serv. said to man that s.
6: 15. s. sacrifices the same day
11: 15. peo. went to Gilgal and s.
2 S. 6: 13. David s. oxen fatlings
1 K. 3: 2. Only peo. s. in hi. places, 3.
2 K. 12: 3.-15: 4, 35.-16: 4. 2 Ch.
28: 4. [gods
11: 8. strange wives wh. s. to their
2 K. 17: 32. lowest priests which s.
23: †20. he s. all priests of high plac.
1 Ch. 21: 28. L. ans-d, then David s.
29: 21. They s. sacrifices un. the L.
2 Ch. 5: 6 all before ark s. sheep
28: 23. Ahaz s. un. gods of Damas.
33: 16. Manasseh s. on altar of Lord
22. Amon s. unto carved images
34: 4. up. graves of them that had s.
Ps. 106. 37. they s. sons unto devils
38. dau-s they s. un. idols of Cana.
Eze. 16: 20. sons and dau-s hast th. s.
39: 19. which I have s. for you
Ho. 11: 2. they s. unto Baalim
Jon. 1: † 16. s. a sacrifice unto Lord
Mk 14: † 12. they s. passover
1 Co. 5: 7. Ch. our passover is s. [20.
Re. 2: 14. to eat things s. unto idols,

SACRIFICEDST.

De. 16: 4. nor shall flesh thou s.

SACRIFICERS.

Ho. 13 † 2. Let s. of men kiss calves

SACRIFICETH.

Ex. 22: 20. He that s. unto any god
Ec. 9: 2. him th. s. and him th. s. not
Is. 65: 3. people that s. in gardens
66. 3. he that s. a lamb as if he cut
Mal 1: 14. and s. a corrupt thing

SACRIFICING.

1 K. 8: 5. Israel with him s. sheep
12: 32. s. unto calves he had made
Ro. 15: † 16. s. of Gentiles might be

SACRILEGE.

Ro. 2: 22. idols, dost thou com. s.?

SAD, SADDER.

Ge. 40: 6. Joseph looked, th. were s.
1 K. 21: 5. Jezebel said, Why so s.?
Ne. 2: 1. I had not been before s.
Eze. 13: 22 with lies ye made right-
eous s. wh. I have not made s.
Da. 1: †10. why he see y-r faces s-r?
Mk. 10: 22. he was s. at that saying
Lu. 24: 17. as ye walk, and are s.?
See COUNTENANCE.

SADDLE. [Noun.]

Le. 15: 9. s. he rideth upon unclean

SADDLE. [Verb.]
2 S. 19 : 26. said, I will s. me an ass
1 K. 13 : 13. prophet said, s. me the
SADDLED. [ass, 27.
Ge. 22 : 3. Abr. rose early and s. his
Nu. 22 : 21. Balaam s. his ass [ass
Ju. 19 : 10. with Levite two asses s.
2 S. 16 : 1. met David with asses s.
17 : 23. Ahithophel s. his ass
1 K. 2 : 40. Shimei s. went after serv.
13 : 13. So they s. the ass, 23, 27.
2 K. 4 : 24. wom. of Shunam s. ass
SADDUCEES.
Mat. 3 : 7. saw S. come to his bapt
16 : 1. the S. came tempting Jesus
6. Beware of leaven of S., 11.
12. Beware of doctrine of the S.
22 : 23. S. say there is no resurrec.
Mk. 12 : 18.-Lu. 20 : 27.-Ac. 23 :
34. he had put S. to silence [8.
Ac. 4 : 1. priests and the S. came
5 : 17. S. laid hands on apostles
23 : 6. Paul perceived one part S.
7. dissension betw. Phari. and S.
SADLY.
Ge. 40 : 7. Whf. look ye so s. today?
SADNESS.
Ec. 7 : 3. by s. of counten. ht. better
SA'DOC.
Mat. 1 : 14. Azor begat S.; S. begat
SAFE.
1 S. 12 : 11. L. deliv., ye dwelled s.
2 S. 18 : 29. Is young man s.? 32.
Jb. 21 : 9. Their houses s. from fear
Ps. 119 : 117. Hold me up, I sh. be s.
Pr. 18 : 10. righte. run into it, are s.
29 : 25. whoso trusteth in L. be s.
Is. 5 : 29. shall carry prey away s.
Eze. 34 : 27. they sh. be s. in land
Lu. 15 : 27. he had received him s.
Ac. 23 : 24. may br. him s. un. Felix
27 : 44. escaped all s. to land
Ph. 3. 1, to write same things, for you
SAFEGUARD. [is s.
1 S. 22 : 23. wi. me thou shalt be in s.
SAFELY.
Le. 26 : 5. ye shall dwell in land s.
Ps. 78 : 53. he led them on s.
Pr. 3 : 23. shalt walk in thy way s.
31 : 11. husb. doth s. trust in her
Is. 41 : 3. He pursued, passed s. [s.
Je. 33 : 16. In ths. days Jerus. dwell
Ho. 2 : 18. will make them lie down s.
Zch. 14 : 11. Jerus. be s. inhabited
Mk. 14 : 44. that is he, lead him aw.
Ac. 16 : 23. jailer to keep th. s. [s.
See **DWELL safely.**
See DWELLETH, DWELT.
SAFETY.
Jb. 3 : 26. I was not in s., nei. had rest
5 : 4. His children are far from s.
11 wh. mourn may be exalt. to s.
11 : 18. thou shalt take rest in s.
24 : 23. Tho. given him to be in s.
Ps. 12 : 5. I will set him in s. from
22 : † 9. in s. on my mother's breasts
33 : 17. An horse vain thing for s.
Pr. 11 : 14. in counsellors is s., 24 : 6.
21 : 31. horse for battle, s. is of L.
Is. 14 : 30. needy shall lie down in s.
Ac. 5 : 23. prison found shut with s.
1 Th. 5 : 3. when they sh. say, Peace
See **DWELL in safety.** [and s.
SAFFRON.
Can. 4 : 14. spikenard s. calamus
SAID. [my
Ge. 2 : 23. Adam s. This is bone of
3. 1. serp. s. Hath G. s. ye shall not
9 : 26. Noah s. Blessed be L. [eat?
21 : 12. all Sarah hath s. hearken
24 : 65. serv. had s. It is my master
41 : 54. dearth began, as Joseph s.
Ex. 5 : 22. Moses unto Lord and s.
12 : 31. go, serve L., as ye have s.
32. take your flocks, as ye have s.
17 : 10. Joshua did as Moses had s.
Le. 10 : 5. car. th. out, as Mos. had s.
Le. 10 : 6 Mos.'s. un. A , Uncover
Nu. 11 : 21. s. I will give flesh [1 : 39.
14 : 31. little ones, ye s. be prey, De.
23 : 30. Balak did as Balaam s.
36 : 5. tribe of sons of Joseph s. well
De. 1 : 21. as God of thy fathers s.
Ju. 1 : 20. Hebron un. Caleb as Mo. s.
6 : 36. save Israel, as thou s., 37.
1 S. 10 : 15. tell me what Samuel s.
11 : 12. Who s. Shall Saul reign?
12 : 1. I have hearkened in all ye s.
27 : 1. David s., I sh. perish by Saul
2 S. 7 : 25 O L., do as thou hast s.
13 : 35. as thy servant s. so it is
23 : 1. Dav., son of Jesse s., and the
sweet psalmist of Israel s.
1 K. 2 : 38. as my king hath s.
8 : 29. place of which thou hast s.
My name be there, 2 Ch. 6 : 20.
12 : 26. Jerob. s. now sh. kingd. re.
17 : 13. Elijah s. unto her, go, do as
thou hast s. [other s.
22 : 20. one s. on this manner, an-
2 K. 7 : 17. he died, as man of G. s.
8 : 14. who s., What s. Elisha [3.
20 : 14. What s. these men? Is. 39 :
1 Ch. 17 : 23. L., do as thou hast s.
Ezr. 10 : 12. As thou s., so must we
Es. 5 : 5. he may do as Esther s.
Ne. 5 : 2. that s. we are many, 3, 4.
8. I will do to morrow as king s.
Jb. 11 : 4. thou hast s. My doctrine
31 : 31. If men of my taberu. s. not
38 : 11. I s. Hitherto shalt come
Ps. 12 : 4. Who s. With our tongue
14. 1. fool s. in heart, is no G., 53 : 1.
27 : 8. my heart s., Thy face will I
Pr. 7 : 13. with impudent face, s.
Is 14 : 13. hast s., I will ascend
28 : 15. ye s., We have made cove.
30 : 16. ye s., No, we will flee upon
41 : 6. Ev. one s. to bro., Be of good
47 : 10. thou hast s., None seeth
Je. 2 : 8. priests s. not, Where is L.?
23 : 25. I heard what prophets s.
28 : 6. prophet Jerem s., Amen
29 : 15. ye s., L. ha. raised prophets
38 : 25. Declare what thou s. unto
king, also what king s. [live
La. 4 : 20. We s., Un. his shad. we sh.
Eze. 12 : 9. hath not rebelli. house s.
26 : 2. Tyrus s. agai. Jerus., 36 : 2.
27 : 3. Tyrus, th. s., I am of beauty
28 : 2. thou hast s., I am a god
29 : 3. drag. who s., My riv. is mine
Da. 3 : 28. Nebuch. s., bless. be G. of
8 : 13. anot. saint s. un. that saint
Jon. 3 : † 7. it to be s. thro. Nineveh
4 : 8. Jonah s., It is better to die
Mi. 7 : 10. her who s., Where is L?
Zph. 2 : 15. city that s. I am
Mal. 3 : 14. Ye s., It is vain to ser. G.
Mat. 17 : 5. wh. s., This is my belov.
Son, Lu. 3. 22. [14 : 31,
26 : 35. Likew. s. all disciples, Mk.
64. Jesus saith, Thou hast s.
27 : 63. we remem. that deceiver s.
Mk. 2 : 14. s. unto Levi, Follow me
Lu. 1 : 13. ang. s., Fear not, 30.-2 : 10.
20 : 39. s., Master, thou hast well s.
23 : 46. having s. he gave up ghost
24 : 23. angels, who s. he was alive
24. found it as the women had s.
Jn. 1 : 23. Make straight, as s. Esaias
5 : 18. s. also, God was his Father
7 : 38. Scrip. ha. s. out of belly flow
12 : 41. These things s. Esaias
50. Even as Father s. unto me
Ac. 2 : 38. then Peter s., Repent
4 : 23. reported all chief priests s. to
7 : 37. This is Moses who s. un. Isr.
17 : 28. as certain of your poets s.
Ro. 7 : 7. law had s., not covet
Ga. 1 : 9. As we s. before, so say I
He. 7 : 21. that s., The Lord sware
10 : 30. him that ha. s., Vengeance
Ja. 2 : 11. he that s., Do not kill
Re. 5 : 14. the four beasts s., Amen
See **ANSWERED and said.**
He SAID or SAID he.
Ge. 9 : 26. h.s. Blessed be L. G. of
19 : 17. h.s. Escape for thy life
20 : 5. s.h. not, She is my sister?
31 : 8. if h.s. thus, speck. thy wages
12. h.s., lift up thine eyes
32 : 26. h.s., Let me go, day break.
27. h.s., Wh. thy name? h.s., Jac.
41 : 51. G., s.h., made me forget toil
Ex. 18 : 24. Moses did all Jethro s.
Nu. 23 : 19. h.s., sh. he not do it
De. 11 : 25. no man be able to st. bef.
you, as h.s., 18 : 2.-29 : 13.- Jos.
13 : 14, 33. [h.s.
Jos. 14 : 10. L. hath kept me alive, as
Ju. 8 : 3. anger was abated, wh. h.s.
1 S. 3 : 17. if hide any thing h. s.
1 K. 2 : 4. not fail, s.h., man on thr.
31. Do as h. s., fall upon him
2 K. 17. 23. as h.s. by his serv. proph.
1 Ch. 22 : 11. build house, as h. s.
2 Ch. 24 : 22. h.s., L., look upon it
Jb. 28 : 28. unto man h.s., fear L.
Ps. 10 : 6. h. s. in heart, 11, 13.
106 : 23. h. s. he would destroy
Is. 28 : 12. To who h.s., This is rest
40 : 6. Cry, h.s., What sh. I cry?
63 : 8. h.s., Surely they are my peo.
Je. 40 : 3. Lord hath done as h. s.
Eze. 9 : 5. h. s. in mine hearing
29 : 9. because h.s. river is mine
Jon. 3 : 10. G. repented of evil h.s.
Mat. 27 : 43. h.s., I am son of God
28 : 6. not here, he is risen, as h.s.
Mk. 14 : 16. came and found as h.s.,
Lu. 19 : 32.-22 : 13. [you
16 : 7. shall ye see him, as h.s. unto
Lu. 9 : 33. Peter, not know. wh. h.s.
13 : 17. when h.s. these, his advers.
Jn. 2 : 22. disciples remem. h.s. this
6 : 6. this h.s. to prove him
59. These th. s.h. in synagogue
9 : 17. Wh. sayest? h.s., He is proph.
11 : 11. These th. s.h., and aft. that
12 : 6 This h.s., not th. he cared
33. This h.s., signifying death
18 : 6. As soon as h.s. I am he
19 : 30. h. s., It is finished
20 : 20. h. had so s., he shew. hands
22. h. had s. this he breathed
Ac. 7 : 60. h. had s. this, fell asleep
9 : 5. h.s., Who art thou, Lord?
20 : 35. h.s., It is more blessed
23 : 7. h. had so s., arose dissension
28 : 29. h.s. th wds., Jesus depart.
2 Co. 12 : 9. h.s., My grace sufficient
He. 1 : 5. un. wh. of angels s.h., 13.
10 : 9. s.h., Lo, I come to do
15. h. had s. before, This is cove.
13 : 5. h. hath s., I will never leave
Re. 22 : 6. h.s., These thi. are faith.
God SAID.
Ge. 1 : 3. G. s. Let there be light
6. G. s. Let, 9, 11, 14, 20, 24, 26,
28, 29. [all flesh
6 : 13. G. s. to Noah, The end of
9 : 12. G. s. This token of cov-t [19.
17 : 9. G. s. to Ab. keep cov-t, 15,
20 : 6. G. s. to Abimelech in dream
21 : 12. G. s. to Abraham, Let it
not be grievous [Bethel
35 : 1. G. s. to Jacob, Arise, go to
10. G. s. Thy name is Jacob
11. G. s. I am God Almighty
Ex. 3 : 14. G. s. I AM THAT I AM [Is.
15. G. s. Thus say to the chil. of
13 : 17. G. s. Lest people repent
when [shalt not go
Nu. 22 : 12. G. s. to Balaam, Thou
1 K. 3 : 5. G. s. Ask what I sh. give
thee, 11. [them
1 Ch. 14 : 14. G. s. Go not up after
28 : 3. G. s. Thou shalt not build
2 Ch. 1 : 11. G. s. to Solomon, Because this in thine

Ho. 1:6. G. s. Call her name Lo-ruha.
9. G. s. Call his name Lo-ammi
Jon. 4: 9. G. s. to Jonah, Doest
thou well to be ⌈night thy
Lu. 12: 20. G. s., Thou fool, this
2 Co. 6: 16. temple of God, as G. s.
See GOD said.
I SAID, or SA D I.
Ge. 26: 9. I s. lest I die for her
Ex. 3: 17. I s., I will bring you out
23: 13. I have s. be circumspect
De. 32:26. I s. I would scatter them
Jos. 1: 3. given, as I s. unto Moses
Ju. 6: 10. I s., I am your God
1 S. 2: 30. I s., thy house sh. walk
9: 23. portion of which I s.
2 S. 19: 29. I s. thou and Ziba div
2 K. 23: 27. hou. of wh. I s., My name
Jb. 9: 22. This is one thing, thf. I s.
29: 18. I s., I shall die in my nest
32: 7. I s., Days should speak
Ps. 30: 6. I s., I sh. never be moved
39: 1. I s., I will take heed to my
40: 7. s. I, Lo, I come, He. 10: 7.
41: 4. I s., Lord, be merciful, heal
82: 6. I have s., Ye are gods, and
94: 18. When I s. foot slippeth
102: 24. I s., O God, take me not
119: 57. I s. I wo. keep thy words
142: 5. I s., Thou art my refuge
Ec. 2: 1. I s. in my heart, 15.-3: 17,
Is. 6: 11. s. I, Lord, how long? ⌊18.
45: 19. I s. not unto seed of Jacob
65: 1. I s., Behold me, un. nation
Eze. 6: 10. I have not s. in vain
9: 8. I s., Ah, Lord, wilt destroy
16: 6. I s. unto thee, Live (2)
Zch. 5: 6. And I s., What is it?
Jn. 1: 30. This is he of whom I s.
3: 7. Marvel not that I s., Ye must
8: 25. same that I s. fr. beginning
10: 36. Because I s. I am son of G.
11: 40. s. I not, if thou believe
42. I s. it, that they may believe
14. 26. to rememb. whatso. I have
28. Ye heard how I s., I go ⌊s.
16: 4. these I s., not at beginning
18: 20. in secret have I s. nothing
21. ask them whi. heard what I s.
Ac. 11: 8. I s., Not so, Lord
2 Co. 7: 3. I s., ye are in our hearts
9: 3. that as I s. ye may be ready
Ga. 2: 14. I s. un. Peter, If thou, be-
Re. 7: 14. I s., thou knowest ⌊ing
See JESUS said.
See LORD said.
SAID she, or she SAID.
Ge. 4: 25. God, s.s., appointed me
20: 5. even s.s., He is my brother
21: 7. s.s., 10, 16.-24: 18, 19, 24,
25, 46. ⌈I will
24: 58. go with this man? s.s.,
25: 22. s.s., If so, why am I thus
29: 32. s.s., Surely L. hath looked
33. s.s., 34, 35.-30: 3, 15.-38:
16, 17, 18, 25, 29.-39: 7. Ex. 2: 10.
Ex. 4: 26. s.s., A bloody husband
Ru. 3: 17. s.s. 1 S. 19: 14.-25: 19.-
28: 14. 1 K. 2: 13.
1 K. 2: 14. to say, s.s., Say on
21. s.s. 3: 26.-17: 12. 2 K. 4:
2, 6.-6: 31. Ho. 2: 5, 12. Mat.
9: 2. Mk. 5: 28. ⌈the dogs eat
Mat. 15: 27. s.s., Truth, Lord, yet
Mk. 14: 67. s.s. Thou wast wi. Jes.
Jn. 8: 11. s.s., No man, L. ⌊6: 24
11: 28, when s. had s. she went
20: 14. when s. had s. she turned
Ac. 5: 8. And s.s., Yea, for so much
They SAID, or SAID they.
Ex. 24: 7. t.s., All L. hath sd. will we
De. 5: 28. t. have well s. all they
1 K. 18: 10. when t.s., He not there
2 Ch. 22: 9. s. t., He is son of Jehosh.
26: 23. for t.s., He is a leper
Ps. 83: 4. t.s., Let us cut them off
122: 1. was glad when t.s. unto me
Je. 2: 6. Neither s.t., Where is L.?
Mat. 9: 28. Believe ye? t.s., Yea, L.
27: 4. t. s. What is that to us?
Mk. 3: 21. t. s. He is beside himself
30. t.s., He hath unclean spirit
16: 8. nei. s.t. any thing to any
Lu. 19: 34. t.s. L. hath need of him
Ac. 12: 15. s.t., It is his angel
SAID. [Passive.]
Ge. 10: 9. it is s., Even as Nimrod
22: 14. is s. to this day, In mt. of L.
Ex. 5: 19. was s., Ye sh. not minish
Nu. 21: 14. it is s. in book of wars
1 S. 9: 10. to serv., Well s., let us go
1 K. 13: 17. was s. by word of Lord
Jb. 3: 3. night perish in wh. it was s.
34: 31. it is meet to be s. unto God
Ps. 87: 5. of Zion it shall be s., This
Pr. 25: 7. better it be s., Come up
Ec. 1: 10. Is thing wh. it may be s.?
Is. 25: 9. be s. that day, This our G.
32: 5. nor churl s. to be bountl.
Je. 4: 11. that time it be s. to peo.
16: 14. no more be s. the L. liveth
Eze. 13: 12. be s., Where is daubing
Ho. 1: 10 where it was s., Ye not my
people, it shall be s.-Ro. 9: 26.
Zph. 3: 16. be s. to Jerus., Fear thou
Mat. 5: 21. s. by them of old, 27, 33.
31. Ye have heard it been s., 38, 43
Mk. 6: 22. when dau. of s. Herodias
Lu. 2: 24. that wh. is s. in law of L.
4: 12. It is s., Thou sht. not tempt
9: 7. was s. of some, John risen
23: 46. having s., he gave up ghost
Ro. 9: 12. it was s. elder shall serve
He. 3: 15. Whilst it is s. to day, 4: 7.
11: 18. Of whom it was s., in Isaac
Re. 6: 11. it was s. they should rest
SAIDST. ⌈sister?
Ge. 12: 19. Why s. thou, She is my
26: 9. how s., She is my sister?
32: 9. Lord, wh. s. unto me, Return
12. thou s., I will do thee good
44: 21. s. unto servts., Bring him, 23
Ex. 32: 13. s., I will multiply seed
Ju. 9: 38. Where mouth whw. thou s.
1 K. 2: 42. thou s. word is good
Jb. 35: 2. s., My righte-n. more than
3. thou s., What advantage ⌊God's
Ps. 27: 8 When s., Seek ye my face
89: 19. in vision to Holy One s.
Is. 47: 7. thou s., I shall be lady
57: 10. s. not, There is no hope
Je. 2: 20. s., I will not transgress
25. thou s., There is no hope, I
22: 21. but thou s., I will not hear
La. 3. 57. I called, thou s., Fear not
Eze. 25: 3. bec. thou s. Aha, ag. my
Ho. 13: 10. of whom s., Give me king
Jn. 4: 18 not thy hush. in that s.
SAIL. [Noun.] ⌊truly
Is. 33: 23. they could not spread s.
Eze 27: 7. spread. forth to be thy s.
Ac 27: 17. strake s. were driven
See MAINSAIL.
SAIL. [Verb.]
Ac. 20: 3. about to s. into Syria
16. Paul determined to s. by Eph.
27: 1. determ. we sho. s. into Italy
2. we launched, meaning to s. by
24. G. hath given thee all that s.
SAILED.
Lu. 8: 23. as they s. he fell asleep
Ac. 13: 4. thence s. to Cyprus, 15: 39
14: 26. And thence s. to Antioch
18: 18. s. thence into Syria, 21: 3.
21. And he s. from Ephesus
20: 6. we s. away from Philippi
13. s. unto Assos | 15. s. fr. thence
27: 4. launched, we s. und Cyprus
5. had s. over sea of Cilicia
7. we had s. slowly many days
13. they s. close by Crete, 7.
SAILING [Noun, Part.]
Ac. 21: 2. finding ship s. unto Phen.
27: 6. found a ship s. into Italy
Ac. 27: 9. when s. was now dangerous
SAILORS ⌈off
Re. 18: 17. ships and s. stood afar
SAINT.
Da. 8: 13. Then I heard one s. speaking, another s. said to that s.
Ph. 4: 21. Salute every s. in Christ
SAINTS. ⌊Jesus
De. 33: 2. he came with ten thous. of
3. all his s. are in thy hand ⌊s.
1 S. 2: 9. He will keep feet of his s.
2 Ch. 6: 41. let s. rejoice in goodness
Jb. 5: 1. to which of s. wilt turn
15: 15. putteth no trust in his s.
Ps. 16: 3. to s. that are in the earth
30: 4. Sing unto the L., O ye s.
31: 23. O love Lord, all ye his s.
34: 9. fear the Lord, ye his s. ⌈s.
37: 28. the Lord forsaketh not his
50: 5. Gather my s. toget. unto me
52: 9. thy name is good bef thy s.
79: 2. flesh of thy s. unto beasts
89: 5. faithfulness in congr. of s.
7. be feared in assembly of s.
97: 10. preserveth souls of his s.
116: 15. Precious is death of his s.
132: 9. and let thy s. shout for joy
16. her s. shall shout for joy ⌈thee
145: 10. works praise, s. shall bless
148: 14. He exalteth praise of s.
149: 1. his praise in congr. of s.
5. Let s. be joyful in glory, let
9. this honor have all his s.
Pr. 2: 8. preserveth way of s.
Da. 7: 18. s. shall take kingd., 22, 27
21. same horn made war with s.
25. wear out s. of Most High
Ho. 11: 12. Judah is faithful wi. s.
Zch. 14: 5. G. shall come and all s.
Mat. 27: 52. bodies of s. that slept
Ac. 9: 13. evil he hath done to thy s.
32. Peter came down also to s.
41. when he had called the s. ⌈up
26: 10. many of the s. did I shut
Ro. 1: 7. beloved of G., called to
8: 27. maketh interces. for s. ⌊be s.
12: 13. Distributing to neces. of s.
15: 25 Jerus. to minister to s.
26. cert. contribution for poor s.
31. service may be accepted of s.
16: 2. receive her as becometh s.
15. Salute all the s., He. 13: 24.
1 Co. 1: 2. sanctified, called to be s.
6: 1. go to law, and not before s.?
2. that the s. shall judge world?
14: 33. as in all churches of the s.
16: 1. concerning collection for s.
15. addicted to ministry of s.
2 Co. 1: 1. with all s. in Achaia
8: 4. upon us ministering to s.
9: 1. the ministering to s.
12. not only supplieth want of s.
13: 13. All s. salute you., Ph. 4: 22.
Ep. 1: 1. to the s. at Ephesus
15. aft. I heard of yr. love unto s.
18. glory of his inheritance in s.
2: 19. fellow citizens with s.
3: 8. am less than least of all s.
18. be able to comprehend with s.
4: 12. For perfecting of the s.
5: 3. not be named, as becometh s.
6: 18. with prayer for all s.
Ph. 1: 1. to all s. in Christ Jesus
Col. 1: 2. To all the s. at Colosse
4. love ye have to all the s.
12. partakers of inheritance of s.
26. mystery made manifest to s.
1 Th. 3: 13. coming of L. wi. his s.
2 Th. 1: 10. to be glorified in his s.
1 Ti. 5: 10. if she washed s.' feet
Phm. 5. love thou hast tow. all s.
7. bowels of s. refreshed by thee
He. 6: 10. ye have ministd. unto s.
Jude 3. faith once delivered unto s.
14. L. cometh with 10,000 of s.
Re. 5: 8. are prayers of s., 8: 3, 4. ⌈s.
11: 18. shouldest give reward unto

Re.13:7. to make war with the s.
10. patience and faith of the s.
14:12. Here is the patience of s.
15:3. Just thy ways, King of s.
16:6. they have shed blood of s.
17:6. woman drunk. with bl. of s.
18:24. in her was blood of s.
19:8. fine linen is right-n. of s.
20:9. compassed camp of the s.

SAITH.

2 S. 14:10. Whoso s. aught, bri. him
1 K. 3:23. one s., This is my son, other s., Nay, thy son is dead
20:2. s. Ben-had., Thy gold is mine
32. Ben-hadad s., let me live
22:27. s. king, Put this fellow in prison. 2 Ch. 18:26. [peace, 19.
2 K. 9:18. thus s. the king, Is it
18:19. thus s. great k. of Assyria
18:29. s. the king, Let not Hezekiah deceive you. 31. 2 Ch. 32:10. Is. 36:14.
19:3. s. Hezekiah, This a day of trouble, Is. 37:3.
2 Ch. 36:23. thus s. Cyrus, Ezr. 1:2
Jb. 28:14. The depth s. sea s. It is
33:24. s., Deliv. him from the pit
35:10. none s., Where is God my
Ps. 36:1. transgr. of the wicked s.
Pr. 9:4. understanding, she s., 16.
20:14. It is naught s. the buyer
22:13. slothful s., is lion, 26:13.
24:24. s. to wicked, Thou righte.
26:19. s., Am not I in sport?
La. 3:37. Who s. and it com. to pass?
Ob. 3. s. in heart, Who shall bring
Mat. 7:21. Not ev. one that s. L. L.
26:18. Master s., My time is at hand
Mk. 8:29. Peter s., Thou art Christ
15:28. Scripture wh. s., Ja. 2:23.
Lu. 18:6. Hear wh. unjust Judge s.
Jn. 4:10. If knewest who s., Give
19:28. After this, Jesus s., I thirst
Ac. 7:48. s. prophet, Heaven is my
21:11. s. Holy Ghost sh. Jews bind
Rom. 3:19. law s. it s. to them und.
10:16. For Esaias s., 20.-15:12.
19. First, Moses s., I will provoke
11:4. what s. the answer of God
1 Co. 3:4. one s. I am of Paul, 1:12.
9:8. s. not the law same also?
14:34. wom. under obed. as s. law
He. 3:7. Holy Ghost s., If ye hear
Re. 2:7. what the spirit s. unto the churches, 11, 17, 29.-3:6, 13,
8. These, s. the first and last [22.
18. These s. the son of God
3:14. s. the Amen | 14:13. s. Spirit
18:7. she s., I sit a queen, no wid.
22:20 he s., Surely I come quickly
See **GOD saith**, SCRIPTURE.

SAITH he, or he SAITH.

Ge. 41:55. what h.s. to you, do
1 S. 9:6. all that h.s. cometh [this
20:3. h.s., Let not Jona. know
2 S. 17:5. let us hear what h.s.
2 K. 5:13. when h.s. to thee, Wash
Jb. 37:6. h.s. to snow, Be thou
39:25. h.s. among the trumpets,
Pr. 23:7. Eat, drink, s.h. [Ha, ha!
Ec. 4:8. nei. s.h., For whom do I
10:3. h.s. to every one he is a fool
Is. 10:8. h.s., 13.-29:11, 12. Mat. 4:19.-8:26.-9:6, 9, 37.-12:13, 44.-16:15.-17:25.-19:8, 18.-20:7, 23.-22:8, 12, 20, 21, 43.-26:38. Mk. 2:10, 17.-3:3, 4, 5.-4:35.-5:36, 39.-6:38.-7:18.-8:17, 29.-10:11.-12:16.
Mk. 11:23. sh. believe things h.s., he sh. have whatso. h.s.
14:32. h.s., 16:6. Lu. 5:39.-7:40.-11:24. [mouth
19:22. h.s. to him, Out of own
Jn. 1:21. Elias? h.s., I am not
36. h.s., 39, 51.-5:6.-6:5, 20, 42.-8:22.-11:7.-16:17.-18:17.-19:14. 26, 27.-20:27. Ac. 2:34.-12:8.-13:35. 1 Co. 15:27. Ep. 4:8.-5:14. He. 1:6, 7.-5:6.-8:8. Ja. 4:6. Re. 2:1, 12.-3:1.-17:15.-19:9.
Re. 22:9. s.h., See thou do it not
10. h.s., Seal not sayings of book
Jn. 2:5. Whatso. h.s. unto you
16:18. What is this h.s.? We cannot tell what h.s. [true
19:35. and he knoweth that h.s.
21:15. h.s. to Peter, Feed my, 16
Ac. 1:4. s.h., Ye have heard of me
22:2. kept more silence, and h.s.
Ro. 9:15. h.s. to Moses, I will have
25. As h.s. in Osee [mercy
10:21. to Israel h.s., All day long
15:10. h.s., Rejoice ye Gentiles
1 Co. 6:16 two, s.h., be one flesh
9:10. s.h., it altog. for our sakes
2 Co. 6:2. h.s., I have heard thee
10:10. letters, s.h., are weighty
Ga. 3:16. not, h.s., And to seeds
He. 8:5. See, s.h., thou make all
13. in that h.s., A new covenant

Jesus SAITH.

Mat. 4:10. s. J., Get thee hence
Mk. 11:33. J. s., Neither do I tell
Jn. 2:7. J. s., Fill the waterpots
4:16. J. s., Go call thy husband, 26.
5:8. J. s., Rise, take thy bed
8:25. J. s., Even same th. I said
11:40. J. s., if thou wouldest believe
20:17. J. s., Touch me not
19. J. s., Peace be unto you
See **JESUS saith.**
See **Saith the LORD, Thus saith the LORD, Saith LORD God of hosts, Saith LORD God of Israel, Saith the LORD of hosts, Thus saith LORD of hosts.**

SAKE.

Ge. 8:21. not curse ground for man's [s.
12:16. entreated Abram for her s.
18:29. will not do it for forty's s.
31. twenty's s. | 32. ten's s.
20:11. will slay me for wife's s.
26:24. mult. thy seed for Abr.'s s.
39:5. bles. Eg'n's hou. for Jos.'s s.
Ex. 18:8. done to Egy. for Isr.'s s.
21:26. let him go free for eye's s.
27. let him go free for tooth's s.
Nu. 11:29. Enviest thou for my s.?
25:11. he was zealous for my s.
18. slain in plague for Peor's s.
1 S. 23:10. to destroy city for my s.
2 S. 5:12. exalteth kingd. for Isr s.
7:21. For thy word's s., 1 Ch. 17:19.
9:1. kindness for Jonathan's s., 7.
18:5. Deal gent. for my s. wi. Abs.
1 K. 11:12. for David thy fa.'s s., 13, 32, 34.-15:4. 2 K. 8:19.-19:34.-20:6. Ps. 132:10.
13. for Jerus.'s s. wh. I have chos.
Ne. 9:31. not cons. for mercies' s.
Jb. 19:17. entreated for child.'s s.
Ps. 6:4. save me for mercies' s., 31:16
25:7. rememb. me for goodn. s.
69:6. not be confounded for my s.
115:1. for thy mer. and truth's s.
Is. 37:35. mine own s. and Da.'s s.
43:14. For your s. I sent to Bab.
25. blotteth thy transgns. for my s.
45:4. for Jacob's s. I called thee
48:11. for mine own s. will I do it
62:1. For Zion's s., for Jerus.'s s.
63:17. Return for thy servant's s.
Da. 9:17. shine upon sanct. for L.'s
19. defer not for own s. O God [s.
Jon. 1:12. for my s. this tempest
Mi. 3:12 Zion for y-r s. be ploughed
Mat. 5:11. ag. you falsely for my s.
10:18. shall be brought bef. kings for my s., Mk. 13:9. Lu. 21:12.
39. that loseth his life for my s. sh. find it, 16:25. Mk. 8:35. Lu. 9:24.
14:3. bound for Herodias' s. Mk. 6:17.
9. for the oath's s., Mk. 6:26.
19:12. for kingdom of heaven's s.
24:22. for elect's s. days shall be shortened, Mk. 13:20.
Mk. 4:17. persecution for word's s.
Lu. 6:22. cast out for Son of m.'s s.
Jn. 12:9. came not for Jesus' s. only
13:38. Wilt lay down life for my s.?
14:11. believe me for works' s.
Ac. 26:7. For hope's s. I am accus.
Ro. 4:23. not writ. for his s. alone
15:30. for L.'s s. strive in prayers
1 Co. 4:10. we are fools for Christ's
9:23. this I do for gospel's s. [s.
10:28. eat not, for his s. that sho.
2 Co. 4:5. your serv-ts for Jesus' s.
11. delivered to death for Jesus' s.
Ph. 1:29. given to suffer for his s.
Col. 1:24. for his body's s. the ch.
3:6. for wh. things' s. wrath of G.
1 Th. 1:5. men we were for your s.
5:13. to esteem them for work's s.
1 Ti. 5:23. wine for thy stomach's s.
Tit. 1:11. teach. things for lucre's s.
Phm. 9. Yet for love's s. I beseech
1 Pe. 2:13. submit to ord. for L.'s s.
2 Jn. 2. for the truth's s. in us
See **For CHRIST, CONSCIENCE.**
See **NAME'S Sake.**
See **For RIGHTEOUSNESS.**

Thy SAKE.

Ge. 3:17. cursed is the ground for [t. s.
12:13. may be well wi. me for t. s.
30:27. L. hath blessed me for t. s.
Ps. 44:22. for t. s. are we killed all day long, Ro. 8:36. [proach
69:7. Bec. for t. s. I have borne re-
Is. 54:15. who ag. thee fall for t. s.
Jer. 2:12. I remem. for t. s. kindn.
15:15. for t. s. I suffered rebuke
Jn. 13:37. I will lay down life for [t. s.

SAKES.

Ge. 18:26. spare place for their s.
Le. 26:45. I will for their s. remem.
De. 1:37. L. angry with me for your s. 3:26.-4:21. [for our s.
Ju. 21:22. Be favourable unto them
Ru. 1:13 it grieveth me for your s.
1 Ch. 16:21. yea, he reproved kings for their s., Ps 105:14 [on high
Ps. 7:7. for their s. thf. return thou
106:32. ill with Moses for their s.
122:8. breth. and companions' s.
Is. 65:8. will I do for servants' s.
Eze. 36:22. I do not for your s., 32
Da. 2:30. for their s. that make kno.
Mal. 3:11. rebuke devour. for y-r s.
Mk. 6:26. their s. wh. sat with him
Jn. 11:15. I am glad for your s.
12:30. This voice came for your s.
17:19. for their s. I sanctify mys.
Ro. 11:28. are beloved for fa.s' s.
28. they are enemies for y-r s.
1 Co. 4:6. I transferred for your s.
9:10. saith he it for our s.? for our
2 Co. 2:10. for y-r s. forgave I [s.
4:15. all things are for your s.
8:9. yet for your s. became poor
1 Th. 3:9. we joy for yr. s. bef. God
2 Ti. 2:10. I endure all for elect's s.

SA'LA, SA'LAH, SHE'LAH.

Ge. 10:24. Arphaxad begat S., S. begat, 11:12, 13. 1 Ch. 1:18. [15.
11:14. S. lived 30 years, begat Eber.
Lu. 3:35. Heber, wh. was the son [of S.

SAL'AMIS.

Ac. 13:5. And when they were at S.

SALA'THIEL.

1 Ch. 3:17. S. son of Jechoniah, Mat. 1:12.
Lu. 3:27. Zorobabel was son of S.

SAL'CAH = SAL'CHAH.

De. 3:10. S and Edrei, cities of Og
Jos. 12:5. reigned in Hermon, S.

Jos. 13:11. Bashan unto S., 1 Ch. 5:[11.
SALE.
Le. 25: 27. let him count yrs. of s.
† 42. not sold wi. s. of bondman
50. price of his s. be acc-g. to yrs.
De. 18: 8. bes. that wh. cometh of s.
SA'LEM.
Ge. 14: 18. Melchizedek king of S.
Ps. 76: 2. in S. is his tabernacle
He. 7: 1. Melchize. k. of S. blessed
2. k. of S. wh. is k. of peace [Ab.
SA'LIM.
Jn. 3: 23. was baptizing near to S.
SAL'LAI.
Ne. 11: 8. sons of Benjamin, S.
12: 20. chief of faths. of S., Kallai
SAL'LU.
1 Ch. 9:7. sons of Benj., S., Ne. 11: 7.
Ne. 12: 7. Iddo, S. chief of priests
SAL'MA, SAL'MON.
Ru. 4: 20. Nahshon begat S-n
21. S-n begat Boaz, 1 Ch. 2: 11.
Mat. 1: 4, 5.
1 Ch. 2: 51. S-a fa. of Bethle. 54.
Lu. 3: 32. Boaz, wh. was the son of
SAL'MON. [Place.] [S-n
Ps. 68: 14. was white as snow in S.
SALMO'NE. [ag. S.
Ac. 27: 7. sailed under Crete over
SALO'ME. [and S.
Mk. 15: 40. wom. looking on Mary
16: 1. M. and S. had bought spices
SALT. [Place.] See NIBSHAN.
SALT. [Noun.]
Ge. 19: 26. Lot's wife a pillar of s.
Le. 2: 13. with thy offer-gs offer s.
De. 29: 23. that the whole land is s.
Ju. 9: 45. city, and sowed it with s.
2 S. 8: 13. smit. Syrians in val. of s.
2 K. 2: 20. Bring new cruse, put s.
21. went to spring, cast the s. in
14: 7. Amaziah slew in valley of s.
10,000, 1 Ch. 18: 12.-2 Ch. 25: 11
Ezr. 4: † 14. salted with s. of palace
6: 9. need of wheat, s. wine
7: 22. s. with-t prescrib. how much
Jb. 6: 6. unsavory be eaten with s.?
39: † 6. made s. places his dwell-gs
Je. 17: 6. sh. inhab. places in s. la.
Eze. 43: 24. priest sh. cast s. upon
47: 11. marshes shall be given to s.
Mat. 5: 13. Ye are the s. of the earth,
but if the s. [with s.
Mk. 9: 49. ev. sacrifice sh. be salted
50. s. is good, but if s. lost saltn-s,
have s. in yourselves, Lu. 14: 34.
Col. 4: 6. speech be seasoned wi. s.
Ja. 3: 12. no fount. yields s. water
and fresh
See **COVENANT of salt.**
SALT pits. See SALTPITS.
SALT sea.
Ge. 14: 3. vale of Siddim, wh. is s.s.
Nu. 34: 12. goings out be at s.s. 3.
De. 3: 17. coast even to s.s. [s.s.
Jos. 3: 16. waters that come toward
12: 3. sea of plain, even to s.s.
15: 2, 5.-18: 19. Nu. 34: 3.
SALTED.
Ex. 30: † 35. make it a perfume s.
Ezr. 4: † 14. we are s. wi. salt of pal.
Eze. 16: 4. thou wast not s. at all
Mat. 5: 13. wherewith shall it be s.
Mk. 9: 49. ev. one sh. be s. with fire,
every sacrifice shall be s.
SALTNESS. [into s.
Ps. 107: † 34. turneth fruitful land
Mk. 9: 50. if the salt have lost his s.
SALTPITS, SALT pits.
Jos. 11: † 8. Isr. chased them to s.p.
Zph. 2: 9. Moab shall be as s.
SA'LU. See ZIMRI.
SALUTATION, S.
Mk. 12: 38. scribes who love s-s in
Lu. 1: 29. what manner of s. this be
41. at s. of Mary, babe leaped, 44
1 Co. 16: 21. The s. of me, Paul

Col. 4: 18. s. by hand of Paul, 2 Th. [3: 17.
SALUTE.
1 Sa. 10: 4. they will s. thee and give
13: 10. Saul to Sam. might s. him
25: 14. David sent to s. our master
2 Sa. 8: 10. Toi sent Joram to s. Da.
2 K. 4: 29. s. him not, if any s. thee
10: 13. we go to s. chil. of the king
1 Ch. 18: † 10. sent to s. of his welfare
Mat. 5: 47. if ye s. your breth. only
10: 12. when come into house, s. it
Mk. 15: 18. began to s. him, Hail, K.
Lu. 10: 4. s. no man by the way
Ac. 25: 13. Agrippa came to s. Festus
Ro. 16: 5. s. my beloved Epenetus
7. s. Andronicus | 9. s. Urbane
10. s. Apelles. s. Aristobulus' ho.
11. s. Herodian | 12. s. bel. Persis
13. s. Rufus chosen of Lord
14. s. Asyncritus | 15. s. Julia
16. s. with holy kiss, churches s.
21. Lucius and Jason s. you [you
22. I, Tertius, who wrote this, s.
1 Co. 16: 19. churches of Asia s.
you, Aquila, Pris. s. you much
2 Co. 13: 13. All saints s. you, Ph.
Ph. 4: 21. s. ev. saint in Christ [4: 22.
Col. 4: 15. s. brethren in Laodicea
2 Ti. 4: 19. s. househ. of Onesiphorus
Tit. 3: 15. All with me, s. thee
Phm. 23. s. thee, Epaphras, Marcus
He. 13: 24. s. them that have the
rule, they of Italy s. you
3 Jn. 14. Our friends s. thee, greet
SALUTED. [Micah
Ju. 18: 15. Danites came and s.
1 S. 17: 22. David s. his brethren
30: 21. Da. came near people and s.
2 K. 10: 15. Jehu s. Jehonadab, and
Mk. 9: 15. people running to Jesus,
Lu. 1: 40. Mary s. Elizabeth [s. him
Ac. 18: 22. Paul, when he had s. ch.
21: 7. came to Ptolemais, s. breth.
19. when Paul had s. James and
SALUTETH.
Ro. 16: 23. Gaius s. and Erastus s.
Col. 4: 10. Aristarchus s. you [you
12. Epaphras, a serv. of C. s. you
1 Pe. 5: 13. church at Bab-n s. you
SALVATION, S.
Ex. 14: 13. See the s. of the Lord,
2 Ch. 20: 17. [his s.
De. 32: 15. lightly esteemed rock of
1 S. 11: 13. Lord wrought s. to day
14: 45. Jona. who wrought great s.
19: 5. L. wrought great s. for Isr.
2 S. 19: † 2. s. turned into mourn-g
22: 51. He is tower of s. for king
1 Ch. 11: † 14. L. saved th. by gt. s.
16: 23. shew from day to day his s.
35. Save us, O God of our s.
2 Ch. 6: 41. priests be clothed wi s.
Ps. 3: 8. s. belongeth unto the Lord
14: 7. O that the s. of Israel were
come, 53: 6.
20: † 6. by the s. of his right hand
24: 5. righteousn. from G. of his s.
28: † 8. The Lord is strength of s-s
35: 9. my soul sh. rejoice in his s.
37: 39. s. of righteous is of L.
42: † 5. praise him, his pres. is s.
50: 23. to him will I shew s. of G.
60: † 11. vain is s. of man, 146: † 3.
65: 5. wilt answer us, O G. of our s.
68: 19. Blessed be God of our s.
20. He that is our God is God of s.
74: 12. working s. in the earth
78: 22. they trusted not in his s.
79: 9. Help us, O God of our s., for
85: 4. Turn us, O God of our s.
9. Surely his s. is nigh th. that fear
95: 1. joyful noise to rock of our s.
96: 2 shew his s. from day to day
98: 2. L. hath made known his s.
3. ends of earth have seen s. of G.
116: 13. I will take cup of s.
118: 15. voice of s. is in tabernacles

Ps. 119: 155. s. is far from wicked
132: 16. I will clothe priests with s.
144: 10. he that giveth s. unto ks.
146: † 3. son of man in wh. is no s.
149: 4. will beautify meek with s.
Is. 12: 3. dr. wat. out of wells of s.
25: 9. we will rejoice in his s.
26: 1. s. will God appoint for walls
33: 2. be thou our s. in trouble
6. wisdom be strength of s. † s-s
45: 8. earth open, let th. bring s.
17. Isr. sh. be saved wi. everl. s.
46: 13. will place s. in Zion
49: 8. in a day of s. I helped thee
52: 7. feet of him that publish. s.
10. ends of earth shall see s. of G
59: 11. we look for s. but it is far
16. his arm brought s. unto him
17. he put helmet of s. upon head
60: 18. shalt call thy walls s. [s.
61: 10. clothed me wi. garments of
62: 1. s. th-f as lamp that burneth
63: 5. mine arm bro-t s. unto me
Je. 3: 23. Truly in vain is s. hoped
for fr. hills, in Lord is s. of Isr.
La. 3: 26. quietly wait for s. of L.
Jon. 2: 9. I vowed. s. is of Lord
Ha. 3: 8. didst ride upon char. of s.
13. wentest forth for s. of thy peo.
for s. with thine anointed
Zch. 9: 9. King, he is just having s.
Lu. 1: 69. raised up horn of s. for us
77. To give knowledge of s. to peo.
3: 6. all flesh shall see the s. of G.
19: 9. Jes. said, This day is s. come
Jn. 4: 22. worship, for s. is of Jews
Ac. 4: 12. Neither is s. in any other
13: 26. to you is word of th. s. sent
47. be for s. unto ends of earth
16: 17. these shew unto us way of s.
28: 28. s. of G. is sent unto Gent.
Ro. 1: 16. gospel power of G. unto s.
10: 10. wi. mouth confess. unto s.
11: 11. thro. th. fall. s. unto Gent.
13: 11. now is our s. nearer than
2 Co. 1: 6. comforted, it is for y-r s.
6: 2. in day of s. I succored thee;
behold now is the day of s.
7: 10. sorrow worketh repent. to s.
Ep. 1: 13. heard gospel of your s.
6: 17. take helmet of s. and sword
Ph. 1. 28. to you evident token of s.
2: 12. work out your own s. wi. fear
1 Th. 5: 8. for helmet the hope of s.
9. appointed us to obtain s. by L.
2 Th. 2: 13. G. hath chos. you to s.
2 Ti. 2: 10. may obtain s. in Christ
3: 15. Scrip. ab. to make wise unto s.
Tit. 2: 11. grace of God bringeth s.
He. 1: 14. who shall be heirs of s.
2: 3. how escape if neg. so great s.?
10. to make captain of s. perfect
5: 9. he became author of eter. s.
6: 9. and things that accompany s.
9: 28. sh. appear with-t sin unto s.
1 Pe. 1: 5. kept through faith un. s.
9. receiving end of your faith, s.
10. Of which s. prophets inquired
2 Pe. 3: 15. longsuffering of L. is s.
Jude 3. to write unto of common s.
Re. 7: 10. saying, s. to our G., 19: 1.
12: 10. Now is come s. and strength
My SALVATION.
Ex. 15: 2. the Lord is become m.s.
2 S. 22: 3. is horn of m.s. [46.
47. exalted be rock of m.s., Ps. 18:
23: 5. this is all m.s., my desire
Jb. 13: 16. He also shall be m.s.
Ps. 22: † 1. why thou so far fr. m.s.
25: 5. thou art G. of m.s. [Is. 12: 2
27: 1. L. is my light and m.s., 62: 6
9. leave me not, O God of m.s.,
51: 14.-88: 1. [m.s.
38: 22. Make haste to help, O Lord
62: 1. God: fr. him cometh m.s.
2. He only is my rock and m.s.
7. In God is m.s. and my glory

Ps.89:26. Thou my G. and rk. of **m.s.**
91 : 16. will satisfy, shew him **m.s.**
118 : 14. L. is become **m.s.**, 21. Is.
140 : 7. O G., streng. of **m.s.** ⌊12:2
Is. 12 : 2. G. is **m.s.**, he is bec. **m.s.**
46 : 13. **m.s.** shall not tarry
49 : 6. may. be **m.s.** to end of earth
51 : 5. **m.s.** is gone forth
6. but **m.s.** shall be forever
8. **m.s.** from generation to gener.
56 : 1. **m.s.** is near to come, and
Mi. 7 : 7. will wait for G. of **m.s.**
Ha. 3 : 18. will joy in God of **m.s.**
Ph. 1 : 19. I know this sh. turn to
Thy SALVATION. ⌊**m.s.**
Ge. 49 : 18. I have waited for **t.s.**
1 S. 2 : 1. enlarged bec. I rej. in **t.s.**
2 S. 22 : 36. Thou hast given me the shield of **t.s.**, Ps. 18 : 35.
Ps. 9 : 14. I will rejoice in **t.s.**
13 : 5. my heart sh. rejoice in **t.s.**
20 : 5. We will rejoice in **t.s.**, and
21 : 1. in **t.s.** how greatly sh. he re-
5. His glory is great in **t.s.** ⌊joice
35 : 3. say unto my soul, I am **t.s.**
40 : 10. I have declared **t.s.** ⌈magn.
16. such as love **t.s.** say, L. be
51 : 12. Restore joy of **t.s.** 70 : 4.
69 : 13. O God, hear me in truth of
29. let **t.s.** set me on high ⌊**t.s.**
71 : 15. My mouth shall shew **t.s.**
85 : 7. O Lord, grant us **t.s.** ⌈**t.s.**
106 : 4. remember, O visit me with
119 : 41. Let **t.s.** come ac. to word
81. My soul fainteth for **t.s.**
123. Mine eyes fail for **t.s.**
166. Lord, I have hoped for **t.s.**
174. I have longed for **t.s.**, O L.
Is. 17 : 10. hast forgotten G. of **t.s.**
62 : 11. say to Zion, **t.s.** cometh
Lu. 2 : 30. mine eyes have seen **t.s.**

SAMA'RIA.

1 K. 16 : 24. Omri bought the hill S.
20 : 1. Ben-hadad besieged S. 2 K.
10. if dust of S. shall suffice ⌊6 : 24
17. are men come out of S.
21 : 1. viney. by palace of k. of S.
22 : 10. Ahab sat in the entrance of gate of S., 2 Ch. 18 : 9. ⌈S.
38. one washed chariot in pool of
2 K. 1 : 3. messengers of king of S.
3 : 6. Jehoram went out of S.
6 : 20. they were in the midst of S.
7 : 1. for a shekel in gate of S., 18.
17 : 6. k. of Assyria took S., 18 : 10
24. placed men in cities of S. (2)
26. nations, placed in cities of S.
28. priests they had carried fr. S.
18 : 9. Shalmaneser came ag-st S.
34. have they deliv-d S., Is. 36:19.
21 : 13. over Jerusalem line of S.
23 : 18. prophet that came out of S.
19. houses that were in cities of S.
2 Ch. 25:13. army upon Judah fr. S.
Ezr. 4 : 10. Asnap. set in cities of S.
Ne. 4 : 2. Sanballat bef. army of S.
Is. 7 : 9. the head of Ephraim is S., head of S. is Remaliah's son
8 : 4. spoil of S. shall be taken
9 : 9 inhabitants of S. shall know
10 : 9. is not S. as Damascus? ⌈S.
10. graven ima. did excel them of
Je. 23 : 13. seen folly in proph. of S.
31 : 5. plant vines upon mts. of S.
41 : 5. certain fr. Shechem and S.
Eze. 16 : 46. thine elder sister is S.
51. Nei. S. committed half thy sins
53. bring captivity of S.
55. S. and daus. shall return to
23 : 4. S. is Aholah, and Jerusa.
33. filled, with cup of thy sis. S.
Ho. 7 : 1. wickedness of S. discov-d
8 : 5. Thy calf, O S., hath cast thee
6. calf of S. shall be broken ⌊off
10 : 5. inhabitants of S. shall fear
7. As for S., her king is cut off
13 : 16. S. shall become desolate
Am. 3 : 9. Assemble upon mts. of S.
4 : 1. kine of Bashan in mt. of S.
6 : 1. Woe to them trust in mt. of S.
8 : 14. that swear by sin of S.
Ob. 19. they sh. possess fields of S.
Mi. 1 : 1. the word he saw conc. S.
5. transg-n of Jacob? Is it not S.
6. I will make S. as a heap of
Lu. 17 : 11. he passed through S.
Jn. 4 : 4. he must needs go thro. S.
5. cometh he to city of S.
9. askest drink of me, a wom. of S.
Ac. 8 : 1. were scattered through S.
5. Philip preached Ch. to them of
9. bewitched the people of S. ⌊S.
14. heard S. received the word
15 : 3. passed thro. Phenice and S.
In SAMA'RIA. ⌈**i.S.**
1 K. 13 : 32. ag. high places wh. are
16 : 28. Omri was buried **i. S.**
29. Ahab reigned **i.S.**
32. house of Baal he had built **i.S.**
18 : 2. there was a sore famine **i.S.**
20 : 34. streets, as my fa. made **i.S.**
21 : 18. Ahab k. of Isr. wh. is **i.S.**
22 : 37. they buried Ahab **i.S.**
51. Ahaziah began to reign **i.S.**
2 K. 1 : 2. chamber that was **i.S.**
3 : 1. Jehoram beg. to reign **i.S.**
5:3. Would G. my lord wi. prophet
6 : 25. was great famine **i.S.** ⌊**i.S.**
10 : 1. Ahab had seventy sons **i.S.**
17. slew all remained to Ahab **i.S.**
35. buried Jehu **i.S.** | 36. Jehu rei.
13 : 1. Jehoahaz reigned **i.S.** | 10.
6. remained grove **i.S.** ⌊Jehoash
9. they buried Jehoahaz **i.S.**
13. Joash was buried **i.S.**, 14 : 16.
14 : 23. Jeroboam reigned **i.S.**
15 : 8. Zechariah reigned **i.S.**, 13.
14. Menahem smote Shallum **i.S.**
17. Menahem reigned 10 yrs. **i.S.**
25. Pekah smote Pekahiah **i.S.** ⌊23.
27. Pekah reigned twenty yrs. **i.S.**
17 : 1. Hoshea to reign nine yrs. **i.S.**
2 Ch. 22. 9. Ahaziah was hid **i.S.**
Ezr. 4 : 17. companions th. dwell **i.S.**
Am. 3 : 12. be tak. out that dw. **i.S.**
Ac. 1 : 8. be witnesses unto me **i.S.**
9 : 31. Then had churches rest **i.S.**
To or unto SAMA'RIA. ⌈**S.**
1 K. 20 : 43. Ahab displeased came **t.**
22 : 37. king died, was bro. **t.S.**
2 K. 2 : 25. Elisha ret-ed fr. Carmel
6 : 19. Elisha led them **t.S.** 20. ⌊**t.S.**
10 : 1. Jehu wrote letters sent **t.S.**
12. Jehu came **t.S.**, 17. ⌈25 : 24.
14 : 14. Jehoash returned **t.S.** 2 Ch.
15 : 14. Menahem **t. S.** and smote
17 : 5. king of Assyria went up **t.S.**
2 Ch. 18 : 2. Jehoshaphat went **t.S.**
28 : 8. Isr. bro-t spoil of Jud. **t.S.**
9. went out bef. host that ca. **t.S.**
15. then they returned **t.S.**
Is. 10. 11. as I have done **u.S.** and
SAMAR'ITAN. ⌊idols
Lu. 10 : 33. a S. came where he was
17 : 16. giv. him thanks, he was S.
Jn. 8 : 48. thou a S. and hast a devil
SAMAR'ITANS.
2 K. 17 : 29. high places S. had made
Mat. 10 : 5. into city of S. enter not
Lu. 9 : 52. entered into village of S.
Jn. 4 : 9. Jews no dealings with S.
39. many of S. of city believed
40. the S. besought him to tarry
Ac. 8 : 25. preached in villages of S.

SAME.

Ge. 2 : 13. **s.** that compasseth Ethio.
5 : 29. **s.** shall comfort us conc-g
6 : 4. **s.** became mighty men ⌊work
10 : 12. Rezem, the **s.** is great city
14 : 8. king of Bela (the **s.** is Zoar)
19 : 37. **s.** is father of Moabites
38. **s.** is father of chil. of Ammon
23 : 2. Kirjath-arba; **s.** is Heb. 19.
24 : 14. **s.** be she thou appointed, 44
Ge. 25 : 30. F-d me with the **s.** pottage
26 : 24. appeared unto Isaac **s.** night
32 : 13. Jacob lodged there **s.** night
41 : 48. food laid he up in the **s.**
44 : 6. overseer spake **s.** words
48 : 7. of Ephrath, **s.** is Bethlehem
Ex. 12 : 6. fourteenth day of **s.** mon.
25 : 31. flowers be of **s.**, 37 : 17.
35. sh. be a knop und. two branches of the **s.**, (3) 36.-37 : 21, 22.
27 : 2. his horns shall be of **s.** 30 : 2.-37 : 25.-38 : 2. ⌈39 : 5.
28 : 8. curious girdle shall be of **s.**,
Le. 23 : 6. fifteenth day of **s.** month
Nu. 9 : 13. **s.** soul shall be cut off
10 : 32. **s.** goodness will we do thee
15 : 30. **s.** reproacheth the Lord
Jos. 11 : 16. mt. of Is. valley of the **s.**
15 : 8. Jebusite, **s.** is Jerusalem
Ju. 7 : 4. **s.** shall go, **s.** shall not go
1 S. 9 : 17. **s.** sh. reign over my peo.
14 : 35. **s.** was first altar built
17 : 23. Goliath spake the **s.** words
2 S. 2 : 23. Asahel died in **s.** place
5 : 7. Zion the **s.** in city of David
23 : 8. **s.** was Adino the Eznite
1 K. 7:35. borders th-f were of the **s.**
13 : 9. nor turn again by **s.** way
2 K. 19: 29. springeth of **s.**, Is. 37:30.
33. by **s.** way return, Is. 37 : 34.
1 Ch. 1 : 27. Abram, the **s.** is Abra-
4 : 33. villages about **s.** cities ⌊ham
16 : 17. confirmed **s.** unto Jacob, Ps. 105 : 10. ⌈than
17 : 3. **s.** night word came to Na-
2 Ch. 13 : 9. **s.** may be a priest of
18 : 7. **s.** is Micaiah son of Imla
20 : 26. **s.** pl was called The valley
32 : 12. hath not **s.** Hez, taken, 30.
34 : 28. bring upon inhabi-ts of **s.**
Ezr. 4 : 15. moved sedition within **s.**
5 : 16. Then came **s.** Sheshbazzar
10 : 23. Kelaiah, **s.** is Kelita
Ne. 10 : 37. **s.** Levites have tithes
Es. 9 : 1. Adar on 13th day of **s.**
17. on day of **s.** rested, 18, 21.
Jb. 4 : 8. that sow wick-ness reap **s.**
13 : 2. What ye know **s.** do I know
Ps. 68 : 23. tongue of thy dogs in **s.**
75 : 8. mixture he poureth out **s.**
102:27. art the **s.** thy yrs., He 1:12.
113 : 3. go. down of the **s.**, Mal. 1 : 11.
Pr. 28 : 24. **s.** is comp-n of destroy-r
Ec. 9:15. no man rememb-d **s.** poor
Je. 27:8. wh. will not serve **s.** Nebuc.
Eze. 3 : 18. **s.** wicked man shall die
10:16. the **s.** wheels also turned not
22. **s.** faces I saw by river Chebar
21 : 26. this sh. not be the **s.** exalt
44 : 3. prince shall go by way of **s.**
Da. 5 : 12. dissolving of doubts in **s.**
7 : 21. **s.** horn made war ⌊Dan.
Am. 2 : 7. man and father to **s.** maid
Mat. 3 : 4. **s.** John had his raiment
5 : 19. **s.** shall be called great in
46. do not publicans the **s.** ⌈8:35.
12 : 50. **s.** is my bro. and sister, Mk.
13 : 20. **s.** is he that heareth word
15:22. woman came out of **s.** coasts
18:4. **s.** is greatest in kingd. of heav.
28. **s.** servant went and found
21 : 42. **s.** is become head of the cor- ner, Lu. 20 : 17. 1 Pe. 2 : 7. ⌊13.
24:13. endure **s.** sh. be saved, Mk. 13:
25 : 16. went and traded with the **s.**
26 : 23. dippeth hand **s.** sh. betray
48. **s.** is he, hold him, Mk. 14 : 44.
27 : 44. thieves cast **s.** in his teeth
Mk. 8 :35. lose life **s.** save it, Lu. 9:24.
9 : 35. first, **s.** sh. be last of all
10 : 10. disciples asked of **s.** matter
Lu. 2 : 8. were in **s.** country shep-rds
25. **s.** man was just and devout
6 : 33. sinners also do even the **s.**
38. with **s.** measure th. ye mete
7:47. little forgiven, **s.** loveth little
9 : 48. least am. you, **s.** sh. be great

Lu. 10:7. in s. house remain; eating
10. go into streets of s. and say
16:1. s. was accused th. he wasted
20:47. s. shall rec greater damna.
23:40. thou art in s. condemnation
51. s. not consented to counsel
Jn. 1:2. The s. was in beginning
7. the s. came for a witness [Gh.
33. s. is he wh. baptizeth with H.
3:2. The s. came to Jesus by night
26. s. baptizeth and all come
5:11. the s. said unto me, Take bed
7:18. that sent him, the s. is true
8:25. s. I s-d unto you fr. beginn-g
10:1. other way, s. is a thief
12:21. The s. came thf. to Philip
48. s. sh. judge him in last day
15:5. in me, s. bringeth much fruit
Ac. 1:11. this s. Jesus shall so come
2:36. G. made s. Jesus both L. and
7:19. s. dealt subtilly with kind-d
35. s. did God send to be ruler
8:35. began at the s. Scripture and
12:6. the s. night Peter was sleep.
13:33. G. hath fulfilled s. unto us
14:9. The s. heard Paul speak
15:27. tell you s. things by month
16:17. s. followed Paul and us
18:3. bec. he was of the s. craft
21:9. the s. man had 4 daughters
24:20. let these s. say if they found
28:7. In s. quarters were posses-ns
Ro. 1:32. knowing not only do the s.
2:1. that judgest doest s. things, 3.
8:20. hath subjected s. in hope
9:17. Even for this s. purpose I
21. of same lump to make one ves.
10:12. s. L. over all is rich unto all
12:4. all members not s. office [s.
13:3. thou shalt have praise of the
1 Co. 1:10. sp-k s. thing in s. judg-t
7:20. Let ev. man abide in s. call-g
8:3. love God s. is known of him
9:8. saith not the law the s. also?
10:3. s. spirit-l meat | 4. s. drink
11:23. s. night in wh. he was betr.
12:4. but the s. spirit, 8, 9. 2 Cor.
4:13.-12:18. [s. God
5. but the s. Lord | 6. but it is the
25. members sho. have the s. care
15:39. All flesh is not the s. flesh
2 Co. 2:2. s. wh. is made sorry by me
3. I wrote this s. unto you, lest
3:14. remaineth s. vail, untaken
18. we are changed into s. image
6:13. Now for a recomp-e in the s.
7:8. s. epistle hath made you sorry
8:6. also finish in you s. grace
16. put s. care into heart of Titus
19. administered to glory of s. L.
9:4. we be ashamed in s. boasting
5. s. might be ready as bounty
Ga. 2:8. the s. was mighty in me
10. the s. wh. I was forward to do
3:7. s. are children of Abraham
Ep. 3:6. of s. body and partakers
4:10. He is the s. that ascended
6:8. the s. shall he receive of the L.
9. ye masters do the s. things
Ph. 1:30. having s. conflict ye saw
2:2. having s. love, being of one
18. For the s. cause do ye joy
3:1. To write the s. things to you
16. walk by s. rule, mind s. thing
Col. 4:2. watch in s. with thanksg.
2 Ti. 2:2. s. commit to faithful men
He. 2:14. he also took part of the s.
4:11. lest any fall aft. s. example
6:11. ev. one shew s. diligence
10:11. priest offer-g the s. sacrifices
11:9. heirs with him of s. promise
13:8. Jes. Ch. s. yesterday, to day
Ja. 3:2. if offend not, s. is perfect
10. out of s. mouth proceedeth
1 Pe. 4:4. th. ye run not to s. excess
10. so minister s. one to another
5:9. s. afflictions are accomplished
2 Pe. 2:19. of the s. is he in bondage
3:7. by s. word are kept in store
1 Jn. 2:23. denieth the Son, s. hath
27. s. anointing teacheth [not Fa.
Re. 3:5. s. shall be clothed in white
14:10. s. shall drink wine of wrath
See Same DAY, Same HOUR.
See MANNER, MIND, PLACE, PURPOSE, SELFSAME, TIME, WAY, YEAR.

SAM'GAR-NE'BO.

Je. 39:3. princes sat in gate, even S.

SAM'LAH.

Ge. 36:36. S. reigned, 1 Ch. 1:47.
37. S. died, Saul reigned, 1 Ch 1:48.

SA'MOS.

Ac. 20:15. next day we arrived at S.

SAMOTHRA'CIA.

Ac. 16:11. came with straight course [to S.

SAM'SON.

Ju. 13:24. wom. called his name S.
14:1. S. went down to Timnath
3. S. said, Get her for me to wife
7. the woman pleased S. well
10. and S. made there a feast
12. S. said, I will put riddle
15. unto S.'s wife, Entice thy hus-
16. S.'s wife wept before him [band
20. S.'s wife was giv. to compau-n
15:1. S. visited his wife with kid
3. S. said, I sh. be blameless | 6, 7.
4. S. caught 300 foxes and took
10. To bind S. are we come | 11.
12. S. said, Swear unto me that
16. S. said, With jawbone of ass
16:1. Then went S. to Gaza and saw
2. was told Gazites S. is come bith.
3. S. at midn-t took doors of gate
6. Delilah said to S., Tell me
7. S. said, If they bind me [14, 20.
9. she said, Philis. upon thee, S., 12,
10. Delilah unto S., thou told lies,
23. G. hath deliv-d S. into our [13.
25. Call S. that he make sport
26. S. said unto lad, Suffer me | 27.
28. S. called, O L. G., remem. me
29. S. took hold of two pillars
30. S. said, Let me die with Philis.
He. 11:32. time fail me to tell of S.

SAM'UEL. [him S.

1 S. 1:20. Hannah bare son, called
2:18. S. ministered before L., 3:1.
21. S. grew bef. Lord, 3:19 | 3:3.
3:4. Lord called S., 6, 7, 8, 9, 10 | 11.
15. S. feared to show Eli vision
16. Eli called S., S., my son | 18.
20. S. was estab-d to be prophet
21. L. revealed to S. in Shiloh
4:1. word of S. to all Israel, 7:3.
7:5. S. said, Gather Isr. to Mizpeh
6. S. judged chil. of Isr., 15 | 8.
9. S. cried unto Lord for Isr., 10.
12. S. set stone bet-n Mizpeh and
13. L. was ag. Philis. all days of S.
8:1. S., old, made his sons judges
6. displ-d S. said, Give us a k. [| 4.
7. L. unto S., Hearken unto peo.,
10. S. told words of L. unto peo. [22.
19. peo. refused to obey S. | 21, 22.
9:14. S. came out ag. them to go
15. L. told S. bef. Saul came | 17, 18.
19. S. answered Saul, I am seer
22. S. took Saul and his serv-t | 23.
24. Saul did eat wi. S. that day
26. S. called S. to top of ho., 25.
27. S. said, Bid serv. pass out [14.
10:1. S. took oil, anointed Saul | 9,
15. Tell me what S. s-d | 16, 20, 24.
25. S. told manner of kingdom
11:7. Whoso-r cometh not aft. S.
12. peo. said unto S., 12:19.
14. S. said to people, 12:6, 20.
12:11. L. sent S. and delivered you
18. people greatly feared L. and S.
13:8. tarried time S. app-ted | 10.
11. S. said, What hast done | 13.
15. S. arose, gat fr. Gilgal [foolishly
1 S. 15:1. S. said unto S., 14, 16, 17,
10. word of L. unto S. [22, 26, 28.
11. it grieved S., he cried unto L.
12. S. rose early to meet Saul (2)
20. Saul s-d unto S., I obeyed, 24.
27. as S. turned, Saul laid hold
31. So S. turned again after Saul
33. S. hewed Agag in pieces | 32.
34. S. went to Ramah; Saul went
35. neverth. S. m-rned for Saul (2)
16:1. L. unto S., How long mourn
2. S. said, How can I go? If Saul
4. S. did that which Lord spake
7. L. said unto S., Look not on his
8. Abinadab pass bef. S. [counten.
10. Jesse made sons pass before S.
13. S. took oil and anointed David
19:18. David fled to S. to Ramah
20. saw S. standing as appointed
22. he said, Where are S. and Dav.
24. Saul prophesied before S.
25:1. S. died; all Isr. lamented, 28:3.
28:11. Saul said, Bring me up S.,
14. Saul perceived th. it was S. [12.
15. S. said, Why hast disquieted
16. said S., Whf. dost ask? [me?
20. Saul afraid bec. of words of S.
1 Ch. 6:28. sons of S.; Vashni, Abi.
9:22. whom S. the seer did ordain
11:3. acc. to word of Lord by S.
26:28. all that S. the seer dedicated
2 Ch. 35:18. no passo. like th. fr. S.
Ps. 99:6. S. among them that call
Je. 15:1. Tho. Moses and S. stood
Ac. 3:24. prophets from S. foretold
13:20. gave judges 450 yrs. till S.
He. 11:32. time wo. fail to tell of S.

SANBAL'LAT. [him, 19.

Ne. 2:10. S. heard of it it grieved
4:1. S. heard he was wroth, 7.-6:1.
6:2. S. sent unto me, say-g, Come,
12. Tobiah and S. had hired him [5.
14. My G., think upon S. acc. to
13:28. son of Joiada son in l. to S.

SANCTIFICATION. [s.

1 Co. 1:30. Ch. who is made unto us
1 Th. 4:3. this is will of God, y-r s.
4. to possess his vessel in s. [1:2.
2 Th. 2:13. thro. s. of spirit, 1 Pe.

SANCTIFIED. [it

Ge. 2:3. God blessed 7th day, and s.
Ex. 19:14. Moses s. the people
29:43. the tabernacle shall be s.
Le. 8:10. s. the tabernacle, and all
15. s. the altar | 30. s. Aaron
10:3. I will be s. in them nigh me
27:15. if he that s. it will redeem
19. if he that s. field redeem
Nu. 7:1. s. tabernacle, instruments
8:17. I s. the firstborn of Israel
De. 32:51. bec. ye s. me not in Isr.
Jos. 20:† 7. they s. cities of refuge
1 S. 7:1. s. Eleazar to keep ark
16:5. he s. Jesse and his sons to
21:5. though it were s. this day
1 Ch. 15:14. priests, Levites, s. thems.
2 Ch. 5:11. all priests pres-t were s.
7:16. I have s. this house, 20.
29:15. gathered brethren, s. thems.
17. s. house of L. in eight days
19. all the vessels have we s.
34. other priests had s. thems.
30:3. the priests had not s. thems.
8. enter sanct-y which he hath s.
15. Levites ashamed, s. thems.
17. many in congregation not s.
24. a gr. numb. of priests s. thems.
31:18. in set office they s. thems.
Ne. 3:1. built and s. sheep gate
12:47. s. holy things unto Levites
Levites s. them unto chil. of
Jb. 1:5. Job s. his sons and dau-s
Is. 5:16. God be s. in righteousn-s
13:3. I have commanded my s. ones
Je. 1:5. I s. and ordained thee
Eze. 20:41. I will be s. in you, 36:23.
28:22. when I shall be s. in her

Eze.28:25.be s. in si-t of hea-n,39:27.
38 : 16. when I shall be s. in thee
48 : 11. sh. be for priests th. are s.
Zph. 1 : † 7. Lord hath s. his guests
Jn. 10 : 36. Say of him whom Fa. s.
17 : 19. might be s. thro. the truth
Ac. 20 : 32. inheritance am. them s.
Ro. 15 : 16. s. by Holy Ghost ⌊26:18.
1 Co. 1 : 2. them th. are s. in Christ
6: 11. ye are s. in name of the Lord
7 : 14. unbelieving husb. is s., wife
1 Ti. 4 : 5. it is s. by word of G. ⌊is s.
2 Ti. 2 : 21. vessel s. for Master's use
He. 2 : 11. who are s. are all of one
10 : 10. By the which will we are s.
14. hath perfected them th. are s.
29. blood wherewith he was s.
Jude 1. to them that are s. by God

SANCTIFIETH. ⌈gold?
Mat. 23 : 17. or temple that s. the
19. greater the gift, or altar th. s.
He. 2 : 11. both he that s. and they
9: 13. if blood of bulls s. to purify-g

SANCTIFY.
Ex. 13 : 2. s. unto me all firstborn
19:10. s. them to day and to mor-w
22. let the priests s. themselves
23. Set bounds about mt. s. it
28 : 41. thou shalt anoint and s.
Aaron and his sons, 29 : 33, 44.-
40 : 13. Le. 8 : 12.-21 : 8.
29 : 27. shalt s. breast of wave off-g
36. shalt s. the altar, 37.-40 : 10.
44. I will s. tabern. and altar
30:29. thou shalt s. tabernacle and
vessels, 40 : 10, 11. Le. 8 : 11.
31 : 13. I am the Lord that doth s.
you, Le. 20:8.-21:8. Eze. 20:12.
Le. 11 : 44. ye shall s. yours., 20 : 7.
Nu. 11 : 18. Jos. 3 : 5.-7 : 13.
21 : 15. I Lord do s. him ⌊1 S. 16:5.
23. I the L. do s. them, 22 : 9, 16.
27 : 14. when man sh. s. his house
16. if a man s. his field, 17, 18, 22.
26. firstl-g, no man sh. s. it⌈27:14.
Nu. 20 : 12. ye bel-d me not, to s. me,
De. 5 : 12. Keep sab.day to s. it, Ne.
15:19. All firstl-g males sh.s.⌊13:22.
Jos. 7 : 13. Up, s. people, s. yours.
2 K. 10 : † 20. s. an assemb. for Baal
1 Ch. 15 : 12. s. yours., 2 Ch. 29 : 5.-
23:13. he sho. s. holy things ⌊35:6.
2 Ch. 29 : 17. began on first day to s.
34. Levites upright in heart, to s.
30 : 17. for ev. one not clean to s.
Ne. 13 : 22. keep gates to s. sabbath
Is. 8 : 13. s. the L. of hosts himself
29 : 23. shall s. Holy One of Jacob
66:17. th. s. themselves in gardens
Eze. 36 : 23. I will s. my great name
37 : 28. heathen know I do s. Israel
38 : 23. thus will I s. myself⌈46:20.
44 : 19. not s. peo. with garments,
Jo. 1 : 14. s. ye a fast, call a, 2 : 15.
2 : 16. s. the congr., assemble⌈men
3 : † 9. s. war, wake up the mighty
Jn. 17 : 17. s. them thro. thy truth
19. for their sakes I s. myself
Ep. 5 : 26. might s. and cleanse ch.
1 Th. 5:23. very God of peace s. you
He. 13 : 12. might s. peo. wi. his bl.
1 Pe. 3 : 15. s. the Lord in y-r hearts

SANCTUARY, IES.
Ex. 15:17. shall plant them in the s.
25 : 8. make me s. that I may dwell
30 : 13. give ev. one aft. shekel of s.
24. 500 shekels aft. shekel of s.
36:1. all manner of work for s. 3, 4.
6. not more work for offering of s.
38 : 24. shekels, after the shekel of
the s. 25, 26. Le. 5 : 15.-27 : 3,
25. Nu. 3 : 47, 50.-7 : 13, 19, 25,
31, 37, 43, 49, 55, 61, 67, 73, 79,
85, 86.-18 : 16.
27. were cast the sockets of the s.
Le. 4 : 6. sprinkle bl. bef. vail of s.
10 : 4. carry brethren from bef. s.
Le. 12 : 4. nor into s. un. her purify-g
16 : 33. sh. make atonement for s.
19 :30. ye sh. reverence my s.,26:2.
21 : 12. Neither sh. he go out of s.,
nor profane s. of his God
23. that he profane not my s-s
26:31. I will bring your s-s to desola.
Nu. 3: 28. keep-g charge of s. 31, 32.
38. Aaron keeping charge of s.
4 : 12. whw. they minister in s.
15. made an end of cov-g the s.
16. all in the s. and ves. th-f.
7 : 9. service of s. belonging unto
8 : 19. when Isr. come nigh unto s.
10 : 21. Kohathites bearing the s.
18 : 1. with thee sh. bear iniq. of s.
3. not come nigh vessels of s.
5. ye shall keep charge of the s.
19 : 20. because he hath defiled s.
Jos. 24 : 26. set up great stone by s.
1 Ch. 9 : 29. oversee instrum-ts of s.
22 : 19. arise, and build ye the s. of
24 : 5. divided, for governors of s.
28 : 10. chosen to build ho for s.
2 Ch 20 : 8. they have built thee a s.
26:18. go out of s., thou hast tresp.
29 : 21. for a sin offering for the s.
30 : 8. yield unto Lord, enter his s.
19. acc. to purification of the s.
36 : 17. king of Bab. slew men in s.
Ne. 10 : 39. where are vessels of s.
Ps. 20 : 2. Lord send thee help fr. s.
28 : † 2. tow. oracle of thy holy s.
29 : † 2. worship L. in his s. 96: † 9.
63 : 2. as I have seen thee in s.
68 : 24. have seen thy goings in s.
73 : 17. Until I went into s. of God
74 : 3. enemy done wickedly in s.
7. They have cast fire into thy s.
77 : 13. Thy way, O God, is in the s.
78:54. he bro-t th. to the border of s.
69. built his s. like high palaces
96 : 6. strength and beauty in his s.
102:19. looked from height of his s.
114 : 2. Judah was his s. Israel his
134 : 2. Lift up your hands in the s.
150:1. Praise the L., praise God in s.
Is. 8 : 14. L. of hosts, sh. be for a s.
16 : 12. shall come to his s. to pray
43 : 28. I profaned princes of s.
60 : 13. to beautify place of my s.
63: 18. our adversa-s trodden thy s.
Je. 17 : 12. from beginning is our s.
51 : 51. strangers are come into s-s
La. 1: 10. the heathen entered her s.
2 : 7. Lord hath abhorred his s.
20. sh. the prophet be slain in s.?
4 : 1. stones of s. are poured out
Eze. 5 : 11. bec. hast defiled my s.
11 : 16. will I be to th. as a little s.
23 : 38. defiled my s. same day
39. same day into s. to profane
28 : 18. hast defiled s-s by iniqui-s
41 : 21. face of the s. was squared
23. temple and s. had two doors
42 : 20. betw. s. and profane place
43 : 21. appointed place without s.
44 : 1. way of gate of outward s.
5. with every going forth of s.
27. in day that he goeth into s.
45 : 2. Of this shall be for the s.
3. in it sh. be s. and ho. place ⌈(2)
4. for houses and place for the s.
18. take young bullock cleanse s.
47 : 12. bec. waters issued out of s.
48 : 8. s. be in midst of it, 10, 21.
Da. 8 : 11. place of s. was cast down
13. s. to be trodden under foot
14. then shall the s. be cleansed
9 : 17. cause thy face to shine upon
26. peo. shall destroy the s. ⌊s.
11 : 31. shall pollute s. of strength
Am. 7:9. s-s of Isr. sh. be laid waste
† 13. Beth-el is the king's s. and
Zph. 3 : 4. priests have polluted s.
He.8:2. A minister of s. and taberu.
9 : 1. first covenant had worldly s.
He. 9 : 2. taberu. wh. is called the s.
13 : 11. whose blood is bro-t into s.

SAND.
Ex. 2 : 12. he hid Egyptian in s.
De. 33 : 19. suck treasures hid in s.
Jb. 29 : 18. sh. mult-y my days as s.
Ps. 139 : 18. more in numb. than s.
Pr. 27 : 3. stone is heavy, s. weighty
Is. 48 : 19. thy seed had been as s.
Ha. 1 : 9. sh. gather the capt-y as s.
Mat. 7:26. man who built ho. upon

SAND with sea. ⌊s.
Ge. 22 : 17. thy seed as s. upon s.
shore, 32 : 12. ⌈of s.
41 : 49. Joseph gathered corn as s.
Jos. 11 : 4. host as s. upon s. shore
Ju. 7 : 12. camels as s. by the s.⌈sh.
1 S. 13 : 5. Philis. gath-d as s. on s.
2 S. 17 : 11. Isr. be gath-d as s. by s.
1 K. 4 : 20. Jud and Isr. as s. by s.
29. largeness of heart as s. on s.
Jb. 6 : 3. heavier than s. of s.⌊shore
Ps. 78 : 27. feathered fowls as s. of s.
Is. 10 : 22. tho. my peo. be as s. of s.
Je. 5 : 22. placed s. for bound of s.
15 : 8. widows incr-d. above s. of s.
33 : 22. s. of s. cannot be measured
Ho.1:10. Isr. be as s. of s.,Ro. 9 : 27.
He. 11 : 12. sprang of one many as
Re. 13: 1. I stood upon s. of s.⌊s.of s.
20:8. number of whom is as s. of s.

SANDALS.
Mk. 6 : 9. But be shod with s., put
Ac. 12 : 8. Gird thys. and bind thy s.

SANG.
Ex. 15 : 1. Then s. Moses this song
Nu. 21 : 17. Isr. s. this song, Spring
Ju. 5 : 1. then s. Deb-h and Barak
1 S. 29: 5. this David of wh. they s.?
2 Ch. 29 : 28. singers s. the trumpet.
30. s. praises with gladness, and
Ezr. 3: 11. they s. together by course
Ne. 12:42. the singers s. aloud, with
Jb. 38 : 7. morning stars s. together
Ps. 106 : 12. they believed, s. praise
Ac. 16 : 25. Paul and Silas s. praises

SANK.
Ex. 15:5. they s. into bot-m as stone
10. they s. as lead in mighty wat.

SANSAN'NAH.
Jos. 15:31. cities of chil. of Judah, S.

SAP.
Ps. 104 : 16. trees of L. are full of s.

SAPH=SIP'PAI.
2 S. 21 : 18. Sibbechai slew S., 1 Ch.

SAPH'IR. ⌊20 : 4.
Mi. 1 : 11. Pass away inhab-t of S.

SAPPHI'RA.
Ac. 5:1. Ananias with S sold poss-n

SAPPHIRE, S.
Ex. 24 : 10. paved work of s. stone
28 : 18. the second row a s. 39 : 11.
Jb. 28 : 6. stones of it are pla. of s-s
16. cannot be valued with s.
Can. 5 : 14. as ivory, overlaid wi s-s
Is. 54 : 11. lay thy founda-s with s-s
La. 4 : 7. their polishing was of s. ⌈s.
Eze. 1 : 26. throne, as appearance of
10 : 1. appear. ov. th. as it were a s.
28 : 13. s. and emerald thy cover-g
Re. 21 : 19. second founda. was s.

SA'RA, SA'RAH. ⌈name
Ge. 17 : 15. not Sarai, but S., her
19. S. shall bear a son, 18 : 10, 14.
21. Isaac, which S. shall bear ⌈S.
18 : 6. Ab. hastened into tent unto
9. said, Where is S. thy wife?⌈wom.
11. ceased with S., aft. man-r of
12. S. laughed | 13. whf. S. laugh
15. S. denied, I laughed not
20 : 2. Ab. said of S. she is my sister
14. Abim. restored Ab. S. his wife
16. unto S. said, I given thy bro.
18. L. closed all wombs bec. of S.
21 : 1. Lord did unto S. as spoken
2. S. bare Ab. son, 3.-24 : 36.
6. S. said, God made me to laugh

Ge.21:7. S. sho.have given chil.suck
9. S. saw son of Hagar mocking
12. In all S. said hearken unto
23:1. S. was 127 years old (2) [S.
2. S. died. Ab. came to mourn for
19. aft. this Ab. buried S. in cave
24:67. Isaac bro-t her into S.'s tent
25:10. was Ab. buried and S., 49:31.
12. son, Hagar S.'s handm-d bare
Is. 51:2. Look unto S. th. bare you
Ro. 4:19. nor deadness of S.'s womb
9:9. I will come, S. sh. have a son
He. 11:11. Thro. faith S-a rec-d str.
1 Pe. 3:6. as S-a obeyed Abraham

SA'RAH. See SERAH.

SA'RAI=SA'RAH.

Ge. 11:29. name of Ab.'s wife was S.
30. But S. was barren, 16:1.
31. Terah took S. his dau. in law
12:5. Ab. took S. his wife and all
11. unto S., I know thou art fair
17. Lord plagued Pha. bec. of S.
16:2. S. said, Behold the L. hath(2)
3. S. gave Hagar to Abraham
5. S. said, My wrong be upon thee
6. S. dealt hardly with Hagar
8. I flee fr. face of mistress S.
17:15. not call her name S. but
[Sarah

SA'RAPH.

1 Ch. 4:22. S. has dominion in Moab

SARDINE. [stone

Re. 4:3. was to look upon like s.

SAR'DIS.

Re. 1:11. write and send it unto S.
3:1. unto angel of ch. in S. write
4. a few names in S. not defiled

SAR'DITES. See SERED.

SARDIUS. [10.

Ex. 28:17. first row shall be a s..39:
Eze. 28:13. s. and diamond thy cov-g
Re. 21:20. sixth found-n of wall was
[s.

SARDONYX.

Re. 21:20. fifth founda. of wall a s.

SAREP'TA. [K.17:†9.

Lu. 4:26. unto S. a city of Sidon, 1

SAR'GON.

Is. 20:1. S. of Assyria sent him

SA'RID. [unto S.

Jos. 19:10. border of their inherit.
12. border turned fr. S. eastward

SA'RON.

Ac. 9:35. all that dwelt at S. saw him

SARSE'CHIM.

Je. 39:3. princes of king of Bab. S.

SA'RUCH. See RAGAU.

SAT.

Ge. 18:1. he s. in tent door in heat
19:1. Lot s. in gate of Sodom
31:34. Rachel had s. upon images
38:14. Tamar wi. vail s. in open pl.
43:33. they s. bef. him the firstb-n
48:2. Isr. strength-d hims. and s.
Ex. 12:29. firsth. of Pha. that s. on
16:3. when we s. by the flesh pots
17:12. a stone, and Moses s. ther-n
18:13. Moses s. to judge the people
Le. 15:6. he s. that hath the issue
22. any thing that she s. upon
Ju. 6:11. angel of L. s. under oak
13:9. angel unto wom. as she s. in
20:26. they wept and s. before L.
Ru. 2:14. Ruth s. beside the reapers
1 S. 1:9. Eli s. by post of temple
4:13. Eli s. upon seat by wayside
19:9. Saul, as he s. in his house
20:25. Saul k. s. upon his seat (2)
28:23. Saul rose, and s. upon bed
2 S. 7:1. Da. s. in his ho., 1 Ch. 17:1.
18. Da. s. before L., 2 Ch. 17:16.
18:24. Da. s. between gates, 19:8.
23:8. Tachmonite s. in seat, chief
1 K. 2:12. s. Sol. upon th-e, 1 Ch. 29:23.
19. Bath-sheba s. on his right hand
13:20. to pass as they s. at table
16:11. soon as Zimri s. on his thr-e
21:13. came in two men s. bef. Nab.
22:10. k. of Isr. k. of Jud. s. on th-e
2 K. 1:9. Elijah s. on top of hill
4:20. s. on her knees till noon
6:32. Elish. s. in his house and (2)
11:19. Jehoiada s. on thr-e of k-s
13:13. Jeroboam s. upon his thr-e
Ezr. 9:4. I s. astonied until even.
10:9. all the people s. in street
Ne. 8:17. they made booths, and s.
Es. 1:2. Ahasuerus s. upon throne
14. wh. s. first in the kingdom
2:19. Mordecai s. in k.'s gate, 21.
5:1. king s. upon throne [chief
Jb. 29:25. I chose their way, and s.
Ps. 26:4. I not s. wi. vain persons
Je. 3:2. in ways hast s. for them
15:17. I s. not in assem-y of mock-s
I s. alone bec. of thy hand
32:12. Jews that s. in the court
36:12. lo, all the princes s. there
22. Now king s. in winter house
39:3. princes s. in middle gate
Eze. 3:15. I saw where they s. and
8:1. I s. in my house, elders s.
14. s. women weeping for Tammuz
20:1. the elders s. bef. me, 14:1.
Da. 2:49. Daniel s. in gate of king
Jon. 3:6. sackcloth, and s. in ashes
4:5. made booth and s. und. it (2)
Mat 4:16. peo. who s. in darkness
saw light; to them wh. s. in sh.
9:10. s. at meat, 26:7. Mk. 2:15.
14:3, 18.-16:14. Lu. 5:29.-7:
36, 37, 49.-14:10, 15.-24:30.
Jn. 12:2. [side
13:1. went Jesus and s. by sea
2. Jesus into ship and s., Mk. 4:1.
14:9. wh. s. with him, Mk. 6:22, 26.
24:3. he s. upon mount, Mk. 13:3.
26:55. I s. daily wi. you, teaching
58. Peter s. wi. serv-s, Mk. 14:54.
69. Peter s. without in palace
28:2. stone fr. door and s. upon it
Mk. 3:32. mult. s. about him, 34.
6:22. pleased Herod, and them that
s., 26. [Jn. 9:8.
10:46. Bartimeus s., Lu. 18:35.
11:2. colt never man s., Lu. 19:30.
7. colt to Jesus, he s. upon, Jn. 12:
12:41. Jes. s. over ag. treasury [14.
14:18. as t-y s., Jes. s-d, One of you
54. Peter s. wi. serv-s and warmed
16:19. he s. on right hand of God
Lu. 7:15. he that was dead s. up
10:39. Mary s. at Jesus' feet, Jn.
22:56. maid beheld as he s. [11:20.
Jn. 4:6. Jesus, wearied, s. on well
6:3. into mt. and s. wi. his discip.
Ac. 2:3. cloven tongues s. upon ea.
3:10. he who s. for alms at gate
6:15. all s. in council saw his face
9:40. when she saw Pe. she s. up
12:21. Herod s. upon his throne
14:8. s. a certain man at Lystra
18:†11. he s. there year and 6 m-s
20:9. s. in window a young man
25:17. I s. on judgment seat
26:30. king rose up and they that s.
Re. 4:2. one s. on the throne, 9, 10.
-5:1, 7.-19:4.-20:11.-21:5.
6:2. he that s. on him had bow
4. power given him th. s. thereon
5. s. on him had pair of balances
8. name that s. on him was death
9:17. horses and they that s. on
11:16. elders wh. s. bef. G. [them
14:14. one s. like unto Son of man
15. cry-g to him th. s. on cl-d, 16.
19:11. s. upon him, called Faithf.
19. ag. him that s. upon horse, 21.
20:4. thrones and they th. s. upon

SAT down. [him

Ge. 21:16. Hagar s. her d. over ag.
37:25. And they s.d. to eat bread
Ex. 2:15. Moses s.d. by a well
32:6. people s.d. to eat and drink
De. 33:3. they s.d. at thy feet
Ju. 19:6. they s.d., did eat and
Ju. 19:15. Levite s.d. in str-t of city
Ru. 4:1. Boaz s. himself d. by gate
2. Sit ye down, and they s.d.
1 S. 20:24. David s.d. to eat
2 S. 2:13. they s.d. one on one side
1 K. 2:19. Sol. vowed, s.d. on thr-e
19:4. Elijah s.d. und. Juniper tree
Ezr. 9:3. heard this, I s.d. aston-d
10:16. they s.d. to examine mat-r
Ne. 1:4. I s.d. and mourned [drink
Es. 3:15. king and Haman s.d. to
Jb. 2:8. Job s.d. among the ashes
13. friends s.d. wi. him upon gro.
Ps. 137:1. there we s.d., we wept
Can. 2:3. I s.d. under his shadow
Je. 26:10. princes s.d. in entry of g-e
Mat. 9:10. many sin-s s.d. wi. him
13:48. drew to shore and s.d.
15:29. Jes. into mountain, and s.d.
26:20. s. d. wi. 12, Mk. 9:35. Lu. 22:
Mk. 6:40. s.d. in ranks by hund-s [14.
Lu. 4:20. book to minister and s.d.
5:3. s.d. and taught the people
29. others that s.d. with them
7:36. went in, s.d. to meat, 11:37.
22:55. Peter s.d. among them
Ju. 6:10. So the men s.d. ab. 5,000
8:2. peo. came he s.d. and tau-t
19:13. Pilate s.d. in judg-t seat
Ac. 13:14. Paul into synag. and s.d.
16:13. we s.d. spake unto women
1 Co. 10:7. people s.d. to eat [10:12.
He. 1:3. s.d. on right hand of God,

SA'TAN. [numb. Isr

1 Ch. 21:1. S. provoked David to
Jb. 1:6. S came also am. them, 2:1.
7. L. said unto S., 8.-2:2, 3, 6.
9. S. answered the Lord, 7.-2:2, 4.
12. S. went fr. presence of L., 2:7.
Ps. 109:6. let S. stand at right hand
Zch. 3:1. S. standing at his right ha.
2. The Lord rebuke thee, O S. (2)
Mat. 4:10. Jes. saith, Get thee h-e S.
12:26. if S. cast out S., Mk. 3:23,
26. Lu. 11:18. [8:33. Lu. 4:8.
16:23. Get thee behind me, S., Mk.
Mk. 1:13. was 40 days tempted of S.
4:15. S. taketh away the word
Lu. 10:18. beheld S. as lightn-g fall
13:16. whom S. hath bound 18 yrs.
22:3. entered S. into Judas Iscari.
31. Simon, S. desired to have you
Jn. 13:27. aft. sop, S. entered him
Ac. 5:3. why S. filled thine heart to
26:18. to turn fr. power of S. [lie?
Ro. 16:20. God shall bruise S. und.
1 Co. 5:5. To deliver such unto S.
7:5. S. tempt you not for incont-y
2 Co. 2:11. Lest S. get advantage
11:14. S. is transformed into angel
12:7. messenger of S. to buffet me
1 Th. 2:18. come, but S. hindered us
2 Th. 2:9. coming is aft. work-g of S.
1 Ti. 1:20. whom I deliv-d unto S.
5:15. some are alr-y turned aft. S.
Re. 2:9. not Jews, but synag. of S.
13. S.'s seat is, where S. dwelleth
24. have not known depths of S.
3:9. will make them of synag. of S.
12:9. dragon was cast out, called S.
20:2. laid hold on dragon, wh. is S.
7. S. shall be loosed out of prison

SATEST.

Ps. 9:4. s. in throne judging right
Eze. 23:41. thou s. upon stately bed

SATIATE, ED.

Je. 31:14. I will s. soul of the priests
25. I have s-d the weary soul
46:10. sword sh. be s-d wi. their bl.

SATISFACTION. [derer

Nu. 35:31. take no s. for life of mur-
32. take no s. for him fled for ref.

SATISFIED. [them

Ex. 15:9. my lust sh. be s. upon
Le. 26:26. ye sh. eat and not be s.
De. 14:29. fatherl-s sh. eat and be s.
33:23. O Naphtali, s. with favor

Jb.19:22. why not s. with my flesh?
27:14. offspring not be s. wi. br-d
31:31. of his flesh! we cannot be s.
Ps. 17:15. I sh. be s. when I awake
22:26. The meek sh. eat and be s.
36:8. They shall be s. with fatness
37:19. in days of famine shall be s.
59:15. let them grudge if not s.
63:5. My soul s. as with marrow
65:4. s. with goodness of thy ho.
81:16. wi. honey sho. I have s. thee
104:13. earth is s. with fruit of [en
105:40. s. them wi. bread of heav-
Pr. 12:11. that tilleth land sh. be s.
14. A man be s. wi. good by fruit
14:14. a good man be s. fr. hims.
18:20. A man's belly be s. wi. fruit
19:23. that hath it shall abide s.
20:13. open eyes, thou shalt be s.
27:20. the eyes of man are never s.
30:15. three things th. are never s.
Ec. 1:8. eye is not s. with seeing
4:8. nei. is his eye s. with riches
5:10. loveth silver, shall not be s.
Is. 9:20. eat and not be s., Mi. 6:14.
44:16. he roasteth roast and is s.
53:11. see of travail of soul, be s.
66:11. be s. wi. the breasts of her
Je. 31:14. peo. be s. with goodness
50:10. all that spoil Chaldea be s.
19. soul sh. be s. upon mt. Ephr.
La. 5:6. hand to Eg-ns to be s. [29.
Eze. 16:28. thou couldest not be s.
Jo. 2:19. wine, oil, and ye sh. be s.
26. sh. eat in plenty and be s. [s.
Am. 4:8. drink water, but were not
Ha. 2:5. he is as death, cannot be s.

SATISFIEST, ETH. [good

Ps. 103:5. Who s-h thy mouth wi.
107:9. For he s-h the longing soul
145:16. thou s-t desire of ev. thing
Is. 55:2. labor for that wh. s-h not

SATISFY.

Jb. 38:27. To s. the desolate ground
Ps. 90:14. O s. us early with mercy
91:16. With long life will I s. him
132:15. I will s. her poor with br-d
Pr. 5:19. let her breasts s. thee
6:30. if steal to s. soul when hungry
Is. 58:10. if thou s. afflicted soul
11. Lord sh. s. thy soul in drou-t
Eze. 7:19. they sh. not s. th-r souls
Mk. 8:4. whence can a man s. these

SATISFYING. [soul

Pr. 13:25. righteous eateth to s. of
Col. 2:23. not in honor to s. of flesh

SATYR, S. [there

Is. 13:21. owls shall dwell, s-s dance
34:14. s. shall cry to his fellow

SAUL = SHAUL. [1:48.

Ge. 36:37. S. of Reho. reigned, 1Ch.
38. S. died, 1 Ch. 1:49.

SAUL. [Son of Kish.]

1 S. 9:2. Kish a son, whose name
was S., 14:51. [27.
3. S. 5, 7, 8, 10, 19, 21, 22, 25, 26,
15. told Sam. day bef. S. came
17. Sam. saw S. | 18. S. drew near
24. set it bef. S. So S. did eat [19:24.
10:11. Is S. also am. prophets? 12.-
14. S. 15, 16, 26.-11:4, 5, 11, 13.
21. S. was taken | 11:12. Sh. S. r-n
11:6. Spirit of God came upon S.
7. Whoso. cometh not forth aft. S.
15. Gilgal, there they made S. k.
13:1. S. reigned one yr. and when
2. S. 4, 9, 11, 13.-14:2, 16, 17, 18,
19, 20, 33, 34, 36, 38, 40, 41, 42,
44, 45, 47.
3. S. blew trumpet thro. land
7. As for S., he was yet in Gilgal
10. S. went out to meet Samuel
15. S. numbered the peo. present
14:24. S. had adjured people [sel
35. S. built altar | 37. S. asked coun-
46. S. went up fr. following Philis.
50. S.'s wife was Ahinoam
1 S. 14:51. and Kish was the fa. of S.
52. when S. saw any strong man
15:1. Sam. to S., The L. hath sent
4. S. 5, 6, 7, 9, 12, 13, 15, 16, 20, 24,
26, 34.-16:15, 17, 19, 20, 21, 22.
15:11. repenteth me I have set up S.
31. Sam. turned again aft. S. (2)
35. Sam. came no more to see S.
16:1. How long wilt thou mourn for
2. If S. hear it he will kill me [S.?
14. Spirit of Lord departed fr. S.
23. evil spirit upon S., 18:10.-19:9.
17:2. S. and men of Isr. were gath.
8. I a Philis., you servants to S.?
11. S. 13, 14, 15, 31, 32, 33, 34, 37,
39, 55, 57, 58.
12. Jesse old man in days of S.
19. S. and all Isr. in valley of Elah
38. S. armed Da. with his armor
18:1. end of speaking unto S.
2. S. 5, 7, 8, 11, 13, 17, 18, 19, 20,
21, 22, 23, 24, 25, 27.
6. wom. dancing to meet king S.
9. S. eyed David from that day
12. S. afraid of David; L. fr. S. 29.
15. S. saw, he behaved wisely, 30.
28. S. knew Lord was with David
29. S. became David's enemy
19:2. S. my fa. seeketh to kill thee
10. S. sought to smite David, 18:11.
11. S. sent messengers to Da. 14, 15,
17. S. 18, 19, 21.-20:26.-21:7. [20.
20:25. Ab-r sat by S.'s side, and Da.
33. S. cast javelin at Da. to smite
21:10. David fled for fear of S.
11. S. hath slain his thou-s, 29:5.
22:6. S. 7, 9, 12, 13.-23:7, 8, 9, 10.
21. that S. had slain L.'s priests
22. I knew that he would tell S.
23:11. will S. come down? He will
12. S. 13, 15, 19, 21, 24, 25, 26, 27.
14. S. sought him every day
17. shall be king, that S. knoweth
28. S. returned fr. pursuing David
24:1. S. 2, 3, 5, 16.-25:44.-26:1,
2, 3, 6, 21, 25.-27:4.
4. David cut off skirt of S.'s robe
7. Da. suffered not to rise ag. S.
8. Da. cried aft. S. | 22. sware to S.
26:4. David unders-d S. was come
5. Da. beheld place where S. lay
7. S. lay sleeping within trench
12. Da. took cruse fr. S.'s bolster
17. S. knew David's voice, and s-d
25. S. s-d to Da., Bles-d be thou (2)
27:1. I shall perish by hand of S.
28:3. S. had put away the wizards
4. S. 5, 6, 7, 8, 13, 15, 21, 25.
9. thou knowest wh. S. hath done
10. S. sware to her by the Lord
12. Why deceived me? Thou art S.
14. S. perceived it was Samuel
20. S. fell straightway on the earth
29:3. Is not this David, serv. of S.
31:2. Philis. followed hard upon
S., slew Jona., 1 Ch. 10:2. [3.
3. battle went sore ag. S., 1 Ch. 10:
4. S. fell upon sword, 1 Ch. 10:4.
6. So S. died, his three sons, and
all his men, 5, 7, 8. 1 Ch. 10:5,
6, 7, 8. [10:11.
11. Philis. had done to S., 1 Ch.
12. men took body of S. 1 Ch. 10:12
2 S. 1:1. S. 2, 22.-2:4, 8, 10, 22.-3:
6, 7, 8, 13, 14.-4:1, 2, 8.-6:20,
23.-9:2, 6, 9.
6. S. leaned upon his spear, and lo
21. vilely cast away shield of S.
24. dau-s of Isr. weep over S. [S.
2:5. Blessed, ye shewed kindn-s to
7. be valiant, your master S. is
3:1. ho. of S. waxed weaker [dead
10. kingd. fr. ho. of S., 1 Ch. 12:23.
4:10. brought tidings, S. is dead
5:2. time, when S. was k., 1 Ch. 11:2.
6:16. Michal, S.'s dau., 1 Ch. 15:29.
7:15. not depart, as I took it fr. S.
2 S. 9:1. Is any left of ho. of S.? 3.
7. I will restore thee land of S.
12:7. thee out of hand of S., 22:1.
16:5. S. 19:17, 24.-21:2, 6, 7, 8,
11, 13.-22:1.
8. on thee blood of house of S.
21:1. It is for S. and his bloody ho.
4. have no silver nor gold of S.
1 Ch. 5:10. in days of S. made war
8:33. S. 9:39.-12:2, 19, 23, 29.
10:13. So S. died for his transgr-n
12:1. David kept close, bec. of S.
13:3. inquired not in days of S.
26:28. all Sam. and S. had dedic-d
Is. 10:29. Gibeah of S. is fled [Cis
Ac. 13:21. G. gave them S. son of

SAUL with Jonathan.

1 S. 13:16. S. and J. abode in Gibeah
14:41. perfect lot, S. and J. were
43. S. said to J., Tell me wh. [taken
49. sons of S. were J., Ishui
19:4. J. spake good of David unto S.
6. S. hearkened unto voice of J.
7. and J. brought David to S.
20:27. S. said to J., Whf. cometh
28. J. ans-d S., Da. asked leave, 32.
2 S. 1:12. they mourned for S. and J.
4:4. when tid-s came of S. and J. [17.
21:12. Da. took bones of S. and J.
1 Ch. 8:33. S. begat J. and, 9:39 [13, 14.
See JONATHAN.

SAUL = PAUL.

Ac. 7:58. at y-g man's feet name S.
8:1. S. consenting unto his death
3. S. he made havoc of church
9:1. S. breathing out threatenings
4. S. why perseo-t me? 22:7.-26:14.
11. inquire for one called S.
17. Brother S., L. sent me, 22:13.
22. S. increased more in strength
24. their laying wait known of S.
26. when S. was come to Jerus.
11:25. Barnabas went to seek S.
30. sent relief by the hands of S.
12:25. Barnabas and S. returned
13:1. prophets brought up with S.
2. Separate me Barnabas and S.
7. Paulus called for Barna. and S.
9. S. set his eyes on him, and said

SAVE. [Conj., Prep.]

Ge. 14:24. s. what young men eaten
39:6. he knew not aught s. bread
Ex. 12:16. s. that ev. man must eat
22:20. that sacrifi-h unto any God,
s. to L. [De. 1:36.
Nu. 14:30. s. Caleb, 26:65.-32:12.
De. 4:† 12. no similitude, s. a voice,
15:4. s. when there sh. be no poor
Jos. 11:13. Isr. burned none, s. Haz.
19. peace with Israel, s. Hivites
14:4. no part unto Levites, s. cities
Ju. 7:14. nothing s. sword of Gideon
1 S. 21:9. none other, s. that here
30:17. escaped none, s. 400 y-g men
22. s. to every man his wife
2 S. 12:3. nothing, s. one ewe lamb
22:32. who is God, s. the L., Ps. 18:31.
1 K. 3:18. no stranger s. we two [10.
8:9. noth. in ark s. 2 tables, 2 Ch. 5:
15:5. s. in matter of Uriah [18:30.
22:31. Fight not, s. with k., 1 Ch.
2 K. 4:2. not thing, s. pot of oil
15:4. s. th. high places not remov.
2 Ch. 2:6. s. only to burn sacrifice
21:17. no son left, s. Jehoahaz
23:6. none into ho. of L. s. priests
Ne. 2:12. nei. any s. beast I rode
Da. 6:7. s. of thee, O king, 12. [Son
Mat. 11:27. nei. know. any the Fa. s.
13:57. honour, s. in his own country
17:8. saw no man s. Jes., Mk. 9:8.
19:11. s. they to wh. it is given
Mk. 5:37. suffered no man to follow
s. Pe., Ja., Jn., Lu. 8:51.
6:5. s. th. he laid h-ds upon few sick
8. should take nothing, s. a staff
Lu. 4:26. sent, s. unto Sarepta

Lu. 17:18. none found, s. this stra-r
18:19. none good, s. one, th. is God
Jn. 6:22. was no other boat, s. that
46. seen Fa., s. he wh. is of God
13:10. needeth not, s. to wash feet
Ac. 20:23. s. that H. Gh. witness-h
21:25. s. to keep from fornication
1 Co. 2:2. not know any thi. s. Jes.
11. s. spirit of man, wh. is in him
2 Co. 11:24. receiv-d 1 40 stripes, s.
Ga. 1:19. I saw none, s. James⌊one
6:14. forbid I glory, s. in cross
Re. 13:17. s. he that had the mark

SAVE. [Verb.]

Ge. 45:7. G. sent me to s. y-r lives
De. 20:4. Lord goeth with you to s.
22:27. she cried, was none to s. her
28:29. spoiled, no man sh. s. thee
Ju. 6:14. Go in might, sh. s. Israel
15. O L., wh.w. sh. I s. Israel?
31. plead for Baal? will ye s. him?
36. If thou wilt s. Isr. by mine h-d
37. sh. I know thou wilt s. Israel
7:7. By 300 that lapped will I s.
10:†1. there arose to s. Isr. Tola
1 S. 9:16. anoint him, th. he s. peo.
10:24. people said, God s. the k., 2 S. 16:16. 2 K. 11:12. 2 Ch. 23:11.
14:6. no restraint to s. by many, or
19:11. If save not thys. this night
23:2. said to David, Go s. Keilah
2 S. 3:18. By David I will s. Israel
14:†4. she fell on face, said, s. O k.
22:28. peo. thou wilt s. Ps., 18:27.
42. was none to s. them, Ps. 18:41.
1 K. 1:12. mayest s. thine own life
25. they say, God s. k. Adonijah
34. say, God s. king Solomon, 39.
20:31. peradv. he will s. thy life
2 K. 6:†27. Let not the Lord s. thee
19:34. will def-d city to s., Is. 37:35.
Ne. 6:11. into temple to s. his life
Jb. 2:6. in thine hand, but s. his life
20:20. sh. not s. of that he desired
22:29. he sh. s. the humble person
40:14. that own hand can s. thee
Ps. 12:†1. s. L., for godly man ceas-
20:9. s. L., let the king hear us⌊eth
28:9. s. thy people, feed, Je. 31:7.
37:40. sh. s. th., bec. t-y trust him
44:3. neither did own arm s. them
60:5. s. with thy right hand, 108:6.
69:35. For God will s. Zion, and
72:4. he sh. s. children of needy
13. he shall s. the souls of needy
76:9. When God arose to s. meek
86:2. O my God, s. thy servant th.
16. s. the son of thine handmaid
109:31. s. him fr. those th. cond-n
118:25. s. I beseech thee, O Lord
145:19. will hear their cry, and s.
Pr. 20:22. wait on Lord, he shall s.
Is. 35:4. God will come and s. you
45:20. pray unto a god cannot s.
46:7. cannot s. him out of trouble
47:13. Let the astrologers s. thee
15. sh. wander, none shall s. thee
49:25. saith L., I will s. thy chil.
59:1. not shortened, th. it can-t s.
63:1. in righteousn. mighty to s.
Je. 2:28. let th. arise, if can s. thee
11:12. sh. not s. them in trouble
14:9. be as mighty man th. can-t s.
15:20. I am with thee to s. thee, saith the L., 30:11.-42:11.-46:27.
30:10. O Isr. I will s. thee fr. afar
48:6. Flee, s. your lives, be like
Eze. 3:18. warn wicked to s. his life
13:19. to s. souls th. sho. not live
†22. not return, th. I sho. s. his life
34:22. Thf. will s. my flock ⌈them
36:29. I will s. you | 37:23. will s.
Ho. 1:7. I will s. them by the Lord, and will not s. them by bow
13:10. where is any th. may s. thee
Ha. 1:2. cry of violence, thou not s.
Zph. 3:17. he will s., rejoice ov. thee
Zph. 3:19. I will s. her th. halt-h, and
Zch. 8:7. I will s. my people fr. east
13. will I s. you, ye sh. be bless-g
9:16. Lord their G. sh. s. them
10:6. I will s. the house of Joseph
12:7. Lord shall s. tents of Judah
Mat. 1:21. Jesus shall s. his people
16:25. whosoever will s. his life, Mk. 8:35. Lu. 9:24.-17:33.
18:11. come to s. th. was lost, Lu. 19:10. ⌈Mk. 15:30.
27:40. destroyest temple, s. thys.,
42. hims. he cannot s., Mk. 15:31.
49. see whe. Elias come to s. him
Mk. 3:4. to s. life, or kill? Lu. 6:9.
Lu. 9:56. not come to destroy but s.
23:35. let him s. himself if be Ch.
37. s. thyself | 39. if Ch. s. thyself
Jn. 12:47. not to jud., but s. world
Ac. 2:40. s. yours. from generation
27:43. centur-n, willing to s. Paul
Ro. 11:14. if I might s. some, 1 Co.
1 Co. 1:21. by preach-g to s. th.⌊9:22.
7:16. shalt s. husb., shalt s. wife
1 Ti. 1:15. Christ came to s. sinners
4:16. in doing this shalt s. thyself
He. 5:7. unto him th. was able to s.
7:25. able to s. them to uttermost
Ja. 1:21. word, is able to s. souls
2:14. have not works, can faith s.
4:12. one lawgiver, who is ab. to s.
5:15. prayer of faith shall s. sick
20. shall s. a soul from death
Jude 23. others s. with fear, pulling
See ALIVE. ⌊them

SAVE me.

2 K. 16:7. s.m. out of hand of king
Ps. 3:7. Arise, O Lord, s.m. O God
6:4. s.m. for thy mercies' sake, 31:16.-109:26. ⌈cute
7:1. s.m. from all them th. perse-
22:21. s.m. from the lion's mouth
31:2. be house of defence to s.m.
44:6. nor shall my sword s.m.
54:1. s.m. O God, by thy name
55:16. will call upon G., L. sh. s.m.
57:3. sh. send from heaven s.m.
59:2. and s.m. from bloody men
69:1. s.m. for waters are come
71:2. incline thine ear and s.m.
3. given commandment to s.m.
119:94. s.m., I sou-t thy precepts
146. I cried unto thee, s.m., and
138:7. thy right hand shall s.m.
Is. 38:20. Lord was ready to s.m.
Je. 17:14. O L. s.m., I sh. be saved
Mat. 14:30. Peter cried, Lord, s.m.
Jn. 12:27. Father s.m. fr. this hour

SAVE us.

Jos. 10:6. come quickly and s.u.
22:22. rebellion (s.u. not th. day)
1 S. 4:3. ark may s.u. fr. enemies
7:8. cry to the Lord, that he s.u.
10:27. said, How shall this man s.
11:3. if no man to s.u. we will⌊u.?
2 K. 19:19. s. thou u., Is. 37:20.
1 Ch. 16:35. s.u. O G. of our salva.
Ps. 80:2. stir up thy strength, s.u.
106:47. s.u., O Lord our God
Is. 25:9. we ha. waited, he will s.u.
33:22. Lord is our king, will s.u.
Je. 2:27. in trouble will say, s.u.
La. 4:17. nation th. could not s.u.
Ho. 14:3. Ashur shall not s.u. ⌈u.
Mat. 8:25. awoke him, saying, L. s.
1 Pe. 3:21. baptism doth also s.u.

SAVED. ⌈lives

Ge. 47:25. said, Thou hast s. our
Ju. 2:†16. L. raised judges which s.
7:2. lest Isr. say, Mine hand s. me
1 S. 23:5. Da. s. inhab-ts of Keilah
27:11. Da. s. nei. man nor woman
2 S. 19:5. servants which s. thy life
9. king s. us, and now he is fled
2 K. 6:10. s. himself, not once nor
Ne. 9:27. gavest saviours, who s. th.
Ps. 33:16. no king is s. by multitude
Ps. 44:7. thou hast s. us fr. enemies
106:8. he s. them for name's sake
10. he s. them fr. him that hated
Is. 43:12. I have declared and s.
45:22. look unto me, and be ye s. all
Je. 4:14. wash heart, that thou be s.
8:20. summer ended, and we not s.
Mat. 19:25. saying, Who then can be s.? Mk. 10:26. Lu. 18:26. ⌈20.
24:22. sho. no flesh be s. Mk. 13:
27:42. He s. others, Mk. 15:31. Lu. 23:35.
Mk. 6:†20. Herod feared Jn. s. him
10:†52. Go thy way; faith hath s.
Lu. 1:71. That we be s. fr. ene-s⌊thee
7:50. Thy faith hath s. thee, 18:42.
8:12. lest they sho. believe and be s.
13:23. Lord, are th. few that be s.?
Jn. 3:17. that world might be s. ⌈s.
5:34. things I say, th. ye might be
Ac. 2:47. added such as should be s.
4:12. name whereby we must be s.
15:1. exc. circumcised cannot be s.
16:30. Sirs, what must I do to be s.
27:20. hope we sho. be s. was taken
31. Exc. abide in ship, ye can-t be
Ro. 8:24. we are s. by hope ⌊s.
10:1. prayer for Isr. that they be s.
1 Co. 1:18. to us who are s. it is power
5:5. that spirit may be s. in day
10:33. profit of many th. they be s.
15:2. By wh. ye are s. if ye keep
2 Co. 2:15. savour in them th. are s.
Ep. 2:5. with Ch. by grace are ye s.
8. By grace are ye s. thro. faith
1 Th. 2:16. Gentiles that they be s.
2 Th. 2:10. not truth, th. they be s.
1 Ti. 2:4. Who will have all to be s.
Tit. 3:5. acc. to his mercy he s. us
1 Pe. 3:20. eight souls s. by water
4:18. if righteous scarcely be s.
2 Pe. 2:5. but s. Noah, eighth per-n
Re. 21:24. nations s. sh. walk in light
See ALIVE.

God or Lord SAVED. ⌈23.

Ex. 14:30. L. s. Isr. th. day, 1 S. 14:
De. 33:29. who like thee, O peo. s.
1 S. 10:19. rej-d G. who s. you ⌊by L.
2 K. 14:27. L. s. them by Jeroboam
1 Ch. 11:14. L. s. th. by gr. deliveran.
2 Ch. 32:22. L. s. Hezekiah fr. Senn.
Ps. 34:6. L. s. him out of troubles
107:13. L. s. them out of distresses
Is. 63:9. Angel of his presence s. th.
2 Ti. 1:9. God who hath s. us
Jude 5. how L. having s. people

Shall or shalt be SAVED.

Nu. 10:9. ye – s. from your enemies
2 S. 22:4. I – s. fr. enemies, Ps. 18:3.
Ps. 80:3. face to shine, we – s., 7, 19.
Pr. 28:18. Whoso walk-h upri-y – s.
Is. 30:15. In retur-g and rest ye – s.
45:17. But Israel – s. in the Lord
64:5. is continuance, and we – s.
Je. 17:14. O Lord save, and I – s.
23:6. in his days Judah – s., 33:16.
30:7. Jacob's trouble, but he – s.
Mat. 10:22. but he that endureth to the end – s., 24:13. Mk. 13:13.
Mk. 16:16. He that believeth – s.
Jn. 10:9. if any man enter, he – s.
Ac. 2:21. whoso. sh. call on name of the Lord, – s., Ro. 10:13.
11:14. wh-y thou and thy ho. – s.
15:11. that through grace we – s.
16:31. Believe on L. Jes. thou – s.
Ro. 5:9. we – s. fr. wrath thro. him
10. reconciled, we – s. by his life
9:27. Tho. Isr. as sand, remn-t – s.
10:9. believe G. raised him, thou – s.
11:26. all Israel – s., as written
1 Co. 3:15. he – s., yet so as by fire
1 Ti. 2:15. she – s. in childbearing, if

SAVEST. ⌈lence

2 S. 22:3. saviour, thou s. me fr. vio-
Jb. 26:2. how s. that hath no str.?
Ps. 17:7. O thou th. s. by right hand

SAVETH.
1 S. 14 : 39. as L. liveth who s. Israel
17 : 47. Lord, s. not with sword and
Jb. 5 : 15. he s. poor from sword
Ps. 7:10. of God, who s. the upright
20 : 6. know I L. s. his anointed
34 : 18. he s. such as be of contrite
107 : 19. he s. th. out of distresses

SAVING. [life
Ge. 19 : 19. mercy shewed in s. my
1 S. 25 : †26. withholden fr. s. thys.
Ps. 20 : 6. s. strength of his hand
28 : 8. he is the s. strength of his
67 : 2. thy s. health am. all nations
Zch. 9:†9. he is just and s. himself
He. 10 : 39. that believe to s. of soul
11 : 7. Noah an ark to s. of his ho.

SAVING. [Conj., Prep.] [off
Ne. 4 : 23. clothes s. that ev. one put
Ec. 5 : 11. s. the beholding of them
Am. 9 : 8. s. I will not destroy Jacob
Mat. 5:32. s. for cause of fornication
Lu. 4 : 27. none cleansed s. Naaman
Re. 2 : 17. no man, s. he th. rec-h it

SAVIOUR, S.
Ju. 3 : †9. Lord raised a s. to Israel
2 S. 22 : 3. my high tower, my s.
2 K. 13 : 5. the Lord gave Israel a s.
Ne. 9 : 27. thou gavest them s-s who
Ps. 106:21. They forgat God their s.
Is. 19 : 20. he shall send them a s.
43 : 3. I am Holy One of Isr., thy S.
11. I am L., beside me is no s.
45 : 15. hidest thyself, O G., the S.
21. a just God, and a S. [S.
49:26. all flesh shall know I am thy
60 : 16. shalt know I L. am thy S.
63 : 8. my peo., so he was their S.
Je. 14:8. S. of Isr. in time of trouble
Ho. 13 : 4. there is no s. beside me
Ob. 21. s-s shall come up on Zion
Lu. 1 : 47. spirit rejoiced in G. my S.
2 : 11. is born in city of Da. a S.
Jn. 4 : 42. This is Christ, S. of world
Ac. 5 : 31. Him God exalted to be S.
13 : 23. G. raised unto Isr. a S. Jes.
Ep. 5 : 23. Christ is S. of the body
Ph. 3 : 20. whence we look for the S.
1 Ti. 1 : 1. by command. of G. our S.
2:3. acceptable in sight of G. our S.
4 : 10. God, who is S. of all men [S.
2 Ti. 1 : 10 manifest by appearing of
Tit. 1 : 3. acc. to com-t of God our S.
4. peace fr. L. Jesus Christ our S.
2 : 10. adorn doctrine of God our S.
13. glorious appearing of our S.
3 : 4. kindness of our S. appeared
6. abundantly thro. Christ our S.
2 Pe. 1:1. thro. righteousn. of our S.
11. into kingdom of our L. and S.
2 : 20. thro. knowledge of L. and S.
3 : 2. of us, apostles of L. and S.
18. in knowledge of our S. Christ
1 Jn. 4 : 14. Father sent Son to be S.
Jude 25. To only wise God our S.

SAVOUR. [horred
Ex. 5 : 21. ye have made our s. ab-
Le. 26:31. not smell s. of y-r odours
Ec. 10 : 1. oint-t to send stinking s.
Can. 1 : 3. Bec. of s. of thy ointment
Jo. 2:20. his stink and ill s. sh. come
Mat. 5 : 13. if salt lost s., Lu. 14 : 34.
2 Co. 2 : 14. manifest s. of his knowl.
16. s. of death unto death, s. of
Ep. 5:2. to G. for sweetsmelling s.

Sweet SAVOUR, S.
Ge. 8. 21. the Lord smelled a s.s.
Ex. 29 : 18. it is a s.s., an offering
unto the Lord, 25, 41. Le. 1 : 9.
13, 17.-2 : 9, 12. -3 : 5, 16. -4 :
31.-6 : 15, 21.-8 : 28.-17 : 6.-23 :
13. Nu. 15:7, 14, 24.-18 : 17.-28 :
2, 6, 13, 27.-29 : 2, 6, 8. Eze. 16 :
19. [13, 36.
Le. 23 : 18. of a s.s., Nu. 28 : 24.-29 :
Nu. 15 : 3. to make a s.s. unto Lord
28 : 13. burnt offer-g of s.s. unto L.

Ezr. 6 : 10. sacrifices of s.s-s unto G
Eze. 6:13. did offer s.s. to their idols
20 : 28. there also made their s.s.
41. will accept you with s.s.
2 Co. 2 : 15. we are unto God a s.s.

SAVOUREST. [8:33.
Mat.16:23. s. not things of God, Mk.

SAVOURY. [17.
Ge. 27 : 4. make me s. meat, 7, 9, 14,
31. Esau, had made s. meat, and
Is. 30:†24. oxen sh. eat s. provender

SAW, S. [Noun.]
2 S. 12 : 31. Ammonites under s-s, 1
Ch. 20:3. [shaketh it
Is. 10 : 15. s. magnify ag. him that

SAW. [Verb.]
Ge. 3:6. woman s. the tree was good
6 : 2. sons of God s. daus. of men
9 : 22. Ham s. nakedness of his fa.
23. they s. not father's nakedness
12:15. princes s. commended her
16:4. when Hagar s. she had conc-d
18 : 2. Ab. s. he ran to meet them
21 : 9. Sarah s. son of Hagar | 19.
22 : 4. Abraham s. the place afar
24 : 30. he s. bracelets upon sister's
64. s. Is. she lighted off came | 163.
26 : 8. Abim. s. Isaac was sporting
28. we s. the Lord was with thee
28 : 6. When Esau s. Is. blessed Ja.
29 : 10. when Jacob s. Rachel [9.
30 : 1. Rachel s. she bare no chil. |
31:10. time cattle conceived, I s. in
32:2. Jacob s. he said, This G.'s host
25. when he s. he prevailed not
33 : 5. Esau lifted eyes s. the wom.
34 : 2. Sheeh. s. Dinah he took her
37 : 4. s. their father loved Joseph
18. when they s. him afar off
38 : 2. Judah s. a daughter Shuah
14. she s. Shelah was grown | 15.
39:3. his master s. L. was with him
13. she s. he had left his garment
16. when chief baker s. interpret.
42 : 1. Jacob s. was corn in Egypt
7. Joseph s. his breth. and knew
21. we s. the anguish of his soul
35. when they s. bundles of money
43 : 16. when Joseph s. Benj-in, 19.
45:27. he s. wagons, Jos. sent [48:
49:15. Issachar s. rest was good [17.
50:11. when Canaanites s. mourn-g
15. brethren s. father was dead
23. Joseph s. Ephraim's chil. [5, 6.
Ex. 2 : 2. she s. he was goodly child |
12. s. there was no man, he slew
8:15. Pha. s. th. was respite | 9 : 34.
10 : 23. they s. not one ano. 3 days
14 : 30. Israel s. Egyptians dead
31. Israel s. great work L. did
16:15. chil. of Isr. s. manna [34:30.
18 : 14. s. 20 : 18.-32 : 1, 5, 19, 25.-
24 : 10. they s. God of Israel, 11.
33 : 10. all people s. cloudy pillar
34 : 35. chil. of Israel s. face of Mo.
Le. 9:24. when peo. s. they shouted
Nu. 13:28. we s. chil. of Anak, 32, 33.
20: 29. cong. s. Aaron was dead [22:
22:23. ass s. angel of L., 25, 27. [2.
31. Balaam s. angel of Lord
33. ass s. and turned from me
24 : 1. Balaam s. it pleased L. | 2.
4. wh. s. vis. of the Almighty, 16.
25 : 7. when Phinehas s. it he rose
32:9. s. land, they discouraged Isr.
De. 1:19. terrible wildern-s ye s. [1.
4 : 12. voice, but s. no similit-e, 15.
7 : 19. temptations thine eyes s.
Jos. 8:14. when k. of Ai s. it, 20, 21.
Ju. 1:24. s. 3:24.-9 : 36, 55.-11 : 35.
-14 : 1, 11.-16 : 1, 18, 24.-18 : 7,
26.-19 : 3, 17.-20:36, 41. Ru. 2 : 18.
19:30. that s. it said, no such deed
Ru. 1 : 18. s. she was steadfastly
1 S. 5:7. men of Ashdod s. it [minded
6 : 13. they s. ark and rejoiced [11.
9:17. when Sams. s. S., L. said | 10:

1 S. 10 : 14. he s. they were no where
12 : 12. when ye s. Nahash came ag.
13:6. when Isr. s. th. were in strait
14 : 52. s. 17 : 51, 55.-19 : 20.-23 : 15.-
25 : 23, 25.-26 : 3.-28 : 5.-31 : 5,
7. 2 S. 4, 7.-6 : 16.-10 : 6, 9, 14,
15, 19.-12 : 19.-14 : 24, 28.-17 :
23.-20 : 12.-24 : 20. 1 Ch. 10 : 5,
7.-15 : 29.-19 : 6, 10, 15, 16, 19.
17 : 24. Isr. when they s. man fled
42. Philis. s. David disdained him
18:28. Saul s. Lord was with David
26 : 12. no man s. it nor knew it
28 : 12. woman s. Sam., she cried
21. woman s. Saul sore troubled
2 S. 11:2. Da. s. wom. washing hers.
17 : 18. lad s. them told Absalom
18 : 10. certain man s. it told Joab
26. watchman s. anoth. man run-g
24 : 17. Da. s. angel th. smote, 1 Ch.
1 K. 3 : 28. s. wisdom of God [21 : 16.
12:16. when Isr. s. k. hearkened not
13 : 25. s. carcass cast in the way
16 : 28. When Zimri s. city taken
18 : 17. Ahab s. Elijah, he said
39. people s. it fell on their faces
19 : 3. s. th. he went for his life [31.
22 : 32. capt-s s. Jehosh-t, 2 Ch. 18 :
2 K. 2 : 12. Elisha s. it, cried, My fa.
15. when sons of prophets s. Elisha
3:22. s. water on other side as blood
26. king of Moab s. battle too sore
4 : 25. when man of God s. her afar
5:21. when Naaman s. him running
6:17. opened eyes of yo. man he s.
20. L. opened eyes and they s. | 21.
9 : 22. s. 27.-11 : 1.-12 : 10. 1 Ch.
12 : 20, 21, 28. 2 Ch. 7 : 3.-10 : 16.
-22 : 10.-24 : 11.-32 : 2.
13 : 4. he s. the oppression of Israel
16 : 10. Ahaz s. altar at Damas., 12.
2 Ch. 15 : 9. they s. L. was with him
25 : 21. s. one another in the face
31:8. princes s. heaps, they blessed
Ne. 6:16. s. these th. were cast down
Es. 1 : 14. princes wh. s. king's face
3:5. Haman s. Mord. bowed not, 5:9.
5 : 2. when king s. Esther queen
7 : 7. he s. evil determined ag. him
Jb. 2:13. they s. his grief very great
3 : 16. as infants wh. never s. light
20 : 9. eye s. him, see him no more
29 : 8. young men s. me, and hid
11. when eye s. me, it gave witu-s
32 : 5. when Elihu s. was no answer
42:16. Job s. his sons' sons&genera.
Ps. 48 : 5. They s. it and marvelled
77 : 16. waters s. thee, O G., waters
95 : 9. y-r fa-s s. my work [s. thee
97 : 4. the earth s. his lightn-s and
114 : 3. sea s. it and fled, Jordan was
Can. 3 : 3. s. ye him my soul loveth ?
6 : 9. daughters s. and blessed her
Is. 1 : 1. wh. he s. cone-g Judah, 2 : 1.
21 : 7. he s. chariot with horsemen
41 : 5. isles s. it, and feared
59 : 16. he s. there was no man
Je. 3 : 7. treacherous sis. Judah s. it
39 : 4. When Zedekiah s. them
41 : 13. wh. all the peo. s. Johanan
44 : 17. we were well and s. no evil
52 : †25. seven of them s. face of k.
La. 1 : 7. adversaries s. her, did mock
Eze. 19 : 5. she s. her hope was lost
20 : 28. then they s. every high hill
23 : 11. when her sister Aholibah s.
14. she s. men portrayed upon
16. soon as she s. them she doted
Da. 3 : 27. s. men upon wh. fire no
4 : 23. k. s. a watcher com-g [power
5 : 5. king s. part of hand th. wrote
7 : † 1. Dan. s. visions of his head
Ho. 5 : 13. Ephraim s. his sickness
Am. 1 : 1. wh. he s. cone-g Isr., Mi.
Ha. 3 : 10. mts. s. thee and trem-d, [1. 1.
Hag. 2 : 3. Who s. ho. in first glory ?
Mat. 2:9. star th. s. went bef. th., 10.

Mat. 2:11. th. s. yo-g child wi. Mary
16. When he s. he was mocked
3:7. when he s. many of Pharisees
16. s. Sp. of G. descend-g, Mk. 1:10.
4:16. people s. great light [16, 19.
18. Jesus s. two brethren, Mk. 1:
8:14. s. 18, 34.-9:8, 9, 11, 23, 36.
9:22. s. her, he said, Dau. [-12:2.
12:22. bl-d and dumb spake and s.
17:8. s. no man save Jesus, Mk. 9:8.
18:31. fel-w serv-ts s. wh. was done
20:3. he s. others standing idle in
21:15. priests and scribes s. wondf.
19. when he s. fig tree in the way
20. disciples s. it and marvelled
38. when husbandmen s. the son
22:11. s. man had not wed-g garm.
25:37. wh. s. we thee hungered, 44.
38. when s. we thee a stranger [39.
26:8. disci. s. it, had indignation
71. another maid s. him, Mk. 14:
69. Lu. 22:58. [demned
27:3. Judas, when s. he was con-
24. Pilate s. he prevailed not [54.
28:17. s. him they worship-d him
Mk. 2:5. Jes. s. th. faith, Lu. 5:20.
14. he s. Levi sitting, Lu. 5:27.
16. s. 3:11.-5:6, 16, 22.-6:33,
34, 48, 49, 50.-7:2.
8:23. he asked if he s. aught
25. he s. every man clearly
9:14. s. 20, 25.-10:14.-11:20.-12:
34.-14:67. [9:49.
38. s. one casting out devils, Lu.
15:39. s. 16:4, 5. Lu. 1:12, 29.-
2:48.-5:2, 8.
Lu. 8:28. s. Jesus, he cried out
34. s. what was done, they fled
36. wh. s. it, told by what means
47. woman s. she was not hid
9:32. wh. awake they s. his glory
54. s. 10:31, 33.-11:38.-13:12.
15:20. father s. him, had compas-n
17:15. when he s. he was healed [14.
18:15. s. 24, 43.-19:5, 7.-20:14.-
21:1.-22:49.
21:2. he s. a certain poor widow
23:47. centu-n s. wh. was done [8.
24:24. as wom. said; him th. s. not
Jn. 1:38. when Jes. s. th. following
39. s. 47.-2:23.-5:6.-6:2, 5, 22, 24.
6:26. not, bec. ye s. miracles
8:10. Jesus s. none but the woman
56. Abraham s. my day, was glad
9:1. s. 11:31, 33.-19:6, 26, 33.
11:32. Mary s. him, she fell at his ft.
12:41. said Esaias when he s. glory
19:6. s. 26, 33.-20:5, 14.-21:9.
35. he that s. it bare record
20:8. other disci. s. and believed
20. disciples glad when s. the Lord
Ac. 3:9. all the peo. s. him walking
12. s. 7:31.-11:6.-12:9, 16.-13:45.
4:13. when s. boldness of Pe. [14:11.
6:15. s. his face as face of angel
7:55. Stephen s. glory of God
8:18. When Simon s. H. Gh. given
39. the eunuch s. him no more
9:8. eyes opened, he s. no man
35. all at Lydda s. him and turned
40. Tabitha s. Peter, she sat up
10:3. Cornelius s. in vision angel
11. Peter s. heaven opened and
12:3. bec. he s. it pleased the Jews
13:12. when deputy s. what was
36. David s. corruption [done
37. whom G. raised s. no corrup-n
16:19. masters s. hope of gain gone
17:16. s. city given to idolatry
20:27. th. s. him in the temple, 32.
22:9. they s. light and were afraid
18. s. him say-g to me, Make haste
28:4. barbarians s. venomous beast
6. looked, s. no harm come to him
15. when Paul s. be thanked God
Ga. 2:7. s. gospel committed to me
Ph. 1:30. same conflict which ye s.

He. 3:9. your fathers s. my works
11:23. s. he was a proper child
Re. 1:2. bare record of all he s.
11:11. gr. fear fell on them who s.
12:13. dragon s. he was cast out
13:1. s. beast rise out of sea
18:18. s. smoke of her burning

God or Lord SAW.

Ge. 1:4. G. s. the light it was good
10. earth, and G. s. it was good, 12,
18, 21, 25, 31. [great
6:5. G. s. wickedness of man was
29:31. when L. s. Leah was hated
Ex. 3:4. when L. s. that be turned
De. 32:19. wh. L. s. it, he abhorred
2 K. 14:26. L. s. affliction of Israel
2 Ch. 12:7. when L. s. they humbled
Is. 59. 15. L. s. it, it displeased him
16. L. s. that there was no man
Jon. 3:10. G. s. their works, th. they
Lu. 7:13. L. s. her, he had compas-n

I SAW.

Ge. 41:19. such as I never s. in Eg.
22. I s. in my dream seven ears
44:28. one went, I s. him not since
Jos. 7:21. I s. am. spoils garment
Ju. 12:3. I s. he delivered me not
1 S. 13:11. bec. I s. peo. were scat-d
22:9. I s. son of Jesse coming
28:13. I s. gods ascending out of
2 S. 18:10. I s. Absalom hanged in
29. I s. gr. tumult, but knew not
1 K. 22:17. I s. all Israel scattered
19. I s. the Lord on his throne, 2
Ch. 18:18. Is. 6:1. [wine presses
Ne. 13:15. s. I in Jud. some tread-g
23. s. I Jews mar-d wives of Ash-d
Jb. 31:21. when I s. help in gate
Ps. 73:3. I s. prosperity of wicked
Pr. 24:32. Then I s. and considered
Ec. 2:13. I s. that wisdom excelleth
24. This I s. from hand of God
3:16. I s. under sun place of judgm.
4:7. I s. vanity under the sun
8:10. so I s. the wicked buried
9:11. I s. race is not to the swift
Je. 3:8. I s. when I had put her aw.
Eze. 1:1. I s. visions of God [27.
28. When I s. I fell upon my face
3:23. I s. 8:4.-10:15, 20, 22.-41:8.-
8:10. I s. abominable beasts [43:3.
11:1. among whom I s. Jaazaniah
16:6. I s. thee polluted in own bl.
50. took them away as I s. good
23:13. Then I s. th. she was defiled
Da. 4:5. I s. 10, 13.-7:2, 7, 13.-8:2,
3, 4, 7.-10:7, 8. Am. 9:1. Ha. 3:7.
Ho. 9:10. I s. your fas. as first ripe
13. Ephr., as I s. Tyrus, is planted
Zch. 1:8. I s. by night man rid-g [18.
Jn. 1:32. I s. the Spirit descending
34. I s. and bare record that this
48. under fig tree I s. thee, 50.
Ac. 11:5. in trance I s. a vision
26:13. I s. in the way a light from
Ga. 1:19. other of apostles s. I none
2:14. I s. th. walked not uprightly
Re. 1:12. I s. golden candlesticks
17. when I s. him, I fell as dead
4:4. I s. 5:1, 2.-6:1, 2, 9.-7:1, 2.-
8:2.-9:1, 17.-10:1, 5.-13:2, 3.-14:
6.-15:1, 2.-16:13.-17:3, 6.-18:1.
-19:11, 17, 19.-20:1, 4, 11, 12.-
21:1, 2, 22.
22:8. I, John, s. these things

SAWED, SAWN. [s-d

1 K. 7:9. these were of costly stones
He. 11:37. stoned, were s-n asunder

SAWEST. [this

Ge. 20:10. What s. that hast done
1 S. 19:5. thou s. it didst rejoice
28:13. king said, for what s. thou
2 S. 18:11. Joab said, thou s. him
Ps. 50:18. s. thief, thou consentedst
Da. 2:31. Thou, O king, s. gr. image
34. Thou s. till stone was cut, 45.
41. thou s. iron mixed wi. clay, 43.

Da. 4:20. The tree thou s. wh. grew
8:20. ram thou s. having 2 horns
Re. 1:20. sev. stars, thou s. sev. (2)
17:8. beast thou s. was, is not
12. 10 horns thou s. are 10 ks., 16.
15. waters thou s. where whore
18. wom. thou s. is gr. city [sitteth

SAWN. See SAWED.

SAY. [wife

Ge. 12:12. they sho. s., This is his
14:23. lest thou s. I made Abram
24:14. she shall s., Drink and I, 44.
26:7. Isaac feared to s. she my wife
32:18. shalt s., They thy servants
34:11. ye sh. s. to me, I will give, 12.
37:17. them s., Let us go to Dothan
20. will s., Some beast devou-d him
41:15. heard s., thou canst interp.
43:7. he would s., Bring your bro.
44:16. Judah said, What sh. we s.
46:31. will s. un. Pha., My breth.
50:17. s. to Jos., Forgive [33, 34.
Ex. 3:14. sh. ye s. unto chil. of Isr.,
I AM hath sent, 15.-19:3.-20:22.
18. what they s., Wh. is his name?
4:12. teach you what shalt s. [1, 22.
5:16. s. unto us, Make brick [17.-
7:9, 16. [1.
12:26. when your chil. s. [27.-13:
14:3. Pha. will s. of chil. of Israel
21:5. if serv. s. I love my master
Le. 20:2. shalt s. unto chil. [17:8.
-25:20. [21.
Nu. 5:19. priest sh. s. unto woman
22. the wom. sh. s., Amen, amen
11:12. shouldest s. unto me, Carry
21:27. s., Come into Heshbon, 18:30.
22:19. may know what L. will s., 20.
38. have I any power to s. anyth.
23:3. shalt s., This is the offering
De. 4:6. sh. s., Surely this gr. nation
5:27. hear all our God shall s. [son
6:21. Then thou shalt s. unto thy
7:17. if s. in thine heart, 8:17.
9:2. a peo. of wh. thou hast heard s.
28. Lest the land s., Bec. the Lord
12:20. s. 18:12.-15:16.-17:14.-
18:21.-20:3, 8.-21:7, 20.-22:
14.-25:7, 8, 9.-26:3.
26:5. shalt s. bef. G., A Syrian, 13.
27:14. Levites sh. s. unto all Israel
15. all the people shall s. Amen,
16, 17, 18, 19, 20, 21, 22, 23, 24,
25, 26. [God
28:67. In morning shalt s., Would
29:22. generation to come sh. s.,
24. s. 25.-30:12, 13.
31:17. so they will s. that day
32:27. lest they s. our hand is high
37. s., Where their gods, 40. [33:27
Jos. 8:6. s. they flee bef. us [22:11.
22:27. your chil. may not s. to our
28. th. s. to us th. we may s. again
Ju. 4:20. s., Is any man here [9:54.
7:11. thou shalt hear what they s.
16:15. How canst s. I love thee?
18:24. what this ye s., What aileth
21:22. will s., Be favourable for our
Ru. 1:12. If I sho. s. I have hope
1 S. 2:36. s. 8:9.-10:2.-11:9.-13:
4.-14:9.-18:25.-19:24.-20:6.
8:7. in all they s. hearken [-25:6.
14:10. if they s., Come, we will go
20:7. if he thus s., It is well [17:7.
2 S. 7:8. shalt s. unto David, 1 Ch.
11:20. if k.'s wrath arise, and he s.
25. s. 14:32.-15:10.-16:10.-17:
9.-19:2.-24:1.
15:26. if he s. I no delight in thee
21:4. What you shall s. will I do
1 K. 1:25. th. s., God save Adonijah
36. L. God of my lord s. so too
2:14. I somewhat to s. unto thee
17. speak, he will not s. thee nay, 20.
5:†6. give hire acc. to all thou s.
9:8. sh. s., Why hath Lord done
thus, 2 Ch. 7:21.

1 K. 12: 10. s. 16: 16. 2 K. 9: 17.-18: 22.
-19: 6, 9.-22: 18. 1 Ch. 21: 18.
2 Ch. 7: 21.-10: 10.-20: 21.-34: 26.
13: 22. Lord did s., Eat no bread
14: 5. thus and thus sh. s. unto her
22: 8. Let not k. s. so, 2 Ch. 18: 7.
2 K. 7: 4. If we s. will enter city
9: 37. shall not s. This is Jezebel
2 Ch. 18: 15. th. s. noth-g but truth
Ezr. 8: 17. I told what they should s.
9: 10. what shall we s. after this
Es. 1: 18. sh. the ladies of Persia s.
Jb. 9: 12. will s., What doest thou,
19: 28. s. 21: 28.-32: 13.-36: 23.
20: 7. wh. have seen him sh. s., Where is he?
21: 14. they s. unto God, Depart
22: 29. thou sh. s., There is lifting
23: 5. I wo. underst. what he wo. s.
28: 22. Destruction and death s., We
32: 11. searched out what to s.
33: 27. if any s., I have sinned and
32. if any thing to s., answer me
34: 18. Is it fit to s. to king, Thou
37: 19. teach what we sho. s. [wicked
38: 35. s. unto thee, Here we are
Ps. 3: 2. many s. of my soul, no help
4: 6. many that s., Who will shew us
11: 1. how s. ye to my soul, Flee
13: 4. s. 35: 10.-40: 15.-41: 8.-42: 3, 9, 10. [him
35: 25. them not s., We swallowed
27. let them s. continually, 40: 16.
42: 9. I will s. unto God my rock
58: 11. man shall s. there is reward
59: 7. for who, s. they, doth hear?
64: 5. they s., Who sh. see them?
70: 3. s. 4.-73: 11.-79: 10.-107: 2.-
115: 2.-118: 2, 3, 4.-122: 8.-124: 1.-129: 1.
94: 7. they s., Lord shall not see
106: 48. let all people s. Amen
129: 8. nei. do they s., The blessing
Pr. 1: 11. If they s. let us lay wait
5: 12. s., How I hated instruction
20: 9. who can s., I am pure fr. sin
23: 35. stricken me, shalt thou s.
30: 9. Lest I s., Who is the Lord
15. four things s. not, It enough
Ec. 8: 4. who may s. unto k., What
12: 1. shalt s., I ha. no pleas. [doest
Is. 2: 3. many peo. sh. s., Come ye
5: 19. that s., Let him make speed
† 20. that s. cone-g evil, It is good
8: 12. s. 19.-9: 9.-12: 1, 4.-19: 11.-
14: 4. s. How oppressor ceased [20: 6.
10. all sh. s., Art thou become weak
29: 15. Woe to them s., Who seeth
16. shall the work s. of him that made it? or thing framed s. of
30: 10. Wh. s. to the seers, See not
22. shalt s. unto it, Get hence
33: 24. inhab-ts not s., I am sick
36: 7. s. 37: 6, 9.-41: 26, 27.-45: 9.
44: 5. One shall s., I am the Lord's
19. s. 20.-45: 9.-49: 9, 20, 21.-51: 16.-56: 12.-57: 14. [righteousn-s
45: 24. sh. one s., In L. have I
48: 5. lest s., Mine idol hath done
7. lest thou s., Behold I knew
58: 3. Whf. have we fasted, s. they
9. thou cry, he shall s., Here I am
65: 5. Which s. come not near to me
Je. 2: 23. s. 31.-3: 1, 12.-5: 2, 19, 24.
-7: 10, 28.-8: 4, 8.-13: 12, 13, 22.-14: 13, 15.-15: 2.-16: 10, 11, 19.-17: 15.-19: 11.-21: 3, 8, 13.
-22: 8.-23: 17, 31, 33, 34, 35, 37, 38.-25: 27.-26: 4.-27: 4.-31: 7.
-32: 3, 36, 43.-33: 10, 11.-36: 29.-37: 7.-38: 22, 25, 26.-42: 13.-43: 2.-45: 3, 4.-48: 14.-51: 35, 62, 64. [us
27. in trouble will s., Arise, save
3: 16. s. no more, The ark of cov-t
5: 15 nei. underst-t what they s.
10: 11. sh. ye s., The gods sh. perish
Je. 13: 21. Wh. s. wh. he sh. punish
14: 17. shalt s. this word unto them
20: 10. Report, s. they, we will rep-t
23: 7. no more s., The Lord liveth
31: 29. s. no more, fa-s eaten [thee
39: 12. do unto him as he s. unto
42: 20. acc-g to all, Lord sh. s. [corn
La. 2: 12. s. to mothers, Where is
Eze. 2: 4. s. 3: 27.-9: 9.-12: 27.-13: 15.-18: 25.-20: 32, 49.-21: 7.-
25: 8.-26: 17.-33: 17, 20.-36: 13, 35.-37: 11.-38: 11, 13.-44: 6.
11: 3. Which s., It is not near; let
13: 7. whereas ye s., Lord saith it
18: 19. Yet s. ye, Why? doth not son
28: 9. wilt s. before him that slayeth
Ho. 2: 7. s. 23.-10: 3, 8.-13: 2 [ber
7: †2. they s. not to hearts I remem-
14: 3. nei. s. to work of our hands
8. Ephr. s., What I to do wi. idols
Jo. 2: 17. s. 19. Am. 4: 1.-5: 16.-6: 13.-8: 14.-9: 10. Mi. 2: 4.
Am. 6: 10. sh. s., Is any with thee? he shall s., No
Mi. 2: 6. prophesy yet not s. they
3: 11. will s., Is not the Lord am. us
4: 2. nations shall s. let us go up
Na. 3: 7. s. Zph. 1: 12. Hag. 1: 2.
Ha. 2: 1. to see what he will s. unto
Zch. 11: 5. th. sell th. s., I am rich [me
12: 5. s. 13: 3, 5, 6, 9.
Mal. 1: 2. Yet ye s., Wherein hast thou loved us, 2: 14, 17.-3: 13.
1: 5. s. 6, 7, 12.-3: 8. [Lu. 3: 8.
Mat. 3: 9. not to s. within yours.,
4: 17. to s., Repent, for kingdom
5: 11. shall s. all manner of evil
22. s. 7: 4.-9: 5.-11: 18, 19.-14: 17.-15: 5, 33.-16: 2, 14.
7: 22. Many will s. unto me in that
13: 51. understood? They s., Yea, L.
16: 13. whom do men s. I am, Mk. 8: 27. Lu. 9: 18.
15. whom s. ye that I am, Mk. 8: 29. Lu. 9: 20. [33.-21: 21.
17: 10. s. 20.-19: 7, 10.-20: 7, 22,
21: 3. if any s. aught, ye shall s.
16. Hearest thou what these s.
25. if we s., From heaven, he will s., Mk. 11: 31. Lu. 10: 5.
26. if we s., Of men we fear, Mk. 11: 32. Lu. 10: 9.
31. s. 41.-22: 21, 23, 42.-23: 16, 30, 39.-24: 23, 26, 48.-25: 34, 40, 41.-26: 13.-27: 33, 46, 64.
28: 3. do not works, th. s., and do not
Mk. 1: 44. see thou s. nothing to any
2: 9. s. 18.-4: 38.-6: 38.-7: 2, 11.
-8: 19, 28.-9: 11.
9: 6. For he wist not what to s.
11: 3. s. 23, 28.-12: 14, 18, 35.-13: 21.-14: 9, 58, 65.
Lu. 4: 23. will surely s., Heal thys.
† 41. not to s. th. knew he was Ch.
5: 23. s. 6; 42.-7: 33, 34.-9: 18, 19, 20.-11: 5, 7, 18.-12: 19, 45, 55.-13: 26, 35.-14: 9, 10, 17.-
15: 18.-17: 6.-19: 31.-20: 41.
-22: 11.-23: 19, 30. [s.
7: 40. Simon, I have somewhat to
12: 11. no thought what ye shall s.
12. H. Gh. teach wh. ye ought to s.
54. ye s., There cometh a shower
13: 25. he sh. s., I know you not, 27.
17: 7 will s. unto him, by and by sit
8. will not rather s. unto him
21. Nei. shall they s., Lo, here! or
23. they shall s. to you, See, here
19: 31. thus sh. ye s., L. hath need
22: 70. Son of God? Ye s. that I am
Jn. 1: 38. s. 9: 17, 19.-11: 8.-20: 13,
4: 20. ye s. Jeru. is pl. [16. Ac. 1: 19.
35. s. not ye, There are yet 4 mos.
7: 26. and they s. nothing unto him
8: 4 they s. unto him, This woman
26. I have many things to s., 16: 12
48. s. we not well, thou a Samari.
Jn. 8: 54. of wh. ye s. he is y-r God
9: 41. but now ye s., We see; theref.
10: 36. s. ye of him, Fa. sanctified
11: 8. His disciples s. unto him
13: 13. and ye s. well; for so I am
Ac. 3: 22. him hear in all he shall s.
4: 14. they could s. nothing ag. it
6: 14. him s. Jesus shall destroy
17: 18. What will this babbler s.?
21: 23. Do this that we s. to thee
23: 18. something to s. unto thee
30. s. what they had against him
24: 20. let these same s. if found evil
26: 22. none but what Moses did s.
Ro. 3: 5. what sh. we s., Is G. unrigh.?
8. affirm that we s., Let us do evil
4: 1. What sh. we s. then, sh. we contin., 6: 1.-7: 7.-8: 31.-9: 14, 30.
9. for we s. faith was reckoned
9: 19. Thou wilt s., Why find fault
20. Shall thing formed s. to him
11: 19. Thou wilt s., The branches
1 Co. 1: 15. Lest any s. I baptized in
10: 28. If any s., This is offered
12: 3. no man can s. Jesus is Lord
15. if foot sh. s., Because | 16, 21.
14: 16. how s. Amen at thy thanks?
23. Will they not s. ye are mad
15: 12. s. is no resurrec-n? Ac. 23: 8.
35. some man will s., How are dead
2 Co. 9: 4. we (that we s. not ye) be
10: 10. letters s. they are weighty
12: 6. for I will s. the truth
1 Th. 4: 15. this we s. by word of L.
5: 3. when they shall s. Peace and
1 Ti. 1: 7. underst-g nei. what they s.
Tit. 2: 8. having no evil to s. of you
Phm. 19. I do not s. how thou owest
He. 5: 11. we ha. many th-s to s. [me
7: 9. as I may s., Levi paid tithes
9: 11. is to s., not of this building
10: 20. vail, that is to s., his flesh
11: 14. that s. such things declare
13: 6. may boldly s., L., my helper
Ja. 1: 13. Let no man s. when temp-d
2: 3. and s. unto him, Sit here (2)
16. one of you s., Depart in peace
18. Yea, a man may s., Hast faith
4: 13. Go to now ye that s., To day
15. ye ought to s., If Lord will
1 Jn 1: 6. If s. we have fellowship
8. If s. we have no sin, we dec., 10.
4: 20. If man s. I love G., and hateth
5: 16. I do not s. he shall pray for it
Re. 2: 2. which s. they are apostles
9. s. they are Jews, are not, 3: 9.
6: 3. heard s., 5, 6, 7.-16: 5, 7.
22: 17. Spirit and bride s. Come

SAY. [Imperative.]

Ge. 12: 13. s. thou art my sister
20: 13. s. of me, He is my brother
32: 20. s. ye, Behold thy serv Jacob
44: 4. s., Whf. have ye revolted
45: 9. s., Thus saith thy son Joseph
17. s. unto thy brethren, This do
Ex. 3: 16. s., The L. G. of y-r fa-s [ye
6: 6. Whf. s. unto children of Israel, I am the Lord [8: 5, 16.
7: 19. s. unto Aaron, Take thy rod
8: 1. s., Thus saith the Lord, 20.-
9: 13. 2 K. 9: 3. Is. 38: 5. Je. 11: 3.-43: 10.-Eze. 11: 16, 17.-12: 10, 19, 28.-13: 18.-14: 4, 6.-16: 3.-17: 3, 9.-20: 3, 5, 27, 30.-21: 3, 9, 28.-22: 3.-24: 3.-33: 25, 27.-34: 2.-35: 3.-36: 3, 6, 22.-
37: 9, 12, 19, 21.-38: 3, 14.-39: 1. Zch. 1: 3.
16: 9. s. unto all the congr. of Isr.
33: 5. s. unto Isr., Ye are stiffneck- [ed
Le. 1: 2. s., If any bring offering
15: 2. s., When any man hath issue
17: 2. s., This is thing L. command.
18: 2. s., I am the Lord your God
19: 2. s., Ye shall be holy
21: 1. s., There sh. none be defiled
22: 3. s., Whoso. be of all your seed

Le.25 :2. s. Wh. ye be come unto land
28 : 10. Nu. 15 :2, 18.-34 :2.[vow
27 :2. s., When man make singular
Nu. 5 : 12. s., If man's wife go aside
6:2. s., When man or wom. separate
8 : 2. s., When lightest the lamps
11:18. s., Sanctify yours. [33 : 11.
14 : 28. s., as I live, saith L., Eze.
15:26. s., When ye take of children
23 : 16. go again into Balak and s.
25 : 12. s., Behold I give him cov-t
28 : 2. s., My offering and my bread
33:51. s., Wh. ye are passed, 35:10.
De 1 : 42. s., Go not up, nei. fight
5 : 30. s., Get ye into your tents
Ju. 7:18. s., the sword of the L. and
12 : 6. s., Shibboleth ; he said[Gid.
1 S. 14 : 34. s., Bring me hither ox
15 : 16. he said unto him s. on, 2 S.
14 : 12. 1 K. 2 : 14, 16. Lu. 7:40.
Ac. 18 : 15.
16 : 2. s., I am come to sacrifice
18:22. s., king hath delight in thee
2 S.11:21. s., Thy serv. Uriah is dead
13: 5. s., Let my sister Tamar come
15 : 34. s. unto Abs. I will be servt.
19 : 13. s., Art thou not of my bone
20 : 16. s. unto Joab, Come near
24:12. s. unto David, Thus saith L.
1 K. 1 : 13. s., Didst not my lord
34. s., God save king Solomon [ot
18:44. s. unto Ahab, Prepare chari-
22 : 8. Let not k. s. so, 2 Ch.18 : 7.
27. s., Put fellow in prison, 2 Ch.
18 : 26. [God
2 K. 1 : 3. s., Is it not bec. is not a
4:13. s. unto her, hast been careful
26. s., Is it well with thee?
8 : 10. s., Thou mayest recover
1 Ch.16: 31. let men s., L. reigneth,
Ps. 96 : 10. [vation
35. s., Save us, O God of our sal-
Ps 35:3. s. unto my soul, I thy salva.
25. Let them not s. in hearts
66 : 3. s. unto God, How terrible
106 : 48. let all people s. Amen
107: 2. Let redeemed of Lord s. so
Pr. 3 : 28. s. not unto neighbor, Go
7 : 4. s. unto wisdom, Thou sister
20 : 22. s. not I will recompense
24 : 29. s. not I will do to him as
Ec. 5:6. neither s. before angel [mer
7:10. s. not, What is cause that for-
Is. 8 : 10. s. to righteous, It be well
7 : 4. s., Take heed, be quiet
8 : 12. s. not, A confederacy to all
22 : 15. s., What hast thou here
35 : 4. s. to them of fearful heart
36 : 4. s. to Hez., Thus saith king
40:9. s. unto cities, Behold your G.
43 : 9. let them s., It is truth
48 : 20. s., The Lord hath redeemed
56 : 3. nei. let eunuch s. I am a dry
62 : 11. s. ye to daughter of Zion
Je. 1 : 7. s. not I am a child
4 : 5. s., Blow ye the trumpet (2)
7: 2. s., Hear word of Lord, 17 : 20.
-19 : 3.-21 : 11.-22 : 2. Eze. 13 :
2.-20 : 47.-25 : 3.-36 : 1.-37 : 4.
13 : 13. s. unto k. and qu., Humble
25:30. s., The Lord shall roar from
31 : 10. s., He that scattered Israel
46 : 14. s. ye, Stand fast, prepare
48:17. s., How is strong staff broken
19. ask her, and s., What is done
50 : 2. publish, s., Babylon is taken
Eze. 6 : 3. s., Ye mts. of Israel [Isr.
11. s., Alas for abominations of
12 : 11. s., I am your sign
23. s., The days are at hand and
13 : 11. s. unto them wh. daub with
17:12. s. to rebel. ho., Know ye not
19 : 2. s., is thy mother? a lioness
21 : 9. s., a sword is sharpened, 28.
22:24. s., Thou ar'. land not cleansed
27 : 3. s. unto Tyrus, O thou that
32 : 2. s., Thou like a young lion

Eze.33 :2. s., When I bri.sword [him
12. s., Righteousness not deliver
37:4. s., O ye dry bones, Hear word
Da. 4 : 35. s. unto him, What doest
Ho. 2 : 1. s. unto your breth., Ammi
14 : 2. s., Take away all iniquity
Jo. 2 : 17. s., Spare thy people, O L.
3 : 10. let weak s. I am strong[mts.
Am. 3: 9. s., Assemble yours. upon
Ha. 2 : 6. s., Woe to him increaseth
th. wh. is not his [time at hand
Mat. 26 : 18. s., Master saith, My
28:13. s., His discip. came by night
Mk.11:3. s. ye that the L. hath need
14 : 14. s. ye to goodman of house
Lu. 7 : 7. s. in a word, and my serv-t
10 : 5. s., Peace be to this house
9. s., kingd. of G. is nigh unto you
10. s. dust of your city we wipe off
11 : 2. s., Our Father which art in
17 : 10. s., We are unprofitable
Jn. 20 : 17. s., I ascend unto my Fa.
Ac.13:15. if word of exhorta-n, s. on
28 : 26. s. ye shall not understand
Ro. 10 : 6. s. not who shall ascend
Col. 4 : 17. s., Take heed to ministry
Ja. 1:13. Let no man s. wh. tempted

See **BEGAN** to say.

I SAY.

Ge. 24 : 14. I sh. s., Let down pitcher
43. when virgin cometh and I s.
Ex. 3 : 13. his name, what shall I s.
Jos. 7 : 8. sh. I s. when Isr. turneth
1 S. 20:21. If I s. unto lad, 22.[ceive
2 K. 4 : 28. did not I s., Do not de-
7 : 13. I s. they are as multitude
2 Ch. 20:11. I s. how they reward us
Jb. 6 : 22. Did I s., Bring unto me
7 : 13. When I s., My bed sh. comf-t
9 :20. If I s. I am perfect, it sh. prove
27. If I s., I will forget complaint
10:2. I will s. unto G., Do not con-
Ps. 27:14. wait, I s., on the L.[demn
73 : 15. If I s. I will speak thus, I
91 : 2. I will s. of L., He my refuge
130:6. I s. more than they th. watch
139:11. If I s. darkness sh. cover me
Ec. 6 : 3. I s. an untimely birth is
Is. 36 : 5. I s. sayest thou (but vain)
38:15. What sh. I s.? He hath spok.
43 : 6. I will s. to north, Give up
Eze. 3 : 18. When I s. to wicked, 33 :
12 : 25. I will s. and perform [8, 14.
21 : 24. I s. ye are come to remem.
33 : 13 When I s. to righteous, he
Ho. 2 : 23. I will s. to them not my
people, Zch. 13 : 9. [Lu. 7 : 8.
Mat. 8 : 9. I s. unto this man, Go,
Lu. 6 : 46. do not the things I s.[eth
7 : 8. I s. unto one, Go, and he go-
Jn. 5:34. I s. that ye might be saved
8 : 46. I s. truth, why not believe
55 if I s. I know him not, be liar
12 : 27. what sh. I s., Fa. save me
49. he gave com-t. what I sho. s.
16 : 26. I s. not I will pray Father
Ac. 10 : 37. That word, I s. ye know
Ro. 3 : 26. To declare, I s. his right-
9 : 1. I s. truth in Christ [eousness
10 : 18. I s., Have they not heard?
19. I s., Did not Israel know?
11 : 1. I s., Hath God cast away his
11. I s., Have they stumbled that
12 : 3. For I s., through the grace
15 : 8. I s., Jesus Ch. was minister
1 Co. 1 : 12. I s. that ev. one of you
7 : 8. I s. thf. to the unmarried
26. I s. it is good for a man
29. I s., brethren, time is short
9 : 8. s. I these things as a man?
10:15. to wise men, judge what I s.
19. What s. I, then? that the idol
20. I s. things Gentiles sacrifice
29. Conscience, I s., not thine own
15 : 50. this, I s., brethren. 2 Co. 9:
6. Ga. 3 : 17.-5 : 16. Ep. 4 : 17.
Col. 2 : 4.

2 Co. 5 : 8. We are confident, I s.
11 : 16. I s., Let no man think
Ga. 1. 9. so s. I, now if any man
4 : 1. I s. the heir as long as he
Ep. 4 : 17. This I s., and testify in
Ph. 4 : 4. and again I s., Rejoice
Col. 1 : 20. by him I s., whe. things
2 : 4. I s., lest any beguile you
2 Ti. 2:7. Consider what I s., L. give
Phm. 21. thou wilt do more than I s.
He. 11 : 32. what shall I more s.

I SAY unto thee.

Ex. 4 : 23. I s. -, Let my son go
6:29. speak unto Pha. all th. I s. -
Ju. 7:4. of whom I s. -, This sh. (2)
Eze 2 : 8. I s. -, Be not rebellious
44:5. mark well all th. I s. - conc-g
Mat. 5:26. I s. -, Thou by no means
16 : 18. I s. -, That thou art Peter
18 : 22. I s. -, Until 7 times seven
26:34. I s. -, Th. this night, Mk. 14:30.
Mk. 2 : 11. I s. -, Arise, and take up
thy bed, go, Lu. 5 : 24.-7 : 14.
5 : 41. Damsel, I s. -, Arise
Lu.7:47. I s. -, Her sins, wh. are many
23:43. I s. -, To day thou sh. be wi.
Jn.3:3. I s. -, Except man be born, 5.
11. I s. -, We speak th. we do know
13:38. I s. -, The cock sh. not crow
21:18. I s. -, When thou wast young

I SAY unto you.

2 S. 13:28. when I s. -, Smite Ammon
2 K. 2 : 18. did I not s. -, Go not
Mat 3: 9. I s. -, God is able, Lu. 3:8.
5 : 18. I s. -, Till heaven and earth
20. I s. -, except y-r righteousness
22. I s. -, that whosoever is angry
28. I s. -, whoso. looketh on wom.
32. I s. -, whoso. sh. put away wife,
34. I s. -, Swear not at all [19 : 9.
39. I s. -, that ye resist not evil[27.
44. I s. -, love y-r enemies, Lu.6:
6:2. I s. -, they have reward, 5, 16.
29. I s. -, Sol. in his glory, Lu. 12:27.
8:10. I s. -, I not found so gr., Lu.7:
11. I s. -, many shall come from[9.
10:15. I s. -, it shall be more tolerable, 11 :22, 24. Mk. 6 : 11. Lu.
23. I s. -, ye sh. not have gone[10:12.
42. I s. -, sh. in no wise lose, Mk.9:41.
11:9. I s. -, more th. proph., Lu.7:26.
11. I s. -, Among th. b. of, Lu.7:28.
12 : 6. I s. -, in this place is one[28.
31. I s. -, all manner of sin, Mk. 3:
36. I s. -, That every idle word
13:17. I s. -, th. many proph. have
16 : 28. I s. -, be some standing,
Mk. 9 : 1. [Mk.9:13.
17:12. I s. -, Elias is come already,
20. I s. -, If ye have faith as, 21:21.
18:3. I s. -, Exc ye be convert., Mk.
10. I s. -, in heav. th. angels [10:15.
13. I s. -, he rejoiceth more of that
18. I s. -, whatsoever ye shall bind
19. I s. -, if two of you shall agree
19:23. I s. -, a rich man shall hardly
24. I s. -, It is easier for camel
28. I s. -, ye which have followed
21:31. I s. -, publicans go before you
43. I s. -, the kingdom of God
23:36. I s. -, All these sh. come upon
39. I s. -, Ye shall not see me till
24 : 2. I s. -, There shall not be left
34. I s. -, This generation, Mk. 13:30.
47. I s. -, sh. make him ruler, Lu. 12
25 : 12. I s. -, I know you not [44.
40. I s. -, Inasmuch as ye have, 45.
26 : 13. I s. -, Whereso this gospel
be preached, Mk. 14 : 9.
21. I s. -, one sh. betray me, Mk. 14:
18. Jn. 13:33.
29. I s. -, I will not drink of this
fruit, Mk. 14:25. Lu. 22:18. [m.
64. I s. -, Hereaf. sh. ye see Son of
Mk. 8 : 12. I s. -, there shall no sign
10:29. I s. -, There is no man hath
left ho. for my sake, Lu. 18 : 29.

Mk. 11 : 23. I s. -, whoso. say unto
24. I s.-, Wh. things ye desire⌊mt.
12:43. I s.-, this poor widow, Lu. 21:
13 : 37. what I s. -, I say unto all⌊3.
Lu. 4:24. I s. -, no prophet is accept.
11: 8. I s.-, Though he will not rise
9. I s. -, Ask, and it shall be given
51. I s. -, It shall be required
12:4. I s.-, my friends, Be not afraid
5. cast into hell, I s. -, Fear him
8. I s. -, Whoso. shall confess me
22. I s. -, Take no thought for
37. I s. -, he shall gird himself
13:24. many, I s.-, will seek to enter
35. I s. -, ye shall not see me ⌈bid
14 : 24. I s.-, none of these wh. were
15 : 7. I s.-, joy shall be in heav., 10.
16: 9. I s. -, make to yours. friends
18 : 17. I s. -, Whoso. shall not rec.
19:26. I s.-, unto ev. one wh. hath sh.
21:32. I s.-, generation sh. not pass
22:16. I s. -, I will not eat th-f until
37. I s.-, this th. is written⌈heaven
Jn. 1:51. I s.-, Hereafter ye shall see
4 : 35. I s. -, Lift up your eyes
5 : 19. I s. -, The Son can do noth.
24. I s. -, He th. heareth my word
25. I s. -, The hour is coming
6:26. I s. -, Ye seek me not because
32. I s. -, Moses gave you not that
47. I s. -, He that believeth, 14: 12.
53. I s. -, Except ye eat the flesh
8:34. I s. -, Whoso. committeth sin
51. I s.-, If a man keep my saying
58. I s. -, Bef. Abraham was I am
10 : 1. I s. -, He that entereth in
7. I s.-, I am the door of the sheep
12:24. I s.-, Except a corn of wheat
13: 16. I s.-, Servant is not greater
20. I s.-, He th. receiveth whomso.
16:20. I s. -, Ye sh. weep and lam-t
23. I s. -, Whatso. ye shall ask
Ac. 5:38. I s.-, Refrain fr. these⌈not
1 Co. 11:22. What sh. I s. -, I praise
Ga. 5: 2. I, Paul, s. -, if circumcised
Re. 2:24. I s.-, As many as have not

SAYEST. ⌈peo.

Ex. 33 : 12. thou s. unto me, Bring
Nu. 22 : 17. I will do whatso. thou s.
Ru. 3 : 5. All thou s. I will do ⌈14.
1 K. 18:11. thou s., Go, tell thy lord,
2 K. 18 : 20. Thou s. but th. are vain words, Is. 36 : 5.⌈smitten Edom
2 Ch. 25 : 19. Thou s., Lo, thou hast
Ne. 5 : 12. so will we do as thou s.
6:8. no such things done as thou s.
Jb. 22 : 13. s., How doth God know?
35 : 14. s. thou shalt not see him
Ps. 90 : 3. s., Return ye chil. of men
Pr. 24 : 12. If thou s. we knew it not
Is. 36 : 5. s. (but are vain words)
40 : 27. Why s. thou, O Jacob
47 : 8. that s. in thine heart, I am
Je. 2 : 35. s., Bec. I am innocent, because thou s. I have not sinned
Am. 7 : 16. s., Prophesy not ag. Isr.
Mat. 26 :70. I know not what thou s.
27 : 11. Art King of Jews? Jes. said. Thou s., Mk 15 : 2. Lu. 23 : 3. Jn. 18 : 37. ⌈45.
Mk. 5 : 31. s., Who touched, Lu. 8 :
14 : 68. Peter denied, I know not what th. s., Lu. 22 : 60. ⌈rightly
Lu. 20 : 21. Master, we know thou s.
Jn. 1 : 22. What s. thou of thyself
8 : 5. such be stoned, what s. thou?
33. s. thou, We shall be made free? 12 : 34.-14 : 9.
52. Abraham is dead, and thou s.
9 : 17, say to blind man, What s. thou of him?
18 : 34. s. thou this of thyself, or
37. Thou s. I am a king
Ro. 2 : 22 s. a man should not steal
1 Co. 14 : 16. thy thanks, seeing he understandeth not what thou s.
Re. 3 : 17. thou s. I am rich

SAYING. [Part.]

Ge. 1:22. G. blessed them, s., Be fruitf.
2 : 16. man s., Thou mayest eat
3 : 17. I com-ded, s., Thou shalt
5 : 29. Noah, s., This sh. comfort us
8:15. God spake unto Noah, s., 9:8.
15:1. unto Abram in a vision, s., 4.
18. L., s., Unto thy seed, 24 : 7.
17 : 3. God talked with Abram, s.
18 : 12. Sarah, s., After I am waxed old, 13. ⌈Arise
19 : 15. Angels hastened Lot, s.,
21 : 22. unto Abr., s., God is with
22:20. told Abr., s., Behold, Milcah
23 : 3. Abr., s., I am a stranger
5. chil. of Heth, s., Thou prince|8.
10. Ephron, Hittite, ans-d Abr.
13. Ab. spake unto Ephron, s.⌊s. 14.
24 : 30. Rebekah, s. | 37.⌈this man
26:11. Ahim., s., He that toucheth
20. herdmen, s., the water is ours
27:6. Rebek., s., I heard thy fa (2)
28 : 6. Esau, s., not take wife of
20. Jacob vowed, s., If G. be wi. me
31 : 1. Laban's sons, s., Jac. tak. all
11. angel spake s., Jac.: I said,
29. G. spake yesternight, s.⌈(2) 19.
32 : 4. Jac. s. speak unto Esau, 17.
34 : 4. Shechem, s., Get me damsel
8. s., my son longeth for y-r dau.
37:15. man asked, s., Wh. seek.⌊|20.
38:13. told Tamar, s., Thy fa. in law
21. Judah, s., Where is harlot, 24.
25. Tamar sent to her fa. in law
28. midwife, s., This came first
39:12. she caught him, s., Lie wi. me
14. she s., he hath bro-t a Hebrew,
19. heard words of his wife, s. ⌊17.
40 : 7. he asked Pha.'s officers, s.
41:9. butler, s., I rememb. my faults
16. Jos. ans-d, s., It is not in me
42 : 14. Joseph, s., Ye are spies
22. Reuben, s., Do not sin ag. child
28. breth. afraid, s., What is this
37. Reuben, s., Slay my 2 sons if
43:3. Judah, s., man did protest(2)
7. The man, s., Is your fa. alive?
44 : 1. s., Fill the men's sacks
19. asked, s., Have ye a father, or
32. surety for the lad, s., If I⌈47:5.
45:16. s., Joseph's breth. are come,
48 : 20. Jacob blessed them, s. (2)
50:4. Joseph unto Ph., s., If now (2)
5. my father made me swear, s.
16. s., Thy father did com-d me
Ex. 1 : 22. Pha. charged, s., Ev. son
3 : 16. God appeared unto me, s.
5 : 6. Pha. commanded officers, s.
8. they cry, s., Let us go sacrifice
10. the taskmasters spake, s.
13. taskmasters hasted them., s.
15. officers of Isr. cried unto Pha. s.
17 : 4. Moses cried unto Lord, s.
21 : † 5. if servant s., say I love ⌈s.
Nu. 6 : 23. Speak unto Aaron and
1 S. 25 : 40. Abigail, s., Da. sent ⌈(2)
2 S. 3 : 12. to Da., s., Whose is land?
1 K. 1 : 6. not displeased him in s.
12:16. s., Wh. portion we in David?
22 : 36. s., Ev. man to his city ⌈not
2 K. 18:36. k.'s com-t s., Ans. him
Je. 6 : 14. s., Peace, when no peace,
42:14. s., No; we will go into Egypt
Mi. 3 : † 11. s., Is not Lord among us
Mat. 21 : 2. s., Go into vil., Lu. 19:30.
26 : 44. Jesus prayed third time, s.
27:23. cried, s., Let him be crucified
Mk. 1 : 15. Jes., s., time is fulfilled
40. came a leper, s., If thou wilt
8 : 27. s., Whom do men say I am?
10:33. s., we go up to Jer.⌊Lu. 9:18.
11 : 17. s., Is it not written, My house, Lu. 19 : 46.
13 : 6. many sh. come, s., I am Ch.
14 : 44. a token, s., Whomso. I kiss
68. But he denied, s., I know not
15:36. s., Let alone; let us see whe.
Lu. 1 : 63. wrote, s., His name is Jn.
66. s., Wh. manner of child this be?
3 : 16. John s., I baptize wi. water
4 :34. s., wh. we to do with thee, Jes.
7 : 6. s., Lord, trouble not thyself
32. s., We have piped unto you
8 : 25 s., Wh. manner of man this?
11 : 45. Master, thus s., thou re-
14:7. s., When art bidden⌊proachest
15:6. s., Rejoice with me, I have, 9.
23 : 2. they began to accuse him, s.
35. rulers derided, s., He saved
37. s., If thou King of Jews⌊others
39. s., If thou be Christ save thys.
47. centurion, s., this was righteous man ⌈came, s.
24 : 23. found not his body, they
34. s., The Lord is risen indeed
Jn. 4 : 51. told, s., Thy son liveth
6:52. s., How th. man give his flesh
7 : 15. s., How knoweth this man
11 : 28. s., The Mas. is come⌊letters
32. Mary, s., If th. hadst been here
18 : 22. struck Jes., s., Answerest
40. s., Not this man, but Bar.⌊th.?
Ac. 1 : 6. s., Lord, wilt thou restore
2 : 7. s., Are not these Galileans?
40. s., save yours. fr. this gener-n
3:25. s., unto Ab. in thy seed shall
4 : 16. s., What shall we do to these
5 : 23. s., The prison we found shut
7 : 27. s., Who made thee a ruler
40. s. unto Aaron, Make us Gods
59. s., Lord Jesus, rec. my spirit
10 : 3. angel of God, s., Cornelius
11 : 7. s., Arise, Peter, slay and eat
12 : 22. s. it is the voice of a god
26 : 22. s. none other things than
Re. 18 : 14. s. to th. dwell on earth
14 : 13. s., Write, Blessed are the

SAYING. [Noun.] ⌊dead

Ge. 37 : 11. but his fa. observed s.
De. 1 : 23. the s. pleased me well
1 S. 18 : 8. the s. displeased Saul
2 S. 17 : 4. s. pleased Absalom well
6. shall we do after his s.? if
24 : 19. Da. acc. to s. of G. went up
1 K. 2 : 38. Shimei said, s. is good
12 : 15. perform his s. by Ahijah
13 : 4. Jerob. heard s. of man of G.
32. s. which he cried sh. come⌈17.
15 : 29. acc unto s. of L., 2 K. 10 :
17:15. acc. to s. of Elijah, 2 K. 2:22.
20 : 4. acc. to s., I am thine
2 K. 5 : 14 to s. of man of G., 8 : 2.
1 Ch. 21 : 19. David went at s. of Gad
Es. 1 : 21. s. pleased k. and princes
Ps. 49 : 4. I will open my dark s.
Jon. 4 : 2. this s. in my country?
Mat. 15 : 12. offended after heard s.
19 : 11. All cannot receive this s.
22. when young man heard s.
28:15. this s. is commonly reported
Mk. 7 : 29. For this s. go thy way
8 : 32. And he spake that s. openly
9 : 10. kept that s. with themselves
32. But they understood not that s., Lu. 2 : 50.-9 : 45. ⌈went
10 : 22. he was sad at that s. and
Lu. 1 : 29. she was troubled at his s.
2 : 17. they made known abroad s.
9 : 45. feared to ask him of that s.
18 : 34. this s. was hid from them
Jn. 4 : 37. that s. true, One soweth
39. many believed, for s. of wom.
42. believe, not because of thy s.
6 : 60. This a hard s., who hear it
7 : 36. What manner of s. is this
40. Many, when th. heard s., said
8 : 51. If a man keep my s., 52.
55. I know him and keep his s.
12 : 38. That s. of Esaias be fulfilled
15 : 20. If they have kept my s.
18:9. That s. of Jes. be fulfilled. 32.
19:8. Pilate heard s. was afraid, 13.
21:23. went this s. among brethren
Ac. 6 : 5. s. pleased whole multitude

Ac. 7 : 29. fled Moses at this s. into
16:36. keeper told this s. to Paul
Ro 13 : 9. comprehended in this s.
1 Co. 15 : 54. sh. be brou-t to pass s.
1 Ti. 1 : 15. This is a faithful s.. 4:
9. 2 Ti. 2 : 11. Tit. 3 : 8. [office
3 : 1. This a true s., if a man desire

SAYINGS.

Nu. 14 : 39. Moses told s. unto peo.
Ju. 13 : 17. when thy s. come to pass
1 S. 25 : 12. Da.'s young men told s.
1 K. 10 : † 6. I heard of thy s., 2 Ch.
2 Ch. 13:22. Abijah's s. written [9:†5.
33:19. are written among s. of seers
Ps. 49 : 13. posterity approve their s.
78 : 2. I will utter dark s. of old
Pr. 1 : 6. understand dark s. of wise
4 : 10. O my son, receive my s.
20. son attend unto my s. [6:47.
Mat. 7:24. heareth these s., 26. Lu.
28 Jesus ended s., people astonished, 19 : 1. -26 : 1. Lu. 7 : 1.
Lu. 1 : 65. all these s. were noised in
2:51. his mo. kept all these s. [Jud.
9 : 28. about 8 days after these s.
44. Let these s. sink into your
Jn. 10: 19. division again for these s.
14 : 24. loveth not, keepeth not s.
Ac. 14 : 18. with s. scarce restrained
19 : 28. heard s. were full of wrath
Ro 3 : 4. mightest be justified in s.
Re 19 : 9. These are true s. of God
22 : 6. These s. are faithf. and true
See **This BOOK.**

SCAB. [s.

Le. 13 : 2. have in skin of his flesh a
6. it is but a s. | 7. if s. spread, 8.
14:56. th. is the law for a s. [Is.3:17.
De 28 : 27. L. will smite thee wi. a s.
5:†7. looked for judgm-t behold a s.

SCABBARD.

Je. 47 : 6. O sword, put thys. into s.

SCABBED.

Le. 21 : 20. he th. is scurvy or s. sh.
22 : 22. scurvy or s. ye sh. not offer

SCAFFOLD. [s.

2 Ch. 6 : 13. Sol. had made a brazen
Ne. 9 : † 4. stood upon s. of Levites

SCALES. [14 : 9.

Le. 11 : 9. these th. have s. eat, De.
10. ha. no s. not eat, 12. De.14:10.
Jb. 41 : 15. His s. are his pride, shut
Is. 40 : 12. weighed mountains in s.
Eze. 29 : 4. cause fish to stick unto s.
Ac. 9:18. fell fr. his eyes as had been

SCALETH. [s.

Pr. 21 : 22. A wise man s. the city

SCALL.

Le. 13 : 30. it is a dry s., even leprosy
31. plague of s. not deeper (2) 33.
32. behold, if s. spread not, 34.
33. but the s. shall he not shave
35. if s. spread he is unclean, 36.
37. if s. be at a stay, s. healed
14 : 54. This is law of all leprosy,

SCALP. [and s.

Ps. 68 : 21. God sh. wound hairy s.

SCANDAL, S. [all s-s

Mat. 13:†41. gather out of his kingd.
1 Jn. 2 : † 10. none occasion of s. in

SCANT. [Adj.] [him

Mi. 6 : 10. s. measure is abominable

SCANT. [Verb.]

2 K. 4 : † 3. borrow vessels, s. not

SCAPEGOAT.

Le. 16 : 8. the other lot for the s.
10. let him go for s. into wildern.
26. th. let go s. sh. wash his clothes

SCARCE.

Ge. 27:30. Jacob s. gone from father
Ac. 14 : 18. wi. sayings s. restrained
27:7. s. come over ag. Cnidus [peo.

SCARCELY.

Ro. 5 : 7. s. for righte. man one die
1 Pe. 4 : 18. if righteous s. be saved

SCARCENESS.

De. 8 : 9. shalt eat bread without s.

SCAREST.

Jb. 7 : 14. Then thou s. me with
dreams

SCARLET. [30.

Ge. 38:28. midwife bound s. thread,
Ex. 25 : 4. blue, and purple, and s.,
26 : 1, 31, 36. -27 : 16. -28 : 5, 6, 8,
15, 33. -35 : 6, 23, 25, 35. -36 : 8,
35, 37. -38 : 18, 23. -39 : 1, 2, 3, 5,
8, 24, 29. [s.
39 : 3. gold into wires, to work it in
Le. 14 : 4. take two birds, s. and
hyssop, 6, 49, 51, 52. Nu. 19 : 6.
Nu. 4 : 8. spread upon th. cloth of s.
Jos. 2 : 18. bind s. thread in window
21. she bound s line in window
2 S. 1 : 24. S., who clothed you in s.
Pr. 31:21. household clothed with s.
Can. 4 : 3. Thy lips like thread of s.
Is. 1 : 18. though your sins be as s.
La. 4 : 5. that were brought up in s.
Eze. 27 : † 7. purple and s. from isles
Da 5 : 7. be clothed with s., 16, 29.
Na. 2 : 3. the valiant men are in s.
Mat. 27 : 28. they put on Jes. s. robe
He. 9 : 19. took water and s. wool
Re. 17 : 3. woman sit upon s. beast
See PURPLE.

SCATTER. [Isr.

Ge. 49 : 7. divide them in Jac., s. in
Le 26 : 33. I will s. you am heathen
Nu. 16 : 37. take censers, s. the fire
De. 4 : 27. L. sh. s. you am. heath.,
28 : 64. Je. 9:16. Eze. 22 : 15.
32:26. I would s. them into corners
1 K. 14 : 15. he sh. s. them bey. river
Jb 18 : † 11. terrors shall s. him
Ps. 59 : 11. s. th. by thy power, O L.
68 : 30. s. peo. that delight in war
106 : 27. he lifted hand to s. them
144:6. Cast forth lightning, s. them
Is 28 : 25. cast fitches, s. cummin
30 : † 22. s. th. as menstruous cloth
41 : 16. whirlwind shall s. them
Je. 13 : 24. I will s. them as stubble
18:17. will s. them as wi. east wind
23:1. Woe unto pastors th. s. sheep
49 : 32. I will s. them in utmost
corners, 36. Eze. 5 : 10, 12.
Eze. 5:2. a third part shalt s. in wind
6 : 5. s. your bones about altars
10 : 2. and s. the coals over the city
12 : 14. I will s. all that help him
15. when I sh. s. them am. nations
20 : 23. I would s. them am. heath.
29:12. I will s. Egyptians, 30:23, 26.
Da. 4 : 14. hew down tree, s. fruit
11 : 24. he sh. s. am. them the prey
12:7. to s. the power of holy people
Ha 3 : 14. out as whirlwind to s. me
Zch 1 : 21. lift horn over Jud. to s.
Mal. 2:† 3. I will s. dung upon faces

SCATTER, ED, ETH, abroad. [earth

Ge. 11 : 4. lest we be s-d a. upon
8. So the Lord s-d them a., 9.
Ex. 5:12. peo. s-d a. to gather stub.
Ne. 1: 8. If transgr. I will s. you a.
Es. 3:8. There is a certain peo. s-d a.
Jb. 4:11. lions' whelps are s-d a.
Is. 24 : 1. L. s-h a. inhab-ts of earth
Eze. 34 : 21. pushed till ye s-d th. a.
Mat. 9 : 36. s-d a. as sheep no shep.
12:30. gath-th not s-h a. Lu. 11:23.
26 : 31. Sheep shall be s-d a.
Jn. 11:52. gather. chil. of G. s-d a.
Ac. 8 : 1. all s-d a. thro-t Judea [19.
4. were s-d a. went preaching, 11 :
Ja. 1: 1. to 12 tribes s-d a greeting

SCATTERED. [68 : 1.

Nu. 10 : 35. let enemies be s., Ps.
De. 30 : 3. whither Lord s. thee
1 S. 11 : 11. the Ammonites were s.
13: 8. the people were s. from Saul
11. I saw people were s. from me
2 S. 18:8. battle was s. over country
20: † 22. they were s. from the city
22 : 15. he sent out arrows and
s. them, Ps. 18 : 14. [18 : 16.
1 K. 22 : 17. I saw all Isr. s., 2 Ch.
2 K. 25 : 5. his army were s., Je.52:8.
Jb. 18 : 15. brimstone s. upon habita.
Ps. 44 : 11. hast s. us am. heathen,
60 : 1. [campeth
53 : 5. G. s. bones of him that en-
68 : 14. Almighty s. kings
89 : 10. hast s. thine enemies
92 : 9. workers of iniquity sh. be s.
141 : 7. Our bones are s. at grave's
Is. 18 : 2. go ye to nation s. peeled
7. present be brought of people s.
33 : 3. lifting thys. nations were s.
Je. 3 : 13. s. thy ways to strangers
10 : 21. all their flocks shall be s.
23 : 2. Ye have s. my flock [thee
30 : 11. end of all nations whi. I s.
31 : 10. He that s. Isr. will gather
40: 15. that all Jews should be s.
50: 17. Israel is a s. sheep [tries
Eze 6 : 8. when ye be s. thro. coun-
11 : 16. tho. I s. them, I a sanct-y
17. out of countries where ye have
been s., 20:34, 41, -28:25. [winds
17 : 21. that remain sh. be s. to all
29 : 13. Eg-ns gathered whi. were s.
34 : 5. flock s. bec. no shepherd (2)
6. my flock was s. upon the earth
12 am. his sheep that are s. where
have been s. in cloudy day
36 : 19. I s. them among heathen
46 : 18. that my people be not s.
Jo. 3 : 2. plead for people they s.
Na. 3 : 18. thy people is s. upon mts
Ha. 3 : 6. everlasting mts. were s.
Zch. 1: 19. horns which have s. Isr.,
7 : 14. I s. th. with whirlwind, [21.
13 : 7. smite Shepherd, sheep shall
be s., Mat. 26 : 31. Mk. 14 : 27.
Lu. 1 : 51. he hath s. proud in imag.
Jn. 16 : 32. hour cometh ye sh. be s.
Ac. 5 : 36. obeyed Theudas were s.
1 Pe. 1 : 1. strangers s. thro-t Pontus

SCATTERETH.

Jb. 37 : 11. he s. his bright cloud
38 : 24. s. east wind upon earth
Ps 147 : 16. s. hoar frost like ashes
Pr. 11 : 24. is that s. yet increaseth
20 : 8. king s. away evil with eyes
26. A wise king s. the wicked
Jn. 10 : 12. wolf catcheth s. sheep

SCATTERING. [winds

Jb. 37 : † 9. cold cometh out of s.
Is. 30:30. L. shall shew anger with s.

SCENT.

Jb. 14:9. thro. s. of water it will bud
Is. 11:†3. make him of s. in fear of L.
Je. 48 : 11. his s. is not changed
Ho. 14 : 7. s. thereof be wine of Leb.

SCEPTRE, S. [Judah

Ge. 49 : 10. s. shall not depart from
Nu 24 : 17. a S. sh. rise out of Israel
Es. 4:11. king sh. hold out golden s.
5: 2. k. held to Es golden s., 8 : 4.
Ps. 45 : 6. s. of thy kingd. is right s.
Is. 14 : 5. L. broken s. of rulers [s-s
Eze. 19 : 11. she had strong rods for
14. hath no strong rod to be s. [8.
Am. 1 : 5. will cut of him holdeth s.,
Zch. 10 : 11. s. of Egypt shall depart
He. 1:8. s. of righteousn. is s. of thy

SCE'VA. [kingd.

Ac. 19 : 14. seven sons of one S., a

SCHISM, S. [you

1 Co. 1 : † 10. I beseech be no s. am.
11 : † 18. I hear be s-s among you
12 : 25. should be no s. in the body

SCHOLAR.

1 Ch. 25 : 8. cast lots, teacher as s.
Mal. 2:12. L. will cut off mas. and s.

SCHOOL. [s.

2 Ch. 34: † 22. she dwelt in Jerus. in
Ac. 19: 9. disput-g in s. of Tyrannus

SCHOOLMASTER.

Ga. 3 : 24. law was our s. to bring

Ga.3 : 25. we are no longer under a
SCIENCE. ⌊s.
Da. 1 : 4. child. skilful in wisdom, s.
1 Ti 6 : 20. avoid-g oppositions of s.
SCOFF.
Ha. 1 : 10. they sh. s. at the kings
SCOFFERS.
2 Pe. 3 : 3. shall come in last days s.
SCORCH, ED. ⌈4 : 6.
Mat. 13 : 6. sun was up were s-d, Mk
Re 16:8. power given him to s. men
9. men were s-d with great heat
SCORN. [Noun.] ⌈37:21.
2 K. 19 : 21 laughed thee to s., Is.
Es 3:6. s. to lay hands on Mordecai
Ps 44 : 13. makest us a s., 79 : 4.
Ha. 1 : 10. princes sh. be a s. unto th.
See LAUGH, LAUGHED.
SCORN. [Verb.] ⌈eye
Jb. 16 : 20. my friends s. me, mine
SCORNER, S.
Jb. 16 : † 20. My friends are my s-s
Pr. 1 : 22. How long will s-s delight
3 : 34. Surely he scorneth the s-s '
9 : 7. reproveth s. getteth shame
8. Reprove not s. lest he hate thee
13 : 1. a s. heareth not rebuke ⌈not
14. 6. s. seeketh wisdom, findeth
15 : 12. s. loveth not that reproveth
19 : 25. Smite s. simple will beware
29. Judgments are prepared for s-s
21. 11. When s. is punished, simple
24. s. is his name, who dealeth in
22 : 10. Cast out s. content-n sh. go
24 : 9. s. is an abomination to men
Is. 29 : 20. s. is consumed and all
Ho 7:5. he stretched out hand wi. s-s
SCORNEST, ETH.
Jb. 39 : 7. He s-h multitude of city
18. ostrich, she s-h horse and rider
Pr 3: 34. Surely he s-h the scorners
9 : 12. if thou s-t thou sh. bear it
19 : 28. ungodly witness s-h judgm.
Eze. 16 : 31. not harlot, in that thou
SCORNFUL. ⌊s-t hire
Ps. 1 : 1. nor sitteth in seat of the s.
Pr. 29 : 8. s. bring city into a snare
Is. 28 : 14. hear word of L ye s. men
SCORNING.
Jb. 34 : 7. Job drinketh s. like water
Ps. 123 : 4. filled wi. s. of th. at ease
Pr. 1 : 22. How long scorners delight
SCORPION. ⌈in s.
Lu. 11 : 12. ask egg, will he offer s.
Re. 9 : 5. their torment was as of a s.
SCORPIONS.
De. 8:15. thro. wilderness wherein s.
1 K 12 : 11. but I will chastise you
with s., 14. 2 Ch. 10 : 11, 14.
Eze. 2 : 6. dwell am. s. be not afraid
Lu 10 : 19. you power to tread on s.
Re 9 : 3. to them given power, as s.
10. th. had tails like unto s., 19.
SCOURED.
Le. 6:28. if in brazen pot, it sh. be s.
1 K 7 : † 45. made of s. brass, 2 Ch.
SCOURGE, S. ⌊4 : † 16.
Jos. 23 : 13. s-s in your sides, thorns
Jb 5:21. shalt be hid fr s. of tongue
9 : 23. if s. slay suddenly, he laugh
Is. 10 : 26. L. shall stir up s. for him
28 : 15. wh. overflowing s. pass, 18.
Jn. 2 : 15. he made s. of small cords
SCOURGE, ED, ETH.
Le. 19:20. lie wi. bondm-d, she be s-d
Jb 5 : † 21. thou hid wh. tongue s-h
Mat. 10 : 17. will s. you in synagog-s
20 : 19. to mock, s., and crucify,
Mk. 10 : 34. Lu 18 : 33. ⌈persec.
23 : 34. some of them ye sh. s. and
27 : 26. s-d Jesus, deliv-d him to be
crucified, Mk. 15 : 15. ⌈Jn. 19 : 1.
Ac 22 : 25. Is it lawful to s. a Roman?
He 12 : 6. L. s-h ev. son he receiveth
SCOURGING, S.
Ac. 22 : 24. th. he be examined by s.
He. 11 : 36. others had trial of s-s

SCRABBLED.
1 S. 21 : 13. David feigned mad and s.
SCRAPE, ED.
Le. 14 : 41. sh. cause ho. to be s-d,
pour out dust they s. off ⌈ho.
43. if plague come aft. he hath s-d
Jb 2:8. Job took potsh-d to s. hims.
Eze. 26 : 4. I will s. dust from her
SCREECH owl. ⌈find
Is. 34 : 14. s. o. shall rest there and
SCRIBE.
2 S. 8 : 17. Seraiah, s., ⌊20 : 25. Sheva was s. ⌈24 : 11.
2 K. 12:10. k.'s s. put money, 2 Ch
18 : 18. came out Shebna, s., 37.-
19 : 2. Is. 36 : 3, 22.-37 : 2.
22 : 3. k. sent Shaphan, s., 8, 9, 10,
12. 2 Ch. 34 : 15, 18, 20 Je. 36 : 10.
25 : 19. principal s. of host, Je. 52 :
1 Ch. 18 : 16. and Shavsha was s. ⌊25.
24 : 6. Shemaiah, s., wrote them
27:32. Jonathan a wise man and s.
2 Ch. 26 : 11. account by Jeiel the s.
Ezr. 4 : 8. Shimshai, s., wrote, 9, 17, 23.
7 : 6. Ezra, a ready s. in law, 11, 12,
21. Ne. 8 : 1, 4, 9, 13.-12:26, 36.
Ne. 8 : 4. Ezra, s., stood upon pulpit
13 : 13. Shelemiah, priest, Zadoc s.
Is. 33 : 18. Where is the s.? where
Je 36 : 12. sat Elishama s., 20, 21. ⌈32.
26. com-ded to take Baruch., s.,
37 : 15. prison in ho of Jona. s., 20.
Mat. 8 : 19. a s. said, Master, I will
13 : 52. s. instructed unto kingdom
Mk. 12 : 32 the s. said, Well, Master
1 Co. 1 : 20. Where is s.? where dis-
SCRIBES. ⌊puter?
1 K. 4 : 3. Ahiah, sons of Shisha, s.
1 Ch 2 : 55. families of s. at Jabez
2 Ch 34 : 13. of Levites there were s.
Es. 3 : 12. were king's s. called, 8 : 9.
Je. 8 : 8. pen of the s. is in vain
Mat 2 : 4. gathe-d chief priests and s.
5 : 20. exceed righteousness of s.
7 : 29. he taught not as s., Mk. 1:22.
9 : 3. certain of s. within thems.
12:38. certain of s. and Phari. ans-d
15 : 1. to Jes. s. and Phari., Mk. 7 : 1.
16 : 21. suffer many things of the s.
17 : 10. Why say s. Elias must first
come, Mk. 9 : 11.
20 : 18. Son of man be betrayed
unto s., Mk 10 : 33.
21 : 15. s. saw, they were displeased
23 : 34. I send unto you wise men, s.
26 : 3. Then assembled chief priests
and s., Mk. 14 : 53. Lu. 22 : 66.
57. wh. s. and elders were assem.
27:41. priests mocking him, with s.
Mk. 2 : 6. went certain s. reasoning
16. s. saw him eat with publicans
3 : 22. s. said, He hath Beelzebub
7 : 5. s. asked, Why walk not disci.
8:31. must be rejected of s., Lu. 9:22.
9 : 14. s. questioning with disciples
16. asked s., what question ye
11 : 18. s. sought how they might
destroy him, Lu. 19 : 47. ⌈thou
28. s. say, By what authority doest
12 : 28. one of s. asked first com-t
35. How say s., Ch. is Son of David
38. said, Beware of s., Lu. 20 : 46.
14 : 1. s. sought how to take him
43. mult. from chief priests and s.
15 : 1. consultation wi. elders and s.
31. chief priests mocking with s.
Lu. 11 : 53. s. began to urge vehe-
20 : 1. chief priests, s., came ⌊mently
19. s. sought to lay hands on him
39. s. ans-g, Master, th. said well
22 : 2. priests and s. sought to kill
23 : 10. s. vehemently accused him
Jn. 8 : 3. s. brought a woman taken
Ac. 4 : 5. the s. gathered ag. apostles
6 : 12. s. brought Steph. to council
23 : 9. s. of Pharisees' part arose
See PHARISEES.

SCRIP.
1 S. 17 : 40. David put stones in a s.
2 K. 4 : † 42. ears of corn in his s.
Mat. 10 : 10. Nor s. for your journey,
Mk. 6 : 8. Lu. 9 : 3.-10 : 4.
Lu. 22 : 35. I sent you without s.
36. let him take his purse and s.
SCRIPTURE.
Da 10 : 21. shew what is noted in S.
Mk. 12 : 10. have ye not read this S.
15 : 28. S. was fulfilled wh. saith,
Jn. 13 : 18.-17 : 12.-19 : 24, 28, 36.
Lu 4 : 21. This day is this S. fulfilled
Jn. 2 : 22. they believed the S and
7 : 38. He th. believeth as S. said
42. Hath not S. said, Ch. cometh
10 : 35. the S. cannot be broken
19:37. S. saith, They shall look on
20 : 9. they know not the S. ⌊him
Ac. 1 : 16. S must needs be fulfilled
8 : 32. The place of S. wh. he read
35. Philip began at the same S.
Ro. 4 : 3. What saith the S.? 10 : 8.
Ga. 4 : 30. ⌈2. 1 Ti. 5 : 18.
9 : 17. For the S. saith, 10 : 11.-11 :
Ga. 3 : 8. S foreseeing G. wo. justify
22. S. hath concluded all und sin
2 Ti. 3 : 16. All S. is given by inspir.
Ja. 2 : 8. royal law, acc to S ⌈lieved
23. S. fulfilled wh saith, Ab. be
4 : 5. ye think S. saith in vain
1 Pe. 2 : 6. It is in S. I lay in Sion
2 Pe 1:20. no S. is of private interp.
SCRIPTURES.
Mat. 21 : 42. Did ye never read in S.
22 : 29. err, not knowing S., Mk.
26 : 54. how sh. S. be fulfil-d ⌊12:24.
56. S. of prophets might be fulfill-
Mk. 14 : 49. S. must be fulfilled ⌊ed
Lu. 24 : 27. he expounded in all S.
32. burn, while he opened to us S.
45. that they might understand S.
Jn. 5 : 39. Search S., for in them ye
Ac. 17 : 2. he reasoned out of S
11. noble, and searched S. daily
18 : 24. a Jew, Apollos, mighty in S.
28. shewing by S. th. Jes. was Ch.
Ro. 1 : 2. promised by prophets in
holy S. ⌈hope
15 : 4. through comfort of S. have
16 : 26. by S. made known to all na.
1 Co. 15 : 3. how Ch. died acc-g to S.
4. th. he rose again acc-g to the S.
2 Ti. 3 : 15. from child hast known S.
2 Pe. 3 : 16. wrest, as th. do other S.
SCROLL.
Is. 34:4. heavens sh. be rolled as a s.
Re. 6 : 14. the heaven departed as a s.
SCUM.
Eze. 24 : 6. Woe to pot whose s. is
11. that s. of it may be consumed
12. her great s. went not out of
her, her s. shall be in the fire
SCURVY. See SCABBED.
SCYTHE, S. ⌈† 3
Is. 2:† 4. beat spears into s-s, Mi. 4 :
Je. 50:† 16. Cut off him th. handl-h s.
Jo. 3 : † 10. beat your s-s into spears
SCYTH'IAN. ⌈S.
Col. 3 : 11. Where is nei. barbarian
SEA. [Molten.] ⌈4 : 2.
1 K. 7 : 23. he made molten s., 2 Ch.
24. were knops compassing s. ⌈4.
25. s. was set upon oxen, 2 Ch. 4 :
39. set the s. on right side of the
house, 2 Ch. 4 : 10. ⌈2 Ch. 4 : 15.
44. one s. and 12 oxen under s.,
2 K. 16 : 17. Ahaz took down the s.
25 : 13. the s. did Chaldeans break
in pieces, Je. 52 : 17. ⌈Je. 52:20.
16. two pillars, one s., and bases,
1 Ch. 18 : 8. wh w. Sol. made brazen s.
2 Ch. 4 : 6. s. for priests to wash in
Je. 27 : 19. saith L. concern-g the s.
SEA of glass. ⌊s. o. g.
Re. 4 : 6. And before throne was a
15 : 2. And I saw as it were a s. o. g.

Re. 15 : 2. on **s.o.g.** having harps
SEA. [s.
Ex. 14 : 2. encamp betw. Migdol and
16. stretch thine hand over s., 27.
21. Lord caused s. to go back (2)
15 : 10. Thou didst blow, s. covered
20:11. L. made the s., Ps.95:5. Jon.
1 : 9. Ac. 4 : 24.-14 : 15. [Philis.
23 : 31. bounds from Red s. to s. of
Nu. 11:31. wind brought quails fr. s.
34 : 5. goings out of it sh. be at the
s., Jos. 15 : 4, 11.-16 : 3, 8.-17 :
9.-19 : 29. [3.-13 : 27.
11. the s. of Chinnereth, Jos. 12 :
De. 30:13. Nei. is it bey-d s. th. thou
say, Who go over the s. for us
Jos. 15 : 46. From Ekron unto the s.
16 : 6. border went toward s., 19:11.
17:10. Manass. and the s. is border
24 : 6. ye came unto s. Eg-ns pur-
7. he brought s. upon them [sued
1 K. 10 : 22. king had at s. a navy
18 : 43. Go up, look tow. s. [-98 : 7.
1 Ch. 16 : 32. Let s. roar, Ps. 96 : 11.
2 Ch. 20:2. multitude ag. thee bey. s.
Ne. 9 : 11. thou didst divide the s.,
went thro. the s., Jb. 26 : 12.
Ps. 74 :13.-78 :13 Is. 51:15. Je.
Jb. 7 :12. Am I a s. or a whale[31:35.
11:9. measure is broader than the s.
14 : 11. As the waters fail from s.
28 : 14. the s. saith, It is not wi. me
38 : 8. Or who shut s. with doors
41 : 31. he maketh the s. like a pot
Ps. 66 : 6. He turned s. into dry land
72 : 8. sh. have dominion fr. s. to s.
78 : 53. s. overwhelmed their enem.
80 : 11. She sent her boughs unto s.
104 : 25. So is this great wide s.
107: † 3. And gathered them fr. the
23. that go down to s. in ships [s.
114 : 3. The s. saw it and fled
5. What ailed thee, O thou s., that
Pr. 8 : 29. he gave to s. his decree
Is. 11 : 9. as waters cover s., Ha. 2:14.
15. destroy tongue of Egyptian s.
16:8. her branches are gone over s.
19 : 5. waters shall fail from the s.
23 : 2. merchants that pass over s.
4. Be ashamed, O Zion, s. hath spok-
11. He stretched hand over s. [en
24 : 14. they sh. cry aloud from s.
42 : 10. Sing unto L. ye th. go to s.
50 : 2. at my rebuke I dry up the s.
51 : 10. Art thou it wh. dried the s.
57 : 20. wicked are like troubled s.
Je. 6 : 23. their voice roareth like s.
25 : 22. kings of isles beyond s.
48:32. O vine, thy plants gone ov. s.
50 : 42. their voice shall roar like s.
51:36. I will dry up her s. and make
42. The sea is come upon Babylon
La. 2 : 13. breach is great like s.
Eze. 26 : 3. s. causeth waves to come
47 : 17. border from s. be Hazar-
18. from border unto east s. [enan
Da. 7 : 3. four beasts came from s.
Jo. 2 : 20. his face toward east s. (2)
Am. 8:12. shall wander from s. to s.
Jon. 1:11. What do unto thee that s.
be calm, for s. tempestuous, 11,
Mi. 7 : 12. he shall come fr. s. to s. [12.
Na. 1:4. He rebuketh the s., maketh
3 : 8. No, whose rampart was the s.
Ha 3 : 8. was thy wrath against s.
15. Thou didst walk thro. the s.
Hag. 2 : 6. I will shake earth and s.
Zch. 9 : 10. dominion be from s. to s.
10 : 11. he shall pass through the s.
14 : 8. toward former s., hinder s.
Mat. 8 : 26. he arose and rebuked s.
27. and s. obey him, Mk. 4:39, 41.
15 : 29. nigh unto s. of Gali., Mk. 7:
17 : 27. go thou to s., cast hook[31.
23:15. hypocrites, ye compass s. and
Mk. 3 : 7. withdrew hims. with disci.
5 : 21. he was nigh unto s. [to s.
Lu. 21 : 25. distress, the s. roaring
Jn. 6 : 1. s. of Gali. is s. of Tiberias
16. disciples went down unto s.
18. s. arose by reason of wind
21 : 1. to disciples at s. of Tiberias
Ac. 17 : 14. sent Paul to go to s.
27 : 5. sailed over s. of Cilicia
40. committed themselves unto s.
28 : 4. this man, tho. he escaped s.
1 Co. 10:1. our fath-s passed thro. s.
Re. 7 : 2. given to hurt earth and s.
3. saying, Hurt not earth nor s.
10:6. who created the s. and things
14:7. worship him that made the s.
20 : 13. and the s. gave up the dead
21 : 1. and there was no more s.
By the SEA. [s.
Ex. 14 : 9. Eg-ns overtook them **b.**
Nu. 13 : 29. Canaanites dwell **b. s.**,
Jos. 5 : 1. [sand **b.s.**
2 S. 17 : 11. all Israel be gathered as
1 K. 4:20. Jud. and Isr. as sand **b.s.**
5 : 9. convey them **b.s.**, 2 Ch. 2:16.
Is. 18 : 2. sendeth ambassadors **b.s.**
Je 46:18. Carmel **b.s.**, so [Mk. 1:16.
Mat. 4:18. Jes. walking **b.s.** of Gali,
Mk. 4 : 1. multitude was **b.s.** [afar off
Re. 18:17. many as trade **b.s.** stood
See **Sea COAST, GREAT Sea.**
In the or into the SEA. [s.
Ex. 14: 28. host of Pha. th. came **i-o**
15 : 1. horse and rider thrown **i-o**
4. Pha.'s host he cast **i-o s.**[s., 21.
19. horse with horsemen **i-o s.**
Ps. 77 : 19. Thy way is **i.s.**, thy path
89 : 25. I will set his hand **i.s.**
Ec. 1 : 7. all rivers run **i-o s.**, yet s. is
Is. 27 : 1. he sh. slay dragon **i.s.**
43 : 16. L., which maketh a way **i.s.**
Eze. 26:17. city that was strong **i.s.**
18. isles **i. s.** shall be troubled
47 : 8. These waters go **i-o s.** which
brought **i-o s.** shall be healed
Jon. 1 : 4. a mighty tempest **i.s.**
5. mariners cast forth wares **i-o s.**
12. Take me, cast me **i-o s.**, 15.
Zch. 9 : 4. will smite her power **i. s.**
10 : 11. shall smite waves **i. s.**
Mat. 4:18. casting net **i-o s.**, Mk. 1:16.
8 : 24. arose great tempest **i. s.**
32. whole herd of swine ran **i-o s.**
13 : 47. kingd. like a net cast **i-o s.**
21:21. be thou cast **i-o s.**, Mk. 11:23.
Mk. 4 : 1. entered ship, sat **i. s.**
5 : 13. herd ran **i-o s.**, choked **i. s.**
9 : 42. he were cast **i-o s.**, Lu. 17:2.
Lu. 17 : 6. be thou planted **i. s.**
Jn. 21 : 7. Peter cast himself **i-o s.**
Ac. 27 : 30. had let down boat **i-o s.**
38. and cast out the wheat **i-o s.**
43. they should cast thems. **i-o s.**
1 Co 10 : 2. baptized **i.** cloud and **s.**
2 Co. 11 : 26. in perils **i. s.** am. false
Ja. 3:7. beasts and things **i.s.** tamed
Re. 5 : 13. every creature **i.s.**, say-g
8 : 8. mt. burning was cast **i-o s.**
9. third part of creatures **i.s.**
16 : 3. ev. living soul died **i.s.** [s.
18 : 19. made rich that had ships **i.**
21. angel cast a millstone **i-o s.**
Of the SEA. [o.s.
Ge. 9 : 2. fear of you upon all fishes
49 : 13. Zeb. dwell at haven **o.s.** [s.
Ex. 14:23. went aft. them to midst **o.**
15 : 8. congealed in heart **o.s.**
19. brought waters **o.s.** upon them
Jos. 15 : 5. bay **o. s.** at uttermost
18:14. compassed corner **o.s.**[part
2 S 22 : 16. channels **o. s.** appeared
1 K. 18 : 44. ariseth a cloud out **o.s.**
2 Ch. 8:18. servants had knowl. **o.s.**
Es. 10 : 1. isles **o.s.**, Is. 11:11.-24.15.
Jb. 9 : 8. treadeth upon waves **o.s.**
36 : 30. he covereth bottom **o.s.**
38 : 16. Hast entered springs **o.s.**
Ps. 8 : 8. Fowl of the air, fish **o.s.**
33 : 7. He gathereth waters **o.s.**
Ps. 68 : 22. my people fr. depths **o.s.**
89 : 9. Thou rulest the raging **o.s.**
93 : 4. L. mightier than waves **o.s.**
139 : 9. dwell in utterm. parts **o.s.**
Is. 5 : 30. ag. them like roaring **o.s.**
9 : 1. afflict her by way **o.s.**
21 : 1. burden of the desert **o.s.**
23 : 4. strength **o.s.** hath spoken
48 : 18. righteousn. as waves **o.s.**
51 : 10. hath made depths **o.s.**
60 : 5. abund. **o.s.** sh. be converted
63 : 11. brought them out **o.s.**
Je. 5 : 22. sand for the bound **o.s.**
Eze. 26 : 16. princes **o.s.** shall come
27 : 3. Tyrus, situate at entry **o.s.**
9. ships **o.s.** in thee to occupy
29. pilots **o.s.** shall come [s.
32. like the destroyed in midst **o.**
39 : 11. of passengers on east **o.s.**
Am. 5 : 8. calleth for waters **o.s.**, 9:
9:3. fr. sight in bottom **o.s.** [6.
Mi. 7 : 19. cast sins into depths **o.s.**
Zph. 1 : 3. I will consume fishes **o.s.**
Mat. 4 : 15. way **o. s.** beyond Jordan
18:6. better drowned in depth **o.s.**
Mk. 5 : 1. unto other side **o.s.** [o.s.
Jn. 6 : 22. peo. stood on other side
25. found him on other side **o.s.**
Ja. 1 : 6. wavereth, is like wave **o.s.**
Jude 13. Raging waves **o.s.** foaming
Re. 8:8. third part **o.s.** became blood
12 : 12. Woe to the inhabiters **o.s.**
13 : 1. I saw a beast rise out **o.s.**
See FISH, FISHES, MIDST.
See **In the MIDST, PLAIN.**
On or Upon the SEA.
Ps. 65 : 5. them th. are afar off **u.s.**
Is. 10 . 26. as his rod was **u.s.**
Je. 49:23. fainthearted, is sorrow **o.s.**
Mat. 14 : 25. Jes. went walking **o.s.**,
26. Mk. 6 : 48, 49. Jn. 6 : 19.
Re. 7 : 1. wind should not blow **o.s.**
10 : 2. he set his right foot **u.s.**
5. angel wh. I saw stand **u.s.**, 8.
16 : 3. angel poured his vial **u.s.**
SEA monsters.
La. 4:3. Even **s.m.** draw out breast
SEA port.
Ju. 5:† 17. Asher continued on **s.p.**
See **RED sea, SALT sea.**
See **SAND** with SEA.
SEA shore. [s.s.
Ge. 22:17. thy seed as sand upon the
Ex. 14 : 30. saw Eg-s dead upon **s.s.**
Jos. 11 : 4. came as sand upon **s.s.**
Ju. 5 : 17. Asher continued on **s.s.**
1 S. 13 : 5. Philistines as sand on **s.s.**
1 K. 4:29. largeness of heart as sand
on **s. s.** [s.s.
Je. 47 : 7. given it a charge against
He. 11 : 12. sprang many as sand by
SEA side. [s.s.
De. 1 : 7. Turn, go by way of **s. s.**
Ju 7 : 12. Midianites lay as sand by
2 Ch. 8 : 17. Sol. to Eloth at **s.s.**[s.s.
Mat. 13 : 1. same day Jes. sat by **s.s.**
Mk. 2 : 13. he went again by **s.s.**
4 : 1. he began to teach by **s.s.**
Ac. 10 : 6. Simon, whose ho. by **s.s.**,
SEAS. [32
Ge. 1 : 10. gath-g of waters called **s.**
22. multiply and fill waters in **s.**
Le. 11 : 9. what hath fins in **s.** eat
10. not fins in **s.** be abomination
De. 33 : 19. suck of abundance of **s.**
Ne. 9 : 6. thou hast made **s.** and all
Ps 8:8. whatso. passeth thro. paths
24:2. hath founded it upon **s.**[of s.
65 : 7. Which stilleth noise of the **s.**
69 : 34. Let the **s.** praise him, and
135 : 6. what L. pleased did he in **s.**
Is. 17 : 12. a noise like noise of **s.**
Je. 15:8. widows are above sand of **s.**
Eze. 26 : † 17. wast inhabited of **s.**
27 : 4. Thy borders in midst of **s.**
25. glorious in midst of the **s.**
26. broken in midst of **s.**, 27, 34.

Eze. 27 : 33. thy wares went out of s.
28 . 2. in seat of God,in midst of s.
8. of them slain in midst of the s.
32 . 2. Pha , thou as a whale in s.
Da. 11:45. taberu. of palace betw. s.
Jon. 2 : 3. cast me into midst of s.
Ac. 27 : 41. place where two s. met

SEAFARING. [men
Eze. 26 : 17. that was inhabited of s.

SEAL, SEALS. [s.
1 K. 21 : 8. Jezebel sealed wi. Ahab's
Jb. 38 : 14. It is turned as clay to s.
41 : 15. scales shut as with close s.
Can. 8 : 6. Set me as a s. upon thy heart, as a s. on thy arm
Jn. 3:33. hath set to his s. G. is true
Ro. 4: 11. circumc. s. of righteousn.
1 Co. 9: 2. s. of mine apostleship, ye
2 Ti. 2 : 19. having this s., The Lord
Re. 5 : 1. a book sealed with 7 s-s
2. Who is worthy to loose the s-s ?
5. Lion of Juda prevailed to loose
9. Thou art worthy to open s-s[s-s
6 : 1. I saw Lamb opened one of s-s
3. opened second s. | 5. third s.
7. opened fourth s. | 9. fifth s.
12. when he had opened sixth s.
7 : 2. angel having s. of living God
8 : 1. he had opened 7th s. [God
9 : 4. hurt those th. have not s. of
20:3. shut him up, set s. upon him

SEAL. [Verb.] [1.
Ne. 9 : 38. princes and priests s., 10:
Is. 8 : 16. s. law among my disciples
Je. 32 : 44. subscribe evidences, s.th.
Da. 9 : 24. 70 weeks to s. vision
12:4. shut up words, s. book [tered
Re. 10: 4. s. things the thunders ut-
22 : 10. s. not sayings of prophecy

SEALED. [ures?
De. 32 : 34. Is not this s. am. treas-
1 K. 21:8. letters s. with Ahab's seal
Ne. 10 : 1. those s. were Nehemiah
Es. 3 : 12. s. with k.'s ring, 8: 8, 10.
Jb. 14 : 17. My transgr-n is s. in bag
Can. 4 : 12. my spouse is fountain s.
Is. 29 : 11. vision is as book s.
Je 32 : 10. I subscribed s. evidence
11. I took that which was s., 14.
Da. 6 : 17. king s. it with his signet
12 : 9. words are s. till the end
Jn. 6 : 27. him hath God the Fa. s.
Ro. 15 : 28. have s. to them this fruit
2 Co. 1 : 22. Who hath s. us and given
Ep. 1 : 13. ye were s. with Holy Spir-
4 : 30. Spirit, whereby ye are s. [it
Re 5 : 1. I saw book s. with seven
7 : 3. hurt not sea, till we s. serv-ts
4. I heard number of them s., were s. 144,000 of tribes
5. of Juda were s. 12,000, of Reuben s. 12,000, of Gad s. 12,000
6. of Aser s. 12,000, of Nephthalim s. 12,000, s. 12,000
7. of Simeon s. 12,000, of Levi s. 12,000, of Issachar s. 12,000
8. of Zabulon s. 12,000, of Joseph s. 12,000, of Benjamin s. 12,000

SEALEST, ETH.
Jb. 9 : 7. com-deth sun, s-h stars
33:16. openeth ears, s-h instruction
37 : 7. He s-h up hand of every man
Eze. 28: 12. Thou s-t sum full of wisd.

SEALING. [Noun, Part.]
Ne. 9 : † 38. priests are at s., 10 : † 1.
Mat. 27:66. s. the stone and setting

SEAM. [watch
Jn. 19:23. coat was with-t s., woven

SEARCH. [Noun.]
De. 13:14. shalt inquire and make s.
Ezr. 4 : 15. That s. be made in records, 5 : 17. [found, 6 : 1.
19. s. hath been made, and it is
Jb. 5 : † 9. gr things, and is no s.
8 : 8. prepare thyself to s. of fa-s
38 : 16. hast walked in s. of depth ?
64 : 6. accomplish a diligent s.

Ps. 77 : 6. my spirit made diligent s.
Je. 2 : 34. not found it by secret s.

SEARCH. [Verb.]
Le. 27:33. sh. not s. whet. it be good
Nu. 10 : 33. to s. out resting place
13 : 2. Send men, that they s. land
32. land which we have gone to s.
14 : 7. land we passed to s. is good
38. Caleb of men th. went to s., 36.
De. 1:22. We will send men, they sh. s.
33. who went to s. out a place
Jos. 2 : 2. came men to s. country, 3.
Ju. 18 : 2. Danites sent to s. land
1 S. 23 : 23. if in land, I will s. him
2 S. 10 : 3. hath not David sent servants to s. city, 1 Ch. 19 : 3. [s.
1 K. 20:6. will send my serv-s, they sh
2 K. 10:23. s. that none of serv-s of L.
Jb. 13 : 9. Is it good he sho. s. you out
Ps. 44 : 21. sh. not God s. this out
139:23. s. me, O G., know my heart
Pr. 25:2. honor of k-s to s. a matter
27. to s. own glory is not glory[25
Ec. 1: 13. my heart to s. by wisd., 7:
Je. 17 : 10. I, the Lord, s. heart
29 : 13. when yes. for me with all your
La. 3 : 40 Let us s. our ways [heart
Eze. 34 : 6. none did s. after them
8. nei. did shepherds s. for flock
11. I will both s. my sheep, and
39 : 14. after 7 months shall they s.
Am. 9 : 3 I will s. and take them
Zph. 1: 12. will s. Jerus. wi. candles
Mat. 2 : 8. s. diligently for yo. child
Jn. 5 : 39. s. Scriptures, they testify
7:52. s., for out of Galilee no proph.

SEARCHED.
Ge 31:34. Laban s. the tent, but, 35.
37. Whereas thou has s. my stuff
44 : 12. steward s. for the cup, and
Nu. 13:21. they went up, s. the land
32. evil report of land they s.
Nu. 14 : 6. Josh. and Caleb s. la., 38.
34. Aft. number of days ye s. land
De. 1 : 24. came unto Eshcol, s. it
1 S. 20 : † 12. When I have s. my fa.
1 K. 7: † 47. nei. weight of brass s. out
Jb. 5 : 27. we have s. it for thy good
28 : 27. he prepared it, and s. it out
29 : 16. cause I knew not, I s. out
32 . 11. whilst ye s. out what to say
36 : 26. can number of his yrs. be s.
Ps. 139 : 1. O Lord, thou hast s. me
Je. 31 : 37. founda-s of earth s. out
46:23. cut forest, tho. it cannot be s.
Ob 6. How are things of Esau s.
Ac. 17 : 11. Bereans s. Script-s daily
1 Pe. 1 : 10. salvation prophets s. diligently

SEARCHEST.
Jb. 10 : 6. that thou s. after my sin
Pr. 2:4. if thou s. for her as treasures

SEARCHETH.
1 Ch. 28 : 9. for the Lord s. all hearts
Jb. 28 : 3. he s. out all perfection
39 : 8. he s. after every green thing
Pr 18 : 17. neighbour s. him [him
28 : 11. poor that hath underst-g s.
Ro. 8 : 27. s. hearts, knoweth Spirit
1 Co. 2 : 10. the Spirit s. all things
Re. 2 : 23. I am he which s. the reins

SEARCHING, S.
Nu. 13 : 25. returned from s. of land
Ju. 5:16. For divis-ns of Reub. gr. s-s
Jb. 11 : 7. Canst by s. find out God ?
34 : † 24. in pieces men without s.
Pr. 20 : 27. s. inward parts of belly
25 : † 3. heart of kings there is no s.
Is. 40 : 28. is no s. of his underst-g
1 Pe. 1 : 11. s. what time Spirit of Ch.

SEARED.
1 Ti. 4:2. conscience s. with hot iron

SEASON. [Noun.]
Ge. 40:4. they continued a s. in ward
Ex. 13 : 10. keep ordinance in his s.
De. 16 : 6. s. thou camest out of Eg.
De 28 : 12. rain unto thy land in s.

Jos. 24 : 7. dwelt in wilderness long s.
2 K. 4 : 16. this s. shall embrace son
17 woman bare a son at that s.
1 Ch. 21 : 29. altar that s. at Gibeon
2 Ch. 15 : 3. for long s. without God
Jb. 5 : 26. shock of corn cometh in s.
30 : 17. bones pierced in night s.
38:32. Canst bring Mazzaroth in s.?
Ps. 1: 3. tree, th. bringeth fruit in s.
22: 2. I cry in nights., am not silent
Pr. 15:23. word in s., how good is it?
Ec. 3 : 1. To every thing there is a s.
Is. 50 : 4. how to speak word in s.
Je. 5:24. former and latter rain in s.
33:20. not day and night in their s.
Eze. 34 : 26. cause shower come in s.
Da. 7 : 12. lives prolonged for a s.
Ho. 2 : 9. take away my wine in s.
Mk. 12 : 2. at s. sent to husbandmen
Lu. 1 : 20. words be fulfilled in s.
4 : 13. devil departed fr. him for a s.
13 : 1. present at th. s. some th. told
20 : 10. at the s. he sent servant
23 : 8. desirous to see him long s.
Jn. 5: 4. angel went down at cert. s.
35. willing for s. to rejoice in his
Ac. 13 : 11. not seeing sun for a s.
19 : 22. he stayed in Asia for a s.
24 : 25. when I have convenient s.
2 Co. 7 : 8. you sorry, tho. but for s.
2 Ti. 4 : 2. be instant in s. out of s.
Phm. 15. he thf. departed for a s.
He. 11 : 25. pleasures of sin for a s.
1 Pe. 1 : 6. tho. for a s. if need be, ye
Re. 6 : 11. should rest yet a little s.
20 : 3. he must be loosed a little s.
See APPOINTED, DUE season.

SEASONS. [s.
Ge. 1 : 14. lights sh. be for signs and
Ex. 18 : 22. judge people at all s., 26.
Le. 23 : 4. feasts proclaim in their s.
Ps. 16 : 7. reins instruct in night s.
104 : 19. appointeth moon for s.
Da. 2 : 21. changeth times and s.
Mat. 21 : 41. render fruits in their s.
Ac. 1 : 7. It is not for you to know s.
14 : 17. gave us rain and fruitful s.
20 : 18. I have been with you all s.
1 Th. 5 : 1. of s. no need that I write

SEASON, ED.
Le. 2: 13. ev. meat off-g shalt thou s.
Mk. 9 : 50. wherewith will ye s. it?
Lu. 14:34. if lost savour, whw. be s-d?
Col. 4:6. Let speech be wi. grace, s-d

SEAT. [Noun.]
Ju. 3 : 20. Eglon rose out of his s.
1 S. 1 : 9. Eli sat upon a s. by, 4 : 13.
4 : 18. he fell from off s. backward
20: 18. because thy s. will be empty
25. k. sat upon his s., a s. by wall
2 S. 23 : 8. Tachmonite that sat in s.
1 K. 2 : 19. s. set for king's mother
10: 19. were stays on place of the s.
Es. 3 : 1. Haman's s. above princes
Jb. 23 : 3. I might come to his s.
29 : 7. I prepared my s. in street
Ps. 1: 1. nor sitteth in s. of scornful
Pr. 9: 14. foolish woman sitteth on s.
Eze. 8 : 3. s. of image of jealousy
28 : 2. I sit in s. of God, in midst
Da. 11 : † 38. the Almighty in his s.
Am. 6 : 3. cause s. of viol-e to come
Mat. 23: 2. Pharisees sit in Moses' s.
Re. 2: 13. dwellest where Satan's s. is
13: 2. dragon gave power and his s.
16 : 10. poured vial upon s. of beast
See JUDGMENT seat.
See MERCY seat.

SEATS.
Je. 18 : † 3. he wrought a work on s.
Mat. 21: 12. he overthrew s. of them sold doves, Mk. 11: 15. [Mk. 12: 39.
23 : 6. love chief s. in synagogues,
Lu. 1 : 52. put down mighty from s.
11: 43. ye love uppermost s.. 20: 46
Re. 4 : 4. four and 20 s., upon s. 24
11 : 16. elders sat before God on s.

SEATED. [he s.
De. 33:21. in portion of lawgiver was
SEATWARD. [ubim
Ex. 37 : 9. to mercy s., face of cher-
SEBA. [Ch. 1 : 9.
Ge. 10 : 7. sons of Cush ; S. and, 1
Ps. 72 : 10. kings of Sheba and S. shall
Is. 43:3. I gave Ethiopia and S. [offer
SEBAT. [month S.
Zch. 1 : 7. eleventh month, which is
SECA'CAH. See MIDDIN.
SE'CHU.
1 S. 19 : 22. came to a great well in S.
SECOND.
Ge. 2 : 13. name of s. river is Gihon
6 : 16. s. and third stories make ark
30 : 7. Bilhah bare Jacob a s. son, 12.
32 : 19. so commanded he the s. and
41 : 43. made him ride in s. chariot
52. the s. called he Ephraim
Ex. 26:4. loops in coupling of s., 5, 10.
20. s. side of tabern. [-36: 11, 12, 17.
28 : 18. s. row be emerald, 39 : 11.
Le. 5 : 10. offer s. for burnt offering
Nu. 2 : 16. shall set forth in s. rank
Jos. 19 : 1. the s. lot came to Simeon
Ju. 6 : 26. take s. bullock and offer,
1 S. 8:2. name of his s., Abiah [25, 28.
15 : † 9. Saul spared best of s. sort
2 S. 3 : 3. his s., Chileab, of Abigail
2 K. 9 : 19. he sent a s. on horseback
22 : † 14. dwelt in Jerus. in s. part
23 : 4. comm-ded priests of s. order
25 : 17. the s. pillar, Je. 52 : 22. [24.
18. took Zeph-h, s. priest, Je. 52 :
1 Ch. 2 : 13. the s., 7 : 15.-8 : 1.-12 :
9.-23 : 11.-24 : 7.-25 : 9.
3 : 1. were the sons, the s., 15. - 8 :
39.- 23 : 19, 20.-24 : 23.-26 : 2, 4,
15 : 18. brethren of s. degree [11.
2 Ch. 28 : † 7. Elkanah, s. to the king
35 : 24. serv-ts put him in s. chariot
Ezr. 1 : 10. silver basins of s. sort
Ne. 11 : 9. Judah, s. over the city
17. Bakbukiah, s. am. his breth-n
Es. 2:14. she into s. house of women
9 : 29. to confirm s. letter of Purim
Jb. 42 : 14. first Jemima, the s. Kezia
Ec. 4 : 8. one alone, there is not a s.
15. s. child that sh. stand instead
Eze. 10 : 14. s. face was face of man
Da. 7 : 5. ano. beast, a s. like a bear
8 : † 3. one horn higher than s.
Zph. 1 : 10. a cry, a howling from s.
Zch. 6 : 2. in s. chariot black horses
Mat. 21 : 30. he came to s. and said
22: 26. likewise the s. had her, Mk.
12 : 21. Lu. 20 : 30. [12 : 31.
39. s. commandment is like it, Mk.
Lu. 6 : 1. came to pass on s. sabbath
12 : 38. if he come in s. watch
19 : 18. s. came saying, L. thy pound
Jn. 4 : 54. this is the s. miracle
Ac. 12 : 10. when past the s. ward
13 : 33. as it is written in s. psalm
1 Co. 15 : 47. the s. man is the Lord
2 Co. 1 : 15. ye might have s. benefit
Ti. 3 : 10. after s. admonition
He. 8 : 7. no place been sought for s.
9 : 3. after s. vail, the tabernacle
7. into the s. went the high priest
10 : 9. first, th. he may establish s.
2 Pe. 3 : 1. s. epistle I now write [6.
Re. 2. 11. not be hurt of s. death, 20:
4 : 7. the s. beast like a calf
6 : 3. I heard s. beast say, Come (2)
8 : 8. s. angel sounded, as it were
11 : 14. The s. woe is past, the third
16 : 3. s. angel poured out vial
20 : 14. This is the s. death, 21 : 8.
21 : 19. s. founda-n of wall sapphire
See **Second DAY, MONTH.**
See **Second TIME, YEAR.**
SECONDARILY.
1 Co. 12 : 28. God set s. prophets
SECRESIES.
Pr 9 : † 17. and bread of s. is pleasant

SECRET. [Adj.]
De. 27 : 15. putteth an idol in s. place
29 : 29. s. things belong unto Lord
Ju. 3 : 19. I have a s. errand, O king
13 . 18. Why askest my name, it is
1 S. 5 : 9. had emerods in s. parts [s. ?
19 : 2. take heed, abide in s. place
2 K. 5 : † 24. Gehazi came to s. place
Jb. 14 : 13. O that thou keep me s.
15 : 11. is any s. thing with thee ?
20 : 26. darkness be hid in s. places
Ps. 10:8. in s. places doth he murder
† 9. He lieth in wait in s. places
17 : 12. yo. lion lurking in s. places
18 : 11. made darkness his s. place
19 : 12. cleanse thou me fr. s. faults
64 : 2. Hide me fr. s. counsel of wick.
81 : 7. I ans-d in s. place of thunder
90 : 8. s. sins in light of thy counten.
91 : 1. dwelleth in s. place of Most
Pr. 27 : 5. rebuke better than s. love
Ec 12 : 14. into judgment ev. s. thing
Can. 2 : 14. dove that art in s. places
Is. 3 : 17. L. will discover s. parts
26 : † 16. poured out a s. speech
45 : 3. give thee riches of s. places
Je. 2 : 34. not found it by s. search
13 : 17. my soul sh. weep in s. places
23 : 24. Can any hide in s. places
49 : 10. I have uncov-d his s. places
La. 3 : 10. unto me as lion in s. places
Eze. 7 : 22. shall pollute my s. place
Da. 2 : 22. revealeth deep s. things
Mat 13 : 35. I will utter things kept
s., Ro. 16 : 25.
24 : 26. he is in s. chambers
Mk. 4 : 22. nei. anything kept s. but it
sho. come, Lu. 8 : 17. [in s. place
Lu. 11 : 33. No man putteth a candle
SECRET. [Noun.] [their s.
Ge. 49 : 6. O my soul, come not into
Jb. 15:8. Hast heard s. of God ? [me
9 : † 19. All men of my s. abhorred
24 : † 15. adulterer setteth face in s.
29 : 4. when s. of G. upon my taber.
40 : 13. Hide and bind faces in s.
Ps. 25 : 14. s. of L. wi. them th. fear
27 : 5. in s. of taberu. hide me, 31 : 20.
64 : 4. may shoot in s. at perfect
139 : 15. not hid when I was made
Pr. 3 : 32. his s. is wi. righteous [in s.
9 : 17. bread eaten in s. is pleasant
21 : 14. a gift in s. pacifieth anger
25 : 9. discover not a s. to another
26 : † 26. Whose hatred is cov-d in s.
Is. 24 : † 16. I said, My s. to me, Woe
45 : 19. I have not spok. in s., 48 : 16.
Je. 23 : † 18. who stood in s. of Lord
Eze. 13 : † 9. not be in s. of my people
28 : 3. no s. that they can hide
Da. 2 : 18. mercies of God cone-g s.
19. was s. revealed to Daniel
27. s. which king hath demanded
30. s. not revealed to me for any
47. th. couldest reveal s. [wisdom
4 : 9. I know no s. troubleth thee
Am. 3 : 7. revealeth s. unto his serv-s
Mat. 6 : 4. that thine alms may be
in s., and Fa. wh. seeth in s.,
6. pray to Father wh. is in s. [6, 18.
18. appear to fast to Fa. wh. is in s,
Jn. 7 : 4. no man doeth thing in s.
10. went unto feast as it were in s.
18 : 20. in s. have I said nothing
Ep. 5 : 12. things which are done in s.
SECRETS.
De. 25 : 11. wife taketh him by the s.
Jb. 11 : 6. would shew thee s. of wisd.
Ps. 44 : 21. he knoweth s. of heart
Pr. 11 : 13. A talebearer revealeth s.
20 : 19. as a talebearer revealeth s.
Da. 2 : 28. is a God that revealeth s.
29. that revealeth s. maketh kno.
47. your God is a revealer of s.
8 : † 13. saint said to number of s.
Ro. 2 : 16. God sh. judge s. of men
1 Co. 14 : 25. s. of his heart manifest

SECRETLY. [away s. ?
Ge. 31 : 27. Wheref. didst thou flee
De. 13 : 6. if thy broth. entice thee s.
27 : 24. that smiteth his neighb. s.
28 : 57. her children she shall eat s.
Jos. 2 : 1. Joshua sent two men to spy
1 S. 18 : 22. Commune with Dav. s. [s.
23 : 9. knew Saul s. practised mis-
2 S. 12 : 12. For thou didst it s. [chief
2 K. 17 : 9. Isr. did s. things not right
Jb. 4 : 12. thing was s. brought to me
13 : 10. reprove, if ye s. accept persons
31 : 27. if my heart been s. enticed
Ps. 10 : 9. He lieth in wait s. as a lion
31 : 20. sh. keep them s. in a pavilion
Je. 37 : 17. Zedekiah asked s., Is any
38 : 16. Zedekiah sware s. unto Jere-h
40 : 15. Johanan spake to Ged-h s.
Ha. 3 : 14. rejoicing to devour poor s.
Jn. 11 : 28. called Mar., her sister s.
19 : 38. Joseph, a disciple, s. for fear
SECT, S.
Ac. 5 : 17. which is s. of Sadducees
15 : 5. rose certain of s. of Pharisees
24 : 5. ringleader of s. of Nazarenes
26 : 5. straitest s. of our religion
28 : 22. s. every where spoken ag-t
1 Co. 11 : † 19. must be s-s am. you
SECUN'DUS. [Asia, S.
Ac. 20 : 4. accompanied him into
SECURE. [Verb.] [you
Mat. 28 : 14. will persuade him and s.
SECURE, LY. [Adj., Adv.]
Ju 8 : 11. smote host, for host was s.
18 : 7. they dwelt careless and s.
10. ye sh. come unto people, s., 27
Jb. 11 : 18. shalt be s. because is
12 : 6. that provoke God are s. [hope
Pr. 3 : 29. seeing he dwelleth s-y by
Am. 6 : † 1. Woe to them s. in Zion [s-y
Mi. 2 : 8. garment fr. them that pass by
SECURITY.
Ac. 17 : 9. when had taken s. of Ja-
SEDITION, S. [son
Ezr. 4 : 15. they moved s. in city, 19.
Lu. 23 : 19. for s. cast into prison, 25.
Ac. 24 : 5. this man a mover of s.
Ga. 5 : 20. works of the flesh are s-s
SEDUCE, ED.
2 K. 21 : 9. Manasseh s-d th. to do evil
Is. 19 : 13. they have also s-d Egypt
Eze. 13 : 10. they have s-d my people
Mk 13 : 22. signs and wonders to s.
1 Ti. 6 : † 10. some been s-d fr. faith
1 Jn. 2 : 26. cone-g them that s. you
Re. 2 : 20. sufferest Jezebel to s. my
SEDUCERS. [servs.
2 Ti. 3 : 13. but s. shall wax worse
SEDUCETH, ING.
Pr. 12 : 26. way of wicked s-h them
1 Ti. 4 : 1. giving heed to s-g spirits
SEE. [call
Ge. 2 : 19. Adam, to s. what he would
8 : 8. sent dove to s. if the waters
11 : 5. Lord came down to s. city
12 : 12. when Egyptians sh. s. thee
18 : 21. I will s. whether they have
19 : 21. said, s. I ha. accepted thee
22 : † 14. name of pl., The L will s.
27 : 27. s., the smell of my son is as
29 : † 32. Leah called name, S. a son
31 : 5. I s. your father's countenance
12. s. all the rams are ringstreaked
50. s., G. witn-s betw. me and thee
34 : 1. Dinah went to s. daus. of la.
37 : 14. s. whe. it be well wi. breth.
39 : 14. s., he hath bro-t an Hebrew
41 : 41. s., I ha. set thee over Egypt
42 : 9. to s. nakedness of land, 12.
44 : 34. lest I s. the evil th. sh. come
45 : 12. your eyes s. and eyes of my
24. s. that ye fall not out by way
28. I will s. Joseph before I die
48 : 11. not thought to s. thy face
Ex. 1 : 16. when ye s. th. upon stools
3 : 3. I will turn s. this gr. sight, 4.
4 : 18. s. whe. my brethren be alive

Ex. 4:21. s. th. do those woud-s bef.
5:19. did s. they were in evil case
6:1. sh. s. wh. I will do to Pharaoh
7:1. s., I ha. made thee god to Pha.
10:5. cannot be able to s. earth
12:13. when I s. blood, I will pass
13:17. peo. repent when they s. war
14:13. stand still and s. salvation
16:29. s., for L. hath giv. you sabb.
32. may s. bread whw. I fed you
22:8. s. whe. he hath put hand
23:5. If thou s. ass of him th. hateth
31:2. s., I called Bezaleel, 35:30.
33:12. s. thou sayest, Br. up peo.
20. shall no man s. me and live
23. thou shalt s. my back parts
34:10. people shall s. work of Lord
Le. 13:8. if priest s. scab spreadeth
10. the priest shall s. him, 17.
15. priest sh. s. the raw flesh, and
30. Then priest sh. s. plague, 14:36.
20:17. if a man s. her nakedn-s, (2)
Nu. 4:20. not go in to s. holy things
11:23. s. whe. word come to pass
13:18. s. the land wh. it is [ne s. it
14:23. nei. sh. any that provoked
22:41. th. he might s. utmost part
23:9. from top of rocks I s. him
13. place thou mayest s. them, thou shalt s. but utmost part
24:17. I shall s. him, but not now
27:12. s. land I have given to Isr.
32:8. I sent your fa-s to s. land
11. none that came out of Egypt shall s. land, De. 1:35.
De. 1:36. save Caleb, he sh. s. land
3:25. I pray, let me s. good land
28. to inherit land thou shalt s.
18:16. nei. let me s. this great fire
23:14. s. no unclean thing in thee
28:10. peo. shall s. thou art called
34. sight which thou shalt s., 67.
68. Thou shalt s. it no more again
29:4. L. not given you eyes to s.
22. when they s. plagues of land
30:15. s., I have set bef. thee life
32:20. I will s. what their end be
39. s. now I am he, there is no G.
52. thou sh. s. land bef. thee, but
34:4. I have caused thee to s. it
Jos. 6:2. s. I have given Jericho and
8:8. sh. do. s., I have commanded
22:10. built a great altar to s. [you
Ju. 9:37. s. there come peo. by mid.
14:8. Samson turned to s. carcass
16:5. s. wh-in his great strength
21:21. s. if dau-s of Shiloh come
1 S. 2:32. s. an enemy in my habita.
6:9. s. if it goeth by his coast
13. ark, and rejoiced to s. it
12:16. s. great thing Lord will do
17. may s. your wickedness is gr.
14:17. Number, and s. who is gone
29. s. how eyes been enlightened
38. s. wherein this sin hath been
15:35. Sam. came no more to s. Saul
17:28. that thou mightest s. battle
19:3. what I s. that I will tell thee
15. Saul sent messengers to s. Da.
20:29. let me, I pray, s. my breth.
21:14. said, You s. the man is mad
23:22. s. place where his haunt is
23. s. where he hideth himself
24:11. my fa. s. skirt of thy robe
15. Lord s. and plead my cause
25:35. s., I hearkened to thy voice
26:16. s. where king's spear is
2 S. 7:2. s., I dwell in hou. of cedar
13:5. thy father cometh to s. thee, say, let Tamar dress meat (2)
6. when king was come to s. him
14:30. s., Joah's field is near mine
15:3. s., thy matters are good and
28. s., I will tarry in the plain
24:3. that eyes of king may s. it
13. advise and s. what answer I sh. return to him that sent me

1 K. 9:12. Hiram, to s. cities Solomon had [Ch. 10:16.
12:16. s. to thy house, David, 2
17:23. Elijah said, s. thy son liveth
20:7. s. how man seeketh mischief
22. proph. said, s. what thou doest
22:25. sh. s. in that day, 2 Ch. 18:24.
2 K. 2:10. if s. when I am taken
5:7. s. how he seeketh quarrel
6:17. open his eyes that he s.
20. open eyes of these that they s.
32. s. how this son of a murderer
7:2. shalt s. it with thine eyes, 19.
13. serv-ts said, Let us send and s.,
14. king sent, saying, Go and s.
8:29. went to s. Joram, 9:16. 2
9:17. said, I s. company [Ch. 22:6.
34. Go, s. now this cursed woman
10:16. come, s. my zeal for the L.
19:16. open, L., eyes, and s., Is. 37:17.
23:17. What title is that I s.
2 Ch. 18:16. I did s. all Is. scattered
20:17. s. the salvation of the Lord
24:5. Go, s. ye hasten the matter
25:17. Come, let us s. one another
Ezr. 4:14. not meet to s. k.'s dishon.
Ne. 9:9. s. affliction of our fathers
Es. 3:4. to s. if Mordecai's matters
5:13. so long as I s. Mordecai sit.
8:6. Es. said, How endure to s. evil on my people? to s. destruction
Jb. 3:9. neither let it s. the dawning
7:7. mine eye shall no more s. good
8. eye that seen me s. me no more
9:25. my days flee, they s. no good
10:15. therefore s. mine affliction
17:15. my hope, who shall s. it?
19:26. yet in my flesh sh. I s. God
27. Whom I shall s. for myself
20:9. eye wh. saw him s. him no more
21:20. His eyes shall s. his destruc.
22:19. righteous s. it, and are glad
24:1. why do they not s. his days?
15. adulterer saith, No eye sh. s. me
28:27. Then did he s. it, declare it
31:4. doth not he see my ways, and
33:28. his life shall s. the light
35:5. Look unto heavens, s. clouds
36:25. Every man may s. it, man
Ps. 10:11. said, God will never s. it
14:2. G. looked to s. if any did, 53:2.
16:10. nei. suffer Holy One to s. corruption, Ac. 2:27, 31.-13:35.
22:7. All they th. s. me laugh. [L.
27:13. had believed to s. goodn. of
31:11. they that did s. me, fled
34:8. O taste and s. Lord is good
12. many days, th. he may s. good
37:34. wicked are cut off, thou sh. s.
40:3. many shall s. it and trust in
41:6. come to s. me, he speak-h van-
49:19. they shall never s. light [ity
52:6. The righte-s shall s. and fear
59:10. God shall let me s. desire upon mine enemies, 92:11.-118:
63:2. To s. thy power and glory [7.
64:5. they say, Who shall s. them?
8. all that s. them shall flee away
66:5. Come and s. works of God
69:32. The humble sh. s. this, be glad
86:17. which hate me may s. it
91:8. shalt s. reward of wicked
97:6. all the people s. his glory
106:5. may s. good of thy chosen
107:24. These s. the works of Lord
42. righteous shall s. it and rejoice
112:8. s. his desire upon enemies
10. wicked shall s. it, be grieved
119:74. will be glad when they s. me
128:5. shalt s. good of Jerusalem
6. thou sh. s. thy children's chil.
139:16. eyes did s. my substance
24. s. if be any wicked way in me
142:† 4. Look on right hand and s.
Pr. 24:18. Lest L. s. and it displease
29:16. righteous shall s. their fall
Ec. 1:10. may be said s., this is new

Ec. 2:3. s. wh. was good for sons of
3:18. s. th. themselves are beasts
22. to s. what shall be after him
7:11. is profit to them that s. sun
8:16. to s. business that is done
9:† 9. s. life with wife thou lovest
Can. 2:14. O my dove, let me s. thy
6:11. into garden of nuts to s. fruits to s. whe. vine flourished, 7:12.
Is. 5:19. hasten work that we s.
6:10. lest they s. with their eyes
13:1. wh. Isaiah, son of Amoz, did s.
14:16. that s. thee sh. narrowly
26:11. they sh. s. and be ash-d [look
29:18. eyes of the blind sh. s. [ers
30:20. thine eyes sh. s. thy teach-
32:3. eyes of them th. s. not be dim
33:17. sh. s. the king in his beauty
20. thine eyes sh. s. Jerus., a quiet
35:2. they sh. s. glory of the L. [it
40:5. glory revealed, all flesh sh. s.
41:20. That they may s. and know
48:6. s. all this | 49:7. Kings sh. s.
52:8. for they shall s. eye to eye
10. the earth shall s. salvation
15. what not been told sh. they s.
53:2. when we s. him, is no beauty
10. he shall s. his seed, he shall
11. He shall s. of travail of his soul
60:4. Lift thine eyes round and s.
5. shalt s. and flow together
61:9. all that s. them sh. acknowl.
62:2. Gent. shall s. thy righeousn.
64:9. s., we are all thy people
66:18. they shall come s. my glory
Je. 1:10. s., I have set thee ov. nat-s
11. I s. a rod | 13. I s. seething pot
2:10. s. if there be such a thing
19. s. it is an evil thing and bitter
23. s. thy way in the valley [with
3:2. s. where hast not been lain
4:21. How long shall I s. standard
5:1. s. now, seek in broad places
6:16. Stand ye, s. and ask for paths
7:12. my place, and s. what I did
11:20. let me s. thy veng-e, 20:12.
20:18. out of womb to s. labour
22:10. no more, nor s. nat. country
12. he shall s. this land no more
30:6. s. whe. man doth travail, why do I s. every man with hands
51:61. sh. s. and read all these words
La. 1:11. s., O L., for I become vile
12. s. if any sorrow like my sorrow
Eze. 8:6. thou sh. s. greater abominations, 13, 15. [of peace
13:9. that s. vanity | 16. s. visions
16:37. they may s. all thy nakedu.
20:48. sh. s. I, L., have kindled it
21:29. While they s. vanity unto
32:31. Pharaoh shall s. them [thee
33:6. if watchman s. sword come
39:21. heathen sh. s. my judgment
Da. 1:10. why sho. he s. your faces
3:25. Lo, I s. four men loose
Jo. 2:28. shall s. visions, Ac. 2:17.
Am. 6:2. Pass ye unto Calneh and s.
Jon. 4:5. s. what wo. become of city
Mi. 6:9. man of wisdom s. thy name
7:10. she mine enemy shall s. it
16. nations sh. s., be confounded
Ha. 1:1. burden which Hab. did s.
2:1. watch to s. what he will say
Zch. 2:2. to s. what is the breadth
4:10. shall s. the plummet in hand
5:2. I answered, I s. flying roll
5. Lift your eyes, s. what is this
9:5. Ashkelon sh. s. it and fear (2)
10:7. their children shall s. it
Mal. 1:5. And your eyes shall s. [G.
Mat. 5:8. pure in heart, they sh. s.
16. they may s. your good works
7:5. shalt thou s. clearly, Lu. 6:42.
8:4. s. thou tell no man, shew, 9:30. Mk. 1:44. Ac. 23:22.
11:4. Go and shew John those things which ye do hear and s.

Mat.11:7. Wh. went you into wildern.
to s., 8, 9. Lu. 7 : 24, 25, 26.
12 : 38. Master, we would s. a sign
13 : 14. seeing, ye sh. s., Mk. 4 : 12.
Ac. 28 : 26. ⌈28 : 27.
15. gross, lest they should s., Ac.
16. blessed are your eyes, they s.
17. desired to s. things which ye s.
15 : 31. saw blind to s., Lu. 7 : 22.
16 : 28. till s. Son of man coming
22 : 11. when k. came in to s. guests
24 : 6. wars, s. ye be not troubled
30. they shall s. Son of man coming, Mk. 13 : 26. Lu. 21 : 27.
26 : 58. Pe. sat wi. serv-ts to s. end
27 : 4. s. thou to that|24. s. ye to it
49. let us s. whe. Elias will come
28 : 1. and the other Mary to s. sepul.
6. Come s. place where Lord lay
10. Galilee, there shall they s. me
Mk. 5 : 14. out to s. what was done
15. s. him possessed with devil
32. to s. her that had done this
6 : 38. how many loaves? Go and s.
8 : 24. I s. men as trees walking ⌈it
12 : 15. bring a penny that I may s.
13 : 1. s. what manner of stones, and
15 : 32. let Ch. descend th. we may s.
Lu. 2 : 15. go unto Bethlehem and s.
3 : 6. all flesh shall s. salvation of G.
8 : 16. who enter may s. light, 11 : 33.
20. brethren, desiring to s. thee
35. they went out to s. wh. was done
9 : 9. he desired to s. him, 23 : 8.
27. not taste of death till they s.
14 : 18. bought ground, I must s. it
17 : 22. desire to s. one of the days
23. shall say, s. here, or s. there
19 : 3. Zaccheus sought to s. Jesus
4. into sycamore tree to s. him
20 : 13. will reverence when they s.
24 : 39. it is I, handle me and s. ⌊him
Jn. 1 : 33. Upon whom s. Sp. descend.
39. Come and s., 46. 11 : 34. Re.
6 : 1, 3, 5, 7. ⌈these
50. shalt s. greater things than
4 : 29. s. a man who told me all
6 : 19. they s. J. walking on the sea
7 : 3. discip. may s. works thou doest
8 : 51. If keep sayings, nev. s. death
56. Abraham rejoiced to s. my day
9 : 15. I washed, and do s.
25. I was blind, now I s.
19. asked, How doth he now s.?
39. that they who s. not might s., and they who s. be made blind
11 : 34. They say, Lord, come and s.
40. if believe, shouldest s. glory of
12 : 9. they might s. Lazarus ⌊God
21. saying, Sir, we would s. Jesus
16 : 22. sorrow, but I will s. you
20 : 25. Exc. I s. the print of nails
Ac. 2 : 17. young men sh. s. visions
7 : 56. I s. the heavens opened
8 : 36. eunuch said, s., here is water
15 : 36. visit breth., s. how they do
19 : 21. been there, I must s. Rome
22 : 14. his will, and s. that Just One
28 : 20. I called you to s. you
Ro. 1 : 11. For I long to s. you, that
7 : 23. I s. ano. law in my members
15 : 21. not spoken of, they shall s.
24. I trust to s. you in my journey
1 Co. 8 : 10. if s. thee wh. hast knowl.
16 : 10. s. that he be with you with-t
2 Co. 8 : 7. s. that ye abound in grace
Ga. 1 : 18. I went to Jerusa. to s. Pet.
Ep. 3 : 9. all s. what is fellowship
5 : 15. s. that ye walk circumspectly
33. wife s. th. she reverence husb.
Ph. 1 : 27. whe. I s. you or be absent
2 : 23. soon as I s. how it will go ⌈you
1 Th. 3 : 6. desiring to s. us, we to s.
5 : 15. s. none render evil for evil
1 Ti. 6 : 16. whom no man can s.
2 Ti. 1 : 4. Greatly desiring to s. thee
He. 8 : 5. s. thou make acc. to pattern
He. 12 : 14. holin. with-t wh. no man s.
25. s. ye refuse not him speak-h ⌊L.
13 : 23. if he come shortly, I will s.
1 Pe. 1 : 22. s. th. ye love one ano. ⌊you
3 : 10. he that will s. good days, let
him refrain ⌈er sin a sin
1 Jn. 5 : 16. If any man s. his broth-
3 Jn. 14. I trust I sh. shortly s. thee
Re. 1 : 7. he cometh, every eye sh. s.
12. I turned to s. voice that spake
3 : 18. eyesalve, that thou mayest s.
6 : 1. beast saying, Come and s., 3,
6. s. thou hurt not the oil ⌊5, 7.
9 : 10. idols which neither can s.
11 : 9. s. their dead bodies 3 days
16 : 15. naked, and th. s. his shame
18 : 7. I, a queen, shall s. no sorrow
9. shall s. smoke of her burning
19 : 10. me, s. thou do it not, 22 : 9.

See FACE with see.

SEE with nor, not, or cannot.

Ge. 21 : 16. let me n.s. death of child
27 : 1. Isaac was old, he could n.s.
48 : 10. eyes of Israel dim, cou. n.s.
Nu. 11 : 15. n.s. my wretchedness
14 : 23. sh. n.s. land I sware unto
23 : 13. utmost part, sh. n.s. them
De. 22 : 1. n.s. brother's ox go astray
4. shalt n.s. thy brother's ass fall
1 S. 3 : 2. Eli, dim, he cou. n.s., 4 : 15.
1 K. 14 : 4. Ahijah could n.s. eyes set
2 K. 3 : 14. I not look tow. n.s. thee
17. Ye shall n.s. wind, n.s. rain
22 : 20. thine eyes n.s. evil I will
Ne. 4 : 11. They sh. n.s. till we come
Jb. 9 : 11. Lo, he goeth, I s. him n.
20 : 17. He sh. n.s. rivers of honey
22 : 11. Or darkness thou canst n.s.
23 : 9. hideth himself that I c.s.
24 : 1. that know him n.s. his days
31 : 4. Doth n. he s. my ways
34 : 32. That I s.n. teach thou me
35 : 14. sayest, thou shalt n.s. him
37 : 21. s.n. bright light in clouds
Ps. 49 : 9. live and n.s. corruption
58 : 8. that they may n.s. the sun
69 : 23. be darkened, that they s.n.
74 : 9. We s.n. our signs, there is
89 : 48. What man shall n.s. death
94 : 7. they say, The Lord sh. n.s.
9. formed eye, shall he n.s.?
115 : 5. eyes, but they s.n., 135 : 16.
Is. 26 : 11. is lifted up, they will n.s.
30 : 10. Which say to the seers, s.n.
33 : 19. Thou shalt n.s. a fierce peo-
38 : 11. I shall n.s. the Lord ⌈ple
44 : 9. s.n., that they be ashamed
18. he shut their eyes, they c.s.
Je. 5 : 21. eyes, and s.n., Eze. 12 : 2.
12 : 4. He shall n.s. our last end
14 : 13. say, Ye shall n.s. the sword
17 : 6. he sh. n.s. when good cometh
8. he sh. n.s. when heat cometh
23 : 24. can any hide that I n.s.?
Eze. 12 : 6. thou s.n. the ground, 12.
13. shall n.s. it, though he die
Da. 5 : 23. gods of gold, wh. s.n., Re.
Zph. 3 : 15. n.s. evil any more|9 : 20.
Mat. 13 : 13. they seeing s.n. ⌈13 : 35.
23 : 39. Ye sh. n.s. me hencef., Lu.
Lu. 2 : 26. n.s. death bef. seen Ch.
8 : 10. that seeing, they might n.s.
17 : 22. desire to s. and ye sh. n.s.
Jn. 3 : 3. he c.s. kingdom of God
36. sh. n.s. life, but wrath abid-h
9 : 39. that they wh. s.n. might s.
12 : 40. should n.s. with their eyes
16 : 16. A little while, n.s. me, 17, 19.
18 : 26. Did I n.s. thee in garden?
Ac. 22 : 11. could n.s. for the glory
Ro. 8 : 25. if we hope for th. we s.n.
11 : 8. eyes, that they should n.s.
10. eyes be darkened th. may n.s.
1 Co. 16 : 7. For I will n.s. you now
He. 2 : 8. we s.n. yet all things put
11 : 5. translated, that he n.s. death
1 Pe. 1 : 8. tho. now ye s. him n., yet
2 Pe. 1 : 9. he is blind, c.s. afar

We SEE.

Ge. 37 : 20. w. sh. s. what will become of his dreams
Ps. 36 : 9. in thy light sh. w.s. light
Is. 5 : 19. hasten work th. w. may s.
53 : 2. when w. sh. s. him, there is no
Je. 5 : 12. nei. shall w. s. sword or
42 : 14. Eg., where w. sh. s. no war
Mat. 12 : 38. Master, w. would s. sign ⌈Jn. 6 : 30.
Mk. 15 : 32. w. may s. and believe,
Jn. 9 : 41. w.s. your sin remaineth
12 : 21. saying, Sir, w. wou. s. Jesus
1 Co. 13 : 12. now w.s. thro. a glass
He. 2 : 9. But w.s. Jesus, who was
3 : 19. So w.s. they could not enter
1 Jn. 3 : 2. w. shall s. him as he is

SEE ye, or Ye SEE.

Ex. 14 : 13. y. shall s. them no more
16 : 7. y. shall s. glory of the Lord
Jos. 3 : 3. When y.s. ark of covenant
1 S. 10 : 24. s.y. him L. hath chosen?
21 : 14. y.s. the man is mad ⌈derer
2 K. 6 : 32. s.y. how this son of mur-
2 Ch. 29 : 8. to hissing, as y.s. with
30 : 7. them to desolation, as y.s.
Ne. 2 : 17. y.s. the distress we are in
Jb. 6 : 21. y.s. my casting down
Can. 6 : 13. What will y.s. in Shula-
Is. 6 : 9. s.y., but perceive not⌊mite
18 : 3. s.y., when he lifteth ensign
42 : 18. look, ye blind, that y. may s.
66 : 14. y.s. your hearts sh. rejoice
Je. 2 : 31. s.y. the word of the Lord
42 : 18. y. sh. s. this place no more
Eze. 13 : 23. y. sh. s. no more vanity
14 : 22. y. sh. s. their way and do-s
23. comfort when y.s. their ways
Da. 2 : 8. y.s. thing is gone from me
Mat. 11 : 4. things y. do hear and s.
13 : 14. seeing y. sh. s., and not perceive, Ac. 28 : 26.
17. many have desired to s. things y.s., Lu. 10 : 23, 24. ⌈things?
24 : 2. Jesus said, s. y. not all these
33. when y. sh. s. all these things, know, Mk. 13 : 29. Lu. 21 : 31.
26 : 64. Hereafter shall y.s. the Son of man, Mk. 14 : 62.
27 : 24. I am innocent, s.y. to it, Mk. 15 : 36. ⌈16 : 7.
28 : 7. in Galilee sh. y.s. him, Mk.
Mk. 8 : 18. having eyes, s.y. not?
13 : 14. y. sh. s. abom-n, Mat. 24 : 15.
Lu. 12 : 54. When y.s. a cloud rise
55. When y.s. south wind blow
13 : 28. when y. shall s. Abraham
21 : 20. when y.s. Jerus. compassed
30. y.s. and know, summer is nigh
24 : 39. not flesh, as y.s. me have
Jn. 1 : 51. y. shall s. heaven open
4 : 48. Exc. y.s. signs not believe
6 : 62. What if y.s. Son of man asc-d
14 : 19. seeth no more; but y.s. me
16 : 10. to my Fa., y.s. me no more
16. a little while y. sh. s. me, 17, 19.
Ac. 2 : 33. shed forth this y. now s.
3 : 16. made this man strong, y.s.
19 : 26. y.s. that not alone at Eph.
25 : 24. y.s. this man about whom
1 Co. 1 : 26. y.s. your calling, breth
Ga. 6 : 11. y.s. how large a letter
Ph. 2 : 28. when y.s. him again, ye
He. 10 : 25. as y.s. day approaching
Ja. 2 : 24. y.s. by works man is just-
Pe. 1 : 8. tho. now y.s. him not⌊ified

SEED. ⌈s.

Le. 12 : 2. If a woman have conceived
15 : 32. This is the law of him whose s. goeth fr. him, 22 : 4. ⌈conc. s.
Nu. 5 : 28. then she shall be free and
He. 11 : 11. Sarah strength to conc. s.
1 Pe. 1 : 23. born not of corrupt-e s.
1 Jn. 3 : 9. Whosoever is born of God his s. remaineth in him

See COPULATION.

SEED, S. [Progeny.] [s.
Ge. 4:25. G. hath appointed me ano.
7:3. to keep s. alive upon earth
15:3. Abr. said, to me given no s.
19:32. may preserve s. of our fa., 34.
38:8. raise up s. to thy brother,
Mat. 22:24. Mk. 12:19. Lu. 20:28.
9. Onan knew s. should not be his
Le. 21:21. a blemish of s. of Aaron
22:4. What man of s. of Aa. is leper
Nu. 16:40. wh. is not of s. of Aaron
De. 1:8. to give it unto their s., 11:9.
4:37. chose their s. after th., 10:15.
31:21. forgott. out of mouths of s.
Ru. 4:12. s. L. sh. give of this wom.
1 S. 1:† 11. unto handm. s. of men
2:20. L. give thee s. of this woman
24:21. thou wilt not cut off my s.
1 K. 11:14. he was of the king's s.
39. I will afflict the s. of David
2 K. 11:1. Athaliah destroyed all s.
royal, 2 Ch. 22:10. [Israel
17:20. Lord rejected all the s. of
25:25. Ishmael of s. royal, Je. 41:1.
1 Ch. 16:13. O ye s. of Isr. [Ne. 7:61.
Ezr. 2:59. could not shew their s.,
9:2. the holy s. have mingled
Ne. 9:2. the s. of Israel separated
Es. 6:13. If Mordecai of s. of Jews
9:27. Jews took upon their s., 31.
28. nor memorial perish fr. their s.
Jb. 21:8. Their s. is established in
Ps. 21:10. their s. sh. thou destroy
22:23. praise him, all ye s. of Jac.,
fear him, all ye s. of Israel
30. A s. sh. serve him, be counted
37:28. s. of wicked shall be cut off
69:36. s. of his serv-ts sh. inherit it
102:28. their s. sh. be established
106:27. To overthrow their s. am.
Pr. 11:21. s. of righteous be deliv-d
Is. 1:4. Ah, nation, s. of evil doers
6:13. holy s. sh. be the substance
14:20. s. of evil doers nev. renowned
45:19. I said not unto s. of Jac., Seek
25. In L. all s. of Isr. be justified
57:3. s. of the adulterer and whore
4. Are ye not a s. of falsehood
61:9. their s. sh be known am. Gentiles th. they are s. L. hath bles-d
65:9. I will bring a s. out of Jacob
23. are s. of the blessed of Lord
Je. 2:21. I planted thee a right s.
7:15. I will cast out s. of Ephraim
23:8. wh. led s. of house of Israel
31:27. sow wi. s. of man s. of beast
36. s. of Israel sh. cease as nation
37. I will cast off s. of Isr., 33:26.
33:22. so will I multiply s. of David
Eze. 17:13. hath taken of king's s.
20:5. I lifted hand unto s. of Jacob
43:19. priests th. be of s. of Zadok
44:22. take maidens of s. of Israel
Da. 1:3. bring of children of k.'s s.
2:43. shall mingle with s. of men
9:1. Darius of the s. of the Medes
Mal. 2:15. he might seek a godly s.
Mk. 12:20. 1st dying left no s., 21, 22.
Jn. 7:42. Ch. cometh of s. of David
Ac. 13:23. Of this man's s. hath
God raised Jesus [2 Ti. 2:8.
Ro. 1:3. was made of the s. of Da.,
4:16. promise be sure to all his s.
9:8. chil. of promise counted for s.
29. Except Lord had left us a s.
Ga. 3:16. saith not to s-s as of many
19. it was added, till s. sho. come
Re. 12:17. make war with remnant
of her s.
See **ABRAHAM** with seed.

His SEED. [h.s.
Ge. 17:19. my cov-t with Isaac and
46:6. Jacob came and all h.s., 7.
48:19. h.s. shall bec. a multitude
Ex. 28:43. a statute of h.s., 30:21.
Le. 20:2. of h.s. unto Molech, 3, 4.
21:15. Neither sh. ye profane h.s.
Nu. 14:24. Caleb and h.s. sh. possess
24:7. h.s. shall be in many waters
25:13. he sh. have it and h.s. aft.
Jos. 24:3. I multiplied h.s. [s.
2 S. 4:8. avenged thee of Saul and h.
22:51. mercy to Da., h.s., Ps. 18:50.
1 K. 2:33. blood upon head of Joab
and h.s., upon Da. h.s. peace
Ne. 9:8. a covenant to give it to h.s.
Es. 10:3. speaking peace to all h.s.
Ps. 25:13. h.s. shall inherit earth
37:25. have I not seen h.s. begging
26. He is merciful, h.s. is blessed
89:29. h.s. will I make endure, 36.
112:2. h.s. shall be mighty
Is. 53:10. sh. see h.s. prolong days
Je. 22:28. whf. cast out, he and h.s.?
30. no man of h.s. shall prosper
29:32. punish Shemaiah and h.s.
33:26. not take of h.s. to be rulers
36:31. punish Jehoiakim and h.s.
49:10. Esau, h.s. is spoiled, and
Ac. 7:5. wo. give it to him and h.s.
6. h.s. sho. sojourn in strange land

Thy SEED. [s.
Ge. 3:15. enmity betw. t.s. and her
12:7. Unto t.s. will I give this land,
13:15.-15:18.-17:8.-24:7.-
26:3.-28:4, 13.-35:12.-48:4.
Ex. 33:1. De. 34:4. [10.-28:14.
13:16. I will make t.s. as dust, 16:
15:5. So shall t.s. be, Ro. 4:18.
13. t.s. shall be a stranger in land
17:7. covenant betw. me and t.s.;
be a God unto thee and t.s., 10.
9. thou and t.s. after thee
12. stranger not of t.s. be circ-d
21:12. in Isaac sh. t.s. be called
He. 11:18. [is t.s.
13. make Ishmael a nation bec. he
22:17. t.s. possess the gate, 24:60.
18. in t.s. shall all nations be
blessed, 26:4.-28:14. Ac 3:25.
26:4. make t.s. to multiply as
stars, 22:17. [sake
24. multiply t.s. for Abraham's
32:12. I will make t.s. as sand
48:11. God hath shewed me t.s.
Le. 18:21. not of t.s. pass thro. fire
21:17. Whoso. of t.s. hath blemish
Nu. 18:19. off-gs I give thee and t.s.
De. 28:46. curses for sign upon t.s.
59. make plagues of t.s. wonderf.
30:6. will circumcise heart of t.s.
19. choose life that t.s. may live
1 S. 20:42. L. be betw. my s. and t.s.
2 S. 7:12. I will set up t.s., 1 Ch.
17:11. [unto t.s.
2 K. 5:27. leprosy of Naaman cleave
Jb. 5:25. know t.s. shall be great
Ps. 89:4. t.s. will I estab-h forever
Is. 43:5. I will bring t.s. from east
44:3. will pour my Spirit upon t.s.
48:19. t.s. had been as the sand
54:3. t.s. shall inherit Gentiles
59:21. Spirit not depart out of
mouth of t.s., nor t.s.'s seed [27.
Je. 30:10. t.s. fr. land of capt-y, 46:
Ga. 3:16. And to t.s. which is Ch.

Your SEED. [y.s.
Ex. 32:13. this land will I give unto
Le. 22:3. Whoso. of y.s. goeth to
Is. 66:22. so sh. y.s. and name rem-n

SEED, S. [Vegetable.]
Ge. 1:11. herbs yielding s., 12, 29.
47:19. give us s. | 23. lo, here is s.
24. four parts your own for s. [7.
Ex. 16:31. like coriander s., Nu. 11:
Le. 11:37. if carcass fall upon any s.
38. if any water be put upon s.
19:19. not sow field wi mingled s.
26:16. ye sh. sow your s. in vain
27:16. thy estimation be acc g to
s., a homer of barley s.
30. all tithe of s. of land is the L.'s
Nu. 20:5. is no place of s. or figs
De. 11:10. Egypt, where sowedst s.
De. 14:22. tithe all increase of thy s.
22:9. sow not with divers s-s, lest
fruit of thy s. be defiled
28:38. carry much s. into field
1 S. 8:15. king will take tenth of s.
1 K. 18:32. contain 2 measures of s.
Jb. 39:12. will unicorn bring thy s.
Ps. 126:6. goeth bearing precious s.
Ec. 11:6. In the morning sow thy s.
Is. 5:10. s. of homer yield ephah
17:11. in morning make s. flourish
23:3. by great waters s. of Sihor
55:10. that it may give s. to sower
Je. 35:7. nor sow s. nor plant viney.
9. neither have we vineyard nor s.
Eze. 17:5. He took of s. of land
Jo. 1:17. s. is rotten under clods
Am. 9:13. overtake him th. soweth s.
Hag. 2:19. Is the s. yet in the barn?
Zch. 8:12. the s. shall be prosperous
Mal. 2:3. I will corrupt your s. and
Mat. 13:4. some s-s fell by way side
19. wh. receive s. by way side
20. received s. into stony places
22. that received s. among thorns
23. that received s. into good gr-d
24. a man which sowed good s.
27. Sir, didst not thou sow good s.?
32. Wh. is least of all s-s, Mk. 4:31.
37. th. soweth good s. is Son of man
38. good s. are child-n of kingdom
Mk. 4:26. if man cast s. into ground
27. s. should spring and grow up
Lu. 8:5. A sower went out to sow s.
11. parable; The s. is word of God
1 Co. 15:38. and to ev. s. his own body
See **SOW, SOWED, SOWER.**

SEEDING. [seed
Ge. 1:† 29. given you every herb s.

SEEDTIME.
Ge. 8:22. s. and harvest sh. not cease

SEEING. [Adj.]
Pr. 20:12. The Lord maketh s. eye

SEEING. [Conj.] [less
Ge. 15:2. wh. give me, s. I go child-
18:18. s. Ab. sh. become great na
22:12. s. hast not withh-d only son
24:56. s. L. hath prospered my way
26:27. Whf. to me, s. ye hate me
44:30. s. his life bound up in lad's
Ex. 21:8. s. he dealt deceitfully [life
23:9. s. ye were strangers in Egypt
Le. 10:17. s. the place is most holy
Nu. 16:3. s. congregation are holy
Jos. 17:14. s. I am a great people
22:18. s. ye rebel to day ag. Lord
Ju. 13:18. askest name, s. it is secret
17:13. do me good, s. I have Levite
21:7. s. we have sworn by the Lord
16. s. wom. destroyed out of Benj.
Ru. 1:21. s. Lord testified ag. me
2:10. s. I am a stranger [ing
1 S. 16:1. s. I rejected him fr. reign-
17:36. s. he defied armies of God
18:23. s. that I am a poor man
24:6. s. he is the anointed of Lord
25:26. s. L. hath withholden thee
28:16. s. Lord is departed from thee
2 S. 13:39. s. Amnon was dead
15:20. s. I go whither I may
18:22. s. thou hast no tidings
19:11. s. the speech of all Israel
2 K. 10:2. s. y-r master's sons wi. you
1 Ch. 12:17. s. is no wrong in mine
2 Ch. 2:6. s. heavens can-t contain
Ezr. 9:13. s. hast furnished us [him
Ne. 2:2. s. thou art not sick
Jb. 14:5. s. his days are determined
19:28. s. root of matter is in me
21:22. s. he judgeth those are high
24:1. s. times not hidden fr. Almi.
Ps. 50:17. s. thou hatest instruct-n
Pr. 3:29. s. he dwelleth securely
17:16. s. he hath no heart to wisd.
Ec. 2:16. s. th. wh. now is be forgot.
6:11. s. many things increase vanity
Is. 49:21. s. I have lost my children

Je. 47 : 7. s. L. hath given it charge
Eze. 16 : 30. s. thou doest these thi-s
17 : 18. s. he despised the oath
21 : 4. s. I will cut off righteous
Da. 2 : 47. s. couldest reveal secret
Ho. 4 : 6. s. thou hast forgotten law
Lu. 1 : 34. How this, s. I know not a man? ⌈nation
23 : 40. s. thou art in same condem-
Jn. 2 : 18. s. thou doest these things
Ac. 2 : 15. s. it is but 3d hour of day
13 : 46. s. ye put word of G. fr. you
17 : 24. s. he is Lord of heaven and
25. s. he giveth to all life, breath
19 : 36. s. these can-t be spoken ag.
24 : 2. s. by thee we enjoy quietness
Ro 3:30. s. it is one God wh. sh. justify
1 Co. 14 : 16. s. he understand-h not
2Co. 3:12. s. then we have such hope
4 : 1. s. we have ministry, faint not
11 : 18. s. that many gone aft. flesh
19. ye suffer fools, s. ye are wise
Col. 3 : 9. s. ye have put off old man
2 Th. 1 : 6. s. it is a righteous thing
He. 4 : 6. s. some must enter therein
14. s. we have great high priest
5 : 11. s. ye are dull of hearing
6 : 6. s. they crucify Son of God
7 : 25. s. he liveth to make interc-n
8 : 4. s. there are priests that offer
12 : 1. s. we are compassed about
1 Pe. 1 : 22. s. ye have purified souls
2 Pe. 3 : 11. s. these things be dissolved
14. s. ye look for such things
17. s. ye know these things, beware

SEEING. [Noun.]

Ex. 4 : 11. who maketh the s. or blind
23 : † 8. the gift blindeth the s. ⌈G.
2 Ch. 26 : † 5. had underst-g in s. of
Ec. 1 : 8 eye not satisfied with s.
Is. 6 : † 9. See ye in s., perceive not
21 : 3. I was dismayed at s. of it
33 : 15. shutteth eyes from s. evil
2 Pe. 2 : 8. in s. Lot vexed his soul

SEEING. [Part.]

Ge 19 : 1. Lot s. them rose to meet
28 : 8. Esau s. that dau-s of Canaan
Ex. 22 : 10. beast driven aw., no man
Nu. 35:23. s. not, cast it upon him⌊s.
1 K 1 : 48. one to sit, mine eyes s. it
11 : 28. s. young man was indust-s
Is. 42:20. s. many thi-s, observest not
Eze. 22 : 28. s. vanity, divining lies
Da. 2:†31. Thou, O k., wast s., 4:†10
Mat. 5 : 1. s. mult. he went into m-t
9 : 2. Jesus s. faith, said unto sick
13:13. parables, bec. they s. see not
14. s. ye shall see and shall not perceive, Mk. 4 : 12. Ac. 28 : 26.
Mk. 11 : 13. And s. fig tree afar off
Lu. 5 : 12. man full of leprosy, s. Jes.
8 : 10. that s. they might not see
Jn. 9 : 7. He went, washed, came s.
21 : 21. Pe. s. him, saith to Jes., L.
Ac. 2:31. s. this, spake of resurrec-n
3 : 3. s. Pe. and John about to go
7 : 24. s. one of them suffer wrong
8 : 6. people s. miracles that he did
9 : 7. hearing voice, but s. no man
13 : 11. not s. the sun for a season
16 : 27. s. the prison doors open⌈ble
He. 11 : 27. endured as s. him invisi-

SEEK. ⌈brethren

Ge. 37 : 16. Joseph said, I s. my
43 : 18. th. he may s. occasion ag.
Le. 19 : 31. nei. s. after wizards ⌊us
Nu. 16 : 10. s. ye priesthood also?
24 : 1. Balaam not to s. enchantm-ts
De. 4 : 29. if s. him with all heart
12 : 5. unto his habitation sh. ye s.
22 : 2. ox with thee until bro. s. it
1 S. 9 : 3. Kish to Saul. go s. the asses
10 : 2. asses thou wentest to s. are
14. Whither went ye? To s. asses
16 : 16. to s. out a cunning player
23 : 15. Saul came to s. his life, 25.-
24 : 2.-26 : 2.

1 S. 25 : 26. s. evil to my lord, be as
29. man risen to s. thy soul⌊Nabal
26 : 20. k. of Isr. is come to s. a flea
27 : 1. Saul shall despair to s. me
28 : 7. s. me woman hath a spirit
2 S. 5 : 17. Philistines came up to s. David, 1 Ch. 14 : 8. ⌈virgin
1 K. 1 : † 2. Let them s. a damsel a
2 : 40. Shimei went to s. servants
18 : 10. whi. my lord not sent to s.
19 : 10. s. my life to take it, 14.⌊thee
2 K. 2:16. let them go, s. thy master
6 : 19 I will bring you to man ye s.
18 : † 31. s. my favour with present
1 Ch. 4 : 39. to s. pasture for flocks
28 : 8. s. commandments of Lord
9. if s. him he be found, 2Ch.15:2.
2 Ch. 19 : 3. prepared heart to s. G.
30 : 19. prepareth his heart to s. G.
31 : 21. to s. his God, did it with all
34 : 3. Josiah began to s. after God
Ezr. 4 : 2. build, for we s. your God
7 : 10. Ezra prepared heart to s. law
8 : 21. to s. him a right way for us
22. name of G. upon them th. s. him
Ne. 2 : 10. a man to s. welfare of Isr.
Jb. 5 : 8. I would s. unto God, and
7 : 21. shalt s. me in morning, but
8 : 5. If thou wouldest s. unto God
20 : 10. His chil. sh. s. to please poor
Ps. 4 : 2. vanity, and s. after leasing
9 : 10. not forsaken them that s. thee
10 : 15. s. out his wickedness till
14 : 2. if any that did s. God, 53:2.
24:6. generation of them th. s. him
27:4. One thing desired, th. will I s.
8. s. ye my face, Thy face, L., will
34 : 14. s. peace, 1 Pe. 3 : 11. ⌊I s.
35 : 4. put to shame that s. my soul
38 : 12. they th. s. my life s. my hurt
40 : 14. that s. after my soul, 70 : 2.
54 : 3. oppressors s. after my soul
63 : 1. art my G., early will I s. thee
9. those that s. my soul go into
69 : 6. not those s. thee be confoun.
32. your heart shall live th. s. God
70:4. Let all those th. s. thee rejoice
71 : 13. wi. dishonour th. s. my hurt
24. unto shame that s. my hurt
83 : 16. that they may s. thy name
104 : 21. young lions s. meat fr. God
109 : 10. let his chil. s. their bread
119 : 2. that s. him wi. whole heart
45. at liberty, for I s. thy precepts
176. astray as sheep, s. thy serv-t
122 : 9. house of God, I s. thy good
Pr. 1 : 28. shall s. me, but not find me
8 : 17. that s. me early sh. find me
21 : 6. to fro of them th. s. death
23 : 30. they th. go to s. mixed wine
35. when I awake I will s. it again
29 : 10. hate upright, just s. his soul
26. Many s. the ruler's favor
Ec. 1 : 13. I gave my heart to s. out
3 : † 6. A time to s. a time to lose⌈dom
7 : 25. applied mine heart to s. wis-
8 : 17. a man labor to s. it, not able
Can. 3 : 2. will s. him my soul loveth
6 : 1. thy beloved, th. we may s. him
Is. 1 : 17. Learn to do well, s. judgm.
8:19. say, s. unto th. have familiar spirits; sho. not a peo. s. unto G.?
11 : 10. root of Jesse, to it Gent. s.
19 : 3. they shall s. to the charmers
26 : 9. wi. spirit will I s. thee early
29 : 15. Woe unto th. s. deep to hide
34 : 16. s. ye out of book of Lord
41 : 12. Thou shalt s. them, not find
17. When the needy s. water ⌈vain
45 : 19. I said not unto Jacob s. me in
58 : 2. they s. me daily, and delight
Je. 2 : 24. that s. her, in her month
33. Why trimmest way to s. love?
4 : 30. lovers despise will s. thy life
11 : 21. men of Anathoth, s. thy life
19 : 7. fall by the s. their lives, 21 : 7.
9. that s. their lives shall straiten

Je. 22 : 25. into hand of th. s. thy life,
29 : 7. s. the peace of city ⌊38 : 16.
13. ye sh. s. me, and find me, when
34 : 20. into hand of th. s. their life,
44:30. Pha. to them th. s. his life⌊21.
46 : 26. Eg-ns to those s. their lives
49 : 37. dismayed bef. them s. their
La. 1 : 11. All her people s. bread⌊life
Eze. 7 : 25. sh. s. peace, shall be none
26. shall they s. vision of prophet
34 : 6. flock scattered, none did s. th.
11. I will search my sheep, and s.
12. so will I s. out my sheep
16. I will s. that wh. was lost⌈pra-r
Da. 9 : 3. my face unto G., to s. by
Ho. 2 : 7. he sh. s., but not find them
Am. 5 : 4. s. me, and ye shall live
8. s. him that maketh seven stars
14. s. good not evil, that ye live
8 : 12. to s. word of L., and not find
Na. 3 : 7. whence sh. I s. comforters?
11. hid, thou shalt s. strength
Zph. 2 : 3. s. ye the Lord, ye meek
Zch. 11 : 16. shepherd nei. s. young
12:9. I will s. to destroy nations⌊one
Mal. 2 : 7. should s. law at his mouth
15. That he might s. a godly seed
Mat. 2 : 13. Herod will s. young child
6 : 32. these things do Gentiles s.
33. s. ye kingd. of God, Lu. 12:31.
7 : 7. s. and ye shall find, Lu. 11 : 9.
28 : 5. I know ye s. Jes., Mk. 16 : 6.
Mk. 1 : 37. said, All men s. for thee
3:32. mother and breth-ns. for thee
8 : 12. s. after a sign, Lu. 11 : 29.
Lu. 12:30. these things do nations s.
13 : 24. many, I say, will s. to enter
15 : 8. doth she not s. diligently?
17: 33. Whoso. s. to save his life sh.
19 : 10. Son of man is come to s. and
24 : 5. Why s. ye living am. dead?
Jn. 1 : 38. Jesus saith, What s. ye?
6:26. s. me not bec. ye saw miracles
7 : 25. Is not this he they s. to kill?
34. ye sh. s. me and not find me, 36.
8 : 21. Ye sh. s. me, and die in sins
37. Ab.'s seed, but s. to kill me, 40.
13 : 33. Ye shall s. me, and whi. I go
18 : 4. Jesus said, Whom s. ye? 7.
8. if ye s. me, let these go th-r way
Ac. 10:19. Behold, three men s. thee
21. Peter said, I am he whom ye s.
11 : 25. Barna. departed, to s. Saul
Ro. 2 : 7. to them who s. for glory
11 : 3. I alone, and they s. my life
1 Co. 1 : 22. Greeks s. after wisdom
10 : 24. Let no man s. his own, but
14 : 12. s. that ye excel to edifying
2 Co. 13 : 3. Since ye s. a proof of Ch.
Ga. 1 : 10. Do I s. to please men?
2 : 17. if while we s. to be justified
Ph. 2 : 21. For all s. their own things
Col. 3 : 1. if risen, s. things above
He. 11 : 6. rewarder of them th. s. him
14. declare plainly they s. country
13 : 14. here no city, but we s. one
Re. 9 : 6. those days sh. men s. death
See **Seek FACE, Seek LORD.**

SEEK not or not SEEK.

Le. 13 : 36. priest sh. n. s. yellow hair
Nu. 15 : 39. ye s. n. after own heart
De. 23 : 6. n. s. their peace, Ezr. 9 : 12.
Ru. 3 : 1. dau., sh. I n. s. rest for thee?
Ps. 10 : 4. wicked will n. s. after God
119 : 155. wicked, s. n. thy statutes
Je. 30 : 14. all thy lovers s. thee n.
45:5. seekest gr. things? s. them n.
Am. 5 : 5. But s. n. Beth-el, nor ent.
Lu. 12 . 29. s. n. what ye shall eat or
Jn. 5 : 30. bec. I s. n. mine own will
44. s. n. honor th. cometh from G.
8 : 50. I s. n. mine own glory ⌈wife
1 Co. 7 : 27. s. n. to be loosed, s. n. a
2 Co. 12 : 14. I s. n. yours, but you

SEEKEST.

Ge. 37 : 15. man asked, What s. thou
Ju. 4 : 22. I will shew the man thou s.

2 Sa. 17 : 3. man thou s. is as if all
20 : 19. s. to destroy mother in Isr.
1 K. 11 : 22. s. to go to thy country
Pr. 2 : 4. If thou s. her as silver, and
Je. 45 : 5. s. gr. things? seek th. not
Jn. 4 : 27. no man said, Whats. thou?
20 : 15. Jes. saith, Woman whom s.
SEEKETH. ⌊thou?
De. 11 : † 12. A land wh. L. thy Gods.
1 S. 19 : 2. Saul my fa. s. to kill thee
20 : 1. what my sin, th. he s. my life?
22 : 23. he th. s. my life, s. thy life
23 : 10. Saul s. to destroy the city
24 : 9. saying, David s. thy hurt?
2 S. 16 : 11. Behold my son s. my life
1 K. 20 : 7. how this man s. mischief
2 K. 5 : 7. see how he s. a quarrel
Jb. 39 : 29. Fr. thence she s. the prey
Ps. 37 : 32. watcheth rights., s. to slay
Pr. 11 : 27. He that s. good procureth favour, he that s. mischief ⌈not
14 : 6. A scorner s. wisd. findeth it
15 : 14. hath understg s. knowledge
17 : 9. covereth transgress-n s. love
11. An evil man s. only rebellion
19. exalteth his gate, s. destruc-n
18 : 1. Thro. desire a man s. all wisd.
15. ear of the wise s. knowledge
31 : 13. virtuous woman s. wool and
Ec. 7 : 28. Wh. my soul s. I find not
Is. 40 : 20. he s. a cunning workman
Je. 5 : 1. if any s. truth, I will pard. it
30 : 17. Zion, whom no man s. after
38 : 4. this man s. not welfare of peo.
La. 3 : 25. L. good to soul th. s. him
Eze. 14 : 10. as punish-t of him th. s.
34 : 12. As shepherd s. his flock ⌊him
Mat. 7 : 8. that s. findeth, Lu. 11 : 10.
12 : 39. generation s. a sign, 16 : 4.
18 : 12. leaveth 99, s. th. gone astray
Jn. 4 : 23. Fa. s. such to worship him
7 : 4. and s. to be known openly
18. s. his own glory ; s. his glory
8 : 50. is one that s. and judgeth
Ro. 3 : 11. is none that s. after God
11. 7. Israel not obtained that he s.
1 Co. 13 : 5. charity s. not her own
SEEKING. ⌈people
Es. 10 : 3. Mordecai s. wealth of his
Is. 16 : 5. s. judgm., hasting rights.
Eze. 34 : † 12. Acc-g to the s. his flock
Mat. 12 : 43. s. rest, and findeth none
Lu. 11 : 24. ⌈pearls
13 : 45. like merchantman s. goodly
Mk. 8 : 11. s. a sign from heaven ⌈him
Lu. 2 : 45. turned back to Jerus. s.
11 : 54. s. to catch something out of
13 : 7. I come s. fruit, find none
Jn. 6 : 24. to Capernaum, s. for Jesus
Ac. 13 : 8. s. to turn deputy fr. faith
11. s. some to lead him by hand
1 Co. 10 : 33. not s. mine own profit
1 Pe. 5 : 8. s. whom he may devour
SEEM.
Ge. 27 : 12. I shall s. as a deceiver
De. 15 : 18. not s. hard, when sendest
25 : 3. then thy bro. should s. vile
Jos. 24 : 15. if it s. evil to serve Lord
Ne. 9 : 32. let not the trouble s. little
Es. 8 : 5. if thing s. right before king
Na. 2 : 4. chariot shall s. like torches
1 Co. 11 : 16. if any man s. contentious
12 : 22. those members wh. s. feeble
2 Co. 10 : 9. not s. as if I wo. terrify
He. 4 : 1. lest any s. to come short of
Ja. 1 : 26. If any s. to be religious
See Seem, ed, eth GOOD.
SEEMED.
Ge. 19 : 14. he s. as one that mocked
29 : 20. s. unto him but a few days
Ec. 9 : 13. wisdom s. great unto me
Je. 27 : 5. earth unto whom it s. meet
Lu. 24 : 11. their words s. as idle tales
Ga. 2 : 6. these who s. to be somewhat
Ga. 2 : 9. Ja., Ceph., Jo., who s. pillars
He. 12 : † 10. they verily chastened us as s. meet to them

SEEMETH.
Le. 14 : 35. It s. is a plague in house
Nu. 16 : 9. s. it but a small thing
1 S. 18 : 23. s. it light to be k.'s son
2 S. 18 : 4. What s. best I will do
Pr. 14 : 12. a way wh. s. right, 16 : 25.
18 : 17. first in his own cause s. just
Eze. 34 : 18. s. it a small thing to
Lu. 8 : 18. taken that he s. to have
Ac. 17 : 18. He s. a setter forth of gods
25 : 27. s. unreasonable to send pris.
1 Co. 3 : 18. If s. wise, let him become
He. 12 : 11. no chastening s. joyous
SEEMLY.
Pr. 19 : 10. Delight is not s. for fool
26 : 1. so honour is not s. for a fool
Da. 4 : † 2. It was s. to shew signs
Ja. 2 : † 3. say unto him, Sit here s.
SEEN. [Active.]
Ge. 31 : 42. G. hath s. mine afflict-n
Ex. 10 : 6. locusts as fathers not s.
Le. 5 : 1. whe. s. or known of swear-g
Nu. 14 : 22. men wh. have s. my glory
23 : 21. nei. s. perverseness in Israel
27 : 13. when hast s. it, sh. be gath-d
De. 1 : 28. have s. sons of Anakim
31. s. how L. bare thee as a man
3 : 21. Thine eyes s. all L. hath done
4 : 3. s. what L. did bec. of Baal-p.
9. lest forget things thine eyes s.
5 : 24. s. God doth talk to man
10 : 21. terrible things thine eyes s.
11 : 2. have not s. chastisem-t of L.
7. your eyes have s. great acts of L.
21 : 7. not shed blood nei. eyes s. it
29 : 3. tempt-ns thine eyes have s.
33 : 9. to mother, I have not s. him
Jos. 24 : 7. s. what I have done in Eg.
Ju. 2 : 7. elders who had s. gr. works
13 : 22. We sh. die, bec. we have s. G.
18 : 9. we have s. land, it is very
1 S. 6 : 16. five lords had s. it ⌊good
23 : 22. and who hath s. him there
24 : 10. this day thine eyes have s.
2 S. 18 : 21. tell k. what thou hast s.
1 K. 10 : 4. queen had s. Sol.'s wisd.
7. till mine eyes had s. 2 Ch. 9 : 3, 6.
13 : 12. sons s. way man of G. went
20 : 13. Hast thou s. all this multi.?
2 K. 20 : 15. What have they s.? all things in mine house s. Is. 39 : 4.
23 : 29. slew Josiah, when had s. him
Ezr. 3 : 12. had s. first house, wept
Es. 9 : 26. had s. cone-g this matter
Jb. 7 : 8. eye hath s. me see no more
8 : 18. place say, I have not s. thee
10 : 18. Oh, that no eye had s. me
13 : 1. mine eye hath s. all this
20 : 7. have s. him say, Wh-e is he?
28 : 7. wh. vulture's eye hath not s.
38 : 17. hast s. doors of shadow of
22. s. treasures of hail? ⌊death?
Ps. 10 : 14. Thou hast s. it, for thou
35 : 21. Aha, aha, our eye hath s. it
22. This thou hast s., O L. ; keep
48 : 8. so have we s. in city of Lord
54 : 7. s. his desire on mine enemies
68 : 24. Th. have s. thy goings, O G.
90 : 15. years wh-in we have s. evil
98 : 3. ends of earth have s. salva-n
Pr. 25 : 7. prince thine eyes have s.
Ec. 4 : 3. who hath not s. evil work
6 : 5. he hath not s. sun, nor known
6. tho. he live, hath he s. no good
Is. 6 : 5. mine eyes have s. Lord of
9 : 2. In darkness have s. a gr. light
64 : 4. nei. eye s. wh. he hath pre-
66 : 8. who hath s. such thi-s? ⌊pared
19. isles that have not s. my glory
Je. 1 : 12. said L., Thou hast well s.
3 : 6. Hast s. what backsliding Isr.?
12 : 3. hast s. me, and tried my heart
La. 1 : 8. bec. have s. her nakedness
10. s. heathen into her sanctuary
2 : 14. Thy prophets have s. vain thi-s, they have s. false burdens
16. thy enemies say, we have s. it

La. 3 : 1. I am man th. hath s. afflic-n
58 : 59. O L., thou hast s. my wrong
60. hast s. their vengeance ag. me
Eze. 8 : 12. hast s. what ancients do
15. Hast thou s. this? 17.–47 : 6.
11 : 24. vision I had s. went fr. me
13 : 3. Woe unto prophets have s.
6. they ha. s. lying divin-n ⌊noth.
7. Have ye not s. a vain vision
Da. 8 : 6. ram I had s. before river
15. when I, Dan., had s. the visions
9 : 21. Gabriel I had s. in vision
Zch. 10 : 2. the diviners have s. a lie
Mat. 2 : 2. have s. his star in the east
13 : 17. many prophets desired to see and have not s., Lu. 10 : 24.
21 : 32. when ye had s. it, repented
Mk. 9 : 1. till ha. s. kingd. of G. ⌊not
9. tell no man things they had s.
16 : 14. believed not th. had s. him
Lu. 1 : 22. perceived he had s. vision
2 : 17. wh. had s. they made known
20. praising God for things had s.
26. not death bef. he had s. L.'s Ch.
30. mine eyes have s. thy salva-n
5 : 26. We have s. strange things
9 : 36. told no man things th. had s.
19 : 37. for mighty works th. had s.
23 : 8. he hoped to have s. miracle
24 : 23. they had s. vision of angels
37. supposed they had s. a spirit
Jn. 1 : 18. No man hath s. God, 1 Jn. 4 : 12.
3 : 11. we testify th. we ha. s. ⌊
32. what he hath s. he testifieth
4 : 45. Galileans had s. all he did
5 : 37. not at any time s. his shape
6 : 14. when they had s. miracle
46. Not that any man hath s. Fa.
8 : 57. not 50 yrs. old, hast s. Abra.
9 : 8. neighbours which had s. him
37. Thou hast s. it is he th. talketh
11 : 45. s. what Jesus did, believed
14 : 9. he that hath s. me s. Father
15 : 24. have s. and hated both me
20 : 18. Mary told she had s. the L.
25. disci. said, We have s. the L.
29. Thomas, because thou hast s.
Ac. 4 : 20. but speak thi-s we have s.
7 : 44. acc-g to fashion he had s.
9 : 12. s. in vision a man, Ananias
27. declared how he had s. Lord
10 : 17. what vision he had s. should
11 : 13. how he had s. angel ⌊mean
23. when he had s. grace of God
16 : 10. aft. he had s. vis-n we went
40. had s. brethren, comforted th.
21 : 29. had s. with him Trophimus
22 : 15. witn-s of wh. hast s., 26 : 16.
1 Co. 2 : 9. Eye hath not s., nor ear
9 : 1. have I not s. Jesus Ch. our L.
Ph. 4 : 9. things ye have s. in me, do
Col. 2 : 18. intruding into things he
1 Ti. 6 : 16. wh. no man hath s. ⌊not s.
1 Jn. 1 : 1. that which we have s.
2. life was manifested, we ha. s. it
3. That wh. we have s. declare we
3 : 6. whoso. sinneth, hath not s. him
4 : 14. we have s. and do testify
20. loveth not bro. he hath s., how love God he hath not s.?
3 Jn. 11. that doeth evil hath not s. G.
Re. 1 : 19. Write things thou hast s.
22 : 8. had heard and s. I fell down
See FACE with seen.
Have I SEEN.
Ge. 7 : 1. thee – s. righteous bef. me
1 Ch. 29 : 17. – s. thy people to offer
Ps. 37 : 25. – not s. right-s forsaken
Ec. 7 : 15. All thi-s – s. in days of my
8 : 9. All this – s., applied my heart
9 : 13. This wisdom – s. under the sun
Je. 46 : 5. Whf. – s. them dismayed
Zch. 9 : 8. now – s. with mine eyes
I have SEEN. ⌈thee
Ge. 31 : 12. – s. all Laban doeth unto
32 : 30. – s. G. face to face, and am
Ex. 3 : 7. – s. affliction of my people

Ex 3: 9. - also s. the oppression, 16.
32:9. L. said, - s. this peo.,De.9:13.
Ju. 6: 22. alas, bec. - s. an angel
14: 2. - s. a woman in Timnath
1 S. 16: 18. - s. a son of Jesse [both
2 K. 9: 26. - s. yesterday bl. of Na-
20: 5. saith L., - s. thy tears, Is.
38: 5. [iquity
Jb. 4: 8. as - s. they that plough in-
5: 3. - s. the foolish taking root
15: 17. hear, that wh. - s. I declare
31: 19. If - s. any perish for want
Ps 37: 35. - s. wicked in gr. power
55: 9. - s. violence, strife in city
63: 2. as - s. thee in the sanctuary
119: 96. - s. an end of all perfect-n
Ec. 1: 14. - s. all works under sun
3: 10. - s. travail God hath given
5: 13. is a sore evil - s. under sun
18. that which - s. it is good to eat
6: 1. is an evil which - s., 10: 5.
10: 7. - s. serv-ts upon horses, and
Is. 44: 16. I am warm, - s. the fire
57: 18. - s. his ways, will heal him
Je. 7: 11. Behold, - s. it, saith the L.
13: 27. - s. thine adulteries and
23: 13. - s. folly in prophets of Sa.,
La. 3: 1. - s. affliction by rod [14.
Da. 2: 26. make known dream - s.
4: 9. visions of dream - s., 18.
Ho. 6: 10. - s. a horrible thing in Isr.
Jn. 8: 38. I speak that - s. with Fa
Ac. 7: 34. - s. affliction of my people
Ye have, or have ye SEEN.
Ge. 45: 13. tell my father all - s.
Ex. 14: 13. Eg-ns whom - s. to day
19: 4. - s. what I did unto Eg-ns
20: 22. - s. I have talked with you
De. 29: 2. - s. all L. did in Eg., Jos.
17. - s. their abominations [23: 3.
Ju. 9: 48. What - s. me do, do as I
1 S. 17: 25. - s. this man th. is come?
Jb. 27: 12. all - s. it, why then vain?
Is. 22: 9. - s. breaches of the city
Je. 44: 2. - s. all evil I have brought
Eze. 13: 8. - s. lies, thf. I am ag. you
Lu. 7: 22. Go, tell John things - s.
Jn. 6: 36. - s. me and believe not
8: 38. do that - s. with your father
14: 7. ye know him, and - s. him
Ac. 1: 11. Jes. come, as - s. him go
Ja. 5: 11. - s. the end of the Lord
SEEN. [Passive.]
Ge. 8: 5. were tops of mountains s.
9: 14. bow shall be s. in the cloud
22: 14. In mount of Lord it sh. be s.
Ex. 13: 7. no leav-d bread s., De. 16:
33: 23. my face shall not be s. [4.
34: 3. nei. let man be s. thro-t mt.
Le. 13: 7. aft. he ha. been s. of priest
Nu. 14: 14. Lord, art s. face to face
Ju. 5: 8. shield or sp-r s. am. 40,000
19: 30. was no such deed done nor s.
2 S. 17: 17. might not be s. to come
22: 11. was s. upon wings of wind
1 K. 6: 18. there was no stone s.
8: 8. ends of staves not s., 2Ch.5:9.
10: 12. no such almug trees were s.
2 Ch. 8: † 1. when Lord was s. of Da.
9: 11. none such s. before in Judah
Jb. 33: 21. His flesh cannot be s.
Ps. 18: 15. channels of water were s.
Is. 1: † 12. when ye come to be s. bef.
16: 12. when s. that Moab is weary
47: 3. yea, thy shame shall be s.
60: 2. his glory sh. be s. upon thee
Zch. 9: 14. Lord sh. be s. over them
Mat. 6: 1. do not y-r alms to be s., 5.
9: 33. It was never so s. in Israel
23: 5. their works they do to be s.
Mk. 16: 11. th. he had been s. of her
Lu. 24: † 31. ceased to be s. of them
Ac. 1: 3. s. of them forty days, 13: 31.
Ro. 1: 20. invisib. thi-s of him are s.
8: 24. hope that is s. is not hope
1 Co. 15: 5. he was s. of Cephas, then
6. after that he was s. of above 500

1 Co. 15: 7. Aft. that was s. of James
8. And last of all was s. of me
2 Co. 4: 18. we look not at things s.,
but thi-s not s., thi-s s. temporal
1 Ti. 3: 16. God in flesh s. of angels
He. 11: 1. evidence of things not s.
3. that things s. were not made
7. Noah warned of things not s.
13. having s. them afar off were
1 Pe. 1: 8. wh. having not s. ye love
Re. 11: 19. was s. in his temple the
SEER. [ark
1 S. 9: 9. let us go to the s. Prophet
was beforetime called a s. [here?
11. said unto maidens, Is the s.
18. Tell me, where the s.'s house
19. Samuel ans. Saul, I am the s.
2 S. 15: 27. king said, Art thou a s.?
24: 11. Gad, David's s., 1 Ch. 21: 9.
1 Ch. 9: 22. Samuel the s. did ordain
25: 5. Heman, k.'s s. in words of G.
26: 28. all Samuel the s. dedicated
29: 29. acts of David in book of
Sam. the s., in b-k of Gad the s.
2 Ch. 9: 29. in visions of Iddo the s.
12: 15. of Rehob. in book of Iddo, s.
16: 7. Hanani the s. came to Asa
10. Asa was wroth with the s.
19: 2. Jehu, son of Hanani the s.
29: 25. com-t of Gad, the king's s.
30. words of Da. and Asaph the s.
35: 15. com-t of Jeduthun, king's s.
Am. 7: 12. Amos, O thou s., flee aw.
SEERS.
2 K. 17: 13. testified ag. Israel by s.
2 Ch. 33: 18. words of s. that spake
19. written among sayings of s.
Is. 29: 10. rulers, s. hath he covered
30: 10. Who say to the s., See not
Mi. 3: 7. Then sh. the s. be ashamed
SEEST.
Ge. 13: 15. land thou s. will I give it
16: 13. that spake, Thou God s. me
31: 43. said, all thou s. is mine [die
Ex. 10: 28. day thou s. my face shalt
De. 4: 19. lest s. sun thou worship
12: 13. offer not in ev. place thou s.
20: 1. when to battle and s. horses
21: 11. s. am. captives beauti-l wom.
Ju. 9: 36. Thou s. shadow of mts.
1 K. 21: 29. s. how Ahab humbleth
Jb. 10: 4. or s. thou as man seeth?
Pr. 22: 29. s. thou man diligent?
26: 12. s. man wise in his conceit?
29: 20. s. thou a man that is hasty?
Ec. 5: 8. If s. oppression of poor
Is. 58: 3. Whf. fasted, and thou s. not?
7. when s. naked, that thou cover
Je. 1: 11. word came unto Jeremiah,
What s. thou? 13. - 24: 3. Am.
7: 8. - 8: 2. Zch. 4: 2. - 5: 2. [Judah?
7: 17. s. thou not what they do in
20: 12. O Lord, that s. the reins
32: 24. is come behold, thou s. it [do?
Eze. 8: 6. Son of man, s. what they
40: 4. declare all thou s. to Israel
Da. 1: 13. as thou s. deal wi. serv-ts
Mk. 5: 31. s. multitude thronging
13: 2. s. thou these gr. buildings?
Lu. 7: 44. Simon, s. thou this wom.?
Ac 21: 20 Thou s. how many believe
Ja. 2: 22. s. thou how faith wrought
Re. 1: 11. What thou s. write in book
SEETH. [s. me?
Ge. 16: 13. Have I looked after him
44: 31. s. lad not wi. us, he will die
Ex. 4: 14. when he s. thee be glad
12: 23. when he s. blood upon lintel
Le. 13: 20. when priest s. plague
De. 32: 36. when he s. power gone
1 S. 16: 7. Lord s. not as man s. [s.
2 K. 2: 19. city pleasant, as my lord
Jb 8: 17. and s. the place of stones
10: 4. or seest thou as man s.?
11: 11. s. wickedn., will he consider
22: 14. clouds a covering, he s. not
28: 10. his eye s. ev. precious thing

Jb. 28: 24. he s. under whole heaven
34: 21. upon man, he s. all his goings
42: 5. but now mine eye s. thee
Ps. 37: 13. s. that his day is coming
49: 10. he s. that wise men die
58: 10. righte-s rejoice, when s. veng.
Ec. 8: 16. nei. day nor night, s. sleep
Is. 21: 6. watchman decl. what he s.
28: 4 when he that looketh, s. it
29: 15. and they say, Who s. us?
23. But when he s. his children
47: 10. thou hast said, None s. me
La. 3: †36. To subvert a man L. s. not
Eze. 8: 12. they say, L. s. us not, 9: 9.
12: 27. vision he s. is for many days
18: 14. son that s. his father's sins
33: 3. If when he s. sword come
39: 15. when any s. a man's bone
Mat. 6: 4. thy Fa. who s. in secret, 6,
Mk. 5: 38. he s. the tumult [18.
Lu. 16: 23. he s. Abraham afar off
Jn. 1: 29. next day John s. Jesus
5: 19. noth. but what he s. Fa. do
6: 40. who s. Son, and believeth
9: 21. by what means he s. we know
10: 12. hireling s. wolf coming [not
11: 9. stumbleth not, bec. s. light
12: 45. that s. me, s. him sent me
14: 17. it s. him not, nei. knoweth
19. a little and world s. me no more
20: 1. s. stone taken fr. sepulchre
6. Peter went in and s. clothes lie
12. s. two angels in white, sitting
21: 20. s. the disciple Jesus loved
Ro. 8: 24. what a man s. why hope
2 Co. 12: 6. above what he s. me to
1 Jn. 3: 17. and s. bro. have need [be
SEETHE, ING. [s.
Ex. 16: 23. sabb. to day s. that ye will
23: 19. shalt not s. a kid in mother's
milk, 34: 26. De. 14: 21. [place
29: 31. shalt s. his flesh in holy
1 S. 2: 13. came, while flesh was s-g
2 K. 4: 38. s. pottage for the sons of
Jb. 41: 20. smoke as out of a s-g pot
Je. 1: 13. What seest thou? a s-g pot
Eze. 24: 5. let them s. bones therein
Zch. 14: 21. that sacrif. sh. s. therein
SE'GUB. [son, S.
1 K. 16: 34. set gates in youngest
1 Ch. 2: 21. begat S. | 22. S. begat Jair
SE'IR. [Person.] [1: 38.
Ge. 36: 20. the sons of S., 21. 1 Ch.
SE'IR. [Place.]
Ge. 32: 3. to Esau unto land of S.
33: 14. lead softly, till I come unto S.
16. Esau returned unto S.
36: 30. are dukes in the land of S.
Nu. 24: 18. S. shall be for enemies
De. 1: 44. Amorites destr-d you in S.
2: 4. breth. wh. dw. in S., 8, 22, 29.
12. The Horim also dwelt in S.
33: 2. Lord fr. Sinai rose up fr. S.
Jos. 11: 17. mount Halak, that go
eth up to S., 12: 7. [ef S.
Ju. 5: 4. Lord, wh. thou wentest out
2 Ch. 20: 23. end of inhab-ts of S.
25: 11. smote of chil. of S. 10,000
14. brought gods of children of S.
Is. 21: 11. calleth to me out of S.
Eze. 25: 8. bec. Moab and S. do say
Mount SE'IR.
Ge. 14: 6. the Horites in their m. S.
36: 8. thus dwelt Esau in m. S., 9.
De. 1: 2. fr. Horeb by way of m. S.
2: 1. we compassed m. S. many
5. given m. S. unto Esau, Jos. 24: 4
Jos. 15: 10. fr. Baalah unto m. S.
1 Ch. 4: 42. of sons of Sim. 500 to m.
2 Ch. 20: 10. m. S. not let invade [S.
22. L. set ambushments ag. m. S
23. and Moab stood against m. S.
Eze. 35: 2. set thy face against m. S.
3. O m. S., I am against thee
7. will I make m. S. desolate, 15.
SE'IRATH.
Ju. 3: 26. And Ehud escaped unto S

SEIZE.
Jos. 8 : 7. ye shall rise and s. city
Jb. 3 : 6. th. night, let darkn-s s. it
Ps. 55 : 15. Let death s. upon them
Mat. 21:38. let us kill him,s.inherit-

SEIZED. [ance
Je. 49 : 24. Damas., fear hath s. on

SE'LA, SE'LAH.
2 K. 14 : 7. Amaziah tookS-h by war
Is. 16 : 1. fr. S-a to wildern. unto mt.

SELAH.
Ps. 3 : 2. is no help for him in G. S.
4. L. heard me out of holy hill, S.
8. thy blessing upon thy peo., S.
4 : 2. S. 4.-7 : 5. -9 : 16, 20. -20 : 3.
-21 : 2.-24 : 6, 10.-32 : 4, 7.-39 :
5, 11.-44 : 8.-46 : 3, 7, 11.-47 : 4.
-48 : 8.-49 : 13, 15.-50 : 6.-52: 3,
5.-54 : 3.-55 : 7, 19. -57 : 3, 6. -
59 : 5, 13.-60 : 4.-61 : 4.-62 : 4,
8.-66 : 4, 7, 15.-67 : 1, 4.-68 : 7,
19, 32.-75 : 3.-76 : 3, 9.-77 : 3,
9, 15.-81 : 7.-82 : 2.-83 : 8.-84 :
4, 8.-85 : 2.-87 : 3, 6.-88 : 7, 10.
-89 : 4, 37, 45, 48.-140 : 3, 5, 8.-
143 : 6. Ha. 3 : 3, 9, 13.
32 : 5. forgavest iniq-y of my sin, S.

SE'LA-HAMMAHLE'-KOTH.
1 S. 23 : 28. they called that place S.

SELDOM. [house
Pr. 25 : †17. be s. in neighbour's

SE'LED. See NADAB.

SELEU'CIA.
Ac. 13 : 4. they departed unto S.

SELF. See **OWN self.**

SELFSAME. [hour
Mat. 8 : 13. servant was healed s.
1 Co. 12 : 11. worketh that s. spirit
2 Co 5 : 5.wrought us for s. thing, is
7 : 11. s. thing ye sorrowed aft. [G.
See **Selfsame DAY.**

SELFWILL. [wall
Ge 49 : 6. in s. they digged down a

SELFWILLED.
Tit. 1 : 7. a bishop must not be s.[s.
2 Pe. 2 : 10. Presumptuous are they,

SELL. [birthright
Ge. 25 : 31. Jacob said, s. me thy
37 : 27. let us s. him to Ishmaelites
Ex. 21 : 7. If man s. his daughter
8. to s. her unto strange nation
35. shall s. live ox, divide money
22 : 1. if man steal an ox, or s. it
Le. 25 : 14. if s. aught unto neighb.
15. fruits he shall s. unto thee, 16.
29. if a man s. a dwellinghouse
47. if bro. s. himself unto stranger
De. 2 : 28. Thou shalt s. me meat
14 : 21. s. that which dieth of itself
21 : 14. shalt not s. her for money
Ju. 4 : 9. s. Sisera into hand of wom.
1K.21:25. Ahab did s. hims. to work
2 K. 4 : 7. Go s. oil, and pay thy debt
Ne. 5 : 8. will ye s. your brethren?
10 : 31. bring victuals on sab. to s.
Pr. 23 : 23. Buy truth, and s. it not
Eze. 30 : 12. will s. land into hand
48 : 14. they shall not s. firstfruits
Jo. 3 : 8. I will s. your sons and
dau-s, they sh. s. th. to Sabeans
Am. 8 : 5. gone, that we may s. corn
6. yea, and s. refuse of the wheat
Zch. 11 : 5. th. s. them say, I am rich
Mat. 19 : 21. go s. that thou hast,
follow me, Mk. 10 : 21. Lu. 12 :
33.-18 : 22.
25 : 9. go ye rather to them that s.
Lu. 22 : 36. s. his garment, buy sw-d
Ja. 4 : 13. we will buy and s. and
Re. 13 : 17. that no man buy or s.

SELLER, S. [save
Ne. 13 : 20. s-s lodged with-t Jerus-m
Is. 24 : 2. as with buyer, so with s.
Eze. 7 : 12. buyer rej-e nor s. mourn
13. s. shall not return to that sold
Ac. 16 : 14. named Lydia, a s. of purple

SELLEST. [nought
Ps. 44 : 12. thou s. thy people for

SELLETH. [De. 24:7.
Ex. 21 : 16. stealeth a man, s. him,
Ru. 4 : 3. Naomi s. a part of land
Pr. 11 : 26. blessing upon him s. corn
31 : 24. She maketh fine linen, s. it
Na. 3 : 4. s. nations thro. whoredoms
Mat. 13 : 44. he s. all, buyeth that

SELVEDGE. [field
Ex. 26 : 4. from s. in coupling, 36 : 11.

SELVES. See **OWN selves.**

SEM. See SHEM.

SEMACHI'AH. [S.
1 Ch. 26 : 7. sons of Shemaiah, Othni,

SEM'EI.
Lu. 3 : 26. Mattathias, the son of S.

SEN'AAH.
Ezr. 2 : 35. children of S., Ne. 7 : 38.

SENATE. [gether
Ac. 5 : 21. they called s. of Isr. to-

SENATORS.
Ps 105 : 22. and teach his s. wisdom

SEND. [thee, 40.
Ge. 24 : 7. God shall s. angel bef.
12. I pray thee s. me good speed
54. s. me aw. unto my master, 56.
30 : 25. Jac. unto Laban, s. me aw.
38 : 17. Wilt give pledge, till s. it?
42 : 16. s. one, let him fetch brother
43 : 4. If s. our brother with us, 5.
8. said unto Isr., s. lad with me
14. may s. y-r other bro. and Benj.
45 : 5. God did s. me before you
Ex. 4 : 13. s. by hand thou wilt s.
7 : 2. he s. chil. of Isr. out of land
9 : 19. s. now and gather thy cattle
12 : 33. might s. them out in haste
33 : 12. not let me know whom thou
Le. 16 : 21. s. him by a fit man [wilts.
Nu. 13 : 2. s. thou men to search
land, shall ye s. a man a ruler
31 : 4. s. a thousand to the war
De. 1 : 22. We will s. men to search
7 : 20. thy G. will s. the hornet am.
19 : 12. elders shall s. and fetch him
24 : 1. bill of divorce, and s. her out
28 : 20. L. shall s. upon thee curs-g
48. serve enemies L. sh. s. ag. thee
Ju. 13 : 8. let man of G. didst s. come
1 S. 5 : 11. s. away ark of God, 6 : 8.
6 : 2. tell us wherew. we shall s. it
3. if ye s. ark of God, s. not empty
9 : 26. Up, that I may s. thee away
11 : 3. respite, that we s. messeng-s
12 : 17. Lord shall s. thunder and
16 : 11. unto Jesse, s. fetch David
19. Saul said, s. me David thy son
20 : 31. now s. fetch him unto me
25 : 25. I saw not yo. men didst s.
2 S. 11 : 6. David saying, s. me Uriah
14 : 32. that I may s. thee to king
15 : 36. ye sh. s. unto me ev. thing
17 : 16. Now s. quickly, tell David
1 K. 5 : †9. timber to pla. thou sh. s.
8 : 44. whither thou sh. s., 2 Ch. 6 : 34.
11 : †21. s. me away that I may go
18 : 19. s., gather to me all Israel
20 : 9. All thou didst s. I will do
2 K. 2 : 16. And he said, Ye sh. not s.
17. when they urged, he said s.
4 : 22. s. me one of the young men
5 : 7. s. unto me to recover a man
6 : 13. spy where he is that I may s.
7 : 13. one said let us s. and see
9 : 17. Take a horseman, s. to meet
15 : 37. Lord began to s. ag. Judah
1 Ch. 13 : 2. let us s. abroad brethren
2Ch. 2 : 3. didst s. him cedars to bui.
7. s. me a man cunning to work
8. s. me also cedar trees, fir trees
15. let him s. unto his servants
6 : 27. and s. rain upon thy land
28 : 16. Ahaz did s. to k. of Assyria
32 : 9. Sennacherib did s. servants
Ezr. 5 : 17. let king s. his pleasure
Ne. 2 : 5. wouldest s. me unto Judah
Ne. 2 : 6. So it pleased the k. to s. me
8 : 10. eat, drink, and s. port-ns, 12.
Jb. 21 : 11. s. little ones as a flock
38 : 35. Canst thou s. lightnings
Ps. 20 : 2. s. thee help fr. sanctuary
43 : 3. O s. out thy light and truth
57 : 3. He shall s. from heaven, God
shall s. forth his mercy
68 : 9. Thou didst s. a plentiful rain
33. he doth s. out his voice
110 : 2. shall s. rod of thy strength
118 : 25. O Lord, s. now prosperity
144 : 7. s. thine hand fr. above [him
Pr. 10 : 26. so sluggard to them s.
22 : 21. truth to them s. unto thee
25 : 13. messenger to them that s.
Ec. 10 : 1. ointment to s. a stinking
Is. 6 : 8. Whom sh. I s.? I said, s. me
10 : 16. sh. s. am. fat ones leanness
16 : 1. s. ye the lamb to the ruler
19 : 20. he shall s. them a saviour
32 : 20. th. s. forth feet of ox and ass
57 : 9. didst s. thy messengers far
Je. 1 : 7. shalt go to all I sh. s. thee
2 : 10. s. unto Kedar, and consider
9 : 17. s. for cunning wom. th. they
27 : 3. s. the yokes to king of Edom
29 : 31. s. to all of the captivity
42 : 5. for wh. L. shall s. thee to us
6. will obey L., to whom we s. thee
Mat. 9 : 38. Pray ye the Lord that he
s. labourers, Lu. 10 : 2. [s. peace
10 : 34. Think not th. I am come to
12 : 20. till he s. forth judgm-t unto
13 : 41. Son of man sh. s. his angels,
24 : 31. Mk. 13 : 27. [Lu. 9 : 12.
14 : 15 s. mult. away, Mk. 6 : 36.
15 : 23. s. her aw., she crieth aft. us
21 : 3. he will s. them, Mk. 11 : 3. [6:7.
Mk. 3 : 14. might s. them to preach,
5 : 10. not s. them aw. out of country
12. saying, s. us into the swine
12 : 13. s. unto him cert-n of Phari.
Lu. 12 : 49. I am come to s. fire on the
16 : 24. s. Lazarus [27. s. to my fa.'s
Jn. 14 : 26. whom the Father will s.
17 : 8. believed thou didst s. me
Ac. 3 : 20. he sh. s. Jes. Christ, who
7 : 35. same did God s. to be ruler
10 : 5. s. men to Joppa, 32.-11 : 13.
22. to s. for thee into his house
11 : 29. to s. relief unto breth. [25.
15 : 22. to s. men of their company,
23. apostles and elders s. greeting
25 : 3. would s. for him to Jerus.
25. I have determined to s. Paul
27. unreasonable to s. a prisoner
Ph. 2 : 19. I trust to s. Timotheus, 23.
25. necessary to s. Epaphroditus
2 Th. 2 : 11. God shall s. delusion
Tit. 3 : 12. When I s. Artemas [bitter?
Ja. 3 : 11. fount-n s. sweet wat. and
Re. 1 : 11. write, s. it unto 7 churches
11 : 10. they sh. s. gifts one to ano.
See **Send FIRE.**

I SEND.
Ex. 23 : 20. I s. angel before thee
Nu. 22 : 37. Did I not earnestly s.
1 S. 20 : 12. if be good, and I s. not
21 : 2. know the business I s. thee
2Ch. 7 : 13. if I s. pestil-e, Eze. 14 : 19.
Is. 6 : 8. Lord, say, Whom sh. I s.?
Je. 25 : 15. all to whom I s. to drink it
Eze. 2 : 3. I s. thee to chil. of Isr., 4.
5 : 16. When I sh. s. evil arrows
14 : 21. I s. my four sore judgm-ts
Mat. 10 : 16. I s. you forth as sheep
11 : 10. I s. my messenger before
thy face, Mk. 1 : 2. Lu. 7 : 27.
23 : 34. I s. you prophets and wise
Mk. 8 : 3. if I s. them away fasting
Lu. 10 : 3. I s. you forth as lambs
24 : 49. I s. promise of my father
Jn. 13 : 20. that receiveth whom I s.
20 : 21. as Fa. sent me, so s. I you
Ac. 25 : 21 kept till I s. him to Cesar
26 : 17. Gentiles, unto wh. I s. thee

I will SEND.
Ge. 27 : 45. I w.s. and fetch thee
37 : 13. and I w.s. thee unto them
38 : 17. I w.s. thee a kid from flock
Ex. 3 : 10. I w.s. thee unto Pha., Ac.
8 : 21. I w.s. swarms of flies⌊7 : 34.
9 : 14. I w.s. all my plagues upon
23 : 27. I w.s. my fear before thee
28. I w.s. hornets before thee wh.
33 : 2. I w.s. an angel before thee
Le. 26 : 22. I w.s. beasts among you
25. I w.s. pestilence among you
36 upon them alive I w.s. faintn.
De. 11 : 15. I w.s. grass in thy fields
32 : 24. I w.s. the teeth of beasts
Jos. 18 : 4. Give 3 men I w.s. them
1 S. 9 : 16. I w.s. thee a man of Benj.
16 : 1. I w.s. thee to Jesse the
20 : 13. I w. shew it, s. thee away
1 K. 18 : 1. I w.s. rain upon earth
20 : 6. I w.s. my serv-ts unto thee
34. I w.s. thee away wi. this cov.
2 K. 5 : 5. I w.s. letter to k of Israel
19 : 7. I w.s. blast upon him, Is. 37 : 7.
Is. 10 : 6. I w.s. him ag. hypocritical
66 : 19. I w.s. those that escape
Je. 8 : 17. I w.s. serpents am. you
9 : 16. I w.s. a sword after them
till consumed, 24 : 10.-25 : 16.
27.-29 : 17.-49 : 37. ⌈hunters
16 : 16. I w.s. for many fishers,
25 : 9. I w.s. and take families of
43 : 10. I w.s. Nebuchadnezzar my
48 : 12. I w.s. unto him wanderers
51 : 2. I w.s. unto Babylon fanners
Eze. 5 : 16. I w.s. famine, 17.-14 : 13.
Am. 8 : 11. ⌈and judge
7 : 3. I w.s. mine anger upon thee
28 : 23. I w.s into her pestilence
Jo. 2, 19. I w.s. you corn and wine
Mal. 2 : 2. I w.s. a curse upon you
3 : 1. I w.s. my messenger, and he
4 : 5. I w.s. you Elijah the prophet
Mat. 15 : 32. I w. not s. them fast-g
Lu. 11 : 49. I w.s. prophets, apostles
20 : 13. I w.s. my beloved son
Jn. 15 : 26. Comforter whom I w.s.,
Ac. 22 : 21. I w.s. thee to Gent. ⌊16 : 7.
1 Co. 16 : 3. whom. ye approve, them

SENDEST. ⌊I w.s.
De. 15 : 13 when s. him out free, 18.
Jos. 1 : 16. whitherso. s. us we will go
2 K. 1 : 6. s. to inquire of Baal-zebub
Jb. 14 : 20. changest countenance,
and s. him away
Ps. 50 : † 19. s. thy mouth to evil
104 : 30. s. spirit, they are created
Is. 27 : † 8. when thou s. it forth

SENDETH.
De. 24 : 3. if latter husb. s. her out
1 K. 17 : 14. day that the Lord s. rain
Jb. 5 : 10. who s. waters upon fields
12 : 15. he s. th., they overt-n earth
Ps. 104 : 10. He s. springs into valleys
147 : 15. He s. forth his com-t, 18.
Pr. 16 : † 28. a froward man s. strife
26 : 6. that s. a message by a fool
Can 1 : 12. spikenard s. forth smell
Is. 18 : 2. Th. s. ambassadors by sea
Mat. 5 : 45. s. rain on just and unjust
Mk. 11 : 1. he s. two disciples, 14 : 13.
Lu. 14 : 32. s. and desireth peace
Ac. 23 : 26. Lysias unto Felix s.

SENDING. ⌈greeting
2 S. 13 : 16. evil in s. me aw. greater
2 Ch. 36 : 15. s. to them by messengers, Jer. 7 : 25.-25 : 4.-26 : 5.-
29 : 19.-35 : 15.-44 : 4. ⌈22.
Es. 9 : 19. of s. portions one to ano.,
Ps. 78 : 49. by s. evil angels am. th.
Is. 7 : 25. for the s. of lesser cattle
Eze. 17 : 15. rebelled in s. ambas-rs
Ro. 8 : 3. God s. his Son in likeness

SE'NEH.
1 S. 14 : 4. name of the rock, S.

SE'NIR or SHE'NIR.
De. 3 : 9. Amorites call it S.
1 Ch. 5 : 23. incr-d fr. Bashan unto S.
Can. 4 : 8. look from top of S. ⌈S.
Eze 27 : 5. ship boards of fir trees of

SENNACH'ERIB. ⌈36 : 1.
2 K. 18 : 13. S. came ag Judah, Is.
19 : 16, hear words of S., Is. 37 : 17.
20. hast prayed ag. S., Is. 37 : 21.
36. S dwelt at Nineveh, Is. 37 : 37.
2 Ch. 32 : 1. S. entered into Judah, 2.
10. saith S., Whereon do ye trust?
22. L. saved Hezekiah from S.

SENSE.
Ne. 8 : 8. read in book, gave the s.
Ph 1 : † 9. your love abound in all s.

SENSES. ⌈his s.
Ec. 2 : † 24. than he should delight
He. 5 : 14. s. exercised to disc-n good

SENSUAL.
Ja. 3 : 15. this wisdom is earthly, s.
Jude 19. be s., having not Spirit

SENT.
Ge 20 : 2. Abim. s. and took Sarah
27 : 42. and she s. and called Jacob
31 : 4. Jacob s. and called Rachel
32 : 23. he s. th. over the brook (2)
37 : 32. th. s. coat of many colours
38 : 20. Judah s. kid by friend
25. Tamar s. to her father in law
41 : 14. Pha. s. and called Joseph
42 : 4. Benj. Jacob s. not wi. breth.
45 : 8. not you that s. me, but God
27. wh. Joseph had s. to carry him
46 : 5 wagons Pha. had s. to him
Ex 2 : 5. s. her maid to fetch ark
3 : 14. I AM hath s. me unto you
5 : 22. Lord, why is it hast s. me
9 : 7. Pha. s. there was not one
27. Pha s. and called for Moses
Nu 13 : 3. Moses s. them fr. wildern.
16. names of men, Moses s. to
spy, 17.-14 : 36.
16 : 12. Moses s. to call Dathan
22 : 10. Balak, k., hath s. unto me
15. Balak s. princes more hon-ble
40. Balak s. to Balaam, Jos. 24 : 9.
31 : 6. Moses s. them to the war
Jos. 2 : 3. k. of Jeri. s. unto Rahab
6 : 17. Rahab hid messengers we s.
7 : 2 s. 10 : 3, 6.-22 : 13. Ju. 1 : 23.
-3 : 15.-4 : 6.-12 : 9.-16 : 18.-18 :
2.-20 : 12.-21 : 13. ⌈11.
14 : 7. 40 yrs. old when Moses s. me,
Ju. 20 : 6. cut in pieces, s. her throughout Israel, 19 : 29. ⌈valiantest
21 : 10. cong-n s. 12,000 men of
1 S. 4 : 4. people s. to Shiloh
5 : 8. s. 10, 11.-11 : 7.-16 : 20, 22.-
18 : 5.-19 : 11.-22 : 11.-25 : 32,
39, 40. ⌈among people
31 : 9. Philistines s. to publish it
2 S. 3 : 15. s. 8 : 10.-9 : 5.-10 : 2, 3, 6,
16.-11 : 1, 3, 5, 6, 14, 18, 22, 27.-
13 : 7.-14 : 2, 29.-15 : 10, 12.-18 :
2, 29.-19 : 11, 14. ⌈that s. me
24 : 13. what answer return to him
1 K. 1 : 44. k. hath s. with him Zadok
53. Solomon s., and they, 2 : 25, 29.
36. s. 42.-5 : 1, 2, 8.-7 : 13.-9 :
14, 27.-12 : 3, 18, 20.-15 : 18. ⌈s.
18 : 10. no nation whi. my lord not
20. s. 20 : 5, 10.-21 : 8, 14. 2 K. 1 :
2, 9, 16.-2 : 17.-3 : 7.-5 : 10, 22.-
21 : 11. did as Jezebel had s. ⌊6 : 9.
2 K. 1 : 6. Go unto king that s. you
6 : 10. king of Israel s. to place, whi.
32. king s. a man before him, son
of a murderer hath s. to take
7 : 14. s. 8 : 9 -10 : 1, 5, 7, 21.-11 : 4
-12 : 18.-14 : 8. (2)⌈2 Ch. 25 : 18.
14 : 9. thistle in Leb. s. to cedar,
19. s. after him to Lachish, 2 Ch.
25 : 27. ⌈20 : 12.-22 : 3.
16 : 8. s. 10.-18 : 14, 27.-19 : 20.-
11. Urijah built as Ahaz s. ⌈12.
18 : 27. Hath master s. me (2). Is. 36 :
19 : 4. his master s. to reproach
God, 16. Is 37 : 4, 17.
2 K. 22 : 15. tell the man s. you, 18
2 Ch. 34 : 23, 26.
23 : 1. s. 16.-24 : 2. 1 Ch. 10 : 9.-19 : 6.
2 Ch. 2 : 3. s. 8 : 18.-10 : 3, 18-16 : 2, 4.
-24 : 23.-25 : 13, 17.-30 : 1.-32 :
31.-34 : 29.-36 : 10, 15. ⌈th. s. me
1 Ch. 21 : 12, what word bring to him
Ezr. 4 : 11. copy of letter they s., 5 : 7.
14. s. 17.-5 : 6.-6 : 13. Ne. 2 : 9.-6 : 2.
Ne. 6 : 4. s. unto me six times
Es. 4 : 4. s. raiment to clothe Mord.
Jb. 1 : 4. Job's sons s. for three sisters
5. Job s. and sanctified them
Ps. 105 : 20. king s. and loosed him
106 : 15. gave request, but s. lean-
135 : 9. who s. tokens, wonders ⌊ness
Is. 20 : 1. when Sargon king s. him
36 : 2. k. of Assyria s. Rabshakeh
Is. 37 : 21, s. 39 : 1. Je. 21 : 1.-26 :
22.-29 : 1, 3.-36 : 14, 21.-37 : 3.
48 : 16. G. and his Spirit hath s. me
Je. 14 : 3. nobles have s. little ones
23 : 21. I have not s. these prophets
37 : 7. thus say unto king th. s. you
17. s. 38 : 14.-39 : 13, 14.-40 : 14. ⌈20.
42 : 9. men ye s. to present supp-n,
Eze. 23 : 40. ye have s. for men fr. far
Da. 3 : 2. Neb-r s. to gather princes
28. who s. his angel and delivered
Ho. 5 : 13. Ephraim s. to king Jareb
Am. 7 : 10. Amaziah s. to Jeroboam
Zch. 7 : 2. had s. unto house of God
Mat. 10 : 40. receiveth me, receiveth
him s. me, Mk. 9 : 37. Lu. 9 : 48.
Jn. 13 : 20.
21 : 1. then s. Jesus two disciples
27 : 19. Pilate's wife s. unto him
Mk. 3 : 31. breth. and mo. s. unto him
6 : 27. king s. execu'r, Mat. 14 : 10.
Lu. 7 : 6. centurion s. friends
19. John s. them to Jes., say-g, Art
20. John Baptist s. us unto thee
10 : 1. Jesus s. them two and two
16. despiseth him that s. me
14 : 17. s. his servant at supper time
19 : 14. they s. a message after him
23 : 11. and s. him again to Pilate
Jn. 1 : 19. Jews s. priests and Levites
22 give answer to them that s. us
33. he that s. me to baptize
4 : 34. to do will of him that s. me
5 : 23. honoureth not Fa. wh. s. him
24. that believeth on him that s.
me, 12 : 44. ⌈38, 39, 40.
30. will of Father which s. me. 6 :
33. Ye s. unto John, he bare witn-s
36. works I do bear witness Father
s. me, 37.-6 : 57.-8 : 16, 18.
6 : 44. except Father wh. s. me draw
7 : 16. doctrine not mine, his th. s. me
18. seeketh his glory that s. him
28. he that s. me is true, 8 : 26.
32. priests s. officers to take him
33. I go unto him that s. me
8 : 29. he that s. me is with me
9 : 4. the works of him that s. me
10 : 36. Say ye of him wh. Fa. hath s.
11 : 3. his sisters s. unto him
42. may believe thou hast s. me
12 : 45 seeth me, seeth him th. s. me
49. Father wh. s. me gave com-nt
13 : 16. neither he that is s. greater
than he that s. ⌈s. me
14 : 24. not mine, but Fa.'s which
15 : 21. bec. know not him th. s. me
16 : 5. I go my way to him th. s. me
17 : 3. to know Jesus whom thou s.
18. As thou hast s. me into the
world, so have I s. them
21. world may believe thou s. me
23. world may know thou s. me
25. have known thou hast s. me
18 : 24. Now Annas had s. him bound
20 : 21. as my Father hath s. me
Ac. 5 : 21. s. to prison to have them
7 : 14. s. Joseph and called his fa.
8 : 14. they s. unto them Pet. and Jn

Ac. 9 : 38. they s. unto Peter 2 men
10:29. what intent ye have s. for me
11 : 30. s. it to elders by Barnabas
13:15. rulers of synag. s. unto them
15 : 27. We have s. Judas and Silas
16 : 36. have s. to let you go, 35.
19 : 31. Paul's friends s. unto him
1 Co. 1 : 17. Christ s. me not to bapt.
2 Co. 8:18. we have s. the brother, 22.
Ph. 4 : 16. in Thessalonica ye s. once
1 Th. 3 : 2. s. Timotheus our brother
1 Jn. 4:14. testify that Fa. s. the Son

SENT away.

Ge. 12 : 20. Pha. s.a. Abra. and wife
21 : 14. Ab. s. Ishmael and Hagar a.
24 : 59. s.a. Rebekah their sister
25 : 6. Ab. s. Keturah's children a.
26 : 27. ye hate and have s. me a.
29. as we have s. thee a. in peace
31. Isaac s. them a., they departed
28 : 5. Isaac s.a. Jacob to Padan-a.
6. Isaac blessed Jacob, s. him a.
31 : 27. I might have s. thee a. with
42. hadst s. me a. empty ⌊mirth
45 : 24. Joseph s. his brethren a.
De. 24 : 4. husband wh. s. her a. not
Jos. 2: 21. Rahab s. spies a.⌊take her
8 : 3. men and s. them a. by night
22 : 6. Joshua s. Reubenites a., 7.
Ju. 3 : 18. s.a. peo th. bare present
11 : 38. Jephthah s. his daughter a.
1 S. 10 : 25. Samuel s. all the peo. a.
19 : 17. Why hast s.a. my enemy?
2 S. 3 : 21. David s. Abner a., 22, 23.
24. why is it thou hast s. him a.?
10 : 4. cut garments, s. them a.,
1 Ch. 19 : 4. ⌈10.
1 K. 8 : 66. he s. people a., 2 Ch. 7 :
20 : 34. he made cov. and s. him a.
2 K. 6 : 23. had eaten, he s. them a.
1 Ch. 8 : 8. after he had s. them a.
12 : 19. lords of Philis. s. David a.
Jb. 22 : 9. hast s. widows a. empty
Mat. 13 : 36. Jesus s. multitude a.,
14 : 22, 23.-15 : 39. Mk. 4 : 36.
Mk. 1:43. charged him and s. him a.
6. 45. while he s.a. people, 46.
8 : 9. about 4,000, and he s. them a.
26. Jesus s. him a. to his house
12 : 3. caught servant, beat him, s.
him a., 4. Lu. 20 : 10, 11.
Lu. 1 : 53. rich he hath s. empty a.
8 : 38. but Jesus s. him a., saying
Ac. 13 : 3. had prayed, they s. them a.
17 : 10. immediately s.a. Paul, 14.

SENT forth.

Ge. 8 : 7. Noah s.f. a raven
8. he s.f. a dove to see, 10, 12.
Jos. 8 : 9. Josh. s. them f.; th. went
Pr. 9 : 3. She hath s. f. her maidens
Eze 10:†7. one cherub s.f. his hand
Zch. 9 : 11. I have s. f. thy prisoners
Mat. 2 : 16. Herod s. f. and slew
10 : 5. These twelve Jesus s.f. and
22 : 3. s.f. his serv-ts to call th., 4.
7. he s. f. his armies and destroyed
Mk. 6 : 17. Herod s.f., laid hold upon
Lu. 20 : 20. priests s.f. spies ⌊John
Ac. 9 : 30. breth. s. him f. to Tarsus
11 : 22. s.f. Barnabas far as Antioch
Ga. 4 : 4. God s.f. his Son made of
6. God s.f. Spirit into your hearts
See GOD sent.

He SENT.

Ge. 37 : 14 So h.s. him out of Hebron
41 : 8. h.s. for all magicians of Egypt
45 : 23. to his father h.s. 10 asses
46 : 28. h.s. Judah unto Joseph
Ex. 18 : 2. Zipporah, after h.s. her
24 : 5. h.s. young men of Israel
Jos. 11 : 1. h.s. to Jobab, k. of Madon
Ju. 7 : 8. h.s. every man unto tent,
1 S. 13 : 2. ⌈h.s.
11 : 28. hearkened not unto words
1 S. 16 : 12. h.s. brought David in
17 : 31. before Saul; h.s. for David
30 : 26. h.s. of spoil unto elders

2 S. 10 : 5. h.s. to meet, 1 Ch. 19 : 5.
7. h.s. Joab and all host, 1 Ch. 19 :
12 : 25. h.s. by hand of Nathan ⌊8.
14 : 29. h.s. again, Joab would not
come ⌈Ps. 18 : 16.
22 : 17. h.s. from above, took me,
1 K. 5 : 14. h.s. them to Lebanon
20 : 7. h.s. unto me for my wives
2 K. 1 : 11. h.s. another captain, 13.
5:8. h.s. to king, Whf. rent clothes?
6 : 14. theref. s.h. horses and char.
17 : 26. theref. h.s. lions am. them
19 : 2. And h.s. Eliakim, Is. 37 : 2
1 Ch. 18 : 10. h.s. 19 : 3 5. 2 Ch. 2 : 11.
2 Ch. 24 : 19. h.s. prophets to⌊-17 : 7.
25 : 15. h.s. unto Amaziah a prophet
34 : 8. h.s. Shaphan to repair house
35 : 21. h.s. ambassadors to him
Es. 5 : 10. h.s. for friends and wife
Ps. 78 : 25. h.s. them meat to the
45. h.s. flies among them ⌊full
105 : 17. h.s. a man before them,
26. h.s. Moses and Aaron⌊Joseph
28. h.s. darkness, made it dark
106 : 15. h.s. leanness into soul
107 : 20. h.s. his word, healed them
111 : 9. h.s. redemption unto peo.
Is. 61 : 1. h.s. me to bind up, Lu. 4 : 18.
Je. 29 : 28. h.s. unto us in Babylon
42 : 21. for which h.s. me unto you
La. 1 : 13. h.s. fire into my bones
Zch. 2 : 8. hath h.s. me unto nations
Mat. 2 : 8. h.s. them to Bethlehem
11 : 2. h.s. two of disci., Lu. 19 : 29.
14 : 10. h.s. and beheaded John
20 : 2. h.s. them into his vineyard
21 : 34. h.s. serv-ts unto the husb-n,
Mk. 12 : 2. Lu. 20 : 10, 11, 12.
36. Again h.s. other serv-ts more,
22 : 4. Mk. 12 : 4, 5. Lu. 20 : 11, 12.
37. last of all h.s. his son, Mk. 12 : 6.
Lu. 7 : 3. h.s. unto Jesus the elders
9 : 2. h.s. them to preach kingdom
15 : 15. h.s. him to feed swine
22 : 8. h.s. Peter, Prepare passover
Jn. 5 : 38. whom h.s. ye believe not
6 : 29. believe on him h. hath s.
7 : 29. I know him, h. hath s. me
8. 42. nei. came I of mys., h.s. me
Ac. 10 : 8. h.s. them to Joppa
19 : 22. h.s. into Macedonia two of
20 : 17. from Miletus h.s. to Ephesus
24 : 24. h.s. for Paul and heard him
26. h.s. for Paul the oftener
Re. 1 : 1. h.s. by his angel unto John

I SENT, or I have SENT.

Ge. 32 : 5. I h.s. to tell my lord
38 : 23. I s. this kid, thou hast not
Ex. 3 : 12. shall be token I h. s. thee
Nu. 32 : 8. did your fa-rs when I s. th.
Jos. 24 : 5. I s. Moses and Aa., Mi. 6 : 4.
Ju. 6 : 14. save Israel h. not I s. thee?
2 S. 14 : 32. Abs. ans-d I s. unto thee
2 K. 5 : 6. I h.s. Naaman to thee
17 : 13. the law which I s. to you
2 Ch. 2 : 13. I h.s. a cunning man
16 : 3. I h.s. thee silver and gold
Ezr. 8 : 16. then s. I for Eliezer
17. I s. them with com-t unto Iddo
Ne. 6 : 8. then I s. unto Sanballat
Is 42 : 19. who deaf, as mess-r I s.?
43 : 14. For y-r sake I h.s. to Bab.
55 : 11. it sh. prosper whereto I s. it
Je. 7 : 25. I s. unto you all my serv-ts
the prophets, 26 : 5.-35 : 15.-44 : 4.
14 : 14. The prophets I s. them not,
15.-23 : 21, 32.-27 : 15.-29 : 9.
23 : 38. I h.s. unto you, saying
29 : 20. all ye whom I h.s. to Bab.
31. I s. him not, he caused you
Eze. 3 : 6. had I s. thee they hearken
Jo. 2 : 25. my great army which I s.
Am. 4 : 10. I h.s. the pestilence
Mal 2 : 4. ye shall know I h.s. this
Lu. 22 : 35. Wh. I s. you with-t purse
23 : 15. for I s. you to Herod
Jn. 4 : 38. I s. you to reap that wh-n

Jn. 17 : 18. so h. I s. th. into world
Ac. 10 : 20. doubting nothing I h.s.
33. Immediately theref. I s. to thee
23 : 30. I s. straightway to thee
1 Co. 4 : 17. For this h. I s. to Timo.
2 Co. 9 : 3. Yet h. I s. brethren, lest
12 : 17. Did I make gain by any I s.
18. Titus, with him I s. a brother
Ep. 6 : 22. Whom I s. for same, Col.
Ph. 2 : 28. I s. him more caref-y⌊4:8.
1 Th. 3 : 5. I s. to know your faith
2 Ti. 4 : 12. Tychicus h. I s. to Eph.
Phm. 12. Whom I h.s. again, receive
Re. 22 : 16. I, Jesus, h.s. mine angel
See LORD with sent.
See LETTER, S, MESSENGER, S.

SENT out.

Ge. 19 : 29. God s. Lot o. of midst
Jos. 2 : 1. Joshua s.o. two men
1 S. 25 : 5. David s.o. ten yo. men
26 : 4. David therefore s.o. spies
2 S. 22 : 15. he s.o. arrows, Ps. 18 : 14.
1 K. 20 : 17. Ben-hadad s.o. ⌈back
2 K. 9 : 19. s.o. a second on horse-
Jb. 39 : 5. Who hath s.o. wild ass
Ps. 77 : 17. the skies s.o. a sound⌊free?
80 : 11. She s.o. her boughs to sea
Je. 24 : 5. wh. I have s.o. of this pla.
Eze. 31 : 4. she hath s.o. little rivers
Mat. 14 : 35. they s.o. into all the
country ⌈ciples
22 : 16. Phari. s.o. unto him dis-
Ac. 7 : 12. Jacob s.o. our fa-s first
Ja. 2 : 25. Rahab s. them o. ano. way

SENT. [Passive.] ⌈Esau
Ge. 32 : 18 it is a present s. unto
Ju. 5 : 15. was s. on foot into valley
1 K. 14 : 6. I am s. wi. heavy tidings
Ezr. 7 : 14. as thou art s. of the king
Je. 49 : 14. ambas-r is s. unto heath.
Eze. 2 : 9. a hand was s. unto me
3 : 5. art not s. to people of strange
Da. 5 : 24. was part of the hand s.
10 : 11. Dan. unto thee am I now s.
Ob. 1. ambassador is s. am. heathen
Mat. 15 : 24. I am not s. but unto lost
23 : 37. stonest them s., Lu. 13 . 34.
Lu. 1 : 19. I am Gabr-l, and am s. to
26. Gabriel was s. unto Nazareth
4 : 26. But unto none was Elias s.
43. preach, for therefore am I s.
7 : 10. th. were s. returned to hou.
19 : 32. that were s. went their way
Jn. 1 : 6. a man s. from God, was Jn
8. John was s. to bear witness of
24. wh. were s. were of Pharisees
3 : 28. I am not Christ, but s. bef.
9 : 7. wash in Siloam, which is S ⌈than
13 : 16. nei. he that is s. greater
Ac. 10 : 17. men s. had made inquiry
21. Pet. went to the men s., 11 : 11.
29. came I as soon as I was s. for
13 : 4. being s. forth by Holy Ghost
26. to you is word of salvation s.
28 : 28. salvation is s. unto Gentiles
Ro. 10 : 15. how preach, except be s.?
Ph. 4 : 18. received things s. fr. you
He. 1 : 14. spirits s. forth to minister
1 Pe. 1 : 12. wi. Holy Gh. s. fr. heav
2 : 14. unto governors, as th. are s.
Re. 5 : 6. seven spirits s. into earth

SENTENCE, S.

De 17 : 9. they sh. shew thee the s.
10. shalt do acc-g to the s., 11.
Ps. 17 : 2. Let my s. come forth
Pr. 16 : 10. A divine s. is in lips of k
Ec. 8 : 11. bec. s. not exec-d speedily
Je. 4 : 12. will I give s. ag-t them
Da. 5 : 12. shewing of hard s-s in Da.
8 : 23. a king underst-g dark s-s⌈as
Lu. 23 : 24. Pilate gave s. that it be
Ac. 15 : 19. my s. is, we trouble not
2 Co. 1 : 9. we had the s. of death

SENTEST.

Ex. 15 : 7. s. forth thy wrath, which
Nu. 13 : 27. land whither thou s. us
24 : 12. not to messengers thou s.

1 K. 5 : 8. Hiram saying, I have considered the things thou s. for
SEN'UAH. [city
Ne. 11 : 9. Judah, son of S., 2d over
SEO'RIM.
1 Ch. 24 : 8. fourth lot came to S.
SEPARATE. [Adj.] [16.
Ge. 49 : 26. was s. fr. breth., De. 33 :
Jos. 16 : 9. the s. cities of Ephraim
Eze. 41 : 12. building before s. place
13. measured house and s. place
14. breadth of the s. pla. tow. east
42 : 1 chamber ag. s. place, 10,13.
2 Co. 6 : 17. come out fr. them, be s.
He. 7 : 26. undefiled, s. from sinners
SEPARATE. [Verb.] [me
Ge. 13 : 9. Abram said, s. thyself fr.
30 : 40. Jacob did s. the lambs, and
Le. 15 : 31. shall ye s. chil. of Israel
22 : 2. to Aaron and sons th. they s.
Nu. 6 : 2. when man or woman s. to vow, to s. thems. unto the L.
3. Nazarite sh. s. himself fr. wine
8 : 14. shalt s. Levites from Israel
16 : 21. s. from this congregation
De. 19 : 2. Thou sh. s. three cities, 7.
29 : 21. Lord shall s. him unto evil
1 K. 8 : 53. didst s. them to be thine
Ezr. 10 : 11. s. from people of land
Je. 37 : 12. Jeremiah went to s. hims.
Mat. 25 : 32. sh. s. them as shepherd
Lu. 6 : 22. blessed when men s. you
Ac. 13 : 2. s. me Barnabas and Saul
Ro. 8 : 35. Who s. us fr. love of Ch.?
39. noth. able to s. us fr. love of G.
Jude 19. be they who s. themselves
SEPARATED.
Ge. 13 : 11. then Abram and Lot s.
14. L. said, aft. Lot was s. fr. him
25 : 23. two peo. be s. fr. thy bowels
Ex. 33 : 16. so we be s. from people
Le. 20 : 24. I am Lord which s. you
25. which I s. from you as unclean
Nu. 16 : 9 God of Israel hath s. you
De. 10 : 8. Lord s. the tribe of Levi
32 : 8. when he s. sons of Adam
33 : 16. him th. was s. fr. his breth.
1 Ch. 12 : 8. of Gadites s. unto David
23 : 13. Aaron was s. th. he sanctify
25 : 1. David s. to the service of
2 Ch. 25 : 10. Then Amaziah s. them
Ezr. 6 : 21. all that had s. thems.
8 : 24. Then I s. twelve of the chief
9 : 1. Levites have not s. thems.
10 : 8. whoso. not come, be s. from
16. all of them by names were s.
Ne. 4 : 19. and we are s. upon wall
9 : 2. Israel s. thems. fr. strangers
10 : 28. that had s. clave to breth.
13 : 3. s. from Israel mixed mult.
Pr. 18 : 1. a man having s. himself
19 : 4. poor is s. from his neighbour
Is. 1 : † 4. forsaken L., they are s.
56 : 3 Lord hath s. me fr. his peo.
59 : 2. iniquities s. betw. you and G.
Ho. 4 : 14. thems are s. wi. whores
9 : 10. they s. thems. unto th. shame
Zch. 14 : † 4. valley of mts. to pla. s.
Ac. 19 : 9. Paul departed, s. discip-s
Ro. 1 : 1. Paul s. unto gospel of God
9 : † 3. could wish I were s. fr. Ch.
Ga. 1 : 15. G. who s. me from womb
2 : 12. Peter withdrew and s. hims.
SEPARATETH.
Nu. 6 : 5. days in which he s. himself unto Lord [dead
6. days he s. himself, come at no
Pr. 16 : 28. whisperer s. chief friends
17 : 9. repeateth a matter s. friends
Eze. 14 : 7. stranger which s. hims
SEPARATING.
Nu. 15 : † 3. unto L. a sacrifice in s.
Zch. 7 : 3. Sho. I weep s. mys. as I
SEPARATION. [mity
Le. 12 : 2. days of s. for her infir-
5. unclean 2 weeks, as in her s.
15 : † 19. shall be in her s. 7 days
Le. 15 : 20. bed she lieth upon in her s.
25. of blood out of time of her s.
26. every bed be as bed of her s.
16 : † 22. iniquities to a land of s.
20 : † 21. take brot.'s wife, it is a s.
25 : † 5. nei. gather grapes of thy s.
Nu. 6 : 4. days of s. sh. eat nothing
5. days of his s. no razor sh. come
† 7. bec. s. of his God is upon head
8. All days of his s. he is holy
12. sh. consecrate days of his s., bring lamb, bec. s. was defiled
13. when days of his s. fulfilled
18. Nazarite sh. shave head of his s., take hair of his s. [shaven
19. after hair of Nazarite's s. is
21. off-g for his s. after law of s.
19 : 9. ashes be kept for water of s.
13. water of s. not sprinkled, 20.
21. he that sprinkleth water of s., that toucheth water of s. [of s.
31 : 23. shall be purified with water
Eze. 7 : † 19. their gold be for a s.
42 : 20. wall round to make a s.
Zch. 13 : † 1. fountain opened for s.
SE'PHAR. [mount
Ge. 10 : 30. as thou goest unto S., a
SEPH'ARAD.
Ob. 20. captiv. of Jerus. which is in S.
SEPHARVA'IM. [fr. S.
2 K. 17 : 24. king of Assyria bro-t men
31. and Anam, Melech, gods of S.
18 : 34. where gods of S.? Is. 36 : 19.
19 : 13. Where is king of S.? Is. 37 : 13.
SE'PHARVITES.
2 K. 17 : 31. S. burnt their chil. in fire
SEPULCHRE.
Ge. 23 : 6. none shall withhold his s.
De 34 : 6. no man knoweth of his s.
Ju. 8 : 32. Gideon buried in fa.'s s.
1 S. 10 : 2. find 2 men by Rachel's s.
2 S. 2 : 32. buried Asahel in fa.'s s.
4 : 12. Ishb-h buried in Abner's s.
17 : 23. Ahithop-l buried in s. of fa.
21 : 14. bones of Saul in s. of Kish
1 K. 13 : 22. thy carcass not unto s.
31. bury me in s. wh-in man of G. is
2 K. 9 : 28. Ahaziah in s. with fa-s
13 : 21. cast man into s. of Elisha
21 : 26. Amon was buried in his s.
23 : 17. It is the s. of man of God
30. Josiah buried in his own s.
Ps. 5 : 9. throat an open s., Ro. 3 : 13.
Is. 22 : 16. hewed thee out a s., as he that heweth out s. on high
Je. 5 : 16. Their quiver is as open s.
Mat. 27 : 60. rolled stone to door of s.
61. other Mary, sitting over ag. s.
64. Command s. be made sure, 66.
28 : 1. other Mary came to see s.
8. departed fr. s. with fear and joy
Mk. 15 : 46. Joseph laid him in s., and rolled stone unto door of s., Lu.
23 : 53. Ac. 13 : 29. [of sun
16 : 2. they came unto s. at rising
3. who sh. roll stone fr. door of s.
5. entering s. they saw young man
8. out quickly and fled from s.
Lu. 23 : 55. women also beheld the s.
24 : 1. in morning they came to s.
2. found stone rolled fr. s., Jn. 20 : 1.
9. they returned from s., told all
12. arose Peter, and ran unto s.
22. certain women early at the s.
24. certain with us went to the s.
Jn. 19 : 41. in garden was a new s.
42. laid Jes., for s. was nigh at ha.
20 : 1. cometh Mary when dark to s.
2. They have taken Lord out of s.
3. other disciple came to s., 4, 8.
6. cometh Peter, went into s.
11. Mary stood at the s. weeping, she stooped and looked into s.
Ac. 2 : 29. his s. with us unto this day
7 : 16. Jacob laid in s. Abr. bought
SEPULCHRES.
Ge. 23 : 6. in choice of our s. bury
2 K. 23 : 16. Josiah spied the s. and took the bones out of the s.
2 Ch. 16 : 14. buried Asa in his own s.
21 : 20. Jehoram not bur. in s. of k-s
24 : 25. buried Joash not in s. of k-s
28 : 27. bro-t Ahaz not into s. of k-s
32 : 33. Hez-kiah in chiefest of s.
35 : 24. Josiah buried in one of s. of
Ne. 2 : 3. place of my fa-s' s. waste
5. send me unto city of my fa-s' s.
3 : 16. Nehemiah unto place ag-t s.
Mat. 23 : 27. Woe, ye are like whited s.
29 bec. ye garnish s. of righteous
Lu. 11 : 47. ye build s. of prophets, 48.
SE'RAH = SA'RAH.
Ge. 46 : 17. Beriah, Se. sister, 1 Ch.
Nu. 26 : 46. dan. of Asher was Sa. [7 : 30.
SERAI'AH = SHAV'SHA.
2 S. 8 : 17. S-h, scribe, 1 Ch. 18 : 16. S-a
SERAI'AH. [† S-h
2 K. 25 : 18. captain of guard took S. and Zeph., Je. 52 : 24. [40 : 8.
23. there came to Gedaliah, S., Je.
1 Ch. 4 : 13. sons of Kenaz, S.
14. S. begat Joab | 35. Josibiah son of S. [Jehozadak
6 : 14. Azariah begat S., and S. begat
Ezr. 2 : 2. came with Zerubbabel, S.
7 : 1. Ezra, son of S., was fr. Bab-n
Ne. 10 : 2. those that sealed were S.
11 : 11. S. was ruler of house of God
12 : 1. S. went up with Zerubbabel
12. chief of fathers of S., Meraiah
Je. 36 : 26. com-ded S. to take Baruch
51 : 59. word Jeremiah com-ded S., this S. was a quiet prince
61. Jeremiah said to S., When comest to Babylon
SERAPHIM.
Is. 6 : 2. Above it stood the s., each
6. flew one of s. having live coal
SE'RED. [26 : 26.
Ge. 46 : 14. sons of Zebulun, S., Nu.
SERGEANTS. See SERJEANTS.
SER'GIUS PAU'LUS.
Ac. 13 : 7. S. P. a prud. man, dep.y
SERJEANTS.
Ac. 16 : 35. sent s. saying, Let men go
38. s. told words unto magistrates
SERPENT.
Ge. 3 : 1. s. was more subtle than any
2. woman said unto s., We may eat
4. s. said unto woman, Ye sh. not
13. The s. beguiled me, 2 Co. 11 : 3.
14. God said unto s., Because thou hast done this
49 : 17. Dan shall be a s. by the way
Ex. 4 : 3. rod became s., 7 : 9, 10, 15.
Nu. 21 : 8. Lord said, Make a fiery s.
9. Moses made a s. of brass; if a s. had bitten any man, he beheld the s. of brass [brazen s.
2 K. 18 : 4. Hezekiah brake in pieces
Jb. 26 : 13. hand formed crooked s.
Ps. 58 : 4. Their poison like pois. of s.
140 : 3. sharpened tongues like s.
Pr. 23 : 32. At last it biteth like a s.
30 : 19. too wonderful, way of a s.
Ec. 10 : 8. breaketh hedge, s. sh. bite
11. s. will bite without enchantm.
Is. 14 : 29. of s.'s root come cockatrice; fruit be as fiery flying s.
27 : 1. L. shall punish s., crooked s.
30 : 6. whence viper and fiery fly-g s.
65 : 25. dust shall be the s.'s meat
Je 46 : 22. The voice shall go like a s.
Am. 5 : 19. hand on wall, a s. bit him
9 : 3. will comm-d s. and he sh. bite
Mi. 7 : 17. shall lick dust like a s.
Mat. 7 : 10. if ask fish, will he give him a s.? Lu. 11 : 11.
Jn. 3 : 14. as Moses lifted up s., so must Son of man be lifted up
Re. 12 : 9. that old s. the devil, 20 : 2.
14. nourished from face of the s.
15. s. cast out water as a flood

SERPENTS. [came s.
Ex. 7 : 12. down their rods, they be-
Nu. 21 : 6. L. sent fiery s. am. them
7. pray Lord that he take s. fr. us
De. 8 : 15. wilderness wherein fiery s.
32 : 24. I will send poison of s. upon
Je. 8 : 17. I will send s. among you
Mat. 10 : 16. be ye theref. wise as s.
23 : 33. Ye s. how can ye escape?
Mk. 16 : 18. They shall take up s.
Lu. 10 : 19. you power to tread on s.
1 Co. 10 : 9. and were destroyed of s.
Ja. 3 : 7. every kind of s. is tamed
Re. 9 : 19. their tails were like unto s.

SE'RUG.
Ge. 11 : 20. Reu. lived 32 years, begat
22. S. begat Nahor [S., 21.
23. S. lived after 200 years
1 Ch. 1 : 26. S., Nahor, Serah, Abram

SERVANT.
Ge. 9 : 25. Canaan a s. of servants
18 : 5. theref. are ye come to your s.
19 : 2. turn into your s.'s house
24 : 9. s. put his hand und. thigh, 2.
10. s. took 10 camels of his master
17. s. ran to meet Rebekah
34. he said, I am Abraham's s.
52. Abr.'s s. heard their words
53. s. bro-t forth jewels of silver
59. sent aw. Rebekah and Ab.'s s.
61. s. took Rebekah and went
65. Rebek. to s., What man is this?
66. s. told Isaac all things done
41 : 12. yo. man, Hebrew, s. to capt.
49 : 15. Issachar bowed became s.
Ex. 21 : 5. if s. say I love master
Nu. 11 : 28. Joshua, s. of Moses, said
De. 5 : 15. remember thou wast a s.
23 : 15. shalt not deliver s. escaped
Ju. 19 : 11. s. said unto his master
Ru. 2 : 6. s. set over reapers answ-d
1 S. 2 : 13. priest's s. came, 15.
9 : 8. s. answered Saul again, I
27. bid the s. pass on before us
25 : 41. let thy handmaid be a s. to
29 : 3. Is not this David, s. of Saul?
30 : 13. I am s. to an Amalekite [17.
2 S. 9 : 2. of Saul, s. named Ziba, 19:
9. king called to Ziba Saul's s.
16 : 1. Ziba the s. of Mephibosheth
18 : 29. When Joab sent king's s.
and me thy s., 2 Ch. 13:6. [hand
1 K. 11 : 26. Jerob., Solo.'s s., lifted
12 : 7. If wilt be s. to this people
2 K. 4 : 24. she said to her s., Drive
5 : 20. Gehazi, s. of Elisha, said
6 : 15. s. of man of God was risen
8 : 4. k. talketh with s. of man of G
22 : 12. Asahiah s. of k., 2 Ch 34:20.
25 : 8. Nebuzar-adan, s. of king of
1 Ch. 2 : 34. Sheshan had a s. Jarha
Ne. 2 : 10. Tobiah the s. heard, 19.
Jb. 3 : 19. there s. is free fr. master
7 : 2. As a s. desireth the shadow
41 : 4. wilt take Leviathan for s.
Ps. 105 : 17. Joseph was sold for a s.
Pr. 11 : 29. fool shall be s. to wise
12 : 9. that is despised and hath a s.
14 : 35. king's favour is tow. wise s.
17 : 2. wise s. sh. have rule over son
19 : 10. much less s. to rule princes
22 : 7. borrower is s. to the lender
29 : 19. A s. not corrected wi. words
30 : 10. Accuse not s. unto his mas.
22. earth cannot bear a s. when
Is. 24 : 2. as with s. so with master
49 : 7. saith the L. to a s. of rulers
53 : 11. my righteous s. justify many
Je. 2 : 14. Is Israel a s.? a slave?
Da. 6 : 20. O Daniel, s. of living God
10 : 17. how can s. talk wi. my lord?
Mal. 1 : 6. s. honoureth his master
Mat. 10 : 24. nor is s. above his lord
25. enough for s. to be as his lord
18 : 26. s. fell down worsh-d him
27. the lord of that s. was moved
32. O thou wicked s. I forgave
Mat. 20 : 27. whoso. will be chief, let
be your s., 23 : 11. Mk. 10 : 44.
24 : 45. Who is a faithful and wise s.
46. Blessed is that s., Lu. 12 : 43.
48. But if evil s. sh. say, Lu. 12:45.
50. lord of s. sh. come, Lu. 12 : 46.
25 : 21. Well done, thou good and
faithful s., 23. Lu. 19 : 17.
26. Thou wicked and slothful s.,
Lu. 19 : 22. [darkness
30. cast unprofitable s. into outer
26 : 51. Peter struck s. of high pri.,
Mk. 14:47. Lu. 22:50. Jn. 18:10.
Mk. 9 : 35. shall be last and s. of all
12 : 2. sent to husbandmen a s., 4.
Lu. 7 : 10. found s. whole been sick
12 : 47. s. which knew lord's will
14 : 21. s. came and shewed his lord
22. s. saith, It is done as comm-ded
23. said unto s., Go into highways
16 : 13. No s. can serve two masters
17 : 7. which having a s. ploughing
9. Doth he thank s.? I trow not
20 : 10. at the season he sent a s., 11.
Jn. 8 : 34. commit-h sin, is s. of sin
35. s. abideth not in house [15:20.
13 : 16. s. not greater than lord,
15 : 15. s. knoweth not wh. his lord
Ro. 1 : 1. Paul, a s. of Jesus Christ
14 : 4. Who thou judgest man's s.?
16 : 1. I commend Phebe, s. of ch.
1 Co. 7 : 21. Art thou called, be-g a s.?
22. being a s. is the Lord's freem-n
9 : 19. I made myself a s. unto all
Ga. 1 : 10. I should not be s. of Ch.
4 : 1. child differeth nothing fr. s.
7. thou art no more a s., but son
Ph. 2 : 7. he took the form of a s.
Col. 4 : 12. Epaphras, a s. of Christ
2 Ti. 2 : 24. s. of L. must not strive
Phm. 16. Not as a s., but above a s.
He. 3 : 5. Moses was faithful as a s.
2 Pe. 1 : 1. Peter, a s. of Jes. Christ
Jude 1. Jude, the s. of Jesus Christ
See BONDSERVANT.

SERVANT David.
2 K. 8 : 19. Lord not destroy Judah
for D. his s.'s sake [sake, 20 : 6.
19 : 34. defend city for my s. D.'s
1 Ch. 17 : 4. tell D. my s., saith L., 7.
Ac. 4 : 25. Who by the mouth of thy
s. D. hast said, Why did the
See **DAVID** with servant.
See **FELLOW** servant, s.
See **Servant, s, of GOD.**
See **HEBREW** servant.
See **HIRED** servant, s.

His SERVANT.
Ge. 9 : 26. Canaan shall be h.s., 27.
Ex. 14 : 31. peo. believed h.s. Moses
21 : 20. if man smite h.s. and he die
26. if he smite eye of h.s. that it
33 : 11. h.s. Joshua departed not
Jos. 5 : 14. What saith my L. to h.s.?
9 : 24. God commanded h.s. Moses
Ju. 7 : 11. Gideon, with Phurah h.s.
19 : 3. Levite went, having h.s.
9. man rose to depart, and his s.
13. He said unto h.s., Come, let us
Ru. 2 : 5. said Boaz unto h.s. over
reapers [7, 10.
1 S. 9 : 5. Saul said to h.s., Come,
22. Samuel took Saul and h.s.
10 : 14. Saul's uncle said unto h.s.
19 : 4. Let not the king sin ag. h.s.
22 : 15. let not king impute to h.s.
25 : 39. L. hath kept h.s. from evil
26 : 18. Whf. doth my lord pursue h.
19. let lord hear words of h.s. [s.?
2 S. 9 : 11. as my lord com-ded h.s.
13 : 17. Amnon called h.s. th. min.
18. h.s. bro-t Tam. out bolted door
14 : 22. king fulfilled request of h.s.
24 : 21. whf. my lord come to h.s.
1 K. 1 : 51. swear, he will not slay h.s.
8 : 56. promised by Moses h.s.
59. he maintain the cause of h.s.
1 K. 14 : 18. spa. by h.s. Ahijah, 15 : 29.
16 : 9. h.s. Zimri conspired ag. him
18 : 43. said to h.s., 2 K. 4 : 12, 25, 38.
19 : 3. Elijah left h.s. at Beer-sh.
2 K. 6 : 15. h.s. said, Alas, my mast.
9 : 36. he spake by h.s. Elijah, 10 : 10.
14 : 25. word he spake by h s. Jon.
17 : 3. Hoshea bec-e h.s., and gave
24 : 1. Jehoiakim became h.s.
1 Ch. 2 : 35. dau. to Jarha h.s. to wife
16 : 13. O ye seed of Israel h.s.
2 Ch. 32 : 16. spake ag. h.s. Hezek.
Ne. 4 : 22. every one with h.s. lodge
6 : 5. sent Sanballat h.s. unto me
Ps. 35 : 27. L. hath pleasure in h.s.
105 : 6. O ye seed of Abraham h.s.
26. He sent Moses h.s. and Aaron
42. he rememb-d Abraham h.s.
136 : 22. a heritage unto Israel h.s.
Pr. 29 : 21. delicately brin-h up h.s.
Is. 44 : 26. confirmeth word of h.s.
48 : 20. L. redeemed h.s. Jacob [s.
49 : 5. formed me fr. womb to be h.
50 : 10. who obeyeth voice of h.s.
Je. 34 : 16. every man h.s. to return
Mat. 8 : 13. h.s. was healed in same
Lu. 1 : 54 He hath holpen h.s. Isr.
7 : 3. beseeching he would heal h.s.
14 : 17. sent h.s. at supper time
21. the master, angry, said to h.s.
Re. 1 : 1. by his angel unto h.s. Jn.
See **Servant, s, of the LORD,**
MAIDSERVANT, MANSERVANT.

My SERVANT.
Ge. 26 : 24. I multiply thy seed for
m.s. Abraham's sake [17.
44 : 10. he with wh. found be m.s.,
Nu. 12 : 7. m.s. Moses is not so [s.?
8. whf. not afraid to speak ag. m.
14 : 24. m.s. Caleb had ano. spirit
Jos. 1 : 2. Moses m.s. is dead
7. law Moses m.s. commanded,
2 K. 21 : 8. [m.s.
1 S. 22 : 8. my son hath stirred up
27 : 12. he shall be m.s. forever
2 S. 19 : 26. O king, m.s. deceived me
2 K. 5 : 6. I have sent Naaman m.s.
Jb. 1 : 8. considered m.s. Job? 2:3.
19 : 16. I called m.s., he gave me no
42 : 7. not spoken right, as m.s. Job
8. go to m.s. Job, he pray for you
Is. 20 : 3. as m.s. Is. walked naked
22 : 20. I will call m.s. Eliakim
41 : 8. thou Isr. m.s. fear not, 9.
42 : 1. Behold m.s. whom I uphold
19. Who is blind but m.s. I sent?
43 : 10. ye are witnesses, and m.s.
44 : 1. Yet now hear, O Jacob, m.s.
2. Fear not, O Jacob, m.s., and
thou, Je. 30 : 10. 46 : 27, 28.
21. Remember thou art m.s., 49 : 3.
45 : 4. For Jacob m.s.'s sake, and
49 : 6. light thi. thou sho. be m.s.
52 : 13. m. s. shall deal prudently
53 : 11 m. righteous s. justify many
Je. 25 : 9. Nebuchadrezzar m. s.
27 : 6. 43 : 10. [Jacob, 37 : 25.
Eze. 28 : 25. land I have given m.s.
Hag. 2 : 23. thee, O Zerubbabel m.s.
Zch. 3 : 8. bring m.s. the BRANCH
Mal. 4 : 4. the law of Moses m.s.
Mat. 8 : 6. m.s. lieth at home sick
8. speak, m.s., be healed, Lu. 7 : 7.
9. and to m.s., Do this, Lu. 7 : 8.
12 : 18. m.s. whom I have chosen
Jn. 12 : 26. where I am sh. m.s. be

Thy SERVANT.
Ge. 18 : 3. L. pass not away from t.s.
19 : 19. t.s. found grace, Ne. 2 : 5.
24 : 14. she thou appointed for t.s.
32 : 4. t.s. Jacob saith, I sojourned
10. not worthy mercies unto t.s.
18. shalt say, They be t.s. Jacob's
20. t.s. Jacob is behind us
33 : 5. children G. hath given t.s.
39 : 19. After this manner did t.s.
43 : 28. t.s., our fa., in good health

Ge.44:18. let t.s. speak in lord's ears, let not anger turn ag. t.s.[fa.,30.
24. when we came unto t.s. our
27. t.s. my father said unto us
31. gray hairs of t.s. our father
32. t.s. became surety for lad, 33.
Ex. 4 : 10. hast spoken unto t.s.
Le. 25 : 6. sabbath be meat for t.s.
Nu. 11 : 11. Whf. hast afflicted t.s.
De. 3 : 24. shew t.s. thy greatness
15 : 7. thro. his ear, he shall be t.s.
Ju. 7 : 10. go down with Phurah t.s.
15 : 18. deliverance into hand of t.s.
1 S. 3 : 9. speak, L., t.s. heareth, 10.
17 : 32. t.s. will fight wi. Philistine
34. t.s. kept his father's sheep
36. t.s. slew the lion and bear
58. I am son of t.s. Jesse, Beth.
20 : 7. If he say t.s. sh. have peace
8. shalt deal kindly with t.s.
22 : 15. t.s. knew nothing of this
23 : 10. t.s. hath certainly heard
11. O L. of Isr., I beseech tell t.s.
27 : 5. sho. t.s. dwell in royal city
28 : 2. Surely know what t.s. can do
29 : 8. what hast thou found in t.s.
2 S. 7 : 19. spoken of t.s.'s house, 1 Ch. 17 : 17. [17 : 18.
20. thou, L., knowest t.s., 1 Ch.
21. to make t.s. know them [23.
25. word concerning t.s., 1 Ch. 17:
27. thou hast revealed to t.s., thf. hath t.s. found in his heart, 1 Ch. 17 : 25. [26.
28. promised unto t.s., 1 Ch. 17 :
29. bless ho. of t.s., 1 Ch. 17 : 27.
9 : 2. Art thou Ziba? t.s. is he
6. Mephib-h answ-d, Behold t.s.
8. What is t.s. th. thou sho-st look
11 : 21. T.s. Uriah is dead also
13 : 24. t.s. hath sheepshearers
35. k.'s sons come; as t.s. said, so
14 : 19. t.s. Joab, he bade me be put
20. hath t.s. Joab done this thing
22. t.s. know-h I have found grace
15 : 2. t.s. is one of tribes of Israel
8. t.s. vowed a vow at Geshur
21. in death or life th-e will t.s. be
34. to Absalom, I will be t.s.
18 : 29. When Joab sent me to t.s.
19 : 19. that wh. t.s. did perversely
20. t.s. doth know I have sinned
26. t.s. said, I will saddle an ass(2)
27. he slandered t.s. unto my lord
28. didst set t.s. at thine own table
35. can t.s. taste what I eat?[dan
36. t.s. will go a little way ov. Jor-
37. Let t.s. turn back again
24 : 10. take away iniquity of t.s., 1 Ch. 21 : 8. [Solomon, 19.
1 K. 1 : 26. But me, t.s., and t.s.
27. hast not shewed it unto t.s.
2 : 38. as king said, so will t.s. do
3 : 8. t.s. is in midst of thy people
9. Give t.s. an underst-g heart
8 : 28. have respect unto prayer of t.s., 2 Ch. 6:19, 20. Ne. 1:6, 11.
30. hearken to supplication of t. s., 52. 2 Ch. 6:21. [s., Ne. 9:14.
53. speakest by hand of Moses t.
11 : 11. will give kingdom to t.s.
18 : 9. deliver t.s. into hand of Ahab
12. I, t.s., fear Lord from youth
36. let it be known, I am t.s.
20 : 9. All thou didst send for to t.s.
32. t.s. Ben-hadad saith, I pray thee, let me live
39. t.s. went out into battle
40. as t.s. was busy here and th-e
2 K. 4 : 1. t.s. my husband is dead, knowest t.s. did fear Lord
5 : 15. now take a blessing of t.s.
17. be given to t.s. two mules, for t.s. will offer sacrifice
18. Lord pardon t.s. in this thing
25. Gehazi said t.s. went no whi-r
8 : 13. Hazael said, Is t.s. a dog?
2 K. 16 : 7. Ahaz sent, saying, I am t.s.
1 Ch. 17 : 18. can Da. speak for honour of t.s.? [done all
19. O Lord, for t.s.'s sake hast
Ne. 1 : 7. commandments thou commandedst t.s. Moses, 8.
11. O Lord prosper t.s. this day
2 : 5. if t.s. have found favour in
Ps. 19 : 11. by them is t.s. warned
13. Keep t.s. from presumpt. sins
27 : 9. put not t.s. away in anger
31 : 16. face to shine upon t.s., 119:
69 : 17. hide not thy face fr. t.s.[135.
86 : 2. O God, save t.s. th. trusteth
4. Rejoice the soul of t.s. for
16. give thy strength unto t.s.
89 : 39. made void covenant of t.s.
109 : 28. them be ashamed; t.s. rejoice [143 : 12.
116 : 16. truly I am t.s., 119 : 125.-
119 : 17. Deal bountifully with t.s.
23. t.s. did meditate in statutes
38. Stablish word unto t.s., 49, 76.
65. Thou hast dealt well with t.s.
84. How many are the days of t.s.?
122. Be surety for t.s. for good
124. Deal wi. t.s. acc-g to thy mer.
140. word pure thf. t.s. loveth it
176. I, like a lost sheep: seek t.s.
143 : 2. ent. not into judgm. wi. t.s.
12. destroy: for I am t. s.
Ec. 7 : 21. lest hear t. s. curse thee
Da. 9 : 17. O God, hear prayer of t.s.
Lu. 2 : 29. Lord, lettest t. s. depart [in peace

SERVANTS.

Ge. 9 : 25. Canaan, a serv. of s. sh. be
21 : 25. a well Abim-h's s. had taken
26 : 14. Isaac had great store of s.
15. wells his father's s. had digged
19. Isaac's s. dig-d in valley, 25, 32.
27 : 37. breth. have I given him for s.
44 : 16. we are my lord's s. we and he
47 : 19. we will be s. unto Phar., 25.
50 : 7. went up wi. Joseph s. of Phar.
Ex. 9 : 20. He that feared L. among s. of Pharaoh [man be snare
10 : 7. Phar.'s s. said, How long this
11 : 3. Moses gr. in sight of Pha.'s s.
13 : † 3. Remember ye came out of house of s., 20 : † 2. De. 6 : † 12.
Le. 25 : 55. unto me chil. of Isr. are s.
Nu. 22 : 18. Bal-m said unto s. of Bal.
Jos. 9 : 11. Go meet, say, We are yr. s.
1 S. 4 : 9. ye be not s. unto Hebrews
9 : 3. take one of s. seek asses
16 : 15. Saul's s. 18 : 5, 23, 24, 30.- 21 : 7.- 22 : 9. [of Jesse
18. one of s. said, I have seen a son
17 : 8. am not I Philis., you s. to
9. if he kill me, we be your s., if I kill him, shall ye be our s.
21 : 11. s. of Achish said, Is this Da.?
22 : 17. s. of king wo. not put forth
25 : 10. be many s. that break away
19. Abigail said unto s., Go on bef.
40. s. of David, 10. 2 S. 2 : 13, 15, 17, 30, 31.- 3 : 22.- 8 : 2, 6, 14.- 10 : 2, 4.- 11 : 17.- 12 : 18.- 16 : 6. - 18 : 7, 9. 1 Ch. 18 : 2, 6, 13.- 19 : 2, 4.
41. to wash feet of s. of my lord
29 : 10. rise early with master's s.
2 S. 2 : 12. s. of Ish-bosheth went out
8 : 7. Da. took shields on s. of, 1 Ch.
9 : 10. Ziba had 20 s., 19 : 17. [18 : 7.
12. house of Ziba, s. to Mephib-h
10 : 19. kings; s. to Hadarezer, 1 Ch. 19 : 19. [13.
11 : 9. Uriah slept wi. s. of his lord,
11. s. of my lord are encamped
12 : 18. s. feared to tell chi. was dead
13 : 29. s. of Abs-m did unto Am-n
14 : 30. Abs.'s s. set field on fire
15 : 15. k.'s s. said thy s. are ready
19 : 6. regardest nei. princes nor s.
20 : 6. take thy lord's s., 1 K. 1 : 33.
1 K. 1 : 9. men of Judah the king's s.
1 K. 1 : 47. k.'s s. came to bless k. Da.
2 : 39. two s. of Shimei ran aw. [12.
10 : 13. queen went and s., 2 Ch. 9 :
11 : 17. fled and cert. of father's s.
20 : 23. s. of k. of Syr. said, Their gods
2 K. 3 : 11. one of s. said, Here Elisha
9 : 11. Jehu came to s. of his lord
18 : 24. capt. of master's s., Is. 36 : 9.
19 : 5. s. of king to Isaiah, Is. 37 : 5.
6. s. of k. of Assyria blasph-d me
20 : † 14. saith L., Even by s. of prin-
21 : 23. s. of Amon conspired [ces
24 : 10. s. of Neb-r came ag. Jerus.
25 : 24. Fear not to be s. of Chaldees
1 Ch. 21 : 3. are they not all my lord's
2 Ch. 8 : 9. of Isr. Sol. made no s. [s.?
18. Huram sent by his s. ships and s. that had knowledge
9 : 10. the s. of Huram and s. of Sol.
21. ships to Tarshish wi. s. of Hur.
36 : 30. to Bab-n where they were s.
Ezr. 2 : 55. chil of Sol.'s s., Ne 7:57.
65. Besides s. and maids of, Ne 7:67.
Ne. 5 : 5. we bring our sons to be s.
15. Even their s. bare rule ov. peo.
9 : 36. Behold, we are s. this day (2)
Es. 2 : 2. said king's s., Let be virgins
3 : 2. all k.'s s. reverenced Haman
3. k.'s s. unto Mord., Why transg.
4 : 11. k.'s s. know that whosoever shall come unto the king
5 : 11. advanced him above s. of k.
6 : 3. said k.'s s. nothing for Mord.
5. said k.'s s. Haman standeth [17.
Jb. 1 : 15. they have slain s. wi sword,
16. fire hath burned sheep and s.
Ps. 123 : 2. eyes of s. look unto mast.
Ec. 2 : 7. got me s. and had s. born
10 : 7. I have seen s. upon horses, princes walking as s. upon earth
Is. 14 : 2. Isr. sh. possess them for s.
Je. 34 : 11. s. they had let go free (2)
La. 5 : 8. s. have ruled over us
Da. 3 : 26. ye s. of most high God
Jo. 2 : 29. upon s. will pour Spirit
Mi. 6 : 4. redeemed out of house of s.
Zch. 2 : 9. they shall be a spoil to s.
Mat. 13 : 27. s. of household came, 28.
21 : 36. Again he sent other s., 22 : 4.
22 : 10. those s. went into highways
13. Then said king to s., Bind him
25 : 19. lord of those s. cometh
26 : 58. Peter sat with s., Mk. 14 : 54.
Mk. 14 : 65 s. did strike Jesus
Lu. 12 : 37. Blessed are those s., 38.
15 : 26. elder son called one of s.
17 : 10. say, We are unprofitable s.
19 : 15. nobleman comm-ded these s. to be called [Whatsoever
Jn 2 : 5. his mother said unto s.,
9. s. which drew the water knew
15 : 15. Henceforth I call you not s.
18 : 18. s. and officers stood there
26. One of the s. of the high priest
Ac. 16 : 17. These are s. of high God
Ro. 6 : 16. ye yield yours. s. to obey
17. be thanked ye were s. of sin
18. ye became the s. of righteousn.
19. yielded your members s. to sin
20. s. of sin, ye were free fr. righte.
22. free from sin, become s. of God
1 Co. 7 : 23. bought, be not s. of men
2 Co. 4 : 5. ours. your s. for Jesus'
Ep. 6 : 5. s. be obedient to masters, Col. 3 : 22. Ti. 2 : 9. 1 Pe 2 : 18
6. not eyeserv., but as s. of Christ
Ph. 1 : 1. Paul and Tim. s. of Christ
Col. 4 : 1. give your s. what is just
1 Ti. 6 : 1. Let as many s. as und. yoke
1 Pe. 2 : 16. liberty, but as s. of God
2 Pe. 2 : 19. they are s. of corruption
Re. 7 : 3. till we have sealed s. of God

See **Servant, s. of GOD.**
See **HIRED Servant, s.**

His SERVANTS.

Ge. 14 : 14. Abram armed h. trained [s.
15. Abram and h.s. smote them

Ge.20:8. Ab-h rose early, called **h.s.**
32:16. Jac. said unto **h.s.**, Pass ov.
40:20. Pha. made feast unto **h.s.**(2)
41 : 10. Pha. was wroth with **h.s.**
38. Pha.said untoh.s.,Can ye find
44 : 19. asked h.s. Have ye a father
50:2. Joseph com-d h.s. to embalm
Ex.9:20. made **h.s.** flee into houses
21. left **h.s.** and cattle in field
Nu.22:22. Balaam riding and **h. 2 s.**
De.32:36. L.sh. repent hims.for **h.s.**
43. he will avenge the bl-d of **h.s.**
Ju.3 : 24. Ehud was gone **h.s.** came
6 :27. Gideon took 10 men of **h.s.**
1 S. 8 : 14. best and give to **h.s.**, 15.
17. will take ten ; ye shall be **h.s.**
16: 17. Saul said unto **h.s.**, 18 : 22.
-22 : 7. -28 : 25. ⌈pleased well
18 :26. When **h.s.** told David, it
19 : 1. Saul to **h.s.** th. they kill Da.
21 : 14. Achish unto **h.s.**, Go ye see
22 : 6. Saul and **h.s.** abo. him⌊man
24 : 7. David stayed **h.s.** with these
28:7. Saul untoh.s.,Seek a wom.(2)
23. h.s.with woman compel-d him
2 S. 3:38. k.unto h.s.,a prince fallen
6 : 20. uncovered in eyes of hand-maids of **h.s.** ⌈by **h.s.**
10 : 2. Dav. sent to comfort Hanun
11 : 1. David sent Joab and **h.s.** and Israel ⌈pered (2)
12 : 19. When David saw **h.s.** whis-
21. said **h.s.** unto David, What hast done? ⌈thy servant
13 : 24. let king and **h.s.** go with
28. Absalom had commanded **h.s.**, 31.-14 : 30. ⌈sore
36. king and all **h.s.** wept very
15 : 14. David unto **h.s.** let us flee
18. all **h.s.** passed on beside him
16 : 11. David to h.s.my son seek-h
21 : 15. David and **h. s.** fought ag.
22. fell by Da. and **h.s.**,1 Ch.20:8.
24:20. Araunah saw king and **h. s.** coming ⌈virgin
1 K. 1 : 2. **h.s.**unto Da.,Let a young
2:40. Shimei to Gath toseek **h.s.**(2)
3:15.Sol. made feast to all **h.s.**⌈27.
5 : 1. Hiram sent **h.s.** unto Sol., 9 :
9 : 22. chil. of Isr. were **h.s.**, his princes ⌈2 Ch. 9 : 4.
10 : 5. queen seen sitting of **h.s.**,
15 : 18. Asa delivered silver to **h.s.**
20 : 12. Ben-hadad to **h.s.**, Set yourselves ❘ 31. ⌈Ramoth is ours
22 : 3. king of Israel said unto **h.s.**
2 K.5 : 13. **h.s.**came near and spake
23. laid 2 talents of silver on **h.s.**
6 : 8. king of Syria took counsel with **h.s.**, 11, 12. ⌈❘ 13.
7 : 12. king arose, said unto **h.s.**,
9 : 28. **h.s.**carried Ahazi-h toJerus.
10 : 19. call all prop-ts of Baal,**h.s.**
12 : 20. **h.s.** arose, slew Joash ❘ 21.
14 : 5. slew **h.s.** which had slain his father, 2 Ch. 25 : 3. ⌈prophets
21 : 10. the Lord spake by **h.s.** the
23 : 30. **h.s.** carried him dead from
24 : 11. Neb-r and **h.s.** did besiege
1 Ch.19: 3. are not **h.s.** come to thee
19. made peace wi. Da., bec. **h.s.**
2 Ch. 2 : 15. the wheat, the oil, wine let him send unto **h.s.** ⌈serv.
8 : 18. Huram sent by **h. s.** ships
12 : 8. Neverthel-s they sh. be **h.s.**
24: 25. **h.** own **s.** conspired ag. him
32 : 9. Sennacherib send **h.s.**toJer.
16. **h.s.** spake yet more ag. L. G.
33 : 24. **h.s.** conspired ag. Amon
35 : 23. Josiah to **h.s.**, Have me away, I am sore wounded
Ne. 2 : 20. we **h.s.** will arise, build
Es. 1 : 3. Ahas-s made feast unto **h.s.**, 2 : 18. ⌈**h.s.**
Jb. 4 : 18. Behold, he put no trust in
Ps. 69 : 36. seed of **h.s.** sh. inherit
105 : 25. to deal subtilely with **h.s.**

Ps.135 : 14.he will repent conc-g **h.s.**
Pr. 29 : 12. to lies,all **h.s.**are wicked
Is. 56 : 6. love name of L., to be **h.s.**
65 : 15. L. sh. call **h.s.**by ano.name
66 : 14. Lord be known toward **h.s.**
Je. 21: 7. will deliver Zedek.and**h.s.**
22 : 4. riding on horses,he and **h.s.**
36 : 24. not afraid, nei. k. nor **h.s.**
31. punish him, his seed, and **h.s.**
37 : 2. nei. he nor **h.s.** did hearken
46: 26. hands of k.of Bab-n and **h.s.**
Eze. 46 : 17. if prince gave gift to**h.s.**
Da. 2 : 7. Let king tell **h.s.** dream
3 : 28.deliv-d **h.s.** that trusted⌈Jn.
Mat. 14 : 2. Herod unto **h.s.**, This is
18 : 23. king take account of **h.s.**
21 : 34. sent **h.s.** to husbandm.,35.
22: 3. sent **h.s.** to call them bidden
6. took **h.s.**, entreated th. spitef-y
8. saith to **h.s.** wedding is ready
13. king to **h.s.**, Bind him hand
25 : 14. called **h.** own **s.** and deliv-d
Mk. 13 : 34. gave authority to **h.s.**
Lu. 15 : 22. fa. to **h.s.**, Bri.best robe
19 : 13. called **h.** ten **s.** and deliv-d
Jn. 4 : 51. **h.s.**,saying, Thy son liv-h
Ac. 10 : 7. Cornelius called 2 of **h.s.**
Ro. 6 : 16. **h.s.** ye are whom ye obey
Re. 1 : 1. to shew **h.s.** things, 22 : 6.
19 : 2. hath avenged blood of **h.s.**
5. Praise God all ye **h.s.**, and ye
22 : 3. and **h.s.** shall serve him

See Pharaoh and his SERVANTS.

See Servants of the LORD, MAIDSERVANTS, MENSERVANTS

My SERVANTS. ⌈55.

Le. 25 : 42. are **m.s.** wh.I bro-t out,
1 S. 21 : 2. I appointed **m.s.** a place
1 K. 5 : 6. **m.s.** shall be with thy servants, 2 Ch. 2 : 8. ⌈morrow
20 : 6.I will send **m.s.** unto thee to
22 : 49. Let **m.s.**go wi.thy servants
2K.9 : 7.I may avenge blood of **m.s.**
Ne. 4 : 16. half of **m.s.** wrought in
23. nei. I nor **m.s.** put off clothes
5 : 10. I and **m.s.** might exact
16. **m.s.** were gathered unto work
13 : 19. some of **m.s.** set I at gates
Is. 65 : 8. so will I for **m.s.**' sake
9. mine elect and **m.s.** sh. dwell
13. **m.s.** shall eat, but ye shall be hungry ⌈for sorrow
14. **m.s.** shall sing, ye shall cry
Je. 7 : 25. sent unto you all **m.s.**,44:
Jn. 18 : 36.then would **m.s.** fight⌊4.
Ac. 2 : 18. on **m.s.** I will pour Spirit
Re. 2 : 20. prophetess to seduce **m.s.**

Pharaoh and his SERVANTS. ⌈of **-s.**

Ge. 41 : 37. thing was good in eyes
45 : 16. Jos. breth. are come : it pleased **-s.** ⌈of **-s.**
Ex. 5 : 21. savour abhorred in eyes
7 : 10. Aaron cast rod before**-s.**, 20.
8 : 24. swarms of flies into **-s.**' houses, 29, 31. ⌈1.
9 : 34. hardened his heart, **-s.**, 10 :
12 : 30. **-s.** rose up. and Egyptians
14 : 5. heart of **-s.** turned ag. peo.
De. 29 : 2. all the Lord did unto **-s.**
34 : 11. Lord sent him to do to **-s.**
Ne. 9 : 10. shewedst signs and wonders upon **-s.**, Ps. 135 : 9.

See Servants with PROPHETS.

Thy SERVANTS.

Ge. 42 : 10. to buy food are **t.s.**come
11. we are true, **t.s.** are no spies
13. **t.s.** are 12 brethren, sons of
44 : 7. G.forbid **t.s.** do acc-g to this
9. with whomso. of **t.s.** it is found
16. G. hath found out iniq-y of**t.s.**
21. saidst untot.s.,Bring him,23.
31. **t.s.** sh. bring down gray hairs
46 : 34. **t.s.** trade been about cattle
47 : 3. **t.s.** are shepherds, we and

Ge.47.4.**t.s.**no past-e for flocks(2)⌈s.
50 . 18. breth said, Behold we be **t.**
Ex. 5 : 15. Whf. dealest thus wi. **t.s.**
16. There is no straw giv. unto **t.s.**
8 : 3. frogs sh. go into ho. of **t.s.**,4.
9. when entreat for thee and **t.s.**
11. frogs shall depart from **t.s.**
21. send swarms of flies upon **t.s.**
9 : 14. send all my plagues upon**t.s.**
30. thee and **t.s.**, I know ye will
10 : 6. locusts sh. fill houses of **t.s.**
11 : 8. **t.s.** sh. bow down unto me
32 : 13. Remember Abraham, Isaac, Israel, **t.s.**, De. 9 : 27. ⌈of men
Nu. 31 : 49. **t.s.** have taken the sum
32 : 4. land for cattle, **t.s.** have cat.
5. let this land be given unto **t.s.**
25. **t.s.** will do as lord commanded, 31. 2 Ch. 34 : 16. ⌈battle
27. **t.s.** will pass over armed for
Jos. 9 : 8.Gibeonites said, We are **t.s.**
9.From a far country**t.s.**are come
24. it was told **t.s.** how L.com-ded
10 : 6. slack not thy hand from **t.s.**
Ju. 19 : 19. for the yo-g man wi. **t.s.**
1 S. 12 : 19. pray for **t.s.** unto L. G.
16 : 16. com-ded **t.s.** to seek a man
22 : 14. who so faithful am. **t.s.** as
25 : 8. cometh to hand, give unto **t.**
2 S. 9 : 10. **t.s.** shall till the land ⌊s.
11 : 24. shot off the wall upon **t.s.**
14 : 31. Whf. **t.s.** set field on fire?
15 : 15. **t.s.** are ready to do whatso.
19 : 5. hast shamed faces of **t.s.** ⌈s.
7. Now speak comfortably unto **t.**
14. unto king, Return,and all **t.s.**
1 K. 2 : 39. they told Shimei, **t.s.** be in Gath ⌈2 Ch. 2 : 8.
5 : 6. my servants sh. be with **t.s.**,
8 : 23. who keepest covenant and mercy with **t.s.**, 2Ch. 6 : 14.⌈23.
32. hear and judge **t.s.**, 2 Ch. 6 :
36. hear thou forgive sin of **t.s.**
10 : 8. Happy are **t.s.**, 2 Ch. 9 : 7.
12 : 7. be **t.s.** for ever, 2 Ch. 10 : 7.
20 : 6. shall search houses of **t.s.**
22 : 49. Let my serv-s go with **t.s.**
2K.1 : 13. life of these 50 **t.s.**be prec
2 : 16. be with **t.s.** 50 strong men
6 : 3. Be content and go with **t.s.**
10 : 5. We are **t.s.**, and will do all
18 : 26. Speak to **t.s.** in Syrian, Is. 22 : 9. **t.s.** gath-d the money⌊36: 11.
2 Ch. 2 : 10. I will give **t.s.** 20,000
Ezr. 4 : 11. **t.s.** men on this side riv.
Ne. 1 : 6. I pray day and night for **t.**
10. Now these are **t.s.** ⌊s.
11. be attentive to prayer of **t.s.**
Ps. 79 : 2. bodies of **t.s.** have th. giv.
10. revenging of blood of **t.s.** shed
89 : 50. Remember reproach of **t.s.**
90 : 13. let it repent thee conc-g **t.s.**
16. Let thy work appear unto **t.s.**
102 : 14. **t.s.** take pleasure in her
28. chil. of **t.s.** shall continue
119 : 91. for all are **t.s.** ⌈Lord
Is. 37 : 24. By **t.s.** hast reproached
Je. 22 : 2. Hear word, O k., and **t.s.**
37 : 18.Wh. have I offended ag. **t.s.**
Da. 1 : 12. Prove **t.s.**, I beseech, ten
13. as thou seest,deal wi. **t.s.**⌊days
2 : 4. tell **t.s.** dream, we will shew
Ac. 4 : 29. grant unto **t.s.** that with

See WOMENSERVANTS.

SERVE. ⌈years

Ge. 15 : 13. seed shall **s.** them 400
14. nation they sh. **s.** will I judge
25 : 23. elder shall **s.** the younger
27 : 29. Let people **s.** thee, nations
40. by sword shalt live, **s.** brother
29 : 15. sho-t thou**s.**me for nought?
18. I will **s.** seven years for Rachel
25. did I not **s.** thee for Rachel
27. thou shalt **s.**seven other years
Ex. 1 : 13.made Isr.to **s.**with rigour,
3 : 12. ye sh. **s.** G. upon this mt.⌊14.
4 : 23. Let my son go th. he **s.** me

Ex. 7 : 16. Let my peo. go that they
may s. me, 8 : 1, 20.-9 : 1, 13.-10 : 3.
14 : 12. Let us alone, th. we may s.
Eg-ns, been better for us to s.
them [De. 5 : 9.
20 : 5. not bow down nor s. them,
21 : 2. servant, six years he shall s.
6. bore ear, he sh. s. him for ever
Le. 25 : 39. not compel to s. as bonds.
40. he sh. s. thee unto jubilee
† 46. ye sh. s. yourselves wi. them
Nu. 4 : 24. fam-s of Gershonites to s.
26. bear all service, so sh. they s.
8 : 25. fr. age of 50 sh. s. no more
18 : 7. within vail; and ye shall s.
21. Levi, tenth, for service they s.
De. 4 : 19. shouldest be driven to s.
5 : 9. sh. not bow down nor s. them
6 : 13. Thou shalt fear the Lord thy
God and s. him, 10 : 12, 20.-11 :
13.-13 : 4. Jos. 22 : 5.-24 : 14, 15.
1 S. 7 : 3.-12 : 14, 20, 24.
15 : 12. if bro. be sold and s. 6 years
20 : 11. be tributa-s, and sh. s. thee
28 : 48. shalt thou s. thine enemies
Jos. 16 : 10. Canaanites s. under
24 : 15. choose whom ye will s. [trib.
Ju. 9 : 28. should s. Shechem, sho.
s. Hamor [him?
38. Who is Abimelech, that we s.
1 S. 10 : 7. do as occasion shall s.
11 : 1. Make covenant, we will s. thee
12 : 10. deliver us, we will s. thee
17 : 9. shall ye be serv-ts, and s. us
2 S. 16 : 19. whom should I s.? should
I not s. [me, Ps. 18 : 43.
22 : 44. people I knew not shall s.
1 K. 12 : 4. make heavy yoke lighter,
we will s. thee, 2 Ch. 10 : 4. [good
7. If thou wilt s. them and speak
2 K. 10 : 18. Jehu shall s. Baal much
25 : 24. dwell in land, s. k. of Bab-n,
Je. 27 : 11, 12, 17.-28 : 14.-40 : 9.
1 Ch. 28 : 9. s. him wi. perfect heart
2 Ch. 29 : 11. L. hath chosen you to s.
34 : 33. Josiah made all to s. Lord
Jb. 21 : 15. What Almighty, that we
s. him? [prosperity
36 : 11. If s. him, spend days in
39 : 9. unicorn willing to s. thee?
Ps. 22 : 30. A seed shall s. him and
72 : 11. kings, all nations sh. s. him
97 : 7. Confounded they th. s. ima.
101 : 6. in perfect way, he sh. s. me
Is. 14 : 3. bondage wast made to s.
19 : 23. Egypt-s shall s. with Assyr-s
43 : 23. I have not caused thee to s.
24. hast made me to s. wi. thy sins
56 : 6. join to the Lord, to s. him
60 : 12. nation not s. thee sh. perish
Je. 2 : † 20. thou saidst I will not s.
5 : 19. so shall ye s. strangers
17 : 4. will cause thee to s. enemies
25 : 11. nations sh. s. king of Bab-n
14. nations shall s. thems., 27 : 7.
27 : 6. beasts have I given to s. him
8. that will not s. k. of Bab-n, 13.
9. that say, Ye shall not s., 14.
30 : 8. strangers no more s. thems.
34 : 9. that none sho. s. hims., 10.
40 : 9. Fear not to s. the Chaldeans
10. as for me, I will s. Chaldeans
Eze. 20 : 32. families to s. wood and
39. Go s. ye every one his idols
40. Israel all of them shall s. me
29 : 18. his army to s. against Tyrus
48 : 18. for food to them that s. city
19. that s. city, sh. s. of all tribes
Da. 3 : 17. God we s. able to deliver
28. not s. any, except their own G.
7 : 14. nat-ns and languages sho. s.
27. all dominions sh. s. him [him
Zph. 3 : 9. may call upon L. to s. him
Mal. 3 : 14. Ye said. It is in vain to s. G.
Mat. 4 : 10. him only sh. s., Lu. 4 : 8.
6 : 24. No man can s. two masters;
ye cannot s. God and, Lu 16 : 13.

Lu. 1 : 74. th. we deliv-d, might s. him
10 : 40. my sister left me to s. alone
12 : 37. he will come and s. them
15 : 29. Lo, many years do I s. thee
17 : 8. will say, gird thyself, s. me
22 : 26. he chief as he that doth s.
Jn. 12 : 26. If any man s. me, let him
Ac. 6 : 2. leave word of G., s. tables
7 : 7. shall they s. me in this place
27 : 23. by me angel of God, wh. I s.
Ro. 1 : 9. God is witness, whom I s.
6 : 6. henceforth we sho. not s. sin
7 : 6. we sho. s. in newness of spirit
25. with mind I s. the law of God
9 : 12. The elder sh. s. the younger
16 : 18. that are such s. not our Lord
Ga. 5 : 13. by love s. one another
Col. 3 : 24. for ye s. the Lord Christ
1 Th. 1 : 9. ye from idols to s. liv. G.
2 Ti. 1 : 3. I thank God whom I s.
He. 8 : 5. s. unto example of heavenly
9 : 14. purge fr. dead works to s. G.
12 : 28. grace ye may s. G. accept-ly
13 : 10. no right to eat, wh. s. taber.
Re. 7 : 15. they s. him day and night
22 : 3. and his servants shall s. him
SERVE, ED with gods.
De. 7 : 16. nei. shalt thou s. their g.
28 : 14. thou shalt not go after other
g. to s. them [and s. them
31 : 20. will turn out unto other g.
Jos. 23 : 16. ye have gone s-d other g.
24 : 14. put away g. your fa-s s-d
Ju. 3 : 6. dau-s to sons and s-d their g.
1 K. 9 : 6. But if ye will s. other g.
2 K. 17 : 33. feared L. and s-d own g.
Je. 5 : 19. as ye have s-d strange g.
11 : 10. went aft. other g. to s. 44 : 3.
16 : 11. walked aft. other g. s-d th.
22 : 9. worshipp-d other g. and s-d
44 : 3. they went to s. other g.
See Serve, ed GODS. [them
See **Serve, ed other GODS.**
See **Serve the LORD.**
SERVED.
Ge. 14 : 4. they s. Chedorlaomer
29 : 20. Jac. s. 7 years for Ra., 30.
30 : 26. my chil. for whom I s. thee
29. Thou knowest how I s. thee
31 : 6. wi. my power I s. your fath.
41. I s. thee 14 yrs. for 2 dau-s.
39 : 4. Jos. found grace and s. him
40 : 4. capt. charged Jos-h he s. them
Jos. 24 : 31. Israel s. Lord, Ju. 2 : 7.
Ju. 2 : 11. Israel s. Baalim, 13.-3 :
7.-10 : 6, 10. 1 S. 12 : 10. 2 K.
17 : 16. [eight years
3 : 8. Isr. s. Chushan-rishathaim
14. Israel s. Eglon king 18 years
8 : 1. said, Why hast thou s. us thus?
10 : 16. put away gods s. L., 1 S. 7 : 4.
2 S. 10 : 19. Syrians made peace s. Isr.
16 : 19. as I s. in thy fa.'s presence
1 K. 4 : 21. bro-t presents and s. Sol.
16 : 31. Ahab s. Baal, 2 K. 10 : 18.
22 : 53. Ahaziah s. Baal
17 : 12. they s. idols wh-f Lord said
41. these nations s. graven images
18 : 7. Hez-h s. not king of Assyria
21 : 3. Manasseh s. host of heaven,
2 Ch. 33 : 3 [Ch. 33 : 22
21. Amon s. idols his father s., 2
1 Ch. 19 : 5. told Da. how men were s
27 : 1 offi-s that s. k. in any matter
2 Ch. 24 : 18. princes of Jud. s. idols
Ne. 9 : 35. not s. thee in kingdom
Es. 1 : 10. they s. in pres. of Ahasu-s
Ps. 106 : 36. And they s. their idols
137 : 8. rewardeth as thou hast s. us
Ec. 5 : 9. king himself is s. by field
Je. 8 : 2. sun and moon whom they s.
34 : 14. s. thee six years, let him go
52 : 12. capt. wh. s. king of Bab-n
Eze. 29 : 18. for service he had s., 20.
34 : 27. out of hand of those that s.
Ho. 12 : 12. Israel s. for a wife
Lu. 2 : 37. Anna s. G. night and day

Jn. 12 : 2. made supper, Martha s.
Ac. 13 : 36. aft. David had s. genera.
Ro. 1 : 25. worsh-d and s. creature
Ph. 2 : 22. he s. with me in gospel
SERVEDST, EST.
De. 28 : 47. thou s-dst not the Lord
Da. 6 : 16. God thou s-est will deliver
20. is God thou s-est able to de-
SERVETH. [liver
Nu. 3 : 36. under Merari all that s.
Mal. 3 : 17. spareth his son that s.
18. him th. s. God, and him s. not
Lu. 22 : 27. greater, he that sitteth
or he th. s.? I am as one that s.
Ro. 14 : 18. he that in these s. Christ
1 Co. 14 : 22. prophesying s. not th.
Ga. 3 : 19. Wheref. then s. the law?
SERVICE. [with me
Ge. 29 : 27. for s. thou shalt serve
30 : 26. knowest s. I have done
Ex. 1 : 14. in all manner of s. in field;
all their s. was with rigor
12 : 25. ye shall keep this s., 13 : 5.
26. What mean ye by this s.?
27 : 19. vessels in all s. be brass
30 : 16. appoint it for s. of tabern.
31 : 10. make clothes of s., 35 : 19,
-39 : 1, 41. [ments
35 : 21. for all his s. and holy gar-
24. word for any work of the s.
36 : 1. work for s. of sanctuary, 3.
5. bring more than enough for s.
38 : 21. counted for s. of the Levites
39 : 1. of blue made clothes of s.
40. vessels for s. of tabernacle
Le. 25 : † 39. not serve thyself wi. s.
Nu. 3 : 7. tribe of Levi to do s. of tabern. 8.-4 : 41.-8 : 15.-18 : 23.
26. charge of Gershonites for s.
4 : 4. the s. of sons of Kohath, 3 : 31.
19. Aaron shall appoint to the s.
23. all that enter to perform s.
24. this is s. of Gershon-s, 27, 28.
26. cords and all instruments of s.
30. s. of sons of Merari, 33, 43.
47. came to do s. of the ministers
49. numb-ed ev. one acc-g to his s.
7 : 5. may do s. of the tabernacle
7. wagons and oxen acc-g to s., 8.
9. s. of same belonging unto them
8 : 11. Levites may execute s. of L.
15. Levites do s. of tabern., 19, 22.
24. in to wait upon s. of tabern.
25. fr. 50 y-rs cease waiting upon s.
26. to keep charge and sh. do no s.
16 : 9. a small thing to do the s.
18 : 4. Levites be joined for all s.
6. Levites are given to do s.
7. priests office as s. of gift [31.
21. given tenth in Isr. for their s.,
Jos. 22 : 27. witn., th. we might do s.
1 K. 12 : 4. make grievous s. lighter
1 Ch. 6 : 31. whom David set over s.
48. Levites appointed unto all s.
9 : 13. able men for work of s., 26 : 8.
23 : 24. that did s. for house of Lord
32. keep charge in s. of house of L.
24 : 3. David distributed them in s.
19. These were orderings in their s.
25 : 1. separated to s. of sons of Asaph
number of workmen acc-g to s.
6. for s. of the house of God
26 : 30. business of L. and s. of king
28 : 13. Levites for all work of s.
21. priests with thee for all s.
29 : 5. who consecrate his s. to L.?
7. gave for s. of house of God, gold
2 Ch. 8 : 14. courses of priests to s.
12 : 8. know my s. and s. of kingd-s
24 : 12. money to such as did the s.
29 : 35 s. of house was set in order
31 : 2. every man according to his s.
16. his daily portion for their s.
21. every work that he began in s.
34 : 13. work in any manner of s.
35 : 2. encouraged them to s. of L.
10. So s. of Lord was prepared, 16.

2 Ch.35.15. might not dep-t fr. th. s.
Ezr.6 : 18. in courses, for s. of G. 7 : 19.
8 : 20. s. of Levites 220 Nethinim
Ne. 10 : 32. third part of shekel for s.
Ps.104 : 14. herb to grow for s. of man
Je. 22 : 13. neigb-'s s. without wages
Eze. 29 : 18. army to serve great s.
44 : 14. keepers of house for all s.
Jn. 16 : 2. will think he doeth G. s.
Ro. 9 : 4. to wh. pertaineth s. of G.
12 : 1. which is your reasonable s.
15 : 31. that my s. may be accepted
2 Co. 9 : 12. for administration of s.
11 : 8. taking wages to do you s.
Ga. 4 : 8. did s. unto th. are no gods
Ep. 6 : 7. doing s. as to the Lord
Ph. 2 : 17. if off-d upon s. of faith
30. to supply your lack of s. tow.
1 Ti. 6 : 2. rather do s. bec. beloved
He. 9 : 1. had ordinances of divine s.
6. priests accomplishing s. of God
9. not make him that did s. perf-t
Re. 2 : 19. I know thy works, and s.
See BONDSERVICE, EYESERVICE.

SERVILE.

Le.23 : 7. ye shall do no s. work therein, 8, 21, 25, 35, 36. Nu. 28 : 18 25, 26.–29 : 1, 12, 35.

SERVING.

Ex. 14 : 5. have let Isr. go fr. s. us
De. 15 : 18. worth double serv-t in s.
Lu. 10 : 40. Martha cumbered about [s.
Ac. 20 : 19. s. L. with all humility
26 : 7. twelve tribes instantly s. G.
Ro. 12 : 11. fervent in spirit, s. Lord
Tit. 3 : 3. foolish, s. divers lusts

SERVITOR.

2 K. 4 : 43. s. said, sho. I set this [bef. 100

SERVITUDE.

2Ch. 10 : 4. ease grievous s. of thy fa.
La. 1 : 3. Judah is gone bec. of gr. s.

SET. [Active.]

Ge. 1 : 17. God s. stars in firmament
4 : 15. Lord s. a mark upon Cain
6 : 16. door of ark shalt s. in side
9 : 13: I do s. my bow in the cloud
18 : 8. Abraham s. calf before them
19 : 16. angels s. Lot with-t city [28.
21 : 29. ewe lambs hast s. by thems.,
28 : 22. stone I s. for pillar [twixt
30 : 36. he s. 3 days' journey be-
38. he s. rods which he had pilled
40. Jacob s. faces of flocks toward
31 : 17. Jac. rose up, and s. his sons
37. s. it bef. my brethren and thy
35 : 20. Jac. s. pillar upon her grave
41 : 33. let Pharaoh s. him over Eg.
41. I have s. thee over all Egypt
43 : 9. if I bring not, and s. him bef.
31. Joseph said, s. on bread, 32.
44 : 21. that I may s. eyes upon him
47 : 7. Joseph s. Jacob bef. Pharaoh
48 : 20. Jac. s. Ephr. bef. Manasseh
Ex. 1 : 11. s. over th. taskmas-rs, 5 : 14.
4 : 20. Mo. s. wife and sons upon ass
7 : 23. nei. did s. his heart to this
9 : † 21. s. not his heart unto word
13 : 12. s. apart all th. open matrix
19 : 12. sh. s. bounds unto peo., 23.
21 : 1. judgm-ts thou sh. s. bef. th.
23 : 31. will s. thy bounds fr. Red Sea
25 : 30. s. upon table shewbr-d bef.
26 : 35. s. the table without the rail
28 : 17. s. it in settings of stones
20. they shall be s. in gold
31 : 5. cutting of stones to s., 35 : 33.
39 : 10. they s. it in 4 rows of stones
40 : 5. s. altar of gold | 6. of burnt of-
7. s. the laver | 20. s. staves [fering
30. s. laver, betw. tent and altar
Le. 24 : 6. shalt s. cakes in two rows
26 : 11. I will s. my tabern. am. you
Nu. 5 : 16. priest sh. s. her before L.,
8 : 13. s. Levites bef. Aaron [18, 30.
11 : 24. s. elders around the tabern.
21 : 8. s. fiery serpent upon pole

Nu. 27 : 16. Let L. s. a man ov. cong-n
19. s. Joshua bef. Eleazar, priest, 22.
De. 1 : 8. I have s. land bef. you, 21.
4 : 8. as all this law I s. bef. you, 44.
7 : 7. Lord not s. his love upon you
11 : 26. I s. bef. you blessing and
32. to do judgments I s. bef. you
14 : 24. choose to s. name, Ne. 1 : 9.
17 : 14. say, I will s. king over me
15. shalt s. him, L. shall choose
19 : 14. landmark they of old have s.
26 : 4. s. down basket bef. altar, 10.
28 : 1. thy God will s. thee on high
56. not s. sole of her foot upon gro.
30 : 1. blessing and curse I s. before
15. have s. bef thee life, death, 19.
32 : 8. s. bounds of peo. by numbers
46. s. your hearts unto words I
Jos. 8 : 12. s. them to lie in ambush
13. when they had s. the people
10 : 18. mouth of cave, and s. men
24 : 25. he s. a statute in Shechem
Ju. 6 : 18. till I s. present bef. thee
7 : 5. that lappeth, him s. by hims.
19. they had but newly s. watch
22. Lord s. every man's sword ag.
8 : † 31. whose name he s. Abim-h
9 : 25. men s. liers in wait for Abim.
33. shalt rise early, s. upon city
15 : 5. he had s. brands on fire
16 : 25. they s. Samson betw. pillars
20 : 29. Israel s. liers in wait, 36.
1 S. 2 : 8. raiseth poor to s. them am princes; he hath s. world
4 : † 20. she answ-d not, s. not her
5 : 2. Philis. s. ark of God by Dagon
3. took Dagon, s. him in his place
6 : 18. whereon they s. ark of Lord
7 : 12. Sam. s. stone betw. Mizpeh
8 : 12. s. them to ear his ground
9 : 20. as for asses, s. not thy mind
23. of whom I said, s. it by thee
24. cook s. it before Saul; Sam. said, s. it before thee and eat
10 : 19. Nay, but s. a king over us
12 : 13. L. hath s. a king over you
13 : † 21. they had a file to s. goads
17 : 2. Saul s. battle in array, 8. 2 S. 10 : 17. 1 K. 20 : 12. 1 Ch 19 : 17.
18 : 5. Saul s. him over men of war
28 : 22. let me s. bread before thee
2 S. 6 : 3. they s. ark upon a new cart
17. brought ark, s. it in his place
11 : 15. s. Uriah in forefront of bat.
12 : 20. they s. bread before him
15 : 24. they s. down the ark of G.
18 : 1. David s. captains of hundr-s
13. wouldest have s. thys. ag. me
19 : 28. didst s. thy serv. at thy tab.
23 : 23. s. him ov. his guard, 1 Ch. [11 : 25.
1 K. 2 : 15. all Isr. s. faces
24. s. me on throne of fa. [throne
5 : 5. Thy son wh. I will s. upon
6 : 19. oracle he prepared to s. ark
27. he s. cherubim within house
7 : 16. chapiters to s. upon pillars
39. s. sea on right side, 2 Ch. 4 : 10.
8 : 21. I s. there a place for ark [19.
9 : 6. statutes I s. bef. you, 2 Ch. 7 :
10 : 9. to s. thee on throne, 2 Ch. 9 :
12 : 29. he s. 1 in Beth-el, other [8.
21 : 9. and s. Naboth on high, 12.
10. s. two men, sons of Belial
2 K. 4 : 4. s. aside that which is full
10. let us s. for him there a bed
38. s. on great pot, seethe pottage
43. sho I s. this bef. 100 men? 44.
6 : 22. s. bread and water bef. them
8 : † 11. settled counten-e, and s. it
10 : 3. s. him on his father's throne
12 : 9. and s. it beside the altar [8.
18 : 23. able to s. riders upon. Is. 36 :
21 : 7. he s. graven image of grove
25 : 28. s. his throne above throne of kings, Je. 52 : 32. [service
1 Ch. 6 : 31. whom David s. over the
11 : 14. s. thems. in midst of parcel

1 Ch. 16 : 1. and s. it in midst of tent
22 : 2. he s. masons to hew stones
19. s. your heart to seek the L. | G.
29 : 3. I s. my affection to house of
2 Ch. 2 : 18. he s. 70,000 to be bearers of burdens, 6,600 overseers to s. people a-work
3 : 5. he s. thereon palm trees
4 : 7. he s. candlesticks in temple
6 : 13. s. scaffold in midst of court
11 : 16. s. their hearts to seek Lord
13 : 3. Ahijah s. bat. in array, 14 : 10
17 : 2. s. garrisons in the land
19 : 5. he s. judges in the land
8. did s. of Levites, and of priests
20 : 3. he s. himself to seek the Lord
17. s. yours. see salvation of God
22. L. s. ambushments ag. Ammon
23 : 10. And he s. all the people
19. he s. the porters at the gates
20. he s. king on throne of kingd.
24 : 8. s. chest at gate of hou. of L.
13. s. house of God in his state
29 : 25. he s. Levites in house of L.
32 : 6. he s. captains of war ov. peo.
33 : 7. he s. carved image in house
35 : 2. Josiah s. priests in charges
Ezr. 4 : 10. nations Asnapper s. in Sa
6 : 18. s. priests in their divisions
Ne. 2 : 6. it pleased king, I s. a time
4 : 9. we s. a watch day and night
13. s. I in lower places, I s. people
5 : 7. I s. great assembly ag. them
9 : 37. increase unto kings s. over us
12 : † 47. they s. apart holy things
13 : 11. I gathered, s. them in place
19. some of servants s. I at gates
Es. 2 : 17. he s. crown upon her head
3 : 1. s. his seat above all princes
8 : 2. Esther s. Mordecai ov. Haman
Jb. 1 : † 8. hast s. thy heart on Job?
6 : 4. terrors of God s. against me
7 : 17. shouldest s. heart upon him
20. why s. me as a mark ag. thee?
9 : 19. who s. me a time to plead?
19 : 8. hath s. darkness in my paths
30 : 1. disdained to s. with the dogs
34 : 14. If he s. his heart upon man
24. break mighty men and s. oth-s
38 : 10. when I s. bars and doors
33. canst s. dominion in earth?
Ps. 2 : 2. kings of earth s. themselves
6. Yet have I s. king upon Zion
3 : 6. I will not be afraid if 10,000 s.
4 : 3. Lord, s. apart him th. is godly
8 : 1. hast s. thy glory ab. heavens
12 : 5. I will s. him in safety from
16 : 8. I have s. Lord always bef. me
17 : 11 have s. their eyes bowing
19 : 4. In them hath he s. a taber'n.
20 : † 1. God of Jac. s. thee on high
21 : † 6. hast s. him to be blessings
† 12. thou shalt s. him as a butt
31 : 8. hast s. my feet in a large room
40 : 2. s. my feet upon a rock [warks
48 : † 13. s. your heart to her bul-
54 : 3. have not s. God before them
59 : † 1. s. me on high from such as
62 : 10. if riches, s. not your heart
73 : 9. s. their mouth ag. heavens
18. didst s. them in slippery places
74 : 17. hast s. all borders of earth
78 : 7. might s. their hope in God
8. genera-n th. s. not heart aright
† 43. s. his signs in Egypt
85 : 13. shall s. us in his steps
86 : 14. violent men not s. thee bef.
89 : 25. I will s. his hand in the sea
90 : 8. hast s. our iniq-s before thee
91 : 14. bec he has s. his love upon me, I will s. him on high [my
101 : 3. I will s. no wicked thi. bef.
104 : 9. s. bound they may not pass
109 : 6. s. thou wicked man ov. him
113 : 8. he may s. him with princes
118 : 5. Lord, s. me in large place
132 : 11. fruit of thy body, will I s.

Ps. 140 : 5. proud have s. gins for me
141 : 3. s. a watch before my mouth
Pr. 8 : 27. he s. compass upon depth
22 : 28. landmark wh. thy fa-s have s.
23 : 5. Wilt s. eyes on that which is
24 : † 32. I saw, and s. mine heart
25 : † 6. s. not thy glory in presence
27 : † 23. s. thy heart to thy herds
29 : † 8. scornful men s. city on fire
Ec. 3 : 11. he s. world in their heart
7 : 14 God hath s. one ag. the other
9 : † 1. For all this I s. to my heart
Can. 8 : 6. s. me as seal upon heart
12 : † 1. my soul s. me on chariots
Is. 7 : 6. let us s. king in midst of it
11 : 11. L. sh. s. hand a second time
14 : 1. L. will s. them in own land
17 : 10. shalt s. it with strange slips
19 : 2. I will s. Egyptians ag. Eg-ns
21 : 6. Go s. a watchman, let him
27 : 4. who would s. briers ag-t me
41 : 19. I will s. in desert, fir tree
42 : 4. till he s. judgment in earth
46 : 7. carry s. him in his place
57 : 7. Upon mt. hast thou s. thy bed
62 : 6. I have s. watchmen, Je. 6 : 17.
66 : 19. I will s. a sign among them
Je. 1 : 10. I have s. thee over nations
15. shall s. every one his throne
5 : 26. they s. a trap, catch men
6 : 27. I have s. thee for a tower
7 : 12. Shiloh place I s. my name
30. s. abominat-s in house, 32 : 34.
9 : 13. forsaken law I s. before them
21 : 8. I s. before you life and death
24 : 6. s. eyes upon them for good
26 : 4. walk in law, I s. bef. you⌈(2)
31 : 21. s. thine heart tow. highway
32 : 20. wh. hast s. signs and wond.
35 : 5. I s. pots of wine bef. Rechab-
38 : 22. friends have s. thee on⌊ites
39 : † 12. s. eyes upon him, do him
no harm ⌈thee
40 : † 4. I will s. mine eyes upon
11. he had s. over them Gedaliah
42 : 15. if ye s. faces to enter Egypt
17. that s. faces to go into Eg., 44 : 12.
43 : 10. I will s. Neb-r's throne upon
44 : 10. nor in statutes I s. bef. you
49 : 38. I will s. my throne in Elam
La. 3 : 6. hath s. me in dark places
12. he s. me as mark for the arrow
Eze. 2 : 2. and s. me upon my feet
4 : 2. s. camp ag. it, s. battering
3. s. it for wall of iron ⌊rams
5 : 5. I s. it in midst of nations
7 : 20. have I s. it far from them
9 : 4. s. a mark upon foreheads of
12 : 6. I s. thee for sign unto Israel
16 : 18. hast s. my oil bef. images, 19.
17 : 4. s. it in city of merchants
5. he s. it as a willow tree
22. off highest branch, I will s. it
19 : 8. nations s. ag. him on ev. side
21 : 15 I have s. a sword ag. gates
22 : 7. in thee s. light by fa. and mo.
23 : 24 s. ag. thee buckler and shield,
25. will s. my jealousy ag. thee⌊(2)
41. thou hast s. mine incense and
24 : 2. king of Bab-n s. ag. Jerusa.
3. s. on a pot, s. it on, pour water
7. her blood, she s. it upon rock, 8.
11. s. pot empty upon coals
25. whereon they s. their minds
25 : 4. they shall s. palaces in thee
26 : 9. he shall s. engines of war
20. I sh. s. glory in land of living
28 : 2. s. thy heart as heart of God, 6.
14. cherub, and I have s. thee so
32 : 8. s. darkness upon thy land
25. s. her a bed in midst of slain
33 : 2. if peo. s. him for watchman
7. I have s. thee watchman unto
37 : 1. Lord s. me in midst of valley
26. I will s. my sanctuary in midst
39 : 21. I will s. my glory am. heath.
40 : 2. L. s. me upon high mountain
Eze. 40 : 4. s. thine heart upon all I
44 : † 5. Son of man s. thine heart
8. have s. keepers in my sanctuary
Da. 1 : 11. prince had s. over Daniel
2 : 49. s. Shad-k over affairs, 3 : † 12.
6 : 1. s. over kingdom 120 princes
3. k. thought to s. him over realm
14. s. his heart on Dan. to deliver
8 : 18. awaked and s. me upright
9 : 10. to walk in laws he s. bef. us
10 : 10. wh. s. me upon my knees
12. s. thine heart to understand
Ho. 2 : 3. lest I s. her as in day she
4 : 8. s. their heart on iniquity ⌊(2)
6 : 11. O Jud. he hath s. an harvest
8 : 1. s. trumpet to thy mouth
11 : 8. how sh. I s. thee as Zeboim
Am. 7 : 8. I will s. plumbline in mid.
9 : 4. I will s. eyes upon th. for evil
Ob. 4. tho. s. thy nest among stars
Na. 3 : 6. s. thee as gazingstock
Ha. 2 : 1. I will s. me upon tower
9. th. he may s. his nest on high
Zph. 3 : † 19. I will s. them for praise
Hag. 1 : † 5. s. heart on your ways
Zch. 3 : 5. s. fair mitre upon his head
6 : 11. crowns, s. them upon Joshua
8 : 10. I s. all men, one ag. neighb.
Mat. 10 : 35. to s. a man at variance
18 : 2. Jesus called little child s.
him in midst, Mk. 9 : 36. Lu. 9 : 47.
25 : 33. he sh. s. sheep on right hand
Mk. 1 : 32. at even when sun did s.
6 : 41. he gave to his disciples to s.
before them, 8 : 6, 7. Lu. 9 : 16.
12 : 1. vineyard, s. a hedge about it
Lu. 4 : 9. s. him on pinnacle of tem.
18. to s. at liberty them bruised
10 : 34. s. him on his own beast
11 : 6. friend come, I nothing to s.
19 : 35. they s. Jes. th-on, Mat. 21 : 7.
Jn. 3 : 33. s. to his seal, God is true
8 : 3. when they had s. her in midst
Ac. 4 : 7. when had s. them in midst
5 : 27. they s. them before council
6 : 6. when they s. before apostles
7 : 5. not so much as to s. his foot
26. would have s. them at one ag.
13 : 9. then Paul s. his eyes on him
47. I have s. thee to be a light
16 : 34. he s. meat before them
17 : 5. Jews s. city on an uproar
18 : 10. no man s. on thee to hurt
22 : 30. bro-t Paul s. him bef. them
23 : 24. beasts, that they may s.
Paul on ⌈esteemed in ch.
1 Co. 6 : 4. s. them to judge, least
12 : 18. G. hath s. members in body
28. G. hath s. some in the church
Ep. 1 : 20. s. him at his right hand
Col. 3 : 2. s. affection on things above
He. 2 : 7. s. him over work of thy
Re. 3 : 8. I have s. open door ⌊hands
10 : 2. he s. his right foot upon sea
20 : 3. shut him up, and s. a seal
See ARRAY. [Noun.]
See Set FACE, Set FIRE.

SET forth.

Nu. 2 : 9. camp of Judah sh. first s. f.
16. camp of Reub. s. f. in 2nd rank
Ps 141 : 2. Let my prayer be s. f.
Eze. 27 : 10. they s. f. thy comeliness
Da. 11 : 11. shall s. f. a great mult., 13.
Am. 8 : 5. sabbath, that we may s. f.
Lu. 1 : 1. to s. f. a declaration⌊wheat
Jn. 2 : 10. at begin-g s. f. good wine
Ac. 21 : 2. And finding a ship we s. f.
Ro. 3 : 25. s. f. to be a propitiation
1 Co. 4 : 9. G. s. f. us the apostles last
Ga. 3 : 1. Christ been s. f. crucified
Jude 7. cities are s. f. an example

SET forward. ⌈(2) 34.

Nu. 2 : 17 So sh. s. f. ev. man in pla.
4 : 15. as the camp is to s. f.⌈tabern.
10 : 17. sons of Merari s. f. bearing
18. s. f. acc-g to their armies, 22, 28.
21. Kohathites s. f. bear-g sanct-y
Nu. 10 : 25. chil. of Dan s. f. rearward
35. when ark s. f. Moses said, Rise
21 : 10. children of Israel s. f., 22 : 1.
1 Ch. 23 : 4. 24,000 to s. f. the work
of houses, 2 Ch. 34 : 12. Ezr. 3 : 8,
Jb. 30 : 13. they s. f. my calamity⌊9.
See In ORDER.

SET up. ⌈earth

Ge. 28 : 12. beheld ladder s. u. on
18. Jacob took stone, s. it u. for
pillar, 22. – 31 : 45. – 35 : 14.
Ex. 40 : 2. shalt s. u. taberu. of tent
8. thou shalt s. u. the court
18. Moses s. u. boards | 21. vail
28. s. u. hanging at door of tab., 33.
Le. 26 : 1. nei. s. u. image of stone
Nu. 1 : 51. tab., Levites sh. s. it u.
7 : 1. Moses had fully s. u. taberu.
10 : 21. did s. u. tab. ag. they came
De. 16 : 22. Nei. shall s. u. any image
27 : 2. shalt s. u. great stones, 4.
Jos. 4 : 9. Joshua s. u. 12 stones in
6 : 26. sh. he s. u. gates, 1 K. 16 : 34.
18 : 1. Israel at Shiloh s. u. tabern.
24 : 26. Josh. s. u. stone under oak
Ju. 18 : 30. Dan s. u. graven image
31. they s. u. Micah's graven im.
1 S. 15 : 11. repenteth me I s. u. S.
12. Saul hath s. him u. a place
2 S. 3 : 10. to s. u. throne of David
7 : 12. will s. u. thy seed after thee
1 K. 7 : 21. he s. u. pillars on porch
15 : 4. to s. u. his son after him⌊(3)
2 K. 17 : 10. they s. them u. images
1 Ch. 21 : 18. s. u. alt. in threshingfl.
2 Ch. 25 : 14. Amaziah s. u. his gods
33 : 19. Manasseh s. u. groves and
Ezr. 2 : 68. freely to s. u. G.'s house
4 : 12. Jews have s. u. walls, 13, 16.
5 : 11. hou. a great king of Isr. s. u.
6 : 11. being s. u., let him be hanged
9 : 9. a reviving to s. u. hou. of God
Ne. 3 : 1. they s. u. doors of sheep-
gate, 3, 6, 13, 14, 15. – 7 : 1. ⌈doors
6 : 1. tho. that time I had not s. u.
Jb. 5 : 11. To s. u. on high those low
16 : 12. hath s. me u. for his mark
Ps. 20 : 5. we will s. u. our banners
27 : 5. he shall s. me u. upon rock
69 : 29. let thy salvation, s. me u.
74 : 4. they s. u. ensigns for signs
89 : 42. hast s. u. hand of adversa-s
Is. 9 : 11. L. s. u. adversar-s of Rezin
11 : 12. he sh. s. u. ensign for nat-s
23 : 13. they s. u. towers thereof
45 : 20. s. u. wood of graven image
49 : 22. I will s. u. my standard
57 : 8. hast s. u. thy remembrance
Je. 4 : 6. s. u. standard toward Zion
6 : 1. s. u. sign of fire in Beth-hac.
10 : 20. none to s. u. my curtains
11 : 13. s. u. altars to shamef. thing?
23 : 4. I will s. u. shepherds over
31 : 21. s. thee u. way marks⌊them
50 : 2. s. u. a standard, 51 : 12, 27.
51 : 12. s. u. the watchmen, prepare
La. 2 : 17. he s. u. horn of adversa-
Eze. 14 : 3. these have s. u. idols⌊ries
31 : 4. the deep s. him u. on high
34 : 23. I will s. u. one shepherd
39 : 15. seeth bone shall s. u. sign
Da. 2 : 44. God shall s. u. kingdom
3 : 14. nor worship golden image I
have s. u., 1, 2, 3, 7, 12, 18.
5 : 19. whom he would he s. u. and
12 : † 11. and to s. u. the abomina-n
Ho. 8 : 4. They have s. u. kings⌈cusa.
Mat. 27 : 37. s. u. over his head ac-
Ac. 6 : 13. And s. u. false witnesses
15 : 16. I will build ruins and s. it

SET. [Passive.] ⌊u.

Ge. 24 : 33. was s. meat before him
28 : 11. he tarried bec. sun was s.
12. a ladder was s. upon the earth
Ex. 25 : 7. stones s. in ephod, 28 : 11.
– 35 : 9, 27. ⌈inclosings
28 : 20. they shall be s. in gold in

Ex.32 : 22. peo.,th. are s. on misch-f
37 : 3. from rings of gold to be s.
Ru. 2 : 5. that was s. over reapers,6.
1 S. 18 : 30. his name was much s. by
22 : 9. Doeg was s. ov. serv-s of Saul
26 : 24. thy life was much s. by [20:2.
2 S. 12 : 30. crown s. on Dav., 1 Ch.
1 K. 2 : 19. a seat s. for king's mother
7 : 25. sea s. upon oxen, 2 Ch. 4 : 4.
14 : 4. Ahi. co. not see, eyes were s.
2 K. 12 : 4. money every man is s. at
25 : 19. officer s. over men of war
1 Ch. 19 : 10. Joab saw bat. was s. ag.
29 : 2. Dav. gave onyx stones to be s.
2 Ch. 4 : 19. whereon shewbread was
6 : 10. I am s. on throne of Isr. [s.
23 : 14. captains th. were s. ov. host
Es. 6 : 8. crown wh. is s. upon head
Jb. 36 : 16. wh. should be s. on table
Ps. 10 : 8. eyes privily s. ag. poor
122 : 5. are s. thrones of Judgment
Pr. 8 : 23. I was s. up fr. everlasting
18 : † 10. righteous is s. aloft
29 : † 25. putteth trust in Lord sh. be s. on high [to do evil
Ec. 8 : 11. heart is fully s. in them
10 : 6. Folly s. in gr. dignity ; rich is
Can. 5 : 12. as eyes of doves fitly s.
14. His hands are as gold rings s.
15. His legs are s. upon sockets
7 : 2. thy belly as wheat s. wi. lilies
Is. 3 : 24. instead of well s. hair
18 : † 4. I will regard my s. dwelling
21 : 8. am s. in my ward who. nights
Je. 6 : 23. s. in array, as men for war
24 : 1. figs were s. before temple[2.
31 : 29. teeth are s. on edge, Eze. 18:
30. his teeth shall be s. on edge
Eze. 22 : 10. her that was s. apart
32 : 23. graves are s. in sides of pit
Da. 7 : 10. judgment was s., books
12 : 11. till abomination be s. up
Jo. 2 : 5. strong people s. in battle
Na. 3 : 13. the gates shall be s. open
Zch. 5 : 11. hou. be s. upon own base
Mal. 3 : 15. work wickedn. are s. up
Mat. 5 : 1. wh. he was s. disci. came
14. city s. on hill cannot be hid
27 : 19. he was s. on judgment seat
Mk. 1 : 32. wh. sun did s. they bro-t
4 : 21. not to be s. on a candlestick
Lu. 2 : 34. this child is s. for fall
7 : 8. I am a man s. under author-y
10 : 8. eat such as are s. before you
22 : 55. were s. down together, Pet.
Jn. 2 : 6. were s. six waterpots of
19 : 29. s. a vessel full of vinegar
Ac. 12 : 21. on s. day Herod arrayed,
1 Co. 10 : 27. whatso. is s. before you
Ga. 3 : 1. Ch. been s. forth crucified
Ph. 1 : 17. I am s. for defence of the
He. 6 : 18. hold upon hope s. bef. us
8 : 1. who is s. on right hand, 12:2.
12 : 1. let us run race is s. before us
2. for joy that was s. before him
Re. 3 : 21. am s. down with my Fa.
4 : 2. a throne was s. in heaven
See Set FEAST, Set TIME.
See LIBERTY, OFFICE, NOUGHT.

SETH or SHETH.

Ge. 4 : 25. she called his name S. †Sh.,
26. to S. was born son, Enos [5 : 3.
5 : 4. had begotten S. [7. S. lived aft.
8. all days of S. were 912 years
Nu. 24 : 17. Sceptre sh. destroy chil.
1 Ch. 1 : 1. Adam, Sh., Enosh [of Sh.
Lu. 3 : 38. Enos, which was son of S.

SETHUR.

Nu. 13 : 13. of tribe of Asher, S.

SETTER. [gods

Ac. 17 : 18. seemeth s. forth of strange

SETTEST. [8, 20.

De. 23 : 20. in all s. thine hand to, 28:
Jb. 7 : 12. I a sea, thou s. a watch?
13 : 27. s. print upon heels of my
Ps. 21 : 3. s. crown on his head [feet
41 : 12. s. me bef. thy face for ever

SETTETH.

Ex. 30 : † 8. when Aaron s. up lamps
Nu. 1 : 51. when taberu. s. forward
4 : 5. when camp s. forward, Aaron
De. 24 : 15. poor, s. his heart upon it
27 : 16. Cursed he th. s. light by fa.
2 S. 22 : 34. He s. me upon my high places, Ps. 18 : 33. [secret
Jb. 24 : † 15. adulterer s. his face in
28 : 3. He s. an end to darkness
40 : † 17. he s. up his tail like cedar
Ps. 36 : 4. s. hims. in way not good
65 : 6. by strength s. fast mounta-s
68 : 6. God s. solitary in families
75 : 7. putteth down one, s. up ano.
83 : 14. as the flame s. mts. on fire
107 : 41. s. poor on high fr. affliction
Is. 44 : † 19. none s. to his heart, nor
Je. 5 : 26. lay wait, as he th. s. snares
43 : 3. Baruch s. thee on against us
Eze. 14 : 4. s. idols in his heart, 7.
Da. 2 : 21. removeth kings s. up k-s
4 : 17. he s. up over it basest of men
Mat. 4 : 5. s. him on pinnacle of tem.
Lu. 8 : 16. but s. it on a candlestick
Ja. 3 : 6. tongue s. on fire course of

SETTING. [Part.]

Mat. 27 : 66. sealing stone, s. watch
Lu. 4 : 40. sun was s. they bro-t sick

SETTING, S.

Ex. 28 : 17. shall set in it s-s of stones
Eze. 43 : 8. In s. of their threshold

SETTLE. [Noun.]

Eze. 43 : 14. from ground to lower s.
17. the s. shall be 14 cubits long
20. put blood on corners of s., 45 :

SETTLE. [Verb.] [19.

1 Ch. 17 : 14. will s. him in mine ho.
Eze. 36 : 11. will s. you aft. old est-es
Lu. 21 : 14. s. it in your hearts, not
1 Pe. 5 : 10. but God strengthen, s.

SETTLED. [you

1 K. 8 : 13. I built s. place for thee
2 K. 8 : 11. he s. his countenance [mt.
Ps. 30 : † 7. hast s. strength for my
89 : † 5. man s. is altogether vanity
119 : 89. For ever, O L., thy word
Pr. 8 : 25. Before mts. were s. [is s.
Je. 48 : 11. Moab he hath s. on his lees
Zph. 1 : 12. that are s. on their lees
Col. 1 : 23. If ye continue in faith s.

SETTLEST.

Ps. 65 : 10. thou s. furrows thereof

SEVEN. [s.

Ge. 7 : † 2. Of every clean beast take
46 : 25. all the souls were s. [dau-s
Ex. 2 : 16. priest of Midian had s.
Nu. 23 : 1. Build me here s. altars prepare s. oxen and s. rams
4. I have prepared s. altars and, 14.
De. 7 : 1. s. nat-s greater th. [6, 8, 13.
Jos. 6 : 4. s. priests bear s. trumpets,
18 : 2. remained of Isr. s. tribes.
Ju. 16 : 7. if bind me wi. s. withs, 8.
1 S. 2 : 5. the barren hath borne s.
16 : 10. Jesse made s. of his sons
2 S. 21 : 9. fell all s. together [pass
1 K. 6 : 6. third was s. cubits broad
7 : 17. s. for 1 chapiter s. for other
1 Ch. 5 : 13. breth. of their fa-s weres.
2 Ch. 13 : 9. consecrate with s. rams
29 : 21. brought s. he goats for off-g
Ezr. 7 : 14. king and his s. counsel-s
Es. 1 : 10. s. chamberlains th. served
14. s. princes wh. saw king's face
2 : 9. he gave her s. maidens meet to
Jb. 5 : 19. in s. troubles no evil shall
Pr. 6 : 16. s. are an abomination
9 : 1. wisdom hath hewn s. pillars
26 : 25. s. abominations in his heart
Ec. 11 : 2. Give a portion to s. [man
Is. 4 : 1. s. women take hold of one
11 : 15. L. sh. smite it in s. streams
Je. 15 : 9. hath borne s. languisheth
Eze. 41 : 3. breadth of door s. cubits
Mi. 5 : 5. raise ag. him s. shepherds
Zch. 3 : 9. upon one stone be s. eyes
Zch. 4 : 2. s. lamps and s. pipes to s.
10. Zerubbabel wi. those s. [lamps
Mat. 15 : 34. How many loaves? said s., and few fishes, 36, Mk. 8:5,6.
37. took up s. baskets full, Mk. 8:8.
16 : 10. Nei. the s. loaves of the 4,000
22 : 25. with us s. breth. : first married, 22 : †26. Mk. 12 : 20. Lu. 20 :
28. whose wife sh. she be of s. [29.
Mk. 12 : 22. And the s. had her and left no seed. 23. Lu. 20 : 31, 33.
16 : 9. out of whom be cast s. devils
Ac. 13 : 19. destroyed s. nations in Ca.
21 : 8. Philip wh. was one of the s.
Re. 1 : 12. I saw s. golden candlest-s
13. in midst of s. candlesticks one
20. s. candlest-s are the s. churches
2 : 1. walketh in mid. of s. candle-ks
5 : 1. book sealed with s. seals, 5.
6. Lamb as slain having s. horns s. eyes which are s. spirits of God
12 : 3. dragon having s. heads s.
17 : 9. s. heads are s. mts. [crowns
10. are s. kings, five fallen [dition
11. beast is of the s. goeth into per-
See ANGELS, CHURCHES.

SEVEN, bullocks, with rams.

Nu. 23 : 29. prepare me s. b., s. r.
29 : 32. on seventh day s. b., two r.
1 Ch. 15 : 26. Levites off-d s. b., s. r.
2 Ch. 29 : 21. they brought s. b., s. r.
Jb. 42 : 8. take now, s. b., s. r. [s. r.
Eze. 45 : 23. prepare burnt off-g s. b.

SEVEN days.

Ge. 7 : 10. after s. d. waters of flood
31 : 23. Lab. pursued after him s. d.
Ex. 7 : 25. s. d. fulfilled aft. L. smit.
Le. 8 : 35. abide at door of tab. s. d.
13 : 4. shut up him hath plag. s. d.
14 : 38. shut up house s. d. [5 : 31.
15 : 13. shall number for cleansing,
24. he shall be unclean s. d. [s. d.
28. she shall number to hers. s. d.
23 : 34. feast of tabernacle for s. d.
36. s. d. ye sh. offer off-g [s. d., 16.
Nu. 19 : 11. toucheth dead be uncl.
28 : 24. ye sh. offer daily thro-t s. d.
31 : 19. abide without camp s. d.
De. 16 : 15. s. d. keep solemn feast
1 K. 20 : 29. pitched one ag. other s. d.
2 K. 3 : 9. a compass of s. d. journey
1 Ch. 9 : 25. breth. to come aft. s. d.
2 Ch. 7 : 8. Solomon kept feast s. d.
30 : 22. did eat through-t feast s. d.
Eze. 3 : 16. end of s. d. word of L. ca.
43 : 25. s. d. shalt prepare ev. day
44 : 26. reckon unto him s. d. [goat
45 : 21. passe-r, feast of s. d., 23, 25.
He. 11 : 30. walls fell compassed s. d.
See DAYS, EARS, HEADS, HUNDRED, KINE, LAMBS, LAMPS, LOCKS, MEN, MONTHS, PARTS, PLAGUES, SABBATHS, SONS, SPIRITS, STARS, STEPS, THIRTY, THOUSAND, THUNDERS, TIMES, TRUMPETS, TWENTY, VIALS, WAYS, WEEKS, YEARS.

SEVENS. [by s.

Ge. 7 : 2. Of every clean beast take
3. Of fowls also of the air, by s., the male and the fe nale

SEVENFOLD. [him s.

Ge. 4 : 15. vengeance be taken on
24. If Cain shall be avenged s. Lamech 70 and s. [proach
Ps. 79 : 12. render s. into bosom re-
Pr. 6 : 31. if found he shall restore s.
Is. 30 : 26. light of the sun shall be s.

SEVENTEEN.

See SHEKELS, THOUSAND, YEARS.

SEVENTEENTH. [Hezir

1 Ch. 24 : 15. lot came forth, s. to
25 : 24. lot came s. to Joshbekashah
See DAY, YEAR.

SEVENTH.

Ex. 21 : 2. in s. he shall go out free

Ex. 31 : 15. in s. is the sabbath of rest
Le. 23 : 16. morrow after s. sabbath
Jos. 6 : 16. s. time when priests blew
10 . 40. s. lot came for tribe of Dan
1 K. 18 : 44. s. time arose a cloud
1 Ch. 2 : 15. Jesse begat David the s.
12 : 11. mighty men, Eliel the s.
24 : 10. lot came forth s. to Hakkoz
25 : 14. lot came s. to Jesharelah
26 : 3. sons, Elioenai the s.
5. sons of Obed-edom Issachar s.
27 : 10. s. capt. for s. month Helez
Mat. 22 : 26. second, and 3d unto s.
Jn. 4 : 52. at s. hour fever left him
Jude 14. Enoch s. fr. Adam proph-d
Re. 8 : 1. he had opened the s. seal
10 : 7. in days of voice of s. angel
11 : 15. the s. angel sounded, voices
16 : 17. s. angel poured out his vial
21 : 20. s. foundation was chrysolite

SEVENTH day. [s.d.
Ex. 16 : 30. So the people rested on
Nu. 7 : 48. On s.d. Elishama offered
29 : 32. on s.d. 7 bullocks, 2 rams
Ju. 14 : 18. said unto Sams. the s.d.
He. 4 : 4. God did rest the s. d. (2)
See **7th DAY, MONTH, YEAR.**

SEVENTY. [and sevenf.
Ge. 4 : 24. If Cain sevenf. Lamech s.
Ex. 1 : 5. of loins of Jacob s. souls
24 : 1. Come Aaron and s. elders, 9.
38 : 29. brass of offering s. talents
Nu. 11 : 25. gave spirit unto s. elders
Ju. 9 : 56. in slaying his s. brethren
1 K. 10 : 1. Ahab had s. sons in Sama.
Ezr. 2 : 40. chil., s. and 4, Ne. 7 : 43.
8 : 35. six rams s. and seven lambs
Eze. 41 : 12. building tow. west s. cub.
Da. 9 : 24. s. weeks are determined
Mat. 18 : 22. but, Until s. times seven
Lu. 10 : 1. the L. appointed other s.
17. the s. returned again with joy
See MALES, MEN, PERSONS, SHEKELS.
See **Seventy THOUSAND.**
See **Seventy YEARS.**

SEVER, ED. [shen
Ex. 8 : 22. I will s. in that day Go-
9 : 4. L. sh. s. betw. cattle of Israel
Le. 20 : 26. I s-d you from other peo.
De. 4 : 41. Moses s-d three cities on
Ju. 4 : 11. Heber had s-d fr. Kenites
Eze. 39 : 14. sh. s. out men of employ-
Mat. 13 : 49. s. wicked fr. just [ment
Jn. 15 : †5. s-d fr. me, ye can do noth.

SEVERAL, LY.
Nu. 28 : 13. And a s. 10th deal of flour
with oil, 21, 29. – 29 : 10, 15.
2 K. 15 : 5. Azariah a leper dwelt in
a s. house, 2 Ch. 26 : 21. [spears
2 Ch. 11. 12. in ev. s. city put shields
28 : 25. in ev. s. city made high places
31 : 19. sons of Aaron in ev. s. city
Zch. 4 : †2. seven s. pipes to lamps
Mat. 25 : 15. acc-g to his s. ability
1 Co. 12 : 11. dividing to ev. man s-y
Re. 21 : 21. ev. s. gate was of pearl

SEVERITY.
Ro. 11 : 22. Behold goodness and s.
of God, on them who fell s. but

SEW, ED, EST, ETH.
Ge. 3 : 7. they s-d fig leaves together
Ezr. 4 : †12. s-d together foundations
Jb. 14 : 17. thou s-t up mine iniquity
16 : 15. s-d sackcloth upon my skin
Ec. 3 : 7. a time to rend time to s.
Eze. 13 : 18. Woe to women s. pillows
Mk. 2 : 21. No man s-h new cloth on

SHAALAB'BIN. [old
Jos. 19 : 42. coast of inherit. was S.

SHAAL'BIM. [S.
Ju. 1 : 35. Amorites would dwell in
1 K. 4 : 9. The son of Dekar in S.

SHAAL'BONITE. [33.
2 S. 23 : 32. Eliahaba the S., 1 Ch. 11 :

SHA'APH.
1 Ch. 2 : 47. sons of Jahdai Regem S.
1 Ch. 2 : 49. S. father of Madmannah

SHAARA'IM, or **SHAR'AIM.** [S.
Jos. 15 : 36. cities of chil. of Judah
1 S. 17 : 52. Philistines fell down to S.
1 Ch. 4 : 31. And they dwelt at S.

SHAASH'GAZ. [S.
Es. 2 : 14. she returned to custody of

SHABBETH'AI. [them
Ezr. 10 : 15. S. the Levite helped
Ne. 8 : 7. S. caused peo. to understand
11 : 16. S. had oversight of business

SHACH'IA. See MIRMA.

SHADE. [hand
Ps. 121 : 5. Lord is thy s. upon right

SHADOW, S.
Ge. 19 : 8. came under s. of my roof
Nu. 14 : †9. their s. is departed fr. th.
Ju. 9 : 15. come put trust in my s.
36. Thou seest the s. of mountains
2 K. 20 : 9. s. go forward 10 degrees
10. light thing for s. to go do. ten
11. bro-t s. ten degrees backward
1 Ch. 29 : 15. days are as s., Jb. 8 : 9.
Jb. 7 : 2. As a servant desireth the s.
14 : 2. he fleeth also as a s. and
17 : 7. all my members are as a s.
40 : 22. trees cover him wi. their s.
Ps. 17 : 8. hide me under s. of wings
36 : 7. trust under s. of thy wings,
57 : 1. in s. of thy wings my refuge
63 : 7. in s. of thy wings I rejoice
80 : 10. hills were covered with s.
91 : 1. abide under s. of the Almi-y
102 : 11. My days are like a s. that
109 : 23. I am gone like a s. when
144 : 4. his days are as a s., Ec. 8 : 13.
Ec. 6 : 12. vain life he spendeth as s.
Ec. 7 : † 12. wisdom is a s. and money
Can. 2 : 3. I sat under s. with delight
17. until daybr-k, and s-s flee, 4 : 6.
Is. 4 : 6. a tabernacle for a s. in day
16 : 3. make thy s. as night in noon.
25 : 4. Lord hast been a s. fr. heat
5. bring heat with s. of a cloud
30 : 2. and trust in the s. of Egypt
3. trust in s. of Eg. y-r confusion
32 : 2. as s. of great rock in weary
34 : 15. owl hatch, gather und. her
38 : 8. I will bring s. of degrees [s.
49 : 2. in s. of hand he hid me, 51 : 16.
Je. 6 : 4. s-s of evening are stretched
48 : 45. under s. of Heshbon
La. 4 : 20. Under his s. we shall live
Eze. 17 : 23. in s. thereof shall dwell
31 : 6. und. his s. dwelt gr. nations
12. people are gone from his s.
17. that dwelt under his s. in
Da. 4 : 12. beasts had s. under it
Ho. 4 : 13. under elms bec. s. is good
14 : 7. dwell under his s. sh. return
Jon. 4 : 5. made a booth, sat in s.
6. that it might be s. over head
Mk. 4 : 32. fowls may lodge under s.
Ac. 5 : 15. th. s. of Pet. might oversh.
Col. 2 : 17. are a s. of things to come
He. 8 : 5. serve unto s. of heavenly
10 : 1. law having s. of good things
Ja. 1 : 17. with whom no s. of turn-g
See **Shadow of DEATH.**

SHADOWING.
Is. 18 : 1. Woe to land s. with wings
Eze. 31 : 3. a cedar with a s. shroud
He. 9 : 5. cherubim of glory s. mercy

SHA'DRACH, [seat
Meshach, and Abednego.
Da. 1 : 7. to Hananiah name of S. ;
to Mishael of M. ; to Azariah
of A. [of Bab-n, 3 : 12.
2 : 49. k. set S., M., A. over affairs
3 : 13. Neb-r in fury commanded
to bring S., M., A.
14. Is it true, O S., M., A. ? do not
ye worship golden image? [29.
16. S., M., A., 19, 20, 23, 26, 28,

SHADY.
Jb. 40 : 21. He lieth under s. trees
Jb. 40 : 22. s. trees cover him with

SHAFT. [shadow
Ex. 25 : 31. his s. and branches shall
be of same, 37 : 17. Nu. 8 : 4.
Is. 49 : 2. he made me a polished s.

SHA'GE. [of S.
1 Ch. 11 : 34. valiant men, Jona. son

SHAHARA'IM.
1 Ch. 8 : 8. S. begat Shachia, Mirma

SHAHAZ'IMAH.
Jos. 19 : 22. the coast reacheth to S.

SHAKE, ED.
Ex. 29 : † 24. s. them for wave off-g
Ju. 16 : 20. Sams. said, I will s. mys-f
Ne. 5 : 13. shook my lap, said, So G. s.
Jb. 4 : 14. fear made my bones s.
15 : 33. He shall s. off unripe grape
16 : 4. I could s. mine head at you
Ps. 22 : 7. they shoot out lip, s. head
46 : 3. tho. the mountains s. with
68 : † 9. didst s. out plentiful rain
69 : 23. make loins continually to s.
72 : 16. fruit shall s. like Lebanon
109 : 25. looked upon me, s-d heads
136 : † 15. But s-d off Pha. and host
Is. 2 : 19. he ariseth to s. earth, 21.
10 : 15. as if rod should s. itself ag.
32. he sh. s. his hand ag. mount
11 : 15. L. shall s. hand over river
13 : 2. exalt the voice, s. the hand
13. Theref. I will s. the heavens,
Jo. 3 : 16. Hag. 2 : 6. 21. [doms?
14 : 16. Is this the man did s. king-
24 : 18. foundations of earth do s.
33 : 9. Bashan, Carmel, s. off fruits
52 : 2. s. thys-f from dust, O Jerus.
Je. 23 : 9. heart broken, my bones s.
Eze. 26 : 10. walls shall s. at noise
15. Shall not isles s. at thy fall?
27 : 28. suburbs shall s. at cry
31 : 16. I made nations s. at his fall
38 : 20. all shall s. at my presence
Da. 4 : 14. s. off his leaves, scatter
Jo. 3 : 16. heaven and earth shall s.
Am. 9 : 1. Smite lintel, that posts s.
Hag. 2 : 7. I will s. all nations [them
Zch. 2 : 9. I will s. my hand upon
Mat. 10 : 14. s. off the dust of your
feet, Mk. 6 : 11. Lu. 9 : 5. [s.
28 : 4. for fear of him the keepers did
Lu. 6 : 48. beat house, could not s. it
He. 12 : 26. once more I s. not earth

SHAKEN. [only
Le. 26 : 36. sound of s. leaf sh. chase
1 K. 14 : 15. smite Isr. as a reed is s.
2 K. 19 : 21. daughter of Jerus. hath
s. head at thee, Is. 37 : 22.
Ne. 5 : 13. thus be he s. out and
Jb. 16 : 12. taken me by neck, s. me
38 : 13. wicked might be s. out of it
Ps. 18 : 7. foundations of hills were s.
Na. 2 : 3. fir trees shall be terribly s.
3 : 12. if s. they fall into mouth [24.
Mat. 11 : 7. A reed s. with wind, Lu. 7 :
24 : 29. powers of heaven shall be
s., Mk. 13 : 25. Lu. 21 : 26.
Lu. 6 : 38. measure, pressed, s. tog-r
Ac. 4 : 31. had prayed, place was s.
16 : 26. foundations of prison s.
2 Th. 2 : 2. ye be not soon s. in mind
He. 12 : 27. removing of things that
are s. that things which cannot
be s. may remain [wind
Re. 6 : 13. as a fig tree when s. of

SHAKETH.
Jb. 9 : 6. Which s. earth out of place
Ps. 29 : 8. voice of L. s. wilderness
60 : 2. heal the breaches, for it s.
Is. 10 : 15. saw magnify ag. him s. it?
19 : 16. hand of the L. he s. over it
33 : 15. he that s. his hand from

SHAKING. [bribes
Jb. 41 : 29. laugheth at s. of spear
Ps. 44 : 14. s. of head among people
Is. 17 : 6. as s. of olive tree, 24 : 13.
19 : 16. shall fear, bec. of s. of hand
30 : 32. in battles of s. will he fight

Eze. 37 : 7. behold a s., bones came together [in Israel
38 : 19. that day shall be great s.

SHA'LEM.

Ge. 33 : 18. Jacob came to S., a city

SHA'LIM. [of S.

1 S. 9 : 4. they passed through land

SHAL'ISHA. [S.

1 S. 9 : 4. he passed through land of

SHAL'LECHETH. [way

1 Ch. 26 : 16. with gate S. by cause-

SHAL'LUM. [Zach., 13.

2 K. 15 : 10. S., son of Jabesh, slew
14. Menahem slew S., son of Jab.
15. acts of S. are written in the b-k
22 : 14. Huldah, prophetess, wife of S., 2 Ch. 34 : 22. [begat Jekamiah
1 Ch. 2 : 40. Sisamai begat S. | 41. S.
3 . 15. sons of Josiah were, fourth S.
4 : 25. of Simeon, S. | 6 : 12. Zadok begat S. [Naphtali, S.
6 : 13. S. begat Hilkiah | 7 : 13. of
9 : 17. S., a porter, 19 | 31. S., Korah-
2 Ch. 28 : 12. Jehizkiah, son of S. [ite
Ezr. 2 : 42. the children of S., 10 : 24. Ne. 7 : 45. Je. 35 : 4. [Ahitub
7 : 2. S., the son of Zadok, son of
10 : 42. S., Amariah taken strange
Ne. 3 : 12. next repaired S., 15. [wives
Je. 22 : 11. thus saith L. touching S.
32 : 7. Hanameel, son of S., uncle

SHAL'LUN.

Ne. 3 : 15. S., son of Colhozeh,

SHAL'MAI. [48.

Ezr. 2 : 46. the children of S., Ne. 7 :

SHAL'MAN. [battle

Ho. 10 : 14. S. spoiled Beth-arbel in

SHALMANE'SER.

2 K. 17 : 3. S. came ag. Samaria, 18 : 9.

SHA'MA. [than

1 Ch. 11 : 44. valiant S., son of Ho-

SHAMARI'AH.

2 Ch. 11 : 19. bare him children, S.,

SHAMBLES. [Zaham

1 Co. 10 : 25. whatso. is sold in s. eat

SHAME. [Noun.]

Ex. 32 : 25. made naked unto their s.
Ju. 18 : 7. none to put them to s.
1 S. 20 : 34. father had done him s.
2 S. 13 : 13. whi. cause my s. to go?
2 Ch. 32 : 21. returned with s. of face
Jb. 8 : 22. hate thee be clothed with s.
Ps. 4 : 2. how long turn my glory in-
35 : 4. to s. th. seek my soul [to s.?
26. let them be clothed with s.
40 : 14. put to s. wish me evil, 83 : 17.
15. desolate for reward of their s.
44 : 7. hast put them to s. hated us,
9. thou hast put us to s. | 53 : 5.
15. s. of face covered me, 69 : 7.
69 : 19. Thou hast known my s.
70 : 3. turned back for reward of s.
71 : 24. bro-t unto s. that seek hurt
83 : 16. Fill their faces with s., O L.
89 : 45. hast covered him with s.
109 : 29. adversaries be clothed wi.
119 : 31. O L., put me not to s. [s.
132 : 18. enemies will I clothe wi. s.
Pr. 3 : 35. s. be promotion of fools
9 : 7. reproveth scorner, getteth s.
10 : 5. sleepeth, is son th. causeth s.
11 : 2. pride cometh, then com-h s.
12 : 16. a prudent man covereth s.
13 : 5. a wicked man cometh to s.
18. s. be to him refuseth instruc.
14 : 35. wrath is ag. him causeth s.
17 : 2. rule over a son causeth s.
18 : 13. ans-h before heareth, it is s.
19 : 26. chaseth mother, causeth s.
25 : 8. neighbour hath put thee to s.
10. lest he heareth it put thee to s.
29 : 15. child left bring. mother to s.
Is. 20 : 4. buttocks uncovered to s.
22 : 18. chariots s. of lord's house
30 : 3. strength of Pha. be y-r s., 5.
47 : 3. uncovered, thy s. sh. be seen
50 : 6. I hid not my face from s.
Is. 54 : 4. th. shalt not be put to s., thou shalt forget s. of thy youth
61 : 7. For s. you shall have double
Je. 3 : 24. s. devoured labour of fa-'s
25. We lie down in s., confusion
13 : 26. that thy s. may appear [s.
20 : 18. th. my days be consumed wi.
23 : 40. perpetual s. not be forgott.
46 : 12. nat-ns have heard of thy s.
48 : 39. Moab turned back with s.
51 : 51. s. hath covered our faces
Eze. 7 : 18. s. shall be upon all faces
16 : 52. bear own s. for sins, 54.
63. never open mouth bec. of s.
32 : 24. yet have borne their s., 25.
30. bear their s. th. go down to pit
34 : 29. nei. bear the s. of heathen
36 : 6. ye have borne s. of heathen
7. heathen sh. bear their s., 44 : 13.
15. to hear in thee s. of heathen
39 : 26. After they have borne s.
Da. 12 : 2. many sh. awake, some to s.
Ho. 4 : 7. will change their glory in-
18. her rulers with s do love [to s.
9 : 10. separated themselves unto s.
10 : 6. Ephraim shall receive s.
Ob. 10. for violence s. cover thee
Mi. 1 : 11. pass ye, having s. naked
2 : 6. sh. not prophesy, not take s.
7 : 10. s. shall cover her which said
Na. 3 : 5. I will shew kingd-s thy s.
Ha. 2 : 10. Thou hast consulted s.
16. Thou art filled with s. for glory
Zph. 3 : 5. the unjust knoweth no s.
19. praise, where been put to s.
Lu. 14 : 9. with s. take lowest room
Ac. 5 : 41. counted worthy to suffer s.
1 Co. 6 : 5. I speak to your s., 15 : 34.
11 : 6. if s. for woman to be shorn
14. if man have long hair, it is s.
14 : 35. s. for woman to speak in ch.
2 Co. 4 : † 2. renounced things of s.
Ep. 5 : 12. s. to speak of things done
Ph. 3 : 19. whose glory is in their s.
He. 6 : 6. and put him to an open s.
12 : 2. endured cross, despising s.
Jude 13. foaming out their own s.
Re. 3 : 18. that s. of thy nakedness
16 : 15. lest naked, they see his s.

SHAME, ED, ETH. [s-d

Ge. 38 : 23. Let her take it lest we be
Ru. 2 : † 15. Let her glean, s. her not
1 S. 25 : † 7. thy shepherds, we s-d
† 15. men good, we were not s-d
2 S. 19 : 5. hast s-d faces of thy serv-s
Ps. 14 : 6. ye have s-d counsel of poor
Pr. 28 : 7. companion of riotous s-h
1 Co. 4 : 14. I write not to s. you [fa.
11 : 22. despise ye ch. and s. them?

SHA'MED. [S.

1 Ch. 8 : 12. Sons of Elpaal, Misham,

SHAMEFACEDNESS.

1 Ti. 2 : 9. that women adorn with s.

SHAMEFUL, LY.

Je. 11 : 13. ye set up altars to s. thing
Ho. 2 : 5. th. conceived, hath done s-y
Ha. 2 : 16. s. spewing on thy glory
Mk. 12 : 4. they sent him away s-y handled, Lu. 20 : 11.
1 Th. 2 : 2. we were s-y entreated

SHAMELESSLY.

2 S. 6 : 20. one of fellows s. uncover-

SHA'MER. [eth

1 Ch. 6 : 46. on left, Bani, son of S.
See SHOMER.

SHAM'GAR.

Ju. 3 : 31. after him S. son of Anath
5 : 6. In days of S. highw-s unoccupi.

SHAM'HUTH = SHAM'MOTH. [rahite

1 Ch. 27 : 8. 5th capt. was S. the Iz-

SHA'MIR. [Person.]

1 Ch. 24 : 24. of the sons of Micah, S.

SHA'MIR. [Place.]

Jos. 15 : 48. And in mountains, S. [in S.
Ju. 10 : 1. Tola dwelt in S. | 2 buried

SHAM'MA. See SHILSHAH.

SHAM'MAH. [1 : 37

Ge. 36 : 13. son of Reuel S., 17. 1 Ch.
2 S. 23 : 11. after him S. Hararite, 33.

SHAM'MAH or SHAM'MOTH. [27.†

2 S. 23 : 25. S. Harodite, 1 Ch. 11 :

SHAM'MAH. See SHIMEA.

SHAM'MAI.

1 Ch. 2 : 28. Sons of Onam, S. and
32. sons of Jada, bro-r of S [Jada
44. Rekem begat S. | 45. son of S
4 : 17. she bare Miriam and S. [Maon

SHAM'MOTH.

See SHAMHUTH, SHAMMAH.

SHAM'MUA.

Nu. 13 : 4. Of the tribe of Reuben S.
Ne. 11 : 17. and Abda the son of S.
12 : 18. were priests. Of Bilgah, S.
See SHEMAIAH, SHIMEA.

SHAM'MUAH.

2 S. 5 : 8. S. and Shobab, etc.
See SHIMEA. [David's son.]

SHAMSHERA'I.

1 Ch. 8 : 26. S., Shehariah, sons of

SHAPE, SHAPES.

Lu. 3 : 22. descended in bodily s. like
Jn. 5 : 37. not heard voice, nor seen s.
Re. 9 : 7. s-s of locusts were like

SHAPEN. [horses

Ps. 51 : 5. Behold, I was s. in iniquity

SHA'PHAM.

1 Ch. 5 : 12. Joel chief, and S. the next

SHA'PHAN.

2 K. 22 : 3. Josiah sent S. the scribe to repair house, 2 Ch. 34 : 8.
8. Hilkiah gave book to S. (2) 2 Ch.
9. S. brought the k. word [34 : 15.
10. S. read the book before the k.
12. commanded Ahikam son of S. and S. scribe to inquire of Lord
14. S. went unto Huldah prophet-s
25 : 22. Ahikam the son of S., Je. 39 :
14. - 40 : 5, 9, 11. - 41 : 2 - 43 : 6.
2 Ch. 34 : 16. S. carried book unto k.
Je. 26 : 24. son of S. was wi. Jeremiah
29 : 3. Jere. sent by Elasah son of S.
36 : 10. Gemariah son of S., 11, 12.
Eze. 8 : 11. stood Jaazaniah son of S.

SHA'PHAT.

Nu. 13 : 5. of Simeon, S. to spy land
1 K. 19 : 16. anoint Elisha son of S.
19. found Elisha son of S. plough.
2 K. 3 : 11. Here is Elisha son of S.
6 : 31. if head of Elisha, son of S.
1 Ch. 3 : 22. the sons of Shemaiah, S.
5 : 12. of Gadites, S. in Bashan chief
27 : 29. over herds was S. son of Adlai

SHA'PHER.

Nu. 33 : 23. they pitched in mount S.
24. And they removed from mount

SHAR'AI. [S.

Ezr. 10 : 40. sons of Bani, Shashai, S.

SHAR'AIM. See SHAARAIM.

SHA'RAR.

2 S. 23 : 33. of the 30, Ahiam son of

SHARE. [S.

1 S. 13 : 20. sharpen every man his s.

SHARE'ZER. [38.

2 K. 19 : 37. S. his son smote. Is. 37 :

SHAR'ON, ITE.

1 Ch. 5 : 16. dwelt in suburbs of S.
27 : 29. ov. herds in S. Shitrai the S-e
Can. 2 : 1. I am the rose of S. the lily
Is. 33 : 9. S. is like a wilderness [of
35 : 2. excellency of Carmel and S.
65 : 10. S. shall be a fold of flocks

SHARP.

Ex. 4 : 25. Zipporah took a s. stone
Jos. 5 : 2. Make s. knives, circumcise
3. s. knives and circumcised Isr.
1 S. 14 : 4. betw. passages was s. rock
Jb. 41 : 30. s. stones under him, he spreadeth s. pointed things
Ps. 52 : 2. thy tongue like a s. razor
Is. 41 : 15. thee a s. threshing instru.
Eze. 5 : 1. take thee a s. knife and
Ha. 1 : †8. horses more s. than wolves

Ac.15:39. contention so s. betw. Paul
See ARROW, S, SICKLE, SWORD
SHARPEN, ED, ETH.
De. 6 : †7. s. them unto thy children
1 S. 13 : 20. to s. every man his share
21. file for axes, and to s. goads
Jb. 16 : 9. mine enemy s-h his eyes
Ps.140 : 3. s-d their tongues like serp
Pr. 27 : 17. Iron s-h iron, so a man
s-h his friend [bished, 10. 11.
Eze. 21 : 9. a sword is s-d and fur-
SHARPER. [hedge
Mi. 7 : 4. upright is s. than a thorn
He. 4 : 12. word of God s. than any
SHARPLY. [sword
Ju. 8 : 1. did chide with Gideon s.
Tit. 1 : 13. rebuke them s. that they
SHARPNESS.
2 Co. 13 : 10. lest present I should
SHARU'HEN. [use s.
Jos. 19 : 6. in their inheritance, S.
SHASH'AI. See SHAR'AI.
SHA'SHAK. [S.
1 Ch. 8 : 14. sons of Beriah, Ahio and
25. and Penuel son of S.
SHAUL, SHAUL'ITES.
Ge. 46 : 10. S. son of Canaanitish wo.
Nu.26:13. of S. family of S-s [Ex.6:15.
1 Ch. 1 : 48. S. of Rehoboth reigned
49. S. dead, Baal-hanan reigned
4 : 24. sons of Simeon, Zerah and S.
6 : 24. sons of Kohath; Uzziah, S. his
See SAUL. [eon, † 36.
SHAVE, ED. [ment
Ge. 41 : 14. Joseph s-d changed rai-
Le. 13 : 33. but scall shall he not s.
14 : 8. unclean person sh. s. hair, 9.
21 : 5. nei. shall s. corner of beard
Nu. 6 : 9. then he shall s. his head
on 7th day shall he s. it [aration
18. Nazarite sh. s. head of his sep-
8 : 7. let them s. flesh, wash clothes
De. 21 : 12. captive shall s. her head
Ju.16 : 19. caused him to s. locks
2 S.10 : 4. s-d off beards, 1 Ch.19 : 4.
Jb. 1 : 20. Job rent mantle s-d head
Is. 7 : 20. Lord shall s. with a razor
Eze. 44 : 20. Nei. shall s. their heads
Ac. 21 : 24. that they s. their heads
SHA'VEH. [dale
Ge. 14 : 17. valley of S. wh. is king's
SHA'VEH KIRIATHA'IM.
Ge. 14 : 5. smote the Emim in S.
SHAVEN. [not
Le. 13 : 33. He shall be s. but scall
Nu. 6 : 19. hair of his separation s.
Ju. 16 : 17. if s. my strength will go
22. hair began to grow after was s.
Je. 41 : 5. fourscore men beards s.
1 Co. 11 : 5. all one as if she were s.
6. if shame to be s. let her be cov-d
SHAV'SHA. See SERAIAH.
SHEAF.
Ge. 37 : 7. my s. arose, your sheaves
made obeisance to my s. [fruits
Le. 23 : 10. shall bring a s. of first
11. ye shall wave s. bef. Lord, 12.
De. 24 : 19. forgot a s. not fetch it
Jb. 24 : 10. they take s. fr. hungry
Zch. 12 : 6. governors like a torch in
SHE'AL. See RAMOTH. [a s.
SHEAL'TIEL.
Ezr. 3 : 2. Zerubbabel son of S., 8. -
5 : 2. Ne. 12 : 1. Hag. 1 : 1, 12, 14.
SHEAR. [-2 : 2, 23.
Ge. 31 : 19. Laban went to s. sheep
38 : 13. Judah goeth to s. sheep
De. 15 : 19. nor s. firstling of sheep
1 S. 25 : 4. David heard Nabal did s.
SHEARER. [sheep
Ac. 8 : 32. like a lamb dumb bef. his
SHEARERS. [s.
1 S. 25 : 7. I have heard thou hast s-s
11. take flesh I killed for my s-s
2 S. 13 : 23. Absalom had s-s in, 24.
Is. 53 : 7. as sheep before s-s is dumb
See SHEEPSHEARERS.

SHEARI'AH.
1 Ch. 8 : 38. sons of Azel, S. Obadiah
SHEARING.
1 S. 25 : 2. Nabal s. sheep in Carmel
SHEARING house. [s.h.
2 K. 10 : 12. brethren of Ahaziah at
14. he slew them at pit of the s.h.
SHEAR-JA'SHUB.
Is. 7 : 3. Go to meet Ahaz, thou and S.
SHEATH. [s-
1 S. 17 : 51. David drew sword out of
2 S. 20 : 8. with sword fastened in s.
1 Ch. 21 : 27. angel put sword into s.
Eze. 21 : 3. his sword out of s., 4, 5.
30. cause it to return into his s.?
Da. 7 : †15. I, Dan. was grieved in mys.
Jn. 18 : 11. Put up thy sword into s.
SHEAVES.
Ge. 37 : 7. we were binding s. in field
Ru. 2 : 7. Let me glean among s., 15.
Ne. 13 : 15. on sabbath bringing in s.
Ps. 126 : 6. he shall come bringing s.
129 : 7. nor he th. bindeth s. his bos
Am. 2 : 13. am pressed, as cart full of s.
Mi. 4 : 12. Lord sh. gather them as s.
SHE'BA. [Person.] [1 : 9.
Ge. 10 : 7. sons of Raamah; S., 1 Ch.
28. Joktan begat S., 1 Ch. 1 : 22.
25 : 3. Jokshan begat S., Dedan, 1
Ch. 1 : 32. [13, 21, 22.
2 S. 20 : 1. S. son of Bichri, 2, 6, 7, 10.
22. they cut off head of S.
1 Ch. 5 : 13. of chil. of Gad S. Joral
SHE'BA, SHE'BAH. [Place.]
Ge. 26 : 33. Isaac called the well S-h
Jos. 19 : 2. Simeon had in inherit-e S.
1 K. 10 : 1. when queen of S. heard
of Sol., 10, 13. 2 Ch. 9 : 1, 3, 9, 12.
Jb. 6 : 19. companies of S. waited for
Ps. 72 : 10. kings of S. and Seba [th.
15. to him gold of S., Is. 60 : 6. [S.?
Je. 6 : 20. what purpose is incense fr.
Eze. 27 : 22. merchants of S. thy, 23.
38 : 13. S. sh. say, Art thou come to
take a spoil?
SHE'BAM. See NIMRAH.
SHEBANI'AH. [pets
1 Ch. 15 : 24. S. did blow with trum-
Ne. 9 : 4. stood up upon stairs, S., 5.
10 : 4. that sealed were S, 10, 12.
12 : 14. were priests, of S, Joseph
SHEB'ARIM. [unto S.
Jos. 7 : 5. men of Ai chased them
SHE'BER. [hanah
1 Ch. 2 : 48. Maachah bare S., Tir-
SHEB'NA.
2 K. 18 : 18. came to Rab-shakeh S.
scribe, 37. Is. 36 : 3. [Is. 36 : 11
26. Then said S., Speak, I pray,
19 : 2. sent S. to Isaiah, Is. 37 : 2.
Is. 22 : 15. Go unto this treasurer, S.
36 : 22. came S., scribe to Hezekiah
SHEB'UEL.
1 Ch. 23 : 16. Of sons of Gershom, S.
25 : 4. sons of Heman, S. and [26 : 24.
SHECANI'AH.
1 Ch. 24 : 11. the tenth lot to S.
2 Ch. 31 : 15. next him were Eden, S.
SHECHANI'AH. [5.
1 Ch. 3 : 21. sons of S., 22. Ezr. 8 : 3,
Ezr. 10 : 2. S., son of Jehiel, ans-d
Ne. 3 : 29. Aft. him Shem-h son of S.
6 : 18. son in law of S., son of Arah
12 : 3. went up with Zerubbabel, S.
SHE'CHEM. [Place.]
Ge. 33 : 18. Jacob to Salem, city of S.
35 : 4. Jac. hid them und. oak by S.
37 : 12. to feed fa.'s flock in S., 13.
14. Jos. came from Hebron to S.
Jos. 17 : 7. Michmethah lieth bef. S.
20 : 7. S. in mount Ephraim, city of
refuge, 21 : 21. 1 Ch. 6 : 67.
24 : 1. Jos. gath-d tribes of Isr. to S.
25. Joseph set an ordinance in S.
32. bones of Joseph buried in S.
Ju. 8 : 31. Gideon's concubine in S.
9 : 1. Abimelech to S., unto moth-s

Ju. 9 : 3. spake in ears of men of S.
6. men of S. gathered together (2)
7. Jotham cried, Hearken, ye of S.
18. made Abim. k. over men of S.
20. let fire co. out fr. men of S. [S.
23. evil spirit betw. Abim.. men of
24. upon men of S. wh. aided him
25. men of S. set liers in wait
26. Gaal went over to S. (2), 39.
31. Gaal and brethren come to S.
34. they laid wait against S.
41. that they sho. not dwell in S.
46. men of the tower of S., 47, 49.
57. evil of men of S. did G. render
21 : 19. highway that goeth up to S.
1 K. 12 : 1. Rehoboam to S., 2 Ch. 10 : 1.
25. Jeroboam built S. in mt. Ephr.
1 Ch. 7 : 28. S. and the towns thereof
Ps. 60 : 6. I will divide S., 108 : 7.
Je. 41 : 5. there came certain from S.
See SICHEM.
SHE'CHEM, ITES. [S.'s fath
Ge. 33 : 19. field of chil. of Hamor,
34 : 2. S. took Dinah, lay with her
4. S. spake, Get me this damsel
6. father of S. went unto Jac. [11.
8. soul of S. longeth for your dau.,
13. sons of Jac. ans-d S. deceitf-y
18. their words pleased S. [20, 24.
26. Dinah's brethren slew Hamor
Nu. 26 : 31. of S. fam-y of S-s [and S.
Jos. 17 : 2. was a lot for children of S.
Ju. 9 : 28. Who S. th. we serve him?
1 Ch. 7 : 19. sons of Shemidah, Likhi,
SHED. [S.
2 S. 20 : 10. Joab s. Amasa's bowels
Mat. 26 : 28. is s. for remiss-n of sins
Ac. 2 : 33. hath s. forth this ye see
Ro. 5 : 5. love of God s. in our hearts
Tit. 3 : 6. Wh. he s. on us thro. Jes.
See **Shed BLOOD.** [Ch.
SHEDDER.
Eze. 18 : 10. If beget son a s. of blood
SHEDDETH.
Ge. 9 : 6. Whoso. s. man's blood, his
Eze. 22 : 3. city s. blood in midst of it
SHEDDING. [mission
He. 9 : 22. without s. of blood no re-
SHED'EUR.
Nu. 1 : 5. of Reuben, Elizur, son of
S., 2 : 10.-7 : 30, 35.-10 : 18.
SHE goat, s. See GOAT, S.
SHEEP.
Ge. 4 : 2. Abel a keeper of s., Cain
29 : 2. three flocks of s. by well [s.
3. stone fr. well's mouth watered
6. Rachel cometh with the s., 9.
7. water ye the s. and feed, 8.
10. when Jac. saw s. of Laban [35.
30 : 32. all brown cattle am. s., 33,
31 : 19. Laban went to shear his s.
34 : 28. They took their s. captive
38 : 13. Judah goeth to shear his s.
Ex. 9 : 3. hand of Lord is upon the s.
12 : 5. ye sh. take it out from the s.
20 : 24. sh. sacrifice thereon thy s.
22 : 1. If a man steal a s., 4, 9.
10. If a man give neighbour a s.
Le. 1 : 10. if his offering be of s. or
22 : 19. Ye sh offer a male of s., 21.
27. When a s. is bro-t forth, it sh.
27 : 26. no man sanctify firstl-g of s.
Nu. 18 : 17. firstl-g of s. not redeem
31 : 28. levy a tribute unto Lord of s.
32. And the booty was 675,000 s.
36. the portion was 337,500 s., 43.
37. the L.'s tribute of s. was 675.
32 : 24. Build ye folds for y-r s., 36.
De. 7 : 13. will bless flocks of thy s.
15 : 19. nor shear firstling of s.
17 : 1. not sacrifice s. wh-in is blem-
18 : 4. first of fleece of s. give [ish
22 : 1. not see brother's s. go astray
28 : 4. Blessed be flocks of thy s. [51.
18. Cursed be flocks of thy s., 31,
32 : 14. Butter of kine, milk of s.
1 S. 8 : 17. king will take tenth of s.

1 S. 15 : 9. peo. spared best of s., 15.
14. What meaneth bleating of s.?
21. people took of the spoil, s.
16 : 11. behold, he keepeth the s.
19. Send me David, who is with s.
17 : 15. Da. returned to feed fa.'s s.
20. left the s. with a keeper [s.?
28. with whom hast left those few
34. Thy servant kept his fa.'s s.
25 : 2. Nabal had 3000 s., he was
shearing his s. in Carmel, 4.
16. a wall while we were keeping s,
18. Abigail took five s. dressed
2 S. 7 : 8. I took thee from following
the s., 1 Ch. 17 : 7. [and s.
17 : 29. Barzillai brought Da. butter
24 : 17. I have sinned, but these s.,
wh. have they done? 1Ch. 21 : 17.
2 K. 10 : † 12. at house of shepherds
binding s. [s.
1 Ch. 5 : 21. from Hagarites 250,000
12 : 40. they bro-t s. abundantly
2 Ch. 14 : 15. Asa carried from Ethi-ns
15 : 11. offered of spoil 7,000 s. [s.
30 : 24. Hezekiah did give 7,000 s.,
princes gave 10,000 s. [s.
Jb. 1 : 3. his substance also was 7,000
16. the fire hath burned up the s.
31 . 20. if not warmed wi. fleece of s.
42 : 12. for he had 14,000 s.
Ps. 8 : 7. thou hast given him all s.
44 : 11. hast given us like s. for meat
49 : 14. Like s. are laid in grave
74 : 1. why anger smoke ag. thy s.?
78 : 52. made people go forth like s.
79 : 13. we thy peo., s. of thy past-e
95 : 7. we are s. of his hand, 100 : 3.
119 : 176. gone astray like lost s.
144 : 13. th. s. bring forth thous-ds
Can. 4 : 2. Thy teeth like flock of s.,
Is. 7 : 21. man sh. nourish two s. [6:6.
22 : 13. joy, gladness, killing of s.
53 : 6. All we like s. are gone astray
Je. 12 : 3. pull th. out like s. for slau.
23 : 1. pastors that scatter the s.
50 : 6. My people hath been lost s.
17. Israel is as scattered s. lions
Eze. 34 : 6. My s. wander thro. m-ts.
11. I will search my s. and, 12.
Ho. 12 : 12. Israel for a wife kept s.
Jo. 1 : 18. flocks of s. are desolate
Mi. 5 : 8. young lion am. flocks of s.
Zch. 13 : 7. Smite the Shepherd, s.
be scattered, Mat. 26 : 31. Mk.
14 : 27. [s.'s clothing
Mat. 7 : 15. Beware of prophets in
10 : 6. go rather to lost s. of Israel
12 : 11. if s. fall into a pit on sab. [s.?
12. How much is man better than
15 : 24. sent but unto lost s. of Isr.
18 : 12. if man have 100 s. and one
13. he rejoiceth more of that s.
than of 90 and 9, Lu. 15 : 4, 6.
25 : 32. as a shepherd divideth s. fr.
33. sh. set s. on right hand [goats
Jn. 2 : 14. in temple those th. sold s.
10 : 2. entereth by door is shepherd
3. the s. hear his voice, 27. [of s.
4. he goeth before and s. follow
7. verily I am the door of the s.
8. but the s. did not hear them
11. shepherd giveth life for his s.
12. a hireling leaveth the s., 13.
14. I am good shepherd, know my
15. I lay down my life for the s. [s.
16. other s. I have, not of this fold
26. because ye are not of my s.
27. my s. hear my voice, and I
21 : 16. unto Peter, Feed my s., 17.
He. 13 : 20. L. Jes., gr. Shepherd of s.
Re. 18 : 13. no man buyeth s. horses

As SHEEP. [herd

Nu. 27 : 17. be not a.s., have no shep-
1 K. 22 : 17. I saw Israel a. s. that
have no shepherd, 2 Ch. 18 : 16.
Ps. 44 : 22. are counted a. s. for
slaughter, Ro. 8 : 36.
Is. 13 : 14. be a. a s. no man taketh
53 : 7. a. a s. bef. shearers is dumb
Mi. 2 : 12. I will put them together
a. the s. of Bozrah, as flock
Mat. 9 : 36. because scattered a.s.
having no sheph., Mk. 6 : 34.
10 : 16. I send you a.s. in midst of
wolves [slaughter
Ac. 8 : 32. He was led a. a s. to the
1 Pe. 2 : 25. ye were a.s. going astray
See **Sheep GATE.**

SHEEP market. [pool

Jn. 5 : 2. at Jerusalem, by s.m., a
See OX, OXEN.

SHEEPCOTE, S.

1 S. 24 : 3. Saul came to s-s aft. Dav.
2 S. 7 : 8. I took thee fr. s., 1 Ch. 17 : 7.

SHEEPFOLD, S.

Nu. 32 : 16. will build s-s for cattle
Ju. 5 : 16. Why abodest th. am. s-s?
Ps. 78 : 70. chose Da., took him fr. s-s
Jn. 10 : 1. th. entereth not s. by door

SHEEPMASTER.

2 K. 3 : 4. Mesha, k. of Moab, was s.

SHEEPSHEARERS. [s.

Ge. 38 : 12. Judah went up unto his

SHEEPSKINS.

He. 11 : 37. wandered in s., goatsk-s

SHEET.

Ru. 3 : † 15. Bring the s. thou hast
Ac. 10 : 11. descen-g as a gr. s., 11 : 5.

SHEETS.

Ju. 14 : 12. I will give you thirty s-s
13. shall give me thirty s-s and

SHEHARI'AH. [fathers

1 Ch. 8 : 26. S, Athaliah, heads of

SHEKEL.

Ge. 24 : 22. took earring of half a s.
Ex. 30 : 13. a s. after s. of sanctuary,
a s. is 20 gerahs, Le. 27 : 25. Nu.
3 : 47.-18 : 16. Eze. 45 : 12. [a s.
15. poor sh. not give less than half
1 S. 9 : 8. I have fourth part of a s.
2 K. 7 : 1. meas. of flour for s., 16, 18.
Ne. 10 : 32. charged with third of s.
Am. 8 : 5. making ephah small, the
See SANCTUARY. [s. great

SHEKELS. [weight

Ge. 24 : 22. two bracelets of ten s.
Ex. 30 : 23. of myrrh 500 s., of cinnamon 250 s., of sweet calamus
24. And of cassia 500 s. [250 s.
38 : 24. the gold of holy place 730 s.
25. silver was 100 talents, 1,775 s.,
29. brass of offer-g was 2,400 s. [28.
Le. 27 : 4. if female, estimation 30 s.
5. if fr. 5 yrs. old, estimation of
male 20 s., of female 10 s.
7. if fr. 60 yrs. old, a male estimation be 15 s., for female 10 s.
Nu. 3 : 47. take 5 s. apiece, 18 : 16.
50. Of the firstb-n took he, 1,365 s.
7 : 13. offering was silver charger,
weight 130 s., one silver bowl of
70 s., after shekel of sanctuary,
19, 25, 31, 37, 43, 49, 55, 61, 67,
73, 79, 85.
14. one spoon of 10 s. of gold full
of incense, 20, 26, 32, 38, 44, 50,
56, 62, 68, 74, 80, 86. [120 s.
86. all the gold of the spoons was
31 : 52. all the gold was 16,750 s.
Ju. 8 : 26. weight of earrings 1,700 s.
1 S. 17 : 5. weight of coat was 5,000 s.
7. spear's head weighed 600 s.
2 S. 14 : 26. Abs. weighed hair, 200 s.
21 : 16. whose spear weighed 300 s.
1 K. 10 : 16. 600 s. of gold to 1 target
1 Ch. 21 : 25. Da. gave to Ornan 600
2 Ch. 3 : 9. weight of nails was 50 s. [s.
Eze. 4 : 10. meat by weight 20 s. a day
45 : 12. 20 s., 25 s. 15 s., your maneh
See SANCTUARY.

SHEKELS of silver.

Ge. 23 : 15. land is worth 400 s. -, 16.
Ex. 21 : 32. give their master 30 s. -
Le. 5 : 15. thy estimation by s. - [s. -
Le. 27 : 3. estima-n sh. of male, 50 s. -
6. if from a month old estimation
be of male 5 s. -, of female 3 s. -
16. homer of barley seed valued at
50 s. - [100 s. -
De. 22 : 19. they shall amerce him in
29. give unto damsel's fa. 50 s. -
Jos. 7 : 21. When I saw among the
spoils 200 s. - [thee, 3.
Ju. 17 : 2. The 1,100 s. - taken from
4. his mother took 200 s. -, gave
10. be priest, I will give thee 10 s. -
2 S. 18 : 11. I would have given thee
10 s. - [s. -
12. though I should receive 1,000
24 : 24. Dav. bought oxen for 50 s. -
1 K. 10 : 29. chariot went out of E
for 600 s. -, horse for 150, 2 Ch.
1 : 17. [s. -
2 K. 15 : 20. exacted of each man 50
Ne. 5 : 15. govern-s had taken 40 s. -
Je. 32 : 9. I bo-t field, weighed 17 s. -

SHE'LAH, SHE'LAMITES.

Ge. 38 : 5. Shuah bare son, name S.
11. remain widow till S. be grown
14. S. was grown and she not wife
26. because I gave her not to S.
46 : 12. sons of Judah, Er, Onan,
S., Nu. 26 : 20. 1 Ch. 2 : 3.-4 : 21.
Nu. 26 : 20. of S. family of the S-s
1 Ch. 1, 18. Arphaxad begat S., and
See SALAH [S. Eber, 24.

SHELEMI'AH.

1 Ch. 26 : 14. lot eastward fell to S.
Ezr. 10 : 39. S., Nathan, strange wives
41. sons of Bani, S., Shemariah [S.
Ne. 3 : 30. Aft. him Hananiah, son of
13 : 13. over the treasuries S., Zadok
Je. 36 : 14. S. the son of Chushi
26. S., son of Abdeel, to take Baruch
37 : 3. king sent Jehucal, son of S.
13. a captain, Irijah, son of S.
38 : 1. Jucal, son of S., heard words

SHE'LEPH. [20.

Ge. 10 : 26. Joktan begat S., 1 Ch. 1:

SHE'LESH. See ZOPHAH.

SHEL'OMI. [of S.

Nu. 34 : 27. the prince Ahihud, son

SHEL'OMITH.

Le. 24 : 11. his mother's name was S.
1 Ch. 3 : 19. Hananiah and S. sister

SHEL'OMITH, or
SHEL'OMOTH. [iel

1 Ch. 23 : 9. sons of Shimei, S, Haz-
18. sons of Izhar, S., the chief, † 18.
24 : 22. Of the Izharites; S.: of
the sons of S.; Jahath † 22.
26 : 25. Zichri his son, S. his son
26. S. and breth. were ov. treas., 28.
2 Ch. 11 : 20 Maachah bare him S
Ezr. 8 : 10. from Bab-n: of sons of S

SHELTER. [s.

Jb. 24 : 8. embrace rock for want of
Ps. 61 : 3. thou hast been s. for me

SHELU'MIEL.

Nu. 1 : 6. of tribe of Simeon; S. son
of Zurishaddai, 2 : 12 - 7 : 36, 41.

SHEM or **SEM.** [-10 : 9.

Ge. 5 : 32. Noah begat S., 6 : 10 -10 :
1. 1 Ch. 1 : 4. [ark
7 : 13. entered Noah and S. into the
9 : 18. forth of ark, S., Ham, Japh.
23. S. took garment, went backw-d
26. Blessed be Lord God of S.
27. he shall dwell in tents of S.
10 : 22. The children of S., 21, 31.-
11 : 10. 1 Ch. 1 : 17. [phaxad
11 : 11. S. lived after he begat Ar-
1 Ch. 1 : 24. S., Arphaxad, Shelah
Lu. 3 : 36. Arphaxad was son of Sem

SHE'MA. [Person.] [S.

1 Ch. 2 : 43. sons of Hebron, Rekem,
44. and S. begat Raham
Ne. 8 : 4. beside Ezra stood S.

SHE'MA or **SHEMAI'AH.**

1 Ch. 5 : 4. The sons of Joel, S-h, † 8.
8. Bela, son of Azaz, son of S-a

SHE'MA or SHIM'HI.
1 Ch. 8 : 13. Beriah and S-a heads of fathers, † 21.
21. Beraiah, Shimrath, sons of S-i

SHE'MA. [Place.] ⌈adah
Jos. 15 : 26. cities of Judah, S., Mol-

SHEM'AAH.
1 Ch. 12 : 3. mighty men, sons of S.

SHEMAI'AH.
1 K. 12 : 22. word of the Lord came unto S., 2 Ch. 11:2.-12 : 7.⌈of S.
1 Ch. 4 : 37. of Simeon, Shimri, son
5 : 4. of Reuben, S., the son of Joel
9 : 14. of the Levites, S., 16.-15 : 8, 11.-24 : 6.-26 : 4, 6, 7. 2 Ch. 17 : 8.-29 : 14.-31 : 15.-35 : 9. Ezr. 8 : 16.-10 : 21, 31. ⌈hoboam
2 Ch. 12 : 5. came S., prophet, to Re-
15. written in the book of S. ⌈up
Ezr. 8 : 13. S. son of Adonikam went
Ne 3 : 29. S., keeper of the east gate
6 : 10. I came to the house of S.
10 : 8. S., a priest, sealed, 12: 34, 42.
11 : 15. of Levites, S., 12:6, 18, 35, 36.
Je. 26 : 20. Urijah, son of S., who
29 : 24. say to S., Nehelamite, 31, 32.
36 : 12. Delaiah, son of S., a prince
See Shema.

SHEMARI'AH.
1 Ch. 12 : 5. am. the mighty men, S.
Ezr. 10 : 32. of the sons of Harim, S.
41. of sons of Bani; Azareel, S.

SHEM'EBER.
Ge. 14 : 2. war with S., k. of Zeboiim

SHE'MER. ⌈S.
1 K. 16 : 24. bought hill Samaria of

SHEMI'DA, SHEMI'DAH.
Nu. 26 : 32. of S-a, fam. of Shemid-s
Jos. 17 : 2. was a lot, for chil. of S-a
1 Ch. 7 : 19. sons of S-h, Ahian, She-

SHEMI'DAITES. ⌈chem
Nu. 26 : 32. of Shemida, family of S.

SHEMINITH. ⌈excel
1 Ch. 15 : 21. with harps on the S. to

SHEMIR'AMOTH.
1 Ch. 15 : 18. breth. of 2d degree, S.
20. S. and Unni wi. psalteries, 16: 5.
2 Ch. 17 : 8. with them he sent Le-

SHEMU'EL. ⌊vites, S.
Nu. 34 : 20. tribe of chil. of Simeon,
1 Ch. 6 : 33. son of Joel, son of S.⌊S.
7 : 2. Jibsam and S., valiant men

SHEN. ⌈and S.
1 S. 7 : 12. set stone between Mizpeh

SHENA'ZAR. ⌈S.
1 Ch. 3 : 18. sons of Jeconiah, Assir,

SHE'NIR. See Senir.

SHE'PHAM. ⌈S.
Nu. 34 : 10. point out east border to
11. coast sh. go from S. to Riblah

SHEPHATHI'AH.
1 Ch. 9 : 8. Meshullam, son of S.

SHEPHATI'AH. ⌈3 : 3.
2 S. 3 : 4. S., fifth son of David, 1 Ch.
1 Ch. 12 : 5. S., Haruphite, came to Dav.
27 : 16. ruler of Simeonites was S.
2 Ch. 21 : 2. Jehoram had breth., S.
Ezr. 2 : 4. the children of S., 372, 57. Ne. 7 : 9, 59. ⌈11 : 4.
8 : 8. of sons of S., Zebadiah, Ne.
Je. 38 : 1. S. heard words of Jerem-h

SHEPHERD. ⌈Eg-ns
Ge. 46:34. ev. s. is abomination unto
49 : 24. thence is s. stone of Israel
1 S. 17 : 40. he put stones into s.'s bag
Ps. 23 : 1. The Lord is my s., I sh. not
80 : 1. Give ear, O S. of Israel, thou
Ec. 12 : 11. words given from one s.
Is. 38 : 12. mine age is departed from me as a s.'s tent ⌈s.
40 : 11. He shall feed his flock like a
44 : 28. L. saith of Cyrus, He is my
63 : 11. bro-t them wi. s. of flock⌊s.
Je. 31 : 10. keep him as s. doth flock
43 : 12. array himself as s. putteth
49 : 19. who is th. s. will stand, 50: 44.
Je. 51 : 23. I will break s. and flock
Eze. 34 : 5. scattered, because is no s.
8. my flock a prey, is no s.
12. As a s. seeketh out his flock
23. I will set up one s. over them, David be their s., 37 : 24.⌈of lion
Am. 3 : 12. As s. taketh out of mouth
Zch. 10 : 2. troubled, bec. was no s.
11 : 15. instruments of a foolish s.
16. lo, I will raise up a s. in land
17. Woe to idol s. th. leaveth flock
Jn. 10 : 12. he th. is hireling, not s.
16. shall be one fold and one s.
1 Pe. 2 : 25. ye are returned unto S.
5 : 4. when the chief S. sh. appear
See Sheep.

SHEPHERDS.
Ge. 46 : 32. And the men are s. for
47 : 3. unto Pha., Thy serv-ts are s.
Ex. 2 : 17. s. came drove them away
19. Eg-n deliv-d out of hand of s.
1 S. 25 : 7. thy s. we hurt not
2 K. 10 : † 12. Jehu was at hou. of s.
Can. 1 : 8. feed kids beside s-s' tents
Is. 13 : 20. nei. s. make folds there
31 : 4. multi. of s. is called ag. him
56 : 11. are s. th. can-t understand
63 : † 11. Where he that bro-t them
Je. 6 : 3. The s. sh. come unto⌊wi. s.
23 : 4. I will set up s. over them
25 : 34. Howl, ye s., and cry and
35. the s. shall have no way to flee
36. cry of the s. and a howling
33 : 12. in cities be habitation of s.
50:6. their s. caused th. to go astray
Eze. 34 : 2. prophesy ag. s. of Israel, Woe be to the s. of Israel, sho. not s. feed the flocks? ⌈Lord, 9.
7. Therefore, ye s., hear word of
8. nor did my s. search for flock, but s. fed thems., not my flock
10. saith Lord, I am against s., nei. sh. s. feed thems. any more
Am. 1 : 2. habita-ns of s. sh. mourn
Mi. 5 : 5. shall we raise ag. him 7 s.
Na. 3 : 18. Thy s. slumber, O king
Zph. 2 : 6. coasts be cottages for s.
Zch. 10 : 3. Mine anger was kindled
11 : 3. voice of howling of s. ⌊ag. s.
5. their own s. pity them not
8. Three s. I cut off in one month
Lu. 2 : 8. in same country s. in field
15. s. said, Let us go unto Beth-m
18. things which were told by s.
20. the s. returned, glorifying God

SHE'PHI, or SHE'PHO.
Ge. 36 : 23. chil. of Shobal, S., 1 Ch.

SHEPHU'PHAN, ⌊1:40.
SHU'PHAM,
SHU'PHAMITES,
SHUP'PIM.
Nu. 26: 39. Of S-am family of S-s, Ge. 46 : † 21. 1 Ch. 7 : † 12.-8 : † 5.
1 Ch. 7 : 12. men of valour, S-im, Ge. 46 : † 21. ⌈S-im
15. Machir took to wife sister of
8 : 5. son of Benjamin, S-n, Huram
See Muppim, Shuppim.

SHE'RAH.
1 Ch. 7 : 24. dau. was S., who built Beth-horon

SHERD, S. ⌈a s.
Is. 30 : 14. there shall not be found
Eze. 23 : 34. thou shalt break the s-s

SHEREBI'AH.
Ezr. 8 : 18. S., with his sons and
24. chief of the priests, S.⌈breth-n
Ne. 8 : 7. S. caused peo. to underst-d
9 : 4. stood up upon stairs, S. ⌊law
5. S. and Pethahiah said, Stand up
10 : 12. that sealed were S. and in
12 : 8. S. was over the thanksgiving
24. chief of Levites, S. wi. breth-n

SHE'RESH. ⌈Rakem
1 Ch. 7 : 16. S; his sons Ulam and

SHERE'ZER. ⌈Lord
Zch. 7 : 2. had sent S. to pray before

SHERIFFS.
Da. 3 : 2. Neb-r sent to gather the s.
3. then s. and rulers were gath-d

SHE'SHACH. ⌈them
Je. 25 : 26. king of S. sh. drink after
51 : 41. How is S. taken! how Bab-n

SHE'SHAI. See Talmai.

SHE'SHAN.
1 Ch. 2 : 31. And the sons of Ishi: S.
34. Now S. had no sons, but dau-s
35. S. gave his dau. to Jarha his

SHESHBAZ'ZAR. ⌊serv.
Ezr. 1 : 8. he numbered them unto S.
11. All these did S. bring fr. Bab-n
5 : 14. delivered unto S. governor
16. S. laid foundation of hou. of G.

SHETH. See Seth.

SHE'THAR. See Meres.

SHE'THAR-BOZ'NAI. ⌈S.
Ezr. 5 : 3. came to them Tatnai and
6. copy of letter Tatnai and S. sent
6 : 6. Tatnai, S. be ye far fr. thence
13. Tatnai and S. did speedily

SHE'VA. ⌈priest
2 S. 20 : 25. S. was scribe, Zadok
1 Ch. 2 : 49. She bare S., fa. of Machb.

SHEW. [Noun.]
Ps. 39 : 6. ev. man walketh in vain s.
Is. 3 : 9. s. of countenance witness
Lu. 17 : † 20. kingd. of God not wi. s.
20 : 47. for a s. make long prayers
Ga. 6 : 12. to make a fair s. in flesh
Col. 2 : 15. made a s. of them openly
23. Which things have s. of wisd.

SHEW. [Verb.]
Ex. 7 : 9. Pharaoh, saying, s. miracle
9 : 16. I raised thee to s. my power
10 : 1. that I might s. my signs bef.
13 : 8. shalt s. thy son in that day
14 : 13. see the salvation L. will s.
18 : 20. thou sh. s. the way, De. 1: 33.
25 : 9. According to all that I s. thee
33 : 13. s. me now thy way, that I
18. I beseech s. me thy glory ⌈his
Nu. 16 : 5. to morrow L. s. who are
De. 3 : 24. to s. servant thy greatness
5 : 5. I stood to s. you word of Lord
7 : 2. make no coven-t, nor s. mercy
13 : 17. that Lord may s. thee mercy
17 : 9. they shall s. thee sentence
10. shalt do as they sh. s. thee, 11.
28 : 50. old, nor s. favour to young
32 : 7. ask thy father, he will s. thee
Jos. 5 : 6. L. sware he wo. not s. land
Ju. 1 : 24. spies said, s. us entrance into city, we will s. thee mercy
6 : 17. s. me a sign that thou talkest
1 S. 3 : 15. Samuel feared to s. Eli
8 : 9. s. them manner of the king
9 : 6. man of God can s. us our way
27. that I may s. thee word of God
10 : 8. I will s. thee what shalt do
14 : 12. Come, we will s. you a thing
20 : 2. fa. do nothing, but he will s.
12. if I send not, and s. it thee⌊me
22 : 17. knew he fled, did not s. it
25 : 8. Ask young men, they will s.
2 S. 15 : 25. he will s. me, both it and
22 : 26. With merciful wilt s. thyself merciful (2), Ps. 18 : 25. ⌈26.
27. wilt s. thyself pure (2), Ps. 18 :
1 K. 1 : 52. If he will s. hims. worthy
2 : 2. be strong, s. thyself a man
18 : 1. Go, s. thyself unto Ahab, 2.
2 K. 6 : 11. Will ye not s. wh. is for k.
1 Ch. 16 : 23. s. forth his salva-n, Ps.
2 Ch. 16 : 9. to s. hims. strong ⌊96: 2.
Ezr. 2 : 59. they could not s. father's house, whe. of Israel, Ne. 7:61.
Ne. 9 : 19. pillar of fire to s. th. light
Es. 1 : 11. to s. people her beauty
2 : 10. charged her not to s. kind-d
4 : 8. copy of writing to s. Esther
Jb. 10 : 2. s. me wh. contendest wi.
11 : 6. s. thee secrets of wisdom⌊me
32 : 6. durst not s. you my opinion
33 : 23. to s. unto man his uprightn.

Ps. 4 : 6. Who will s. us any good?
9 : 14. That I may s. praise in gates
16 : 11. wilt s. me the path of life
17 : 7. s. thy marvellous lovingkin.
25 : 4. s. me thy ways, O Lord, teach
14. Lord will s. them his covenant
51 : 15. my mouth sh. s. thy praise
71 : 15. My mouth s. thy righteousn.
79 : 13. we thy peo. will s. thy praise
85 : 7. s. us mercy, O Lord, grant
86 : 17. s. me a token for good, that
88 : 10. Wilt s. wonders to the dead?
92 : 15. To s. that Lord is upright
94 : 1. O G., to wh. vengeance s. thys.
106 : 2. who can s. all his praise? [ly
Pr. 18 : 24. man must s. hims. friend-
Is. 27 : 11. he will s. them no favour
30 : 30. L. sh. s. lightning of his arm
41 : 22. let them s. us what shall
happen, let them s. former thi-s
23. s. thi-s th. are to come hereaf.
43 : 9. who can s. us former things?
21. peo. I formed sh. s. my praise
44 : 7. things coming, let them s. to
46 : 8. Remember, s. yours. men
49 : 9. say to th. in darkn., s. yours.
58 : 1. s. my people their transgr-n
60 : 6. they sh. s. praises of the Lord
Je. 16 : 10. s. them all these words
13. where I will not s. you favour
42 : 3. thy God may s. us the way
51 : 31. to s. king of Babylon city is
Eze. 22 : 2. s. all her abominations
33 : 31. wi. mouth they s. much love
37 : 18. Wilt not s. us wh. meanest?
40 : 4. set heart upon all I shall s.
43 : 10. s. the house to house of Isr.
11. s. them form of the house and
Da. 2 : 2. sorcerers to s. k. his dreams
4. we will s. the interpreta-n, 7, 9.
6. if ye s. dream and interpreta-n,
theref. s. dream and interpre-n
10. not a man can s. k.'s matter
11. is none other that can s. it
16. he would s. king interpreta-n
27. secret cannot wise men s. king
4 : 2. I thought it good to s. signs
5 : 7. whoso. sh. s. me interpretation
15. wise men could not s. interp-n
9 : 23. and I am come to s. thee
Ha. 1 : 3. Why dost s. me iniquity?
Mat. 8 : 4. go, s. thyself to the priest,
Mk. 1 : 44. Lu. 5 : 14.-17 : 14.
11 : 4. Go and s. John thi-s ye hear
12 : 18. he sh. s. judgment to Gent.
14 : 2. mighty works do s. themselves in him, Mk. 6 : 14. [s. sign
16 : 1. Pharisees desired he would
21. began Jes. to s. unto disciples
22 : 19. s. tribute money, Lu. 20 : 24.
24 : 1. came to s. him buildings
24. false Christs shall s. gr. signs,
and wonders, Mk. 13 : 22.
Mk. 14 : 15. he will s. you a large
upper room, Lu. 22 : 12. [tidings
Lu. 1 : 19. I am sent to s. thee glad
8 : 39. s. how great things God hath
Jn. 5 : 20. he will s. greater works
7 : 4. If do these things s. thyself
11 : 57. if any knew he should s. it
14 : 8. s. us Father, it sufficeth, 9.
16 : 13. he will s. things to come
14. sh. rec. of mine, and s. it, 15.
25. I sh. s. you plainly of Father
Ac. 1 : 24. L. s. whe. of these chosen
7 : 3. come into land I sh. s. thee
12 : 17. Go, s. these thi-s unto Jas.
16 : 17. who s. unto us way of salva.
24 : 27. Felix willing to s. Jews a
26 : 23. should s. light unto people
Ro. 2 : 15. Who s. work of the law [er
9 : 17. raised th. I might s. my pow-
22. if God, willing to s. his wrath
1 Co. 11 : 26. ye do s. the L.'s death
12 : 31. s. I more excellent way
15 : 51. I s. you a mystery, we shall
2 Co. 8 : 24. s. ye proof of your love
Ep. 2 : 7. might s. exceeding riches
1 Th. 1 : 9. For they thems. s. of us
1 Ti. 1 : 16. Ch. might s. longsuffer-g
5 : 4. learn first to s. piety at home
6 : 15. Which in his times he sh. s.
2 Ti. 2 : 15. Study to s. thys. approved
He. 6 : 11. that ev. one s. diligence
17. God willing to s. unto heirs of
Ja. 2 : 18. s. me thy faith without
3 : 13. s. out of good conversa. works
1 Pe. 2 : 9. ye sho-d s. praises of him
1 Jn. 1 : 2. s. unto you eternal life
Re. 1 : 1. sent angel to s. servants,

I will SHEW. [22 : 6.

Ge. 12 : 1. Get unto land I w. s. thee
46 : 31. I w. go up and s. Pharaoh
Ju. 4 : 22. I w. s. man thou seekest
1 S. 16 : 3. I w. s. thee what shalt do
20 : 13. do thee evil, I w. s. it thee
1 K. 18 : 15. I w. s. myself unto Ahab
2 K. 7 : 12. I w. s. you what Syrians
Jb. 15 : 17. I w. s. that I have seen
32 : 10. Hearken, I also w. s. mine
opinion, 17.-36 : 2. [works
Ps. 9 : 1. I w. s. all thy marvellous
50 : 23. I w. s. salva. of God, 91 : 16.
Je. 18 : 17. I w. s. them the back
33 : 3. I w. s. thee mighty things
42 : 12. I w. s. mercies unto you
Da. 2 : 24. I w. s. king interpreta-n
10 : 21. I w. s. thee what is noted
11 : 2. I w. s. thee the truth [2 : 19.
Jo. 2 : 30. I w. s. woud-s in heav., Ac.
Mi. 7 : 15. I w. s. marvellous things
Na. 3 : 5. I w. s. thy nakedness
Zch. 1 : 9. I w. s. thee what these be
Lu. 6 : 47. I w. s. you wh. he is [suf.
Ac. 9 : 16. I w. s. him how he must
Ja. 2 : 18. I w. s. my faith by works
Re. 4 : 1. I w. s. thee things must be
17 : 1. I w. s. judgment of the whore
21 : 9. I w. s. bride the Lamb's wife
See KINDNESS.
See **MERCY,** with
shew, ed, est, eth, ing.

SHEWBREAD.

Ex. 25 : 30. shalt set upon table s.
35 : 13. make table and s., 39 : 36.
Nu. 4 : 7. on table of s. spread cloth
1 S. 21 : 6. was no bread, but the s.
1 K. 7 : 48. table of gold whereupon s.
1 Ch. 9 : 32. Kohathites to prepare s.
23 : 29. service for s. and fine flour
28 : 16. gave gold for tables of s. (2)
2 Ch. 2 : 4. a house for continual s.
4 : 19. made tables whereon s. was
13 : 11. s. also set they in order
29 : 18. We have cleansed s. table
Ne. 10 : 33. to charge ourselves for s.
Mat. 12 : 4. how David entered and
did eat s., Mk. 2 : 26. Lu. 6 : 4.
He. 9 : 2. tabernacle wherein was s.

SHEWED. [priest, 49.

Le. 13 : 19. a spot, and it be s. to
Nu. 13 : 26. s. them fruit of land
De. 4 : 35. Unto thee it was s. that
34 : 12. Moses s. in sight of Israel
Ju. 1 : 25. he s. them the entrance
4 : 12. s. Sisera that Barak was gone
8 : 35. goodness he had s. unto Isr.
13 : 10. the woman s. her husband
16 : 18. he hath s. me all his heart
Ru. 2 : 11. been s. me all thou hast
19. she s. her mother in law [done
1 S. 11 : 9. s. it to men of Jabesh
19 : 7. Jonathan s. all those things
22 : 21. s. Da. Saul had slain priests
24 : 18. Saul said to David, hast s.
thou hast dealt well with me?
2 S. 11 : 22. messenger s. David all
1 K. 1 : 27. hast not s. it unto serv-t
16 : 27. and his might th. he s., 22 : 45.
2 K. 6 : 6. Where fell it? he s. place
11 : 4. took oath, and s. king's son
20 : 13. Hezekiah s. all house of his
precious things, Is. 39 : 2. [39 : 4.
15. Is nothing I have not s. th., Is.
2 K. 22 : 10. Shaphan the scribe s. the
Es. 1 : 4. When he s. riches of kingd.
2 : 10. Es. had not s. her people, 20.
3 : 6. had s. him people of Mordecai
Jb. 6 : 14. to afflicted pity sho. be s.
Ps. 71 : 18. until I have s. thy stren.
98 : 2. righteousn. hath he openly s.
105 : 27. they s. his signs, Ac. 7 : 36.
142 : 2. I s. before him my trouble
Pr. 26 : 26. his wickedn. shall be s.
Ec. 2 : 19. labour, I s. myself wise
Is. 40 : 14. Who s. way of underst.-g?
Eze. 22 : 26. s. no difference between
Mat. 28 : 11. s. to chief priests all
Lu. 4 : 5. devil s. him all kingdoms
7 : 18. disciples of John s. him these
14 : 21. servant came and s. his lord
20 : 37. dead are raised, Moses s.
24 : 40. he s. th. his hands, Jn. 20 : 20.
Jn. 10 : 32. Many good works I s.
21 : 1. Jes. s. hims. again, 14. Ac. 1 : 3.
Ac. 4 : 22. miracle of healing was s.
7 : 26. Moses s. himself as th. strove
36. after he had s. wonders and
52. wh. s. of coming of Just One
11 : 13. s. how he had seen an angel
19 : 18. many that believed s. deeds
20 : 20. s. and taught you publicly
35. I have s. you all things, how
23 : 22. tell no man thou hast s. me
26 : 20. Paul s. unto them of Damas.
28 : 21. nei. breth. s. harm of thee
1 Co. 10 : 28. eat not, for his sake
that s. it [name
He. 6 : 10. love ye have s. toward his
Re. 21 : 10. angel s. me great city
22 : 1. s. pure river of water of life
8. to worship angel which s. me

God or Lord SHEWED.

Ge. 19 : 19. mercy s. in saving my life
32 : 10. not worthy of mercies s.
41 : 25. G. s. Pha. what about to do
39. as G. hath s. thee all this
48 : 11. G. hath s. me also thy seed
Ex. 15 : 25. he cried, L. s. him a tree
25 : 40. make them after pattern s.
in mount, 26 : 30.-27 : 8. He. 8 : 5.
Le. 24 : 12. that mind of L. be s.
Nu. 8 : 4. pattern L. had s. Moses
14 : 11. all signs I have s., De. 6 : 22.
De. 4 : 36. he s. thee his great fire
5 : 24. L. our G. s. us his glory
34 : 1. L. s. him all land of Gilead
Ju. 13 : 23. nei. wo. have s. all these
2 K. 8 : 10. L. hath s. me, he sh. die
13. L. hath s. me thou sh. be king
2 Ch. 7 : 10. goodness L. had s. Dav.
Ezr. 9 : 8. grace s. from Lord our God
Ps. 60 : 3. hast s. thy peo. hard thi-s
71 : 20. Thou hast s. me sore troubles
78 : 11. forgat wonders he had s.
98 : 2. righteousn. hath s. in sight
111 : 6. he s. people power of works
118 : 27. G. the L. who s. us light
Is. 26 : 10. Let favour be s. to wicked
43 : 12. I s. when no strange god
48 : 3. I s. them I did th. suddenly
5. before it came to pass I s. thee
6. I have s. thee new things
Je. 24 : 1. L. s. me 2 baskets of figs
38 : 21. this is the word the L. s. me
Eze. 11 : 25. all that L. hath s. me
20 : 11. and s. them my judgments
Am. 7 : 1. Thus hath the L. s. me, 4,
7.-8 : 1. [is good
Mi. 6 : 8. hath s. thee, O man, what
Zch. 1 : 20. the L. s. me 4 carpenters
3 : 1. he s. me Joshua stand-g bef.
Lu. 1 : 51. s. strength with his arm
Ac. 3 : 18. things wh. G. bef. had s.
10 : 28. G. s. not call any man com-
40. G. raised him and s. him [mon
Ro. 1 : 19. manifest, for G. hath s. it
2 Pe. 1 : 14. as our L. Jes. hath s. me
See KINDNESS.

SHEWEDST. [Pha.

Ne. 9 : 10. s. signs and wonders upon

Je. 11 : 18. thou s. me their doings

SHEWEST. [on me
Jb. 10 : 16. s. thyself marvellous up-
Je. 32 : 18. s. lovingkindn. to thou-s
Jn. 2 : 18. What sign s. thou? 6:30.

SHEWETH. [to Pha.
Ge. 41 : 28. What God is to do, he s.
Nu. 23 : 3. whatso. he s. I will tell
1 S. 22:8. none s. my son made league
Jb. 36 : 9. he s. them their work, and
33. noise thereof s. concerning it
Ps. 19 : 1. firmament s. handywork
2. night unto night s. knowledge
112 : 5. good man s. favour, lend-h
147 : 19. He s. his word unto Jacob
Pr. 12 : 17. speaketh truth, s. right-sn.
27 : 25. hay appear-h, tender grass s.
Is. 41 : 26. is none that s. y-r words
Mat. 4 : 8. s. him all kingdoms of
Jn. 5 : 20. Father s. Son all things

SHEWING.
Ps. 78 : 4. s. to generation praises of
Can. 2 : 9. My beloved s. thro. lattice
Da. 5 : 12. s. of hard sentences in Dan.
Lu. 1 : 80. in deserts till day of his s.
8 : 1. s. glad tidings of kingdom
Ac. 9 : 39. s. the coats Dorcas made
18 : 28. s. by Scriptures Jes. was Ch.
2 Th. 2 : 4. as God, s. that he is God
Tit. 2 : 7. In all things s. thys. pat-n
10. Not purloining, but s. fidelity
3 : 2. s. all meekness unto all men

SHIB'BOLETH. [leth
Ju. 12 : 6. say now S., be said Sibbo-

SHIB'MAH = SHE'BAM.
Nu. 32 : 38. chil. of Reuben built S.,

SHIC'RON. [† 3.
Jos. 15 : 11 border was drawn to S.

SHIELD.
Ge. 15 : 1. I am thy s. and gr. reward
De. 33 : 29. the Lord, s. of thy help
1 S. 17 : 7. one bearing a s. went, 41.
2 S. 1 : 21. s. of mighty is cast away,
s. of Saul as tho. not anointed
22 : 3. he is my s., my tower, my
refuge, my saviour, Ps. 3 : 3.-28 :
7.-119 : 114.-144 : 2. [Ps. 18 : 35.
36. given me s. of thy salvation,
1 K. 10 : 17. 3 pounds of gold to 1 s.
2 K. 19 : 32. he shall not come before
it with a s., Is. 37 : 33. [dle s.
1 Ch. 12 : 8. Gadites that could han-
2 Ch. 9 : 16. 300 shekels of gold to 1 s.
17 : 17. men wi. bow and s., 200,000
Ps. 5 : 12. wilt compass him as wi. s.
33 : 20. the Lord is our s., 59 : 11.-
84 : 9.-89 : † 18.
35 : 2. Take hold of the s. and buckler
76 : 3. brake he arrows of bow, s.
84 : 11. Lord God is sun and s.
91 : 4. his truth shall be thy s., and
115 : 9. he is their help and s., 10, 11.
Pr. 24 : † 34. want come like man of s.
30 : 5. s. unto them put trust in him
Is. 21 : 5. ye princes, anoint the s.
22 : 6. quiver, Kir uncovered the s.
37 : † 33. nor come bef. Jerus. wi. s.
Je. 46 : 3. Order buckler and s. draw
9. Libyans, that handle the s. [s.
Eze. 23 : 24. set ag. thee buckler and
27 : 10. they hanged s., helmet, 11.
38 : 5. all of th. with s. and helmet
Na. 2 : 3. s. of mighty is made red
Ep. 6 : 16. Above all taking s. of faith

SHIELD, S, with spear, s.
Ju. 5 : 8. was there s. or s. am. 40,000?
1 S. 17 : 45. comest to me wi. s. and s.
2 K. 11 : 10. to captains did priests
give Da.'s s-s and s-s, 2 Ch. 23 : 9.
1 Ch. 12 : 24. that bare s. and s. were
34. wi. s. and s. were 37,000 [6,800
2 Ch. 11 : 12. ev. city put s-s and s-s
25 : 5. 300,000 co. handle s. and s.
26 : 14. Uzziah prepared s-s and s-s
Ne. 4 : 16. half held the s-s the s-s
Jb. 39 : 23. ag. him glitter-g s. and s.
Eze. 39 : 9. they sh. burn s-s and s-s

SHIELDS.
2 S. 8 : 7. David took s. of gold on
servants, 1 Ch. 18 : 7.
1 K. 10 : 17. Solomon made 300 s. of
gold, 2 Ch. 9 : 16.
14 : 26. Shishak took all s. of gold
Sol. made, 2 Ch. 12 : 9. [2 Ch. 12 : 10.
27. Rehoboam made brazen s.,
2 Ch. 14 : 8. of Benj. th. bare s., 17 : 17.
32 : 5. Hezek. made darts and s., 27.
Jb. 41 : † 15. pieces of s. are his pride
Ps. 47 : 9. s. of earth belong unto G.
Can. 4 : 4. bucklers all s. of mighty
Je. 51 : 11. arrows gather the s. [men
Eze. 38 : 4. great company with s., 5.
Ho. 4 : † 18. her s. with shame do love

SHIGGA'ION.
Ps. 7.* S. of David which he sang

SHIGIO'NOTH. [on S.
Ha. 3 : 1. A prayer of Habakkuk up-

SHI'HON. [tow. S.
Jos. 19 : 19. Issachar, their border

SHI'HOR. [S.
1 Ch. 13 : 5. David gathered Isr. from

SHI'HOR-LIB'NATH.
Jos. 19 : 26. Asher, border reach-h to

SHIL'HI. See AZUBAH. [S.

SHIL'HIM. See RIMMON.

SHIL'LEM, ITES. [7 : † 13.
Ge. 46 : 24. sons of Naphtali; S., 1 Ch.
Nu. 26 : 49. of S.; the family of S-s

SHIL'OAH = SIL'OAH.
Is. 8 : 6. people refuseth waters of S.
See SILOAH, SILOAM.

SHI'LOH. [MESSIAH.] [S.
Ge. 49 : 10. sceptre not depart until

SHI'LOH. [Place.] [22 : 12.
Jos. 18 : 1. all Israel assembled at S.,
8. I may cast lots for you in S., 10.
9. men came again to Joshua at S.
19 : 51. for inheritance by lot in S.
21 : 2. They spake unto them at S.
22 : 9. Reub. departed fr. Isr. ont of
Ju. 18 : 31. hou. of God was in S. [S.
21 : 12. brought young virgins to S.
19. feast of the Lord in S. yearly
21. if dau-s of S. come to dance (2)
1 S. 1 : 3. Elka-h up to worship in S.
9. Hannah rose after had eaten in
24. Sam. unto house of L. in S. [S.
2 : 14. So did priests in S. unto all
3 : 21. the Lord appeared ag. in S.
4 : 3. Let us fetch ark out of S., 4.
12. a man to S. with clothes rent
14 : 3. Ahitub, the L.'s priest in S.
1 K. 2 : 27. word ag. the hou. of Eli
14 : 2. get thee to S. to Ahijah [in S.
4. Jeroboam's wife went to S. [S.
Ps. 78 : 60. he forsook tabernacle of
Je. 7 : 12. go ye to my place in S.
14. I will do to this house as to S.
26 : 6. will I make this ho. like S., 9.
41 : 5. there came certain from S.

SHILO'NI.
Ne. 11 : 5. Of Zechariah, son of S.

SHILO'NITE, S. [way
1 K. 11 : 29. Ahijah, S., found him in
15 : 29. spake by Ahijah, S., 12 : 15.
1 Ch. 9 : 5. of S-s; Asaiah [1 Ch. 10 : 15
2 Ch. 9 : 29. in prophecy of Ahijah, S.

SHIL'SHAH. [ma, S.
1 Ch. 7 : 37. sons of Zophah; Sham-

SHIM'EA.
1 Ch. 6 : 30. sons of Merari, S. [of S.
39. Asaph, son of Berechiah, son

SHIM'EA, SHIM'EAH, SHAM'MAH, or SHIM'MA.
[David's brother.] [† S-eah
1 S. 16 : 9. Jesse made S-mah pass by,
17 : 13. eldest sons of Jesse, third,
S-mah, 1 Ch. 2 : 13, S-ma, † S-mah
2 S. 13 : 3. Jonadab, son of S-ah, David's brother, 32.-21 : 21. S-eah.
1 Ch. 20 : 7. S-a, † S-mah

SHIM'EA, SHAM'MUA, SHAM'MUAH. [David's son.]
2 S. 5 : 14. born unto David in Jerusalem, S-h, † S-ea, 1 Ch. 3 : 5,
S-ea, † S-us, 14 : 4, S-ua

SHIM'EAH, SHIM'EAM.
1 Ch. 8 : 32. Mikloth begat S-h, 9 : 38,

SHIM'EATH, ITES. [S-m
2 K. 12 : 21. Jozachar, son of S., smote
1 Ch 2 : 55. families at Jabez; the S-s
2 Ch. 24 : 26. conspired; Zabad, son

SHIM'EI. [of S.
2 S. 16 : 5. S., son of Gera of, 19 : 16, 18.
7. thus said S. when he cursed
13. S. went along on hill's side
19 : 21. shall not S. be put to death
23. said unto S., Thou sh. not die
1 K. 1 : 8. S. and mighty men not wi.
2 : 8. hast wi. thee S. who cursed me
36. king sent and called for S., 42.
38. S. said, The saying is good (2)
39. two of the servants of S. ran aw.
40. S. arose and saddled his ass (2)
41. was told Solomon, S. had gone
44. k. said to S., Thou knowest all
4 : 18. S., the son of Elah, officer
1 Ch. 3 : 19. sons of Pedaiah; were S.
4 : 26. sons of Mishma; Zacchur, S.
27. S. had 16 sons and 6 daughters
5 : 4. sons of Joel; Shemaiah, S. [23 : 7.
6 : 17. sons of Gershom; S., 42.-
29. sons of Merari, Libni, S. [10.
23 : 9. sons of S.; Shelomith, Haran,
25 : 17. they cast lots, 10th to S. [ite
27 : 27. over vineyards S., Ramath-
2 Ch. 29 : 14. sons of Heman, Jehiel,
31 : 12. ov. dedicated thi-s, S., 13. [S.
Ezr. 10 : 23. S. a strange wife, 33, 38.
Es. 2 : 5 Mordecai of Jair, son of S.
Zch. 12 : 13. fam. of S. sh. mourn apart
See SHIMI.

SHIM'EON.
Ezr. 10 : 31. of the sons of Harim, S.

SHIM'HI. See SHEMA.

SHIM'I, or SHIM'EI.
Ex. 6 : 17. Sons of Gershon, Libni,
and S-mi, Nu. 3 : 18. S-ei, 1 Ch.
6 : 17, S-ei

SHIM'ITES. [S.
Nu. 3 : 21. Of Gershon, family of the

SHIM'MA. See SHIMEA.

SHI'MON. [and
1 Ch. 4 : 20. sons of S. were Amnon

SHIM'RATH. See SHEMA.

SHIM'RI, SIM'RI. [45.
1 Ch. 4 : 37. Jedaiah, son of Sh., 11 :
26 : 10. Also Hosah had sons, Si.
2 Ch. 29 : 13. of sons of Elzaph., S-h.

SHIM'RITH = SHO'MER.
2 Ch. 24 : 26. Jehozabad, son of S-h,
a Moabitess, 2 K. 12 : 21, S-r,

SHIM'ROM, or [† S-h

SHIM'RON, ITES.
Ge. 46 : 13. sons of Issachar, S-n, 1
Ch. 7 : 1, S-m
Nu. 26 : 24. of S-n, family of S-s

SHIM'RON. [Place.]
Jos. 11 : 1. Jabin sent to king of S.
19 : 15. S. inheritance of Zebulun

SHIM'RON-ME'RON.
Jos. 12 : 20. gave unto king of S. one

SHIM'SHAI.
Ezr. 4 : 8. S., scribe wrote a letter, 9.
17. the king sent an answer to S.
23. letter was read before S.

SHI'NAB.
Ge. 14 : 2. war with S., k. of Admah

SHI'NAR.
Ge. 10 : 10. Calneh, in the land of S.
11 : 2. found a plain in the land of S.
14 : 1. days of Amraphel, king of S.
Is. 11 : 11. recover remnant from S.
Da. 1 : 2. which he carried into land
Zch. 5 : 11. house in land of S. [of S.

SHINE.
Nu. 6 : 25. L. make his face s. upon
Jb. 3 : 4. day be dark; nei. let light s.
10 : 3. s. upon counsel of wicked?
11 : 17. thou shalt s. forth, thou be
18 : 5. spark of his fire shall not s.

Jb. 22 : 28. light sh. s. upon thy ways
36 : 32. he commandeth it not to s.
37 : 15. caused the light of cloud to s.
41 : 18. By his neesings light doth s.
32. he maketh path to s. aft. him
Ps. 31 : 16. Make thy face to s. upon
thy servant, 119 : 135. [3, 7, 19.
67 : 1. cause face to s. upon us, 80 :
80 : 1. between cherubim s. forth
94 : † 1. O God of revenges s. forth
104 : 15. oil to make his face to s.
Ec. 8 : 1. wisdom maketh face to s.
Is. 13 : 10. moon not cause light to s.
60 : 1. Arise, s., thy light is come
Je. 5 : 28. They are waxen fat, they s.
Da. 9 : 17. cause face to s. upon
12 : 3. that be wise shall s. as stars
Mat. 5 : 16. Let your light so s. bef.
13 : 43. shall righteous s. as sun
17 : 2. his face did s. as sun, and
2 Co. 4 : 4. lest light of gospel sho. s.
6. God, who com-ded light to s.
Ph. 2 : 15. am. whom ye s. as lights
Re. 18 : 23. candle shall s. no more
21 : 23. city no need of sun to s. in it

SHINED.

De. 33 : 2. Lord s. from mount Paran
Jb. 29 : 3. his candle s. upon my head
31 : 26. If I beheld sun when it s.
Ps. 50 : 2. Out of Zion God hath s.
Is. 9 : 2. upon them hath the light s.
Eze. 43 : 2. earth s. with his glory
Ac. 9 : 3. suddenly s. about him light
12 : 7. and a light s. in the prison
2 Co. 4 : 6. God hath s. in our hearts

SHINETH.

Jb. 25 : 5. to the moon, and it s. not
Ps. 139 : 12. the night s. as the day
Pr. 4 : 18. as shining light th. s. more
Mat. 24 : 27. as lightning s. unto west
Lu. 17 : 24. s. to other part under
Jn. 1 : 5. the light s. in darkness
2 Pe. 1 : 19. light th. s. in dark place
1 Jn. 2 : 8. darku. past, true light s.
Re. 1 : 16. his countenance as sun s.

SHINING.

2 S. 23 : 4. by clear s. after rain
Ezr. 8 : † 27. two vessels of s. brass
Pr. 4 : 18. path of just as the s. light
Is. 4 : 5. s. of flaming fire by night
Jo. 2 : 10. stars sh. withdraw s., 3 : 15.
Ha. 3 : 11. s. of thy glittering spear
Mk. 9 : 3. his raiment became s.
Lu. 11 : 36. s. of candle giveth life
24 : 4. two men stood in s. garm-ts
Jn. 5 : 35. a burning and s. light
Ac. 26 : 13. above brightn. of sun, s.

SHIP.

Pr. 30 : 19. way of s. in the sea
Is. 33 : 21. no gallant s. shall pass
Jon. 1 : 3. Jonah found a s. going to
4. tempest, s. was like to be broken
5. mariners cast wares into the s.
Mat. 4 : 21. in a s., with Zebedee
22. they left s. and followed him
8 : 23. when he was entered into
s., 9 : 1. -13 : 2. Mk. 4 : 1. -5 : 18.
-8 : 10, 13. Lu. 8 : 22, 37. [waves
24. the s. was covered with the
14 : 13. Jesus heard, he dep-d by s.
22. constrained disciples to get into s., Mk. 6 : 45. [4 : 37. -6 : 47.
24. s. was tossed with waves, Mk.
29. when Peter was come out of s.
32. were come into s. wind ceased
33. th in s. came worshipped him
15 : 39. he took s., came into Mag-a
Mk. 1 : 19. in s. mending their nets
20. left their father Zebedee in s.
3 : 9. a small s. should wait on him
4 : 36. took him as he was in the s.
38. he in hinder part of s. asleep
5 : 2. when he was come out of s.
21. wh. Jesus was passed ov. by s.
6 : 32. departed into desert place by
47. the s. was in midst of sea [s.
51. he went up unto them into s.
Mk. 6 : 54. out of s., straightway they
8 : 14. had they in s. but one loaf
Lu. 5 : 3. taught people out of s.
7. partners which were in other s.
Jn. 6 : 17. disciples entered a s., 21 : 3.
19.. Jesus drawing nigh unto s.
21. immediately s. was at land
21 : 6. Cast net on right side of s.
8. other disciples came in little s.
Ac. 20 : 13. we went before to s.
38. they accompanied him unto s.
21 : 2. a s. sailing unto Phenicia
3. s. was to unlade her burden
6. had taken our leave, we took s.
27 : 2. entering s. of Adramyttium
6. then centurion found a s.
10. damage of lading and of s.
11. centurion believed owner of s.
15. s. was caught, and could not
17. used helps, undergird-g the s.
18. next day they lightened s., 38.
19. we cast out tackling of s.
22. be no loss of life, but of s.
30. shipmen about to flee out of s.
31. except these abide in the s.
37. we were in all in s. 276 souls
39. if possible to thrust in the s.
41. they ran the s. aground
44. some on broken pieces of s.
28 : 11. departed in s. of Alexandria

SHIP boards.

Eze. 27 : 5. made all thy s.b. of fir
[trees

SHIPS.

Ge. 49 : 13. Zebulun be haven for s.
Nu. 24 : 24. s. shall come fr. Chittim
De. 28 : 68. L. shall bring thee wi. s.
Ju. 5 : 17. why did Dan remain in s.?
1 K. 9 : 26. Solomon made navy of s.
22 : 48. made s. of Tharshish go to
Ophir, s. broken, 2 Ch. 20 : 36, 37.
49. Let my servants go in the s.
2 Ch. 8 : 18. Huram sent him s.
9 : 21. king's s. went to Tarshish
Jb. 9 : 26. are passed away as swift s.
Ps. 48 : 7. breakest s. of Tarshish
104 : 26. There go the s. there is
107 : 23. that go down to sea in s.
Pr. 31 : 14. She is like the merch-ts' s.
Is. 2 : 16. day of L. upon s. of Tarsh.
23 : 1. Howl, ye s. of Tarshish, 14.
43 : 14. Chaldeans, whose cry is in s.
60 : 9. the s. of Tarshish first
Eze. 27 : 9. all s. of sea wi. mariners
25. s. of Tarshish did sing of thee
29. Pilots shall come from their s.
30 : 9. messengers go from me in s.
Da. 11 : 30. s. of Chittim shall come
40. king of north sh. come with s.
Mk. 4 : 36. with him other little s.
Lu. 5 : 2. saw two s. stand-g by lake
3. he entered one of the s., Simon's
7. filled both s. they began to sink
11. when had bro-t their s. to land
Ja. 3 : 4. s., tho. so great, are turned
Re. 8 : 9. third part of s. destroyed
18 : 17. company in s. stood afar off
19. were made rich all that had s.

SHI'PHI.

1 Ch. 4 : 37. Ziza, the son of S, son of

SHIPH'MITE.

1 Ch. 27 : 27. over wine cellars, Zab-
[di, S.

SHIPH'RAH.

Ex. 1 : 15. midwives, one S., other
[Puah

SHIPH'TAN.

Nu. 34 : 24. prince of Kemuel, son of S.

SHIPMASTER. [sleeper?

Jon. 1 : 6. s. said, What meanest, O
Re 18 : 17. every s. and sailors cried

SHIPMEN. [edge

1 K. 9 : 27. Hiram sent s. had knowl-
Ac. 27 : 27. s. deemed they drew near
30. as s. about to flee out of ship

SHIPPING. [um

Jn. 6 : 24. took s., came to Caperna-

SHIPWRECK. [s.

2 Co. 11 : 25. stoned, thrice suffered
1 Ti. 1 : 19. concerning faith, made s.

SHIRTS.

Ju. 14 : † 12. I will give you thirty s.

SHI'SHA. [18 : † 16.

1 K. 4 : 3. sons of S., scribes, 1 Ch.

SHI'SHAK. [12 : 2.

1 K. 14 : 25. S., king of Egypt, 2 Ch.
2 Ch. 12 : 5. princes were gath-d bec.
of S., I left you in hand of S.
7. wrath not be poured on Jerusalem by S. [of Lord
9. S. took away treasures of house

SHIT'RAI. See SHARON.

SHIT'TAH tree.

Is. 41 : 19. will plant in wildern. s.t.

SHIT'TIM.

Nu. 25 : 1. Israel abode in S., people
Jos. 2 : 1. out of S. two men to spy
3 : 1. they removed fr. S. to Jordan
Jo. 3 : 18. shall water valley of S.
Mi. 6 : 5. Balaam anew-d him fr. S.

SHIT'TIM wood. [35 : 7.

Ex. 25 : 5. badgers' skins and s.w.,
10. ark of s.w., 37 : 1. De. 10 : 3.
13. shalt make staves of s.w., 28.
-27 : 6. -30 : 5. -37 : 4, 15, 28. -38 : 6.
23. shalt make table of s.w., 37 : 10.
26 : 15. boards for taber. of s.w., 36 :
26. make bars of s.w., 36 : 31. [20.
32. pillars of s.w., 37. -36 : 36.
27 : 1. thou shalt make an altar of
s.w., 30 : 1. -37 : 25. -38 : 1.
35 : 24. man with whom was found
[s.w.

SHIVERS.

Re. 2 : 27. as vessels of potter be
broken to s.

SHI'ZA. [son of S.

1 Ch. 11 : 42. valiant men ; Adina,

SHO'A. [men

Eze. 23 : 23. S. : all desirable young

SHO'BAB.

2 S. 5 : 14. those born unto David in
Jerus., S., Sol-n, 1 Ch. 3 : 5. -14 : 4.
1 Ch. 2 : 18. Azubah, her sons ; S.

SHO'BACH, or SHO'PHACH

2 S. 10 : 16. S, captain of host, went,
1 Ch. 19 : 16. [Ch. 19 : 18.
18. David smote S., who died, 1

SHO'BAI. [Ne. 7 : 45.

Ezr. 2 : 42. Nethinim, children of S.,

SHO'BAL.

Ge. 36 : 20. sons of Seir, Horite ; S.
23. chil. of S., 1 Ch. 1 : 40 [29. duke S.
1 Ch. 2 : 50. S., father of Kirjath-jear-
4 : 1. the sons of Judah, S. [im, 52.
2. Reaiah, son of S., begat Jahath

SHO'BEK. See PILEHA.

SHO'BI. [beds

2 S. 17 : 27 S. son of Nahash bro-t

SHO'CHO, SHO'CHOH, SHO'CO, SO'CHOH, or SO'COH.

Jos. 15 : 35. cities in the valley Socoh
48. And in the mountains, Socoh
1 S. 17 : 1. Philistines gathered their
armies at Shochoh (2) [Socoh
1 K. 4 : 10. The son of Hesed ; to him
2 Ch. 11 : 7. cities for defence, Shoco
28 : 18. Philistines had taken Sho-
[cho

SHOCK, S.

Ju. 15 : 5. Samson burnt up the s-s
Jb. 5 : 26. like as a s. of corn cometh

SHOD. [them

2 Ch. 28 : 15. took captives and s.
Eze. 16 : 10. I s. thee with badgers'
Mk. 6 : 9. But be s. with sandals [skin
Ep. 6 : 15. s. with preparation of
[gospel

SHOE.

De. 25 : 9. bro.'s wife sh. loose his s.
10. house of him th. hath s. loosed
29 : 5. thy s. is not waxen old upon
Jos. 5 : 15. Loose thy s. from off foot
Ru. 4 : 7. plucked off his s. and gave
8. Buy it. So he drew off his s. [it
Ps. 60 : 8. ov. Edom I cast my s., 108 :
Is. 20 : 2. put off thy s. from foot [9.

SHOE'S latchet. [unl.

Jn. 1 : 27. whose s.l. I not worthy to

SHOES. [Ac. 7 : 33.
Ex. 3 : 5. put s. from off thy feet,
Ex. 12 : 11. eat it with s. on your feet
De. 33 : 25. s. sh. be iron and brass
Jos. 9 : 5. old s., and clouted upon
13. our s. old with long journey
1 K. 2 : 5. put the blood in his s.
Can. 7 : 1. beautiful thy feet with s.
Is. 5 : 27. nor latchet of s. be broken
11 : † 15. L. make men go over in s.
Eze. 24 : 17. put s. upon thy feet, 23.
Am. 2 : 6. sold the poor for pair of s.
8 : 6. may buy needy for pair of s.
Mat. 3 : 11. s. am not worthy to bear
10 : 10. provide neither s., Lu. 10:4.
Mk. 1 : 7. latchet of whose s. I am not worthy, Lu. 3:16. Ac. 13:25.
Lu. 15 : 22. ring on hand, s. on feet
22 : 35. I sent you without purse [and s.

SHOELATCHET.
Ge. 14 : 23. not take from thread to s.
See SHOE.

SHO'HAM.
1 Ch. 24 : 27. The sons of Merari; S.

SHO'MER, or SHA'MER.
1 Ch. 7 : 32. Heber begat Sho., † Sha.
34. † sons of Sha., Rohgah, Jehub- [bah
See SHIMRITH.

SHONE.
Ex. 34 : 29. wist not that his face s.
30. his face s., they afraid, 35.
2 K. 3 : 22. they rose early, sun s.
Lu. 2 : 9. glory of L. s. round them
Ac. 22 : 6, suddenly s. great light
Re. 8 : 12. day s. not for third part

SHOOK.
Ex. 14 : † 27. L. s. off Egypt-s in sea
2 S. 6 : 6 oxen s the ark, 1 Ch. 13: † 9.
22 : 8. the earth s., Ps. 18:7.-68:8.
-77 : 18. [God shake
Ne. 5 : 13. I s. my lap, and said, So
Is. 23 : 11. he s. the kingdoms [feet
Ac. 13:51. they s. off the dust of their
18 : 6. he s. his raiment, and said
28 : 5 he s. off beast into the fire
He. 12 : 26. Whose voice s. the earth

SHOOT.
Ex. 26 : 33. he made middle bar to s.
1 S. 20 : 36. find out arrows wh. I s.
2 S. 11 : 20. knew ye not they wo. s.?
2 K. 13 : 17. Elisha said, s. And he
1 Ch. 5 : 18. men able to s. wi. bow
Ps 11 : 2. may privily s. at upright
22 : 7. they s. out lip, shake head
64 : 4. may s. in secret at perfect
7. God sh. s. at them with arrow
Je. 50 : 14. that bend bow, s. at her
Eze. 31 : 14. nei. s. up top am. boughs
36 : 8. ye shall s. forth branches
Lu. 21:30. When th. s. forth, ye know
See ARROW, ARROWS.

SHOOTERS.
2 S. 11 : 24. s. shot from wall upon [serv-s

SHOOTETH.
Jb. 8 : 16. branch s. forth in garden
Is. 27 : 8. In measure when it s. forth
Mk. 4 : 32. mustard seed s. out great [branches

SHOOTING.
1 Ch. 12 : 2. co. use right and left in s.
Am. 7 : 1. in s. up of latter growth

SHO'PHACH. See SHOBACH.

SHO'PHAN.
Nu. 32 : 35. children of Gad built S.

SHORE.
Jos. 15 : 2. border from s. of salt sea
1 K. 9 : 26. Eloth, on s. of Red sea
Mat. 13 : 2. multitude stood on the s.
48. it was full, they drew to s. [s.
Mk. 6 : 53. of Gennes-t, and drew to
Jn. 21 : 4. morning, Jesus stood on s.
Ac. 21 : 5. we kneeled on s., prayed
27 : 39. discovered creek with a s.
40. hoised mainsail, made tow. s.
See **SEA shore.**

SHORN. [even s.
Can. 4 : 2. teeth like sheep that are
Na. 1 : † 12. so sho. they have been s.
Ac. 18:18. having s. his head in [be s.
1 Co. 11 : 6. wom. be s.: if a shame to

SHORT.
Nu. 11 : 23. Is the L.'s hand waxed s.
2 K. 19 : † 26. The inhabitants were s. of hand, Is. 37 : † 27. [trouble
Jb. 14 : † 1. man is s. of days, full of
17 : 12. light is s. bec. of darkness
20 : 5. triumphing of wicked is s.
Ps. 89 : 47. Rememb. how s. my time
Pr. 14 : † 29. s. of spirit exalteth folly
Ro. 3 : 23. all have come s. of glory
9 : 28. a s. work will Lord make on
1 Co. 7 : 29. brethren, the time is s.
1 Th. 2 : 17. taken fr. you for s. time
Re. 12 : 12. knoweth he hath s. time
17 : 10. ye must continue s. space
See **COME short, CUT short.**

SHORTENED.
Nu. 21 : † 4. soul of people much s.
Ju. 10 : † 16. soul was s. for misery
16 : † 16. his soul was s. unto death
Jb. 21 : † 4. why not my spirit be s.
Ps. 89 : 45. days of his youth hast s.
102 : 23. my strength, he s. my days
Pr. 10 : 27. years of wicked sh. be s.
Is. 50 : 2. Is my hand s. at all, that
59 : 1. The Lord's hand is not s.
Mi. 2 : † 7. is the Spirit of the Lord s.
Mat. 24 : 22. except those days be s., but for elect's sake s., Mk. 13:20.

SHORTER.
Is. 28 : 20. bed is s. than th. a man [s.
Eze. 42 : 5. the upper chambers were

SHORTLY.
Ge. 41 : 32. G. will s. bring it to pass
Je. 27 : 16. vessels s. be brought from
Eze. 7 : 8. will I s. pour out my fury
Ac. 25 : 4. that he would depart s.
Ro. 16 : 20. G. of peace bruise Sat. s.
1 Co. 4 : 19. I will come to you s., if
Ph. 2 : 19. I trust to send Timoth. s.
24. I trust th. I also shall come s.
1 Ti. 3 : 14. I write, hoping to come
2 Ti. 4 : 9. Do diligence to come s. [s.
He. 13 : 23. if he come s. I will see
2 Pe. 1 : 14. s. I must put off my tab.
3 Jn. 14. I trust I shall s. see thee
Re. 1 : 1. must s. come to pass, 22: 6.

SHORTNESS. [spirit
Ex. 6 : † 9 hearkened not for s. of

SHOT. [Noun.]
Je. 6 : † 6. Hew down trees, pour out engine of s., Eze. 26 : † 8.
32 : † 24. Behold, engines of s. come
See BOWSHOT.

SHOT. [Verb.]
Ge. 40 : 10. her blossoms s. forth
49 : 23. archers s. at him, hated him
Ex. 19 : 13. he sh. be stoned or s.
Nu. 21 : 30. We have s. at th. [thro.
1 S. 20 : 37. arrow which Jona. had s.
2 S. 11 : 24. shooters s. from the wall
2 K. 13 : 17. Elisha said, Shoot, He s.
2 Ch. 35 : 23. archers s. at Josiah
Ps. 18 : 14. s. out lightnings, and
Je. 9 : 8. Their tongue is an arrow s.
Eze. 17 : 6. a vine, and s. forth sprigs
7. vine s. forth branches tow. him
31 : 5. of waters when he s. forth
10. he hath s. his top am. boughs

SHOULDER. [s.
Ge. 21:14. putting bread on Hagar's
24 : 15. pitcher upon her s., 45, 46.
49 : 15. Issachar bowed s. to bear
Ex. 29 : 27. sanctify s. of heave of. [3.
Nu. 6 : 19. sodden s. of ram, De. 18 :
34 : † 11. border, unto s. of sea
Jos. 4 : 5. take ev. man stone upon s.
Ju. 9 : 48. Abim. laid bough on his s.
1 S. 9 : 24. the cook took up the s.
10 : † 9. Saul had turned s. to go
1 K. 6 : † 8. door was in right s. of ho.
7 : † 39. bases on right s. of house
2 K. 11 : † 11. guard with his weapons fr. the right s., 2 Ch. 23: † 10.
Ne. 9 : 29. withdrew s., hardened
Jb. 31 : 36. I wo. take it upon my s.
Ps. 21 : † 12. make them turn th. ir s.
81 : 6. I removed his s. from burden
Is. 9 : 4. hast broken staff of his s.
6. government sh. be upon his s.
10 : 27. burden be taken fr. thy s.
22 : 22. key of Da. will I lay upon his
46 : 7. They bear him upon s. [s.
Eze. 12 : 7. I bare it upon my s.
12. prince shall bear upon his s.
24 : 4. gather pieces, the thigh and
25 : † 9. I will open s. of Moab [s.
29 : 7. thou didst rend their s., 18.
34 : 21. ye thrust with side and s.
Ho. 6 : † 9. priests murder wi. one s.
Zph. 3 : † 9. to serve Lord with one s.
Zch. 7 : 11. they pulled away the s.

SHOULDER blade.
Jb. 31 : 22. let mine arm fall fr. s. b.

Heave SHOULDER. [20.
Le. 7 : 34. h. s. have I taken, Nu. 6:
10 : 14. h. s. eat in a clean place
15. h. s. and wave breast sh. they

Right SHOULDER. [br.
Ex. 29 : 22. shalt take of ram r. s.
Le. 7 : 32. r. s. give unto the priest
33. offereth, shall have the r. s.
8 : 25. Moses took the fat and r. s.
26. put cake and wafer upon r. s.
9 : 21. r. s. waved is thine, Nu. 18:18.

SHOULDERS.
Ge. 9:23. laid garment upon their s.
Ex. 12 : 34. troughs bound upon s.
28 : 12. stones on s. of ephod, 39:7.
Nu. 7 : 9. of Kohath, bear upon s.
De. 33 : 12. he sh. dwell betw. his s.
Ju. 16 : 3. Sams. took bar upon his s.
1 S. 9:2. fr. s. upward higher, 10 : 23.
17:6. he had a target between his s.
1 Ch. 15:15. Levites bare ark upon s.
2 Ch 35:3. not a burden upon y-r s.
Is. 11 : 14. sh. fly upon s. of Philis.
14 : 25. his burden from their s.
30 : 6. carry riches upon s. of asses
49:22. dau-s be carried upon th-r s.
Eze. 12 : 6. shall bear it upon thy s.
Mat. 23 :4. burdens, lay th. on men's
Lu. 15:5. layeth it on his s. rejoicing [s.

SHOULDERPIECES.
Ex. 28 : 7. ephod shall have two s.,
39 : 4, 18. [ephod
25. put ends of chains on s. of

SHOUT. [Noun.]
Nu. 23 : 21. s. of a king is am. them
Jos. 6 : 5. peo. shouted with great s.,
1 S. 4 : 5. great s., so earth rang [20.
6. What meaneth this great s.?
2 Ch. 13 : 15. men of Judah gave a s.
Ezr. 3 : 11. a gr. s. when they praised Lord, peo. shouted with loud s.
13. could not discern s. of joy from
Ps. 47 : 5. God is gone up with s.
Je. 25 : 30. Lord shall give a s. as
51 : 14. shall lift a s. against Bab-n
Ac. 12 : 22. peo. gave s., saying, voice
1 Th. 4 : 16. L. shall descend with a

SHOUT. [Verb.] [s.
Ex. 32 : 18. them that s. for mastery
Jos. 6 : 5. hear trumpet, all shall s.
10. shall not s. till I bid you s., then shall ye s. [you city
16. s., for the Lord hath given
Ps. 47 : 1. s. unto God with triumph
Is. 12 : 6. s., thou inhabitant of Zion
42 : 11. let them s. from top of mts.
44 : 23. s., ye lower parts of earth
Je. 31 : 7. s. among chief of nations
50 : 15. Bab. had sinned, s. ag. her
La. 3 : 8. I s., he shutteth out prayer
Zph. 3 : 14. s., O Israel, be glad
Zch. 9 : 9, s., O daughter of Jerusa.
See **Shout, ed for JOY.**

SHOUTED.
Ex 32 : 17. as peo. s., Joshua said
Le. 9 : 24. when fire consumed, they s.
Jos. 6 : 20. people s. when priests
Ju. 15 : 14. Philistines s. ag. Samson

1 S. 4 : 5. all Israel s. because of ark
10 : 24. people s., G. save the king
17 : 20. as host going s. for battle
52. men of Israel and Judah s.
2 Ch. 13 : 15. as Judah s., God smote
Ezr. 3 : 11. when praised Lord they s.
13. the people s. with a loud shout

SHOUTETH.

Ps. 78 : 65. like mighty man that s.

SHOUTING, S. [15:28.

2 S. 6 : 15. bro-t up ark with s., 1 Ch.
2 Ch. 15 : 14. sware unto Lord wi. s.
Jb. 8 : † 21. he fill thy lips with s.
39 : 25. he smelleth battle, and the s.
Ps. 27 : † 6. will I offer sacrifice of s.
Pr. 11 : 10. when wicked perish is s.
Is. 16 : 9. s., for summer fruits is, 10.
Je. 20 : 16. let th. hear s. at noontide
48 : 33. none shall tread with s.,
their s. shall be no s. [s.
Eze. 21 : 22. to lift up the voice with
Am. 1 : 14. sh. devour Rabbah wi. s.
2 : 2. Moab sh. die with tumult, s.
Zch. 4 : 7. sh. bring headstone wi. s-e

SHOVEL.

Is. 30 : 24. hath been winnowed with

SHOVELS. [13.

Ex. 27 : 3. sh. make his pans and s.,
38 : 3. he made the pots and the s.
Nu. 4 : 14. put upon purple cloth s.
1 K. 7 : 40. Hiram made the lavers,
the s., 45. 2 Ch. 4 : 11, 16.
2 K. 25 : 14. pots and s. he took away,

SHOW. [Je. 52 : 18.

Na. 2 : † 4. their s. like torches

SHOWER.

Eze. 13 : 11. sh. be overflow-g, s., 13.
34 : 26. I will cause s. in his season
Lu. 12 : 54. ye say, There cometh a s.

SHOWERS.

De. 32 : 2. my speech sh. distil as s.
Ezr. 10 : † 9. peo sat in streets bec.
Jb. 24 : 8. poor are wet with s. [of s.
Ps. 65 : 10. makest earth soft with s.
72 : 6. king shall come like s. [en
Je. 3 : 3. Thf. s. have been withhold-
14 : 22. or can the heavens give s.?
Eze. 34 : 26. in season s. of blessing
Mi. 5 : 7. Jac. sh. be as s. upon grass
Zch. 10 : 1. Lord shall give them s.

SHRANK.

Ge. 32 : 32. Isr. eat not of sinew th. s.

SHRED. [tage

2 K. 4 : 39. s. wild gourds into pot-

SHRILL.

Is. 10 : † 30. Cry s., O dau. of Gallim

SHRINES.

Ac. 19 : 24. Demetrius made silver s.

SHROUD.

Eze. 31 : 3. Assyrian a cedar with s.

SHRUBS.

Ge. 21 : 15. Hagar cast child under s.

SHU'A, or SHU'AH. [32.

Ge. 25 : 2. Keturah bare S., 1 Ch. 1 :
38 : 2. Judah married daughter of a
Canaanite named S., 12. 1 Ch. 2 : 3.
1 Ch. 4 : 11. Chelub, bro. of S., begat
7 : 32. Heber begat Hotham and S.

SHU'AL. [Person.]

1 Ch. 7 : 36. sons of Zophah, Suah, S.

SHU'AL. [Place.] [of S.

1 S. 13 : 17. spoilers turned unto land

SHU'BAEL.

1 Ch. 24 : 20. Of the sons of Amram, S.
25 : 20. thirteenth, lot came to S.

SHU'HAM, ITES.

Ge. 46 : † 23. the sons of Dan ; S. S-s
Nu. 26 : 42. of S., the family of the
43. All the families of S-s, 64,400

SHU'HITE. See BILDAD.

SHU'LAMITE.

Can. 6 : 13. Return, O S. What will
ye see in the S.?

SHU'MATHITES. [im, S.

1 Ch. 2 : 53. families of Kirjath-jear-

SHUN, SHUNNED. [of G.

Ac. 20 : 27. not s-d to declare counsel
2 Ti. 2 : 16. But s. profane babblings

SHU'NAMMITE.

1 K. 1 : 3. a fair damsel, Abishag, a S.
1 : 15. Abishag, S., ministered
2 : 17. give me Abishag, S., to wife
21. Let Ab-g, S., be given Adonij.
22. why ask Ab-g S. for Adonijah?
2 K. 4 : 12. said to Gehazi, Call this
25. Behold, yonder is th. S. [S., 36.

SHU'NEM.

Jos. 19 : 18. their border was tow. S.
1 S. 28 : 4. Philis. came, pitched in S.
2 K. 4 : 8. Elisha passed to S., where

SHU'NI, SHU'NITES.

Ge. 46 : 16. sons of Gad, Ziphion, S.
Nu. 26 : 15. of S., the family of S-s

SHUNNED. See SHUN.

SHU'PHAM, ITES.

See SHEPHUPHAN.

SHUP'PIM. [lot came

1 Ch. 26 : 16. To S. and Hosah the
See SHEPHUPHAN.

SHUR. [S.

Ge. 16 : 7. by the fountain in way to
20 : 1. Ab. dwelt betw. Kadesh and S.
25 : 18. Ish. dwelt fr. Havilah unto S.
Ex. 15 : 22. Isr went into wildern. of S.
1 S. 15 : 7. Saul smote Amalekites to S.
27 : 8. land, as thou goest to S.

SHU'SHAN. [unto S.

Es 2 : 8. many maidens were gath-d
3 : 15. the city S. was perplexed
4 : 16. gather all Jews in S., and fast
8 : 15. city of S. rejoiced and was
9 : 11. number slain in S. was bro-t
15. Jews slew in S. 300 men [to k-g
See PALACE.

SHUT.

Ge. 7 : 16. went in, Lord s. him in
Ex. 14 : 3. wilderness s. them in
Nu. 12 : 14. let her be s. from camp
15. Miriam was s. out from camp
24 : † 3. man who had his eyes s.
De. 15 : 7. nor s. hand from poor bro.
Jos. 2 : 7. they s. the gate of Jericho
Ju. 3 : † 15 Ehud was s. of right ha.
9 : 51. they s. the tower to them
1 S. 23 : 7. he is s. in, by ent-g town
Ne. 13 : 19. I com-ded gates to be s.
Ps. 69 : 15. let not the pit s. upon me
Is. 6 : 10. s. their eyes, lest they see
22 : 22. he shall open, none shall s.,
he shall s., none shall open
44 : 18. for he hath s. their eyes
45 : 1. and gates shall not be s.
52 : 15. kings shall s. mouths at him
60 : 11. thy gates shall not be s.
66 : 9. shall I s. womb, saith God?
Eze. 3 : 24. Spirit said, Go, s. thyself
44 : 1. gate toward the east was s.
2. this gate shall be s., God hath
entered, theref. it shall be s.
46 : 1. gate sh. be s. 6 working days
2. gate sh. not be s. until evening
12. after his going, one sh. s. gate
Da. 6 : 22. God hath s. lions' mouths
Ac. 5 : 23. prison truly found we s.
Re. 11 : 6. have power to s. heaven
21 : 25. gates shall not be s. by day
See DOOR, DOORS, with shut.

SHUT up.

Le. 13 : 4. priest shall s. him u. hath
plague, 5, 21, 26, 31, 33, 50, 54.
11. the priest shall not s. him u.
14 : 38. priest shall s. u. house 7 days
46. goeth in while house is s. u.
De. 11 : 17. he s. u. heav., th. no rain
32 : 30. except the L. had s. them u.
36. when he seeth is none s. u.
Jos. 6 : 1. when Jericho was s. u.
1 S. 1 : 5. L. had s. u. Han-h's womb
6. bec Lord had s. u. her womb
6 : 10. s. u. their calves at home
17 : † 46. this day will L. s. thee u.
23 : † 12. Will men of Keilah s. me u.?
24 : † 18. when Lord had s. me u.
26 : † 8. G. hath s. u. thine enemy
2 S. 18 : † 28. Blessed be L., who s. u.
20 : 3. concubines were s. u. to day
1 K. 6 : † 20. overlaid ark wi. s. u. gold
8 : 35. When heaven is s. u., if they
pray, 2 Ch. 6 : 26.-7 : 13.
14 : 10. I will cut off from Jerob.
him s. u., 21 : 21. 2 K. 9 : 8.
2 K. 14 : 26. there was not any s. u.
17 : 4. k-g of Assyria s. him u. [s. u.
1 Ch. 12 : † 1. came to Da., being yet
2 Ch. 9 : † 20. vessels of s. u. gold
Ne. 6 : 10. Shemaiah, who was s. u.
Jb. 11 : 10. If he s. u., who can hin.?
16 : † 11. G. s. me u. to the ungodly
41 : 15. His scales are s. u. together
Ps. 31 : 8. not s. me u. into hand of
77 : 9. hath he s. u. tender mercies?
78 : † 48. he s. u. also their cattle
88 : 8. I am s. u., I cannot come
Can. 4 : 12. a spring s. u., a fount-n
Is. 19 : † 4. s. u. into hand of a cruel
24 : 10. every house is s. u., no man
22. they shall be s. u. in prison
Je. 13 : 19. cities of south sh. be s. u.
20 : 9. word as fire s. u. in my bones
32 : 2. prophet was s. u., 3. [15.
33 : 1. word, while he was s. u., 39 :
36 : 5. I am s. u., I can-t go into ho.
Da. 8 : 26. Wheref. s. thou u. vision
12 : 4. thou, O Dan., s. u. the words
Ob. † 14. nei. s. u. those that remain
Mat. 23 : 13. ye s. u. kingd. of heaven
Lu. 3 : 20. he s. u. John in prison
4 : 25. heaven was s. u. three years
Ac. 26 : 10. many saints did I s. u.
Ro. 11 : † 32. s. them u. in unbelief
Ga. 3 : 23. s. u. unto the faith that
Re. 20 : 3. s. u. the devil, set a seal

SHU'THALHITES. [S.

Nu. 26 : 35. sons of Ephraim, fam. of

SHU'THELAH. [bites

Nu. 26 : 35. of S., family of Shuthal-
36. And these are the sons of S.
1 Ch 7 : 20. the sons of Ephraim ; S.
21 Zabad, his son, S., his son

SHUTTETH.

Jb. 12 : 14. he s. up a man, be no
Pr. 16 : 30. He s. his eyes to devise
17 : 28. s. lips is a man of underst-g
Is. 33 : 15. s. his eyes fr. seeing evil
La. 3 : 8. I cry, he s. out my prayer
1 Jn. 3 : 17. s. up bowels of compas-n
Re. 3 : 7. openeth, no man s., and s.

SHUTTING.

Jos. 2 : 5. about time of s. the gate

SHUTTLE.

Jb. 7 : 6. days swifter th. weaver's s.

SI'A, SI'AHA. [7 : 47.†

Ezr. 2 : 44. †Nethinim ; chil. of S., Ne.

SIB'BECAI, SIB'BECHAI.

2 S. 21 : 18. S. slew Saph, 1 Ch. 20 : 4.
1 Ch. 11 : 29. valiant men, S., Hush-e
27 : 11. The 8th capt. for 8th mo., S.

SIB'BOLETH.

Ju. 12 : 6. Say Shibboleth. He said S.

SIB'MAH.

Jos 13 : 19. their coast was from S.
Is. 16 : 8. fields languish, vine of S.
9. vine of S. ; I will water thee
Je. 48 : 32. O vine of S. I will weep

SIB'RAIM. [mascus

Eze. 47 : 16. S., betw. border of Da-

SI'CHEM, SY'CHEM.

Ge. 33 : † 18. Jac. came to city of Sy.
Ge. 12 : 6. Ab. passed thro. land unto Si.
Ac. 7 : 16. And were carried over un-
to Sy., Emmor, father of Sy.
See SECHEM.

SICK. [s.

Ge. 48 : 1. told Joseph, thy father is
Le. 15 : 33. that is s. of her flowers
De. 29 : † 22 Lord hath made it s.
1 S. 19 : 14. sent, she said, He is s.
30 : 13. master left me, bec. I fell s.
2 S. 12 : 15. L. struck child, it was s.
13 : 2. Amnon vexed, fell s. for Ta-r
5. Jonadab said, make thyself s.

2 S.13 : 6. So Amnon made himself s.
1 K. 14 : 1. Abijah son of Jerob. fell s.
5. wife of Jerob. for son, he is s.
17 : 17. the son of the woman fell s.
1K. 22 : † 34. Carry me out, for I am
made s., 2 Ch. 18 : †33.-35 : †23.
2 K. 1 : 2. Ahaziah fell thro. lattice,
8:7. Ben-hadad k. of Syria s.⌊was s.
29. to see Joram, was s., 2Ch. 22:6.
13 : 14. Elisha was fallen s. of sickn.
20 : 1. was Hezekiah s. unto death,
2 Ch. 32:24. Is. 38:1. ⌈Is. 39:1.
12. heard Hezekiah had been s.,
2 Ch: 18 : † 33. carry me out of the
host, for I am made s., 35 : † 23.
Ne. 2 : 2. Why sad : thou art not s.?
Ps. 35 : 13. when they s., my cloth-g
41 : † 1. Blessed is he considereth s.
Pr. 13 : 12. Hope deferred, heart s.
23 : 35. stricken me, and I was not s.
Can. 2 : 5. comfort me, I am s. of love
5 : 8. I tell him that I am s. of love
Is. 1 : 5. whole head is s., heart faint
33 : 24. inhabitant not say, I am s.
38 : 9. when Hezek. had been s. and
Je. 14 : 18. that are s. with famine
Eze. 34 : 4. nei. healed th. wh. was s.
16. will strengthen that wh. was s.
Da. 8 : 27. I, Dan., fainted, and was s.
Ho. 7 : 5. princes made him s. wi wine
Mi. 1: †9. she grievously s. of wounds
6 : 13. make thee s. in smiting thee
Mal. 1 : 8. if ye offer s., is it not evil?
13. ye brought th. torn, and the s.
Mat. 4 : 24. bro-t unto him all s. peo.
8 : 14. Peter's wife's mother s. of a
fever, Mk. 1 : 30. ⌈Mk. 1 : 34.
16. healed all that were s., 14 : 14.
9 : 12. whole need not a physician,
but they s., Mk. 2:17. Lu. 5:31.
10 : 8. Heal the s., cleanse the lepers, Lu. 9 : 2.-10 : 9. ⌈43.
25 : 36. I was s., and ye visited me,
39. when saw we thee s. in prison? 44 ⌈a few s. folk, Ac. 5 : 16.
Mk. 6 : 5. th. he laid his hands upon
13. anointed wi. oil many th. were s.
55. carry about in beds those s.
56. they laid s. in streets, Ac. 5:15.
16 : 18. lay hands on s., they recover
Lu. 4 : 40. all that had s. bro-t them
7 : 2. centurion's servant was s.
10. found serv-t whole had been s.
Jn. 4 : 46. a nobleman's son was s.
11 : 1. man was s. named Lazarus, 2.
3. Lord, he whom thou lovest is s.
6. heard he was s., abode two days
Ac. 9 : 37. Dorcas was s., and died
19 : 12. bro-t unto s. handkerchiefs
28 : 8. the father of Publius lay s.
Ph. 2 : 26. ye heard th. he had been s.
27. For he was s. nigh unto death
1 Ti. 6 : † 4. he is s. about questions
2 Ti. 4 : 20. Trophimus have I left s.
Ja. 5 : 14. any s., let him call elders
15. prayer of faith shall save the s.
See PALSY.

SICKLE.

De. 16 : 9. beginnest to put s. to corn
23 : 25. not move a s. unto thy
neighbour's standing corn
Je. 50 : 16. cut off him handleth s.
Jo. 3 : 13. Put in s., harvest is ripe
Mk. 4 : 29. immediately putteth in s.
Re. 14 : 14. and in his hand sharp s.
15. Thrust in thy sharp s., 16, 18.
17. ano. angel, hav-g a sharp s.⌊19.
18. cried to him that had sharp s.

SICKLY. ⌈s.

1 Co. 11 : 30. For this cause many are

SICKNESS, ES.

Ex. 23 : 25. I will take s. aw. fr. thee
Le. 20 : 18. if lie with wom. having s,
De. 7 : 15. L. will take from thee all s.
28 : 59. sore s-s of long continuance
61. every s. not written in this law
29 : 22. when they see the s-s L. laid

1 K. 8 : 37. whatsoever s., 2 Ch. 6:28.
17 : 17. s. was so sore, was no breath
2 K. 13 : 14. Elisha sick of s., he died
2 Ch. 21 : 15. thou shalt have great
s. by reason of the s. day by day
19. bowels fell out by reason of s.
Ps. 41 : 3. wilt make all his bed in s.
Ec. 5 : 17. much sorrow with his s.
Is. 38 : 9. Hezek. was recovered of s.
12. will cut me off with pining s.
Ho. 5 : 13. When Ephraim saw his s.
Mat. 4 : 23. Jesus went about healing all manner of s., 9 : 35. ⌈s-s
8 : 17. spoken, say-g, Hims. bare our
10 : 1. power to heal all s., Mk. 3:15.
Jn. 11 : 4. said, This s. is not unto

Vale of SID'DIM. ⌊death

Ge. 14 : 3. All are joined in v. o. S.
8. they joined battle in v. o. S.
10. v. o. S. was full of slimepits

SIDE. ⌈s.

Ge. 6 : 16. door of ark sh. set in the
Ex. 2:5. maidens walked by river's s.
26 : 20. for sec. s. of tabern. 20 b-ds
35. candlest. on s. of tab., 40 : 24.
28 : 26. is s. of ephod inward, 39:19.
32 : 26. Who is on the Lord's s.? let
27. put every man sword by his s.
36 : 11. in uttermost s. of curtain
40:22. table upon s. of taber. northw.
Le. 1 : 11. shall kill it on s. of altar
15. blood wrung out at s. of altar
5 : 9. blood sprinkled on s. of altar
Nu. 3 : 29. pitch on s. of tabern., 35.
32 : 19. not inherit on yond. s. Jor.
De. 31 : 26. book of law in s. of ark
Jos. 5 : 1. all kings on s. of Jordan
15 : 10. border unto s. of m-t Jearim
11. border went unto s. of Ekron
18 : 12. border went to s. of Jericho
16. border to s. of Jebusi on south
18. passed tow. s., ov. ag. Arabah
19. passed to s. of Beth-hoglah
Ju. 19 : 1. a Levite on s. of Ephr., 18.
1 S. 4 : 18. Eli fell by s. of the gate
6 : 8. mice in coffer by s. of ark⌈th-f
20 : 20. I will shoot 3 arrows on s.
25. and Abner sat by Saul's s.
2 S. 2 : 16. sword into his fellow's s.
13 : 34. people came by way of hill s.
16 : 13. Shimei went on the hill s.
1 K. 7 : 30. molten at s. of addition
10 : 19. stays on eit. s., 2 Ch. 9 : 18.
2K. 9:32. Jehu said, Who is on my s.?
1Ch. 12:18. Thine are we, D., on thy s.
2Ch. 11:12. Judah and Benj. on his s.
Ne. 4 : 18. ev. one had sword by his s.
Jb. 18 : 12. destruc-n ready at his s.
Ps. 91 : 7. thousand sh. fall at thy s.
118 : 6. The Lord is on my s., I will
124 : 1. If not been Lord on our s., 2.
Ec. 4 : 1. on s. of oppressors power
Is. 60 : 4. dau-s be nursed at thy s.
Je. 25 : † 22. kings of region by sea s.
41 : † 9. had slain by s. of Gedaliah
52 : 23. were 96 pomegranates on a s.
Eze. 4 : 8. not turn thee fr. one s. to
9. days shalt lie upon thy s. ⌊ano.
9 : 2. writer's inkhorn by s., 3, 11.
25 : 9. I will open the s. of Moab
34 : 21. Bec. ye have thrust with s.
40 : 18. pavement by s. of the gates
40. at s. without, as one goeth (2)
41. by the s. of gate; eight tables
44. wh. was at s. of gate (2) 46:19.
Da. 7 : 5. it raised up itself on one s.
11 : 17. she shall not stand on his s.
Mk. 10 : 1. Jesus came by farther s. of
Jn. 19 : 18. thieves, on either s. one
34. one of soldiers pierced his s.
20 : 20. he shewed unto them his s.
25. Except I thrust my hand into s.
27. reach hand, thrust into my s.
Ac. 12 : 7. angel smote Pet. on the s.

SIDE chamber, s. ⌈cubits

Eze. 41 : 5. breadth of every s. c. 4
6. the s. c-s were three, one ov. (2)

Eze. 41:7. wind-g about upw-d to s. c-s
8. foundations of s. c-s were a reed
9. thickness of wall for s. c-s five
11. doors of s. c-s were toward⌈c-s
26. narrow windows upon the s.

East SIDE. ⌈50 cubits

Ex. 27 : 13. breadth of court on e. s.
38 : 13. for e. s. hangings 50 cubits
Nu. 2 : 3. on e. s. shall Judah pitch
34 : 11. go to Riblah on e. s. of Ain
35 : 5. meas. on the e. s. 2,000 cub.
Jos. 7 : 2. men to Ai on e. s. of Bethel
16 : 5. border of inheritance on e. s.
18 : 20. Jordan was border on e. s.
Ju. 11 : 18. Isr. came by e. s. of Moab
21 : 19. feast of L. on e. s. of highw.
1 Ch. 4 : 39. went unto e. s. of valley
6 : 78. on e. s. of Jordan were given
Eze. 11 : 23. upon mt. on e. s. of city
42 : 9. und. chambers entry on e. s.
16. He measured the e. s. wi. reed
45 : 7. city from e. s. eastward ⌈e. s.
47 : 18. e. s. ye sh. measure, This is
48 : 16. measures; on e. s. 4,500, 32.
Jon. 4 : 5. Jonah sat on e. s. of city
See West SIDE.

Every SIDE. ⌈on e. s.

Nu. 16 : 27. fr. tabernacle of Abiram
Ju. 7 : 18. blow ye trumpets, on e. s.
8:34. L. deliv-d th. on e. s., 1S. 12:11.
1 S. 14 : 47. S. fought enemies on e.
1 K. 5 : 3. wars about him on e. s.⌊s.
4. Lord given me rest on e. s.
1Ch. 22 : 18. not giv. you rest on e. s.?
2 Ch. 14 : 7. given us rest on e. s.
32 : 22. Lord guided them on e. s.
Jb. 1 : 10. put hedge about all on e.
18 : 11. make him afraid on e. s. ⌊s.
19 : 10. He destroyed me on e. s.
Ps. 12 : 8. The wicked walk on e. s.
31 : 13. fear was on e. s. while they
65 : 12. little hills rejoice on e. s.
71 : 21. shalt comfort me on e. s.
Je. 6 : 25. fear is on e. s., 20:10.-49:29.
Eze. 16 : 33. come unto thee on e. s.
19 : 8. nations set ag. him on e. s.
23 : 22. I bring them ag. thee on e.
28 : 23. sword upon her on e. s. ⌊s.
36 : 3. they swallowed you on e. s.
37 : 21. I will gather them on e. s.
39 : 17. gather to my sacri. on e. s.
41 : 5. round about ho. on e. s., 10.
Lu. 19 : 43. shall keep thee in on e. s.
2 Co. 4 : 8. We are troubled on e. s.,

Left SIDE. ⌊7 : 5.

1 K. 7 : 39. five bases on l. s. of hou.
49. five candlesticks on the l. s.
2 Ch. 23 : 10. weapon fr. right to l. s.
Eze. 1 : 10. had face of an ox on l. s.
4 : 4. Lie upon thy l. s., lay iniquity
Zch. 4 : 3. olive tree upon l. s., 11.

North SIDE. ⌈boards

Ex. 26 : 20. tabernacle on n. s., 20
35. thou shalt put table on n. s.
27 : 11. for n. s. hangings of 100
cubits long, 38 : 11.
Nu. 2 : 25. camp of Dan be on n. s.
35 : 5. measure on n. s. 2,000 cubits
Jos. 8 . 11. peo. pitched on n. s. of Ai
15 : 10. unto mount Jearim on n. s.
16:6. border to Michmethah on n. s.
17 : 9. of Manasseh, on n. s. of river
18 : 12. to side of Jericho on n. s. (2)
19 : 14. border on n. s. to Hanna-
27. tow. n. s. of Beth-emek ⌊thon
24 : 30. buried Joshua on n. s. of
the hill of Gaash, Ju. 2 : 9.
Ju. 7 : 1. Midianites were on n. s.
21 : 19. feast on n. s. of Beth-el ⌈alt.
2 K. 16 : 14. brazen altar on n. s. of
Eze. 42 : 17. measured n. s. 500 reeds
47 : 15. border tow. n. s. fr. great
17. And this is the n. s. ⌊sea
48 : 16. the measures on n. s. 4,500
30. goings out of city on the n. s.

On this SIDE.

Nu. 11 : 31. quails a day's jour. - s.

Nu. 22 : 1. pitched in Moab - s. Jordan, by Jericho, De. 1 : 1, 5.
1 S. 20 : 21. if I say, the arrows are -s.
1 K. 4 : 24. over region - s. river (2)
1 Ch. 26 : 30. 1,700 officers - s. Jord.
2 Ch. 20 : 2. mult-e ag. thee - s. Syria
Ezr. 4 : 10. rest that are - s. the riv., 11.
16. thou sh. have no portion - s.
5 : 3. Tatnai, governor - s. the riv.
6. - 6 : 13. - 8 : 36. [governor - s.
Ne. 3 : 7. repaired unto throne of
See **On this side JORDAN.**

On this SIDE, with on that SIDE.

Ex. 26 : 13. sh. hang over tabernacle - s. and - s. [cherub - s.
37 : 8. one cherub - s., another
Nu. 22 : 24. wall being - s., wall - s.
Jos. 8 : 22. midst of Isr., some - s., some - s. [- s.
33. Isr. and judges stood, - s., and
1 S. 23 : 26. Saul - s. of mt., Da. - s.
Eze. 1 : 23. 2 which cov-d - s., 2 - s.
40 : 10. little chambers of the gate were, 3 - s., 3 - s. (2), 21. [- s. (2)
12. chambers one cubit - s., one
26. had palm trees, one - s. another - s. [- s., 37.
34. palm trees upon posts - s., and
39. were 2 tables - s., 2 tables - s.
41. Four tables - s., 4 - s. by side
48. each post 5 cubits - s., 5 - s. (2)
49 pillars by posts, one - s., another - s. [grow
47 : 12. by river - s. and - s. shall
Da. 12 : 5. one - s.. other - s. of river
Zch. 5 : 3 th. stealeth, be cut off as - s., and ev. one th. sweareth as

The other SIDE. [- s.

Nu. 11 : 31. a day's journey on - s.
21 : 13. From thence pitched on - s. of Arnon, Ju. 11 : 18.
Jos. 24 : 2. fathers dwelt on - s. of flood, 3, 14, 15.
1 S. 14 : 1. Philis. garrison on - s.
40. I am Jonathan, will be on - s.
26 : 13. David went over to - s.
31 : 7. men of Isr. on - s. of valley (2)
2 K. 3 : 22. water on - s. red as blood
Eze. 40 : 40. on - s. at gate 2 tables
Ob. 11. In day thou standest on - s.
Mat. 8 : 18. com-t to depart into - s.
28. he was come to - s., Mk. 5 : 21.
14 : 22. his disciples to go before him unto - s., Mk. 4 : 35. [- s.
16 : 5. when disciples were come to
Mk. 5 : 1. they came over unto - s.
6 : 45. his disciples to go to - s.
8 : 13. into ship, he departed to - s.
Lu. 8 : 22. Let us go unto - s. of lake
10 : 31. priest passed by on - s., 32.
Jn. 6 : 22. peo. which stood on - s. of
25. had found him on - s. [sea
See **On the other side JORDAN.**

One SIDE with the other.

1 K. 7 : 7. porch with cedar fr. o.s. of floor to the o. [the o., 2 Ch. 9 : 19.
10 : 20. twelve lions on o.s. and on
Eze. 45 : 7. portion for prince on o. s. and on o., 48 : 21. [and on o.
47 : 7 bank of riv. many trees on o.s.

One SIDE, with the other SIDE.

Ex. 25 : 12. two rings shall be in o.s. and 2 rings in - s., 37 : 3. [27 : 9.
32. three branches of candlestick out of o.s., 3 out of - s., 37 : 18.
26 : 13. cub. on o.s. and cubits on - s.
27 : 14. the hangings of o.s. of gate 15 cubits, and on - s. 15 cubits, 15. - 38 : 14, 15. [tables written
32 : 15. on o.s. and on - s. were
1 S. 14 : 4. betw. passages was sharp rock on o.s., sharp rock on - s.
17 : 3. Philistines stood on o.s., and Israel stood on - s.

Eze. 41 : 1. measured posts 6 cubits on o.s., 6 cubits on - s.
2. door 5 cubits on o.s., 5 on - s.
15. galleries on o.s., on - s., 100 cu.
19. face of man o.s. of lion, - s.
26. palm trees on o.s. and on - s.
See **ONE with other.**
See **Side POSTS.**

Right SIDE.

2 S. 24 : 5. pitched in Aroer, on r.s.
1 K. 6 : 8. door was in r.s. of house
7 : 39. put 5 bases on r.s. of house; set sea on r.s., 2 Ch. 4 : 10.
49. 5 candlesticks on r.s., 2 Ch. 4 : 8.
2 K. 12 : 9. set it beside altar on r.s.
2 Ch. 23 : 10. fr. r.s. of temple to left
Eze. 1 : 10. had face of lion on r.s.
4 : 6. lie again on thy r.s., and shalt
10 : 3. the cherubim stood on r.s.
47 : 1. under r.s. of hou. waters, 2.
Zch. 4 : 3. olive trees, one on r.s., 11.
Mk. 16 : 5. men on r.s. of sepulchre
Lu. 1 : 11. angel on r.s. of altar
Jn. 21 : 6. Cast net on r.s. of ship
See RIVER, **SEA side.**

South SIDE.

Ex. 26 : 18. boards for tabernacle, twenty on s. s., 36 : 23. [38 : 9.
27 : 9. make court of tabern. for s.s.,
Nu. 2 : 10. on s.s. standard of Reub.
10 : 6. camps on s.s. go forward
35 : 5. measure on s.s. 2,000 cubits
Jos. 15 : 3. went to s.s. to Maaleh (2)
7. up to Adummim, on s.s. of riv.
8. unto s.s. of the Jebusite [horon
18 : 13 hill lieth on s.s. of Beth-
19 : 34. reacheth to Zebulon on s.s.
Eze. 42 : 18. measured s.s. 500 reeds
47 : 1. waters came at s.s. of altar
19. fr. Tamar, that is s.s., (2) 48 : 28.
48 : 16. the measures; the s.s., [4,500, 33.
See **WAY side.**

West SIDE.

Ex. 27 : 12. w.s. hangings of 50 cubits, 38 : 12. [Ephraim
Nu. 2 : 18. On the w. s. standard of
35 : 5. city on the w.s. 2,000 cubits
Jos. 8 : 9. lie in ambush on w.s., 12.
19 : 34. coast reacheth to Asher on the w.s. [to w.s.
2 Ch. 32 : 30. brought watercourse
33 : 14. built wall on w.s. of Gihon
Eze. 42 : 19. He turned about to w.s.
45 : 7. city from w.s. westward
47 : 20. w.s. shall be the gr. sea (2)
48 : 2. from the east side unto the w.s. a portion, 3, 4, 5, 6, 7, 8, 23, 24, 25, 26, 27. [s., 4,500, 34.
16. be the measures th-f; the w.

SIDES. [cle

Ex. 26 : 13. hang over s. of taberna-
22. for s. of tabern. sh. make, 36 : 27.
23. corners of tabern. in 2 s., 36 : 28.
27. bars for 2 s. westward, 36 : 32.
27 : 7. staves upon 2 s. of altar, 38 : 7.
28 : 27. put them on 2 s. of ephod, [39 : 20.
30 : 3. sh. overlay s., 37 : 26.
32 : 15. tables written on both s.
37 : 5. put rings by s. of ark [30 : 4
27. made 2 rings of gold upon 2 s.
Nu. 33 : 55. thorns in y-r s., Ju. 2 : 3.
Jos. 23 : 13. be scourges in your s.
Ju. 5 : 30. needlework on both s.
1 S. 24 : 3. David in s. of the cave
1 K. 4 : 24. Sol-n had peace on all s.
6 : 16. built 20 cubits on s. of house
2 K. 19 : 23. to s. of Leb-n, Is. 37 : 24.
Ps. 48 : 2. beautiful is Zion on s. of
128 : 3. wife as vine by s. of house
Is. 14 : 13. I will sit in s. of north
15. shall be brought to s. of pit
66 : 12. we sh. be borne upon her s.
Je. 6 : 22. gr. nation from s. of earth
48 : 28. her nest in s. of the holes
49 : 32. bring their calamity fr. all s.
Eze. 1 : 8. hands of man under wings on four s., 17. - 10 : 11.

Eze. 1 : 17. the wheels went upon their four s., 10 : 11.
32 : 23. graves are set in s. of pit
39 : † 2. to come up from s. of north
41 : 2. s. of door were five cubits
26. palm trees on s. of porch
42 : 20. He measured it by four s.
46 : 19. was a place on two s. west-d
48 : 1. these are his s. east and west
Da. 2 : † 32. his s. were of brass
Am. 6 : 10. him that is by s. of hou.
Jon. 1 : 5. Jonah down to s. of ship
Ha. 3 : † 4. bright beams out of his s.

SI'DON = ZI'DON. [Person.]

Ge. 10 : 15. Canaan begat S., 1 Ch. 1 : 13.

SI'DON = ZI'DON. [Place.] [Z.

Ge. 10 : 19. border of Canaanites fr. S.
Ju. 18 : 28. Laish was far from Z [S.
Mat. 11 : 21. if works been done in Tyre and S., Lu. 10 : 13. [Lu. 10 : 14.
22. more tolerable for Tyre and S.,
15 : 21. Jesus departed into coasts of Tyre and S., Mk. 7 : 24.
Mk. 3 : 8. they about Tyre and S. came, Lu. 6 : 17. [and S.
7 : 31. depart-g from coasts of Tyre
Lu. 4 : 26. unto Sarepta, city of S.
Ac. 12 : 20. Herod was displeased with them of Tyre and S.
27 : 3. next day we touched at S.
See ZIDON.

SIDO'NIANS. [Sirion

De. 3 : 9. Which Hermon the S. call
Jos. 13 : 4. all the land beside the S.
6. all the S. will I drive out
Ju. 3 : 3. five lords of Philis. and S.
1 K. 5 : 6. skill to hew timber like S.
See ZIDONIANS.

SIEGE.

De. 20 : 19. shalt not cut them in s.
28 : 53. shalt eat thy children in s.
55. nothing left him in s., 57.
1 K. 15 : 27. Isr. laid s. to Gibbethon
2 K. 24 : † 10. the city came into s.
2 Ch. 32 : 9. hims. laid s. ag. Lachish
10. Wh-n trust that ye abide in s.
Is. 29 : 3. I will lay s. against thee
Je. 19 : 9. eat flesh of friend in s.
Eze. 4 : 2. lay s. ag. it build fort, 3.
7. sh. set thy face tow. s. of Jerus.
8. till thou hast ended days of s.
5 : 2. when days of s. are fulfilled
Mi. 5 : 1. he hath laid s. against us
Na. 3 : 14. Draw thee waters for s.
Zch. 12 : 2. cup of trembling in the s.

SIEVE. [vanity

Is. 30 : 28. to sift nations wi. s. of
Am. 9 : 9. sift, as corn is sifted in a s.

SIFT, SIFTED.

Is. 30 : 28. to s. nations with sieve of
Am. 9 : 9. I will s. Isr. as corn is s-d
Lu. 22 : 31. Simon, Satan desired to [s. you

SIGH.

Is. 24 : 7. all merryhearted do s.
La. 1 : 4. priests, s. | 11. her peo. s.
21. They have heard that I s. [s.
Eze. 9 : 4. upon foreheads of men that
21 : 6. s. with breaking of thy loins, with bitterness s. bef. their eyes

SIGHED, EST, ETH. [age

Ex. 2 : 23. Isr. s. by reason of bond-
La. 1 : 8. she s-h, turneth backward
Eze. 21 : 7. they say, Whf. s-t thou?
Mk. 7 : 34. looking to heaven, he s-d
8 : 12. s-d deeply in his spirit and

SIGHING.

Jb. 3 : 24. my s. cometh before I eat
Ps. 12 : 5. for s. of needy will I arise
31 : 10. life wi. grief, my yrs. wi. s.
79 : 11. Let s. of prisoner come bef.
Is. 21 : 2. all s. have I made cease
35 : 10. sorrow and s. shall flee away
Je. 45 : 3. I fainted in my s., I find [no rest

SIGHS.

La. 1 : 22. my s. are many, heart faint

SIGHT, SIGHTS.

Ge. 2 : 9. every tree is pleasant to s.

Ge.21 : 11. thi. was griev-s in Abr.'s s.
Ex. 3 : . . I will turn and see great s.
24 : 17. s. of glory of Lord, like fire
Le. 13 : 3. the plague in s. be deeper, 20, 25, 30. [31, 32, 34.
4. in s. be not deeper than skin,
14 : 37. if plague in s. lower than
De.28 : 34. mad for s. of thine eyes, 67.
Jos. 23 : 5. God drive them out of s.
2 S. 23 : † 21. slew Eg-n, a man of s.
1 K. 7 : † 4. s. was ag. s. in 3 ranks
2 K. 2 : † 7. 50 sons of prophets in s.
Jb. 18 : 3. Whf. we reputed vile in y-r
41 : 9. not cast down at s. of him ? [s.
Ec. 6 : 9. Better is s. of the eyes than
Is. 11 : 3. sh. not judge aft. s. of eyes
Je.51 : 24. evil done in Zion in y-r s.
Eze. 20: 9. in whose s. I made known
14. in whose s. I bro-t th. out, 22.
43. loathe yours. in own s., 36 : 31.
23 : † 16. at s. of her eyes she doted
Da.4 : 11. s. of tree to end of earth, 20.
8 : † 5. the goat had a horn of s.
Ho. 2 : 2. her whoredoms out of s.
Lu. 4 : 18. recovering of s. to blind
21 : 11. fearful s-s signs from heaven
23 : 48. came to th. s. smote breasts
Jn. 9 : 11. washed, and I received s.
Ac. 7 : 31. Moses saw, wondered at s.
9 : 9. was three days without s.
18. he received s. forthwith, arose
2 Co. 5 : 7. we walk by faith, not by s.
He. 12 : 21. so terrible was s., Moses
Re. 4 : 3. rainbow in s. like emerald
See EYESIGHT, FAVOUR.
See **FIND grace, FOUND grace.**

His SIGHT. [of h.s.
Ju. 6 : 21. angel of Lord departed out
2 K. 17 : 18. Lord angry removed Israel out of **h.s.**, 20, 23.–24 : 3.
Es. 2 : 17. Esther obtained favour in **h.s.**, 5 : 2. [of **h.s.**
Ps. 10 : 5. thy judgments are far out
Ec. 8 : 3. not hasty to go out of **h.s.**
Mk. 10 : 52. Bartimeus immediately rec-d **h.s.**, Lu. 18:43. [**h.s.**, 18.
Jn. 9 : 15. asked how he had received
Ac. 9 : 12. that he might receive **h.s.**

In his SIGHT.
Ex. 15 : 26. if wilt do th. is right - **s.**
Le. 13 : 5. if plague - **s.** be at a stay
37. if scall be - **s.** at a stay
Nu. 19 : 5. one shall burn heifer - **s.**
De. 4 : 37. bro-t thee - **s.** out of Eg-t
2 S. 12 : 9. despised L., to do evil - **s.**
13 : 8. Tamar went, made cakes - **s.**
1 Ch. 19 : 13. L. do what is good - **s.**
Jb. 15 : 15. heavens are not clean - **s.**
25 : 5. the stars are not pure - **s.**
40 : † 24. will any take him - **s.** ?
Ps. 72 : 14. precious their blood - **s.**
Ec. 2 : 26. G. giveth to man good - **s.**
Ho. 6 : 2. will raise us, we sh. live - **s.**
Ro. 3 : 20. by law, no flesh just-d - **s.**
Col. 1 : 22. to present you holy - **s.**
He. 4 : 13. ev. creature is manifest - **s.**
13 : 21. which is well pleasing - **s.**
1 Jn. 3 : 22. do those thi-s pleas-g - **s.**

In the SIGHT. [lord
Ge. 33 : 15. let me find grace - **s.** of
47 : 18. not aught left - **s.** of my lord
Ex. 7 : 20. he smote waters - **s.** of Pha.
9 : 8. Moses sprinkled ashes - **s.** of Pharaoh [servants
11 : 3. Moses great - **s.** of Pharaoh's
Nu. 3 : 4. ministered - **s.** of Aaron
20 : 27. Eleazar went - **s.** of cong-n
25 : 6. Midianitish wom. - **s.** of Mo.
33 : 3. with high hand - **s.** of Eg-ns
De. 4 : 6. your wisdom - **s.** of nations
2 S. 12 : 11. lie with wives - **s.** of sun
2 Ch. 32 : 23. Hez. magnified - **s.** of nat.
Ezr. 9 : 9. shewed mercy - **s.** of kings
Ne. 1 : 11. mercy - **s.** of this man
Jb. 34 : 26. striketh th. - **s.** of others
Ps. 78 : 12. Marvel-s thi-s - **s.** of fa-s
Pr. 1 : 17. in vain net spread - **s.** of
4 : 3. beloved - **s.** of my moth. [bird
Ec. 11 : 9. walk - **s.** of thine eyes
Je. 19 : 10. break bottle - **s.** of men
32 : 12. I gave evidence - **s.** of Hana.
43 : 9. hid stones - **s.** of men of Jud.
Eze. 5 : 8. judgments - **s.** of nations
14. Jerus. a reproach - **s.** of all
16 : 41. judgments upon thee - **s.** of many women [all
28 : 18. bring thee to ashes - **s.** of
36 : 34. lay desolate - **s.** of all [ers
Ho. 2 : 10. discover lewdn. - **s.** of lov-
Ac. 7 : 10. gave him wisd. - **s.** of Pha.
Ro. 12 : 17. things honest - **s.** of all
2 Co. 2 : † 10. I forgave it - **s.** of Christ
Re. 13 : 13. fire come down - **s.** of
14. had power to do - **s.** of beast

In the SIGHT of God.
Pr. 3 : 4. find good underst-g - **s.** -
Lu. 16 : 15. th. is abomination - **s.** -
Ac. 4 : 19. Whe. right - **s.** - to heark.
8 : 21. thy heart is not right - **s.** -
10 : 31. thy alms in rememb-e - **s.** -
2 Co. 2 : 17. - **s.** - speak we in Christ
4 : 2. to ev. man's conscience - **s.** -
7 : 12. our care for you - **s.** -
Ga. 3 : 11. no man justified by law - **s.** -
1 Th. 1 : 3. Rememb-g work of faith
1 Ti. 2 : 3. this acceptable - **s.** - [- **s.** -
6 : 13. I give thee charge - **s.** -
1 Pe. 3 : 4. which is - **s.** - of gr. price

In the SIGHT of heathen.
Le. 26 : 45. whom I brought out of Egypt - **s.** - [- **s.** -
Ps. 98 : 2. righteousness he shewed
Eze. 20 : 22. name not be polluted - **s.** -
22 : 16. shalt take inheritance in thyself - **s.** - [39 : 27.
28 : 25. be sanctified in them - **s.** -,

In the SIGHT of Israel.
Ex. 17 : 6. smite rock. Moses did so - **s.** - [- **s.** -
40 : 38. fire on tabernacle by night
De. 31 : 7. Moses said unto Jos. - **s.** -
34 : 12. gr. terror Mo. shewed - **s.** -
Jos. 3 : 7. will I magnify thee - **s.** -,
10 : 12. he said - **s.** -, Sun, stand [4 : 14.
1 Ch. 28 : 8. Now - **s.** - keep commandments of Lord [- **s.** -
29 : 25. Lord magnified Solomon
See **Sight of the LORD.**

In the SIGHT of the people.
Ex. 4 : 30. Aaron did signs - **s.** -
19 : 11. Lord will come down - **s.** -
Le. 20 : 17. they shall be cut off - **s.** -
1 S. 18 : 5. David was accepted - **s.** -
Ne. 8 : 5. Ezra opened the book - **s.** -

Mine own, or my SIGHT.
Ge. 23 : 4. may bury my dead out of **m.s.**, 8. [**s.**, 17.
Ex. 33 : 12. hast found grace in **m.**
1 S. 16 : 22. he found favour in **m.s.**
29 : 6. thy coming is good in **m.s.**
9. I know thou art good in **m.s.**
2 S. 6 : 22. I will be base in **m.o.s.**
13 : 5. let Tamar dress meat in **m.s.**
6. make a couple of cakes in **m.s.**
1 K. 8 : 25. shall not fail thee, a man in **m.s.** to sit, 2 Ch. 6 : 16.
9 : 7. house will I cast out of **m.s.**, 2 Ch. 7 : 20. [in **m.s.**
11 : 38. if thou wilt do that is right
2 K. 21 : 15. have done evil in **m.s.**
23 : 27. remove Judah out of **m.s.**
1 Ch. 22 : 8. shed much blood in **m.s.**
Ps. 101 : 7. lies, sh. not tarry in **m.s.**
Is. 43 : 4. thou wast precious in **m.s.**
Je. 4 : 1. put abominations out of **m.**
7 : 15. I will cast you out of **m.s.** [s.
30. of Jud. have done evil in **m.**
15 : 1. cast them out of **m.s.** [s.
18 : 10. If it do evil in **m.s.** that
34 : 15. ye had done right in **m.s.**
Eze. 10 : 2. he went in **m.s.** to fill
19. cherubim mounted up in **m.s.**
Am. 9 : 3. be hid from **m.s.** in sea
Mk. 10 : 51. What wilt thou ? Lord, th. I might receive **m.s.**, Lu. 18 : [41.

Our or their SIGHT.
Nu. 13 : 33. we were in **o.s.** as grasshoppers, so we were in **t.s.**
27 : 19. and give him charge in **t.s.**
Jos. 24 : 17. L. did great signs in **o.s.**
Jb. 19 : 15. I am an alien in **t.s.**
21 : 8. seed is established in **t.s.** [s.
Ps. 79 : 10. known am. heathen in **o.**
Is. 5 : 21. are prudent in **t. own s.**
Eze. 4 : 12. bake it with dung in **t.s.**
12 : 3. remove by day in **t.s.**, 4.
5. Dig thou thro. wall in **t.s.** [7.
6. In **t.s.** bear it upon shoulders,
21 : 23. as a false divination in **t.s.**
43 : 11. shew the forms write in **t.s.**
Mat 11 : 5. The blind receive **t.s.**, the lame walk, 20 : 34. Lu. 7 : 21.
Lu. 24 : 31. knew him, he vanished out of **t.s.** [**t.s.**
Ac. 1 : 9. cloud received him out of

Thine own or Thy SIGHT.
Ge. 21 : 12. not be grievous in **t.s.**
Ex. 33 : 16. be known I found grace in **t.s.** [over him in **t.s.**
Le. 25 : 53. shall not rule with rigour
Nu. 11 : 11. whf. I not found fav. in **t.**
32 : 5. if we found grace in **t.s.** [s. ?
1 S. 1 : 18. handm. find grace in **t.s.**
15 : 17. When wast little in **t.o.s.**
2 S. 7 : 9. cut off enemies out of **t.s.**
19. this was small thing in **t.s.**
14 : 22. I have found grace in **t.s.**
2 K. 1 : 13. life be precious in **t.s.**, 14.
20 : 3. done good in **t.s.**, Is. 38 : 3.
Ps. 5 : 5. foolish not stand in **t.s.**
9 : 19. let heathen be judged in **t.s.**
19 : 14. medita-n acceptable in **t.s.**
51 : 4. I have done this evil in **t.s.**
76 : 7. who may stand in **t.s.** art
90 : 4. 1,000 years in **t.s.** are but
143 : 2. in **t.s.** no man be justified
Is. 26 : 17. so have we been in **t.s.**
Je. 18 : 23. nei. blot their sin from **t.**
Jon. 2 : 4. I am cast out of **t.s.** [s.
Mat. 11 : 26. Father ; for so it seemed good in **t.s.**, Lu. 10 : 21. [in **t.s.**
Lu. 15 : 21. I have sinned ag. heaven
18 : 42. Jesus said, Receive **t.s.** [s.
Ac. 9 : 17. th. thou mightest rec-e **t.**
22 : 13. Brother Saul, receive **t.s.**

SIGN. [Noun.]
Ex. 4 : 8. if they believe not first **s.**, they will believe latter **s.**
8 : 23. to morrow shall this **s.** be
13 : 9. it sh. be a **s.** upon thine hand
31 : 13. my sabbaths a **s.** betw. me and you, 17. Eze. 20 : 12, 20.
Nu. 16 : 38. they sh. be a **s.** unto Isr.
26 : 10. fire devoured, they bec. a **s.**
De. 6 : 8. bind for **s.** upon hand, 11 : [18.
13 : 1. if a prophet giveth a **s.**
2. **s.** come whereof he spake
28 : 46. they sh. be upon thee for **s.**
Jos. 4 : 6. this may be a **s.** am. you
Ju. 6 : 17. shew me a **s.** thou talkest
20 : 38. appointed **s.** betw. Isr. and
1 S. 2 : 34. this be a **s.**, in one day they shall die, 2 K. 19 : 29.
14 : 10. we will go up, this sh. be a **s.**
1 K. 13 : 3. gave a **s.** same day, This is **s.** Lord hath spoken [given
5. according to **s.** man of God hath
2 K. 20 : 8. What sh. be **s.** L. will heal
9. This **s.** shalt thou have of Lord, Is. 38 : 30.–38 : 7, 22. [a **s.**
2 Ch. 32 : 24. he spake, he gave him
Is. 7 : 11. Ask thee a **s.** of the Lord
14. L. himself shall give you a **s.**
19 : 20. it shall be for a **s.** unto Lord
20 : 3. Isaiah walked barefoot for **s.**
55 : 13. name, for an everlasting **s.**
66 : 19. I will set a **s.** among them
Je. 6 : 1. set up **s.** of fire in Beth-hac.
44 : 29. this shall be a **s.**, Lu. 2 : 12.
Eze. 4 : 3. This shall be a **s.** to Israel

Eze. 12:6.set thee for s. unto Isr., 11.
14: 8. I will make him a s., a prov.
24: 24. Thus Ezekiel is unto you a s.
27. thou shalt be a s. unto them
39: 15. then shall he set up a s. [s.
Zch. 3: † 8. men bef. thee are men of
Mat. 12: 38. Master, we would see a
s., 16: 1. Mk. 8: 11. Lu. 11: 16.
39. evil generation seeketh after a
s.; there shall no s. be given
but s. of prophet Jonas, 16: 4.
Mk. 8: 12. Lu. 11: 29, 30. [Lu. 21: 7.
24: 3. what sh. be s. of thy coming?
30. shall appear s. of Son of man
26: 48. he th. betrayed him gave s.
Mk. 13: 4. what s. when all these be
Lu. 2: 34. s. which sh. be spoken ag.
11: 30. as Jonas was s. unto Nine-s
Jn. 2: 18. Wh. s. shewest thou? 6: 30.
Ac. 28: 11. ship, whose s. was Castor
Ro. 4: 11. he received s. of circum-n
1 Co. 1: 22. Jews require s., Greeks
11: † 10. woman to have cov-g in s.
14: 22. Wherefore tongues are a s.
Re. 12: † 1. appeared gr. s. in beav., † 3.
15: 1. I saw another s. in heaven

SIGNS. [ons

Ge. 1: 14. let them be for s. fer seas-
Ex. 4: 9. if not believe these two s.
17. with this rod thou shalt do s.
28. Moses told Aaron all words of
Lord, and all s., 30. Jos. 24: 17.
7: 3. I will multiply my s. in Eg.
10: 2. mayest tell thy son my s. wh.
Nu. 14: 11. all the s. I have shewed
De. 7: 19. gr. s. thine eyes saw, 29: 3.
1 S. 10: 7. when these s. are come
9. those s. came to pass that day
2 K. 23: † 5. th. burned inc. to the 12 s.
Jb. 38: † 32. Canst bring forth the 12
Ps. 74: 4. th. set up ensigns for s. [s.?
9. We see not our s., is no prophet
Je. 10: 2. be not dismayed at the s.
Da. 4: 3. How gr. are his s.! mighty
Mat. 16: 3. can ye not discern the s.?
Mk. 16: 17. s. follow them th. believe
20. confirming the word with s.
Lu. 1: 62. they made s. to Zacharias
21: 11. great s. shall there be
25. be s. in sun, moon, and stars
Jn. 20: 30. many other s. did Jesus
Ac. 8: 13. Simon wondered, behold-
ing the miracles and s.

SIGNS and wonders, or Wonders and SIGNS.

De. 4: 34. G. to take a nation by s. -
6: 22. Lord shewed s. - upon Egypt,
Ne. 9: 10. Ps. 78: 43. Ac. 7: 36.
7: 19. the great s. - thine eyes saw
26: 8. L. bro-t us out of Eg. wi. s. -
34: 11. s. - L. sent him to do in Eg.
Ps. 105: 27. shewed s. - in land of
Is. 8: 18. I and chil. are for s. - [Ham
Je. 32: 20. hast set s. - in Egypt, 21.
Da. 4: 2. I thought good to shew s. -
6: 27. he worketh s. - in heaven and
Mat. 24: 24. false Christs shall shew
great s. -, Mk. 13: 22. [believe
Jn. 4: 48. Exc. ye see s. - will not
Ac. 2: 19. I will shew w. in heav. a. s.
22. man approved of God by - s.
43. many - s. were done by apostles, 5: 12. - 14: 3. [Jesus
4: 30. s. - may be done by name of
Ro. 15: 19. Thro. mighty s. - by Sp.
2 Co. 12: 12. Truly the signs of an
apostle wrought am. you in s. -
2 Th. 2: 9. working of Satan with s.
a. lying w. [s. -
He. 2: 4. God bearing witness with

SIGN, ED. [writing

Da. 6: 8. O king, establish decree, s.
9. Whf. king Darius s-d writing
10. When Dan. knew writing was
12. Hast thou s-d a decree? [s-d, 13.

SIGNET, S. [25.

Ge. 38: 18. give me thy s. and staff,
Ex. 28: 11. like the engravings of a
s., 21, 36. - 39: 14, 30.
39: 6. onyx stones graven as s-s are
Je. 22: 24. Though Coniah were s. on
Da. 6: 17. king sealed it with his s.
Hag. 2: 23. I will make thee as a s.

SIGNIFICANT. [s.

1 Co. 14: † 9. except ye utter words

SIGNIFICATION. [s.

1 Co. 14: 10. none of th. is without

SIGNIFIED, ETH.

Ac. 11: 28. Agabus s-d sho. be dearth
He. 12: 27. s-h the removing of thi-s
Re. 1: 1. s-d by his angel to John

SIGNIFY, ING.

Jn. 12: 33. s-g by what death he
sho. glorify God, 18: 32. - 21: 19.
Ac. 21: 26. to s. accomplishment of
23: 15. s. to captain he bring Paul
25: 27. not to s. crimes laid ag. him
2 Th. 3: † 14. s. th. man by an epistle
He. 9: 8. Holy Ghost s-g that the way
1 Pe. 1: 11. Searching what Spirit

SI'HON. [did s.

Nu. 21: 23. S. not suffer Israel to,
Ju. 11: 20. [S. be built
27. Come into Heshbon, let city of
34. do to him as thou didst unto
S., De. 3: 2, 6. [his land
De. 2: 31. I have begun to give S. and
32. S. came out against us, 29: 7.
Ju. 11: 20. [did to S.
31: 4. L. shall do unto them as he
Jos. 2: 10. S., Og whom ye destroyed
13: 21. dukes of S. dwel-g in coun-y
Ju. 11: 21. God delivered S. into hand
Je. 48: 45. stood under shadow of
Heshbon; but a fire out of Hesh-
bon, a flame from S., Nu. 21: 28.

SI'HON, king of Amorites.

Nu. 21: 21. and Israel sent messengers unto S. -, Ju. 11: 19.
26. Heshbon was the city of S. -,
34. De. 1: 4. - 3: 2. - 4: 46. Jos.
12: 2. - 13: 10, 21. [to S. -
29. his daughters into captivity
34. As thou didst unto S. -, De. 3: 2.
32: 33. Mos. gave th. kingdom of S. -
De. 1: 4. after he had slain S. -, Ps.
135: 11. - 136: 19. [Jos. 13: 21.
4: 46. S. -, whom Moses smote,
Jos. 13: 10. Mo. gave cities of S. - [S. -
1 K. 4: 19. Gebar, officer in country of

SI'HON, king of Heshbon.

De. 2: 24. give into thine hand S. -
26. I sent messengers unto S. -
30. S. - would not let us pass
3: 6. S. - 29: 7. Jos. 12: 5. - 13: 27.
Jos. 9: 10. all that he did to S. -
Ne. 9: 22. so possessed land of S. -

SI'HOR.

Jos. 13: 3. S., which is bef. Egypt
Is. 23: 3. by great waters seed of S.
Je. 2: 18. to drink the waters of S.

SI'LAS. [breth., 27.

Ac. 15: 22. sent S., chief among
32. Judas and S. exhorted breth-n
34. it pleased S. to abide there
16: 29. fell down before Paul and S.
17: 10. sent aw. Paul and S. by night
See PAUL, TIMOTHEUS.

SILENCE.

Jb. 4: 16. an image before me, was s.
29: 21. men kept s. at my counsel
Ps. 22: † 2. in night is no s. to me
31: 18. Let lying lips be put to s.
39: 2. dumb with s. I held my peace
94: 17. my soul almost dwelt in s.
115: 17. neither any that go into s.
Is. 15: 1. Moab is laid waste, brought
to s., Kir is brought to s. [lish
62: † 7. give him no s. till he estab-
Je. 8: 14. our God hath put us to s.
La. 3: 28. He sitteth alone, keep-h s.
Am. 8: 3. sh. cast them forth with s.
Mat. 22: 34. had put Sadducees to s.
Ac. 21: 40. was made gr. s., he spake
Ac. 22: 2. spake in Hebrew, th. kept s.
1 Ti. 2: 11. Let women learn in s.
12. not a woman to teach, but be
in s. [foolish men
1 Pe. 2: 15. put to s. ignorance of
Re. 8: 1. s. in heaven half an hour
See KEEP silence.
See KEPT silence.

SILENT. [Gibeon

Jos. 10: † 12. said, Sun, be s. upon
Ju. 16: † 2. they were s. all the night
1 S. 2: 9. wicked sh. be s. in darku.
7: † 8. Be not s. fr crying unto L.
2 S. 19: † 10. why s. in bringing k.?
1 K. 22: † 3. Ramoth is ours, we be s.
Jb. 13: † 13. Be s., that I may speak
Ps. 22: 2. I cry in night, am not s.
28: 1. be not s. to me, if thou be s.
30: 12. sing praise to thee, not be s.
31: 17. let wicked be s. in grave
37: † 7. Be s. to the Lord, and wait
62: † 1. Truly my soul is s. upon G.
65: † 1. Praise is s. for thee, O God
Pr. 26: † 20. no talebearer, strife is s.
Is. 23: † 2. Be s., ye inhab-ts of isle
47: 5. Sit thou s., get into darkness
Je. 8: 14. enter cities, let us be s.
38: † 27. they were s. from him [ing
Eze. 24: † 17. Be s., make no mourn-
Am. 8: † 3. sh. cast forth dead, be s.
Jon. 1: † 11. that the sea may be s.
4: † 8. God prepared s. east wind
Ha. 2: † 20. be s. all the earth before
Zph. 3: † 17. will be s. in his love
Zch. 2: 13. Be s. O all flesh, bef. Lord

SILK. [eph in s.

Ge. 41: † 42. Pharaoh arrayed Jos-
Ex. 25: † 4. this off-g take, scarlet, s.
Pr. 31: 22. her clothing is s., purple
Eze. 16: 10. I covered thee with s.
13. thy raiment was of s. and
Re. 18: 12. no man buyeth their s.

SIL'LA. [to S.

2 K. 12: 20. Millo which goeth down

SILLY.

Jb. 5: 2. envy slayeth the s. one
Ho. 7: 11. Ephraim is like a s. dove
2 Ti. 3: 6. who lead captive s. women

SIL'OAH or SIL'OAM.

Ne. 3: 15. repaired wall of pool of S-h
Lu. 13: 4. upon wh. tower in S-m fell
Jn. 9: 7. Go wash in pool of S-m, 11.
See SHILOAH.

SILVA'NUS. [and S.

2 Co. 1: 19. preached am. you by me
1 Th. 1: 1. S. unto the church, 2 Th.
1 Pe. 5: 12. By S., a faithf. bro. [1: 1.

SILVER. [Adj.] [mouth

Ge. 44: 2. put my s. cup in sack's
Nu. 7: 13. his offering was one s.
charger, 1 s. bowl, 19, 25, 31, 37,
43, 49, 55, 61, 67, 73, 79. [bowls
84. twelve chargers of silver, 12 s.
Es. 1: 6. s. rings, pillars of marble
Pr. 26: 23. potsherd cov-d wi. s. dross
Ec. 12: 6. Or ever s. cord be loosed
Is. 40: 19. golds-h casteth s. chains
Mat. 27: 6. priests took the s. pieces
Ac. 19: 24. Demetrius made s. shrines

SILVER vessels. [shek-s

Nu. 7: 85. all the s. v. weighed 2 400
Ezr. 6: 5. golden and s. v. be restored
8: 26. I weighed s. v. 100 talents
Da. 5: 2. to bring golden and s. v.
See Vessels of SILVER.

SILVER. [Noun.] [s.

Ex. 20: 23. Ye sh. not make gods of
26: 19. make forty sockets of s.,
21, 25, 32. - 36: 24, 26, 30, 36.
27: 17. filleted wi. s.; hooks sh. be
of s., 10, 11. - 38: 10, 11, 12, 17,
35: 24. did offer offering of s. [19
38: 25. s. of them th. were numb-d
Nu. 7: 84. 12 chargers of s., 12 silver
85. Each charger of s. weighing
10: 2. Make thee 2 trumpets of s.
Jos. 7: 22. hid in his tent, s. und. it,

Ju. 17 : 2. the s. is with me, I took it
1 S. 9 : 8. fourth part of shekel of s.
1 K. 10:21. none were of s., 2Ch. 9:20.
27. s. in Jerus. as stones, 2 Ch. 9:
2 K. 12:13. not for ho. bowls of s. [27.
18 : 15. Hezekiah gave him all the s.
22 : 4. Hilkiah may sum s. brought
1 Ch. 22 : 16. Of s. is no number
28 : 14. s. for instruments of s., 29:2,
15. candlesticks of s. by weight [5.
16. likewise s. for the tables of s.
17. s. by weight for ev. basin of s.
2 Ch. 17 : 11. Jehoshaphat presents
Ks. 3 : 11. The s. is giv. to thee [of s.
Jb. 3 : 15. princes filled houses wi. s.
22 : 25. thou shalt have plenty of s.
27 : 16. Tho. he heap up s. as dust
17. innocent shall divide the s.
28 : 15. nei. s. be weighed for wisd.
Ps. 12 : 6. words of L. are as s. tried
66 : 10. hast tried us, as s. is tried
Pr. 2 : 4. If thou seekest her as s.
8 : 14. of wisdom is better than of s.
8 : 10. Receive my instruction, not
19. my revenue than choice s. [s.
10 : 20. tongue of just as choice s.
16 : 16. get underst-g rather than s.
17 : 3. fining pot is for s., furnace
25 : 4. Take away dross from the s.
Ec. 5 : 10. he that loveth s. shall not
be satisfied with s. [of s.
Can. 8 : 9. will build upon her palace
Is. 1 : 22. Thy s. is become dross
30 : 22. shall defile thy images of s.
48 : 10. I have refined thee, not with
60 : 17. for iron I will bring s. [s.
Je. 6 : 30. Reprobate s. sh. men call
10 : 9. s. spread into plates is bro-t
Eze. 22 : 18. Isr. are dross of s. [from
20. As they gather s., brass, iron
22. As s. is melted in furnace
27 : 12. with s. Tarshish traded in
Da. 2 : 32. breast and arms were of s.
Ho. 9 : 6. pleasant places for their s.
13 : 2. made molten images of s.
Am. 2 : 6. they sold righteous for s.
8 : 6. That we may buy poor for s.
Zph. 1 : 11. all that bear s. are cut off
Zch. 9 : 3. Tyrus heaped s. as dust
13 : 9. I will refine them as s. is
Mal. 3 : 3. refiner and purifier of s.
Lu. 19 : † 15. serv-ts to wh. he had giv.
See FILLETS, PIECE, S. [s.

SILVER with gold.

1 Ch. 18 : 11. Da. dedicated unto L.
wi. s. and g., 2 Ch. 5:1. [numb.
22 : 16. Of g. and s. and brass is no
Ezr. 7 : 16. all s. and g. find in Bab-n
18. with s. and g. do aft. will of G.
8 : 28. s. and g. are freewill offer-g
30. took Levites weight of s. and g.
Ne. 7 : 71. gave 20,000 drams of g.,
22,000 pounds of s.
72. rest gave 22,000 of g., 2,000
Zch. 9:3. heaped s. as dust, g. as mire
Re. 18 : 12. merchandise of g. and s.
See GOLD with silver.
See SHEKELS of silver.

Talent, s of SILVER.

1 K. 16 : 24. bought hill Samaria for
20 : 39. th. shalt pay a - s. [two -s.
2 K. 5 : 5. Naaman took ten - s.
22. give them, I pr'y thee a - s.
23. bound two - s. in two bags
15 : 19. Menahem gave Pul 1,000 - s.
1 Ch. 19 : 6. Hanun sent 1,000 - s.
22 : 14. house of Lord a thousand
29 : 4. and 7 thous. - s. [thous. - s.
2 Ch. 25 : 6. hired men for 100 - s.
27 : 5. Ammon gave Jotham 100 - s.
36 : 3. condemned land in 100 - s.
Ezr. 7 : 22. I decree it unto 100 - s.
8 : 26. I weighed unto hand 650 - s.
See TALENTS with silver.

Vessels of SILVER.

2 S. 8 : 10. Joram brought - s. and
vessels of gold, vessels of brass

1 K. 10 : 25. brought every man his
present, - s. and gold, 2Ch. 9:24.
2 K. 12 : 13. not made v. of gold or s.
1 Ch. 18 : 10. with him all manner of
- s., gold, brass, 2 Ch. 24:14. [11.
Ezr 1:6. strengthened wi. - s., gold,
5 : 14. v. of gold and s. of ho. of G.
Da. 11 : 8. their precious - s. and gold
2 Ti. 2 : 20. in gr. house v. of gold, s.

SILVERLINGS.

Is. 7 : 23. were 1,000 vines at 1,000 s.

SILVERSMITH.

Ac. 19:24. Demet-s, a s., made shrines

SIM'EON.

Ge. 29 : 33. Leah bare son, name S.
34 : 25. S. and Levi took each sword
30. Jac. said to S., Ye have troub-d
35 : 23. sons of Leah; Reub. and S.
42 : 24. Joseph took from them S.
36. Joseph is not, S. is not
43 : 23. he bro-t S. out unto them
46 : 10. sons of S., Ex. 6 : 15. Nu.
1 : 22.-26 : 12. 1 Ch. 4 : 24, 42.-
12 : 25. [be mine
48 : 5. as Reuben and S. they shall
49 : 5. S. and Levi are brethren
Ex. 1 : 2. chil. of Isr.; S., 1 Ch. 2:1.
Nu. 1 : 6. prince of S. was Shelumiel, 2 : 12.-7 : 36. [stand to bless
De. 27 : 12. S., Levi, and Judah,
Jos. 19 : 1. second lot came to S.
9. S. had inheritance within Judah
Ju. 1 : 3. S. went with Judah (2)
17. Judah wi. S. slew Canaanites
2 Ch. 15 : 9. strangers out of S. fell to
34 : 6. so did Josiah in cities of S.
Eze. 48 : 24. S. shall have a portion
25. And by border of S. from east
33. one gate of S., one gate of Iss.
Zch. 12 : † 13. fam. of S apart and
Lu. 2 : 25 man in Jerus., name was S.
34. S. blessed Joseph and Mary
3 : 30. Levi, which was the son of S.
Ac. 13 : 1. at Anti-h, S. called Niger
15 : 14. S. hath declared how G. did
See SYMEON. [visit

Tribe of SIMEON.

Nu. 1 : 23. of the - S. numb-d 59,300
2 : 12. the - S. sh. pitch by Reuben
10 : 19. over host of - S. Shelumiel
13 : 5. of - S. Shaphat to spy land
34 : 20. of - S. Shemuel to divide la.
Jos. 19 : 1. second lot came for - S.
8. This is the inheritance of - S.
21 : 4. Levites had of - S., 9. - 1Ch. 6:65.
Re. 7 : 7. of - S. were sealed 12,000

SIM'EONITES. [S.

Nu. 25 : 14. prince of chief house am
26 : 14. These are families of the S.
1 Ch. 27 : 16. ruler of S. Shephatiah

SIMILITUDE, S.

Nu. 12 : 8. s. of Lord shall he behold
De. 4 : 12. heard voice, saw no s., 15.
16. lest ye make s. of any figure
2 Ch. 4 : 3. under it was s. of oxen
Ps. 106 : 20. glory into s. of ox [ace
144 : 12. stones polished aft. s. of pal-
Da. 10 : 16. one like s. of sons of men
Ro. 5 : 14. aft. s. of Adam's transg-n
He. 7 : 15. after s. of Melchisedec
Ho. 12 : 10. I used s-s by ministry
Ja. 3 : 9. men made after s. of God

SI'MON.

Mat. 10 : 4. S., Canaanite, Mk. 3:18.
13 : 55. James, Joses, S., Mk. 6 : 3.
16 : 17. Blessed art thou, S. Bar-jona
17 : 25. What thinkest thou, S.?
26 : 6. house of S., leper, Mk. 14 : 3.
27 : 32. man of Cyrene, S., to bear
cross, Mk. 15 : 21. Lu. 23 : 26.
Mk. 1 : 16. by sea of Gal. Jes. saw S.
29. entered house of S., Lu. 4 : 38.
30. S.'s wife's mother sick, Lu. 4:38.
36. S. they with him followed Jes.
14 : 37. S., sleepest thou? couldst
Lu. 5 : 3. into one of ships, wh. was S.'s
4. unto S., Launch out into deep

Lu. 5 : 5. S. We have toiled all night
10. James, John, partners with S.
Jesus said unto S., Fear not,
6 : 15. S. called Zelotes, Ac. 1 : 13.
7 : 40. S., I have somewhat to say
43. S. said, he wh. he forgave most
44. Jes. unto S., Seest this woman?
22 : 31. S., S., Satan hath desired
24 : 34. Lord hath appeared to S.
Jn. 1 : 41. He first findeth his bro. S.
42. Jesus said, Thou art S., son of
6 : 71. Judas Iscariot, the son of S.,
12 : 4.-13 : 2, 26. [me? 16, 17.
21 : 15. S., son of Jonas, lovest thou
Ac. 8 : 9. man, S., who used sorcery
13. Then S. himself believed also
18. when S. saw H. Gh. was given
24. S. said, Pray ye to Lord for me
9 : 43. wi. one S. a tanner, 10 : 6, 32.
10 : 17. made inquiry for S.'s hou.
See PETER.
See Simon PETER.

SIMPLE. [the s.

Ps. 19 : 7. testimony of L. making wise
116 : 6. Lord preserveth the s.
119 : 130. giveth understanding to
Pr. 1 : 4. To give subtilty to s. [s.
22. How long, s. ones, will ye love
32. turning away of s. sh. slay th.
7 : 7. I beheld am. s. ones yo. man
8 : 5. O ye s. understand wisdom
9 : 4. Whoso is s. let him turn in, 16.
13. A foolish woman is s. and
14 : 15. s. believeth every word
18. s. inherit folly, but prudent
19 : 25. Smite scorner s. will beware
21 : 11. is punished, s. made wise
22 : 3. s. pass on are punished, 27:12.
Eze. 45 : 20. so do for him that is s.
Mat. 10 : † 16. as serpents, s. as doves
Ro. 16 : 18. fair speeches deceive s.
19. wise unto good, s. conc-g evil

SIMPLICITY. [not

2 S. 15 : 11. went in their s., knew
1 K. 22 : † 34. man drew a bow in his
s., 2 Ch. 18 : † 33.
Pr. 1 : 22. How long will ye love s.?
Ro. 12 : 8. giveth let him do it with s.
2 Co. 1 : 12. in s. had our conversa-n
8 : † 2. poverty abounded unto rich-
9 : † 11. enriched to all s. [es of s.
11 : 3. corrupted from s. in Christ

SIM'RI. See SHIMRI.

SIN. [Place.]

Ex. 16 : 1. they came unto the wilderness of S., Nu. 33 : 11. [33 : 12.
17 : 1. Israel journeyed fr. S., Nu.
Eze. 30 : 15. I will pour fury upon S.
16. S. shall have great pain, No

SIN. [Noun.] [door

Ge. 4 : 7. if doest not well, s. lieth at
Ex. 34 : 7. forgiving iniquity and s.
Le. 4 : 3. if priest sin according to
the s. of people [shall offer
14. When s. is known, cong-n
6 : 26. priest offereth it for s., 9:15.
19 : 17. not suffer s. upon neighb-r
22. s. he hath done be forgiven
Nu. 5 : 6. When man or wom. commit
12 : 11. lay not the s. upon us [s.
19 : 9. it is a purification for s., 17.
De. 15 : 9. cry unto L. it be s., 24:15.
19 : 15. one witn. not rise up for s.
21 : 22. if man have committed s.
22 : 26. damsel no s. worthy of death
23 : 21. L. require it, it would be s.
22. if forbear to vow, it be no s.
24 : 16. every man be put to death
for own s., 2 K. 14:6. 2Ch. 25:4.
1 S. 14 : 38. see wh-n this s. hath been
15 : 23. rebellion as s. of witchcraft
1 K. 12 : 30. this thing became s., 13:
2 K. 12 : 16. s. money was priests' [34.
Jb. 20 : 11. His bones are full of s.
Ps. 32 : 1. Blessed whose s. is cov-d
51 : 5. in s. did mother conc-e me
59 : 12. For s. of mouth be taken

Ps. 109 : 7. and let his prayer bec. s.
14. let not s. of mother be blotted
Pr. 10 : 16. of wicked tendeth to s.
19. In words there wanteth not s.
13 : † 6. wickedness overthroweth s.
14 : 9. Fools make a mock at s., but
34. s. is reproach to any people
21 : 4. ploughing of wicked is s.
24 : 9. thought of foolishness is s.
Is. 5 : 18. draw s. as with cart rope
30 : 1. they may add s. to s. [for s.
31 : 7. idols which y-r hands made
53 : 10. make his soul offering for s.
12. he bare the s. of many, and
Je. 17 : 1. s. of Jud. written with pen
3. I will give high places for s.
51 : 5. tho. land was filled with s.
La. 4 : 6. punishment of s. of Sodom
Ho. 4 : 8. They eat up s. of my peo.
10 : 8. s. of Israel sh. be destroyed
12 : 8. none iniquity in me th. were s.
Am. 8 : 14. that swear by s. of Sama-a
Mi. 1 : 13. she beginning of s. to Zi.
6 : 7. fruit of body for s. of soul
Zch. 13 : 1. a fountain opened for s.
14 : † 19. this shall be s. of Egypt
Jn. 1 : 29. taketh aw. s. of the world
8 : 7. He without s. let him cast [s.
34. Whoso committeth s. serv-t of
46. Wh. of you convinceth me of s.
9 : 41. blind, ye should have no s.
15 : 22. If I had not come, they not
had s., 24. [world of s.
16 : 8. Comforter, he will reprove
9. Of s. bec. they believe not on
19 : 11. delivered me hath greater s.
Ac. 7 : 60. lay not s. to their charge
Ro. 3 : 9. Jews, Gentiles, all under s.
20. by the law is knowledge of s.
4 : 8. to wh. L. will not impute s.
5 : 12. s. entered world, death by s.
13. uutil the law s. was in the world
20. where s. abounded, grace more
21. That as s. reigned unto death
6 : 1. What, shall we continue in s.?
2. How sh. we th. are dead to s. live?
6. that body of s. be destroyed th.
we should not serve s. [s.
7. For he that is dead is freed fr.
10. in th. he died, he died to s. once
11. reckon yours. to be dead unto
12. Let not s. reign in y-r body [s.
13. nei. yield your members to s.
14. s. shall not have dominion
16. his servants ye are, whe. of s.
17. G. be thanked, ye were serv-ts
18. Being made free from s. [of s.
20. when ye were servants of s. ye
23. For wages of s. is death, but
7 : 7. Is law s.? God forbid. I had
not known s. but by the law
8. s. taking occasion wrought in
me; without the law s. was dead
9. com-t came, s. revived, I died
11. s. by commandment slew me
13. But s. that it might appear s.,
that s. by com-t might become
14. but I am carnal, sold under s.
17. no more I, but s. dwelleth in
23. into captiv-y to law of s. [me, 20.
25. but with the flesh the law of s.
8 : 2. made me free fr. the law of s.
3. for s. condemned s. in the flesh
10. if C. in you, body dead bec. of s.
14 : 23. whatso. is not of faith is s.
1 Co. 6 : 18. Every s. a man doeth is
15 : 56. The sting of death is s.,
and the strength of s. is the law
2 Co. 5 : 21. made him to be s. for us,
who knew no s. [ter of s.?
Ga. 2 : 17. is therefore Christ minis-
3 : 22. Scripture conclud. all und. s.
2 Th. 2 : 3. th. man of s. be revealed
He. 3 : 13. thro. the deceitfuln. of s.
4 : 15. tempted as we are, yet with-t s.
9 : 26. he appeared to put away s.
28. sh. appear with-t s. to salva-n

He. 10 : 6. In sacrifices for s. no pleas.
8. offering for s. thou wouldst not
18. where remission, no off-g for s.
11 : 25. enjoy pleasures of s. for sea.
12 : 1. lay aside s. th. doth beset us
4. Ye not resisted, striving ag. s.
13 : 11. bodies of beasts for s. burned
Ja. 1 : 15. it bringeth forth s., and
s. finished, bringeth forth death
2 : 9. if respect to pers-s, ye com-t s.
4 : 17. doeth not good, to him it is s.
1 Pe. 2 : 22. did no s. nor was guile
4 : 1. suffered in flesh ceased from s.
2 Pe. 2 : 14. eyes th. can-t cease fr. s.
1 Jn. 1 : 7. cleanseth us from all s.
8. If say we have no s. we deceive
3 : 4. Whoso committeth s. transgresseth, s. is transgr-n of law
5. manifested, and in him is no s.
8. that committeth s. is of devil
9. born of God doth not commit s.
5 : 16. If man see his brother sin a
s. There is a s. unto death
17. All unrighteousness is s., and
there is a s. not unto death
See **BEAR sin.**
See FORGIVE, FORGIVEN.

Great SIN. [s.
Ge. 20 : 9. bro-t on me and kingd. g.
Ex. 32 : 21. that hast bro-t this g.s.
30. Mo. said, Ye have sinned g.s.
31. this people have sinned a g.s.
1 S. 2 : 17. s. of y-g men was very g.
2 K. 17 : 21. Jerob. made th. sin a g.s.

His SIN. [lock
Le. 4 : 3. bring for h.s. young bul-
23. if h.s. come to knowledge, 28.
26. priest shall make atonement
for h.s., 35.-5 : 6, 10, 13. [(2)
28. sh. bring kid of goats for h.s.
5 : 6. sh. bring trespass off-g for h.
Nu. 27 : 3. our father died in h.s. [s.
De. 24 : 16. every man shall be put
to death for h. own s., 2 K. 14 :
6. 2 Ch. 25 : 4.
1 K. 15 : 26. Nadab walked in way of
his father and in h.s. [h.s.
34. Baasha in way of Jerob. and
16 : 19. Zimri in way of Jerob. h.s.
26. Omri in way of Jerob. and h.s.
2 K 21 : 16. h.s. wherewith made Ju-
17. acts of Manasseh and h.s. [dah
2 Ch 25 : 4. Ev. man die for h. own s.
Jb. 34 : 37. addeth rebel-n unto h.s.
Is. 27 : 9. is fruit to take away h.s.
Eze. 3 : 20. he shall die in h.s., 18 : 24.
33 : 14. if turn from h.s. do right
Ho. 13 : 12. iniquity bound, h.s. hid
Mi. 3 : 8. full to declare to Isr. h.s.

My SIN. [sued me?
Ge. 31 : 36. what is m.s. thou pur-
1 S. 15 : 25. I pray thee, pardon m.s.
20 : 1. what is m.s. before thy father
1 K. 17 : 18. to call m.s. to remembr.
Jb. 10 : 6. thou searchest aft. m.s.
13 : 23. make me to know m.s. [s.
14 : 16. dost thou not watch ov. m.
35 : 3. What if cleansed from m.s.?
Ps. 32 : 5. I acknowledged m. s.,
thou forgavest iniquity of m.s.
38 : 3. nei. rest in my bones bec. of m.
18. for I will be sorry for m.s. [s.
51 : 2. Wash, cleanse me from m.s.
3. m.s. is ever before me
59 : 3. mighty ag. me; not for m.s.
Pr. 20 : 9. who say, I am pure fr. m.s.?
Da. 9 : 20. whilst I was confes-g m.s.

SIN offering, with bullock, s.
Ex. 29 : 36. offer ev. day b. for s.o.
Le. 4 : 3. bring a young b. for s.o.,
16 : 3. Nu. 8 : 8. Eze. 43 : 19.
8. take all fat of b. for s.o.
20. do with bullock as b. for s.o.
8 : 2. Take Aaron, his sons, and a
b. for s.o. 14. (2) [s.o., 11, 27.
16 : 6. Aaron shall offer his b. of

2 Ch. 29 : 21. th. bro-t 7 b-s for s.o.
Eze. 43 : 21. shall take b. of the s.o.
45 : 22. prince prepare b. for s.o.
See **Sin OFFERING, S.**

Our SIN. [o.s.
Ex. 34 : 9. pardon our iniquity and
Je. 16 : 10. what is o.s. we committed

Their SIN.
Ge. 18 : 20. bec. t.s. is grievous [7 : 14.
50 : 17. forgive, I pray, t.s., 2 Ch.
Ex. 32 : 32. if thou wilt forgive t.s.,
34. when I visit, I will visit t.s.
Nu. 5 : 7. they shall confess t.s.
De. 9 : 27. look not unto t.s.
1 K. 8 : 35. if turn fr. t.s., 2 Ch. 6 : 26.
Ne. 4 : 5. let not t.s. be blotted out
Ps. 85 : 2. thou hast covered all t.s.
Is. 3 : 9. they declare t.s. as Sodom
Je. 16 : 18. will recompense t.s. doub-
18 : 23. neither blot out t.s. [le
31 : 34. will remember t.s. no more
36 : 3. may forgive their iniq-y, t.s.
Jn. 15 : 22. th. have no cloak for t.s.

Thy SIN.
2 S. 12 : 13. Lord hath put aw. t.s.
Is. 6 : 7. thine iniq-y, t.s. is purged

Your SIN. [for y.s.
Ex. 32 : 30. I shall make atonement
Nu. 32 : 23. sure y.s. will find you out
De. 9 : 21. I took y.s., calf ye made
Jn. 9 : 41. say, We see, y.s. remain-h

SINS. [Rehob.
1 K. 15 : 3. Abijam walked in s. of
16 : 13. For s. of Baasha, s. of Elah
19. For his s. which Zimri sinned
2 K. 24 : 3. remove Jud. for s. of Manas.
2 Ch. 28 : 10. are there not wi. you s.?
33 : 19. all his s. and his trespass
Ne. 1 : 6. confess the s. of Israel [s.?
Jb. 13 : 23. How many mine iniq-s and
Ps. 19 : 13. Keep fr. presumptuous s.
25 : 7. Remember not s. of my youth
Pr. 5 : 22. holden with cords of his s.
10 : 12. strifes, love covereth all s.
28 : 13. cover-h his s. sh. not prosp.
Is. 40 : 2. received double for her s.
43 : 24. hast made me serve wi. thy s.
25. I will not remember thy s.
44 : 22. blotted out as cloud thy s.
Je. 15 : 13. will give to spoil for thy s.
30 : 14. bec. thy s. were increased, 15.
50 : 20. s. of Judah sought not found
La. 3 : 39. man for punishment of s.
4 : 13. For the s. of her prophets
22. O Edom, he will discover thy s.
Eze. 16 : 51. Nei. Samaria com-ted thy
52. bear own shame for thy s. [s.
18 : 14. if son that seeth father's s.
21. if wicked will turn from his s.
23 : 49. he sh. bear s. of your idols
33 : 16. None of his s. be mentioned
Da. 4 : 27. break off thy s. by rightn.
9 : 24. 70 weeks to make end of s.
Mi. 1 : 5. for the s. of Israel is all this
6 : 13. thee desolate bec. of thy s.
Lu. 7 : 49. Who is this forgiveth s.?
Jn. 9 : 34. said, Thou wast born in s.
20 : 23. Whosesoever s. ye remit,
whosesoever s. ye retain [on na.
Ac. 22 : 16. wash away thy s. calling
Ro. 4 : 7. Blessed whose s. are covered
7 : 5. motions of s. did work [s., 5.
Ep. 2 : 1. quickened who were dead in
Col. 2 : 11. in putting off body of s.
1 Ti. 5 : 22. nei. partakers of men's s.
24. Some men's s. open beforeha.
2 Ti. 3 : 6. silly women laden with s.
He. 2 : 17. reconciliation for s. of peo.
5 : 1. may offer sacrifices for s.
3. for peo., for hims. to offer for s.
7 : 27. for his own s., then for peo-'s
9 : 28. Christ was offered to bear s.
10 : 2. had no more conscience of s.
3. remembrance again made of s.
4. not blood of goats take away s.
11. same sacrifices nev. take aw. s.
12. he offered one sacrifice for s.

He. 10 : 26. rema-h no sacrifice for s.
Ja. 5 : 20. shall hide a multitude of s.
1 Pe. 2 : 24. we being dead to s. sho.
3 : 18. Christ once suffered for s.
4 : 8. charity cover multitude of s.
2 Pe. 1 : 9. was purged from his old s.
1 Jn. 2 : 2. also for s. of whole world
Re. 18 : 4. be not partakers of her s.
5. her s. have reached unto heaven
See FORGIVE, FORGIVEN.

Forgiveness of SINS.

Ac. 5 : 31. exalted to give f.o.s. [o.s.
13 : 38. through him is preached f.
26 : 18. that they may receive f.o.s.
Ep. 1 : 7. in wh. we have f.o.s., Col. [1:14.

SINS of Jeroboam.

1 K. 14 : 16. he shall give Israel up because of s. - [of s. -
15 : 30. smote house of Jerob. bec.
2 K. 13 : 6. Isr. departed not from s. -
17 : 22. Israel walked in the s. - [11.

SINS of Jeroboam, son of Nebat.

1 K. 16 : 31. light thing to walk in s. -
2 K. 3 : 3. Jehoram cleaved unto s. -
10 : 29. fr. s. - Jehu departed not, 31.
13 : 2. Joash followed the s. -, 6.
11. Jehoa. departed not fr. all s. -
14 : 24. Jerob. departed not fr. s. -
15 : 9. Zach-h departed not from s. -
18. Menahem departed not fr. s. -
24. Pekahiah departed not fr. s. -
28. Pekah departed not from s. -

My SINS.

Ps. 51 : 9. Hide thy face from m.s.
69 : 5. O God, m.s. are not hid
Is. 38 : 17. th. hast cast m.s. behind

Our SINS.

1 S. 12 : 19. added unto o.s. this evil
2 Ch. 28 : 13. ye intend to add to o.s.
Ne. 9 : 37. kings over us bec. of o.s.
Ps. 79 : 9. purge aw. o.s. for thy na.
90 : 8. o.s. in light of thy counten.
103 : 10. hath not dealt acc. to o.s.
Is. 59 : 12. for o.s. testify against us
Eze. 33 : 10. If o.s. upon us we pine
Da. 9 : 16. bec. of o.s. thy people are
1 Co. 15 : 3. how Christ died for o.s.
Ga. 1 : 4. Who gave himself for o.s.
He. 1 : 3. had purged o.s. sat down
1 Pe. 2 : 24. Who bare o.s. in his body
1 Jn. 1 : 9. If we confess o.s. he is faithful to forgive us o.s.
2 : 2. is propitiation for o.s., 4 : 10.
3 : 5. manifested to take away o.s.
Re. 1 : 5. washed us fr. o.s. in blood
See REMISSION.

Their SINS.

Le. 16 : 16. bec. of transgr-ns in t.s.
21. sh. confess over goat all t.s.
34. to make atonement for t.s.
Nu. 16 : 26. lest consumed in t.s.
1 K. 14 : 22. provoked him with t.s.
16 : 2. provoke me to anger with t.s.
Ne. 9 : 2. Israel confessed t.s.
Is. 58 : 1. shew house of Jacob t.s.
Je. 14 : 10. visit t.s., Ho. 8 : 13.-9 : 9.
Mi. 7 : 19. cast all t.s. into the sea
Mat. 1 : 21. save his peo. from t.s.
3 : 6. baptized, confes-g t.s., Mk. 1 : 5.
Ro. 11 : 27. when I take away t.s.
1 Th. 2 : 16. to fill up t.s. always
He. 8 : 12. I will be merciful to t.s.
10 : 17. t.s. I will remember no more

Your SINS.

Le. 16 : 30. may be clean fr. y.s. [28.
26 : 18. punish 7 times for y.s., 24,
21. plagues upon you acc. to y.s.
De. 9 : 18. nor drink wat., bec. of y.s.
Is. 1 : 18. though y.s. be as scarlet
59 : 2. y.s. have hid his face fr you
Je. 5 : 25. y.s. have withholden good
Eze. 21 : 24. in all y-r doings y.s. ap.
Am. 5 : 12. I know y. transg. mighty s.
Jn. 8 : 21. seek me, and die in y.s., 24.
Ac. 3 : 19. that y.s. be blotted [y.s.
1 Co. 15 : 17. if Ch. not raised, ye in

Col. 2 : 13. you being dead in y.s.
1 Jn. 2 : 12. bec. y.s. are forgiv. you

SIN. [Verb] [ag. God

Ge. 39 : 9. How can I do this and s.
42 : 22. said, Do not s. ag. the child
Ex. 20 : 20. his fear that ye s. not
23 : 33. lest th. make thee s. ag. me
Le. 4 : 2. If a soul s. thro. ignorance
3. If priest s. 1 13. if congreg-n s.
27. If any of peo. s. thro. ignoran.
5 : 1. If a soul s. and hear swearing
15. if a soul s. through ignorance in holy things, 17. Nu. 15 : 27.
6 : 2. If a soul s. and lie unto neighb
Nu. 16 : 22. shall one s. thou wroth
De. 20 : 18. so sho. ye s. ag. L. [wi. all?
24 : 4. shalt not cause land to s.
1 S. 2 : 25. If one man s. ag. another, if a man s. ag. the Lord [pray
12 : 23. G. forbid I s. in ceasing to
14 : 33. the people s. ag. the Lord
34. s. not in eating with the blood
19 : 4. Let not king s. ag. his servant
5. whf. wilt s. ag. innocent blood
1 K. 8 : 46. If they s. against thee, and thou angry, 2 Ch. 6 : 36.
2 K. 17 : 21. Jerob. made them s. gr.
21 : 11. Manasseh made Judah s. [sin
16. sin wh w. he made Judah s.
2 Ch. 6 : 22. If a man s. ag neighb.
Ne. 6 : 13. that I sho. be afr. and s.
13 : 26. Did not Sol. s. by these thi.?
Jb. 2 : 10. In all this did not Job s.
5 : 24. shalt visit habita. and not s.
10 : 14. If I s. thou markest me [s.
31 : 30. Nei. suffered my mouth to
Ps. 4 : 4. Stand in awe and s. not
39 : 1. take heed I s. not wi. tongue
119 : 11. th. I might not s. ag. thee
Ec. 5 : 6. mou. to cause thy flesh to s.
Je. 32 : 35. do this abomination to cause Jud. to s. [he doth not s.
Eze. 3 : 21. that righteous s. not, and
Ho. 8 : 11. Ephraim made altars to s., altars shall be unto him to s.
13 : 2. And now they s. more and
Mat. 18 : 21. Lord, how oft broth. s.?
Jn. 5 : 14. s. no more, lest worse thi.
8 : 11. Nei. I condemn, s. no more
9 : 2. who did s., man or parents?
Ro. 6 : 15. sh. we s. bec. not und. law?
1 Co. 8 : 12. when ye s. so against the brethren, ye s. against Christ
15 : 34. Awake to righteousn., s. not
Ep. 4 : 26. Be ye angry, and s. not
1 Ti. 5 : 20. Them th. s. rebuke bef. all
He. 10 : 26. if we s. wilfully aft. knol.
1 Jn. 2 : 1. I write that ye s. not, if any s. we have advocate
3 : 9. he cannot s. bec. born of God
5 : 16. If any man see his brother s. he shall give him life for them that s. not unto death
See **Made ISRAEL sin.**

SI'NA.

See **Mount SINAI.**

SI'NAI. [S.

Ex. 16 : 1. Sin, wh. is betw. Elim and
19 : 1. the wilderness of S., 2. Le. 7 : 38. Nu. 1 : 1, 19.-3 : 4, 14.-9 : 1, 5.-10 : 12.-26 : 64.-33 : 15, 16. Ac. 7 : 30.
De. 33 : 2. The Lord came from S.
Ju. 5 : 5. mts. melted, even that S.
Ps. 68 : 8. S. was moved at pres. of G.
17. Lord is among them as in S.

Mount SI'NAI, or SI'NA.

Ex. 19 : 11. sight of all the people upon m. S. [the Lord
18. m. S. was on a smoke because
20. Lord came down upon m. S.
23. peo. cannot come up to m. S.
24 : 16. glory of L. abode upon m. S.
31 : 18. L. gave Mo. upon m. S. two
34 : 2. come up in morning to m. S.
4. Moses rose early, went to m. S
29. when Mo. came down fr. m. S.

Ex. 34 : 32. L. had spoken with him in m. S., Le. 25 : 1. Nu. 3 : 1.
Le. 7 : 38. L. com-ded Mo. in m. S.
26 : 46. in m. S. by hand of Moses
27 : 34. for chil. of Israel in m. S.
Nu. 28 : 6. offering ordained in m. S.
Ne. 9 : 13. camest down upon m. S.
Ac. 7 : 38. angel which spake to him in m. S-a, 30. [m. S-i, † S-a
Ga. 4 : 24. two covenants, one from
25. this Agar is m. S. in Arabia

SINCE. [coming

Ge. 30 : 30. L. blessed thee s. my
44 : 28. went out, I saw him not s.
46 : 30. lot me die, s. I have seen thy
Ex. 4 : 10. s. hast spoken unto serv.
5 : 23. s. I came to Phar. to speak
9 : 18. hail not in Eg. s. foundation
24. in Egypt s. it became nation
Nu. 22 : 30. ridden on s. I was thine
De. 34 : 10. not a prophet s. in Israel
Jos. 2 : 12. swear, s. I shewed kindn.
3 † 4. ye not this way s. yesterday
14 : 10. L. kept me alive, s. L. spake
Ru. 2 : 11. done, s. death of thy husb.
1 S. 9 : 24. s. I said, I invited people
21 : 5. three days s. I came out
29 : 3. no fault s. he fell unto me
2 S. 7 : 6. s. I brought up Israel
11. s. I com-ded judges, 1 Ch 17 : 10.
13 : † 28. will you not, s. I com-ded
2 Ch. 30 : 26. s. Sol. not the like in Je.
31 : 10. s. peo. began to bring off-gs
Ezr. 4 : 2. s. the days of Esar-haddon
5 : 16. s. that time been in building
9 : 7. s. days of fathers we in trespass
Ne. 9 : 32. s. time of kings of Assyria
Jb. 20 : 4. s. man was placed upon
38 : 12. com-ded morn-g s. thy days?
Is. 14 : 8. s. thou laid down, no feller
16 : 13. cone-g Moab s. that time
43 : 4. s. wast precious in my sight
44 : 7. s. I appointed ancient people
64 : 4. s. beginning men not heard
Je. 7 : 25. s. day your fathers came
15 : 7. s. they return not from
20 : 8. s. I spake I cried out [ways
23 : 38. s. ye say, The burden of L.
31 : 20. s. I spake ag. him I rememb.
44 : 18. s. we left off to burn incense
48 : 27. s. thou speakest of him
Da. 12 : 1. never was s. was a nation
Hag. 2 : 16. s. days when one came
Mat. 24 : 21. as was not s. beginning
Mk. 9 : 21. How long s. this came
Lu. 1 : 70. been s. the world began, Jn. 9 : 32. Ac. 3 : 21. Ro. 16 : 25.
7 : 45. s. time I came in she not
16 : 16. s. kingd. of G. is preached
24 : 21. is 3d day s. these things
Ac. 19 : 2. Holy Gh. s. ye believed?
24 : 11. 12 days s. I went to Jerus.
1 Co. 15 : 21. s. by man came death
2 Co. 13 : 3. s. ye seek proof of Christ
Col. 1 : 4. s. we heard of your faith
He. 7 : 28. word of oath s. the law
9 : 26. s. foundation of the world
2 Pe. 3 : 4. s. the fathers fell asleep
Re. 16 : 18. as was not s. men upon
See **Since the Day.** [earth

SINCERE. [be thou s.

Ge. 17 : † 1. walk thou bef. me and
De. 18 : † 13. Thou shalt be s. with L.
Ps. 119 : † 1. Blessed are s. in way
Ep. 4 : † 15. s. in love may grow into
Ph. 1 : 10. be s. till day of Ch., 2 : † 15.
1 Pe. 2 : 2. babes desire s. milk of word

SINCERELY.

Ju 9 : 16. if ye have done truly, s., 19.
Ph. 1 : 16. The one preach Ch., not s.

SINCERITY.

Ge. 20 : † 5. in s. of my heart have I
Jos. 24 : 14. fear and serve the L. in s.
1 Co. 5 : 8. unleavened bread of s.
2 Co. 1 : 12. in godly s. we have had
2 : 17. but as of s. in sight of God
8 : 8. and to prove s. of your love

Ep. 6 : 24. with th. love our L. in s.
Tit. 2 : 7. in doctrine shewing grav-

SINEW, S. [ity, s.

Ge. 32 : 32. Isr. eat not of s., because
he touched Jacob in s.
Jb. 10 : 11. hast fenced me with s-s
30 : 17. pierced my s-s, take no rest
40 : 17. s-s of his stones are wrap-d
Is. 48 : 4. bec. thy neck is an iron s.
Eze. 37 : 6. I will lay s-s upon you
8. s-s and flesh came upon them

SINFUL.

Nu. 32 : 14. ye an increase of s. men
Is. 1 : 4. Ah, s. nation, a peo. laden
Am. 9 : 8. eyes of L. are on s. kingd.
Mk. 8 : 38. ashamed in s. generation
Lu. 5 : 8. Depart, I am s. man, O L.
24 : 7. deliv-d into hands of s. men
Ro. 7 : 13. that sin become exc-g s.
8 : 3. his Son in likeness of s. flesh

SING.

Ex. 15 : 21. s. to the Lord, 1 Ch. 16 :
23. Ps. 30 : 4.-95 : 1.-96 : 1, 2.-98 :
1, 5.-147 : 7.-149 : 1. Is. 12 : 5.-
42 : 10. Je. 20 : 13. [I hear
32 : 18. the noise of them that s. do
Nu. 21 : 17. Spring up, O well, s. ye
De. 32 : † 43. s., O nations, wi. his peo.
1 S. 21 : 11. did they not s. one to ano.
1 Ch. 16 : 9. s. unto him, s. psalms
unto him, Ps. 105 : 2. [s. out
33. Then sh. the trees of the wood
2 Ch. 20 : 22. when they began to s.
Jb. 29 : 13. I caused widow's heart
Ps. 21 : 13. so will we s. and [to s.
33 : 2. s. to him with the psaltery
3. s. unto him new song, Is. 42 : 10.
51 : 14. s. of thy righteousn., 145 : 7.
65 : † 8. outgoings of morning to s.
13. the valleys shout, they also s.
66 : 2. s. forth honour of his name
4. All the earth shall s. to thee,
they shall s. to thy name [joy
67 : 4. let nations be glad and s. for
68 : 32. s. unto God, ye kingdoms
71 : 22. will I s. with harp, 98 : 5.
81 : 1. s. aloud unto G. our strength
104 : 12. fowls which s. am. branches
105 : 2. s. unto him, s. psalms, talk
137 : 3. s. us one of songs of Zion
4. How shall we s. Lord's song in
138 : 5. they shall s. in ways of Lord
149 : 5. let saints s. aloud upon beds
Pr. 29 : 6. but the righteous doth s.
Is. 23 : 15. 70 years Tyre s. as harlot
24 : 14. they sh. s. for majesty of L.
26 : 19. s., ye that dwell in dust
27 : 2. In that day s. ye unto her
35 : 6. shall the tongue of dumb s.
38 : 20. we will s. my songs all days
42 : 11. let inhabitants of rock s.
44 : 23. s., O ye heavens, for L., 49 : 13.
52 : 8. with the voice shall they s.
9. s. to Lord, ye waste places of
54 : 1. s., O barren, didst not bear
65 : 14. my servants shall s. for joy
Je. 31 : 7. s. with gladness for Jacob
12. they shall s. in height of Zion
51 : 48. all shall s. for Babylon
Eze. 27 : 25. ships of Tarshish did s.
Ho. 2 : 15. she shall s. as in youth
Zph. 2 : 14. voice shall s. in windows
3 : 14. s., O dau. of Zion, Zch. 2 : 10.
Ja. 5 : 13. merry? let him s. psalms
Re. 15 : 3. they s. song of Moses and

I will SING. [Lamb

Ex. 15 : 1. I w. s. unto the Lord,
Ju. 5 : 3. Ps. 18 : 6. [I w. s., 108 : 1.
Ps. 57 : 7. my heart is fixed, O God,
9. I w. s. unto thee am. nations
59 : 16. I w. s. of thy power, 89 : 1.
17. Unto thee, my strength, w. I s.
101 : 1. I w. s. of mercy and judgm.
104 : 33. I w. s. unto Lord, as long
144 : 9. I w. s. new song unto thee
Is. 5 : 1. w. I s. to my well beloved
Ro. 15 : 9. for this cause w. I s. to
1 Co. 14 : 15. I w. s. with the spirit,
I w. s. wi. the understanding
See PRAISE, PRAISES.

SINGED.

Da. 3 : 27. nor was hair of their head s.

SINGER.

1 Ch. 6 : 33. Heman, a s., son of Joel
Ha. 3 : 19. To chief s. on instruments

SINGERS.

1 K. 10 : 12. psalteries for s., 2 Ch. 9 : 11.
1 Ch. 9 : 33. these are s. chief, 15 : 16.
15 : 19. s. were appointed to sound
27. Levites and s. had fine lin. [(2)
2 Ch. 5 : 12. Also Levites whi. were s.,
13. trumpeters and s. were as one
20 : 21. Jehosaphat appointed s.
23 : 13. peo. rejoiced and s., 29 : 28.
35 : 15. s. sons of Asaph, Ne. 7 : 44.
Ezr. 2 : 41. s. hundred twenty eight
70. So the s. dwelt in their cities,
Ne. 7 : 73.-10 : 28. [Jerusalem
7 : 7. some of the s. went up unto
24. not be lawful to impose toll
10 : 24. s. to put aw. wives [upon s.
Ne. 7 : 1. porters and s. appointed
10 : 28. s. clave to their brethren
39. of the sanctuary, priests and
11 : 22. s. over business of house [s.
23. a portion sh. be for s., 12 : 47.-
12 : 28. sons of s. gathered [13 : 5
29. s. had builded them villages
42. s. sang aloud with Jezrahiah,
45. s. kept ward of th-r G. [overseer
46. in days of Da. were chief of s.
13 : 10. Levites and s. were fled
Ps. 68 : 25. s. went bef., players aft.
87 : 7. as well s. as players be there
Ec. 2 : 8. I gat me men s., women s.
Eze. 40 : 44. chambers of s. in court

SINGETH.

Pr. 25 : 20. he that s. songs to heavy

SINGING. [heart

1 S. 18 : 6. women out of cities s.
1 Ch. 6 : 32. they ministered with s.
13 : 8. all Isr. played bef. G. with s.
2 Ch. 20 : † 22. when they began in s.
23 : 18. to offer burnt off-gs with s.
30 : 21. s. with loud instruments
Ne. 12 : 27. kept dedication with s.
Ps. 30 : † 5. s. cometh in the morn-g
100 : 2. before his presence with s.
105 : † 43. bro-t his chosen with s.
107 : † 22. declare his works with s.
126 : 2. was our tongue filled with s.
† 5. that sow in tears sh. reap in s.
Can. 2 : 12. time of the s. of birds
Is. 14 : 7. they break forth into s.
16 : 10. in vineyards shall be no s.
35 : 2. it sh. rejoice with joy and s.
44 : 23. break forth into s. ye mts.
48 : 20. flee from Chaldeans with s.
49 : 13. O earth, break forth into s.
51 : 11. redeemed shall come with s.
54 : 1. break forth into s., O barren
55 : 12. mts. sh. break forth into s.
Da. 3 : † 5. time ye hear s. fall down
Zph. 3 : 17. will joy over thee with s.
Ep. 5 : 19. s. in your heart to Lord,
Col. 3 : 16.

SINGING men and SINGING women. [s. w.?

2 S. 19 : 35. can I hear voice of s. m.,
2 Ch. 35 : 25. all s. m., s. w. spake of
Ezr. 2 : 65. 200 s. m., 200 s. w. [Josiah
Ne. 7 : 67. they had 245 s. m. and

SINGLE. [Adj.] [s. w.

Mat. 6 : 22. if thine eye be s., thy
whole body full of light, Lu 11 :

SINGLE. [Verb.] [34.

Eze. 23 : † 47. company shall s. them

SINGLENESS. [out

Ac. 2 : 46. eat meat with s. of heart
Ep. 6 : 5 obey in s. of heart, Col. 3 : 22.

SINGULAR. [vow

Le. 27 : 2. When man sh. make s.

SI'NIM.

Is. 49 : 12. and these from land of S.

SIN'ITE. [1 : 15.

Ge. 10 : 17. the Arkite and S., 1 Ch.

SINK.

Jb. 38 : † 6. are foundations made to
Ps. 69 : 2. I s. in deep mire [s.
14. Deliver me, and let me not s.
Je. 51 : 64. Thus sh. Babylon s. and
Mat. 14 : 30. beginning to s., he cried
Lu. 5 : 7. ships, so they began to s.
9 : 44. Let these sayings s. into y-r

SINNED. [ears

Ex. 9 : 34. Pha. s. yet more, harden-
32 : 30. Ye have s. a great s., 31. [ed
33. Whoso. s., him will I blot out
Le. 4 : 3. for sin he hath s. a bullock
14. when the sin cong-n have s.
22. When ruler s. thro. ignor., 23.
28. If his sin which he hath s. (2)
5 : 5 sh. confess he s. in that thing
6. for sin he hath s. bring female
10. priest make atonement for sin
he hath s., 11, 13. Nu. 6 : 11.
6 : 4. bec. he s. sh. restore what he
Nu. 32 : 23. ye have s. against Lord
De. 9 : 16. behold ye had s. ag. Lord
18. sins ye s. in doing wickedly
Jos. 7 : 11. Isr. hath s. and transg-d
Ju. 11 : 27. I have not s. against thee
1 S. 19 : 4. he hath not s. ag. thee
24 : 11. know I have not s. ag. thee
1 K. 8 : 33. bec. th. have s. ag. thee,
35. 2 Ch. 6 : 24, 26. [6 : 39.
50. forgive thy peo. that s., 2 Ch.
15 : 30. sins of Jerob. he s., 16 : 13,
18 : 9. what have I s. that [19.
2 K. 17 : 7. Israel had s. ag. Lord
21 : 17. sin Manasseh s. is written
Ne. 9 : 29. but s. ag. thy judgments
Jb. 1 : 5. It may be my sons have s.
22. In all Job s. not, nor charged
8 : 4. If chil. have s. ag. him [s.
24 : 19. so doth grave those wh. have
Ps. 78 : 17. they s. yet more, 32.
Is. 43 : 27. Thy first father hath s.
Je. 2 : 35. thou sayest, I have not s.
33 : 8. whereby they have s. ag. me
40 : 3. because ye have s., 44 : 23.
50 : 7. bec. they have s., Zph. 1 : 17.
14. Babylon hath s. ag. the Lord
La. 1 : 8. Jerus. hath grievously s.
5 : 7. Our fa-s have s. and are not
Eze. 18 : 24. in sin he hath s. in th.
28 : 16. violence, and thou hast s.
37 : 23. dwellingplaces wh-n they s.
Ho. 4 : 7. As they were increased, so
they s. against me
10 : 9. Isr. thou hast s. fr. days of
Ha. 2 : 10. thou hast s. ag. thy soul
Jn. 9 : 3. Nei. this man s. nor parents
Ro. 2 : 12. as have s. without law;
as have s. in the law [5 : 12.
3 : 23. all have s. and come short,
5 : 14. death over them had not s.
16. not as it was by one that s.
1 Co. 7 : 28. if thou marry, hast not
s., if virgin marry, she not s. [s.
2 Co. 12 : 21. bewail many that have
13 : 2. I write to them which have s.
He. 3 : 17. was it not wi. them th. s.?
2 Pe. 2 : 4. G. spared not angels that s.
1 Jn. 1 : 10. if we say we have not s.

I have SINNED. [16.

Ex. 9 : 27. Pharaoh said, I h. s., 10 :
Nu. 22 : 34. Balaam said, I h. s.
Jos. 7 : 20. Indeed I h. s. ag. Lord
1 S. 15 : 24. S. said, I h. s., 30.-26 : 21.
2 S. 12 : 13. David said unto Nathan, I
h. s., 24 : 10, 17. 1 Ch. 21 : 8, 17.
19 : 20. thy serv. doth know I h. s.
Jb. 7 : 20. I h. s.; what shall I do?
33 : 27. if any say I h. s., he will
Ps. 41 : 4. heal my soul, for I h. s.
51 : 4. Ag. thee, thee only h. I s.
Mi. 7 : 9. I h. s. ag. him till he plead
Mat. 27 : 4. Judas said, I h. s. in betr.
Lu. 15 : 18. I will say, Father, I h. s.
ag. heaven and before thee, 21.

We have SINNED.
Nu. 12 : 11. lay not sin wherein w. h. s. [for w.h.s., De. 1 : 41.
14 : 40. we will go up unto the place,
21 : 7. w.h.s., we have spok. ag. L.
Ju. 10 : 10. w.h.s. because we have forsaken God, 1 S. 12 : 10. [good
15. w.h.s., do to us wh. seemeth
1 S. 7 : 6. fasted and said w.h.s.
1 K. 8 : 47. w.h.s., done perversely
2Ch. 6 : 37. w.h.s., have done amiss
Ne. 1 : 6. confess the sins w.h.s.
Ps. 106 : 6. w.h.s. with our fathers
Is. 42 : 24. L., he ag. whom w.h.s.
64 : 5. thou art wroth, for w.h.s.
Je. 3 : 25. down in our shame, w.h.s.
8 : 14. given us gall, for w.h.s. [s.
14 : 7. our backslid-gs many, w.h.
20. acknowledge wickedn. w.h.s.
La. 5 : 16. woe unto us that w.h.s.
Da. 9 : 5. w.h.s., committed iniq-y
8. to us confusion, because w.h.
11. curse upon us, bec. w.h.s. [s.
15. O Lord, w.h.s., done wickedly

SINNER.
Pr. 11 : 31. more the wicked and s.
13 : 6. wickedness overthroweth s.
22. wealth of s. laid up for just
Ec. 2 : 26. to s. he giveth travail
7 : 26. the s. shall be taken by her
8 : 12. Tho. s. do evil 100 times, yet
9 : 2. as is the good, so is the s.
18. one s. destroyeth much good
Is. 65 : 20. s. being 100 years old, sh.
Lu. 7 : 37. woman in city wh. was s.
39. wh. wom. this is ; for she is s.
15 : 7. joy in heaven over one s., 10.
18 : 13. God be merciful to me a s.
19 : 7. to be guest wi. man th. is a s.
Jn. 9 : 16. How can s. do such mir-
24. we know th. man is a s. [acles?
25. Whe. he be a s. I know not
Ro. 3 : 7. why yet am I judged as a s.
Ja. 5 : 20. he that converteth a s.
1 Pe. 4 : 18. where sh. ungodly and s.

SINNERS. [appear
Ge. 13 : 13. men of Sod. s. exceed-y
Nu. 16 : 38. take censers of these s.
1S. 15 : 18. utterly destroy s., Amalek-s
1 K. 1 : † 21. I and Sol. sh. be count-
Ps. 1 : 1. stand-h not in way of s. [ed s.
5. nor s. in cong-n of righteous
25 : 8. will he teach s. in the way
26 : 9. Gather not my soul with s.
51 : 13. and s. sh. be converted unto
104 : 35. Let the s. be consumed [three
Pr. 1 : 10. if s. entice, consent not
13 : 21. Evil pursueth s., but righte.
23 : 17. Let not thine heart envy s.
Is. 1 : 28. destruction of s. shall be
13 : 9. he shall destroy s. thereof
33 : 14. The s. in Zion are afraid
Am. 9 : 10. All s. of my peo. sh. die by
Mat. 9 : 10. many s. sat down with Jesus and disciples, Mk. 2 : 15.
11. Why eateth your master with s.? Mk. 2 : 16. Lu. 5 : 30.-15 : 2.
13. not come to call righteous, but s., Mk. 2 : 17. Lu. 5 : 32 [Lu. 7 : 34.
11 : 19. friend of publicans and s.,
26 : 45. and Son of man is betrayed into hands of s., Mk. 14 : 41. [th.
Lu. 6 : 32. for s. love those that love
33. thank have ye? for s. do same
34. s. lend to s. to receive again
13 : 2. that these were s. ab. all, 4.
15 : 1. publicans and s. to hear him
Jn. 9 : 31. we know G. heareth not s.
Ro. 5 : 8. while we were s. Ch. died
19. by one man's disobed. many s.
Ga. 2 : 15. We Jews, not s. of Gent.
17. if we ourselves are found s.
1 Ti. 1 : 9. the law is made for s.
15. Christ Jesus came to save s.
He. 7 : 26. high priest separate fr. s.
12 : 3. such contradiction of s.
Ja. 4 : 8. ye s., purify your hearts
Jude 15. speeches ungodly s. have

SINNEST. [spoken
Jb. 35 : 6. If s., what doest ag. him?

SINNETH. [norantly
Nu. 15 : 28. atonement for soul s. ig-
29. one law for him s. thro. ignor.
De. 19 : 15. one witn. not in sin he s.
1 K. 8 : 46. there is no man that s. not, 2 Ch. 6 : 36. Ec. 7 : 20. [soul
Pr. 8 : 36. he that s. ag. me wrongeth
14 : 21. that despiseth neighbour s.
19 : 2. that hasteth with his feet s.
20 : 2. whoso provoketh a king s.
Eze. 14 : 13. when la. s. will I stretch
18 : 4. soul that s. it shall die, 20.
33 : 12. for righteousn. in day he s.
1 Co. 6 : 18. fornicator s. ag. his body
7 : 36. let him do what he will, s. not
Tit. 3 : 11. such is subverted and s.
1 Jn. 3 : 6. Whoso. abideth in him s. not, whoso. s. hath not seen him
8. for devil s. from the beginning
5 : 18. whoso. is born of God s. not

SINNING. [me
Ge. 20 : 6. I withheld thee fr. s. ag.
Le. 6 : 3. in these th. a man doeth s.

SI'ON.
De. 4 : 48. From Aroer unto mount S.
See ZION.

SIPH'MOTH. [S.
1 S. 30 : 28. and to them wh. were in

SIP'PAI. See SAPH.

SIR.
Ge. 43 : 20. s., we came to buy food
Mat. 13 : 27. s., didst not sow good
21 : 30. he said, I go, s., went not
27 : 63. s., we rememb. deceiver said
Jn. 4 : 11. s., hast noth. to draw with
15. s., give me this water that I
19. s., I perceive thou art prophet
49. s., come ere my child die
5 : 7. s., I have no man to put me
12 : 21. saying, s., we would see Jes.
20 : 15. s., if have borne him hence
Re. 7 : 14. I said, s., thou knowest

SIRS.
Jn. 21 : † 5. s., have ye any meat?
Ac. 7 : 26. s., ye are brethren, why do
14 : 15. s., why do ye these [wrong
16 : 30. s., wh. must I do to be saved?
19 : 25. s., ye know th. by this craft
27 : 10. s., I perceive this voyage
21. s., ye should have hearkened
25. Wheref., s., be of good cheer

SI'RAH.
2 S. 3 : 26. bro-t him ag. fr. well of S.

SIR'ION. [S.
De. 3 : 9. wh. Hermon Sidonians call
Ps. 29 : 6. S. like a young unicorn

SIRNAME. See SURNAME.

SIRNAMED. See SURNAMED.

SISAM'AI.
1 Ch. 2 : 40. Eleasah begat S., S. begat

SIS'ERA.
Ju. 4 : 2. capt. of Jabin's host was S.
7. I will draw unto thee S.
9. sh. sell S. into hand of woman
12. shewed S. that Barak was gone
13. S. gathered together his char-s
14. L. hath deliv-d S. into thine ha.
15. Lord discomfited S. and all (2)
16. host of S. fell upon edge of sw.
17. S. fled away on his feet to, 15.
18. Jael went out to meet S., and
22. S. lay dead, and nail in temple
5 : 20. stars in courses fought ag. S.
26. with hammer she smote S.
28. mo. of S. looked out at window
30 to S. a prey of divers colours
1 S. 12 : 9. sold them into hand of S.
Ezr. 2 : 53. children of S., Ne. 7 : 55.
Ps 83 : 9. Do unto them as to S.

SISTER. [mah
Ge. 4 : 22. s. of Tubal-Cain was Naa-
24 : 30. bracelets upon his s.'s hands
59. sent away Rebekah their s.
60. Thou art our s., be mother of
Ge. 25 : 20. Reb-h, s. of Laban, Syrian
28 : 9. s. of Nebajoth to be wife
29 : 13. heard of Jacob his s.'s son
30 : 1. Rachel envied her s. [27.
34 : 13. had defiled Dinah, their s.,
14. can-t give our s. to one uncirc.
31. deal with our s. as a harlot
36 : 3. Bashemath, s. of Nebajoth
22. Lotan's s. was Timna, 1Ch. 1 : 39.
46 : 17. Serah their s., 1 Ch. 7 : 30.
Ex. 2 : 4. his s. stood afar off to witn.
7. said his s. to Pha.'s daughter
6 : 20. Amram took fa.'s s. to wife
23. Aaron took Elish. s. of Naashon
15 : 20. Miriam, s. of Aa. took timb.
Le. 18 : 9. nakedn. of thy s. not unc.
11. fa.'s wife's dau., she is thy s.,
12. not uncov. nakedn. of fa.'s s.
13 not uncov. nakedn. of moth-
18. Nei. take wife to her s. [er's s.
20 : 17. If man take s., see nakedn.
19. nakedn. of thy mo.'s s., fa.'s s.
21 : 3. for his s., a virgin, be defiled
Nu. 6 : 7. Nazarite not defiled for s.
25 : 18. dau. of prince of Midian, s.
26 : 59. Jochebed bare Miriam th. s.
De. 27 : 22. Cursed that lieth with s.
Ju. 15 : 2. is not younger s. fairer th.
2 S. 13 : 1. Abs. had a fair s., Tamar
2. Amnon fell sick for his s. Tamar
4. I love Tamar, my bro. Abs.'s s.
22. he had forced his s. Tamar, 32.
17 : 25. Abigail, s. to Zeruiah
21 : † 8. took five sons of Michal's s.
1 K. 11 : 19. gave him s. of his wife (2)
20. s. of Taphenes bare Genubath
2 K. 11 : 2. Jehosheba, s. of Ahaziah, took Joash, 2 Ch. 22 : 11.
1 Ch. 3 : 9. sons of David and Tamar
19. and Shelomith their s. [their s.
4 : 3. name of their s. Hazel-elponi
19. his wife Hodiah, s. of Naham
7 : 15. Machir took to wife s. of Hup-
18. And his s. bare Ishod [pim
32. Hotham and Shuah their s.
Can. 8 : 8 We have a little s., what shall we do for our s.? [it
Je. 3 : 7. her treacherous s. Judah saw
8. her treacherous s. feared not
10. her s. Jud. hath not turned [s.
22 : 18. not lament, saying, Ah, my
Eze. 16 : 45. thou art s. of thy sisters
46. thine elder s. is Samaria, thy younger s. Sodom [thou hast
48. Sodom thy s. hath not done as
49. this was iniquity of s. Sodom
56. thy s. Sod. was not mentioned
22 : 11. ano. hath humbled his s.
23 : 4. Aholah elder, Aholibah her
11. when her s. Aholibah saw [s.
18. my mind alienated fr. her s.
31. hast walked in way of thy s.
32. drink of thy s.'s cup deep, 33.
44 : 25. s. that hath no husb. defile
Lu. 10 : 39. s. called Mary, Jn. 11 : 1, 5.
Jn. 11 : 28. called Mary her s. secretly
39. the s. of him that was dead
19 : 25. stood by cross mother's s.
Ac. 23 : 16. Paul's s.'s son heard of
Ro. 16 : 1. I commend Phebe our s.
15. Salute Nereus and his s.
1 Co. 7 : 15. a s. is not under bondage
9 : 5. Have we not power to lead about a s. [nabas
Col. 4 : 10. Marcus, s.'s son to Bar-
Ja. 2 : 15. If brother or s. be naked
2 Jn. 13. the children of thy elect s.

SISTER in law.
Ru. 1 : 15. thy s. i. l. is gone back, return thou after thy s. i. l.

My SISTER.
Ge. 12 : 13. Say, I pray, thou art m.s.
19. Why saidst thou, She is m.s.?
20 : 2, 5, 12.-26 : 7, 9.
30 : 8. I have wrestled wi. m.s. and
2 S. 13 : 5. let m.s. Tamar come, 6.
11. Amnon said, lie with me, m.s.

2 S. 13:20. said, hold thy peace, m.s.
Jb. 17 : 14. said to worm, Thou m.s.
Pr. 7 : 4. Say unto wisd., Thou m.s.
Can. 4 : 9. ravished my heart, m.s.
10. How fair is thy love, m. s.
12. A garden inclosed is m.s.
5 : 1. am come into my gard., m.s.
2. Open to me, m.s., my love
Mk. 3 : 35. same is my brother, m.s.
Lu. 10 : 40. not care that m.s. left [me?

SISTERS.

Jos. 2 : 13. swear ye will save my s.
1 Ch. 2 : 16. Whose s. were Zeruiah
Jb. 1 : 4. called for their 3 s. to eat
42 : 11. came all his brethren and s.
Eze. 16 : 45. thou art sister of thy s.
51. justified s. in thy abom., 52.
55. When thy s. and dau-s return
61. ashamed when receive thy s.
Ho. 2 : 1. say unto your s., Ruhamah
Mat. 13 : 56. And his s., are they not
all with us? Mk. 6 : 3.
19 : 29. forsaken s. or father for my
sake, Mk. 10 : 29. Lu. 14 : 26. [s.
Mk. 10 : 30. shall receive 100 fold,
Jn. 11 : 3. Lazarus' s. sent unto him
1 Ti. 5 : 2. entreat younger wom. as s.

SIT.

Ge. 27 : 19. s. and eat of my venison
Nu. 32 : 6. Sh. breth. to war ye s. here
Ju. 5 : 10. Speak ye that s. in judgm.
Ru. 3 : 18. s. still, my daughter, till
4 : 1. Ho, such a one, s. down here, 2.
1 S. 9 : 22. made s. in chiefest place
16 : 11. we will not s. till he come
20 : 5. I not fail to s. with king
2 S. 19 : 8. the king doth s. in gate
2 K. 7 : 3. Why s. we until we die, 4.
18 : 27. men wh. s. on wall, Is. 36 : 12.
Ps. 26 : 5. will not s. with wicked
69 : 12. that s. in gate speak ag. me
107 : 10. Such as s. in darkness and
110 : 1. said, s. at my right hand
119 : 23. Princes did s. speak ag. me
127 : 2. vain for you to s. up late
Ec. 10 : 6. and rich s. in low place
Is. 3 : 26. shall s. upon the ground
14 : 13. I will s. upon mt. of cong-n
30 : 7. Their strength is to s. still
42 : 7. bring them that s. in darku.
47 : 1. s. in dust, s. on ground, 52 :
5. s. thou silent, O daughter [2.
8. sayest, I shall not s. as a widow
14. shall not be a fire to s. bef. it
Je. 8 : 14. Why do we s. still?
13 : 18. Say unto k., s. down, 36 : 15.
16 : 8. to s. with them to eat and
48 : 18. Thou daughter, s. in thirst
La. 1 : 1. How doth city s. solitary?
2 : 10. elders of Zion s. upon ground
Eze. 26 : 16. th. shall s. upon ground
28 : 2. hast said, I s. in seat of God
33 : 31. s. before thee as my people
44 : 3. prince shall s. to eat bread
Da. 7 : 9. till Ancient of days did s.
26. But the judgment shall s.
Jo. 3 : 12. will I s. to judge heathen
Mi. 4 : 4. s. ev. man under his vine
7 : 8. when I s. in darkn. L. be light
Zch. 3 : 8. fellows that s. before thee
Mal. 3 : 3. he shall s. as a refiner and
Mat. 8 : 11. many sh. s. down wi. Abr.
14 : 19. he commanded mult. to s.
down, 15 : 35. Mk. 6 : 39.-8 : 6.
20 : 21. sons may s., 1 on thy right
23. to s. on my right hand, not
mine to give, Mk. 10 : 37, 40.
22 : 44. s. thou on my right hand
till I make thine enemies, Mk. 12 :
36. Lu. 20 : 42. Ac. 2 : 34. He. 1 : 13.
23 : 2. Pharisees s. in Moses' seat
26 : 36. s. ye while I pray, Mk. 14 : 32.
Lu. 1 : 79. light to them s. in darku.
9 : 14. s. by fifties in a company
12 : 37. make them to s. down, and
13 : 29. sh. s. down in kingd. of God
14 : 8. s. not down in highest room
14 : 10. go, s. down in lowest room
16 : 6. Take thy bill, s. down quickly
17 : 7. will say, Go, s. down to meat
22 : 69. sh. Son of man s. on right ha.
Jn. 6 : 10. Jes. said, Make men s. do.
Ac. 8 : 31. that he come s. with him
1 Co. 8 : 10. s. at meat in idol's temple
Ep. 2 : 6. us s. in heavenly places
Ja. 2 : 3. say s. thou in a good place
Re. 17 : 3. I saw woman s. upon beast
18 : 7. saith in heart, I s. a queen
19 : 18. horses, and them that s. on

SIT, with throne, s.

1 K. 1 : 13. Solomon shall s. upon
my t., 17, 24, 30, 35. [on t., 27.
20. shouldest tell them who sh. s.
48. given one to s. on my t., 3 : 6.
8 : 25 shall not fail a man to s. on
t. of Isr., 20. 2 Ch. 6 : 16. Je. 33 : 17.
2 K. 10 : 30. thy sons sh. s. on t., 15 : 12.
1 Ch. 28 : 5. chosen Sol. to s. upon t.
Ps. 132 : 12. chil. sh. s. upon thy t.
Is. 16 : 5. he shall s. upon t. in truth
Je. 13 : 13. kings th. s. upon Da.'s t.
36 : 30. none to s. upon t. of David
Zch. 6 : 13. he shall s. upon his t.
Mat. 19 : 28. when Son of man shall
s. in t. of his glory, ye shall s.
on 12 t-s, 25 : 31. Lu. 22 : 30.
Ac. 2 : 30. raise up Ch. to s. on his t.
Re. 3 : 21. grant to s. wi. me in my t.

SITH. [blood

Eze. 35 : 6. s. thou hast not hated

SIT'NAH.

Ge. 26 : 21. called name of well S.

SITTEST. [alone?

Ex. 18 : 14. why s. thou thyself
De. 6 : 7. talk of them when thou s.
in thine ho., and walkest, 11 : 19.
28 : † 13. when thou s. down sh. dig
Ps. 50 : 20. Thou s. speakest ag. bro.
Pr. 23 : 1. When s. to eat wi. a ruler
Je. 22 : 2. Hear, O k. of Judah, th. s.
Ac. 23 : 3. s. thou to judge me after

SITTETH. [law?

Le. 15 : 4. thi. wh-n he s. be unclean
6. whereon he or she s. be unclean, 20, 23, 26. [at gate
Es. 6 : 10. do so to Mordecai that s.
Ps. 1 : 1. nor s. in seat of scornful
2 : 4. that s. in heavens shall laugh
10 : 8. He s. in the lurking places
29 : 10. Lord s. upon the flood; yea,
the Lord s. king for ever
99 : 1. Lord s. betw. the cherubim
Pr. 9 : 14. s. at the door of her house
31 : 23. when he s. am. elders of la.
Can. 1 : 12. While king s. at his table
Is. 28 : 6. to him that s. in judgment
40 : 22. It is he that s. upon circle
Je. 17 : 11. As partridge s. on eggs
La. 3 : 28. He s. alone and keepeth
Zch. 1 : 11. all the earth s. still, and
5 : 7. a woman that s. in the ephah
Mat. 23 : 22. sweareth by him that s.
Lu. 14 : 28. s. not down first and, 31.
22 : 27. greater, he that s. at meat
or serveth? is not he that s. [by
1 Co. 14 : 30. If revealed to ano. th. s.
Col. 3 : 1. Ch. s. on right ha. of God
2 Th. 2 : 4. he, as God, s. in tem. of G.
Re. 17 : 1. whore th. s. upon waters, 15.
9. seven mts. on which woman s.

SITTETH, SITTING, in, on or upon throne.

Ex. 11 : 5. from firstborn that s-h -
De. 17 : 18. when he s-h - he sh. write
1 K. 1 : 46. Solomon s-h - of kingdom
22 : 19. I saw the Lord s-g - and
the host, 2 Ch. 18 : 18. Is. 6 : 1.
Ps. 47 : 8. God s-h - of his holiness
Pr. 20 : 8. A king that s-h - of judgm.
Je. 17 : 25. kings s-g - of Da., 22 : 4, 30.
29 : 16. saith of king th. s-h - of Da.
Re. 5 : 13. glory, power unto him s-h-
6 : 16. hide from face of him s-h -
7 : 10. salvation to our God wh. s-h-
Re. 7 : 15. he that s-h - sh. dwell am.

SITTING. [Noun.] [them

1 K. 10 : 5. queen of Sheba had seen
s. of servants, 2 Ch. 9 : 4. [going
2 K. 19 : † 27. I know thy s. and thy
La. 3 : 63. their s. down and rising
See DOWNSITTING. [up

SITTING. [Part.]

De. 22 : 6. the dam s. upon young
Ju. 3 : 20. Eglon was s. in parlour
1 K. 13 : 14. found man of G. s. und.
2 K. 4 : 38. sons of proph-s s. bef. [oak
9 : 5. captains of the host were s.
Ne. 2 : 6. king said, queen s. by him
Es. 5 : 13. long as I see Mordecai s.
Ps. 17 : † 12. as young lion s. in secret
Can. 5 : † 12. His eyes are s. in fuln.
Je. 38 : 7. king s. in gate of Benj.
Mat. 9 : 9. s. at receipt of cust., Mk.
2 : 14. Lu. 5 : 27. [Lu. 7 : 32.
11 : 16. like children s. in markets,
20 : 30. two blind men s. by way side
21 : 5. Behold, thy King cometh unto thee s. upon an ass, Jn. 12 : 15.
26 : 64. shall see the Son of man s.
on right hand of God, Mk. 14 : 62.
27 : 36. And s. down, they watched
61. Mary s. over ag. the sepulchre
Mk. 2 : 6. certain scribes s. there
5 : 15. see him th. was possessed s.
16 : 5. saw a young man s. on right
Lu. 2 : 46. s. in midst of doctors [by
5 : 17. Phar., doctors of the law s.
8 : 35. s. clothed, in his right mind
10 : 13. s. in sackcloth and ashes
Jn. 2 : 14. the changers of money s.
20 : 12. Mary seeth two angels s.
Ac. 2 : 2. filled house they were s.
8 : 28. eunuch was s. in his chariot
25 : 6. Festus s. on judgment seat
Re. 4 : 4. upon the seats I saw 24 eld.

SITTING-place. [ers s.

2 Ch. 9 : 18. stays on each side of s.p.

SITUATE.

1 S. 14 : 5. forefront of one s. northw.
Eze. 27 : 3. Tyrus, s. at entry of sea
Na. 3 : 8. populous No s. am. rivers

SITUATION.

2 K. 2 : 19. s. of the city is pleasant
Ps 48 : 2. Beautiful for s. is Zion

SIVAN. See MONTH.

SIX. [36 : 16.

Ex. 26 : 9. shalt couple s. curtains,
22. westw. shalt make s. boards
28 : 10. s. of names on one stone (2)
36 : 27. for sides of tabern. s. boards
Le. 24 : 6. set s. cakes on a row
Nu. 7 : 3. s. covered wagons, 12 oxen
2 S. 6 : 13. gone s. paces he sacrificed
21 : 20. man had on every hand s.
fingers, on every foot s. toes,
1 Ch. 20 : 6. [5 or s. times
2 K. 13 : 19. shouldest have smitten
1 Ch. 3 : 4. These s. were born in Heb.
4 : 27. Shimei had 16 sons, s. dau-s
25 : 3. s. under hands of their father
26 : 17. eastward were s. Levites
Ne. 5 : 18. for me daily, 1 ox, s. sheep
Jb. 5 : 19. sh deliv. thee in s. troub-s
Pr. 6 : 16. these s. things doth L. hate
Eze. 9 : 2. s. men came fr. higher gate
Jn. 2 : 6. were set s. waterpots [me
Ac. 11 : 12. s. brethren accompanied
See BRANCHES, Six CITIES.

SIX cubits. [and span

1 S. 17 : 4. Goliath's height was s.c.
1 K. 6 : 6. mid. chamber s. c. broad
Eze. 40 : 5. a measuring reed of s.c.
12. the little chambers were s.c.
41 : 1. measured posts s.c. broad
3. door s.c. | 5. wall of house s.c.
8. foundations were s. great c.
Da. 3 : 1. breadth of image of gold s.c.
See DAYS, HUNDRED, LAMBS,
MEASURES, MONTHS, SONS,
STEPS, THOUSAND, WINGS,
YEARS.

SIXSCORE. [talents
1 K. 9 : 14. Hiram sent Solomon s.
SIXTEEN. [s. souls
Ge. 46 : 18. Zilpah bare unto Jacob
Ex. 26 : 25. of silver s. sockets, 36:30.
Jos. 15:41. s. cities wi. villages, 19:22.
1 Ch. 4 : 17. Shimei s. sons, 6 dau-s
24 : 4. were s. chief men of the hou.
2Ch. 13:21. Abi. begat 22 sons s. dau-s
See Sixteen THOUSAND.
See Sixteen YEARS.
SIXTEENTH. See DAY, LOT.
SIXTH.
Ge. 30 : 19. Leah bare Jacob s. son
Ex. 26 : 9. shalt double s. curtain
2 S. 3 : 5. the s., 1 Ch. 2 : 15.-3 : 3.-
12 : 11.-24 : 9.-25 : 13.-26 : 3, 5.
1 Ch. 27 : 9. The s. captain was Ira
Ne. 3 : 30. Hanun, the s. son of Zal.
Re. 6 : 12. opened s. seal, was earthq.
16 : 12. s. angel poured vial upon
21 : 20. s. foundation was sardius
See ANGEL, DAY, HOUR, LOT, MONTH, PART, YEAR.
SIXTY.
Nu. 7 : 88. for the sacrifice, rams s.,
he goats s., lambs s. [Mk. 4:8, 20.
Mat. 13 : 23. some 100 fold, some s.,
See CUBITS, YEARS.
SIXTYFOLD. [s.
Mat. 13 : 8. some an hund.-fold, some
SIZE. [15.
Ex. 36 : 9. curtains were all of oue s.,
1 K. 6 : 25. both cherubim of one s.
7 : 37. bases of one measure, and s.
1 Ch. 23 : 29. for all manner of s. Da.
SKEWED. [dows
1 K. 6 : † 4. for house made s. win-
SKIES.
2 S. 22 : 12. made thick clouds of s.
his pavilion, Ps. 18:11. [a sound
Ps. 77 : 17. clouds poured, s. sent out
Is. 45 : 8. let s. pour righteousness
Je. 51 : 9. her judgment is lifted to s.
See SKY.
SKILFUL, LY.
1 Ch. 5 : 18. sons of Reuben s. in war
15 : 22. Chenaniah, bec. he was s.
28 : 21. with thee ev. willing s. man
2 Ch. 2 : 14. cunning man, s. to work
Ps. 33 : 3. sing a new song, play s-y
Is. 3 : † 3. L. taketh aw. s. of speech
Eze. 21:31. into hand of s. to destroy
Da. 1 : 4. children s. in all wisdom
9 : † 22. to make thee s. of underst.
Am. 5 : 16. such are s. of lamenta-n
SKILFULNESS. [hands
Ps. 78 : 72. guided them by s. of his
SKILL. [Noun.]
Ec. 9 : 11. nor favour to men of s.
Da. 1 : 17. G. gave them s. in wisdom
9 : 22. I am come to give thee s.
SKILL. [Verb.]
1 K. 5 : 6. not any that can s. to hew
timber like Sidonians, 2 Ch. 2:8.
2 Ch. 2 : 7. send man that can s. to
34 : 12. all th. co. s. of music [grave
SKIN.
Ex. 22 : 27. it is his raiment for s.
29 : 14. bullock's s. burn, Le. 4 : 11.
34 : 29 wist not that s. shone, 30, 35.
Le. 7 : 8. priest that offereth have s.
11 : 32. if dead fall on s. be unclean
13 : 2. have in s. rising like plague
3. priest shall look on plague in s.,
if deeper than the s. of his flesh,
25, 30, 31, 32. [38, 39.
4. If bright spot be white in s., 24,
5. if the plague spread not in the
s., 6, 22, 28. [27, 35, 36.
7. if scab spread abroad in s., 8,
10. rising white in s. is leprosy
11. It is an old leprosy in s., 12.
18. in s. was a boil, and is healed
20. in sight lower than s., 21, 26.
48. whether in s. or anything made
of s., 49, 51, 52, 53, 57, 58.

Le. 13:56. rend it out of garment or s.
15 : 17. s. whereon is seed washed
Nu. 19 : 5. burn heifer, her s., flesh
Jb. 2 : 4. s. for s., all th. a man hath
7 : 5. my s. is broken, loathsome
10 : 11. hast clothed me wi. s., flesh
16 : 15. I sewed sackclo. upon my s.
18 : 13. devour strength of his s.
19 : 20. bone cleaveth to my s., I
am escaped wi. s. of teeth [body
26. after my s. worms destroy this
30 : 30. My s. is black upon me
41 : 7. Canst fill his s. with irons?
Ps. 102 : 5. my bones cleave to my s.
Je. 13 : 23. Can Ethiopian change s.?
La. 3 : 4. My flesh and s. he made old
4 : 8. s. cleaveth to their bones
5 : 10. Our s. was black like oven
Eze. 37 : 6. I will cover you with s.,
Mi. 3 : 2. who pluck off their s. [8.
3. who eat flesh, and flay their s.
Mk. 1 : 6. John had a girdle of a s.
SKINS.
Ge. 3 : 21. Lord made coats of s. and
27 : 16. she put s. of kids upon hand
Ex. 25 : 5. rams' s. dyed red, 26 : 14.
-35 : 7.-36 : 19.-39 : 34. [ers' s.
Ex. 35 : 23. red s. of rams and badg-
Le. 13 : 59. is the law of plague of s.
16 : 27. shall burn in fire their s.
Nu. 31:20. raiment made of s. [goat s.
He. 11 : 37. wandered in sheep s.,
SKIP, PED, PEDST, PING.
Ps. 29 : 6. maketh them s. like calf
114 : 4. the mts. s-d like rams, 6.
Can. 2 : 8. he cometh s-g upon hills
Je. 48 : 27. spakest of him, s-t for joy
SKIRT. [s.
De. 22 : 30. sh. not discover father's
27 : 20. he uncovereth his fath.'s s.
Ru. 3 : 9. spread thy s. over handm.
1 S. 15 : 27. he laid hold upon the s.
24 : 4. Da. cut off s. of Saul's robe
5. heart smote bec. cut off S.'s s.
11. father, see s. of thy robe in my
Eze. 16 : 8. I spread my s. over thee
Hag. 2 : 12. If one bear holy flesh in
s., and wi. his s. touch bread, or
Zch. 8 : 23. sh. take hold of s. of Jew
SKIRTS. [ments
Ps. 133 : 2. went down to s. of gar-
Is. 6 : † 1. s. filled the temple [poor
Je. 2 : 34. in s. is found blood of
13 : 22. for iniq-y thy s. discovered
26. will I discover thy s. Na. 3 : 5.
La. 1 : 9. Her filthiness is in her s.
Eze. 5 : 3. bind a few hairs in thy s.
SKULL.
Ju. 9 : 53. millstone to brake his s.
2 K. 9 : 35. no more of Jezebel than s.
Mat. 27 : 33. Golgotha, place of a s.,
Mk. 15:22. Lu. 23:†33. Jn. 19:17.
SKY. [s.
De. 33 : 26. rideth in excellency on
Jb. 37 : 18. Hast thou spread the s.?
Mat. 16:2. fair weather, for s. is red, 3.
Lu. 12 : 56. ye can discern face of s.
He. 11 : 12. so many as the stars of s.
See SKIES.
SLACK. [Adj.] [eth him
De. 7 : 10. not be s. to him that hat-
Jos. 18 : 3. How long s. to possess la.
Pr. 10:4. poor th. dealeth with s. hand
Zph. 3 : 16. Zion, Let not hands be s.
2 Pe. 3:9. Lord not s. concerning his
SLACK, ED. [prom.
De. 23 : 21. vow shalt not s. to pay
Jos. 10 : 6. s. not thy hand fr. serv-ts
2 K. 4 : 24. s. not riding for me
Ha. 1 : 4. law is s., judgm-t doth nev.
SLACKNESS. [s.
2 Pe. 3:9. L. not slack, as some count
SLAIN. [Active.]
Ge. 4 : 23. s. a man to my wounding
Nu. 14:16. he hath s. th. in wildern.
22 : 33. surely now I had s. thee
De. 1 : 4. After he had s. Sihon, king

De. 21:1. not known who hath s. him
Ju. 9 : 18. s. his sons upon 1 stone
15 : 16. jaw of ass have I s. 1,000
20 : 5. men of Gibeah to have s. me
1S. 18:7. Saul s. his thousands, 21:11.
22:21. that Saul had s. L.'s priests
2 S. 1 : 16. I have s. Lord's anointed
3 : 30. Abner, bec. he had s. Asahel
4 : 11. when wicked have s. righte-s
13 : 30. Abs. hath s. all king's sons
32. not s. all, Amnon only is dead
21 : 12. when Philistines had s. Saul
16. Ishbi-benob to have s. David
1 K. 1 : 19. Adonijah hath s. oxen, 25.
9 : 16. Pharaoh had s. Canaanites
13 : 26. lion hath torn and s. him
16 : 16. heard Zimri hath s. king
2 K. 14 : 5. slew serv-s who had s. k.
2 Ch. 21: 13. hast s. thy breth., better
22 : 1. band of men had s. eldest
9. when they had s. Ahaziah [liah
23 : 21. city quiet aft. had s. Atha-
28 : 9. have s. them in rage that
Es. 9 : 12. Jews have s. 500 men
Jb. 1: 15. Sabeans have s. serv-ts, 17.
Pr. 7 : 26. many strong men s. by her
Is. 14 : 20. because thou hast s. peo.
Je. 33 : 5. men I have s. in anger
41:4. aft. he had s. Geda-h, 9, 16, 18.
La. 2 : 21. hast s. them in anger, 3:43.
Eze. 16 : 21. thou hast s. my child-n
23 : 39. had s. their children to idols
Ho. 6 : 5. I have s. them by words
Ac. 2 : 23. ye by wicked hands have s.
7 : 52. s. them shewed com-g of Just
23 : 14. eat nothing till have s. Paul
SLAIN. [Passive.] [s.
Ge. 34 : 27. sons of Jacob came upon
Le. 14 : 51. dip in blood of s. bird
26 : 17. ye sh. be s. before enemies
Nu. 11:22. Sh. flocks and herds be s.
23:24. drink blood of the s.
25 : 14. Israelite th. was s. was Zim.
15. woman th. was s. was Cozbi, 18.
31 : 8. besides the rest that were s.
De. 21 : 1. if one be found s. in land
2. cities round about him th. is s.
3. elders of city next to s. man, 6.
28 : 31. ox sh. be s. bef. thine eyes
32:42. arrows drunk with blood of s.
Jos. 11 : 6. will I deliver them all s.
13 : 22. Balaam am. them th. were s.
Ju. 16 : † 24. who multiplied our s.
20 : 4. husband of the woman s.
1 S. 4 : 11. Hophni and Phinehas s.
19 : 6. As Lord liveth, he not be s.
11. to morrow thou shalt be s.
20 : 32. Whf. sh. he be s., what done
31 : 1. men of Israel fell down s. in
mt. Gilboa, 1Ch. 10:1. [1Ch. 10:8.
8. when Philis. came to strip s.,
2 S. 1 : 19. beauty of Israel is s.
22. From the blood of s., from fat
25. O Jonathan, thou wast s. in
18 : 7. Isr. s. bef. David's servants
23 : † 8. ag-t 800 s. at one time, †18.
1 K. 11: 15 Joab was gone to bury s.
2K. 3: 23. is blood, kings are surely s.
11 : 2. stole Joash fr. among them
were s., 2 Ch. 22 : 11. [be s.
8. cometh within ranges, let him
15. Let her not be s. in house of L.
16. laid hands, there was she s.
1 Ch. 5 : 22. many s. war was of God
11 : 11. 300 s. by him at one time
2 Ch. 13 : 17. fell s. of Israel 500,000
28:14. whoso. follow-h, let him be s.
Es. 7 : 4. sold, I and my peo., to be s.
9 : 11. number of the s. in Shushan
Jb. 39 : 30. where s. are, there is she
Ps. 62 : 3. ye shall be s., all of you
88 : 5. like the s. that lie in grave
89 : 10. hast broken Rahab as one s.
Pr. 22 : 13. slothful saith, I sh. be s.
24 : 11. deliver those ready to be s.
Is. 10 : 4. they shall fall under the s.
26 : 21. earth no more cover her s.

Is. 27 : 7. he s. acc. to slaughter of s.
34 : 3. Their s. also shall be cast out
66 : 16. s. of the Lord shall be many
Je. 9 : 1. weep for s. of my people
25 : 33. s. of L. be from end of earth
41 : 9. Ishmael filled pit with the s.
51 : 4. s. sh. fall in land of Chald-s
47. her s. sh. fall in midst of her
49. As Babylon caused s. of Isr.
to fall, at Bab. sh. fall s. of earth
La. 2 : 20. sh. prophet be s. in sanct-y
Eze. 6 : 7. s. shall fall in midst of you
13. s. men sh. be among their idols
9 : 7. Defile house, fill courts wi. s.
11 : 6. Ye have multiplied s. in
city, filled streets wi. s. ⌈cald-n
7. Your s. are flesh, this city the
21 : 14. sword of s., it is the sword
of great men s. ⌈them s.
29. to bring thee upon necks of
28 : 8. shalt die deaths of them s.
30 : 4. great pain when s. sh. fall in
11. shall fill land with s. ⌊Egypt
35 : 8. I will fill mts. with s. men
37 : 9. O breath, breathe upon s.
Da. 2 : 13. decree that wise men be
s., sought Daniel to be s. ⌈k. s.
5 : 30. that night was Belshazzar
7 : 11. I beheld, till beast was s.
11 : 26. army overfl., and many s.
Na. 3 : 3. there is multitude of s.
Zph. 2 : 12. Ye Ethiopians shall be s.
Lu. 9 : 22. Son of man must be s.
Ac. 5 : 36. Theudas was s. and many
7 : 42. O Isr. have ye off-d s. beasts?
13 : 28. desired Pilate that he be s.
1 Co. 5 : † 7. Ch., our passover, s. for us
Ep. 2 : 16. cross, having s. enmity
Re. 2 : 13. Antipas, who was s. amo.
5 : 6. in midst stood Lamb, as s. ⌈s.
9. Thou art worthy, for thou wast
12. Worthy is Lamb that was s.,
13 : 8. ⌈word of God
6 : 9. souls of them that were s. for
11. 13. in earthquake were s. 7,000
13 : † 3. one of his heads s. to death
18 : 24. in her found blood of all s.
See **Slain by** or **with SWORD.**

SLANDER, S. ⌈land

Nu. 14 : 36. by bringing up a s. on
Ps. 31 : 13. I have heard s. of many
Pr. 10 : 18. th. uttereth a s. is a fool
Je. 6 : 28. revolters walking with s-s
9 : 4. neighbour will walk with s-s
Eze. 22 : † 9. In thee are men of s-s

SLANDERED.

2 S. 19 : 27. he hath s. thy servant

SLANDERERS.

1 Ti. 3 : 11. th. wives be grave, not s.

SLANDEREST, ETH.

Ps. 50 : 20. s-t thine own mo.'s son
101 : 5. s-h his neigh. him will I cut

SLANDEROUSLY. ⌊off

Ro. 3 : 8. not rather, as we be s. re-

SLANG. ⌊ported

1 S. 17 : 49. Da. took a stone and s. it

SLAUGHTER.

Ge. 14 : 17. return fr. s. of Chedor-r
1 S. 14 : 14. first s. wh. Jona-n made
30. had there not been greater s.
17 : 57. as David returned fr. s. of
Phils., 18 : 6. 2 S. 1 : 1. ⌈shearers
25 : † 11. Shall I take my s. for my
2 S. 17 : 9. s. am. peo. th. follow Abs.
2 Ch. 25 : 14. Amaziah was come fr. s.
Es. 9 : 5. with stroke of sword and s.
Ps. 44 : 22. counted as sheep for s.
Pr. 7 : 22. goeth aft. her, as ox to s.
Is. 10 : 26. acc-g to the s. of Midian
14 : 21. Prepare s. for his chil. for
27 : 7. acc-g to s. of them are slain
34 : 2. he hath delivered them to s.
53 : 7. brought as lamb to s., Je. 11 : 19.
65 : 12. ye shall all bow down to s.
Je. 7 : 32. The valley of s., 19 : 6.
12 : 3. pull them out like sheep for
s., prepare them for day of s.
Je. 25 : 34. days of s. are accompl-d
48 : 15. young men are gone down
50 : 27. let them go down to s. ⌊to s.
51 : 40. bring them like lambs to s.
Eze. 9 : 2. and every man a s. weapon
21 : 10. is sharpened to make sore s.
15. it is wrapped up for the s.
22. to open the mouth in the s.
28. sword is drawn, for s. furbished
26 : 15. s. is made in midst of thee
39 : † 17. gather on ev. side to my s.
Ho. 5 : 2. are profound to make s.
Ob. 9. of Esau may be cut off by s.
Zch. 11 : 4. saith Lord, Feed flock of s.
7. I will feed flock of s., O poor
Ac. 8 : 32. He was led as a sheep to s.
9 : 1. Saul yet breathing out s. ag.
Ro. 8 : 36. counted as sheep for s.
He. 7 : 1. Abr. returning fr. s. of k-s
Ja. 5 : 5. nourished hearts, as in day
See **GREAT slaughter.** ⌊of s.

SLAUGHTERMEN.

Je. 39 : † 9. Then Nebuzar-adan, chief
of the s., Je. 52 : † 12. Da. 2 : † 14.

SLAVE, S.

Je. 2 : 14. Is Israel a homeborn s.
Re. 18 : 13. no man buyeth their s-s

SLAY.

Ge. 4 : 14. that every one shall s. me
20 : 4. wilt thou s. righteous nat-n?
11. will s. me for my wife's sake
27 : 41. will I s. my brother Jacob
34 : 30. they shall gather and s. me
37 : 20. Come now, let us s. him
26. What profit if we s. brother?
42 : 37. s. my 2 sons if I bring him not
43 : 16. Bring men, s., make ready
Ex. 4 : 23. I will s. thy son, firstborn
23 : 7. innoc-t and righteous s. not
29 : 16. sh. s. ram and sprinkle bl.
32 : 12. did bring them out to s. th.
27. s. every man his brother and
Le. 4 : 29. he sh. s. the sin off-ing, 33.
14 : 13. he shall s. the lamb in
20 : 15. man lie with beast, s. beast
Nu. 19 : 3. one shall s. red heifer
25 : 5. s. ye every one his men
35 : 19. revenger sh. s. murderer, 21.
De. 19 : 6. lest avenger of blood s. him
Ju. 8 : 19. saved them wo. not s. you
20. said to Jether, Up and s. them
9 : 54. s. me, that men say not, A
1 S. 2 : 25. L. would s. them ⌊woman
5 : 11. Send aw. ark that it s. us not
14 : 34. Bring ev. man his ox, s. here
15 : 3. spare not, s. man and woman
19 : 15. Bring him, that I may s. him
20 : 8. if be in me iniq-y, s. me thys.
22 : 17. king said, s. priests of Lord
2 S. 1 : 9. Saul said, Stand upon, s. me
1 K. 3 : 26. child, in no wise s. it, 27.
15 : 28. Nadab did Baasha s.
18 : 12. cannot find thee, he sh. s. me
14. Elijah is here, he shall s. me
19 : 17. escapeth Hazael shall Jehu
s., escapeth Jehu sh. Elisha s.
20 : 36. soon as departed, lion s. thee
2 K. 10 : 25. Go in, s. them, let none
17 : 26. God sent lions, they s. them
2 Ch. 20 : 23. utterly to s. and destroy
23 : 14. s. her not in hou. of L.
Ne. 4 : 11. we will s. them
Jb. 9 : 23. If scourge s. suddenly, he
13 : 15. Tho. he s. me, will I trust
20 : 16. viper's tongue shall s. him
Ps. 34 : 21. Evil shall s. wicked that
59 : 11. s. them not, lest peo. forget
94 : 6. They s. widow and stranger
109 : 16. might s. broken in heart
139 : 19. Surely thou wilt s. wicked
Pr. 1 : 32. turning of simple sh. s. th.
Is. 11 : 4. with breath sh. he s. wicked
14 : 30. and he shall s. thy remnant
27 : 1. Lord shall s. dragon in sea
65 : 15. for Lord God shall s. thee
Je. 5 : 6. a lion shall s. them ⌈them
29 : 21. shall s. Ahab and Zedekiah
Je. 40 : 15. Let me go, I will s. Ishmael; wheref. should he s. thee?
41 : 8. ten found that said, s. us not
50 : 27. s. her bullocks, woe unto
Eze. 9 : 6. s. utterly old and young
23 : 47. sh. s. their sons and dau-s
44 : 11. they shall s. burnt offering
Ho. 2 : 3. dry land s. her with thirst
9 : 16 bring forth, yet will I s. fruit
Am. 2 : 3. I will s. all princes thereof
9 : 4. I com-d sword, it sh. s. them
Zch. 11 : 5. Whose possessors s. them
Lu. 11 : 49. some of them they sh. s.
19 : 27. bri. hither, s. them bef. me
Ac. 11 : 7. Arise, Peter, s. and eat

To SLAY. ⌈cone

Ge. 18 : 25. far from thee t. s. right-
22 : 10. Ab. stretched hand t. s. son
37 : 18. they conspired t. s. him
Ex. 2 : 15. Pha. sought t. s. Moses
5 : 21. sword in their hand t. s. us
21 : 14. if man upon neighbour t. s.
De. 9 : 28. bro-t them out t. s. them
27 : 25. taketh reward t. s. innocent
1 S. 5 : 10. have brought ark t. s. us
19 : 5. whf. then sin, t. s. David
11. Saul went t. s. him in morning
20 : 33. determined of fa. t. s. David
2 S. 3 : 37. was not of king t. s. Abn.
21 : 2. Saul sought t. s. them in ⌈son?
1 K. 17 : 18. art thou come t. s. my
18 : 9. me into hand of Ahab t. s. me?
2 Ch. 20 : 23. utterly t. s., destroy th.
Ne. 6 : 10. they will come t. s. thee,
in night t. s. thee ⌈sault them
Es. 8 : 11. t. s. power that would as-
Ps. 37 : 14. t. s. such as be of upright
32. watcheth righte., seeketh t. s.
Je. 15 : 3. appoint sword t. s. dogs
18 : 23. thou knowest counsel t. s. me
40 : 14. Baalis sent Ishm. t. s. thee
Eze. 13 : 19. t. s. souls that should
40 : 39. t. s. burnt offering ⌊not die
Da. 2 : 14. Arioch gone t. s. wise men
Ha. 1 : 17. continually t. s. nations
Jn. 5 : 16. Jews sought t. s. Jesus
Ac. 5 : 33. took counsel t. s. the apos.
9 : 29. th. went about t. s. him ⌈part
Re. 9 : 15. angels prepared t. s. third
See **Slay by** or **with SWORD.**

SLAYER.

Nu. 35 : 11. cities of refuge for you;
that s. may flee thither, De. 4 :
42.–19 : 3, 4. Jos. 20 : 3.
24. judge between s. and revenger
25. cong-n deliver s. from avenger
26. if s. shall come without city
27. the revenger of blood kill s.
28. after death of high priest s.
shall return, Jos. 20 : 6. ⌈sue s.
De. 19 : 6. Lest avenger of blood pur-
Jos. 20 : 5. they shall not deliver s.
21 : 13. Hebron city of refuge for s.
21. Shechem for s. | 27 Golan for s.
32. Kedesh in Galilee for the s.
38. Ramoth, a city of refuge for s.
Eze. 21 : 11. sword is furbished, given

SLAYETH. ⌊to s.

Ge. 4 : 15. Lord said, whoso. s. Cain
De. 22 : 26. riseth ag. neighb. and s.
Jb. 5 : 2. wrath killeth, envy s. silly
Eze. 28 : 9. Wilt say bef. him that s.
thee, I am God? thou shalt be a
man in hand of them th. s. thee

SLAYING.

Jos. 8 : 24. Isr. made end of s., 10 : 20.
Ju. 9 : 56. wickedness in s. his breth.
1 K. 17 : 20. evil upon widow by s. her
Is. 22 : 13. s. oxen, killing sheep ⌊son
57 : 5. s. the children in the valleys
Eze. 9 : 8. while s. them, and I was

SLEEP. [Noun.] ⌊left

Ge. 28 : 16. Jacob awaked out of his
31 : 40. that I was, my s. departed ⌊s.
Ju. 16 : 14. Sam. awaked out of s. 20.
Jb. 14 : 12. nor be raised out of s.
Ps. 13 : 3. lest I sleep the s. of death

Ps. 76 : 5. stouthearted slept their s.
6. chariot and horse into deep s.
78 : 65. Lord awaked as out of s.
90 : 5. them away, they are as a s.
127 : 2. so he giveth his beloved s.
132 : 4. I will not give s. to eyes
Pr. 3 : 24. and thy s. shall be sweet
4 : 16. their s. is taken away, unless
6 : 4. Give not s. to thine eyes, nor
9. O sluggard, when arise out of thy
10. Yet a little more s., 24 : 33. ⌊s.
20 : 13. Love not s., lest to poverty
Ec. 5 : 12. s. of labouring man sweet
8 : 16. nei. day nor night seeth s.
Je. 31 : 26. my s. was sweet unto me
51 : 39. may sleep perpetual s., 57.
Da. 2 : 1. spirit troubled, his s. brake
6 : 18. passed night, his s. went fr.
Zch. 4 : 1. as a man wakened out of s.
Mat. 1 : 24. Joseph being raised fr. s.
Lu. 9 : 32. they were heavy with s.
Jn. 11 : 11. that I awake him out of s.
13. spoken of taking of rest in s.
Ac. 13 : 36. David fell on s., was laid
16 : 27. keeper awaking out of his s.
Ro. 13 : 11. high time to awake out
See **DEEP sleep.** ⌊of s.

SLEEP. [Verb.]

Ge. 28 : 11. Jacob lay down to s.
Ex. 22 . 27. raiment, wh-in sh. he s.?
De. 24 : 12. not s. with his pledge
13. he may s. in his own raiment
31 : 16. shalt s. with fa-s, 2 S. 7:12.
Ju. 16 : 19. made him s. upon her kne.
1 S. 3 : 3. Samuel was laid down to s.
1 K. 1 : 21. king shall s. with his fa-s
Es. 6 : 1. that night could not king s.
Jb. 7 : 21. now shall I s. in the dust
Ps. 4 : 8. I will lay me down and s.
13 : 3. lest I s. the sleep of death
121 : 4. shall neither slumber nor s.
Pr. 4 : 16. s. not except done mischief
6 : 9. How long wilt thou s., O slug.?
10. a folding of hands to s., 24:33.
Ec. 5 : 12. but abundance of the rich
will not suffer him to s.
Can. 5 : 2. I s., but my heart waketh
Is. 5 : 27. none shall slumber nor s.
Je. 51 : 39. may s. perpetual sleep, 57.
Eze. 34 : 25. they shall s. in woods
Da. 12 : 2. that s. in dust sh. awake
Mat. 26 : 45. s. on now, Mk. 14 : 41.
Mk. 4 : 27. should s. and seed spring
Lu. 22 : 46. Why s. ye? rise, pray
Jn. 11 : 12. if he s. he shall do well
1 Co. 11 : 30. For this cause many s.
15 : 51. We shall not all s., but be
changed ⌈will God bring
1 Th. 4 : 14. them which s. in Jesus
5 : 6. let us not s. as do others
7. they that s. sleep in night ⌈or s.
10. died for us, that whe. we wake

SLEEPER. ⌈arise

Jon. 1 : 6. What meanest thou, O s.,

SLEEPEST. ⌈Lord?

Ps. 44 : 23. Awake, why s. thou, O
Pr. 6 : 22. thou s. it shall keep thee
Mk. 14 : 37. Simon, s. thou? couldest
Ep. 5 : 14. Awake, thou that s., and

SLEEPETH. ⌈s.

1 K. 18 : 27. Elijah said, peradven. he
Pr. 10 : 5. that s. in harvest is a son
Ho. 7 : 6. their baker s. all night ⌊th.
Mat. 9 : 24. Give place, for maid is
not dead, but s., Mk. 5 : 39. Lu.
Jn. 11 : 11. Our friend Laz-s s. ⌊8:52.

SLEEPING.

1 S. 26 : 7. Saul lay s. within trench
Is. 56 : 10. watchmen blind, s. ⌈s.
Mk. 13 : 36. Lest coming he find you
14 : 37. cometh and findeth them s.
Lu. 22 : 45. found discip. s. for sor-w
Ac. 12 : 6. Peter was s. betw. 2 sold-s

SLEIGHT.

Ep. 4 : 14. carried about by s. of men

SLENDER.

Le. 21 : † 20 a man too s. not to offer

SLEPT. ⌈s.

Ge. 2 : 21. deep sleep upon Adam, he
41 : 5. Pharaoh s., and dreamed
2 S. 11 : 9. Uriah s. at door of k.'s ho.
1 K. 3 : 20. while thine handmaid s.
19 : 5. as he s. angel touched him
Jb. 3 : 13. I sho. have s. then had I
Ps. 3 : 5. I laid me down and s.
76 : 5. stouthearted have s. sleep
Mat. 13 : 25. while men s. his enemy
25 : 5. bridegroom tarried, they s.
27 : 52. bodies of saints whi. s. arose
28 : 13. discip. stole him while we s.
1 Co. 15 : 20. firstfruits of them th. s.
See **Slept with FATHERS.**

SLEW. ⌈Cain s.

Ge 4 : 25. instead of Abel, whom
34 : 25. they s. all the males ⌈son
26. they s. Hamor and Shechem,
49 : 6. in anger they s. a man, and
Ex. 2 : 12. Moses s. the Egyptian
13 : 15. Lord s. all firstborn in Egy.
Le. 8 : 15. s. bullock, took blood, 23.
9 : 8. Aaron s. calf of sin off-g, 15.
12. s. burnt off-g, presented blood
18. He s. the bullock and the ram
Nu. 31 : 7. they s. all males of Midian
Jos. 8 : 21. turned and s. men of Ai
9 : 26. Gibeonites, they s. them not
10 : 10. Lord s. them with great
slaughter, 1 S. 19 : 8. 2Ch. 13:17.
26. Joshua s. the five kings, 11:17.
Ju. 1 : 4. they s. in Bezek 10,000
10. they s. Sheshai and Talmai ⌈5.
17. Judah with Simeon s. Canaan.,
3 : 29. they s. of Moab 10,000 men
31. Shamgar s. of Philistines 600
7 : 25. s. Oreb and Zeeb, 2 princes
8 : 17. Gideon s. men of Penuel ⌈s.?
18. What manner of men whom ye
21. Gideon s. Zebah and Zalmunna
9 : 5. Abimelech s. breth., 70 pers-s
24. blood upon Abimelech wh. s. th.
44. ran upon peo. in fields, s. th.
14 : 19. Sams. s. 30 men of Askelon
15 : 15. with jawbone Sams. s. 1,000
16 : 24. our enemy, who s. many of
30. dead he s. at his death more ⌊us
20 : 45. they s. 2,000 men of them
1 S. 1 : 25. Elkanah, Hannah s. bul-k
4 : 2. Philis. s. of Israel 4,000 men
11 : 11. Isr. s. Ammonites until heat
14 : 13. his armourbearer s. aft. him
32. the people s. oxen and calves
34. ev. man brought ox and s.
17 : 36. Thy serv-t s. lion and bear
18 : 27. David s. of Philis. 200 men
19 : 5. life in hand, and s. Philistine
22 : 18. Doeg s. 85 persons that did
29 : 5. they sang, Saul s. thousands
30 : 2. Amalekites s. not any, gr. or
31 : 2. Philistines s. Jonathan and
2 S. 3 : 30. Joab, Abishai, s. Abner
4 : 12. David s. them, cut off hands
8 : 5. David s. of Syrians 22,000
10 : 18. David s. men of 700 chariots
14 : 7. kill him for life of bro. he s.
21 : 1. Saul, bec. he s. Gibeonites
18. Sibbechai s. Saph, of sons of
giant, 1 Ch. 20 : 4. ⌈1 Ch. 20 : 5.
19. Elhanan s. brother of Goliath,
23 : 8. spear ag. 800 whom he s.
12. Shammah defended ground,
s. Philistines ⌈Ch. 11 : 20.
18. spear ag. 300 and s. them, 1
20. he s. two lionlike men of Moab, he s. lion, 1 Ch 11 : 22. ⌈11:23.
21. he s. Egyp-n, goodly man, 1 Ch.
1 K. 1 : 9. Adonijah s. sheep, oxen
2 : 5. Joab did to Amasa, whom he s.
11 : 24. David s. them of Zobah
16 : 11. Zimri s. all house of Baasha
18 : 13. when Jez. s. prophets of L.
40. and Elijah s. prophets of Baal
19 : 21. Elisha s. yoke of oxen and
20 : 20. they s. every one his man
21. King of Israel s. Syrians, 29.
2 K. 9 : 31. Zimri peace, who s. mas.?
10 : 7. s. 70 persons and put heads
9. I s. him, but who s. all these?
11. Jehu s. all that remained, 17.
14. they took them alive and s. ⌈17.
11 : 18. peo. s. Mattan, priest of Baal,
12 : 20. his serv-s s. Joash in house
14 : 5. Amaziah s. servants that had
slain his father, 2 Ch. 25 : 3.
6. their chil. he s. not, 2 Ch. 25:4.
7. he s. of Edom in valley, 1Ch. 18:
16 : 9. king of Assyria s. Rezin ⌊12.
17 : 25. L. sent lions which s. some
21 : 23 the servants of Amon s. him
24. people s. them, 2 Ch. 33 : 25.
23 : 20. Josiah s. all priests of high
25 : 7. Nebuchadnezzar s. sons of
Zedekiah, Je. 39 : 6.-52 : 10.
1 Ch. 7 : 21. whom men of Gath s.
10 : 2. the Philistines s. Jonathan
11 : 14. deliv-d parcel and s. Philis.
18 : 5. Da. s. of Syr-s 22,000, 19:18.
2 Ch. 22 : 8. Jehu s. princes of Judah
24 : 22. remembered not, but s. son
28 : 6. Pekah s. in Judah, 120,000
7. Zichri s. Maaseiah king's son
Ne. 9 : 26. they s. thy prophets, whi.
Es. 9 : 6. in Shushan Jews s. 500 men
10. The ten sons of Haman s. they
15. Jews s. 300 men at Shushan
16. Jews s. of their foes 75,000
Ps. 78 : 31. wrath of God s. fattest
34. When he s. them they sought
105 : 29. waters into blood, s. fish
135 : 10. smote nations, s. mighty k-s
136 : 18. And s. famous kings: for
Is. 66 : 3. killeth ox as if he s. man
Je. 20 : 17. Bec. he s. me not fr. womb
41 : 3. Ishm s. all Jews wi. him, 7.
8. he forbare, and s. them not
La. 2 : 4. s. all pleasant to the eye
Eze. 9 : 7. they went and s. in city
40 : 42. instruments whw. s. sac. 41.
Da. 3 : 22. fire s. men took up Sha-
5 : 19. wh. he would Neb-r s. ⌊drach
Mat. 2 : 16. Herod s. all the children
22 : 6 remnant took servants and s.
23 : 35. whom ye s. betw. temple and
Lu. 13 : 4. whom tower in Siloam s.
Ac. 5 : 30. raised Jesus, whom ye s.
10 : 39. Jesus, wh. they s. and hanged
Ro. 7 : 11. For sin by com-t s. me
1 Jn. 3 : 12. not as Cain, who s. his

SLEW him. ⌊brother

Ge. 4 : 8. Cain rose ag. Abel, s. h.
38 : 7. Er was wicked, Lord s. h.
10. displeased Lord, he s. h. ⌈h.
Ju. 9 : 54. say not of me, A woman s.
12 : 6. s. h. at passages of Jordan
1 S. 17 : 35. I caught him and s. h.
50. Da. smote Philis. and s. h., 51.
2 S. 1 : 10. I stood upon him and s. h.
4 : 7. smote Ish-bosheth and s. h.
10. I took hold and s. h. in Ziklag
14 : 6. one smote other and s. h.
18 : 15. ten compassed Abs. and s. h.
21 : 21. Jonathan s. h., 1 Ch. 20 : 7.
23 : 21. s. h. wi. own spear, 1Ch. 11:23.
1 K. 2 : 34. Benaiah upon Joab, s. h.
13 : 24. lion met him, s. h., 20 : 36.
2 K. 10 : 9. I consp-d ag. master, s. h.
14 : 19. Amaziah fled, but they sent
and s. h., 2 Ch. 25 : 27. ⌈and s. h.
15 : 10. Shallum conspired ag. him
14. Menahem smote Shallum, s. h.
30. Hoshea ag. Pekah, and s. h.
23 : 29. Pharaoh-necho s. h. at Meg.
1 Ch. 2 : 3. Er was evil, Lord s. h.
10 : 14. inquired not of Lord, he s. h.
2 Ch. 22 : 11. hid Joash, Atha. s. h. not
24 : 25. servants s. h. on his bed
32 : 21. that came of his bowels s. h.
33 : 24. servants s. h. in own house
Je. 41 : 2. Ishm. s. h. king made gov.
Mat. 21 : 39. cast out of viney. s. h.
Ac. 22 : 20. I kept raiment of th. s. h.
See **Slew by** or **with SWORD.**

SLEWEST. [thou s.
1 S. 21 : 9. sword of Goliath whom
SLICE, S.
1 Ch. 9 : † 31. office over things in s-s
Eze. 4 : † 3. take a s., set it for wall
SLIDDEN, [back?
Je. 8 : 5. Why is peo. of Jerus. s.
SLIDE, SLIDETH.
De. 32 : 35. foot shall s. in due time
Ps. 26 : 1. trusted in L., I shall not s.
37 : 31. none of his steps shall s.
Ho. 4 : 16. Israel s-h back as a heifer
SLIGHT, LY. [11.
Je. 6 : 14. healed hurt of peo. s-y, 8 :
Eze. 13 : † 10. one built s. wall, others
SLIME. [tar
Ge. 11 : 3. brick for stone, s. for mor-
Ex. 2 : 3. she daubed the ark with s.
SLIMEPITS. [s.
Ge. 14 : 10. vale of Siddim was full of
SLING. [Verb.] [hair
Ju. 20 : 16. ev. one co. s. stones at a
1 S. 25 : 29. thine enemies sh. he s. out
Je. 10 : 18. I will s. out inhab-ts at
SLING stones. [ble
Jb. 41 : 28. s. s. are turned into stub-
Zch. 9 : 15. they shall subdue wi. s. s.
SLING, S.
1 S. 17 : 40. David had his s. in hand
50. David prevailed with a s.
25 : 29. sling enemies as out of a s.
2 Ch. 26 : 14. Uzziah prepared s-s to
cast stones [a s.
Pr. 26 : 8. As he that bindeth stone in
SLINGERS. [haraseth
2 K. 3 : 25. s. went and smote Kir-
SLIP, SLIPPED. [ence
1 S. 19 : 10. Da. s-d out of Saul's pres-
2 S. 22 : 37. my feet did not s., Ps. 18 : 36.
Jb. 12 : 5. ready to s. with his feet
Ps. 17 : 5. that my footsteps s. not
73 : 2. my steps had well nigh s-d
Je. 37 : † 12. Jeremy went to s. away
He. 2 : 1. lest we should let them s.
SLIPPERINESS.
Ps. 35 : † 6. Let their way be darku. s.
SLIPPERY.
Ps. 35 : 6. Let their way be dark and s.
73 : 18. didst set them in s. places
Je. 23 : 12. their way sh. be as s. ways
SLIPPETH.
De. 19 : 5. head s. from the helve
Ps. 38 : 16. my foot s., they magnify
94 : 18. I said my foot s., thy mercy
SLIPS. [held me
Is. 17 : 10. thou sh. set it wi. strange
SLOTHFUL. [s.
Ju. 18 : 9. be not s. to possess land
Pr. 12 : 24. s. shall be under tribute
27. s. roasteth not that he took
15 : 19. The way of s. is as a hedge
18 : 9. s. is brother to great waster
19 : 24. s. hideth hand in bosom, 26 :
21 : 25. desire of s. killeth him [15.
22 ; 13. s. man saith, a lion, 26 : 13.
24 : 30. I went by field of the s.
26 : 14. so doth the s. upon his bed
Mat. 25 : 26. Thou wicked and s. serv
Ro. 12 : 11. Not s. in business, fervent
He. 6 : 12. That ye be not s., but fol-
SLOTHFULNESS. [low-s
Pr. 19 : 15. s. casteth into deep sleep
Ec. 10 : 18. By s. building decayeth
SLOW. [tongue
Ex. 4 : 10. I am s. of speech, of s.
Ne. 9 : 17. thou art a God s. to anger
Pr. 14 : 29. He that is s. to wrath is
Lu. 24 : 25. O fools and s. of heart
Tit. 1 : 12. Cretians liars, s. bellies
Ja. 1 : 19. s. to speak, s. to wrath
SLOW to anger.
Ne. 9 : 17. but thou art a God s. –
Ps. 103 : 8. L. is gracious s. –, 145 : 8.
Pr. 15 : 18. th. is s. – appeaseth strife
16 : 32. th. is s. – better than mighty
Jo. 2 : 13. s. –, of gr. kindness, Jon.
Na. 1 : 3. L. is s. –, of gr. power [4 : 2.

SLOWLY.
Ac. 27 : 7. we had sailed s. many days
SLUGGARD. [sider
Pr. 6 : 6. Go to the ant, thou s., con-
9. How long wilt thou sleep, O s.
10 : 26. as smoke to eyes, so is s. to
13 : 4. soul of s. desireth hath noth.
20 : 4. s. will not plough, therefore
shall he beg
26 : 16. s. is wiser in his own conceit
SLUICES.
Is. 19 : 10. all that make s. for fish
SLUMBER. [Noun.]
Ps. 132 : 4. not give s. to mine eyelids
Pr. 6 : 4. not sleep nor s. to eyelids
10. Yet little sleep, little s., 24 : 33.
Zch. 12 : † 2. make Jerus. a cup of s.
Ro. 11 : 8. God hath given spirit of s.
SLUMBER, ED, ETH.
Ps. 121 : 3. keepeth thee will not s.
4. th. keepeth Israel sh. nei. s. nor
Is. 5 : 27. none shall s. nor sleep
56 : 10. his watchmen loving to s.
Na. 3 : 18. Thy shepherds s. O king
Mat. 25 : 5. bridegr-m tarried they s-d
2 Pe. 2 : 3. their damnation s-h not
SLUMBERINGS. [bed
Jb. 33 : 15. God speaketh in s. upon
SMALL. [ed
Ge. 41 : † 23. seven ears s. and blast-
Ex. 9 : 9. it sh. become s. dust in Eg.
16 : 14. a s. thing, s. as hoar frost
30 : 36. shalt beat spices very s.
Le. 16 : 12. sweet inc. beaten s. [you
Nu. 16 : 9. a s. thing th. G. separated
13. Is it s. thing that thou bro-t us
32 : 41. Jair took s. towns th-f [up?
De. 9 : 21. I ground the calf s.; even
as s. as dust [rain
32 : 2. My doctrine shall distil as s.
2 S. 7 : 19. and this was yet a s. thing
in thy sight, 1 Ch. 17 : 17.
17 : 13. until be not 1 s. stone found
22 : 43. I beat them s. as dust, Ps.
1 K. 2 : 20. I desire s. petition [18 : 42.
19 : 12. after the fire, a still s. voice
2 K. 19 : 26. their inhabitants were of
s. power, Is. 37 : 27. [powder, 15.
23 : 6. high place he stamped s. to
2 Ch. 24 : 24. Syrians with s. comp-y
35 : 8. gave for off-gs 2,600 s. cattle
9. to chief gave 5,000 s. cattle [s.
Jb. 8 : 7. Though thy beginning was
15 : 11. Are consolations of God s.
36 : 27. maketh s. the drops of wat.
Ps. 119 : 141. I am s. yet do not forget
Pr. 24 : 10. If faint, strength is s.
Is. 1 : 9. Exc. L. hath left s. remnant
7 : 13. Is it s. thing to weary men?
: 14. remnant shall be very s.
: 24. hang vessels of s. quantity
: 5. strangers sh. be like s. dust
: 15. nations counted as s. dust
: 15. sh. thresh mts., beat them s.
: 23. not brought me s. cattle
16 : 7. For s. moment have I forsak.
[illegible] : 22. a s. one sh. become nation
Je. 30 : 19. and they shall not be s.
44 : 28. a s. number shall return [en
49 : 15. will make thee s. am. heath-
Eze. 16 : † 47. was loathed as a s. thing
34 : † 17. I judge betw. s. cattle [ture
18. s. thing to have eat. good pas-
Da. 11 : 23. become strong with s. peo.
Am. 7 : 2. by wh. Jac. arise? he is s., 5.
Ob. 2. made thee s. among heathen
Zch. 4 : 10. despised day of s. things?
Mk. 3 : 9. that a s. ship wait on him
8 : 7. they had a few s. fishes
Jn. 2 : 15. made scourge of s. cords
6 : 9. five barley loaves, two s. fishes
Ac. 12 : 18. was no s. stir am. soldiers
15 : 2. Paul and Bar. no s. dissens-n
19 : 23. arose no s. stir ab. that way
24. Demetrius brought no s. gain
27 : 20. no s. tempest lay on us [you
1 Co. 4 : 3. s. thing that I be judged of

Ja. 3 : 4. ships are turned with s. helm
See **GREAT** with **small.**
See MATTER.
SMALLEST. [tribes?
1 S. 9 : 21. not 1 Benjamite, of s. of
1 Co. 6 : 2. ye unworthy to judge s.
SMART. [matters?
Pr. 11 : 15. He surety for stranger sh.
SMELL. [Noun.] [s. for it
Ge. 27 : 27. Isaac smelled s. of rai-
ment, s. of my son is as s. of field
Can. 1 : 12. my spikenard sendeth s.
2 : 13. vines with grape give good s.
4 : 10. s. of thy ointm-t better than
11. s. of thy garments like s. of
7 : 8. s. of thy nose like apples [Leb.
13. The mandrakes give a s., and at
Is. 3 : 24. instead of sweet s. stink [L.
11. † 3. make him of quick s. in fear of
Da. 3 : 27. nor s. of fire had passed
Ho. 14 : 6. as olive, his s. as Lebanon
Ph. 4 : 18. things sent odour of sweet
SMELL. [Verb.] [s.
Ex. 30 : 38. make like unto that to s.
Le. 26 : 31. I will not s. your odours
De. 4 : 28. gods, which nei. see nor s.
1 S. 26 : † 19. L. stirred thee, let him s.
Ps. 45 : 8. All thy garm. s. of myrrh
115 : 6. noses have they, s. not
Am. 5 : 21. I will not s. in your as-
SMELLED, ETH. [semb-s
Ge. 8 : 21. L. s-d a sweet savour and
27 : 27. Isaac s-d raiment, blessed
Ju. 16 : † 9. he brake withs as tow is
broken when it s-h fire
Jb. 39 : 25. he s-h the battle afar off
SMELLING. [Noun.] [s.?
1 Co. 12 : 17. If hearing, where were
See **SWEET smelling.**
SMITE. [and s.
Ge. 32 : 8. If Esau to one company
11. I fear him, lest he will s. me
Ex. 7 : 17. I will s. upon the waters
8 : 16. Say unto Aaron, s. the dust
12 : 23. not suf-r destroyer to s. you
17 : 6. thou shalt s. rock in Horeb
21 : 18. if men strive, one s. another
20. if man s. his serv. and he die
26. if man s. eye of his servant or
27. if he s. out manserv-'s tooth
Nu. 22 : 6. prevail, that we s. them
24 : 17. Sceptre out of Isr. s. Moab
25 : 17. Vex Midianites and s. them
35 : 16. if he s. him wi. instrument
17. if he s. him with a stone
18. Or if he s. him with weapon
21. Or in enmity s. him with hand
De. 7 : 2. thou shalt s. Canaanites
19 : † 6. Lest avenger s. him in life
11. if any s. neighbour mortally
Jos. 7 : 3. let two or 3 thousand s. Ai
10 : 4. help, that we may s. Gibeon
19. pursue and s. the hindmost
12 : 6. did Moses and Isr. s., 13 : 12.
Ju. 6 : 16. shalt s. the Midianites
20 : 31. then Benj. began to s., 39.
21 : 10. s. inhab-ts of Jabesh-gilead
1 S. 15 : 3. s. Amalek, spare them not
17 : 46. I will s. thee, take thy head
18 : 11. Saul said, I will s. David
19 : 10. Saul sought to s. David
20 : 33. Saul cast a javelin to s. him
23 : 2. Shall I go s. Philis.? Go, s.
26 : 8. let me s. him to earth at
once, I will not s. second time
2 S. 2 : 22. wh'f. should I s. thee?
5 : 24. Lord shall go before thee to
s. Philistines, 1 Ch. 14 : 15.
13 : 28. when I say, s. Amnon, kill
17 : 2. and I will s. the k. only [him
18 : 11. Joab said, Why not s. him?
1 K. 20 : 35. in word of the L. s. me,
the man refused to s. him, 37.
2 K. 3 : 19. sh. s. every fenced city
6 : 21. father, shall I s. them? (2)
22. Thou shalt not s. them, wouldest thou s. those captive?

2 K. 9 : 7. thou sh. s. the house of
27. Jehu said, s. him in chariot
13 : 17. sh. s. Syrians, till consumed
18. said unto king, s. upon ground
19. now shalt s. Syria but thrice
Ps. 121 : 6. sun sh. not s. thee by day
141 : 5. Let righteous s. me, it shall
Pr. 19 : 25. s. a scorner, simple will
Is. 10 : 24. he shall s. thee with rod
49 : 10. nei. sh. heat nor sun s. th.
58 : 4. ye fast to s. with fist of wick.
Je. 18 : 18. let us s. him with tongue
43 : 11. sh. s. land of Egypt, 46 : 13.
49 : 28. Kedar, Hazor, Neb-r shall s.
Eze. 5 : 2. take a 3d part of hair, and s.
6 : 11. s. with thy hand, and stamp
9 : 5. Go ye aft. him thro. city and s.
21 : 12. son of man, s. upon thigh
14. prophesy, s. thi. hands togeth.
Am. 9 : 1. he said, s. lintel of door
Mi. 5 : 1. they shall s. judge of Israel
Na. 2 : 10. heart melteth, the knees s.
Zch. 10 : 11. shall s. waves in the sea
11 : 6. deliver men, they sh. s. land
Mat. 5 : 39. whoso s. thee on cheek
24 : 49. begin to s. his fellow serv-ts
Ac. 23 : 2. commanded to s. Paul on
2 Co. 11 : 20. if man s. you on face
Re. 11 : 6. witnesses power to s. earth

SMITE. [God the agent.]

Ge. 8 : 21. nei. will I s. any more
Ex. 3 : 20. out my hand and s. Egypt
8 : 2. will s. all thy borders wi. frogs
9 : 15. that I may s. thee with pestil.
12 : 12. I will s. all firstborn in Eg.
13. pass over you, when I s. Eg., 23.
Nu. 14 : 12. I will s. with pestilence
De. 28 : 22. Lord sh. s. with consumption and sword [with madness
27. L. will s. with botch | 28. s.
35. Lord shall s. thee in knees and
33 : 11. s. thro. loins of them ag. him
1 S. 26 : 10. Da. said, L. shall s. him
2 S. 5 : 24. bestir, for sh. L. go out to s. Philis., 1 Ch. 14 : 15.
1 K. 14 : 15. L. sh. s. Israel as a reed
2 K. 6 : 18. s. this peo. with blindness
2 Ch. 21 : 14. with plague will Lord s.
Is. 3 : 17. Lord will s. dau-s of Zion
11 : 4. he shall s. earth with rod of
15. shall s. Eg. in 7 streams, 19 : 22.
Je. 21 : 6. I will s. inhab-ts of city
Eze. 21 : 17. I will s. hands together
32 : 15. when I shall s. them in Eg.
39 : 3. I will s. bow out of thy hand
Am. 3 : 15. I will s. the winter house
6 : 11. Lord will s. great house
Zch. 9 : 4. L. will s. her power in sea
12 : 4. I will s. every horse and rider
13 : 7. Awake, O sword, s. the Shepherd, Mat. 26 : 31. Mk. 14 : 27.
14 : 12. plague whw. L. will s. peo., [18.
Mal. 4 : 6. lest I s. earth wi. curse
Ac. 23 : 3. G. sh. s. thee, whited wall
Re. 19 : 15 wi. it he sho. s. nations

See **Edge of the SWORD.**
See **Smite with SWORD.**
See **TWOEDGED sword.**

SMITERS.

Is. 50 : 6. I gave my back to the s.

SMITEST.

Ex. 2 : 13. Wherefore s. thy fellow?
Jn. 18 : 23. if I have spok. well, why [s. me?

SMITETH.

Ex. 21 : 12. s. man so he die, be put to death, Le. 24 : † 17. [death
15. s. fa. or mother, surely put to
De. 25 : 11. wife to deliver husband out of hand that s. him [cretly
27 : 24. Cursed he th. s. neighb. se-
Jos. 15 : 16. He that s. Kirjath-sepher, Ju. 1 : 12. [11 : 6.
2 S. 5 : 8. that s. the Jebusites, 1 Ch.
Jb. 26 : 12. by underst-g he s. proud
Is. 9 : 13. peo. turn not unto him th. s.
La. 3 : 30. cheek to him that s. him
Eze. 7 : 9. know I am Lord that s.
Lu. 6 : 29. that s. thee on one cheek

SMITH, SMITHS.

1 S. 13 : 19. no s. found in land of Isr.
2 K. 24 : 14. Neb-r carried away craftsmen and s-s, 16. Je. 24 : 1.
Is. 44 : 12. s. with tongs worketh in
54 : 16. I created the s. th. bloweth
Je. 29 : 2. s-s were departed fr. Jerus.

See COPPERSMITH, SILVERSMITH.

SMITING.

Ex. 2 : 11. Mo. spied Eg-n s. Hebrew
2 S. 8 : 13. returned fr. s. the Syrians
1 K. 20 : 37. so in s. he wounded him
2 K. 3 : 24. went forward s. Moabites
Is. 41 : † 7. smootheth wi. hammer the [s.
Mi. 6 : 13. make thee sick in s. thee

SMITTEN.

Ex. 7 : 25. after Lord had s. the river
9 : 31. flax and the barley was s.
32. wheat and the rye were not s.
22 : 2. If a thief be found, and be s.
Nu. 14 : 42. Go not up, that ye be not s., De. 1 : 42. [hast s. me?
22 : 28. What have I done that thou
32. Whf. hast s. thine ass 3 times?
33 : 4. buried firstborn Lord had s.
De. 28 : 7. Lord cause enemies to be s.
25. L. cause thee be s. bef. enemies
Ju. 1 : 8. Judah had s. Jerus. and set
20 : 32. Benj. said, They are s. bef. us
36. chil. of Benj. saw they were s.
39. Surely they are s. before us
1 S. 4 : 2. Isr. was s. before Philis., 10.
3. Whf. L. s. us to day bef. Philis.?
5 : 12. the men were s. wi. emerods
6 : 19. lamented bec. L. had s. many
7 : 10. Philis. were s. before Israel
13 : 4. Saul s. garrison of Philistines
30 : 1. Amalekites had s. Ziklag
2 S. 2 : 31. s. of Abner's men, 360 died,
8 : 9. Toi heard David had s. host of Hadadezer, 10. 1 Ch. 18 : 9. 10.
10 : 15. Syrians saw they were s., 19.
11 : 15. retire ye, that he may be s.
1 K. 8 : 33. When thy peo. Israel be s.
11 : 15. aft. he had s. ev. male in Edom
2 K. 2 : 14. when he had s. waters
3 : 23. kings have s. one another
13 : 19. Thou shouldest have s. five or 6 times, then hadst s. Syria till consumed [2 Ch. 25 : 19.
14 : 10. Thou hast indeed s. Edom,
† 12. Judah was s. before Israel
2 Ch. 6 : † 24. if thy people Isr. be s.
20 : 22. Moab and mt. Seir were s.
25 : 16. why shouldest thou be s.?
† 22. Judah was s. bef. Isr. and fled
26 : 20. Uzziah hasted, bec. L. s. him
28 : 17. Edomites had s. Judah
Jb. 16 : 10. have s. me upon cheek
Ps 3 : 7. thou hast s. all mine ene-s
69 : 26. persecute him thou hast s.
102 : 4. My heart is s. and withered
143 : 3. he hath s. my life to ground
Is. 5 : 25. the Lord hath s. his people
24 : 12. gate is s. with destruction
27 : 7. Hath he s. him, as he smote
53 : 4. yet we did esteem s. of God
Je. 2 : 30. In vain have I s. children
14 : 19. why hast s. us and no heal-
37 : 10. tho. ye had s. army [ing
Eze. 22 : 13. s. my hand at thy dishon.
33 : 21. one came saying, The city is s.
40 : 1. in 14th year after city was s.
Ho. 6 : 1. he hath s. he will bind up
9 : 16. Ephraim is s., their root is
Am. 4 : 9. I have s. you, ye not retur.
Ac. 23 : 3. com-dest me to be s. ag. law
Re. 8 : 12. third part of sun was s.

SMOKE. [Noun.]

Ge. 19 : 28. Sodom, and s. of country went up as s. of furnace
Ex. 19 : 18. mount Sinai was on a s.
Jos. 8 : 20. s. of Ai ascended to, 21.
Ju. 20 : 38. make s. rise out of city
40. when pillar of s. began to rise
2 S. 22 : 9. went up a s. out of his nostrils, Ps. 18 : 8. [s. as
Jb. 41 : 20. Out of his nostrils goeth
Ps. 37 : 20. wicked sho. consume into
68 : 2. As s. is driven aw., so drive [s.
102 : 3. my days are consumed like s.
119 : 83. I am like bottle in s.
Pr. 10 : 26. as s. to eyes, so sluggard
Can. 3 : 6. cometh like pillars of s.
Is. 4 : 5. L. upon her assemblies a s.
6 : 4. the house was filled with s.
9 : 18. mount up like lifting up of s.
14 : 31. shall come from north a s.
34 : 10. the s. shall go up for ever
51 : 6. heavens shall vanish like s.
65 : 5. These are a s. in my nose
Ho. 13 : 3. they shall be as s. out of
Jo. 2 : 30. in earth, fire, pillars of s.
Na. 2 : 13. I will burn chariots in s.
Ac. 2 : 19. signs, fire, vapour of s.
Re. 8 : 4. s. of the incense ascended
9 : 2. a s. out of bottomless pit
3. there came out of the s. locusts
17. out of mouths issued fire, s.
18. third part of men killed by s.
14 : 11. s. of their torment ascend-h
15 : 8. temple was filled with s.
18 : 9. kings lament for her when see
18. when saw s. of her burning [s.
19 : 3. her s. rose up for ever and ev.

SMOKE. [Verb.]

De. 29 : 20. anger of L. shall s. ag-t
Ps. 74 : 1. O G., why thine anger s.?
80 : † 4. how long s. ag. prayer of peo.
104 : 32. he toucheth hills, they s.
144 : 5. touch mountains, they sh. s.

SMOKING.

Ge. 15 : 17. behold a s. furnace
Ex. 20 : 18. all peo. saw mountain s.
Is. 7 : 4. tails of these s. firebrands
42 : 3. s. flax not quench, Mat. 12 : [20.

SMOOTH, ER. [Adj.]

Ge. 27 : 11. Esau hairy, I am a s. man
1 S. 17 : 40. David chose five s. stones
Ps. 55 : 21. words were s-r than butter
Pr. 5 : 3. her mouth is s-r than oil
Is. 30 : 10. speak unto us s. things
57 : 6. Among s. stones of stream
Lu. 3 : 5. rough ways sh. be made s.

SMOOTH. [Noun.] [neck

Ge. 27 : 16. put skins upon s. of his

SMOOTH, ETH.

Is. 41 : 7. he that s-h with hammer
Je. 23 : † 31. am ag. prophets s. their [tongues

SMOTE.

Ge. 14 : 5. s. the Rephaim in Ashte-h
7. s. all the country of the Amalekites, 1 S. 14 : 48. -15 : 7. 1 Ch. 4 : 43.
15. Abraham s. them and pursued
19 : 11. s. the men with blindness
36 : 35. Hadad s. Midian in field of Moab, 1 Ch. 1 : 46.
Ex. 7 : 20. he lifted up rod, s. waters
8 : 17. Aaron s. dust, became lice
9 : 25. hail s. thro-t Eg. man and (2)
12 : 27. passed over, when he s. Eg-ns
29. L. s. all firstborn in land of Egypt, Nu. 3 : 13. -8 : 17. Ps. 78 : 51. -105 : 36. -135 : 8. -136 : 10.
Nu. 11 : 33. L. s. peo. with gr. plague
14 : 45. Amalekites came and s.
20 : 11. Mo. s. rock twice, Ps. 78 : 20.
22 : 23. Balaam s. the ass, 25, 27.
24 : 10. Balak s. his hands together
32 : 4. country Lord s. is land for
De. 4 : 46. whom Moses s., Jos. 13 : 21.
25 : 18. Amalek s. hindmost of thee
29 : 7. Sihon and Og came, we s. th.
Jos. 7 : 5. men of Ai s. about 36 men
8 : 22. they s. them, let none escape
9 : 18. Isr. s. them not, bec. princes
10 : 10. Lord s. them to Azekah
26. afterward Joshua s. the 5 k-s
40. s. and utterly destroyed all, 30, 32, 35, 37, 39, 41. -11 : 8. 18.
11 : 11. they s. all the souls [22 : 19.
12 : 1. are kings of land Isr. s., 7.

Jos.20 : 5. s. his neighb. unwittingly
Ju. 3 : 13. Eglon went and s. Israel
4 : 21. Jael s. nail into his temple
5 : 26. she s. Sisera, s. off his head
7 : 13. cake came into tent and s. it
8 : 11. and Gideon s. the host
9 : 48. Abim-h rose up and s. them
11 : 21. Sihon and his people they s.
33. Jephthah s. them from Aroer
12 : 4. men of Gilead s. Ephraim
15 : 8. Samson s. them hip and thi.
20 : 35. Lord s. Benj. before Israel
1 S. 4 : 8. are the gods that s. Eg-ns
5 : 6. Lord s. them with emerods
9. s. men of city small and great
6 : 9. know it is not his hand s. us
19. s. men of Beth-shemesh, s. peo.
7 : 11. pursued Philistines, s. them,
14 : 31.-23 : 5. 2 S. 5 : 20. 1 Ch. 14 :
19 : 10. Saul s. javelin into wall⌊11.
25 : 38. Lord s. Nabal that he died
27 : 9. Da. s. land, left nei. man nor
30 : 17. David s. them from twilight
2 S. 8 : 2. And David s. Moab ⌈18 : 3.
3. David s. Hadad-ezer, k. of, 1 Ch.
10 : 18. Da. s. Shobach, capt. of ho.
11 : 21. Who s. Abim-h? did not a
14 : 6. one son s. other, slew⌊woman
7. Deliver him that s. his brother
24 : 17. when he saw angel s. people
1 K. 15 : 20. s. Ijon and Dan. 2 Ch. 16 : 4.
29. Baasha s. all house of Jerob-m
20 : 21. k. of Isr. s. horses, chariots
22 : 24. Zedekiah s. Micaiah on
cheek, 2 Ch. 18 : 23. ⌈of Isr.
34. drew bow at venture, s. king
2 K. 2 : 8. Elijah s. the waters ⌈ers
14. Elisha took mantle s. the wat-
3 : 24. Israelites s. Moab-s 1 Ch. 18 : 2.
25. slingers went about it, s. it
6 : 18. Lord s. them with blindness
8 : 21. Joram s. Edomites, 2 Ch. 21 : 9.
9 : † 15. wounds wh. Syrians s. him
24. Jehu s. Jehoram between arms
10 : 32. Hazael s. them in all coasts
15 : 5. Lord s. king so he was leper
16. Menahem s. Tiphsah (2) ⌊14.
19 : 35. angel of L. s. 185,000, Is.
25 : 25. Ishmael s. Gedaliah⌊37 : 36.
1 Ch. 4 : 41. these s. tents and hab-ns
20 : 1. Joab s. Rabbah, destroyed it
21 : 7. God displeased; he s. Israel
2 Ch. 13 : 15. God s. Jerob-m and Isr.
14 : 12. Lord s. Ethiopians bef. Asa
14. s. all in cities round Gerar
15. They s. also tents of cattle
22 : 5. the Syrians s. Joram
25 : 11. Amaziah s. chil. of Seir, 13.
Ne. 13 : 25. I cursed and s. certain
Jb. 1 : 19. gr. wind s. 4 corners of ho.
2 : 7. Satan s. Job with sore boils
Ps. 78 : 31. God s. chosen men of Isr.
66. he s. enemies in hinder parts
105 : 33. He s. their vines, fir trees
135. 10. Who s. great nations and
136 : 17. To him which s. gr. kings
Can. 5 : 7. watchm. found me, s. me
Is. 10 : 20. no more stay upon him th.
14 : 6. who s. peo. is persecuted ⌊s.
29. rod of him that s. thee is brok.
30 : 31. Assyrian be beaten which s.
41 : 7. encouraged him that s. anvil
60 : 10. in my wrath I s. thee, but
Je. 20 : 2. Then Pashur s. Jeremiah
31 : 19. was instructed, I s. my thigh
46 : 2. army of Pharaoh-necho, wh.
47 : 1. bef. Pharaoh s. Gaza⌊Neb-rs.
52 : 27. king of Babylon s. them
Da. 2 : 34. a stone cut out s. image 35.
5 : 6. Belshazzar's knees s. one ag-t
8 : 7. he goat with choler s. the ram
Jon. 4 : 7. a worm s. the gourd, that
Ha. 2 : 17. I s. you with blasting
Mat. 26 : 51. Peter s. off his ear, Mk.
14 : 47. Lu. 22 : 50. Jn. 18 : 10.
68. prophesy, Who is he that s.
thee, Lu. 22 : 64.

Lu. 18 : 13. publi-n s. upon his breast
23 : 48. beholding Jesus, s. breasts
Ac. 7 : 24. David avenged him and s.
12 : 7. angel s. Peter on side ⌊Eg-n

SMOTE him.

Ex. 21 : 19. shall he that s. h. be quit
Nu. 21 : 35. s. h. and sons, De. 2 : 33.
35 : 21. that s. h. be put to death
De. 3 : 3. we s. h. until none was left
Jos. 10 : 33. Horam, k.; Jos. s. h. and
1 S. 17 : 35. I went aft. and s. h.⌊peo.
24 : 5. Da.'s heart s. h., 2 S. 24 : 10.
2 S. 1 : 15. one of young men s. h. he
died, 2 K. 2 : 21. ⌈4 : 6.-20 : 10.
2 : 23. s. h. under 5th rib, 3 : 27.-
4 : 7. they s. and beheaded h.
6 : 7. God s. h. for error, 1 Ch. 13 : 10.
1 K. 15 : 27. Baasha s. h. at Gibbe-n
16 : 10. Zimri s. h. and killed
20 : 37. man s. h. so th. he wounded
2 K. 15 : 10. Shallum s. h. bef. people
25. Pekah s. h. in Samaria, 30.⌈ease
2 Ch. 21 : 18. s. h. wi. incurable dis-
28 : 5. Syria s. h., king of Isr. s. h.
23. unto gods of Damas., wh. s. h.
Is. 27 : 7. Hath he smitten him as
he s. them that s. h.
57 : 17. for his covetous. I s. h.⌈s. h.
Je. 37 : 15. princes wroth with Jer.,
Mat. 26 : 67. others s. h. with hands
27 : 30. th. took reed, s. h. on head,
Mk. 15 : 19. Lu. 22 : 63. Jn. 19 : 3.
Ac. 12 : 23. immediately angel of L.
See PHILISTINE, s. ⌊s. h.
See **Smote with SWORD.**

SMOTEST.

Ex. 17 : 5 take rod whw. thou s. river

SMYR'NA. ⌈in S.

Re. 1 : 11. write and send unto church
2 : 8. unto angel of church in S. write

SNAIL.

Le. 11 : 30. lizard, s., and mole uncl.
Ps. 58 : 8. As a s. let ev. one pass aw.

SNARE. ⌈a s.?

Ex. 10 : 7. How long sh. this man be
23 : 33. if serve their gods, it will be
a s., De. 7 : 16. Ju. 2 : 3. ⌈a s.
34 : 12. make no covenant lest it be
Ju. 8 : 27. became a s. unto Gideon
1 S. 18 : 21. give him her, th. she be a
28 : 9. whf. layest s. for my life? ⌊s.
Jb. 18 : 8. net, he walketh upon a s.
10. s. is laid for him in the ground
Ps. 69 : 22. Let their table become a
s. unto them, Ro. 11 : 9. ⌈fowler
91 : 3. he shall deliver thee fr. s. of
106 : 36. served idols, wh. were a s.
119 : 110. wicked have laid s. for me
124 : 7. escaped as bird out of s.; s.
is broken, we are escaped
140 : 5. proud have hid a s. for me
142 : 3. have privily laid s. for me
Pr. 7 : 23. as a bird hasteth to s. and
18 : 7. fool's lips are s. of his soul
20 : 25. s. to man who devoureth
22 : 25. lest learn his ways, get a s.
29 : 6. In transg-n of evil man is a s.
8. Scornful men bring city into s.
25. The fear of man bringeth a s.
Ec. 9 : 12. as birds caught in the s.
Is. 8 : 14. a s. to inhabit-s of Jerus.
24 : 17. fear, pit, and the s. are
upon thee, 18. Je. 48 : 43, 44.⌈eth
29 : 21. lay a s. for him that reprov-
Je. 50 : 24. I laid a s. for thee, O Bab.
La. 3 : 47. a s. is come upon us ⌈20.
Eze. 12 : 13. he be taken in my s., 17 :
Ho. 5 : 1. ye have been a s. on Miz-
9 : 8. prophet is a s. of a fowler⌊pah
Am. 3 : 5. Can a bird fall in a s.
where no gin is for him? shall
one take up a s. from earth?
Lu. 21 : 35. For as a s. shall it come
1 Co. 7 : 35. not that I may cast a s.
1 Ti. 3 : 7. lest we fall into s. of devil
6 : 9. that will be rich, fall into a s.
2 Ti. 2 : 26. may recov. out of s. of devil

SNARES.

Jos. 23 : 13. be s. and traps unto you
2 S. 22 : 6. s. of death prevented me,
Ps. 18 : 5. ⌈about thee
Jb. 22 : 10. Therefore s. are round
40 : 24. behemoth's nose pierceth s.
Ps. 11 : 6. Upon wicked he sh. rain s.
38 : 12. seek my life lay s. for me
64 : 5. commune of laying s. privily
141 : 9. Keep me from the s. laid for
Pr. 13 : 14. depart fr. s. of death, 14 : 27.
22 : 5. s. are in way of froward
Ec. 7 : 26. woman whose heart is s.
Je. 5 : 26. wait as he that seeketh s.
18 : 22. digged and hid s. for my feet

SNARED. ⌈s.

De. 7 : 25. not take silver of idols lest
12 : 30. Take heed thou be not s. by
Ps. 9 : 16. wicked s. in work of his ha.
Pr. 6 : 2. art s. with words of, 12 : 13.
Ec. 9 : 12. so are the sons of men s.
Is. 8 : 15. many shall fall and be s.
28 : 13. they might be s. and taken
42 : 22. they are all s. in holes, hid

SNARING.

Is. 42 : † 22. in s. all the young men

SNATCH.

Is. 9 : 20. he shall s. on right hand

SNEEZED.

2 K. 4 : 35. child s. 7 times and opened

SNORTING. ⌈Dan

Je. 8 : 16. s. of his horses heard from

SNOUT.

Pr. 11. 22. As a jewel in a swine's s.

SNOW.

Ex. 4 : 6. his hand was leprous as s.
Nu. 12 : 10. Miriam became white as
2 S. 23 : 20. slew lion in time of s. ⌊s.
2 K. 5 : 27. Gehazi went white as s.
Jb. 6 : 16. and wherein the s. is hid
9 : 30. If I wash myself in s. water
24 : 19. heat consumeth s. waters
37 : 6. saith to s., Be thou on earth
38 : 22. entered into treasures of s.?
Ps. 51 : 7. I shall be whiter than s.
68 : 14. it was white as s. in Salmon
147 : 16. He giveth s. like wool
148 : 8. Fire, s., fulfilling his word
Pr. 25 : 13. As cold of s. in harvest
26 : 1. As s. in summer, so honour
31 : 21. She is not afraid of the s.
Is. 1 : 18. sins as scarlet be white as s.
55 : 10. s. fr. heaven returneth not
Je. 18 : 14. Will man leave s. of Leb.
La. 4 : 7. Her Nazarites purer than s.
Da. 7 : 9. garment was white as s.⌈3.
Mat. 28 : 3. raim-t white as s., Mk. 9 :
Re. 1 : 14. his head and hairs white

SNOWY. ⌊as s.

1 Ch. 11 : 22. he slew a lion in a s. day

SNUFFDISHES. ⌈37 : 23.

Ex. 25 : 38. s. shall be of pure gold,
Nu. 4 : 9. take cloth, cover his s.

SNUFFED.

Je. 14 : 6. wild asses s. up the wind
Mal. 1 : 13. ye have s. at it, saith Lord

SNUFFERS.

Ex. 37 : 23. he made his s. of pure
gold, 1 K. 7 : 50. 2 Ch. 4 : 22.
2 K. 12 : 13. s. not made of money
25 : 14. pots, s. took they away, Je.

SNUFFETH. ⌊52 : 18.

Je. 2 : 24. a wild ass that s. up wind

SO. [Person.] ⌈Egypt

2 K. 17 : 4. sent messengers to S. of

SO.

Ge. 25 : 22. If it be s., why am I thus?
43 : 11. If it must be s., now do this
Ex. 4 : 26. s. he let him go
10 : 10. Let Lord be s. with you
25 : 9. even s. shall ye make it, 27 : 8.
39 : 43. as L. com-ded s. had th. done
Le. 24 : 19. as he hath done, s. to him,
Nu. 13 : 33. s. we in their sight ⌊20.
De. 17 : 7. s. thou shalt put the evil
aw., 19 : 19.-21 : 21.-22 : 21, 22, 24.
22 : 26. as when man riseth, s. is this

De. 25 : 9. s. sh. it be done unto them
33 : 25. as thy days, s. thy strength
Jos. 14 : 11. as strength then, s. now
22 : 28. when they sho. s. say to us
Ju. 8 : 18. As thou art, s. were they
21. as the man is, s. his strength
15 : 11. As they did to me, s. have I
1 S. 11 : 7. s. it be done unto his oxen
25 : 25. as his name, s. is he, Nabal
26 : 24. s. let my life be much set by
2 S. 13 : 35. as thy serv-ts said, s. it is
16 : 10. s. let him curse. Who shall
say, Whf. hast done s.? 1 K. 1 : 6.
1 K. 1 : 30. s. will I do this day
22 : 8. Let not king say s., 2 Ch. 18 : 7.
2 K. 2 : 10. it shall be s. unto thee,
but if not, it shall not be s.
4 : 44. s. he set it before them
7 : 20. s. it fell out to him, peo. trode
2 Ch. 18 : 21. go out and do even s.
34 : 26. s. shall ye say unto him [do
Ezr. 10 : 12. As hast said, s. must we
Es. 4 : 16. s. will I go in unto king
9 : 27. s. as it should not fail that
Jb. 5 : 27. s. it is, hear it and know
21 : 4. if it were s., why not my soul
Ps. 35 : 25. not say, s. we wo. have it
37 : 3. do good, s. shalt thou dwell
80 : 18 s. will we not go back fr. thee
81 : 12. s. I gave them up [wrath
90 : 11. acc-g to thy fear, s. is thy
12. s. teach us to number our days
109 : 17. s. let it come, s. let it be
far from him [any nation
147 : 20. He hath not dealt s. with
Pr. 23 : 7. as he thinketh, s. is he
Ec. 3 : 19. as one dieth, s. dieth other
5 : 16. as he came, s. shall he go
9 : 2. as is the good, s. is the sinner
Is. 24 : 2. as with people, s. wi. priest
26 : 17. s. have we been in thy sight
47 : 12. if s. be thou be able to profit;
if s. be thou mayest prevail
63 : 8. s. he was their saviour
Je. 5 : 31. my peo. love to have it s.
10 : 18. that they may find it s.
42 : 17. s. be with all that set faces
La. 3 : 29. if s. be, there may be hope
Eze. 1 : 28. As the bow, s. was brightn.
12 : 11. as I have done, s. be done
16 : 16. nei. shall it be s. [unto them
44. As mother, s. is the daughter
24 : 19. what these are thou doest s.
28 : 14. cherub, I have set thee s.
35 : 15. s. will I do unto thee
45 : 20. s. thou sh. do, s. reconcile
Da. 3 : 17. If it be s., our God is able
Ho. 3 : 3. for me, s. will I be for thee
Am. 5 : 14. s. Lord shall be with you
Zch. 8 : 13. s. will I save you, and ye
Mat. 3 : 15. Suffer it to be s. now
5 : 16. Let your light s. shine [thee
8 : 13. believed, s. be it done unto
9 : 33. It was never s. seen in Israel
11 : 26. Even s., Father, for s. it
seemed, Lu. 10 : 21.
12 : 40. s. shall Son of man be, Lu.
11 : 30.-17 : 24. [generation
45. s. sh. it be unto this wicked
13 : 40. s. sh. it be in end of world, 49.
19 : 10. If case of man be s. with
24 : 33. s. when ye shall see all
these things, Lu. 21 : 31.
Mk. 10 : 43. s. shall it not be am. you
Lu. 12 : 54. cometh shower, and s. it
14 : 33. s., whoso. he be of you [is
17 : 10. s. when ye sh. have done all
Jn. 3 : 16. God s. loved the world
13 : 13. ye say well, for s. I am. [you
33. cannot come; s. now I say to
14 : 31. Fa. gave com-t, even s. I do
15 : 9. As Fa. loved me, s. have I
loved you [like manner
Ac. 1 : 11. this Jesus shall s. come in
7 : 1. said, Are these things s.?
14 : 1. they s. spake that a gr. multi.
17 : 11. whether those things were s.
Ac. 24 : 9. saying these things were s.
Ro. 1 : 15. s. as much as in me is
5 : 15. not as the offence, s. gift [eth
9 : 16. s. it is not of him that will-
1 Co. 6 : 5. Is it s., is not wise man am.
7 : 26. good for a man s. to be [you?
9 : 15. that it be s. done unto me
15 : 11. s. we preached, s. ye believed
2 Co. 10 : 7. as he is Ch.'s, s. are we
Christ's [burdensome
11 : 9. s. I keep myself from being
22. Are they Hebrews? s. am I;
Israelites? s. am I [den you
12 : 16. But be it s., I did not bur-
Ga. 3 : 9. s. they which be of faith
4 : 29 persecuted, even s. it is now
Ph. 3 : 17. mark them which walk s.
4 : 1. s. stand fast in the Lord
1 Th. 4 : 17. s. shall we ever be with L.
1 Jn. 4 : 17. as he is, s. are we in world
Re. 1 : 7. wail bec. of him. Even s.,
22 : 20. Even s., come, L. Jes. [Amen

SO be it.

Jos. 2 : 21. Acc-g unto your words s. -
Je. 11 : 5. Then ans-d I, s. -, O Lord

SO, with did.

Ge. 45 : 21. children of Israel d.s.
Ex. 16 : 17. Nu. 5 : 4.-8 : 20.-9 :
5. Jos. 4 : 8.-14 : 5.
Ex. 7 : 20. Moses and Aa. d.s. [14 : 4.
8 : 17. they d. s.; for Aaron, 24.-
17 : 6. Mos. d.s.; as L. commanded
Jos. 5 : 15. Joshua d.s., 9 : 26. [s.d.
10 : 23. they d.s., and bro-t 5 kings
39. As to Hebron s. he d. to Debir
Ju. 6 : 20. pour out broth. And he
11 : 23. children of Benj. d.s. [d.s.
1 S. 6 : 10. men d.s. and took 2 kine
2 S. 5 : 25. David d.s., as Lord had
1 K. 7 : 18. s. he d. for oth. chapiters
20 : 25. Ben-ha. hearkened and d.s.
2 K. 9 : 27. Smite him. And they d.s.
2 Ch. 35 : 12. s.d. they with the oxen
Ezr. 10 : 16. children of captivity d.s.
Es. 2 . 4. thing pleased king, he d.s.
Lu. 9 : 15. they d.s., made them sit
Ac. 7 : 51. as your fa-s d., s. do ye
12 : 8. bind on sandals; and s. he d.
19 : 14. seven sons of Sceva, wh. d.s.
See DID, DIED, DO, DOING.

SO it was, or It was SO.

Ge. 1 : 7. and - s., 9, 11, 15, 24, 30.
41 : 13. as he interpreted to us, s. -
45 : 8. s. - not you that sent me
Nu. 9 : 16. s. - always, cloud cov-d it
20. s. - when cloud was on taberu.
21. s. - when cloud abode fr. even
Ju. 6 : 38. dew be on fleece only, - s.
19 : 30. - s. th. all said, no such deed
1 S. 5 : 7. men of Ashdod saw th. - s.
9. - s. after they had carried ark
10 : 9. - s. th. when he turned from
11 : 11. - s. Saul put peo. in 3 comp-s
30 : 25. - s. fr. that day made a stat.
2 S. 15 : 2. - s. when any came to king
5. - s. th. when any man came nigh
1 K. 8 : 54. - s. when Sol. made an end
13 : 9. s. - charged me by word of L.
2 K. 17 : 7. s. - that Isr. had sinned?
25. s. - at beginning of their dwell-g
Jb. 42 : 7 - s. after Lord had spoken
Je. 41 : 7. - s. when came into city
Ac. 12 : 15. Rhoda constantly af-
See So it WAS. [firmed - s.
See GREAT, LONG, MUCH.

Not SO. [wickedly

Ge. 19 : 7. I pray, brethren, do n.s.
Nu. 12 : 7. my servant Moses is n.s.
1 S. 20 : 2. why hide this? it is n.s.
Ps. 1 : 4. The ungodly are n.s.
Pr. 15 : 7. heart of foolish doeth n.s.
Is. 10 : 7. Howbeit he meaneth n.s.
16 : 6. but his lies shall n. be s. [s.
Mat. 25 : 9. the wise ans-d, saying n.
Lu. 1 : 60. his mother ans-d, n.s., he
Ep. 4 : 20. ye have n.s. learned Ch.
See NOT.

SO that. [with me

Ge. 21 : 6. s.t. all th. hea[r w]ill laugh
27 : 1. s.t., 28 : 21.-47 : 13.-49 : 17.
Ex. 10 : 20.-11 : 10.-21 : 12. De.
28 : 34.-30 : 17. Ju. 10 : 9. 1 S.
4 : 5.-11 : 11.-18 : 30. 1 K. 8 : 25.
2 K. 8 : 15.-18 : 5. 2 Ch. 6 : 16.
Ezr. 9 : 14. Ne. 4 : 10. Jb. 1 : 3-
7 : 20. Ps. 40 : 12.-58 : 11.-78 :
60.-102 : 4.-106 : 32.-107 : 29.
Pr. 31 : 11. Ec. 6 : 2. Is. 47 : 7.-
60 : 15. Je. 33 : 26.-44 : 22.-52 :
6. La. 4 : 14. Eze. 14 : 15.-21 : 24.
-23 : 27.-31 : 9.-38 : 20.-41 : 19.
Da. 5 : 6.-8 : 4. Jon. 1 : 4. Zch. 1 :
21. Mat. 8 : 28.-13 : 2, 32. Mk.
4 : 1, 32, 37.-15 : 15. Ro. 15 : 19.
1 Co. 1 : 7. 2 Co. 2 : 7.-7 : 7. Ga.
5 : 17. 1 Th. 1 : 7, 8. He. 11 : 3.-

SO they. [13 : 6.

Le. 10 : 5. s.t. went near and carried
Nu. 2 : 34. s.t., 13 : 21. Jos. 19 : 51.
Ju. 21 : 14. 1 S. 2 : 14.-5 : 11.-
9 : 10. 2 K. 2 : 2, 4-7 : 10.-17 :
32. 2 Ch. 29 : 17.-34 : 28. Ezr. 6 :
13. Ps. 48 : 5.-64 : 8.-78 : 29. Je.
38 : 23, 27.-43 : 7. Eze. 23 : 44.
Da. 2 : 2. Ho. 4 : 7.-11 : 2. Jon.
1 : 7, 15. Mi. 2 : 2.-7 : 3. Zch. 6 :
7.-7 : 13.-11 : 12. Mat. 27 : 66.-
28 : 15. Mk. 8 : 8. Jn. 20 : 4.

SO that they. [door

Ge. 19 : 11. s.- wearied thems. to find
De. 31 : 17. s. - will say in that day
Ju. 1 : 35. s. - became tributaries
2 : 14. s.- could not stand bef. enem.
2 K. 2 : 8. s. - two went over on dry
9 : 37. s. - not say, This is Jezebel
Ps. 78 : 53. led them s. - feared not
80 : 12. s.- wh. pass by do pluck her
107 : 38. s. - are multiplied greatly
Eze. 39 : 10. s. - sh. take no wood out
Da. 10 : 7. s. - fled to hide thems. [eat
Mk. 3 : 20. s. - could not so much as
Lu. 16 : 26. s. - wh. would pass from
20 : 20. s. - might deliver him [hence
Ac. 7 : 19. s. - cast out young chil.
19 : 10. s. - wh. dwelt in Asia heard
Ro. 1 : 20. s. - are without excuse

SOAKED.

Is. 34 : 7. land shall be s. with blood

SOAP. [much s.

Je. 2 : 22. tho. thou wash and take
Mal. 3 : 2. for he is like fullers' s.

SOBER. [cause

2 Co. 5 : 13. whe. we be s. it is for y-r
1 Th. 5 : 6. not sleep, but watch be s.
8. let us who are of the day be s.
1 Ti. 3 : 2. A bishop must be s., Tit. 1 : 8.
11. must deacons' wives be s.
Tit. 2 : 2. That aged men be s.
4. teach the young women to be s.
1 Pe. 1 : 13. gird loins of y-r mind, be s.
4 : 7. be ye s., watch unto prayer
5 : 8. Be s., be vigilant, bec. devil

SOBERLY. [of faith

Ro. 12 : 3. think s., acc-g to measure
Tit. 2 : 12. teaching we should live s.

SOBERMINDED.

Tit. 2 : 6. exhort young men to be s.

SOBERNESS. [s.

Ac. 26 : 25. speak forth the words of

SOBRIETY. [to s.

Ro. 12 : † 3. ev. man ought to think
1 Ti. 2 : 9. that women adorn with s.
15. if continue in holiness with s.

SO'CHO.

1 Ch. 4 : 18. Heber the father of S.

SO'CHOH. See SHOCHO.

SOCIABLE. [s.

1 Ti. 6 : † 18. be ready to distribute,

SOCIETY, IES. [† 9, † 17.

Ezr. 4 : † 7. wrote Bishlam and s-,
6 : † 6. your s-s wh. are beyond river
Pr. 21 : † 9. brawling wem. in ho. of s.

SOCKET. [for s.

Ex 38 : 27. hundred talents, talent

SOCKETS.
Ex. 26 : 19. make forty s. of silver,
two s. under one board, two s.
under, 21, 25.-36 :24, 26, 30, 36.
25. s. of silver, sixteen s., 36 : 30.
37. shalt cast 5 s. of brass, 36 : 38.
27 : 10. twenty s. of brass, 38 : 10, 11.
12. pillars ten, their s. ten, 38 : 12.
14. hangings of one side : s. three
15. other side, s. three, 38 : 14, 15.
16. pillars shall be four, their s.
four, 26 :32.-36 :36.-38 : 19. ⌈18.
17. hooks sh. be of silver, s. brass
35 : 11. s. of the tabernacle, 39 : 33.
17. hangings, pillars, and s., 39 :40.
38 : 27. s. of the sanctuary, s. of
the vail, hundred s. ⌈s., 17.
30. of the brass of offering he made
31. s. of court, s. of court gate ⌈s.
40 : 18. reared tabernacle, fastened
Nu. 3 : 36. under charge of sons of
Merari be s., 37.-4 : 31, 32. ⌈ed
Jb. 38 : †6. Whereupon are s. fasten-
Can. 5 : 15. pillars set upon s. of gold

SO'COH. See SHOCHO.

SOD. ⌈came
Ge. 25 :29. Jacob s. pottage, and Esau
2 Ch. 35 : 13. offerings s. they in pots

SODDEN. ⌈water
Ex. 12 : 9. Eat not of it raw, nor s. wi.
Le. 6 :28. earthen vessel wh-in it is s.
be broken ; if s. in a brazen pot
Nu. 6 : 19. priest sh. take s. shoulder
1 S. 2 : 15. not have s. flesh of thee
La. 4 : 10. women have s. own chil-

SO'DI. See GADDIEL.⌊dren

SOD'OM, SOD'OMA. ⌈S.
Ge. 13 : 12. Lot pitched his tent tow.
13. men of S. wicked exceedingly
14 : 12. took Lot, who dwelt in S.
17. king of S. went out to meet Ab.
21. king of S. said unto Ab. ⌊ 22.
18 :22. men turned, went tow. S., 16.
26. If I find fifty righteous in S.
19 : 1. came two angels to S. at even
4. men of S. compassed the house
Is. 3 : 9. shall declare their sin as S.
La. 4 : 6. the punishment of sin of S.
Eze. 16 : 46. thy younger sister is S.,
48, 49, 55, 56. ⌈of S.
53. When I bring again captivity
Mat. 11 : 23. if works in thee done in
Lu. 17 :29. day Lot went out of S.⌊S.
Ro. 9 : 29. seed, we had been as S-a
Re. 11 :8. gr. city, spiritually called S.

SODOM with Gomorrah.
Ge. 10 :19. as thou goest unto S. and G.
13 : 10. bef. Lord destroyed S. and G.
14 : 2. Bera, k. of S., Birsha, k. of G. 8.
10. kings of S. and G. fled and fell
11. took all the goods of S. and G.
18 : 20. Bec. cry of S. and G. is great
19 : 24. L. rained upon S. and G. fire
28. Ab. looked toward S. and G.
De. 29 : 23. like the overthrow of S.
and G., Is. 13 : 19. Je. 49 : 18.-
50 : 40. ⌈G.
32 : 32. their vine is of vine of S. and
Is. 1 : 9. we should have been as S.,
and like G., Ro. 9 : 29.
10. Hear Lord, ye rulers of S., give
ear, people of G.
Je. 23 : 14. they are all as S. and G.
Am. 4 :11. as God overthrew S. and G.
Zph. 2 : 9. Surely Moab shall be as
S., and children of Ammon as G.
Mat. 10 : 15. more tolerable for land
of S. and G., 11 : 24. Mk. 6 : 11.
Lu. 10 : 12. ⌈ashes
2 Pe. 2 : 6. turning S. and G. into
Jude 7. Even as S. and G. and cities

SOD'OMA. See SODOM.

SODOMITE, S. ⌈Isr.
De. 23 : 17. shall be no s. of sons of
1 K. 14 : 24. were s-s in the land
15 : 12. Asa took s-s out of land
22 :46. remnant of s-s Jehoshaphat
2 K. 23 :7. Josiah brake houses of s-s
Jb. 36 : † 14. their life is amo. the s-s

SOEVER. ⌈be
2 S. 24 : 3. people how many s. they
See **WHAT** with soever.
See **WHEREWITH** soever.

SOFT, SOFTER, SOFTLY.
Ge. 33 : 14. I will lead s-y, as cattle
Ju. 4 : 21. Jael went s-y and smote
Ru. 3 : 7. she came s-y, uncov-d feet
1 K. 21 :27. Ahab, in sackcl., went s-y
Jb. 23 : 16. God maketh my heart s.
Ps. 65 : 10. makest it s. wi. showers
Pr. 15 : 1. A s. answer turneth wrath
25 : 15. a s. tongue breaketh bone
Is. 8 : 6. waters of Shiloah th. go s-y
38 : 15. I shall go s-y all my years
Ac. 27 :13. wind blew s-y, they sailed
See CLOTHING, RAIMENT.
See **Soft** or **Softer WORDS.**

SOIL. ⌈own s.
Ps. 37 : † 35. like tree that groweth in
Eze. 17 :8. It was planted in a good s.

SOJOURN. ⌈to s.
Ge. 12 : 10. Abram went into Egypt
19 : 9. said, This fellow came in to s.
26 : 3. s. in this land, I will be with
47 : 4. to s. in the land are we come
Ex. 12 : 48. when stranger sh. s. with
thee, Le. 19 :33. Nu. 9 : 14 -15 : 14.
Le. 17 :8. of strangers wh. s. that off-h
10. of strangers that s. that eateth
13. th. s. among you wh. hunteth
20 : 2. of strangers that s. that giv-
25 : 45. of strangers that s. buy⌊eth
Ju. 17 : 8. Levite to s. where find, 9.
Ru. 1 : 1. Elim-h went to s. in Moab
1 K. 17 :20. upon widow wi. whom I s.
2 K. 8 :1. s. wheresoev. thou canst s.
Ps. 15 : † 1. who s. in thy tabern.?
120 : 5. Woe is me, I s. in Meshech
Is. 23 : 7. feet sh. carry her afar to s.
52 : 4. My people went into Eg. to s.
Je. 42 : 15. If ye set your faces to s.
there, 17.-44 : 12, 14, 28. ⌈to s.
22. sh. die in place whi. ye desire
43 : 2. Go not into Egypt to s.
La. 4 : 15. They sh. no more s. there
Eze. 20 :38. bring from where they s.
47 :22. unto you and strangers th. s.
Ac. 7 : 6. his seed sho. s. in strange

SOJOURNED. ⌊land
Ge. 20 : 1. Abraham s. in Gerar ⌈s.
21 : 23. to the land wherein th. hast
34. s. in the Philistines' land
32 : 4. I s. with Laban, and stayed
35 : 27. Hebron, where Abraham s.
De. 18 : 6. if Levite from where he s.
26 : 5. Jacob s. in Egypt with a few
Ju. 17 : 7. Levite s. in Bethlehem-
19 : 16. an old man s. in Gibeah⌊ju.
2K. 8 :2. she s. in land of Philistines
Ps. 105 : 23. Jacob s. in land of Ham
He. 11 : 9. By faith he s. in land of

SOJOURNER, S. ⌊prom.
Le. 22 : 10. s. of priest not eat holy
25 : 40. thy brother shall be as a s.
2 S. 4 : 3. Beerothites s-s in Gittaim
See **STRANGER, S,** with
Sojourner, s.

SOJOURNETH. ⌊s.
Ex. 3 : 22. woman borrow of her th.
12 : 49. One law to homeborn and
stranger that s., Le. 16 : 29.
Le. 17 : 12. nei. shall stranger that
s. eat blood ⌈statutes
18 : 26. s. among you shall keep
25 : 6. sab. meat for stranger that s.
Nu. 15 : 15. One ordinance for you
and stranger th. s., 16, 29.-19 : 10.
26. sh. be forgiven stranger that s.
Jos. 20 : 9. cities for stranger that s.
Ezr. 1 : 4. whoso. remain, where he s.
Eze. 14 : 7. every one that s. in Isr.
47. 23. in what tribe stranger s. give

SOJOURNING, S. ⌈† 4.
Ge. 17 : †8. give thee land of s-s, 28 :
Ge. 37 : †1. Jac. dwelt in la. of fa-'s s-s
Ex. 12 : 40. s. of Israel was 430 years
Ju. 19 : 1. a Levite s. on m-t Ephraim
1 Pe. 1 : 17. pass time of y-r s. in fear

SOLACE.
Pr. 7 : 18. let us s. ourselves wi. loves

SOLD.
Ge. 25 : 33. Esau s. his birthright
31 : 15. our father hath s. us
37 :28. they s. Joseph to Ishmaelites
36. Midianites s. him into Egypt
41 : 56. Joseph s. corn unto Eg-ians
42 :6. he it was th. s. to all the peo.
45 : 4. I am your brother whom ye
5. be not angry that ye s. me ⌊s.
47 : 20. Eg-ns s. every man his field
22. the priests s. not their lands
Ex. 22 :3. then shall he be s. for theft
Le. 25 : 23. land sh. not be s. for ev.
25. sh. redeem that wh. brother s.
27. restore overplus to wh. he s. it
28. that which is s. shall remain
29. redeem ho. within year aft. s.
33. house s. shall go out in jubilee
34. field of suburbs may not be s.
39. if bro. poor and be s. unto thee
42. brethren not be s. as bondmen
48. after he is s., may be redeemed
50. from year he was s. unto him
27 : 20. if s. field to another man
27. be s. acc-g to thy estimation
28. no devoted thing shall be s.
De. 15 :12. if brother be s. unto thee
28 : 68. shall ye be s. unto enemies
32 : 30. exc. their Rock had s. them
Ju. 2 : 14. he s. them into hands of
3 : 8. L. s. them to Chushan-risha.
10 : 7. L. s. th. into hands of Phil.
1 S. 12 : 9. L. s. them into hands of
1 K. 21 : 20. s. thyself to work evil
2 K. 6 : 25. ass's head was s. for 80
7 : 1. fine flour s. for a shekel, 16.
17 : 17. Israel s. thems. to do evil
Ne. 5 :8. redeemed brethren wh. were
s., or shall they be s. unto us
13 : 15. in day wh-in they s. victuals
16. bro-t ware and s. on sabbath
Es. 7 : 4. we are s. I and my peo. ; if
we had been s. for bondmen
Ps. 105 : 17. Joseph was s. for serv-t
Is. 50 : 1. which is it to whom I s.
you? for iniq-s have ye s. yours.
52 : 3. Ye have s. yours. for nought
Je. 34 : 14. let go bro. wh. hath been s.
La. 5 : 4. our wood is s. unto us ⌈s.
Eze. 7 : 13. seller not return to this
Jo. 3 : 3. they have s. a girl for wine
6. children of Judah have ye s.
7. raise out of place which ye s. th.
Am. 2 : 6. they s. righteous for silver
Mat. 10 : 29. Are not two sparrows s.
13 : 46. went and s. all that he had
18 :25. lord commanded him to be s.
21 : 12. cast out them that s. and
bought, overthrew seats of them.
th. s. doves, Mk. 11: 15. Lu. 19: 45.
26 :9. For this ointment might have
been s. Mk. 14 : 5. Jn. 12 : 5.
Lu. 12 : 6. Are not five sparrows s. for
17 : 28. they bought, they s., they
Jn. 2 : 14. in temple those th. s. oxen
16. said unto them that s. doves
Ac. 2 : 45. s. their possessions, 4 :34.
4 : 37. Joses having land, s. it, and
5 : 1. Ananias and wife s. possess-n
4. aft. it was s., was it not in thine
8. ye s. the land for so much?
Ro. 7 : 14. I am carnal, s. under sin
1 Co. 10 : 25. Whatso. is s. in shamb.
He. 12 : 16. for one morsel s. birth-

SOLDER. ⌊right
Is. 41 † 7. saying of s., It is good

SOLDERING.
Is. 41 : 7. It is ready for the s.

SOLDIER.
Jn. 19 : 23. parts, to every s. a part
Ac. 10 : 7. Cornel. called a devout s.

Ac. 28 : 16. suff-d Paul to dwell wi. s.
2 Ti. 2 : 3. endure as good s. of Christ
4. who hath chosen him to be a s.

SOLDIERS.

1 Ch. 7 : 4. bands of s. for war, 36,000
11. s. fit to go out for battle ⌈dah
2 Ch. 25 : 13. s. fell upon cities of Ju-
Ezr. 8 : 22. I ashamed to require s.
Is. 15 : 4. armed s. of Moab shall ⌊cry
Mat. 8 : 9. s. under me, Lu. 7:8. ⌊out
27 : 27. the s. took Jesus, and gathered to him s., Mk. 15 : 16. ⌈s.
28 : 12. they gave large money unto
Lu. 3 : 14. s. demanded, saying ⌈gar
23 : 36. s. mocked, offering him vine-
Jn. 19 : 2. s. platted crown of thorns
23. s. took his garments, and coat
24. These things the s. did
32. came the s., brake legs of first
34. one of the s. pierced his side
Ac. 12 : 4. Peter to 4 quaternions of s.
6. Peter sleeping between two s.
18. was no small stir among the s.
21 : 32. when they saw capt. and s.
35. that he was borne of the s.
23 : 10. capt. com-ded s. to take Paul
23. make ready 200 s. to go to Cesa.
31. s., as it was com-ded, took Paul
27 : 31. Paul said to the s., Except
32. s. cut off the ropes of the boat
42. s.' counsel was to kill prisoners
See **FELLOW soldier.**

SOLE, S. See **Sole of FOOT.**
See **FEET** with **sole, s.**

SOLEMN. ⌈trumpets
Nu. 10 : 10. in your s. days blow
Ps. 92 : 3. sing praise with s. sound
Is. 1 : 13. is iniquity, the s. meeting
La. 2 : 22. hast called as in a s. day
Ho. 9 : 5. What will ye do in s. day?
Zch. 8 : † 19. fast be joy and s. times

SOLEMN assembly, ies.
Le. 23 : 36. on the eighth day is a s.
a., Nu. 29 : 35. Ne. 8 : 18. ⌈to L.
De. 16 : 8. on seventh day be a s.a.
2 K. 10 : 20. Proclaim a s.a. for Baal
2 Ch. 7 : 9. 8th day they made a s.a.
Am. 5 : 21. I not smell in your s.a-s
Jo. 1 : 14. Sanctify fast, call s.a., 2:15.
Zph. 3 : 18. they are sorrowf. for s.a.
See Solemn **FEAST, FEASTS**

SOLEMNITY, IES.
De. 31 : 10. in the s. of year of release
Is. 30 : 29. as when a holy s. is kept
33 : 20. upon Zion, city of our s-s
Eze. 45 : 17. burnt off-gs in s-s of Isr.
46 : 11. in s-s meat off-g be an ephah

SOLEMNLY.
Ge. 43 : 3. The man did s. protest
1 S. 8 : 9. yet protest s. unto them

SOLITARILY. ⌈wood
Mi. 7 : 14. Feed people wh. dwell s. in

SOLITARY. ⌈him
Nu. 23 : † 3. Balaam went s., G. met
Jb. 3 : 7. let that night be s., let no
30 : 3. For famine they were s.
Ps. 68 : 6. God setteth s. in families
107 : 4. They wandered in a s. way
Is. 35 : 1. wildern. and s. place be glad
La. 1 : 1. How doth city sit s.
Mk. 1 : 35. Jesus departed into s. pla.

SOLOMON.
2 S. 5 : 14. born unto David in Jerusalem, S., 1 Ch. 3 : 5.–14 : 4.
12 : 24. called his name S., G. loved
1 K. 1 : 10. S. he called not, 19, 26.
13. S. thy son sh. reign aft. me, 17, 30.
21. I and S. be counted offenders
33. cause S. to ride upon Da.'s mule,
34. God save king S., 39. ⌊38.
37. L. with David, so be he with S.
43. Verily David hath made S. king
47. God made the name of S. bet.
50. Adonijah feared king S., 51.
51. Let S. swear he will not slay me
52. S. said, If he shew hims. worthy
53. S. said, Go to thine house
1 K. 2 : 1. David charged S. his son
13. S., 17, 19, 22, 25, 27, 29, 41.
23. king S. sware, God do so to me
46. kingdom estab-d in hand of S.
3 : 1. S. made affinity with Pharaoh
3. S. loved the Lord, walking in
4. a thous. burnt off-gs did S. offer
5. Lord appeared to S., 9 : 2. 2 Ch.
1 : 7.–7 : 12 ⌈this
10. pleased the Lord that S. asked
15. S. awoke; behold it was dream
4 : 1. So king S. was king over all Isr.
7. S., 11, 15, 21, 25, 26, 27.
22. S.'s provision for one day was
29. God gave S. wisdom exc-g, 5 : 12.
30. S.'s wisd. excelled wisd. of all
34. came to hear wisdom of S. fr.
all kings, Mat. 12 : 42. Lu. 11 : 31.
5 : 1 Hiram of Ty. sent serv-ts unto
2. S., 7, 8, 10, 11, 12, 15, 16, 18. ⌊S.
13. S. raised a levy out of Israel
6 : 1. S., 2, 11, 21.–7 : 1, 8, 13, 14,
40, 45, 47, 48.
14. So S. built the house, finished
it, 2 Ch. 7 : 11.–35 : 3. Ac. 7:47.
7 : 51. So was ended all work S. made
8 : 1. S. assemb-d elders, 2 Ch. 5 : 2.
2. S., 63.–9 : 1, 10, 11, 12, 15, 16.
19, 21, 22, 23, 24, 25, 27, 28 ⌈6.
5. S. and cong-n sacrificing, 2 Ch. 5:
12. Then spake S., 2 Ch. 6 : 1.
22. S. stood before altar of Lord
54. S. made end of praying, 2 Ch. 7:
65. at that time S. held a feast ⌊1.
9 : 2. L. appeared unto S. sec. time
17. S. built Gezer, Beth-heron
26. king S. made a navy of ships
10 : 1. queen of Sheba heard of the
fame of S., 2 Ch. 9 : 1.
2. S., 4, 10, 13, 14, 16, 21, 23, 26, 28.
3. S. told queen all her questions,
2 Ch. 9 : 2. ⌈2 Ch. 9 : 22.
23. S. exceeded all kings of earth,
24. all the earth sought to S., 2
Ch. 9 : 23 ⌈en
11 : 1. S. loved many strange wom-
2. S. clave unto these in love
4. S. was old, wives turned his h-t
5. S. went after Ashtoreth goddess
6. S. did evil in sight of the Lord
7 S. build high pla. for Chemosh
9. Lord was angry with S. ⌈ite
14. advers-y unto S. Hadad Edom-
25. S., 26, 31, 41, 42. ⌈breaches
27. S. built Millo and repaired
28. S. seeing the yo. man industri-
40. S. sought to kill Jeroboam ⌈ous
43. S. slept with his fathers, 2 Ch.
9 : 31. ⌈Ch. 10 : 2.
12 : 2. Jeroboam fled from k. S., 2
6. S., 21, 23. 2 K. 23 : 13.–24 : 13.–
25 : 16. ⌈2 Ch. 12 : 9.
14 : 26. took shields of gold S. made,
2 K. 21 : 7. Lord said to Da. and S., I
will put my name, 2 Ch. 33 : 7.
1 Ch. 3 : 10. S., 6 : 10, 32.–14 : 4.–18 : 8.
22 : 6. S., 7.–28 : 5.–29 : 22, 24, 28. ⌈S.
9. his name sh. be S. | 17. to help
23 : 1. he made S. his son king
28 : 6. S. thy son sh. build my house
11. Da. gave to S. his son pattern of
20. David said to S., Be strong
29 : 22. S., 24, 28. 2 Ch. 1 : 3, 5, 6, 8,
11, 13, 14.–2 : 11.–4 : 11, 16, 18,
19.–5 : 1, 2, 6.–6 : 1, 13.–7 : 8, 10.
23. S. sat on throne of Lord as k.
25. Lord magnified S. exceedingly
2 Ch. 1 : 1. S. son of Da. was strength-
2. Then S. spake unto Israel ⌊ened
7. that night did G. appear unto S.
2 : 1. S. determined to build house
2. S. told out 70,000 men to bear
2 Ch. 2 : 3. S. sent to Huram of Tyre
17. S. numbered all the strangers
3 : 1. S. began to build house of L.
3. things wh-n S. was instructed.
7 : 1. S. had made end of praying
2 Ch. 7 : 5. S. offered sacri. of 22,000
7. S. hallowed mid. of court ⌊oxen
12. L. appeared unto S. by night
8 : 1. S., 2, 3, 6, 8, 9, 10, 11, 12, 16,
17, 18. ⌈pared
16. all the work of S. was pre-
9 : 3. S., 9, 10, 12, 13, 14, 15, 20.
28, 29, 30.–11 : 17.–13 : 6, 7.
25. S. had 4,000 stalls for horses
30 : 26. since time of S. not such joy
35 : 4. prepare yours. acc-g to writing of S. ⌈58. Ne. 7 : 57, 60.–11 : 3.
Ezr. 2 : 55. The children of S. serv-ts,
Ne. 12 : 45. acc-g to command-t of S.
13 : 26. Did not S., k., sin by these;
Pr. 1 : 1. proverbs of S., 10 : 1.–25 : 1.
Can. 1 : 1. The song of songs, wh. is S.'s
5. but comely, as curtains of S.
3 : 7. Behold, his bed, which is S.
9. King S. made himself a chariot
11. S. with crown whw-h his moth.
8 : 11. S. had viney. at Baal-hamon
12. thou, O S., must have a thous.
Je. 52 : 20. sea S. made was carried
Mat. 1 : 6. David begat S. of her that
7. S. begat Roboam ⌈Lu. 12 : 27.
6 : 29. S. in all his glory not arrayed,
12 : 42. a greater than S. is here,
See Porch, My SON. ⌊Lu. 11 : 31.

SOME. ⌈me
Ge. 19 : 19. Lot said, Lest s. evil take
33 : 15. let me leave s. of the folk
37 : 20. let us cast him into s. pit,
and say, s. evil beast hath
47 : 2. took s. of his brethren and
Ex. 16 : 17. gathered s. more, s. less
20. s. left of it till the morning ⌈er
27. s. went out on 7th day to gath-
Le. 4 : 7. put s. of bl. upon horns, 18.
17. priest dip finger in s. of blood
Nu. 21 : 1. Arad took s. prisoners
27 : 20. put s. of honour upon him
De. 24 : 1. s. uncleanness in her ⌈her
Ru. 2 : 16. let fall s. of handfuls for
1 S. 24 : 10, s. bade me kill thee ⌈(2)
2 S. 17 : 9. hid in s. pit, or s. place, 12,
1 K. 14 : 13. in him is s. good thing
2 K. 7 : 9. s. mischief will come ⌈ance
2 Ch. 12 : 7. I will grant s. deliver-
Ezr. 10 : 44. s. had wives by whom
Ne. 5 : 3. s. said, We mortgaged ⌈es
13 : 15. saw I s. treading winepress-
19. s. of my servants set I at gates
Jb. 24 : 2. s. remove landmarks
Ps. 20 : 7. s. trust in chariots, s. horses
69 : 20. I looked for s. to take pity
Pr. 4 : 16. unless they cause s. to fall
Je. 49 : 9. not leave s. gleaning
Da. 8 : 10. it cast down s. of host
11 : 35. s. of understanding sh. fall
12 : 2. s. to everl-g life, s. to shame
Am. 4 : 11. overth-n s. as God overth.
Ob. 5. wo. they not leave s. grapes?
Mat. 13 : 4. s. fell by the wayside,
Mk. 4 : 4. Lu. 8 : 5. ⌈5.
5. s. fell upon stony places, Mk. 4:
7. s. am. thorns, Mk. 4 : 7. Lu. 8 : 7.
16 : 14. s. say, Thou art John Baptist, s. Elias, Mk. 8 : 28. Lu. 9 : 19.
28. be s. standing here, who not
taste, Mk. 9 : 1. Lu. 9 : 27. ⌈made
19 : 12. s. eunuchs were so born, s.
23 : 34. s. ye sh. kill, s. ye sh. scourge
27 : 47. s. said, This man calleth
for Elias, Mk. 15 : 35. ⌈into city
28 : 11. behold s. of the watch came
17. worshipped him, but s. doubted
Mk. 4 : 8. s. thirty, s. sixty, s. a
hundred, 20. Mat. 13 : 8, 23. ⌈(2)
7 : 2. s. of disciples. | 12 : 5. killing s.,
14 : 4. were s. that had indignation
65. And s. began to spit on him
Lu. 8 : 6. s. fell upon a rock, withered
9 : 7. was said of s., John was risen
8. of s., that Elias had appeared
11 : 15. s. said, He casteth out devils
13 : 1. s. that told him of Galileans

Lu. 19 : 39. s. of the Pharisees,Jn.9:
21 : 5. as s. spake of the temple[16.
16. s. sh. cause to be put to death
28 : 8. to have seen s. miracle
Jn. 6 : 64. s. of you that believe not
7 : 25.said s.of Jerus.,Is not this he
41.s.said,Sh. Ch.come out of Gal.?
44. s. would have taken him ; but
9 : 9. s. said, This is he ; others said
11 : 37. s. said, Could not this man
46. s. went their ways to Pharisees
13 : 29. s. thought bec. Judas had
Ac. 5 : 15. of Pet. overshad. s. of th.
8 : 9. that himself was s. great one
31. How, except s. man guide me?
34. of himself, or of s. other man ?
11 : 20. s. were men of Cyprus and
13 : 11. seek-g s. to lead him by ha.
15 : 36. s. days after Paul said, Let
17 : 4. s. believed and consorted
18. s. said,What will babbler say?
21. to tell or hear s. new thing[s.
32.heard of resurrec-n, s. mocked
18 : 23. after he had spent s. time
19 : 32. s. cried one thing, s., 21:34.
27 : 27. th. drew near to s. country
34. Whf., I pray you, take s. meat
44. s. on boards, s. on pieces of
28 : 24. s. believed, s. believed not
Ro.1:11.may impart s. spiritual gift
13. I might have s. fruit am. you
3 : 3.For what if s. did not believe?
8. s. affirm we say, Let us do evil
5 : 7. for good man s.wo.dare to die
11 : 14. if by any means I save s.
17. if s. of branches be broken
15 : 15. writt. more boldly in s. sort
1 Co. 4 : 18. now s. are puffed up as
6 : 11. such were s. of you, but ye
8 : 7. s. with conscience of idol eat
9 : 22. I might by all means save s.
10 : 7. nei. be idolaters as were s.
8. Nei. commit fornication as s. of
9. as s. tempted Ch.were destroy-
10. Nei. murmur ye as s. of th.[ed
12 : 28. God hath set s. in church
15 : 6. but s. are fallen asleep
12. how say s. is no resurrection ?
34. s. have not knowledge of God
35. s. man will say, How are dead
37.chance of wheat or s.oth.grain
2 Co. 3 : 1. or need we, as s. others.
10 : 2. I think to be bold ag.s.[epis.
12. dare not compare ours. with s.
Ga. 1 : 7. there be s. that trouble you
Ep. 4 : 11. gave s. prophets, s. past-s
Ph. 1 : 15. s. preach Christ of envy
2 Th.3:11.s. am.you walk disorderly
1Ti.1 : 3. charge s. th. they teach no
6. from which s. having swerved
19. s. have made shipwreck [faith
4 : 1. in latter times s.sh.depart fr.
5 : 15. s. are turned aside aft. Satan
24.s. men's sins open beforehand,
s. men they follow [forehand
25. good works of s. manifest be.
6 : 10. which while s. coveted after
21.s. professing erred cone-g faith
2 Ti. 2 : 18. overthrow the faith of s.
20.s.vessels to honour,s. to disho.
He. 3 : 4. ev. hou. builded by s. man
16.s. when th. heard, did provoke
4 : 6. it remaineth th. s. must enter
10:25.Not forsaking as manner of s.
11 : 40. provided s. better thing for
13 : 2. thereby s. entertained angels
1 Pe. 4 : 12. as tho. s. strange thing
2 Pe. 3 : 9. L. is not slack, as s. count
16. s. things hard to be underst.
Jude 22. of s. have compassion
Re. 2 : 10.devil sh. cast s. into prison

See Of the PEOPLE.

SOMEBODY. [ed me
Lu. 8 : 46.Jesus said, s. hath touch-
Ac. 5 : 36.Theudas, boasting to be s.

SOMETHING. [falicn
1 S. 20 : 26. he thought, s. had be-
Mk. 5 : 43. th. s. be given her to eat
Lu.11 : 54.to catch s.out of his mou.
Jn. 13 : 29. he give s. to poor [them
Ac. 3 : 5. expecting to receive s. of
23 : 15 wo.inquire s.more perfectly
18. this young man hath s.to say
Ga. 6 : 3. if man think hims. to be s.

SOMETIME, S.
Ep. 2 : 13. ye who were s. afar off
5 : 8. ye were s. darkness, but now
Col. 1 : 21.you that were s. alienated
3 : 7. In which ye walked s. when
Tit. 3 : 3.we ourselves were s. foolish
1 Pe.3 :20.Which s.were disobedient

SOMEWHAT.
Le. 4 : 13.have done s. ag. com-ts,27.
22. ruler hath done s. thro. ignor.
13 : 6. if plague s.dark,21,26,28,56.
19. bright spot, s. reddish, 24.
1S.2 :†36.put me s.about priesthood
1 K. 2 : 14. I have s. to say unto thee
2 K. 5 : 20. I will run, take s. of him
2 Ch. 10 : 4. ease s. grievous servitu.
9. Ease s. the yoke thy father put
10. make yoke s. lighter for us
Lu. 7 : 40. Simon, I have s. to say
Ac. 23 : 20. inquire s. more perfectly
25 : 26. th. I might have s. to write
Ro. 15 : 24. s. filled with y-r comp-y
2 Co. 5 : 12. you may have s. to ans.
10 : 8. tho. I should boast s.more of
Ga. 2 : 6. those who seemed to be s.
He. 8 : 3. this man have s. to offer
Re.2 : 4.Neverthel., I have s.ag. thee

SON. [cised
Ge. 16 : † 12. s. of 8 days be circum-
17 : 16. I will give thee s.of Sarah,19.
-18 : 10, 14. [age, 7.
21 : 2. Sarah bare Ab. a s. in his old
10. Cast out bondwom. and her s.
24 : 36. Sarah,master's wife,bare s.
44.L.appointed for my master's s.
51.let her be thy master's s.'s wife
29 : 33.he hath given me this s. also
30 : 6. God hath heard me, given
me a s. [6th s.
17. Leah bare Jacob 5th s. | 19.
24. Lord sh. add to me another s.
35 : 17. thou shalt have this s. also
† 18. the s. of my sorrow ; s. of
the right hand [old age
37 : 3. because he was the s. of his
Ex. 1 : 16. if it be s. ye shall kill him
22. Every s. born cast into river
2 : 10. child grew, became her s.[s.
4 : 25. Zipporah cut foreskin of her
12 : † 5. your lamb shall be s. of a
year, Le. 12 : † 6.[or a daughter
21 : 31.Whether he have gored a s.
23 : 12. s. of handmaid be refreshed
29 : 30. s. that is priest in his stead
Le. 12 : 6. days of purifying for a s.
24 : 10. s. of Israelitish wom. strove
11. Israelitish wom.'s s. blasph-d
25 : 49. uncle's s. may redeem [por
Nu. 23 : 18. hearken, thou s. of Zip-
27 : 4.Why name done away bec. no
8. If a man die and have no s. [s.
De. 13 : 6. If s. of thy mother entice
21 : 16. not make s. of beloved,
firstborn, before s. of hated, 17.
18. If a man have a stubborn s.
20. our s. is stubborn, rebellious
28 : 56.eye sh. be evil toward her s.
Jos. 6 :26.in youngest s. set up gates
15 : 8. by valley of s. of Hinnom
Ju.5 : 12. lead captive s.of Abinoam
9 : 18. made s. of his maidserv.king
28. is not he the s. of Jerubbaal ?
11 : 2. thou art s. of strange woman
34. beside her nei. s. nor daughter
13 : 3. shalt conceive, bear s., 5, 7.
24. bare a s.,called him Samson[s.
Ru. 4 : 13. Boaz took Ruth, she bare
17. There is a s. born to Naomi
1 S. 1 : 23. Hannah gave her s. suck
4 : 20. Fear not, thou hast borne s.
1 S. 9 : 2.Kish had a s.whose name
10 : 11. What is come to s. of Kish ?
13 : †1. Saul,s. of 1 year in reigning
16 : 18. I have seen a s. of Jesse[16.
17 : 55.Abner,whose s. is th.youth?
58. Saul said,Whose s. art thou ?
18 : † 17.only be s. of valour for me
20 : 27.Whf.cometh not s.of Jesse ?
30. Thou s.of the perverse woman
†31. fetch him, he is the s.of death
22 : 7.will s. of Jesse give you fields
9. Doeg said, I saw s. of Jesse[tub
12. Saul said, Hear, th. s. of Ahi-
25 : 10. Who is David ? Who s. of
17. he is such a s. of Belial [Jesse ?
2 S. 1 : 13. I am s. of a stranger
3 : 3. s. of, 14, 15.-4 : 4, 8. 2 Ch. 11:
17, 22. [Ch. 3 : 2.
4. Adonijah, s. of Haggith (2) 1
4 : 2. Saul's s. had two captains
9 : 3. Jonathan hath s. who is lame
9. given s. all that pertained to S.
10. master's s. may have food ;
but Mephibosheth thy mast-'s s.
10 :2.shew kindness to s. of Nahash
12 : † 5. the man is a s. of death
16 : 3. where is thy master's s. ?
18 : 12. not put hand ag. king's s.
18. I have no s. to keep my name
20. no tidings, bec. king's s. dead
20 : 1.nei. inheritance in s. of Jesse,
1 K. 12 : 16. 2 Ch. 10 : 16.
1 K. 3 : 6. given him s. to sit on thr.
26.her bowels yearned upon hers.
5 : 7. hath given Da. a wise s. [Nap.
7 : 14. Hiram was a widow's s. of
14 : 1. Abijah s. of Jerob. fell sick
5. cometh to ask thing for her s.
17 : 17. s. of mistress of house sick
20. evil upon widow by slaying s.
22 : 26. Joash king's s., 2Ch.18:25.
2 K. 1 :17.Jehoram reigned bec. no s.
4 : 6. she said unto s.,Bring a vessel
16. this season shalt embrace a s.
17. woman bare a s. that season
28. Did I desire a s. of my lord ?
37. she took up her s., went out
6 : 29. Give thy s. that we may eat
him, she hath hid her s.
32. See ye how this s. of murderer
8 : 1. woman, whose s. he restored.
5. this is her s. Elisha restored !
11 : 1 saw her s. was dead,2 Ch. 22:
4. Jehoiada shewed king a s. [10.
12. he bro-t king's s., put crown
1 Ch. 12 : 18. are we on thy side, s. of
20 : 6. he was s. of the giant [Jesse
22 : 9. a s. shall be born to thee
2 Ch. 21 : 17. was never a s. left him
22 : 9.buried him. Bec.s.of Jehosh.
23 : 3. behold, king's s. shall reign
Ne. 11 : 14. Zabdiel, s. of great man
Jb. 18 : 19. He shall nei. have s. nor
Ps. 2 : 12.Kiss the S. lest he be angry
50 : 20. slanderest own mother's s.
72 : 1.thy righteous. unto king's s.
† 17. a s. to continue his fa.'s name
86 : 16. save s. of thine handmaid
89 :22.nor s. of wickedn. afflict him
116 : 16. I am s. of thine handmaid
Pr. 3 : 12. s. in whom he delighteth
4 : 3. I was my fa.'s s., beloved [20.
10 : 1. A wise s. maketh glad fa., 15:
5. gathereth in summer is wise s.,
sleepeth in harvest, s. causeth
shame, 17 : 2.-19 : 26.[struction
13 : 1. A wise s. heareth fa.'s in-
17 : 25. foolish s. is grief to father
19 : 13. A foolish s. calamity of fa.
28 : 7. Whoso keepeth law is wise s.
31 : 2. s. of my womb, s. of vows ?
Ec. 5 : 14.begetteth s. nothing in his
10 : 17.when king is the s. of nobles
Is. 5 : † 1. in the horn of s. of oil
7 : 4.not afraid of s.of Remaliah, 5.
6. let us set a king, s. of Tabeal
9. head of Samaria, Remaliah's s.

Is. 7:14. virgin sh. bear a s., Mat. 1:23.
8:3. prophetess conceived, bare a s.
9:6. child born, unto us a s. given
14:12. O Lucifer, s. of the morning
22. I will cut off fr. Babylon s. and
19:11. I am s. of wise, s. of kings
21:† 10. my thresh-g, s. of my floor
49:15. compassion on s. of womb
56:3. Nei. let s. of stranger speak
Je. 6:26. mourning, as for only s.
33:21. sho. not have a s. to reign
Eze. 14:20. sh. deliv. nei. s. nor dau.
18:4. soul of the s. is mine, soul
10. If he beget s. that is a robber
14. a s. that seeth father's sins
19. doth not s. bear iniquity of father? when s. hath done right
20. The s. sh. not bear iniquity of father, nei. father iniquity of s.
44:25. for s. or dau. defile thems.
46:† 13. unto L. of a s. of his year
Ho. 1:3. Gomer, wh. bare him a s., 8.
13:13. unwise s., for he should not
Am. 7:14. nei. was a prophet's s. [s.
8:10. make it as mourning of only
Jon. 4:† 10. gourd was s. of the night
Mi. 7:6. the s. dishonoureth father
Mal. 1:6. s. honoureth his father
Mat. 1:21. bring forth s., Lu. 1:31.
25. bro-t forth firstborn s., Lu 2:7.
9:2. s., be of good cheer, Mk. 2:5.
10:37. that loveth s. or dau. more
11:27. no man knoweth S. but Fa., nor any the Fa. save S., Lu. 10:22.
13:55. Is not this the carpenter's s.
21:28. s., go work in my vineyard
38. when husbandmen saw s.
22:42. What think of Ch.? whose s.
23:35. blood of Zacharias, s. of Bar-s
28:19. baptizing in name of Fa., S.
Mk. 6:3. Is this carpenter, s. of Mary
10:46. Bartimeus s. of Timeus
12:6. Having one s. well beloved
13:12. father shall betray the s.
32. that hour knoweth not the S.
14:61. Art thou the Christ, the S.?
Lu. 1:13. Elisabeth sh. bear thee s.
32. shall be called S. of the Highest
36. Elisabeth conceived s., in age
57. and Elisabeth brought forth s.
2:48. s., why hast th. dealt with us?
3:2. came unto Jn. s. of Zacharias
23. Jesus, s. of Joseph, s. of Heli,
4:22. Is not this Joseph's s.? [24.+
7:12. the only s. of his mother
10:6. if s. of peace be there, your
11:11. If a s. ask bread of you [s.
12:53. father sh. be divided against
15:13. the younger s. gathered all
31. s., thou art ever with me, all
16:25. s., remember, in thy lifetime
19:9. he also is s. of Abraham
Jn. 1:18. only begotten S. in bosom
42. Thou art Simon s. of Jonah
45. Jesus of Nazareth, s. of Joseph
3:35. Father loveth the S., 5:20.
36. that believeth on S. hath life, that believeth not S. hath not
4:46. nobleman whose s. was sick
5:19. S. can do nothing of himself, what things Father doeth doeth
21. S. quickeneth whom he will [S.
22. committed all judgm-t unto S.
23. all men sho. honour S. He th. honoureth not S. honoureth not
26. given to S. to have life in hims.
6:40. wh. seeth S. and believeth on
42. Is not this Jes., s. of Joseph?
8:35. but the S. abideth for ever
36. If S. shall make you free
9:19. Is this your s., born blind?
20. We know that this is our s. [S.
14:13. Father may be glorified in
17:12. none lost but s. of perdition
21:15. Simon, s. of Jonas, lovest
Ac. 4:36. Barna., s. of consol-n [me
7:21. nourished for her own s.
Ac. 13:21. God gave th. Saul, s. of
22. I found David, s. of Jesse [Cis
16:1. Timotheus s. of a Jewess
23:6. I am Pharisee, s. of Pharisee
16. Paul's sister's s. heard of their
Ro. 9:9. this time Sarah sh. have s.
1 Co. 15:28. then shall S. be subject
Ga. 4:7. no more a servant, but s., and if s., then an heir of God
30. Cast out the bondwoman and her s., for s. of bondwoman not be heir with s. of free woman
Ph. 2:22. as a s. he served in gospel
Col. 4:10. Marcus sister's s. to Barn.
2 Th. 2:3. man of sin, s. of perdit-n
1 Ti. 1:18. charge unto thee, s. Tim.
He. 1:5. I a father, he shall be a s.
8. to the S. he saith, thy throne
3:6. Christ as s. over his own hou.
5:8. Tho. a s., learned obedience
7:28. word of the oath maketh s.
11:24. refused to be called s. of Ph.
12:6. scourgeth ev. s. he receiveth
7. what s. father chasteneth not?
2 Pe. 2:15. way of Balaam s. of Bosor
1 Jn. 2:22. He is antichrist that denieth the Father and S.
23. Whoso. denieth S. hath not Fa.; he that acknowledgeth S.
24. ye shall continue in S. and Fa.
4:14. Father sent S. to be Saviour
5:12. He that hath the S. hath life; he that hath not S. hath not life
2 Jn. 3. Jesus Christ S. of Father [S.
9. he th. abideth hath both Fa. and

See Son of ABINOAM.
See DAVID, NADAB, NEBAT.

SON of God.

Da. 3:25. form of fourth like S. -
Mat. 4:3. If thou be S. - com-d that these, 6.-27:40.-Lu. 4:3, 9.
8:29. What we to do with thee, Jesus, thou S. -, Lu. 8:28. [16.
14:33. Of a truth thou art S. -, 16:
26:63. tell whether thou be Christ
27:43. he said, I am the S. - [S. -
54. this was the S. -, Mk. 15:39.
Mk. 1:1. gospel of Jesus Christ, S. -
3:11. Thou art the S. -, Jn. 1:49.
Lu. 1:35. holy thing be called S. -
3:38. was s. of Adam, the s. -
4:41. devils, crying out, Thou art Christ, S. -, Jn. 6:69.-11:27.
22:70. said, Art thou then the S. -?
Jn. 1:34. I bare record, this is S. -
3:18. not believed in only begot. S. -
5:25. dead shall hear voice of S. -
9:35. Dost thou believe on S. -?
10:36. because I said, I am the S. -
11:4. that the S. - be glorified
19:7. because made himself S. -
20:31. believe Jesus is Christ, S. -
Ac. 8:37. I believe Jesus is the S. -
9:20. preached Ch., that he is S. -
Ro. 1:4. declared to be the S. -
2 Co. 1:19. S. - was not yea and nay
Ga. 2:20. I live by faith of the S. -
Ep. 4:13. unity of knowledge of S. -
He. 4:14. high priest, Jesus the S. -
6:6. they crucify the S. - afresh
7:3. made like S. - abideth a priest
10:29. trodden under foot the S. -
1 Jn. 3:8. For this S. - manifested
4:15. Whoso. confess Jesus is S. -
5:5. believeth Jesus is the S. -
10. that believeth on the S. -
12. hath not the S. - hath not life
13. that ye may believe on the S. -
20. We know that the S. - is come
Re. 2:18. write these saith the S. -

His SON.

[Enoch
Ge. 4:17. city after name of h.s.
9:24. Noah knew what h.s. had
11:31. Terah took Ab. h.s.(3) [26.
16:15. called h.s.'s na. Ishm., 17:25,
21:3. called name of h.s. Isaac, 4, 5.
11. thing grievous because of h.s.
Ge. 22:3. Abr. took Isaac h.s., 6, 9
10. Abra. took knife to slay h.s.
13. for burnt off-g instead of h.s.
24:48. brother's daughter to h.s.
25:6. sent from Isaac h.s. while
11. aft. death of Abr., G. bles-d h.s.
27:1. Isaac called Esau h.s., 5, 20.
31. let my fa. eat h.s.'s venison
34:20. Shechem h.s. came to gate
24. to Shechem h.s. hearkened all
26. slew Hamor and Shechem h.s.
37:34. Jacob mourned for h.s.
47:29. Jacob called h.s. Joseph
Ex. 21:9. if betrothed her unto h.s.
32:29. conse-rate ev. man upon h.s.
Le. 21:2. for h.s. may be defiled
Nu. 20:25. h.s. De. 10:6. Jos. 24:33. Ju. 6:11. 1 S. 7:1.-9:3.-13:16, 22.-16:20.-17:17.-19:1.-20:27. 2 S. 1:4, 5, 12, 17.-8:10.-10:1.-21:12, 13, 14. 1 K. 2:1.-11:20. [28.
26. put them upon Eleazar h.s.,
De. 1:31. G. bare thee, as a man h.s.
7:3. thy dau. not give unto h.s.
8:5. as man chasteneth h.s., so L.
18:10. not any maketh h.s. pass
Jos. 6:26. in h.s. shall set up gates
2 S. 13:37. David mourned for h.s.
16:19. I not serve in pres. of h.s.?
19:2. king was grieved for h.s.
1 K. 11:43. h.s. reigned, 14:20, 31.-15:8, 24-16:6, 28.-22:40, 50. 2 K. 8:24-10:35.-12:21.-13:9, 24.-14:16, 29.-15:17, 22, 38.-16:20.-19:37.-20:21.-21:24, 26.-24:6. 1 Ch. 19:1.-23:1.-29:28.-2 Ch. 9:31.-12:16.-14:1.-17:1.-24:27.-26:23.-27:9.-28:27.-32:33.-33:20, 25.-36:8. Is. 37:38.
11:35. kingdom out of h.s.'s hand
36. unto h.s. will I give one tribe
13:† 11. old prophet h.s. told him
15:4. give a lamp to set up h.s.
16:13. for all the sins of Elah h.s.
21:29. in h.s.'s days will I bri. ev.
2 K. 3:27. h.s. for burnt offering
16:3. Ahaz made h.s. pass through
21:6. Manasseh made h.s. pass
7. of which Lord said to David and to Solomon h.s., 2 Ch. 33:7.
23:10. no man make h.s. pass
1 Ch. 3:10. h.s., 11, 12, 13, 14, 16, 17.-4:25, 26.-5:4, 5, 6.-6:20, 21, 22, 23, 24, 26, 27, 29, 30, 50, 51, 52, 53.-7:20, 21, 25, 26, 27.-8:37.-9:43.-18:10.-22:6, 17.-26:6, 14, 25.-27:6, 7.-28:11, 20.-29:28. 2 Ch. 26:21.-35:4. Ne. 12:45. [h.s.
2 Ch. 24:22. Joash the king slew
Pr. 13:24. spareth rod hateth h.s.
29:21. shall have him become h.s.
30:4. what is h.s.'s name, if thou
Je. 27:7. all nations shall serve him h.s. and h.s.'s son [humbled
Da. 5:22. thou h.s., O Belshaz., not
Mal. 3:17. as a man spareth h.s.
Mat. 7:9. what man, if h.s. ask bread, give stone? Lu. 11:11.
21:37. last of all he sent unto them
22:2. k. made marr for h.s. [h.s.
45. how is he then h.s.? Mk. 12:37. Lu. 20:44. [the field
Lu. 15:25. Now h. elder s. was in
Jn. 3:16. gave h. only begotten S.
17. God sent not h. S. to condemn
4:5. ground Jacob gave to h.s.
47. that he would come heal h.s.
Ac. 3:13. God hath glorified h. S.
26. God having raised up h. S.
Ro. 1:3. Cone-g h. S. Jesus Christ
9. I serve in gospel of h. S.
5:10. reconciled to God by h. S.
8:3. G. sending h. own S. in liken.
29. conformed to image of h. S.

Ro. 8 : 32. He th. spared not h. own S.
1 Co. 1 : 9. fellowship of h. S. Jesus
Ga. 1 : 16. pleased G. to reveal h. S.
4 : 4. God sent forth h. S. made of
6. God sent Spirit of h. S. into
Col. 1 : 13. into kingd. of h. dear S.
1 Th. 1 : 10. And to wait for h. S. fr.
He. 1 : 2. G. hath spok. to us by h. S.
11 : 17. Abr. offered up h. only s.
Ja. 2 : 21. had offered Isaac h. s.
1 Jn. 1 : 3. fellows. wi. Fa. and h. S.
7. blood of Ch. h. S. cleanseth us
3 : 23. believe on name of h. S. Jes.
4 : 9. God sent h. only begotten S.
10. sent h. S. to be propitiation
5 : 9. which he testified of h. S.
10. believeth not record God gave
11. this life is in h. S. [of h. S.
20. we are in h. S. Jesus Christ

SON in law. [s. -
Ge. 19 : 12. Hast here any besides?
Ju. 15 : 6. Samson, s. - of the Timnite
19 : 5. damsel's fa. said unto his s. -
1 S. 18 : 18. I sho. be s. - to king, 23.
21. Saul said, Thou sh. be my s. -
22. now be the king's s. -
26. it pleased David to be k.'s s. -
27. that he might be king's s. -
22 : 14. who faithful as king's s. -
2 K. 8 : 27. Jehoram was s. - of Ahab
Ne. 6 : 18. Tobiah was s. - to Shecha.
13 : 28. was s. - to Sanballat
See **Son of MAN.**

Mine own, or my SON.
Ge. 21 : 10. Ishm. not be heir wi. m.s.
23. wilt not deal falsely with m.s.
22 : 7. and he said, Here am I, m.s.
8. m.s., God will provide a lamb
24 : 3. not wife to m.s. of Cana., 37.
4. go, take a wife unto m.s., 7, 38.
6. thou bring not m.s. again, 8.
27 : 1. Isaac called Esau, said, m.s.
8. Now, m.s., obey my voice, 43.
13. Upon me be thy curse, m.s.
18. Here am I, who art thou, m.s.?
20. how found it so quickly, m.s.?
21. whe. thou be m.s. Esau, 24.
25. I will eat of m.s.'s venison, 26.
27. smell of m.s. is as a field
37. what sh. I do unto thee, m.s.?
30 : 15. take m.s.'s mandrakes, 16.
34 : 8. m.s. longeth for your dau.
37 : 33. he said, It is m.s.'s coat
35. go into grave to m.s. mourn-g
38 : 11. till Shelah m.s. be grown
26. I gave her not to Shelah m.s.
42 : 38. m.s. shall not go with you
43 : 29. God be gracious unto thee,
45 : 28. Joseph m.s. is alive [m.s.
48 : 19. Jacob said, I know it m.s.
49 : 9. from prey, m.s., thou art
Ex. 4 : 22. Israel is m.s., firstborn
23. Let m.s. go, that he serve me
Jos. 7 : 19. m.s., give glory to God
Ju. 8 : 23. neither shall m.s. rule
17 : 2. Blessed be thou of L., m.s.
3. for m.s. to make graven image
1 S. 3 : 6. I called not m.s. lie down
16. Eli called and said, Samu. m.s.
4 : 16. What is there done, m.s.?
10 : 2. What shall I do for m.s.?
14 : 39. tho. Jonathan m.s. he sh.
40. I and Jona. m.s. will be [die
42. Cast lots betw. me and J. m.s.
22 : 8. m.s. made league with son of Jesse, or m.s. hath stirred
24 : 16. Is this thy voice, m.s. David? 26 : 17.
26 : 21. I sinned, return, m.s. Da.
25. Blessed be thou, m.s. David
2 S. 7 : 14. I will be his fa., he shall be m.s., 1 Ch. 17 : 13.-22 : 10.
13 : 25. Nay, m.s., let us not all go
14 : 11. revengers, lest destroy m.s.
16. destroy m.s. out of inherit-e
16 : 11. m.s. wh. came of my bowels
18 : 22. Joab said, Whf. run, m.s.
2 S. 18 : 33. king said, O m.s. Abs. m.s., m.s. Absalom! 19 : 4.
1 K. 1 : 21. I and m.s. be offenders
33. m.s. to ride upon Da.'s mule
3 : 20. she took m.s. fr. beside me
21. it was not m.s. wh. I did bear
22. wom. said Nay; living is m.s.
23. thy son dead, m.s. the living
17 : 12. dress it for me and m.s.
18. Art thou come to slay m.s.
2 K. 6 : 28. we will eat m.s. to mor.
29. we boiled m.s., did eat him, I said, Give thy son [2 Ch. 25 : 18.
14 : 9. Give thy daughter to m.s.,
1 Ch. 22 : 5. Sol. m.s. is yo. and ten-
7. m.s., it was in my mind to [der
11. m.s., Lord will be with thee
28 : 5. chosen Sol. m.s. to sit upon
6. I have chosen him to be m.s.
9. Sol., m.s., know God of thy fa.
29 : 1. Sol., m.s., whom God hath
19. give Sol. m.s. perfect heart
Ps. 2 : 7. Thou art m.s., this day have I, Ac. 13 : 33. He. 1 : 5.-5 : 5.
Pr. 1 : 8. m.s. hear instruct-n of fa.
10. m.s., if sinners entice consent
15. m.s., walk not with them [not
2 : 1. m.s., if wilt receive my words
3 : 1. m.s., forget not my law
11. m.s., despise not chastening of Lord, He. 12 : 5. [thine eyes
21. m.s., let not them depart fr.
4 : 10. Hear, O m.s., rec. my say-s
20. m.s., attend to my words
5 : 1. m.s., attend unto my wisdom
20. why, m.s., be ravished with a strange woman
6 : 1. m.s., if surety for thy friend
3. Do this, m.s., deliver thyself
20. m.s., keep thy father's com-t
7 : 1. m.s., lay up my com-ts with
19 : 27. Cease, m.s., to hear instruc.
23 : 15. m.s., if thine heart be wise
19. m.s., be wise, guide thine h-t
26. m.s., give me thine heart
24 : 13. m.s., eat honey bec. good
21. m.s., fear thou the L. and k.
27 : 11. m.s., be wise, make my h-t
31 : 2. What, m.s.? and what, the s. of my vows? [monished
Ec. 12 : 12. by these, m.s., be ad-
Je. 31 : 20. Is Ephraim, m. dear s.?
Eze. 21 : 10. it contem-h rod of m.s.
Ho. 11 : 1. I called m.s. out of Egypt
Mat. 2 : 15. out of Eg. I called m.s.
17 : 15. Lord, have mercy on m.s.
21 : 37. saying, They will reverence m.s., Mk. 12 : 6. [thee m.s.
Mk 9 : 17. Master, I have bro-t to
Lu. 9 : 38. Master, look upon m.s.
15 : 24. m.s. was dead and is alive
1 Ti. 1 : 2. Timothy, m.o.s. in faith
2 Ti 2 : 1. m.s., be strong in grace
Tit. 1 : 4. Titus, m.o.s. after faith
Phm. 10. I beseech for m.s. Onesi.
1 Pe. 5 : 13. Marcus, m.s., saluteth
Re. 21 : 7. I will be his G., he be m.s.
See **My BELOVED,** Sixth.

Thine only, or Thy SON.
Ge. 22 : 2. Take t.s., t.o.s. Isaac
12. hast not withh. t.s., t.o.s., 16.
24 : 5. must I bring t.s. again.
27 : 32. he said, I am t.s., Esau
30 : 14. give me of t.s.'s mandrakes
15. lie with thee for t.s.'s mandr-s
37 : 32. know. whe. it be t. s.'s coat
45 : 9. say, Thus saith t.s. Joseph
48 : 2. Behold, t.s. Joseph cometh
Ex. 4 : 23. I will slay t.s., firstborn
10 : 2. tell in ears of t.s. and t.s.'s
13 : 8. thou shalt shew t.s. [son
14. when t.s. asketh, What is this? say, De. 6 : 20. [t.s., De. 5 : 14.
20 : 10. sabbath, not do work, nor
Le. 18 : 10. nakedness of t.s.'s dau.
15. nakedness of daughter in law t.s.'s wife
De. 6 : 2. I commanded thee, t.s.,
21. Th. sh. say unto t.s. [t.s.'s son
7 : 3. nor his dau. take unto t.s.
4. will turn t.s. fr. following me
12 : 18. eat before the Lord, thou, and t.s., 16 : 11, 14.
13 : 6. if t.s. entice thee secretly
Ju. 6 : 30. Bring out t.s. that he die
8 : 22. Rule over us, thou, t.s., t.
1 S. 16 : 19. Send me Da. t.s. [s.'s son
25 : 8. give servants and t.s. David
2 S. 14 : 11. not one hair of t.s. fall
15 : 27. Ahimaaz t.s., and Jonathan
16 : 8. kingd. into hands of Abs. t.s.
1 K. 1 : 12. save thy life, life of t.s.
13. t.s. Sol. shall reign, 17, 30.
3 : 22. dead is t.s., living my son, 23.
5 : 5. t.s. I will set upon throne
11 : 12. rend it out of hand of t.s.
13. I will give one tribe to t.s.
17 : 13. make for thee and for t.s.
19. Elijah said, Give me t.s.
23. Elijah said, See, t.s. liveth
2 K. 4 : 36. he said, Take up t.s.
6 : 28. Give t.s. that we eat him, 29.
8 : 9. t.s. Ben-hadad hath sent me
16 : 7. I am thy servant and t.s.
1 Ch. 28 : 6. Solomon t.s. shall build my house, 2 Ch. 6 : 9. [is hope
Pr. 19 : 18. Chasten t.s. while there
29 : 17. Correct t.s., he sh. give rest
Is. 7 : 3. Isa-h and Shear-jashub
Lu. 9 : 41. Jes. said, Bring t.s. [t.s.
15 : 19. no more worthy to be t.s., 21.
30. as soon as this t.s. was come
Jn. 4 : 50. Go, t.s. liveth, 51, 53.
17 : 1. glorify t. S. that t. S. glorify
19 : 26. he saith, Wom., behold t.s.

SONS.
Ge. 7 : 13. s. of Noah entered the ark
9 : 18. s. of Noah that went forth
10 : 1. s. born after the flood (2)
2. The s. of Japheth, 1 Ch. 1 : 5.
3. And the s. of Gomer. 1 Ch. 1 : 6.
4. And the s. of Javan, 1 Ch. 1 : 7.
6. And s. of Ham; Cush and, 1 Ch. 1 : 8. [1 : 9.
7. s. of Cush s. of Raamah, 1 Ch.
20. the s. of Ham after families
29. these were s. of Joktan, 1 Ch.
31. s. of Shem aft. families [1 : 23.
32. are families of s. of Noah [(2)
19 : 14. Lot spake unto his s. in law
23 : 3. Abraham spake unto s. of Heth, 16, 20. [give I
11. in presence of s. of my people
25 : 3. And the s. of Dedan were
4. And the s. of Midian, 1 Ch. 1 : 33.
6. unto s. of concubines Abr. gave
13. names of s. of Ishm., 16. [gifts
27 : 29. let thy mother's s. bow down
31 : 1. Jac. heard words of Laban's s.
32 : 22. Jacob took 11 s. ov. Jabbok
34 : 13. s. of Jacob ans-d Shechem
27. s. of Jacob came upon slain
35 : 5. did not pursue s. of Jacob
22. the s. of Jacob were twelve, 23, 24, 25, 26. [18, 19.
36 : 5. s. of Esau, 10, 12, 14, 16, 17,
11. the s. of Eliphaz, Teman, 13, 15
20. these are s. of Seir the Horite
37 : 2. lad was wi. the s. of Bilhah (2,
42 : 5. s. of Israel came to buy corn
11. We are all one man's s., 13, 32.
46 : 5. s. of Isr. carried Jac. in wag-s
9. the s. of, 10, 11, 12, 13, 14, 15, 16, 17, 18, 19, 21, 22, 23, 24, 25, 26, 27. Ex. 6 : 14. 15, 16, 17, 18, 19, 21, 22, 24. Nu. 2 : 14, 18, 22.-3 : 17, 18, 19, 20, 25, 29, 36.-4 : 22, 27, 28, 29, 33, 34, 38, 41, 42.-7 : 7, 8, 9.-10 : 17.-13 : 33.-16 : 1, 8, 10, 12.-26 : 8, 9, 12, 19, 20, 21, 23, 26 28, 29, 30, 35, 36, 37, 38, 40, 41, 42, 45, 47, 48.-36 : 1, 5, 11, 12. De. 1 : 28.-11 : 6.-21 : 5.-31 : 9. Jos. 17 : 6. -24 : 32. Ju. 9 : 2, 5, 24.-11 : 1.

Ge. 49 : 2. Gather yours, ye s. of Jac.
Ex. 32 : 2. Break off earrings of s.
Le. 26 : 29. ye sh. eat flesh of your s.
Nu. 4 : 2. Take sum of s. of Kohath
4. service of the s. of Kohath, 15.
16 : 7. ye take too much s. of Levi
27. in door of tents wives and s.
27 : 3. Our father died and had no s.
36 : 3. married to s. of other tribes
De. 23 : 17. nor sodomite of s. of Isr.
32 : 8. he separated s. of Adam
Jos. 15 : 14. Caleb drove three s. of Anak, Ju. 1 : 20. [my mother
Ju. 8 : 19. there were even the s. of
30. Gid-n had 70 s., many wives [24.
9 : 2. s. of Jerubbaal, which are 70,
5. he slew s. of Jerubb. 70 persons
10 : 4. Jair had 30 s. th. rode on 30
11 : 2. Gilead's wife bare s.; his wife's s. thrust out Jephthah
12 : 9. Ibzan 30 s. and 30 daus. (2)
14. Abdon had 40 s. and 30 neph-s
18 : † 2. children of Dan sent 5 s. of valour, 2 S. 2 : † 7.-13 : † 28.
19 : 22. certain s. of Belial beset ho.
Ru. 1 : 11. any more s. in my womb?
1 S. 1 : 8. am not I better than 10 s.?
2 : 12. s. of Eli were s. of Belial
8 : 11. He will take your s. for hims.
14 : 49. s. of, 22 : 20. 2 S. 4 : 2, 5, 9.-23 : 32. 1 K. 4 : 3.-12 : 31.-18 : 31. 1 Ch. 1 : 17.+2 : 1.+3 : 1.+4 : 1.+5 : 1, 3, 4, 18.-6 : 1.+7 : 1.+8 : 3.+9 : 6, 7, 14, 32, 41, 44.-11 : 34, 44, 46.-12 : 3, 7, 14.-15 : 5, 6, 7, 8, 9, 10, 17.-16 : 42.-23 : 6.+24 : 3.+25 : 2, 3, 4, 5.-26 : 1, 4, 7, 8, 9, 11. 2 Ch. 5 : 12.-11 : 21.-21 : 2.-22 : 8.-29 : 11, 13, 14.-34 : 12.-35 : 15. Ezr. 8 : 9, 10.-8 : 2.+10 : 2.+Ne. 10 : 9, 36.-11 : 6, 7, 22.
17 : 12. name was Jesse; he had 8 s.
26 : † 16. L. liveth, ye are s. of death
31 : 2. Philistines slew Saul's s. (2), I Ch. 10 : 2. [there
2 S. 2 : 18. were three s. of Zeruiah
3 : 2. unto David's s. born in Heb-n
39. s. of Zeruiah too hard for me
6 : 3. s. of Abinadab drave new cart
8 : 18. David's s. were chief rulers
9 : 10. Now Ziba had 15 s., 19 : 17.
11. Mephib-th eat as one of k.'s s.
13 : 23. Absalom invited all k.'s s.
27. let all king's s. go wi. him, 29.
30. Absalom slain all king's s., 33.
35. Behold, the king's s. come, 36.
16 : 10. What with you, s. of Zeruiah? 19 : 22. [5 s. of Michal
21 : 8. king took 2 s. of Rizpah and
16. which was of the s. of the giant, 18. [mit
22 : † 45. s. of stranger shall sub-
23 : 6. s. of Belial shall be as thorns
1 K. 1 : 9. called all king's s., 19, 25.
2 : 7. shew kindness to s. of Barzillai
4 : 31. he wiser than s. of Mahol
11 : 20. Genubath was am. s. of Pha.
21 : 10. set two men, s. of Belial
2 K. 2 : † 16. fifty s. of strength
4 : 5. she shut door upon her s.
10 : 1. Ahab had 70 s. in Samaria, 6.
2. seeing your master's s. are with
3. look out meetest of master's s.
7. they took king's s. and slew 70
8. they have bro-t heads of k.'s s.
11 : 2. stole him fr. k.'s s., 2 Ch. 22 : 11.
25 : 7. slew s. of Zedekiah before his eyes, Je. 39 : 6.-52 : 10.
1 Ch 2 : 6. s. of Zerah five in all
5 : 1. his birthright to s. of Joseph
† 18. tribe of Manasseh s. of valour
7 : 1. the s. of Issachar were four
21 : 20. Ornan and his four s. hid
23 : 10. These 4 were s. of Shimei, 9.
17. s. of Rehabiah very many (3)
24 : 28. came Eleazar, who had no s.
28 : 4. am. s. of my fa. he liked me
1 Ch. 28 : 5. L. ha. given me many s.
29 : 24. s. of Da. submitted unto Sol.
2 Ch. 23 : 3. as L. said of s. of David
24 : 7. s. of Athaliah brok. house of
25. for blood of s. of Jehoiada [G.
25 : † 13. s. of band fell on cities of
28 : † 6. slew 120,000, all s. of val-r
32 : 33. Hez-h in sepul. of s. of Da.
35 : † 5. your breth., s. of the peo.
Ezr. 4 : † 1. s. of transporta-n, 6 : † 16.
Ne. 3 : 3. gate s. of Hassenaah build
12 : 23. s. of Levi writt. in Chron-s
28. s. of the singers gathered [ets
35. certain of priests' s. wi. trump-
13 : 28. one of the s. of Joiada [12.
Es. 9 : 10. ten s. of Haman slew they,
13. Haman's ten s. be hanged, 14.
Jb. 1 : † 3. greatest of s. of the east
5 : † 7. as the s. of burning coal
Ps. 18 : † 44. s. of stranger sh. yield
29 : † 1. ye s. of mighty give unto L.
89 : 6. who among s. of mighty be
144 : 12. That our s. may be as plants
Pr. 7 : † 7. am. s. a yo. man void of
31 : † 5. pervert Judgment of s. of
† 8. in cause of s. of destruction
Ec. 2 : † 7. I got maidens, and had s.
Can. 2 : 3. so is my beloved among s.
Is. 51 : 18. none to guide her am. all s.
56 : 6. s. of stranger that join to L.
57 : 3. draw near, ye s. of sorcerers
60 : 10. s. of the stranger sh. build
14. s. of them that afflicted thee
61 : 5. s. of alien be y-r ploughmen
62 : 8. s. of stranger not drink wine
Je. 6 : 21. fa-s and s. sh. fall upon th.
13 : 14. even fa-s and s. will I dash
19 : 5. built high places to burn s.
26 : † 23. into graves of s. of the peo.
29 : 6. beget s., take wives for y-r s.
35 : 4. into chamber of s. of Hanan
5. bef. s. of Rechabites pots of wine
6. Ye sh. drink no wine, nor y-r s.
16. s. of Jonadab performed commandment (2) [10.
39 : 6. king slew s. of Zedekiah, 52 :
49 : 1. Hath Israel no s.? no heir?
La. 3 : † 13. caused s. of his quiver to
4 : 2. precious s. of Zion, comparab.
Eze. 5 : 10. fa-s sh. eat s., s. fathers
20 : 31. make your s. pass thro. fire
23 : 37. caused s. to pass thro. fire
40 : 46. s. of Zadok among s. of Levi
44 : 15. s. of Zadok charge of sanct-y
48 : 11. are sanctified of s. of Zadok
Ho. 1 : 10. Ye are s. of the living God
Jo. 3 : † 6. chil. sold unto s. of Grec.
Am. 2 : 11. raised y-r s. for prophets
Mi. 6 : † 6. with calves, s. of year old
Zch. 4 : † 14. These are the 2 s. of oil
Mal. 3 : 3. he shall purify s. of Levi
6. ye s. of Jacob not consumed [s.
Mat. 20 : 20. moth. of Zeb-'s chil., her
Mk. 3 : 17. Boanerges, s. of thunder
10 : 35. James and John, s. of Zebedee, Lu. 5 : 10. Jn. 21 : 2. [th. out
Lu. 11 : 19. by whom do your s. cast
Ac. 7 : 16. sepul. Abr. bought of s. of
Ga. 4 : 5. receive the adoption of s.
6. bec. ye are s. God hath sent Spi.
Ep. 3 : 5. not made known to s. of men
He. 2 : 10. bringing many s. to glory
7 : 5. s. of Levi, who rec. priesthood
11 : 21. Jacob blessed both s. of Jos.
12 : 7. God dealeth with you as s.
8. then are ye bastards, and not s.
See **AARON** with sons.

SONS with brethren.

Nu. 16 : 10. brought thee and thy b., s. of Levi [16. 17.
1 Ch. 6 : 44. b., s. of Merari stood,
9 : 32. b., s. of Kohathites, over shewbread [daughters
23 : 22. their b., s. of Kish, took
32. charge of s. of Aaron, their b.
1 Ch. 25 : 9. who with his b. and s. were twelve, 10, 11, 12, 13, 14, 15, 16, 17, 18, 19, 20, 21, 22, 23, 24, 25, 26, 27, 28, 29, 30, 31. [men
26 : 7. s. of Shemaiah, whose b. str.
8. s. of Obed-edom and b., able
9. Meshel. had s. and b. [men
11. s. and b. of Hosah, thirteen
2 Ch. 21 : 2. Jehoram had b. s. of Jehoshaphat [ziah
22 : 8. Jehu found s. of b. of Aha-
Ezr. 3 : 9. Joshua with his s. and b., the s. of Henadad, their s. and b.
8 : 18. Sherebiah, his s. and b. 18
19. Jeshaiah his b. and their s. 20
Ne. 4 : 14. fight for your b., your s.

SONS with daughter, s.

Ge. 5 : 16. he begat s. and d-s, 19, 22, 26, 30.-11 : 13, 15, 17. 19, 21, 23, 25. [d-s
36 : 6. Esau took his wives, s., and
46 : 7. came into Egypt, Jacob, his s.s' s., his d-s and his s-s' d-s
Ju. 12 : 9. Ibzan had 30 s. and 30 d-s
2 S. 14 : 27. unto Abs. three s. one d.
Is. 60 : 4. thy s. sh. come fr. far and thy d-s shall be nursed at thy
2 Co. 6 : 18. ye sh. be my s. and d-s
See **DAUGHTERS** with sons.
See ELEAZAR, UZZIEL.

SONS of God.

Ge. 6 : 2. the s. - saw dau-s of men
4. the s. - came in to dau-s of men
Jb. 1 : 6. s. - to present thems., 2 : 1.
38 : 7. when the s. - shouted for joy
Ho. 1 : 10. said, Ye are s. o. living G.
Jn. 1 : 12. them power to become s.-
Ro. 8 : 14. led by Spirit of G., are s.-
19. waiteth for manifesta-n of s.-
Ph. 2 : 15. ye may be harml., the s.-
1 Jn. 3 : 1. that we sho. be called s.-
2. Beloved, now we are the s.-

His SONS. [h.s.

Ge. 7 : 7. Noah went into ark and
8 : 18. Noah went forth and h.s.
9 : 1. God blessed Noah and h.s.
8. God spake to Noah and h.s.
19 : 14. Lot spake unto h.s. in law as one th. mocked to h.s. in law
25 : 9. h.s. Isaac, Ishm. buried him
30 : 35. gave th. into hands of h.s.
31 : 17. Jacob rose, set h.s. upon camels [eleven s.
32 : 22. Jac. took his two wives, h.
34 : 5. h.s. wi. cattle in field [him
35 : 29. h.s. Esau, Jacob buried
36 : 6. Esau took h. wives and s.
42 : 1. Jacob said unto h.s., Why
46 : 8. Israel into Eg. Jac. and h.s.
49 : 1. Jac. called h.s., said, Gather
33. an end of commanding h.s.
50 : 12. h.s. did as he commanded
13. h.s. carried him into Canaan
Ex. 4 : 20. Moses took wife and h.s.
18 : 5. Jethro came with h.s. and
28 : 1. Aaron and h.s. to minister
41. put garments upon h.s., 29 : 8.
29 : 20. upon tip of right ear of h.s.
21. sprinkle the blood upon h.s.
† 30. And he of h.s. that is priest
40 : 14. sh. bring h.s., clothe them
Le. 6 : 22. priest of h.s. that is
Nu. 21 : 35. they smote Og and h.s.
De. 2 : 33. we smote Sihon, h.s. and
18 : 5. L. hath chosen him and h.s.
21 : 16. he maketh h.s. to inherit
Ju. 9 : 18. have slain h.s., 70 pers-s
17 : 5. Micah consecrated 1 of h.s.
14. the Levite was as one of h.s.
18 : 30. he and h.s. were priests to
1 S. 2 : 22. Eli heard all that h.s. did
3 : 13. bec. h.s. made thems vile
8 : 1. Sam. when old made h.s.
3. h.s. walked not in ways [judges
16 : 1. provided me a king am. h.s.
5. Sam. sanctified Jesse and h.s.
30 : 6. grieved, every man for h.s.
31 : 2. Philistines followed hard up on Saul and h.s., 1 Ch. 10 : 2.

2 S. 21 : 6. Let seven men of h.s. be
1 K. 13 : 11. h.s. told him all works
12. h.s. seen way man of G. went
13. said unto h.s., Saddle ass, 27.
31. spake to h.s., When I am dead
2 K. 9 : 26. blood of Naboth and h.s.
19 : 37. h.s. smote him, Is. 37 : 38.
1 Ch. 7 : 16. h.s. were Ulam and Rak.
8 : 10. These, h.s., heads of fathers
9 : 5. Asaiah firstborn and h.s.
23 : 14. concerning Moses, h.s. were named ⌈and s. 12.
25 : 9. Gedaliah, with h. brethren
10. he, h.s., and brethren were twelve, 11, 12, 13, 14, 15, 16, 17, 18, 19, 20, 21, 22, 23, 24, 25, 26, 27, 28, 29, 30, 31. ⌈cast them off
2 Ch. 11 : 14. Jerob. and h.s. had
13 : 5. to h.s. by covenant of salt
21 : 7. a light to him and to h.s. for
17. carried away h.s., save the youngest of h.s. ⌈Joash
23 : 11. Jehoiada and h.s. anointed
24 : 27. conc-g h.s. and the greatn.
36 : 20. servants to him and h.s.
Ezr. 3 : 9. stood Jeshua with h.s.(2)
6 : 10. for life of king and h.s. ⌈s.
7 : 23. wrath ag. realm of k. and h.
Es. 9 : 25. th. he and h.s. be hanged
Jb. 1 : 4. And h.s. went and feasted
14 : 21. h.s. come to honour, he
38 : 32. guide Arcturus with h.s.?
42 : 16. Job saw h.s. and h.s.' sons
Je. 35 : 3. I took h.s. and Rechabites
14. h.s. not to drink wine⌈17, 18.
Eze. 46 : 16. if prince give unto h.s.,
Da. 11 : 10. h.s. shall be stirred up
See **Sons of MEN.**

My SONS. ⌈s.
Ge. 48 : 9. Joseph said, They are m.
1 S. 2 : 24. m.s., it is no good report
12 : 2. Sam. said, m.s. are with you
1 Ch. 28 : 5. of all m.s. chosen Solo.
2 Ch. 29 : 11. m.s., be not negligent
Jb. 1 : 5. It may be m.s. have sin-d
Is. 45 : 11. Ask me concerning m.s.
1 Co. 4 : 14. as m. beloved s. I warn
See **Of the PROPHETS.**

Thy SONS. ⌈t.s.
Ge. 6 : 18. come into ark, thou and
8 : 16. go forth of ark, thou, t.s.
Ex. 12 : 24. ordinan. to t.s., Nu. 18 : 8.
22 : 29. firstborn of t.s. give to me
34 : 16. t.s. go a whoring aft. gods
20. firstborn of t.s. shalt redeem
Le. 10 : 9. not drink wine, nor t.s.
14. it is thy due, and t.s.' due, 13.
15. it sh. be thine and t.s. for ev.
Nu. 18 : 1. Thou, t.s. sh. bear iniq-y
2. thou and t.s. shall minister
7. thou and t.s. sh. keep y-r office
9. most holy for thee and t.s.
11. given them unto thee and t.s.
De. 4 : 9. teach t.s. and t.s.' sons
1 S. 2 : 29. honourest t.s. above me
8 : 5. t.s. walk not in thy way ⌈me
28 : 19. tomorrow thou, t.s. be with
2 S. 9 : 10. Thou, t.s. shall till land
2 K. 4 : 4. shalt shut door upon t.s.
15 : 12. L. said unto Jehu, t.s. sh. sit on throne of Isr., 1 Ch. 17 : 11.
20 : 18. t.s. shall be eunuchs in Babylon, Is. 39 : 7.
Is. 49 : 22. bring t.s. in their arms
51 : 20. t.s. have fainted, they lie
60 : 4. t.s. shall come from far, 9.
62 : 5. as young man marrieth virgin, so shall t.s. ⌈against t.s.
Zch. 9 : 13. raised up t.s., O Zion,

Two SONS. ⌈1 Ch. 1 : 19.
Ge. 10. 25. unto Eber were born t.s.,
34 : 25. t. of s. of Jacob slew males
41 : 50. unto Joseph were born t.s.
42 : 37. Slay my t.s. if I bring not
44 : 27. Ye know my wife bare t.s.
48 : 1. he took with him t.s., 5.
Ex. 18 : 3. took Zipporah, her t.s., 6.
Le. 16 : 1. death of t.s. of Aaron
Ru. 1 : 1. he, wife, t.s., Mahlon, 2.
3. and she was left and her t.s.
5. woman left her t.s. and husb.
1 S. 1 : 3. the t.s. of Eli, 4 : 11.
2 : 34. that shall come upon thy t.s.
4 : 4. t.s. of Eli were with ark
17 thy t.s. Hophni and Phin. dead
2 S. 14 : 6. thy handmaid had t.s.
15 : 27. return in peace and y-r t.s.
36. had with them their t.s.
21 : 8. king took the t.s. of Rizpah
2 K. 4 : 1. creditor to take t.s. to be
Mat. 20 : 21. Grant my t.s. may sit
21 : 28. man had t.s., Lu. 15 : 11.
26 : 37. took Peter and t.s. of Zebed.
Ac. 7 : 29. Midian, where he begat t.s.
Ga. 4 : 22. written that Abr. had t.s.

Three SONS.
Ge. 6 : 10. Noah begat t.s., 9 : 19.
29 : 34. bec. I have borne him t.s.
Jos. 15 : 14. Caleb drove thence t.s. of Anak, Ju. 1 : 20.
1 S. 2 : 21. Hannah conceived and bare t.s., two daughters⌈(2) 14.
17 : 13. t.s. of Jesse followed Saul
31 : 6. Saul died and t.s., 1 Ch. 10 : 6.
8. found Saul and t.s. fallen
2 S. 2 : 18. were t.s. of Zeruiah
14 : 27. unto Abs. were born t.s.
1 Ch. 2 : 16. and the s. of Zeruiah, t.
3 : 23. And the s. of Neariah, t.
23 : 23. The s. of Mushi; Mahli

Four SONS. ⌊and, t.
1 Ch. 7 : 1. the s. of Issachar were f.
23 : 10. These f. were the s. of Shi-i
12. s. of Kohath; Amram and f.

Six SONS. ⌈s.s.
Ge. 30 : 20. good dowry; I have borne
1 Ch. 3 : 22. And the s. of Shech-h, s.
8 : 38. And Azel had s.s., 9 : 44.
25 : 3. the s. of Jeduthun, s.

Seven SONS.
Ru. 4 : 15. thy dau. better than s.s.
1 S. 16 : 10. Jesse made s. of s. pass
1 Ch. 3 : 24. the s. of Elioenai were s.
Jb. 1 : 2. were born unto him s.s.
42 : 13. he had s.s. and three dau-s
Ac. 19 : 14. were s.s. of one Sceva

SONG.
Ex. 15 : 1. Then sang Moses this s. unto the Lord, Nu. 21 : 17.
2. The Lord is my strength and s., Ps. 118 : 14. Is. 12 : 2. ⌈witness
De. 31 : 19. write this s. that s. be
21. this s. shall testify ag. them
22. Moses wrote this s. ⌈44.
30. Mo. spake words of this s., 32:
Ju. 5 : 12. Awake, Deborah, utter a s.
2 S. 22 : 1. Da. spake unto L. this s.
1 Ch. 6 : 31. Da. set over service of s.
15 : 22. Chenaniah was for a s., 27
25 : 6. were under their father for s.
2 Ch. 29 : 27. s. began with trumpets
†28. cong-n worshipped and s. sang
Jb. 30 : 9. I am their s., I am by word
Ps. 28 : 7. with s. will I praise him
33 : 3. Sing unto him new s., Is. 42 : 10.
40 : 3. put a new s. in my mouth
42 : 8. in night his s. be with me
69 : 12. I was the s. of drunkards
30. I will praise God with a s.
77 : 6. to remembrance my s. in night
96 : 1. O sing unto the Lord a new s., 98 : 1. -149 : 1. ⌈mirth
137 : 3. they required of us a s. and
4. How sing L.'s s. in strange land?
144 : 9. I will sing a new s. unto
Ec. 7 : 5. a man to hear the s. of fools
Can. 1 : 1. The s. of songs, Solomon's
Is. 5 : 1. will I sing s. of my beloved
23 : †15. be unto Tyre as s. of harlot
24 : 9. not drink wine with a s.
26 : 1. In that day this s. be sung
30 : 29. Ye shall have a s. as in night
La. 3 : 14. I was a derision and s. all
Eze. 33 : 32. art us a very lovely s.
Re. 5 : 9. a new s., Thou art worthy,
14 : 3. no man could learn s. ⌊14 : 3.
15 : 3. they sing s. of Moses and s.

SONGS. ⌊of Lamb
Ge. 31 : 27. sent thee away with s.
Ju. 9 : †27. they trod grapes, made s.
1 K. 4 : 32. his s. a thousand and five
1 Ch. 13 : † 8. David prayed with s.
25 : 7. were instructed in s. of Lord
Ne. 12 : 46. in days of David were s.
Jb. 35 : 10. God, who giv-h s. in night
Ps. 32 : 7. compass wi. s. of deliver-e
119 : 54. my s. in hou. of pilgrimage
137 : 3. Sing us one of the s. of Zion
Pr. 25 : 20. singeth s. to heavy heart
Can. 1 : 1. The song of s., Solomon's
Is. 23 : 16. make melody, sing many s.
24 : 16. Fr. utterm. part we heard s.
35 : 10. shall come to Zion with s.
38 : 20. will sing my s. to stringed
Eze. 26 : 13. the noise of thy s. to cease
Am. 5 : 23. Take away noise of thy s.
8 : 3. s. of the temple sh. be howl-gs
10. all your s. into lamentation
Ha. 3 : † 1. prayer acc-g to variable s.
Ep. 5 : 19. in psalms and spiritual s.
Col. 3 : 16. admon. one ano. in spirit-

SOON. ⌊ual s.
Ex. 2 : 18. How is it ye are come so s.?
De. 4 : 26. ye sh. s. perish from land
Jb. 32 : 22. my Maker s. take me aw.
Ps. 37 : 2. they shall s. be cut down
68 : 31. s. stretch her hands unto G.
81 : 14. I should s. have subdued
90 : 10. it is s. cut off, we fly away
106 : 13. They s. forgat his works
Pr. 14 : 17. He that is s. angry deal-h
Mat. 21 : 20. How s. is fig tree with-d
Ga. 1 : 6. I marvel ye are so s. remov.
2 Th. 2 : 2. be not s. shaken in mind
Tit. 1 : 7. not s. angry, not given to

As SOON as.
Ge. 18 : 33. a.s.a. he left commun-g
27 : 30. a.s.a. Isaac made an end
44 : 3. a.s.a. morning was light
Ex. 9 : 29. a.s.a. I am gone out of city
32 : 19. a.s.a. he came nigh camp
Jos. 2 : 7. a.s.a. they pursued them
11. a.s.a. we heard, hearts melt
3 : 13. a.s.a. soles of feet of priests
8 : 19. they ran a.s.a. he stretched
29. a.s.a. sun was down Joshua
Ju. 8 : 33. a.s.a. Gideon was dead
9 : 33. a.s.a. sun is up set ag. city
1 S. 9 : 13. a.s.a. ye come into city
13 : 10. a.s.a. he had made end of offering, 2 S. 6 : 18. 2 K. 10 : 25.
20 : 41. a.s.a. lad was gone David
29 : 10. a.s.a. ye have light depart
2 S. 13 : 36. a.s.a. end of speaking
15 : 10. a.s.a. ye hear sound of
22 : 45. a.s.a. they hear, shall be obedient unto me, Ps. 18 : 44.
1 K. 16 : 11. a.s.a. Zimri sat on thr.
18 : 12. a.s.a. I am gone fr. thee
20 : 36. a.s.a. departed lion slew
2 K. 10 : 2. a.s.a. this letter cometh
14 : 5. a.s.a. kingd. was confirmed
2 Ch. 31 : 5. a.s.a. com-dment came
Ps. 58 : 3. go astray a.s.a. be born
Is. 66 : 8. a.s.a. Zion travailed ⌈ed
Eze. 23 : 16. a.s.a. she saw she dot-
Mk. 1 : 42. a.s.a. had spok. leprosy
5 : 36. a.s.a. Jes. heard, saith, Be
11 : 2. a.s.a. ye be entered sh. find
14 : 45. a.s.a. come, he saith, Mas.
Lu. 1 : 23. a.s.a. ministr-n accomp.
44. a.s.a. voice of thy salutation
8 : 6. a.s.a. sprung up it withered
15 : 30. a.s.a. this thy son was come
22 : 66. a.s.a. day the elders came
23 : 7. a.s.a. he knew he belonged
Jn. 11 : 20. a.s.a. Martha heard
29. a.s.a. Mary heard that, she
16 : 21. a.s.a. she is deliv-d of child
18 : 6. a.s.a. he had said, I am he
21 : 9. a.s.a. they were come to la.

Ac. 10 : 29. came I a.s.a. sent for
12 : 18. a.s.a. day no small stir
Ph. 2 : 23. a.s.a. I see how it will go
Re. 10 : 10. a.s.a. I had eaten it, my
12 : 4. devour her child a.s.a.born

SOONER.

He. 13 : 19. be restored to you the s.
Ja. 1 : 11. sun is no s. risen but it

SOOTHSAYER, S.

Jos. 13 : 22. Balaam, s., did Isr. slay
Is. 2 : 6. forsaken thy people bec. s-s
Da. 2 : 27. secret cannot s-s shew, 4 : 7.
5 : 7. king cried aloud to bring s-s
11. king made master of s-s [s-s
Mi. 5 : 12 thou shalt have no more

SOOTHSAYING. [by s.

Ac. 16 : 16. wh. bro-t masters gain

SOP.

Jn. 13 : 26. He to whom I shall give
s.; had dipped s., he gave it Jud.
27. after s. Satan entered him, 30

SOP'ATER. [S.

Ac. 20 : 4. accomp-d him into Asia,

SOPH'ERETH.

Ezr. 2 : 55. children of S., Ne. 7 : 57.

SORCERER.

Ac. 13 : 6. found a certain s., a Jew
8. Elymas the s. withstood them

SORCERERS. [and s.

Ex. 7 : 11. Phara. called wise men
Je. 27 : 9. hearken not to your s.
Da. 2 : 2. Neb-r com-ded to call s.
Mal. 3 : 5. I will be a witness ag-t s-
Re. 21 : 8. s. shall have part in lake
22 : 15. without are dogs, s., murd.

SORCERESS.

Is. 57 : 3. draw near, ye sons of the s.

SORCERY, IES.

Is. 47 : 9. come upon thee for thy s-s
12. Stand with multit-e of thy s-s
Ac. 8 : 9. Simon, who beforet. used s.
11. that bewitched them with s-s
Re. 9 : 21. Nei. repented they of s-s
18 : 23. by thy s-s all nations decei-d

SORE. [Adj.] [s.

Ge. 34 : 25. third day when th. were
41 : 56. famine waxed s. in Egypt
57. famine so s. in the land, 43 : 1.
47 : 13. fam. was very s. in Canaan, 4.
50 : 10. mourned with s. lamenta-n
De. 6 : 22. L. shewed signs s. upon Eg.
28 : 35. L. smite thee with s. botch
59. s. sicknesses of long continu.
Ju. 20 : 34. 10,000 ag. Gibeah, the
battle was s., 1 S. 31 : 3. 2 S. 2 : 17.
1 S. 14 : 52. was s. war ag. Philistines, 2 K. 3 : 26. 1 Ch. 10 : 3.
1 K. 17 : 17. sickness so s. no breath
18 : 2. was a s. famine in Samaria
2 Ch. 21 : 19. Jehoram died of s. dis.
Jb. 2 : 7. Satan smote Job wi. s. boils
5 : 18. he maketh s., bindeth up
Ps. 2 : 5. vexeth in his s. displeasure
71 : 20. hast shewed me s. troubles
Ec. 1 : 13. s. travail hath G. giv., 4 : 8.
5 : 13. s. evil ha. I seen und. sun, 16.
Is. 27 : 1. s. sword punish leviathan
Je. 52 : 6. famine was s. in city
Eze. 14 : 21. send my four s. judgm-s
21 : 10. to make a s. slaughter
Mi. 2 : 10. destroy you with s. destruc.

SORE. [Adv.]

Ge. 19 : 9. they pressed s. upon Lot
31 : 30. s. longest aft. father's hou.
Ju. 10 : 9. Israel was s. distressed
14 : 17. told her, bec. she lay s. upon
15 : 18. Samson was s. athirst
1 S. 1 : 6. adversary provoked her s.
5 : 7. his hand is s. upon us [21.
28 : 15. Saul ans-d, I am s. distres-d,
2 K. 6 : 11. king of Syria s. troubled
2 Ch. 28 : 19. Ahaz transg-d s. ag. L.
35 : 23. away, for I am s. wounded
Ne. 13 : 8. it grieved me s., therefore
Ps. 38 : 2. thy hand presseth me s.
8. I am feeble and s. broken
44 : 19. hast s. broken us in place
Ps. 55 : 4. My heart is s. pained
118 : 13. Thou hast thrust s. at me
18. L. hath chastened me s., but
Pr. 11 : † 15. surety, sh. be s. broken
Is. 59 : 11. we mourn s. like doves
64 : 9. Be not wroth very s., O Lord
12. wilt thou afflict us very s. ?
La. 1 : 2. She weepeth s. in the night
3 : 52. Mine enemies chased me s.
Mat. 21 : 15. they were s. displeased
Mk. 9 : 26. spirit cried, rent him s.
See Sore **AFRAID.**
See AMAZED, DISPLEASED,
WEEP, WEPT, VEXED.

SORE, S. [Noun.]

Le. 13 : 42. if reddish s. it is leprosy
43. if rising of s. be white reddish
2 Ch. 6 : 28. whatso. s. or sickness
29. every one sh. know his own s.
Ps. 38 : 11. friends stand aloof fr. mys.
77 : 2. my s. ran in the night and
Is. 1 : 6. bruises and putrifying s-s
Eze. 47 : † 12. leaf be for bruises, s-s
Lu. 16 : 20. Lazarus full of s-s, 21.
Re. 16 : 2. fell grievous s. upon men
11. blasphemed God bec. of pains

SOREK. [and s-s

Ju. 16 : 4. Samson loved a wom. in S.

SORELY.

Ge. 49 : 23. archers s. grieved him
Is. 23 : 5. s. pained at report of Tyre

SORER.

He. 10 : 29. Of how much s. punishm-t

SORROW. [Noun.]

Ge. 3 : 16. will greatly multiply thy
s., in s. shalt bring forth chil.
17. in s. shalt eat of it all thy life
35 : † 18. his name, the son of my s.
42 : 38. bring down my gray hairs
with s. to grave, 44 : 29, 31.
Ex. 15 : 14. s. take hold of inhab-ts
Le. 26 : 16. terror cause s. of heart
De. 28 : 65. Lord shall give s. of mind
1 Ch. 4 : 9. Because I bare him wi. s.
Ne. 2 : 2. is nothing but s. of heart
Es. 9 : 22. mouth turned fr. s. to joy
Jb. 3 : 10. it hid not s. fr. mine eyes
6 : 10. I would harden myself in s.
17 : 7. Mine eye dim by reason of s.
41 : 22. s. is turned into joy
Ps. 13 : 2. having s. in my heart daily
38 : 17. my s. is continually bef. me
39 : 2. I held peace, s. was stirred
55 : 10. mischief and s. in midst [s.
90 : 10. their strength, labour, and
107 : 39. they are bro-t low thro. s.
116 : 3. I found trouble and s.
Pr. 10 : 10. He th. winketh causeth s.
22. L. maketh rich, addeth no s.
15 : 13. by s. of heart spirit broken
17 : 21. begetteth fool, doeth it to s.
23 : 29. Who hath woe? who hath s.?
Ec. 1 : 18. increaseth knowl. incr-h s.
5 : 17. he hath much s. with sickn.
7 : 3. s. is better than laughter
11 : 10. remove s. from thy heart
Is. 5 : 30. if look unto land behold s.
14 : 3. L. shall give thee rest from s.
17 : 11. heap in day of desperate s.
29 : 2. will distress Ariel, shall be s.
35 : 10. s. and sighing sh. flee away
50 : 11. ye shall lie down in s.
51 : 11. s. and mourning shall flee
65 : 14. serv-ts sing, ye sh. cry for s.
Je. 8 : 18. would comfort mys. ag. s.
20 : 18. out of the womb to see s. ?
30 : 15. why criest? s. is incurable
31 : 13. make them rejoice from s.
45 : 3. L. hath added grief to my s.
49 : 23. there is s. on the sea, it
La. 1 : 12. see if be any s. like my s. ?
18. hear all people, behold my s.
3 : 65. Give them s. of heart
Eze. 23 : 33. Thou sh. be filled wi. s.
Lu. 22 : 45. found th. sleeping for s.
Jn. 16 : 6. s. hath filled your heart
20. your s. shall be turned into joy
Jn. 16 : 21. A wom. in travail hath s.
22. ye now therefore have s., but
Ro 9 : 2. I continual s. in my heart
2 Co. 2 : 3. I should have s. fr. them
7. swallowed up with overmuch s.
7 : 10. godly s. worketh repentance,
but s. of world worketh death
Ph. 2 : 27. me, lest I have s. upon s.
Re. 18 : 7. so much torment and s.
give her; she saith I shall see
no s. [ther s.
21 : 4. shall be no more death, nei-

SORROWS.

Ex. 3 : 7. I heard cry, know their s.
2 S. 22 : 6. s. of hell compassed me
about, Ps. 18 : 4, 5.-116 : 3.
Jb. 9 : 28. I am afraid of all my s.
21 : 17. God distributeth s. in anger
39 : 3. They bow, they cast out s.
Ps. 16 : 4. Then s. sh. be multiplied
32 : 10. Many s. shall be to wicked
127 : 2. vain to eat bread of s.
Ec. 2 : 23. For all his days are s. and
Is. 13 : 8. pangs and s. sh. take hold
53 : 3. a man of s. and acquainted
4. Surely he hath carried our s.
Je. 13 : 21. s. take thee as a woman
49 : 24. s. taken her as a woman
Da. 10 : 16. by vision my s. are turned
Ho 13 : 13. s. of travailing woman
Mat. 24 : 8. beginning of s., Mk. 13 : 8.
1 Ti. 6 : 10. pierced thems. wi. many s.

SORROW. [Verb.]

Je. 31 : 12. they sh. not s. any more
51 : 29. the land sh. tremble and s.
Ho. 8 : 10. they sh. s. for the burden
1 Th. 4 : 13. that ye s. not as others

SORROWED, ETH.

1 S. 10 : 2. lo, thy father s-h for you
2 Co. 7 : 9. I rejoice ye s-d to repent
11. that ye s-d after a godly sort

SORROWFUL.

1 S. 1 : 15. I am a woman of a s. spirit
1 Ch. 4 : † 9. they called his name S.
Jb. 6 : 7. things are as my s. meat
Ps. 69 : 29. I am poor and s., let [s.
Pr. 14 : 13. Even in laughter heart is
Je. 31 : 25. I replenished ev. s. soul
Zph. 3 : 18. I will gather them are s.
Zch. 9 : 5. Gaza shall see it and be s.
Mat. 19 : 22. young man heard he
went away s., Lu. 18 : 23, 24.
26 : 22. were exceeding s., Mk. 14 : 19.
37. he began to be s. and heavy
38. My soul exc-g s., Mk. 14 : 34.
Jn. 16 : 20. ye shall be s., but sorrow
2 Co. 6 : 10. As s., yet always rejo-g
Ph. 2 : 28. and I may be the less s.

SORROWING. [s.

Lu. 2 : 48. thy fa. and I sought thee
Ac. 20 : 38. s. sho-d see face no more

SORRY. [me

1 S. 22 : 8. none of you that is s. for
Ne. 8 : 10. this day holy, nei. be ye s.
Ps. 38 : 18. I will be s. for my sin
Is. 51 : 19. who shall be s. for thee
Mat. 14 : 9. the king was s., Mk. 6 : 26.
17 : 23. th. were exceeding s., 18 : 31.
2 Co. 2 : 2. if I make you s., same
which is made s. [made you s.
7 : 8. tho. I made you s., epistle
9. I rejoice not that ye were made
s., for ye were s. after godly

SORT.

Ge. 6 : 19. two of every s. into ark, 20.
7 : 14. bird of ev. s. went into ark
1 S. 15 : † 9. they spared of second s.
1 Ch. 24 : 5. divided one s. wi. another
29 : 14. be able to offer after this s.
2 Ch. 30 : 5. in such s. as was written
Ezr. 1 : 10. silver basins of second s.
4 : 8. wrote to Artax-s after this s.
Ne. 6 : 4. sent four times after this s.
Is. 28 : † 26. bindeth in such s. as G.
Eze. 23 : 42. with men of common s.
39 : 4. to ravenous birds of every s.
44 : 30. first of every s. of oblations

Da. 1 : 10. worse than chil. of your s.
3 : 29. no other G. deliver aft. this s.
Ac. 17 : 5. lewd fellows of baser s. [s.
Ro. 15 : 15. I written boldly in some
1 Co. 3 : 13. try work, of what s. it is
2 Co. 7 : 11. sorrowed after godly s.
2 Ti. 3 : 6. of this s. who creep into
3 Jn. 6. on journey after a godly s.

SORTS. [vers s.

De. 22 : 11. not wear garment of di-
Ne. 5 : 18. store of all s. of wine
Ps. 78 : 45. divers s. of flies, 105 : 31. [s.
Ec. 2 : 8. musical instruments of all
Eze. 27 : 24. merchants in all s. of
things [mour
38 : 4. all clothed with all s. of ar-

SOSIP'ATER. See LUCIUS.

SOS'THENES. [him

Ac. 18 : 17. Greeks took S. and beat
1 Co. 1 : 1. Paul and S. to church at

SO'TAI. [Corinth

Ezr. 2 : 55. the chil. of S., Ne. 7 : 57.

SOTTISH.

Je. 4 : 22. my people are s. children

SOUGHT.

Ge. 43 : 30. he s. where to weep
Ex. 2 : 15. Pharaoh s. to slay Moses
4 : 19. men are dead which s. thy life
24. Lord met him and s. to kill him
33 : 7. that s. Lord went to taberu.
Le. 10 : 16. Moses diligently s. goat
Nu. 35 : 23. not enemy, nor s. his
De. 13 : 10. he s. to thrust thee from
Jos. 2 : 22. pursuers s. the spies [L.
Ju. 14 : 4. Sams. s. occasion ag. Phil.
18 : 1. Danites s. an inheritance to
1 S. 14 : 4. passages by wh. Jona. s.
19 : 10. Saul s. to smite David [to go
27 : 4. Saul s. no more ag. for him
2 S. 3 : 17. ye s. for David to be king
4 : 8. head of enemy that s. thy life
17 : 20. had s. and could not find
21 : † 1. David s. the face of Lord
2. Saul s. to slay them in his zeal
1 K. 1 : 2. Let be s. a young virgin
3. s. for a fair damsel thro. Israel
10 : 24. all the earth s. to Solomon
11 : 40. Solomon s. to kill Jeroboam
2 K. 2 : 17. s. three days for Elijah
1 Ch. 26 : 31. am. Hebronites were s.
2 Ch. 1 : 5. Sol. and congregation s.
9 : 23. kings s. the presence of Sol.
14 : 7. bec. we have s. the L. our G.
16 : 12. in disease he s. not the Lord
17 : 3. Jehosh-t s. not unto Baalim
4. s. to Lord God of his father
22 : 9. he s. Ahaziah, they caught
him ; bec. Jehosh-t s. Lord with
25 : 15. Why s. aft. gods of Edom? 20
26 : 5. he s. G. in days of Zech. ;
long as he s., L. G. made him
Ezr. 2 : 62. These s. their register,
Ne. 12 : 27. they s. Levites [Ne. 7 : 64.
Es. 2 : 2. Let fair young virgins be s.
21. s. to lay hand on king, 6 : 2.
3 : 6. Haman s. to destroy all Jews
9 : 2. hand on such as s. their hurt
Ps. 34 : 4. I s. Lord, he heard, 77 : 2.
86 : 14. violent men s. aft. my soul
111 : 2. s. out of all that have pleas
119 : 10. With my whole heart I s.
94. save me, I have s. thy precepts
142 : † 4. no man s. after my soul
Pr. 28 : † 12. wicked rise, a man is s.
Ec. 2 : 3. I s. to give myself unto wine
7 : 29. have s. out many inventions
12 : 9. preacher s. out many prov-s
10. preacher s. acceptable words
Is. 62 : 12. sh. be called, S. out, city
65 : 1. I am s. of them th. asked not,
found of them that s. not, Ro. 10 :
10. place for my peo. th. s. me [20.
Je. 8 : 2. sun and moon whom they s.
10 : 21. pastors have not s. the Lord
26 : 21. king s. to put him to death
44 : 30. Zedekiah to Neb. that s. his
50 : 20. iniquity of Israel shall be s.

La. 1 : 19. s. meat to relieve souls
Eze. 22 : 30. I s. for a man am. them
26 : 21. s., yet shalt never be found
34 : 4. nei. ye s. that which was lost
Da. 2 : 13. th. s. Dan. and his fellows
4 : 36. my counsellors s. unto me
6 : 4. princes s. occasion ag. Daniel
8 : 15. when I had s. for meaning
Ob. 6. how Esau's hidden things s.
Zph. 1 : 6. those that have not s. L.
Zch. 6 : 7. the bay s. to go thro. earth
Mat. 2 : 20. they are dead which s.
the child's life [12 : 12. Lu. 20 : 19.
21 : 46. s. to lay hands on him, Mk.
26 : 16. he s. opportunity to betray
him, Lu. 22 : 6. [Mk. 14 : 55.
59. they s. false witness ag. Jesus,
Mk. 11 : 18. scribes s. how might
destroy him, 14 : 1. Lu. 19 : 47.-
22 : 2. [rowing
Lu. 2 : 48. thy fa. and I s. thee sor-
49. How is it that ye s. me?
5 : 18. they s. means to bring him
6 : 19. multitude s. to touch him
11 : 16. others s. a sign from heaven
13 : 6. he s. fruit and found none
19 : 3. Zaccheus s. to see Jesus [7 : 1.
Jn. 5 : 16. Jews s. to slay him, 18.-
7 : 11. Jews s. him at feast, 11 : 56.
30. they s. to take him, 10 : 39.
11 : 8. Master, Jews s. to stone thee
19 : 12. Pilate s. to release him
Ac. 12 : 19. when Herod s. for Peter
17 : 5. s. to bring them out to peo.
Ro. 9 : 32. Bec. s. it not by faith, but
1 Th. 2 : 6. Nor of men s. we glory
2 Ti. 1 : 17. in Rome he s. me out
He. 8 : 7. no place sho. have been s.
12 : 17. tho. he s. it carefully with

SOUGHT him. [tears

1 S. 10 : 21. s.h., could not be found
13 : 14. L. s.h. a man to be captain
23 : 14. Saul s.h. every day, God
1 Ch. 15 : 13. we s.h. not after due
2 Ch. 14 : 7. s.h., he hath given rest
15 : 4. when they s.h. he was found
15. they s.h. with whole desire
Ps. 37 : 36. I s.h., cou. not be found
78 : 34. when he slew th. they s.h.
Can. 3 : 1. I s.h. whom my soul loveth ; I s.h., found him not, 2.-
Lu. 2 : 44. they s.h. am. kinsfolk [5 : 6.
4 : 42. people s.h., came unto him

SOUL. [hath s.

Ge. 1 : † 20. moving creature that
† 30. to every thing wherein is a s.
2 : 7. man became a living s.
34 : 8. s. of my son longeth for dau.
35 : 18. as her s. was in departing
Ex. 12 : † 16. that wh. every s. must
23 : † 9. ye know s. of stranger [eat
Le. 4 : 2. If s. sh. sin thro. ignorance
† 27. if any s. of common people sin
5 : 1. if a s. sin and hear swearing
2. if s. touch any unclean thing
4. if a s. swear to do evil or good
15. If a s. commit trespass through
17. if a s. commit any of these [ig-
6 : 2. If a s. lie unto his neighbour
7 : 18. s. that eateth of it shall bear
20. s. eateth of it be cut off 21, 27.
21. s. that shall touch any [for s.
17 : 11. blood maketh atonement
12. No s. of you shall eat blood
15. s. that eateth that which died
be unclean, 22 : 6. Nu. 19 : 22.
20 : 6. s. that turneth after spirits
22 : 11. if priest buy s. with money
23 : 30. whatso. s. doeth work, 29.
26 : 15. if your s. abhor my judgm.
43. their s. abhorred my statutes
Nu. 9 : 13. same s. shall be cut off
15 : 27. if any s. sin thro. ignor., 28.
19 : † 11. dead body of any s. of man
21 : 4. s. of people was discouraged
30 : 4. every bond she hath bound
her s., 5, 6, 7, 8, 9, 10, 11, 12, 13.

Nu. 31 : 28. one s. of five hundred for
De. 11 : 13. serve him with all your s.
18. lay up these my words in y-r s.
13 : 3. whe. ye love the L. with all
your s., Jos. 22 : 5. 1 K. 2 : 4.
1 S. 18 : 1. s. of Jona. knit to s. of Da.
25 : 29. s. of my lord bound up in
30 : 6. s. of all people was grieved
2 S. 5 : 8. blind hated of David's s.
13 : 39. s. of Da. longed to go to Abs.
1 K. 8 : 48. return to thee with all s.
17 : 21. let child's s. come again, 22.
2 K. 4 : 27. Let her alone, her s. is
23 : 3. to keep com-ts with all s.
1 Ch. 22 : 19. set your s. to seek Lord
2 Ch. 6 : 38. If return to thee with all
15 : 12. to seek L. wi. all their s. [s.
Jb. 12 : 10. In whose ha. s. of ev. thing
24 : 12. s. of wounded crieth out
31 : † 39. caused s. of owners to ex-
36 : † 14. th. s. dieth in youth [pire
Ps. 17 : † 9. hide me fr. enemies ag. s.
19 : 7. law perfect, converting s.
33 : 19. to deliver their s. fr. death
34 : 22. L. redeemeth s. of his serv.
49 : 8. redemption of s. is precious
† 19. The s. sh. go to genera. of fa-s
72 : 14. sh. redeem their s. fr. deceit
74 : 19. deliver not s. of turtledove
78 : 50. spared not their s. fr. death
86 : 4. Rejoice s. of thy servant, O L.
94 : 21. They gather ag. s. of righte.
106 : 15. sent leanness into their s.
107 : 5. Hungry their s. fainted
9. satisfieth longing s., filleth hun-
18. Their s. abhorreth meat [gry s.
26. s. is melted because of trouble
Pr. 10 : 3. not s. of righteous to fam-
11 : 25. liberal s. sh. be made fat [ish
13 : 2. s. of transg-rs eat violence
4. s. of sluggard desireth hath not
19. desire accompl-d is sweet to s.
16 : 24. Pleasant words sweet to s.
19 : 2. s. without knowl. it is not
15. idle s. sh. suffer hunger [good
21 : 10. s. of wicked desireth evil
22 : 23. Lord will spoil s. of those
25 : 13. refresheth s. of his masters
25. As cold waters to thirsty s., so
27 : 7. full s. loatheth honeycomb ;
to hungry s. bitter is sweet
† 9. So man's friend by counsel of s.
Ec. 6 : † 7. labour for his mouth, yet
s. not filled [walking of s.
† 9. Better is sight of eyes than
Is. 3 : 9. Woe unto their s., they have
† 20. I will take away hou. of the s.
10 : 18. † sh. consume fr. s. to flesh
32 : 6. to make empty s. of hungry
46 : † 2. their s. is gone into captiv.
49 : † 7. saith L. to him despised in s.
55 : 2. let your s. delight itself in
3. come unto me, your s. sh. live
66 : 3. their s. delighteth in abom-s
Je. 4 : 10. sword reacheth unto the s.
20 : 13. he hath delivered s. of poor
31 : 12. s. sh. be as watered garden
14. I will satiate the s. of priests
25. saith L., I have satiated weary
s., replenished sorrowful s. [s.
38 : 16. As L. liveth, that made this
40 : † 14. Ishm. to strike thee in s.
44 : † 14. to la. of Jud. lift their s.
La. 1 : 11. for meat to relieve the s.
2 : 12. s. was poured into bosom
3 : 25. L. good to s. th. seeketh him
Eze. 18 : 4. all souls are mine, as s.
of father, so s. of son is mine, s.
that sinneth it shall die, 20.
24 : 21. what your s. pitieth sh. fall
† 25. I take fr. them lifting up of s.
25 : † 6. thou hast rejoiced in s.
Ho. 4 : † 8. lift s. to their iniquity
9 : 4. their s. not in to house of Lord
Jon. 2 : 5. waters compassed me to s.
Mat. 10 : 28. not able to kill s., fear
him can destroy s. and body

Mk. 12 : 33. to love him wi. all the s.
Ac. 2 : 43. fear came upon every s.
3 : 23. ev. s. wh. will not hear proph.
4 : 32. mult. that believed of one s.
Ro. 2 : 9. anguish upon ev. s. of man
13 : 1. Let every s. be subject to
1 Co. 15 : 45. Adam was made living s.
1 Th. 5 : 23. your s. and body preser.
He. 4 : 12. piercing to dividing of s.
6 : 19. hope we have as anchor of s.
10 : 39. that believe to saving of s.
Ja. 5 : 20. he sh. save a s. fr. death [s.
1 Pe. 2 : 11. fleshly lusts wh. war ag.
2 Pe. 2 : 8. Lot vexed his righteous s.
Re. 16 : 3. every living s. died in sea
See AFFLICT, AFFLICTED,
BITTER, BITTERNESS.

His SOUL.

Ge. 34 : 3. h.s. clave unto Dinah
42 : 21. when we saw anguish of h.s.
Ex. 30 : 12. sh. give ransom for h.s.
Nu. 30 : 2. or swear oath to bind h.s.
De. 24 : †15. is poor, and lifteth h.s.
Ju. 10 : 16. h.s. was grieved for mis.
16 : 16. she urged so h.s. was vexed
2 K. 23 : 25. Josiah turned unto L.
with all h.s., 2 Ch. 34 : 31.
Jb. 14 : 22. and h.s. shall mourn
18 : † 4. He teareth h.s. in anger
23 : 13. what h.s. desireth he doeth
27 : 8. when God taketh away h.s.
31 : 30. by wishing a curse to h.s.
32 : †2. justified h.s. rather than G.
33 : 18. keepeth back h.s. from pit
20. h.s. abhorreth dainty meat
22. h.s. draweth near unto grave
28. He will deliver h.s. fr. pit, 30.
Ps. 10 : † 3. wicked boasteth of h.s.'s
11 : 5. wicked h.s. hateth [desire
24 : 4. not lifted h.s. unto vanity
25 : 13. h.s. shall dwell at ease [s.
49 : 18. while he lived he blessed h.
89 : 48. sh. he deliver h.s. fr. grave?
105 : † 18. with fetters, h.s. came
into iron [h.s.
109 : 31. from those that condemn
Pr. 6 : † 16. 7 an abomin-n unto h.s.
30. if he steal to satisfy h.s.
13 : 25. eateth to satisfying of h.s.
14 : † 10. knoweth bitterness of h.s.
16 : 17. keepeth his way preserveth
18 : 7. fool's lips snare of h.s. [h.s.
21 : 23. keepeth mou., keepeth h.s.
22 : 5. doth keep h.s. be far fr. them
23 : 14. shalt deliver h.s. from hell
29 : 10. hate upright, just seek h.s.
Ec. 2 : 24. sho. make h.s. enjoy good
6 : 2. he wanteth nothing for h.s.
3. and h.s. be not filled with good
Is. 29 : 8. awaketh and h.s. empty;
is faint and h.s. hath appetite
44 : 20. he cannot deliver h.s. nor
53 : 10. make h.s. offering for sin
11. He shall see of travail of h.s.
12. he poured out h.s. unto death
Je. 50 : 19. h.s. shall be satisfied
51 : 6. deliver every man h.s., 45.
†14. L. of hosts hath sworn by h.s.
Eze. 18 : 27. when wicked man doeth right, he shall save h.s.
33 : 5. taketh warning, deliver h.s.
Am. 2 : † 14. nei. mighty deliv. h.s.
Mi. 7 : † 3. uttereth mischief of h.s.
Ha. 2 : 4. h.s. that is lifted up, is
Mat. 16 : 26. if gain world and lose
h.s., what can man give in exchange for his s.? Mk. 8 : 37.
Ac. 2 : 31. h.s. was not left in hell

My SOUL. [of thee

Ge. 12 : 13. m.s. shall live because
19 : 20. let me escape, m.s. sh. live
27 : 4. m.s. bless thee bef. I die, 25.
49 : 6. O m.s., come not into their
Le. 26 : 11. m.s. not abhor you, 30.
Nu. 23 : † 10. let m.s. die death of
Ju. 5 : 21. O m.s. thou hast trodden
16 : † 30. Let m.s. die with Philis.
1 S. 1 : 15. poured out m.s. bef. L.
24 : 11. yet thou huntest m.s.
26 : 21. m.s. was precious in thine
2 S. 4 : 9. As the Lord liveth, who
hath redeemed m.s., 1 K. 1 : 29.
Jb. 6 : 7. The things m.s. refused
7 : 15. So m.s. chooseth strangling
9 : 21. yet would I not know m.s.
10 : 1. m.s. is weary of life, I will
speak in bitterness of m.s.
16 : 4. if your s. were in m.s.'s stead
19 : 2. How long will ye vex m.s.?
27 : 2. Almighty, who hath vexed
m.s. [wind
30 : 15. they pursue m.s. as the
16. m.s. is poured out upon me
25. was not m.s. grieved for poor?
Ps. 3 : 2. who say of m.s., is no help
6 : 3. m.s. is sore vexed, but, O L.
4. O Lord, deliver m.s., 17 : 13.-
22 : 20.-116 : 4.-120 : 2.
7 : 2. Lest he tear m.s. like a lion
5. Let the enemy persecute m.s.
11 : 1. how say ye to m.s., Flee as
13 : 2. How long take counsel in m.s.
16 : 2. O m.s. thou hast said unto
10. wilt not leave m.s. in hell, Ac.
23 : 3. He restoreth m.s. [2 : 27.
25 : 1. Unto thee, O L., I lift m.s.
25 : 20. O keep m.s. and deliver me
26 : 9. Gather not m.s. wi. sinners
30 : 3. hast brought m.s. fr. grave
†12. that m.s. may sing praise
31 : 7. hast known m.s in adversit.
9. m.s. and belly are consumed
34 : 2. m.s. shall make boast in L.
35 : 3. say unto m.s., I am thy salv.
4. be put to shame that seek m.s.
7. witho. cause digged pit for m.s.
9. m.s. shall be joyful in L. [m.s.
12. rewarded me to spoiling of
13. I humbled m.s. with fasting
17. rescue m.s. from destructions
40 : 14. confounded that seek m.s.
41 : 4. heal m.s., for I have sinned
42 : 1. As the hart, so panteth m.s.
2. m.s. thirsteth for God, 143 : 6.
4. When I remember, I pour out
m.s. in me [s.? 11.-43 : 5.
5. Why art thou cast down, O m.
6. O my God, m.s. is cast down
49 : 15. G. will redeem m.s. fr. grave
54 : 3. oppressors seek after m.s.
4. L. is with them uphold m.s.
55 : 18. He hath delivered m.s. in
56 : 6. mark my steps, wait for m.s.
13. hast delivered m.s. fr. death
57 : 1. be merciful, O G., for m.s.
4. m.s. is among lions [pit
6. m.s. is bowed down, th. digged
59 : 3. lo, they lie in wait for m.s.
62 : 1. Truly, m.s. waiteth upon G.
5. m.s., wait thou only upon God
63 : 1. O G., m.s. thirsteth for thee
5. m.s. shall be satisfied as with
8. m.s. followeth hard after thee
9. that seek m.s. to destroy it
66 : 16. wh. God hath done for m.s.
69 : 1. waters are come in unto m.s.
10. When I wept and chast-d m.s.
18. Draw nigh unto m.s., redeem
70 : 2. confounded that seek m.s.,
71 : 10. that lay wait for m.s. [71. 13.
23. m.s. shall rejoice which thou
77 : 2. m.s. refused to be comforted
84 : 2. m.s. longeth for courts of
86 : 2. Preserve m.s., for I am holy
4. unto thee, O L., do I lift m.s.,
13. th. hast delivered m.s. [143 : 8.
14. valiant men sought aft. m.s.
88 : 3. m.s. is full of troubles, my
14. L., why castest thou off m.s.?
94 : 17. m.s. almost dwelt in silence
19. thy comforts delight m.s.
103 : 1. Bless the Lord, O m.s., 2,
22.-104 : 1, 35. [against m.s.
109 : 20. reward of them that speak
Ps. 116 : 7. Return unto thy rest, O m.
8. hast delivered m.s. fr. death [s.
119 : 20. m.s. breaketh for longing
25. m.s. cleaveth to the dust
28. m.s. melteth for heaviness
81. m.s. fainteth for salvation
109. m.s. is continually in hand
129. theref. doth m.s. keep them
167. m.s. hath kept thy testim-s
175. Let m.s. live, it shall praise
120 : 2. Deliver m.s. fr. lying lips
6. m.s. dwelt wi. him hateth peace
130 : 5. for Lord m.s. doth wait, 6.
131 : 2. m.s. is as a weaned child
138 : 3. strengthen me in m.s.
139 : 14. that m.s. knoweth right
141 : 8. leave not m.s. destitute
142 : 4. no man cared for m.s.
7. Bring m.s. out of prison, that
143 : 3. en-y hath persecuted m.s.
11. Lord, bring m.s. out of troub.
146 : 1. Praise the Lord, O m.s.
Ec. 4 : 8. For whom do I bereave m.s.
7 : 28. m.s. seeketh, but I find not
Can. 1 : 7. Tell me, O thou whom
m.s. loveth, 3 : 1, 2, 3, 4.
5 : 6. m.s. failed when he spake
6 : 12. m.s. made me like chariots
Is. 1 : 14. your feasts m.s. hateth
26 : 9. With m.s. have I desired
38 : 17. hast in love to m.s. deliv-d
42 : 1. elect, in wh. m.s. delighteth
61 : 10. m.s. shall be joyful in my
Je. 4 : 19. hast heard, O m.s., sound
31. m.s. is wearied bec. of murd-s
5 : 9. shall not m.s. be avenged on
nation? 29.-9 : 9. [m.s. depart
6 : 8. be instructed, O Jerus., lest
12 : 7. beloved of m.s. into hand of
13 : 17. m.s. shall weep in secret
18 : 20. they digged a pit for m.s.
32 : 41. rejoice over them wi. m. s.
La. 1 : 16. that should relieve m.s.
3 : 17. removed m.s. far fr. peace
20. m.s. hath them in remembra.
24. L. is my portion, saith m.s.
†51. Mine eye affecteth m.s.
58. L. hast pleaded causes of m.s.
Eze. 4 : 14. m.s. not been polluted
Jon. 2 : 7. When m.s. fainted within
Mi. 6 : 7. of my body for sin of m.s.
7 : 1. m.s. desired first ripe fruit
Zch. 11 : 8. shepherds m.s. loathed
Mat. 12 : 18. beloved, in whom m.s.
is well pleased [Mk. 14 : 34.
26 : 38. m.s. exceeding sorrowful,
Lu. 1 : 46. m.s. doth magnify Lord
12 : 19. I will say to m.s., Soul, eat
Jn. 12 : 27. m.s. is troubled, what
2 Co. 1 : 23. G. for record upon m.s.
He. 10 : 38. m.s. shall have no pleas.

Our SOUL.

Nu. 11 : 6. o.s. is dried aw., nothing
21 : 5. o.s. loatheth light bread
Ps. 33 : 20. o.s. waited for Lord [it
35 : † 25. not say, Ah, o.s. wo. have
44 : 25. o.s. is bowed to the dust
66 : 9. God who holdeth o.s. in life
123 : 4. o.s. is filled with scorning
124 : 4 stream had gone ov. o.s., 5.
7. o.s. is escaped as a bird [name
Is. 26 : 8. desire of o.s. is to thy

Own SOUL. [o.s.

De. 13 : 6. if friend which is as thine
1 S. 18 : 1. he loved him as his o.s.,
3.-20 : 17. [his o.s.
Ps. 22 : 29. and none can keep alive
Pr. 6 : 32. doeth it, destroyeth his o.s.
8 : 36. sinneth, wrongeth his o.s.
11 : 17. merciful doeth good to o.s.
15 : 32. refus. instruc-n despis. o.s.
19 : 8. getteth wisdom, loveth o.s.
16. keep. com-ts keepeth his o.s.
20 : 2. provoketh k. sinneth ag. o.s.
29 : 24. partner wi. thief, hateth o.s.
Mat. 16 : 26. if he gain whole world
and lose his o.s.? Mk. 8 : 36.

Lu. 2 : 35. sword shall pierce thro.
That SOUL. ⌊thy o.s.
Ge. 17 : 14. not circumcised, t.s. sh.
be cut off, Ex. 31 : 14. Le. 7 : 20,
21, 25, 27.–19 : 8. Nu. 15 : 30.
Ex. 12 : 15. eateth leavened bread,
t.s. shall be, 19. Nu. 19 : 13, 20.
Le. 17 : 10. I will set my face ag. t.s.,
22 : 3. t.s., be cut off from ⌊20 : 6.
23 : 30. t.s. will I destroy ⌈off
Nu. 15 : 31. t.s. shall utterly be cut
Thy SOUL.
Ge. 27 : 19. eat, that t.s. bless me, 31.
De. 4 : 9. and keep t.s. diligently
29. find, if seek him with all t.s.
6 : 5. love L. G. with all t.s., 30 : 6.
10 : 12. to serve L. G. with all t.s.
: 15. whatso. t.s. lusteth, 20, 21.–
12 : 16. do them wi. all t.s.⌊14 : 26.
30 : 2. obey his voice with all t.s., 6.
10. if turn unto Lord wi. all t.s.
1 S. 2 : 16. as much as t.s. desireth
20 : 4. Whatso. t.s. desireth I will
23 : 20. come acc. to desire of t.s.
25 : 29. man is risen to seek t.s.
1 K. 11 : 37. acc. to all t.s. desireth
Ps. 121 : 7. Lord shall preserve t.s.
Pr. 2 : 10. knowl. is pleas. unto t.s.
3 : 22. So shall they be life unto t.s.
19 : 18. let not t.s. spare for his
22 : 25. and get a snare to t.s.
24 : 12. keepeth t.s., doth not he
14. So shall wisdom be unto t.s.
29 : 17. shall give delight unto t.s.
Is. 51 : 23. which said to t.s., Bow
58 : 10. if draw out t.s. to hungry
11. L. sh. satisfy t.s. in drought
Je. 14 : 19. hath t.s. loathed Zion?
38 : 17. go forth, t.s. shall live, 20.
Eze. 3 : 19. hast delivered t.s., 21.–
Ha. 2 : 10. hast sinned ag. t.s.⌊33 : 9.
Mat. 22 : 37. shalt love Lord with all
t.s., Mk. 12 : 30. Lu. 10 : 27.
Lu. 12 : 20. this night t.s. be requir-
3 Jn. 2. mayest prosper as t.s. ⌊ed
Re. 18 : 14. fruits t.s. lusted after
See **As thy soul LIVETH.**
SOULS. ⌈Haran
Ge. 12 : 5. Abr. took s. they got in
14 : † 21. Give me the s., take goods
36 : † 6. Esau took all s. of his hou.
46 : 15. Leah bare; all the s., thirty
and three ⌈teen s.
18. Zilpah bare unto Jacob six-
22. sons of Rachel; all s. were 14
25. sons of Bilhah; all the s. were 7
26. s. that came wi. Jac. into Eg.
27. sons of Joseph were two s., all
s. of house of Jacob were 70 s.,
Ex. 1 : 5. De. 10 : 22. ⌈ber of s.
Ex. 12 : 4. take a lamb acc. to num-
16 : † 16. homer acc. to numb. of s.
30 : 15. to make an atonement for
your s., 16. Le. 17 : 11. Nu. 31 : 50.
Le. 11 : † 43. Ye sh. not make your s.
18 : 29. s. th. commit them be cut
20 : 25. not make y-r s. abominable
Nu. 16 : 38. sinners ag. their own s.
30 : 9. vow wherew. bound their s.
Jos. 10 : 28. utterly destroyed all s.
therein, 30, 32, 35, 37, 39.–11 : 11.
23 : † 11. Take good heed unto y-r s.
14. Ye know in all your s. ⌈out
1 S. 25 : 29. s. of enemies sh. he sling
2 K. 12 : † 4. Money of s. of his estima.
1 Ch. 5 : † 21. they took of s. 100,000
Es. 9 : † 31. days decreed for their s.
Ps. 72 : 13. shall save s. of needy
97 : 10. preserveth s. of his saints
Pr. 11 : 30. he that winneth s. is wise
14 : 25. A true witness delivereth s.
Is. 47 : † 14. shall not deliver their s.
57 : 16. spirit sho. fail and s. I made
Je. 2 : 34. in thy skirts is blood of s.
6 : 16. rest for your s., Mat. 11 : 29.
26 : 19. procure great evil ag. our s.
37 : † 9. saith L., Deceive not y-r s.
Je. 42 : † 20. ha. used deceit ag. y-r s.
44 : 7. why commit evil ag. y-r s.?
52 : † 29. Neb-r carried capt. 832 s.
La. 1 : 19. meat to relieve their s.
Eze. 7 : 19. shall not satisfy their s.
13 : 18. to hunt s. Will ye hunt s.
of my peo., will ye save the s.? 20.
19. to slay s. that should not die
14 : 14. sho. deliver their own s., 20.
18 : 4. Behold, all s. are mine
22 : 25. they have devoured s.
27. her princes wolves to destroy s.
Lu. 21 : 19. In patience possess y-r s.
Ac. 2 : 41. added unto them 3,000 s.
7 : 14. Jacob and his kindred 75 s.
14 : 22. Confirming s. of disciples
15 : 24. troubled you, subverting s.
27 : 37. were in all in ship 276 s.
2 Co. 12 : † 15. I be spent for your s.
1 Th. 2 : 8. imparted our own s. unto
He. 13 : 17. they watch for your s.
Ja. 1 : 21. word able to save your s.
1 Pe. 1 : 9. end of faith salv. of y-r s.
22: Seeing have purified your s.
2 : 25. unto the Shepherd of your s.
3 : 20. few, that is 8, s. were saved
4 : 19. commit keeping of s. to him
2 Pe. 2 : 14. beguiling unstable s.
Re. 6 : 9. I saw und. altar s. of them
18 : 13. no man buyeth s. of men
20 : 4. I saw the s. of them behead-
See AFFLICT, AFFLICTED. ⌊ed
SOUND. [Adj.]
Ps. 119 : 80. Let my heart be s. in
Pr. 14 : 30. s. heart is life of flesh
Lu. 15 : 27. received him safe and s.
2 Ti. 1 : 7. G. hath given us s. mind
13. hold fast the form of s. words
Tit. 1 : 13. that they be s. in faith
2 : 2. th. aged men be s. in faith ⌈ed
8. s. speech th. can-t be condemn-
See **Sound DOCTRINE.**
See WISDOM.
SOUND, S. [Noun.]
Ex. 28 : 35. his s. shall be heard
Le. 25 : † 9. trumpet loud of s. to
26 : 36. s. of shaken leaf sh. chase
2 S. 5 : 24. s. of a going in tops of
mulberry trees, 1 Ch. 14 : 15.
1 K. 1 : 40. earth rent with s. of these
14 : 6. Ahijah heard s. of her feet
18 : 41. s. of abundance of rain
2 K. 6 : 32. is not s. of master's feet
1 Ch. 16 : 5. Asaph made s. with cym-
42. those that sho. make a s.⌊bals
2 Ch. 5 : 13. as one, to make one s.
Jb. 15 : 21. A dreadful s. in his ears
21 : 12. rejoice at the s. of organ
37 : 2. s. that goeth out of his mou.
Ps. 77 : 17. water, skies sent out a s.
89 : 15. people that know joyful s.
92 : 3. sing upon harp wi. solemn s.
98 : 6. Wi. trumpets and s. of cornet
Ec. 7 : † 6. as s. of thorns under pot
12 : 4. when s. of grinding is low
Je. 8 : 16. trembled at s. of neighing
25 : 10. I will take s. of the millst-s
50 : 22. s. of battle is in the land
51 : 54. A s. of a cry from Babylon
Eze. 10 : 5. s. of cherubim's wings
26 : 13. s. of thy harps be no more
15. isles shake at s. of thy fall?
27 : 28. suburbs sh. shake at s. of
31 : 16. I made nat-s to shake at s.
Da. 3 : 5. time ye hear s. of, 7, 10, 15.
Am. 6 : 5. that chant to the s. of the
Mat. 24 : 31. send angels with gr. s.
Jn. 3 : 8. hearest s., canst not tell
Ac. 2 : 2. suddenly a s. from heaven
Ro. 10 : 18. s. went into all the earth
1 Co. 14 : 7. things without life giving s., whether pipe or harp,
exc. they give distinction in s-s
8. if trumpet give an uncertain s.
Re. 1 : 15. voice as s. of many waters
9 : 9. s. of wings as s. of chariots
18 : 22. s. of millstone be heard no
SOUND of the trumpet.
Jos. 6 : 5. when ye hear s. – people
shall shout, 20. Ju. 20 : † 37.
2 S. 6 : 15. bro-t up ark with s. –, 1
Ch. 15 : 28. ⌈lom reigneth
15 : 10. as ye hear s. –, say, Absa-
1 K. 1 : 41. when Joab heard s. –
Ne. 4 : 20. In what place ye hear s. –
Jb. 39 : 24. nei. believeth be it is s. –
Ps. 47 : 5. Lord is gone up with s. –
150 : 3. Praise him wi. the s. – ⌈s. –
Je. 4 : 19. hast heard, O my soul, the
21. How long shall I hear s. –
6 : 17. Hearken to the s. –
42 : 14. where we shall hear no s. –
Eze. 33 : 4. heareth s. – taketh not
5. heard s. – took not warning
Am. 2 : 2. Moab shall die with s. –
He. 12 : 19. ye are not come unto s. –
SOUND. [Verb.]
Le. 25 . 9. trumpet of jubilee to s.,
make the trumpet s. thro. land
Nu. 10 : 7. ye shall not s. an alarm
1 Ch. 15 : 19. Heman and Asaph to s.
Is. 16 : 11. wherefore my bowels shall
s. for Moab, Je. 31 : † 20. ⌈Moab
Je. 48 : 36. mine heart shall s. for
Jo. 2 : 1. s. an alarm in my holy mt.
Mat. 6 : 2. do not s. a trumpet before
1 Co. 15 : 52. trumpet sh. s., dead be
Re. 8 : 6. seven angels prepared to s.
13. trumpet of 3 angels wh. are to s.
10 : 7. when 7th angel sh. begin to
SOUNDED. ⌊s.
Ex. 19 : 19. voice of trumpet s. long
2 Ch. 7 : 6. priests s. trumpets, 13 : 14.
23 : 13. people s. with trumpets
29 : 28. singers sang, trumpeters s.
Ne. 4 : 18. he that s. trumpet was by
Mat. 6 : † 2. cause not trumpet be s.
Lu. 1 : 44. salutation s. in my ears
1 Th. 1 : 8. fr. you s. out the word of
Re. 8 : 7. The first angel s. and hail
8. second angel s. | 10. third s. ⌈s.
12. 4th angel s. | 9 : 1. 5th angel
9 : 13. 6th angel s. | 11 : 15. seventh
SOUNDED. ⌊angel s.
1 S. 20 : 12. When I have s. my father
Ac. 27 : 28. s. and found it 20 fath-s,
s. again, found it 15 fathoms
SOUNDETH.
Ex. 19 : 13. when trumpet s. long
SOUNDING.
1 Ch. 15 : 16. instruments of music s.
2 Ch. 5 : 12. with them 120 priests s.
13 : 12. wi. s. trumpets to cry alarm
Ps. 150 : 5. praise him upon s. cymb.
Is. 63 : 15. where is s. of thy bowels
Eze. 7 : 7. not the s. of mountains
1 Co. 13 : 1. not charity, I am as s.
SOUNDNESS. ⌊brass
Ps. 38 : 3. There is no s. in my flesh,
Is. 1 : 6. is no s. in it, but wounds⌊7.
Ac. 3 : 16. given him this perfect s.
SOUR. ⌈flower
Is. 18 : 5. when s. grape is ripening
Je. 31 : 29. the fathers have eaten a
s. grape, Eze. 18 : 2.
30. ev. man th. eateth the s. grape
Ho. 4 : 18. Their drink is s., they have
SOUTH. [Adj.]
Nu. 34 : 3. s. quarter from Zin by
coast of Edom, and s. border sh.
Jos. 11 : 2. of the plains s. of Chin-h
15 : 2. s. border of Judah fr. salt sea
19. given me s. land, Ju. 1 : 15.
18 : 15. s. quarter fr. Kirjath-jear.
19. salt sea at s. end of Jordan
1 S. 30 : 27. to them which were in s.
Ramoth, and to them which
Eze. 20 : 46. prophesy ag. forest of s.
40 : 28. inner court by s. gate ⌊field
42 : 13. north and s. chambers be
46 : 9. entereth by north go out by
s. gate; entereth by s. gate
Zch. 14 : 10. fr. Geba to Rimmon s.
See **South COAST.**

SOUTH country.

Ge. 20 : 1. Abr. sojourned tow. s. c.
24 : 62. Isaac dwelt in the s. c. , [8.
Jos. 11 : 16. Joshua took all s. c., 12 :
Zch. 6 : 6. grisled go forth tow. s. c.
See South SIDE.

SOUTH with wind.

Jb. 37 : 17. quieteth earth by s. w.
Ps. 78 : 26. by power bro-t in s. w.
Can. 4 : 16. Awake, O north w. ; and
come, thou s., blow upon my
Lu. 12 : 55. see s. w. blow [garden
Ac. 27 : 13. when s. w. blew, 28 : 13.

SOUTH. [Noun.]

Ge. 12 : 9. Abr. journeyed toward s.
13 : 1. Abram went up into the s.
3. Abram on his journeys fr. the s.
28 : 14. shalt spread to north, and s.
Ex. 26 : 35. side of tabern. toward s.
Nu. 13 : 22. they ascended by the s.
29. Amalekites dwell in the s.
21 : 1. Arad, wh. dwelt in s., 33 : 40.
34 : 4. border sh. turn fr. the s. (2)
De. 1 : 7. on the hills and in the s.
33 : 23. O Naph. possess west and s.
34 : 3. Lord shewed Moses the s.
Jos. 10 : 40. Josh. smote country of s.
12 : 3. fr. the s. under Ashdoth-pis.
13 : 4. Fr. the s. all land of Canaan-s
18 : 5. Judah shall abide on the s.
16. to side of Jebusi on the s.
19 : 8. Ramath of the s.
Ju. 1 : 9. fight Canaanites in the s.
16. wilderness in the s. of Arad
21 : 19. a place on s. of Lebonah [s.
1 S. 20 : 41. Da. arose out of pla. tow.
23 : 19. hill on the s. of Jeshi-n, 24.
27 : 10. ag. s. of Jud., s. of Jerahm-s
30 : 1. Amalekites invaded the s., 14.
2 S. 24 : 7. they went to s. of Judah
1 K. 7 : 25. three looking toward the
s., 2 Ch. 4 : 4. [2 Ch. 4 : 10.
39. set sea on side of house, ag. s.,
1 Ch. 9 : 24. porters were tow. the s.
2 Ch. 28 : 18. Phil. invaded s. of Jud.
Jb. 9 : 9. maketh chambers of the s.
37 : 9. Out of s. cometh whirlwind
39 : 26. stretch her wings toward s.
Ps. 75 : 6. promotion not fr. east nor
89 : 12. north and s. hast created [s.
107 : 3. gathered th. fr. north and s.
126 : 4. turn captivity as streams in
Ec. 1 : 6. wind goeth toward s. [s.
11 : 3. if tree fall toward s. or north
Is. 21 : 1. As whirlwinds in s. pass
30 : 6. burden of beasts of the s.
43 : 6. I will say to s., Keep not
Je. 13 : 19. cities of s. shall be shut
17 : 26. fr. s. bringing burnt off-gs
32 : 44. buy fields in cities of the s.
33 : 13. in cities of s. sh. flocks pass
Eze. 20 : 46. set thy face tow. s., drop
thy word toward s., prophesy
47. say to forest of s., Hear word of
L., all faces from s. sh. be burned
21 : 4. sword ag. all from s. to north
40 : 2. was as frame of city on s.
24. After that he bro-t me tow. s.
27. gate in court tow. the s. (2), 28.
44. their prospect was tow. s., 45.
41 : 11. ano. door tow. s., 42 : 12, 13.
48 : 10. tow. the s. 25,000 in length
17. suburbs of city, tow. s. 250 [s.
Da. 8 : 9. little horn waxed great tow.
11 : 5. king of the s. sh. be strong
6. king's daughter of s. sh. come
9. king of s. sh. come into kingd.
11. king of s. be moved wi. choler
14. many stand up ag. king of s.
15. arms of s. shall not withstand
25. king of s. shall be stirred up
29. he shall return, come tow. s.
40. king of s. shall push at him
Ob. 19. they of s. shall possess m-t
20. captivity sh. possess cities of s.
Ha. 3 : † 3. God came from s., from
Zch. 7 : 7. when men inhabited the s.
Zch. 9 : 14. G. sh. go wi. whirlwind of s.
14 : 4. half of mt. remove toward s.
Mat. 12 : 42. queen of s. shall rise in
judgment, Lu. 11 : 31. [wi. Abr.
Lu. 13 : 29. come from s. to sit down
Ac. 8 : 26. Arise, and go tow. the s.
Re. 21 : 13. on s. three gates, on west

SOUTHWARD.

Ge. 13 : 14. Lord said to Abr., Look s.
Nu. 3 : 29. pitch on side of tabern. s.
13 : 17. Mo. said, Get you th. way s.
De. 3 : 27. L. said, Lift thine eyes s.
Jos. 15 : 1. wilderness of Zin s. was
2. the bay that looketh s. [coast
21. cities toward coast of Edom s.
17 : 9. coast unto river Kanah, s.
10. s. it was Ephraim's ; northw.
18 : 13. tow. Luz, wh. is Beth-el s.
14. border compassed corner of sea
1 S. 14 : 5. other s., ag. Gibeah [s. (2)
1 Ch. 26 : 15. cast lots. To Obed-ed. s.
17. Levites s. four a day [(2) 48 : 28.
Eze. 47 : 19. south side s. fr. Tamar,
Da. 8 : 4. I saw ram pushing s.

SOUTHWEST.

Ac. 27 : 12. Phenice lieth toward s.

SOW. [Noun.] [ing

2 Pe. 2 : 22. s. washed to her wallow-

SOW. [Verb.]

Ge. 47 : 23. is seed, and ye sh. s. land
Ex. 23 : 10. 6 years s. land, Le. 25 : 3.
Le. 25 : 4. in 7th year sh. not s., 11.
20. we shall not s. nor gather in
22. And ye shall s. the eighth yr.
2 K. 19 : 29. in 3d year s., Is. 37 : 30.
Jb. 4 : 8. th. s. wickedness reap same
31 : 8. let me s., let another eat
Ps. 107 : 37. s. fields, plant viney-ds
126 : 5. s. in tears shall reap in joy
Ec. 11 : 4. observeth wind sh. not s.
Is. 28 : 24. ploughman plough to s. ?
30 : 23. give rain of seed th. shalt s.
32 : 20. Blessed th. s. beside all wat.
Je. 4 : 3. Break fallow ground, s. not
31 : 27. I will s. the house of Israel
Ho. 2 : 23. I will s. her unto me in
10 : 12. s. to yours. in righteousness
Mi. 6 : 15. Thou sh. s., but not reap
Zch. 10 : 9. I will s. them am. people
Mat. 6 : 26. fowls of air s. not, Lu. 12 : 24.
13 : 3. sower went forth to s. ; when
he, Mk. 4 : 3. Lu. 8 : 5. [s., 22.
Lu. 19 : 21. reapest th. thou didst not
See SEED. [Vegetable.]

SOWED.

Ge. 26 : 12. Isaac s. in land same year
Ju. 9 : 45. Abim. s. Shechem wi. salt
Mat. 13 : 4. when he s. some fell by
way side, Mk. 4 : 4. Lu. 8 : 5.
24. s. good seed | 25. s. tares, 39.
31. grain of mustard seed a man s.
25 : 26. reap where I s. not. See SOW.

SOWEDST. [s.

De. 11 : 10. not as Egypt, where thou

SOWER.

Is. 55 : 10. it may give seed to the s.
Je. 50 : 16. Cut off s. from Babylon
Mat. 13 : 18. Hear ye parable of the s.
Mk. 4 : 14. s. soweth the word, these
2 Co. 9 : 10. that ministereth seed to
See SOW [Verb.] [s.

SOWEST. [fened

1 Co. 15 : 36. th. thou s. is not quick-
37. thou s. not that body th. shall

SOWETH. [cord

Pr. 6 : 14. naughty person s. dis-
19. he th. s. discord am. brethren
11 : 18. to him th. s. righteousness
16 : 28. A froward man s. strife
22 : 8. that s. iniquity reap vanity
Am. 9 : 13. overtake him that s. seed
Mat. 13 : 37. that s. good seed is Son
Mk. 4 : 14. sower s. the word, these
Jn. 4 : 36. he that s. and th. reapeth
37. true, One s. and ano. reapeth
2 Co. 9 : 6. He wh. s. sparingly, he
which s. bountifully
Ga. 6 : 7. whatsoev. a man s. shall he
8. s. to his flesh, reap corruption ;
but he that s. to the Spirit

SOWING.

Le. 11 : 37. if carcass fall upon any s.
26 : 5. vintage sh. reach unto s. time

SOWN.

Ex. 23 : 16. firstfruits of labours s.
Le. 11 : 37. carcass upon seed to be s.
De. 21 : 4. valley nei. eared nor s.
22 : 9. fruit of seed s. be defiled
29 : 23. generations see land not s.
Ju. 6 : 3. Isr. had s. Midianites came
Ps. 97 : 11. Light is s. for righteous
Is. 19 : 7. things s. by brooks wither
40 : 24. not be planted, not be s.
61 : 11. causeth things s. to spring
Je. 2 : 2. after me in a land not s.
12 : 13. s. wheat shall reap thorns
Eze. 36 : 9. ye shall be tilled and s.
Ho. 8 : 7. s. wind shall reap whirlw.
Na. 1 : 14. no more of thy name be s.
Hag. 1 : 6. Ye s. much, bring in little
Mat. 13 : 19. catcheth away that was
s., Mk. 4 : 15. [hast not s.
25 : 24. man, reaping where thou
Mk. 4 : 16. wh. are s. on stony ground
18. they which are s. am. thorns
20. th. wh. are s. on good ground
31. wh. s. is less than all seeds, 32.
1 Co. 9 : 11. s. unto you spiritual thi.
15 : 42. It is s. in corruption, it is
43. It is s. in dishonour, it is
44. It is s. a natural body, raised
2 Co. 9 : 10. multiply your seed s.
Ja. 3 : 18. fruit of righteousness is s.

SPACE, SPACES.

Ge. 29 : 14. Jac. with him s. of month
32 : 16. put a s. betwixt drove and
Le. 25 : 8. s. of 7 sabbaths of years
30. if not redeemed in s. of year
De. 2 : 14. s. in which we came, 38.
Jos. 3 : 4. be a s. between you and it
1 S. 26 : 13. s. betw. Dav.'s company
1 K. 7 : † 5. s-s and pillars were squ.
Ezr. 9 : 8. little s. grace been shewed
Ne. 7. † 4. city was broad in s-s
Is. 22 : † 18. into country large of s-s
33 : † 21. to us a place broad of s-s
Je. 28 : 11. within s. of 2 full years
Eze. 40 : 12. The s. was one cubit (2)
Lu. 22 : 59. about s. of one hour aft.
Ac. 5 : 7. s. of 3 hours his wife came
34. to put apostles forth a little s.
7 : 42. slain beasts by s. of 40 years
13 : 20. gave judges s. of 450 years
21. G. gave them Saul s. of 40 yrs.
15 : 33. after they had tarried a s.
19 : 8. spake boldly s. of 3 months
10. this continued s. of two years
34. all about s. of two hours cried
20 : 31. by s. of 3 years I ceased not
Ja. 5 : 17. rained not by s. of 3 years
Re. 2 : 21. I gave her s. to repent
8 : 1. was silence s. of half an hour
14 : 20. blood by s. of 1,600 furlongs
17 : 10. he must continue a short s.

SPAIN.

Ro. 15 : 24. I take my journey into S.
28. I will come by you into S.

SPAKE. [found

Ge. 18 : 29. Abr. s., Peradv. be forty
19 : 14. Lot s. to his sons in law
21 : 22. Abim-h Phichol s. unto Ab.
22 : 7. Isaac s. unto Abr., My father
23 : 3. Abr. s. unto the sons of Heth
13. Abr. s. unto Ephron in audi-
24 : 30. Thus s. the man unto [ence
27 : 5. Rebekah heard when Isaac
6. Rebekah s. to Jacob [s. to Esau
29 : 9. while he yet s., Rachel came
31 : 11. angel s. to Jacob in dream
34 : 3. he s. kindly to the damsel
4. Shechem s. to his father Hamor
39 : 10. As she s. to Jos. day by day
14. she called men of house and s.
17. she s., saying, The Hebrew

Ge. 39 :19. when master heard words
41 : 9. Then s. chief butler ⌊wife s.
42 : 7. Jos-h s. roughly unto breth.
14. that is it that I s. unto you
22. s. I not unto you, Do not sin
23. he s. unto them by interpreter
30. lord of land s. roughly unto
37. Reuben s. unto his fa., Slay
43 : 3. Jud. s., The man did protest
27. old man of wh. ye s., Is he
29. Is this y-r bro. of whom ye s.?
44 : 6. steward overtook th. and s.
47 : 5. Pha. s., Thy fa. and breth-n
49 : 28. this their fa. s. unto them
50 : 4. days of mourning past, Jos.
17. Joseph wept when they s. ⌊s.
21. he comforted th. and s. kindly
Ex. 1 : 15. k. of Egypt s. to Heb. mid-
4:30. Aaron s. the words, 16: 10.⌊wiv
5 : 10. taskmasters s. to the people
6 : 9. Moses s. unto children of Israel, 19 : 25.-34 : 34.-35 : 4. Le.
24 : 23. Nu. 9 : 4, 9.-16 : 26.-30 :
1.-31 : 3. De. 1 : 1, 3.-4 : 45.-27:
9.-31 : 1, 30. ⌈Nu. 27 : 15.
12. Moses s. bef. the Lord, 19 : 19.
27. These are th. wh. s. to Pha., 7:7.
15 : 1, sang Israel this song and s.
16 : 9. Moses s. unto Aaron, Say
35 : 5. wise men s. unto Moses, The
Le. 10 : 12. Moses s. unto Aaron and
Nu. 12 : 1. Miriam and Aaron s. ag.
14 : 7. Joshua, Caleb s. unto comp.
16 : 5. Mos. s. unto Korah and comp.
17 : 12. chil. of Isr. s. unto Mos., 20:3.
21 . 5. the peo. s. ag. God and Mos.
22 : 7. elders of Moab s. words⌈I not
24 : 12. Balaam said unto Balak, s.
26 : 3. Moses and Ele-r s. wi. them
32 : 2. chil. of Gad s. unto Mos., 25.
36 : 1. fa-s of families s. unto Moses
De. 1 : 9. I s. unto you at that time
43. So I s. ye would not hear
5 : 28. Lord heard words when ye s.
13 : 2. sign come wh-f he s. unto⌈s.
28 : 68. L. bring thee by way wh-f I
32 : 44. Moses s. words of this song
Jos. 1 : 12. to Reubenites s. Joshua
3 : 6. Joshua s. unto priests, Take
4 : 12. Mo. s. unto 40,000 prepared
21. Joshua s., When your chil. ask
7 : 2. Joshua s., Go up, view the
9 : 11. our elders s., Take victuals
22. Josh. s., Whf. have ye beguiled
10 . 12. s. Joshua, Sun, stand thou
17 : 14. chil of Jos. s. unto Josh. ⌊17
20 : 2. appoint cities whereof I s.
21 : 2. heads of fathers s. at Shiloh
22 : 8. Joshua s., Return wi. much
15. unto land of Gilead, s. wi. them
30. words chil. of Gad s., it pleased
Ju. 8:9. Gid. s. unto men of Penu., 8.
9 : 3. mother's brethren s. of him
37. Gaal s., See, there come people
15 : 13. s. unto Samson, No ; we
19 : 22. sons of Belial s. to master
Ru. 4 : 1. kinsman of whom Boaz s.
1 S. 1 : 13. Hannah s. in her heart
7 : 3. Samuel s. unto Israel, If ye
9 : 9. to inquire of God ; thus he s.
10 : 16. of kingdom wh-f Sam. s.
17 : 23. came Goliath s. same words
26. Dav. s. to men th. stood, 28, 30.
31. words Da. s. rehearsed before
18 : 23. Saul's servants s. words in
24. On this manner s. David ⌊ears
19 : 1. Saul s. to Jona. th. they kill
4. Jona. s. good of David unto Saul
20 : 26. Saul s. not anything th. day
25 : 9. David's yo. men s. to Nabal
40. serv-ts of Da. s. unto Abigail
28 : 12. woman s. to Saul, Why hast
thou deceived ⌈stoning him
30 : 6. Da. distressed ; people s. of
2 S. 3 : 19. Abner s. in ears of Benj-n
5 . 1. tribes of Isr. to David and s.
6. Jebusites s. unto Da., Exc. thou
2 S. 12 : 18. child alive, we s. unto
13 : 22. Absalom s. unto bro. Am-n
14 : 4. woman of Tekoah s. to king
17 : 6. Absalom s. unto Hushai
20 : 18. wise woman out of city s.
22 : 1. David s. unto Lord this song
24 : 17. Da. s. unto Lord, Lo, I have
1 K. 1 : 11. Nathan s. unto Bath-she.
42. while Joab s. Jona. priest came
3 : 22. dead is thy son. Thus they s.
4 :32. And Sol. s. 3,000 proverbs⌊26.
33. And he s. of trees ; s. of beasts
8 : 12. s. Sol., The Lord said he wou.
12 : 3. Jeroboam and cong-n s. unto Rehob., 2 Ch. 10:3.⌈2Ch. 10:7.
6 : 8. Then cried he unto me and s.
7. the old men s. unto Rehoboam,
10. the young men grown up with
him s. (2), 2 Ch. 10 : 10. ⌈men
14. Reh-m s. aft. the counsel of yo.
13 : 18. angel s. unto me by Lord
27. prophet s. to sons, Saddle the
31. s. to sons, When dead bury me
20 : 28. came a man of G., s. unto k.
21 : 2. Ahab s. to Naboth, Give me, 6.
22 : 13. messenger to call Micaiah, s.
2 K. 1 : 9. captain s., Thou man of
God, come down, 2 Ch. 18 : 12.
2 :22. healed acc-g to say-g Elisha s.
5 : 13. serv-s s., My fa. if proph. had
7:17. trode upon him as man of G. s.
8 : 1. s. Elisha unto wom. whose son
9 : 12. Thus and thus s. he unto me
14 : 25. word of God he s. by Jonah
17 : 26. s. to k. of Assyria, The nat-s
18 : 28. Rab-shakeh s., Hear word
25 : †6. s. judgment wi. k., Je. 39:†5.
28. Evil-mer-h s. kindly to Jehoia.
1 Ch. 15 :16. Da. s. to chief of Levites
21 :19. saying of Gad, he s. in name
2 Ch. 1 : 2. Then Sol. s. unto all Isr.
18 : 19. Who entice Ahab? And I s.
30 : 22. Hez-h s. comfortably unto
32 : 6. Hez-h s. comfortably to peo.
16. serv-s s. more ag. L and Hez., 19.
33 : 18. seers that s. to Manas. in
34 :22. Hilkiah s. to Huldah proph.
35 :25. s. of Josiah in lamentations
Ne. 4 : 2. Sanballat s. bef. his breth.
8 : 1. peo. s. unto Ezra to bri. book
13:24. chil. s. half in speech of Ash-d
Es. 3 : 4. they s. daily unto Mordecai
4 : 10. Es. s. unto Hatach, gave
8 :3. Es. s. unto king, fell at his feet
Jb. 2 : 13. none s. a word unto Job
3 : 2. After this Job s., Let the day
19 : 18. yea, young chil. s. ag. me
29 : 22. After my words they s. not
32 : 16. th. s. not and ans-d no more
35 : 1. Elihu s., Thinkest this right
Ps. 39 : 3. My heart was hot, then s.
78 : 19. Yea, they s. against God ⌊1
Pr. 30 : 1. the man s. unto Ithiel
Can. 2 : 10. My beloved s., Rise, my
5 : 6. my soul failed when he s.
Je. 8 : 6. I heard ; they s. not aright
20 : 8. since I s., I cried violence
25 : 2. which Jere-h s. unto Judah
26 : 11. s. priests unto princes, This
12. s. Jere-h unto princes, 27 : 16.
17. certain elders s. to the assem-y
27 : 12. I s. unto Zedekiah, k., 34:6.
28 : 1. Hananiah s. unto me in⌊11.
38 : 8. Ebed-melech s. to king ⌈fly
40 : 15, Johan. s. to Gedal-h secret-
43 : 2. s. Azariah, Thou speakest
45 : 1. Jer-h s. unto Baruch⌊falsely
Eze. 11 : 25. s. I unto them of captiv.
24 : 18. So s. I in morning ; at even
Da. 1:3. k. s. unto Ashpenaz⌊wife died
2 : 4. s. Chaldeans to king in Syriac
3 : 9. they s., O king, live for ever
14. Neb. s., Is it true, O Shadrach, 19, 24, 26, 28. ⌈of Shadr-h
28. Then Neb. s., Blessed be God
4 : 19. k. s., Beltes-r, let not dream
30. k. s., Is not this gr. Babylon
5 : 7. k. s. to wise men of Babylon
Da. 5 : 10. queen s., O king, live for
13. king s., Art thou that Daniel
6 : 12. they s. conc-g king s decree
16. k. s. unto Dan., Thy G. will deliv.,
7 : 2. Dan. s., I saw in my vis-n⌊20.
11. gr. words wh. the horn s., 20.
8 : 13. saint said unto saint wh. s.
9 : 6. prophets wh. s. to our kings
12. confirmed words wh. he s. ag.
10 : 16. touched my lips then I s.
Ho. 13 : 1. When Ephr. s. trembling
Hag. 1 : 13. s. Haggai, L.'s messen-r
Zch. 3 : 4. angel s., Take away filthy
4 : 4. So I s. to the angel wi. me | 6.
Mal. 3 :16. they th. feared L. s. often
Mat. 9 : 18. while he s. these things unto
them, 17 : 5.-26 : 47. Mk. 5 : 35.
-14 : 43. Lu. 8 : 49.-11 : 27, 37.
-22 : 47, 60. ⌈12:22. Lu. 11:14
33. devil was cast out, dumb s.,
13 : 3. he s. many things in parables, 33, 34.-22 : 1. Mk. 4 : 33,
34. Lu. 5 : 36.-6 : 39.-8 : 4.-12:
16.-13 : 6.-15 : 3.-18 : 1, 9.-19:
11.-21 : 29. ⌈28 : 18.
14 : 27. Jesus s., Be of good cheer,
16 : 11. I s. not unto you conc. br-d
17 : 13. he s. unto th. of John Bap-t
21 : 45. perceived that he s. of them
23 : 1. s. Jes. to multitude, Lu. 7:24.
Mk. 3 : 9. s. to disciples that a ship
7 : 35. he s. plain | 8 : 32. s. openly
9 : 18. I s. to disciples that they ⌈ly
14 :31. Peter s. the more vehement-
39. Jes. prayed and s. same words
Lu. 1 : 42. Elis-h s. with loud voice
55. As he s. to our fathers, to Abr.
64. Zach-s s. and praised God
2 : 38. Anna s. of him to all that
50. they understood not wh. he s.
4 : 36. s. am. thems., What word is
7 :39. Pharis. s. within hims., This
9 : 11. he s. of kingdom of God⌊man
31. s. of his decease to be at Jerus-
34. while he s. came cloud ⌊alem
11 : 27. as he s. these a woman ⌈ful
14 : 3. s. Jes. unto lawyers, Is it law-
20 : 2. s., Tell us by what authority
21 : 5. as some s. of the temple⌈him
22 : 65. blasphemously s. they ag.
23 : 20. Pil. willing to release Jes. s.
24 : 6. remember how he s. in Gali.
36. as they s. Jesus stood in midst
Jn. 1 : 15. This was he of whom I s.
2 : 21. he s. of temple of his body
6 : 71. he s. of Judas Iscariot
7 : 13. no man s. openly of him
39. But this s. he of the Spirit
46. Never man s. like this man
8 : 12. s. Jes., I am light of world
20. These words s. Jes. in treas-y
27. understood not he s. of Father
30. As he s. many believed
9 : 22. These words s. his parents
10 : 6. understood not things he s.
41. all John s. of this man true
11 : 13. Howbeit Jes. s. of his death
51. s. he not of hims., he proph-d
56. s. am. thems. as stood in temple
12 : 29. others said angel s. to him
36. These thi-s s. Jes., 17 : 1.⌈9, 32.
38. saying be fulfilled wh. he s. 18 :
41. saw his glory and s. of him ⌈s.
13 : 22. disciples doubting of wh. he
24. should ask of whom he s.
28. no man knew for what intent
he s. ⌈kept the door
18 : 16. disciple s. unto her that
20. Jesus answered, I s. openly to
21 : 19. s. signifying by what death
Ac. 1 : 16. Holy Gh. s. conc-g Judas
2 : 31. He s. of the resurrec-n of Ch.
4 : 1. as they s., priests, Sadd-s came
31. s. word of God with boldness
6 : 10. not resist spirit by wh. he s.
7 : 38. angel wh. s. to him in Sina-

Ac. 8 : 6. heed unto things Philip s.
26. angel of Lord s. unto Philip
9 : 29. he s. boldly in name of Lord
10 : 7. angel which s. unto Cornel.
15. voice s. unto Peter second time
44. while Peter s., Holy Ghost fell
11 : 20. s. unto Grecians, preaching
13 : 45. Jews s. against things [L. J.
14 : 1. so s. gr. multitude believed
16 : 13. s. to women which resorted
32. s. unto him word of L. [gently
18 : 25. fervent in spirit he s. dili-
19 : 6. s. wi. tongues and prophes-d
8. in syna. Paul s. boldly 3 months
9. s. evil of that way before multi.
26 : 24. as he s., Festus said, Paul
28 : 19. when Jews s. ag. it I was
21. neither any s. harm of thee
25. well s. Holy Ghost by Esaias
1 Co. 13 : 11. when child I s. as child
14 : 5. I would ye all s. wi. tongues
2 Co. 7 : 14. we s. all things in truth
Ga. 4 : 15. Where blessedness ye s. of?
He. 7 : 14. of wh. tribe Mos. s. noth.
12 : 25. refused him that s. on earth
2 Pe. 1 : 21. holy men of God s. as
Re. 1 : 12. voice th. s. with me, 10:8.
13 : 11. another beast s. as a dragon

God SPAKE.

Ge. 8 : 15. G. s. unto Noah, Go forth
of ark, thy wife and sons | 9 : 8.
35 : 15. called pla. where G. s. Beth-
46 : 2. G. s. unto Isr. in visions [el
Ex. 6 : 2. G. s. unto Moses, I am the
20 : 1. G. s. all these words, saying
De. 1 : 6. our G. s. unto us in Horeb
Jos. 23 : 14. not failed of things G. s.
Mk. 12 : 26. in bush G. s. unto him
Jn. 9 : 29. We know G. s. unto Mos.
Ac. 7 : 6. G. s. on this wise, That his
He. 1 : 1. G. who s. in time past unto
See **LORD** with **spake.**

SPAKE.

[Referring to God or Lord.] [ing
Ge. 24 : 7. G. who s. and sware, say-
Jos. 24 : 27. words of L. which he s.
1 S. 9 : 17. man whom I s. to thee of
28 : 17. L. hath done to him as he s.
2 S. 7 : 7. s. I word with any of the
tribes of Israel, 1 Ch. 17 : 6.
23 : 2. The Spirit of the L. s. by me
3. The rock of Israel s. to me
1 K. 6 : 12. word wh. I s. unto David
2 K. 22 : 19. what I s. ag. this place
2 Ch. 6 : 4. hath fulfilled that he s.
32 : 24. L. s. unto him, gave a sign
Ps. 33 : 9. he s. and it was done [lar
99 : 7. He s. unto th. in cloudy pil-
105 : 31. He s., there came flies
34. He s., and locusts came
Is. 65 : 12. I s., ye did not hear, 66:4.
Je. 7 : 13. I s. unto you, rising early
22. I s. not unto your fathers, I
14 : 14. I sent not, nei. s. unto them
19 : 5. I commanded not nor s. it
22 : 21. I s. unto thee in prosperity
31 : 20. since I s. ag. him I rememb.
37 : 2. words of L. wh. he s. by Jer-h
Eze. 1 : 28. I heard voice of one th. s.
2 : 2. spirit entered when he s. 3:24.
10 : 2. he s. unto the man clothed
Da. 9 : 12. confirmed words he s.
Ho. 12 : 4. in Beth-el he s. with us
Lu. 1 : 70. As he s. by prophets
24 : 44. are words I s. unto you
He. 4 : 4. he s. in a certain place

SPAKEST.

Ju. 13 : 11. Art man s. unto woman?
17 : 2. silver s. of in mine ears [s.
1 S. 28 : 21. hearkened unto words th.
1 K. 8 : 24. thou s. and hast fulfilled
it, 2 Ch. 6 : 15. [David
26. word be verified thou s. unto
53. separate as thou s. by Moses
Ne. 9 : 13. s. with them from heaven
Ps. 89 : 19. s. in vision to Holy One
Je. 48 : 27. since s. of him skippedst

SPAN.

Ex. 28 : 16. a s. the length, a s. the
breadth of breastplate, 39 : 9.
1 S. 17 : 4. Goliath's height 6 cub. and s.
Is. 40 : 12. meted out heaven with s.?
La. 2 : 20. woman eat children s. long
Eze. 43 : 13. border of altar sh. be a s.

SPANGLED. [ments

Is. 3 : † 19. I will take away s. orna-

SPANNED. [ens

Is. 48 : 13. my hand hath s. the heav-

SPARE. [eous

Ge. 18 : 24. not s. place for 50 right-
26. I will s. place for their sakes
45 : † 20. let not y-r eye s. y-r stuff
De. 13 : 8. not s. nor conceal him
29 : 20. Lord will not s. him, but
1 S. 15 : 3. destroy Amalek, s. not
Ne. 13 : 22. s. me acc-g to thy mercy
Jb. 6 : 10. let him not s., I have not
16 : 13. cleav-h my reins, doth not s.
20 : 13. Tho. he s. it and forsake not
27 : 22. G. sh. cast upon him, not s.
30 : 10. they s. not to spit in my face
Ps. 39 : 13. O s. me that I may recover
72 : 13. He shall s. poor and needy
Pr. 6 : 34. not s. in day of vengeance
19 : 18. let not soul s. for his crying
Is. 9 : 19. no man shall s. brother
13 : 18. their eye sh. not s. children
30 : 14. he shall break it, sh. not s.
54 : 2. s. not, lengthen cords, stren.
58 : 1. Cry aloud, s. not, lift up voi.
Je. 13 : 14. I will not s. th., Eze. 24 : 14.
21 : 7. he shall not s. them
50 : 14. all shoot at her, s. no arrows
51 : 3. s. ye not her young men
Eze. 5 : 11. neither shall mine eye s.,
7 : 4, 9.–8 : 18.–9 : 10. [pity
9 : 5. let not your eye s., nei. have
Jo. 2 : 17. say, s. thy people, O Lord
Jon. 4 : 11. should not I s. Nineveh
Ha. 1 : 17. not s. to slay the nations
Mal. 3 : 17. I will s. as man spareth
Lu. 15 : 17. have bread enough to s.
Ro. 11 : 21. heed, lest he s. not thee
1 Co. 7 : 28. ha. trouble, but I s. you
2 Co. 1 : 23. to s. you I came not unto
13 : 2. if I come again, I will not s.

SPARED.

1 S. 15 : 9. But Saul and peo. s. Agag
15. people s. best of the sheep [s.
24 : 10. bade me kill thee, mine eye
2 S. 12 : 4. s. to take of own flock
21 : 7. king s. Mephibosheth because
2 K. 5 : 20. master hath s. Naaman
Ps. 78 : 50. s. not their soul fr. death
Eze. 20 : 17. mine eye s. them from
Jon. 4 : † 10. Thou hast s. the gourd
Ro. 8 : 32. He th. s. not his own Son
11 : 21. if G. s. not natural branches
2 Pe. 2 : 4. if God s. not angels that
5. s. not old world, but saved Noah

SPARETH.

Pr. 13 : 24. He that s. rod hateth son
17 : 27. hath knowledge, s. his words
21 : 26. righteous giveth, and s. not
Mal. 3 : 17. I will sp-re as man s. son

SPARING.

Ac. 20 : 29. wolves enter, not s. flock
Col. 2 : † 23. humility, . . not s. of body

SPARINGLY. [reap s.

2 Co. 9 : 6. He who soweth s. shall

SPARK.

Jb. 18 : 5. s. of his fire sh. not shine
Is. 1 : 31. maker of it shall be as a s.

SPARKS. [ward

Jb. 5 : 7. unto trouble, as s. fly up-
41 : 19. Out of mouth go s. of fire
Pr. 26 : † 18. madman who casteth s.
Is. 50 : 11. compass yours. with s.
Da. 3 : † 22. s. of fire slew those men

SPARKLED.

Eze. 1 : 7. s. like the colour of brass

SPARROW, S.

Le. 14 : † 4. take for him 2 s-s alive
Ps. 84 : 3. Yea, s. hath found house
Ps. 102 : 7. I am as a s. upon housetop
Mat. 10 : 29. Are not two s-s sold for
31. value than many s-s, Lu. 12 : 7.
Lu. 12 : 6. five s-s sold for 2 farthings?

SPAT.

Jn. 9 : 6. thus spoken, he s. on ground

SPEAK. [God, 31.

Gen. 18 : 27. taken on me to s. unto
24 : 50. we can-t s. unto thee bad or
27 : 6. I heard thy fa. s. unto Esau
31 : 24. heed thou s. not to Jacob
32 : 4. thus s. unto my lord Esau, 19.
37 : 4. not s. peaceably unto him
44 : 16. What sh. we say? what s.?
18. Judah said, Let thy servant s.
Ex. 4 : 14. I know th. he can s. well
15. s. and put words in his mouth
5 : 23. since I came to s. to Pharaoh
7 : 2. thou shalt s. all I command
9. when Pharaoh shall s. unto you
19 : 6. thou sh. s. unto chil. of Isr.,
30 : 31. Le. 9 : 3.–24 : 15. Nu. 27 : 8.
23 : 2. not s. in a cause to decline
28 : 3. shalt s. unto all wise hearted
29 : 42. where I will meet you to s.
32 : 12. wheref. should Egyptians s.
34 : 35. he went in to s. wi. the L., 34.
Nu. 7 : 89. Moses into taber. to s.
12 : 8. ye not afraid to s. ag Moses
14 : 15. wh. heard fame of thee will
21 : 27. that s. in proverbs, say [s.
22 : 8. I will bring word, as L. sh. s.
35. word I s., that thou shalt s.
23 : 5. Return unto Balak, and s.
12. Must I not s. that which Lord
27 : 7. dau-s of Zelophehad s. right
De. 18 : 18. he sh. s. all that I com-d
19. words he sh. s. in my name [(3)
20. sh. presume to s. in my name
20 : 2. priest shall s. unto the people, 5, 8. Jos. 4 : 10. [to him
25 : 8. elders of the city shall s. un-
26 : 5. thou shalt s. before the Lord
27 : 14. Levites shall s. unto Israel
Jos. 22 : 24. your chil. might s. unto
Ju. 19 : 3. to s. friendly unto her
21 : 13. to s. to chil. of Benjamin
1 S. 25 : 17. such a son of Belial that
a man cannot s. to him [ence
24. Let handmaid s. in thine audi-
2 S. 3 : 19. Abner went to s. to David
27. Joab took him aside to s.
7 : 17. acc. to vision Nathan s. to
14 : 12. let handmaid s. unto k., 15.
13. king doth s. th. thing as faulty
18. Let my lord the king now s.
19 : 10. why s. ye not of bringing
20 : 18. were wont to s. in old time
1 K. 2 : 19. she went to s. unto him
12 : 7. wilt s. good words, 2 Ch. 10 : 7.
10. Thus shalt s. unto this people
21 : 19. shalt s. unto Ahab, Thus
22 : 24. Which way went Spirit of L.
for me to s. unto? 2 Ch. 18 : 23.
2 K. 18 : 27. my master sent me to
thee to s. words? Is. 36 : 12. [10.
19 : 10. Thus s. to Hezekiah, Is. 37 :
1 Ch. 17 : 15. so did Nathan s. unto
18. What can Dav. s. more to thee?
2 Ch. 32 : 17. wrote letters to s. ag.
Ne. 13 : 24. not s. in Jews' language
Es. 6 : 4. to s. unto k. to hang Mord.
Jb. 8 : 2. How long wilt s. these thi-s?
11 : 5. oh that G. would s. ag. thee
13 : 7. Will ye s. wickedly for God
22. let me s., and answer thou me
18 : 2. mark and afterw-d we will s.
27 : 4. My lips sh. not s. wickedness
32 : 7. I said, Days should s. [half
36 : 2. I have yet to s. on G.'s be-
37 : 20. if man s. be swallowed up
41 : 3. will he s. soft words unto
Ps. 2 : 5. Then sh. he s. in his wrath
5 : 6. destroy them that s. leasing
12 : 2. They s. vanity, s. wi. double
17 : 10. wi. mouth s. proudly [heart
28 : 3. which s. peace to neighbours

Ps. 29 : 9.doth ev. one s. of his glory
31 : 18. which s. grievous things ag.
35 :20. they s. not peace, but devise
28.My tongue shall s. of thy right.
38 : 12. they s. mischievous things
40 : 5. if I would declare and s. of
41 : 5. enemies s. evil of me ⌊them
49 : 3. my mouth shall s. of wisdom
52:3.lying rather th. s. righteousn.
58 :1.Do ye s.righteousn.cong-n⌈s.
59 : 12. cursing and lying wh. they
63 : 11. that s. lies shall be stopped
69 : 12.They th. sit in gate s. ag. me
71 : 10. mine enemies s. against me
73 : 8. they s. wickedly, s. loftily
85 : 8. I will hear what L. will s. ;
he will s. peace to his people
94 : 4.How long sh. th. s. hard thi-s
109 : 20.be reward of th. that s. evil
115 : 5. mouths, but they s. not,7.–
7. nei.s. thro.their throat⌊135:16.
119 : 23. Princes did s. against me
172. My tongue sh. s. of thy word
127 : 5. sh. s. with enemies in gate
139 ; 20. they s. ag. thee wickedly
145 : 6. sh. s. of thy terrible acts
11. sh. s. of glory of thy kingdom
21 My mouth shall s. praise of L.
Pr. 8 : 7. my mouth shall s. truth
23 : 16. rejoice, when lips s. right
Ec. 3 : 7. to be silent, and time to s.
Can. 7 : 9. lips of those asleep to s.
Is. 8 : 20. if s. not acc. to this word
14 : 10. all they shall s. and say
19 : 18. cities in Eg. sh. s. language
28 : 11. with ano. tongue sh. he s.
29 : 4. thou shalt s. out of ground
32 : 4. of stammerers sh. s. plainly
6. vile person will s. villany ⌈on
41 : 1. come near, then let them s.
50 :4. I sho. know how to s. in seas-
52 : 6. shall know I am he doth s.
56 : 3. nei. let son of stranger s.
59 : 4. trust in vanity, and s. lies ⌈s.
Je. 1 : 7. whatso. I command thou sh.
5 : 14. saith L., Bec. ye s. this word
7 : 27. sh. s. these words unto them
9 : 5. not s. truth, taught to s. lies
10 : 5. idols upright as tree, s. not
12 : 6.believe not, tho. s. fair words
13 : 12. shalt s. this word to them
18 : 7. I shall s. conc-g a nation, 9.
20. I stood before thee to s. good
20 : 9. I said I will not s. any more
23 :16. s. a vision of their own heart
28. let him s. my word faithfully,
26 : 15. L. sent me to s. these words
27 : 9. sorcerers which s. unto you
14. hearken not unto proph-s th. s.
29 : 24. Thus shalt s. to Shemaiah
32 : 4. and sh. s. wi. him mouth to
34 : 3. sh. s. wi. thee mouth to mou.
Eze. 2 :7.sh. s. my words unto them
3 : 10.words I sh. s. receive in heart
20 :49. say, Doth he not s. parab-s?
24 : 27. shalt s., be no more dumb
32 : 21. strong am. mighty, shall s.
33 : 8. if dost not s. to warn wicked
10. Thus ye s., If our sins be upon
24.th. s., Abr. was one, he inherited
30. peo. are talking ag. thee and s.
37 : 18. when chil. of thy people s.
Da. 2 : 9.prepa-d corrupt words to s.
3 : 29. s. amiss ag. God of Shadrach
7 : 25. sh. s. gr. words ag. Most Hi.
10 : 19. I said, Let my lord s.
11 : 27. shall s. lies at one table
36. king sh. s. marvellous things
Ha. 2 : 3. at end it sh. s. and not lie
Zph. 3 : 13. not do iniquity nor s. lies
Zch. 7 : 3. And to s. unto priests
9 : 10.sh. s. peace unto the heathen
† 17. corn shall make young men s.
Mat.10 :19.what ye sh. s., Mk.13:11.
20.For it is not ye th.s., Mk.13:11.
12 : 34.how being evil s. good thi-s?
36. ev. idle word that men shall s.
Mat. 12 : 46. moth. desiring to s., 47.
15 : 31. th. saw dumb s., Mk. 7 : 37.
Mk. 1 : 34. suffered not devils to s.
2 : 7. Why doth man s. blasphe-s?
9 : 39. that can lightly s. evil of me
12 : 1. he began to s. by parables
14 :71.know not man of whom ye s.
16 : 17. th. shall s. wi. new tongues
Lu. 1 : 19. I am sent to s. unto thee
20. not able to s. until these be
22. when came out he could not s.
4 : 41. he suffered them not to s.
6 : 26. Woe, when all s. well of you
7 : 15. he that was dead began to s.
24. began to s. unto people, 20 : 9.
11 : 53. provoke him to s. of many
12 : 10. whoso. sh. s. word ag. Son
Jn. 1 : 37.two disci. heard him s.,40.
3 : 11.verily, We s. that we do know
9 : 21. is of age, ask him, he shall s.
12 : 49. Fa. gave com-t wh. I sho. s.
16 : 13. shall not s. of himself;
whatso. hear that sh. he s.⌈erbs
25. sh. no more s. to you in prov-
Ac. 2 :7.are not these wh. s. Galil-s?
11.we hear them s.in our tongues,
4. 6.–10 : 46. ⌈David
2 : 29. let me s. to you of patriarch
4 : 17. they s. to no man in this na.
18. com-ded them not to s., 5 : 40.
20.can-thut s.things we have seen
18 : 26. Ph. 1 : 14. 1 Th. 2 : 2.
29. with all boldness s. thy word,
6 : 11. have heard him s. blasphe-s
13. ceaseth not to s. blasphemous
10 : 32. cometh shall s. unto thee
11 : 15. I began to s. Holy Gh. fell
14 : 9. The same heard Paul s.
21 :37.Who said, Canst thou s. G-k
39. I beseech suffer me s. to peo.
23 : 5. Thou sh. not s. evil of ruler
24 : 10. gov-r beckoned him to s.
26 :1.Paul, thou art permitted to s.
25. I s.words of truth and sobern.
28 : 20. have I called to s. with you
Ro 15 : 18. I will not dare to s. of
1 Co. 1 : 10. ye all s. same thing
2 : 6. Howbeit we s. wisdom, 7, 13.
3 : 1. not s. unto you as to spiritual
12 : 30. do all s. with tongues?
14 : 9. for ye shall s. into the air
23. If theref. all s. wi. tongues,27.
28. let him s. to hims. and to God
29. Let prophets s. two or three
35. shame for wom. to s. in ch.,34.
39. forbid not to s. with tongues
2 Co. 2 : 17. in sight of God s. we in
4 : 13. we believe and therefore s.
12 : 19. we s. before God in Christ
Ep. 5 : 12. shame to s. of those thi-s
Ph. 1 : 14. much more bold to s.
Col. 4 : 3. utterance to s. mystery
4. make manifest, as I ought to s.
1 Th. 1 : 8. so that we need not s.
2 : 4. we s. not as pleasing men
16. Forbidding us to s. to Gentiles
1 Ti. 5 : 14.occasion to s. reproachf-y
Tit. 3 : 2. mind, to s. evil of no man
He. 2 : 5. world to come, wh-f we s.
6 : 9. But, beloved, tho. we thus s.
9 : 5. of wh. we cannot s. particu-ly
Ja. 1 : 19. let every man be slow to s.
1 Pe. 2 : 12. they s. ag. you as evil
3 : 10. his lips that they s. no guile
16 s. evil of you as of evil doers
4 : 11. If s., let him s. as oracles
2 Pe. 2 : 10. they are not afraid to s.
12. s. evil of things that they⌊evil
18. they s. great swelling words of
1 Jn. 4 : 5. of world, s. they of world
2 Jn. 12. s. face to face. 3 Jn. 14.
Jude 8. dreamers s. evil of dignities
10. s. evil of things they know not
Re. 2 : 24. depths of Satan as they s.
13 : 15. that image of beast sho. s.

SPEAK. [Imperative.]

Ge. 24 : 33 told errand. He said, s. on
Ex. 11 : 2. s. in ears of people
12 : 3. s. unto cong-n of Isr., Le. 19 : 2.
14 2. s. unto children of Israel,
15.–16 : 12.–25 : 2.–31 : 13. Le.
1 : 2.–4 : 2.–7 : 23, 29.–11 : 2.–12 :
2.–15 : 2.–17 : 2.–18 : 2.–19 : 2.–
23 : 2, 10, 24, 34.–25 : 2.–27 : 2.
Nu. 5 : 6, 12.–6 : 2.–9 : 10.–15 :
2, 18, 38.–17 : 2.–19 : 2.–33 : 51.–
35 : 10. Jos. 20 : 2.
20 : 19. s. thou with us, we will hear
Nu. 16 : 24. s. unto the congregation
37. s. unto Eleazar son of Aaron
18 : 26. Thus s. unto the Levites
20 : 8. s. unto rock before their eyes
De. 3 : 26. L. said, s. no more of this
5 : 27. s. unto us all Lord shall s.
9 : 4. s. not thou in thine heart
Ju. 5 : 10. s. ye that ride on asses
9 : 2. s. ye in ears of men of Shech.
19 : 30. take advice, s. your minds
1 S. 3 : 9. s., L., thy serv-t heareth, 10.
2 S. 18 : 13. s. unto king, 1 K. 2 : 17.
14 : 3. come to king and s.
17 : 6. do after his saying? if not, s.
19 : 7. s. comfortably unto servants
11. s. unto elders of Judah, Why
1 K. 12 : 23. s. to Rehobo., 2 Ch. 11 : 3.
22 : 13. s. that is good, 2 Ch. 18. 12.
2 K. 18 : 19. s. ye now to Hezekiah
26. s. in Syrian language. Is 36 : 11.
Es. 5 : 14. to morrow s. thou to king
Jb. 12 : 8. Or s. to earth, it sh. teach
33 : 32. s., I desire to justify thee
34 : 33. therof. s. wh. thou knowest
Ps. 75 : 5. s. not with a stiff neck
Pr. 23 : 9. s. not in the ears of fool
Is. 8 : 10. s. word, it shall not stand
30 : 10. who say, s. smooth things
36 : 11. s. not in the Jews' language
40 : 2. s. ye comfortably to Jerus.
Je. 1 : 17. s. unto th. all I command
9 : 22. s., Even carcasses shall fall
11 : 2. s. unto the men of Judah
22 : 1. Go to ho. of Jud., s. this word
26 : 2. s. unto all cities of Judah all
words I command thee to s., 8.
34 : 2. Go, s. to Zedekiah, king
35 : 2. Go unto Rechabites and s.
39 : 16. Go s. to Ebed-melech⌈38 : 2.
Eze. 3 : 11. unto chil. of thy peo. s.,
11 : 5. Spirit of L. said unto me, s.
14 : 4. s. unto elders of Israel, 20 : 3.
29 : 3. s., I am ag. thee, Pharaoh
39 : 17. s. to every feathered fowl
Hag. 2 : 2. s. now to Zerubbabel, 21.
Zch. 2 : 4. Run, s. to this young man
6 : 12. s. unto Joshua, Behold the
7 : 5. s. unto all the people of the la.
8 : 16. s. ev. man truth, Ep. 4 : 25.
Mat. 8 : 8. s. word, my servant be
10 : 27. What I tell in darkness s. ye
Mk. 13 : 11. given in that hour, s. ye
Lu. 12 : 13. s. to bro. that he divide
Ac. 5 : 20. Go, s. in the temple
18 : 9. Be not afraid, but s., hold
Tit. 2 : 1. s. things become sound doc.
15. these things s. and exhort
Ja. 2 : 12. so s., as they th. shall be
4 : 11. s. not evil one of another

See AARON with sons.
See HOUSE of Israel.
See PHARAOH.

I SPEAK.

Ex. 19 : 9. peo. may hear when I s.
23 : 22. if thou shalt do all that I s.
Nu. 22 : 35. I sho. s. unto thee that
38. G. putteth in mouth th. sh. I s.
De. 5 : 1. hear judgments which I s.
11 : 2. I s. not with your chil. who
31 : 28. that I may s. these words
2 S. 20 : 16. Come near that I may s.
1 K. 22 : 14. what Lord saith, will I s.
Jb. 9 : 19. If I s. of strength, lo, he
35. Then wo. I s. and not fear him
13 : 3. Surely I would s. to Almighty
13. let me alone, that I may s.

16 : 4. I could s. as ye do, I could
6. Though I s., my grief is not
21 : 3. Suffer me that I may s.
37 : 20. Shall it be told him th. I s.?
Ps. 40 : 5. I would declare and s.
45 : 1. I s. of things wh. I have made
77 : 4. I am so troubled I cannot s.
120 : 7. when I s. they are for war
Is. 45 : 19. I, the L., s. righteousness
63 : 1. I that s. in righteousness
Je. 1 : 6. L., I cannot s., I am a child
6 : 10. To wh. sh. I s., give warn-g?
18 : 7. I sh. s. concerning nation, 9.
28 : 7. hear word I s. in thine ears
38 : 20. obey voice of Lord wh. I s.
Eze. 3 : 10. words I shall s. receive
27. when I s. with thee I will [I s.
Da. 10 : 11. O Dan., underst. words
Mat. 13 : 13. Theref. s. I in parables
Jn. 4 : 26. Jes. saith, I that s. am he
6 : 63. words that I s. they are spirit
7 : 17. of G., or wheth. I s. of mys.
8 : 26. I s. to world things I heard
28. as my Father taught me I s.
38. I s. that which I have seen
12 : 49. gave com-t what I should s.
50. wh. I s., as Father said, so I s.
13 : 18. I s. not of all, I know whom
14 : 10. words I s. I s. not of myself
16 : 25. I sh. no more s. in proverbs
17 : 13. these things I s. in world
Ac. 21 : 37. May I s. unto thee?
26 : 26. king before whom I s. freely
Ro. 3 : 5. Is G. unrighteous? I s. as
6 : 19. I s. aft. manner of, Ga. 3 : 15.
7 : 1. I s. to them that know the law
11 : 13. I s. to you Gentiles
1 Co. 6 : 5. I s. to your shame, 15:34.
7 : 6. I s. this by permission, not
12. to the rest s. I, not the Lord
35. this I s. for your own profit
10 : 15. I s. as to wise men, judge
13 : 1. Tho. I s. with tongues of men
14 : 6. exc. I s. to you by revelation
18. I s. wi. tongues more than you
19. I had rather s. five words with
2 Co. 6 : 13. I s. as unto my children
7 : 3. I s. not this to condemn you
8 : 8. I s. not by command-t but by
11 : 17. that wh. I s. I s. not aft. Lord
21. I s. as concern-g reproach, I s.
23. ministers? I s. as a fool, I am
Ep. 5 : 32. I s. concern-g Christ and
6 : 20. I may s. boldly, as I ought to
Ph. 4 : 11. not that I s. of want [s.
1 Ti. 2 : 7. I s. the truth in Christ

I will SPEAK. [32.

Ge. 18 : 30. not L. be angry, I w. s.,
Nu. 12 : 6. I w. s. unto him in dream
8. With him w. I s. mouth to mou.
24 : 13. what Lord saith, that w. I
s., 1 K. 22: 14. 2 Ch. 18:13 [w. s.
De. 5 : 31. stand thou here and I
32 : 1. Give ear, O heavens, I w. s.
Ju. 6 : 39. Gideon said, I w. s. once
2 S. 14 : 15. handmaid said, I w. s.
1 K. 2 : 18. I w. s. for thee unto king
Jb. 7 : 11. I w. s. in anguish of spirit
10 : 1. I w. s. in bitterness of soul
32 : 20. I w. s. that I be refreshed
33 : 31. hold thy peace, I w. s.
42 : 4. Hear, I beseech, and I w. s.
Ps. 50 : 7. Hear, O people, I w. s.
73 : 15. If say I w. s. thus, I should
119 : 46. I w. s. of thy testimonies
145 : 5. I w. s. of honour of thy
Pr. 8 : 6. I w. s. of excellent things
Je. 5 : 5. unto great men, and I w. s.
Eze. 2 : 1. stand, I w. s. to thee
12 : 25. I w. s., and word I s. shall
Ho. 2 : 14. I w. s. comfortably to her
1 Co. 14 : 21. with other lips w. I s.

SPEAKER.

Ps. 140 : 11. Let not evil s. be estab-d
Ac. 14 : 12. bec. he was the chief s.

SPEAKEST.

1 S. 9 : 21. wheref. s. thou so to me?
2 S. 19 : 29. Why s. of thy matters?
2 K. 6 : 12. words thou s. in bedcham.
Jb. 2 : 10. s. as one of foolish women
Ps. 50 : 20. sittest and s. ag. thy bro.
51 : 4. be justified when thou s.
Is. 40 : 27. Why s. thou, O Israel
Je. 40 : 16. thou s. falsely of Ishmael
43 : 2. s. falsely, the L. not sent thee
Eze. 3 : 18. givest not warning, nor s.
Zch. 13 : 3. thou s. lies in name of L.
Mat. 13 : 10. Why s. thou in parables?
Lu. 12 : 41. s. this parable unto us?
Jn. 16 : 29. s. plainly, s. no proverb
19 : 10. Pilate saith, s. not unto me?
Ac. 17 : 19. know this wh-of thou s.?

SPEAKETH.

Ge. 45 : 12. it is my mouth that s.
Ex. 33 : 11. Mos. as man s. to friend
Nu. 23 : 26. All th. Lord s. must I do
De. 18 : 22. When prophet s. in name
1 S. 20 : † 4. Whatso. thy soul s., I
1 K. 20 : 5. Thus s. Benhadad [will
Jb. 17 : 5. s. flattery to his friends
33 : 14. For God s. once, yea, twice
Ps. 12 : 3. cut off tongue s. proud
15 : 2. that s. truth in his heart
37 : 30. mouth of righteous s. wisd.
41 : 6. come to see me, he s. vanity
144 : 8. Whose mouth s. vanity, 11.
Pr. 2 : 12. man that s. froward thi-s
6 : 13. he s. with his feet, teacheth
19. a false witness that s. lies and
10 : 32. the wicked s. frowardness
12 : 17. s. truth, shew-h righteousn.
18. that s. like piercings of sword
14 : 25. a deceitful witness s. lies
16 : 13. they love him that s. right
19 : 5. that s. lies shall not escape
9. he that s. lies shall perish
21 : 28. man that heareth, s. const-y
26 : 25. When he s. fair, believe not
Is. 9 : 17. and every mouth s. folly
32 : 7. even when the needy s. right
33 : 15. s. uprightly sh. dwell on high
Je. 9 : 8. s. deceit; one s. peaceably
10 : 1. Hear word which L. s. unto
Eze. 10 : 5. as voice of G. when he s.
Am. 5 : 10. abhor him th. s. uprightly
Mat. 10 : 20. Spirit of Fa. which s. in
12 : 32. whoso. s. word ag. Son of
man; whoso. s. ag. Holy Ghost
34. abundance of heart mouth s.,
Lu. 6 : 45. [phemies
Lu. 5 : 21. Who is this which s. blas-
Jn. 3 : 31. he of the earth s. of earth
34. wh. God sent, s. words of God
7 : 18. s. of hims. seek-h own glory
26. he s. boldly they say nothing
8 : 44. When he s. a lie, s. of his own
19 : 12. maketh hims. k., s. ag. Ce.
Ac. 2 : 25. David s. concerning him
8 : 34. of whom s. the prophet this?
Ro. 10 : 6. righteousness of faith s.
1 Co. 14 : 2. th. s. in unknown tongue;
in spirit he s. mysteries
3. prophesieth s. to edification
4. s. in unknown tongue edifieth
5. greater th. prophesi-h, than th.
11. be to him that s. barbarian [s.
13. that s. in unknown tongue
1 Ti. 4 : 1. Spirit s. expressly, that in
He. 11 : 4. by it, he being dead, yet s.
12 : 5. exhortation which s. unto
24. s. better thi-s than th. of Abel
25. See ye refuse not him that s.,
if we turn fr. him s. fr. heaven
Ja. 4 : 11. He that s. evil of his bro.,
s. evil of the law [words
Jude 16. mouth s. great swelling

See **LORD of hosts.**
See **LORD God of Israel.**

SPEAKING. [Part.] [on

Ex. 34 : 33. s. with them he put vail
Nu. 7 : 89. s. from off mercy seat
De. 5 : 26. God s. out of the fire
11 : 19. s. of them when sittest in
2 Ch. 36 : 12. s. from mouth of Lord
Es. 10 : 3. s. peace to all his seed [18.
Jb. 1 : 16. while s. still ano. came, 17,
58 : 3. astray soon as born, s. lies
Is. 58 : 13. nor s. own words on holy
65 : 24. while they are s. I will hear
Je. 7 : 13. rising up early and s., 25:
3.—35 : 14. [these words
26 : 7. people heard Jeremiah s.
Eze. 43 : 6. I heard him s. unto me [5.
Da. 7 : 8. mouth s. gr. things, Re. 13:
8 : 13. I heard one saint s., ano. said
18. as he was s. I was in sleep [21.
9 : 20. while I was s., praying, and,
Ac. 1 : 3. s. of things pertaining to
7 : 44. s. unto Mo. that he make it
13 : 43. Paul and Barn. s. unto th.
14 : 3. they abode, s. boldly in Lord
20 : 30. s. perverse things, to draw
26 : 14. heard voice s. unto me
1 Co. 12 : 3. no man s. by Spirit calleth Jesus accursed [what profit
14 : 6. if I come s. with tongues
2 Co. 13 : 3. seek a proof of Ch. s. in
Ep. 4 : 15. s. the truth in love may
5 : 19. s. to yours. in psalms, hymns
1 Ti. 4 : 2. depart from faith, s. lies
5 : 13. busybodies s. things ought n.
1 P. 4 : 4. excess of riot, s. evil of you
2 Pe. 2 : 16. dumb ass s. with man's
3 : 16. As in all epistles s. of these

SPEAKING, S. [Noun.]

Ge. 24 : 15. before he had done s., 45.
Ru. 1 : 18. Naomi left s. unto her
Jb. 4 : 2. who can withhold from s.?
32 : 15. were amazed; th. left off s.
Ps. 34 : 13. keep lips from s. guile
Is. 58 : 9. if thou take away the yoke,
the s. vanity [s. oppression
59 : 13. In lying ag. the Lord and
Je. 38 : 4. he weakeneth the hands
of the people in s. such words
27. So they left off s. with him [s.
Mat. 6 : 7. think sh. be heard for much
Lu. 5 : 4. left s., he said unto Simon
Ep. 4 : 31. let all evil s. be put away
1 Pe. 2 : 1. lay-g aside all guile, evil s-s

See **Made an END.**

SPEAR, S. [s., 26.

Jos. 8 : 18. L. said, Stretch out thy
1 S. 17 : 7. staff of his s. was like
a weaver's beam; his s.'s head
weighed, 2 S. 21 : 19. 1 Ch. 20:5.
22 : 6. Saul, having his s. in hand
26 : 7. Saul's s. stuck at bolster, 11.
8. let me smite him with the s.
16. see where king's s. is, 12, 22.
2 S. 1 : 6. Saul leaned upon his s.
2 : 23. Abner with s. smote Asahel
21 : 16. s. weighed 300 shek-s of bra.
23 : 7. must be fenced wi. staff of s.
8. he lifted up his s. against 800
18. Abishai lifted s. ag. 300 and
slew them, 1 Ch. 11 : 11, 20.
21. slew Egyp-n wi. s., 1 Ch. 11:23.
2 Ch. 14 : 8. men th. bare 300,000 s.
Ne. 4 : 21. half held s-s fr. morning
Jb. 41 : 7. Canst fill his head wi. fish s-s
26. s. of him that layeth at him
29. leviathan laugheth at the s.
Ps. 35 : 3. Draw out the s., stop the
46 : 9. breaketh bow and cutteth s.
57 : 4. whose teeth are s-s [4 : 3.
Is. 2 : 4. s-s into pruninghooks, Mi.
Je. 6 : 23. sh. lay hold on bow and s.
46 : 4. furbish the s-s, put [on s-s
Jo. 3 : 10. beat your pruninghooks
Ha. 3 : 11. at shining of glittering s.
Jn. 19 : 34. soldier with s. pierced
See **SHIELD, S, with spear, s.**
See **SWORD, S, with spear, s.**

SPEARMEN.

Ps. 68 : 30. Rebuke company of s.
Ac. 23 : 23. Make ready two hundred [s.

SPECIAL.

De. 7 : 6. L. chosen thee to be a s. peo.
Mal. 3 : † 17. I make up my s. treas.
Ac. 19 : 11. s. miracles done by Paul

SPECIALLY. [Lord
De. 4 : 10. s. day thou stoodest bef.
Ac. 25 : 26. s. bef. thee, O k. Agrippa
1 Ti. 4 : 10. Saviour of all, s. of those
5 : 8. s. for those of his own house
Tit. 1 : 10. deceivers s. of circumc-n
Phm. 16. a brother beloved s. to me
See ESPECIALLY.

SPECKLED. [35, 39.
Ge. 30 : 32. removing s. cattle, 33,
31 : 8. The s. shall be thy wages;
cattle bare s., 10, 12. [as s. bird
Je. 12 : 9. Mine heritage is unto me
Zch. 1 : 8. red horses, s. and white

SPECTACLE. [world
1 Co. 4 : 9. we are made a s. unto the

SPED.
Jn. 5 : 30. Have they not s. ? have

SPEECH.
Ge. 4 : 23. ye wives, hearken to my s.
11 : 1. the whole earth was of one s.
7. may not underst. one ano.'s s.
Ex. 4 : 10. Mos. said, I am slow of s.
De. 22 : 14. occas-s of s. ag. her, 17.
32 : 2. my s. shall distil as dew [s.
1 S. 16 : † 18. son of Jesse, prudent in
2 S. 14 : 20. To fetch about form of s.
19 : 11. s. of all Isr. is come to king
1 K. 3 : 10. Sol.'s s. pleased the Lord
2 Ch. 32 : 18. cried in Jews' s. [dod
Ne. 13 : 24. spake half in s. of Ash-
Jb. 12 : 20. He removeth s. of trusty
13 : 17. Hear diligently my s., 21 :
2. Ps. 17 : 6. Is. 28 : 23.
15 : † 4. restrainest s. before God
24 : 25. make my s. nothing worth ?
29 : 22. my s. dropped upon them
37 : 19. we cannot order our s. by
Ps. 19 : 2. Day unto day uttereth s.
3. there is no s. where voice is not
64 : † 5. encourage thems. in evil s.
Pr. 1 : † 6. understand eloquent s.
7 : 21. With her fair s. she caused
17 : 7. Excellent s. becometh not a
Can. 4 : 3. lips like scarlet, s. comely
Is. 3 : † 3. take away skilful of s.
14 : † 4. take up taunting s. ag. k.
26 : † 16. have poured out secret s.
29 : 4. thy s. sh. be low out of dust;
thy s. shall whisper out of dust
32 : 9. ye dau-s give ear unto my s.
33 : 19. deeper s. than canst perceive
Je. 31 : 23. shall use this s. in Judah
Eze. 1 : 24. voice of s. as noise of host
3 : 5. not sent to peo. of strange s., 6.
Ha. 3 : 2. O L., I have heard thy s.
Mat. 26 : 73. thy s. bewrayeth thee
Mk. 7 : 32. had impediment in his s.
14 : 70. art Galilean, thy s. agreeth
Jn. 8 : 43. Why not understand my s.?
Ac. 14 : 11. saying in s. of Lycaonia
20 : 7. continued s. until midnight
1 Co. 1 : † 17. not with wisdom of s.
2 : 1. I came not with excell-y of s.
4. s. was not with enticing words
4 : 19. will know, not s., but power
2 Co. 3 : 12. we use great plainness of
7 : 4. Great is my boldness of s. [s.
10 : 10. weak, his s. is contemptible
11 : 6. though I be rude in s., yet
Col. 4 : 6. Let s. be always wi. grace
Tit. 2 : 8. Sound s. that cannot be

SPEECHES.
Nu. 12 : 8. will speak not in dark s.
Jb. 6 : 26. s. of one that is desperate
15 : 3. with s. he can do no good ?
32 : 14. nei. will I answer with s.
† 15. they removed s. from thems.
33 : 1. Job, I pray thee, hear my s.
Ro. 16 : 18. by fair s. deceive hearts
Jude 15. convince them of hard s.

SPEECHLESS. [was s.
Mat. 22 : 12. not wedding garm., he
Lu. 1 : 22. Zacharias remained s.
Ac. 9 : 7. men wh. journeyed stood s.

SPEED.
Ge. 24 : 12. O Lord, send me good s.
1 K. 12 : 18. Rehoboam made s., 2
Ch. 10 : 18. [s.
Ezr. 6 : 12. decree, let it be done with
Is. 5 : 26. they shall come with s.
8 : † 1. conc. making s. to the spoil
Ac. 17 : 15. to come to him wi. all s.
2 Jn. 10. receive not, nor bid God s.
11. biddeth him God s. is partaker
See MAKE speed.

SPEEDILY. [sack
Ge. 44 : 11. s. took every man his
1 S. 27 : 1. I sho. s. escape to Philis.
2 S. 17 : 16. lodge not in plains, s. pass
2 Ch. 35 : 13. offer-gs divided they s.
Ezr. 6 : 13. as k. sent, so they did s.
7 : 17. mayest buy s. wi. this money
21. whatso. Ezra require, it be done
26. let judgment be executed s. [s.
Es. 2 : 9. he s. gave her things for
Ps. 31 : 2. O Lord, deliver me s. [7.
69 : 17. in trouble hear me s., 143 :
79 : 8. let mercies s. prevent us
102 : 2. in day I call, answer me s.
Ec. 8 : 11. sentence not executed s.
Is. 58 : 8. health shall spring forth s.
Jo. 3 : 4. recomp. me, s. will I return
Zch. 8 : 21. Let us go s. and pray
Lu. 18 : 8. he will avenge them s.

SPEEDY.
Zph. 1 : 18. shall make a s. riddance

SPELT.
Is. 28 : † 25. doth he not cast in the s.
Eze. 4 : † 9. Take unto thee barley

SPEND. [and s.
De. 32 : 23. I will s. mine arrows
Jb. 21 : 13. th. s. their days in wealth
36 : 11. s. their days in prosperity
Ps. 90 : 9. we s. our yrs. as a tale [bread
Is. 55 : 2. Whf. s. money for that not
Ac. 20 : 16. would not s. time in Asia
2 Co. 12 : 15. I will very gladly s.

SPENDEST, ETH.
Pr. 21 : 20. but a foolish man s-h it
29 : 3. with harlots, s-h substance
Ec. 6 : 12. life, wh. he s-h as shadow
Lu. 10 : 35. whatso. thou s-t more, I

SPENT.
Ge. 21 : 15. water was s. in bottle
47 : 18. not hide th. our money is s.
Le. 26 : 20. strength shall be s. in
Ju. 19 : 11. by Jebus, day was far s.
1 S. 9 : 7. bread is s. in our vessels
Jb. 7 : 6. my days s. without hope
17 : † 1. My spirit is s., my days are
Ps. 31 : 10. my life is s. with grief
Is. 49 : 4. s. my strength for nought
Je. 37 : 21. all bread in city was s.
Mk. 5 : 26. s. all th. she had, Lu. 8 : 43.
6 : 35. day was far s., Lu. 24 : 29. [all
Lu. 15 : 14. when younger son had s.
Ac. 17 : 21. s. time to tell some new
27 : 9. much time was s., 18 : 23.
Ro. 13 : 12. night is far s., the day
2 Co. 12 : 15. I will gladly be s. for

SPEW, ED.
Le. 18 : 28. That land s. not you out
as it s-d out nations, 20 : 22.
Je. 25 : 27. drink, s., and rise no more
Re. 3 : 16. I will s. thee out of my

SPEWING. [mouth
Ha. 2 : 16. shameful s. on thy glory

SPHERES.
Am. 9 : † 6. It is he that buildeth s.

SPICE. [Noun.]
Ex. 35 : 28. rulers bro-t s. for light
Can. 5 : 1. gathered my myrrh with s.

SPICE merchants.
1 K. 10 : 15. of the traffick of s.-m.

SPICES. [s.
Ge. 43 : 11. carry present, balm and
Ex. 25 : 6. s. for anointing oil, 35 : 8.
30 : † 7. Aaron shall burn inc. of s.
34. Moses, Take unto thee sweet s.,
37 : 29. made pure inc. of sweet s. [23.
39 : † 38. bro-t incense of sweet s.
1 K. 10 : 2. she came with camels that
bare s., 10. 2 Ch. 9 : 1.
1 K. 10 : 25. they brought to Solomon
s., 2 Ch. 9 : 24. [s., Is. 39 : 2.
2 K. 20 : 13. Hezekiah shewed them
1 Ch. 9 : 29. appointed to oversee s.
30. priests made the ointment of s.
2 Ch. 2 : † 4. burn bef. him inc. of s.
9 : 9. queen of Sheba gave s.
16 : 14. divers s. for burial of Asa
32 : 27. Heze. made treasures for s.
Can. 4 : 10. thine ointments than s.
14. myrrh and aloes, with chief s.
16. blow upon my garden, that s.
8 : 14. like hart on mountains of s.
Eze. 27 : 22. in fairs with chief of s.
Mk. 16 : 1. Mary bought sweet s.,
Lu. 24 : 1. [ointments
Lu. 23 : 56. the women prepared s.,
Jn. 19 : 40. wound it in linen with s.
See BED, S, of spices

SPICE, ED. [s-d wine
Can. 8 : 2. would cause thee to drink
Eze. 24 : 10. consume flesh and s. it

SPICERY.
Ge. 37 : 25. Ishmaelites bearing s.
2 K. 20 : † 13. shewed his s., Is. 39 : † 2.

SPIDER. [web
Jb. 8 : 14. whose trust shall be a s-'s
Pr. 30 : 28. s. taketh hold with hands
Is. 59 : 5. They weave the s-'s web

SPIED. [Hebrew
Ex. 2 : 11. he s. Egyptian smiting
Jos. 6 : 22. two men had s. country
2 K. 9 : 17. a watchman s. company
13 : 21. behold, they s. a band of
23 : 16. he s. sepulchres that were
See SPY. [Verb.]
See ESPY, ESPIED.

SPIES. [16.
Ge. 42 : 9. Joseph said, Ye are s., 14,
11. thy servants are no s., 31.
30. lord of the land took us for s.
34. then shall I know ye are no s.
Nu. 21 : 1. Israel came by way of s.
Jos. 6 : 23. the young men s. went in
Ju. 1 : 24. s. saw man come out of city
1 S. 26 : 4. David theref. sent out s.
2 S. 15 : 10. Absalom sent s. thro. Isr.
Lu. 20 : 20. they watched and sent s.
He. 11 : 31. Rahab had received s.
See SPY. [Noun.]

SPIKENARD.
Can. 1 : 12. my s. sendeth forth smell
4 : 13. fruits, camphire with s., 14.
Mk. 14 : 3. box of s. very precious,

SPILLED. [Jn. 12 : 3.
Ge. 38 : 9. Onan s. his seed on ground
Mk. 2 : 22. bottles burst, wine is s.,

SPILT. [Lu. 5 : 37.
2 S. 14 : 14. as wat. s. on the ground

SPIN. [s.
Ex. 35 : 25. women wise hearted did
Mat. 6 : 28. they toil not, neither s.,

SPINDLE. [Lu. 12 : 27.
Pr. 31 : 19 layeth her hands to the s.

SPIRIT.
Ge. 7 : † 22. in wh. breath of s. of life
26 : † 35. a bittern. of s. unto Isaac
41 : 8. Pharaoh's s. was troubled
45 : 27. s. of Jacob revived [s.
Ex. 6 : 9. heark-d not for anguish of
35 : 21. whom his s. made wil-g [30.
Nu. 5 : 14. s. of jealousy upon him,
11 : 17. will take of s. upon thee, 25.
26. s. rested upon them] [them
29. Lord would put his S. upon
14 : 24. Caleb, bec. he had another s.
27 : 18. take Joshua, in whom is s.
De. 2 : 30 L. thy God hardened his s.
Jos. 5 : 1. nei. s. in them any more
Ju. 8 : † 3. s. was abated tow. him
15 : 19. he had drunk, his s. came
1 S. 1 : 15. I am woman of sorrowful s.
30 : 12. he had eaten, his s. came
1 K. 10 : 5. was no s. in her, 2 Ch. 9 : 4.
21 : 5. said, Why is thy s. so sad ?
22 : 21. came forth a s., 2 Ch. 18 : 20.
2 K. 2 : 9. let double portion of s.

2 K. 2 : 15. s. of Elijah doth rest on
1 Ch. 5 : 26. L. stirred up s. of Pul
12 : 18. the s. came upon Amasai
28 : 12. pattern of all he had by S.
2 Ch. 21 : 16. ag. Jehoram s. of Phil.
36 : 22. L. stirred s. of Cyrus, Ezr. 1:
Ezr. 1 : 5. whose s. God raised ⌊1.
Ne. 9 : 20. gavest good S. to instruct
30. testifiedst against th. by thy S.
Jb. 4 : 15. a s. passed before my face
15 : 13. thou turnest thy s. ag. God
17 : † 1. My s. is spent, days extinct
20 : 3. s. of underst-g causeth me to
26 : 4. whose s. came from thee?
13. By his S. he garnished heavens
32 : 8. is a s. in man, inspiration of
18. the s. within me constraineth
34 : 14. If he gather s. and breath
Ps. 32 : 2. in whose s. is no guile
51 : 10. renew a right s. within me
12. uphold me with thy free S.
76 : 12. He sh. cut off s. of princes
78 : 8. whose s. was not stedfast
104 : 30. Thou sendest forth thy S.
106 : 33. they provoked his s., so
139 : 7. Whither sh. I go fr. thy S.?
143 : 10. Thy S. is good, lead me
Pr. 11 : 13. he of faithf. s. concealeth
14 : 29. he that is hasty of s.
15 : 4. perverseness is breach in s.
16 : 18. haughty s. goeth bef. a fall
32. that ruleth s. better than he
18 : 14. s. of man sustain infirmity; but wounded s. who can bear?
20 : 27. s. of a man is candle of Lord
25 : 28. hath no rule ov. his s. ⌈in s.
29 : 23. honour sh. uphold humble
Ec. 3 : 21. Who knoweth the s. of man, s. of beast ⌈proud in s.
7 : 8. patient in s. is better than
9. Be not hasty in s. to be angry
8 : 8. no man hath power over s. to retain the s. ⌈against thee
10 : 4. If the s. of the ruler rise
11 : 5. knowest not the way of s.
12 : 7. the s. sh. return unto God
Is. 4 : 4. purged Jerus. by s. of burn.
11 : 2. the s. of wisdom and understanding; the s. of counsel and might; s. of knowledge
19 : 3. the s. of Egypt shall fail
14. L. hath mingled a perverse s.
28 : 6. L. be for s. of judgm. to him
29 : 10. L. poured upon you s. of
24. they that erred in s. ⌊sleep
31 : 3. their horses flesh and not s.
32 : 15. until S. be poured upon us
34 : 16. his s. it hath gathered them
37 : † 7. I will put a s. into him
42 : 5. giveth s. to them that walk
48 : 16. Lord God and his S. sent me
54 : 6. as a woman grieved in s.
57 : 16. s. should fail before me ⌈18.
61 : 1. S. of L. God is upon me, Lu. 4:
3. of praise for s. of heaviness
Je. 51 : 11. Lord raised s. of king
Eze. 1 : 12. s. was to go, they went, 20.
21. s. was in the wheels, 10 : 17.
2 : 2. s. entered me when he spake, and set me upon my feet, 3 : 24.
3 : 12. Then s. took me up, 11 : 24
14. So s. lifted me up, I went in heat of my s., 8 : 3.–11 : 1. ⌈26.
11 : 19. put a new s. within you, 36:
13 : 3. Woe unto prophets that follow their own s. ⌈a new s.
18 : 31. make you a new heart and
21 : 7. every s. shall faint ⌈court
43 : 5. s. brought me into inner
Da. 2 : 1. Neb-r's s. was troubled
4 : 8. in whom is the s. of the holy gods, 9, 18.–5 : 11, 14. ⌈6 : 3.
5 : 12. excellent s. found in Daniel,
Ho. 9 : † 7. a fool, man of s. is mad
Am. 4 : † 13. lo, he that createth s.
Mi. 2 : 11. If man walking in the s.
Hag. 1 : 14. Lord stirred s. of Zerub.

Zch. 7 : 12. sent in his S. by prophets
12 : 1. formeth s. of man within him
10. pour on ho. of David s. of grace
Mal. 2 : 15. Yet had he residue of S.; take heed to y-r s., 16. ⌈Lu. 4 : 1.
Mat. 4 : 1. Jesus was led up of the S.,
5 : 3. blessed are the poor in s.
10 : 20. not ye that speak, but S. of
14 : 26. saying, it is a s., Mk. 6 : 49.
22 : 43. doth Dav. in s. call him L.?
26 : 41. the s. is willing, Mk. 14 : 38.
Mk. 1 : 10. S. descending, Jn. 1 : 32.
12. S. driveth him into wilderness
2 : 8. When Jes. perceived in his s.
8 : 12. he sighed deeply in his s.
9 : 17. my son, who hath a dumb s.
20. straightway the s. tare him
26. the s. cried and rent him
Lu. 1 : 17. shall go bef. in s. of Elias
80. child waxed strong in s., 2 : 40.
2 : 27. he came by S. into temple
4 : 14. Jes. returned in power of S.
8 : 55. her s. came again, she arose
9 : 39. a s. taketh him, he crieth
55. know not what s. ye are of
10 : 21. that hour Jes. rejoiced in s.
13 : 11. a woman had s. of infirmity
24 : 37. supposed they had seen a s.
39. a s. hath not flesh and bones
Jn. 1 : 33. on wh. see S. descend-g, 32.
3 : 34. giveth not S. by measure
4 : 23. worship the Father in s.
24. God is a S., worship him in s.
6 : 63. It is the S. that quickeneth; words that I speak they are s.
7 : 39. But this spake he of the S.
11 : 33. Jesus groaned in the s. and
13 : 21. he was troubled in s. and
Ac. 2 : 4. spake as S. gave utterance
6 : 10. not able to resist wisd. and s.
8 : 29. S. said unto Philip, Go near
10 : 19. S. said unto Peter, 11 : 12.
11 : 28. Agabus signified by the S
16 : 7. assayed, but S. suffered not
16. a damsel with s. of divination
18. Paul turned and said to the s.
17 : 16. his s. was stirred when he
18 : 5. Paul was pressed in the s.
25. This man being fervent in s.
20 : 22. I go bound in the s., 19 : 21.
21 : 4. disciples said to Saul thro. S.
23 : 8. Sadducees say there is no s.
9. if a s. or angel hath spoken
Ro. 1 : 4. Son of God acc-g to the S.
2 : 29. circumcision is of heart in s.
7 : 6. we sho. serve in newness of s.
8 : 1. walk not after flesh, but S., 4.
2, law of the S. of life hath made
5. after the S., the things of the S.
9. ye are not in the flesh, but S., if so be the S. of God dwell in you. Now if any man have not S. of C.
10. S. is life bec. of righteousness
11. if S. of him that raised up Jes. quicken your bodies by S.
13. if ye through S. mortify deeds
15. ye have not rec-d s. of bondage, but ye have rec-d S. of adop.
16. S. beareth witness with our s.
23. ourselves have firstfruits of S.
26. S. also helpeth our infirmities; but S. maketh intercession
27. know-h what is mind of the S.
11 : 8. God hath given s. of slumber
12 : 11. fervent in s., serving the L.
15 : 30. I beseech for love of the S.
1 Co. 2 : 4. but in demonstration of S.
10. G. hath revealed them by his S., for the S. searcheth all things
11. save s. of a man wh. is in him
12. not s. of world, but S. of God
4 : 21. sh. I come in s. of meekness?
5 : 3. absent in body, present in s.
5. s. may be saved in day of L. Jes.
6 : 17. he joined unto Lord is one s.
20. glorify G. in your body and s.
7 : 34. she be holy in body and s.

1 Co. 12 : 4. but same S., 8, 9, 11.
7. the S. is given to every man to
8. given by the S. word of wisdom
13. by one S. are we all baptized, made to drink into one S. ⌈ies
14 : 2. in the s. he speaketh myster-
15. I will pray with the s., I will sing with the s. ⌈with the s.
16. Else, when thou shalt bless
15 : 45. last Adam a quickening s.
2 Co. 3 : 6. but of the s.: the letter killeth, but s. giveth life
8. how shall not ministration of s.
17. L. is that S.: where S. of Lord
4 : 13. We having same s. of faith
7 : 1. fr. all filthiness of flesh and s.
13. his s. was refreshed by you
11 : 4. ano. s. wh. ye have not rec-d
12 : 18. walked we not in same s.
Ga. 3 : 2. Received ye the S. by works
3. foolish? having begun in the S.
5. He th. ministereth to you the S.
14. might receive promise of S.
4 : 6. God sent forth S. of his Son
5 : 5. For we thro. S. wait for hope
16. This I say then, Walk in the S.
17. flesh lusteth ag. S., and S. ag.
18. But if ye be led of the S. ⌊flesh
22. fruit of S. is love, joy, peace
25. If we live in the S., walk in S.
6 : 8. soweth to S., shall of S. reap
18. grace be wi. your s., Phm. 25.
Ep. 2 : 2. s. that worketh in children
18. we have access by one S. to Fa.
22. habitation of God thro. the S.
3 : 5. revealed unto apostles by S.
16. strengthened wi. might by S.
4 : 3. to keep unity of the S. in
4. There is one body, and one S.
23. renewed in s. of your mind
5 : 9. fruit of S. is in all goodness
18. be not drunk, but filled with S.
6 : 17. take sword of S., wh. is word
18. Praying with all prayer in S.
Ph. 1 : 19. supply of S. of Jesus Ch.
27. that ye stand fast in one s.
2 : 1. if be any fellowship of the S.
3 : 3. which worship God in the s.
Col. 1 : 8, declared y-r love in the S.
2 : 5. tho. absent, yet am I wi. you
1 Th. 5 : 19. Quench not the S. ⌊in s.
23. pray God your s. and body be
2 Th. 2 : 2. troubled, nei. by s. nor
8. L. sh. consume with s. of mouth
13. chosen you thro. sancti-n of S.
1 Ti. 3 : 16. G. manifest, justified in S.
4 : 1. Now the S. speaketh expressly
12. be an example in s., in faith
2 Ti. 1 : 7. God not given us s. of fear
4 : 22. Lord Jesus Ch. be with thy s.
He. 4 : 12. to dividing of soul and s.
9 : 14. thro. eternal S. offered hims.
10 : 29. done despite to S. of grace
Ja. 2 : 26. body with-t the s. is dead
4 : 5. The s. in us lusteth to envy
1 Pe. 1 : 2. thro. sanctification of S.
11. what the S. of Ch. did signify
22. in obeying truth thro. the S.
3 : 4. the ornament of a meek s. ⌈S.
18. death in flesh, quickened by
4 : 6. but live acc-g to God in the s.
14. S. of glory resteth upon you
1 Jn. 3 : 24. by S. he hath given us
4 : 1. Beloved, believe not every s.
2. Every s. that confesseth Jesus
3. every s. that confesseth not th. Jesus is come, is s. of antichrist
6. Hereby know we the s. of error
13. bec. he hath given us of his S.
5 : 6. S. beareth witness, S. is truth
8. the s., the water, and the blood
Jude 19. sensual, not having the S.
Re. 1 : 10. I was in S. on Lord's day
2 : 7. Hear wh. S. saith unto churches, 11, 17, 29.–3 : 6, 13, 22.
4 : 2. immediately I was in the S.
11 : 11. S. of life from God entered

Re. 14 : 13. Bles-d are the dead, saith S.
17 : 3. So he carried me away in the
s., 21 : 10. [of prophecy
19 : 10. testimony of Jesus is the s.
22 : 17. S. and the bride say, Come

Born of or after the SPIRIT.

Jn. 3 : 5. Except man be b.o.S. he
6. that which is b.o.S. is spirit
8. so is every one that is b.o.S.
Ga. 4 : 29. persecuted him b.a.S.
See BROKEN, CONTRITE, DUMB,
EARNEST, FOUL.
See **EVIL spirit, s.**
See **FAMILIAR spirit, s.**

SPIRIT of God.

Ge. 1 : 2. S. - moved upon face of
41 : 38. a man in whom the S. - is
Ex. 31 : 3. Basaleel with S. -, 35 : 31.
Nu. 24 : 2. the S. - came upon Balaam
1 S. 10 : 10. the S. - came upon Saul,
he prophesied, 11 : 6.-19 : 23.
19 : 20. S. - upon messengers of Saul
2 Ch. 15 : 1. S. - came upon Azariah
24 : 20. the S. - came upon Zeeba-h
Jb. 27 : 3. the S. - is in my nostrils
33 : 4. S. - hath made me, breath of
Eze. 11 : 24. in a vision by the S. -
Mat. 3 : 16. he saw S. - descending
12 : 28. if I cast out devils by S. -
Ro. 8 : 9. if so be S. - dwell in you
14 as many as are led by S. -
15 : 19. mighty signs by the S. -
1 Co. 2 : 11. knoweth no man, but S. -
14. receiveth not things of S. -
3 : 16. that the S. - dwelleth in you
6 : 11. ye are sanctified by the S. -
7 : 40. I think also that I have S. -
12 : 3. no man speaking by the S. -
2 Co. 3 : 3. epistle written with S. -
Ep. 4 : 30. And grieve not Holy S. -
1 Pe. 4 : 14. the S. - resteth upon
1 Jn. 4 : 2. Hereby know ye the S. -
See **HOLY Spirit.**
See HUMBLE [Adj.], MEEKNESS.
See **Spirit of the LORD.**

Lying SPIRIT.

1 K. 22 : 22. I will be a l.s. in mouth
of proph., 2 Ch. 18 : 21. [18 : 22.
23. L. put a l.s. in prophets, 2 Ch.

My SPIRIT.

Ge. 6 : 3. m. S. shall not alw. strive
Jb. 6 : 4. the poison drinketh m.s.
7 : 11. I speak in anguish of m.s.
10 : 12. thy visita-n preserved m.s.
17 : † 1. m.s. is spent, my days
21 : 4. why not m.s. be troubled [s.
Ps. 31 : 5. Into thine hand com-t m.
77 : 3. m.s. was overwhelmed
6. m.s. made diligent search
142 : 3. when m.s. was overwhelmed
143 : 4. is m.s. overwhelmed
7. Hear me, O Lord, m.s. faileth
Pr. 1 : 23. I will pour m.s. unto you
Is. 26 : 9. with m.s. will I seek thee
30 : 1. a covering, but not of m. S.
38 : 16. in all these is life of m.s.
42 : 1. I have put m. S. upon him
44 : 3. will pour m. S. upon thy seed
59 : 21. m. S. upon thee sh. not dep.
Eze. 3 : 14. I went in heat of m.s.
36 : 27. put m. S. within you, 37 : 14.
39 : 29. have poured m. S. upon
Da. 2 : 3. m.s. was troubled [Israel
7 : 15. I, Dan., was grieved in m.s.
Jo. 2 : 28. I will pour out m. S. upon all flesh, 29. Ac. 2 : 17, 18.
Hag. 2 : 5. so m. S. remaineth am.
Zch. 4 : 6. Not by might, but by m. S.
6 : 8. quieted m.s. in north coun-y
Mat. 12 : 18. will put m. S. upon
Lu. 1 : 47. m.s. hath rejoiced in G.
23 : 46. thy hands I commend m.s.
Ac. 7 : 59. Lord Jesus, receive m.s.
Ro. 1 : 9. whom I serve with m.s.
1 Co. 5 : 4. when gathered and m.s.
14 : 14. m.s. prayeth, my underst-g
1 Co. 16 : 18. have refreshed m.s.
2 Co. 2 : 13. I had no rest in m.s.

SPIRIT of truth. [ceive

Jn. 14 : 17. S. - wh. world cannot re-
15 : 26. S. - wh. proceedeth fr. Fath-
16 : 13. when S. - is come he will [er
1 Jn. 4 : 6. Hereby know we the S. -
See **Spirit of WISDOM.**

Unclean SPIRIT. [land

Zch. 13 : 2. cause u.s. to pass out of
Mat. 12 : 43. When the u.s. is gone
out of a man, Lu. 11 : 24.
Mk. 1 : 23. In synagogue a man with
u.s., Lu. 4 : 33.
26. when the u.s. had torn him
3 : 30. they said, He hath an u.s.
5 : 2. met him a man with an u.s.
8. Come out, thou u.s., Lu. 8 : 29.
7 : 25. whose daughter had an u.s.
Lu. 9 : 42. Jesus rebuked the u.s.
See VEXATION, WHOREDOMS.

SPIRITS. [27 : 16.

Nu. 16 : 22. O God, the God of s.,
Ps. 104 : 4. maketh angels s., He. 1 : 7.
Pr. 16 : 2. Lord weigheth the s.
Zch. 6 : 5. These are the 4 s. of heav-s
Mat. 8 : 16. he cast out s. with word
Lu. 10 : 20. rejoice not s. are subject
1 Co. 12 : 10. to ano. discerning of s.
14 : † 12. as ye are zealous of s. seek
32. s. of the proph-s are subject to
Ep. 6 : † 12. we wrestle ag. wicked s.
1 Ti. 4 : 1. giving heed to seducing s.
He. 1 : 14. Are not all ministering s.
12 : 9. in subjection unto Fa. of s.
23. to s. of just men made perfect
1 Pe. 3 : 19. preached unto s. in pris.
1 Jn. 4 : 1. try the s., whether of G.
Re. 16 : 14. they are the s. of devils
See EVIL, FAMILIAR.

Seven SPIRITS.

Mat. 12 : 45. taketh with himself s.
other s. more wicked, Lu. 11 : 26.
Re. 1 : 4. fr. s.s. bef. the throne of G.
3 : 1. he that hath the s.s. of God
4 : 5. seven lamps, are the s.s. of G.
5 : 6. seven eyes, are the s.s. of God

Unclean SPIRITS.

Mat. 10 : 1. he gave power ag. u.s.,
Mk. 6 : 7. [Lu. 4 : 36.
Mk. 1 : 27. he commandeth u. s.,
3 : 11. u.s., when saw him, fell do.
5 : 13. the u.s. entered into swine
Lu. 6 : 18. vexed with u.s., Ac. 5 : 16.
Ac. 8 : 7. for u.s. came out of many
Re. 16 : 13. I saw 3 u.s. like frogs

SPIRITUAL. [mad

Ho. 9 : 7. prophet a fool, s. man is
Ro. 1 : 11. I may impart some s. gift
7 : 14. we know that the law is s.
15 : 27. partakers of their s. things
1 Co. 2 : 13. comparing s. thi-s wi. s.
15. he that is s. judgeth all things
3 : 1. I not speak to you as unto s.
9 : 11. if sown unto you s. things
10 : 3. did all eat the same s. meat
4. same s. drink, drank of s. rock
12 : 1. now conc-g s. gifts, brethren
14 : 1. Follow charity, desire s. gifts
12. as ye are zealous of s. gifts
37. if any man think himself s.
15 : 44. raised a s. body, is a s. body
46. not first which is s., but natural; afterward th. which is s.
Ga. 6 : 1. ye wh. are s. restore such
Ep. 1 : 3. blessed us with s. blessings
5 : 19. Speak-g to yours. in s. songs
6 : 12. wrestle ag. s. wickedness
Col. 1 : 9. be filled with s. underst-g
3 : 16. admon. one ano. in s. songs
1 Pe. 2 : 5. are built s. hou. to offer s.

SPIRITUALLY. [sacrifi.

Ro. 8 : 6. to be s. minded is life
1 Co. 2 : 14. because are s. discerned
Re. 11 : 8. which s. is called Sodom

SPIT.

Le. 15 : 8. s. upon him that is clean
Nu. 12 : 14. If fa. but s. in her face
De. 25 : 9. she shall s. in his face
Jb. 30 : 10. spare not to s. in my face
Mat. 26 : 67. they did s. in his face
27 : 30. th. s. upon and smote him
Mk. 7 : 33. he s. and touched tongue
8 : 23. when he had s. on his eyes
10 : 34. they shall s. upon and kill
14 : 65. began to s. on him, 15 : 19.

SPITE.

Ps. 10 : 14. beholdest s. to requite it

SPITEFULLY.

Mat. 22 : 6. they entreated them s.
Lu. 18 : 32. he shall be s. entreated

SPITTED. [s. on

Lu. 18 : 32. spitefully entreated and

SPITTING.

Is. 50 : 6. I hid not my face from s.

SPITTLE.

1 S. 21 : 13. he let s. fall upon his beard
Jb. 7 : 19. till I swallow down my s.
30 : † 10. they withhold not s. from
Jn. 9 : 6. he made clay of s. [my face

SPOIL. [Noun.]

Ge. 49 : 27. at night he shall divide s.
Ex. 15 : 9. enemy said, I will divide s.
Nu. 31 : 9. Israel took s. of cattle, 11.
12. bro-t the prey and s. unto Mos.
53. men of war had taken s.
De. 2 : 35. s. of cities which we took,
3 : 7. Jos. 8 : 27.-11 : 14.
13 : 16. shalt gather all the s. and
20 : 14. s. thou shalt take, Jos. 8 : 2.
Ju. 5 : 30. necks of them that take s.
14 : 19. Samson slew 30 men, took s.
1 S. 14 : 30. if had eaten freely of s.
32. the people flew upon the s.
15 : 19. didst fly upon the s. and
21. people took of s. sheep and
30 : 16. great s. they had taken
19. nei. s. nor anything lacking
20. David said, This is David's s.
22. will not give them aught of s.
26. sent of s. unto elders of Judah; a present of s. of enemies
2 S. 2 : † 21. 10. men, and take his s.
8 : 12. s. of Hadadezer, k. of Zobah
3 : 22. Joab brought in a great s.
12 : 30. He brought the s. of Rab-h
2 K. 3 : 23. now theref., Moab, to s.
21 : 14. shall become a s. to enemies
1 Ch. 20 : 2. fr. Rabbah he brought
much s. [opians, 14.
2 Ch. 14 : 13. carried s. from Ethi-
15 : 11. offered unto Lord of the s.
20 : 25. Jehosh-t came to take s.,
were three days in gathering s.
24 : 23. Syrians sent s. unto king
25 : 13. smote 3,000, took much s.
28 : 8. took much s., bro-t s. to Sa.
14. So armed men left capt-s and s.
15. with s. they clothed all naked
Ezr. 9 : 7. kings been delivered to s.
Es. 3 : 13. to take s. of them, 8 : 11.
9 : 10. on s. laid they not hand
Jb. 29 : 17. I plucked s. out of teeth
Ps. 68 : 12. she at home divided s.
119 : 162. rejoice, as one find-h gr. s.
Pr. 1 : 13. sh. fill our houses with s.
16 : 19. to divide s. with the proud
31 : 11. he shall have no need of s.
Is. 3 : 14. s. of poor in your houses
8 : † 1. In making speed to the s.
4. s. of Samaria shall be taken
9 : 3. as men rejoice when divide s.
10 : 6. him charge to take the s.
33 : 4. your s. shall be gathered
23. is prey of a great s. divided
42 : 22. they are for a s. none saith
24. Who gave Jacob for a s.? did
53 : 12. he sh. divide s. with strong
Je. 2 : † 14. why is Isr. become a s.?
6 : 7. violence and s. is heard in her
15 : 13. thy treasures will I give to s.
17 : 3. I will give thy substance to s.
20 : 8. I cried violence and s.
30 : 16. that spoil thee sh. be a s.

Je. 49:32. multi. of cattle sh. be a s.
50:10. Chaldea sh. be a s. saith L.
Eze. 7:21. I give it to wicked for s.
23:†46. I will give them for a s.
25:7. deliver thee for s. to heathen
26:5. Tyrus shall become a s.
29:19. Neb-r shall take s. of Egypt
38:12. I will go up to take a s.
13. say, Art thou come to take a s.
45:9. remove violence and s.
Da. 11:24. he sh. scatter am. them s.
33. they shall fall by s. many days
Ho. 7:†13. Woe! s. unto them!
9:†6. lo, they are gone, bec. of s.
Am. 3:†10. store up s. in palaces
5:†9. strengtheneth s. ag. strong
Na. 2:9. Take s. of silver, s. of gold
Ha. 2:17. s. of beasts sh. cover thee
Zch. 2:9. they shall be a s. to serv-s
14:1. thy s. shall be divided in the

SPOILS. [ment

Jos. 7:21. I saw am. s. a goodly gar-
1 Ch. 26:27. Out of s. did th. dedicate
Is. 25:11. bring down pride with s.
Lu. 11:22. taketh armour divideth
He. 7:4. Abr. gave tenth of s. [his s.

SPOIL. [Verb.]

Ex. 3:22. ye shall s. Egyptians
1 S. 14:36. s. them until morning
2 S. 23:10. peo. returned only to s.
Ps. 44:10. they who hate us s. for
89:41. All that pass by way s. him
109:11. let stranger s. his labour
Pr. 22:23. s. soul of those that spoil.
24:15. O, s. not his resting place
Can. 2:15. Take us foxes that s. vines
Is. 11:14. they shall s. them of the
17:14. is portion of them th. s. us
33:1. cease to s. thou sh. be spoiled
Je. 5:6. wolf of evening sh. s. them
20:5. give Jerus. to them sh. s. it
30:16. that s. thee shall be a spoil
47:4. day that cometh to s., Philis.
49:28. go to Kedar, s. men of the
50:10. all that s. her shall be satis.
Eze. 14:15. s. it so th. it be desolate
16:†57. dau-s of Philis. wh. s. thee
28:†26. judgm-ts upon those th. s.
29:†19. Neb. shall s. her spoil, 38:
32:12. they shall s. pomp of Eg. [12.
39:10. shall s. those spoiled them
Ho. 10:2. sh. break altars, s. images
13:15. sh. s. treas. of all pleasant
Ha. 2:8. remnant of peo. sh. s. thee
Zph. 2:9. residue of peo. sh. s. them
Mat. 12:29. how enter strong man's house, s. his goods? Mk. 3:27.
Col. 2:8. Bew. lest any man s. you

SPOILED.

Ge. 34:27. sons of Jacob s. the city
29. they s. all was in Hamor's ho.
Ex. 12:36. they s. the Egyptians
De. 28:29. shalt be oppressed and s.
Ju. 2:14. into hand of spoilers th. s.
16. out of hand of those th. s. th.
1 S. 14:48. Israel from them that s.
17:53. they s. Philistines' tents
2 K. 7:16. Israel s. tents of Syrians
2 Ch. 14:14. Asa s. cities of Gerar
Jb. 12:17. leadeth counsellors aw. s.
19. He leadeth princes away s.
Ps. 76:5. The stouthearted are s.
Pr. 22:23. spoil soul of those th. s.
Is. 13:16. their houses shall be s.
18:2. whose land rivers have s., 7.
24:3. the land shall be utterly s.
33:1. Woe to thee that wast not s.
42:22. this is a peo. robbed and s.
Je. 2:14. Is Isr. a serv.? why is he s.?
4:13. Woe unto us, for we are s.
20. whole land is s., my tents are s.
30. when s. what wilt thou do?
9:19. voice out of Zion, How are we
10:20. My tabernacle is s. [s.
21:12. deliver him that is s., 22:3.
25:36. Lord hath s. their pasture
48:1. Nebo is s. | 15. Moab is s., 20.
Je. 49:3. Ai is s. | 10. Esau, his seed s.
51:55. Bec. Lord hath s. Babylon
Eze. 18:7. hath s. none by violence,
12. oppressed poor, hath s. [16.
18. bec. he cruelly s. his brother
23:46. I will give them to be s.
39:10. sh. spoil those that s. them
Ho. 10:14. thy fortresses shall be s.
Am. 3:11. thy palaces shall be s.
5:9. strengtheneth the s. ag. strong
Mi. 2:4. shall say, We be utterly s.
Ha. 2:8. thou hast s. many nations
Zch. 2:8. unto nations which s. you
11:2. Howl, bec. the mighty are s.
3. glory is s., pride of Jordan is s.
Col. 2:15. having s. principalities

SPOILER.

Is. 16:4. covert fr. face of s., the s.
21:2. s. spoileth, Go up, O Elam
Je. 6:26. the s. shall suddenly come
15:8. I have brought upon th. a s.
48:8. s. shall come upon every city
18. s. of Moab sh. come upon thee
32. s. is fallen upon thy fruits
51:56. bec. s. is come upon Baby-n

SPOILERS. [2 K. 17:20.

Ju. 2:14. he deliv. th. into ha. of s.,
1 S. 13:17. s. came out of camp of
14:15. garrison and s. trembled
Je. 12:12. s. are come upon hi. pla.
51:48. s. come unto her fr. north
53. fr. me shall s. come unto her

SPOILEST, ETH.

Ps. 35:10. needy from him th. s-h
Is. 21:2. spoiler s-h; Go up, Elam
33:1. Woe to thee that s-t and
Ho. 7:1. troop of robbers s-h [away
Na. 3:16. cankerworm s-h, flieth

SPOILING.

Ps. 35:12. me evil, to s. of my soul
Is. 22:4. s. of daughter of my peo.
Je. 15:†8. ag. city a young man s.
48:3. a voice fr. Horonaim, s. and
Ha. 1:3. s. and violence are bef. me
He. 10:34. took joyfully s. of your

SPOKEN. [goods

Nu. 14:28. as ye have s. so will I do
21:7. we have s. ag. Lord and thee
De. 5:28. I heard words they have s., well said all that they have s.
13:5. he hath s. to turn you fr. L.
18:17. have well s. th. they have s.
2 S. 2:27. unless had s. people had
14:19. turn fr. aught king hath s.
17:6. Ahithophel hath s. aft. this
1 K. 2:23. if Adonijah not s. this
12:9. may answer this people who have s. to me? 2 Ch. 10:9.
18:24. all the peo. said, It is well s.
22:28. If in peace L. not s. by me
2 K. 4:13. wouldest be s. for to k.?
2 Ch. 2:15. wine my lord hath s. of
36:22. word s. by Jer-h, Je. 36:1.
Jb. 33:2. tongue hath s. in my mou.
34:35. Job hath s. without knowl.
42:7. ye not s. of me as serv. Job, 8.
Ps. 66:14. hath s. when in trouble
87:3. Glorious things are s. of thee
109:2. s. ag. me with a lying tongue
Pr. 15:23. a word s. in due season
25:11. word fitly s. is like apples
Ec. 7:21. no heed unto all words s.
Can. 8:8. day when she sh. be s. for
Is. 23:4. for the sea hath s.
59:3. defiled, your lips have s. lies
Je. 26:16. s. to us in name of Lord
29:23. s. lying words in my name
33:24. Considerest not what people have s. [your mouths
44:25. Ye and wives have s. with
Eze. 13:7. have ye not s. lying div-
8. Bec. ye have s. vanity [ination
Da. 4:31. O Neb-r, to thee it is s.
Ho. 7:13. they have s. lies ag. me
10:4. s. words, swearing falsely [s.
Am. 5:14. L. be wi. you, as ye have
Ob. 12. nei. shouldest have s. proudly
Mi. 6:12. inhabitants have s. lies
Zch. 10:2. for the idols have s. vanity
Mal. 3:13. What have we s. ag. thee
Mat. 26:65. He hath s. blasphemy
Mk. 5:36. Jesus heard word was s.
14:9. be s. of for memorial of her
Lu. 2:33. marvelled at things s. of
34. for a sign which shall be s. ag.
12:3. whatso. s. in darkness, s. in
18:34. nei. knew they things s.
Ac. 3:24. many as have s. foretold
8:24. none of things s. come on me
13:40. lest that come upon you s. of
45. Jews spake ag. things s. by P.
46. word sho. first been s. to you
16:14. Lydia attended unto thi-s s.
19:36. these things cannot be s. ag.
23:9. if a spirit or angel s. to him
27:11. more than things s. by Paul
35. when had thus s. took bread
28:22. know every where it is s. ag.
24. some believed the things s.
Ro. 1:8. your faith is s. of thro-out
4:18. acc. to that s., so thy seed be
14:16. Let not your good be evil s.
15:21. To whom he was not s. of
1 Co. 10:30. why am I evil s. of
14:9. how sh. it be known wh. is s.?
2 Co. 9:†5. bounty been so much s.
He. 2:2. if the word s. by angels was
3:5. a testimony of things to be s.
4:8. would not have s. of ano. day
7:13. he of whom these thi-s are s.
8:1. of things s. this is the sum
11:†4. he being dead is yet s. of [s.
12:19. entreated word sho. not be
13:7. have s. unto you word of God
1 Pe. 4:14. on their part he is evil s.
2 Pe. 2:2. way of truth be evil s. of
3:2. ye may be mindful of words s.
Jude 15. ungodly sinners s. ag. him
17. remember words which were s.

SPOKEN. [By God or Lord.]

Ge. 18:19. upon Abr. that he hath s.
21:2. time of wh. G. had s. to Abr.
28:15. I have done which I have s.
Ex. 32:13. land I have s. of will give
34. lead people unto pla. I have s.
Nu. 23:19. s., sh. he not make it good
De. 26:19. holy people as he hath s.
1 S. 3:12. ag. Eli all things I have s.
25:30. L. hath done all he hath s.
2 K. 19:21. word L. hath s. conc-g Sennacherib, Is. 37:22. [hath s.
2 Ch. 6:10. Lord performed word he
Ps. 60:6. G. s. in his holin. 108:7.
62:11. G. hath s. once; twice have
Is. 38:15. he hath s. unto me
45:19. I have not s. in secret, 48:16.
46:11. I have s. it, will also bring
48:15. I have s., I have called him
Je. 4:28. I have s. it, will not repent
23:21. I have not s., yet they proph.
30:2. Write words I have s., 36:2.
35:17. I have s., they have not
Eze. 12:28. word I have s. shall be
13:7. L. saith, albeit I have not s.
26:5. I have s. it, saith L., 28:10.
36:5. Surely in fire of my jealousy have I s., 6.—38:19. [in old time
38:17. Art thou he of wh. I have s.
39:8. this is the day wh-of I have s.
Ho. 12:10. I have s. by the prophets
Mat. 22:31. not read th. was s. by G.
Ac. 3:21. G. hath s. by his prophets
He. 1:2. G. hath s. unto us by Son
2:3. which began to be s. by the L.

See **LORD** with spoken.

Mouth of the LORD Had SPOKEN.

Ge. 44:2. acc. to word Joseph h. s.
Nu. 23:2. Balak did as Balaam h. s.
Jos. 6:8. Joshua h. s. unto people
1 K. 13:11. words he h. s. they told
21:4. wh. Naboth, Jezreelite, h. s.
2 K. 1:17. acc. to word Elijah h. s.
7:18. it came as man of God h. s.

Ezr. 8 : 22. bec. we h.s. unto king
Ne. 2 : 18. I told k.'s words he h.s.
Es. 7 : 9. Mordecai, who h.s. for k.
Jb. 32 : 4. waited till Job h.s.
Je. 36 :4.Baruch wrote words L.h.s.
38 : 1. words Jer-h h.s. unto peo.
Da. 10 : 11. when he h.s. this word
15. h.s. words I became dumb
19. he h.s. I was strengthened
Mk. 1 : 42. he h.s. leprosy departed
12 : 12. knew he h.s. the parable against them, Lu. 20 : 19.
Lu. 19 : 28. when he h. thus s., 24 : 40. Jn. 9 : 6.-11 : 43.-18 : 1, 22.
Ac. 1 : 9.-19 : 41.-20 : 36.-26:30.
Jn. 4 : 50. believed word Jesus h.s.
11 : 13. tho-t he h.s. of taking rest
15 : 22. If I h. not s. unto them
20 : 18. that Lord h.s. these things
21 : 19. h.s. this, he saith, Follow [me
Ac. 9 : 27.that Lord h.s. to Saul
27 : 35. h. thus s. he took bread
28 : 25. departed, after Paul h.s.
He. 9 : 19. Mos. h.s. ev. prec.to peo.

I have SPOKEN. [Pha.
Ge. 41 : 28. This is thing I h.s. unto
1 S. 1 : 16. out of my grief h. I s.
20 : 23. touching mat. of wh. I h.s.
Jb. 21 : 3. aft. that I h.s., mock on
40 : 5. Once h. I s., but I will not answer [I s., 2 Co. 4 : 13.
Ps. 116 : 10. I believed, therefore h.
Je. 25 : 3. I h.s. unto you, rising early, 35 : 14. [him
Jn. 12 : 48. word I h.s. shall judge
49. I h. not s. of myself, but Fa.
14 : 25. These things h. I s., 15 : 11. -16 : 1, 25, 33. [s. to you
15 : 3. ye are clean thro. word I h.
18 : 23. If I h.s. evil, bear witness.

SPOKEN, with prophet, s.
De. 18 : 22. p.s. it presumptuously
Eze. 14 : 9. if p. be deceived when he hath s. [the p., 27 : 9.
Mat. 2 : 17. which was s. by Jeremy
23. be fulfilled which was s. by the p., 13:35.-21:4.-27:35. [have s.
Lu. 24 : 25.to believe all that the p-s
Ja. 5 : 10. Take, brethren, p-s who s.
See Esaias, Joel.

Thou hast SPOKEN.
Ge. 19 : 21. this city for which - s.
Ex. 4 : 10. nor since - s. unto serv-t
10 : 29. Moses said, - s. well, I will
33 : 17. I will do this thing that - s.
Nu. 14 : 17. power of L. great as - s.
De. 1 : 14. thing which - s. is good
Ru 2 : 13. - s. friendly unto handm.
2 S. 6 : 22. maidservants which - s. of
7 : 19. - s. of thy servant's house, 25. 1 Ch. 17 : 17, 23. [Is. 39 : 8.
2 K. 20 : 19. Good is word of L. - s.,
2 Ch. 6 : 17. O G., word be verified - s.
Es. 6 : 10. let nothing fail of all - s.
Jb. 33 : 8. surely - s. in mine hear-g
Je. 3 : 5. - s. and done evil things
32 : 24. that wh. - s. is come to pass
44 : 16. As for the word - s. unto us
51 : 62. O Lord, - s. ag. this place
Eze. 35 : 12. have heard blasphemies [- s.

SPOKES.
1 K. 7 : 33. felloes and s. were all mol- [ten

SPOKESMAN.
Ex. 4 : 16. he sh. be thy s. unto peo.

SPONGE.
Mat. 27 : 48. one took a s., filled it wi. vinegar, Mk. 15:36. Jn. 19:29.

SPOON.
Nu. 7 : 14. One s. of ten shekels of gold, 20, 26, 32, 38, 44, 50, 56, 62.

SPOONS.
Ex. 25 : 29. make the dishes and s.
37 : 16. he made his dishes and s.
Nu. 4 : 7. put thereon dishes and s.
7 : 84. silver bowls, 12 s. of gold, 86.
1 K. 7 : 50. s. were gold, 2 Ch. 4 : 22.
2 K. 25 : 14. s. took he, Je. 52 : 18, 19.
2 Ch. 24 : 14. rest of money s. were

SPORT. [Noun.] [s.
Ju. 16 : 25. Sams. make s., he made
27. beheld while Samson made s.
Pr. 10 : 23. s. to fool to do mischief
21 : † 17. loveth s. sh. be poor man
26 : 19. deceiveth, and saith, Am not [I in s.?

SPORT, ING.
Ge. 26 : 8. Isaac s-g with Rebekah
Is. 57 : 4. Ag. whom do ye s. yours.?
2 Pe. 2 : 13. s-g with own deceivings

SPOT, SPOTS.
Le. 13 : 39. it is freckled s. in skin
Nu. 19 : 2. bring heifer without s.
28 : 3. two lambs without s., 9, 11.-29 : 17, 26. [children
De. 32 : 5. their s. is not the s. of his
Jb. 11 : 15. shalt lift face without s.
Can. 4 : 7. art all fair, no s. in thee
Je 13 : 23. can leopard change s-s?
Eph. 5 : 27. glorious ch., not having s.
1 Ti. 6 : 14. keep command-t witho. s.
He. 9 : 14. who offered hims. without s.
1 Pe. 1 : 19. as of a lamb without s.
2 Pe. 2 : 13. s-s they are, blemishes
3 : 14. ye may be found without s.
Jude 12. These are s-s in your feasts
See Bright.

SPOTTED. [35-
Ge. 30 : 32. removing all the s. cattle,
33. ev. one not s. counted stolen
39. bro-t forth cattle speckled, s.
Jude 23. hating garment s. by flesh

SPOUSE, S. [s.
Can. 4 : 8. Come from Lebanon, my
9. hast ravished my heart, my s.
10. How fair is thy love, my s.
11. Thy lips, my s., as honeycomb
12. garden inclosed is my s. [s.
5 : 1. I am come into garden, my
Ho. 4 : 13. s-s sh. commit adultery
14. will not punish your s-s when

SPOUTS. See Waterspouts.

SPRANG.
Mk. 4 : 8. fruit that s. up, 5. Lu. 8 : 8.
Lu. 8 : 7. thorns s. up and choked it
Ac. 16 : 29. called for light and s. in
He. 7 : 14. evident L. s. out of Juda
11 : 12. s. of one so many as the stars
See Sprung.

SPREAD. [35 : 21.
Ge. 33 : 19. where Jacob had s. tent,
Le. 13 : 5. plague s. not in skin, 6,
32. if the scall s. not, 34. [23, 28.
35. if scall s. much in skin, 36. [44.
51. if plague be s. in garm., 14 : 39,
53. if plague be not s., 55.-14 : 48.
Nu. 4 : 7. on table s. clo. of blue, 11.
8. they shall s. a cloth of scarlet
13. they shall s. a purple cloth
14. sh. s. cover-g of badgers' skins
De. 22 : 17. s. cloth bef. elders of city
Ju. 8 : 25. s. garm. cast in earrings
15 : 9. Philistines s. thems. in Lehi
1 S. 4 : † 2. when the battle was s.
23 : † 27. Philis. s. thems. upon land
2 S. 5 : 18. Philistines s. themselves in Rephaim, 22. 1 Ch. 14 : 9, 13.
16 : 22. they s. Absalom a tent on
17 : 19. woman s. covering over
21 : 10. Rizpah s. sackcloth for her
1 K. 6 : 32. he s. gold upon cherubim
8 : 54. with hands s. up to heaven
2 K. 8 : 15. Hazael s. cloth on his face
19 : 14. s. letter bef. Lord, Is. 37 : 14.
Ps. 105 : 39. He s. cloud for covering
140 : 5. have s. a net by way side
Pr. 1 : 17. in vain net is s. in sight of
Is. 14 : 11. worm is s. under thee
19 : 8. th. s. ne s upon waters shall
33 : 23. they could not s. sail
58 : 5. to s. sackcloth under him
Je. 8 : 2. they sh. s. them bef. the sun
10 : 9. Silver s. into plates fr. Tarsh.
La. 1 : 13 he hath s. net for my feet
Eze. 2 : 10. he s. the ro. before me
12 : 13. net will I s. upon him, 17 : 20.
Eze. 26 : 14. shalt be pla. to s. nets
Ho. 5 : 1. ye been a net s. upon Tabor
7 : 12. I will s. my net upon them
14 : 6. His branches sh. s. his beauty
Jo. 2 : 2. as morn-g s. upon the mts.
Ha. 1 : 8. horsemen sh. s. themselves
Mal. 2 : 3. I will s. dung upon your
Mat. 21 : 8. gr. multitude s. garm-ts in way, Mk. 11 : 8. Lu. 19 : 36.
Jn. 9 : † 6. s. clay upon eyes of blind
Ac. 4 : 17. th. it s. no further am. peo.

SPREAD abroad. [s.a.
Ge 10 : 18. the families of Canaanites
28 : 14. shalt s.a. to west and east
Ex. 9 : 29. will s.a. my hands unto
33. Moses s.a. his hands unto L.
40 : 19. he s.a. tent over tabern.
Le. 13 : 7. if scab s. much a., 22, 27.
Nu. 11 : 32. s.a. quails round camp
1 S. 30 : 16. were s.a. upon the earth
2 S 22 : 43. I did s.a. mine enemies
1 Ch. 14 : 13. Philistines s. thems. a.
2 Ch. 26 : 8. Uzziah's name s.a., 15.
Zch. 1 : 17. thro. prosperity be s.a.
2 : 6. I s. you a. as the four winds
Mat. 9 : 31. they s.a. his fame in all that country, Mk. 1 : 28.-6 : 14.
1 Th. 1 : 8. your faith to God-ward is [s.a.

SPREAD forth.
Nu. 24 : 6. As valleys are they s.f.
1 K. 8 : 7. cherubim s.f. their two wings, 2 Ch. 3 : 13.-5 : 8. [12, 13.
22. Solo-n s.f. his hands, 2 Ch. 6 :
38. and s.f. his hands toward this house, 2 Ch. 6 : 29.
Is. 1 : 15. when ye s.f. your hands, I
25 : 11. s.f. hands, as he th. swim-h
42 : 5. God, he that s.f. the earth
Eze. 47 : 10. shall be a place to s.f. [nets

SPREAD out.
Ex. 37 : 9. the cherubim s.o. their wings on high, 1 Ch. 28 : 18.
Ezr. 9 : 5. I s.o. my hands unto L.
Jb. 29 : 19. My root was s.o. by wat.
37 : 18. Hast thou s.o. the sky?
Is. 48 : † 13. hand hath s.o. heaven
65 : 2. s.o. my hands to rebel. peo.
La. 1 : 10. adversary s.o. his hand
Eze. 32 : 3. I will s.o. my net ov. thee

SPREAD over.
Nu. 4 : 6. shall s.o. it a cloth of blue
Ru. 3 : 9. s. thy skirt o. handmaid
Is. 25 : 7. vail that is s.o. all nations
Je. 43 : 10. sh. s. his pavilion o. th.
48 : 40. he sh. s. his wings o. Moab
49 : 22. shall s. his wings o. Bozrah
Eze. 16 : 8. I s. my skirt o. thee
19 : 8. nations s. their net o. him

SPREADEST.
Eze. 27 : 7. linen thou s. for thy sail

SPREADETH.
Le. 13 : 8. if priest see that scab s.
De. 32 : 11. as an eagle s. her wings
Jb. 9 : 8. God who alone s. out heav-
26 : 9. he s. his cloud upon it [ens
36 : 30. Behold, he s. light upon it
41 : 30. he s. sharp pointed things
Pr. 13 : † 16. but a fool s. his folly
29 : 5. th. flattereth neighb. s. net
31 : † 20. she s. out her hand to poor
Is. 25 : 11. th. swimmeth s. his hands
40 : 19. goldsmith s. it over wi. gold
22. that s. the heavens as a tent
44 : 24. I, the L., s. abroad the earth
Je. 4 : 31. dau. of Zion s. her hands
17 : 8. a tree that s. roots by river
La. 1 : 17. Zion s. forth her hands
Na. 3 : † 16. cankerworm s. himself

SPREADING. [Adj. Part.]
Le. 13 : 57. appear, it is s. plague
Ps. 37 : 35. I have seen wicked s.
Eze. 17 : 6. it grew, became a s. vine

SPREADING, S. [clouds?
Jb. 36 : 29. can any underst-d s-s of
Eze. 26 : 5. be a place for s. of nets

SPRIGS.
Is. 18 : 5 afore harvest shall cut s.

Eze. 17 : 6. a vine, and shot forth s.
SPRING. [Noun.]
1 S. 9 : 26. about s. of day Samuel
See DAYSPRING.
SPRING. [Noun.]
Eze. 17 : 9. Wither in all leaves of s.
SPRING. [Noun.]
2 K. 2 : 21. he went forth unto the s.
Pr. 25 : 26. a troubled and corrupt s.
Can. 4 : 12. my spouse is a s. shut up
Is. 58 : 11. thou shalt be like a s.
Ho. 13 : 15. his s. shall become dry
SPRINGS.
De. 4 : 49. plain under s. of Pisgah
Jos. 10 : 40. Josh. smote country of s.
12 : 8. kings in plains and in s.
15 : 19. give me s. of water, gave her upper s., nether s., Ju. 1 : 15.
Jb. 38 : 16. Hast entered into s. of
Ps. 87 : 7. all my s. are in thee [sea?
104 : 10. He sendeth s. into valleys
Is. 35 : 7. thirsty land s. of water
41 : 18. I make dry land s. of water
49 : 10. by s. of water shall he guide
Je. 51 : 36. I will make her s. dry
See WATERSPRING.
SPRING. [Verb.]
Nu. 21 : 17. Israel sang, s. up, O well
De. 8 : 7. depths th. s. out of valleys
Ju. 19 : 25. when day began to s. they
Jb. 5 : 6. nei. doth trouble s. out of
38 : 27. bud of tender herb to s.
Ps. 85 : 11. Truth shall s. out of earth
92 : 7. When wicked s. as the grass
Is. 42 : 9. bef. they s. forth, I tell you
43 : 19. new thing, it shall s. forth
44 : 4. they shall s. up as am. grass
45 : 8. let righteousn. s. up togeth.
58 : 8. thine health shall s. forth
61 : 11. as garden causeth things to s., Lord will cause praise to s. [s.
Jo. 2 : 22. not afraid for pastures do
Mk. 4 : 27. seed s. he knoweth not
SPRINGETH. [wall
1 K. 4 : 33. unto hyssop th. s. out of
2 K. 19 : 29. eat in second year that which s. of same, Is. 37 : 30.
Ho. 10 : 4. judgment s. as hemlock
SPRINGING. [Adj. Part.]
Ge. 26 : 19. found a well of s. water
2 S. 23 : 4. as tender grass s. out of
Jn. 4 : 14. in him a well of water s.
He. 12 : 15. lest root of bitterness s.
SPRINGING. [Noun.] [up
Ps. 65 : 10. thou blessest the s. th-of
SPRINKLE.
Ex. 9 : 8. let Mos. s. ashes tow. heav.
Le. 14 : 7. s. upon him to be cleansed
16. priest s. of oil with finger, 27.
51. shall s. the house seven times
16 : 14. he sh. s. on mercy seat, 15.
Nu. 8 : 7. s. water of purifying upon
19 : 18. sh. s. it upon the tent, and
19. clean shall s. it upon unclean
Is. 52 : 15. So sh. he s. many nations
Eze. 36 : 25. I s. clean wat. upon you
SPRINKLE, ED, ETH, with blood.
Ex. 24 : 6. half of b. Moses s-d upon altar, Le. 8 : 19, 24. [people
8. Moses took b. and s-d upon the
29 : 16. thou shalt take ram's b. and s. upon altar, 20. Le. 1 : 5, 11.–3 : 2, 8, 13.–7 : 2.–17 : 6. Nu. 18 : 17.
Le. 4 : 6. priest sh. s. b. seven times bef. Lord, 17.–16 : 14, 19. [altar
5 : 9. he shall s. b. of sin off-g upon
6 : 27. when is s-d of b. upon garment (2) [ings
7 : 14. that s-h the b. of peace offer-
8 : 30. Mos. took b., s-d upon Aaron
9 : 12. sons presented b., he s-d, 18.
14 : 51. shall dip bird in b., and s. (
16 : 14. take of b. of bullock and s.
Nu. 19 : 4. s. b. of heifer bef. tabern.
2 K. 9 : 33. Athaliah's b. was s-d on
2 K. 16 : 13. Ahaz s-d b. of his peace?
15. Ahaz commanded Urijah s. upon altar b. of sacrifice (2)
2 Ch. 29 : 22. killed lambs, s-d b. upon altar (3), 30 : 16.
35 : 11. killed passov. s-d b. [ments
Is. 63 : 3. that b. be s-d upon my gar-
Eze. 43 : 18. make altar to s. b. th-on
He. 9 : 21. he s-d with b. tabernacle
SPRINKLED.
Ex. 9 : 10. Moses s. ashes tow. heav.
Le. 8 : 11. he s. upon altar 7 times
Nu. 19 : 13. wat. not s. upon him, 20.
Jb. 2 : 12. s. dust upon their heads
Is. 59 : † 5. that which is s. as if there
Ho. 7 : † 9. gray hairs are s. here and
He. 9 : 19. he s. book and all the peo.
10 : 22. hearts s. fr. an evil conscien.
SPRINKLETH, ING.
Nu. 19 : 21. s-h water of separation
He. 9 : 13. ashes of heifer s-g unclean
SPRINKLING with blood.
He. 11 : 28. Thro. faith he kept s. of b.
12 : 24. b. of s. th. speaketh better
1 Pe. 1 : 2. s. of the b. of Jes. Christ
SPROUT.
Jb. 14 : 7. hope of a tree th. it will s.
SPRUNG.
Ge. 41 : 6. seven thin ears s. up, 23.
Le. 13 : 42. leprosy s. up in his head
Mat. 4 : 16. in shadow of death light
13 : 5. forthwith they s. up [is s. up
7. thorns s. up and choked them
26. but when blade was s. up
Lu. 8 : 6. as it was s. up it withered
See SPRANG.
SPUE, ED. See SPEW, ED.
SPUN. [had s.
Ex. 35 : 25. women bro-t that they
35 : 26. all the women s. goats' hair
SPUNGE. See SPONGE.
SPY.
Nu. 13 : 16. Moses sent to s. land, 17.
21 : 32. Moses sent to s. out Jaazer
Jos. 2 : 1. Josh. sent men to s., 6 : 25.
Ju. 18 : 2. Danites sent to s., 14, 17.
2 S. 10 : 3. David sent servants to s. out city, 1 Ch. 19 : 3. [he is
2 K. 6 : 13. he said, Go and s. where
Ga. 2 : 4. privily to s. out our liberty
SQUARE.
1 K. 7 : 5. all doors and posts were s.
Eze. 45 : 2. s. round about, 50 cubits
See FIVESQUARE, FOURSQUARE.
SQUARED. [s.
Eze. 41 : 21. posts of the temple were
SQUARERS.
See STONESQUARERS.
SQUARES.
Eze. 43 : 16. broad, square in four s.
17. fourteen broad in the four s.
STABILITY.
Is. 33 : 6. knowl. be s. of thy times
Je. 32 : † 41. plant them in land in s.
STABLE. [Adj. Noun.]
1 Ch. 16 : 30. world sh. be s. not moved
Is. 7 : † 9. it is because ye are not s.
Eze. 25 : 5. make Rab-h s. for camels
STABLENESS. [fed
Ps. 37 : † 3. in truth and s. shalt be
Es. 9 : 21. to s. the days of Purim
STABLISH. [ever
1 Ch. 17 : 12. I will s. his throne for
18 : 3. Hadarezer went to s. domin.
29 : † 18. O Lord God, s. their heart
2 Ch. 7 : 18. s. throne of thy kingd.
Ps. 119 : 38 s. thy word unto servant
Ro. 16 : 25. th. is of power to s. you
1 Th. 3 : 13. he may s. your hearts
2 Th. 2 : 17. s. you in ev. good word
3 : 3. L shall s., keep you from evil
Ja. 5 : 8. Be patient, s. your hearts
1 Pe. 5 : 10. God of all grace, s. you
STABLISHED, ETH.
2 Ch. 17 : 5. L. s-d kingd. in his hand
Ps. 93 : 1. the world also is s-d that
148 : 6. He hath s-d them for ever
Ha. 2 : 12. s-h a city by iniquity [Ch.
2 Co. 1 : 21. he wh. s-d us with you is
Col. 2 : 7. Rooted in him, s-d in faith
See ESTABLISH, ED, ETH.
STA'CHYS. See URBANE.
STACKS.
Ex. 22 : 6. so s. of corn be consumed
STACTE.
Ex. 30 : 34. Take sweet spices, s. and
STAFF. [Jordan
Ge. 32 : 10. with my s. I passed over
38 : 18. Give me thy signet and s.,
Ex. 12 : 11. eat it, wi. s. in hand [25.
21 : 19. If he rise, and walk upon s.
Nu. 13 : 23. grapes betw. two upon s.
22 : 27. Balaam smote ass with a s.
Ju. 6 : 21. angel put forth end of s.
1 S. 17 : 7. s. of his spear was like a weaver's beam, 2 S. 21 : 19.
40. David took his s. in hand, and
21 : † 16. whose s. weighed 300 shek.
2 S. 3 : 29. not fail one leaneth on s.
23 : 7. be fenced with s. of a spear
21. went to him wi. s., 1 Ch. 11 : 23.
2 K. 4 : 29. take my s., lay my s. upon
31. Gehazi laid the s. on face of
18 : 21. trustest s. of reed, Is. 36 : 6.
Ps. 23 : 4. thy rod and s. comfort me
Is. 3 : 1. Lord will take from Judah s.
9 : 4. hast broken s. of his shoulder
10 : 5. s. in their hand mine indign.
15. as if s. should lift up itself
24. shall lift up his s. against thee
14 : 5. L. hath broken s. of wicked
28 : 27. fitches are beaten out wi. s.
30 : 32. where grounded s. sh. pass
Je. 48 : 17. How is strong s. broken
Eze. 29 : 6. been a s. of reed to Israel
Ho. 4 : 12. their s. declareth unto th.
Zch. 8 : 4. ev. man with his s. for age
11 : 10. I took my s., even Beauty
14. I cut asunder mine other s.
Mat. 10 : † 10. for journey nei. a s.
Mk. 6 : 8. nothing for journey save s.
He. 11 : 21. worship-d, leaning upon
STAFF of bread. [s.
Le. 26 : 26. When I have broken s. –
Ps. 105 : 16. he brake the whole s. –
Eze. 4 : 16. I will break the s. – in Jerusalem, 5 : 16. [break the s. –
14 : 13. when land sinneth I will
STAGGER, ED, ETH.
Jb. 12 : 25. maketh them to s. like drunken man, Ps. 107 : 27.
Ps. 99 : † 1. L. reigneth, let earth s.
Is. 19 : 14. as a drunken man s-h in
29 : 9. s. but not with strong drink
Ro. 4 : 20. He s-d not at promise of
STAGGERING. [G.
1 S. 25 : † 31. this shall be no s.
STAIN.
Jb. 3 : 5. Let shadow of death s. it
Is. 23 : 9. L. purposed to s. pride of
63 : 3. their blood, I will s. my rai-
STAIRS. [ment
1 K. 6 : 8. went up with winding s.
2 K. 9 : 13. put under him on top of s.
2 Ch. 9 : † 11. k made of almug trees s.
Ne. 3 : 15. s. that go down from city
9 : 4. stood upon s. Jeshua and
12 : 37. went by s. of city of David
Can. 2 : 14. art in secret places of s.
Eze. 38 : † 20. s. shall fail and ev. wall
40 : 6. man went up by s. and meas.
43 : 17. his s. shall look toward east
Ac. 21 : 40. Paul stood on s., 35.
STAKES.
Is. 33 : 20. not one of s. be removed
54 : 2. lengthen cords, strengthen
STALK, S. [thy s.
Ge. 41 : 5. 7 rank ears in one s., 22.
Jos. 2 : 6. hid them with s. of flax
Je. 11 : † 19. Let us destroy s. with
Ho. 8 : 7. hath no s. but yield no meal
STALL, S.
1 K. 4 : 26. Solomon had forty thousand s. of horses, 2 Ch. 9 : 25.

2 Ch. 32 : 28. Hezekiah had s-s for all
Je. 46 : †21. men like bullocks of s.
Am. 6 : 4. eat the calves out of s.
Ha. 3 : 17. altho. be no herd in s-s
Mal. 4 : 2. ye grow up as calves of s.
Lu. 13 : 15. on sabbath loose ox fr. s.

STALLED.

Pr. 15 : 17. than a s. ox and hatred

STAMMERERS.

Is. 32 : 4. tongue of s. sh. speak plain-⌊ly

STAMMERING.

Is. 28 : 11. with s. lips and another
33 : 19. sh. not see peo. of s. tongue

STAMP.

2 S. 22 : 43. I did s. them as the mire
Eze. 6 : 11. smite wi. hand, s. wi. foot

STAMPED.

De. 9 : 21. I s. calf and ground it
2 Ch. 15 : 16. Asa cut down idol, s. it
Eze. 25 : 6. Bec. hast s. with the feet
Da. 7 : 7. fourth beast s. residue, 19.
8 : 7. the he goat s. upon the ram
10. cast down stars, s. upon them
See POWDER.

STAMPING.

Je. 47 : 3. At noise of s. of horses

STANCHED.

Lu. 8 : 44. woman's issue of blood s.

STAND. [Noun.]

Eze. 29 : 7. madest loins to be at a s.
Na. 2 : †7. there was a s. made

STAND. [Verb.]

Ge. 19 : 9. said, s. back. This fellow
Ex. 33 : 10. peo. saw cloudy pillar s.
Le. 27 : 14. house, as the priest shall estimate it, so shall it s., 17.
Nu. 1 : 5. men that shall s. with you
11 : 16. they may s. there with thee
30 : 4. her vows shall s., 5, 7, 11.
12. her vows or bond shall not s.
De. 5 : 31. But s. thou here by me
18 : 5. chosen him to s. to minister
24 : 11. s. abroad, man shall bring
25 : 8. if he s. to it, and say, I like
Jos. 20 : 4. he shall s. at gate of city
1 S. 12 : 16. s. and see this great thi.
19 : 3. I will s. beside my fa. in field
1 K. 8 : 11. priests could not s. to minister, because of, 2 Ch. 5 : 14.
17 : 1. As Lord liveth, before whom I s., 18 : 15. 2 K. 3 : 14.-5 : 16.
2 K. 5 : 11. I tho-t he will come and s.
10 : 4. k-s stood not, how sh. we s.?
1 Ch. 21 : 16. David saw angel s.
23 : 30. to s. ev. morning to thank
2 Ch. 34 : 32. caused all present to s.
Ezr. 10 : 14. Let rulers of cong-n s.
Es. 8 : 4. see if Mordecai's matters s.
8 : 11. and to s. for their life ⌈s.
Jb. 8 : 15. lean upon house, it not
19 : 25. that he sh. s. at latter day
38 : 14. and they s. as a garment
Ps. 30 : 7. hast made mt. to s. strong
38 : 11. my lovers and friends s. aloof, my kinsmen s. afar off
45 : 9. upon right hand did s. queen
73 : 7. their eyes s. out with fatness
78 : 13. he made waters s. as heap
102 : †26. they sh. perish, thou sh. s.
107 : †25. maketh to s. stormy wind
109 : 6. let Satan s. at his right ha.
31 shall s. at right hand of poor
122 : 2 Our feet sh. s. within gates
130 : 3. If mark iniq-s, who sh. s.?
Pr. 12 : 7. house of righteous sh. s.
19 : 21. counsel of the Lord shall s.
25 : 6. s. not in place of great men
Ec. 8 : 3. s. not in an evil thing
Is. 7 : 7. saith L., it shall not s., 8 : 10.
11 : 10. root of Jesse, s. for ensign
14 : 24. as I purposed, it shall s.
21 : 8. I s. upon watchtower ⌈not s.
28 : 18. your agreement with hell
32 : 8. by liberal things shall he s.
40 : 8. word of our God shall s.
46 : 10 My counsel shall s., I will
47 : 12. s. with thine enchantments
Is. 50 : 8. let us s. togeth., who mine
61 : 5. strangers sh. s. feed flocks
Je. 6 : 16. s. ye in the ways and see
44 : 28. whose word sh. s., mine or
46 : 4. s. forth with your helmets
21. did not s. bec. day was come
Eze. 17 : 14. keep-g of cov-t it might s.
Da. 2 : 44. the kingdom shall s. for
11 : 6. king of the north sh. not s.
25. king of the south shall not s.
Am. 2 : 15. Nei. he s. th. handleth bow
7 : †2. who of Jac. s.? he is small
Mi. 5 : 4. he sh. s. in strength of L.
Na. 2 : 8. s., shall they cry, but none
Mal. 3 : 2. who s. when he appeareth
Mat. 12 : 25. house divided shall not s., 26. Mk. 3 : 24, 25. Lu. 11 : 18.
Mk. 3 : 3. saith unto man had withered hand, s. forth, Lu. 6 : 8.
11 : 25. when ye s. praying, forgive
Ac. 1 : 11. why s. gazing into heav.?
5 : 20. Go, s., and speak in temple
25 : 10. Paul said, I s. at Cesar's
26 : 6. I s. and am judged for hope
Ro. 5 : 2. this grace wherein we s.
9 : 11. purpose acc. to election might
14 : 4. God is able to make him s. ⌊s.
1 Co. 15 : 1. I decla. gospel wh-in ye s.
30. why s. we in jeopardy ⌈s.
2 Co. 1 : 24. helpers, for by faith ye
Ep. 6 : 13. and having done all to s.
14. s. having your loins girt about
Col. 4 : 12. ye may s. perfect complete
Ja. 2 : 3. say to the poor, s. there ⌈s.
1 Pe. 5 : 12. true grace of G. wh-in ye
Re. 3 : 20. Behold, I s. at door and
6 : 17. great day, who be able to s.?
18 : 15. merchants s. afar off for fear

STAND against.

Le. 19 : 16. nei. s.a. blood of neighb.
Nu. 30 : 9. vow of widow sh. s.a. her
Je. 44 : 29. my words shall s.a. you
Ep. 6 : 11. be able to s.a. wiles of

STAND before.

Ex. 8 : 20. Rise up early, s.b., 9 : 13.
9 : 11. magicians not s.b. Moses
17 : 6. I will s.b. thee in Horeb
Le. 18 : 23. nei. sh. wom. s.b. beast
26 : 37. ye sh. have no power to s. b. enemies, Jos. 7 : 12, 13. Ju. 2 : 14.
Nu. 16 : 9. to s.b. congregation to minister, 35 : 12. Jos. 20 : 6.
27 : 21. and he shall s.b. Eleazer
De. 7 : 24. no man able to s.b. thee, 11 : 25 : Jos. 1 : 5.-10 : 8.-23 : 9.
9 : 2. Who can s.b. chil. of Anak?
10 : 8. tribe of Levi to s.b. Lord, 2 Ch. 29 : 11. Eze. 44 : 11, 15. ⌈L.
18 : 7. Levites who s. there b. the
19 : 17. both the men shall s.b. L.
29 : 10. Ye s. this day all b. the L.
1 S. 6 : 20. Who able to s.b. Lord G.?
16 : 22. Let David, I pray, s.b. me
1 K. 1 : 2. Let young virgin s.b. king
10 : 8. happy are thy servants who s.b. thee, 2 Ch. 9 : 7. ⌈L.
19 : 11. go, and s. upon mount b.
2 Ch. 20 : 9. we s.b. this house in
Ezr. 9 : 15. we cannot s.b. thee bec.
Jb. 41 : 10. who is able to s.b. me?
Ps. 5 : †5. foolish not s.b. thine eyes
147 : 17. who can s.b. his cold?
Pr. 22 : 29 a man diligent shall s.b. kings, not s.b. mean men
27 : 4. but who is able to s.b. envy?
Je. 7 : 10. s.b. me in this house
15 : 19. If thou return, sh. s.b. me
35 : 19. not want a man to s.b. me
40 : †10. at Mizpah, to s.b. Chald-ns
49 : 19. who is shepherd that will s. b. me? 50 : 44.
Da. 1 : 5. that they might s.b. king
8 : 4. that no beasts might s.b. him
7. no power in ram to s.b. him
11 : 16. none shall s.b. him, he sh.
Na. 1 : 6. Who s.b. his indignation?
Lu. 21 : 36. worthy to s.b. Son of m.
Ro. 14 : 10. all sh. s.b. judgment
Re. 20 : 12. I saw dead s.b. God

STAND by.

Ge. 24 : 43. Behold I s.b. the well
Ex. 7 : 15. shalt s.b. river's brink
18 : 14. people s.b. thee till even
Nu. 23 : 3. s.b. thy burnt offering
Ne. 7 : 3. while they s.b. shut doors
Is. 65 : 5. s.b. thyself, I am holier
Je. 48 : 19. s.b. the way, and ask
Eze. 46 : 2. prince shall s.b. post of
Zch. 3 : 7. to walk am. these th. s.b.
4 : 14. anointed ones that s.b. Lord
Jn. 11 : 42. bec. of people wh. s.b.

STAND fast.

Ps. 89 : 28. my covenant shall s.f.
111 : 8. all his com-ts s.f. for ever
Je. 46 : 14. say ye, s.f. and prepare
1 Co. 16 : 13. Watch ye, s.f. in faith
Ga. 5 : 1. s.f. in liberty Christ made
Ph. 1 : 27. that ye s.f. in one spirit
4 : 1. beloved, so s.f. in the Lord ⌈L.
1 Th. 3 : 8. we live, if ye s.f. in the
2 Th. 2 : 15. s.f. hold the traditions

STAND here.

Ge. 24 : 13. I s.h. by well of water
Nu. 23 : 15. s.h. by thy burnt off-g
De. 5 : 31. as for thee, s.h. by me
2 S. 18 : 30. king said, Turn, and s.h.
Mat 20 : 6. Why s. ye h. all day?
Mk. 9 : 1. s.h., who not taste death
Ac. 4 : 10. by him doth this man s.h.

STAND in.

Ju. 4 : 20. s.i. door of tent, and say
2 Ch. 35 : 5. s.i. holy place acc-g to
Ps. 1 : 5. ungodly not s.i. judgment
4 : 4. s.i. awe, sin not, commune
5 : 5. foolish sh. not s.i. thy sight
24 : 3. who sh. s.i. his holy place?
33 : 8. inhabitants of world s.i. awe
76 : 7. who s.i. sight when angry?
89 : 43. not made him s.i. battle
134 : 1. by night s.i. hou. of Lord
Je. 7 : 2. s.i. gate of L.'s hou. ⌊135 : 2.
14 : 6. asses did s.i. high places
17 : 19. s.i. gate of chil. of people
26 : 2. s.i. court of the L.'s house
Eze. 13 : 5. not gone to s.i. battle
22 : 30. should s.i. gap before me
44 : 24. they shall s.i. judgment
Da. 1 : 4. ability to s.i. king's palace
11 : 16. he shall s.i. glorious land
12 : 13. shall s.i. thy lot at the end
Zch. 14 : 4. shall s.i. in m-t of Olives
Mat. 24 : 15. abomina. s.i. holy place
Lu. 1 : 19. am Gabriel, that s.i. pres.
1 Co. 2 : 5. faith not s.i. wisdom of
Ga. 4 : 20. for I s.i. doubt of you

STAND on.

Ex. 17 : 9. tomorrow I will s.o. hill
2 K. 6 : 31. if head of Elisha s.o. him
Da. 11 : 17. she shall not s.o. his side
31. arms sh. s.o. his part, pollute
Re. 15 : 2. s.o. sea of glass, having

STAND still.

Ex. 14 : 13. Moses said, s.s., and see the salvation of G., 2 Ch. 20 : 17.
Nu. 9 : 8. s.s., I will hear what Lord
Jos. 3 : 8. ye shall s.s. in Jordan
10 : 12. sun, s.s. upon Gibeon and
1 S. 9 : 27. s. thou s. a while, that
12 : 7. s.s. that I may reason with
14 : 9. we will s.s. in our place and
Jb 37 : 14. s.s. consider works of G.
Je. 51 : 50. escaped sword, s. not s.
Ac. 8 : 38. commanded chariot to s. ⌊s.

STAND up.

Ex. 9 : †16. for this I made thee s.u.
Ne. 9 : 5. s.u., and bless Lord your
Jb. 30 : 20. I s.u., thou regardest not
33 : 5. set thy words in order, s.u.
Ps. 35 : 2. s.u. for my help
94 : 16. who s.u. for me ag. workers?
Ec. 4 : 15. child shall s.u. in stead
Is. 27 : 9. images shall not s.u.
44 : 11. let them s.u., they sh. fear
47 : 13. Let the prognosticators s.u.

Is. 48 : 13. when I call they s.u.
51 : 17. Awake, awake, s.u., Jerus.
Eze. 31 : 14. nei. trees s.u. in height
Da. 8 : 22. four kingdoms shall s.u.
23. king of fierce counten. sh. s.u.
25. he shall s.u. against prince of
11 : 2. shall s.u. 3 kings in Persia
3. a mighty king shall s.u., 4.
7. of her roots shall one s.u.
14. many sh. s.u. ag. king of sou.
20. shall s.u. a raiser of taxes
21. and shall s.u. a vile person
12 : 1. that time shall Michael s.u.
Na. 1 : † 6. who s.u. in his anger
Ac. 10 : 26. Peter said, s.u., I am a

STAND upon.

Ex. 33 : 21. Thou shalt s.u. a rock
De. 27 : 12. shall s.u. m-t Gerizim
13. shall s.u. m-t Ebal to curse
Jos. 3 : 13. they shall s.u. a heap
2 S. 1 : 9. Saul said, s.u. me, slay me
1 K. 19 : 11. s.u. mount bef. the Lord
Eze. 2 : 1. Son of man, s.u. thy feet, I will speak, Ac. 26 : 16. [land
27 : 29. the pilots of sea shall s.u.
33 : 26. Ye s.u. your sword, ye work
47 : 10. fishers sh. s.u. it fr. Engedi
Da. 7 : 4. made s.u. feet as a man
8 : † 18. made me s.u. my standing
Ha. 2 : 1. I will s.u. my watch
Zch. 14 : 4. his feet shall s.u. mount
12. consume, while they s.u. feet
Re. 10 : 5. angel I saw s.u. sea, lifted

STAND upright.

Ps. 20 : 8. but we are risen and s.u.
Da. 10 : 11. O Dan., man belov., s.u.
Ac. 14 : 10. Paul said to cripple, s.u.

STAND without.

Ezr. 10 : 13. we are not able to s.w.
Mat. 12 : 47. s.w. to speak, Lu. 8 : 20.
Lu. 13 : 25. ye begin to s.w. and to

STANDARD, S.

Nu. 1 : 52. ev. man by own s., 2 : 2, 17.
2 : 3. east side sh. s. of Judah pitch
10. on south s. of Reuben, 10 : 18.
18. on west s. of Ephraim, 10 : 22.
25. on north s. of Dan, 10 : 25.
31. Dan shall go hindmost with s-s
34. pitched by their s-s and set
10 : 14. In first place s. of Judah
Is. 49 : 22. will set up my s. to peo.
59 : 19. Lord shall lift s. ag. him
62 : 10. Go through, lift up a s. for
Je. 4 : 6. Set up a s. toward Zion
21. How long shall I see the s. [27.
50 : 2. set ye up a s. in land, 51 : 12,

STANDARDBEARER. [s.

Can. 5 : † 10. My beloved is ruddy as a
Is. 10 : 18. be as when a s. fainteth

STANDEST.

Ge. 24 : 31. come in, wh. s. without
Ex. 3 : 5. place whereon thou s. is holy ground, Jos. 5 : 15. Ac. 7 : 33.
Ps. 10 : 1. Why s. thou afar off, O L.
Ro. 11 : 20. they broken off, thou s.

STANDETH. [by faith

Nu. 14 : 14. th. thy cloud s. ov. them
De. 1 : 38. Joshua, who s. bef. thee
17 : 12. hearken unto priest that s.
29 : 15. with him that s. with us
Ju. 16 : 26. feel pillars wh-on house s.
Es. 6 : 5. Behold, Haman s. in court
7 : 9. gallows s. in Haman's house
Ps. 1 : 1. nor s. in way of sinners
26 : 12. My foot s. in an even place
33 : 11. counsel of Lord s. for ever
82 : 1. God s. in cong-n of mighty
119 : † 90. establi-d earth, and it s.
161. my heart s. in awe of thy word
Pr. 8 : 2. wisdom s. in high places
Can. 2 : 9. beloved s. behind wall
Is. 3 : 13. L. s. to plead, s. to judge
46 : 7. set him in place, and he s.
59 : 14. Justice s. afar off, truth is
Da. 12 : 1. prince who s. for people
Zch. 11 : 16. nor feed that that s. still
Jn. 1 : 26. s. one am. you ye know not
Jn. 3 : 29. friend of bridegr. s. hear-h
Ro. 14 : 4. to his own master he s. or
1 Co. 7 : 37. he that s. stedf-t in heart
8 : 13. eat no flesh while world s.
10 : 12. th. thinketh he s. take heed
2 Ti. 2 : 19. foundation of G. s. sure
He. 10 : 11. ev. priest s. daily minist-g
Ja. 5 : 9. the judge s. before the door
Re. 10 : 8. angel wh. s. upon the sea

STANDING. [Part.]

Ex. 26 : 15. tabernacle s. up, 36 : 20.
Nu. 22 : 23. angel of L. s. in way, 31.
1 S. 19 : 20. Samuel s. as appointed
22 : 6. servants were s. about him
1 K. 13 : 25. lion s. by the carcass, 28.
22 : 19. host of heaven s., 2 Ch. 18 : 18.
2 Ch. 9 : 18. two lions s. by stays
Es. 5 : 2. king saw Esther s. in court
Da. 8 : 6. ram seen s. before river
Am. 9 : 1. I saw Lord s. upon altar
Zch. 3 : 1. Joshua s. before angel of the Lord, and Satan s. at his
6 : 5. wh. go forth fr. s. before Lord
Mat. 6 : 5. love to pray s. in synag-s
16 : 28. be some s. here, Lu. 9 : 27.
20 : 3. he saw others s. idle in, 6.
Mk. 3 : 31. breth., mother s. without
13 : 14. abomi-n s. wh. it ought not
Lu. 1 : 11. angel s. on right of altar
5 : 2. saw two ships s. by lake
18 : 13. publican s. afar off smote
Jn. 8 : 9. Jesus alone, and woman s.
19 : 26. his mother and discip. s. by
20 : 14. she saw Jesus s. and knew
Ac. 2 : 14. But Peter s. up with the
4 : 14. beholding the man healed s.
5 : 23. We found keepers s. without
25. men are s. in temple teaching
7 : 55. Jes. s. on right hand of G., 56.
22 : 20. I was s. by and consenting
24 : 21 I cried, s. am. them, Touch-g
He. 9 : 8. while first tabern. was s.
2 Pe. 3 : 5. earth s. out of water and
Re. 7 : 1. four angels s. on 4 corners
11 : 4. two candlesticks s. bef. God
18 : 10. s. afar for fear of torment
19 : 17. I saw an angel s. in the sun

STANDING. [Adj.]

Le. 26 : 1. nei. rear you up s. image
1 K. 14 : † 33. they built s. images
Ps. 107 : 35. wilderness into s. water
114 : 8. turned rock into s. water
Ho. 10 : † 1. made goodly s. images
Mi. 5 : 13. I will cut off s. images

STANDING corn. [ed

Ex. 22 : 6. If fire so s.c. be consum-
De. 23 : 25. into s.c. of neighb. (2)
Ju. 15 : 5. foxes into s.c., burnt s.c.
Ho. 8 : † 7. it hath no s. c.; bud sh.

STANDING. [Noun.] [ters

1 K. 10 : † 5. queen saw s. of minis-
2 Ch. 30 : † 16. stood in s. acc-g to
Ne. 13 : † 11. I set them in their s.
Ps. 69 : 2. I sink in mire where no s.
Da. 8 : † 18. me stand upon my s.
10 : † 11. O Dan., stand upon thy s.
Ho. 3 : † 4. of Isr. abide without a s.
Mi. 1 : 11. he sh. receive of you his s.

STANK.

Ex. 7 : 21. fish in river died, river s.
8 : 14. they gathered frogs, land s.
16 : 20. manna bred worms and s.
2 S. 10 : 6. Ammon saw they s. bef.

STAR. [David

Nu. 24 : 17. sh. come a s. out of Jac.
Am. 5 : 26. have borne s. of your god
Mat. 2 : 2. have seen his s. in east
7. inquired what time s. appeared
9. s. they saw in east, went before
10. When they saw s. they rejoiced
Ac. 7 : 43. ye took up s. of your god
1 Co. 15 : 41. s. differeth from ano. s.
Re. 8 : 10. fell great s. fr. heaven, 11.
9 : 1. a s. fell fr. heaven unto earth
See DAYSTAR.

Morning STAR, S.

Jb. 38 : 7. When m. s-s sang togeth.
Re. 2 : 28. I will give him the m.s.
22 : 16. I am the bright and m.s.

STARS.

Ge. 1 : 16. God made 2 lights, s. also
15 : 5. tell the s. if thou be able to
37 : 9. sun, moon, eleven s. made
De. 4 : 19. seest sun, moon, and s.
Ju. 5 : 20. s. in their courses fought
1 Ch. 27 : 23. wo. increase Isr. like s.
Ne. 4 : 21. fr. morning till s. appeared
Jb. 3 : 9. Let s. of twilight be dark
9 : 7. com-deth sun, sealeth up s.
22 : 12. behold height of s., how
25 : 5. s. are not pure in his sight
Ps. 8 : 3. moon and s. thou ordained
136 : 9. moon and s. to rule by ni.
147 : 4. He telleth number of the s.
148 : 3. praise him, sun, moon, all ye s. of light [be not darkened
Ec. 12 : 2. While sun, or moon, or s.
Is. 13 : 10. s. shall not give light, sun shall be darkened and the moon, Eze. 32 : 7. Jo. 2 : 10.-3 : 15. Mat. 24 : 29. Mk. 13 : 24, 25.
14 : 13. exalt my throne above s. of
Je. 31 : 35. moon and s. for light by
Eze. 32 : 7. I will make the s. dark
Da. 8 : 10. it cast down some of s. to
12 : 3. they shall shine as s. for ev.
Jo. 2 : 10. s. shall withdraw, 3 : 15.
Ob. 4. tho. set thy nest am. the s.
Lu. 21 : 25. signs in sun, moon, and s.
Ac. 27 : 20. nei. sun nor s. appeared
1 Co. 15 : 41. is one glory of the sun, ano. of moon, ano. of the s.
He. 11 : 12. so many as s. of the sky
Jude 13. raging waves, wander-g s.
Re. 8 : 12. third part of the sun was smitten, third part of moon and s. [s.
12 : 1. upon her head crown of 12
See HEAVEN with star, s.

Seven STARS.

Jb. 38 : † 31. Canst thou bind s.s.
Am. 5 : 8. Seek him th. maketh s.s.
Re. 1 : 16. in right ha. s.s., 2 : 1.-3 : 1.
20. mystery of s.s. thou sawest; s.s. are angels of 7 churches

STARE.

Ps. 22 : 17. they look and s. upon me

STARGAZERS.

Is. 47 : 13. Let s. stand up and save

STATE.

Ge. 43 : 7. the man asked us of our s.
2 Ch. 24 : 13. set house of G. in his s.
Es. 1 : 7. acc-g to s. of king, 2 : 18.
Ps. 39 : 5. man at his best s. is vanity
Pr. 27 : 23. to know s. of thy flocks
28 : 2. by man of knowl. s. prolonged
Is. 22 : 19. from thy s. pull thee down
Mat. 12 : 45. last s. of that man is worse than the first, Lu. 11 : 26.
Ph. 2 : 19. comf-t when I know y-r s.
20. will naturally care for your s.
4 : 11. whatso. s., I am, to be content
Col. 4 : 7. my s. sh. Tychicus declare
See ESTATE.

STATELY.

Eze. 23 : 41. And satest upon a s. bed

STATER. [a s.

Mat. 17 : † 27. opened mouth sh. find

STATION. [of Aaron

1 Ch. 23 : † 28. s. was at hand of sons
2 Ch. 35 : † 15. sons of Asaph in s.
Is. 22 : 19. I will drive thee fr. thy s.

STATUE, S.

Ex. 34 : † 13. ye sh. break their s-s, 2 K. 18 : † 4.-23 : † 14. 2 Ch. 14 : † 3.
De. 7 : † 5. destroy altars, break s-s
16 : † 22. neither set thee up any s.
1 K. 14 : † 23. built s-s on ev. high hill
2 K. 3 : † 2. Jeho. put away s. of Baal
10 : † 26. brought s-s out of house
2 Ch. 31 : † 1. all Israel brake the s-s
Ho. 3 : † 4. Israel abide without a s.
Ho. 10 : † 1. th. have made goodly s-s
Mi. 5 : † 13. I will cut off thy s-s

STATURE. [great s.
Nu. 13 : 32. people we saw are men of
1 S. 16 : 7. Look not on height of s.
28 : † 20. Saul fell with fulness of s.
2 S. 21 : 20. man of great s., six fingers on each, 1 Ch. 11 : 23.-20 : 6.
23 : † 21. slew Eg-n man of great s.
Can. 7 : 7. thy s. is like a palm tree
Is. 10 : 33. high ones of s. hewn down
45 : 14, men of s. shall come unto
Eze. 13 : 18. kerchiefs upon head of
17 : 6. became a vine of low s. [ev. s.
19 : 11. her s. was exalted am. bran.
31 : 3. Assyrian a cedar of high s.
Mat. 6 : 27. Which of you can add one cubit to his s., Lu. 12 : 25.
Lu. 2 : 52. Jesus increased in wisd. s.
19 : 3. Zaccheus, little of s. climbed
Ep. 4 : 13. measure of s. of Christ

STATUTE. [nance
Ex. 15 : 25. he made a s. and ordi-
Le. 16 : 34. everl-g s. to make atonem.
Nu. 27 : 11. for s. of judgment, 35 : 29.
Jos. 24 : 25. he set th. a s. in Shechem
1 S. 30 : 25. Dav. made it a s. for Isr.
Ps. 81 : 4. this was a s. for Israel
Da. 6 : 7. consulted to estab. royal s.
15. no s. king establ-h be changed
See **Statute for EVER.**
See PERPETUAL.

STATUTES.
Ex. 18 : 16 make them know s. of G.
Le. 10 : 11. may teach Isr. all the s.
Nu. 30 : 16. Th. are the s. L. com-ded
De. 4 : 6. which shall hear all these s.
6 : 24. Lord commanded us to do s.
16 : 12. sh. observe and do these s.
17 : 19. may learn to keep these s.
1 K. 3 : 3. walking in the s. of David
2 K. 17 : 8. walked in s. of heath., 19.
34. neither do they after their s.
37. s. he wrote, ye shall observe
2 Ch. 33 : 8. they take heed to do s.
Ne. 9 : 14. thou commandedst them
Ps 19 : 8. s. of Lord are right [s.
Je. 10 : † 3. s. of the people are vain
Eze. 20 : 25. I gave them s. not good
33 : 15. if wicked walk in s. of life
Mi. 6 : 16. s. of Omri are kept, and

His STATUTES. [13.
De. 6 : 17. diligently keep h. s., 10 :
27 : 10. do h. s. which I command
28 : 15. if thou wilt not do h. s., 45.
2 S. 22 : 23. h. s. I did not depart fr.
1 K. 8 : 61. be perfect to walk in h. s.
2 K. 17 : 15. they rejected h. s. and his covenant [2 Ch. 34 : 31.
23 : 3. made covenant to keep h. s.,
Ezr. 7 : 11. to Ezra a scribe of h. s. to
Ps. 18 : 22. I did not put away h. s.
105 : 45. That they might observe h.
Je. 44 : 23. in his law, nor in h. s. [s.
See **Statutes** with **JUDGMENTS, KEEP** statutes.

My STATUTES.
Ge. 26 : 5. Abr. kept m. s. and laws
Le. 25 : 18. Wheref. ye shall do m. s.
26 : 3. If ye walk in m. s., 1 K. 3 : 14.
15. if ye shall despise m. s. [-11 : 38.
43. bec. their soul abhorred m. s.
1 K. 3 : 14. if will keep m. s. as Dav.
9 : 6. if ye will not keep m. s.
11 : 11. hast not kept m. cov. and s.
34. David kept m. com-ts and s.
2 K. 17 : 13. keep m. s., Eze. 18 : 21.
2 Ch. 7 : 19. if ye forsake m. s. [-44 : 24.
Ps. 50 : 16. What hast thou to declare
89 : 31. If they break m. s. [m. s.
Je. 44 : 10. nei. have walked in m. s.
Eze. 5 : 6. have changed m. s. more
7. Bec. ye have not walked in m. s.
11 : 20. they may walk in m. s.
18 : 19. when son hath kept m. s.
36 : 27. cause you to walk in m. s.
Zch. 1 : 6. m. s. did take hold of y-r

Thy STATUTES. [fa-s
1 Ch. 29 : 19. give heart to keep t. s.
Ps. 119 : 12. O Lord, teach me t. s., 26, 33, 64, 68, 124, 135.
16. I will delight myself in t. s.
23. thy serv-t did meditate in t. s.
48. and I will meditate in t. s.
54. t. s. have been my songs in my
71. afflicted, I might learn t. s.
80. Let my heart be sound in t. s.
83. yet do I not forget t. s. [t. s.
112. inclined my heart to perform
117. I will have respect unto t. s.
118. trodden them that err fr. t. s.
155. for the wicked seek not t. s.
171. My lips praise when taught

STATUTEMAKER. [t. s.
Is. 33 : † 22. Lord is our s., L. our K.

STAVES.
Ex. 25 : 13. shalt make s. of shittim-wood, 28.-27 : 6.-30 : 5.-37 : 4.
14. put s. into rings, 15.-27 : 7.-37 : 5.-38 : 7.
27. rings be for places for the s., 30 : 4.-37 : 14, 27.-38 : 5. [39 : 35.
35 : 12. The ark, s. with mercy seat,
13. The table his s., and vessels
15. altar his s. and oil, 16.-39. 39.
37 : 15. he made s. of shittim wood, 28.-38 : 6. [mercy seat
40 : 20. he set s. on ark, and put
Nu. 4 : 6. shall put in s., 8, 11, 14.
21 : 18. nobles digged with their s.
1 S. 17 : 43. Am I a dog, thou comest with s.? [5 : 8.
1 K. 8 : 7. covered ark and s., 2 Ch.
8. drew out s., the s. seen, 2 Ch. 5 : 9.
1 Ch. 15 : 15. Levites bare ark with s.
Ha. 3 : 14. didst strike with his s.
Zch. 11 : 7. I took unto me two s.
Mat. 10 : 10. two coats nor s., Lu. 9 : 3.
26 : 47. multitude with s., Mk. 14 : 43.
26 : 55. Are ye come with s. to take me? Mk. 14 : 48. Lu. 22 : 52.
See HANDSTAVES.

STAY, S. [a s.
Le. 13 : 5. if plague in his sight be at
37. if scall in his sight be at a s.
2 S. 22 : 19. L. was my s., Ps. 18 : 18.
1 K. 10 : 19. s-s on either side throne; two lions beside s-s, 2 Ch. 9 : 18.
Is. 3 : 1. Lord doth take away the s., whole s. of bread, the s. of water
19 : 13. they that are the s. of tribes
Je. 50 : † 36. a sword upon chief s-s
1 Ti. 3 : † 15. church, pillar, and s. of [truth

STAY. [Verb.]
Ge. 18 : † 5. fetch bread, s. y-r hearts
19 : 17. neither s. thou in plain
Ex. 9 : 28. ye shall s. no longer [28.
Le. 13 : 23. if bright spot s. in place,
Jos. 10 : 19. s. not, pursue enemies
Ru. 1 : 13. wo. ye s. fr. having husb-ds
1 S. 15 : 16. s. and I will tell thee wh.
20 : 38. Jona. cried, haste, s. not
2 S. 24 : 16. s. thine hand, 1 Ch. 21 : 15.
Jb. 37 : 4. he will not s. them when
38 : 37. who can s. bottles of heaven
Ps. 59 : † 15. they will s. all night
Pr. 28 : 17. flee to pit, let no man s.
Can. 2 : 5. s. me with flagons, I am
Is. 10 : 20. sh. no more s. upon him
29 : 9. s. yourselves and wonder
30 : 12. Because ye s. on oppression
31 : 1. Woe to them s. on horses
48 : 2. they s. themselves upon God
50 : 10. let him s. upon his God
Je. 4 : 6. s. not, for I will bring evil
20 : 9. I was weary, I could not s.
Da. 4 : 35. none can s. his hand, or
Ho. 13 : 13. not s. in place of break-g

STAYED.
Ge. 8 : 10. Noah s. seven days, 12
32 : 4. with Laban, and I have s.
Ex. 10 : 24. let flocks and herds be s.
17 : 12. Aa. and Hur s. up M.'s hands
Nu. 16 : 48. plague was s., 50.-25 : 8. 2 S. 24 : 25. Ps. 106 : 30.
De. 10 : 10. I s. in mount forty days
Jos. 10 : 13. sun stood still, moon s.
1 S. 20 : 19. when thou hast s. 3 days
24 : 7. David s. his serv-ts wi. words
30 : 9. where those that were left s.
2 S. 17 : 17. Jonathan s. by En-rogel
24 : 21. that plague be s., 1 Ch 21 : 22.
1 K. 22 : 35. king was s. up in his chariot, and died, 2 Ch. 18 : 34.
2 K. 4 : 6. is not a vessel more. And the oil s. [and s.
13 : 18. Smite. And he smote thrice,
15 : 20. k. of Assyria s. not in land
Jb. 38 : 11. here thy proud waves be
Is. 26 : 3. whose mind is s. on thee [s.
La. 4 : 6. and no hands s. on Sodom
Eze. 31 : 15. the great waters were s.
Hag 1 : 10. heaven is s., earth is s.
Lu. 4 : 42. people came and s. him
Ac. 19 : 22 he s. in Asia for a season

STAYETH. [day
Is. 27 : 8. he s. his rough wind in a
Je. 48 : † 30. on whom he s. do not

STEAD, STEADS. [right
Ge. 22 : 13. offered ram in s. of son
30 : 2 Jacob said, Am I in God's s.
Ex. 29 : 30. that son that is priest in his s. shall put, Le. 16 : 32.
Le. 6 : 22. priest anointed in his s.
Nu. 32 : 14. ye are risen in father's s.
De. 2 : 12. children of Esau in their s.
21. Ammonites in their s., 22, 23.
10 : 6. Eleazer ministered in his s.
Jos. 5 : 7. chil. be raised in their s.
1 K. 14 : 27. Rehob. made in their s. brazen shields, 2 Ch. 12 : 10.
1 Ch. 5 : 22. dwelt in their s-s until captivity [in David's s.
2 Ch. 1 : 8. Thou hast made me reign
Jb. 16 : 4. if your soul in my soul's s.
33 : 6. I am acc. to thy wish in G.'s s.
34 : 24. he sh. set others in their s.
Pr. 11 : 8. wicked cometh in his s.
Ec. 4 : 15. child sh. stand up in his s.
Je. 29 : 26. Lord made thee priest in the s. of Jehoiada [God of forces
Da : 11 : † 38. in his s. shall honour
2 Co. 5 : 20. We pray you in Ch.'s s.
Phm. 13. in thy s. might have minist.

King in STEAD. [30.
1 K. 1 : 35. Sol. shall be k. i. my s.,
2 K. 21 : 24. made Josiah k. i. Amon's s., 2 Ch. 33 : 25.
23 : 30. made Jehoahaz k. i. father's s., 2 Ch. 36 : 1.
24 : 17. made Mattaniah k. i. his s.

Reigned in STEAD.
2 S. 10 : 1.-16 : 8. 1 K. 11 : 43.-14 : 20, 31.-15 : 8, 24, 28.-16 : 6, 10, 28.-22 : 40, 50. 2 K. 1 : 17.-3 : 27.-8 : 15, 24.-10 : 35.-12 : 21.-13 : 9, 24.-14 : 16, 29.-15 : 7, 10, 14, 22, 30, 38.-16 : 20.-19 : 37.-20 : 21.-21 : 18, 26.-24 : 6. 1 Ch. 19 : 1.-29 : 28. 2 Ch. 9 : 31.-12 : 16.-14 : 1.-17 : 1.-21 : 1.-22 : 1.-24 : 27.-26 : 23.-27 : 9.-28 : 27.-32 : 33.-33 : 20.-36 : 8. Is. 37 : 38. Je. 22 : 11.-37 : 1.
See REIGNED.

STEADFAST.
Jb. 11 : 15. shalt be s. and not fear
Ps. 78 : 8. whose spirit not s. wi. God
37. nei. were they s. in his cov-nt
Da. 6 : 26. he is living God, and s.
1 Co. 7 : 37. standeth in his heart s.
15 : 58. beloved brethren, be ye s.
2 Co. 1 : 7. our hope of you is s. [s.
He. 2 : 2. if word spok. by angels was
3 : 14. if we hold our confidence s.
6 : 19. hope as an anchor sure and s.
1 Pe. 5 : 9. Whom resist s. in the faith

STEADFASTLY.
Ru. 1 : 18. saw she was s. minded [s.
2 K. 8 : 11. settled his countenance
Lu. 9 : 51. he s. set face to go to Jeru.
Ac. 1 : 10. while they looked s. 2 men
2 : 42. s. in the apostles' doctrine

Ac. 6 : 15. all looking s. on him, saw
7 : 55. Steph. looked s. into heaven
14 : 9. who s. beholding him and
2 Co. 3 : 7. Isr. not s. behold face of
13. could not s. look to the end

STEADFASTNESS.

Ps. 5 : † 9. is no s. in their mouth
Col. 2 : 5. beholding s. of your faith
2 Pe. 3 . 17. beware, lest ye fall from

STEADY. ⌊your s.

Ex. 17 : 12. Moses' hands were s.
until ⌈standeth s.
2 Ti. 2 : † 19. foundation of God

STEAL. ⌈me?

Ge. 31 : 27 whf. didst s. away from
44 :8. how sho. we s. silver or gold?
Ex. 20 : 15. Thou shalt not s., Le.
19 : 11. De. 5 : 19. Mat. 19 : 18.
Ro 13 : 9. ⌈oxen
22 : 1. If man s. ox, sh. restore five
2 S. 19 : 3. as peo. s. away in battle
Pr. 6 : 30. if he s. to satisfy his soul
30 : 9. or lest I be poor and s., and
Je. 7 : 9. Will ye s., murder, commit
23 : 30. I am ag. the prophets th. s.
Mat. 6 :19. thieves break thro. and s.
20. thieves do not break nor s.
27 : 64. lest his disciples s. him aw.
Mk. 10 : 19. do not s., Lu. 18 : 20. ⌈s.
Jn. 10 : 10. thief cometh not, but to
Ro. 2 : 21. thou that preachest sho.
not s., dost thou s. ⌈more
Ep. 4 : 28. Let him that stole, s. no

STEALERS.

See MENSTEALERS.

STEALETH.

Ex. 21 : 16. that s. a man and selleth
Jb. 21 : † 18. chaff that storm s. aw.
27 : 20. tempest s. him aw. in night
Zch. 5 : 3. ev. one that s. be cut off

STEALING. ⌈breth.

De. 24 : 7. If a man be found s. his
Ho. 4 : 2. By swearing and s. they

STEALTH. ⌊break

2 S. 19 : 3. people gat by s. into city
Jb. 4 : † 12. thing was by s. bro-t to

STEEDS. ⌈me

Je. 50 : † 11. ye are fat and neigh as s.

STEEL. ⌈18 : 34.

2 S. 22 : 35. bow of s. is broken, Ps.
Jb. 20 : 24. bow of s. shall strike him
Je. 15:12. Sh. iron break north-n s.?

STEEP.

Eze. 38 : 20. the s. places shall fall
Mi. 1 : 4. as waters down a s. place
Mat. 8 : 32. swine ran violently down
a s. place, Mk. 5 : 13. Lu. 8 : 33.

STEM.

Is. 6 : † 13. oak whose s. is in them
11 : 1. come a rod out of s. of Jesse

STEP.

1 S. 20 :3. but s. betw. me and death
Jb. 31 :7. If my s. turned out of way
Eze. 40 : † 40. at the s. were 2 tables

STEPS. ⌈altar

Ex. 20 : 26. Neither go up by s. unto
2 S. 22 : 37. Thou hast enlarged my
s., Ps. 18 : 36. ⌈s.
Jb. 14 : 16. now thou numberest my
18 : 7. s. of his strength straitened
23 : 11. My foot hath held his s.
29 : 6. I washed my s. with butter
31 :4. Doth he not see, count my s.
37. I would declare numb. of my s.
Ps. 17:11. they compassed us in ours.
37 : 23. s. of good man are ordered
31. none of his s. shall slide ⌈way
44 : 18. nei. have our s. declined fr.
56 : 6. they mark my s. when they
57 : 6. they prepared net for my s.
73 : 2. my s. had well nigh slipped
85 : 13. shall set us in way of his s.
119 : 133. Order my s. in thy word
Pr. 4 :12. thy s. sh. not be straitened
5 : 5. her s. take hold on hell
16 : 9. but the Lord directeth his s.
Is. 26 : 6. s. of needy sh. tread it do
Je. 10 :23. not in man to direct his s.
La. 4 : 18. They hunt our s., that we
Eze. 40 : 22. went up by seven s., 26.
31. going up had eight s., 34, 37.
49. he brought me by s. whereby
Da. 11 : 43. Ethiopians be at his s.
Ro. 4 :12. walk in s. of that faith ⌈s.?
2 Co. 12 : 18. walked we not in same
1 Pe. 2 : 21. that ye sho. follow his s.

Six STEPS.

1 K. 10 : 19. The throne had s. s.,
and the top, 2 Ch. 9 : 18.
20. twelve lions stood on the s.
s., 2 Ch. 9 : 19.

STEPH'ANAS. ⌈S.

1 Co. 1 : 16. I baptized household of
16 : 15. ho. of S., firstfruits of Ach.
17. I am glad of the coming of S.

STE'PHEN. ⌈8.

Ac. 6 : 5. chose S., man full of faith,
9. them of Asia disputing with S.
7 : 59. stoned S., calling upon God
8 : 2. devout men carried S. to bur-
11 : 19. persecution about S. ⌊ial
22 : 20. blood of martyr S. was shed

STEPPED, PETH.

Jn. 5 :4. whoso. first s-d in was made
7. while I am coming ano. s-h bef.

STERN. ⌊me

Ac. 27 : 29. cast 4 anchors out of s.

STEWARD, S.

Ge. 15 : 2. s. of my house is Eliezer
43 : 19. s. of Joseph's hou., 44:1, 4.
1 K. 16 : 9. drunk in house of his s.
1 Ch. 28 : 1. Da. assemb-d capt-s s-s
Da. 1 : † 11. Then said Daniel to s.
Mat. 20 : 8. lord of vineyard unto s.
Lu. 8 : 3. wife of Chuza, Herod's s.
12 : 42. Who then is that faithful s.
16 : 1. certain rich man had a s.
2. thou mayest be no longer s., 3.
8. the lord commended unjust s.
1 Co. 4 : 1. s-s of mysteries of God
2. required in s-s man be faithful
Ti. 1 : 7. bishop blameless as s. of G.
1 Pe. 4 : 10. good s-s of grace of God

STEWARDSHIP.

Lu. 16 : 2. give an account of thy s.
3. my lord taketh from me the s.,

STICK. [Noun.] ⌊4.

2 K. 6 : 6. cut down a s., cast it in
La. 4 : 8. their skin is become like s.
Eze. 37 : 16. take one s., write, take
17. Join th. into one s., 19. ⌊ano. s.

STICKS. ⌈bath

Nu. 15 : 32. gathered s. upon sab-
33. that found him gathering s.
1 K. 17 : 10. widow was gathering s.
12. I am gathering two s. to go in
Eze. 37 : 20. the s. wh-n thou writest
Ac. 28 : 3. Paul gathered bundle of s.

STICK, ETH.

Jb. 33 : 21. his bones not seen, s. out
41 :17. scales joined, they s. togeth.
Ps. 38 : 2. thine arrows s. fast in me
Pr. 18 : 24. is a friend s-h closer than
Eze. 29 : 4. cause fish to s. unto thy

STIFF.

Eze. 3 : † 7. all hou. of Isr. s. of fore-
See NECK. ⌊head

STIFFENED. ⌈heart

2 Ch. 36 : 13. s. his neck, hardened

STIFFHEARTED.

Eze. 2 : 4. are impudent chil. and s.

STIFFNECKED.

Ex. 32 : 9. this people is a s. people
33 : 3. thou art s. people, De. 9 : 6.
5. Say unto Israel, Ye are a s. peo.
34 : 9. it is a s. people, De. 9 : 13.
De. 10 :16. Circumcise, be no more s.
2 Ch. 30 : 8. be not s. as your fathers
Ac. 7 : 51. Ye s. always resist H. Gh.

STILL. [Adj.]

Ex. 15 : 16. shall be as s. as a stone
Ju. 18 : 9. land good : and are ye s.?
Ru. 3 : 18. Sit s., my dau., until thou
1 S. 14 : † 9. Be s. until we come to
1 K. 19 : 12. after fire s. small voice
22 : 3. Ramoth is ours and we be s.
2 K. 7 : 4. if we sit s. here we die
Jb. 3 : 13. now should I have lain s.
4 : † 16. was silence, I heard a voice
Ps. 4 : 4. commune with heart, be s.
23 : 2. leadeth me beside s. waters
46 : 10. Be s., and know I am God
76 : 8. earth feared, and was s. ⌈God
83 : 1. hold not peace, be not s., O
107 : 29. that waves thereof are s.
Is. 23 : 2. Be s., ye inhabitants of isle
30 : 7. Their strength is to sit s.
42 :14. I have been s., and refrained
Je. 8 :14. Why do we sit s.? assemble
47 : 6. O sword of L., rest and be s.
Mk. 4 : 39. said unto sea, Peace, be s.
See **STAND, STOOD still.**

STILL. [Adv.] ⌉s.

Ge. 12 : 9. Abr. Journeyed, going on
41 : 21. they were s. ill favoured
Ex. 9 : 2. if thou wilt hold them s.
Le. 13 : 57. if it appear s. in garment
Nu. 14 : 38. Josh. and Caleb lived s.
Jos. 24 : 10. thf. Balaam blessed you s.
1 S. 12 : 25. if ye sh. s. do wickedly
26 : 25. Thou also shalt s. prevail
2 S. 14 : 32. good to ha. been there s.
16 : 5. Shimei cursed s. as he came
2 K. 2 :11. they s. went on and talked
12 : 3. people sacrificed s., burnt
incense, 15 : 4, 35. 2 Ch. 33 : 17.
2 Ch. 22:9. no power to keep s. kingd.
Jb. 2 : 3. s. holdeth fast his integrity
9. Dost s. retain thine integrity?
20 : 13. though he keep it s. within
Ps. 49 : 9. he should s. live for ever
68 : 21. as goeth on s. in trespasses
78 : 32. for all this they sinned s.
84 : 4. they will be s. praising thee
92 : 14. s. bri. forth fruit in old age
139 : 18. awake, I am s. with thee
Ec. 12 :9. he s. taught people knowl.
Is. 5 : 25. his hand is stretched out
s., 9 : 12, 17, 21.–10 : 4. ⌈that
Je. 23 : 17. They say s. unto them
27 : 11. I let remain s. in own land
31:20. I do earnestly rememb. him s.
42 : 10. if ye will s. abide in land
La. 3 : 20. hath them s. in remembr.
Eze. 33 : 30. peo. s. are talking ag.
41 : 7. winding about s. upward ⌈s.
Zch. 11 :16. nor feed that th. stand-h
Jn. 7 : 9. he abode s. in Galilee, 11:
11 : 20. Mary sat s. in the house ⌊6.
Ac. 15 : 34. Silas to abide s., 17 : 14.
Ro. 11 : 23. if bide not s. in unbelief
1 Ti. 1 : 3. thee to abide s. at Ephe-s
Re. 22 : 11. be unjust s. : filthy s. :
righteous s. : holy s.

STILL, ED, EST, ETH.

Nu. 13 . 30. Caleb s-d peo. bef. Mos.
Ne. 8 : 11 Levites s-d all the people
Ps. 8 :2. mightest s. enemy, avenger
65 : 7. which s-h noise of the seas
89 : 9. waves arise thou s-t them

STING, S. ⌈s.?

1 Co. 15 : 55. O death, where is thy
56. The s. of death is sin
Re. 9 : 10. s-s in their tails, power to

STINGETH. ⌊hurt men

Pr. 23 : 32. at last it s. like an adder

STINK. [Noun.]

Is. 3 : 24. instead of sweet smell, be s.
34 : 3. s. sh. come out of carcasses
Jo. 2 : 20. his s. shall come up, and
Am. 4 : 10. made s. of your camps to

STINK, ETH, ING. ⌈s.

Ge. 34 : 30. Ye ha. made made me to
Ex. 5 : † 21. made our savour to s.
7 : 18. fish shall die, river shall s.
16 : 24. manna laid up did not s.
1 S. 13 : † 4. Israel did s. with Philis
27 : † 12. he hath made Israel to s.
1 Ch. 19 : † 6. they made them to s.
Ps. 14 : † 3. they are become s-g
38 : 5. My wounds s., are corrupt

Ec. 10 : 1. ointment to send s-g sav-
Is. 50 : 2. fish s-h bec. is no water [our
Jn. 11 : 39. Lord, by this time he s-h

STIR, S. [city
Is. 22 : 2. art full of s-s, a tumultu-s
Ac. 12 : 18. no small s. am. soldiers
19 : 23. arose no small s. ab. that way

STIR. [Verb.]
Nu. 24 : 9. who shall s. him up?
Jb. 17 : 8. innocent s. ag. hypocrite
41 : 10. None so fierce th. dare s. him
Ps. 35 : 23. s. up thyself, awake to
78 : 38. did not s. up all his wrath
80 : 2. s. up thy strength, save us
Pr. 15 : 1. grievous words s. anger
Can. 2 : 7. that ye s. not up my love,
3 : 5.–8 : 4. [for him
Is. 10 : 26. L. shall s. up a scourge
13 : 17. I will s. up Medes ag. them
42 : 13. he shall s. up jealousy like
Da. 11 : 2. shall s. up all ag. Grecia
25. shall s. up his power ag. king
2 Ti. 1 : 6. s. up gift of God in thee
2 Pe. 1 : 13. I think it meet to s. you,

STIRRED. [3 : 1.
Ex. 35 : 21. heart s. him, 26.–36 : 2.
1 S. 22 : 8. son hath s. up serv. ag. me
26 : 19. If Lord have s. thee ag. me
1 K. 11 : 14. Lord s. up an adversary
23. God s. him up ano. adversary
21 : 25. whom Jezebel his wife s. up
1 Ch. 5 : 26. God s. up spirit of Pul
2 Ch. 21 : 16. L. s. ag. Jehoram Phil.
36 : 22. L. s. spirit of Cyrus, Ezr. 1 : 1.
Ps. 39 : 2. dumb, my sorrow was s.
Da. 11 : 10. his sons shall be s. up
25. k. of south be s. up to battle
Hag. 1 : 14. L. s. spirit of Zerubbabel
Ac. 6 : 12. they s. up the people, 17 :
13.–21 : 27. [women
13 : 50. but Jews s. up the devout
14 : 2. unbelieving Jews s. Gentiles
17 : 16. Paul, his spirit was s. in him

STIRRETH.
De. 32 : 11. As an eagle s. up her nest
Pr. 10 : 12. Hatred s. up strifes, love
15 : 18. wrathf. man s. up strife, 29 : 22.
28 : 25. He of a proud heart s. up
Is. 14 : 9. Hell beneath s. dead for
64 : 7. none s. to take hold on thee
Lu. 23 : 5. He s. up people teaching

STOCK.
Le. 25 : 47. s. of stranger's family
Jb. 14 : 8. though the s. thereof die
Is. 6 : † 13. as oak whose s. is in them
40 : 24. their s. shall not take root
44 : 19. sh. I fall down to s. of tree?
Je. 2 : 27. Saying to s. Thou, my fa.
10 : 8. s. is a doctrine of vanities
Ac. 13 : 26. chil. of s. of Abraham
Ph. 3 : 5. of s. of Israel, a Hebrew
See GAZINGSTOCK.

STOCKS. [s.
Jb. 13 : 27. Thou puttest my feet in
33 : 11. He putteth my feet in s.
Pr. 7 : 22. fool to correction of s. [s.
Je. 3 : 9. committed adultery with
20 : 2. Pashur put Jerem-h in s., 3.
29 : 26. put him in prison and s.
Ho. 4 : 12. My peo. ask counsel at s.
Ac. 16 : 24. made their feet fast in s.

STOICS. [tered him
Ac. 17 : 18. certain of S. encoun-

STOLE.
Ge. 31 : 20. Jacob s. away to Laban
2 S. 15 : 6. Absalom s. hearts of Isr.
2 K. 11 : 2. Jehosheba s. Joash from
am. king's sons, 2 Ch. 22 : 11.
Mat. 28 : 13. disciples s. him while
Ep. 4 : 28. Let him that s. steal no

STOLEN. [more
Ge. 30 : 33. that shall be counted s.
31 : 19. Rachel had s. fa.'s images,
26. hast s. aw. unawares to me [32.
30. whf. hast thou s. my gods?
39. whe. s. by day, or s. by night
40 : 15. I was s. away out of the la.
Ex. 22 : 7. if stuff be s. out of house
12. if it be s. from him, he shall
Jos. 7 : 11. have s. and dissembled
2 S. 19 : 41 Why men of Jud. s. thee
21 : 12. men of Jabesh s. bones of
Pr. 9 : 17. s. waters are sweet [Saul
Ob. 5. wo. th. not have s. till enough?

STOMACH. [sake
1 Ti. 5 : 23. use a little wine for s.'s

STOMACHER. [cloth
Is. 3 : 24. instead of s., gird-g of sack-

STONE. [Noun.]
Ge. 2 : 12. is bdellium and onyx s.
11 : 3. they had brick for s. and
28 : 18. Jacob set up a s., 22.–31. 45.
29 : 3. rolled s. fr. well's mou., 8, 10.
35 : 14. Jacob set up a pillar of s.
49 : 24. is the shepherd, s. of Israel
Ex. 4 : 25. Zipporah took a sharp s.
15 : 5. they sank into bottom as a s.
16. by thy arm shall be still as s.
17 : 12. they took s., put it und. him
20 : 25. if make me an altar of s.
21 : 18. if one smite ano. with a s.
28 : 10. Six names on one s., six on
11. work of engraver in s. [ano. s.
† 17. shalt fill in it fillings of s.
Le. 26 : 1. neither set up image of s.
Nu. 35 : 17. if he smite him with
throwing a s., 23.
De. 25 : † 13. shalt not have in thy
bag a s., and a s. [s.
Jos. 4 : 5. take you up every man a
15 : 6. border went to s. of Bohan
18 : 17. descended to s. of Bohan
24 : 27. this s. shall be a witness
Ju. 9 : 5. slew 70 persons upon s., 18.
1 S. 6 : 18. s. remain-h unto this day
7. 12. Samuel set up s., called it
17 : 49. David took from his bag a
s., s. sunk into Philistine's [s.
50. Da. prevailed over Philis. with
20 : 19. shalt remain by s. Ezel [a s.
25 : 37. Nabal's heart, he became as
2 S. 17 : 13. until be not one small s.
1 K. 1 : 9. cattle by s. of Zoheleth
6 : 7. house built of s. made ready
18. all was cedar, was no s. seen
2 K. 3 : 25. on land cast ev. man his s.
1 Ch. 22 : 14. timber, s. have I pre-
15. hewers of s., 2 K. 12 : 12. [pared
2 Ch. 2 : 14. skilf. to work in gold, s.
Ne. 9 : 11. threwest as a s. into the
Es. 1 : † 6. pavement of s. of blue
Jb. 28 : 2. brass is molten out of s.
38 : 30. waters are hid as with a s.
41 : 24. His heart is as firm as a s.
Ps. 91 : 12. angels, lest thou dash thy
foot ag. s., Mat. 4 : 6. Lu. 4 : 11.
118 : 22. s. which builders refused,
is become head s., Mat. 21 : 42.
Mk. 12 : 10. Lu. 20 : 17. Ac. 4 :
11. 1 Pe. 2 : 7.
Pr. 11 : † 1. perfect s. is his delight
20 : † 10. a s. and a s. are abomin.
26 : 8. that bindeth a s. in a sling
27. that rolleth a s. it will return
27 : 3. A s. is heavy, fool's wrath is
Is. 28 : 16. I lay in Zion a tried s. (2)
Je. 2 : 27. to a s. hast bro-t me forth
51 : 26. not take a s. for corner,
nor a s. for foundations
63. shalt bind a s. to this book
La. 3 : 53. have cast a s. upon me
Da. 2 : 34. s. was cut out of mt., 45.
35. s. that smote image became
6 : 17. s. was upon mouth of den
Am. 9 : † 9. shall not least s. fall
Ha. 2 : 19. Woe unto him, saith to s.
Hag. 2 : 15. bef. a s. was laid upon s.
Zch. 3 : 9. s. I have laid before Joshua, upon one s. be seven eyes
4 : 7. shall bring forth the head s.
7 : 12. their hearts as adamant s.
12 : 3. make Jerus. burdensome s.
Mat. 7 : 9. if his son ask bread, will
he give him a s.? Lu. 11 : 11.
Mat. 21 : 44. whoso. shall fall on this
s. shall be broken. Lu. 20 : 18.
24 : 2. shall not be left one s. upon
ano., Mk. 13 : 2. Lu. 19 : 44.–21 : 6.
27 : 66. sealing the s., Mk. 15 : 46.
28 : 2. angel rolled back s., Mk. 16 : 3.
Lu. 4 : 3 command this s. be bread
22 : 41. withdrawn fr. them s.'s cast
24 : 2. found s. rolled away, Mk.
16 : 4. Jn. 20 : 1. [pretation a s.
Jn. 1 : 42. Cephas, wh. is by inter-
2 : 6. were set six waterpots of s.
8 : 7. sin, let him first cast s. at her
11 : 38. was a cave, a s. lay upon it
39. Jesus said, Take ye away the s.
41. took s. fr. where the dead was
Ac. 17 : 29. Godhead is like s. graven
1 Pe. 2 : 4. To whom as unto living s.
Re. 2 : 17. I will give him a white s.
16 : 21. hail fell, ev. s. weight of [stone
18 : 21. angel took up s. like a mill-
See CORNER stone, s.
See GREAT stone, s.
See HEADSTONE.

Hew, Hewed, or Hewn STONE, S. [s.
Ex. 20 : 25. shalt not build it of h-n
1 K. 5 : 17. h-d s-s to lay foundation
6 : 36. inner court 3 rows of h-d s.,
7 : 12. [11.
7 : 9. acc-g to measures of h-d s-s,
2 K. 12 : 12. to buy h-d s. to repair
house, 22 : 6. 2 Ch. 34 : 11. [s-s
1 Ch. 22 : 2. masons to h. wrought
Is. 9 : 10. we will build with h-n s-s
La. 3 : 9. inclosed my ways with h-n s.
Eze. 40 : 42. 4 tables were of h-n s.
Am. 5 : 11. have built ho. of h-n s.
Lu. 23 : 53. a sepulchre h-n in s.

Hewer, s, of STONE. [s.
2 K. 12 : 12. laid out money to h-s o.
1 Ch. 22 : 15. h-s and workers o. s.

Precious STONE. [it
Pr. 17 : 8. A gift is p.s. to him hath
26 : † 8. a p.s. in a heap of stones
Can. 5 : † 12. his eyes as a p.s. in ring
Is. 28 : 16. I lay in Zion a p. corner
s., 1 Pe. 2 : 6. [ering
Eze. 28 : 13. every p.s. was thy cov-
Re. 21 : 11. her light was like a s.
most p.
See Stone of STUMBLING.
See STUMBLINGSTONE, WALL.
See TABLES of stone.
See WOOD and stone.

STONES.
Ge. 28 : 11. Jac. took s. for his pillow
31 : 46. Jac. unto breth., Gather s.
Ex. 25 : 7. Onyx s. to be set, 35 : 9,
27. 1 Ch. 29 : 2. [them, 39 : 6.
28 : 9. two onyx s. and grave on
11. shalt engrave the two s., 12.
17. set it in settings of s., 4 rows
of s., 39 : 10. [rael, 39 : 14.
21. s. shall be with names of Is-
31 : 5. cut-g of s. to set them, 35 : 33.
39 : 7. should be s. for a memorial
Le. 14 : 40. command they take aw. s.,
42. put s. in place of those s. [43.
45. sh. break down house, s. of it
19 : † 36. just s., just ephah, sh. ye
De. 8 : 9. a land whose s. are iron
27 : 4. set up these s. in m-t Ebal
6. build altar of whole s., 5. Jos.
8. write upon s. words of law [8 : 31.
Jos. 4 : 3. take you hence 12 s., 9.
6. What mean ye by these s.? 21.
8. took twelve s. out of Jordan
20. 12 s. did Josh. pitch in Gilgal
8 : 32: he wrote upon s. copy of law
Ju. 20 : 16. co. sling s. at hairbreadth
1 S. 17 : 40. David chose 5 smooth s.
2 S. 16 : 6. Shimei cast s. at David, 13.
18 : 17. laid gr. heap of s. upon Abs.
1 K. 5 : 18. so they prepared timber
and s. to build the house
7 : 10. s. of eight cubits, s. of ten

1 K. 10 : 27. king made silver to be in
Jerus. as s., 2 Ch. 1. 15.-9 : 27.
15 : 22. took away s. of Ramah, 2
Ch. 16 : 6. [to number
18 : 31. Elijah took 12 s. according
32. with s. he built an altar, 38.
2 K. 3 : 19. mar every good piece of
land with s. [s.
25. only in Kir-haraseth left they
16 : 17. put it upon pavement of s.
1 Ch. 12 : 2. in hurling of s., shoot-g
22 : 2. masons to hew wrought s.
29 : 2. I have prepared onyx s., s.
to be set, glistering s., precious
s., marble s. in abundance [s.
2 Ch. 26 : 14. prepared slings to cast
Ezr. 5 : †8. hou. of God wi. s. of roll.
Ne. 4 : 2. will they revive the s. out
Jb. 5 : 23. shalt be in league with s.
6 : 12. Is my strength strength of s.?
8 : 17. His roots seeth the place of s.
14 : 19. the waters wear the s. thou
22 : 24. gold of Ophir as s. of brooks
28 : 3. searcheth out s. of darkness
6. s. of it are place of sapphires
41 : 30. Sharp s. are under him
Ps. 102 : 14. servants take pleasure
in her s. [the s.
137 : 9. dasheth little ones against
Pr. 16 : † 11. s. of bag are his work
26 : † 8. precious stone in heap of s.
Ec. 3 : 5. A time to cast s., to gather s.
10 : 9. Whoso. removeth s. sh. be hurt
Is. 5 : 2. he fenced it, gathered out s.
14 : 19. that go down to s. of the pit
27 : 9. the s. of altar as chalkstones
34 : 11. str-h upon it s. of emptiness
54 : 11. lay thy s. with fair colours
12. make thy borders of pleas-t s.
57 : 6. Among smooth s. of stream
60 : 17. I will bring for s. iron
62 : 10. cast up; gather out the s.
Je. 3 : 9. she com-ted adultery with s.
43 : 10. will set his throne upon s.
La. 3 : 16. broken teeth with gravel s.
4 : 1. s. of sanctuary are poured
Eze. 26 : 12. shall lay thy s. in water
28 : 14. thou hast walked in midst
of s. of fire [of s. of fire
16. I will destroy thee from midst
40 : † 43. within were two hearth s.
Mi. 1 : 6. I will pour s. into valley
Zch. 4 : †10. see s. in hand of Zeruh-l
5 : 4. shall consume it with the s.
9 : 16. they shall be as s. of a crown
Mat. 3 : 9. of these s. to raise up
children, Lu. 3 : 8. [made bread
4 : 3. command that these s. be
Mk. 5 : 5. crying, cutting hims. wi. s.
12 : 4. and at him they cast s., and
13 : 1. Master, see what s. are here
Lu. 19 : 40. s. wo. immediately cry
21 : 5. adorned with goodly s. [out
Jn. 8 : 59. s. to cast at him, 10 : 31.
2 Co. 3 : 7. ministra-n engraven in s.
1 Pe. 2 : 5. ye as lively s. are built up
See CORNER stone, s.
See COSTLY, HEAP.
See GREAT stone, s.

Precious STONES.

2 S. 12 : 30. talent of gold with p.s.,
1 Ch. 20 : 2. [p.s., 10.-2 Ch. 9 : 1, 9.
1 K. 10 : 2. queen of Sheba came with
11. navy of Hiram brought p.s.,
2 Ch. 9 : 10. [p.s.
1 Ch. 29 : 2. prepared all manner of
8. with whom p.s. were found [s.
2 Ch. 3 : 6. garnished house with p.
32 : 27. made treasuries for p.s.
Eze. 27 : 22. occupied in fairs wi. p.s.
Da. 11 : 38. a god honour with p.s.
1 Co. 3 : 12. if any man build upon
this foundation gold, p.s.
Re. 18 : 12. no man buyeth p.s. [4
16. decked with gold and p.s., 17 :
21 : 19. foundation garnished with
See SLING stones. [p.s.

See STONE, ED, with stones.

STONES. [broken

Le. 21 : 20. scabbed, or hath his s.
De. 23 : 1. wounded in s. sh. not enter
Jb. 40 : 17. sinews of his s. are wrapped

STONE. [Verb.]

Ex. 8 : 26. and will they not s. us?
17 : 4. they be almost ready to s. me
Le. 24 : 14. let congregation s. him
that cursed, 16. [die
1 K. 21 : 10. Naboth s. him that he
Lu. 20 : 6. if we say, Of men, all the
people will s. us [do ye s. me
Jn. 10 : 32. for which of those works
33. For a good work we s. thee not
11 : 8. Jews of late sought to s. thee
Ac. 14 : 5. an assault made to s. them.

STONE, ED, with stones.

Le. 20 : 2. thy peo. sh. s. him w.s.
27. familiar spirit or wizard s.w.s.
24 : 23. him that had cursed s.w.s.
Nu. 14 : 10. bade s. Josh., Caleb, w.s.
15 : 35. man, gathering sticks upon
sab. day cong. sh. s. him w.s., 36.
De. 13 : 10. thou shalt s. him w.s.
17 : 5. that woman shalt thou s. w.s.
21 : 21. drunkard, men of city s.w.s.
22 : 21. damsel men of city sh. s.w.s.
24. ye sh. s.w.s. damsel and man
Jos. 7 : 25. all Israel s-d Achan w.s.
1 K. 12 : 18. all Israel s-d Adoram
w.s., 2 Ch. 10 : 18.
21 : 13. they s-d Naboth w.s., 14, 15.
2 Ch. 24 : 21. s-d Zechariah w.s. in
Eze. 16 : 40. they shall s. thee w.s.
23 : 47. company sh. s. them w.s.
Jn. 10 : 31. Jews took s. ag. to s. him

STONED.

Ex. 19 : 13. he shall surely be s. or
21 : 28. ox shall be surely s., 29, 32.
Mat. 21 : 35. husbandmen beat one,
s. another [should be s.
Jn. 8 : 5. Moses commanded th. such
Ac. 5 : 26. lest they sho. have been s.
7 : 58. they s. Stephen, calling, 59.
14 : 19. having s. Paul, drew him out
2 Co. 11 : 25. beaten, once was I s.
He. 11 : 37. They were s., were sawn
12 : 20. beast touch mount, it be s.

STONESQUARERS.

1 K. 5 : 18. builders and s. did hew

STONEST, ING.

1 S. 30 : 6. people spake of s-g David
Mat. 23 : 37. O Jerus., that s-t them
are sent unto thee, Lu. 13 : 34.

STONY. [places

Ps. 141 : 6. judges overthrown in s.
Eze. 11 : 19. I will take s. heart, 36 : 26.
Mat. 13 : 5. fell upon s. places, 20,

STOOD. [Mk. 4 : 5, 16.

Ge. 18 : 22. Abraham s. before Lord
29 : † 35. and Leah s. from bearing
37 : 7. my sheaf arose, s. upright
Ex. 14 : 19. pillar of cloud s. behind
15 : 8. floods s. upright as an heap
Nu. 16 : 48. s. betw. dead and living
De. 4 : 11. ye came and s. under m-t
5 : 5. I stood between the Lord and
Jos. 3 : 16. the waters s. and rose up
4 : 3. stones where priests' feet s., 9.
21 : 44. s. not a man of their enem.
Ju. 6 : 31. Joash said unto all that
s. against him, Will ye plead
7 : 21. s. every man in his place
9 : 7. Joth. stood in top of m-t Ger.
16 : 29. two pillars upon wh. hou. s.
1 S. 3 : 10. Lord s. and called Samuel
4 : † 15. Eli's eyes s. he co. not see
10 : 23. s. am. the peo., he was higher
17 : 8. Goliath s., cried unto armies
1 K. 8 : 14. all the congregation of
Israel s., 2 Ch. 6 : 3.-7 : 6.
55. Solo. s. and blessed the cong-n
14 : †4. Ahijah, eyes s. for hoariness
2 K. 10 : 9. Jehu s. and said to people
13 : † 6. s. the grove in Samaria
23 : 3. all the people s. to covenant

2 Ch. 6 : 13. on brazen scaffold Sol. s.
20 : 5. Jehosh-t s. in cong. of Judah,
Ne. 8 : 4. beside him s. Shema [ac.
9 : 2. s. and confessed their sins, 12 :
Es. 9 : 16. other Jews s. for lives [40.
Ps. 33 : 9. he commanded, it s. fast
Isa. 6 : 2. above it s. the seraphim
36 : 13. Rabshakeh s. and cried
Je. 46 : 15. they s. not bec. Lord did
48 : 45. s. under shadow of Heshbon
Eze. 1 : 21. when those s., these s.,
10 : 17. [their wings
24. when they s. they let down
25. there was a voice when they s.
47 : 1. forefront of house s. toward
Da. 8 : 17. Gabriel came where I s.
10 : 11. he had spoken, I s. tremb-g
11 : 1. I s. to confirm and strength-
12 : 5. Behold, s. other two [en him
Jon. 1 : † 15. The sea s. from raging
Ha. 3 : 6. He s. and measured earth
Zch. 1 : 8. s. am. myrtle trees, 10, 11.
Mat. 12 : 46. mother, breth. s. with-t
Lu. 6 : 8. had withered hand s. forth
18 : 11. Pharisee s. and prayed thus
19 : 8. Zach-s s. and said, Behold L.
23 : 10. priests s. and accused him
35. the people s. beholding
Jn. 1 : 35. next day John s. and two
7 : 37. Jesus s. and cried, If any
18 : 25. Simon Peter s. and warmed
20 : 11. Mary s. with-t at sepulchre
Ac. 3 : 8. lame man leaping up, s.
9 : 7. the men wi. him s. speechless
11 : 13. angel wh. s. and said, Send
16 : 9. There s. a man of Macedonia
22 : 13. Ananias s. and said, Brother
27 : 21. Paul s. forth in the midst
He. 9 : 10. s. only in meats, drinks

STOOD about. [s.a.

1 S. 22 : 7. Saul said unto serv-s that
17. king said unto footmen th. s.a.
Ac. 14 : 20. as the disciples s.a. him

STOOD above.

Ge. 28 : 13. the Lord s.a. the ladder
2 Ch. 24 : 20. Zechariah s.a. the peo.
Ps. 104 : 6. the waters s.a. mount-s

STOOD afar.

Ex. 2 : 4. his sister s.a. off, to wit
20 : 18. people removed, s.a. off, 21.
1 S. 26 : 13. David s. on top of hill a.
2 K. 2 : 7. sons of prophets s. to view
Lu. 17 : 12. 10 lepers who s.a. off [a. off
23 : 49. all his acquaintance s.a. off
Re. 18 : 17. many as trade by sea s.a.

STOOD at. [m-t

Ex. 19 : 17. they s.a. nether part of
33 : 8. s. every man a. his tent door
9. cloudy pillar s.a. door of taber.
2 K. 5 : 9. Naaman s.a. door of hou.
2 Ch. 5 : 12. singers s.a. east end of
23 : 13. king s.a. his pillar, at the
Eze. 10 : 19. cherubim s.a. door of
21 : 21. king s.a. parting of the way
Lu. 7 : 38. woman s.a. his feet behind
Jn. 18 : 16. Pet. s.a. the door with-t
Re. 8 : 3. ano. angel came s.a. altar.

STOOD before.

Ge. 19 : 27. place where he s.b. Lord
43 : 15. went to Egypt, s.b. Joseph
Ex. 9 : 10. took ashes and s.b. Pha.
Le. 9 : 5. the congregation s.b. Lord
Nu. 27 : 2. dau-s of Zeloph-d s.b.
Jos. 20 : 9. until he s.b. cong. [Moses
Ju. 20 : 28. Phinehas s.b. ark in days
1 S. 16 : 21. David came and s.b. Saul
1 K. 1 : 28. Bath-sheba s.b. k. Dav.
3 : 15. Solomon s.b. ark of coven-t
16. two women, harlots, s.b. him
8 : 22. Sol. s.b. altar, 2 Ch. 6 : 12.
12 : 6. old men that s.b. Sol., 2 Ch.
10 : 6. [s.b., 2 Ch. 10 : 8.
8. consulted with young men that
22 : 21. spirit s.b. Lord, 2 Ch. 18 : 20.
2 K. 4 : 12. Shunammite s.b. Elisha
5 : 15. Naaman returned, s.b. Elisha
25. Gehazi s.b. his master

2 K. 8 : 9. Hazael came, s.b. Elisha
10 : 4. two kings s. not b. him [L.
2 Ch. 20 : 13. And all Judah s.b. the
Es. 5 : 4. So Esther arose s.b. king
Ps. 106 : 23. had not Moses s.b. him
Je. 15 : 1. Tho. Mos. and Samuel s.b.
18 : 20. I s.b. thee to speak good
52 : † 12. captain which s.b. king
Eze. 8 : 11. s.b. them seventy men
Da. 1 : 19. they s.b. the king, 2 : 2.
2 : 31. this great image s.b. thee
3 : 3. they s.b. image Neb. set up
7 : 10. times ten thousand s.b. him
8 : 3. there s.b. the river a ram
15. s.b. me as appearance of man,
Zch. 3 : 3. Joshua s.b. angel [10 : 16.
4. spake unto those that s.b. him
Mat. 27 : 11. Jesus s.b. the governor
Ac. 10 : 17. three men s.b. the gate
30. man s.b. me in bright clothing
12 : 14. told how Peter s.b. gate
24 : 20. say, while I s.b. council
Re. 7 : 9. great multitude s.b. throne
8 : 2. I saw 7 angels which s.b. God
12 : 4. the dragon s.b. the woman

STOOD beside.

2 S. 15 : 2. Absalom s.b. way of gate
1 K. 10 : 19. two lions s.b. the stays
Je. 36 : 21. princes which s.b. king
Eze. 9 : 2. six men s.b. brazen altar
10 : 6. he went in s.b. wheels

STOOD by.

Ge. 18 : 2. and lo, three men s.b. him
8. Abr. s.b. them under the tree
24 : 30. he s.b. the camels at well
41 : 1. Pha. dreamed, he s.b. river
3. s.b. the other kine upon the
45 : 1. not refrain bef. all that s.b.
Ex. 18 : 13. the people s.b. Moses
Nu. 23 : 6. Balak s.b. burnt sacr., 17.
Ju. 3 : 19. all that s.b. him went
18 : 16. men s.b. entering of gate
1 S. 1 : 26. woman th. s.b. thee, pray-
4 : 20. women th. s.b. her said [ing
17 : 26. Da. spake to men that s.b.
2 S. 13 : 31. s.b. with clothes rent
18 : 4. And the king s.b. gate side
20 : 11. one of Joab's men s.b. him
1 K. 13 : 1. Jeroboam s.b. the altar
24. ass s.b. it, lion s.b. carcass
2 K. 2 : 7. they two s.b. Jordan, 13.
11 : 14. the king s.b. a pillar, 23 : 3.
18 : 17. they s.b. conduit, Is. 36 : 2.
1 Ch. 21 : 15. angel s.b. threshingfl.
Je. 44 : 15. women that s.b. answ-d
Eze. 43 : 6. man s.b. me and said
Da. 7 : 16. I came near one that s.b.
Zch. 3 : 5. the angel of the Lord s.b.
Mat. 26 : 73. that s.b. said to Peter,
Thou art one of, Mk. 14 : 69, 70.
Mk. 14 : 47. one th. s.b. drew sword
15 : 35. some th. s.b. when th. heard
Lu. 5 : 1. s.b. lake of Gennesaret
19 : 24. said unto them that s.b.
24 : 4. two men s.b. them in shin-g
Jn. 12 : 29. that s.b. said it thund-d
18 : 22. officer that s.b. struck Jes.
19 : 25. s.b. cross of Jes. his mother
Ac. 1 : 10. two men s.b. in white app.
9 : 39. all widows s.b. him weeping
22 : 25. Paul unto centurion s.b.
23 : 2. com-ded them s.b. to smite
4. that s.b. said, Revilest thou
11. night following Lord s.b. him
27 : 23. s.b. me this night angel of

STOOD in. [God

Ex. 5 : 20. Moses and Aaron, who s.i.
32 : 26. Moses s.i. gate of the camp
Nu. 12 : 5. Lord s.i. door of tabern.
16 : 18. laid incense, and s.i. the
27. Dath. and Abiram s.i. door of
22 : 22. angel of Lord s.i. way, 24.
26. angel s.i. a narrow pla. [4 : 10.
Jos. 3 : 17. priests s.i. midst of Jord.,
Ju. 9 : 7. Jotham s.i. top of Gerizim
35. Gaal s.i. entering of the gate
44. Abim. s.i. the entering of gate
Ju. 18 : 17. priests s.i. the entering
2 S. 23 : 12. he s.i. midst of ground
1 K. 19 : 13. he s.i. entering in of
2 K. 3 : 21. Moabites s.i. border
4 : 15. Shunammite s.i. the door
2 Ch. 30 : 16. s.i. their place, 35 : 10.
34 : 31. k. s.i. his place, made cov-t
Ne. 8 : 7. the people s.i. their place
Es. 5 : 1. Esther s.i. inner court
Je. 19 : 14. Jere s.i. court of L.'s ho.
23 : 18. who s.i. counsel of Lord
22. if they had s.i. in my counsel
Eze. 8 : 11. Jaazaniah s.i. the midst
Ob. 14. Nei. sho. have s.i. crossway
Lu. 6 : 17. he s.i. plain and company
24 : 36. Jesus s.i. midst and saith,
Peace unto you, Jn. 20 : 19, 26.
Jn. 11 : 56. spake as they s.i. temple
Ac. 17 : 22. Paul s.i. midst Mars' hill
Re. 5 : 6. i. midst of elders s. a Lamb

STOOD on. [ark

Jos. 8 : 33. judges s.o. this side of
1 S. 17 : 3. Philistines s.o. a mountain, Israel s.o. a mountain
26 : 13. David s. o. the top of a hill
2 S. 2 : 25. Benj. s.o. top of a hill
2 K. 9 : 17. s. watchman o. tower in
1 Ch. 6 : 39. Asaph, who s.o. right
44. sons of Merari s.o. left hand
2 Ch. 3 : 13. cherubim s.o. their feet
Eze. 10 : 3. cherubim s.o. right side
Mat. 13 : 2. multitude s.o. the shore
Jn. 6 : 22. people wh. s.o. other side
21 : 4. morning, Jesus s.o. shore
Ac. 21 : 40. Paul s.o. stairs, beck-d
Re. 14 : 1. lo, a Lamb s.o. m-t Sion

STOOD over. [bered

Nu. 7 : † 2. s.o. them th. were num-
De. 31 : 15. pillar of cloud s.o door
Jos. 5 : 13. a man s.o. against him
2 K. 2 : † 7. fifty of sons s.o. against
Eze. 10 : 4. glory of L. s.o. threshold
18. glory of Lord s.o. cherubim
Mat. 2 : 9. star s.o. where child was
Mk. 15 : 39. centurion s.o. ag. him
Lu. 4 : 39. he s.o. her, rebuked fever

STOOD round.

Ge. 37 : 7. your sheaves s.r. about
Ac. 14 : 20. as the disciples s. r. him
25 : 7. Jews s.r. about Paul, and
Re. 7 : 11. all the angels s.r. throne

STOOD still.

Jos. 10 : 13. sun s.s., moon stayed
11 : 13. cities that s.s. in their stren.
2 S. 2 : 23. as many as came s.s.
28. Joab blew trumpet, peo. s.s.
18 : 30. he turned aside and s.s.
20 : 12. when man saw people s.s.
Ne. 12 : 39. they s.s. in prison gate
Jb. 4 : 16. spirit s.s., I co. not discern
32 : 16. for they spake not, but s.s.
Ha. 3 : 11. sun and moon s.s. in their
Mat. 20 : 32. Jesus s.s., called them
Mk. 10 : 49. Jesus s.s., Lu. 18 : 40.
Lu. 7 : 14. they that bare him s.s.

STOOD there.

Ex. 34 : 5. Lord descended and s.t.
1 S. 6 : 14. ark came into field, s.t.
1 K. 10 : 20. 12 lions s.t., 2 Ch. 9 : 19.
Eze. 3 : 23. glory of the Lord s.t. [S.
Ho. 10 : 9. fr. days of Gibeah t. they
Mat. 27 : 47. some that s.t., Mk. 11 : 5.
Jn. 18 : 18. servants and officers s.t.

STOOD up. [dead

Ge. 23 : 3. Abraham s.u. before his
7. Abraham s.u., bowed to people
Ex. 2 : 17. Moses s.u., helped them
Nu. 11 : 32. people s.u. all that day
2 K. 13 : 21. man revived and s.u.
1 Ch. 21 : 1. Satan s.u. ag. Israel
28 : 2. David, k., s.u. upon his feet
2 Ch. 13 : 4. Abijah s.u., said, Hear
20 : 19. Levites s.u. to praise Lord
23. Moab s.u. ag. mount Seir
28 : 12. s.u. that came fr the war
Ezr. 2 : 63. s.u. a priest with Urim and Thummim, Ne. 7 : 65.
Ezr. 3 : 2. s.u. Jeshua and builded
10 : 10. Ezra, priest, s.u. and said
Ne. 8 : 5. opened book people s.u.
9 : 3. s.u. in their place, read law
4. s.u. upon stairs, of the Levites
Es. 5 : 9. Haman saw Mord. s. not u.
7 : 7. Haman s.u. to make request
Jb. 4 : 15. the hair of my flesh s.u.
29 : 8. yo. men saw me, aged s.u.
30 : 28. I s.u. and cried in cong-n
Ps. 106 : 30. Then s.u. Phinehas
Eze. 37 : 10. s.u. exceeding gr. army
Da. 8 : 22. whereas four s.u. for it
Mk. 14 : 60. high priest s.u. in mid-t
Lu. 4 : 16. Jesus s.u. to read in sy n.
10 : 25. a lawyer s.u. and tempted
Ac. 1 : 15. in those days Peter s.u.
4 : 26. kings of earth s.u. ag. the L.
5 : 34. Then s.u. Gamaliel, a doctor
11 : 28. Agabus s.u. and signified
13 : 16. Paul s.u., and beckoning
25 : 18. Ag. whom when accusers s.

STOOD upon. [Lu.

Ge. 41 : 17. I s.u. bank of the river
1 S. 17 : 51. David ran and s.u. Phil.
2 S. 1 : 10. I s.u. Saul and slew him
1 K. 7 : 25. sea s.u. oxen, 2 Ch. 4 : 4.
2 K. 13 : 21. he revived, s.u. his feet
2 Ch. 6 : 13. u. it he s. and kneeled
Ne. 8 : 4. Ezra, scribe, s.u. a pulpit
Eze. 11 : 23. glory of Lord s.u. mt.
Am. 7 : 7. Lord s.u. a wall made by
Re. 11 : 11. two prophets s.u. feet
13 : 1. I s.u. sand of sea and saw

STOOD with.

Ge. 45 : 1. there s.w. him no man
2 K. 11 : 11. ev. man s.w. his weapons
2 Ch. 29 : 26. Levites s.w. instrum-ts
Ezr. 3 : 9. Josh. s.w. sons and breth.
La. 2 : 4. he s.w. his right hand
Lu. 9 : 32. saw 2 men that s.w. him
Jn. 18 : 5. Judas also s.w. them
18. Peter s.w. them and warmed
2 Ti. 4 : 16. no man s.w. me, but all
17. Lord s.w. and strengthened

STOODEST. [Lne

Nu. 22 : 34. I knew not thou s. in
De. 4 : 10. day that thou s. bef. Lord
Ob. 11. In day thou s. on other side

STOOL, STOOLS. [s-s

Ex. 1 : 16. when ye see them upon
2 K. 4 : 10. set for him bed, table and s.

STOOP. [fulm

Jb. 9 : 13. proud helpers s. under
Pr. 12 : 25. maketh heart of man s.
Is. 46 : 2. They s., they bow down
Mk. 1 : 7. I am not worthy to s. and

STOOPED.

Ge. 49 : 9. Judah s. down, couched
1 S. 24 : 8. David s. [28 : 14. Saul s.
2 Ch. 36 : 17. no compassion upon maiden or him that s. for age [S.
Jn. 8 : 6. Jesus s. down and wrote,
20 : 11. as she wept, she s. down

STOOPETH, ING. [s-h

Is. 46 : 1. Bel boweth down, Nebo
Lu. 24 : 12. s-g down, saw clothes,

STOP. [Jn. 20 : 5.

1 K. 18 : 44. that the rain s. thee not
2 K. 3 : 19. ye shall s. all wells, 25.
2 Ch. 32 : 3. took counsel to s. waters
Ps. 35 : 3. s. way ag. them persecute
107 : 42. iniquity sh. s. her mouth
Eze. 39 : 11. sh. s. noses of passengers
2 Co. 11 : 10. no man shall s. me of

STOPPED. [boasting

Ge. 8 : 2. windows of heaven were s.
26 : 15. Philistines had s. wells, 18.
Le. 15 : 3. his flesh be s. from issue
2 Ch. 32 : 30. Hezekiah s. watercourse
4. who s. all fountains and brook
Ne. 4 : 7. breaches began to be s.
Ps. 63 : 11. mouth speaketh lies be s.
Je. 51 : 32. that the passages are s.
Zch. 7 : 11. refused, and s. their ears
Ac. 7 : 57. s. their ears, ran upon him
Ro. 3 : 19. that ev. mouth may be s.

2 Co. 11 : † 10. this boasting not be s.
Tit. 1 : 11. Whose mouths must be s.
He. 11:33. Who thro. faith s. mouths
STOPPERS. [of lions
Eze. 27: †9. wise men were s. of chinks
STOPPETH.
Jb. 5 : 16. and iniquity s. her mouth
Ps. 58 : 4. like adder that s. her ear
Pr. 21 : 13. whoso s. his ears at cry
Is. 33 : 15. s. ears from hearing of
STORE. [Noun.]
Ge. 26 : 14. Isaac had gr. s. of ser-ts
41 : 36. food sh. be for s. in famine
Le. 25 : 22. ye sh. eat of old s., 26: 10.
De. 28 : 5. Blessed be basket and s.
17. Cursed be thy basket and s.
32 : 34. Is not this laid up in s. wi.
1 K. 10 : 10. gave king of spices gr. s.
2 K. 20 : 17. fathers have laid up in
s. to this day, Is. 39 : 6. [hand
1 Ch. 29 : 16. this s. cometh of thine
2 Ch. 11 : 11. he put s. of victuals
31 : 10. which is left in this great s.
Ne. 5 : 18. s. of all sorts of wine
Ps. 144 : 13. our garners affording s.
Na. 2 : 9. there is none end of the s.
1 Co. 16 : 2. let every one lay by in s.
1 Ti. 6 : 19. laying in s. good founda.
2 Pe. 3: 7. by same word are kept in s.
STORE, with cities. [6.
1 K. 9 : 19. c. of s. Sol. had, 2 Ch. 8:
2 Ch. 8 : 4. s. c. which he built
16 : 4. they smote s. c. of Naphtali
17 : 12. Jehosh-t built c. of s. in
STORE. [Verb.] [aces
Am. 3 : 10. who s. up violence in pal-
STOREHOUSE.
Mal. 3 : 10. Bring all tithes into s.
Lu. 12 : 24. the ravens have no s.
STOREHOUSES.
Ge. 41 : 56. Joseph opened all the s.
De. 28 : 8. command blessing in s.
1 Ch. 9 : † 26. Levites were ov. the s.
27 : 25. over s. was Jehonathan
Ne. 13: †12. bro-t Judah tithe unto s.
2 Ch. 31 : † 11. Hez. com-ded to pre-
32 : 28. Hezekiah made s. [pare s.
Ps. 33 : 7. he layeth up depth in s.
Je. 50 : 26. open her s. cast her up
STORK. [14 : 18.
Le. 11 : 19. s. thou shalt not eat, De.
Jb. 39 : † 13. gavest feathers to s.?
Ps. 104 : 17. s., fir trees are her hou.
Je. 8 : 7. s. knoweth her appointed
Zch. 5 : 9. they had wings like a s.
STORM, S. [away
Jb. 21 : 18. as chaff that s. carrieth
27 : 21. s. hurleth him out of place
Ps. 55 : 8. I would hasten my escape
from the windy s. [s.
83 : 15. make them afraid with thy
107 : 29. He maketh the s. a calm
Is. 4 : 6. and for a covert from s. and
25 : 4. thou hast been refuge fr. s.
28 : 2. as destroying s. sh. cast down
29 : 6. thou shalt be visited with s.
La. 5: †10. Our skin black bec. of s.
Eze. 38 : 9. Thou shalt come like a s.
Na. 1 : 3. Lord hath his way in the s.
Mk. 4 : 37. arose a great s. of wind
Lu. 8 : 23. came a s. of wind on lake
STORMY. [wind
Ps. 107 : 25. he commandeth the s.
148 : 8. s. wind fulfilling his word
Eze. 13 : 11. and s. wind sh. rend it
13. I will rend it with a s. wind
STORIES.
Ge. 6 : 16. with s. make the ark
Eze. 41 : 16. galleries three s. ov. ag.
42 : 3. gallery ag. gallery in 3 s., 6.
Am. 9 : 6. buildeth his s. in the heav.
STORY. [Iddo
2 Ch. 13 : 22. acts of Abijah in s. of
24 : 27. written in s. of book of k-s
STOUT. [tered
Jb. 4 : 11. s. lion's whelps are scat-
Is. 10 : 12. punish fruit of s. heart

Da. 7 : 20. whose look was more s.
Mal. 3 : 13. Your words been s. ag. me
STOUTHEARTED.
Ps. 76 : 5. s. are spoiled, they slept
Is. 46 : 12. Hearken unto me, ye s.
STOUTNESS.
Is. 9 : 9. that say in s. of heart
STRAIGHT. [him, 20.
Jos. 6 : 5. ascend every man s. bef.
1 S. 6 : 12. kine took s. way to Beth.
2 Ch. 32 : 30. bro-t waterco-e s. down
Ps. 5 : 8. make way s. bef. my face
Pr. 4 : 25. let thine eyelids look s.
Ec. 1 : 15. crooked cannot be made s.
7 : 13. who can make that s. he
Is. 40 : 3. make s. in desert highway
4. the crooked shall be made s.,
42 : 16.-45 : 2. Lu. 3 : 5.
45 : † 13. I will make s. all his ways
Je. 31 : 9. cause to walk in s. way
Eze. 1 : 7. their feet were s. feet [22.
9. went ev. one s. forward, 12.-10:
23. under firmament were wings s.
Mat. 3 : 3. make his paths s., Mk. 1:
3. Lu. 3 : 4. Jn. 1 : 23. [glorified
Lu. 13 : 13, she was made s., and
Ac. 9 : 11. go into street called S
16 : 11. came wi. a s. course, 21 : 1.
He. 12 : 13. make s. paths for y-r feet
STRAIGHTLY. [s.
Can. 7 : †9. like wine th. goeth down
STRAIGHTWAY.
1 S. 9 : 13. ye shall s. find him before
28 : 20. Saul fell s. along on earth
Pr. 7 : 22. He goeth aft. her s. as an ox
Da. 10 : 17. s. no strength in me
Mat. 3 : 16. Jes. went up s. out of the
water, Mk. 1 : 10. [Mk. 1 : 18.
4 : 20. and they s. left their nets,
14 : 22. s. Jesus constrained disciples, Mk. 6 : 45.
27. s. Jes. spake, Be of good cheer
21 : 2. s. ye shall find an ass tied
3. s. he will send them hither,
25 : 15. s. took his journey [Mk. 11 : 3.
27 : 48. s. one ran and took a sponge
Mk. 1 : 20. And s. Jesus called them
21. s. on sab. day he ent-d synag.
2 : 2. s. many were gath-d together
3 : 6. s. took counsel with Herodi-s
5 : 29. s. fountain of her blood was
42. s. damsel arose, walked [dried
6 : 25. she came s. wi. haste unto k.
54. out of ship, s. they knew him
7 : 35. s. his ears were opened
8 : 10. s. Jesus entered into a ship
9 : 15. s. all the people were amazed
20. s. the spirit tare him
24. s. father of child cried, Lord
14 : 45. he goeth s. to him and saith
15 : 1. s. chief priests held consult-n
Lu. 5 : 39. old wine, s. desireth new
8 : 55. spirit came, and she arose s.
12 : 54. s. ye say, cometh a shower
14 : 5. not s. pull him out on sab.?
Jn. 13 : 32. God shall s. glorify him
Ac. 5 : 10. Then fell she s. at his feet
9 : 20. s. he preached Chist in syna.
16 : 33. Jailer was baptized and his
22 : 29. s. they departed fr. him [s.
23 : 30. was told me, I sent s. to thee
Ja. 1 : 24. s. forgetteth what man he
STRAIN. [was
Mat. 23 : 24. guides s. at a gnat and
STRAIT. [Adj.] [us
2 K. 6 : 1. place we dwell is too s. for
Is. 49 : 20. The place is too s. for me
Mat. 7 : 13. Enter ye in at s. gate
14. Because s. is gate, Lu. 13 : 24.
STRAIT, STRAITS.
1 S. 13 : 6. Isr. saw they were in a s.
2 S. 24 : 14. I am in a s., 1 Ch. 21 : 13.
Jb. 20 : 22. In his sufficiency be in s-s
36 : 16. removed thee out of the s.
La. 1 : 3. overtook her betw. the s-s
Da. 9 : † 25. wall built in s. of times
Ph. 1 : 23. I am in a s. betwixt two

STRAITEN. [them
Je. 19 : 9. that seek their lives sh. s.
STRAITENED. [be s.
Jb. 18 : 7. steps of his strength shall
37 : 10. breadth of the waters is s.
Pr. 4 : 12. goest, thy steps sh. not be s.
Eze. 42 : 6. building was s. more than
Mi. 2 : 7. is Spirit of the Lord s.?
Lu. 12 : 50. how am I s. till it be ac.
2 Co. 6 : 12. Ye are not s. in us, s. in
STRAITENETH. [s.
Jb. 12 : 23. he enlargeth nations and
STRAITEST. [ligion
Ac. 26 : 5. aft. most s. sect of our re-
STRAITLY.
Ge. 43 : 7. man asked s. of our state
Ex. 13 : 19. Joseph had s. sworn Isr.
Jos. 6 : 1. Jericho was s. shut up
1 S. 14 : 28. thy fa. s. charged people
Mat. 9 : 30. he s. charged them, say-
ing, Mk. 3 : 12.-5 : 43. Lu. 9 : 21.
Mk. 1 : 43. s. charged and sent him
Ac. 4 : 17. let us s. threaten them
5 : 28. Did not we s. command you
STRAITNESS. [for s.
Ex. 6 : † 9. hearkened not unto Mos.
De. 28 : 53. shalt eat chil. in s., 55, 57.
Jb. 36 : 16. broad place where is no s.
Is. 42 : † 16. crooked things into s.
Je. 19 : 9. eat flesh of friend in s.
He. 1 : † 8. sceptre of s. is sceptre of
STRAKE.
Ac. 27 : 17. fearing s. sail and so were
See STRUCK. [driven
STRAKES. See STREAKS.
STRANGE. [unto th.
Ge. 42 : 7. Joseph made himself s.
Ex. 21 : 8. to sell her unto s. nation
30 : 9. Ye shall offer no s. incense
Le. 10 : 1. Nadab, Abihu, off-d s. fire
2 K. 19 : 24. I have drunk s. waters
Jb. 19 : 3. are not ashamed that ye
make yourselves s. to me
17. my breath is s. to my wife
31 : 3. s. punishment to workers of
Ps. 114 : 1. Jacob fr. peo. of s. langu.
Pr. 21 : 8. way of man is froward, s.
Is. 17 : 10. shalt set it with s. slips
28 : 21. that he may do his s. work
28 : 21. may bring to pass his s. act
Je. 2 : 21. degenerate plant of s. vine
8 : 19. provoked me with s. vanities
18 : † 14. shall running waters be
forsaken for the s. cold waters?
Eze. 3 : 5. sent to a peo. of s. speech, 6.
Zph. 1 : 8. are clothed with s. apparel
Ac. 7 : 6. should sojourn in s. land
26 : 11. I persecuted th. to s. cities
He. 11 : 9. sojourned in s. country
13 : 9. not carried ab. wi. s. doctrines
1 Pe. 4 : 4. think it s. ye run not to
12. think it not s. concerning trial
Jude 7. as Sodom going aft. s. flesh
See **Strange CHILDREN.**
See **Strange GOD, GODS.**
See **Strange LAND.**
STRANGE thing, s.
Ho. 8 : 12. they were counted as s. t.
Lu. 5 : 26. We have seen s. t-s to day
Ac. 17 : 20. bringest s. t-s to our ears
1 Pe. 4 : 12. as tho. some s. t. happ-d
See **Strange WIVES.** See
Strange WOMAN, WOMEN.
STRANGELY.
De. 32 : 27. lest adversaries behave s.
STRANGER. [land
Ge. 15 : 13. thy seed shall be a s. in
17 : 8. give thee land wherein thou
art a s., 28 : 4.-37 : 1. [any s.
12. or that is bought wi. money of
27. men bo-t with money of the s.
Ex. 2 : 22. I been a s. in strange land
12 : 19. be cut off, whe. a s., or born
in, Le. 16 : 29.-17 : 15. Nu. 15 : 30.
43. shall no s. eat thereof, 29 : 33.
48. s. will keep passover, Nu. 9 : 14.
49. One law shall be to him that is

homeborn and the s., Le.24 :22.
Nu. 9 : 14.-15 : 15, 16, 29. [a s.
Ex. 18 : † 3.the name of the one was
20 : 10.nor s. within gates, De.5:14.
22 : 21. shalt not vex or oppress a s.
23 : 9. ye know heart of a s., seeing
12. that the s. may be refreshed
30 : 33. whoso. putteth it upon a s.
Le. 17 : 12. neither shall s. eat blood
19 : 10. neither gather every grape
leave for poor and s.,23:22.-25:6.
33. if s. in land, ye shall not vex
34. s. be as one born am.,Nu.15:15.
22 : 10. no s. eat of holy thing, 13.
12. if married to s. sh. not eat of-g
25. Nei. from s. hand offer bread
24 : 16. as well s. when blasphemeth
Nu. 1 : 51. s. that cometh nigh be
put to death, 3 : 10, 38.-18 : 7.
15 : 14. if a s. sojourn offer offering
16 : 40. that no s. come near to offer
18 : 4. s. shall not come nigh unto
19 : 10. to Isr. and s. statute for ev.
De. 1 : 16. Judge righteously betw. s.
10 : 18. L. loveth s. in giving food
19. s., for ye were strangers [to s.
14 : 21. give th. wh. dieth of its.un-
17 : 15. not set a s. over thee
23 : 7. bec. thou wast a s. in his land
20. Unto a s. lend upon usury [s.
25 : 5. wife not marry with-t unto a
26 : 11. shalt rejoice, thou and s.
28 : 43. s. shall get above thee high
29 : 11. thy s. to enter into covenant
22. s. sh. say, Why hath Lord done
31 : 12. Gather thy s. that he hear
Jos. 8 : 33. bef. priests, as well the s.
Ju. 19 : 12. will not turn to city of s.
Ru. 2 : 10. why found grace, I am a s.?
2 S. 1 : 13. I am the son of a s., an
15 : 19. thou art a s. and an exile
1 K. 8 : 18. was no s. with us in hou.
8 : 41. concerning a s., 2 Ch. 6 : 32.
43. acc-g to all s. calleth, 2Ch.6:33.
Jb. 15 : 19. no s. passed am. them
19 : 15. my maids count me for a s.
†27. eyes shall behold, and not a s.
31 : 32. s. did not lodge in street
Ps. 18 : † 44. sons of s. yield feigned
69 : 8. I am become s. unto breth.
94 : 6. They slay the widow and s.
137 : †4. How sing L.'s song in la. of
119 : 19. I am a s. in the earth [s.?
Pr. 2 : 16. To deliver thee from the s.
5 : 10. thy labours be in house of s.
20. why embrace bosom of s.?
6 : 1. if hast stricken hand with s.
7 : 5. keep thee fr. s. who flattereth
11 : 15. he is surety for a s. sh. smart
14 : 10. a s. doth not intermeddle
20 : 16. that is surety for a s., 27:13.
27 : 2. Let a s. praise thee, not own
Ec. 6 : 2. not power to eat, s. eateth
Is. 56 : 3. nei. let son of a s. speak
6. sons of the s. that join thems.
62 : 8. sons of s. not drink thy wine
Je. 14 : 8. why thou be as s. in land
Eze. 14 : 7. ev. s. th. setteth up idols
22 : 7. dealt by oppression wi. s., 29.
44 : † 7. into sanctuary chil. of a s.
9. No s. uncirc-d enter sanctuary
47 : 23. in what tribe s. sojourneth
Ob. 12. in the day he became a s.
Mal. 3 : 5. turned aside s. fr. his right
Mat. 25 : 35. I was s., ye took me in, 43.
38. when saw we thee a s.? 44.
Lu. 17 : 18. not found, save this s.
24 : 18. Art thou only a s. in Jerus.
Jn. 10 : 5. s. will they not follow
Ac. 7 : 29. Moses a s. in land of Midian
See **FATHERLESS**, with
stranger, strangers.

STRANGER, S, with
sojourner, s.

Ge. 23 : 4. I am a s. and s. with you
Le. 25 : 23. ye are s-s and s-s with me
35. if poor, relieve him, tho. s. or s.
Le. 25 : 47. if s. or s. wax rich, and
bro. wax poor, sell hims. to s. or s.
Nu. 35 : 15. cities refuge for s. and s.,
Jos. 20 : 9. [fathers
1 Ch. 29 : 15. we s-s and s-s as our
Ps. 39 : 12. I am s. and s. as all my

STRANGERS. [fa-s

Ge. 31 : 15. are we not counted s.?
36 : 7. wh-n they were s., Ex. 6 : 4.
Ex. 22 : 21. for ye were s. in land of
Eg., 23 : 9. Le. 19 : 34.-25 : 23.
De. 10 : 19. [22 : 18.
Le. 17 : 8. s. that offer an oblation
10. whatso. man of s. eateth blood
13. whatso. man of s. hunteth fowl
20 : 2. s. that give seed to Molech
25 : 45. of chil. of s. shall ye buy
De. 24 : 14. not oppress a serv. of s.
31 : 16. go a whoring aft. gods of s.
Jos. 8 : 35. s. that were conversant
Ju. 10 : † 16. they put aw. gods of s.
2 S. 22 : 45. s. shall submit unto me
46. s. sh. fade aw., Ps. 18 : 44, 45
1 Ch. 16 : 19. ye were s., Ps. 105 : 12.
22 : 2. David com-ded to gather s.
2 Ch. 2 : 17. Sol. numbered all the s.
15 : 9. Asa gathered Judah and s.
30 : 25. s. of Isr. and Jud. rejoiced
Ne. 9 : 2. seed of Isr. separated fr. s.
13 : 30. cleansed I them from all s.
Ps. 54 : 3. For s. are risen up ag. me
109 : 11. let the s. spoil his labour
146 : 9. The Lord preserveth the s.
Pr. 5 : 10. Lest s. be filled wi. wealth
17. let them be thine own, not s.,
Is. 1 : 7. your land, s. devour it (2)
2 : 6. they please themselves in s.
5 : 17. places of fat ones shall s. eat
14 : 1. s. shall be joined with them
25 : 2. hast made a palace of s.
5. shall bring down the noise of s.
29 : 5. mult. of s. shall be like dust
60 : 10. sons of s. shall build walls
61 : 5. And s. shall feed your flocks
Je. 2 : 25. I have loved s., and after
3 : 13. hast scattered thy ways to s.
5 : 19. so shall ye serve s. in a land
30 : 8. s. shall no more serve thems.
35 : 7. live in land where ye be s.
51 : 51. s. are come into sanctuaries
La. 5 : 2. Our inherit. is turned to s.
Eze. 7 : 21. I give it into hand of s.
11 : 9. deliver you into hands of s.
16 : 32. wife wh. taketh s. instead of
28 : 7. will bring s. upon thee [husb.
10. thou shalt die by hand of s.
30 : 12. I will make land waste by s.
31 : 12. s. have cut him off, and ha.
44 : 7. bro-t into my sanctuary s.
47 : 22. inheritance unto you and s.
Ho. 7 : 9. s. have devour. his strength
8 : 7. the s. shall swallow it up
Jo. 3 : 17. shall no s. pass thro. her
Ob. 11. the day s. carried aw. captive
Mat. 17 : 25. tribute? of chil. or s.?
26. Peter saith unto him, of s.
27 : 7. potter's field to bury s.
Jn. 10 : 5. they know not voice of s.
Ac. 2 : 10. s. of Rome, Jews, and
13 : 17. they dwelt as s. in la. of Eg.
17 : 21. Athenians and s. spent time
Ep. 2 : 12. s. fr. covenants of promise
19. theref. ye are no more s., but
1 Ti. 5 : 10. if she have lodged s., if
He. 11 : 13. confessed they were s.
13 : 2. not forgetful to entertain s.
1 Pe. 1 : 1. to s. scattered thro. Pontus
2 : 11. I beseech you as s., pilgrims
3 Jn. 5. doest faithfully whatsoever
thou doest to s.

STRANGLED.

Na. 2 : 12. the lion s. for lionesses
Ac. 15 : 20. abstain fr. things s., 29.-

STRANGLING. [21 : 25.

Jb. 7 : 15. So that my soul chooseth

STRAW. [Noun.] [s.

Ex. 5 : 7. no more give s., 10, 13, 16, 18.
Ex. 5 : 11. Go, get s. where ye can
12. gather stubble instead of s.
1 K. 4 : 28. brought s. for the horses
Jb 41 : 27. esteemeth iron as s., brass
Is. 11 : 7. lion eat s. like ox, 65 : 25.
25 : 10. Moab shall be trodden as s.
See PROVENDER.

STRAWED. See STREWED.

STREAKS. [rods

Ge. 30 : 37. Jacob pilled white s. in
Le. 14 : 37. if plague with hollow s.
Eze. 1 : † 18. their s. full of eyes

STREAM.

Nu. 21 : 15. what he did at s. of brooks
Jb. 6 : 15. as s. of brooks they pass
Ps. 124 : 4. s. had gone over our soul
Is. 27 : 12. L. shall beat off unto s. of
30 : 28. breath as overflowing s.
33. like a s. of brimstone, kindle
57 : 6. Am. stones of s. thy portion
66 : 12. glory of Gent. like flowing s.
Da. 7 : 10. fiery s. issued forth [s.
Am. 5 : 24. righteousness as mighty
Lu. 6. 48. s. beat vehemently, 49.

STREAMS. [8 : 5.

Ex. 7 : 19. stretch hand on their s.,
Ps. 46 : 4. s. make glad city of God
78 : 16. He brought s. out of rock
20. waters gushed, s. overflowed
126 : 4. Turn our captivity as s. in
Can. 4 : 15. living waters, s. fr. Leb-n
Is. 11 : 15. L. shall smite in seven s.
30 : 25. upon ev. high hill sh. be s.
33 : 21. place of broad rivers and s.
34 : 9. s. shall be turned into pitch
35 : 6. waters break out, and s. in

STREET. [desert

Ge. 19 : 2. we will abide in s. all night
De. 13 : 16. gather all spoil into s.
Jos. 2 : 19. out of thy house into s.
Ju. 19 : 15. he sat down in a s., 17.
20. old man said, lodge not in s.
2 S. 21 : 12. stolen fr. s. of Beth-shan
2Ch. 29 : 4. gath-d L. into east, s., 32:6.
Ezr. 10 : 9. all the people sat in s.
Ne. 8 : 1. people gathered into the s.
3. he read therein before the s.
16. So people made booths in s.
Es. 4 : 6. So Hatach went unto s.
6 : 9. him on horseback thro s. 11.
Jb. 18 : 17 shall have no name in s.
29 : 7. I prepared my seat in the s.
31 : 32. stranger did not lodge in s.
Pr. 7 : 8. through s.. near her corner
Is. 42 : 2. not heard in s. Mat 12 : 19.
51 : 23 hast laid thy body as the s.
59 : 14. truth is fallen in the s.. and
Je 37 : 21. give bread out of bakers' s.
La. 2 : 19. faint for hunger in ev. s.
4 : 1. stones are poured out in ev. s.
Eze. 16 : 24. a high place in ev. s., 31.
Da. 9 : 25. s. shall be built again
Ac. 9 : 11. go into s. called Straight
12 : 10. Peter passed through one s.
Re. 11 : 8. dead bodies shall lie in s.
21 : 21. s. of the city was pure gold
22 : 2. In midst of s. was tree of life
See Mire.

STREETS.

Nu. 22 : † 39. they came to city of s.
2 S. 1 : 20. publish it not in the s. of
1 K. 20 : 34. shalt make s. in Damas.
Ps 18 : 42. I cast them as dirt in s.
55 : 11. guile depart not from her s.
144 : 13. sheep bring forth 10,000 in
14. be no complaining in our s. [s.
Pr. 1 : 20. wisdom uttereth voice in s.
5 : 16. and rivers of water in the s.
7 : 12. How is she in s., and lieth
22 : 13. is a lion, I sh. be slain in s.
26 : 13. slothful saith, A lion is in s.
Ec. 12 : 4. doors shall be shut in s.
5. the mourners go about the s.
Can. 3 : 2. I will go about city in s.
Is. 5 : 25. carcasses were torn in s.
15 : 3. In s. they shall gird thems.
24 : 11. is a crying for wine in s.

Is. 51 : 20. sons lie at head of all s.
Je. 9 : 21. cut off young men from s.
48 : 38. be lamentation in s. of Moab
49 : 26. yo. men sh. fall in s., 50 : 30.
51 : 4. are thrust through in her s.
La. 2 : 11. sucklings swoon in s., 12.
21. The young and old lie in the s.
4 : 5. did feed delicately, are in s.
8. Nazarites are not known in s.
14. wandered as blind men in s.
18. They hunt our steps in our s.
Eze. 7 : 19. shall cast silver in the s.
11 : 6. ye have filled s. with slain
26 : 11. hoofs of horses tread thy s.
28 : 23. I will send blood into her s.
Am. 5 : 16. Wailing shall be in all s.
Na. 2 : 4. chariots shall rage in s.
3 : 10. dashed in pieces at top of s.
Zph. 3 : 6. I made their s. waste
Zch. 8 : 4. old women sh. dwell in s.
5. s. shall be full of boys and girls
10 : 5. who tread enemies in the s.
Mat. 6 : 2. do not sound trumpet in s.
5. pray standing in corners of s.
Mk. 6 : 56. laid sick in s., Ac. 5 : 15.
Lu. 10 : 10. go out into s. of same
13 : 26. thou hast taught in our s.
14 : 21. Go quickly into s. and lanes
See MIRE.

STREETS of Jerusalem.

Je. 5 : 1. Run ye to and fro thro. s. -
7 : 17. seest not what they do in s. -
34. cause to cease from s. - mirth
11 : 6. Proclaim these words in s. -
13. acc-g to the number of the s.-
14 : 16. peo. shall be cast out in s.-
33 : 10. mirth shall be heard in s. -
44 : 6. my anger was kindled in s. -
9. wickedness they com-ted in s. -
21. incense that ye burn in s. -

STRENGTH. [s.

Ge. 4 : 12. ground shall not yield her
Ex. 13 : 3. by s. L. bro-t you out, 14, 16.
Nu. 23 : 22. hath s. of unicorn, 24 : 8.
Ju. 5 : 21. O my soul, hast trodden s.
1 S. 2 : 4. th. stumbled are girded with
9. for by s. sh. no man prevail [s.
10. he shall give s. unto his king
15 : 29. S. of Israel will not lie
28 : 22. eat, th. thou mayest have s.
2 S. 22 : 40. thou hast girded me with
s. to battle, Ps. 18 : 32, 39.
1 K. 7 : † 21. he called the left pillar.
In it is s., 2 Ch. 3 : † 17. [sons of s.
2 K. 2 : † 16. there be with us fifty
18 : 20. I have counsel and s. for
war, Is. 36 : 5. [Is. 37 : 3.
19 : 3. there is no s. to bring forth,
1 Ch. 16 : 27. s. and gladness are in
28. give unto Lord glory and s.,
Ps. 29 : 1.-96 : 7. [able men for s.
26 : 8. they, sons, and brethren
29 : 12. in thine hand it is to give s.
† 14. obtain s. to offer willingly
2 Ch. 2 : † 6. obtained s. to build ho.
13 : 20. Nei. did Jeroboam recov. s.
30 : † 21. sing-g with instruments of
Ezr. 4 : † 13. endamage s. of kings [s.
Ne. 4 : 10. s. of bearers of burdens
Es. 9 : † 29. Esther wrote with all s.
Jb. 9 : † 13. helpers of s. do stoop
19. If I speak of s., lo, he is strong
12 : 13. With him is wisdom and s.,
21. he weakeneth s. of mighty [16.
17 : † 9. hath clean hands, sh. add s.
18 : 13. It sh. devour s. of his skin
22 : † 25. thou shalt have silver of s.
23 : 6. but he would put s. in me
30 : 2. whereto might s. profit me
† 21. with s. thou opposest me
31 : † 39. if eaten the s. with-t money
36 : 19. will not esteem forces of s.
39 : 19. Hast thou given horse s.?
41 : 22. In his neck remaineth s.
Ps. 8 : 2. Out of babes ordained s.
20 : 6. with saving s. of right hand
27 : 1. Lord is the s. of my life
Ps. 28 : 8. is saving s. of his anointed
29 : 11. L. will give s. unto his peo.
30 : † 7. hast settled s. for my mt.
31 : † 2. be to me for a rock of s. [s.
33 : 16. mighty is not delivered by
39 : 13. spare, th. I may recover s.
46 : 1. G. is our refuge and s., 81 : 1.
60 : 7. Ephraim is s. of mine head,
† 9. bring me into city of s. [108 : 8.
62 : † 11. s. belongeth unto God
68 : 34. Ascribe ye s. unto G., his s.
35. G. of Isr. is he that giveth s.
73 : 26. God is the s. of my heart
74 : † 15. thou driedst up rivers of s.
81 : 1. Sing aloud unto God our s.
84 : 5. Blessed is man whose s. is
7. They go fr. s. to s. every one [s.
89 : † 10. scattered enemies wi. thy
90 : 10. if by reason of s. fourscore
93 : 1. the Lord is clothed with s.
95 : 4. the s. of the hills is his also
96 : 6. s. and beauty in his sanct-y
99 : 4. king's s. loveth judgment
138 : 3. strengthenedst me with s.
140 : 7. O God, s. of my salvation
Pr. 8 : 14. I am underst-g; I have s.
10 : 29. way of Lord s. to upright
14 : 4. much increase is by s. of ox
21 : 22. a wise man casteth down s.
24 : 5. man of knowl. increaseth s.
27 : † 24. For s. is not for ever
31 : 17. She girdeth her loins with s.
25. s. and honour are her clothing
Ec. 8 : † 1. s. of his face be changed
9 : 16. Wisdom is better than s.
10 : 10. If iron blunt, put to more s.
17. princes eat for s., not drunken.
Is. 5 : 22. men of s. to mingle drink
10 : 13. By s. of hand I have done it
23 : 4. spoken, even s. of the sea
25 : 4. hast been a s. to poor, a s. to
the needy in his distress [s.
26 : 4. in L. JEHOVAH is everlasting
28 : 6. s. to them that turn battle
30 : 3. s. of Pha. sh. be your shame
33 : 6. wisdom sh. be stability and s.
40 : 9. O Jeru., lift up voice with s.
29. have no might, he increas-h s.
42 : 25. poured upon him s. of bat.
44 : 12. worketh it with s. of arms
45 : 24. in L. have I righteousn. and
51 : 9. Awake, put on s., O arm [s.
Je. 20 : 5. I will deliver s. of city
51 : 53. tho. she fortify height of s.
La. 1 : 6. they are gone without s.
Eze. 30 : 15. my fury upon Sin, the s.
18. pomp of her s., 33 : 28. [of Eg.
Da. 2 : 37. God hath given thee s.
41. shall be in it of s. of the iron
3 : † 20. com-ded the mighty of s.
11 : 15. nei. be any s. to withstand
17. to enter wi. s. of his kingdom
31. shall pollute sanctuary of s.
Jo. 3 : 16. Lord, the s. of Isr. [by s.?
Am. 6 : 13. Have we not taken horns
Na. 1 : † 7. L. is s. in day of trouble
3 : 9. Ethi-a and Egypt were her s.
11. thou sh. seek s. bec. of enemy
Hag. 2 : 22. I will destroy s. of kingd.
Mk. 12 : 33. love him with all the s.
Lu. 1 : 51. He shewed s. with his arm
Ac. 3 : 7. his ankle bones received s.
Ro. 5 : 6. when with-t s. Christ died
1 Co. 15 : 56. the s. of sin is the law
2 Co. 1 : 8. we were pressed, above s.
He. 11 : 11. Sarah received s. to conc.
Re. 3 : 8. thou hast a little s., hast
5 : 12. Worthy is Lamb to receive s.
12 : 10. Now is come salvation and s.
17 : 13. these sh. give s. unto beast

His STRENGTH.

Ex. 14 : 27. the sea returned to h.s.
De. 21 : 17. he is beginning of h.s.
Ju. 8 : 21. as the man is, so is h.s.
16 : 5. see wherein h. great s. lieth
9. So h.s. was not known [went
19. she began to afflict him, h.s.
2 K. 9 : 24. Jehu drew bow with h.s.
1 Ch. 16 : 11. Seek the Lord and h.
s., Ps. 105 : 4. [ened
Jb. 18 : 7. steps of h.s. shall be strait-
12. h.s. shall be hunger bitten
13. firstborn of death shall devour
21 : 23. One dieth in h. full s. [h.s.
37 : 6. saith to great rain of h.s.
39 : 11. Wilt trust him bec. h.s. is
21. He rejoiceth in h.s. [great?
40 : 16. Lo, now h.s. is in his loins
Ps. 33 : 17. nei. deliver by h. great s.
52 : 7. man that made not G. h.s.
59 : 9. Because of h.s. will I wait
65 : 6. Wh. by h.s. setteth fast mts.
68 : 34. Ascribe s. unto G., h.s. is
78 : 4. shewing to generation h.s.
61. delivered h.s. into captivity
Is. 31 : † 9. he shall pass over to h.s.
44 : 12. he is hungry, h.s. faileth
62 : 8. Lord hath sworn by h.s. [s.
63 : 1. travelling in greatness of h.
Da. 11 : 2. by h.s. shall stir up all
Ho. 7 : 9. strangers devoured h.s.
12 : 3. by h.s. had power with God
Re. 1 : 16. his countenance as sun in

In STRENGTH. [h.s.

Ge. 49 : 24. But his bow abode i.s.
1 K. 19 : 8. i.s. of that meat, 40 days
Jb. 3 : † 17. wearied i.s. be at rest
9 : 4. He is wise, mighty i.s., 36 : 5.
Ps. 71 : 16. I will go i.s. of the Lord
103 : 20. his angels that excel i.s.
147 : 10. delighteth not i.s. of horse
Pr. 24 : † 5. A wise man is i.s., yea
increaseth s. [hand
Is. 8 : † 11. Lord spake to me i.s. of
30 : 2. strengthen thems. i.s. of Pha.
Mi. 5 : 4. he shall feed i.s. of Lord
Ac. 9 : 22. Saul increased the more

My STRENGTH. [i.s.

Ge. 49 : 3. Reuben beginn-g of m.s.
Ex. 15 : 2 : Lord is m.s. and song, 2
S. 22 : 33. Ps. 18 : 2.-28 : 7.-118 :
14. Is. 12 : 2. [m.s. now
Jos. 14 : 11. as m.s. was then, so is
Ju. 16 : 17. if shaven, m.s. will go
Jb. 6 : 11. What is m.s. that I hope?
12. Is m.s. of stones? is my flesh
Ps. 18 : 1. I will love thee, O L., m.s.
19 : 14. O Lord, m.s. and redeemer
22 : 15. m.s. is dried like potsherd
19. O m.s., haste thee to help me
31 : 4. pull me out of the net, for
thou art m.s. [38 : 10.-71 : 9.
10. m.s. fails bec. of my iniquity,
43 : 2. thou art the God of m.s.
59 : 17. Unto thee, O m.s., will I
62 : 7. rock of m.s. is in God [way
102 : 23. He weakened m.s. in the
139 : † 15. m.s. was not hid fr. thee
144 : 1. Blessed be L., m.s., which
Is. 27 : 5. let him take hold of m.s.
49 : 4. have spent m.s. for nought
5. glorious, my God shall be m.s.
Je. 16 : 19. O Lord, m.s. and fortress
La. 1 : 14. he hath made m.s. to fall
3 : 18. m.s. and hope is perished
Ha. 3 : 19. The Lord God is m.s.
Zch. 12 : 5. be m.s. in Lord of hosts
2 Co. 12 : 9. m.s. is made perfect in

No STRENGTH.

1 S. 28 : 20. there was n.s. in Saul
Jb. 26 : 2. how savest that hath n.s.
Ps. 88 : 4. I am as man th. hath n.s.
Da. 10 : 8. remained n.s. in me, 17.
16. are turned upon, I have n.s.
He. 9 : 17. otherwise it is of n.s.

Their STRENGTH. [t.s.

Jos. 11 : 13. cities that stood still in
Ps. 37 : 39. is t.s. in time of trouble
49 : † 14. t.s. shall consume
73 : 4. no bands in death, t.s. firm
78 : 51. smote chief of t.s., 105 : 36.
89 : 17. thou art the glory of t.s.
90 : 10. is t.s. labour and sorrow [s.
Pr. 20 : 29. glory of young men is t.

Is. 30 : 7. I cried, t.s. is to sit still[s.
40 : 31. that wait upon L., renew t.
41 : 1. let the people renew t.s.
63 : 6. I will bri. down t.s. to earth
Eze. 24 : 25. when I take fr. them t.s.
Jo. 2 : 22. fig tree and vine yield t.s.

Thine own or thy STRENGTH.

Ex. 15 : 13. hast guided them in t.s.
De 33 : 25. as thy days, so shall t.s.
Ju. 16 : 6. Tell wherein t.s. lieth, 15.
2 Ch. 6 : 41. ark of t.s., Ps. 132 : 8.
Ps. 21 : 1. king shall joy in t.s., O L.
13. Be exalted, O. L., in t.o.s.
54 : 1. Save me, judge me by t.s.
68 : 28. Thy God commanded t.s.
71 : 18. until I have shewed t.s.
74 : 13. didst divide the sea by t.s.
77 : 14. declared t.s. am. the peo.
80 : 2. stir up t.s., come and save
86 : 16. give t.s. unto thy servant
110 : 2. send rod of t.s. out of Zion
Pr. 5 : † 10. lest strangers be filled with t.s. [small
24 : 10. if faint in adversity t.s. is
31 : 3. Give not t.s. unto women[s.
Is. 17 : 10. not mindful of rock of t.
52 : 1. Awake, put on t.s., O Zion
63 : 15. where is thy zeal and t.s.
Am. 3 : 11. he shall bring down t.s.
Mk. 12 : 30. thou shalt love the Lord thy God wi. all t.s., 33. Lu. 10 : [27.

Your STRENGTH.

Le. 26 : 20. y.s. sh. be spent in vain
Ne. 8 : 10. the joy of the Lord is y.s.
Is. 23 : 14. ships, y.s. is laid waste
30 : 15. in confidence shall be y.s.
Eze. 24 : 21. sanct-y, excellency of [y.s.

STRENGTHS.

Is. 23 : † 11. ag. city to destroy the s.

STRENGTHEN. [s. him

Le. 25 : † 35. if thy brother be poor,
De. 3 : 28. charge Joshua, s. him
Ju. 16 : 28. s. me, I pray thee, once
19 : † 5. s. thine heart with a morsel
1 K. 20 : 22. go, s. thyself, mark
Ezr. 6 : 22. to s. their hands in work
Ne. 6 : 9. Now, O God, s. my hands
Jb. 16 : 5. wo. s. you with my mouth
Ps. 20 : 2. Lord s. thee out of Zion[24.
27 : 14. L., he sh. s. thine heart, 31 :
41 : 3. Lord will s. him upon bed of
68 : 28. s. that thou hast wrought
89 : 21. mine arm also shall s. him
119 : 28. s. me acc-g unto thy word
Is. 22 : 21. I will s. him with girdle
30 : 2. to s. thems. in strength of
33 : 23. co. not s. their mast [Pha.
35 : 3. s. ye the weak hands, confirm
41 : 10. I am thy God : I will s. thee
54 : 2. lengthen cords, s. thy stakes
Je. 4 : † 6. Set standard, s., stay not
23 : 14. they s. hands of evil doers
Eze. 7 : 13. nei. sh. any s. in iniquity
16 : 49. nei. did she s. hand of poor
30 : 24. I will s. arms of the k., 25.
34 : 16. I will s. that which was sick
Da. 11 : 1. even I stood to s. him
Am. 2 : 14. strong sh. not s. his force
Zch. 10 : 6. I will s. house of Judah
12. I will s. them in the Lord
Lu. 22 : 32. when converted, s. breth-
1 Pe. 5 : 10. God stablish, s. you[ren
Re. 3 : 2. Be watchful and s. things

STRENGTHENED.

Ge. 48 : 2. Isr. s. hims., sat upon bed
Ju. 3 : 12. Lord s. Eglon ag. Israel
7 : 11. afterward thine hands be s.
9 : † 24. s. his hands to kill breth.
Ru. 1 : † 18. saw she s. herself to go
1 S. 23 : 16. Jonathan s. hand in God
2 S. 2 : 7. now let your hands be s.
1 K. 12 : † 18. Rehob. s. hims., 2 Ch.
1 Ch. 11 : 10. s. thems. wi. Da.[10 : † 18.
2 Ch. 1 : 1. Sol. was s. in his kingdom
10 : † 18. Rehob. s. himself to flee
11 : 17. they s. kingdom of Judah
2 Ch. 12 : 1. wh. Rehob. had s. hims.
13 : 7. s. themselves ag. Rehoboam
17 : 1. Jehosh. s. himself ag. Israel
21 : 4. Jehoram s. hims., slew breth.
23 : 1. Jehoiada s. hims. took capt-s
24 : 13. set house of God, and s. it
25 : 11. Amaziah s. himself, and led
26 : 8. Uzziah s. himself exceedingly
28 : 20. distressed Ahaz, s. him not
29 : † 34. Levites s. them till work
32 : 5. Hezekiah s. hims., built wall
Ezr. 1 : 6. all about them s. hands
7 : 28. I was s., as hand of my God
Ne. 2 : 18. s. their hands for work
Jb. 4 : 3. thou hast s. the weak hands
4. thou hast s. the feeble knees
Ps. 52 : 7. s. himself in wickedness
147 : 13. hath s. bars of thy gates
Pr. 7 : † 13. she s. her face and said
8 : 28. he s. fountains of the deep
Is. 45 : † 1. Cyrus, whose hand I s.
Eze. 13 : 22. ye have s. hands of wick.
34 : 4. The diseased have ye not s.
Da. 10 : 18. touched me, s. me, 19.
11 : 6. he that begat her and s. her
12. cast down many, but not be s.
Ho. 7 : 15. Tho. I have s. their arms
Ac. 9 : 19. received meat, Saul was s.
Ep. 3 : 16. s. with might by Spirit
Col. 1 : 11. s. with all might acc-g to
2 Ti. 4 : 17. L. stood with and s. me

STRENGTHENEDST.

Ps. 138 : 3. s. me wi strength in soul

STRENGTHENETH.

Jb. 15 : 25. he s. hims. ag. Almighty
Ps. 104 : 15. bread wh. s. man's heart
Pr. 24 : † 5. man of knowl. s. might
31 : 17. girdeth her loins, s. her arms
Ec. 7 : 19. Wisdom s. the wise more
Is. 44 : 14. cypress and oak he s. [el
Da. 10 : † 21. none s. hims. but Micha-
Am. 5 : 9. That s. spoiled ag. strong
Ph. 4 : 13. do all thro. Christ wh. s.

STRENGTHENING. [me

Lu. 22 : 43. appeared an angel s. him
Ac. 18 : 23. Paul s. all the disciples

STRENGTHENERS. [s.

Eze. 27 : † 9. wise men of Gebal, thy

STRETCH. [of Egypt

Ex. 7 : 19. s. out hand upon waters
8 : 16. s. out thy rod, smite dust of
25 : 20. cherubim sh. s. their wings
Jos. 8 : 18. s. out the spear to Ai
2 K. 21 : 13. I will s. over Jerus. line
1 Ch. 21 : † 10. I s. out three things
Jb. 11 : 13. If thou s. hands tow. him
39 : 26. Doth hawk s. her wings tow.
Ps. 68 : 31. soon s. her hands unto
143 : 6. I s. forth my hands unto G.
Is. 28 : 20. shorter than a man can s.
34 : 11. s. upon it line of confusion
54 : 2. s. curtains of thy habitation
Je. 10 : 20. none to s. forth my tent
Eze. 30 : 25. k. of Bab. s. out my sword
Am. 6 : 4. s. thems. upon couches
Jn. 21 : 18. shalt s. forth thy hands
2 Co. 10 : 14. we s. not ours. beyond
See Stretch, ed forth HAND.

STRETCHED.

Ge. 48 : 14. Israel s. out right hand
Ex. 9 : 23. Moses s. rod tow., 10 : 13.
Jos. 8 : 18. Joshua s. out spear, 26.
19. ran soon as he s. out his hand
2 S. 6 : † 17. set ark in tab., David s.
1 K. 6 : 27. cherubim s. forth wings
17 : 21. s. himself upon, 2 K. 4 : 34, 35.
1 Ch. 21 : 16. angel with a sword s.
Jb. 38 : 5. who hath s. line upon it?
Ps. 44 : 20. s. hands to strange god
88 : 9. I have s. hands unto thee
136 : 6. to him that s. out the earth
Is. 3 : 16. walk with s. forth necks
16 : 8. her branches are s. out, are
42 : 5 s. out heavens, 45 : 12.-51 : 13.
Je. 6 : 4. shadows of evening s. out
10 : 12. he s. out the heavens by his
51 : 15. s. out heaven by underst-g
La. 2 : 8. Lord hath s. out a line
Eze. 1 : 11. their wings were s. upw.
16 : 27. I have s. out hand ov. thee
Ho. 7 : 5. s. out hands with scorners
Am. 6 : 7. that s. shall be removed
Zch. 1 : 16. line be s. upon Jerus.
Mat. 12 : 13. s. forth his hand, Mk. 3 :
14 : 31. Jesus s. forth his hand [5.
Lu. 22 : 53. ye s. no hands ag. me
Ac. 12 : 1. Herod s. hands to vex ch.
26 : 1. Paul s. forth hand and ans-d
Ro. 10 : 21. All day long I s. forth ha-s

STRETCHED out arm.

Ex. 6 : 6. I will redeem you with s. -
De. 4 : 34. G. to take him nation wi. s. -
5 : 15. Lord bro-t thee out by s. -,
7 : 19.-9 : 29.-26 : 8. Je. 32 : 21.
11 : 2. y-r chil. have not seen his s. -
1 K. 8 : 42. hear of thy hand and s. -
2 K. 17 : 36. bro-t out of Eg. with s. -
2 Ch. 6 : 32. stranger is come for thy s. -
Ps. 136 : 12. With a s. - for his mercy
Je. 32 : 17. thou hast made the earth and man by thy s. - [over you
Eze. 20 : 33. with a s. - will I rule
34. I will gather you with s. - and
See OUTSTRETCHED.

STRETCHEDST.

Ex. 15 : 12. Thou s. thy right hand

STRETCHEST. [tain

Ps. 104 : 2. who s. heavens like cur-

STRETCHETH.

Jb. 15 : 25. he s. out hand ag. God
26 : 7. He s. north over empty pla.
Pr. 31 : 20. She s. out her hand to
Is. 40 : 22. that s. out the heavens
44 : 13. carpenter s. out his rule[1.
24. that s. forth heavens, Zch. 12 :

STRETCHING.

Is. 8 : 8. s. of his wings fill land
Ac. 4 : 30. By s. forth hand to heal

STREW, ED. [on

Ex. 32 : 20. he ground calf, s-d it up-
2 Ch. 34 : 4. he s-d dust upon graves
Can. 2 : † 5. s. me with apples
Mat. 21 : 8. others cut branches and s-d them, Mk. 11 : 8. [not s-d
25 : 24. gathering where thou hast
26. and gather where I have not s-d

STRICKEN. [1.

Ge. 18 : 11. Sarah well s. in age, 24 :
Jos. 13 : 1. Joshua s. in yrs., 23 : 1, 2.
Ju 5 : 26. Jael had s. thro temples
1 K. 1 : 1. David was old, s. in years
Pr. 6 : 1. if s. thy hand wi. stranger
23 : 35. s. me, and I was not sick
Is. 1 : 5. Why she. ye be s. any more?
16 : 7. ye mourn ; surely they are s.
53 : 4. yet we did esteem him s. [s.
8. for transgression of peo. was he
Je. 5 : 3. thou hast s. them, they have
La. 4 : 9. s. thro for want of fruits
Lu. 1 : 7. Elisabeth, well s. in yrs, 18.

STRIFE.

Ge. 13 : 7. was a s. between herdmen
8. Abr. said, Let there be no s.
Ex. 17 : † 7. he called the place S.
Nu. 20 : † 13. This is the water of S.
27 : 14. ye rebelled in s. of congre.
De. 1 : 12. How can I bear your s.?
Ju. 12 : 2. I and people at s. with
2 S. 19 : 9. all the people were at s.
Ps. 31 : 20. keep from s. of tongues
55 : 9. I have seen s. in the city
80 : 6. makest us a s. unto neighb-s
81 : † 7. proved thee at waters of S
106 : 32. angered him at waters of s.
Pr. 15 : 18. wrathful man stirreth up s. ; but he that is slow to anger appeaseth s., 29 : 22.
16 : 28. A froward man soweth s.
17 : 1. a house full of sacri. with s.
14. beginning of s. is as when one
19. loveth transgr-n that loveth s.
20 : 3. honour for man to cease fr s.
22 : 10 Cast out scorner s. sh. cease
26 : 17. he that meddleth with s.

Pr. 26 : 20. is no talebearer, the s.
21. contentious man to kindle s.
28 : 25. a proud heart stirreth up s.
30 : 33. forcing of wrath bringeth s.
Is. 41 : † 11. men of thy s. sh. perish
58 : 4. ye fast for s. and debate
Je. 15 : 10. hast borne me man of s.
Eze. 47 : 19. to waters of s., 48 : 28.
Ha. 1 : 3. there are that raise up s.
Lu. 22 : 24. was a s. among disciples
Ro. 13 : 13. walk honestly, not in s.
1 Co 3 : 3. there is among you s.
Ga. 5 : 20. works of the flesh are s.
Ph. 1 : 15. some preach Christ of s.
2 : 3. Let nothing be done thro. s.
1 Ti. 6 : 4. whereof cometh envy, s.
He. 6 : 16. an oath is end of all s.
Ja. 3 : 14. if bitter envying and s.
16. where s. is, is confusion and

STRIFES.

Pr. 10 : 12. Hatred stirreth up s. [s.
2 Co. 12 : 20. lest there be envyings,
1 Ti. 6 : 4. doting about s. of words
2 Ti. 2 : 23. knowing they gender s.

STRIKE.

Ex. 12 : 7 s. blood on the posts, 22.
De. 21 : 4. shall s. off heifer's neck
2 K 5 : 11. will s. his hand over pla.
Jb. 17 : 3. who will s. hands with me?
20 : 24. bow of steel shall s. him
Ps. 110 : 5 s. thro. kings in wrath
Pr. 7 : 23. Till dart s. thro his liver
11 : † 15. hateth those th. s. hands
17 : † 10. than to s. fool 100 times
17 : 26. it is not good to s. princes
22 : 26. Be not of them th. s. hands
Je. 40 : † 14. sent Ishmael to s. thee
Eze. 39 : † 2. s. thee with six plagues
Ho. 14 : † 5. he sh. s. forth his roots
Ha. 3 : 14. didst s. thro. with staves
Mk. 14 : 65. did s. Jesus with palms

STRIKER. [1 : 7.

1 Ti. 3 : 3. bishop must be no s., Tit.

STRIKETH.

Jb. 34 : 26. He s. them as wicked men
Pr. 17 : 18. void of underst-g s. hands
Re. 9 : 5. scorpion, when he s. a man

STRING, STRINGS.

Ps. 11 : 2. make ready arrow upon s.
21 : 12. ready thine arrows upon s-s
33 : 2. sing with the psaltery, and an
instrument of ten s-s, 92 : 3.-
144 : 9. [loosed
Mk. 7 : 35. the s. of his tongue was

STRINGED instruments.

1 S. 18 : † 6. women came with 3 s.i.
Ps. 150 : 4. praise him with s.i. and
Is. 38 : 20. will sing songs to s.i.
Ha. 3 : 19. To chief singer on my s.i.

STRIP.

Nu. 20 : 26. s. Aaron of garments [S.
1 S. 31 : 8. Philis. to s. slain, 1 Ch. 10:
Is. 32 : 11. s. ye, make ye bare, gird
Eze. 16 : 39. they shall s. thee, 23 : 26.
Ho. 2 : 3. Lest I s. her naked, and

STRIPE. [s. for s.

Ex. 21 : 25. give wound for wound,

STRIPES.

De. 25 : 3. Forty s. he may give him :
if he beat him with many s.
2 S. 7 : 14. with s. of chil. of men [s.
Ps. 89 : 32. visit their iniquity with
Pr. 17 : 10. than 100 s. into a fool
19 : 29. s. are prepared for fools
20 : 30. so do s. the inward parts of
Is. 53 : 5. with his s. we are healed,
1 Pe. 2 : 24. [with many s.
Lu. 12 : 47. which knew, be beaten
48. knew not be beaten with few s.
Ac. 16 : 23. laid many s. upon them
33. took them, washed their s.
2 Co. 6 : 5. in s., in imprisonments
11 : 23. in s. above measure, in
24. five times received I 40 s., save

STRIPLING.

1 S. 17 : 56. And the king said, Inquire thou whose son the s. is

STRIPPED.

Ge. 37 : 23. they s. Joseph of coat
Ex. 33 : 6. Israel s. of ornaments
Nu. 20 : 28 Mo. s. Aaron of garm-ts
1 S. 18 : 4. Jonathan s. hims. of robe
19 24. Saul s. off his clothes, and
31 : 9. Philis. s. Saul, 1 Ch 10 : 9.
2 Ch. 20 : 25. precious jewels they s.
Jb. 19 : 9. He s. me of my glory
22 : 6. thou hast s. the naked of
Mi. 1 : 8. I will go s. and naked
Mat. 27 : 28. they s. Jesus, put on
Lu. 10 : 30. thieves which s. him

STRIPPETH. [out

Ho. 7 : † 1. troop of robbers s. with-

STRIPT=STRIPPED.

STRIVE. [s.

Ge 6 : 3. My Spirit shall not always
26 : 20. herdmen of Gerar did s. wi.
Ex. 21 : 18. if men s., and one smite
22. If man s. and hurt a woman
with child, De. 25 : 11. [at Mer.
De. 33 : 8. with whom thou didst s.
Ju. 11 : 25. did he ever s. ag. Israel
Jb. 33 : 13. Why dost thou s. ag. him?
Ps. 35 : 1. Plead with them th. s. with
Pr. 3 : 30. s. not without cause [me
25 : 8. Go not forth hastily to s.
Is. 41 : 11. that s. with thee sh. perish
45 : 9. Let potsherd s. with potsherds
Ho. 4 : 4 let no man s. : thy people
are as they that s. with priest
Mat. 12 : 19. He shall not s. nor cry
Lu 13 : 24. s. to enter at strait gate
Ro. 15 : 30. s. in your prayers for me
2 Ti. 2 : 5. if a man s. for masteries
14. that they s. not about words
24. servant of Lord must not s.

STRIVED, EN, ETH.

Is. 45 : 9. Woe unto him that s-h wi.
Je. 50 : 24. bec. hast s-n ag. L. [Maker
Ro. 15 : 20. so I s-d to preach gospel
1 Co. 9 : 25. ev. man th. s-h for mas- [tery

STRIVING.

Ph. 1 : 27. with one mind s. for faith
Col. 1 : 29. s. acc-g to his working
4 : † 12. always s. for you in prayers
He. 12 : 4. not resisted unto blood,
s. against sin.

STRIVINGS.

2 S. 22 : 44. hast delivered me from
s. of people, Ps. 18 : 43.
Tit. 3 : 9. avoid contentions and s.

STROKE, STROKES.

De. 17 : 8. If a matter arise too hard
between s. and s. [axe
19 : 5. and his hand fetched s. with
21 : 5. by word every s. be tried
2 S. 20 : † 10. Joab doubled not his s.
2 Ch. 21 : † 14. with gr. s. will L. smite
Es. 9 : 5. Jews smote enemies with s.
Jb. 23 : 2. my s. is heavier than my
36 : 18 lest he take thee with his s.
Ps 38 : † 11. stand aloof from my s.
39 : 10. Remove thy s. from me
Pr. 18 : 6. fool's mouth calleth for s-s
Is. 14 : 6. smote the people with s.
27 : † 7. smitten acc. to s. of those
30 : 26. Lord healeth s. of wound
53 : † 8. for transgression of my people was s. upon him [with a s.
Eze. 24 : 16. I take desire of thine eyes

STRONG. [ing

Ge. 49 : 14. Issa-r is a s. ass, couch-
24. arms of hands were made s.
Ex. 10 : 19. L. turned a s. west wind
14 : 21. sea to go back by s. east wind
Nu. 21 : 24. border of Ammon was s.
24 : 21. s. is thy dwellingplace
28 : 7. s. wine to be poured unto L.
De. 2 : 36. not one city too s. for us
22 : † 25. if man take s. hold of her
28 : † 50. a nation s. of face, which
Jos. 14 : 11. I am s. this day, as I was
17 : 13. Israel were waxen s., Ju. 1 : [28.
19 : 29. coast turneth to s. city
23 : 9. L. driven gr. nations and s.

Ju. 6 : † 2. hand of Midian s. ag. Isr.
† 26. altar upon top of this s. place
9 : 51. was a s. tower within city
14 : 14. out of the s. came sweetness
18 : 26. Micah saw they were too s.
1 S. 14 : 52. when Saul saw s. man
2 S. 2 : † 16. called field of s. men
3 : 6. Abner made hims. s. for Saul
11 : † 15. Uriah in forefront of s. bat.
25. make thy bat. more s. ag. city
15 : 12. the conspiracy was s., the
22 : 18. He delivered me fr. my s.
enemy, they too s. for, Ps. 18 : 17.
1 K. 2 : † 8. cursed me with a s. curse
19 : 11. great s. wind rent the mts
2 K. 2 : 16. with thy serv-ts 50 s. men
24 : 16. all s. and apt for war [9.
1 Ch. 26 : 7. whose breth. were s. men.
2 Ch. 11 : 12. made the cities exc-g s.
17. made Rehoboam s. 3 years
16 : 9 eyes run to shew himself s.
26 : 15. was helped till he was s.
16. Uzziah was s., he was lifted up
Ne. 9 : 25. they took s. cities and fat
Jb 8 : 2. words be like a s. wind [s.
9 : 19. If I speak of strength, he is
33 : 19. his bones with s. pain [s.
37 : 18. Hast spread out sky that is
39 : 28. she dwelleth upon s. place
40 : 18. bones as s. pieces of brass
Ps. 10 : † 10. th. poor fall into s. parts
19 : 5. rejoiceth as s. man to run
24 : 8. Lord s. and mighty in battle
30 : 7 hast made my mt. to stand s.
31 : 2. be thou my s. rock, and hou
21. shewed me kindness in s. city
35 : 10. poor from him that is too s.
† 18. I will praise thee am. s. people
38 : 19. mine enemies lively and s.
60 : 9. Who bring me into s. city?
61 : 3. hast been a s. tower [108 : 10.
71 : 3. Be thou my s. habitation
7. but thou art my s. refuge [17.
80 : 15. the branch thou madest s.,
89 : 8. who is a s. L., like unto thee?
10. scatter thine enem. with s. arm
Pr. 7 : 26. many s. men slain by her
10 : 15. man's wealth his s. city, 18:
11 : 16. s. men retain riches [11.
14 : 26. In fear of L. is s. confidence
18 : 10. name of Lord is a s. tower
19. A bro. harder to be won than s.
21 : 14. rew-d pacifieth s. wrath [city
24 : 5. A wise man is s. ; yea
30 : 25. The ants are a people not s.
Ec. 9 : 11. the battle is not to the s.
12 : 3. when the s. men shall bow
Can. 8 : 6. seal, for love is s. as death
Is. 1 : 31. the s. shall be as tow
8 : 7. bringeth on them waters, s.
17 : 9. s. cities shall be as forsaken
25 : 3. shall s. people glorify thee
26 : 1. this song, We have a s. city
27 : 1. wi. s. sword punish leviathan
28 : 2. L. hath a mighty and s. one
22. not mockers, lest hands be s.
31 : 1. trust in horsemen, bec. s.
40 : 26. For that he is s. in power
41 : † 6. ev. one said to broth., Be s.
21. bring forth your s. reasons
53 : 12. he shall divide spoil with the
56 : † 11. they are s. of appetite [s.
60 : 22. small one become a s. nation
Je. 5 : † 6. their backslidings are s.
21 : 5. I will fight you with s. arm
47 : 3. the stamping of his s. horses
48 : 14. We are mighty, s. men for
17. say, How is the s. staff broken!
49 : 19. he shall come against habitation of the s., 50 : 44. [hosts
50 : 34. Their Redeemer is s., L. of
51 : 12. make the watch s., set up
Eze. 3 : 8. made thy face s., foreh. s.
14. hand of Lord was s. upon me
7 : 24. make pomp of the s. to cease
26 : 11. thy s. garrisons shall go
17. renowned city s. in the sea.

Eze. 30 : 21. to make it s. to hold sw-d
22. I will break s. arm of Pharaoh
32 : 21. s. shall speak to him out of
34 : 16. destroy the fat and s. [hell
Da. 4 : 11. The tree grew, was s., 20.
22. thou, O king, art become s.
7 : 7. the fourth beast terribly s.
8 : 8. when s. great horn was broken
11 : 23. sh. become s. wi. small peo.
Jo. 1 : 6 nation is on my land, s., 2 : 2.
2 : 5. noise of s. people set in battle
11 he is s. that executeth word
3 · 10. let the weak say, I am s.
Am. 2 : 9. Amorite was s. as the oaks
14 s. sh not strengthen his force
† 16. he that is s. of heart shall flee
5 · 9. strengtheneth spoiled ag. the s.
Mi 4 : 3 he shall rebuke s. nations
7. her that was cast off, s. nation
6 · 2. hear, ye s., foundations
Na. 2 . 1 make thy loins s., fortify
Zch. 6 . † 3. grisled and s. horses
8 : 22. s. nations shall seek the L.
Mat. 12 · 29. how enter a s. man's
hou. except bind s. man? Mk. 3:
14 : † 30. saw wind s. he was afr-d [27.
Lu 1 : 80 the child waxed s., 2 : 40.
11 21. s. man armed keepeth pal
Ac 3 : 16 thro. faith made this man
Ro. 4 : 20. but was s. in faith [s.
15 : 1. We that are s. ought to bear
1 Co 4 : 10. we are weak, ye are s.
2 Co. 12 . 10. when weak, then am I s.
13 : 9. glad we are weak, and ye s.
2 Th. 2 : 11. sh. send them s. delus-n
He 5 : 7. off-d prayers with s. crying
12 need of milk, not of s. meat
14. s. meat to them of full age
6 : 18 we might have s. consolation
11 : 34. out of weakness made s.
1 Jn. 2 : 14. young men, bec. yo are s.
Re. 5 · 2. I saw a s. angel proclaim
18 : 2. cried with s. voice, Babylon
8. for s. is L. G., who judgeth her

Be STRONG. [weak

Nu. 13 : 18. see whe. they b. s. or
28. peo. b. s. that dwell in land
De. 11 : 8. keep com-ts that ye b. s.
12 : † 23. only b. s., eat not blood
Jos. 17 : 18. Canaanites, tho. they b. s.
1 S. 4 : 9. b. s., quit yours. like men
2 S. 10 : 11. if Syrians b. too s. for
me, if Ammon b. too s. for thee,
I will help thee, 1 Ch. 19 : 12.
16 : 21. of all with thee shall b. s.
1 K. 2 : 2. b. s., shew thyself a man
1 Ch. 28 : † 7. if he b. s. to do com-ts
10. Lord hath chosen thee, b. s.
2 Ch. 15 : 7. b. s., your work sh. be
25 : 8. if thou go, b. s. for battle
Ezr. 9 : 12. that ye b. s. and eat good
Ps. 144 : 14. Th. oxen b. s. to labour
Is. 35 . 4. them of fearf. heart, b. s.
Eze. 22 : 14. can thine hands b. s.
Da. 2 : 40. kingdom sh. b. s. as iron
42. kingd. sh. b. partly s., partly
10 : 19. he said, peace, b. s., yea, b. s.
11 : 5. king of the south shall b. s.,
and he shall b. s. above him
32. that know their God shall b. s.
Hag. 2 : 4. b. s., O Zerubbabel, b. s.,
O Joshua, b. s., all ye people
Zch 8 : 9. Let hands b. s. ye th. hear
13. fear not, let hands b. s.
1 Co. 16 : 13. quit you like men, b. s.
Ep. 6 : 10. brethren, b. s. in the Lord
2 Ti. 2 : 1. my son, b. s. in grace
See **Good COURAGE, Strong DRINK, Strong HAND, Strong HOLD, S, Strong ONES.** See ROD, RODS.

STRONGER. [than

Ge. 25 : 23. one people shall be s.
30 : 41. s. cattle did conceive
42. feebler Laban's, and s. Jacob's
Nu. 13 : 31. we not able, they are s.
Ju. 14 : 18. what is s. than a lion?
2 S. 1 : 23. Saul, Jona., s. than lions
3 : 1. David waxed s. and s., Saul
13 : 14. Amnon, s. than she, forced
1 K. 20 : 23. they s. than we; fight
in plain; we be s. than they. 25.
Jb. 17 : 9. hath clean hands shall be
s. and s. [enies
Ps. 105 : 24. made them s. than en-
142 : 6 deliver me, for they are s.
Je. 20 : 7. thou art s. than I, and
31 : 11. ransomed fr him that was s.
Lu. 11 : 22. when a s. come upon him
1 Co. 1 : 25. weakness of God is s.
10 · 22. Do we provoke Lord? are we

STRONGEST. [s.

Pr. 30 · 30. A lion, which is s. among

STRONGLY.

Ju. 8 · † 1. Ephr-s did chide Gideon s.
1 Ch. 11 : † 10. men held s. wi. David
2 Ch. 16 : † 9. s. to hold with them
Ezr. 6 : 3. let foundation be s. laid

STROVE. [they s., 21.

Ge 26 : 20. called well Ezek, because
22. ano. well, for that they s. not
Ex. 2 : 13. two men of Hebrews s.
Le. 24 : 10. man of Israel s. in camp
Nu. 20 : 13. chil of Isr. s. with Lord
26 : 9. Dathan, who s. ag. Moses
2 S. 14 : 6. they two s. in the field
Da. 7 : 2. winds s. upon great sea
Jn. 6 : 52. the Jews s. am. thems [s.
Ac. 7 : 26. Mos shewed hims. as they
23 : 9. s., saying, We find no evil in

STROWED. See STREWED.

STRUCK.

1 S. 2 : 14. he s. it into pan or pot
2 S. 12 : 15 Lord s. child, it was sick
20 : 10 Joab s. him not again
2 Ch. 13 : 20. Lord s. Jerob, he died
Mat. 26 : 51. one of them s. a servant
Lu. 22 : 64. s. Jesus on face, Jn 18 :

STRUGGLED. [22.

Ge. 25 : 22. children s. within her

STUBBLE. [straw

Ex. 5 : 12. to gather s. instead of
15 · 7. wrath consumed them as s.
Jb. 13 : 25. wilt thou pursue dry s.?
21 : 18. They are as s. before wind
41 : 28. slingstones are turned into s.
29. Darts are counted as s.
Ps. 83 : 13. make them as s. bef. wind
Is. 5 : 24. as fire devoureth s., so
33 : 11. conceive chaff bring forth s.
40 : 24. whirlw. sh. take them as s.
41 : 2. he gave them as driven s. to
47 : 14. they shall be as s. fire shall
Je. 13 : 24. will I scatter them as s.
Jo. 2 : 5. flame that devoureth the s.
Ob. 18. house of Esau shall be for s.
Na. 1 : 10. devoured as s. fully dry
Mal. 4 : 1. all the proud shall be as s.
1 Co. 3 : 12. on this foundation hay, s.

STUBBORN.

De. 21 : 18. If a man have a s. son
20. say unto elders, our son is s.
Ju. 2 : 19. they ceased not fr. s. way
Ps. 78 : 8. not as fathers, s. genera-n
Pr. 7 : 11. she is loud and s.; her feet

STUBBORNNESS.

De. 9 : 27. look not unto s. of people
29 : † 19. peace, though I walk in s.
1 S. 15 : 23. and s. is as iniquity and
Je. 3 : † 17. nei. walk after s. of heart
7 : † 24. walked in s. of evil heart,
9 : † 14. - 11 : † 8. - 13 : † 10. - 16 : † 12.
23 : † 17. one that walketh after s.

STUCK. [of heart

1 S. 26 : 7. his spear s. in the ground
Ps. 119 : 31. I have s. unto testimon.
Ac. 27 : 41. fore part of the ship s.

STUDIETH. [ans.

Pr. 15 : 28. heart of righteous s. to
24 : 2. their heart s. destruction

STUDS. [of silver

Can. 1 : 11. borders of gold with s.

STUDY. [Noun.]

Ec. 12 : 12. much s. is a weariness

STUDY. [Verb.]

1 Th. 4 : 11. that ye s. to be quiet
2 Ti. 2 : 15. s. to shew thys. approved

STUFF.

Ge. 31 : 37. hast searched all my s.
45 : 20. also regard not your s.
Ex. 22 : 7. if man deliver s. to keep
36 : 7. s. they had was sufficient
Jos. 7 : 11. they put it among own s.
1 S 10 : 22. he hath hid among the s.
25 : 13. two hundred abode by the s.
30 : 24. his part that tarrieth by s.
Ne. 13 . 8. I cast househ. s. of Tobiah
Eze. 12 : 3. prepare s. for removing
4. bring forth thy s. by day, 7.
Lu. 17 : 31. upon housetop, his s. in
See **HOUSEHOLD stuff.**

STUMBLE.

Pr. 3 : 23. sh. walk, foot not s., 4 : 12
4 : 19. know not at what they s.
Is. 5 : 27. None shall be weary nor s.
8 : 15. many am. them shall s. and
28 : 7. err in vision, s. in judgment
59 : 10. we s. at noonday as in night
63 : 13. led them th. they sho. not s.
Je. 13 : 16. bef. feet s. upon dark mts.
18 : 15. caused them to s. in ways
20 : 11. thf. my persecutors shall s.
31 : 9 to way wh-in they sh. not s.
46 . 6. sh. s. and fall toward north
50 : 32. most proud shall s. and fall
Da. 11 : 19. but he shall s. and fall
Na. 2 : 5. they shall s. in their walk
3 : 3. they s. upon their corpses
Mal. 2 : 8. caused many to s. at law
1 Pe. 2 : 8. offence to them wh. s. at

STUMBLED. [word

1 S. 2 : 4. they that s. are girded
1 Ch. 13 : 9. for the oxen s., 2 S. 6 : † 6.
Ps. 27 : 2. to eat my flesh, they s.
Je. 46 : 12. mighty man s. ag. mighty
Ro. 9 : 32. they s. at stumblingstone
11 : 11. Have they s. that they fall?

STUMBLETH. [he s.

Pr. 24 : 17. let not heart be glad when
Jn. 11 : 9. If any walk in day, s. not
10. if man walk in the night he s.
Ro. 14 : 21. not to eat wh-by brother

STUMBLING. [s.

1 S. 25 : † 31. this be no s. unto thee
1 Jn. 2 : 10. is none occasion of s. in

Stone of STUMBLING.

Is. 8 : 14. he sh. be for s. o. s. to Isr.
1 Pe. 2 : 8. s. o. s. to them s. at word
See STUMBLINGSTONE.

STUMBLINGBLOCK, S.

Le. 19 : 14. sh. not put a s. bef. blind
Ps. 119 : † 165. love thy law have no s.
Is. 57 : 14. take s. out of the way
Je. 6 : 21. I will lay s-s before people
Eze. 3 : 20. and I lay a s. before him
7 : 19. it is the s. of their iniquity
14 : 3. they put s. of iniquity, 4, 7
44 : † 12. were s. of iniq-y unto Isr.
Zph. 1 : 3. I will consume the s-s
Ro. 11 : 9. Let table be made a s.
14 : 13. no man put s. in bro.'s way
1 Co. 1 : 23. we preach Christ crucified, unto Jews a s. [come a s.
8 : 9. lest this liberty of yours be-
Re. 2 : 14. Balak to cast s. bef. Israel

STUMBLINGSTONE.

Ro 9 : 32. they stumbled at that s.
33. I lay in Sion a s. and rock

STUMP.

1 S. 5 : 4. only s. of Dagon was left
Da. 4 : 15. leave s. in the earth, 23,

SU'AH. See SHUAL. [26.

SUBDUE. [s. it

Ge. 1 : 28. God said, replenish earth,
1 Ch. 17 : 10. I will s. thine enemies
Ps. 47 : 3. He sh. s. people under us
127 : † 5. they sh. s. thine enemies
Is. 45 : 1. I have holden to s. nations
Da. 7 : 24. he shall s. three kings
Mi. 7 : 19. he will s. our iniquities
Zch. 9 : 15. they sh. s. wi. slingstones

Ph. 3 : 21. he is able to s. all things

SUBDUED.

Nu. 32 : 22. land be s. bef. the Lord
29. land shall be s. bef. you[be s.
De. 20 : 20. build bulwarks until it
33 : † 29. thine enemies shall be s.
Jos. 18 : 1. land was s. before them
Ju. 3 : 30. So Moab was s. | 4 : 23.
God s. Jabin | 8 : 28. Midian was
11 : 33. Ammon was s. [s.
1 S. 7 : 13. the Philistines were s. 2 S.
8 : 1. 1 Ch. 18 : 1.-20 : 4. [he s.
2 S. 8 : 11. gold of all nations which
22 . 40. that rose up against me hast
thou s., Ps. 18 : 39. [fore the L.
1 Ch. 22 : 18. and the land is s. be-
Ps. 81 : 14. soon have s. their enemies
1 Co. 15 : 28. when all be s. unto him
He. 11 : 33. Who thro. faith s. kingd-s

SUBDUEDST, ETH.

Ne. 9 : 24. thou s-t inhab-ts of land
Ps. 18 : 47. It is G. s-h peo., 144 : 2.
Da. 2 : 40. as iron breaketh and s-h

SUBJECT. [all thi-s

Ge. 3 : † 16. thy desire be s. to husb.
4 : † 7. his desire sh. be s. unto thee
Lu. 2 : 51. Jesus was s. unto them
10 : 17. L., even devils are s. unto us
20. rejoice not that spirits are s.
Ro. 3 : † 19. world be s. to judgment
8 : 7. for it is not s. to the law of God
20. creature was made s. to vanity
13 : 1. Let every soul be s. to higher
5. Whf. ye must needs be s. not[s.
1 Co. 14 : 32. spirits of prophets are
15 : 28. then sh. Son be s. unto him
Ep. 5 : 24. as church is s. unto Christ
Col. 2 : 20. why, ye s. to ordinances
Tit. 3 : 1. mind to be s. unto powers
He. 2 : 15. all lifetime s. to bondage
Ja. 5 : 17. Elias s. to like passions
1 Pe. 2 : 18. Servants be s. to masters
3 : 22. angels being made s. unto him
5 : 5. all of you be s. one to another

SUBJECTED.

Ro. 8 : 20. who hath s. same in hope

SUBJECTION. [s.

Ps. 106 : 42. enemies were bro-t into
Je. 34 : 11. brought them into s., 16.
1 Co. 9 : 27. I bring my body into s.
2 Co. 9 : 13. glorify God for your s.
Ga. 2 : 5. gave place by s. not an hour
1 Ti. 2 : 11. Let women learn with s.
3 : 4. having his children in s. with
He. 2 : 5. put in s. world to come
8. hast put all in s. under his feet
12 : 9. rather be in s. unto the Fath.
1 Pe. 3 : 1. wives be in s. to husb., 5.

SUBMIT.

Ge. 16 : 9. s. thys. under her hands
2 S. 22 : 45. strangers shall s. themselves unto me, Ps. 18 : 44.
Ps. 66 : 3. sh. thine enemies s. unto
68 : 30. till every one s. with silver
1 Co. 16 : 16. That ye s. unto such
Ep. 5 : 22. Wives s. yourselves unto
your husbands, Col. 3 : 18.
He. 13 : 17. s. yours. for they watch
Ja. 4 : 7. s. yourselves theref. to God
1 Pe. 2 : 13. s. to every ordinance
5 : 5. ye younger, s. yours. to elder

SUBMITTED, TING.

1 Ch. 29 : 24. sons of Dav. s-d unto Sol.
Ps. 81 : 15. haters of L. sho. have s-d
Ro. 10 : 3. not s-d unto righteousn-s
Ep. 5 : 21. s-g one to ano. in fear of G.

SUBORNED.

Ac. 6 : 11. then they s. men who said

SUBSCRIBE, ED. [L.

Is. 44 : 5. another shall s. unto the
Je. 32 : 10. I s-d evidence, sealed it
12. presence of witnesses that s-d
44. men sh. s. evidences, and seal

SUBSTANCE.

Ge. 7 : 4. I will destroy ev. living s.
23. every living s. was destroyed
12 : 5. Abram took s. they gathered
Ge. 13 : 6. their s. was great, so that
15 : 14. they sh. come with great s.
34 : 23. Shall not their s. be ours ?
36 : 6. Esau took his cattle and s.
De. 11 : 6. earth swallowed their s.
33 : 11. Bless, L., his s., accept work
Jos. 14 : 4. unto Levites cities for s.
1 S. 9 : † 1. Kish a mighty man of s.
1 Ch. 27 : 31. these were rulers of s.
28 : 1. stewards over all s. of king
2 Ch. 21 : 17. carried aw. s. in k.'s ho.
31 : 3. appointed k.'s portion of s.
32 : 29. God given Heze. s. very much
35 : 7. bullocks, these were of k.'s s.
Ezr. 8 : 21. seek right way for our s.
10 : 8. not come, his s. be forfeited
Jb. 1 : 3. Job's s. was 7,000 sheep
10. his s. is increased in the land
5 : 5. robber swalloweth their s.
6 : 22. say, Give reward of your s. ?
15 : 29. not be rich, nei. s. continue
20 : 18. acc-g to s. sh. restitution be
22 : 20. whereas our s. is not cut do.
30 : 22. liftest and dissolvest my s.
Ps. 17 : 14. leave their s. to babes
52 : † 7. strengthened hims. in his s.
105 : 21. made Joseph ruler over s.
139 : 15. My s. was not hid from thee
16. Thine eyes did see my s., yet
Pr. 1 : 13. We sh. find all precious s.
3 : 9. Honour the Lord with thy s.
6 : 31. he sh. give all s. of his house
8 : 21. those th. love me to inherit s.
10 : 3. casteth away s. of wicked
12 : 27. s. of diligent man precious
28 : 8. He that by usury increas-h s.
29 : 3. with harlots spendeth his s.
Can. 8 : 7. if man give his s. for love
Is. 6 : 13. as oak whose s. is in th.,
so holy seed be s. thereof
Je. 15 : 13. thy s. will I give to spoil,
Ho. 12 : 8. have found me out s. [17 : 3.
Ob. 13. nor laid hands on their s.
Mi. 4 : 13. I will consecrate their s.
Lu. 8 : 3. ministered unto him of s.
15 : 13. younger son wasted his s.
He. 10 : 34. ye have in heaven bet. s.
11 : 1. faith is s. of things hoped for

SUBTILE.

Ge. 3 : 1. serpent more s. than any
2 S. 13 : 3. Jonadab, a very s. man
Pr. 7 : 10. attire of harlot, and s. of

SUBTILELY. [heart

1 S. 23 : 22. told me he dealeth very s.
Ps. 105 : 25. to deal s. with servants
Ac. 7 : 19. same dealt s. wi. our kin-

SUBTILTY. [dred

Ge. 27 : 35. Thy brother came with s.
2 K. 10 : 19. Jehu did it in s. that he
Pr. 1 : 4. To give s. to the simple
8 : † 12. I wisdom dwell with s. [s.
Mat. 26 : 4. they might take Jes. by
Ac. 13 : 10. Paul said, O full of all s.
2 Co. 11 : 3. serpent beguiled Eve

SUBURBS. [thro. s.

Jos. 21 : 11. they gave to children of
Aaron city with s., 13, 14, 15,
16, 17, 21, 23, 25, 27, 28, 30, 34,
36, 38. 1 Ch. 6 : 55, 57, 58, 59,
60, 67, 68, 69, 70, 71, 72, 73, 74,
75, 76, 77, 78, 79, 80, 81.
2 K. 23 : 11. took away horses by
chamber in s. [on
1 Ch. 5 : 16. dwelt in the s. of Shar-
2 Ch. 11 : 14. Levites left s. and came
Eze. 27 : 28. s. shall shake at sound
45 : 2. fifty cubits round for s. th-of
48 : 15. place for dwelling and for s.
17. s. of city shall be toward north

SUBURBS with cities.

Le. 25 : 34. s. of the c. may not be
Nu. 35 : 2. give to Levites s. for c.
3. shall have c. to dwell in and s.
for cattle, Jos. 14 : 4.-21 : 2. [cubits
4. s. of c. sh. reach outward 6,000
5. this shall be to them s. of the c.
7. c. to Levites shall be 48, with s.
Jos. 21 : 3. chil. of Isr. gave Levites
these c. and s., 8. 1 Ch. 6 : 64.
18. with her s. ; four c., 22, 24, 29,
31, 32, 35, 37, 39. [with s.
19. all c. of the priests were 13 c.
25. with her s. ; 2 c., 27. [Kohath
26. c. were ten with s., for chil. of
32. and Kartan with her s. ; 3 c.
33. all c. of Gershonites 13 c. wi. s.
41. c. of Levites were 48 c. with s.
42. These c. were ev. one wi. s. (2)
1 Ch. 13 : 2. send to Levites in c. and s.
2 Ch. 31 : 19. priests in the s. of their

SUBVERT, ED, ING. [c.

La. 3 : 36. To s. a man L. approv. not
Ac. 15 : 24. troubled you s-g y-r souls
2 Ti. 2 : 14. no profit but s-g of hear-
Tit. 1 : 11. who s. whole houses [ers
3 : 11. he th. is such is s-d and sin-h

SUCCEED, ED, EST.

De. 2 : 12. chil. of Esau s-d them, 22.
21. Ammonites s-d them and dw-t
12 : 29. when s-t them in land, 19 : 1.
25 : 6. firstborn shall s. his brother

Good SUCCESS. [dead

Jos. 1 : 8. then thou shalt have g. s.
Jb. 22 : † 2. doth his g. s. depend
Ps. 111 : † 10. g. s. that do his com-ts
Pr. 3 : † 4. So shalt thou find g. s.

SUC'COTH.

Ge. 33 : 17. Jacob journeyed to S.,
therefore it is called S. [see to S.
Ex. 12 : 37. Isr. journeyed fr. Rame-
13 : 20. journey fr. S., Nu. 33 : 5, 6.
Jos. 13 : 27. Gad had in valley, S.
Ju. 8 : 5. Gideon said unto men of S.
6. the princes of S. said [S., 15.
8. men of Penuel ans-d as men of
14. Gideon caught a yo. man of S.
16. with them he taught men of S.
1 K. 7 : 46. in clay ground between
S. and Zarthan, 2 Ch. 4 : 17. [7.
Ps. 60 : 6. mete out valley of S., 108 :

SUC'COTH-BE'NOTH.

2 K. 17 : 30. men of Babylon made S.

SUCCOUR, ED.

2 S. 8 : 5. Syrians came to s. Hadad-r
18 : 3. better thou s. us out of city
21 : 17. Abishai s-d him, smote Phil.
2 Co. 6 : 2. in day of salva. I s-d thee
He. 2 : 18. he is able to s. tempted

SUCCOURER.

Ro. 16 : 2. she hath been s. of many

SUCH. [in tents

Ge. 4 : 20. Jabal, father of s. as dwell
21. Jubal, fa. of s. as handle harp
27 : 4. sav-y meat, s. as I love, 9, 14.
46. wife of dau-s of Heth, s. as
30 : 32. spotted of s. sh. be my hire
41 : 19. s. as I never saw in Egypt
44 : 15. wot ye not that s. a man
Ex. 9 : 18. s. hail as not in Egypt, 24.
10 : 14. no s. locusts, nor sh. be s.
11 : 6. great cry, s. as was none like
18 : 21. able men, s. as fear God [it
34 : 10. s. as have not been done in
Le. 11 : 34. on which s. water cometh be uncl., all drink in s. ves.
14 : 22. pigeons s. as he is able, 30, 31.
20 : 6. turneth after s., I will cut
22 : 6. touched any s. shall be unc.
27 : 9. giveth of s. unto L., be holy
Nu. 8 : 16. inst. of s. as open womb
De. 5 : 29. O that th. were s. a heart
13 : 11. shall do no more s. wickedness, 19 : 20. [you, 17 : 4.
14. that s. abomination among
16 : 9. s. time as to put the sickle
Ju. 3 : 2. s. as before knew nothing
19 : 30. was no s. deed done or seen
1 S. 25 : 17. he is s. a son of Belial
2 S. 9. 8. look upon s. dead dog as I
11 : † 25. sword devoureth so and s.
13 : 18. with s. robes were virgins
16 : 2. that s. as be faint may drink
19 : 36. why recompense me with s.
1 K. 10 : 10. no more s. abundance of

1 K. 10 : 12. no s. almug trees, 2 Ch. 9 : 11.
2 K. 6 : 9. thou pass not s. a place
21 : 12. bringing s. evil upon Jerus.
23 : 22. not holden s. a passover
1 Ch. 12 : 33. s. as went to battle, 36.
29 : 25. L. bestowed s. royal majesty
2 Ch. 1 : 12. s. as none of kings had
9 : 9. nei. s. spice as queen gave, 11.
11 : 16. s. as set hearts to seek Lord
23 : 13. and s. taught to sing praise
24 : 12. gave it to s. as did work of
30 : 5. had not done it in s. sort
Ezr. 4 : 10. peace, and at s. a time, 11, 17.-7 : 12. [selves unto them
6 : 21. all s. as had separated them-
7 : 25. all s. as know laws of God
8 : 31. s. as lay in wait by the way
9 : 13. hast given s. deliverance as
10 : 3. put aw. wives, and s. as are
Ne. 6 : 11. Should s. a man as I flee?
Es. 4 : 11. exc. s. to wh. k. shall hold
14. art come to kingdom for s. time
9 : 2. lay hand on s. as sought hurt
27. upon all s. as joined themselves
Jb. 18 : 21. s. are dwellings of wicked
Ps. 25 : 10. to s. as keep cov-t, 103 : 18.
27 : 12. s. as breathe out cruelty
37 : 14. to slay s. as be of upright
22. s. as be blessed of him inherit
40 : 4. nor s. as turn aside to lies
16. let s. as love thy salv. say, 70 : 4.
55 : 20. ag-t s. as be at peace wi. him
73 : 1. God good to s. as are of clean
107 : 10. s. as sit in darkness, and
125 : 5. s. as turn unto crooked ways
139 : 6. s. knowl. is too wonderful
144 : 15. Happy that peo. in s. a case
Pr. 11 : 20. s. as are upright are his
28 : 4. s. as keep the law contend
31 : 8. s. as are appointed to destr-n
Ec. 4 : 1. tears of s. as were oppressed
Is. 9 : 1. dimness not be s. as was in
10 : 20. s. as are escaped of Jacob
20 : 6. s. is our expectation whither
37 : 30. eat s. as groweth of itself
58 : 5. Is it s. a fast I have chosen?
Je. 5 : 9. avenged on s. na., 29.-9 : 9.
15 : 2. s. as are for death to death, s. as are for sword, s. as are for famine, s. as are for cap-y, 43 : 11.
21 : 7. deliver s. as are left in city
44 : 14. none return, but s. as escape
Da. 1 : 4. s. as had ability to stand
11 : 32. s. as do wickedly be corrupt
12 : 1. time of trouble, s. as nev. was
Am. 5 : 16. s. as are skilful to wail-g
Mi. 5 : 15. in fury s. they not heard
Zph. 1 : 8. s. as are clothed wi. strange
Mat. 9 : 8. G. who had given s. power
18 : 5. whoso shall receive one s. little child, Mk. 9 : 37.
19 : 14. of s. is the kingdom of God, Mk. 10 : 14. Lu. 18 : 16.
24 : 21. tribulation, s. as, Mk. 13 : 19.
44. in s. an hour as ye think not
26 : 18. Go into the city to s. a man
Mk. 4 : 18. sown am. thorns s. as hear
20. in good ground, s. as hear
33. with many s. parables spake he
6 : 2. s. mighty works are wrought
Jn. 4 : 23. Fa. seeketh s. to worship
8 : 5. Moses commanded s. be stoned
9 : 16. can a sinner do s. miracles?
Ac. 2 : 47. Lord added daily s. as be
3 : 6. s. as I have, give I thee, rise
15 : 24. we gave no s. commandm-t
16 : 24. having received s. a charge
18 : 15. will be no judge of s. mat-s
22 : 22. said, Away with s. a fellow
25 : 20. I doubted of s. questions
26 : 29. and altogether s. as I am
Ro. 16 : 18. s. serve not our L. Jesus
1 Co. 5 : 1. s. fornication as is not
6 : 11. s. were some of you [case
7 : 15. sister not under bond in s.
28. s. shall have trouble in flesh
10 : 13. no temptation, but s. as is

1 Co. 11 : 16. we have no s. custom
15 : 48. s. are they th. are earthy (2)
16 : 16. Th. ye submit yours. unto s.
18. acknowledge them that are s.
2 Co. 2 : 6. Sufficient to s. a man is
3 : 4. such trust have we thro. Ch.
12. Seeing that we have s. hope
10 : 11. Let s. a one think, s. as we in word by letters, s. will we be
11 : 13. For s. are false apostles
12 : 3. I knew s. a man, whether
20. not find you s. as I would; and be found s. as ye would not
Ga. 5 : 23. Meekness ag. s. is no law
Ph. 2 : 29. and hold s. in reputation
1 Th. 4 : 6. bec. L. is avenger of all s.
2 Th. 3 : 12. that are s. we command
1 Ti. 6 : 5. corrupt men, fr. s. withdr.
2 Ti. 3 : 5. heady, from s. turn away
Tit. 3 : 11. he that is s. is subverted
He. 5 : 12. ye s. as have need of milk
7 : 26. s. a high priest became us
8 : 1. s. a high priest, who is set on
12 : 3. endured s. contradiction of
13 : 16. wi. s. sacrifi-s G. well pleased
Ja. 4 : 13. to morrow go into s. a city
16. all s. rejoicing is evil
2 Pe. 1 : 17. came s. a voice to him
3 Jn. 8. We thf. ought to receive s.
Re. 5 : 13. s. as are in sea heard I
16 : 18. s. as was not since men were
20 : 6. on s. sec. death hath no power
See **Such LIKE, Such a ONE.**

SUCH AND SUCH.

1 S. 21 : 2. my servants to s.-a.-s. place
2 S. 12 : 8. have given s.-a.-s. things
2 K. 6 : 8. in s.-a.-s. place be my camp
See THING, WORDS.
See **Such THINGS.**

SU'CHATHITES.

1 Ch. 2 : 55. families of scribes, the S.

SUCK. [Noun.] [s.

Ge. 21 : 7. Sarah sho. have given chil.
1 S. 1 : 23. Hannah gave her son s.
1 K. 3 : 21. I rose to give child s. [s.
Is. 40 : † 11. gently lead those th. give
La. 4 : 3. the sea monsters give s. to
Mat. 24 : 19. woe unto them give s. in those days, Mk. 13 : 17. Lu. 21 : 23.
Lu. 23 : 29. Blessed are the paps which never gave s.

SUCK, ED, ING. [rock

De. 32 : 13 made him s. honey out of
33 : 19. they sh. s. of abund. of seas
1 S. 7 : 9. Sam. took a s-g lamb [s.?
Jb. 3 : 12. why breasts that I should
20 : 16. He sh. s. the poison of asps
39 : 30. Her young ones s. up blood
Can. 8 : 1. s-d breasts of my mother
Is. 60 : 16. Thou shalt s. milk of Gentiles, shalt s. breast of kings
66 : 11. ye may s. and be satisfied
12. then sh. ye s., ye sh. be borne
Eze. 23 : 34. Thou shalt even s. it out
Jo. 2 : 16. gather chil. and those th. s.
Lu. 11 : 27. Blessed are paps thou
See **Sucking CHILD.** [hast s-d

SUCKLING, S.

De. 32 : 25. s. with man of gray hairs
1 S. 15 : 3. slay woman, infant, and s.
22 : 19. Doeg smote s-s of Nob
Ps. 8 : 2. Out of mouth of babes and s-s, Mat. 21 : 16. [s.
Je. 44 : 7. to cut off fr. you child and
La. 2 : 11. s-s swoon in streets of city

SUDDEN.

Jb. 22 : 10. s. fear troubleth thee
Pr. 3 : 25. Be not afraid of s. fear
1 Th. 5 : 3. then s. destruction com-

SUDDENLY. [eth

Nu. 6 : 9. if any man die very s.
12 : 4. Lord spake s. unto Moses
35 : 22. if thrust him s. with-t enmity
De. 7 : 4. anger of L. will destroy you
Jos. 10 : 9. Joshua came s., 11 : 7. [s.
2 S. 15 : 14. Lest he overtake us s.
2 Ch. 29 : 36. for the thing was done s.

Jb. 5 : 3. s. I cursed his habitation
9 : 23. If scourge slay s. he will laugh
Ps. 6 : 10. let them be ashamed s.
64 : 4. s. do they shoot at him and
7. with arrow s. they be wounded
Pr. 6 : 15. his calamity shall come s., he shall be broken s. [ox
7 : † 22. he goeth after her s. as an
24 : 22. their calamity shall rise s.
29 : 1. shall s. be destroyed, and that
Ec. 9 : 12. it falleth s. upon them
Is. 29 : 5. it shall be at an instant s.
30 : 13. whose breaking cometh s.
47 : 11. desolation come upon thee s.
48 : 3. I did them s. and they came
Je. 4 : 20. s. are my tents spoiled
6 : 26. spoiler sh. s. come upon us
15 : 8. caused him to fall upon it s.
18 : 22. sh. bring troop s. upon them
49 : 19. s. make him run aw., 50 : 44.
51 : 8. Bab. is s. fallen and destroy.
Ha. 2 : 7. rise up s. that sh. bite thee
Mal. 3 : 1. L. shall s. come to temple
Mk. 9 : 8. s. saw no man save Jesus
13 : 36. coming s. he find you sleep
Lu. 2 : 13. s. with angel a multitude
9 : 39. spirit taketh, he s. crieth out
Ac. 2 : 2. s. came a sound fr. heaven
9 : 3. s. shined light fr. heav., 22 : 6.
16 : 26. s. was a great earthquake
28 : 6. he should have fallen dead s.
1 Ti. 5 : 22. Lay hands s. on no man

SUE. [law

Mat. 5 : 40. if any man will s. thee at

SUFFER. [come

Ex. 12 : 23. L. will not s. destroyer to
22 : 18. shalt not s. a witch to live
Le. 2 : 13. nei. s. salt of cov-t lacking
19 : 17. shalt rebuke him, not s. sin
22 : 16. Or s. them to bear iniquity
Nu. 21 : 23. Sihon not s. Isr. to pass
De. 21 : † 12. sh. s. her nails to grow
Jos. 10 : 19. s. th. not to enter cities
Ju. 1 : 34. not s. to come to valley
15 : 1. her father would not s. him
16 : 26. s. me that I may feel pillars
2 S. 14 : 11. not s. revengers of blood
1 K. 15 : 17. might not s. any to go
Es. 3 : 8. not king's profit to s. them
6 : † 10. s. not a whit to fail of all
Jb. 9 : 18. not s. me to take breath
21 : 3. s. me that I may speak
24 : 11. tread winepresses, s. thirst
36 : 2. s. me a little, I will shew thee
Ps. 9 : 13. consider trouble I s.
16 : 10. nor s. Holy One to see corruption, Ac. 2 : 27.-13 : 35. [ger
34 : 10. yo. lions do lack and s. hun-
55 : 22. never s. righteous to be mov.
88 : 15. while I s. thy terrors, I am
89 : 33. nor s. my faithfuln. to fail
101 : 5. a proud heart will not I s.
121 : 3. not s. thy foot to be moved
Pr. 10 : 3. L. not s. righteous to famish
19 : 15. an idle soul shall s. hunger
19. man of wrath sh. s. punishm.
Ec. 5 : 6. s. not thy mouth to cause
12. abund. of rich not s. to sleep
Eze. 44 : 20. nor s. locks to grow
Ho. 5 : † 4. doings not s. th. to turn
Mat. 3 : 15. Jesus said, s. it to be so
8 : 21. s. me to bury fa., Lu. 9 : 59.
31. s. to go into swine, Lu. 8 : 32.
16 : 21. that he must s. many things of the elders, 17 : 12. Mk. 8 : 31.-9 : 12. Lu. 9 : 22.-17 : 25.
17 : 17. how long shall I s. you? Mk. 9 : 19. Lu. 9 : 41. [Lu. 18 : 16.
19 : 14. s. little children, Mk 10 : 14.
23 : 13. neither s. ye them to go in
Mk. 7 : 12. ye s. him no more to do
11 : 16. Jes. not s. any man to carry
Lu. 22 : 15. to eat passover before I s.
51. s. ye thus far., touched his ear
24 : 46. It behooved Christ to s., Ac.
3 : 18.-26 : 23. [should s.
Ac. 3 : 18. God before shewed Christ

Ac. 5 : 41. counted worthy to s. sha.
7 : 24. seeing one s. wrong he def-d
9 : 16. things he must s. for my na.
21 : 39. s. me to speak unto people
Ro. 8 : 17. if so be we s. with him
1 Co. 3 : 15. if work be burned s. loss
4 : 12. being persecuted, we s. [ed
6 : 7. Why not s. y-rs. to be defraud-
9 : 12. not used power but s. all thi-s
10 : 13. God not s. you to be tempt-
12 : 26. if one member s., all s. [ed
2 Co. 1 : 6. same sufferings wh. we s.
11 : † 16. as a fool, s. me that I may
19. For ye s. fools gladly [age
20. ye s. if man bring into bond-
Ga. 5 : 11. why do I s. persecution?
6 : 12. lest sho. s. persecut. for cross
Ph. 1 : 29. given you to believe and s.
4 : 12. to abound and to s. need
1 Th. 3 : 4. we told you we should s.
2 Th. 1 : 5. kingd. of God for wh. ye s.
1 Ti. 2 : 12. I s. not woman to teach
4 : 10. therof. we both labour and s.
2 Ti. 1 : 12. For which cause I also s.
2 : 9. I s. trouble as an evil doer
12. If we s. we shall also reign
3 : 12. all that live godly shall s.
He. 11 : 25. Choosing to s. affliction
13 : 3. Remember them who s. adver-
22. s. word of exhortation [sity
Ja. 5 : † 7. s. with long patience
1 Pe. 2 : 20. if when ye do well, and s.
3 : 14. if ye s. for righteousn-s' sake
17. better ye s. for well doing than
4 : 15. let none s. as a murderer
16. if any man s. as a Christian
19. that s. according to will of God
Re. 2 : 10. Fear none of those things
thou shalt s. [in graves
11 : 9. not s. dead bodies to be put

SUFFERED.

Ge. 20 : 6. s. I thee not to touch her
31 : 7. God s. him not to hurt me
28. hast not s. me to kiss my sons
De. 8 : 3. he s. thee to hunger
18 : 14. Lord not s. thee so to do
Ju. 2 : † 23. Thf. L. s. those nations
3 : 28. s. not a man to pass over
1 S. 24 : 7. David s. them not to rise
2 S. 21 : 10. s. not the birds to rest
1 Ch. 16 : 21. He s. no man to do them
wr-ng, Ps. 105 : 14. [to sin
Jb. 31 : 30. Nei. have I s. my mouth
Je. 15 : 15. for thy sake I s. rebuke
Mat. 3 : 15. suffer it to be so; he s.
19 : 8. s. you to put away wives
24 : 43. nor s. his house, Lu. 12 : 39.
27 : 19. I have s. many things this
Mk. 1 : 34. he s. not devils, Lu. 4 : 41.
5 : 19. Jesus s. him not, but said
26. s. many things of physicians
37. s. no man to follow save Peter
10 : 4. Moses s. to write a bill of
Lu. 8 : 32. he s. them to enter swine
51. s. no man to go in save Pe., Ja.
13 : 2. sinners, bec. s. such things?
24 : 26. Ought not Christ to have s.?
Ac. 13 : 18. forty years s. their man-rs
14 : 16. s. nations to walk in own
16 : 7. they essayed, Spirit s. th. not
17 : 3. that Christ must needs have s.
19 : 30. disciples s. him not to enter
28 : 16. Paul was s. to dwell by hims.
2 Co. 7 : 12. not for his cause that s.
11 : 25. thrice I s. shipwreck
Ga. 3 : 4. Have ye s. things in vain?
Ph. 3 : 8. for whom I have s. loss of
1 Th. 2 : 2. even after we had s.
14. ye have s. like things of own
He. 2 : 18. he hath s. being tempted
5 : 8. learned obed. by things he s.
7 : 23. not s. to continue by reason
9 : 26. then must he often have s.
13 : 12. Jesus s. without the gate
1 Pe. 2 : 21. Christ s. for us, leaving
23. when he s. he threatened not
3 : 18. Christ hath once s. for sins
1 Pe. 4 : 1. Christ hath s. for us in
flesh, he that hath s. in the flesh
5 : 10. after ye have s. a while

SUFFEREST. [ebel

Re. 2 : 20. bec. thou s. th. wom. Jez-

SUFFERETH. [moved

Ps. 66 : 9. God s. not our feet to be
107 : 38. s. not cattle to decrease
Mat. 11 : 12. kingdom of heaven s.
Ac. 28 : 4. vengeance s. not to live
1 Co. 13 : 4. Charity s. long, is kind

SUFFERING. [Part.]

Ac. 27 : 7. wind not s. us, we sailed
Ja. 5 : 10. example of s. affliction
1 Pe. 2 : 19. endure grief, s. wrongf-y
Jude 7. s. vengeance of eternal fire

SUFFERING. [Noun.]

He. 2 : 9. for s. of death, crowned

SUFFERINGS.

Ro. 8 : 18. I reckon that s. of this time
2 Co. 1 : 5. as s. of Christ abound in
6. enduring same s. we suffer [us
7. ye are partakers of the s. of [s.
Ph. 3 : 10. may know fellowship of his
Col. 1 : 24. Who now rejoice in my s.
He. 2 : 10. capt. of salv. perfect thro.
1 Pe. 1 : 11. it testified s. of Christ [s.
4 : 13. ye are partakers of Ch.'s s.
5 : 1. I am a witness of s. of Christ

SUFFICE.

Nu. 11 : 22. Shall herds be slain to s.
them? fish gathered to s. them?
De. 3 : 26. Let it s. thee, sp-k no more
1 K. 20 : 10. if dust of Samaria sh. s.
Eze. 44 : 6. let it s. you of all your
abominations, 45 : 9.
Ho. 12 : † 8. All my labours s. me not
1 Pe. 4 : 3. time passed may s. to have

SUFFICED, ETH. [wro-t

Ju. 21 : 14. wives, yet they s-d th. not
Ru. 2 : 14. she did eat, and was s-d
18. gave her that, aft. she was s-d
Jn. 14 : 8. Lord, shew the Fa. it s-h us

SUFFICIENCY.

Le. 5 : † 7. if his hand cannot reach
to s. of a lamb, 12 : † 8. [to redeem
25 : † 26. If his hand hath found s.
De. 16 : † 10. keep feast with a s.
Jb. 20 : 22. In his s. sh. be in straits
Je. 49 : † 9. if thieves destroy their s.
2 Co. 3 : 5. but our s. is of God
9 : 8. always having s. in all things

SUFFICIENT. [work

Ex. 36 : 7. stuff they had was s. for
De. 15 : 8. shalt lend s. for his need
33 : 7. let his hand be s. for him
Pr. 25 : 16. eat so much honey as s.
Is. 40 : 16. Lebanon is not s. to burn,
nor beasts s. for burnt offering
Mat. 6 : 34. s. unto the day is the evil
Lu. 14 : 28. whe. he have s. to finish
Jn. 6 : 7. 200 pennyworth is not s.
2 Co. 2 : 6. s. to such is this punishm.
16. And who is s. for these things?
3 : 5. Not that we are s. of ourselves
12 : 9. said, My grace is s. for thee

SUFFICIENTLY. [s.

2 Ch. 30 : 3. priests not sanct-d thems.
Is. 23 : 18. th. dwell bef. L. to eat s.

SUIT. [apparel

Ju. 17 : 10. I will give thee a s. of
2 S. 15 : 4. every man who hath any s.
Jb. 11 : 19. many shall make s. unto

SUITS.

Is. 3 : 22. changeable s. of apparel

SUK'KIIM. See LUBIM.

SUM. [Noun.] [ey

Ex. 21 : 30. If laid on him s. of mon-
30 : 12. When thou takest s. of chil.
38 : 21. This is the s. of tabernacle
Nu. 1 : 2. Take the s. of cong-n, 26 : 2.
49. shalt not take s. of Levites
4 : 2. Take the s. of sons of Kohath
22. Take s. of the sons of Gershon
26 : 4. Take s. of people fr. 20 years
31 : 26. Take the s. of the prey that
49. have taken s. of men of war
2 S. 24 : 9. Joab gave s. of people unto king, 1 Ch. 21 : 5.
Es. 4 : 7. s. of money that Haman
Ps. 139 : 17. how great is s. of them
Eze. 28 : 12. Thou sealest up the s.
48 : † 10. let them measure the s.
Da. 7 : 1. Daniel told s. of the dream
Ac. 7 : 16. Abraham bought for a s.
22 : 28. With gr. s. obtained I freed.
He. 8 : 1. of things spoken this is s.

SUM. [Verb.]

2 K. 22 : 4. that he may s. the silver

SUMMER. [Adj.]

Ju. 3 : 24. covereth his feet in his s.
chamber [floors
Da. 2 : 35. as chaff of s. threshing-

SUMMER fruit, s.

2 S. 16 : 1. bro-t 100 bunches of s. f-s
2. bread and s. f. for young men
Is. 16 : 9. shouting for s. f-s is fallen
Je. 40 : 10. gather ye wine s. f-s, 12.
48 : 32. spoiler is fallen upon s. f s
Am. 8 : 1. behold, basket of s. f-s, 2.
Mi. 7 : 1. I am as when they gathered

SUMMER house. [s. f-s

Am. 3 : 15. Will smite winter house

SUMMER parlour. [wi s. h.

Ju. 3 : 20. Eglon was sitting in s. p.

SUMMER. [Noun.]

Ge. 8 : 22. s. and winter sh. not cease
Ps. 32 : 4. moisture into drought of s.
74 : 17. hast made s. and winter
Pr. 6 : 8. Provideth meat in s., 30 : 25.
10 : 5. gathereth in s. is wise son
26 : 1. As snow in s., rain in harvest
Is. 28 : 4. as hasty fruit before the s.
Je. 8 : 20. the harvest past s. is ended
Zch. 14 : 8. in s. and winter sh. it be
Mat. 24 : 32. putteth forth leaves, ye
know s. is nigh, Mk. 13 : 28. Lu.

SUMMER. [Verb.] [21 : 30.

Is. 18 : 6. fowls shall s. upon them

SUMPTUOUSLY.

Lu. 16 : 19. rich man fared s. ev. day

SUN. [down

Ge. 15 : 17. to pass when the s. went
19 : 23. s. risen when Lot entered
28 : 11. Jac. tarried, bec. s. was set
32 : 31. as he passed Penuel, s. rose
Ex. 16 : 21. s. waxed hot it melted
22 : 3. If s. be risen, blood be shed
Le. 22 : 7. when the s. is down, he
shall be clean, De. 23 : 11. [the s.
Nu. 25 : 4. hang them bef. the L. ag.
De. 11 : 30. way where s. goeth down
17 : 3. hath worshipped s. or moon
24 : 15. nei. shall s. go down upon it
33 : 14. precious fruits brought by s.
Jos. 1 : 4. toward going down of s.
8 : 29. soon as s. was down Joshua
10 : 12. s., stand thou still upon Gib.
13. the s. stood still, and the moon
Ju. 5 : 31. them that love him be as s.
8 : 13. Gid-n returned bef. s. was up
9 : 33. soon as s. is up rise early
14 : 18. said to him bef. s. went down
19 : 14. s. went do. when by Gibeah
1 S. 11 : 9. time s. be hot, ye ha. help
2 S. 2 : 24. s. went down, they at Am.
3 : 35. if taste bread or aught till s.
12 : 11. neighbour lie wi. thy wives
in sight of s. [and before the s.
12. I will do this before all Israel,
23 : 4. as the light when s. riseth
2 K. 3 : 22. s. shone upon the water
23 : 5. that burn incense to s. and
11. burned chariots of the s. [moon
Ne. 7 : 3. gates opened until s. hot
Jb. 8 : 16. hypocrite is green bef. s.
9 : 7. commandeth s. it riseth not
30 : 28. I went mourning without s.
31 : 26. If I behold s. when it [s.
Ps. 19 : 4. In them hath set tabern. for
58 : 8. pass away, may not see the s.
72 : 5. shall fear thee as long as s.
17. name be continued long as s.
74 : 16. hast prepared light and the s.

Ps. 84 : 11. Lord God is a s. and shield
89 : 36. his throne sh. endure as s.
104 : 22. s. ariseth, they gath. thems.
121 : 6. The s. shall not smite thee
by day, nor moon by night
136 : 8. made the s. to rule by day
Ec. 1 : 5 The s. ariseth, s. goeth do.
6 : 5. he hath not seen s. nor known
7 : 11. is profit to them that see s.
11 : 7. pleasant for eyes to behold s.
Can. 1 : 6. bec. s. hath looked upon
6 : 10. fair as moon, clear as the s.
Is. 19 : † 18. be called city of the s.
24 : 23. s. be ashamed when L. shall
30 : 26. light of moon be as light of
s., light of s. sh. be sevenfold
38 : 8. down in s. dial of Ahaz ten
degrees. So s. returned 10 deg-s
49 : 10. nei. sh. the heat nor s. smite
60 : 19. s. be no more light by day
20. s. no more go down, nei. moon
Je. 8 : 2. shall spread bones before s.
15 : 9. her s. gone down while yet
19 : † 2. is by entry of s. gate [day
43 : † 13. He shall break house of s.
Eze. 8 : 16. worshipped the s. tow.
Jo. 2 : 31. The s. be turned into darkness, moon into blood, Ac. 2 : 20.
Am. 8 : 9. will cause s. to go down
Jon. 4 : 8. when the s. did arise, s.
beat upon the head of Jonah [ets
Mi. 3 : 6. s. sh. go down over proph-
Na. 3 : 17. when s. ariseth, they flee
Ha. 3 : 11. s. and moon stood still [s.
Zch. 8 : † 7. country of going down of
Mal. 4 : 2. unto you s. of righteousn.
Mat. 5 : 45. s. to rise on evil and good
13 : 6. s. up were scorched, Mk. 4 : 6.
43. shall righteous shine as the s.
17 : 2. his face did shine as the s.,
Re. 1 : 16.-10 : 1. [the sick
Mk. 1 : 32. when s. did set they bro-t
Lu. 4 : 40. s. was setting brought sick
Ac. 13 : 11. sh. be blind, not seeing s.
26 : 13. light above brightness of s.
Ep. 4 : 26. let not s. go down upon
Ja. 1 : 11. s. is no sooner risen with
Re. 6 : 12. s. became black as sackc.
7 : 16. nei. shall s. light on them
9 : 2. the s. and air were darkened
12 : 1. a woman clothed with the s.
16 : 8. angel poured vial upon the s.
19 : 17. I saw an angel stand-g in s.
21 : 23. city had no need of s., nei.
of the moon, 22 : 5.
See Goeth, Going, Stars.

SUN images. [and s. i.
2 Ch. 14 : † 5. Asa took high places
34 : † 4. Josiah brake down s. i. on
Is. 17 : † 8. nei. shall respect the s. i.
27 : † 9. the s. i. shall not stand
Eze. 6 : † 4. your s. i. sh. be broken
See **RISING of sun.**

Under the SUN.
Ec. 1 : 3. What profit of all labour u.
s.? 2 : 18, 19, 20, 22.-5 : 18.-9 : 9.
9. and there is no new thing u. s.
14. I have seen all the works done
u. s., 2 : 17.-4 : 3.-8 : 17.-9 : 3.
2 : 11. and there was no profit u. s.
3 : 16. I saw u. s. place of judgment
4 : 1. all the oppressions done u. s.
7. I returned, saw vanity u. s.
5 : 13. an evil I have seen u. s., 6 : 1.-
6 : 12. tell what shall be u. s. [10 : 5.
8 : 9. my heart unto ev. work u. s.
15. man hath no better thing u. s.
9 : 6. nei. portion in any thing u. s.
9. days he hath given thee u. s.
11. I saw u. s. race is not to swift
13. This wisdom have I seen u. s.

SUNDER. [in s.
Ps. 46 : 9. break-h bow, cut-h spear
107 : 14. he brake their bands in s.
16. he hath cut bars of iron in s.
Is. 27 : 9. as stones beaten in s.
45 : 2. I will cut in s. bars of iron
Na. 1 : 13. I will burst thy bonds in s.
Lu. 12 : 46. he will come, cut him in

SUNDERED. [s.
Jb. 41 : 17. his scales stick, cannot
Ps. 22 : † 14. all my bones are s. [be s.

SUNDRY.
He. 1 : 1. God, who at s. times spake

SUNG.
Is. 26 : 1. In that day this song be s.
Mat. 26 : 30. when they had s. a
hymn, they went out, Mk. 14 : 26.
Re. 5 : 9 they s. a new song, saying
14 : 3. they s. as it were a new song
See **SANG.**

SUNK.
Nu. 11 : † 2. Moses prayed, the fire s.
1 S. 17 : 49. stone s. into his forehead
2 K. 9 : 24. Jehoram s. down in chari-
Ps. 9 : 15. heathen are s. in the pit [ot
Je. 38 : 6. so Jeremiah s. in the mire
22. thy feet are s. in the mire
La. 2 : 9. Her gates are s. into ground
Ac. 20 : 9. Eutychus s. down wi. sleep

SUNRISING.
Nu. 21 : 11. wilderness before Moab
toward s., 34 : 15 De. 4 : 41, 47.
Jos. 1 : 15.-13 : 5.-19 : 12, 27, 34.
Ju. 20 : 43. trode Benjamites down
toward s., [ard s.
21 : † 19. place north of Beth-el tow-
Lu. 1 : † 78. s. from on high visited us
See **RISING of sun.**

SUNSET. [unto s.
Jos. 23 : † 4. nations I have cut off

SUP, SUPPED. [at once
Is. 42 : † 14. I will destroy and s. up
Ob. † 16. all the heathen shall s. up
Ha. 1 : 9. faces sh. s. up as east wind
Lu. 17 : 8. Make ready whw. I may s.
1 Co. 11 : 25. took cup when he had s-d
Re. 3 : 20 I will s. with him, and he

SUPERFLUITY, IES.
Am. 6 : † 4. lie on beds of ivory and
abound with s-s [ness
Ja. 1 : 21. lay apart all s. of naughti-

SUPERFLUOUS. [thing s.
Le. 21 : 18. whatsoever man hath any
22 : 23. lamb that hath any thing s.
2 Co. 9 : 1. it is s. for me to write to

SUPERIOR. [you
La. 3 : † 35. To turn aside man fr. a

SUPERSCRIPTION. [s.
Mat. 22 : 20. Whose is this image and
s.? Mk. 12 : 16. Lu. 20 : 24.
Mk. 15 : 26. s. of his accusation, Lu.

SUPERSTITION. [23 : 38.
Ac. 25 : 19. had questions against
him of their s.

SUPERSTITIOUS.
Ac. 17 : 22. I perceive ye are too s.

SUPPED. See Sup.

SUPPER.
Mk. 6 : 21. Herod made s. to his lords
Lu. 14 : 12. When makest dinner or s.
16. A certain man made a great s.
17. sent his servant at s. time
24. none bidden sh. taste of my s.
22 : 20. Likewise also the cup aft. s.
Jn. 12 : 2. There they made Jes. a s.
13 : 2. s. being ended, the devil
4. Jesus riseth from s., laid aside
21 : 20. leaned on his breast at s. [s.
1 Co. 11 : 20 this is not to eat the L.'s
21. taketh before other his own s.
Re. 19 : 9. are called unto marriage s.
17. Come unto s. of the great God

SUPPING. [east wind
Ha. 1 : † 9. s. up of their faces as the

SUPPLANT, ED. [times
Ge. 27 : 36. he hath s-d me these two
Je. 9 : 4. every brother will utterly s.

SUPPLANTER. [a s.
Ge. 27 : † 36. Is not he rightly named

SUPPLE. [thee
Eze. 16 : 4. nei. washed in water to s.

SUPPLIANTS. [fering
Zph. 3 : 10. my s. sh. bring mine of-

SUPPLICATION.
1 K. 8 : 28. have thou respect to his
s., O Lord, 2 Ch. 6 : 19.
30. hearken thou to the s., 45,
49. 2 Ch. 6 : 35. [vants
52. eyes be open unto s. of thy ser
54. made end of praying this s. [s.
2 Ch. 33 : 13. Lord heard Manasseh's
Ps. 6 : 9. The Lord hath heard my s.
55 : 1. hide not thyself from my s.
119 : 170. Let my s. come bef. thee
Je. 36 : 7. may be will present s. to
37 : 20. O k., let my s. be accepted
38 : 26. I presented my s. bef. king
42 : 2. Let our s. be accepted before
9. ye sent me to present your [s.
Da. 6 : 11. men found Dan. making
9 : 20. while I was presenting my s.
Ac. 1 : 14. one accord in prayer and
Ep. 6 : 18. with all prayer and s. [s.
Ph. 4 : 6. in ev. thing by prayer and

Made or Make SUPPLICATION, S. [L.
1 S. 13 : 12. I have not m. s. unto the
1 K. 8 : 33. When Israel shall m. s.
unto thee, 47. 2 Ch. 6 : 24. [nigh
59. let these whw. I have m. s. be
9 : 3. I have heard s. thou hast m.
2 Ch. 6 : 29. what s. be m. of any man
Es. 4 : 8. sho. m. s. for her people
Jb. 8 : 5. wouldest m. s. to Almighty
9 : 15. I would m. s. to my judge
41 : 3. Will leviathan m. many s-s?
Ps. 30 : 8. unto L. I m. my s., 142 : 1.
Is. 45 : 14. they shall m. s. unto thee
Ho. 12 : 4. he wept and m. s. unto
1 Ti. 2 : 1. first, s-s be m. for all

SUPPLICATIONS. [serv.
2 Ch. 6 : 21. Hearken unto s. of thy
39. hear thou their prayer and s.
Ps. 28 : 2. Hear voice of my s. when
I cry, 140 : 6. [116 : 1.
6. heard voice of my s., 31 : 22.-
86 : 6. attend to the voice of my s.
130 : 2. be attentive to my s., 143 : 1.
Je. 3 : 21. weeping and s. of Israel
31 : 9. and with s. will I lead them
Da. 9 : 3. set my face to seek by s.
17. hear prayer of serv. and his s.
18. not present s. for our righto-s
23. At begin-g of s. the command
Zch. 12 : 10. pour spirit of grace and s.
1 Ti. 5 : 5. she continueth in s. night
He. 5 : 7. when he had offered up s.

SUPPLIED, ETH.
1 Co. 16 : 17. lacking on your part,
they s-d [saints
2 Co. 9 : 12. not only s-h want of the
11 : 9. lacking to me, the breth. s-d
Ep. 4 : 16 by that wh. every joint s-h

SUPPLY. [Verb.]
Ph. 2 : 30. to s. your lack of service
4 : 19. my God shall s. all your need

SUPPLY. [Noun.]
2 Co. 8 : 14. that your abundance be
a s. for their want, that their
abundance a s. for your want
Ph. 1 : 19. thro. prayer and the s. of
the Spirit of Jesus

SUPPORT, ED. [s-d him
Ge. 27 : † 37. with corn and wine I
Ps. 20 : † 2. Lord s-d thee out of Zion
Ac. 20 : 35. ye ought to s. weak, 1 Th.

SUPPOSE. [5 : 14.
2 S. 13 : 32. Let not my lord s. they
Lu. 7 : 43. I s. he to whom he forgave
12 : 51. s. ye I am come to give peace
13 : 2. s. ye these Galileans were
Jn. 21 : 25. I s. world not contain
Ac. 2 : 15. are not drunken, as ye s.
1 Co. 7 : 26. I s. this good for present
2 Co. 11 : 5. I s. I was not behind the
He. 10 : 29. Of how much sorer punishment s. ye [as I s.
1 Pe. 5 : 12. Sylvanus, faithful bro.,

SUPPOSED. [more
Mat. 20 : 10. s. sho. have received

Mk. 6 : 49. s. it had been a spirit
Lu. 3 : 23. Jes., as was s., the son of
24 : 37. s. they had seen a spirit
Ac. 7 :25. s. breth. wo. have underst-d
21 :29. whom they s. Paul had bro-t
25 : 18. none accusa. of things as I s.
Ph. 2 : 25. I s. it necessary to send
⌊Epaph.

SUPPOSING.

Lu. 2 : 44. s. him in the company
Jn. 20 :15. She s. him to be gardener
Ac. 14 : 19. drew Paul out, s. he dead
16 : 27. keeper s. prisoners been fled
27 :13. s. they had obtained purpose
Ph. 1 : 16. s. to add affliction to my
1 Ti. 6 : 5. men, s. gain is godliness
⌈s.

SUPREME.

1 Pe. 2 : 13. submit, whe. to king as

SUR.

2 K. 11 :6. part shall be at gate of S.
⌈20.

SURE.

Ge. 23 · 17. field, cave were made s.,
Ex. 3 : 19. am s. king not let you go
Nu. 32 : 23. be s. y-r sin will find you
De. 12 : 23. be s. eat not the blood
1 S. 2 : 35. will build him a s. house
20 : 7. be s. that evil is determined
25 : 28. will make my lord a s. hou.
2 S. 1 : 10. I was s. he could not live
23 : 5. with me cov-t ordered and s.
1 K. 11 :38. I will hold thee s. house
Ezr. 9 : † 8. and to give us a s. abode
Ne. 9 : 38. we make a s. covenant
11 : † 23. a s. ordinance for singers
Jb. 24 : 22. and no man is s. of life
Ps. 19 : 7. testimony of the Lord is s.
93 : 5. Thy testimonies are very s.
111 : 7. all his commandm-ts are s.
Pr. 6 : 3. and make s. thy friend
11 : 15. he th. hateth suretiship is s.
18. to him soweth rightn. s. reward
Is. 22 : 23. as a nail in a s. place, 25.
28 : 16. I lay in Zion for s. founda.
32 : 18. my people in s. dwellings
33 : 16. bread be given, waters be s.
55 :3. s. mercies of Dav., Ac. 13 :34.
Je. 15 : † 18. unto me as waters not s.
Da. 2 : 45. interpretation thereof s.
4 : 26. kingd. shall be s. unto thee
Mat. 27 :64. sepulchre be made s., 66.
65. he said, make it s. as you can
Lu. 10 : 11. be s. kingdom of God is
Jn. 6 : 69. we are s. thou art Christ
16 : 30. we are s. thou knowest all
Ro. 2 : 2. are s. judgm. of G. is true
4 : 16. promise be s. to all the seed
15 : 29. I am s. that when I come
2 Ti. 2 : 19. founda. of G. standeth s.
He. 6 : 19. hope we have as anchor s.
2 Pe. 1 : 10. diligence to make call-g s.
19. We ha. a more s. word of proph-
⌊ecy

SURELY.

Ge. 2 : 17. day thou eatest shalt s. die
3 : 4. serpent said, Ye sh. not s. die
9 : 5. s. your blood will I require
18 : 18. Abr. s. become great nation
20 : 7. if restore her not shalt s. die
11. s. fear of God is not in this pla.
28 : 16. Jac. said, s. L. is in this pla.
22. I will s. give tenth unto thee
29 : 14. s. th. art my bone and flesh
32. s. L. looked upon my affliction
30 : 16. unto me, s. I have hired
31 : 42. s. hadst sent me away⌊ thee
32 : 12. saidst, I will s. do thee good
42 : 16. fetch bro., or s. ye are spies
43 : 10. s. we had returned sec. time
44 : 28. I said s. he is torn in pieces
46 : 4. I will s. bring thee up again
50 : 24. I die, God will s. visit you,
25. Ex. 13 : 19. ⌈known
Ex. 2 : 14. Moses said, s. this thing is
3 : 7. I have s. seen afflic. of Isr., 16.
4 : 25. s. a bloody husband art thou
11 : 1. he shall s. thrust you out
18 : 18. Thou wilt s. wear away, and
19 : 13. he shall s. be stoned, or shot
21 : 20. die, he sh. be s. punished, 22.
Ex. 21 :28. If ox gore, ox sh. be s. st-d
36. he sh. s. pay ox for ox ⌈titu-n
22 : 6. kindleth fire sh. s. make res-
14. if it die, he sh. s. make it good
16. if lie with her, sh. s. endow her
23. if cry, I will s. hear their cry
23 : 4. shalt s. bring it back to him
5. If thou see, thou shalt s. help
33. gods, will s. be snare, 1K. 11 :2.
40 : 15. anointing sh. s. be an overl-g
Nu. 13 : 27. s. it floweth with milk
14 :23. s. they shall not see the land
35. I will s. do it unto all this cong.
18 : 15. firstb. shalt thou s. redeem
22 : 33. s. I had slain thee, saved
23 : 23. s. no enchantment ag. Jac.
26 : 65. They shall s. die in wildern.
27 : 7. shalt s. give them a posses-n
32 : 11. s. none from 20 years old
shall see land, De. 1 : 35. ⌈people
De. 4 · 6. s. this great nation is a wise
8 : 19. that ye shall s. perish, 30 : 18.
13 : 9. thou shalt s. kill the idolater
15. Thou shalt s. smite inhabit-ts
15 : 8. shalt s. lend him sufficient
10. shalt s. give thy poor brother
16 : 15. s. rejoice in feast of tabern.
22 : 4. shalt s. help him to lift them
23 : 21. Lord will s. require thy vow
31 : 18. I will s. hide my face in
Jos. 14 : 9. s. the land shall be thine
Ju. 3 : 24. s. covereth his feet ⌈thee
4 : 9. Deborah said, I will s. go with
6 : 16. Gideon, s. I will be with thee
11 : 31. to meet me, shall s. be the
15 :13. will bind, but s. not kill thee
20 : 39. s. they are smitten bef. us
Ru. 1 : 10. s. we will return with thee
1 S. 9 : 6. he saith cometh s. to pass
15 : 32. s. bitterness of death is past
17 : 25. s. to defy Isr. is he come up
20 : 26. Saul tho-t, s. he is not clean
22 : 22. I knew Doeg wo. s. tell Saul
24 : 20. I know thou shalt s. be king
25 : 21. s. in vain have I kept all
34. s. not been left to Nabal any
28 : 2. s. sh. know what serv. can do
29 :6. s. as Lord liveth thou upright
30 : 8. thou shalt s. overtake them
2 S. 2 : 27. s. the people had gone up
9 :7. s. shew kindn. for Jona.'s sake
11 : 23. s. the men prevailed ag. us
15 : 21. s. where k. sh. be, will I be
18 : 2. I will s. go forth with you
20 : 18. They sh. s. ask counsel at
24 : 24. but I will s. buy it of thee
1 K. 8 : 13. I have s. built thee hou.
11 : 11. I will s. rend kingd. fr. thee
13 : 32. saying shall s. come to pass
18 : 15. I will s. shew mys. unto him
20 : 23. s. we shall be stronger, 25.
22 : 32. s. it is the king of Israel
2 K. 3 :14. s. were it not I regard Jeh.
23. This is blood, kings are s. slain
5 :11. I thought, he will s. come out
8 : 14. He told me thou s. recover
9 : 26. s. I have seen blood of Nab-h
18 : 30. The Lord will s. deliver us,
Is. 36 : 15. ⌈over
23 :22. s. was not holden such a pass-
24 : 3. s. at command of the Lord
Es. 6 : 13. shalt not prevail, s. fall
Jb. 8 :6. if pure s. wo. awake for thee
13 :3. s. I would speak to Almighty
10. he will s. reprove you, if ye
14 :18. s. the mt. cometh to nought
18 :21. s. such are dwellings of wick.
20 :20. s. he shall not feel quietness
28 : 1. s. there is a vein for silver
31 :36. s. take it upon my shoulder
33 : 8. s. hast spoken in my hear-g
34 : 12. yea, s. G. will not do wick-y
31. s. it is meet to be said unto G.
35 : 13. s. God will not hear vanity
37 :20. if man speak s. be swallowed
40 : 20. s. the mts. bring forth food
Ps. 32 : 6. s. in floods they shall not
Ps. 39 : 6. s. man walketh in a vain
11. consume, s. ev. man is vanity
62 : 9. s. men of low degr. are vanity
73 : 18. s. didst set them in slippery
76 : 10. s. wrath of man shall praise
77 :11. s. I will rememb. thy wond-s
85 : 9. s. his salvation is nigh them
91 : 3. s. he sh. deliver thee fr. snare
112 :6. s. he sh. not be moved for ev.
131 : 2. s. I have behaved as a child
132 : 3. s. I will not come into taber.
† 15. I will s. bless her provision⌈ed
139 : 19. s. thou wilt slay the wick.
140 :13. s. righteous sh. give thanks
Pr. 1 · 17. s. in vain net is spread in
3 : 34. s. he scorneth the scorners
10 :9. walketh uprightly, walketh s.
22 : 16. giveth to rich, sh. s. come to
23 : 18. for s. there is an end ⌊want
30 : 2. s. I am more brutish than
33. s. churning of milk bringeth b.
Ec. 4 : 16. s. this is vanity, vexation
7 :7. s. oppression maketh man mad
8 : 12. s. be well wi. them th. fear G.
10 : 11. s. serpent will bite without
Is. 7 : 9. not believe, s. ye shall not
14 :24. s. as I have thought so sh. it
16 : 7. foundations s. are stricken
19 : 11. s. princes of Zoan are fools
22 : 14. s. this iniquity not be purg.
17. the Lord will s. cover thee
18. he will s. violently toss thee
29 : 16. s. your turning of things
40 : 7. s. the peo. is grass ⌊ups. do.
45 : 14. s. G. is in thee, is none else
24. s. in the L. have I righteousn.
49 : 4. s. my judgment is with the L.
53 : 4. s. he hath borne our griefs
54 : 15. sh. s. gather, but not by me
60 : 9. s. the isles shall wait for me
62 :8. s. I will no more give thy corn
63 : 8. s. they are my people ⌈me
Je. 2 : 35. s. his anger sh. turn from
3 : 20. s. as wife treacherously deps.
4 : 10. s. hast greatly deceived peo.
5 : 2. say, L. liveth ; s. they swear
4. I said, s. these are poor ⌊falsely
8 : 13. I will s. consume them, saith
16 : 19. s. our fa.'s have inherited
22 : 6. s. I will make thee a wildern.
22. s. be ashamed for thy wicked-s
24 : 8. s. so will I give Zedekiah
26 : 15. s. bring innocent blood
31 : 18. s. heard Ephraim bemoan-g
19. s. after I was turned, I repent.
20. I will s. have mercy upon him
32 : 4. Zedekiah s. be delivered into
34 : 3. shalt s. be taken and deliv-d
36 : 16. s. tell king of all these words
37 : 9. Chaldeans sh. s. depart fr. us
38 : 3. this city sh. s. be given to k.
15. wilt th. not s. put me to death?
39 : 18. I will s. deliver thee, thou
44 : 25. we will s. perform our vows
29. my words shall s. stand ag. you
46 : 18. s. as Carmel by the sea, so
49 : 12. thou s. drink of cup⌈50 :45.
20. s. least of flock sh. draw them,
51 : 14. s. I will fill thee with men
56. G. of recompences sh. s. requite
La. 3 : 3. s. against me is he turned
Eze. 3 : 6. s. had I sent thee to them
21. he shall s. live, because he is
warned. 18 : 9, 17, 19, 21, 28.-
33 : 13, 15, 16. ⌈sanctuary
5 : 11. s., bec. thou hast defiled my
17 : 16. s. in place king dwelleth
19. s. mine oath will I recompense
20 : 33. s. with mighty hand I rule
31 : 11. he shall s. deal with him
33 : 27. s. they in wastes fall by sw.
34 :8. s. bec. my flock became a prey
36 : 5. s. in the fire of my jealousy
7. s. heathen sh. bear their shame
38 : 19. s. in that day great shaking
Ho. 5 : 9. made known that wh. sh. s.
12 : 11. s. they are vanity, they ⌊be

Am. 3 : 7. s. the L will do nothing
5 : 5. Gilgal sh. s. go into captivity
7 : 11. Israel shall s. be led away, 17.
8 : 7. s. I will never forget any of
Mi. 2 : 12. I will s. assemble, O Jacob,
I will s. gather remnant of Isr.
Ha. 2 : 3. it will s. come, not tarry
Zph. 2 : 9. s. Moab shall be as Sodom
3 : 7. s. then wilt fear me, and recei.
Mat. 26 : 73. s. thou art one of them,
Mk. 14 : 70. [believed am. us
Lu. 1 : 1. things which are most s.
4 : 23. Ye will s. say, Heal thyself
Jn. 17 : 8. known s. I came out from
He. 6 : 14. s. blessing, I will bless
Re. 22 : 20. s. I come quickly, even
See **Surely DIE.**

SURELY be put to death.
Ge. 26 : 11. toucheth this man sh. s. -
Ex. 19 : 12. toucheth mount sh. s. -
21 : 12. that smiteth a man sh. s. -
15. that smiteth his father sh. s. -
16. that stealeth a man shall s. -
17. that curseth his father or his mother shall s. -, Le 20 : 9.
22 : 19. Whosoever lieth with a beast s. -, Le. 20 : 15, 16. [15.
31 : 14. that defileth sabbath sh. s. -,
Le. 20 : 2. Whosoever giveth his seed unto Molech, shall s. -
10. adulterer, adulteress, sh. s. -
11. lieth with fa.'s wife, both s. -
12. lie with dau. in law, both s. -
13. man lie wi. mankind, both s. -
24 : 16. he that blasphemeth, s. -
17. he that killeth any man shall s. -, Nu. 35 : 16, 17, 18, 21, 31.
27 : 29. not be redeemed, but s. -
Ju. 21 : 5. Who came not up, sh. s. -

SURETIES.
Pr. 22 : 26. be not of them that are s.

SURETISHIP.
Pr. 11 : 15. he that hateth s. is sure

SURETY.
Ge. 43 : 9. I will be s. for him, shalt
44 : 32. thy serv. became s. for lad
Jb. 17 : 3. put me in a s. with thee
Ps. 119 : 122. Be s. for thy servant for
Pr. 6 : 1. if thou be s. for thy friend
11 : 15. He that is s. for stranger
17 : 18. becometh s. in presence of
20 : 16. th. is s. for a stranger, 27 : 13.
He. 7 : 22. was Jes. made s. of better

Of a SURETY. [ger
Ge. 15 : 13. - s. thy seed sh. be a stran-
18 : 13. Shall I - s. bear a child?
26 : 9. Abim. said, - s. she is thy wife
Ac. 12 : 11. I know - s. L. hath sent
See SURETIES. [angel

SURFEITING.
Lu. 21 : 34. lest be overcharged with

SURMISINGS. [s.
1 Ti. 6 : 4. wh-f cometh strife, evil s.

SURNAME. [Noun.]
Mat. 10 : 3. Lebbeus, s. was Thad-s
Ac. 10 : 5. Simon, whose s. is Peter,
32. - 11 : 13. [25. - 15 : 37.
12 : 12. John, whose s. was Mark,

SURNAME. [Verb.] [rael
Is. 44 : 5. s. himself by name of Is-

SURNAMED. [not
Is. 45 : 4. I have s. thee, thou hast
Mk. 3 : 16. And Simon he s. Peter,
Ac. 10 : 18. [thunder
17. s. them Boanerges, the sons of
Lu. 22 : 3. into Judas, s. Iscariot
Ac. 1 : 23. Barsabas, who was s. Jus.
4 : 36. Joses, who was s. Barnabas
15 : 22. to send Judas, s. Barsabas

SURPLUSAGE. [in s.
Ex. 26 : † 13. a cubit on the other side

SURPRISED.
Is. 33 : 14. fearfulness s. hypocrites
Je. 48 : 41. taken, strong holds are s.
51 : 41. how is praise of whole earth

SU'SANCHITES. [s.
Ezr. 4 : 9. wrote Rehum, and the S.

SUSAN'NA.
Lu. 8 : 3. and S., which ministered

SU'SI. [unto him
Nu. 13 : 11. of tribe of Manasseh,

SUSPENSE. [son of S.
Lu. 3 : † 15. peo. in s., and all mused
12 : † 29. live not in careful s.
Jn. 10 : † 24. How long hold us in s.

SUSTAIN.
1 K. 17 : 9. a widow woman to s. thee
Ne. 9 : 21. forty years didst s. them
Ps. 55 : 22. Cast burden upon Lord,
he shall s. thee [infirmity
Pr. 18 : 14. spirit of man will s. his

SUSTAINED. [him
Ge. 27 : 37. with corn and wine I s.
Ps. 3 : 5. I awaked, for the L. s. me
Is. 59 : 16. his righteousness s. him

SUSTENANCE. [Israel
Ju. 6 : 4. Midianites left no s. for
2 S. 19 : 32. Barzillai provided k. of s.
Ac. 7 : 11. dearth, our fa-s found no s.

SWADDLED. [with
La. 2 : † 20. women eat children s.
22. those I have s. and brought up
Eze. 16 : 4. wast not salted nor s. at

SWADDLING. [all
Jb. 38 : 9. darkness a s. band for it
Lu. 2 : 7. wrapped him in s. clothes

SWALLOW. [Noun.]
Ps. 84 : 3. the s. hath found a nest
Pr. 26 : 2. as s. by flying, so the curse
Is. 38 : 14. like a s. so did I chatter
Je. 8 : 7. crane and s. observed time

SWALLOW. [Verb.] [of
Nu. 16 : 30. if earth open and s. them
34. Lest the earth s. us up also
2 S. 20 : 19. why s. up inherit-e of L.
20. far be it from me I sho. s. up
Jb. 2 : † 3. movedst me to s. him up
7 : 19. alone till I s. down my spittle
20 : 18. he sh. restore, not s. it down
Ps. 21 : 9. the Lord sh. s. them up
56 : 1. O God, man would s. me up
2. Mine enemies wo. daily s. me up
57 : 3. reproach of him wo. s. me up
69 : 15. nei. let the deep s. me up
Pr. 1 : 12. Let us s. them up alive
Ec. 10 : 12 lips of fool will s. up hims.
Is. 8 : † 12. s. up way of thy paths
19 : † 3. I will s. up counsel thereof
25 : † 7. he will s. up face of cover-g
8. will s. up death in victory
42 : † 14. I will destroy and s. up
Ho. 8 : 7. the strangers shall s. it up
Am. 8 : 4. O ye that s. up the needy
Ob. 16. they shall drink and s. down
Jon. 1 : 17. prepared fish to s. Jonah
Mat. 23 : 24. strain at a gnat, and s.

SWALLOWED. [camel
Ex. 7 : 12. Aaron's rod s. their rods
15 : 12. stretchedst thy right hand,
the earth s. them [10. De. 11 : 6.
Nu. 16 : 32. earth opened and s., 26 :
2 S. 17 : 16. pass over, lest k. be s. up
Jb. 6 : 3. theref. my words are s. up
20 : 15. hath s. riches, he sh. vomit
37 : 20. if man speak, he sh. be s. up
Ps. 35 : 25. let them not say, We
have s. him up [Dathan
106 : 17. The earth opened and s.
107 : † 27. all their wisdom is s. up
124 : 3. Then they had s. us up quick
Is. 9 : † 16. th. are led of them are s.
28 : 7. priest, proph., are s. up [aw.
49 : 19. that s. thee up, shall be far
Je. 51 : 34. hath s. me like dragon
44. out of his mouth th. he hath s.
La. 2 : 2. L. hath s. up habit-n of Jac.
5. hath s. up Isr., s. up her palaces
16. Hiss and say, We have s. her
Eze. 36 : 3. have s. you up on ev. side
Ho. 8 : 8. Israel is s. up am. Gentiles
1 Co. 15 : 54. Death is s. up in victory
2 Co. 2 : 7. lest be s. up with sorrow
5 : 4. that mortality be s. up of life
Re. 12 : 16. earth opened s. up flood

SWALLOWETH.
Jb. 5 : 5. robber s. up their substance
39 : 24. He s. the ground with rage
Is. 28 : † 4. while in hand, he s. it up

SWALLOWING. [up
La. 2 : † 8. not withdrawn hand fr. s.

SWAN. [De. 14 : 16.
Le. 11 : 18. the s., the pelican uncl.,

SWARE. [both
Ge. 21 : 31. Beer-sheba, bec. they s.
24 : 7. the Lord God that s. unto me
9. servant s. to him cone-g that
25 : 33. Swear to me, and he s. unto
26 : 3. perform oath I s. unto Ab-.
31. Abim. and Isaac s. to one an.
31 : 53. Jac. s. by fear of his father
47 : 31. Joseph s. unto Jacob his fa.
50 : 24. you unto land he s. to Abr.
Ex. 13 : 5. the land which the Lord s.
unto thy fathers to give thee, 11
- 33 : 1. Nu. 14 : 16, 23, 30. - 32 :
11. De. 1 : 8. 35. - 6 : 10, 18, 23. -
7 : 13. - 8 : 1. - 11 : 9, 21. - 26 : 3. -
28 : 11. - 30 : 20. - 31 : 21, 23. - 34 :
4. Jos. 1 : 6. - 5 : 6 - 21 : 43.
Nu. 32 : 10. he s., saying, None of the
men shall enter, De. 1 : 34.
De. 2 : 14. men of war were wasted,
as Lord s.. [Jordan
4 : 21. Lord s. I should not go over
31. not forget coven-t which he s.
7 : 12. keep mercy he s. unto fa-s
8 : 18. establish covenant he s.. 9 : 5.
Jos. 6 : 22. bring out Rahab, as ye s.
9 : 15. princes of congreg-n s. unto
20. oath which we s. unto them
14 : 9. Moses s. on that day, saying
21 : 44. rest acc-g to all that he s.
Ju. 2 : 1. land wh. I s. to your fathers
1 S. 19 : 6. Saul s. Da. not be slain
20 : 3. David s. moreover to Jona.
24 : 22. David s. unto Saul.
28 : 10. Saul s. to her by the Lord
2 S. 3 : 35. David s. he would not eat
19 : 23. Da. s. unto Shimei, 1 K. 2 : 8.
1 K. 1 : 29. David s. to Bathsheba, 30.
2 : 23. Sol. s. that Adonijah sho. die
2 K. 25 : 24. Gedaliah s., Je. 40 : 9.
2 Ch. 15 : 14. they s. unto the Lord
Ezr. 10 : 5. s. to put aw. strange wives
Ps. 95 : 11. Unto whom I s. in my
wrath, He. 3 : 11.
132 : 2. How he s. unto L. and vowed
Je. 38 : 16. king s. secretly unto Jer.
Eze. 16 : 8. I s. and entered into cov.
20 : † 5. when I s. to the seed of Jacob, 47 : † 14. [Re. 10 : 6
Da. 12 : 7. s. by him liveth for ever,
Mk. 6 : 23. Herod s. unto dau-r of
Lu. 1 : 73. rememb. oath he s. to Abr.
He. 3 : 18. s. he they sho. not enter
6 : 13. by no greater, he s. by hims.
7 : 21. The L. s. and will not repent
See **Our, Your FATHERS.**

SWAREST.
Ex. 32 : 13. to whom s. by own self
De. 26 : 15. as thou s. to our fathers
1 K. 1 : 17. thou s. Sol. shall reign
Ps. 89 : 49. kindnesses thou s. unto
See **Their FATHERS.** [Da.

SWARM of bees.
Ju. 14 : 8. a s. - and honey in carcass

SWARM, S of flies.
Ex. 8 : 21. I will send s-s -, houses
of Egyptians sh. be full of s-s -
22. th. no s-s - shall be in Goshen
24. there came a grievous s. -
29. that s-s - may depart fr. Pha-h
31. he removeth s-s - from Pha-h

SWEAR. [to me
Ge. 21 : 23. Abim. said to Abr., s. un-
24. and Abraham said, I will s.
24 : 3. I will make thee s. by the L.
37. my master made me s., saying
25 : 33. Jac. said, s. to me, he sware
47 : 31. Jac. said unto Joseph, s.
50 : 5. My father made me s., 6.

Ex. 6 8. land conc-g which I did s.
Le. 5 : 4. if a soul s. whatso. it be
19 : 12. not s. by my name falsely
Nu. 30 : 2. If a man s. oath to bind
De. 6 : 13. shalt s. by his name, 10 : 20.
Jos. 2 : 12. Rahab said to spies, s.
17. oath thou hast made us s., 20.
23 : 7. nor cause to s. by their gods
Ju. 15 : 12. s. ye will not fall upon
1 S. 20 : 17. Jona. caused David to s.
24 : 21. s. thou not cut off my seed
30 : 15. s. by God thou wilt nei. kill
2 S. 19 : 7. I s. by L. if thou go not
1 K. 1 : 13. Didst not s. Sol. sh. reign
51. Let king Sol. s. unto me to day
2 : 42. Did I not make thee to s. by
8 : 31. an oath be laid upon him to
cause him to s., 2 Ch. 6 . 22.
2 Ch. 36 : 13. Neb. made him s. by G.
Ezr. 10 : 5. Ezra made all Israel to s.
Ne. 13 : 25. I made them s. by God
Is. 3 : 7. sh. he s. I will not be healer
19 : 18. five cities in Eg, sh. s. to L.
45 : 23. unto me every tougue sh. s.
48 : 1. s. by Lord, but not in truth
65 : 16. shall s. by the God of truth
Je. 4 : 2. shalt s., The Lord liveth
5 : 2. say, The L. liveth, th. s. falsely
7 : 9. Will ye steal, murder, and s.
12 : 16. to s. by my name, as they
taught people to s. by Baal
22 : 5. I s., saith L., this house shall
32 : 22. given th. land thou didst s.
Ho. 4 : 15. nei. to Beth-aven nor s.
Am. 8 : 14. that s. by sin of Samaria
Zph. 1 : 5. that s. by the Lord, that s.
Mat. 5 : 34. s. not at all ⌊by Malcham
36. Nei. s. by thy head, bec. thou
23 : 16. Whoso. shall s. by temple ;
whoso. sh. s. by gold of temp., 21.
18. whoso. shall s. by the altar, 20.
22. he th. sh. s. by heaven, sweareth
26 : 74. Then began he to curse and
s., Mk. 14 : 71 ⌈sware
He. 6 : 13. could s. by no greater, he
16. men verily s. by the greater
Ja. 5 : 12. above all things, s. not

SWEARERS. ⌈false s.
Mal. 3 : 5. I will be a witness against

SWEARETH. ⌈falsely
Le. 6 : 3. found what was lost, and s.
Ps. 15 : 4. s. to his hurt, changeth not
63 : 11. ev. one s. by him sh. glory
Ec. 9 : 2. he that s. as he that feareth
Is. 65 : 16. he th. s. shall swear by G.
Zch. 5 : 3. ev. one s. shall be cut off
4. sh. enter house of him s. falsely
Mat. 23 : 18. whoso. s. by gift guilty
20. whoso. sh. swear by altar s. by
21. whoso. sh. swear by temple s.
22. s. by throne of God, and him

SWEARING. [Noun, Part.]
Le. 5 : 1. if soul sin, hear voice of s.
Je. 23 : 10. bec. of s. land mourneth
Ho. 4 : 2. By s. and lying, and steal.
10 : 4. s. falsely in making covenant
He. 7 : † 21. priests made without s.

SWEAT. ⌊oath
Ge. 3 : 19. In the s. of thy face ⌈s.
Eze. 44 : 18. not gird wi. thing causeth
Lu. 22 : 44. his s. was as it were great

SWEATING. ⌈places
Eze. 44 : † 18. not gird thems. in s.

SWEEP, ING. ⌈food
Pr. 28 : 3. s-g rain which leaveth no
Is. 14 : 23. I will s. it with the besom
28 : 17. shall s. away refuge of lies
Lu. 15 : 8. not s. hou. and seek dili-

SWEET. ⌊gently
Ex. 15 : 25. the waters were made s.
30 : 23. Take of s. cinnamon half so
much ; of s. calamus 250 shek-s
Ju. 8 : † 26. besides s. jewels and
2 S. 1 : † 23. Saul, Jona., s. in lives
23 : 1. David s. psalmist of Israel
Ne. 8 : 10. eat the fat and drink the s.
Jb. 20 : 12. Tho. wickedn. be s. in his
Jb. 21 : 33. clods of valley shall be s.
38 : 31. bind s. influences of Plei-s?
Ps. 55 : 14. We took s. counsel tog-r
104 : 34. My meditation of him be s.
119 : 103. How s. are thy words
141 : 6. hear my words, they are s.
Pr. 3 : 24. and thy sleep shall be s.
9 : 17. Stolen waters are s., bread in
13 : 19. desire accomplished is s.
16 : 24. Pleasant words are s. to soul
20 : 17. Bread of deceit is s. to man
23 : 8. shalt vomit, lose thy s. words
24 : 13. eat honeycomb, which is s.
27 : 7. to hungry bitter thing is s.
Ec. 5 : 12. sleep of a labouring man s.
11 : 7. light is a s., a pleasant thing
Can. 2 : 3. his fruit was s. to my taste
14. O my dove, s. is thy voice
5 : 13. cheeks, as spices, s. flowers
16. His mouth is most s., yea, he
Is. 3 : † 19. L. will take away s. balls
24. instead of s. smell, be stink
5 : 20. put bitter for s., s. for bitter
23 : 16. make s. melody, sing songs
Je. 6 : 20. nor sacrifices s. unto me
31 : 26. I awaked, my sleep was s.
Ja. 3 : 11. send s. water and bitter?
Re. 10 : 9. in mouth s. as honey, 10.
18 : † 12. no man buy-h their s. wood
See CANE, ODOURS.
See Sweet INCENSE.
See Sweet SAVOUR, S.

SWEET smelling. ⌈myrrh
Can. 5 : 5. fingers dropped with s.s.
13. his lips like lilies dropping s.s.
See SWEETSMELLING. ⌊myrrh
See Sweet SPICES.

SWEET wine. ⌈s.w.
Is. 49 : 26. drunken with blood as wi.
Am. 9 : 13. the mount sh. drop s.w.
Mi. 6 : 15. s.w., but shalt not drink

SWEETENED. ⌊w.
Ps. 55 : † 14. we s. counsel together

SWEETER.
Ju. 14 : 18. What is s. than honey?
Ps. 19 : 10. thy word s. than houeye.
119 : 103. thy words s. than honey

SWEETLY.
Jb. 24 : 20. worm sh. feed s. on him
Can. 7 : 9. hke best wine, goeth down

SWEETNESS. ⌊s.
Ju. 9 : 11. Should I forsake my s.
14 : 14. out of strong came s. ⌈ing
Pr. 16 : 21. s. of lips increas-h learn-
27 : 9. so doth s. of a man's friend
Eze. 3 : 3. the roll was as honey for s.

SWEETSMELLING. ⌈our
Eph. 5 : 2. himself to G. for a s. sav-
See SWEET smelling.

SWELL, ED. ⌈s., 22.
Nu. 5 : 21. thy thigh to rot, belly to
27. her belly shall s., thigh sh. rot
De. 8 : 4. nei. did thy foot s. 40 years
Ne 9 : 21. 40 years their feet s-d not

SWELLING. [Adj., Part.]
Is. 30 : 13. breach s. out in high wall
2 Pe. 2 : 18. speak great s. words
Jude 16. mouth speak. great s. words

SWELLING, S.
Le. 13 : † 2. a man have in skin a s.
Ps. 46 : 3. tho. mount-s shake with s.
Je. 12 : 5. how do in s. of Jordan ⌈44.
49 : 19. like lion from s. of Jord., 50 :
2 Co. 12 : 20. lest be s-s tumults am.

SWEPT. ⌈you
Ju. 5 : 21. river of Kishon s. th. aw.
Je. 46 : 15. Why thy valiant s. away
Mat. 12 : 44. house, s. and garnish-
ed, Lu. 11 : 25.

SWERVED. ⌈s.
1 Ti. 1 : 6. From which some having

SWIFT.
De. 28 : 49. a nation as s. as the eagle
1 K. 4 : † 28. straw for the s. beasts
1 Ch. 12 : 8. as s. as roes upon mts.
Jb. 9 : 26. are passed away as the s.
24 : 18. he is s. as the waters ⌊ships
Pr. 6 : 18. s. in running to mischief
Ec. 9 : 11. I saw race is not to the s.
Is. 18 : 2. Go s. messengers to nation
19 : 1. the L. rideth upon s. cloud
30 : 16. said, We will ride upon the
s. ; sh. they th. pursue you be s.
66 : 20. bring breth. upon s. beasts
Je. 2 : 23. thou art a s. dromedary
46 : 6. Let not the s. flee away, nor
Am. 2 : 14. flight sh. perish fr. the s.
15. he s. of foot not deliver hims.
Mi. 1 : 13. bind the chariot to s. beast
Mal. 3 : 5. I s. witness ag. sorcerers
Ro. 3 : 15. Their feet s. to shed blood
Ja. 1 : 19. let every man be s. to hear
2 Pe. 2 : 1. bring on thems. s. de-

SWIFTER. ⌊struction
Jb. 7 : 6. My days s. than a shuttle
9 : 25. my days are s. than a post
Ha. 1 : 8. Their horses also are s. than
See EAGLES. ⌊leopards

SWIFTLY. ⌈s.
Ps. 147 : 15. his word runneth very
Is. 5 : 26. they sh. come with speed s.
Da. 9 : 21. Gabriel being caused to fly
Jo. 3 : 4. if ye recompense me s. ⌊s.

SWIM. ⌈s.
2 K. 6 : 6. cast in the stick, iron did
Ps. 6 : 6. all night make my bed to s.
Is. 25 : 11. spread forth hands to s.
Eze. 47 : 5. were risen, waters to s. in
Ac. 27 : 42. lest any s. out and escape
43. com-ded th. they who could s.

SWIMMEST, ETH.
Is. 25 : 11. he th. s-h spreadeth hands
Eze. 32 : 6. water land wh-in thou s-t

SWIMMING. ⌈thy s.
Eze. 32 : † 6. water with blood land of
47 : † 5. waters of s. not be passed

SWINE. ⌈14 : 8.
Le. 11 : 7. s. is unclean to you, De.
Pr. 11 : 22. As a jewel in a s.'s snout
Is. 65 : 4. wh. eat s.'s flesh and broth
66 : 3. as if he offered s.'s blood
17. eating s.'s flesh, and abomina.
Mat. 7 : 6. nei. cast ye pearls bef. s.
8 : 30. a herd of s. feeding, Mk. 5 :
11. Lu. 8 : 32. ⌈s., Mk. 5 : 12.
31. suffer us to go into the herd of
32. they went into the herd of s. ;
herd of s. ran violently down,
Mk. 5 : 13. Lu. 8 : 33.
Mk. 5 : 14. they that fed the s. fled
16. they told them conc-g the s.
Lu. 15 : 15. he sent him to feed s.
16. his belly with husks s. did eat

SWOLLEN. ⌈have s.
Ac. 28 : 6. looked when he should

SWOON, ED.
La. 2 : 11. children s. in the streets
12. when they s-d as the wounded

SWORD. ⌈ing s.
Ge. 3 : 24. he placed cherubim, flam-
34 : 25. took each man his s.
Ex. 5 : 21. put s. in hands to slay us
32 : 27. Put every man s. by his side
Le. 26 : 6. nei. shall s. go thro. land
25. I will bring a s. upon you th.
shall avenge, Eze. 5 : 17.-6 : 3.-
14 : 17.-29 : 8.-33 : 2.
37. they shall fall before a s.
Nu. 22 : 29. I would there were a s.
in mine hand ⌈within
De. 32 : 25. The s. without, terror
33 : 29. who is s. of thy excellency
Jos. 24 : 12. not with thy s. nor bow
Ju. 7 : 14. nothing save s. of Gideon
18. s. of the Lord, and Gideon, 20.
22. Lord set every man's s. against
his fellow, 1 S. 14 : 20. ⌈childless
1 S. 15 : 33. thy s. hath made women
17 : 39. David girded his s., 25 : 13.
50. there was no s. in hand of Da.
51. David took s. and slew him
18 : 4. even to his s., bow, and girdle
21 : 9. s. of Goliath wrapped in cloth
22 : 10. gave him the s. of Goliath

1 S. 22:13. given him bread, and a s.
25:13. Gird ye on every man his s.,
they girded on every man his s.
31:4. Saul took a s., fell upon it, 1
Ch. 10:4. [Ch. 10:5.
5. armourbearer fell upon his s., 1
2 S. 1:22. s. of Saul returned not
2:16. thrust his s. in fellow's side
26. Shall the s. devour for ever?
3:29. not fail one that falleth on s.
11:25. s. devoureth one as another
12:10. the s. never fr. thine house
18:8. wood devoured more than s.
20:8. Joab with a s. upon his loins
10. Amasa took no heed to s. in
23:10. his hand clave unto the s.
1 K. 3:24. Bring me s.; they bro-t s.
19:17. that escapeth s. of Hazael
1 Ch. 5:18. able to bear buckler, s.
21:12. s. of thine enemies overtake, or three days s. of the L.
30. he afraid because of s. of angel
2 Ch. 20:9. If evil cometh, as the s.
Ezr. 9:7. we and our kings to the s.
Ne. 4:18. ev. one had his s. girded
Jb. 5:20. to deliver from power of s.
15:22. he is waited for of the s.
19:29. Be ye afraid of the s., for wrath bringeth punishm-t of s.
20:25. glittering s. out of his gall
27:14. If children be, it is for the s.
40:19. can make his s. approach
41:26. s. of him that layeth at him
Ps. 7:12. If turn not, will whet his s.
17:13. from wicked, which is thy s.
37:15. Their s. sh. enter own heart
45:3. Gird thy s. upon thy thigh
57:4. and their tongue a sharp s.
64:3. whet their tongue like a s.
76:3. brake he the shield and s.
78:62. He gave his people unto s.
Pr. 12:18. speak-h like piercings of s.
25:18. man beareth false witn. is s.
Can. 3:8. ev. man s. upon his thigh
Is. 2:4. nation not lift s. ag. nation
31:8. s. not of a mean man shall
34:6. s. of Lord is filled with blood
41:2. he gave them as dust to s.
49:2. made my mouth like sharp s.
51:19. famine and the s. are come
65:12. will I number you to the s.
Je. 2:30. your s. devoured prophets
4:10. the s. reacheth unto the soul
5:12. nei. see s. nor famine, 14:13.
6:25. s. of the enemy is on ev. side
9:16. I will send a s. aft. them till
24:10.-25:27.-29:17.-49:37.
12:12. s. of the Lord shall devour
14:13. say, Ye shall not see the s.
15. s. and famine not be in land
16. be cast in streets because of s.
15:2. such as are for s. to s., 43:11.
3. I will appoint s. to slay, and
9. residue will I deliver to the s.
18:21. pour out their blood by s.
25:16. they sh. be mad bec. of the s.
29. I will call for s., Eze. 38:21.
31. he will give wicked to the s.
31:2. people left of s. found grace
32:24. city is given bec. of the s.
34:17. I proclaim a liberty to the s.
42:16. s. ye feared sh. overtake you
44:28. a small number wh. escape s.
46:10. s. sh. devour, be satiate, 14.
47:6. O thou s. of Lord, how long
48:2. O Madmen, s. shall pursue
10. cursed that keepeth back his s.
50:16. for fear of oppressing s. they
35. A s. is upon the Chaldeans
36. A s. is upon the liars, a s. is on her mighty men [her treasures
37. A s. is upon their horses, s. on
51:50. Ye that have escaped s. go
La. 5:9. we gat bread by peril bec. of the s. [thee, 6:3.
Eze. 5:17. I will bring the s. upon
6:8 some that shall escape the s.

Eze. 7:15. s. without, pestilence wi-in
11:8. ye have feared the s., and I will bring a s. [through
14:17. If I bring a s. and say, s. go
21. my four sore judgments, the s.
21:9. say, A s., a s. is sharpened,
12. terrors, by reason of the s. [11.
13. what if the s. contemn rod?
14. let their s. be doubled, the s. of the slain: it is the s. of great
15. set the point of the s. ag. gates
19. appoint two ways that s. may
20. that s. may come to Rabbath
30:4. the s. shall come upon Egypt
21. to make it strong to hold s.
22. cause s. to fall out of his hand
32:11. s. of k. of Babylon sh. come
33:3. If when he seeth s. come
4. if the s. come and take him, 6.
6. if watchman see the s. come, if s. come and take any [file
26. ye stand upon your s. and de-
35:5. thou hast shed blood by s.
Ho. 2:18. I will break bow and s.
11:6. s. shall abide on his cities
Am. 9:4. will I command the s.
Mi. 4:3. nation sh. not lift up s. ag.
6:14. that wh. thou deliverest, will I give up to s. [lions
Na. 2:13. s. shall devour the young
3:15. there the s. shall cut thee off
Zch. 9:13. made thee as s. of mighty
11:17. the s. shall be upon his arm
13:7. Awake, O s., ag. my shepherd
Mat. 10:34. not to send peace, but s.
26:52. Put up thy s., Jn. 18:11.
Lu. 2:35. s. shall pierce thy soul
22:36. he th. hath no s. let him buy
Ro. 8:35. sh. s. separate us from love
13:4. he beareth not the s. in vain
Ep. 6:17. s. of Spirit, which is word
Re. 2:12. hath sharp s. wi. two edges
6:4. was given to him a great s.
19:15. out of his mouth sharp s., 21.

By SWORD. [serve
Ge. 27:40. b. s. thou shalt live and
2 S. 1:12. bec. they were fallen b. s.
Jb. 33:18. his life fr. perishing b. s.
36:12. obey not, shall perish b. s.
Ps. 44:3. they got not land b. s.
78:64. their priests fell b. s.
Is. 66:16. b. s. will thy Lord plead
Je. 11:22. saith Lord, Their young men sh. die b. s., 18:21. La. 2:21.
14:12. but I will consume b. s.
15. b. s. sh. prophets be consumed
16:4. they shall be consumed b. s. and famine, 44:12, 18, 27.
21:9. He that abideth in city shall die b. s., 38:2.-42:17, 22.
27:13. Why will ye die b. s., by
32:36. city shall be delivered b. s.
33:4. houses thrown down b. s.
34:4. O Zedekiah, sh. not die b. s.
44:13. I punished Jerusalem b. s.
Eze. 28:23. wounded be judged b. s.
39:23. trespassed, so they fell b. s.
Ho. 1:7. I will not save them b. s.
Am. 7:11. Jeroboam shall die b. s.
9:10. sinners of my peo. sh. die b. s.
Hag. 2:22. every one b. s. of his bro.
Re. 13:14. had wound b. s., and did

See DRAW, DRAWN, DREW.
See FALL, with sword.
See FALLEN, FELL.

Edge of the SWORD.
Ge. 34:26. slew Hamor, Shechem, with - s. [- s.
Ex. 17:13. discomfited Amalek with
Jos. 6:21. destroyed all in city with
Ju. 1:8. Jud. smit-n Jerus. wi. - s. [- s.
4:16. host of Sisera fell upon - s., 15.
1 S. 15:8. destroyed people with - s.
Jb. 1:15. slain serv-ts with - s., 17.
Ps. 89:43. Thou hast turned - s.
Lu. 21:24. people sh. fall by - s. [- s.
He. 11:34. Who thro. faith escaped

See **Smite with edge of SWORD.**

From SWORD. [aoh
Ex. 18:4. delivered me f. s. of Phar-
Le. 26:36. shall flee, as fleeing f. a s.
1 K. 19:17. escapeth f. s. of Jehu
2 Ch. 36:20. escaped f. s. carried to
Jb. 5:15. he saveth poor f. s. [Bab.
39:22. neither turneth he back f. s.
Ps. 22:20. Deliver my soul f. s. [s.
144:10. delivereth Dav. f. hurtful
Is. 31:8. but he shall flee f. s. [s.
Je. 21:7. deliver such as are left f.
46:16. let us go f. oppressing s.
Eze. 12:16. will leave few men f. s.
38:8. land that is bro-t back f. s.

My SWORD. [m. s.
Ge. 48:22. I took from Amorite wi.
De. 32:41. If I whet m. glittering s.
42. and m. s. shall devour flesh
1 S. 21:8. neither brought m. s. nor
Ps. 44:6. neither sh. m. s. save me
Is. 34:5. m. s. shall be bathed in
Eze. 30:24. I put m. s. in his ha., 25.
32:10. afraid when I brandish m. s.

Slay, Slew, or Slain by or with SWORD.
Nu. 19:16. whosoever toucheth one that is s-n w. s., 18.-31:19.
31:8. s-w kings of Midian, Balaam also they s-w w. s., Jos. 13:22.
Jos. 10:11. more died wi. hailstones than they whom Isr. s-w w. s.
2 S. 12:9. hast s-n Uriah w. s. [w. s.
1 K. 1:51. k. swear he not s-y serv-t
2:32. Joab, who s-w w. s. Abner
19:1. Elijah had s-n prophets w. s.
10. Isr. s-n thy prophets, w. s., 14.
2 K. 8:12. yo. men wilt thou s-y w. s.
11:20. s-w Athaliah w. s. beside king's house, 2 Ch. 23:15, 21.
2 Ch. 21:4. Jehoram s-w breth. w. s.
23:14. followeth her be s-n w. s.
32:21. s-w Sennacherib w. s. [w. s.
36:17. k. of Chaldees s-w yo. men
Is. 14:19. as raiment of those s-n w.
22:2. thy s-n men not s-n w. s. [s.
Je. 14:18. if I go into field, behold the s-n w. s. [in battle
18:21. let young men be s-n b. s.
20:4. carry Judah captive s-y w. s.
26:23. Jehoiakim s-w Urijah w. s.
La. 4:9. They that be s-n w. s. are better than they s-n wi. hunger
Eze. 23:10. took sons, s-w her w. s.
26:6. dau-s in field sh. be s-n b. s.,
11. he shall s-y thy people b. s. [8.
31:17. into hell, unto them s-n w. s.
18. sh. lie wi. them s-n b. s., 32:28.
32:20. sh. fall in midst of s-n b. s.
21. they lie s-n b. s., 22, 23, 24, 29.
25 all uncirc-d s-n b. s., 26, 30, 32.
31. Phar. and his army s-n b. s., 32.
35:8. in rivers sh. th. fall s-n w. s.
Am. 4:10. yo. men have I s-n w. s.
9:1. I will s-y the last of them w. s.
Zph. 2:12. Ethiop-s be s-n b. my s.
Lu. 22:49. Lord shall s. us w. s.
He. 11:37. were stoned, were s-n w. s.
Re. 19:21. remnant s-n w. s. of him

See SHEATH.

Smite or Smote with SWORD.
De. 28:22. Lord shall s. thee w. s.
Jos. 11:10. Josh. took Hazor, s. king w. s. [w. s., Is. 37:38.
2 K. 19:37. his sons s. Sennacherib
Es. 9:5. Thus the Jews s. all their enemies w. stroke of s.
Je. 41:2. Ishmael s. Gedaliah w. s.
Lu. 22:49. Lord, sh. we s. him w. s.

Smite or smote with edge of SWORD.
Nu. 21:24. Israel s. Sihon w. - s.
De. 13:15. shall s. that city w. - s.
20:13. thou sh. s. ev. male w. - s.
Jos. 8:24. Israelites s. Ai w. - s.

Jos. 10 : 28. Joshua s. it w. - s., 30, 32, 35, 37, 39. [w. - s.
11 : 11. they s. all the souls therein
12. cities of kings Joshua s. w. - s.
14. every man Israel s. w. - s.
19 : 47. chil. of Dan s. Leshem w. - s.
Ju. 1 : 25. spies s. the city w. - s.
18 : 27. chil. of Dan s. peo. w. - s.
20 : 37. liers in wait s. city w. - s.
48. Israel s. chil. of Benj. w. - s.
21 : 10. Go, s. Jabesh-gilead w. - s.
1 S. 22 : 19. Nob, the city, Doeg s. w. - s. [w. - s.
2 S. 15 : 14. flee, lest Absalom s. city
2 K. 10 : 25. they s. worshippers of Baal w. - s. [them w. - s.
Je. 21 : 7. Nebuchadrezzar shall s.

With SWORD. [s.

Ge. 31 : 26. dau-s as captives tak. w.
Ex. 22 : 24. I will kill you w. s. [s.
Nu. 20 : 18. lest I come ag. thee w.
2 S. 20 : 8. Joab w. a s. upon his loins
21 : 16. Ishbi-benob girded w. s.
1 K. 2 : 8. not put thee to death w. s.
2 K. 6 : 22. hast taken captive w. s.
11 : 15. that followeth Athaliah kill w. s., 2 Ch. 23 : 14.
Ps. 42 : 10. As w. a s. in my bones mine enemies reproach me
Is. 1 : 20. ye shall be devoured w. s.
27 : 1. Lord, w. strong s. sh. punish
Je. 5 : 17. impoverish thy cities w. s.
27 : 8. th. nation will I punish w. s.
29 : 18. I will persecute them w. s.
Eze. 7 : 15. he in field shall die w. s.
Am. 1 : 11. did pursue his bro. w. s.
7 : 9. rise ag. house of Jerob. w. s.
Mi. 5 : 6. shall waste Assyria w. s.
Mat. 26 : 52. th. take s. sh. perish w. s.
Ac. 12 : 2. Herod killed James w. s.
Re. 2 : 16. I will fight ag. them w. s.
6 : 8. power to kill w. s. and hunger
13 : 10. that killeth w. s. must be killed w. s.

SWORD, S, with spear, s.

1 S. 13 : 19. Lest Hebrews make s-s or s-s [people
22. nei. s. nor s. found in any of
17 : 45. Thou comest with s. and s.
47. Lord saveth not with s. and s.
21 : 8. is not und. thine hand s. or s.?
Ne. 4 : 13. I set peo. with s-s and s-s
Na. 3 : 3. horseman lifteth s. and s.
See **TWOEDGED sword.**

SWORDS. [s.

2 K. 3 : 26. took 700 men that drew
2 Ch. 32 : †5. Hez-h made s. in abund.
Ps. 55 : 21. his words were drawn s.
59 : 7. belch out, s. are in their lips
Pr. 30 : 14. a genera., teeth are as s.
Can. 3 : 8. all hold s., being expert
Is. 2 : 4. they shall beat their s. into ploughshares, Mi. 4 : 3. [bow
21 : 15. they fled fr. the s. and the
Eze. 16 : 40. thrust thee thro. with s.
23 : 47. shall dispatch them with s.
28 : 7. strangers shall draw their s.
30 : 11. sh. draw their s. ag. Egypt
32 : 12. By s. of the mighty will I
27. have laid s. under their heads
38 : 4. all of them handling s.
Jo. 3 : 10. Beat ploughshares into s.
Mi. 5 : †6. waste land with naked s.
Mat. 26 : 47. with Judas was a great multitude with s., Mk. 14 : 43.
55. Are ye come out as ag. a thief with s., Mk. 14 : 48. Lu. 22 : 52.
Lu. 22 : 38. L., behold here are 2 s.

SWORE. [give

Eze. 47 : †14. land conc-g wh. I s. to

SWORN.

Ge. 22 : 16. By myself have I s., saith the Lord, Is. 45 : 23. Je. 49 : 13. -51 : 14. Am. 6 : 8. [Israel
Ex. 13 : 19. Joseph had straitly s.
17 : 16. hath s. he will have war
Le. 6 : 5. which he hath s. falsely
De. 7 : 8. would keep the oath he had s., Je. 11 : 5. [unto fathers
13 : 17. multiply thee, as he hath s.
19 : 8. if he enlarge thy coast as he hath s. [hath s., 29 : 13.
28 : 9. shall establish thee, as he
31 : 7. bring thee unto land Lord hath s., Ne. 9 : 15. [unto them
Jos. 9 : 18. bec. the princes had s.
19. We have s. unto them by the Lord, 2 S. 21 : 2. [s.
Ju. 2 : 15. against them, as Lord had
21 : 1. men of Isr. had s. in Mizpeh
7. s. not to give them wives, 18.
1 S. 3 : 14. I have s. unto hou. of Eli
20 : 42. Go in peace, as we have s.
2 S. 3 : 9. exc. as L. hath s. to David
21 : 2. Israel had s. unto Gibeonites
2 Ch. 15 : 15. s. with all their hearts
Ne. 6 : 18. many in Judah s. unto him
9 : 15. land thou hadst s. to give
Ps. 24 : 4. who hath not s. deceitfully
89 : 3. I have s. unto David my [2.
35. have s. by my holiness, Am. 4 :
102 : 8. mad ag. me, are s. ag. me
110 : 4. L. hath s., will not repent
119 : 106. I have s., I will perform it
132 : 11. L. hath s. in truth unto Da.
Is 14 : 24. The Lord of hosts hath s.
45 : 23. I have s. by mys., the word
54 : 9. I have s. waters of Noah no more go, have s. I would not be
62 : 8. L. hath s. by his right hand
Je. 5 : 7. s. by them that are no gods
44 : 26. I have s. by my great name
Eze. 21 : 23. to them th. have s. oaths
Am. 8 : 7. s. by excellency of Jacob
Mi. 7 : 20. perform mercy thou hast s.
Ac. 2 : 30. G. hath s. he wo. raise Ch.
7 : 17. time of promise wh. G. had s.
He. 4 : 3. I have s. in my wrath

SYCAMINE. [up

Lu. 17 : 6. say to s. tree, be plucked

SYCAMORE. [Adj.]

Am. 7 : 14. and a gatherer of s. fruit

SYCAMORE tree, s.

1 K. 10 : 27. Solo. made cedars to be as s. t-s, 2 Ch. 1 : 15. -9 : 27.
1 Ch. 27 : 28. over s. t. was Baal-ha.
Ps. 78 : 47. he destroyed their s. t-s
Lu. 19 : 4. Zaccheus climbed into a

SYCAMORES. [s. t.

Is. 9 : 10. s. are cut down, but we will

SY'CHAR. [S.

Jn. 4 : 5. cometh he to a city called

SY'CHEM. See SICHEM.

SYE'NE. [of S.

Eze. 29 : 10. land desolate fr tower
30 : 6. fr tower of S. shall they fall

SYM'EON = SIM'EON.

2 Pe. 1 : †1. S. Peter, an apostle of

SYMPHONY. [s.

Da. 3 : †5. hear sound of cornet, flute,

SYNAGOGUE.

Mat. 12 : 9. he went into their s.
13 : 54. he taught them in their s., Mk. 1 : 21. -3 : 1. -6 : 2. Lu. 6 : 6. Ac. 18 : 19.
Mk. 1 : 23. there was in their s. man with an unclean spirit, Lu. 4 : 33.
29. when they were come out of s., Lu. 4 : 38.
5 : 22. Jairus, one of rulers of s., besought, 35, 36, 38. Lu. 8 : 41, 49.
Lu 4 : 16. went into s. on sabbath
20. eyes of all in s. on him, 28.
7 : 5. loveth our nation, built a s.
13 : 14. ruler of s. answ-d wi. indig.
Jn. 6 : 59. These things said he in s.
9 : 22. that he be put out of the s.
12 : 42. lest they be put out of the s.
18 : 20. I ever taught in s. and tem.
Ac. 6 : 9. Then arose certain of the s., wh. is called s. of Libertines
13 : 14. th. went into s. on sabbath
15. rulers of s. sent unto them
42. when Jews were gone out of s.
Ac. 14 : 1. Paul and Barnabas into s.
17 : 1. Thessalonica, where was a s.
10. Paul and Silas into s. of Jews
17. he disputed in s. with Jews
18 : 4. reasoned in s. every sabbath
7. Justus, house joined hard to s.
8. Crispus, ruler of the s., believed
17. Sosthenes, chief ruler of the s.
26. Apollos began to speak boldly in the s., 19 : 8. [lieved, 26 : 11.
22 : 19. beat in every s. such as be-
Ja. 2 : †2. if come into s. a man with
Re. 2 : 9. but are the s. of Satan
3 : 9. I will make them of s. of Satan

SYNAGOGUES.

Ps. 74 : 8. they have burned s. of G.
Mat. 4 : 23. Jesus went teaching in their s., 9 : 35. Mk. 1 : 39. Lu.
6 : 2. as hypocrites do in s. [13 : 10.
5. love to pray standing in the s.
10 : 17. will scourge you in s., 23 : 34.
23 : 6. love chief seats in the s., Mk. 12 : 39. Lu. 11 : 43. -20 : 46.
Mk. 13 : 9. in s. ye shall be beaten
Lu. 4 : 15. he taught in the s., being
44. he preached in s. of Galilee [s.
12 : 11. when they bring you unto
21 : 12. delivering you up to the s.
Jn. 16 : 2. shall put you out of s.
Ac. 9 : 2. Saul desired letters to s.
20. he preached Christ in s.
13 : 5. Paul, Barna. preached in s.
15 : 21. being read in s. ev. sabbath
24 : 12. nei. raising up people in s.

SYN'TYCHE.

Ph. 4 : 2. I beseech S. they be of same

SYR'ACUSE.

Ac. 28 : 12. landing at S., we tarried

SYR'IA.

Ju. 10 : 6. Israel served gods of S.
2 S. 8 : 6. Da. put garrisons in S., 1
12. Of S., Moab, Ammon [Ch. 18 : 6.
15 : 8. a vow while at Geshur in S.
1 K. 10 : 29. for kings of S. did they
11 : 25. Rezon reigned over S. [13 : 3.
19 : 15. Hazael to be king of S., 2 K.
22 : 1. without war betw. S. and Isr.
2 K. 5 : 1. deliverance given unto S.
6 : 23. the bands of S. came no more
7 : 5. was no man in camp of S. [of S.
8 : 13. L. shewed me thou sh. be k.
13 : 7. king of S. had destroyed them
17. The arrow of deliverance fr. S.
19. thou shalt smite S. but thrice
16 : 6. k. of S. recovered Elath to S.
2 Ch. 1 : 17. horses for kings of S.
18 : 10. with these shalt push S.
20 : 2. beyond sea, on this side S.
24 : 23. host of S. came ag. Joash
28 : 23. gods of kings of S, help them
Is. 7 : 2. S. is confederate with Ephr.
4. fierce anger of Rezin with S.
5. Bec. S. has taken evil counsel
8. for head of S. is Damascus, and
17 : 3. fortress shall cease from S.
Eze. 16 : 57. reproach of dau-s of S.
27 : 16. S. was thy merchant for thy
Ho. 12 : 12. Jacob fled into S. [wares
Am. 1 : 5. people of S. into captivity
Mat. 4 : 24. his fame through-t all S.
Lu. 2 : 2. Cyrenius, governor of S.
Ac. 15 : 23. greeting unto breth. in
41. he went thro. S. and Cilicia [S.
18 : 18 sailed into S., 21 : 3. Ga. 1 : 21.
20 : 3. as was about to sail into S.
See **DAUGHTERS of Syria.**
See **KING of Syria.**

SYR'IAC. [S.

Da. 2 : 4. Chaldeans spake to king in

SYR'IA-DAMAS'CUS.

1 Ch. 18 : 6. Da. put garrisons in S.

SYR'IA-MA'ACHAH.

1 Ch. 19 : 6. to hire chariots out of S.

SYR'IAN.

Ge. 25 : 20. Bethuel the S., Laban the S., 28 : 5. -31 : 20, 24. [my fa.
De. 26 : 5. A S. ready to perish was

2 K. 5 : 20. spared Naaman this S.
18 : 26. Speak in S. lang., Is. 36 : 11.
Ezr. 4 : 7. letter was written in S.
tongue, and interpreted in S.
Lu. 4 : 27. cleansed, saving Naaman
[the S.

SYR'IANS.

2 S. 8 : 5. when S. of Damascus came,
David slew of S. 22,000 men
6. the S. became David's servants,
1 Ch. 18 : 5, 6. [ing of the S.
13. when he returned from smit-
10 : 6. the Ammonites hired the S.
8. S. were by thems. in the field
9. put them in array against the S.
11. S. be too strong, 1 Ch. 19 : 12.
13 drew nigh unto battle ag. S.
14. saw the S. were fled, 1 Ch. 19. 15.
15. when S. saw they were smitten
16. Hadarezer brought out the S.
17. S. set thems. in array ag. David
18. S. fled; David slew men of S.
2 S. 10 : 19. S. feared to help chil. of
Ammon any more, 1 Ch. 19 : 19.
1 K. 20 : 20. S. fled, and Isr. pursued
21. slew S. with great slaughter
26. numbered S. and went to fight
27. but S. filled the country
28. S. said, The L. is G. of the hills
29. Israel slew of the S. 100,000 [S.
22 : 11. With these shalt push the
35. k. was stayed in chariot ag. S.
2 K. 5 : 2. S. had taken a maid captive
6 : 9. thither the S. are come down
7 : 4. let us fall unto host of the S.
5. rose to go unto camp of the S.
6. Lord made S. to hear a noise
10. We came to camp of S., no man
12. shew you what S. have done to
14. king sent after host of S. [us
15. garments S. had cast away
16. people spoiled tents of the S.
8 : 28. S. wounded Joram, 29.—9 :
15. 2 Ch. 22 : 5. [hand of S.
13 : 5. Israel went out from under
17. thou shalt smite S. in Aphek
16 : 6. S. came to Elath and dwelt
24 : 2. Lord sent ag. him bands of S.
1 Ch. 19 : 10. put them in array ag. S.
14. Drew nigh before S. unto battle
16. S. saw they were put to worse
17. Da. put battle in array ag. S. [(2)
18. S. fled. David slew of S. 7,000
2 Ch. 18 : 34. king stayed hims. ag. S.
24 : 24. army of S. wi. small comp-y
Is. 9 : 12. S. before, Philist-s behind
Je. 35 : 11. to Jerus. for fear of the S.
Am. 9 : 7. have not I bro-t S. fr. Kir?

SYROPHENI'CIAN.

Mk. 7 : 26. The woman was a S. by
nation

T.

TA'ANACH, TA'NACH.

Jos 12 : 21. unto k. of T. one poss-n
17 : 11. Manasseh had inhabitants
of T., 21 : 25. [out T.
Ju. 1 : 27. Nei did Manasseh drive
5 : 19. fought the kings in T.
1 K. 4 : 12. to Baana pertained T.

TA'ANATH-SHILOH.

Jos. 16 : 6. the border went unto T.

TAB'BAOTH.

Ezr. 2 : 43. children of T., Ne. 7 : 46.

TAB'BATH.

Ju. 7 : 22. and the host fled unto T.

TA'BEAL. [T.

Is. 7 : 6. set king in midst of it, son of

TA'BEEL. [of T.

Eze. 4 : 7. set king in midst, even son

TAB'ERAH.

Nu. 11 : 3. he called the place T.
De. 9 : 22. at T. he provoked Lord to
[wrath

TABERING.

Na. 2 : 7. her maids t. upon their
[breasts

TABERNACLE.

Ex. 25 : 9. make it after pattern of t.
26 : 1. make t. wi. 10 curtains [13.
6. couple the curtains, be 1 t., 36 :
7. curtains of goats' hair to be a
covering upon t., 35 : 11.—36 : 14.
9. curtain in forefront of t.
12. sh. hang ov backside of t., 13.
15. make boards for t., 17, 18, 20,
22, 23, 26.—36 : 20, 22, 23, 25,
27, 28, 31, 32. [of t., 27.
26. five bars for boards of one side
30. rear t. accord-g to the fashion
35. table on side of t. toward south
27 : 9 thou shalt make court of t.
19. all vessels of t. of brass, 39 : 40.
29 : 43. t. be sanctified by my glory
31 : 7. make all furniture of the t.
33 : 7. Moses pitched t. with-t camp
9. as Moses entered t. the pillar, 8.
11. Joshua departed not out of t.
35 : 15. door at entering in of t.
18. the pins of the t., 38 : 20, 31.
36 : 8. that wrought the work of t.
38 : 21. This the sum of t., even of t.
39 : 32. Thus was work of t. finished
33. they brought t. unto Moses
40 : 2. thou shalt set up the t.
9. shall anoint t. and all therein
17. the t. was reared, 18. Nu. 7 : 1.
19. he spread the tent over the t.
21. he brought the ark into the t.
22. put table upon side of t. [ward
24. candlestick on side of t., south-
33. he reared the court ab-t the t.
34. glory of the Lord filled t., 35.
36. cloud was taken up from over
the t., Nu. 9 : 17.—10 : 11.—12 : 10.
38. cloud of the Lord was on t. by
day, Nu. 9 : 18, 19, 20, 22.
Le. 8 : 10. Moses anointed the t.
15 : 31. die not when they defile my t.
17 : 4. bringeth not offering bef. t.
26 : 11. I will set my t. among you
Nu. 1 : 50. appoint Levites over t.,
shall bear the t., shall encamp
round about the t., 53.
51. when the t. setteth forward,
and when t. is to be pitched
53. Levites shall keep charge of t.,
3 : 7, 8, 25.—18 : 3, 4.—31 : 30, 47.
3 : 23. Gershonites pitch behind t.
26. curtain for door of court by t.
29. of Kohath on side of t., southw.
35. of Merari on side of t., northw.
36. charge of Merari boards of t.
4 : 16. oversight of t. pertaineth to
25. they shall bear curtains of t.
26. hang-gs for door of court by t.
31. shall bear the boards of the t.
5 : 17. priest shall take of dust of t.
7 : 3. they brought offering bef. t.
9 : 15. day that t. was reared, cloud
covered the t. [shon bearing t.
10 : 11. t. taken down, sons of Ger-
21. the Kohathites did set up t.
11 : 24. Moses set 70 elders round t.
26. they went not out unto the t.
16 : 9 Seemeth it small to do the
service of the t. [Korah, 27.
24. Get you up from about t. of
17 : 13. cometh near t. shall die
De. 31 : 15. L. appeared in t. in pillar
Jos. 22 : 19. wherein L.'s t. dwelleth
29. altar of G. that is before his t.
1 S. 2 : † 32. see the affliction of t.
2 S. 6 : 17. they set the ark in the t.
7 : 6. I have walked in tent and t.
1 K. 1 : 39. took horn of oil out of t.
8 : 4. vessels in t. bro-t, 2 Ch. 5 : 5.
1 Ch. 6 : 48. Levites for service of t.
9 : 19. Korahites keepers of gates of
23. oversight of house of t. [t.
17 : 5. have gone from one t. to ano.
23 : 26. they shall no more carry t.
Jb. 5 : 24. that thy t. sh. be in peace
18 : 6. light shall be dark in his t. [t.
14. confidence be rooted out of his
15. destruction shall dwell in his t.
19 : 12. troops encamp ab. my t.
20 : 26. go ill with him left in his t.
29 : 4. secret of God was upon my t.
31 : 31. If men of my t. said not
36 : 29. understand noise of his t.?
Ps. 15 : 1. L., who sh. abide in thy t.?
19 : 4. In them hath set a t. for sun
26 : † 8. have loved t. of thy honour
27 : 5. in secret of his t. hide me
6. I will offer in his t. sacrifices
61 : 4. I will abide in thy t. for ever
76 : 2. In Salem is his t., his [Shiloh
78 : 60. So that he forsook the t. of
67. he refused the t. of Joseph
132 : 3. not come into t. of my hou.?
Pr. 14 : 11. t. of upright sh. flourish
Is. 4 : 6. sh. be t. for shadow fr. heat
16 : 5. sh. sit upon it in t. of David
33 : 20. a t. that shall not be taken
Je. 10 : 20. my t. is spoiled, my cords
La. 2 : 4. he slew all pleasant in t.
6. he hath violently taken away t.
Eze. 23 † 4. Samaria is his t., and
Jerusalem is my t. in her
37 : 27. My t. also sh. be with them
41 : 1. was breadth of the t. [loch
Am. 5 : 26. ye have borne t. of Mo-
9 : 11. will I raise up t. of David
Ac. 7 : 43. Ye took up t. of Moloch
46. desired to find t. for G. of Jac.
15 : 16. will build again t. of David
2 Co. 5 : 1. if our house of this t. be
4. we that are in this t. do groan
He. 8 : 2. true t. wh. the Lord pitched
5. when Moses about to make t.
9 : 2. was a t. made, called sanctu-y
3. t. which is called holiest of all
6. priests always into the first t.
8. while first t. was yet standing
11. a high priest by a greater t.
21. he sprinkled with blood the t.
13 : 10. no right to eat wh. serve t.
2 Pe. 1 : 13. as long as I am in this t.
14. shortly I must put off my t.
Re. 13 : 6. blaspheme his name and t.
15 : 5. temple of t. was opened
21 : 3. Behold t. of God is with men

TABERNACLE of the congregation.

Ex. 27 : 21. lamp to burn always in
t. —, Le. 24 : 3. [29 : 30.
28 : 43. Aaron and sons unto t. —,
29 : 10. bullock to be bro-t bef. t. —
44. I will sanctify t. — and altar [t. —
30 : 16. appoint atonem. money for
18. put laver betw. t. — and altar
20. When go into t. — they sh. wash
26. shalt anoint t. — and ark [t. —
36. put incense bef. testimony in
31 : 7. wisdom that they make t. —
33 : 7. Moses called it the T. — (2)
35 : 21. bro-t offering to work of t. —
40 : 2. first day of mo. set up t. —
12. bring Aaron and sons into t. —
Le. 1 : 1. Lord spake unto Moses out
of the t. —, Nu. 1 : 1. [t. —, 13.
3 : 8. he shall kill the lamb before
4 : 5. priest shall bring bullock's
blood to t. —, 14, 16, 18. [in t. —
7. altar of sweet incense bef. Lord
6 : 16. in court of t. — eat meat offering, 26. [eaten
30. no sin offering into t. —, be
9 : 5. brought that which Moses
commanded before t. —
23. Mos. and Aaron went into t. —
10 : 9. not drink wine when into t. —
16 : 16. atonement for t. —, 20, 33.
17. be no man in t. — wh. Aaron 23.
Nu. 2 : 2. Every man pitch far off t. —
17. Then t. — shall set forward
3 : 7. charge bef. t. — to do service
8. shall keep all instruments of t. —
25. charge of sons of Gershon in
t. —, 4 : 23, 25, 28, 39, 41.
38. those that encamp before t. —
eastward (2)

Nu. 4 : 4. serv. of sons of Kohath in
t. -, 3, 15, 35, 37. ⌈30, 33, 43
31. of Merari, their service in t. -,
47. Levites to do service in t. -, 8 :
15, 19, 22, 24, 26,-18 : 4, 6, 21, 23,
7 : 5. offer-gs to do service of t. - ⌊31.
89. when Moses was gone into t. -
8 : 9. shalt bring Levites before t. -
11 : 16. Gather 70 men, elders, into
12 : 4. Come out ye 3 into t. - ⌊t. -
14 : 10. glory of L. appeared in t. -
16 : 42. against Aaron they looked
toward the t. - ⌈t. -
43. Moses and Aaron came before
17 : 4. thou sh. lay up rods in t. -
18 : 22. Nei. must Isr. come nigh t. -
19 : 4. sprinkle heifer's blood bef. t. -
31 : 54. gold into t. - for memorial
De 31 : 14. presented thems. in t. - ,(2)
Jos. 18 : 1. Isr. at Shiloh set up t. -
1 K. 8 : 4. bro-t up the t. -, 2 Ch. 5 : 5.
1 Ch. 6 : 32. they ministered bef. t. -
23 : 32. Levites sh. keep charge of t. -
2 Ch. 1 : 3. high place at Gibeon t. -
6. Sol. up to altar bef. Lord at t. -
See **DOOR of tabernacle.** ⌊13.

TABERNACLE of the Lord.

Le. 17 : 4. to offer unto Lord bef. t. -
Nu. 17 : 13. Whoso. cometh near t. -
19 : 13. touch. dead body defileth t. -
31 : 30. Levites keep charge of t. -,
1 K. 2 : 28. Joab fled into t. -, 29. ⌊47.
30. Benaiah came to t. -, and said
1 Ch. 16 : 39. Zadok and priests bef. t. -
21 : 29. t. - wh. Mos. made in wild-s
2 Ch. 1 : 5. brazen altar Da. put bef.

TABERNACLE of testimony. ⌊t. -

Ex. 38 : 21. This is the sum of the t. -
Nu. 1 : 50. appoint Levites over t. -
53. Levites th. keep charge of t. -
10 : 11. cloud was taken off t. - ⌊(2)

TABERNACLE of witness.

Nu. 17 : 7. Moses laid up rods in t. -
8. on morrow Moses went into t. -
18 : 2. shall minister before the t. -
2 Ch. 24 : 6. bring collection for t. -
Ac. 7 : 44. Our fathers had the t. -

TABERNACLES. ⌈Isr.

Nu. 24 : 5. How goodly are thy t., O
Jb. 11 : 14. let not wickedn. dwell in t.
12 : 6. t. of robbers prosper
15 : 34. fire consume t. of bribery
22 : 23. put iniquity far from thy t.
Ps. 43 : 3. let them bri. me unto thy t.
46 : 4. make glad the t. of Most Hi.
78 : 51. smote strength in t. of Ham
83 : 6. t. of Edom have consulted
84 : 1. How amiable are thy t., O L.
118 : 15. salvation in t. of righteous
132 : 7. We will go into his t. and
Da. 11 : 45. sh. plant t. of his palace
Ho. 9 : 6. thorns shall be in their t.
12 : 9. I will make thee dwell in t.
Mal. 2 : 12. Lord cut off man out of t.
Mat. 17 : 4. Lord, if thou wilt, let us
make 3 t., Mk. 9 : 5. Lu. 9 : 33.
He. 11 : 9. Abr. dwelling in t. with
See **FEAST of tabernacles.**

TAB'ITHA. ⌈T.

Ac. 9 : 36. at Joppa a disciple named
40. Peter, turning to body, said,

TABLE. ⌊T., arise

Ex. 25 : 23. make a t. of shittim wood
27. places of staves to bear the t.,
28.-37 : 14. ⌈out the vail
26 : 35. thou shalt set the t. with-
30 : 27. thou shalt anoint the t. and
31 : 8. Bezaleel shall make the t.
35 : 13. make t., staves, and shewb.
37 : 10. made the t. of shittim wood
15. the staves with gold to bear t.
16. made vessels upon t. of gold
39 : 33. they bro-t t. unto Moses, 36.
40 : 4. sh. bring in t. set in order
22. put the t. in tent of congre-n
Ex. 40 : 24. put candlest. over ag. t.
Le. 24 : 6. six on a row upon pure t.
Nu. 3 : 31. Kohathites' charge be t.
Ju. 1 : 7. k-s gathered meat und. my
1 S. 20 : 29. cometh not unto k.'s t. ⌊t.
34. Jona. arose fr. t. in fierce anger
2 S. 9 : 7. Mephib-h sh. eat bread at
my t. contin-y, 10, 11, 13.-19 : 28.
1 K. 2 : 7. be of those th. eat at thy t.
4 : 27. all that came unto Sol.'s t.
10 : 5. when queen of Sheba saw
meat of his t., 2 Ch. 9 : 4. ⌈L. came
13 : 20. as they sat at t. the word of
18 : 19. prophets eat at Jezebel's t.
2 K. 4 : 10. set for him a t. and stool
1 Ch. 28 : 16. he gave gold for every t.
2 Ch. 13 : 11. shewbread upon pure t.
Ne. 5 : 17. were at my t. 150 Jews
Jb. 36 : 16. wh. sho. be set on thy t.
Ps. 23 : 5. Thou preparest a t. before
69 : 22. Let their t. become a snare
78 : 19. Can G. furnish t. in wildern.
128 : 3. like olive plants about thy t.
Pr. 3 : 3. upon t. of thy heart, 7 : 3.
9 : 2. wisdom hath furnished her t.
Can. 1 : 12. While k. sitteth at his t.
Is. 21 : 5. Prepare the t., eat, watch
30 : 8. go, write before them in a t.
65 : 11. prepare a t. for that troop
Je. 17 : 1. graven on t. of their heart
Eze. 23 : 41. a t. prepared before it
39 : 20. Thus ye sh. be filled at my t.
41 : 22. This is the t. bef. the Lord
44 : 16. they sh. come near to my t.
Da. 6 : †18. nei. was t. of music bro-t
11 : 27. they sh. speak lies at one t.
Mal. 1 : 7. t. of Lord is contemptible
12. ye say t. of Lord is polluted
Mat. 15 : 27. dogs eat crumbs from
their master's t., Mk. 7 : 28.
Lu. 16 : 21. crumbs which fell from
rich man's t. ⌈on t.
22 : 21. that betrayeth, is with me
30. That ye may drink at my t.
Jn. 12 : 2. Lazarus one that sat at t.
13 : 28. no man at t. knew for what
Ro. 11 : 9. let their t. be made a snare
1 Co. 10 : 21. ye cannot be partakers
of Lord's t. and of t. of devils
He. 9 : 2. tabern-e wh-n candlestick
See SHEWBREAD. ⌊and t.
See **WRITING table.**

TABLES. ⌈sides

Ex 32 : 15. t. were written on both
16. t. were the work of God, grav-
en upon the t. ⌈and brake
19. he cast the t. out of his hands,
34 : 1. I will write upon these t. the
words in first t., 28. De. 10 : 2.
De. 10 : 4. he wrote on t. acc. to first
5. put the t. in the ark, He. 9 : 4.
1 Ch. 28 : 16. gave silver for t. of silv.
2 Ch. 4 : 8. Sol. made 10 t. and placed
Is. 28 : 8. all t. are full of vomit ⌈43.
Eze. 40 : 41. 8 t. wh-n slew sacrifices,
42. four t. were of hewn stone 41.
Ha. 2 : 2. Write vision plain upon t.
Mat. 21 : 12. he overthrew t. of money changers, Mk. 11 : 15. Jn. 2 : 15.
Mk. 7 : 4. as washing of cups, pots, t.
Ac. 6 : 2. leave word of God, serve t.
2 Co. 3 : 3. not in t. of stone, but
See SHEWBREAD. ⌊fleshly t.

TABLES of stone.

Ex. 24 : 12. I will give thee t. -, 31 : 18.
34 : 1. L. said, Hew two t. -, De. 10 : 1.
4. he hewed two t. - (2) De. 10 : 3.
De. 4 : 13. wrote upon two t. -, 5 : 22.
9 : 9 I was gone up to receive t. -
10. L. delivered unto me two t. -
11. the Lord gave me the two t. -
1 K. 8 : 9. nothing in ark save two t. -
2 Co. 3 : 3. not in t. -, but in fleshly

Two TABLES. ⌊tables

De. 9 : 15. t. t. of cov-t in my 2 hands
17. I took t. t., cast them out
2 Ch. 5 : 10. nothing in ark save t. t.
Eze. 40 : 39. t. t. on this side | 40. t. t.
See **TABLES of stone.**
See TESTIMONY.

TABLETS.

Ex. 35 : 22. they bro-t t. all jewels
Nu. 31 : 50. we brought t. to make
Is. 3 : 20. I will take away the t.

TA'BOR.

Jos. 19 : 22. the coast reacheth to T.
Ju. 4 : 6. Lord said, draw tow. m-t T.
12. Barak was gone to m-t T., 14.
8 : 18. Wh. men whom ye slew at T.?
1 S. 10 : 3. shalt come to plain of T.
1 Ch. 6 : 77. given T. with suburbs
Ps. 89 : 12. T., Hermon shall rejoice
Je. 46 : 18. as T. is among mountains
Ho. 5 : 1. ye have been a net spread
upon T.

TABRET. ⌈t.

Ge. 31 : 27. have sent thee away with
1 S. 10 : 5. coming fr. high pla. wi. t.
Jb. 17 : 6. and aforetime I was as a t.
Is. 5 : 12. t. pipe, and wine in feasts

TABRETS. ⌈t.

1 S. 18 : 6. women to meet Saul with
Is. 24 : 8. The mirth of t. ceaseth
30 : 32. it shall be with t. and harps
Je. 31 : 4. shalt be adorned with t.
Eze. 28 : 13. workmanship of thy t.

TAB'RIMON. ⌈T.

1 K. 15 : 18. sent to Benhadad son of

TACHES.

Ex. 26 : 6. shalt make fifty t. of gold
11. make fifty t. of brass., 35 : 11.
33. shalt hang up vail under t.
36 : 13. he made fifty t. of gold, 18.
39 : 23. they bro-t his t., his boards

TACH'MONITE.

2 S. 23 : 8. The T. that sat in seat

TACKLING, S.

Is. 33 : 23. Thy t-s are loosed ⌈of ship
Ac. 27 : 19. third day we cast out t.

TAD'MOR. ⌈ness

1 K. 9 : 18. Baalath and T. in wilder-
2 Ch. 8 : 4. Sol. built T. in wilderness

TA'HAN, ITES.

Nu. 26 : 35. of T. the family of T.-s
1 Ch. 7 : 25. Telah his son, T. his son

TAHAP'ANES, TAH'PANHES, TEHAPH'NEHES.

Je. 2 : 16. chil. of T. broken crown
43 : 7. thus came they even to T.
8. word came unto Jeremiah in T.
9. clay wh. is at Phar.'s hou. in T.
44 : 1 conc-g Jews which dwell at T.
46 : 14. publish in Noph, and T., say
Eze. 30 : 18. At T. day sh. be dark-d

TA'HATH. [Person.]

1 Ch. 6 : 23. Assir, T. his son, 37. ⌈son
7 : 20. Bered, T. his son, Eladah, T.

TA'HATH. [Place.] ⌈at T.

Nu. 33 : 26. fr. Makheloth, encamped
27. departed fr. T., pitched at Tarah

TAH'PANHES.

See TAHAPANES.

TAH'PENES.

1 K. 11 : 19. gave him sister of T.
20. sister of T. bare Genubath,
whom T. weaned

TAH'REA. See TAREA.

TAH'TIM-HOD'SHI. ⌈T.

2 S. 24 : 6. Then they came to land of

TAIL, S.

Ex. 4 : 4. Put out hand, take it by t.
De. 28 : 13. make the head, not t., 44.
Jos. 10 : † 19. pursue, cut off t. of
Ju. 15 : 4. Samson caught foxes and
turned t. to t., put firebrand
between two t-s ⌈like cedar
Jb. 40 : 17. behemoth moveth his t.
Is. 7 : 4. two t-s of smoking firebr-ds
9 : 14. L. cut off fr. Isr. head and t.
15. that teacheth lies, he is the t.
19 : 15. no work head or t. may do
Re. 9 : 10. t. like unto scorpions,
and there were stings in their t-s

Re. 9 : 19. power is in their t-s, their t-s were like serpents
12 : 4. his t. drew third part of stars

TAKE.

Ge. 3 : 22. t. also of tree of life
6 : 21. t. thou of all food is eaten
7 : 2. of clean beast t. by sevens [go
12 : 19. behold thy wife, t. her and
13 : 9. if thou wilt t. left hand
14 : 21. Give me persons, t. goods
23. I will not t. from a thread, I will not t. anything thine, lest
24. men, let them t. their portion
15 : 9. t. me a heifer of 3 years old
19 : 15. Arise, t. thy wife, 2 dau-s
19. lest some evil t. me, and I die
21 : 30. these 7 ewe lambs sh. thou t.
22 : 2. t. now thy son, only son Isaac
23 : 13. t. money, I will bury my dead
24 : 3. not t. a wife unto my son of Canaanites, 37. [7, 38, 40.
4. go unto my kindred, t. a wife,
48. to t. my master's brother's daughter unto his son
51. Rebekah is before thee, t. her
27 : 3. t. thy weapons, t. venison
46. if Jac. t. a wife of dau-s of Heth
28 : 1. sh. not t. wife of daughters of Canaan, 6. [Laban, 6.
2. t. thee a wife from daughters of
31 : 31. afraid thou t. thy dau-s fr.
32. discern what is thine, t. it [me
50. if thou t. other wives besides
33 : 11. t., I pray thee, my blessing
12. Jacob said, let us t. our journey
34 : 9. give your dau-s, t. our dau-s
16. we will t. your dau-s to us, 21.
17. will t. our dau. if not circumc.
38 : 23. Let her t. it lest we be sham-
41 : 34. t. 5th part of land of Eg. [ed
42 : 33. t. food for famine of househ.
43 : 11. t. of best fruits of the land
12. t. double money in your hand
13. t. also your brother and go
18. that he may t. us for bondmen
44 : 29. if ye t. this also from me
45 : 18. t. your father, households
19. t. your wagons out of Egypt
Ex. 4 : 4. Lord said, t. it by the tail
9. t. river, pour it upon dry land
17. sh. t. this rod in thine hand,
6 : 7. I will t. you for a people [7 : 15.
7 : 9. t. thy rod, cast it bef. Pharaoh
19. t. rod, stretch hand upon wat.
9 : 8. t. to you handfuls of ashes
10 : 26. th-f must we t. to serve L.
12 : 3. they shall t. ev. man a lamb, 4, 5, 7, 21, 22, 32. [his tents
16 : 16. t. ye fr. ev. man for them in
33. t. a pot and put manna therein
17 : 5. t. of elders of Isr. and thy rod
20 : 7. Thou shalt not t. name of Lord thy God in vain, De. 5 : 11.
21 : 10. If he t. him ano. wife, her
14. t. him fr. mine altar th. he die
22 : 26. if thou t. neighbour's raim.
23 : 8. thou shalt t. no gift; gift blindeth, De. 16 : 19. [fering, 3.
25 : 2. of ev. man ye shall t. my of-
28 : 1. t. Aaron thy bro. and his sons
5. they shall t. gold and blue and
9. t. 2 onyx stones and grave names
29 : 1. t. 1 young bullock and 2 rams
5. t., 7, 12, 13, 15, 16, 19, 20, 21, 22, 26, 31.-30 : 23.
30 : 16. t. atonement money [ance
34 : 9. Lord, t. us for thine inherit-
16. lest thou t. of their dau-s, De.
35 : 5. t. ye an off-ing unto L. [7 : 3.
40 : 9. thou shalt t. anointing oil
Le. 2 : 2. t., 9.-3 : 9.-4 : 5, 8, 19, 25, 30, 34.-6 : 15.-8 : 2.-9 : 2, 3.-10 : 12.-14 : 4, 6, 10, 12, 14, 15, 21, 24, 25, 42, 49, 51.-15 : 14, 29.-16 : 5, 7, 12, 14.-24 : 5. [daughter
18 : 17. nei. shalt thou t. her son's
18. neither t. a wife to her sister

Le. 20 : 14. if man t. wife and her mo.
17. if man t. his sister, fa.'s dau.
21. if a man t. his brother's wife
21 : 7. priests shall not t. a wife th. is a whore, nor t. a woman put away, Eze. 44 : 22. [virginity, 14.
13. high priest shall t. a wife in
14. divorced woman; harlot not t.
22 : 5. man of whom t. uncleanness
23 : 40. sh. t. boughs of goodly trees
25 : 36. t. no usury of thy brother
46. ye sh. t. them as inheritance
Nu. 1 : 2. t. ye the sum of congregation, 26 : 2, 4. [Levi
49. neither t. the sum of tribe of
51. tabernacle, Levites sh. t. it do.
3 : 40. firstborn of males t. number
41. thou shalt t. the Levites for me
45. t. Levites instead of firstborn
47. t. five shekels apiece by poll (2)
4 : 2. t. the sum of sons of Kohath
5. Aaron and sons sh. t. down vail
9. sh. t. cloth and cover candlest.
12. t. all instruments of ministry
22. t. the sum of sons of Gershon
5 : 17. priest shall t. holy water (2)
25. Then priest sh. t. jealousy off-g
26. priest sh. t. a handful of off-g
6 : 18. Nazarite sh. t. hair of head
19. priest t. sodden shoul. of ram
7 : 5. t. offering of them to do service, 8 : 8.-10 : 6.-19 : 4, 6, 17, 18.-20 : 25. [Israel
8 : 6. t. Levites from among chil. of
11 : 17. I will t. of spirit upon thee
16 : 3. Ye t. too much upon you, 7.
6. t. censers, Korah and com-y, 17.
37. that Eleazar t. up the censers
46. Moses unto Aaron, t. a censer
17 : 2. t. ev. one a rod acc-g to house
18 : 26. When ye t. of Israel tithes
20 : 8. t. rod, gather the assembly
27 : 18. t. Joshua, a man in whom
31 : 26. t. the sum of the prey taken
29. t. tribute of their half and give
30. of Israel t. one portion of fifty
34 : 18. ye t. one prince of ev. tribe
35 : 31. t. no satisfaction for life, 32.
De. 1 : 7. Turn you, t. your journey, 40.-2 : 24.-10 : 11. [am. tribes
13. t. your wise men, and known
4 : 34. t. him a nation from nations
7 : 25. nor t. gold on graven images
12 : 26. Only holy things and vows t.
15 : 17 t. an awl, thrust it thro. ear
16 : 19. nei. t. a gift; gift doth blind
20 : 7. lest he die, and anoth. t. her
14. all the spoil t. unto thyself
19. When thou besiege city to t. it
21 : 3. elders of city shall t. a heifer
22 : 6. sh. not t. dam wi. the young
7. let the dam go and t. young
13. If a man t. wife and hate her
15. t. tokens of damsel's virginity
18. elders of city shall t. that man
30. man sh. not t. his father's wife
24 : 4. former husb. may not t. her
6. No man sh. t. millst-e to pledge
17. nor t. widow's raim-t to pledge
25 : 5. husb.'s brother sh. t. her to
7. if man like not to t. bro.'s wife
8. if he say, I like not to t. her
26 : 2. shalt t. of first of all fruit
4. priest sh. t. basket out of thine
31 : 26. t. this book of the law [hand
Jos. 3 : 12. t. 12 men out of tribes, 4 : 2.
4 : 3. t. out of Jordan 12 stones, 5.
6 : 18. when ye t. of accursed thing
7 : 14. family which the L. shall t., household which the L. shall t.
8 : 1. t. all people of war with thee
2. cattle shall ye t. for a prey [tree
29. they sho. t. his carcass from
9 : 11. t. victuals wi. you for journey
10 : 42. their land did Joshua t. [t.
11 : 12. cities and kings did Joshua
20 : 4. they shall t. him into the city

Jos. 22 : 19. t. ye possession among
Ju. 4 : 6. t. with thee 10,000 men
5 : 30. necks of them that t. spoil
6 : 20. t. flesh and unleavened cakes
25. t. thy fa.'s young bullock, 26.
7 : 24. Come, t. waters unto Jor. [8.
14 : 3. to t. a wife of uncircumcised
15. ye called us to t. that we have
15 : 2. younger sister fairer, t. her
19 : 30. consider, t. advice, speak
20 : 10. we will t. ten men of a 100.
Ru. 2 : 10. sho. t. knowledge of me, 19.
1 S. 2 : 16. t. as thy soul desireth, if not I will t. it by force [kine
6 : 7. make cart, and t. two milch
8. t. ark of Lord upon the cart
8 : 11. He will t. your sons for hims.
13. will t. your dau-s to be cooks
14. and he will t. your fields and
15. will t. 10th of your seed [work
16. will t. your young men to his
17. he will t. tenth of your sheep
9 : 3: t. one of servants, seek asses
5. lest my father t. thought for us
16 : 2. t. a heifer, say I am come to
17 : 17. t. for brethren parched corn
18. how breth. fare, t. their pledge
46. t. thine head from thee [26.
19 : 14. Saul sent to t. David, 20.-23:
20 : 21. arrows on this side, t. them
21 : 9. if wilt t. that, t. it, no other
23 : 23. t. knowl. of all lurking places
24 : 11. thou huntest my soul to t. it
25 : 11. Sh. I t. my bread and water
39. Dav. sent to t. Abigail to wife,
26 : 11. t. spear at his bolster [40.
2 S. 2 : 21. Abner said, t. his armour
12 : 4. spared to t. of his own flock
11. I will t. thy wives before thine
28. t. it, lest I t. the city [eyes
13 : 33. let not king t. the thing to heart, 19 : 19. [ren
15 : 20. return, t. back thy breth-
16 : 9. let me go and t. off his head
19 : 30. Mephibo-h said, let him t. all
20 : 6. t. thy lord's servants, pursue
24 : 22. Let k. t. what seemeth good
1 K. 1 : 33. Da. said, t. wi. you serv-ts
11 : 31. said to Jerob., t. ten pieces
34. I will not t. the whole kingdom
35. I will t. kingdom out of his
37. I will t. thee, thou shalt reign
14 : 3. t. ten loaves, go to prophet
18 : 40. said, t. the prophets of Baal
20 : 18. for war or peace, t. th. alive
21 : 15. t. possession of vineyard, 16.
22 : 3. t. it not out of hand of king
26. t. Micaiah back, 2 Ch. 18 : 25.
2 K. 4 : 1. creditor is come to t. my
29. t. my staff and go thy way
5 : 15. t. a blessing of thy servants
16. urged him to t. it; but he ref.
20. I will run, t. somewhat of him
23. Naaman said, t. two talents
6 : 2. unto Jordan t. ev. man a beam
7 : 13. t. five of horses left in city
8 : 8. king unto Hazael, t. a present
9 : 1. t. this box of oil in hand, 3.
17. Joram said, t. a horseman and
26. t. cast him into plat of ground
10 : 6. t. ye heads of master's sons
14. t. them alive. They slew them
12 : 5. Let priests t. money to them
13 : 15. Elisha said, t. bow, arrows, 18.
20 : 7. Isaiah said, t. lump of figs
1 Ch. 21 : † 11. t. 3 years' famine or
23. Ornan said unto Da. t. the place
24. I will not t. that wh. is thine
2 Ch. 19 : † 11. t. courage, L. wi. good
32 : 18. that they might t. the city
Ezr. 5 : 14. the vessels did Cyrus t.
15. t. vessels to temple in Jeru-m
9 : 12. give not your daughters, nei. t. their dau-s, Ne. 10 : 30.-13 : 25.
Ne. 10 : 38. when the Levites t. tithes
Es. 3 : 13. t. the spoil for prey, 8 : 11.
6 : 10. t. apparel, do so to Mordecai

Jb. 9 : 18. not suffer me to t. breath
10 : 20. th. I may t. comfort a little
11 : 18. shalt t. thy rest in safety
13 : 14. Whf. t. my flesh in my teeth
18 : 12. gin shall t. him by the heel
21 : 12. They t. the timbrel and harp
23 : 10. he knoweth the way I t.
24 : 3. they t. widow's ox for pledge
9. they t. a pledge of the poor
30 : 17. and my sinews t. no rest
31 : 36. I wo. t. it upon my shoulder
38 : 20. thou sho. t. it to the bound
41 : 4. wilt t. him for a serv. for ever?
42 : 8. t. unto you seven bullocks
Ps. 7 : 5. Let enemy persecute my soul and t. it [thy house
50 : 9. I will t. no bullock out of
16. sho t. my cov-t in thy mouth
51 : 11. t. not thy Holy Spirit fr. me
69 : 20. I looked for some to t. pity
71 : 11. t. him, for is none to deliver
75 : 2. When I shall t. a set time
81 : 2. t. a psalm, bring the timbrel
83 : 12. Let us t. houses of God
89 : 33. my kindness not utterly t.
102 : 14. t. pleasure in her stones
109 : 8. and let another t. his office
116 : 13. I will t. cup of salvation
119 : 43. t. not word of truth utterly
139 : 9. If I t. wings of the morning
20. enemies t. thy name in vain
Pr. 5 : 22. His iniquities sh. t. wicked
6 : 25. nei. let her t. thee wi. eyelids
27. Can a man t. fire in his bosom
7 : 18 let us t. our fill of love until
20 : 16. t. his garment th. is surety, t. a pledge of him for, 27 : 13.
30 : 9 and t. the name of G. in vain
Ec. 5 : 15. sh. t. nothing of his labour
19. to t. his portion and rejoice
Can. 2 : 15. t. us the foxes, lit. foxes
Is. 10 : 6 to t. the spoil, to t. prey
14 : 2. t. them captives, whose cap.
18 : 4. I will t. my rest only [(2)
23 : 16. t. a harp, go about the city
28 : 19. from time it goeth sh. t. you
29 : 9. t. your pleasure and riot
30 : 14. not shred to t. fire fr hearth
33 : 23. divided, the lame t. the prey
44 : 15. will t. th-f and warm hims.
47 : 2. t. the millstones, grind meal
3. I will t. vengeance, I will not
57 : 13. vanity shall t. them, wind
58 : 2. t. delight in approaching G.
66 : 21. I will t. of them for priests
Je. 2 : 22. thou t. much soap, yet
3 : 14. I will t. you one of a city
13 : 4. t. the girdle thou hast got, 6.
21. sh. not sorrow t. thee as a wom.
15 : 19. if thou t. precious from vile
16 : 2. not t. thee wife in this place
18 : 22. have digged a pit to t. me
19 : 1. t. of the ancients of people
20 : 5. enemies sh. t. them to Bab-n
10. we shall t. our revenge on him
25 : 9. I will t. all families of north
10 I will t. from th. voice of mirth
15. t. the wine cup of this fury
28. if refuse to t. cup at thine hand
29 : 6. t. ye wives and beget sons
32 : 3. the king of Babylon shall t. the city, 28.-37 : 8.-38 : 3.
14. t. these evidences of purchase
24. are come unto city to t. it
25. Buy the field, t. witnesses, 44.
: 26. not t. his seed to be rulers
: 22. they sh. t. city and burn it
: 26. king com-ded to t. Jeremiah
: 10. t. fr. hence 30 men wi. thee
39 : 12. t. Jere-h, look well to him
43 : 9. t. great stones, hide them in
10. I will t. Neb. and set his throne
: 12. I will t. remnant of Judah
44 : 11. into Gilead, t. balm, 51 : 8.
46 : 29. sh. t. to themselves vessels
49 : 15. t. vengeance upon her, as
51 : 26. shall not t. of thee a stone

Je. 51 : 36. I will t. vengeance for
La. 2 : 13. What t. to witn. for thee?
Eze. 4 : 1. t. thee a tile | 3. t. an iron pan
9. t. unto thee wheat, barley, and
5 : 1. t. a sharp knife, a barber's razor, t. balances [knife
2. t. third part and smite with
3. t. a few, bind them in thy skirts
4. t. of them again, cast into fire
10 : 6. t. fire from between wheels
11 : 19. I will t. the stony heart out
14 : 5. that I may t. house of Israel
15 : 3. will men t. a pin of it to hang
16 : 16. of thy garm-ts thou didst t.
39. sh. strip thee, t. thy fair jewels
17 : 22. I will t. highest branch
21 : 26. remove diadem, t. off crown
22 : 16. thou shalt t. thine inherit.
23 : 25. they shall t. thy sons and
24 : 5. t. the choice of the flock [daus.
8. fury come up to t. vengeance
25. when I t. fr. them their streng.
29 : 19. he shall t. her multitude, t. her spoil, t. her prey [coast
33 : 2. if people t. a man of their
36 : 24. I will t. you fr. am. heathen
37 : 16. t. one stick, t. another, write
19. I will t. the stick of Joseph
38 : 13. art thou come to t. prey, to t. a great spoil? 12. [of field
39 : 10. So they shall t. no wood out
43 : 20. shalt t. blood of bullock or sin offering, 21.-45 : 18, 19.
46 : 18. prince not t. people's inheri.
Da. 7 : 18. saints sh. t. the kingdom
11 : 15. king sh. t. most fenced cities
18. to the isles, and shall t. many
Ho. 1 : 2. Go, t. a wife of whoredoms
11 : 4. I was as they that t. off yoke
14 : 2. t. with you words, turn to L.
Am. 5 : 11. ye t. from him burdens
12. they afflict the just, t. a bribe
9 : 2. shall mine hand t. them, 3.
Jon. 4 : 3. t., I beseech thee, my life
Mi. 2 : 2. covet fields, t. them by vio-
6. that they sh. not t. shame [lence
Na. 1 : 2. the Lord will t. vengeance
2 : 9. t. ye spoil of silver, t. spoil of
Ha. 1 : 10. shall heap dust and t. it
Hag. 1 : 8. house, I will t. pleas. in it
2 : 23. will I t. thee, O Zerubbabel
Zch. 6 : 10. t. of them of the captivity
11. Then t. silver, gold, make cr-ns
11 : 15. t. instrum-s of foolish shep.
14 : 21. that sacrifice shall t. of pot
Mat 1 : 20. fear not to t. Mary, wife
2 : 13. t. young child and moth., 29.
6 : 25. t. no thought for your life, 28, 31, 34.-10 : 19. Mk. 13 : 11. Lu. 12 : 11, 22, 26. [by force
11 : 12. the violent t. the kingdom
29. t. my yoke, and learn of me
15 : 26. not meet to t. the children's bread, Mk. 7 : 27. [Mk. 8 : 14.
16 : 5. they had forgot. to t. bread,
17 : 25. of whom kings t. custom
27. sh find piece of money, that t.
18 : 16. t. wi. thee one or two more
23. k. would t. account of serv-ts
20 : 14. t. that thine is, go thy way
24 : 17. let him not come down to t. out of his hou., 18. Mk. 13 : 15, 16.
25 : 28. t. the talent fr. him, give it
26 : 4. might t. Jesus, Mk. 14 : 1, 44.
26. Jesus took bread and said, t., eat, Mk. 14 : 22. 1 Co. 11 : 24.
45. Sleep on now, t. your rest, Mk. 14 : 41. [by the sword
52. that t. the sword shall perish
55. with staves to t. me, Mk 14 : 48.
Mk. 6 : 8. t. nothing for their journey, Lu. 9 : 3. [Lu. 20 : 28.
12 : 19. his brother sho. t. his wife,
15 : 24. lots what every man sho. t.
36. whether Elias will t. him down
Lu. 6 : 4. Da. did t. and eat shewbr.
29. forbid him not to t. thy coat

Lu. 10 : 35. two pence, t. care of him
12 : 19. will say, Soul, t. thine ease
14 : 9. with shame to t. lowest room
16 : 6. t. thy bill, write fifty, 7.
19 : 24. t. from him the pound [it
22 : 17. cup, and said, t. this, divide
36. that hath a purse, let him t. it
Jn. 2 : 16. Jes. said, t. these hence
6 : 7. that every one may t. a little
15. that they wo. t. him by force
7 : 30. Then they sought to t. him: but no man, 32.-10 : 39.-11 : 57.
10 : 17. bec. lay down my life, that I might t. it again, 18. [it
16 : 15. he sh. t. of mine, and shew
17 : 15. shouldest t. th. out of world
18 : 31. t. ye him, judge him acc-g
19 : 6. Pilate saith, t., crucify him
Ac. 1 : 20. his bishoprick let anoth. t.
25. That he may t. part of ministry
12 : 3. Herod proceeded to t. Peter
15 : 14. to t. a people for his name
37. Barnabus determined to t. J-n
38. Paul tho-t not good to t. him
20 : 13. there intending to t. in Paul
26. I t. you to record this day.
21 : 24. Them t. and purify thyself
23 : 10. to t. Paul by force fr. them
24 : 8. mayest t. knowl. of things
27 : 33. Paul beso-t to t. meat, 34.
Ro. 15 : 24. I t. my journey into Spain
1 Co. 6 : 7. Why not rather t. wrong?
15. shall I t. members of Christ
9 : 9. Doth God t. care for oxen?
2 Co. 8 : 4. t. upon us ministering to
11 : 20. ye suffer, if a man t. of you
12 : 10. I t. pleasure in infirmities
Ep. 6 : 13. t. unto you whole armour
17. And t. the helmet of salvation
1 Ti. 3 : 5. how sh. he t. care of chur.
2 Ti. 4 : 11. t. Mark, and bring him
He. 7 : 5. a com-t to t. tithes of peo.
Ja. 5 : 10. t., the prophets an examp.
1 Pe. 2 : 20. if ye t. it patiently, it is
Re. 3 : 11. that no man t. thy crown
5 : 9. Thou art worthy to t. the book
6 : 4. power to t. peace from earth
10 : 8. t. the little book wh. is open
9. angel said, t. it and eat it up
22 : 17. let him t. of water of life

TAKE away. [mandr.

Ge. 30 : 15. wo. thou t. a. my son's
42 : 36. and ye will t. Benjamin a.
Ex. 2 : 9. t. this child a., nurse it
8 : 8. that he may t. a. frogs fr. me
10 : 17. may t. a. from me this death
23 : 25. will t. sickness a., De. 7 : 15.
33, 23. I will t. a. mine hand, and
Le. 3 : 4. it shall he t. a., 10. 15.-4 : 9.
4 : 31. he sh. t. a. all the fat, 35.-7 : 4.
14 : 40. com-d th. they t. a. stones
Nu. 4 : 13. sh. t. a. ashes from altar
17 : 10. quite t. a. their murmur-gs
21 : 7. that he t. a. serpents from us
Jos. 7 : 13. until ye t. a. accursed thi.
2 S. 4 : 11. sh. I not t. you a. fr. earth
5 : 6. Except thou t. a. the blind
24 : 10. t. a. iniquity of thy servant
1 K. 2 : 31. mayest t. a. innoc. blood
14 : 10. t. a. remnant of hou. of Jer-
16 : 3. t. a. posterity of Baasha [ob.
19 : 4. enough, O Lord, t. a. my life
10. they seek my life to t. it a., 14.
20 : 6. pleasant, shall my serv. t. a.
24. t. the kings a., and put capt-s
21 : 21. will t. a. posterity of Ahab
2 K. 2 : 3. L. will t. a. thy master, 5.
6 : 32. hath sent to t. a. mine head
18 : 32. until I t. you a., Is. 36 : 17.
20 : 18. And of thy sons shall they t. a., Is. 39 : 7. [tle, Eze. 38 : 13.
1 Ch. 7 : 21. came down to t. a. cat-
17 : 13. I not t. my mercy a. fr. him
2 Ch. 20 : 25. peo. came to t. a. spoil
Es. 4 : 4. sent to t. a. his sackcloth
Jb. 7 : 21. Why not t. a. mine iniquity?
9 : 34. Let him t. his rod a. fr. me

Jb. 24 : 2. they violently t.a. flocks
10. they t.a. sheaf from hungry
32 :22. my maker wo. soon t. me a.
36 : 18. lest he t. thee a. wi. stroke
Ps. 26 : † 9. t. not a. my soul wi. sin-
31 : 13. devised to t.a. my life⌊ners
52 : 5. sh. t.a. and pluck thee out
58 : 9. t. them a. with a whirlwind
102 : 24. t.me not a. in midst of days
Pr. 22 : 27. why sho. he t.a. thy bed
25 : 4. t.a. the dross from the silver
5. t.a. the wicked from bef. king
Is. 1 : 25. and I will t.a. all thy tin
3 : 1. Lord doth t.a. stay and staff
18. L. t.a. bravery of ornaments
4 : 1. name, to t.a. our reproach
5 : 5. vineyard, I will t.a. hedge
23. t.a. righteousness of righteous
10 : 2. to t.a. the right fr. the poor
18 : 5. t.a. and cut down branches
25 : 8. rebuke of his peo. sh. he t.a.
27 : 9. all the fruit to t.a. his sin
39 : 7. of thy sons shall they t.a.
40 : 24. whirlwind shall t. them a.
58 : 9. If thou t.a. fr. midst of thee
Je. 4 : 4. t.a. foreskins of your heart
5 :10. destroy, t.a. her battlements
15 :15. t.me not a. in thy longsuf-g
49 : 29. tents, flocks shall they t.a.
Eze. 11 :18. sh. t.a. detestable things
23 : 25. shall t.a. thy nose and ears
26. strip thee, t.a. thy fair jewels
29. they shall t.a. all thy labour
24 :16. I t.a. the desire of thine eyes
30 :4. they shall t.a. her multitude
33 : 4. if sword come, t. him a., 6.
36 : 26. I will t.a. the stony heart
45 : 9. t.a. your exactions fr. peo.
Da. 7 : 26. shall t.a. his dominion
11 : 31. they sh. t.a. daily sacrifice
Ho. 1 : 6. I will utterly t. them a.
2 : 9. and t.a. my corn in the time
17. I will t.a. names of Baalim
4 : 11. Whoredom, wine, t.a. heart
5 : 14. I will t.a., none shall rescue
14 : 2. say unto him, t.a. all iniqu.
Am. 4 : 2. will t. you a. with hooks
5 :23. t.a. from me noise of thy viols
Mi. 2 : 2. covet houses, and t. th. a.
Zph. 3 : 11. I will t.a. out of midst
Zch. 3 : 4. t.a. the filthy garments
9 : 7. I t.a. blood out of his mouth
Mal. 2 : 3. one sh. t. you a. wi. dung
Mat. 5 : 40. t.a. thy coat, let him ha.
22 :13. t.a., cast him into outer dar.
Mk. 14 : 36. Father, t.a. this cup
Lu. 1 : 25. t.a. my reproach am. men
17 : 31. let him not come to t. it a.
Jn. 11 :39. Jesus said t.a. the stone
48. Romans shall t.a. our place
19 :38. might t.a. body of Jes.,20 :15.
Ro. 11 : 27. when I sh. t.a. their sins
He. 10 :4. blood of bulls t.a. sins, 11.
1 Jn. 3 : 5. manifested to t.a. sins
Re. 22 :19. if any man t.a. fr. words
of book, God shall t.a. his part
See Take COUNSEL.

TAKE heed. ⌈Jac., 29.
Ge. 31 : 24. t.h. thou speak not to
Ex. 10 : 28. t.h. to thyself, 34 : 12.
De. 4 : 9.-12 : 13, 19, 30. 1 S. 19 :
2. 1 Ti. 4 : 16.
19 : 12. t.h. to yourselves, De. 2 : 4.
-4 : 15, 23.-11 : 16. Jos. 23 : 11.
Je. 17 : 21. ⌈that which
Nu. 23 : 12. Must I not t.h. to speak
De. 24 : 8. t.h. in plague of leprosy
27 : 9. t.h. and hearken, O Israel
Jos. 22 : 5. t. diligent h. to do com-t
1 K. 2 : 4. If thy children t.h. to
their way, 8 : 25. 2 Ch. 6 : 16.
1 Ch. 28 :10. t.h. for L. hath chosen
2 Ch. 19 : 6. t.h. wh. ye do, ye judge
7. fear of the Lord be on you, t.h.
33 :8. they will t.h. to do, Ezr. 4 :22.
Jb. 36 :21. t.h., regard not iniquity
Ps. 39 : 1. I will t.h. to my ways

Ec. 7 : 21. t. no h. unto all words
Is. 7 : 4. t.h. and be quiet, fear not
Je. 9 : 4. t.h. ev. one of his neighb-r
Ho. 4 :10. left off to t.h. to the Lord
Mal. 2 : 15. t.h. to your spirit, 16.
Mat. 6 : 1. t.h. ye do not alms before
16 : 6. t.h. of the leaven of Pharisees, Mk. 8 : 15. ⌈these
18 : 10. t.h. ye despise not one of
24 :4. t.h. no man deceive, Mk. 13 : 5.
Mk. 4 : 24. he said, t.h. what ye hear
13 : 9. t.h. to yourselves, Lu. 17 : 3.
-21 : 34. Ac. 5 : 35.-20 : 28.
23. t.h., I have foretold you all
33. t. ye h., ye know not wh. time
Lu. 8 : 18. t.h. theref. how ye hear
11 :35. t.h. light in thee be not dar.
12 : 15. t.h., beware of covetousn-s
21 : 8. t.h. that ye be not deceived
Ac. 22 :26. t.h., this man is a Roman
Ro. 11 : 21. t.h. lest he spare not
1 Co. 8 : 10. every man t.h. how he
8 : 9. t.h. lest this liberty of yours
10 : 12. let him that standeth t.h.
Ga. 5 : 15. t.h. ye be not consumed
Col. 4 :17. t.h. to ministry thou hast
He. 3 : 12. t.h. of an evil heart of
2 Pe. 1 : 19. whereunto ye do well to

TAKE hold. ⌊t.h.
Ex. 15 :14. sorrow sh. t.h. on inhab-ts
15. trembling sh. t.h. upon them
26 : 5. that loops t.h. one of anoth.
De. 32 :41. if mine hand t.h. of judg.
Jb. 27 : 20. Terrors t.h. on him as
36 :17. judgm., justice t.h. on thee
38 : 13. t.h. on ends of the earth
Ps. 35 : 2. t.h. of shield and buckler
69 : 24. let thy anger t.h. of them
Pr. 2 : 19. nei. t. they h. of paths of
4 : 13. t. fast h. of instruction ⌊life
5 : 5. her steps t.h. on hell ⌈this
Ec. 7 : 18. It is good thou t.h. of
Can. 7 : 8. I will t.h. of the boughs
Is. 3 : 6. When a man sh. t.h. of bro.
4 : 1. 7 women sh. t.h. of one man
13 : 8. pangs shall t.h. of them
27 : 5. let him t.h. of my strength
56 :4. eunuchs that t.h. of my cov-t
64 : 7. stirreth up hims. t.h. of thee
Mi. 6 : 14. shalt t.h., but not deliver
Zch. 1 : 6. not t.h. of your fathers?
8 : 23. ten men shall t.h. of a Jew
Lu. 20 : 20. might t.h. of his words
26. could not t.h. of his words
See FIGS, ROLL, ROOT.

TAKE up.
Ge. 41 : 34. t.u. fifth part of Egypt
Le. 6 : 10. priest shall t.u. the ashes
Nu. 16 : 37. t.u. the censers out of
Jos. 3 : 6. t.u. ark of covenant, 6 : 6.
4 : 5. t.u. ev. man stone out of Jor.
2 K. 2 : 1. when L. would t.u. Elijah
4 : 36. Elijah said, t.u. thy son ⌈u.
6 : 7. iron did swim, said he, t. it
9 : 25. t.u. and cast him into field
Ne. 5 : 2. we t.u. corn for them that
Jb. 27 : † 1. Job added to t.u. his
parable, Jb. 29 † 1. ⌈my lips
Ps. 16 :4. nor t.u. their names into
27 : 10. then the Lord will t.me u.
Is. 14 : 4. thou sh. t.u. this proverb
57 : 14. t.u. the stumblingblock
Je. 7 :29. O Jerus., t.u. lamentation
9 : 10. mountains will t.u. weeping
18. let them t.u. wailing for us
38 :10. t.u. Jeremiah out of dungeon
Eze. 19 : 1. t.u. lament-n for princes
26 : 17. shall t.u. a lamentation
for Tyrus, 27 : 2, 32. ⌈k. of Tyrus
28 : 12. t.u. a lamentation upon
32 : 2. t.u. a lament-n for Pharaoh
Da. 6 : 23. sho. t. Dan. u. out of den
Am. 3 : 5. shall one t.u. a snare from
5 : 1. Hear this word I t.u. ag. you
6 : 10. A man's uncle sh. t. him u.
Jon. 1 : 12. t.me u., cast me into sea
Mi. 2 : 4. shall one t.u. a parable

Ha. 1 : 15. They t.u. all wi. the angle
2 : 6. Shall not all t.u. parable ag.
Mat. 9 : 6. Arise, t.u. thy bed, Mk. 2 :
9, 11. Lu. 5 : 24. Jn. 5 : 8, 11, 12.
16 :24. let him t.u. his cross and follow, Mk. 8 : 34.-10 : 21. Lu. 9 : 23.
17 : 27. t.u. fish that first cometh
Mk. 16 : 18. They shall t.u. serpents

TAKEN.
Ge. 2 : 22. rib God had t. from man
23. called Woman, bec. t. out of
3 :19. out of ground wast thou t., 23.
4 :15. vengeance t. on him sevenfold
12 : 15. woman t. into Pha.'s house
19. so I might have t. her to wife
14 : 14. Abr. heard his bro. was t.
18 :27. t. upon me to speak unto L
20 : 3. wom. thou hast t. is wife⌊31.
27 : 33. where is he hath t. venison
30 : 15. that thou hast t. my husb
31 : 16. riches G. hath t. fr. our fa.
26. dan-s as captives t. with sword
34. Now Rachel had t. images
Ex. 25 : 15. staves not t. from rings
Le. 4 : 10. As it was t. from bullock
7 : 34. heave shoulder have I t.
24 : 8. t. fr. chil. of Israel by cov-t
Nu. 3 : 12. I have t. the Levites for
firstborn of Isr., 8 : 16, 18.-18 : 6.
5 :13. nei. she be t. with the manner
10 : 17. the tabernacle was t. down
12 : † 1. Mo. had t. Ethiopian woman
16 :15. I have not t. one ass fr. them
21 : 26. t. his land out of his hand
31 : 49. we have t. the sum of men
53. men of war had t. spoil ⌊of war
36 :3. inheritance be t. from the lot
De. 4 :20. L. t. you out of the furnace
20 : 7. betrothed a wife, and not t.
21 : 10. thou hast t. th. captive⌊her
24 : 1. When a man hath t. a wife
5. When a man hath t. a new wife
cheer wife he hath t. ⌈thing
Jos. 7 : 11. they have t. of accursed
15. he that is t. shall be burnt
16. and the tribe of Judah was t.
17. Zabdi was t. | 18. Achan was t.
8 : 8. when ye have t. city, 21.
10 : 1. heard how Joshua had t. Ai
Ju. 1 :8. Jud. fought ag. Jerus., t. it
11 : 36. Lord hath t. vengeance
14 : 9. told not he had t. the honey
15 : 6. he had t. his wife, and given
17 :2. The 1,100 shekels t. from thee
1 S. 4 : 11. the ark of God was t., 17,
19, 21, 22. ⌈tines had t.
7 : 14. the cities which the Philis-
10 : 20. tribe of Benjamin was t.
21. Saul was t. | 12 : 3. whose ox
have I t.? ⌈man's hand
12 : 4. neither hast t. aught of any
14 : 41. Saul and Jonathan were t.
42. said, Cast lots, and Jona-n was t.
21 :6. shewbread was t. from bef. L.
30 : 2. had t. the women capt-s, 3.
5. David's two wives t. captives
16. bec. of great spoil they had t.
19. noth-g lacking th. they had t.
2 S. 12 : 9. t. his wife to be thy wife,
27. I have t. city of waters ⌊10.
16 : 8. thou art t. in thy mischief
18 : 18. Abs. had t. and reared pillar
23 : 6. they cannot be t. with hands
1 K. 7 : 8. Pha.'s dau. he had t. to
9 : 16. For Pha. had t. Gezer ⌊wife
16 : 18. Zimri saw that city was t.
21 : 19. Hast thou killed, t. poss-n
2 K. 2 :10. if thou see me when I am
4 : 20. had t. him to his mother ⌊t.
6 :22. wouldest smite those t. capt
13 : 25. took cities Ben-hadad had t.
18 : 10. year of Hoshea, Samaria t.
24 :7. king of Bab. had t. from river
1 Ch. 24 : 6. one household t. for
Eleazar, one t. for Ithamar
2 Ch. 15 : 8; put away idols he had t.
17 : 2. cities Asa his father had t.

2 Ch. 28 : 11. deliv. captives ye have t.
18. Philis. had t. Beth-shemesh
Ezr. 9 : 2. they have t. of their dau-s
10 : 2. we t. strange wives, 14, 17, 18.
44. All these had t. strange wives
Ne. 5 : 15. had t. bread and wine
6 : 18. Johanan had t. dau. of Mes.
Es. 2 : 15. had t. Esther for his dau.
16. Esther was t. unto king Ahas-s
8 : 2. off ring he had t. from Haman
Jb. 16 : 12. hath t. me by my neck
19 : 9. hath t. crown fr. mine head
22 : 6. hast t. a pledge from thy bro.
24 : 24. they are t. out of the way
28 : 2. Iron is t. out of the earth
38 : † 30. the face of the deep is t. [t.
Ps. 9 : 15. in net hid is their own foot
10 : 2. let them be t. in the devices
59 : 12. let them be t. in their pride
83 : 3. have t. crafty counsel ag. peo.
119 : 111. Thy testimonies have I t.
Pr. 3 : 26. L. keep thy foot fr. being t.
6 : 2. art t. with words of thy mouth
7 : 20. He hath t. a bag of money
11 : 6. transg-rs be t. in own naugh-s
Ec. 2 : 18. I hated labour I had t. [t.
3 : 14. noth. put to it, nor any thing
7 : 26. the sinner shall be t. by her
9 : 12. as fishes t. in an evil net
Is. 6 : 6. coal he had t. from altar
8 : 15. many shall be snared and t.
14 : † 2. take capt. that had t. them
24 : 18. be t. in snare, Je. 48 : 44.
28 : 13. th. they might be snared, t.
33 : 20. tabern. th. sh. not be t. down
41 : 9. Thou whom I have t. fr. euds
49 : 24. sh. prey be t. from mighty
51 : 22. I have t. cup of trembling
53 : 8. He was t. from prison and
Je. 6 : 11. husband with wife sh. be t.
8 : 9. wise men are dismayed and t.
12 : 2. hast planted, they have t. root
34 : 3. thou shalt surely be t., 38 : 23.
38 : 28. until day Jerusalem was t.
39 : 5. had t. him, they brought him
40 : 1 had t. him, being bound
10. dwell in cities ye have t. [be t.
48 : 1. Kiriathaim is t. | 7. thou sh.
33. joy and gladness is t. from [t.
41. Kirioth is t. | 46. thy sons are
49 : 20. counsel of Lord t. ag. Edom
24. anguish, sorrow have t. Dama.
50 : 2. Babylon is t., 24-51 : 31, 41.
9. from thence she shall be t.
45. hear counsel of L. t. ag. Bab.
51 : 56. Bab-n, her mighty men are t.
La. 4 : 20. anointed of Lord was t.
Eze. 12 : 13. prince be t. in my snare
15 : 3. Sh. wood be t. to do any work?
16 : 17. Thou hast t. thy fair jewels
20. thou hast t. thy sons and dau-s
37. with whom thou hast t. pleas.
17 : 12. k. of Bab-n hath t. the king
13. hath t. of the king's seed, hath
t. an oath of him; he hath t.
the mighty of the land
20. and he shall be t. in my snare
18 : 8. not upon usury, nei. t. incr.
13. given upon usury, t. increase
†16. Nei. oppressed nor t. to pledge
17. hath t. off his hand from poor
19 : 4. he was t. in their pit, 8. [t.
21 : 23. call to remembr. th. they be
24. ye shall be t. with the hand
22 : 12. they t. gifts, hast t. usury
25. have t. precious things [heart
25 : 15. t. vengeance with despiteful
27 : 5. have t. cedars from Lebanon
Da. 5 : 2. vessels his father had t., 3.
Jo. 3 : 5. Bec. ye have t. my silver
Am. 3 : 4. lion cry out, if t. noth.? 5.
12. Isr. be t. that dwell in Samaria
6 : 13. Have we not t. to us horns
Zch. 14 : 2. the city shall be t. and
Mat. 4 : 24. peo t. wi. diseases came
9 : 15. the bridegroom shall be t.
fr. them, Mk. 2 : 20. Lu. 5 : 35.

Mat. 16 : 7. It is bec. we have t. no br.
21 : 43. kingdom of God be t. fr. you
24 : 40. the one shall be t. and the
other left, 41. Lu. 17 : 34, 35, 36.
27 : 59. when Joseph had t. the body
Mk. 4 : 25. fr. him t. that wh. he hath
6 : 41. when he had t. five loaves
9 : 36. when had t. him in his arms
Lu. 1 : 1. as many have t. in hand
4 : 38. Simon's wife's moth. t. wi. fev-
5 : 5. toiled all night, t. nothing [er
9. draught of fishes they had t.
18. man which was t. wi. the palsy
36. piece that was t. out of the new
8 : 37. they were t. with great fear
19 : 8. if I have t. anything fr. any
Jn. 7 : 44. some would have t. him
8 : 3. bro-t woman t. in adultery, 4.
19 : 12. after he had t. his garments
Ac. 2 : 23 ye have t., and by wicked
8 : 7. many t. with palsies he healed
33. his life is t. from the earth [son
17 : 9. when they had t. secur. of Ja-
21 : 6. had t. our leave one of ano.
23 : 27. This man was t. of the Jews
27 : 33. fasting, having t. nothing
Ro. 9 : 6. Not as tho. word t. none eff.
1 Co. 10 : 13. hath no temp-n t. you
1 Th. 2 : 17. t. fr. you for short time
2 Th. 2 : 7. will let, until he be t.
1 Ti. 5 : 9. Let not a widow be t. into
2 Ti. 2 : 26. are t. captive by him at
He. 5 : 1. high priest t. fr. am. men
2 Pe. 2 : 12. made to be t., destroyed
Re. 5 : 8. when he had t. the book
11 : 17. thou hast t. thy great power
19 : 20. beast was t., and with him

TAKEN away. [t.a.

Ge. 21 : 25. a well Abim's serv-ts had
27 : 35. Jacob hath t.a. thy bless-g
36. now he hath t.a. my blessing
30 : 23. God hath t.a. my reproach
31 : 1. Jacob t.a. all is our father's
9. God hath t.a. cattle of your fa.
Ex. 14 : 11. hast thou t. us a. to die
Le. 4 : 31. fat is t.a. fr. sacrifice, 35.
6 : 2. in a thing t.a. by violence
14 : 43. after he hath t.a. stones
De. 26 : 14. nei. t.a. aught for uncl.
28 : 31. thine ass be violently t.a.
Ju. 18 : 24. Ye have t.a. my gods wh.
1 S. 21 : 6. in day when it was t.a.
2 S. 14 : † 14. bec. G. not t.a. his life
1 K. 22 : 43. the high places were not
t.a., 2 K. 12 : 3.-14 : 4. 2 Ch.
15 : 17.-20 : 33. [thee
2 K. 2 : 9. ask, before I be t.a. from
18 : 22. whose altars Hezekiah hath
t.a., 2 Ch. 32 : 12. Is. 36 : 7.
2 Ch. 19 : 3. th. thou hast t.a. groves
Jb. 1 : 21. Lord gave, Lord hath t.a.
20 : 19. hath violently t.a. a house
27 : 2. who hath t.a. my judgment
34 : 5. God hath t.a. my judgment
20. mighty sh. be t.a. with-t hand
Ps. 85 : 3. hast t.a. all thy wrath
Pr. 4 : 16. their sleep is t.a. unless
Can. 4 : † 9. Thou hast t.a. my heart
Is. 6 : 7. thine iniquity is t.a., thy
8 : 4. spoil of Samaria shall be t.a.
10 : 27. burden be t.a. fr. shoulder
16 : 10. gladness is t.a. | 17 : 1. Da-
mascus is t.a. [be t.a.
49 : 25. captives of the mighty shall
52 : 5. my people is t.a. for nought
57 : 1. merciful men are t.a., righteous is t.a. [t. us a.
64 : 6. our iniquities like wind have
Je. 16 : 5. I have t.a. my peace fr. peo.
La. 2 : 6. violently t.a. his taberu-e
Eze. 33 : 6. is t.a. in his iniquity
34 : †29. no more be t.a. wi. hunger
Da. 7 : 12. had their dominion t.a.
8 : 11. daily sacrifice was t.a., 12 : 11.
11 : 12. wh. he hath t.a. the multi.
Ho. 4 : 3. fishes of the sea be t.a.
Am. 4 : 10. I have t.a. your horses

Mi. 2 : 9. ye have t.a. my glory for
Zph. 3 : 15. L. hath t.a. thy judgm-ts
Mat. 13 : 12. from him shall be t.a.
even that he hath, 25 : 29. Lu.
8 : 18.-19 : 26. [Lu. 5 : 35.
Mk. 2 : 20. bridegroom shall be t.a.,
Lu. 10 : 42. th. good part not be t.a.
11 : 52. ye have t.a. key of knowl.
Jn. 19 : 31. that they might be t.a.
20 : 1. seeth the stone t.a. fr. sepul.
2. They have t.a. the Lord out
13. Bec. they have t.a. my Lord
Ac. 8 : 33. In his humiliation his
judgment was t.a. [was t.a.
27 : 20. all hope we should be saved
1 Co. 5 : 2. done this might be t.a.
2 Co. 3 : 16. the veil shall be t.a.
See COUNSEL.

TAKEN hold.

1 K. 9 : 9. have t.h. upon other gods
Jb. 30 : 16. of affliction t.h. upon me
Ps. 40 : 12. mine iniqu-s t.h. upon me
119 : 143. Trouble, anguish, t.h. on
Is. 21 : 3. pangs have t.h. upon me
Je. 6 : 24. anguish hath t.h. of us

TAKEN up.

Ex 40 : 36. cloud t.u. fr. ov. taberu.
37. if cloud not t.u., journeyed
not till t.u., Nu. 9 : 22.-10 : 11.
Nu. 9 : 17. when cloud was t.u., 21.
2 S. 18 : 9. Abs. was t.u. betw. heav.
2 K. 2 : 16. lest Spirit of L. t. him u.
Is. 10 : 29. t.u. lodging at Geba
Je. 29 : 22. sh. be t.u. a curse by Jud.
Eze. 36 : 3. t.u. in lips of talkers
Da. 6 : 23. So Dan. was t.u. out of den
Lu. 9 : 17. was t.u. of fragments
Ac. 1 : 2. until the day he was t.u.
9. while they beheld, he was t.u.
11. this same Jesus which is t.u.
22. unto th. same day he was t.u.
20 : 9. Eutychus fell, was t.u. dead
27 : 17. when had t.u. the boat
40. when they had t.u. the anch-

TAKEST. [ors

Ex. 4 : 9. water thou t. out of river
30 : 12. When thou t. sum of Israel
Ju. 4 : 9. journey thou t. not be for
1 Ch. 22 : 13. if t. heed to fulfil stat-
Ps. 104 : 29. t. aw. their breath [utes
144 : 3. what is man thou t. knowl.
Ec. 9 : 9. in thy labour which thou t.
Is. 58 : 3. afflicted thou t. no knowl.
Lu. 19 : 21. t. up that thou layedst

TAKETH. [5 : 11.

Ex. 20 : 7. t. his name in vain, De.
De. 10 : 17. not persons nor t. reward
24 : 6. he t. a man's life to pledge
25 : 11. putteth her hand and t. him
27 25. that t. reward to slay innoc.
32 : 11. As an eagle t. beareth them
Jos. 7 : 14. tribe the L. t. shall come
15 : 16. Kirjath-sepher and t. it, Ju.
1 : 12. [from Israel
1 S. 17 : 26. and t. away reproach
1 K. 14 : 10. as a man t. away dung
Jb. 5 : 5. t. it even out of the thorns
13. He t. the wise in their craftiness, 1 Co. 3 : 19. [him?
9 : 12. he t. away, who can hinder
12 : 20. t. away underst-g of aged
24. He t. away heart of the chief
27 : 8. wh. hope, when G. t. his soul?
40 : 24. t. it with his eyes, his nose
Ps. 15 : 3. nor t. up reproach ag. ne.
5. nor t. reward ag. the innocent
118 : 7. Lord t. my part with them
137 : 9. t. and dasheth little ones
147 : 10. he t. not pleasure in legs
11. L. t. pleasure in them th. fear
149 : 4. Lord t. pleasure in his people
Pr. 1 : 19. which t. away life of owners
11 : † 30. and he that t. souls is wise
16 : 32. is better than he th. t. a city
17 : 23. A wicked man t. gift out of
25 : 20. th. t. away a garment in cold
26 : 17. one that t. a dog by the ears

Pr. 31 : † 16. she considereth field, t.
Ec. 1 : 3. labour he t. und.sun, 5:18.
2 : 23. his heart t. not rest in night
Is. 13 : 14. a sheep that no man t. up
40 : 15. he t. up isles as a very little
44 : 14. the carpenter t. the cypress
51 : 18. is there any that t. her by
Eze. 16 : 32. wh. t. strangers instead of her husband [warning
33 : 4. t. not warning | 5. he that t.
Am. 3 : 12. shepherd t. out of mouth
Mat. 4 : 5. devil t. him into holy city
8. t. him up into high mountain
9 : 16. t. from garment, Mk. 2 : 21.
10 : 38. t. not his cross and follow-h
12 : 45. t. 7 other spirits, Lu. 11 : 26.
17 : 1. Jesus t. Pet., Ja., John, into high mt., Mk. 9 : 2.-14 : 33.
Mk. 4 : 15. Satan t. aw. word, Lu. 8 :
5 : 40. he t. father of the damsel[12.
9 : 18. whereso. he t. he teareth him
Lu. 6 : 29. him that t. thy cloak
30. of him that t. thy goods, ask
9 : 39. a spirit t. him, he crieth out
11 : 22. a stronger t. all his armour
16 : 3. my lord t. fr. me stewardship
Jn. 1 : 29. Lamb of God who t. away
10 : 18. No man t. it from me, I lay
15 : 2. beareth not fruit, he t. aw.
16 : 22. your joy no man t. from you
21 : 13. Jes. t. bread and giv. them
Ro. 3 : 5. Is God unrighteous, who t. vengeance? [before another
1 Co. 11 : 21. in eating, every one t.
He. 5 : 4. no man t. honour to hims.
10 : 9. He t. away first that he may

TAKETH hold. [estab.

Jb. 21 : 6. trembling t.h. on my flesh
Pr. 30 : 28. spider t.h. wi. her hands
Is. 56 : 6. that t.h. of my covenant
He. 2 : † 16. he t. not h. of angels(2)

TAKING.

2 Ch. 19 : 7. with God is no t. of gifts
Jb. 5 : 3. I have seen foolish t. root
Ps. 119 : 9. by t. heed thereto, acc-g
Je. 50 : 46. At noise of t. of Babylon
Eze. 25 : 12. dealt ag. Jud. by t. venge.
Ho. 11 : 3. I taught Ephr-m to go, t. them by their arms [Lu. 12 : 25.
Mat. 6 : 27. Which of you by t. tho-t,
Mk. 13 : 34. as a man t. a far journey
Lu. 4 : 5. devil t. him up into high
19 : 22. t. up that I laid not down
Jn. 11 : 13. spoken of t. rest in sleep
Ro. 7 : 8. sin t. occasion by com-t, 11.
2 Co. 2 : 13. t. my leave of them, I
11 : 8. t. wages of them to do you
Ep. 6 : 16. Above all t. shield of faith
2 Th. 1 : 8. in flaming fire t. vengean.
1 Pe. 5 : 2. t. the oversight willingly
3 Jn. 7. went, t. nothing of Gentiles

TALE. [Reckoning.]

Ex. 5 : 8. t. of bricks they did make
18. no straw, deliver t. of bricks
1 S. 18 : 27. gave foreskins in full t.
1 Ch. 9 : 28. bring vessels in and out

TALE, TALES. [by t.

Ps. 90 : 9. our years as a t. th. is told
Eze. 22 : 9. carry t-s to shed blood
Lu. 24 : 11. words seemed as idle t-s

TALEBEARER. [t.

Le. 19 : 16. not go up and down as a
Pr. 11 : 13. t. revealeth secrets, 20 : 19.
18 : 8. words of t. are wounds, 26 : 22.
26 : 20. where no t. strife ceaseth

TALENT, S. [t-s

Ex. 38 : 24. gold of offering was 29
27. hundred sockets, a t. for socket
29. brass of the offering was 70 t-s
2 K. 18 : 14. unto Hez-h 30 t-s of gold
1 Ch. 29 : 7. gave for service of house of God, of gold 5,000 t-s, of silver 10,000 t-s, of brass 18,000 t-s, and 100,000 t-s of iron
2 Ch. 3 : 8. gold amounting to 600 t-s
Zch. 5 : 7. was lifted up a t. of lead
Mat. 18 : 24. wh. owed him 10,000 t-s
Mat. 25 : 15. unto one he gave 5 t-s, to ano. two, to ano. one, 16, 20, 22,
25. I hid thy t. in the earth [24.
28. Take thf. the t. from him, and give it unto him wh. hath 10 t-s
Re. 16 : 21. ev. stone ab. weight of a t.

TALENTS with silver. [100 t.

Ex. 38 : 25. s. of them numbered was
27. of 100 t. of s. were cast sockets
2 K. 18 : 14. unto Hez-h 300 t. of s.,
30 t. of | 1 Ch. 29 : 7. of s. 10,000 t.
Es. 3 : 9. I will pay 10,000 t. of s.

See Talent, s of GOLD.
See Talent, s of SILVER.
See HUNDRED, TALENTS, THOUSAND.

TAL'ITHA-CU'MI. [arise

Mk. 5 : 41. said unto her, T., Damsel,

TALK. [Noun.]

Jb. 11 : 2. sho. a man full of t. be justified? [able t.?
15 : 3. Should reason with unprofit-
Pr. 14 : 23. t. of lips tend-h to penury
Ec. 10 : 13. end of his t. is madness
Mat. 22 : 15. might entangle him in

TALK. [Verb.] [his t.

Nu. 11 : 17. I will come t. with thee
De. 5 : 24. that God doth t. wi. man
6 : 7. shalt t. of them when sittest
Ju. 11 : † 40. dau-s of Isr. to t. with
1 S. 2 : 3. t. no more so proudly [dau.
2 K. 18 : 26. t. not in Jews' language
1 Ch. 16 : 9. sing, t. ye of all his wondrous works, Ps. 105 : 2. [him?
Jb. 13 : 7. will ye t. deceitfully for
Ps. 69 : 26. they t. to grief of wound-
71 : 24. My tongue sh. t. of thy [ed
77 : 12. I will t. of thy doings
119 : 27. sh. I t. of thy wondr. works
145 : 11. thy kingd., t. of thy power
Pr. 6 : 22. awakest, it sh. t. with thee
24 : 2. and their lips t. of mischief
Je. 12 : 1. let me t. of thy judgments
Eze. 3 : 22. Arise, and I will t. wi. thee
Da. 10 : 17. how servant t. wi. my lord
Jn. 14 : 30. I will not t. much wi. you

TALKED.

Ge. 4 : 8. Cain t. with Abel his bro.
17 : 3. Abr. on his face : G. t., 35 : 13
45 : 15. his brethren t. with him
Ex. 20 : 22. that I have t. with you,
33 : 9. the L. t. with Moses[De. 5 : 4:
34 : 29. his face shone while he t., 31.
Ju. 14 : 7. Samson t. with the woman
1 S. 14 : 19. while Saul t. unto priest
17 : 23. as he t. there came champion
1 K. 1 : 22. while he t., Nathan came
2 K. 2 : 11. as they t. appeared chariot
6 : 33. while he t. the messenger
8 : 4. the king t. with Gehazi [came
2 Ch. 25 : 16. it came to pass as he t.
Je. 38 : 25. if princes hear I have t.
Da. 9 : 22. the man Gabriel t. wi. me
Zch. 1 : 9. angel that t. with me, 13, 19.-2 : 3.-4 : 1, 4, 5.-5 : 5, 10.-6 :
4. Re. 17 : 1. [people
Mat. 12 : 46. While he yet t. to the
Mk. 6 : 50. immed-y he t. with them
Lu. 9 : 30. t. with him, Moses, Elias
24 : 32. heart burn wh. he t. wi. us, 14.
Jn. 4 : 27. marvelled he t. wi. woman
Ac. 10 : 27. as Peter t. with Cornelius
20 : 11. t. long, even till break of day
26 : 31. they t. between themselves
Re. 21 : 15. th. t. with me had golden

TALKERS. [reed, 9.

Eze. 36 : 3. are taken up in lips of t.
Tit. 1 : 10. are many unruly, vain t.

TALKEST, ETH. [me

Ju. 6 : 17. shew me a sign thou t-t wi.
1 K. 1 : 14. while thou t-t with king
2 K. 18 : † 20. Thou t-t, I have counsel
Ps. 37 : 30. his tongue t-h of judgm.
Jn. 4 : 27. no man said, Why t-t thou?
9 : 37. and it is he that t-h with thee

TALKING. [Part.]

1 K. 18 : 27. a god, he is t. or pursuing
Es. 6 : 14. while they were t. wi. him
Is. 56 : † 10. watchmen are t. in sleep
Eze. 33 : 30. thy people are t. ag. thee
Mat. 17 : 3. Moses t. wi. him, Mk. 9 : 4.
Re. 4 : 1. voice of trumpet t. with me

TALKING. [Noun.]

Ge. 17 : 22. he left off t. with him
Jb. 29 : 9. The princes refrained t.
Ep. 5 : 4. Nei. filthiness nor foolish t.

TALL, TALLER.

De. 1 : 28. The people is t-r than we
2 : 10. peo. t. as Anakim, 21.-9 : 2.
2 K. 19 : 23. cut t. cedar trees, Is. 37 : 24.

TALLNESS.

2 K. 19 : † 23. will cut down t. [dars
Is. 37 : † 24. will cut down t. of ce-

TAL'MAI. [Anak

Nu. 13 : 22. Sheshai, T., children of
Jos. 15 : 14. Caleb drove Sheshai and T.
Ju. 1 : 10. Judah slew Sheshai and T.
2 S. 3 : 3. Maacah, dau. of T., 1 Ch. 3:
13 : 37. Abs. fled and went to T. [2.

TAL'MON.

1 Ch. 9 : 17. the porters were Akkub and T., Ne. 11 : 19.-12 : 25.
Ezr. 2 : 42. children of T., Ne. 7 : 45.

TALONS. [having t.

Je. 12 : † 9. Mine heritage as bird

TA'MAH = THA'MAH.

Ne. 7 : 55. The Nethinim : chil. of T.

TA'MAR. [Person.] [was T.

Ge. 38 : 6. wife for Er, whose name
11. said Jud. to T., Remain a wid.
13. told T., thy father in law goeth
24. told Jud., T. hath played harlot
Ru. 4 : 12. Pharez, whom T. bare to Judah, 1 Ch. 2 : 4. Mat. 1 : 3.
2 S. 13 : 1. Abs. had a fair sister, T.
2. Amnon fell sick for sister T.
4. Amnon said, I love T., Abs.'s sis.
5. say unto fa., let sis. T. come, 6.
7. Da. sent to T., Go to bro.'s house,
10. T. took cakes into chamber[8
19. T. rent garments, went on cry.
20. T. desolate in Absalom's house
22. Abs. hated Am. bec. he forced
14 : 27. Abs. a dau named T.[T. 32.
1 Ch. 3 : 9. sons of Da. besides T. sis.

TA'MAR. [Place.] [48 : 28.

Eze. 47 : 19. fr. T. to waters of strife,

TAME, TAMED.

Mk. 5 : 4. nei. could any man t. him
Ja. 3 : 7. ev. kind of beasts, and serpents is t-d, and hath been t-d
8. but the tongue can no man t.

TAM'MUZ. [for T.

Eze. 8 : 14. there sat women weeping

TAN'HUMETH. [40 : 8.

2 K. 25 : 23. Seraiah, son of T., Jer.

TA'NIS = ZO'AN.

Eze. 30 : † 14. I will set fire in T.

TANNER. [mon, a t.

Ac. 9 : 43. Peter tarried with one Si-
10 : 6. lodgeth wi. one Simon, a t., 32.

TAPESTRY. See COVERINGS.

TA'PHATH.

1 K. 4 : 11. had T. dau. of Sol. to wife

TAP'PUAH. [session

Jos. 12 : 17. The king of T. one pos-
15 : 34. in the valley T. and Enam
16 : 8. border went from T. westw.
17 : 8. Manasseh had land of T. (2)
1 Ch. 2 : 43. the sons of Hebron, T.

TA'RAH. [1 28.

Nu. 33 : 27. fr. Tahath pitched at T.

TAR'ALAH. [T.

Jos. 18 : 27. cities of Benj-n, Rekem,

TARE. [Verb.]

2 S. 13 : 31. the king t. his garments
2 K. 2 : 24. two she bears t. 42 chil.
Mk. 9 : 20. straightway spirit t. him,
Lu. 9 : 42. devil threw him and t. him

TA'REA, or TAH'REA.

1 Ch. 8 : 35. † sons of Micah were, T.,

TARES. [9 : 41.

Mat. 13 : 25. his enemy sowed t. am
26. blade sprung up, then the t.

Mat. 13 : 27. seed, whence hath it t.?
29. lest ye gather up t., ye root,30
36. Declare the parable of the t.,

TARGET, S. [38, 40.

1 S. 17 : 6. Goliath had t. of brass
1 K. 10 : 16. Solomon made 200 t-s,
600 shekels of gold to one t., 2
Ch. 9 : 15. [and spears
2 Ch. 14 : 8. an army that bare t-s

TAR'PELITES. [T.

Ezr. 4 : 9. Then wrote Rehum, and

TARRIED.

Ge. 24 : 54. Abr.'s servant t. all night
28 : 11. Jacob t. there all night and
31 : 54. Jac., Laban t. all night in
Nu. 9 : 19. when cloud t. long, 22. [m-t
Ju. 3 : 25. And they t. till ashamed
26. Ehud escaped while they t.
19 : 8. t. until afternoon and did eat
Ru. 2 : 7. she t. a little in the house
1 S. 13 : 8. he t. seven days according
14 : 2. Saul t. in uttermost Gibeah
2 S. 11 : 1. David t. still at Jerusalem
15 : 17. king t. in a place far off
29. Zadok, Abiathar t. at Jerus.
20 : 5. he t. longer than set time
2 K. 2 : 18. for Elisha t. at Jericho
1 Ch. 20 : 1. But David t. at Jerus.
Ps. 68 : 12. she th. t. at home divided
Mat. 25 : 5. While the bridegroom t.
Lu. 1 : 21. marvelled he t. so long
2 : 43. child Jesus t. in Jerusalem
Jn. 3 : 22. he t. and baptized [Joppa
Ac. 9 : 43. Peter t. many days in
15 : 33. Judas, Silas t. at Antioch
18 : 18. Paul t. a good while at Cor.
20 : 5. going bef., t. for us at Troas
15. next day we t. at Trogyllium
21 : 4. finding disciples, we t. 7 days
10. as we t. many days at Cesarea
25 : 6. Festus t. at Jerusa. 10 days
27 : 33. 14th day ye have t. fasting
28 : 12. landing at Syracuse, we t.

TARRIEST, ETH.

1 S. 30 : 24. his part that t-h by stuff
Mi. 5 : 7. that t-h not for a man [ed
Ac. 22 : 16. why t-t thou? be baptiz-

TARRY. [feet

Ge. 19 : 2. t. all night, wash your
27 : 44. t. with Laban a few days
30 : 27. if favour in thine eyes, t.
45 : 9. saith thy son, come, t. not
Ex. 12 : 39. thrust out, could not t.
24 : 14. t. ye for us until we come
Le. 14 : 8. leper t. out of tent 7 days
Nu. 22 : 19. I pray you t. this night
Ju. 5 : 28. why t. wheels of his char-
6 : 18. I will t. until thou come [iot?
19 : 6. Be content and t. all night
10. the man would not t. th. night
Ru. 1 : 13. ye t. for them till grown?
3 : 13. t. this night, it sh. be in morn.
1 S. 1 : 23. t. until thou have weaned
10 : 8. seven days t. till I come
14 : 9. If they say, t. until we come
2 S. 10 : 5. t. at Jericho until your
beards, 1 Ch. 19 : 5. [t. in plain
11 : 12. t. here to day | 15 : 28. I will
18 : 14. Joab said, I not t. with thee
19 : 7. will not t. one with thee [6.
2 K. 2 : 2. t. here, L. hath sent me, 4,
7 : 9. lepers said, if we t. till morn-g
9 : 3. open the door, flee, and t. not
14 : 10. glory of this, and t. at home
Ps. 101 : 7. liar sh. not t. in my sight
Pr. 23 : 30. They that t. long at wine
Is. 46 : 13. my salvation shall not t.
Je. 14 : 8. turn aside to t. for a night?
Ha. 2 : 3. though it t. wait for it,
for it will not t. [Mk. 14 : 34.
Mat. 26 : 38. t. ye here and watch,
Lu. 24 : 29. he went in to t. wi. them
49. t. ye in Jerus-m until endued
Jn. 4 : 40. besought that he would t.
21 : 22. if I will he t. till I come, 23.
Ac. 10 : 48. they prayed Peter to t.
18 : 20. they desired Paul to t. longer
Ac. 28 : 14. were desired to t. 7 days
1 Co. 11 : 33. whf. t. one for another
16 : 7. I trust to t. a while with you
8. I will t. at Ephesus until Pent.
1 Ti. 3 : 15. if I t. long, that thou
He. 10 : 37. he th. sh. come, will not t.

TARRYING. [70 : 5.

Ps. 40 : 17. make no t., O my God,

TAR'SHISH, or **THAR'SHISH.**

[Person.] [1 : 7.

Ge. 10 : 4. sons of Javan, T., 1 Ch.
1 Ch. 7 : 10. sons of Bilhan, Zethan,
Es. 1 : 14. next unto king was T. [Th.

TAR'SHISH, or **THAR'SHISH.**

1 K. 10 : 22. Sol. had at sea a navy of
Th., with a navy, 2 Ch. 9 : 21.
22 : 48. Jehosh. made ships of Th.
2 Ch. 20 : 36. to make ships to go to T.
37. ships were not able to go to T.
Ps. 48 : 7. Thou breakest ships of T.
72 : 10. kings of T. sh. bring presents
Is. 2 : 16. day of L. upon ships of T.
23 : 1. Howl, ye ships of T., 14.
6. Pass over to T., howl, ye inhab-ts
10. Pass thro. thy land, O dau. of
60 : 9. ships of T. sh. wait for me [T.
66 : 19. send those that escape to T.
Je. 10 : 9. Silver spread into plates fr.
Eze. 27 : 12. T. was thy merchant [T.
25. ships of T. did sing of thee in
38 : 13. merchants of T. shall say
Jon. 1 : 3. Jonah rose to flee unto T.
4 : 2. I fled bef. unto T., for I knew

TAR'SUS.

Ac. 9 : 11. inquire for one Saul of T.
30. brethren sent him forth to T.
11 : 25. Barnabas departed to T. to
21 : 39. I who am a Jew of T., 22 : 3.

TAR'TAK. [T.

2 K. 17 : 31. Avites made Nibhaz and

TAR'TAN.

2 K. 18 : 17. king of Assyria sent T.
Is. 20 : 1. year that T. came unto Ash.

TASK, TASKS. [t-s

Ex. 5 : 13. Fulfil your works, daily
14 Whf. not fulfilled t. in making
19. Ye sh. not minish y-r daily t.

TASKMASTERS.

Ex. 1 : 11. set over them t. to afflict
3 : 7. heard cry by reason of their t.
5 : 6. and Pharaoh commanded t.
10. t. told them | 13. t. hasted them
14. officers which t. set over them

TASTE. [Noun.]

Ex. 16 : 31. t. of manna like wafers
Nu. 11 : 8. t. of it as t. of fresh oil
Jb. 6 : 6. any t. in white of an egg?
30. cannot my t. discern perverse
Ps. 119 : 103. How sweet are thy
words unto my t.! [the t.
Pr. 24 : 13. honeycomb is sweet to
Can. 2 : 3. his fruit sweet to my t.
Je. 48 : 11. thf. his t. remained in

TASTE. [Verb.] [him

1 S. 14 : 43. I did but t. little honey
2 S. 3 : 35. if I t. bread till sun down
19 : 35. can thy serv. t. what I eat
Jb. 12 : 11. doth not mouth t. meat?
Ps. 34 : 8. O t., see that Lord is good
Jon. 3 : 7. neither herd nor flock t.
Mat. 16 : 28. some here shall not t.
of death, Mk 9 : 1. Lu. 9 : 27.
Lu. 14 : 24. none bidden t. of my sup.
Jn. 8 : 52. my saying, he sh. never t.
Col. 2 : 21. Touch not, t. not [death
He. 2 : 9. sho. t. death for every man

TASTED.

1 S. 14 : 24. So none t. any food [hon.
29. enlightened bec. I t. a little
Da. 5 : 2. Belshazz. whilst he t. wine
Mat. 27 : 34. when he had t. thereof
Jn. 2 : 9. ruler had t. wat. made wine
He. 6 : 4. have t. of heavenly gift
5. have t. the good word of God
1 Pe. 2 : 3. If t. that Lord is gracious

TASTETH. [meat

Jb. 34 : 3. trieth words as mouth t.
Pr. 31 : †18. t. that her merchandise

TAT'NAI. [is good

See SHETHAR-BOZNAI.

TATTLERS.

1 Ti. 5 : 13. not only idle, but t. and

TAUGHT.

De. 4 : 5. I have t. you statutes
31 : 22. Mo. t. chil. of Isr. this song
Ju. 8 : 16. he t. the men of Succoth
2 K. 17 : 28. t. them how to fear Lord
2 Ch. 6 : 27. has t. th. the good way
17 : 9. Levites t. people in Judah
23 : 13. such as t. to sing praise
30 : 22. t. the good knowl. of the L.
35 : 3. the Levites that t. all Israel
Ne. 8 : 9. Levites that t. the people
Ps. 71 : 17. O God, thou hast t. me,
119 : 102. [statutes
119 : 171. when thou hast t. me thy
Pr. 4 : 4. He t. me also and said, Let
11. I have t. thee in way of wisdom
31 : 1. prophecy that his moth. t. him
Ec. 12 : 9. he still t. peo. knowl. [cept
Is. 29 : 13. fear tow. me is t. by pre-
40 : 13. his counsellor t. him, 14.
54 : 13. thy chil. shall be t. of L.
Je. 2 : † 24. A wild ass t. to wildern.
33. theref. hast thou t. the wicked
9 : 5. t. their tongues to speak lies
14. after Baalim, wh. their fa-s t.
12 : 16. t. my peo. to swear by Baal
13 : 21. hast t. them to be captains
†23. do good that are t. to do evil
28 : 16. hast t. rebellion ag. Lord
29 : 32. he hath t. rebellion ag. L.
32 : 33. tho. I t. them, rising up
Eze. 23 : 48. women t. not to do lewdn.
Ho. 10 : 11. Ephr-m as a heifer th. is t.
11 : 3. t. Ephr. to go, taking by arms
Zch. 13 : 5. man t. me to keep cattle
Mat. 5 : 2. opened his mouth and t.
them, Mk. 2 : 13.-11 : 17.
7 : 29. he t. them as one having authority, Mk. 1 : 22.
13 : 54. he t. them in their synagogue, Mk. 1 : 21. Lu. 4 : 15, 31.
-6 : 6. [were t.
28 : 15. took money, did as they
Mk. 4 : 2. t. many things by para-
6 : 30. told him all they had t. [bles
9 : 31. t. disciples, The Son of man
10 : 1. as he was wont he t. them
Lu. 5 : 3. t. the people out of ship
11 : 1. teach us to pray, as John t.
13 : 26. thou hast t. in our streets
Jn. 6 : 45. they shall be all t. of God
59. as he t. in Capernaum
8 : 2. all the people came, he t. th.
28. but as my father hath t. me, I
Ac. 4 : 2. grieved that they t. people
11 : 26. Paul and Barna. t., 14 : 21.
15 : 1. certain men t. the brethren
18 : 25. Apollos t. diligently things
20 : 20. I have shewed and t. you
22 : 3. t. acc. to perfect man-r of law
Ga. 1 : 12. was t. it but by revelation
6 : 6. Let him th. is t. communicate
Ep. 4 : 21. if ye have been t. by him
Col. 2 : 7. stablished in faith, as t.
1 Th. 4 : 9. ye are t. of God to love
2 Th. 2 : 15. traditions ye have been t.
Tit. 1 : 9. holding the word, as been t.
1 Jn. 2 : 27. as anointing hath t. you
Re. 2 : 14. t. Balak to cast stumbling b.
See In the TEMPLE.

TAUNT. [t.

Je. 24 : 9. I will deliver them to be a
Eze. 5 : 15. So it shall be a reproach

TAUNTING. [and t.

Is. 14 : † 4. sh. take up this t. speech
Ha 2 : 6. all take t. proverb ag. him

TAVERNS. [T.

Ac. 28 : 15. came as far as the Three

TAXATION. [to t.

2 K. 23 : 35. exacted of ev. one acc-g

TAXED.
2 K. 23 : 35. Jehoiakim t. the land to
Lu. 2 : 1. a decree that world be t.
3. all went to be t. | 5. Jos. to be t.
TAXES. [t.
Da. 11 : 20. shall stand up a raiser of
TAXING.
Lu. 2 : 2. t. first made when Cyren-s
Ac. 5 : 37. rose Judas in days of t.
TEACH. [he t.
Ex. 35 : 34. G. hath put in heart that
Le. 10 : 11. ye may t. Isr. all statutes
14 : 57. To t. when it is unclean and
De. 4 : 10. th. they may t. their chil.
31 : 19. t. children of Isr. this song
33 : 10. sh. t. Jacob thy judgments
Ju. 13 : 8. t., us what do unto child
2 S. 1 : 18. bade them t. use of bow
2 Ch. 17 : 7. to t. in cities of Judah
Ezr. 7 : 10. to t. in Israel statutes
Jb. 21 : 22. Shall any t. God knowl.
32 : 7. multi. of years sho. t. wisd.
37 : 19. t. us what we shall say unto
Ps. 25 : 8. he will t. sinners in way
9. the meek will he guide and t.
12. him that feareth Lord sh. he t.
51 : 13. will I t. transgr-s thy ways
90 : 12. So t. us to number our days
105 : 22. and t. his senators wisdom
Pr. 9 : 9. t. a just man, he will incr.
Is. 2 : 3. will t. us his ways, Mi. 4 : 2.
28 : 9. Whom shall he t. knowledge
26. his God doth t. him discretion
Je. 9 : 20. t. your daughters wailing
31 : 34. shall t. no more ev. man his neighbour, He. 8 : 11. [between
Eze. 44 : 23. t. my people difference
Da. 1 : 4. t. the learning of Chalde-s
Mi. 3 : 11. priests thereof t. for hire
Ha. 2 : 19. to stone, Arise, it shall t.
Mat. 5 : 19. Whoso. break com-t and t.
28 : 19. Go ye thf. and t. all nations
Lu. 11 : 1. Lord, t. us to pray, as Jn.
Jn. 7 : 35. will he go t. Gentiles
9 : 34. born in sins, dost thou t. us?
Ac. 4 : 18. not t. in name of Jes., 5 : 28.
5 : 42. ceased not to t. and preach
16 : 21. t. customs which are not
1 Co. 4 : 17. as I t. every where in ev.
14 : 19. that I might t. others
1 Ti. 1 : 3. charge they t. no other
2 : 12. But I suffer not woman to t.
3 : 2. a bishop must be apt to t., 2 Ti. 2 : 24. [t.
4 : 11. these things command and
6 : 2. these things t. and exhort
3. If man t. otherwise he is proud
2 Ti. 2 : 2. faithf. men, able to t. oth-s
Tit. 2 : 4. t. young women to be sober
Re. 2 : 20. sufferest woman Jezebel to
Began to TEACH. [t.
Mk. 4 : 1. Jesus again -t. by sea side
6 : 2. he -t. in the synagogue
34. he -t. them many things
8 : 31. -t. that Son of man must suf-
Ac. 1 : 1. treatise of all Jesus -t. [fer
TEACH me.
Jb. 6 : 24. t. m. I will hold my tongue
34 : 32. Th. wh. I see not t. thou m.
Ps. 25 : 4. O Lord, t. m. thy paths
5. Lead me in thy truth and t. m.
27 : 11. t. m. thy way, O L., 86 : 11.
119 : 12. t. m. thy statutes, 26, 33, 64, 68, 124, 135. [m. thy judgm-ts
66. t. m. good judgments | 108. t.
143 : 10. t. m. to do thy will, thou
TEACH thee.
Ex 4 : 12. I will t. t. what shalt say
De. 17 : 11. sentence they shall t. t.
Jb. 8 : 10. fa-s, Shall not they t. t.?
12 : 7. ask the beasts, they sh. t. t.
8. Or speak to the earth, it sh. t. t.
33 : 33. hold peace, I sh. t. t. wisdom
Ps. 32 : 8. I will t. t. way thou sh. go
45 : 4. hand sh. t. t. terrible things
TEACH them. [laws
Ex. 18 : 20. shall t. t. ordinances and
Ex. 24 : 12. ha. writ. thou mayest t. t.
De. 4 : 9. t. t. thy sons, thy sons' sons
5 : 31. judgments wh. thou sh. t. t.
6 : 7. t. t. diligently unto chil., 11 : 19.
Ju. 3 : 2. might know to t. t. war
1 K. 8 : 36. thou t. t. the good way
2 K. 17 : 27. t. t. manner of G. of land
Ezr. 7 : 25. t. ye t. that know th. not
Ps. 132 : 12. keep testimony I sh. t. t.
Mat. 5 : 19. whoso. shall t. t. shall
TEACH you.
Ex. 4 : 15. I will t. y. what ye sh. do
De. 4 : 1. hearken unto stat-s I t. y.
14. Lord com-ded me to t. y., 6 : 1.
20 : 18. they t. y. not to do aft. abom-
24 : 8. all that Levites t. y. [inations
1 S. 12 : 23. I will t. y. the good way
Jb. 27 : 11. I will t. y. by hand of God
Ps. 34 : 11. I will t. y. fear of Lord
Lu. 12 : 12. Holy Ghost t. y. what to
Jn. 14 : 26. Holy Ghost t. y. all thi-s
1 Co. 11 : 14. Doth not nature t. y.
He. 5 : 12. ye have need th. one t. y.
1 Jn. 2 : 27. need not th. any man t. y.
TEACHER. [scholar
1 Ch. 25 : 8. cast lots, as well t. as
Jo. 2 : † 23. given a t. of righteousn.
Ha. 2 : 18. the image, a t. of lies
Jn. 3 : 2. thou art a t. come fr. God
Ro. 2 : 20. that thou art a t. of babes
1 Ti. 2 : 7. I am a t. of Gentiles, 2 Ti.
TEACHERS. [1 : 11.
Ps. 119 : 99. more underst-g than my
Pr. 5 : 13. have not obeyed my t. [t.
Is. 30 : 20. sh. not thy t. be removed, thine eyes shall see thy t. [me
43 : 27. thy t. have transgressed ag
Da. 12 : † 3. they that be t. sh shine
Ac. 13 : 1. at Antioch were certain t.
1 Co. 12 : 28. hath set prophets, t.
29. Are all apostles? are all t.?
Ep. 4 : 11. he gave some evangelists,
1 Ti. 1 : 7. Desiring to be t. of law [t.
2 Ti. 4 : 3. sh. heap to themselves t.
Tit. 2 : 3. aged women be t. of good
He. 5 : 12. when ye ought to be t.
2 Pe. 2 : 1. shall be false t. am. you
TEACHEST. [t.
Ps. 94 : 12. Blessed is the man thou
Mat. 22 : 16. we know thou t. way of God, Mk. 12 : 14. Lu. 20 : 21. [Mo.
Ac. 21 : 21. thou t. Jews to forsake
Ro. 2 : 21. that t. another, t. thou
TEACHETH. [not thys.?
2 S. 22 : 35. He t. my hands to war, Ps. 18 : 34. -144 : 1. [iniquity
Jb. 15 : † 5. For thy mouth t. thine
35 : 11. Who t. more than the beasts
36 : 22. G. exalteth, who t. like him?
Ps. 94 : 10. he that t. man knowledge
Pr. 6 : 13. wicked man t. wi. fingers
16 : 23. heart of the wise t. his mou.
Is. 9 : 15. the prophet that t. lies, he
48 : 17. thy G., wh. t. thee to profit
Ac. 21 : 28. the man that t. all men
Ro. 12 : 7. or he that t. on teaching
1 Co. 2 : 13. not in words man's wis- dom t., but wh. Holy Gh. t. [t.
Ga 6 : 6. communicate unto him th.
1 Jn. 2 : 27. same anointing t. you all
TEACHING. [Part.]
2 Ch 15 : 3. Israel without a t. priest
Je. 32 : 33. I rising early and t. them
Mat. 4 : 23. Jesus went about Gali- lee, t., 9 : 35. Lu. 13 : 10.
15 : 9. t. for doctrines the com- mandments of men, Mk. 7 : 7.
21 : 23. elders came as he was t.
28 : 20. t. them to observe all things
Lu. 23 : 5. t. throughout all Jewry, 5 : 17. -13 : 22. Mk. 6 : 6. [ioch, t.
Ac. 15 : 35. Paul, Barnabas in Anti-
18 : 11. Paul t. word of God at Cor.
28 : 31. Paul t. at Rome with all
Col. 1 : 28. warning and t. every man
3 : 16. t., admonishing one another
Tit. 1 : 11. t. things they ought not
Tit. 2 : 12. t. us, that denying ungod
See In the TEMPLE.
TEACHING. [Noun.]
Ro. 12 : 7. or he that teacheth on t.
Tit. 1 : † 9. holding fast the word in t.
TEAR. [Verb.]
Ju. 8 : 7. will I t. y-r flesh wi. thorns
Ps. 7 : 2. Lest he t. my soul like a lion
35 : 15. they did t. me, ceased not
50 : 22. consider this, lest I t. you
Je. 15 : 3. I will appoint dogs to t.
16 : 7. Nei. sh. men t. thems. for th.
Eze. 13 : 20. pillows I will t. fr. arms
21. your kerchiefs will I t. and de-
Ho. 5 : 14. I will t. and go away [liver
13 : 8 wild beast shall t. them [ally
Am. 1 : 11. his anger did t. perpetu-
Na. 2 : 12 lion did t. for his whelps
Zch. 11 : 16. shepherd shall t. their
TEARETH. [claws
De. 33 : 20. Gad as a lion, t. the arm
Jb. 16 : 9. He t. me in his wrath
18 : 4. He t. himself in his anger
Mi. 5 : 8. as young lion t. in pieces
Mk. 9 : 18. wheresoever he taketh him, he t. him, Lu. 9 : 39.
TEAR. [Noun.] [t.
Ex. 22 : † 29. first of ripe fruits, and
TEARS. [on my t.
2 S. 16 : † 12. may be Lord will look
2 K. 20 : 5. I have seen thy t., Is 38 : 5.
Es. 8 : 3. Es. besought king with t.
Jb. 16 : 20. mine eye poureth out t.
Ps. 6 : 6. I water my couch with t.
39 : 12. L., hold not peace at my t.
42 : 3. My t. my meat day and night
56 : 8. put thou my t. in thy bottle
80 : 5. feedest them with bread of t., and givest t. to drink [t.
116 : 8. hast delivered mine eyes fr.
126 : 5. They that sow in t. sh. reap
Ec. 4 : 1. behold the t. of the oppres-d
Is. 16 : 9. I will water thee with t.
25 : 8 L. will wipe aw. t. fr. all faces
Je. 9 : 1. Oh that mine eyes were a fountain of t. [t. and eyelids
18. th. our eyes may run down wi.
13 : 17. mine eyes sh. run down wi.
14 : 17. Let mine eyes run with t. [t.
31 : 16. Refrain thine eyes from t.
La. 1 : 2. her t. are on her cheeks
2 : 11. Mine eyes do fail with t.
18. let t. run down like river, day
Eze. 24 : 16. nei. shall thy t. run do.
Mal. 2 : 13. covering the altar with t.
Mk. 9 : 24 father said with t., Lord
Lu. 7 : 38. to wash his feet with her t.
44 she hath washed my feet wi. t.
Ac. 20 : 19. serving Lord wi many t.
31. I ceased not to warn with t.
2 Co. 2 : 4. I wrote you with many t.
2 Ti 1 : 4. being mindful of thy t.
He. 5 : 7. off-d supplications with t.
12 : 17. he sought it carefully wi. t.
Re. 7 : 17. God shall wipe away all t., [21 : 4.
TEATS.
Is 32 : 11. They shall lament for t.
Eze. 23 : 3. there they bruised t., 21.
TE'BAH. See REUMAH
TEBALI'AH. [3d
1 Ch. 26 : 11. sons of Hosah, T. the
TE'BETH. [T.
Es. 2 : 16. in 10th month, which is
TEDIOUS. [thee
Ac. 24 : 4. that I be not further t. to
TEETH. [milk
Ge. 49 : 12. his t. shall be white with
Nu 11 : 33. flesh yet between their
De. 32 : 24. I will send t. of beasts [t.
1 S. 2 : 13. a fleshhook of three t.
1 K. 10 : † 22. elephants' t., 2 Ch. 9 : † 21.
Jb 4 : 10. t. of young lions are brok.
13 : 14. Whf. take my flesh in my t.?
19 : 20 am escaped wi. skin of my t.
29 : 17. the spoil out of t. of wicked
41 : 14. Leviathan's t. are terrible
Ps. 3 : 7 hast broken t. of ungodly

Ps. 57 : 4. whose **t.** are spears, arrows
58 : 6. Break **t.**, O G., in their mou.
124 : 6. not given us prey to their **t.**
Pr. 10 : 26. As vinegar to **t.**, so slugg.
30 : 14. whose **t.** are swords, their jaw **t.** as knives [sheep, 6 : 6.
Can. 4 : 2. thy **t.** are like a flock of
Is. 41 : 15. an instrument having **t.**
Je. 31 : 29. children's **t.** are set on edge, Eze. 18 : 2. [be set on edge
30. eateth sour grapes, his **t.** shall
La. 3 : 16. broken my **t.** with gravel
Eze. 39 : †2. draw thee wi. hook of 6 **t.**
Da. 7 : 5. three ribs between **t.** of it
7. 4th beast had great iron **t.**, 19.
Jo. 1 : 6. hath cheek **t.** of great lion
Am. 4 : 6. given you cleanness of **t.**
Mi. 3 : 5. bite with **t.** and cry Peace
Zch. 9 : 7. abomina-s fr. betw. his **t.**
Mat 27 : 44. cast the same in his **t.**
Re. 9 : 8. their **t.** were as **t.** of lions
See GNASH, ED, ETH, ING.

TEHAPH'NEHES.
See TAHAPANES.

TEHIN'NAH. See RECHAH.

TEIL tree.
Is. 6 : 13. as a **t. t.**, and as an oak

TEKEL.
Da. 5 : 25. this is the writing, MENE, MENE, T., UPHARSIN
27. T., thou art weighed in balan-s

TEKO'A. [Person.] [T.
1 Ch. 2 : 24. Abiah bare Ashur, fa. of
4 : 5. Ashur, father of T., had 2 wiv.

TEKO'A, TEKO'AH.
2 S. 14 : 2. to T-h to fetch a wise wom.
4. woman of T-h spake to king, 9.
2 Ch. 11 : 6. Rehob. built Etam, T-a
20 : 20. army into wilderness of T-a
Je. 6 : 1. O Benj., blow trumpet in T-a
Am. 1 : 1. Amos, am. herdmen of T-a

TEKO'ITE, S. [28.-27 : 9.
2 S. 23 : 26. Ikkesh the T., 1 Ch. 11 :
Ne. 3 : 5. next unto them T-s repaired, [27.

TEL-A'BIB.
Eze. 3 : 15. I to them of captivity at

TE'LAH. See TAHAN. [T.

TEL'AIM. [T.
1 S. 15 : 4. Saul numbered people in

TELAS'SAR. See THELASAR.

TE'LEM. [Person.]
Ezr. 10 : 24. porters, Shallum and T.

TE'LEM. [Place.] See ZIPH.

TEL-HARE'SHA, or TEL-HAR'SA.
Ezr. 2 : 59. Went up from Tel-melah,

TELL. [T., Ne. 7 : 61.
Ge. 15 : 5. **t.** the stars if thou be able
32 : 5. I have sent to **t.** my Lord
43 : 6. to **t.** man whe. ye had a bro.
22. we can-t **t.** who put our money
45 : 13. **t.** my father of all my glory
Ex. 9 : 1. **t.** Pha., Let my people go
10 : 2. mayest **t.** in ears of thy son
19 : 3. **t.** chil of Isr., Ye have seen
Le. 14 : 35. **t.** priest, saying, It seem-h
Nu. 14 : 14. will **t.** it to inhabitants
1 S. 6 : 2. **t.** us wh-w. we shall send it
9 : 8. man of God to **t.** us our way
17 : 55. thy soul liveth, I cannot **t.**
22 : 22. I knew he would **t.** Saul
23 : 11. O G., I beseech, **t.** thy serv.
27 : 11. Lest they should **t.** on us
2 S. 1 : 20. **t.** it not in Gath [Ch 17 : 4
7 : 5. Go, **t.** my servant David, 1
12 : 18. feared to **t.** him child was
22. child alive, I said, Who can **t.**
15 : 35. **t.** to Zadok and Abiathar,
18 : 21. **t.** k. what hast seen [17 : 16.
1 K. 1 : 20 **t.** who shall sit on throne
14 : 7. **t.** Jerob., as I exalted thee
18 : 8. **t.** thy lord, Elijah is here, 11, 14. [me
12. when I **t.** Ahab, he will slay
20 : 9. **t.** king, All thou didst send
11. **t.** him, Let not him th. girdeth
2 K. 7 : 9 we may **t.** k.'s household
2 K. 9 : 12. said, It is false; **t.** us now
15. let none escape to **t.** it in Jez-l
20 : 5. **t.** Hez. I have heard thy [23.
22 : 15. **t.** man th. sent you, 2 Ch. 34 :
1 Ch. 21 : 10. **t.** David I offer 3 things
Ps. 22 : 17. I may **t.** all my bones
26 : 7. **t.** of all thy wondrous works
48 : 12. go round ab. her, **t.** towers
13. ye may **t.** generation following
Pr. 30 : 4. his son's name, if canst **t.**
Ec. 6 : 12. who can **t.** wh. sh. be, 10 : 14.
8 : 7. who can **t.** when it shall be?
10 : 20. hath wings sh. **t.** the matter
Can. 5 : 8. **t.** him th. I am sick of love
Is. 6 : 9. go and **t.** this people
45 : 21. **t.** ye, and bring them near
48 : 20. **t.** this, Lord hath redeemed
Je. 15 : 2. **t.** such as are for death
23 : 27. by dreams wh. they **t.**, 28, 32.
28 : 13. Go, **t.** Han., Thou hast brok.
34 : 2. Go, **t.** Zed-h, I will give city
35 : 13. **t.** men of of Judah. Will ye
36 : 16. We will **t.** king of all these
17. **t.** us, How th. didst write these
48 : 20. **t.** it in Arnon, Moab is spoil.
Eze. 3 : 11. **t.** chil. of thy peo., Thus
12 : 23. **t.** them, The days are at ha.
17 : 12. **t.** them, Behold k. of Bab-n
24 : 19. Wilt thou not **t.** us what?
Da. 2 : 4. **t.** thy servants dream, 7, 9.
36. we will **t.** the k. interpretation
Jo. 1 : 3. **t.** ye your children, let your children **t.** [evil
Jon. 1 : 8. **t.** us for whose cause this
3 : 9. Who can **t.** if God will turn
Mat. 8 : 4. See thou **t.** no man, but go thy way, Mk. 8 : 26, 30.-9 : 9. Lu. 5 : 14.-8 : 56. Ac. 23 : 22.
16 : 20. charged his disciples they **t.** no man, Mk. 7 : 36. Lu. 9 : 21.
17 : 9. **t.** the vision to no man, until
18 : 15. go, **t.** him his fault alone
17. if he neglect to hear, **t.** church
21 : 5. **t.** ye the daughter of Sion
22 : 4. **t.** them which are bidden
17. **t.** us thf., What thinkest thou?
24 : 3. **t.** us, when shall these things be? Mk. 13 : 4.
26 : 63. **t.** us whether thou be the Christ, Lu. 22 : 67. Jn. 10 : 24.
28 : 7. go, **t.** his disciples he is risen
9. went to **t.** his discip., Mk. 16 : 7.
10. **t.** my broth. that they go into
Mk. 1 : 30. anon they **t.** him of her
5 : 19. **t.** them how gr. things the L.
11 : 33. We cannot **t.**, Mat. 21 : 27.
10 : 32. began to **t.** what things sho. happen unto him [Lu. 20 : 7.
Lu. 7 : 22. **t.** Jn. things ye have seen
13 : 32. **t.** that fox I cast out devils
20 : 2. **t.** us by wh. authority [eth
Jn 3 : 8. canst not **t.** whence it com-
4 : 25. when come, he will **t.** us all
8 : 14. ye cannot **t.** whence I come
16 : 18. we cannot **t.** what he saith
18 : 34. did others **t.** it thee of me?
Ac. 15 : 27. who sh. **t.** you the same
17 : 21. to **t.** or hear some new thing
23 : 17. hath certain thing to **t.** him
2 Co. 12 : 2. whether out of body I cannot **t.**, 3. [Gideon
He. 11 : 32. time would fail to **t.** of

TELL me. [thy wife?
Ge. 12 : 18. why not **t. m.** she was
21 : 26. nei. didst **t. m.**, nei. heard I
24 : 23. **t. m.**, Whose dau. art thou?
49 if ye will deal truly **t. m.**, and if not, **t. m.**, that I may turn
29 : 15 **t. m.**, wh. sh thy wages be?
31 : 27. steal away, and not **t. m.**
32 : 29. Jacob said **t. m.** thy name
37 : 16. **t. m.** where breth. feed floc.
40 : 8. **t. m.** interpret-us I pray you
Jos. 7 : 19. **t. m.** what thou hast done
Ju. 16 : 6. **t. m.** wh-n thy strength, 10, 13. [I may know
Ru. 4 : 4. if not redeem it, **t. m.** that
1 S. 9 : 18. **t. m.** where seer's house
10 : 15. **t. m.** what Samuel said
14 : 43. Saul said, **t. m.** wh. hast done
20 : 10. Da. to Jona., Who sh. **t. m.**?
2 S. 1 : 4. How went the matter, **t. m.**?
13 : 4. Why lean, wilt thou not **t. m.**?
1 K. 22 : 16. **t. m.** nothing but truth
2 K. 4 : 2. Wh. sh. I do for thee, **t. m.**?
8 : 4. **t. m.** great things that Elisha
Jb. 34 : 34. Let men of underst-g **t. m.**
Can. 1 : 7. **t. m.**, thou whom my soul
Da. 2 : 9. **t. m.** the dream [loveth
Mat. 21 : 24. one thing wh if ye **t. m.**
Lu. 7 : 42. **t. m.** which will love most
Jn. 20 : 15. **t. m.** where hast laid him
Ac. 5 : 8. **t. m.** whe. ye sold land for
22 : 27. **t. m.**, art thou a Roman?
23 : 19. Wh. is th. thou hast to **t. m.**?
Ga. 4 : 21. **t. m.** ye that desire to be

TELL thee. [und. law
Ge. 22 : 2. one of mts. I will **t. t.** of
26 : 2. dwell in land I will **t. t.** of
Ex. 14 : 12. word we did **t. t.** in Egypt
Nu. 23 : 3 he sheweth me I will **t. t.**
De. 17 : 11. judgment wh. they sh. **t. t.**
32 : 7. ask thy elders, they will **t. t.**
Ju. 14 : 16. not told it, sh. I **t.** it **t.**?
Ru. 3 : 4. he will **t. t.** what thou do
1 S. 9 : 19. I will **t. t.** all in thine hea.
15 : 16. I will **t. t.** what L. hath said
19 : 3. what I see, that I will **t. t.**
20 : 9 if I knew, would not I **t.** it **t.**?
1 K. 14 : 3. **t. t.** what become of child
22 : 18. Did I not **t. t.** that he would prophesy evil, 2 Ch. 18 : 17.
1 Ch. 17 : 10. I **t. t.** that L. will build
Jb. 1 : 15. I am escaped alone to **t. t.**, 16, 17, 19. [and **t. t.**
8 : 10. Shall not thy fathers teach
12 : 7. ask fowls, they shall **t. t.** [t.
Ps. 50 : 12. If hungry, I would not **t.**
Is. 19 : 12. let thy wise men **t. t.** now
Je. 19 : 2. proclaim words I sh. **t. t.**
Lu. 12 : 59. I **t. t.** thou not depart
22 : 34. I **t. t.**, cock not crow this day
Ac. 10 : 6. **t. t.** what to do, 11 : 14
Re. 17 : 7. I will **t. t.** mystery of wom.

I TELL you, or TELL I you.
Ge. 49 : 1. I may **t. y.** what sh. befall
Is. 5 : 5. I will **t. y.** what I will do
42 : 9. bef. they spring forth, I **t. y.**
Mat. 10 : 27. What I **t. y.** in darkn-s
21 : 27. Nei. **t.** I **y.** by what authority I do these, Mk. 11 : 33. Lu. 20 : 8.
Mk. 11 : 29. I will **t. y.** by what authority I do, Mat. 21 : 24.
Lu. 4 : 25. But I **t. y.** of a truth, 9 : 27.
10 : 24. I **t. y.** many prophets [sion
12 : 51. I **t. y.** nay, but rather divi-
13 : 3. I **t. y.** nay, exc. ye repent, 5.
27. I **t. y.** I know you not, depart
17 : 34. I **t. y.** sh. be two in one bed
18 : 8. I **t. y.** he will avenge them
14. I **t. y.** this man went to his ho.
19 : 40. I **t. y.** if these sho. hold peace
22 : 67. If I **t. y.** ye not believe [ly
Jn. 3 : 12. believe if I **t. y.** of heaven-
8 : 45. bec. I **t. y.** truth, Ga. 4 : 16.
13 : 19. Now I **t. y.** before it come
16 : 7. I **t. y.** the truth It is expd.
Ga. 5 : 21. I **t. y.** before, as I have
Ph. 3 : 18. of whom I now **t. y.**, weep-

TELLEST. [ing
Ps. 56 : 8. Thou **t.** my wanderings
Is. 40 : †9. O thou that **t.** good tid-

TELLETH. [ings
2 S. 7 : 11. Lord **t.** thee he will build
2 K. 6 : 12. Elisha **t.** king the words
Ps 41 : 6. he goeth abroad he **t.** it
101 : 7. **t.** lies not tarry in my sight
147 : 4. he **t.** the numb. of the stars
Je. 33 : 13. und. hands of him that **t.**
Jn 12 : 22. Philip cometh **t.** Andrew

TELLING. [Noun, Part.]
Ju 7 : 15. when Gideon heard the **t.**
2 S. 11 : 19. made an end of **t.** matters
2 K. 8 : 5. as he was **t.** the king how

TEL-ME'LAH.
See TEL-HARESHA.
TE'MA. [1 : 30.
Ge. 25 : 15. sons of Ishm., T., 1 Ch.
Jb. 6 : 19. troops of T. looked for th.
Is. 21 : 14. inhab.s of T. bro-t water
Je. 25 : 23. I made T. drink the cup
TE'MAN.
Ge. 36 : 11. sons of Eliphaz were T.,
Omar, Zepho, 1 Ch. 1 : 36.
15. duke T., duke Omar, d. Zepho
42. duke T., d. Mibzar, 1 Ch. 1 : 53.
Jos. 12 : † 3. Sihon ruled fr. T. under
Je. 49 : 7. Is wisdom no more in T.?
20. that L. hath purposed ag. T.
Eze. 25 : 13. will make it desol. fr. T.
Am. 1 : 12. I will send a fire upon T.
Ob. 9. thy mighty men, O T., sh. be
Ha. 3 : 3. God came fr. T., Holy One
TEM'ANI, ITES.
Ge. 36 : 34. Husham of the land of
T-i reigned, 1 Ch. 1 : 45. T-s
TE'MANITE.
Jb. 2 : 11. Job's friends, Eliphaz the
T., 4 : 1.-15 : 1.-22 : 1.-42 : 7, 9.
TEM'ENI.
1 Ch. 4 : 6. And Naarah bare him T.
TEMPER.
Eze. 46 : 14. hin of oil to t. with fine
TEMPERANCE. [flour
Ac. 24 : 25. as he reasoned of t. and
Ga. 5 : 23. Meekness, t. : ag. such no
2 Pe. 1 : 6. add to knowl. t., and to t.
TEMPERATE. [t.
1 Co. 9 : 25. striveth for mastery, is
Tit. 1 : 8. a bishop must be holy, t.
2 : 2. aged men be sober, grave, t.
TEMPERED.
Ex. 29 : 2. take cakes t. with oil
30 : 35. a perfume t., pure and holy
1 Co. 12 : 24. God hath t. body toge-
TEMPEST. [ther
Jb. 9 : 17. he breaketh me with a t.
27 : 20. t. stealeth him aw. in night
Ps. 11 : 6. Upon wicked he sh. rain t.
55 : 8. I would hasten from windy t.
83 : 15. So persecute them wi. thy t.
Is. 28 : 2. L. hath a strong one, as a t.
29 : 6. thou shalt be visited with t.
30 : 30. Assyrian be beaten with a t.
32 : 2. a man sh. be a covert from t.
54 : 11. O thou afflicted, tossed wi. t.
Am. 1 : 14. a t. in day of whirlwind
Jon. 1 : 4. was a mighty t. in the sea
12. for my sake this gr. t. is come
Mat. 8 : 24. arose great t. in the sea
Ac. 27 : 18. exceedingly tossed wi. a t.
20. no small t. lay on us, all hope
He. 12 : 18. ye are not come to t.
2 Pe. 2 : 17. clouds that are carried
TEMPESTUOUS. [with t.
Ps. 50 : 3. shall be very t. about him
Jon. 1 : 11. sea wrought and was t., 13.
Ha. 3 : † 14. they were t. to scat. me
Ac. 27 : 14. arose against it a t. wind
TEMPLE.
2 S. 22 : 7. he did hear my voice out
of his t., Ps. 18 : 6.
1 K. 6 : 3. porch before the t. of hou.
5. walls both of t. and of oracle
17. t. before it was 40 cubits long
33. for door of t. posts of olive [17.
7 : 21. pillars in porch of t., 2 Ch. 3 :
50. hinges of gold for doors of t.
2 K. 11 : 11. guard stood from right
corner of t. to left of t., along
by altar and t., 2 Ch. 23 : 10.
2 Ch. 4 : 22. doors of t. were of gold
35 : 20. when Josiah had prepared t.
36 : 7. put vessels in his t. at Baby.
Ezr. 4 : 1. they builded t. unto Lord
5 : 14. vessels which Neb-r took out
of the t. in Jerusalem and bro-t
into t. in Babylon, (3) 15.-6 : 5.
Ne. 6 . 10. hid ourselves in the t.,
shut doors of the t.
Ps. 27 : 4. and to inquire in his t.

Ps. 29 : 9. in his t. doth ev. one speak
48 : 9. thought of thy lovingkindness in midst of thy t. [sh. kings
68 : 29. Bec. of thy t. at Jerusalem
Is. 6 : 1. and his train filled the t.
44 : 28. to the t., Thy founda-n sh.
66 : 6. a voice fr. the t., voice of Lord
Je. 50 : 28. vengeance of his t., 51 : 11.
Eze. 41 : 1. he brought me to the t.
4. breadth of door 20 cubits bef. t.
15. inner t. and porches of court
20. cherubim, palm trees on wall
21. posts of t. were squared [of t.
23. t. and sanctuary had 2 doors
25. on doors of t. cherubim, palm
42 : 8. before the t. were 100 cubits
Da. 5 : 2. golden vessels out of t., 3.
Am. 8 : 3. songs of t. sh. be howlings
Zch. 8 : 9. be strong that t. be built
Mal. 3 : 1. Lord suddenly to his t.
Mat. 4 : 5. on a pinnacle of t., Lu. 4 : 9.
12 : 6. is one greater than the t.
23 : 16. Whoso. shall swear by the
t., or by the gold of the t., 17, 21.
35. slew betw. t. and altar, Lu. 11 : 51
24 : 1. to shew him the buildings of
the t., Mk. 13 : 1. Lu. 21 : 5. [G.
26 : 61. am able to destroy the t. of
27 : 40. th. destroyest t., Mk. 15 : 29.
51. behold vail of the t. was rent,
Mk. 15 : 38. Lu. 23 : 45.
Mk. 11 : 16. carry any vessel thro. t.
13 : 3. sat upon m-t over ag. the t.
14 : 58. I will destroy this t. made
Lu. 2 : 37. Anna departed not from t.
22 : 52. Jes. said unto captains of t.
Jn. 2 : 15. he drove all out of the t.
19. Destroy this t. I will raise it
20. 46 years was this t. in building
21. he spake of the t. of his body
8 : 59. out of t., going thro. midst
Ac. 3 : 2. at gate of t. to ask alms of
them that entered the t., 10.
4 : 1. captain of t. came upon them
5 : 24. when captain of t. heard these
19 : 27. t. of Diana sho. be despised
† 35. city of Eph. t. keeper of Diana
21 : 30. took Paul, drew him out of t.
24 : 6. gone about to profane the t.
25 : 8. nei. ag. the t. nor ag. Cesar
1 Co. 3 : 16. Know not ye are t. of G.
17. if any man defile t. of God, him
shall God destroy, for the t. of
God is holy, which t. ye are
6 : 19. your body is t. of Holy Gho.
8 : 10. These sit at meat in idol's t.
9 : 13. minister live of things of t.
2 Co. 6 : 16 what agreement hath the
t. of God with idols? ye are t.
of the living God [in his t.
Re. 7 : 15. serve him day and night
11 : 1. Rise and measure t. of God
2. court without the t., leave out
19. t. of God was opened in heav-
en, seen in t. ark of testament [17.
14 : 15. ano. angel came out of t.,
15 : 5. t. of tabernacle was opened
6. seven angels came out of the t.
8. t. was filled with smoke fr. [17.
16 : 1. I heard great voice out of t.,
21 : 22. I saw no t. therein, for the
L. and the Lamb are the t. of it
See **HOLY temple.**
In or Into the TEMPLE.
2 K. 11 : 10. Da.'s spears that were i. t.
1 Ch. 6 : 10. executed priest's office
i. t. that Solomon built [Dagon
10. 10. fastened Saul's head i. t. of
2 Ch. 4 : 7. set ten candlest-s i. t., 8.
Ezr. 5 : 15. carry these vessels i-o t.
Ne. 6. 11. who wo. go i-o t. to save life?
Mat. 12 : 5. priests i. t. profane sab-h
21 : 12. went i-o t., cast out all that
sold i. t., Mk. 11 : 15. Lu. 19 : 45.
Jn 2 : 14. [him i. t.
14. blind and the lame came to
15. children crying i. t., Hosannah

Mat. 26 : 55. sat daily wi. you teaching i. t., Mk. 14 : 49. Lu. 21 : 37.
27 : 5. he cast down pieces of silv. i. t.
Mk. 11 : 11. Jesus entered i-o Jerus.
alem and t., Mat. 21 : 23. [10 : 23.
27. as he walking i. t. priests, Jn.
Lu. 1 : 21. marvelled he tarried i. t.
22. perceived he had seen vis-n i. t.
2 : 27. and he came by Spirit i-o t.
46. found him i. t. sitting in midst
18 : 10. Two men went i-o t. to pray
21 : 38. peo. came to him i. t. to hear
22 : 53. when I was daily wi. you i. t.
24. 53. continually i. t. praising G.
Jn. 5 : 14. Jesus findeth him i. t.
7 : 14. Jes. went up i-o t. and taught,
28. Mk. 12 : 35. Lu. 19 : 47.-20 :
1. Jn. 8 : 2, 20.
11 : 56. spake as they stood i. t.
18 : 20. I ever taught i. the synagogue and the t. [cord i. t.
Ac. 2 : 46. continuing with one ac-
3 : 1. Peter and John went up i-o t.
3. Pet. and John about to go i-o t.
8. leaping, entered wi. them i-o t.
5 : 20. Go, stand, speak i. t. to peo.
21. i-o t. in morning and taught
25. men are standing i. t. teach-g
42. daily i. t. and every house they
ceased not to teach [tered i-o t.
21 : 26. Paul, purifying himself, en-
27. Jews when they saw him i. t.
28. brought Greeks also i-o t., 29.
22 : 17. prayed i. t. I was in a trance
24 : 12. nei. found me i. t. disputing
18. Jews found me purified i. t. [t.
26 : 21 For causes Jews caught me i.
2 Th. 2 . 4. he as God sitteth i. t. of G.
Re. 3 : 12. make a pillar i. t. of my G.
15 : 8. no man able to enter i-o t.
See **Temple of the LORD.**
TEMPLES.
Ho. 8 : 14. Israel forgotten Maker,
buildeth t. [ant things
Jo. 3 : 5. into y-r t. my goodly pleas-
Ac. 7 : 48. the Most High dwelleth
not in t. made wi. hands, 17 : 24.
TEMPLES. [Of the head.]
Ju. 4 : 21. Jael smote nail into t., 22.
5 : 26. she had stricken thro. his t.
Can. 4 : 3. thy t. like a pomegr., 6 : 7.
TEMPORAL. [are t.
2 Co. 4 : 18. things which are seen
TEMPT.
Ge. 22 : 1. God did t. Abraham and
Ex. 17 : 2. Moses said, Whf. do t. L.?
De. 6 : 16. Ye shall not t. the Lord
Is. 7 : 12. I will not ask, nei. t. the L.
Mal. 3 : 15. that t. God are delivered
Mat. 4 : 7. Thou sh. not t. the Lord
thy God, Lu. 4 12. [Lu. 20 : 23.
22 : 18. Why t. ye me? Mk. 12 : 15.
Ac. 5 : 9. have agreed to t. the Spirit
15 : 10. why t. ye God to put a yoke
1 Co. 7 : 5. that Satan t. you not for
10 : 9. Neither let us t. Ch. as some
TEMPTATION
Ex. 17 : † 7. Mos. called the place T.
Ps. 95 : 8. as in the day of t. in the
wilderness, He. 3 : 8. [11 : 4.
Mat. 6 : 13. lead us not into t., Lu.
26 : 41. Watch th. ye enter not into
t., Mk. 14 : 38. Lu. 22 : 40, 46.
Lu. 4 : 13. when devil had ended t.
8 : 13. no root and in time of t. fall
1 Co. 10 : 13 hath no t. taken you;
with t. make a way to escape
Ga. 4 : 14. my t. ye despised not
1 Ti. 6 : 9. th. will be rich fall into t.
Ja. 1 : 12. Blessed is man endur-h t
Re. 3 : 10. I will keep thee fr. hour of t.
TEMPTATIONS.
De. 4 : 34. hath G. assayed to take a
nation fr. another nation by t.
7 : 19. great t. thine eyes saw, 29 : 3.
Lu. 22 : 28. ye have continued with
me in my t.

Ac. 20 : 19. serving God with many
tears and t.
Ja. 1 : 2. when ye fall into divers t.
1 Pe. 1 : 6. heaviness thro. manif-d t.
2 Pe. 2 : 9. how to deliver godly out

TEMPTED. [of t.

Ex. 17 : 7. because they t. the Lord
Nu. 14 : 22. have t. me now ten times
De. 6 : 16. not tempt God as ye t. him
Ps. 78 : 18. t. God in their heart, 41.
56. Yet they t. the most high God
95 : 9. When your fa-s t. me, He. 3 : 9.
106 : 14. lusted, and t. G. in desert
Mat. 4 : 1. to be t. of the devil, Mk.
1 : 13. Lu. 4 : 2. [Master
Lu. 10 : 25. a lawyer t. him, saying,
1 Co. 10 : 9. some t. were destroyed
13. not suffer you to be t. above
Ga. 6 : 1. considering, lest thou be t.
1 Th. 3 : 5. lest tempter have t. you
He. 2 : 18. he hath suffered, be-g t. (2)
4 : 15. in all points t. like as we are
11 : 37. were sawn asunder, were t.
Ja. 1 : 13. Let no man say when he is
t., I am t. of God, for God cannot be t. with evil, nor [lust
14. every man is t. when drawn of

TEMPTER.

Mat. 4 : 3. when the t. came to him
1 Th. 3 : 5. lest t. have tempted you

TEMPTETH.

Ja. 1 : 13. cannot be tempted, nei. t.

TEMPTING.

Mat. 16 : 1. Pharisees t. Christ, and
seeking a sign, Mk. 8 : 11. Lu.
19 : 3. Pharisees came, t. him [11 : 16
22 : 35. lawyer asked quest-n, t. him
Mk. 10 : 2. lawful to put away wife ? t.
Jn. 8 : 6. this they said t. him [him

TEN.

Ge. 18 : 32. Peradv. t. sh. be found,
I will not destroy it for t. sake
24 : 10. serv. took t. camels [least t.
55. Let damsel abide few days, at
42 : 3. Joseph's t. breth. to buy corn
Ex. 26 : 1. tabern. with t. curtains,
Jos. 15 : 57. t. cities wi. villages [36 : 8.
21 : 5. Kohath had out of Eph., Dan,
Manas. t. cities, 26. 1 Ch. 6 : 61.
2 S. 15 : 16. David left t. concubines
20 : 3. king took his t. concubines
1 K. 7 : 24. t. in a cubit compassing
sea, 2 Ch. 4 : 3. [months t. days
2 Ch. 36 : 9. Jehoiachin reigned three
Ezr. 8 : 24. t. brethren with them
Ne. 11 : 1. bring one of t. to dwell at
Am. 5 : 3. leave t. to house of Israel
Hag. 2 : 16. when one came to heap
of 20 measures, there were but t.
Mat. 20 : 24. when t. heard it, Mk.
Lu. 17 : 17. were not t. cleansed [10 : 41.
Re. 17 : 12. t. horns are t. kings
See ACRES, ASSES, BASES, BATHS,
BULLOCKS, BULLS, CANDLE-
STICKS, CHANGES, CHARIOTS,
CHEESES, COMMANDMENTS.

TEN cubits. [board

Ex. 26 : 16. t. c. shall be length of
1 K. 6 : 3. t. c. breadth of porch [25, 26.
23. two cherubim each t. c. high,
24. from one wing unto other t. c.
7 : 10. foundation of stones of t. c.
23. sea t. c. fr. one brim, 2 Ch. 4 : 2.
2 Ch. 4 : 1. altar t. c. the height
Eze. 40 : 11 the breadth of gate t. c.
41 : 2. breadth of door was t. c. [c.
42 : 4. before chambers a walk of t.
Zch. 5 : 2 breadth of flying roll t. c.

See Ten DAYS.

See DEGREES, FOALS, HOMERS,
HORNS, LAVERS, LOAVES,
MEN, OXEN, PARTS, PIECES,
PILLARS, PORTIONS, POUNDS,
PRINCES, SHEKELS, SOCK-
ETS, SONS, STRINGS, TABLES,
TALENTS, TRIBES, VIRGINS,
WOMEN.

See Ten THOUSAND, S.
See Ten TIMES, Ten YEARS.

TENS. [t., 25.

Ex. 18 : 21. over them to be rulers of
De. 1 : 15. I made them captains over

TEND. [t.

Pr. 21 : 5. thoughts of diligent t. to

TENDER. [grass

Ge. 1 : † 11. Let earth bring forth t.
18 : 7. Abr. fetched calf t. and good
29 : 17. Leah was t. eyed ; but Ra.
33 : 13. My lord knoweth chil. are t.
41 : † 43. cried before him, t. father
De. 20 : † 3. Let not your hearts be t.
28 : 54. the man that is t. am. you
56. t. and delicate woman am. you
32 : 2 as the small rain upon t. herb
2 S. 3 : † 39. I am this day t. tho. king
23 : 4. as the t. grass springeth out
2 K. 22 : 19. thy heart t., 2 Ch. 34 : 27.
1 Ch. 22 : 5. Sol. is young and t., 29 : 1.
Jb. 38 : 27. bud of t. herb to spring
Pr. 4 : 3. t., beloved in sight of moth.
Is. 7 : † 4. neither let thy heart be t.
47 : 1. shalt no more be called t.
53 : 2. he sh. grow up as a t. plant
Eze. 17 : 22. I will crop off a t. one
Da. 1 : 9. G. bro-t Daniel into t. love
4 : 15. leave stump in t. grass, 23.
See BRANCH, GRAPE, S, GRASS.

See Tender MERCIES,
MERCY.

TENDERHEARTED.

2 Ch. 13 : 7. when Rehoboam was t.
Ep. 4 : 32. be kind and t. one to ano.

TENDERNESS. [for t.

De. 28 : 56. set her foot on ground

TENDETH. [life

Pr. 10 : 16. labour of righteous t. to
11 : 19. As righteousness t. to life
24. withholdeth, but it t. to pov.
14 : 23. talk of the lips t. to penury
19 : 23. fear of the Lord t. to life

TENONS.

Ex. 26 : 17. Two t. in one board, 19.-

TENOR. [36 : 22, 24.

Ge. 43 : 7. acc. to t. of these words
Ex. 34 : 27. after t. of these words I

TENT.

Ge. 9 : 21. Noah was uncovered in t.
13 : 3. Abr. went where t. had been
18. Abr. removed his t. and dwelt
18 : 1. Abr. sat in t. door in heat
2. Abr. ran to meet them from t.
6. Abr. hastened into the t. [10.
9. Where is Sarah ? he said, in t.,
24 : 67. Isaac bro-t her into Sarah's
26 : 17. Isaac pitched t. in valley [t.
25. pitched his t. at Beer-sheba
31 : 25. Jac. pitched his t. in mount
33. Laban went into Jacob's t.,
Leah's t., Rachel's t., 34.
33 : 19. Jacob bought field where
he had spread his t. [tower
35 : 21. Israel spread his t. beyond
Ex. 18 : 7. Moses and Jethro into t.
26 : 11. couple the t. together that
12. remnant of curtains of t., 13.
14. covering for t. of ram's skins
36. hanging for door of t., 36 . 19.
33 : 8. stood ev. man at his t. door
10. worship-d ev. man in his t. do.
35 : 11. make the tabernacle, his t.
36 : 18. made taches to couple the t.
39 : 33. they bro-t the t. unto Mos.
40 : 19. he spread t. over taberu.,
and put covering of t. above
Le. 14 : 8. leper sh. tarry out of his t.
Nu. 3 : 25. charge of Gershon be t.
9 : 15. cloud covered t. of testimony
11 : 10. peo. weep ev. man in his t.
19 : 14. law when a man dieth in a
t., all th. come into t., and is
in t., shall be unclean [t.
18. a clean person sh. sprinkle the
25 : 8. after the man of Isr. into t.
Jos. 7 : 21. hid in the earth in my t.
Jos. 7 : 22. they ran into the t., and
it was hid in his t. [the t.
23. they took them out of midst of
24. Joshua took Achan and his t.
Ju. 4 : 17. Sisera fled to t. of Jael, 18,
20. said, Stand in door of t. [22.
21. Jael took nail of t. and hammer
5 : 24. blessed she be ab. wom. in t.
7 : 8. ev man unto his t., 1 S. 13 : 2.
13. a cake of bread unto a t. [t.
19 : † 9. to morrow mayest go to thy
20 : 8. not any of us go to his t.
1 S. 4 : 10. fled every man into his t.,
2 S. 18 : 17.-19 : 8. [into his t.
17 : 54. Dav. put Goliath's armour
2 S. 7 : 6. I have walked in a t., 1 Ch.
16 : 22. spread Absalom a t. [17 : 5
20 : 22. retired every man to his t.
2 K. 7 : 8. lepers into one t., ano. t.
2 Ch. 25 : 22. fled every man to his t.
Jb. 21 : † 28. where is t. of tabern-es
Ps. 78 : 60. the t. he placed am. men
Is. 38 : 12. Mine age as shepherd's t.
40 : 22 spreadeth them out as a t.
54 : 2. Enlarge the place of thy t.
Je. 10 : 20. is none to stretch my t.
37 : 10. sho. rise ev. man in his t.
Eze. 23 : † 4. their names ; Samaria
See PITCH, PITCHED. [is His t.

TENT of the congregation.

Ex. 39 : 32. tabern-e of t.-finished
40. vessels of service for t.- [t.-
40 : 2. on 1st day set up tabern. of
6. set altar before tabern. of t.-
7. set laver betw. t.-and altar, 30.
22. he put table in t.- upon side of
24. he put candlestick in the t.-
26. he put golden altar in the t.-
29. altar of burnt offering by t.-
32. Wh. went into t.- they washed
34. Then a cloud covered the t.-
35. Moses not able to enter t.-

TENTS. [in t.

Ge. 4 : 20. Jabal, fa. of such as dwell
9 : 27. Jap-h sh. dwell in t. of Shem
13 : 5. Lot had flocks, herds, and t.
25 : 27. Jac. a plain man, dwel-g in t.
31 : 33. Laban into maidservants' t.
Ex. 16 : 16. gather ye for them in t.
Nu. 1 : 52. Israel shall pitch their t.
9 : 17. cloud abode, they pitched t.
18. cloud abode, they rested in
their t., 20, 22. 23. [strongholds
13 : 19. whether they dwell in t. or
16 : 26. Depart fr. t. of these wicked
27. stood in the door of their t.
24 : 2. saw Israel abiding in his t.
5. How goodly are thy t., O Jacob
De. 1 : 27. ye murmured in your t.
33. search place to pitch your t.
5 : 30. say, Get ye into your t. again
11 : 6. earth swallowed them and t.
16 : 7. shalt turn and go unto thy t.
33 : 18. Rejoice, Issachar, in thy t.
Jos. 3 : 14. when people remove fr. t.
22 : 4. return, get into your t., 6. [7.
8. Return wi. much riches unto t.,
Ju. 6 : 5. Midianites came with t.
8 : 11. way of them that dwelt in t.
1 S. 17 : 53. they spoiled Philistines' t.
2 S. 11 : 11. Isr. and Judah abide in t.
20 : 1. every man to his t., 1 K. 12 :
16. 2 Ch. 10 : 16. [2 Ch 7 : 10.
1 K. 8 . 66. Israel went unto their t.,
20 : † 12. drinking, he and k-s, in t.
2 K. 7 : 7. Syrians left their t. ; 10.
16. Israel spoiled t. of Syrians
8 : 21. peo. fled into their t., 14 : 12.
13 : 5. children of Israel dwelt in t
1 Ch. 4 : 41. th. smote the t. of Ham
5 : 10 they dwelt in Hagarites' t.
2 Ch 14 : 15. They smote t. of cattle
31 : 2. to praise in the t. of the Lord
Ezr. 8 : 15. at Ahava in t. three days
Ps. 69 : 25. let none dwell in their t.
78 : 55. made Isr. dwell in their t.
84 : 10. than dwell in t. of wickedn

Ps.106 : 25. murmured in their t. [K.
120 : 5. Woe, that I dwell in t. of
Can. 1 : 5. but comely, as t. of Kedar
8. feed kids beside shepherds' t.
Je. 4 : 20. suddenly are my t. spoiled
6 : 3. they shall pitch their t. ag. her
30 : 18. again captivity of Jacob's t.
35 : 7. all your days sh. dwell in t.
10. we have dwelt in t. and obeyed
49 : 29. their t. shall they take aw.
Ha. 3 : 7. t. of Cushan in affliction
Zch. 12 : 7. L. save t. of Judah first
14 : 15. be plague of all in these t.

TENTH.

Ge. 28 : 22. I will surely give the t.
Le. 27 : 32. t. sh. be holy unto Lord
Nu. 18 : 21. given chil. of Levi the t.
1 S. 8 : 15. k. will take t. of your seed
17. will take t. of your sheep [ah t.
1 Ch. 12 : 13. men of might, Jeremi-
24 : 11. lot came, t. to Shecaniah
25 : 17. lot came forth, t. to Shimei
Is. 6 : 13. yet in it shall be a t.
Jn. 1 : 39. it was about the t. hour
Re. 21 : 20. t. founda. a chrysoprasus
See CAPTAIN, DAY, DEAL, DEALS,
GENERATION, MONTH, PART,
SPOILS, YEAR.

TENTMAKERS.

[t.
Ac. 18 : 3. by occupation they were

TE'RAH = THA'RA.

Ge. 11 : 24. Nahor begat T., 1 Ch. 1 :
25. Nahor lived after begat T. [26.
26. T. begat Abram, 27, Jos. 24 : 2.
28. Haran died bef. his father T.
31. T. took Abram his son and Lot
32. days of T. 205 years, T. died

TERAPHIM.

Ge. 31 : † 19. Rachel had stolen the t.
Ju. 17 : 5. Micah made an ephod, t.
18 : 14. in these houses ephod and t.
17. took the ephod and t., 18, 20.
1 S. 19 : † 13. Michal took a t. and
2 K. 23 : † 24. the t. that were spied
Eze. 21 : † 21. he consulted with t.
Ho. 3 : 4. Isr. shall abide without t.
Zch. 10 : † 2. the t. have spoken van-

TE'RESH.

[ity
Es. 2 : 21. Bigthan and T. were wroth,

TERMED.

[6 : 2.
Is. 62 : 4. shalt no more be t. Forsaken, nei. thy land be t. Desol.

TERRACES.

[house
2 Ch. 9 : 11. of algum trees t. to the

TERRESTRIAL.

1 Co. 15 : 40. bodies t. the glory of t.

TERRIBLE.

Ex. 34 : 10. it is a t. thing I will do
De. 1 : 19. from Horeb we went thro.
that t. wilderness, 8 : 15.
7 : 21. L. thy G. is a mighty G., and
t., 10 : 17. Ne. 1 : 5.–4 : 14.–9 : 32.
10 : 21. hath done for thee t. things,
2 S. 7 : 23. [t.
Ju. 13 : 6. like an angel of God, very
Jb. 37 : 22. with God is t. majesty
39 : 20. the glory of his nostrils is t.
41 : 14. his teeth are t. round about
Ps. 45 : 4. shall teach thee t. things
47 : 2. the Lord Most High is t., he
65 : 5. by t. things in righteousness
66 : 3. Say unto God, How t. art
5. t. in his doing toward chil. of
68 : 35. art t. out of thy holy places
76 : 12. he is t. to kings of earth
86 : † 14. of t. men sought my soul
99 : 3. Let them praise thy t. name
106 : 22. done t. things by Red sea
145 : 6. speak of might of thy t. acts
Can. 6 : 4. t. as an army wi. banners
Is. 13 : 11. lay low haughtiness of t.
18 : 2. to a people t. fr. beginning,
21 : 1. it cometh from a t. land [7.
25 : 3. city of t. nations shall fear
49 : 25. prey of the t. sh. be deliv-d
64 : 3. when thou didst t. things
Je. 15 : 21. thee out of hand of the t.
La. 5 : 10. black, because of t. famine
Eze. 1 : 22. as colour of t. crystal
28 : 7. I will bring the t. of nations
upon thee, 30 : 11.–31 : 12. [tions
32 : 12. cause to fall the t. of na-
Da. 2 : 31. form of the image was t.
7 : 7. I saw a fourth beast t., strong
Jo. 2 : 11. day of the Lord is very t.
31. bef. great and t. day of the L.
Ha. 1 : 7. Chaldeans are t., dreadful
Zph. 2 : 11. Lord will be t. unto Moab
He. 12 : 21. so t. was sight that Moses

TERRIBLE one, s.

Is. 25 : 4. blast of t. o-s is as a storm
5. branch of t. o-s sh. be bro-t low
29 : 5. multitude of t. o-s as chaff
20. the t. o. is brought to nought
Je. 20 : 11. Lord is with me as t. o.

TERRIBLENESS.

[t.
De. 26 : 8. Lord bro-t us out wi. great
1 Ch. 17 : 21. to make thee name of t.
Je. 49 : 16. Thy t. hath deceived thee

TERRIBLY.

Is. 2 : 19. to shake t. the earth, 21.
Na. 2 : 3. fir trees shall be t. shaken

TERRIFIED.

Ge. 45 : † 3. were t. at his presence
De. 20 : 3. nei. be t. because of them
Ju. 8 : † 12. Gideon t. all the host
1 S. 16 : † 14. an evil spirit fr. Lord t.
Lu. 21 : 9. hear of wars, be not t.
24 : 37. they were t. and affrighted
Ph. 1 : 28. in nothing t. by advers-s

TERRIFIEST.

Jb. 7 : 14. thou t. me thro. visions

TERRIFY.

Jb. 3 : 5. let blackn. of the day t. it
9 : 34. his rod, and let not his fear t.
31 : 34. contempt of families t. me?
Ps. 10 : † 18. man of earth no more t.
2 Co. 10 : 9. as if I would t. you by

TERROR.

Ge. 35 : 5. t. of God was upon cities
Le. 26 : 16. I will appoint over you t.
De. 32 : 25. sword without, t. within
34 : 12. in the great t. Mos. shewed
Jos. 2 : 9. your t. is fallen upon us
Jb. 31 : 23. destruction from God a t.
33 : 7. my t. sh. not make thee afr.
Ps. 91 : 5. not afraid for t. by night
Is. 10 : 33. L. will lop bough with t.
19 : 17. Judah sh. be a t. unto Egypt
33 : 18. Thine heart sh. meditate t.
54 : 14. thou shalt be far from t.
Je. 17 : 17. Be not a t. unto me
20 : 4. I will make thee a t. to thys.
32 : 21. bro-t forth Isr. with great t.
Eze. 26 : 17. cause t. to be on all th.
21. I will make thee a t., and those,
27 : 36.–28 : 19.
32 : 23. wh. caused t. in the land,
24, 25, 26, 27.
30. with their t. they are ashamed
32. I have caused my t. in the land
Ro. 13 : 3. rulers are not a t. to good
2 Co. 5 : 11. Knowing the t. of the L.
1 Pe. 3 : 14. be not afraid of their t.

TERRORS.

[t.
De. 4 : 34. to take a nation by great
Jb. 6 : 4. t. of God do set themselves
18 : 11. t. shall make him afraid
14. it shall bring him to king of t.
20 : 25. sword cometh, t. are upon
24 : 17. in t. of the shadow of death
27 : 20. t. take hold on him as wat-s
30 : 15. t. are turned upon me
39 : † 20. glory of his nostrils are t.
Ps. 55 : 4. t. of death are upon me
73 : 19. are utterly consumed wi. t.
88 : 15. I suffer thy t. I am dis-
16. thy t. have cut me off [tracted
Je. 15 : 8. caused t. to fall upon city
La. 2 : 22. Thou hast called my t.
5 : † 10. our skin black because of t.
Eze. 21 : 12. t. by reason of sword
27 : † 36. thou sh. be t. and never
shalt be any more, 28 : † 19.

TER'TIUS.

[epistle
Ro. 16 : 22. I, T., who wrote this

TERTUL'LUS.

Ac. 24 : 1. a certain orator, named T.
2. T. began to accuse Paul

TESTAMENT, S.

Mat. 26 : 28. this is my blood in the
new t., Mk. 14 : 24. [1 Co. 11 : 25.
Lu. 22 : 20. This cup is the new t.,
Ro. 9 : † 4. to whom pertaineth t-s
2 Co. 3 : 6. able ministers of new t.
14. same vail in reading old t.
Ga. 3 : † 15. tho. it be but a man's t.
4 : † 24. for these are the two t-s
He. 7 : 22. Jesus a surety of better t.
8 : † 6. he is mediator of a better t.
9 : 15. he is mediator of the new t.
for redemption under first t.
16. where a t. is must be the death
17. t. is of force aft. men are dead
18. nei. first t. dedicated with-t bl.
20. This is the blood of the t. God
12 : † 24. Jesus, Mediator of new t.
13 : † 20. thro. blood of everlasting t.
Re. 11 : 19. seen in his temple, ark of

TESTATOR.

[his t.
He. 9 : 16. must be the death of the t.
17. is of no strength while t. liveth

TESTIFIED.

Ex. 21 : 29. it hath been t. to owner
De. 19 : 18. hath t. falsely ag. broth.
Ru. 1 : 21. the Lord hath t. ag. me
2 S. 1 : 16. thy mou. hath t. ag. thee
2 K. 17 : 13. Yet the Lord t. ag. Isr.
15. testimonies wh. he t. ag. them
2 Ch. 24 : 19. prophets t. ag. them,
Ne. 13 : 15. I t. ag. them, 21. [Ne. 9 : 26.
Je. 42 : † 19. I know I have t. ag. you
Jn. 4 : 39. saying which the wom. t.
44. Jesus t. that a prophet, 13 : 21.
Ac. 8 : 25. when they had t., preached
18 : 5. Paul t. to Jews that Jesus
23 : 11. thou hast t. of me at Jerus.
28 : 23. to wh. he t. kingd. of God
1 Co. 15 : 15. false, because we have t.
1 Th. 4 : 6. we forewarned you and t.
1 Ti. 2 : 6. who gave himself, to be t.
He. 2 : 6. one in a certain place t.
1 Pe. 1 : 11. t. beforehand sufferings
1 Jn. 5 : 9. wh. God hath t. of his Son
3 Jn. 3. t. of truth that is in thee

TESTIFIEDST.

[30.
Ne. 9 : 29. t. ag. them by thy Spirit,

TESTIFIETH.

Ho. 7 : 10. pride of Isr. t. to his face
Jn. 3 : 32. what he hath seen he t.
21 : 24. discip. wh. t. of these things
He. 7 : 17. t., Thou art a priest for
Re. 22 : 20. he which t. these things

TESTIFY.

[any person
Nu. 35 : 30. one witness not t. ag.
De. 8 : 19. I t. that ye shall perish
19 : 16. If a false witness t. ag. any
31 : 21. this song shall t. ag. them
32 : 46. Set hearts unto words which
Ne. 9 : 34. thou didst t. ag. them [I t.
Jb. 15 : 6. thine own lips t. ag. thee
Ps. 50 : 7. O Isr., I will t. ag. thee, 81 :
Is. 59 : 12. our sins t. against us [8.
Je. 14 : 7. tho. our iniqui-s t. ag. us
Ho. 5 : 5. pride of Isr. doth t. to his
Am. 3 : 13. Hear ye, t. in Jacob [face
Mi. 6 : 3. what have I done? t. ag. me
Lu. 16 : 28. send Lazarus that he t.
Jn. 2 : 25. needed not any sho. t. of
3 : 11. We t. that we have seen [man
5 : 39. Script-s are they wh. t. of me
7 : 7. me it hateth because I t. of it
15 : 26. Comforter, he shall t. of me
Ac. 2 : 40. with many words did he t.
10 : 42. to t. that it is he who was
ordained of God [God
20 : 24. to t. the gospel of grace of
26 : 5. my life know they, if wou. t.
Ga. 5 : 3. I t. to ev. man circumcised
Ep. 4 : 17. This I say, and t. in Lord
1 Jn. 4 : 14. we have seen and do t.

Re. 22 : 16. I, Jesus, have sent angel
to t. ⌈eth words
18. I t. unto every man that hear-

TESTIFYING. ⌈Greeks
Ac. 20 : 21. t. both to the Jews and
He. 11 : 4. witness, God t. of his gifts
1 Pe. 5 : 12. t. th. this is true grace of

TESTIMONIES. ⌊God
De. 4 : 45. These are the t. Mo. spake
6 : 17. Ye sh. diligently keep the t.
20. What mean the t. God com-ded
1 K. 2 : 3. to keep his statutes and his
t., 2 K. 23 : 3. 1 Ch. 29 : 19. 2 Ch.
2 K 17 : 15. they rejected his t.⌊34 : 31.
Ne. 9. 34. Nei. k-s hearkened unto thy
Ps 25 : 10. to such as keep his t. ⌊t.
78 : 56. Yet they kept not his t.
93 : 5. Thy t. are very sure ⌈nance
99 : 7. they kept his t. and the ordi-
119 . 2. Blessed they that keep his t.
14. I have rejoiced in way of thy t.
22. I have kept thy t., 167, 168.
24. Thy t. also are my delight
31. I have stuck unto thy t., O L.
36. Incline my heart unto thy t.
46. I will speak of thy t. bef. kings
59. I turned my feet unto thy t.
79. Let those have known thy t.
95. I will consider thy t. ⌊turn to
99. for thy t. are my meditation
111. Thy t. have I taken as heri-
119. therefore I love thy t. ⌊tage
125. underst g that I may know
129. Thy t. are wonderful ⌊thy t.
138. thy t. are righteous and very
144. righteousness of thy t. everl.
146. save me, and I sh. keep thy t.
152. thy t. I have known of old
157. do I not decline from thy t.
Je. 44 : 23. have not walked in his t.

TESTIMONY. ⌈the t.
Ex. 16 : 34. laid pot of manna before
25 : 16. thou shalt put into the ark
the t., 21.-40 : 20. ⌈24 : 3.
27 . 21. vail which is bef. the t., Le.
30 : 6. mercy seat over the t., Le. 16 :
36. beat small, put it before t. ⌊13.
31 : 18. gave to Moses 2 tables of t.
32 : 15. 2 tables of t. in hand, 34 : 29.
Nu. 9 : 15. cloud covered tent of t.
17 : 4. shalt lay up rods bef. the t.
10. Bring Aaron's rod bef. the t.
Ru. 4 : 7. gave his shoe, a t. in Israel
2 K. 11 : 12 gave k. the t., 2 Ch 23 : 11.
Ps. 78 : 5. established a t. in Jacob
81 : 5. ordained in Joseph for a t.
119 : 88. so I keep t. of thy mouth
122 : 4. tribes go up to t. of Israel
132 : 12. If thy chil. will keep my t.
Is. 8 : 16. Bind up the t., seal the law
20. To the law and to the t.
Mat. 8 : 4. gift Moses commanded for
a t., Mk. 1 : 44. Lu. 5 : 14
10 : 18. for a t. ag. them, Mk 13 : 9.
Mk. 6 : 11. shake off the dust for a
t., Lu. 9 : 5. ⌈for a t.
Lu. 21 : 13. And it shall turn to you
Jn. 3 : 32. no man receiveth his t.
33. He that hath received his t.
hath set to his seal that God
5 : 34. But I receive not t. fr. man
8 : 17. the t. of two men is true
21 : 24. we know that his t. is true
Ac. 13 : 22. to whom also he gave t.
14 : 3. gave t. unto word of his grace
22 : 18. they will not receive thy t.
1 Co. 1 : 6. as the t. of Christ was
confirmed in you ⌈t. of God
2 : 1. I came, declaring unto you the
2 Co. 1 : 12. the t. of our conscience
2 Th. 1 : 10. bec. our t. was believed
1 Ti. 2 : † 6. gave himself to be a t.
2 Ti. 1 : 8. Be not ashamed of t. of L.
He. 3 : 5. a t. of things which were
11 : 5. Enoch had this t. that he
Re. 1 : 2. who bare record of t. of Jes.
9. in isle of Patmos for t. of Jesus

Re. 6 : 9. souls of them slain for the t.
11 : 7. when have finished their t.
12 : 11. overcame by word of their t.
17. war wi. them wh. have t. of Jes.
15 : 5. tabernacle of the t. in heaven
19 : 10. that have the t. of Jesus,
for the t. of Jesus is spirit of

Ark of the TESTIMONY.
Ex. 25 : 22. cheru-m wh. are upon - t.
26 : 33. mayest bri. within vail - t.
34. put mercy seat upon the - t.
30 : 6. put altar bef. vail by the - t.
26. thou shalt anoint the - t.
31 : 7. wisdom that they make - t.
39 : 35. they bro-t unto Moses - t.
40 : 3. shalt put in tabernacle - t.
5. set altar of gold for me bef. - t.
21. Moses covered - t. as L. com-d
Nu. 4 : 5. Aaron and sons sh. cov. - t.
7 : 89. mercy seat was upon - t.⌈- t.
Jos. 4 : 16. command priests th. bare
See **TABERNACLE of testimony.**

TETRARCH.
Lu. 3 : 1. brother Philip, t. of Iturea
and Lysanias t. of Abilene

Herod the TETRARCH.
Mat. 14 : 1. H., t., heard fame of Jes.
Lu. 3 : 1. H., being t. of Galilee
19. H., t. being reproved by John
9 : 7. H., t., heard of all th. was done
Ac. 13 : 1. Manaen bro-t up wi. H., t.

THAD'DEUS. ⌈was T.
Mat. 10 : 3. Lebbeus, whose surname
Mk. 3 : 18. T. and Simon, Canaanite

THA'HASH. See REUMAH.

THA'MAH = TA'MAH.
Ezr. 2 : 53. The Nethinim ; chil. of T.

THA'MAR = TA'MAR.
Mat. 1 : 3. Judas begat Phares of T.

THAN.
Le. 14 : 37. in sight lower t. the wall
1 S. 27 : 1. nothing better for me t.
Ec. 5 : 8. he that is higher t. highest regardeth ; be higher t. they
Mat. 10 : 15. for Sodom t. for that
city, 11 : 22, 24. Mk. 6 : 11. Lu.
10 : 12, 14 ⌈Lu. 15 : 7.
18 : 13. t. of the ninety and nine,
19 : 24. easier t. for a rich man to
enter, Mk. 10 : 25. Lu 18 : 25.
Mk. 9 : 43. t., 45. 47. Lu 18 : 14. Jn.
1 : 50.-4 : 1.-5 : 20. Ac. 15 : 28 -
25 : 6. 1 Co. 7 : 9.-14 : 5, 19. Ga.
4 : 27. He. 11 : 25, 26. 1 Pe. 3 :
17. 2 Pe 2 : 21. ⌈light
Lu. 16 : 8. are wiser t. children of
17. t. one tittle of the law to fail
17 : 2. t. that he should offend one
Ro. 13 : 11. nearer t. when we believ.
1 Co. 3 : 11. founda. can no man lay t.
2 Co. 1 : 13. none other t. what ye read
Ga. 1 : 8. preach other gospel t., 9.
He. 2 : 7. madest him little lower t., 9.
3 : 3. worthy of more glory t. Moses
4 : 12. sharper t. twoedged sword
11 : 4. excellent sacrif. t. Cain, 9 : 23.
See BETTER, GREATER, MORE, RATHER, THESE, THEY, THOSE.

THANK.
Lu. 6 : 32. if ye love them wh. love
you, wha' t. have ye ? 33, 34.
1 Pe. 2 : † 19. this is t. if a man endure grief ⌈t.
†20. if ye take it patiently, this is
See **Thank OFFERINGS.**

THANKS.
Ezr. 3 : 11. sang, giving t. unto Lord
Ne. 12 : 31. companies th. gave t., 38.
40. stood 2 companies th. gave t.
Ps. 42 : † 5. for I shall yet give t.
Da. 6 : 10. he prayed and gave t.
Mat. 26 : 27. he took the cup, gave
t., †26. Lu. 22 : 17. ⌈Mat. 15 : 36.
Mk. 8 : 6. took seven loaves, gave t.,
14 : 23. had given t. he gave it to
Lu. 2 : 38. Anna gave t. unto the L.

Lu. 17 : 16. fell at his feet giving t.
22 : 19. he took bread, and gave t.
Jn. 6 : 11. had given t. he distrib-d
23. did eat bread, aft. L. had giv. t.
Ac. 27 : 35. Paul took bread, gave t.
Ro. 14 : 6. He th. ea-eth giveth G. t. ;
he eateth not, and giveth G. t.
1 Co. 11 : 24. had given t. he brake it
14 : 16. say Amen at thy giving of t.
17. For thou verily givest t. well
15 : 57. t. be to G., wh. giveth vict-y
2 Co. 1 : 11. t. be given on our behalf
2 : 14. t. unto God who causeth us
8 : 16. t. to God who put same care
9 : 15. t. unto God for his unspeak.
Ep. 5 : 20. Giving t. for all things, 4.
Col. 1 : 12. Giving t. unto the Father
3 : 17. giving t. to God and the Fa.
1 Th. 3 : 9. what t. can we render to
1 Ti. 2 : 1. intercessions, giving of t.
He. 13 : 15. sacrif. of praise, giving t.
Re. 4 : 9. give t. to him on throne
See **GIVE thanks.**

THANK, ED.
2 S. 14 : 22. Joab bowed and t-d king
1 K. 8 : † 66. the people t-d the king
1 Ch. 16 : 4. appointed Levites to t. L.
7. Da. delivered this psalm to t. L.
23 : 30. every morning to t. the L
29 : 13. we t. thee and praise thy na.
Da. 2 : 23. I t. and praise thee, O G.
Mat. 11 : 25. I t. thee, O Fa., Lu. 10 : 21.
Lu. 17 : 9. Doth he t. that servant ?
18 : 11. I t. thee I am not as other
Jn. 11 : 41. I t. thee, thou heardest
Ac. 28 : 15. Paul t-d God, took cour.
Ro. 1 : 8. I t. my God thro. Jes., 7 : 25.
6 : 17. God be t-d ye were servants
1 Co. 1 : 4. I t. my God on y-r behalf
14. I t. God I baptized none of you
14 : 18. I t. G. I speak wi. tongues
Ph. 1 : 3. I t. God upon ev. rememb.
1 Th. 2 : 13. For this cause also t. we
2 Th. 1 : 3. bound to t. God for you
1 Ti. 1 : 12. I t. Jes. Ch. who enabled
2 Ti. 1 : 3. I t. God whom I serve
Phm. 4. I t. my God, making men-

THANKFUL. ⌊tion
Ps. 100 : 4. be t. unto him, Col. 3 : 15.
Ro. 1 : 21. glorified him not, nei. were

THANKFULNESS. ⌊t.
Ac. 24 : 3. we accept it, noble Felix.

THANKING. ⌊with t.
2 Ch. 5 : 13. singers as one in t. the

THANKSGIVING, S. ⌊L.
Le. 7 : 12. If he offer it for a t., 13, 15.
-22 : 29. ⌈prayer
Ne. 11 : 17. principal to begin t. in
12 : 8. over the t., he and his breth.
27. to keep the dedication with t-s
46. songs of praise and t. unto G.
Ps. 26 : 7. That I may publish with t.
50 : 14. Offer unto God t., pay vows
69 : 30. I will magnify him with t.
95 : 2. Let us come bef. his face wi. t.
100 : 4. Enter into his gates with t.
107 : 22. sacrifice sacrifices of t.
116 : 17. I will offer sacrifices of t.
147 : 7. Sing unto the Lord with t.
Is. 51 : 3. t. and melody sh. be found
Je. 30 : 19. out of them sh. proceed t.
Am. 4 : 5. offer a sacrifice of t.
Jon. 2 : 9. sacrifice with voice of t.
1 Co. 10 : † 30. if I by t. be partaker
2 Co. 4 : 15. grace thro. the t. of many
9 : 11. causeth thro. us t. to God
12. abundant by many t-s unto G.
Ph. 4 : 6. with t. let your requests
Col. 2 : 7. in the faith, abound. wi. t.
4 : 2. Continue and watch with t.
1 Ti. 4 : 3. created to be rec-d with t.
4. creature good if received with t.
Re. 7 : 12. t. and honour be to our G.

THANKWORTHY.
1 Pe. 2 : 19. is t. if man endure grief

THA'RA = TE'RAH.
Ge 11 : †24. Nahor begat T., Lu. 3 : 34.

THAR'SHISH. See TARSHISH.

THAT, or THAT which.
Ge. 1 : 31. ev. thing t. he had made
2 : 11. t. is it w. compasseth land
19. What Adam called t. was name
3 : 13. what is this t. thou hast done
18 : 25. t. far fr. thee, to slay righte.
30 : 33. t. shall be counted stolen
Ex. 13 : 8. t. 20 : 4. 2 S. 17 : 12. 1 K.
3 : 4. Ezr. 4 : 11. Ps. 10 : 2.-17 :
9.-132 : 12. Is. 42 : 17.-43 : 8.
Da. 7 : 20. Mat. 2 : 6.-18 : 28.-
27 : 62. Mk. 9 : 39. Lu. 7 : 29.
Jn. 3 : 31 (3).-8 : 25.-10 : 41.-16 :
15. Ro. 6 : 2.-7 : †6.-11 : 7. Ph.
1 : 10. 1 Ti. 5 : 4. Re. 1 : 12.-17 : 8.
30 : 38. Whosoever make like unto t.
34 : 34. Moses spake t. w. he was
Le. 6 : 5. t. about w. he hath sworn
10 : 20. Moses heard t. was content
Nu. 6 : 21. besides t. his hand sh. get
22 : 20. word w. I say, t. sh. thou do
24 : 13. what the Lord saith, t. will
I speak, 1 K. 22 : 14.
32 : 24. do t. w. proceeded out of
mouth, Ju. 11 : 36. [t.
Ju. 8 : 3. anger abated when he said
21 : 25. did t. w. was right in own
1 S. 9 : 24. t. w. is left set it before
13 : 14. not kept t. w. L. com-ded
21 : 9. Goliath's sword, if thou taket.
24 : 19. for t. thou hast done unto
30 : 23. with t. w. L. hath given us
31 : 11. heard t. w. Philis. had done
2 S. 12 : 8. if t. had been too little, I
19 : 6. in t. thou lovest enemies and
7. t. worse than evil t. befell thee
24 : 10. I sinned in t. I have done
24. offer of t. w. doth cost nothing
1 K. 14 : 8. to do t. w. was right, 2 K.
2 K. 19 : 20. t. w. thou prayed ag. [15 : 3.
23 : 17. What title is t. t. I see
1 Ch. 4 : 10. G. granted t. w. he request.
2 Ch. 6 : 15. t. w. thou hast prom., 16.
28 : 1. Ahaz did not t. w. was right
Ezr. 6 : 9. t. w. they have need of
7 : 18. t. do after will of your God
Jb. 3 : 25. t. w. I was afraid of is co.
15 : 17. t. w. I have seen I declare
20 : 20. not save of t. w. he desired
23 : 13. soul desireth t. he doeth
34 : 32. t. w. I see not, teach me
Ps. 24 : 6. t. seek him, t. seek thy face
27 : 4. t. will I seek t. I may dwell
69 : 4. restored t. w. I took not aw.
10. I wept, t. was to my reproach
Ec. 1 : 9. thing t. hath been, it is t.
w. shall be; t. w. is done, is t.
w. shall be done [numbered
15. t. w. is wanting cannot be
2 : 3. see what was t. good for men
12. t. w. hath been already done
3 : 9. profit in t. wh-n he labour-h
15. God requireth t. w. is past (2)
5 : 4. pay t. w. thou hast vowed
8 : 7. he knoweth not t. w. shall be
11 : 6. knowest not this or t. prosper
Is. 17 : 8. neither respect t. w. his fin-
21 : 10. t. w. I heard of L. [gers made
52 : 15. t. w. had not been told sh.
they see, t. not heard sh. they
55 : 11. So my word be t. goeth forth
Je. 15 : 4. t. w. Manasseh did in Jeru.
37 : 15. they had made t. the prison
45 : 4. t. w. I built, t. w. I planted
Da. 11 : 36. t. t. is determined sh. be
Zeh. 11 : 9. t. t. dieth, let it die (2)
Mat. 1 : 20. t. w. is conceived in her
13 : 12. be taken away t. he hath,
25 : 29. Mk. 4 : 25. Lu. 8 : 18.-19 : 26.
15 : 11. not t. w. goeth into mou. (2)
17 : 27. t. take, gi. for me and thee (2)
20 : 7. whatso. right t. ye sh. receive
23 : 3. All they bid, t. observe and
26 : 12. in t. she hath poured oint.
27 : 4. Wh. is t. to us? See thou to t.
9. price of him t. was valued [ful?
Mk. 2 : 24. why do t. w. is not law-
Mk. 4 : 15. Satan taketh word t. was
7 : 20. t. w. cometh out, t. defileth
13 : 11. be given in t. hour, t. speak
Lu. 4 : 6. for t. is delivered unto me
5 : 25. took up t. whereon he lay
6 : 2. Why do ye t. w. is not lawful
11 : 40. Ye fools, did not he t. made
t. w. is without make t. within?
16 : 12. not faithf. in t. w. is anoth.
15. t. w. is highly esteemed [man's
17 : 10. have done t. w. was our duty
19 : 21. takest up t. layest not do.,
reapest t. thou didst not sow, 22.
23 : 48. people t. came to t. sight
24 : 12. wondering at t. w. was come
Jn. 1 : 9. t. was the true Light w.
2 : 10. good wine, then t. w. is worse
3 : 6. t. w. is born of flesh, t. w. is
11. we speak t. we know, testify t.
32. what he hath seen t. testifieth
4 : 18. not husband in t. saidst truly
38. to reap t. wherein ye no labour
39. He told me all t. ever I did [11.
5 : 12. What man is t. w. said, Take,
8 : 38. I speak t. w. I have seen wi.
my Fa.; ye do t. w. ye have seen
11 : 4. Jes. heard t., said, This sickn.
29. soon as she heard t. she arose
52. gather chil. of G., t. were scat.
13 : 27. t. thou doest, do quickly
14 : 13. whatso. ye ask t. will I do
16 : 13. Whatso. he sh. hear, t. speak
17. what this t. he saith unto us
19. do ye inquire of t. I said [24.
21 : 22. What is t. to thee, follow me,
Ac. 2 : 16. is t. w. was spoken by Joel
3 : 10. with wonder at t. w. happ-d
4 : 21. glorified G. for t. w. was done
24. heard t. they lifted up, 5 : 21, 33.
Ro. 1 : 19. t. w. may be known of G.
6 : 10. in t. he died, in t. he liveth
7 : 6. t. being dead wherein we were
13. Was then t. w. is good made
15. t. w. I do, I allow not; what I
would, t. do I not, 20. (3) [cons-t
16. If, then, I do t. w. I wou. not I
18. perform t. w. is good I find not
19. For the good t. I would I do
not; the evil I would not t. I do
13 : 11. And t. 1 Co. 6 : 6, 8. Ep. 2 :
8. Ph. 1 : 28. [t. w. is good
16 : 19. would have you wise unto
1 Co. 10 : 19. idol, or t. w. is off-d [w.
30. why am I evil spoken of for t.
11 : 23. t. w. I delivered unto you
13 : 10. t. w. is perfect, t. in part
15 : 37. t. w. thou sowest thou sowest not t. body w. sh. [but t. w.
46. t. was not first w. is spiritual,
16 : 17. t. w. was lacking on your
2 Co. 3 : 11. if t. w. was done away
8 : 11. performance out of t. w. ye
11 : 12. what I do, t. I will do [Lord
17. t. w. I speak I speak not after
Ga. 6 : 7. man soweth t. sh. he reap
Ep. 1 : 21. every name t. is named
2 : 11. t. w. is called circumcision
3 : 20. acc-g to the power t. work-h
Ph. 3 : 12. apprehend t. for w. I am
1 Th. 3 : 10. perfect t. w. is lacking
5 : 21. hold fast t. w. is good [come
1 Ti. 4 : 8. life t. now is and t. w. is to
6 : 20. keep t. w. is committed to thy
Phm. 8. enjoin t. w. is convenient
18. oweth put t. on mine account
He. 2 : 18. in t. he hath suffered, is
able to succour them t. are
5 : 7. was heard in t. he feared (2)
6 : 19. entereth into t. within vail
8 : 13. In t. he saith, A new covenant. Now t. w. waxeth old is
12 : 20. not endure t. w. was comm.
13 : 17. t. unprofitable for you [t.
Ja. 4 : 15. If L. will, we sh. do this or
1 Pe. 3 : 13. who t. will harm you if
followers of t. w. is good, 3 Jn. 11.
1 Jn. 1 : 1. t. w. was fr. the beginning
1 Jn. 1 : 3. t. w. we have seen we decl.
2 : 24. Let t. abide in you, w. ye
2 Jn. 5. com-t t. w. we had fr. beg'n-g
3 Jn. 11. follow not t. w. is evil. He
t. doeth good is of God (4)
See **That WHICH.**

Above THAT. [written
1 Co. 4 : 6. not think of men a. t. is
10 : 13. not tempted a. t. ye are able
2 Co. 12 : 6. lest any think of me a. t.

Above all THAT. [16 : 30.
1 K. 14 : 9. done evil – t. were before
22. sins committed – t. their fathers
2 K. 21 : 11. wickedly – t. Amorites
1 Ch. 29 : 3. gold above – t. I prepar.
Ec. 2 : 7. posses-ns – t. were in Jerus.
Lu. 13 : 4. sinners – t. dwelt in Jerus.
Ep. 3 : 20. do – t. we ask or think
2 Th. 2 : 4. himself – t. is called God

According to THAT.
Ge. 27 : 8. Now obey – t. I command
Jos. 24 : 5. – t. which I did am. them
Ju. 11 : 36. do to me – t. wh. proceeded
2 K. 14 : 6. slew not – t. is written
2 Ch. 35 : 26. goodness – t. was writ.
Ezr. 6 : 13. Tatnai did – t. Darius sent
Ro. 4 : 18. – t. was spoken. So they
2 Co. 5 : 10. – t. he hath done, good
8 : 12. – t. a man hath; not – t. he

According to all THAT.
Ge. 6 : 22. Noah did – t. God, 7 : 5.
Ex. 25 : 9. – t. I shew thee aft. pattern
31 : 11. – t. I have commanded thee,
36 : 1.-39 : 32, 42.-40 : 16. Nu.
2 : 34.-8 : 20.-9 : 5.-29 : 40. De.
1 : 3, 41.-26 : 14.-30 : 2. 1 K. 9 :
4. 2 K. 21 : 8. (2) 1 Ch. 6 : 49. 2
Ch. 7 : 17. Je. 11 : 4.-50 : 21.
Nu. 30 : 2. if vow he sh. do – t. proceedeth out of his mouth [4 : 34.
De. 1 : 30. – t. he did for you in Eg.
17 : 10. sh. do – t. they inform thee
18 : 16. – t. thou desiredst of the L.
24 : 8. – t. the priests sh. teach you
Jos. 1 : 8. to do – t. is written, 8 : 34.
1 Ch. 16 : 40. [Libnah, 35.
10 : 32. smote it – t. he had done to
11 : 23. – t. the L. said unto Moses
Ru. 3 : 6. did – t. her mother bade
2 S. 7 : 22. – t. we have heard
9 : 11. – t. king hath commanded
1 K. 5 : 6. give hire – t. thou shalt
8 : 43. do – t. stranger calleth for
56. rest unto peo., – t. he prom-d
11 : 37. reign – t. thy soul desireth
22 : 53. he provoked the Lord, – t.
his father had done, 2 K. 23 : 32,
37.-24 : 9, 19. 2 Ch. 26 : 4.-27 : 2.
2 K. 10 : 30. unto Ahab – t. was in
mine heart [18 : 3. 2 Ch. 29 : 2.
15 : 3. did right – t. his fa. had done,
16 : 11. Urijah built altar – t. Ahaz
22 : 13. not hearkened to do – t.
24 : 3. sins of Manasseh – t. he did
1 Ch. 6 : 49. atonement – t. Moses
Ne. 5 : 19. – t. I have done for this peo.
Es. 3 : 12. – t. Haman commanded
4 : 17. Mord. did – t. Esther comm
8 : 9. written – t. Mordecai com-ded
Is. 63 : 7. – t. L. hath bestowed on us
Je. 35 : 10. done – t. Jonadab commanded, 18. [commanded
36 : 8. Baruch did – t. Jeremiah
42 : 20. – t. Lord our God shall say
50 : 29. – t. she hath done, do unto
52 : 2. evil – t. Jehoiakim had done
Eze. 24 : 24. – t. Ezekiel hath done

After THAT.
Ge. 6 : 4. a. t., when sons of G. came
13 : 14. a. t., Le. 13 : 55. Nu. 30 : 15.
2 S. 1 : 10. 1 Ch. 2 : 24. 2 Ch. 25 :
14. Je. 12 : 15.-24 : 1.-28 : 12.-
29 : 2.-34 : 8.-36 : 27.-51 : 46.
Mk. 12 : 34. He. 7 : 2.-10 : 15, 26.
18 : 5. a. t. ye shall pass on [sh. go
24 : 55. with us few days: a. t. she
25 : 26. a. t. came his brother out

Ge. 45 : 15. a.t. breth-n talked with
Ex. 3 : 20. a.t. he will let you go
7 : 25. a.t. Lord had smitten river
11 : 8. a.t. I will go out. He went
Le. 14 : 8. a.t. he sh. come into camp
43. a.t. he hath taken away stones
15 : 28. a.t. she shall be clean
25 : 48. a.t. he is sold be redeemed
Nu. 4 : 15. a.t. sons of Kohath shall
6 : 20. a.t. Nazar-e may drink wine
7 : 88. dedica. a.t. altar was anoint-
8 : 15. a.t. sh. Levites go in, 22.[ed
9 : 17. a.t. chil. of Israel journeyed
12 : 14. a.t. let her be received again
De. 21 : 13. a.t. go in unto her
24 : 4. not take her a.t. she is defiled
Jos. 24 : 20. a.t. he hath done you
Ju. 15 : 7. Samson said a.t. I cease
1 S. 10 : 5. a.t. thou come to hill of G.
2 S. 21 : 14. a.t. God was entreated
1 K. 3 : 18. 3d day a.t. I was deliv-d
2 K. 14 : 22. a.t. king slept with fa-s
Ezr. 5 : 12. a.t. our fa-s had provoked
Jb. 21 : 3. a.t. I have spoken, mock
Ec. 9 : 3. a.t. they go to the dead[on
Je. 31 : 19. a.t. I was turned, repent-
40 : 1. a.t. Neb-n let him go [ed (2)
Da. 4 : 26. a.t. thou sh. have known
Mat. 27 : 31. a.t. they had mocked
Mk. 1 : 14. a.t. John was put in pris.
4 : 28. a.t. the full corn in the ear
8 : 25. a.t. put his hands upon eyes
9 : 31. a.t. he is killed sh. rise[20 : 40.
12 : 34. no man a.t. durst ask, Lu.
14 : 28. a.t. am risen I will go[form
16 : 12. a.t. he appeared in another
Lu. 12 : 4. a.t. no more t. they can
13 : 9. a.t. thou shalt cut it down
15 : 4. go a.t. which is lost until
Jn. 6 : 23. a.t. L. had given thanks
11 : 7. a.t. saith to disciples, Let
11. a.t. he saith, Our friend Laz.
13 : 5. a.t. poureth water into basin
21 : 14. a.t. he was risen from dead
Ac. 1 : 2. a.t. he thro. Holy Ghost
8. receive power a.t. Holy Ghost
7 : 7. a.t. sh. they serve me in this
36. a.t. he had shewed wonders
9 : 23. a.t. many days were fulfilled
13 : 20. a.t. he gave them judges
1 Co. 1 : 21. For a.t. in wisdom of G.
7 : 7. one aft. this manner, ano. a.
12 : 28. a.t. miracles, then gifts [t.
15 : 6. a.t. he was seen of above 500
7. a.t. he was seen of James; then
Ga. 3 : 25. But a.t. faith is come we
4 : 9. now a.t. ye have known God
Ep. 1 : 13. a.t. ye heard the word(2)
1 Th. 2 : 2. a.t. we had suffered bef.
Tit. 3 : 4. a.t. the kindness of God
He. 7 : 2. being a.t. king of Salem
10 : 15. for a.t. he had said before
Re. 15 : 5. a.t. I looked and behold
20 : 3. a.t. he must be loosed

All THAT.

Ge. 7 : 22. a.t. was in dry land died
9 : 2. fear of you upon a.t. moveth
10. from a.t. go out of the ark
17 : 23. (2) a. t. 32 : 19. -34 : 24,
29. -39 : 8. -42 : 29. -45 : 11. -50 :
14. Ex. 18 : 12. -23 : 22. -34 : 19.
Le. 7 : 9. -27 : 9. Nu. 4 : 23, 37. -
11 : 32 (2). -19 : 14 (2). De. 3 :
18. -5 : 27, 28. -25 : 18. -Jos. 10 :
40. Ju. 9 : 25. Ru. 4 : 9. 1 S. 2 :
22. -9 : 6. -10 : 11. -15 : 3. -30 : 18,
19. 2 S. 3 : 19. -11 : 22. -16 : 4. -
18 : 32. 1 K. 11 : 41. 2 K. 10 : 11.
-18 : 12. -20 : 13, 17. -24 : 7. 1 Ch.
10 : 11. -26 : 28. 2 Ch. 7 : 11. -28 :
15 (2). -29 : 29. -34 : 12, 16, 32,
33. Ne. 8 : 2. -10 : 28. Es. 1 : 13. -
4 : 1. Jb. 1 : 11. Ps. 5 : 11. -74 : 3. -86 :
5. -89 : 41. Ec. 9 : 1. -11 : 8. Is.
19 : 10. -22 : 3. -29 : 7, 20 -39 : 2,
6. -45 : 24. -61 : 2. Je. 17 : 13. -20 :
6, -30 : 16, 20. -50 : 7, 10, 33. La.

1 : 8. -2 : 4, 15. Eze. 14 : 22, 23. -
20 : 26. -27 : 29. -31 : 14. Zch. 12 :
3. Mal. 4 : 1. Mat. 8 : 16. -13 : 46.
-14 : 35. -18 : 32. Mk. 1 : 32. Lu.
2 : 47. -5 : 9. -14 : 29. -24 : 25. Jn.
5 : 28. -6 : 37. Ac. 2 : 44. -4 : 23. -
6 : 15. -9 : 14, 21, 35. -10 : 38. -
14 : 27 -16 : 3. -28 : 30. 2 Th. 2 : 4.
2 Ti. 3 : 12. 1 Pe. 5 : 14. Re. 18 :
8. -18 : 19, 24. [are thine
Ge. 20 : 7. shalt die, thou and a. t.
16. covering of eyes unto a.t. are
21 : 6. a.t. hear will laugh with me
12. in a.t. Sarah hath said heark.
22. God wi. thee in a.t. thou doest
23 : 10. audience of a.t. went in, 18.
28 : 22. of a.t. thou sh. give me, 10th
31 : 1. Jac. taken a.t. was our fa-'s
12. I have seen a.t. Laban doeth
43. Laban ans-d a.t. seest is mine
35 : 2. Jacob unto a.t. were wi. him
39 : 3. Lord made a.t. he did prosp.
45 : 10. be near me a.t. thou hast, 11.
Ex. 7 : 2. thou shalt speak a. t. I
command, 6 : 29. -34 : 32. [dren's
9 : 4. noth. die of a.t. is the chil-
10 : 12. locusts eat a.t. hail hath left
18 : 1. a. t. G. had done for Isr., 8.
24. Mos. did a.t. Jethro had said
19 : 8. a.t. L. spoken we do, 24 : 7.
20 : 11. heaven, earth, sea, and a.t.
is therein, De. 10 : 14 Ne. 9 : 6.
Ps. 146 : 6. Ac. 4 : 24. -14 : 15. Re.
23 : 22. if th. do a.t. I speak [5 : 13.
31 : 6. wisdom th. they may make
a.t. I comm-ded, 35 : 10. -38 : 22.
40 : 9. a.t. is therein, Le. 8 : 10.
Nu. 4 : 16. De. 13 : 15. Jos. 6 :
17, 24. 2 K. 15 : 16. 1 Ch. 16 : 32.
Ps. 96 : 12. Is. 34 : 1. -42 : 10.
Je. 8 : 16. -47 : 2 (2). -51 : 48. Eze.
12 : 19 (2). -30 : 12. Am. 6 : 8.
Mi. 1 : 2. Ha. 2 : 8, 17. [done
Le. 6 : 7. be forgiven for a.t. he hath
11 : 9. These shall ye eat of a.t. are
in waters, De. 14 : 9. [ination
10 a.t. have not fins sh. be abom-
31. unclean to you am. a.t. creep
14 : 36. a.t. is in house be not uncl.
23 : 42. a.t. are Israelites born shall
26 : 44. for a.t. I will not cast away
Nu. 1 : 3. a.t. are able to go to war,
20, 22, 24. 2 K. 3 : 21. -24 : 16.
2 : 9. a.t. were numbered, 16, 24,
31, 32. -3 : 39. -4 : 46. -14 : 29.
4 : 41. of a.t. might do service [33.
16 : 30. swallow them up with a.t.
22 : 4. shall lick up a.t. is about us
23 : 26. a.t. Lord speaketh must I
De. 3 : 21. seen a.t. Lord hath done
unto two kings, 29 : 2. Jos. 9 : 10.
8 : 13. a.t. thou hast is multiplied
12 : 11. a.t. I command you, 14. -
18 : 18. Jos. 1 : 16. Ju. 13 : 14. 2 Ch.
33 : 8. [thou doest, 10. -24 : 19.
15 : 18. Lord shall bless thee in a.t.
18 : 12. a.t. do these things are
abomina-n, 22 : 5. -25 : 16. [take
20 : 14. women and a.t. is in city
29 : 9. may prosper in a.t. ye do,
1 K. 2 : 3. [est, 22 : 2. Je. 32 : 23.
Jos. 1 : 18. in a.t. thou command-
2 : 13. save brethren a.t. they have
9 : 9. fame of him a.t. he did in Eg.
Ju. 8 : 10. a.t. were left of host[ware
13 : 13. Of a.t. I said to woman be-
19 : 30. a.t. saw it, said no such deed
20 : 48. smote men and a.t. came to
Ru. 2 : 11. a.t. thou done unto moth.
3 : 5. a.t. thou sayest I will do, 11.
16. she told her a.t. man had done
1 S. 8 : 7. Hearken unto the people
in a.t. they say, 12 : 1.
9 : 19. tell a.t. is in thine heart[7 : 3.
14 : 7. Do a.t. is in thine heart, 2 S.
15 : 9. Saul spared best of a.t. was
19 : 18. told Sam. a.t. Saul had do.

1 S. 25 : 21. a.t. this fellow hath, 22.
2 S. 3 : 21. reign ov. a.t. heart desireth
25. Abner came to know a.t. thou
16 : 21. of a.t. are wi. thee be strong
21 : 14. performed a.t. king comm.
1 K. 4 : 27. victuals for a.t. came
8 : 52. hearken in a.t. they call for
10 : 2. communed of a.t. was in her
heart, 2 Ch. 9 : 1. [mand
11 : 38. hearken unto a.t. I com-
41. acts of Sol-n and a.t. he did
14 : 9. evil above a.t. were, 16 : 25,
22. above a.t. their fa-s had [30.
20 : 4. I am thine and a.t. I have
9. a.t. thou didst send for I will do
2 K. 8 : 6. saying, Restore a.t. was
10 : 5. we will do a.t. thou bid[hers
12 : 12. for a.t. was laid out for hou.
1 Ch. 5 : 20. Hagarites, a.t. were wi.
29 : 3. a.t. I prepared for house
11. a.t. is in the heaven and in
2 Ch. 31 : 19. a.t. were reckoned by
32 : 31. know a.t. was in his heart
34 : 13. overseers of a.t. wrought
21. aft. a.t. is written in book
Ezr. 1 : 6. a.t. was willingly offered
9 : 13. aft. a.t. is come upon us
Ne. 9 : 33. just in a.t. is bro-t upon
Es. 4 : 7. Mord. told a.t. had happ-d
6 : 10. fail of a.t. thou hast spoken
Jb. 2 : 4. a.t. a man hath will he give
8 : 13. So are paths of a.t. forget G.
Ps. 41 : 7. a.t. hate me whisper tog.
64 : 8. a.t. see them shall flee away
76 : 11. let a.t. be about him bring
103 : 1. a.t. is within me bless
145 : 14. Lord upholdeth a.t. fall
Ec. 2 : 7. above a.t. were in Jerus., 9.
6 : 2. wanteth noth. of a.t. he desir.
9 : 3. a.t. are done under the sun
Is. 36 : 6. so is Pha. to a.t. trust in
39 : 4. a.t. is in mine house [edge
61 : 9. a.t. see them sh. acknowl-
Je. 9 : 26. a.t. are in utmost, 25 : 23.
25 : 13. a.t. is written in this book
26 : 8. Jer. speaking a.t. L. comm.
28 : 6. a.t. is carried captive, 29 : 4.
31 : 37. will cast off Isr. for a.t. [ed
35 : 8. obeyed a.t. Jonadab charg-
38 : 9. a.t. they have done to Jer-h
Eze. 5 : 14. make thee a reproach in
sight of a.t. pass by, 36 : 34.
12 : 14. scatter a.t. are about him
16 : 54. confounded in a.t. thou hast
63. pacified for a.t. th. hast done
26 : 17. terror on a.t. haunt it
28 : 24. nor thorn of a.t. are about
40 : 4. set heart upon a.t. I shall
shew; declare a.t. thou seest
43 : 11. ashamed of a.t. they have
44 : 5. hear a.t. I say unto thee[in
14. keepers for a.t. be done there-
Na. 3 : 19. a.t. hear bruit of thee
Zph. 3 : 19. I will undo a.t. afflict
Mat. 5 : 15. light unto a.t. are in hou.
18 : 31. told their lord a.t. was done
34. till he sho. pay a.t. was due
Lu. 1 : 65. fear came on a.t. dwelt
71. saved fr. hand of a.t. hate us
5 : 9. astonished, and a.t. were wi.
9 : 7. Herod heard of a.t. was done
10. apost. told him a.t. they had
15 : 31. Son, a.t. I have is thine
18 : 12. give tithes of a.t. I possess
22. sell a.t. thou hast, distribute
Jn. 4 : 39. told me a.t. ever I did, 29.
10 : 8. a.t. came bef. me are thieves
Ac. 1 : 1. of a.t. Jesus began to do
2 : 39. promise to a.t. are afar off
13 : 29. fulfilled a.t. was written of
39. by him a.t. believe are justified
16 : 32. spake unto a.t. were in hou.
26 : 29. I wo. thou and a.t. hear me
Ro. 1 : 7. To a.t. be in Rome [call
10 : 12. same Lord is rich unto a.t.
1 Co. 1 : 2. with a.t. call upon our L.
14 : 21. for a.t. th. will not hear me

Ep. 3 : 20. to do above **a.t.** we ask
1 Th. 1 : 7. ensamples to **a.t.** believe
1 Ti. 2 : 2. for **a.t.** are in authority
Tit. 3 : 15. **a.t.** are with me salute
He. 3 : 16. not **a.t.** came out of Eg.
1 Jn. 2 : 16. For **a.t.** is in the world
Jude 15. convince **a.t.** are ungodly

All THAT
he had, or she had.

Ge. 12 : 20. sent Abr. away, his wife, and **a.t.** - ⌈wife, **a.t.** -
13 : 1. Abr. went out of Egypt, his
24 : 2. serv-t that ruled over **a.t.** -
25 : 5. Abr. gave **a.t.** - unto Isaac
31 : 21. Jacob fled with **a.t.** - ⌈5, 6.
39 : 4. **a.t.** - into Joseph's hand,
5. blessing of Lord was upon **a.t.** -
Mat. 13 : 46. sold **a.t.** - and bou-t it
18 : 25. him to be sold, chil., **a.t.** -
Mk. 5 : 26. woman had spent **a.t.** -
12 : 44. did cast in all **a.t.** -, Lu. 21: ⌊4.

All THAT
he hath, or she hath.

Ge. 24 : 36. unto him hath giv. **a.t.** -
39 : 8. com-ted **a.t.** - into my hands
Le. 27 : 28. devote unto Lord of **a.t.** -
De. 21 : 17. double portion of **a.t.** -
Jos. 6 : 22. bring out woman **a.t.** -
7 : 15. shall be burnt, he and **a.t.** -
Jb. 1 : 10. hedge about him **a.t.** - ?
11. touch **a.t.** - he will curse thee
12. Behold **a.t.** - is in thy power
Ps. 109 : 11. extortioners catch **a.t.** -
Mat. 13 : 44. for joy selleth **a.t.** -
Lu. 12 : 44. make him rule over **a.t.** -
14 : 33. whoso. forsaketh not **a.t.** -

All them THAT.

Ge. 45 : 1. Joseph not refrain bef. - **t.**
De. 7 : 15. lay th. upon - **t.** hate thee
2 S. 22 : 31. is buckler, to - **t.** trust in him, Ps. 18 : 30. ⌈Ch. 33 : 25.
2 K. 21 : 24. slew - **t.** conspired, 2
Ezr. 8 : 22. hand of God upon - **t.** seek him (2) ⌈secute
Ps. 7 : 1. O Lord, save me fr. - **t.** per-
73 : 27. destroyed - **t.** go a whoring
86 : 5. in mercy unto - **t.** call upon
89 : 7. to be had in reverence of - **t.**
111 : 2. sought of - **t.** have pleasure
119 : 63. I am a companion of - **t.** fear thee (2) ⌈thy statutes
118. trodden down - **t.** err from
143 : 12. destroy - **t.** afflict my soul
145 : 18. Lord is nigh unto - **t.** call
20. Lord preserveth - **t.** love him
Je. 46 : 25. punish - **t.** trust in Pha.
Eze. 12 : 19. violence of - **t.** dwell
16 : 37. gather - **t.** thou hast loved with - **t.** thou hast hated ⌈hold
28 : 18. to ashes in sight of - **t.** be-
32 : 15. sh. smite - **t.** dwell therein
Mat. 21 : 12. Jesus cast out - **t.** sold
Lu. 2 : 38. - **t.** looked for redempt-n
4 : 20. eyes of - **t.** were in synagogue
21 : 35. snare on - **t.** dwell on earth
Ac. 4 : 16. manif-t to - **t.** dwell in Jer.
5 : 5. great fear on - **t.** heard, 11.
27 : 24. G. hath given thee - **t.** sail
Ro. 3 : 22. righteousness of God upon - **t.** believe, 1 Th. 1 : 7. 2 Th. 1:
4 : 11. might be fa. of - **t.** believe⌊10.
Ep. 6 : 24. Grace with - **t.** love our L.
He. 5 : 9. of salvation unto - **t.** obey
13 : 24. Salute - **t.** have rule over
See **THEM that, THEY that.**

All they THAT.

Ezr. 1 : 6. - **t.** were about strength-d
Ne. 10 : 28. - **t.** had separated fr. peo.
Jb. 42 : 11. Then came - **t.** had been
Ps. 2 : 12. Blessed are - **t.** put trust
22 : 7. - **t.** see me laugh to scorn
29. - **t.** be fat upon earth sh. eat (2)
97 : 7. Confounded be - **t.** serve ima.
111 : 10. understanding have - **t.**
Pr. 8 : 36. - **t.** hate me love death
Ec. 1 : 16. I more wisdom than - **t.**
Is. 19 : 8. - **t.** cast angle shall lament
Is. 30 : 18. blessed are - **t.** wait for
41 : 11. - **t.** were incensed ag. thee
60 : 14. - **t.** despised thee sh. bow at
Je. 30 : 16. - **t.** devour thee shall be
Eze. 28 : 19. - **t.** know thee astonished
Na. 3 : 7. - **t.** look upon thee sh. flee
Zph. 1 : 11. - **t.** bear silver are cut off
Zch. 14 : 21. - **t.** sacrifice sh. take of
Mat. 26 : 52. - **t.** take sword sh. perish
Lu. 1 : 66. - **t.** heard laid up in hearts
2 : 18. - **t.** heard it wondered⌈eases
4 : 40. - **t.** had any sick with dis-
Ac. 5 : 17. high priest rose and - **t.**
2 Jn. 1. not I only but - **t.** have kno.

All those THAT. ⌈4 : 46.

Nu. 1 : 45. So were - **t.** were num-b,
Ps. 5 : 11. Let - **t.** put trust in thee
18 : 30. he a buckler to - **t.** trust
40 : 16. Let - **t.** seek thee be glad,
70 : 4. ⌈captives
106 : 46. pitied of - **t.** carried them
145 : 14. Lord raiseth - **t.** be bowed
Je. 49 : 5. fear from - **t.** be about thee
Eze. 28 : 26. judgments on - **t.** despi.
Zph. 1 : 9. punish - **t.** leap on threshh.
See **THOSE that.**

THAT is. ⌈t.i.

2 S. 3 : 13. one thing I require of thee,
Ac. 19 : 4. **t.i.**, Ro. 1 : 12.-7 : 18.-9 : 8.
Ro. 10 : 6. **t.i.**, to bring Christ down
7. **t.i.**, to bring up Christ again
8. **t.i.**, word of faith we preach
Phm. 12. receive him, **t.i.** mine own
He. 2 : 14. **t.i.**, 7 : 5.-11 : 16.-13 : 15.
1 Pe. 3 : 20.

THAT is to say. ⌈t. -

Mat. 27 : 46. Eli, lama sabachthani?
Mk. 7 : 2. **t.** -, 11. Ac. 1 : 19. He. 9 : 11.-10 : 20.
See DAY, HOUR, MAN, PLACE, PROPHET, SOUL, THING, TIME.
See **SO that, SO that they.**

THEATRE.

Ac. 19 : 29. they rushed into the **t.** ⌈t.
31. th. he wo. not adventure into
1 Co. 4 : † 9. we are made a **t.** unto

THE'BEZ. ⌈T.

Ju. 9 : 50. Abimelech to T. and took
2 S. 11 : 21. smote Abim. th. he died in T.

THEE.

Ge. 7 : 1. **t.** have I seen righteous
17 : 2. I will multiply **t.** exceeding-
22 : 17. in bles-g I will bless **t.**⌊ly,
23 : 11. the field give I **t.**, and the cave give I **t.** ⌈me but **t.**
39 : 9. nei. kept back anything from
De. 28 : 43. stranger sh. get above **t.**
1 S. 8 : 7. have not rejected **t.** but me
20 : 22, arrows are beyond **t.**, 37.
2 S. 18 : 11. I wo. have giv. **t.** 10 shekels
12. king charged **t.** and Abishai
Ps. 86 : 14. have not set **t.** bef. them
Is. 14 : 11. and the worms cover **t.**
Je. 15 : 11. enemy to entreat **t.** well
Eze. 7 : 9. I will recompense **t.** acc-g
Lu. 14 : 9. he that bade **t.** and him
Ro. 10 : 8. The word is nigh **t.**, even
11 : 21. heed, lest he spare not **t.**
See BESEECH, DESPISE, HEAR, HEARD, LEAVE, ROOT, SAW.

About THEE.

Jb. 11 : 18. dig **a.t.** and take thy rest
Is. 26 : 20. shut thy doors **a.t.**, hide
Je. 46 : 14. sword devour **a.t.**, Eze.
49 : 5. bring fear fr. all **a.t.** ⌊5 : 12.
Eze. 5 : 14. am. nations that are **a.t.**
15. astonishment to nations **a.t.**
Lu. 19 : 43. shall cast a trench **a.t.**
Ac. 12 : 8. Cast thy garment **a.t.**, fol- ⌊low me

After THEE.

Ge. 17 : 7. to thy seed **a.t.**, 8, 9, 10.-
35 : 12.-48 : 4, ⌈25. 28.
De. 4 : 40. with thy children **a.t.**, 12:
Ju. 5 : 14. **a.t.** Benjamin among peo.
Ru. 1 : 16. or return from following
4 : 4. tell me, for I am **a.t.** ⌊**a.t.**
2 S. 7 : 12. I will set up thy seed **a.t.**
1 K. 1 : 14. I also will come in **a.t.**
3 : 12. nei. **a.t.** shall any arise like thee, 2 Ch. 1 : 12. ⌈**a.t.**
1 Ch. 17 : 11. I will raise up thy seed
Jb. 39 : 10. will he harrow valleys **a.t.**?
Ps. 42 : 1. so panteth my soul **a.t.**
63 : 8. My soul followeth hard **a.t.**
143 : 6. my soul thirsteth **a.t.** as a
Can. 1 : 4. Draw me, we will run **a.t.**
Is. 45 : 14. shall come **a.t.** in chains
Je. 12 : 6. called a multitude **a.t.**
Da. 2 : 39. **a.t.** rise another kingdom
Ho. 5 : 8. cry at Beth-aven, **a.t.**, O ⌊Benj.

Against THEE.

Ex. 23 : 29. lest the beast multiply **a.t.**
Nu. 20 : 18. **a.t.** De. 20 : 12. Ju. 9 : 33. Ps. 41 : 4.-53 : 5.-83 : 5. Is. 41 : 11, 12.-54 : 15, 17. Je. 11 : 17.-15 : 6.-22 : 7.-37 : 18.-38 : 22.-50 : 42.-51 : 14. Eze. 16 : 37, 40, 44.-21 : 31.-23 : 22, 24, 25.-27 : 30. Da. 9 : 8. Ob. 7. Mi. 4 : 11.
De. 15 : 9. he cry unto L. **a.t.** 24 : 15.
23 : 4. bec. they hired Balaam **a.t.**
28 : 7. shall come out **a.t.** one way
48. enemies Lord sh. send **a.t.**, 49.
31 : 26. be there for a witness **a.t.**
Ju. 9 : 31. they fortify the city **a.t.**
10 : 10. We have sinned **a.t.**, Ne. 1 : 6. Je. 14 : 7, 20 ⌈**a.t.**
2 S. 12 : 11. behold I will raise up evil
1 K. 8 : 50. forgive thy people that have sinned **a.t.**, 2 Ch. 6 : 39.
20 : 22. k. of Syria will come up **a.t.**
2 Ch. 20 : 2 cometh great multi. **a.t.**
35 : 21. I come not **a.t.** this day, but
Ne 1 : 7. dealt very corruptly **a.t.**
Jb. 7 : 20. why set me as a mark **a.t.**
11 : 5. th G. would open his lips **a.t.**
42 : 7. My wrath **a.t.** and thy friends
Ps. 21 : 11. they intended evil **a.t.**
139 : 20. they speak **a.t.** wickedly
Is. 7 : 5. have taken evil counsel **a.t.**
10 : 24. Assyrian shall lift staff **a.t.**
Je. 21 : 13. Behold I am **a.t.**, 50 : 31.-51 : 25. Eze. 5 : 8.-21 : 3.-26 : 3.-28 : 22.-29 : 3, 10.-35 : 3.-38 : 3.-39 : 1. Na. 2 : 13.-3 : 5. ⌈t.
La. 2 : 16. enemies opened mouth **a.**
Eze. 26 : 8. make a fort **a.t.**, cast mount **a.t.**, lift buckler **a.t.**
33 : 30. people still are talking **a.t.**
Am. 7 : 10. Amos hath conspired **a.t.**
Na. 2 : 13. I am **a.t.**, saith the Lord
Mat. 5 : 23. th. thy bro. hath aught **a.**
Re. 2 : 4. I have somewhat **a.t.** ⌊t.
14. I have a few things **a.t.**, 20.
See COME UP, ENCAMPETH, FIGHT, PREVAIL, REBELLED, RISE, ROSE, SIN, SINNED, SPOKEN, TESTIFIED, TESTIFY, TRESPASS, TRESPASSED, WAR [Verb], WITNESS [Verb].

At THEE.

2 K. 19 : 21. hath shaken her head **a.t.**, Is. 37 : 22. ⌈and cedars
Is. 14 : 8. the fir trees rejoice **a.t.**,
52 : 14. as many were astonied **a.t.**
La. 2 : 15. all that pass by clap their hands **a.t.** ⌈27 : 35.-28 : 19.
Eze. 26 : 16. shall be astonished **a.t.**
27 : 36. the merchants sh. hiss **a.t.**
32 : 10. make many people amazed ⌊a.t.

Before THEE.

Ge. 13 : 9. Is not the whole land **b.t.**
17 : 18. **b.t.** 20 : 15.-31 : 35.-47 : 6.-49 : 8. Ex 33 : 19. De 1 : 21, 38.-2 : 31.-4 : 32.-7 : 2, 22, 24.-9 : 3.-12 : 29, 30.-22 : 6.-23 : 14.-28 : 66.-30 : 1, 15.-32 : 52.-33 : 10, 27. 1 S. 16 : 16. 2 S. 7 : 15, 16, 26. 1 K. 8 : 6.-8 : 28. 2 K. 20 : 3. 1 Ch. 17 : 8, 13, 25, 27.-29 : 15. 2 Ch. 6 : 24. Ne. 1 : 6.-4 : 5.-9 : 8, 28, 32 Ps. 22 : 27.-39 : 5.-69 : 19.-73 : 22.-79 : 11.-86 : 9.-88 : 1, 2.-90 : 8.-102 : 28.-119 : 169.-141:

2. Pr. 4 : 25. Is. 9 : 3.-45 : 2.-58 : 8.
-59 : 12. Je. 17 : 16.-18 : 20, 23.-
34 : 5.-37 : 20 -39 : 16.-42 : 2. La.
1 : 22. Eze. 4 : 1. Da. 1 : 13.-2 :
31.-5 : 23.-6 : 22.-9 : 18. Mat. 6 :
2. Re. 15 : 4.
Ge. 24 : 7. Lord send his angel **b.t.**,
Ex. 23 : 20, 23.-32 : 34.-33 : 2.
51. Rebekah is **b.t.**, take her, go
32 : 17. asketh, whose are these **b.t.**
33 : 12. I will go **b.t.**, Is. 45 : 2.
43 : 9. if I bring him not **b.t.**, let
Ex. 23 : 28. I will send hornets **b.t.**,
which shall drive out the Canaanites **b.t.**, 29, 30, 31.-34 : 11.
De. 4 : 38.-9 : 4, 5.-18 : 12.
34 : 24. I will cast out **b.t.**, De. 6 :
19.-7 : 1.-9 : 4. ⌈good
De. 30 : 15. I have set **b.t.** life and
31 : 3. Joshua shall go over **b.t.**, 8.
Ju. 4 : 14. is not Lord gone **b.t.**?
2 S. 5 : 24. shall Lord go out **b.t.**
7 : 15. Saul, I put aw. **b.t.** ⌈17 : 24.
16. be established **b.t.**, 26. 1 Ch.
1 K. 3 : 12. was none like thee **b.t.**
14 : 9. hast done evil above all **b.t.**
1 Ch. 14 : 15. for G. is gone forth **b.t.**
17 : 13. I took it from him was **b.t.**
2 Ch. 1 : 12. none that have been **b.t.**
Ps. 38 : 9. Lord, all my desire is **b.t.**
119 : 168. for all my ways are **b.t.**
169. Let my cry come **b.t.** ⌈is **b.t.**
Pr. 23 : 1. consider diligently what
Je. 28 : 8. proph-s th. have been **b.t.**
40 : 4. all the la. is **b.t.**, go whither
Mi. 6 : 4. I sent **b.t.** Moses, Aaron
Zch. 3 : 8. thy fellows that sit **b.t.**
Lu. 15 : 18. Father, I have sinned **b.t.**
Ac. 23 : 30. say **b.t.** what they had
24 : 19. ought to have been here **b.t.**
25 : 26. especially **b.t.** Agrippa ⌈t.
26 : 2. I shall answer for myself b.
Re. 3 : 8. I have set **b.t.** open door
See COME, FLEE, GO, GONE, PASS, SET, SIT, STAND, STOOD, WALK, WALKED, WAY, WENT.

Behind THEE. ⌈b.t.
Ge. 19 : 17. Escape for life, look not
De. 25 : 18. Amalek smote feeble **b.t.**
Ps. 50 : 17. th. castest my words **b.t.**
Is. 30 : 21. ears shall hear a word **b.t.**

Besides THEE.
Ru. 4 : 4. is none to redeem it **b.t.**
1 S. 2 : 2. holy as Lord; is none **b.t.**,
2 S. 7 : 22. 1 Ch. 17 : 20. ⌈**b.t.**
Ps. 73 : 25. none upon earth th. I desire
Is. 26 : 13. lords **b.t.** have had domin.
64 : 4. nei. hath eye seen, O G., **b.t.**

Between or Betwixt THEE.
Ge. 31 : 49. Lord watch **b-n** me and **t.**
51. this pillar cast **b-t** me and **t.**
1 S. 20 : 23. L. be **b-n t.** and me, 42.
Eze. 4 : 3. wall of iron **b-n t.** and city
Mat. 18 : 15. tell him his fault **b-n t.**
See ENMITY, ME, WITNESS.

By THEE.
Ex. 18 : 14. why all peo. stand **b.t.**
22 : 25. If lend money to poor **b.t.**
Le. 25 : 39. if thy bro. **b.t.** be waxen
47. if stranger wax rich **b.t.** ⌊poor
1 S. 1 : 26. I am woman stood **b.t.**
9 : 23. of which I said, Set it **b.t.**
2 S. 22 : 30. **b.t.** I ran through a
troop, Ps. 18 : 29. ⌈fr. the womb
Ps. 71 : 6. **b.t.** have I been holpen
Pr. 3 : 28 Say not, Go, wh. hast it **b.t.**
29. neighb. dwelleth securely **b.t.**
Is. 26 : 13. **b.t.** we will make mention
Eze. 16 : 6. when I passed **b.t.**, 8.
Ac. 24 : 2. **b.t.** we enjoy quietness
Phm. 7. the saints are refreshed **b.t.**

Concerning THEE. ⌈me
Jos. 14 : 6. thing the L. said **c.t.** and
1 S. 25 : 30. good he hath spoken **c.t.**
2 S. 14 : 8. said, I will give charge **c.t.**
1 K. 22 : 23. Lord hath spok evil **c.t.**
Na. 1 : 14. L. hath given com-nt **c.t.**
Mat. 4 : 6. give his angels charge **c.t.**
Ac. 21 : 24. they were informed **c.t.**
28 : 21. nei. received we letters **c.t.**

For THEE.
Ge 6 : 21. sh be for food **f.t.** and them
20 : 7. sh. pray **f.t.** and thou live
Ex. 2 : 7. **f.t.** 8 : 9.-9 : 30.-15 : 17.-18 :
18. Le. 25 : 6. Nu. 18 : 9. De. 5 :
31.-10 : 21.-14 : 24.-17 : 8.-18 :
14.-19 : 2, 7. Jos. 17 : 15. Ju. 11 :
36.-13 : 15.-18 : 19. Ru. 3 : 1.-4 :
8. 1 S. 9 : 24.-20 : 4. 2 S. 1 : 26.-
10 : 11.-13 : 13.-18 : 33. 1 K. 2 :
18.-8 : 13.-19 : 7.-20 : 34. 2 K. 4 :
2, 13. 1 Ch. 19 : 12. 2 Ch. 6 : 2.
Jb. 8 : 6.-18 : 4. Ps. 63 : 1.-65 :
1.-119 : 126. Pr. 25 : 16. Can. 7 :
13. Is. 14 : 9.-26 : 8.-33 : 2.-43 :
3, 4.-48 : 9.-51 : 19. Je. 32 : 17.-
34 : 5.-48 : 32.-50 : 24.-51 : 36.
La. 2 : 13, 14. Eze. 7 : 6.-26 : 17.-
27 : 5, 31, 32.-32 : 10. Da. 2 : 29.
Ho. 6 : 11. Na. 3 : 7. Zch. 9 : 11.
Mat. 11 : 24.-14 : 4.-17 : 4.-18 :
8, 9.-26 : 17. Mk. 1 : 37.-3 : 32.-
6 : 18.-9 : 5, 43, 45, 47. Lu. 22 :
32. Jn. 5 : 10. Ac. 9 : 5.-10 : 22.-
22 : 10.-24 : 25.-26 : 14.
De. 17 : 8. if a matter too hard **f.t.**
Ju. 7 : 4. I will try them **f.t.** there ⌈t.
2 S. 19 : 38. thou sh require will I do **f.**
1 K. 17 : 13 after make **f.t.** and son
2 K. 2 : 9. Elijah said, Ask what I sh.
do **f.t.**, 4 : 2, 13. ⌈Zch. 9 : 11.
2 Ch. 7 : 17. and as **f.t.**, Da. 2 : 29.
Ho. 3 : 3. not for ano. so will I be **f.t.**
Mat. 5 : 29. is profitable **f.t.**, 30.
17 : 27. give unto them **f.** me and **t.**
Mk. 5 : 19. things L. hath done **f.t.**
Jn. 11 : 28. The master calleth **f.t.**
2 Co. 12 : 9. My grace sufficient **f.t.**

From THEE.
Ge. 18 : 25. that be far **f.t.** to slay
28 : 6. **f.t.**. 27 : 45.-30 : 2. Ex. 8 : 9.
-33 : 5.-De. 7 : 15, 10.-13 : 7.-15 :
13, 18.-20 : 15.-23 : 13, 14. Ju.
17 : 2. 1 S. 1 : 14.-15 : 28.-17 : 46.
-28 : 16. 2 S. 13 : 13. 1 K. 11 : 11.
-18 : 12. 2 K. 2 : 9, 10.-20 : 18.
Ezr. 4 : 12. Jb. 13 : 20.-26 : 4.-
42 : 2. Ps. 38 : 9.-69 : 5.-139 : 12,
15. Pr. 4 : 24. Is. 39 : 7.-54 : 8,
10. Jer. 11 : 15.-34 : 14.-Eze. 16 :
9, 42.-21 : 3, 4.-23 : 27.-24 : 16.-
28 : 3. Da. 4 : 31. Am. 3 : 11.
Mi. 1 : 16. Na. 3 : 7. Zch. 3 : 4.
Mat. 5 : 29, 30.-12 : 38.-18 : 8, 9.
Jn. 17 : 8. Ac. 23 : 21. Re. 18 : 14.
Ex. 8 : 29. Behold I go out **f.t.** ⌈24.
De. 12 : 21. If place too far **f.t.**, 14 :
15 : 12. let him go free **f.t.**, 13, 18.
16. I will not go away **f.t.**
1 S. 20 : 9. Far be it **f.t.**, Mat. 16 : 22.
Ps. 73 : 27. they th. are far **f.t.** perish
80 : 18. So will we not go back **f.t.**
Eze. 22 : 5. those far **f.t.** shall mock
See **DEPART from**, DEPARTED, HID, HIDE, HIDETH.

In THEE.
Ge. 12 : 3. **i.t.** 28 : 14.-48 : 20. Ex. 9 :
16. De. 23 : 14, 21, 22. 1 S 25 :
28.-29 : 6. 1 K. 10 : 9. 2 Ch. 9 :
8.-19 : 3. Ps. 7 : 1.-9 : 2, 10.-16 :
1.-17 : 7.-22 : 4, 5.-25 : 2, 20.-
31 : 1, 14, 19.-39 : 7.-40 : 16.-
55 : 23.-56 : 3.-57 : 1.-70 : 4.-71 :
1.-81 : 9.-84 : 5, 12.-85 : 6.-86 :
2.-87 : 7.-141 : 8.-143 : 8. Can.
1 : 4.-4 : 7. Is. 22 : 3.-26 : 3.-
45 : 14.-62 : 4. Je. 2 : 19. Eze.
5 : 10, 15.-16 : 34.-20 : 47.-22 :
6, 7, 9, 10, 11, 12.-25 : 4.-27 : 8,
9, 10. 27 -28 : 13, 15.-36 : 15.-
38 : 16. Da. 4 : 9.-5 : 14. Ho.
14 : 3. Mi. 1 : 13. Mat. 6 : 23.-
11 : 23. Lu. 3 : 22.-11 : 35.-19 :
44. Ro. 9 : 17. Ga. 3 : 8. 1 Ti. 4 :
14. 2 Ti. 1 : 5, 6. 3 Jn. 3. Re. 18 :
22, 23. ⌈not done
Eze. 5 : 9. will do **i.t.** what I have
Mi. 4 : 9. cry? is there no king **i.t.**
Jn. 17 : 21. as thou in me and I **i.t.**
Re. 18 : 22 sh. be heard no more **i.t.**
See DELIGHT, FOUND, HOPE, JOYFUL, REJOICE, TRUST [Noun], TRUST, ED, ETH.
See **Put TRUST.**

Into THEE. ⌈cumc-d
Is. 52 : 1. no more come **i.t.** uncir.

Of THEE.
Ge. 12 : 2. And I will make **o.t.** a
great nation and bless, 17 : 6.-
35 : 11.-46 : 3.-48 : 4. Eze. 32 : 10.
12 : 13. **o.t.** 17 : 6.-35 : 11.-41 : 15.-
46 : 3.-48 : 4. Ex. 23 : 25.-32 : 10.
-33 : 3, 5.-34 : 12. Nu. 14 : 15.
De. 2 : 25.-10 : 12.-13 : 5.-18 :
15.-23 : 21.-25 : 18.-28 : 10. Ju.
4 : 20. Ru. 2 : 19. 1 S. 2 : 15.
-19 : 3.-24 : 12. 2 S. 3 : 13.-24 :
24. 1 K. 2 : 16, 20. 1 Ch. 22 : 11.
-29 : 12, 14. Jb. 11 : 6.-22 : 4.-
38 : 3.-40 : 7.-42 : 4, 5. Ps. 6 : 5.
-21 : 4.-22 : 25.-71 : 6.-87 : 3.-
116 : 19.-119 : 120.-135 : 9. Pr.
25 : 17.-30 : 7. Is. 12 : 6.-26 : 8.
-49 : 17.-58 : 9, 12.-64 : 7. Je.
30 : 11.-34 : 4.-46 : 28.-51 : 26.
Eze 5 : 8, 10, 12.-7 : 4, 9.-22 : 7,
9, 13, 15.-26 : 15.-27 : 25, 27,
34.-28 : 16, 18, 22.-29 : 8.-32 :
6.-39 : 2. Da. 2 : 23.-5 : 14, 16.-
6 : 7, 12. Ho. 11 : 9. Mi. 2 : 12.-
5 : 2, 10, 13, 14.-6 : 8, 14.-7 : 17.
Na. 1 : 11.-3 : 13, 19. Zph. 3 : 11,
12, 15, 17, 18. Zch. 2 : 10, 11.-
14 : 1. Mat. 2 : 6.-3 : 14.-5 : 42.-
Mk 11 : 14. Lu. 1 : 35.-6 : 30.-
12 : 20. Ac. 10 : 22.-21 : 21.-28 :
21, 22. 1 Co. 12 : 21. 2 Ti. 1 : 3.
Phm. 4. ⌈done **o.t.**
1 K. 11 : 11. the Lord said, as this is
Is. 58 : 12. that shall be **o.t.** sh. build
Lu. 16 : 2. How is it I hear this **o.t.**?
Jn. 17 : 7. all whatsoever thou hast
given me are **o.t.** ⌈Lord
Phm. 20. let me have joy **o.t.** in the
See **In the MIDST.**

Off THEE.
Ge. 40 : 19. Pha. shall lift thy head
from **o.t.**, birds shall eat thy
flesh from **o.t.** ⌈**o.t.**
Na. 1 : 13. will I break his yoke from

On or Upon THEE.
Ge. 16 : 5.-38 : 29. Ex. 8 : 4, 21.-15 :
26. Le. 19 : 19. Nu. 6 : 25, 26.-
11 : 17. De. 4 : 30.-7 : 15, 22.-8 :
4.-13 : 17.-19 : 10.-28 : 2, 8, 15,
20, 24, 45, 46, 60, 61.-30 : 1,
3. Ju. 12 : 1.-16 : 9, 12, 14, 20.-
18 : 25. Ru. 3 : 3, 15. 1 S. 10 : 6.
-16 : 16.-20 : 9.-24 : 12, 13. 2 S.
16 : 8. 1 K. 1 : 20.-13 : 2.-21 : 21.
2 K. 4 : 4. 2 Ch. 14 : 11.-19 : 2.-
20 : 12. Jb. 4 : 5.-33 : 7.-36 : 17.
Ps. 22 : 10.-25 : 3, 5, 21.-59 : 9.
63 : 6.-69 : 6.-104 : 27.-145 : 15.
Can. 6 : 13.-7 : 5. Is. 1 : 25.-7 :
17.-14 : 16.-24 : 17.-26 : 3.-43 :
2.-47 : 9, 11, 13.-49 : 18.-54 : 8,
10.-59 : 21.-60 : 1, 2, 10. Je. 14 :
22.-15 : 5.-22 : 23.-30 : 16.-48 :
18, 43.-49 : 5.-51 : 25. Eze. 3 :
25.-4 : 8.-5 : 17.-7 : 3, 4, 8.-16 :
8, 14, 41.-21 : 31.-24 : 13, 17.-
25 : 7.-26 : 19.-28 : 7.-29 : 7, 8.-
32 : 4, 11. Na. 3 : 6, 7. Mat. 18 :
33.-21 : 19. Mk. 5 : 19 Lu. 1 :
35.-19 : 43. Ac. 13 : 11.-18 : 10.
-22 : 19. 1 Tim. 1 : 18. Re. 3 : 3.
1 S. 9 : 20. Is it not **o.t.** and fa.'s hou.
Ps. 17 : 6. I have called **u.t.**, O God,
31 : 17.-86 : 5, 7.-88 : 9 La. 3 : 57.
See CALL, CALLED, COME, WAIT.

Over THEE.

Ge. 3 : 16. husband and he rule o.t.
De. 15 : 6. they shall not reign o.t.
17 : 15. set him k. o.t., 28 : 36. [10.
Ps 91 : 11.angels charge o.t., Lu.4:
Je. 13 :21.taught th. to be chief o.t.
La. 2 : 17. enemy to rejoice o.t.
Eze. 16 : 8. I spread my skirt o.t.
27. I have stretched my hand o.t.
27:32.lament o.t. saying, What city
32 : 3. I will spread my net o. t.
8. All lights will I make dark o.t.
Da. 4 : 25. 7 times sh. pass o.t., 32.
Na. 3 : 19. all shall clap hands o.t.
See REJOICE.

I pray THEE.

Ge. 12:13 I p.t.,13:8,9 -16:2.-18:3.-
23: 13.-24 : 2, 12, 14, 17, 23, 43,
45.-25 : 30.-27 : 3, 19, 21.-30 :
14, 27.-32 : 11, 29.-33 : 10, 11,
14.-37 : 14, 16.-38 : 16, 25.-40 :
14.-44 : 18, 33.-47 : 29.-48 : 9 -
50 : 5, 17. Ex. 4 : 13, 18.-10 : 17
-32 : 32.-33 : 13.-34 : 9. Nu. 10:
31.-11 : 15.-20 : 17.-22 : 6,16,17.
-23 : 13, 27. De. 3 : 25. Jos 7 :
19. Ju. 4 : 19.-6 : 18, 39.-9 : 38
-11 : 17.-13 : 4, 15.-15 : 2 -16 :
6, 10, 28.-19 : 6, 8, 11. 1 S. 2.
36.-3 : 17.-9 : 18.-10 : 15.-15 :
25, 30.-16 : 22.-19 : 2.- 20 :29.-
22 : 3.-25 : 8, 24, 25, 28.-26 : 8,
11, 19.-28 : 8, 22.-30 : 7. 2 S. 1.
4.-13 : 5, 6, 13, 26.-14 : 2, 11.12,
18.-15 : 7, 31.-16 : 9.-18 : 22.-
19 : 37.-24 : 17. 1 K. 1 : 12 -2 :
17, 20.-8 : 26.-14 : 2.-17 :10, 11,
21.-19 : 20.-20 : 31, 32, 35, 37.-
22 : 5, 13. 2 K. 1 : 13.-2 : 2, 4, 6,
9, 19.-4 : 10, 22, 26.-5 : 15, 17,
22.-6 : 3, 17,18.-7 : 13.-8 : 4 -
18 : 23, 26. 1 Ch. 21 : 17. 2 Ch
18 : 4.-18 : 12. Ne. 1 : 11. Jb. 4 :
7.-8 : 8.-22 : 22.-33 : 1. Ps. 119:
76. Is. 29 : 11, 12.-36 : 8, 11.
Je. 21 : 2.-32 : 8.-37 :20.-40 :15.
Jon. 4 : 2. Mk. 5 : 23. Lu. 14 :
18, 19.-16 : 27. Ac. 8 : 34.-24 :4.

We pray THEE.

Ge. 47 : 4. w.p.t., 50 : 17. Ex. 5 : 3.
Ju. 1 : 24.-10 : 15.-11 : 19.-18 :
5. 2 K. 2 : 16.-6 : 2. Jon. 1 : 8.

See

TEACH thee, TELL thee.

Through THEE. [enemies

Ps. 44 : 5. t.t. will we push down

To or Unto THEE.

Ge. 3 : 18.-4 : 7, 12.-6 : 20, 21.-7 : 2.
-18 : 10, 14.-19 : 5.-20 : 16.-21 :
12, 23.-24 : 50.-26 : 29.-27 : 29,
37.-28 : 15, 22.-29 : 19.-31 : 12,
16, 39, 52.-33 : 11.-35 : 1.-37 :
10.-38 : 16.-43 : 29.-47 : 5.-48 :
2, 5, 22.-50 : 17. Ex. 2 : 7.-3 :12.
-4 : 1, 5, 16, 23.-6 : 29.-7 : 16.-
12 :24.-18 : 11.-18 : 6, 22.-20 :4.
-23 : 27, 33.-28 : 1.-29 : 42.-30 :
23.-32 : 21, 34. Le. 21 : 8.-24 : 2.
-25 : 8, 15, 16, 39. Nu. 6 : 25.-
10 : 3, 4, 32.-11 : 23.-18 : 2, 4,
19.-22 : 37, 38. De. 4 : 35 -5 :
27, 31.-7 : 16, 23, 25.-13 : 7.-15:
9, 12, 13.-16 : 9.-18 : 15, 18 -20:
11.-22 : 2, 7.-23 : 15.-24 : 11,15.
-25 : 3.-28 : 9, 21. 31, 44, 68.
Jos. 1 : 17.-2 : 18.-9 : 25. Ju. 8:
19.-6 : 18.-10 : 15.-17 : 3. Ru.
3 : 13.-4 : 15. 1 S. 1 : 8.-2 : 34 -
3 : 17.-9 : 17.-10 : 2, 7, 8.-11 : 3.
-14 : 36, 40.-16 : 3.-17 : 45 -20 :
21.-24 : 4.-25 : 6, 31, 40.-28 : 8,
10, 11, 18. 2 S. 3 : 12.-12 : 14.-
17 : 3.-19 : 7, 37, 38.-20 : 21 1
K. 3 : 12.-8 : 52.-11 : 31, 38.-14:
6.-20 : 6.-21 : 3.-22 : 24. 2 K. 5:
6, 10, 27.-6 : 7.-8 : 9, 14.-9 : 5,
11.-18 : 27.-20 : 14. 1 Ch. 12 :
18.-16 : 18. 2 Ch. 26 : 18. Ezr.
7 : 18.- 9 : 6.-10 : 4. Ne. 9 : 26.
Es. 3 : 11. Jb. 10 : 3.-11 : 19.-
22 : 21, 28.-35 : 3.-38 : 17, 35.-
41 : 3. Ps. 5 : 2, 3.-10 :14 -16 :2.
-22 : 5.- 27 : 8. - 28 : 2. - 32 : 5,
6, 9.-40 : 5.-45 : 14.-51 : 13.-54.
6.-62 : 12 -65 : 1, 2.-66 : 3, 15.-
68 : 29.-69 : 13.-81 : 8.-88 : 9.-
89 : 8.-102 : 1.-105 : 11.-120 : 3.
-123 : 1.-130 : 12.-141 : 8.-142 :
5.-143 : 6. Pr. 3 : 2.-4 : 9.-22 .
19, 20, 21.-23 : 7.-25 : 7. Is. 14
10.-30 : 19.-36 : 12.-39 : 3.-45 :
14.-47 : 9, 15.-48 : 5 -49 :18, 23.
-51 : 19.-55 : 5.-60 : 5, 7, 10, 11,
13, 14, 19. Je. 2 : 31.-3 : 22.-4 .
18.-10 : 7.-11 : 20.-12 : 6.-13 :
12, 27.-15 : 2, 19.-16 : 10, 19.-
20 : 12, 15.-22 : 21.-30 : 2, 15,
17.-32 : 7.-34 : 14.-38 : 15, 20,
25.-39 : 12, 18.-40 : 4, 5, 15.-44.
16.-45 : 5.-48 :27, 46.-49 :9. La
2 : 13.-4 : 21.-5 : 21. Eze. 2 : 1.
8.-3 : 6, 7, 10.-4 : 3, 9.-7 : 7.-12:
9.-16 : 8, 33, 34, 60, 61.-21 : 7,
29.-23 : 30.-38 : 7, 13.-40 : 4 -
44 : 5. Da. 2 :29, 39 -3 : 18.-4 ·
26, 27, 31.-10 : 11, 19.-Jo. 1 :
19, 20. Ob. 5, 15. Jon. 2 : 7, 9
Mi. 2 : 11.-4 : 8.-7 : 12. Ha. 1 :2
-2 : 16. Zch. 2 : 11.-9 : 9, 12.
Mat. 1 : 20.-5 : 26.-16 : 17, 19.-
18 : 17, 22.-21 : 5.-23 : 37.-25 :
44, 39.-26 : 34. Mk. 5 : 41 -9 :17.
-14 : 30, 36. Lu. 1 : 3, 19.-6 : 24.
-7 : 7, 14, 20, 40, 47.-8 : 39 -
-10 : 13.-14 : 9, 10.-17 : 4.-18 :
41.-23 : 43. Jn. 1 : 50.-3 : 3, 5,
7, 11.-4 : 10, 26.-5 : 14.-18 : 38.
-17 : 11, 13.-18 : 30.-19 : 11.-21:
18, 23. Ac. 9 : 17.-10 : 32, 33.-
21 : 37.-24 : 4, 8, 14.-26 : 16. Ro.
15 : 9. 2 Ti. 1 : 14. Phm. 11, 19,
21. 3 Jn. 14. Re 11 : 17.
Ge. 13 : 15. the land thou seest, t.t.,
will I give it, 17.-17 : 8.-26 :3.-
28 : 4, 13.-35 : 12. [t.t.
31 : 32.what is thine with me, take
42 : 37. slay my two sons if I bring
him not t.t., 43 : 9.-44 : 32.
Ex. 13 : 9. and it shall be for a sign
u.t. and, 2 K. 19 : 29. Is. 38 : 7.
33 : 5. I may know what to do u.t.
De. 33 : 29. who is like u.t., 1 S. 26 :
15. Ps. 35 : 10.-71 : 19.
1 S. 8 : 7. in all that they say u.t.
8. forsaken me, so do they u.t.
2 S. 24 :12. one, that I may do it u.t.
1 K. 19 :20.go, what have I done u.t.
2 K. 2 : 10. if see me it sh. be so u.t.
Jb. 7 : 20. sinned, what sh. I do u.t.
Ps. 25 : 1. u.t., O Lord, do I lift my
soul, 86 : 4.-143 : 8.
28 : 1. u.t. will I cry, O Lord, my
rock, 2.-30 : 8.-31 : 22.-56 : 9.-
61:2.-86:3.-88: 13.-130: 1.-141:1.
30 : 12. may sing praise t.t., 56 :12.
-59 : 17.-66 : 4.-71 : 22, 23.
86 : 8. none like u.t., Je. 10 : 6.
101 : 1. u.t., O Lord, will I sing,
108 :3.-138 : 1.-144 :9. He.2:12.
Eze. 16 : 5. to do any of these u.t.
6. I said u.t. when in thy blood
Ho. 6:4. O Ephr., what sh. I do u.t. ?
Am. 4 : 12. thus will I do u.t., because I will do this u.t. [u.t.
Jon. 1 : 11. said, What shall we do
Mi. 6 : 3. what have I done u.t.
Mat. 8 : 13. so be it done u.t. [u.t.
16 :22. far from thee this sh. not be
20 : 14. give unto last, even as u.t.
Mk. 10 : 51. what will I do u.t., Lu.
Jn. 9 : 26. what did he t.t. [18 : 41.
11 :40.said I not u.t. that if believe
Jn. 21 :22.What is th. t.t., 23.[u.t.
Phm. 16. to me, but how much more
See BRING, COME, CRY, DO, GIVE,
SENT, WELL.

See GIVE thanks.

See I SAY unto thee.

Toward THEE.

2 K. 3 : 14. I would not look t.t. nor
Je. 12 : 3. hast tried mine heart t.t.
Eze. 16 :42.make my fury t.t. to rest
63. when I am pacified t.t. for
Ro. 11 : 22. t.t. goodness, if thou

Under THEE. [continue

De. 28 : 23. earth u.t. shall be iron
Ps. 45 : 5. whereby people fall u.t.
Pr. 22 :27.why take thy bed fr.u.t. ?
Is. 14 : 11.worm is spread u.t. [u.t.
Ob. 7. that eat thy bread laid wound

With THEE.

Ge. 6 : 18. w.t. 19.-8 : 16, 17.-19 :9.-
-28 :4.-29 :25.-30 :5.-31 :3.-32:9.
-40 :14.-Ex. 12 : 48.-18 :7.-17 :5.
-18 : 18.-19 : 9, 24. Le. 10 :9, 14,
15.-19 :33.-25 :6, 35, 36, 40. Nu.
11 : 16, 17 -16 : 10.-18 : 1, 2, 7,
11, 19. De. 14 : 27, 29.-16 : 4.-
20 : 12, 20.-22 : 2, 7. Jos. 8 : 1.
Ju. 6 : 12.-9 : 32.-12 : 1. Ru. 1 :
10. 1 S. 9 : 3.-15 : 26.-16 : 2.-20:
8.-27 : 5.-28 : 19.-29 : 10. 2 S. 3 :
13, 21.-15 : 35.-16 : 21.-20 : 16.
1 K. 3 : 6.-6 : 12.-11 : 38.-13 :
18.-14 : 3. 2 K. 3 : 13.-5 : 26.- 6:
1. 1 Ch. 17 : 2, 8.-22 : 15.-28 :
21. 2 Ch. 25 : 7, 19. Ezr. 7 : 13.
Jb. 4 : 2.-14 : 3, 5.-15 : 11.-17 :
3.-22 : 4.-35 : 4.-36 : 4.-40 : 15.-
41 : 4. Ps. 36 : 9.-39 : 12.-78 : 23.
-94 : 20.-116 : 7.-128 : 2. Pr. 2 :
1.-5 : 17.-7 : 1.-23 : 11. Is. 33 : 1.
37 : 9.-41 : 11, 12.-49 : 25.-54 : 9.
Je. 2 : 35.-12 : 1, 6.-19 : 10.-34 :
3.-38 : 10, 25. Eze. 3 : 27.-16 :
60.-23 : 25, 29.-27 : 21.-32 : 4.
Ho. 4 : 5. Mal. 1 : 8. Mat. 12 : 47.
Lu. 1 : 28.-14 : 10. Ac. 27 : 24. 2
Ti. 4 : 11, 13.
Ge. 17 : 4. my covenant is w.t., Ex.
34 : 27. De. 29 : 12. [to all w.t.
20 : 16. he is a covering of eyes un-
21 : 22 God is w.t. in all thou doest
24 : 40. L. will send his angel w.t.
26 : 3. I will be w.t. and bless thee
24. I am w.t., 28 : 15.-31 : 3.-46 :
4. Ex. 3 :12. De. 31 : 8, 23. Ju. 6:
16. Jos. 1 : 5.-3 : 7. 1 K. 11 : 38.
Is. 43 : 2. [was w.t.
28. We saw certainly that the Lord
31 : 38. 20 years have I been w.t.
33 : 5. Who are those w.t. [wi. me
15. Let me leave w.t. some th. are
46 : 4. I will go down w.t. into Eg.
Ex. 18 : 19. Hearken, G. sh. be w.t.
25 : 22. I will meet w.t., 30 : 6, 36.
33 : 14. My presence shall go w.t.,
De. 31 : 6, 8. Ju. 6 : 16.[all night
Le. 19 : 13. wages sh. not abide w.t.
Nu. 22 : 9. Wh. men are these w.t.?
De. 2 : 7 L. thy God hath been w.t.
20 : 1. Lord thy God is w.t., De.
31 : 6. Jos. 1 : 9, 17. Ju. 6 : 12.
2 S. 7 : 3, 9. [w.t.
20. against city that maketh war
22 : 2. it shall be w.t. until thy
brother seek after it
Jos. 2 : 14. we will deal truly w.t.
19. whoso. shall be w.t. in house
Ju. 1 : 3. I will go w.t. into thy lot
4 : 9. she said, I will surely go w.t.
7 : 2. people w.t. are too many
4. of whom I say, This shall go w.
t., the same shall go w.t.
1 S. 10 : 7. for God is w.t., 1 Ch.
17 : 2. Lu. 1 : 28. [heart
14 : 7. I am w.t. according to thy
17 : 37. the Lord be w.t., 20 : 13.
1 Ch. 22 : 11, 16. [man w.t.?
21 : 1. Why art thou alone, and no
26 : 6. I will go down w.t.

1 S.29:8.so long as I have been **w.t.**
2 S.3:12.behold my hand sh. be **w.t.**
7 : 9.I was **w.t.**, 1 Ch. 17 : 8.[**w.t.**
13 : 20. Hath Amnon thy bro. been
26. Why should he go **w.t.** ? [20.
14 : 17. God will be **w.t.**, 1 Ch. 28 :
15 : 20. mercy and truth be **w.t.**
35. hast thou not **w.t.** Zadok [me
1 K. 2 : 8. **w.t.** Shimei who cursed
13 : 8.I will not go in **w.t.**, nor, 16
17 : 18. What have I to do **w.t.**, 2
K. 3 : 13. 2 Ch. 35 : 21. Mk. 5 :
7. Lu. 8 : 28. Jn. 2 : 4.
2 K. 14 : 10. even thou and Judah
w.t., 2 Ch. 25 : 19. [to help
2 Ch. 14 : 11. L., it is nothing **w.t.**
18 : 3. we will be **w.t.**, Ezr. 10 : 4.
Jb. 10 : 13. I know that this is **w.t.**
Ps. 130 : 4. there is forgiveness **w.t.**
139 : 18. when I awake, I am **w.t.**
Pr. 23 : 7. but his heart is not **w.t.**
Can.6 :1. that we may seek him **w.t.**
Is. 41 : 10. I am **w.t.**, 43 : 5. Je. 1 :
8, 19.-15 : 20.-30 : 11.-46 : 28.
Ac. 18 : 10. [**w.t.**, 9, 15.-39 : 4.
Eze. 38 : 6. his bands and many peo.
Am. 6 : 10. Is there yet any **w.t.**
Ob. 7. men that were at peace **w.t.**
Zch. 14 : 5.come, and all saints **w.t.**
Mat. 8 : 29. cried out, What have we
to do **w.t.**, Mk. 1 : 24. Lu.4:34.
18 : 16. take **w.t.** one or two more
26 :35. Peter said, Though I should
die **w.t.**, Mk. 14 : 31. [to prison
Lu. 22 : 33.I am ready to go **w.t.** in-
Jn. 3 : 26. he th. was **w.t.** bey. Jord.
17 : 5. glory which I had **w.t.** bef.
21 : 3. They say, We also go **w.t.**
Ac. 8 : 20. Thy money perish **w.t.**
1 Ti. 6 : 21. Grace be **w.t.** Amen.
See **BREAK in pieces**,
BRING, COMMUNE, COVENANT,
DEAL, DEALT, DWELL, GO,
LAIN, LIE, LIVE, PEACE, PRES-
ENCE, RETURN, SPEAK, TALK,
TALKETH, TARRY, WELL.

Within THEE. [above
De. 28 : 43. stranger **w.t.** shall get
Ps. 122 :8. I now say, Peace be **w.t.**
147 :13.hath blessed thy chil. **w.t.**
Pr. 22 : 18.pleasant, if keep th. **w.t.**
Je. 4 :14.vain thoughts lodge **w.t.** ?
Lu. 19 : 44. shall lay thy chil. **w.t.**

Without THEE. [hand
Ge. 41 : 44. **w.t.** sh. no man lift his

THEEWARD. [good
1 S. 19 : 4. his works been to **t.** very

THEFT, S.
Ex. 22 : 3. he shall be sold for his **t.**
4. if **t.** be found in his hand alive
Mat. 15 : 19. out of the heart proceed
t-s, Mk. 7 : 22. [their t-s
Re. 9 : 21. neither repented they of

THEIR own.
1 S. 14 : 46. Philis. went to **t.o.** pla.
2 S. 7 : 10. dwell in a place of **t.o.**
2 K. 18 : 27. men may eat **t.o.** dung,
drink **t.o.**, Is. 36 : 12. [cities
2 Ch. 31 : 1. Israel returned into **t.o.**
Ezr. 7 : 13. minded of **t.o.** freewill
Ps. 9 : 15. in net they hid is **t.o.** foot
17 : 10. inclosed in **t.o.** fat
44 : 3. got not land by **t.s.** sword,
neither did **t.o.** arm save them
49 : 11. call lands after **t.o.** names
64 : 8. **t.o.** tongue to fall on thems.
81 :12.gave th. up unto **t.o.** hearts'
94 : 23. upon them **t.o.** iniquity,(2)
106 : 39. defiled with **t.o.** works, a
whoring with **t.o.** inventions
109 : 29.cover thems. wi. **t.o.** confu.
140 :9.mischief of **t.o.** lips cover th.
141 : 10. wicked fall into **t.o.** nets
Pr. 1 : 18. lay wait for **t.o.** blood,
lurk privily for **t.o.** lives
31. sh. be filled with **t.o.** devices
25 :27. search **t.o.** glory is not glory
Is. 2 : 8. worship work of **t.o.** hands,
which **t.o.** fingers have made
5 : 21. Woe unto them wise in **t.o.**
eyes, prudent in **t.o.** sight
44 : 9. they are **t.o.** witnesses ; they
49 : 26. And I will feed them that
oppress with their **t. o.** flesh,
and sh. be drunken wi. **t.o.** bl.
65 : 2. peo. walketh aft. **t.o.** tho-ts
Je. 7 : 19. to confusion of **t.o.** faces
25 : 14. acc-g to works of **t.o.** hands
31 : 17. shall come to **t.o.** border
Eze. 13 :2. proph-y out of **t.o.** hearts
3. prophets that follow **t.o.** spirit
14 :14.sho. deliver but **t.o.** souls,20.
20 : 26. polluted them in **t.o.** gifts
Da. 3 : 28.not serve any god exc. **t.o.**
Ho. 13 :2. idols acc. to **t.o.** underst-g
Zch. 11 : 5. **t.o.** shepherds pity not
Mk. 8 : 3. fasting to **t.o.** houses[ence
Jn. 8 : 9. convicted by **t.o.** consci-
20 : 10. disciples went to **t.o.** home
Ac. 4 : 23. went to **t.o.** company
7 : 41. rejoiced in works of **t.o.** ha-s
25 : 19. questions of **t.o.** supersti-n
Ro. 1 : 24. thro lusts of **t.o.** hearts
to dishonour **t.o.** bodies
10 : 3. to establish **t.o.** righteousn.
11 : 24. graffed into **t.o.** olive tree
16 :4. for my life laid do. **t.o.** necks
18. serve not Christ, but **t.o.** belly
Ep. 5 : 24. so wives be to **t.o.** hush-s
28. to love wives as **t.o.** bodies
1 Th. 2 :15.killed Jos. and **t.o.** proph.
2 Th. 3 : 12. work and eat **t.o.** bread
1 Ti 3 : 12. ruling **t.o.** houses well
6 : 1. count **t.o.** masters worthy
2 Ti. 4 :3. after **t.o.** lusts heap to
Tit. 2 : 5. obedient to **t.o.** husbands
9. be obedient unto **t.o.** masters
He. 12 :10.chastened us aft. **t.o.** ple.
1 Pe. 3 :5.subjection unto **t.o.** husb.
2 Pe. 2 : 12. perish in **t.o.** corrupt-n
13. sporting with **t.o.** deceivings
3 : 3. scoffers walking aft. **t.o.** lusts
16. wrest unto **t.o.** destruction
Jude 6. but left **t.o.** habitation
13. foaming out **t.o.** shame
18. walk after **t.o.** ungodly lusts
See DOINGS, HOME, STUFF.
See OWN, **OWN selves**, SOULS.

THEIRS. [is not **t.**
Ge. 15 : 13. be stranger in land that
34 : 23. sh. not beast of **t.** be ours?
43 : 34. mess 5 times as much as **t.**
Ex. 29 : 9. priests' office shall be **t.**
Le. 18 : 10. **t.** is thine own nakedn-s
Nu. 16 : 26. depart, touch noth. of **t.**
18 : 9. every oblation of **t.**, every
meat offering of **t.** [1 Ch. 6 : 54.
Jos. 21 : 10. for **t.** was the first lot,
2 Ch. 18 : 12. let thy word be like **t.**
Je. 44 : 28. words stand, mine or **t.**
Eze. 7 :11.none remain, nor any of **t.**
44 : 29. delicate thi. in Isr. sh. be **t.**
Ha. 1 :6.dwellingplaces th. are not **t.**
Mat. 5 :3. **t.** is kingdom of heav.,10.
1 Co. 1 : 2. our L., both **t.** and ours
2 Ti. 3 : 9. folly manifest, as **t.** was

THELAS'AR, TELAS'SAR.
2 K. 19 : 12. delivered chil. of Eden
wh. were in Th.? Is.37 : 12. Te.

THEM.
Ge. 1 : 22. And God blessed **t.**, 28.
27. male and female created he **t.**
Nu. 14 : 31. **t.**, De. 28 : 61. Jos. 10 :
28. Ju. 11 : 24. 1 S. 25 : 29. 1 K.
13 : 11. 1 Ch. 15 : 2. 2 Ch. 8 : 8.
Ps. 5 : 11.-35 : 19. Is. 56 : 7. Da.
6 : 24. Mat. 13 : 41.-24 : 16. Mk.
13 : 14.-16 : 13. Lu. 21 : 21. Jn.
10 : 16, 35. Ac. 5 : 16.-15 : 19.-
18 : 19.-21 : 24. Ro. 11 : 14. 1 Co.
6 : 4, 13.-16 :3. He. 2 : 15. Re. 7:
14.-10 : 4.
Ro. 8 : 30. **t.** he called, **t.** he also
justified, **t.** he also glorified

About THEM. [**a.t.**
Ge. 35 : 5. terror was upon the cities
Ru. 1 : 19. all city was moved **a.t.**
2 K. 17 : 15. heathen that were **a.t.**
2 Ch. 14 : 7. make **a.t.** walls, towers
Ezr. 1 :6.all **a.t.** strengthened hands
Eze. 1 : 18.were full of eyes **a.t.** four
28 : 26. all that despise them **a.t.**
Mk. 9 : 14. saw great multitude **a.t.**
Lu. 1 : 65. fear on all that dwelt **a.t.**
2 : 9. glory of the Lord shone **a.t.**
Jude 7.the cities **a.t.** in like manner

Above THEM. [**a.t.**
Ex. 18 : 11. dealt proudly, he was
Nu. 3 :49. of them th. were **a.t.**[me
2 S. 22 : 49. lifted **a.t.** that rose ag.
2 Ch. 34 : 4.images **a.t.** he cut down

After THEM. [19, 27.
Ge. 41 : 3. other kine came up **a.t.**,
23. **a.t.**, 30.-48 : 6. Ex. 10 : 14.-
14 : 4, 9, 10, 23, 28. Le. 26 : 6.
Ju. 2 : 10. Ru. 2 : 9. 1 S. 6 : 12.-
14 : 22. 1 K. 9 : 21.-20 : 15. 2 K.
7 : 15.-10 : 29. 1 Ch. 14 : 14. 2
Ch. 8 : 8. Ne. 3 : 27, 29.-12 : 32,
38. Je. 25 : 26.-32 : 18, 39.-39 :
5.-50 : 21. Eze. 29 : 16.-34 : 6.-
Da. 7:24. Zch. 6:6.-7:14.[-10:15.
De. 1 : 8. unto their seed **a.t.**, 4 : 37.
12 : † 30. that thou be not snared
Jos. 2 : 5. pursue **a.t.** quickly [**a.t.**
7. men pursued **a.t.**, 8 : 16. Ju.8:
12.-20 : 45. [battle
1 S. 14 :22. followed hard **a.t.** in the
Jb. 30 : 5. cried **a.t.** as after thief
Je. 2 : 25. strangers **a.t.** will I go
9 : 16. I will send a sword **a.t.**, 49:
37. Eze. 5 : 2, 12.-12 : 14. [21 : 8.
Lu. 17 :23.say, See here, go not **a.t.**,
Ac. 20 : 30. to draw away disciples

Against THEM. [**a.t.**
Ge. 14 : 15. he divided himself **a.t.**
Ex. 32 : 10. that my wrath may wax
hot **a.t.**, Nu. 12 : 9. De. 2 : 15.-
31 : 17. Ju. 2 : 15.
Nu. 16 : 19. **a.t.**, 21 : 33. De. 20 : 19.
Jos. 8 : 22.-11 : 7.-22 : 12. Ju. 6:
3, 4.-9 : 43.-18 : 9.-20 : 20, 25. 1
S. 9 : 14.-12 : 9.-15 : 18. 2 S. 24 :
1. 1 K. 20 : 27. 2 K. 3 : 21. 1 Ch.
14 : 8.-19 : 17. 2 Ch. 14 : 9.-27 :
5. Ne. 13 : 2. Ps. 35 : 3, 20. Is.
5 :30.-63 :10. Je. 51 :1. La. 1 :13.
Eze. 44 : 12. Da. 11 :7. Jon.1:13.
De. 28 :25. shalt go out one way **a.t.**
31 : 28. call heaven to record **a.t.**
1 Ch. 5 :11.chil. of Gad dwelt ov. **a.t.**
20. were helped **a.t.** for they cried
8 : 32. dwelt with brethren in Jerusalem over **a.t.**, 9 :38.[**a.t.**, 17.
2 Ch. 20 : 16. To morrow go ye down
28 : 12. stood **a.t.** that came fr. war
Ezr. 4 :5.hired counsellors **a.t.**[him
8 : 22. his wrath is **a.t.** th. forsake
Ne. 4 : 9. watch **a.t.** day and night
5 : 7. I set a great assembly **a.t.**
9 : 10. that they dealt proudly **a.t.**
12 : 9. breth. over **a.t.** in watches
24. breth. ov. **a.t.** to praise, 37, 38.
Ps. 34 : 16. The face of the Lord is **a.**
t. that do evil, 1 Pe. 3 : 12. [**a.t.**
Is. 8 :9. their countenance doth witn.
5 :25.stretched forth his hand **a.t.**
13 : 17. I will stir up the Medes **a.t.**
Je 1 : 16. I will utter my judgments
4 :12. I will give sentence **a.t.**[**a.t.**
23 : 32. I am **a.t.** th. prophesy false
25 : 30. Therefore prophesy **a. t.**,
Eze. 6 : 2.-13 : 17.-25 : 2.
26 : 19. evil he pronounced **a.t.**, 35:
17.-36 : 31. [**t.**, 21.-8 : 13.
Eze. 1 : 20.wheels were lifted over **a.**
15 : 7. I will set my face **a.t.** (2)
20 : 8. to accompl. my anger **a.t.**(2)
35 : 11. used out of thy hatred **a.t.**
38 : 17. th. I would bring thee **a.t.**
Da. 7 : 21. same horn prevailed **a.t.**

Ho. 10 : 10. people sh. be gath-d **a.t.**
Mat. 10 : 18. for a testimony **a.t.**,
Mk. 6 : 11.-13 : 9. Lu. 9 : 5. [19.
Mk. 12 : 12. spok. parable **a.t.**, Lu. 20 :
Ac 13 : 51. shook off the dust **a.t.**
16 : 22. the multitude rose up **a.t.**
19 : 16. man in wh. ev. spirit, prevail-
26 : 10. I gave my voice **a.t.** [ed **a.t.**
11. being exceedingly mad **a.t.**
Ro. 2 : 2. judgment of God is **a.t.** [t.
Col. 3 : 19. love wives, be not bitter **a.**
2 Pe. 2 : 11. not railing accusat. **a.t.**
Re. 11 : 7. beast shall make war **a.t.**
See **ANGER kindled, FIGHT against, GO up, RISE up,** TESTIFIED, ST, TESTIFY.

THEM all, All THEM, or All of THEM.

Ge. 42 : 17. he put **t.a.** into ward
45 : 22. To **a.t.** gave changes of rai.
Nu. 23 : 13. Thou shalt not see **t.a.**
Jos. 11 : 6. I will deliver **t.a.** slain
1 S. 22 : 11. they came **a.t.** to the k.
1 K. 7 : 37. **a.t.** had one casting
1 Ch. 7 : 3. sons of Uzzi; **a.t.** chief
12 : 15. put to flight **a.t.** of valleys
2 Ch. 5 : 12. singers **a.t.** of Asaph
31 : 1. altars, utterly destroyed **t.a.**
36 : 17. Lord gave **t.a.** into his hand
Ezr. 6 : 20. priests, Levites, **a.t.** pure
8 : 20. **a.t.** expressed by name [wives
10 : 14. let **a.t.** wh. have taken stra.
Ne. 4 : 8. conspired **a.t.** to fight ag.
9 : 6. art Lord, preservest **t.a.** [Jeru.
Jb. 1 : 5. offered acc. to number of **t.a.**
Ps. 34 : 19. delivereth him out of **t.a.**
102 : 26. **a.t.** sh. wax old like garm.
104 : 24. in wisd. hast thou made **t.a.**
129 : 5. Let **t.a.** be confounded that
147 : 4. calleth **t.a.** by their names
Pr. 22 : 2. Lord is the maker of **t.a.**
30 : 27. locusts go **a.t.** by bands
31 : 29. dau-s, thou excellest **t.a.** [a.
Ec. 7 : 18. feareth G. come forth of **t.**
Is. 7 : 19. sh. rest **a.t.** in desolate val.
14 : 18. the kings **a.t.** lie in glory
: 26. host he calleth **t.a.** by na-s
: 22. are **a.t.** snared in holes [11.
40 : 9. make image are **a.t.** vanity,
45 : 16. They shall be ashamed **a.t.**
49 : 18. shalt clothe thee with **t.a.**
57 : 13. wind shall carry **t.a.** away
65 : 8. that I may not destroy **t.a.**
Je. 9 : 25. I will punish **a.t.** circumc.
23 : 14. are **a.t.** unto me as Sodom
29 : 31. Send to **a.t.** of captivity
48 : 39. Moab a derision to **a.t.** abo.
Eze. 7 : 16. **a.t.** mourning for iniq-y
20 : 40. in holy mt. sh. **a.t.** serve me
23 : 6. **a.t.** desirable young men, 12,
15. **a.t.** princes to look to [23. (2)
32 : 12. terrible of the nations **a.t.**
22. **a.t.** slain by sw., 24, 25, 26, 30.
37 : 22. one king sh. be king to **t.a.**
38 : 4. **a.t.** clothed with armour (2)
8. they shall dwell safely **a.t.** [5.
11. **a.t.** dwelling without walls
15. **a.t.** upon horses, mighty army
Da. 1 : 19. among **t.a.** none like Dan.
2 : 38. beasts, made thee ruler ov. **t.a.**
Ho. 5 : 2. have been a rebuker of **t.a.**
Am. 9 : 1. cut in the head **a.t.** [ness
Na. 2 : 10. faces of **t.a.** gather black-
Ha. 1 : 15. Take up **a.t.** wi. the angle
Mat. 12 : 15. multit-s, he healed **t.a.**
24 : 39. flood took **t.a.** aw., Lu. 17 :
26 : 70. Pet. denied bef. **t.a.** [27, 29.
Mk. 2 : 12. he took up the bed, went forth before **t.a.** [8 : 54.
5 : 40. when had put **t.a.** out, Lu.
6 : 41. two fishes divided he am. **t.a.**
Lu. 3 : 16. John answered, unto **t.a.**
6 : 10. looking upon **t.a.**, Jes. said
19. went virtue out and healed **t.a.**
9 : 15. they made **t.a.** sit down
23. said to **t.a.**, If any man will
Jn. 2 : 15. he drove **t.a.** out of temple
Ac. 4 : 33. great grace was upon **t.a.**
9 : 40. Peter put **t.a.** forth, kneeled
10 : 44. Holy Gh. fell on **a.t.** which
11 : 23. Barnabas exhorted **t.a.** [fied
20 : 32. among **a.t.** wh. are sancti-
36. Paul kneeled, prayed with **t.a.**
27 : 33. besought **t.a.** to take meat
35. gave thanks in presence of **t.a.**
Ro. 11 : 32. concluded **t.a.** in unbeli.
Ga. 2 : 14. I said unto Pet. bef. **t.a.**
2 Ti. 3 : 11. out of **t.a.** L. deliv-d me
4 : 8. **a.t.** that love his appearing

Among THEM.

Ge. 47 : 6. any man of activity **a.t.**
Ex. 7 : 5. **a.t.**, 29 : 46.-30 : 13, 14.-36 : 8. Le. 15 : 31.-16 : 16. Nu. 1 : 47.-11 : 1, 3, 4.-13 : 2.-14 : 11, 13. -15 : 26, 29.-19 : 10.-25 : 11.-33 : 4.-35 : 15. De. 7 : 20.-29 : 17.-31 : 16. Jos. 8 : 35.-9 : 16,-10 : 1.-13 : 22.-19 : 49.-20 : 4, 9. Ju. 1 : 29, 30.-2 K. 17 : 26.-Ps. 68 : 18.-Je. 37 : 10. La. 1 : 17. Eze. 33 : 6. Zch. 12 : 8. Jn. 12 : 20. Ac. 23 : 10. -24 : 21.-25 : 6. 2 Co. 6 : 17. 2 Pe. 2 : 8.-3 Jn. 9. Jude 15. Re. 7 : 15.
Ex. 10 : 2. tell signs I have done **a.t.**
30 : 12. that there be no plague **a.t.**
Nu. 16 : 3. Lord is **a.t.**, Ps. 68 : 17.
18 : 20. Aaron no part **a.t.**, Jos. 14 :
23 : 21. shout of a king is **a.t.** [3.
Jos. 8 : 33. stranger, as he born **a.t.**
24 : 5. acc. to that which I did **a.t.**
Ju. 10 : 16. put strange gods fr. **a.t.**
1 S. 6. 6. he wrought **a.t.**, Ne 9 : 17.
9 : 22. them sit in chiefest place **a.t.**
10 : 10. and Saul prophesied **a.t.**
2 S. 19 : 28. servant **a.t.** that did eat
2 K. 17 : 25. Lord sent lions **a.t.** [a.t.
1 Ch. 21 : 6. Levi, Benj., not counted
26 : 31. were found mighty men **a.t.**
2 Ch. 20 : 25. **a.t.** abundance of spoil
28 : 15. clothed all were naked **a.t.**
Ezr. 2 : 65. **a.t.** 200 singing men
Ne. 4 : 11. till we come **a.t.** and slay
Es. 9 : 21. establish the Purim **a.t.**
Jb. 1 : 6. Satan came also **a.t.**, 2 : 1.
15 : 19. no stranger passed **a.t.**
Ps. 22 : 18. They part my garm-ts **a.t.**, Mat. 27 : 35. Jn. 19 : 24. [a.t.
55 : 15. Let death seize, wickedn. is
57 : 4. I lie **a.t.** that are set on fire
68 : 25, **a.t.** were damsels playing
78 : 45. sent divers sorts of flies **a.t.**
49. by sending evil angels **a.t.**
99 : 6. Sam. **a.t.** that call upon na.
105 : 27. they shewed his signs **a.t.**
136 : 11. brought out Isr. from **a.t.**
Can. 4 : 2. none is barren **a.t.**, 6 : 6.
Is. 5 : 27. None shall be weary **a.t.**
8 : 15. many **a.t.** sh. stumb. and fall
41 : 28. I beheld, was no man **a.t.**
43 : 9. who **a.t.** can declare this
48 : 14. wh. **a.t.** hath declared these
66 : 19. I will set a sign **a.t.**, and
Je. 6 : 15. sh. fall **a.t.** th. fall, 8 : 12.
18. know, O coug-n, what is **a.t.**
12 : 14. pluck hou. of Judah fr. **a.t.**
24 : 10. famine and pestilence **a.t.**
25 : 16. bec. of sword I will send **a.t.**
41 : 8. ten **a.t.** that said, Slay us not
Eze. 3 : 15. I remained **a.t.** 7 days
25. thou shalt not go out **a.t.**
9 : 2. man **a.t.** had writer's inkhorn
12 : 10, concerneth all Israel **a.t.**
12 the prince that is **a.t.** sh. bear
22 : 26. and I am profaned **a.t.**
30. And I sought for a man **a.t.**
34 : 24. servant David a prince **a.t.**
35 : 11. make myself known **a.t.**
Da. 1 : 19. **a.t.** none like Daniel
7 : 8. came up **a.t.** ano. little horn
11 : 24. he sh. scatter **a.t.** the prey
Ho. 7 : 7. none **a.t.** th. calleth unto
Zch. 12 : 8. feeble **a.t.** be as David
14 : 13. tumult fr. Lord sh. be **a.t.**
Mat. 11 : 11. I say, **a.t.** born of wom.
Mk. 6 : 41. two fishes divided he **a.t.**
Lu. 9 : 46. Then arose a reason-g **a.t.**
22 : 24. there was also a strife **a.t.**
55. Peter sat down **a.t.** in the hall
Jn. 9 : 16. there was division **a.t.**
15 : 24. If I had not done **a.t.** works
Ac. 4 : 34. Nei. any **a.t.** that lacked
17 : 33. So Paul departed from **a.t.**
18 : 11. teaching word of God **a.t.**
Ro. 11 : 17. thou wert graffed in **a.t.**
1 Co. 2 : 6. we speak wisdom **a.t.**
2 Co. 6 : 17. come out from **a.t.** and
Jude 15. convince all ungodly **a.t.**
See DWELL, DWELT, DWELLING, PROPHET, SANCTIFIED.

At THEM.

Nu. 21 : 30. We have shot **a.t.**, Hesh- [bon
De. 7 : 21. shalt not be affrighted **a.t.**
Ps. 10 : 5. enemies, he puffeth **a.t.**
59 : 8. thou, O Lord, sh. laugh **a.t.**
64 : 7. God sh. shoot **a.t.** wi. arrow
Je. 10 : 2. heathen are dismayed **a.t.**

Before THEM.

Ge. 18 : 8. **b.t.**, Jos. 8 : 5, 6, 15.-18 : 1.-21 : 44. Ju. 2 : 21.-3 : 27.-7 : 24.-18 : 21.-1 S. 21 : 13. 2 S. 10 : 16. -20 : 8. 1 K. 7 : 6.-20 : 27. 2 K. 3 : 24.-6 : 22. 1 Ch. 19 : 16 2 Ch 7 : 6.-25 : 14. Ne. 9 : 35.-12 : 36. Ps. 54 : 3.-69 : 22.-86 : 14 Je. 32 : 13. -49 : 37. Eze. 8 : 11.-16 : 18, 19.-23 : 24.-40 : 22, 26 -42 : 11. Da. 4 : 7. Am. 2 : 9. Mat. 14 : 6.-26 : 70. Mk. 2 : 12.-6 : 41.-8 : 6, 7.-10 : 32. Lu. 5 : 25.-24 : 43. Jn. 12 : 37.
Ex. 10 : 14. **b.t.** were no such locusts
Nu. 14 : 14. thou goest **b.t.** by dayti.
27 : 17. go out and in **b.t.**, 1 S. 18 : 16.
De. 2 : 12. destroyed them from **b.t.**, 21, 22. 1 Ch. 5 : 25. Ne. 9 : 24.
28 : 25. shalt flee seven ways **b.t.**
1 S. 10 : 5. with tabret and harp **b.t.**
1 K. 8 : 50. give them compassion **b.t.**, 2 Ch. 30 : 9. [2 Ch. 18 : 9.
22 : 10. prophets prophesied **b.t.**,
2 K. 17 : 11. whom L. carried aw. **b.t.**
Ps. 22 : 25. I will pay my vows **b.t.**
78 : 55. he cast out heathen **b.t.**
105 : 17. He sent a man **b.t.**, Joseph
Ec. 4 : 16. no end of all people **b.t.**
9 : 1. or hatred by all that is **b.t.**
Is. 30 . 8. go write it **b.t.** in table
42 : 16 I will make darkn. light **b.t.**
63 : 12. dividing the water **b.t.**
Je. 33 : 24. no more be a nation **b.t.**
Eze. 8 : 11. there stood **b.t.** 70 men
23 : 24. I will set judgment **b.t.**
32 : 10. when I brandish sword **b.t.**
44 : 11. shall stand **b.t.** to minister
Jo. 2 : 3. A fire devoureth **b.t.**, land is as garden of Eden **b.t.**
10. The earth shall quake **b.t.**
Mi. 2 : 13. breaker is come up **b.t.**
Zch. 12 : 8. David as angel of L. **b.t.**
Mt. 17 : 2. transfig-d **b.t.**, Mk. 9 : 2.
Jn. 10 : 4. shepherd goeth **b.t.** sheep
Ga. 2 : 14. I said unto Peter **b.t.** all
See **PASSED over,** PASS, PASSED, SET, WENT.

Behind THEM.

Ex. 14 : 19. pillar removed, stood **b.t.** [t.
Jos. 8 : 20. men of Ai looked **b.t.**
Ju. 20 : 40. Benjamites looked **b.t.**
2 S. 5 : 23. fetch a compass **b.t.**
2 Ch. 13 : 13. ambushm-t to come **b.t.**
Jo. 2 : 3. **b.t.** flame burneth, **b.t.** [wildern.

Beside THEM.

Jb. 1 : 14. the asses were feeding **b.t.**
Eze. 10 : 16. wheels turned not from **b.t.**, 19.-11 : 22. [talents, 22.
Mat. 25 : 20. I have gained **b.t.** five

Between THEM.

Ex. 22 : 11. oath of the L. sh. be **b.t.**
28 : 33. and bells of gold **b.t.** round
Jos. 8 : 11. was a valley **b.t.** and Ai
1 S. 17 : 3. a valley **b.t.** and Philis.
26 : 13. David stood; a gr. space **b.t.**

2 S. 14 : † 6. there was no deliv-r **b.t.**
21 : 7. because of Lord's oath **b.t.**
1 K. 18 : 6. So divided the land **b.t.**
Jb. 41 : 16. no air ean come **b.t.**
Zch. 6 : 13. counsel of peace be **b.t.**
Ac. 15 : 39. content-n was sharp **b.t.**

THEM both.

Ge. 3 : 7. eyes of **t.b.** were opened
48 : 13. Jo. took **t.b.**, Ephr., Manas.
Ex. 22 : 11. oath of Lord between **t.b.**
26 : 24. thus shall it be for **t.b.**
De. 22 : 24. sh. bring **t.b.** out to gate
2 K. 2 : 11. parted **t.b.**, Elijah went
Pr. 24 : 22. who knoweth ruin of **t.b.**
27 : 3. fools' wrath heavier than **t.b.**
Zch. 6 : 13. counsel of peace betw. **t.b.**
Lu. 7 : 42. he frankly forgave **t.b.**

Both of THEM.

Ge. 21 : 27. **b.o.t.** made a covenant
31. bec. there they sware **b.o.t.**
22 : 6. Abra-m, Isaac went, **b.o.t.**, 8.
40 : 5. dreamed a dream, **b.o.t.**
Ex. 36 : 29. thus he did to **b.o.t.**
Le. 20 : 11. **b. o. t.** shall be put to
death, 12. De. 22 : 22 (2).
13. **b.o.t.** have committed abom-n
18. **b.o.t.** sh. be cut off from people
Nu. 7 : 13. **b.o.t.** full of fine flour,
19, 25, 31, 37, 43, 49, 55, 61, 67, 73, 79.
25 : 8. Phinehas thrust **b.o.t.** thro.
Ju. 19 : 6. did eat, drink, **b.o.t.**, 8.
Ru. 1 : 5. Mahlon, Chilion died, **b.**
1 S. 2 : 34. in 1 day sh. die **b.o.t.** [**o.t.**
9 : 26. went on **b.o.t.**, he and Sam.
14 : 11. **b. o. t.** discovered themselves unto Philistines [**t.**
20 : 11. Jona., David went out **b.o.**
25 : 43. were **b.o.t.** David's wives
2 S. 17 : 18. went **b.o.t.** away quickly
Pr. 20 : 10. **b.o.t.** abom-n to the Lord
12. ear, eye, L. hath made **b.o.t.**

By THEM.

Le. 19 : 31. **b.t.**, Jos. 13 : 22.-23 : 7.
Ju. 8 : 1, 4.-9 : 25. 2 S. 15 : 36. 2
Ch. 24 : 13. Ne. 4 : 12. Ps. 104 :
12. Je. 5 : 7. Eze. 1 : 19.-37 : 2.
Ha. 1 : 16. Mk. 6 : 48. Lu. 24 : 4.
Ac. 1 : 10.-4 : 16.-15 : 12. Ro. 10 :
19. 1 Ti. 1 : 18. He. 2 : 3. 1 Pe. 1 : 12.
Jb. 36 : 31. **b.t.** judgeth he the peo.
Ps. 19 : 11. **b.t.** is thy servant warned
Is. 7 : 20. **b.t.** beyond the river [**t.**?
Eze. 14 : 3. sho. I be inquired of **b.**
Mat. 5 : 21. said **b.t.** of old, 27, 33.
Ro. 10 : 5. doeth those shall live **b.t.**
1 Co. 1 : 11. **b.t.** of house of Chloe

Concerning THEM.

Nu. 32 : 28. **c.t.** Moses commanded
Ju. 15 : 3. **c.t.** I shall be blameless
Ne. 11 : 23. it was king's comm-t **c.t.**
1 Th. 4 : 13. to be ignorant **c.t.** asleep
1 Jn. 2 : 26. written **c.t.** that seduce

For THEM. [47 : 24.

Ge. 6 : 21. be for food **f.** thee and **t.**,
34 : 21. land, it is large enough **f.t.**
43 : 32. and they set on bread **f.t.**
Ex. 14 : 25. **f.t.** 16 : 16.-26 : 37.-28 :
40 (2).-36 : 36. Le. 4 : 20.-7 : 7.-
9 : 7.-10 : 17. Nu. 4 : 26.-8 : 21.-
10 : 33.-11 : 22.-16 : 46. De. 28 :
32.-33 : 2. Jos. 9 : 22. Ju. 21 :
16, 17. Ru. 1 : 13. 2 K. 6 : 23.-
17 : 32. 1 Ch. 12 : 39. 2 Ch. 28 :
14.-30 : 18.-35 : 15.- Ne. 5 : 2.-
9 : 15. Es. 5 : 8. Jb. 6 : 19.-24 : 5.
Ps. 104 : 8.-106 : 45. Is. 4 : 2.-
28 : 13. Je. 16 : 6, 7.-18 : 20.-28 :
13. Eze. 7 : 11.-16 : 21.-20 : 6.-
28 : 37.-34 : 10.-45 : 15.-46 : 17.
Zch. 10 : 8, 10. Mat. 5 : 44. Lu.
6 : 28. Jn. 17 : 9, 20. Ac. 8 : 15.-
10 : 24.-17 : 16.-1 Co. 2 : 9. 2 Co.
5 : 15. He. 6 : 7.-11 : 16. Re. 20 : 11.
Le. 4 : 20. priest shall make atonement **f.t.**, 9 : 7,-10 : 17. Nu. 8 :
21.-16 : 46. [Shiloh
Jos. 18 : 10 Joshua cast lots **f.t.** in
Jos. 19 : 9. part of Jud. too much **f.t.**
47. the coast of Dan too little **f.t.**
2 Ch. 34 : 21. Go, inquire of Lord **f.t.**
Ne. 1 : 5. G. keepeth mercy **f.t.** [**f.t.**?
Jb. 22 : 17. what can Almighty do
Ps. 31 : 19. hast laid up **f.t.** that fear
thee, **f.t.** that trust in thee
126 : 2. L. hath done great thi-s **f.t.**
Is. 23 : 18. merchandise shall be **f.t.**
34 : 17. he hath cast the lot **f.t.**
35 : 1. solitary place be glad **f.t.**
Je. 3 : 2. in the ways hast sat **f.t.**
7 : 16. nei. lift up cry nor prayer **f.t.**
Eze. 11 : 21. as **f.t.** whose heart
34 : 29. raise **f.t.** plant of renown
36 : 37. I will be inquired of to do it
48 : 10. **f.t.** shall be oblation [**f.t.**
Da. 2 : 35. no place **f.t.**, Re. 20 : 11.
Ho. 2 : 18. covenant **f.t.** with beasts
Mat. 12 : 4. nei. lawful **f.t.** with him
18 : 19. be done **f.t.** of my Father.
Mk. 10 : 24. hard **f.t.** trust in riches
Lu. 2 : 7. no room **f.t.** in the inn
Jn. 6 : 7. bread is not sufficient **f.t.**
1 Co. 7 : 8. good **f.t.** if they abide as
14 : 22. prophesying serveth **f.t.**
Col. 2 : 1. what gr. conflict I have **f.t.**
4 : 13. great zeal **f.t.** in Laodicea
He. 1 : 14. sent forth to minister **f.t.**
6 : 7. bringeth forth herbs meet **f.t.**
7 : 25. to make intercession **f.t.**
2 Pe. 2 : 21. it had been better **f.t.**
1 Jn. 5 : 16. give life **f.t.** that sin not
See DIED, FOUND, FOUNDED,
PRAY, PREPARED, WAITED.

From THEM. [f.t.

Ge. 11 : 6. nothing will be restrained
42 : 24. he took **f.t.** Simeon and
Nu. 18 : 26. tithes I have given **f.t.**
35 : 8. **f. t.** that have many give
many ; **f.t.** that have few give
De. 8 : 4. **f.t.**, 22 : 1, 4.-31 : 17.-32 : 20.
1 S. 6 : 7. 2 S. 22 : 18, 23. 2 K.
17 : 22. 1 Ch. 2 : 23. 2 Ch. 28 : 8.
Ps. 18 : 17.-69 : 14. Mk. 14 : 52.
Lu. 2 : 15.-4 : 42.-22 : 41. Ac.
15 : 38.-21 : 1. Ro. 15 : 31.
22 : 1. shall not see sheep go astray,
and hide thyself **f.t.**, 4.
31 : 17. hide my face **f.t.**, 32 : 20.
Eze. 7 : 22. Mi. 3 : 4. [secute me
Ps. 31 : 15. deliver me **f.t.** that per-
Ec. 2 : 10. eyes desired I kept not **f.t.**
Je. 8 : 13. things given sh. pass **f.t.**
9 : 2. I might leave peo. and go **f.t.**
Eze. 23 : 17. mind was alienated **f.t.**
39 : 23. hid I my face **f.t.**, 24.
29. nei. will I hide my face **f.t.**
Mi. 2 : 8. ye pull off the robe **f.t.**
Mat. 8 : 30. good way off **f.t.** a herd
Mk. 14 : 52. yo. man fled **f.t.** naked
Lu. 9 : 45. saying was hid **f.t.**, 18 : 34.
24 : 51. was parted **f.t.** and carried
Jn. 12 : 36. did hide himself **f.t.**
2 Co. 2 : 3. I should have sorrow **f.t.**
11 : 12. I may cut off occasion **f.t.**
He. 7 : 6. descent is not counted **f.t.**
2 Pe. 2 : 18. **f.t.** who live in error
Re. 9 : 6. desire to die, death flee **f.t.**
See DEFEND, DELIVERED, DE-
PART, ED, ING, FAR, PASSED,
TAKE, TAKEN, THRUST, TURN,
TURNED, WENT, WITHDRAWN,
WITHHOLD.

In THEM.

Ge. 30 : 37. **i.t.**, Ex. 12 : 16. Le. 22 :
25. Nu. 16 : 7, 17, 18. Ju. 21 :
23. 1 S. 31 : 7. 1 Ch. 10 : 7. 2 Ch.
4 : 6.-11 : 11.-14 : 14. Ec. 2 : 5.
Eze 5 : 13.-10 : 17.-28 : 25.-46 :
23. Da. 1 : 4. Ob. 18. Hag. 2 : 22.
Ex. 20 : 11 L. made heaven, earth, sea,
and all that **i. t.** is, Ac. 4 : 24.
29 : 29. to be consecrated **i. t.**
Le. 10 : 3. I will be sanctified **i. t.**
Le. 18 : 5. he shall livo **i.t.**, Ne. 9 : 29.
Eze. 20 : 11, 13, 21. Ga. 3 : 12.
Nu. 20 : 13. and he was sanctified **i.t.**
De. 5 : 29. O were such a heart **i.t.**
32 : 28. nei. any understanding **i.t.**
Jos. 5 : 1. nei. was spirit **i.t.** more
Jb. 4 : 21. Doth not excellency **i.t.**
Pr. 8 : 8. is nothing froward **i.t.**
Ec. 3 : 12. I know is no good **i.t.**
Is. 6 : 13. oak, whose substance is **i.t.**
8 : 20. it is bec. there is no light **i.t.**
Je. 2 : 37. thou shalt not prosper **i.t.**
5 : 13. prophets, the word is not **i.t.**
8 : 9. wise, what wisdom is **i.t.** [good
10 : 5. cannot do evil, nei. **i.t.** to do
Eze. 5 : 13. accomplished my fury **i.t.**
10 : 17. spirit of living creature **i.t.**
18 : 24. his sin, **i.t.** shall he die, 26.
28 : 25. when I sh. be sanctified **i.t.**
33 : 10. our sins, if pine away **i.t.**
Da. 5 : 3. his wives drank **i.t.**, 23.
Ob. 18. kindle **i.t.** and devour them
Mal. 2 : 17. doeth evil, delighteth **i.t.**
Mat. 13 : 14. **i.t.** is fulfilled prophecy
Lu. 13 : 14. six days, **i.t.** be healed
Jn. 5 : 39. **i.t.** think ye have eternal
17 : 10. I am glorified **i.t.** [life
23. I **i.t.**, and thou in me, th. they
26. th. love may be **i.t.** and I **i.t.**
Ro. 1 : 19. known of God, manif. **i.t.**
Ep. 4 : 18. alienated thro. ignor. **i.t.**
He. 4 : 2. not mixed with faith **i.t.**
1 Pe. 1 : 11. spirit of Christ wh. was **i.**
2 Pe. 3 : 16. speaking **i.t.** of these [**t.**
Re. 5 : 13. all that are **i.t.** heard I
15 : 1. **i.t.** is filled up wrath of God
20 : 13. delivered up the dead **i.t.**
21 : 14. **i.t.** names of twelve apostles
See BREATH, CONTINUE, DWELL,
FAINTED, LIVED, PERISH,
PLEASURE, SET, TRUSTETH,
WALK, WALKED, WASH.

Into THEM. [lived

Eze. 37 : 10. breath came **i.t.** they
Mk 5 : 12. may enter **i.t.**, Lu. 8 : 32.
Re. 11 : 11. spirit from God entered

Of THEM. [i.t.

Ge. 2 : 1. **o.t.**, 19 : 13.-22 : 8.-42 : 9.
Ex. 14 : 7.-19 : 21.-20 : 5, 6.-21 :
34.-25 : 3.-32 : 18.-35 : 35.-38 :
25. Le. 4 : 2.-10 : 1.-11 : 4, 22,
24, 28, 32, 33.-22 : 22.-25 : 44,
45.-26 : 43. Nu. 1 : 49.-3 : 32,
48, 49, 51.-7 : 5.-11 : 26.-14 : 23.
-16 : 3, 15, 34.-17 : 2.-18 : 12.-
21 : 1.-26 : 64.-27 : 3.-33 : 55.
De. 2 : 6.-5 : 9, 10.-20 : 19.-28 :
8.-25 : 5.-31 : 4.-33 : 11 (2). Jos.
10 : 8, 19, 20.-19 : 9. Ju. 5 : 30.-
11 : 35.-20 : 42 2 S. 6 : 22. 1 K.
1 : 40. 2 K. 2 : 24.-10 : 14.-11 : 4.
12 : 11.-16 : 17.-17 : 32.-22 : 9.-
23 : 12.-25 : 19. 1 Ch. 2 : 6, 53.-
5 : 20.-24 : 19. 2 Ch. 28 : 15. Ezr.
10 : 3, 6. Ne. 4 : 9.-5 : 10, 11, 12.
-7 : 5.-8 : 17.-10 : 31.-13 : 25. Es.
3 : 13.-8 : 11.-9 : 2, 28. Jb. 14 : 21.-
22 : 20.-30 : 31. Ps. 9 : 13.-19 :
11.-21 : 12.-24 : 6.-33 : 6.-34 :
16, 22.-40 : 5.-49 : 7.-58 : 3.-68 :
11.-65 : 5.-69 : 9, 24.-78 : 31.-
84 : 5.-101 : 3.-105 : 3, 38.-107 :
34.-109 : 15, 20.-119 : 63.-127 :
5.-139 : 16, 17. Pr. 21 : 6.-22 :
26.-Ec. 5 : 11.-7 : 18.-9 : 5. Is.
9 : 16.-10 : 22.-13 : 8.-17 : 14.-
19 : 22.-24 : 8.-25 : 11.-28 : 1.-
31 : 2, 4.-32 : 3.-39 : 2.-41 : 22,
28.-42 : 9.-51 : 23.-60 : 14.-65 :
1, 22.-66 : 19, 21. Je 6 : 13.-8 :
3, 19.-11 : 23.-12 : 4.-15 : 9.-22 :
25.-25 : 14.-29 : 5, 22, 28.-30 :
19, 21.-31 : 4, 34.-32 : 39.-33 : 11.
34 : 9, 10, 20.-37 : 5.-40 : 7.-41 :
18.-42 : 17.-44 : 27, 30.-50 : 28,
43.-51 : 1.-52 : 17, 25. Eze. 5 : 4.
7 : 11.-8 : 11.-12 : 16, 19.-16 :
27, 53.-19 : 11.-20 : 17.-21 : 29.-
23 : 28.-28 : 8.-29 : 21.-32 : 20,

25.-34 : 27 -36 : 23.-37 : 26, 28.-
39 : 12, 28.-43 : 9 -46 : 10, 24.
Da. 1 : 20.-6 : 24 -12 : 2. Ho 5 :
4.-6 : 8.-13 : 2. Jo. 2 : 4. Am. 5 :
11.-6 : 7.-9 : 14. Jon. 1 : 5.-3 : 5.
Mi. 2 : 13.-3 : 2, 3.-7 : 4, 13.
Zch. 6 : 10.-11 : 13.-14 : 8, 21.-
Mat. 2 : 4, 7.-4 : 8.-17 : 12.-18 :
2, 20.-21 : 3, 12, 31, 45.-23 : 31.-
26 : 2. Mk. 8 : 3.-9 : 36.-11 : 5,
15.-12 : 23.-16 : 12. Lu. 4 : 6, 26,
27, 30, 40.-5 : 2.-6 : 13.-7 : 42.-
9 : 46.-14 : 10.-15 : 12 -20 : 33.-
22 : 23, 24, 58.-23 : 1, 23, 51.-24 :
13, 24, 35, 36. Jn. 4 : 52.-8 : 59.
-10 : 20.-16 : 4.-17 : 12.-18 : 9.-
Ac. 1 : 3.-2 : 3.-3 : 2, 5 -4 : 4, 13,
32.-5 : 9, 24.-6 : 9.-8 : 16.-10 : 7.
-13 : 31.-15 : 2, 14.-19 : 12, 19.-
21 : 26.-22 : 11, 20.-23 : 21, 27.-
27 : 35. Ro. 2 : 19.-10 : 15, 20.-
11 : 12, 15.-15 : 3. 1 Co. 4 : 19.-10 :
5, 27.-12 : 18.-14 : 10.-15 : 20. 2
Co. 11 : 8.-12 : 17. Ep. 5 : 12.
Col. 2 : 15. 1 Ti. 3 : 7.-4 : 3. He.
6 : 12,-10 : 33, 39.-11 : 6, 13. Ja.
3 : 18.-5 : 3, 4. 1 Pe. 2 : 14.-4 : 17.
Re. 2 : 9.-4 : 8.-5 : 8, 11.-6 : 9, 11.
7 : 4.-9 : 16.-20 : 4 -21 : 24 -22 : 9.
Ps. 40 : 5. if I would speak **o.t.** they
65 : 5. **o.t.** afar off on the sea
Lu. 22 : 23. which **o.t.** sho. do this?
58. ano. said, Thou art also **o.t.**
He. 10 : 39. we are not **o.t.** who draw
back, but **o.t.** that believe
See AFRAID, NUMBERED,

All of THEM, One of THEM.

Some of THEM. [ing
Ex. 16 : 20. **-t.** left manna until morn-
2 S. 17 : 9. when **-t.** be overthrown
2 K. 17 : 25. L. sent lions wh. slew **-t.**
1 Ch. 4 : 42. And **-t.**, 500 men, went
Ezr. 10 : 44. **-t.**, Da. 11 : 35. Mat.
28 : 34 (2).-27 : 47. Mk. 9 : 1.
15 : 35. Lu. 11 : 15. Jn. 7 : 25, 44,
-11 : 37, 46.-13 : 29. Ac. 5 : 15.-
11 : 20.-17 : 4. Ro. 11 : 14. 1 Co.
10 : 7, 8, 9, 10. [persecute
Lu. 11 : 49. **-t.** they shall slay and
See SOME.

On, or Upon THEM.

Ge. 19 : 3.-31 : 34.-40 : 6.-45 : 15.-
48 : 16. Ex. 5 : 8.-9 : 19.-15 : 9,
15, 16, 19.-18 : 8.-19 : 22, 24.-
28 : 9.-29 : 8, 9, 13, 22. Le. 3 : 4,
10, 15.-4 : 9.-8 : 13.-26 : 36. Nu.
4 : 8.-10 : 34.-11 : 17, 25, 26, 29.
-16 : 33.-31 : 27. De. 7 : 16, 25.-
9 : 10.-27 : 3, 5.-30 : 7.-32 : 23,
24, 35. Jos. 9 : 5.-10 : 11.-11 : 7.
Ju. 9 : 49, 57.-16 : 26.-19 : 14.-
20 : 41. 1 S. 2 : 8, 10.-5 : 6.-9 :
20.-25 : 14.-26 : 12. 2 S. 5 : 23.-
11 : 23.-16 : 1.-21 : 10. 1 K. 7 :
25.-8 : 50.-9 : 9.-18 : 28. 2 K. 2 :
24.-4 : 33.-13 : 23.-18 : 23.-23 :
20. 1 Ch. 9 : 27.-14 : 14.-19 : 17
2 Ch. 4 : 4.-7 : 22.-14 : 14.-32 :
26.-33 : 11.-36 : 17. Ezr. 3 : 3.-
7 : 24. Ne. 9 : 1. Es. 8 : 17.-9 : 3,
27. Jb. 1 : 15.-21 : 9, 17.-29 : 22,
24. Ps. 33 : 18.-48 : 6.-49 : 14.-
55 : 15.-62 : 10.-69 : 24.-78 :
24, 27, 31, 49.-103 : 17.-105 :
38.-106 : 29.-118 : 7.-119 : 84.
-140 : 10. Ec. 9 : 12. Is. 8 : 7.-
9 : 2.-18 : 6.-26 : 16.-27 : 11.-
33 : 4.-36 : 8.-40 : 24.-49 : 10.-
63 : 7.-66 : 4. Je. 6 : 21.-11 : 20.-
12 : 15.-14 : 16.-15 : 8.-18 : 22.-
20 : 12.-24 : 6.-29 : 17.-32 : 23,
42.-33 : 26.-42 : 17.-46 : 21. Eze.
5 : 13, 16.-6 : 12, 14.-13 : 15.-
20 : 8, 13, 21.-22 : 31.-23 : 16,
46.-25 : 12, 17.-30 : 9.-36 : 18.-
37 : 8.-39 : 21.-41 : 25.-43 : 24.-
44 : 17. Da. 8 : 27.-8 : 10.-10 : 7.
Ho. 5 : 10.-7 : 12. Am. 9 : 4.
Ha. 1 : 13. Zph. 3 : 8. Zch. 2 :
9.-10 : 6.-14 : 17. Mat. 9 : 36.-
19 : 15.-20 : 25, 34.-21 : 7. Mk
3 : 5, 34.-10 : 27, 42.-15 : 24. Lu.
1 : 50.-2 : 9.-6 : 10.-22 : 25. Jn.
6 : 2.-20 : 22. Ac. 4 : 1, 33.-5 : 5.
11 : 15.-16 : 23 -19 : 6, 13, 16.-21 :
23. Ro. 11 : 22. Ga. 6 : 16. 1 Th.
2 : 16.-5 : 3. 2 Th. 1 : 8. He. 9 :
10. Re. 6 : 10.-7 : 16.-9 : 17.-11 :
11.-16 : 2.-19 : 18.-20 : 4.
Ex. 32 : 34. I will visit their sin **u.t.**,
21. Ps. 94 : 23. [12, 13, 16, 27.
Le. 20 : 11. then blood sh. be **u.t.**,
2 Ch. 29 : 23. they laid their hands
o.t., Ac. 4 : 3.-6 : 6.-8 : 17.-13 : 3.
Je. 11 : 11. I will bring evil **u.t.**, 8.-
2 : 3.-23 : 12.-36 : 31.-49 : 37
Mat. 19 : 13. should put his hands
u.t., Mk. 10 : 16. [way
He. 5 : 2. **o.t.** that are out of the
See FELL, MERCY, SET.

Over THEM.

Ge. 47 : 20. Ex. 18 : 21. Nu. 7 : 2.-
11 : 16.-14 : 14. Ju. 9 : 8.-11 : 11.
1 S. 8 : 9.-19 : 20.-22 : 2. 2 S. 2 :
7.-18 : 1. 1 K. 12 : 17. 2 K. 25 :
22. 1 Ch. 9 : 20.-27 : 26. 2 Ch.
2 : 11.-9 : 8 -10 : 17. Ne. 9 : 28.
Es. 9 : 1. Ps. 49 : 14.-106 : 41.
Pr. 20 : 26. Is. 52 : 5. Je. 15 : 3.-
23 : 4.-31 : 28.-32 : 41.-40 : 11.-
43 : 10.-44 : 27 Eze. 10 : 1, 19.-
11 : 22.-34 : 23.-37 : 24. Mi. 3 :
6.-4 : 7. Ha. 1 : 14. Zch. 9 : 14.
Mat. 20 : 25. Mk. 10 : 42. Lu.
11 : 44.-19 : 27.-22 : 25. Ac. 19 :
13. Ro. 5 : 14. Col. 2 : 15. Re. 9 :
11.-11 : 10.
See REIGN, RULE, RULER, SET.

THEM that.

Ge. 12 : 3. **t.t.**, 1 S. 2 : 30 -10 : 18. 2
S. 19 : 28. 2 K. 11 : 9.-23 : 5. 2
Ch. 14 : 11.-23 : 8. Ps. 5 : 11.-
25 : 14.-35 : 1 -54 : 4.-57 : 4.-68 :
1.-88 : 4.-99 : 6.-103 : 11.-118 : 7.
Pr. 21 : 6. Ec. 8 : 12. Is. 41 : 12.-
49 : 9.-60 : 14. Je. 6 : 15.-25 : 16.
Eze. 26 : 20 (2)-31 : 14, 16, 18,
32 : 18, 21, 24, 25, 28, 29, 30, 32.-
38 : 11. Ho. 7 : 7. Zph. 1 : 5.-3 :
11. Mk. 1 : 32.-5 : 40.-6 : 22.-
15 : 7. Lu. 4 : 18.-11 : 52.-19 :
45. Ac. 4 : 34.-5 : 16.-17 : 17.-
21 : 24.-22 : 11, 19. Ro. 12 : 15.
1 Co. 16 : 3. Ep. 6 : 24. Col. 4 :
13. 1 Th. 4 : 14. 1 Ti. 5 : 20. 2
Ti. 2 : 22. He. 2 : 18.-3 : 17.-10 :
14.-11 : 6. Ja. 1 : 12.-2 : 5. 1 Pe.
4 : 19. Re. 9 : 17.-11 : 1.-13 : 6.
Je. 5 : 7. sworn by **t.t.** are no gods
Eze. 32 : 25. **t.t.** go do. to the pit, 29.
Zph. 1 : 6. **t.t.** are turned from the L.
Mk. 4 : 11. but unto **t.t.** are without
Lu. 1 : 79. light to **t.t.** are in darkn.
24 : 33. found the eleven and **t.t.**
Ac. 5 : 32. Holy Ghost to **t.t.** obey
20 : 34. ministered to **t.t.** were wi.
22 : 11. led by **t.t.** were wi. me [me
Ro. 10 : 19 jealousy by **t.t.** are no
1 Co. 5 : 12. I to judge **t.t.** are without? 13. Col. 4 : 5. 1 Th. 4 : 12.
16 : 18 acknowledge **t.t.** are such,
2 Th. 3 : 12. [thee
1 Ti. 4 : 16. Save thyself and **t.t.** hear
He. 5 : 2. compassion on **t.t.** are out
14. meat to **t.t.** are of full age
11 : 6. a rewarder of **t.t.** seek him
1 Pe. 1 : 12. reported by **t.t.** preached
See **All them THAT.**
See **TEACH them.**

Through THEM. [t.t.

Ge. 6 : 13. earth filled with violence
Ju. 2 : 22. that **t.t.** I may prove Isr.
Je. 9 : 10. because they are burned
up, so that none can pass **t.t.**

To, or Unto THEM.

Ge. 37 : 13. -40 : 6, 22.-42 : 7. 23, 25
43 : 23.-44 : 4 -45 : 27.-49 : 28.-
50 : 21. Ex. 1 : 19.-3 : 13.-6 : 3.-
7 : 13, 22.-8 : 15.-9 : 12.-12 : 36.-
14 : 20, 22.-30 : 21. Le. 6 : 17.-
-17 : 7.-26 : 41 Nu. 4 : 27.-16 :
30.-20 : 6 -35 . 6. De 1 : 8.-4 : 7.
-7 : 2.-18 : 18.-31 : 23.-33 : 2.-
Jos. 11 : 9 Ju. 2 : 17 -9 : 33, 51.
1 S. 14 : 8.-30 : 19, 27, 28, 29, 30,
31. 2 S. 20 : 3. 1 K. 12 : 7. 2 K.
9 : 18, 20.-10 : 1.-12 : 5.-20 : 13.
-23 : 19. 1 Ch. 9 : 27. 2 Ch 32 :
6. Ezr. 4 : 20.-5 : 1.-6 : 21. Ne.
8 : 4, 5, 7, 9, 10.-5 : 11.-6 : 17.
Es. 9 : 22. Jb. 24 : 12, 17. Ps 28 :
4.-34 : 9, 18.-36 : 10.-44 : 3, 13.
-60 : 4.-73 : 10.-83 : 9.-115 : 8.-
125 : 4.-135 : 18. Pr. 2 : 7.-3 : 18.
-8 : 9 :-10 : 26.-14 : 22.-22 : 21.-
24 : 25.-25 : 13.-30 : 5. Ec. 7 : 11,
12. Is. 1 : 23.-19 : 3.-24 : 9.-28 :
13.-34 : 17.-35 : 4.-40 : 29.-42 :
5, 16.-50 : 6.-56 : 5.-57 : 6.-59 :
20.-61 : 7. Je. 5 : 5 -6 : 10.-7 :
27.-11 : 11.-14 : 13.-15 : 19.-18 :
8.-23 : 17, 21.-24 : 10.-26 : 2, 3.
-29 : 19.-30 : 9.-31 : 32.-33 : 6.-
35 : 17.-36 : 3, 32.-38 : 4.-40 : 9.
49 : 29. La. 3 : 25, 65.-4 : 15.
Eze. 2 : 4, 7.-3 : 4, 6, 11, 26.-6 :
10.-11 : 16.-13 : 11.-16 : 20, 37,
54.-20 : 6, 9, 15.-21 : 23.-23 : 27.
-24 : 27.-33 : 7.-39 : 13, 24.-44 :
12.-48 : 12, 18. Da. 1 : 14 -2 : 21.
4 : 19.-6 : 2 -9 : 4.-11 : 34. Ho.
2 : 13.-4 : 12.-7 : 13.-9 : 4. Mi. 2 :
6. Ha. 1 : 10 Zph. 2 : 11. Mat.
6 : 8.-7 : 11.-8 : 4, 15.-13 : 11,
24, 34.-17 : 3, 13.-20 : 4.-21 : 27,
36.-25 : 9, 34.-26 : 27, 71.-27 :
26. Mk. 1 : 31, 44.-2 : 2, 26.-4 :
11, 13.-6 : 48, 50 -8 : 29.-10 : 36,
40.,-12 : 6.-14 : 10.-15 : 6, 8, 11,
-16 : 19. Lu. 1 : 22.-2 : 50, 51.-4 :
39 -5 : 14.-6 : 4, 34.-9 : 11, 17.-
11 : 13.-15 : 12.-16 : 28.-19 : 24,
32.-20 : 15.-22 : 6.-23 : 17, 20,
28.-24 : 11. 27, 30, 36. Jn. 1 : 12,
22.-2 : 16, 22 24.-4 : 32 -6 : 11,
13, 17, 61.-7 : 9, 50.-8 : 27.-10 :
6.-15 : 22.-17 : 8, 26.-18 : 6, 21,
29.-19 : 4, 5.-20 : 22, 23. Ac. 1 :
7, 16.-2 : 3, 41.-3 : 11.-5 : 13, 32.
6 : 2.-7 : 26.-8 : 5.-9 : 27. 38.-11.
4.-12 : 17, 21.-13 : 42.-14 : 18.-
16 : 10.-17 : 2.-18 : 2.-20 : 34.-
25 : 11. Ro. 1 : 19.-2 : 7, 8.-8 :
28.-10 : 20.-11 : 27. 1 Co. 1 : 2,
24.-9 : 3 -10 : 11.-14 : 34. 2 Co.
4 : 3, 4.-9 : 13. Ga. 1 : 17 -4 : 8.-
6 : 10. Ep. 2 : 17. Ph. 1 : 28. 2
Th. 1 : 6. 1 Ti. 4 : 15. 2 Tim. 4 :
8. Tit. 3 : 13 He. 3 : 18.-4 : 2.-
12 : 11, 19. Ja. 1 : 12.-2 : 5, 16.-
1 Pe 4 : 6 2 Pe. 1 : 1.-2 : 22. Re.
9 : 3, 5.-11 : 12.-20 : 4. [K. 13 : 23.
Ex. 2 : 25. God had respect **u.t.**, 2
20 : 5. sh not bow down thys. **t.t.**,
De. 5 : 9. Jos. 23 : 7. 2 K. 17 : 35.
Nu. 4 : 19. thus do **u.t.** that they
8 : 22. so did they **u.t.** [may live
33 : 56. unto you as I thought to do
Jos. 9 : 20 This will we do **t.t.** [**u.t.**
26 so he did **u.t.** and delivered
Ju. 15 : 11. As unto me, so have I
done **u.t.** [yourselves
Is. 49 : 9. say **t.t.** in darkness, Shew
Je. 5 : 13. thus shall it be done **u.t.**
La. 1 : 22. **u.t.** as thou hast unto me
Eze. 12 : 11. as I have done so be **u.t.**
33 : 32. art **u.t.** as lovely song [yoke
Ho. 11 : 4. I **t.t.** as they th. take off
Jon. 3 : 10. evil he said he wo. do **u.t.**
Mat. 4 : 16. **t.t.** which sat in shad-
ow of death, Lu. 1 : 79.

Lu. 6 : 31. would that men do to you,
do t.t., Mat. 7 : 12. [to you
33 if do good t.t. which do good
Ac. 20 : 34. and t.t. that were wi.me
He. 8 : 10. I will be t.t. a God, they
See SAID, SAY.

Say to or unto THEM.

Ge. 44 : 4. s.u.t., Ex 3 : 16. Le. 1 :
2.-15 : 2.-17 : 2.-18 : 2.-19 : 2.-
21 : 1.-22 : 3, 18.-23 : 2, 10.-25 :
2.-27 : 2. Nu. 5 : 12.-6 : 2.-14 :
28.-15 : 2, 18.-18 : 26.-28 : 2.-
33 : 51.-34 : 2.-35 : 10. De. 1 :
42.-5 : 30. Jos. 9 : 11. 1 S. 14 :
34. 2 K. 1 :3. Is. 35 :4. Je. 11 :3.
17 : 20.-25 : 30.-43 : 10. Eze. 12 :
10, 23, 28.-13 : 2, 11.-14 : 4.-20:
3, 5, 27.-24 : 3.-33 : 2, 11, 25,27.
-34 :2.-37 :4,12,19,21. Zch. 1 : 3.
Lu. 10 : 9. Jn. 20 : 17.

Toward THEM. [th.fear

Ps. 103 : 11. so great his mercy t.t.
Mat. 14 : 14. compassion t.t., Mk. 6 : 34.
Col. 4 : 5. walk in wisdom t.t. with-t
1 Th. 4 : 12. honestly t.t. without

Under THEM. [u.t.

Nu. 16 : 31. ground clave asunder
Jb. 26 : 8. the cloud is not rent u.t.

With THEM.

Ge. 7 : 13 -14 : 8.-18 : 16.-19 : 9.-23:
8.-29 : 9.-34 : 8.-40 : 4.-42 : 24.-
43 : 16. Ex. 1 : 10.-6 : 4.-12 :38.
-16 : 20.-23 : 32.-25 : 14, 28.-34:
31, 33. Le. 11 : 43.-26 : 39, 44.
Nu. 10 : 3.-22:20 -26 : 3.-32 : 19.
De. 2 : 5, 9, 19.-5 :29.-7 :2, 3, 5,
9.-29 : 1, 25.-31 : 16. Jos. 4 : 8.
-9 : 15, 16.-11 : 4.-22 : 15.-23 :
12. Ju. 8 : 10, 16.-9 : 1, 38:-16 :
3, 8. 1 S. 10 : 6.-13 : 16.-14 : 21.
-15 : 6.-17 : 23.-25 : 15. 2 S. 3 :
22.-5 : 3.-12 : 17. 1 K. 8 : 46.-
11 : 18.-15 : 22. 2 K. 6 : 33.-11 :
4, 9.-22 : 7. 1 Ch. 7 : 4.-9 : 25.-
11 : 3.-12 : 34.-13 : 2.-15 : 18.-
16 : 41, 42. 2 Ch. 5 : 12.-6 : 36.-
15 : 9.-17 : 8, 9.-20 : 1.-22 : 12.-
23 : 8. Ezr. 1 : 11.-5 : 2 -8 : 13,
14, 24.-10 : 14. Ne. 9 : 13.-13 :
25.-Jb. 1 : 4.-21 : 8 -Ps. 9 : 6.-
25 :14 -35 :1.-42:4.-54:4.-88:4.-
118 : 7.-119 : 93. Pr. 28 : 4. Ec.
8 : 12. Is. 14 : 1, 20 -34 : 7.-49 :
18.-57 : 8.-59 : 21.-60 : 9.-61 : 8.
-65 : 23. Je. 16 : 8.-18 : 23.-27 :
18.-31 : 8.-32 : 40.-41 : 9.-49 :
20.-50 : 45. Eze. 3 : 25.-16 : 17,
28.-23 : 7, 17, 23, 43.-30:5.-31 :
16, 18.-32 : 21, 28, 30, 32 -34 :
25.-37 : 26, 27.-38 : 5. Da. 1 :
19.-11 : 30. Ho. 5 : 5. Jo. 3 : 2.-
Jon. 1 : 3. Mat. 9 : 15.-13 : 29.-
15 : 30.-23 : 30 -25 : 3, 19.-26 :
36.-27 : 7. Mk. 2 : 19 (2).-6 : 50.
-9 : 14, 16.-15 : 7.-16 : 20. Lu. 2:
51.-5 : 29, 34.-6 : 17.-7 : 6.-15 :
2.-18 : 7.-23 : 35.-24 : 1, 10, 15,
29, 30. Jn. 3 :22.-4 :40.-18 :5, 18.
-20 : 24, 26. Ac. 1 : 4.-3 : 8.-4 :
14.-8 : 7.-9 : 28, 19.-10 : 20, 23.-
11 : 3, 12, 21.-12 : 20, 25.-14 :
27.-15 : 2, 4, 37, 38.-17 : 2, 17,
34.-18 : 3, 20.-20 : 36.-21 : 7, 16,
24, 26.-26 : 30.-28 : 14. Ro. 11 :
17.-12 : 15.-16 : 14, 15. 2 Co. 8 :
22. Ep. 5 : 7.-6 : 24. 1 Th. 4 : 17.
2 Tim. 2 : 22. He. 8 : 8.-10 : 16.
-11 : 31.-13 : 3. 1 Pe. 3 : 7.-4 :
4. 2 Pe. 2 : 20. Re. 9 : 19.
Nu. 22 : 12. Thou shalt not go w.t.
Ju. 1 : 22. went, and Lord was w.t.
19 : 24. do w.t. what seemeth good
unto you, Es. 3 : 11. [t.
1 S. 25 : 16. all the while we were w.
2 S. 15 : 36. have w.t. their 2 sons
2 K. 6 : 16. more than they th. be w.t.
1 Ch. 5 : 20. and all that were w.t.
2 Ch. 14 : 11. whe. with many or w.t.
Ne. 9 : 24. do w.t. as they would
Pr. 1 : 15. walk not in way w.t. [t.
24 : 1. evil men, nei. desire to be w.
Eze. 26 : 20. w.t. that go down to
the pit, 31 : 14.-32 : 18, 24, 25, 29.
34 : 30. I the L. am w.t., Zch. 10 : 5.
Mk. 8 : 14. nei. w.t. more than half
Lu. 24 : 33. eleven and them w.t.
Jn. 17 : 12. while I was w.t. in [sinn.
He. 3 : 17. was it not w.t. that had
Re. 21 : 3. God himself shall be w.t.
See COVENANT, DEAL, GO,
JOINED, MEDDLE, PEACE, SAT,
SPAKE, TALKED, TARRY,
WELL, WENT.

Without THEM. [w.t.

Le. 26 : 43. while she lieth desolate
See **WOE to them.**

THEMSELVES. [rons

Ge 3 : 7. fig leaves, and made t. ap-
8. Adam and his wife hid t. fr. L.
13 : 11. Lot and Abram separated t.
19 : 11. they wearied t. to find door
30 : 40. he put his own flocks by t.
32 : 16. delivered every drove by t.
43 : 32. for them by t., for Egyptians wh. did eat wi. him, by t.
Ex. 5 : 7. go and gather straw for t.
12 :39. nei. prepared for t. victuals
18 : 26. small matter they judge t.
26 :9. couple 6 curtains by t., 36 : 16.
32 : 7. thy people have corrupted
t., De. 9 : 12.-32 : 5. Ju. 2 : 19.
Ho. 9 : 9. [naments
33 :6. Israel stripped t. of their or-
Le. 15 : 8. shall both bathe t. [things
22 : 2. that they separate t. from holy
Nu. 8 : 7. let Levites make t. clean
11 : 32. spread quails for t. ab. camp
De. 31 : 14. Moses, Josh., presented t.
20. should have eaten and filled t.
32 : 27. lest adversaries behave t.
31. our enemies t. being judges
Jos. 8 : 27. Isr. took for prey unto t.,
10 : 13. until peo. avenged t. [11 : 14.
Ju. 7 : 2. lest Israel vaunt t. ag. me
1 S. 2 : 5. hired out t. for bread
3 : 13. because his sons made t. vile
14 : 11. both discov-d t. to garrison
21 : 4. if yo. men have kept t. from
2 S. 10 : 8. Syrians by t., 1 Ch. 19 : 9.
16 : 14. people weary refreshed t.
1 K. 8 : 47. if bethink t., 2 Ch. 6 : 37.
18 : 23. choose bullock for t. [21 : 8.
2 K. 8 : 20. Edom made k. ov t., 2 Ch.
17 : 17. sold t. to do evil in sight of
32. made unto t. of lowest priests
19 : 29. eat such things as grow of t.
1 Ch. 12 : 8. Gadites separated t. un-
19 : 6. made t. odious to Da. [to Da.
29 : 24. sons of Da. submit-d t. un.
2 Ch. 3 : 13. wings of cherub. spread t.
14 : 13. Ethiopians not recover t. [t.
20 : 25. jewels they stripped off for
30 : 18. many had not cleansed t.
32 : 8. peo. rested t. upon words of
35 : 14. made ready for t. and priests
Ezr. 6 : 20. killed passover for t. [t.
9 : 2. taken of their daughters for
Ne. 4 : 2. Jews, will they fortify t.?
8 : 16. So the people made t. booths
9 : 25 delighted t. in thy goodness
13 : 22. Levites that they cleanse t.
Es. 8 : 13. Jews be ready to avenge t.
9 : 27. such as joined t. unto them
31. as they had decreed for t. [2 : 1.
Jb. 1 : 6. sons of God to present t.,
3 : 14. built desolate places for t.
24 : 16. houses th. had marked for t.
30 : 14. in desolation rolled t. upon
41 : 23. firm in t. cannot be moved
Ps. 3 : 6. I not afraid if 10,000 set t.
Ps. 9 : 20. may know t. to be but men
37 : 11. delight t. in abund. of peace
44 : 10. they whi. hate us spoil for t.
57 : 6. into the midst are fallen t.
Ps. 61 : 5. encourage t. in ev. matter
8. make their tongue fall upon t.
66 : 3. sh. thine enemies submit t.
80 : 6. our enemies laugh among t.
81 : 15. The haters of Lord should
have submitted t. unto him
97 : 7. all that boast t. of idols
106 : 28 they joined t. to Baal-peer
109 : 29. cover t. with confusion
Pr. 23 : 5. for riches make t. wings
Ec. 3 : 18. see that they t. are beasts
11 : 3. clouds full they empty t.
Is. 2 : 6. please t. in chil. of strangers
3 : 9. have rewarded evil unto t.
8 : 21. shall fret t. and curse God
15 : 3. shall gird t. with sackcloth
46 : 2. t. are gone into captivity
47 : 14. shall not deliver t. fr. flame
48 : 2. they call t. of the holy city
56 : 6. of stranger, that join t. to L.
Je. 2 : 24. seek her will not weary t.
4 : 2. nations shall bless t. in him
5 : 22. though the waves toss t.
7 : 19. do they not provoke t. to
9 : 5. weary t. to commit iniquity
11 : 17. evil they have done ag t.
12 : 13. they have put t. to pain
16 : 6. nor cut t. nor make t. bald
7. Nei. shall men tear t. in mourn.
27 : 7. kings shall serve t. of him
30 : 8. strangers no more serve t. of
21. their nobles shall be of t. [him
34 : 10. none sho. serve t. any more
41 : 5. came 80 men, having cut t.
49 : 29. sh. take to t. their curtains
La. 2 : 10. girded t. wi. sackol., Eze.
4 : 14. polluted t. wi. blood [7 : 18.
Eze. 6 : 9. shall loathe t. for the evils
10 : 17. these lifted up t. also [t.
22. same faces, appearances, and
14 : 18. they only shall be deliv-d t.
26 : 16. sh. clothe t. with trembling
27 : 30. shall wallow t. in the ashes
31. shall make t. utterly bald
31 : 14. none of all trees exalt t.
34 : 2. Woe to shepherds do feed t.
8. shepherds fed t., fed not flock
10. nei. sheph-ds feed t. any more
27. out of ha. of those th. served t.
37 : 23. Nei. defile t. with idols [t.
43 : 26. purge altar and consecrate
44 : 18. not gird t. with anything
25. come at no dead person to defile t. ; for fa. or son may defile t.
45 : 5. Levites of house have for t.
Da. 2 : 43. mingle t. wi. seed of men
11 : 6. in end of years shall join t.
14. robbers of thy peo. sh. exalt t.
Ho. 1 : 11. Israel shall appoint t. one
10 : 10. when sh. bind t. in furrows
Am. 2 : 8. lay t. down upon clothes
6 : 4. stretch t. upon couches
5. invent to t. instrum-s of music
6. anoint t. with chief ointments
7. banquet of them th. stretched t.
Mi. 3 : 4. as they behaved t. ill
Ha. 1 : 7. judgments proceed of t.
2 : 13. people sh. weary t. for vanity
Zch. 4 : 12. empty golden oil out of t.
11 : 5. slay and hold t. not guilty
Mat. 9 : 3. scribes said within t.
14 : 2. mighty works do shew forth
t. in him, Mk. 6 : 14.
15. into villages and buy t. victuals, Mk. 6 : 36.
16 : 7. they reasoned among t., 21 :
25. Mk. 2 : 8.-8 : 16.-11 : 31. Lu.
20 : 5, 14. [nuchs
19 : 12. eunuchs which made t. eu-
21 : 38. husbandmen said among t.,
This is the heir, Mk. 12 : 7.
23 : 4. they t. will not move them
Mk 1 : 27. all questioned among t.
4 : 17. have no root in t. [measure
6 : 51. sore amazed in t. beyond
9 : 2. into high mountain apart by t.
8. saw no man save Jes. only wi. t.

Mk. 9 : 10. they kept th. saying wi. t.
34. disputed am. t., Who be great.
10 : 26. saying am. t., Who can be
14 : 4. some had indigna. within t.
15 : 31. priests mocking, said am. t.
16 : 3. said am. t., Who roll stone
Lu. 4 : 36. spake am. t., What word is
7 : 30. rejected counsel of God ag. t.
49. began to say within t., Who is
18 : 9. certain which trusted in t.
20 : 20. spies sho. feign t. just men
22 : 23. inquire am. t. which should
23 : 12. were at enmity between t.
24 : 12. linen clothes laid by t.
Jn. 6 : 52. The Jews strove among t.
7 : 35. said Jews am. t., Whither
11 : 56. sought Jes. and spake am. t.
12 : 19. Phari. said am. t., Perceive
16 : 17. said some of his disci. am. t.
17 : 13. have my joy fulfilled in t.
18 : 18. was cold, and they warmed t.
28. they t. went not into judgm-t
19 : 24. said am. t., Let us not rend
Ac. 4 : 15. they conferred among t.
5 : 36. to whom about 400 joined t.
15 : 32. Judas and Silas prophets t.
16 : 37. let them come t. fetch us
18 : 6. opposed t. and blasphemed
21 : 25. keep t. fr. things offered to
23 : 12. Jews bound t. und. curse, 21.
24 : 15. a resurrection t. also allow
26 : 31. talked between t., This man
27 : 40. committed t. unto the sea
28 : 4. said am. t., No doubt this
25. when they agreed not am. t.
29. Jews had gr-t reasoning am. t.
Ro. 1 : 22. Professing t. to be wise
24. dishonour own bodies betw. t.
27. receiv-g in t. that recompense
2 : 14. not having law, are a law unto t. [eousness
10 : 3. not submitted t. to right-
13 : 2. resist sh. rec. to t. damnat-n
1 Co. 6 : 9. abusers of t. with mankind
16 : 15. addicted t. to the ministry
2 Co. 5 : 15. should not live unto t.
8 : 3. bey. their power willing of t.
10 : 12. measuring t. by t., comparing t. with t. [les of Christ
11 : 13. transforming t. into apost-
Ga. 6 : 13. neither do they t. keep law
Ep. 4 : 19. given t. unto lasciviousn.
Ph. 2 : 3. esteem other better than t.
1 Th. 1 : 9. t. shew of us what manner
1 Ti. 1 : 10. that defile t. with mank.
2 : 9. th. women adorn t., 1 Pe. 3 : 5.
3 : 13. purchase to t. good degree
6 : 10. pierced t. wi many sorrows
19. laying up for t. good founda-n
2 Ti. 2 : 25. instr-g those th. oppose t.
26. recover t. out of snare of devil
4 : 3. they shall heap to t. teachers
Tit. 1 : 12. one of t. even a prophet
He. 6 : 6. crucify to t. Son of God
9 : 23. heavenly things t. with better sacrifices [minister
1 Pe. 1 : 12. not unto t. but us did
2 Pe. 2 : 1. upon t. swift destruction
13. sporting t. wi. own deceivings
19. t. are the servants of corrupt-n
Jude 7. giving t. over to fornication
10. in those things they corrupt t.
12. feeding t. without fear [Spirit
19. separate t. sensual, having not
Re. 6 : 15. hid t. in dens and caves
8 : 6. 7 angels prepared t. to sound
See ADORNED, ARRAY [Noun].

Assemble, Assembled THEMSELVES. [a.t.
Nu. 10 : 3. when blow, assembly sh.
Ju. 10 : 17. Isr. a-d t. and encamped
1 S. 14 : 20. Saul and all peo. a-d t.
1 K. 8 : 2. men of Israel a-d t. unto Solomon, 2 Ch. 5 : 3.
2 Ch. 20 : 26. on fourth day a-d t. in valley of Berachah [houses
Je. 5 : 7. thy chil. a-d t. in harlots'
Ho. 7 : 14. a.t., for wine they rebel
Ac. 11 : 26. whole year a-d t. with ch.

Bow, ed THEMSELVES.
Ge. 33 : 6. handmaidens and children b-d t. [Rachel b-d t.
7. Leah with chil. b-d t., Joseph,
42 : 6. Joseph's brethren b-d t. before him, 43 : 26.
Ex. 11 : 8. servants shall b. t. to me
Ju. 2 : 12. b-d t. unto other gods, 17.
2 K. 2 : 15. sons of prophets b-d t.
2 Ch. 7 : 3. saw glory of L. Isr. b-d t.
29 : 29. king and all present b-d t.
Jb. 39 : 3. They b. t., they bri. forth
Ec. 12 : 3. the strong men shall b. t.
Is. 60 : 14. all they sh. b. t. at thy f-t
See BOAST [Verb], CUT, EXALT.

Gather, ed THEMSELVES.
Nu. 10 : 4. princes sh. g. t. unto thee
1 S. 22 : 2. every one in debt g-d t.
1 Ch. 11 : 1. all Isr. g-d t. to David
13 : 2. th. Levites may g. t. unto us
Is. 10 : 31. inhabitants of Gebim g. t.
See **HIDE themselves.**
See HUMBLE, ED, MAGNIFY, IED, OFFERED, PREPARE, PRESENTED, PURIFY, SANCTIFY, IED, SEPARATE, ED, SET, SPREAD, STRENGTHEN, ED, SUBMIT.
See **Themselves TOGETHER**

THEN. [name
Ge. 4 : 26. t. began men to call upon
13 : 7. t., 16.-27 : 41.-37 : 28.-38 : 11, 21.-39 : 9.-41 : 9, 14.-42 : 34, 38.-48 : 9.-44 : 11, 13, 18, 26, 32. -45 : 1.-47 : 1, 6.-49. 4. Ex. 40 : 37. Le. 17 : 16.-20 : 5.-26 : 41, 42. Nu. 5 : 27. De. 29 : 20. Jos. 14 : 11. Ju. 5 : 8, 11.-6 : 37.-11 : 31. -17 : 13. 1 S. 6 : 9.-15 : 14.-20 : 7, 9, 13.-25 : 31.-26 : 8.-28 : 16, 25.-30 : 22.-31 : 4. 2 S. 15 : 33. 1 K. 1 : 13.-3 : 14.-9 : 24.-11 : 7.-12 : 5.-19 : 5.-22 : 47. 2 K. 1 : 10. -4 : 14.-5 : 17.-7 : 2, 9.-8 : 1, 16, 22.-9 : 3.-13 : 28.-20 : 2, 19.-23 : 17. 1 Ch. 6 : 32.-11 : 16. 2 Ch. 33 : 13. Ezr. 5 : 1, 2. Es. 5 : 9, 14. -7 : 9, 10. Jb. 3 : 13.-11 : 11.-22 : 26, 29.-38 : 21. Ps. 27 : 10.-51 : 13, 19.-55 : 12.-69 : 4.-96 : 12.-106 : 12.-119 : 6. Pr. 2 : 5, 9. -20 : 24.-24 : 14. Ec. 2 : 15. Is. 28 : 18.-32 : 16.-58 : 8, 9. Je. 4 : 1.-8 : 22.-11 : 15, 18.-23 : 22.-33 : 26.-Eze. 39 : 28. Da. 5 : 24. Mal. 3 : 16. Mat. 5 : 24.-7 : 11.-9 : 15.-12 : 29.-13 : 27, 26.-16 : 27.-17 : 26.-21 : 25.-23 : 32.-24 : 10, 14, 21, 30.-25 : 27, 31, 34, 41, 44, 45.-26 : 54, 56, 67.-27 : 3, 9, 16. Mk. 2 : 20.-3 : 27, 31.-4 : 28.-11 : 31.-13 : 14, 21, 26, 27. Lu. 5 : 35.-6 : 42.-12 : 28, 42.-13 : 7, 26.-14 : 10.-20 : 44.-21 : 20, 21, 28. Jn. 1 : 25.-2 : 20. -4 : 35.-6 : 30.-8 : 28.-13 : 14, 30.-14 : 9.-19 : 16.-20 : 20. Ac. 2 : 38, 41.-5 : 34.-7 : 1, 42.-10 : 48.-11 : 16, 18.-12 : 3, 15.-26 : 20. Ro. 6 : 21.-8 : 17.-11 : 5. 1 Co. 4 : 5.-6 : 4.-9 : 18.-12 : 28.-13 : 10.-14 : 26.-15 : 5, 7, 24, 28, 29. 2 Co. 2 : 2.-5 : 20.-6 : 1. Ga. 4 : 29, 31.-5 : 11.-6 : 4. Ep. 5 : 15. Col. 3 : 1. 1 Th. 5 : 3. 2 Th. 2 : 8. He. 7 : 27.-12 : 26. Ja. 2 : 4. 1 Jn. 3 : 21. [God
Ge. 28 : 21. t. shall the Lord be my
Nu. 15 : 19. t. it shall be when ye eat
Jos. 14 : 12. if L. with me t. I be able
2 S. 2 : 26. how long it be t. ere thou
19 : 12. whf. t. are ye the last [bid
1 K. 8 : 32. t. hear thou in heaven, 34, 36, 39, 45, 49.
2 K. 4 : 14. what t. to be done for her
Jh. 28 : 27. t. did he see it and declare it
Ps. 40 : 7. t. said I, Lo, I co.
Is. 44 : 15. t. it be for man to burn
Mat. 13 : 56. whence, t., this man
19 : 25. disciples, saying, Who t. be saved? Mk. 10 : 26. Lu. 18 : 26.
22 : 21. t. saith he unto them, 26 : 31, 38. Lu. 21 : 10. Jn. 11 : 14.-20 : 27. [called Christ
27 : 22. What shall I do t. with Jes.
Mk. 12 : 37. whence is he t. his son?
15 : 12. what will ye t. I shall do to
Lu. 3 : 10. What shall we do t.? [him
Jn. 1 : 21. What t.? Art thou Elias?
7 : 33. t. I go unto him th. sent me
9 : 19. how t. doth he now see?
18 : 37. Art thou a king, t., Jesus
Ro. 7 : 7. What shall we say, t., 9 : 14.
1 Co. 5 : 10. t. must ye needs go out
10 : 19. What say I t.? that idol
13 : 12. t. face to face; t. sh. I know
14 : 15. what is it t.? I will pray
15 : 14. t. is our preaching vain and
13. dead, t. is Christ not risen, 16.
2 Co. 5 : 14. if died for all, t. all dead
12 : 10. when weak, t. am I strong
Ga. 2 : 21. t. Christ is dead in vain
3 : 29. if Ch.'s, t. are ye Abr.'s seed
He. 12 : 8. t. are ye bastards, not
Ja. 3 : 17. first pure, t. peaceable
2 Pe. 3 : 6. Whereby world th. t. was
Re. 22 : 9. t. saith he unto me, Do it [not

THENCE.
Ge. 2 : 10. fr. t.. the river was parted
11 : 8. t., 9.-18 : 16, 22.-20 : 1.-24 : 7.-28 : 2, 6.-30 : 32.-42 : 2.-49 : 24. Nu. 13 : 23, 24.-22 : 41.-23 : 13, 27. De. 4 : 29.-5 : 15.-6 : 23.-10 : 7.-22 : 8.-24 : 18. Jos. 6 : 22. -15 : 4, 14.-18 : 14.-19 : 13, 34. Ju. 1 : 20.-18 : 13.-19 : 18. 1 S. 4 : 4.-10 : 3, 23.-17 : 49. 2 S. 16 : 5.-21 : 13. 1 K. 1 : 45.-2 : 36.-9 : 28. 2 K. 2 : 21.-6 : 2.-7 : 8.-17 : 27, 33.-23 : 12.-24 : 13. 2 Ch. 26 : 20. Ezr. 6 : 6. Jb. 39 : 29. Is. 52 : 11.-65 : 20. Je. 5 : 6.-13 : 6.-22 : 24.-36 : 29.-37 : 12.-38 : 11. 43 : 12.-49 : 16, 38.-50 : 9. Eze. 11 : 18. Ho. 2 : 15. Am. 6 : 2.-9 : 2, 3, 4. Ob. 4. Mat. 4 : 21.-5 : 26.-9 : 9.-10 : 11.-12 : 15. Mk. 1 : 19.-7 : 24.-10 : 1. Lu. 16 : 26. Ac. 16 : 12.-21 : 1.-27 : 4.-28 : 13, 15.
Ge. 12 : 8. removed from t., 26 : 22. Nu. 21 : 12, 13. Ac. 7 : 4.
26 : 17. departed t., 42 : 26. Ju. 21 : 24. 1 S. 22 : 1. 1 K. 19 : 19. 2 K. 10 : 15. Mat. 9 : 27.-11 : 1.-12 : 9.-13 : 53.-14 : 13.-15 : 21, 29.-19 : 15. -Mk. 9 : 30. Jn. 4 : 43. Ac. 18 : 7.
23. went from t., Nu. 21 : 16. Jos. 15 : 15.-18 : 13. Ju. 1 : 11.-18 : 11.-21 : 24. 1 S. 22 : 3.-23 : 29. 1 K. 12 : 25. 2 K. 2 : 23, 25. Mat. 15 : 21. Mk. 6 : 1.-7 : 24. Jn. 11 : 54. 2 Co. 2 : 13.
27 : 9. fetch from t., 45. De. 19 : 12. -30 : 4. 2 S. 14 : 2.
De. 5 : 15. the Lord brought thee out t., 6 : 23.-24 : 18. [am I
Ju. 19 : 18. to m-t Ephraim, from t.
1 S. 4 : 4. might bring from t. ark of covenant, 2 S. 6 : 2. 1 Ch. 13 : 6.
1 K. 2 : 36. go not t. any whither
2 K. 2 : 21. not be from t. any death
7 : 8. carried t., 17 : 33.-24 : 13. [t.
Ezr. 6 : 6. Now theref be ye far from
Is. 52 : 11. depart, go ye out from t.
65 : 20. sh. be no more t. an infant
Je. 5 : 6. ev. one that goeth t. be torn
36 : 29. cause to cease from t. man
43 : 12. he shall go from t. in peace
49 : 16. I will bring thee down fr. t.
50 : 9. from t. he shall be taken
Am. 9 : 2. dig into hell, t. shall my hand take them, 3.

Ob 4. among stars, t. will I bring
Mat. 5 : 26. by no means come out t.
Mk. 1 : 19. gone little further t.
6 : 11. depart t., Lu. 9 : 4.-12 : 59.
Ac. 27 : 12. [come from t.
Lu. 16 : 26. neither pass that would
See SAILED.

THENCEFORTH. [for you
Le. 22 : 27. t. it shall be acceptable
2 Ch. 32 : 23. Hez. was magnified fr. t.
Mat. 5 : 13. is t. good for nothing
Jn. 19 : 12. t. Pilate sought to re-

THEOPH'ILUS. [lease
Lu. 1 : 3. unto thee, most excel-t T.
Ac. 1 : 1. treatise have I made, O T.

THERE.
Ge. 2 : 6. t., 13 : 4.-18 : 29.-21 : 31,
33.-22 : 2, 9.-23 : 13.-26 : 8, 17,
25.-28 : 11.-33 : 20.-43 : 25. Ex.
8 : 22.-15 : 27. Le 8 : 31.-16 : 23.
Nu. 21 : 32.-33 : 9. De. 13 : 12.-
26 : 5.-27 : 7.-28 : 68. Jos. 18 :
10.-Ju. 16 : 27.-18 : 2.-19 : 2.-
20 : 27.-21 : 9. 1 S 1 : 3, 28.-4 :
4, 7, 12.-5 : 11.-7 : 17.-11 : 13,
14.-14 : 34.-21 : 6.-23 : 22.-27 : 5.
-31 : 12. 2 S. 3 : 27.-10 : 18.-13 :
38.-15 : 29, 36.-16 : 14.-18 : 11.-
24 : 25. 1 K. 19 : 3. 2 K. 5 : 18.-
7 : 4.-9 : 16 -14 : 19 -15 : 20.-16 :
6 -17 : 25, 27. 1 Ch. 4 : 23, 41,
43.-12 : 39.-13 : 10. 2 Ch 25 :
27.-32 : 21. Ezr. 5 : 17. Ps. 69 :
35.-87 : 6.-137 : 3. Pr. 9 : 18. Is.
28 : 13.-34 : 12, 15. Je. 8 : 14.-
13 : 6.-22 : 1, 26.-37 : 16, 20.-38 :
26.-41 : 3.-43 : 2.-47 : 7. La. 4 :
15.-Eze. 1 : 3.-8 : 4.-20 : 28.-39 :
28.-42 : 13.-47 : 23. Da 10 : 13.
Ho. 12 : 4. Hag. 2 : 14. Zch. 5 :
11. Mat: 2 : 15.-8 : 12.-10 : 11.-
12 : 45.-13 : 58.-14 : 23.-15 : 29
-19 : 2.-21 : 17.-22 : 11, 13 -24 :
28, 51.-26 : 13, 71.-27 : 55.-28 :
10. Mk. 1 : 13, 35 -2 : 6.-3 : 1.-
5 : 11.-6 : 10.-14 : 13, 15. Lu.
2 : 6.-8 : 32.-9 : 4.-11 : 26.-12 :
34, 54, 55.-15 : 13.-17 : 21, 23.-
22 : 12 -23 : 33.-24 : 18. Jn. 2 : 1,
6, 12 -3 : 22.-5 : 5.-6 : 3, 22, 24.
-10 : 42.-11 : 15, 31, 54.-12 : 2,
9.-19 : 42.-21 : 9. Ac. 9 : 33, 38.-
10 : 18.-14 : 7, 28.-16 : 1.-17 : 21.
18 : 19, 23 -20 : 13.-21 : 3, 4.-
22 : 5.-25 : 9, 20.-27 : 6 2 Co. 3 :
17. Tit. 3 : 12. He. 7 : 8. Ja. 3 :
16.-4 : 13. Re. 2 : 14.-12 : 6.
Ge. 2 : 8. t. he put the man he formed
18 : 28 If I find t. 45 I will not dest-y
32 : 29. And he blessed him t. [it
35 : 7. bec. t. G. appeared unto him
49 : 31 t. they buried Abr., Sarah (2)
Ex. 15 : 25. t. he made a statute, t. he
17 : 6. I will stand before thee t. in
24 : 12. Come into m-t, be t., 34 : 2.
34 : 28. he was t. with Lord 40 days
Nu. 11 : 17. I will talk with thee t.
13 : 28. we saw the children of Anak
t., 33. De. 1 : 28. Jos. 14 : 12. [t.
20 : 1. Miriam died t., was buried
26. Aaron sh. die t., 28. De. 10 : 6.
De. 4 : 28. t. ye sh. serve gods work
of men's, 28 : 36, 64. Je. 16 : 13.
10 : 5. t. they be unto this day, Jos.
4 : 9. 1 K 8 : 8.
12 : 5. your God shall choose to put
his name t., 11.-14 : 23.-16 : 2,
11. 1 K 8 : 29.-9 : 3. [ag. thee
31 : 26. it may be t. for a witness
Ju. 5 : 27. t. he fell down dead
7 : 4. I will try them for thee t.
Ru. 1 : 17. Where thou diest, t. will
1 S. 5 : 11. hand of God very heavy t.
7 : 17. his house, t. he judged (3)
2 S. 6 : 7. G smote Uzzah t., t. he died
15 : 21. even t. will thy servant be
35. hast thou not t. Zadok and

1 K. 11 : 36. I have chosen to put my
name t., 2 K. 23 : 27. 2 Ch. 6 :
5, 6.-7 : 16. Ne. 1 : 9. [thee t.
17 : 4. I commanded ravens to feed
18 : 10. He is not t., he took an oath
2 K. 2 : 21. Elisha cast the salt in t.
4 : 11. famine in city, we sh. die t.
7 : 5. were come, was no man t., 10.
1 Ch. 14 : 12. they left their gods t.
2 Ch. 28 : 9. prophet of the L. was t.
Jb. 3 : 17. t. the weary be at rest (2)
18. t. the prisoners rest together
19. small and great are t., servant
23 : 7. t. the righteous might dispute
35 : 12. t. they cry, none giveth ans.
39 : 30. where the slain are, t. is she
Ps. 14 : 5. t. were they in gr. fear, 53 :
45 : 12. daughter of Tyre sh. be t. [5.
48 : 6. Fear took hold upon them t.
66 : 6. thro. flood, t. did we rejoice
87 : 7. singers and players sh. be t.
104 : 26. t. go the ships, t. is th. Le.
133 : 3. t. L. commanded blessing
139 : 8. if my bed in hell thou art t.
10. even t. sh. thy hand lead me
Pr. 8 : 27. prepared heavens I was t.
9 : 18. he knoweth not the dead are t.
26 : 20. no wood, t. fire goeth out
Ec. 3 : 16. that wickedness was t. (2)
17. is a time t. for every purpose
11 : 3. the tree falleth t. it shall be
Can. 8 : 5. t. thy mother bro-t forth
Is 13 : 20. nei. shepherds make fold t.
21. beasts of the desert shall lie t.
22 : 18. t. shalt thou die, t. chariots
23 : 12. t. shalt thou have no rest
28 : 10. here a little and t. a little
33 : 21. t. glorious L. will be a place
35 : 8. a highway shall be t., and
9. but the redeemed shall walk t.
48 : 16. from the time it was t. am I
Je. 8 : 22. Is t. no balm in Gilead (2)
18 : 2. t. will I cause thee to hear
20 : 6. t. thou shalt die, be buried t.
22 : 26. t. shall ye die, 42 : 16. [th.
27 : 22. t. shall they be until I visit
38 : 28. he was t. when Jerus. was ta.
Eze. 3 : 22. I will t. talk with thee
12 : 13. sh. not see it tho. he die t.
17 : 20. I will plead with him t.
20 : 35. t. will I plead with you, face
40. t. will I accept them, t. require
22 : 20. I will leave you t. and melt
23 : 3. t. were their breasts pressed
29 : 14. they sh. be t. a base kingd.
32 : 22. Ashur is t., all her company
35 : 10. whereas the Lord was t.
48 : 35. name of city, The Lord is t.
Ho 2 : 15. sh. sing t. as in her youth
7 : 9. gray hairs here and t. upon
9 : 15, in Gilgal, t. I hated them
12 : 4. in Bethel, t. he spake with us
Jo. 3 : 2. I will plead with them t.
Am. 6 : 12. will one plough t. wi. oxen
7 : 12. t. eat bread and prophesy t.
Mi. 4 : 10. t. Lord shall redeem thee
Zph. 1 : 14. mighty man cry t. bitter-
Mat. 2 : 13. be t. until I bri. word [ly
5 : 23. t. remember bro. hath aught
24. Leave t. thy gift bef. the altar
6 : 21. where treasure is, t. will heart
be, Lu. 12 : 34. [t., Mk. 6 : 5.
13 : 58. did not many mighty works
18 : 20. t. am I in the midst of them
24 : 23. Lo, here is Christ, or t.,
Mk. 13 : 21. Lu. 17 : 21. [thine
25 : 25. I hid thy talent, t. thou hast
27 : 36. sitting, they watched him t.
61. t. was Mary Magdalene, Mary
28 : 7. t. shall ye see him, Mk. 16 : 7.
Mk 1 : 38. that I may preach t. also
Lu. 10 : 6. if son of peace be t., your
12 : 18. t. will I bestow all my fruits
17 : 23. sh. say, See here; or see t.
Jn. 3 : 23. t. was much water t.
4 : 6. Now Jacob's well was t. [be
12 : 26. where I am t. my servant

Jn. 14 : 3. th. where I am, t. ye may
Ac. 19 : 21. Aft. I have been t. I must
20 : 22. things that sh. befall me t.
22 : 10. t. it shall be told thee of all
Ro. 9 : 26. t. be called chil. of God
Re. 21 : 25. sh. be no night t., 22 : 5.
See ABIDE, ABODE, BORN,
DWELL, GNASHING, IS, NONE,
ONE, STAND, STOOD, WAS,
WEEPING.

Is THERE or THERE is.
Ge. 24 : 23. i. t. room in thy fa.'s hou.
40 : 8. dream, t. i. no interpreter of
42 : 2. heard t. i. corn in Egypt
Ex. 5 : 16. t. i. no straw given serv-ts
32 : 17. t. i. a noise of war in camp
33 : 21. Lord said, t. i. place by me
Le. 11 : 36. t. i. plenty of wat. [31, 37.
13 : 24. skin wh-f t. i. hot burning,
14 : 35. t. i. as it were plague in hou.
Nu. 11 : 6. t. i. noth-g besides manna
20 : 5. nei. i. t. any water, 21 : 5. (2)
22 : 5. t. i. a people come fr. Eg., 11.
23 : 23. nei. i. t. divination ag. Isr.
De. 22 : 26. t. i. in damsel no sin
32 : 39. t. i. no god with me; I kill
Ju. 18 : 10. place where t. i. no want
14. t. i. in these houses an ephod
19 : 18. t. i. no man receiveth me
19. Yet t. i. straw and provender
21 : 19. t. i. feast of Lord in Shiloh
Ru. 3 : 12. t. i. a kinsman nearer
4 : 17. t. i. a son born to Naomi
1 S. 14 : 6. t. i. no restraint to Lord
17. 46. know t. i. a God in Israel
20 : 3. t. i. but a step betw. me and
21. come, for t. i. peace to thee [(2)
21 : 4. t. i. no common bread under
8. i. t. not und. thine ha. a sword?
9. t. i. no other save that here
24 : 11. t. i. nei. evil nor transgr-n
27 : 1. t. i. noth. better for me than
28 : 7. t. i. woman hath familiar spi.
2 S. 3 : 38. t. i. a prince fallen in Isr.
13 : 16. she said, t. i. no cause
15 : 3. t. i. no man deputed of king
18 : 13. t. i. no matter hid fr. king
1 K. 5 : 4. rest so t. i. nei. adversary
8 : 23. t. i. no God like thee in heav-
en, 2 Ch. 6 : 14.
35. t. i. no rain because they have
sinned, 2 Ch. 6 : 26. [2 Ch. 6 : 36.
46. t. i. no man that sinneth not,
14 : 2. t. i. Ahijah the prophet who
13. in him t. i. found some good
18 : 10. t. i. no nation which my L.
41. t. i. sound of abundance of rain
22 : 8. t. i. one man, Micaiah, by who.
2 K. 1 : 16. is it not bec. t. i. no G. in
5 : 8. he shall know t. i. a prophet
15. I know t. i. no God but in Isr.
9 : 23. t. i. treachery, O Ahaziah
20 : 15. t. i. noth-g among my treasures not shewed, Is. 39 : 4.
1 Ch. 12 : 17. seeing t. i. no wrong in
17 : 20. nei. i. t. any God besides
22 : 16. Of gold, silver, t. i. no numb.
2 Ch. 28 : 13. t. i. fierce wrath ag. Isr.
Ezr. 10 : 2. t. i. hope in Isr., Jb. 11 : 18.
Es. 3. 8. t. i. a people scattered
Jb. 3 : 3. was said, t. i. a man child
5 : 4. nei. i. t. any to deliver them
6 : 6. i. t. taste in white of an egg?
7 : 1. i. t. not an appointed time
9 : 33. Neither i. t. any daysman
betwixt us, 11 : 18.
12 : 24. wander in wildern. where
t. i. no way, Ps. 107 : 40. [ment
19 : 7. I cry aloud, but t. i. no judg-
29. th. ye may know t. i. a judgm-t
22 : 29. Thou sh. say t. i. a lift-g up
25 : 3. i. t. any numb. of his armies?
28 : 1. Surely t. i. a vein for silver
31 : 2. portion of God i. t. fr. above?
32 : 8. But t. i. a spirit in man
34 : 22. t. i. no darkn. where workers
36 : 16. place t. i. no straitness

Ps. 6 : 5. in death t.i. no remembr-c
14 : 1. fool said, t.i. no God, 53 : 1.
19 : 6. t.i. nothing hid from heat
11. keeping them t.i. great reward
33 : 16. t.i. no king saved by host
34 : 9. t.i. no want to them that
36 : 1. t.i. no fear of God before his
eyes, Ro. 3 : 18. ⌈sh. make glad
46 : 4. t.i. a river, streams whereof
58 : 11. t.i. a reward for righteous
68 : 27. t.i. little Benj-n with ruler
69 : 2. I sink where t.i. no stand-g
92 : 15. t.i. no unrighteousn. in him
146 : 3. in man in whom t.i. no help
Pr. 11 : 24. t.i. that scattereth, t.i.
12 : 18. t.i. th. speaketh like piercings
28. in pathway th-f t.i. no death
13 : 7. t.i. that maketh hims. rich,
t.i. maketh himself poor, yet
14 : 9. among righteous t.i. favour
12. t.i. a way seemeth right, 16 :
23. in all labour t.i. profit ⌊25.
16 : 27. his lips t.i. as burning fire
20 : 15. t.i. gold, multi. of rubies
21 : 30. t.i. no wisdom against Lord
22 : 13. slothful saith t.i. a lion wi-t
23 : 18. for surely t.i. an end
28 : 12. righteous rejoice t.i. glory
29 : 6. In transg-n of man t.i. snare
18. Where t.i. no vision peo. per-h
30 : 11. t.i. a generation curseth fa.
12. t.i. a genera. pure in own eyes
13. t.i. a generation, O how lofty
14. t.i. a generat., teeth are swords
31. a king ag. wh. t.i. no rising up
Ec. 2 : 16. t.i. no remembr. of wise
21. t.i. a man whose lab-r is wisd.
3 : 1. To every thing t.i. a season
4 : 16. t.i. no end of all the people
5 : 13. t.i. a sore evil I have seen,
6 : 1.-10 : 5. ⌈that see sun
7 : 11. by wisdom t.i. profit to them
15. t.i. a just man, t.i. a wicked
8 : 4. Where word of king, t.i. power
6. Bec. to ev. purpose t.i. a time
14. t.i. a vanity upon earth ⌈sleep
16. t.i. that day nor night seeth
9 : 3. that t.i. one event with all, 2.
4. to him joined to living t.i. hope
10. t.i. no work in the grave, whi.
Can. 4 : 7. love ; t.i. no spot in thee
Is. 8 : 20. is bec. t.i. no light in th.
15 : 6. faileth, t.i. no green thing
23 : 1. Tyre is laid waste ; t.i. no
28 : 8. of vomit, t.i. no place clean
40 : 28. t.i. no search-g his underst.
43 : 11. beside me t.i. no saviour
44 : 6. beside me t.i. no G., 8.-45 : 5.
47 : 1. t.i. no throne, O dau. of Chal.
48 : 22. t.i. no peace unto wicked,
50 : 2. bec. t.i. no water ⌊57 : 21.
53 : 2. t.i. no beauty we sho. desire
57 : 10. saidst thou, t.i. no hope,
Je. 2 : 25.-18 : 12. ⌈peace, 8 : 11.
Je. 6 : 14. Peace, peace, when t.i. no
10 : 14. t.i. no breath in them, 51 : 17.
14 : 19. and t.i. no healing for us ;
we looked for peace, t.i. no good
16 : 19. things wh w-h t.i. no profit
31 : 17. t.i. hope in thine end
37 : 17. i.t. any word from L. ? t.i.
Eze. 13 : 16. peace for her, t.i. no pea.
22 : 25. t.i. a conspiracy of prophets
28 : 3. t.i. no secret they can hide
32 : 24. t.i. Elam about her grave
26. t.i. Meshech and all her multi.
29. t.i. Edom and all her princes
34 : 5. scat-d bec. t.i. no shepherd
Da. 2 : 10. t.i. not a man can shew (2)
28. t.i. a God th. revealeth secrets
3 : 29. t.i. no other God can deliver
5 : 11. t.i. a man in wh. is sp. of God
Ho. 4 : 1. bec. t.i. no truth in land
Na. 3 : 19. t.i. no healing of bruise
Ha. 2 : 19. t.i. no breath at all in it
Zph. 3 : 6. destroyed, so t.i. no man
Zch. 11 : 3. t.i. a voice of howling

Mat. 22 : 23. Sadducees say t.i. no
resurrection, Mk. 12 : 18. 1 Co
15 : 12. ⌈shall not
Mk. 4 : 22. t.i. nothing hid which
9 : 39. t.i. no man shall do miracle
10 : 18. t.i. none good but one
29. t.i. no man hath left house,
Lu. 18 : 29. ⌈not be
Lu. 12 : 2. t.i. nothing covered shall
14 : 22. it is done, yet t.i. room
15 : 10. t.i. joy in presence of ang.
Jn. 5 : 2. t.i. at Jerusalem a pool
6 : 9. t.i. a lad wh. hath five loaves
7 : 4. t.i. no man doeth in secret
8 : 44. your fa. t.i. no truth in him
11 : 10. stumbleth bec. t.i. no light
Ac. 17 : 7. t.i. ano. king, one Jesus
Ro. 3 : 22. upon all, t.i. no difference
5 : 13. not imputed wh. t.i. no law
1 Co. 3 : 3. t.i. among you strife and
5 : 1. it is reported t.i. fornication
8 : 6. but to us t.i. but one God
15 : 44. t.i. a nat-l body, t.i. a sp-l
2 Co. 3 : 17. Spirit of L., t.i. liberty
Ga. 3 : 28. t.i. nei. Jew nor Greek, t.
i. nei. bond nor free (3), Col. 3 : 11.
5 : 23. against such t.i. no law
Col. 3 : 25. t.i. no respect of persons
1 Jn. 4 : 18. t.i. no fear in love ; but
5 : 16. t.i. a sin unto death ; I do
17. and t.i. a sin not unto death
See **IS there, There IS not.**

THEREABOUT.

Lu. 24 : 4. were much perplexed t.

THEREAT. ⌈40 : 31.

Ex. 30 : 19. wash hands and feet t.,
Mat. 7 : 13. many there be wh. go in t.

THEREBY. ⌈shewed

Ge. 24 : 14. t. sh. I know thou hast
Le. 11 : 43. that ye sho. be defiled t.
Jb. 22 : 21. with G. t. good will come
Pr. 20 : 1. is deceived t. is not wise
Ec. 10 : 9. cleaveth wood endang-d t.
Is. 33 : 21. nei. gallant ship pass t.
Je. 18 : 16. passeth t. astonished, 19 : 8.
51 : 43. nei. any son of man pass t.
Eze. 12 : 5. Dig thro. wall, carry out
33 : 12. wicked sh. not fall t. ⌊t., 12.
18. righteous shall even die t.
19. if do that is right he sh. live t.
Zch. 9 : 2. Hamath shall border t.
Jn. 11 : 4. Son of God be glorified t.
Ep. 2 : 16. having slain the enmity t.
He. 12 : 11. them wh. are exercised t.
15. root spring-g, t. many be defiled
13 : 2. t. some have entertained ang.
1 Pe. 2 : 2. milk of word that ye may

THEREFORE. ⌊grow t.

Ge. 2 : 24. t. shall man leave his fa.
3 : 23. t. God sent him forth fr. gard.
4 : 15. t. whoso. slayeth Cain, veng.
11 : 9. t. is the name of it called, 19 :
22.-26 : 33.-31 : 48.-33 : 17. Ex.
15 : 23. 1 Ch. 14 : 11.
12 : 12. t. it shall come to pass, Jos.
23 : 15. Zch. 7 : 13. ⌈and seed
17 : 9. keep my covenant, t., thou
25 : 30. t. was his name called, 29 :
34, 35.-30 : 6.-38 : 29. ⌈heaven
27 : 28. t. God gave thee of dew of
29 : 15. thou t. serve me for nought ?
33. he hath t. given me this son
30 : 15. t. Le 8 : 35.-16 : 4.-17 : 12,
14. Nu. 21 : 7. De. 16 : 15. Jos.
22 : 26, 28. 1 S. 13 : 12. 2 K. 5 :
27.-19 : 32. ⌈of sinew
32 : 32. t. children of Israel eat not
33 : 10. for t. I have seen thy face
34 : 21. t. let them dwell in land ⌈us
42 : 21. t. is this distress come upon
22. t. also his blood is required
Ex. 1 : 11 t. did set taskmasters
20. t. God dealt well with midwiv.
5 : 8. idle ; t. cry, Let us go, 17, 18.
13 : 10. Thou shalt t. keep this ordinance, Le. 18 : 30.-22 : 9. ⌈rix
15. t. I sacrifice all th. openeth mat-

Ex. 16 : 29. t. he giveth on 6th day
31 : 14. Ye shall keep sabbath t. ;
for it is holy, De. 5 : 15.
Le. 11 : 44. ye shall t. be holy, for I
am, 45.-21 : 6. ⌈of
18 : 25. t. I do visit iniquity there-
26. ye shall t. keep my statutes,
19 : 37.-20 : 22. ⌈bear iniquity
19 : 8. t. every one that eateth shall
20 : 23. and t. I abhorred them
25. t. put difference between clean
21 : 8. Thou sh. sanctify priests t.
25 : 17. Ye shall not t. oppress one
Nu. 3 : 12. t. Levites shall be mine
11 : 18. t. the L. will give you flesh
14 : 16. t. he ha. slain them in wild.
18 : 7. t. thou and sons keep office
De. 15 : 15. t. I command thee this
thing, 11.-24 : 18, 22. ⌈giv. rest
25 : 19. t. it shall be when L. hath
27 : 4. t. it shall be when ye be gone
28 : 48. t. th. sh. serve thine enemies
Jos. 8 : 6. t. we will flee before them
Ju. 3 : 8. t. anger of L. hot ag. Isr.
11 : 8. said, t. we turn to thee now
26. why t. did ye not recover them
Ru. 3 : 3. Wash thyself t. and anoint
1 S. 1 : 28. t. I have lent him to the L.
10 : 12. t. it became proverb, Is Saul
20 : 8. t. deal kindly with serv. ⌈ing
23 : 23. See, t., take knowl. of lurk-
24 : 15. L. t. be judge betw. me and
26 : 4. David t. sent out spies ⌊thee
27 : 12. t. he sh. be my serv. for ev.
28 : 2. t. will I make thee keeper
18. t. hath Lord done this thing
31 : 4. t. Saul took sword, fell upon it
2 S. 6 : 21. t. will I play bef. the Lord
23. t. Michal, dau. of Saul had no
22 : 50. t. I will give thanks unto thee
1 K. 2 : 2. be strong, t., shew thyself
14 : 10. t. evil upon house of Jacob
20 : 42. t. thy life sh. go for his life
2 K. 1 : 14. t. let my life be precious
6 : 11. t. head of k. was sore troubled
17 : 18. t. Lord was angry with Isr.
26. t. he hath sent lions am. them
19 : 18. were no gods ; t. they destroyed them, Is. 37 : 19. ⌈thy fa-s
22 : 20. t. I will gather thee unto
1 Ch. 10 : 14. Saul inquired not, t. L.
11 : 3. t. came elders to David ⌊slew
2 Ch. 7 : 22. t. he bro-t evil upon th.
18 : 18. t. hear word of Lord
19 : 2. love them that hate Lord ?
t. is wrath ⌈tion
30 : 7. who t. gave them to desola-
35 : 14. t. Levites prep-d for thems.
Ezr. 4 : 14. t. have we certified king
Ne. 2 : 20. t. we will arise and build
13 : 28. t. I chased him from me
Jb. 20 : 2. t. tho-ts cause me to ans.
21 : 14. t. they say unto G., Depart
22 : 10. t. snares are round ab. thee
35 : 14. judgment is bef. him, t. trust
42 : 8. t. take unto you 7 bullocks
Ps. 16 : 9. t. my heart is glad ⌈me
31 : 3. t. for thy name's sake lead
36 : 7. t. chil. of men put their trust
45 : 2. t. God hath blessed thee for
7. t. God hath anointed thee
17. t. shall the people praise thee
55 : 19. no changes, t. fear not God
63 : 7. t. in shadow of thy wings
73 : 10. t. his people return ⌈liver
91 : 14. his love upon me, t. will I de-
106 : 23. t. he said he would destroy
116 : 10. I believed, t. spoken, 2 Co.
119 : 104. t. I hate ev. false way ⌊4 : 13.
129. wonderful, t. doth my soul
139 : 19. depart, t., ye bloody men
Pr. 17 : 11. t. a cruel messenger ag.
14 t. leave off contention before
Ec. 5 : 2. God in heav. t. words be few
8 : 6. t. misery of man is great
11. t. heart of men is set in them
Is. 3 : 17. t. L. will smite with scab

Is 10 : 16. t. Lord sh. send leanness
22 : 4. t. said I, Look away from me
24 : 6. t. hath curse devoured earth
28 : 16. t. saith the Lord God, Je.
7 : 20.-9 : 15.-22 : 18.-23 : 38.-
35 : 19. Zch. 1 : 16. [you be swift
30 : 16. t. shall they that pursue
42 : 25. t. he hath poured the fury
59 : 16. t. his arm brought salvat-n
Je. 5 : 4. t. I said, These are poor
6 : 15. t. they sh. fall am. them th.
40 : 3 ye obeyed not, t. this thing
La. 3 :24. L. my port-n, t. will I hope
Da. 2 : 6. t. shew me the dream, 9.
10. t. is no king nor ruler | 3:7, 22.
Jon. 4 : 2. t. I fled unto Tarshish
Zch. 1 :16. t. I am returned to Jerus.
7 : 12. t. great wrath from Lord
Mal. 3 :6. t. sons of Jac. not consumed
Mat. 3 : 8. t., 10.-5 : 19, 23.-6 : 2, 8,
9, 22, 23, 31, 34.-7 : 12, 24.-9 :
38.-10 : 16, 26.-13 : 18, 40, 52.-
18 : 4, 26.-21 : 40.-22 : 17, 21, 28.
-23 : 3, 20.-25 :27, 28.-27 :17, 64.
Mk. 10 : 9,-12 : 6, 23, 37.-Lu. 3 :
8.-7 : 42.-8 : 18.-10 : 2 (2).-11 :
34, 35, 36.-12 : 7, 40.-15 : 28.-
16 : 27.-19 : 12.-20 : 25, 29, 44.-
21 : 8, 14, 36.-23 : 16.-Jn. 4 : 6,
33.-5 : 16, 18.-6 : 13, 15, 24, 30,
43, 45, 52, 60, 65.-7 : 3, 22, 40.-
8 : 13, 24, 36.-9 : 8.-10 : 19, 39.-
11 : 3, 33, 38, 54.-12 : 17, 19, 21,
29.-13 : 11, 24, 31.-16 : 15, 18,
22.-18 : 4, 37.-19 : 1, 4, 6, 8, 11,
13, 16, 30, 31, 38, 42.-20 : 3, 25.-
21 : 6, 7. Ac. 1 : 6.-2 : 33.-8 : 4,
22.-10 :20, 29, 32 -12 : 5.-13 :38,
40.-14 : 3.-15 : 2, 27.-16 : 11.-
17 : 12, 17, 20, 23.-19 :32.-20 :28.-
21 : 22, 23.-25 : 5, 17.-26 : 22.-
28 : 20, 28. Ro. 2 : 21, 26.-3 : 28.
-4 : 16.-5 : 1.-6 : 4. 12.-11 : 22.-
12 : 1.-13 : 7, 10, 12.-14 : 8, 13.-
15 : 17.-16 : 19. 1 Co. 5 : 7, 8.-7 :
8, 26.-8 : 4.-10 : 31.-11 : 20.-14 :
11.-15 : 11, 58.-16 : 11, 18. 2 Co.
1 : 17.-4 : 1.-5 : 6, 11.-7 : 1, 13.-
11 : 15.-12 : 9.-13 : 10. Ga. 3 : 5.
-5 : 1.-6 : 10. Col. 2 : 6, 16.-3 :
5, 12. 1 Th. 3 : 7. 1 Ti. 2 : 1, 8.-
5 : 14. 2 Ti. 2 : 1, 3, 10, 21.-4 : 1.
Phm. 15, 17. He. 1 : 9.-2 : 1.-4 :
1, 6, 11, 16.-7 : 11.-9 : 23.-10 :
19, 35.-13 : 13, 15. Ja. 4 : 4, 7,
17.-5 : 7. 1 Pe. 2 : 7.-4 : 7.-5 : 6.
2 Pe. 3 : 17. 1 Jn. 2 : 24. 3 Jn. 8.
Re. 2 : 5.-3 :3, 19.-12 :12. [y-r Fa.
Mat. 5 : 48. Be ye t. perfect, even as
6 : 25. t. I say unto you, 21 : 43.
Mk. 11 : 24. Lu. 12 : 22. [value
10 : 31. Fear ye not, t., ye of more
32. Whoso. t. shall confess me bef.
12 : 27. t. they y-r judges, Lu. 11 :19.
13 :13. t. speak I to them in parab-s
14 : 2. t. mighty works do shew
forth in him, Mk. 6 : 14. [ened
18 :23. t. is kingdom of heaven lik-
19 :6. what t. G. hath joined togeth.
27. forsak. all, what sh. we have t. ?
22 :9. go ye t. into the highways
23 : 14. t. ye sh. rec. greater damna.
24 : 15. When ye t. see abomination
42. Watch, t., 25 : 13 Mk. 13 :35.
44. t. be ye ready, for in such an
28 : 19. Go ye t. teach all nations
Mk. 1 :38. may preach ; for t. came I
2 : 28. t. Son of man is Lord of sab.
8 : 38. Whoso. t. sh. be ashamed of
12 : 9. What sh. t. lord of vineyard
do ? Lu. 20 : 15 [greatly err
27. not God of the dead ; ye do t.
Lu. 1 : 35. t. that holy thi. wh. sh be
3 : 9 every tree t. wh bringeth not
4 : 7. if thou t. wilt worship me
43. I must preach, for t. am I sent
6 : 36. Be ye t. merciful as your Fa.

Lu. 10 : 40. bid her t. that she help
11 : 49. t. also said the wisd. of God
12 : 3. t. whatso. ye have heard in
13 ; 14. in th. t. come and be healed
14 : 20. I married, t. I cannot come
16 : 11. If t. ye have not been faitht.
20 :33. t. in resurrection whose wife
Jn. 1 : 31. t. am I come baptizing
3 : 29. this my joy t. is fulfilled
4 : 1. When t. L. knew how Pharis-s
5 : 10. Jes. t. said unto him was cur-
8 : 47. ye t. hear them not bec. [ed
9 :7. He went his way, t., and washed
10. t. said they, How eyes opened ?
16. t. said Pharis., This man not
23. t. said his parents, He is of age
41. We see ; t. your sin remaineth
10 : 17. t. doth my Father love me
11 : 6. Wh. he heard t. Laz. was sick
12 : 39. t. they could not believe
50. what I speak t. as Father said
15 : 19. chosen you t. world hateth
18 : 8. if t. ye seek me, let these go
25. said t. unto Pet., Art not thou
31. Jesus t. said, not lawful for us
39 will ye t. I release k of Jews ?
19 :24. these thi-s t. soldiers did (2)
26. When Jesus t. saw his mother
Ac. 2 : 26. t. did my heart rejoice
30. t. bring prophet, knowing th.
36. t. let all house of Israel know
3 :19. Repent ye t. and be converted
20 : 31. t. remember that by space
Ro. 2 : 1. t. thou art inexcusable, O
3 : 20. t. by deeds of the law [man
4 : 16. t. it is of faith that it might
22. t. was imputed to him for righ.
5 : 18. t. as by offence of one [to
8 : 12. t. breth we are debtors, not
9 : 18. t. hath he mercy on whom
12 : 20. t. if thine enemy hunger
13 : 2. Whoso. t. resisteth the pow.
14 : 19. Let us t. follow aft. things
1 Co. 3 : 21. t. let no man glory in
4 : 5. t. judge nothing bef. the time
6 : 20. t. glorify God in your body
9 : 26. I t. so run, not uncertainly
12 : 15. is it t. not of the body ? 16.
14 : 23. if t. whole church become
15 : 58. t. be ye stedfast, unmoveab.
2 Co. 4 : 1. t. seeing we have ministry
13. we also believe, and t. speak (2)
5 : 17 t. if any man be in Christ
7 :13. t. we were comforted in your
8 : 7. t. as ye abound in every thing
9 : 5. t. I thought it nec-y to exhort
12 : 10. t. I take pleasure in infirmi.
Ga. 2 : 17. is t. Christ minist. of sin ?
3 : 7. know ye t. they wh. are of fai.
4 : 16. am I t. become your enemy
Ep. 5 : 7. Be not ye t. partakers with
24. t. as church is subject to Ch.
Ph. 4 :1. t., brethren beloved, stand
fast in L., 2 Th. 2 : 15.
1 Th. 4 : 8. t., he that despiseth
5 : 6. t. let us not sleep as others
1 Ti. 4 : 14. t. we both labour and
2 Ti. 1 :8. Be not t. ashamed of testi.
2 : 10 t. I endure all for the elect's
He. 1 :9 t. God thy G. hath anointed
2 : 1. t. ought we to give more heed
4 : 9. There remaineth t. a rest to
11 : 12. t. sprang there even of one
1 Jn. 3 : 1. t. world knoweth us not
4 : 5. of the world : t. speak of world
Re. 7 : 15. t. are they bef. the throne
18 : 8. t. her plagues come in 1 day

Now THEREFORE.

Ge. 12 : 19. n. t. behold thy wife
20 :7. n. t. restore the man his wife
21 :23. n. t. swear to me here by G.
27 :3. n. t. take thy weapons and go
8. n. t., my son, obey my voi., 43.
29 : 32. n. t. my husb. will love me
31 : 44. n. t. let us make a covenant
37 : 20 n. t. let us cast him into pit
41 : 33. n. t. let Pha. look out a man

Ge. 44 : 30. n. t. when I come to my
33. n. t. let thy serv-t abide inst-d
45 :5. n. t. be not grieved ye sold me
Ge. 47 : 4. n. t. serv-ts dwell in Gosh.
50 :5. n. t. let me go bury my father
21. n. t. fear not, I will nourish
Ex. 3 : 9. n. t. cry of Isr is co. unto
4 :12. n. t. I will be with thy mouth
9 : 19. Send t. n., gather thy cattle
10 :17. n. t. forgive my sin this once
19 : 5. n. t. if ye will obey my voice
33 : 13. n. t. if I have found grace
De. 4 : 1. n. t. hearken, O Isr. unto
Jos. 14 :12. n. t. give me this mount.
24 : 14. n. t. fear Lord, serve him
Ju. 9 : 16. n. t. if ye have done truly
11 : 13. n. t. restore lands peaceably
14 : 2. n. t. get her for me to wife
1 S. 6 : 7. n. t. make a new cart and
9 : 13. n. t. get you up ; ye sh. find
10 : 19. n. t. present yours. bef. L.
12 :7. n. t. stand still th. I may rea-
13. n. t. behold the k. chosen [son
16. n. t. stand, see this gr. thing
15 : 1. n. t. hearken unto voice of L.
25. n. t. pardon my sin and turn
18 : 22. n. t. be the king's son in law
19 : 2. n. t. take heed until morn-g
21 : 3. n. t. what is under th. hand ?
23 :20. n. t., O k., come acc. to desire
24 :21. Swear n. t. unto me by the L.
25 : 17. n. t. consider what wilt do
26. n. t., my lord, as the L. liveth
26 : 8. n. t. let me smite him
19. n. t. let king hear his servant
20. n. t. let not my blood fall to
28 : 22. n. t. hearken unto handm.
2 S. 2 :7. t. n. hands be strengthened
4 : 11. sh. I not t. n. require his bl.
7 : 8. n. t., so shalt say unto David
29. t. n. let it please thee to bless
12 : 10. n. t. sword sh. never depart
28. n. t. encamp ag. the city, take
13 : 13. n. t. speak unto the king
33. n. t. let not king take to heart
14 : 15. n. t. I am come to speak to
32. n. t. let me see king's face [k.
17 : 16. n. t. send quickly, tell Dav.
18 : 3. t. n. better thou succour us
19 :7. n. t. speak comfortably [king
10. n. t. why speak not of bring-g
1 K. 1 : 12. n. t. let me give counsel
2 : 9. n. t. hold him not guiltless
24. n. t. Adoni-h eb. be put to death
5 : 6. n. t. command they hew cedar
8 :25. t. n. L. G keep with Dav. that
promised, 2 Ch 6 : 16. [lighter
12 : 4. n. t. make grievous service
18 :19. n. t. gather Isr. unto Carmel
22 : 23. n. t. Lord hath put lying
spirit, 2 Ch 18 : 22.
2 K. 1 : 4 n. t. Thou shalt not come
from that bed, 6, 16.
3 : 23. n. t. Moab to the spoil [vant
5 : 15. n. t. take blessing of thy ser-
7 : 4. n. t. let us fall unto Syrians
9. n. t. that we tell k.'s household
9 :26. n. t. cast him into plot of gro
10 : 19. n. t. call prophets of Baal
12 : 7. n. t. rec. no more money of
18 : 23 n. t. give pledges to king of
Assyria, Is. 36 : 8.
19 : 19. n. t. O Lord, save us out of
his hand, Is. 37. 20.
1 Ch. 17 : 7. n. t. thus say unto Dav.
23. n. t., Lord, do as thou hast said
27. n. t. let it please thee to bless
21 : 12. n. t. advise thys. what word
28 : 8. n. t. keep all the com-ts of G.
29 :13. n. t. our God, we thank thee
2 Ch. 2 : 7. n. t. a man cun-g to work
15. n. t. wheat and oil let him send
6 : 41. n. t., O Lord, into thy resting
10 : 4. n. t. ease grievous servitude
28 : 11. n. hear me, t. deliver capt-s
32 : 15. n. t. let not Hez-h deceive
Ezr. 5 : 17. n. t. let search be made

Ezr. 6 : 6. **n.t.** Tatnai and compa-ns
9 : 12. **n.t.** give not dau-s unto th.
10 : 3. **n.t.** let us make covenant
10 : 11. **n.t.** make confes-n unto L.
Ne. 6 : 7. **n.t.** let us take counsel
9. **n.t.**, O G, strengthen my hands
9 : 32 **n.t.** our God, let not trouble
Jb. 6 : 28 **n.t.** be content, look upon
Ps. 2 : 10. Be wise, **n.t.**, O ye kings
Pr. 5 : 7. Hear me, **n.t.**, O ye children, 7 : 24.-8 : 32. [waters
Is. 8 : 7. **n.t.** Lord bringeth upon th.
28 : 22. **n.t.** be ye not mockers, lest
52 : 5. **n.t.**, what have I here, saith
Je. 18 : 11. **n.t.** speak to men of Jud.
26 : 13. **t.n.** amend your ways and
29 : 27. **n.t.** why not reproved Jere.
32 : 36. **n.t.**, saith Lord, conc-g city
42 : 15. **n.t.**, hear L., remn-t of Jud.
22. **n. t.** know ye sh. die by sword
44 : 7. **t.n.**, saith L., Whf. commit
Da. 9 : 17. **n.t.**, O G., cause thy face
Jo. 2 : 12. **t.n.** turn ye to me with all
Am. 6 : 7. **t.n.** shall they go captive
7 : 16. **n.t.** hear thou word of Lord
Jon. 4 : 3. **t.n.**, O Lord, take my life
Hag. 1 : 5. **n.t.**, saith Lord, consider
Ac. 10 : 33. **n.t.** we are here bef. God
15 : 10. **n.t.** why tempt ye God to
16 : 36. **n.t.** depart and go in peace
23 : 15. **n.t.** ye with council signify
Ro. 8 : 1. There is **t.n.** no condemna.
1 Co. 6 : 7. **n.t.** there is fault am. you
2 Co. 8 : 11. **n.t.** perform, doing of it
Ep. 2 : 19. **n.t.** ye are no more strang- [ers

THEREFROM.

Jos. 23 : 6. that ye turn not aside **t.**
2 K. 3 : 3. sins of Jeroboam, he departed not **t.**, 13 : 2.

THEREIN. [tiply t.

Ge. 9 : 7. bring forth in earth, mul-
18 : 24. not spare for 50 righteous **t.**?
23 : 11. field **t.** I give thee, 17, 20.
34 : 10. trade **t.** and get possessions
t., 21.-47 : 27.
Ex. 2 : 3., **t.**, 5 : 9.-16 : 33.-21 : 33.-
29 : 29.-30 : 18.
16 : 24. nei. was there any worm **t.**
40 : 3. put **t.** ark of testimony
9. tabernacle, and all **t.**, Le. 8 : 10.
Nu. 4 : 16. [passing **t.**
Le. 6 : 3. sinning **t.** | 7. done in tres-
13 : 21. be no white hairs **t.** | 37.
18 : 30. that ye defile not yours. **t.**
22 : 21. be no blemish **t.**, De. 15 : 21.
Nu. 13 : 20. whe. there be wood **t.** or
16 : 7. put fire, put incense **t.**, 46.
35 : 53. cannot be cleansed of blood
De. 7 : 25. not gold, lest snared **t.** [t.
17 : 19. he shall read **t.** all his life
20 : 11. peo. found **t.** be tributaries
29 : 23. salt, nor grass groweth **t.**
Jos. 1 : 8. meditate **t.** day and night
6 : 17. city accursed and all **t.**, 24.
10 : 28. smote all souls that were **t.**,
30, 32, 35, 37, 39. Ju. 9 : 45. 2 K.
15 : 16. (2)
Ju. 8 : 25. cast **t.** every man earrings
16 : 30. house fell upon all **t.**
18 : 7. came to Laish, saw people **t.**
1 S. 30 : 2. women captives th. were **t.**
2 S. 12 : 31. people **t.** put under saws
1 K. 8 : 16. that my name might be **t.**
2 K. 2 : 20. Bring a cruse, put salt **t.**
Ezr. 4 : 19. rebellion been made **t.**
Ne. 6 : 1. there was no breach left **t.**
7 : 4. city large, but people few **t.**
8 : 3. he read **t.** before the street
Jb. 3 : 7. let no joyful voice come **t.**
20 : 18. restitution, sh. not rejoice **t.**
Ps. 104 : 26. leviat-n made to play **t.**
111 : 2. sought of all have pleasure **t.**
119 : 35. com-ts; for **t.** do I delight
Pr. 15 : 4. perverseness **t.** is breach
22 : 14. abhorred of L. shall fall **t.**,
26 : 27. Je. 28 : 12. Ho. 14 : 9. [t.
Ec. 2 : 21. man th. hath not laboured
Is. 5 : 2. he made a winepress **t.**
7 : 6. let us make a breach **t.** for us
34 : 1. let the earth hear and all **t.**
35 : 8. men, tho. fools, sh. not err **t.**
42 : 10. go down to sea and all **t.**
44 : 23. slug-g, O forest, every tree **t.**
51 : 3. joy, gladn-s shall be found **t.**
59 : 8. goeth **t.** shall not know peace
Je. 47 : 2. overflow land and all **t.**
Eze. 2 : 9. roll of a book was **t.**
7 : 20. images of detestable things **t.**
12 : 19. land desolate fr. all that is **t.**
14 : 22. **t.** shall be left a remnant
20 : 47. all faces shall be burned **t.**
24 : 5. let them seethe bones of it **t.**
6. Woe to pot whose scum is **t.**
30 : 12. make land waste and all **t.**
40 : 33. windows **t.** and in arches
44 : 14. keepers for th. sh. be done **t.**
Da. 5 : 2. concubines might drink **t.**
Ho. 14 : 9. transgressors shall fall **t.**
Am. 6 : 8. deliver up city with all **t.**
Mi. 1 : 2. hearken, O earth, all **t.** is
Ha. 2 : 18. maker of work trusteth **t.**
Zch. 2 : 4. **t.**, 6 : 6.-13 : 8 (2).-14 : 21.
Lu. 10 : 9. heal the sick that are **t.**
19 : 45. cast out them that sold **t.**
Jn. 12 : 6. bag, bare what was put **t.**
Ac. 27 : 6. centurion put us **t.**
Ro. 1 : 17. **t.** is righteousness of God
6 : 2. dead to sin live any longer **t.**?
1 Co. 7 : 24. wh-in he is called **t.** abide
Ep. 6 : 20. th. **t.** I may speak boldly
Ph. 1 : 18. I **t.** do rejoice and will
Col. 2 : 7. abounding **t.** wi. thanksg.
He. 4 : 6. Seeing some must enter **t.**
10 : 8. offer-gs nei. hadst pleasure **t.**
13 : 9. not profited them occupied **t.**
Ja. 1 : 25. continueth **t.** sh. be blessed
2 Pe. 2 : 20. they are ag. entangled **t.**
3 : 10. earth and works **t.** be burned
Re. 11 : 1. meas. them that worship **t.**
21 : 22. I saw no temple **t.** God is
See **All That.** [temple

Dwell, Dwelt, or Dwelleth THEREIN. [t., 21.

Ge. 34 : 10. land bef. you; **d.**, trade
Le. 25 : 19. ye shall **d.t.** in safety
26 : 32. ene-s wh. **d.t.** be astonished
Nu. 13 : 18. peo. wh. **d-h t.** whe. few
14 : 30. I sware to make you **d.t.**
32 : 40. Gilead unto Machir, he **d-t t.**
33 : 53. ye shall dispossess the inhabitants and **d.t.**, De. 11 : 31.-17 :
14.-26 : 1. Jos. 21 : 43. [and tall
De. 2 : 10. Emim **d-t t.**, people many
20. giants **d-t t.** in old time, and
8 : 12. built goodly houses, **d-t t.**
28 : 30. sh. build hou. and not **d.t.**
Jos. 19 : 47. Leshem children of Dan
d-t t., Ju. 18 : 28. [t.
50. Joshua built the city and **d-t**
1 K. 11 : 24. went to Damascus, **d-t t.**
12 : 25. Jerob. built Shechem, **d-t t.**
2 Ch. 2 : 3. cedars to build ho. to **d.t.**
20 : 8. **d-t t.** and built sanctuary **t.**
Ne. 13 : 16. **d-t** men of Tyre **t.**, which
Ps. 24 : 1. The earth is the Lord's;
the world, and they that **d.t.**,
69 : 34. Ac. 17 : 24. Re. 10 : 6.
37 : 29. righteous shall **d.t.** for ever
68 : 10. Thy congreg-on hath **d-t t.**
69 : 36. that love his name sh. **d.t.**
98 : 7. Let world roar, they th. **d.t.**
107 : 34. for wickedness of them th.
d.t., Je. 12 : 4. [are desolate
Is. 24 : 6. the earth, they that **d.t.**
33 : 24. peo. that **d.t.** are forgiven
34 : 17. fr. genera. to genera. sh. **d.t.**
51 : 6. th. **d.t.** sh. die in like man-r
Je. 4 : 29. city forsaken, not man **d.t.**
8 : 16. devoured city and all **d.t.**
27 : 11. they shall till land and **d.t.**
44 : 2. a desolation, no man **d-h t.**
47 : 2. overflow land, all that **d.t.**
48 : 9. the cities without any to **d.t.**
50 : 3. land desolate, none sh. **d.t.**
Je. 50 : 39. Thf. beasts and owls sh. **d.t.**
40. nei. shall any son of man **d.t.**
Eze. 12 : 19. because of violence of
them th. **d.t.**, Mi. 7 : 13. Ha. 2 : 8, 17.
28 : 26. they sh. **d.** safely **t.**, build
32 : 15. when I smite them that **d.t.**
37 : 25. shall **d.t.** they and children
Ho. 4 : 3. every one **d-h t.** shall languish, Am. 8 : 8. [t. sh. mourn
Am. 9 : 5. land shall melt, all th. **d.**
Na. 1 : 5. is burned, world, all **d.t.**
Mat. 23 : 21. sweareth by him **d-h t.**
Ac. 1 : 20. ble habita., let no man **d.t.**
Re. 13 : 12. them wh. **d.t.** to worship
See Enter, walk, walked,
work, write, written,
wrote.

THEREINTO. [enter t.

Lu. 21 : 21. not them in countries

THEREOF. [3 : 5.

Ge. 2 : 17. in the day thou eatest **t.**,
19. Adam called, that was name **t.**
21. Lord closed up flesh instead **t.**
3 : 6. woman took of the fruit **t.**
4 : 4. **t.**, 6 : 16.-9 : 4 (2).-40 : 10, 18.
-41 : 8.-45 : 16.-47 : 21. [midst **t.**
Ex. 3 : 20. wonders I will do in the
5 : 8. ye sh. not diminish aught **t.**
9 : 18. not in Egypt since founda. **t.**
10 : 26. **t.** must we take to serve L.
12 : 9. roast head wi. purtenance **t.**
43. There shall no stranger eat **t.**,
45, 48. 2 K. 7 : 2. [t.
44. when circumcised shall he eat
46. nei. shall ye break a bone **t.**
16 : 31. **t.**, 25 : 9, 10. (8), 12, 17, 19,
23, 26, 29. (4), 37. (2), 38. (2).-28 :
27. (2).-30 : 2. (4).-36 : 29.-37 : 6.
(2). 18, 25, 27. (2).-38 : 1. (8) -39 :
9. (2). Le. 2 : 2. (3), 16. (2) -11 : 39.
-19 : 23, 24, 25.-24 : 5.-25 : 7.-
27 : 21. Nu. 3 : 31, 36. (4).-4 : 31.
De. 26 : 14. 1 K. 6 : 2. (3), 3. (2).-
7 : 36. (2).-16 : 34. 2 K. 4 : 43, 44.
-19 : 29. Ne. 8 : 3, 6, 13. (2), 14,
15.-11 : 25. (2). Es. 2 : 22.
2 K. 13 : 14. chariot of Israel and
horsemen **t.** [earth
Jb. 11 : 9. measure **t.** longer than
14 : 8. Tho. stock **t.** die in ground
24 : 13. they know not the ways **t.**
28 : 22. We have heard the fame **t.**
31 : 38. If the furrows **t.** complain
39. If I have eaten fruits **t.** without money, or caused owners **t.**
Ps. 34 : 2. humble sh. hear **t.** be glad
46 : 3. Though the waters **t.** roar
65 : 10. Thou waterest the ridges
t.: thou settlest the furrows **t.**:
thou blessest the springing **t.**
Pr. 16 : 33. disposing **t.** is of the L.
Ec. 6 : 2. G. giveth not power to eat **t.**
Mat. 12 : 36. They sh. give account **t.**

THEREON. [t. (2)

Ge. 35 : 14. Jacob poured drink off-g
Ex. 17 : 12. stone und. Moses, he sat **t.**
20 : 24. An altar, sacrifice **t.** burnt
offerings, peace off-gs, De. 27 : 6.
Jos. 8 : 31.-22 : 23. 2 Ch. 33 : 16.
Ezr. 3 : 2, 3. Eze. 40 : 39.-43 : 18 (2).
26. that nakedn. be not discov-d **t.**
30 : 7. Aaron sh. burn sw. incense
t., 40 : 27. Nu. 16 : 18. [t. (2)
9. ye shall offer no strange incense
40 : 35. not enter tent bec. cloud
abode **t.**, Nu. 9 : 22. [t., 6, 15.
Le. 2 : 1. offering put frankincense
6 : 12. burn **t.** fat of peace offerings
10 : 1. Nadab, Abihu put incense **t.**
11 : 38. if carcass fall **t.** unclean
Nu. 4 : 6. put **t.** covering of badger's
skins, 7, 13.-5 : 15. [sh. be **t.**
7. put **t.** dishes, spoons; bread
Jos. 8 : 29. raise **t.** gr. heap of stones
2 S. 17 : 19. spread ground corn **t.**
19 : 26. saddle ass that I may ride **t.**
1 K. 13 : 13. saddled ass; he rode **t.**

2 K. 16 : 12. king saw altar offered t.
1 Ch. 12 : 17. God of our fa-s look t.
15 : 15 Levites bare ark wi. staves t.
2 Ch. 3 : 5. set t. palm trees, chains
14. made vail, wrought cherubim
Ezr. 6 : 11. let him be hanged t. ⌊t.
Es. 5 : 14. th. Mordecai be hanged t.
7 : 9. king said, Hang Haman t. ⌈t.
Is. 30 : 12. in perverseness and stay
35 : 9. nor ravenous beast go up t.
Eze. 15 : 3. pin of it to hang vessel t.
Mat. 21 : 7. they set him t., Lu. 19 :
35. Jn. 12 : 14. ⌈13. Lu. 13 : 6.
19. and found nothing t., Mk. 11.
23 : 20. by altar, sweareth by all t.
22. sweareth by him th. sitteth t.
Mk. 14 : 72. when thought t. he wept
Jn. 21 : 9. saw fire and fish laid t.
1 Co. 3 : 10. foundation, buildeth t.
Re. 5 : 3. not open book or look t., 4.
6 : 4. power given him that sat t.
21 : 12 twelve gates, names written

THEREOUT. ⌊t.

Le. 2 : 2. sh. take t. handful of flour
Ju. 15 : 19. in the jaw, came water t.

THERETO.

Ex. 25 : 24. make t. a crown of gold
29 : 41. do t. acc-g to meat offering
30 : 38. like unto that to smell t.
Le. 5 : 16. add the fifth part t., 6 : 5.
-27 : 15, 27, 31. ⌈down t.
18 : 23. nei. stand bef. a beast to lie
20 : 16. if wom. lie down t. kill wom.
Nu. 3 : 36. vessels and all th. serv. t.
19 : 17. running water sh. be put t.
De. 12 : 32. not add t. nor diminish
Ju. 11 : 17. k. of Edom not heark. t.
1 Ch. 22 : 14. and thou mayest add t.
2 Ch. 10 : 14. yoke heavy, I will add t.
21 : 11. Jehoram compelled Jud. t.
Ps. 119 : 9. by taking heed t. acc-g
Is. 44 : 15. an image, falleth down t.
Mk. 14 : 70. thy speech agreeth t.
Ga. 3 : 15. no man disannulleth or

THEREUNTO. ⌊addeth t.

Ex. 32 : 8. molten calf sacrificed t.
36 : 39. made t. 4 pillars of shittim
37 : 11. he made t. a crown of gold
12. made t. border of handbreadth
De. 1 : 7. go to all the places nigh t.
Ep. 6 : 18. watching t. with persever.
1 Th. 3 : 3. know we are appointed t.
He. 10 : 1. nev. make comers t. perf.
1 Pe. 3 : 9. knowing ye are t. called

THEREUPON. ⌈t.

Eze. 16 : 16. thou playedst the harlot
Zph. 2 : 7. remnant of Judah feed t.
1 Co. 3 : 10. heed how he buildeth t.
14. If work abide he hath built t.

THEREWITH. ⌈t.

Ex. 22 : 6. so th. stacks be consumed
30 : 26. anoint taberu. of cong-n t.
38 : 30. t. be made sockets to door
Le. 7 : 7. priest th. maketh atone-t t.
8 : 7. bound ephod unto him t.
15 : 32. is defiled t., 18 : 23.-22 : 8.
De. 16 : 3. 7 days eat unl-d bread t.
23 : 13. wilt ease thys. abroad, dig t.
Ju. 16 : 12. Delilah bound him t.
1 S. 12 : 3. bribe to blind mine eyes t.
17 : 51. drew sw., cut off his head t.
31 : 4. thrust me thro. t., 1 Ch. 10 : 4.
2 S. 20 : 10. smote him t. in 5th rib
2 K. 5 : 6. I have t. sent Naaman
12 : 14. repaired t. house of the L.
2 Ch. 16 : 6. Asa built t. Geba, Miz.
Pr. 15 : 16. treasure and trouble t.
17. than stalled ox, and hatred t.
17 : 1. dry morsel and quietness t.
25 : 16. lest be filled t. and vomit it
Ec. 1 : 13. travail to be exercised t.
10 : 9. removeth stones be hurt t.
Eze. 4 : 15. prepare thy bread t.
Jo. 2 : 19. oil, wine, be satisfied t.
Ph. 4 : 11. I learned t. to be content
1 Ti. 6 : 8. food, raiment, be t. content
Ja. 3 : 9. t. bless we God, t. curse we
3 Jn. 10. prating ag. us, not content

THESE. [Adj.] ⌊t.

Ge. 26 : 3. t., 4.-27 : 36.-31 : 43.(3).-
43 : 16.-45 : 6. Ex. 10 : 1. Nu. 1 :
17. De. 6 : 25.-28 : 65. Ru. 3 : 17.
1 S. 17 : 17, 18.-21 : 5. 2 S. 23 :
17. 1 K. 10 : 8.-17 : 1.-22 : 23. 2
Ch. 18 : 22. Ezr. 5 : 9, 15.-6 : 8.
Ne. 6 : 14. Es. 1 : 5.-4 : 11.-9 :
27, 31. Je. 10 : 11. Eze. 40 : 24,
28, 32, 33, 35.-43 : 27. Da. 2 : 44.
(2).-6 : 5, 6.-7 : 17. Zch. 8 : 6.-
14 : 15. Mat. 5 : 19.-13 : 53.-20 :
21.-22 : 40. Mk. 13 : 2.-16 : 17.
Lu. 1 : 19.-13 : 2.-19 : 15.-20 : 16.
Jn. 3 : 2. Ac. 11 : 12.-21 : 38.-
24 : 20.-25 : 20.-26 : 21, 29. Ro. 15 :
23. 2 Co. 7 : 1. 1 Th. 3 : 3. He. 1 :
2 Re. 9 : 20.-11 : 10-16 : 9. ⌈her
Ex. 21 : 11. if he do not t. three unto
1 Ch. 3 : 4. t. six were born in Hebron
Je. 31 : 21. O Isr., turn to t. thy cities
38 : 9. t. men have done evil to Jere.
16. nei. give thee into ha. of t. men
Da. 3 : 13. they bro-t t. men bef. king
21. t. men were cast into furn., 23.
27. t. men upon whose bodies fire
6 : 11. t. men found Dan. pray-g ⌊15.
Zch. 4 : 11. what t. two olive trees, 12.
Mat. 20 : 21. Grant t. my sons may sit
25 : 40. one of least of t. my breth.
Mk. 8 : 4. whence satisfy t. men in
Ac. 1 : 21. t. men wh. companied with
24. shew whe. of t. 2 hast chosen
4 : 16. What shall we do to t. men?
24 : 20. let t. same say if they have
See These ABOMINATIONS.

THESE days.

Jos. 22 : 3. t. d., 1 S. 29 : 3. Es. 4 :
11.-9 : 27. He. 1 : 2. ⌈t. d.
1 S. 29 : 3. Is not this David, with me
Es. 1 : 5. t. d. were expired k. made
9 : 26. Whf. they called t. d. Purim
28. t. d. sho. be kept thro-t every
generation, t. d. should not fail
31. to confirm t. d. of Purim
Eze. 43 : 27. when t. d. are expired
Zch. 8 : 6. If it be marvellous in t. d.
9. be strong, ye that hear in t. d.
10. bef. t. d. was no hire for man
15. I tho-t in t. d. to do well unto
Lu. 21 : 22. t. be d. of veng-e ⌊Jeru.
24 : 18. not known thi-s co. in t. d.?
Ac. 3 : 24. prophets foretold of t. d.
5 : 36. before t. d. rose up Theudas
11 : 27. in t. d. came proph-s fr. Jer.
21 : 38. Egypt-n before t. d. madest
He. 1 : 2. G. hath spok. in t. last d.
See These NATIONS, Little
ONES, These THINGS,
These WORDS,
MEN, SAYINGS, STONES, THREE,
TIMES, YEARS.

THESE. [Pronoun.]

Ge. 10 : 5. By t. were isles divided, 32
29. All t. were sons of, 25 : 4.-36 :
12, 13, 14, 15, 17, 18, 19, 40.-46 :
15. Nu. 3 : 17. 1 Ch. 2 : 23.-3 : 1,
9.-4 : 6.-6 : 17.-9 : 44.-23 : 10.-26 : 8.
14 : 2. t. made war with k. of Sodom
3. All t. were joined in vale of Sid.
13. t. were confederate wi. Abram
15 : 10. Abram took unto him all t.
23 : 1. t. were years of life of Sarah
27 : 46 if Jac. take wife of such as t.
36 : 15. t. were dukes of, 16, 19, 21,
29, 30, 40, 43. ⌈teen souls, 25.
46 : 18. t. she bare unto Jacob, six-
Ex. 6 : 14. t. be the heads of father's
house (2), 1 Ch. 8 : 28.-23 : 9. ⌈to t.
14 : 20. but cloud ga. light by night
32 : 4. t. be thy gods, O Israel, 8.
Le. 5 : 13. hath sinned in one of t.
11 : 4. t. sh. ye not eat of them th.
9. t. shall ye eat, 21, 22. De. 14 : 9
24. And for t. ye shall be unclean
29. t. sh. be unclean am. creeping
Le. 18 : 24. in all t. nations are defiled
22 : 22. ye shall not offer t. unto L.,
Nu. 2 : 9. t. shall first set forth ⌊25,
13 : 4. t. were names of heads of Isr.
26 : 51 t. were the numbered of Isr.
53. unto t. land shall be divided
64. among t. was not a man ⌈pass
31 : 16. t. caused Isr. to com-t tres-
De. 27 : 12. t. upon Gerizim to bless
13. t. sh. stand upon Ebal to curse
Jos. 13 : 12. t. did Moses smite, cast
17 : 2. t. were the chil. of Manasseh
Ju. 13 : 23. nei. would he have told
us such things as t. ⌈35, 44.
20 : 17. all t. were men of war, 25,
46. all t. were men of valour ⌈t.
1 S. 16 : 10. The L. hath not chosen
17 : 39. Dav. said, I cannot go wi. t.
2 S. 5 : 14. t. be the names of those
born in Jerus., 1 Ch. 3 : 5. ⌈by t.?
16 : 2. king said, What meanest th.
23 : 1. t. be the last words of David
8. t. be names of mighty men Da.
1 K. 4 : 2. t. princes Sol-n had ⌊had
7 : 9. All t. were of costly stones
11 : 2. Sol-n clave unto t. in love
10 : 10. as t. wh. queen of Sheba ga.
22 : 11. saith L., With t. shalt thou
push Syrians, 2 Ch. 18 : 10.
17. L. said, t. have no master, 2 Ch.
2 K. 10 : 9. who slew all t.? ⌊18 : 16.
25 : 20. Neb-n took t., bro-t them
1 Ch. 4 : 3. t. were of the fa. of Etam
23. t. were potters | 31. t. their cities
33. t. their habitations, genealogy
38. t. were princes in their families
41. t. writ. by name came in days
7 : 29. in t. dwelt children of Joseph
8 : 32. t. dwelt with breth. in Jeru.
9 : 22. All t. wh. were chosen porters
2 Ch. 29 : 32. All t. for burnt offer-g
35 : 7. t. were of king's substance
36 : 18. All t. he bro-t to Babylon
Ezr. 2 : 62. t. sought their register
10 : 44. All t. had taken stra. wives
Ne. 7 : 6. t. co. not shew their house
12 : 26. t. were in days of Joiakim, 7
Jb 12 : 3. who knoweth not such as t.
Ps. 104 : 27. t. wait all upon thee
Ec. 12 : 12. by t., my son, be admonish-
Is. 34 : 16. no one of t. shall fail ⌊ed
44 : 21. Remember t., O Jac. and Isr.
49 : 12. t. shall come from far, t.
fr. north and west, t. fr. Sinim
21. Who hath begotten me t.? who
brought up t.? I was left alone;
t., where had they been? ⌊t.?
57 : 6. Should I receive comfort in
Je. 2 : 34. not found bl., but upon all
5 : 5. t. have broken the yoke ⌊t.
52 : 22. pomegr-s were like unto t.
La. 4 : 9 for t. pine away, stricken
Eze. 1 : 21. When those went, t. went,
when those stood, t. st., 10 : 17.
16 : 5. none pitied, to do t. unto thee
20. t. hast thou sacrificed unto th.
23 : 10. t. discovered her nakedness
27 : 21. in t. were they thy merch-s
37 : 18. Shew us what meanest by t.
48 : 16. t. shall be the measures th-f
Da. 1 : 6. am. t. were of chil. of Jud.
2 : 40. iron that breaketh all t.
6 : 2. ov. t. Darius set 3 presidents
Hag. 2 : 13. if one unclean touch t.
Zch. 1 : 9. I will shew what t. be
19. I said unto angel, What be t.?
21. said I, What come t. to do?
3 : 7. to walk am. t. th. stand by ⌈13.
4 : 5. Knowest thou not what t. be?
6 : 8. t. that go tow. north country
Mat. 6 : 29. Sol. not arrayed like one
of t., Lu. 12 : 27. ⌈saying, Go
10 : 5. t. twelve Jesus sent forth,
20 : 12. t. last have wrought but 1 hr.
21 : 16. Hearest thou what t. say?
28 : 23. t. ought ye to have done
and not left, Lu. 11 : 42.

Mat.25:45.did it not to one of least of
46.t.sh. go into everl-g punish. ⌊t.
26 : 62.What is it t. witness against
thee, Mk. 14 : 60.
Mk. 10 : 20. All t. have I observed
from youth, Lu. 8 : 21. ⌈nation
12 : 40.t. shall receive greater dam-
Lu. 8 : 13. t. have no root, fall away
19 : 40. if t. hold peace stones cry
21 : 4. all t. of abundance cast in
12. bef. all t. they sh. lay hands on
22. t. be the days of vengeance
Jn. 5 : 3.In t. lay multi. of impotent
19. what he doeth, t. doeth Son
6 : 5. Whence buy bread t. may eat
17 : 20. Neither pray I for t. alone
25. t. have known thou sent me
18 : 8. if ye seek me, let t. go their
Ac. 1 :14. t. all continued wi. one ac.
10 :47.Can any forbid t. be baptized
17 :6.t.that have turned world ups.
7. t. all do contrary to decrees of
11. t.more noble than those in Th.
20 : 5. t. tarried for us at Troas
27:31. Exc. t.abide in ship, ye can-
Ro. 2 : 14. t. having not the law⌊not
11 : 24.much more sh. t. be graffed
31. Even so have t. not believed
1 Co.12 : 11. all t. worketh one spi.
23. upon t. we bestow more hon.
13 : 13. t. 3, greatest of t. is charity
Col. 3 : 8. put off all t. anger,malice
1 Ti. 3 : 10. let t. also first be proved
2 Ti. 2 : 21. If man purge hims. fr. t.
3 : 8. as Jannes so t. resist truth
He.9:23.patterns be purified with t.
10 :18. Now where remission of t. is
11 : 13. t. all died in faith, not, 39.
2 Pe.1 :4.by t. be partakers of divine
2 : 12. t. as brute beasts ⌈know not
Jude 12. t. speak evil of things they
14. Enoch prophesied of t., say-g
19.t. be they who separate thems.
Re. 11 :6.t.have power to shut heav.
14 : 4. t. were redeemed fr. am.men
17 :13.t.have one mind and sh.give
14. t. sh.make war with the Lamb
16. t. shall hate whore, burn her

Are THESE, or THESE are.

Ge: 2 : 4. t.a. the generations, 6 :9.-
10 : 1.-11 : 10, 27.-25 : 12, 19.-
36 :1,9.-37 :2. Nu. 3:1. Ru.4:18.
9 : 19 t.a.the sons, 10:20, 31, 32 -
25 : 16.(2).-35 : 26.-36 : 10, 18,
19, 20.-46 : 22, 25. Nu. 3 : 2, 3,
18.-26 : 30, 35, 36, 41, 42. 1 Ch.
2 : 1, 18.-7 : 8.-8 : 40.
10 : 32. t.a. the families, Nu. 3 :
20, 21.-26 : 7, 14, 18, 22, 25, 27,
34, 37, 47, 50, 58.
25 :7. t.a. the years of Abr-.'s life,
17.t.a. the years of life of Ishmael
32 :17. asketh, Whose a.t. bef.thee?
33 : 8. t.a. to find grace in sight of
36 : 24. t.a. children of, 25, 26, 27,
28. Jos. 17 : 2. ⌈of Edom
31. t.a. kings that reigned in land
38 : 25. By the man whose t.a. am
I with child. Discern whose a.t.
46 : 8. t.a. names of chil. of Israel
48 : 8. Israel said, Who a.t.?
49 : 28. all t.a. 12 tribes of Israel
Ex. 6 : 25.t.a.heads of fa-s of Levites
26. t.a. that Aaron and Moses
27. t.a. they which spake to Pha.
21 : 1. t.a. judgments thou shalt
set, Le. 26 : 46. De. 6 : 1.
Le. 11 :2.t.a. the beasts ye shall eat,
De. 14 : 4. ⌈ination, De. 14 : 12.
13. t.a. they ye sh. have in abom-
31. t.a. unclean to you ⌈wash
16 : 4. t.a. holy garments; therof.
23 : 2.convocat-s, t.a. my feasts, 4.
Nu. 1 :5.t.a.men sh. stand with you
44.t.a. those which Mos.number-
22 : 9. God said, What men a.t. ⌊ed
33 : 2. t.a. their journeys acc-g

Nu. 34 :17. t.a. names of, 19. 1K.4:8.
De.22 : 17. t.a. tokens of dau-'s vir-
23 : 18. both t.a. abomina. ⌊ginity
Jos. 12 : 1. t.a.the kings of the la.,7.
14 : 1. t.a. countries Isr. inherited
17:3.t.a. names of Zeloph-d's dau-s
19 : 51.t. a. the inheritances⌈nam.
1 K. 4 : 8. Sol-n had 12 officers, t.a.
9 : 13. What cities a.t. given me?
10 :8.Happy a.t. wh.stand bef.thee
1 Ch. 2 : 55. t.a. the Kenites that
4 : 22. And t.a. ancient things
6 : 31. t.a. set over service of song
33. t.a. they which waited with
7 : 8. All t.a. sons of, 8 : 40. ⌊chil.
11 : 10. t.a. chief of mighty men
12:1.t.a.they came to Da.at Ziklag
15. t.a.they th.went over Jordan
2 Ch. 24 : 26. t.a. they th. conspired
Ezr. 2 : 1. t.a. chil. of the province
8 :1. t.a.chief of their fathers⌈a.t.
13. sons of Adon-m whose names
Ne. 1 : 10. Now t.a. thy servants
Jb. 26 :14. t.a. part of his ways, but
Ps. 73 : 12.Behold, t.a. the ungodly
Pr. 25 : 1. t.a. also proverbs of Sol-n
Is. 60 : 8.Who a.t. that flee as cloud
65 : 5. t.a. a smoke in my nose
Je. 5 : 4. Surely t.a. poor, a. foolish
7 : 4. The temple of the Lord a.t.
Eze. 11 : 2. t.a. men devise mischief
36 : 20. t.a. the people of the Lord
43 : 13. t.a. measures of the altar
18. t.a. ordinances of the altar
46 : 24. t.a. places of them th. boil
48 : 1. Now t.a. names of the tribes
29. unto tribes t.a. their portions
30. t.a. the goings out of the city
Da. 2 : 28. visions upon thy bed a.t.
Mi. 2 :7.straitened? a.t.his doings?
Zch. 1:9.O my L.,wh. a.t.? 4:4.-6:4.
10. t.a. they L. hath sent to walk
21.t.a. the horns which scattered
Jud., but t.a. co.to fray th.,19.
4 : 14. t.a. two anointed ones, 11.
8 : 16. t.a. the things ye shall do
17. All t.a. things I hate, saith L.
Mat. 10 : 2.names of 12 apostles a.t.
24 : 8. All t.a. beginning of sorrows, Mk. 13 : 8.
Mk. 4 : 15. t.a. they by way side
16.t.a.they sown on stony ground
18. t.a. they sown among thorns
20 t.a.they sown on good ground
Lu. 8 :21. my moth. and breth. a.t.
24 :17. What communicat-s a.t. ye
Jn. 10 : 21. t.a. not words of him
17 : 11. t.a. in the world, and I co.
20 : 31. t.a. written that ye believe
Ac. 2 : 7.a.not all t.wh.speak Gali-s
15.t.a.not drunken,as ye suppose
Ro. 9 : 8. t.a. not children of God
Ga. 4 : 24. t.a. the two covenants
5 : 17. t.a. contrary one to other
19. works of the flesh, which a.t.
Col. 4 :11.t. only a. my fel. workers
2 Pe. 2 : 17. t.a. wells without water
1 Jn. 5 : 7. and t. three a. one, 8.
Jude 12. t.a. spots in your feasts
16. t.a. murmurers, walking aft.
Re. 7 :13.Wh.a.t. arrayed in white?
14. t.a. they out of great tribula.
11 : 4. t.a. two olive trees bef. God
14:4.t.a. they not defiled wi.wom.,
t.a. they wh. follow the Lamb
19 : 9. t.a. the true sayings of God,
See THREE. ⌊22 : 6.

Than THESE.

Ec. 7 : 10. former days better t.t.?
Eze. 8 : 15. see greater abomin. t.t.
16 : 47. wast corrupted more t.t.
42 : 5. galleries were higher t.t.
Mat. 5 : 37. more t.t. cometh of evil
Mk. 12 : 31. none com-t greater t.t.
Jn. 1 : 50. sh. see greater things t.t.
5 : 20. greater works t.t., 14 : 12.
7 : 31. will he do more miracles t.t.

Jn. 21 : 15. Lovest th. me more t.t.?
He. 9 : 23. with better sacrifices t.t.

THESSALO'NIANS.

Ac. 20 : 4. of the T. Aristarchus and
1 Th. 1 : 1. unto ch. of T., 2 Th. 1 :1.

THESSALONI'CA.

Ac. 17 : 1. at T. was a synagogue of
11. more noble than those in T.
13. wh. Jews of T. had knowledge
27 : 2. Aristarchus of T. with us
Ph. 4 :16. even in T. ye sent once⌈T.
2 Ti. 4 : 10. Demas is departed unto

THEU'DAS.

Ac. 5 : 36. bef. these days rose up T.

THEY. ⌈sewed

Ge. 3 : 7. t. knew t. were naked, t.
6 : 2. t. took wives of all t. chose
7 : 14. t. and ev. beast aft. his kind
Ex. 1 : 10. t. join unto our enemies
9 :32.not smitten; for t. not grown
Nu. 16 :33.t. and theirs went into pit
18 : 3. that nei. t. nor you also die
2 K. 25 : 23. when t. and men heard
1 Ch. 9 :23.t.and chil. had oversight
Jb. 36 : 14. t. die in youth and their
Ps. 31 :4.net that t. have laid for me
Ec. 3 : 18. might see th. t. are beasts
Can. 6 : 5. thine eyes, t. have over-
Is. 9 : 21. t. toge. ag. Jud. ⌊come me
28 : 7. t. also have erred thro. wine
57 : 6.t. are thy lot, to them offered
58 : 12. t. sh. build old waste places
Je. 2 : 26. so ashamed t., their kings
5 : 28. t.are waxen fat, t. shine (4).
9 : 16. whom neither t. nor fathers
have known, 19 :4.-44 :3.⌈lies (8)
23 : 14. a horrible thing; t. walk in
44 : 12. t. shall be an execration(3)
49 : 12.t.whose judgm.not to drink
Eze. 2 :3. t. and fathers transgressed
5. whether t. will hear or forbear
34 : 30. shall know t. are my people
Zch. 1 : 5. y-r fa-s, where are t.? (2)
Mat. 5 : 4. t., 11 :7. Mk.16: 13,14,17,
19, 20. Lu. 9 : 34.-13:4.Jn.7:45.
-10 : 6.-11 : 13.-18 : 21.-20 : 13.
Ac. 5 : 21.(3).-10 : 9, 10.-18:4.-
21 : 6.-24 : 15. 1 Co. 9 : 25.-10 :
6.-16 : 17. Ga. 6 : 12.
9 : 31, t. spread abroad his fame in
15 : 18. fr. the heart, t. defile man
19 : 11. save t. to whom it is given
Mk. 1 : 5. t. of Jerus. were baptized
16 : 11. when t. heard he was alive
Lu. 12 : 4. no more that t. can do
Jn. 4 : 45.t. also went unto the feast
6 :9. fishes,wh. are t.am. so many?
10 : 25. works I do t. bear witn. of
17 :16. t. are not of the world, even
19. that t. might be sanctified
23. that t. be made perfect in one
24. Fa., I will that t. be with me,
that t. may behold my glory
18 :28.went not in, lest t. be defiled
Ac.5 :41.th. t. were counted worthy
13 : 28. t. found no cause of death
15 : 11.thro. grace we be saved as t.
21 : 12. we and t. besought him
Ro. 8 :14.led by Spi.,t. are sons of G.
23. not only t., but oursel. groan
11 : 23. And t. also, if t. abide not
still in unbelief, sh.be graffed in
1 Co. 15 : 11. whether I or t., so we
Ga. 2 : 6. t. who seemed somewhat
9.t. gave right hand of fellowship
6 : 13. nei. t. circumcised keep law
1 Th. 1 : 9. t. shew what entering in
1 Ti. 6 :17.t. who labour in the word
He. 1 : 12. t. shall be changed, but
4 : 6. t. to wh. it was first preached
11 :40.that t. should not be perfect
12 :25.if t. escaped not who refused
13 : 24. Salute all, t. of Italy salute
1 Jn. 2 :19. t. went out from us, but
t. were not of us (7)
4 : 5. t. are of the world, t. speak
Jude 19. be t. who separate thems.

Re. 2 : 9. say t. are Jews, and are
not, 3 : 9. [16 : 6.
3 : 4. with me, for t. are worthy,
7 : 13. in white robes, whence ca. t.
14 : 4. not defiled, for t. are virgins

All THEY, or THEY all.

Ge 11 : 6. t.a. have one language
47 : 1. breth.and a.t.have are come
1 S. 22 : 11. t. came a. of them to k.
26 : 12. t. were a. asleep, because
2 K. 19 : 35. behold t. were a. dead
corpses, Is. 37 : 36. [servants
1 Ch. 21 : 3. are t. not a. my lord's
5. a.t. of Isr. were 1,100,000 men
2 Ch. 25 : 12. t.a. were broken in piec.
Ezr. 7 : 13. a.t. wh. are minded go
Ne. 6 : 9. t.a. made us all afraid
Jb. 34 : 19. t.a. are work of his hands
Ps. 14 : 3. t. are a. gone aside, t. are
a. together become filthy
80 : 12. a.t. wh. pass by pluck her
Pr. 8 : 9. t.a. plain to him underst-h
30 : 27. go t. forth a. by bands
Ec. 3 : 19. yea t. have a. one breath
Can. 3 : 8. t.a. hold swords expert
Is. 14 : 10. a.t.sh.say, Art thou weak
30 : 5. t.a. ashamed of peo. [as we
31 : 3. t.a. sh. fall together [45 : 16.
41 : 29. Beh-d t. are a.vanity, 44 : 9.-
42 : 22. t. are a. snared in holes
56 : 10. t.a. ignorant, a. dumb dogs
11. greedy dogs, t.a. look to their
own way
60 : 4. a.t. gather thems. they co.
6. a.t. from Sheba shall come
Je. 5 : 16. t. are a. mighty men
6 : 28. t. are a. grievous revolters
9 : 2. t. be a. adulterers, Ho. 7 : 4.
10 : 9. t. are a. work of cun-g men
12 : 1. whf. a.t. happy that deal
23 : 14. t.a. unto me as Sodom
31 : 34. t. sh. a. know me from least
44 : 12. t. sh. a. be consumed in Eg.
Eze. 14 : 5. t. are a. estranged thro.
22 : 18. Israel is dross : a.t. are tin
31 : 14. t. are a. deliv-d unto death
37 : 24. t.a. sh. have one shepherd
38 : 8. t. sh. dwell safely a. of them
39 : 23. so fell t.a. by the sword
Ho. 7 : 7. t. are a. hot as an oven
Mi. 3 : 7. seers t. shall a. cover their
7 : 2. t.a. lie in wait for blood [lips
Ha. 1 : 9. t.'sh. come a. for violence
15. t. take a. of them the angle (3)
Zph. 3 : 9. th. t. may a. call upon L.
Mat. 13 : 56. sisters are t. not a. wi. us?
14 : 20. And t. did a. eat and were
filled, 15 : 37. Mk. 6 : 42. Lu. 9 : 17.
22 : 28. whose wife, for t.a. had her
25 : 5. bridegroom tarried, t.a. slept
27 : 22. t.a. say, Let him be crucified
Mk. 1 : 27. And t. were a. amazed,
2 : 12. Lu. 4 : 36.-5 : 26.-9 : 43.
Ac. 2 : 7, 12. [fled
6 : 50. t.a. saw him and were troub-
12 : 44. a.t. did cast in of abnud-ce
14 : 23. gave cup ; t.a. drank of it
31. I not deny thee, also said t.a.
50. t.a. forsook him and fled
64. t.a. condemned him guilty of
Lu. 1 : 63. t. marvelled a. [wrath
4 : 28. a.t. in synagogue filled with
8 : 40. for t. were a. waiting for him
14 : 18. t.a. began to make excuse
19 : 7. when saw it t. a. murmured
22 : 70. said t.a., Art thou Son of G.
23 : 18. t. cried a., Aw.wi.this man
Jn. 6 : 45. t. sh. be a. taught of God
17 : 21. that t.a. be one as thou
18 : 40. cried t.a. again, Not this
Ac. 2 : 1. t.a. with one accord, 5 : 12.
4. t. were a. filled wi. Holy Ghost,
8 : 1. t. were a. scat. abroad[4 : 31.
10. To whom t.a. gave heed from
9 : 26. t. were a. afraid of him
16 : 3. t. knew a. his fa. was Greek
19 : 10. a.t. in Asia heard the word
Ac. 20 : 37. t.a. wept, fell on P.'s neck
21 : 5. t.a. brought us on our way
20. and t. are a. zealous of the law
27 : 36. Then were t.a. of good cheer
44. that t. escaped a. safe to land
Ro. 3 : 9. proved that t. are a. und. sin
12. t. are a. gone out of the way
9 : 6 t. not a. Israel wh. are of Isr.
7. nei. bec. seed of Abr. are t.a. ch.
10 : 16. t. have not a. obeyed gosp.
1 Co. 12 : 19. if t. were a. one member
2 Th. 2 : 12. Th. t.a. might be damn.
2 Ti. 1 : 15. a.t. be turned from me
He. 1 : 11. t.a. shall wax old as garm.
14. Are t. not a. minist-g spirits?
1 Jn. 2 : 19. manifest t. were not a.
See **All they THAT.** [of us

Blessed are THEY.

Ps. 2 : 12. - t. that put trust in him
84 : 4. - t. that dwell in thy house
106 : 3. - t. that keep judgment
119 : 2. - t. that keep his testimon-s
Pr. 8 : 32. - t. that keep my ways
Is. 30 : 18. - t. that wait for him
Mat. 5 : 4. - t. that mourn, for they
6. - t. which do hunger and thirst
10. - t. which are persecuted for
Lu. 11 : 28. - t. that hear word of God
Jn. 20 : 29. - t. th. have not seen, yet
Ro. 4 : 7. - t. whose iniqu-s forgiven
Re. 19 : 9. - t. called unto marriage
22 : 14. - t. th. do his commandm-ts

Than THEY. [t.t.

Nu. 14 : 12. of thee, nation mightier
22 : 15. princes more hon-able t.t.
1 K. 20 : 23. surely we stronger t.t.,
2 K. 6 : 16. they wi. us more t.t. [25.
Ec. 1 : 16. I more wisdom t. all t.
5 : 8. there be higher t.t. [52.
Eze. 16 : 51. multi. abom-s more t.t.,
Da 11 : 2. 4th sh. be far richer t.t.
Mk. 12 : 43. poor widow cast more in
t. all t., Lu. 21 : 3. [t.t. ? No
Ro. 3 : 9. What, then? Are we better
1 Co. 15 : 10. I laboured more t.t. all
He. 1 : 4. more excellent name t.t.

THEY that, or which.

2 K. 6 : 16. t.t. be with us more t.t.
2 Ch. 32 : 21. t.t. came of his bowels
Jb. 18 : 20. t.t. come aft. him astonied, as t.t. went bef. were affright.
Ps. 24 : 1. earth is L.'s and t.t. dw-l
69 : 4. t.t. hate me with-t cause (2)
Is. 19 : 8. t.t. spread net languish
30 : 16. sh. t.t. pursue you be swift
41 : 11. t.t. strive wi. thee sh. perish
12. t.t., war ag. thee sh. be as noth.
44 : 9. t.t. make image are vanity
58 : 12. t.t. sh. be of thee sh. build
Je. 30 : 16. t.t. sh. spoil thee sh. be spoil'
Mat. 12 : 3. what David did and t.t.
were with him, Mk. 2 : 25. Lu. 6 : 3.
20 : 25. t.t. are gr. exerc. author-y
25 : 3. t.t. were foolish took no oil
26 : 57. t.t. had laid hold on Jesus
Mk. 2 : 17. t.t. are whole, Lu. 5 : 31.
4 : 10. t.t. were about him asked
7 : 15. those are t.t. defile the man
8 : 9. t.t. had eaten were ab. 4,000
10 : 23. how hardly t.t. ha. riches
11 : 9. t.t. went bef., cried Hosan. (2)
14 : 70. t.t. stood by said to Peter
Lu. 7 : 10. t.t. were sent found serv.
8 : 12. Those by way side are t.t. hear
13. They on rock are t.w. rec. w-d
14. t.w., when they have heard
15. t.w., having heard word keep
45. Peter and t.t. were with him
22 : 28. ye are t.w. continued with
Jn. 5 : 25. and t.t. hear shall live
29. t.t. have done good unto life (2)
39. t. are t.w. testify of me [(2)
9 : 39. that t.w. see not might see
Ac. 5 : 21. priest and t.t. were wi. him
11 : 2. t.t. were of circumc. cont-d
19. t.w. were scat-d abr. travelled
13 : 27. For t.t. dwell at Jerusalem
Ro. 4 : 14. if t.w. are of the law are
8 : 5. t.t. are aft. flesh do mind (2)
8. t.t. are in flesh can-t please G.
9 : 8. t.w. are children of the flesh
16 : 18. t.t. are s h serve n Jes.
1 Co. 7 : 29. t.t. have wives be as
30. t.t. weep as tho. t. wept not (3)
31. t.t. use world as not abus-g it
9 : 24. t.w. run in a race run all
11 : 19. that t.w. are approved may
15 : 18. t.w. are fallen asleep are
23. afterward t.t. are Christ's
48. such are t.t. are earthy (2) [9.
Ga. 3 : 7. t.w. are of faith are of Abr.,
5 : 12. wo. t. were cut off w. trouble
21. t.w. do such things not inher.
24. t.t. are Ch.'s have crucified
2 Th. 5 : 7. t.t. sleep, sleep in ni. (2)
1 Ti. 3 : 13. t.t. used office of deacon
5 : 25. t.t. are otherwise can-t be hid
6 : 9. t.t. will be rich fall into temp.
2 Ti. 3 : 6. t.w. creep into houses
Tit. 3 : 8. t.w. have believed in God
He. 13 : 17. as t.t. must give account
Ja. 2 : 12. do as t.t. sh. be judged by
Re. 1 : 7. and t. also w. pierced him
14 : 12. here are t.t. keep comm-ts
21 : 27. t.w. are writ. in Lamb's b-k
See **SO they, SO that they, THESE are.**

THICK. [t.

De. 32 : 15. waxen fat, thou art grown
2 S. 18 : 9. mule went und. t. boughs
1 K. 7 : 6. pillars and t. beam before
26. And sea was a handbreadth t.
2 K. 8 : 15. he took t. cloth dipped it
Ne. 8 : 15. of t. trees to make booths
Jb. 15 : 26. t. bosses of his bucklers
Ps. 74 : 5. lifted up axes upon t. trees
Eze. 6 : 13. slain be under ev. t. oak
19 : 11. her stature am. t. branches
20 : 28. they saw all the t. trees
31 : 3. his top am. t. boughs, 10, 14.
41 : 12. the wall was five cubits t.
25. t. planks upon face of porch
Ha. 2 : 6. ladeth himself with t. clay
Lu. 11 : 29. when peo. were gath-d t.

THICK cloud, s. [t.c.

Ex. 19 : 9. Lo, I come unto thee in a
16. third day, t.c. upon the m-t
Jb 22 : 14. t.c-s a covering to him
26 : 8. He bindeth up wat-s in t.c-s
37 : 11. by water-g he weareth t.c-s
Ps. 18 : 11. his pavilion dark waters,
t.c-s of the skies, 2 S. 22 : 12.
12. before him his t.c-s passed
Is. 44 : 22. I have blotted as t.c-s
thy transg-ns, as a c. thy sins
Eze. 8 : 11 a t.c. of incense went up

THICK darkness.

Ex. 10 : 22. a t.d. in all Eg. 3 days
20 : 21. Moses drew near unto t.d.
De. 4 : 11. m-t burned wi. clouds t.d.
5 : 22. L. spake out of cloud and t.d.
1 K. 8 : 12. Lord said he would dwell
in t.d., 2 Ch. 6 : 1. [for it
Jb. 38 : 9. sea, t.d. a swaddling band
Jo. 2 : 2. A day of clouds and t.d.,
Zph. 1 : 15.

THICKENED. [lees

Zph. 1 : † 12. punish men t. on their

THICKER.

1 K. 12 : 10. My little finger sh. be t.
than my fa.'s loins, 2 Ch. 10 : 10.

THICKET, S.

Ge. 22 : 13. ram caught in t. by horns
1 S. 13 : 6. Isr. did hide thems. in t-s
Is. 9 : 18. wickedn. sh. kindle in t-s
10 : 34. he shall cut down the t-s
Je. 4 : 7. lion is come from his t.
29. the whole city shall go into t-s

THICKNESS, ES.

1 K. 7 : † 46. cast them in the t. of
2 Ch. 4 : 5. t. of sea was a handbreadth
† 17. k. cast them into t-s of ground
Je. 52 : 21. t. of the pillar 4 fingers
Eze. 41 : 9. t. of wall was five cubits

... 42 : 10. chamb-s were in t. of wall
Zch. 14 : † 6. light shall not be clear
THIEF. [nor t.
Ex. 22 : 2. If a t. be found break-g, 7.
8. If the t. be not found, then
De. 24 : 7. stealing, that t. shall die
Jb. 24 : 14. murderer in night is as t.
30 : 5. cried after them as after a t.
Ps. 50 : 18. when thou sawest a t.
Pr. 6 : 30. Men do not despise t. if
29 : 24. Whoso. is partner with a t.
Je. 2 : 26. t. is ashamed when found
Ho. 7 : 1. t. cometh in, robbers wi-t
Jo. 2 : 9. enter at windows, like a t.
Zch. 5 : 4. it sh. enter into hou. of t.
Mat. 24 : 43. if had known in what
watch t. would come, Lu. 12 : 39.
26 : 55. Are ye come as ag. a t. wi.
swords, Mk. 14 : 48. Lu. 22 : 52.
Lu. 12 : 33. in heaven, where no t.
Jn. 10 : 1. the same is a t. and rob-r
10. The t. cometh not but to steal
12 : 6. he was a t. and had the bag
1 Th. 5 : 2. day of the L. cometh as
a t., 2 Pe. 3 : 10. [you as a t.
4. that that day should overtake
1 Pe. 4 . 15. let none of you suf- as t.
Re. 3 : 3. I will come on thee as a t.,
THIEVES. [16 : 15.
Is. 1 : 23. princes, companions of t.
Je. 48 : 27. was not Isr. found am. t.?
49 : 9. if t. by night, they will destroy, Ob. 5. [and steal
Mat. 6 : 19. where t. break through
20. where t. do not break through
21 : 13. ye have made it a den of t.,
Mk. 11 : 17. Lu. 19 : 46. [15 : 27.
27 : 38. two t. crucified wi. him. Mk.
44. the t. cast same in his teeth
Lu. 10 : 30. to Jericho, and fell am. t.
36. neighbour to him th. fell am. t.
Jn. 10 : 8. All that came bef. me are t.
1 Co. 6 : 10. Nor t. inherit kingd. of G.
THIGH, S.
Ge. 24 : 2. Put thy hand under my
t., 9.-47 : 29. [t.
32 : 25. touched hollow of Jacob's
31. he halted upon his t. [t.
32. eat not of sinew upon hollow
46 : † 26. that came out of Jacob's
t., Ex. 1 : † 5. [loins to t-s
Ex. 28 : 42. breeches sh. reach from
Nu. 5 : 21. the Lord maketh thy t.
to rot, 22; 27. [right t.
Ju. 3 : 16. Ehud did gird dagger on
21. Ehud took dagger from right t.
8 : † 30 Gideon 70 sons out of his t.
15 : 8. Samson smote th. hip and t.
Ps. 45 : 3. Gird thy sword on thy t.
Can. 3 : 8. ev. man his sword upon t.
7 : 1. joints of thy t-s like jewels
Is. 47 : 2. uncover t., pass over rivers
Je. 31 : 19. I smote upon my t. [t.
Eze. 21 : 12. Cry, howl, smite upon
24 : 4. Gather t., shoulder into pot
Da. 2 : 32. his belly and t-s of brass
Re. 19 : 16. on his t. a name written
THIM'NATHAH.
Jos. 19 : 23. coast of their inherit-
THIN. [ance was T.
Ge. 41 : 6. behold 7 t. ears, 7, 23, 24.
27. seven t. kine are seven years
Ex. 39 : 3. beat gold into t. plates
Le. 13 : 30. be in it a yellow t. hair
2 S. 13 : † 4. Why art thou t. fr. day
1 K. 7 : 29. additions made of t. work
Is. 17 : 4. glory of Jacob be made t.
THINE. [is t.
Ge 14 : 23. I will not take any thing
20 : 7. shalt die, thou and all are t.
31 : 32. discern what is t., take it
33 : † 9. be that to thee, that is t.
48 : 6. thy issue aft. them sh. be t.
Le. 10 : 15. it sh. be t. and thy sons,
Nu. 18 : 9, 11, 13, 14, 15, 18. [t.
Nu. 22 : 30. hast ridden on since I was
De. 15 : 3. what is t. with bro., release
De. 28 : † 41. sh. beget sons, but not be
30 : 4. if t. be driven unto out. [t.
Jos. 17 : 18. the mountains shall be
t., outgoings of it shall be t. [t.
Ju. 15 : † 2. younger sister, let her be
1 S. 2 : 33. man of t. whom I not cut
15 : 28. given it to neighb. of t. [off
2 S. 16 : 4. t. all pertained to Mephib.
1 K. 3 : 26. Let it nei. be mine nor t.
20 : 4. O king, I am t. and all I have
21 : 19. dogs sh. lick blood, even t.
1 Ch. 12 : 18. t. are we, David [t.
21 : 24. I will not take that which is
29 : 11. t., O Lord, is the greatness,
the earth is t., t. the kingdom
Ps 71 : 16. mention righteousn. t. only
74 : 16. the day is t., the night is t.
89 : 11. The heavens are t., the
earth also is t. [thy precepts
119 : 94. I am t., save me, I sought
Is. 45 : 14. labour of Egypt sh. be t.
63 : 19. we are t., thou never bearest
Je. 32 : 8. right of inheritance is t.
Mat. 6 : 13. for t. is the kingdom and
20 : 14. Take that t. is, go thy way
25 : 25. lo, there thou hast th. is t.
Lu. 4 : 7. if worship me, all sh. be t.
5 : 33. discip. fast, t. eat and drink
15 : 31. Son with me, all I have is t.
22 : 42. not my will but t. be done
Jn. 17 : 6. t. they were, gavest th. me
9. I pray for them, for they are t.
10. all mine are t., and t. are mine
See Thine EYE, Thine EYES.
THINE Own.
2 S. 19 : 28. that did eat at t. o. table
1 K. 1 : 12. mayest save t. o. life
2 : 44. wickedness upon t. o. head
Ps. 21 : 13. Be exalted, Lord, in t. o.
74 : 22. O G., plead t. o. cause [stren.
138 : 8. forsa. not works of t. o. ha-s
Pr. 3 : 5. lean not unto t. o underst-g
5 : 15. Drink out of t. o. cistern,
running waters out of t. o. well
17. Let them be t. o., not strangers'
23 : 4. cease from t. o. wisdom
27 : 2. Let ano. praise thee, not t.
o. mouth, a stranger, not t. o.
Is. 58 : 7. hide not fr. t. o. flesh [lips
Je. 2 : 19. t. o. wickedn. correct thee
Eze. 16 : 6. saw thee polluted in t. o.
15. didst trust in t. o. beauty [bl.
52. Thou also bear t. o. shame. 54.
Da. 9 : 19. defer not for t. o. sake, O
Ob. 15 thy reward upon t. o. head
Lu. 19 : 22. Out of t. o. mou judge thee
Jn. 17 : 11. Fa., keep thro. t. o. name
18 : 35. t. o. nation delivered thee
See OWN, OWN self.
See Thine only, or Thy SON.
THING. [Abr.
Ge. 21 : 11. t. was very grievous to
24 : 50. The t. proceedeth fr. Lord
34 : 7. wh. t. ought not to be done
19. yo. man deferred not to do t.
38 : 10. t. displeased L., 2 S. 11 : 27.
41 : 32. the t. is established by God
37. The t. was good in eyes of Phar.
Ex. 18 : 11. t. wh-in th. dealt proudly
22 : 9. for any lost t. wh another
15. if a hired t. it came for hire
34 : 10. terrible t. I will do with thee
Le. 2 : 3. t. most holy of y-r off-gs. 10
4 : 13. the t. be hid from assembly
6 : 2. trespass in t. tak. by violence
4. t. deceitfully gotten, or lost t.
13 : 54. wash the t. wh-in plague is
58. whatsoever t. of skin it be
De. 12 . 32. What t. I com-d, observe
18 : 22. if the t. follow not [Moses
Jos. 14 : 6. knoweth t. L. said unto
22 : 33. t. pleased children of Israel
Ju. 8 : 27. which t. became a snare
19 : 24. but do not so vile a t.
20 . 9. shall be the t. we will do
Ru. 3 : 18. until he have finished t.
1 S. 3 : 11. I will do a t. in Isr. at wh.
1 S. 3 : 17. What is the t. L. h[ath] said
4 : 7. not been such a t. her[e]tofore
† 16. What is the t. done, my son?
8 : 6. t. displeased Samuel, when
14 : 12. Come, we will shew you a t.
18 : 20. told Saul, the t. pleased him
2 S. 13 : 12. no such t. ought to be
33. let not king take t. to heart
14 : 13. Wh. hast thought such a t.?
18. hide not the t. I sh. ask thee
15 : 35. what t. thou hear tell Zadok
17 : 19. spread corn, t. was not kn.
1 K. 8 : † 59. the t. of a day in his day
14 : 5. wife of Jeroboam to ask a t.
2 K. 2 : 10. Thou hast asked a hard t.
3 : 18. but a light t. in sight of Lord
7 : 19. windows in heav., such a t. be?
20 : 9. sign, that the L will do the t.
1 Ch. 17 : 23. let t. spoken be estab-d
2 Ch. 29 : 36. t. was done suddenly
30 : 4. t. pleased the king, Es 2 : 4.
Ezr. 7 : 27. put such a t. in k.'s heart
Es. 2 : 22. t. was known to Mordecai
5 : 14. t. pleased Haman, he caused
Jb. 3 : 25. t. I greatly feared is come
4 : 12. a t. was secretly bro-t to me
6 : 8. O th. G. wo. grant me t. I long
13 : 28. he as a rotten t. consumeth
14 : 4. Who can bring clean t. out
22 : 28. Thou sh. decree a t. it sh. be
23 : 14. performeth t. appointed
26 : 3. hast declared the t. as it is
42 : 7. not spoken t. th. is right, 8.
Ps. 41 : † 11. A t. of Belial, say they,
cleaveth unto him [of my lips
89 : 34. nor alter t. that is gone out
119 : † 42. th. reproacheth me in a t.
Pr. 4 : 7. Wisdom is the principal t.
22 : 18. a pleasant t. if thou keep th.
25 : 2. glory of God to conceal a t.
Ec. 1 : 9. The t. that hath been shall
be, there is no new t. under sun
7 : 8. Better end of a t. than beginn.
8 : 1. knoweth interpreta-n of a t.?
15. no better t. than to eat and dri.
11 : 7. pleasant t. it is to behold sun
Is. 17 : 13. like rolling t. bef. whirlw.
29 : 16. sh. the t. framed say of him
40 : 15. taketh isles as very little t.
55 : 11. prosper in t. whereto I sent
66 : 8. Who hath heard such a t.?
Je. 2 : 10, see if there be such a t.
11 : 13. ye set altars to shameful t.
23 : † 13. I seen absurd t. in proph-s
38 : 14. I will ask thee a t., hide noth.
42 : 3. that God may shew us the t.
4. whatso. t. Lord shall ans. you
44 : 17. do what t. goeth out of our
La. 2 : 13. What t. sh. I take to witness, what t. sh. I liken to thee?
Eze. 14 : 9. when he hath spoken a t.
16 : 47. as if it were a very little t.
Da. 2 : 5. The t. is gone from me, 8.
11. it is a rare t. king requireth
15. Arioch made t. known to Dan.
17. Dan. made t. known to Hanan.
4 : 33. was the t. fulfilled upon Neb.
5 : 15. cou. not shew interpre-n of t.
26 This is interpretation of the t.
6 : 12. The t. is true acc. to the law
10 : 1. a t. was revealed to Daniel,
t. was true, he understood the t.
Mal. 1 : 14. sacrificeth to L. corrupt t.
Mk. 7 : 18. whatso. t. entereth into
Lu. 12 : 11. how or what t. ye ans.
Jn. 5 : 14. sin no more, lest a worse t.
9 : 30. herein is a marvellous t.
Ac. 10 : 28. it is unlawful t. for a Jew
12 : 12. Pet. had consid-d t. he came
21 : 25. that they observe no such t.
26 : 8. Why be thought t. incredible
10. Which t. I also did in Jerus.
Ro. 9 : 20. Shall t. formed say to him
1 Co. 8 : 7. eat it as t. off-d unto idol
2 Th. 1 : 6. seeing it is righteous t.
He. 10 : 29. blood of cov. t unholy t.
31. fearf. t. to fall into hands of G.

1 Jn. 2 : 8. t. is true in him, and you
Re. 2 : 15. doctrine of Nicolaitans, which t. hate

Accursed or Cursed THING.

De. 7 : 26. lest be c.t. ; for it is c.t.
13 : 17. nought of c.t. to thine ha.
Jos. 6 : 18. And ye keep fr. a.t., lest make yours. a. wh. ye take a.t.
7 : 1. Isr. committed trespass in a. t., for Achan took of a.t., 11.
13. an a.t. in midst, not stand bef. ene-s until ye take aw. a.t.
15. he taken with a.t. sh. be burnt
22 : 20. Achan a trespass in a.t.
1 Ch. 2 : 7. Achar who transg-d in t. a. [thine

Any THING.

Ge 14 : 23. I will not take a.t. th. is
18 : 14. Is a.t. too hard for the Lord
19 : 22. cannot do a.t. till thou be
22 : 12. nei. do thou a.t. unto lad
30 : 31. Thou shalt not give me a.t.
39 : 9. nei. kept back a.t. from me
23. looked not to a.t. und. his ha.
Ex. 20 : 4. shalt not make likeness of a.t., De. 4 : 18, 23, 25.-5 : 8.
17. not covet a.t. that is thy neighbour's, De. 5 : 21.
Le. 6 : 7. forgiven him for a.t. done
13 : 48. in a.t. made of skin, 49, 52, 53, 57, 59. [he sat, 23.
15 : 6. that sitteth on a.t. wh-on
10. toucheth a.t. that was under him, 22.-22 : 4, 5. [blood
19 : 26. Ye sh. not eat a.t. with the
21 : 18. hath a.t. superfluous, 22 : 23.
Nu. 20 : 19. I will without doing a. t. else go through [a.t.?
22 : 38. have I now any power to say
35 : 22. if he have cast upon him a.t.
De. 4 : 32. whe. hath been a. such t.
8 : 9. sh. not lack a.t. in the land
14 : 3. sh. not eat a. abominable t.
21. Ye shall not eat a.t. th. dieth
16 : 4. nor a.t. of the flesh remain
23 : 19. usury of a.t. that is lent
24 : 10. when dost lend broth. a.t.
31 : 13. chil. wh. have not kno. a.t.
Jos. 21 : 45. failed not aught of a.t.
Ju. 11 : 25. thou a.t. better th. Balak?
18 : 7. put them to shame in a.t.
10. a place where there is no want of a.t., 19 : 19. [hide a.t.
1 S. 3 : 17. God do so to thee, if thou
20 : 26. Saul spake not a.t. th. day
39. lad knew not a.t., only Jona.
21 : 2. Let no man know a.t. of busi.
22 : 15. let not the king impute a.t.
25 : 15. not hurt, nei. missed we a.t.
30 : 19. there was not lacking a.t.
2 S. 13 : 2. it hard to do a.t. to her
15 : 11. simplicity, they knew not a.
1 K. 10 : 3. was not a.t. hid fr. k. [t.
15 : 5. turned not fr. a.t. com-ded
20 : 33. whe. a.t. come from him
2 K. 4 : 2. not a.t. save pot of oil
1 Ch. 26 : 28. whoso. had dedicated
2 Ch. 9 : 20. silver was not a.t. [a.t.
23 : 19. none unclean in a.t. enter
Jb. 15 : 11. is a. secret t. with thee?
33 : 32. If a.t. to say, answer me
Ec. 1 : 10. a.t. wh-f said, this is new
3 : 14. noth. put to it, nor a.t. taken
5 : 2. not hasty to utter a.t. bef. G.
6 : 5. not seen sun, nor known a.t.
9 : 5. dead know not a.t., nei. have
6. no more portion in a.t. done
Je. 32 : 27. is a.t. too hard for me?
38 : 5. king not he that can do a.t.
42 : 21. nor a.t. for wh. he sent me
Eze. 44 : 18. not gird thems. wi. a.t.
31. priests not eat of a.t. dead of
Da. 3 : 29. which speak a.t. ag. God
Jon. 3 : 7. man nor beast taste [a.t.
Mat. 18 : 19. if 2 agree touching a.t.
24 : 17. not come down to take a.t. out of house, Mk. 13 : 15.
Mk. 4 : 22. nei. was a.t. kept secret,
Lu. 8 : 17. [passion on
9 : 22. if canst do a.t. have com-
11 : 13. if haply he might find a.t.
16 : 8. nei. said they a.t. to any man
18. if drink a. deadly t. it sh. not
Lu. 19 : 8. if I taken a.t. fr. any man
22 : 35. lacked ye a.t.? said, Noth.
Jn. 1 : 3. without him not a.t. made
7 : 4. no man doeth a.t. in secret
14 : 14. If ye ask a.t. in my name
Ac. 10 : 14. never eaten a.t. common
17 : 25. as though he needed a.t.
19 : 39. if inquire a.t. conc. matter
25 : 8. nor ag. Cæsar I offended a.t.
11. or if I a.t. worthy of death
Ro. 8 : 33. Who lay a.t. to G.'s elect
13 : 8. Owe no man a.t., but to love
14 : 14 esteemeth a.t. to be unclean
21. nor a.t. wh-by bro. stumbleth
1 Co. 2 : 2. not to know a.t. save Jesus
3 : 7. neither he that planteth a.t.
8 : 2. if any think he knoweth a.t.
10 : 19. What say I? th. idol is a.t.
14 : 30. If a.t. be revealed to anoth.
35. if learn a.t. ask husbands
2 Co. 2 : 10. To whom ye forgive a.t. I forgive, for if I forgive a.t.
3 : 5. not sufficient to think a.t. as
6 : 3. Giving no offence in a.t. [of
7 : 14. if I have boasted a.t. of you
Ga. 5 : 6. neither circumcision availeth a.t. nor, 6 : 15. [such t.
Ep. 5 : 27. not having wrinkle or a.
Ph. 3 : 15. if in a.t. ye be otherwise
1 Th. 1 : 8. we need not to speak a.t.
1 Ti. 1 : 10. if there be a. other t.
Ja. 1 : 7. not receive a.t. of the Lord
1 Jn. 5 : 14. if we ask a.t. acc-g to
Re. 21 : 27. in no wise enter a.t. th.

Certain THING, S.

De. 13 : 14. if t.c., that such abom-n,
Mat. 20 : 20. desir-g c.t. of him [17 : 4.
Ac. 17 : 20. bringest c. strange t-s to
23 : 17. he hath a c.t. to tell him
25 : 26. Of wh. I have no c.t. to write

THING, S, with creep, creepeth, or creeping.

Ge. 1 : 24. Let earth bring forth c-g
25. God made every t. that c-h [t.
26. dominion over every c-g t. th. c-h, 28.† [green herb
30. to every t. that c-h have given
6 : 7. c-g t. and fowls of the air
20. of every c-g t. after his kind
7 : 14. into ark ev. c-g t. that c-h, 8.
21. all died of every c-g t. that c-h
23. c-g t-s and the fowl of the [c-h
8 : 17. Bring forth of ev. c-g t. that
19. Every c-g t. and whatso. c-h
Le. 5 : 2. carcass of unclean c-g t-s
11 : 21. eat of ev. flying c-g t. that
23. c-g t-s wh. have 4 feet abomi-n
29. These unclean among c-g t-s that c. [43, 44.-20 : 25.
41. ev. c-g t. that c-h be an abom.
42. hath more feet among c-g t-s that c-h an abomina-n [unclean
22 : 5. whoso. toucheth any c-g t.
De. 4 : 18. likeness of any t. th. c-h
14 : 19. every c-g t. that flieth uncl.
1 K. 4 : 33. he spake of beasts, c-g t-s
Ps. 69 : †34. praise him ev. t. th. c-h
104 : 25. wide sea, wherein c-g t-s
148 : 10. Praise the L., c-g t-s and
Eze. 8 : 10. every form of c-g t-s and
38 : 20. all c-g t-s that c. sh. shake
Ho. 2 : 18. a covenant with c-g t-s
Mi. 7 : †17. out of holes like c-g t-s
Ha. 1 : 14. makest men as c-g t-s
Ac. 10 : 12. Peter saw c-g t-s, 11 : 6.
Ro. 1 : 23. G. into image like c-g t-s
See DEVOTED.

Every THING. [eth

Ge. 1 : 28. dominion over e.t. mov-
31. God saw e.t. he had made
6 : 17. e.t. in the earth shall die
Ge. 8 : 1. God rememb-d e. living t.
9 : 3. e. mov-g t. that liveth be meat
Le. 11 : 35. e.t. whereupon carcass
15 : 4. e.t. whereon he sitteth uncl.
20. e.t. she sitteth upon unclean
23 : 37. ye shall offer e.t. upon his
Nu. 18 : 7. office for e.t. of altar [day
15. e.t. that openeth the matrix
31 : 23. e.t. that may abide fire [t.
De. 23 : 9. keep thee from e. wicked
Jos. 4 : 10. priests stood until e.t.
1 S. 15 : 9. e.t. vile they destroyed
2 S. 15 : 36. unto me e.t. ye can hear
Es. 6 : 13. told e.t. had befallen him
Jb. 28 : 10. his eye seeth e. prec-s t.
39 : 8. he searcheth aft. e. green t.
42 : 2. I know th. canst do e.t. [eth
Ps. 69 : 34. praise him e.t. that mov-
150 : 6. Let e.t. hath breath praise
Pr. 27 : 7. to hungry e. bit-r t. sweet
Ec. 3 : 1. To e.t. there is a season
11. made e.t. beautiful in his time
12 : 14. into judgment e. secret t.
Is. 19 : 7. e.t. by brooks sh. wither
Eze. 44 : 29. e. dedicated t. be theirs
47 : 9. e.t. shall live where rivers
Mat. 8 : 33. told e.t. was befallen
1 Co. 1 : 5. in e.t. enriched, 2 Co 9 : 11.
2 Co. 8 : 7. are bound in e.t. in faith
10 : 5. e. high t. th. exalteth itself
Ep. 5 : 24. subject to husbands in e.
Ph. 4 : 6. in e.t. by prayer and [t.
1 Th. 5 : 18. In e.t. give thanks, for
Phm. 6. acknowl-g of e. good t. in

See **EVIL thing, GOOD thing, GREAT thing, HOLY thing, s,** GREEN, HALLOWED, HORRIBLE, LIGHT, LIVING, NEW.

One THING. [all

Jos. 23 : 14. not o.t. hath failed of
2 S. 3 : 13. o.t. I require of thee
Jb. 9 : 22. This is o.t., th. I said it
Ps. 27 : 4. o.t. have I desired of L.
Ec. 3 : 19. even o.t. befalleth them
7 : †27. weighing o.t. with another
Mat. 21 : 24. I will ask you o.t., Mk. 11 : †29. Lu. 6 : 9.-20 : 3. [18 : 22.
Mk. 10 : 21. o.t. thou lackest, Lu.
Lu. 10 : 42. But o.t. is needful [blind
Jn. 9 : 25. o.t. I know, wh-as I was
Ac. 19 : 32. Some cried o.t., 21 : 34.
Ph. 3 : 13. but this o.t. I do, I press
2 Pe. 3 : 8. be not ignorant of that o.

See RIGHT. [Adj.], SAME, SELFSAME, SMALL, STRANGE. [t.

That THING.

Ge. 18 : 17. hide from Abr. t.t. I do
Ex. 9 : 6. L. did t.t. on the morrow
Le. 5 : 5. confess he sinned in t.t.
Je. 11 : 13. altars to t. shameful t. [t.
Lu. 9 : 21. charged to tell no man t.
12 : 26. if not able to do t.t. is least
Ro. 14 : 22. in t.t. which he alloweth

This THING. [t.t.

Ge. 19 : 21. I have accept. thee conc.
30 : 31. if do t.t. I will feed flock
34 : 14. We can-t do t.t. to give sister
44 : 7. th. we should do acc. to t.t.
Ex. 2 : 14. Moses said, t.t. is known
15. Pha. heard t.t. sought slay M.
9 : 5. To morrow Lord shall do t.t.
12 : 24. observe t.t. for ordinance
18 : 14. What is t.t. thou doest to
18. t.t. is too heavy for thee [peo.
23. If thou shalt do t.t., and God
33 : 17. I will do t.t. thou hast spo.
Nu. 32 : 20. If ye will do t.t., if go
De. 1 : 32. in t.t. ye did not believe G.
15 : 10. for t.t. God shall bless thee
22 : 20. if t.t. be true, and tokens
32 : 47. thro. t.t. prolong your days
Jos. 22 : 24. not done it for fear of t.t.
1 S. 20 : 2. why sho. my father hide
24 : 6 Lord forbid th. I do t.t. [t.t.
28 : 10. no punishm. to thee for t.t.

2 S. 11 : 11. I will not do t.t.
25. Let not t.t. displease thee
12 : 6. bec. he did t.t. had no pity
12. I will do t.t. before all Israel
13 :20.he is thy bro.,regard not t.t.
14 : 13. k. doth speak t.t. as faulty
15. I to speak of t.t. unto king
24 : 3.why king delight in t.t.?⌈11.
1 K.3 : 10. pleased L. Sol. asked t.t.,
11 : 10. commanded him conc. t.t.
12 : 24. return ev. man, t.t. is from
30. made 2 calves, t.t. became sin
13 : 33.Aft. t.t.Jerob.returned not
34. t.t.bec. sin to house of Jerob.
20 : 9. tell king t.t. I may not do
24. do t.t., Take the kings away
2 K. 5:18. In t.t. the Lord pardon(2)
6 : 11. king was troubled for t.t.
7 : 2. make windows, might t.t. be
17 : 12. L. said, ye shall not do t.t.
1 Ch. 11 :19. God forbid that I do t.t.
21 : 3. why my lord require t.t.?
7. God was displeased with t.t.
2 Ch. 16 : 10. Asa in rage bec. of t.t.
Ezr. 9 : 3. heard t.t. I rent garment
10 : 2. is hope in Israel cone-g t.t.
13.many that transgressed in t.t.
Ne. 2 : 19. What is t.t. that ye do?
Is. 38 :7. L.will do t.t.he hath spok.
Je. 7 : 23. t.t. commanded I them
22 : 4. if ye do t.t., sh. enter kings
40 :3. theref. t.t. is come upon you
16.Gedaliah said, thou not do t.t.
44 :4. Oh do not t. abominable t.
Lu. 2 : 15. see t.t. which is come
22 : 23. which it was should do t.t.
Jn. 18 : 34. Sayest t.t. of thyself?
Ac. 5 : 4. why hast conceived t.t.
Ro. 13 : 6. attending upon t. very t.
1 Co. 9 : 17. if I do t.t. willingly, I
2 Co. 12 :8.For t.t.I besought the L.
Ph. 1 :6.Being confident of t.very t.
See **DONE** with **this thing.**

This is the THING, or **THING is this.**

Ge.41 :28.t.i.t-g I have spok.toPha.
Ex. 16 : 16. t.i.t-g which the Lord commanded, 32.-35 : 4 Le. 8 : 5. -9 : 6.-17 : 2. Nu. 30 : 1.-36 : 6. De. 15 : 15.-24 : 18, 22.
29 :1.t.i.t-g thou sh. do unto them
Nu. 36 : 6. t.i.t-g cone-g daughters
Jn. 8 :† 1. What t-g i.t. thou hast done unto us, 2 S. 12 : 21.
21 : 11. t.i. t-g that ye shall do, 2 K. 11 : 5. 2 Ch. 23 : 4.
Ne. 13 : 17. what evil t-g i.t. ye do
Mk.1:27.What t-g i.t.? wh.doctrine
See **UNCLEAN thing**, s.
See VAIN, WICKED.

THINGS.

Ex. 40 : 4. set in order t. are to be
Le. 4 : 2. if a soul sin through ignorance concerning t., 13, 22, 27.
De. 4 : 9. lest thou forget t. eyes ha.
10 : 21. these great and terrible t.
32 : 35. t. that shall come upon th.
33 : 15. chief t. of ancient mount-s
Ju. 18 : 27. took the t. Micah made
1 S. 12 : 21. should ye go after vain
15 : 21. people took chief of t. ⌊t.
1 K. 5 :8. Consider the t.thou sentest
11 : † 41. rest of t. of Sol. written in
2 K. 17 : 11.Israel wrought wicked t.
1 Ch. 4 :22. And these are ancient t.
9 : 31. office over t. made in pans
29 : 2. prepared gold for t. of gold, silver for t. of silver, brass for t. of brass, iron for t. of iron
2 Ch. 12 : 12. in Judah t. went well
29 : 33.consecrated t., 600 oxen⌈12.
Es. 2 : 3. t. for purification be given,
Jb. 6 :7.t. my soul refuseth to touch
13 : 20. Only do not two t. unto me
26. thou writest bitter t. ag. me
14 : 19. t. which grow out of dust
26 : 5. Dead t. are formed fr. under

Jb. 41 : 30. spreadeth sharp pointed
Ps. 12 : 3. that speaketh proud t.⌊ t.
17 : 2.thine eyes behold the t.equal
31 : 18. speak grievous t. proudly
35 : 11. laid to my charge t. I knew
38 : 12. speak mischievous t. ⌊not
45 : 1. I speak of t. I have made
60 : 3. hast shewed people hard t.
87 :3.Glorious t. are spoken of thee
94 : 4. How long they sp-k hard t.?
113 : 6.hims. to behold t. in heaven
131 : 1. or in t. too high for me ⌈t.
Pr. 2 : 12. man th. speaketh froward
16 : 30. his eyes to devise froward t.
30 : 7.Two t. have I requi-d of thee
24. four t. are little upon earth
Ec. 1 : 11.nor remembr.of t. to come
7 : 25. to seek out reason of t., † 27.
Is. 25 : 6. unto all peo. feast of fat t.
29 : 16. turning of t. upside down
32 : 8. the liberal deviseth liberal t.,by liberal t.sh.he stand⌈22(2)
41 : 23. Shew the t. th. are to come,
42 : 16. I make crooked t. straight
43 : 18.nei. consider the t. of old (2)
44 :7. t.th.are coming and sh. come
9. delectable t. shall not profit
45 : 11. Ask me of t. conc. my son
46 :10.Declaring the t.not yet done
56 : 4. eunuchs choose t. th. please
58 :† 3. t. wherew. ye grieve others
61 : 11. garden causeth t. sown to
65 : 4. broth of abom-e t. is in ves.
Je. 2 :8. t. that do not profit, 16 : 19.
8. 13. t. I have given sh. pass away
31 : 5. shall eat them as common t.
La. 2 : 14. prophets seen foolish t.
Eze. 11 : 5. I know t. in your mind
16 : 16. the like t. shall not come
38 : 10. shall t. come into thy mind
Da. 7 :16. me know interpret-n of t.
† 18.saints of the high t.take kingd.
Jo. 3 : 5. into your temples goodly t.
Am. 4 : † 3. cast t. of palace away
Ob. 6. How are t. of Esau searched! how are his hidden t. sought!
Zch. 4 : 10. despised day of small t.?
Mat. 6 : 34. morrow take tho-t for t.
13 : 52. bringeth out of treasure t.
16 : 23. thou savourest not t. that be of God, Mk. 8 : 33.
22 : 21. Render to Cæsar t. that are Cæsar's, unto God t. that are God's, Mk. 12 : 17. Lu. 20 : 25.
Mk. 4 : 19. lusts of other t. entering
7 : 15. t. wh. come out of him defile
Lu. 6 :46 call me L., do not t. I say
10 : 23.Blessed wh. see the t. ye see
12 :15. abundance of t. he posses-h
48. commit t. worthy of stripes
13 : 17. peo. rejoiced for glorious t.
17 :9. thank serv. bec. he did the t.?
18 : 27. the t. impossible with men
34. nei. knew they the t. spoken
19 :42. t.wh. belong unto thy peace
22 : 37. t. conc-g me have an end
23 :48.all peo. beholding the t.wh.
24 : 18.hast not known the t.which
27. expounded the t. conc. hims.
Jn. 1 : 50. thou shalt see greater t.
3 : 12. If I have told you earthly t., how if tell you of heavenly t.
11 : 45. Jews wh.had seen t.Jes.did
16 : 13. Spirit will shew t. to come
Ac. 1 : 3. of t. pertaining to kingdom
4 : 20. we cannot but speak t. seen
25. why people imagine vain t.?
32. aught of the t. he possessed
34. bro-t the prices of the t. sold
8 :12. preaching t. cone-g kingdom
15 : 20. abstain fr. t. strangled, 29.
27.Silas who shall tell you same t.
16 :14. she attended unto t. spoken
18 : 25. Apollos taught t. of the L.
19 : 8. persuading t. conc. kingd. of
20 : 22. not knowing t. sh. befall me
21 : 25. keep from t. offered to idols

Ac. 24 : 13.Nei. can they prove the t.
26 : 22. saying none other t. than
28 :24. some believed the t. spoken
Ro. 1 : 20. the invisible t. of him are seen, understood by the t.made
2 : 14. Gentiles do by nature t. in
8 : 5. mind the t. of the flesh, mind t. of the Spirit ⌈1 Co. 3 : 22.
38. nor t. present, nor t. to come,
12 : 16. Mind not high t., condesc-d
† 16. be contented with mean t.
17. Provide t. honest in sight of all men, 2 Co. 8 : 21. ⌈peace
14 : 19.follow after t. that make for
15 : 4. whatsoever t. were written
27. if Gentiles partakers of spirit-l t., duty to minister in carnal t.
1 Co. 1 : 27. God hath chosen foolish t. of world, weak t. to confound t. which are mighty ⌈chosen
28. base t. and t. despised hath G.
2 : 9. t. which God hath prepared
11. what man knoweth t. of man, so t. of God knoweth no man
12.might know the t. freely giv.us
13. which t. we speak, comparing spiritual t. ⌈Spirit of God
14. man receiveth not the t. of the
6 : 3. t. that pertain to this life, 4.
7 : 1. cone-g t. whereof ye wrote
32. unmarried careth for t. of the Lord, 34. ⌈world
33. married careth for t. of the
8 : 1. Now as touching t. offered
9 : 11. If we have sown spiritual t., if we reap carnal t. ⌈rifice
10 :20. that the t. wh. Gentiles sac-
13 : 11. a man, I put aw. childish t.
14 : 7. t. without life giving sound
37. acknowledge that t. I write
2 Co. 1 : 13. we write none other t.
17. t. I purpose, do I according to
4 : 18. while we look not at t. seen, t. seen are temporal, t. not
5 : 10. may rec. t. done in his body
10 :7. Do ye look on t. after the out-
13.we will not boast of t.,15.⌊ward
16. not to boast in ano man's t.
11 : 30. I will glory of t. wh. conc-n
Ga. 1 : 20. t. which I write, I lie not
2 :18.If I build t.which I destroyed
4 : 24. Which t. are an allegory,for
5 : 17. so ye cannot do t. ye would
Ph. 1 : 12. t. wh. happened unto me
2 : 4. Look not ev. man on his own t.,but on the t. of others⌈under
10. of t. in heaven, t. in earth, t.
21. all seek not t. which are Ch.'s
3 : 19. shame, who mind earthly t.
4 : 8.whatsoever t. are true, honest
18. I am full,having t. sent fr.you
Col. 1 : 20. whe. t. in earth, or t. in
2 :17.shadow of t.to come,He 10 : 1.
23. Wh. t. have a shew of wisdom
3 : 2. Set your affection on t. above, not on t. on earth ⌈cometh
6. For which t. sake wrath of God
1 Th. 2 : 14. ye have suffered like t.
2 Th. 3 : 4. will do the t. we com.m-d
1 Ti. 5 :13.speak-g t.they ought not
2 Ti. 2 : 2. t. thou hast heard of me
3 :14.continue in t.th.hast learned
Tit. 1 : 5. set in order the t. wanting
† 8. a lover of good t., sober, just
11. teach-g t. for lucre's sake⌈Joc.
2 : 1. speak t. which become sound
He. 2 : 1. give heed to the t. heard
17. faithful high priest in t., 5 : 1.
5 : 8. obedience by the t. he suff-d
6 : 9. we are persuaded better t. of you, t. th.accompany salvation
18. that by two immutable t.
8 : 1. of t. spoken this is the sum
5. unto the shadow of heavenly t.
9 : 23. that the patterns of t. in the heavens be purified, but heavenly t. with better sacrifices

He. 11 : 1. Now faith is substance of
t. hoped for, the evidence of t.
not seen ⌈appear
3. t. seen, not made of t. which do
7. Noah warned of G. of t. not seen
20. blessed Jac. conc-g t. to come
12:24. speaketh bet. t. than th. of A.
27. signifieth the removing of t.
shaken as of t. that are made,
that those t. which cannot be
Ja. 3 : 7. t. in the sea are tamed of
1 Pe. 1 : 12. did minister t. now reported; wh. t. angels desire to
18. not redeemed with corrupt-e t.
2 Pe. 2 : 12. evil of t. understand not
3 : 16. some t. hard to be understood
1 Jn. 2 : 15. neither the t. in world
Re. 1 : 1. of Christ to shew unto his
serv-s t. must shortly come, 22:6
19. Write the t. thou hast seen, t.
wh. are, and t. which shall be
2 : 14. I have a few t. ag. thee, to
eat t. sacrif-d, and fornica-n, 20.
3 : 2. strengthen the t. which remain
4 : 1. I will shew thee t. wh. must be
10 : 6. earth, sea, and all t. therein
22 : 19. his part fr. t. writ-n in book

All THINGS. ⌈t.

Ge. 9 : 3. as green herb given you a.
24 : 1. L. hath blessed Abr. in a.t.
66. servant told Isaac a.t. done
Ex. 23 : 13. in a.t. be circumspect
29 : 35. do according to a.t. I commanded thee, 25 : 22. ⌈com-ded
Le. 8 : 36. Aaron and sons did a.t.
Nu. 1:50. Levites over a.t. th. belong
31 : 20. purify a.t. made of wood
De. 1 : 18. I commanded a.t. ye sho.
4 : 7. as God is in a.t. we call for
12 : 8 Ye shall not do after a.t. ⌈t.
28 : 47. servedst not for abund. of a.
48. serve enemies in want of a.t.
57. eat them for want of a.t. ⌈a.t.
Jos. 1 : 17. hearkened unto Moses in
2 : 23. spies told a.t. that befell th.
Ru. 4 : 7. manner, to confirm a.t.
1 S. 3 : 12. perform a.t. conc. Eli's ho.
17. if thou hide any of a.t. said
19 : 7. Jonathan shewed Dav. a.t.
2 S. 11 : 18. Joab told David a. the t.
14 : 20. to know a.t. in the earth
23 : 5. a covenant ordered in a.t.
1 K. 21 : 26. he did a.t. as Amorites
2 K. 11 : 9. captains did acc-g to a.t.
commanded, 2 Ch. 23 : 8. ⌈did
14 : 3. Amaziah, acc-g to a.t. Joash
20 : 15. have seen a.t. in my house
1 Ch. 29 : 14. a.t. come of thee, and
2 Ch. 5 : 1. Sol. bro-t a.t. dedicated
31 : 5. tithe of a.t. bro-t they in
Ne. 9 : 6. Lord made a.t., Ac. 14 : 15.
-17 : 24, 25. Col. 1 : 16. Re. 4 :
Es. 6 : 11. Haman told them a.t.⌊11.
Jb. 41 : 34. He beholdeth a. high t.
Ps. 8 : 6. thou hast put a.t. under
his feet, 1 Co. 15 : 27. Ep. 1 : 22.
57 : 2. unto G. th. performeth a.t.
119 : 128. precepts conc a.t. right
Pr. 3 : 15. wisdom is more precious
than a.t., 8 : 11. ⌈himself
16 : 4. The Lord hath made a.t. for
26 : 10. that formed a.t. rewardeth
28 : 5. seek the Lord understand a.
Ec. 1 : 8. a.t. are full of labour ⌊t.
13. to search out a.t. und. heaven
7 : 15. a.t. have I seen in days of
9 : 2. a.t. come alike to all, there
3. This is an evil among a.t. done
10 : 19. but money answereth a.t.
Is. 34 : 1. world, and a.t. that come
44 : 24. I am the Lord that maketh
a.t., 66 : 2. ⌈t., 51 : 19.
Je. 10 : 16. for he is the former of a.
17 : 9. heart is deceitful above a.t.
21 : 14. fire, shall devour a.t. round
42 : 5. if we do not according to a.t.
44 : 18. we have wanted a.t., and

Eze. 11 : 25. I speak a.t. L. shewed
38 : 20. a. creeping t. sh. shake at
44 : 30. first of a.t. be the priest's
Da. 2 : 40. as iron subdueth a.t. ⌈land
Zph. 1 : 2. I will consume a.t. from
Mat. 7 : 12. a.t. ye would that men
should do to you ⌈Lu. 10 : 22.
11 : 27. a.t. are delivered unto me,
13 : 41. shall gather a.t. th. offend
17 : 11. Elias sh. restore a.t., Mk. 9 : 12.
19 : 26. but with God a.t. are possible, Mk. 10 : 27.-14 : 36.
21 : 22. a.t. whatso. ye sh. ask in
22 : 4. Tell them bidden, Behold,
a.t. are ready, Lu. 14 : 17.
23 : 20. sweareth by it, and by a.t.
28 : 11. watch shewed priests a.t.
20. Teaching them to observe a.t.
Mk. 4 : 34. he expounded a.t. to his
6 : 30. told him a.t. they had done
7 : 37. say-g, He hath done a.t. well
9 : 23. a.t. are possible to him that
11 : 11. wh. he had looked upon a.t.
13 : 23. I have foretold you a.t. ⌈t.
Lu. 1 : 3. perfect understanding of a.
2 : 20. praising God for a.t. heard
39. performed a.t. acc-g to the law
9 : 43. wondered at a.t. Jesus did
11 : 41. a.t. are clean unto you ⌈t.
13 : 17. peo. rejoiced for a. glorious
18 : 31. a.t. written conc-g Son of
man shall be, 21 : 22.-24 : 44. Jn.
Jn. 1 : 3. a.t. made by him ⌊19 : 28.
3 : 35. given a.t. into his ha., 13 : 3.
4 : 25. is come, he will tell us a.t.
29. who told me a.t. th. ever I did
45. having seen a. the t. he did
5 : 20. Fa. sheweth Son a.t. he do-
10 : 41. a.t. John spake of him⌊eth
14 : 26. Comforter, sh. teach you a.
t., and bring a.t. to rememb-e
15 : 15. a.t. I heard, I made known
16 : 15. a.t. Father hath are mine
30 Now sure thou knowest a.t.
17 : 7. a.t. given me, are of thee
18 : 4. Jes. thf. knowing a.t., 19 : 28.
21 : 17. said, L., thou knowest a.t.
Ac. 2 : 44. had a.t. common, 4 : 32.
3 : 21. until times of restitu-n of a.t.
22. him hear in a.t. he shall say
10 : 33. to hear a.t. comm-ded thee
39. we witnesses of a.t. he did
13 : 39. believe are justified fr. a.t.
14 : 15. G., who made heav. and a.t.
15 : 4. declared a.t. God had done
17 : 22. in a.t. ye are too supersti-s
20 : 35. shewed a.t. how ye ought
22 : 10. there be told thee of a.t.
24 : 14. believing a.t. wh. are writ.
26 : 2. a. the t. wh-f I am accused
Ro. 8 : 28 we know a.t. work for
32. sh. he not freely give us a.t.?
11 : 36. of him, thro. him, are a.t.
14 : 2. believeth he may eat a.t.
20. a.t. are pure, but evil for him
1 Co. 2 : 10. the Spirit searcheth a.t.
15. he th. is spiritual judgeth a.t.
3 : 21. no man glory, a.t. are yours
4 : 13. the offscouring of a.t.
6 : 12. a.t. are lawful unto me, but
a.t. are not expedient, a.t. are
lawful for me, 10 : 23.
8 : 6. one Father, of whom are a.t.
one Christ, by whom are a.t.
9 : 12. suffer a.t., lest hinder gospel
22. I am made a.t. to all men
25. striveth is temperate in a.t.
10 : 33. as I please all men in a.t.
11 : 2. that ye remember me in a.t.
12. a.t. are of God, 2 Co. 5 : 18.
13 : 7. Charity beareth a.t., believeth a.t., hopeth a.t., endureth
14 : 26. Let a.t. be done unto edify.
40. Let a.t. be done decently and
15 : 28. when a.t. be subdued, sh.
Son be subject to him th. put a.t.
16 : 14. Let a.t. be done wi. charity

2 Co. 2 : 9. whe. ye be obedi-t in a.t.
4 : 15. For a.t. are for your sakes
5 : 17. passed away, a.t. beco. new
6 : 4. in a.t. approv-g ours. as min.
10. having noth., yet possess. a.t.
7 : 11. In a.t. approved yourselves
14. we spake a.t. to you in truth
16. have confidence in you in a.t.
9 : 8. having all sufficiency in a.t.
11 : 6. made manifest to you in a.t.
9. in a.t. I kept fr. being burdens.
12 : 19. we do a.t. for your edifying
Ga. 3 : 10. that continueth not in a.t.
Ep. 1 : 10. gather in one a.t. in Ch.
11. worketh a.t. after his will
22. gave him to be head over a.t.
3 : 9. created a.t. by Jesus Christ
4 : 10. ascended, that he might fill
15. grow up into him in a.t. ⌊a.t.
5 : 13. a.t. that are reproved are
20. Giving thanks for a.t. unto G.
6 : 21. sh. make known a.t., Col. 4 : 9.
Ph. 2 : 14. Do a.t. wi-t murmurings
3 : 8. I count a.t. but loss for Ch.,
for whom I suffered loss of a.t.
21. he is able even to subdue a.t.
4 : 12. and in a.t. I am instructed
13. I can do a.t. thro. Christ, who
Col. 1 : 16. by him were a.t. created
17. he is bef. a.t., by him a.t. ⌊(2)
18. in a.t. might have the preemin.
20 to reconcile a.t. to himself
3 : 20. obey your parents in a.t.
22. obey in a.t. your masters
1 Th. 5 : 21. Prove a.t., hold fast th.
1 Ti. 3 : 11. wives be faithful in a.t.
4 : 8. godliness profitable unto a.t.
† 15. profiting may appear in a.t.
6 : 13. of God, who quickeneth a.t.
17. God, who giveth us richly a.t.
2 Ti. 2 : 7. give thee underst-g in a.t.
10. I endure a.t. for elect's sake
4 : 5. watch thou in a.t., endure
Ti. 1 : 15. Unto the pure a.t. pure
2 : 7. In a.t. shewing a pattern of
9. to please them well in a.t.
10. adorn doctrine of God in a.t.
He. 1 : 2. hath appointed heir of a.t.
3. upholding a.t. by his power
2 : 8. a.t. in subjection under his
feet; we see not yet a.t. ⌊a.t.
10. for whom are a.t., by wh. are
17. in a.t. it behoved him to be
3 : 4. he that built a.t. is God⌈eyes
4 : 13. a.t. are naked opened unto
8 : 5. make a.t. accord-g to pattern
9 : 22. a.t. are purged by blood
13 : 18. in a.t. willing to live honestly
Ja. 5 : 12. above a.t., breth., swear not
1 Pe. 4 : 7. end of a.t. is at hand⌈14.
8. above a.t. have charity, Col. 3 :
11. that God in a.t. be glorified
2 Pe. 1 : 3. given us a.t. th. pertain
3 : 4. a.t. continue as they were⌈t.
1 Jn. 2 : 20. unction, and ye know a.
27. anointing teacheth you a.t.
3 : 20. God is greater, knoweth a.t.
3 Jn. 2. I wish abo. a.t. thou prosper
Re. 1 : 2. bare record of a.t. he saw
4 : 11. created a.t. for thy pleasure
21 : 5. Behold, I make a.t. new⌈a.t.
7. He that overcometh sh. inherit
See DEDICATED, DEEP, DETEST-
ABLE, EXCELLENT,
EVIL things, GOOD things,
FORMER, HIDDEN, HALLOWED.

Holy THING, S. ⌈Jerus.

Eze. 36 : † 38. As the flock of h.t. of
Ac. 13 : † 34. give you h.t. of David

Most holy THINGS. ⌈t.

Nu. 4 : 4. service of Kohath about -
19. may not die wh. approach - t.
18 : 9. This sh. be thine of - t. ⌈- t.
1 Ch. 23 : 13. Aaron that he sanctify
2 Ch. 31 : 14. Kore to distribute - t.
Ezr. 2 : 63. not eat of - t. till stood a
priest with Urim, Ne. 7 : 65.

Eze. 42 : 13. where priests shall eat
- t. there shall they lay - t.
See **HOLY things.**

Many THINGS. [such t.
Jb. 16 : 2. Job said, I have heard m.
23 : 14. m. such t. are with him
Ec. 6 : 11. m.t. that increase vanity
Is. 42 : 20. see-g m.t., observest not
Mat. 13 : 3. he spake m.t., Mk. 4 :2.
16 : 21. and suffer m.t., Mk. 8 : 31.
-9 : 12. Lu. 9 : 22.-17 :25.[t., 23.
25 :21. will make thee ruler ov. m.
27 : 13. Hearest thou not how m.t.
they witness ag. thee ? Mk.15 :4.
19. I have suffered m.t. this day
Mk. 5 : 26. suffered m.t. of phys-ns
6 : 20. did m.t., heard him gladly
34. Jes. began to teach them m.t.
7 : 4. m.t., as wash-g of cups, 8,13.
15 : 3. priests accused him of m.t.
Lu. 3 : 18. m. other t. in his exhort.
10 :41. thou art troubled ab-t m.t.
11 : 53. Pharisees to provoke him to
speak of m.t. [spake they
22 : 65. m. other t. blasphemously
23 : 8. he had heard m.t. of him
Jn. 8 : 26. I have m.t. to say, 16:12.
21 : 25. are m. other t. wh. Jes. did
Ac. 26 :9. ought to do m.t. contrary
2 Co. 8 : 22. we diligent in m.t.
Ga. 3 : 4. suffered so m.t. in vain ?
2 Ti. 1 : 18. m.t. he ministered unto
He. 5 : 11. of whom we m.t. to say
Ja. 3 :2. for in m.t. we offend all [13.
2 Jn. 12. having m.t. to write, 3 Jn.
See NEW, PERVERSE, PLEASANT, PRECIOUS, RIGHT [Adj.], SAME, SECRET, SPAKE, STRANGE, TERRIBLE.

Such THINGS. [ed
Ex. 12 : 36. lent s.t. as they requir-
Le. 10 : 19. s.t. have befallen me
De. 25 :16. that do s.t. are abomina-n
Ju. 13 :23. nor wou. have told us s.t.
1 S. 2 : 23. Eli said, Why do ye s.t. ?
2 S. 12 : 8. I would have given s.t.
2 K. 19 : 29. eat s.t. as grow of thems.
25 : 15. took s.t. as were of gold
Ne. 6 : 8. no s.t. done as thou sayest
Es. 2 : 9. wi. s.t. as belonged to her
Jb. 12 : 3. yea, who knoweth not s.
Is. 66 : 8. who hath seen s.t. ? [t.
Je. 18 : 13. Ask who hath heard s.t.
Eze. 17 :15. sh. he escape doeth s.t. ?
Da. 2 : 10. is no king that asked s.t.
Mk. 7 : 8. many other s. like t. ye do,
13 . 7. s.t. must needs be [13.
Lu. 9 : 9. who this of wh. I hear s.t.
10 : 7. eating s.t. as they give, 8.
11 : 41. give alms of s.t. as ye have
13 : 2. sinners, bec. they suff-d s.t.?
Jn. 7 : 32. that peo. murmured s.t.
Ac. 25 :18. bro-t no accusat-n of s.t.
28 : 10. laded us with s.t. as neces-y
Ro. 1:32. commit s.t. worthy of death
2 : 2. judgment ag. them wh. com-it
3. judgest them wh. do s.t. [s.t.
Ga. 5 : 21. do s.t. not inherit kingd.
He. 11 : 14. say s.t. declare plainly
13 : 5. content with s.t. as ye have
2 Pe. 3 : 14. seeing ye look for s.t.
See **Many THINGS.**

These THINGS.
Ge. 24 : 28. damsel ran and told t.t.
Le. 2 : 8. meat offering made of t.t.
5 : 5. when guilty in one of t.t., 17.
18 : 24. Defile not yourselves in t.t.
26 : 23. and if not reformed by t.t.
Nu. 4 :15. t.t. burden of sons of Koh.
15:13. All born of country sh. do t.t.
29 : 39. t.t. ye sh. do to L. in feasts
35 : 29. t.t. shall be for a statute of
De. 18 :12. all that do t.t. are abomi.
Jos. 2 : 11. we heard t.t., our hearts
1 S. 25 : 37. when his wife told t.t.
2 S. 23:17. t.t. did these three mighty
men, 1 Ch. 11 : 19.
2 S. 23 : 22. t.t. did Benaiah and had
name, 1 Ch. 11 :24.
24 :23. t.t. did Araunah give to king
2 K. 23 : 17. proclaimed t.t. thou
2 Ch. 3 :3 in t.t. was Sol. instructed
Ezr. 9 : 1. t.t. done, princes came to
Ne. 13 : 26. Did not Sol. sin by t.t. ?
Jb. 8:2. How long wilt th. speak t.t.?
10 : 13. t.t. hast hid in thine heart
Es. 9 : 20. Mordecai wrote t.t. and
Ps. 15 : 5. doeth t.t. never be moved
42 : 4. I remember t.t., I pour out
50 : 21. t.t. hast thou done and I
107 : 43. observe t.t., sh. underst-d
Pr. 6 : 16. t. six t. doth Lord hate
24 : 23. t.t. also belong to the wise
Ec. 11 : 9. for t.t. G. will bring thee
Is. 38 : 16. O Lord, by t.t. men live,
in all t.t. is life of my spirit [t.?
40 : 26. behold, who hath created t.
42 : 16. t.t. will I do, not forsake
45 : 7. I form light, I do all t.t.
47 : 7. didst not lay t.t. to heart
9. t. two t. shall come to thee
13. let astrologers save thee fr. t.t.
48 : 14. which hath declared t.t.
51 :19. t. two t. are come unto thee
64 : 12. Wilt refrain for t.t., O Lord
Je. 4 :18. thy doings have procur. t.t.
5 : 9. Sh. I not visit for t.t.? 29.-9:9.
25. Your iniquities turned aw. t.t.
9 : 24. in t.t. do I delight, saith L.
13 : 22. Wheref. come t.t. upon me
20 : 1. heard Jer-h prophesied t.t.
26 : 10. princes of Judah heard t.t.
30 : 15. bec. thy sins t.t. unto thee
La. 1 : 16. For t.t. I weep, mine eye
5 : 17. for t.t. our eyes are dim
Eze. 17 : 12. Know ye what t.t. mean
18 : 10. doeth like to any one of t.t.
23 :30. I will do t.t. unto thee, bec.
24 : 19. Wilt tell what t.t. are to us ?
Da. 10 : 21. holdeth with me in t.t.
12 : 8. Lord, what sh. be end of t.t.?
Ho. 14 :9. wise, he sh. understand t.t.
Zch. 8 :12. Cause peo. to possess t.t.
16. t. are the t. which ye shall do
Mat. 1 : 20. while he thought on t.t.
2 :3 Herod heard t.t. was troubled
9 : 18. While he spake t.t. unto
them, Lu. 8 : 8.-11 : 27, 53.-13 :
17. Jn. 6 : 59.-11 : 11.-12 : 36.-
14 : 25.-15 : 11.-16 : 1. 4, (2), 6,
25, 33.-20 : 18. Ac. 1 : 9. [10 : 21.
11 : 25. hast hid t.t. from wise, Lu.
15 : 20. t. are t. which defile a man
21 : 23. By what authority doest
thou t.t., Mk. 11 :28. Lu. 20 :2.
24. I will tell by what authority I
do t.t., 27. Mk. 11 : 29, 33. Lu.
20 : 8. [4. Lu. 21 : 7 (2).
24 :3. when shall t.t. be ? Mk. 13 :
Mk. 2 : 8. Why reason ye t.t. in
Lu. 1 : 20. be dumb until t.t. sh. be
4 : 28. they heard t.t., 14 : 15.-16 :
14.-19 : 11. Ac. 5 : 5, 11, 24.-11 :
18, 22.-17 : 8.-21 : 12.
7 : 9. When Jesus heard t.t., 18:22.
12 : 30. knoweth ye ha. need of t.t.
14 : 6. could not answer him to t.t.
15. one at meat wi. him heard t.t.
21. servant shewed his lord t.t.
15 : 26. he asked what t.t. meant
18 :34. they understood none of t.t.
21 : 6. As for t.t. which ye behold
23 : 31. if they do t.t. in green tree
49. stood afar off beholding t.t.
24 : 10. Mary told t.t. unto apostles
21. third day since t.t. were done
26. Ought not Ch. to have suffered
48. ye are witnesses of t.t. [t.t. ?
Jn. 1 : 28. t.t. were done in Bethab-
2 : 16. he said, Take t.t. hence [ara
18. Wh. sign, seeing thou doest t.t.
3 :9. Nicod-s said, How can t.t. be?
10. master of Isr., knowest not t.t.?
5 : 16. he had done t.t. on sabbath
Jn. 5 :34. t.t. I say ye might be saved
7 : 4. If thou do t.t. shew thyself
12 : 16. t.t. understood not discip.,
but remembered t.t. were written, and they had done t.t.
41. t.t. said Esaias, when he saw
13 : 17. If know t.t. happy if ye do
15 : 17. t.t. I command, th. ye love
17 : 13. t.t. I speak in the world th.
19 : 24. t.t., theref., the soldiers did
36. t.t. were done, that Scriptures
20:18. Mary told th. L. had spok. t.t.
21 : 24. This is the disciple wh. testifieth of t.t. and wrote t.t.
Ac. 5 : 32. we are witnesses of t.t.
7 : 1. said high priest, Are t.t. so ?
54. heard t.t. they were cut to h-t
8 : 24. Pray for me, none of t.t. co.
12 : 17. Go, shew t.t. unto James
14 : 15. saying, Sirs, why do ye t.t. ?
15 : 28. no greater burden than t.t.
17 :20. we wou. know wh. t.t. mean
19 : 36. see-g t.t. can-t be spok. ag.
20 : 24. none of t.t. move me [t.
23 : 22. tell no man thou shewed t.
24 : 9. Jews assented, t.t. were so
22. Felix heard t.t. he deferred
25 : 9. there be judged of t.t. bef.
11. if none of t.t. wh-f these accu.
26 : 16. to make thee witness of t.t.
26. king knoweth of t.t., none of
t.t. are hidden from him
Ro. 8 : 31. What sh. we say to t.t. ?
14 : 18. he that in t.t. serveth Ch.
1 Co. 4 :6. t.t. I have in a figure
14. I write not t.t. to shame you
9 : 8. Say I t.t. as a man, or saith
15. I have used none of t.t., nei.
have I written t.t. that
10 : 6. t.t. were our examples, to
2 Co. 2 : 16. who is sufficient for t.t. ?
13 : 10. I write t.t. being absent
Ep. 5 : 6. bec. of t.t. wrath of God
Ph. 4 : 8. if any praise, think on t.t.
2 Th. 2 :5. when with you, I told t.t.
1 Ti. 3 :14. t.t. write I, hoping to [t.
4 : 6. put brethren in rememb. of t.
11. t.t. command and teach [self
15. meditate upon t.t. ; give thy-
5 : 7. t.t. give in charge th. they be
21. I charge thee observe t.t. [15.
6 : 2. t.t. teach and exhort, Tit. 2 :
11. O man of God, flee t.t. [t.t.
2 Ti. 1 : 12. For which cause I suffer
2 : 14. Of t.t. put them in rememb.
Tit. 3 :8. t.t. I will thou affirm constantly, t.t. are good and [en
He. 7 : 13. he of whom t.t. are spok-
9 : 6. when t.t. were thus ordained
Ja. 3 : 10. t.t. ought not so to be
2 Pe. 1 : 8. if t.t. be in you and abou.
9. he that lacketh t.t. is blind
10. if ye do t.t. ye shall never fall
12. will put you in rememb. of t.t.
15. to have t.t. always in rememb.
3 : 16. in epistles, speaking of t.t.
17. seeing ye know t.t. beware
1 Jn. 1 : 4. t.t. write we unto you,
2 : 1, 26.-5 : 13. [the seven stars
Re. 2 : 1. t.t. saith he that holdeth
8. write t.t. saith first and last
12 t.t. saith he which hath sharp
18, t.t. saith Son, who hath eyes
3 : 1. t.t. saith he that hath 7 spirits
7. t.t. saith he that is holy, true
14. t.t. saith the Amen [wailing
18 : 15. merchants of t.t. sh. stand
22 : 8 I John saw t.t., fell down
bef. feet of angel wh. shewed t.t.
16. to testify t.t. in the churches
18. If any man sh. add unto t.t.
20 He wh. testifieth t.t. saith, I

After these THINGS.
Ge. 15 : 1. - t. word of Lord came
22 : 1. - t. God did tempt Abr., 20.
39 : 7. - t. his master's wife cast eyes
40 : 1. - t. butler of k. had offended

Ge. 48 : 1. - t. one told Jos., thy fa.
Jos. 24 : 29. -t. Josh. died 110 yrs. old
1 K. 17 : 17. - t. son of wom. fell sick
21 : 1. - t. Naboth had a vineyard
2 Ch. 32 : 1. -t. Sennach-b ent-d Jud.
Ezr. 7 : 1. - t. in reign of Artaxerxes
Es. 2 : 1. - t. wrath of k. was appeas.
3 : 1. - t. did king promote Haman
Jb. 33 : 29. - t. worketh God wi. man
Lu. 5 : 27. - t. Jesus saw publican
9 : † 28. - t. Jesus took Pet. and Jn.
10 : 1. - t. Lord appointed seventy
Jn. 3 : 22. - t. came Jes. into Judea,
7 : 1. - t. Jes. walked in Galilee⌊6 : 1.
21 : 1. - t. Jes. shewed hims. to disc.
Ac. 18 : 1. - t. Paul departed fr. Ath.
19 : 21. - t. Paul purposed to go to
Re. 7 : 1. - t. I saw 4 angels standing
18 : 1. - t. I saw another angel come
19 : 1. - t. I heard gr. voice in heav.

All these THINGS.

Ge. 20 : 8. Abim-h told - t. in their
29 : 13. Jacob told Laban - t. ⌊ears
42 : 36. Jacob said - t. are ag. me
Le. 20 : 23. they committed - t. thf.
De. 4 : 30. when - t. are come upon
30 : 1 when - t. are come upon thee
Ju. 13 : 23. nei. have shewed us - t.
2 S. 13 : 21. Da. heard - t. was wroth
1 K. 18 : 36. I have done - t. at thy
1 Ch. 17 : 19. in making known -great
29 : 17. I willingly offered - t. ⌊t.
19. give unto Sol. heart to do - t.
Je. 3 : 7. after she had done - t.
5 : 19. Whf. doeth L. - t. unto us?
14 : 22. for thou hast made - t.
Eze. 16 : 30. How weak, seeing thou
doest - t., 17 : 18. ⌈in - t.
43. because thou hast fretted me
Da. 12 : 7. - t. shall be finished ⌈L.
Zch. 8 : 17. - t. are t-s I hate, saith
Mat. 4 : 9. - t. will I give thee
6 : 32. after - t. Gentiles seek; Fa.
knoweth ye have need of - t.,
Lu. 12 : 30. ⌈12 : 31.
33. - t. be added unto you, Lu.
13 : 34. - t. spake Jesus, Lu. 8 : 8.-
11 : 27, 53.-13 : 17. Jn. 6 : 59.-
8 : 28.-11 : 11.-12 : 36.-14 : 25.-
15 : 11.-16 : 1, 4, 6, 25, 33.-17 :
13.-20 : 18. Ac. 1 : 9. ⌈- t.?
51. Jesus saith, Have ye underst.
56. Whence hath this man - t.?
Mk. 6 : 2. ⌈youth
19 : 20. - t. have I kept from my
23 : 36. - t. sh. come on this gener.
24 : 2. Jes. said, See ye not - t.?⌈28.
6. -t. must come to pass, Lu. 21 : 9,
33. when ye see - t. know it is
near, Mk. 13 : 29. Lu. 21 : 31.
34. till - t. be fulfilled, Mk. 13 : 30.
Mk. 4 : 11. - t. are done in parables
13 : 4. what sign when - t. be fulfil.
Lu. 1 : † 65. - t. were noised abroad
2 : 19. Mary kept - t. in her heart
7 : 18. disciples of John shewed - t.
12 : 30 - t. do nat-ns of world seek
16 : 14. who were covetous heard -t.
21 : 36. accounted worthy to esc. -t.
24 : 9. told - t. unto the eleven, 10.
14. talked of - t. wh. had happened
Jn. 15 : 21. - t. will they do, 16 : 3.
Ac. 7 : 50. Hath not my hand made -
10 : 8. declared - t. he sent them⌊t.
15 : 17. saith the L., who doeth - t.
24 : 8. mayest take knowledge of - t.
Ro. 8 : 37. in - t. more than conq-rs
1 Co. 10 : 11. -t. happ-d for ensamples
Col 3 : 14. above - t. put on charity
2 Pe. 3 : 11. Seeing - t. sh. be dissolv-

Those THINGS. ⌊ed

Ex. 29 : 33. eat t.t. whw. atonement
Le. 15 : 27. whoso. touch-h t.t. uncl.
22 : 2. t.t. they hallow unto me, 14 :
De. 29 : 29. t.t. revealed belong ⌊11.
Jos 11 : 1. Jabin heard t.t. he sent
1 S. 19 : 7. David, Jona. shewed t.t.
2 K. 17 : 9. Israel did secretly t.t.
Ec. 2 : † 12. in t.t. wh. have been do.
Is. 66 : 2. all t.t. mine hand made, all
t.t. have been, saith the Lord
Eze. 42 : 14. approach to t.t. for peo.
Mat. 11 : 4. Go, shew Jn. t.t. ye see
13 : 17. desired to see t.t. ye see.
and hear t.t. ye hear, Lu. 10 : 24.
27 : 54. saw earthq. and t.t. th. feared
Mk. 1 : 44. offer t.t. Mos. commanded
Lu. 1 : 1. t.t. wh. are believed am. us
4. mightest know certainty of t.t.
45. of t.t. told her from the Lord
2 : 18. wond-d at t.t. told by shep-s
33. his mother marvelled at t.t.
9 : 36. they told no man any of t.t.
12 : 20. whose t.t. thou hast provid.
17 : 10. when ye have done all t.t.
21 : 26. looking after t.t. coming
23 : 14. touching t.t. whf. ye accuse
Jn. 8 : 26. I speak t.t. I have heard
29. I do always t.t. that please
Ac. 3 : 18. t.t. he hath so fulfilled
8 : 6. heed unto t.t. Philip spake
13 : 45. spake against t.t. spoken
17 : 11. searched whe. t.t. were so
18 : 17. Gallio cared for none of t.t.
21 : 24. t.t. conc-g thee are nothing
26 : 16. of t.t. in wh. I will appear
22. none oth. t. than t. Mo. did say
27 : 11. more than t.t. spok. by Pilate
28 : 31. teaching t.t. wh. concern Jes.
Ro. 1 : 28. t.t. wh. are not convenient
4 : 17. calleth t.t. which be not as
6 : 21. What fruit had ye in t.t., for
the end of t.t. is death
10 : 5. man which doeth t.t. sh.
live by th.
15 : 17. in t.t. which pertain to G.
18. not dare to speak of any of t.t.
1 Co. 8 : 4. eating of t.t. offered, 10.
2 Co. 11 : 28. Beside t.t. without
Ep. 5 : 12. a shame to speak of t.t.
Ph. 3 : 13. forgetting t.t. behind,
reaching unto t.t. wh. are bef.
4 : 9. t.t. which ye have learned
Col. 2 : 18. intruding into t.t. not
3 : 1. seek t.t. which are above
He. 3 : 5. for a testimony of t.t.
12 : 27. removing of t.t. shaken,
th. t.t. wh. can-t be shak. remain
Ja. 2 : 16. ye give not t.t. needful
1 Jn. 3 : 22. do t.t. that are pleasing
2 Jn. 8. lose not t.t. we have wrought
Jude 10. speak evil of t.t. they know
not; in t.t. they corrupt thems.
Re. 1 : 3. Blessed they that keep t.t.
2 : 10. Fear none of t.t. shalt suffer
10 : 4. Seal up t.t. thunders utt-d
20 : 12. dead judged out of t.t. writ.
See THREE, UNCLEAN.

What THINGS.

Ex. 10 : 2. tell thy son w.t. I have
Mat. 6 : 8. Fa. knoweth w.t. ye have
Mk. 9 : 9. tell no man w.t. had seen
10 : 32. began to tell w.t. sho. happ.
11 : 24. w.t. ye desire when ye pray
Lu. 7 : 22. tell Jn. w.t. ye have seen
24 : 19. w.t. They said, conc. Jes.
35. told w.t. were done in the way
Jn. 5 : 19. w.t. he doeth doeth Son
10 : 6. underst. not w.t. they were
11 : 46. told w.t. Jesus had done
Ac. 21 : 19. w.t. God wrought among
Ph. 3 : 7. w.t. were gain to me⌊Gen.
See WONDERFUL, WONDROUS.

THINK.

Ge. 40 : 14. t. on me when it be well
Nu. 36 : 6. marry to wh. they t. best
2 S. 13 : 33. to t. king's sons are dead
2 Ch. 13 : 8. ye t. to withstand kingd.
Ne. 5 : 19. t. on me, my God, for good
6 : 6. thou and the Jews t. to rebel
14. My God, t. thou on Tobiah
Es. 4 : 13 t. not thou shalt escape in
Jb. 31 : 1. why sho. I t. upon a maid?
41 : 32. one would t. the deep hoary
Ec. 8 : 17. tho. wise man t. to know it
Is. 10 : 7. nei. doth his heart t. so
Je. 23 : 27. t. to cause peo. to forget
29 : 11. I know thoughts I t. toward
Eze. 38 : 10. shalt t. an evil thought
Da. 7 : 25. he shall t. to change times
11 : † 24. t. his thoughts ag. strong
Jon. 1 : 6. if so be G. will t. upon us
Zch. 11 : 12. if ye t. good give price
Mat. 3 : 9. t. not to say within yours.
5 : 17. t. not I am come to destroy
6 : 7. t. be heard for much speaking
9 : 4. Whf. t. ye evil in your hearts?
10 : 34. t. not I am come to send p.
18 : 12. How t. ye? if man 100 sheep
21 : 28. what t. you? A certain man
22 : 42. What t. ye of Christ? 26 :
66. Mk. 14 : 64.⌈not, Lu. 12 : 40.
24 : 44. in such an hour as ye t.
Lu. 13 : 4. t. ye th. were sinners abo.
Jn. 5 : 39. ye t. ye have eternal life
45. Do not t. I will accuse you
11 : 56. What t. ye, th. he not come
16 : 2. will t. he doeth God service
Ac. 13 : 25. Whom t. ye that I am?
17 : 29. not t. Godhead is like gold
26 : 2. I t. myself happy, k. Agrippa
Ro. 12 : 3. not to t. of himself more
highly than he ought to t., but
to t. soberly as God hath dealt
1 Co. 4 : 6. learn in us not to t. of men
9. I t. that God hath set forth us
7 : 36. if any t. he behaveth uncome-
40. I t. I have Spirit of God ⌊ly
8 : 2. if any t. he knoweth any thi.
12 : 23. members we t. less honourab.
14 : 37. If any t. himself a prophet
2 Co. 3 : 5. of ourselves to t. any thi.
10 : 2. I t. to be bold ag. some wh. t.
7. th. he is Christ's, let him t., 11.
11 : 16. Let no man t. me a fool; if
12 : 6. lest any t. of me above what
19. t. ye that we excuse ourselves
Ga. 6 : 3. if a man t. himself somethi.
Ep. 3 : 20. able to do above all we t.
Ph. 1 : 7. meet to t. this of you all
4 : 8. if be any praise, t. on these
Ja. 1 : 7. let not man t. he sh. receive
4 : 5. Do ye t. Scripture saith in va.?
Pe. 4 : 4. they t. strange ye run not
12. t. it not strange conc-g the trial
2 Pe. 1 : 13. I t. it meet as long as I am

THINKEST.

2 S. 10 : 3. t. thou David doth hon-
our thy father? 1 Ch. 19 : 3.
Jb. 35 : 2. t. thou this right th. thou
Mat. 17 : 25. What t. thou? 22 : 17.
26 : 53. t. thou I cannot pray to Fa.
Lu. 10 : 36. Wh. t. thou was neighb.
Ac. 28 : 22. desire to hear wh. thou t.
Ro. 2 : 3. t. thou this, O man, that

THINKETH. ⌊judgest

1 S. 20 : † 4. whatso. thy soul t. I do
2 S. 18 : 27. Me t. running of foremost
Ps. 40 : 17. poor, yet Lord t. on me
Pr. 23 : 7. as he t. in heart, so is he
Lu. 8 : † 18. taken that he t. he hath
1 Co. 10 : 12. let him th. t. he stand.
13 : 5. Charity t. no evil ⌈flesh
Ph. 3 : 4. If any t. he might trust in

THINKING. ⌈ings

2 S. 4 : 10. t. to have bro-t good tid-
5 : 6. t. David cannot come in hither

THIRD. ⌈kel

Ge. 2 : 14. name of t. river is Hidde-
6 : 16. second and t. stories make it
32 : 19. com-ded the second t. and all
50 : 23. Ephr.'s chil. of t. generation
Ex. 20 : 5. unto t. and fourth generation, 34 : 7. Nu. 14 : 18. De. 5 : 9.
De. 23 : 8. Edomite enter in t. gen-n
1 S. 17 : 13. sons of Jesse to battle,
t. Shammah, 1 Ch. 2 : † 13.
2 S. 3 : 3. unto David sons, t. Absalom, 1 Ch. 3 : 2. ⌈8.
1 K. 6 : 6. t. chamber 7 cubits broad,
2 K. 1 : 13. he sent captain of t. 50(2)

1 Ch. 2 : 13. Jesse begat Shimma t.
3 : 15. sons of Josiah, t. Zedekiah
8 : 1. Benjamin begat Aharah the t.
39. sons of Eshek, Eliphelet t.
12 : 9. men of might ; Eliab t.
23 : 19. sons of Hebron, Jahaziel
the t., 24 : 23. [Harim
24 : 8. first lot to Jehoiarib, t. to
25 : 10. lot to Joseph, t. to Zaccur
26 : 2. sons of Meshele-h, Zebadiah
4. sons of Obed-edom ; Joah t. [t.
11. Hosah had sons, Tebaliah t.
27 : 5. t. captain of host, Benaiah
2 Ch. 23 : 5. a t. part shall be at k.'s
hou., a t. part at gate of founda.
Jb. 42 : 14. Job 3 dau-s ; t. Keren-h
Is. 19 : 24. Israel sh. be t. wi. Egypt
Je. 38 : 14. k. took Jer-h into t. entry
Eze. 10 : 14. t. was face of a lion
Zch. 6 : 3. in t. chariot white horses
Mat. 22 : 26. likewise second and t.,
unto the seventh, Mk. 12 : 21.
Lu. 20 : 31. [ed him
Lu. 20 : 12. sent the t., they wound-
Re. 16 : 4. t. angel poured out vial
21 : 19. t. foundation a chalcedony
See ANGEL, BEAST.

THIRD day. [t.d.
Ge. 1 : 13. evening and morning were
22 : 4. t.d. Abr. saw place afar off
31 : 22. told Laban t.d. Jac. was fled
34 : 25. t.d. when they were sore
40 : 20. t.d., wh. was Pha.'s birthd.
42 : 18. Joseph said unto th. t.d.
Ex. 19 : 11. be ready against t.d.,
t.d. L. will come upon Sinai, 15.
16. on t.d. in morning thunders
Le. 7 : 17. flesh of sacrifice on t.d.
be burnt. 19 : 6. [abom-n, 19 : 7.
18. if any be eaten t.d., it be an
Nu. 7 : 24. t.d. Eliab prince did offer
19 : 12. purify himself t.d.., 31 : 19.
19. clean sh. sprinkle uncl. on t.d.
29 : 20. on t.d. 11 bullocks, 2 rams
Jos. 9 : 17. Isr. came unto cities t.d.
Ju. 20 : 30. Isr. went ag. Benj. t.d.
1 S. 20 : 5. may hide mys. unto t.d.
12. when I have sounded fa. t.d.
30 : 1. Dav. and men to Ziklag t.d.
2 S. 1 : 2. on t.d. man came fr. Saul
1 K. 3 : 18. t.d. after I was delivered
12 : 12. Jeroboam and peo. came to
Rehoboam t.d., 2 Ch. 10 : 12.
2 K. 20 : 5. t.d. thou shalt go unto
house of Lord, 8. [dar
Ezr. 6 : 15. house finished t.d. of A-
Es. 5 : 1. t.d. Es. put on royal app-l
Ho. 6 : 2. in t.d. he will raise us up
Mat. 16 : 21. be killed and raised
again t.d., 17 : 23. Lu. 9 : 22.
20 : 19. t.d. he shall rise, Mk. 9 :
31.-10 : 34. Lu. 18 : 33.-24 : 7, 46.
27 : 64. sepulch. made sure until t.d.
Lu. 13 : 32. the t.d. I sh. be perfected
24 : 21. to day is the t.d. since these
Jn. 2 : 1. t.d. a marriage in Cana
Ac. 10 : 40. Him G. raised up on t.d.
27 : 19. t.d. we cast out tackling
1 Co. 15 : 4. he rose t.d. acc. to Scrip.
See **Yesterday and third DAY.**
See HEAVEN, HOUR, KINGDOM,
LOFT, LOT, MONTH, PART,
RANK, ROW, RULER, SEAL,
TIME, WATCH, WOE, YEAR.

THIRDLY. [acles
1 Co. 12 : 28. t., teachers, aft. th. mir-

THIRST. [Noun.]
Ex. 17 : 3. to kill us and chil. with t.
De. 28 : 48. sh. serve thine enemies in
29 : 19. to add drunkenness to t. [t.
Ju. 15 : 18. now I shall die for t. [t.
2 Ch. 32 : 11. persuade you to die by
Ne. 9 : 15. broughtest water for t., 20.
Jb. 24 : 11. tread winepres-s suffer t.
Ps. 69 : 21. in my t. gave me vinegar
104 : 11. wild asses quench their t.
Is. 5 : 13. multitude dried up with t.
Is. 41 : 17. their tongue faileth for t.
50 : 2. th. fish stinketh, dieth for t.
Je. 2 : 25. withhold thy throat fr. t.
48 : 18. down fr. thy glory, sit in t.
La. 4 : 4. cleaveth to his mouth for
Ho. 2 : 3. lest I slay her with t. [t.
Am. 8 : 11. not a t. for water, but of
13. young men shall faint for t.
2 Co. 11 : 27. in t., in fastings often

THIRST. [Verb.] [t.
Is. 49 : 10. They sh. not hunger nor
Mat. 5 : 6. which t. after righteousn.
Jn. 4 : 13. drinketh of this t. again
14. whoso. drinketh, never t., 6 : 35.
15. me this water, that I t. not [nie
7 : 37. If any t. let him come unto
19 : 28. after this, Jesus saith, I t.
Ro. 12 : 20. if enemy t., give him dri.
1 Co. 4 : 11. to this present hour we t.
Re. 7 : 16. they shall not t. any more

THIRSTED, ETH.
Ex. 17 : 3. people t-d for water, and
Ps. 42 : 2. My soul t-h for God, 63 : 1.
Is. 48 : 21. t-d not when he led [143 : 6.
55 : 1. Ho, every one that t-h, come

THIRSTY. [am t.
Ju. 4 : 19. Give me a little water, I
2 S. 17 : 29. The people t. in wildern.
Ps. 63 : 1. longeth in t. land, 143 : 6.
107 : 5. Hungry, t., their soul fainted
Pr. 25 : 21. if thine enemy be t. give
25. As cold water to a t. soul, so is
Is. 21 : 14. water to him that was t.
29 : 8. be as when t. man dreameth
32 : 6. cause drink of the t. to fail
35 : 7. t. land shall become springs
44 : 3. I will pour water upon him t.
65 : 13. my serv-ts sh drink, ye be t.
Eze. 19 : 13. she is planted in t. gr-d
Mat. 25 : 35. I was t., ye gave me d-k
37. when saw we thee t. and gave
42. I was t., ye gave me no drink
See BLOODTHIRSTY.

THIRTEEN. [14.
Nu. 29 : 13. offer t. young bullocks,
Jos. 19 : 6. Simeon had t. cities and
21 : 4. out of tribe of Benj. t. cities
6. out of half tribe of Manas. t. cit-
19. t. cities with suburbs, 33. [ies
1 Ch. 6 : 60. their cities were t., 62.
26 : 11. sons and breth. of Hosah t.
Eze. 40 : 11. length of gate t. cubits
See SONS, YEARS.

THIRTEENTH.
See DAY, LOT, YEAR.

THIRTIETH. See YEAR.

THIRTY.
Ge. 18 : 30. Peradv. be t. found, he
said I will not do it if I find t.
Ju. 10 : 4. Jair had t. sons that rode
on t. ass colts, and had t. cities
12 : 9. Ibzan had t. sons, t. dau-s,
took in t. dau-s for his sons [13.
14 : 12. changes of raim-t, t. sheets,
2 S. 23 : 13. 3 of t. chief, 1 Ch. 11 : 15.
23. Benaiah more honourable th.
the t., 1 Ch. 11 : 25.-27 : 6. (2) [t.
24. Asahel bro. of Joab, was one of
1 Ch. 11 : 42. captain of Reubenites
and t. with him [the t.
12 : 4. Ismaiah am. the t. and over
Ezr. 1 : 9. number was t. chargers
10. t. basins of gold, silver, 410
Je. 38 : 10. Take hence t. men with
Eze. 40 : 17. t. chambers on pavem-t
41 : 6. side chambers were t. in order
Mat. 13 : 23. some 60, some t., Mk. 4 : 8.
See CAMELS, COMPANIONS.

THIRTY cubits.
Ge. 6 : 15. height of ark was t.c. [15.
Ex. 26 : 8. length of curtain t.c., 36 :
1 K. 6 : 2. height of house of L. t.c.
7 : 2. height of house of forest t.c.
6. porch, length 50 c., breadth t.c.
23. a line of t.c. did compass the
molten sea, 2 Ch. 4 : 2. [broad
Eze. 46 : 22. courts of 40 c. long, t.
See DAYS, FOLD, FURLONGS,
MEASURES, MEN, NEPHEWS,
PERSONS, PIECES, SHEK-
ELS, TALENTS, THOUSAND,
YEARS.

THIRTY first. See YEAR.

THIRTY, with one or two.
1 K. 22 : 31. king commanded his
t.t. captains
See KINGS, PERSONS, YEARS.

THIRTY, with three or four.
See DAYS, SOULS, YEARS.

THIRTY, with five or six.
Jos. 7 : 5. men of Ai smote t.s. of Isr
2 Ch. 3 : 15. two pillars t.f. cubits
See YEARS.

THIRTY, with seven or eight.
2 S. 23 : 39. over his guard t.s. in all
See YEARS.

THIRTY, and seventh, eighth, or ninth.
See YEAR.

THIS. [Adj.]
Ge. 19 : 9. t. fellow came to sojourn
31 : 38. t. 20 years I been with thee
39 : 9. t., Nu. 5 : 30.-11 : 12. De. 3 :
8. Ju. 19 : 23, 24 -20 : 16 1 S. 6 :
9.-12 : 20.-17 : 47 2 S. 13 : 12.-
14 : 20. 1 Ch. 29 : 16 2 Ch 7 : 21,
22. Ne 13 : 27. Ps. 51 : 4. Je. 7 :
14.-11 : 2, 6.-18 : 6.-19 : 12.-32 :
35, 42. Eze 6 : 10. Da. 9 : 13.
Mk. 11 : 28. Lu. 4 : 6, 21.-28 : 41.
Jn. 7 : 31.-12 : 18. [be reckoned
Nu. 18 : 27. t. your heave offering
De. 21 : 20. t. our son is stubborn
Ju. 16 : 18. Come t. once, he hath
1 S. 9 : 17. t. same shall reign ov. peo.
1 K. 3 : 9. who judge t. so gr. people
1 Ch. 17 : 19. hast done all t. greatn-s
Ps. 48 : 14. for t. G. is our G. for ev.
149 : 9. t. honour have all his saints
Can. 7 : 7. t. thy stature like palm t.
Je. 16 : 21. t. once cause them to know
La. 5 : 17. t. our heart is faint [28.
Da. 6 : 5. not find occasion ag. t. Dan.
10 : 17. can serv. talk wi. t. my lord
Lu. 15 : 24. t. my son was dead, is
30. as soon as t. thy son was come
32. t. thy bro. was dead, is alive
Jn. 3 : 29. t. my joy thf is fulfilled
Ac. 1 : 11. t. Jesus sh. so come in like
2 : 32. t. Jesus hath God raised up
6 : 14. that t. Jes. sh. destroy t. pla
7 : 35. t. Moses they refused did G.
40. as for t. Moses, we not what
8 : 22. Repent of t. thy wickedness
19 : 26. t. Paul hath turned people
27. t. our craft is in danger [row
2 Co. 2 : 3. I wrote t. same, lest sor-
See BOOK, CAUSE, CHILD, CITY.

THIS day.
Ge. 4 : 14. hast driven me t.d. fr. [d.
19 : 37. same is fa. of Moab-s unto t.
38. fa. of chil. of Ammon unto t.d.
22 : 14. is said to t.d., In the mount
24 : 12. I pray send good speed t.d.
42. I came t.d. unto the well
25 : 31. Sell me t.d. thy birthright
33. Swear to me t.d., and he sware
26 : 33. name Beer-sheba unto t.d.
31 : 43. what do t.d. unto my dau-s
48. a witn. betw. me and thee t.d.
32 : 32. eat not of sinew unto t.d.
35 : 20. pillar of Ra.'s grave unto t.d.
41 : 9. I remember my faults t.d.
42 : 13. youngest t.d. wi. our fa., 32.
47 : 23. I have bought you t.d. for
26. Joseph made it a law unto t.d.
48 : 15. God who fed me unto t.d.
50 : 20. as it is t.d. to save people
Ex. 10 : 6. since upon earth unto t.d.
12 : 14. t.d. shall be for a memorial
17. observe t.d. in your genera-ns
13 : 3. Remember t.d., ye came, 4.
32 : 29. upon you a bless-g t.d. [t.d.
34 : 11. observe th. I command thee

Le. 8 :34. As he hath done **t.d.**,so L.
10 : 19. **t.d.** have offered sin off-g
Nu. 22 : 30. since I was thine unto **t.**
De. 1: 10. ye are **t.d.** as stars [d.
2 : 18. art to pass over Moab **t.d.**
22. dwelt in their stead unto **t.d.**
25. **t.d.** will I put dread of thee
30. into thy hand as appear-h **t.d.**
3 : 14. after his own name unto **t.d.**
4 : 4. cleave unto L. are alive **t.d.**,
8. law wh. I set bef.you **t.d.**[5 : 3.
20. unto him a peo. as ye are **t.d.**
26. I call heaven and earth to witness ag. you **t.d.**, 30 : 19.
38. to give their land as it is **t.d.**
39. know **t.d.** that Lord he is God
40. shalt keep his statutes and commandments wh. I command **t.d.**, 6 : 6.-7 : 11.-8 : 1, 11.-10 : 13.-11 : 8, 13, 27, 28.-13 :18.-15: 5.-19 : 9.-26 : 16.-27 : 1, 4, 10.- 28 : 1, 13, 14, 15.-30 : 2, 8, 11.[d.
5 : 1. Hear, O Isr., statutes I speak t.
24. seen **t.d.** God doth talk wi. man
6 : 24. as it is **t.d.**, 8 : 18.-10 : 15.- 29 : 28. Ezr. 9 : 7.
8 : 19. I testify **t.d.** ye shall perish
9 : 1. Thou art to pass ov. Jord. **t.d.**
3. understand **t.d.** thy God is he
10 :8. to bless in his name unto **t.d.**
11 : 2. know ye **t.d.**; for I speak
4. how L. destroyed th. unto **t.d.**
26. I set before you **t.d.** a blessing
32. do all statutes I set bef. you **t.d.**
12 : 8. not do aft. things we do **t.d.**
20 :3. ye approach **t.d.** ag. enemies
26 : 3. I profess **t.d.** unto God that
17. avouched the L. **t.d.** thy God
18. L. hath avouched **t.d.** his peo.
27 : 9. **t.d.** thou art beco. peo. of G.
29 : 4. not given you ears unto **t.d.**
10. Ye stand **t.d.** all before Lord
12. oath God maketh wi. thee **t.d.**
15. covenant with him here **t.d.**, and with him not with us **t.d.**
18. whose heart turneth **t.d.** fr. L.
30 : 15. I set before thee **t.d.** life
16. I command thee **t.d.** to love G.
18. I denounce, **t.d.** ye shall per-h
31 : 2. Mos. said, I am 121 years old
27. while I am yet alive **t.d.** [**t.d.**
32 : 46. words I testify **t.d.** [**t.d.**
34 : 6. no man know-h sepulch. unto
Jos. 3 : 7. **t.d.** will I magnify thee
4 : 9. stones in Jordan, unto **t.d.**
5 : 9. **t.d.** I rolled reproach of Eg. off you, place is Gilgal unto **t.d.**
6 :25. Rahab dwel-h in Isr. unto **t.d.**
7 : 25. Lord shall trouble thee **t.d.**
26. ov. him heap of stones unto **t. d.** The valley of Achor unto **t.d.**
8 :28. made Ai desolation unto **t.d.**
29. great heap of stones that remaineth unto **t.d.**, 10 : 27.
9 : 27. hewers of wood unto **t.d.**
13 : 13. dwell among Isr-s until **t.d.**
14 :10. I am **t.d.** fourscore five yrs.
11. strong **t.d.** as when Mos. sent
14. Hebron inheritance of Caleb unto **t.d.**[until **t.d.**, Ju. 1 : 21.
15 : 63. Jebusites dwell at Jerus.
16 : 10. Canaanites dwell am. Ephraimites unto **t.d.** [d.
22 : 3. Ye not left brethren unto **t.**
16. th. ye might rebel **t.d.** ag. L.(2)
17. we are not cleansed until **t.d.**
18. away **t.d.** from following Lord
22. if in transg-n (save us not **t.d.**)
29. God forbid ye turn **t.d.** fr. L.
31. **t.d.** we perceive Lord is am. us
23 : 8. cleave unto L. as unto **t.d.**
9. no man stand bef. you unto **t.d.**
14. **t.d.** I am going way of all earth
24 : 15. choose you **t.d.** whom ye
Ju. 1 : 26. Luz: the name unto **t.d.**
6 : 24. unto **t.d.** it is in Ophrah
9 : 18. ye **t.d.** ag. my father's hou.
Ju. 9 : 19. If ye have dealt truly **t.d.**
10 : 4. called Havoth-jair unto **t.d.**
15. deliver us only we pray **t.d.**
11 :27. Lord be judge **t.d.** betw Isr.
12 : 3. whf. come **t.d.** to fight me?
15 : 19. wh. is Lehi unto **t.d.** [**t.d.**
18 :12. th. place Mahaneh-dan unto
19 : 30. from day Israel came out of Egypt unto **t.d.**, 1 S. 8 : 8. 2 S. 7 : 6. 2 K. 21 : 15. 1 Ch. 17 : 5. Je. 7 : 25.
21 : 6. There is one tribe cut off **t.d.**
Ru. 3 : 18. he have finished thing **t.**
4 : 9. Ye are witnesses **t.d.**, 10. [d.
14. not left **t.d.**, without kinsman
1 S. 5 : 5. threshold of Dagon unto **t.**
6 : 18. stone of Abel unto **t.d.** [d.
10 : 19. ye **t.d.** rejected God [**t.d.**
11 : 13. not a man be put to death
12 :2. bef. you fr. childhood unto **t.**
5. Lord is witness ag. you **t.d.**[d.
14 : 28. cursed be man eateth **t.d.**
33. roll a great stone unto me **t.d.**
38. wh-n this sin hath been **t.d.**
45. Jona. wrought with God **t.d.**
15 : 28. rent kingdom fr. thee **t.d.**
17 : 10. I defy armies of Israel **t.d.**
46. **t.d.** will L. deliver thee into mine hand; host of Philistines **t.d.** unto fowls
18 : 21. Thou **t.d.** be my son in law
21 : 5. though it were sanctified **t.d.**
22 : 8. to lie in wait as at **t.d.**, 13.
24 : 10. **t.d.** thine eyes seen how L.
18. shewed **t.d.** how thou dealt
19. thou hast done unto me **t.d.**
25 : 32. sent thee **t.d.** to meet me
33. **t.d.** fr. coming to shed blood
26 : 8. enemy into thine hand **t.d.**
19. driven me out **t.d.** fr. abiding
21. bec. my soul was precious **t.d.**
24. thy life was much set by **t.d.**
27 : 6. Ziklag unto Judah unto **t.d.**
28 :18. hath done this unto thee **t.d.**
29 :3. no fault in Dav. unto **t.d.**, 6, 8.
30 :25. ordinance for Isr. unto **t.d.**
2 S. 3 : 8. kindness **t.d.** unto Saul
38. a great man fallen **t.d.** in Isr.
39. I am **t.d.** weak though king
4 :3. Beerothites sojourners until **t.**
8. avenged king **t.d.** of Saul [d.
6 : 8. name of place Perez-uzzah to **t.d.**, 1 Ch. 13 : 11. [with us
15 : 20. should I **t.d.** make thee go
16 : 12. requite me for his cursing
18 : 18. called **t.d.** Abs.'s pla. [**t.d.**
20. sh. bear no tidings **t.d.** bec. (2)
31. Lord avenged thee **t.d.** of all
19 : 5. hast shamed **t.d.** faces of all
6. declared **t.d.** thou regardest nei. princes nor servants for **t. d.** I perceive if Absalom had lived and all we had died **t.d.**
20. I am come the first **t.d.** of all
22. ye **t.d.** be adversaries unto me? any be put to death **t.d.** in Israel? do not I know I am **t.d.** king over Israel?
35. I am **t.d.** fourscore years old
1 K. 1 : 25. he is gone **t.d.**, slain oxen
30. so will I certainly do **t.d.**[3:6.
48. one to sit on my throne **t.d.**,
2:24. Adonijah be put to death **t.d.**
5 7. Blessed be Lord **t.d.**, wh. hath
8 : 8. there unto **t.d.**, 2 Ch. 5 : 9.
24. hast fulfilled it as it is **t.d.**, 2 Ch. 6 : 15.[at **t.d.**, 1 Ch. 28 : 7.
61. to keep his commandments as
9 :13. land of Cabul unto **t.d.**[8 : 8.
21. bond service unto **t.d.**, 2 Ch.
10 : 12. no such almug trees unto **t.**
12 : 7. If be serv. unto peo. **t.d.** [d.
19 Israel rebelled ag. house of David unto **t.d.**, 2 Ch. 10 : 19.
18 : 36. be known **t.d.** thou art God
20 :13. deliver into thine hand **t.d.**
2 K. 2 : 22. waters healed unto **t.d.**
2 K. 6 : 31. if head of Elisha stand **t.**
7 : 9. **t.d.** is day of good tidings [d.
8 : 22. Yet Edom revolted fr. Judah unto **t.d.**, 2 Ch. 21 : 10. [**t.d.**
10 : 27. made it draught house unto
14 : 7. called it Joktheel unto **t.d.**
16 :6. Syrians dwelt there unto **t.d.**
17 : 23. Israel to Assyria unto **t.d.**
34. Unto **t.d.** do aft. former man.
41. as fathers so do they unto **t.d.**
19 : 3. **t.d.** a day of trouble, of rebuke, Is. 37 : 3. [Is. 39 : 6.
20 : 17. laid up in store unto **t.d.**,
1 Ch. 4:41. destroyed them unto **t.d.**
43. they dwelt there unto **t.d.**[d.
5 : 26. bro-t th. unto Gozan unto **t.**
29 : 5. who consecrate his serv. **t.d.**
2 Ch. 20 : 26. valley of Ber-h unto **t.**
35 : 21. I come not ag. thee **t.d.**[d.
25. spake of Josiah in lamentations to **t.d.**
Ezr. 9 : 7. we in great trespass unto **t.d.**, confus-n of face (2) Da. 9 : 7.
15. we remain escaped as it is **t.d.**
Ne. 1 : 11. prosper thy servant **t.d.**
5 : 11. Restore **t.d.** their lands [10.
8 : 9. **t.d.** is holy unto the Lord,
9 : 10. didst get a name, as it is **t.d.**, Je. 32 : 20. Da. 9 : 15.[unto **t.d.**
32. since time of kings of Assyria
36. Behold we are servants **t.d.**
Es. 1 : 18. ladies of Persia say **t.d.**
5 :4. let king and Haman come **t.d.**
9 :13. Jews to do acc. to **t.d.**'s decree
Ps. 2 : 7. my Son **t.d.** have I begotten thee, Ac. 13 : 33. He. 1 : 5.
119 : 91. They continue **t.d.** acc-g
Pr. 7 : 14. **t.d.** have I paid my vows
22 : 19. I made known to thee **t.d.**
Is. 38 : 19. living sh. praise as I do **t.d.**
56 : 12. to morrow shall be as **t.d.**
58 : 4. ye sh. not fast as ye do **t.d.**
Je. 1: 10. I **t.d.** set thee over nations
18. made thee **t.d.** a defenced city
3 : 25. sinned we and fa-s unto **t.d.**
11 : 5. land with honey as it is **t.d.**
7. protested unto fa-s unto **t.d.**(2)
25 : 3. 13th year of Josiah unto **t.d.**
18. to make them a curse as it is **t.d.**, 44 : 2, 6, 22. [d., and in
32 : 20. wonders in Egypt unto **t.**
31. fr. day they built city unto **t.**
35 : 14. unto **t.d.** they drink none
36 :2. from days of Josiah unto **t.d.**
40 : 4. I loose thee **t.d.** from chains
42 : 19. I have admonished you **t.d.**
21. **t.d.** I have declared it to you
44 : 10. are not humbled unto **t.d.**
23. this evil unto you as at **t.d.**
Eze. 2 :3. transgressed ag. me to **t.d.**
20 : 29. is called Bamah unto **t.d.**
31. pollute yourselves with idols unto **t.d.** [**t.d.** (3)
24 : 2. Son of man, write name of
Da. 9 : 7. confusion of faces as **t.d.**
Hag. 2 : 15. consider from **t.d.**, 18.
19. from **t.d.** will I bless you
Mat. 6 : 11. Give us **t.d.** daily bread
11 : 23. Sod. have remain. until **t.d.**
27 :8. called field of blood unto **t.d.**
19. I have suffered **t.d.** in a dream
28 : 15. reported am Jews unt. **t.d.**
Mk. 14 : 30. **t.d.** thou shalt deny me
Lu. 2 : 11. unto you born **t.d.** a Sav.
4 :21. **t.d.** is this Scripture fulfilled
19 :9. **t.d.** is salva. come to this ho.
42. If hadst known in **t.** thy **d.**
22 : 34. cock not crow **t.d.** bef. thou
Ac. 2 : 29. sepulchre is wi. us unto **t.**
4 : 9. If we **t.d.** be examined [d.
19 : 40 in question for **t.d.** uproar
20 : 26. I take you to record **t.d.**
22 : 3. was zealous as ye all are **t.d.**
23 :1. I in good conscience unt. **t.d.**
24 : 21. I am called in question **t.d.**
26 : 2. I sh. answer for myself **t.d.**
22. I continue unto **t.d.** witness-g

Ac. 26 :29.I wou. all th.hear me **t.d.**
27 : 33. **t.d.** is the 14th day fasting
Ro. 11 : 8. ears not hear unto **t.d.**(2)
1 Co. 4 : 13. we offscouring unto **t.d.**
2 Co.3:14.unt.**t.d.**remained vail,15.
See **THIS is the day.**
See DOCTRINE, EVIL, HOUSE, LAND, LAW, LIFE, MAN, MATTER, MONTH, ONCE, PEOPLE, PLACE, THING, TIME, WAY, WISE, WORD, WORLD.

THIS. [Pronoun.]

Ge. 3:14. Bec.hast done **t.**art cursed
5 :29. **t.**sh.comfort us conc.woman
15 : 4. **t.** shall not be thine heir,but
20 : 6. thou didst **t.** in integrity of
29 : 27. we will give **t.** for service
34 : 15. in **t.** will we consent unto
36:24.**t.**wasAnah that found mules
37 : 32. sent coat, said, **t.** we found
38 : 28. thread, saying, **t.** came 1st
41 : 24. I told **t.** unto magicians
44 : 29. if ye take **t.** from me, and
Ex. 3 : 12. **t.** a token that I sent thee
7 : 17. in **t.** sh. know I am the Lord
*23. nei. did he set his heart to **t.**
16 : 8. **t.** shall be in the evening
17 :14.Write **t.** for memorial in b-k
30 : 13. **t.** they sh. give, each half a
31. **t.** sh. be anointing oil unto me
Le. 14 : 2. **t.** shall be law of leper
15 : 3.**t.**sh.be his uncleann.in issue
16 :29.**t.**a statute for ever,34.-17:7.
Nu. 4 : 4. **t.** be service of sons of Ko.
7 : 17. **t.** was the offering of, 23, 29, 35,41,47,53,59,65,71,77,83,84,88.
18 : 9. **t.** sh. be thine of most holy things, De. 18 : 3. [doeth **t.**?
24 : 23. alas, who sh. live when God
34 : 6. **t.** be your west border | 7, 9.
12. **t.** sh. be your land with coasts
35 : 5. **t.** shall be suburbs of cities
De. 18 : 3. **t.** shall be priest's due
32 : 29. O that they understood **t.**
Jos. 4 : 6. **t.** may be a sign am. you, 1 S. 2 : 34.-14 : 10. 2 K. 19 : 29. Is. 37 : 30.-38 : 7. Je. 44 : 29. Eze. 4 : 3. [Judah
15 : 1. **t.** was the lot of children of
4. **t.** sh. be your south coast,18:19.
Ju. 7 :4.of wh.I say,**t.**sh.go wi.thee, of whomso. I say **t.** shall not go
20 : 9. **t.** sh. be the thing we will do
Ru. 4 : 7. **t.** was the manner in former time, **t.** was a testimony in
1 S. 8 : 11. **t.** sh. be manner of king
16 : 8. nei. hath Lord chosen **t.**,9.
20 : 3. Let not Jonathan know **t.**
25 : 31.that **t.** be no grief unto thee
2 S. 7 : 19.**t.**small thing in thy sight
19 : 21.Shim. be put to death for **t.**?
1 K. 11 : 27.**t.** the cause he lifted ha.
39. I will for **t.** afflict seed of Dav.
17 : 24.by **t.**I know thou man of G.
2 K. 4 : 43. sho. I set **t.** bef. 100 men
9 : 27. when Ahaziah saw **t.** he fled
14 :10.glory of **t.** and tarry at home
15 : 12. **t.** was word of the Lord [**t.**
24 : 3. at commandment of L. came
1 Ch. 17 : 17.**t.** was small thing,O G.
2 Ch. 1: 11.Bec. **t.**was in thine heart
25 :9.Lord able to give more than **t.**
29 : 9. our wives in captivity for **t.**
Ezr. 6 : 11. house be dunghill for **t.**
Ezr. 7 :27.put such as **t.** in k.'s heart
8 : 23. So we besought our G. for **t.**
9 : 13. given such deliverance as **t.**
15. we cannot stand because of **t.**
Ne. 7 : 7. numb. of men of Isr. was **t.**
13 : 14. Remember me conc. **t.**, 22.
Es. 4:14.to kingd. for such time as **t.**
6 : 3.What honour to Mord. for **t.**?
Jb. 5 : 27. Lo **t.**, we have searched it
12 : 9. hand of L. hath wrought **t.**
17 :8.Upright men be astonied at **t.**
20 : 2. answer ; for **t.** I make haste
4. Knowest thou not **t.** of old

Jb. 21 :2. Hear let **t.** be y-r consola-n
31 :28. **t.** an iniquity to be punished
33 : 12. in **t.** thou art not just, I
34 :16. If hast understand-g hear **t.**
35 : 2. Thinkest thou **t.** to be right
36 : 21. **t.** hast thou chosen rather
37 : 1. At **t.** my heart trembleth
14. Hearken unto **t.**, O Job, stand
Ps. 11 : 6. **t.** be portion of their cup
27 : 3. war, in **t.** will I be confident
32 : 6. For **t.** shall every one pray
35 :22.**t.** hast seen,keep not silence
41 : 11. By **t.**I know thou favourest
44 : 21. Shall not God search **t.** out
49 : 1. Hear **t.** all ye people, give ear
50 : 22. consider **t.**ye th.forget God
56 : 9. **t.** I know, for God is for me
62 : 11. twice have I heard **t.** that
69 : 31. **t.** also shall please the Lord
32. humble shall see **t.** and be glad
73 : 16. When I thought to know **t.**
74:18.Rememb.**t.**,enemy reproach.
78 : 21. Lord heard **t.**was wroth, 59.
81 : 4.For **t.** was a statute for Israel
5. **t.** he ordained in Joseph for a
92 : 6.nei.doth a fool understand **t.**
102 :18.**t.** sh.be written for gener-n
109 :20. Let **t.**be reward of advers-s
119 : 56.**t.**I had bec.I kept precepts
Ec. 2 : 10.**t.**my portion of my labour
24. **t.** I saw, that it was from God
4 : 4. for **t.** a man is envied of his
6 : 5.**t.** hath more rest than oth.[**t.**
7 : 10. dost not inquire wisely conc.
18. It is good that thou take hold of **t.**,from **t.**withdraw not hand
27. **t.** have I found, counting one
29 Lo **t.** only have I found[by one
11 :6. whether sh. prosper **t.** or th.
Is. 1 :12.who required **t.** at your ha.
6 : 7. said, **t.** hath touched thy lips
9 : 5. **t.** shall be with burning and.
7. zeal of the Lord will perform **t.**
27 : 9.By **t.** iniquity of Jac. purged
28 : 29.**t.** also cometh forth fr.Lord
29 : 11. saying, Read **t.** I pray, 12.
30 : 7. theref. have I cried conc. **t.**
38 : 7. **t.** shall be a sign unto thee
42 : 23. Who am. you give ear to **t.**
43 : 9. who can declare **t.**? 45 : 21
46:8.Remember **t.**,shew yours.men
47 : 8. Therefore hear now **t.**, 48 : 1, 16.-51 : 21. [The Lord
48 :20.tell **t.**to the end of the earth,
50 : 11. **t.** sh. ye have of mine hand
51 : 21. hear **t.** thou afflicted, and
56 : 2. Blessed is man that doeth **t.**
58 : 5. wilt thou call **t.** a fast, an
63 : 1. **t.** that is glorious in apparel
66 :14.see **t.** your hearts sh. rejoice
Je. 2 :12.Be astonished heavens at **t.**
17. hast not procured **t.**unto thys.
4 : 8.For **t.** gird you with sackcloth
28. For **t.** shall the earth mourn
5 :7. How sh. I pardon thee for **t.**?
9. be avenged on such a nation as **t.**, 29.-9 : 9. [ob, publish
20. Declare **t.** in the house of Jac-
21. Hear now **t.**, O foolish people
9 : 12.Who is man may underst. **t.**?
24. him that glorieth, glory in **t.**
22 : 16.was not **t.** to know me, saith
21. **t.** been thy manner fr. youth
23:26.How long sh. **t.**be in proph-ts
31 : 26.Upon **t.**I awaked and beheld
33. **t.** shall be the covenant I will
32 : 8. I knew **t.** was word of Lord
La. 3 :21. **t.** I call to mind,thf. hope
5 : 17. For **t.** our heart is faint, our
Eze. 1 :5.**t.**was their appearance, 28.
8 : 15. Hast thou seen **t.**? 17.-47:6.
16 : 49. **t.** was the iniquity of Sod.
20 : 27. in **t.** your fa-s blasphemed
21 :26. saith Lord, **t.** sh. not be the
23 : 11. when sister Aholibah saw **t.**
24 :24. **t.**cometh ye sh. know,33:33.
36 : 37. I will for **t.** be inquired of

Eze. 45 :1.**t.**be holy in all the borders
2. Of **t.** there sh. be for sanctuary
47 : 6. Son of man hast th. seen **t.**?
13. **t.** be border wh-by inherit,15.
Da. 2 : † 43. shall not cleave **t.** wi. **t.**
Ho. 5 : 1. Hear ye **t.**, O priest, and
7 : 16. **t.** be their derision in Egypt
Jo. 1 : 2. Hear **t.** ye old men, all ye
3 : 9. Proclaim ye **t.** am. Gentiles
Am. 4 :5.**t.**liketh you, O chil. of Isr.
7 : 3. L. repented for **t.**,it sh.not,6.
8 : 4.Hear **t.**O ye th.swallow needy
8.Sh. not the land tremble for **t.**?
9 : 12. saith the Lord that doeth **t.**
Jon. 4 : 2. **t.** saying in my country?
Mi. 3 : 9. Hear **t.** ye heads of Jacob
Zph. 2 : 10.**t.** sh. they have for pride
Zch. 6 : 15. **t.** shall come if ye obey
14 : 12. **t.** shall be the plague, 15.
19. **t.** sh be punishment of Egypt
Mal.1 :9.**t.**hath been by your means
13. sho. I accept **t.** of your hand?
2 : 12. cut off the man doeth **t.**[eth
Mat. 12 : 7. if known what **t.** mean-
15 :11.out of mouth **t.** defileth man
16 : 22. Lord **t.** sh. not be unto thee
22:33.multitude heard**t.**astonished
24 : 43. know **t.**, that if goodman of house, Lu. 12 : 39.
27 : 54. Truly **t.** was the Son of God
28 : 14. if **t.** come to governor's ears
Mk. 9 : 21. How long since **t.** came
12 : 11. **t.** was the Lord's doing [**t.**
31. And the second is like,namely
Lu. 1 : 18. Whereby shall I know **t.**
29. what salutation **t.** should be
34. How **t.** be, I know not a man?
66.What manner of child sh. **t.**be?
2 : 12. **t.** shall be a sign unto you
3 : 20. added yet **t.** above all, he
6 :3 Have ye not read so much as **t.**
9 : 54. when disci. Jas., Jn., saw **t.**
10 :11.be sure of **t.**, th. kingdom of
20.notwithstand-g in **t.**rejoice not
16 : 2 How is it I hear **t.** of thee
18:23.heard **t.** he was very sorrowf.
22 :17. Take **t.**, divide it am. yours.
37. that **t.** must be accomplished
23 : 47. Certainly **t.** was righteous
Jn. 1 : 15, **t.** was he of whom I spake
2: 22.discip.remembered he said **t.**
4 : 27. upon **t.** came his disciples
5 : 28.Marvel not at **t.**, for the hour
6 : 6. **t.** he said to prove him, for
61. Jes. said, Doth **t.** offend you?
7 : 39. But **t.** spake he of the Spirit
8 : 6. **t.** they said, tempting him
40. ye seek to kill me ; **t.** did not
11 :26. never die. Believest thou **t.**?
51. **t.** spake he not of himself
12 : 6. **t.** he said, not that he cared
7. against day of my burying she kept **t.** [death, 21 : 19.
33. **t.**, he said, signifying what
13 : 28. for what intent he spake **t.**
35. By **t.** sh. all know ye my disci.
15 : 13.Greater love no man than **t.**
25. **t.** cometh to pass that word be
16 : 30. by **t.** we believe thou camest
18 : 38. when Pilate had said **t.**[th.
20 : 22. had said **t.**, he breathed on
21 . 19. spoken **t.**, he saith, Follow
Ac. 2 : 6. when **t.** was noised abroad
12. one to ano.,What meaneth **t.**?
14. Ye men of Judea, Be **t.** known
31. He, seeing **t.** bef., spake of [see
33. he hath shed forth **t.** ye now
37. heard **t.** they were pricked
3 :12.men of Isr.,why marvel at **t.**?
5 :24. doubted wh-to **t.** would grow
7 : 60.Stephen said **t.**, he fell asleep
8 : 32.Scripture wh.he read was **t.**
34. of whom speaketh prophet **t.**?
13 : 48. Gentiles heard **t.**were glad
15 : 15. to **t.** agree words of proph-s
16 : 18. **t.** did she many days, but
19 : 5. heard **t.** they were baptized

Ac. 19:10. t. continued space of 2 yrs.
17. t. known to all Jews in Asia
20:29. I know t., aft. my departfng
24:14. t. I confess, that aft. the way
Ro. 2:3. thinkest thou t., O man
6:6. Knowing t., that our old man
9:10. not only t., ; when Rebecca
13:9. For t., Thou shalt not steal
14:13. judge t. rather, that no man
15:28. When I have performed t.
1 Co. 1:12. t. I say, every one saith
7:6. I speak t. by permission, not
29. But t. I say, The time is short
35. t. I speak for your own profit
9:3. mine answer to them is t.
11:17. in t. that I declare, I praise
22. shall I praise you in t.? ⌊not
15:34. I speak t. to your shame
50. t. I say, flesh cannot inherit
2 Co. 2:1. I determined t. with mys.
5:2. in t. we groan, earnestly
7:3. I speak not t. to condemn you
8:5. t. they did, not as we hoped
20. avoiding t., th. no man blame
9:6. But t. I say, He which soweth sparingly ⌈again, 11.
10:7. let him of himself think t.
13:9. t. we wish, your perfection
Ga. 3:2. t. would I learn of you ⌈ed
17. t. I say, cove-t th. was confirm-
5:14. fulfilled in one word, even t.
Ep. 4:17. t. I say, and testify in L.
5:5. t. ye know, no whoremonger
Ph. 1:7. meet for me to think t. of
9. t. I pray, that your love abound
19. t. shall turn to my salvation
Col. 2:4. t. I say, lest any beguile
1 Th. 4:15. t. we say unto you by
2 Th. 3:10. wi. you, t. we commanded
1 Ti. 1:9 knowing t., Ja. 1:3. 2 Pe. 1:20.-3:3. ⌈thyself and
4:16. in doing t. shall both save
2 Ti. 1:15. t. knowest, they in Asia
3:1. t. know, in last days perilous
He. 7:21. hut t. with an oath by him
27. t. he did once wh. offered hims.
9:8. The Holy Ghost t. signifying
2 Pe. 1:5. besides t. giving diligence
3:5. For t. they are ignorant of
1 Jn. 3:10. In t. chil of G. manifest
4:9. In t. was manifested love of G.
5:2. By t. we know we love chil.
Jude 5. in remembr. tho. ye knew t.
Re. 2:6. t. thou hast, hatest deeds

After THIS. ⌈rah

Ge. 23:19 a.t. Abraham buried Sa-
2 S. 2:1. a.t. Dav. inquired of Lord
2 Ch. 21:18. a. all t. L. smote him
Da. 7:6. a.t., lo, ano., like leopard
7. a.t. I saw in the night visions
Jn. 2:12. a.t. he went to Capernaum
5:1. a.t. was a feast of the Jews
19:28. a.t. Jesus saith, I thirst
38. a.t. Joseph besought Pilate
Ac. 15:16. a.t. I will build tabern.
He. 9:27. to die, but a.t. the judgm.
Re. 4:1. a.t. I looked, and a door
7:9. a.t., lo, a great multitude

All THIS. ⌈a.t.

Ge. 41:39. as God hath shewed thee
Le. 26:18. And if ye not for a.t., 27.
Ju. 6:13. why is a.t. befallen us?
1 S. 22:15. serv. knew nothing of a.t.
2 S. 14:19. Joab with thee in a.t.
1 Ch. 28:19. a.t. L. made me under-
2 Ch. 29:28. a.t. continued till ⌊st-d
31:1. a.t. was finished Israel went
Ezr 8:35. a.t. was burnt off-g unto
Ne. 9:38. bec of a.t. we make cov-t
Es. 5:13. Yet a.t. availeth me noth
Jb 1:22. In a.t. Job sinned not, 2:10.
13:1. So, mine eye hath seen a.t.
Ps. 44:17. a.t. is come upon us, yet
78:32. for a.t. they sinned still
Ec. 7:23. a.t. have I proved by wisd.
8:9. a.t. have I seen and applied
9:1 a.t. I consid-d to declare a.t.
Is. 5:25. For a.t. his anger is not turned, 9:12, 17, 21.-10:4.
48:6. Thou hast heard, see a.t.
Je. 3:10. yet for a.t. her sister Jud.
Da. 4:28. a.t. came upon Neb. ⌈a.t.
5:22. Belshaz-r, tho. thou knewest
7:16. I asked him truth of a.t.
Ho. 7:10. do not seek Lord for a.t.
Mi. 1:5. For transg-n of Jac. is a.t.
Lu. 16:26. beside a.t. betw. us and
24:21. beside a.t., to day is third

See **DO with this, DONE with this, Thou hast DONE.**

THIS is.

Ge. 2:23. t.i. now bone of my bones
5:1. t.i. book of the generations
6:15. t.i. fashion thou shalt make
9:12. t.i. the token of the coven-t
12:12. they shall say, t.i. his wife
17:10. t.i. my covenant ye sh. keep
20:13. t.i. kindness shalt shew me
28:17. t.i. none other but house of God, t.i. the gate of heaven
32:2. Jacob, he said, t.i. G.'s host
40:12. Joseph said, t.i. interpret-n
41:28. t.i. thing spok. unto Pha. ⌊18.
38. Can we find such a one as t.i.
48:18. Not so, fa., t.i. the firstborn
49:28. t.i. it their father spake
50:11. t.i. grievous mourning to
Ex. 2:6. t.i. one of Hebrews' chil.
3:15. t.i. my name for ever, and
8:19. said, t.i. the finger of God
12:42. t.i. night of L. to be observ-
43. t.i. ordinance of passover ⌊ed
16:15. t.i. bread L. hath given you
23. t.i. that which Lord hath said
29:38. t.i. that thou shalt offer
38:21. t.i. the sum of the tabern-e
Le. 7:35. t.i. portion of anointing
10:3. t.i. that the Lord spake
Nu. 4:24. t.i. the service of, 28, 33
31. t.i. charge of their burden
8:24. t.i. it belongeth unto Levites
13:27. they said, t.i. fruit of it
18:11. t.i. thine, heave off-g of gift
20:13. t.i. the water of Meribah
28:3. t.i. the offering made by fire
31:21. t.i. ordinance of the law
De. 13:11. no more wickedness as t.
15:2. t.i. the manner of release ⌊i.
33:1. t.i. blessing wherew. Moses
Jos 16:8. t.i. inheritance of Ephra.
18:29 t.i. the inheritance of, 19: 8, 16, 23, 31, 39, 48. ⌈i. he
1 S. 16:12. Arise, anoint him, for t.
30:20. took herds said t.i. David's
1 K 1:45. t.i. noise ye have heard
13:3. t.i. sign Lord hath spoken
2 K. 3:18. t.i. but a light thing ⌈city
6:19 t.i. not the way, neither i.t.
8:5. t.i. the woman, t.i. her son
9:36. Jehu said, t.i. word of Lord
37. they shall not say t.i. Jezebel
1 Ch. 11:11. t.i. number of mighty
2 Ch. 2:4. t.i. an ordinance forever
28:22. t.i. that king Ahaz
Ezr 1:9. vessels of L., t.i. number
4:11. t.i. letter unto Artax., 7:11.
Ne. 2:2. t.i. nothing but sorrow of
9:18 t.i. God bro-t thee out of Eg.
Es. 1:1. t.i. Ahaz-s reigned fr. India
Jb. 8:19. t.i. the joy of his way
9:22 t.i. one thing, thf. I said it
10:13 I know t.i. with thee ⌈God
18:21 t.i. pla. of him know-h not
20:29. t.i. the portion of a wicked man from God, 27:13. ⌈be pun.
31:11. For t.i. a heinous crime to
Ps. 24:6. t.i. generation of them
68:16. t.i. the hill God desireth
77:10. t.i. my infirmity, but I will
109:27. may know t.i. thy hand
118:23. t.i. Lord's doing; marvellous, Mat 21:42. ⌈affliction
119:50. t.i. my comfort in mine
132:14 t.i. my rest for ever, here
Ec. 1:10. it may be said, t.i. new
17. I perceived t.i. vexation of spi.
2:1. behold t. also i. vanity, 15, 19, 21, 23, 26.-4:4, 8, 16.-5:10.-6:2, 9.-7:6.-8:10, 14. ⌈came
5:16 t. also i. sore evil that as he
19. to rejoice in labour, t.i. gift
9:3. t.i. an evil th. one event unto
12:13. t.i. whole duty of man ⌊all
Can. 5:16. t.i. my beloved, and t.i.
Is 12:5. Sing unto L., t.i. known
14:26. t.i. the purpose upon the earth, t.i. the hand stretched
17:14. t.i. portion of them th. spoil
25:9. Lo, t.i. our God, we waited
27:9. t.i. the fruit, to take aw. sin
28:12. t.i. the rest, t.i. refreshing
30:9. t.i. a rebellious people
21. t.i. the way, walk ye in it
54:9 t.i. as the waters of Noah
17. t.i. heritage of serv-ts of Lord
59:21. t.i. my covenant with them
Je. 4:18. t.i. thy wickedn., bitter
7:28. t.i. nation obeyeth not Lord
10:19. Truly t.i. a grief, I must
13:25. t.i. thy lot, saith the Lord
23:6. t.i. name he sh. be called, The L. our Righteousn., 33:16.
30:17. t.i. Zion, no man seeketh
46:10. t.i. day of Lord of hosts
50:25. t.i. work of L. in land of C.
La. 2:16. t.i. day we looked for
Eze. 5:5. t.i. Jerusalem, I set it in
10:15. t.i. the living creature I saw
31:18. t.i. Pha. and his multitude
32:16. t.i. the lamentation, 19:14.
41:4. t.i. the most holy place
22. t.i. table that is bef. the Lord
45:13. t.i. oblation ye shall offer
47:19. t.i. south side | 20. west side
Da. 2:36. t.i. dream; we will tell
4:24. t.i. interpretation. t.i., 5:26.
5:25. t.i. the writing, MENE
Mi. 2:10. Arise, t.i. not your rest
Zph. 2:15. t.i. the rejoicing city
Zch. 5:3. t.i. the curse that goeth
6. he said, t.i. an ephah ⌊forth
7. t.i. a woman in midst of ephah
8. he said, t.i. wickedness ⌈Esaias
Mat. 3:3. t.i. he was spoken of by
17. t.i. my beloved Son, 17:5. Mk. 9:7. Lu. 9:35. 2 Pe. 1:17.
11:10. t.i. he of whom it is written, Lu. 7:27. ⌈come
14. t.i. is Elias, which was for to
13:19. t.i. he received seed ⌈6:35.
14:2. t.i. Jn. the Baptist risen, Mk.
15. t.i. desert place; time is past
19:26. With men t.i. impossible
21:11. t.i. Jesus, prophet of Naz.
38. t.i. the heir, let us kill him, Mk. 12:7. Lu. 20:14. ⌈12:30.
22:38. t.i. first command-t, Mk.
26:26. Jesus said, Take, eat, t.i.
28. t.i. my blood, Mk. 14:22, 24. Lu. 22:19, 20. 1 Co. 11:24, 25.
27:37. t.i. Jesus the king of the Jews, Lu. 23:38 ⌈ried again
Mk. 14:69. t.i. one of them, he de-
Lu. 1:36. t.i. sixth month with her
7:39. what manner of woman t.i.
11:29. t.i. an evil generation; seek
22:53. t.i. your hour and power of
Jn. 1:19. t.i. the record of John
30. t.i. he of wh. I said, After me
34. record that t.i. Son of God
3:19. t.i. condemnation, th. light
4:42. t.i. indeed Christ, 7:26, 41.
54. t.i. the second miracle
6:29. t.i. work of God th. ye believe
39. t.i. the Father's will which, 40.
50. t.i. the bread from heaven, 58.
60. t.i. a hard saying, who hear it?
7:26. Do rulers know t.i. very Ch.?
40. of a truth t.i. the prophet, 6:14
9:9. Some said t.i. he; others
20. We know that t.i. our son and

Jn. 15 : 12. t.i. com-nt, that ye love
17 : 3. t. i. life eternal, that they
21 : 14. t.i. third time Jesus shewed
24. t.i. the disciple wh. testifieth
Ac. 2 : 16. t.i. that spoken by Joel
4 : 11. t.i. the stone set at nought
7 : 37. t.i. that Moses which said
38. t.i. he in church in wilderness
9 : 22. proving that t.i. very Christ
21 : 28. t.i. the man teacheth ag. law
27 : 34. take meat ; t.i. for y-r health
Ro. 9 : 9. t.i. the word of promise
Ro. 11 : 27. t.i. my covenant, He. 8 :
10.-10 : 16. ⌈tress
1 Co. 7 : 26. t.i. good for present dis-
10 : 28. if say t.i. offered in sacrifice
11 : 20. t.i. not to eat L.'s supper
2 Co. 8 : 10. t.i. expedient for you
13 : 1. t.i. the 3d time I am coming
Ep. 5 : 32. t.i. a great mystery ; but
6 : 1. obey parents, for t.i. right
Ph. 1 : 22. t.i. the fruit of my labour
Col. 3 : 20. t.i. well pleasing unto L.
1 Th. 4 : 3. t.i. the will of God, 5 : 18.
1 Ti. 1 : 15. t.i. a faithful saying, 3 :
1.-4 : 9. Tit. 3 : 8. ⌈of God
2 : 3. For t.i. acceptable in the sight
He. 9 : 20. t.i. blood of the testam-t
1 Pe. 1 : 25. t.i. word preached unto
2 : 19. t.i. thankworthy, if man
20. take it patiently, t.i. accepta.
5 : 12. t.i. the true grace of God
1 Jn. 1 : 5. t.i. the message, 3 : 11.
2 : 25. t. i. the promise, eternal life
3 : 23. t.i. command-t th. we believe
4 : 3. t.i. that spirit of antichrist
5 : 3. t.i. love of God, that we keep
4. t.i. the victory, even our faith
6. t.i. he that came by water and
9. t.i. the witness of God which
11. t.i. record, God hath given life
14. t.i. confidence we have in him
20. t.i. true God, and eternal life
2 Jn. 6. t.i. love, that we walk after
his com-ts, t.i. the command-t
7. t.i. a deceiver and an antichrist
Re. 20 : 5. t.i. the first resurrection
14. into lake of fire, t.i. 2d death

THIS is the day.

Ju. 4 : 14. t. - L. hath deliv-d Sisera
Ps. 118 : 24. t. - wh. Lord hath made
La. 2 : 16. t. - that we looked for
Eze. 39 : 8. t. - wh-f I have spoken

See **This is the LAW.**
See **This is the THING.**

Is or Is not THIS.

Ge. 24 : 65. What man i.t. in field ?
43 : 29. i.t. your younger brother?
44 : 5. i.n.t. in wh. my lord drink-h
Ex. 13 : 14. say-g, Wh. i.t.? Ju. 18 : 24.
17 : 3. Wht. i.t. thou bro-t us out
De. 32 : 34. i.n.t. laid up in store
Jos. 10 : 13. i.n.t. in book of Jasher ?
22 : 16. What trespass i.t. ye commit
Ju. 20 : 12. What wickedn-s i.t. am.
Ru. 1 : 19. all city said i.t. Naomi ?
2 : 5. said Boaz, Whose damsel i.t. ?
1 S. 10 : 11. What i.t. unto son of Kish
24 : 16. i.t. thy voice son David ?
29 : 3. i.n.t. David servant of Saul
5. i.n.t. Dav. of whom they sang
2 S. 7 : 19. i.t. the manner of man
16 : 17. i.t. thy kindness to friend?
23 : 17. i.n.t. blood of men th. went
2 K. 18 : 19. Wh. confidence i.t. wh-n
Ezr. 10 : 13. nei. i.t. work of one day
Ne. 13 : 17. Wh. evil thing i.t. ye do
Jb. 4 : 6. i.n.t. thy fear, thy hope
38 : 2. Who i.t. darkeneth counsel ?
Can. 3 : 6. Who i.t. out of wilderness
8 : 5. who i.t. cometh fr. wilderness
Is. 23 : 7. i.t. your joyous city ⌈en
58 : 6. i.n.t. the fast I have chos-
63 : 1. Who i.t. cometh from Edom
Je. 30 : 21. who i.t. engaged heart?
46 : 7. Who i.t. cometh up as flood
Eze. 16 : 20. i.t. of thy whoredoms a
Da. 4 : 30. i.n.t. great Babylon
Zch. 3 : 2. i.n.t. a brand plucked
5 : 5. see what i.t. that goeth forth
Mat. 8 : 27. Wh. manner of man i.t.
th. winds obey, Mk. 4 : 41. Lu. 8 : 25.
12 : 23. i.n.t. the son of David ?
13 : 55. i.n.t. the carpenter's son ?
Mk. 6 : 3. Lu. 4 : 22. Jn. 6 : 42.
21 : 10. All city saying, Who i.t. ?
Mk. 1 : 27. they questioned, What
thing i.t.? wh. new doctrine i.t.?
Lu. 1 : 43. whence i.t. to me that
4 : 36. Wh. a word i.t. he com-doth
5 : 21. Who i.t. speaketh blasphem-s
7 : 49. Who i.t. forgiveth sins ?
8 : 11. Now the parable i.t., The
9 : 9. who i.t. I hear such things ?
20 : 17. What i.t. that is written
Jn. 4 : 29. Come, see, i.n.t. Christ ?
7 : 25. i.n.t. he they seek to kill ?
7 : 36. What manner of saying i.t.
9 : 8. i.n.t. he that sat and begged?
19. i.t. your son was born blind ?
16 : 17. What i.t. he saith, 18.
Ac. 9 : 21. i.n.t. he that destroyed
2 Co. 1 : 12. For our rejoicing i.t.
Ja. 1 : 27. Pure religion undefiled i.

See **Done with THIS.** ⌊t.
See **Thou hast DONE.**

THISTLE, S. ⌈forth

Ge. 3 : 18. thorns, t-s shall it bring
Ju. 9 : † 14. said the trees unto the t.
2 K. 14 : 9. The t. in Lebanon, wild
beast trod down t., 2 Ch. 25 : 18.
Jb. 31 : 40. Let t-s grow inst. of wheat
Ho. 10 : 8. thorn and t. upon altars
Mat. 7 : 16. Do men gather figs of t-s ?

THISTLE down.

Is. 17 : † 13. like t.d. before whirlw.

THITHER. ⌈t.

Ge. 19 : 20. city near, let me escape
22. escape t. until thou be come t.
24 : 6. bring not my son t. again, 8.
29 : 3. t. were all the flocks gathered
39 : 1. Ishm-s brought him down t.
42 : 2. get you t. and buy for us ⌈t.
Ex. 10 : 26. know not until we come
26 : 33. mayest bring in t. the ark
Nu. 35 : 6. slayer may flee t., 11, 15.
De. 4 : 42.-19 : 3, 4. Jos. 20 : 3, 9.
De. 1 : 37. Th. sh. not go in t., 38, 39.
12 : 5. his habitation, t. thou come
6. t. sh. bring burnt offerings, 11.
32 : 52. not go t. unto land, 34 : 4.
Jos. 7 : 3. make not all peo. labour t.
4. went up t. about 3,000 men
Ju. 8 : 27. Israel went t. a whoring
9 : 51. t. fled the men and women
18 : 3. the men turned in t., 17.
19 : 15. turned t. to lodge in Gibeah
21 : 10. cong-n sent t. 12,000 men
1 S. 2 : 14. did to Israelites th. came t.
5 : 8. carried ark of God about t.
9 : 6. let us go t. ; he can shew way
10 : 5. art come t. sh. meet company,
10 : 22. inquired if man come t. ⌊10.
19 : 23. Saul went t. to Naioth in
22 : 1. his brethren went down t. to
30 : 7. Abiathar brought t. ephod to
2 S. 2 : 2. Dav. went up t. and wives
4 : 6. came t. and smote Ish-bosheth
1 K. 6 : 7. ready before it was bro-t t.
19 : 9. Elijah came t. unto a cave
2 K. 2 : 8. waters hither and t., 14,
4 : 8. Elisha turned in t. to eat, 10, 11.
5 : † 25. servant went not hither t.
6 : 6. cast stick in t., iron did swim
9. t. the Syrians are come down
14. king sent t. horses and gr. host
17 : 27. Carry t. one of the priests
2 Ch. 1 : 6. Sol. went t. to altar bef. L.
Ezr. 10 : 6. when Ezra came t. did eat
Ne. 4 : 20. resort ye t. unto us, God
13 : 9. t. brought I vessels of house
Jb. 1 : 21. naked shall I return t.
6 : 20. came t. and were ashamed
Ec. 1 : 7. whence rivers come t. retur.
Is. 7 : 24. with bows sh. men come t.
25. not come t. fear of briers and
32 : 20. send t. feet of ox and ass
55 : 10. rain returneth not t. again
57 : 7. t. wentest thou to offer sacri.
Je. 22 : 11. he not return t. any more
27. to the land, t. they not return
31 : 8. great company sh. return t.
40 : 4. seemeth good for thee t. go
Eze. 1 : 20. t. was their spirit to go
11 : 18. Israel sh. come t. and take
40 : 1. hand of L. brought me t., 3.
47 : 9. these waters shall come t.
Jo. 3 : 11. t. cause thy mighty ones
Mat. 2 : 22. he was afraid to go t.
Mk. 6 : 33. many ran t. out of cities
Lu. 17 : 37. t. will eagles be gathered
21 : 2. widow casting in t. 2 mites
Jn. 7 : 34. I am, t. ye can-t come, 36.
11 : 8. to stone thee, goest t. again?
18 : 2. Jesus ofttimes resorted t.
3. Judas cometh t. with lanterns
Ac. 8 : 30. Philip ran t. to him ⌈ed t.
16 : 13. spake to women wh. resort-
17 : 13. came t. and stirred up peo.

THITHERWARD. ⌈hou.

Ju. 18 : 15. turned t. came to Micah's
Je. 50 : 5. way to Zion, with faces t.
Ro. 15 : 24. bro-t on my way t. by you

THOMAS.

Mat. 10 : 3. T., and Matthew publican, Mk. 3 : 18. Lu. 6 : 15. Ac. 1 : 13.
Jn. 11 : 16. T. said, Let us go die wi.
14 : 5. T. said unto him, Lord we
20 : 24. T. was not with them when
26. disciples within and T. with th.
27. T., Reach hither thy finger ⌈G.
28. T. answered, My Lord and my
29. T., bec. seen me hast believed
21 : 2. were Peter and T. called Did.

THONGS. ⌈t.

Ac. 22 : 25. as they bound him with

THORN. ⌈cedar

2 Ch. 25 : † 18. t. in Lebanon sent to
Jb. 41 : 2. canst bore his jaw with t. ?
Pr. 26 : 9. As a t. goeth into hand of
Is. 55 : 13. Instead of t. the fir tree
Eze. 28 : 24. no more any grieving t.
Ho. 10 : 8. t. shall come up on altars
Mi. 7 : 4. upright is sharper than t.
2 Co. 12 : 7. was given me t. in flesh

THORNS.

Ge. 3 : 18. t. and thistles sh. it bring
Ex. 22 : 6. If fire catch in t. ⌈2 : 3.
Nu. 33 : 55. be t. in your sides, Ju.
Jos. 23 : 13. shall be t. in your eyes
2 S. 23 : 6. sons of Belial sh. be as t.
2 Ch. 33 : 11. took Manasseh am. t.
Jb. 5 : 5. hungry taketh it out of t.
Ps. 58 : 9. Before your pots can feel t.
118 : 12. are quenched as fire of t.
Pr. 15 : 19. slothf. man is hedge of t.
22 : 5. t. snares in way of froward
24 : 31. it was all grown over with t.
Ec. 7 : 6. as crackling of t. und. pot
Can. 2 : 2. At lily am. t. so my love
Is. 7 : 19. rest upon all t. and bushes
33 : 12. as t. cut up they be burned
34 : 13. t. sh. come up in her palaces
Je. 4 : 3. break ground, sow not am. t.
12 : 13. sown wheat, but sh. reap t.
Ho. 2 : 6. I will hedge thy ways wi. t.
9 : 6. t. shall be in their tabernacles
Na. 1 : 10. while they be folden as t.
Mat. 7 : 16. Do men gather grapes of
t., or figs of thistles ? Lu. 6 : 44.
13 : 7. fell among t., and t. sprang,
22. Mk. 4 : 7, 18. Lu. 8 : 7, 14.
27 : 29. when they had platted a
crown of t., Mk. 15 : 17. Jn. 19 :

THORNS and briers. ⌊2, 5.

Ju. 8 : 7. tear your flesh with t.a.b.
16. he took elders of city t.a.b.
Is. 5 : 6. there shall come up b.a.t.
7 : 23. it shall even be for b.a.t.
24. all the land sh. become b.a.t.
25. on all hills nor fear of b.a.t.

Is. 9 : 18 it sh. devour **b.a.t.**, 10 : 17.
27 : 4. who would set **b.a.t.** ag. me
32 : 13. Upon the land come **t.a.b.**
Eze. 2 : 6. tho. **b.a.t.** be not afraid
He. 6 : 8. beareth **t.a.b.** is rejected

THOROUGHLY = THROUGHLY.

Ge. 11 : 3. make brick, burn them **t.**
Ex 21 : 19. cause him to be **t.** healed
2 K. 11 : 18. his images brake they **t.**
Jb. 6 : 2. Oh that my grief **t.** weighed
Ps. 51 : 2. Wash me **t.** from iniquity
Je. 6 : 9. sh. **t.** glean remnant of Isr.
7 : 5. if ye **t.** amend your ways, if ye **t.** execute judgment between
50 : 34. he shall **t.** plead their cause
Eze. 16 : 9. I **t.** washed away thy bl.
Mat. 3 : 12. **t.** purge floor, Lu. 3 : 17.
2 Co 11 : 6. we have been **t.** manifest
2 Ti. 3 : 17. man of God **t.** furnished

THOROW. See THROUGH.

THOSE. [Adj.]

Ge. 19 : 25. **t.**, Nu. 14 : 22, 27. De. 7: 22. 1 S. 17 : 28.-27 : 8.-30 : 20. 2 Ch. 32 : 13, 14 Ezr. 5 : 9. Da. 3 : 22.-6 : 24. Mat. 21 : 40.-22 : 7, 10.-25 : 7, 19. Mk. 12 : 7. Lu. 12 : 37, 38.-14 : 24.-19 : 27. Jn. 8: 10, 29, 31.-10 : 32. Ac. 16 : 3, 35.-20 : 2. He. 10 : 1.-13 : 11.

THOSE days.

Ge. 6 : 4. were giants in the earth in **t.d.**
Ex. 2 : 11. in **t.d.** when Mos. grown
De. 17 : 9. judge that shall be in **t.d.**
19 : 17. stand before the priests and judges in **t.d.**, 26 : 3. Jos. 20 : 6.
Ju. 17 : 6. In **t.d.** there was no king in Israel, 18 : 1.-19 : 1.-21 : 25.
18 : 1. in **t.d.** Danites sought inheri.
20 : 27. ark of cov-t was there in **t.d.**
28. Eleazar stood bef. it in **t.d.**
1 S. 3 : 1. word of L. precious in **t.d.**
28 : 1. in **t.d.** Philis. gath-d armies
2 S. 16 : 23. Ahith. counselled in **t.d.**
1 K. 3 : 2. no house unto L. until **t.d.**
2 K. 10 : 32. In **t.d.** Lord began to cut Israel short
15 : 37. In **t.d.** Lord began to stand up ag. Judah
18 : 4. unto **t.d.** Isr. did burn inc.
20 : 1. In **t.d.** was Hez-h sick unto death, 2 Ch. 32 : 24. Is. 38 : 1.
Ne. 6 : 17. in **t.d.** nobles sent letters
13 : 15. In **t.d.** saw I some treading
23. In **t.d.** saw I Jews th. married
Es. 1 : 2. in **t.d.** Ahaz sat on throne
2 : 21. In **t.d.** Mord. sat in k.'s gate
Je. 3 : 16. in **t.d.** say no more, ark
18. In **t.d.** Judah sh. walk with Isr.
5 : 18. in **t.d.** I not make full end
31 : 29. In **t.d.** say no more, fathers
33. After **t.d.** I will put my law in
33 : 15. In **t.d.** will I cause Branch
16. In **t.d.** shall Judah be saved
50 : 4. In **t.d.** chil of Isr. sh. come
20. In **t.d.** iniq-y of Isr. be sought
Eze. 38 : 17. prophesied in **t.d.** many
Da. 10 : 2. In **t.d.** I, Dan, was mourn.
Jo. 2 : 29. in **t.d.** will I pour out my spirit, Ac. 2 : 18.
3 : 1. in **t.d.** shall I bring captivity of Judah
Hag. 2 : 16. since **t.d.** were when one came to heap of 20 measures
Zch. 8 : 23. In **t.d.** ten men shall take
Mat. 3 : 1. In **t.d.** came John Baptist
24 : 19. woe to them that give suck in **t.d.**, Mk. 13 : 17. Lu. 21 : 23.
24 : 22. except **t.d.** be shortened for elect's sake **t.d.** be, Mk. 13 : 20.
29. aft. tribula-n of **t.d.**, Mk. 13 : 24.
Mk. 1 : 9. in **t.d.** Jesus came fr. Naz.
2 : 20. shall fast in **t.d.**, Lu. 5 : 35.
8 : 1. In **t.d.** mult. hav:ng noth. to eat
13 : 19. in **t.d.** sh. be affliction
Lu. 1 : 24. after **t.d.** Elisabeth conceived
39. Mary arose in **t.d.** and
2 : 1. in **t.d.** a decree from Cesar
4 : 2. in **t.d.** he did eat nothing
Lu. 6 : 12. in **t.d.** he went out to pray
9 : 36. they told no man in **t.d.**
20 : 1. on one of **t.d.** as he taught
Ac. 1 : 15. in **t.d.** Peter stood up
6 : 1. in **t.d.** arose a murmuring
7 : 41. they made a calf in **t.d.**
9 : 37. in **t.d.** she was sick and died
21 : 5. accomplished **t.d.** we depar.
15. aft. **t.d.** we took our carriages
He. 8 : 10. covenant aft. **t.d.**, 10 : 16.
Re. 2 : 13. in **t.d.** Antipas a martyr
9 : 6. in **t.d.** shall men seek death
See MEN, THINGS.

THOSE. [Pronoun.]

Ge. 33 : 5. Esau said, Who **t.** with thee
50 : 3. days of **t.** wh. are embalmed
Le. 11 : 27. goeth upon paws **t.** are
1 K. 8 : 4. vessels, **t.** did priests bring
9 : 21. upon **t.** did Sol. levy tribute
2 K. 6 : 22. thou smite **t.** taken capt.?
Ezr. 5 : 14. **t.** did Cyrus take out of temple of Babylon, 1 : 8.
Jb. 5 : 11. **t.** wh. mourn may be exalted
24 : 19. so doth grave **t.** wh have sin.
Ps. 68 : 6. **t.** wh. are bound wi. chains
69 : 26. grief of **t.** th. hast wounded
Ec. 7 : 28. wom. am. all **t.** not found
Is. 35 : 8. a highway it shall be for **t.**
64 : 5. in **t.** is continuance; we sh.
Je. 27 : 11 **t.** will I let remain in land
Eze. 1 : 21. When **t.** went these went; when **t.** stood these stood; wh. **t.**
Da. 11 : 4. kingd. for others besides **t.**
Zch. 13 : 6. **t.** with wh. I was wounded
Mat. 4 : 24. **t.** with devils, **t.** lunatic
Mk. 7 : 15. **t.** are they that defile man
Lu. 8 : 12. **t.** by way side are they th.
13 : 4. Or **t.** 18 upon wh. tower fell
14 : 7. parable to **t.** wh. were hidden
Jn. 17 : 11. keep thro. own name **t.**
Ac. 17 : 11. These more noble than **t.**
26 : 22. **t.** Moses did say sho. come
2 Cor. 7 : 6. comforteth **t.** cast down
Ph. 3 : 7. things gain **t.** I counted loss
He 5 : 14. **t.** who have senses exercised
6 : 4. impossible for **t.** enlightened

THOSE that.

Nu. 3 : 38. But **t.t.** encamp bef. tabernacle
46. **t.t.** are to be redeemed, 18 : 16.
1 S. 28 : 3. **t.t.** had familiar spirits
30 : 9. Besor, where **t.t.** were left
1 K. 2 : 7. be of **t.t.** eat at thy table
Ezr. 2 : 62. am. **t.t** were reckoned by
9 : 4. transg-n of **t.t.** had been carried away, 10 : 8. Ne. 7 : 6.
10 : 3. **t.t.** tremble at commandm-t of G.
Ne. 5 : 17. **t.t.** came fr. the heathen
8 : 3. read bef. **t.t.** could underst-d
10 : 1. **t.t.** sealed were Nehemiah
Es. 3 : 9. **t.t.** have charge of business
9 : 5. what they wou. to **t.t.** hated
11. of **t.t.** were slain in Shushan
Jb. 5 : 11. To set on high **t.t.** be low
21 : 22. he judgeth **t.t.** are high
24 : 13. of **t.t.** rebel ag. the light
27 : 15. **t.t.** remain of him be buried
Ps. 17 : 7. save from **t.t.** rise ag. them
18 : 48. liftest me above **t.t.** rise ag.
21 : 8. hand sh. find **t.t.** hate thee
37 : 9. **t.t.** wait upon the L. inherit
50 : 5. **t.t.** have made covenant wi.
61 : 5. heritage of **t.t.** fear thy name
63 : 9. **t.t.** seek my soul to destroy
68 : 11. company of **t.t.** published it
69 : 6. not **t.t.** seek thee be confou.
74 : 23. tumult of **t.t.** rise ag. thee
79 : 11. **t.t.** are appointed to die
92 : 13. **t.t.** be planted in house of L.
102 : 20. to loose **t.t.** are appointed
103 : 18. to **t.t.** rememb. his com-ts
109 : 31. from **t.t.** condemn his soul
119 : 79. Let **t.t.** fear thee turn unto me, **t.t.** ha. known testimon.
132. as unto **t.t.** love thy name
123 : 4. scorning of **t.t.** are at ease
125 : 4. do good unto **t.t.** be good
139 : 21. grieved wi. **t.t.** rise ag. thee
Ps. 140 : 9. head of **t.t.** compass me
143 : 3. as **t.t.** have been long dead
147 : 11. in **t.t.** hope in his mercy
Pr. 1 : 12. as **t.t.** go down into pit
8 : 17. **t.t.** seek me early shall find
21. cause **t.t.** love me to inherit
22 : 23. spoil soul of **t.t.** spoiled th.
24 : 11. **t.t.** are ready to be slain
31 : 6. wine to **t.t.** be of heavy heart
Ec. 1 : 11. nei. remembr. with **t.t.** come
8 : 8. nei. wickedn. deliv. **t.t.** are giv.
12 : 3. **t.t.** look out of the windows
Can. 7 : 9. lips of **t.t.** are asleep to
8 : 12. **t.t.** keep the fruit th-f 200
Is. 14 : 19. raiment of **t.t.** are slain
56 : 8. **t.t.** are gathered unto him
64 : 5. **t.t.** remember thee in thy
66 : 19. send **t.t.** escape unto nations
Je. 8 : 16. devoured city and **t.t.** dw.
21 : 7. hand of **t.t.** seek their life
39 : 9. captive **t.t.** fell away, 52 : 15.
La. 2 : 22. **t.t.** I have swaddled and
3 : 62. lips of **t.t.** rose against me
Eze. 22 : 5. **t.t.** be near, **t.t.** be far
34 : 27. **t.t.** served thems. of them
Da. 4 : 37. **t.t.** walk in pride he is able
Jo. 2 : 16. gather chil. and **t.t.** suck
Ob. 14. nei. cut off **t.t.** did escape (2)
Zph. 1 : 6. **t.t.** have not sought Lord
Mat. 4 : 24. and **t.t.** had the palsy
15 : 30. with them **t.t.** were lame
16 : 23. not of God, but **t.t.** be of
Mk. 6 : 55. carry in beds **t.t.** were sick
10 : 13. rebuked **t.t.** brought them
Lu. 6 : 32. sinners love **t.t.** love them
7 : 28. Among **t.t.** are born of wom.
Jn. 2 : 14. in temple **t.t.** sold oxen
17 : 12. **t.t.** thou gavest I have kept
Ac. 3 : 24. fr. Samuel and **t.t.** follow
1 Co. 14 : 23. come in **t.t.** are unlearn.
1 Ti. 4 : 10. Saviour of **t.t.** believe
2 Ti. 3 : 3 despisers of **t.t.** are good
2 Pe. 2 : 6. unto **t.t.** sho. live ungodly
18. allure **t.t.** were clean escaped
See **All those THAT.**
See NUMBERED.

THOU.

Ge. 2 : 16. Of every tree **t.** mayest eat
3 : 11. Hast **t.** eaten of the tree (2)
12. woman **t.** gavest to be with me
17. Bec. **t.** hearkened unto wife
6 : 18. **t.** sh. come into ark, **t.** and
17 : 9. **t.** shalt keep my covenant (2)
20 : 7. if not restore, **t.** shalt surely die, **t.** and all thine, 1 S. 22 : 16.
10. What sawest **t.** that **t.** hast
24 : 6. Beware **t.** bring not my son
31. Come in **t.** blessed of the Lord
40 : 13. **t.** shalt deliver Pha.'s cup
41 : 40. in throne, I greater than **t.**
43 : 8. that we may live, we and **t.**
45 : 10. **t.** shalt be near unto me, **t.**
Ex. 3 : 18. **t.** sh. come unto k. of Eg.
18 : 18. **t.** wilt surely wear away (3)
19 : 24. **t.** shalt come up, **t.** and Aa.
Le. 10 : 9. Do not drink wine, **t.** nor
14. **t.**, thy sons and thy dau-s
Nu. 16 : 11. **t.** and company are ag. L.
16. Be **t.** bef. Lord, **t.**, they, Aa., 17.
18 : 1. **t.** and thy sons wi. thee, 2, 7.
De. 5 : 14. servant rest as well as **t.**
7 : 1. nations mightier than **t.**, 20 : 1.
13 : 6. gods **t.** hast not known, 28 : 64.
14 : 26. **t.** and thine household, 15: 20.-16 : 11, 14.-26 : 11.
28 : 36. nation **t.** nor thy fa.'s have known
30 : 19 th. **t.** and thy seed may live
1 S. 15 : 28. neighbour better than **t.**
20 : 2. God forbid; **t.** shalt not die
25 : 33. Blessed be **t.** that kept me
2 S. 19 : 29. **t.** and Ziba divide land
1 K. 8 : 30. **t.** knowest hearts of all (3)
18 : 18. **t.** and fa.'s hou. trouble Isr.
20 : 14. who order battle? he said **t.**
2 K. 9 : 25. I and **t.** rode after Ahab
14 : 10. why meddle that **t.** shouldest fall, **t.** and Jud., 2 Ch. 25 : 19.

Ne. 6 : 6. t. and Jews think to rebel
Es.4 :14.t.and fa.'s ho. be destroyed
Jb. 35 : 5. clouds are higher than t.
Ps. 55 : 13. it was t. a man, mine eq.
92 : 4. For t. L. hast made me glad
109 : 27. may know t., L.hast done
28. Let them curse, but bless t.⌊it
119 : 98.t. hast made me wiser than
123 : 1. O t. that dwellest in heav-s
132 : 8. Arise into thy rest, t. and
Cant. 1 :7.O t. whom my soul loveth
Is. 7 :3.unto Isai., Go,meet Ahaz, t.
23 : 2. t.wh.merchants replenished
65 : 5. not near, I am holier than t.
Je. 17 : 4.t. sh. continue fr. heritage
20 :6.t.shalt die, t. and thy friends
27 : 13. why will ye die, t. and peo.
La. 5 : 19. t., O L., remainest for ev.
Eze. 3 : 25. t., O son of man, behold
7 : 7. O t. that dwellest in land
16 : 52. are more righteous than t.
Da. 2 :31. t., O king, 3 :10.-5 :18, 23.
5 :22. t. hast not humbled thine(2)
6 : 16. God wh. t. servest will deliv.
Mi. 4 :8. t., O tower of flock, to thee
Mat. 2 : 6. t. Bethlehem in la. of Ju.
6 : 3. when t. doest alms let not
6. t. when t. prayest enter closet
17. t. when t. fastest, anoint head
17 : 25. What thinkest t., Simon?
18 : 33. Sho. not t. have compas-n
19 :21.If t. be perfect sell th. t.hast
26 : 39. not as I will, but as t. wilt
69. t. also wast wi.Jes., Mk.14:67.
Lu. 10 : 15. t. Capernaum exalted to
14 :8. lest more honourable than t.
14. t. sh. be blessed, recompensed
16 : 5. said, How much owest t.? 7.
19 :42.If t. hadst known,in thy day
Jn. 1 : 25. if t. be not Ch. nor Elias
4 : 9. t., being a Jew, askest drink
8 : 5. such be stoned, Wh. sayest t.
13. t. bearest record of thyself
9 : 37. t. hast seen him, he talketh
17 : 23.I in them and t. in me, that
Ac. 1 :24.t., L., who knowest hearts
11 : 14.t. and thy house sh. be saved
13 : 10. t. child of the devil, t. enemy, wilt t. not cease to pervert
17 : 19. new doctr-e wh-f t. speakest
24 : 11. Bec. t. mayest understand
26 : 29. I would not only t., but all
Ro. 2 : 21. t.which teachest another
1 Ti. 1 : 18.t.mightest war good war-
4 : 12. be t. an example of ⌊fare
6 : 11. t., O man of God, flee these
2 Ti. 1 : 8.Be not t. ashamed of testi.
18. unto me at Eph., t. knowest
2 : 1. t., my son, be strong in grace
Phm. 12. t. receive him th. is mine
He. 1 : 10. t., Lord,hast laid founda.

THOU alone.

Ex. 18 :14.Why sittest t.a. and peo.
18. t. art not able to perform it a.
Nu. 11 : 17. t. bear it not thyself a.
1 S. 21 : 1. Why art t.a., no man wi.
2 K. 19 : 15.t. art the God, even t.a.
Ne. 9 : 6.-Ps. 86 : 10. Is. 37 : 16.
Pr. 9 : 12. if scornest, t.a. sh. bear it

Art THOU, or THOU art.

Ge. 3 : 9. said to Adam, Where a.t.?
14.Bec. hast done this t.a.cursed
19.dust t.a.,unto dust sh. t. retu.
4 : 6. unto Cain, Why a.t. wroth?
12 : 11. I know t.a. a fair woman
13. say, I pray, t.a. my sister
13 :14. look fr. the place where t.a.
16 :11 said unto Hagar,t.a.wi.child
17 : 8.land wh-n t.a.stranger,28:4.
20 : 3. Behold t.a. but a dead man
23 : 6. t.a. a mighty prince am. us
24 : 23. Whose daughter a.t.? 47.
60. t.a. our sister, be t. mother
26 : 16. Isaac, Go, t.a. mightier th.
29. t.a. blessed of the Lord ⌊we
27 : 18. Here am I; who a.t., 32.
24. said, a.t. my son Esau? I am

Ge. 29 : 14. Surely t.a. my bone
15.Bec.t.a. my bro.serve for nou.
32 : 17. Whose a.t.? whither goest
39 : 9. but thee, bec. t.a. his wife
41 : 39. Joseph, none so wise as t.a.
44 : 18. for t.a. even as Pharaoh
45 : 19. Now t.a. com-ded, this do
46 : 30. let me die bec. t.a. yet alive
47 :8.Pha. unto Jac.,How old a.t.?
49 : 3. Reuben, t.a. my firstborn
8. t.a. he wh. brethren sh. praise
Ex. 4 : 26. A bloody husband t.a.
34 : 10. people among whom t.a.
De. 2 : 18. t.a. to pass thro. Ar this
7 :6.t.a. a holy people unto G.⌊day
33 : 29. Happy a.t., O Israel; who
Jos. 5 : 13. a.t. for us or adversaries
Ju.8 :18.ans-d, As t.a.,so were they
11 : 2. t.a. son of a strange woman
35. t.a.one of them th.trouble me
12 : 5.a.t. an Ephraimite? said⌈an
13 : 11.a.t.man spakest unto wom-
Ru. 2 : 9. when t.a. athirst, drink
1 S. 17 :28.t.a. come th. t. see battle
58. Whose son a.t. young man?
19 : 3. I stand in field where t.a.
24 : 17. t.a. more righteous than I
28 : 12. why deceived me? t.a. Saul
30 : 13.belongest t.? Whence a.t.?
2 S. 1 : 8. Who a.t.? I Amalekite,
2 : 20.Abner said,a.t. Asahel?⌊13.
12 : 7. Nathan said, t.a. the man
13 : 4.Why a.t. lean fr. day to day?
15 : 2. Abs. said, Of what city a.t.?
19.t.a. a stranger and exile⌈seer?
27. k. said unto Zadok, a.t. not a
16 :21.hear t.a. abhorred of thy fa.
20 : 9. a.t. in health, my brother?
17. the woman said, a.t. Joab?
1 K.13 :14. a.t.man of God fr. Jud.?
18. I am a prophet also as t.a.
18 : 7. a.t. that my lord Elijah?
17. a.t. he that troubleth Israel?
22 : 4. I am as t.a., my people as thy people, 2 K. 3 : 7. 2 Ch. 18:3.
2K.19 :19.th.all kingdoms may know t.a.Lord G., even t., Is 37:20.
2 Ch. 20 : 7. a. not t. our God who
25 : 16. a.t. made of king's counsel
Ne. 2 : 2. Why sad, t.a. not sick?
9 : 7. t.a. the God who didst choose
17. t.a. God ready to pardon
Es. 4 : 14. when t.a. come to kingd.
Jb.35 :8.wickedn.hurt a man as t.a.
Ps.2 :7. t.a.my Son; this day have I begotten,Ac. 13:33. He.1:5.-5:5.
23 : 4. fear no evil, t.a. wi. me⌈er's
71 :6.a.t. he took me out of moth-
76 : 7.t., even t., a. to be feared (2)
83 : 18. t. Jehovah a. the Most Hi.
97 . 9. t., Lord, a. high above the earth; t.a. exalted ab. all gods
102 : 27. t.a. same,thy yrs. no end
118 : 28. t.a. my God, I will praise
119 : 12. Blessed a.t. O Lord, teach
114. t.a. my hiding place and⌈th.
139 : 8. If I ascend into heaven t.a.
Is. 14 : 10. a.t. become weak as we?
a.t. become like unto us? ⌈sen
41 :9.t.a. my servant; I have cho-
44 : 17. deliver me, for t.a my God
21. Rememb..O Isr.,t.a. my serv.
45 : 15. a.t.a God th. hidest thyself
51 : 9. a.t. not it that hath cut Ra.
10. a.t. not it wh. hath dried sea?
12. who a.t. that t. afraid of man
63 : 16. t. O Lord,a.our Fa.(2)⌈God
Je. 14 : 22. a. not t. he, O Lord, our
Eze. 28 :14.t.a.the anointed cherub
31 : 18. To whom a.t. like in glory
38 : 17. a.t. he of wh. I have spok.
Da. 2 : 37. t. O king a. a k. of kings
38. t.a. this head of gold
4 : 18. but t.a. able; for the spirit
22. t., O king, a. become strong
5 : 13. a.t. that Daniel of captivity
Jon. 1 :8.whence t.? of wh.peo.a.t.?

Mi. 2 : 7. O t. that a. named Jacob
Ha. 1 : 12. a. not t. from everlasting
Zch. 4 :7.Who a.t.,O gr. mountain?
Mat. 8 : 29. a.t. come to torment us before time, ⌈Lu. 7 : 19, 20.
11 : 3. a.t.he that should come, or,
16 : 16. t.a. the Christ, the Son of the living God, Mk. 8 : 29. Lu. 4:41.-22:67, 70. Jn.6 :69.-11:27.
18. t.a. Peter, upon this rock ⌈58.
26 :73.Surely t.a.one of th.,Lu.22 :
27 : 11. a. t.k.of the Jews? Mk. 15 : 2. Lu. 23 : 3. Jn. 18 : 33. ⌈3 :22.
Mk. 1 : 11. t.a. my beloved Son, Lu.
24.a.t.come to destroy us? I know who t.a., the Ho. One,Lu. 4:34.
3 : 11. unclean spirits cried, t.a. the Son of God ⌈Blessed?
14 : 61. a.t. the Christ, Son of the
Lu. 1 : 28. t. that a. highly favoured
42. said, Blessed a.t. am. women
10 : 41.t.a.careful ab. many things
12 : 58. as t.a. in the way give dil-
14 :10.when t.a. bidden,sit⌊igence
15 : 31. Son, t.a. ever with me, all
16 : 25. but now t.a. tormented
22 : 32. when t.a. converted stren.
23 : 40. t.a. in same condemnation
24 : 18. a.t. only a stranger in Jer.
Jn. 1 : 19. sent priests to ask, Who a.t.? 22.-8 : 25.-21 : 12. ⌈et?
21. a.t. Elias? a.t. that Proph-
42. t.a. Simon, t. sh. be Cephas
49. t.a. Son of God, t.a. king of
3 : 2. we know t.a. teacher fr.God
10. a.t. a master of Israel and
4 : 12 a.t. greater than our fa.Jac.
19. Sir, I perceive t.a. a prophet
7 : 52. a.t. also of Galilee? Search
8 : 48.t.a. a Samaritan,hast a devil
53. a.t. greater than our fa. Abr.
57. t.a. not yet fifty years old
9 : 28. t.a. his disciple, we are Mos.
11 :27. she saith, I believe t.a. Ch.
18 : 17.a. not t. one of disciples,25.
37. Pilate said, a.t. a king then?
19 : 9. Whence a.t.? Jesus gave no
12.let this man go,t.a.not Cesar's
Ac. 4 : 24. Lord, t.a. God wh. made
8 : 23. t.a. in the gall of bitterness
9 : 5. Saul said, Who a.t., Lord,
22 : 8.-26 : 15. ⌈madest
21 : 38. a. no. t. that Egyptian wh.
22 : 27. Tell me, a.t. a Roman? ⌈r.
26 : 24. Paul, t. a. beside thyself,
Ro. 2 : 17. Behold, t.a. called a Jew
19. that t.a. a guide of the blind
3 : 4. overcome when t.a. judged
9 :20. O man, who a.t. that repliest
14 :4. Who a.t. th. judgest another
He. 1 : 12. they be changed, t.a. same
5 : 6. t.a. a priest forever, 7:17,21.
Ja. 2 : 11 if t. kill t.a. a trangressor
4 : 11. t.a. not a doer of law,but ju.
12. who a.t. th. judgest another?
Re. 3 : 17. bec. t.a. lukewarm I will
4 : 11. t.a. worthy, O Lord to recei.
5 : 9. t.a. worthy to take the book
15 : 4. Who not fear thee? t. only a. holy ⌈art and wast
16 : 5 t.a. righteous, O Lord, which

See Hast thou DONE.
See Thou hast DONE.

THOUGH. ⌈be gone

Ge. 31 : 30. t. thou wouldest needs
33 : 10. as t. I had seen face of God
40 : 10. the vine was as t. it budded
Le. 5 : 17. t. he wist not,is he guilty
11 : 7. swine, t. he divide hoof
25 : 35.sh. relieve him t. a stranger
De. 29 : 19. t. I walk in imagination
Jos. 17 : 18. shall drive out Canaanites,t.have iron chariots,t.stro.
Ju. 13 : 16. t. detain me, I not eat
15 : 3. t. I do them a displeasure
7. t. ye have done this, yet will I
Ru. 2 : 13. t. not like handmaidens

1 S.14:39.t.it be in Jonaathan,he die
20 : 20. arrows, as t. I shot at mark
21 : 5. t. it were sanctified this day
2 S. 1 : 21. as t.he not been anointed
3 : 39. I weak t. anointed king ⌈els
18 : 12. t.I receive a thousand shek-
1 K.2:28.t.Joab turned not aft. Abs.
2 Ch. 30 : 19. t. he be not cleansed
Ne 1 : 9. t. were of you cast out to
6 : 1. t. I had not set up doors of
Jb. 8 : 7. t. thy beginning small,yet
9 : 15 t.righteous, I would not ans.
21. t. perfect, yet I would despise
10 : 19. I as t. I had not been ⌊life
11 : 12. t. born like wild ass's colt
13 : 15.t. he slay me yet will I trust
14 : 8. t. the root wax old in earth
16 : 6. t. I speak, yet grief not assuaged, t. forbear what am I
19 : 17.t.I entreated for chil.'s sake
26.t. after my skin worms destroy
27. t. my reins be consumed
20 : 6. t. his excellency mount to
12.t.wickedness sweet in his mou.
t. he hide it under his tongue
13. t. he spare it, forsake it not
24 : 23. t. given him to be in safety
27 : 8. hypocrite, t. he hath gained
16. t. he heap up silver as dust
30 : 24. t. they cry in his destruc-n
39 : 16. ag.young ones as t.not hers
Ps. 23 : 4. t. I walk thro. the valley
27 : 3. t. a host encamp against me
35 :14.I behaved as t. he my broth.
37 : 24. t. he fall not be utterly cast
44 : 19. t. thou hast sore broken us
46 : 2. not fear, t. earth be removed
3.t.the waters roar, t. mts. shake
49 : 18. t. while he lived he blessed
68 : 13. t. ye have lain am.the pots
78 :23.t.he had com-ded the clouds
99 : 8. forgavest t.tookest venge-ce
138 : 6. t. Lord be high, unto low-
7.t. I walk in midst of trouble ⌊ly
Pr. 6 : 35.nei. content, t. many gifts
11 : 21. t. hand join in hand, 16 : 5.
27 :22.t. thou bray a fool in mortar
28 : 6.than he th. is perverse t.rich
29 :19.t. serv.underst-d,he not ans.
Ec. 6 : 6. t. he live 1,000 years twice
8 : 12. t. a sinner do evil 100 times
17. t. man labour to seek it out, t.
wise man think to know it, yet
Is. 1 : 18. t. your sins be as scarlet
10 : 22. t. Isr. be as sand of the sea
12 : 1. t. thou wast angry with me
30 : 20. t. L. give bread of adversity
35 : 8. wayfaring men, t. fools, not
45 : 4. surnamed thee, t. not,5.⌊err
49:5. t. Isr. be not gath-d yet sh. I
63 :16. ourFa.,t.Abr.ignorant of us
Je. 2 : 22. t. thou wash thee wi.nitre
4 :30.t.clothest thys.with crimson,
t. thou deckest thee with gold,
t.rentest thy face with painting
5 : 2. t. they say, The Lord liveth
22. waves toss, t. they roar, yet
11 : 11.t.they cry, I will not heark.
12 : 6.believe not, t. they speak fair
14 :7. t. our iniquities testify ag. us
15 : 1.t. Moses and Sam-l stood bef.
22 : 24. t. Coniah were the signet
30 : 11.t.I make full end of nations
32 : 5. t. ye fight with Chaldeans
33. t. I taught them, rising early
46 :23.forest, t.it can-t be searched
51 : 5. t. land was filled with sin
53. t. Babylon mount to heaven,
t.she fortify the height⌈passion
La. 3 : 32. t. he cause grief, yet com-
Eze. 2 : 6. be not afraid t. thorns be
with thee, t. they be, 3:9.-12:3.
8 : 18. t. they cry, I will not hear
12 : 13. sh. not see it t. he die there
14 : 14. t. Noah, Daniel, Job were
in it, 16, 18, 20. ⌈found
26 : 21. t.thou sought for, never be

Eze. 28 : 2.t. th. set heart as heart of
32 : 25. t. terror in land, 26, 27. ⌊G.
Da. 5 : 22. not humbled t. knewest
9 : 9. forgiveness t. we rebelled ag.
Ho. 4 : 15. t. Israel play the harlot
5 : 2.t. I have been rebuker of them
7 : 13.t.I redeemed them, yet spok.
15. t. I strengthened their arms
8 : 10. t. have lived among nations
9 : 12. t. bri. up chil., yet I bereave
16. t. bring forth, I slay fruit of
11 :7.t.called them to Most Hi.⌊wo.
13 : 15. t. fruitful am. his brethren
Am. 5 :22. t. ye offer burnt offerings
9 : 2. t. they dig into hell, t. they
climb to heaven, thence will I
3. t. they hide in the top of Carmel; t.they be hid in bottom of
4. t. they go into captivity before
Ob. 4. t. exalt thyself as the eagle;
t.thou set thy nest am. the stars
16.shall be as t.they had not been
Mi. 5 :2.t. thou little am. thousands
Na. 1 : 12.t.they be quiet, and many
Ha. 1 : 5. ye not believe, t. told you
2 : 3. t. it tarry, wait for it, it will
Zch. 9 : 2. Zidon, t. it be very wise
10 : 6. be as t. I had not cast th. off
12 : 3. t. all people be gathe-d ag. it
Mat. 26 : 33.t.all men sh. be offended
35. t. I die with thee,yet not deny
60. t. false witn-es, yet found none
Lu. 9 : 53. face as t. go to Jerusalem
11 : 8. t. he will not rise bec. friend
16 : 31. neither be persuaded t. one
rose from dead. ⌈man
18 : 4. t. I fear not God nor regard
7.avenge his elect, t. he bear long
24 :28.made as t. he wou.have gone
Jn. 4 : 2. t. Jesus hims. baptized not
8 : 6. wrote on the ground, as t. he
14. t. I bear record of myself yet
10 : 38. t. ye believe not me, believe
11 : 25. t. he were dead, yet sh. live
12 :37.t.he had done so many mira.
Ac. 3 : 12. as t. we made him walk
13 : 28.t. found no cause of death
41. not believe, t. a man declare it
17 : 25. as t. he needed anything
27. t. he be not far from every one
23 : 15. as t. ye would inquire, 20.
27 : 30. as t. they would have cast
28 : 4. t. he hath escaped sea ⌈toms
17. t.I committed nothing ag.cus-
Ro. 4 : 11. believe,t. not circumcised
17. thi-s wh. be not as t. they were
7 : 3. no adult-s t. married to ano.
9 : 6. Not as t. word taken none eff.
27. t. chil. of Isr. be as sand of sea
1Co.4:15.t.ye have10,000instructors
18. as t. I would not come to you
5 : 3. judged as t. present conc.him
7 : 29. have wives be as t. had none
30. that weep as t. wept not; that
rejoice as t. rejoiced not; that
buy as t. they possessed not
8 : 5. t. there be th. are called gods
9 : 16. t. I preach gospel, I noth.to
19. t. I be free from all men⌊glory
13 : 1. t. I speak with the tongues
of angels | 2 (2), 3(2). ⌈perish
2 Co. 4 : 16. but t. our outward man
5 : 16. t. we have known Christ aft.
20.as t.God did beseech you by us
7 :8. t. I made you sorry with a letter, t. I did repent (8) ⌈for his
12.t. I wrote unto you, I did it not
8 : 9.t.he was rich, he became poor
10 : 3.t. walk in flesh we do not war
8. t. I sho. boast of our authority
14. as t. we reached not unto you
11 : 6. t. I be rude in speech
21. cone-g reproach, as t. we had
12 : 6. t. desire to glory, I not a fool
11. in noth. behind apostles, t. I
15. t. more I love you less I be lo.
13 : 4. t. crucified thro. weakness

2 Co. 13 : 7. t. we be as reprobates
Ga. 1 :8.t. we or angel preach anoth.
3 :15. t. it be but a man's covenant
4 : 1. heir differeth noth. t. lord of
Ph. 3 : 4. t. I might have confidence
12. as t. I had attained or were
Col. 2 : 5. t. I be absent in the flesh
20. as t. living, are ye subject to
Phm. 8. t. I might be bold in Christ
He. 5 :8.t. he were a son, yet learned
6 : 9.better things, t. we thus speak
7 : 5.t.they come out of loins of Ab.
12 : 17. t. he sought it with tears.
Ja. 2 : 14. t. a man say he hath faith
3 : 4. ships, t. so great, are turned
1 Pe.1 :6.t.now for season in heavin.
8. t. ye see him not, ye rejoice
4 : 12.as t. some strange thing hap.
2 Pe. 1 :12.put in remembrance,t.ye
2 Jn. 5.not as t.I wrote a new com-t
Jude 5. in remembrance, t. ye once

THOUGHT.

De. 15 :9.not a t.in thy wicked heart
1 S. 9 :5. lest my father take t. for us
Jb. 12 :5.despised in t.of him at ease
42 : 2. no t. be withholden fr. thee
Ps. 49 :11.their t.is,their houses sh.
64 : 6. inward t. of them is deep
139 : 2. understandest my t.afar off
Pr. 24 : 9.The t. of foolishness is sin
Ec. 10 :20. Curse not the k. in thy t.
Is. 26 : † 3.whose t. is stayed on thee
Eze. 38 : 10. thou sh. think an evil t.
Am. 4 : 13. unto man what is his t.
Mat. 6 :25.I say, Take no t. for your
life, 31. Lu. 12 : 22.
27. Which of you by taking t. can
add 1 cub., Lu.12:25.⌈Lu. 12:26.
28. why take ye t. for raiment,
34.Take th-f. no t.for the morrow,
for morrow shall take t. for its.
10 : 19. take no t. how or what ye
shall speak, Mk. 13:11. Lu.12:11.
Ac. 8 : 22. if the t. may be forgiven
2 Co. 10 :5. into captivity every t. to

THOUGHTS. ⌊Christ

Ge. 6 : 5. imagination of t. was evil
Ju. 5 : 15. For Reuben were great t.
1 K. 18 : † 21. How long halt betw.
1 Ch. 28 : 9.Lord underst-eth t. ⌊2 t.
29 : 18. keep this in imagina-n of t.
Jb. 4 : 13.In t. from visions of night
17 : † 7. all my t. are as a shadow
11. are broken off, even my t.
20 :2. thf. my t. cause me to answer
21 : 27. I know your t. and devices
Ps. 10 : 4. God is not in all his t.
33 : 11. t. of his heart to all genera-s
40 :5. thy t. cannot be reckoned up
56 : 5. all their t. are against me
73 : † 7. they pass the t. of heart
92 : 5. and thy t. are very deep
94 : 11. Lord knoweth the t. of man
19. in multitude of my t. within
119 :113.I hate vain t., but thy law
139 : 17, How precious are thy t.
23. O God, try me know my t.⌈ish
146 : 4. in that very day his t. per-
Pr. 12 : 5. t. of righteous are right
15 : 26.t.of wicked are abomination
16 : 3. thy t. shall be established
21 : 5. The t. of diligent tend to ⌈t.
Is. 55 : 7. let unrighteous forsake his
8. my t. are not your t.,saith Lord
9. so are my t.higher than your t.
59 :7.evil, their t. are t. of iniquity
65 : 2. people walketh after own t.
66 : 18. I know their works and t.
Je. 4 : 14. How long vain t. in thee?
6 : 19. evil, even fruit of their t.
23 :20. till performed t.of his heart
29 : 11.I know the t.I think toward
you, saith the Lord, t. of peace
Da. 2 :29. thy t.came into thy mind
30. mightest know t. of thy heart
4 : 5. Neb-r's t. upon bed troubled
19. Daniel astonied, t. troubled

Da. 5 :6. Belshazzar's t. troubled him
10. queen said, let not t. trouble
11 :†24. think his t. ag. strong holds
Mi. 4 : 12. they know not t. of Lord
Mat. 9 :4. And Jesus, knowing their
t., said, 12 : 25. Lu. 5 : 22.-6 :8.
-9 : 47.-11 : 17. [t., Mk. 7 : 21.
15 : 19. out of the heart proceed evil
Lu. 2 : 35. t. of hearts be revealed
24 : 38. why t. arise in your hearts?
Ro. 2 : 15. t. accusing, or excusing
14 : † 1. not to judge his doubtful t.
1 Co. 3 : 20. L knoweth t. of wise
He. 4 :12. word of G. a discerner of t.
Ja. 2 : 4. ye are become judges of evil

THOUGHT. [Verb.] ⌊t.
Ge. 20 . 11. I t. fear of G. not in this
38 : 15. Judah t. her to be a harlot
48 : 11. I had not t. to see thy face
50 : 20. as for you, ye t. evil ag. me
Ex. 32 : 14. L. repented of evil he t.
Nu. 24 : 11. I t. to promote thee
33 : 56. do unto you as I t. unto th.
De. 19 :19. sh. ye do unto him as ye t.
Ju. 15 : 2. I t. thou hadst hated her
20 : 5. of Gibeah t. to have slain me
Ru. 4 : 4. I t. to advertise thee [en
1 S. 1 :13. Eli t. she had been drunk-
18 : 25. Saul t. to make David fall
20 :26. Saul t., Something befallen
2 S. 4 :10. t. I would have given rew.
13 :2. Amnon t. it hard to do to her
14 :13. t. such a thing ag. peo. of G.
19 : 18. to do what king t. good[Da.
21 : 16. Ishbi-benob t. to have slain
2 K. 5 : 11. I t., He will come to me
2 Ch. 11 . 22. Rehob. t. to make Abi.
32 : 1. Sennacherib t. to win th.⌊k.
Ne. 6 : 2. they t. to do me mischief
Es. 3 : 6. he t. scorn to lay hands on
6 : 6. Haman t. in heart ⌊Mordecai
Ps. 48 : 9. We have t. of thy lovingk.
73 :16. When I t. to know this, pain-
119 : 59. I t. on my ways and ⌊ful
Pr. 30 : 32. if thou hast t. evil, lay
Is. 14 : 24. as I have t. so sh. it come
Je. 18 : 8. I will repent of evil I t.
Da. 4 : 2. I t. it good to shew signs
6 : 3. king t. to set him over realm
Jon. 1 : † 4. ship was t. to be broken
Zch. 1 : 6. as Lord of hosts t. to do
8 : 14. As I t. to punish you ⌊unto
15. I have t. to do well unto Jerus.
Mal. 3 :16. they that t. upon his name
Mat 1 : 20. while he t. on these thi-s
Mk. 14 :72. when he t. th-on he wept
Lu. 7 : 7. nei. t. I myself worthy to
12 : 17. he t., What sh. I do?⌊come
19 : 11. t. kingdom of G. sho. appear
Jn. 11 : 13. t. he had spoken of rest
Ac. 8 : 20. t. gift of G. be purchased
10 : 19. While Peter t. on the vision
12 : 9. true; but t. he saw a vision
15 :38. Paul t. not good to take him
26 :8. Why be t. a thing incredible?
9. I t. I ought to do thi-s contrary
1 Co. 13: 11. When a child, I t. as child
2 Co. 9 : 5. I t. it necessary to exhort
Ph. 2 : 6. t. it not robbery to be equal
1 Th. 3 : 1. we t. it good to be left at
He. 10 : 29. sorer punishment be t.

THOUGHTEST. ⌊worthy
Ps. 50 : 21. thou t. I was as thyself

THOUSAND. [pieces
Ge. 20 : 16 given thy brother a t.
Nu. 31 : 4. Of ev. tribe a t. to war, 5, 6.
35 : 4. suburbs of cities t. cubits
De. 1 : 11. L. make you t. times more
7 :9. G. keepeth coven-t to t. genera.
32 : 30. How should one chase a t.
and two, Jos. 23 : 10. [Manasseh
Ju. 6 : † 15. my t. is the meanest in
9 :49. men of Shechem died, ab. a t.
15 : 15. Samson slew a t. men, 16.
20 : 10. a hundred of a t., a t. out of
1 S. 13 : 2. a t. were with Jonathan
17 : 18. ten cheeses unto capt. of t.
1 S. 18 : 13. S. made David capt. over
25 : 2. Nabal had a t. goats ⌊a t.
2 S. 8 :4. Da. took t. chariots, 1 Ch. 18:
10 : 6. of king Maacah a t. men ⌊4.
18 :12. Though I receive a t. shekels
19 : 17. a t. men of Benj-n with him
1 K. 3 : 4. a t. burnt offerings did
Sol. offer, 2 Ch. 1 : 6. [talents
2 K. 15 : 19. Menahem gave Pul a t.
24 : 16. craftsmen and smiths a t.
1 Ch. 12 : 14. greatest was over a t.
34. of Naphtali a t. captains
16 : 15. com-ded to a t. generations
19 : 6. chil. of Ammon sent t. talents
29 : 21. sacrificed unto Lord a t.
bullocks, a t. rams, a t. lambs
2 Ch. 30 :24. Hez-h did give t. bul-ks
Ezr. 1 :9. Cyrus did bring t. chargers
10. thirty basins, other vessels a t.
8 : 27. Also 20 basins of a t. drams
Ne. 3 : 13. a t. cubits on the wall
7 : 70. gave a t. drams of gold [a t.
Jb. 9 : 3. cannot answer him one of
33 : 23. an interpreter, one am. a t.
42 : 12. Job had a t. yoke of oxen,
a t. she asses [mine
Ps. 50 : 10. cattle upon t. hills are
84 :10. day in thy courts better th. a
90 : 4. a t. years in thy sight are⌊t.
91 : 7. A t. sh. fall at thy side, ten t.
105 :8. word he com-ded to a t. gen.
Ec. 6 : 6. tho. he live a t. years twice
7 :28. one man am. a t. have I found
Can. 4 : 4. there hang a t. bucklers
8 : 11. fruit was to bring a t. pieces
12. thou, O Sol-n, must have a t.
Is. 7 : 23. t. vines, at a t. silverlings
30 : 17. One t. shall flee at rebuke
60 : 22. A little one sh. become a t.
Eze. 47 :3. man measured a t. cubits
4. he measured a t. and brought, 5.
Da. 5 : 1. Belshazzar made feast to a
t. lords, drank wine bef. the t.
Am. 5 : 3. city that went out by a t.
2 Pe. 3 : 8. one day is with Lord as a
t. years, a t. years as one day
Re. 20 : 2. he bound Satan a t. years
3. deceive nations no more till t.
4 reigned with Ch. a t. years⌊yrs.
5. until the t. years were finished
6. shall reign with him a t. years
7. when the t. years are expired

THOUSAND and five.
1 K. 4 : 32. his songs were a t. -

THOUSAND and seventeen.
Ezr 2:39 chil. of Harim t. -, Ne. 7:42.

THOUSAND fifty and two.
Ezr. 2 : 37. chil. of Immer, t. -, Ne.

THOUSAND two ⌊7 : 40.
hundred twenty and two.
Ezr. 2 : 12. children of Azgad, a t. -

THOUSAND two
hundred forty and seven.
Ezr. 2 :38. chil. of Pashur, a t. -, Ne.

THOUSAND ⌊7 :41.
two hundred fifty and four.
Ezr. 2 : 7. The children of Elam, a
t. -, Ne. 7 : 12, 34.

THOUSAND
two hundred and threescore.
Re. 11 :3. shall prophesy a t. - days
12 : 6. They sho. feed her a t. - days

THOUSAND
two hundred and ninety.
Da. 12 : 11. there shall be a t. - days

THOUSAND three
hundred five and thirty.
Da. 12 : 12. Blessed is he that cometh to the t. - days

THOUSAND three hundred
threescore and five.
Nu. 3:50. of firstborn he took t. - shek.

THOUSAND four hundred.
1 K. 10 :26. Sol-n had a t. - chariots,
2 Ch. 1 : 14.

THOUSAND six hundred.
Re. 14 :20. by space of a t. - furlongs

THOUSAND seven hundred
Ju. 8:26. weight of earrings a t. - sh-s
1 Ch. 26 :30. a t. - men were officers

THOUSAND
seven hundred and thirty.
Nu. 26 :51. numbered of Israel a t. -

THOUSAND seven
hundred and threescore.
1 Ch. 9 : 13. a t. - able men for work

THOUSAND seven hundred
threescore and fifteen.
Ex. 38 :25. silver was a t. - shek-s, 28.

Two THOUSAND.
Nu. 35 : 5. ye shall measure on east
side t. t. cubits, on west side t.
t., on south side t. t., and on
north side t. t. [t. t. cubits
Jos. 3 :4. space between you and ark
7 :3. let t. or three t. men smite Ai
Ju. 20 : 45. men of Israel slew t. t.
1 S. 13 : 2. t. t. with Saul in Mickm-h
1 K. 7 : 26. sea contained t. t. baths
2 K. 18 : 23. give pledges and I will
deliver t. t. horses, Is. 36 : 8.
1 Ch. 5 : 21. took away of asses t. t.
Ne. 7 : 72. gave t. t. pounds of silver
Mk. 5 : 13. t. t. swine were choked

Two THOUSAND
fifty and six.
Ezr. 2 : 14. children of Bigvai, t. t. -

Two THOUSAND
threescore and seven.
Ne. 7 : 19. children of Bigvai, t. t. -

Two THOUSAND
a hundred seventy and two.
Ezr. 2:3. chil. of Parosh t. t. -, Ne. 7:8.

Two THOUSAND and
two hundred. [silv.
Ne. 7 : 71. fa-s gave t. t. - pounds of

Two THOUSAND and
three hundred.
Da. 8 : 14. Unto t. t. - days; then sh.
sanctuary be cleansed

Two THOUSAND three
hundred twenty and two.
Ne. 7 : 17. children of Azgad, t. t. -

Two THOUSAND and
four hundred.
Ex. 38 :29. brass of off-s t. t. - shek-s
Nu. 7 : 85. vessels weighed t. t. - sh-s

Two THOUSAND and
six hundred. [t. t. -
2 Ch. 26 :12. number of mighty men
35 : 8. for offer-gs t. t. - small cattle

Two THOUSAND and
six hundred and thirty.
Nu. 4 : 40. of sons of Gershon, t. t. -

Two THOUSAND and
seven hundred.
1 Ch. 26 :32. men of valour were t. t. -

Two THOUSAND seven
hundred and fifty.
Nu. 4 : 36. sons of Kohathites t. t. -

Two THOUSAND eight
hundred and twelve.
Ezr. 2 :6. chil. of Pahath-moab t. t. -

Two THOUSAND eight
hundred and eighteen.
Ne. 7 :11. chil. of Pahath-moab t. t. -

Three THOUSAND.
Ex. 32 : 28. fell of the people t. t.
Jos. 7 : 3. let two or t. t. smite Ai
4. there went to Ai about t. t. men
Ju. 15 : 11. t. t. went to bind Samson
16 : 27. were upon the roof t. t. men
1 S. 13 : 2. Saul chose t. t. men of Isr.
24 :2. Saul took t. t. chos. men, 26:2.
25 : 2. Nabal had t. t. sheep and
1 K. 4 : 32. Sol. spake t. t. proverbs
1 Ch. 12 : 29. of kindred of Saul t. t.
29 : 4. t. t. talents of gold of Ophir
2 Ch. 4:5. molten sea held t. t. baths
25 : 13. smote t. t. of them, took
29:33. consecrated things, t. t. sheep
35 : 7. Josiah gave t. t. bullocks
Jb. 1 : 3. his substance t. t. camels
Ac. 2 :41 added unto them t. t. souls

Three THOUSAND and three and twenty.
Je. 52 :28. carried captive Jews t.t. -
Three THOUSAND and two hundred.
Nu 4 :44. of the sons of Merari, t.t.-
Three THOUSAND and three hundred.
1 K. 5 :16. t.t.- which ruled ov. peo.
Three THUOSAND and six hundred. [18.
2 Ch. 2 :2. t.t.- men to oversee them,
Three THOUSAND and six hundred and thirty.
Ezr. 2 :35. The chil. of Senaah, t.t. -
Three THOUSAND and seven hundred. [t.t.-
1 Ch. 12 :27. with leader of Aaronites,
Three THOUSAND nine hundred and thirty.
Ne. 7 :38. The chil. of Senaah t.t. -
Four THOUSAND.
1 S. 4 : 2. slew of Isr. about f.t. men
1 Ch. 23 :5. f.t. porters, f.t. praised L.
2 Ch. 9 : 25. Sol-n had f.t. stalls for
Mat. 15 : 38. they that did eat were f.t., beside, Mk. 8 : 9. [Mk. 8:20.
16 : 10. Nei. seven loaves of the f.t.,
Ac. 21 : 38. leddest f.t. murderers
Four THOUSAND and five hundred.
Eze. 48 : 16. on north side of city f.t. - measures, east side, south side, west side, f.t.-, 30, 32, 33, 34.
Four THOUSAND and six hundred.
1 Ch. 12 :26. of children of Levi f.t. -
Je. 52 :30. all the persons were f.t.-
Five THOUSAND.
Jos. 8 : 12. he took about f.t. men
Ju. 20 : 45. gleaned of them f.t. men
1 S. 17 : 5. weight of coat f.t. shekels
1 Ch. 29 : 7. of gold f.t. talents
2 Ch. 35 : 9. for offerings f.t. cattle
Ezr. 2 : 69. gave f.t. pounds of silver
Eze. 45 :6. possess-n of city f.t. broad
48 : 15. f.t. that are left in breadth
Mat. 14 : 21. had eaten were ab. f.t.
16 : 9. five loaves of the f.t., Mk. 6 : 44.-8 : 19. Lu. 9 : 14. Jn. 6 : 10.
Ac. 4 : 4. number that believed f.t.,
Five THOUSAND and four hundred. [f.t. -
Ezr. 1 : 11. vessels of gold and silver
Six THOUSAND.
1 S. 13 : 5. ag. Isr. with s.t. horsem.
2 K. 5 : 5. Naaman took s.t. pieces
1 Ch. 23 : 4. s.t. officers and judges
Jb. 42 : 12. Job had s.t. camels
Six THOUSAND and two hundred.
Nu. 3 : 34. of Merari were s.t. -
Six THOUSAND seven hundred and twenty.
Ezr. 2 : 67. their asses, s.t.-, Ne. 7:69.
Six THOUSAND and eight hundred. [s.t. -
1 Ch. 12 :24. of Judah th. bare shield,
Seven THOUSAND.
1 K. 19 : 18. I have s.t. in Isr. who have not bowed to Baal, Ro. 11:4.
1 K. 20 :15. chil. of Israel, being s.t.
2 K. 24 : 16. away men of might, s.t.
1 Ch. 12 :25. of Sim., mighty men, s.t.
18 : 4. Da. took fr. him s.t. horsem.
19 : 18. Da. slew of Syrians s.t. men
29 : 4. I prepared s.t. tal-ts of silv.
2 Ch. 15 : 11. they offered s.t. sheep
30 : 24. Hez. gave cong. s.t. sheep
Jb. 1 :3. His substance was s.t. sheep
Re. 11 : 13. in earthquake slain s.t.
Seven THOUSAND three hundred thirty and seven.
Ezr. 2 :65. servants, maids, s.t. -, Ne. [7:67.
Seven THOUSAND and five hundred.
Nu. 3 :22. Of Gershonites were s.t.-

Seven THOUSAND and seven hundred.
2 Ch. 17 :11. Arabians bro-t Jehosh-t s.t. - rams, s.t. - he goats
Eight THOUSAND and five hundred and fourscore.
Nu. 4 :48. numbered of Levites, e.t.-
Eight THOUSAND and six hundred.
Nu. 3 : 28. of the Kohathites, e.t. -
Ten THOUSAND.
Le. 26 : 8. a 100 sh. put t.t. to flight
Nu. 10 : † 36. Return, O Lord, unto the t.t. thousands of Israel
De. 32 :30. How sh. 2 put t.t. to flight?
Ju. 1 : 4. Jud. slew in Bezek t.t. men
3 : 29. slew of Moab t.t. men, all
4 : 6. take t.t. men of Naphtali
10. he went up with t.t. men, 14.
7 : 3. there remained to Gideon t.t.
20 : 10. we will take a t. out of t.t.
34. came against Gibeah t.t. men
1 S. 15 : 4. Saul numbered t.t. men
2 S. 18 : 3, thou art worth t.t. of us
1 K. 5 : 14. to Lebanon, t.t. a month
2 K. 13 : 7. to Jehoahaz t.t. footmen
14 : 7. Amaziah slew of Edom t.t.
24 : 14. he carried away even t.t.
1 Ch. 29 : 7. gave of gold t.t. drams, of silver t.t. talents
2 Ch. 2 : 2. t.t. to bear burdens
25 : 11. smote of chil. of Seir t.t.
12. t.t. left alive, did Judah carry
27 : 5. the Ammonites gave t.t. measures of wheat, t.t. of barley
30 :24. Heze. gave cong-n t.t. sheep
Es. 3 : 9. I will pay t.t. talents of sil.
Ps. 91 : 7. t.t. shall fall at thy right
Can. 5 : 10. beloved chiefest am. t.t.
Eze. 45 : 1. breadth of the land sh be t.t., 3, 5.-48 : 9, 10. (2), 13. (2), 18. (2). [fore him
Da 7 : 10. t.t. times t.t. stood be-
Mat. 18 : 24. owed him t.t. talents
Lu. 14:31. whe. able with t.t. to meet
1 Co. 4 : 15. for tho. t.t. instructors
14 : 19. than t.t. words in an unknown tongue
Re. 5 :11. number was t.t. times t.t.
Twelve THOUSAND.
Nu. 31 : 5. were t.t. armed for war
Jos. 8 :25. all that fell of Ai were t.t.
Ju. 21 : 10. sent t.t. men to Jabesh-gil.
2 S. 10 : 6. hired of Ish-tob, t.t. men
17 : 1. Let me now choose t.t. men
1 K. 4 : 26. Sol. had t.t. horsemen, 10: 26. 2 Ch. 1 : 14.-9 : 25. [salt t.t.
Ps. 60 : * Joab smote in valley of
Re. 7 : 5. Of tribe of Juda, Reuben. Gad, were sealed t.t. (3)
6. Of Aser, Nephthalim, Manasses, were sealed t.t. (3)
7. Of Simeon. Levi, Issachar, were sealed t.t. (3) [sealed t.t. (3)
8. Of Zabulon, Joseph, Benjamin,
21 : 16. measured city t.t. furlongs
Fourteen THOUSAND.
Jb. 42 : 12. for Job had f.t. sheep
Fourteen THOUSAND and seven hundred.
Nu. 16 :49. that died in plague f.t. -
Fifteen THOUSAND.
Ju. 8 : 10. hosts wi. them ab. f.t. men
Sixteen THOUSAND.
Nu. 31 : 40. the persons were s.t., 46
Sixteen THOUSAND seven hundred and fifty.
Nu. 31 :52 gold of offer-g s.t.-shek-s
Seventeen THOUSAND and two hundred.
1 Ch. 7 : 11. sons of Jediael s.t. -
Eighteen THOUSAND.
Ju. 20 : 25. destroyed of Israel e.t.
44. fell of Benjamin e.t. men [e.t.
2 S. 8 : 13. smiting in valley of salt
1 Ch. 12 : 31. of tribe of Manas. e.t.
18 : 12. Abishai slew Edomites e.t.

1 Ch. 29 :7. gave of brass e.t. talents
Eze. 48 :35. city round e.t. measures
Twenty THOUSAND.
2 S. 8 : 4. David took from Hadadezer t.t. footmen, 1 Ch. 18 : 4.
10 : 6. chil. of Ammon hired Syrians, t.t. [t.t. men of Israel
18 : 7. great slaughter that day of
2 Ch. 2 : 10. I will give t.t. measures of wheat, t.t. of barley, t.t. baths of wine, t.t. baths of oil, 1 K. 5:11.
Ne. 7:71. gave to work t.t. drams, 72.
Ps. 68 : 17. chariots of God are t.t.
Lu. 14 : 31. meet him th. cometh wi. [t.t.
Twenty THOUSAND and two hundred. [t.t.
1 Ch. 7 : 9. number of mighty men,
Twenty THOUSAND and eight hundred.
1 Ch. 12 : 30. of Ephraim t.t. - men
Twenty two THOUSAND.
Nu. 3 : 39. number of Levites - t. [t.
Ju. 7 :3. returned of Gideon's army -
20 : 21. Benj-n destroyed of Isr. - t.
2 S. 8 : 5. David slew of the Syrians - t. men, 1 Ch. 18 : 5. [2 Ch. 7:5.
1 K. 8 :63. Solomon offered - t. oxen,
Twenty two THOUSAND and thirty four. [- t. -
1 Ch. 7 :7. sons of Bela; mighty men,
Twenty two THOUSAND and two hundred. [t. -
Nu. 26 : 14. families of Simeonites -
Twenty two THOUSAND two hundred and threescore and thirteen.
Nu. 3 :43. firstborn males were - t. -
Two and twenty THOUSAND six hundred.
1 Ch. 7 : 2. sons of Tola, valiant -t.-
Twenty three THOUSAND.
Nu. 26 : 62. numbered of Levites, -t.
1 Co. 10 : 8. and fell in one day - t.
Twenty four THOUSAND.
Nu. 25 : 9. died in the plague - t.
1 Ch. 23 :4. - t. to forward the work
27 : 1. officers that served king - t., 2, 4, 5, 7, 8, 9, 10, 11, 12, 13, 14, 15.
Five and twenty THOUSAND. [men
Ju. 20 : 46. wh. fell of Benjamin - t.
Eze. 45 : 1. offer a holy portion of land; length shall be - t. reeds 3, 5, 6.-48 :8, 9, 10. (2), 13. (2), 15.
48 :20. oblation sh. be - t. by - t., 21.
Twenty five THOUSAND and a hundred.
Ju. 20 :35. destroyed of Benj-s - t. -
Twenty six THOUSAND.
Ju. 20 : 15. of Benj. - t. drew sword
1 Ch. 7 :40. of Asher, apt to war, - t.
Twenty seven THOUSAND.
1 K. 20 : 30. wall fell upon - t. men
Twenty eight THOUSAND and six hundred. [- t. -
1 Ch. 12 : 35. Danites, expert in war,
Thirty THOUSAND.
Jos. 8 : 3. Joshua chose -t. mighty
1 S. 4 : 10. fell of Israel - t. footmen
11 : 8. the men of Judah were - t.
13 : 5. Philis. gathered - t. chariots
2 S. 6 : 1. Da. gath-d - t. chosen men
1 K. 5 : 13. Sol. raised levy; - t. men
Thirty THOUSAND and five hundred. [45.
Nu. 31 :39. and the asses were t.t.-,
Thirty two THOUSAND.
Nu. 31 : 35. - t. women taken capt-s
1 Ch. 19 : 7. Ammon hired - t. chari.
Thirty two THOUSAND and two hundred. [2 :21.
Nu. 1 :35. go to war of Manas - t. -,
Thirty two THOUSAND and five hundred. [t. -
Nu. 26 : 37. of Ephraim numbered -
Thirty three THOUSAND.
2 Ch. 35 :7. Josiah gave - t. bullocks

Thirty five THOUSAND and four hundred.
Nu. 1 :37. to war, of Benj. were - t. -
2 : 23. host of Abidan were - t. -
Thirty six THOUSAND.
Nu. 31 : 38 And the beeves - t.
44. pertained to cong-n - t. beeves
1 Ch. 7 :4. bands of soldiers were - t.
Thirty seven THOUSAND.
1 Ch. 12 :34. of Naphtali wi. spear - t.
Thirty eight THOUSAND.
1 Ch. 23 : 3. Levites from 30 yrs. - t.
Forty THOUSAND. [war
Jos. 4 : 13. about f.t. prepared for
Ju. 5 : 8. was there shield am. f.t. ?
2 S. 10 : 18. David slew f.t. horsem.
1 K. 4 : 26. Solomon had f.t. stalls
1 Ch. 12 :36. Asher, expert in war, f.t.
19 : 18. David slew of Syrians f.t.
Forty THOUSAND and five hundred. [2 : 19.
Nu 1 : 33. to war of Ephraim f.t. -,
26 : 18. of Gad were numbered f.t. -
Forty and one THOUSAND and five hundred. [2 : 28.
Nu. 1 :41. go to war, of Asher - t. -,
Forty two THOUSAND.
Ju 12 : 6. fell of Ephraimites - t.
Forty two THOUSAND three hundred threescore.
Ezr. 2:64. whole cong-n - t. -, Ne. 7:66.
Forty three THOUSAND seven hundred and thirty.
Nu. 26 : 7. of Reubenites - t. -
Four and forty THOUSAND seven hundred and threescore. [war, - t. -
1 Ch. 5 : 18. of Reuben, skilful in
Forty five THOUSAND and four hundred.
Nu. 26 : 50. of Naphtali were - t. -
Forty five THOUSAND and six hundred.
Nu. 26 : 41. sons of Benj. were - t. -
Forty five THOUSAND six hundred and fifty.
Nu. 1 : 25. war of Gad, - t. -, 2 : 15.
Forty and six THOUSAND and five hundred.
Nu. 1: 21. war of Reuben - t. -, 2: 11.
Fifty THOUSAND.
1 Ch. 5 : 21. of Hagarites' camels f.t.
12 :33. Of Zebulun f.t. co. keep rank
Ac. 19 : 19. price of books f.t. pieces
Fifty THOUSAND and threescore and ten.
1 S. 6 :19. the Lord smote f.t. - men
Fifty two THOUSAND and seven hundred.
Nu. 26 :34. of Manass. numbered - t. -
Fifty three THOUSAND and four hundred.
Nu 1 : 43. of Naphtali - t. -, 2 : 30.
26 : 47. of sons of Asher were - t. -
Fifty four THOUSAND and four hundred. [2 : 6.
Nu 1 : 29. to war, of Issachar - t. -,
Fifty seven THOUSAND and four hundred.
Nu 1 : 31. of Zebulun - t. -, 2 : 8.
Fifty nine THOUSAND and three hundred.
Nu. 1 : 23. of Simeon - t. -, 2 : 13.
Threescore THOUSAND.
2 Ch. 12 :3. Shishak came with 1,200 chariots and t.t. horsemen
Threescore THOUSAND and five hundred.
Nu. 26 : 27. of the Zebulunites t.t. -
Threescore and one THOUSAND.
Nu. 31 : 34. And booty was - t. asses
Ezr. 2 : 69. gave - t. drams of gold
Threescore and two THOUSAND and seven hundred. [26.
Nu. 1 : 39. of tribe of Dan - t. -, 2 :

Threescore and four THOUSAND and three hundred.
Nu. 26 :25. of Issachar numb-d - t. -
Threescore and four THOUSAND four hundred.
Nu. 26 :43. Shuhamites numbered -
Seventy THOUSAND. [t. -
2 S. 24 :15. there died of the peo. s.t.
1 Ch. 21 : 14. there fell of Israel s.t.
Threescore and ten THOUSAND.
1 K. 5 : 15. Solomon had - t. that bare burdens, 2 Ch. 2 : 2, 18.
Threescore and twelve THOUSAND.
Nu. 31 : 33. booty of beeves was - t.
Threescore and fourteen THOUSAND six hundred.
Nu. 1 : 27. of Judah were - t. -, 2 : 4.
Seventy five THOUSAND.
Es. 9 : 16. Jews slew of their foes - t.
Threescore and sixteen THOUSAND five hundred.
Nu. 26 : 22. of Jud. numbered - t. -
Fourscore THOUSAND.
1 K. 5 : 15 f.t. hewers, 2 Ch. 2 : 2, 18.
Fourscore and seven THOUSAND.
1 Ch. 7 : 5. Issachar reckoned - t.
Hundred THOUSAND.
Nu. 2 :9. all numb-d in Judah a h.t.
16. in the camp of Reuben a h.t.
1 K. 20 :29. slew of Syrians h.t. foot.
2 K. 3 : 4. Mesha unto king of Israel a h.t. lambs, a h.t. rams [men
1 Ch. 5 : 21. took fr. Hagarites h.t.
22 : 14. for house of L. h.t. talents
29 : 7. gave a h.t. talents of iron
2 Ch. 25 : 6. hired h.t. men of valour
A hundred and eight THOUSAND and a hundred.
Nu: 2 : 24. of camp of Ephraim - t. -
A hundred and twenty THOUSAND.
Ju. 8 : 10. fell of the Midianites - t.
1 K. 8 : 63. Solomon offered a sacrifice of - t. sheep, 2 Ch. 7 : 5.
1 Ch. 12 : 37. of Reubenites, Gadites, and Manasseh, - t.
2 Ch. 28 : 6. Pekah slew in Judah - t.
Sixscore THOUSAND.
Jon. 4 : 11. in Nineveh s.t. cannot
A hundred and forty and four THOUSAND.
Re. 7 : 4. sealed - t. of tribes of Isr.
14 : 1. - t. having Father's name
3. no man learn that song but - t.
A hundred and fifty and one THOUSAND and four hundred and fifty.
Nu. 2 : 16. in camp of Reuben, - t. -
A hundred and fifty three THOUSAND six hundred.
2 Ch. 2 : 17. strangers in Israel - t. -
A hundred and fifty seven THOUSAND six hundred.
Nu. 2 : 31. All in camp of Dan - t. -
A hundred and fourscore THOUSAND.
1 K. 12 : 21. of Judah and Benjamin - t. - warriors, 2 Ch. 11 : 1.
2 Ch. 17 : 18. with Jehozabad - t. -
A hundred fourscore and five THOUSAND.
2 K. 19 : 35. angel of Lord smote in camp of Assyrians - t., Is. 37 : 36.
A hundred fourscore and six THOUSAND and four hundred. [- t. -
Nu. 2 : 9. All in camp of Judah were
Two hundred THOUSAND.
1 S. 15 : 4. Saul numb-d - t. footmen
2 Ch. 17 : 16. with Amaziah - t. men
17. with Eliada - t. armed men
28 : 8. carried captive of breth. - t.

Two hundred and fifty THOUSAND.
1 Ch. 5 : 21. they took of sheep - t.
Two hundred fourscore THOUSAND. [bows
2 Ch. 14 : 8. out of Benj-n - t. drew
17 : 15. next was Jehohanan and - t.
Three hundred THOUSAND
Nu. 31 : 36. that went out to war - t.
1 S. 11 : 8. Isr. were - t., 2 Ch. 14 : 8.
2 Ch. 17 : 14. with Adnah chief - t.
25 : 5. throughout Judah and Benj. Amaziah found - t. choice men
Three hundred and seven THOUSAND and five hundred.
2 Ch. 26 :13. Uzziah had army of - t. -
Three hundred thirty seven THOUSAND five hundred.
Nu. 31 : 43. unto cong-n - t. - sheep
Four hundred THOUSAND.
Ju. 20 : 2. Isr. besides Benj. - t., 17.
2 Ch. 13 : 3. battle in array with - t.
Four hundred threescore and ten THOUSAND.
1 Ch. 21 : 5. Judah was - t. th. drew
Five hundred THOUSAND.
2 S. 24 : 9. of Judah were - t. men
2 Ch 13 : 17. slain of Israel - t. men
Six hundred THOUSAND.
Ex. 12 :37. Isr. journeyed - t. on foot
Nu. 11 : 21. The peo. are - t. footm.
Six hundred THOUSAND, a thousand seven hundred and thirty. [Isr. - t. -
Nu. 26 :51. These were numbered of
Six hundred and three THOUSAND and five hundred and fifty. [- t. -
Ex. 38 : 26. A bekah for ev. man for
Nu. 1 : 46. all that were able to go to war in Israel - t. -, 2 : 32
Six hundred and seventy and five THOUSAND.
Nu. 31 :32. rest of prey was - t. sheep
Eight hundred THOUSAND
2 S. 24 : 9. in Israel - t. valiant men
2 Ch. 13 : 3. Jeroboam with - t. men
THOUSAND THOUSAND.
1 Ch. 22 : 14. I prepared t. t. talents
2 Ch. 14 :9. Ethiopian wi. host of t.t.
THOUSAND THOUSAND and hundred THOUSAND.
1 Ch. 21 : 5. all they of Israel were t.t. and h.t. that drew sword
Two hundred THOUSAND THOUSAND.
Re. 9 : 16. army of horsemen - t.t.
THOUSANDS. [lions
Ge. 24 :60. be thou moth. of t. of mil-
Ex. 18 : 21. place rulers of t., 25 [10.
20 : 6. shewing mercy unto t., De. 5:
34 :7. Keeping mercy for t., forgiv-g
Nu. 1 :16. princes of tribes, heads of t. in Isr., 10 : 4. Jos. 22 : 14, 21, 30.
10 : 36. Ret., O L., unto the many t.
31 : 5. were delivered out of the t.
De. 33 :17. they are the t. of Manas-h
1 S. 10 :19. present yourselves by t.
18 : 8. to me have ascribed but t.
23 : 23. search him thro-t t. of Jud.
29 : 2. lords of Philis. passed by t.
2 S. 18 : 4. all the people came by t.
Ps. 68 : 17. The chariots of God are 20,000, even t. of angels [gold
119 : 72. thy law is better than t. of
Je. 32 :18. shewest lovingkindn. to t.
Mi. 5 : 2. tho. little am. the t. of Jud.
6 : 7. L. be pleased with t. of rams ?
Ac. 21 : 20. how many t. of Jews bel.
Re. 5 : 11. numb. of them was t. of t.
THOUSANDS, with captains.
Nu. 31 : 14. Moses wroth with c. over
48. c. of t. came unto Moses [t.
52. all the gold of c. of t., 54.
De. 1 : 15. I made them c. over t. [t.
1 S. 8 : 12. he will appoint him c. ov.

1 S. 22 : 7. will son of Jesse make you
2 S. 18 : 1. David set c. of t. [c. of t. ?
1 Ch. 12 : 20. c. of the t. of Manas-h
13 : 1. David consulted with c. of t.
15 : 25. c. of t. went to bring ark
26 : 26. wh. c. over t. had dedicated
27 : 1. c. of t. wh. came in month
28 : 1. David assembled c. ov. t. [by
29 : 6. c. of t. offered willingly
2 Ch. 1 : 2. Solomon spake to c. of t.
17 : 14. Of Judah the c. of t., 25 : 5.

Ten THOUSANDS. [Jude 14.

De. 33 : 2. came with t.t. of saints,
33 : 17. they are the t.t. of Ephraim
1 S. 18 : 7. Saul hath slain his t., Da.
his t.t., 8.-21 : 11.-29 : 5.
Ps. 3 : 6. I will not be afraid of t.t.
144 : 13. sheep may bring forth t.t.
Da. 11 : 12 sh. cast down many t.t.
Mi. 6 : 7. pleased with t.t. of rivers

THOUSAND THOUSANDS.

Da. 7 : 10. t.t. ministered unto him

THREAD. [latchet

Ge. 14 : 23. I not take from a t. to a
38 : 28. she bound up a scarlet t., 30.
Jos 2 : 18. bind scarlet t. in window
Ju. 16 : 9. brake withs as a t. of tow
12. brake ropes fr. his arms like t.
Can. 4 : 3. Thy lips like t. of scarlet
Je. 52 : †21. a t. of 12 cubits did com-

THREATEN. [pass

Ac. 4 : 17. let us straitly t. them

THREATENED.

1 Pe. 2 : 23. wh. he suffered he t. not

THREATENING, S.

Ac. 4 : 29. Lord, behold their t-s
9 : 1. Saul breath-g out t-s and slan.
Ep. 6 : 9. do same things, forbear-g t.

THREE. [her

Ex. 21 : 11. if do not these t. unto
25 : 33. t. bowls made like (2), 37 : 19.
Nu. 12 : 4. Come out ye t. ; t. came
28 : 12. And t. tenth deals of flour
Jos. 17 : 11. Manas. had t. countries
1 S. 1 : 24. Hannah took t. bullocks
10 : 3. carrying t. kids, ano. t. loaves
17 : 14. t. eldest followed Saul, 13.
2 S. 23 : 9. Eleazer was one of the
t. mighty, 1 Ch. 11 : 12.
13. t. of 30 chief went down to
David, 1 Ch. 11 : 15.
16. t. mighty men brake through
host of Philis s, 17. 1 Ch. 11 : 18.
18. Abishai was chief among t. (2),
1 Ch. 11 : 18. 20. (2).
19. Was he not most honourable
of t. ? attained not unto first
t., 1 Ch. 11 : 21.
22. Benaiah had name among t.
mighty men, 1 Ch. 11 : 24.
23. he attained not to the first t.,
1 Ch. 11 : 25. [52 : 24.
2 K. 25 : 18. t. keepers of door, Je.
1 Ch. 2 : 3. sons wh. t. born of dau.
7 : 6. sons of Benjamin t. [of Shua
23 : 8. The sons of Laadan ; t.
9. The sons of Shimei ; Haziel, t.
Jb. 1 : 17. Chaldeans made t. bands
32 : 1. So these t. men ceased to answer Job, 5. [bough
Is. 17 : 6. two or t. berries in top of
Eze. 14 : 14. Tho. these t. men, Noah, Dan., Job, were in it, 16, 18.
40 : 10 little chambers, t. on one
side, t. on, 21. [over another
41 : 6. side chambers were t., one
Da 7 : 8. t. of first horns plucked
20. of ten horns in his head t. fell
Mat. 18 : 20. where two or t. are gath-d
Lu. 10 : 36. wh. of these t. was neighb-r
11 : 5. say, Friend, lend me t. loaves
12 : 52. divided t. ag. two, two ag. t.
1 Co. 13 : 13. now abideth these t. [t.
14 : 27. let it by two, or at most by
29. Let prophets speak two or t.
1 Jn. 5 : 7. are t. that bear record in
heaven, these t. are one

1 Jn. 5 : 8. are t. th. bare witness in
earth, and these t. agree in one
Re. 9 : 18. By these t. third part killed
16 : 13. I saw t. unclean spirits
See ANGELS, ARROWS, BASKETS

THREE branches.

Ge. 40 : 10. in the vine were t.b.
12. interpretation, t.b. are 3 days
Ex. 25 : 32. t.b. of candlestick out
of the one side, and t.b., 37 : 18.

THREE cities.

Nu. 35 : 14. Ye sh. give t.c. on this
side Jordan, and t.c. in Canaan
De. 4 : 41. Moses severed t.c. on this
19 : 2. Thou sh. separate t.c. for, 7.
9. shalt add t.c. more for thee [c.
Jos. 21 : 32. Kartan with suburbs t.
Am. 4 : 8. 2 or t.c. unto one for water

THREE companies.

Ju. 7 : 16. Gideon divided 300 men
into t.c. [chers
20. t.c. blew trumpets, brake pit-
9 : 43. Abim. divided peo. into t.c.
1 S. 11 : 11. Saul put the peo. in t.c.
13 : 17. the spoilers came in t.c.

THREE cubits. [1.

Ex. 27 : 1. height of altar be t.c., 38:
1 K. 7 : 27. t.c. the height of base
2 K. 25 : 17. height of chapiter t.c.
2 Ch. 6 : 13. made scaffold t.c. high
Eze. 40 : 48. gate t.c. on this side, t.
41 : 22. altars t.c. high, two c. [c. on
See DARTS, DAUGHTERS.

THREE days. [t.d.

Ge. 40 : 12. The three branches are
13. wi-n t.d. Pha. lift thy head, 19
18. The three baskets are t.d.
42 : 17. put them all into ward t.d.
Ex. 10 : 22. thick darkness in Eg. t.d.
23. They saw not one ano. for t.d.
15 : 22. they went t.d. in wilderness
Jos. 1 : 11. within t.d. pass ov. Jord.
2 : 16. hide there t.d., 22. [host
3 : 2. aft. t.d. officers went through
9 : 16. t.d. aft. they had made leag
Ju. 14 14. not in t.d. expound ridd.
19 : 4. Levite abode with him t.d.
1 S. 9 : 20. asses lost t.d. ago, found
20 : 19. hast stayed t.d.. then go
21 : 5. women been kept fr. us t.d.
30 : 12. he had eaten no bread t.d.
13. bec. t. d. agone I fell sick
2 S. 20 : 4 Assemble me men of Judah in t.d. [21 : 12.
24 : 13. be t.d. pestilence, 1 Ch.
1 K. 12 : 5 Depart for t.d., 2 Ch. 10 : 5.
2 K. 2 : 17. sought him t.d., but not
1 Ch 12 : 39. with David t.d. eating
2 Ch 20 : 25. t.d. in gathering spoil
Ezr. 8 : 15. abode we in tents t.d.
32. to Jerus., abode t.d., Ne. 2 : 11.
10 : 8. whoso. not come in t.d., 9.
Es. 4 : 16. eat nor drink t. d. [12 : 40.
Jon. 1 : 17. Jonah in fish t.d., Mat
Mat. 12 : 40. so shall Son of man be
t.d. and 3 nights in the earth
15 : 32. compassion on multitude
bec. with me t.d., Mk. 8 : 2.
26 : 61. to destroy temple of God
and build it in t.d., 27 : 40. Mk.
14 : 58 -15 : 29. Jn. 2 : 19. [31.
27 : 63, aft. t.d. I will rise, Mk. 8 :
Lu. 2 : 46. aft. t.d. found in temple
Jn. 2 : 20. wilt thou rear it in t.d. ?
Ac. 9 : 9. Saul was t.d. with-t sight
17 : 2. Paul t. sabbath d. reasoned
25 : 1. after t.d. Festus ascended
28 : 7. Publius lodged us t.d. cour-
12. at Syracuse t.d. [teously
17. after t.d. Paul called chief of
Re. 11 : 9. dead bodies t.d. and half
11. after t.d. Spirit of life entered
See **Three days' JOURNEY.**
See DEALS, EUNUCHS, FIRK-
INS, FLOCKS, FRIENDS, GATES,
HOURS, HUNDRED, KINGS,
LOAVES, MEN, MEASURES,

MIGHTIEST, NIGHTS, OXEN,
PARTS, PILLARS, POUNDS,
PRESIDENTS, RANKS, RIBS,
ROWS, SHEKELS, SHEPHERDS,
SISTERS, SOCKETS, STO-
RIES, TABERNACLES, TEETH,
THINGS, THOUSAND, TRANS-
GRESSIONS, WEEKS, WITNES-
SES, WIVES.
See **Three MONTHS, Three SONS, Three TIMES,**

THREE things. [10.

2 S. 24 : 12. I offer thee t.t., 1 Ch. 21 :
Pr. 30 : 15. t.t. that are nev. satisfied
18. be t.t. which are too wonderf.
21. For t.t. the earth is disquieted
29. There be t.t. which go well
See **Three YEARS.**

THREE Taverns.

See TAVERNS.

THREEFOLD. [en

Ex. 4 : 12. t. rod is not quickly brok-

THREESCORE.

De. 3 : 4. we took of them t. cities,
Jos. 13 : 30. 1 Ch. 2 : 23. [cities
1 K. 4 : 13. to him pertained t. great
6 : 2. house for Lord, length there-
of t. cubits, 2 Ch. 3 : 3.
2 Ch. 11 : 21. Rehob. took t. concu-
bines and begat t. daughters
Ezr. 6 : 3. Let house be, length th-of
t. cubits, breadth t. cubits
Eze. 40 : 14. He made posts of t. cub-s
Da. 3 : 1. image of gold, height t. cub-s
1 Ti. 5 : 9. not widow be taken und. t.
See FURLONGS, HUNDRED,
MALES, MEASURES, MEN,
QUEENS, SIXTY, THOUSAND,
YEARS.

THREESCORE and one, two, five, or six.

Le. 12 : 5. her purifying t.a.s. days
Nu. 31 : 39. of asses, L.'s trib. t.a.o.
1 Ch. 26 : 8. able men t.a.t. of Obed.
See SOULS, WEEKS, YEARS.

THREESCORE and seven.

Ne. 7 : 72. people gave t. - garments

THREESCORE and eight.

1 Ch. 16 : 38. Obed-edom with their
brethren, t. -

THREESCORE and ten.

Ge. 50 : 3. mourned for Isr. t. - days
Ex. 15 : 27. to Elim where were t. -
palm trees, Nu. 33 : 9.
Ju. 12 : 14. rode on t. - ass colts
2 Ch. 29 : 32. of offerings t. - bull-ks
See HORSEMEN, KINGS, PER-
SONS, PIECES, SEVENTY, SONS,
SOULS, THOUSAND, YEARS.

THREESCORE and twelve or fifteen.

Nu. 31 : 38. of beeves, L.'s trib. t.a.t.
Ac. 7 : 14. Jac. and kind-d t.a.f. souls

THREESCORE and seventeen.

Ju. 8 : 14. elders of Succoth t. - men

THRESH, ED, ETH. [t-h

De. 25 : † 4. not muzzle ox when he
Ju. 6 : 11. Gideon t-d wheat by winep.
8 : † 7. wilt t. your flesh wi. thorns
Is. 25 : † 10. Moab shall be t-d down
28 : 27. fitches not t-d wi. threshing
41 : 15. thou shalt t. the mountains
Je 51 : 33. Bab-n it is time to t. her
Am. 1 : 3. t-d Gilead wi. instruments
Mi. 4 : 13. Arise and t. O dau. of Zion
Ha. 3 : 12. didst t. heathen in anger
1 Co. 9 : 10. t-h in hope, be partaker

THRESHING. [vintage

Le. 26 : 5. your t. shall reach unto
2 S. 24 : 22. here be oxen and t. instruments, 1 Ch. 21 : 23.
2 K. 13 : 7. king had made them like
dust by t. [wheat
1 Ch. 21 : 20. Now Ornan was t.
Is. 21 : 10. O my t. and corn of my floor
28 : 27. fitches not threshed with t.

Is. 28 : 28. he will not ever be t. it
41 : 15. a new sharp t. instrument
Jo 3 : †14. multitudes in valley of t.

THRESHINGFLOOR, S.

Ge. 50 : 10. they came to t. of Atad
Nu. 15 : 20. as ye do heave off-g of t.
18 : 27. as tho· it were corn of t.
30. be counted as increase of t.
Ru. 3 : 2. he winnoweth in the t.
1 S. 23 : 1. Philistines rob the t-s
2 S. 6 :6. to Nachon's t., 1 Ch. 13 : 9.
24 : 18. rear altar in t. of Araunah,
1 Ch. 21 : 18, 21, 22. 2 Ch. 3 : 1.
21. Da. said, To buy t. of thee, 24.
1 Ch. 21 :15. angel of Lord stood by t.
28. L. answered Da. in t. of Ornan
2 Ch. 3 : 1. Da. prepared iu t. of Or.
Je. 51 : 33. dau. of Bab-n is like a t.
Da. 2 : 35. like chaff of summer t-s

THRESHINGPLACE.

2 S. 24 : 16. angel of the L. was by t.

THRESHOLD, S. ⌈t.

Ju. 19 : 27. her hands were upon the
1 S. 5 : 4. palms of his hands cut off
5. tread not on t. of Dagon ⌊on t.
1 K. 14 : 17. when she came to t.
2 K. 12 : † 9. keeper of t. 22 : † 4.-
25 : † 18. Es. 2 : † 21.-6 : † 2.
Je. 35 : † 4.-52 : † 24.
1 Ch. 9 : † 19. keepers of the t-s, 2
Ch. 23 : † 4. ⌈of the gates
Ne. 12 : 25. keeping ward at the t-s
Ps. 84 : † 10. I choose to sit at the t.
Is. 6 : † 4. posts of the t. moved at
Eze. 9 : 3. glory of God was gone up
to t., 10 : 4. ⌈the t.
10 : 18. glory of God departed from
40 : 6. measured the t. of gate (2) 7.
43 : 8. In their setting of their t.
by my t-s and posts ⌈the gate
46 : 2. prince shall worship at t. of
47 : 1. waters issued from under t.
Zph. 1 : 9. punish all that leap on t.
2 : 14. desolation shall be in the t-s

THREW.

2 S. 16 : 13. Shimei t. stones at David
2 K. 9 : 33. t. Jezebel down and trod
2 Ch. 31 : 1. they t. down high places
Mk. 12 : 42. widow, she t. in two mites
Lu. 9 : 42. devil t. him down and
Ac. 22 : 23. as they cried and t. dust

THREWEST.

Ne. 9 : 11. their persecutors thou t.

THRICE. ⌊into deep

Ex. 34 : 23. t. in year all appear, 24.
2 K. 13 : 18. Joash smote t. and stayed
19. thou shalt smite Syria but t.
Jb. 33 : † 29. worketh G. twice and t.
Mat. 26 : 34. thou shalt deny me t.,
75. Mk. 14 : 30, 72. Lu. 22 : 34,
61. Jn. 13 : 38. ⌈was received
Ac. 10 : 16. This was done t.; vessel
2 Co. 11 : 25. t. was I beaten wi rods,
t. I suffered shipwreck ⌈t.
12 : 8. For this I besought the Lord

THROAT. ⌈Ro. 3 : 13.

Ps. 5 : 9. their t. an open sepulchre,
69 : 3. I am weary, my t. is dried
115 : 7. nei. speak they thro. their t.
149 : † 6. let praises be in their t.
Pr. 23 : 2. put a knife to thy t.
Is. 58 : † 1. cry with t., lift up voice
Je. 2 : 25. withhold thy t. fr. thirst
Mat. 18 : 28. servant took him by t.

THRONE.

Ge. 41 : 40. in the t. will I be greater
1 S. 2 : 8. them inherit t. of glory
2 S. 3 : 10. to set t. of David ov. Isr.
7 : 13. I will stablish t. of his kingdom for ever, 16. 1 Ch 22 : 10.
1 K. 2 : 4. shall not fail thee a man
on the t. of Israel, 8 : 25.-9 : 5.
2 Ch. 6 : 16. Je. 33 : 17.
12. Solomon sat upon t. of David,
24.-8 : 20.-10 : 9. 1 Ch. 29 : 23 2
Ch. 6 : 10. ⌈where might judge
7 : 7. Solomon made a porch for t.
1 K. 10 : 18. king made a great t. of
iron, 2 Ch. 9 : 17. ⌈Ch. 9 : 18.
19. t. had six steps. top of t., 2
2 K. 11 : 19. Jehoash sat on t. of
kings, 2 Ch. 23 : 20. ⌈28 : 5.
1 Ch. 29 : 23. Sol-n sat on t. of Lord,
Ne. 3 : 7. repaired unto t. of gover-r
Jb. 36 : 7. with kings are they on t.
Ps. 11 : 4. Lord's t. is in heaven
45 : 6. Thy t., O God, is for ever,
La. 5 : 19. He. 1 : 8. ⌈erations
89 : 4. I will build thy t. to all gen-
14. Justice and judgment are the
habitation of thy t.
94 : 20. Shall t. of iniquity have fellowship with thee ⌈thy t.
132 : 11. Of thy body will I set upon
Is. 9 : 7. of peace no end upon t. of
14 : 13. I will exalt my t. ⌊David
22 : 23. Eliakim sh. be for glorious t.
47 : 1. is no t., O dau. of Chaldeans
66 : 1. The heaven is my t., Ac. 7 : 49.
Je. 3 : 17. call Jerus t. of the Lord
14 : 21. not disgrace t. of thy glory
17 : 12. A glorious high t. fr. begin-g
22 : 2. O ki , th. sittest upon t., 29 : 16.
Eze. 1 : 26. was likeness of t. (2) 10 : 1.
43 : 7. my t. shall Isr. no more defile
Hag. 2 : 22. I will overthrow the t.
of kingdoms ⌈t., 23 : 22.
Mat. 5 : 34. by heaven, for it is God's
Lu. 1 : 32. L. sh. give him t. of Dav.
He. 4 : 16. come boldly to t. of grace
8 : 1. right hand t. of God, 12 : 2.
Re. 4 : 2. a t. in heaven, one sat on t.
3. was a rainbow round about t.
4 about t. four and twenty seats
5. out of t. proceeded lightnings,
there were seven lamps bef. t.
6. before the t. was a sea of glass,
in t. and round the t. four beasts
9. thanks to him that sat on t.
10. fall before him that sat on t.,
and cast their crowns bef. the t.
5 : 1. in hand of him on t. a book
6. in midst of t. stood a Lamb
7. book out of hand of him on t.
11. voice of many angels ab. the t.
7 : 9. a great multitude stood bef. t.
11. all the angels stood about t.
and fell before t. on their faces
15. they are before the t. of God
17. lamb in midst of t. sh. feed th.
8 : 3. golden altar which was bef. t.
14 : 3. they sung a new song bef. t.
5. without fault bef. the t. of God
16 : 17. came a voice fr. the t., 19 : 5.
19 : 4. worshipped God th. sat on t.
20 : 11. I saw great white t. and
21 : 5. he that sat upon t. said ⌈t.
22 : 1. pure river proceeding out of
3 t. of God and Lamb sh. be in it

His THRONE. ⌈t.

Ex. 12 : 29. firstborn th. sat upon h.
2 S. 14 : 9. king and h. t. be guiltless
1 K. 1 : 37. his t. greater than t. of Da.
2 : 19. Sol-n bowed, sat on h. t. ⌊47.
33. upon his seed and h. t. sh. be
22 : 10. king of Israel and king of
Jud., sat each on h. t., 2 Ch. 18 : 9.
Jb. 26 : 9. He hold-h back face of h. t.
Ps. 9 : 7. prepared h. t. for judgment
89 : 29. h. t. to endure as days of
36. h. t. shall endure as the sun
44. thou hast cast h. t. down to
97 : 2. judgment habitation of h. t.
103 : 19. L. prepared h. t. in heavens
Pr. 20 : 28. h. t. upholden by mercy
Je. 1 : 15. set each h. t. at gates of J.
33 : 21. Da. not have son upon h. t.
43 : 10. set h. t. upon these stones
Da. 5 : 20. deposed from h. kingly t.
7 : 9. h. t. was like the fiery flame
Jon. 3 : 6. king of Nin-h rose fr. h. t.
Zch. 6 : 13. sh. be a priest upon h. t.
Re. 1 . 4. fr. seven spirits before h. t.
3 : 21. as I am with my Fa. in h. t.
Re. 12 : 5. her child up to G., to h. t.

THRONES. ⌈ment

Ps. 122 : 5. there are set t. of judg-
Is. 14 : 9. raised up fr. their t. kings
Eze. 26 : 16. princes down fr. their t.
Da. 7 : 9. I beheld till t. were cast
Col. 1 : 16. all created by him whe. t.
See ESTABLISH, ED, STABLISH.
See SAT, SATEST, SET.
See **SIT** with **throne, s.**
See **SITTETH** or **SITTING**
in, on, or upon throne, s.

THRONG, ED, ING.

Mk. 3 : 9. multitude, lest they t. him
5 : 24. much peo t-d him, Lu. 8 : 42.
31. Thou seest multitude t-g thee
Lu. 8 : 45. multitude t. thee and

THROUGH. ⌈t. them

Ge. 6 : 13. earth filled with violence
41 : 36. th. land perish not t. famine
Ex. 10 : 15. not any green thi. t. Eg.
14 : 24. L. looked upon Eg-ns t. pil-r
19 : 13. be be stoned or shot t. ⌊of fire
36 : 33. middle bar to shoot t. board
Nu. 24 : 8. pierce them t. with arrows
De. 29 : 16. how we came t. the nat-s
Jos. 2 : 15. she let them down t. win.
2 S. 4 : 7. gat them away t. plain
22 : 13. t. the brightness before him
30. I have run t. a troop, Ps. 18 : 29.
2 K. 1 : 2. Ahaziah fell t. lattice
Jb. 14 : 9. t. scent of water it bud
22 : 13. can he judge t. the dark
cloud? ⌈t. proud
26 : 12. by understanding smiteth
Ps 10 : 4. wicked t. pride of counten.
19 : 4. line is gone out t. all earth
32 : 3. bones waxed old t. my roar-g
44 : 5. t. thee push down enemies (2)
60 : 12. t. God we shall do valiantly
66 : 3. t. thy power enemies submit
68 : 7. when didst march t. wildern.
106 : 9. he led them t. the depths
110 : 5. sh. strike t. kings in wrath
115 : 7. Neither speak they t. throat
119 : 104. t. thy precepts I get und-g
Pr. 18 : 1. t. desire man seek-h wisd.
Ec. 10 : 18. t. idlen. house droppeth t.
Can. 2 : 9. shewing himself t. lattice
Is. 9 : 19. t. wrath of L. is land dark-d
28 : 7. they have erred t. wine; t.
strong drink are out of way (4)
30 : 31. t. will of L. Assyr-s be beaten
43 : 2. when t. the waters, t. the fire
Je. 51 : 52. t. land wounded sh groan
52 : 3. t. anger of L. it came to pass
Eze. 46 : 19. he brought me t. entry
47 : 4. and brought me t. waters
Zch. 4 : 12. t. two golden pipes empty
9 : 15. make a noise as t. wine, 10 : 7.
13 : 9. I will bring third part t. fire
Mat. 9 : 34. he casteth out devils t.
prince, Lu. 11 : 15, 18.
19 : 24. camel t. eye of needle, Mk.
10 : 25. Lu. 18 : 25. ⌈capolis
Mk. 7 : 31. unto sea of Galilee t. De-
11 : 16. not carry vessel t. temple
Lu. 1 : 78. t. tender mercy of our G.
5 : 19. they let him down t. tiling
17 : 1. woe unto him t. whom they
Jn. 4 : 4. he must needs go t. Sam-a
17 : 17. Sanctify th. t. the truth, 19.
Ac. 1 : 2. t. Holy Ghost given com-t
3 : 17. I wot t. ignorance ye did it
4 : 2. preached t. Jesus resurrect-n
8 : 18. saw th. t. laying on of hands
13 : 38. t. this man is preached
14 : 22. we must t. much tribula-n
20 : 3. purposed to return t. Maced.
Ro. 1 : 8. I thank my God t. Jesus
Christ, 7 : 25. ⌈hearts
24. uncleanness t. lusts of their
2 : 23. t. break-g law dishonourest G.
24. name of God blasphemed t. you
3 : 7. if truth of G. abounded t. my
24. by his grace t. redemption ⌊lie
4 : 13. not t. law, but t. righteousn.

Ro. 5 : 1. peace with God t. our Lord
11. we joy in God t. our L. Jesus
21. so might grace reign t. righte.
6 : 11. but alive unto God t. Jesus
23. gift of God is eternal life t. Jes.
8 : 3. law cou. not do, weak t. flesh
15 : 4 t. patience, comfort of Scrip.
13 abound in hope t. power of Holy Ghost [Jesus Christ
17. I have whereof I may glory t.
19. t. mighty signs and wonders
16 : 27. To only wise G. be glory, t.
1 Co. 1 : 1. Paul, apostle t. will of G
8 : 11. t. thy knowl. sh. weak broth.
13 : 12. now we see t. a glass darkly
15 : 57. giveth us victory t. our L.
2 Co. 3 : 4. such trust have we t. Ch.
4 : 15. might t. thanksg-g of many
9 : 11. causeth t. us thanksg-g to G.
11 : 3. serpent beguiled Eve t. subtil- [ty
33. t. window in a basket was I
13 : 4. tho. crucified t. weakness he
Ga. 2 : 19. I t. the law am dead to law
3 : 14. blessing on Gentiles t. Jes. Ch.
4 : 7. if son then heir of God t. Ch.
13. know how t. infirmity I prea.
5 : 10. I have confidence in you t. L.
Ep. 1 : 7. redemption t. his blood, Col. 1 : 14. [Christ
2 : 7. his kindness toward us t.
4 : 6. One G. and Fa. t. all in you all
18. alienated fr. life of God t. igno.
Ph. 1 : 19. my salvat-n t. y-r prayer
2 : 3. Let nothing be done t. strife
4 : 7. sh. keep your hearts t. Ch. Jes.
Col. 1 : 20. peace t. blood of his cross
22. In the body of his flesh t. death
2 : 8. spoil you t. philosophy [rows
1 Ti. 6 : 10. pierced thems. t. wi. sor-
Tit. 1 : 3. manifested word t. preach-g
3 : 6 shed on us t. Jesus Christ
Phm. 22. I trust t. y r prayers I sh.
He. 2 : 10. captain perfect t. suffer-gs
14. t. death might destroy him th.
9 : 14. t. Spirit offered hims. to God
10 : 10. sanctified t. offering of Jes.
20. new way t. the vail, his flesh
13 : 20. t. blood of everl-g covenant
21. working in you t. Jes. Christ
1 Pe. 1 : 6 heaviness t. manifold temp.
2 Pe. 1 : 1. faith, t. righteousn. of G.
2. Grace and peace t. knowl. of G.
4. corruption in the world t. lust
2 : 3. t. covetousn. wi. feigned words
18. they allure t. lusts of flesh, t. much wantonness [edge of L.
20. escaped pollutions t. knowl-
Re. 8 : 13. angel flying t. heaven
18 : 3 waxed rich t. her delicacies

See **BREAK through, Through FAITH, Through HIM, PASS through, PASSED, WENT through.**
See GO, GOING, GOSPEL, GRACE, NAME, PASSING, SPIRIT, THEM, THRUST, US, WALKETH, WORD.

THROUGHLY.

See THOROUGHLY.

THROUGHOUT.

Ex. 35 : 3. no fire t. habitations on [sab.
37 : 19. So t. 6 branches of candlest.
Nu. 1 : 52. ev. man by stand-d t. hosts
2 : 3. they of Judah pitch t. armies
9 in Judah were 186,400 t. armies
16. all of Reuben 151,450 t. armies
24. all of Ephr-m 108,100 t. armies
32. those of camps t. hosts 603,550
3 : 39. of Levites t. families 22,000
4 : 22. sons of Gershon, t. houses of fathers, 38, 40. [6 : 63.
42. sons of Merari t. families, 1 Ch.
10 : 25. Dan rearward of camps t. [hosts
11 : 10. people weep t. fam-s
28 : 14. burnt off-g t. months of yr.
21. offer for every lamb t. 7 lambs
24. ye sh. offer daily t. seven days
29 : 4 for one lamb t. 7 lambs, 10.
Jos. 16 : 1. fr. Jericho t. m-t Bethel
1 K. 22 : 36. went a proclamat-n t. host
1 Ch. 6 : 54. dwellingplaces t. castles
60. All their cities t. fam-s were 13
62 to sons of Gershon t. families
7 : 40. number t. genealogy of them
12 : 30. men, famous t. hou. of fa-s
26 : 6. ruled t. house of their fath-s
2 Ch. 16 : 9. eyes of Lord run t. earth
30 : 22. did eat t. the feast 7 days
Ezr. 10 : 7. proclamation t. Judah
Es. 3 : 6. to destroy Jews t. kingdom
Lu. 8 : 1. he went t. ev. city and vil- [lage
39. he published t. city how
Jn. 19 : 23. coat woven fr. the top t.
Ac. 8 : 1. scattered t. Judea, Samaria
1 Pe. 1 : 1. strangers scattered t. Pon- [tus

THROUGHOUT all.

Ge. 41 : 29. t. a. the land of Egypt, 45 : 8. Ex. 5 : 12.-7 : 19, 21.-8 : 16, 17.-9 : 9, 25.-11 : 6.
Ex. 9 : 16. my name may be declared t. a. the earth, Ro. 9 : 17.
34 : 3. nei. let man be seen t. a. m-t
40 : 38. in sight of Isr. t. a. journeys
Le. 3 : 17. statute t. a. y-r dwellings
25 : 9. make trumpet sound t. a. la.
10. proclaim liberty t. a. the land
De. 28 : 52. besiege thee t. a. thy la.
Jos. 6 : 27. Josh.'s fame t. a. country
24 : 3. I led Abr. t. a. land of Canaan
Ju. 6 : 35. messeng-s t. a. land of M.
7 : 22. ev. man ag. fellow t. a. host
24. sent messengers t. a. m-t Eph.
20 : 6. I sent her t. a. the country
1 S. 5 : 11. deadly destruc. t. a. city
11 : 7. oxen in pieces t. a. Israel
13 : 19. no smith t. a. land of Israel
23 : 23. search him out t. a. thous.
2 S. 8 : 14. t. a. Edom Da. put garri-s
1 K. 6 : 38 house finished t. a. parts
15 : 22. Asa made proclamat-n t. a. J.
2 K. 17 : 5. king of Assyria t. a. land
1 Ch. 5 : 10. tents t. a. land of Gilead
21 : 4. Joab went t. a. Isr., 2 S. 20 : 14.
22 : 5. house of glory t. a. countries
27 : 1. courses t. a. months of year
2 Ch. 11 : 23. his chil. t. a. countries
17 : 9. priests went t. a. cities of J.
19. put in fenced cities t. a. Judah
20 : 3. Jehosh. proclaimed fast t. a.
25 : 5. houses of fa-s t. a. Jud [Jud.
26 : 14. prepared t. a. host shields
30 : 5. to make proclamation t. a. Is.
6. posts went with letters t. a. Ju.
31 : 20. thus did Hez-h t. a. of Jud.
34 : 7. Josiah cut down idols t. a. la.
36 : 22. Cyrus made proclamation t. a. kingdom, Ezr. 1 : 1. [empire
Es. 1 : 20. k.'s decree published t. a.
Je. 17 : 3. places for sin t. a. borders
Eze. 38 : 21. sword ag. him t. a. mts.
Mat. 4 : 24. his fame went t. a. Syria
Mk. 1 : 28. his fame t. a. region, 39.
Lu. 1 : 65. noised t. a. hill country
4 : 25. great famine was t. a. land
7 : 17. rumour of him went t. a. Judea and t. a. region [Jewry
23 : 5. stirreth peo., teaching t. a.
Ac. 9 : 31. churches rest t. a. Judea
32. as Peter passed t. a. quarters
42. it was known t. a. Jop. [13 : 49.
10 : 37. word published t. a. Judea,
19 : 26. t. a. Asia this Paul turned
2 Co. 8 : 18. praise is t. a. churches
Ep. 3 : 21. Unto him glory in church t. a. ages, world without end

See CAMP, COASTS.

THROUGHOUT generation, s.

Ex. 30 : 21. a statute for ever t. their g-s, Le. 7 : 36.-10 : 9.-17 : 7.-23 : 14, 21, 31. Nu. 18 : 23.-35 : 29.
Nu. 1 : 42. children of Naphtali t.
Es. 9 : 28. days kept t. every g. [g-s
Ps. 145 : 13. thy dominion endureth t. all g-s

See GENERATIONS, PROVINCES, TRIBES, WORLD.

THROW down.

Ju. 2 : 2. ye shall t. d. their altars
6 : 25. t. d. the altar of Baal
2 S. 20 : 15. battered wall to t. it d.
2 K. 9 : 33. t. her d. So they threw
Je. 1 : 10. I have set thee to t. d.
31 : 28 watched over them to t. d.
Eze. 16 : 39. sh. t. d. eminent place
Mi. 5 : 11. I will t. d. strong holds
Mal. 1 : 4. They sh. build, I will t. d.

THROWING. [stone

Nu. 35 : 17. if he smite him with t. a
Ps. 78 : †9. children of Ephr. t. bows

THROWN.

Ex. 15 : 1. horse and rider hath t., 21.
2 S. 20 : 21. his head be t. over wall
Eze. 29 : 5. leave thee t. into wildern
Lu. 4 : 35. when the devil had t. him

THROWN down.

Ju. 6 : 32. bec. he hath t. d. his altar
1 K. 19 : 10. Isr. have t. d. altars, 14.
Je. 31 : 40. sh. not be t. d. any more
33 : 4. houses of kings of Jud. t. d.
50 : 15. foundat-ns fallen, walls t. d.
La. 2 : 2. Lord hath t. d. in his wrath
17. he hath t. d., hath not pitied
Eze. 38 : 20. mountains shall be t. d.
Na. 1 : 6. the rocks are t. d. by him
Mat. 24 : 2. not one stone left th. sh. not be t. d., Mk. 13 : 2. Lu. 21 : 6.
Re. 18 : 21. city of Bab-n sh. be t. d.

THRUM. [the t.

Is. 38 : † 12 he will cut me off from

THRUST, ETH.

Ex. 11 : 1. he shall surely t. you out
12 : 39. bec. they were t. out of Eg.
Nu. 22 : 25. Balaam's ass t. herself
25 : 8. Phinehas t. both of them thro.
35 : 20. but if he t. him of hatred
22. But if he t. him with-t enmity
De. 13 : 5. hath spoken to t. thee out
10. he sought to t. thee fr. the Lord
15 : 17. t. awl thro. his ear to door
33 : † 14. things t. forth by moon
27 he shall t. out the enemy from
Ju. 3 : 21. Ehud t. dagger into belly
6 : 38. t. fleece togeth., wringed dew
9 : 41. Zebul t. out Gaal and breth.
54. young men t. Abim-h through
11 : 2. wives' sons t. out Jephthah
1 S. 11 : 2. t. out all your right eyes
31 : 4. Saul said t. me thro., lest uncircumcised t. me, 1 Ch. 10 : 4.
2 S. 2 : 16. t. sword in his fel-w's side
15 : † 14. lest Abs. t. upon us [Abs.
18 : 14. Joab t. 3 darts thro. heart of
23 : 6. sons of Belial as thorns t. aw.
1 K. 2 : 27. Sol. t. Abiathar fr. priesth.
2 K. 4 : 27. Gehazi came near to t. her
2 Ch. 26 : 20. they t. Uzziah out from
Jb. 32 : 13. God t-h him down, not [man
Ps. 118 : 13. thou hast t. at me
Is. 13 : 15. Ev. one found sh. be t. thro.
14 : 19. as raiment of those t. thro.
Je. 51 : 4. are t. thro. in her streets
Eze. 16 : 40. sh. t. thee thro. wi. swords
21 : † 12. princes are t. down to the
34 : 21. ye have t. with side [forth
44 : † 22. nei. take for wives her t.
46 : 18. to t. them out of possess-ns
Jo. 2 : 8. Neither sh. one t. another
Zch. 13 : 3. shall t. him thro. when he prophesieth [kingdom
Mat. 11 : † 12. they that t. men take
Lu. 4 : 29. they t. him out of city
5 : 3. prayed he would t. out a little
10 : 15. Capernaum be t. down to h
13 : 28. Jacob in heaven, you t. out
Jn. 20 : 25. t. my hand into his side,
Ac. 7 : 27. he th. did wrong t. him [27.
39. our fathers t. him from them
16 : 24. who t. them into inner pris.
37. do they t. us out privily?
27 : 39. if possible to t. in the ship
He. 12 : 20. it sh. be stoned or t. thro.

Re. 14 : 15. t. in thy sickle, harvest
16. he that sat on cloud t. in sickle
18. t. in thy sharp sickle, gather
19. angel t. in his sickle into the
THUMB, S, and toe, s. ⌊earth
Ex. 29 : 20. put blood upon t. of
right hand, a. great t. of right
foot, Le. 8:23, 24.-14. 14, 17, 25, 28.
Ju. 1 :6. cut off his t-s a. great t-s
7. 70 kings their t-s a. t-s cut
THUMMIM with Urim.
Ex. 28 : 30. shalt put in breastplate
of judgment, U. and T., Le. 8 :8.
De. 33 : 8. Let thy T. and U. be with
Ezr. 2 : 63. stood up priest with U.
and T., Ne. 7 : 65.
THUNDER, S. [Noun.]
Ex. 9 : 23. the Lord sent t. and hail
29. t. shall cease, nor be hail
33. and the t-s and hail ceased, 34.
19 :16. t-s and lightnings, Re. 16: 18.
1 S. 7 :10. Lord thundered wi. great t.
12 : 17. sh. send t. | 18. Lord sent t.
Jb. 26 : 14. the t., who understand?
28 :26. way for lightning of t., 38: 25.
39 : 19. hast clothed his neck wi. t.?
25. he smelleth t. of captains afar
Ps. 77 : 18. The voice of thy t. was
81: 7. I answ-d in secret pla. of thy t.
104 : 7. at voice of t. hasted away
Is. 29 : 6. be visited of Lord with t.
Mk. 3 : 17. Boanerges, The sons of t.
Re. 6 : 1. I heard the noise of t.
10 : 3. seven t-s uttered voices, 4. (2)
14 : 2.. I heard voice as of great t.
THUNDER. [Verb.] ⌈th.
1 S. 2 : 10. out of heaven he t. upon
Jb. 40 : 9. or canst thou t. like him?
THUNDERBOLTS. ⌈t.
Ps. 78 :48. he gave their flocks to hot
THUNDERED, ETH.
1 S 7 : 10. L t-d with a gr. thunder
2 S. 22 : 14. The L. t-d from heaven,
Ps. 18 : 13. ⌈excellency
Jb. 37 : 4. he t-h with voice of his
5. God t-h marvellously with voice
Ps. 29 : 3. the God of glory t-h
Jn. 12 : 29. that heard it said it t-d
THUNDERINGS. ⌈t.
Ex. 9 : 28. there be no more mighty
20 : 18. all the people saw the t.
Re 4 : 5. out of throne proceeded t.
8: 5. were voices and t., 11: 19. ⌊19:6.
THUS.
Ge. 2 : 1. t., 19 : 36.-20 : 16.-21 :32.
-24 : 30.-25 : 34.-31 : 8, 9, 40.-
32 : 4.-36 : 8.-45 . 9. Ex. 3 : 14,
15.-5 : 15.-12 : 50.-14 : 11, 30.-
19 : 3.-20 : 22.-26 ; 17.-29 : 35.-
36 : 22.-40 : 16. Le. 15 : 31.-16 :
3. Nu. 4 : 49 -8 : 14, 26.-10 : 28.
-11 : 15.-15 : 11.-18 : 26, 28.-20:
21. - 21 : 31 - 23 : 5, 16. - 32 : 8.
De. 7 : 5.-32 : 6. Jos. 2 : 4.-6 :3.
-10 : 25.-21 : 13. 42.-22 :16. Ju.
8 : 28.-9 : 56.-11 : 33.-20 : 43. 1
S. 9 : 9.-18 : 25.-25 : 6.-26 : 18
2 S. 11 : 25.-12 : 31.-15 : 26 -16:
7.-17 : 21.-18 : 14, 33. 1 K. 1 :
48.-3 : 22.-5 : 11.-12 : 10.-16 :
12.-20: 2, 5. 2 K. 1 : 11 -9 : 18.-
10 : 28.-16 : 16.-18 : 29, 31.-19 :
3, 6, 10.-22 : 18. 1 Ch. 15 : 28.-
17 : 7.-18 : 6.-29 : 26. 2 Ch. 5: 1.
-10 : 10.-13 : 18 -19 : 9.-24 : 11,
22.-31 : 20.-32 : 10, 22.-36 : 23.
Ezr. 5 : 3, 7, 9.-6 : 2. Ne. 5 : 13.
-13 : 18. Es. 1 : 13.-2 : 13.-9 : 5.
Jb. 1 : 5 Ps. 38 : 14 -73 : 15.-
106 : 29, 39.-128 : 4. Is. 8 : 11 -
21 : 6, 16.-31 : 4. Je 4 : 27.-5 :
13.-6 : 6.-10 : 11.-18 :23.-19: 12.
-21 : 3.-22 : 8.-23 : 35, 37.-26 :
19.-27 : 4.-28 : 2.-29 : 24, 25.-
30 : 2.-33 : 24.-35 : 8.-37 : 21.-
43 : 7.-45 : 4 -48 : 47.-51 : 4, 64.
-52 : 27. Eze. 5 : 13.-6 : 12.-11 :
5.-13 : 15.-16 : 19.-23 : 4, 7, 21,
27, 39, 48.-24 : 24.-30 : 19.-31 :
7, 18.-33 : 10, 27.-34 : 30.-35 :7.-
38 : 14.-39 : 16.-43 : 20.-46 : 15.
Da. 1 : 16 -2 : 24, 25.-4 : 10, 14.
-6 : 6.-7 : 5, 23.-11 : 17, 39. Ho.
10 : 4. Am. 5 : 16.-7 : 1, 4, 7.-8 :
1. Mi. 5 : 6. Hag. 1 : 2. Zch. 6 :
12.-7 : 9, 14. Mal. 1 : 13. Mat.
2 : 5.-3 : 15.-15 : 6.-26 : 54. Mk.
2 : 7. Lu. 1 : 25.-2 : 48.-9 : 34.-
11 : 45.-17 : 30.-18 : 11.-19 : 28
-23 : 46.-24 : 36, 40, 46. Jn. 4.
6.-9 : 6.-11 : 48.-13 : 21.-18 :22
-20 : 14 Ac 19 : 41.-20 :36.-21
11.-26 : 24, 30.-27 : 35. 2 Co. 1
17. Ph. 3 : 15. He. 6 : 9.-9 : 6.
Re. 9 : 17.-18 : 21. ⌈all God
Ge. 6 : 22. t. did Noah according to
25 :22. she said, If so, why am I t.?
31 : 40. t. it was; in the day drought
41. t. have I been 20 yrs. in thy ho.
37 : 35. t. his father wept for him
Ex. 5 : 10. t. saith, Nu. 20 : 14.-22 :
16. Jos. 22 : 16. Ju. 11 : 15. 1 K.
2 : 30.-22 :27. 2 Ch. 24 : 20. Ezr.
1 : 2. Is. 30 : 12.-36 : 4, 16.-37 :
6.-42 : 5.-57 : 15. Am. 7 : 11.
12 : 50. t. did all the chil. of Israel
12 : 11. t. shall ye eat it, girded
26 : 24. t. shall it be for them both
39 : 32. t. was all the work finished
Nu. 4 : 19. t. do that they may live
8 : 7. t. sh. thou do to cleanse them
15 : 11. t. it be done for one bullock
De. 9 : 25. t. I fell bef. Lord 40 days
Jos. 2 : 4. t. said, 2 S. 16 : 7. 1 K. 1 :
48. Ezr. 5 : 3, 9. Is. 21 : 6. Eze.
11 : 5. Da. 2 : 24, 25.-4 : 14.-6:
6.-7 : 5, 23. Jn. 13 : 21.-20 : 14.
7 : 10. wheref. liest t. upon thy face
Ju. 8 : 1. Why hast served us t.?
13 :18. why askest t. aft. my name?
1 S. 14 : 9. If they say t. unto us,
10. If say t., Come unto us ⌊Tarry
20 :7. if he say t., It is well, 2 S. 15:
22. if I say t. to young man ⌊26.
2 S. 6 : 22. I be yet more vile than t.
18 : 33. t. he said, O my son Absa.
1 Ch. 24 : 4. t. were they divided, 5.
Ezr. 5 : 11. t. they returned answer
Es. 6 : 11. t. be done to man wh. k., 9.
Ne. 5 : 13. even t. he be shaken out
Jb. 27 : 12. why ye t. altogeth. vain?
Ps. 38 : 14. t. I was as man th. hear-h
63 : 4. t. will I bless thee while ⌊not
73 :21. t. was my heart grieved ⌈ry
106 : 20. t. they changed their glo-
Is. 24 :13. when t. it shall be in land
47 : 15. t. shall they be unto thee
Je. 31 : 18. Ephr. bemoaning hims. t.
33 : 24. t. have ye despised my peo.
38 : 4. t. he weakeneth the hands of
Eze. 1 : 11. of an eagle; t. their faces
4 : 13. even t. sh. chil. of Israel eat
16 : 13. t. wast thou decked in gold
19. and t. it was, saith Lord God
31 : 7. t. was he fair in his greatn-s
18 to wh. art thou t. like in glory
39 : 20. t. ye sh. be filled at my table
Da. 11 : 17. upright with him; t. sh.
Am. 2 : 11. Is it not t., O Israel ⌈day
Lu. 17 : 30. Even t. shall it be in the
Jn. 11 : 43. if we let him t. alone
Ro 9 : 20. say, Why hast made me t.
1 Co. 14 :25. t. all secrets of his heart
2 Co. 5 : 14. we t. judge if one died
Re. 16 : 5 bec. thou hast judged t.
See DEAL, DEALT, DID, DO,
DONE, FAR, SAID, SAY, SAITH,
SPAKE, SPOKEN, WRITTEN.
See **Thus saith the LORD,**
Thus saith the LORD of
hosts.
THUS and THUS.
Jos. 7 :20. Achan said, t. - ha. I done
Ju. 18 : 4. t. - dealeth Micah wi. me
2 S. 17 :15. t. - did Ahithophel coun.
sel Absalom. t. - I counselled
1 K. 14 :5. t. - sh. say to Jerob.'s wife
2 K. 5 : 4. t. - said the maid of Israel
9 : 12. he said, t. - spake he to me
THYATI'RA. ⌈God
Ac. 16 : 14. Lydia of T. worshipped
Re. 1 :11. send it unto 7 ch-s, unto T.
2 : 18. unto angel in ch. in T. write
24. unto you I say and rest in T.
THYINE. ⌈wood
Re. 18 : 12. no man buyeth their t.
THYSELF. ⌈from me
Ge 13 : 9. separate t., I pray thee,
14 : 21. me the persons, goods to t.
16 : 9. submit t. under her hands
33 : 9. brother, keep that unto t.
Ex. 9 : 17. exaltest t. ag. my people
10: 3. How long refuse to humble t.?
18 : 14. said, Why sittest t. alone?
18. not able to perform it t.
22. so shall it be easier for t.
20 : 5. not bow t. to them, De. 5 : 9.
34 : 2. present t. there before me
Le. 9 : 7. Go make atonement for t.
18 : 20. wi. neighb-'s wife to defile t.
23. Nei. lie with beast to defile t.
19 :34. stranger, shalt love him as t.
Nu. 11 : 17. bear it not t. alone
16 : 13. exc. make t. a prince ov. us
De. 9 : 1. nations greater than t.
20 : 14. all the spoil shalt take to t.
22 : 12. vesture wherew. coverest t.
23 : 13. wilt ease t. thou shalt dig
28 :40. but thou shalt not anoint t.
Jos. 17 : 15. cut down for t. in land
Ru. 3 :3. wash t., make not t. known
4 : 6. redeem thou my right to t.
1 S. 20 : 8. if iniq-y in me, slay me t.
25 : 26. withholden fr. avenging t.
2 S. 5 : 24. then thou shalt bestir t.
7 :24. hast confirmed to t., thy peo.
13 : 5. Lay down and make t. sick
14 : 2. feign t. to be a mourner, and
anoint not t. with oil ⌈me
18 : 13. wouldest have set t. against
1 K. 2 :3. prosper whitherso. turn-t t.
3 :11. not asked for t. long life, but
understanding, 2 Ch. 1 : 11. ⌈t.
13 : 7. Come home with me, refresh
14 :2. Arise, I pray, and disguise t.
6. why feignest t. to be another?
20 :22. strengthen t., see what thou
40. judgment, t. hast decided it
21 : 20. bec. hast sold t. to work ev.
1 Ch. 21 : 12. advise t. what word
2 Ch. 20 : 37. joined t. with Ahaziah
21 : 13. slain breth. better than t.
Es. 4 :13. Think not wi. t. thou sh. es-
Jb. 5 : † 27. hear, know it for t. ⌊cape
8 : 8. prepare t. to search of fathers
15 : 8. dost restrain wisdom to t.
22 : 21. Acquaint t. with him and
30 :21. with hand opposest t. ag. me
40 : 10. deck t. now with majesty,
array t. with glory and beauty
Ps. 7 : 6. in thine anger lift up t.
10 : 1. why hidest t. in times of
35 : 23. Stir up t. and awake ⌊troub.
37 : 1. Fret not t. because of evil
doers, Pr. 24 : 19.
4. Delight t. also in the Lord
7. Fret not t. bec. of him who pros-
8. fret not t. to do evil ⌊pereth
49 : 18. praise when doest well to t.
50 : 21. that I was such a one as t.
52 : 1. why boastest t. in mischief
80: 15. branch madest stro. for t., 17.
85 :3. turned t. fr. fierceness of ang.
94 : 2. Lift up t., Judge of the earth
104 : 2. Who coverest t. with light
Pr. 6 :3. Do this, my son, deliver t., 5.
9 : 12. If wise, shalt be wise for t.
24 : 27. make it fit for t. in the field
25 : 6. Put not t. in presence of k.
27 : 1. Boast not t. of to morrow ⌈t.
30 : 32. done foolishly in lifting up

Ec. 7 : 16. nor make t. over wise, why shouldest thou destroy t. ?
22. thou t. hast cursed others
Is. 33 : 3. lifting up t. nations were
52 : 2. Shake t. from dust, loose t.
57 : 8. hast discovered t. to another
9. thou didst debase t. unto hell
58 : 14. shalt delight t. in the L. rd
63 : 14. to make t. a glorious name
64 : 12. Wilt th. refrain t. for these
65 : 5. say, Stand by t., com: not
Je. 2 : 17. Hast not procured unto t.
4 : 30. Tho. clothest t. wi. crimson, in vain shalt thou make t. fair
6 :26. sackcloth, wallo t. in ashes
17 : 4. t.sh. discontinue fr. heritage
20 : 4. I will make thee terror to t.
22 :15. bec. thou closest t. in cedar
32 : 8. the redemption, buy it for t.
45 : 5. seekest great things for t.
46 : 19. furnish t. to go into capt-y
47 : 5. how long wilt thou cut t. ?
6. O sword, put t. into scabbard
La. 2 : 18. give t. no rest, let not eye
3 : 44. hast covered t. with cloud
4 : 21. be drunken, make t. naked
Eze. 3 : 24. Go shut t. within house
16 : 17. madest to t. images of men
22 : 4. hast defiled t. in thine idols
23 : 40. they for whom didst wash t. and deckest t. wi. ornaments
31 : 10. Bec. thou hast lifted up t.
38 :7. prepare for t. and company
Da. 5 : 17. said, Let thy gifts be to t.
23. hast lifted up t. ag. the Lord
10 :12. to chasten t. before thy God
Ho. 13 : 9. O Israel hast destroyed t.
Ob. 4. Though exalt t. as the eagle
Mi. 1 : 10. in house of Aphrah roll t.
5 : 1. gather t. in troops, O daugh-r
Na. 3 : 15. make t. many as canker-worm, make t. many as locusts
Zch. 2 : 7. Deliv. t., O Zion[Lu. 4 : 9.
Mat. 4 : 6. If Son of G., cast t. down,
5 : 33. shalt not forswear t. [37, 39.
27 : 40. save t., Mk. 15 : 30. Lu. 23 :
Lu. 4 : 23. say, Physician, heal t.
6 : 42. t. beholdest not the beam
7 : 6. Lord, trouble not t. for I am
10 : 27. shalt love thy neighb. as t.
17 : 8. will say, Gird t. and serve me
Jn. 1 :22. Who art thou? What of t. ?
8 : 13. Thou bearest record of t. [t.
53. prophets dead, whom makest
10 : 33. being man, makest t. God
14 : 22. L., how manifest t. unto us
18 : 34. Sayest thou this of t. ? or
21 : 18. When young, thou girdedst
Ac. 8 : 29. join t. to this chariot [t.
12 : 8. angel said unto him, Gird t.
16 : 28. Paul cried, Do t. no harm
21 : 24. purify t. with them, that all may know t. walkest or lerly
24 : 8. t. mayest take knowledge
26 : 1. art permitted to speak for t.
24. said, Paul, thou art beside t.
Ro. 2 : 1. judgest ano., condemnest t.
19. that t. art guide of the blind
21. that teachest, teachest not t.
14:22. Hast thou faith? have it to t.
Ga. 6 : 1 considering t., lest be temp.
1 Ti. 3 : 15. oughtest to behave t.
4 : 7. exercise t. unto godliness
15. things, give t. wholly to them
16. shalt save t. and them th. hear
5 : 22. oth. men's sins, keep t. pure
6 : 5. corrupt, fr. such withdraw t.

THYSELF with hide, est.

De. 22 : 1. not see bro.'s ox astray
3. thou mayest not h.t. [and h.t.
4. shalt not see ass fall and h.t.
1 S. 19 : 2. abide in secret place, h.t.
20 : 19. place where didst h.t.
1 K. 17 : 3. turn thee eastward, h.t.
22 :25. into inner chamber to h.t., 2 Ch. 18 : 24. [cation
Ps. 55 : 1. h. not t. from my suppli-
Ps. 89 :46. L., wilt thou h.t. forever?
Is. 26 : 20. h.t. for a little moment
45 : 15. thou art a God that h.t t.
58 : 7. h. not t. fr. thine own flesh
See HUMBLE, LOVE [Verb], SHEW, SHEWEST, SHEWING, TAKE heed, TURN again.

TIBE'RIAS. [T.

Jn. 6 : 1. sea of Galilee, wh. is sea of
23. came other boats from T. [T.
21 : 1. shewed to disciples at sea of

TIBE'RIUS CE'SAR.

Lu. 3 : 1. Now in 15th year of T. C.

TIB'HATH = BE'TAH.

2 S. 8 : 8.† from T. and Chun David took much brass, 1 Ch. 18 : 8.†

TIB'NI. [T

1 K. 16 : 21. half of the peo. followed
22. Omri prevailed ag. those fol-

TI'DAL. [lowed T.

Ge. 14 : 1. T., king of nations, made

TIDE. [war, 9.

See EVENINGTIDE, EVENTIDE.

TIDINGS.

Ge. 29 : 13. Laban heard t. of Jacob
Ex. 33 : 4. when people heard evil t.
1 S. 4 : 19. Phinehas's wife heard t.
11 : 4. told t. of men of Jabesh, 5, 6.
27 : 11. David saved none to bring t.
2 S. 4 : 4. when t. came of Saul[his t.
10. would have given reward for
13 :30. t. came, Absalom hath slain the king's sons [t., 25, 26, 31.
18 : 19. Let me run bear the king
20. Joab said, Thou shalt not bear t. this day, but bear t. ano. day
22. why run? thou hast no t. ready
31. Cushi said, t. my lord the king
1 K. 2 : 28. t. came to Joab, Joab fled
14 : 6. am sent to thee wi. heavy t.
1 Ch. 10 : 9. to carry t. to their idols,
Ps. 112 : 7. not be afraid of evil t. [t.
Je. 20 : 15. Cursed be man th. bro-t
37 : 5. Chaldeans heard t. of them
49 : 23. for they have heard evil t.
Eze. 21 : 7. Wherefore sighest thou? For the t. [him
Da. 11 :44. t. of the east shall trouble
Ac. 11 :22. t. came unto the church
21 : 31. t. came unto chief captain
See GLAD, GOOD tidings.

TIE, TIED. [blue

Ex. 39 : 31. they t-d to it a lace of
1 S. 6 : 7. t. the kine to the cart, 10.
1 K. 18 : † 44. t. thy chariot, get down
20 : † 14. Who shall t. the battle?
2 K. 7 : 10. no man there, but horses t-d, asses t-d [neck
Pr. 6:21. bind upon thy heart, t. about
Mat. 21 : 2. ye shall find an ass t-d, and a colt, Mk. 11:2, 4. Lu. 19:30.

TIERCE. [in a t.

Is. 40 : † 22. comprehended the dust

TIG'LATH-PILE'SER.

2 K. 15 : 29. T. took Ijon and Kedesh
16 : 7. Ahaz sent messengers to T.
10. Ahaz went to Damas. to meet T.
See TILGATH-PILNESER.

TIKVAH, TIKVATH.

2 K. 22 : 14.† wife of Shallum son of T., 2 Ch. 34 : 22. [empioyed
Ezr. 10 : 15. Only Jahaziah son of T.

TILE.

Eze. 4 : 1. thou son of man take the t.

TILING. [the t.

Lu. 5 : 19. they let him down thro.

TIL'GATH-PILNE'SER.

1 Ch. 5 : 6. Beerah T. carried captive
26. God stirred up the spirit of T.
2 Ch. 28 : 20. T. came and distressed
See TIGLATH-PILESER.

TILL. [eturu

Ge. 3 : 19. in sweat eat bread t. thou
19:22. I cannot do any thing t. thou
29 : 8. t. they rolled stone fr. wells
38 : 11. a widow t. Shelah be grown
17. wilt give me pledge t. th. send
Ex. 15 :16. sh. be still t. thy peo. pass
34 : 33. t. Moses had done speak-g
40 : 37. journeyed not t. day it was
Nu. 12 : 15. journeyed not t. Miriam
De. 17 : 5. sh. stone them t. they die
28 : 45. pursue t. thou be destroyed
Ju. 3 :25. tarried t. they were asham.
11 : 33. smote t. thou come to Min.
19 :26. woman at door t. it was light
Ru. 1 : 13. ye tarry t. th. were grown
1 S. 16 : 11. we not sit t. he come[me
22 : 3. t. I know what G. will do for
2 S. 3 :35. if I taste bread t. sun be d.
1 K. 14 : 10. taketh aw. dung t. it all
18 : 28. cut thems. t. blood gushed
2 K. 2 : 17. urged t. he was ashamed
7 : 9. if we tarry t. morning light
10 : 17. slew Ahab t. destroyed him
21 :16. shed blood t. he filled Jerus.
2 Ch. 26 : 15. helped t. he was strong
29 : 34. breth. did help t. work was
36 :16. th. mocked t. was no remedy
Ezr. 2 : 63. t. a priest wi. Urim, Ne.
5 : 5. t. mat-r came to Darius[7:65.
Ne. 2 : 7. convey t. I come into Jud.
4 : 11. nei. see t. we come am. them
21. held spears t. stars appeared
13 : 19. gates not opened t. aft. sab.
Jb. 7 : 19. t. I swallow my spittle?
8 :21. t. fill thy mouth wi. laughing
14 : 6. rest t. he accomplish his day
12. man riseth not t. the heavens
14. will I wait t. my change come
27 : 5. t. I die, not remove integrity
32 : 4. Elihu waited t. Job had spok.
Ps. 10 :15. seek wickedn. t. find none
68 : 30. t. every one submit himself
Pr. 7 :23. t. dart strike thro. his liver
29 : 11. wise keepeth it in t. afterw.
Ec. 2 : 3. t. might see wh. was good
Can. 2 : 7. my love, t. he please, 3: 5.
Is. 5 : 8. field to field, t. be no place
22 : 14. not be purged t. ye die
23 : 13. t. Assy-n founded it for th.
30 : 17. t. ye be left as a beacon
42 : 4. sh. not fail t. he set judgm-t
62 : 7. no rest t. he make Jerus. a
Je. 7 : 32. sh. bury in Tophet t. be no place, 19 : 11. [Ob. 5.
49 : 9. destroy t. they have enough
52 : 3. anger of L. t. he cast th. out
11. Zed-h in prison t. day of death
La. 3 :50. t. L. looked down fr. heav.
Eze. 4 : 8. not turn from one side to another t. ended siege [fury
24 : 13. thou not be purged t. my
28 : 15. wast perfect t. iniq-y found
34 : 21. t. ye have scattered them
39 : 15. t. buriers have buried it in
19. ye shall eat fat t. ye be full, and drink blood t. be drunk. (2)
47 : 20. t. a man come ov. ag. Ham.
Da. 2 :9. to speak t. time be changed
34. sawest t. a stone was cut out
4:23. with beasts t. 7 times pass over
25. t. know Most High ruleth, 5:21.
33. t. his hairs grown like eagles'
6 :14. laboured t. going down of sun
7 :4. I beheld t. wings were plucked
9. I beheld t. thrones were cast
11. I beheld t. beast was slain [ed
10 : 3. nei. anoint t. 3 weeks fulfill-
11 : 36. k. exalt hims. t. indignat-n
12 : 9. words sealed t. time of end
13. go thou thy way t. the end be
Ho. 5 : 15. t. they acknowl. offence
10 :12. t. he rain righteousn. upon
Jon. 4 : 5. t. see what become of city
Zph. 3 : 3. gnaw not bones t. mor-w
Mat. 1 : 25. he knew her not t. she
2 : 9. t. it stood over where child
5 : 18. t. heaven and earth pass, one jot in no wise pass t. all be
26. by no means come out t. hast
10 : 11. there abide t. ye go thence,
23. t. Son of man be come[Mk. 6:10.
12 : 20. t. he send judgm. unto vict.

Mat. 13 : 33. leaven in meal t. whole was leavened, Lu. 13 : 21.
16 : 28. not taste of death t. they see Son of man, Mk. 9 : 1. Lu. 9 : 27
18 : 21. I forgive him? t. 7 times? 30. t. he sho. pay debt, 34. Lu. 12 : 59.
22 : 44. t. I make enemies footstool, Mk. 12 : 36. Lu. 20 : 43. He. 10 : 13.
23 : 39. not see me t. ye say, Blessed
24 : 34. this generation not pass t. all these things be fulfilled, 5 : 18. Mk. 13 : 30. Lu. 21 : 32.
Mk. 9 : 9. t. Son of man were risen
Lu. 1 : 80. in deserts t. day of his
12 : 50. how am I straitened t. it be
13 : 8. t. I shall dig about it and
15 : 8. not sweep house t. she find it
17 : 8. serve me t. I have eaten and
19 : 13. he said, Occupy t. I come
Jn. 13 : 38. not crow t. hast denied
21 : 22. If I will that he tarry t. I
Ac. 7 : 18. t. ano. k. arose [coms, 23.
8 : 40. cities t. he came to Cesarea
20 : 11. Paul talked t. break of day
21 : 5. bro-t on our way t. out of city
23 : 12. nei. eat t. had killed P., 21.
25 : 21. t. I might send him to Cesar
28 : 23. persuading fr. morn. t. ev-g
1 Co. 11 : 26. shew L.'s death t. he
15 : 25. reign t. put all enemies und
Ga. 3 : 19. t. seed come to wh. prom- [ise
Ep. 4 : 13. t. we all come in unity
Ph. 1 : 10. with-t offence t. day of Ch.
1 Ti. 4 : 13. t. I come give attendance
Re. 2 : 25. that hold fast t. I come
7 : 3. t. we sealed servants of our G.
15 : 8. t. seven plagues were fulfilled
20 : 3. t. the thous. yrs. be fulfilled
See **CONSUMED** with till, Till the **MORNING**, UNTIL.

TILL. [Verb.] [23

Ge. 2 : 5. not a man to t. ground, 3 :
2 S. 9 : 10. thy servants shall t. land
Je. 27 : 11. they shall t. it and dwell

TILLAGE. [for t.

1 Ch. 27 : 26. Ezri over them th. were
Ne. 10 : 37. Levites have tithes of t.
Pr. 13 : 23. Much food is in t. of poor
1 Co. 3 : † 9. ye are God's t., ye are

TILLED.

Eze. 36 : 9. I am for you, ye sh. be t.
36 : 34. the desolate land shall be t.

TILLER.

Ge. 4 : 2. Cain was a t. of the ground

TILLEST, ETH.

Ge. 4 : 12. When thou t-t the ground
Pr. 12 : 11. t-h his land sh. be satisf.
28 : 19. t-h his land sh. have plenty

TI'LON. See RINNAH.

TIMBER.

Ex. 31 : 5. And in carving of t.
Le. 14 : 45. he sh. break down the t.
1 K. 5 : 6. not any that can skill to hew t. like, 2 Ch. 2 : 8. [6 : 10.
8. thy desire conc. t. of cedar (2),
18. prepared t. and stones to build house, 2 K. 12 : 12.-22 : 6. 1 Ch. 22 : 14, 15. 2 Ch. 2 : 9. [2 Ch. 16 : 6.
15 : 22. they took aw. t. of Ramah,
1 Ch. 14 : 1. Hiram sent t. of cedars
2 Ch. 2 : 10. I will give to hewers th.
14. sent a man skilful in t. [cut t.
34 : 11. to buy stone, t. for couplings
Ezr. 5 : 8. and t. is laid in the walls
6 : 4. g-t stones and a row of new t.
11. let t. be pulled from his house
Ne. 2 : 8. give me t. to make beams
Eze. 26 : 12. shall lay thy t. in water
Ha. 2 : 11. beam out of t. sh. answer
Zch. 5 : 4. It shall consume it with [the t.

TIMBREL, S.

Ex. 15 : 20. Miriam took a t. in her hand; the wom. went aft. wi. t-s
Ju. 11 : 34. his dau. came out wi. t-s
2 S. 6 : 5. David and Israel played before Lord on t-s, 1 Ch. 13 : 8.
Jb. 21 : 12. They take the t. and harp
Ps. 68 : 25. damsels playing with t-s
81 : 2. Take a psalm, bring hither t.
149 : 3. let sing praises with the t.
150 : 4. Praise him wi. t. and dance
Je. 31 : † 4. shalt be adorned with t-s

TIME. [water

Ge. 24 : 11. t. th. women go to draw
29 : 7. nei. is it t. cattle be gathered
31 : 10. at the t. cattle conceived
39 : 5. from t. he made him overseer
47 : 29. t. drew nigh Israel must die
Ex. 21 : 19. shall pay for loss of his t.
Le. 15 : 25. if beyond t. of her separ.
26 : 5. vintage reach unto sowing t.
Nu. 13 : 20. was t. of first ripe grapes
26 : 10. t. the fire devoured 250 men
De. 16 : 9. t. thou put sickle to corn
Jos. 6 : 16. 7th t. when priests blew
10 : 27. at t. of going down of sun, Joshua com-d-d, 2 Ch. 18 : 34.
42. land did Joshua take at one t.
22 : 27. not say in t. to come, Ye
Ju. 9 : 8. The trees went forth on a t.
14 : 8. aft. t. he returned to take her
18 : 31. all t. house of G. in Shiloh
Ru. 4 : 7. was manner in former t.
1 S. 1 : 4. t. was th. Elkanah offered
† 7. fr. t. she went up to hou. of L.
18 : 19. t. Merab been given to Dav.
27 : 7. t. Da. dwelt in country of Phi.
2 S. 2 : 11. t. Da. was king in Hebron
7 : 6. since t. I bro-t chil. of Israel
11. since t. I commanded judges, 1 Ch. 17 : 10. [battle
11 : 1. at t. when kings go forth to
23 : 8. against 800 he slew at one t.
20. Benaiah slew lion in t. of snow
1 K. 11 : 42. t. Sol. reigned was 40 yrs.
18 : 29. prophesied until t. of offering, 36. [tle cloud
44. at 7th t. he said, Behold, a lit-
2 K. 5 : 26. Is it t. to receive money
10 : 36. t. Jehu reigned was 28 yrs.
1 Ch. 9 : 25. were to come from t. to t.
11 : 11. 300 slain by him at one t.
20 : 1. at the t. kings go to battle
4. at wh. t. Sibbechai slew Sippai
29 : 27. t. David reigned was 40 yrs
2 Ch. 24 : 11. t. chest was brought
25 : 27. aft. t. Amaziah did turn from
30 : 26. since t. of Sol. not the like
Ezr. 4 : 17. Peace, and at such a t., 10, 11.-7 : 12. [t. of rain
10 : 13. peo. are many, and it is a
Ne. 2 : 6. when return? I set him a t.
5 : 14. fr. t. I was appointed gover- [nor
6 : 5. Sanballat sent fifth t.
9 : 32. since t. of kings of Assyria
Jb. 6 : 17. t. they wax warm vanish
9 : 19. who shall set me a t. to plead
15 : 32. he accomplished bef. his t.
22 : 16. wicked, cut down out of t.
30 : 3. in former t. desolate, waste
39 : 1. Knowest t. they bri. forth, 2.
18. What t. she lifteth up herself
Ps. 32 : 6. a t. thou mayest be found
38 : † 4. I may know what t. I have
56 : 3. t. I am afraid, I will trust
69 : 13. my prayer in acceptable t.
78 : 38. many a t. turned anger aw.
81 : 15. their t. sho. have endured
89 : 47. Remember how short my t.
105 : 19. Until t. that his word came
119 : 126. It is t. for thee, L., to work
129 : 1. many a t. ha. afflicted me, 2.
Ec. 3 : 1. there is a t. to every purpose under the heaven, 17.-8 : 6.
2. A t. to be born, a t. to die, a t. to plant, and a t., 3, 4, 5, 6, 7, 8.
3 : 11. every thing beautiful in his t.
7 : 17. why shouldest die bef. thy t.
8 : 5. wise man's heart discerneth t.
9. a t. one man ruleth to his hurt
9 : 11. t. and chance happ-th to all
12. For man knoweth not his t.
Is. 26 : 17. near t. of her delivery
28 : 19. Fr. t. it goeth forth it sh. take
Is. 45 : 21. who declared this fr. anc-t
48 : 16. from t. that it was am I [t.?
49 : 8. In an acceptable t. have I heard thee, 2 Co. 6 : 2. [his t.
60 : 22. I the Lord will hasten it in
Je. 6 : 15. t. I visit they be cast down
8 : 7. swallow observe t. of coming
15. for t. of health, behold troub.
14 : 19. for t. of healing, trouble
49 : 8. t. th. I will visit him, 50 : 31.
19. who appoint me the t.? 50 : 44.
51 : 33. Bab., it is t. to thresh her (2)
Eze. 4 : 10. fr. t. to t. sh. thou eat it, 11.
16 : 8. thy t. was t. of love, I spread
57. at t. of thy reproach of dau-s
30 : 3. it shall be t. of the heathen
Da. 2 : 8. I know ye would gain t.
9. lying words till the t. be changed
16. Daniel desired he would give t.
3 : 5. at t. ye hear the cornet, 15.
7 : 12. lives were prolonged for a t.
22. t. came, saints posses-d kingd.
25. until a t. and divid-g of t.. 12 : 7.
8 : 17. at t. of end the vision, 23.
11 : 24. forecast his devices for a t.
35. make white, to t. of the end
40. at t. of end shall king of south
12 : 4. seal book to t. of the end, 9.
11. from t. daily sacrifice be taken
Ho. 9 : 10. ripe in fig tree at first t.
10 : 12. it is t. to seek the Lord
13 : † 13. not stay a t. in the place
Mi. 5 : 3. until t. she wh. travaileth
Hag. 1 : 2. t. Lord's house be built
4. is it t. to dwell in ceiled houses
Zch. 14 : 7. at evening t. it sh. be light
Mal. 3 : 11. nei. vine cast fruit bef. t.
Mat. 2 : 7. Herod inquired wh. t. star
8 : 29. art to torment us bef. the t.?
21 : 34. when t. of fruit drew near
26 : 18. master saith, My t. is at ha.
Mk. 1 : 15. The t. is fulfilled, repent
4 : 17. no root, so endure but for t.
6 : 35. This is desert, t. is far passed
11 : 13. the t. of figs was not yet
13 : 33. ye know not when the t. is
Lu. 1 : 10. peo. praying at t. of incen.
57. Elisabeth's t. to be delivered
4 : 5. shewed kingd-s in mom-t of t.
7 : 45. this woman, since t. I came
14 : 17. sent his servant at supper t.
21 : 8. t. draweth near, go not after
Jn. 7 : 6. My t. is not come, your t.
16 : 2. t. cometh whoso. killeth you
25. t. cometh I shall no more spe.
Ac. 1 : 21. t. the L. went in and out
7 : 17. when t. of promise drew nigh
20. in which t. Moses was born
17 : 21. spent t. in nothing, but to
18 : 20. desired him to tarry longer
23. spent some t. he departed [t.
20 : 16. be wou. not spend t. in Asia
27 : 9. Now when much t. was spent
Ro. 13 : 11. it is high t. to awake
1 Co. 4 : 5. Judge nothing bef. the t.
7 : 5. except with consent for a t.
29. I say, brethren, the t. is short
16 : 12. he come when convenient t.
2 Co. 6 : 2. I heard thee in a t. accepted; now is the accepted t.
Ep. 5 : 16. Redeeming the t., Col. 4 : 5.
1 Th. 2 : 17. taken from you for a short
2 Th. 2 : 6. be revealed in his t. [t.
1 Ti. 4 : † 8. bodily exercise profiteth a little t. [hand
2 Ti. 4 : 6. t. of my departure is at
He. 5 : 12. t. ye ought to be teachers
9 : 10. on them until t. of reforma- [tion
11 : 32. t. fail to tell of Gideon
Ja. 4 : 14. that appeareth a little t.
1 P. 1 : 11. searching what t. Spirit
17. t. of your sojourning in fear
4 : 2. no longer live rest of his t.
Re. 1 : 3. the t. is at hand, 22 : 10.
10 : 6. sware, should be t. no longer
11 : 18. t. of dead, th. they be judged
12 : 12. know-h he hath but short t.

Re. 12 : 14. she is nourished for a t.
and times, and half a t. [reap
14 : 15. the t. has come for thee to

TIME with about.

Ge. 39 : 11. a. this t. Joseph went
Jos 2 : 5. a.t. of shutting of gate
1 S. 4 :20. a.t. of her death wom. said
2 Ch. 18 :34. a.t. of sun down he died
Da. 9 : 21. touched me a.t. of obla-n
Mat. 1 : 11. a.t. carried aw. to Bab-n
Ac. 12 : 1. a. that t. Herod began to
13 : 18. a.t. of 40 years suffered he

According to TIME. [life, 14.

Ge. 18 : 10. return unto thee - t. of
Le. 25 : 50. - t. of an hired servant
Nu. 23 : 23. - this t. it be said of Jac.
2 K. 4 :16. - t. of life thou shalt em-
brace a son, 17. [wise men
Mat. 2 : 16. - t. he had inquired of
See **TIME with appointed.**

Any TIME. [t.

Le. 25 : 32. Levites may redeem at a.
Nu. 35 : 26. if slayer at a.t. come
1 S. 20 : 12. sounded my father a.t.
1 K. 1 : 6. not displeased him at a.t.
Mat. 4 : 6. lest at a.t. thou dash thy
foot ag. a stone, Lu. 4 : 11.[thee
5 :25. lest at a.t. adversary deliver
13:15. lest at a.t. they see, Mk. 4 : 12.
Lu. 15 :29. nei. transgressed I at a.t.
21 : 34. lest at a.t. your hearts be
overcharged. [1 Jn. 4 : 12
Jn. 1 : 18. No man seen God at a.t.,
5 : 37. nei. heard his voice at a.t.
Ac. 11 : 8. nothing unclean at a.t.
1 Co. 9 : 7. Who goeth a warfare a.t.
at own charges [tering words
1 Th. 2 : 5. nei. at a.t. used we flat-
He. 1 : 5. unto wh. said he at a.t., 13.
2 : 1. lest at a.t. we let them slip

TIME, S., with appointed.

Ge. 18 : 14. At the t.a. will I return
Ex. 9 : 5. the Lord a. a set t., saying
23 :15. eat unleavened bread in t.a.
Jos. 8 :14. king of Ai to battle at t.a.
1 S. 13 : 8. acc. to set t. Sam-l had a.
20 : 35. Jonathan went at t.a. [a.
2 S. 20 : 5. tarried longer than set t.
24 : 15. pestilence upon Israel from
morning to t.a.
Ezr. 10 : 14. all which have strange
wives come at a. t-s [13 : 31.
Ne. 10 : 34. wood offering at t-s a.,
Es. 9 : 27. keep acc. to a.t. ev. year
31. confirm days of Purim in t-s a.
Jb. 7 : 1. Is there not an a.t. to man
14 : 14. all the days of my a.t. I
Ps. 81 : 3. Blow up trumpet in t.a.
Is. 14 :31. none be alone in his a.t-s
40 : † 2. her a.t. is accomplished
Je 8 : 7. stork knoweth her a. t-s
46 : 17. Pharaoh hath passed t.a.
Da. 8 : 19. at t.a. end sh. be, 11 : 27.
10 : 1. thing was true, but t.a. long
11 : 29. At t.a. he sh. return [t.a.
35. time of end : because it is for
Ha. 2 : 3. vision is for an a.t., wait
Ac. 17 : 26. he determined t-s bef. a.
Ga. 4 : 2. under tutors until t.a. of
See BEFORETIME, DAYTIME.
See **COME** with **time,**
DUE time, s, EVIL time,
HARVEST with time.

In or In the TIME.

Ge. 38 : 27. - t. of her travail twins
Ex. 34 : 18. commanded - t. of Abib
Ju. 10 : 14. deliver - t. of tribulat-n
1 K. 15 : 23. - t. of old age diseased
2 Ch. 28 :22. - t. of distress did tresp.
29 : † 27. - t. when burnt offering
Ps. 4 : 7. than - t. when corn increa.
21 : 9. fiery oven - t. of thine anger
71 : 9. Cast me not off - t. of old age
Je. 11 : 14. I not hear - t. they cry
15 : 11. enemy to entreat thee well
- t. of evil, and - t. of affliction
15 : 15. deal thus - t. of thine anger

Eze. 27 :34. - t. when thou be broken
35 : 5. - t. of their calamity, - t.
that their iniquity had an end
Ho. 2 : 9. I will take aw. corn - t. th-f
Zph. 3 : 20. - t. that I gather you
Zch. 10 : 1. Ask rain - t. of latter rain
Lu. 4 : 27. lepers - t. of Eliseus
8 : 13. i.t. of temptation fall away
He. 4 : 16. grace to help i.t. of need

Last TIME, S.

1 Pe. 1 :5. ready to be revealed in l.t.
20. manifest in these l.t-s for you
1 Jn. 2 : 18. it is l.t., are many antichrists, wh-by we know it is l.t.
Jude 18. sho. be mockers in the l.t.

LIFE time. See LIFETIME.

Long TIME. [l.t.

Ge. 26 : 8. when he had been there a
Nu. 20 : 15. we dwelt in Egypt a l.t.
De. 20 : 19. when besiege city a l.t.
Jos. 11 : 18. Joshua made war a l.t.
23 : 1. a l.t. after Joshua waxed old
1 S. 7 : 2. while ark abode t. was l.
2 S. 14 : 2. woman that l.t. mourned
2 Ch. 30 : 5. had not done it of l.t.
Is. 42 : 14. I have l.t. holden peace
La. 5 : 20. Wheref. forsake us so l.t.
Mat. 25 : 19. After a l.t. lord of those
servants cometh, Lu. 20 : 9.
Lu. 8 : 27. a man wh. had devils l.t.
20 : 9. into a far country for a l.t.
Jn. 5 : 6. had been a l.t. in that case
14 : 9. Have I been so l.t. with you
Ac. 8 : 11. bec. of l.t. he bewitched
14 : 3. l.t. abode with disciples, 28.
He. 4 : 7. To day after so l. a t. [not
2 Pe. 2 :3. judgment of l.t. lingereth

Meal TIME. See MEALTIME.

Old TIME.

De. 2 : 20. giants dwelt there in o.t.
19 : 14. of o.t. set in thy inherit-e
Jos. 24 : 2. fa-s on other side in o.t.
2 S. 20 :18. were wont to speak in o.t.
Ezr. 4 : 15. moved sedition of o.t., 19.
Ec. 1 : 10. hath been already of o.t.
Je. 2 : 20. of o.t. I have broken yoke
Eze. 26 : 20. down with peo. of o.t.
38 : 17. of wh. I have spoken in o.t.
Mat. 5 : 21. said by th. of o.t., 27, 33.
Ac. 15 : 21. Mos. of o.t. hath in ev. city
1 Pe. 3 :5. in o.t. holy wom. adorned
2 Pe. 1 : 21. prophecy not in o.t. by
See PAST, PRESENT, PROCESS.

Same TIME. [s.t.

Nu. 32 : 10. L.'s anger was kindled
De. 9 : 20. I prayed for Aaron s.t.
2 K. 3 :6. Jehoram out of Sama s.t.
8 : 22. Edom revolted, then Libnah
at s.t., 2 Ch. 21 : 10. [feast
2 Ch. 7 : 8. at s.t. Solomon kept the
15 : 11. they offered s.t. 700 oxen
16 : 10. Asa oppressed peo. at s.t.
Ezr. 5 : 3. At the s.t. came Tatnai
Ne. 4 : 22. s.t. said I unto people [ah
Is. 20 :2. At s.t. spake Lord by Isai-
Je. 31 : 1. At s.t. will I be God of all
39 : 10. gave vineyards at the s.t.
Eze. 38 : 10. at s.t. thou think evil
18. s.t. when Gog sh. come ag Isr.
Da. 4 :36 At s.t. my reason returned
12 : 1. trouble, as never to th. s.t.
Mat. 18 : 1. at s.t. came disciples
Ac. 19 : 23. s.t. arose no small stir

Second TIME. [s.t.

Ge. 22 : 15. Angel called unto Abr.
41 : 5. Pha. slept, and dreamed s.t.
43 : 10. we had returned this s.t.
Le. 13 : 58. it sh. be washed the s.t.
Nu. 10 : 6. When ye blow alarm s.t.
Jos. 5 : 2. circumcise Israel the s.t.
1 S. 26 : 8. I will not smite him s.t.
2 S. 14 : 29. Abs. sent to Joab the s.t.
1 K. 9 : 2. L. appeared to Sol-n s.t.
18 : 34. Do it the s.t. they did it s.t.
19 : 7. angel came to Elijah the s.t.
2 K. 10 : 6. Jehu wrote a letter s.t.
1 Ch. 29 : 22. made Sol. king the s.t.

Es. 2 : 19. virgins were gathered s.t.
Is. 11 : 11. Lord set his hand s.t.
Je. 1 : 13. word of Lord came unto
me the s.t., 13 : 3. -33 : 1.
Jon. 3 : 1. word came unto Jon. s.t.
Na. 1 : 9. affliction not rise up s.t.
Mat. 26 : 42. went s.t. and prayed
Mk. 14 : 72. the s.t. the cock crew
Jn. 3 : 4. can he enter s.t. womb?
21 : 16. Jesus saith to Peter the s.t.
Ac. 7 :13. at s.t. Jos. was made known
10 : 15. voice spake unto Peter s.t.
2 Co : 13 : 2. as if I were present s.t.
He. 9 : 28. he appear s.t. with-t sin
See SEEDTIME, SHORT.

Set TIME, S. [t.

Ge. 17 : 21. Sarah sh. bear at this s.
21 : 2. at s.t. of wh. G. had spoken
2 K. 4 : † 16. s.t. sh. embrace a son
Jb. 14 :13. wouldest appoint me s.t.
Ps. 75 : † 2. When I shall take a s.t.
102 : 13. s.t. to favour her is come
Zch. 8 : † 19. fast of tenth sh. be s.t-s
See **TIME with appointed.**

That TIME. [in t.t.

Ju. 11 : 26. why did ye not recover
1 S. 3 : 2. at t.t. wh. Eli was laid do.
11 : 9. by t.t. the sun be hot [t.t.
14 : 21. Hebrews with Philis. before
Ezr. 5 :16. since t.t. been in build-g
Ne. 4 : 16. fr. t.t. forth my servants
13 : 21. Fr. t.t. forth came no more
Is. 16 : 13. spoken conc. Moab since
18 : 7. In t.t. present be bro-t [t.t.
44 : 8. have I not told thee fr. t.t.
45 : 21. who hath told it from t.t. ?
48 : 8. from t.t. thine ear was not
Je. 50 : 4. t.t. Isr. sh. come weeping
20. t.t. iniquity of Isr. not found
Jo. 3 : 1. t.t. when I bring captivity
Am. 5 : 13. prudent keep silence t-t.
Mat. 4 :17. t.t. Jes. began to preach
16 : 21. From t.t. began Jesus to
shew unto disciples [portunity
26 : 16. from t.t. Judas sought op-
Lu. 16 : 16. since t.t. kingd. of God
Jn. 6 : 66. Fr. t.t. many went back
Ac. 12 : 1. about t.t. Herod, to vex

At that TIME. [Abr.

Ge. 21 : 22. - t. Abim-h spake unto
38 : 1. - t. Judah went from breth.
Nu. 22 : 4. Balak was k. of Moab - t.
De. 1 : 9. And I spake unto you - t.
16. I charged your judges - t.
18. I commanded you - t., 3 : 18.
2 : 34. took all his cities - t., 3 : 4.
3 : 8. we took - t. the land on side
12. this land we possessed - t.
21. I commanded Joshua - t. [ing
23. I besought the Lord, - t., say-
4 : 14. L. com-ded me - t. to teach
5 : 5. I stood betw. L. and you - t.
9 : 19. Lord hearkened - t., 10 : 10.
10 : 1. - t. Lord said, Hew 2 tables
8. - t. L. separated tribe of Levi
Jos. 5 : 2. - t. L. said, Make sharp k.
6 : 26. Joshua adjured them - t.
11 :10. Joshua - t. turned, took H.
21. - t. Joshua cut off the Anakim
Ju. 3 : 29. slew of Moab - t. 10,000
4 : 4. Deborah judged Israel - t.
12 : 6. fell - t. 42,000 [ion ov. Isr.
14 : 4. - t. Philistines had domin-
20 : 15. chil. of Benj. numbered - t.
21 : 14. Benjamin came again - t.
24. chil. of Isr. departed thence - t.
1 S. 3 :2. - t. when Eli was laid down
14 : 18. the ark was - t. with Israel
1 K. 8 : 65. - t. Solomon held a feast
11 : 29. - t. Jerob. went out of Jeru.
14 : 1. - t. Abijah fell sick [to Syria
2 K. 16 : 6. - t. Rezin recov-d Elath
18 : 16. - t. Hez. cut off gold [Is. 39 : 1.
20 : 12. - t. Berodach sent letters,
24 : 10. - t. servants of Neb. came
1 Ch. 12 : 22. - t. came to Da. to help
21 : 28. - t. when Da. saw L. ans-d

2 Ch. 13 : 18. Israel bro-t under - t.
16 : 7. - t. Hanani, seer, came to Asa
28 : 16. - t. did Ahaz send unto k-s
30 : 3. could not keep passover - t.
35 : 17. Israel kept the passov. - t.
Ezr. 8 : 34. weight was written - t.
Ne. 6 : 1. - t. I had not set up doors
12 : 44. - t. were some appointed
Es. 8 : 9. king's scribes called - t.
Je. 3 : 17. - t. they shall call Jerus.
4 : 11. - t. be said, A dry wind
8 : 1. - t. shall they bring out bones
33 : 15. - t. cause Branch of righte.
Da. 3 : 7. - t. when peo. heard sound
8 - t. cert-n Chaldeans came near
12 : 1. - t. sh. Michael stand up (2)
Mi. 3 : 4. Lord will hide his face - t.
Zph. 1 : 12. - t. I will search Jerus.
3 : 19. - t. I will undo all th. afflict
20. - t. will I bring you again
Mat. 11 : 25. - t. Jesus answ-d, I thank
12 : 1. - t. Jes. went on sabb-h day
14 : 1. - t. Herod heard of fame of
Lu. 23 : 7. Herod at Jerusalem - t.
Ac. 8 : 1. - t. was great persecution
Eph. 2 : 12. - t. ye were with-t Christ

THIRD time. [t.
1 S. 3 : 8. Lord called Samuel the t.
19 : 21. Saul sent messengers t.t.
1 K. 18 : 34. Do it the t.t., they did it the t.t. [the t.t.
Eze. 21 : 14. let the sword be doubled
Mat. 26 : 44. prayed t.t., Mk. 14 : 41.
Lu. 23 : 22. said t.t., Why, wh. evil
Jn. 21 : 14. t.t. Jesus shewed hims.
17. saith t.t., l vest thou me? Peter grieved bec. he said t.t.
2 Co. 12 : 14. t.t., I am ready to co., [13 : 1.

This TIME.
Ge. 29 : 34. t.t. will my husband be
Ex. 8 : 32. Ph. hardened heart at t.t.
9 : 14. I will t.t. send my plagues
27. Phar. said, I have sinned t.t.
Nu. 23 : 23. acc. to t.t. it sh. be said
Ju. 13 : 23. nor as at t.t. ha. told us
21 : 22. did not give unto th. at t.t.
1 S. 9 : 13. about t.t. ye sh. find him
24. unto t.t. hath it been kept
2 S. 17 : 7. counsel is not good at t.t.
1 K. 2 : 26. not at t.t. put thee to dea.
Ne. 13 : 6. all t.t. was not I at Jerus.
Es. 4 : 14. if holdest thy peace at t.t.; whe. to kingd. for such t. as t.?
Ps. 113 : 2. Blessed be the Lord from t.t. forth, 115 : 18.
121 : 8. Lord sh. preserve thy going out from t.t. forth [t.t.
Is. 48 : 6. I shewed new things from
Je. 3 : 4. Wilt not from t.t. cry unto
51 : 6. t. is the t. of the L.'s veng-e
Mi. 2 : 3. nei. haughtily, t.t. is evil
Mat. 24 : 21. tribulation such as was not to t.t., Mk. 13 : 19.
Mk. 10 : 30. receive hundredfold now in t.t., Lu. 18 : 30. [cern t.t.?
Lu. 12 : 56. how is it ye do not dis-
Jn. 11 : 39 Lord, by t.t. he stinketh
Ac. 1 : 6. wilt at t.t. restore kingd.?
24 : 25. Go thy way for t.t. [ousn.
Ro. 8 : 26. declare at t.t. his righte-
9 : 9. At t.t. will I come, Sara shall
1 Co. 16 : 12. will not to come at t.t.
2 Co. 8 : 14. at t.t. your abundance

To morrow about this TIME.
Ex. 9 : 18. - t. I will rain grievous hail
Jos. 11 : 6. - t. will deliv. them slain
1 S. 9 : 16. - t. I will send thee man
1 K. 19 : 2. thy life as one of them - t.
20 : 6. - t. search thine house [18.
2 K. 7 : 1. - t. me-s of flour be sold,
10 : 6. come to me to Jezreel by - t.

TIME, S, of trouble.
Ne. 9 : 27. in t. - thou heardest them
Jb. 38 : 23. hail, I have reserved ag. t. -
Ps. 9 : 9. Lord will be refuge in t-s -
10 : 1. why hidest thyself in t-s -?
Ps. 27 : 5. in t. - sh. hide me in pavil.
37 : 39. he is their strength in t. -
41 : 1. L. will deliver in t. - [in t. -
Pr. 25 : 19. confidence in unfaithf.
Is. 33 : 2. be our salvation in t. -
Je. 2 : 27. in t. - they will say, save
28. gods, if they can save in t. -
11 : 12. not save them at all in t. -
14 : 8. hope of Isr., Saviour in t. -
30 : 7. Alas! it is t. o. Jacob's t.
Da. 12 : 1. shall be a t. - as nev. was
See VISITATION.

TIMES. [t.
Le. 19 : 26. neither shall ye observe
Nu. 24 : 1. Balaam not as at other t.
De. 1 : 11. L. make you thous. t. as
18 : 10. an observer of t., 14. [many
Ju. 13 : 25. Spirit to move him at t.
16 : 20. I will go out as at other t.
20 : 30. put in array as at other t.
31. began to kill as at other t.
1 S. 3 : 10. L. called as at other t. Sa.
18 : 10. David played as at other t.
20 : 25. k. sat upon seat as at oth. t.
2 K. 19 : 25. Hast not heard how of ancient t. I formed it? Is. 37 : 26.
21 : 6. Manasseh observed t., dealt with wizards, 2 Ch. 33 : 6. [the t.
1 Ch. 12 : 32. had understanding of
21 : 3. make his peo. 100 t. so many
29 : 30. t. th. went ov. him and ov.
2 Ch. 15 : 5. in those t. was no peace
Es 1 : 13. wise men wh. knew the t.
Jb 24 : 1. t. are not hidden from Almi.
Ps. 31 : 15. My t. are in thy hand
44 : 1. works thou didst in t. of old
77 : 5. considered years of ancient t.
Pr. 17 : †10. than to strike fool 100 t.
Is. 33 : 6. knowledge stability of thy t.
46 : 10. fr. ancient t. things not yet
Eze. 12 : 27. prophesied of t. far off
Da. 2 : 21. changeth t. and seasons
7 : 25. think to change t. and laws
9 : 25. street be built in troublous t.
11 : 6. strengthened her in these t.
†13. king of north come at end of t.
14. in those t. sh. many stand up
12 : 7. time, t. and a half, Re. 12 : 14.
Mat. 16 : 3. ye not discern signs of t.
Lu. 21 : 24. t. of Gentiles be fulfilled
Ac. 1 : 7. not for you to know the t.
3 : 19. when t. of refresh-g sh. come
21. until t. of restitution of all
17 : 30. t. of ignorance G. winked at
Ga. 4 : 10. Ye observe months, t. [t.
Ep. 1 : 10. dispensation of fulness of
1 Th. 5 : 1. of t., ye have no need that I
1 Ti. 4 : 1. latter t. some sh. depart
6 : 15. in his t. he sh. shew, who is K.
2 Ti. 3 : 1. in last days perilous t.
He. 1 : 1. God who at sundry t. spake
Re. 12 : 14. a time and t. and half [time

All TIMES.
Le. 16 : 2. come not at a.t. within vail
1 K. 8 : 59. cause of his people at a.t.
Ps. 34 : 1. I will bless Lord at a.t.
62 : 8. Trust in him at a.t. ye peo.
106 : 3. th. doeth righteousn. at a.t.
119 : 20. longing unto thy judgments at a.t. [at a.t.
Pr. 5 : 19. let her breasts satisfy thee
17 : 17. A friend loveth at a.t., a
See DUE, PAST.

Many TIMES.
1 K 22 : 16. How m.t. sh. I adjure th. thou tell, 2 Ch. 18 : 15. [Ps. 106 : 43.
Ne. 9 : 28. m.t. didst deliver them,

Two TIMES. [t.t.
Ge. 27 : 36. he supplanted me these

Three TIMES.
Ex. 23 : 14. t.t. keep a feast unto me
17. t.t. a year all thy males shall appear before bef. L., De. 16 : 16.
Nu. 22 : 32. Whf. smitten ass t.t., 28.
33. ass turned from me these t.t.
24 : 10. thou hast blessed them t.t.
Ju. 16 : 15. thou hast mocked me t.t.
1 S. 20 : 41. David arose, bowed t.t.
1 K. 9 : 25. Sol-n offered t.t. a year
17 : 21. stretched hims. on child t.t.
2 K. 13 : 25. t.t. Joash beat Hazael
2 Ch. 8 : 13. offering t.t. in the year
Da. 6 : 10. on his knees t.t. a day
13. Dan maketh petition t.t. a d.
Ac. 11 : 10. this was done, t.t. and

Four, Five, or Six TIMES.
Ge. 43 : 34. Benj.'s mess f-e t. so mu.
2 K. 13 : 19. sho. have smitten f-e or s.
Ne. 6 : 4. they sent unto me f-r t. [t.
2 Co. 11 : 24. f-e t. received I 40 stripes

Seven TIMES.
Ge. 33 : 3. Jac. bowed bef. Esau s.t.
Le. 4 : 6. priest sh. sprinkle of the blood s.t., 17.–8 : 11.–14 : 7.–16 : 14, 19. Nu. 19 : 4. [ger s.t., 27.
14 : 16. sh. sprinkle oil with his fin-
51. dip in blood, sprinkle hou. s.t.
25 : 8. numb. s.t. seven yrs. [24, 28.
26 : 18. punish you s.t. more, 21,
Jos. 6 : 4. he sh. compass city s.t., 15.
1 K. 18 : 43. to serv-t, Go again s.t.
2 K. 4 : 35. child sneezed s.t. [s.t., 14.
5 : 10. Elisha sent, Go wash in Jor.
Ps. 12 : 6. are as silver purified s.t.
119 : 164. s.t. a day I praise thee
Pr. 24 : 16. a just man falleth s.t.
Da. 3 : 19. heat furnace one s.t. more
4 : 16. let s.t. pass ov. him, 23, 25, 32.
Mat. 18 : 21. how oft forgive? till s.t.
22. I say not, Until s.t., but 70 t.s.
Lu. 17 : 4. if brother trespass s.t. a day, and s.t. a day turn again

Ten TIMES. [41.
Ge. 31 : 7. changed my wages t.t.,
Nu. 14 : 22. tempted me these t.t.
Ne. 4 : 12. when Jews came they said unto us t.t. [me
Jb. 19 : 3. t.t. have ye reproached
Da. 1 : 20. t.t. better than all magi- [cians

TIME'US.
Mk. 10 : 46. son of T. sat by highway

TIM'NA. [phaz
Ge. 36 : 12. T. was concubine to Eli-
22. Lotan's sister was T., 1 Ch. 1 : 39.
1 Ch. 1 : 36. sons of Eliphaz T. and

TIM'NAH. [Person.] [T.
Ge. 36 : 40. dukes came of Esau, duke
1 Ch. 1 : 51. dukes of Edom, duke T.

TIM'NAH. [Place.] [57.
Jos. 15 : 10. border passed on to T.,
2 Ch. 28 : 18. Philistines had taken T.

TIM'NATH. [ers to T.
Ge. 38 : 12. Judah unto sheepshear-
13. father in law goeth up to T. [T.
14. she sat in place by the way to
Ju. 14 : 1. Samson went down to T. (2)
2. said, I have seen a woman in T.
5. Samson down to T., to viney-ds

TIM'NATH-HE'RES. [of T.
Ju. 2 : 9. they buried Joshua in T.

TIM'NATH-SE'RAH.
Jos. 19 : 50. gave Joshua the city, even T. [Ju. 2 : †9.
24 : 30. they buried Joshua in T.,

TIM'NITE. [T.
Ju. 15 : 6. Samson, son in law of the

TI'MON. See PROCHORUS.

TIMO'THEUS=TIMOTHY
Ac. 16 : 1. a certain disciple named T.
17 : 14. Silas and T. abode there still
15. com-t unto Silas and T. to come
18 : 5. Silas and T. were come fr. M.
19 : 22. So he sent into Macedonia T
20 : 4. Accompan-d him into Asia, T
Ro. 16 : 21. T. my workfel-w saluteth
1 Co. 4 : 17. for this cause I sent T.
16 : 10. if T. come [2 Co. 1 : 1. T. our b.
2 Co. 1 : 19. was preached by me and T.
Ph. 1 : 1. Paul, T., serv-ts of Jes. Ch.
2 : 19. I trust in the Lord to send T.
Col. 1 : 1. T. our broth. to the saints
1 Th. 1 : 1. T. unto church, 2 Th. 1 : 1.
3 : 2. sent T. our broth. to establish
6. when T. came from you unto us

TIM'OTHY.

1 Ti. 1 : 2. Unto T., my own son in the faith, Grace, 2 Ti 1 : 2. [T.
18. This chargeI commit unto thee
6 . 20. T. keep that wh. is commit-d
Phm. 1. T. our bro. unto Philemon
He. 13 : 23. brother T. is set at liberty

TIN.

Nu. 31 : 22. t. that may abide fire
Is. 1 : 25. I will take away all thy t.
Eze. 22 : 18. all they are brass and t.
20. gather lead and t. into furnace
27 : 12. Tarshish thy merch-t in t.
Zch. 4 : †10. sh. see store of t. in ha.

TINGLE.

1 S. 3 : 11. at which ears of every one shall t., 2 K. 21 : 12. Je. 19 : 3.

TINKLING.

Is. 3 : 16. making a t. with their feet
18. bravery of their t. ornaments
1 Co. 13 : 1. I am become as a t. cym- [bal

TIP.

Lu. 16 : 24. dip t. of his finger in wa.
See **Right EAR.**

TIPH'SAH.

1 K. 4 : 24. Sol. had dominion fr. T.
2 K. 15 : 16. Th. Menahem smote T.

TI'RAS. [1 : 5.

Ge. 10 : 2. sons of Japhet, T., 1 Ch.

TI'RATHITES. [the T.

1 Ch. 2 : 55. families of the scribes,

TIRE, TIRES.

Is. 3 : 18. Lord will take aw. their t-s
Eze. 24 : 17. bind the t. of thy head
23. your t-s sh. be upon y-r heads

TIRED. [Attired.]

2 K. 9 : 30. Jezebel t. her head

TIRED. [Wearied.] [t.

Mat. 9 : †36. compas-n bec. they were

TIRHA'KAH. [Is. 37 : 9.

2 K. 19 : 9. Rab-shakeh heard of T.,

TIRHA'NAH. See SHEBER

TIR'IA. [phah, T.

1 Ch. 4 : 16. sons of Jehaleleel, Zi-

TIR'SHATHA. [7 : 65.

Ezr. 2 : 63. T. said sho. not eat, Ne.
Ne. 7 : 70. T. gave to treasure gold
8 : 9. Nehemiah, which is the T.
10 : 1. that sealed were Nehe. the T.

TIR'ZAH. [Person.]

See NOAH. [Woman.]

TIR'ZAH. [Place.]

Jos. 12 : 24. Joshua smote king of T.
1 K. 14 : 17. Jerob.'s wife came to T.
15 : 21. Baasha dwelt in T, | 33. reign- [ed
16 : 6. Baasha was buried in T.
8. Began Elah to reign ov. Isr. in T.
9. in T. drinking himself drunk (2)
15. did Zimri reign 7 days in T.
17. Omri and Israel besieged T.
23. six years reigned Omri in T.
2 K. 15 : 14. Menahem went up fr. T.
16. Menahem smote coast from T.
Can. 6 : 4. beautiful, O my love, as T.

Elijah the TISH'BITE.

1 K. 17 : 1. E. t. T. said unto Ahab
21 : 17, word of L. came to E. t. T.
2 K. 1 : 3. angel said to E. t. T., Arise
8. Ahaziah said, It is E. t. T. [T.
9 : 36. word which L. spake by E. t.

TITHE. [Noun.]

Le. 27 : 30. t. of the land is the L.'s
32. conc. t. of the herd or the flock
Nu. 18 : 26. offer tenth part of the t.
De. 12 : 17. not eat the t. of corn
14 : 23. eat t. in place L. sh. choose
28. at end of 3 years bring forth t.
2 Ch. 31 : 5. they brought in the t. of all things, 6, 12. Ne. 13 : 12.
Ne. 10 : 38. Levites sh. bring up t. of
Mat. 23 : 23. ye pay t. of mint, anise

TITHES. [of all

Ge. 14 : 20. Abr. gave Melchizedek t.
Le. 27 : 31. if man will redeem his t.
Nu. 18 : 24. t. I have given to Levites
26. when ye take of Israel the t.
28. offer heave offering of all t.
De. 12 : 6. thither bring your t., 11.
26 : 12. made an end of tithing t.
2 Ch. 31 : 12. bro-t in offerings and t.
Ne. 10 : 37. t. of our ground unto Levites, th. same ha. t. in all cit.
38. priest with Levites when take t. ; Levites sh. bri. up tithe of t.
12 : 44. some were appointed for t.
13 : 5. where they laid the t. of corn
Am. 4 : 4. bring your t. after three years, Mal. 3 : 10 [offerings
Mal. 3 : 8. ye have robbed me of t.
Lu. 18 : 12 I give t. of all I possess
He. 7 : 5. priests have com-t to take t.
6. he received t. of Abraham
8 men that die receive t. [Abr.
9. Levi who received t. paid t. in

TITHE. [Verb.] [seed

De: 14 : 22. surely t. increase of thy
Lu. 11 : 42. ye t. mint, rue, and all [herbs

TITHING.

De. 26 : 12. made end of t. tithes the third year, which is year of t.

TITLE.

2 K. 23 : 17. What t. is that that I see
Jn. 19 : 19. Pilate wrote a t. and put
20. This t. read many of the Jews

TITLES. See FLATTERING.

TITTLE.

Mat 5 : 18. one t. sh. in no wise pass
Lu. 16 : 17. than for one t. of law to [fail

TI'TUS.

2 Co 2 : 13. no rest, bec. I found not [T.
7 : 6. comforted us by com-g of T.
13. more joyed we for joy of T. [T.
14. our boasting wh. I made before
8 : 6. Insomuch that we desired T.
16. same care into heart of T.
23. inquire of T., he is my partner
12 : 18. Did T. make a gain of you?
Ga. 2 : 1. to Jerus., and took T. wi. me
3. nei. was T. circumcised [matia
2 Ti. 4 : 10. T. is departed from Dal-
Tit. 1 : 4. To T. mine own son after

TI'ZITE. [T.

1 Ch. 11 : 45. valiant men, Joha the

TO day.

Ge. 21 : 26. nei. heard I of it but t.d.
30 : 32. will pass thro. thy flock t.d.
40 : 7. Wheref. look ye so sadly t.d.?
Ex. 2 : 18. How ye are come so soon [t.d.
5 : 14. task making brick t.d.
14 : 13. salvat. he will shew you t. d.; Egyp-ns seen t.d, see no m.
16 : 23. bake that ye will bake t.d.
25 Moses said, Eat that t.d. ; t. d. is a sab-h, t.d. ye not find it
32 : 29. Consecrate yours. t.d. to L.
Le. 9 : 4. t.d. the Lord will appear
10 : 19. if I had eaten sin off-g t.d.
De. 15 : 15. I comm-d thee this t.d.
29 : 13. may estab. thee t.d. for peo.
Jos. 22 : 18. ye rebel t.d. ag. Lord
Ju. 21 : 3. why t.d. one tribe lacking
Ru. 2 : 19. Where hast gleaned t.d.?
1 S. 4 : 3. Whf. hath L. smitten us t.d.
9 : 12. he came t.d. to the city ; is sacrifice of people t.d. [him
† 13. get you up : t.d. ye sh. find
† 27. stand still t.d. th. I may shew
10 : 2. When thou art departed t.d.
11 : 13. t.d. Lord wrought salvat-n
12 : 17. Is it not wheat harvest t.d.
14 : 30. if people eaten t.d. of spoil
24 : 10. Lord had delivered thee t. d. into mine hand, 26 : 23.
27 : 10. Whither made road t.d.?
2 S. 3 : 8. chargest me t.d. conc. wom?
6 : 20. How glorious the king t.d.
14 : 22. t.d. thy servant knoweth I
16 : 3. t.d. shall restore me kingd.
1 K. 1 : 51. Let Sol. swear unto me t.d.
8 : 28. wh. thy servant prayeth t.d.
18 : 15. shew myself unto him t.d.
22 : 5. Inquire of L. t.d., 2 Ch. 18 : 4.
2 K. 2 : 3. take master fr. head t.d.,
4 : 23. Whf. wilt go to him t.d. [5.
2 K. 6 : 28. Give son, may eat him t.d.
Jb. 23 : 2. t.d. is my complaint bitter
Ps. 95 : 7. t.d. if ye will hear his voice, He. 3 : 7, 15.-4 : 7.
Je. 34 : †15. ye were t.d. turned and
Zch. 9 : 12. t.d. declare I will render
Mat. 16 : 3. It be foul weather t.d.
21 : 28. go work t.d. in vineyard
Lu. 5 : 26. seen strange things t.d.
19 : 5. t.d. I must abide at thy hou.
23 : 43. t.d. be with me in paradise
24 : 21. t.d. is 3d d. since th. thi-s
He. 3 : 13. exhort, while it is called t.
5 : 5. t.d. have I begotten thee [d.
See YESTERDAY.

TO day with to morrow.

Ex. 19 : 10. sanct. peo. t.d. and t.m.
1 S. 9 : 19. ye sh. eat with me t.d. ; t.m. I will let thee go [I will
2 S. 11 : 12. Tarry here t.d. and t.m.
Mat. 6 : 30. grass wh. t.d. is and t.m. is cast into oven, Lu. 12 : 28.
Lu. 13 : 32. I do cures t.d. and t.m., and third day [day following
33. I must walk t.d., t.m., and
Jas. 4 : 13. ye that say t.d. or t.m.

TO and fro. See FRO.

TO morrow.

See **To MORROW.**

TO wit. See **To WIT.**

TO'AH. [34.

1 Ch. 6 : † 26. Zophai and T. his son,

TOB. [T., 5.

Ju. 11 : 3. Jephthah dwelt in land of

TOB-ADONI'JAH.

2 Ch. 17 : 8 he sent Levites, even T.

TOBI'AH. [hou., 7 : 62.

Ezr. 2 : 60. chil. of T. not shew fa.'s
Ne. 2 : 10. Sanballat and T. heard, 19.-4 : 7.-6 : 1. [if fox
4 : 3. T. said that which they build
6 : 12. T. and Sanballat hired him
14. My G., think thou upon T. [T.
17. nobles sent many letters unto
19. T. sent letters to put me in fear
13 : 4. Eliashib was allied to T.
7. evil that Eliashib did for T. [T.
8. I cast forth household stuff of

TOBI'JAH.

2 Ch. 17 : 8. he sent Levites, even T.
Zch. 6 : 10. Take of captivity even of
14. the crowns shall be to T. [T.

TO'CHEN. [and T.

1 Ch. 4 : 32. their villages, Rimmon

TOES. [20 : 6.

2 S. 21 : 20. on ev. foot six t., 1 Ch.
Da. 2 : 41. sawest t., part of iron, 42.
See **THUMB, S, and toe, s.**

TOGAR'MAH. [1 : 6.

Ge. 10 : 3. sons of Gomer, T., 1 Ch.
Eze. 27 : 14. they of house of T. traded
38 : 6. house of T. of north quar- [ters

TOGETHER.

Ge. 1 : 10. t. Ex. 2 : 13.-21 : 18.-26 : 3, 6, 11, 24.-28 : 7.-36 : 29.-39 : 4. Le. 24 : 10. De. 25 : 11. Jos. 17 : 10.-18 : 1. 1 S. 10 : 17.-23 : 8. 2 S. 2 : 13.-14 : 6. 2 K. 3 : 10, 13. Ne. 6 : 7. Jb. 24 : 4. Ps. 2 : 2.-31 : 13.-37 : 38.-55 : 14.-71 : 10.-85 : 10. Pr. 29 : 13. Is. 45 : 21.-48 : 13.-52 : 8, 9. Je. 50 : 29.-51 : 27. Da. 11 : 6. Na. 2 : 10. Mat 19 : 6. Mk. 10 : 9.-14 : 56, 59.-15 : 16. Lu. 15 : 6. Jn. 4 : 36. Ac. 1 : 15.-5 : 9, 21.-10 : 24.-19 : 25.-21 : 30. Ro 15 : 30. 1 Co : 1 : 10. 2 Th. 2 : 1.
Ge. 25 : 22. chil. struggled t. within
42 : 17. he put them all t. into ward
Ex. 19 : 8. all the people answered t.
30 : 35. perfume tempered t. pure
Nu. 26 : 10. earth swallowed them t.
De. 22 : 10. not plough wi. ox and ass t.
11. not wear garment of woollen and linen t. [to ends
33 : 17. Joseph shall push people t.
Jos. 11 : 5. kings met t., pitched t.

Jn. 6 : 38. Gideon thrust the fleece t.
19 : 6. they did eat and drink both t.
20. divided her t. with her bones
1 S. 11 : 11. so that two were not left t.
17 : 10. give me a man that we may fight t. [compelled Saul
28 : 23. his servants t. with woman
31 : 6. Saul and all his men died th. day t., 1 Ch. 10 : 6. [him
2 S. 12 : 3. ewe lamb grew up t. with
1 K. 3 : 18. we were t., no stranger in
5 : 12. Hiram and Sol. made league t.
11 : 1. Sol. loved many women, t.
2 K. 2 : 8. Elijah wrapped his mantle t.
9 : 25. thou and I ride t. aft. Ahab
Ezr. 2 : 64. whole congregation t. was 42,360, Ne. 7 : 66.
3 : 9. stood Jeshua, Kadmiel t. [ing
11. they sang t. by course in prais-
4 : 3. we t. will build unto G. of Isr.
6 : 20. priests, Levites were purified t.
Ne. 4 : 8. conspired t. to fight ag. Jer.
6 : 2. Sanballat say-g, let us meet t.
10. Let us meet t. in house of God
Jb. 2 : 11. appointment t. to mourn
3 : 18. There prisoners rest t. [t.
6 : 2. my calamity laid in balances
10 : 8. made me and fashioned me t.
17 : 16. when our rest t. is in dust
24 : 4. poor of earth hide thems. t.
34 : 15. All flesh shall perish t. [t.
38 : 7. When the morn-g stars sang
38. When clods cleave fast t. [seal
41 : 15. his scales shut up t. as with
17. They are joined, th. stick t., 23.
Ps. 2 : 2. rulers take counsel t. ag. L.
14 : 3. all t. become filthy, Ro. 3 : 12.
34 : 3. let us exalt his name t. [t.
35 : 26. them be bro-t to confusion
37 : 38. transgres-rs be destroyed t.
40 : 14. Let them be confounded t.
41 : 7. All that hate whisper t. ag.
48 : 4. For lo, kings passed by t. [me
49 : 2. low and high, rich and poor t.
74 : 8. said, Let us destroy them t.
83 : 5. consulted t. wi. one consent
88 : 17. they compass me about t.
98 : 8. let the hills be joyful t.
122 : 3. Jerus. as a city compact t.
147 : 2. L. gath-h t. outcasts of Isr.
Ec. 4 : 5. fool foldeth his hands t.
11. if two lie t. they have heat
Pr. 22 : 2. The rich and poor meet t.
29 : 13. The poor and deceitf. meet t.
Is. 1 : 18. Come now let us reason t.
28. destruction of sinners sh. be t.
31. and they shall both burn t.
9 : 11. Lord shall join his enem-s t.
21. Ephr., Manas. t. sh be ag. Jud.
11 : 6. and young lion and fatling t.
14. shall spoil them of the east t.
18 : 6. be left t. unto fowls of mts.
22 : 3. All thy rulers are fled t., (2)
25 : 11. sh. bring down their pride t.
26 : 19. t. wi. my dead body sh. arise
27 : 4. briers and thorns I wou. burn
31 : 3. they all shall fail t. [t.
34 : 4. heavens be rolled t. as scroll
40 : 5. glory of L., all flesh sh. see t.
41 : 1. let us come t. to judgment
19. I will set pine and box tree t.
20. they may see and understand t.
23. that we may behold it t.
43 : 26. in remembr-e let us plead t.
44 : 11. th. sh. fear, sh be ashamed t.
45 : 8. let righteousn. spring up t.
16. makers of idols to confusion t.
20. draw near t. ye th. are escaped
46 : 2. They stoop, they bow down t.
52 : 9. B-k forth into joy, sing t., 8
60 : 13. fir tree and box t. to beautify
65 : 7. your and iniquity of fath-s t.
25. The wolf and lamb shall feed t.
66 : 17. They eating the mouse shall be consumed t. [t.
Je. 6 : 11. pour fury upon young men
12. houses unto oth-s, and wives t.

Je. 6 : 21. fa-s and sons t. sh. fall upon
13 : 14. I will dash fa-s and sons t.
31 : 8. wom. and her th. travaileth t.
12. shall flow t. to goodn. of the L.
13. in dance young men and old t.
24. in all the cities t. husbandmen
41 : 1. they did eat bread t. in Miz.
46 : 12. mighty, th. are fallen both t.
21. they are turned and fled aw. t.
48 : 7. into captivity, priests and princes t., 49 : 3. Am. 1 : 15.
50 : 4. chil. of Isr., Jud., weeping t.
50 : 33. Isr. and Jud. were oppres-d t.
51 : 38. They shall roar t. like lions
44. nations sh. not flow t. unto him
La. 2 : 8. rampart and wall languished
Eze. 29 : 5. thou sh. not be bro-t t. [t.
Da. 2 : 35. iron, brass, gold, broken t.
6 : 7. governors, capt-s, consulted t.
Ho. 11 : 8. my repentings kindled t.
Am. 3 : 3 Can two walk t. exc agreed?
Mi. 2 : 12. put them t. as sheep of B.
Na. 1 : 10. be folden t. as thorns [t.
Zch. 10 : 4. out of him ev. oppressor
Mat. 13 : 30 Let both grow t. until
Mk 3 : 20. multitude cometh t. again
12 : 28 one heard them reason-g t.
Lu. 6 : 38. Give good meas. shaken t.
13 : 11. behold, was a wom., bowed t.
17 : 35. Two wom. sh. be grinding t.
22 : 55. when they were set down t.
23 : 12. Pilate, Herod, made friends t.
24 : 14 talked t. of all wh. happened
Jn. 20 : 7. napkin wrapped t. in place
21 : 2. were t. Peter, Thomas, Nath.
Ac. 1 : 15. (number of names t. 120)
2 : 44. And all that believed were t.
3 : 11. peo. ran t. unto Pet. and Jn.
16 : 22. multitude rose t. ag. them
23 : 12. certain of Jews banded t.
Ro. 1 : 12. th. I be comforted t. wi. you
3 : 12. are all t. become unprofitable
6 : 5. if we have been planted t. in
8 : 17. that we may be glorified t.
22. creation travaileth in pain t.
28. all things work t. for good to
1 Co. 3 : 9. we are labourers t. with G.
2 Co. 1 : 11. Ye helping t. by prayer
6 : 1. We then as workers t. wi. him
14. Be not unequally yoked t. [13.
Ep. 2 : 5. hath quickened us t., Col. 2 :
6. raised us up t., made us sit t.
21. In wh. building fitly framed t.
22. In which ye also are builded t.
Ph. 1 : 27. striving t. for faith of gos.
3 : 17. Breth. be followers t. of me
Col. 2 : 2. hearts being knit t. in love
19. all the body knit t. increaseth
1 Th. 4 : 17. we sh. be caught up t. in
5 : 10. that we sho. live t. with him
11. Wheref. comfort yourselves t.
2 Th. 2 : 1. by our gather-g t. unto him
He. 10 : 25. Not forsaking assemb-g t.
Ja. 5 : 3. heaped treas. t. for last days
1 Pe. 3 : 7. as heirs t. of grace of life
See **CAME, COME together.**

Dwell TOGETHER.

Ge. 13 : 6. land not able to bear th. that they might **d. t.**, (2)
36 : 7. their riches more than that they might **d. t.** [die
De. 25 : 5. If brethren **d. t.**, and one
Ps. 133 : 1. pleasant for breth. to **d. t.**
See DESTROY, FELL.
See **GATHERED together.**
See **GATHER, ED, themselves together, LIE down.**
See HIDE, JOINED, RAN, SMITE, SMOTE, STAND, WENT.

TO'HU. See ZUPH.

TO'I or TO'U.

2 S. 8 : 9.† When T. heard David had smitten, 1 Ch. 18 : 9.† [18 : 10.
10. T sent unto Da. to salute, 1 Ch.

TOIL. [Noun.]

Ge. 5 : 29. comfort us conc. our t. [t.
41 : 51. G. hath made me forget my

TOIL, ED, ING. [12 : 27.

Mat. 6 : 28. they t. not nor spin, Lu.
Mk. 6 : 48. saw them t-g in rowing
Lu. 5 : 5. Master we have t-d all night

TOKEN. [17.

Ge. 9 : 12. This is t. of covenant, 13,
17 : 11. it shall be t. of the covenant
Ex. 3 : 12. this be a t. I sent thee
12 : 13. the blood shall be for a t.
13 : 16. it shall be for a t. upon ha.
Nu. 17 : 10. be kept for t. ag. rebels
Jos. 2 : 12. swear, give me a true t.
Ps. 86 : 17. Shew me a t. for good
Mk. 14 : 44. Judas had given th. a t.
Ph. 1 : 28. an evident t. of perdition
2 Th. 1 : 5. a manifest t. of judgment
3 : 17. which is the t. in ev. epistle

TOKENS. [17, 20.

De. 22 : 15. t. of damsel's virginity,
Jb. 21 : 29. do ye not know their t.?
Ps. 65 : 8. they are afraid of thy t.
135 : 9. sent t. in midst of thee O Eg.
Is. 44 : 25. frustrateth the t. of the [liars

TO'LA.

1 Ch. 7 : 2. sons of T.; Jeriel, Jahmai, and Jibsam, valiant men (2)
See PUA, PUAH, TOLAITES.

TO'LAD.

1 Ch. 4 : 29. they dwelt at Ezem and T.

TO'LAITES.

Nu. 26 : 23. of Tola, family of T.

TOLD. [naked?

Ge. 3 : 11. Who t. that thou wast
9 : 22. And Ham t. his two breth-n
14 : 13. one that escaped t. Abr-m
20 : 8. Abim-h called serv-s, t. all
24 : 28 damsel t. th. of moth.'s ho.
33. I not eat until have t. errand
66. serv-t t. Isaac all he had done
27 : 42. words of Esau t. to Rebek-h
29 : 12. Jacob t. Rachel he was her father's bro.; she t. her father
13. Jacob t. Laban all these things
37 : 5. t. dream to his breth., 9. 10.
40 : 9. chief butler t. dream to Jos.
41 : 8. t. magicians his dream, 24.
47 : 1. Jos t. Pha. my breth. are co.
48 : 1. t. Joseph, thy father is sick
2. t. Jacob thy son Joseph cometh
Ex. 4 : 28. Moses t. Aaron words of L.
5 : 1. Moses and A. t. Pha., Let peo.
16 : 22. rulers of cong-n t. Moses
18 : 8. Mos. t. fa. in law all L. had done
19 : 9. Moses t. words of the people unto the Lord [Nu. 11 : 24.
24 : 3. Moses t. people words of L.,
Le. 21 : 24. Moses t. it unto Aaron and Israel, Nu. 14 : 39.-29 : 40.
Nu. 11 : 27. young man t. Moses [all
23 : 26. Balaam said, t. not I thee
De. 17 : 4. it be t. thee, and be true
Jos. 2 : 23. two men t. Josh. all that
Ju. 6 : 13. miracles our fathers t. of
7 : 13. man th. t. dream unto his fel.
9 : 7. t. it to Jotham, he went to top
42. people went into field t. Abim.
13 : 6. I asked not, nei. t. his name
23. nor wou have t. us such things
14 : 2 he came, t. his fa. and moth.
6. t. not his father, 9, 16. 1 S. 14 : 1.
17. on the seventh day he t. her, she t. the riddle [heart, 18.
16 : 17. she urged him, he t. all his
Ru. 3 : 16. she t. all the man had do.
1 S. 4 : 14. man came hastily t. Eli
8 : 10. Sam. t. words of L. unto peo.
9 : 15. L. had t. Samuel a day before
10 : 16. he t. us asses were found
25. Sam. t. peo. manner of kingd.
11 : 4. messengers t. tidings in ears
14 : 33. t. Saul, the peo. sin ag. Lord
18 : 20. Michal loved Da.; they t. S.
26. servants t., it pleased Da. well
19 : 2. Jonath. t. David, Saul seeketh to kill thee, 23 : 25. [Keilah
23 : 1. t. David Philistines fight ag.
25 : 14. one of young men t. Abigail

1 S. 25 : 19. Abigail t. not her husb.
2 S. 2 : 4. t. David men of Jabesh-gil.
3 : 23. t. Joab, Abner came to the k.
10 : 5. t. Dav., he sent to meet them
11 : 5. woman conceived and t. Dav.
10. t. Da. Uriah went not unto ho.
18. Joab t. David all things concerning war [spirators
15 : 31. t. Da. Ahith-l is among con-
17 : 17. a wench t. them, they t. Da.
18. lad saw them, and t. Absalom
21. they came out of well t. David
18 : 10. t. Joab, I saw Abs. hanged
25. watchman cried and t. the king
19 : 8. t. peo. king doth sit in gate
1 K. 1 : 23. t. the k., Behold Nathan
2 : 39. t. Shimei thy serv-s be in Ga.
10 : 3. Solomon t. all her questions, not thing he t. not, 2 Ch. 9 : 2.
13 : 11. words they t. to their father
25. t. it in city where old prophet
19 : 1. Ahab t. Jezebel all Elijah had
2 K. 4 : 7. She came and t. man of G.
5 : 4. one t. his lord, Thus said maid
7 : 10. t. them, We came to camp
11. porters t. it to king's house
15. messengers returned, t. king
9 : 18. watchman t., The messenger came, 20. [build house
1 Ch. 17 : 25. t. thy servant thou wilt
19 : 5. t. Da. how men were served
2 Ch. 20 : 2. t. Jehosh-t cometh mult.
34 : 18. Shaphan the scribe t. the k.
Ezr. 8 : 17. I t. what they should say
Ne 2 : 12. nei. t. I what G. put in my
16. nei. had I as yet t. it to Jews
18. Then I t. them of ha. of my G.
Es. 2 : 22. Mordecai t. it unto Esther
3 : 4. t. Haman to see whe. Mordecai's matters: had t. he was Jew
4 : 4. So Esther's maids t. it her
9. Hatach t. Esther words of Mord.
12. they t. Mord. Esther's words
5 : 11. Haman t. them of his riches
6 : 2. Mord. had t. of Bigthana and
13. Haman t. Zeresh his wife all
8 : 1. Esther t. what he was unto
Jb. 15 : 18. wise men have t. fr. fa-s
Ps. 44 : 1. our fa-s have t. us, 78 : 3.
90 : 9. our years as tale that is t.
Is. 44 : 8. have not I t. thee fr. time?
45 : 21. who hath t. it fr. that time?
52 : 15. not been t. them, sh. they see
Je. 36 : 20. they t. all in ears of king
38 : 27. Jerem-h t. princes acc-g to
Eze. 20 : †29. I t. what high pla. was
Da. 4 : 7. I t. the dream bef. magi-
8. before king I t. the dream [cians
7 : 1. Dan. wrote the dream and t.
Jon. 1 : 10. men knew bec. he had t.
Zch. 10 : 2. diviners t. false dreams
Mat. 8 : 33. went into city, t. ev. thi.
14 : 12. buried it went and t. Jesus
18 : 31. serv-s sorry, t. their lord all
26 : 13. sh. this be t. for a memorial
Mk. 5 : 14. that fed swine, fled and t. it in city, Lu. 8 : 34.
16. saw, t. how it befell, Lu. 8 : 36.
9 : 12. t. them Elias verily cometh
16 : 10. Mary t. them as they wept
13. they went, t. it unto residue
Lu. 1 : 45. shall be performance of things which were t. her
2 : 18. they wondered at things t.
9 : 36. kept it close, t. no man [10.
24 : 9. sepulc., and t. all unto elev.,
35. t. how he was known of th. in
Jn. 5 : 15. man t. it was Jesus [had
11 : 46. some t. Phari. what Jesus
20 : 18. Mary Magdalene t. disciples
Ac. 5 : 22. officers found them not,
25. one t., men are in temp. [and t.
9 : 6. be t. what th. must do, 22 : 10.
12 : 14. she ran in, t. how Pet. stood
16 : 36. keeper of prison t. this to Pa.
38. sergeants t. unto magistrates
22 : 26. t. chief captain, Take heed
Ac. 23 : 16. he entered castle. t. Paul
2 Co. 7 : 7. he t. us your earnest desire

TOLD him. [h., 9.

Ge 22 : 3. place of wh:ch God had t.
26 : 32. Isaac's serv-ts t. h. conc. well
31 : 20. Jacob t. h. not that he fled
41 : 12. we t. h. he interp-d dreams
42 : 29. they t. h. all that befell th.
43 : 7. we t. h. acc. to tenor of words
44 : 24. we t. h. the words of my lord
45 : 26. they t. h. Joseph is alive
27. they t. h. all the words of Jos.
Nu. 13 : 27. t. h., We came unto land
1 S. 3 : 13. I have t. h. I will judge
18. and Samuel t. h. every whit
10 : 16. of the kingdom he t. h. not
11 : 5. t. h. tid-gs of men of Jabesh
14 : 43. Jonath. t. h. I did but taste
18 : 24. servants of S. t. h. [thy life
19 : 11. Da.'s wife t. h., If save not
18. David t. h. all Saul had done
24 : 1. was t. h., David is in wildern.
25 : 12. David's young men t. h.
36. Abigail t. h. nothing until morning light, 37. [t. h., 6, 13.
2 S. 1 : 5. Dav. said unto yo. man th.
14 : 33. Joab came to king and t. h.
18 : 11. Joab said unto man that t. h.
24 : 13. Gad came to David and t. h.
1 K. 13 : 11. old proph., his sons t. h.
18 : 16. Obad. to meet Ahab, and t. h.
20 : 17. t. h., These are out of Sama.
2 K. 4 : 31. t. h., Child is not awaked
6 : 10. place man of God t. h. of
13. it was t. h., he is in Dothan
8 : 6. when k. asked wom. she t. h.
7. it was t. h. man of God is come
9 : 36. they came again and t. h.
10 : 8. and t. h., saying, They have brought heads of king's sons
18 : 37. Joah t. h. words of Rabshakeh, Is. 36 : 22. [chre of
23 : 17. men of city t. h., It is sepul-
Es. 4 : 7. Mord. t. h. all had happ-d
Jb. 37 : 20. sh. it be t. h. th. I speak
Mat. 12 : 48. Jes. said unto him th. t. h.
Mk. 5 : 33. woman t. h. all the truth
6 : 30. apostles t. h. all, Lu. 9 : 10.
Lu. 8 : 20. was t. h., Thy mother and
13 : 1. some that t. h. of Galileans
18 : 37. t. h. Jes. of Naz. passeth by
Jn. 4 : 51. servants t. h., Thy son liv- [eth

TOLD me.

Ju. 13 : 6. neith. t. m. his name [13.
16 : 10. hast mocked and t. m. lies,
15. not t. m. wh-n strength lieth
1 S. 23 : 22. t. m. he dealeth subtilely
2 S. 4 : 10. one t. m. Saul is dead
1 K. 10 : 7. half not t. m., 2 Ch. 9 : 6.
14 : 2. t. m. I sho. be king ov. peo.
2 K. 4 : 27. hid it and hath not t. m.
8 : 14. He t. m. thou sho. recover
Da. 7 : 16. t. m., made me know [39.
Jn. 4 : 29. man wh. t. m. all things,
Ac. 23 : 30. when it was t. m. how Jes.
27 : 25. it shall be as it was t. m.

Was TOLD. [borne

Ge. 22 : 20. w. t. Abr., Milcah hath
31 : 22. w. t. Laban, Jacob was fled
38 : 13. w. t. Tamar, thy fa. in law
24. w. t. Judah, Tamar hath play.
Ex. 14 : 5. w. t. king that. peo. fled
Jos. 2 : 2. it w. t. king of Jericho
9 : 24. w. t. thy servants how the L.
10 : 17. w. t. Josh., The 5 k-s are fled
Ju. 9 : 25. robbed all; it w. t. Abim.
47. w. t. Abim-h men of Shechem
16 : 2. w. t. Gazites, Samson is come
1 S. 15 : 12. w. t. Sam-l, Saul came to
19 : 19. w. t. Saul, Da. is at Naioth
21. w. t. Saul, he sent messengers
23 : 7. w. t. S. Da. was co. to Ke-h
13. w. t. Saul David was escaped
27 : 4. w. t. Saul Da. was fled to Ga.
2 S. 6 : 12. w. t. Da. L. hath blessed
10 : 17. when w. t. David, he gathered all Israel, 1 Ch. 19 : 17.
2 S. 19 : 1. w. t. Joab k. weepeth fo.
21 : 11. w. t. Da. what Rizpah done
1 K 1 : 51. w. t. Sol. Adonij. feareth
2 : 29. w. t. Sol. Joab was fled [S.
41. w. t. Sol. that Shimei had gone
18 : 13. w. it not t. my lord what I
Is. 7 : 2. w. t. house of David, Syria
Da. 8 : 26. vision which w. t. is true
Lu. 2 : 17. which w. t. conc. this chld
20. praising God for all as w. t. th.

TOLD you. [words

2 K. 1 : 7. What man was he t. y. these
Is. 40 : 21. hath it not been t. y.
Ha. 1 : 5. not believe tho. it be t. y.
Mat. 24 : 25. Behold I have t. y. bef.
28 : 7. ye sh. see him, lo, I have t. y.
Jn. 3 : 12. If I have t. y. earthly thi-s
8 : 40. to kill me th. hath t. y. truth
9 : 27. I have t. y. already, 10 : 25.
14 : 2. if not so, I would have t. y.
29. I have t. y. bef. it come to pass
16 : 4. these things have I t. y. that ye may remember that I t. y.
18 : 8. Jesus said, I have t. y. that
2 Co. 13 : 2. I t. y., and foretell you
Ga. 5 : 21. as I also t. y. in time past
Ph. 3 : 18. walk of whom I have t. y.
1 Th. 3 : 4. we t. y. we should suffer
2 Th. 2 : 5. when with you, I t. y.
Jude 18. t. y. there sho. be mockers

TOLD.

[Counted or numbered.]

1 K. 8 : 5. sheep, oxen, th. could not be t. for multitude, 2 Ch. 5 : 6.
2 K. 12 : 10. t. money found in hou.
11. gave money, being t. [of Lord
2 Ch. 2 : 2. Sol. t. out 70,000 men to
Ec. 6 : 6. tho. he live 1,000 yrs. twice t.

TOLERABLE.

Mat. 10 : 15. It shall be more t. for Sodom and Gomorrah, 11 : 24.
Mk. 6 : 11. Lu. 10 : 12. [Lu. 10 : 14.
11 : 22. more t. for Tyre and Sidon,

TOLL. [custom

Ezr. 4 : 13. will they not pay t. and
20. t., tribute, custom was paid
7 : 24. not be lawful to impose t.

TOMB, TOMBS. [t.

Jb. 21 : 32. and he sh. remain in the
Mat. 8 : 28. two possessed with devils, out of t-s, Mk. 5 : 2, 3, 5. Lu. 8 : 27.
23 : 29. ye built the t-s of prophets
27 : 60. Joseph laid body in his t.
Mk. 6 : 29 laid John's corpse in a t.

TONGS.

Ex. 25 : 38. make thee t. of pure gold
Nu. 4 : 9. cover t. with cloth of blue
1 K. 7 : 49. and t. of gold, 2 Ch. 4 : 21.
Is. 6 : 6. coal he had taken with t.
44 : 12. smith with t. worketh in

TONGUE. [it

Jos. 7 : †21. I saw a t. of gold, coveted

TONGUE. [Bay.] [ward

Jos. 15 : †2. fr. t. th. looketh south-
18 : †19. at the north t. of salt sea
Is. 11 : 15. L. destroy t. of Eg-n sea

TONGUE, S. [t.

Ex. 4 : 10. I am slow of speech of slow
11 : 7. ag. Isr. not a dog move his t.
Jos. 10 : 21. none moved t. ag. Israel
Ju. 7 : 5. lappeth of water with his t.
Jb. 5 : 21. sh. be hid fr. scouge of t.
15 : 5. thou choosest t. of the crafty
20 : 12. tho. he hide wickedness und.
16. the viper's t. shall slay him [t.
41 : 1. draw out his t. with a cord?
Ps. 5 : 9. they flatter with their t.
10 : 7. under his t. is mischief and
12 : 3. cut off t. that speaketh proud
4. said, With our t. will we prevail
15 : 3. that backbiteth not wi. his t.
31 : 20. keep them fr. strife of t-s [10.
34 : 13. Keep thy t. fr. evil, 1 Pe. 3:
37 : 30. his t. talketh of judgment
50 : 19. and thy t. frameth deceit
52 : 2. Thy t. deviseth mischiefs
55 : 9. Destroy, O L., divide their t-s

Ps. 57 : 4. their t. is a sharp sword
64:3. Who whet their t. like a sword
8. make their t. to fall upon thems.
68 : 23. t. of thy dogs be dipped in
73 : 9. their t. walketh thro. earth
78 : 36. lied unto him with their t-s
120 : 3. wh. be done to thee, false t. ?
126 : 2. was our t. filled with sing-g
140 : 3. sharpened t-s like serpent
† 11. let not a man of t. be estab-d
Pr. 6 : 24. from t. of strange woman
10 : 20. t. of the just as choice silver
31. froward t. shall be cut out
12 : 18. the t. of the wise is health
15 : 2. t. of the wise useth knowl.
4. A wholesome t. is a tree of life
16 : 1. answer of the t. is from Lord
17 : 4. liar giveth ear to naughty t.
20. perverse t. falleth into mischief
18:21. Death and life in power of t.
21:23. keepeth his t. keepeth his soul
25 : 15. a soft t. breaketh the bone
23. so doth an angry countenance a backbiting t. [with t.
28 : 23. favour than he th. flattereth
30 : †10. hurt not wi. thy t. a serv.
31 : 26. in her t. is law of kindness
Ec. 10 : † 11. master of the t. is no
Can. 4 : 11. honey and milk und. t.
Is. 3 : 8. bec. their t. is ag. the Lord
5 : † 24. t. of fire devoureth stubble
28 : 11. with ano. t. will he speak to
30 : 27. his t. is as devouring fire
32 : 4. t. of stammerers shall speak
33 : 19. not see peo. of stammer-g t.
35 : 6. Then sh. t. of the dumb sing
41 : 17. their t. faileth for thirst
45 : 23. unto me every t. sh. swear
50 : 4. given me t. of the learned
54 : 17. ev. t. that sh. rise ag. thee
57 : 4. ag. whom draw ye out the t.
59 : 3. your t. muttered perversen.
Je. 9 : 3. bend t-s like bow for lies
5. taught their t. to speak lies
8. Their t. is as an arrow shot out
18 : 18. Come, let us smite him wi. t.
23 : 31. prophets that use their t-s
36 : †3. made to come upon lip of t.
Ho. 7 : 16. sh. fall for rage of their t.
Ha. 1 : 13. holdest t. when wicked
Zch. 14 : 12. their t. shall consume
Mk. 7 : 33. he spit, and touched his t.
35. and straightway his t. was loosed, Lu. 1 : 64.
Ro. 3 : 13. with their t-s used deceit
14 : 11. every t. shall confess to God
1 Co. 14: 9. except ye utter by the t.
Ph. 2 : 11. every t. confess Jes. is L.
Ja. 1 : 26. and bridleth not his t.
3 : 5. so the t. is a little member
6. t. is a fire, a world of iniquity ; so is the t. among our members
8. But the t. can no man tame [evil
1 Pe. 3 : 10. let him refrain his t. fr.
1 Jn. 3 : 18. nei. let us love in t. but
Re. 16 : 10. gnawed their t-s for pain
See DECEITFUL, HOLD.

Lying TONGUE.

Ps. 109 : 2. spoken ag. me with l. t.
Pr. 6 : 17. L. hateth proud look, l. t.
12 : 19. a l. t. is but for a moment
21 : 6. getting of treasures by l. t.
26 : 28. l. t. hateth those afflicted by [it
See MOUTH with roof.

My TONGUE.

2 S. 23 : 2. and his word was in m. t.
Es. 7 : 4. If sold, I had held m. t.
Job. 6 : 30. Is there iniquity in m. t.
27 : 4. nor shall m. t. utter deceit
33 : 2. m. t. hath spoken in my mo.
Ps. 22 : 15. m. t. cleaveth to my jaws
30 : †12. that m. t. may sing praise
35 : 28. and m. t. sh. speak of thy righteousness, 51 : 14.-71 : 24.
39 : 1. take heed I sin not wi. m. t.
3. was hot, then spake I wi. m. t.
45 : 1. m. t. is pen of ready writer
Ps. 66 : 17. G. was extolled with m. t.
119 : 172. m. t. sh. speak of thy word
139 : 4. not a word in m. t. but th.
Lu. 16 : 24. may dip finger, cool m. t.
Ac. 2 : 26. did rejoice, m. t. was glad

TONGUE. [Language.]

Ge 10 : 5. divided every one aft. his [t.
De. 28 : 49. nation whose t. thou sh. not understand [Syrian t. (2)
Ezr. 4 : 7. the letter was written in
Is. 28 : 11. with ano. t. will he speak
Eze. 3 : †5. not to a peo. heavy of t. †6.
Da. 1 : 4. might teach t. of Chalde-s
Jn. 5 : 2. a pool, called in Hebrew t.
Ac. 1 : 19. called in prop. t. Aceldama
2 : 8. how hear we every man in our [t.
21 : 40. P-l spake in Heb. t., 22: 2.
26 : 14. saying in Hebrew t., Saul
1 Co. 14 : 2. that speaketh in unknown t., 4, 13, 14, 19, 27. [t.
26. every one hath a psalm, hath a
Re. 5 : 9. redeemed us out of every t.
9 : 11. name in Hebrew t. is Abad-n
14 : 6. gospel to preach to every t.
16 : 16. called in Hebrew t. Armageddon

TONGUES.

Ge. 10 : 20. sons of Ham aft. their t.
31. the sons of Shem after their t.
Is. 66 : 18. gather all nations and t.
Je. 23 : 31. that use their t. and say
Mk. 16 : 17. they sh. speak wi. new t.
Ac. 2 : 3. appeared unto th. cloven t.
4. began to speak with other t.
11. we hear in our t. the wonderf.
10 : 46. they heard them speak wi. t.
19 : 6. spake with t. and prophesied
1 Co. 12 : 10. to ano. divers kinds of t., to ano. interpretation of t., 28.
30. do all speak with t. ? do all
13 : 1. Tho. I speak with t. of men
8. whether be t. they shall cease
14 : 5. I would ye all spake with t., but greater than he th. speaketh [wi. t.
6. if I come speaking wi. t.
18. I speak wi. t. more th. you all
21. With men of other t. will I spe.
22. t. are for a sign [come
23. if all speak with t. and there
39. forbid not to speak with t.
Re. 7 : 9. peo. and t. stood bef. throne
10 : 11. prophesy bef. nations and t.
11 : 9. t., nations sh. see their dead
13 : 7. power given him over all t.
17 : 15. The waters are nations and [t.

TONGUED.

See DOUBLE-TONGUED.

TOO. See Too MUCH.

TOOK.

Ge. 2 : 15. God t. man put him into [Eden
21. Lord t. one of his ribs and
3 : 6. she t. of the fruit and did eat
4 : 19. Lamech t. unto him 2 wives
5 : 24. Enoch was not ; God t. him
6 : 2. t. wives of all which th. chose
8 : 9. t. her and pulled her into ark
20. Noah t. of every clean beast
9 : 23. Shem and Japhet t. garment
11 : 29. Abram and Nahor t. wives
31. Terah t. Abr. and Lot into Ca.
12 : 5. Abr. t. Sarai and Lot into C.
14 : 11. they t. all goods of Sodom
12. they t. Lot, Abr.'s bro.'s son
16 : 3. Sarai t. Hagar, gave her to A.
17 : 23. Abr. t. Ishmael, circumc-d [him
18 : 8. Abr. t. butter and milk
20 : 2. Abim-h k. of Gerar t. Sarah
14. Abim-h t. sheep gave unto A.
21 : 14. Abr. t. bread and water
21. mother t. him wife out of Eg.
27. Abr. t. sheep, oxen, gave Abim.
22 : 3. Abr. t. two of his young men
6. Abr. t. the fire and a knife (2) 10.
13. Abr. t. the ram and offered
24 : 7. God, wh. t. me fr. fa.'s house
10. And the servant t. ten camels
22. the man t. a golden earring
61. serv. t. Rebekah, went his way
Ge. 24 : 65. Rebekah t. vail, covered
67. Isaac t. Rebekah, she bec. wife,
25 : 1. again Abr. t. a wife [25 : 20.
26 : 34. Esau 40 yrs. old he t. Judith
27 : 15. Rebekah t. raiment of Esau
28 : 9. Esau t. Mahalath dau. of Ish.
11. Jac. t. stones for his pillows, 18.
29 : 23. Laban t. Leah, bro-t her to
30 : 9. Leah t. Zilpah to Jacob
37. Jac. t. rods of poplar and hazel
31 : 23. Laban t. his breth. pursued
45. Jac. t. a stone set it for pillar
46. they t. stones and made a heap
32 : 13. Jac. t. of that came to hand
22. Jac. t. his 2 wives ov. Jabbok, [23.
34 : 2. Shechem t. Dinah, lay wi.
25. Sim. and Levi t. each his sword
26. th. t. Dinah out of Shech.'s ho.
28. They t. their sheep, oxen, asses
36 : 2. Esau t. wives of dau-s of Ca.
6. Esau t. wives, sons, went fr. Jac.
37 : 24. t. Joseph cast him into pit
31. t. Joseph's coat dipped it in bl.
38 : 2. Judah took Shua, went in
6. Judah t. wife from Er, name T.
28. midw. t. bound scarlet thread
39 : 20. Joseph's master t. him into
40 : 11. I t. grapes, pressed them
42 : 24. Jos. t. Simeon, bound him
30. lord of the land t. us for spies
43 : 15. men t. double money and
46 : 6. t. cattle, goods, into Egypt
47 : 2. Jos. t. some of brethren unto
48 : 13. Joseph t. Ephr, Manasseh, 1.
22. wh. I t. out of hand of Amorite
Ex. 2 : 1. a man t. to wife dau. of Levi
3. she t. for him ark of bulrushes
9. the woman t. child and nursed
4 : 6. t. it out, his hand was leprous
20. Mos. t. his wife returned to Eg. Moses t. rod of God in his hand
25 Zipporah t. stone, cut off fores.
6 : 20. Amram t. Jochebed to wife
23. Aaron t. Elisheba to wife
25. Eleazar t. one of dau-s of Putiel
9 : 10. they t. ashes, stood bef. Pha.
13 : 19. Moses t. bones of Jos. wi. him
14 : 6. Pharaoh t. his peo. with him
7. he t. 600 chosen chariots and
17 : 12. t. a stone, put under Moses
18 : 2. Jethro t. Zipporah, Moses' [wife
12. Jethro t. sacrifices for G.
24 : 6. Moses t. bl-d, put it in basins
7. Moses t. book of cove-t and read
8. Mos. t. bl-d sprinkled it on peo.
32 : 20. he t. calf wh. they had made
33 : 7. Moses t. tabernacle, pitched
34 : 4. Moses t. two tables of stone
34. he t. vail off until he came out
40 : 20. M. t. put testim-y into ark
Le. 8 : 10. Moses t. anointing oil, 30.
15. Moses t., 16, 23, 25, 26, 28, 29.
9 : 15. Aaron t. the goat and slew it
10 : 1. Nadab and Abihu t. censer
Nu. 1 : 17. M. Aa. t. men expressed
3 : 49. Mos. t. redempt-n money, 50.
7 : 6. Moses t. wagons, gave Levites
11:25. L. t. of spirit th. was upon him
16 : 18. they t. every man his censer
39. Eleazar t. the brazen censers
47. Aaron t. as Moses commanded
17 : 9. they t. every man his rod
20 : 9. M. t. rod fr. before the Lord
21 : 1. Arad t. some of them prisoners
25. Israel t. all these cities
32. to spy out Jazer, and t. villages
22 : 41. Balak t. Balaam into high
23 : 11. I t. thee to curse enemies
25 : 7. Phinehas t. a javelin in hand
27 : 22. t. Joshua, set him bef. Elea-r
31 : 11. Israel t. the spoil and all
47. Moses t. one portion of fifty
51. M. and Eleazar t. the gold, 54.
De. 1 : 15. I t. chief of y-r tribes, 23.
25. they t. of the fruit of the land
2 : 34 And we t. all his cities, 3: 4. (2)
35. Only cattle we t. for a prey

De 3 : 8. we t. land this side of Jor.
14. Jair t. all the country of Argob
9 : 21. I t. your sin, and calf ye made
22 : 14. I t. this wom., found not maid
24 : 3. if latter husb die wh. t. her
29 : 8. we t. their land, gave it unto
Jos. 2 : 4. woman t. two men and hid
4 : 20. 12 stones they t. out of Jor.
6 : 20. people went up, t. the city
7 : 1. Achan t. of accursed thing
17. Joshua t. family of Zarhites
21. then I coveted and t. them
23. t. th. out of tent unto Joshua
24. Joshua and Israel t. Achan
8 : 12. Josh. t. 5,000 men to lie in
19. ambush entered city, t. it ⌊am.
23. king of Ai they t. alive and
9 : 4. t. old sacks upon their asses
14. men t. of victuals, asked not
10 : 28. Josh. t. Makkedah, smote it
32. Isr. t. Lachish on second day
35. Joshua t. Eglon and king th-f
37. t. Hebron, smote it with sword
39. Joshua t. Debir and king th-f
11 : 10. Josh. t. Hazor, smote k. th-f
16. Joshua t. all that land, 23.
17. all their kings he t. and slew
19. Hivites; all other they t. in
15 : 17. Othniel t. Kirjath-sepher,
24 : 3. I t. your fa. Abr. ⌊Ju. 1 : 13.
26. Josh. t. stone, set it und. oak
Ju. 1 : 18. Judah t. Gaza with coast
3 : 6. Isr. t. their dau-s to be wives
21. Ehud t. dagger from thigh
25. servants t. key, opened doors
5 : 19. kings t. no gain of money
6 : 27. Gideon t. ten men of his
7 : 8. people t. victuals, trumpets
24. men of Ephr. t. waters unto D.
25. t. two princes, Oreb and Zeeb
8 : 12. Gideon t. two kings of Midian
16. he t. elders of city and thorns
9 : 43. Abim-h t. peo., divided into
45. Ahim. t. city and slew people
48. Abim. t. an axe, cut bough (2)
50. Abim-h against Thebes, t. it
12 : 5. Gileadites t. passages of Jor.
13 : 19. Manoah t. kid, offered it
14 : 19. Sams. slew 30 men, t. spoil
15 : 4. S. caught foxes, t. firebrands
and turned tail to ⌈men
15. t. jawbone of an ass, slew 1,000
16 : 3. S. t. doors of the gate of city
12. Delilah t. new ropes, bound him
21. Philis t. Samson, put out eyes
17 : 2. the silver is with me, I t. it
4. his mother t. 200 shekels of silv.
18 : 17. the 5 men t. graven image
20. priest t. ephod, teraphim, and
27. they t. things wh. Micah made
19 : 1. a Levite who t. concubine
15. no man t. them into his house
25. man t. hi. concubine unto th.
29. t. knife, laid hold on concubine
20 : 6. I t. my concubine, cut her
Ru. 4 : 2. he t. ten men of elders of
13. Boaz t. Ruth, she was his wife
16. Naomi t. child, laid it in bosom
1 S. 2 : 14. all fleshhook brought up
the priest t. for himself ⌈2.
5 : 1. Philistines t. the ark of God,
3. t. Dagon, set him in his place
6 : 10. men t. two milch kine, tied
7 : 9. Sam-l t. sucking lamb, off-d it
12. S t. stone, set it betw Mizpeh
8 : 3. his sons t. bribes, perverted
9 : 22. Samuel t. Saul into parlour
10 : 1. S. t. vial of oil, poured upon
11 : 7. t. a yoke of oxen ⌊Saul
14 : 32. peo. flew upon spoil, t. sheep
47. Saul t. kingdom over Israel
52. S. saw valiant man, he t. him
15 : 8. he t. Agag k. of Amalekites
21. people t. of spoil, sheep, oxen
16 : 13. Sam. t. oil, anointed David
20. Jesse t. an ass laden with bread
23. David t. harp, played wi. hand

1 S. 17 : 40. Da. t. staff, chose 5 stones
49. David t. a stone and slang it
51. Dav. t. his sword, slew Philis.
54. Dav. t. head of Philis. to Jerus.
57. Abner t. David, bro-t bef. Saul
18 : 2. Saul t. David, not let him go
19 : 13. Michal t. image, laid in bed
24 : 2. Saul t. 3,000 chos. men of Isr.
25 : 18. Abigail t. 200 loaves
43. David t. Ahinoam of Jezreel
26 : 12. Dav. t. spear fr. Saul's bols.
28 : 24. the wom. t. flour, kneaded it
30 : 20. Dav. t. all the flock and herd
31 : 4. Theref. Saul t. a sword, fell
upon it, 1 Ch. 10 : 4. ⌈1 Ch. 10 : 12.
12. valiant men t. body of Saul,
13. t. their bones and buried them
2 S. 1 : 10. I t. crown, bro-t it hither
2 : 8. Abner t. Ish-bosh. son of Saul
3 : 15. Ish-bosheth t. Michal fr. hus.
4 : 7. smote Ish-bosh., t. his head
5 : 7. David t. the strong hold of
Zion, 1 Ch. 11 : 5. ⌈1 Ch 17 : 7.
7 : 8. I t. thee from the sheepcote,
15. mercy not depart fr. him as I
t. it from Saul, 1 Ch. 17 : 13.
8 : 1. David t. Metheg-ammah out
4. David t. from Hadad-ezer 1,000
chariots, 1 Ch. 18 : 4. ⌈18 : 7
7. Dav. t. shields of gold, 1 Ch.
8. David t. exceeding much brass
10 : 4. Hanun t. David's servants,
shaved half of beards, 1 Ch 19 : 4.
11 : 4. Da. sent messeng-s t. Bath-s.
12 : 4. rich man t. poor man's lamb
26. Joab fought and t. royal city
30 Dav. t. king's crown, 1 Ch. 20 : 2.
13 : 8. Tamar t. flour, made cakes, 9.
10. Tamar t. cakes into chamber
15 : 5. any man, Absalom t. him
17 : 19. woman t. and spread cov-g
18 : 14. he t. 3 darts, thrust them
17. they t. Abs., cast him into pit
20 : 3. Dav. t. his concubines, put
9. Joab t. Amasa by beard to kiss
21 : 8. Dav. t. the two sons of Rizpah
10. Rizpah t. sackcloth, spread it
12. Dav. t. bones of Saul and Jona.
22 : 17. he t. me; he drew me out of
many waters, Ps. 18 : 16. ⌈Sol.
1 K. 1 : 39. Zadok t. oil; anointed
3 : 1. Sol. t. Pha.'s dau. into city of
20. she t. my son from beside me
4 : 15. Ahimaaz t. Basmath to wife
11 : 18. t. men with th. out of Paran
15 : 18. Asa t. gold left in treasures
16 : 31. Ahab t. to wife Jezebel, dau.
17 : 19. he t. her son out of her bos.
23. Elijah t. child unto his moth.
18 : 4. Obadiah t. 100 prophets, hid
26. proph-s of Baal t. the bullock
31. Elijah t. 12 stones, acc. to tribes
40. Take prophets of Baal; they t.
19 : 21. Elisha t. yoke of oxen, slew
20 : 34. cities my father t. I restore
2 K. 2 : 8. Elijah t. his mantle smote
14. he t. mantle of Elijah ⌊waters
3 : 26. k. of Moab t. 700 men to break
27. t. his eldest son and offered
5 : 5. Naaman t. wi. him ten talents
24. he t. them from their hand
6 : 7. put out his hand and t. iron
7 : 14. k.'s servants t. chariot horses
8 : 9. Hazael t. present with him
15. he t. cloth, dipped it in water
9 : 13. t. every man his garment
10 : 7. t. king's sons, slew 70 persons
14. they t. them alive and slew th.
31. Jehu t. no heed to walk in law
11 : 2. Jehosheba t. Joash, stole
him fr. among sons, 2 Ch. 22 : 11.
9. captains t. every man his men
19. Jehoiada t. rulers over hundreds, 2 Ch. 23 : 1, 20.
12 : 9. Jehoiada t. a chest, bored
18. Jehoash t. all the hallowed
13 : 15. Joash king t. bow and arr.

2 K. 13 : 25. Jeho-h t. again the cities
14 : 7. Amaziah t. Selah by war
13. Jehoash t. Amaziah the king
of Judah, 2 Ch. 25 : 23. ⌈ho. of L.
14. Jehoash t. all gold and silv. fr.
21. all peo. of Judah t. Azariah,
made him king; 2 Ch. 26 : 1.
15 : 29. Tiglath-pileser t. Ijon and
16 : 8. Ahaz t. silver, gold in house
9. king of Assyria t. Damascus
17. Ahaz t. down sea from off oxen
17 : 6. k. of Assyria t. Samaria and
18 : 10. at end of 3 yrs. th. t. Sam-a
13. Sennach-b ag. cities of Judah,
t. them, Is. 36 : 1. ⌈sepulchres
23 : 16. Josiah t. bones out of the
30. people t. Jehoahaz and made
him king, 2 Ch. 36 : 1. ⌈in 8th yr.
24 : 12. king of Bab-n t. Jehoiachin
25 : 6. armies of the Chaldees t. Zedekiah to Babylon, Je. 52 : 9.
18. captain of guard t. Seraiah,
priest, Je. 52 : 24. ⌈war, 20.
19. he t. an officer over men of
1 Ch. 2 : 19. Caleb t. Ephrath wh. bare
†21. dau. of Machir, Hezron t. ⌊Hur
23. he t. Geshur with towns of Jair
4 : 18. sons of Bithiah wh. Mered t.
7 : 15. Machir t. to wife Maachah
10 : 9. Philis. t. Saul's head, arm-r
11 : 18. three drew water, t. it to Da.
14 : 3. Dav. t. more wives at Jerus.
18 : 1. David t. Gath out of hands
2 Ch. 8 : 18. to Ophir t. 450 talents
11 : 18. Reho-m t. Mahalath to wife
20. aft. her he t. Maachah dau. of
21. he t. 18 wives, 60 concubines
12 : 4. Shishak t. fenced cities
13 : 19. Abijah pursued Jerob-m, t.
16 : 6. Asa, k., t. all Judah ⌊cities
23 : 8. Levites t. every man his men
24 : 3. Jehoiada t. two wives, begat
11. k.'s scribe and officers t. chest
25 : 13. the soldiers t. much spoil
28 : 15. men expressed by name t.
33 : 11. wh. t. Manasseh am. thorns
35 : 24. his servt-s t. Josiah out of
36 : 4. Necho t. Jehoahaz to Egypt
Ezr. 2 : 61. which t. a wife of dau-s of
Barzillai, Ne. 7 : 63. ⌈6 : 5.
5 : 14. vessels Neb-r t. out of temple,
Ne. 9 : 25. chil. of Isr. t. strong cities
Es. 2 : 7. Mordecai t. for his dau.
3 : 10. k. t. ring, gave it unto Haman
6 : 11. t. Haman apparel, arrayed
8 : 2. k. t. off ring, gave it to Mord.
9 : 27. t. upon them they would
Jb. 2 : 8. t. a potsherd to scrape hims.
10 : † 8. Thine hands t. pains upon
Ps. 22 : 9. t. me out of womb, 71 : 6.
78 : 70. He chose Dav. t. fr. sheepf-s
Pr. 12 : 27. roasteth not that he t.
Is. 8 : 2. I t. me faithful witnesses ⌈it
20 : 1. Tartan fought ag. Ashdod, t.
Je. 13 : 7. t. girdle fr. place wh. I hid
25 : 17. t. I cup at Lord's hand ⌈die
26 : 8. t. Jere-h saying, Thou shalt
27 : 20. vessels which Neb-r t. not
28 : 10. Hananiah t. yoke off Jeremiah's neck ⌈He. 8 : 9.
31 : 32. day I t. them by the hand,
32 : 11. I t. evidence of purchase
35 : 3. Then I t. Jaazaniah and sons
36 : 14. Baruch t. the roll in hand
21. Jehudi t. roll out of Elishama's
32. t. Jere-h another roll, gave to
37 : 13. Irijah t. Jeremiah, saying
14. Irijah t. Jeremiah to princes
17. Zedekiah k. sent t. Jere-h out
38 : 6. t. Jere-h, cast him into du.
11. Ebed-melech t. men into hou.
13. t. Jeremiah out of dungeon
14. Zed-h sent t. Jerem. unto him
39 : 14. they t. Jerem. out of prison
40 : 2. captain of guard t. Jeremiah
41 : 12. captains t. men to fight wi.
16. t. Johanan rem-t of peo., 43 : 5.

Je. 52 :25. capt. t. out of city eunuch
26. Neb-n t. them to king of Bab-n
La. 5 :13. they t. young men to grind
Eze. 8 : 3. he t. me by lock of head
10 : 7. he t. fire fr. betw. cherubim
17 : 3. a gr. eagle t. highest branch
5. he t. also of seed of the land
19 :5. then she t. ano. of her whelps
23 : 10. t. her sons and dau-s, slew
13. I saw they t. both one way ⌊her
33 : 5. heard trumpet, t. not warn-g
Da. 5 : 20. they t. his glory from him
31. Darius the Median t. kingdom
Ho. 1 : 3. t. Gomer dau. of Diblaim
12 : 3. t. his bro. by heel in womb
Am. 7 :15 L. t. me as I followed flock
Zch. 11 : 7. I t. two staves. Beauty
10. I t. staff, Beauty cut it asund.
13. I t. 30 pieces and cast to potter
Mat. 1 : 24. Joseph t. unto him his
2 : 14. he t. young child, 21. ⌊wife
8 : 17. Himself t. our infirmities
9 : 25. he t. her by the hand, maid
arose, Mk. 1:31.-5 :41. ⌈Lu. 13:19.
13 : 31. mustard seed wh. a man t.,
33. kingdom is like leaven which a
woman t., Lu. 13 : 21. ⌈Jn. 6:11.
14 :19. t. 5 loaves, 2 fishes, Lu. 9:16.
15 :36. he t. seven loaves, Mk. 8 :6.
39. he took ship, came unto coasts
16 : 22. Peter t. him and began to
rebuke him, Mk. 8 : 32. ⌈apart
20 :17. Jesus t. the twelve disciples
21 : 35. husbandman t. servants
46. bec. they t. him for a prophet
22 : 6. remn-t t. servants. slew th.
25 : 1. ten virgins wh. t. th. lamps
3. they that were foolish t. no oil
4. But the wise t. oil in vessels
35. I was stranger, ye t. me in, 38.
43. I was stranger, ye t. me not in
26 : 26. Jesus t. bread and blessed
it, gave it, Mk. 14 :22. Lu. 22 :19
-24 :30. Ac. 27 :35. 1 Co. 11 : 23
27. he t. the cup and gave thanks
Mk. 14:23. Lu. 22:17. 1 Co. 11:25
37. he t. Peter and two sons of
Zebedee, Lu. 9 : 28. ⌈of silver, 6
27 : 9. And they t. the thirty pieces
24 Pilate t. water, washed hands
27. Then soldiers t. Jesus into hall
30. th. t. reed, smote him on head
31. they t. robe off him, Mk. 15:20.
48. t. sponge, filled it with vinegar
28 :15. t. the money, did as taught
Mk. 4 : 36. t. him even as he was in
7 : 33. he t. him aside fr. multitude
8 :23. he t. blind man by the hand
9 : 27. Jesus t. him by hand, lifted
36. t. a child, set him in midst
10 : 32. he t. again the 12 ⌊Lu. 9:47.
12 : 8. they t., killed, cast him out
20 first t. a wife, and dying left no
seed, Lu. 20 : 29.
21, second t. her and died; third
likewise, Lu. 20 : 30, 31. ⌈him
14 : 46. they laid hands on and t.
49. in temple teach-g, ye t. me not
15 : 46. he t. him down, Lu. 23 :53
Lu. 9 : 10. Jesus t. them privately
10 :35. he t. two pence, gave to host
14 : 4. he t. him and healed him
18 :31 Then he t. him unto twelve
22:54. they t. him, led him, Jn 19:16
24:43. he t. it, and did eat bef. them
Jn. 6 : 24. t. ship-g, came to Capero.
10 : 31. Jews t. stones to stone him
12 : 3. t. Mary pound of ointment
13. peo. t. branches of palm trees
13 : 4. he t. a towel, girded himself
18 : 12. Then officers of Jews t. Jes.
19 : 1. Pilate t. Jesus, scourged him
16. they t. Jesus and led him aw.
23. Then soldiers t. his garments
27. disciple t. her to his own hou
38 He came and t. body of Jesus
40. Then they t. the body of Jesus
Ac. 1 : 16. guide to them th. t. Jesus
3 : 7. Pet. t. him by the right hand
4 : 13. they t. knowledge of them th.
7 : 21. Pha.'s daughter t. him and
9 :25. disciples t. him by night and
27. Barnabas t. him and declared
12 25. t. John, surname was Mark
13 29. t. him fr. tree, laid him in
15 39. so Barnabas t. Mark ⌊sepul.
16 3. Paul t. and circumcised him
33. he t. th., washed their stripes
17 : 5. Jews t. lewd fellows of baser
19. they t. Paul unto Areopagus
18 : 17. all the Greeks t. Sosthenes
18. Paul t. his leave of brethren
26. th. t. him and expounded way
19 : 13. exorcists t. upon th. to call
20 : 14. when Paul met us we t. him
21 : 6. we t. ship, they returned
11. he t. Paul's girdle, bound ha-s
26. Paul t. the men, and next day
30. they t. Paul out of the temple
32. immediately t. soldiers and ran
33. chief captain t. him, 24 : 7.
23 : 18. centurion t. him to captain
19. chief captain t. him by hand
31. Then soldiers t. Paul and bro-t
24 : 6. whom we t. and would have
27 : 36. all of good cheer, t. meat
28 :15. Paul thanked God, t. courage
Ga. 2 :1 14 yrs. after I t. Titus wi. me
Ph. 2 :7. t. upon him form of servant
Col. 2 : 14. and t. it out of the way
He. 2 : 14. he also t. part of the same
16 t. not on him nature of angels;
but t. the seed of Abraham
9 : 19. he t. blood of calves, goats
10 : 34. ye t. joyfully the spoiling
Re. 5 :7. he t. book out of right hand
8 : 5. angel t. censer and filled it
10 : 10. I t. book out of angel's hand

TOOK away.

Ge. 27 : 36. he t.a. my birthright
Ex. 10 : 19. a west wind t.a. locusts
13 : 22. He t. not a. pillar of cloud
Le. 6 : 4. shall restore that he t.a.
Ju. 8 : 21. Gideon t.a. ornaments
11 :13. Israel t.a. my land wh. they
15. Israel t. not a. and of Moab
1 S. 27 : 9. David t.a. sheep and oxen
1 K. 14 : 26 Shishak t.a. treasures
of house of Lord; he t.a. all,
(3) 2 Ch. 12 : 9. ⌈the land
15 : 12. Asa t.a. Sodomites out of
22. they t.a. the stones of Ramah
2 K. 23 :11. t.a. horses given to sun
34. Pharaoh-nechoh t. Jehoahaz a.
25 :14. all the vessels the Chaldeans
t.a., 15. Je. 52 : 18, 19. ⌈250,000
1 Ch. 5 : 21. t.a. their cattle; sheep
2 Ch 14 : 3. Asa t.a. altars of gods
5. he t.a. out of cities images
17 : 6. Jehosaphat t.a. high places
28 : 8. chil. of Isr. t.a. much spoil
30 : 14. Hez h t.a. altars in Jerus
33 :15. Manasseh t.a. strange gods
34 :33. Josiah t.a. all abominations
Jb. 1 :15. Sabeans fell upon, t. th. a.
Ps. 69 : 4. I restored that I t. not a.
Can. 5 : 7. keepers t.a. veil from me
Je. 28 : 3. bring all vessels Neb-r t.a.
Eze. 3 : 14. spirit lifted and t. me a.
16 : 50. I t. them a. as I saw good
Da. 1 : 16. Melzar t.a. their meat
Ho. 13 : 11. I t. king a. in my wrath
Mat. 24 : 39. flood came, t. th. all a.
Jn. 11 : 41. they t.a. stone fr. place
Ac. 24 :7. Lysias with gr. violence t.
See COUNSEL. ⌊him a.

TOOK hold. ⌈heel

Ge. 25 : 26. his hand t.h. of Esau's
Ju. 16 : 29. Samson t.h. of pillars
2 S. 1 :11. t.h. on his clothes, 2 K. 2
4 : 10. I t.h. of and slew him ⌊12
6 : 6. Uzzah t.h. of ark, 1 Ch. 13 :9.
13 : 11. he t.h. of her, said, lie with
Ps. 48 : 6. Fear t.h. upon them ⌊me
Je. 50 : 43. anguish t.h. of him
Eze. 29 : 7. When they t.h. of thee

TOOK up.

Nu. 23 : 7. Balaam t.u. his parable
and said, 18.-24 : 3, 15, 20, 21, 23
Jos. 3 :6. the priests t.u. the ark, 6 :
12. 1 K. 8 : 3. ⌈upon ass
Ju. 19 : 28. man t. his concubine u.
1 S. 9 : 24. cook t.u. the shoulder
2 S. 2 : 32. t.u. Asahel, buried him
4:4. Mephibosheth's nurse t. him u.
1 K. 8 : 3. priests t.u. ark, 2 Ch. 5 :4.
13 : 29. prophet t.u. the carcass of
2 K. 2 : 13. He t.u. mantle of Elijah
4 : 37. Shunammite t.u. her son
10 : 15. Jehu t. him u. into chariot
Ne. 2 : 1. I t.u. wine, gave it unto k.
Je. 38 : 13. they t. Jeremiah u. out
Eze. 3 : 12. Then the Spirit t. me u.,
11 : 24.-43 : 5. ⌈rach
Da. 3 : 22. slew men that t.u. Shad-
Jon. 1 : 15. t.u. Jonah, and cast him
Mat. 14:12. t.u. body of Jn., Mk. 6:29.
20. they t.u. of the fragments,
15 : 37. Mk. 6 : 43.-8 : 8, 20.
16 : 9. how many baskets ye t.u.,
10. Mk. 8 : 19, 20. ⌈Lu. 5 : 25.
Mk. 2 : 12. t.u. the bed, went forth,
10 : 16. he t. them u. in his arms
Lu. 2 : 28. t. him u. in his arms and
Jn. 5 :9. t.u. his bed and walked ⌈31.
8 :59. t.u. stones to cast at him, 10:
Ac. 7 : 21. Pha.'s dau. t. Moses u.
43. ye t.u. tabernacle of Moloch
10 : 26. Peter t. him u., saying
21 : 15. t.u. our carriages, went to
Re. 18 :21. mighty angel t.u. a stone

TOOKEST.

Ps 99 : 8. t. vengeance of inventions
Exe. 16 :18. t. thy broidered garm-ts

TOOL. ⌈luted it

Ex. 20 : 25. if lift up thy t. hast pol-
32 : 4. fashioned it with graving t.
De. 27 : 5. not lift iron t. upon them
1 K. 6 : 7. nor t. of iron heard in the

TOOTH. ⌊house

Ex. 21 : 24. thou shalt give t. for t.,
Le. 24 :20. De. 19 :21. Mat. 5:38.
27. if he smite out manservant's t.
let him go free for t.'s sake
1 S. 14 : † 5. t. of one was northward
Pr. 25 :19. unfaithful man like brok-

TOP, TOPS. ⌊en t.

Ge. 11 :4. t. may reach unto heaven
28 : 12. t. of ladder reached to heav.
18. Jac. poured oil upon t. of stone
Ex. 19 :20. L. came upon t. of Sinai,
called Mos. to t. of mount, 34:2.
24 : 17. like fire on t. of mount
28 : 32. shall be a hole in t. of it ⌈26.
30 : 3. overlay t. wi. pure gold. 37:
Nu 20 :28. Aaron died in t. of mount
De. 28 : 35. sole of foot to t. of head
33 : 16. upon t. of the head of him
Jos. 15 : 8. to t. of mt. bef. Hinnom
Ju. 9 :7. Jotham stood in t. of Geriz-
51. peo. gat up to t. of tower ⌊im
2 S. 5 : 24. sound of a going in t-s of
mulberry trees, 1 Ch. 14 : 15.
15 : 32. when David was come to t.
1 K. 7 : 16. two chapiters of brass
upon the t-s of pillars, 17, 18,
19, 22, 41. (2) 2 Ch. 3 :15.-4:12. (2)
35. in t. of base a compass (2)
10 : 19. t. of the throne behind
21 : † 9. set Naboth in t. of people
2 K. 9 : 13. under him on t. of stairs
2 Ch. 25 : 12. cast them fr. t. of rock
Es. 5 : 2. Esth. touched t. of sceptre
Jb. 24 : 24. are cut off as t-s of corn
Pr. 8 : 2. she standeth in t. of high
23 :34. he th. lieth upon t. of a mast
Can. 4 :8. look from the t. of Amana,
from the t. of Shenir ⌈howl
Is. 15 : 3. on t-s of houses ev. one sh.
La. 2 : 19. hunger in t. of ev. street
4 : 1. stones of sanct-y in t. of street

Na. 3 : 10. chil. dashed at t. of streets
Zch. 4 : 2. candlest. wi. bowl on t.(2)
Jn. 19 : 23. woven from t. through-t
He. 11 : 21. leaning upon t. of staff
See BOTTOM, BOUGH, BOUGHS,
CARMEL, CHAPITER, HILL.
See **HOUSE** with **top.**
See HOUSETOP, S, MOUNTAIN.
See **Of the MOUNTAINS,**
PEOR, PILLARS, PISGAH, ROCK,
ROCKS, TWIGS.

TOPAZ. [39 : 10.

Ex. 28 : 17. first row a sardius, a t.,
Jb. 28 : 19. t. of Ethiopia not equal it
Eze. 28 : 13. t. was thy covering
Re. 21 : 20. eighth, beryl, ninth, a t.

TO'PHEL.

De. 1 : 1. words Moses spake between
Paran and T.

TO'PHET, or TO'PHETH.

2 K. 23 : 10. Josiah defiled T-h in val.
Is. 30 : 33. T. is ordained of old, for
Je. 7 : 31. built the high places of T.
32. sh. no more be called T., (2) 19:
19 : 11. bury in T. till be no place[6.
12. I will even make this city as T.
13. Jerus-m shall be defiled as T.
14. came Jere-h from T., whither

TORCH, ES. [sent

Ju. 7 : † 16. put t-s within pitchers
15 : † 4. caught 300 foxes, took t-s
Na. 2 : 3. chariots shall be with t-s
4. the chariots shall seem like t-s
Zch. 12 : 6. governors of Judah like t.
Jn. 18 : 3. Judas with lanterns and t-s

TORMENT, S. [t-s

Mat. 4 : 24. with divers diseases and
Lu. 16 : 23. in hell, he being in t-s
28. lest come into this place of t.
1 Jn. 4 : 18. no fear, bec. fear hath t.
Re. 9 : 5. their t. as t. of scorpion
14 : 11. smoke of their t. ascendeth
18 : 7. so much t. sorrow give her
10. afar off for fear of her t., 15.

TORMENT. [Verb.] [time?

Mat. 8 : 29. art come to t. us before
Mk. 5 : 7. thou t. me not, Lu. 8 : 28.

TORMENTED.

Is. 53 : †4. he was t. for our transg-ns
Mat. 8 : 6. servant lieth grievously t.
Lu. 16 : 24. send Lazarus, for I am t.
25. now he is comforted, thou art
He. 11 : 37. wandered, afflicted, t.[t.
Re. 9 : 5. they should be t. 5 months
11 : 10. these two prophets t. them
14 : 10. be t. with fire and brimstone
20 : 10. be t. day and night for ever

TORMENTORS.

Mat. 18 : 34. lord delivered him to t.

TORN. [bro-t not

Ge. 31 : 39. which was t. of beasts I
44 : 28. said, Surely he is t. in pieces
Ex. 22 : 13. If t. in pieces he sh. not
make good what was t.
31. nor sh. eat any flesh t. of beasts
Le. 7 : 24. fat of that t. may be used
17 : 15. if eat that wh. was t. he sh.
22 : 8. wh. is t. with beasts not eat
1 K. 13 : 26. lion which hath t. him
28. lion not eaten carcass, nor t. ass
Is. 5 : 25. carcasses t. in the streets
Je. 5 : 6. that goeth out shall be t.
Eze. 4 : 14. I eaten of that which is t.
44 : 31. priests shall not eat th. is t.
Ho. 6 : 1. hath t. and he will heal us
Mal. 1 : 13. ye brought that wh. was t.
Mk. 1 : 26. when unclean spirit hath

TORTOISE. [t.

Le. 11 : 29. t. shall be unclean unto

TORTURED. [you

Ac. 22 : †29. who should have t. him
He. 11 : 35. t., not accepting deliver-

TOSS. [ance

Is. 22 : 18. he will turn and t. thee
Je. 5 : 22. though the waves t. thems.

TOSSED.

Ps. 109 : 23. I am t. up and down
Pr. 21 : 6. is a vanity t. to and fro
Is. 54 : 11. O afflicted, t. with tempest
Mat. 14 : 24. ship was now t. wi. waves
Ac. 27 : 18. exceed-y t. with tempest
Ep. 4 : 14. be no more chil. t. to and
Ja. 1 : 6. th. wavereth is like a wave t.

TOSSINGS. [of day

Jb. 7 : 4. I am full of t. to dawning
2 Co. 6 : † 5. approving ourselves in

TOTTERING. [t.

Ps. 62 : 3. ye shall be as a t. fence

TO'U. See TOI.

TOUCH.

Ge. 3 : 3. nei. shall ye t. it lest ye die
20 : 6. suffered I thee not to t. her
Ex. 19 : 12. that ye t. not border of it
13. not a hand t. it but shall die
Le. 5 : 2. if soul t. any unclean thing
3. if he t. uncleanness of man, 7 : 21.
6 : 27. Whatsoever shall t. the flesh
11 : 8. carcass ye sh. not t., De. 14 : 8.
31. doth t. them dead, be unclean
12 : 4. she sh. t. no hallowed thing
Nu. 4 : 15. sh. not t. any holy thing
16 : 26. depart, t. nothing of theirs
Jos. 9 : 19. now we may not t. them
Ru. 2 : 9. that they sho. not t. thee
2 S. 14 : 10. he shall not t. thee any
18 : 12. Beware th. none t. Absalom
23 : 7. t. th. must be fenced wi. iron
1 Ch. 16 : 22. t. not mine anointed,
Ps. 105 : 15. [curse thee
Jb. 1 : 11. t. all he hath and he will
2 : 5. t. his bone, he will curse thee
5 : 19. in seven shall no evil t. thee
6 : 7. things my soul refused to t.
Ps. 144 : 5. t. the mts. they sh. smoke
Is. 6 : † 7. caused it to t. my mouth
52 : 11. t. no uncl. thing, 2 Co. 6 : 17.
Je. 12 : 14. t. inheritance of my peo.
La. 2 : † 2. strong holds to t. ground
4 : 14. could not t. their garments
15. they cried, it is unclean, t. not
Hag. 2 : 12. If one with skirt t. bread
13. If one unclean t. any of these
Zch. 14 : † 4. when he shall t. the
valley of mountains [Mk. 5 : 28.
Mat. 9 : 21. if I may but t. his garm-t,
14 : 36. they might t. hem of his
garment, Mk. 5 : 28.-6 : 56.-8 : 22.
Mk. 3 : 10. pressed to t. him, Lu. 6 : 19.
8 : 22. besought him to t. blind man
Lu. 11 : 46. ye t. not the burdens
18 : 15. bro-t infants that he would
t. them, Mk. 10 : 13. [me not
Jn. 20 : 17. Jesus saith unto her, t.
1 Co. 7 : 1. is good not to t. a woman
Col. 2 : 21. t. not, taste not, handle
He. 11 : 28. lest he that destroyed
firstborn should t. them [mt.
12 : 20. if so much as a beast t. the

TOUCHED. [t. thee

Ge. 26 : 29. Do us no hurt, have not
32 : 25. t. hollow of Jac.'s thigh, 32.
Le. 22 : 6. soul wh. hath t. any such
Nu. 19 : 18. upon him that t. a bone
31 : 19. whosoev. hath t. any slain
Ju. 6 : 21. angel of Lord t. the flesh
20 : †41. amazed, they saw evil t. th.
1 S. 10 : 26. whose hearts God had t.
1 K. 6 : 27. wing of one t. one wall,
wing of other cherub. t. other
wall; their wings t. one anoth.
19 : 5. angel t. him, Arise, eat, 7.
2 K. 13 : 21. man t. bones of Elisha
Es. 5 : 2. Esther t. top of sceptre
Jb. 19 : 21. the hand of God hath t.
Is. 6 : 7. lo, this hath t. thy lips [me
Je. 1 : 9. then the Lord t. my mouth
Eze. 3 : 13. wings of creatures t. one
Da. 8 : 5. he goat t. not ground[ano.
18. he t. me, 9 : 21.-10 : 10, 16, 18.
Mat. 8 : 3. and Jesus t. him, Mk. 1 :
41. Lu. 5 : 13. [left her
15. And he t. her hand, and fever
9 : 20. a woman t. hem of his garment, Mk. 5 : 27. Lu. 8 : 44.
Mat. 9 : 29. Th. t. he their eyes, 20 : 34.
14 : 36. as many as t. were made
whole, Mk. 6 : 56. [not afraid
17 : 7. Jesus t. them, and said, Be
Mk. 5 : 30. Who t. my clothes, 31.
Lu. 8 : 45, 47. [his tongue
7 : 33. was deaf, and he spit, and t.
Lu. 7 : 14. he came and t. the bier
8 : 46. Jesus said, Somebody t. me
47. for what cause she had t. him
22 : 51. Jesus t. his ear and healed
Ac. 27 : 3. next day we t. at Sidon[t.
He. 4 : 15. not a priest wh. cannot be
12 : 18. not unto m-t th. might be t.

TOUCHETH. [die

Ge. 26 : 11. t. this man shall surely
Ex. 19 : 12. whoso. t. mount be put
29 : 37. whatso. t. altar sh. be holy
30 : 29. t. them be holy, Le. 6 : 18.
Le. 7 : 19. flesh that t. any unclean
11 : 24. whoso. t. carcass, 27, 36, 39.
26. ev. one th t. them be unclean
15 : 5. whoso. t. his bed shall wash
7. that t. flesh of him shall wash
10. whoso. t. any thing under him
11. whomso. he t. that hath issue
12. vessel he t. shall be broken
19. whoso. t. her shall be unclean
21. whoso. t. her bed shall wash
22. whoso. t. any thi. she sat upon
23. if on her bed, when he t. it, 27.
-22 : 4, 5. Nu. 19 : 22. (2) [16.
Nu. 19 : 11. He that t. dead body, 13,
18. sprinkle upon him th. t. bone
21. t. water of separation, unclean
Ju. 16 : 9. as thread when it t. fire
Jb. 4 : 5. it t. thee thou art troubled
Ps. 104 : 32. he t. hills they smoke
Pr. 6 : 29. whoso. t. her not innocent
Eze. 17 : 10. wither when east wind t.
Ho. 4 : 2. break out, blood t. blood
Am. 9 : 5. Lord is he that t. land
Zch. 2 : 8. t. you, t. apple of his eye
Lu. 7 : 39. known what wom. t. him
1 Jn. 5 : 18. th. wicked one t. him not

TOUCHING. [fort

Ge. 27 : 42. Esau, as t. thee doth com-
Le. 5 : 13. as t. sin he hath sinned
Nu. 8 : 26. Levites t. their charge
1 S. 20 : 23. t. matter thou and I have
2 K. 22 : 18. t. words thou hast heard
Ezr. 7 : 24. t. priests not lawful to
Jb. 37 : 23. t. Almighty, we cannot
Ps. 45 : 1. things made t. the king
Is. 5 : 1. my beloved. t. his vineyard
Je. 1 : 16. judgments t. their wickedn.
21 : 11. t. house of king of Judah
22 : 11. saith Lord, t. Shallum, king
Eze. 7 : 13. vision is t. the multitude
Mat. 18 : 19. as t. any thing they ask
22 : 31. as t. resurrection of the
dead, Mk. 12 : 26. Ac. 24 : 21.
Lu. 23 : 14. t. things wh-f ye accuse
Ac. 5 : 35. ye intend as t. these men
21 : 25. As t. Gentiles who believe
26 : 2. t. things wh-f I am accused
Ro. 11 : 28. as t. the election, they
1 Co. 8 : 1. as t. things offered unto
16 : 12. as t. our brother Apollos
2 Co. 9 : 1. as t. ministering to saints
Ph. 3 : 5. as t. the law, a Pharisee
6. t. the righteousness in the law
Col. 4 : 10. t. wh. ye received com-ts
1 Th. 4 : 9. as t. brotherly love, ye
2 Th. 3 : 4. confidence in Lord, t. you

TOW. [t.

Ju. 16 : 9. brake withs, as thread of
Is. 1 : 31. And the strong sh. be as t.
43 : 17. are extinct, quenched as t.

TOWARD, or TOWARDS.

Ge. 2 : 14. river wh. goeth t. east of A.
13 : 12. Lot pitched tent t. Sodom
18 : 2. Abr. bowed hims. t. ground
16. men rose, looked t. Sodom, 22.
19 : 1. Lot bowed himself t. ground
28. Abr. looked t. Sod. and Gom. (2)
25 : 18. Shur, as thou goest t. As-s

Ge. 28 : 10. And Jac. went t. Haran
30 : 40. Jac. set flocks t. ringstreak-
31 : 21. Jacob set face t. Gilead [ed
48 : 13. Ephraim t. Isr.'s left hand,
Manasseh t. Israel's right hand
Nu. 2 : 3. t. rising of sun shall pitch
21 : 20. Pisgah, wh. looketh t. Jesh.
23 : 28. Peor that looketh t. Jesh.
24 : 1. he set his face t. wilderness
De. 28 : 54. eye evil t. his brother
56. be evil t. her husband, daugh.
Jos. 8 : 18. Stretch out spear t. Ai
15 : 4. border passed t. Azmon
7. border went t. Debir, passed t.
waters of Enshemesh (3)
19 : 11. their border went up t. sea
Ju. 5 : 9. My heart is t. governors
1 S. 20 : 12. if there be good t. David
2 S. 14 : 1. king's heart t. Absalom
15 : 23. peo. passed over t. wildern.
1 K. 8 : 29. prayer thy serv. sh. make
t. this pla., 30, 35. 2 Ch. 6 : 21.
2 Ch. 24 : 16. Jehoi-a had done good
in Isr. t. God and t. his house
31 : 14. Kore, porter t. east, ov. off-gs
Ezr. 3 : 11. his mercy endureth t. Isr.
Es. 8 : 4. king held sceptre t. Esther
Ps. 5 : 7. worship t. thy holy temple,
25 : 15. Mine eyes ever t. L. [138 : 2.
28 : 2. my hands t. thy holy oracle
98 : 3. remembered his truth t. Isr.
Pr. 14 : 35. k.'s favour is t. wise serv-t
Is. 7 : 1. Pekah went t. Jerus. to war
63 : 7. the great goodness t. Israel
Je. 15 : 1. my mind cou. not be t. peo.
Eze. 40 : 32. court t. the east, 42 : 10.
41 : 19. face of man t. palm tree,
face of lion t. palm tree [cubits
42 : 7. wall t. outer court was fifty
12. way bef. the wall t. east [43 : 4.
15. t. gate, wh. prospect is t. east,
Da. 6 : 10. his windows open t. Jerus.
Jon. 2 : 4. I will look t. holy temple
Mat. 12 : 49. his hand t. his disciples
14 : 14. Jesus, moved with compassion t. them, Mk. 6 : 34. [day
28 : 1. as it began to dawn t. first
Lu. 2 : 14. peace, good will t. men
12 : 21. treasure, and not rich t. G.
13 : 22. he went journeying t. Jerus.
24 : 29. Abide with us, it is t. even
Jn. 6 : 17. over sea t. Capernaum [L.
Ac. 20 : 21. repentance t. G., faith t.
24 : 15. and have hope t. God [men
16. void of offence t. God and t.
27 : 12. Phenice, wh. lieth t. south w.
40. hoised mainsail, made t. shore
28 : 14. and so we went t. Rome [er
Ro. 1 : 27. in their lust one t. anoth-
11 : 22. severity; but t. thee goodn.
12 : 16. Be of the same mind one t.
another, 15 : 5. [his virgin
1 Co. 7 : 36. if behaveth uncomely t.
2 Co. 1 : 16. bro-t on my way t. Judea
Ga. 2 : 8. was mighty in me t. Gent.
Ph. 3 : 14. I press t. the mark
1 Th. 3 : 12. abound in love one t.
another and t. all men, as we
do t. you [in peace
4 : 10. ye do it t. all the brethren
5 : 14. brethren, be patient t. all men
2 Th. 1 : 3. charity t. each aboundeth
Phm. 5. love and faith thou hast t.
Lord Jesus and t. all saints
He. 6 : 1. foundation of faith t. God
10. love ye have shewed t. his na.
1 Pe. 3 : 21. of good conscience t. G.
1 Jn. 3 : 21. have we confidence t. G.
See EAST, NORTH, SOUTH, WEST.
See FOREPART, HEAVEN, HIM,
ME, SUNRISING, THEE, THEM,
US, YOU.

TOWEL. [hims.

Jn. 13 : 4. he took a t. and girded
5. he began to wipe their feet wi. t.

TOWER.

Ge. 11 : 4. let us build us city and t.
Ge. 11 : 5. L. came to see city and t.
35 : 21. Isr. spread tent bey. t. of E.
Ju. 8 : 9. I will break down this t.
17. he beat down the t. of Penuel
9 : 46. men of t. of Shechem, 47, 49.
51. was a strong t. within the city;
all of city gat up to top of t. [(2)
52. Abim. came unto t. and fought
2 S. 22 : 51. He t. of salvation for king
2 K. 5 : 24. came to t. he took them
9 : 17. a watchman on t. in Jezreel
17 : 9. from t. of watchmen, to city,
2 Ch. 2 : † 3. The t. he built [18 : 8
Ne. 3 : 1. t. of Meah they sanctified
it, unto t. of Hananeel, 12 : 39.
11. repaired the t., 25, 26, 27.
† 26. Noth. dwelt in the t., 11 : † 21.
8 : † 4. Ezra stood upon t. of wood
12 : 38. fr. beyond t. of the furnaces
Ps. 61 : 3. hast been a strong t. from
Pr. 18 : 10. name of Lord is strong t.
Can. 4 : 4. Thy neck like t. of David
7 : 4. Thy neck is as a t. of ivory,
thy nose is as t. of Lebanon
Is. 5 : 2. he built a t. in vineyard
Je. 6 : 27. I have set thee for a t. [eel
31 : 38. city be built fr. t. of Hanan-
Eze. 29 : 10. Eg. desolate fr. t. of Sy-e
30 : 6. fr. t. of Syene shall they fall
Mi. 4 : 8. O t. of the flock, to thee sh.
Ha. 2 : 1. I will set me upon t. and
Zch. 14 : 10. inhabited fr. t. of Han-l
Mat. 21 : 33. built a t., let it, Mk. 12 : 1
Lu. 13 : 4. the t. in Siloam fell [t.
14 : 28. which, intending to build a

High TOWER. [-144 : 2.

2 S. 22 : 3. God is my h. t., Ps. 18 : 2.
Is. 2 : 15. day of the L. upon ev. h. t.

TOWERS. [t.

2 Ch. 14 : 7. Let us build cities, make
26 : 9. Uzziah built t. in Jerusalem
10. he built t. in the desert and
15. engines to be on the t. and
27 : 4. Jotham built castles and t.
32 : 5. Hezekiah raised up wall to t.
Ps. 48 : 12. go about Zion, tell her t.
Can. 5 : † 13. His cheeks as t. of per-
8 : 10. and my breasts like t. [fume
Is. 23 : 13. the Assyrian set up the t.
30 : 25. upon hill, rivers, when t. fall
32 : 14. forts and t. sh. be for dens
33 : 18. where is he that counted t.?
Eze. 26 : 4. sh. break down her t., 9.
27 : 11. Gammadim were in thy t.
36 : † 20. the t. sh. fall and every wall
Zph. 1 : 16. day of alarm ag. high t.
3 : 6. t. are desolate, streets waste

TOWN. [t. wall

Jos. 2 : 15. Rahab's house was upon
1 S. 16 : 4. elders of the t. trembled
23 : 7. entering a t. that hath gates
27 : 5. give me a place in some t.
Ha. 2 : 12. buildeth a t. with blood
Mat. 10 : 11. into whatso. t. ye enter
Mk. 8 : 23. led blind man out of t.
26. Nei. go into t., nor tell it in t.
Lu. 5 : 17. were come out of every t.
Jn. 7 : 42. Christ cometh out of t.
11 : 1. the t. of Mary and her sister
30. Jesus was not yet come into t.

TOWNS. [t.

Ge. 25 : 16. these are names by their
Nu. 32 : 41. Jair took the small t.
De. 3 : 5. beside unwalled t. gr. many
Jos. 13 : 30. unto Manasseh all t. of
15 : 45. Ekron with t. and villages
47. Ashdod, her t. and villages (2)
17 : 11. Manasseh had Bethshean
and t. (6), 16. Ju. 1 : 27. 1 Ch. 7 : 29.
Ju. 11 : 26. Israel dwelt in Heshbon
and her t., Aroer and her t.
1 K. 4 : 13. to him pertained t. of
Jair, 1 Ch. 2 : 23. (2) [and her t.
1 Ch. 5 : 16. they dwelt in Bashan
7 : 28. possessions, Beth-el and t. (4)
8 : 12. built Ono and Lod, with the t.
18 : 1. David took Gath and her t.
2 Ch. 13 : 19. Abijah took Bethel wi.
Es. 9 : 19. Jews in unwalled t. [t. (3)
Je. 19 : 15. upon all her t. the evil
Zch. 2 : 4. Jerus. be as t. with-t walls
Mk. 1 : 38. Let us go into the next t.
8 : 27. Jes. and disci. into t. of Ces-a
Lu. 9 : 6. went thro. the t. preaching
12. may go into the t. and lodge

TOWNCLERK. [peo.

Ac. 19 : 35. when the t. had appeased

TRACHONI'TIS.

Lu. 3 : 1. Philip being tetrach of T.

TRADE, S.

Ge. 46 : 32. their t. to feed cattle, 34.
Tit. 3 : † 14. learn to profess honest t.

TRADE, ED, ING. [21.

Ge. 34 : 10. dwell and t. ye therein,
Eze. 27 : 12. Tarshish t-d in thy fairs
13. Javan, Tubal, t-d persons of
14. They of Togar-h t-d wi. horses
17. Judah, Isr. t-d in thy market
Mat. 25 : 16. five talents, went and t-d
Lu. 19 : 15. how much every man
had gained by t-g [afar off
Re. 18 : 17. many as t. by sea, stood

TRADITION, S.

Mat. 15 : 2. Why do thy disciples
transgress t. of elders, Mk. 7 : 5.
6. ye have made com-nt of God of
none effect by your t., Mk. 7 : 13.
Mk. 7 : 3. hold-g the t. of elders, 8, 9.
1 Co. 11 : † 2. keep t-s as I delivered
Ga. 1 : 14. zealous of t-s of my fathers
Col. 2 : 8. spoil you after t. of men
2 Th. 2 : 15. hold t-s ye have been
3 : 6. not after t. he received of us
1 Pe. 1 : 18. received by t. fr. fathers

TRAFFICK. [Noun.]

1 K. 10 : 15. that had t. of merchants
Eze. 17 : 4. carried it into land of t.
28 : 5. by t. hast increased thy riches
18. defiled sanctuaries by iniq-y of

TRAFFICK. [Verb.] [t.

Ge. 42 : 34. and ye shall t. in the land

TRAFFICKERS.

Is. 23 : 8. whose t. are the honour-

TRAIN. [Noun.] [able

1 K. 10 : 2. she came with a great t.
Is. 6 : 1. and his t. filled the temple

TRAIN, TRAINED.

Ge. 14 : 14. Abram armed t-d serv-ts
Pr. 22 : 6. t. up a child in the way

TRAITOR, S.

Lu. 6 : 16. Judas Iscariot, wh was t.
2 Ti. 3 : 4. in last days sh. men be t-s

TRAMPLE. [feet

Ps. 91 : 13. dragon sh. thou t. under
104 : † 20. beasts do t. on the forest
Is. 63 : 3. I will t. them in my fury
Mat. 7 : 6. pearls, lest they t. them

TRAMPLINGS.

Ju. 5 : † 22. horsehoofs broken by t.

TRANCE.

Nu. 24 : 4. vision falling into a t., 16.
Ac. 10 : 10. fell into a t., saw heaven
11 : 5. praying, in a t. I saw vision
22 : 17. while I prayed I was in a t.

TRANQUILLITY. [t.

Da. 4 : 27. if it be lengthening of thy

TRANSFERRED. [self

1 Co. 4 : 6. I have in figure t. to my-

TRANSFIGURED.

Mat. 17 : 2. Jesus was t., Mk. 9 : 2.

TRANSFORMED.

Ro. 12 : 2. be ye t. by renew-g of mind
2 Co. 11 : 14. Satan is t. into an angel
15. no great thing if his ministers

TRANSFORMING. [be t.

2 Co. 11 : 13. t. thems. into apos. of

TRANSGRESS. [Christ

Nu. 14 : 41. Wheref. do ye t. com-ts
of the Lord ? 2 Ch. 24 : 20. [t.
1 S. 2 : 24. ye make the L.'s people to
Ne. 1 : 8. If ye t. I will scatter you
13 : 27. sh. we hearken unto you to
Ps. 17 : 3. my mouth shall not t. [t.
25 : 3. let them be ashamed wh. t.

Pr. 28 : 21. for bread this man will t.
Je. 2 : 20. thou saidst I will not t.
Eze. 20 : 38. I purge out them t. ag.
Am. 4 : 4. Come to Beth-el and t. [me
Mat. 15 : 2. why disciples t. tradition?
3. Why do ye t. comm-nt of God?
Ro. 2 : 27. by circumcision dost t.

TRANSGRESSED. [law
De. 26 : 13. I have not t. thy com-ts
1 S. 14 : 33. Ye have t.; roll a stone
15 : 24. I have t. com-t of the Lord
1 K. 8 : 50. they have t. against thee
1 Ch. 2 : 7. Achar t. in thi. accursed
5 : 25. t. ag. God of their fathers
10 : † 13. Saul died for transgr. he t.
2 Ch. 12 : 2. because they t. ag. Lord
26 : 16. Uzziah t. ag. the L. his God
28 : 19. Ahaz t. sore ag. the Lord
36 : 14. priests and people t. much
Ezr. 10 : 10. Ye have t. and taken strange wives [this thing
13. we are many that have t. in
Is. 24 : 5. bec. they have t. the laws
43 : 27. thy teachers have t. ag. me
66 : 24. upon men's carcasses that t.
Je. 2 : 8. the pastors t. ag. me and
29. ye all have t. against me [t.
3 : 13. only acknowledge thou hast
33 : 8. I will pardon iniqu-s they t.
La. 3 : 42. We have t. and rebelled
Eze. 2 : 3. they and fathers t. ag. me
18 : 31. cast aw. transgressions ye t.
Da. 9 : 11. all Israel have t. thy law
Ho. 7 : 13. bec. they have t. ag. me
Zph. 3 : 11. not ashamed for doings wherein thou t. [command-t
Lu. 15 : 29. nei. t. I at any time thy

TRANSGRESSED, ING covenant. [his c.
De. 17 : 21. wrought wickedn. in t-g
Jos. 7 : 11. Israel hath t-d my c. [L.
15. be burnt, bec. he hath t-d c. of
23 : 16. When ye have t-d c. of Lord
Ju. 2 : 20. anger hot bec. people t-d c., 2 K. 18 : 12. Ho. 8 : 1. [laud of
Je. 34 : 18. men that t-d my c. into
Ho. 6 : 7. they like men have t-d c.

TRANSGRESSEST.
Es. 3 : 3. Why t. thou the k.'s com-t?

TRANSGRESSETH.
Pr. 16 : 10. his mouth t. not in judg-t
Ha. 2 : 5. bec. t. by wine, he is proud
1 Jn. 3 : 4. committ-h sin, t. the law
2 Jn. 9. Whoso. t. and abideth not in

TRANSGRESSING.
Is. 59 : 13. In t. and lying ag. Lord

TRANSGRESSION. [18.
Ex. 34 : 7. forgiv-g t. and sin, Nu. 14:
Jos. 22 : 22. if it be in t. ag. the Lord
1 S. 24 : 11. is no t. in my hand [t.
1 Ch. 9 : 1. carried to Bab-n for their
10 : 13. So Saul died for his t. [in t.
2 Ch. 29 : 19. vessels Ahaz cast away
Ezr. 9 : 4. t. of those carried away
10 : 6. he mourned bec. of their t.
Jb. 7 : 21. why dost not pardon my t.
8 : 4. he have cast them away for t.
13 : 23. make me to know my t.
14 : 17. My t. is sealed up in a bag
21 : † 34. seeing in your answers t.
33 : 9. I am clean without t. [t.
34 : 6. my wound incurable with-t
Ps. 19 : 13. I be innocent fr. great t.
32 : 1. Blessed whose t. is forgiven
36 : 1. The t. of the wicked saith
59 : 3. gathered ag. me, not for my t.
89 : 32. will I visit their t. wi. a rod
107 : 17. Fools bec. of t. are afflicted
Pr. 12 : 13. is snared by t. of his lips
17 : 9. that covereth t. seeketh love
19. He loveth t. that loveth strife
19 : 11. his glory to pass over a t.
28 : 2. For t. of a l[a]. many are princes
24. robbeth fath., saith, It is no t.
29 : 6. In t. of an evil man, a snare
16. wicked multiplied, t. increaseth
22. furious man aboundeth in t.

Is. 24 : 20. the t. sh. be heavy upon it
53 : 8. for t. of my peo. was stricken
57 : 4. are ye not children of t.?
58 : 1. and shew my people their t.
59 : 20. them that turn fr. t. in Jac.
Eze. 33 : 12. not deliver him in day of
Da. 8 : 12. ag. daily sacrifice by t. [t.
13. conc. sacrifice and t. of desolat.
9 : 24. seventy weeks to finish the t.
Am. 4 : 4. at Gilgal multiply the t.
Mi. 1 : 5. For t. of Jacob is all this, What is the t. of Jacob? [t.
3 : 8. power to declare unto Jac. his
6 : 7. sh. I give firstborn for my t.
7 : 18. that passeth by the t. of his
Ac. 1 : 25. fr. which Judas by t. fell
Ro. 4 : 15. where no law there is no t.
5 : 14. aft. similitude of Adam's t.
1 Ti. 2 : 14. the woman was in the t.
He. 2 : 2. ev. t. received just recomp.
1 Jn. 3 : 4. sin is the t. of the law

TRANSGRESSIONS.
Ex. 23 : 21. he will not pardon y-r t.
Le. 16 : 16. make atonem-t bec. of t.
21. confess over the goat all their t.
Jos. 24 : 19. he will not forgive y-r t.
1 K. 8 : 50. forgive thy people all t.
Jb. 31 : 33. If I cov-d my t. as Adam
35 : 6. if thy t. be multiplied, what
36 : 9. he sheweth them their t. [t.
Ps. 5 : 10. cast them out in mult. of
25 : 7. Remember not the sins of my youth, nor my t.
32 : 5. I will confess my t. unto Lord
39 : 8. Deliver me from all my t. [t.
51 : 1. Have mercy, blot out all my
3. I acknowledge my t., my sin
65 : 3. as for our t. thou shalt purge
103 : 12. so far hath removed our t.
Is. 43 : 25. I am he blotteth out thy t.
44 : 22. I have blotted out thy t.
50 : 1. for your t. is mother put aw.
53 : 5. he was wounded for our t.
59 : 12. our t. are multiplied before thee, our t. are with us [many
Je. 5 : 6. sh. be torn bec. their t. are
La. 1 : 5. for the multitude of her t.
14. The yoke of my t. is bound [t.
22. unto them as unto me for my
Eze. 14 : 11. nei. be polluted with t.
18 : 22. his t. sh. not be mentioned
28. he turneth away from all his t.
30. Repent and turn from your t.
31. Cast away all your t. whereby
21 : 24. in that your t. are discov-d
33 : 10. If our t. be upon us and we
37 : 23. nor defile themselves with t.
39 : 24. acc. to their t. have I done
Ho. 10 : † 10. I sh. bind them for two t.
Am. 1 : 3. For three t. of Damascus
11. For 3 t. of Edom | 13. of Ammon
2 : 1. For 3 t. of Moab | 4. of Judah
6. For 3 t. of Israel, and for four
3 : 14. in day I shall visit t. of Israel
5 : 12. I know your manifold t.
Mi. 1 : 13. t. of Israel found in thee
Ga. 3 : 19. law was added because of t.
He. 9 : 15. for redemption of the t.

TRANSGRESSOR.
Pr. 21 : 18. the t. shall be a ransom
22 : 12. he overthrow-h words of t.
Is. 48 : 8. wast called a t. from womb
Ga. 2 : 18. if I build, make myself t.
Ja. 2 : 11. if thou kill, thou art a t.

TRANSGRESSORS.
Ps. 37 : 38. the t. shall be destroyed
51 : 13. Then will I teach t. thy ways
59 : 5. be not merciful to wicked t.
119 : 158. I beheld t. and was griev.
Pr. 2 : 22. t. shall be rooted out of it
11 : 3. perverseness of t. sh. destroy
6. t. be taken in own naughtiness
13 : 2. soul of t. shall eat violence
15. but the way of t. is hard
23 : 28. she increaseth the t. am. men
26 : 10. God rewardeth fool and t.
Is. 1 : 28. destruction of t. shall be

Is. 46 : 8. bring it again to mind, ye t.
53 : 12. he was numbered with the t., made intercession for the t.
Da. 8 : 23. t. are come to the full
Ho. 14 : 9. the t. shall fall therein
Mk. 15 : 28. he was numbered wi. t.,
Lu. 22 : 37. [as t.
Ja. 2 : 9. ye are convinced of the law

TRANSLATE, ED.
2 S. 3 : 10. To t. the kingdom fr. Saul
Col. 1 : 13. t-d us into kingdom of Son
He. 11 : 5. Enoch was t-d that he

TRANSLATION. [mony
He. 11 : 5. bef. t. he had this testi.

TRANSPARENT.
Re. 21 : 21. street of city as t. glass

TRANSPORTATION.
Ezr. 1 : † 11. did Sheshbazzar bring of
4 : † 1. sons of t. builded temple [t.
6 : † 16. sons of the t. kept dedica-n

TRAP, S. [you
Jos. 23 : 13. they shall be t-s unto
Jb. 18 : 10. t. is laid for him in way
Ps. 69 : 22. welfare, let it become a t.
Je. 5 : 26. they set a t. catch men [t.
Ro. 11 : 9. Let their table be made a

TRAVAIL. [Noun.]
Ge. 38 : 27. in her t. behold, twins
Ex. 18 : 8. Moses told t. by the way
Nu. 20 : 14. knowest the t. befallen us
Ps. 48 : 6. Fear took hold upon them and pain as of a woman in t., Je. 6 : 24.-13 : 21.-22 : 23.-49 : 24.-50 : 43. Mi. 4 : 9, 10. [to men
Ec. 1 : 13. this sore t. hath God giv.
2 : 23. his days sorrows, his t. grief
26. to the sinner he giveth t. [men
3 : 10. I have seen the t. G. given to
4 : 4. I considered all t. every work
6. than both hands full wi. t. and
8. This is vanity, yea a sore t.
5 : 14. these riches perish by evil t.
Is. 53 : 11. shall see of t. of his soul
Je. 4 : 31. voice as of a woman in t.
30 : 6. why ev. man as woman in t.
La. 3 : 5. He compassed me with t.
Jn. 16 : 21. A woman in t. hath sor.
1 Th. 2 : 9. for ye remember our t.
5 : 3. destruction as t. on a woman
2 Th. 3 : 8. wrought wi. t. night and d.

TRAVAIL, ED. [t-d
Ge. 35 : 16. Rachel t-d | 38 : 28. Tamar
1 S. 4 : 19. Phinehas' wife bowed and
Is. 23 : 4. sea spoken, I t. not [t-d
54 : 1. that didst not t. with child
66 : 7. Bef. she t-d she brought forth
8. as soon as Zion t-d she brought
Je. 30 : 6. whe. a man doth t. [forth
Ga. 4 : 19. My children, of wh. I t. in

TRAVAILEST. [birth
Ga. 4 : 27. break forth, cry, thou that

TRAVAILETH. [t. not
Jb. 15 : 20. wicked man t. with pain
Ps. 7 : 14. Behold he t. with iniquity
Is. 13 : 8. be in pain as woman that t.
21 : 3. as pangs of a woman that t.
Je. 31 : 8. and with them her that t.
Mi. 5 : 3. till she who t. hath brought
Ro. 8 : 22. whole creation t. in pain

TRAVAILING.
Is. 42 : 14. will I cry like a t. woman
Ho. 13 : 13. sorrows of a t. woman
Re. 12 : 2. woman cried, t. in birth

TRAVEL. [Noun.]
Ac. 19 : 29. Paul's companion in t.

TRAVEL, LED.
Ac. 11 : 19. they t-d far as Phenice
2 Co. 8 : 19. was chosen to t. with us

TRAVELLER, S.
Ju. 5 : 6. the t-s walked thro. byways
2 S. 12 : 4. came t. to the rich man [t.
Jb. 31 : 32. I opened my doors to the

TRAVELLETH. [24 : 34.
Pr. 6 : 11. poverty come as one t.

TRAVELLING.
Is. 21 : 13. lodge, O ye t. companies
63 : 1. Who is this t. in greatness

Mat. 25 : 14. kingdom of heaven is as [man t.

TRAVERSING.

Je. 2 : 23. thou a swift dromedary t.

TREACHEROUS.

Is. 21 : 2. t. dealer dealeth treach-ly,
Je. 3 : 7. t. sister Jud. saw it [24 : 16.
8. her t. sister Judah feared not
10. t. sister Judah hath not turned
11. Isr justified more than t. Jud.
9 : 2. they be an assembly of t. men
Zph. 3 : 4. Her proph-s are light and [t.

TREACHEROUSLY.

Ju. 9 : 23. men of Shechem dealt t.
1 S. 14 : † 33. Ye have dealt t., roll
Is. 21 : 2. dealer dealeth t., 24 : 16.
33 : 1. Woe to thee dealest t., they
dealt not t. wi. thee ! when thou
make end to deal t. they shall
deal t. with thee [deal very t.
48 : 8. I knew that thou wouldest
Je. 3 : 20. as a wife t. departeth from
her husband, and so have ye
dealt t. with me [11.
5 : 11. Judah hath dealt t.. Mal. 2 :
12 : 1. whf. all happy that deal t. ?
6. they have dealt t. with thee
La. 1 : 2. all her friends have dealt t.
Ho. 5 : 7. They have dealt t. ag. Lord
6 : 7. have they dealt t. against me
Mal. 2 : 10. why do we deal t. ev. man
14. thy wife ag. whom hast dealt t.
15. let none deal t. ag. wife of his
16. take heed ye deal not t. [youth

TREACHERY.

2 K. 9 : 23. There is t., O Ahaziah

TREAD. [yours

De. 11 : 24. place soles of your feet t.
25. dread of you upon land ye t.
33 : 29. t. upon their high places
Jos. 1 : 3. ev. place foot shall t. upon
1 S. 5 : 5. priests nor any t. on the
threshold of Dagon [thirst
Jb. 24 : 11. t. winepresses and suffer
40 : 12. t. down wicked in th. place
Ps. 7 : 5. let him t. down my life on
44 : 5. thro. thy name will we t. th.
60 : 12. t. down our enemies, 108 : 13.
91 : 13. Thou shalt t. upon the lion
Is. 1 : 12. required to t. my courts
10 : 6. to t. th. down, like the mire
14 : 25. upon my mountains t. him
16 : 10. treaders sh. t. out no wine
26 : 6. the foot shall t. it down [6.
63 : 3. I will t. them in mine anger,
Je. 25 : 30. shout, as they th. t. grapes
48 : 33. none shall t. with shouting
50 : † 26. t. her as heaps, and destroy
Eze. 26 : 11. With his horses sh. he t.
34 : 18. t. the residue with your feet
Da. 7 : 23. fourth beast sh. t. it down
Ho. 10 : 11. Ephr. loveth to t. out corn
Mi. 1 : 3. L. will t. upon high places
5 : 5. Assyrian sh. t. in our palaces
6 : 15. t. olives, but not anoint thee
Na. 3 : 14. t. the mortar, make strong
Zch. 10 : 5. mighty men, wh. t. enemies
Mal. 4 : 3. ye sh. t. down the wicked
Lu. 10 : 19. power to t. on scorpions
Ro. 16 : † 20. God sh. t. Satan under
Re. 11 : 2. holy city sh. they t. under

TREADER, S. [foot

Is. 16 : † 4. t-s down are at an end
10. the t-s shall tread out no wine
Am. 9 : 13. t. of grapes overtake sower

TREADETH.

De. 25 : 4. not muzzle ox when he t.
out corn, 1 Co. 9 : 9. 1 Ti. 5 : 18.
Jb. 9 : 8. which t. upon the waves
Pr. 27 : † 7. t. under foot honeycomb
Is. 18 : † 2. a nation that t. down
41 : 25. come as the potter t. clay
63 : 2. like him that t. in winefat
Am. 4 : 13. he th. t. upon high places
Mi. 5 : 6. he t. within our borders
8. if he go thro., t. down and tear.
Re. 19 : 15. he t. winepress of wrath
of God

TREADING.

De. 2 : † 5. even to t. of sole of foot
2 Ch. 22 : † 7. t. down of Ahaziah
Ne. 13 : 15. t. winepresses on sabbath
Is. 5 : † 5. break wall, it be for a t.
7 : 25. for the t. of lesser cattle [t.
10 : † 6. give charge to lay them a
18 : † 2. a nation of t. under foot
22 : 5. a day of trouble and t. down
28 : † 18. th. ye sh. be a t. down to it
42 : † 22. they are for a t., and none
Am. 5 : 11. as your t. is upon poor
Mi. 7 : † 10. she sh. be for a t. down

TREASON.

1 K. 16 : 20. acts of Zimri and his t.
2 K. 11 : 14. Athaliah cried, t., t., 2
Ch. 23 : 13.

TREASURE. [Noun.]

Ge. 43 : 23. given you t. in y-r sacks
De. 28 : 12. L. open unto thee good t.
1 Ch. 29 : 8. gave to t. of hou. of Lord
Ezr. 2 : 69. gave after their ability to
t. of work [1,000 drams
Ne. 7 : 70. The Tirshatha gave to t.
71. fathers gave to t. of the work
Ps. 17 : 14. belly fillest with hid t.
Pr. 15 : 6. In hou. of righte. much t.
16. a little, than gr. t. and trouble
21 : 20. There is a t. to be desired
Is. 33 : 6. fear of the Lord is his t.
Eze. 22 : 25. prophets have taken t.
Ho. 13 : 15. he shall spoil t. of all
pleasant vessels [my special t.
Mal. 3 : † 17. be mine, when I make up
Mat. 6 : 21. For where your t. is,
there your heart, Lu. 12 : 34.
12 : 35. A good man out of the good
t. of his heart, an evil man out
of evil t., Lu. 6 : 45. [hid
13 : 44. kingdom of heaven is like t.
52. out of his t. things new and old
19 : 21. sell that thou hast, have t.
in heav., Mk. 10 : 21. Lu. 18 : 22.
Lu. 12 : 21. th. layeth up t. for hims.
33. provide a t. in the heavens wh.
Ac. 8 : 27. had charge of all her t.
2 Co. 4 : 7. this t. in earthen vessels
Ja. 5 : 3. Ye have heaped t. for last
See PECULIAR. [days

TREASURE cities. [c.

Ex. 1 : 11. they built for Pharaoh t.

TREASURE house. [h.

Ezr. 5 : 17. search be made in k.'s t.
7 : 20. bestow it out of king's t. h.
Ne. 10 : 38. Levites bri. tithe into t. h.
Da. 1 : 2. vessels into t. h. of his God

TREASURES. [t.

De. 32 : 24. Is not this sealed am. my
33 : 19. sh. suck of t. hid in the sand
1 K. 7 : 51. dedicated things among t.
14 : 26. Shishak took t. of house of
L. and t. of king's house, 2 Ch.
12 : 9.-16 : 2.-25 : 24. (2)
15 : 18. Asa took gold left in the t.,
2 Ch. 16 : 2. [14 : 14.
2 K. 12 : 18. Jehoash t. gold in t.,
16 : 8. Ahaz took gold found in t.
18 : 15. Hez. gave silver found in t.
20 : 13. Hez. shewed them all that
was found in t., 15. Is. 39 : 2, 4.
24 : 13. Neb-r carried out all the t.
of house of Lord, and t. of k.'s
house, 2 Ch. 36 : 18.
1 Ch. 26 : 20. Ahijah over t. of the
house of God (2), 22.
24. Shebuel was ruler of the t. [t.
26. Shelomith and brethren over
27 : 25. over k.'s t., Azmaveth [of L.
2 Ch. 5 : 1. instruments am. t. of house
8 : 15. king's com-t concerning t.
Ne. 12 : 44. some appointed for the t.
Ezr. 6 : 1. t. were laid up in Babylon
Jb. 3 : 21. for it more than for hid t.
38 : 22. Hast entered into t. of the
snow ? hast seen t. of hail ? [t.
Pr. 2 : 4. if searchest for her as for hid
8 : 21. fill the t. of those th. love me

Pr. 10 : 2. t. of wickedn. profit nothing
21 : 6. getting of t. by lying tongue
Is. 2 : 7. neither is any end of their t.
10 : 13. I have robbed their t. [els
30 : 6. carry t. on bunches of cam-
45 : 3. will give thee t. of darkness
Je. 10 : 13. he bringeth wind out of
his t., 51 : 16 [17 : 3.-20 : 5.
15 : 13. thy t. I will give to the spoil,
41 : 8. Slay us not, for we have t. in
48 : 7. bec. hast trusted in thy t.
49 : 4. daugh. that trusted in her t.
50 : 37. a sword is upon her t., they
51 : 13. that dwellest abundant in t.
Eze. 28 : 4. gotten gold into thy t.
Da. 11 : 43. he sh. have power over t.
Mi. 6 : 10. Are t. of wickedn. in house
Mat. 2 : 11. wh. had opened their t.
6 : 19. Lay not up t. upon earth [en
20. But lay up for y-rs. t. in heav.
Col. 2 : 3. In whom all the t. of wisd.
He. 11 : 26. greater riches than t. in

TREASURED. [Egypt

Is. 23 : 18. her merchandise not be t.

TREASURER, S. [t.

Ezr. 1 : 8. Cyrus brought vessels by
7 : 21. make a decree to all the t-s
Ne. 13 : 13. I made t-s ov. treasuries
Is. 22 : 15. get thee unto t., Shebna
Da. 3 : 2. Neb-r gathered the t-s, 3.

TREASUREST.

Ro. 2 : 5. t. up wrath ag. day of wrath

TREASURIES.

1 Ch. 9 : 26. Levites were over the t.
28 : 12. David gave Sol-n pattern of
t. of house of Lord (2), 11. [ver
2 Ch. 32 : 27. Heze-h made t. for sil.
Ne. 12 : † 25. porters keep-g ward at t.
13 : 12. Judah brought tithe unto t.
13. I made treasurers over the t.
Es. 3 : 9. to bring it into king's t.
4 : 7. Haman promised to pay to t.
Ps. 135 : 7. he bring-h wind out of t.

TREASURY. [L., 24.

Jos. 6 : 19. gold and silver into t. of
Je. 38 : 11. into house under the t.
Mat. 27 : 6. not lawful to put into t.
Mk. 12 : 41. Jesus over ag. t. beheld
how people cast money into t.
43. more than they wh. cast into t.
Lu. 21 : 1. rich men cast-g gifts into t.
Jn. 8 : 20. words spake Jes. in the t.

TREATISE.

Ac. 1 : 1. former t. have I made, O

TREE.

Ge. 1 : 12. the t. yielding fruit, 11.
29. I have given you ev. t. for meat
2 : 9. God made every t. to grow, the
t. of life, the t. of knowledge
16. Of ev. t. of garden mayest eat
17. of t. of knowledge not eat, 3 : 1, 3
3 : 6. when woman saw t. was good
11. Hast thou eaten of the t. ? 17.
12. The woman gave me of the t.
22. take of t. of life, 24. Keep
18 : 4. wash your feet, rest under t.
8. Abr. stood by them und. the t.
21 : † 33. Abr. planted t. in Beer-sh.
40 : 19. Pha. sh. hang thee on a t.
Ex. 9 : 25. the hail brake every t. of
10 : 5. the locusts shall eat every t.
15 : 25. he cried, and Lord shewed t.
Le. 27 : 30. seed or fruit of t. is Lord's
De. 19 : 5. stroke to cut down the t.
20 : 19. t. of the field is man's life
21 : 22. if thou hang him on a t.
23. His body not all night upon t.
22 : 6. bird's nest chance in any t.
Jos. 8 : 29. take king of Ai down fr. t.
1 S. 22 : 6. Saul abode und. t. in Ra
31 : 13. buried them und. t. at Jab.
2 K. 3 : 19. shall fell every good t.
Es. 2 : 23. were both hanged on a t.
5 : † 14. Let t. be made 50 cubits hi
7 : † 9. t. 50 cubits high wh. Haman
Jb. 14 : 7. is hope of a t. if cut down
19 : 10. mine hope he removed like t.
24 : 20. wickedn-s be broken as a t.

Ps. 1 : 3. like a t. planted by rivers
Ec. 11 : 3. if t. fall toward the south ;
where t. falleth there it shall be
Is. 30 : † 17. ye be left as a t. bereft
40 : 20. chooseth a t. will not rot
44 : 19. I fall down to stock of a t. ?
23. into singing, O forest and ev. t.
56 : 3. nei. eunuch say, I am dry t.
65 : 22. as days of t. days of my peo.
66 : 17. purify thems. behind one t.
Je. 10 : 3. cutteth a t. out of forest
11 : 19. Let us destroy t. with fruit
17 : 8. be as a t. planted by waters
Eze. 15 : 2. Is vine t. more than any t.
17 : 24. brought down the high t.,
exalted the low t., dried up the
green t., made dry t. to flourish
21 : 10. contem-h rod of son, as ev. t.
31 : 8. not any t. in garden of G. like
34 : 27. t. of field sh. yield fruit [him
36 : 30. I will multiply fruit of the t.
Da. 4 : 10. visions in bed, I saw a t.
11. t. grew and was strong, 20. [26.
14. He cried, Hew down the t., 23,
Jo. 2 : 22. Be not afraid, for t. beareth
Mat. 3 : 10. t. that bringeth not forth
good fruit, 7 : 19. Lu. 3 : 9.
7 : 17. good t. bringeth forth good
fruit, corrupt t. evil, Lu. 6 : 43.
18. good t. cannot bring forth evil
12 : 33. Either make the t. good,
t. is known by fruit, Lu. 6 : 44.
13 : 32. grain of must. rd seed becometh a t., Lu. 13 : 19. [a t.
Ac. 5 : 30. Jesus whom ye hanged on
10 : 39. Jesus wh. they hanged on t.
13 : 29. took him from t. and laid
Ga. 3 : 13. Cursed that hangeth on t.
1 Pe. 2 : 24. bare our sins on the t.
Re. 2 : 7. give to eat of the t. of life
7 : 1. wind sho. not blow on any t.
9 : 4. not hurt any green thi. nor t.
22 : 2. leaves of t. were for healing
14. that they may have right to t.
See ALMOND, APPLE, BAY, BOX.

Cedar TREE, S.

Nu. 24 : 6. Israel's tabern-s as c. t-s
2 S. 5 : 11 Hiram sent c. t-s to David
1 K. 4 : 33. he spake fr. c. t. to hyssop
5 : 6. they hew me c. t-s out of Leb-n
10. So Hiram gave Sol. c. t-s, 9 : 11.
2 K. 19 : 23. I will cut down tall c. t-s
1 Ch. 22 : 4. David prepared c. t-s in
2 Ch. 1 : 15. c. t-s as sycamore, 9 : 27.
2 : 8. send me c. t-s out of Lebanon
Ezr. 3 : 7. gave money to bring c. t-s
See ALGUM, ALMUG, CHEST-
NUT, EDEN, FIG, FIR, FRUIT,
GREEN, JUNIPER, LIGNAL-
OES, MULBERRY, MYRTLE,
OIL, OLIVE, PALM, PINE,
POMEGRANATE, SHITTAH,
SYCAMINE, SYCAMORE, TEIL,
THICK, VINE, WILLOW.

TREES.

Ge. 3 : 2. We may eat of fruit of t.
8. hid amongst the t. of garden
23 : 17. t. were made sure to Abr.
Ex. 10 : 15. locusts did eat fruit of t.
not any green thing in t.
Le. 19 : 23. planted all manner of t.
23 : 40. take the boughs of goodly t.
26 : 4. the t. of the field shall yield
20. nei. sh. the t. of the land yield
De. 16 : 21. not plant grove of any t.
20 : 19. shalt not destroy t. by axe
20. the t. thou knowest not to be
t. for meat [cust consume
28 : 42. all thy t. and fruit shall lo-
34 : 3. Jericho, city of palm t.
Jos. 10 : 26. hanged them on five t.
27. they took them down off t.
Ju. 9 : 8. t. went to anoint a king
9. to be promoted ov. the t., 11, 13.
10. t. said to fig tree, reign over us
12. t. said unto vine, reign over us
14 said all t. unto bramble, reign
Ju. 9 : 15. bramble said unto t., If ye
48. Abimelech cut bough fr. the t.
1 K. 4 : 33. he spake of t. from cedar
6 : † 23. made cherubim of t. of oil
2 K. 3 : 25. they felled all the good t.
1 Ch. 16 : 33. shall t. of wood sing at
presence of L., Ps. 96 : 12. [37.
Ne. 10 : 35. bring firstfruits of all t.,
Jb. 40 : 21. lieth under shady t., 22.
Ps. 104 : 16. t. of Lord are full of sap
105 : 33. brake the t. of their coasts
148 : 9. fruitful t. praise the Lord
Ec. 2 : 5. I planted t. of all kinds [t.
6. water, wood, that bring-h forth
Can. 2 : 3. As apple tree among t.
4 : 14. with all t. of frankincense
Is. 7 : 2. his heart was moved as t.
† 19. rest upon all commendable t.
10 : 19. the rest of the t. sh. be few
44 : 14. he strengtheneth am. the t.
55 : 12. all t. of the fields shall clap
61 : 3. be called t. of righteousness
Je. 6 : 6. Lord said, Hew down t.
7 : 20. fury shall be poured upon t.
Eze. 15 : 2. What is vine tree more
than branch among the t., 6.
17 : 24. all t. of the field shall know
31 : 4. sent her rivers unto all t.
5. his height exalted above all t.
14. none of all t. by waters exalt
15. all t. fainted for him [thems. (2)
47 : 7. many t. on one side and on
12. by the rivers shall grow all t.
Jo. 1 : 12. all t. of field are withered
19. the flame hath burned all t.
Mat 3 : 10. the axe is laid unto the
root of t., Lu. 3 : 9. [11 : 8.
21 : 8. cut branches from t., Mk.
Mk. 8 : 24. I see men as t. walking
Lu. 21 : 29. Behold fig tree and all t.
Jude 12. t. whose fruit withereth
Re. 7 : 3. hurt not t. till we ha. sealed
8 : 7. third part of the t. was burnt
See THREESCORE and ten.

TREMBLE. [thee

De. 2 : 25. nations shall t. because of
20 : 3. and do not t. because of them
Ezr. 10 : 3. those that t. at the com-t
Jb. 9 : 6. shaketh earth, the pillars t.
26 : 11. The pillars of heaven t. and
Ps. 60 : 2. Thou hast made earth to t.
99 : 1. Lord reigneth, let the peo. t.
114 : 7. t. earth at presence of Lord
Ec. 12 : 3. keepers of the house sh. t.
Is. 5 : 25. hills did t., their carcasses
14 : 16. man th. made the earth to t.
32 : 11. t. ye women th. are at ease
64 : 2. nations may t. at thy presen.
66 : 5. Hear word of Lord, ye that t.
Je. 5 : 22. will ye not t. at my pres.
10 : 10. at his wrath earth shall t.
33 : 9 they shall t. for all the goodn.
51 : 29. land of Babylon shall t.
Eze. 26 : 16. t. at every moment, 32 : 10.
18. shall isles t. in day of thy fall
Da. 6 : 26. men t. bef. God of Daniel
Ho. 11 : 10. chil. shall t. fr. the west
11. They sh. t. as a bird out of Eg.
Jo. 2 : 1. let all the inhabitants t.
10. earth shall quake, heavens t.
Am. 8 : 8. Shall not the land t. for
Ha. 3 : 7. captains of Midian did t.
Ja. 2 : 19. devils also believe and t.

TREMBLED.

Ge. 27 : 33. Isaac t. very exceedingly
Ex. 19 : 16. the people in the camp t.
Ju. 5 : 4. the earth t. and the heavens dropped, 2 S. 22 : 8. Ps. 18 :
7.-77 : 18.-97 : 4. [of God
1 S. 4 : 13. Eli's heart t. for the ark
14 : 15. the garrison t. [coming
16 : 4. elders of town t. at Samson's
28 : 5. Saul afraid, his heart t. [t.
Ezr. 9 : 4. assembled to me ev. one th.
Je. 4 : 24. mountains t., Ha. 3 : 10.
8 : 16. whole land t. at neighing of
Da. 5 : 19. peo. and nations t. before
Ha. 3 : 16. When I heard, my belly
t., I t. in myself th. I might rest
Mk. 16 : 8. fled fr. sepulchre, they t.
Ac. 7 : 32. Moses t., durst not behold
24 : 25. as Paul reasoned, Felix t.

TREMBLETH. [moved

Jb. 37 : 1. At this my heart t. and is
Ps. 104 : 32. He looketh on earth it t.
119 : 120. My flesh t. for fear of thee
Is. 66 : 2. to him that t. at my word

TREMBLING. [Adj., Part.]

De. 28 : 68. L. sh. give thee a t. heart
1 S. 13 : 7. the peo. followed him t.
Ezr. 10 : 9. all people sat t. bec. of
Da. 10 : 11. had spok. this I stood t.
Ho. 13 : 1. When Ephraim spake t.
Mk. 5 : 33. the woman t., Lu. 8 : 47.
Ac. 9 : 6. Saul t. said, L., what wilt
16 : 29. keeper came t., fell down

TREMBLING. [Noun.]

Ge. 27 : † 33. Isaac trembled with a
great t. [t. take hold
Ex. 15 : 15. upon mighty men shall
1 S. 14 : 15. in the host a very gr. t.
Jb. 4 : 14. Fear came upon me and t.
21 : 6. I am afraid, t. taketh hold
Ps. 2 : 11, Serve Lord, rejoice with t.
55 : 5. Fearfulness and t. upon me
Is. 51 : 17. hast drunk. the cup of t.
22. out of thy hand the cup of t.
Je. 30 : 5. We have heard a voice of t.
Eze. 12 : 18. drink thy water with t.
26 : 16. shall clothe thems. with t.
Zch. 12 : 2. make Jerus. a cup of t.
1 Co. 2 : 3. I was with you in much t.
2 Co. 7 : 15. how with t. ye rec-d him
Ep. 6 : 5. be obedient wi. fear and t.
Ph. 2 : 12. your salvation with fear

TRENCH. [and t.

1 S. 17 : 20. David to t. and shouted
26 : 5. Saul lay sleeping within t., 7.
2 S. 20 : 15. the bank stood in the t.
1 K. 18 : 32. Elijah made t. ab. altar
35. he filled t. with water, 38.
Lu. 19 : 43. enemies sh. cast a t. ab.

TRESPASS. [Noun.] [thee

Ge. 31 : 36. What is my t. that thou
50 : 17. Forgive the t. of thy serv-ts
Ex. 22 : 9. For all t., whether for ox
Le. 5 : 7. he shall bring for his t., 15.
22 : 16. suffer them to bear iniq. of t.
Nu. 5 : 6. when any do a t. ag. Lord
7. recompense his t. wi. principal
8. if no kinsman to recompense t.
27. if she have done t. ag. husb-d
1 S. 25 : 28. forgive t. of handmaid
1 Ch. 21 : 3. why cause of t. to Isr. ?
2 Ch. 24 : 18. wrath upon Jud. for t.
28 : 13. ye intend to add to our t.
33 : 19. Manasseh's prayer and t.
Ezr. 9 : 2. rulers been chief in this t.
6. our t. is grown unto heaven
7. we have been in a great t., 13.
10 : 10. strange wives to increase t.
19. they offered a ram for their t.
See COMMIT, TED trespass.
See Trespass OFFERING.
See TRESPASSED.

TRESPASS money.

2 K. 12 : 16. The t. m. was not bro-t

TRESPASSES.

Ezr. 9 : 15. we are bef. thee in our t.
Ps. 68 : 21. as goeth on still in his t.
Eze. 39 : 26. borne their shame and t.
Mat. 6 : 14. if ye forgive men their t.
15. if ye forgive not men their t.,
nei. will fa. forgive y-r t., 18 : 35.
Mk. 11 : 25. your father may forgive t.
26. nei. will your fath. forgive your
2 Co. 5 : 19. not imputing their t. [t.
Ep. 2 : 1. who were dead in t. and sins
Col. 2 : 13. having forgiven you all t.

TRESPASS. [Verb.]

1 K. 8 : 31. If any man t. ag. neighb.
2 Ch. 19 : 10. warn that they t. not ag.
Lord : this do, and ye sh. not t.
28 : 22. Ahaz did t. more ag. Lord

Mat. 18 : 15. if bro. t. ag. thee tell him
Lu. 17 : 3. If bro. t. ag. thee rebuke
4. if he t. ag. thee 7 times in a day

TRESPASSED. [Lord
Le. 5 : 19. he hath certainly t. ag.
26 : 40. if confess t. wh. they t. [t.
Nu. 5 : 7. recompensed ag. whom he
De. 32 : 51. Bec. ye t. ag. me am. Isr.
2 Ch. 26 : 18. go out of sanct-y, thou
29 : 6. our fathers have t. [hast t.
30 : 7. be not like fa-s who t. ag. L.
33 : 23. but Amo t. more and more
Ezr. 10 : 2. We ha t. ag. our God
Eze. 15 : † 8. desolate bec. they t. a
trespass, 20 : † 27. [he t. ag. me
17 : 20. plead wi. him for trespass
18 : 24. in trespass he hath t. sh. die
39 : 23. because they t. ag. me, 26.
Da. 9 : 7. trespass th. they t. ag. thee
Ho. 8 : 1. bec. they have t. ag. my law

TRESPASSING. [t.
Le. 6 : 7. any thing he hath done in
Eze. 14 : 13. land sinneth ag. me by t.

TRIAL. [t.
Ge. 44 : † 5. cup whereby he maketh
† 15. such a man as I can make t.
Jb 9 : 23. laugh at t. of the innocent
Eze. 21 : 13. Bec. it is a t. wh. if sword
2 Co. 8 : 2 in a great t. of affliction
He. 11 : 36. had t. of cruel mockings
1 Pe. 1 : 7. th. the t. of your faith be
4 : 12. think it not strange conc-g

TRIBE. [fiery t.
Nu. 1 : 4. with you shall be a man of
every t., 13 : 2.-34 : 18. [ites
4 : 18. Cut ye not off t. of Kohath-
18 : 2. t. of thy father bring wi. thee
31 : 4. Of ev. t. a thous. to war, 5, 6.
36 : 3. be put to inheritance of t., 4.
5. The t. of Joseph hath said well
6. only to family of t. marry, 8.(2)
7. So shall not inheritance remove
from t. to t., 9. [of father
12. inheritance remained with t.
De. 1 : 23. I took twelve men, one of
a t., Jos. 3 : 12. [Lord, Jos. 4 : 2, 4.
29 : 18. t. whose heart turneth fr
Jos. 7 : 14. t. the L. taketh sh. come
18 : 4. Give out three men for each t.
Ju 18 : 1. t. of Danites sought inher-
19. thou be priest unto a t. [itance
21 : 3. why one t. lacking in Isr. ? 6.
17. a t. be not destroyed out of Isr.
24. every man to his t. and family
1 K. 11 : 13. give one t. to son, 32, 36.
12 : 21. Judah wi. t. of Benj. 180,000
1 Ch. 6 : 61. wh. were left of that t.
Ps. 74 : † 2. Rememb. t. of thine in.
Eze. 47 : 23. in what t. the stranger
He. 7 : 13. for he pertaineth to ano. t.
14. of wh. t. Moses spake nothing
See ASHER, BENJAMIN, DAN,
EPHRAIM, GAD, ISSACHAR,
JOSEPH, JUDAH, LEVI, MAN-
ASSEH, NAPHTALI, REUBEN,
SIMEON, ZEBULON.
See COAST, S. [Of the tribes.]

Half TRIBE.
Nu. 34 : 13. This is the land unto 9
tribes and h.t., Jos. 13 : 7.-14 : 2.
15. The two tribes and h.t. received inheritance, Jos 14 : 3.
Jos. 22 : 1. Josh. called h.t. of Manas.
7. to one h. of t. of M. Moses had
given; unto other h. gave Josh.
See Tribe of MANASSEH.

TRIBE, S, with fathers.
Nu 1 : 16. princes of t-s of their f.
47. Levites aft. t. of f. not numb-d
26 : 55. acc-g to names of t-s of f.
32 : 28. chief f. of t-s of Israel, Jos.
14 : 1.-21 : 1. 1 K. 8 : 1. 2 Ch. 5 : 2.
33 : 54. acc. to t-s of your f. inherit.
36 : 4. from inheritance of t. of f.
7. ev. one keep to inherit. of t. of f.

TRIBES. [39 : 14.
Ex. 28 : 21. his name acc-g to 12 t.,
Nu. 7 : 2. were princes of the t. [t.
24 : 2. Isr. abiding in tents acc-g to
30 : 1. Moses spake unto heads of t.
31 : 4. of ev. tribe 1,000 thro-t t. [t.
De. 1 : 13. Take wise men known am.
15. I took chief of your t., made
officers among your t. [t.
5 : 23. came near me all heads of y-r
12 : 5. place L. sh. choose out of t.,
16 : 18. Judges make thro-t t. [14.
18 : 5. G. hath chosen him out of t.
29 : 10. Ye stand bef. L. capt-s of t.
31 : 28. Gather all the elders of t.
Jos. 7 : 14. Ye sh. be brought acc. to t.
11 : 23. land acc-g to divisions by t.
13 : 7. divide land into 9 t. and half
14 : 2. By lot inheritance for 9 t.
3. Moses had given inherit. of 2 t.
4. children of Joseph were two t.
18 : 2. seven t. not received inherit.
21 : 16. 9 cities out of those two t.
23 : 4. nations are inherit. of your t.
1 S. 10 : 19. present before Lord by t.
1 K. 11 : 31. will give 10 t. to thee, 35.
18 : 31. twelve stones according to t.
1 Ch. 28 : 1. Dav. assembled princes of
Ps. 105 : 37. not one feeble am. t. [t.
122 : 4. Whi. t. go up, the t. of L.
Is. 19 : 13. they that are the stay of t.
49 : 6. to raise up the t. of Jacob
63 : 17. for t. of thine inheritance
Eze. 45 : 8. give to Israel acc-g to t.
48 : 1. Now these are names of t.
23. As for rest of t., Benj. sh. have
Ha. 3 : 9. acc. to the oaths of the t.
Mat. 24 : 30. sh all t. of earth mourn
Ac. 26 : 7. Unto promise 12 t. hope
Ja. 1 : 1. twelve t. which are scat-
Re. 7 : 4. sealed 144,000 of t. [tered

TRIBES of Israel. [of B.
Ju. 20 : 12. t. - sent men thro. tribe
2 S. 20 : 14. Joab went thro. all t. -
1 Ch. 27 : 16. over the t. - the ruler
22. These were the princes of t. -
29 : 6. chief of the princes of the t. -
Eze. 48 : 29. This land divide unto t. -
Re. 21 : 12. gates wi. names of 12 t. -
See Tribes of ISRAEL.

TRIBULATION, S. [L.
De. 4 : 30. When in t., if thou turn to
Ju. 10 : 14. let them deliver you in t.
1 S. 10 : 19. saved you out of all y-r t-s
26 : 24. let him deliver me out of t.
Mat. 13 : 21. t. ariseth, he is offended
24 : 21. sh. be great t., such as not
29. Immediately aft. t., Mk. 13 : 24.
Jn. 16 : 33. In world ye sh. have t.
Ac. 14 : 22. thro. much t. ent. kingd.
Ro. 2 : 9. t., anguish upon every soul
5 : 3. we glory in t-s also, knowing
that t. worketh patience [Christ
8 : 35. shall t. separate us fr. love of
12 : 12. Rejoic-g in hope, patient in t.
2 Co. 1 : 4. Who comforteth us in t.
7 : 4. I am exceeding joyful in all t.
Ep. 3 : 13. that ye faint not at my t-s
1 Th. 3 : 4. told you we should suffer
2 Th. 1 : 4. for your faith in all t-s [t.
6. recompense t. to them th. troub-
Re. 1 : 9. I John, companion in t. [le
2 : 9. I know thy works, t., and pov-
10. ye shall have t. ten days [erty
22. I will cast them into great t.
7 : 14. are they which came out of t.

TRIBUTARY, IES.
De. 20 : 11. the people found sh. be t-s
Ju. 1 : 30. Canaan-s became t-s, 33, 35.
Is. 31 : †8. his young men shall be t.
La. 1 : 1. great, how is she become t.

TRIBUTE.
Ge. 49 : 15. Issachar a serv-t unto t.
Nu. 31 : 28. levy a t. of men of war, 41.
37. Lord's t. of sheep was 675 [72
38. beeves 36,000, the L.'s t. was
39. asses 30,500 ; Lord's t. was 61
40. persons 16,000, Lord's t. 32.
De. 16 : 10. t. of a freewill offering
Jos. 16 : 10. the Canaanites serve under t., 17 : 13. Ju. 1 : 28.
2 S. 20 : 24. Adoram was over the t.,
1 K. 4 : 6.-12 : 18. 2 Ch. 10 : 18.
1 K. 5 : † 13. Sol. raised a t. of men
9 : 21. upon those did Sol. levy a t.
2 K. 17 : † 3. Hoshea gave t. [t.
23 : 33. Pharaoh-necho put land to
2 Ch. 8 : 8. did Sol. make to pay t.
17 : 11. some of Philis. bro-t t. silv.
Ezr. 4 : 13. then will they not pay t.
20. toll, t., and custom was paid
6 : 8. of the t. expenses be given
7 : 24. to impose t. upon Levites
Ne. 5 : 4. borrowed money for k.'s t.
Es. 10 : 1. Ahasuerus laid t. upon la.
Pr. 12 : 24. slothful shall be under t.
Is. 31 : † 8. young men sh. be for t.
Mat. 17 : 24. that received t. money,
said, Doth not your master pay
25. of whom do kings take t. [t. ?
22 : 17. Is it lawful to give t. to Cesar, or no ? Mk. 12 : 14. Lu. 20 : 22.
19. Shew me the t. money [Cesar
Lu. 23 : 2. forbidding to give t. to
Ro. 13 : 6. For this cause pay ye t.
7. Render thf. t. to whom t. is due

TRICKLETH. [not
La. 3 : 49. Mine eye t. down, ceaseth

TRIED. [t.
De. 21 : 5. by Levites every stroke be
2 S. 22 : 31. the word of the Lord is
t., Ps. 18 : 30. [as gold
Jb. 23 : 10. when he hath t. me I
34 : 36. My desire is that Job be t.
Ps. 12 : 6. as silver is t. in furnace
17 : 3. hast t. me, shalt find noth-g
66 : 10. For thou, O God, hast t. us,
as silver is t. [him
105 : 19. the word of the Lord t.
119 : † 140. thy word is t., I love it
Is. 28 : 16. I lay in Zion a t. stone
Je. 12 : 3. thou hast t. mine heart
Da. 12 : 10. Many shall be purified, t.
Zch. 13 : 9. will try them as gold is t.
He. 11 : 17. Abraham when he was t.
Ja. 1 : 12. when t. sh. receive crown
1 Pe. 1 : 7. than of gold, tho. t. wi. fire
Re. 2 : 2. t. them wh. say are apostles
10. you into prison, that ye be t.
3 : 18. buy of me gold t. in the fire

TRIEST. [heart
I Ch. 29 : 17. I know th. thou t. the
Je. 11 : 20. O Lord, that t. the reins
20 : 12. O Lord, that t. the righte-s
Ro. 2 : † 18. thou t. things that differ

TRIETH. [tasteth
Jb 34 : 3. ear t. words as the mouth
Ps. 7 : 9. righteous God t. the hearts
11 : 5. The Lord t. the righteous
Pr. 17 : 3. gold, but Lord t. the hearts
1 Th. 2 : 4. but God, who t. our hearts

TRIMMED, EST.
2 S. 19 : 24. Mephib-h had not t-d
Je. 2 : 33. Why t-t thou to seek love ?
Mat. 25 : 7. virgins arose t-d lamps

TRIPPING.
Is. 3 : † 16. and t. nicely as they go

TRIUMPH. [Noun.] [t.
Ps. 47 : 1. shout unto G. wi. voice of

TRIUMPH, ED.
Ex. 15 : 1. he hath t-d gloriously, 21.
2 S. 1 : 20. lest dau-s of uncircumc-d t.
Ps. 25 : 2. let not enemies t. over me
41 : 11. enemy doth not t. over me
60 : 8. Philistia, t. thou bec. of me
92 : 4. will t. in works of thy hands
94 : 3. Lord, how long sh. wicked t. ?
106 : 47. gather us to t. in thy praise
108 : 9. over Philistia will I t.
2 Co. 2 : 14. causeth us to t. in Chr.

TRIUMPHING. [Noun, Part.]
Jb. 20 : 5. t. of the wicked is short
Col. 2 : 15. made a shew, t. ov. them

TRO'AS. [T.
Ac. 16 : 8. passing by Mysia came to
11. loosing fr. T., we came to Sam.

Ac. 20 : 5. These tarried for us at T.
6. we came to T. in five days [Ch.
2 Co. 2 : 12. I came to T. to preach
2 Ti. 4 : 13. cloak I left at T. bring

TRODDEN.

De. 1 : 36. to Caleb will I give land
he hath t. upon, Jos. 14 : 9.
Ju. 5 : 21. O my soul, hast t. down
Jb. 22 : 15. old way wicked men ha. t.
28 : 8. lion's whelps have not t. it
Ps. 119 : 118. hast t. down all th. err
Is. 5 : 5. vineyard shall be t. down
14 : 19. art cast out as a carcass t.
18 : 2. Go to a nation meted out and
t. down, 7. [as straw is t.
25 : 10. Moab shall be t. under him
28 : 3. drunkards of Ephr. sh. be t.
18. scourge pass thro., ye be t. do.
63 : 3. I have t. winepress alone
18. have t. down thy sanctuary
Je. 12 : 10. they have t. my portion
La. 1 : 15. L. hath t. the mighty men,
he hath t. the virgin dau. of Jud.
Eze. 16 : † 6. saw thee t. under foot,
27 : † 6. thy hatches of ivory well t.
34 : 19. my flock eat what ye ha. t.
Da. 8 : 13. sanct-y and host to be t.
Mi. 7 : 10. now shall she be t. as mire
Mat. 5 : 13. salt to be t. under foot
Lu. 8 : 5. fell by way side, was t. down
21 : 24. Jesusalem shall be t. down
He. 10 : 29. t. under foot Son of God
Re. 14 : 20. winepress was t. without

TRODE. [Abim-h

Ju. 9 : 27. they t. grapes and cursed
20 : 43. Israel t. Benjamites down
2 K. 7 : 17. peo. t. upon him in gate,
9 : 33. Jehu t. Jezebel und. foot [20.
14 : 9. t. down thistle, 2 Ch. 25 : 18.
Lu. 12 : 1. th. they t. one upon ano.

TROGYL'LIUM. [T.

Ac. 20 : 15. we sailed, and tarried at

TROOP.

Ge. 30 : 11. † Leah said, A t. cometh;
she called his name A t.
49 : 19. Gad, a t. sh. overcome him
1 S. 30 : 8. Sh. I pursue after this t.?
2 S. 2 : 25. Benjamin became one t.
3 : 22. Joab came fr. pursuing a t.
22 : 30 by thee have I run through
a t., Ps. 18 : 29. [into a t.
23 : 11. Philistines were gathered
13. t. pitched in valley of Reph-m
Is. 65 : 11. prepare a table for that t.
Je. 18 : 22. shalt bring a t. suddenly
Ho. 7 : 1. t. of robbers spoileth with-t
Am. 9 : 6. hath founded t. in earth

TROOPS.

Ex. 38 : † 8. of women assembled by
t. at the door, 1 S. 2 : † 22.
Jb. 6 : 19. The t. of Tema looked
19 : 12. His t. come together and
Je. 5 : 7. by t. in the harlots' houses
Ho. 6 : 9. as t. of robbers wait [of t.
Mi. 5 : 1. gather thyself in t., O dau.
Ha. 3 : 16. he will invade them with

TROPH'IMUS. [his t.

Ac. 20 : 4. accomp-d him into Asia, T.
21 : 29. for they had seen wi. Paul T.
2 Ti. 4 : 20. T. I left at Miletum

TROUBLE. [Noun.]

Jos. 7 : † 26. called The valley of T.
unto this day [house of Lord
1 Ch. 22 : 14. in my t. I prepared for
2 Ch. 15 : 4. when they in t. did turn,
Lord was found, Ne. 9 : 27.
29 : 8. hath delivered them to t. [tle
Ne. 9 : 32. let not all the t. seem lit-
Jb 3 : 26. nei. was I quiet, yet t. came
5 : 6. nei. doth t. spring out of gr-d
7. man is born unto t. as sparks
14 : 1. Man is of few days, full of t.
15 : 24. t. shall make him afraid
27 : 9. Will G. hear when t. cometh
30 : 25. Did not I weep for him in t.?
34 : 29. giveth quietness, who make
Ps. 9 : 13. O Lord, consider my t. [t.?
Ps. 22 : 11. Be not far fr. me, t. is near
31 : 7. thou hast considered my t.
9. Have mercy, O Lord, I am in t.
32 : 7. thou shalt preserve me fr. t.
46 : 1. God is a present help in t. [t.
54 : 7. he hath delivered me out of
60 : 11. Give us help fr. t. : for vain
is help of man, 108 : 12. [in t.
66 : 14. mouth spoken when I was
69 : 17. hide not thy face, I am in t.
73 : 5. They are not in t. as oth. men
78 : 33. years did he consume in t.
49. upon them indignation and t.
81 : 7. Thou calledst in t., I deliv-d
91 : 15. I will be with him in t., I
102 : 2. hide not face when I am in t.
107 : 6. cried unto Lord in t., 13, 19.
26. their soul is melted bec. of t.
28. cry unto Lord in their t. [t.
116 : 3. pains of h. gat hold, I found
119 : 143. t. and anguish taken hold
138 : 7. Tho. I walk in midst of t.
142 : 2. I shewed bef. him my t. [t.
143 : 11. O L. bring my soul out of
Pr. 11 : 8. righte-s is deliv-d out of t.
12 : 13. the just shall come out of t.
15 : 6. in revenues of wicked is t. [t.
16. little, than great treasure and
Is. 1 : 14. Your new moons, are a t.
8 : 22. behold t., darkness, dimness
17 : 14. behold, at eveningtide, t.
26 : 16. L., in t. they visited thee
30 : 6. into land of t. carry riches
46 : 7. can not save him out of t.
65 : 23. shall not bring forth for t.
Je. 8 : 15. looked for health, behold t.
11 : 14. in time they cry for their t.
14 : 19. time of healing, behold t.
30 : 7. that day is time of Jacob's t.
La 1 : 21. enem-s have heard of my t.
1 Co. 7 : 28. such sh. have t. in flesh
2 Co. 1 : 4. able to comfort them in t.
8. not have you ignorant of our t.
2 Ti. 2 : 9. I suffer t. as an evil doer

Day of TROUBLE. [3.

2 K. 19 : 3. This day is a - t., Is. 37 :
Ps 20 : 1. The Lord hear thee in - t.
50 : 15. call upon me in - t., I will
59 : 16. thou hast been my refuge in
77 : 2. In - t. I sought the L. [- t.
86 : 7. In - t. I will call upon thee
Is. 22 : 5. it is a - t., of treading down
Je. 51 : 2. in - t. they shall be ag. her
Eze. 7 : 7. time is come, - t. is near
Na. 1 : 7. Lord is a strong hold in - t.
Ha. 3 : 16. that I might rest in - t.
Zph. 1 : 15. That day is a - t., day of
See **TIME, S, of trouble.**

TROUBLES. [21.

De. 31 : 17. many t. sh. befall them,
Jb. 5 : 19. He deliver thee in six t.
Ps. 25 : 17. t. of mine heart enlarged
22. Redeem Israel, O God, out of t.
34 : 6. the L. saved him out of all t.
17. L. deliver-h righteous out of t.
71 : 20. Thou hast shewed me sore t.
88 : 3. thine ear, my soul full of t.
Pr. 21 : 23. keepeth mouth, keepeth
Is. 65 : 16. former t. forgotten [fr. t.
Mk. 13 : 8. there sh. be famine and t.

TROUBLE. [Verb.]

Jos. 6 : 18. lest ye t. camp of Israel
7 : 25. Joshua said, Lord sh. t. thee
Ju. 11 : 35. art one of them th. t. me
2 Ch. 32 : 18. they cried in Jews'
speech to t. them [pleasure
Ps. 2 : † 5. t. them in his sore dis-
3 : 1. L., how are increased th. t. me?
13 : 4. those that t. me, rejoice wh.
Eze. 32 : 13. nei. shall foot of man t.
them, nor hoofs of beasts t. [thee
Da 4 : 19. let not interpretation t.
5 : 10. O k., let not thoughts t. thee
11 : 44. tidings of north sh. t. him
Mat. 26 : 10. Why t. ye the woman?
Mk. 14 : 6. [not worthy
Lu. 7 : 6. Lord, t. not thyself, I am
Lu. 8 : 49. Thy dau. is dead; t. not
11 : 7. t. me not, door is shut [Mas.
Ac. 15 : 19. t. not Gentiles turned to
16 : 20. These men do t. our city [G.
20 : 10. t. not yours., life is in him
Ga 1 : 7. there be some that t. you
5 : 12. I would were cut off who t.
6 : 17. hencef. let no man t. me [you
2 Th. 1 : 6. tribulation to them that t.
He. 12 : 15. lest root of bitterness t.

TROUBLED. [you

Ge. 34 : 30. Ye have t. me, to make
41 : 8. Pha.'s spirit was t. [me stink
45 : 3. breth. were t. at his presence
Ex. 14 : 24. Lord t. host of Egyptians
Jos. 7 : 25. Joshua said, Why t. us?
1 S. 14 : 29. My fa. hath t. the land
16 : 14. evil spirit fr. the L. t. him
28 : 21. woman saw Saul was sore t.
2 S. 4 : 1. Abner dead, Israelites were
1 K. 18 : 18. I have not t. Israel [t.
2 K. 6 : 11. king of Syria was sore t.
Ezr. 4 : 4. people t. them in building
Jb. 4 : 5. toucheth thee thou art t.
21 : 4. why sho. not my spirit be t.?
23 : 15. theref. am I t. at his pres-e
34 : 20. people sh. be t. at midnight
Ps. 30 : 7. hide thy face, and I was t.
38 : 6. I am t.; I go mourning all
39 : † 2. I held peace, sorrow was t.
46 : 3. Tho. the waters roar and be t.
48 : 5. kings were t. and hasted aw.
77 : 3. I rememb-d God and was t.
4. I am so t. I can not speak [t.
16. waters afraid, the depths were
83 : 17. Let them be confounded and
90 : 7. by thy wrath are we t. [t.
104 : 29. hidest thy face, they are t.
Pr. 25 : 26. is as a t. fountain and
Is. 32 : 10. many years shall ye be t.
11. women, be t. ye careless ones
57 : 20. the wicked are like t. sea
Je. 31 : 20. my bowels are t. for him
La. 1 : 20. my bowels are t., 2 : 11.
Eze. 7 : 27. hands of people sh. be t.
26 : 18. the isles in the sea sh. be t.
27 : 35. kings sh. be t. in counten.
Da. 2 : 1. Neb-zar's spirit was t., 3.
4 : 5. visions of my head t. me, 7 : 15.
19. Daniel astonied, tho-ts t. him
5 : 6. Belshaz-'s thoughts t. him, 9.
7 : 28. my cogitations much t. me
Zch. 10 : 2. t. bec. was no shepherd
Mat. 2 : 3. Herod was t. and all Jerus.
14 : 26. saw him on sea, they were
t., Mk. 6 : 50. [Jn. 14 : 1, 27.
24 : 6. see ye be not t., Mk. 13 : 7.
Lu. 1 : 12. Zach-s saw angel was t.
29. wh. Mary saw angel she was t.
10 : 41. Martha thou art t. about
24 : 38. Why are ye t., and why do
Jn. 5 : 4. an angel went t. the water
7. I have no man when water is t.
11 : 33. Jesus groaned and was t.,
12 : 27.-13 : 21. [mind
Ac. 2 : † 6. the multitude were t. in
15 : 24. some from us have t. you
17 : 8. they t. the people and rulers
2 Co. 4 : 8. We are t. on ev. side. 7 : 5.
2 Th. 1 : 7. to you that are t. rest
2 : 2. th. ye be not t. nei. by spirit
1 Pe. 3 : 14. not afraid of terror, nor

TROUBLEDST. [be t.

Eze. 32 : 2. t. waters with thy feet

TROUBLER.

1 Ch. 2 : 7. Achar, the t. of Israel

TROUBLESOME.

Jb. 16 : † 2. t. comforters are ye all
20 : † 22. hand of t. sh. come upon

TROUBLEST. [him

Mk. 5 : 35. why t. thou the Master

TROUBLETH.

1 S. 16 : 15. evil spirit fr. God t. thee
1 K. 18 : 17. Art thou he th. t. Isr.?
Jb. 22 : 10. theref. sudden fear t. thee
23 : 16. my heart soft, Almi-ty t. me
Pr. 11 : 17. is cruel t. his own flesh

Pr. 11 : 29. He that t. his own house
15 : 27. He greedy of gain, t. house
Da. 4 : 9. I know no secret t. thee
Lu. 18 : 5. because this widow t. me
Ga. 5 : 10. t. you sh. bear his judg- [ment

TROUBLING.

Jb. 3 : 17. There wicked cease fr. t.
Jn. 5 : 4. stepped in first after t. of [water

TROUBLOUS.

Da. 9 : 25. wall be built again in t. [times

TROUGH, S.

Ge. 24 : 20. she emptied pitcher into t.
30 : 38. Jac. set rods in watering t-s
Ex. 2 : 16. filled t-s to water flock
See KNEADINGTROUGHS.

TROW.

Lu. 17 : 9. thank that servant? I t. [not

TRUCEBREAKERS.

2 Ti. 3 : 3. in last days men sh. be t.

TRUE.

Ge. 42 : 11. we are t. men, no spies
19. If ye t. men, let one be bound
33. Thereby I sh. know ye are t.,
De. 17 : 4. if ye be t., 22 : 20. [34.
Jos. 2 : 12. swear, give me a t. token
Ru. 3 : 12. is t. I am thy kinsm. [t.
2 S. 7 : 28. art th. God, thy words be
1 K. 10 : 6. It was t. report I heard,
2 Ch. 9 : 5. [which is t.
22 : 16. tell me nothing but that
Ne. 9 : 13. thou gavest them t. laws
Ps. 19 : 9. judgments of Lord are t.
119 : 160. Thy word is t. fr. begin-g
Pr. 14 : 25. A t. witness deliv-h souls
Je. 42 : 5. L. be a t. witness betw. us
Eze. 18 : 8. hath executed t. judgm.
Da. 3 : 14. Is it t., O Shadrach, do
24. They said unto Neb., t., O king
6 : 12. the king said, The thing is t.
8 : 26. vision which was told is t.
10 : 1. was revealed and thing was t.
Zch. 7 : 9. Execute t. judgm. [12 : 14.
Mat. 22 : 16. know thou art t., Mk.
Lu. 16 : 11. to your trust t. riches
Jn. 1 : 9. That was the t. light which
3 : 33. set to his seal that God is t.
4 : 23. when t. worshippers worship
37. Is that saying t., One soweth
5 : 31. of myself, my witness not t.
32. witness he witnesseth of me t.
6 : 32. my Father giveth t. bread
7 : 18. his glory th. sent, same is t.
28. he that sent me is t., 8 : 26.
8 : 13. Phari-s said, thy record not t.
14. tho. of myself my record is t.
16. if I judge my judgment is t.
17. the testimony of two men is t.
10 : 41. all John spake of this man t.
15 : 1. I am the t. vine, my Father
19 : 35. and his record is t., 21 : 24.
Ac. 12 : 9. wist not that it was t.
Ro. 3 : 4. let God be t., but ev. man
2 Co. 1 : 18. But as God is t., our word
6 : 8. as deceivers, and yet t. [liness
Ep. 4 : 24. new man created in t. ho-
Ph. 4 : 3. I entreat t. yokefellow
8. whatso. things are t., think on
1 Ti. 3 : 1. This a t. saying, If a man
Tit. 1 : 13. This witness is t. Wheref.
He. 8 : 2. t. tabernacle Lord pitched
9 : 24. holy places figures of the t.
10 : 22. draw near with a t. heart
1 Pe. 5 : 12. this is the t. grace of G.
2 Pe. 2 : 22. acc. to the t. proverb
1 Jn. 2 : 8. which thing is t. in him,
and you, t. light now shineth
5 : 20. that we may know him that
is t., and we are in him th. is t.
3 Jn. 12. know our record is t. [t.
Re. 3 : 7. saith the holy, he that is
14. These things saith t. witness
6 : 10. How long, O L., holy and t.?
15 : 3. just and t. are thy ways, th.
16 : 7. t. are thy judgments, 19 : 2.
19 : 9. These the t. sayings of God
11. he was called Faithful and T.
21 : 5. Write, for these words are t.
Re. 22 : 6. These sayings are faithful
See **True GOD.** [and t.

TRULY.

Ge. 4 : 24. t. Lamech 70 and 7 fold
24 : 49. now if ye will deal t., 47 : 29.
48 : 19. t. younger bro. sh. be greater
Nu. 14 : 21. t. as I live, saith L., 28.
De. 14 : 22. t. tithe the increase of seed
Jos. 2 : 14. we will deal t. with thee
24. t. Lord hath delivered the land
Ju. 9 : 16. if ye have done t. and, 19.
1 S. 20 : 3. t. but step betw. me and
Jb. 36 : 4. t. my words not be false
Ps. 62 : 1. t. my soul waiteth upon
73 : 1. t. God is good to Israel [God
116 : 16. t. I am thy servant, I am
Pr. 12 : 22. th. deal t. are his delight
Ec. 11 : 7. t. the light is sweet, and
Je. 3 : 23. t. in vain is salva-n hoped,
t. in Lord is salvation of Israel
10 : 19. t. this is a grief I must bear
28 : 9. be known that L. t. sent him
Eze. 18 : 9. my judgments to deal t.
Mi. 3 : 8. t. I am full of power to
Mat. 9 : 37. The harvest t. is plenteous, Lu. 10 : 2. [restore all thi-s
17 : 11. Elias t. shall first come and
27 : 54. t. this was Son of God. Mk.
Mk. 14 : 38. spirit t. is ready [15 : 39.
Lu. 11 : 48. t. ye allow deeds of your
20 : 21. teachest way of God t. [fa.
22 : 22. t. Son of man goeth, as it
Jn. 4 : 18. no husband, saidst thou t.
17 : † 19. they might be t. sanctified
20 : 30. other signs t. did Jesus
Ac. 1 : 5. John t. baptized wi. water
3 : 22. Moses t. said unto fathers
5 : 23. The prison t. found we shut
2 Co. 12 : 12. t. signs of an apostle
He. 7 : 23. they t. were many priests
11 : 15. t. if been mindf of country
1 Jn. 1 : 3. t. our fellowship with Fa.
3 Jn. † 1. Gaius, wh. I love t.

TRUMP. [raised

1 Co. 15 : 52. at last t. dead shall be
1 Th. 4 : 16. Lord sh. descend with t.

TRUMPET. [of God

Ex. 19 : 16. voice of t. exceeding loud
20 : 18. people heard noise of the t.
Nu. 10 : 4. if they blow with one t.
Ju. 3 : 27. he blew t. in mt. of Ephr.
6 : 34. Spirit upon Gid-n ; he blew t.
7 : 16. put a t. in every man's hand
18. when I blow with a t., blow ye
1 S. 13 : 3. Saul blew t. thro-t land
2 S. 2 : 28. Joab blew t., peo. stood,
18 : 16.-20 : 22. [no part in Dav.
20 : 1. Sheba blew t., said, We have
1 K. 1 : 34. blow ye wi. t. G. save Sol.
39. they blew t., God save Solo-n
Ps. 81 : 3. Blow up t. in new moon
Is. 18 : 3. when he bloweth a t. hear
27 : 13. the great t. shall be blown
58 : 1. Cry aloud, lift voice like a t.
Je. 4 : 5. Blow ye the t. in the land
6 : 1. blow t. in Tekoah, set up sign
51 : 27. blow the t. among nations
Eze. 7 : 14. blown t. to make ready
33 : 3. if he blow t. and warn people
6. if watchman blow not the t.
Ho. 5 : 8. Blow ye the t. in Ramah
8 : 1. Set the t. to thy mouth, he sh.
Jo. 2 : 1. Blow t. in Zion, 15. [come
Am. 3 : 6. t. be blown, peo. not afraid?
Zph. 1 : 16. day of the t. ag. cities
Zch. 9 : 14. Lord G. shall blow the t.
Mat. 24 : 31. his angels, with great
sound of t. [sound
1 Co. 14 : 8. if the t. give uncertain
Re. 1 : 10. great voice, as of t., 4 : 1.
8 : 13. by the other voices of the t.
9 : 14. sixth angel which had the t.
See **SOUND of the trumpet,**
SOUND, SOUNDED, SOUNDETH.

TRUMPETS. [Nu. 29 : 1.

Le. 23 : 24. memorial of blowing t.,
Nu. 10 : 2. Make two t. of silver
Nu. 10 : 8. sons of Aaron sh. blow with
9. then blow an alarm with t. [t.
10. blow with t. over burnt off-gs
31 : 6. with t. to blow in his hand
Jos. 6 : 4. seven priests sh. bear 7 t.;
priests shall blow with t., 6, 13.
8. priests bearing seven t. of rams'
horns, blew t.
9. bef. the priests that blew with t.;
priests blowing wi. t., 13, 16, 20.
Ju. 7 : 8. people took victuals and t.
18. when I blow, then blow ye t.
20. three companies blew t., brake
pitchers, held t. in right hands
to blow, 19. [the t.
22. And the three hundred blew
2 K. 9 : 13. blew with t. ; Jehu is k.
11 : 14. all the people blew with t.
12 : 13. not made bowls, t. of money
1 Ch. 13 : 8. Da. and Isr. played wi. t.
15 : 24. the priests did blow with t.
before the ark of God, 16 : 6, 42.
2 Ch. 5 : 12.-7 : 6.-13 : 12, 14.
28. all Israel bro-t up ark with t.,
2 Ch. 15 : 14. [t.
2 Ch. 5 : 13. lifted up their voice with
13 : 12. priests with t. to cry alarm
20 : 28. harps and t. unto hou. of L.
23 : 13. king stood, princes and t.
29 : 27. song of L. began with t., 26.
Ezr. 3 : 10. set priests in apparel wi. t.
Ne. 12 : 35. certain of priests' sons
with t. [with t.
41. priests, Eliakim, Zechariah,
Jb. 39 : 25. horse saith am. t., Ha, ha!
Ps. 98 : 6. with t. make a joyful noise
Re. 8 : 2. to 7 angels given 7 t., 6.

TRUMPETERS. [k.

2 K. 11 : 14. princes and t. stood by
2 Ch. 5 : 13. t. and singers were as one
29 : 28. singers sang, t. sounded
Re. 18 : 22. voice of t. be heard no

TRUST. [Noun.] [more

1 Ch. 9 : †22. wh. Dav. did ordain in t.
† 26. four chief porters in their t.
† 31. Mattithiah had t. over pans
2 Ch. 31 : †15. their t. to give to breth.
† 18. in their t. sanctified thems.
Jb. 8 : 14. whose t. be a spider's web
Ps. 40 : 4. Blessed is he that maketh
the Lord his t. [my youth
71 : 5. O Lord, thou art my t. from
141 : 8. in thee is my t., leave not
Pr. 22 : 19. That thy t. may be in L.
Is. 30 : 3. t. in Egypt be confusion
Lu. 16 : 11. to your t. true riches?
2 Co. 3 : 4. such t. have we thro. Ch.
1 Ti. 1 : 11. was committed to my t.
6 : 20. keep that committed to thy t.

Put, putteth TRUST.

Ju. 9 : 15. come p. t. in my shadow
2 K. 18 : 24. How p. thy t. on Egypt
for chariots, Is. 36 : 9. [him
1 Ch. 5 : 20. bec. they p. their t. in
Jb. 4 : 18. he p. no t. in his servants
15 : 15. he p-h no t. in his saints
Ps. 2 : 12. Blessed are all that p. t. in
4 : 5. p. your t. in the Lord [him
5 : 11. let all th. p. t. in thee rejoice
7 : 1. my God, in thee do I p. my t.,
11 : 1.-16 : 1.-25 : 20.-31 : 1, 6.-
71 : 1.-73 : 28. [t. in thee
9 : 10. that know thy name will p.
17 : 7. savest them wh. p. t. in thee
36 : 7. p. t. under shadow of wings
56 : 4. in God I have p. my t., 11.
73 : 28. I have p. my t. in Lord G.
146 : 3: p. not your t. in princes
Pr. 28 : 25. p-h t. in L. be made fat
29 : 25. p-h t. in Lord shall be safe
30 : 5. shield unto them p. t. in him
Is. 57 : 13. p-h t. in me possess land
Je. 39 : 18. bec. hast p. thy t. in me
1 Th. 2 : 4. to be p. in t. with gospel
He. 2 : 13. ag. I will p. my t. in him

TRUST. [Verb.] [to t.

Ru. 2 : 12. und. wings thou art come

2 S. 22 : 3. God, in him I t., Ps. 18 :
2.-91 : 2. [Ps. 18 : 30.
31. a buckler to all that t. in him,
2 K. 18 :20. Now on whom dost thou
t., 2 Ch. 32 : 10. Is. 36 : 5.
21. so is Pharaoh unto all that t.
in him, Is. 36 : 6.
Jb. 13 : 15. Tho. he slay, yet will I t.
15 : 31. Let not him t. in vanity
35 : 14. judgment is bef. him, thf. t.
39 :11. Wilt t. him bec. he is strong?
Ps. 20 : 7. Some t. in chariots, and
25 : 2. I t. in thee, 31 : 6.-55 : 23.-
56 : 3.-143 : 8. [t. in thee
31 : 19. hast wrought for them that
34 :22. none that t. in him be desol.
37 : 5. way unto L.; t. in him [him
40. he shall save, bec. they t. in
44 : 6. I will not t. in my bow, nor
49 : 6. They that t. in their wealth
52 : 8. I t. in the mercy of G. [thee
56 : 3. time I am afraid, I will t. in
61 : 4. I will t. in the covert of thy
62 : 8. t. in him at all times [wings
10. t. not in oppression, become
64 : 10. righteous sh. be glad, and t.
91 : 2. my God; in him will I t.
4. under his wings shalt thou t.
119 :42. answer, for I t. in thy word
144 : 2. my fortress, he in whom I t.
Pr. 31 : 11. heart of her husb. doth t.
Is. 12 : 2. God my salvation, I will t.
14 : 32 Zion, the poor shall t. in it
30 : 2. to t. in the shadow of Egypt
12. because ye t. in oppression
31 : 1. t. in chariots, bec. are many
36 :5. on whom dost thou t. ag. me
6. so is Phs. to all that t. in him
42 : 17. be ashamed th. t. in images
50 : 10. let him t. in name of Lord
51 : 5. and on mine arm sh. they t.
59 : 4. they t. in vanity, speak lies
Je. 7 : 4. t. ye not in lying words
8. ye t. in lying words that cannot
14. called by my name wh-in ye t.
9 : 4. take heed, t. ye not in any bro.
28 : 15. people to t. in a lie, 29 : 31.
46 : 25. punish Phs. and all that t.
49 : 11. let thy widows t. in me [him
Eze. 16 : 15. didst t. in own beauty
33 : 13. if he t. to his own righteousn.
Ho. 10 : 13. bec. didst t. in thy way
Am. 6 : 1. that t. in mt. of Samaria
Mi. 7 : 5. t. ye not in a friend, put
Na. 1 : 7. Lord knoweth them that t.
Zph. 3 :12. they sh. t. in name of Lord
Mat. 12 : 21. in his name shall the
Gentiles t., Ro. 15 :12. [in riches
Mk. 10 : 24. how hard for th. that t.
Jn. 5 : 45. Moses in whom ye t. [ney
Ro. 15 :24. I t. to see you in my jour-
1 Co. 16 : 7. I t. to tarry awhile with
2 Co. 1 :9. not t. in ours., but in God
10. we t. he will yet deliver us
13. I t. ye sh. acknowl. to the end
5 : 11. t. are made manifest in your
10 : 7. If man t. that he is Christ's
13 : 6. I t. ye shall know we are not
reprobates [whereof to t.
Ph. 3 : 4. If any thinketh he hath
1 Ti. 4 : 10. bec. we t. in living God
6 : 17. t. not in uncertain riches
Phm. 22. I t. thro. your prayers I
He. 13 :18. t. we have a good consci.
2 Jn. 12. I t. to come unto you and
3 Jn. 14. I t. I shall shortly see thee

TRUST, ED, ETH in the Lord.

2 K. 18 : 5. he t-d - God of Israel
22. if ye say, We t. -, Is. 36 : 7.
30. nei. let Hez-h make you t. -,
saying, L. will deliver, Is. 36 :15.
Ps. 21 : 7. For the king t-h - [14.
26 : 1. I have also t-d -, 28 : 7.-31 :
32 : 10. he that t-h - mercy shall
compass him, Pr. 16 :20. Je. 17 : 7.
37 : 3. t. -, do good; thou sh. be fed

Ps. 40 : 3. many shall see it, and t. -
115 : 9. O Israel, t. -; he is, 10, 11.
118 : 8. It is better to t. - than, 9.
125 : 1. that t. - sh. be as m-t Zion
Pr. 3 : 5. t. - with all thine heart
Is. 26 : 4. t. - for ever; for in Lord
Zph. 3 :2. she t-d not in L.; drew not
Ph. 2 : 24. t. -, I sh. come shortly, 19.

TRUSTED. [t.?

De. 32 : 37. where is rock in wh. they
Ju. 11 : 20. Sihon t. not Isr. to pass
20 : 36. they t. unto liers in wait
Ps. 13 : 5. But I have t. in thy mercy
22 : 4. Our fathers t. in thee; they
t., thou didst deliver, 5. [liver
8. He t. on Lord that he would de-
31 : 14. But I t. in thee, O Lord
33 : 21. we have t. in his holy name
41 : 9. familiar friend in whom I t.
52 : 7. t. in abundance of his riches
78 : 22. they t. not in his salvation
Is. 47 : 10. hast t. in thy wickedness
Je. 13 : 25. thou hast t. in falsehood
48 : 7. thou hast t. in thy works
49 : 4. O dau. that t. in treasures
Da. 3 : 28. G. delivereth serv-ts th. t.
Mat. 27 :43. He t. in G., let him deliv.
Lu. 11 : 22. taketh armour wh-in he
18 : 9. certain which t. in thems. [t.
24 : 21. we t. it had been he that
Ep. 1 : 12. his glory, who first t. in C.
13. In whom ye t. after ye heard
2 Ti. 1 : † 12. I know whom I have t.
1 Pe. 3 : 5. holy women who t. in God

TRUSTEDST. [thou t.

De. 28 : 52. walls come down wh-in
Je. 5 :17. impover-h cities wh-n th. t.
12 : 5. if in land of peace wh-in thou

TRUSTEST. [t.

2 K. 18 : 19. What confidence is this
wherein thou t.? Is. 36 : 4.
21. t. upon staff of bruised reed,
Is. 36 : 6. [t., Is. 37 : 10.
19 : 10. Let not God in whom thou

TRUSTETH.

Jb. 24 : † 22. he t. not his own life
40 :23. t. he can draw up Jord. [12.
Ps. 34 : 8. blessed is man t. in him, 84 :
57 : 1. be merciful, my soul t. in thee
86 : 2. save servant that t. in thee
115 : 8. so is every one th. t., 135 : 18.
Pr. 11 : 28. t. in his riches shall fall
28 : 26. that t. in own heart is a fool
Is. 26 : 3. in peace, bec. he t. in thee
Je. 17 : 5. Cursed be man th. t. in man
Hs. 2 : 18. maker of his work t. th-in
1 Ti. 5 : 5. a widow indeed t. in God

TRUSTING.

Ps. 112 : 7. his heart is fixed, t. in L.

TRUSTY. [the t.

Jb. 12 : 20. He removeth speech of

TRUTH.

Ge. 24 : 27. hath not left destitute
my master of his t. [least of t.
32 : 10. I am not worthy of the
42 : 16. be proved, whe. any t. in you
Ex. 18 : 21. provide able men, men of
34 : 6. The Lord, abundant in t. [t.
De. 13 : 14. if it be t. that such abom-
32 : 4. a God of t. is he [ination
2 S. 2 : 6. Lord shew kindness and t.
15 : 20. mercy and t. be with thee
1 K. 17 :24. word of L. in mouth is t.
2 K. 20 : 19. if peace and t., Is. 39 : 8.
2 Ch. 18 :15. th. thou say noth. but t.
31 :20. Hez. wrought that wh. was t.
Ne. 9 : † 13. gavest them laws of t.
Ps. 15 : 2. speaketh t. in his heart
25 : 10. paths of L. are mercy and t.
31 : 5. redeemed me, O Lord G. of t.
45 : 4. ride prosperously bec. of t.
51 : 6. desirest t. in inward parts
57 : 3. God shall send forth his t.
60 : 4. banner be displayed bec. of t.
61 : 7. O prepare mercy and t. whi.
85 : 10. Mercy and t. are met toget.
11. t. shall spring out of the earth

Ps. 86 : 15. art plenteous in mercy and
89 : 14. mercy and t. sh. go bef. [t.
91 : 4. his t. shall be thy shield
96 : 13. shall judge people with t.
98 : 3. remembered his mercy and t.
100 : 5. his t. endureth to all, 117 : 2.
119 : 30. I have chosen the way of
142. and thy law is the t., 151. [t.
146 : 6. God who keepeth t. for ever
Pr. 3 : 3. Let not t. forsake thee
8 : 7. For my mouth shall speak t.
12 : 17. speaketh t. sheweth righte.
19. lip of t. shall be established
14 : 22. t. be to them th. devise good
16 : 6. By t. iniquity is purged; by
20 : 28. Mercy and t. preserve king
23 : 23. Buy the t. and sell it not
Is. 25 : 1. thy counsels faithfuln., t.
26 : 2. nation which keepeth t. may
42 : 3. sh. bring forth judgm. unto t.
43 : 9. let them hear and say, It is t.
59 : 4. nor any pleadeth for t.
14. t. is fallen in the street and
15. Yea t. faileth; he th. depart-h
65 : 16. shall bless himself in God of
t.; sh. swear by the God of t. [t.
Je. 5 : 1. if there be any that seeketh
3. O L., are not thine eyes upon t.?
7 : 28. t. is cut off from their mouth
9 : 3. they are not valiant for the t.
5. they will deceive, not speak t.
10 : † 10. the Lord is the God of t.
14 : † 13. I will give you peace of t.
33 : 6. I will reveal abundance of t.
Da. 4 : 37. King, whose works are t.
7 : 16. I asked him t. of all this, 19.
8 : 12. it cast down the t. to ground
10 : 21. wh. is noted in Script. of t.
11 : 2. now will I shew thee the t.
Ho. 4 : 1. no t. nor mercy in land
Mi. 7 : 20. wilt perform t. to Jacob
Zch. 7 : † 9. Judge judgment of t.
8 : 3. Jerus. sh. be called A city of t.
16. Speak ye every man the t., execute the judgment of t. and
19. therefore love the t. and peace
Mal. 2 : 6. law of t. was in his mouth
Mat. 15 : 27. she said, t. Lord, yet [t.
Mk. 5 : 33. woman fearing, told the
12 : 32. Well, Master, th. hast said t.
Jn. 1 : 14. only begotten, full of t.
17. grace and t. came by Jesus Ch.
3 :21. that doeth t. cometh to light
5 : 33. John, he bare witness unto t.
8 : 32. ye sh. know t., t. make free
40. ye seek to kill me, that told t.
44. abode not in t., bec. no t. in him
45. bec. I tell you t. ye believe not
46. If I say t., why not believe?
14 : 6. I am the way and the t. and
16 : 7. I tell you t., it is expedient
13. Spirit of t. guide you into all t.
17 : 19. be sanctified thro the t., 17.
18 : 37. should bear witness unto t.
Every one that is of t. heareth
38. Pilate saith unto him, Wh. is t.?
Ro. 1 : 18. hold t. in unrighteousn.
25. changed t. of God into a lie
2 : 2. judgment of God is acc. to t.
8. unto them that do not obey t.
20. which hast the form of the t.
3 : 7. if t. of God more abounded
9 : 1. I say the t. in Christ, I lie not
15 : 8. minister of circumc-n for t.
1 Co. 5 : 8. with unleav-d bread of t.
2 Co. 4 : 2. by manifestation of the t.
7 : 14. boasting I made is found a t.
11 : 10. As the t. of Christ is in me
12 : 6. I sh. not be fool, I will say t.
13 : 8. we can do nothing against
t., but for the t. [tinue
Ga. 2 : 5. t. of the gospel might con-
14. walked not acc. to t. of gospel
3 : 1. that ye sho. not obey t., 5 : 7.
4 : 16. enemy, bec. I tell you the t.?
Ep. 4 : 15. speaking the t. in love
21. taught by him as t. is in Jesus

Ep. 4 : † 24. is created in holin. of **t.**
4 : 25. speak ev. man **t.** with neigh-
5 : 9. fruit of Spirit is in all **t.** ⌊bour
6 : 14. your loins girt about with **t.**
2 Th. 2 : 10. received not love of **t.**
12. damned, who believed not **t.**
13. to salvation, thro. belief of **t.**
1 Ti. 2 : 4. unto knowledge of the **t.**
7. I speak **t.** in Christ and lie not
3 : 15. church, pillar, ground of **t.**
4 : 3. received of them wh. know **t.**
6 : 5. corrupt minds, destitute of **t.**
2 Ti. 2 : 18. Who cone-g the **t.** erred
25. to acknowledging of the **t.**
3 : 7. not able to come to knowl. of **t.**
8. as Jannes, so do these resist **t.**
4 : 4. shall turn away ears from **t.**
Tit. 1 : 1. acc. to acknowledging of **t.**
14. com-ts of men th. turn from **t.**
He. 10 : 26. after we received knowl.
Ja. 3 : 14. and lie not ag. the **t.** ⌊of **t.**
5 : 19. if any of you err from the **t.**
1 Pe. 1 : 22. purified in obeying the **t.**
2 Pe. 2 : 2. way of **t.** be evil spoken of
1 Jn. 1 : 6. we lie and do not the **t.**
8. say we ha. no sin **t.** is not in us
2 : 4. is a liar, and **t.** is not in him
21. I ha. not written. bec. ye know not **t.**, but bec. no lie is of the **t.**
27. as anointing is **t.** ye sh. abide
3 : 19. hereby we know we are of **t.**
5 : 6. witness because the Spirit is **t.**
2 Jn. 1. all they that have known **t.**
2. For **t.**'s sake that dwelleth in us
3 Jn. 3. breth. testified of **t.** in thee
8. might be fellow helpers to the **t.**
12. good report of all and of the **t.**

In TRUTH. ⌈24.

Jos. 24 : 14. serve him **i.t.**, 1 S. 12 :
Ju. 9 : 15. If **i.t.** ye anoint me king
1 K. 2 : 4. if thy children walk **i.t.**
3 : 6. as he walked before thee **i.t.**
2 K. 20 : 3. how I have walked **i.t.**
Ps. 33 : 4. all his works **i.t.**, 111 : 8.
37 : † 3. shalt dwell, and **i.t.** be fed
132 : 11. Lord sworn **i.t.** unto Dav.
145 : 18. all that call upon him **i.t.**
Is. 10 : 20. shall stay upon Lord **i.t.**
16 : 5. shall sit upon it **i.t.**, judging
38 : 3. I have walked bef. thee **i.t.**
48 : 1. mention of God, but not **i.t.**
61 : 8. I will direct their work **i.t.**
Je. 4 : 2. swear, The Lord liveth **i.t.**
32 : † 41. plant them in this land **i.** ⌊**t.**
Zch. 8 : 8. I will be their God **i.t.**
Mat. 22 : 16. teachest the way of God **i.t.**, Mk. 12 : 14. ⌈and **i.t.**, 24.
Jn. 4 : 23. sh. worship him in spirit
2 Co. 7 : 14. we speak all things **i.t.**
Ph. 1 : 18. whe. **i.t.** Christ is preached
Col. 1 : 6. ye knew grace of God **i.t.**
1 Th. 2 : 13. as it is **i.t.** word of God
1 Jn. 3 : 18. not love in tongue, but
2 Jn. 3. Son of the Father **i.t.** ⌊**i.t.**
4. I found thy children walking **i.t.**, 3 Jn. 4.

In the TRUTH.

Ps. 69 : 13. hear me **- t.** of thy salva.
Jn. 8 : 44. murderer. abode not **- t.**
1 Co. 13 : 6. charity rejoiceth **- t.**
2 Pe. 1 : 12. tho. ye be established **- t.**
2 Jn. 1. elect lady whom I love **- t.**, 3
3 Jn. 3. as thou walkest **- t.** ⌊Jn. 1.

Of a TRUTH. ⌈fr. us

1 S. 21 : 5. **o. a t.** women been kept
2 K. 19 : 17. **o. a t.** kings of Assyria destroyed nations, Is. 37 : 18.
Jb. 9 : 2. I know it is so **o. a t.**, but
Is. 5 : 9. **o. a t.** many houses desolate
Je. 26 : 15. **o. a t.** Lord hath sent me
Da. 2 : 47. **o. a t.** your God is a God
Mat. 14 : 33. **o. a t.** thou art Son of G.
Lu. 4 : 25. But I tell you **o. a t.**, 9 : 27.
12 : 44. **o. a t.** I say unto you, 21 : 3.
22 : 59. **o. a t.** this fellow was wi. him
Jn. 6 : 14. **o. a t.** that prophet, 7 : 40.
Ac. 4 : 27. **o. a t.** ag. holy child Jes.
Ac. 10 : 34. **o. a t.** God is no respect-
1 Co. 14 : 25. God is in you **o. a t.** ⌊er
See **SPIRIT of truth.**

Thy TRUTH.

Ps. 25 : 5. Lead me in **t.t.**, teach me
26 : 3. and I have walked in **t.t.**
30 : 9. shall the dust declare **t.t.**
40 : 10. I have not concealed **t.t.**
11. let **t.t.** continu-y preserve me
43 : 3. send out thy light and **t.t.**
54 : 5. mine enemies cut off in **t.t.**
57 : 10. **t.t.** unto the clouds, 108 : 4.
71 : 22. I will praise thee, even **t.t.**
86 : 11. Teach me, I will walk in **t.**
89 : 49. swarest unto Dav. in **t.t.** ⌊**t.**
115 : 1. give glory for **t.t.** sake, 138 : 2.
Is. 38 : 18. cannot hope for **t.t.** ⌈**t.t.**
19. father to chil. sh. make known
Da. 9 : 13. we might understand **t.t.**
Jn. 17 : 17. Sanctify through **t.t.**

Word of TRUTH. ⌈mouth

Ps. 119 : 43. take not **- t.** out of my
2 Co. 6 : 7. approving ours. by **- t.**
Ep. 1 : 13. trusted after ye heard **- t.**
Col. 1 : 5. wh-f ye heard before in **- t.**
2 Ti. 2 : 15. rightly dividing the **- t.**
Ja. 1 : 18. Of his own will begat us by

Words of TRUTH. ⌊- t.

Es. 9 : 30. letters unto Jews with **- t.**
Pr. 22 : 21. make thee know certainly of **- t.**; that thou answer **- t.**
Ec. 12 : 10. that wh. was written was
Ac. 26 : 25. I speak forth the **- t.** ⌊**- t.**

TRY.

Ju. 7 : 4. and I will **t.** them for thee
2 Ch. 32 : 31. God left him to **t.** him
Jb. 7 : 18. th. thou shouldest **t.** him
12 : 11. Doth not the ear **t.** words
Ps. 11 : 4. his eyelids **t.** chil. of men
26 : 2. **t.** my reins and my heart
139 : 23. **t.** me and know my tho-ts
Je. 6 : 27. thou mayest **t.** their way
9 : 7. I will melt, **t.** them, Zch. 13 : 9.
17 : 10. I the Lord **t.** the reins
La. 3 : 40. Let us **t.** our ways, turn
Da. 11 : 35. some shall fall to **t.** them
1 Co. 3 : 13. fire sh. **t.** ev. man's work
Ph. 1 : † 10. may **t.** things excellent
1 Pe. 4 : 12. fiery trial wh. is to **t.** you
1 Jn. 4 : 1. **t.** the spirits whe. of God
Re. 3 : 10. hour of temptation to **t.** th.

TRYING. ⌈patience

Ja. 1 : 3. **t.** of your faith worketh

TRYPHE'NA, TRYPHO'SA

Ro. 16 : 12. Salute T. and T. who lab.

TU'BAL. ⌈T.

Is. 66 : 19. send those that escape to
See MESHECH.

TU'BAL-CAIN. ⌈T. was

Ge. 4 : 22. Zillah bare T.; sister of

TUMBLED.

Ju. 7 : 13. a cake **t.** into the host

TUMULT, S.

1 S. 4 : 14. What meaneth this **t.** ?
14 : † 19. the **t.** in the host increased
2 S. 18 : 29. I saw a **t.**, but knew not
2 K. 19 : 28. bec. thy rage ag. me and thy **t.** is come, Is. 37 : 29. ⌈peo.
Ps. 65 : 7. Which stilleth the **t.** of
74 : 23. **t.** of those that rise ag. thee
83 : 2. lo, thine enemies make a **t.**
Is. 33 : 3. At noise of **t.** people fled
Je. 11 : 16. with gr. **t.** kindled fire ⌈**t.**
Eze. 7 : † 11. none remain, nor of their
Ho. 10 : 14. shall **t.** rise am. thy peo-
Am. 2 : 2. Moab shall die with **t.** ⌊ple
3 : 9. behold great **t.** in midst ⌈them
Zch. 14 : 13. great **t.** fr. Lord among
Mat. 27 : 24. but rather a **t.** was made
Mk. 5 : 38. seeth **t.** and them th. wept
Lu. 22 : † 6. to betray him without **t.**
Ac. 21 : 34. not know certainty for **t.**
24 : 18. nei. with multitude nor **t.**
1 Co. 14 : † 33. G. is not author of **t.**
2 Co. 6 : 5. ministers in stripes in **t-s**
12 : 20. lest be swellings, **t-s** ⌈**t.**
Ja. 3 : † 16. where strife is, there is

TUMULTUOUS, LY. ⌈the

Ps. 2 : † 1. Why do heathen **t-y** assem-
Is. 13 : 4. a **t.** noise of the kingdoms
22 : 2. art a **t.** city, a joyous city
Je. 48 : 45. devour head of the **t.** ones
Eze. 7 : † 1. nor any of **t.** persons
Da. 6 : † 6. princes came **t-y** together

TUNES. ⌈to **t.**

Ha. 3 : † 1. prayer of Habakkuk acc-g
1 Co. 14 : † 7. exc. give distinct-n in **t.**

TURBANS. ⌈in **t.**

Da. 3 : † 21. These men were bound

TURN. [Noun.] ⌈go in

Es. 2 : 12. when every maid's **t.** to
15. when the **t.** of Esther was come

TURN. [Verb.] ⌈or left

Ge. 24 : 49. that I may **t.** to the right
Ex. 14 : 2. Speak unto Isr. that th. **t.**
23 : 27. make enemies **t.** their backs
32 : 12. **t.** from thy fierce wrath and
Le. 19 : 4. **t.** ye not unto idols, nor
Nu. 14 : 25. To morrow **t.** you, get
20 : 17. we will not **t.** to right hand
21 : 22. we will not **t.** into fields or
22 : 23. he smote the ass to **t.** her
26. was no way to **t.** to the right
34 : 4. your border sh. **t.** from south
De. 1 : 7. **t.** ye, go to mount of Amor.
40. **t.** ye, take journey into wilder.
2 : 3. enough, **t.** you northward
27. I will nei. **t.** unto right nor left
13 : 17. that Lord may **t.** fr. fiercen.
14 : 25. Then shall **t.** it into money
16 : 7. **t.** in morning unto thy tents
30 : 3. Lord will **t.** their captivity
31 : 20. will they **t.** unto other gods
Jos. 1 : 7. **t.** not from it to right or l.
22 : 23. an altar to **t.** from Lord, 29.
24 : 20. he will **t.** and do you hurt
Ju. 20 : 8. nei. will **t.** into his house
1 S. 14 : 7. **t.** thee, I am with thee
22 : 17. **t.** and slay priests of L., 18.
2 S. 14 : 19. none can **t.** to right or l.
24. Let him **t.** to his own house
15 : 31. Lord, **t.** Ahithophel's coun.
1 K. 8 : 35. if they **t.** from their sin, 2 Ch. 6 : 26, 37.-7 : 14. ⌈ing me
9 : 6. if you shall at all **t.** fr. follow-
17 : 3. **t.** eastward and hide thyself
22 : 34. **t.** thine hand, 2 Ch. 18 : 33.
2 K. 9 : 18. Jehu said, **t.** behind me,
17 : 13. **t.** ye fr. your evil ways ⌊19.
Je. 18 : 8.-26 : 3. Zch. 1 : 3, 4.
1 Ch. 12 : 23. to **t.** kingdom of Saul
2 Ch. 35 : 22. Josiah wou. not **t.** face
Ne. 1 : 9. if ye **t.** and keep my commandments, Eze. 3 : 20.-18 : 21.
-33 : 11, 14, 19. ⌈their own head
4 : 4. and **t.** their reproach upon
9 : 26. prophets which testified to **t.**
Jb. 5 : 1. to wh. of saints wilt thou **t.** ?
14 : 6. **t.** from him that he may rest
23 : 13. in one mind, who can **t.** him?
24 : 4. They **t.** needy out of the way
Ps. 4 : 2. will ye **t.** my glory into sha.?
7 : 12. If he **t.** not, he will whet swo.
20 : † 3 Lord **t.** to ashes thy sacrifice
21 : 12. sh. make them **t.** their back
25 : 16. **t.** unto me, 69 : 16.-86 : 16.
41 : † 3. wilt **t.** all his bed in sickn-s
85 : 4. **t.** us, O God of our salvation
119 : 79. those that fear thee **t.** unto
132 : 11. L. sworn unto Da., will not
Pr. 1 : 23. **t.** you at my reproof ⌊**t.**
4 : 15. pass not by it, **t.** from it and
27. **t.** not to the right hand nor to
Can. 2 : 17. **t.** my beloved, be like roe
Is. 1 : 25. will **t.** my hand upon thee
13 : 14. every man **t.** to own people
19 : 6. shall **t.** the rivers far away
22 : 18. he will violently **t.**, toss thee
23 : 17. she shall **t.** to her hire and
28 : 6. strength to them th. **t.** battle
30 : 21. when ye **t.** to right hand
31 : 6. **t.** ye unto him fr. whom Isr.
59 : 20. **t.** from transgression in Jac.
Je. 2 : 35. his anger shall **t.** from me

Je.3:7.t.unto me; she returned not,
13 : 16. t.it into shadow of death[14.
31 : 13. I will t.their mour-g into joy
18. t. me and I shall be turned
44 : 5. heark-d not to t. fr. wickedn.
50 : 16. shall t.every one to his peo.
La. 5 : 21. t. us unto thee, O Lord
Eze.3 : 19.he t.not fr.wickedn., 33:9.
4 : 8. shalt not t. thee from one side
7 : 22. My face will I t. from them
14 : 6. Repent and t. yourselves fr.
your idols, 18 : 30, 32.-33 : 9,
11. Ho. 12 : 6. Jo. 2 : 12. [live
33 : 14. if he t. from his sin, he sh.
19. if wicked t. from wickedness
36 : 9. I will t., and ye shall be tilled
38 : 12.to t. thine hand upon desol.
Da. 9 : 13. that we might t. fr. iniq-s
11 : 18 sh. t. his face unto the isles,
cause reproach to t. upon him
19.shall t. his face toward the fort
12 : 3. that t. many to righteousn.
Ho. 5 : 4.not frame their doings to t.
12 : 6. Therefore t. thou to thy God
Am. 1 : 8. I will t. mine hand ag. Ek.
5 : 7.who t. judgment to wormwood
8 : 10. I will t. feasts into mourn-g
Jon. 3 : 8. t. every one from evil way
Na. 2 : † 8. none shall cause th. to t.
Zph. 3 : 9. I t.to peo.a pure language
Zch. 9 : 12. t.to strong hold, ye pris.
13 : 7. t. mine hand upon little ones
Mal. 4 : 6. he shall t. the heart of
fathers to children, Lu. 1 : 17.
Mat. 5 : 39.smite on thy right cheek,
t. to him the other [timony
Lu. 21 : 13. shall t. to you for a tes-
Ac. 13 : 46. lo, we t. to the Gentiles
14 : 15.ye sho. t.from these vanities
26 : 18. to t. them fr.darkn-s to light
20. should repent and t. to God
Ph. 1 : 19. this sh. t. to my salvation
Tit.1 : 14.com-ts of men th.t.fr.truth
Ja. 3 : 3. and we t. their whole body
2 Pe 2 : 21. to t. from holy comm-t
Re. 11 : 6. have power to t. waters to

TURN again. [blood

Le. 13 : 16. if raw flesh t.a. and be
Ju. 11 : 8. Thf. we t.a. to thee now
Ru. 1 : 11. said, t.a., my dau-s. 12.
1 S. 15 : 25. I pray, t.a. with me.30.
1 K. 8 : 33. when Israel t.a. to thee
12 : 27. people t.a. unto their lord
13 : 9.eat not, nor t.a.same way,17.
2 K. 1 : 6. Go, t.a. to k. th. sent you
20 : 5. t.a. and tell Hezekiah, capt.
2 Ch. 30 : 6. Isr. t.a. unto the Lord
9. if ye t.a.unto L.,find compas-n
Jb. 34 : 15. man shall t.a.unto dust
Ps. 18 : 37. neither did I t.a. till they
60 : 1. O God t. thyself to us a.
80 : 3. t. us a., O Lord God, 7, 19.
85 : 8.but let them not t.a. to folly
104 : 9.they t. not a. to cover earth
126 : 4. t.a.our captivity as streams
Ec. 3 : 20. of dust, all t. to dust a.
Je. 25 : 5.t. ye a. ev. one fr. evil way
31 : 21. t.a., O virgin of Israel, t.
a. to these thy cities [to the L.
La. 3 : 40. let us try our ways, t.a.
Eze. 8 : 6. t.a., thou shalt see, 13,15.
Mi.7 : 19.He will t.a.,have compas-n
Zch. 10 : 9. live wi. children and t.a.
Mat. 7 : 6. lest th. t.a. and rend you
Lu. 10 : 6. if not, it shall t. to you a.
17 : 4.seven times in day t.a.to thee
Ga. 4 : 9. how t. ye a. to weak ele-

TURN aside. [ments

Ex. 3. 3.I will t.a. and see the sight
De. 5 : 32. sh. not t.a. to right hand
11 : 16. ye t.a. serve other gods,28.
17 : 20. that he t. not a. fr. com-nt
31 : 29. after my death ye will t.a.
Jos. 23 : 6. that ye t. not a. to right
or left, 1 S. 12 : 20, 21. [ger
Ju. 19 : 12.not t.a.into city of stran-
Ru. 4 : 1. Ho, t.a., sit down here

2 S. 2 : 21. Asahel, t.a., take armour,
23. howbeit he refused to t.a. [22.
18 : 30. king said, t.a., stand here
Jb. 36 : † 18.ransom can-t t. thee a.
Ps. 40 : 4. not such as t.a. to lies[a.
101 : 3. I hate work of them that t.
125 : 5.such as t.a. to crooked ways
Is. 10 : 2. To t.a. needy fr. judgment
29 : 21. t.a. just for thing of nought
30 : 11.say to seers, t.a. out of path
La. 3 : 35. to t.a. the right of a man
Am. 2 : 7. that t.a. the way of meek
5 : 12.they t.a. the poor in the gate
Mal. 3 : 5. that t.a. stranger fr. his

TURN away. [right

Ge. 27 : 44.until thy bro.'s fury t.a.
45. until thy brother's anger t.a.
Nu. 32 : 15. For if ye t.a. fr.aft.him,
De.30 : 17.Jos.22 : 16,18.2Ch.7 : 19.
De. 7 : 4. they will t.a. thy son from
13 : 5. spoken to t. you a. fr. Lord
17 : 17. Nei. multiply wives, that
his heart t. not a. [and t.a.
23 : 14. that he see no unclean thi.
1 K. 2 : † 16. I ask, t. not a. my face
11 : 2. surely will t.a. your heart
2 K. 18 : 24. how wilt thou t.a. face
of one captain? Is. 36 : 9. [them
1 Ch. 14 : 14. Go not up, t.a. from
2 Ch. 6 : 42. O Lord t. not a. face of
thine anointed, Ps. 132 : 10.
25 : 27.Amaziah did t.a. from Lord
29 : 10. a covenant with God that
wrath may t.a., 30 : 8. Ps. 106:
23. Pr. 24 : 18. [you
30 : 9. Lord will not t.a. face from
Jb. 9 : †12.who can t.him a.?11:†10.
Ps. 119 : 37. t.a. mine eyes fr.vanity
39. t.a. my reproach which I fear
Pr. 25 : 10.lest thine infamy t. not a.
29 : 8. but wise men t.a. wrath
Can. 6 : 5. t.a. thine eyes fr. me [a.
Is. 47 : †10.wisdom caused thee to t.
58 : 13. If t.a. foot from sabbath
Je. 2 : 24. in her occasion who t. her
3 : 19. thou sh. not t.a. fr. me[a. ?
8 : 4. shall he t.a. and not return ?
18 : 20. I stood to t.a. thy wrath
29 : 14.I will t.a. your capt-y,Zph.
32 : 40. I will not t.a. fr. them[2:7.
La. 2 : 14. to t.a. thy captivity
Eze. 14 : 6. t.a. your faces fr. abom.
Am. 1 : 3. for four I will not t.a.
punishm-t, 6,9,11,13.-2 : 1,4,6.
Jon. 3 : 9. God will t.a. fr. his anger
Mal. 2 : 6. did t. many a. fr. iniquity
Mat. 5 : 42. borrow of thee, t. not a.
Ac. 13 : 8.to t.a. the deputy fr. faith
Ro. 11 : 26. t.a. ungodlin-s fr. Jacob
2 Ti. 3 : 5. traitors, from such t.a.
4 : 4. shall t.a.their ears from truth
He. 12 : 25. how escape if we t.a. fr.

TURN back. [him

De. 23 : 13. t.b., cover that which
2 S. 19 : 37. t.b. that I may die in
2 K. 19 : 28. I will put a hook in thy
nose and t. thee b., Is. 37 : 29.
Ps. 44 : 10. makest us to t.b. fr. ene.
56 : 9. shall mine enemies t.b. [my
Is. 14 : 27. his hand, who sh.t.it b.?
43 : † 13.I will work, who sh.t.it b.
Je. 4 : 28. neither will I t.b. from it
6 : 9. t.b. hand as a grapegatherer
21 : 4.I will t.b.the weapons of war
49 : 8. Flee ye, t.b., O ye inhabit-ts
Eze. 38 : 4. and I will t. thee b.,39:2.
Zph. 3 : 20.when I t.b. your captiv-y
Mk. 13 : 16.not t.b. to take up garm.
Ga. 4 : † 9. how t. ye b. to beggarly

TURN in. [elements?

Ge. 19 : 2.Behold now,my lords, t.i.
Ju. 4 : 18. t.i., my lord, t.i. to me
19 : 11. Let us t.i. to city of Jebus.
2 K. 4 : 10. man of G. sh. t.i.[i., 16.
Pr. 9 : 4. Whoso is simple, let him t.

TURN to or unto the Lord.

De. 4 : 30. if thou t. - thy G., 30:10.

2 Ch. 15 : 4. in their trouble did t. -
Ps. 22 : 27. ends of the world sh. t. -
La. 3 : 40. let us try our ways, t. -
Ho. 14 : 2.Take with you words, t. -
Jo. 2 : 13. rend your heart and t. -
Lu. 1 : 16. many of Israel sh. he t. -
2 Co. 3 : 16. neverthel.when it sh.t.-

TURNED. [way

Ge. 3 : 24.flaming sword wh. t. every
18 : 22. men t. and went tow. Sod.
38 : 16. he t. unto her by the way
42 : 24. Joseph t. fr.them and wept
Ex. 7 : 15. rod wh. was t. to serpent
17. waters in the river sh. be t. to
blood, 20. Ps. 78 : 44.-105 : 29.
23. Pha-h t., went into his house
10 : 6. Moses t., went out fr. Pha-h
19. Lord t. a strong west wind
14 : 5. heart of Pha.was t. ag. peo.
32 : 15. Moses t.,went down fr. m-t
Le. 13 : 3. when the hair is t. white,
10, 13, 17, 20, 25. [white
4. if the hair thereof be not t.
Nu. 21 : 33. they t. by way of Bashan
22 : 33. ass t. from me three times
De. 1 : 24. they t. and went up mt.
2 : 1. we t.,took journey into wilder.
8.we t.,passed by way of Moab,3:1.
9 : 15. So I t., came down fr., 10 : 5.
23 : 5. t. curse into blessing, Ne. 13:
31 : 18. are t. unto other gods [2.
Jos. 7 : 12. Isr. t. back bef. enemies
26. Lord t. fr. fierceness of anger
19 : 12. border t. from Sarid eastw.
Ju. 2 : 17. t. quickly out of the way
15 : 4. firebrands and t. tail to tail
18 : 15. t., came to house of Levite
21. they t., and put little ones, 26.
23. they t. faces, said unto Micah
20 : 42. t. their backs before Israel
45. they t. and fled, 47. 2 K. 9 : 23.
Ru. 3 : 8. man was afraid and t. [t.
1 S. 4 : † 19.travailed, her pains were
10 : 6. thou sh. be t. into ano. man
9. when he had t. his back to go
13 : 17. comp-y t. unto way, 18. (2)
14 : 21. they t. to be wi. Israelites
47. whitherso. he t. he vexed them
15 : 27. as Samuel t. to go away
17 : 30. David t. from him toward
22 : 18. Doeg t. and fell upon priests
25 : 12. David's young men t.[Abn.
2 S. 2 : 19. Asahel t. not fr. following
19 : 2. victory was t. into mourn-g
1 K. 2 : 15. the kingdom is t. about
28. Joab t. after Adonijah, though
8 : 14. king t. his face and blessed
10 : 13. queen t.,went to own coun.
11 : 9. his heart was t. fr. the Lord
2 K. 5 : 12. Naaman t., went in rage
9 : 23. Joram t. his hands and fled
16 : 18. Ahaz t. covert fr. hou. of L.
20 : 2. t. his face to the wall,Is.38:2.
23 : 16. as Josiah t. hims. he spied
25. king that t. to Lord like him
26. Lord t. not from his wrath
34. t. his name to Jehoi-m, 2 Ch.
24 : 1. Jehoiakim t., rebelled[36 : 4.
1 Ch. 10 : 14. he t. kingd. unto Dav.
2 Ch. 6 : 3. king t. face,blessed cong.
9 : 12. queen t. went to her own la.
12 : 12. wrath of Lord t. from him
20 : 10. chil. of Ammon t. from him
29 : 6. our fath-s have t. their backs
Ezr. 6 : 22 t. heart of king of Assyria
10 : 14. until wrath of our God be t.
Ne. 9 : 35.nei. t. they fr. wicked works
Es. 9 : 1. though it was t. to contrary
22. month which was t. fr. sorrow
Jb. 16 : 11. God t. me into hands of
19 : 19. whom I loved are t. ag. me
20 : 14. his meat in his bowels is t.
28 : 5. und. it is t. up as it were fire
30 : 15. Terrors are t. upon me
31. my harp is t. to mourning
31 : 7. If my step hath t. out of way
37 : 12. cloud is t. by his counsels

Jb. 38 : 14. It is t. as clay to the seal
41 : 22. sorrow is t. into joy bef. him
28. slingstones are t. into stubble
42 : 10. Lord t. captivity of Job[hell
Ps. 9 : 17. The wicked sh. be t. into
30 : 11. Thou hast t. my mourning
32 : 4. moisture is t. into drought
66 : 6. He t. the sea into dry land
81 : 14. t. my hand ag. their adver-s
85 : 3. t. thys. fr. fierceness of anger
89 : 43. Thou hast t. edge of sword
105 : 25. He t. their heart to hate peo.
114 : 8. t. rock into standing water
119 : 59. I t. my feet unto thy testim.
Ec. 2 : 12. I t. mys. to behold wisdom
Is. 21 : 4. my pleasure he t. into fear
29 : 17. Leb. be t. into fruitful field
34 : 9. streams shall be t. into pitch
38 : 2. Hez-h t. his face to the wall
53 : 6. t. every one to his own way
60 : † 5. noise of sea be t. tow. thee
63 : 10. he was t. to be their enemy
Je. 2 : 21. how art thou t. into degen.
27. t. their backs unto me. 32 : 33.
3 : 10. not t. unto me wi whole heart
6 : 12. their houses be t. unto oth-s
8 : 6. every one t. to his course, as
23 : 22. should have t. from evil way
30 : 6. all faces are t. into palenesss
31 : 18. turn me, and I shall be t.
19. Surely after I was t. I repented
34 : 15. ye were t., had done right
16. but ye t., polluted my name, 11.
48 : 39. how hath Moab t. the back
La. 1 : 20. L. mine heart is t. within
3 : 3. Surely against me is he t.[me
5 : 2. Our inherit-e is t. to strangers
15. our dance is t. into mourning
21. Turn us unto thee, O Lord,
and we shall be t. [12.-10 : 11.(2)
Eze. 1 : 9. they t. not when th. went,
9 : † 2. gate, wh. is t. toward north
10 : 16. same wheels t. not fr. beside
17 : 6. a vine, whose branches t.
26 : 2. she is t. unto me [tow. him
42 : 19. We t. about to west side
Da. 10 : 8. my comeliness was t. into
16. by the vision my sorrows are t.
Ho. 7 : 8. Ephraim is a cake not t.
11 : 8. Ephraim, mine heart is t.
Jo. 2 : 31. sun t. into darkn., Ac. 2 : 20.
Am. 6 : 12. have t. judgm. into gall
Jon. 3 : 10. that they t. from evil way
Ha. 2 : 16. cup of L.'s hand be t. to
Hag. 2 : 17. I smote, ye t. not to me
Zch. 5 : 1. I t., lifted mine eyes, 6 : 1.
14 : 10. land shall be t. into a plain
Mat. 9 : 22. Jesus t. him and said
16 : 23. t., said unto Pe., Mk. 8 : 33.
Mk. 5 : 30. Jesus t. in the press and
Lu. 7 : 9. he t., said, I have not found
44. he t. to woman, said to Simon
9 : 55. he t. and rebuked them
10 : 23. he t. unto disciples, said
14 : 25. he t., said unto multitude
22 : 61. Lord t., looked upon Peter
Jn. 1 : 38. Jes. t., saw them follow-g
16 : 20. your sorrow be t. into joy
20 : 16. She t. hers., saith, Rabboni
Ac. 7 : 42. God t. and gave them up
9 : 35. all at Lydda t. to the Lord
11 : 21. a great numb. t. to the Lord
15 : 19. which fr. Gent. are t. to God
16 : 18. Paul t., and said to spirit
17 : 6. have t. the world upside down
1 Th. 1 : 9. how ye t. to G. from idols
2 Ti. 4 : 4. they sh. be t. unto fables
He. 11 : 34. t. to flight the armies of
12 : 13. lest lame be t. out of way
Ja. 3 : 4. are t. with very small helm
4 : 9. y-r laughter be t. to mourn-g
2 Pe. 2 : 22. dog is t. to his own vomit
Re. 1 : 12. I t. to see the voice which

TURNED again.

Ex. 4 : 7. was t.a. as his other flesh
33 : 11. Moses t.a. into the camp
Nu. 33 : 7. they t.a. into Pi-hahiroth
Jos. 8 : 21. they t.a., slew men of Ai
Ju. 3 : 19. Ehud t.a. from quarries
8 : 33. Israel t.a., went a whoring
20 : 41. Isr. t.a., Benjam-s amazed,
1 S. 15 : 31. So Samuel t.a. [48.
2 S. 22 : 38. I t. not a. until I had[a.
1 K. 18 : 37. thou hast t. their hearts
2 K. 5 : 26. when man t.a. fr. chariot
Ps. 126 : 1. When L. t.a. captivity of

TURNED aside. [Zion

Ex. 3 : 4. Lord saw he t.a. to see
32 : 8. They have t.a. quickly out
of the way, De. 9 : 12, 16.
Nu. 22 : 23. ass saw angel, t.a. out
Ju. 14 : 8. t.a. to see lion's carcass
19 : 15. they t.a. to lodge in Gibeah
Ru. 4 : 1. he t.a. and sat down
1 S. 6 : 12. kine t. not a. to the right
8 : 3. t.a. after lucre, took bribes
2 S. 18 : 30. Ahimaaz t.a., stood still
1 K. 15 : 5. David t. not a. from any
20 : 39. a man t.a., bro-t man unto
22 : 32. t.a. to fight ag. Jehosh-t
43. Jehosh-t t. not a., doing right
2 K. 22 : 2. Josiah t. not a. to right
Jb. 6 : 18. paths of their way are t.a.
Ps. 78 : 57. t.a. like a deceitful bow
Can. 6 : 1. whith. is thy beloved t.a.?
Is. 44 : 20. deceived heart t. him a.
La. 3 : 11. He hath t.a. my ways
Mat. 2 : 22. he t.a. into parts of Gali.
1 Ti. 1 : 6. t.a. unto vain jangling
5 : 15. For some are t.a. after Satan

TURNED away.

Nu. 14 : 43. bec. ye are t.a. fr. Lord
20 : 21. wheref. Israel t.a. from him
25 : 4. that anger of Lord be t.a.
11. Phinehas hath t. my wrath a.
1 K. 11 : 3. wives t.a. his heart, 4.
21 : 4. Ahab t.a., would eat no bread
2 Ch. 29 : 6. fathers t.a. their faces
Ps. 66 : 20. not t.a. his mercy fr. me
78 : 38. many a time t. his anger a.
90 : † 9. our days t.a. in thy wrath
Is. 5 : 25. For all this, anger not t.a.,
but, 9 : 12, 17, 21.-10 : 4.[t. I a.
12 : 1. thine anger is t.a. [50 : 5. nor
59 : 14. A judgment is t.a. backw-d
Je. 5 : 25. Your iniq-s have t.a. these
38 : 22. thy feet are t.a. back
46 : 5. have I seen them t.a. [mts.
50 : 6. shepherds have t. them a. on
Da. 9 : 16. thy fury be t.a. fr. Jerus.
Ho. 14 : 4. mine anger is t.a. fr. him
Na. 2 : 2. L. t.a. excellency of Jacob
Ac. 19 : 26. Paul hath t.a. much peo.
2 Ti. 1 : 15. all they in Asia be t.a. fr.

TURNED back. [me

Jos. 8 : 20. people t.b. upon pursu-
11 : 10. Joshua at th. time t.b.[ers
1 S. 15 : 11. Saul is t.b. fr. following
2 S. 1 : 22. bow of Jonathan t. not b.
1 K. 18 : 37. thou hast t. their heart b.
22 : 33. saw it was not k. they t.b.
2 K. 1 : 5. when the messengers t.b.,
he said, Why are ye t.b.?
2 : 24. he t.b., looked on them, and
15 : 20. So the king of Assyria t.b.
1 Ch. 21 : 20. Ornan t.b., saw angel
2 Ch. 18 : 32. they t.b. fr. pursuing
Ne. 2 : 15. I viewed the wall and t.b.
Jb. 34 : 27. Because they t.b. fr. him
Ps. 9 : 3. When mine enemies are t.b.
35 : 4. let them be t.b. that devise
my hurt, 70 : 3. [thy way
44 : 18. Our heart is not t.b. from
78 : 9. Ephraim t.b. in day of battle
41. they t.b. and tempted God, 57.
129 : 5. them be t.b. that hate Zion
Is. 42 : 17. be t.b. that trust in ima.
Je. 4 : 8. anger of Lord is not t.b.
11 : 10. are t.b. to iniq-s of fathers
46 : 21. they are t.b. and are fled
La. 1 : 13. he hath t. me b. and made
Zph. 1 : 6. that are t.b. fr. the Lord
Lu. 2 : 45. t.b. to Jerus. seeking him
17 : 15. one of lepers t.b., glorified
Jn. 20 : 14. she t. herself b., saw Jes.
Ac. 7 : 39. in their hearts t.b. into

TURNED in or into. [Eg.

Ge. 19 : 3. two angels t.i. unto Lot
38 : 1. Judah t.i. to Hirah, Adull-e
Ju. 4 : 18. Sisera had t.i. unto Jael
18 : 3. Danites t.i. and said to him
2 K. 4 : 8. Elisha t.i. to eat bread
11. he t.i-o chamber and lay there

TURNEST. [thou t.

1 K. 2 : 3. mayest prosper whitherso.
Jb. 15 : 13. thou t. thy spirit ag. God
Ps. 90 : 3. Thou t. man to destruct n

TURNETH.

Le. 20 : 6. soul that t. after wizards
De. 23 : † 11. when it t. tow. evening
29 : 18. whose heart t. away fr. God
Jos. 7 : 8. when Israel t. their backs
19 : 27. border t. toward sunrising
29. coast t. to Ramah, t. to Hosah
34. then the coast t. westward to
2 K. 21 : † 13. wipeth t. it upon face
Jb. 39 : 22. horse t. not from sword
Ps. 107 : 33. He t. rivers into wildern.
35. He t. wilderness into water
146 : 9. way of wicked he t. upside
Pr. 15 : 1. A soft answer t. aw. wrath
17 : 8. gift, whitherso. it t. prosper.
21 : 1. he t. the king's heart [eth
26 : 14. as door t. upon his hinges
28 : 9. t. his ear from hearing law
30 : 30. a lion that t. not aw. for any
Ec. 1 : 6. wind t. about unto north
Can. 1 : 7. why I be as one th. t. aside
Is. 9 : 13. people t. not unto him
24 : 1. Lord t. the earth upside down
44 : 25. that t. wise men backward
Je. 14 : 8. that t. to tarry for a night
49 : 24. Damascus feeble, t. to flee
La. 1 : 8. she sigheth, t. backward
3 : 3. he t. his hand ag. me all day
Eze. 18 : 24. when righteous t. from
righte-sn., 26.-33 : 18.[28.-33 : 12.
27. when wicked man t. fr. his
Am. 5 : 8. t. shadow of death into

TURNING. [Adj., Part.]

2 K. 21 : 13. wipe Jerus., as a dish t. it
Is. 57 : † 17. I wroth, went on t. aw.
Eze. 41 : 24. doors had two t. leaves
Mi. 2 : 4. t. away, he divided fields
Lu. 23 : 28. Jesus t., said, Dau-s of
Jn. 21 : 20. Peter t., seeth disci.[Jeru.
Ac. 9 : 40. Peter t. said, Tabitha arise
2 Pe. 2 : 6. God t. Sodom into ashes
Jude 4. t. grace of God into lascivi-

TURNING. [Noun.] [ousness

2 Ch. 36 : 13. hardened fr. t. unto L.
Pr. 1 : 32. t. away of simple sh. slay
Is. 29 : 16. your t. of things upside
Ac. 3 : 26. bless in t. you fr. iniquit-s
Ja. 1 : 17. with wh. is no shadow of t.

TURNING of the wall.

2 Ch. 26 : 9. Uzzah built towers at t. -
Ne. 3 : 19. repaired Ezer at t. -, 20,

TURTLE, S. [24, 25.

Le. 12 : 8. she sh. bring two t-s, 15 : 29.
Nu. 6 : 10. eighth day bring two t-s
Can. 2 : 12. voice of the t. is heard in
Je. 8 : 7. t. and crane observe time

TURTLEDOVE, S.

Ge. 15 : 9. take a t. and young pigeon
Le. 1 : 14. sh. bring his offering of t-s
5 : 7. he sh. bring 2 t-s, 14 : 22, 30.-15 :
11. if not able to bring two t-s[14.
12 : 6. shall bring a t. for sin offer-g
Ps. 74 : 19. deliver not soul of thy t.
Lu. 2 : 24. sacrifice acc. to law, pair

TUTORS. [of t-s

Ga. 4 : 2. heir while a child is under

TWAIN. [t.

1 S. 18 : 21. my son in law in one of t.
2 K. 4 : 33. shut door upon them t.
Is. 6 : 2. with t. he covered his face,
with t. he covered his feet, and
with t. he did fly [t.
Je. 34 : 18. when they cut the calf in
Eze. 21 : 19. t. sh. come out of one la.

Mat. 5: 41 go a mile, go with him t.
19 5. and they t. sh be one flesh
6. they are no more t.. Mk 10: 8.
21: 31. Whe. of t. did will of fath.?
27 21. Whe. of t. will ye I release
51. the vail of temple was rent in
t., Mk. 15 · 38 [one new man
Ep. 2: 15 to make in himself of t.

TWELFTH.

1 K 19: 19. 12 yoke of oxen, he wi. t.
Re. 21 20. t. foundation an ameth
See CAPTAIN, DAY, LOT,
MONTH, YEAR.

TWELVE. [spoons

Nu. 7 · 84 t. chargers, t. bowls, t-
87. t. bullocks, t. rams, t. lambs
29 · 17. on 2nd day offer t. bullocks
33: 9. in Elim were t. fountains
2 S 2: 15 went over t. of Benjamin
and t. of servants of David
Ezr. 8 · 24 I separated t. of chief of
35 offered t. bullocks for all Israel
Mat 10 5 These t. Jesus sent forth
14: 20 of fragments t. baskets,
Mk.6 43.-8 19 Lu.9: 17. Jn 6 13.
26: 14. Then one of t. called Judas
20. even was come, he sat down
with the t., Mk. 14: 17 Lu. 22 14
47 Judas one of the t. came, Mk.
14: 10,43. Lu. 22 3,47 Jn. 6·71.
Mk 3: 14. And he ordained t. that
4 · 10. they about him with the t.
6: 7. called unto him the t., 9 · 35
10: 32 took again the t., Lu. 18 31.
11 · 11. went unto Bethany wi. the t.
14: 20. It is one of the t. that dip-
Lu. 8. 1. the t. were with him [peth
9 · 12. came the t., said, Send mult
Jn 6· 67. Jesus unto the t., Will
70. Have I not chosen you t.?
20 · 24. Thomas, one of the t., not
Ac 6. 2. Then the t. called multitude
19 · 7. all the men were about t. [t.
1 Co 15 · 5. seen of Cephas, then of
Re. 21 12. city had t. gates, at gates
21. t. gates were t. pearls [t. angels
See APOSTLES, BRETHREN,
BULLS, CAKES

TWELVE cities. [19 15.

Jos. 18 24 t. c. with their villages,
21 7 children of Merari had t. c.,
40 (2) 1 Ch. 6 63.

TWELVE cubits.

1 K. 7 15 a line of t. c. did compass
either, Je. 52 · 21 [t. broad
Eze. 43 16. altar shall be t. c. long,
See DAYS, DISCIPLES, FOUNDATIONS, GOATS, HOURS, HUNDRED, LEGIONS, LIONS, MANNER, MEN, MONTHS, OFFICERS, OXEN, PATRIARCHS, PIECES, PILLARS, PRINCES, RODS, STARS, SIGNS, SONS
See SONS with brethren,
STONES, THOUSAND, THRONES,
TRIBES, WELLS, YEARS, YOKE.

TWENTIETH.

See DAY, LOT, YEAR.

One, Two, Three, or Four and TWENTIETH.

See DAY, LOT, YEAR

Five or Seven and TWENTIETH. See DAY, YEAR

TWENTY.

Ge. 18: 31. Peradventure be t. found,
will not destroy it for t.'s sake
32: 14 for Esau t. goats, t. rams
37: 28. sold Joseph for t. pieces of
Ex. 26: 18 t. boards on south side,
19, 20.-36: 23, 24, 25
27: 10. t. pillars, t. sockets of brass,
11 -38: 10, 11. [sons t.
Ezr. 8. 19. his brethren and their
See ASSES, BASINS, DAYS.

TWENTY cities. [c.

Ju. 11: 33 Jephthah smote even t.
1 K. 9: 11 Sol gave Hiram t. c. in

TWENTY cubits.

Ex. 27 · 16 for the gate of court a
hanging of t. c., 38: 18.
1 K. 6: 2 house for the Lord, the
breadth t. c., 2 Ch. 3 3 [3 4.
3. porch, t. c. was the length, 2 Ch.
16. he built t. c. on sides of house
20. oracle in forepart was t. c. (2)
2 Ch. 3: 11 wings of cherub. t. c., 13.
8. the most holy house, length
was t. c., and breadth t. c. [c. the
4· 1. made altar, t. c. the length, t.
Eze. 40· 49 length of porch was t. c.
41: 2. breadth of door was t. c., 4.
10. between the chambers was t. c.
42: 3. Over ag. the t. c. was gallery
Zch 5: 2. length of flying roll t. c.
See FATHOMS, GERAHS, LOAVES,
MALES, MEASURES, MEN, OXEN, SERVANTS, SHEKELS.
See Twenty YEARS.

One and TWENTY. [days

Da. 10: 13. prince withstood me -t.

TWENTY two or three

Jos 19 30. t. t-o cities with villages
1 Ch. 2· 22 Jair had t-e and t. cities
12 · 28 of fa.'s house t. t-o captains
2 Ch 13 21. Abijah begat t. and t-o
See YEARS. [sons

TWENTY third. See YEAR.

Four and TWENTY.

Nu 7· 88. offerings were f. a. t. bul-ks
2 S 21 · 20. fingers and toes f. a. t.
See ELDERS, SEATS, YEARS.

TWENTY fifth. See DAY.

Five and TWENTY.

Eze. 40: 13. measured gate; breadth
f. a. t. cubits, 21, 25, 29, 30, 33, 36
See FURLONGS, MEN, SHEKELS,
YEARS

TWENTY sixth. See YEAR.

TWENTY seventh. See YEAR.

Eight and TWENTY.

Ex. 26 2. length of curtain -t. cub-s,
2 Ch. 11· 21 Rehob begat-t. sons [36: 9

TWENTY nine. [ents

Ex 38. 24. gold of offering t. n. tal-
Jos 15· 32. cities t. n. with villages
See MALES, YEARS
See Twenty THOUSAND.

TWICE. [t.

Ge. 41 · 32 the dream was doubled
43 † 10. we had returned t. by this
Ex. 16: 5. shall be t. as much, 22.
Nu. 20: 11 with rod smote rock t.
1 S 18. 11. Da. out of his presence t.
1 K 11. 9. had appeared unto him t
Jb. 40 5. t., but I proceed no further
42 · 10. Lord gave Job t. as much
Ps 62· 11. t. have I heard this; that
Ec. 6: 6. tho live 1,000 years t. told
Mk 14· 30 cock crow t.. deny me. 72.
Lu 18 · 12. I fast t. in the week, I
Jude 12. t. dead plucked up by the
See ONCE. [roots

TWIGS. [young t.

Eze 17 · 4. He cropped off top of his
22. I will crop off from top of his

TWILIGHT. [young t.

1 S 30 17. David smote them from t.
2 K 7 · 5 lepers rose in the t. to go
7 Syrians fled in the t., left tents
Jb 3 9. Let the stars of t. be dark
24 · 15 adulterer waiteth for the t.
Pr 7: 9. he went to her house in t.
Eze. 12 · 6. shalt carry it forth in t.
7 I digged, and bro t it forth in t.
12 prince shall bear it in the t.

TWINED. See **FINE Linen.**

TWINKLING. [eye

1 Co. 15 · 52. be changed in t. of an

TWINNED.

Ex 26 · † 24. boards shall be t. together, 36: † 29.

TWINS. [womb

Ge. 25 · 24 behold t. in Rebekah's
38· 27 behold t. in Tamar's womb

Can. 4: 2. every one beareth t., 6 6.
5. breasts like two roes th are t.,

TWO. [7: 3.

Ge. 6: 19 t. of every sort into ark, 20.
7 · 2. of beasts not clean by t.
9 There went t. and t. into ark, 15.
22: 3. Abr. took t. of his young men
25: 23. t. manner of people fr. thy
31: 33. Laban into t. maids-ts' tents
33 · 1 Jac. divided chil. unto t. hand-
Ex. 21 · 21. if contin. a day or t. [maids
25: 18. make t. cherubim in t. ends
of mercy seat, 19-37· 7, 8
35 sh be a knop and t. branches
of candlestick, (3) 37: 21 (3)
26 23 t. boards for corners of tabernacle in t. sides, 36 · 28.
24. they shall be for t. corners
28 7 ephod have t. shoulderpieces
12. Aa-n bear names upon t. shoul-
14 sh. make t. chains of gold [ders
23. make t. rings of gold, put on
t. ends of breastpl., 26-39. 16, 19.
25 t. ends of t. wreathen chains
fasten in the t. ouches, 39: 17, 18.
27. t. other rings put upon the t.
side of the ephod, 39 20.
30: 4 t. rings make to it by t. corners upon t. sides [rings upon
37: 3. t. rings upon one side, t.
27 t. rings by t. corners upon t.
39: 16 made t. ouches, t. gold rings
Le 12: 5. if maid unclean t. weeks
Nu. 7 · 3. wagon for t. of princes
7. t. wagons unto sons of [bly
10· 2 t. trumpets for calling assem-
18: 23. bare it between t. upon staff
22· 22. Balaam, t. servants wi. him
28: 11. offered t. y-g bullocks, 19, 27.
29 · 13 t. rams, 17, 20, 23, 26, 29, 32
De 9· 15. t. tables in my t. hands, 17.
14 · 6. cleaveth cleft into t. claws
32. 30. How t. put 10,000 to flight
Ju. 5. 30 to every man damsel or t.
9· 44. t. companies ran upon people
15: 13 bound Sams. wi. t. new cords
16: 28 I be avenged for my t. eyes
19: 10 with Levite t. asses saddled
Ru 1 19 they t. went to Beth-lehem
4: 11. wh. t. did build house of Isr.
1 S 11: 11. so th t. not left together
23: 18. t. made cov-t before L [wine
25: 18. Abigail took t. bottles of
30 · 12 gave t. clusters of raisins
2 S. 8: 2 with t. lines measured he
18: 24 David sat betw. the t. gates
1 K 8: 18. none save we t. in house
25. Divide the living child in t.
5: 12 Hiram, Sol, they t. made leag.
6. 32. The t. doors were of olive tree
34 the t. doors were of fir tree, the
t. leaves of door were folding
7: 16. he made t. chapiters of brass
41 The t. pillars and t. bowls on
top of the t. pillars, and the t.
networks to cover the t. bowls,
42. 2 Ch. 4 12, 13. [houses
9: 10. when Solo-n had built the t.
10 19 and t. lions stood beside the
stays, 2 Ch. 9 · 18 [field
11· 29. they t. were alone in the
16: 24. hill Samaria for t. talents
17: 12. I am gathering t. sticks to
18· 23. Let them give us t. bullocks
20 · 27 Isr. pitched like t. flocks of
2 K 2: 6 And they t. went on [kids
7 And they t. stood by Jordan
8 they t. went over on dry ground
12. Elisha rent clothes in t. pieces
24. came t. she bears out of wood
5: 17 to servant t. mules' burden
22. give t. changes of garments
23. Naaman said, Take t. talents;
he bound t. talents of silver in
t. bags, with t. changes of garments, and laid upon t. of his
7: 14 took t. chariot horses [serv-s

2 K.9: 32. looked out t.or 3 eunuchs
10: 8 king's sons. Lay in t. heaps
23: 12. altars Manasseh made in t.
courts, 2 Ch.33:5. [than the t.
1 Ch. 11: 21. he more honourable
26: 17. and tow Asuppim t. and t.
18. four at causeway, t. at Parbar
2 Ch. 4: 12. t. wreaths to cover, t.
pommels of chapiters, 13.
Ne. 12: 31. t. companies that gave
thanks, 40. [berlains
Es 6: 2. told t. of the king's cham-
Jb.42: 7 My wrath ag thy t. friends
Ec. 4: 9. t. are better than one
11. if t. lie together they have heat
12. if one prevail t. sh. withstand
Can. 4: 5. Thy t. breasts like t. roes,
6: 13. company of t. armies [7: 3.
Is. 7: 21 nourish yo. cow, t. sheep
Je. 2: 13. my people committed t.
3: 14. I will take t. of a family [evils
24: 1. t. baskets of figs were set bef.
33: 24 The t. families Lord cast off
Eze. 35: 10. t. countries sh be mine
37: 22. nei. into t. kingd-s any more
41: 18. every cherub had t. faces
23 The temple had t. doors
24 doors had t. leaves apiece (3)
47: 13 Joseph shall have t. port-ns
Da. 12: 5 behold there stood other t.
Ho. 10: 10 bind thems. in t. furrows
Am 3: 3 Can t. walk togeth. except
12 out of mouth of lion t. legs or
Zch. 4: 3. t. olive trees by candlest., 11.
12 What be these t. olive branches
wh. thro. t. golden pipes empty
14. These are the t. anointed ones
6: 1. 4 chariots from betw. t. mts.
11: 7 I took t. staves and fed flock
Mat. 8: 28 met him, t. possessed
18: 8. than having t. hands and t.
feet, Mk 9: 43, 45 [9: 47.
9. rather than having t. eyes, Mk.
16. not hear, then take one or t.
19. if t. of you shall agree [more
22: 40. On these t. com-ts hang the
24: 40 be t. in field, one taken [law
25: 15 to one 5 talents, to anoth. t.
17. rec'd t. he gained oth. t., 22(3)
Mk. 6: 7. began to send them by t.
and t., Mat. 21: 1. Lu. 10: 1.
12: 42. she threw in t. mites, farth.
16: 12. Aft. that Jes. appeared unto
Lu. 7: 41. creditor had t. debtors [t.
10: 35. took t. pence, gave to host
23: 32. t. malefactors led with him
24: 13. t. of them went to Emmaus
Jn. 1: 35 John stood and t. dis-ip.
37. the t. disciples followed Jesus
40. One of the t. wh. heard John
19: 18. crucified him and t. others
Ac. 1: 23. appointed t., Joseph and
24. shew whe. of these t. hast chos.
10: 7. Cornelius called t. of serv-ts
12: 6. Peter bound with t. chains
19: 22. Paul sent into Macedonia t.
34. all, about t. hours, cried out
21: 33. to be bound with t. chains
1 Co. 6: 16. t. sh. be one flesh, Ep. 5: 31.
Ga. 4: 24. these are the t. covenants
Ph. 1: 23 I am in a strait betwixt t.
Re. 9: 12. there come t. woes more
11: 4. these are t. olive trees and
t. candlesticks stand-g bef. God
10. these t. prophets tormented
See ANGELS, BAYS, BANDS, BIRDS, BRACELETS, BRETHREN, CALVES, CAPTAINS, CENTURIONS, CHERUBIM.

TWO cities. [villages
Jos. 15: 60. inherit of Jud t.c. wi.
21: 25. out of half tribe t.c., 27.
Am. 4: 8. t. or three c. wandered
See COATS, COURTS.

TWO cubits. [earth
Nu. 11: 31. as it were t.c. high upon
Eze. 40: 9 measured posts, t.c., 41: 3
Eze. 41: 22. altar of wood, length t.c.
43: 14. bottom to lower settle, t.c.
Ex 25: 10 ark of shittim wood; t.
c. and half the length, 17.-37: 6
23 make table; t.c. shall be the
length, 37: 10. [height, 37: 25
30: 2. make an altar, t.c. the
See DAUGHTERS, DAYS, DEALS, DISCIPLES, EDGES, FIRKINS, FISHES, GOATS, HORNS, HUNDRED, KIDNEYS, KIDS, KINE, KINGS, LAMBS, LOAVES, MASTERS, MEASURES, MEN, MITES, MONTHS, NATIONS, OFFICERS, OMERS, OPINIONS, OXEN, PARTS, PIGEONS, PILLARS, POSTS, RAMS, ROWS, SEAS, SHIPS, SIDES, SIGNS, SOCKETS, SOLDIERS, SONS, SOULS, SPARROWS, STONES, SWORDS, TABLES, TAILS, TENONS, THIEVES, THINGS, THOUSAND, THREE, TIMES, TRIBES, TRUMPETS, TURTLEDOVES, TURTLES, VESSELS, WALLS, WAYS, WINGS, WITNESSES, WIVES, WOMEN, YEARS.

TWOEDGED sword.
Ps. 149: 6. Let be a t.s. in their hand
Pr. 5: 4. her end is sharp as t.s. [s.
He 4: 12. word of G. sharper than t.
Re 1: 16. out of his mouth went t.s.

TWOFOLD
Mat 23: 15. make him t. more child

TWOLEAVED. [of hell
Is 45: 1. to open before him t. gates

TYCH'ICUS.
Ac. 20: 4. T. of Asia accompanied P.
Ep 6: 21. T. shall make known all
Col 4: 7. All my state sh. T declare
2 Ti 4: 12. T. have I sent to Ephesus
Tit 3: 12. When I sh. send T unto

TYPES. [thee
1 Co 10: †11. things happened for t.

TYRAN'NUS.
Ac. 19: 9. disputing in school of one

TYRE. [T.
Jos. 19: 29. coast turneth to city T.
2 S. 24: 7. came to strong hold of T.
1 K. 7: 13. S. fetched Hiram out of T
14. his fa. a man of T., 2 Ch 2: 14.
9: 12 Hiram came fr T. to see cities
1 Ch 22: 4. they of T bro-t cedar to
Ezr. 3: 7. gave meat to them of T
Ne 13: 16. dwelt men of T therein
Ps. 45: 12. dau of T. shall be there
83: 7. Philistines. wi inhabitants of
87: 4. behold Philistia and T. [T
Is. 23: 1. The burden of T, Howl
5. shall be pained at report of T
8 Who taken this counsel ag. T.
15. T shall be forgotten 70 years
17 after 70 yrs L will vi-it T., 15.
Jo. 3: 4. Yea, what have ye to do
with me, O T. and Zidon
Ac 21: 3. into Syria, landed at T
7 when we finished course from T.
See KING of Tyre. SIDON.

TY'RUS
or TY'RUS and Zidon.
Je. 25: 22. I made all the kings of
T a. Z to drink [a. Z
27: 3 send yokes to the kings of T.
47: 4. cut off from T. a. Z ev helper
Eze. 26: 2. because T said ag Jerus.
3 Behold I am against thee, O T.
4. they sh destroy the walls of T
7 I will bring upon T Nebuchad
15. saith L to T, Shall not isles
27: 2. take up lamentation for T.
3. T., O thou at entry of the sea (2)
8. wise men, O T, were thy pilots
32. What city like T. the destroved
28: 2 Son of man, say unto prince
12. lamenta-n upon k. of T [of T.
29: 18. a great service ag T. (3) [ed
Ho. 9: 13. Ephr., as I saw T., is plant-
Am. 1: 9. For transgressions of T
10. I will send a fire on wall of T.
Zch. 9: 2. T. a. Z. tho. it be very wise
3 T. heaped up silver as dust and

U.

U'CAL.
Pr. 30: 1. man spake unto Ithiel and

U'EL. [U
Ezr 10: 34. sons of Bani; Amram,

U'LAI. [U.
Da 9: 2. in vision I was by river U.
16. I heard voice betw. banks of U.

U'LAM. [Rem 17.
1 Ch. 7: 16 sons of Machir, U., Ra.
8: 39. sons of Eshek, U. his firstb-n
40. sons of U were mighty men

UL'LA. See REZIA.

UM'MAH.
Jos. 19: 30 for Asher, U and 22 cit.

UMPIRE. [ies
Jb 9: †33 Nei. any u. betwixt us

UNACCUSTOMED.
Je. 31: 18 Ephraim, as bullock u. to

UNADVISEDLY. [yoke
Ps. 106: 33. he spake u. with his lips

UNAWARES.
Ge 31: 26. Jacob stole away u., 26.
Nu 35: 11 slayer may flee thither,
who killeth person u., 15. De.
4: 42 Jos. 20: 3, 9. [him at u.
Ps. 35: 8 Let destruct-n come upon
Lu 21: 34. th day come upon you u.
Ga. 2: 4. false brethren u. brought in
He. 13: 2 have entertained angels u.
Jude 4. are certain men crept in u.

UNBELIEF. [of u.
Mat 13: 58 did not many works bec.
17: 20. not cast him out bec of u.
Mk. 6: 6 marvelled bec of their u.
9: 24. Lord, I believe, help mine u.
16: 14 upbraided them wi. their u.
Ro. 3: 3. u. make faith with-t effect?
4: 20. he staggered not through u.
11: 20 bec of u. were broken off
23. if they abide not still in u. sh.
30. obtained mercy thro' their u.
32. God hath concluded all in u.
Eph. 5: †6. wrath of G. on chil. of u.
1 Ti. 1: 13 I did it ignorantly in u.
He. 3: 12. in you an evil heart of u.
19. not enter in bec. of u., 4: 6
4: 11 any fall after same example

UNBELIEVERS. [of u.
Lu. 12: 46 appoint his portion wi u.
1 Co. 6: 6. bro goeth to law before u.
14: 23. there come in those th. are u.
2 Co. 6: 14 not unequally yoked with

UNBELIEVING. [u.
Ac 14: 2. u. Jews stirred up Gent-s
1 Co 7: 14. u. husband is sanctified
by wife, u. wife is sanctified by
15. if the u. depart, let him depart
Tit. 1: 15. unto u. is nothing pure
Re. 21: 8. u. shall have part in lake

UNBLAMEABLE.
Col. 1: 22. to present you holy, u.
1 Th. 3: 13. may stablish your hearts

UNBLAMEABLY. [u.
1 Th 2: 10. how u. we have behaved

UNCERTAIN. [sound
1 Co. 14: 8 if the trumpet give an u.
1 Ti. 6: 17 nor trust in u. riches, but

UNCERTAINLY.
1 Co. 9: 26 I theref. so run, not as u.

UNCERTAINTY.
1 Ti 6: †17. trust not in u. of riches

UNCHANGEABLE. [hood
He. 7: 24. this man hath u. priest-

UNCIRCUMCISED. [off
Ge 17: 14. u. man child sh. be cut
34: 14. cannot give sister to one u.
Ex. 6: 12. Pha. hear me of u. lips? 30
12: 48. no u. person eat of passover
Le. 19: 23. count the fruit u. 3 years

Le. 26 : 41. if their u. hearts humb.
Jos. 5 : 7. for their children were u.
Ju. 14 : 3. goest to take a wife of u.
15 : 18. shall I fall into hands of u.
1 S. 14 : 6. us go unto garrison of u.
17 : 26. who is this u. Philist-e? 36.
31 : 4. lest these u. thrust me thro.,
1 Ch. 10 : 4. [triumph
2 S. 1 : 20. lest daughters of the u.
Is. 52 : 1. no more come into thee u.
Je. 6 : 10. ear u., they can-t hearken
9 : 25. punish circumcised with u.
26. these nations are u., all u.
Eze. 28 : 10. shalt die death of the u.
31 : 18. shalt lie ' . midst of u., 32 ;
19, 21, 24, 25, 26, 27, 28, 29, 30, 32.
44 : 7. bro-t strangers u. in heart
and u. in flesh into sanct-y, 9.
Ac. 7 : 51. Ye stiffnecked, u. in heart
11 : 3. wentest into men u., didst eat
Ro. 4 : 11. faith he had being u., 12.
1 Co. 7 : 18. let him not become u.

UNCIRCUMCISION. [u.
Ro. 2 : 25. thy circumcision is made
26. if the u. keep righteousn. of
law, shall not his u. be counted
27. sh. not u. by nature judge thee?
3 : 30. sh. justify the u. thro. faith
4 : 9. blessedn-s on circumc-n or u.
10. when he was in circumcision
or u.? Not in circumc-n but u.
1 Co. 7 : 18. Is any man called in u.?
19. Circumc. is nothing, u. is noth.
Ga. 2 : 7. they saw gospel of u. committed unto me [nor u., 6 : 15.
5 : 6. neither circumcision availeth
Ep. 2 : 11. who are called U. by Circ.
Col. 2 : 13. you, dead in the u. of flesh
3 : 11. nei. circumcision nor u., but

UNCLE. [Ch.
Le. 10 : 4. son of Uzziel, u. of Aaron
20 : 20. if man lie with his u.'s wife,
hath uncov-d his u.'s nakedn-s
25 : 49. his u. or u.'s son may rede.
1 S. 10 : 14. Saul's u. said unto him,
14 : 50. son of Ner, Saul's u. [15, 16.
1 Ch. 27 : 32. Jonathan David's u.
Es. 2 : 7. Mord. bro-t up u.'s dau., 15.
Je. 32 : 7. son of Shallum thine u.
8. Hanameel my u.'s son, 9, 12.
Am. 6 : 10. man's u. sh. take him up

UNCLEAN.
Le. 10 : 10. that ye may put difference betw. u. and clean, 11 : 47
11 : 4. he is u. unto you, 5, 6, 7, 29.
De. 14 : 19. [14 : 7.
8. are u. to you, 26, 27, 28, 31. De.
24. for these ye shall be u.; whosoever toucheth carcass of them
shall be u. until the even, 25,
26, 27, 28, 29, 31, 32, 39, 40.-14:
46.-15 : 5, 6, 7, 8, 10, 11, 16, 17,
18, 19, 21, 22, 23, 27.-17 : 15.-
22 : 6. Nu. 19 : 7, 8, 10, 21, 22.
32. upon whatso. any of them fall
it shall be u., 33, 34, 35, 36, 38.-
13 : 51, 55.-15 : 4, 9, 20, 24, 26.
43. not with creeping thing make
yourselves u.
12 : 2. then she shall be u. 7 days,
5.-15 : 25. Nu. 19 : 11, 16. [u.
13 : 11. not shut him up; for he is
14. raw flesh appeareth, he be u.
45. leper in wh. plague cry, u., u.
14 : 36. all in house be not made u.
40. cast them into u. place, 41, 45.
44. leprosy in house it is u. [clean
57. To teach when it is u. and wh.
15 : 2. hath running issue he is u.
24. if lie with her he sh. be u. (2)
27. whoso. toucheth these things
be u., 22 : 4, 5. Nu. 19 : 13.
33. that lieth with her that is u.
20 : 25. difference betw. clean beasts
and u., and u. fowls and cle. (3)
22 : 5. or toucheth creeping thing
whereby made u.

Nu. 6 : 7. not make himself u. for fa.
9 : 10. be u. by reason of dead body
18 : 15. firstling of u. beasts redeem
; 14. all in the tent be u. 7 days
15. vessel wh. hath no covering u.
17. for u. person take ashes of hei.
19. clean shall sprinkle upon u.
20. man u. and not purify hims. (2)
21. toucheth water of separa-n u.
22. whatso. u. person toucheth
be u. (2) [th-f, 22.-15 : 22.
De. 1 . 15. u. and clean may eat
14 : 8. the swine it is u. unto you
10. whatsoever hath not fins is u.
19. creeping thing that flieth is u.
26 : 14. nei. aught for any u. use
Jos. 22 : 19. if land of possession u.
2 Ch. 23 : 19. house of God none u.
Ezr. 9 : 11. land is an u. land [enter
Jb. 14 : 4. Who bring clean out of u.?
36 : 14. hypocrites, their life am. u.
Ec. 9 : 2. is one event to clean and u.
Is. 6 : 5. I am a man of u. lips, and I
dwell in midst of peo. of u. lips
35 : 8. the u. shall not pass over it
52 : 1. no more come into thee the u.
La. 4 : 15. Depart ye, it is u., depart
Eze. 22 : 26. put no difference between clean and u. [u. and clean
44 : 23. cause them to discern betw.
Hag. 2 : 13. if one that is u. touch it
it shall be u. [is u.
14. and that which they offer there
Lu. 4 : 33. had a spirit of an u. devil
Ac. 10 : 28. not call any man u., 11 : 8
Ro. 14 : 14. nothing is u. of itself,
but to him that esteemeth any
thing to be u. to him it is u.
1 Co. 7 : 14. else were your children u.
Ep. 5 : 5. no u. person hath inherit-e
He. 9 : 13. ashes sprinkling the u.
Re. 18 : 2. Babylon cage of ev. u. bird
See Beast, Priest, Pronounce.
See Unclean SPIRIT.
See Unclean SPIRITS.

UNCLEAN thing, s.
Le. 5 : 2. if a soul touch any u. t., the
carcass of u. cattle, u. creeping
t-s, he shall be u. (5) 7 : 21.-22 : 4.
7 : 19. flesh that toucheth u. t. not
be eaten [u. t.
20 : 21. take brother's wife, it is an
De. 23 : 14. th he see no u. t. in thee
Ju. 13 : 4. eat not any u. t., 7, 14.
Is. 52 : 11. touch no u. t., 2 Co. 6 : 17.
64 : 6. we are all as an u. t., we fade
Eze. 7 : † 20. have I made it an u. t.
Ho. 9 : 3. shall eat u. t-s in Assyria
Ac. 10 : 14. have never eaten any t. u.

UNCLEANNESS, ES.
Le. 5 : 3. if he touch the u. of man,
whatso. u. it be, a man shall be
defiled, 7 : 21.-22 : 5. [22 : 3.
7 : 20. eateth, hav-g his u. upon him,
14 : 19. is to be cleansed from his u.
15 : 3. this be his u. in his issue
25. all the days of her u. sh. be, 26.
30. atonement for issue of her u.
31. sh. separate Isr. from their u.
16 : 16. atonement because of u. of
Israel; so do for tabernacle of
congregation in midst of u.
19. shall hallow it from u. of Isr.
18 : 19. long as she is put apart for u.
Nu. 5 : 19. if not gone aside to u.
19 : 13. unclean, his u. is upon him
De. 23 : 10. by reason of u. th. chanc.
24 : 1. bec. he found u. in her [eth
2 S. 11 : 4. was purified from her u.
2 Ch. 29 : 16. priests bro-t out all u.
Ezr. 9 : 11. filled land with their u.
Eze. 7 : † 19. their gold sh. be for u.
36 : 17. way as u. of removed wom.
29. I will save you fr. all your u-s
39 : 24. Acc. to their u. have I done
Zch. 13 : 1. fountain opened for u.

Mat. 23 : 27. full of bones and all u.
Ro. 1 : 24. God also gave th. up to u.
6 : 19. your members servants to u.
2 Co. 12 : 21. have not repented of u.
Ga. 5 : 19. works of flesh, u., strife
Ep. 4 : 19. work all u. with greedin-s
5 : 3. all u. let not be once named
Col. 3 : 5. Mortify fornication, u.
1 Th. 2 : 3. exhortation was not of u.
4 : 7. God hath not called us to u.
2 Pe. 2 : 10. that walk in the lust of u.

UNCLOTHED. [u.
2 Co. 5 : 4. not for that we would be

UNCOMELY. [virgin
1 Co. 7 : 36. behaveth u. toward his
12 : 23. our u. parts have more com.

UNCONDEMNED.
Ac. 16 : 37. have beaten us openly u.
22 : 25. to scourge a man a Roman u.

UNCORRUPTIBLE. [God
Ro. 1 : 23. changed glory of the u.
See Incorruptible.

UNCORRUPTNESS.
Tit. 2 : 7. in doctrine shewing u.

UNCOVER.
Le. 10 : 6. u. not your heads, neith.
18 : 6. None shall approach near of
kin to u. nakedness, 7, 8, 9, 10,
11, 12, 13, 14, 15, 16, 17, 18, 19.-
20 : 18. [to u. nakedn.
18. Neither take wife to her sister
21 : 10. high priest sh. not u. head
Nu. 5 : 18. priest sh. u. wom.'s head
Ru. 3 : 4. shalt go in and u. his feet
1 S. 20 : † 2. father will u. mine ear
Is. 47 : 2. u. thy locks, u. the thigh
† 12. and I then not u. thine ear
Zph. 2 : 14. he shall u. the cedar work
See Nakedness.

UNCOVERED. [tent
Ge. 9 : 21. Noah was u. within his
Le. 20 : 11. u. his father's nakedn-s
17. u. his sister's | 20. u. his uncle's
18. she u. fountain of her blood
21. hath u. his brother's nakedn.
Ru. 3 : 7. came softly and u. his feet
2 S. 6 : 20. u. himself as vain fellows
Is. 20 : 4. led away with buttocks u.
22 : 6. bare quiver, Kir u. shield
47 : 3. Thy nakedness shall be u.
Je. 49 : 10. I have u. his secret places
Eze. 4 : 7. and thine arm shall be u.
Ha. 2 : 16. let thy foreskin be u.
Mk. 2 : 4. they u. roof where he was
1 Co. 11 : 5. prophesieth with head u.
13. is it comely that a woman pray

UNCOVERETH. [u.?
Le. 20 : 19. he u. his near kin [skirt
De. 27 : 20. bec. he u. his father's
1 S. 22 : † 8. is none that u. mine ear
2 S. 6 : 20. as one of vain fellows u.
Jb. 33 : † 16. he u. the ears of men

UNCTION. [One
1 Jn. 2 : 20. ye have an u. fr. Holy

UNDEFILED. [way
Ps. 119 : 1. Blessed are the u. in the
Can. 5 : 2. open to me, my love, my u.
6 : 9. My dove, my u. is one [u.
He. 7 : 26. a high priest who is holy,
13 : 4. Marriage honourable, bed u.
Ja. 1 : 27. Pure religion and u. bef.
1 Pe. 1 : 4. To an inheritance u. [God

UNDER. [ment
Ge. 1 : 7. divided waters u. firma-
21 : 15. cast child u. one of shrubs
39 : 23. looked not to anythi. u. Jos.
49 : 25. blessings of deep th. lieth u.
Ex. 6 : 6. bring you out fr. u. burdens
26 : 19. sockets of silver u. twenty
boards, (3) 21. (2) 25. (2) [38 : 4.
27 : 5. put it u. compass of altar,
37 : 27. rings of gold u. crown [ari
Nu. 3 : 36. u. custody of sons of Merari
6 : 18. put hair in fire u. sacrifice
Jos. 7 : 21. in my tent and silver u. it
13 : 5. from Baal-gad u. m. t Hermon
Ru. 2 : 12. God, u. whose wings thou

1 S.7:11.smote Philis. until u. Beth-
21 : 3. what is u. thine hand ? ⌊car
2 S. 2 : 23. smote him u. fifth rib
1 K. 7 : 32. u. the borders 4 wheels
18 : 23. lay it on wood, no fire u. 25.
2 K. 8 : 20. Edom revolted fr.u.Jud.
13 : 5.Isr. went out from u. Syrians
16 : 17. sea from brazen oxen u. it
1 Ch.24 :19.these the order-gs u.Aa.
27 :23.Da. took not fr.20 yrs.and u.
2 Ch. 28 :10.purpose to keep u. Jud.
Ne. 8 : 17. all congr-n sat u. booths
Jb. 26 : 5. Dead thi-s formed u.water
28 : 5. and u. it is turned up as fire
30 : 7.u. nettles they were gathered
Ps. 44 :5.thro.thy name tread th. u.
Can. 8 :3. his hand sh.be u.my head
Is. 10:16. u.his glory kindle burn-g
Je. 38 :11. house of king u. treasury
12. Put rotten rags u. armholes
u. the cords ⌈cherub
Eze. 10 : 2. Go in between wheels u.
20.creature I saw u. God of Israel
17 : 23. u. it shall dwell all fowl
42 : 9. u. these chambers was entry
46 : 23. with boiling places u. rows
47 :1.waters issued fr. u. threshold
Da. 4 : 12.beasts had shadow u.it,21.
14. let beasts get away from u. it
Ho. 4 :12.gone a whoring from u. G.
Jon. 4 : 5. Jon. made booth, sat u.it
Mi. 4 : 4. sh.sit ev.man u.his vine(2)
Mat. 2 : 16. slew chil.fr.2 yrs.and u.
8 : 8. thou come u. my roof,Lu.7:6.
23 : 37. chickens u. her, Lu. 13:34.
Mk. 6 :11.shake off dust u. your feet
7 : 28. dogs u. table eat the crumbs
Lu. 8 : 16. No man putteth it u. bed
Ro. 3 : 13.poison of asps u. their lips
6 : 15. we not u. law, but u. grace
1 Co. 6 : 12. I will not be brought u.
9 : 27.I keep my body u. and bring
10 : 1. all our fathers were u. cloud
14 : 34. women to be u. obedience
2 Co. 11 : 32. governor u. Aretas
Ga. 3 : 10.of the law are u. the curse
25.we no longer u. a schoolmaster
4 : 2.But is u. tutors and governors
3. so we u. elements of the world
Ph. 2 : 10. and things u. the earth
1 Ti. 5 : 9. Let not a widow u. three-
6 : 1. as many as u. the yoke⌊score
He. 7 : 11. u. it people received law
9 : 15. transg-rs u. first testament
10 : 28. died u. two or three witn-es
Ja. 2 : 3. or sit here u. my footstool
1 Pe. 5 : 6. u. mighty hand of God
Jude 6. reserved in chains u. darkn.
Re.5 :3.nor in earth,nei.u.earth,13.
6 : 9. I saw u. the altar the souls
See AUTHORITY, BUSHEL, HAND, HEAVENS, JUNIPER, OAK, S, SHADOW, SIN, THIGH, TONGUE, TREE.
See Under FEET, FIG tree, GREEN tree, s, Under HEAVEN, HIM, LAW, ME, SUN, THEE, THEM, US, WHOLE Heaven.

UNDERGIRDING. ⌈ship
Ac. 27 : 17. they used helps u. the

UNDERNEATH. ⌈39:20.
Ex. 28 : 27.on two sides of ephod u.,
De. 33 : 27. u. are everlasting arms

UNDERSETTERS.
1 K. 7 : 30. four corners had u., 34.

UNDERSTAND. ⌈speech
Ge. 11 : 7. may not u. one another's
41 : 15.I heard thou canst u.dream
Nu.16 :30.sh.u.these have provoked
De. 9 : 3. u. that L.goeth bef.thee,6.
28 :49.whose tongue they sh.not u.
2 K 18 : 26. Speak in Syrian language, for we u. it, Is. 36 : 11.
1 Ch. 28 : 19.L.made me u. in writ-g
Ne. 8 :3. read bef.those th. could u.
7.caused people to u.the law,8,13.
Jb. 6 : 24.me to u. wh-n I have erred
23 : 5. I would u. what he wou. say
26:14.thunder of his power who u.?
32:9. nei. do the aged u. judgment
36 : 29. can any u. the clo. ? ⌈2.
Ps. 14 : 2. if were any that did u.,53:
19 : 12. Who can u. his errors ? ⌈u.
82 : 5. know not, neither will they
92 : 6. neither doth a fool u. this
94 : 8. u. ye brutish am. the people
107 : 43. shall u. lovingkindn. of L.
119 : 27.Make me u.way of thy prec.
100. I u. more than the ancients
Pr. 1 : 6. To u. a proverb and interp.
2 : 5. shalt thou u. fear of the Lord
9. then shalt thou u. righteousn-s
8 : 5. O ye simple, u. wisdom, and
14 : 8. of prudent is to u. his way
19 : 25. reprove one, will u. knowl.
20 : 24. how can a man u. his way ?
28 : 5. Evil men u. not judgment, they that seek Lord u.all things
29 : 19.tho. he u.he will not answer
Is. 6 : 9. Hear ye indeed, but u. not
10. lest they u.wi. heart,Jn.12:40.
28 : 9. whom make to u. doctrine ?
19. be vexation only to u. report
32 :4. heart of rash sh.u. knowledge
33 : 19. a stammering tongue not u.
40 : †14. made him u. and taught
41 : 20. u. that Lord hath done this
43 : 10. that ye may u. that I am he
44 :18.shut hearts,th.they can-t u.
56 : 11. shepherds that cannot u.
Je.9 :12.Who is the wise may u.this
Eze. 3 :6. to people thou canst not u.
Da. 8 : 16. make this man to u. vis-
17. he said, u., O son of man ⌊ion
9 : 13. that we might u. thy truth
23. beloved ; thf.u.the matter,25.
10 :11. O Dan.,u. the words I speak
12. day thou didst set heart to u.
14. make thee u. what shall befall
11 : 33. that u. shall instruct many
12 : 10. the wicked shall not u., the wise shall u. ⌈u. shall fall
Ho. 4 : 14. the people that doth not
14 : 9. Who is wise, he sh. u. these
Mi. 4 :12.nei. u.they counsel of Lord
Mat.13 :13. they hear not,neither u.
14. ye shall hear and shall not u.
15 :10.said, Hear, and u., Mk 7 :14.
15 : 17. Do not ye u.? 16 : 9, 11. Mk. 8 : 17, 21. ⌈Mk. 13 : 14.
24 : 15. whoso readeth, let him u.,
Mk. 4 : 12. that hearing they may hear and not u., Mat. 13 : 15. Lu. 8 :10. Jn. 12 :40. Ac. 28 :26.
14 : 68. I know not, nei. u. I what
Lu. 24 : 45.th. they might u. Script.
Jn. 8 : 43. Why not u. my speech ?
Ac. 24 :11. mayest u. are but 12 days
28 : 27. lest they u.with their heart
Ro. 15 :21.that have not heard sh.u.
1 Co.12:3.I give you to u.th.no man
13 : 2. tho. I u. mysteries am noth.
2 Co 10:†12 comparing thems.u.not
Ep. 3 :4.ye may u. my knowledge in
Ph. 1 : 12.I would ye sho. u., breth.
He.11 :3.Through faith we u.worlds
2 Pe. 2 : 12. speak evil of things they

UNDERSTANDEST. ⌈u. not
Jb. 15 :9.what u.,which is not in us?
Ps. 139 : 2.thou u.my thoughts afar
Je. 5 : 15.nei. u. thou what they say
Ac. 8 : 30. Philip said, u. what thou

UNDERSTANDETH.
1 Ch. 28 : 9.Lord u.the imaginations
Jb. 28 : 23. God u. the way thereof
Ps. 49 :20.man in honour and u. not
Pr. 8 : 9. are all plain to him that u.
14 :6. knowl easy unto him that u.
16 : †20.He that u. a matter wisely
Je. 9 : 24. let him glory th. he u. me
Mat. 13 : 19. heareth the word u.not
23. he that heareth word and u.
Ro. 3 :11.There is none that u.,none
1 Co. 14 :2.not unto men, no man u.
16. how say Amen, see-g he u.not

UNDERSTANDING. [Part.]
Da. 1 :4 skilful in wisdom,u. science
8 : 23. king u. dark sentences
Ep. 5 : 17. u. what will of L. is ⌈say
1 Ti. 1 :7. teachers u. nei.what they

UNDERSTANDING. [Adj.]
De. 1 : 13. Take ye wise men and u.
4 : 6. this great nation is an u. peo.
1 K. 3 : 9. Give thy serv. an u. heart
12. I have given thee an u. heart
Pr. 8 : 5. ye fools, be of an u. heart

UNDERSTANDING, S.
De. 32 : 28.neither is any u. in them
1 K. 3 : 11. hast asked u. to discern
1 Ch. 12 : 32. were men that had u.
2 Ch. 2 : 12.given Da. wise son wi.u.
26 : 5. Zech. had u. in visions of G.
Ezr. 8 :16.Joiarib,Elnath. men of u.
Ne. 8 : 2. all that could hear with u.
10 :28.ev.one having knowl.and u.
Jb. 12 :3.But I have u.as well as you
12. in length of days is u. ⌈aged
20. he taketh away the u. of the
17 : 4. hast hid their hearts from u.
20 : 3. my u. causeth me to answer
26 :12.by u.he smiteth thro. proud
28 : 12. where is the place of u. ? 20.
28. he said, to depart fr. evil is u.
32 : 8. inspiration of Almighty giv-
† 11. I gave ear to your u-s ⌊eth u.
34 : 10. hearken to me, men of u.
16. If now thou hast u. hear this
34. Let men of u. tell me ⌈hast u.
38 : 4. where wast thou ? declare if
36. or who given u. to the heart ?
39 :17.nei. hath imparted to her u.
Ps. 32 : 9. as the mule th.hath no u.
47 : 7. God is K., sing praises wi. u.
49 : 3. meditation of heart be of u.
119 : 34.Give me u.,73,125,144,169.
99.I have more u. than my teach-
104.Thro thy precepts I get u.⌊ers
130. it giveth u. unto the simple
147 : 5. our Lord, his u. is infinite
Pr. 2 : 2. so apply thine heart to u.
3. if thou liftest thy voice for u.
6. out of his mouth knowl. and u.
11. discret-n preserve, u. sh. keep
3:5.Trust in L.,lean not to thine u.
13. Happy is man that getteth u.
19. by u. established the heavens
4 :1.ye children, attend to know u.
5 :1.My son,bow thine ear to my u.
6 : 32. committeth adultery, lack-
7 : 4.call u. thy kinswoman⌊eth u.
8 : 1. doth not u. put forth voice ?
9 : 4.as for him that wanteth u.,16.
6. Forsake foolish; go in way of u.
10.the knowledge of the holy is u.
14 : 29. He slow to wrath,is of gr.u.
15 : 14. that hath u.seeketh knowl.
32. th. heareth reproof getteth u.
16 : 16. to get u. rather than silver
22. u. is wellspring of life to him
18 : 2. A fool hath no delight in u.
19 : 8. keepeth u. shall find good
25. reprove one that hath u. he
21 : 16. wandereth out of way of u.
24 : 3. by u. a house is established
28 : 11. poor th. hath u. searcheth
16. prince th. want-h u. is oppres-
30 : 2. have not the u. of a man⌊sor
Ec.9 : 11. nor yet riches to men of u.
Is.11 : 3. him of quick u.in fear of L.
27 : 11. it is a people of no u.
29 : 14. u. of their prudent be hid
16. framed say, He had no u. ?
24. erred in spirit shall come to u.
40 : 14. who shewed way of u.? † u-s
28. there is no searching of his u.
44 : 19. nei. is their knowl. nor u.
Je. 3 : 15. which sh. feed you with u.
4 : 22.my peo. is foolish, have no u.
5 : 21. O foolish people, without u.
51 : 15. stretched out heaven by u.

Eze. 28 : 4. with **u.** hast got riches
Da. 1 : 17. Daniel had **u.** in visions
2 : 21. giveth knowl. to them that
4 : 34. mine **u.** returned ⌊know u.
5 :12.excellent spirit and u. in Dan.
9 : 22. I am come to give thee u.
10 : 1. Daniel had **u.** of the vision
11 :35. some of them of u. shall fall
Ho. 13 : 2. idols acc. to their own u.
Ob. 7. all is no **u.** in him ⌈of Esau?
8. Sh. I not destroy u. out of m-t
Mat. 15 :16.Are ye without u.? Mk.
Mk.12 :33.love him with all u.⌊7:18.
Lu. 1 : 3.having had perf. u. of thi-s
2 : 47. all were astonished at his **u.**
24 : 45. Then opened he their **u.**
Ro. 1 :31. Without **u.**,cov-t breakers
1 Co.1:19.bring to nothing u.of pru-
14 : 14. but my **u.** is unfruitf. ⌊dent
15. I will pray with the u., sing
with the **u.** ⌈with my **u.**
19. I had rather speak five words
20. be not chil. in **u.**, in **u.** be men
Ep. 1 :18. eyes of your **u.** enlighten-
4 : 18. Having the **u.** darkened ⌊ed
Ph. 4 : 7. peace which passeth all **u.**
Col. 1:9.be filled with all spiritual **u.**
2 : 2. of the full assurance of **u.**
2 Ti. 2 : 7. Lord give thee **u.** in all
1 Jn. 5 : 20. Son hath given us an **u.**
Re. 13 : 18. him that hath **u.** count
See **GOOD understanding.**

Man of UNDERSTANDING

Ezr. 8:18.they brought us a **m.o.u.**
Pr.1 :5.**m.o.u.** sh.attain wise coun-
10 : 23. **m.o.u.** hath wisdom ⌊sels
11 : 12. a **m.o.u.** holdeth his peace
15 :21. **m.o.u.** walketh uprightly
17 : 27.**m.o.u.** is of excellent spirit
28.shutteth lips esteemed **m.o.u.**
20 :5. **m.o.u.** will draw out couns.
28 : 2. by **m.o.u.** state prolonged

Void of UNDERSTANDING

Pr. 7 :7. I discerned young man -u.
10 : 13. a rod for back of him - **u.**
12 : 11. followeth vain persons - **u.**
17 : 18. A man - **u.** striketh hands
24 : 30. by vineyard of the man - **u.**
See **WISDOM** with
understanding.

UNDERSTOOD. ⌈them

Ge. 42 : 23. knew not that Joseph **u.**
De. 32 : 29. O that they **u.** this, that
1 S. 4 : 6. they **u.** the ark was come
26 :4. David **u.** that Saul was come
2 S. 3 : 37. people **u.** it was not of Da.
Ne. 8 : † 2. the law before all that **u.**
12. they had **u.** the words that
13 : 7. I **u.** of the evil that Eliashib
Jb. 13 : 1. lo, mine ear hath **u.** it
42 : 3. I uttered that I **u.** not ⌈end
Ps.73:17.into sanct-y,then u. I their
81 : 5. I heard a language I **u.** not
106 : 7.Our fa-s **u.** not thy wonders
Is.40 :21.have ye not **u.**fr.foundat-s
44 :18.They have not known nor **u.**
Da. 8 : 27. I astonished, but none **u.**
9 :2. I Daniel **u.** by books the years
10 : 1. Daniel **u.** the thing and had
12 : 8. I heard, but I **u.** not, then
Mat. 13 : 51. Have ye **u.** all these?
16 : 12. **u.** they how he bade them
17 : 13. they **u.** he spake of John
26 : 10. When Jes. **u.**, he said, Why
Mk. 9 : 32. they **u.** not that saying,
Lu. 2 : 50.-9 : 45. Jn. 10 : 6.
Lu. 18 : 34. **u.** none of these things
Jn. 8 : 27. **u.** not he spake of Father
12 . 16.these things **u.** not disciples
Ac. 7 : 25 would have **u.** that God
by his hand would deliver them,
but they **u.** not ⌈man
23 :27. having **u.** that he was a Ro-
34. When I **u.** he was of Cilicia
Ro. 1 : 20. being **u.** by things made
1 Co. 13 : 11. a child, I **u.** as a child
14 : 9. except words easy to be **u.**
2 Pe. 3 :16.some things hard to be **u.**

UNDERTAKE.

Is. 38 :14. I am oppressed, **u.** for me

UNDERTOOK. ⌈begun

Es. 9 : 23. Jews **u.** to do as they had

UNDO. ⌈burdens

Is. 58 : 6. is not this the fast? to **u.**
Zph. 3 : 19. I will **u.** all that afflict

UNDONE. ⌊thee

Nu. 21 : 29. thou art **u.**, O Chemosh
Jos. 11 : 15. Joshua left nothing **u.**
Is. 6 : 5. Woe is me, for I am **u.**, I
Mat. 23 : 23. not to leave other **u.**,

UNDRESSED. ⌊Lu.11:42.

Le. 25 : 5. nei. gather grapes of vine

UNEQUAL. ⌊u., 11.

Eze. 18 : 25. are not your ways **u.**?

UNEQUALLY. ⌊29.

2 Co. 6 : 14. Be not **u.** yoked with

UNFAITHFUL, LY.

Ps. 78 : 57.dealt **u-y** like their fath-s
Pr. 25 : 19. Confidence in an **u.** man
Mal.2 : †15.let none deal **u-y** ag. wife

UNFEIGNED.

2 Co. 6 :6. by Holy Ghost, by love **u.**
1 Ti. 1 : 5. charity out of a faith **u.**
2 Ti. 1 : 5. to remembr-e the **u.** faith
1 Pe. 1 : 22. unto **u.** love of brethren

UNFRUITFUL. ⌈19.

Mat. 13 : 22. he becometh **u.**, Mk. 4:
1 Co. 14 : 14. spirit prayeth, my understanding is **u.** ⌈**u.** works
Ep. 5 : 11. have no fellowship with
Tit.3:14.maintain good works,not **u.**
2 Pe. 1 :8.ye sh.nei.be barren nor **u.**

UNGIRDED.

Ge. 24 : 32. the man **u.** the camels

UNGODLINESS. ⌈u.

Ro. 1 : 18. wrath of God against all
11 :26. he sh.turn away **u.**from Ja-
2 Ti.2:16.increase unto more **u.**⌊cob
Tit. 2 : 12. denying **u.** and worldly

UNGODLY. ⌊lusts

2 S. 22 : 5.floods of **u.** men made me
afraid, Ps. 18 : 4. ⌈**u.**
2 Ch. 19 : 2. Shouldest thou help the
Jb. 8 : †20.God nei. take **u.** by hand
16 : 11. God delivered me to **u.**⌈**u.**?
34 : 18. fit to say to princes, Ye are
Ps. 1 : 1. not in the counsel of the **u.**
4. The **u.** are not so ⌈ment
5. Thf. **u.** shall not stand in judg-
6. the way of the **u.** shall perish
3 : 7. hast broken teeth of the **u.**
43 :1. plead my cause ag. **u.** nation
73 :12.these are the **u.** who prosper
Pr. 16 : 27. **u.** man diggeth up evil
19 :28. **u.** witness scorneth judgm-t
Ro. 4 : 5. him that justifieth the **u.**
5 : 6. in due time Christ died for **u.**
1 Ti. 1 : 9. the law is for the **u.** and
1 Pe. 4 :18.where sh. the **u.** appear?
2 Pe. 2 : 5.flood upon world of the **u.**
6. those who after should live **u.**
3 :7. ag. day of perdition of **u.** men
Jude 4.**u.** men turning grace of God
15. to convince all that are **u.** of
their **u.** deeds ⌈own **u.** lusts
18. who should walk after their

UNHOLY. ⌈and u.

Le. 10 : 10. put difference betw.holy
1 Ti. 1 :9. law was made for the **u.**
2 Ti. 3 : 2. men sh. be unthankful **u.**
He. 10 : 29. blood of covenant an **u.**

UNICORN, S. ⌊thing

Nu. 23 : 22. strength of a **u.**, 24 : 8.
De. 33 : 17. horns like horns of **u-s**
Jb. 39 :9.Will **u.** be willing to serve?
10. Canst thou bind **u.** in furrow?
Ps. 22 :21. heard me fr. horns of **u-s**
29 : 6. and Sirion like a young **u.**
92 :10.my horn exalt like horn of **u.**
Is. 34 :7.**u-s** sh. come down wi.them

UNITE, ED. ⌈u-d

Ge. 49 : 6. to their assembly be not
Ps. 86:11.**u.** my heart to fear thy na.
He. 4 : †2.they were not **u-d** by faith

UNITY.

Ps.133 :1.for brethren to dwell in **u.**
Ep. 4 :3. to keep the **u.** of the Spirit
13. Till we come in the **u.** of the

UNJUST. ⌊faith

Ps. 43:1.deliver me from the **u.**man
Pr. 11 : 7. hope of **u.** men perisheth
28 : 8. who by **u.** gain increaseth
29 : 27. An **u.** man is an abomin-n
Zph. 3 : 5.the **u.** knoweth no shame
Lu. 16 : 8. commended **u.** steward
10. he **u.** in the least, **u.** in much
18 : 6.Hear what the **u.** judge saith
11. I am not as other men are, **u.**
1 Co. 6 :1.Dare any go to law bef.**u.**?
2 Pe. 2 : 9. reserve **u.** to day of judg.
Re. 22 : 11. He th.is **u.** let him be **u.**
See JUST. ⌊still

UNJUSTLY.

Ps. 82 : 2. How long will ye judge **u.**
Is. 26 :10. in land of uprightn-s deal

UNKNOWN. ⌊u.

Ac. 17 : 23.inscription to the **u.** God
1 Co. 14 : 2. that speaketh in an **u.**
tongue, 4, 13, 27. ⌈prayeth
14.if I pray in an **u.**tongue, spirit
19.than 10,000 words in **u.**tongue
2 Co. 6 :9. As **u.** and yet well known
Ga. 1 : 22. I was **u.** by face unto

UNLADE. ⌊churches

Ac. 21 : 3. ship was to **u.** her burden

UNLAWFUL.

Ac. 10 : 28. an **u.** thing for a Jew
2 Pe. 2 : 8. vexed his soul with their

UNLEARNED. ⌊u. deeds

Ac. 4 : 13. perceived they were **u.**
1 Co.14 :16.occupieth room of the **u.**
23. come in those that are **u.**, 24.
2 Ti. 2 : 23. But **u.** questions avoid
2 Pe. 3 : 16. which they that are **u.**

UNLEAVENED. ⌊wrest

Ex. 12 : 39. they baked **u.** cakes of
Le. 2 :4. be an **u.** cake of flour, with
oil, or **u.** wafers, 5. ⌈oil
7 : 12. offer **u.** cakes mingled with
8 : 26. and Moses took one **u.** cake
Nu. 6 :19. one **u.** cake, one **u.** wafer
Jos. 5 :11. did eat old corn of land u.
Ju. 6 :19.Gid-n made ready **u.** cakes
20. Take the flesh and the **u.** cakes
21. angel touched flesh and **u.**
cakes ; fire consumed **u.** cakes
1 Ch. 23 : 29.their office for **u.** cakes
1 Co. 5 : 7. be a new lump as ye are u.

UNLEAVENED bread.

Ge. 19 : 3. Lot did bake **u.b.**, they
Ex. 12 : 8. they sh. eat the flesh th.
night, roast and **u.b.**, Nu.9:11.
15. Seven days shall ye eat **u.b.**,
13 : 6, 7.-23 :15.-34 : 18. Le. 23:
6. Nu. 28 : 17. De. 16 : 3.
18. 1st month, 14th day, at even,
ye shall eat **u.b.**, Eze. 45 : 21.
20. in all habitations eat **u.b.**
29 : 2. to hallow priests take **u.b.**
23. of basket of **u.b.**, Le. 8: 2, 26.
Le. 6 : 16. off-g Aaron eat with **u.b.**
Nu. 6 :15. Nazarite sh. offer basket of
u.b., cakes, wafers of **u.b.**, 17.
De. 16 :8. Six days thou sh. eat **u.b.**
1 S. 28 : 24. wom. at En-dor bake **u.**
2 K. 23 : 9. priests did eat **u.b.** ⌊b.
Mk. 14 :12.day of **u.b.** disciples said
Lu.22 :7.Then came day of **u.b.**,Ac.
Ac. 20 : 6. aft. the days of **u.b.**⌊12:3.
1 Co. 5 : 8. with **u.b.** of sincerity
See **FEAST of**
unleavened bread.

UNLESS. ⌈flesh

Le. 22 :6. be unclean **u.** he wash his
Nu. 22 :33. **u.** she had turned fr. me
2 S. 2 : 27. **u.** thou hadst spoken
Ps. 27 : 13. fainted, **u.** I had believed
94 : 17. **u.** the L. had been my help
119 : 92. **u.** thy law been my delight
Pr. 4 : 16. **u.** they cause some to fall
1 Co. 15 :2. saved, **u.** believed in vain

UNLOOSE.
Mk. 1 : 7 latchet of whose shoes I
am not worthy to u., Lu. 3 : 16.
UNMARRIED. [Jn. 1 : 27.
1 Co. 7 :8. I say thi. to u. and widows
11. if wife depart let her remain u.
32. He u. careth how may please
34. u. wom. careth th. she be holy
UNMERCIFUL. [tion
Ps. 43 : † 1. plead my cause ag u. na-
Ro. 1 : 31. with-t natural affection,
UNMINDFUL. [u.
De. 32 : 18. Of rock th. begat thee, u.
UNMOVEABLE. [u.
Ac. 27 :41. forepart of ship remained
1 Co. 15 : 58. breth., be steadfast, u.
UN'NI. [U., Eliab
1 Ch. 15 : 18. breth. of second degree,
20. U. and Eliab with psalteries
Ne. 12 :9. U. ov. ag. them in watches
UNOCCUPIED. [u.
Ju. 5 : 6. days of Shamgar highways
UNPERFECT. [u.
Ps. 139 :16. did see my substance, yet
UNPREPARED. [u.
2 Co 9 . 4. if they come and find you
UNPROFITABLE.
Jb. 15 : 3 Sho. be reason wi. u. talk ?
Mat. 25 : 30. cast u. serv. into outer
Lu. 17 : 10. say, We are u. servants
Ro. 3 : 12. are altogether become u.
Tit. 3 : 9. genealogies, for they are u.
Phm. 11. Which was to thee u.
He. 13 :17. not with grief, that is u.
UNPROFITABLENESS.
He. 7 : 18. for the weakness and u.
UNPUNISHED.
Pr. 11 :21. the wicked shall not be u.
16 : 5. the proud shall not be u.
17 : 5. is glad at calamities not be u.
19 : 5. A false witness not be u., 9.
28 : † 20. haste to be rich not be u.
Je. 25 : 29. should ye be utterly u. ?
Ye shall not be u. [gether u.
30 : 11. I will not leave thee alto-
46 : 28. I not leave thee wholly u.
49 : 12. shalt thou go u. ? sh. not go
UNQUENCHABLE. [u.
Mat. 3 : 12. gather wheat, but burn
chaff with u. fire, Lu. 3 : 17.
UNQUIETNESS. [u.
1 Co. 14 : † 33. God is not author of
Ja. 3 : † 16. where strife there is u.
UNREASONABLE. [oner
Ac. 25 : 27. seemeth u. to send pris-
2 Th. 3 : 2. may be deliv-d fr. u. men
UNREBUKEABLE. [u.
1 Ti. 6 : 14. th. thou keep this com-t
UNREPROVEABLE.
Col. 1 : 22. to present you holy, u.
UNRIGHTEOUS. [ness
Ex. 23 : 1. put not hand to be u. wit-
Jb. 27 :7. riseth ag. me, be as the u.
Ps 71 :4. Deliv. me out of hand of u.
Is. 10 : 1. Woe that decree u. decrees
55 : 7. u. man forsake his thoughts
Lu. 16 :11. not faithf. in u. mammon
Ro. 3 : 5. Is G. u. who taketh veng.
1 Co 6 : 9. u. sh. not inherit kingd.
He 6 :10 G. is not u. to forget your
UNRIGHTEOUSLY. [works
De. 25 : 16. all th. do u. are abomi-n
UNRIGHTEOUSNESS.
Le. 19 : 15. do no u. in judgment, 35.
Ps. 92 : 15. my rock, is no u. in him
Je. 22 : 13. buildeth his house by u.
Lu. 16 : 9. friends of mammon of u.
Jn. 7 : 18. is true, no u. is in him
Ro. 1 : 18. all u. of men who hold
the truth in u. [cation, envy
29. Being filled with all u., forni-
2 : 8. to them that obey u., wrath
3 :5. if our u. commend righteousn.
6 : 13. nor yield members as instru.
9 :14. Is there u. wi. G. ? [m-ts of u.
2 Co 6 : 14. what fellowship righteousness with u. ?

2 Th. 2 : 10. with all deceiveableness
12. but had pleasure in u. [of u.
He. 8 :12. will be merciful to their u.
2 Pe. 2 :13. shall receive reward of u.
15. Balaam, who loved wages of u.
1 Jn. 1 : 9. to cleanse us from all u.
5 : 17. All u. is sin ; is a sin not un-
UNRIPE. [to death
Jb. 15 : 33. sh. shake off his u. grape
UNRULY. [are u.
1 Th. 5 : 14. breth., warn them that
Tit. 1 : 6. not accused of riot, or u.
10. are many u. and vain talkers
Ja. 3 · 8. the tongue is an u. evil, full
UNSATIABLE. [u.
Eze. 16 :28. whore wi. Assyrians, bec.
UNSAVOURY. [u.
2 S. 22 :27. with froward shew thys.
Jb. 6 . 6. u. be eaten without salt ?
Je. 23 : †13. an u. thing in prophets
UNSEARCHABLE. [u.
Jb. 5 : 9. God, wh. doeth great thi-s,
Ps. 145 : 3. Lord, his greatness is u.
Pr. 25 : 3. the heart of kings is u.
Ro. 11 : 33. how u. are his judgm-ts
Ep. 3 : 8. preach u. riches of Christ
UNSEEMLY. [is u.
Ro. 1 : 27. men working that which
1 Co. 13 : 5. charity doth not behave
UNSHOD. [u.
Je. 2 : 25. Withhold foot from being
UNSKILFUL. [u.
He. 5 : 13. babe is u. in the word of
UNSOCIABLE.
Ro. 1 : † 31 covenant-breakers, u.
UNSPEAKABLE. [gift
2 Co. 9 : 15. Thanks unto God for u.
12 :4. into paradise, heard u. words
1 Pe. 1 :8. in whom ye rejoice wi. joy
UNSPOTTED. [u.
Ja. 1 : 27. to keep hims. u. fr. world
UNSTABLE. [cel
Ge. 49 : 4 u. as water, shalt not ex-
Ja. 1 : 8. A doubleminded man is u.
2 Pe. 2 : 14. beguiling u. souls [u.
3 · 16. they that are unlearned and
UNSTOPPED.
Is. 35 : 5. ears of the deaf shall be u.
UNTAKEN. [away
2 Co. 3 : 14. remaineth same vail u.
UNTEMPERED.
Eze. 13 . 10. lo, others daubed it wi.
u. mortar, 11, 14, 15.–22 : 28.
UNTHANKFUL. [evil
Lu. 6 : 35. he is kind to the u. and
2 Ti. 3 : 2. men sh. be blasphemers,
UNTIL. [u.
Ge. 8 :5. wat-s decreased u. 10th mo
24 : 19. u. camels have done drink-g
33. not eat u. have told my errand
26 : 13. Isaac grew u. became great
28 :15. not leave thee u. I have done
29 :8. cannot u. flocks be gathered
32 : 24. wrestled with Jacob u.
34 :5. held peace u. they were come
41 : 49. corn, very much, u. he left
Ex. 10 : 26. know not u. we come
17 :12 his hands steady u. down of
24 : 14. Tarry for us u. we come [son
33 : 8. looked after Moses u. be was
34 : 35. vail upon face u. he went in
Le. 22 : 4. not eat of holy things u.
30. leave none of it u. morr. [clean
25 : 22. eat of old fruit u. ninth yr.
Nu. 4 : 3. From 30 years old u. 50, 23.
14 : 33. u. your carcasses be wasted
20 :17. not turn u. passed thy bord-s
23 : 24. not lie down u. he eat prey
24 :22. u. Asshur carry thee captive
32 : 17. go armed bef. Israel u. we
De. 2 :14. u. we were come ov. brook
3 :20. u. Lord given rest unto breth.
20 : 20. ag. city u. it be subdued
22 : 2. with thee u. thy bro. seek it
28 :22. they sh. pursue u. thou per-
31 : 30. Mos. spake this song u. [ish
Jos. 7 : 13. u. ye take aw. accursed

Jos. 20 :9. not die by avenger u. [rah
Ju. 5 :7. inhabi-ts ceased u. I Debo.
6 : 18. Depart not u. I come unto
13 :15. u. made ready a kid for thee
19 : 8. they tarried u. afternoon [u.
Ru. 2 : 21. keep fast by young men
3 : 18. Sit still, my dau. u. thou (2)
1 S. 1 : 22. not go u. child be weaned
7 :11. smote Philis. u. under Beth.
15 : 7. smote Amal-s u. comest to
19 : 23. prophesied u. came to Nai.
20 :41. and they kissed and wept u.
David exceeded [had no power
30 : 4. David and peo. wept u. they
2 S. 15 : 24. u. all people out of city
28. I will tarry in plain u. word
17 : 13. u. not be one stone found
19 : 24. nor trimmed beard u. king
23 : 10. smote Philis. u. hand weary
1 K 11 :16. u. he had cut off ev. male
40. Jerob. in Egypt u. death of Sol.
18 : 26. called on Baal fr. m. u. noon
2 K. 6 : 25. u. ass's head was sold for
7 : 3. Why sit we here u. we die ?
8 :11. settled countenance u. asha-d
10 :11. slew house of Ahab u. none
17 : 20. u. Lord had cast them out
of sight, 23.–24 : 20. [captivity
1 Ch. 5 : 22. dwelt in their steads, u.
6 : 32. u. Sol. had built house of L.
12 : 22. came to David u. a gr. host
2 Ch. 18 :26. fellow in prison u. I retu.
35 : 14. sons of Aaron busied u. ni.
36 : 20. servants u. reign of kingd.
21. u. land had enjoyed sabbaths
Ezr. 4 : 5. to frustrate u. reign of D.
21. city not be builded u. com-t
8 :29. u. ye weigh them bef. priests
Ne. 7 :3. not gates be opened u. sun
8 :3. read from morning u. midday
Jb. 14 : 13. keep me secret u. wrath
Ps. 36 : 2. u. iniq-y be found hateful
57 : 1. u. calamities be overpast
71 :18. u. I have shewed thy stren.
73 :17. u. I went into sanct-y of G.
94 : 13. u. pit be digged for wicked
123 : 2. u. he have mercy upon us
132 : 5. u. I find out place for Lord
Can. 3 :4. u. I brought him into my
8 :4. nor awake my love u. he ple.
Is. 5 :11. that continue u. night, till
6 : 11. u. cities be wasted [wine
26 :20. hide u. indignation overpast
32 :15. u. Spirit be poured upon us
62 : 1. u. the righteousn-s go forth
Je. 23 · 20. anger of Lord u. he have
executed, 30 : 24. (2) [come
27 : 7. u. the very time of his land
32 : 5. Zedekiah to Bab-n u. I visit
37 : 21. give Jere. bread u. all spent
44 :27. consumed u. an end [ruleth
Da. 4 : 32. u. thou know Most High
9 : 27. desolate u. consummation
Ho. 7 : 4. kneadeth dough u. leav-d
Mi. 7 : 9. bear u. he plead my cause
Mat. 1 : 17. fr. Dav. u. carrying aw.
2 : 13. be there u. I bri. thee word
15. Jos. was there u. death of Her.
11 :13. prophesied u. Jn., Lu. 16. 16.
13 : 20. Let both grow u. harvest
17 : 9. Tell no man u. Son of man
24 : 39. knew not u. the flood came
Mk. 15 :33. darkn. u. 9th h., Lu. 23:44.
Lu. 15 : 4. which is lost u. he find it
24 : 49. u. ye be endued with power
Ju. 9 : 18. u. they called parents of
Ac. 2 : 35. u. I make thy foes thy
footstool, He. 1 :13. [u. this hr.
10 : 30. Four days ago I was fasting
13 : 20. Judges 450 years u. Samuel
20 : 7. continued speech u. midni-t
21 : 26. u. an offering for every one
23 : 14. eat nothing u. slain Paul
Ro. 5 :13. u. the law sin in the world
11 : 25. u. fulness of Gentiles beco.
1 Co. 16 : 8. tarry at Eph. u. Pentec.
Ga. 4 : 19. u. Christ be formed in

Ep. 1 : 14. **u.** the redemption of pur-
2 Th. 2 : 7. **u.** he be taken [chased
1 Ti. 6 : 14. **u.** appearing of our Lord
Ja. 5 : 7. **u.** be receive latter rain
See **Until CONSUMED.**
See CAME, COME, DAY, DAYS.

UNTIL destroyed. [he d.
De. 7 : 20. Lord send hornet **u.** they
Jos. 8 : 26. **u.** had **d.** inhab-ts of Ai
11 : 14. smote with sword **u.d.** th.
23 : 15. upon you evil things **u.d.**
Ju. 4 : 24. **u.** Israel had **d.** Jabin k.
1 K. 15 : 29. **u.** Baasha had **d.** Jerob.
2 Ch. 31 : 1. **u.** Israel had utterly **d.**
See DESTROYED, EVENING, FINISHED, FULFILLED,

Until MORNING.

UNTIL now.
Ge. 32 : 4. I have stayed there **u.n.**
46 : 34. our trade from youth **u.n.**
Ex. 9 : 18. hail such not in Eg. **u.n.**
Nu. 14 : 19 forgiven peo. fr. Eg-t **u.n.**
2 S. 19 : 7. befell thee fr. youth **u.n.**
2 K. 8 : 6. since she left the land **u.n.**
Ezr. 5 : 16 **u.n.** hath been in build-g
Mat. 11 : 12. fr. days of Jn. Bapt. **u.n.**
Jn. 2 : 10. hast kept good wine **u.n.**
Ro. 8 : 22. creation travaileth **u.n.**
Ph. 1 : 5. fellowship fr. first day **u.n.**
1 Jn. 2 : 9. hateth bro., in darkn. **u.n.**
See TILL, TIME, TIMES, TURN, TURNED,

UNTIMELY.
See BIRTH, **FIG tree.**

UNTO.
See ALL, DAY, DEATH, END, FATHERS, HOUR, ME, THEE, THEM, US, YOU.

UNTOWARD. [oration
Ac. 2 : 40. Save yours. fr. this **u.** gen-

UNWALLED. [towns
De. 3 : 5. took sixty cities besides **u.**
Es. 9 : 19. Jews th. dwell in **u.** towns
Eze. 38 : 11. up to land of **u.** villages

UNWASHEN.
Mat. 15 : 20. but to eat with **u.** hands defileth not a man, Mk. 7 : 2, 5.

UNWEIGHED.
1 K. 7 : 47. Sol. left all the vessels **u.**

UNWISE. [people?
De. 32 : 6. thus requite Lord, O **u.**
Ho 13 : 13. he is an **u.** son, he should
Ro. 1 : 14. I am debtor to wise and **u.**
Ep. 5 : 17. be ye not **u.** but underst-g

UNWITTINGLY. [u.
Le. 22 : 14. if a man eat of holy thing
Jos. 20 : 3. th. killeth any person **u.**, 5.

UNWORTHILY. [u.
1 Co. 11 : 27. shall drink cup of Lord
29. he th. eateth and drinketh **u.**

UNWORTHY.
Ac. 13 : 46. ye judge yours **u.** of life
1 Co. 6 : 2. **u.** to judge smallest mat-

UNWROUGHT. [ter?
Mat. 9 : † 16. No man putteth **u.** cloth into old garm-ts, Mk. 2 : 21.

UP. [Interj.]
Ge. 19 : 14. Lot said, **u.**, get ye out
44 : 4. Joseph said, **u.**, follow men
Ex. 32 : 1. **u.**, make us gods th. shall
Jos. 7 : 13. **u.**, sanctify the people
Ju. 4 : 14. **u.**, this is day in wh. Lord
8 : 20. to his firstborn, **u.**, slay them
9 : 32. **u.** thou and people with thee
19 : 28. **u.**, and let us be going, but
1 S. 9 : 26. **u.**, that I may send thee

UP. [Adv.]
Nu. 14 : 40. they rose **u.**, gat them **u.** into mt., saying, we will go **u.**
42. Go not **u.**, Lord is not am. you
44. presumed to go **u.** unto hill top
Ju. 8 : 13. Gideon returned from battle before sun **u.** [rise early
9 : 33. soon as sun is **u.** thou shalt
1 S. 29 : 10. soon as ye be **u.**, depart
2 S. 24 : 11 Dav. was **u.**, word came
Ne. 4 : 7. walls of Jerus. were made **u.**
Eze. 41 : 16. fr. ground **u.** to windows
Mat. 13 : 6. when sun was **u.**, Mk.
Jn. 2 : 7. they filled waterpots **u.** [4 : 6.
17. zeal of thine house eaten me **u.**
He. 12 : 15. springing **u.** trouble you
See BREAK, CAST, COMETH, DELIVERED, DOWN, GAVE, GIVE.
See **Up to JERUSALEM.**
See LAID, LAY, LIFTED, RISE, SET, SHUT, STAND, STOOD, SWALLOW, ED, TAKE, TAKEN, TOOK, WENT, YOUTH.

UPBRAID, ED, ETH.
Ju. 8 : 5. Zebah, with wh. ye did **u.** me
Mat. 11 : 20. began to **u.** the cities
Mk. 16 : 14. **u-d** them with unbelief
Ja. 1 : 5. to all liberally, and **u-h** not

UPHARSIN.
Da. 5 : 25. MENE, MENE, TEKEL, U.

U'PHAZ. [from U.
Je. 10 : 9. silver from Tarshish, gold
Da. 10 : 5. loins girded wi. gold of U.

UPHELD. [u. me
Is. 63 : 5. arm bro-t salvation, fury

UPHOLD. [thee
Jb. 36 : † 17. judgm., justice sho. **u.**
Ps. 51 : 12. **u.** me wi. thy free Spirit
54 : 4. with them that **u.** my soul
119 : 116. **u.** me acc-g unto thy word
Pr. 29 : 23. honour shall **u.** humble
Is. 41 : 10. I will **u.** thee wi. right ha.
42 : 1. serv. whom I **u.**, mine elect
63 : 5. I wondered was none to **u.**
Eze. 30 : 6. that **u.** Egypt shall fall

UPHOLDEN, EST.
Jb. 4 : 4. thy words have **u-n** him
Ps. 41 : 12. **u-t** me in mine integrity
Pr. 20 : 28. king's throne is **u-n** by

UPHOLDETH. [mercy
Ps. 37 : 17. the Lord **u.** the righteous
24. the Lord **u.** him with his hand
63 : 8. thy right hand **u.** me
145 : 14. The Lord **u.** all that fall

UPHOLDING.
He. 1 : 3. **u.** all things by the word

UPON.
Ge. 2 : 21. deep sleep to fall **u.** Adam
3 : 14. **u.** thy belly shalt thou go
12 : 11. art fair woman to look **u.**,
24 : 16.–26 : 7. [tell thee
22 : 2. **u.** one of mts. which I will
28 : 11. Jac. lighted **u.** certain place
Ex. 7 : 19. hand **u.** waters of Eg. (5)
9 : 3. hand of L. is **u.** thy cattle (6)
10. wi. blains **u.** man and **u.** beast
29 : 20. put blood **u.** tip of ear (4).
Le. 8 : 23, 24.–14 : 14, 17, 25, 28.
21. blood that is **u.** altar, sprinkle **u.** Aaron (5) [table
40 : 4. things to be set in order **u.**
19. he put covering of tent **u.** it
22. put table **u.** side of tabernacle
23. he set the bread in order **u.** it
Le. 6 : 12. burnt off-g in order **u.** it
15 : 9. saddle she rideth **u.** unclean
20. ev. thing she lieth **u.** uncl. (2)
22. toucheth any thing she sat **u.**
26. whatso. she sitteth **u.** be uncl-n
23 : 37. offer, every thing **u.** his day
Nu. 19 : 18. sprinkle **u.** tent, vessels
De. 1 : 36. to Caleb land trodden **u.**
1 S. 9 : 24. cook took shoulder and that **u.** it [her sons
2 K. 4 : 5. shut door **u.** her and **u.**
2 Ch. 20 : 14. **u.** Jahaziel Spirit of L.
29 : 8. wrath of L. **u.** Judah and Je.
Ne. 2 : 12. nei. any, save beast I rode
5 : 4. borrowed money **u.** lands [u.
Jb. 29 : 4. secret of G. **u.** my tabern.
Ps. 80 : 17. **u.** man of thy right hand
Is. 7 : 19. rest **u.** thorns, **u.** all bushes
22 : 25. burden **u.** it shall be cut off
Je. 7 : 20. fury be poured **u.** man (5)
Mat. 9 : 18. lay hand **u.** her she live
10 : 13. **u.** it, 23 : 18.–28 : 2. Lu. 10 : 6. Ju. 11 : 38. He. 6 : 7. [u. her
Lu. 1 : 58. Lord shewed great mercy
Lu. 5 : 36. of new garment **u.** an old
Jn. 4 : 27. **u.** this came his disciples
Ac. 2 : 3. as of fire, it sat **u.** each
5 : 11. fear **u.** as many as heard (2)
8 : 16. he was fallen **u.** none of them
11 : 6. **u.** wh. when I fastened eyes
Ro. 13 : 6. attending continually **u.**
2 Co. 5 : 2. desir-g to be clothed **u.**, 4.
See ALL, ALTAR, BED, EARTH, FACE, FACES, FEET, GROUND, HEAD, HEADS, HIM, HOUSETOP, ME, MEN, ROCK, SOUL, STOOD, THEE, THEM, THRONE, US, WHOM, YOU.

UPON. [With Nouns.]
Ge. 22 : 9, 12. Le. 16 : 14. Ju. 8 : 22. 2 K. 4 : 4. Ezr. 5 : 5.–7 : 17. Jb. 40 : 4. Je. 48 : 10. Da. 4 : 24, 28, 33.–5 : 5.–6 : 17,–7 : 6.–12 : 6, 7. Mat. 12 : 2.–18 : 5.–19 : 28.–21 : 5.–23 : 36.–24 : 3.–25 : 31. Mk. 6 : 39, 48.–8 : 25.–13 : 3. Lu. 5 : 19, 36.–8 : 43.–9 : 38.–18 : 13.–19 : 35. –20 : 18.–21 : 23. Jn. 1 : 51.–9 : 15.–19 : 31. Ac. 1 : 26.–2 : 17.–10 : 9.–11 : 19–15 : 10.–20 : 7.–21 : 35.–27 : 26, 29. Ro. 4 : 9. (2)–15 : 20. 1 Co. 3 : 12.–16 : 2. 2 Co. 1 : 23.–3 : 15. Ga. 6 : 16. Ep. 2 : 20.–4 : 26.–5 : 6. Ph. 1 : 3.–2 : 17, 27. He. 8 : 6.–11 : 21. Ja. 4 : 3. Re. 4 : 4.–5 : 7.–8 : 3, 10. (2).–10 : 2, 5. (2).–13 : 1. (2).–14 : 14.–16 : 3, 4, 8, 10, 12.–17 : 1, 3, 5, 16.–19 : 14, 21.–20 : 4. (2).

UPPER. [posts
Ex. 12 : 7. strike blood on **u.** door-
Le. 13 : 45. a covering built on **u.** lip
De. 24 : 6. No man sh. take **u.** millstone to pledge [Ju. 1 : 15.
Jos. 15 : 19. gave her the **u.** springs,
2 K. 18 : 17. they stood by conduit of **u.** pool, Is. 7 : 3.–36 : 2.
1 Ch. 7 : 24. built Beth-horon nether and **u.**, Jos. 16 : 5. 2 Ch. 8 : 5.
2 Ch. 32 : 30. stopped **u.** watercourse
Eze. 24 : † 17. and cover not thy **u.** lip
Zph. 2 : 14. cormorant in **u.** lintels
Ac. 19 : 1. Paul having passed thro.
See CHAMBER, ROOM. [u. coasts

UPPERMOST.
Ge. 40 : 17. in **u.** baskets were meats
Is. 17 : 6. two or three in **u.** bough
9. his cities sh. be as an **u.** branch
Mat. 23 : 6. they love the **u.** rooms at feasts, Mk. 12 : 39. Lu. 11 : 43.

UPRIGHT.
Ge. 6 : † 9. Noah was an **u.** man
17 : † 1. I am God, and be thou **u.**
Le. 26 : 13. broken your yoke and made you go **u.** [Lord thy God
De. 18 : † 13. Thou sh. be **u.** with the
Jos. 10 : † 13. Is not this in book of the **u.**, 2 S. 1 : † 18. [2 Ch. 29 : 34.
1 S. 29 : 6. thou hast been **u.** wi. me,
2 S. 22 : 24. I was also **u.** bef. him, Ps. 18 : 23. [u., Ps. 18 : 25.
26. with **u.** man wilt shew thys.
Jb. 1 : 1. Job was **u.** man, 8.–2 : 3.
8 : 6. If **u.** he would awake for thee
12 : 4. **u.** man is laughed to scorn
17 : 8. **u.** men be astonished at this
Ps. 11 : 7. his counten-e doth behold
19 : 13. then shall I be **u.** [u.
25 : 8. Lord is good and **u.**, 92 : 15.
33 : 1. praise is comely for the **u.**
37 : 14. slay such as of **u.** conversa.
18. Lord knoweth days of the **u.**
37. Mark perfect man, behold **u.**
49 : 14. the **u.** shall have dominion
111 : 1. praise Lord in assembly of **u.**
112 : 2. generation of **u.** be blessed
4. Unto the **u.** there ariseth light
119 : 137. and **u.** are thy judgments
125 : 4. do good to them **u.** in hearts
140 : 13. **u.** sh. dwell in thy presence
Pr. 2 : 21. **u.** shall dwell in the land

Pr 10 :29. way of L. is strength to **u.**
11 : 3. integrity of **u.** shall guide
6. righteousness of **u.** shall deliver
11. By the **u.** the city is exalted
20. **u.** in their way are his delight
12 : 6. mouth of **u.** shall deliver [u.
13 : 6. Righteousness keepeth the
14 : 11. tabernacle of **u.** sh. flourish
15 : 8. prayer of **u.** is his delight
16 : 17. highway of **u.** is from evil
21 : 18. transgre-r be ransom for **u.**
29. as for **u.** he directeth his way
28 : 10. the **u.** shall have good thi-s
29 : 10. The bloodthirsty hate the **u.**
27. he **u.** is an abomi-n to wicked
Ec. 7 : 29. God hath made man **u.**
12 : 10. that which was written, **u.**
Can. 1 : 4. the **u.** love thee [of just
Is. 26 : 7. thou **u.**, dost weigh path
Jer. 10 : 5. they are **u.** as palm trees
Da. 8 : 18. he touched and set me **u.**
11 : 17. to enter and **u.** ones wi. him
Mi. 2 : †7. good to him th. walketh **u.**
7 : 2. is none **u.** among men, all lie
4. most **u.** is sharper than a thorn
Ha. 2 : 4. his soul lifted up is not **u.**
See **Upright in HEART.**
See **STAND upright,** Stood.

UPRIGHTLY.

Ps. 15 :2. that walketh **u.** shall never
58 : 1. Do ye judge **u.** ? [be moved
75 :2. I will judge **u.** [th. walk **u.**
84 :11. withhold no good from them
Pr. 2 : 7. he a buckler to them walk
10:9. walketh **u.** walketh surely [u.
15:21. man of underst-g walketh **u.**
28 : 18. Whoso walketh **u.** be saved
Can. 1 : † 4. they love thee **u.** [high
Is. 33 : 15. speaketh **u.** sh. dwell on
Am. 5:10. abhor him th. speaketh **u.**
Mi. 2 : 7. do good to him walketh **u.**
Ga. 2 : 14. I saw they walked not **u.**

UPRIGHTNESS, ES.

1 K. 9 : 4. If wilt walk as David in **u.**
1 Ch. 29 :17. thou hast pleasure in **u.**
Jb. 4 : 6. is not this **u.** of thy ways?
33 : 23. interpreter, to shew man
Ps. 9 :8. judgm. to peo. in **u.** [his **u.**
25 :21. Let integrity, **u.** preserve me
111 :8. stand fast and are done in **u.**
143 : 10. lead me into land of **u.**
Pr. 2 : 13. Who leave the paths of **u.**
14 :2. that walketh in **u.** feareth L.
28 : 6. Better is the poor in his **u.**
Is. 26 : 7. The way of the just is **u.**
10. in land of **u.** will deal unjustly
33 : † 15. He that speaketh **u**-s that
57 : 2. each one walking in his **u.**
Da. 11 : † 17. to enter and **u.** wi. him

UPRIGHTNESS of heart.

De. 9 : 5. Not for the **u.o.** thine h.
1 K. 3 : 6. he walked in **u.o.h.**, 9 : 4.
Jb. 33 :3. My words be of **u.o.** my **h.**
Ps. 119:7. will praise thee wi **u.o.h.**

UPRISING. [and **u.**

Ps. 139 : 2. knowest my downsitting

UPROAR.

1 K. 1 : 41. noise of the city in an **u.**
Mat. 26 : 5. lest be an **u.**, Mk 14 : 2.
Ac. 17 : 5. Jews set all city on an **u.**
19 : 40. in question for this day's **u.**
20 : 1. after **u.** was ceased, paul
21 : 31. that all Jerus. was in an **u.**
38. Art not thou Eg-n who madest

UPSIDE down. [an **u.**?

2 K. 21 : 13. wiping Jerusalem as a
dish, turning it **u.d.** [eth **u.d.**
Ps. 146 : 9. way of wicked he turn-
Is. 24 : 1. Lord turneth earth **u.d.**
29 : 16. your turning of thi-s **u.d.**
Ac. 17 : 6. have turned world **u.d.**

UPWARD. [ers

Ge. 7 : 20. Fifteen cubits **u.** did wat-
Nu. 3 : 15. shalt number every male
from a month old and **u.**, 22,
28, 34, 39, 40, 43.-26 : 62.
Ju. 1 : 36. coast was fr. rock and **u.**
1 S. 9 : 2. Saul was higher fr. shoulders **u.**, 10 : 23. [and **u.**
2 K. 3 : 21. all able to put on armour
19 :30. shall bear fruit **u.**, Is. 37 : 31.
2 Ch. 31 : 16. males 3 years old and **u.**
Jb. 5 :7. unto trouble as sparks fly **u.**
Ec. 3 : 21. spirit of man th. goeth **u.**
Is. 8 : 21. curse God and look **u.** [u.
38 : 14. mine eyes fail with looking
Eze. 1 : 11. wings were stretched **u.**
27. from his loins **u.**, 8 : 2.
41 : 7. was a winding about still **u.**
43 : 15. fr. altar and **u.** sh. be 4 horns
Hag. 2 : 15. consider fr. this day **u.**, 18.

UR. [Person.]

1 Ch. 11 : 35. Eliphal, son of U.

UR of the Chaldees. [U.-

Ge. 11 : 28. Haran died bef his fa. in
31. They went forth wi. them fr. U.-
15 : 7. I bro-t thee out of U.-, Ne.

UR'BANE. [9 : 7

Ro. 16 : 9. Salute U. our helper and

URGE. [Stachys

Lu. 11 : 55 Pharisees began to u.

URGED. [him

Ge. 33 : 11. Jacob **u.** Esau, he took
Ju. 16 : 16. Delilah **u.** Samson, he
19 : 7. his father in law **u.** him [ed
2 K 2 :17. **u.** him till he was asham-
5 :16. Naaman **u.** Elisha | 23. he **u.**

URGENT. [Gehazi

Ex. 12 :33. Egyptians were **u.** on peo.
Da. 3 : 22. king's commandm. was **u.**

U'RI.

Ex. 31 : 2. I called Bezaleel the son
of U., 35 : 30.-38 : 22. 1 Ch. 2 :
20. 2 Ch. 1 : 5. [Gilead
1 K. 4 : 19. Geber son of U. was in
Ezr. 10 : 24. Telem and U. porters

URI'AH, or URI'AS. [tite

2 S. 11 : 3. Bath-sheba, wife of U. Hit-
6. David to Joab, Send me U. Hit.
7. when U. was come, Da. demanded
8. Da. said to U., Go to the hou. (2)
9. U. slept at door of king's house
10. U. went not. David said to U.
11. U. said unto David, The ark
12. Dav. said to U., Tarry here (2)
14. letter to Joab Dav. sent by U.
15. Dav. wrote, Set U. in forefront
16. Joab assigned U. unto place
17. U. the Hittite died also, 21, 24.
26. wife of U. mourned for husb.
12 : 9. thou hast killed U. Hittite
10. hast taken wife of U. Hittite
15. L. struck child U.'s wife bare
23 : 39. mighty men whom Da. had,
U. Hittite, 1 Ch. 11 : 41. [Hittite
1 K. 15 : 5. save only in matter of U.
Mat. 1 :6. Dav. begat Sol. of wife of
See Urijah or Uriah. [U-s

U'RIEL. [son

1 Ch. 6 : 24. Tahath his son, U. his
15 :5. sons of Kohath, U. the chief
11. David called for Levites for U.
2 Ch. 13 : 2. was Michaiah dau. of U.

URI'JAH or URI'AH. [altar

2 K. 16 : 10. Ahaz sent U. fashion of
11. U. built altar acc. to all A-z (2)
15. Ahaz commanded U., Upon alt.
16. did U. acc. to all Ahaz com-ded
Ezr. 8 : 33. vessels weighed by Merimoth son of U. [son of U., 21.
Ne. 3 : 4. next repaired Merimoth
Is. 8 :2. I took me witnesses, U. priest

URI'JAH.

Ne. 8 : 4. beside Ezra stood U. [U.
Je. 26 : 20. a man that prophesied,
21. U. afraid, fled into Egypt, 23.

U'RIM. [of U.

Nu. 27 : 21. ask counsel after judgm.
1 S. 28 : 6. neither by dreams, by U.
See **THUMMIM with Urim.**

US. [rifices

Ex. 10 : 25. Thou must give **u.** sac-
1 S. 8 : 20. that king may judge u.
2 S. 20 : 6. Sheba do **u.** more harm
Mat. 3 : 15. it becometh **u.** to fulfil
6 : 11. give **u.** this day our daily br.
12. forgive **u.** our debts as we
13. lead **u.** not into temptation (2)
Lu. 23 :39. If Christ, save thys. and **u.**
Jn. 10 : 24. How long make **u.** doubt
11 : 16. Let **u.** also go that we die
Ro. 9 : 24. **u.** whom he hath called
1 Co. 4 : 9. God set forth **u.** apostles
6 :14. raise up **u.** by his own power
2 Co. 1 :14. ye have acknowledged **u.**
21. he which establisheth **u.** is God
5 : 18. reconciled **u.** to hims. by Ch.
Ph. 3 :17. as ye have **u.** for ensample
1 Th. 5 : 8. let **u.** of the day be sober
9. God not appointed **u.** to wrath
Ja. 1 :18. Of his own will begat he **u.**

About US.

Nu. 22 : 4. lick up all that are **a.u.**
Ne. 5 : 17. came from heathen **a.u.**
6 : 16. heathen **a.u.** saw these thi-s
Da. 9 :16. people a reproach to all **a.**

After US. [u.

Jos. 8 : 6. they will come out **a. u.**
22 : 27. witness to generations **a.u.**
Mat. 15 : 23. Send her aw., she crieth

Against US. [a.u.

Ge. 43 : 18. may seek occasion **a.u.**
Ex. 1 : 10. join enemies fight **a.u.**
16 :7. what we th. ye murmur **a.u.**?
8. your murmurings not **a.u.** but
De. 2 : 32. Sihon came out **a.u.**, 29 : 7.
3 : 1. Og, king of Bashan **a.u.**
Jos. 8 : 5. men of Ai came out **a.u.**
10 : 6. kings of the Amorites **a.u.**
22 : 19. rebel not ag. Lord nor **a.u.**
Ju. 15 : 10. Why are ye come up **a.u.**?
1 S. 30 : 23. company that came **a.u.**
2 S. 11 : 23. the men prevailed **a.u.**
21 : 5. the man that devised **a.u.**
2 K. 7 :6. k. hired **a.u.** kings of Eg-ns
22 : 13. great is wrath of Lord **a.u.**
2 Ch. 20 : 12. this gr-t company **a.u.**
Ps. 44 : 5. tread them that rise **a.u.**
79 : 8. remember not **a.u.** iniquit-s
124 : 2. Lord for us when men **a.u.**
3. when wrath was kindled **a.u.**
Is. 14 :8. no feller is come **a.u.** [14 : 7.
59 : 12. our sins testify **a.u.**, Je.
Je. 16 : 10. L. pronounced evil **a.u.**
21 : 2. Neb-r maketh war **a.u.** [u.?
13. say, Who shall come down **a.**
43 : 3. Baruch setteth thee on **a.u.**
La. 3 : 46. opened their mouth **a.u.**
5 : 22. thou art very wroth **a.u.**
Da. 9 : 12. confirmed words he spake
Mi. 5 : 1. he hath laid siege **a.u.** [a.u.
Mk. 9 : 40. he that is not **a.u.** is on
our part, Lu. 9 : 50. [be **a.u.** ?
Ro 8 : 31. If God be for us, who can
Col. 2 :14. blotting handwriting **a.u.**
3 Jn. 10. prating **a.u.** wi. malicious

Among or Amongst US.

Ge. 23 :6. thou a mighty prince **a.u.**
34 :22. if ev. male **a.u.** be circum-d
Ex. 17 : 7. Is the Lord **a.u.** or not?
34 : 9. let my lord, I pray, go **a.u.**
De. 31 : 17. bec. our God is not **a.u.**
Jos. 9 : 7. peradv. ye dwell **a.u.**, 22.
22 : 19. and take possession **a.u.**
31. we perceive the Lord is **a.u.**
Ju. 18 :25. Let not thy voice be heard
1 S. 4 : 3. ark **a.u.** it may save [a.n.
1 K. 5 : 6. not **a.u.** any can skill to
Jb. 34 : 37. clappeth his hands **a.u.**
Ps. 74 :9. not **a.u.** any that knoweth
Pr. 1 : 14. Cast in thy lot **a.u.**, let
Is. 33 : 14. Who **a.u.** sh. dwell with
the devouring fire? [L. **a.u.** ?
Mi. 3 : 11. they will say, Is not the
Lu. 1 : 1. most surely believed **a.u.**
7 : 16. gr prophet is risen up **a.u.**
Jn. 1 : 14. made flesh and dwelt **a.u.**
Ac. 1 : 21. Jes. went in and out **a.u.**
15 : 7. God made choice **a. u.** that

At US. [Gentiles

1 Pe 4 : 17. if first begin **a.u.**, what

Before US.

Ex. 32 : 23. Make us gods which sh. go **b.u.**, Ac. 7 : 40. [**b.u.**
De. 1 : 22. ye said, We will send men
2 : 33. our God delivered him **b.u.**
Jos. 4 : 23. which he dried up **b.u.**
8 : 6. will say, They flee **b.u.**
24 : 18 L. drave out **b.u.** Amorites
Ju. 11 : 24. Lord shall drive out **b.u.**
20 : 32. They are smitten **b.u.**, 39.
1 S. 8 : 20. that king may go out **b.u.**
9 : 27. Bid thy servant pass on **b.u.**
2 S. 2 : 14. Let young men play **b.u.**
2 Ch. 14 : 7. while land is yet **b.u.**
Ec. 1 : 10. of old time, what was **b.u.**
Is. 30 : 11. cause Holy One cease **b.u.**
Da. 9 : 10. walk in laws he set **b.u.**
He. 6 : 18. lay hold upon hope set **b.u.**
12 : 1. let us run the race set **b.u.**

Behind US. [20.

Ge. 32 : 18. behold, also, he is **b.u.**,

Between or **Betwixt US.**

Ge. 26 : 28. Let there be an oath **b-t u.**
31 : 37. they may judge **b-t u.** both
53. God of Abraham judge **b-t u.**
Jos. 22 : 25. made Jord. border **b-n u.**
27. be a witn-s **b-n u.**, 28, 34. [42 : 5.
Ju. 11 : 10. L. be witness **b-n u.**, Je.
Jb. 9 : 33. Nei. is any daysman **b-t u.**
Lu. 16 : 26. **b-n u.** and you, a gr. gulf
Ac. 15 : 9. put no difference **b-n u.**
Ep. 2 : 14. middle wall of partition **b-n** [**u.**

By US.

Nu. 12 : 2. Hath not L. spoken **b.u.**?
2 K. 4 : 9. this man of G. passeth **b.u.**
2 Co. 1 : 19. Jesus was preached **b.u.**
20. Amen, unto glory of God **b.u.**
2 : 14. savour of his knowledge **b.u.**
3 : 3. epistle of Ch. ministered **b.u.**
5 : 20. as tho. God did beseech **b.u.**
7 : 9. receive damage **b.u.** in noth.
8 : 19. administered **b. u.** to glory

Concerning US. [of L., 20.

2 K. 22 : 13. do acc. to all written **c.u.**

See **DELIVERED us.**

For US. [lodge

Ge. 24 : 23. is there room **f. u.** to
26 : 22. Lord hath made room **f.u.**
31 : 14. Is yet any inheritance **f.u.**
42 : 2. corn in Eg-t : buy **f.u.** from
Ex. 2 : 19. An Egyp-n drew wat. **f.u.**
14 : 12. better **f.u.** to serve Egyp-s
24 : 14. Tarry ye here **f.u.** [Egypt
Nu. 14 : 3. better **f.u.** to return into
9. fear not people, they bread **f.u.**
De. 1 : 14. thing is good **f.u.** to do
2 : 36. not one city too strong **f.u.**
30 : 12. Who go up **f.u.** to heaven?
13. Who sh. go over the sea **f.u.**?
Jos. 5 : 13. Art thou **f.u.** or our adv.
17 : 16. The hill is not enough **f.u.**
22 : 17. iniq-y of Peor too little **f.u.**?
Ju. 1 : 1. Who go **f.u.** ag. Canaan-s?
1 S. 7 : 8. to cry unto the Lord **f.u.**
9 : 5. lest my fa. take thought **f.u.**
14 : 6. may be Lord will work **f.u.**
2 S. 18 : 3. If flee, will not care **f.u.**
21 : 4. nei. **f.u.** shalt kill any man
2 K. 4 : 13. thou hast been caref **f.u.**
6 : 1. the place is too strait **f.u.** [u.
2 Ch. 10 : 10. make thou it lighter **f.**
13 : 10. as **f.u.**, Lord is our God
Ezr. 4 : 14. not meet **f.u.** to see [u.
8 : 21. to seek of him a right way **f.**
Ne. 4 : 20. our God shall fight **f.u.**
10 : 32. we made ordinances **f.u.**
Ps. 47 : 4. sh. choose inheritance **f.u.**
62 : 8. Trust, God is a refuge **f.u.**
68 : 28. strengthen th. wrought **f.u.**
126 : 3. hath done great things **f.u.**
Is. 6 : 8. whom send, who will go **f.u.**
7 : 6. let us make breach th-in **f.u.**
26 : 12. thou wilt ordain peace **f.u.**
Je. 9 : 18. take up a wailing **f.u.** [u.
14 : 19. smitten, there is no heal-g **f.**
21 : 2. inquire, I pray, of Lord **f.u.**
35 : 9. Not to build houses **f.u.**
Je. 37 : 3. Pray unto God **f.u.**, 42 : 2,
La. 4 : 17. as **f.u.**, our eyes failed [20.
19. laid wait **f.u.** in wilderness
Mat. 17 : 4. Lord, it is good **f.u.** to be here, Mk. 9 : 5. Lu. 9 : 33.
25 : 9. lest there be not enough **f.u.**
Mk. 10 : 35. Master do **f.u.** whatso-r
14 : 15. room, there make ready **f.u.**
Lu. 1 : 69. raised horn of salvation **f.**
9 : 50. he not against us is **f.u.** [u.
20 : 22. lawful **f.u.** to give tribute
Jn. 11 : 50. expedient **f.u.** one die
18 : 31. not lawf. **f.u.** to put to dea.
Ac. 16 : 21. customs not lawful **f.u.**
Ro. 4 : 24. **f.u.**, to whom it shall be
5 : 8. while sinners, Christ died **f.u.**
8 : 26. Spirit maketh interces-n **f.u.**
31. If God be **f.u.**, who be ag. us?
32. but delivered him up **f.u.** all
34. Christ maketh interces-n **f.u.**
1 Co. 5 : 7. Christ is sacrificed **f.u.**
2 Co. 1 : 11. helping by prayer **f.u.**
4 : 17. light affliction worketh **f.u.**
5 : 21. he made him to be sin **f.u.**
Ga. 3 : 13. Christ made a curse **f.u.**
Ep. 5 : 2. loved us, given hims. **f.u.**
Col. 4 : 3. praying **f.u.** th. God would
1 Th. 5 : 10. who died **f.u.**, 1 Jn. 3 : 16.
25. pray **f.u.**, 2 Th. 3 : 1. He. 13 : 18.
Tit. 2 : 14. Who gave himself **f.u.**
He. 6 : 20. forerunner is **f.u.** entered
9 : 12. obtained eternal redemp-n **f.**
24. in the presence of God **f.u.** [u.
10 : 20. he hath consecrated **f.u.**
11 : 40. G. provided better thing **f.u.**
1 Pe. 2 : 21. bec. Christ suffered **f.u.**, [4 : 1.

From US.

Ge. 26 : 16. said unto Isaac, Go **f.u.**
Nu. 21 : 7. that he take serpents **f.u.**
1 S. 6 : 20. to whom shall he go **f.u.**?
14 : 17. numb., see who is gone **f.u.**
21 : 5. women kept **f.u.** three days
2 Ch. 29 : 10. that his wrath may turn **f.u.**, Ezr. 10 : 14.
Ps. 2 : 3. cast away their cords **f.u.**
103 : 12. removed our transgr-s **f.u.**
Is. 59 : 9. Theref. is judgment far **f.u.**
11. for salvation, but it is far **f.u.**
64 : 7. thou hast hid thy face **f.u.**
Je. 4 : 8. anger of L. not turned **f.u.**
21 : 2. that Neb-r may go up **f.u.**
38 : 25. princes say, Hide it not **f.u.**
Ac. 1 : 22. day he was taken up **f.u.**
15 : 24. certain who went out **f.u.**
2 Th. 2 : 2. by word, nor letter, as **f.u.**
1 Jn. 2 : 19. went out **f.u.**, but not [of us

See **DEPART from.**

In US. [he will

Nu. 14 : 8. If the Lord delight **i.u.**
Jb. 15 : 9. what understandest thou, which is not **i.u.** [i.u.
Is. 26 : 12. hast wrought all our works
Jn. 17 : 21. that they may be one **i.u.**
Ro. 8 : 4. law might be fulfilled **i.u.**
18. glory wh. sh. be revealed **i.u.**
1 Co. 4 : 6. learn **i.u.** not to think
2 Co. 1 : 5. sufferings of Ch. abound **i.**
4 : 12. So death worketh **i.u.** [u.
6 : 12. Ye are not straitened **i.u.**
Ep. 3 : 20. power that worketh **i.u.**
2 Ti. 1 : 14. Holy Gh. wh. dwelleth **i.u.**
Ja. 4 : 5. spirit **i.u.** lusteth to envy
1 Jn. 1 : 8. If we say, no sin, truth not
10. and his word is not **i.u.** [i.u.
3 : 24. we know th. he abideth **i.u.**
4 : 12. If love, God dwelleth **i.u.**,
2 Jn. 2. for the truth's sake **i.u.** [13.

Of US. [o.u.

Ge. 3 : 22. the man is become as one
23 : 6. none **o.u.** withhold fr. thee
Nu. 31 : 49. lacketh not a man **o.u.**
De. 5 : 3. are all **o.u.** alive this day
Jos. 2 : 24. inhabit-ts faint bec. **o.u.**
Ju. 16 : 5. give thee ev. one **o.u.** 1,100
24. our enemy, wh. slew many **o.u.**
20 : 8. not any **o.u.** go to his tent(2)
18. Which **o.u.** go first to battle?
Ju. 21 : 1. not any **o.u.** give daughter
1 S. 20 : 42. as have sworn both **o.u.**
2 S. 18 : 3. nei. if half **o.u.** die will they care: thou worth 10,000 **o.u.**
2 K. 6 : 11. which **o.u.** is for king
Ezr. 8 : 23. he was entreated **o.u.**
Ne. 4 : 15. returned all **o.u.** to wall
23. none **o.u.** put off our clothes
Ps. 115 : 12. Lord been mindful **o.u.**
Is. 53 : 6. on him iniquities **o.u.** all
63 : 16. tho. Abraham ignorant **o.u.**
Je. 6 : 24. anguish taken hold **o.u.**
14 : 9. O Lord, art in the midst **o.u.**
Ac. 17 : 27. not far fr. every one **o.u.**
28 : 15. brethren heard **o.u.** came
Ro. 4 : 16. Abraham, father **o.u.** all
6 : 3. so many **o.u.** as were baptized
14 : 7. none liveth to himself **o.u.**
1 Co. 4 : 1. account **o.u.** as ministers
2 Co. 2 : 11. Satan get advantage **o.u.**
4 : 7. power may be of God not **o.u.**
10 : 2. think **o.u.** as if we walked
Ga. 4 : 26. Jerusalem, moth. **o.u.** all
Ep. 4 : 7. unto every one **o.u.** grace
1 Th. 1 : 6. ye became followers **o.u.**
9. they shew **o.u.** what entering
2 : 13. the word wh. ye heard **o.u.**
3 : 6. ye have good remembr-e **o.u.**
4 : 1. ye received **o.u.** how to walk
2 Th. 3 : 6. tradition he received **o.u.**
2 Pe. 3 : 2. command-t **o.u.** apostles
1 Jn. 2 : 19. they were not **o.u.** (8)

On or **Upon US.**

Ge. 26 : 10. brought guiltiness **u.u.**
42 : 21. is this distress come **u.u.**
43 : 18. fall **u.u.**, take us for bondm.
Ex. 5 : 3. he fall **u.u.** with pestilence
Nu. 12 : 11. beseech, lay not sin **u.u.**
Jos. 2 : 9. your terror is fallen **u.u.**
9 : 20. let them live lest wrath be **u.**
Ju. 8 : 21. Rise thou and fall **u.u.** [u.
1 S. 5 : 7. his hand is sore **u.u.** and
2 S. 15 : 14. lest he bring evil **u.u.**
1 K. 12 : 4. make thou yoke be put **u.u.** lighter, 9, 10. 2 Ch. 10 : 4, 9.
2 K. 7 : 6. kings of Eg-ns to come **u.**
9. mischief will come **u.u.** [u.
1 Ch. 15 : 13. G. made a breach **u.u.**
2 Ch. 20 : 9. If when evil cometh **u.u.**
34 : 21. great is wrath poured **u.u.**
Ezr. 8 : 18. good hand of G. **u.u.**, 31.
Ne. 9 : 32. trouble th. hath come **u.u.**
33. just in all that is brought **u.u.**
13 : 18. did not G. bring evil **u.u.**?
Jb. 9 : 33. lay his hand **u.u.** both
Ps. 4 : 6. light of countenance **u.u.**
33 : 22. Let thy mercy, O L., be **u.u.**
67 : 1. cause his face to shine **u.u.**
90 : 17. beauty of the Lord be **u.u.**
123 : 2. until he have mercy **u.u.**
3. Have mercy **u.u.**, O Lord, have mercy **u.u.**, Mat. 9 : 27.-20 : 30, 31. Lu. 17 : 13. [**u.u.**
Is. 32 : 15. until the Spirit be poured
63 : 7. all Lord hath bestowed **u.u.**
Je. 5 : 12. nei. shall evil come **u.u.**
6 : 26. the spoiler shall come **u.u.**
La. 3 : 47. Fear and a snare **u.u.**
Eze. 33 : 10. If our transg-s be **u.u.**
Da. 9 : 11. thf. curse is poured **u.u.**
12. bringing **u.u.** gr. evil, 13, 14.
Ho. 10 : 8. they shall say to hills, fall **o.u.**, Lu. 23 : 30. Re. 6 : 16.
Jon. 1 : 6. if so be God will think **u.u.**
Jon. 1 : 7. cause this evil is **u.u.**, 8.
14. lay not **u.u.** innocent blood
Mi. 3 : 11. none evil can come **u.u.**
7 : 19. will have compassion **u.u.**
Mat. 27 : 25. His blood be **o.u.** and
Lu. 10 : 11. dust **o.u.** do we wipe off
Ac. 3 : 4. And Peter said, Look **o.u.**
12. why look ye so earnestly **o.u.**
5 : 28. bring this man's blood **u.u.**
11 : 15. Holy Gh. fell on th. as **o.u.**
24 : 7. chief capt. Lysias came **u.u.**
27 : 20. no small tempest lay **u.u.**
Ro. 16 : 6. Mary bestowed labour **o.u.**

2 Co. 1 : 11. for gift bestowed u.u.
8 : 4. u.u. fellowship of ministering
Tit. 3 : 6. he shed o.u. abundantly
1 Jn. 3 : 1. love the Fa. bestowed u.
See COME. [Passive.] ⌊u.

Over US.

Ge. 37 : 8. Sh. thou indeed reign o.u.
Ex. 2 : 14. Who made thee a judge
o.u., Ac. 7 : 27. ⌈a prince o.u.
Nu. 16 : 13. except thou make thys.
Ju. 8 : 22. unto Gideon, Rule o.u.
15 : 11. Knowest Philis. are rulers
1 S. 8 : 19. have k.o.u., 10 : 19.⌊o.u.?
2 S. 5 : 2. time when Saul was k.o.u.
19 : 10. Absalom we anointed o.u.
Ne. 9 : 37. kings thou hast set o.u.
Ps. 12 : 4. lips our own: who lord o.u.
Is. 26 : 13. other lords dominion o.u.
La. 5 : 8. servants have ruled o.u.
See REIGN [Verb.], SAVE us.

Through US. ⌈to God

2 Co. 9 : 11. causeth t.u. thanksg-g

To or Unto US. ⌈u.u.

Ge. 19 : 31. is not a man to come in
20 : 9. What hast done u.u.? 26 : 10.
34 : 9. give y-r dau-s u.u.⌊Ju. 15 : 11.
14. for that were a reproach u.u.
16. we will take your daugh-s t.u.
17. But if ye will not hearken u.u.
21. let us take their daugh-s t.u.
22. herein will men consent u.u.
39 : 14. bro-t Hebrew u.u. to mock
17. the serv. thou hast bro-t u.u.
41 : 12. he interp-d u.u. dreams, 13.
42 : 28. What is this that God hath
done u.u.? Je. 5 : 19. ⌈u.u., 33.
30. lord of the land spake roughly
43 : 3. The man did protest u.u.
44 : 27. servant my father said u.u.
Ex. 5 : 16. they say u.u., Make brick
10 : 7. How long th. man snare u.u.?
Nu. 10 : 31. be t.u. instead of eyes
32. goodness, Lord, shall do u.u.
De. 1 : 25. took fruit brought it u.u.
5 : 27. speak thou u.u., we will hear
29 : 29. things revealed belong u.u.
30 : 12. to heaven and bring it u.u.
13. over the sea and bring it u.u.
Jos. 9 : 25. as it seemeth right to do
u.u. do, Ju. 10 : 15. ⌈u. or to
22 : 28. when they should so say t.
Ju. 13 : 8. let man of God come u.u.
15 : 10. to him as he hath done t.u.
18 : 19. go with us, be t.u. a father
Ru. 2 : 20. the man is near of kin u.u.
1 S. 4 : 3. ark out of Shiloh u.u.
8. Woe u.u.! who shall deliver
us, 7. Je. 4 : 13.-6 : 4. La. 5 : 16.
6 : 9. he hath done u.u. great evil
14 : 9. If they say u.u., Tarry until
10. this shall be a sign u.u. (2)
12. Come up t.u.. we will shew
25 : 15. the men were very good u.u.
16. they were a wall u.u. by night
29 : 4. lest he be an adversary t.u.
2 S. 19 : 42. king is near of kin t.u.
21 : 6. 7 of his sons be deliv-d u.u.
2 K. 1 : 6. man said u.u., Go unto k-g
4 : 10. when cometh t.u. sh. turn in
7 : 12. what Syrians have done t.u.
1 Ch. 13 : 2. may gather thems. u.u.
3. bring again ark of God t.u. ⌈u.
Ezr. 4 : 12. Jews wh. came fr. thee t.
18. letter ye sent u.u. been read
5 : 17. let k. send his pleasure t.u.
Ne. 4 : 12. whence ye return u.u.(2)
15. ene-s heard it was known u.u.
20. hear trumpet, resort ye u.u.
22. in night may be guard u.u.
5 : 8. shall brethren be sold u.u.
17. those th. came u.u. fr. heathen
Jb. 34 : 4. Let us choose t.u. judgm.
Ps. 60 : 1. O turn thyself t.u. again
115 : 1. Not u.u., O Lord, not u.u.
Is. 1 : 9. exc. had left u.u. remnant
9 : 6. u.u. a child is born, u.u. son
14 : 10. Art thou become like u.u.?

Is. 28 : 15. scourge sh. not come u.u.
30 : 10. Prophesy not u.u. right
things, speak u.u. smooth
33 : 2. O Lord, be gracious u.u.
21. L. u.u. a place of broad rivers
36 : 11. Speak not t.u. in Jews' lang.
Je. 5 : 24. u.u. the appointed weeks
26 : 16. spoken t.u. in name of L.⌈k.
38 : 25. Declare u.u. what said unto
40 : 10. Chaldeans wh. will come u.
42 : 5. Lord shall send thee t.u.⌊u.
44 : 16. word thou hast spok. u.u.
La. 5 : 4. water, our wood is sold u.u.
Eze. 11 : 15. u.u. in this land given
24 : 19. tell us what these are t.u.?
Da. 2 : 23. known u.u. king's matter
9 : 7. but u.u. confusion of faces, 8.
Ho. 6 : 3. he sh. come u.u. as rain
10 : 3. what should a king do t.u.?
Jon. 1 : 11. that sea be calm u.u.
Zch. 1 : 6. as Lord thought to do u.u.
Mal. 1 : 9. beseech G. be gracious u.u.
Mat. 13 : 36. Declare u.u. the parable of the tares, 15 : 15. ⌈u.u.
20 : 12. thou hast made them equal
21 : 25. he will say u.u., Why did
25 : 11. Lord, open t.u., Lu. 13 : 25.
26 : 68. Prophesy u.u., thou Christ
27 : 4. What is that t.u.? see to th.
Mk. 12 : 19. Mos. wrote u.u., Lu. 20 : 28.
Lu. 1 : 2. as they delivered them u.u.
74. grant u.u. that we serve him
2 : 15. Lord hath made known u.u.
10 : 17. even devils are subject u.u.
11 : 4. forgive ev. one indebted t.u.
12 : 41. speakest this parable u.u.?
16 : 26. neither can they pass t.u.
24 : 32. while he opened t.u. Script.
Jn. 2 : 18. What sign shewest u.u.?
14 : 22. wilt manifest thyself u.u.
16 : 17. What is this he saith u.u.?
Ac. 7 : 38. lively oracles to give u.u.
10 : 41. t.u. who did eat with him
11 : 17. gave them like gift as u.u.
13 : 33. G. hath fulfilled same u.u.
14 : 11. The gods are come t.u.
15 : 8. giving Holy Ghost as u.u.
25. It seemed good u.u., 28.⌈girdle
21 : 11. come u.u. he took Paul's
Ro. 5 : 5. by Holy Ghost given u.u.
1 Co. 1 : 18. u.u. it is the power of G.
30. Christ, who is made u.u. wisd.
2 : 10. God revealed them u.u. by
12. things freely given t.u. of God
8 : 6. t.u. there is but one God⌈Asia
2 Co. 1 : 8. trouble wh. came t.u. in
5 : 5. given u.u. earnest of Spirit
19. u.u. word of reconciliation
8 : 5. gave thems. u.u. by will of G.
7. as ye abound in your love t.u.
10 : 13. rule G. hath distributed t.u.
Ep. 1 : 9. made known u.u. mystery
Col. 1 : 8. declared u.u. your love
2 : 14. handwriting contrary t.u.
4 : 3. God would open u.u. a door
1 Th. 2 : 8. bec. ye were dear u.u.
He. 2 : 3. salvation confirmed u.u.
4 : 2. u.u. was the gospel preached
10 : 15. Holy Ghost is witness t.u.
1 Pe. 1 : 12. u.u. they did minister
1 Jn. 4 : 16. love that God hath t.u.
See US-WARD.

Toward US. ⌈cease

Ps. 85 : 4. cause thine anger t.u. to
117 : 2. his kindness is great t.u.
Ro. 5 : 8. commendeth his love t.u.
Ep. 1 : 8. he hath abounded t.u.
2 : 7. in his kindness t.u. thro. Ch.
1 Jn. 4 : 9. was manifested love of G.

Under US. ⌊t.u.

Ps. 47 : 3. he shall subdue people u.

With US. ⌊u.

Ge. 24 : 55. Let damsel abide w.u.
31 : 50. no man w.u., G. is witness
34 : 9. make ye marriages w.u.
10. ye shall dwell w.u., land bef.
21. These men are peaceable w.u.

Ge. 34 : 23. they will dwell w.u., 22.
41 : 12. w.u. a young man, Heb-w
43 : 4. if send our bro. w.u., 44 : 26.
44 : 30. seeth the lad is not w.u., 31.
Ex. 3 : 18. G. of Hebrews met w.u., 5:
10 : 26. Our cattle shall go w.u.⌊3.
14 : 11. whf. hast dealt thus w.u.?
20 : 19. Speak thou w.u., let not
God speak w.u. lest we die⌈u.?
33 : 16. is it not in that thou goest w.
Nu. 10 : 29. come w.u., we will do
32. if thou go w.u., what goodn.
11 : 18. it was well w.u. in Egypt
14 : 9. L. is w.u., fear them not⌈u.
22 : 14. Balaam refuseth to come w.
De. 5 : 2. L. made covenant w.u., 3.
29 : 15. him that standeth here w.
u., wi. him that is not here w.u.
Jos. 9 : 6. thf. make a league w.u., 11.
Ju. 6 : 13. O my lord, if Lord be w.u.
11 : 8. we turn, that thou go w.u.
18 : 19. Hold thy peace and go w.u.
1 S. 5 . 7. ark shall not abide w.u.
11 : 1 Make cov-t w.u. we will serve
10. To morrow ye sh. do w.u. all
23 : 19. Doth not David hide w.u.?
25 : 7. shepherds w.u. we hurt not
29 : 4. him not go w.u. to battle, 9.
30 : 22. Bec. they went not w.u.
2 S. 13 : 26. let bro. Amnon go w.u.
15 : 19. Thf. goest thou w.u. ⌈u.?
20. make thee go up and down w.
21 : 17. sh. go no more w.u. to bat.
1 K. 3 : 18. no stranger w.u. in hou.
8 : 57. the Lord our God be w.u.
2 K. 6 : 16. they that be w.u. more
than they with them, 2 Ch. 32 : 7.
18 : 26. talk not w.u. in Jews' lang.
2 Ch. 13 : 12. behold, G. is w.u., 32 : 8.
Ezr. 4 : 3. nothing to do w.u.⌈w.u.
9 : 14. wouldest not thou be angry
Jb. 15 : 10. w.u. are the grayheaded
Ps. 46 : 7. Lord of hosts is w.u., 11.
85 : 5. thou be angry w.u. for ever?
103 : 10. He hath not dealt w.u.
Pr. 1 : 11. If they say, Come w.u.
Is. 8 : 10. sh. not stand; God is w.u.
59 : 12. our transgressions are w.u.
Je. 8 : 8. We wise, law of L. is w.u.
14 : 21. break not thy cov-t w.u.
21 : 2. if Lord will deal w.u. acc-g
42 : 6. be well w.u. when we obey
Ho. 12 : 4. Beth-el, he spake w.u.
Zch. 1 : 6. doings, so he dealt w.u.
Mat. 1 : 23. interpreted is, God w.u.
13 : 56. his sisters w.u., Mk. 6 : 3.
22 : 25. were w.u. seven brethren
Lu. 2 : 48 Son, why thus dealt w.u.
9 : 49. bec. he followeth not w.u.
24 : 24. certain w.u. went to sepulc.
29. Abide w.u.; day is far spent
32. while he talked w.u. by way
Ac. 1 : 17. For he was numbered w.u.
21. which have companied w.u.
22. witness w.u. of his resurrect-n
2 : 29. his sepulchre w.u. unto this
20 : 14. when Paul met w.u. at As.
21 : 16. went w.u. certain disciples
18. Paul went w.u. unto James
25 : 24. Agrippa and all here w.u.
27 : 2. one Aristarchus being w.u.
1 Co. 16 : 16. ev. one th. helpeth w.u.
2 Co. 8 : 19. was chos. to travel w.u.
2 Th. 1 : 7. are troubled, rest w.u.
2 Pe. 1 : 1. obtained like faith w.u.
1 Jn. 1 : 3. may have fellowship w.u.
2 : 19. would have continued w.u.
2 Jn. 2. truth shall be w.u. for ever

Within US. ⌈w.u.

Lu. 24 : 32. Did not our heart burn

Without US. ⌈w.u.

1 Co. 4 : 8. ye have reigned as kings
He. 11 : 40. w.u. not be made perfect

USE, USES. ⌈u.

Le. 7 : 24. fat may be used in any oth.
De. 26 : 14. nei. taken for unclean u.
2 S. 1 : 18. teach Judah u. of the bow

1 Ch. 28 : 15 acc. to u. of candlest-k
Ro 1 :26. women did change nat-l u.
27. men leaving nat-l u. of women
Ep 4 . 29 good to the u. of edifying
2 Ti 2:21. vessel meet for master's u.
Tit. 3 :14. good works for neces-y u-s
He.5 :14. by u. have senses exercised

USE. [Verb.] [ment
Le. 19 . 26 nei. shall ye u. enchant.
Nu. 10 : 2. u. trumpets for calling of
15 : 39. aft. wh. ye u. to go whoring
De. 2 : † 9 u. no hostility ag. Moab
1 Ch. 12 : 2. cou. u. right ha and left
Je. 23 : 31. u. their tongues and say
31 : 23. shall u. this speech in Jud
46 : 11. in vain u. many medicines
Eze. 12 : 23. no more u. it as proverb
16 ; 44. sh. u. this proverb ag. thee
18 :2 What mean ye, u. this prov-b
3. not have occasion to u. proverb
21 : 21. king stood to u. divination
Jo 2 . † 17. u. a by-word ag. them
Mat 5 : 44. pray for them that despitefully u. you, Lu. 6 : 28.
6 : 7. when ye pray, u. not repetitions
Ac. 14 : 5 to u. apostles despitefully
1 Co. 7 : 21 if made free, u. it rather
31 u. this world as not abusing it
2 Co. 1 : 17. minded, did I u. lightn-s?
3 : 12. we u. gr. plainness of speech
13 : 10. lest I should u. sharpness
Ga. 5 : 13. u. not liberty for occasion
1 Ti 1 : 8. law good if u. it lawfully
3 : 10. let them u. office of deacon
1 Ti. 5 : 23 u. a little wine for thy
1 Pe. 4 : 9. u. hospitality one to ano.

USED.
Ex. 21 : 36. if the ox hath u. to push
Le. 7 : 24. fat may be u. in any other
Ju. 14 : 10. so u. the young men to do
20. whom Samson had u. as friend
2 K. 17 : 17 u. enchantments, 21 : 6.
2 Ch 33 : 6. [derness
Je. 2 : 24. A wild ass u. to the wil-
Eze. 22 : 29. The people of land have u. oppression [hast u.
35 : 11. acc-g to envy which thou
Ho. 12 : 10. u. similitudes by proph-s
Mk. 2 : 18. disciples of Jn. u. to fast
Ac. 8 : 9. Simon Magus u. sorcery
19 : 19. many which u. curious arts
27 : 17. u. helps, undergirding ship
Ro. 3 : 13. wi. tongues they u. deceit
1 Co. 9 : 12. we have not u. this power
15. I have u. none of these things
1 Th 2 : 5. nei. u. we flattering words
† 6. we might have u. authority
1 Ti. 3 : 13. have u. office of a deacon
He. 10 : 33. companions of them so u.

USEST. [name
Ps. 119 : 132. u. to those th. fear thy

USETH.
De. 18 : 10. not any th. u. divination
Es. 6 : 8. apparel king u. to wear
Pr 15 : 2 tongue of wise u. knowledge
18 . 23 the poor u. entreaties, but
Je. 22 : 13. u. his neighbour's serv-e
Eze. 16 : 44. that u. proverbs, sh. use
He. 5 : 13. ev. one that u. milk is un-

USING. [skilful
Col. 2 : 22. all are to perish wi. the u.
1 Pe. 2 : 16. not u. your liberty for

USURER. [cloak
Ex. 22 : 25. shall not be to him as u.
Pr. 29 : † 13. The poor and u. meet

USURP. [u.
1 Ti. 2 : 12. I suffer not a woman to

USURY. [u.
Ex. 22 : 25. nei. shalt lay upon him
Le. 25 : 36. Take thou no u. of him, 37.
De. 23 : 19. Thou sh. not lend upon u. to brother; u. of money, u. of victuals, u. of any thing lent upon u., 20. [upon u.
20. Unto a stranger mayest lend
Ne. 5 : 7. Ye exact u., ev one of his
10. let us leave off this u. [bro.
Ps. 15 : 5. putteth not his money to u.
Pr. 28 : 8. He that by u. increaseth
Is. 24 : 2. as with the taker of u., so with the giver of u. to him
Je. 15 : 10. I have neither lent on u., nor men have lent to me on u.
Eze. 18 . 8. not given forth upon u.,
13 Hath given forth upon u. [17.
22 : 12. thou hast taken u. and inc.
Mat. 25 ; 27. should have received mine own with u., Lu. 19 23.

US-WARD. [u.
Ps. 40 : 5. thy thoughts which are to
Ep. 1 : 19. greatn. of his power to u.
2 Pe. 3 : 9. his longsuffering to u.

UTHAI.
1 Ch. 9 : 4. in Jerus. dwelt U. son of
Ezr. 8 : 14 sons of Bigvai, U., Zabbud

UTMOST, OUTMOST.
Ge 49 : 26. u. bound of everlasting
Ex 26 : 10. edge of curtain o. [hills
Nu. 22 : 36. Arnon, wh. is in u. coast
41. might see the u. of peo., 23 : 13.
34 : 3. border be o. coast of salt sea
De. 34 : 2. land of Judah unto u. sea
Je. 9 : 26. I will punish all in u. corners, 25 : 23.-49 : 32. [border
50 : 26. Come against her from u.
Jo. 2 . 20. his hinder part tow u. sea
Lu. 11 : 31. came fr. u. parts to hear
See OUTMOST. [Sol.

UTTER. [Adj.]
Na. 1 : 8. he will make u. end of place

UTTER destruction.
Nu 21 : † 3. he called place U. d.
1 K 20 : 42. man I appointed to u. d.
Zch. 14 : 11. there sh. be no more u. d.

UTTER = OUTER.
See OUTER

UTTER. [Verb.]
Le. 5 : 1. if not u. it sh. bear iniquity
Jos. 2 : 14 Our life if ye u. not this
20. if thou u. it, we will be quit of
Ju. 5 : 12. awake, Deborah, u. song
Jb. 15 : 2. Sho. wise man u. vain knowl.
27 : 4 nor my tongue u. deceit
33 : 3. lips sh u. knowledge clearly
Ps 78 : 2 I will u. dark sayings of
94 : 4 How long sh. they u. hard
106 : 2. Who can u. the mighty acts
119 : 171. my lips shall u. praise
145 : 7. sh. u. memory of thy goodn.
Pr. 14 : 5. false witness will u. lies
23 : 33 heart sh. u. perverse things
Ec. 1 : 8. All things full of labour; man cannot u. it [God
5 : 2. heart not be hasty to u. bef.
Is. 32 : 6. a vile person will u. error
48 : 20. u. it even to end of earth
Je. 1 : 16. I will u. my judgments ag.
4 : † 12. now will I u. judgments
51 : † 14. sh. u. a shout ag. Babylon
Eze. 24 : 3. u. parable unto rebellious
Mat. 13 : 35. I will u. things secret
2 Co. 12 : 4. not lawful for man to u.
See VOICE, S, with utter, ed, eth.
See WORDS, with utter, ed, eth, ing.

UTTERANCE. [gave u.
Ac. 2 : 4. they spake as the Spirit
1 Co. 1 : 5. enriched by him in all u.
2 Co. 8 : 7. as ye abound in u. and
Ep. 6 : 19. that u. be given unto me
Col. 4 : 3. wou. open to us door of u.

UTTERED, ETH.
Nu. 30 : 6. if had husband when she u-d aught, 8. [ties
Jb. 15 : 5. thy mouth u-h iniqui-
42 : 3. I u-d that I understood not
Ps. 19 : 2. Day unto day u-h speech
29 : † 9. ev. whit of it u-h his glory
66 : 14. What my lips u-d in trouble
Pr. 10 : 18. that u-h slander is fool
29 : 11. fool u-h all his mind [desire
Mi. 7 : 3. gr. man u-h mischievous
Ro. 8 : 26. groanings cannot be u-d
He. 5 : 7. many things had to be u-d
Re. 10 : 4 Seal up things, thunders

UTTERLY. [u-d
Ex. 17 : 14. u. put out remem b. of Am
22 : 17. If father u. refuse to give her
23 : 24 sh u. overthrow their idols
Le. 13 : 44. pronounce him u. unclean
Nu. 15 : 31. soul shall be u. cast off
30 : 12 if husb. u. made them void
De. 4 : 26. if corrupt yours. u. perish
7 : 26. sh. u. detest gold of images
31 : 29 ye will u. corrupt yourselves
Jos. 17 : 13. chil. of Israel did not u. drive Canaanites out, Ju. 1 : 28.
Ju. 15 : 2. I tho-t thou u. hated her
1 S. 27 : 12. He made Israel u. abhor
2 S 17 : 10. that is valiant sh. u. melt
23 : 7 sons of Belial sh. be u. burned
Ne. 9 : 31. didst not u. consume them
Ps. 37 : 24. not be u. cast down [rors
73 : 19. wicked u. consumed wi. ter-
89 : 33. lovingkindness not u. take
119 8. O forsake me not u. [fr. him
43 take not word of truth u. out
Can 8 : 7. for love, it u. be contem-d
Is. 2 : 18. the idols he sh. u. abolish
6 : 11. until the land be u. desolate
24 : 3. The land be u. emptied
19. the earth is u. broken down
32 : † 19. the city shall be u. abased
40 : 30. the young men shall u. fall
56 : 3. u. separated me fr. his people
60 : 12. nations shall be u. wasted
Je. 9 : 4. ev. brother will u. supplant
12 : 17 not obey, I will u. pluck up
14 : 19. Hast thou u. rejected Judah
23 : 39. I, even I, will u. forget you
25 : 29. sho. ye be u. unpunished?
46 : † 28. will I not u. cut thee off
51 : 58. walls of Bab. be u. broken
La. 5 : 22. thou hast u. rejected us
Eze. 9 : 6. Slay u. old and young
17 : 10. planted, shall it not u. wither
27 : 31. shall make thems. u. bald
29 : 10. I will make Egypt u. waste
Da 11 : 44. go u. to make away many
Ho 1 : 6. I will u. take them away
10 : 15 sh. king of Isr. be u. cut off
Mi 2 : 4 one say, We be u. spoiled
Na. 1 : 15. the wicked he is u. cut off
Zph. 1 : 2. I will u. consume all thi-s
Zch. 11 : 17. right eye be u. darkened
2 Co. 6 : 7. is u. a fault among you
2 Pe. 2 : 12. u. perish in their corrup.
Re. 18 : 8. Babylon sh. be u. burned

UTTERLY destroy, ed, ing.
Le. 26 : 44. nei. will I abhor them to
Nu. 21 : 2. I will u. d. cities [d. u.
De. 3 : 6. u. d-g men, women, chil.
7 : 2. sh. u. d. Canaanites, 20 : 17.
12 : 2. ye shall u. d. all high places
13 : 15 d-g u. the city of idolators
Jos. 11 : 11. smote all souls, u. d-g
20. so that he might d. them u.
Ju. 21 : 11. Ye shall u. d. every male
1 S. 15 : 3. smite Amalek, u. d.. 18.
9. Saul spared the best, would not u. d.; but every thi. vile d. d u.
1 K. 9 : 21. chil. Isr. not able u. to d.
2 K. 19 : 11. kings of Assyria to all lands by d-g them u., Is. 37 : 11.
2 Ch. 20 : 23. inhab-s of Seir u. to d.
Is. 11 : 15. u. d. tongue of Eg-n sea
Je. 25 : 9. Behold, I will u. d. them
50 : 21. Go ag. Pekod; waste, u. d.
26. Babylon, cast up as heaps, d. u.
51 : 3. spare not young men, d. u.
Am. 9 : 8. will not u. d. hou. of Jac.
See Utterly DESTROYED.

UTTERMOST. [17.
Ex. 26 : 24. u. edge of curtain, 36 : 11,
Nu. 20 : 16. Kadesh, city in u. of
De. 11 : 24. fr. riv. unto u. sea [border
Jos. 15 : 21. u. cities of Judah
Mat. 5 : 26. till hast paid u. farthing
Ac. 24 : 22. I will know u. of matter
1 Th. 2 : 16. wrath upon them to u.

He. 7 : 25. be able to save them to u.
See UTMOST.

UTTERMOST part, s.

Nu. 11 : 1. consumed them in u.p-s
Jos. 15 : 1. Zin was u.p. of south coast
5. from bay of sea at u.p. of Jord.
1 S. 14 : 2. Saul tarried in u.p. of Gib.
1 K. 6 : 24. from u.p. of one wing to u.p. of other, ten cubits [8.
2 K. 7 : 5. lepers came to u.p. of camp,
Ne. 1 : 9. were of you cast out to u.p.
Ps. 2 : 8. u.p-s for thy possession
65 : 8. in u.p-s are afraid at tokens
139 : 9. If I dwell in u.p-s of sea
Is. 7 : 18. hiss for fly in u.p. of Egypt
24 : 16. from u.p. have heard songs
Mat. 12 : 42. she came from u.p-s to hear Solomon, Lu. 11 : 31.
Mk. 13 : 27. shall gather his elect fr. u.p. of earth to u.p. of heaven
Ac. 1 : 8. witnesses unto u.p. of the [earth

UZ. [Person.]

Ge. 10 : 23. chil. of Aram; U., Mash
36 : 28. chil. of Dishan; U., 1 Ch. 1 : 42.
1 Ch. 1 : 17. sons of Shem; Lud, U.

UZ. [Place.]

Jb. 1 : 1. man in the land of U., Job
Je. 25 : 20. king of U. to drink the
La. 4 : 21. Rejoice, O dau. of Edom, in [U.

U'ZAI. See PALAL.

U'ZAL. [1 : 21.

Ge. 10 : 27. sons of Joktan, U., 1 Ch.

UZ'ZA, UZ'ZAH.

2 S. 6 : 3. U-h and Ahio drave the cart, 1 Ch. 13 : 7. [1 Ch. 13 : 9.
6. U-h put forth his hand to ark,
7. anger of L. ag. U-h, 1 Ch. 13 : 10.
8. Lord had made a breach upon U-h, 1 Ch. 13 : 11. [garden of U-a
2 K. 21 : 18. Manasseh was buried in
26. Amon buried in garden of U-a
1 Ch. 6 : 29. sons of Merari; Mahli, U-a
8 : 7. he removed them, begat U-a
Ezr. 2 : 49. children of U-a, Ne. 7 : 51.

UZ'ZEN-SHE'RAH. [U.

1 Ch. 7 : 24. his dau. Sherah, built

UZ'ZI. [7 : 4.

1 Ch. 6 : 5. Bukki begat U., 51. Ezr.
6. U. begat Zerakiah, 51. [of U.
7 : 2. the sons of Tola, U. | 3. the sons
7. sons of Bela, U., men of valour
9 : 8. sons of Benj.; Elah son of U.
Ne. 11 : 22. overseer of Levites was U.
12 : 19. priests, of Jedaiah, U., 42.

UZZI'A. [U.

1 Ch. 11 : 44. valiant men of armies,

UZZI'AH = OZI'AS.

2 K. 14 : †21. people took U. 16 years old, made him king, 2 Ch. 26 : 1, 3.
15 : 13. to reign in 39th year of U.
30. Jotham son of U., 32. Is. 7 : 1.
34. Jotham did as his fath. U. had, 2 Ch. 27 : 2. [gifts to U.
2 Ch. 26 : 8. the Ammonites gave
9. U. built towers in Jerusalem
11. U. had a host of fighting men
14. U. prepared shields and spears
18. priests withstood U., said (2)
19. U. was wroth, and had a censer
21. U. a leper to day of his death
22. acts of U. did Isaiah write
23. So U. slept with his fathers
Is. 1 : 1. saw concerning Judah in days of U., Ho. 1 : 1. Am. 1 : 1.
6 : 1. year king U. died I saw Lord
Zch. 14 : 5. earthquake in days of U.
See OZIAS.

UZZI'AH.

1 Ch. 6 : 24. sons of Kohath were; U.
27 : 25. ov. storehouses the son of U.
Ezr. 10 : 21. taken strange wives; U.
Ne. 11 : 4. at Jerus. Athaiah, son of U.

UZZI'EL.

Ex. 6 : 18. sons of Kohath; Amram, U., Nu. 3 : 19. 1 Ch. 6 : 2, 18.-23 : 12.
22. the sons of U., Le. 10 : 4. Nu. 3 : 30. 1 Ch. 15 : 10.-23 : 20.-24 : 24.
1 Ch. 4 : 42. for captains, Neariah, U., sons of Ishi
7 : 7. sons of Bela; U. | 25 : 4. sons of Heman; U. [Shemaiah, U.
2 Ch. 29 : 14. sons of Jeduthun;
Ne. 3 : 8. Next repaired U. of gold- [smiths

UZZI'ELITES.

Nu. 3 : 27. of Kohath, family of U.
1 Ch. 26 : 23. of Hebronites, and U.

V.

VAGABOND, S. [be

Ge. 4 : 12. a fugitive and v. sh. thou
14. I shall be a fugitive and v. in
Ps. 109 : 10. Let his chil. be v-s, beg
Ac. 19 : 13. certain v. Jews took on

VAIL, S. [herself

Ge. 24 : 65. Rebek. took v., covered
38 : 14. Tamar covered herself wi. v.
Ex. 26 : 31. thou sh. make a v. of blue
33. shalt hang up v. under taches, within v. ark of testimony: v. shall divide between holy and
35. shall set table without the v.
27 : 21. In tabernacle without the v., 40 : 22. [26. Le. 4 : 6, 17.
30 : 6. shalt put altar before v., 40 :
34 : 33. Moses put v. upon his face, 34, 35. [39 : 34.-40 : 21.
35 : 12. make the v. of the covering,
36 : 35. made a v. of blue, 2 Ch. 3 : 14.
38 : 27. were cast the sockets of v.
40 : 3. shalt cover the ark with v.
Le. 16 : 2. come not into holy place within the v., 12. Nu. 18 : 7.
15. kill goat, and bring his blood within the v. [v.
21 : 23. he shall not go in unto the
24 : 3. without the v. shall Aaron
Nu. 4 : 5. sh. take down covering v.
Ru. 3 : 15. Bri. the v. that thou hast
Can. 5 : 7. keepers of walls took my v.
Is. 3 : 23. the Lord will take away v-s
25 : 7. destroy v. over all nations
Mat. 27 : 51. v. of the temple was rent in twain, Mk. 15 : 38. Lu. 23 : 45.
1 Co. 11 : †15. her hair is given for a v.
2 Co. 3 : 13. Mos. wh. put v. over face
14. until this day remaineth same v., which v. is done away in Ch.
15. unto this day v. upon their
16. v. shall be taken away [heart
He. 6 : 19. entereth that within the v.
9 : 3. after second v. the tabernacle
10 : 20. thro. the v., that is, his flesh

VAILED. [v.

Can. 1 : † 7. Why should I be as one

VAIN.

De. 32 : 47. it is not a v. thing for you
Ju. 9 : 4. Abimelech hired v. persons
11 : 3. gathered v. men to Jephthah
1 S. 12 : 21. then sho. ye go after v. things, for they are but v. [eth
2 S. 6 : 20. as one of v. fellows uncover-
2 K. 17 : 15. v. and went aft. heathen
2 Ch. 13 : 7. gath-d unto Jerob. v. men
Jb. 11 : 11. he knoweth v. men, he
12. v. man would be wise, though
15 : 2. Sho. wise man utter v. knowl.?
27 : 12. why are ye altogether v.?
Ps. 2 : 1. people imagine a v. thing
26 : 4. I have not sat with v. persons
33 : 17. A horse is v. thing for safety
39 : 6. every man walketh in v. shew
60 : 11. v. is the help of man, 108 : 12.
62 : 10. become not v. in robbery if
119 : 113. I hate v. thoughts, but
127 : 2. It is v. for you to rise early
Pr. 12 : 11. that followeth v. persons is void of, 28 : 19. [is v.
31 : 30. Favour is deceitful, beauty
Ec. 6 : 12. his v. life wh. he spendeth
Is. 1 : 13. Bring no more v. oblations
Je. 2 : 5. aft. vanity, and are become v.
4 : 14. How long v. thoughts within
Je. 10 : 3. customs of people are v.
23 : 16. the prophets make you v.
La. 2 : 14. prophets have seen v. thi-s
4 : 17. our eyes failed for our v. help
Eze. 12 : 24. be no more any v. vision
13 : 7. Have ye not seen a v. vision
Mal. 3 : 14. said, it is v. to serve God
Mat. 5 : †22. whoso. say to bro. v. fel. [low
6 : 7. pray, use not v. repetitions
Ac. 4 : 25. people imagine v. things
Ro. 1 : 21. became v. in imaginations
1 Co. 3 : 20. thoughts of wise are v.
15 : 14. if Christ be not risen, our preaching v., your faith v., 17.
Col. 2 : 8. lest any spoil you through philosophy and v. deceit [ling
1 Ti. 1 : 6. turned aside unto v. jang-
6 : 20. avoiding profane and v. babblings, 2 Ti. 2 : 16. [v. talkers
Tit. 1 : 10. there are many unruly,
3 : 9. they are unprofitable and v.
Ja. 1 : 26. this man's religion is v.
2 : 20. wilt know, O v. man, th. faith
1 Pe. 1 : 18. redeemed fr. v. conver- [sation

In VAIN.

Ex. 20 : 7 Thou shalt not take the name of Lord i.v., De. 5 : 11.
Le. 26 : 16. ye sh. sow your seed i.v.
20. your strength be spent i.v.
1 S. 25 : 21. i.v. I kept all Nabal hath
Jb. 9 : 29. If wicked, why labour I i. [v.?
21 : 34. How comf. ye me i.v.
35 : 16. doth Job open his mou. i.v.
39 : 16. her labour i.v. with-t fear
41 : 9. Behold, hope of him is i.v.
Ps. 39 : 6. they are disquieted i.v.
73 : 13. have cleansed my heart i.v.
89 : 47. wheref. made all men i.v.?
127 : 1. they labour i.v. that build, watchman waketh i.v. [i.v.
139 : 20. thine enemies take name
Pr. 1 : 17. i.v. net is spread in sight
30 : 9. lest take name of my G. i.v.
Is. 30 : 7. Egyptians shall help i.v.
45 : 18. he created it not i.v., he
19. I said not, Seek ye me i.v.
49 : 4. I have laboured i.v., I have spent my strength i.v.
65 : 23. They shall not labour i.v.
Je. 2 : 30. i.v. have I smit. your chil.
3 : 23. i.v. is salvation hoped from
4 : 30. i.v. shalt make thyself fair
6 : 29. the founder melteth i.v.
8 : 8. We are wise. Lo. i.v. made he it; pen of the scribes is i.v.
46 : 11. i.v. sh. use many medicines
50 : 9. arrows, none sh. return i.v.
51 : 58. the people shall labour i.v.
Eze. 6 : 10. that I have not said i.v.
Ha. 2 : †13. people weary thems. i.v.
Zch. 10 : 2. the diviners comfort i.v.
Mat. 15 : 9. But i.v. they worship me, Mk. 7 : 7. [sword i.v.
Ro. 13 : 4. for he beareth not the
1 Co. 15 : 2. unless ye believed i.v.
10. his grace upon me was not i.v.
58. your labour is not i.v. in Lord
2 Co. 6 : 1. ye receive not grace of G. i.
9 : 3. our boast-g of you be i.v. [v.
Ga. 2 : 2. lest by any means I run i.v.
21. Then Christ is dead i.v.
3 : 4. Have ye suffered so many thi-s i.v. ? if it be yet i.v. [bour i.v.
4 : 11. lest I bestowed upon you la-
Ph. 2 : 16. may rejoice I have not run i.v., nor laboured i.v. [i.v.
1 Th. 2 : 1. our entrance, it was not
3 : 5. tempted you, our lab. be i.v.
Ja. 4 : 5. Do ye think Script. saith i.v.
See Vain WORDS.

VAINGLORY. [v.

Ga. 5 : 26. Let us not be desirous of
Ph. 2 : 3. Let noth. be done thro. v.

VAINLY. [mind

Col. 2 : 18. v. puffed up by his fleshly

VAJEZ'ATHA.

Es. 9 : 9. V. slew they, but on spoil

VALE. [Siddim, 8.
Ge. 14 : 3. kings were joined in v. of
10. v. of Siddim full of slimepits
37 : 14. Joseph out of v. of Hebron
De.1:7.unto all places in hills and v.
Jos.10 :40.Josh. smote country of v.
1 K. 10 : 27. Sol. made cedars as sycamore trees in the v.,2 Ch.1:15.
Je.33:13. in cities of v.sh.flocks pass

VALIANT, EST. [the v-st
Ju. 21 : 10. to Jabesh 12,000 men of
1 S. 14 : 52. Saul saw any v. man, he
16 : 18.son of Jesse a mighty v.man
18 : 17. be v. for me, fight the L.'s
26 :15.Ab-r,Art not thou a v.man ?
31 : 12. All the v. men took body of
Saul, 1 Ch. 10 : 12. [13 : 28.
2 S. 2 : 7. be ye v., for Saul is dead,
11 : 16. Uriah, where v. men were
17 :10. he that is v. sh. utterly melt
23 : 20. Jehoiada, son of a v. man
of Kabzeel, 1 Ch. 11 : 22.
24 :9. were in Israel 800,000 v. men
1 K. 1 :42. Come in, thou art v. man
1 Ch. 5 : 18. of v. men, able to bear
7 : 2. sons of Tola ; v. men[buckler
5.of Issachar were v.men of might
11 : 26. v. men of the armies were
28 :1. Da. assembled all the v. men
2 Ch. 13 :3.Abijah set bat. wi. v.men
26 : 17. with him 80 priests, v. men
28 :6.Pekah slew 120,000,all v.men
Ne. 11 : 6. sons of Perez 468 v. men
Can. 3 : 7. his bed which is Sol.'s,
threescore v. men are about it,
of the v. of Israel [a v. man
Is. 10 :13. put down inhabitants like
33 :7. their v. ones sh. cry without
Je. 9 :3.they are not v. for the truth
46 : 15.Why thy v. men swept aw.?
Na. 2 : 3. the v. men are in scarlet
3 : † 18. v. ones shall dwell in dust
He. 11 : 34.who thro. faith waxed v.

VALIANTLY. [in fight
Nu. 24 : 18. and Israel shall do v.
1 Ch. 19 : 13. let us behave ours. v.
Ps. 60 : 12. Through God we shall do
v., 108 : 13. [v., 16.
118 : 15. right hand of Lord doeth

VALLEY. [Gerar
Ge. 26 :17. Isaac pitched in the v. of
19. serv-s digged in v., found well
Nu. 13 : † 23.to the v. of Eshcol,†24.
14 : 25. Canaanites dwelt in v., Jos.
21 :20. went fr. Bamoth in v.[17:16.
De. 2 : † 13. get you over v. Zered
3 : 16.unto Gadites gave half the v.
29 So we abode in the v. over
against Beth-peor, 4 : 46. [(2) 6.
21 : 4. bring heifer unto rough v.,
34 : 3.shewed plain of v. of Jericho
Jos. 8 : 11.a v. between them and Ai
13. Joshua went into midst of v.
11 : 2. Jabin sent to kings in the v.
16. Joshua took all v.and plain(2)
17.unto Baal-gad in v.of Lebanon
13 : 19. Zareth-shahar in m-t of v.
27.gave unto Gad in v. Beth-aram
15 : 8. of v. of giants, (3). 18 :16. (3)
33. in the v. 14 cities with villages
17 :16. Canaanites in v. have chariots, and they of v. of Jezreel
Ju. 1 : 9. Judah to fight against the
Canaanites in v. [ants in v.
19. could not drive out inhabit-
34. not suffer Dan to come to v.
5:15.Barak was sent on foot into v.
6 : 33. Midianites in v. of Jezreel
7 : 8. host of Midian in the v.. 1,12.
16 : 4. loved a woman in v. of Sorek
18 :28. v. that lieth by Beth-rehob
1 S. 6 :13.reap-g wheat harvest in v.
15 : 5. Saul laid wait in the v. [19.
17 : 2. Saul pitched by the v.Elah,
3. there was a v. between them
† 40. chose 5 smooth stones out of
52. Isr. pursued Philis. to v. [v.
1 S. 21 : 9. thou slewest in v. of Elah
31 : 7. men on other side of v. saw
2 S. 24 :†5.city that lieth in v.of Gad
2 K. 2 : 16. lest cast him into some v.
3 : 16. Make this v. full of ditches
17. that v. shall be filled wi. water
1 Ch. 4 : 39.side of v. to seek pasture
10 : 7.when men in v. saw they fled
14 : 13.Philis. again spread in v.[v.
2 Ch. 20 :†16. sh find them at end of
26. assembled in v. of Berachah ;
called The v. of B.unto this day
33 : 14. Manasseh built wall in v.
35 : 22. to fight in v. of Megiddo
Ne. 11 : 35. and Ono, v. of craftsmen
Jb. 21 :33. clods of v. shall be sweet
39 :21.he paweth in v.and rejoiceth
Ps. 23:4.tho.I walk thro. v. of death
60.* Joab smote in v. of salt 12,000
Pr. 30 : 17. ravens of the v. sh. pick
Can. 6 : 11. I went to see fruits of v.
Is. 15 : † 7. abund. to v. of Arabians
22 :1. The burden of the v.of vision
5. day of trouble in v. of vision
28 : 4. beauty on head of the fat v.
40 : 4. Every v. shall be exalted
63 : 14. As a beast goeth into the v.
Je. 2 : 23. See thy way in the v.
7 : 32. no more be called v. of Hinnom, but v. of slaughter, 19 :6.
21 : 13. I am ag. thee, O inhab.of v.
31 : 40. whole v. of the dead bodies
32 :44. take witnesses in cities of v.
47 : 5. Ashkelon cut off wi. their v.
48 : 8. the v. also shall perish, and
49 :4.why gloriest in thy flowing v.
Eze. 37 :1.v. which was full of bones
2. bones very many in open v.[(2)
39 : 11. unto Gog v. of passengers,
47 : † 19. fr. v. to great sea [Jezreel
Ho. 1 : 5. break bow of Israel in v. of
Jo.3 :14.multitudes in v.of decision;
day of Lord in v. of decision
Mi. 1 : 6. stones of Samaria into v.
Zch.12 :11.mourning in v. of Megid-
14 : 4. there shall be a great v.[don
5. ye shall flee to v. of mount-s (2)
Lu. 3 : 5. every v. be filled, ev. hill
See **GATE** with **valley.**
See ACHOR, AJALON, BACA,
BERACHAH, CHARASHIM,
CRAFTSMEN, ESHCOL, GIBE-
ON, HAMON-GOG, HINNOM,
JEHOSHAPHAT, JIPHTHAH-
EL, KEZIZ, MIZPEH, MOAB,
REPHAIM, SALT, SHAVEH,
SHITTIM, SUCCOTH, ZARED,
ZEBOIM, ZEPHATHAH.

VALLEYS. [forth
Nu. 24 :6. As the v.are they spread
De. 8 :7.depths that spring out of v.
11 : 11.land is a land of hills and v.
Jos. 9 :1.wh. kings in v. heard,12:8.
2 S. 23 : † 30. Hiddai of v. of Gaash
1 K. 20 : 28. God of hills, but he is
not God of v. [the v.
1 Ch. 12 : 15. put to flight them of
27:29.over herds in v.was Shaphat
Jb. 30 : 6. To dwell in cliffs of v., in
39 : 10. will he harrow v.after thee?
Ps. 65 : 13. v. are covered with corn
104 : 8.they go down by the v.unto
10. He sendeth springs into the v.
Can. 2 : 1. I am the lily of the v.
Is. 7 :19 they sh. rest in desolate v.
22 : 7. v. shall be full of chariots
24 : † 15. glorify the Lord in the v.
28 : 1. beauty on the head of fat v.
41 : 18. I will open fountains in v.
57 : 5. slaying chil. in v. und.rocks
Je. 49 :4. Whf.gloriest thou in the v.
Eze. 6 : 3. saith Lord to v., 36 : 4. 6.
7 :16.on mountains like doves of v.
31 : 12. in all v. his branches fallen
32 : 5. I will fill v. with thy height
35 : 8. in thy v. shall they fall slain
36 : 6. say unto v.,Thus saith Lord
Mi. 1 : 4. v. shall be cleft as wax

VALOUR. [of v.
Ju. 3 : 29. slew of Moab 10,000 men
18 : 2. sent 5 men of v. to spy land
20 :44. fell 18,000, all men of v.,46.
1 S. 18 : †17.be thou son of v.for me
2 S. 2 : † 7. be ye sons of v., 13 : †28.
1 Ch. 5 : † 18. sons of v. able to bear
26 : 30. his brethren men of v., 32.
2 Ch. 28 :†6.slew 120,000, sons of v.

Mighty man of VALOUR.
Ju. 6 : 12. L. is with thee, thou - v.
11 : 1. Jephthah, Gileadite, a - v.
1 K. 11 : 28. Jeroboam was a - v.
2 K. 5 : 1.Naaman a - v., but a leper
1 Ch. 12 :28. Zadok,young man,a - v.
2 Ch. 17 : 17. Eliada, a - v., armed

Mighty men of VALOUR.
Jos. 1 : 14. ye shall pass before your
brethren, all the - v. [and - v.
6 : 2. given into thine hand Jericho
8:3. ag. Ai Joshua chose 30,000 - v.
10 :7. Joshua fr. Gilgal and all - v.
2 K 24 :14.he carried aw.all the - v.
1 Ch. 5 : 24. And these were - v.,
famous men, 7 : 7, 9, 11, 40.-12:
21, 25, 30.-26 : 6, 30, 31, 32.
8 : 40. the sons of Ulam were - v.
9 : † 13.- v. for service of hou. of G.
2 Ch. 13 : 3. Jerob-m set battle with
800,000 -v., 14 :8.-17 :13,14,16.
14:8. Asa an army of 280,000, all -v.
17:13.men of war -v.were in Jerus.
14. Adnah,chief,with -v.,300,000
16. Amaziah, wi. him 200,000 - v.
25 : 6. Amaziah hired 100,000 - v.
26 :12.number of chief of fa-s of -v.
32 : 21. an angel which cut off - v.
Ne. 11 :14.And their breth., -v. 128

VALUE. [Noun.] [v.
Jb. 13 : 4. ye are all physicians of no
Mat. 10 : 31. ye are of more v. than
many sparrows, Lu. 12 : 7.

VALUE, ED, EST.
Le. 27 : 8. the priest shall v. him
12. priest shall v. it, whe. good or
bad ; as thou v-t it so shall it be
27 :16.hom. of barley seed v-d at 50
Jb.28:16.wisdom not be v-d wi.gold
19. nei. sh. it be v-d wi. pure gold
Mat. 27 :9.price of him that was v-d,
whom they of chil. of Isr.did v.

VANI'AH.
Eze. 10 : 36. Of the sons of Bani, V.

VANISH, ED, ETH. [v.
Jb. 6 : 17. time they wax warm, they
7 : 9. As cloud is consumed and v-h
Is. 51 : 6. the heavens shall v. away
Je. 49 :7. saith, is their wisdom v-d?
Lu. 24 : 31. he v-d out of their sight
1 Co. 13 : 8.whe. knowledge, it sh.v.
He. 8 : 13. waxeth old, is ready to v.
Ja.4:14.life is even a vapour that v-h

VANITIES.
De. 32 : 21. they have provoked me
with their v., 1 K. 16 : 13, 26.
Ps. 31 : 6. I hated them that regard
lying v. [12 : 8.
Ec.1 :2.Vanity of v., saith preacher,
5 : 7. in multitude of dreams are v.
Je. 8 : 19. provoked me with strange
10 : 8. stock is a doctrine of v. [v.
14 :22.are any v. th. can cause rain
Jon. 2 :8. they that observe lying v.
Ac. 14 : 15. ye should turn fr. these

VANITY. [v.
2 K. 17 : 15.followed v. became vain
Jb. 7 : 3. made to possess months of
16.let me alone,my days are v.[v.
15 : 31. not trust in v., for v. shall
be his recompense [forth v.
35. conceive mischief and bring
31 : 5. If I have walked with v. or
35 : 13. Surely God will not hear v.
Ps. 4 : 2. how long will ye love v.
10 : 7 und. his tongue mischief,v.
12 : 2. speak v. ev. one to neighb-r

Ps. 24 : 4. not lifted his soul unto v.
36: † 4. wicked deviseth v. upon bed
39 : 5. man at his best state is v.
11. surely every man is v. [8, 11.
41 :6. if come, he speaketh v., 144 :
62 : 9. Surely men of low degree are
v. ; they are lighter than v. [v.
78 :33. their days did he consume in
94 : 11. Lord knoweth thoughts of
man are v. [v.
119 :37. Turn away mine eyes from
144 : 4. Man is like to v., his days
Pr. 13 : 11. Wealth gotten by v. shall
be diminished [tongue is v.
21 : 6. getting of treasures by lying
22 : 8. soweth iniquity shall reap v.
30 : 8. Remove from me v. and lies
Ec. 1 : 2. v. of vanities, saith the
Preacher, v. of vanities, all is
v., 14.-3 : 19.-11 : 8.-12 : 8.
2 : 1. this is also v., 15, 19, 21, 23.-4:
8, 16.-5: 10.-6: 2, 9.-7 :6.-8: 10, 14.
11. all v. and vexation, 17, 26 -4 :4.
4 : 7. Then I saw v. under the sun
6 : 4. For he cometh in with v. [v.
11. be many things that increase
† 12. numb. of days of life of his v.
7 : 15. have I seen in days of my v.
8 : 14. There is a v. upon the earth
9 :9. joyfully wi. wife days of thy v.
11 : 10. childhood and youth are v.
Is. 5 : 18. draw iniq-y wi. cords of v.
30 : 28. sift nations with sieve of v.
40 : 17. All nations are counted v.
23. maketh judges of earth as v.
41. :29. Behold, they are all v., 44:9.
57 : 13. v. shall take them [ing v.
58 : 9. If thou take away the speak-
59 : 4. they trust in v., speak lies
Je. 2 : 5. fathers have walked aft. v.
10 : † 3. statutes of the people are v.
15. Th. are v., work of errors, 51: 18.
16: 19. our fathers have inherited v.
18 : 15. peo. have burned inc. to v.
Eze. 13 :6. They have seen v., 22: 28.
8. Bec. ye have spoken v., seen lies
9. Prophets that see v. and divine
lies, 21 : 29. [v.
23. Therefore ye shall see no more
Ho. 12 : 11. surely they are v., they
Ha. 2 : 13. sh. weary thems. for v.
3 : † 7. I saw tents of Cushan und. v.
Zch. 10 : 2. For idols have spoken v.
Ro. 8 : 20. creature made subj. to v.
Ep. 4 : 17. not as Gentiles walk in v.
2 Pe. 2 : 18. speak gr. swelling words

VAPOUR, S. [of v.

Jb. 36 :27. pour down rain acc. to v.
33. cattle also concerning the v.
Ps. 135 :7. He causeth v-s to ascend,
Je. 10 : 13.-51 : 16. [word
148 : 8. hail, snow, v. fulfilling his
Ac. 2 :19. signs in earth, v. of smoke
Ja. 4 : 14. your life? It is even a v.

VARIABLE.

Ha. 3 : † 1. a prayer acc. to v. songs

VARIABLENESS. [v.

Ja. 1 :17. Fa. of lights, with wh. is no

VARIANCE. [v.

Mat. 10 : 35. I am come to set man at
Ga. 5:20. works of flesh are hatred, v.

VASH'NI = JOEL.

1 Ch. 6 : 28. sons of Samuel ; V. and
Abiah, 1 S. 8 : † 2.

VASH'TI. [women

Es. 1 : 9. V., queen, made feast for
11. To bring V. queen, before king
12. queen V. refused to come at
15. what shall we do unto queen V.
16. V. not done wrong to king only
17. king com-ded V. to be brought
19. That V. come no more before k.
2 : 1. k. rememb-d V. what she had
4. let maid. be queen instead of V.
17. k made Es. queen instead of V.

VAULT. [dar

1 K. 6 :† 9. covered v. beams with ce-

VAUNT, ETH.

Ju. 7 : 2. lest Israel v. thems. ag. me
1 Co. 13 : 4. charity v-h not itself

VEHEMENT. [flame

Can. 8 :6. love is as fire that hath v.
Jon. 4 : 8. prepared a v. east wind
2 Co. 7: 11. what v. desire it wrought

VEHEMENTLY.

Mk. 14 : 31. Peter spake the more v.
Lu. 6 : 48. beat v. upon house, 49.
11 : 53. Phari. began to urge him v.
23 : 10. scribes stood and v. accused

VEIL. See VAIL. [him

VEIN.

Jb. 28 : 1. there is a v. for the silver

VENERABLE.

Ph. 4 : † 8. whatsoever things are v.

VENGEANCE, S. [fold

Ge. 4 : 15. v. be taken on him seven-
De. 32 : 35. To me belongeth v., Ps.
94 : 1. He. 10 : 30. [mies
41. I will render v. to mine ene-
43. render v. to his adversaries
Ju. 11 : 36. Lord taken v. for thee
Ps. 58 : 10. rejoice when he seeth v.
79 :† 10. by v. of blood of thy serv-ts
99 :8. tookest v. of their inventions
149 :7. To execute v. upon heathen
Pr. 6 : 34. not spare in the day of v.
Is. 34 : 8. it is the day of the Lord's
v., 61 : 2. Je. 51 : 6. [with v.
35 : 4. behold your God will come
47 : 3. I will take v., Je. 51 : 36. [v.
59 : 17. he put on the garments of
63 :4. the day of v. is in mine heart
Je. 11 : 20. let me see thy v., 20 : 12.
46 : 10. day of the Lord a day of v.
50 : 15. it is the v. of the Lord : take
v. upon her [ple, 51 : 11.
28. v. of the Lord, v. of his tem-
La. 3 : 60. hast seen all their v. ag. me
Eze. 24 : 8. fury come up to take v.
25 : 12. Edom by v. hath offended
14. I will lay my v. upon Edom (2)
15. bec. Philistines have taken v.
17. wh. I lay my v. upon Philis. (2)
Mi. 5 : 15. I will execute great v.,
Eze. 25 : 17. † v-s [versaries
Na. 1 : 2. Lord will take v. on his ad-
Lu. 21 : 22. these be the days of v.
Ac. 28 :4. wh. v. suffereth not to live
Ro. 3 : 5. unrighteous who taketh v.
12 : 19. v. is mine, I will repay [v.
2 Th. 1 : 8. L. in flaming fire taking
Jude 7. suffering v. of eternal fire

VENISON.

Ge. 25 :28. Isaac loved Esau, because
he eat of his v. [5, 7.
27 : 3. go to field, take me some v.,
19. arise, and eat of my v., 31. [v.
25. Bring it, I will eat of my son's
33. where is he th. hath taken v.?

VENOM. [of asps

De. 32 : 33. their wine is the cruel v.

VENOMOUS. [hang

Ac. 28 : 4. barbarians saw v. beast

VENT. [hath no v.

Jb. 32 : 19. my belly as wine which

VENTURE.

1 K. 22 : 34. certain man drew a bow
at a v., and smote k., 2 Ch. 18:33.

VERIFIED.

Ge. 42 : 20. so shall your words be v.
1 K. 8 : 26. let thy word be v., 2 Ch.

VERILY. [6 : 17.

Ge. 42 : 21. v. guilty conc. our broth-
Ex. 31 : 13. v. my sabbaths keep [er
Ju. 15:2. I v. thought thou hated her
1 K. 1 : 43. v. L. hath made Sol. king
2 K. 4 : 14. v. she hath no child, and
1 Ch. 21 : 24. I will v. bring for price
Jb. 19 : 13. mine acquaintance are
v. estranged from me [be fed
Ps. 37 :3. do good, and v. thou shalt
39 : 5. v. every man is vanity
58 : 11. v. is a reward for righteous,
v. he is a God that judgeth
Ps. 66: 19. v. God hath heard me [vain
73 : 13. v. I cleansed my heart in
Is. 45 :15. v. thou a God that hidest
Je. 15 : 11. v. it shall be well with
thy remnant, v. I will [the poor
Zch. 11 : † 7. flock of slaughter, v.
Mat. 5 : 18. v. I say unto you, 6 : 2,
5, 16.-8 : 10.-10 : 15, 23, 42.-11 :
11.-13 : 17.-16 : 28.-17 : 20.-18 :
3, 13, 18.-19 : 23, 28.-21 : 21, 31.
-23 : 36.-24 : 2, 34, 47. -25 : 12,
40, 45.-26 : 13, 21, 34. Mk. 3:28,
-6 : 11.-8 : 12.-9 : 1, 12, 41.-10 :
15, 29.-11 : 23.-12 : 43.-13 : 30.-
14 : 9, 18, 25, 30. Lu. 4 : 24.-11 :
51.-12 : 37.-13 : 35.-18 : 17, 29.-
21 : 32. [14 : 30. Lu. 23 : 43.
26. v. I say unto thee, 26 :34. Mk.
Mk. 9 : 12. Elias v. cometh first and
Ac. 16 : 37. nay, v. let them fetch us
19 :4. John v. baptized wi. baptism
22 : 3. am v. a man which am a Jew
26 : 9. I v. thought I ought to do
Ro. 2 : 25. circumc-n v. profiteth if
10 : 18. v. their sound went into all
15 : 27. It hath pleased them v.
1 Co. 5 :3. I v. as absent in body, but
14 : 17. thou v. givest thanks well
Ga. 3 : 21. v. righteousness had been
He. 2 : 16. v. he took not nature of
3 : 5. Mos. v. was faithful in all his
6 : 16. men v. swear by the greater
7 : 5. v. they that are sons of Levi
18. is v. a disannulling of comm-t
9 : 1. v. first cove-t had ordinances
12 :10. they v. few days chastened us
1 Pe. 1 : 20. who v. was foreordained
1 Jn. 2 :5. in him v. love of God per-

VERILY, VERILY. [fected

Jn. 1 : 51. v., v., I say unto you, 5 :
19, 24, 25.-6 : 26, 32, 47, 53.-8 :
34, 51, 58.-10 : 1, 7.-12 : 24.-13 :
16, 20, 21.-14 : 12 -16 : 20, 23.
3 : 3. v., v., I say unto thee, 5, 11.-
13 : 38.-21 : 18.

VERITY.

Ps. 111:7. works of his hands are v.
1 Ti. 2 : 7. a teacher in faith and v.

VERMILION.

Je. 22 : 14. and painted with v. [v.
Eze. 23 : 14. images portrayed with

VERY.

Ge. 1 : 31. and behold it was v. good
12 : 14. woman that she was v. fair
13 : 2. Abram was v. rich in cattle
18 : 20. bec. their sin is v. grievous
24 : 16. damsel v. fair to look upon
27 : 24. Art th. my v. son Esau? 21.
33. Isaac trembled v. exceedingly
41 : 19. other kine v. ill favoured
50: 10. mourned with v. sore lament.
Ex. 1 : 20. people waxed v. mighty
8 : 28. ye shall not go v. far away
9 : 3. sh. be a v. grievous murrain
30 :36. beat some of it v. small [him
Nu. 6 : 9. if any die v. suddenly by
12 :3. Moses was v. meek, above all
De. 20 : 15. do unto cities v. far from
27 :8. write this law v. plainly [thee
28 : 43. stranger sh. get above thee
v. high ; thou come down v. low
54. man that is tender, v. delicate
30 : 14. word is v. nigh unto thee
32 : 20. are a v. froward generation
Jos. 1 : 7. be thou v. courageous
9 : 9. From a v. far country come
13. garm-s old by v. long journey
22. saying, We are v. far from you
10 : 20. with v. great slaughter
23 : 6. Be ye v. courageous to do all
Ju. 3 : 17. Eglon was a v. fat man
18 : 9. seen the land ; it is v. good
Ru. 1 : 20. dealt v. bitterly with me
1 S. 5 : 11. hand of G. v. heavy there
14 : 31. and the people were v. faint
18 : 15. S. saw he behaved v. wisely
19: 4. his works to thee-ward v. good

1S. 25 : 36. for Nabal was v. drunken
2 S. 1 : 26. v. pleasant hast thou been
2 : 17. was a v. sore battle that day
11 : 2. the woman was v. beautiful
12 : 15. the Lord struck the child; it was v. sick [man
13 : 3. Jonadab was a v. subtile
19 : 32. Barzillai was a v. aged man
24 : 10. have done v. foolishly, 1 Ch.
1 K. 1 : 6. he a v. goodly man[21 :8.
4. Abishag v. fair, cherished king
15. king was v. old; and Abishag
21 : 26. Ahab did v. abominably
2 K. 14 : 26. affliction of Isr. v. bitter
1 Ch. 9 : 13. v. able men for service
2 Ch. 6 : 18. God in v. deed dwell with
20 : 35. Ahaziah did v. wickedly
Ne. 1 : 7. We have dealt v. corruptly
Ps. 5 : 9. inward part is v. wickedn.
35 : 8. into v. destruct. let him fall
46 : 1. God is a v. present help[him
50 : 3. sh. be v. tempestuous about
89 : 2. thy faithfuln. in v. heavens
92 : 5. O Lord, thy thoughts v. deep
93 : 5. Thy testimonies v. sure, 119:
105 : 12. When v. few, strangers[138.
119 : 140. Thy word is v. pure, thf.
147 : 15. His word runneth v. swiftly
Pr. 17 : 9. he separateth v. friends
27 : 15. dropping in a v. rainy day
Is. 1 : 9. Exc. had left v. small rem-t
5 : 1. vineyard in a v. fruitful hill
16 : 6. heard of Moab; he is v. proud
14. the remnant shall be v. small
24 : 16. have dealt v. treacherously
30 : 19. will be v. grievous unto thee
31 : 1. trust in horsem. bec. v. strong
33 : 17. behold land v. far off[yoke
47 : 6. upon ancient v. heavily thy
48 : 8. wouldest deal v. treacher-sly
Je 2 : 12. be ye v. desolate, saith Lord
4 : 19. I am pained at my v. heart
12 : 1. happy th. deal v. treacher-ly
14 : 17. peo. broken wi. v. grievous
18 : 13. virgin done v. horrible thi.
20 : 15. child, making him v. glad
24 : 2. One basket had v. good figs; other basket v. naughty, 3.
27 : 7. until the v. time of his land
46 : 20. Eg. like v. fair heifer[come
Eze. 27 : 25. v. glorious in the seas
33 : 32. art as a v. lovely song [ous
Da. 2 : 12. for this, king was v. furi-
6 : 19. king arose v. early and went
Ha. 2 : 13. people shall labour in v. fire, weary thems. for v. vanity
Zch. 8 : 4. ev. man wi. staff for v. age
9 : 2. Zidon, though it be v. wise
5. Gaza sh. see it, be v. sorrowful
Mat. 10 : 30. v. hairs of head, Lu. 12 : 7.
15 : 28. whole fr. that v. hour, 17 : 18.
18 : 31. serv-s v. sorry, and told lord
24 : 24. if possible, deceive v. elect
Mk. 16 : 2. v. early in morning unto sepulchre, Lu. 24 : 1. [v. first
Lu. 1 : 3. perfect understanding fr.
9 : 5. shake off v. dust fr. feet, 10 : 11.
12 : 59. till hast paid v. last mite
18 : 23. v. sorrowful, for v. rich, 24.
19 : 48. the people were v. attentive
Jn. 7 : 26. this is v. Christ, Ac. 9 : 22.
8 : 4. taken in adultery in v. act
12 : 3. pound of spikenard v. costly
14 : 11. believe me for v. works' sake
Ac. 10 : 10. Peter became v. hungry
24 : 2. v. worthy deeds are done by
2 Co. 11 : 5. I was not behind the v. chiefest apostles, 12 : 11.
12 : 15. v. gladly be spent for you
1 Th. 5 : 13. to esteem them v. highly
23. v. God of peace sanctify you
He. 10 : 1. not the v. image of things
Ja. 3 : 4. turned with v. small helm
5 : 11. the Lord is v. pitiful, and of
See ANGRY, DAY, DEED, FAR.

VERY great. [comp-y

Ge. 50 : 9. wi. him horsemen, v.g.
Nu. 32 : 1. children of Gad had v.g. multitude of cattle [Ju. 11 : 33.
Jos. 10 : 20. an end of v.g. slaughter,
1 K. 10 : 10. gave of spices v.g. store
2 Ch. 7 : 8. kept feast a v.g. congr-n
9 : 1. queen of S. with v.g. company
Ezr. 10 : 1. unto Ezra v.g. congreg-n
Mk. 16 : 4. stone rolled aw. was v.g.
See Very GREAT.
See GRIEVOUS, HEAVY, HIGH, LITTLE, LOW.

VERY many. [v.m.

Jos. 11 : 4. kings wi. horses, chariots,
1 Ch. 23 : 17. sons of Rehabiah v.m.
2Ch. 16 : 8. huge host wi v.m. char-ts
Eze. 37 : 2. bones v.m. in open valley
47 : 7. at bank of river v.m. trees
2 Co. 9 : 2. zeal hath provoked v.m.
See Very MUCH.
See OLD, SORE, TERRIBLE, THING, WROTH.
See This THING, Very WELL

VESSEL. [wood (2)

Le. 11 : 32. unclean, whe. any v. of
34. all drink in such v. be unclean
13 : † 49. if plague in any v. of skin
15 : 12. v. of earth he toucheth (2) † 4.
Nu. 19 : 15. open v. wh. hath no cov-g
17. running water be put in a v.
31 : † 20. purify your v. of skins[v.
De. 23 : 24. eat grapes, not put any in
1 S. 17 : † 40. stones in shepherd's v.
21 : 5. tho. sanctified this day in v.
1 K. 17 : 10. Fetch me water in a v.
2 K. 4 : 6. Bring yet a v. There is not a v. more [a broken v.
Ps. 31 : 12. I am forgotten, I am like
Pr. 25 : 4. sh. come a v. for the finer
Is. 66 : 20. bring offering in clean v.
Je. 22 : 28. is he v. wh-n no pleasure?
25 : 34. ye sh. fall like a pleasant v.
35 : † 4. Maaseiah, keeper of the v.
48 : 11. Moab not emptied fr. v. to v.
38. I have broken Moab like a v.
51 : 34. Neb-r made me an empty v.
Eze. 4 : 9. put in one v., make bread
15 : 3. will men take pin to hang v.?
Ho. 8 : 8. as a v. wh-n no pleasure
Mk. 11 : 16. not carry v. thro. temple
Lu. 8 : 16. no man cover-h candle wi.
Jn. 19 : 29. a v. full of vinegar [v.
Ac. 9 : 15. he is a chosen v. unto me
10 : 11. Peter saw a certain v. descending, 16.-11 : 5. [to honour
Ro. 9 : 21. power to make one v. un-
1 Th. 4 : 4. possess his v. in sanctifi-n
2 Ti. 2 : 21. he sh. be a v. unto honour
1 Pe. 3 : 7. honour unto wife as weaker

Earthen VESSEL, S. [v.

Le. 6 : 28. e.v. wherein it is sodden
11 : 33. e.v. whereinto any falleth
14 : 5. birds be killed in an e.v., 50.
Nu. 5 : 17. take holy water in e.v.
2 S. 17 : 28. Shobi brought beds, e.v-s
Je. 32 : 14. this evidence, put in e.v.
2 Co. 4 : 7. we have this treasure in
See POTTER. [e.v-s

VESSELS. [v.

Ge. 43 : 11. take of best fruits in y-r
Ex. 7 : 19. in v. of wood, v. of stone
25 : 39. make it wi. these v., 37 : 24.
27 : 19. All the v. of the tabernacle,
31 : † 7. - 39 : 40. - 40 : 9. Nu. 1 : 50. (2). -3 : 36 1 K. 8 : 4. 1 Ch. 23 : 26. 2 Ch. 5 : 5.
30 : 27. table and his v., candlest-k and his v., 35 : 13. -37 : 16. -39 : 36, 37. Nu 4 : 9, 10.
28. the altar with his v., 35 : 16.- 38 : 3, 30.-39 : 39. Nu. 4 : 14.-7 : 1.
40 : 10. anoint altar and v., Le. 8 : 11.
Nu. 3 : 31. v. of sanctuary, 4 : 15, 16. Ne. 10 : 39. [uary
18 : 3. not come nigh v. of sanct-
19 : 18. sprinkle water upon all v.
Ru. 2 : 9. when athirst go unto the v.
1 S. 9 : 7. bread is spent in our v.
1 S. 17 : † 22. David left v. in hand of
21 : 5. v. of young men are holy
1 K. 7 : 45. all v. which Hiram made
47. Solomon left all v. unweighed
48. Sol. made v. th. pertained unto hou. of L., 51. 2 Ch. 4 : 18, 19.
1 K. 10 : 21. v. of house of Leb-n were of pure gold, 2 Ch. 9 : 20. [18.
15 : 15. bro-t gold and v., 2 Ch. 15 :
2 K. 4 : 3. Go, borrow v. of all thy neighbours, empty v. not a few
4. shalt pour into all those v., 5.
6. When v. were full she said, Bri.
7 : 15. way full of garments, v. [24.
14 : 14. v. found in house, 2 Ch. 25 :
20 : † 13. Hezekiah shewed all the house of his v., Is. 39 : † 2.
23 : 4. bring out all v. made for Baal
1 Ch. 9 : 28. had charge of ministering v., 2 Ch. 24 : 14. (2) [see v.
29. Some were appointed to over-
22 : 19. holy v. of God, Ezr. 8 : 28.
28 : 13. pattern for all v. of service
2 Ch. 15 : 18. Asa brought into house of God silver, and gold, and v.
24 : 14. of money were made v. for hou. of L., v. to minist., v. of gold
28 : 24. Ahaz gathered v. of hou. of God, cut in pieces v. [with v. (2)
29 : 18. we have cleansed house of L.
19. v. Ahaz cast out we sanctified
36 : 7. carried v. of hou. of Lord to Babylon, 10, 18. Je. 27 : 18, 21.
19. destroyed all the goodly v. th-f
Ezr. 1 : 7. Cyrus brought forth the v.
10. silver basins 410, other v. 1,000
5 : 15. v. carry to temple in Jerus.
7 : 19. v. deliver bef. God of Jerus.
8 : 25. I weighed unto th. v., 30, 33.
27. two v. of fine copper, precious
28. the v. are holy unto the Lord
Ne. 13 : 5. chamber where they laid
9. thither bro-t I v. of hou. [the v.
Eze. 1 : 7. v. of gold (v. being diverse)
Is. 18 : 2. v. of bulrushes upon waters
22 : 24. all v. of small quantity, from v. of cups to v. of flagons
52 : 11. be ye clean that bear v. of
65 : 4. broth of abominable things
Je. 14 : 3. returned wi. v. empty[in v.
27 : 16. v. of Lord's house shall be brought from Babylon, 28 : 3, 6.
18. v. at Jerus. go not to Bab-n, 21.
19. saith Lord conc. v. in this city
40 : 10. wine, fruits, oil, put in v.
48 : 12. wanderers sh. empty his v.
49 : 29. shall take to thems. all v.
Da. 1 : 2. v. of house of God Neb-r carried to house of his god[thee
5 : 23. bro-t v. of his house before
Ho. 13 : 15. spoil treasure of pleasant
Na 2 : † 9. glory out of v. of desire[v.
Hag. 2 : 16. to draw 50 v. out of press
Mat. 13 : 48. gathered the good into
25 : 4. wise took oil in their v. [v.
Ro. 9 : 22. if God endured v. of wrath
23. riches of glory on v. of mercy
He. 2 : † 1. lest we run out as leaking
9 : 21. sprinkled v. of ministry [v.
Re. 18 : 12. v. of ivory, all man. of v.
See **Vessels of BRASS, Vessels of GOLD, Vessels of SILVER, SILVER vessels.**
See GOLDEN, POTTER.

VESTMENTS.

2 K. 10 : 22. Bring v. for worshippers

VESTRY. [the v.

2 K. 10 : 22. Jehu said unto him over

VESTURE, S.

Ge. 41 : 42. Joseph in v-s of fine linen
De. 22 : 12. fringes on quarters of v.
Ps. 22 : 18. garments, they cast lots upon my v., Mat. 27 : 35. Jn. 19 : 24.
102 : 26. as a v. sh. thou change th.
He. 1 : 12. as a v. shalt thou fold th.
Re. 19 : 13. with a v. dipped in blood
16. on his v. and thigh a name

VEX.

Ex. 22 : 21. shalt nei. v. a stranger, nor oppress, Le. 19 : 33. [v. her
Le. 18 : 18. nor a wife to her sister to
Nu. 25 : 17. v. Midianites and smite
18. they v. you with their wiles
Nu. 33 : 55. those ye let remain sh. v.
2 S. 12 : 18. how v. himself if we tell
2 Ch. 15 : 6. G. did v. with adversity
Jb. 19 : 2. How long ye v. my soul
Ps. 2 : 5. v. them in sore displeasure
Is. 7 :6. Let us go ag. Judah and v. it
11 : 13. Judah shall not v. Ephraim
Eze. 32 : 9. I will v. hearts of many
Ha. 2 : 7. not awake that sh. v. thee?
Ac. 12 :1. Herod v. certain of church

VEXATION, S. [v.

De. 28 :20. Lord shall send upon thee
2 Ch. 15 : 5. great v-s were upon all
Ec. 1 : 14. All is vanity and v. of spirit, 2 : 11, 17. [4, 16.-6 : 9.
17. this is v. of spirit, 2 : 26.-4 :
2 : 22. what hath man of the v. of his heart? [v. of spirit
4 : 6. than both the hands full with
Is. 9 : 1. not be such as was in her v.
28 : 19. be a v. to understand report
65 : 14. ye shall howl for v. of spirit
Je. 24 : †9. will deliver them for a v.
Eze 22 : †5. mock thee, which art

VEXED. [much in v.

Nu. 20 :15. Egy-ns v. us and fathers
Ju. 2 :18. by reason of them that v.
10 : 8. that year Ammonites v. Isr.
16 : 16. his soul was v. unto death
1 S. 14 : 47. Saul v. his enemies on
2 S. 13 : 2. Amnon so v. he fell sick
2 K. 4 : 27. let her alone, soul is v.
Ne. 9 : 27. to enemies who v. them
Jb. 27 : 2. Almighty, hath v. my soul
Ps. 6 : 2. heal me: for my bones are
3. my soul also is sore v. [v.
10. let mine enemies be sore v.
Is. 63 : 10. they v. his Holy Spirit
Eze. 22 :5. art infamous and much v.
7. in thee they v. fatherless and
29. people of land v. the poor [devil
Mat. 15 : 22. dau. is grievously v. wi.
17 : 15. for he is lunatic and sore v.
Lu. 6 : 18. were v. with uncl. spirits, and healed, Ac. 5 : 16. [conver-n
2 Pe. 2 : 7. delivered just Lot, v. with
8. v. his righteous soul from day to

VIAL, VIALS. [day

1 S. 10 : 1. Samuel took a v. of oil
Re. 5 : 8. golden v-s full of odours
15 : 7. gave 7 angels 7 golden v-s
16 :1. pour out v-s of wrath of God
2. first angel poured his v. upon
3. second poured. v. upon the sea
4. third poured v. upon the rivers
8. fourth poured v. upon sun
10. fifth poured v. upon seat of b.
12. sixth poured v. upon Euphra-
17. seventh poured v. into air [tes
17 : 1. one of the angels had 7 v-s,

VICTORY. [21 : 9.

1 S. 15 : † 29. v. of Israel will not lie
2 S. 19 : 2. v. was turned into mourn-
23 : 10. L. wrought great v., 12 [ing
2 K. 5 :†1. L. had given v. unto Syria
1 Ch. 29 : 11. Thine, O Lord, is the v.
Ps. 98 :1. his holy arm hath gotten v.
Pr. 21 : † 31. battle, but v. is of Lord
Is. 25 : 8. he will swallow up death in v., 1 Co. 15 : 54. [m-t unto v.
Mat. 12 : 20. till he send forth judg-
1 Co. 15 : 55. O grave, where thy v.?
57. thanks to God, who giveth us
1 Jn. 5 : 4. this is the v. our faith [v.
Re. 15 :2. th. had gotten v. over beast

VICTUAL, S. [v-s

Ge. 14 : 11. took goods of Sodom and
Ex. 12 :39. nei. had prepared any v.
Le. 25 : 37. nor lend v-s for increase
De. 23 : 19. not lend upon usury of v-s
Jos. 1 : 11. command peo., Prepare v-s
Jos. 9 : 11. Take v-s wi. you for journey
14. men took of their v-s asked not
Ju. 7 : 8. So people took v-s in hand
17 : 10. I will give apparel and v-s
20 : 10. 1,000 to fetch v. for people
1 S. 22 : 10. he gave him v-s and sword
1 K. 4 : 7. provided v-s for king, 27.
11 : 18. Pharaoh appointed him v.
1 Ch. 12 :†40. that were nigh bro-t v.
2 Ch. 11 : 11. captains and store of v.
23. gave them v. in abundance
Ne. 10 :31. if people bring v-s on sab-h
13 :15. ag them in day they sold v-s
Je. 40 : 5. captain gave Jeremiah v-s
44 : 17. for then had we plenty of v-s
Mat. 14 : 15. into villages to buy v-s

VICTUALLED. [Lu. 9 : 12.

1 K. 20 : † 27. chil. of Israel were v.

VIEW, VIEWED. [cho

Jos. 2 : 1. Go, v. the land, even Jeri-
7 : 2. Go, v. the country. The men went up and v-d Ai [v., 15.
2 K. 2 : 7. sons of prophets stood to
Ezr. 8 : 15. I v-d people and priests
Ne. 2 : 13. I v-d walls of Jerus., 15.

VIEWERS. [up

Is. 47 : † 13. Let v. of heavens stand

VIGILANT. [behav-r

1 Ti. 3 :2. A bishop must be v. of good
Tit 2 : †2. That the aged men be v.
1 Pe. 5 :8. be v. bec. your adversary

VIGOUR. [corruption

Da. 10 : † 8. my v. was turned into

VILE. [unto thee

De. 25 : 3. lest thy brother seem v.
Ju. 19 : 24. but do not so v. a thing
1 S. 3 : 13. bec. his sons made thems. v.
15 :9. every thing v. they destroyed
2 S. 6 :22. I will be more v. than thus
Jb. 18 : 3. why are we reputed v.
40 : 4. I am v., what shall I answer?
Je. 15 : 19. take precious from the v.
29 : 17. I will make them like v. figs
La. 1 : 11. see; O L., I am become v.
Na 1 : 14. thy grave, for thou art v.
3 : 6. I will cast filth, make thee v.
Ro. 1 : 26. them unto v. affections
Ph. 3 : 21. Who change our v. body
Ja. 2 : 2. come in a poor man in v.
See PERSON. [raiment

VILELY. [away

2 S. 1 :21. shield of mighty is v. cast

VILER, VILEST.

Jb. 30 : 8. they were v-r than earth
Ps. 12 : 8. when v-t men are exalted

VILLAGE. [coast

Eze. 47 : †16. The middle v. wh. is by
Mat. 21 : 2. Go into the v., ye shall find an ass, Mk. 11 :2. Lu. 19 :30.
Lu. 8 : 1. went thro-t ev. city and v.
10 :38. he entered into a certain v.,
9 : 52, 56.-17 : 12. [to a v.
24 : 13. two of them went same day
28. they drew nigh unto the v.

VILLAGES.

Ex. 8 : 13. frogs died out of v. [fields
Le. 25 : 31. houses of v. counted as
Nu. 21 : 32. took v., drove out Am.
32 : 42. Nobah took Kenath and v.
Jos. 15 : 46. all near Ashdod with v.
21 : 12. fields and v. gave they to Caleb, 1 Ch. 6 : 56. [11.
Ju. 5 : 7. inhabitants of v. ceased,
1 Ch. 9 : 16. dwelt in v. of Netoph-ites
22. reckoned by genealogy in v.
25. their breth. in v. were to come
Ne. 6 : 2. let us meet in one of the v.
11 : 25. for the v. some of Judah dwelt (4) 27, 28, 30 (2) [and v.
31. chil. of Benj. dwelt at Beth-el
12 :29. singers had builded them v.
Es. 9 : 19. Jews of v. made 14th day
Ps. 10 : 8. in lurking places of v.
Can. 7 : 11. beloved, let us lodge in v.
Is. 42 : 11. v. that Kedar doth inhabit
Eze. 38 : 11. I will go to unwalled v.
Ha. 3 : 14. didst strike head of his v.
Mat. 14 : 15. may go into v. and buy victuals, Mk. 6 : 36. [teaching
Mk. 6 : 6. Jesus went about the v.
Ac. 8 :25. preached gospel in many v.
See TOWNS.
See **CITIES** with **villages.**

VILLANY.

Is. 9 : †17. every mouth speaketh v.
32 : 6. the vile person will speak v.
Je. 29 : 23. have committed v. in Isr.
Ho. 2 : †19. now will I discov. her v.

VINE. [fore me

Ge. 40 : 9. In my dream a v. was be-
10. in the v. were three branches
49 :11. Binding his foal unto the v., his ass's colt unto choice v. [11.
Le. 25 :5. nei. gather grapes of thy v.,
De. 32 : 32. their v. is of v. of Sodom
Ju. 9 :12. said trees unto v., reign, 13.
13 : 14. she not eat any thing of v.
1 K. 4 : 25. safely ev. man under his v.
2 K. 4 : 39. found wild v. and gourds
18 : 31. eat ye every man of his own v., Is. 36 : 16. [as the v.
Jb 15 :33. shake off his unripe grape
Ps. 80 : 8. Thou hast brought a v.
14. look down, and visit this v.
128 : 3. Thy wife be as a fruitful v.
Can. 6 : 11. whe. the v. flourished,
7 :8. breasts as clusters of v. [7 :12.
Is 5 : 2. he planted it wi. choicest v.
24 :7. wine mourneth, v. languish-
32 : 12. lament for fruitful v. [eth
34 : 4. as leaf falleth from v. as a fig
Je. 2 : 21. I planted thee a noble v., how turned into plant of strange
6 : 9. glean remnant of Isr. as v. [v.?
8 : 13. shall be no grapes on the v.
Eze. 17 :6. it became a spread-g v. (2)
7. v. did bend her roots tow. him
8. that it might be a goodly v.
19 : 10. mother like v. in thy blood
Ho. 10 : 1. Israel is an empty v.
14 : 7. shall revive as corn, grow as
Jo. 1 : 7. he laid my v. waste [v.
12. The v. is dried up, the fig tree
2 : 22. fig tree and v. yield strength
Mi. 4 : 4. sit every man under his v.
Na. 2 : 2. have marred v. branches
Ha. 2 : 19. v. hath not brought forth
Zch. 3 : 10. ev. man neighbour und.
8 : 12. the v. shall give her fruit [v.
Mal. 3 : 11. nei. shall v. cast her fruit
Mat. 26 :29. I will not drink of fruit of v. till, Mk. 14 : 25. Lu. 22 :18.
Jn. 15 : 1. I am the true v. and, 5.
4. cannot bear fruit, exc. it abide
Ja. 3 : 12. can a v. bear figs? [in v.
Re. 14 : 18. gather clusters of the v.
19. angel gathered v. of the earth
See SIBMAH.

VINE tree. [of v.t.

Nu. 6 : 4. he shall eat nothing made
Eze. 15 : 2. What is v.t. more than any t. or than branch am. t-s
6. As v.t. am. t-s of forest for fuel

VINES.

Nu. 20 : 5. it is no place of v. or
De. 8 : 8. land of wheat, barley, v.
Ps. 78 : 47. He destroyed their v.
105 :33. He smote their v., fig trees
Can. 2 : 13. the v. give a good smell
15. little foxes, that spoil the v., for our v. have tender grapes
Is. 7 : 23. there were a thousand v.
Je. 5 : 17. they shall eat up thy v.
31 : 5. shalt yet plant v. upon mts.
Ho. 2 : 12. I will destroy her v. and
Ha. 3 : 17. nei. shall fruit be in the v.

VINEDRESSERS.

2 K. 25 : 12. left the poor of the land to be v., Je. 52 : 16. [men and v.
2 Ch. 26 : 10. Uzziah had husband-
Is. 61 : 5. sons of alien be your v.
Jo. 1 :11. Be ashamed, howl, O ye v.

VINEGAR. [of wine

Nu. 6 : 3. a Nazarite sh. drink no v.

Ru 2 : 14. dip thy morsel in the v.
Ps. 69 : 21. in my thirst they gave me
v. to drink, Mat. 27 : 34.
Pr. 10 : 26. As v. to the teeth so is
25 : 20. as v. upon nitre [sluggard
Mat. 27 : 48. they took a sponge and
filled it with v., Mk. 15 : 36. Lu.
23 : 36. Jn. 19 : 29, 30.

VINEYARD.

Ex. 22 : 5. If man cause v. to be eaten
23 : 11. In like manner deal with v.
Le. 19 : 10. thou sh. not glean thy v. (2)
25 : 3. six years shalt prune thy v.
4. nei. sow field, nor prune thy v.
De. 22 : 9. not sow v. with divers
seeds, lest fruit of v. be defiled
23 : 24. When into neighbour's v.
24 : 21. When gatherest grapes of v.
1 K. 21 : 1. Naboth had a v. hard by
2. Give me thy v., I will give thee
a better v., 6. [15, 16, 18.
7. I will give thee v. of Naboth,
Pr. 24 : 30. I went by v. of man void
Can. 1 : 6. own v. have I not kept
8 : 11. Sol-n had a v., he let the v.
12. My v., which is mine, is before
Is 1 : 8. dau. of Zion as cottage in v.
3 : 14. for ye have eaten up the v.
5 : 1. my beloved, touch-g his v. (2)
3. judge betwixt me and my v.
4. What more to my v. that I have
7. v. of Lord is the house of Israel
10. ten acres of v. yield one bath
27 : 2. sing to her, A v. of red wine
Je. 12 : 10. pastors destroyed my v.
35 : 9. nei. have we v., nor field, nor
Mi. 1 : 6. Samaria as plantings of v.
Mat. 20 : 1. hire labourers into v., 2.
4. he said, Go ye also into the v., 7.
8. lord of v. saith unto his steward
21 : 28. Son, go work to day in my v.
39. they cast him out of v. and
slew him, Mk. 12 : 8. Lu. 20 : 10, 15.
40. when lord of v. cometh, what
will he do, Mk. 12 : 9. Lu. 20 : 15.
41. He will let out his v. unto
other, Mk. 12 : 9. Lu. 20 : 16.
Mk. 12 : 2. might receive fruit of v.
Lu. 13 : 7. Then said he unto dresser
of his v., Lu. 20 : 13.

Plant, ed, edst, eth

VINEYARD, S. [wine

Ge. 9 : 20. Noah p-d v. and drank
De. 6 : 11. give thee v-s thou p-d not
20 : 6. wh. man p-d a v. and not eaten
28 : 30. shalt p. v. and not gather
39. Thou sh. p. v-s, but nei. drink
Jos. 24 : 13. of v-s ye p-d not, ye eat
2 K. 19 : 29. p. v-s and eat, Is. 37 : 30.
Ps 80 : 15. v. right hand hath p-d
107 : 37. may sow the fields, p. v-s
Ec. 2 : 4. I builded houses, p-d v-s
Pr. 31 : 16. with fruit of hands p-h v.
Is. 65 : 21. they shall build houses
and p. v-s, Eze. 28 : 26. Am. 9 : 14.
Je. 35 : 7. Neither shall ye build
house, nor p. v., 9.
Am. 5 : 11. ye have p-d pleasant v-s
Zph. 1 : 13. they sh. p. v-s, not drink
Mat. 21 : 33. A householder p-d a v.,
Mk. 12 : 1. Lu. 20 : 9. [his v.
Lu. 13 : 6. A man had fig tree p-d in
1 Co. 9 : 7. who p-h v., eateth not?

VINEYARDS. [of v.

Nu. 16 : 14. not given us inheritance
20 : 17. will not pass thro. v., 21 : 22.
22 : 24. angel stood in a path of v.
Ju. 9 : 27. gath-d v. and trode grapes
11 : 33. from Aroer unto plain of v.
14 : 5. Samson came to v. of Tim-h
15 : 5. burnt standing corn with v.
21 : 20. Go and lie in wait in the v.
21. then come out of v., catch wife
1 S. 8 : 14. he will take your v. and
15. he will take the 10th of your v.
22 : 7. will son Jesse give ev. one v.?
2 K. 5 : 26. Is it a time to receive v.?
2 K. 18 : 32. Until I take you to land
of bread and v., Is. 36 : 17.
1 Ch. 27 : 27. over v. Shimei, over
increase of v. Zabdi [v., 4.
Ne. 5 : 3. We have mortgaged our
5. oth. men have our lands and v.
11. Restore to them their v. and
9 : 25. possessed houses, wells, v.
Jb. 24 : 18. beholdeth not way of v.
Can. 1 : 6 they made me keeper of v.
14. as camphire in v. of En-gedi
7 : 12. Let us get up early to the v.
Is. 16 : 10. in v. shall be no singing
Je. 32 : 15. v. shall be possessed again
39 : 10. Neb-n gave the poor v. and
Ho. 2 : 15. I will give her her v. fr.
Am. 4 : 9. palmer worm devoured v.
5 : 17. in all v. shall be wailing

VINTAGE.

Le. 26 : 5. your threshing shall reach
unto v., and v. unto sowing
Ju. 8 : 2. better than v. of Abiezer?
Jb. 24 : 6. they gather v. of the wicked
Is 16 : 10. I made v. shouting cease
24 : 13. as grapes when v. is done
32 : 10. v. shall fail, gathering not
Je. 48 : 32. spoiler is fallen upon v.
Mi. 7 : 1. I am as gleanings of the v.
Zch. 11 : 2. forest of the v. is come

VIOL, VIOLS.

Is. 5 : 12. v. and wine in their feasts
14 : 11. noise of thy v-s is bro-t down
22 : †24. upon him instrum-ts of v-s
Am. 5 : 23. not hear melody of v-s
6 : 5. that chant to sound of the v.

VIOLATED. [law

Eze. 22 : 26. Her priests have v. my

VIOLENCE, S. [13.

Ge. 6 : 11. earth was filled with v.,
49 : † 5. their swords, weapons of v.
Le. 6 : 2. any thing taken away by v.
2 S. 22 : 3. thou savest me from v.
1 Ch. 12 : † 17. is no v. in my hands
Jb. 19 : † 7. I cry out of v., not heard
Ps. 11 : 5. loveth v. his soul hateth
18 : † 48. delivered me fr. man of v.
25 : † 19. hate me with hatred of v.
55 : 9. I have seen v., strife in city
58 : 2. weigh v. of your hands [v.
72 : 14. He sh. redeem their soul fr.
73 : 6. v. covereth them as garment
140 : † 1. preserve me fr. man of v-s
† 11. let not man of v. be establ-d
Pr. 3 : †31. Envy thou not a man of v.
4 : 17. for they drink the wine of v.
10 : 6. v. cov-h mouth of wicked, 11.
13 : 2. soul of transgr-rs sh. eat v.
26 : †6. message by fool drinketh v.
28 : 17. that doeth v. to blood of any
Is. 53 : 9. bec. he had done no v. nor
59 : 6. the act of v. is in their hands
60 : 18. v. shall no more be heard
Je. 6 : 7. v. and spoil is heard in her
20 : 8. for since I spake, I cried v.
22 : 3. do no v. to the stranger [v.
17. thine eyes, thy heart are for
23 : †10. their v. is evil, their force
51 : 35. v. done to me and my flesh
46. v. in the land, ruler ag ruler
Eze. 7 : 11. v. is risen up into a rod
23. make a chain, city is full of v.
8 : 17. have filled land wi. v., 28 : 16.
12 : 19. bec. of v. of them th. dwell
18 : 7. if man spoiled none by v., 16.
12. if he hath oppressed by v., 18.
22 : †26. priests offered v. to my law
45 : 9. O princes of Israel remove v.
Jo. 3 : 19 Edom a wilderness for the
Am. 3 : 10. store up v. in palaces [v.
6 : 3. ye that cause the seat of v. to
Ob. 10. For thy v. shame shall cover
Jon. 3 : 8. turn every one from the v.
Mi. 2 : 2. covet fields, take them by v.
6 : 12. rich men thereof are full of v.
Ha. 1 : 2. how long shall I cry of v.
3. spoiling and v. are before me
9. They shall come all for v.
Ha. 2 : 8. v. of the land, of the city, 17.
17. v. of Lebanon shall cover thee
Zph. 1 : 9. fill masters' houses with v.
3 : 4. her priests have done v. to law
Mal. 2 : 16. covereth v. with arm-t
Mat. 11 : 12. the kingdom suffereth v.
Lu. 3 : 14. Do v. to no man, nor accuse
Ac. 5 : 26. brought them without v.
21 : 35. Paul borne of soldiers for v.
of the people, 24 : 7.
27 : 41. part broken for v. of waves
He. 11 : 34. Quenched the v. of fire
Re. 18 : 21. with v. sh. Babylon be

VIOLENT. [thrown down

2 S. 22 : 49. hast delivered me from
v. man, Ps. 18 : 48. [pate
Ps. 7 : 16. his v. dealing upon own
86 : 14. assemblies of v. men sought
140 : 1. preserve me from v. man, 4.
11. evil shall hunt the v. man
Pr. 16 : 29. A v. man enticeth neighb.
Ec. 5 : 8. if thou seest v. perverting
Mat. 11 : 12. the v. take it by force

VIOLENTLY. [taken

Ge. 21 : 25. Abim.'s servants had v.
Le. 6 : 4. shall restore that he took v.
De. 28 : 31. thine ass sh. be v. taken
Jb. 20 : 19. he hath v. taken a house
24 : 2. they v. take away flocks and
† 19. heat v. take snow waters
Is. 22 : 18. He will v. turn, toss thee
Je. 13 : †22. thy heels sh. be v. taken
La. 2 : 6. he hath v. taken tabernacle
Mat. 8 : 32. whole herd of swine ran
v. into sea, Mk. 5 : 13. Lu. 8 : 33.

VIOLET. [ings

Es. 1 : † 6. were green and v. hang-
8 : † 15. Mordecai in apparel of v.

VIPER, VIPERS.

Jb. 20 : 16. v.'s tongue shall slay him
Is. 30 : 6. whence the v. and serpent
41 : †24. y-r work worse than of a v.
59 : 5. crushed breaketh out into v.
Mat. 3 : 7. O generation of v-s, who
warned, 12 : 34.-23 : 33. Lu. 3 : 7.
Ac. 28 : 3. v. and fastened on P.'s hand

VIRGIN.

Ge. 24 : 16. Rebekah was fair, a v.
43. when v. cometh to draw water
Le. 21 : 3. for sister, a v., he be defiled
14. a v. of his own people to wife
De. 22 : 19. he bro-t evil name upon v.
23. If v. be betrothed, and man lie
28. If man find v. not betrothed
32 : 25. destroy young man and v.
2 S. 13 : 2. sick for Tamar, she was a v.
2 K. 19 : 21. The v. dau. of Zion hath
despised thee, Is. 37 : 22. [23.
Is. 7 : 14. a v. shall conceive, Mat. 1 :
23 : 12. no more rejoice, O thou v.
47 : 1. sit in the dust, O v. of Bab-n
62 : 5. as a young man marrieth a v.
Je. 14 : 17. v. dau. of peo. is broken
18 : 13. v. of Isr. done horrible thi.
31 : 4. shalt be built, O v. of Israel
13. shall v. rejoice in the dance
21. turn, O v. of Israel to thy cities
46 : 11. take balm, O v., dau. of Eg.
La. 1 : 15. Lord trodden v. dau. of Jud.
2 : 13. that I may comfort thee, O v.
Jo. 1 : 8. Lament like a v. with sackcl.
Am. 5 : 2. the v. of Israel is fallen
Lu. 1 : 27. the angel from God to a v.
1 Co. 7 : 28. if a v. marry, not sinned
34. is difference betw. a wife and v.
36. if behaveth uncomely tow. v.
37. that will keep his v., doeth well
2 Co. 11 : 2. present you as a chaste

Young VIRGIN, S. [v.

Ju. 21 : 12. of Jabesh-gilead 400 y. v-s
1 K. 1 : 2. Let be sought for king y. v.
Es. 2 : 2. Let be y. v-s sought for king
3. they may gath. all the fair y. v-s

VIRGINS. [v.

Ex. 22 : 17. pay accord-g to dowry of
2 S. 13 : 18. king's dau-s v. apparelled
Es. 2 : 17. Es. found fav. above all v.

Es. 2 : 19. when v. were gathered the second time, Mord. sat [brought
Ps. 45 : 14. the v. companions sh. be
Can. 1 : 3. theref. do the v. love thee
6 : 8. queens and v. without number
Is. 23 : 4. I travail not nor bring up
La. 1 : 4. her v. are afflicted [v.
18. my v. and young men are gone
2 : 10. v. of Jerus. hang their heads
21. v. and young men are fallen
Am. 8 : 13. that day shall fair v. faint
Mat 25 : 1. kingdom likened to ten v.
7. all those v. arose and trimmed
11. Afterw. came also the other v.
Ac. 21 : 9. Philip had 4 daughters, v.
1 Co. 7 : 25. conc. v. I have no com-t
Re. 14 : 4. not defiled, for they are v.

VIRGINITY. [v.

Le. 21 : 13. shall take a wife in her
De. 22 : 15. tokens of her v., 17, 20.
Ju. 11 : 37. I may bewail my v., 38.
Eze. 23 : 3. bruised teats of their v., 8.
Lu. 2 : 36. Anna lived 7 yrs. from her

VIRTUE, S. [v.

Mk. 5 : 30. Jesus, knowing v. had gone out of him, Lu. 6 : 19.-8 : 46.
Ph. 4 : 8. if be any v. think on these
1 Pe. 2 : † 9. th. ye shew forth v-s of
2 Pe. 1 : 3. called us to glory and v.
5. add to y-r faith v., to v. knowl-

VIRTUOUS woman. [edge

Ru. 3 : 11. all know thou art a v. w.
Pr. 12 : 4. A v. w. is a crown to husb.
31 : 10. Who can find a v. w.?

VIRTUOUSLY.

Pr. 31 : 29. Many daughters have

VISAGE. [done v.

Is. 52 : 14. his v. was marred more
La. 4 : 8. Their v. blacker than coal
Da. 3 : 19. form of his v. was changed

VISIBLE.

Col. 1 : 16. by him were all things v.

VISION.

Nu. 24 : 4. saw v. of Almighty, 16.
1 S. 3 : 1. word precious, no open v.
15. Sam. feared to shew Eli the v.
2 S. 7 : 17. acc. to all this v. did Na- than speak unto Da., 1 Ch. 17 : 15.
2 Ch. 32 : 32. written in v. of Isaiah
Ps. 89 : 19. spakest in v. to Holy One
Pr. 29 : 18. Where no v. peo. perish
Is. 1 : 1. The v. of Isaiah [to me
21 : 2. A grievous v. is declared un-
22 : 1. burden of the valley of v., 5.
28 : 7. they err in v., they stumble
29 : 11. v. is become as book sealed
Je. 14 : 14. they prophesy a false v.
23 : 16. they speak a v. of own heart
La. 2 : 9. her prophets find no v.
Eze. 7 : 13. v. is touching multitude
26. shall they seek a v. of prophet
8 : 4. acc. to v. I saw, 11 : 24.-43 : 3.
12 : 22. days prolonged, ev. v. faileth
23. say effect of every v. is at hand
24. shall be no more any vain v.
27. v. he seeth is for many days
13 : 7. Have ye not seen a vain v.
Da. 8 : 1. a v. appeared unto me, 15.
13. How long the v. conc. sacrif.?
16. make this man understand v.
17. at time of the end sh. he the v.
26. v. of the evening and morning is true; wheref. shut up the v.
27. I was astonished at the v.
9 : 21. whom I had seen in the v.
23. the mat-r, and consider the v.
24. seventy weeks to seal up v.
10 : 1. he had understanding of v.
7. I saw v., men with me saw not
14. yet v. is for many days [v., 8.
16. by v. my sorrows are turned
11 : 14. exalt thems. to establish v.
Ob. 1. The v. of Obadiah. Thus saith
Na. 1 : 1. The book of v. of Nahum
Ha. 2 : 2. Write the v., make it plain
3. v. is yet for an appointed time
Zch. 13 : 4. ashamed ev. one of his v.
Mat. 17 : 9. Tell the v. to no man
Lu. 1 : 22. perceived he had seen a v.
24 : 23. they had seen v. of angels
Ac. 10 : 17. while Pet. doubted of v., 19.
11 : 5. I saw a v. a vessel descend
12 : 9. but thought he saw a v. [v.
26 : 19. not disobed-t unto heavenly
Re. 9 : 17. thus I saw the horses in v.

In a VISION.

Ge. 15 : 1. word of L. unto Abram i. v.
Nu. 12 : 6. make myself known i. v.
Eze. 11 : 24. bro-t me i. v. by Spirit
Da. 8 : 2. I saw i. v., I was by Ulai (2)
Ac. 9 : 10. to Ananias said Lord i. v.
12. Saul hath seen i. v. Ananias
10 : 3. Cornelius saw i. v. an angel

VISION, S, with night. [n

Ge. 46 : 2. G. spake unto Isr. in v-s of
Jb. 4 : 13. In thoughts from v-s of n.
20 : 8. chased away as v. of the n.
33 : 15. In a dream, in a v. of the n
Is. 29 : 7. be as a dream of a n. v.
Da. 2 : 19. revealed to Daniel in n. v.
7 : 2. I saw in my v. by n.
7. I saw in n. v-s a 4th beast [man
13. I saw in n. v-s one like Son of
Mi. 3 : 6. n. unto you, sh. not have a v.
Ac. 16 : 9. a v. to Paul in n., 10.-18 : 9.

VISIONS. [do

2 Ch. 9 : 29. written in the v. of Id-
26 : 5. Zech. had underst-g in v. of G.
Jb. 7 : 14. thou terrifiest me thro. v.
Eze. 1 : 1. heavens opened, saw v. of G.
8 : 3. bro-t me in the v. of God to J
13 : 16. prophets wh. see v. of peace
40 : 2. In v. he brought me to land of
43 : 3. v. were like vision I saw [Isr
Da. 1 : 17. Dan. had underst-g in all v.
2 : 28. v. of thy head upon bed, are
4 : 5. v. of my head troubled me, 7
9. tell me the v. of my dream [15.
10. the v. of mine head; I saw tree
13. I saw in v. of my head holy one
7 : 1. Daniel had v. upon his bed
Ho. 12 : 10 I have multiplied v. [17.
Jo. 2 : 28. young men sh. see v., Ac. 2 :
2 Co. 12 : 1. I will come to v. and rev- [elations

VISIT.

Ge. 50 : 24. God will surely v. you
25. Ex 13 : 19. [sin upon them
Ex. 32 : 34. when I v., I will v. their
Le. 18 : 25. I do v. the iniquity th-f
Jb. 5 : 24. thou sh. v. thy habitation
7 : 18. shouldest v. him ev. morning
Ps. 59 : 5. O L., awake to v. heathen
80 : 14. look down and v. this vine
89 : 32. Then will I v. their transg.
106 : 4. O v. me with thy salvation
Is. 10 : † 12. I will v. stout heart of k.
23 : 17. Lord will v. Tyre, she shall
24 : † 21. Lord shall v. upon host
Je. 3 : 16. nei. shall they v. the ark
5 : 9. Shall I not v.? 29.-9 : 9. [do
6 : 15. at the time I v. them, be cast
9 : † 25. I will v. upon all circumc-d
11 : † 22. I will v. upon men of Ana
13 : † 21 wilt say when he shall v.
14 : 10. remember iniq-y and v. sins
15 : 15. O Lord, remember and v.
23 : 2. I will v. upon you the evil of
† 34. I will v. upon that man and
25 : † 12. I will v. upon k. of Bab-n
27 : 22. there sh. they be until I v.
29 : 10. I will v. you and perform
32 : 5. there sh. he be until I v. him
36 : † 31. I will v. him for his in- iquities, Am. 3 : † 2. [v. him
49 : 8. calamity of Esau, time I will
50 : 31. day is come I will v. Bab-n
La. 4 : 22. he will v. iniq-y, O Edom
Ho. 1 : † 4. I will v. blood of Jezreel
2 : 13. v. upon her days of Baalim
4 : † 9. I will v. them for their ways
8 : 13. now will he v. their sins, 9 : 9.
12 : † 2. L. will v. Jacob acc. to ways
Am. 3 : 14. day I sh. v. transgression of Israel will v. altars of Beth-el
Zph. 1 : † 8. I will v. upon princes
2 : 7. Lord sh. v. and turn captivity
Zch. 11 : 16. sh. not v. those cut off
Ac. 7 : 23. into his heart to v. breth.
15 : 14. how God did v. the Gentiles
36. let us go and v. our brethren
Ja. 1 : 27 is this, To v. fatherless and

VISITATION. [men

Nu. 16 : 29. if visited after v. of all
Jb. 10 : 12. thy v. preserved my spirit
Is. 10 : 3. what do in day of v.?
Je. 8 : 12. in time of v. be cast down
10 : 15. in time of v. sh. perish, 51 : 18.
11 : 23. evil upon men of Anathoth in year of v., 23 : 12.-48 : 44.
46 : 21. time of v. was come, 50 : 27.
50 : † 21. Go up ag. inhabitants of v.
Ho. 9 : 7. The days of v. are come
Mi. 7 : 4. v. cometh, now perplexity
Lu. 19 : 44. knewest not time of v.
1 Pe. 2 : 12. may glorify G. in day of v.

VISITED.

Ge. 21 : 1. Lord v. Sarah as he said
Ex. 3 : 16. I have surely v. you
4 : 31. heard the Lord had v. Israel
Nu. 16 : 29. if be v. after visitation
Ju. 15 : 1. that Samson v. his wife
Ru. 1 : 6. heard how L. v. his people
1 S. 2 : 21. L. v. Hannah, she conceiv- [ed
Jb. 35 : 15. hath v. in his anger
Ps. 17 : 3. hast v. me, hast tried me
Pr. 19 : 23. he shall not be v. wi. evil
Is. 24 : 22. aft. many days they be v.
26 : 14. hast v. and destroyed them
16. L., in trouble have they v. thee
29 : 6. Thou shalt be v. of the Lord
Je. 6 : 6. Jerusalem is the city to be v.
23 : 2. my flock, ye have not v. them
Eze. 38 : 8. After many days thou be
Zch. 10 : 3. Lord hath v. his flock [v.
† anger ag. shepherds I v. upon
Mat. 25 : 36. was sick, ye v. me [goats
43. sick, ye v. me not [his people
Lu. 1 : 68. he hath v. and redeemed
78. the dayspring hath v. us
7 : 16. That God hath v. his people

VISITEST, ETH, ING.

Ex. 20 : 5. v-g iniq-y of fathers upon chil., 34 : 7.-Nu. 14 : 18. De. 5 : 9.
Jb. 31 : 14. when he v-h what shall I answer him? [He. 2 : 6.
Ps. 8 : 4. Son of man that thou v-
65 : 9. Thou v-t earth and waterest it

VOCATION.

Ep. 4 : 1. that ye walk worthy of v.

VOICE. [crieth

Ge. 4 : 10. v. of thy brother's blood
27 : 22. The v. is Jacob's v., but
Ex. 4 : 8. believe the v. of latter sign
19 : 19. v. of the trumpet sounded, Moses spake, God ans-d by a v.
24 : 3. people answered with one v.
32 : 18. It is not v. of them th. shout
De. 4 : 30. if obedient unto his v. [v.
5 : 22. These words L. spake wi. gr.
8 : 20. ye not obedient unto his v.
Jos. 6 : 10. nor make noise wi. your v.
Ju. 18 : 3. they knew v. of Levite
1 S. 24 : 16. Is this thy v. my son David? 26 : 17. (2) [answered, 29.
1 K. 18 : 26. was no v. nor any that
† 27. Elijah said, Cry with great v.
19 : 12. after fire a still small v., 13.
2 K. 4 : 31. was neither v. nor fearing
7 : 10. no v. of man, but horses tied
19 : 22. against whom hast thou ex- alted thy v.? Is. 37 : 23. [wi. joy
1 Ch. 15 : 16. by lifting up the the v.
2 Ch. 24 : † 9. made a v. thro. Judah
Ezr. 1 : † 1. Cyrus caused a v. to pass
Ne. 12 : † 42. singers made v. be heard
Jb. 3 : 7. let no joyful v. come there
4 : 10. v. of the fierce lion broken
29 : † 10. v. of nobles was hid [weep
30 : 31. my organ into v. of them th.
37 : 4. a v. roareth; he thundereth
5. God thundereth with v. [wi. v.

Jb 40 : 9. canst thou thunder with a
v. like him? [77 : 1.-142 : 1.
Ps. 3 : 4. I cried unto L. with my v.,
Ps. 18 : 13. the Highest gave his v.
26 : 7 publish wi. v. of thanksgiving
27 : 7. Hear, O L., when I cry wi v.
31 : 22. thou heardest the v. of my
supplications, Jon. 2 : 2. [of joy
42 : 4. I went to house of God wi. v.
44 : 16. v. of him that reproacheth
47 : 1. shout unto G. wi. v. of triumph
55 : 3. Because of v. of the enemy
66 : 19. attended to v. of my prayer
68 : 33. he doth send out his v., and
that a mighty v. [enemies
74 : 23. Forget not the v. of thine
86 : 6. attend to v. of my supplica-s
98 : 5. sing with v. of a psalm [ing
102 : 5. By reason of v. of my groan-
104 : †12. fowls wh. give v. am. bran.
118 : 15. v. of rejoicing in tabern-s
141 : 1. give ear to my v. when I cry
Pr. 2 : 3. if liftest v. for understand-g
8 : 1 understand-g put forth her v.?
4. O men, my v. is to sons of men
26 : † 25. maketh his v. gracious
Ec. 5 : 3. fool's v. is known by words
6. wheref. God be angry at thy v.?
10 : 20. bird of the air shall carry v.
12 : 4. he shall rise at v. of the bird
Can. 2 : 8. The v. of my beloved
5 : 2. it is the v. of my beloved that
Is. 6 : 4. posts moved at v. of him
13 : 2. exalt the v. unto them
29 : 4. thy v. as one that hath a spirit
30 : 19. gracious at the v. of thy cry
31 : 4. lion not be afraid of their v.
40 : 3. The v. of him that crieth in
wilderness, Mat. 3 : 3. Mk. 1 : 3.
6. The v. said, Cry [Lu. 3 : 4.
48 : 20. with v. of singing tell this
50 : 10. Who obeyeth v. of his serv.
51 : 3. gladness and the v. of melody
52 : 8. with the v. shall they sing
66 : 6. A v. of noise from city, a v.
from temple, a v. of Lord [v.
Je. 2 : † 15. yo. lions gave out their
4 : 15. a v. declareth from Dan, and
16. give their v. ag. cities of Jud.
31 v. of daugh. of Zion, Woe is me
6 : 23. v. roareth like the sea, 50 : 42.
7 : 34 the v. of mirth, the v. of
gladness, v. of the bridegroom,
v. of bride, 16 : 9.-25 : 10.-33 : 11.
8 : 19. v. of the cry of my people
12 : † 8. it giveth out its v. ag. me
25 : 36. A v. of cry of shepherds
30 : 19. v. of them that make merry
31 : 16. saith L., Refrain v. fr. weep-g
46 : 22. The v. shall go like serpent
48 : 3. A v. of crying from Horonaim
50 : 28. The v. of them that flee and
51 : 55. destroyed out of her great v.
Eze. 1 : 25. v. fr. firmament ov. heads
10 : 5. as the v. of Almighty God
23 : 42. a v. of a multitude at ease
33 : 32. of one that hath pleasant v.
43 : 2. his v. was like the noise of
many waters, Re. 1 : 15. [en
Da. 4 : 31. there fell a v. from heav-
6 : 20. he cried with a lamentable v.
7 : 11. because of v. of great words
10 : 6. v. of his words like the v. of
a multitude [forth his v.?
Am. 3 : † 4. will the young lion give
Mi. 6 : 9. Lord's v. crieth unto city
Jo. 2 : 9. sacrifice wi. v. of thanksg-g
Na. 2 : 7. lead her as with v. of doves
Ha. 3 : 16. my lips quivered at v.
Zph. 1 : 14. v. of the day of the Lord
2 : 14. their v. sh. sing in windows
Zch. 11 : 3. v. of howling of shepherds
Mat. 3 : 17. a v. fr. heaven, This my
beloved Son, Mk. 1 : 11. Lu. 3 : 22.
17 : 5. a v. out of cloud, This is
my beloved Son, Mk. 9 : 7. Lu.
9 : 35 36.

Mat. 24 : †31. send angels wi. great v.
Lu. 1 : 44. soon as v. of thy saluta-n
Jn. 1 : 23. v. of one crying in wildern.
10 : 4. sheep follow, they know his v.
5. they know not v. of strangers
12 : 28. v. saying, I have glorified it
30. This v. came not bec. of me [v.
18 : 37. he of the truth heareth my
Ac. 2 : †6. Now when this v. was made
9 : 7. hearing a v., but see-g no man
10 : 13. came a v. saying, Rise, Pe.
15. v. spake unto him again, 11 : 9.
12 : 14. when she knew Peter's v.
22. It is v. of a god, not of man
19 : 34. all with one v. cried, Great
24 : 21. Except it be for this one v.
26 : 10. I gave my v. against them
1 Co. 14 : 11 if I know not meaning of
19. that by my v. might teach [v.
Ga. 4 : 20. I desire to change my v.
1 Th. 4 : 16. Lord shall descend with
v. of archangel [of words
He. 12 : 19 ye are not come unto v.
26. Whose v. then shook the earth
2 Pe. 1 : 17. a v. from excellent glory
2 : 16. dumb ass speak-g wi. man's v.
Re. 1 : 12. I turned to see the v. [ers
15. his v. as sound of many wat-
10 : 7. days of v. of the seventh angel
16 : 17. a great v. saying. It is done
18 : 2. cried with strong v., Bab-n
19 : 5. a v. out of throne, Praise G.

VOICE
of bridegroom and bride.

Je. 7 : 34. cause to cease from Jeru-s-
alem v. -, 16 : 9.-25 : 10. [v. -
33 : 11. Again sh. be heard in Jerus.
Jn. 3 : 29. rejoiceth because of b.'s v.
Re. 18 : 23. v. - be heard no more in

Hear VOICE. [tions

Ps. 28 : 2. h. the v. of my supplica-
64 : 1. h. my v., O God, in my prayer
119 : 149. h. my v. acc. to lovingk.
130 : 2. Lord h. my v.; be attentive
to v. of my supplications, 140 : 6
Is. 28 : 23. Give ye ear and h. my v.
Re. 3 : 20. if any man h. my v. and
See **HEAR voice.** [open

VOICE, with heard, est.

Ps. 31 : 22. h-t v. of my supplications
Is. 65 : 19 v. of weeping shall be no
more h. in her, nor v. of crying
Je. 33 : 11. be h. in Jerus. v. of bride
Eze. 1 : 24. I h. as v. of Almighty
Jon. 2 : 2. out of belly of hell cried
I, thou h-t my v. [up hither
Re. 11 : 12. they h. a great v., Come
12 : 10. I h. a loud v. in heaven [in
18 : 22. v. of harpers be h. no more
23. v. of bridegroom be h. no more
19 : 6. I h. v. of gr. multitude, v. of
many waters, v. of thunderings
See **HEARD with voice.**

VOICE
with hearken, ed, edst, ing.

Ge. 3 : 17. hast h-d unto v. of wife
16 : 2. Abram h-d to the v. of Sarai
21 : 12. in all Sarah said, h. unto
Ex. 3 : 18. shall h. to thy v. [her v.
4 : 1. they will not h. unto my v.
8. if not h. to v. of the first sign
9. if will not h. unto thy v. take
15 : 26. if diligently h. to v. of Lord
18 : 19. h. unto my v., I will give
24. Moses h-d to the v. of Jethro
Nu. 14 : 22. have tempted me 10 times
and not h-d to my v., De. 9 : 23.
21 : 3. Lord h-d to the v. of Israel
De. 1 : 45 L. would not h. to your v.
13 : 18. When thou sh. h. to v. of L.
15 : 5. if thou carefully h. unto v. of
Lord, 26 : 17.-28 : 1, 2.-30 : 10.
26 : 14. I have h-d to v. of L. my G.
28 : 15. if wilt not h. unto v. of L.
45. thou h-t not unto v. of L. thy G.
Jos. 10 : 14. Lord h-d unto v. of a man
Ju. 2 : 20. people not h-d unto my v.

Ju. 13 : 9. God h-d to v. of Manoah
20 : 13. Benj. not h. to v. of Israel
1 S. 2 : 25. h-d not unto v. of father
8 : 7. h. unto the v. of people, 9, 22.
12 : 1. I have h-d unto your v. in
15 : 1. Now h. unto v. of words of L.
19 : 6. Saul h-d unto v. of Jonathan
25 : 35. go in peace, I h-d to thy v.
28 : 22. h. unto v. of thy handmaid
23. Saul h-d unto their v. [our v.
2 S. 12 : 18. he would not h. unto
13 : 14. he would not h. unto her v.
1 K. 20 : 25. Ben-hadad h-d unto v.
2 K. 10 : 6. if ye will h. unto my v.
Jb. 9 : 16. not believe he h-d unto my
34 : 16. h. to the v. of my words [v.
Ps. 5 : 2. h. unto the v. of my cry
58 : 5. will not h. to v. of charmers
81 : 11. my people not h. to my v.
103 : 20. h-g unto the v. of his word
106 : 25. they h-d not unto v. of L.
Can. 8 : 13. companions h. to thy v.
Je. 18 : 19 h. to v. of them th. contend
See **LIFT, LIFTED voice, s.**
See **Voice of the LORD.**

Loud VOICE, S. [l.

Ex. 19 : 16. v. of trumpet exceeding
De. 27 : 14. Levites speak with l. v.
2 S. 15 : 23. country went with l. v.
1 K. 8 : 55. he blessed cong. with l. v.
2 Ch. 15 : 14. sware unto L. with l. v.
20 : 19. praise L. with l. v., Lu. 19 : 37.
Ezr. 3 : 12. many wept with a l. v.
10 : 12. congr. answered with a l. v.
Pr. 27 : 14. blessed friend with l. v.
Eze. 8 : 18. tho. they cry with a l. v.
9 : 1. He cried with l. v., Cause them
Lu. 1 : 42. she spake out with a l. v.
8 : 28. with l. v., What have I to do
17 : 15. with a l. v. glorified God
23 : 23. they were instant with l. v-s
Ac. 8 : 7. uncl. spirits crying with l. v.
14 : 10. Said with l. v., Stand upright
26 : 24. Festus said with a l. v., Paul
Re. 5 : 2. angel proclaiming wi l. v.
12. angels saying wi. l. v., Worthy
8 : 13. angel with l. v., Woe, woe
12 : 10. I heard a l. v. in heaven [God
14 : 7. angel saying with l. v., Fear
9. angel wi. l. v., If any man worsh.
15. angel wi. l. v., Thrust in sickle
See **CRIED**
with a loud voice.

Obey, ed, edst VOICE.

Ge. 22 : 18. all nations be blessed bec.
hast o-d my v., 26 : 5. [his v.?
Ex. 5 : 2. Who is Lord, I should o.
2 K. 18 : 12. they o-d not v. of Lord
Je. 22 : 21. from youth o-t not my v.
See OBEY, OBEYED, THUNDER.

VOICE, S,
with utter, ed, eth.

2 S. 22 : 14. the Most High u-d his v.,
Ps. 46 : 6. [streets
Pr. 1 : 20. Wisdom u-h her v. in the
Je. 10 : 13. When he u-h his v., 51 : 16.
25 : 30. u. his v. from holy habit-n
48 : 34. even unto Jahaz u-d their v.
51 : 55. a noise of their v. u-d [my
Jo. 2 : 11. L. shall u. his v. bef. ar-
3 : 16. Lord u. his v. fr. Jerus., Am.
Ha. 3 : 10 the deep u-d his v. [1 : 2.
Re. 10 : 3. seven thunders u-d their

VOICES. [v-s, 4.

Ex. 9 : †28. there be no more v. of G.
Lu. 23 : 23. the v. of priests prevailed
Ac. 13 : 27. knew not v. of prophets
1 Co. 14 : 10. are so many v. in world
Re. 4 : 5. out of the throne v., 16 : 18.
8 : 5. were v., thunderings, earthq.
13. woe, by reason of the other v.
11 : 15. there were great v. in heaven
19. temple was opened, there were

VOID. [v.

Ge. 1 : 2. the earth was without form
and v., Je. 4 : 23. [them v., 15.
Nu. 30 : 12. But if her husband made

Nu. 30 : 13. Ev. vow, husb. may make
De. 32 : 28. people v. of counsel [it v.
1 K. 22 : 10. king and Jehosh-t sat in
a v. place, 2 Ch. 18 : 9. [and v.
Ne. 5 : † 13. thus be ye shaken out
Jb. 15 : † 4. makest v. fear and [v.
Ps. 89 : † 33. lovingkindn. not make
39. made v. covenant of thy serv.
107 : † 40. to wander in a v. place
119 : 126. they have made v. thy law
Pr. 11 : 12. v. of wisdom despiseth
15 : † 21. folly joy to him v. of heart
Is. 55 : 11. my word sh. not return v.
Je. 19 : 7. I make v. counsel of Judah
Eze. 45 : † 2. 50 cubits for v. places
Na. 2 : 10. Nineveh is empty, v. and
Ac. 24 : 16. a conscience v. of offence
Ro. 1 : † 28. over to mind v. of judgm.
3 : 31. Do we then make v. the law?
4 : 14. if they of law heirs, faith v.
1 Co. 9 : 15. lest any should make
my glorying v. [judgment
Tit. 1 : † 16. to every good work v. of
See **Void of UNDERSTANDING.**

VOLUME.

Ps. 40 : 7. Lo I come, in v. of book
it is written of me, He. 10 : 7.

VOLUNTARY.

Le. 1 : 3. he shall offer it of his v. will
7 : 16. a v. offering eaten same day
Ps. 47 : † 9. The v. of peo. are gath-d
Eze. 46 : 12. princes shall prepare v.
Col. 2 : 18. in a v. humility [offer-g

VOLUNTARILY. [Lord

Eze. 46 : 12. prepare offerings v. unto

VOMIT. [Noun.] [v.

Pr. 26 : 11. As dog returneth to his
Is. 19 : 14. man staggereth in his v.
28 : 8. all tables are full of v. and
Je. 48 : 26. Moab sh. wallow in his v.
2 Pe. 2 : 22. dog turned to his own v.

VOMIT, ED, ETH.

Le. 18 : 25. land v-h out inhabitants
Jb. 20 : 15. swallowed riches, shall v.
Pr. 23 : 8. morsel eaten thou shalt v.
25 : 16. lest filled wi. honey and v. it
Jon. 2 : 10. fish v-d out Jonah on

VOPH'SI. See NAHBI.

VOUCHSAFE.

2 Th. 1 : † 11. that God would v. you

VOW. [Noun.] [worthy

Ge. 28 : 20. Jacob vowed a v., 31 : 13.
Le. 7 : 16. If the sacrifice of his offering be a v., 22 : 18, 21. [cepted
22 : 23. but for a v. it sh. not be ac-
27 : 2. When man make singular v.
Nu. 6 : 2. to vow a v. of a Nazarite
5. All days of the v. shall no rasor
21. acc. to v. vowed so he must do
15 : 3. of sacrifice in perform-g v., 8
21 : 2. Israel vowed a v. unto Lord
30 : 2. If a man vow a v. unto Lord
3. If a woman vow a v. unto Lord
4. If her father hear her v. and
9. every v. of a widow shall stand
13. Ev. v. her husb. may establish
De. 23 : 18. not price of dog for a v.
21. When vow a v. not slack to pay
Ju. 11 : 30. Jephthah vowed v. unto
39. who did with her acc. to his v.
1 S. 1 : 11. Hannah vowed a v., and
21. Elkanah went to offer his v.
2 S. 15 : 7. let me go and pay my v.
8. thy serv-t vowed a v. at Geshur
Ps. 65 : 1. unto thee v. be performed
Ec. 5 : 4. vowest a v. defer not to pay
Is. 19 : 21. shall vow a v. unto Lord
Ac. 18 : 18. Paul, for he had a v.
21 : 23. We have four men wh. have

VOWS. [a v.

Le. 22 : 18. his oblation for all his v.
23 : 38. beside gifts and all your v.
Nu. 29 : 39. ye shall do beside your v.
30 : 4. all her v. shall stand, 7, 9, 11.
5. not any of her v. sh. stand, 8, 12.
† 6. if she had husb. when her v.
Nu. 30 : 14. he established all her v.
De. 12 : 6. thi. bring your v., 11, 17, 26.
Jb. 22 : 27. thou shalt pay thy v.
Ps. 22 : 25. I will pay my v., 66 : 13.
-116 : 14, 18. [Most High
50 : 14. and pay thy v. unto the
56 : 12. Thy v. are upon me, O God
61 : 5. thou, O G., hast heard my v.
8. that I may daily perform my v.
Pr. 7 : 14. this day have I paid my v.
20 : 25. snare after v. to make inqui-
31 : 2. and what the son of my v. [ry
Je. 44 : 25. will surely perform v. (3)
Jon. 1 : 16. men feared L. and made v.
Na. 1 : 15. keep thy feasts, perform v.

VOW. [Verb.] [a vow

Nu. 6 : 2. separate themselves to v.
De. 23 : 22. if forbear to v. be no sin
Ps. 76 : 11. v. and pay unto the Lord
Ec. 5 : 5. Better thou shouldest not v.
See VOW. [Noun.] [(2)

VOWED.

Le. 27 : 8. acc. to his ability that v.
Nu. 6 : 21. law of Nazarite who v.
30 : 6. if she had husb. when she v.
10. if she v. in husband's house
De. 23 : 23. keep acc. as thou hast v.
Ps. 132 : 2. v. unto mighty G. of Jac.
Ec. 5 : 4. pay that which thou hast v.
Jon. 1 : † 16. men v. vows unto Lord
2 : 9. I will pay that that I have v.
See VOW. [Noun.]

VOWEST. See VOW. [Noun.]

VOWETH. [thing

Mal. 1 : 14. who v. unto Lord corrupt

VOYAGE. [hurt

Ac. 27 : 10. I perceive v. will be with

VULTURE, S.

Le. 11 : 14. the v. and the kite not
be eaten, De. 14 : 13. [not seen
Jb. 28 : 7. a path which v.'s eye hath
Is. 34 : 15. there sh. v-s be gathered

W.

WAFER, S. [like w-s

Ex. 16 : 31. manna, taste of it was
29 : 2. w-s unleavened, anointed
23. one w. out of the basket of unleavened bread, Le. 8 : 26.
Le. 2 : 4. w-s anointed with oil, 7 :
12. Nu. 6 : 15. [arite
Nu. 6 : 19. one w. upon hands of Naz-

WAG. [his head

Je. 18 : 16. that passeth by shall w.
La. 2 : 15. w. their heads at dau. of
Zph. 2 : 15. that passeth sh. w. hand

WAGES. [be?

Ge. 29 : 15. tell me, what shall thy w.
30 : 28. Appoint thy w., I will give it
31 : 7. changed my w. ten times, 41.
8. The speckled shall be thy w.
Ex. 2 : 9. nurse child, I will give w.
Le. 19 : 13. w. of hired not abide with
thee all night [without w.
Je. 22 : 13. useth neighbour's service
Eze. 29 : 18. had no w. nor his army
19. her spoil shall be w. for army
Hag. 1 : 6. earneth w. to put into
Mal. 3 : 5. oppress hireling in his w.
Lu. 3 : 14. be content with your w.
Jn. 4 : 36. he th. reapeth receiveth w.
Ro. 6 : 23. For the w. of sin is death
2 Co. 11 : 8. taking w. of them to do
2 Pe. 2 : 15. Balaam loved w. of un-

WAGGING. [right.

Mat. 27 : 39. they that passed by reviled him, w. their heads, Mk.

WAGON. [15 : 29.

Nu. 7 : 3. bro-t a w. for two of princes

WAGONS. [21.

Ge. 45 : 19. take you w. out of Egypt,
27. Jac. saw w. Joseph sent, 46 : 5.
Nu. 7 : 3. six w. and twelve oxen, 6.
7. 2 w., 4 oxen to sons of Gershon
8. 4 w., 8 oxen to sons of Merari
Eze. 23 : 24. shall come ag. thee with

WAIL, ED. [w.

Eze. 32 : 18. w. for multitude of Eg.
Mi. 1 : 8. I will w., howl, go stripped
Mk. 5 : 38. seeth them th. w-d great-
Re. 1 : 7. all kindreds shall w. [ly

WAILING. [was w.

Es. 4 : 3. whither his decree came
Je. 9 : 10. For the mts. will I take up w.
18. let them take up a w. for us
19. voice of w. is heard out of Zion
20. O women, teach your dau-s w.
Eze. 7 : 11. nei. shall be w. for them
27 : 31. weep for thee with bitter w.
32. in w. sh. take up lamentation
Am. 5 : 16. w. shall be in all streets;
call skilful of lamentation to w.
17. And in all vineyards sh. be w.
Mi. 1 : 8. I will make w. like dragons
Mat. 13 : 42. w. gnashing of teeth, 50.
Re. 18 : 15. merchants stand afar, w.,

WAIT. [Noun.] [19.

See **LAID wait, LAY wait.**
See LAYETH, LAYING.
See **LIE, LIERS, LIETH, LYING in wait.**

WAIT. [Verb.]

Nu. 8 : 10. Aaron and sons shall w.
on their priest's office, 8 : 24. 1
Ch. 23 : 28. 2 Ch 5 : 11.-13 : 10.
2 K. 6 : 33. sho. I w. for the Lord any
Jb. 8 : † 21. w. for death, but it
14 : 14. I will w. till my change
17 : 13. If I w. the grave is my house
Ps. 25 : 3. let none that w. on thee
be ashamed, 69 : 6. [w. all day
5. God of salvation, on thee do I
21. let integrity preserve me, for
I w. on thee [Pr. 20 : 22.
27 : 14. w. on the Lord, 37 : 34.
37 : 7. Rest in the Lord, w. patiently
9. that w. upon Lord inherit earth
38 : † 15. For in thee, O L., do I w.
39 : 7. Lord, what w. I for? [ever
52 : 9. I will w. on thy name for
56 : 6. mark my steps when they w.
59 : 9. Bec. of his strength will I w.
62 : 5. My soul, w. thou only upon
69 : 3 eyes fail while I w. for my G.
104 : 27. These w. upon thee, 145 : 15.
123 : 2. so our eyes w. upon the L.
130 : 5. I w. for Lord, my soul doth
Is. 8 : 17. I will w. upon the Lord [w.
30 : 18. will L. w. to be gracious to
you: blessed all they that w.
40 : 31. w. upon L. renew strength
42 : 4. isles shall w. for his law [me
49 : 23. not be ashamed that w. for
51 : 5. the isles shall w. upon me
59 : 9. we w. for light, but obscurity
60 : 9. Surely the isles sh. w. for me
Je. 14 : 22. thf. we will w. upon thee
La. 3 : 25. L. is good unto them th. w.
26. good th. man hope, quietly w.
Ho. 6 : 9. as robbers w. for a man
12 : 6. and w. on thy G continually
Mi. 7 : 7. will w. for God of my salva.
Ha. 2 : 3. tho. vision tarry, w. for it
Zph. 3 : 8. w. ye upon me, saith Lord
Mk. 3 : 9. small ship would w. on him
Lu. 12 : 36. like men that w. for lord
Ac. 1 : 4. w. for promise of Father
20 : † 23. bonds, afflictions w. for
Ro. 8 : 25. we with patience w. for it
12 : 7. let us w. on our ministering
1 Co. 9 : 13. which w. at the altar are
Ga. 5 : 5. we thro. Spirit w. for hope
1 Th. 1 : 10. to w. for his Son fr. heaven

WAITED. [tion

Ge. 49 : 18. I have w. for thy salva-
1 K. 20 : 38. the prophet w. for king
2 K. 5 : 2. maid w. on Naaman's wife
1 Ch. 6 : 32. they w. on their office, 33.
9 : 18. w. in king's gate, 2 Ch. 35 : 15.
2 Ch. 7 : 6. priests w. on their offices
17 : 19. These w. on the k. besides
Ne. 12 : 44. priests and Levites th. w.

Jb. 6 : 19. companies of Sheba w.
15 : 22. and he is w. for of the sword
29 : 21. Unto men gave ear, w.[rain
23. And they w. for me as for the
30 : 26. when I w. for light, darku.
32 : 4. Elihu had w. till Job, 11, 16.
Ps. 40 : 1. I w. patiently for the Lord
106 : 13. they w. not for counsel
119 : 95. The wicked have w. for me
Is. 25 : 9. our G., we have w. for him
26 : 8. in thy judgm-ts we w. for thee
33 : 2. be gracious, we w. for thee
Eze. 19 : 5. saw she had w., hope lost
Mi. 1 : 12. inhabitants of Maroth w.
Zch. 11 : 11. the poor th. w. upon me
Mk. 15 : 43. Joseph of Arimathea,
w. for kingd. of G., Lu. 23 : 51.
Lu. 1 : 21. people w. for Zacharias
Ac. 10 : 7. Cornelius called soldier th.
24. Cornelius w. for Peter [w.
17 : 16. Paul w., his spirit stirred
1 Pe. 3 : 20. longsuffering of G. w. in

WAITETH.

Jb. 24 : 15. adulterer w. for twilight
Ps. 33 : 20. Our soul w. for Lord
62 : 1. my soul w. upon God, 130 : 6.
65 : 1. Praise w. for thee, O God of
Pr. 27 : 18. he that w. on his master
Is. 64 : 4. hath prepared for him that
Da. 12 : 12. Blessed that w. [w.
Mi. 5 : 7. as showers that w. not for
Ro. 8 : 19. w. for manifestation of
Ja. 5 : 7. husbandman w. for fruit

WAITING. [w.

Nu. 8 : 25. from age of fifty sh. cease
Pr. 8 : 34. w. at gates, w. at posts
Lu. 2 : 25. Simeon w. for consola-n
8 : 40. they were all w. for him [er
Jn. 5 : 3. folk w. for moving of wat-
Ro. 8 : 23. we groan, w. for adoption
1 Co. 1 : 7. w. for coming of our Lord
2 Th. 3 : 5. Lord direct your hearts
into the patient w. for Christ

WAKE, WAKED.

Je. 51 : 39. may sleep and not w., 57.
Jo. 3 : 9. w. up the mighty men
Zch. 4 : 1. the angel came and w-d me
1 Th. 5 : 10. whether we w. or sleep

WAKEN, ED, ETH.

Is. 7 : † 6. go up ag. Judah and w. it
50 : 4. he w-h morning by morning,
w-h mine ear to hear as learned
Jo. 3 : 12. Let heathen be w-d and
Zch. 4 : 1. as a man w-d out of sleep

WAKETH, ING. [w-g

Ps. 77 : 4. Thou holdest mine eyes
127 : 1. except Lord keep the city
watchman w-h in vain
Can. 5 : 2. I sleep, but my heart w-h
Ho. 7 : † 4. baker who ceaseth fr. w-g
Mal. 2 : † 12. L. will cut off him w-h

WALK, WALKS. [lars

Eze. 41 : † 15. measured w-s with pil-
42 : 4. bef. chambers was w. of ten
Na. 2 : 5. stumble in their w.[cubits
Zch. 3 : † 7. give thee w-s to walk

WALK. [Verb.] [am.

Ge. 24 : 40. The Lord, bef. whom I w.
48 : 15. G., bef. whom my fa-s did w.
Ex. 16 : 4. whe. they will w. in my
21 : 19. If he w. abroad, he th. smote
Le. 18 : 3. nei. shall ye w. in their
ordinances, 20 : 23. [therein
4. keep mine ordinances to w.
26 : 12. I will w. am. you and be y-r G.
21. if w. contrary unto me, 23, 27.
24. will I w. contrary unto you, 28.
De. 8 : 19. if ye w. after other gods
29 : 19. tho. I w. in the imagina-n
1 S. 2 : 30. thy house sho. w. bef. me
35. he sh. w. bef. mine anointed
25 : † 27. young men th. w. at feet
1 K. 2 : 4. if take heed to w. bef. me
6 : 12. if keep com-ts to w. in them
8 : 23. keepest covenant with servants th. w. bef. thee, 2 Ch. 6 : 14.
25. that they w. bef. me as thou
1 K. 9 : 4. if thou wilt w. bef. me as Da.
thy father walked, 2 Ch. 7 : 17.
16 : 31. light thing to w. in sins of
2 K. 10 : 31. Jehu no heed to w. in law
23 : 3. Josiah made covenant to w.
after Lord, 2 Ch. 34 : 31. [in law
2 Ch. 6 : 16. that chil. take heed to w.
Ne. 5 : 9. ought ye not to w. in fear
10 : 29. an oath to w. in God's law
Ps. 12 : 8. The wicked w. on ev. side
23 : 4. tho. I w. thro. valley of shad-w
26 : 11. I will w. in mine integrity
56 : 13. I may w. bef. God in light
78 : 10. They refused to w. in his
82 : 5. they w. on in darkness [law
86 : 11. O Lord, I will w. in thy tru.
89 : 15. w. in light of thy counten.
30. if chil. w. not in my judgm-ts
101 : 2. I will w. in my house with
104 : † 10. springs wh. w. am. hills
115 : 7. feet have they, but w. not
116 : 9. I will w. bef. L. in land of
119 : 1. undefiled who w. in law of
45. I will w. at liberty, for I seek
131 : † 1. nei. do I w. in gr. matters
138 : 7. Tho. I w. in midst of troub.
Ec. 4 : 15. I considered living wh. w.
6 : 8. what hath poor that knoweth
to w. before the living? [4 : 2.
Is. 2 : 3. we will w. in his paths, Mi.
5. O Jacob, let us w. in light of L.
3 : 16. w. wi. stretched forth necks
30 : 2. That w. to go down into Eg.
35 : 9. redeemed sh. w. there[faint
40 : 31. th. wait upon L. sh. w., not
42 : 5. giveth spirit to them that w.
59 : 9. for brightn. but w. in darkn.
Je. 3 : 17. nor w. after imagination
18. house of Judah sh. w. with Isr.
6 : 16. said, We will not w. therein
7 : 6. if ye w. not after other gods
9. will ye w. after other gods wh.
9 : 4. ev. neighb. will w. wi. slanders
13 : 10. people, which w. in imagination of heart, and w. after other gods, 16 : 12.-18 : 12. [in lies
23 : 14. commit adultery, and w.
26 : 4. If not hearken to w. in my l.
La. 5 : 18. Zion, foxes w. upon it
Eze. 13 : † 3. prophets that w. after
36 : 12. cause men to w. upon you
37 : 24. they sh. w. in my judgm-s
Da. 4 : 37. those that w. in pride he
9 : 10. Nei. obeyed God to w. in laws
Ho. 11 : 10. shall w. after the Lord
Jo. 2 : 8. shall w. ev. one in his path
Am. 3 : 3. Can two w. together exc.
Mi. 2 : † 11. If a man w. with wind
4 : 5. ev. one will w. in na. of his god
and we will w. in name of Lord
6 : 8. but to w. humbly with thy G.
16. ye w. in the counsels of Omri
Ha. 3 : 15. Thou didst w. thro. sea
19. make me w. upon high places
Zph. 1 : 17. shall w. like blind men
Zch. 1 : 10. whom Lord sent to w. to
and fro thro. earth, 6 : 7. [stand
3 : 7. places to w. among these that
10 : 12. they shall w. up and down
Mat. 11 : 5. the lame w., Lu. 7 : 22.
15 : 31. saw lame w., glorified God
Mk. 7 : 5. Why w. not thy disciples
Lu. 11 : 44. men that w. over them
13 : 33. I must w. to day and to m.
20 : 46. desire to w. in long robes
24 : 17. what communica-s as ye w.
Jn. 7 : 1. Jes. would not w. in Jewry
8 : 12. shall not w. in darkness
11 : 9. If any man w. in the day
10. if man w. in night, stumbleth
Ac. 3 : 12. as tho. we made man to w.
21 : 21 neither to w. after customs
Ro. 4 : 12. w. in steps of faith of Abr.
6 : 4. we should w. in newn. of life
8 : 1. who w. not after flesh, but, 4.
13 : 13. Let us w. honestly as[men
1 Co. 3 : 3. are ye not carnal, w. as
1 Co. 7 : 17. as L. called so let him w.
2 Co. 5 : 7. we w. by faith, not sight
6 : 16. I will dwell and w. in them
10 : 3. though we w. in the flesh
Ga. 5 : 25. let us w. in the Spirit
6 : 16. many as w. acc. to this rule
Ep. 2 : 10. ordained we sho. w. in th.
4 : 1. that ye w. worthy of vocation
17. th. ye w. not as other Gentiles
5 : 15. See that ye w. circumspectly
Ph. 3 : 16. let us w. by the same rule
17. breth., mark them wh. w. so
18. many w. of whom I told you
Col. 1 : 10. that ye might w. worthy
of the Lord, 1 Th. 2 : 12.
1 Th. 4 : 1. how ye ought to w. and
12. That ye may w. honestly tow.
2 Th. 3 : 11 some wh. w. disorderly
2 Pe. 2 : 10. them that w. after flesh
1 Jn. 1 : 6. If say we have fellowship
and w. in darkness [the light
7. if we w. in the light as he is in
2 : 6. ought so to w. as he walked
2 Jn. 6. w. after his comm-ts, as ye
have heard ye should w.[truth
3 Jn. 4. that my children w. in the
Jude 18. w. after their ungodly lusts
Re. 3 : 4. shall w. with me in white
9 : 20. idols that cannot see nor w.
16 : 15. watcheth, lest he w. naked
21 : 24. nations shall w. in light of

WALK. [Imperative.][city

Ge. 13 : 17. Arise, w. thro. the land
17 : 1. I Almighty God, w. before me
Jos. 18 : 8. Joshua charged, w. thro.
Ps. 48 : 12. w. about Zion, go round
Is. 50 : 11. w. in light of your fire
Eze. 20 : 18. w. ye not in statutes of
Mat. 9 : 5. easier, or to say, Arise
and w.? Mk. 2 : 9. Lu. 5 : 23.
Jn. 5 : 8. Jesus saith, Rise, w., 11, 12.
12 : 35. w. while ye have the light
Ac. 3 : 6. Peter said, In name of Ch.,
Ga. 5 : 16. w. in the Spirit, 25. [w.
Ep. 5 : 2. w. in love, as Christ hath
8. are ye light: w. as chil. of light
Col. 2 : 6. as ye received Christ, so w.
4 : 5. w. in wisdom tow. them with-t
See STATUTES, UPRIGHTLY.
See WAY, S, with walk.

WALKED.

Ge. 5 : 24. Enoch w. with God, 22.
6 : 9. Noah, a just man, w. wi. God
Ex. 2 : 5. maidens w. by river side
14 : 29. Israel w. upon dry land in
Le. 26 : 40. have w. contrary unto me
Jos. 5 : 6. Isr. w. 40 years in wildern.
8 : † 35. strangers that w. am. them
14 : † 10. while Israel w. in wildern.
Ju. 5 : 6. in days of Jael travellers w.
11 : 16. when Israel w. thro. wild.
2 S. 2 : 29. Abner and men w. all ni.
11 : 2. David w. upon roof of house
1 K. 3 : 6. Dav. w. bef. thee in truth
8 : 25. walk bef. me as thou hast w.
9 : 4. as David thy father w., 2 Ch.
6 : 16.-7 : 17. [Jeroboam
13 : † 2. Jehoaz w. after the sins of
15 : 3. Abijam w. in sins of his father, 2 K. 21 : 21. [to and fro
2 K. 4 : 35. Then Elisha w. in house
13 : 11. sins of Jerob. he w. th-n, 6.
17 : 19. Judah w. in statutes of Isr.
22. Israel w. in sins of Jeroboam
1 Ch. 17 : 8. I with thee whi. thou w.
2 Ch. 17 : 4. Jehosh. w. in G.'s com-ts
22 : 5. Ahaziah w. after their coun.
Es. 2 : 11. Mord. w. ev. day bef. court
Jb. 29 : 3. by his light I w. thro. dark.
31 : 7. mine heart w. aft. mine eyes
38 : 16. hast w. in search of depth?
Ps. 35 : † 14. w. as tho. he my friend
55 : 14. w. unto hou. of G. in compa-
81 : 12. w. in their own country[ny
Is. 9 : 2. w. in darkness seen gr. light
20 : 3. as Isaiah hath w. naked for
Je. 2 : 5. they have w. aft. vanity, 8.

Je.7 : 24. but w. in counsels of their evil heart, 9 : 14.-11 : 8. [11.
8 : 2. after whom they have w., 16:
9 : 13. forsaken my law, neither w. therein, 32 : 23.-44 : 10, 23.
Eze. 5 : 6. my statutes, have not w.
23 : 14. w. in midst of stones of fire
Da. 4 : 29. Neb. w. in palace of Bab-l
Ho. 5 : 11. Ephraim w. after comm t
Am 2 : 4. after the which fathers w.
Na. 2 : 11. where the old lion w.
Ha. 3 : † 11. arrows w. in light of sun
Zch. 1 : 11. We have w. to and fro through earth, 6 : 7.
Mal. 2 : 6. he w. with me in peace
3 : 14. what profit th. we w. mournf-y
Mat. 14 : 29. Peter w. on water [lee
Mk 1 : 16. as he w. by sea of Gali-
5 : 42. the damsel arose and w.
16 : 12. Jesus appeared as they w.
Jn. 1 : 36. looking upon Jes. as he w.
5 : 9. man took up his bed and w.
6 : 66. disciples w. no more wi. him
7 : 1. After these things Jesus w. in
10 : 23. Jesus w. in temple [Galilee
11 : 54. Jesus w. no more openly
Ac. 3 : 8. he, leaping up, w., 14 : 10.
14 : 8. a cripple, who never had w.
2 Co 10 : 2. as if we w. acc. to flesh
12 : 18. w. we not in same spirit? w. we not in same st ps? [upri.
Ga. 2 : 14. when I saw they w. not
Ep. 2 : 2. Wherein in time past ye w.
Col. 3 : 7. w. when ye lived in them
1 Pe. 4 : 3. when we w. in lasciviousn.
1 Jn. 2 : 6. ought so to walk as he w.

I have WALKED.

Le. 26 : 41. th. I h.w. contrary unto
1 S. 12 : 2. I h.w. bef. you fr. childh.
2 S. 7 : 6. I h.w. in a tent [rael
7. places wherein I h.w. with Is-
2 K. 20 : 3. remember how I h.w. before thee, Is. 38 : 3. [Israel
1 Ch. 17 : 6. Whereso. I h.w. with
Jb. 31 : 5. If I h.w. with vanity
Ps. 26 : 1. for I h.w. in my integrity
3. I h.w. in thy truth, Is. 38 : 3.
See STATUTES,
Statutes with **JUDGMENTS.**
See **WAY, S, wi. walked.**

WALKEDST. [wouldest

Jn. 21 : 18. when young, w. whither

WALKERS.

Ju. 5 : † 6. In days of Shamgar w. of paths walked through byways

WALKEST. [11 : 19.

De. 6 : 7. talk of them when thou w.,
1 K. 2 : 42. on the day thou w. abr.
Is. 43 : 2. w. thro. fire not be burned
Ac. 21 : 24. thou thyself w. orderly
Ro. 14 : 15. now w. not charitably
3 Jn. 3. even as thou w. in truth

WALKETH. [field?

Ge. 24 : 65. What man is this w. in
De. 23 : 14. God w. in midst of camp
1 S. 12 : 2. behold, king w. bef. you
Jb. 18 : 8. into net, he w. upon snare
22 : 14. he w. in circuit of heaven
34 : 8. and w. with wicked men
Ps. 1 : 1. w. not in counsel of ungodly
39 : 6. every man w. in a vain shew
73 : 9. their tongue w. thro. earth
91 : 6. pestilence that w. in darkn-s
104 : 3. who w. upon wings of wind
Pr. 6 : 12. wicked man w. wi. froward
11 : † 13. He th. w. being a talebearer
13 : 20 w. with wise men sh. be wise
14 : 2. that w. in uprightn. feareth
19 : 1. poor th. w. in integrity, 28 : 6.
20 : 7. just man w. in his integrity
28 : 26. whoso w. wisely be deliv-d
Ec. 2 : 14. the fool w. in darkness
Is. 33 : 15. w. righteously shall dwell
50 : 10. that w. in darkness [direct
Je. 10 : 23. not in man that w. to
23 : 17. that w. after the imagina-n
Eze. 11 : 21. w. aft. detestable things
Mat. 12 : 43. unclean spirit w. thro. dry places, Lu 11 : 24. [eth not
Jn. 12 : 35. that w. in darkn. know-
2 Th. 3 : 6. brother th. w. disorderly
1 Pe. 5 : 8. devil w. about seeking
1 Jn. 2 : 11. hateth bro. w. in darkness
Re. 2 : 1. w. in midst of 7 golden can-
See UPRIGHTLY. [dlesticks
See **WAY, S, with walketh.**

WALKING. [garden

Ge. 3 : 8. heard voice of Lord w. in
De. 2 : 7. Lord knoweth thy w. thro.
1 K. 3 : 3. Sol. loved L., w. as David
16 : 19. Zimri w. in way of Jerob-m
Jb. 1 : 7. from w. up and down, 2 : 2.
31 : 26. beheld moon w. in brightn.
Ec. 6 : † 9. Better is sight than w. of
10 : 7. princes w. as servants [soul
Is. 3 : 16. w. and mincing as they go
20 : 2. Isaiah w. naked and barefoot
57 : 2. each one w. in uprightness
Je. 6 : 28. revolters w. with slanders
Da. 3 : 25. I see four men w. in fire
Mi. 2 : 11. If a man w. in fa[lsehood
Mat. 4 : 18. Jesus w. by sea of Galilee
14 : 25. Jes. went to them w. on sea
26. they saw him w. on sea were troubled, Mk. 6 : 48, 49. Jn. 6 : [19.
Mk 8 : 24. I see men as trees w.
11 : 27. as he was w. in the temple
Lu. 1 : 6. w. in all the commandm-ts
Ac. 3 : 8. lame man w., leaping, 9.
9 : 31. w. in the fear of the Lord
2 Co. 4 : 2. not w. in craftiness [16.
2 Pe. 3 : 3. scoffers w. aft. lusts, Jude
2 Jn 4. found thy chil. w. in truth

WALL. [w.

Ge. 49 : 6. in selfwill digged down a
22. whose branches run over w.
Ex. 14 : 22. waters were w. unto them
Le. 14 : 37. if plague lower than w.
Nu. 22 : 24. a w. being on this side, a w. on that side [the w. (2)
25. ass crushed Balaam's foot ag.
35 : 4. suburbs reach from w. of city
Jos. 2 : 15. Rahab dwelt upon town w.
6 : 5. w. of city shall fall down, 20.
1 S. 18 : 11. I will smite Da. to w. [(2)
19 : 10. Saul smote javelin into w.
20 : 25. king sat upon seat by the w.
25 : 16. a w. to us by night and day
22. if I leave any that pisseth ag. the w., 34. 1 K. 14 : 10.-16 : 11. -21 : 21. 2 K. 9 : 8. [the w.
31 : 10. they fastened Saul's body to
12. took body of S. fr. w. of Beth.
2 S. 5 : † 11. sent hewers of stone of w.
11 : 20. knew ye not they would shoot from w., 24. [nigh w.
21. millstone fr. w., why went ye
18 : 24. watchm. up to roof unto w.
20 : 15. the people battered the w.
21 his head be thrown ov. the w.
22 : 30. by my God have I leaped over a w., Ps. 18 : 29. [of w.
1 K. 4 : 33. hyssop that springeth out
6 : 5 ag. w. of house built chambers
27. wing of one touched one w., (2)
20 : 30. a w. fell upon 27,000 men
21 : 23. dogs shall eat Jezebel by w.
2 K. 3 : 27. k. offered his son upon w.
4 : 10. make a little chamber on w.
6 : 26. k. of Isr. passing by upon w.
30. king passed by upon the w.
9 : 33. Jezebel's blood on the w.
18 : 26. talk not in ears of people on w., 27. 2 Ch. 32 : 18. Is. 36 : 11, 12.
20 : 2. Hezekiah turned his face to the w., Is 38 : 2. [house, 12.
2 Ch. 3 : 11. wing reaching to w. of
26 : 6. Uzziah brake down w. of Gath, w. of Jabneh, w. of Ash.
32 : 5. Hez. raised ano. w. without
Ezr. 5 : 3. Who com-ded you make w.
Ne. 2 : 8. make beams for w. of city
15. Then I in night viewed the w.
3 : 13. 1,000 cubits on w. unto gate
Ne. 3 : 15. w. of pool of Siloah by gard-
27. repaired unto w. of Ophel [en
4 : 3. a fox sh. break down stone w.
13. Thf. set I behind w. the pe
15. we returned all of us to the w.
19. we are separated upon the w.
5 : 16. I continued in work of this w.
6 : 15 w. was finished in month E.
12 : 30. priests purified gates and w.
31. I bro-t up princes upon w. (2)
37. stairs at going up of w. [w.
38. half of peo. upon w. unto br-d
13 : 21. Why lodge ye about the w.
Ps. 62 : 3. as a bowing w. shall ye be
Pr. 18 : 11. as high w. in own conceit
24 : 31. stone w. was broken down
Can. 2 : 9. My beloved behind our w.
8 : 10. I am a w.; breasts like towers
Is. 5 : † 2. made w. about it and gath-d
5. I will break w. of my vineyard
22 : 10. houses down to fortify w.
25 : 4. blast is as a storm ag. the w.
30 : 13. breach swelling out in high
59 : 10. grope for w. like blind [w.
Je. 49 : 27. kindle fire in w. of Dam.
51 : 44. the w. of Babylon shall fall
La. 2 : 8. destroy w. of dau. of Zion
18. cried, O w. of daughter of Zion
Eze. 4 : 3. w. of iron betw. thee and
8 : 7. behold a hole in the w. [city
8. Son of man, dig now in the w.,
10. idols portrayed on w., [12 : 5.
12 : 7. in the even I digged thro. w.
12. they shall dig thro. w. to carry
13 : 12 Lo, when the w. is fallen, 15.
14. and break down w. ye daubed
15. accomplish my wrath upon w. and say, The w. is no more, nei.
23 : 14. saw men portrayed upon w.
38 : 20. every w. sh. fall to ground
40 : 5. behold w. on outside of ho.
41 : 5. Aft. he measured w. of hou.
6. they entered into w. of house, but had not hold of the w. [12.
9. The thickn. of the w. five cubits,
17. by all the w. round about, 20.
42 : 7. the w. without was 50 cubits
10 chambers in the thickn. of w.
12. way directly bef w. tow. east
20. it had a w. 500 reeds long
43 : 8. in setting w. betw. me and
Da 5 : 5 wrote upon plaster of w.
Ho. 2 : 6. a w. th. she not find paths
Jo. 2 : 7. climb w. like men of war
9 shall run upon w. and climb
Am. 1 : 7 I will send a fire on w. of
10. on the w. of Tyrus [Gaza
14. will kindle fire in w. of Rab h
5 : 19. leaned on w. serpent bit him
7 : 7. Lord stood upon a w. made by
Na 2 : 5. shall make haste to the w.
3 : 8 and her w. was from the sea
Ha 2 : 11. stone shall cry out of w.
Zch 2 : 5. I be unto her a w. of fire
Ac. 9 : 25. disciples let Saul down by the w., 2 Co. 11 : 33 [whited w.
23 : 3. God shall smite thee, thou
Ep. 2 : 14. Ch. broken down mid. w.
Re 21 : 12. city had w. gr. and high
14. w. of city had 12 foundations
15. reed to measure w. of city, 17.
19. founda-s of w. were garnished

WALL, S with build, ed, est, ing, or built.

1 K. 6 : 15. Solo-n b-t w-s with cedar
2 Ch. 27 : 3. on w. of Ophel Joth. b-t
32 : 5. Hez-h b-t up all w. broken and another w. without [city
33 : 14. Manasseh b-t w. without
Ne. 4 : 1. Sanballat heard we b-d w.
6. So we b-t w.; all w. was joined
10. rubbish, we not able to b. w.
17. they wh. b-d on the w. held
6 : 1. enemies heard I had b-d w.
6. b-st w. that thou mayest be k.
7 : 1. w. was b-t I gave charge
Can. 8 : 9. If she is a w. we will b.

Is. 60 : 10. strangers sh. b. thy w-s
Eze. 13 : 10. one b-t w., oth-s daubed
Da. 9 : 25. w. b-t in troublous times
Mi. 7 : 11. day thy w-s are to be b-t
Re. 21 : 18. b-g of the w. was of jasper
See **WALL, S** with **Jerusalem.**
See **FENCED wall, s.**

WALL, S with Jerusalem.

1 K. 3 : 1. end of building w. of J.
9 : 15. levy raised to build w. of J.
2 K. 14 : 13. Jehoash brake down the w. of J., 2 Ch. 25 : 23.
25 : 10. army of Chaldees brake down w-s of J., Je. 39 : 8.-52 : 14.
2 Ch. 32 : 18. cried unto peo. of J. on w.
36 : 19. brake down w. of J., burnt
Ezr. 4 : 12. Jews unto J. have set w-s
9 : 9. mercy to give us a w. in J.
Ne. 1 : 3. w. of J. also is broken do.
2 : 13. by night I viewed w-s of J., 17. let us build up w. of J. [15.
3 : 8. they fortified J. unto broad w.
4 : 7. heard th. w-s of J. were made
12 : 27. at dedication of w. of J.
Ps. 51 : 18. build thou the w-s of J.
Is. 62 : 6. watchm. upon thy w-s, O J.
Je. 1 : 15 throne at gates of J. ag. w-s
Zch. 2 : 4 J. sh. be as towns wi-t w-s
See **TURNING of the wall.**

WALLS.

Ex. 30 : † 3. overlay w. wi. pure gold
Le 14 : 37. if plague be in the w., 39.
De. 3 : 5. cities fenced with high w.
28 : 52. thy fenced w. come down
1 K. 4 : 13. gr. cities with w. and gates
6 : 5. built chambers ag. w. of hou.
6. beams not be fastened in the w.
29. he carved all the w. of house
1 Ch. 29 : 4. to overlay w. of house
2 Ch. 3 : 7. He graved cherubim on w.
8 : 5. Sol. built fenced cities wi. w.
14 : 7. make about cities, w., gates
Ezr. 4 : 13. if this city be builded and w. set up, 12, 16. [eth fast
5 : 8. timber is laid in w. work go-
9. Who com-ded you to make w.?
Jb. 24 : 11. make oil within their w.
Ps 55 : 10. Day and night go upon w.
122 : 7. Peace be within thy w.
Pr. 25 : 28. is like a city without w.
Can. 5 : 7. keepers of w. took my vail
Is. 22 : 5. a day of breaking down w.
11. ye made ditch between two w.
25 : 12. fortress of thy w. bri down
26 : 1. salvation God appoint for w.
49 : 16. w. are continually bef. me
56 : 5. within my w. a name better
60 : 18. shalt call thy w. Salvation
Je. 1 : 18. brazen w. ag. whole land
4 : † 19. I pained at w. of my heart
5 : 10. Go ye upon her w., destroy
21 : 4. wh. besiege you without w.
39 : 4. fled by the gate betwixt the two w., 52 : 7. [down, 51 : 58.
50 : 15 Babylon's w. are thrown
51 : 12. Set the standard upon w.
La. 2 : 7. given up w. of her palaces
Eze. 26 : 4. destroy w. of Tyrus, 12
9. sh. set engines of war ag. thy w.
10. w. sh. shake at noise of horsem.
27 : 11. men of Arvad upon thy w., hanged their shields upon w.
33 : 30. are talking ag. thee by w.
38 : 11. all dwelling without w. or
41 : 13. he measured house with w.
22 w. of altar were of wood [w.
25. cherubim like as made upon
He. 11 : 30. By faith w. of Jericho fell

WALL, WALLED. [city

Le 25 : 29. if sell dwelling ho. in w-d
30 house in w-d city be establ-ed
Nu. 13 : 28. cities w-d and gr., De. 1 : 28.
Ho. 2 : † 6. I will w. a wall, she not
Am. 9 : † 11. I will w. up the breaches

WALLOW, ED.

2 S. 20 : 12. Amasa w-d in blood
Je. 6 : 26. dau. of people w. in ashes
25 : 34. shepherds w. in the ashes
48 : 26. Moab shall w. in his vomit
Eze. 27 : 30. they sh. w. in the ashes
Mk. 9 : 20. he fell and w-d foaming

WALLOWING.

2 Pe. 2 : 22. the sow to w. in mire

WANDER, ED.

Ge. 20 : 13. God caused me to w. from my father's house
De. 27 : 18. Cursed that causeth the blind to w. [with us?
2 S. 15 : † 20. should I make thee w.
Jb. 12 : † 25. them to w. like drunken
38 : 41. when his young ravens w.
Ps. 55 : 7. then would I w. far off
59 : 15. Let them w. up and down
119 : 10. O let me not w. fr. com-ts
Is. 21 : † 4. my mind w-d, fearfuln-s
47 : 15 sh. w. ev. one to his quarter
Je. 14 : 10. Thus have th. loved to w.
48 : 12. that shall cause him to w.
La. 4 : 14. They w-d as blind men
15. when they fled away and w-d
Eze. 34 : 6. My sheep w-d thro. mts.
Am. 4 : 8. two cities w-d unto one
8 : 12. shall w. from sea to sea [city
He. 11 : 37. w-d about in sheepskins
38. they w-d in deserts, in moun- [tains
See **WILDERNESS** with **wander, ed.**

WANDERERS. [w.

Je. 48 : 12. days that I will send him
Ho. 9 : 17. they sh. be w. am. nations

WANDEREST. [thou w.

Je. 2 : 20. when under ev. green tree

WANDERETH.

Jb. 15 : 23. He w. abroad for bread
Pr. 21 : 16. w. out of way of underst-g
27 : 8. as a bird that w. from her nest, so is man that w. fr. place
Is. 16 : 3. bewray not him that w.
Je. 49 : 5. none sh. gath. up him that [w.

WANDERING, S.

Ge. 37 : 15. he was w. in the field
Ps. 56 : 8. Thou tellest my w-s, put
Pr. 26 : 2. As bird by w., as a swallow
Ec. 6 : 9. Better is sight than the w.
Is. 16 : 2. sh. be as a w. bird cast out
La. 1 : † 8. Jerusalem is become a w.
1 Ti. 5 : 13. idle, w. from hou. to hou.
Jude 13. w. stars to wh. is reserved

WANT, WANTS.

De. 28 : 48. serve thine enemies in w.
57. she shall eat them for w. of
Ju. 18 : 10. place where no w., 19 : 19.
19 : 20. let all thy w-s lie upon me
Jb. 24 : 8. the rock for w. of shelter
30 : 3. For w. they were solitary [w.
31 : 19. If I have seen any perish for
Ps. 34 : 9. is no w. to them that fear
Pr. 6 : 11. thy w. as armed man, 24 : [34.
10 : 21. fools die for w. of wisd.
13 : 23. destroyed for w. of judgm.
14 : 28. in w. of peo. is destruction of the prince [only to w.
21 : 5. of every one that is hasty
22 : 16. giveth to rich sh. come to w.
La. 4 : 9. stricken for w. of fruits of
Am. 4 : 6. have giv. you w. of bread
Mk. 12 : 44. she of her w. cast in all
Lu. 15 : 14. he began to be in w. [(2)
2 Co. 8 : 14. your abund. for their w.,
9 : 12. not only supplieth w. of saints
Ph. 2 : 25. that ministered to my w-s
4 : 11. Not that I speak in respect of

WANT, ED. [w.

Ps. 23 : 1. my shepherd, I sh. not w.
34 : 10. seek L. sh. not w. any good
Pr. 13 : 25. belly of the wicked sh. w.
Is. 34 : 16. none shall w. her mate
Je. 33 : 17. David not w. a man to
18. nei. sh. Levites w. a man bef.
35 : 19. Jonadab shall not w. man
44 : 18. we have w-d all things
Eze. 4 : 17. may w. bread and water
Jn. 2 : 3. w-d wine, mother of Jesus
2 Co. 11 : 9. when I w-d, chargeable

WANTETH. [to no

De. 15 : 8. sh. lend him in that he w.
Pr. 9 : 4. him th. w. underst-ing, 16.
10 : 19. In multi. of words w. not
28 : 16. prince that w. understand-g
Ec. 6 : 2. he w. nothing for his soul
Can. 7 : 2. goblet that w. not liquor

WANTING.

2 K. 10 : 19. call prophets of Baal, let none be w.: whoso. be w.
Pr. 19 : 7. they are w. to the poor
Ec. 1 : 15. is w. cannot be numbered
Is. 24 : † 23. aft. many days found w.
Da. 5 : 27. art weighed and found w.
Tit. 1 : 5. sho. set in order things w.
3 : 13. th. nothing be w. unto them
Ja. 1 : 4. may be perfect w. nothing

WANTON. [eyes

Is. 3 : 16. dau. of Zion walk with w.
1 Ti. 5 : 11. wax w. ag. Christ, marry
Ja. 5 : 5. lived in pleasure, been w.

WANTONNESS. [w.

Ro. 13 : 13. not in chambering and
2 Pe. 2 : 18. allure thro. lusts and w.

WAR. [Noun.]

Ge. 14 : 2. these made w. with Bera
Ex. 1 : 10. is w. they join our enemies
13 : 17. lest peo. repent when see w.
17 : 16. Lord will have w. wi. Amalek
32 : 17. is a noise of w. in the camp
Nu. 1 : 2. from 20 years old all able to go forth to w., 20, 22, 26, 28, 30, 32, 34, 36, 38, 40, 42, 45.-26 : 2. 2 Ch. 25 : 5. [an alarm
10 : 9. if ye go to w. ye shall blow
31 : 3. Arm some of yours, unto w.
4. of ev. tribe 1,000 send to the w.
5. out of Isr. 12,000 armed for w.
6. Moses sent them to the w. (2)
† 14. wroth wi. capt-s fr. host of w.
27. prey betw. them th. took the w.
36. portion that went to w. [sit
32 : 6. Shall breth. go to w. and ye
20. if go armed bef. Lord to w., 27.
32 : 27. pass over, every man armed for w., De. 3 : 18. [nation by w.
De. 4 : 34. hath God assayed to take
20 : 12. if make w. ag. thee, then
19. in making w. not destroy trees
20. bulwarks ag. city maketh w.
21 : 10. When goest to w. ag. enem.
24 : 5. taken a wife sh. not go to w.
Jos. 4 : 13. About 40,000 prep. for w.
8 : 1. take all the people of w. with thee, 3, 11.-10 : 7.-11 : 7. [Gib-n
10 : 5. kings and hosts made w. ag.
11 : 18. Joshua made w. long time
23. the land rested from w., 14 : 15.
14 : 11. so is my strength now for w.
22 : 12. Israel gathered to go to w.
Ju. 3 : 2. might know to teach th. w.
5 : 8. chose new gods, then was w.
11 : 4. Ammon made w. ag. Isr., 5.
21 : 22. not to each his wife in the w.
1 S. 23 : 8. Saul called the peo. to w.
14 : 52. was sore w. ag. Philis., 19 : 8.
28 : 15. Philistines make w. ag. us
2 S. 3 : 1. w. betw. Saul and Dav., 6.
11 : 7. David demanded how the w.
18. Joab told David conc. w., 19.
21 : 15. Phils. had w. ag., 1 Ch. 20 : 5.
1 K. 2 : 5. Joab shed blood of w. in peace, put blood of w. in shoes
14 : 30. w. between Rehoboam and Jeroboam, 15 : 6. [oboam
15 : 7. w. between Abijam and Jer-
16. w. betw. Asa and Baasha, 32.
20 : 18. whe. come for w. take them
† 26. Ben-hadad went up to w.
22 : 1. continued 3 years with-t w.
2 K. 8 : 28. went wi. Joram to the w.
13 : 25. out of hand of Jeho-z by w.
14 : 7. He took Selah by w., called
18 : 20. I have counsel and strength for w., Is. 36 : 5. [5 : 18.-7 : 11, 40.
24 : 16. that were apt for w., 1 Ch.

1 Ch. 5 : 10. made w. wi. Hagarites, 19.
22. many slain, bec. w. was of G.
7 : 4. bands of soldiers for w., 36,000
12 : 1. mighty men helpers for w.
23. bands ready armed to w., 24.
25. mighty men of val. for w., 7,100
33. Of Zebulun expert in w., with all instruments of w., 50,000
35. of Danites exp-t in w., 28,600
36. of Asher expert in w., 40,000
37. with instrum-ts of w. 120,000
20 : 4. arose w. at Gezer with Philis.
6. yet again there was w. at Gath
2 Ch. 6 : 34. If thy people go to w.
13 : 2. w. betw. Abijah and Jerob-m
14 : 6. Asa had no w. in those years
15 : 19. no w. unto 35th y-r of Asa
17 : 10 they made no w. ag. Jehosh.
18. with Jehozabad, 180,000 for w.
18 : 3. we will be with thee in w.
22 : 5. Ahaziah went to w. against
26 : 11. Uzziah had host went to w.
13. made w. with mighty power
28 : 12. stood ag. them th. came fr w.
32 : 6. set capt-s of w. ov. peo. 33 : 14.
35 : 21. ag. house wherewi. I have w.
Jb. 5 : 20. in w. redeem fr. the sword
10 : 17. changes and w. are ag. me
38 : 23. I have reserved ag. day of w.
Ps. 27 : 3. tho. w. should rise ag. me
55 : 21. words smooth, w. in heart
68 : 30. scatter peo. th delight in w.
120 : 7. when I speak they are for w.
140 : 2. continu-y are gath-d for w.
Pr 20 : 18. with good advice make w.
24 : 6. by wise counsel make thy w.
Ec. 3 : 8. a time of w., time of peace
8 : 8. death, no discharge in that w.
Can. 3 : 8. all hold swords exp-t in w.
Is. 2 : 4. neither shall they learn w. any more, Mi. 4 : 3. [men, in w.
3 : 25. Thy men sh. fall, thy mighty
21 : 15. fled from grievousness of w.
37 : 9. He is come forth to make w.
Je. 4 : 19. hast heard the alarm of w.
6 : 4. Prepare ye w. against her
23. in array as men for w. ag. thee
21 : 2. Nebuch-r maketh w. ag. us
28 : 8. prophets prophesied of w.
42 : 14. Egypt, where we sh. see no w.
48 : 14. how say, We mighty men for
49 : 2. alarm of w. in Rabbah [w.?
Eze. 17 : 17. Nei. Pha-h for him in w.
26 : 9. set engines of w. ag. walls
Da. 7 : 21. horn made w. with saints
9 : 26. unto end of w. are desolat-s
Jo. 3 : 9. Prepare w., wake up mighty
Mi. 2 : 8. as men averse from w.
3 : 5. they even prepare w. ag him
Lu. 14 : 31 what king going to make
Ac. 12 : †20 Herod, intending w. [w.
Re. 11 : 7. beast sh. make w. ag. them
12 : 7. was w. in heaven ag. dragon
17. to make w. with remnant of
13 : 4. who able to make w. wi. beast?
† 5. power given him to make w.
7. to make w. with saints [Lamb
17 : 14. These shall make w. with the
19 : 11. in righteousn. doth make w.
19. beast and kings gath-d to make
See MAN of war, s. [w.
See MEN of war.
See WEAPONS of war.

WARS.

Nu. 21 : 14 said in book of w. of L.
Ju. 3 : 1 not known all w. of Canaan
2 S. 8 : 10. for Hadadezer had w. with Toi, 1 Ch. 18 : 10 [ev side
1 K. 5 : 3. w. wh. were about him on
1 Ch. 22 : 8. made gr. w. sh. not build
2 Ch. 12 : 15. w. betw. Rehob. and Jerob.
16 : 9. from hencef. shall have w.
27 : 7. w. written in book of kings
Ps 46 : 9. He maketh w. to cease
Mat. 24 : 6. ye shall hear of w., rumours of w., Mk. 13 : 7. Lu. 21 : 9.
Ja. 4 : 1. From whence come w.

WAR. [Verb.]

Ju. 11 : 27. doest wrong to w. ag. me
2 S. 22 : 35. Lord teacheth my hands to w., Ps. 18 : 34.-144 : 1.
2 K. 16 : 5. kings came to Jerusalem to w. against it, Is. 7 : 1. [ing
Is. 41 : 12. th. w. ag. thee be as noth-
Da. 11 : † 10. But his sons shall w.
2 Co. 10 : 3 do not w. after the flesh
Ja. 4 : 1. lusts that w. in members
2. ye fight and w. yet have not
1 Pe. 2 : 11. lusts which w. ag. soul
See WARFARE.

WARD, S.

Ge. 40 : 3. Pha. put them in w., 4, 7.
41 : 10. Pha-h wroth, put me in w.
42 : 17. Joseph put his breth. in w.
Le. 24 : 12. woman's son blasphemed; they put him in w.
Nu. 15 : 34. man gathered sticks upon sabbath, they put him in w.
2 S. 20 : 3. David put concubines in w.
1 Ch. 9 : 23. oversight of tabern. by
12 : 29. kept w. of hou of Saul [w-s
25 : 8. they cast lots, w. ag. w.
26 : 12. having w-s one ag. another
16. lot came westward, w. ag. w.
Ne. 12 : 24. to give thanks w. ag. w.
25. porters keeping w. at gates
45. kept w. of their God and w.
13 : 30. I appointed w-s of priests
Is. 21 : 8. I in my w. whole nights
Je. 37 : 13. Irijah captain of the w.
52 : † 11. put Zedekiah in the w.
Eze. 19 : 9. Zedekiah in w. in chains
40 : † 45. for priests, keepers of w.
44 : † 8. have set keepers of my w.
Ac. 12 : 10. were past first and second

WARDROBE. [w.

2 K. 22 : 14. Huldah the prophetess, keeper of the w., 2 Ch. 34 : 22.

WARE. [Adj.]

Ac. 14 : 6. were w. of it and fled to
2 Ti. 4 : 15. of coppersmith be thou w.
See AWARE.

WARE. [Verb.] [clothes

Lu. 8 27. man had devils and w. no

WARE, S. [Noun.]

Ne. 10 : 31. if peo. bring w. on sabb
13 : 16 brought all manner of w.
20. sellers of all kind of w. lodged
Je 10 : 17. Gather thy w-s out of la.
Eze. 27 : 16. of multitude of w-s, 18.
33. When thy w-s went out of seas
Jon. 1 : 5 mariners cast w-s into sea

WARFARE.

Nu. 4 : † 23. that enter in to war the w., 8 : † 24. [w.
† 30. every one that entereth into
18 : † 25. sh. return from w. of serv.
1 S 28 : 1. Philis. gath d armies for w.
Jb. 7 † 1. Is there not a w. to man
Is. 40 2. her w. is accomplished
1 Co. 9 : 7 goeth a w. at own charges
2 Co. 10 : 4. weapons of w. not carnal
1 Ti. 1 : 18 mightest war a good w.

WARM. [Adj.]

2 K. 4 : 34. flesh of child waxed w.
Jb. 6 : 17. time they wax w. vanish
37 : 17. How thy garments are w.
Ps. 51 : † 5. in sin did mother w. me
Ec. 4 : 11. how can one be w. alone?
Is. 44 : 16. and saith, Aha, I am w.
Hag. 1 : 6. clothe you, but is none w.

WARM, ED.

Jb. 31 : 20 if not w-d with fleece
Is. 44 : 15. he will take and w. hims.
47 : 14 shall not be a coal to w. at
Mk 14 : 54 Peter w-d himself, Jn 18 : 18, 25. [and filled
Ja. 2 : 16. Depart in peace, be ye w-d

WARMETH, ING.

Jb. 39 : 14. ostrich that w-h eggs
Is. 44 : 16. he w-h himself and saith
Mk. 14 : 67. when she saw Peter w-g

WARN. [not

2 Ch. 19 : 10. w. that they trespass
Eze. 3 : 18. nor speakest to w. the wicked fr. his wicked way, 33 : 8.
19. Yet if thou w. wicked, 33 : 9.
21. if thou w. the righteous man
33 : 3. If he w. the people, 7. [one
Ac. 20 : 31. I ceased not to w. every
1 Co. 4 : 14. as beloved sons I w. you
1 Th. 5 : 14. w. them that are unruly

WARNED.

2 K 6 : 10. place man of God w. him
Ps. 19 : 11. by them is thy servant w.
Eze. 3 : 21. shall surely live bec. w.
33 : 6. if the people be not w. [22.
Mat. 2 : 12 Joseph being w. of G.,
3 : 7. O generation of vipers, who hath w. you to flee, Lu. 3 : 7.
Ac. 10 : 22. Cornelius w. from God
He. 11 : 7. By faith Noah being w.

WARNING.

Je. 6 : 10. To whom shall I give w.?
Eze. 3 : 17. hear the word, give w.
18. thou givest him not w., 20.
33 : 4. heareth and taketh not w.
5. heard trumpet, took not w. (2)
Col. 1 : 28. w. and teaching ev. man

WARP or woof.

Le. 13 : 48. Whether the plague is w. o. w., 49, 51, 53, 57.
52. burn th. garm-t whe. w. o. w.
56. sh send plague out of w. o. w.
58. garment w. o. w. thou sh. wash
59 This law of leprosy in w. o. w.

WARRED. [ag. Isr.

Nu. 24 : † 20. Amalek first that w.
31 : 7. And they w. ag Midianites
42 wh. Mos. divided fr. men th. w.
Jos. 24 : 9. Balak king w. ag. Israel
1 K. 14 : 19. Jeroboam, how he w.
20 : 1. besieged Samaria, w. ag it
22 : 45. acts of Jehoshaphat, how he w., 2 K 14 : 28. [Israel
2 K. 6 : 8. king of Syria w. against
2 Ch. 26 : 6. Uzziah w. ag. Philistines

WARRETH, ING.

2 K. 19 : 8. found king of Assyria w-g against Libnah, Is. 37 : 8.
Ro. 7 : 23. see law in my memb-s w-g
2 Ti. 2 : 4. No man that w-h entan-

WARRIOR, S. [gleth

1 K. 12 : 21. chosen men who were w-s, 2 Ch. 11 : 1. [noise
Is. 9 : 5. battle of w. is wi. confused

WARY.

He. 11 : † 7. By faith Noah being w.

WAS. [he w. not

Ge. 5 : 24. Enoch walked with God:
12 : 18. did not tell she w. thy wife
18 : 10. tent door which w. behind
21 : 20 G. w. with the lad, he grew
26 : 28. We saw the Lord w. wi. thee
29 : 12. told he w. her fath-'s bro.
31 : 1. Jac taken all that w. fath-'s
40. Thus I w. in the day, drought
35 : 3. God w. with me in the way
37 : 29. Joseph w. not in the pit
39 : 2. Lord w. with Joseph, he w. prosperous, 3, 21, 23. [fore me
40 : 9. In my dream a vine w. be-
44 : 14. Joseph's house; he w. yet
Ex. 20 : 21 drew near where God w.
Le. 9 : 8. slew calf wh. w. for himself
Nu 27 : 3 w. not in comp-y of Korah
Jos 1 : 5 as I w. with Moses, so I
17. L. with thee as he w. wi. Moses
6 : 27. the Lord w. with Joshua
14 : 11. I am as strong as I w. for
Ju 13 : 6. I asked not whence he w.
20 : 3. tell, how w. this wickedn.?
Ru. 1 : 7. out of place where she w.
1 S. 9 : 10. went where man of G. was
2 S 12 : 3. ewe lamb w. as daughter
16 : 23 counsel of Ahithophel w. (2)
1 K 3 : 26 whose the living child w.
8 : 57. God be with us as he w. with
19 : 11. Lord w. not in the wind (2)
12. but the Lord w. not in the fire
20 : 41. discerned he w. of prophets

2 K.10:30.unto Ahab all **w.** in heart
Es.8:1. Es.told what he **w.** unto her
Jb. 3 : 26.I **w.** not in safety, neither
29 : 4. As I **w.** in days of my youth
Ps.37 : 36. passed away, lo he **w.** not
38 : 14. I **w.** as a man heareth not
53 : 5. in gr. fear, where no fear **w.**
124 : 1. Lord who **w.** on our side, 2.
Pr. 8 : 30. Then I **w.** by him : **w.**
daily his delight [in her
Is. 9 : 1. dimness not be such as **w.**
23 : 13. people **w.** not till Assyrian
Je. 48 : 27. **w.** not Israel a derision ?
w. he found among thieves ?
La. 3 : 10. He **w.** unto me as a bear
Am. 7 : 14.I **w.** no prophet, nei. **w.**
I a prophet's son, but I **w.** a
Jon. 4 : 2. Lord, **w.** not my saying
Mal.1 : 2.**w.** not Esau Jacob's bro. ?
Mat. 11 : 14.Elias wh. **w.** for to come
24 : 21. such as **w.** not since beginning of the world, Mk. 13 : 19.
Mk.1:45. Jesus **w.** without in desert
2 : 4. uncovered roof where he **w.**
4 : 10.when he **w.** alone they asked
36. took him even as he **w.** in ship
5 : 5. night and day he **w.** in mts.
9 : 26. and he **w.** as one dead [way
33. What **w.** it ye disputed by
11 : 30. The baptism of John, **w.** it
from heaven, Lu. 20 : 4. [alive
16 : 11.when they heard that he **w.**
Lu. 6 : 16.Judas, wh. also **w.** traitor
7 : 6. when he **w.** not far fr. house
9 : 53. face **w.** as tho. he would go
10 : 36. Which of these **w.** neighb.
15 : 20. when he **w.** yet gr. way off
17 : 10. done that wh. **w.** our duty
19 : 4. for he **w.** to pass that way
24 : 13. wh. **w.** fr. Jerus. threescore
19. **w.** a prophet mighty in deed
23. angels which said he **w.** alive
Jn. 1 : 1. the Word **w.** with God,
and the Word **w.** God [light
4.In him **w.** life ; and the life **w.**
9. That **w.** true light, th.lighteth
15. John cried, he **w.** bef. me, 30.
2 : 25. for he knew what **w.** in man
3 : 26.he that **w.** wi.thee bey.Jord.
6 : 62. ascend up where he **w.** bef.
8 : 58. Verily before Abr. **w.** I am
11 : 15. I am glad I **w.** not there
12 : 9. much peo. knew he **w.** there
16 : 4. I said, bec. I **w.** with you
17: 5.'glory I had bef. the world **w.**
20 : 24. Thomas **w.** not with them
21 : 11. yet **w.** not the net broken
Ac. 4 : 34. Nei. **w.** any that lacked
5 : 4. sold, **w.** it not in own power?
7 :9. sold Joseph, God **w.** with him
38. This is he that **w.** in church
9 : 39. Dorcas made, while she **w.**
11 : 17.what **w.** I, I withstand G. ?
21 : 33. capt. demanded who he **w.**
23 : 34. asked of wh. province he **w.**
26 : 4. My life, which **w.** at first
1 Co. 2 : 3. I **w.** with you in fear and
15 : 10. his grace **w.** not in vain
16 : 12.his will **w.** not at all to come
2 Co.1 : 18.word **w.** not yea,nay,19.
11 : 5. **w.** not whit behind chiefest
Ga. 3 : 17. law wh. **w.** 430 yrs. after
1 Th. 2 : 3.exhort-n **w.** not of deceit
2 Ti.3 : 9.folly manifest as theirs **w.**
He. 7 : 4. how great this man **w.**
11 : 38.Of wh. world **w.** not worthy
Ja.1 :24.forgetteth what man he **w.**
2 Pe. 3 : 6. world then **w.** perished
1 Jn. 1 : 1.That wh. **w.** fr. beginning
Re. 1 : 4. from him which is and
which **w.**, 8.-4 : 8. [and is alive
2 : 8. first and last, which **w.** dead
17:8.The beast **w.** and is not.(2),11.
See AFRAID, CALLED, FILLED, FOUND, GOOD, GREAT, TOLD.

It WAS.

Ge. 31 : 2. **i.w.** not toward him as [before
Ge.40 : 10. **i.w.** as though it budded
42 : 6. he **i.w.** sold to all the people
Ex. 16 : 15. they wist not what **i.w.**
Jos. 11 : 20. **i.w.** of Lord to harden
Ju. 14 : 4.knew not **i.w.** of the Lord
2 S. 3 : 37.**i.w.** not of k. to slay Abn.
18 :29.tumult, I knew not wh.**i.w.**
1 K. 2 :15.my bro-'s, **i.w.** from Lord
8 : 17. **i.w.** in heart of Da. to build,
18. (2) 1 Ch. 22 : 7. 2 Ch. 6 : 7, 8.
22 : 33. perceived **i.w.** not k. of Isr.
2 Ch. 20 : 25.the spoil, **i.w.** so much
Ezr. 4 : 14. **i.w.** not meet for us
Es. 4 : 5. command to Mordecai to
know what **i.w.**, and why **i.w.**
Can. 3 : 4. **i.w.** but a little I passed
Is. 48 :16. from time **i.w.** there I am
Eze. 16 : 15. bec. of thy renown his **i.**
19. Thus **i.w.**, saith the Lord [**w.**
43 : 3. **i.w.** acc-g to vision I saw
Mat. 9 :33. **i.w.** never so seen in Isr.
Mk. 4 : 37. so that **i.w.** now full
5 : 14. they went to see what **i.w.**
10 : 47. when he heard **i.w.** Jesus
Lu. 20 : 7.could not tell whence **i.w.**
22 :23.began to inquire which **i.w.**
Jn. 2:9. ruler knew not whence **i.w.**
5 :13.was healed wist not who **i.w.**
15. The man told Jews **i.w.** Jesus
6 : 71. he **i.w.** should betray him
20 : 14. knew not **i.w.** Jesus, 21 : 4.
21 : 7. when Peter heard **i.w.** Lord
12. disciples knowing **i.w.** the L.
Ac. 3 : 10. knew **i.w.** he which sat
1 Th. 2 : 1. entrance, **i.w.** not in [vain
See DARK, DAY.

As it WAS.

Jos. 14 : 7.brought word - **w.** in my [heart
1 S. 12 : 15. hand of the Lord against
you - **w.** against your fathers
1 K. 13 : 6.his hand became - **w.** bef.
2 K. 7 : 7.left camp - **w.**, fled for life
2 Ch.30 : 5.not in such sort - **w.** writ.
Ec.12:7.sh.dust return to earth - **w.**
Is.11 :16. - **w.** to Israel day he came
Lu. 17 : 26. - **w.** in days of Noe
28. Likewise - **w.** in days of Lot
22 : 22. Son goeth - **w.** determined
66. soon - **w.** day priests led him
Ac. 12 : 18.soon - **w.** day no sma.stir
Ro. 5 : 16.not - **w.** by one th.sinned

Behold it WAS.

Ge. 1 : 31.God saw everything, - **w.** [good
6 : 12. G. looked on earth, - **w.** cor- [rupt
29 : 25.in morning, - **w.** Leah
31 : 2,- **w.** not toward Jacob as bef.
41 :7.Pharaoh awoke, - **w.** a dream
42 : 27. - **w.** in the sack's mouth
Le. 10 : 16. goat,-**w.** burnt, 1 S.30:3.
1 K. 3 : 15. Sol. awoke - **w.** a dream
21. - **w.** dead, - **w.** not my son
See **Was** or **Was not RIGHT.**

So it WAS.

Jos. 8 : 25. - **w.** that all that fell th. [day
Ju. 6 : 3. - **w.** when Israel had sown
27. - **w.** bec. he feared father's ho.
1 S. 14 : 15. - **w.** very gr. trembling
2 S. 1 : 2. - **w.** when he came to Dav.
1 K. 20 : 29. - **w.** in 7th day, battle
2 K. 4 : 8. - **w.** as oft as he passed
17 : 7. - **w.** that Israel had sinned
25. - **w.** at beginning of dwelling
Lu. 2 : 6. - **w.** while they were there
Ac. 21 : 35. - **w.** he was borne of sol- [diers
See **SO it was.**

WAS so or WAS not so.

1 S. 25 : 20. it **w.s.** as she rode on
2 K. 12 : 6. it **w.s.** that in 23d year
Mat. 19 : 8.from beginning it **w.n.s.**
See **It was SO.**

WAS so when.

Ju.7 :15.it **w.**- Gideon heard dream
11 : 5. it **w.**- Ammon made war ag.
12 :5. it **w.** -, Ephraimites said,Let
2 S. 6 : 13. it **w.** -, they bare ark six
1 K. 14 : 6.it **w.** -, Ahijah heard feet
28. it **w.** -,k, went into house of L.
1 K.18:4. **w.**-,Jezebel cut off proph-s
19 : 13. it **w.** -, Elijah heard it
2 K. 5 : 8.it **w.** -, Elisha heard th.k.,
12:10.it **w.** -. they saw much money
Es. 5 : 2. it **w.** -, king saw Esther in
Jb. 1 : 5. it **w.** - days of feast-g gone

There WAS.

Ge. 1 :3.Let there be light, and **t.w.** [light
2 : 5. **t.w.** not a man to till ground
20. **t.w.** not found a help meet for
41 : 12. **t.w.** with us a young man
Ex. 12 : 30. **t.w.** great cry in Egypt,
for **t.w.** not house where **t.w.**
24:10.**t.w.** und. his feet paved work
Nu. 9 : 15. **t.w.** as fire upon tabern.
26 : 64. **t.w.** not a man of them
65. **t.w.** not left a man save Caleb
De. 2 : 36. **t.w.** not one city too
strong for us, 3 : 4. [him
32 : 12. **t.w.** no strange god with
Jos. 8 : 17. **t.w.** not a man left in Ai
35. **t.w.** not a word Josh. read not
11 : 11. **t.w.** not any left to breathe
19. **t.w.** not a city made peace wi.
Ju. 4 . 16.host of, **t.w.** not man left
17 : 6. in those days **t.w.** no king
in, 18 : 1.-21 : 25. 1 K. 22 : 47.
1 S. 7 : 17. for **t.w.** his house, he [k.
1 K. 10 : 3. **t.w.** not thing hid from
20. **t.w.** not the like made in any
kingdom, 2 Ch. 9 : 19. [came not
2 K. 10 : 21. **t.w.** not a man that
11 : 16.hands on her, **t.w.** she slain
14 : 26. **t.w.** not any shut up [save
2 Ch 21 : 17.so **t.w.** never a son left
30 : 26. since Sol. **t.w.** not the like
Ps.106 : 11. **t.w.** not one of them left
Is. 43 : 10.bef. me **t.w.** no G. formed
12. when **t.w.** no strange god am.
Eze. 13 : 10. Peace, and **t.w.** no pea.
Da. 12 : 1.as never since **t.w.** nation
Ha. 3 : 4. **t.w.** hiding of his power
Lu. 2 : 13. **t.w.** with angel a multit.
2 Co. 8 : 11. as **t.w.** readiness to will

Behold there WAS.

Ex. 9 : 7. - **w.** not one of cattle dead
Ju. 7 : 13. - **w.** a man told a dream
14 : 8. - **w.** a swarm of bees in lion
1 S. 19 : 16. - **w.** an image in the bed
1 K.19 : 6.- **w.** a cake baken on coals
2 K. 7 : 5. camp, - **w.** no man, 10.
Eze. 40 : 3. - **w.** a man with a line
46 : 19.- **w.** a place on the two sides
Zch.5:7. - **w.** lifted up talent of lead
Mat. 28 : 2. - **w.** a great earthquake
Lu. 2 : 25. - **w.** a man in Jerus.,Sim.
7 : 12. - **w.** a dead man carried out
13 : 11. - **w.** woman had infirmity
14 : 2. - **w.** a man wh.had dropsy
19 : 2. - **w.** a man named Zaccheus
23 : 50. - **w.** a man Jos.,counsellor

There WAS none.

Ex. 9 : 24. hail such as **t.w.n.** in all [Eg.
11 : 6. be cry such as **t.w.n.** like
Jn. 6 : 22. saw **t.w.n.** other boat
See **There was NONE.**
See **WHICH was the son of.**

WASH.

Ex. 2 : 5. daughter of Pharaoh came [to **w.**
29:4.Aaron and sons thou sh. **w.** wi.
water, 30 : 19, 20, 21.-40 : 12.
17.shalt **w.** inwards,legs, Le.9:14.
30 : 18. make laver of brass to **w.**,
and put water therein, 40 : 30.
Le. 1 : 9. his inwards **w.** in water,13.
6 : 27. **w.** th.wh-n it was sprinkled
13 : 54. **w.** thing wherein plague is
58. whatso. of skin thou sh. **w.** it
14 : 8. shall shave and **w.** himself
in water, De. 23 : 11. [24.-22:6.
9. **w.** his flesh in water, 15:16.-16:4,
17 : 16. if he **w.** not, sh. bear iniq-y
De. 21 : 6.shall **w.** hands over heifer
Ru. 3 : 3.**w.** thyself and anoint thee
2 K. 5 : 10. Go **w.** in Jordan 7 times
12, may I not **w.** in th., be clean?
13. wh. he saith **w.**, and be clean?

2 Ch. 4 : 6. lavers to w. in, sea for priests to w. in ⌈water
Jb. 9 : 30. If I w. myself with snow
Ps. 26 : 6. w. mine hands in innoc-y
51 : 2. w. me thoroughly fr. iniq-y
7. w. me, I be whiter than snow
Is. 1 : 16. w. ye, make you clean
Je. 2 : 22. tho. thou w. thee wi. nitre
4 : 14. O Jerusalem, w. thy heart fr.
Eze. 23 : 40. for whom didst w. thys
Mat. 6 : 17. when thou fastest w. face
15 : 2. w. not hands when they eat
Mk. 7 : 3. except w. oft, eat not, 4.
Jn. 9 : 7. Go w. in pool of Siloam, 11.
Ac. 22 : 16. be baptized, w. aw. thy

WASH, ED clothes. ⌊sins
Ge. 49 : 11. Judah w-d c. in blood of grapes ⌈Nu. 8 : 7.
Ex. 19 : 10. and let them w. their c.,
14. people : they w-d their c.
Le. 11 : 25. shall w. his c., and be unclean until the even, 28, 40. (2).-15 : 5, 6, 7, 8, 10, 11, 13, 21, 22, 27.-17 : 15.
13 : 6. he sh. w. his c. and be clean, 34. - 14 : 8, 9, 47. (2).-16 : 26, 28. Nu. 19 : 7, 8, 10, 19, 21.
Nu. 8 : 21. Levites purified, w-d c.
31 : 24. shall w. your c. on 7th day
2 S. 19 : 24. Mephib-h nei. w-d his c.
See **FEET** with **wash, ed.**

WASHED.
Ge. 43 : 31. Joseph w. face, went out
Ex. 40 : 32. w. as L. com ded Moses
Le. 8 : 6 Moses w. Aaron wi. water
21. he w. inwards and legs in wat.
13 : 55. look on plague after it is w.
58. it shall be w. the second time
15 : 17. be w. with water, be unclean
2 S. 12 : 20. Then David arose, w.
1 K. 22 : 38. one w. chariot in pool
2 Ch. 4 : 6. things they off-d they w.
Jb. 29 : 6. I w. my steps with butter
Ps. 73 : 13. w. my hands in innocency
Pr. 30 : 12. a generation not w. from
Can. 5 : 12. his eyes are w. with milk
Is. 4 : 4. w. aw. filth of dau-s of Zion
Eze. 16 : 4. neither wast w. in water
9. Then w. I thee with water; I thoroughly w. away thy blood
40 : 38. gates where they w. offering
Mat. 27 : 24. Pilate took wat. w. hands
Lu 11 : 38. marvelled he had not w.
Jn. 9 : 7. He w., came seeing, 11, 15.
13 : 10. He that is w., needeth not
Ac. 9 : 37. Dorcas, whom they had w.
16 : 33. he took them, w. stripes
1 Co. 6 : 11. but ye are w., sanctified
He. 10 : 22. bodies with w. pure water
2 Pe. 2 : 22. sow th. was w. to wallow-g
Re. 1 : 5. w. us from sins in his blood
7 : 14. have w. their robes white

WASHEST, ING. ⌈hers.
2 S. 11 : 2. David saw a woman w-g
Jb. 14 : 19. thou w-t aw. the things
Lu. 5 : 2. fishermen were w-g nets

WASHING, S.
Le. 13 : 56. if plague be dark after w.
Ne. 4 : 23. ev. one put them off for w.
Can. 4 : 2. like sheep fr. the w., 6 : 6.
Mk. 7 : 4. as the w. of cups, pots, 8.
Ep. 5 : 26. cleanse it with w. of wat.
Tit. 3 : 5. saved us by w. of regener-n
He. 9 : 10. stood only in meats and

WASHPOT. ⌊divers w-s
Ps. 60 : 8. Moab is my w., 108 : 9.

WAST.
Ge. 3 : 11. Who told thou w. naked?
40 : 13. manner when w. his butler
De. 5 : 15. thou w. a servant in Egypt
15 : 15. w. a bondm., 16 : 12.-24 : 18, 22.
23 : 7. bec. thou w. a stranger in la.
25 : 18. when thou w. faint, weary
28 : 60. diseases of Eg. thou w. afraid
Ru. 3 : 2. wi. whose maidens thou w.
1 S. 15 : 17. When thou w. little in own sight w. not made head of
2 S. 5 : 2. w. he that leddest out Isr.
Jb. 38 : 4. w. thou when I laid founda.
Ps. 99 : 8. thou w. a God th. forgavest
Is. 43 : 4. thou w. precious in sight
Je. 50 : 24. art taken, w. not aware
Eze. 16 : 6. when thou w. in thy blood
28 : 15. Thou w. perfect in thy ways
Ob. 11. even thou w. as one of them
Mat. 26 : 69. thou also w. with Jesus of Galilee, Mk. 14 : 67. ⌈tree I saw
Jn. 1 : 48. when thou w. under fig
9 : 34. w. altogether born in sins
Re. 11 : 17. which w. and art to come,

WASTE. [Adj.] ⌊16 : 5.
De. 32 : 10. he found him in w. wild.
Jb. 30 : 3. fleeing into w. wilderness
38 : 27. To satisfy desolate w. ground
Is. 24 : 1. Lord maketh the earth w.
49 : 17. th. made thee w. sh. go forth
19. thy w. places be too narrow
Je. 2 : 15. young lions made land w.
46 : 19 Noph sh. be w. and desolate
Eze. 29 : 9. Egypt sh. be w., 10.-30 : 12.
38 : 8. mountains wh. have been w.
Na. 2 : 10. Nineveh is empty and w.
Zph. 3 : 6. have made their streets w.
Hag. 1 : 9. Bec. of mine house that is
See **CITIES** with **waste,** ⌊w.
LAID waste, LAY waste, LIE waste, LIETH waste.
See **MAKE waste,**
Waste PLACES.

WASTE. [Noun.] ⌈w.
Je. 49 : 13. Bozrah shall become a
Mat. 26 : 8. To what purpose is this w.? Mk. 14 : 4.

WASTES. ⌈thereof
Is. 44 : † 26. I will raise up the w.
61 : 4. they shall build the old w.
Je. 49 : 13. cities of Bozrah sh. be w.
Eze. 29 : † 10. make Eg. w. of waste
33 : 24. that inhabit those w. of Isr.
27. they in w. shall fall by sword
36 : 4. thus saith Lord to desolate w.
10. the w. shall be builded, 33.

WASTE. [Verb.] ⌈w.
1 K. 17 : 14. barrel of meal shall not
1 Ch. 17 : 9. neither shall children of wickedness w. them ⌈w. me
Ps. 17 : † 9. hide me from wicked th.
80 : 13. boar out of wood doth w. it
Je. 50 : 21. w. inhabitants of Pekod
Mi. 5 : 6 they sh. w. land of Assyria

WASTED. ⌈wildern.
Nu. 14 : 33. your carcasses be w. in
24 : 22. the Kenite shall be w. ⌈w.
De. 2 : 14. until all men of war were
1 K. 17 : 16. the barrel of meal w. not
1 Ch. 20 : 1. Joab w. country of Am.
Ps. 137 : 3. they that w. us required
† 8. O dau. of Bab. who art to be w.
Is. 6 : 11. Until the cities be w.
19 : 5. river sh. be w. and dried up
60 : 12. nations shall be utterly w.
Je. 44 : 6. cities are w. and desolate
Eze. 30 : 7. in midst of cities that are
Jo. 1 : 10. field is w., corn is w. ⌊w.
Lu. 15 : 13. younger son w. substa.
16 : 1. accused th. he had w. goods
Ga. 1 : 13. I persecuted church and

WASTENESS. ⌈w. it
Zph. 1 : 15. a day of w., desolation

WASTER. ⌈w.
Pr. 18 : 9. bro. to him that is a great
Is. 54 : 16. I have created the w. to

WASTETH.
Jb. 14 : 10. man dieth and w. away
Ps. 91 : 6. destruction th. w. at noond.
Pr. 19 : 26. He that w. his father

WASTING. ⌈paths
Is. 59 : 7. w., destruction in their
60 : 18. w. nor destruction in thy

WATCH, ES. ⌊borders
Ju. 7 : 19. Gideon and men came in middle w., had but newly set
2 S. 13 : 34. yo. man th. kept w. ⌊w.
2 K. 11 : 5. keepers of w. of K.'s hou., 6.
2 K. 11 : 7. two parts keep w. of hou.
2 Ch. 23 : 6. people sh. keep w. of L.
Ne. 4 : 9. prayer unto G. and set w.
7 : 3. appoint w-s of inhabitants of Jerusalem, every one in his w.
12 : 9. breth. over ag. them in w-s
Jb. 7 : 12. Am I a sea, thou settest w.
Ps. 90 : 4. 1,000 years as w. in night
141 : 3. Set a w., Lord, bef. my mouth
Je. 51 : 12. make the w. strong, set
La. 2 : 19. in beginning of w-s pour
Ha. 2 : 1. I will stand upon my w.
Mat. 14 : 25. in 4th w. of night Jes. went walk-g upon sea, Mk. 6 : 48.
24 : 43. if had known what w. thief
27 : 65. Pilate said, Ye have a w.
66. sealing the stone and setting w.
28 : 11. some of the w. came into
Lu. 2 : 8. shepherds keeping w. ov.
12 : 38. if he shall come in second w., or come in third w., and

Morning WATCH. ⌈host
Ex. 14 : 24. in m. w. L. looked unto
1 S. 11 : 11. came into host in m. w.

Night WATCHES. ⌈w.
Ps. 63 : 6. I meditate on thee in n.
119 : 148. Mine eyes prevent n. w.
Lu. 2 : † 8. keeping n. w. over flock

WATCH. [Verb.] ⌈thee
Ge. 31 : 49. Lord w. between me and
1 S. 19 : 11. Saul sent to w. David
Ezr. 8 : 29. w. ye, keep vessels until
Jb. 14 : 16. dost not w. over my sin?
21 : † 32. to the grave sh. w. in the
Ps. 71 : † 10. that w. for my soul ⌊heap
102 : 7. I w. and am as a sparrow
130 : 6. than they th. w. for morn-g,
Is. 21 : 5. w. in the watchtower ⌊6.
29 : 20. th. w. for iniquity are cut off
Je. 5 : 6. leopard shall w. over cities
31 : 28. so will I w. over them to
44 : 27. I will w. over them for evil
Na. 2 : 1. keep munition, w. the way
Ha. 2 : 1. I will w. to see what he say
Mat. 24 : 42. w. therefore, ye know not the hour, 25 : 13. Mk. 13 : 35. Lu. 21 : 36. Ac. 20 : 31.
26 : 38. Jesus saith : tarry ye here, and w. with me ⌈14 : 34, 37.
40. could ye not w. with me, Mk.
41. w. and pray, Mk. 13 : 33.-14 : 38. Col. 4 : 2. ⌈to w.
Mk. 13 : 34. commanded the porter
37. I say unto you, I say unto all,
1 Co. 16 : 13. w. ye, stand fast ⌊w.
1 Th. 5 : 6. let us w., be, 1 Pe. 4 : 7.
2 Ti. 4 : 5. w. thou in all things
He. 13 : 17. for they w. for your souls
Re. 3 : 3. If theref. thou shalt not w.

WATCHED.
Ps. 59. * w. the house to kill David
Je. 20 : 10. familiars w. for my halt-g
31 : 28. as I w. over them to pluck
La. 4 : 17. w. for nation co. not save
Da. 9 : 14. Lord w. upon evil, and
Mat. 24 : 43. if goodman had known would have w., Lu. 12 : 39. ⌈him
27 : 36. And sitting down they w.
Mk. 3 : 2. they w. him whether he would heal on sabbath day, Lu.
Lu. 20 : 20. They w. him ⌊6 : 7.-14 : 1.
Ac. 9 : 24. w. the gates to kill him

WATCHER, S.
Je. 4 : 16. published that w. come from far country ⌈from heaven
Da. 4 : 13. a w. and a holy one came
17. by decree of the w-s ⌈heaven
23. king saw a w. coming from

WATCHETH.
Ps. 37 : 32. The wicked w. righteous
Eze. 7 : 6. end is come, it w. for thee
Re. 16 : 15. Blessed is he that w. and

WATCHFUL.
Re. 3 : 2. Be w., strengthen things

WATCHING.
1 S. 4 : 13. Eli sat upon a seat w.
Pr. 8 : 34. w. daily at my gates

La. 4 : 17. in our **w.** for a nation
Mat 27 : 54. centurion **w.** Jesus, saw
Lu. 12 : 37. whom Lord shall find **w.**
Ep. 6 : 18. **w.** with all perseverance

WATCHINGS. ⌈w.
2 Co. 6 : 5. in tumults, in labours, in
11:27. in **w.** often, in hunger, thirst

WATCHMAN.
2 S. 18 : 25. **w.** cried, told king, 27.
26. **w.** saw another man run-g, 24.
2 K. 9 : 18. **w.** told, he cometh not, 17,
Ps. 127 : 1. the **w.** waketh in vain⌊20.
Is. 21 : 6. hath Lord said, Go set a **w.**
11. calleth, **w.** what of the night (2)
12. **w.** said, The morning cometh
Eze. 3 : 17. made thee a **w.**, 33 : 7.
33 : 2. if people set him up for **w.**
6. But if the **w.** see sword come (2)
Ho. 9 : 8. **w.** of Ephr. was with my

WATCHMEN. ⌊God
1 S. 14 : 16. **w.** of Saul in Gibeah
2 K. 17 : 9. from tower of **w.** to city,
Can. 3 : 3. **w.** ab. city found me ⌊18:8.
5:7. The **w.** smote me, wounded me
Is. 52 : 8. Thy **w.** shall lift up voice
56:10. His **w.** are blind, all ignorant
62:6. I have set **w.** upon thy walls
Je. 6 : 17. Also I set **w.** over you
31 : 6. **w.** upon Ephraim shall cry
51 : 12. Set up **w.**, prepare am.
Mi. 7 : 4. the day of thy **w.** cometh

WATCHTOWER. ⌈w.
2 Ch. 20 : 24. when Judah came tow.
Is. 21 : 5. watch in the **w.**, eat, drink
8. I stand continually on the **w.**
32 : † 14. **w.** sh. be for dens for ever

WATER. ⌈of w.
Ge. 16 : 7. found Hagar by fountain
18 : 4. Let a little **w.** be fetched
21 : 14. Abr. took bottle of **w.**, gave
15. **w.** was spent in bottle ⌊Hagar
19. Hagar filled the bottle with **w.**
24 : 19. I will draw **w.** for camels
32. Laban ga. man **w.** to wash feet
43. when virgin cometh to draw
w., and I say, Give me little **w.**
26 : 20. herdmen saying, The **w.** is
32. said, We have found **w.** ⌊ours
43 : 24. steward of Joseph gave **w.**
49:4. Unstable as **w.** shalt not excel
Ex. 4 : 9. **w.** of river pour upon land,
7 : 15. he goeth out unto the **w.**⌊(2)
19. stretch forth hand upon pools
8 : 20. lo, he cometh to **w.** ⌊of w.
12 : 9. Eat it not sodden with **w.**
17 : 3. people thirsted there for **w.**
6. shall come **w.** out of the rock
20 : 4. any likeness that is in the **w.**
30 : 18. laver, put **w.** th-in, 40:7, 30.
32:20. burnt calf, strewed it upon **w.**
Le. 6:28. vessel sh. be rinsed in **w.**, 15:
11 : 32. vessel must be put in **w.**⌊12.
34. on wh. such **w.** cometh be un-
36. a pit wh-in plenty of **w.**⌊clean
38. if any **w.** be put upon the seed
15 : 11. not rinsed hands in **w.**, 12.
12. ev. vessel shall be rinsed in **w.**
Nu. 5 : 17. priest shall take holy **w.**
22. **w.** that causeth curse shall go
8 : 7. Sprinkle **w.** of purifying upon
19 : 9. for **w.** of separation, 13, 20,
18. hyssop, dip it in **w.**⌊21.-31 : 23.
20 : 8. thou shalt bring **w.** out of
rock, 10, 11. Ne. 9:15. Ps. 114:8.
13. **w.** of Meribah, 24.-27 : 14 (2).
21 : 16. people, I will give them **w.**
24:7. He sh. pour **w.** out of buckets
27 : 14. com-t to sanctify me at **w.**
31:23. ye shall make go through **w.**
33 : 9. in Elim were 12 fount-s of **w.**
De 11:4. made **w.** of Red sea overflow
11. land drinketh **w.** of heaven
12 : 16. ye shall pour the blood upon earth as **w.**, 24.-15 : 23.
Jos. 2 : 10. L. dried up **w.** of Red sea
3 : 8. When come to brink of **w.**, 15.
7 : 5. hearts of people became as **w.**
Jos. 15 : 9. fount. of **w.** of Nephtoah
16 : 1. unto **w.** of Jericho on east
Ju. 5 : 4. the clouds also dropped **w.**
11. archers in place of drawing **w.**
25. He asked **w.**, she gave milk
6 : 38. out of fleece bowl full of **w.**
7 : 4. bring them down unto **w.**, 5.
15 : 19. **w.** came out of the jaw
1 S. 26 : 11. take cruse of **w.**, let us
go, 12, 16. 1 K. 19:6. ⌈on ground
2 S. 14 : 14. we must die, and are as **w.**
17 : 21. Arise, pass quickly ov. **w.**, 20.
21 : 10. until **w.** dropped upon them
1 K. 14 : 15. as reed is shaken in **w.**
17 : 10. fetch me, I pray, a little **w.**
18 : 33. Fill 4 barrels with **w.**, and
35. **w.** ran about the altar; he
filled trench with **w.** ⌈the w.
38. fire of Lord fell and licked up
2 K. 2 : 19. **w.** is naught, ground bar-n
3 : 11. poured **w.** on Elijah's hands
17. that valley sh. be filled with **w.**
20 there came **w.** by way of Edom
22. rose early, sun shone upon **w.**
6 : 5. the axe head fell into the **w.**
8 : 15. he dipped a thick cloth in **w.**
18 : † 27. may drink **w.** of their feet
20 : 20. a conduit bro-t **w.** into city
2 Ch. 32 : 4. Why kings find much **w.**
Ne. 4 : †23. went with weapon for **w.**
9 : 20. gavest them **w.** for thirst
Jb. 8 : 11. can flag grow without **w.**
14 : 9. thro. scent of **w.** it will bud
15 : 16. who drinketh iniq-y like **w.**
34 : 7. who drink-h scorning like **w.**
36 : 27. maketh sm. the drops of **w.**
Ps. 22 : 14. I am poured out like **w.**
63 : † 10. make him run out like **w.**
65 : 9. river of God that is full of **w.**
66 : 12. we went through fire and **w.**
77 : 17. The clouds poured out **w.**
79 : 3. blood have they shed like **w.**
88 : 17. came round me daily like
109 : 18. into his bowels like **w.**⌊w.
Pr. 17 : 14. as when one letteth out **w.**
20 : 5. Counsel in heart like deep **w.**
27 : 19. As in **w.** face answereth to
30 : 16. earth that is not filled wi. **w.**
Ec. 2 : 6. I made pools of **w.**, Is. 14 :
Is. 1 : 22. thy wine mixed wi. **w.**⌊23.
3 : 1. Lord doth take aw. stay of **w.**
21 : 14. Tema bro-t **w.** to the thirsty
22 : 11. ditch for **w.** of old pool ⌈pit
30 : 14. not sherd to take **w.** out of
37 : 25. I ha. digged and drunk **w.**
41 : 17. When the poor seek **w.** and
18. make wildern. a pool of **w.** (2)
44 : 3. I will pour **w.** upon thirsty
58 : 11. thou sh. be like spring of **w.**
63 : 12. led, dividing **w.** bef. them
Je. 13 : 1. girdle and put it not in **w.**
23 : 15. make them drink **w.** of gall
La. 1 : 16. eye runneth wi. **w.**, 3 : 48.
2 : 19. pour out thy heart like **w.**
5 : 4. ha. drunken our **w.** for money
Eze. 7 : 17. knees be weak as **w.**, 21 : 7.
24 : 3. Set pot, pour **w.** into it ⌈w.
26 : 12. lay thy dust in midst of
36 : 25. I sprinkle clean **w.** upon you
Ho. 2 : 5. aft. my lovers th. give me **w.**
5 : 10. my wrath upon them like **w.**
10 : 7. king cut off as foam upon **w.**
Na. 2 : 8. Nineveh is like pool of **w.**
Ha. 3 : 10. overflowing of **w.** passed
Mat. 3 : 16. Jesus went up out of **w.**,
Mk. 1 : 10. ⌈w., Mk. 9 : 41.
10 : 42. whoso. shall give cup of cold
14 : 28 bid me come on the **w.**, 29.
17 : 15. falleth oft into fire and **w.**
Mk. 14 : 13. shall meet you a man
bearing pitcher of **w.**, Lu. 22 : 10.
Lu. 8 : 23. they were filled with **w.**
24. he rebuked raging of the **w.**
25. winds and **w.** they obey him
16 : 24. may dip tip of finger in **w.**
Jn. 2 : 7. Fill the waterpots with **w.**
9. tasted **w.** that was made wine
Jn. 3 : 5. Exc. a man be born of **w.** ⌈w.
23. near to Salim, bec. was much
4 : 13. whoso. drink. of this **w.** thirst
14. whoso. drink. of **w.** I sh. give
15. woman saith, Give me this **w.**
46. came where he made **w.** wine
5 : 3. waiting for moving of **w.** ⌈(2)
4. angel went down, troubled **w.**,
7. I have no man wh. **w.** is troub-d
13 : 5. he poureth **w.** into a basin
19 : 34. came thereout blood and **w.**
Ac. 8 : 36. they came unto a certain
w.: eunuch said, See, here is **w.**
38. they went down both into **w.**
39. when were come up out of **w.**
10 : 47. Can any man forbid **w.** ⌈w.
Ep. 5 : 26. cleanse it with washing of
He. 9 : 19. took blood of calves wi. **w.**
1 Pe. 3 : 20. eight souls saved by **w.**
2 Pe. 3 : 5. earth standing out of **w.**
6. world overflowed wi. **w.** perished
1 Jn. 5 : 6. is he that came by **w.** (2)
5 : 8. bear witness, Spirit, **w.**, and
Jude 12. clouds are they without **w.**
Re. 12 : 15. cast out of his mouth **w.**
16 : 12. Euphrates, **w.** was dried up
21 : 6. I will give of the **w.** of life
22 : 1. shewed me river of **w.** of life
17. let him take **w.** of life freely
See BAPTIZE, ED, ING.

Bathe himself in WATER.
Le. 15 : 5. he shall wash his clothes
and - **w.**, 6, 7, 8, 10, 11, 13, 18,
21, 22, 27. - 16 : 26, 28. - 17 : 15.
Nu. 19 : 7, 8, 19.

Bitter WATER, S.
Ex. 15 : 23. could not drink **w-s** of
Marah, they were **b.** ⌈19, 24.
Nu. 5 : 18. **b. w.** that causeth curse,
23. sh. blot out curses with **b. w.**
24. cause woman to drink **b. w.**,
w. shall enter and become **b.**
Ja. 3 : 11. fountain send forth sweet
w. and **b.**? ⌈because b.
Re. 8 : 11. many men died of **w-s**

WATER, S with bread. ⌈H.
Ge. 21 : 14. Abr. took **b.** and **w.** unto
Ex. 23 : 25. L. sh. bless thy **b.** and **w.**
34 : 28. Moses 40 days did nei. eat
b. nor drink **w.**, De. 9 : 9, 18.
Nu. 21 : 5. there is no **b.** nei. any **w.**
De. 23 : 4. Because they met you not
with **b.** and **w.**, Ne. 13 : 2. ⌈w.
1 S. 25 : 11. Shall I take my **b.** and
30 : 12. eaten no **b.** nor drunk **w.**
1 K. 13 : 8. neither will I eat **b.** nor
drink **w.** in this pl., 9, 16, 17, 22.
18. Bring him back that he may
eat **b.** and drink **w.**
19. so man of God did eat **b.** and
drank **w.**, 22. ⌈and w., 13.
18 : 4. fed 100 prophets with **b.**
22 : 27. feed him with the **b.** and
w. of affliction, ⌈2 Ch. 18 : 26.
2 K. 6 : 22. set **b.** and **w.** that they
Ezr. 10 : 6. eat no **b.** nor drink **w.**
Pr. 9 : 17. Stolen **w-s** are sweet, **b.**
Ec. 11 : 1. Cast thy **b.** upon the **w-s**
Is. 30 : 20. though Lord give you **b.**
of adversity and **w.** of affliction
33 : 16. **b.** be given; his **w-s** be sure
Ho. 2 : 5. lovers th. give me **b.** and **w.**
Eze. 4 : 17. they may want **b.** and **w.**
Am. 8 : 11. fam. of **b.** nor thirst of **w.**

WATER with brooks.
De. 8 : 7. thee into a land of **b.** of **w.**
Ps. 42 : 1. As hart panteth after **w. b.**
See DRAWER, DRAWERS, DREW.
See **DRINK water, s,**
FACE of the water, s,
Water GATE.
See FOUNTAIN, S. LIVING.

No WATER. ⌈it
Ge. 37 : 24 pit empty, was **n. w.** in
Ex. 15 : 22. they went three days in
wilderness, and found **n. w.**,
17 : 1. Nu. 20 : 2.-33 : 14. De. 8 : 15.

1 K. 13 : 22. Eat no bread, drink **n. w.**
2 K. 3 : 9. there was **n. w.** for host
Ps. 63 : 1. thirsty land where **n. w.** is
Is. 1 : 30. ye be as garden hath **n. w.**
44 : 12. smith drink-h **n. w.** is faint
50 : 2. their fish stinketh bec. **n. w.**
Je. 2 : 13. cisterns that can hold **n. w.**
14 : 3. they came to pits, found **n. w.**
38 : 6. in dungeon was **n. w.**, mire
Zch. 9 : 11. out of pit wh-in is **n. w.**
Lu. 7 : 44. gavest me **n. w.** for feet
See RIVER, RIVERS, RUNNING.
See SPRINGS, STANDING [Adj.], STRIFE, WASH, WASHED, WATERSPRINGS.
See **WELL, S with water, s.**

WATERS.

Ge. 1 : 6. Let firmament divide the **w.** from **w.**, 7. [place
9. Let **w.** be gathered unto one
10. gathering of **w.** called he Seas
20. Let **w.** bring forth abundant-
22. fill the **w.** in the seas [ly, 21.
6 : 17. I do bring a flood of **w.**, 7 : 10.
7 : 6. Noah 600 yrs. old when **w.** ca.
7. Noah into ark bec. of **w.** of flood
17. **w.** increased and bare ark [19.
18. **w.** prevailed exceedingly (2),
20. Fifteen cubits upward did **w.**
24. **w.** prevailed 150 days [prevail
8 : 1. wind, **w.** assuaged, 3. (2). 5, 11.
7. raven to and fro until **w.** dried
8. sent dove to see if **w.** abated
9. **w.** upon face of whole earth
13. in 601st year **w.** were dried
9 : 11. nei. be cut off any more by **w.**
Ex. 7 : 17. will smite upon **w.**, 19. [15.
20. Mos. smote **w.**; **w.** turned bl.
8 : 6. Aaron stretched hand over **w.**
14 : 21. by east wind **w.** were divided
22. the **w.** were a wall unto them
26. **w.** may co. again upon Eg-ns
28. **w.** covered host of Pha., 15 : 19.
15 : 8. **w.** were gathered, flood stood
27. to Elim, they encamped by **w.**
Nu. 24 : 6. as cedar trees beside **w.**
Jos. 3 : 16. **w.** which came down, 13.
4 : 7. **w.** of Jord. cut off bef. ark (3)
18. **w.** of Jordan returned unto
23. L. dried up **w.** of Jordan, 5 : 1.
11 : 5. pitched at the **w.** of Merom, 7.
15 : 7. border passed toward **w.** of En-shemesh [Megiddo
Ju. 5 : 19. kings of Canaan by **w.** of
7 : 24. Come, take the **w.** unto (2)
2 S. 5 : 20. Lord as a breach of **w.** upon mine enemies, 1 Ch. 14 : 11.
12 : 27. said, I have taken city of **w.**
22 : 12. pavilions round about him, dark **w.**, Ps. 18 : 11. [smote **w.**
2 K. 2 : 8. Elijah smote **w.** | 14. Elisha
21. he went unto spring of **w.**; saith Lord, I have healed **w.**, 22.
5 : 12. Are not rivers of Damascus better than all **w.** of Israel?
19 : 24. I have drunk strange **w.**
2 Ch. 32 : 3. took counsel to stop **w.**
Jb. 3 : 24. my roarings like the **w.**
5 : 10. who sendeth **w.** upon fields
11 : 16. thy misery as **w.** pass away
12 : 15. he withholdeth **w.**, they dry
14 : 11. As the **w.** fail from the sea
19. The **w.** wear the stones, thou
22 : 11. abundance of **w.** cover thee,
24 : 18. He is swift as **w.**, [38 : 34.
26 : 5. Dead things fr. under the **w.**
8. bindeth up **w.** in thick clouds
10. He compassed **w.** with clouds
27 : 20. Terrors take hold on him as
28 : 4. **w.** forgotten of the foot [**w.**
25. he weighed the **w.** by measure
29 : 19. My root was spread by **w.**
30 : 14. upon me as break-g in of **w.**
37 : 10. breadth of **w.** is straightened
38 : 25. course for the overflow of **w.**
30. The **w.** are hid as with a stone
Ps. 18 : 15. channels of **w.** were seen
Ps. 23 : 2. leadeth me beside still **w.**
29 : 3. The voice of Lord is upon **w.**
46 : 3. Though the **w.** thereof roar
58 : 7. Let them melt away as **w.**
69 : 1. **w.** are come in unto my soul
73 : 10. **w.** of a full cup are wrung
77 : 16. The **w.** saw thee, O God (2)
78 : 13. made **w.** to stand as a heap
20. he smote the rock that the **w.** gushed, 105 : 41.-114 : 8. Is. 48 : 21.
104 : 6. **w.** stood above the mts.
105 : 29. He turned **w.** into blood
106 : 11. **w.** covered their enemies
124 : 4. the **w.** had overwhelmed us
5. proud **w.** had gone ov. our soul
136 : 6. stretched earth above **w.**
147 : 18. he causeth wind, **w.** flow
148 : 4. ye **w.** above heavens praise
Pr. 5 : 15. Drink **w.** out of own cistern
8 : 29. that **w.** not pass his comm-t
9 : 17. Stolen **w.** are sweet, bread
25 : 25. As cold **w.** to a thirsty soul
30 : 4. who bound **w.** in a garment
Is. 8 : 6. refuseth the **w.** of Shiloah
11 : 9. as **w.** cover sea, Ha. 2 : 14.
15 : 6. For the **w.** of Nimrim shall be desolate, Je. 48 : 34. [blood
9. the **w.** of Dimon shall be full of
18 : 2. in vessels of bulrushes upon
19 : 5. **w.** sh. fail from the sea [**w.**
8. spread nets upon **w.** languish
22 : 9. ye gathered **w.** of lower pool
28 : 2. one, as a flood of mighty **w.**
17. **w.** shall overflow hiding place
30 : 25. upon every hill rivers of **w.**
32 : 20. are ye that sow beside all **w.**
35 : 6. in wilderness shall **w.** break
40 : 12. Who hath measured the **w.**
43 : 2. When thou passest thro. **w.**
20. bec. I give **w.** in the wilderness
48 : 1. are come out of **w.** of Judah
21. caused **w.** to flow out of rock
51 : 10. hath dried **w.** of great deep
54 : 9. this is as **w.** of Noah unto me; **w.** of Noah no more go ov.
55 : 1. come ye to the **w.** [earth
57 : 20. whose **w.** cast up mire, dirt
58 : 11. like spring, whose **w.** fail not
64 : 2. the fire causeth **w.** to boil
Je. 2 : 18. thou to drink **w.** of Sihor
6 : 7. as fountain casteth out **w.**
9 : 1. O that my head were **w.** and
18. our eyelids gush out with **w.**
10 : 13. is a multitude of **w.**, 51 : 16.
14 : 3. nobles sent little ones to **w.**
15 : 18. unto me as a liar, as **w.** fail
17 : 8. be as a tree planted by the **w.**
18 : 14. cold flowing **w.** be forsaken?
31 : 9. cause to walk by rivers of **w.**
47 : 2. **w.** rise up out of the north
50 : 38. a drought is upon her **w.**
La. 3 : 54. **w.** flowed over mine head
Eze. 19 : 10. Thy mother like vine by
27 : 34. broken in depths of **w.** [**w.**
31 : 4. The **w.** made him great [**w.**
5. became long bec. of multit. of
14. that none of trees by **w.** exalt
32 : 2. troublest the **w.** wi. thy feet
47 : 1. **w.** issued fr. under threshold
2. ran out **w.** on the right side
3. he brought me through **w.**: the **w.** were to ankles, 4. (2)
5. for **w.** were risen, **w.** to swim in
8. These **w.** issue toward east (2)
9. these **w.** shall come thither
12. bec. **w.** issued out of sanctuary
Da. 12 : 6. said to man upon **w.**, 7.
Am. 5 : 24. let judgm. run down as **w.**
Jon. 2 : 5. **w.** compassed me to soul
Mi. 1 : 4. as **w.** down a steep place
Na. 3 : 8. No, that had **w.** round it
14. Draw the **w.** for the siege
2 Co. 11 : 26. in perils of **w.**, in perils
Re. 7 : 17. unto liv-g fountains of **w.**
8 : 11. third of **w.** became wormw-d
11 : 6. power over **w.** to turn to bl.
14 : 7. th. made the fountains of **w.**
Re. 16 : 4. angel poured vial upon **w.**
5. I heard angel of the **w.** say
17 : 15. **w.** where the whore sitteth
See DEEP, FOUNTAIN, S, GREAT

In or Into WATERS.

Ex. 15 : 10. as lead **i.** the mighty **w.**
25. a tree **i. w.** they were sweet
Le. 11 : 9. These eat, of all **i. w.**: whatso. hath fins and scales **i. w.** shall ye eat (2). De. 14 : 9.
10. all th. have not fins and scales that move **i. w.** an abomination (2), 12. [ure **i. w.**
46. This is the law of every creat-
De. 4 : 18. likeness of fish **i. w.**, 5 : 8.
Jos. 3 : 13. as the feet rest **i. w.** [**w.**
Ne. 9 : 11. threwest stone **i-o** mighty
Ps. 74 : 13. brakest heads of dragons
104 : 3. beams of chamb-s **i. w.** [**i. w.**
Mat. 8 : 32. the swine perished **i. w.**
Mk. 9 : 22. oft it cast him **i-o** fire, **w.**

Living WATERS.

See LIVING.

Many WATERS.

Nu. 24 : 7. his seed sh. be in **m. w.**
2 S. 22 : 17. he drew me out of **m. w.**, Ps. 18 : 16. [upon **m. w.**
Ps. 29 : 3. the voice of the Lord is
93 : 4. mightier than noise of **m. w.**
Can. 8 : 7. **m. w.** can t quench love
Is. 17 : 13. nations like rush-g of **m.**
Je. 51 : 13. dwellest upon **m. w.** [**w.**
Eze. 19 : 10. fruitf. by reason of **m. w.**
43 : 2. his voice was like a noise of **m. w.**, Re. 1 : 15.-14 : 2.-19 : 6.
Re. 17 : 1. whore th. sitteth on **m. w.**
See MIGHTY, MERIBAH, MERIBAH-KADESH, RIVER, RIVERS, STRIFE.
See **Of the SEA.**

WATER. [Verb.]

[gard.
Ge. 2 : 10. river out of Eden to **w.**
29 : 7. **w.** ye the sheep, feed th., 8.
Ex. 2 : 16. filled troughs to **w.** flock
Ps. 6 : 6. I **w.** my couch with tears
72 : 6. as showers that **w.** the earth
Pr. 5 : † 19. let her breasts **w.** thee
Ec. 2 : 6. I made pools to **w.** the wood
Is. 16 : 9. I will **w.** thee with tears
27 : 3. I will **w.** it every moment
Eze. 17 : 7. he might **w.** it by furrows
32 : 6. will **w.** with my blood the la.
Jo. 3 : 18. shall **w.** valley of Shittim

WATERCOURSE, S.

2 Ch. 32 : 30. Hezekiah stopped **w.**
Jb. 38 : 25. Who hath divided a **w.**
Is. 44 : 4. spring as willows by **w-s**

WATERED.

Ge. 2 : 6. a mist that **w.** the ground
13 : 10. plain of Jordan was well **w.**
29 : 2. of that well they **w.** flocks, 3.
10. Jacob **w.** the flock of Laban
Ex. 2 : 17. Moses **w.** their flocks, 19.
Ps. 36 : † 8. **w.** with fatness of thy h.
Pr. 11 : 25. he th. watereth sh. be **w.**
Is. 58 : 11. shalt be like a **w.** garden
Je. 31 : 12. their soul be as **w.** garden
1 Co. 3 : 6. I have planted, Apollos

WATEREDST, EST.

[**w.**
De. 11 : 10. **w-dst** it with thy foot
Ps. 65 : 9. Thou visitest earth, **w-est**
10. Thou **w-est** ridges abundantly

WATERETH.

[bers
Ps. 104 : 13. He **w.** hills fr. his cham-
Pr. 11 : 25. he that **w.** sh. be watered
Is. 55 : 10. rain return. not, **w.** earth
1 Co. 3 : 7. nei. he th. **w.** anything, 8.

WATERFLOOD.

[me
Ps. 69 : 15. Let not the **w.** overflow

WATERING.

[troughs
Ge. 30 : 38. Jacob laid rods in **w.**
Jb. 37 : 11. by **w.** he wearieth cloud
Pr. 3 : † 8. it sh. be **w.** to thy bones
Lu. 13 : 15. doth not each lead his ass to

WATERPOT, S.

[**w.**
Jn. 2 : 6. were set six **w-s** of stone
7. Jes. saith, Fill **w-s** with water

Jn. 4 : 28. woman left her w., went to
WATERSPOUTS. ⌊city
Ps. 42 : 7. Deep calleth at noise of
WATERSPRINGS. ⌊thy w.
Ps. 107 : 33. he turn. w. into dry gro.
35. he turneth dry ground into w.
WAVE. [Adj.] ⌈loaves
Le. 23 : 17. Ye sh. bring out two w.
WAVE breast. ⌈Isr.
Le. 7 : 30. the w. b. have I taken of
10 : 14. w. b. sh. ye eat in clean pl.
15. w. b. shall they bring wi. off-gs
Nu. 6 : 20. holy for priest, with w. b.
18 : 18. as w. b. and right shoulder
See **Wave OFFERING, S.**
WAVE. [Noun.] ⌈sea
Ja. 1 : 6. that wavereth is like w. of
WAVES. ⌈passed me
2 S. 22 : 5. When w. of death com-
Jb. 38 : 11. here proud w. be stayed
Ps. 42 : 7. all thy w. are gone over
me, Jon. 2 : 3. ⌈9.-107 : 29.
65 : 7. stilleth noise of their w., 89 :
88 : 7. hast afflicted me with thy
93 : 3. floods lift up their w. ⌊w.
107 : 25. wind which lifteth up w.
29. storm a calm so th. w. are still
Is. 51 : 15. divided the sea, whose w.
roared, Je. 31 : 35. ⌈not prevail
Je. 5 : 22. though w. toss, yet can
51 : 42. Babylon is covered with w.
55. Babylon when her w. roar
Eze. 26 : 3. as sea causeth w. to come
27 : † 28. w. sh. shake at cry of pi-
Zch. 10 : 11. sh. smite w. in sea⌊lots
Mat. 8 : 24. ship was covered wi. w.
14 : 24. but the ship was tossed
with w., Mk. 4 : 37. ⌈roaring
Lu. 21 : 25. be signs, the sea and w.
Ac. 27 : 41. hinder part broken with
See **Of the SEA.** ⌊w.
WAVE, ED. ⌈is w-d
Ex. 29 : 27. breast of wave off-g wh.
Le. 7 : 30. that breast be w-d bef. L.
Nu. 8 : † 11. Aaron sh. w. Levites bef. L.
27. he w-d them for wave offering,
29.-9 : 21. ⌈w-d
14 : 21. he shall take one lamb to be
23 : 11. he sh. w. sheaf bef. Lord, 12.
Nu. 5 : 25. priest sh. w. jealousy off-g
See **Wave OFFERING.**
WAVERETH, ING. ⌈w-g
He. 10 : 23. hold fast profession wi-t
Ja. 1 : 6. ask in faith, nothing w-g :
he that w-h is like a wave of sea
WAX. [Noun.] ⌈melted
Ps. 22 : 14. my heart is like w., it is
68 : 2. as w. melteth, wicked perish
97 : 5. hills melted like w. at pres.
Mi. 1 : 4. valleys cleft as w. bef. fire
WAX. [Verb.] ⌈32 : 10.
Ex. 22 : 24. my wrath shall w. hot,
32 : 11. L., why thy wrath w. hot
22. Let not anger of my lord w. hot
Le. 25 : 47. a stranger w. rich by
thee, thy bro. by him w. poor
1 S. 3 : 2. his eyes began to w. dim
Jb. 6 : 17. time they w. warm, vanish
14 : 8. Tho. the root thereof w. old
Ps. 102 : 26. all sh. w. old as a garment, Is. 50 : 9.-51 : 6. He. 1 : 11.
Is 17 : 4. fatn-s of his flesh sh. w. lean
29 : 22. nei. shall his face w. pale
Je. 6 : 24. our hands w. feeble ⌈cold
Mat. 24 : 12. love of many shall w.
Lu. 12 : 33. bags which w. not old
1 Ti. 5 : 11. to w. wanton ag. Christ
2 Ti. 3 : 13. seducers shall w. worse
WAXED. ⌈pleasure ?
Ge. 18 : 12. After w. old shall I have
26 : 13. Isaac w. great and grew
41 : 56. famine w. sore in Egypt
Ex. 1 : 7. Isr. w. exceed-g mighty, 20.
16 : 21. and when the sun w. hot
19 : 19. when trumpet w. louder
32 : 19. Moses' anger w. hot, cast
Nu. 11 : 23. is Lord's hand w. short ?

De. 8 : 4. Thy raiment w. not old,
29 : 5. Ne. 9 : 21. ⌈kicked
32 : 15. But Jeshurun w. fat and
Jos. 23 : 1. Joshua w. old, stricken
1 S. 2 : 5. she that hath many children is w. feeble ⌈Ch. 11 : 9.
2 S. 3 : 1. but David w. stronger, 1
21 : 15. David fought and w. faint
2 K. 4 : 34. flesh of the child w. warm
2 Ch. 13 : 21. Abijah w. mighty and
17 : 12. Jehosh-t w. great exceed-y
24 : 15. Jehoiada w. old, 130 years
Es. 9 : 4. Mordecai w. greater and
Ps. 32 : 3. kept silence my bones w.
Je. 49 : 24. Damasc. is w. feeble⌊old
50 : 43. k. of Bab-n's hands w. feeble
Da. 8 : 8. the he goat w. great ⌈10.
9. little horn w. great tow. south,
Mat. 13 : 15. For this people's heart
is w. gross, Ac. 28 : 27. ⌈it, 2 : 40.
Lu. 1 : 80. the child w. strong in spir-
13 : 19. mustard seed w. great tree
Ac. 13 : 46. Paul, Barnabas w. bold
He. 11 : 34. w. valiant in fight ⌈rich
Re. 18 : 3. merchants of earth are w.
WAXEN.
Ge. 19 : 13. cry of Sodom is w. great
Le. 25 : 25. If thy brother be w.
poor, and hath sold, 35, 39.
De. 29 : 5. clothes are not w. old (2)
31 : 20. w. fat, will turn unto gods
32 : 15. thou art w. fat, grown thick
Jos. 17 : 13. chil. of Isr. were w. stro.
Je. 5 : 27. are become gr. and w. rich
28. They are w. fat, they shine
Eze. 16 : 7. hast increased, w. great
WAXETH, ING. ⌈enem.
Ps. 6 : 7. Mine eye w-h old bec. of
85 : † 3. turned thine anger fr. w-g
He. 8 : 13. w-h old, ready to van. ⌊hot
Ph. 1 : 14. brethren w-g confident
WAY. ⌈of life
Ge. 3 : 24. sword to keep w. of tree
18 : 16. Abr. wi. them to bri. on w.
21 : 16. Hagar sat down good w. off
24 : 42. if thou prosper w. wh. I go
62. Isaac came from w. of the well
35 : 16. little w. to Ephrath, 48 : 7.
42 : 25. give provision for w., 45 : 21.
Ex. 13 : 17. led not thro. w. of Phil.
21. in pillar of cloud to lead w.
18 : 20. sh. shew them w., Ne. 9 : 19.
Nu. 11 : † 31. as it were w. of a day
21 : 4. people discouraged bec. of w.
22 : 23. smote ass to turn her into w.
26. no w. to turn to right or left
De. 1 : 22. bring word by what w. we
must go, 33. Jos. 3 : 4. ⌈plain
2 : 8. we passed through the w. of
8 : 2. remember w. Lord led you
14 : 24. if the w. be too long for thee
17 : 16. shall return no more th. w.
19 : 3. Thou shalt prepare thee a w.
6. lest overtake him, bec. w. long
28 : 7. come ag. thee one w., flee 7
25. shalt go out one w. ag. them
31 : 29. ye will turn aside fr. the w.
Jos. 2 : 7. pursued them w. to Jord.
22. pursuers sought them all w.
10 : 10. chased them along w. to Bet.
12 : 3. unto salt sea w. to Beth-jesh.
23 : 14. I am going w. of all earth
Ju. 9 : 25. robbed all came that w.
18 : 5. whe. w. we go be prosperous
22. when good w. fr. house of Mi.
1 S. 6 : 12. kine took straight w. to B.
9 : 6. peradv. he can shew us our w.
8. to man of God to tell us our w.
12 : 23. I will teach you the good w.
13 : 17. one company unto w. to O.
18. another company w. to Beth-
horon, another to w. of border
15 : 20. I have gone w. Lord sent me
20 : † 19. by stone that sheweth w.
2 S. 15 : 2. Abs. stood beside w. of gate
19 : 36. will go a little w. ov. Jordan
1 K. 2 : 2. I go the w. of all the earth

1 K. 8 : † 44. pray unto Lord tow. w.
13 : 26. prophet that bro-t him fr. w.
2 K. 3 : 8. he said, Wh. w. sh. we go ?
5 : 19. he departed fr. him a little w.
6 : 19. Elisha said, This is not the w.
7 : 15. all the w. full of garments
2 Ch. 6 : 27. thou hast taught good w.
Jb. 3 : 23. light to man who. w. is hid
12 : 24. causeth to wander where
is no w., Ps. 107 : 40. ⌈return
16 : 22. I shall go the w. whence not
22 : 15. Hast thou marked the old w.
23 : 10. he knoweth the w. I take
24 : 18. beholdeth not w. of viney-s
28 : 23. God understandeth w. th-of
26. made a w. for lightning, 38 : 25.
31 : † 32. I opened my doors to w.
38 : 19. Where is w. light dwelleth?
24. By what w. is the light parted
Ps. 1 : 6. L. knoweth w. of righteous
2 : 12. Kiss Son, lest ye perish fr. w.
36 : 4. setteth hims. in w. not good
37 : † 14. bow to slay upright of w.
78 : 50. He made a w. to his anger
101 : 2. I will behave in perfect w., 6.
107 : 4. wandered in a solitary w.
119 : 27. underst-d w. of thy precepts
29. Remove from me w. of lying
30. I have chosen the w. of truth
32. I will run w. of commandm-ts
33. Teach me w. of thy stat-s, 143 :
104. I hate every false w., 128. ⌊8.
139 : 24. see if any wicked w. in me
146 : 9. w. of wicked he turneth ups.
Pr. 2 : 8. preserveth w. of his saints
12. To deliver from w. of evil man
4 : 19. w. of wicked is as darkness
6 : 23. reproofs are the w. of life
7 : 27. Her house is the w. to hell
12 : 15. w. of a fool right in his eyes
26. w. of wicked seduceth them
13 : 15. w. of transgressors is hard
14 : 12. is a w. seemeth right, 16 : 25.
15 : 9. w. of wicked is abomination
10. grievous unto him forsak-h w.
19. w. of slothful man is a hedge;
w. of righteous is made plain
24. The w. of life is above to wise
16 : 29. leadeth him into w. not good
21 : 8. The w. of man is froward ⌈(4)
30 : 19. The w. of an eagle, the w.
20. Such is w. of adulterous wom.
Ec. 11 : 5. knowest not w. of spirit
Is. 3 : 12. they destroy w. of thy paths
26 : 7. w. of the just is uprightness
35 : 8. a highway and a w., it shall
be called, The w. of holiness
40 : 14. who shewed him w. of understanding ? ⌈51 : 10.
43 : 16. Lord maketh a w. in sea,
49 : 11. I will make all my mts. a w.
57 : 14. prepare a w., take stumblingblock out of w., 62 : 10. ⌈17.
59 : 8. w. of peace know not, Ro. 3 :
Je. 10 : 2. Learn not the w. of heathen
23. I know the w. of man is not in
12 : 1. Wheref. w. of wicked prosper
21 : 8. bef. you w. of life, w. of de.
25 : 35. shepherds have no w. to flee
32 : 39. I give them one heart, one w.
42 : 3. That Lord may shew us w.
50 : 5. They sh. ask the w. to Zion
Eze. 8 : 5. lift eyes w. tow. north (2)
9 : 2. six men came from w. of gate
16 : 25. high place at ev. head of w.
27. dau-s of Philis. ashamed of thy
21 : 16. Go thee one w. or⌊lewd w.
19. choose place at head of w. to
20. Appoint a w. that sword may
21. k. of Bab. stood at part-g of w.
28 : 13. I saw that they took one w.
40 : † 6. gate whose face w. tow. east
42 : 1. he bro-t me w. toward north
4. bef. chambers a w. of one cubit
11. w. bef. them like appearance
12. a door in the head of the w. (2)
43 : 2. glory of G. came fr. w. of east

Eze. 44 : 1. bro-t me back w. of gate of sanctuary, 4,-47 : 2. (3)[48 :1.
47 : 15. border the w. of Hethlon,
Am. 2 : 7. turn aside w. of the meek
8 : † 14. swear, The w. of Beer-sh.
Na. 2 : 1. keep munition, watch w.
Mal. 3 : 1. he sh. prepare w. bef. me
Mat. 2:12.into own country ano. w.
7 : 14. narrow is the w. unto life
8 :28. no man might pass by th. w.
30. there was a great w. off a herd
10 : 5. Go not into w. of Gentiles
22 : 16. we know thou teachest w. of God, Mk. 12 : 14. Lu. 20 : 21.
Mk. 10 : 17. when gone into the w.
Lu. 1 : 79. our feet into w. of peace
5 : 19.by what w. might bring him
10 : 31.came certain priest that w.
14 : 32. while other is great w. off
15 :20. yet a great w. off, fath. saw
19 : 4.ran, for he was to pass th. w.
Jn. 10 : 1. up some other w. is a thief
14 : 4.whither I go and w. ye know
5.Lord, how can we know the w.?
6. I am the w., the truth, the life
Ac. 8:26. w. from Jerus. unto Gaza
16 : 17.shew unto us w. of salvat-n
18 :26. expounded unto him w. of
19 : 9. divers spake evil of that w.
23.arose no small stir about th. w.
21 :5.bro-t us on our w. with wives
24 : 14. w. which they call heresy
22. more perfect knowl.of that w.
Ro. 14 : 13. occasion to fall in bro-'s
1 Co. 10 : 13. a w. to escape [w.
12 : 31. shew I a more excellent w.
1 Th. 3 : 11. Lord, direct our w. unto
He. 9 :8. w. into holiest not manifest
10 : 20. by a living w., consecrated
12 ; † 17. no w. to change his mind
Ja. 2 : 25. she sent them out ano. w.
2 Pe. 2 : 2. w. of truth evil spoken of
15. have forsaken the right w., following w. of Balaam [eousn.
21. better not known w. of right-
3 :1.stir up minds by w. of remem.
Re. 16 : 12. that w. of kings be pre- [pared

Broad WAY, S.

Can. 3 : 2. in b. w-s I will seek him
Na. 2 : 4. chariots justle in b. w-s
Mat. 7 : 13. b. is the w. leadeth to [destruction

By the WAY.

Ge. 38 : 14. Tamar sat -w. to Timu.
16. Judah turned unto her - w.
42 : 38. if mischief befall him - w.
45 : 23. bread and meat for father -
24. See ye fall not out - w. [w.
49 : 17. Dan shall be a serpent - w.
Ex. 4 : 24.- w. in the inn L. met him
18 : 8. all travail upon them - w.
Nu. 21 : 1. heard Israel came - w. of
De. 1 : 2. eleven days' journey - w. of mount Seir unto Kadesh
6 : 7. shalt talk of them when walk-est - w., 11 ; 19. [down
11 , 30. - w. where the sun goeth
22 : 4. not see brother's ox fall - w.
24 : 9. wh.L. did unto Miriam - w.
25 ; 17. Amalek did unto thee - w.
18.how he met thee - w., 1 S.15:2.
28 : 68. L. bring thee - w. I spake
Jos. 5 : 4. all men of war died - w.
5. all born - w. as they came out
7. bec. not circumcised them - w.
1 S. 6 : 9. if it goeth up - w. of coast
17 : 52. wounded fell - w. to Shaa.
24 : 3. Saul came to sheepcotes - w.
26 : 3. Saul pitched in Hach-h - w.
2 S. 13 :34. much people - w. of hill
18 : 23. Ahimaaz ran - w. of plain
1 K. 13 : 9. nor turn again - w. that thou camest, 10, 17. [him
24. a lion met him - w., and slew
20 : 38. prophet waited for k. - w.
2 K. 2 : 23. Elisha - w. unto Beth-el
3 : 20. came water - w. of Edom
9 : 27. Ahaziah fled - w. of garden
2 K. 11 : 19. they came - w. of gate
19 : 28. I will turn thee back - w. thou camest, Is.37:29.[Is.37:34.
33. - w. he came by same return,
2 Ch. 6 : 34. if people go to war - w.
Ezr. 8 : 31. such as lay in wait - w.
Jb. 21 : 29.Have ye asked them - w.
Ps. 80 : 12. that pass - w. pluck her
89 : 41. All that pass - w. spoil him
Pr. 8 : 2. wisdom standeth - w. in
Is 9 : 1. did afflict her - w. of sea
41 : 3. - w. that he had not gone
42 : 16. bring blind - w. knew not
48 : 17. Lord God wh. leadeth - w.
Je. 2 : 17. forsaken God when he led thee - w. [- w.
48 : 19. inhabitant of Aroer, stand
La. 1 : † 12.ye that pass - w. behold
2 : †15.All th. pass - w. clap hands
Eze. 43 : 4. glory of Lord - w. of gate
44 : 3. prince shall enter - w. of porch, sh. go out - w. of same,
46 : 2, 8. (2) [north gate, (5)
46 : 9. he that entereth - w. of the
47 : 2. he led me - w. look-h eastw.
Ho. 13 : 7. as leopard - w. will I ob-
Mat.4 : 15.Zabulon - w. of sea[serve
Mk. 8 : 3. if I send them, faint - w.
27. - w. he asked his disciples
9:33.What was it ye disputed - w.?
Lu. 10 : 4. salute no man - w. [34.
24 :32.while he talked with us - w.
1 Co. 16 : 7. I will not see you - w.
See **WENT with way.**

Every WAY.

[w.
Ge. 3 : 24. flaming sword turned e.
Ps. 119 : 101. refrained fr. e. evil w.
104.theref. I hate e. false w.,128.
Pr. 21 : 2. e.w. of man right in own
Eze. 16 : 31. eminent place in e.w.
Ro. 3 : 2. Much e.w. because to th.
Ph. 1 : 18. e.w. whe. in pretence or
See **EVIL way, s, HIGHWAY.**
See **WENT her way.**

His WAY.

Ge. 6 : 12. all flesh corrupted h.w.
32 : 1. on h.w. angels met him
33 : 16. Esau returned on h.w.
Ju. 17 : † 8. to mount Ephraim in making h.w. [w.
19 : 27. her lord went out to go h.
2 S.22:31. h.w. is perfect, Ps.18:30.
1 K. 8 : 32. wicked, to bring h.w. upon his own head, 2 Ch. 6 : 23.
Jb. 8 : 19 this is the joy of h.w.[w.
17 : 9. The righteous sh. hold on h.
21 : 31. Who declare h.w. to face?
23 : 11. h.w. have I not declined
36 : 23. Who hath enjoined him h.
Ps.25:9.meek will he teach h.w.[w.
37 : 7.him who prospereth in h.w.
23. good man, L. delighteth in h.
34. Wait on Lord, keep h.w. [w.
50 : †23. disposeth h.w. aright[w.
119 : 9.Wherew.yo. man cleanse h.
Pr. 8 : 22. Lord possessed me in be-ginning of h.w. [direct h.w.
11 : 5. righteousness of perfect sh.
14 : 8. wisdom is to underst. h.w.
16 : 9 A man's heart deviseth h.w.
17. keepeth h.w. preserveth soul
19 : 3. foolishness perverteth h.w.
20 : 14.gone h.w. then he boasteth
21 : 29. upright, he directeth h.w.
Is. 48 : 15.sh. make h.w. prosperous
55 ; 7.Let wicked forsake h.w.[w.
Je. 4 : 7. destroyer of Gentiles on h.
Eze. 3 :18.nor speakest to warn from h. wicked w., 33 : 8, 9. [33 : 9.
19. if turn not from h.wicked w.
13 : 22. not return fr. h.wicked w.
33 : 11. wicked turn fr. h.w., live
Na. 1 : 3.L.hath h.w. in whirlwind
Lu. 11 : † 6. friend out of h.w. come
Ja. 1:24.beholdeth hims.goeth h.w.
5 : 20. converteth sinner fr. error of
See **WENT his way.** [h.w.

In the WAY. [- w.

Ge. 16 : 7. found Hagar by fountain
24 : 27.I being - w. the Lord led me
35 : 19. Rachel died, was buried - w. to Ephrath, 48 : 7. (2) [w.
Ex. 5 : 20. Moses and Aaron stood -
23 : 20.send angel to keep thee - w.
33 : 3. lest I consume thee - w.
Nu. 22 : 22.angel of Lord stood - w., 23, 31, 34. [- w.
De. 22 : 6. If bird's nest before thee
23 : 4.met you not with bread - w.
2 S. 18 : 30. - w. tidings to Dav. [w.
1 K. 11 : 29. Ahijah found Jerob. -
13 :24. carcass was cast - w., 25, 28.
18 : 7. As Obadiah was - w. Elijah
2 K 10 : 12. Jehu at shearingh. - w.
Ezr. 8 : 22.to help us ag. enemy - w.
Ne. 9 : 12. to give light - w. they go
19. pillar of cloud to lead th. - w.
Jb.18:10.snare and trap for him - w.
Ps. 1 :1.nor standeth - w. of sinners
25 :8.will he teach sinners - w. th-f
12. him sh. he teach - w. he choo.
32 : 8. I will teach - w. thou sh. go
85 : 13. sh. set us - w. of his steps
102:23.weakened my strength - w.
110 : 7.He shall drink of brook - w.
119 : 1. Blessed are undefiled - w.
14. I rejoiced - w. of testimonies
139 : 24. lead me - w. everlasting
142 : 3. - w. privily laid a snare
Pr. 4 : 11. I have taught thee - w. of
14. go not - w. of evil men [wisd.
8 : 20. I lead - w. of righteousness
9 : 6. and go - w. of understanding
10 : 17.He is - w. of life th. keepeth
12 : 28. - w. of righteousness is life
13 : 6. keepeth him is upright - w.
16 : 31. if found - w. of righteousn.
22 : 5. Thorns are - w. of froward
6. Train up a child - w. he sho.go
23 : 19. son, guide thine heart - w.
26 : 13.The slothful saith, lion - w.
29 :27.upright - w. abom. to wicked
Ec. 12 : 5. and fears shall be - w.
Is. 15 : 5. - w. of Horonaim a cry
26 : 8. - w. of thy judgm-ts waited
Je. 2 : 18. what hast thou to do - w. of Egypt ? or - w. of Assyria ?
Ho. 6 : 9. so priests murder - w.
Am.4:†10.I sent pestil-ce - w. of Eg.
Mat. 5 : 25.Agree quickly while - w.
15 : 32. lest they faint - w. Mk 8:3.
20 : 17.Jes. took disciples apart - w.
21 : 8. spread their garments - w., cut branches, strewed them - w., Mk. 11 : 8. Lu. 19 : 36.
19. when he saw fig tree - w.
32.John came - w. of righteousn.
Mk. 10 :32.they - w. up to Jerus-m
52. blind man followed Jesus - w.
Lu. 12 : 58. art - w. give diligence
24 : 35. told what things done - w.
Ac. 9 : 17. Jesus that appeared - w.
27. how he had seen the Lord - w.
25 : 3. laying wait - w. to kill him
26 : 13. I saw - w. light fr. heaven
Jude 11. they have gone - w. of Cain
See **JEROBOAM.**
See **Way of the LORD.**

My WAY. [m.w.

Ge. 24 : 56. seeing Lord prospered
2 S 22 : 33. God, he maketh m.w. Perfect, Ps 18 : 32.[cannot pass
Jb. 19 : 8. fenced up m.w. that I
Is. 40 : 27. m.w. is hid from Lord?
Eze. 18 : 25.Isr., Is not m.w. equal?
Jn. 8 : 21. I go m.w., ye die in sins
Ro. 15 :24.brought on m.w. by you
2 Co.1 :16.bro-t on m.w. tow. Judea

Out of the WAY.

Ex. 32 : 8. They have turned aside - w., De. 9 : 12, 16. Ju. 2 : 17.
Nu.22 : 23. the ass turned aside - w.
De. 11 : 28 cursed if turn aside - w.
13 : 5. thrust thee - w. L. comm-d

De 27 : 18. the blind to wander - w.
Jb. 24 : 4. They turn the needy - w.
24.they are taken - w. and cut off
31 . 7. If my step hath turned - w.
Pr.21 : 16.wandereth -w.of underst.
Is. 28 : 7. thro. strong drink are -w.
30 : 11. Get you - w., turn aside
57 : 14. stumblingblock -w. of peo.
Eze. 47 : 2. bro-t heme - w. of gate
Mal. 2 : 8. But ye are departed - w.
Ro. 3 : 12. They are all gone - w.
Col. 2 : 14. he took handwriting - w.
2 Th. 2 :7.let,until he be taken - w.
He. 5 : 2. compassion on them - w.
12 :13.lest that wh. is lame be turn-

Own WAY. ⌊ed - w.
Pr. 1 : 31. sh. eat fruit of their o.w.
20 : 24.how man understand o.w.?
Is. 53 : 6. turned every one to his o.
56 : 11. all look to their o.w. ⌊w.
Eze.22 : 31.o.w.have I recompensed
36 : 17. defiled Israel by their o.w.
See RIGHT, STRAIGHT.

WAY side. ⌈w.s.
Ge. 38 : 21. Where is harlot was by
1 S. 4 : 13. Eli sat upon seat by w.s.
Ps.140 : 5.have spread a net by w.s.
Mat. 13 : 4. some seeds fell by w.s.,
19. Mk. 4 :4, 15. Lu. 8 :5, 12.⌈s.
20 : 30.two blind men sitting by w.
Lu. 18 : 35. sat by the w.s. begging

Their WAY. ⌈w.
Ju. 2 : 19. ceased not fr. t. stubborn
1 S.25 : 12.David's men turned t.w.
1K. 2 : 4. If thy children take heed
to t.w., 8 :25. 2 Ch. 6 :16.⌈aside
Jb. 6 : 18. paths of t.w. are turned
19 : 12. his troops raise t.w. ag. me
29 : 25. I chose out t.w., sat chief
Ps. 35 : 6. Let t.w. be dark, slippery
49 : 13. This t.w. is their folly, yet
Pr.11 :20.upright in t.w.his delight
Je. 3 : 21. they have perverted t.w.
6 : 27. that thou mayest try t.w.
23 :12. t.w. be unto them as slip-ry
Eze. 7 : 27. I will do unto them after
t.w., 9 : 10.-11 : 21. ⌈doings
14 : 22. ye shall see t.w. and their
33 :17.as for them t.w. is not equal
36 : 17.t.w. bef. me as uncleanness
19. according to t.w. I judged th.
Jn.18 :8.if seek me let these go t.w.
Ac.15 :3.brought on t.w.by church
See WENT their way, s.

This WAY. ⌈w. I go
Ge. 28 : 20. If God will keep me in t.
Ex. 2 : 12.Mos.looked t.w. and that
Jos. 3 : 4. ye have not passed t.w.
8 : 20. nó power to flee t.w.or that
2 K. 6 :19.Elisha said, t. not the w.
Ac. 9 : 2. if he found any of t.w.
22 : 4.I persecuted t.w.unto death

Thy WAY.
Ge. 24 : 40. Lord will prosper t.w.
Ex. 33 : 13. Now, I pray, shew me t.
Nu. 22 : 32. t.w. is perverse ⌊w.
Jos.1 :8. shalt make t.w.prosperous
1 S. 28 : 22.have strength when thou
goest on t.w. ⌈derness
1 K. 19 : 15. return on t.w. to wil-
Ps.5 : 8. make t.w.straight bef.face
27 : 11. Teach me t.w., O L., 86:11.
37 : 5. Commit t.w. unto the Lord
44 : 18. nei. our steps declined fr. t.
67 :2.That t.w.may be known⌊w.
77 : 13.t.w., O God, is in sanctuary
19. t.w. is in the sea, thy path in
119 : 37. quicken thou me in t.w.
Pr. 3 : 23. shalt walk in t.w. safely
5 : 8. Remove t.w. far from her
Is. 57 :10. wearied in greatn.of t.w.
Je. 2 : 23.see t.w. in the valley⌈love
33. Why trimmest t.w. to seek
36. Why gaddest to change t.w.?
4 : 18. t.w. procured these things
Eze. 16 : 43. I will recompense t.w.
Ho. 2 : 6. I will hedge up t.w. with

Ho. 10 : 13. thou didst trust in t.w.
Mat. 11 : 10.my messenger, wh. shall
prepare t.w., Mk. 1:2. Lu.7:27.

Go thy WAY. ⌈- w.
Ge. 12 :19.behold thy wife, take her,
1 S. 20 : 22. if I say to yo. man, - w.
1 K. 19 : 15. -w. to the wilderness of
2 K.4 : 29.said to Gehazi, -w.⌊Dam.
Ec. 9 : 7.-w., eat thy bread with joy
Can. 1 : 8. O fairest am.women, -w.
Da. 12 : 9. - w., Dan. ; words closed
13. But - w. till end be : shalt rest
Mat. 5 : 24. - w. ; be reconciled to
8 : 4. - w. ; shew thyself to priest,
Mk. 1 : 44. ⌈- w.
13. Jesus said unto the centurion
20 : 14. Take that thine is, - w.
Mk. 2 :11.Arise, - w. into thine ho.
7 : 29. - w. ; devil out of thy dau-r
10 : 21.- w., sell whatso. thou hast
52.Jesus said, -w.; thy faith hath
made thee whole, Lu. 17 : 19.
Jn. 4 : 50. Jes.saith, - w.; son liveth
Ac. 9 : 15. - w. ; he is chosen vessel
24 : 25. Felix ans-d, - w. this time

WAY, S
with **walk, ed, eth, ing.** ⌈w.
Ex. 18 : 20. shew w.wh-n they must
De. 5 : 33. Ye sh. w. in all the w-s
of Lord, 13:4.-28:9. Eze. 37:24.
8 : 6. keep commandments of Lord
to w. in his w-s and fear him,
10 : 12.-11 : 22.-19 : 9.-26 : 17.-
30 : 16. Jos. 22 : 5. 1 K. 2 : 3.
2 Ch. 6 : 31. ⌈thee to w.
13 : 5. out of w. Lord commanded
Jos. 22 : 5. diligent heed to w. in
his w-s ⌈thers w-d
Ju. 2 : 17.quickly out of w. their fa-
22. whether they will keep w. or
the Lord to w. therein
5 : 10. Speak ye that w. by the w.
1 S. 8 :3.Sam-l's sons w-d not in w-s
5. art old, sons w. not in thy w-s
1 K. 2 : 4. if take heed to their w. to
w. before me in truth with all
3 : 14. If thou wilt w. in my w-s
as thy fa. David did w., 11 : 38.
8 : 25. heed to their w. that they
w. before me as thou hast w-d
36. teach them the good w. wh-n
they sho. w., 2 Ch. 6 : 27. ⌈w-s
58. incline our hearts to w. in his
11 : 33. have not w-d in my w-s
15 :26.Nadab w-d in w. of his fath.
34. he did evil and w-d in the w.
of Jerob., 16: 2,19,26,31.-22:52.
16 :19. Zimri w-g in w. of Jerob-m
22 : 43. Jehoshaphat w-d in all
the w-s of Asa his fa.,2Ch.20:32.
52. Ahaziah w-d in w. of his father, w. of his mother, w. of
Jerob., 2 K. 8:27. 2 Ch. 22 : 3,5.
2 K. 8 : 18. Jehoram w-d in the w.
of kings of Israel, 2 Ch. 21 :6,13.
16 :3. Ahaz w-d in the w.of kings
of Isr., 2 Ch. 28 : 2. ⌈father w-d
21 : 21.Amon w-d in all the w. his
22. Amon w-d not in w. of the L.
22 : 2. Josiah w-d in all the w. of
Da., 2 Ch.34 :2 w-s⌈as they live
2 Ch. 6 : 31. to w. in thy w-s long
11 : 17. three years w. in w. of Da.
17:3. Jehosh. w-d in first w-s of D.
21 : 12. Because thou hast not w-d
in w-s of Jehosh-t (2) ⌈Israel
13. But w-d in the w. of kings of
22 : 3. Ahaziah w-d in w-s of Ahab
Ps.81 :13.th.Isr.had w-d in my w-s
101 : 6. w-h in a perfect w. shall
119 : 3.they w. in his w-s⌊serve me
128 :1.Blessed ev.one w-h in his w-s
142 : 3. in w. I w-d they laid snare
143 : 8. cause to know w. I sho.w.
Pr. 1 : 15 My son, w. not in w. with
2 : 13.to w. in w-s of darkn.⌊them
20. Th.thou w.in w. of good men

Pr. 3 : 23. shalt w. in thy w. safely
8 : † 20. I w. in w. of righteousn-s
Ec. 10 : 3. when fool w-h by the w.
11 : 9. yo. man, w. in w-s of thine
Is. 8 : 11. not w. in w. of peo.⌊heart
30 : 21. This is the w., w. ye in it
42 : 24. they won.not w.in his w-s
65 : 2. peo. wh. w-h in w.not good
Je. 6 : 16. ask where is good w. and
w. th-n ; said, We not w. th-n
25. Go not into field nor w.by w.
7 : 23.w. ye in all w-s I comm-ded
18 : 15. caused them to stumble in
their w-s, to w. in a w. not
31 :9.cause th. to w.in straight w.
42 : 3.That God shew us w. we w.
Eze. 16 : 47. not w-d after their w-s
23 : 31. hast w-d in w.of thy sister
Ho. 14 : 9. the w-s of Lord are right,
the just shall w. in them
Zch.3 : 7. If thou wilt w. in my w-s
Ac. 14 : 16. suffered nations to w.in
See **WENT** with **way.**⌊own w-s
See **WILDERNESS** with **way.**
See **Way of the WILDERNESS.**

Your WAY.
Ju. 18 : 6. before the Lord is y.w.
19 : 9. to morrow get early on y.w.

Go your WAY.
Jos. 2 : 16. hide three days ; after-
ward may - w. ⌈erward - w.
Ju. 19 : 5. with morsel of bread aft-
Ru. 1 : 12.Turn again my dau-s, - w.
Ne. 8 : 10. - w., eat fat, drink sweet
Mat. 27 : 65. - w., make sure as ye
Mk. 11 :2. -w. into village over⌊ean
16 : 7. - w., tell disciples and Peter
Lu.7 :22. -w.,tell John what things

WAYS. ⌈light
Jb. 24 : 13. they know not w. of the
30 : 12. raise up w. of their destr-n
34 :21.his eyes upon the w. of man
40 : 19. behemoth, chief of w.of G.
Ps. 84 : 5. in whose heart are the w.
Pr. 1 : 19.So are w.of ev.one greedy
2 : 15. Whose w. are crooked, and
3 : 17. Her w. are w. of pleasantn.
5 : 6. her w. moveable, canst not
21. w. of man are before the Lord
6 :6.Go to the ant, consider her w.
7 : 25.Let not heart deoli. to her w.
14 :12. end th-f w. of death, 16 :25.
16 : 2. w. of man clean in own eyes
7.When man's w.please the Lord
17:23.a gift to pervert w.of judgm.
31 : 27. well to w. of her household
Is. 49 : 9. They shall feel in the w.
Je. 2 : 23. dromedary traversing w.
3 :2. In the w. hast thou sat for th.
6 : 16. Stand in the w. and see, ask
7 : 3. Amend your w., 5.-26 : 13.
12 : 16. if they learn w. of my peo.
18 : 11. make your w.,doings good
23 : 12. unto them as slippery w.
32 : 19. thine eyes open upon w. of
La. 1 : 4. The w. of Zion do mourn
3 : 40. Let us search and try our w.
Eze. 21 : 19. son of man appoint two
21. k.stood at head of two w.⌊w.
Zch. 1 : 6. do unto us acc. to our w.
Mk. 11 :4.found colt where 2 w. met
Lu. 3 : 5. rough w. shall be smooth
Ac. 2 : 28. made known w. of life
13 :10.cease to pervert the right w.
Ro. 15 : † 22. I many w. hindered

Any WAYS. ⌈man
Le. 20 : 4. if a.w. hide eyes from the
Nu.30 : 15 if ye a.w.make them void
2 Ch.32 : 13.a.w.able to deliv. lands
See BYWAYS, HIGHWAYS.
See **EVIL ways.**

His WAYS. ⌈37.
De.32 :4. all h.w.are judgm.,Da. 4 :
1 S. 18 : 14. behaved wisely in h.w.
1 K.8 : 39. give to every man according to h.w., 2 Ch. 6 . 30.

2 Ch. 13 : 22. acts of Abijah, h.w.
27 :6.Jotham prepared h.w. bef.L.
7.h.w. writ. in book of k-s,28:26.
Jb. 26 : 14. these are parts of h.w.
34 : 11. every man find acc.to h.w.
27.wou. not consider any of h.w.
Ps. 10 : 5.h. w. are always grievous
108 : 7.made known h.w. unto Mo.
145 : 17. L. is righteous in all h.w.
Pr. 3 : 31. and choose none of h.w.
10 : 9. perverteth h.w. be known
14 :2.perverse in h.w. despiseth L.
19 : 16. that despiseth h.w. sh. die
22 : 25. Lest thou learn h.w. ⌈w.
28 : 6.better than he perverse in h.
18. he perverse in h.w. shall fall
Is. 2 : 3. will teach us h.w., Mi. 4:2.
45 : 13. I will direct all h.w. ⌈him
57 : 18. I have seen h.w., will heal
Je.17 :10.ev.man acc.to h.w.,32:19.
Eze. 18 : 23. that he return fr. h.w.
30. judge Isr. acc. to h.w., 33:20.
Da.4 :37.works truth, h.w. judgm.
Ho. 9 : 8. snare of fowler in all h.w.
12 : 2. L. punish Jacob acc.to h.w.
Jo. 2 : 7. march on ev. one h.w.⌊(2)
Ha. 3 : 6. h.w. are everlasting ⌈w.
Lu. 1 :76. go bef. Lord to prepare h.
Ro.11 : 33. h.w.are past finding out
Ja.1 : 8. man is unstable in all h.w.
11. so shall rich man fade away in
See **Ways of the LORD.**⌊h.w.
See **WAY, S with walk, ed.**

My WAYS.

Jb. 31 : 4. Doth not he see m.w.
Ps. 39 : 1. I will take heed to m.w.
95 : 10. not known m.w.,He. 3:10.
119 : 5. O that m.w. were directed
26. I have declared m.w. and
59. I thought on m.w., turned
168. all m.w. are before thee ⌈w.
139 : 3. art acquainted with all m.
Pr. 8 :32.blessed they th.keep m.w.
23 : 26.let thine eyes observe m.w.
Is. 55 : 8. nei. are your ways m.w.
9. so m.w.higher than your ways
58 : 2.seek me daily to know m.w.
La. 3 : 9. He hath inclosed m.w.
11. he turned aside m.w., pulled
Eze. 18 :29.Isr., are not m.w. eq-l ?
Mal. 2 : 9. acc. as ye not kept m.w.
1 Co. 4 : 17. into rememb-e of m.w.

Own WAYS. ⌈bef. him

Jb. 13 : 15. will maintain mine o.w.
Pr. 14 : 14. backslider be filled with
Is. 58 : 13. not doing o.w. ⌊o.w.
66 :3.they have chosen their o.w.
Eze. 36 : 31. remember your o. evil
32 be ashamed for your o.w.⌊w.
Ac. 14 : 16. suffered nations to walk

Seven WAYS. ⌈in o.w.

De. 28 : 7. sh. come out against thee
one way, flee before thee s.w.
25. thou shalt go one way against
them, and flee s.w.before them

Their WAYS. ⌈w.

2Ch.7:14.If peo.turn from t.wicked
Jb 24:23.yet his eyes are upon t.w.
Ps.125:5.as turn unto t.crooked w.
Pr. 9 :15.passengers who go on t.w.
Je. 15 : 7.they return not from t.w.
16 : 17.mine eyes are upon all t.w.
18 : 15. they have caused them to
stumble in t.w. ⌈see t.w.
Eze. 14 : 23. comfort you when ye
Ho.4 :9.I will punish them for t.w.
Ro.3:16.Destruction,misery in t.w.
2 Pe. 2 : 2. many shall follow t.w.
See **WENT their ways.**

Thy WAYS.

De. 28 :29. shalt not prosper in t.w.
Jb.4 : 6. hope and uprightn. of t.w.
21 :14.we desire not knowl.of t.w.
22 : 3. is it gain to him t.w. perfect
28. the light shall shine upon t.
Ps. 25 :4. Shew me t.w., O Lord⌊w.
51 :13.will I teach transgr-ors t.w.
Ps.91:11.angels to keep thee in t.w.
119 : 15.will have respect unto t.w.
Pr.3: 6.In all t.w. acknowledge him
4 : 26. let t.w. be established ⌈eth
31 :3. nor t.w. to that wh.destroy-
Is. 63 : 17. why made us err fr. t.w.
64 : 5. that remember thee in t.w.
Je. 2 : 33. hast taught wicked t.w.
3 : 13. scattered t.w. to strangers
Eze. 7 : 3. judge thee acc.to t.w., 8.
9. recompense thee acc.to t.w.,4.
16 : 47. corrupted more than they
61. remember t.w. ⌊in all t.w.
24 : 14. acc. to t.w. sh. judge thee
28 : 15. Thou wast perfect in t.w.
Da. 5 :23.G., in whose hand all t.w.
Re. 15 :3. just and true are t.w., K.

Your WAYS.

Is. 55 : 8. neither are y.w. my w.
9.so my w. higher than y.w.⌈29.
Eze. 18 : 25. are not y.w. unequal ?
20 :43.there sh ye remember y.w.
44. not according to y. wicked w.
Hag.1 : 5.saith L., Consider y.w., 7.

Go your WAYS.

Ge.19 : 2.ye shall rise early and -w.
Lu.10 : 3. -w.,I send you as lambs
10.receive you not, - w. into st-ts
Re. 16 : 1 - w., pour out vials of

WAYFARING. ⌊wrath

Ju. 19 : 17. he saw a w. man in city
2 S. 12 : 4. own flock to dress for w.
Is. 33 : 8. the w. man ceaseth ⌊man
35 :8 w. men, though fools, not err
Je. 9 : 2. a lodging place of w. men
14 : 8. why shouldest thou be as a

WAYMARKS. ⌊w. man. ?

Je. 31 : 21. Set thee up w., make

WE.

Ge. 3 : 2. w. may eat of fruit of trees
19 : 13. w. will destroy this place
44 : 9. w. will be my lord's bondm.
46 : 34. trade about cattle, w. and
Ex. 16 :7.what w.th. ye murmur, 8.
Nu. 13 : 31. w. be not able to go up ;
they stronger than w. ⌈Lord
32 : 32. w. will pass over armed bef.
De. 1 : 28. people is greater than w.
5 : 27. w. will hear it and do it
1 S. 8 : 20. that w. be like nations
2 S. 17 : 12. w. will light upon him
19 : 43. w. more right in David ⌊(2)
1 K. 20 : 23. w. sh. be stronger than
2 Ch. 20 : 12. nei. know w. wh.to do
Ezr. 4 : 16. w. certify king, if city be
5 : 11.w. are serv-ts of God of hosts
9 : 7.w. have been in great trespass
10 : 4. w. will be with thee : do it
Ne. 2 : 20. w. will arise and build
5 :2. w., our sons and dau-s many
8. w. aft. ability have redeemed
Jb. 8 : 9. w. are but of yesterday
Ps. 100 : 3. w. are his people ⌈gold
Can. 1 : 11. w. will make borders of
Is. 14 :10. Art thou weak as w. are ?
63 : 19. w. are thine : they were not
Je. 26 :19. might w. procure gr.evil
42 : 6.our God, to wh. w. send thee
La. 3 : 42. w. have transgressed
Da. 3 : 16. w. are not careful to ans.
17. God wh.w. serve able to deliv.
Mat. 6 : 12. forgive us as w. forgive
8 : 29. What have w. to do with
thee, Jesus, Mk. 1 :24. Lu. 4:34.
9 : 14. Why do w. and Phari. fast
15 : 33. Whence should w. have so
much bread ? ⌈out ? Mk. 9 : 28.
17 : 19. Why could not w. cast him
19 :27.w. forsak all (2), Mk. 10 :28.
28 : 13. stole him aw.while w.slept
14. w. will persuade him, secure
Mk. 5 : 9. Legion ; for w. are many
14 : 58.w. heard him say, I will de.
Lu. 1 : 74. w. being delivered from
3 : 14. w., 18 : 28.-23 : 41.-24 : 21.
Jn. 1 : 16.-4 : 22.-6 : 42, 69.-7 :
35.-8 : 41, 48.-9 : 21, 24, 29.-12:
34.-17 : 11.-19 : 7.-21 : 3. Ac. 2:
8, 32.-3 : 15.-4 : 9, 20.-6 : 4.-10:
33, 39.-13 : 32.-20 : 6, 13.-21 : 2,
3.(2), 4, 7.(2), 15, 16, 25.-24 : 5,
6, 8.-27 : 2, 3, 4.(2), 5.(2), 7. (2),
19, 29.-28 : 11, 12, 13 (2), 16, 21.
Ro. 1 : 5.- 2 : 2.- 5 : 3.-6 : 4. - 7 :
5. - 8 : 23, 28. 1 Co. 1 : 23. - 2 :
12, 16.-4 : 8.-9 : 11.(3), 25 -11 :
16.-12 : 13.-15 : 30, 52. 2 Co. 1 :
6.-3 : 18.-4 : 11, 13.-5 : 16, 21.-
10 : 13.-11 : 12, 21.-13 : 4, 6, 7.
(2), 9. Ga. 2 : 9, 16.-5 : 5. Ep. 2 :
3. Ph. 3 : 3. Col. 1 : 9, 28. 1 Th.
2:13, 17.-3:12.-4:15.-5:10. 2 Th.
2 : 13. Tit. 3 : 5. He. 2 : 3.-12 :
25. 2 Pe. 1 : 18. 1 Jn. 1 : 1.(3), 2,
3.(2), 4, 5.(2), 6.(2), 7.(2), 8, 9.-
2 : 1, 5, 18, 28.-3 : 1, 11, 14.(2),
16.(2), 21, 22.(3), 23, 24.-4 : 6,
10, 11, 14, 16, 17, 19.-5 : 2.(8), 9,
14.(2), 15 (5), 18, 19.(2), 20.(3) .2
Jn. 4, 5, 6, 8.(3). 3 Jn. 8.(2), 12, 14.
Lu. 9 : 13. w. have no more but five
Jn. 8 : 33. w. be Abraham's seed
9 :28. Thou his disciple, w. are M.'s
40. Phari. said, Are w. blind also?
41. ye say, w.see : theref. your sin
14 : 23. and w. will come unto him
17 : 11. they may be one as w., 22.
Ac. 4 : 12. wh-by w. must be saved
5 ; 32. w. are his witnesses, 10 : 39.
6 : 2. not reason th. w. leave word
10 : 47.received H. Gh.as well as w.
14 : 15 w. are men of like passions
22. w. must thro. much tribula-n
15 : 10.yoke nei. fath-s nor w. able
16 : 16. And as w. went to prayer
17 : 28. For in him w. live and
move ; For w. are his offspring
21 : 1. w. came unto Coos, thence
5. w. kneeled down on shore (4)
6. when w. had taken leave one
8. w. entered into hou. of Phil.(2)
10. as w. tarried there many days
12. w.besought P.not to go to Jer.
17. when w. were come to Jerus.
23.w.have 4 men wh. have a vow
23 : 9, w. find no evil in this man
14. w. have bound ourselves (2)
15. and w. are ready to kill him
27 : 1. that w. sho. sail into Italy
18. w. being tossed with a tempest
20. all hope that we sho. be saved
26. w. must be cast upon cert.isl.
27. as we were driven up and down
28 : 22. w. desire to hear what (2)
Ro. 5 : 1. w. have peace with God
2. w. have access by faith into (2)
3 :8.w.be slanderously reported(2)
5 : 6. when w. were without stren.
8. while w. were sinners Ch. died
6 : 6. that w. should not serve sin
7 : 6. now w. are deliv-d fr. law (2)
7.What shall w. say then ? 8 : 31.
12 : 5. w. being many are one body
15 : 1. w. that are strong ought to
1 Co.3 : 9. w. are labourers with G.
4 : 8.that w. might reign with you
10. w. are fools for Christ's sake ;
w. are weak ; w. are despised
12. reviled, w. bless ; persecuted,
13. Being defamed w. entreat ;
w. are made as the filth
8 : 6. one God and w. in him ; one
Lord and w. by him ⌈(4)
8. nei. if w. eat are w. the better
9 : 12. w. have not used power (2)
10 : 6 w. sho. not lust aft. evil thi-s
17. w. being many are one bread ;
for w. are all partakers
22. Do w. provoke Lord to jealousy ? are w. stronger ⌈(2)
2 Co. 1 :4.that w. be able to comfort
8. w. were pressed out of meas.(3)
14. w. are your rejoicing, as ye
2 : 15. w. are unto G. sweet savour

2 Co. 2 : 17. For w. are not as many;
speak w. in Christ ⌈side (2)
4 : 8. w. are troubled on every
18. While w. look not at things s.
5 : 13. whether w. be sober, it is (2)
7 : 5. when w. were come into Mac.
8 : 4. Praying that w. receive gift
6. Insomuch that w. desired Titus
18. w. have sent him wi. the bro.
9 : 4. w. (that w. say not, ye) be
10 : 7 as he is Christ's, even so w.
11 : 12. may be found even as w.
13 : 4. w. also are weak in him, but
w. sh. live with him ⌈other (2)
Ga. 1 : 8. though w. or angel preach
2 : 10. that w. sho. remember poor
15. w. who are Jews by nature
17. if w. also are found sinners (2)
4 : 3 so w. when w. were children
28. w., as Isaac, chil. of promise
Ep. 1 : 4. th. w. be holy without blame
12. th. w. be to praise of his glory
2 : 5. Even when w. were dead in
10. For w. are his workmansh. (2)
6 : 12. For we wrestle not ag. flesh
1 Th. 1 : 8. w. need not to speak any
2 : 7. w. were gentle among you
3 : 6. desiring to see us as w. to see
8. w. live if ye stand fast ⌊yon
4 : 6. w. also have forewarned you
17. w. wh. are alive be caught up
so shall w. ever be with the Lord
5 : 5. w. are not of the night nor
2 Th. 1 : 4. So that w. glory in you
Tit. 3 : 3. w. were sometime foolish
He. 2 : 1. w. ought to gi. more earnest
3 : 6. house are w. if w. hold fast
4 : 13, him with wh. w. have to do
5 : 11. of wh. w. have many things
10 : 39. w. not of them draw back
12 : 1. Whf. seeing w. are compassed
13 : 6. w. may boldly say, The Lord
10. w. an altar wh-f they no right
Ja. 1 : 18. w. sho. be a kind of first
5 : 17. subject to like passions as w.
2 Pe. 3 : 13. w. look for new heavens
1 Jn. 1 : 10. if w. say w. not sinned, w.
2 : 3. w. know w. know him if w.
3 : 2. now are w. sons of God (5)
19. hereby w. know w. are of tru.
4 : 6. w. of God : hereby know w.
17. bec. as he is, so are w. in world
5 : 19. w. know that w. are of G. ⌊(2)
20. w. know Son of God is come;
and w. are in him th. is true (3)

See ALL, **We DIE,**
We have HEARD,
We KNOW, We SEE,
We have SINNED.

WEAK. ⌈or w.
Nu. 13 : 18. see whe. they be strong
Ju. 16 : 7. sh. I be w. as other, 11, 17.
19 : † 9. Behold now the day is w.
2 S. 3 : 39. I am this day w. tho. k:
2 Ch. 15 : 7. let not your hands be w.
Jb. 4 : 3. hast strengthened w. hands
Ps. 6 : 2. Have mercy, O L.; I am w.
41 : † 1 Blessed that con-idereth w.
109 : 24. My knees w. thro. fasting
Is. 14 : 10. Art thou become w. as we?
35 : 3. Strengthen ye the w. hands
Eze. 7 : 17. all knees sh. be w., 21 : 7.
16 : 30. How w. is thine heart, saith
Jo. 3 : 10. let the w. say, I am strong
Mat. 26 : 41. the flesh w., Mk. 14 : 38.
Ac. 20 : 35. ye ought to support w.
Ro. 4 : 19. being not w. in faith, he
8 : 3. the law was w. thro. the flesh
14 : 1. Him w. in the faith receive
2. another who is w. eateth herbs
21. whereby thy bro. is made w.
15 : 1. to bear infirmities of the w.
1 Co. 1 : 27. w. things to confound
4 : 10. We are w., ye are strong
8 : 7. conscience w. is defiled, 10.
9. stumblingblock to them are w.
11 thro. thy knowl. w. bro. perish?

1 Co. 8 : 12. wound their w. conscience
9 : 22. To the w. I became as w.
that I might gain the w.
11 : 30. For this cause many are w.
2 Co. 10 : 10. his bodily presence is w.
11 : 21. I speak as tho. we been w.
29. Who is w. and I am not w.?
12 : 10. when I am w. am I strong
13 : 3. which to you-ward is not w.
4. we are w. in him, but shall live
9. glad when we are w., ye strong
Ga. 4 : 9. how turn ye to w. elements
1 Th. 5 : 14. support the w., be patient

WEAK handed. ⌊tow. all
2 S. 17 : 2. upon him while he is w. h.

WEAKEN, ED, ETH.
Ezr. 4 : 4. people of land w-d Judah
Ne. 6 : 9. Their hands shall be w-d
Jb. 12 : 21. w-h strength of mighty
14 : † 10. but man dieth and is w.
Ps. 102 : 23. He w-d my strength in
106 : † 43. w-d for their iniquities
Is. 14 : 12. down, wh. didst w. nations
Je. 38 : 4. w-h hands of men of war

WEAKER. ⌈and w.
2 S. 3 : 1. house of Saul waxed w.
1 Pe. 3 : 7. honour unto wife as, w.

WEAKNESS. ⌊vessel
Ex. 32 : † 18. of them that cry for w.
1 Co. 1 : 25. w. of God is stronger
2 : 3. I was with you in w. and fear
15 : 43. it is sown in w., it is raised
2 Co. 12 : 9. my strength perfect in w.
13 : 4. crucified through w., yet he
He. 7 : 18. disannulling of commandment for the w. thereof
11 : 34. out of w. were made strong

WEALTH. ⌈their w.
Ge. 34 : 29. sons of Jacob took all
De. 8 : 17. my power got me this w.
18. L. giveth thee power to get w.
Ru. 2 : 1. Naomi had kinsman, of w.
1 S. 2 : 32. enemy in all the w. ⌈of w.
2 K. 15 : 20. exacted money of men
2 Ch. 1 : 11. not asked w. nor honour
12. I will give thee w. and honour
Ezr. 9 : 12. nor seek their peace or w.
Es. 10 : 3 seeking the w. of his peo.
Jb. 21 : 13. They spend days in w.
31 : 25. If I rejoiced bec. my w. great
Ps. 44 : 12. dost not increase w. by
49 : 6. They that trust in w. and
10. wise men die, leave w. to oth-s
112 : 3. w., riches shall be in house
Pr. 5 : 10. Lest strangers be filled
with thy w. ⌈city, 18 : 11.
10 : 15. rich man's w. his strong
13 : 11. w. gotten by vanity shall
22. w. of sinner is laid up for just
19 : 4. w. maketh many friends ⌈w.
30 : † 15. yea, four things say not,
Ec. 5 : 19. to wh. God given w., 6 : 2.
Is. 60 : † 5 : w. of Gentiles to thee, 11
Zch. 14 : 14. w. of heathen be gath-d
Ac. 19 : 25. by this craft we have w.
1 Co. 10 : 24. seek ev. man another's
See COMMONWEALTH. ⌊w.

WEALTHY. ⌈w. pla.
Ps. 66 : 12. broughtest us out into
Je. 49 : 31. get you up unto w. nation

WEANED.
Ge. 21 : 8. Isaac grew and was w.,
1 S. 1 : 22. I will not go up until child
be w., 23, 24. ⌈Pha.'s house
1 K. 11 : 20. whom Tahpenes w. in
Ps. 131 : 2. I behaved as child that
is w., my soul is as w. child
Is. 11 : 8. w. child put his hand on
28 : 9. them that are w. from milk
Ho. 1 : 8. when she w. Lo-ruhamah

WEAPON. ⌈w.
Nu. 35 : 18. if he smite thee with hand
De. 23 : 13. have a paddle upon w.
2 Ch. 23 : 10. ev. man having w. in ha.
Ne. 4 : 17. with other hand held w.
† 23. ev. one went wi. his w. for wat.
Jb. 20 : 24. He shall flee from iron w.

Is. 54 : 17. No w. ag. thee sh. prosper
Eze. 9 : 1. with destroying w. in

WEAPONS. ⌊hand, 2.
Ge. 27 : 3. take thy w., thy quiver
1 S. 21 : 8. nei. sword nor w. with me
2 K. 11 : 8. compass the king every
man with his w., 11. 2 Ch. 23 : 7, 10.
2 Ch. 32 : † 5. Hez. made w. in abund.
Ec. 8 : † 8. no casting off w. in war
Is. 13 : 5. the Lord and w. of his indignation, Je. 50 : 25.
Je. 22 : 7. destroyers ag. thee, every
one with his w. ⌈w., 10.
Eze. 39 : 9. they in cities shall burn
Jn. 18 : 3. Judas wi. lanterns and w.
Ro. 6 : † 13. nor yield members as w.
2 Co. 10 : 4. w. of warfare not carnal

WEAPONS of war.
De. 1 : 41. when ye had girded on w.
Ju. 18 : 11. 600 appointed wi. w., 16,
2 S. 1 : 27. How are w. perished ! ⌊17.
Ec. 9 : 18. Wisdom is better than w.
Je. 21 : 4. I will turn back the w.
51 : 20. Thou art my battle axe, w.
Eze. 32 : 27. are gone down to hell

WEAR. ⌊with w.
Ex. 18 : 18. Thou wilt surely w. aw.
De. 22 : 5. wom. not w. th. pertain-h to
11. not w. garments of divers ⌊man
1 S. 2 : 28. choose him to w. an ephod
22 : 18. slew 85 th. did w. an ephod
Es. 6 : 8. royal apparel k. useth to w.
Jb. 14 : 19. The waters w. the stones
Is. 4 : 1. We will w. our own apparel
65 : † 22. elect shall w. out work of
Da. 7 : 25. he shall w. out the saints
Zch. 13 : 4. nei. sh. w. rough garm-t
Mat. 11 : 8. that w. soft clothing are
Lu. 9 : 12. when day began to w. aw.

WEARETH, ING.
1 S. 14 : 3. priest in Shiloh w-g ephod
Jn. 19 : 5. Jes. came w-g purple robe
Ja. 2 : 3. ye respect him w-h the gay
1 Pe. 3 : 3. adorning, let it not be

WEARIED. ⌊w-g of gold.
Ge. 19 : 11. they w. to find the door
Jb. 3 : † 17. there the w. be at rest
Is. 43 : 23. nor w. thee with incense
24. hast w. me wi. thine iniquities
47 : 13. art w. in multi. of counsels
57 : 10. art w. in greatn. of thy way
Je. 4 : 31. soul w. bec. of murderers
12 : 5. If run with footmen and they
w. thee, if in the land of peace
they w. thee ⌈with lies
Eze. 24 : 12. She hath w. herself
Mi. 6 : 3. wherein have I w. thee?
Mal. 2 : 17. Ye have w. the Lord.
Yet ye say, Wherein have we
w. him? ⌈on the well
Jn. 4 : 6. Jesus being w., sat thus
He. 12 : 3. lest ye be w. and faint in

WEARIETH. ⌈cloud
Jb. 37 : 11. by watering he w. thick
Ec. 10 : 15. labour of foolish w. ev.

WEARINESS. ⌊one
Ne. 9 : † 32. let not w. seem little
Ec. 12 : 15. much study is a w. of
Da. 9 : † 21. Gabriel, to fly with w.
Mal. 1 : 13. Ye said, what a w. is it!
2 Co. 11 : 27. In w. and painfulness

WEARISOME. ⌈me
Jb. 7 : 3. w. nights are appointed to

WEARY. [Adj.]
Ge. 27 : 46. said, I am w. of my life
De. 25 : 18. Amalek smote thee w.
Ju. 4 : 21. Jael smote Sisera when w.
8 : 15. bread unto men that are w.?
2 S. 16 : 14. king and people came w.
17 : 2. will come upon him while w.
29. peo. is hungry and w., 14 : † 28.
23 : 10. he smote Philist-s until w.
Jb. 3 : 17. there the w. be at rest
10 : 1. My soul is w. of my life
16 : 7. now he hath made me w.
22 : 7. Thou not given water to w.
Ps. 6 : 6. I am w. with my groaning

Ps. 63 : †1.longeth for thee in w. la.
68 : 9.confirm thy inherit-e wh. w.
69 : 3. I am w. of my crying [tion
Pr. 3 : 11. be not w. of L.'s correc-
25 : 17. lest he be w. of thee[is w.
26 : † 15. slothful hideth hand ; he
Is. 1 : 14. feasts, I am w. to bear th.
5 : 27. None shall be w.nor stumble
16 : 12.that Moab is w.in high pla.
28 : 12.ye may cause the w. to rest
32 : 2. as shadow of rock in w. land
40 : 28. God fainteth not, nei. is w.
30.Even the youths sh.faint,be w.
31.wait on L. shall run, not be w.
43 :22.thou been w. of me, O Israel
46 : 1. are a burden to the w. beast
50:4.word in season to him th.is w.
Je. 6 : 11. I am w. with holding in
15 : 6. I am w. with repenting
20 : 9. I was w. with forbearing, I
31 : 25. I have satiated the w. soul
51 : 58. sh. labour in fire and be w.
64.Babylon sink, they shall be w.
Ga. 6 :9. not be w. in well doing, 2

WEARY. [Verb.] [Th. 3 :13.
Is. 7 :13. Is it small thing for you to
w. men, will ye w. my God?
Je. 2 :24.seek her will not w.thems.
9 : 5.w. thems. to commit iniquity
Ha. 2 : 13. shall w.thems.for vanity
Lu. 18 : 5. continual coming she w.

WEASEL. [me
Le.11 : 29.the w.and mouse unclean

WEATHER. [north
Jb. 37 : 22. Fair w. cometh out of
Pr. 25 : 20.taketh a garm.in cold w.
Mat. 16 : 2. ye say, It will be fair w.
3. in morning, It will be foul w.

WEAVE. [founded
Is. 19 : 9. that w. networks be con-
59 : 5.eggs and w. the spider's web

WEAVER. [of w.
Ex. 35 : 35.wisdom to work the work
1 S. 17 : 7.staff of Goliath's spear was
like a w.'s beam, 2 S. 21 : 19. 1
Ch. 11 : 23.-20 : 5. [w.'s shuttle
Jb. 7 : 6. My days are swifter than a
Is. 38 :12.I have cut off like a w. my

WEAVEST. [life
Ju. 16 : 13. If thou w. locks of my

WEB, WEBS. [head
Ju.16 :13.If weavest 7 locks with w.
14. went with pin of beam and w.
Jb. 8 : 14. trust sh. be a spider's w.
Is. 59 : 5.they weave the spider's w.
6. their w-s sh.not become garm.

WEDDING. [the w.
Mat. 22 : 3. to call them bidden to
8. w. is ready, they not worthy
10. w. was furnished with guests
11.a man that had not a w.garm.
12.how camest thou in not having
a w. garment? [the w.
Lu. 12 : 36.when he will return from
14 : 8.when thou art bidden to a w.

WEDGE.
Jos. 7 :21. Achan saw a w. of gold
24.Joshua took Achan and the w.
Is. 13 : 12. precious than golden w.

WEDLOCK. [of Ophir
Eze.16 : 38.as women that break w.

WEEDS. [barley
Jb. 31 : † 40. let w. grow instead of
Jon. 2 : 5. w. were wrapped about

WEEDY. [my head
Je. 49 : † 21. noise was heard in w.

WEEK. [sea
Ge. 29 : 27.Laban said, Fulfil her w.
28. Jacob did so, fulfilled her w.
Da. 9 : 27. shall confirm covenant
for one w. ; and in midst of w.
Lu. 18 : 12. I fast twice in the w., I
Ac. 13 : †42. be preached in w.betw.

First day of the WEEK.
Mat. 28 : 1. began to dawn toward
- w., Mk. 16 : 2, 9. Lu. 24 : 1.
Jn. 20 : 1, 19.
Ac. 20 : 7. upon - w. Paul preached
1 Co. 16 : 2.Upon - w.let ev. one lay

WEEKS. [by him
Le. 12 : 5. if a maid unclean two w.
Nu.28 : 26.meat offering aft. your w.
De. 16 : 9. 7 w. sh. thou number (2)
Je. 5 : 24. appointed w. of harvest
Da. 9 : 24. Seventy w.are determined
25. unto Messiah sh. be seven w.
and threescore and two w.
26. after threescore and two w.
Messiah be cut off [w.
10 : 2. I Daniel mourning three full
3. nor anoint myself till three w.
See **FEAST** of **weeks.**

WEEP. [Sarah
Ge. 23 : 2. Abraham came to w. for
43 : 30. Joseph sought where to w.
Nu. 11 : 10. Moses heard people w.
13. they w., saying, Give us to eat
1 S. 11 : 5. What aileth peo. they w.?
30:4.until had no more power to w.
2 S. 1 : 24. dau-s of Isr. w.over Saul
12 : 21. didst w. for the child alive
2 Ch. 34 : 27. didst rend clothes, w.
Ne. 8 : 9. day is holy, mourn not,
Jb.27:15.widows sh not w.[nor w.
30 : 25. Did not I w. for him that
was in trouble? [them that w.
31. and my organ into the voice of
31 : † 38. if the furrows likewise w.
Ec. 3 : 4. A time to w. and time to
Is. 15 : 2. gone to high places to w.
22 : 4. I will w.bitterly, labour not
30 : 19. thou shalt w. no more, he
33 7.ambassadors of peace shall w.
Je. 9 : 1. w. day and night for slain
13 : 17. my soul shall w. in secret
for your pride, mine eye sh. w.
22 : 10. w. ye not for the dead, w.
sore for him that goeth away
48 : 32.vine of Sibmah, I will w.for
La. 1 : 16. For these things I w.[23.
Eze.24 : 16. nei.thou mourn nor w.,
27 : 31. w. for thee with bitterness
Jo. 1 : 5. ye drunkards w. and howl
2 : 17. let priests w.between porch
Mi. 1 :10.Declare not at Gath, w.not
Zch.7 : 3.Should I w.in fifth month
Mk. 5 : 39. Why make this ado, w.?
14 : † 72. when he thought, began
Lu. 6 : 21. Blessed ye that w.[to w.
25. Woe unto you that laugh now,
ye shall w. [not, 8 : 52.
7 : 13. Lord saw her and said, w.
23 : 28.w. not for me,w. for yours.
Jn. 11 : 31. goeth unto grave to w.
16 :20.ye shall w.,world sh.rejoice
Ac. 21 : 13.What mean ye to w.[w.
Ro. 12 : 15. and w. with them that
1 Co. 7 : 30.w. as tho. they wept not
Ja. 4 : 9. Be afflicted,mourn, and w.
5 : 1. Go to, ye rich men, w. and
Re. 5 : 5. one of elders saith w. not
18 :11.merchants of earth shall w.

WEEPERS.
Ju. 2 : † 5. they called that place W.

WEEPEST, ETH.
1 S. 1 : 8. Hannah, why w-t thou?
2 S. 19 : 1.was told Joab, the k. w-h
2 K.8 :12.Hazael said,Why w-h lord
Ps.126:6.He th.goeth forth and w-h
La. 1 : 2. She w-h sore in the night
Jn. 20 : 13. said, Woman, why w-t
thou? 15.

WEEPING. [w.
Ge. 35 : † 8. was called, The oak of
45 : † 2.Jos-h gave forth voice in w.
Nu. 25 : 6. w. before door of tabern.
De. 34 :8.days of w. for Moses ended
2 S.3 : 16.husband went with her w.
13 : † 36. king and serv-s with a gr
15 : 30. w. as they went up [w.
2 K. 20 : † 3. Hezekiah wept with a
great w., Is. 38 : † 3. [from w.
Ezr. 3 : 13. not discern noise of joy
10 : 1. when Ezra had prayed, w.
Es. 4 : 3. in ev. province fasting, w.
Jb. 16 : 16. My face is foul with w.
28 :†11.He bindeth the floods fr. w
Ps. 6 : 8. the L. hath heard my w.
30 : 5. w. may endure for a night
102 : 9. mingled my drink with w.
Is. 15 : 3.in their streets sh.howl, w.
5. with w. shall they go it up
16 : 9. I will bewail with w.of Jazer vine of Sibmah, Je. 48 : 32.
22 : † 4. Look away from me, I will
be bitter in w. [hosts call to w.
12. in that day did the Lord of
65 : 19.voice of w.be no more heard
Je. 3 :21.voice upon high places, w.
9 : 10. For mts. will I take up a w.
31 : 9. They shall come with w.
15. voice in Ramah, bitter w.,
Rachel w. for chil., Mat. 2 : 18.
16. saith L., Restrain voice fr. w.
41 : 6. Ishm. went to meet them w.
48 : 5. continual w. shall go up[L.
50 : 4. Judah going and w. to seek
Eze. 8:14.sat women w.for Tammuz
Jo.2 : 12. turn ye to me with w.[w.
Mal.2 :13.covering altar of Lord with
Mat. 8 : 12. there shall be w. and
22 : 13.-24:51.-25:30. Lu.13:28.
Lu.7 :38.woman stood at his feet w.
Jn. 11 : 33. When Jesus saw her w.,
and Jews also w., he groaned
20 : 11.Mary stood at sepulchre, w.
Ac. 9 : 39. widows stood by him w.
Ph. 3 :18.told often,now tell you w.
Re.18 : 15.merchants shall stand w.
19. ev. shipmaster and sailors w.

WEIGH. [money
Ex. 22 : † 17. If fa. refuse he sh w.
2 S. 18 : † 12.Tho.I w. 1,000 shekels
1 K. 20 : † 39. sh. w. talent of silver
1 Ch. 20 :2. Dav. found crown to w.
Ezr. 8 : 29. keep until ye w. them
Es. 3 : † 9. I will w. 10,000 talents
Jb. 31 : † 6.Let him w. me in balan.
Ps. 58 : 2. w. violence of your hands
Is. 26 : 7. thou dost w. path of just
46 : 6.They w. silver in the balance
55:†2.w.money for what not bread
Eze.5:1.take balances to w. the hair

WEIGHED. [ver
Ge. 23 : 16. Abr. w. to Ephraim sil-
Nu. 7 : 85. vessels w. 2,400 shekels
1 S. 2 : 3. by the Lord actions are w.
17 :7.Goliath's spear's head w. 600
shekels, 2 S. 21 : 16. [head
2 S. 14 : 26. Absalom w. hair of his
Ezr.8 : 25. priests w.unto them gold
26. I w. into their hands silv., 33.
Jb. 6 : 2. Oh that my grief were w.
28 : 15. nei. silver be w. for price
31 : 6. Let me be w.in even balance
Ps. 78 : † 50. w. a path to his anger
Is. 40 : 12. who hath w. mountains
Je. 32 : 9. I w. him the money, 10.
Da. 5 : 27.Tekel, Thou art w. in bal.
Zch.11 : 12. So they w. thirty pieces

WEIGHER.
Is. 33 : † 18. Where is the scribe?
where is the w.?

WEIGHETH.
Jb. 28 :25. he w. waters by measure
Pr. 16 : 2. the Lord w. the spirits

WEIGHING. [shekels
Nu. 7 : 85. each charger w. 130
86. golden spoons w. 10 shekels
Ec. 7 : † 27. this I found, w. one aft.

WEIGHT. [another
Ge. 24 : 22.earring of half shekel w.,
two bracelets of 10 shekels w.
43 : 21. money in sack in full w.
Ex. 30 : 34. of each shall be a like w.
Le.19 :35.do no unrighteousn.in w.
26 : 26.sh. deliver you bread by w.
Nu. 7 : 13.his offering a silver charger, w. was 130 shekels, 19, 25,
31, 37, 43, 49, 55, 61, 67, 73, 79.
De. 25 : 15. thou shalt have just w.

Jos.7:21.wedge of gold,50 shek-s w.
Ju. 8 : 26. w. of golden earrings was
1 S. 17 : 5. w. of coat 5,000 shekels
2 S. 12 :30. king's crown w. a talent
14 : 26. hair 200 shekels aft. k.'s w.
21 : 16. w. of spear 300 skekels w.
1 K.7 : 47.all the vessels unweighed,
nei. was w. of the brass found
out, 2 K. 25 :16. 1 Ch. 22 : 3, 14.
2 Ch. 4 : 18. Je. 52 :20. ⌈Ch.9:13.
10 : 14. w. of gold came to Sol-n, 2
1 Ch. 21 : 25.Da.gave 600 shekels w.
28 : 14. gave gold by w. for things
of gold, silver also by w. for⌈(3)
15. Even the w. of candlesticks
16. by w. he gave gold for tables
17. gold by w. for every basin;
and likewise silver by w. for
18 for altar refined gold by w.
2 Ch 3 :9. w. of nails 50 shek-s gold
Ezr 8 : 30. took priests w. of silver
34. By number and w. of ev.one;
all the w. written at that time
Jb. 28 : 25. To make w. for winds
Pr. 11 : 1. just w. is his delight⌈L.'s
16 : 11. just w. and balance are the
Eze. 4 : 10. thy meat shall be by w.
16.shall eat bread by w., with care
Zch. 5 : 8.cast w. of lead upon mou.
Jn. 19 : 39. mixture 100 pounds w.
2 Co.4 :17.for us a more exceed-g w.
He. 12 : 1. let us lay aside every w.
Re. 16 : 21. hail, every stone w. of
WEIGHTS. ⌊talent
Le. 19 : 36. just w. shall ye have
De. 25 : 13. shalt not have divers w.
Pr.16 :11 w. of the bag are his work
20 : 10. Divers w. abomination, 23.
Mi. 6 : 11. with bag of deceitful w.
WEIGHTY, IER. ⌈w.
Pr. 27 :3. A stone is heavy and sand
Zch. 5 : † 7. lifted up w. piece of lead
Mat. 23 : 23. omitted w-r matters of
2 Co. 10 : 10.his letters, say they, are
WELFARE. ⌊w.
Ge. 43 : 27. he asked of their w.
Ex.18 :7.asked each other of w.⌈w.
1 Ch. 18 : 10. to Da. to inquire of his
Ne. 2 : 10.a man to seek w. of Israel
Jb. 30 : 15. my w. passeth as cloud
Ps 69 :22.sho.have been for their w.
Je. 38 : 4. seeketh not w. of his peo.
WELL. [Adj. or adv.] ⌈me
Ge. 12 : 13. that it may be w. with
16. entreated Abram w. for her
13 :10.Jordan was w. watered⌊sake
18 : 11.Abraham and Sarah old, w.
stricken in age, 24 : 1.
29: 6. Jacob said, Is he w.? they
said, He is w. ⌈brethren (2)
37 : 14. Go see whe. it be w. with
43 : 27. Is your father w.? ⌈w.
Ex. 4 : 14. I know that he can speak
10 : 29. Thou hast spoken w., I
Nu. 11 : 18. it was w. with us in Eg.
13 : 30. Caleb said, we are w. able
36 : 5. tribe of Joseph hath said w.
De. 5 :28.people have w. said, 18:17.
29. that it might be w. with them
33. that it may be w. with you
7 : 18. w. remember what Lord did
18 : 17. L. said, Thou hast w. spok.
Ju. 14 : 3. for she pleaseth me w., 7.
Ru. 2 : 13.if perform part of kinsman
1 S. 9 : 10. Saul to his serv., w. ⌊w.
16:16.he play, thou shalt be w., 17.
23.Saul was refreshed and was w.
18 :26. pleased Dav. w. to be called
20 : 7. If he say, It is w. ⌈away?
24 : 19. will he let his enemy go w.
20. I know w. thou shalt be king
2 S. 3 : 13. w.; I will make league
18 : 28. Ahimaaz said, All is w.⌈w.
19 : 6. if we had died, pleased thee
1 K. 2 : 18. w., I will speak for thee
8:18. in thine heart to build house,
thou didst w., 2 Ch. 6 : 8.

1 K. 18 : 24. people answ-d, It is w.
2 K.4:23.she said, It sh. be w. ⌊spok.
26. Is it w. with thy husband?
is it w. with the child? It is w.
5 : 21. and Naaman said, Is all w.?
22. And Gehazi said, All is w.⌈w.
7 : 9. said one to another, We do not
9 : 11. said unto Jehu, Is all w.?
10 : 30. L. unto Jehu, bec. done w.
25 : 24. serve king of Babylon it sh.
be w. with you, Je. 40 : 9. ⌈w.
2 Ch. 12 : 12. in Judah things went
Jb. 33 : 31.Mark w., O Job, hearken
Ps. 48 :13.Mark ye w. her bulwarks
73 : 2.my steps had w. nigh slipped
78 : 29. did eat and were w. filled
139 : 14. my soul knoweth right w.
Pr. 11 : 10.When w. with righteous
13 : 10. with w. advised is wisdom
14 : 15. prudent looketh w. to his
24 : 32. Then I saw and considered
27 : 23. look w. to thy herds⌊it w.
30 : 29.be three things which go w.
31 : 27.She looketh w. to househo.
Ec. 8 : 12. be w. with them fear God
13. it shall not be w. with wicked
Is. 3 :10.say to righteous it sh. be w.
24. instead of w. set hair, baldn-s
25 :6.of wines on the lees w.refined
33 : 23. co.not w. strengthen mast
Je. 1 : 12.L. said, Thou hast w. seen
7 : 23. that it may be w. unto you
15 :11. sh. be w. with thy remnant
22 : 15. it was w. with him, he, 16.
38 : 20. so it shall be w. unto thee
39 : 12. take him, look w. to him
40 : 4. come, I will look w. to thee
42 : 6. that it may be w. with us
44 : 17. for we were w., saw no evil
Eze. 24 : 5. make it boil w., seethe
10. consume the flesh, spice it w.
33 :32.can play w. on an instrum-t
44 : 5. mark w. behold and hear
Da. 3 : 15. if worship the image; w.
Mat. 15 : 7. Ye hypocrites, w. did
Esaias prophesy of you, Mk. 7 :
6. Ac. 28 : 25. ⌈23. Lu. 19 : 17.
25 :21. w. done, thou faithf. serv-t,
Mk. 7 : 9. Full w. ye reject comm-t
37. He hath done all things w.
12 : 28. perceiving he had ans-d w.
32. w., Master, thou hast said tru.
Lu. 1:7.both w. stricken in years, 18.
6 : 26. woe when all speak w. of you
13 : 9.if it bear fruit, w., if not, cut
20 : 39. Master, thou hast w. said
Jn. 2 : 10.when men have w. drunk
4 :17. hast w. said, I have no husb.
8:48.Say we not w., thou hast devil
13 : 13. Ye call me Lord, ye say w.
18 : 23.if w., why smitest thou me?
Ac.10 :33. hast w. done, th.art come
15 : 29. ye shall do w. Fare ye w.
Ro.11: 20.w.; bec.of unbelief brok.
1 Co. 7 :37 keep his virgin, doeth w.
38. giveth in marriage, doeth w.
14:17.thou verily givest thanks w.
2 Co. 6 :9. As unknown yet w. kno.
11 : 4. ye might w. bear with him
Ga.4 :17.zealously affect, but not w.
5:7.Ye did run w.; who did hinder
Ph. 4 : 14. ye have w. done, that
ye did communicate ⌈house
1 Ti. 3 : 4. One that ruleth w. his
12. ruling own houses w. ⌈chase
13. used office of deacon w., pur-
5 : 17. elders that rule w., worthy
Tit. 2 : 9. to please them w. in all
Ja. 2 : † 3.and say, Sit thou here, w.
As WELL. ⌈in land
Le. 24 : 16.a.w. stranger as he born
22. one law a.w. for stranger as
De. 1 :17. sh. hear small a.w. as gr.
3 : 20. rest unto breth. a.w.as you
5 : 14. maidserv. rest a.w. as thou
20 : 8. lest heart faint a.w. as his
Ju. 20 : 48.smote a.w. men as beast

2 S. 6 : 19. a.w. to women as men
11 : 25. devoureth one a.w. as ano.
1 Ch. 25 : 8.a.w. the small as great,
the teacher as the scholar⌈small
2 Ch. 31 :15. to give a.w. to great as
Jb.12 : 3. I understand a.w. as you
Ps. 87 : 7. a.w. singers as players
Eze.47 : 14.inherit, one a.w. as ano.
Ac.10 : 47.which have received Holy
Ghost a.w. as we⌈oth. apostles
1 Co. 9 : 5. to lead sister a.w. as
He. 4 : 2. unto us gospel a.w. as
WELL beloved. ⌈w.b.
Can. 1 : 13. A bundle of myrrh is my
Is. 5 : 1. I will sing to my w.b. a
song. My w.b. hath a vineyard
Mk. 12 : 6. Having one son, his w.
b., he sent him
Ro. 16 : 5.Salute my w.b. Epenetus
3 Jn. 1. elder unto the w.b. Gaius
See DEALT, DOEST, FAREWELL.
See **DO well, Well DOING,**
Well FAVOURED,
Well PLEASED,
Well PLEASING.
See PLEASED, REPORTED.
WELL with thee. ⌈w.-
Ge. 32 : 9. Return, and I will deal
40 : 14. think on me when w.-
De. 4 : 40. that it may go w.- and
thy children, 5 : 16.-6 : 3, 18.-
12 : 25, 28.-19 : 13.-22 : 7. Ru.
3 : 1. Ep. 6 : 3. ⌈he is w.-
15 : 16. will not go away; because
2 K. 4 : 26.Is it w.-? she ans-d, It is
Ps. 128 : 2. and it shall be w.- ⌊w.
Very WELL knowest.
Ac. 25 : 10. have I done no wrong, as
thou v.w.k. ⌈k.v.w,
2 Ti. 1 : 18.ministered unto me, thou
WELL. [Noun.]
Ge. 16 : 14. w. called Beer-lahai-roi
21 : 30. witn. I have digged this w.
24 :16.damsel went down to the w.
20.she ran again unto w. to draw
29. Laban ran out unto the w.
30. he stood by camels at the w.
42. I came this day unto the w.
45. Rebekah went down unto w.
62.Isaac came fr. way of w. Lahai.
25 : 11.Isaac dwelt by w. Lahai-roi
26 : 20. Isaac called the w. Esek
21. Isaac's servants digged another w., 22, 25. ⌈cerning w.
32. Isaac's servants told him con-
29 : 2. Jacob looked, and behold a
w., out of that w. they watered
flocks (3) ⌈mouth, (2) 8, 10.
3. they rolled the stone from w.'s
49 : 22. Joseph fruitful bough by a
Ex.2 : 15.Moses sat down by w.⌊w.
Nu. 21 : 16. is w. wh-f the L. spake
17. Isr. sang this song, Spring up,
18. princes digged w. ⌊O w.
Ju.7 : 1.Gid-n pitched by w. of Ha.
1 S.19 :22.Saul to great w. in Sechu
2 S.3 :26.bro-t Abner fr. w. of Sirah
17 : 18. man had w. in his court
19. covering over the w.'s mouth
21. they came out of w., told Da.
1 K. 1 : † 9. slew sheep by w. Rogel
Ps. 84 : 6.who passing through Baca
make it a w. ⌈is w. of life
Pr. 10 : 11. mouth of righteous man
Jn. 4 : 6. Now Jacob's w. was there,
Jesus, wearied, sat thus on w.
11. woman saith, the w. is deep
12.greater than Jacob wh.gave the
See **DRAGON well.** ⌊w.?
WELL, S, with water, s.
Ge. 21 : 19. Hagar saw a w. of w.
25.reproved Abimelech because of
w. of w. ⌈of w.
24 : 11. made camels kneel by w.
13.I stand here by a w. of w., 43.
26 : 18. Isaac digged again the w-s
of w.; Philis. had stopped them

Ge. 26 : 19. servants found a w. of
springing w. ⌈w-s of w.
Ex. 15 : 27. Elim, where were twelve
Nu. 20 : 17. nei. will we drink of w.
of w-s, 21 : 22. ⌈of Nephtoah
Jos. 18 : 15. went out to w. of w-s
2 S. 23 : 15. Oh that one would give
me drink of w. of w. of Bethlehem, 1 Ch. 11 : 17.
16. three mighty men drew w.
out of w. of Beth-m, 1 Ch. 11. 18.
2 K. 3 : 19. sh. stop all w-s of w., 25.
Pr. 5 : 15. Drink w-s out of own w.
Can. 4 : 15. w. of living w-s fr. Leb-n
Is. 12 : 3. draw w. out of w-s of salva.
Jn. 4 : 14. shall be in him a w. of w.
2 Pe. 2 : 17. These are w-s with-t w.

WELLS. ⌈digged
Ge. 26 : 15. all w. Abr.'s servants
De. 6 : 11. to give thee w. which
thou diggedst not, Ne. 9 : 25.
2 Ch. 26 : 10. Uzziah digged many w.

WELLSPRING. ⌈life
Pr. 16 : 22. Understanding is w. of
18 : 4. w. of wisd. as flowing brook

WEN.
Le. 22 : 22. maimed, or having a w.

WENCH.
2 S. 17 : 17. a w. told Jonathan and

WENT.
Ge. 7 : 18. ark w. upon face of waters
9 : 23. Shem, Japheth w. backward
13 : 3. Abr. w. on his journeys to B.
5. Lot, wh. w. with Abram, had
herds, 12 : 4. ⌈with me
14 : 24. portion of men which w.
18 : 22. men turned, w. tow. Sodom
21 : 16. Hagar w. sat down ov. ag.
19. she w., filled bottle with water
22 : 3. Abr. w. unto place God told
6. Abr. and Isaac w. both, 8. ⌈sheba
19. Abr., young men w. to Beer-
25 : 22. Rebekah w. to inquire of L.
26 : 1. Isaac w. unto Abimelech k.
26. Abim. w. to Isaac from Gerar
27 : 5. Esau w. to hunt venison
14. Jacob w. bro-t them to mother
22. Jacob w. near Isaac his father
28 : 5. Jacob w. to Padan-aram
10. Jacob w. toward Haran ⌈came
29 : 1. Jacob w. on his journey,
10. Jacob w. near, rolled stone fr.
30 : 14. Reub. w., found mandrakes
31 : 19. Laban w. to shear his sheep
35 : 22. Reuben w., lay with Bilhah
36 : 6. Esau took wives, w. fr. Jacob
37 : 12. brethren w. to feed flock
17. Joseph w. after his brethren
38 : 11. Tamar w., dwelt in father's
50 : 18. brethren w. fell bef. his face
Ex. 2 : 8. maid w. called child's moth.
4 : 18. Mos. w. to Jethro his fa. in law
27. Aaron w., met Moses in mount
29. Moses, Aaron w. gath-d elders
14 : 19. pillar of cloud w. fr. before
15 : 22. w. 3 days in wildern., Nu. 33:
38 : 26. that w. to be numbered ⌊8.
40 : 36. Isr. w. onward in journeys
Le. 9 : 8. Aa. w. unto altar, slew calf
10 : 5. they w. near, carried them out
Nu. 10 : 14. first w. standard of Jud.
13 : 26. Mos. sent to spy la.: they w.
14 : 24. Caleb into land wh-into he
16 : 25. Moses w. unto Dathan ⌊w.
20 : 6. Moses, Aaron w. fr. assembly
21 : 16. from thence they w. to Beer
22 : 14. princes of Moab w. unto B.
21. Balaam, w. wi. princes of Moab,
22. God's anger bec. he w. ⌊35. 39.
26. angel of L. w. further, stood
23 : 3. Balaam w. to a high place
24 : 1. Balaam w. not to seek en-
25. Balaam w. to his pl. ⌊chantm-ts
31 : 21. said unto men wh. w. to bat.
33 : 23. w. from and pitched in, 29, 33.
De. 29 : 26. they w. served oth. gods
31 : 1. Moses w. spake unto Israel
De. 31 : 14. Joshua w. presented
33 : 2. from right hand w. fiery law
Jos. 2 : 5. whi. men w., I wot not (2)
22. men w. unto mt. abode 3 days
5 : 13. Josh. w., said, Art thou for
6 : 13. seven priests w. on continu-
8 : 9. they w. to lie in ambush ⌊ally
9 : 4. w. made as if ambassadors
6. they w. to Joshua at Gilgal ⌈w.
10 : 24. Joshua said to captains wh.
18 : 8. them th. w., to describe land
22 : 6. Gadites w. unto tents ⌊(2) 9.
Ju. 1 : 3. So Simeon w. with Judah
17. Judah w. with Simeon his bro.
2 : 6. w. ev. man unto his inherit-e
3 : 13. Eglon w. and smote Israel
4 : 21. Jael w. softly, smote the nail
8 : 29. Jerub. w. dwelt in own hou.
9 : 1. Abimelech w. to Shechem
5. Abimelech w. slew his brethren
6. men of Shechem w. made A. k.
7. Jotham w., stood in top of Ger.
21. Jotham w. to Beer for fear of
52. Abim-h w. unto door of tower
11 : 5. elders w. to fetch Jeph-h, 11.
38. she w. bewailed her virginity
40. dau-s of Isr. w. yearly to lament
12 : 1. men of Ephr. w. northward
14 : 9. Samson took and w. on eating
15 : 4. Samson w. caught 300 foxes
11. then 3,000 men w. to top of E.
16 : 1. Then w. Samson to Gaza
19. and his strength w. from him
18 : 11. there w. of Danites 600 men
14. ans-d the 5 men th. w. to spy, 17.
19 : 18. Levite said, I w. to Beth-leh.
21 : 23. chil. of Benj. w. unto inherit.
Ru. 1 : 1. certain man w. to Moab
19. they two w. to Beth-lehem
2 : 3. Ruth w. gleaned in the field
3 : 7. Boaz w. to lie down at heap
1 S. 2 : 11. Elkanah w. to Ramah
20. Elkanah and wife w. home
3 : 5. Samuel w. and lay down, 9.
7 : 16. Sam-l w. in circuit to Beth-el
9 : 9. when man w. to inquire of G.
10. w. unto city where man of God
10 : 14. Saul's uncle said, Whi. w.
26. Saul w. home to Gibeah 15 :
34.–24 : 22. ⌈Saul king
11 : 15. people w. to Gilgal, made
14 : 16. w. on beat-g down one ano.
19. noise in host of Philis. w. on
46. Philis. w. to their own pla. (2)
15 : 34. Samuel w. to Ramah, 16 : 13.
17 : 12. Jesse w. for an old man in
13. eldest sons of Jesse w. to bat.
15. David w. to feed father's sheep
20. David w. as Jesse commanded
19 : 12 Michal let Dav. down : he w.
18. Dav., Sam. w. dwelt in Naioth
22. w. Saul to Ramah and asked
23. Saul w. to Naioth in Ramah (2)
22 : 3. David w. to Mizpeh ⌈fought
23 : 5. David and men w. to Keilah,
13. David and men w. whitherso.
18. Jonathan w. to his own hou.
25. Saul and men w. to seek him,
26. Saul w. on this side mt ⌊24 : 2.
28 : 8. Saul w. to the woman by ni.
30 : 9. Dav. w. and 600 men to Besor
22. men of Belial that w. with
David said, Bec. they w. not
2 S. 1 : 4. David said, How w. matter
2 : 32. Joab w. all night to Hebron
3 : 19. Abner w. to speak in ears of
21. Dav. sent Ab. aw.; w. in peace
4 : 5. sons of Rimmon w. to Ish-bo.
5 : 6. king and his men w. to Jerus.
10. David w. on and grew great
6 : 12. Dav. w., bro-t up ark of God
7 : 23. what nation like Israel wh.
God w. to redeem, 1 Ch. 17 : 21.
8 : 3. David smote Hadadezer as he
w. to recover, 1 Ch. 18 : 3.
6. Lord preserved David whithersoever he w., 14. 1 Ch. 18 : 6, 13.
2 S. 11 : 21. Why w. ye nigh wall?
22. messenger w. shewed Dav. all
13 : 8. Tamar w. to Amnon's house
19. rent her garment, w. on cry-g
37. Absalom fled, w. to Talmai | 38.
15 : 11. with Abs. w. 200 men out
of Jerus.; they w. in simplicity
16 : 13. Shimei cursed as he w. (3)
17 : 17. wench w., told them (2). 21.
18 : 9. mule w. und. boughs of oak
33. as he w., he said, O my son A.
19 : 40. k. w. to Gilgal, Chim-m w.
20 : 5. Amasa w. to assemble Judah
22. woman w. unto peo. in wisdom
23 : 17. blood of men th. w. in jeop-
1 K. 2 : 8. cursed me when I w. ⌊ardy
19. Bath-sheba w. unto Sol. for A.
3 : 4. king w. to Gibeon to sacrifice
8 : 66. people blessed king, w. joyf.
10 : 13. q. of Sheba w. to her country
16. 600 shekels of gold w. to one
target, 2 Ch. 9 : 15.
17. three pounds of gold w. to one
shield, 2 Ch. 9 : 16. ⌈dwelt
11 : 24. they w. to Damascus, and
12 : 1. Rehoboam w. to Shechem,
2 Ch. 10 : 1. ⌈before the one
30. for the people w. to worship
13 : 28. w., found her carcass in way
16 : 31. Ahab w. and served Baal
17 : 5. Elijah w. acc. unto word of
L.; he w. dwelt by brook Cher.
15. she w., did acc. to saying of E.
18 : 2. Elijah w. to shew himself
16. Obadiah w. to meet Ahab (2)
45. Ahab rode, w. to Jezreel ⌈ed
20 : 43. king w. to house displeas-
21 : 27. Ahab heard, he w. softly
22 : 24. Zed-h w. near smote Mic-h
48. they w. not, ships were broken
2 K. 2 : 1. Elijah w. with Elisha from
6. And they two w. on, 11. ⌊Gilgal
7. fifty sons of prophets w. to view
25. Elisha w. fr. thence to Carmel
3 : 7. Jehoram w., sent to Jehosh-t
9. k. of Israel w. and k. of Judah
4 : 5. she w. fr. him and shut door
25. w. unto man of G. to Carmel
5 : 25. Gehazi said, Thy serv. w. no
26. w. not mine heart with thee?
6 : 4. w. with them, they cut wood
23. eaten, they w. to their master
7 : 8. lepers w., hid silver, gold (3)
8 : 2. w. with her household in land
9. Hazael w. to meet Elisha ⌊of P.
28. Ahaziah w. to war ag. Hazael
9 : 4. yo. prophet w. to Ramoth-gil.
16. Jehu w. to Jezreel; Joram lay
18. w. one on horseback to meet
35. they w. to bury Jezebel ⌊him
10 : 25. captains w. to city of Baal
16 : 10. Ahaz w. to Damas. to meet
19 : 36 Sennacherib w. and dwelt
at Nin-h, Is. 37 : 37. ⌈1 Ch. 34 : 22.
22 : 14. w. unto Huldah prophetess,
1 Ch. 4 : 39. w. to Gedor to seek past.
42. sons of Simeon, 500 w. to m-t
7 : 23. name Beriah bec. it w. ill ⌊Seir
11 : 4. Dav. and all Isr. w. to Jerus.
12 : 20. as David w. to Ziklag ⌈ark
15 : 25. David with elders w. to bri.
16 : 20. when they w. from nation
to nation, Ps. 105 : 13. ⌈men
19 : 5. w. certain told David how
2 Ch. 1 : 3. Sol-n and congr-n w. to
8 : 3. Sol. w. to Hamath-zobah ⌊Gib.
17. w. Sol-n to Eloth, at sea side
18. w. with serv-s of Sol. to Ophir
9 : 21. king's ships w. to Tarshish
10 : 16. all Israel w. to their tents
12 : 12. in Judah things w. well
18 : 12. messenger w. to call Mic.
23 : 17. peo. w. to hou. of Baal, brake
25 : 11. Amaziah w. to valley of salt
30 : 6. posts w. with letters fr. king
Ne. 2 : 14. I w. on to gate of fountain
16. rulers knew not whither I w.

Ne. 12 : 31. one w. on right hand
32. after them w. half of princes
Es.2 :14.In evening she w., on mor.
Jb. 1 :4.his sons w.feasted in houses
30 : 28.I w. mourning without sun
42 : 9. Zophar w. did acc-g as Lord
Ps. 42 : 4.I w. wi. them to ho. of God
106 : 32. w. ill with Moses lor their
Pr. 24 : 30. I w. by field of slothful
Is. 8 : 3. I w. unto the prophetess
Je. 3 : 8. sister w. played the harlot
7 : 24. Isr.w.backward,not forward
13 : 5. I w. hid it by Euphrates, 7.
31 :2.when I w. to cause Isr.to rest
40 : 6. w. Jeremiah unto Gedaliah
41 : 6. Ishmael w. as he w. (2)⌈|14.
12.took men, w. to fight Ishmael,
15.Ishmael escaped,w. to Amm-s
44 : 3. they w. to burn incense and
Eze. 1 : 9.they turned not when they
w.; they w. every one straight
forward, 12, 17.-10 : 11. (2) 22.
12. whither the spirit was to go,
they w., 20. ⌈10 : 11. (2)
17. they w. upon four sides (2).
19. living creatures w.,wheels w.
21. When those w. these w.
24. when they w. I heard wings
3 : 14. I w. in bitterness, in heat of
10 : 16. cherubim w. wheels w.
36 : 20. whither they w. they profaned my name, 21, 22. ⌈post
41 : 3. w. he inward measured
7.winding about of house w.upw.
Da. 2 : 17. Daniel w. to his house
6 : 18. king w. to his palace; his
sleep w. from him⌈to Assyrian
Ho. 5 : 13.Ephr. saw his sickness w.
9 :10. your fathers w. to Baal-peor
11 : 2. called them, so they w.from
IIa. 3 : 5. Bef. him w. pestilence (2)
11.at light of thine arrows they w.
Mat. 13 : 46. w. and sold all he had
14 : 12.buried it, w. and told Jesus
18 : 30. w. and cast him into prison
21 : 6.disciples w.did as Jes.comm.
29. afterward he repented and w.
30. he said, I go, sir, but w. not
25 : 10. w.to buy,bridegroom came
16.five talents, w. traded wi.same
18.received one,w.hid money, 25.
26 : 14. Judas w. unto the chief
priests, Mk. 14 : 10.⌈Mk. 14 : 35.
39. w. a little further and prayed,
27 : 5. Judas w. hanged himself
58. Joseph w. to Pilate, begged
body of Jesus, Lu. 23 : 52. ⌈sure
66. So w. and made the sepulchre
28 : 9. w. to tell disciples, Jesus met
Mk. 2 : 23.began as they w.to pluck
6 : 27. he w. and beheaded John in
16 : 10. Mary w.and told them that
13.w. and told it unto the residue
Lu. 2 : 3. w. to be taxed, every one
41.parents w.to Jerus. every year
44. supposing him in company w.
5 : 19. w. upon housetop, let him
8 : 2.Mary M.out of whom w.seven
34. fled and w. and told it in city
42. as he w. people thronged him
9 : 56. they w. to another village
10 :34.w.to him,bound up wounds
38. as they w. he entered village
14 : 25.w. great multitudes wi.him
15 : 15. w.joined hims. to a citizen
16 :30.if one w. unto them fr. dead
17 : 11. as he w. to Jerus.he passed
14. as they w. they were cleansed
19 :36. as he w.they spread clothes
22 : 13. they w. found as he said
39.w. as was wont to m-t of Olives
24 :13.two w. that day to Emmaus
15. Jesus drew near w.with them
24. certain of them w.to sepulch.
28. drew nigh village whi. they w.
Jn. 4 : 45. Galileans w. unto feast
47. nobleman w. unto Jesus

Jn. 6 : 21. ship at land whi. they w.
7 : 53.every man w. unto own hou.
9 : 11. I w., washed, received sight
11 : 20. Martha w. and met Jesus
13 :3. he was fr. God and w. to God
18 : 6.they w.backw.fell to ground
Ac. 4 : 23. w. to their own company
5 :26.w.captain and brought them
8 : 4. they w. everywhere preach-g
9 : 1. Saul w. unto the high priest
10 : 9. as they w. on their journey,
Peter w. up to pray ⌈the work
15 : 38. Mark w. not with them to
16 : 16.as we w. to prayer a damsel
21 : 2. finding a ship we w. aboard
16.w.with us disciples of Cæsarea
22 : 5. I w. to Damascus to bring
26. centurion w. and told captain
26 : 12. I w. to Damascus with au-
28 : 14.so we w.tow. Rome⌊thority
1 Co. 10 : † 4. drank of Rock that w.
2 Co. 8 : 17. of own accord Titus w.
1 Pe. 3 : 19. he w.preached unto the
Re. 10 : 9. I w. unto angel ⌈spirits
12 : 17. dragon w. to make war
16 : 2. first w. poured out his vial

WENT about. ⌈it

Nu. 11 : 8.people w.a. and gathered
Jos. 16 : 6.the border w.a. eastward
1 K. 18 : † 35. water w.a. the altar
2 K. 3 : 25. slingers w.a. it, smote it
2 Ch.17 : 9.they w.a. taught people
23 : 2. they w.a. gathered Levites
Ec. 2 : 20. I w.a. to cause my heart
Can. 5 : 7. the watchmen that w.a.
found me ⌈21 : 31.-26 : 21.
Ac. 9 : 29. they w.a. to slay him,
13 : 11. he w.a. seeking some to
See Jesus WENT. ⌊lead

WENT abroad.

1 S. 9 :26.w. out, Saul and Sam-l a.
2 Ch. 26 : † 8. Uzziah's name w.a.
Ps. 77 : 17. thine arrows also w.a.
Mat. 9 : 26. fame hereof w.a. into
Lu. 5 : 15. much more w. fame a.
Jn. 21 : 23. w. this saying a. among

WENT after. ⌊breth.

Ge. 37 : 17. Joseph w.a. his breth.
Ex.15 : 20.women w. out a. Miriam
Nu. 25 : 8. he w.a. the man of Isr.
Jos. 8 : 17. not a man in Ai that w.
not out a. Israel ⌈the kine
1 S. 6 : 12. lords of Philistines w.a.
25 : 42.five damsels that w.a. her;
Abigail w.a. messengers of Da.
2 S. 11 : †8. w.out a. Uriah meat fr.
20 :7.w.out a.ShebaJoab's men(2)
13. all the peo. w. on a. Joab, 14.
1 K.11 : 5. Solomon w.a. Ashtoreth
6. Sol-n w. not fully a. the Lord
13 : 14. prophet w.a. man of God
2 K. 7 : 15. they w.a. them unto J.
17 : 15. became vain w.a. heathen
Je. 11 : 10. they w.a. other gods
Eze. 20 : 16. their heart w.a. idols
Ho. 2 :13. w.a. her lovers, forgat L.
Mk.1 : 20.left fath.in ship,w.a. Jes.
See WENT with arose, in, out.

WENT again. ⌈s.

1 S. 25 : 12. David's young men w.
2 K. 4 : 31.Gehazi w.a. to meet him
2Ch.19:4.Jehosh-t w.a.thro.people
Mk. 2 : 13. he w.forth a.by sea side
Jn. 10 : 40. he w.a. beyond Jordan
19 : 4. Pilate w. forth a. and saith
9. Pilate w.a. into judgment hall

WENT against.

Nu. 21 : 23. Sihon w. out a. Israel
33. Og of Bashan w. out a. them
Jos. 8 : 14. men of Ai w. out a. Isr.
Ju. 1 : 10. Judah w.a. Canaanites
11. he w.a. inhabitants of Debir
22. ho. of Joseph w.up a. Beth-el
20 :20.men of Israel w. out a.Benj.
25. Benj. w.forth a. them of Gib.
30. chil. of Israel w. up a. Benj.
31. chil. of Benj. w. out a. people

1 S. 4 : 1. Israel w.out a.Philistines
7 : 7. lords of Philist-s w.up a. Isr.
23 : 28.Saul w.a.Philistines⌈10 : 3.
31 : 3. battle w. sore a. Saul, 1 Ch.
2 S. 18 : 6. peo. w. into field a. Israel
21 : 15. David w. down a. Philist-s
1 K. 15 : 17. Baasha w. up a. Judah
20 : 27.chil.of Isr. w.a. the Syrians
2 K. 9 : 21. Joram and Ahaziah w.
out a. Jehu, (2). 2 Ch. 22 : 7.
23 : 29. Pharaoh-nechoh w. up a.
king of Assyria, Josiah w. a.
him, 2 Ch. 35 : 20. ⌈tines
1 Ch. 14 : 8. David w. out a. Philis-
2 Ch. 14 : 10. Asa w. out a. Zerah
22 : 5. Ahaziah w. to war a. Hazael
7. Ahaziah w. out wi. Jehoram a.
26 : 6. Uzziah w. forth a. Philist-s
Ne.12 : 38.other company w.over a.
See WENT and took.

WENT along. ⌈hand

Jos. 17 : 7. border w.a. on the right
Ju. 11 :18.they w. a. thro. wildern.
1 S.6 :12.kine w.a.,lowing as th. w.
2 S. 3 : 16. husband w. with her a.
16 : 13. Shimei w.a. on hill's side,
cursed as he w. ⌈a. as he w.
Je. 41 : 6. Ishmael w. weeping all

Arose and WENT.

Ge. 24 : 10. he - w. to Mesopotamia
38 : 19. Tamar - w. away, laid by
Jos. 18 : 8. the men - w. away ⌊vail
Ju. 4 : 9. Deborah - w. with Barak
13 : 11. Manoah - w. after his wife
19 : 3.husband - w. aft. her to spe.
20 :18.Israel - w. up to house of G.
1 S. 3 : 6. Samuel - w. to Eli, 8.⌈200
18 : 27. David - w., slew Philist-s
21 : 10. David - w. to Achish king
23 ; 16. Jonathan - w. unto David
24. Ziphites - w. to Ziph bef. Saul
24 : 8. David - w. out of the cave
25 : 1. David - w. down to wildern.
26 : 2. Saul - w.down to wild-s of Z.
31 : 12. valiant men - w. all night
2 S. 2 : 15. Then - w. ov. 12 of Benj.
6 : 2.David - w. to bring ark of God
12 : 17. elders - w. to David to raise
14 : 23. Joab - w. and brought Abs.
15 : 9. So Absalom - w. to Hebron
1 K.1 : 50.Adonijah -w. and caught
hold on horns of altar ⌈servants
2 : 40. Shimei - w. to Gath to seek
14 : 4. Jerob-'s wife - w. to Shiloh
17 : 10. Elijah - w. to Zarephath
19 : 3.Elijah -w. for his life to Bee.
8. Elijah - w. in strength of meat
21.Elisha -w. after Elijah,minist.
2 K. 1 : 15.Elijah - w. down to king
9 : 6. Jehu - w. into the house ⌈L.
Eze. 3 : 23.I - w. into plain: glory of
Da. 6 : 19.king -w.in haste unto den
Jon. 3 : 3.Jonah - w. unto Nineveh
Mk. 2 : 12.he - w. forth before them
7 : 24. he - w. into borders of Tyre
Lu. 1 : 39. Mary - w.into hill coun.
Ac. 8 : 27. Philip -w. ; beh. eunuch
9 : 39. Then Peter - w. with them.

WENT aside.

Lu. 9 : 10.Jesus took them and w.a.
Ac. 23 :19. chief capt. took him,w.a.

WENT astray. ⌈w.a.

Ps. 119 : 67. Before I was afflicted I
Eze. 44 : 10. Isr. w.a. aft. idols, 15.
48 : 11.be for priests which w. not
a. when children of Israel w.
a. as Levites w.a. ⌈w. not a.
Mat. 18 : 13. of ninety and nine wh.

WENT away. ⌈did

Ex. 12 : 28. chil. of Israel w.a. and
Ju. 16 : 3. Samson w.a. with doors
14. w.a. with the pin of the beam
19 : 2. his concubine w.a. fr. him
1 S. 28 : 25. they rose, w.a. th. night
2S.17 :18.w. both of them a. quickly
18 : 9.mule that was und.him w.a.
2 K. 5 : 11.Naaman wroth, w.a.,12.

2 K.12 :18. Hazael w.a. from Jerus.
2 Ch.9 : 12.queen of Sheba w.a.[22.
Mat.19 : 22.w.a. sorrowful, Mk.10 :
26 :42.he w.a. second time,prayed
44. he w.a. third time, Mk.14:39.
28 : 16. eleven w.a. into Galilee
Jn. 10 : 40. he w.a. beyond Jordan
12 : 11. by him many Jews w.a.
20:10.discip-s w.a.unto own home
Ac. 10 :23. on the morrow Pet. w.a.
See Arose and WENT.

WENT back.

Ju. 18 :26.Micah w.b. into his hou.
1 K. 13 : 19. So he w.b. did eat and
2 K. 2 :13.Elisha w.b.,stood by Jor.
8 :29.king Joram w.b.to be healed
Jn. 6 : 66. time many disciples w.b.

WENT before. [cloud

Ex. 13 : 21. Lord w.b. them in a
14 : 19.Angel of God wh.w.b.camp
Nu. 10 : 33.ark w.b. them, Jos.3:6.
Jos.6 :9. armed men w.b.priests,13.
1 S.17:7.one bearing shield w.b.,41.
2 S. 6 : 4. Ahio w.b.the ark[19 : 16.
10 : 16. Shobach w.b. them, 1 Ch.
20 : 8.at Gibeon, Amasa w.b. them
2 Ch. 20 : 21.as they w. out b.army
28 : 9 Oded w. out b. host [ed
Jb. 18 :20. that w.b. were affright-
Ps. 68 : 25.The singers w.b.,players
Mat. 2 : 9. star they saw w.b. them
21 : 9. multitudes that w.b. them
cried, Hosanna, Mk. 11 : 9.
Mk. 2 : 12. took bed, w. forth b. all
10 : 32. to Jerus.; Jesus w.b. them
Lu.18 :39.they which w.b. rebuked
19 :28.he w.b. ascending to Jerus.
22 : 47. Judas w.b., drew near to
Ac. 20 : 13. we w.b. to ship, sailed
1 Ti. 1 : 18. acc. to prophecies which

WENT behind. [w.b.

Ex. 14 : 19. Angel of God removed,

WENT down. [w.b.

Ge. 12 : 10. Abram w.d. into Egypt
24 : 16. damsel w.d. to well, 45.
38 : 1. Judah w.d. fr. his brethren
42 : 3. ten breth. w.d. to buy corn
43 : 15. w.d. to Eg., stood bef. Jos.
Ex. 19 :14.Moses w.d. from mount,
25.-32 : 15. [into pit
Nu. 16 : 33. They and all w.d. alive
20 : 15.and fathers w.d. into Eg-t,
dwelt, De. 10:22.-26:5. Jos.24:4.
Jos.15 : 10.border w.d.to Beth-she.
16 : 7. border w.d. from Janohah
18 : 18. border w.d. unto Arabah
Ju. 1 : 9.Judah w.d. to fight Can-s
3 : 27. Israel w.d. after Ehud, 28.
4 : 14. Barak w.d. from m-t Tabor
7 : 11. Gideon w.d. with Phurah
14:1.Samson w.d.to Timnath,5,7.
10. his father w.d. unto woman
19. he w.d. to Ashkelon, slew 30
15 : 8. he w.d. dwelt in rock Etam
† 11. Then 3,000 men w.d. to top
Ru. 3 : 6. Ruth w.d. unto the floor
1 S.13 :20.Israelites w.d.to sharpen
22 : 1. his brethren w.d. to David
2 S. 5 : 17. David w.d. to the hold
11 :9.Uriah w.not d. to ho .,10,13.
17 : 18. a well, whither they w.d.
23 : 13. three of the thirty chief w.
d. to David, 1 Ch. 11 : 15.
20. Benaiah w.d., slew a lion in
21. Benaiah w.d. to Egyptian,
slew him, 1 Ch. 11 : 22, 23.
1 K. 1 : 38. Zadok w.d. caused Sol.
2 K. 1 : 15. Elijah w.d. with him to
2 :2. Elijah, Elisha w.d.to Beth-el
3 : 12.king of Edom w.d. to Elisha
5 :14.Naaman w.d.dipped in Jord.
8 : 29. Ahaziah w.d. to see Joram,
bec. sick, 2 Ch. 22 : 6. [bones
13 : † 21.when man w.d., touched
2 Ch. 18 : 2. Jehosh-t w.d. to Ahab
Ps. 133 : 2.ointm-t th. w.d. to skirts
Can. 6 : 11.I w.d. into gard.of nuts

Is. 52 : 4. My peo. w.d. into Egypt
Je 18 : 3. I w.d. to potter's house
36:12.Michaiah w.d. into k-'s ho.
Eze. 31 : 15. when he w.d. to grave
31 : 17.They w.d. into hell wi.him
Jon. 1 : 3. Jonah w.d. to Joppa and
2 : 6. I w.d. to bottoms of the mts.
Lu. 2 :51. And he w.d. to Nazareth
10 : 30. certain man w.d.fr.Jerus.
18 : 14. this man w.d. justified
Jn. 2 : 12 Aft.this he w.d.to Caper.
5 : 4. angel w.d. troubled water
6 : 16. his disciples w.d. unto sea
Ac. 7 : 15.So Jacob w.d.into Egypt,
8 : 5. Philip w.d. to Samaria[died
38.they both w.d. into the water
10 : 21.Peter w.d. to the men, said
12 : 19. Herod w.d. to Cesarea
14 : 25. preached,w.d.into Attalia
18 : 22. Paul w.d. to Antioch[him
20 : 10. Paul w.d., and embracing
25 : 6. Festus w.d. unto Cesarea
See WENT with against, arose.

SUN went down.
See SUN.

WENT forth. [f.

Ge. 8 : 7. Noah sent raven which w.
18. Noah w.f., his sons, wife, 19.
9 : 18. sons of Noah that w.f. were
10.11. Out of that land w.f.Asshur
11 : 31.they w.f. fr. Ur of Chaldees
12 : 5. they w.f. to go into Canaan
Nu. 11 : 31. w.f. a wind fr. the Lord
Nu. 26 : 4. children of Egypt which
w.f. out of Egypt, 33 : 1. [meet
31 : 13. Moses and princes w.f. to
Jos. 16 : † 1.lot of chil. of Jos-h w.f.
18 : 17. border w.f. to En-shemesh
Ju.3 : 23. Ehud w.f. thro. porch[(2)
9 : 8. trees w.f. to anoint a king
Ru.1 : 7. Naomi w.f.out of the place
1 S. 18 : 30. princes of Philist-s w.f.
30 : 21.they w.f. to meet David[(2)
2 S.15 : 16.king w.f.and househ.,17.
20 : 8. as Joab w. f. sword fell out
2 K. 2 : 21. Elisha w.f. into waters
8 : 3. woman w.f. to cry unto king
12:†12. all that w.f. for the house
18 :7.prospered whithers o. he w.f.
1 Ch. 12 : 33.such as w.f.to bat.,36.
2 Ch 20 : 20. w.f. into wildern-s of
Tekoa; as they w.f.Jehosh. st.
21 : 9. Jehoram w.f. with princes
Ne. 8 : 16. So peo. w.f. made booths
Es. 4 :6. Hatach w.f.unto Mordecai
5 : 9. w. Haman f. that day joyful
Jb. 1 : 12. Satan w.f. fr. Lord, 2 : 7.
Is. 37 : 36. angel w.f. smote 185,000
48 : 3.things w.f. out of my mouth
Je. 22 : 11.Shallum w.f. out of this
37 : 12.Jeremiah w.f. out of Jerus.
38 : 8.Ebed-melech w.f. out of k-'s
39 : 4.w.f. out of city by night, 52:
41 : 6. Ishmael w.f.from Mizpah[7.
Eze. 1 : 13 out of fire w.f. lightning
9 : 7. they w.f. and slew in city[en
16 : 14.thy renown w.f. am.heath-
24 :12. gr. scum w.not f.out of her
27 : 33. thy wares w.f. out of seas
47 : 3. when the man w.f. eastw-d
Da. 2 : 13. w.f. th. wise men be slain
Am. 5 : 3. The city wh w. out by a
thousand shall leave a hundred,
that which w.f. by a hundred
shall leave ten [feet
Ha. 3 : 5. burning coals w.f. at his
Zch. 2 : 3. angel that talked with me
w.f.,ano. w. out to meet him,
6 : 7. the bay w.f. thro.earth[5 : 5.
Mat. 13 : 3. Behold a sower w.f.
25 : 1.virgins w.f. to meet bridegr.
Mk. 6 : 24. she w.f. said unto moth.
14 : 16. his disciples w.f. into city
16 : 20. w.f. preached every where
Lu. 5 : 27. he w.f., saw a publican
8 : 27. when he w.f. to land, met

Jn. 12 : 13. Took branches, w.f. to
18 : 1. w.f. with discip-s ov Cedron
19 : 17. he bearing cross w.f. into
20 : 3.Peter w.f. and other disciple
21 : 3. They w.f. entered into ship
3 Jn. 7. for his name's sake w.f.
Re. 6 : 2. he w.f.conquering and to
See WENT with again, against, before, Jesus, through.

WENT forward.

Ge 26 : 13. Isaac w.f.,grew great
2 K. 3 : 24. w.f. smiting Moabites
Je. 7 : 24 Your fathers w.backward
and not f. [12.-10 : 22.
Eze. 1 : 9. w. every one straight f.,
Mk. 14 : 35 Jes. w.f.,fell on ground

WENT in or into. [sons

Ge. 7 : 7. Noah w.i-o ark and his
15. w.i. two and two of all flesh,9.
16. that w.i., w.i. male and fem.
19 : 33.firstborn w.i. lay with fath.
23 : 10.audience of all that w.i.,18.
31 : 33. Laban w.i-o Jacob's tent
36 : 6.Esau w.i-o country fr.Jacob
39 : 11. Joseph w.i-o house to do
Ex.5 : 1.Moses,w.i.told Pha-h,7 : 10.
7 : 23. Pha-h turned, w.i-o house
14 : 22. Israel w.i-o midst of sea
upon dry ground, 15 : 19. [19
23. Egyptians w.i. after them, 15:
15 : 22. w.out i-o wildern. of Shur
24 : 18. Moses w.i-o midst of cloud
34 : 34. when Moses w.i. bef. Lord
35.until Moses w.i. to speak with
40 : 32. When they w.i-o tent
Le. 9 : 23. Moses and Aaron w.i-o
tabernacle, Nu. 17 : 8. [place
16 : 23. when Aaron w.i-o the holy
Nu.8 : 22.w. Levites i. to do service
22 : 23. ass turned w.i-o the field
Jos. 2 : 1. they w.i-o harlot's house
6 :23.spies w.i.brought out Rahab
8 : 13. Joshua w. that night i-o val.
Ju. 1 :26. man w.i-o land of Hittites
3 : 22. haft w.i. after the blade
6 : 19. Gid. w.i. made ready a kid
9 : 27. men of She. w. out i-o fields,
and w.i-o house of their god
42. people w. out i-o the field [1.
17 : 10. Dwell with me. Levite w.
18 : 18. these w.i-o Micah's house
20. priest w.i. the midst of people
19 : 15. Levite w.i. to lodge in Gib.
Ru. 2 : 18. Ruth took it, w.i-o city,
1 S.20 .11.w.out both i-o field[3:15.
35. Jonathan w. out i-o the field
42. And Jonathan w.i-o the city
24 : 3. Saul w.i. to cover his feet
2 S. 7 : 18. w. David i., sat bef. Lord
12 :16. Dav. w.i. lay all night upon
1 K. 1 : 15. Bath-sheba w.i. unto k.
14 : 28. when king w.i-o hou. of L.
16 : 10. Zimri w.i. and killed Elah
18. Zimri w.i-o palace and burnt
19 : 4. Elijah w. day's journey i-o
20 : 39. Thy serv. w. out i-o battle
22 : 30. king disguised w.i o battle
2 K. 4 : 33. Elisha w.i. and prayed
37.Then she w.i. fell at his feet(2)
39. one w. out i-o field to gather
5 : 4. one w.i. told his lord, Thus
25. Gehazi w.i. stood bef. master
7 : 8. lepers w.i-o one tent, did eat
10 : 23. Jehu w.i-o house of Baal
24. they w.i. to offer sacrifices
11 : 18. w.i-o house of Baal, brake
19 : 1. Hezekiah rent clothes, w.
i-o house of Lord. Is. 37 : 1.
1 Ch.6:15.Jehozadak w.i-o captiv-y
14 : 17.fame of Dav. w.i-o all lands
2 Ch. 26 : 16. Uzziah w.i-o temple
17. Azariah priest w.i. after him
29 :16.w.i-o ho. of L. to cleanse,18.
Ezr. 5 :8.we w.i-o province of Judea
10 : 6.Ezra w.i-o chamb. of Johan.
Ne. 9 : 24. children w.i., possessed

Es. 7 : 7. king w.i-o palace garden
Ps. 73 : 17. Until I w.i-o sanctuary
Je. 26 : 21. Urijah fled, w.i-o Egypt
28 : 4. captives that w.i-o Babylon
36 : 20. they w.i. to king i-o court
38 : 11. Ebed-melech w.i-o ho. of k.
51 : 59. when Seraiah w.i-o Bab-n
Eze. 8 : 10. I w.i. and saw upon wall
9 : 2. six men w.i. stood by altar
10 : 2. man clothed wi. linen w.i.,
25 : 3. when Jud. w.i-o capt-y ⌊3,6.
39 : 23. w.i-o captivity for iniquity
Da. 2 : 16. Daniel w.i., desired of k.
24. Daniel w.i. unto Arioch
6 : 10. Daniel w.i-o house, prayed
Am. 5 : 19. man w.i-o house, serpent
Na. 3 : 10. she w.i-o captivity ⌊bit
Mat. 8 : 32. devils w.i-o the herd
11 : 7. What w. ye out i-o wilderness to see? Lu. 7 : 24.
12 : 9. he w.i-o their synagogue
13 : 2. that he w.i-o ship and sat
21 : 33. householder w.i-o a far country, Mk. 12 : 1. Lu. 19 : 12. -20 : 9. ⌈highways
22 : 10. those servants w. out i-o
25 : 10. ready w.i. to the marriage
26 : 30. they w. out i-o mount of Olives, Mk. 14 : 26. ⌈vants
58. Peter w.i. sat with the ser-
27 : 53. out of graves, w.i-o holy
Mk. 1 : 21. w.i-o Capernaum ⌊city
35. bef. day he w. out i-o solitary place, Lu. 4 : 42. ⌈God, Lu. 6 : 4.
2 : 26. how David w.i-o house of
3 : 19. twelve; they w.i-o a house
5 : 13. uncl. spirits w. out i-o swine
6 : 1. w. out i-o his own country
14 : 68. Peter w. out i-o the porch
15 : 43. Jos. w.i. boldly unto Pilate
16 : 12. two as they w.i-o country
Lu. 1 : 9 burn incense when he w.i.
4 : 16. he w. i-o synagogue on sab.
37. fame w. out i-o every place, 14.
6 : 12. w. out i-o mount-n to pray
7 : 11. he w.i-o city Nain, many disciples w. with him ⌈37.-14 : 1.
36. he w.i-o Pharisee's house, 11:
8 : 22. he w.i-o ship with disciples
9 : 52. they w.i-o village of Samaria
19 : 45. w.i-o temple, began to cast
24 : 29. he w.i. to tarry with them
Jn. 4 : 43. aft. two days w.i-o Galilee
18 : 15. that disciple w.i. with Jesus
28. they w. not i-o judgment hall
20 : 5. saw linen clothes, yet w. not i.
6. Then Peter w.i-o sepulchre
8. then w.i. that other disciple
Ac. 10 : 27. as Peter talked he w.i.
12 : 17. Peter w.i-o another place
13 : 14. they w.i-o synagogue on sa.
14 : 1. w. both i o synagogue of Jews
17 : 2. P. w.i-o synagogue, 10.-19 : 8.
21 : 18. Paul w.i. wi. us unto James
23 : 16. he w.i-o castle, told Paul
Ro. 10 : 18. sound w.i-o all the earth
2 Co. 2 : 13. I w. from thence i-o Macedonia, 1 Ti. 1 : 3. ⌈tabern.
He. 9 : 6. priests w. always i-o first
7. i-o second w. high priest alone

See **WENT** with **abroad, again, arose, down, forth, Jesus, out, took, up.**

WENT in to or in unto.

Ge. 16 : 4. Abram w. - Hagar ⌈- her
29 : 23. bro-t Leah to Jacob, he w.
30 And he w. - Rachel, loved R.
30 : 4. gave him Bilhah, he w. - her
38 : 2. Judah saw Shuah, w. - her
9. when Onan w. - brother's wife
Ju. 16 : 1. Sam-n saw harlot w. - her
Ru. 4 : 13. Boaz w. - Ruth, she conc.
2 S. 12 : 24. David w. - Bath-sheba, she bare Solomon ⌈concubines
16 : 22. Absalom w. - his father's
17 : 25. Ithra that w. - Abigail
20 : 3. Da. fed, but w. not i.u. them
1 Ch. 2 : 21. Hezron w. - daughter of
7 : 23. Ephraim w. - his wife ⌊Mac.
Eze. 23 : 44. Yet they w. - her as har- ⌊lot

Jesus WENT.

Mat. 3 : 16. J. w. up out of the water
4 : 23. J. w. about all Galilee teaching, 9 : 35. Mk. 6 : 6.
12 : 1. J. w. on sabbath day thro. the corn, Mk. 2 : 23. Lu. 6 : 1.
13 : 1. J. w. out of house, sat by sea
36. J. sent multitude, w. into ho.
14 : 14. J. w. forth, saw great multi.
25. J. w. unto them walk-g on sea
15 : 21. J. w. into coasts of Tyre
21 : 12. J. w. into temple, cast out all that sold, Mk. 11 : 15. ⌈8 : 59.
24 : 1. J. w. out from temple, Jn.
Mk. 5 : 24. J. w. with him; people
8 : 27. J. w. into towns of Cesarea
10 : 32. J. w. before them; they
Lu. 7 : 6. J. w. with them; centurion
24 : 15. J. drew near and w. wi. them
Jn. 2 : 13. J. w. up to Jerus-m, 5 : 1.
6 : 1. J. w. over sea of Galilee, 17.
3. J. w. up into a mt., there he sat
22. J. w. not wi. disciples into boat
7 : 14. J. w. up into temple, taught
8 : 1. J. w. unto mount of Olives
11 : 54. J. w. unto country near
18 : 4. J. w. forth, said, Whom seek
Ac. 1 : 21. time J. w. in and out am.
10 : 38. J. w. about doing good ⌊us

WENT out.

Ge. 2 : 10. And a river w.o. of Eden
4 : 16. Cain w.o. from presence of L.
13 : 1. Abram w. up o. of Egypt
14 : 8. w.o. king of Sodom and king
17. king of Sodom w.o. to meet
19 : 6. Lot w.o. at door unto them
14. Lot w.o. spake to sons in law
30. Lot w. up o. of Zoar and dwelt
24 : 63. Isaac w.o. to meditate in
28 : 10. Jacob w.o. fr. Beer-sheba
30 : 16. Leah w.o. to meet Jacob
31 : 33. Laban w.o. of Leah's tent
34 : 1. Dinah w.o. to dau-s of land
6. Hamor w.o. to commune with
24. all that w.o. of gate of city (2)
26. sons of Jacob took Dinah w.o.
41 : 46. Joseph w.o. from Pharaoh
43 : 31. Joseph w.o. refrained hims.
44 : 28. bare two sons: one w.o.
45 : 25. they w. up o. of Egypt into
47 : 10. Jacob w.o. from bef. Pha.
Ex. 2 : 11. Moses w.o. unto brethren
5 : 10. taskmasters of people w.o.
8 : 12. Moses and Aaron w.o. from Pha., 30.-9 : 33.-10 : 6, 18.-11 : 8.
12 : 41. hosts of L. w.o. from Egypt
13 : 18. Israel w. up o. of Egypt
14 : 8. children of Israel w.o. with a high hand, Nu. 33 : 3. ⌈(2)
15 : 22. w.o. into wilderness of Shur
16 : 27. w.o. some of peo. on 7th day
18 : 7. Moses w.o. to meet fa. in law
33 : 7. w.o. unto tabern. of congr-n
8. when Moses w.o. unto tabern.
Le. 10 : 2. then w.o. fire from Lord
24 : 10. son of Israelitish wom. w.o.
Nu. 10 : 34. cloud upon them when w.o. of camp ⌈words of L.
11 : 24. Moses w.o. told the people
26. two of men they w. not o.
22 : 32. I w.o. to withstand thee
36. Balak w.o. to meet Balaam
31 : 27. who w.o. to battle, 28. ⌈war
36. portion of them that w.o. to
Jos. 2 : 5. when dark, men w.o. (2)
6 : 1. Jericho; none w.o., none
11 : 4. they w.o. and all their hosts
15 : 3. border w.o. to Maaleh-acra.
4. thence it w.o. unto river of E.
9. border w.o. unto cities of Eph-n
11. border w.o. unto side of Ek. (2)
16 : 6. border w.o. to Michmethah on the north: w.o. ⌈Jordan
7. border came to Jericho, w.o. at
Jos. 16 : 8. border w.o. from Tappuah westw. unto river Kanah
18 : 15. the border w.o. to well of Nephtoah (2) ⌈for them
19 : 47. coast of Dan w.o. too little
Ju. 1 : 16. chil. of Kenite w. up o. of city of palm trees (2). ⌈them
2 : 15. Whitherso. they w.o. L. ag.
3 : 10. Othniel judged Israel, w.o.
19. all by Ehud w.o. from him
4 : 18. Jael w.o. to meet Sisera
9 : 35. Gael w.o. stood in gate, 39.
11 : 3. vain men to Jephthah, w. o. with him ⌈them
19 : 23. master of house w.o. unto
27. her lord w.o. to go his way
20 : 1. all Israel w.o. as one man
21 : 24. w.o. every man to inherit.
Ru. 1 : 21. I w.o. full, Lord bro-t me
1 S. 3 : 3. ere lamp of G. w.o. in tem.
7 : 11. men of Israel w.o. of Mizpeh
9 : 26. w.o. both, Saul and Samuel
18 : 10. Saul w.o. to meet Samuel
23. Philis. w.o. to passage of Mich.
17 : 4. w.o. champion of Philistines
35. I w.o. after him, smote him
18 : 5. David w.o. whitherso. Saul
13. he w.o., came in bef. peo., 16.
19 : 8. David w.o. fought wi. Philis.
2 S. 2 : 12. Abner w.o. to Gibeon ⌈o.
13. Joab and servants of David w.
11 : 13. Uriah w.o. to lie on his bed
17. men of city w.o. fought Joab
13 : 9. w.o. every man from Amnon
19 : 19. day my lord w.o. of Jerus.
24 : 4. Joab and captains w.o. from
7. w.o. even to Beer-sheba ⌊king
20. Araunah w.o. bowed bef. king
1 K. 2 : 46. Benaiah w.o. fell upon
10 : 29. w.o. of Eg. for 600 shekels
11 : 29. when Jerob. w.o. of Jerus.
12 : 25. Jeroboam w.o. built Penuel
19 : 13. Elijah face in mantle, w.o.
20 : 16. And they w.o. at noon
17. young men of provinces w.o.
21. king of Isr. w.o. slew Syrians
2 K. 3 : 6. Jehoram w.o. of Samaria
4 : 18. child w.o. to his father
21. she shut door upon him, w.o.
37. she took up her son and w.o.
5 : 27. he w.o. leper white as snow
7 : 16. people w.o. spoiled tents of
9 : 21. Joram, Ahaziah w.o. ag. (2)
24. arrow w.o. at his heart ⌈peo.
10 : 9. morning Jehu w.o. said to
13 : 5. Isr. w.o. from under Syrians
19 : 35. angel w.o. smote 185,000
24 : 12. k. of Judah w.o. to k. of B.
1 Ch. 5 : 18. 44,760 that w.o. to war
12 : 17. David w.o. to meet them
21 : 21. Ornan w.o. of threshingfl.
27 : 1. came in, w.o. month by m.
2 Ch. 15 : 2. Azariah w.o. to meet Asa
5. no peace to him that w.o. nor to him that came in, Zch 8 : 10.
19 : 2. Jehu w.o. to meet Jehosh-t
26 : 11. Uzziah had host w.o. to war
31 : 1. all Israel w.o. to cities of J.
Ne. 2 : 13. I w.o. by night, viewed
Es. 3 : 15. posts w.o., being hastened by king's comm-t, 8 : 14.
4 : 1. Mordecai w.o. into city, cried
7 : 8. as word w.o. of king's mouth
8 : 15. Mord. w.o. in royal apparel
Jb. 31 : 34. Did I fear that I w. not o.
Ps. 114 : 1. when Israel w.o. of Eg.
Je. 37 : 4. Jerem. came in w.o. am.
Eze. 10 : 7. took the fire, w.o. ⌊peo.
19. cherubim w.o. wheels were
Jon. 4 : 5. Jonah w.o. of city, sat
Mat. 8 : 5. w.o. to him Jerus. and
9 : 32. As they w.o. bro-t dumb man
12 : 14. Pharisees w.o. held couns.
18 : 28. servant w.o. and found one
20 : 1. w.o. early to hire labourers
3. he w.o. about 3d hour saw oth-s
21 : 17. he w.o. of city into Beth-y

Mat.26 : 75. Peter w.o. and wept bitterly, Lu. 22 : 62. [of Judea
Mk. 1 : 5. w.o. to him all the land
45. he w.o., began to blaze abroad
3 : 21. they w.o. to lay hold on him
4 : 3. w.o. a sower to sow, Lu. 8 : 5.
5 : 14. they w.o. to see what it was
6 : 12. w.o. preached that men re-
10 : 46. as he w.o. of Jericho [pent
11 : 11. w.o. unto Bethany with 12
19. even was come he w.o. of city
13 : 1. as he w.o. of temple one of di.
16 : 8. w.o. quickly, fled for sepulc.
Lu. 2 : 1. w.o. a decree from Cesar
6 : 19. w. virtue o. of him, healed
8 : 2. Mary o. of whom w. 7 devils
17 : 29. day Lot w.o. of Sodom fire
21 : 37. at night he w.o., abode in
Jn. 4 : 30. they w.o. of city unto him
8 : 9. convicted, w.o. one by one
11 : 31. Jews saw Mary w.o. follo-d
55. many w.o. of country to Jeru.
13 : 30. Judas then w.o.; it was ni.
18 : 16. Then w.o. th. other disciple
29. Pilate w.o. unto them, 38.
Ac. 12 : 9. Pet. w.o. followed angel
10. they w.o., passed thro. street
15 : 24. certain wh. w.o. troubled
16 : 13. on sab. we w.o. by river si.
40. w.o. of prison into hou. of Ly.
19 : 12. evil spirits w.o. of them
He. 11 : 8. Abr. w. o., not knowing
1 Jn. 2 : 19. They w.o. fr. us (2)[(2)
Re. 1 : 16. o. of his mouth w. sword
6 : 4. w.o. another horse, was red
See **WENT** with **after, against, arose, before, forth, into, Jesus, over, through, way.**

WENT over. [him
Ge. 32 : 21. So w. the present o. bef.
41 : 45. Joseph w. out o. all land
of Egypt, 46. Ps. 81 : 5. [of Eg.
Ex. 10 : 14. locusts w. up o. all land
De. 2 : 13. we w.o. the brook Zered
Jos. 18 : 13. border w.o. toward Luz
24 : 11. ye w.o. Jordan unto Jeric.
Ju. 6 : 33. chil. of east w.o., pitched
9 : 26. And Gaal w.o. to Shechem
1 S. 13 : 7. some of Hebrews w.o. Jor.
26 : 13. David w.o. to the other side
2 S. 19 : 17. w.o. Jordan before king
18. w.o. ferry boat to carry king's
31. Barzillai w.o. Jordan wi. king
39. all the people w.o. Jordan
2 K. 2 : 8. they two w.o. on dry gro.
14. Elisha smote waters and w.o.
8 : 21. Joram w.o. to Zair, and all
1 Ch. 12 : 15. w.o. Jordan overflown
29 : 30. times that w.o. David [o.
Is. 51 : 23. body as street to them w.
Ac. 18 : 23. Paul w.o. all Galatia
See **WENT** with
against, arose, Jesus.

WENT through or throughout.
Ge. 41 : 46. Joseph w.t. all land of
Egypt, Ps. 81 : 5. [derness
De. 1 : 19. we w.t. that terrible wil-
Jos. 3 : 2. officers w.t. the host
18 : 9. men w.t. land, described it
2 S. 2 : 29. Abner and men w.t. Bith.
Ne. 9 : 11. they w.t. midst of sea on
dry land, Ps. 66 : 6. [provinces
Es. 9 : 4. Mordecai's fame w. out t.
Jb. 29 : 7. When I w. out t. the city
Ps. 66 : 12. we w.t. fire, thro. water
Is. 60 : 15. forsak., no man w.t. thee
Lu. 4 : 14. w. out a fame of him t. all
9 : 1. he w.t. every city [region
9 : 6. they w.t. the towns preach-g
Ac. 15 : 41. Paul w.t. Syria confirm-g
16 : 4. w.t. cities, delivered decrees
See **THROUGHOUT all.**
See **Jesus WENT.**

WENT and took.
Ge. 22 : 13. Abraham w. & the ram
28 : 9. w. Esau a.t. Mahalath wife

Ex. 2 : 1. w. a man a.t. dau. of Levi
Nu. 32 : 39. children of Machir w. -
41. Jair w. - small towns [Gilead
42. Nobah w. - Kenath and vill-s
Jos. 19 : 47. chil. of Dan w. - Leshen
Ju. 3 : 28. they w. - fords of Jordan
9 : 50. Then w. Abim-h a.t. Thebez
18 : 17. five men that w. to spy land
w. up a.t. ephod and image [it
2 S. 12 : 29. David w. to Rabbah a.t.
21 : 12. David w. - bones of Saul
2 K. 12 : 17. Hazael w. ag. Gath, a.t. it
16 : 9. w. up ag. Damascus a.t. it
Ho. 1 : 3. So he w. - Gomer dau. of
Mat. 9 : 25. he w. in a.t. her by ha.
22 : 15. w. Pharisees a.t. counsel,

WENT up. [Mk. 3 : 6.
Ge. 2 : 6. w.u. a mist from earth
17 : 22. God w.u. from Abraham
19 : 28. smoke of country w.u. as
26 : 23. Isaac w.u. to Beer-sheba
35 : 13. God w.u. fr. Jacob in place
where he talked [shearers
38 : 12. Judah w.u. unto his sheep-
46 : 29. Joseph w.u. to meet his fa.
49 : 4. he w.u. to my couch [(2)
50 : 7. Joseph w.u. to bury his fath.
9. w.u. with him great company,
Ex. 12 : 38. a mixed multi. w.u. [14.
17 : 10. Moses, Aaron w.u. to top
19 : 3. Moses w.u. unto God, 20.
24 : 9. Then w.u. Moses, 70 elders
13. Moses w.u. into the mount of
God, 15. Ex. 34 : 4. [lot w.u.
Le. 16 : † 9. goat upon which Lord's
Nu. 13 : 21. w.u. and searched land
31. that w.u. said, We not able
20 : 27. they w.u. into mount Hor
32 : 9. when they w.u. unto valley
of Eshcol, De. 1 : 24. [and died
33 : 38. Aaron w.u. into m-t Hor
De. 1 : 24. they w.u. into mountain
43. ye w. presumptuously u. into
5 : 5. afraid, ye w. not u. into m-t
10 : 3. I w.u. into m-t, having two
34 : 1. Mos. w.u. unto mts. of Nebo
Jos. 6 : 20. wall fell, peo. w.u. into
7 : 2. men w.u. and viewed Ai [city
4. there w.u. about 3,000 men
8 : 10. Josh. w.u. and elders to Ai
11. all peo. of war with him w.u.
10 : 5. kings w.u. encamped bef. G.
9. Joshua w.u. fr. Gilgal all night
36. Joshua w.u. unto Hebron
14 : 8. brethren that w.u. with me
15 : 3. border w.u. to Adar [(2)
6. border w.u. to stone of Bohan
7. border w.u. tow. Debir fr. Achor
8. border w.u. by val-y of Hin. (2)
15. Caleb w.u. to inhab-s of Debir
18 : 12. border w.u. to Jericho (2)
19 : 11. border w.u. toward sea
47. Dan w.u. to fight ag. Leshem
Ju. 1 : 4. Judah w.u.; L. delivered
4 : 10. Barak w.u. wi 10,000 men;
Deborah w.u. with him
8 : 8. Gideon w.u. to Penuel, 11.
13 : 20. when flame w.u. fr. off altar
14 : 19. Samson w.u. to fa-'s house
15 : 9. Philis. w.u. pitched in Jud.
18 : 12. Danites w.u., pitched in Kir.
20 : 23. Isr. w.u., wept before L., 26.
Ru. 4 : 1. Then w. Boaz u. to gate
1 S. 1 : 3. man w.u. yearly to worship
7. Hannah w.u. to house of Lord
21. Elkanah and house w.u. to of-
22. But Hannah w. not u. [fer
5 : 12. cry of city w.u. to heaven
9 : 11. as they w.u. hill to city, 14.
14 : 21. Hebrews with Philis. which
w.u. into camp [Philis. (2)
46. Saul w.u. from following the
15 : 34. Saul w.u. to hou. to Gibeah
23 : 29. David w.u. dwelt at En-ge.
25 : 13. w.u. after David about 400
27 : 8 David and men w.u., invaded
29 : 11. Philistines w.u. to Jezreel

2 S. 2 : 2. David w.u. and two wives
15 : 24. Abiathar w.u., until peo.
30. David w.u. by ascent of Olivet,
wept as he w.u., he w. barefoot; all the people with him w.
u., weeping as they w.u. [gate
18 : 24. watchman w.u. to roof ov.
33. king w.u. to chamber, wept (2)
20 : 2. every man w.u. from David
22 : 9. w.u. a smoke out of his nostrils, Ps. 18 : 8. [manded
24 : 19. David w.u. as Lord com-
1 K. 2 : 34. Benaiah w.u., slew him
6 : 8 they w.u. with wind-g stairs
10 : 5. ascent by which Sol. w.u.
unto house of Lord, 2 Ch. 9 : 4.
12 : † 32. Jeroboam w.u. to altar
16 : 17 Omri w.u. from Gibbethon
18 : 42. Ahab w.u. to eat and drink
Elijah w.u. to top of Carmel
43. servant w.u., said, There is
20 : 1. Ben-hadad w.u., besieged
Samaria, 2 K. 6 : 24. [fight
26. Ben-hadad w.u. to Aphek to
22 : 29. Jehoshaphat w.u. to Ramoth-gilead, 2 Ch. 18 : 28. [13.
2 K. 1 : 9. capt of 50 w.u. to Elijah,
2 : 11. Elijah w.u. by a whirlwind
23. Elisha w.u. unto Beth-el [(2)
4 : 21. she w.u., laid him on bed
34. he w.u., lay upon child, 35.
14 : 11. Therefore Jehoash king of
Israel w.u., 2 Ch. 25 : 21.
15 : 14. Menahem w.u. from Tirzah
17 : 5. k. of Assyria w.u. to Sama.
18 : 17. gr. host, they w.u. to Jerus.
19 : 14. Hezekiah w.u. into house
of the L., 2 Ch. 29 : 20. Is. 37 : 14.
23 : 2. Josiah w.u. into house of
the Lord, 2 Ch. 34 : 30. [chief
1 Ch. 11 : 6. Joab w.u. first, was
13 : 6. David w.u. and Isr. to Baalah
14 : 8. Philis. w.u. to seek Dav. (2)
21 : 19. David w.u. at saying of G.
2 Ch. 1 : 6. Sol. w.u. to brazen altar
Ezr. 2 : 1. these are children that w.
u. out of captivity, Ne. 7 : 6.
59. were they which w.u. from
Tel-melah, Ne. 7 : 61. [salem
4 : 23. they w.u. in haste to Jeru-
7 : 6 This Ezra w.u. from Babylon
7. w.u. some of priests, singers
8 : 1. genealogy of them that w.u.
Ne. 2 : 15. w. I u. in night, viewed
12 : 1. priests that w.u. with Zeru.
37. w.u. by stairs of city of David
Is. 7 : 1. Rezin, Pekah w.u. tow. Jer.
Eze. 1 : 13. it w.u. and down am. (2)
8 : 11. thick cloud of incense w.u.
10 : 4. glory of L. w.u. fr. cherub
11 : 23. glory of L. w.u. from city
24. vision I had seen w.u. fr. me
19 : 6. he w.u. and down am. lions
40 : 6. w.u. the stairs, measured
22. they w.u. unto it by 7 steps
49. bro-t me by steps wh-by w.u.
Mat. 5 : 1. he w.u. into a mountain,
14 : 23.-15 : 29. Lu. 9 : 28. Jn. 6 : 3.
Mk. 6 : 51. he w.u. unto them into
Lu. 2 : 4. Joseph w.u. from Galilee
42. he 12 years old, they w.u. to
8 : 37. he w.u. into the ship [Jerus.
18 : 10. Two men w.u. into temple
Jn. 7 : 10. then w. he u. unto feast
21 : 11. Peter w.u., drew net [u.
Ac. 1 : 10. looked tow. heaven as he w.
13. they w.u. into upper room
3 : 1. Peter, John w.u. into temple
10 : 9. Peter w.u. upon housetop
21 : 15. after these days we w.u. to
24 : 11. 12 days since I w.u. to Jer.
Ga. 1 : 17. Nei. w. I u. to Jerus. to
apostles; but I w. into Arabia
18. aft. 3 years I w.u. to see Peter
2 : 1. 14 years after I w.u. again to
2. I w.u. by revelation [Jerus.
Re. 20 : 9. w.u. on breadth of earth

See **WENT** with
against, arose, into, Jesus, out, over, took.

WENT with way. [on w.
Ge. 18 : 16. Abr. w. to bring them
35 : 3. Lord with me in w. [w.
Nu. 21 : 33. Israel w. up by the w.
of Bashan, De. 3 : 1. [ye w.
De. 1 : 31. God bare thee in all w.
33. Who w. in w. bef. you in fire
Jos. 24 : 17. preserved us in w. we w.
Ju. 8 : 11. Gideon w. up by w. east
Ru. 1 : 7. she, two dau-s, w. on w.
2 S. 16 : 13. as Dav. and men w. by w.
1 K. 13 : 10. man of God w. ano. w.
12. father said, What w. w. he?
sons seen wh. w. man of G. w.
18 : 6. Ahab w. one w., Obadiah
w. another w. by himself
22 : 24. said, What w. w. Spirit of
Lord from me, 2 Ch. 18 : 23.
2 K. 11 : 16. she w. by w. horses came
Pr. 7 : 8. Young man w. w. to her h.
Is. 57 : 17. w. on in w. of his heart
Je. 39 : 4. men of war w. out of city
by w. of king's garden ; he w.
out the w. of the plains. 52 : 7.
2 K. 25 : 4. [tain man
Lu. 9 : 57. as they w. in the w. cer-
Ac. 21 : 5. we departed and w. our w.

WENT her way.
1 S. 1 : 18. woman w. - no more sad
Jn. 4 : 28. woman left waterpot, w. -
11 : 28. Martha had so said she w. -

WENT his way. [left
Ge. 18 : 33. Lord w. - soon as he had
24 : 61. servant took Rebekah w. -
25 : 34. Esau did eat, drink, w. -
32 : 1. Jacob w. - angels met him
Ex. 18 : 27. Jethro w. - into his own
Nu. 24 : 25. Balak also w. - [land
1 S. 24 : 7. Saul rose out of cave w. -
26 : 25. David w. -, Saul returned
1 K. 1 : 49. guests w. ev. man h. w.
Es. 4 : 17. So Mordecai w. -, did as
Je. 28 : 11. prophet Jeremiah w. -
Mat. 13 : 25. enemy sowed tares w. -
Lu. 4 : 30. passing thro. midst w. -
8 : 39. he w. - published gr. things
22 : 4. w. -, communed with priests
Jn. 4 : 50. the man believed, w. -
9 : 7. He w. -, washed, came seeing
Ac. 8 : 39. eunuch w. - rejoicing
9 : 17. Ananias w. - entered house

WENT their way, s. [w.
Ge. 14 : 11. took goods of Sod., w. t.
Ju. 18 : 26. children of Dan w. t. w.
19 : 14. w. t. w. ; sun went down
1 S. 30 : 2. burned Ziklag w. t. w.
Ne. 8 : 12. all the people w. t. w.
Zch. 10 : 2. they w. t. w. as a flock
Mat. 8 : 33. that kept swine w. t. w-s
20 : 4. right I will give; they w. t. w.
22 : 5. made light of it and w. t. w-s
22. heard these words, w. t. w.
Mk. 11 : 4. w. t. w., found colt, Lu.
12 : 12. left him and w. t. w. [19 : 32.
Jn. 11 : 46. some w. t. w-s to Pharis.
Ac. 8 : 36. w. on t. w., came to water
See **Went a WHORING.**

WENTEST. [bed
Ge. 49 : 4. Reuben, thou w. to fa-'s
Ju. 5 : 4. L., when thou w. out of Seir
8 : 1. called us not when w. to fight
1 S. 10 : 2. asses thou w. to seek [w.
2 S. 7 : 9. I with thee whitherso. thou
16 : 17. why w. not wi. thy friend?
19 : 25. Whf. w. thou not with me
Ps. 68 : 7. O God, when thou w. bef.
Is. 57 : 7. w. thou up to offer sacrifi.
9. thou w. to king with ointment
Je. 2 : 2. w. after me in wilderness
31 : 21. set heart tow. way thou w.
Ha. 3 : 13. Thou w. forth for salva-n
Ac 11 : 3. Thou w. in to men uncir-

WEPT. [cumcised
Ge. 33 : 4. Esau kissed Jacob, they w.
Ge. 37 : 35. his father w. for Joseph
42 : 24. Joseph turned fr. them, w.
43 : 30. Jos. entered his chamb., w.
45 : 2. Joseph w. aloud; Eg-ns heard
14. he fell upon Benj-'s neck and
w. ; Benj. w. upon his neck
15. he kissed all his breth. and w.
46 : 29. Jos. w. on fa-'s neck, 50 : 1.
17. Joseph w. when they spake
50 : †3. Eg-ns w. for Joseph 70 days
Ex. 2 : 6. and, behold, the babe w.
Nu. 11 : 4. the children of Israel also
w. again, 18, 20.-14 : 1. De. 1 :
45. Ju. 20 : 23, 26.-21 : 2. [Moab
De. 34 : 8. w. for Moses in plains of
Ju. 14 : 16. Samson's wife w. bef. him
17. she w. before him the 7 days
21 : 2. people to house of G. w. sore
1 S. 1 : 7. Hannah w., did not eat
10. she prayed unto Lord, and w.
20 : 41. Jonathan, David w. [sore
30 : 4. David and people with him w.
2 S. 1 : 12. Dav. and men w. for Saul
3 : 32. David w. at grave of Abner;
all the people w., 34.
12 : 22. While child was alive I w.
13 : 36. king w. sore for Amnon (2)
15 : 23. country w. with loud [foot
30. David w. as he went up, bare-
18 : 33. w. and said, O my son Abs.
2 K. 8 : 11. and the man of God w.
13 : 14. Joash w. over Elisha and
20 : 3. Hezekiah w. sore, Is. 38 : 3.
22 : 19. bec. king of Judah w. bef. me
Ezr. 3 : 12. priests that had seen the
first house w. [Ne. 8 : 9.
10 : 1. for the people w. very sore,
Ne. 1 : 4. when I heard these words
I w. before God [him
Es. 8 : †3. Esther w. and besought
Ps. 69 : 10. I w. and chastened my
137 : 1. By rivers of Babylon we w.
Ho. 12 : 4. Jacob w., made supplic-n
Mat. 26 : 75. Peter went out, w. bitterly, Mk. 14 : 72. Lu. 22 : 62.
Mk. 5 : 38. Jesus seeth them that
w., and wailed, Lu. 8 : 52.
16 : 10. Mary told them as they w.
Lu. 7 : 32. we mourned, ye ha. not w.
19 : 41. he beheld the city and w.
Jn. 11 : 35. Jesus w. [sepulchre
20 : 11. as she w. she looked into
Ac. 20 : 37. w. sore, fell on P.'s neck
1 Co. 7 : 30. weep, as tho. they w. not
Re. 5 : 4. I w. bec. no man worthy
See **LIFT, LIFTED voice.**

WERE.
Ge. 1 : 5. evening and morning w.
the first day, 8, 13, 19, 23, 31.
7. waters which w. under the firmament from (2) [his wife
2 : 25. w. both naked ; man and
4 : 8. when they w. in field, Cain
5 : 4. days of Adam aft. w. 800 years
5. all days Adam lived w. 930 yrs.
8. all the days of . . . . w., 11, 14,
17, 20, 23, 27, 31. [they w. fair
6 : 2. saw daughters of men that
4. w. giants in earth in these days
7 : 10. aft 7 days waters w. upon
19. hills that w. under heaven w.
23 Noah alive, they th. w. wi. him
8 : 9. waters w. on face of the earth
9 : 18. sons of Noah w. Shem, Ham
23. faces w. backward, saw not
29. all the days of Noah w. 950 yrs.
10 : 29. all these w. sons of Joktan
11 : 32. days of Terah w. 205 years
13 : 13. men of Sodom w. wicked
14 : 5. that w. with him, 17.-24 :
32, 54.-35 : 6.-40 : 7. Ju. 9 : 48.
1 S. 13 : 22.-14 : 17, 20.-30 : 29.
2 S. 1 : 11.-10 : 13.-15 : 22.-17 :
22. 2 K. 25 : 25, 28. 1 Ch. 5 : 20.
Je. 41 : 7.-52 : 32. Mat. 12 : 1, 3.-
27 : 54. Mk. 1 : 36.-5 : 40. Lu. 5 :
9.-8 : 45. Jn. 9 : 40. Ac. 5 : 17, 21.
Ge. 14 : 13. w. confederate wi. Abram
18 : 11. Abraham and Sarah w. old
19 : 36. w. both dau-s of Lot wi. child
20 : 8. and the men w. sore afraid
23 : 1. these w. years of life of Sarah
17. all the trees that w. in field (2)
24 : 10. goods of master w. in his ha.
25 : 3. sons of Dedan w. Asshurim
4. All these w. children of Keturah
24. behold, there w. twins in her
womb, 38 : 27. [and Rebekah
26 : 35. Which w. a grief unto Isaac
27 : 1. his eyes w. dim, so that he
15. raiment of Esau wh. w. in hou.
29 : 2. w. 3 flocks of sheep by well
30 : 35. goats that w. spotted, 31 : 10.
42. cattle w. feeble, put not in (2)
31 : 19. images that w. her father's
34 : 5. his sons w. wi. cattle in field
14. for that w. a reproach unto us
25. third day when they w. sore
35 : 2. Jac. said to all that w. wi. him
4. gave earrings wh. w. in ears (2)
5. terror upon cities that w. about
22. now the sons of Jac. w. twelve
28. days of Isaac w. 180 years
36 : 7. their riches w. more than (2)
11. sons of Eliphaz w. Teman, Omar
13. these w. sons of Bashemath
14. these w. sons of Aholibamah
22. chil. of Lotan w. Hori, Hemam
37 : 27. and his breth. w. content
40 : 6. Jos. looked upon th.; w. sad
10. and in the vine w. 3 branches
41 : 21. but they w. still ill favoured
48. gath-d all food wh. w. in Egypt
43 : 18. men w. afraid bec. w. bro't
34. drank and w. merry with Jos.
46 : 25. of Bilhah ; souls w. seven
26. out of Jacob's loins souls w. 66
27. souls of hou. of Jac. into E. w. 70
48 : 10. eyes of Isr. w. dim for age
Ex. 5 : 19. see they w. in evil case
6 : 4. give land wh-n they w. strang-
16. years of life of Levi w. 137 [ers
20. years of life of Amram w. 137
7 : 20. w. (2)-37 : 14, 17, 22, 25.-
39 : 14. Le. 18 : 27, 28. De. 29 : 17.
Jos. 8 : 16. Ju. 9 : 44. Ezr. 5 : 6.
8 : 18. w. lice upon man and beast
10 : 6. since day they w. upon earth
14. grievous w. they ; bef. w. no
14 : 11. Bec. w. no graves in Egypt
22. waters w. a wall unto them
15 : 23. waters of Marah, w. bitter
27. Elim, where w. 12 wells water
17 : 12. Moses' hands w. heavy (2)
22 : 21. nei. vex a stranger, for ye
w. strangers, Le. 19 : 34. De. 10 : 19.
32 : 15. two tables w. in his hand
16. the tables w. the work of God
36 : 30. w. 8 boards ; sockets w. 16
38. their five sockets w. of brass
37 : 9. mercy seatward w. faces of
Nu. 6 : 12. days that w. before be lost
7 : 2. w. over them th. w. numb-d
9 : 6. w. certain men who w. defiled
10 : 28. Thus w. journeyings of Isr.
12 : 8. w. ye not afraid to speak ag.
13 : 3. all those w. heads of Israel
4. And these w. their names
33. we w. in our sight as grasshoppers, so w. we in their sight
14 : 3. w. it not better to return
15 : 26 seeing peo. w. in ignorance
19 : 18. hyssop upon persons th. w.
21 : 32. drove out Amorites th. w.
22 : 29. wou. w. sword in mine hand
De. 5 : 29. Oh w. such heart in them
6 : 21. we w. Pha.'s bondmen in Eg.
7 : 7. nor bec. ye w. more in number ; for ye w. fewest of all peo.
9 : 15. two tables w. in my hands
25 : 18. smote all that w. feeble
28 : 62. ye w. as the stars of heaven
67. sh. say, Would G. it w. even (2)
32 : 27. w. it not I feared the enemy

De. 32 : 29. O that they w. wise
Jos. 2 : 4. I wist not whence they w.
16 : 8. goings out th-f w. at the sea
Ju. 3 : 4. w. to prove Israel by them
8 : 21. ornaments that w. on necks
9 : 36. seest mts. as if they w. men
15 : 14. cords that w. upon his arms
16 : 27. all lords of Philis. w. there
30. he slew at his death w. more
17 : 4. they w. in the hou. of Micah
18 : 3. When they w. by hou. of M.
7. they w. far from Zidonians (2)
22. w. good way fr. house of Micah,
men that w. in houses ⌈Rim-n
21 : 13. of Benjamin that w. in rock
1 S. 9 : 4. Shalim, there they w. not
14 : 21. Hebrews th. w. with Philis-s
22 : 2. w. with David 400 men ⌊(2)
25 : 7. shepherds which w. with us
15. men w. very good unto us, as
long as we w. conversant (3)
16. w. a wall unto us all while (2)
30 : 2. women captives th. w. th-in
21. 200 w. so faint could not follow
2 S. 1 : 23. Saul, Jonathan w. lovely
in lives, w. swifter than (3)⌈w.
11 : 16. where he knew valiant men
23. we w. upon them unto gate
12 : 31. brought peo. that w. th-n
13 : 30. while they w. in the way
19 : 9. all the people th. w. at strife
22 : 18. they w. too strong for me
1 K. 1 : 8. mighty men w. not with
3 : 18. woman was delivered ; we w.
4 : 28. place where officers w.⌊toge.
5 : 14. a month they w. in Lebanon
7 : 29. on the borders w. lions (3)
12 : 31. priests which w. not of Levi
16 : 30. evil above all that w. bef., 33.
2 K. 3 : 14. w. it not I regard Jehosh.
7 : 3. w. four leprous men at gate
10 horses tied, tents as they w.
15 : 16. Menahem smote all w. th-n
17 : 2. not as kings that w. bef. him
19 : 18. they w. no gods, but work
of men's hands, Is. 37 : 19.
23 : 7. houses of sodomites w. by
house of Lord ⌈Jerusalem (2)
13. the high places that w. before
1 Ch. 4 : 14. for they w. craftsmen
9 : 26. four porters w. in their set
office and w. over treasuries
12 : 8. whose faces w. like faces of
lions, and w. as swift as roes
32. w. men wh. had understanding of times; heads w. 200⌈days
39. then they w. wi. David three
2 Ch. 13 : 13. so they w. before Judah
28 : 23. gods of Syria w. ruin of him
29 : 31. as many as w. of free heart
30 : 8. not stiffnecked as fathers w.
31 : 19. priests wh. w. in the fields
32 : 18. cried unto peo. th. w. on wall
34 : 4. images th. w. on high he cut
36 : 20. Bab., where they w. serv-s
Ezr. 5 : 2. with them w. prophets
Ne. 1 : 9. tho. there w. of you cast out
5 : 2. w. that said, We many, 3, 4.
17. w. at my table, 150 Jews, and
7 : 61. these w. they wh. went up (2)
Jb. 16 : 4. if your soul w. in my soul's
29 : 2. O that I w. as in months past
Ps. 14 : 2. to see if there w. any that
did understand, 53 : 2. ⌈fa-s w.
39 : 12. I am a stranger as all my
53 : 5. There w. they in great fear
105 : 12. When they w. but a few
Pr. 8 : 24. when there w. no depths
I was brought forth (2) ⌈briers
Is. 7 : 23. where w. 1,000 vines, be
14 : 2. them, whose captives they w.
Je. 9 : 1. Oh that my head w. waters
24 : 2. figs not be eaten, w. so bad
31 : 15. for her chil. bec they w. not
34 : 5. the kings wh. w. before thee
44 : 17. then we had plenty, w. well
49 : 2. Isr. heir unto th. w. hie heirs

Eze. 10 : 20. I knew they w. cherubim
14 : 14. Though Noah, Daniel, Job
w. in it, 16, 18, 20.
20 : 9. not polluted before heathen,
among whom they w. ⌈idols
24. their eyes w. aft. their fathers'
25. Whf. gave statutes w. not good
23 : 2. Son of man, there w. 2 wom.
4. names of them w. Aholah and
Aholibah ; and they w. mine (3)
27 : 8. wise men, O Tyrus, that w.
in thee, w. thy pilots (3)
9. wise men of Gebal w. calkers ;
all the ships of sea w. in thee
Hag. 2 : 16. days w. when one came
to heap of 20 measures w. but
Zch. 8 : 13. w. curse am. heath.⌊10 (2)
Mat. 5 : 12. prophets that w. before
12 : 3. what David did and they that
w. with him, 4. Mk. 2 : 25, 26.
Lu. 6 : 3, 4. ⌈him
14 : 33. that w. in ship worshipped
24 : 37. as days of Noe w., so sh., 38.
26 : 51. one of them wh. w. wi. Jesus
Mk. 1 : 19. w. in ships mending nets
2 : 15. w. many, they followed him
4 : 10. they th. w. about him asked
36. w. with him other little ships
10 : 32. w. in the way to Jerus. ; as
they followed w. afraid ⌈born
14 : 21. good w. it for th. man if nev.
Lu. 1 : 2. unto us wh. from beginning
w. eyewitnesses ⌈complished
2 : 6. while w. there days w. ac-
8. w. in same country shepherds
3 : 15. all mused whe. he w. Ch. (2)
4 : 20. eyes of all that w. in synag.
25. many widows w. in Israel in
5 : 7. partners wh. w. in other ships
7 : 39. This man if he w. a prophet
8 : 1. every city ; twelve w. wi. him
9 : 18. praying, disciples w. wi. him
30. wi. him two, wh. w. Mos., Elias
13 : 2. Galileans w. sinners ab. all ? 4.
16 : 14. Pharisees wh. w. covetous
17 : 17. w. there not ten cleansed ?
22 : 49. they wh. w. about him saw
23 : 5. and they w. the more fierce
6. asked whe. the man w. Galilean
12. friends, bef. they w. at enmity
24 : 5. as they w. afraid and bowed
10. other women th. w. with them
22. women wh. w. early at sepulc.
24. certain which w. with us went
Jn. 1 : 24. which w. sent w. of Phari.
9 : 33. If this man w. not of God
40. Pharisees which w. with him
10 : 6. what things they w. he spake
11 : 31. Jews wh. w. wi. her in hou.
57. if any man knew where he w.
13 : 1. loved his own wh. w. in world
15 : 19. If ye w. of the world
17 : 6. thine they w., thou gavest
18 : 30. If he w. not a malefactor
36. if my kingdom w. of this world
20 : 26. aft. 8 days disciples w. within
21 : 2. w. together Pet., Thom. and
8. they w. not far from land (2)
11. for all w. so many, was not net
Ac. 2 : 1. they w. all with one accord
44. all that believed w. together
4 : 6. as many as w. of kindred of
13. perceived they w. ignor-t men
32. that believed w. of oue heart
34. many as w. possessors of lands
9 : 19. disciples wh. w. at Damascus
10 : 12. w. all manner of fourfooted
17 : 11. These w. more noble than
19 : 28. heard, they w. full of wrath
20 : 12. w. not a little comforted
22 : 9. that w. with me saw the light
11. led by them that w. with me
24 : 9. Jews assented, things w. so
26 : 29. would all that hear w. as I
27 : 36. w. they all of good cheer
28 : 7. w. possessions of chief man
Ro. 4 : 17. that be not as tho. they w.

Ro. 9 : 25. call th. my peo. th. w. not
16 : 7. who w. in Christ before me
1 Co. 6 : 11. And such w. some of you
10 : 6. these things w. our examples
7. Nei., idolaters, as w. some of
12 : 17. If whole body w. an eye,
where w. hearing ? if whole w.
hearing (4) ⌈preach
15 : 11. whe. it w. I or they, so we
2 Co. 7 : 8. sorry tho. it w. but a season
Ga. 2 : 6. whatso. they w. no matter
Ep. 2 : 3. w. by nature chil. of wrath
1 Th. 1 : 5. know what we w. am. you
7. So that ye w. ensamples to all
2 : 7. we w. gentle am. you as nurse
8. we w. willing to have imparted
our souls bec. ye w. dear unto us
2 Th. 3 : 10. when we w. with you
2 Pe. 1 : 16. we w. eyewitnesses of
2 : 1. w. false prophets am. people
3 : 4. All things continue as they w.
Re. 6 : 11. should be killed as they w.
8 : 5. there w. voices, thunderings,
lightnings, 11 : 15, 19.–16 : 18. (2)

As it WERE. ⌈shot

Ge. 21 : 16. good way off, - w. bow-
Ex. 24 : 10. under his feet - w. paved
work of sapphire, - w. body of
28 : 32. - w. hole of an habergeon
Le. 14 : 35. is - w. a plague in house
26 : 37. one upon ano., - w. before
Nu. 9 : 15. upon tabern. - w. of fire
11 : 31. - w. a day's journey, and
- w. two cubits high (3)
23 : 22. he hath - w. strength of
a unicorn, 24 : 8.
1 S. 14 : 14. - w. half an acre ⌈fire
Jb. 28 : 5. under it is turned up - w.
Can. 6 : 13. - w. the company of two
Is. 5 : 18. draw sin - w. wi. cart rope
26 : 18. we ha. - w. bro-t forth wind
20. hide thyself - w. for moment
53 : 3. we hid - w. our faces fr. him
Eze. 1 : 16. - w. a wheel in a wheel
27. I saw - w. appearance of fire
10 : 1. over them - w. sapphire st.
Lu. 22 : 44. his sweat - w. blood
Jn. 7 : 10. not openly, - w. in secret
21 : 8. from land - w. 200 cubits
Ac. 17 : 14. sent Paul to go - w. to sea
Ro. 9 : 32. - w. by works of the law
1 Co. 4 : 9. - w. appointed to death
2 Co. 11 : 17. I speak it - w. foolishly
Phm. 14. thy benefit not be - w. of
necessity, but willingly⌈w. fire
Ja. 5 : 3. rust shall eat your flesh -
Re. 4 : 1. voice was - w. of trumpet
6 : 1. I heard - w. noise of thunder
8 : 8. - w. gr. mt. was cast into sea
10. fell a star, burning - w. a lamp
9 : 7. on heads - w. crowns like gold
9. they had - w. breastpl-s of iron
10 : 1. his face was - w. the sun
13 : 3. one of his heads - w. wounded
14 : 3. they sung - w. a new song
15 : 2. I saw - w. a sea of glass
19 : 6. I heard - w. voice of multit.
21 : 21. street gold, - w. transpar-

If it WERE.⌊ent glass

Jb. 21 : 4. - w. so, why not my spirit
be troubled ? ⌈very elect
Mat. 24 : 24. - w. possible to deceive
Mk. 6 : 56. might touch - w. border
Jn. 14 : 2. - w. not so I wo. have told
Ac. 18 : 14. - w. a matter of wrong
20 : 16. - w. possible to be at Jerus.

As if it WERE. ⌈wood

Is. 10 : 15. if staff lift its. - w. no
La. 2 : 6. taken taberu. - w. a garden

WERT. ⌈brother

Can. 8 : 1. O that thou w. as my
Re. 3 : 15. I wo. thou w. cold or hot

WEST. [Noun.]

Ge. 12 : 8. having Bethel on the w.
28 : 14. shalt spread abroad to w.
De. 33 : 23. possess the w. and south
Jos. 8 : 13. liers in wait on w. of city

Jos. 11 : 2. k-s in borders of Dor on **w.**
3. and to the Canaanite on the **w.**
12 : 7. country Josh. smote on **w.**
18 : 15. border went out on the **w.**
1 K. 7 : 25. oxen looking tow. the **w.**
1 Ch. 9 : 24. porters toward east, **w.**,
north, and south, 2 Ch. 4 : 4.
12 : 15. put to flight them toward
east and **w.** ⌈from the **w.**
Ps. 75 : 6. promotion cometh neither
103 : 12. far as the east is fr. the **w.**
107 : 3. gathered them from east, **w.**
Is. 11 : 14. fly upon Philis. toward **w.**
43 . 5. and gather thee from the **w.**
45 : 6. that they may know from **w.**
49 : 12. shall come from north, **w.**
59 : 19. shall fear Lord from the **w.**
Eze. 41 : 12. building tow. **w.** 70 cub.
48 : 1. these his sides east and **w.**
10. tow. the **w.** 10,000 in breadth
17. suburbs of city tow. **w.** 250 m.
Da. 8 : 5. a he goat came from the **w.**
Ho. 11 : 10. chil. shall tremble fr. **w.**
Zch. 14 : 4. mount of Olives tow. **w.**
Mat. 8 : 11. many fr. east and **w.** sit
down with Abraham, Lu. 13 : 29.
24 : 27. as lightn-g shineth unto **w.**
Lu. 12 : 54. see a cloud rise out of **w.**
Re. 21 : 13. on south 3 gates, on **w.**

WEST. [Adj.] ⌊3 gates
Ex. 10 : 19. **w.** wind took aw. locusts
Jos. 18 : 14. Kirjath-baal, **w.** quarter
Zch. 8 : 7. save my peo. from **w.** coun
WEST border. ⌊try
Nu. 34 : 6. great sea shall be **w. b.**
Jos. 15 : 12. **w. b.** was to great sea
Eze. 45 : 7. for prince, from **w. b.**
48 : 21. over ag. 25,000 toward **w.**
See **West SIDE.**

WESTERN. ⌈sea
Nu. 34 : 6. for **w.** border, the great

WESTWARD. ⌈and **w.**
Ge. 13 : 14. Abram looked eastward
Ex. 26 : 22. for sides of tabernacle
w. make, 27.-36 : 27, 32. ⌈**w.**
Nu. 3 : 23. pitch behind tabernacle
De. 3 : 27. lift thine eyes **w.**, behold
Jos. 5 : 1. kings on side of Jordan **w.**
15 : 8. mt. bef. valley of Hin-m **w.**
10. bord. compassed fr. Baalah **w.**
16 : 3. lot of Joseph **w.** to coast of
8. border went **w.**, 18 : 12.-19 : 26,
34.-22 : 7.-28 : 4. 1 Ch. 26 : 16,
18, 30. ⌈zer, with towns
1 Ch. 7 : 28. possessions were **w.** Ge-
Eze. 45 : 7. possession of city from
west side **w.**, 48 : 21. ⌈**w.**
46 : 19. was a place on the two sides
48 : 18. residue sh. be 10,000 **w.** (21)
Da. 8 : 4. I saw the ram pushing **w.**

WET. [Adj.] ⌈of mts.
Jb. 24 : 8. They are **w.** with showers
Da. 4 : 15. let it be **w.** with dew, 23.
33. his body was **w.** with the dew
of heaven, 5 : 21.

WET. [Verb.]
Da. 4 : 25 they sh. **w.** thee with dew

WHALE, S.
Ge. 1 : 21. God created great **w-s**
Jb. 7 : 12. Am I a **w.**, thou settest a
41 : † : 1. Canst thou draw out a **w.**
Ps. 74 : † 13. brakest heads of **w-s**
Eze. 32 : 2. Pha-h, Thou art as a **w.**
Mat. 12 : 40. Jonas 3 days in **w.**'s

WHAT. [Adj.] ⌊belly
Ge. 27 : 46. **w.**, 38 : 18. Nu. 10 : 32.-
13 : 19.-22 : 9. De. 1 : 22.-3 : 24.-
4 : 7, 8. Jos. 22 : 16. Ju. 20 : 12.
2 S. 15 : 2, 21.-19 : 28. - 24 : 13.
1 K. 9 : 13.-12 : 9. 2 K. 9 : 18.-
18 : 19.-23 : 17. 1 Ch. 21 : 12. 2
Ch. 10 : 6, 9. Ne. 4 : 20. Es. 6 : 3.
Jb. 21 : 21. Ps. 46 : 8.-56 : 3. Ec.
5 : 11.-11 : 2. Is. 40 : 18. Je. 2 : 5.
-8 : 9.-18 : 7, 9. Eze. 47 : 23. Da.
3 : 5, 15. Am. 5 . 18. Mat. 5 : 46.
-7 : 2,-24 : 43. Mk. 1 : 27.-2 : 25.
-4 : 30.-6 : 2.-13 : 1. Lu. 4 : 36.-5 :
22.-8 : 47.-12 : 39.-14 : 31 -15 : 8.
-21 : 7. Jn. 2 : 18.-6 : 30.-13 : 28.
18 : 29. Ac. 4 : 7.-7 : 49.-10 : 29.
-15 : 12.-23 : 34. Ro. 8 : 1, 19, 27.
-6 : 21. 1 Co. 3 : 13.-15 : 35. 2
Co. 6 : 14. (2) 15. (2) 16.-7 : 11.
(5). Col. 2 : 1. 1 Th. 4 : 2. 2 Ti.
3 : 11. He. 12 : 7. 1 Pe. 2 : 20.
Re. 3 : 3.-18 : 18. ⌈to Lord
Ju. 21 . 8. **w.** one of tribes came not
Lu. 4 : 36. saying, **w.** a word is this
See AUTHORITY, DEATH, EVIL,
MAN, MANNER, MEANS, NEED,
PROFIT, PORTION, PURPOSE.

WHAT with soever. ⌈eth
Le. 15 : 9. upon **w.** saddle **s.** he rid-
17 : 3. **w.** man **s.** killeth ox or lamb
22 : 4. **w.** man **s.** is a leper or hath
De. 12 : 32. **w.** thing **s.** I command
2 S. 15 : 35. **w.** thing **s.** thou sh. hear
1 K. 8 : 38. **w.** prayer **s.** by man or
2 Ch. 19 : 10. **w.** cause **s.** come to you
Mk. 6 : 10. In **w.** place **s.** ye enter ho.
11 : 24. **w.** things **s.** ye desire, ye
Jn. 5 : 19. **w.** things **s.** he doeth, do-
Ro. 3 : 19. **w.** things **s.** law saith⌊eth
See THANK, THANKS, THING,
WAY.
See **What THINGS.**

WHAT. [Interj.] ⌈men?
2 K. 4 : 43. **w.**, sho. I set this bef. 100
8 : 13. But **w.**, is thy servant a dog
Jb. 2 : 10. **w.**? shall we receive good
Pr. 31 : 2. **w.**, my son? and **w.**, the
son of my womb? and **w.**, the
son of my vows? ⌈one hour?
Mat. 26 : 40. **w.**, could ye not watch
1 Co. 6 : 16. **w.**! know ye not, he wh.
is joined to harlot ⌈temple
19. **w.**! know ye not your body is
11 : 22. **w.**! have ye not houses to
14 : 36. **w.**! came word of G. fr. you

WHAT. [Pronoun.] ⌈call
Ge. 2 : 19. Adam, to see **w.** he would
15 : 2. Abr. said, L., **w.** wilt give me
20 : 9. Abim-h said, **w.** hast thou
done, **w.** have I offended thee?
23 : 15. **w.** is that betw. me and thee
29 ; 15. tell me, **w.** sh. thy wages be?
30 : 21. Laban said, **w.** sh. I give thee
31 : 32. discern **w.** is thine with me
36. **w.** is my trespass? **w.** my sin?
37. **w.** hast found of thy stuff?
32 : 27. **w.** is thy name? said Jacob
33 : 15. **w.** needeth it? Let me find
34 : 11. **w.** ye shall say I will give
37 : 10. **w.** is this dream thou hast
15. man asked him, **w.** seekest th.
20. see **w.** become of his dreams
38 : 16. **w.** give that thou mayest
39 : 8. wotteth not **w.** is with me⌈do
41 : 55. Go unto Joseph, **w.** he saith,
44 : 16. **w.** sh. we say unto my lord (2)
46 : 33. **w.** is your occupation?
Ex. 3 : 13. shall say, **w.** is his name?
w. shall I say unto them? ⌈rod
4 : 2. **w.** is that in thine hand? A
12. I will teach thee **w.** shalt say
10 : 26. with **w.** we must serve Lord
13 : 14. when son asketh **w.** is this?
15 : 24. murmured **w.** shall we drink
16 : 7. **w.** are we that ye murmur
15. manna; they wist not **w.** it
19 : 4. have seen **w.** I did unto Eg-s
23 : 11. **w.** they leave beasts sh. eat
32 : 1. wot not **w.** is become of him,
21. Aaron, **w.** did peo. unto ⌊23.
33 : 5. I may know **w.** to do unto
Le. 25 : 20 **w.** shall we eat 7th year?
Nu. 9 : 8. I will hear **w.** L. will com-d
13 : 18. see the land, **w.** it is, 19, 20.
16 : 11. **w.** is Aaron that ye mur-
21 : 14. **w.** he did in Red sea ⌊mur
22 : 19. I may know **w.** L. will say
23 : 17. **w.** hath the Lord spoken?
23. be said, **w.** hath G. wrought?
Nu. 24 : 13. **w.** L. saith will I speak,
1 K. 22 : 14. 2 Ch. 18 : 13. ⌈peor
De. 4 : 3. **w.** Lord did bec. of Baal-
7 : 18. remember **w.** L. did unto Pha.
8 : 2. know **w.** was in thine heart
10 : 12. **w.** doth Lord require of thee
11 : 5. **w.** he did in the wilderness
6. **w.** he did unto Dathan, Abiram
25 : 17. remember **w.** Amalek did
32 : 20. I will see **w.** their end sh. be
Jos. 2 : 10. **w.** ye did unto two kings
5 : 14. **w.** saith my lord unto serv.
7 : 8. **w.** sh. I say when Isr. turneth
15 : 18. Caleb said unto her, **w.**
wouldest thou? Ju. 1 : 14. ⌈this
Ju. 7 : 11. thou sh. hear **w.** they say
8 : 3. **w.** was I able to do in compar.
9 : 48. **w.** ye have seen me do, do
11 : 12. **w.** hast thou to do with me
13 : 17. Manoah said, **w.** thy name
14 : 18. **w.** is sweeter than honey,
w. is stronger than a lion? ⌈(2)
18 : 3. **w.** makest thou in this place
8. their brethren said, **w.** say ye?
24. **w.** have I more? **w.** is this ye
say? **w.** aileth thee? ⌈gleaned
Ru. 2 : 18. mother saw **w.** she had
1 S. 3 : 17. **w.** is the thing Lord said
6 : 4. **w.** sh. be the trespass offer-g
9 : 7. **w.** shall we bri. the man? (2)
10 : 8. till I shew **w.** thou shalt do
11. **w.** this is come unto son of K.?
15. Tell me **w.** Sam-l said unto you
15 : 16. I will tell **w.** Lord hath said
18 : 8. **w.** he have more but kingd.?
18. David said unto Saul, **w.** am I
19 : 3. **w.** I see that will I tell thee
20 : 1. **w.** have I done? **w.** is mine
iniquity? **w.** is my sin? ⌈ly
10. **w.** if thy father answer rough-
21 : 3. **w.** is under thine hand?
give me 5 loaves, or **w.** is pres-t
25 : 17. consider **w.** thou wilt do
28 : 9. knowest **w.** Saul hath done
13. Be not afraid; for **w.** sawest
29 : 3. **w.** do these Hebrews here?
8. **w.** have I done? **w.** hast found
2 S. 7 : 18. Who am I? **w.** is my
house that thou, 2 Ch. 17 : 16.
20. **w.** can David say more unto
thee? 2 Ch. 17 : 18. ⌈look upon
9 : 8. **w.** is thy servant thou should
17 : 5. let us hear **w.** Hushai saith
18 : 21. Go tell k. **w.** thou hast seen
29. tumult, I knew not **w.** it was
19 : 18. to do **w.** he thought good
35. taste **w.** I eat or **w.** I drink?
21 : 4. **w.** ye shall say, that will I do
11. told David **w.** Rizpah had done
1 K. 1 : 16. king said, **w.** wouldest
2 : 5. thou knowest **w.** Joab did to
me, **w.** he did unto Abner and
9. knowest **w.** thou oughtest to
3 : 5. God said, Ask **w.** I shall give
thee, 2 Ch. 1 : 7. ⌈with me
11 : 22. But **w.** hast thou lacked
14 : 3. tell **w.** shall become of child
14. cut off hou. of Jerob.; but **w.**?
16 : 5. acts of Baasha and **w.** he did
18 : 9. Obad. said, **w.** have I sinned
13. **w.** I did when Jezebel slew⌈er
2 K. 6 : 33. **w.** sho. I wait for L. long-
7 : 12. shew **w.** Syrians have done
8 : 14. **w.** said Elisha to thee? ⌈19.
9 : 18. **w.** hast thou to do wi. peace?
20 : 8. **w.** be sign Lord will heal me
14. Isaiah unto Hezekiah, **w.** said
these men? Is. 39 : 3. ⌈4.
15. **w.** seen in thine house, Is 39 :
22 : 19. **w.** I spake against this place
1 Ch. 12 : 32. to know **w.** Isr. ought
Ezr. 5 : 4. **w.** are names of the men
6 : 8. decree **w.** ye shall do to elders
8 : 17. told **w.** they should say⌈this?
9 : 10. O God, **w.** shall we say after
Ne. 2 : 4. For **w.** dost make request?
12. nei. told I **w.** God had put in

Ne. 2 : 16. rulers knew not w. I did
4 : 2. said, w. do these feeble Jews?
Es. 2 : 1. w. was decreed ag. her (2)
11. know w. sho. become of Esther
4 : 5. to know w. it was, why it was
5 : 3. w. wilt thou, queen Esther?
6. w. is thy petition? it shall be granted. w. is thy request? 3.-7 : 2.-9, 12. [her
8 : 1. Esther told w. he was unto
9 : 5. did w. they would unto those
12. w. have Jews done in provinces
Jb. 6 : 11. w. is my strength that I hope? w. is mine end [prove?
25. but w. doth your arguing re-
7 : 17. w. is man that thou magnify
11 : 8. high as heaven, w. canst thou do? deeper than hell, w. canst thou know? [also
13 : 2. w. ye know, same do I know
13. and let come on me w. will
15 : 9. w. knowest thou we know
12. w. do thy eyes wink at? [not (2)
14. w. is man that he be clean?
16 : 3. w. emboldeneth thee, thou
6. though forbear, w. am I eased?
21 : 15. w. is Almighty that we sho.
23 : 5. I would underst. w. he wou.
13. w. soul desireth, he doeth [say
27 : 8. w. is the hope of hypocrite
31 : 14. w. sh. I do when God riseth? when he visiteth, w. shall I
32 : 11. whilst ye searched w. to say
34 : 4. let us know w. is good [est
33. therefore speak w. thou know-
35 : 7. righteous, w. givest him? (2)
37 : 19. Teach us w. we shall say
40 : 4. I am vile; w. sh. I ans thee?
Ps. 8 : 4. w. is man thou art mindful of him? He. 2 : 6. [w. it is
39 : 4. make me to know mine end,
7. now, Lord, w. wait I for? [stat.
50 : 16. w. hast thou to declare my
66 : 16. w. he hath done for my soul
85 : 8. I will hear w. Lord will spe.
116 : 12. w. shall I render unto Lord
120 : 3. w. shall be given unto thee, false tongue? (2) [est knowl.
144 : 3. Lord, w. is man, thou tak-
Pr. 4 : 19. know not at w. they stum.
10 : 32. righteous know w. is accept-
23 : 1. consider w. is bef. thee [able
25 : 8. lest thou know not w. to do
27 : 1. knowest not w. a day may
30 : 4. w. is his name, w. his son's
Ec. 2 : 2. I said of mirth, w. doeth it?
3. w. was that good for sons of m.
22. w. hath man of all his labour
6 : 8. w. hath wise more than fool? w. hath the poor? [better?
11. increase vanity, w. is man the
12. who knoweth w. is good for m.
7 : 10. w. is cause former days bet-r
10 : 14. a man cannot tell w. shall be; w. shall be after him, who tell him? 8 : 22.-6 : 12. [of spirit
11 : 5. thou knowest not w. is way
Can. 5 : 9. w. is my beloved more
6 : 13. w. will ye see in Shulamite?
Is. 5 : 4. w. more to my vineyard
10 : 3. w. will ye do in visitation
14 : 32. w. sh. one ans. messengers
19 : 12. w. L. hath purposed upon E.
21 : 6. let him declare w. he seeth
11. Watchman, w. of the ni.? (2)
22 : 16. w. hast thou here and who.
38 : 15. w. sh. I say? he hath spok.
22. w. is sign I sh. go up to house
40 : 6. And he said, w. shall I cry?
41 : 22 Let them shew us w. shall happen, former thi-s w. they be
45 : 9. Sh. the clay say, w. makest
10. Woe unto him, that saith unto father, w. begettest thou? (2)
52 : 5. w. have I here, saith Lord
64 : 4. w. he hath prepared for him
Je. 1 : 11. Jere-h, w. seest thou? 13.

Je. 5 : 15. nei. underst-st w. they say
6 : 18. know, O cong-n w. is among
7 : 12. in Shiloh, see w. I did to it
8 : 6. no man saying, w. ha. I done
9 : 12. for w. the land perisheth
11 : 15. w. hath my beloved to do
13 : 21. w. say when he sh punish
16 : 10. w. is our iniquity? w. our
23 : 25. I heard w. prophets said
28. w. is the chaff to the wheat?
33. when people ask w. is the burden of the Lord? (2) [(2)
35. sh. say, w. hath the L. ans-d?
24 : 3. w. seest thou, Jeremiah?
32 : 24. w. thou hast spok. is come
33 : 24. Considerest not w. this peo.
37 : 18. w. have I offended ag. thee?
38 : 25. Declare w. thou said unto king; also w. king said [thee
La. 2 : 13. Jerus., w. shall I equal to
5 : 1. Remember w. is come upon us
Eze. 2 : 8. son of man, hear w. I say
8 : 12. w. ancients of Isr. do in dark
12 : 22. Son of man, w. this proverb
15 : 2. Son of man, w. is vine tree
19 : 2. And say, w. is thy mother?
20 : 29. w. is the high place ye go?
21 : 13. w. if sword contemn the rod
24 : 19. Wilt tell w. these are to us
33 : 30. Come, hear w. is word fr. L.
Da. 2 : 22. he knoweth w. is in darkn.
23. known w. we desired of thee
28. known to Neb-r w. sh. be in lat. days, 29. (2) 45.-8 : 19.-10 : 14.
12 : 8. O Lord, w. sh. be end of these
Ho. 9 : 14 w. give? miscarry-g womb
Am. 4 : 13. unto man, w. his thought
7 : 8. said, Amos, w. seest thou, 8 : 2.
Jon. 1 : 8. Tell us, w. is thine occupation? w. is thy country? (3)
4 : 5. see w. would become of city
Mi. 1 : 5. w. is the transgression of Jac.? w. high places of Judah?
6 : 1. Hear ye now w. the Lord saith
8. shewed thee, O man, w. is good, and w. doth the Lord require
Ha. 2 : 1. I will watch to see w. be will say, and w. I shall answer
18. w. profiteth the graven image
Zch. 1 : 9. O my lord, w. are these? (2) 19.-4 : 4.-6 : 4. [w. is length
2 : 2. Jerus., to see w. is breadth,
4 : 2. angel said, w. seest thou? 5 : 2.
5. knowest not w. these be? 13.
11. w. are these two olive trees
5 : 5. see w. is this that goeth forth
6. And I said, w. is it? an ephah
13 : 6. w. these wounds in hands?
Mal. 1 : 13. w. a weariness is it?
3 : 13. w. have we spoken ag. thee?
Mat. 5 : 47. w. do ye more than oth.
6 : 3. not left hand know w. right
25. Take no thought w. ye shall eat, w. drink (3), 31. Lu. 12 : 22. (2) 29. (2) [possessed of devils
8 : 33. told w. was befallen to the
10 : 19. take no thought w. ye shall speak (2), Mk. 13 : 11. Lu. 12 : 11.
27. w. I tell you in darkness that speak; w. ye hear, that preach
11 : 7. w. went ye out into wilderness to see, 8, 9. Lu. 7 : 24, 25, 26.
12 : 3. Have ye not read w. David did, Mk. 2 : 25. Lu. 6 : 3.
16 : 26. w. is a man profited if he shall gain the whole world, (2), Mk. 8 : 36, 37. Lu. 9 : 25.
17 : 25. w. thinkest thou, Simon?
19 : 6. w. therefore G. hath joined
20. young man saith, w. lack I
27. forsaken all, w. shall we have
20 : 15. lawful to do w. I will with
21. he said unto her, w. wilt thou?
22. Ye know not w. ye ask. Mk.
21 : 16. Hearest w. these say? [10 : 38.
28 But w. think ye? A cert. man
22 : 17. w. thinkest thou? Is it lawf.

Mat. 22 : 42. w. think ye of Christ?
24 : 3. w. shall be sign of thy coming, Mk. 13 : 4. Lu. 21 : 7. [liver
26 : 15. w. will ye give me and I de-
62. w. is it which these witness ag. thee? Mk. 14 : 60. [Mk. 14 : 64.
66. w. think ye? He is guilty,
70. I know not w. thou sayest, Mk. 14 : 68. Lu. 22 : 60.
27 : 4. they said, w. is that to us?
22. w. sh. I do with Jesus, Mk. 15 :
Mk. 4 : 24. Take heed w. ye hear [12.
5 : 7. w. have I to do with thee, Jesus, Lu. 8 : 28. [8 : 30
9. he asked, w. is thy name? Lu.
6 : 24. w. shall I ask? The head of
30. told w. they had done, w. tau.
9 : 6. he wist not w. to say [them?
16. scribes, w. question ye with
33. w. was it ye disputed by way?
10 : 3. w. did Moses command you?
17. w. shall I do that I may inherit eternal, Lu. 10 : 25.-18 : 18.
36. w. wou. ye I sho. do for you?
51. w. wilt I should do for thee?
11 : 5. w. do ye loosing the colt?
13 : 37. w. I say unto you, I say
14 : 36. not w. I will, but w. thou
40. nei. wist they w. to answer
15 : 24. casting lots, w. ev. man take
Lu. 5 : 22. w. reason ye in y-r hearts
7 : 31. this generation, to w. are
8 : 9. w. this parable be? [they like
9 : 33. Pet., not knowing w. he said
10 : 26. He said, w. is writ. in law?
12 : 12. Holy G. teach you w. to say
49. w. will I if already kindled?
57. why judge ye not w. is right?
13 : 18. w. is kingdom of God like?
15 : 26. asked w. these things meant
18 : 6. Hear w. unjust judge saith
36. hearing, he asked w. it meant
41. w. wilt thou I should do unto
20 : 13. w. shall I do? send my belov.
17. w. is this is written, The stone
21 : 14. not meditate w. sh. answer
22 : 49. When they saw w. would
Jn. 1 : 21. asked, w. then? thou Elias
22. w. sayest thou of thy self?
38. Jesus saith, w. seek ye? [thee
2 : 4. Woman, w. have I to do with
25. for he knew w. was in man
3 : 32. w. he hath seen he testifieth
4 : 22. ye worship ye know not w.; we know w. we worship
27. no man said, w. seekest thou?
5 : 19. Son do nothing but w. seeth
6 : 9. w. are they among so many?
28. w. do that we work works of G.?
30. They said, w. dost thou work?
62. w. if ye see Son of man ascend
7 : 51. judge bef. it know w. he doeth
8 : 5. such be stoned: w. say-t thou?
9 : 17. w. sayest thou of him, that
26. said again, w. did he to thee?
11 : 56. w. think, that he not come
12 : 6. Judas bare w. was put th-in
27. soul troubl-d; w. shall I say
49. Fa. gave com-t w. I sho say (2)
15 : 7. If abide in me, ask w. ye will
15. serv. knoweth not w. lord doeth
16 : 17. w. is this he saith? 18. (2)
18 : 21. they know w. I said (2)
35. Pilate ans-d, w. hast thou done?
38. Pilate saith, w. is truth?
19 : 22. w. I have written, I have
21 : 22. if tarry, w. is th. to thee? 23.
Ac. 5 : 35. take heed w. ye intend to
7 : 40. we wot not w. is become of
49. saith Lord, w. is pl. of my rest?
8 : 30. understandest w. readest?
36. w. doth hinder me to be bap.
9 : 6. L., w. wilt thou have me to do
10 : 4. afraid, said, w. is it, Lord?
15. w. God hath cleansed call not
21. w. is cause whf. ye are come?
11 : 17. w. was I that I withstand G.

Ac. 12 : 18. w. was become of Peter
14 : 11 people saw w. Paul had done
16 : 30. Sirs, w. must I do to be sa
17 : 18. w. will this babbler say?
19. May we know w. new doct. is?
19 : 3. Unto w. were ye baptized?
21 : 22. w. is it? multitude must
22 10. I said, w. shall I do, Lord?
15. be witness of w. thou hast seen
23 : 19. w. is it thou hast to tell me
30. say before thee w. had ag. him
28 : 22. desire to hear w. th. thinkest
Ro. 3 : 3. w. if some did not believe
5. w. sh. we say? Is G. unright-s
9. w. then? are we better than
4 : 1. w. shall we say then, 6 : 1.-
7 : 7.-9 : 14, 30. ⌈believed
3. For w. saith the Scripture? Abr.
21. w. he had promised was able
6 : 15. w. then? shall we sin ⌈I do
7 : 15. w. I wo., do I not, w. I hate
8 : 24. w. a man seeth, why hope
26. we know not w. we sho. pray
27. knoweth w. is mind of Spirit
31. w. sh. we say to these things?
9 : 22. w. if G. willing to shew wrath
10 : 8. w. saith it? word is nigh thee
11 : 2. Wot ye not w. Scripture saith
4. w. saith the answer of God?
7. w. then? Israel not obtained
15. w. receiving of th. be but life
12 : 2. prove w. is perfect will of God
1 Co. 4 : 7. w. hast thou, didst not
21. w. will ye? Sh. I come with rod
5 : 12. w. have I to judge them with-
7 : 16. w. knowest thou, O wife⌊out
9 : 18. w. is my reward, then?
10 : 15. wise men, judge ye w. I say
19. w. say I then? that the idol
11 : 22. w. shall I say to you? ⌈speak
14 : 6. w. shall I profit you except I
7. how known w. is piped, harped?
9. how sh. it be known w. is spok.?
15. w. is it then? I will pray with
16. understandeth not w. sayest
15 : 2. if in memory w. I preached
29. w. sh. they do wh. are baptized
32. w. advantageth it me if dead
2 Co. 1 : 13 none other than w. ye
12 : 13. w. is it wherein ye inferior
Ga. 4 : 30. w. saith the Scripture?
Ep 1 : 18. know w. is hope of his calling, w. the riches of his glory
19. w. is greatness of his power
3 : 9. make all see w. is fellowship
18. w. is the breadth and length
4 : 9. w. is it but that he descended
5 : 10. Proving w. is acceptable ⌈is
17. understanding w. will of Lord
Ph. 1 : 18. w. then? Ch. is preached
22 yet w. I sh. choose I wot not
Col. 1 : 27. known w. is riches of glory
1 Th. 2 : 19. w. is our hope or joy
2 Th. 2 : 6. ye know w. withholdeth
1 Ti. 1 : 7. understanding nei. w. they
2 Ti. 2 : 7. Consider w. I say ⌊say
He. 11 : 32. w. sh. I say more? ⌈16.
Ja. 2 : 14. w. doth it profit tho. man.
4 : 14. ye know now w. shall be on morrow. For w. is your life?
1 Pe. 1 : 11. Searching w., or w. time
4 : 17. w. shall the end be of them
1 Jn. 3 : 2. not appear w. we shall be
Jude 10. w. th. know as brute beasts
Re. 1 : 11. w. thou seest, write in bo.
2 : 7. hear w. the Spirit saith unto churches, 11, 17, 29.-3 : 6, 13, 22.
7 : 13. w. are these arrayed in white

See AILED, AILETH, DO, DOEST, DONE, MEAN, MEANEST, MEANETH.

See Seem, ed, eth, GOOD.

WHATSOEVER. ⌈ure

Ge. 2 : 19. w. Adam called ev. creat-
8 : 19. w. creepeth upon earth went
19 : 12. w. thou hast in city, bring
31 : 16. w. God hath said unto thee
Ge. 39 : 22. w. they did, he was doer
Ex. 13 : 2. Sanctify w. open-h womb
21 : 30. for ransom w. is laid upon
29 : 37. w. toucheth be holy, 30 : 29.
Le. 5 : 3. w. uncleanness that a man
4. w. a man pronounce with oath
6 : 27. w. sh. touch flesh th-f be ho-
7 : 27. w. soul eateth any blood⌊ly
11 : 3. w. parteth the hoof, that eat
9. w. hath fins and scales sh. eat
12. w. hath no fins nor scales be an abomination, De. 14 : 10.
27. w. goeth upon his paws uncl.
32. upon w. any dead doth fall (2)
33. w. is in vessel shall be unclean
42. w. goeth upon belly, w. hath more feet not eat (3) ⌈unclean
15 : 26. w. she sitteth upon sh. be
17 : 8. w. man offereth sacrifice⌈bl.
10. w. man eateth any manner of
13. w. man catcheth fowl or beast
21 : 18. w. man hath a blemish
22 : 5. w. uncleanness he hath
18. w. he be th. will offer oblation
20. w. hath blemish, ye not offer
23 : 29. w. soul not afflicted th. day
30. w. soul doeth any work th. day
27 : 32. of w. passeth under the rod
Nu. 5 : 10. w. any man giveth priest
18 : 13. w. is first ripe be thine
19 : 22. w. unclean person toucheth
22 : 17. I will do w. thou sayest
23 : 3. w. he sheweth I will tell thee
30 : 12. w. proceeded out of her lips
De. 2 : 37. w. Lord our God forbade
12 : 8. every man w. is right in own
15. kill, eat w. thy soul lusteth, 20.
32. w. I command you, observe
14 : 26. money for w. soul lusteth (2)
Ju. 10 : 15. do unto us w. seemeth good unto thee, 1 S. 14 : 36.
11 : 31. w. cometh forth of my hou.
1 S. 20 : 4. w. thy soul desireth, I
25 : 8. give w. cometh to thine hand
2 S. 3 : 36. w. k. did, pleased people
15 : 15. ready to do w. king appoint
19 : 39. w. thou sh. require will I do
1 K. 8 : 37. w. plague, w. sickness there be, 2 Ch. 6 : 28.
10 : 13. Solomon gave unto queen w. she asked, 2 Ch. 9 : 12.
20 : 6. w. is pleasant in thine eyes
Ezr. 7 : 18. w. sh. seem good to thee
20. w. sh. be needful for house of
21. w. Ezra require, it be done⌊G.
23. w. is com-ded by G. it be done
Es. 2 : 13. w. she desired was given
Jb. 37 : 12. may do w. he com-deth
41 : 11. w. is under heaven is mine
Ps. 1 : 3. w. he doeth shall prosper
8 : 8. w. passeth through the sea
115 : 3. he hath done w. he hath pleased, 135 : 6. ⌈not from
Ec. 2 : 10. w. mine eyes desired I kept
3 : 14. w. God doeth, it ho for ever
8 : 3. king doeth w. pleaseth him
9 : 10. w. thy hand findeth to do
Je. 1 : 7. w. I command thee, speak
15 : †7. bereave them of w. is dear
Mat. 5 : 37. w. is more than these
7 : 12. w. ye would men sho. do to
10 : 11. w. city ye enter inquire
14 : 7. an oath to give her w. she would ask, Mk. 6 : 22. ⌈Mk. 7 : 11.
15 : 5. by w. mightest be profited,
17. w. entereth mouth, Mk. 7 : 18.
16 : 19. w. thou shalt bind on earth, w. thou shalt loose, 18 : 18. ⌈13.
17 : 12. done to him w. listed, Mk. 9 :
20 : 4. w. is right I will give you, 7.
21 : 22. w. ye shall ask in prayer
23 : 3. w. they bid you, that observe
Mk. 6 : 22. Ask w. thou wilt, 23.
10 : 21. sell w. thou hast gi. to poor
35. that thou do w. we shall desire
11 : 23. he shall have w. he saith
13 : 11. w. shall be given you, speak
Lu. 4 : 23. w. we have heard done
9 : 4. w. house ye enter there abide
10 : 5. w. house ye enter say, Peace
35. w. spendest more I will repay
12 : 3. w. ye have spoken in darkn.
Jn. 2 : 5. w. he saith unto you, do it
5 : 4. made whole of w. disease he
11 : 22. w. wilt ask of God, G. give
12 : 50. w. I speak, as Father said
14 : 13. w. ye shall ask in my name will I do, 15 : 16.-16 : 23. ⌈said
26. to y-r remembrance w. I have
15 : 14. my friends, if ye do w. I com.
16 : 13. w. he sh. hear sh. he speak
Ac. 4 : 28. to do w. hand and counsel
Ro. 14 : 23. w. is not of faith is sin
16 : 2. assist in w. busin. she hath
1 Co. 10 : 25. w. is sold in shambles
27. w. is set before you eat, asking
31. w. ye do, do all to the glory⌈me
Ga. 2 : 6. w. they were, no matter to
6 : 7. w. a man soweth sh. he reap
Ep. 5 : 13. w. doth manifest is light
Ph. 4 : 11. learned in w. state I am
Col. 3 : 17. w. ye do, do all in name
23. w. ye do, do it heartily as to L.
1 Jn. 3 : 22. w. we ask we rec., 5 : 15.
5 : 4. w. is born of God overcometh
3 Jn. 5. faithfully w. thou doest ⌈be
Re. 18 : 22. craftsman of w. craft he
21 : 27. nei. w. worketh abomination

See **WHAT** with **soever.**

WHATSOEVER thing, s.

La. 13 : 58. or w. t. it be, if plague
Je. 42 : 4. w. t. Lord sh. answer you
44 : 17. do w. t. goeth out of mouth
Mat. 21 : 22. all t-s w. ye shall ask
28 : 20. observe all t-s w. I comm-d
Mk. 7 : 18. w. t. entereth man can-t
Jn. 17 : 7. all t-s w. given me are of
Ac. 3 : 22. him sh. ye hear in all t-s w.
Ro. 15 : 4. w. t-s written aforetime
Ep. 6 : 8. w. good t. any man doeth
Ph. 4 : 8. Finally, brethren, w. t-s are true, w. t-s are honest (5)

WHEAT. ⌈harvest

Ge. 30 : 14. found mandrakes in w.
Ex. 9 : 32. w. and rye were not smit.
34 : 22. first fruits of w. harvest
Nu. 18 : 12. All the best of wine, w.
De. 32 : 14. with fat of kidneys of w.
Ju. 6 : 11. Gid. threshed w. to hide
15 : 1. time of w. harvest Samson
1 S. 6 : 13. they of Beth-sh. reap-g w.
12 : 17. Is it not w. harvest to day?
2 S. 4 : 6. as tho. wou. have fetched w.
1 K. 5 : 11. Solomon gave Hiram w.
1 Ch. 21 : 20 Ornan was threshing w.
23. I give thee w. for meat offering
Ezr. 6 : 9. wh. they have need of, w.
7 : 22. speedily, to 100 meas. of w.
Ps. 81 : 16. fed them with finest of w.
147 : 14. filleth thee wi. finest of w.
Pr. 27 : 22. Tho. bray fool among w.
Can. 7 : 2. thy belly like heap of w.
Je. 12 : 13. have sown w., but reap
23 : 28. What is the chaff to the w.
31 : 12. flow togeth. for w., for wine
Eze. 27 : 17. Judah traded in w. of
Jo. 2 : 24. floors shall be full of w.
Am. 5 : 11. ye take from him burdens
8 : 5. th. we may set forth w.⌊of w.
6. buy the poor, sell refuse of w.
Mat. 3 : 12. he will gather his w. into garner, Lu. 3 : 17. ⌈the w.
13 : 25. the enemy sowed tares am.
29. lest ye root up w. with them
30. but gather the w. into my barn
Lu. 16 : 7. he said 100 measures of w.
22 : 31. that he may sift you as w.
Jn. 12 : 24. Except a corn of w. fall
Ac. 27 : 38. cast out the w. into sea
1 Co. 15 : 37. it may chance of w. or
Re. 6 : 6. A meas. of w. for a penny
18 : 13. merchandise of w. departed

WHEAT with **barley.**

De. 8 : 8. A land of w., b., and vines

Ru. 2 : 23. to glean unto end of b.
harvest and w. harv. [for Dav.
2 S. 17 : 28. Brought w., b., flour
2 Ch. 2 : 10. I will give 20,000 measures of w., 20,000 meas. of b.
15. w., b., and oil let him send
27 : 5. gave Jotham 10,000 measures of w., 10,000 of b.
Jb. 31 : 40. thistles instead of w.; cockle instead of b. [and b.
Is. 28 : 25. doth he not cast in w.
Je. 41 : 8. have treasures of w., b.
Eze. 4 : 9. Take w., b., make bread
45 : 13. offer sixth part of ephah of homer of w., sixth part of b.
Jo. 1 : 11. howl, O ye, for w. and b.

WHEATEN. [flour

Ex. 29 : 2. cakes, wafers, make of w.

WHEEL. [and half

1 K. 7 : 32. height of w. was cubit
33. work was like a chariot w. [w.
Ps. 83 : 13. O God, make them like a
Pr. 20 : 26. wise k. bringeth w. over
Ec. 12 : 6. w. brok. at cistern [wicked
Is. 28 : 27. neither is cart w. turned upon the cummin [cart
28. nor break corn with w. of his
Eze. 1 : 15. one w. upon the earth
16. was as it were a w. in middle of a w., 10 : 10. [another w.
10 : 9. one w. by one cherub and
13. for wheels it was cried, O w.
Ja. 3 : †6. tongue setteth on fire w.

WHEELS. [of nature

Ex. 14 : 25. took off their chariot w.
Ju. 5 : 28. why tarry w. of his char.
1 K. 7 : 30. ev. base had 4 brazen w.
32. under the borders were four w., and the axletrees of w. were
33. work of w. was like chariot wh.
Pr. 25 : † 11. word spok. upon his w.
Is. 5 : 28. their w. like a whirlwind
Je. 18 : 3. he wrought work on w.
47 : 3. at the rumbling of his w.
Eze. 1 : 16. appearance of w., 10 : 9.
19. when living creatures went, w. went; the w. were lifted up from the earth, 10 : 16, 19.
20. w. were lifted up, for spirit of creature was in the w., 19, 21.
3 : 13. I heard also the noise of w.
10 : 2. Go in betw. w. under cherub
6. Take fire from between the w.; he went in, stood beside the w.
9. behold the four w. by cherub.
12. the w. were full of eyes (2) [(2)
11 : 22. did cherubim lift wings, w.
23 : 24. Babylonians ag. thee wi. w.
26 : 10. walls shake at noise of w.
Da. 7 : 9. Ancient of days; his w. as
Na. 3 : 2. noise of rattling of w. [fire

WHELP, S.

2 S. 17 : 8. as bear robbed of her w-s
Pr. 17 : 12. Let a bear robbed of w-s
Eze. 19 : 2. she nourished her w-s
3. she brought up one of her w-s
5. took another of her w-s, made
Ho. 13 : 8. as a bear bereaved of w-s
Na. 2 : 11. lion walked and lion's w.
12. The lion did tear enough for
See **LION'S whelp, s.** [his w-s

WHEN.

Ge. 4 : 12. w. thou tillest the ground
6 : 4. w. sons of God came in unto
12 : 11. w. he was near Eg. [dau-s
19 : 15. w. morning arose, the angels
24 : 36. bare a son w. she was old
29 : 31. w. L. saw Leah was hated
30 : 30. w. I shall provide for mine
31 : 49. w. we are absent, one from
37 : 18. w. they saw Joseph afar off
23. w. Joseph was come unto his
38 : 9. w. he went in unto bro-'s wife
25. w. Tamar was brought forth
28 w. she travailed, one put out h.
39 : 13. w. she saw he left garment
15. w. he heard I lifted my voice
Ge. 40 : 13. w. thou wast butler [thee
14. think on me w. it be well with
16. w. baker saw interpret-n was
43 : 16. w. Joseph saw Benj. [good
21. w. we came to the inn [bro-t
26. w. Joseph came home they
44 : 31. w. he seeth lad not wi. us, 30.
45 : 27. w. he saw wagons Jos-h sent
46 : 33. w. Pha. shall call you and
47 : 18. w. th. year was ended [died
48 : 7. w. I came fr. Padan Rachel
17. w. Jos. saw his fath. laid hand
49 : 33. w. Jacob had made an end
50 : 4. w. days of his mourn-g past
17. Joseph wept w. they spake [E.
Ex. 3 : 12. w. hast bro-t people out of
4 : 21. w. thou goest to return into
8 : 9. w. I shall entreat for thee [E.
13 : 8. L. did when I came out of E.
11. w. L. sh. bring thee into land
15. w. Pha. would hardly let us go
17. w. Pharaoh had let people go
16 : 8. w. L. sh. give you in evening
Le. 5 : 3. w. he knoweth of it, guilty
5. w. he shall be guilty in one of
9 : 24. w. people saw they shouted
10 : 20. w. Moses heard, was cont-t
13 : 14. w. raw flesh appeareth, he
14 : 57. To teach w. unclean, w. cl.
15 : 23. w. he toucheth it be uncl-n
31. w. they defile my tabernacle
26 : 17. ye sh. flee w. none pursueth
26. w. I have broken staff of bread
Nu. 10 : 35. w. ark set forward, Mos.
36. w. it rested, he said, Return, L.
De. 6 : 7. teach w. thou sittest in house, w. walkest (4) 11 : 19. (4)
8 : 12. Lest w. full thou forget, 13.
21 : 16. w. he maketh sons to in-
25 : 19. w. L. hath given rest [herit
Jos. 23 : 16. w. ye transgressed cov.
1 S. 1 : 7. w. she went to house of L.
3 : 12. w. I begin will make an end
10 : 2. w. thou art departed from me
12 : 12. w. the L. was your king (2)
30 : 26. w. David came to Ziklag
2 S. 21 : 12. w. Philis. had slain Saul
1 K. 8 : 30. w. thou hearest, forgive
11 : 4. w. Sol-n was old, his wives
14 : 28. w. king went into house of
2 K. 5 : 13. w. he saith, Wash, be cl-n
2 Ch. 12 : 11. w. king entered house
20 : 22. w. they began to sing [of L.
29 : 27. w. the burnt offering began
Ezr. 4 : 23. w. copy of Artaxerxes' let-
Ne. 2 : 6. w. wilt thou return? [ter
Jb. 7 : 4. w. I lie down I say, w. sh. I
22 : 29. w. men are cast down [arise
36 : 13. cry not w. he bindeth them
Ps. 41 : 5. w. sh. he die and his name
42 : 2. w. sh. I appear before God?
49 : 16. be not afraid w. one is rich
71 : 18. w. I am old and grey headed
94 : 8. ye fools, w. will ye be wise?
101 : 2. O w. wilt thou come unto
119 : 82. w. wilt thou comfort me?
126 : 1. w. L. turned captiv-y of Z.
Pr. 4 : 12. w. runnest, not stumble
Ec. 8 : 7. who can tell w. it sh. be? [(2)
Je. 2 : 17. w. he led thee by the way
5 : 7. w. I fed them to the full [est
11 : 15. w. doest evil, thou rejoic-
13 : 27. made clean? w. shall it be
Eze. 21 : 25. w. iniquity have an end
38 : 18. w. Gog shall come ag. land
Da. 3 : 7. w. peo. heard sound of mu.
Am. 8 : 5. w. will new moon be gone
Zch. 7 : 5. w. ye fasted and mourned
6. w. ye did eat, did not ye eat (2)
14 : 3. ag. nations as w. he fought
Mat. 2 8. w. ye have found him
10. w. they saw the star, rejoiced
5 : 11. Blessed are ye w. men shall revile you, Lu. 6 : 22. (2) [sound
6 : 2. w. doest thine alms, do not
5. w. thou prayest, not be as, 6.
16. w. ye fast, be not as hypocr-s
Mat. 7 : 28. w. Jesus had ended say.
9 : 15. w., 25. - 11 : 1. - 12 : 3. -
13 : 26, 32, 46. -15 : 2. - 17 : 25. -
21 : 1, 34, 40. - 24 : 15. - 26 : 29.
Mk. 1 : 32. - 2 : 20, 25. -3 : 11. -
4 : 10, 15, 16, 29, 31, 32. -7 : 17.
-8 : 19, 20, 38. - 11 : 1, 19, 25. -
12 : 23, 25. - 13 : 7, 11, 14 - 14 :
12. - 15 : 20, 41. Lu. 2 : 21, 22,
42. - 4 : 25 - 5 : 35. -6 : 13. - 8 :
13. -9 : 26. -11 : 2, 21, 36. -12 : 11,
54, 55. -13 : 12, 28, 35. -14 : 8, 12,
13. -16 : 4, 9. -17 : 22. -21 : 9, 20,
30, 31. - 22 : 14, 35. - 23 : 33, 42.
Jn. 1 : 19. - 2 : 10, 22. -4 : 21, 23,
45. -5 : 7, 25. -6 : 24. - 7 : 27, 31. -
8 : 28, 44. -9 : 4, 14. -10 : 4. - 12 :
16, 17, 41. - 13 : 19, 31. -14 : 29. -
15 : 26 -16 : 4, 13, 21, 25. -19 : 6,
8, 23, 30. - 20 : 24. - 21 : 15, 18.
Ac. 1 : 13. -8 : 18, 39. -11 : 2. -12 :
6. -21 : 5, 35. -22 : 20. -23 : 30, 33,
34. (2) 35. - 24 : 22. -27 : 39. -28 :
16. Ro. 2 : 14. 1 Co. 14 : 26. -15 :
27. - 16 : 5, 12. 2 Co. 10 : 6. Ga.
2 : 11, 12, 14. Ph. 4 : 15. 1 Ti. 5 :
11. Tit. 3 : 12. Jude 9. Re. 4 : 9.
-9 : 5. -10 : 7. -11 : 7. -17 : 10.
Mat. 10 : 19. w. they deliver you up
23. w. persecute you in one city
12 : 43. w. unclean spirit, Lu. 11 : 24.
13 : 4. w. he sowed, some seeds fell
53. w. Jes. had finished, 19 : 1. -26 : 1.
19 : 28. w. Son of man sh., 25 : 31.
21 : 23. w. he was come into temple
23 : 15. w. he is made, ye make him
24 : 3. Tell us, w. sh. these thi-s be? Mk. 13 : 4. Lu. 21 : 7. [Mk. 13 : 14.
15. w. ye shall see abomination,
32. w. branch is yet tender. Mk. 13
33. w. ye sh. see all, Mk. 13 : 29. [28.
50. shall come, w. he looketh not
25 : 37. Lord, w. saw we thee an hungered, and fed thee? 44.
38. w. saw we thee a stranger [on
39. w. saw we thee sick or in pris-
26 : 30. w. they had sung a hymn
27 : 12. w. he was accused of priests
19. w. he was set on judgment seat
26. w. Pilate had scourged Jesus
34. w. had tasted would not drink
Mk. 4 : 15. w. they have heard, Satan
16. w. they have heard word, rec.
34. w. alone he expounded to disc.
5 : 18. w. he was come into the ship
6 : 20. w. heard John, he did many
41. w. he had taken the five loaves
8 : 19. w. I brake the five loaves
20. And w. the seven among 4,000
38. w. he cometh in glory of Fath.
9 : 20. w. he saw him, the spirit tare
10 : 17. w. he was gone forth, came
12 : 14. w. were come they say, M.
25. w. they shall rise fr. dead, 23.
13 : 7. w. ye hear of wars, be not
11. w. they shall deliver you up
33. watch, for ye know not w., 35.
14 : 11. w. they heard it, they were
15 : 45. w. he knew it of centurion
Lu. 1 : 41. w. Elis-h heard salutation
2 : 27. w. parents bro-t in child Jes.
39. w. they had performed all
48. w. they saw him, were amazed
3 : 21. w. all the peo. were baptized
4 : 25. w. great famine thro-t land,
5 : 4. w. he had left speaking [(2)
6. w. they had this done, inclosed
12. w. he was in a certain city, a
6 : 3. what David did w. hungered
13. w. it was day, called disciples
26. Woe unto you w. all men spe.
7 : 1. w. he had ended his sayings
12. w. he came nigh gate of city
8 : 40. w. Jesus was returned, peo.
9 : 36. w. the voice was past, Jesus
51. w. time, he be received up, he
10 : 35. w. I come again I will repay

Lu. 11 : 1. w. he ceased, one of his
2. w. ye pray, say, Our Father
22. w. stronger than he sh. come
34. w. thine eye is evil (2) [ding
12 : 36. w. he will return from wed-
58. w. thou goest with adversary
14 : 10. w. he th. bade thee com-h (2)
16 : 4. w. I am put out of stewardsh.
9. w. ye fail they may receive you
17 : 10. w. ye shall have done all
20. demanded w. kingdom of God
18 : 43. peo. w. they saw, gave praise
19 : 5. w. Jesus came he saw Zacc.
15. w. he was returned, received
29. w. he was come nigh to Bethp.
41. w. come near, he beheld city
20 : 37. w. he calleth Lord, the G.
22 : 7. w. passover must be killed
32. w. converted, strengthen bre.
35. w. I sent you without purse
23 : 42. remember me w. comest
Jn. 2 : 9. w. ruler of the feast tasted
23. w. he was in Jerus. at passover
4 : 1. w. the Lord knew how Phari.
25. w. he is come, will tell us all
40. w. Samaritans were come
52. of hour w. he began to amend
6 : 12. w. they were filled he said
16. w. even was come his disciples
25. w. they found him on oth. side,
Rabbi, w. camest thou hither?
7 : 10. w. his brethren were gone
8 : 7. So w. they continued asking
28. w. ye have lifted up Son of m.
11 : 6. w. he had heard he was sick
32. w. Mary was come where Jes.
33. w. Jesus saw her weeping
13 : 19. that w. it is come ye may
believe I am he, 14 : 29. [troubl.
21. w. Jesus had thus said, he was
31. w. Judas was gone out, Jesus
16 : 4. w. time is come, may rememb.
8. w. he is come, he will reprove
19 : 33. w. they came to Jesus and
20 : 20. w. he had said, shewed ha.
24. Thomas not with them w. Jes.
21 : 15. w. they had dined, Jesus
18. w. young, thou girdedst (2)
Ac. 1 : 13. w. they were come in
2 : 1. w. day of Pentecost was come
37. w. they heard this were pricked
3 : 19. w. the times of refreshing
4 : 13. w. they saw boldn. of John
31. w. they had prayed, pl. shaken
5 : 7. three hours, w. his wife came
22. w. officers found th. not in, 23.
24. w. the chief priests heard
33. w. they heard that, they were
cut to the heart, 7 : 54.
6 : 6. w. they had prayed, 13 : 3.
7 : 4. w. father was dead he remov.
17. w. time of promise drew nigh
23. w. he was full forty years old
60. when had said this, fell asleep
8 : 12. w. they believed Philip [them
15. w. they were come, prayed for
10 : 7. w. angel which spake unto
12 : 25. w. had fulfilled ministry
13 : 17. w. they dwelt as strangers
29. w. they had fulfilled all writ.
14 : 5. w. there was an assault made
16 : 15. w. she was baptized and her
17 : 13. w. Jews of Thess. had knowl.
18 : 5 w. Silas and Tim. were come
19 : 9. w. divers were hardened and
20 : 14. w. he met with us at Assos
18. w. elders were come, Paul said
21 : 12. w. we heard, besought him
27. w. the seven days were ended
22 : 11. w. I could not see for glory
25 : 14. w. they had been many days
27 : 1. w. it was determined th. we
27. w. 14th night was come [ous
28 : 4. w. barbarians saw venom-
Ro. 2 : 16. In day w. God sh. judge
3 : 4. overcome w. thou art judged
5 : 13. sin not imputed w. no law

Ro. 6 : 20. w. ye were servants of sin
7 : 5. For w. we were in the flesh
11 : 27. w. I sh. take aw. their sins
13 : 11. nearer than w. we believed
1 Co. 9 : 27. lest w. I have preached
11 : 25. took cup w. he had supped
32. w. we are judged are chasten-
34. will set in order w. I come [ed
13 : 10. w. th. wh. is perfect is come
11. w. I was a child I spake (2)
14 : 16. w. thou sh. bless wi. spirit
15 : 24. w. he sh. have put down all
54. w. this corruptible [(2), 28.
16 : 2. no gatherings w. I come, 3.
3. w. I come, whomso. ye approve
2 Co. 3 : 15. w. Moses is read, the vail
16. w. it shall turn to the Lord
12 : 10. w. I am weak then am I st.
13 : 9. we are glad w. we are weak
Ga. 1 : 15. w. it pleased God, who
4 : 3. we, w. children, were in bond.
4. w. fulness of time was come
18. not only w. I am with you
Col. 3 : 4. w. Christ shall appear, ye
7. ye walked w. ye lived in them
4 : 16. w. this epistle is read among
1 Th. 3 : 4. w. with you, we told you
5 : 3. w. they shall say, Peace and
2 Th. 1 : 7. w. L. Jesus sh. be revealed
10. w. he shall come to be glorified
3 : 10. w. we were with you we com.
2 Ti. 4 : 3. w. not endure sound doct.
He. 1 : 6. w. he bringeth in firstbegot.
3 : 9. w. your fathers tempted me
7 : 10. w. Melchisedec met him
Ja. 1 : 2. w. ye fall into divers temp.
1 Pe. 2 : 23. w. reviled, reviled not (2)
3 : 20. w. longsuffering of G. waited
4 : 13. w. his glory shall be revealed
1 Jn. 2 : 28. w. he shall appear, we
3 : 2. w. he shall appear, we be like
5 : 2. we love chil. of G. w. we love G.
Re. 1 : 17. w. I saw, I fell as dead, 22:
5 : 8. w. he had taken book [8.
6 : 1. I saw w. Lamb opened, 3,
5, 7, 9, 12.-8 : 1. [thunders, 4.
10 : 3. and w. he had cried, seven
12 : 13. w. dragon saw he was cast
18 : 9. w. see smoke of her burning
20 : 7. w. 1,000 years are expired
22 : 8. w. I had seen I fell down

WHENCE.

Ge. 3 : 23. to till ground w. he was
29 : 4. Jac. said, brethren, w. be ye?
Nu. 11 : 13. w. flesh to give people?
23 : 13. place w. thou mayest see th.
De. 9 : 28. Lest land w. thou bro-t us
11 : 10. land is not as Eg. w. ye ca.
Jos. 2 : 4. came men, but I wist not w.
20 : 6. slayer unto city, w. he fled
Ju. 13 : 6. I asked not w. he was
1 S. 25 : 11. I know not w. they be?
30 : 13. David said unto him w. art
thou? 2 S. 1 : 3, 13. [shall I?
2 K. 6 : 27. If Lord not help thee, w.
20 : 14. Isaiah said, w. came they
unto thee? Is. 39 : 3. [turn
Ne. 4 : 12. all places w. ye shall re-
Jb. 1 : 7. Satan, w. comest thou? 2 : 2.
10 : 21. Bef. I go w. I not ret., 16 : 22.
Ec. 1 : 7. w. rivers come they return
Is. 30 : 6. land w. the viper, serpent
47 : 11. shalt not know w. evil ris-h
51 : 1. look unto rock w. ye are
hewn, to hole of pit w. [carried
Je. 29 : 14. you again into place w.
Na. 3 : 7. w. shall I seek comforters
Mat. 12 : 44. return into my house
w. I came, Lu. 11 : 24
13 : 27. from w. then hath it tares?
54. w. hath this man this wisdom,
and these works? 56. Mk. 6 : 2.
15 : 33. w. so much bread in wilderness, Mk. 8 : 4. [it?
21 : 25. baptism of John, w. was
Mk. 12 : 37. w. is David then his son?
Lu. 1 : 43. w. is this to me, th. mother

Lu. 13 : 25. I know you not w. ye are,
20 : 7. could not tell w. it was [27
Jn. 1 : 48. Nath. saith, w. knowest
2 : 9. of feast knew not w. wine was
4 : 11. w. hast thou living water?
6 : 5. w. sh. we buy bread th. these
7 : 27. w. know this man, w. he is;
no man knoweth w. Christ is
28. Ye both know me and w. I am
8 : 14. I know w. I came; but ye
cannot tell w. I come [he is, 30.
9 : 29. this fellow, we know not w.
19 : 9. Pilate saith, w. art thou?
Ac. 14 : 26. Antioch, w. recommend-
Ph. 3 : 20. w. we look for Saviour [ed
He. 11 : 15. if mindful of country w.
19. w. Abr. received him in figure
Ja. 4 : 1. w. come fightings am. you
Re. 2 : 5. Remember w. thou art fal-n
7 : 13. in white robes, w. came they?
See CAMEST, COMEST, COMETH.

WHENSOEVER. [good

Mk. 14 : 7. w. ye will, may do them
Ro. 15 : 24. w. I take journey into

WHERE. [Spain

Ge. 2 : 11. w., 13 : 3, 14.-19 : 27.-
20 : 13.-21 : 17.-31 : 13. (2).-33 :
19.-35 : 13, 15, 27.-39 : 20. - 40 :
3.-43 : 30. Ex. 5 : 11.-9 : 26.-12 :
13, 30.-15 : 27. - 18 : 5. - 20 : 21.
Le. 4 : 12, 24, 33.-6 : 25. - 7 : 2.-
14 : 13. Nu. 9 : 17.-17 : 4.-22 : 26.
-33 : 14, 54. De. 1 : 31.-8 : 15.-11:
10, 30.-18 : 6.-23 : 16. Jos. 4 : 3.
Ju. 5 : 27.-6 : 13.-17 : 8, 9.-18 :
10.-19 : 26. Ru. 1 : 7.-3 : 4. 1 S.
3 : 3.-9 : 10. - 10 : 5. - 14 : 11. -
19 : 3.-20 : 19. - 23 : 22, 23.-26 :
5. (2) 16 -30 : 9, 31. 2 S. 2 : 23.-
11 : 16.-15 : 32.- 17 : 12.-18 : 7.
1 K. 7 : 8.-17 : 19 2 K. 4 : 8.-6 :
1. - 23 : 7. 2 Ch. 36 : 20. Ezr. 1 :
4. Ne. 13 : 5 Jb. 10 : 22.-38 : 26.
Ps. 26 : 8.-58 : 5.-68 : 1.-69 : 2.-
84 : 3.-107 : 40. Pr. 15 : 17. Ec.
1 : 5.-8 : 10. Is. 35 : 7.-57 : 8. Je.
22 : 26. - 35 : 7. - 38 : 9. - 39 : 5.
Eze. 8 : 3. - 11 : 16, 17.-17 : 10,
16. - 21 : 30.-34 : 12.-48 : 7.-46 :
20, 24. - Da. 8 : 17. Ho. 13 : 10.
Am. 3 : 5. Na. 3 : 17. Zph. 3 : 19.
Mat. 6 : 19. (2) 20. (2). - 8 : 20. -
13 : 5.-25 : 24. (2) 26. (2).-26 : 57.
-28 : 6, 16. Mk. 2 : 4.-4 : 5, 15.-
5 : 40.- 13 : 14.-15 : 47. - 16 : 6.
Lu. 4 : 16, 17.-12 : 17, 33.-22 : 10.
Jn. 1 : 28, 39. - 3 : 8.-4 : 20, 46.-
6 : 23.-7 : 42.-10 : 40.-11 : 6, 30.
32, 41, 57.-12 : 1.-18 : 1.-19 : 18,
20, 41.-20 : 19. Ac. 1 : 13.-2 . 2.
-4 : 31. - 7 : 29, 33. - 12 : 12.-15 :
36.-17 : 1.-20 : 6, 8.-25 : 10. Ro.
4 : 15.-9 : 26.-15 : 20. Re. 11 : 8.
-12 : 6.-17 : 15.-20 : 10. [art thou?
Ge. 3 : 9. God said unto Adam, w.
4 : 9. Cain, w. is Abel thy brother?
18 : 9. w. is Sarah thy wife?
19 : 5. w. are the men wh. came in
22 : 7. w. is lamb for burnt off-g?
27 : 33. w. is he hath taken venison
37 : 16. tell me w. they feed flocks
38 : 21. w. is the harlot was by way
Ex. 2 : 20. unto his dau-s, w. is he?
20 : 24. places w. I record my name
29 : 42. w. I will meet you to speak
unto thee, 30 : 6, 36. [rock
De. 32 : 37. w. are their gods, their
Ju. 5 : 27. w. he bowed, he fell dead
9 : 38. w. is thy mouth, wherewith
Ru. 1 : 16. w. thou lodgest I will lo.
17. w. thou diest, will I die and
2 : 19. w. hast thou gleaned to
day? w. wroughtest thou? [is
1 S. 9 : 18. Tell me w. the seer's hou.
10 : 14. wh. we saw they were no w.
19 : 22. w. are Samuel and David?
2 S. 9 : 4. the king said, w. is he?

2 S. 16 : 3. king said, w. thy master's
17 : 20. w. is Ahimaaz and Jon. ⌊son
2 K. 2 : 14. w. is Lord God of Elijah ?
6 : 6. man of God said, w. fell it ?
13. spy w. he is, that I may fetch
18 : 34. w. are the gods of Hamath ?
w. are gods of, Is 36 : 19. ⌈37 : 13.
19 : 13. w. is the k. of Hamath, Is.
Est. 6 : 1. w. treasures were laid up
Es. 7 : 5. Who is he, w. is he th. ⌈off ?
Jb. 4 : 7. w. were the righteous cut
9 : 24. if not, w., and who is he ?
14 : 10. giveth up ghost, and w. is
15 : 23. for bread, saying, w. is it ?
17 : 15. And w. is now my hope
20 : 7. seen him shall say, w. is he ?
21 : 28. w. is the hou. of the prince ?
w. dwelling places of wicked ?
28 : 12. w. shall wisdom be found ?
w. is place of understand-g, 20.
35 : 10. none saith, w. is God my
38 : 4. w. thou when I laid founda.
19. w. is the way w. light dwelleth ? darkness, w. is the place
39 : 30. w. the slain are, there is she
Ps. 19 : 3. w. their voice is not heard
42 : 3. they say, w. is thy God ? 10.
79 : 10. whf. heathen say, w. is
their God ? 115 : 2. Jo. 2 : 17.
Pr. 11 : 14. w. no counsel is, peo. fall
14 : 4. w. no oxen are crib is clean
26 : 20. w. no wood, fire goeth out ;
w. no talebearers strife ceaseth
29 : 18. w. is no vision, peo. perish
Ec. 8 : 4. w. word of k. is, is power
11 : 3. w. tree faileth there it sh. be
Can. 1 : 7. Tell me w. thou feedest,
w. makest flock to rest ? ⌈ry ?
Is. 10 : 3. w. will ye leave your glo-
19 : 12. w. are they ? w. wise men ?
33 : 18. w. is the scribe ? w. is receiver ? w. is he that counted
49 : 21. w. had they been ⌊towers ?
50 : 1. w. is the bill of divorcement
51 : 13. w. is fury of the oppressor ?
63 : 11. w. is he bro-t them out of
sea ? w. is he th. put Holy Spirit
15. w. is thy zeal, thy strength
66 : 1. w. is house ye build unto
me ? w. is the place of my rest ?
Je. 2 : 6. Nei. said they, w. is Lord
8. priests said not, w. is the Lord ?
28. But w. are thy gods ? ⌈with
3 : 2. see w. thou hast not been lain
6 : 16. ask, w. is the way, walk th-n
7 : 12. Shiloh, w. I set my name
13 : 20. w. is flock was given thee
16 : 13. w. I will not shew you fav.
17 : 15. they say, w. is word of L. ?
22 : 26. w. not born, there sh. die
36 : 19. let no man know w. ye be
37 : 19. w. are now your prophets
La. 2 : 12. say, w. is corn and wine ?
Eze. 13 : 12. w. is the daubing ye
Ho. 1 : 10. w. it was said, Ye not my
13 : 10. w. is any may save thee
Mi. 7 : 10. w. is the Lord thy God ?
Na. 2 : 11. w. is dwelling of lions (2)
Zch. 1 : 5. Your fathers, w. are they
Mal. 1 : 6. if a father, w. is mine
honour ? if a master, w. my fear
2 : 17. ye say, w. God of judgment ?
Mat. 2 : 2. w. is he born king of Jews
4. demanded w. Christ be born
9. star stood over w. yo. child was
6 : 21. w. your treasure is, there
will your heart, Lu. 12 : 34.
8 : 20. Son of man hath not w. to
lay his head, Lu. 9 : 58. ⌈ered
18 : 20. w. two or three are gath-
26 : 17. w. wilt thou we prepare for
thee, Mk. 14 : 12. Lu. 22 : 9.
28 : 6. Come see place w. Lord lay
Mk. 6 : 55. carry those sick w. he ⌈48.
9 : 44. w. their worm dieth not, 46.
14 : 14. Master saith, w. is the
guestchamber, w., Lu. 22 : 11.

Lu. 8 : 25. he said w. is your faith ?
10 : 33. Samaritan came w. he was
17 : 17. ten cleansed, but w. nine ?
37. they answered, w., Lord ?
Jn. 1 : 38. Master, w. dwellest, 39.
6 : 62. ascend up w. he was before ?
7 : 11. Jews sought him, said, w. is
34. w. I am, ye cannot come, 36.
8 : 10. Woman, w. are thine accus-
19. said, w. is thy Father ? ⌊ers ?
9 : 12. w. is he ? He said, I know
11 : 34. w. have ye laid him ? ⌊not
57. th. if any man knew w. he was
12 : 26. w. I am there sh. my serv.
14 : 3. w. I am there ye may be also
17 : 24. given me, be with me w. I
20 : 2. and we know not w. they
have laid him, 13, 15. ⌈had lain
12. angels sitting w. body of Jes.
Ac. 11 : 11. men unto house w. I was
16 : 13. w. prayer was wont to be
20 : 6. Troas, w. we abode 7 days
28 : 14. Puteoli, w. we found breth.
Ro. 3 : 27. w. is boasting then ?
4 : 15. w. no law is, no transgression
5 : 20. w. sin abounded, grace more
15 : 20. preach, not w. Ch. is named
1 Co. 1 : 20. w. is the wise ? w. is
the scribe ? w. is disputer ?
12 : 17. If the body an eye, w. were
the hearing ? (2) ⌈body ?
19. if all one member, w. were the
15 : 55. O Death, w. is thy sting ?
O grave, w. is thy victory ?
2 Co. 3 : 17. w. Spirit of the Lord is
Ga. 4 : 15. w. is the blessedness ye
Col. 3 : 1. w. Christ sitteth on right
11. w. their is nei. Greek nor Jew
He. 9 : 16. w. a testament is, must
10 : 18. w. remission of these is
Ja. 3 : 16. w. strife is, there ev. evil
1 Pe. 4 : 18. w. shall ungodly appear ?
2 Pe. 3 : 4. w. promise of his coming ?
Re. 2 : 13. I know w. thou dwellest,
even w. Satan's seat is (3) ⌈time
12 : 14. w. she is nourished for a

Every WHERE. ⌈w.

Ge. 13 : 10. all plain well watered e.
Ex. 27 : 18. of court, breadth 50 e. w.
1 Ch. 13 : 2. sent unto brethren e. w.
Mk. 16 : 20. they preached e. w.
Lu. 9 : 6. preaching gospel, healing
e. w., Ac. 8 : 4. ⌈w. to repent
Ac. 17 : 30. commandeth all men e.
21 : 28. teacheth all e. w. ag. law
28 : 22. know it is e. w. spoken ag.
1 Co. 4 : 17. I teach e. w. in church
Ph. 4 : 12. e. w. I am instructed
1 Ti. 2 : 8. I will, that men pray e. w.

WHEREABOUT.

1 S. 21 : 2. Let no man know w. I

WHEREAS. ⌊send thee

Ge. 31 : 37. w. hast searched my stuff
De. 19 : 6. w. he not worthy of death
28 : 62. w. ye were as the stars for
1 S. 24 : 17. w. I reward thee evil for
2 S. 7 : 6. w. I have not dwelt in ho.
15 : 20. w. thou camest but yesterd.
1 K. 8 : 18. w. in thine heart to build
12 : 11. w. my father did lade you
with heavy yoke, 2 Ch. 10 : 11.
2 K. 13 : 19. w. thou sh. smite Syria
2 Ch. 28 : 13. w. we have offended L.
Jb. 22 : 20. w. our substance is not
Ec. 4 : 14. w. he also becometh poor
Is. 37 : 21. w. hast prayed ag. Senn-b
60 : 15. w. thou hast been forsaken
Je. 4 : 10. w. sword reacheth soul
Eze. 13 : 7. w. ye say, The L. saith it
16 : 7. w. thou wast naked and bare
34. w. none followed thee to com-
35 : 10. w. the Lord was there ⌊mit
36 : 34. be tilled, w. it lay desolate
Da. 2 : 41. w. thou sawest feet, toes
43. w. thou sawest iron with clay
4 : 23. w. king saw watcher ⌈stump
26. w. they commanded to leave

Da. 8 : 22. w. four stood up for it
Mal. 1 : 4. w. Edom saith, We impov.
Jn. 9 : 25. w. I was blind, now I see
1 Co. 3 : 3. w. there is am. you strife
Ja. 4 : 14. w. ye know not what shall
1 Pe. 2 : 12. w. they speak against
you as evil doers, 3 : 16. ⌈er in
2 Pe. 2 : 11. w. angels wh. are great-

WHEREBY. ⌈herit

Ge. 15 : 8. w. shall I know I sh. in-
44 : 5. Is not this w. he divineth ?
Le. 22 : 5. w. he may be made uncl-n
Nu. 5 : 8. w. atonement be made
17 : 5. w. they murmur ag. you
De. 7 : 19. arm, w. L. bro-t thee out
28 : 20. doings, w. thou forsak. me
1 S. 20 : 33. w. Jonathan knew it was
Ps. 45 : 5. arrows w. peo. fall under
8. palaces, w. they made thee glad
68 : 9. rain, w. didst confirm inher.
Je. 3 : 8. w. Isr. committed adultery
17 : 19. stand in gate w. kings come
23 : 6. is name w. he shall be called
33 : 8. w. they have sinned ag. me (3)
Eze. 18 : 31. w. ye have transgressed
20 : 25. judgments w. sho. not live
39 : 26. w. they have trespassed
40 : 49. brought me by steps w. they
46 : 9. not return by gate w. came
47 : 13. border, w. ye sh. inherit la.
Zph. 2 : 8. w. have reproached peo.
Lu. 1 : 18. w. shall I know this ?
78. w. the dayspring fr. on high
Ac. 4 : 12. none other na. w. be saved
11 : 14. w. thou and house be saved
19 : 40. no cause w. we give account
Ro. 8 : 15. w. we cry, Abba, Father
14 : 21. w. thy brother stumbleth
Ga. 6 : † 14. w. world is crucified
Ep. 3 : 4. w. ye may understand my
4 : 14. w. they lie in wait to deceive
30. w. we are sealed unto the day
Ph. 3 : 21. w. he is able to subdue
He. 12 : 28. grace w. we may serve G.
2 Pe. 1 : 4. w. are giv. prec. promises
3 : 6. w. world that was, perished
1 Jn. 2 : 18. w. we know it is last time

WHEREFORE.

Ge. 10 : 9. w. it is said, as Nimrod
16 : 14. w. well was called Beer-la.
18 : 13. w. did Sarah laugh ⌈woman
21 : 10. w. she said, Cast out this
31. w. he called place Beer-sheba
24 : 31. Come in, w. standest wi-t ?
26 : 27. w. come ye, seeing ye hate
29 : 25. w. hast thou beguiled me ?
31 : 27. w. didst flee away secretly
30. w. hast thou stolen my goods ?
32 : 29. w. dost ask after my name ?
38 : 10. w. Lord slew Onan also
40 : 7. w. look ye so sadly to day !
43 : 6. w. dealt ye so ill with me ?
44 : 4. w. ye rewarded evil for good ?
7. w. saith my Lord these words
47 : 19. w. sh. we die bef. thine eyes
22. w. they sold not their lands
50 : 11. w. name of it was Abel-miz.
Ex. 2 : 13. w. smitest thy fellow
5 : 4. w. do ye let peo. from works
14. w. have ye not fulfilled task
15. w. dealest thus with servants ?
22. Lord, w. hast so evil entreated
6 : 6. w. say unto Israel, I am Lord
14 : 11. w. dealt thus with us, 17 : 3.
15. Moses, w. criest thou unto me ?
17 : 2. w. people did chide wi. Mos.
20 : 11. w. the Lord blessed sab. day
31 : 16. w. Israel shall keep sabbath
32 : 12. w. Eg-ns say, For mischief
Le. 10 : 17. w. not eaten sin offering
13 : 25. w. priest shall pronounce
25 : 18. w. ye shall do my statutes
Nu. 9 : 7. w. are we kept back, that
11 : 11. L., w. hast afflicted serv. ?
12 : 8. w. not afraid to speak ag. M. ?
14 : 3. w. L. bro-t us into this land
41. w. do ye transgress command.

Nu.16 :3.w. lift yours. above cong.
20 : 5. w. have ye made us to come
up out of Egypt, 21 : 5. [Edom
21. w. Israel turned away from
21 : 14. w. it is said in book of wars
27. w. they th. speak in proverbs
22 : 32. w. hast smitten ass 3 times?
25 : 12. w. say, I give my covenant
32 : 5. w. if we have found grace
7. w. discourage ye chil. of Israel
De. 7 : 12. w. it shall come to pass
10 : 9. w. Levi no part with breth.
19 :7. w. I command, separate 3 cit-
29 . 24. w. hath Lord done thus [ies
Jos. 5 : 9. w. place is called Gilgal
7 : 5. w. hearts of people melted
7. O Lord, w. bro-t peo. over Jor.
10. L. said, w. liest upon thy face?
26. w. name, The valley of Achor
9 :11. w. elders spake, Take victuals
22. w. have ye beguiled us [ham
10 :3. w. Adoni-zedek sent unto Ho-
Ju. 2 : 3. w. I will not drive th. out
10 : 13 w. I will deliv. you no more
11 :27. w. I have not sinned ag. thee
12 : 1. w. passedst to fight ag. Am.
3. w. are ye come to fight ag. me?
15 : 19. w. he called name En-hak.
18 : 12. w. called pl. Mahaneh-dan
Ru. 1 : 7. w. Naomi went forth out
1 S. 1 : 20. w. Hannah bare a son
2 : 17. w. sin of young men was gr.
29 w. kick ye at my sacrifice
4 : 3. w. hath Lord smitten us
6 : 5. w. make images of emerods
6. w. do ye harden your hearts
9 : 21. w. speakest thou so to me?
15 : 19. w. didst not obey voice of L.
16 : 19. w. have sent messengers
18 : 15. w. when Saul Dav. behaved
21. w. Saul said to David, be my
27. w. David slew of Philist. 200
19 : 5. w. sin ag. innocent blood
24. w. they say, Is Saul am. proph-s
20 : 27. w. cometh not son of Jesse
31. w. fetch David, he sh. surely die
32. Jonathan said, w. sh. he be slain?
21 : 14. w. have ye brought him to
23 : 25. w. he came down into rock
28. w. Saul returned fr. pursuing
24 :9. w. hearest thou men's words
19. w. the Lord reward thee good
25 : 8. w. let young men find favour
36. w. Abigail told him noth. until
26 : 15. w. hast not kept thy lord, k.?
18. w. doth my lord pursue serv.?
27 :6. w. Ziklag pertaineth unto k-s
28 : 9. w. layest a snare for my life
16. said Samuel, w. dost ask of me
29 : 7. said Achish, w. go in peace
10. w. rise up early and depart
2 S. 2 : 16. w. place was called Hel-
kath-hazzurim [ground?
22. w. should I smite thee to the
23. w. Abner smote him under
5 : 8. w. they said the blind sh. not
7 : 22. w. thou art great, O Lord
10 : 4. w. Hanun took David's serv.
11 : 20. w. approached ye so nigh
12 : 23. he is dead, w. should I fast
14 : 13. w. thought such thing ag.
31. w. serv-s set my field on fire?
32. w. am I come from Geshur?
15 :19. Ittai, w. goest thou with us?
16 :10. who shall say, w. hast done
18 : 22. w. wilt thou run, my son
19 : 12. w. are ye last to bring king?
25. w. wentest not with me, Mep.
35. w. thy servant be a burden
42. w. be ye angry for this matter?
21:3. w. David said unto Gibeonites
24 : 21. w. is my Lord come to his
1 K. 1 : 2. w. servants said unto Da.
11. w. Nathan spake unto Bath-sh.
41. w. this noise of city in uproar?
11 : 11. w. Lord said unto Solom-n
12 : 15. w. king hearkened not

1 K. 16 : 16. w. Israel made Omri k.
22 : 34. w. said unto driver of char.
2 K. 4 : 23. w. wilt go to him to day?
31. w. Gehazi went again to meet
5 : 7. w. see how he seeketh quarrel
8. w. hast thou rent thy clothes?
7 : 7. w. they fled in twilight, left
9 : 11. w. came this fellow to thee?
36. w. they came again and told
17 : 26. w. they spake to king of As.
19 : 4. w. lift up thy prayer for
the remnant, Is. 37 : 4. [Perez.
1 Ch. 13 : 11. w. that place is called
2 Ch. 19 : 7. w. fear of Lord be upon
25 : 10. w. anger was kindled ag. Ju.
15. w. anger of Lord ag. Amaziah
28 : 5. w. Lord delivered him into
29 : 8. w. wrath of Lord was upon
34. w. brethren Levites did help
33 : 11. w. Lord brought upon them
Ne. 2 : 2. w. king said, Why sad
Es. 3 : 6. w. Haman sought to destr.
9 : 26. w. called these days Purim
Jb. 3 : 20. w. is light given to him
10 : 2. shew w. thou contendest
18. w. hast bro-t me out of womb?
13 : 14. w. do I take my flesh in my
24. w. hidest thou thy face [teeth
18 : 3. w. are we counted as beasts
21 : 7. w. do the wicked live [ion
32 :6. w. durst not shew mine opin-
33 : 1. w. Job, I pray, hear my spee.
42 : 6. w. I abhor myself, repent
Ps. 10 : 13. w. wicked contemn God?
44 : 24. w. hidest thou thy face
49 : 5. w. sho. I fear in days of evil
79 : 10. w. should the heathen say,
Where their God, 115 : 2. Jo. 2:17.
89 : 47. w. hast made all men in v.
Pr. 17 : 16. w. is price in hand of fool
Ec. 3 : 22. w. I perceive is nothing
4 : 2. w. I praised the dead [better
5 : 6. w. God be angry at thy voice
Is. 5 : 4. w. bro-t it forth wild grapes?
10 : 12. w. I will punish the fruit
16 : 11. w. my bowels should sound
24 : 15. w. glorify Lord [like harp
29 : 13. w. L. said, as this peo. draw
30 : 12. w., Because ye despise word
50 :2. w., when I came, was no man
55 : 2. w. spend money for that not
58 : 3. w. have we fasted, say they,
and thou seest not? [parel?
63 : 2. w. art thou red in thine ap-
Je. 2 : 9. w. I will plead with you
29. w. will ye plead with me?
31. w. say my people, We are lords
5 : 6. w. a lion sh. slay them [word
14. w. saith L., Bec. ye speak this
19. w. doeth our God these things
12 : 1. w. doth way of wicked prosp.?
13 : 22. w. come these things upon
16 : 10. w. L. pronounced evil ag. us
20 : 18. w. came I out of the womb?
22 : 8. w. hath Lord done thus
28. w. are they cast out he and his
23 : 12. w. their way be as slippery
27 : 17. w. this city be laid waste?
30 : 6. w. do I see every man as
woman in travail [prophesy
32 : 3. Zed-h, saying, w. dost thou
37 : 15. w. princes wroth with Jere.
40 : 15. w. should he slay thee
44 : 6. w. my fury was poured forth
7. w. commit this evil ag. souls
46 : 5. w. have I seen them turned?
49 : 4. w. gloriest thou in valleys
51 : 52. w. days come I will do judg.
La. 3 : 39. w. doth a man complain
5 : 20. w. dost thou forget us for ev.
Eze. 5 : 11. w. bec. defiled sanctuary
7 : 24. w. I bring worst of heathen
13 : 20. w. saith L., I am ag. your
16 :35. w., O harlot, hear word of L.
18 : 32. w. turn yourselves, live ye
20 : 25. w. I gave statutes not good
30. w. say unto house of Israel

Eze 21 : 7. say, w. sighest thou? [city
24 : 6. w. saith Lord, Woe to bloody
33 : 25. w. say, Ye eat with blood
43 : 8. w. I have consumed them
Da. 3 : 8. w. certain Chaldeans [be
4 : 27. w. O king, let my counsel
6 : 9. w. k. Darius signed writing
10 : 20. knowest w. I come unto [ish
Jon. 1 : 14. w. cried, let us not per-
Ha. 1 : 13. w. lookest upon them
that deal treacherously [the L.
Mal. 2 : 14. Yet ye say w.? Because
15. And w. one? Th. a godly seed
Mat. 6 : 30. w. if God so clothe grass
7 : 20. w. by their fruits ye shall
9 : 4. w. think evil in your hearts?
12 : 12. w. it is lawful to do well on
31. w. I say, All manner of sin
14 : 31. O thou w. didst thou doubt
18 : 8. w. if hand or foot offend thee
19 : 6. w. they are no more twain
23 : 31. w. ye be witnesses unto
34. w. I send unto you prophets
24 : 26. w. if they say, Behold, he
26 : 50. Friend, w. art thou come?
27 : 8. w. was called, Field of blood
Lu. 7 :7. w. nei. tho-t myself worthy
47. w. I say, Her sins are forgiven
19 : 23. w. gavest not my money
Jn. 9 : 27. w. would ye hear it again?
Ac. 1 : 21. w. of these men which
6 : 3. w. breth., look ye out 7 men
10 :21. what is cause w. ye are come
13 : 35. w. he saith in ano. psalm
15:19. w. my sentence is, trouble not
19 :32. knew not w. they were come
38. w. if Demetrius have a matter
20 : 26. w. I take you to record this
22 : 24. know w. they cried so ag.
30. know certainly w. he was accused of the Jews, 23 :28. [tener
24 : 26. w. Felix sent for him the of-
25 : 26. w. I have bro-t him bef. you
26 : 3. w. I beseech hear patiently
27 : 25. w. sirs, be of good cheer
34. w. I pray you to take some m.
Ro. 1 : 24. w. God gave them up to
5 : 12. w. as by one man sin [uncl-s
7 : 4. w. ye are become dead to law
12. w. the law is holy, and com-t
9 : 32. w.? Bec. they sought it not
13 : 5. w. ye must needs be subject
15 : 7. w. receive one ano. as Christ
1 Co. 4 : 16. w. be ye followers of me
8 : 13. w. if meat make my brother
10 : 12. w. let him that thinketh
14. w., beloved, flee from idolatry
11 : 27. w. whoso. sh. eat this bread
33. w., breth., tarry one for ano.
12 : 3. w. I give you to understand
14 : 13. w. let him that speaketh in
22. w. tongues are for a sign [unkn.
39. w., breth., covet to prophesy
2 Co. 2 : 8. w. confirm your love
5 : 9. w. we labour that whe. pres.
16. w. know we no man aft. flesh
6 : 17. w. come out from am. them
7 : 12. w., tho. I wrote unto you, I
8 : 24. w. shew ye to them, proof
11 : 11. w.? Bec. I love you not?
Ga. 3 :19. w., then, serveth the law?
24. w. the law was our schoolm-r
4 : 7. w. thou art no more a serv-t
Ep. 1:15. w. I cease not to give thanks
2 :11. w. remember, ye being Gen-s
3 : 13. w. I desire that ye faint not
4 :8. w. he saith, When he ascended
25. w., putting away lying, speak
5 : 14. w., Awake thou that sleep-
17. w. be ye not unwise, but [est
6:13. w. take unto you armour of G.
Ph. 2 : 9. w. G. hath highly exalted
12. w., as ye have always obeyed
Col. 2 : 20. w. if ye be dead wi. Christ
1 Th. 2 : 18. w. we would have come
3 : 1. w., when ye could no longer
4 : 18. w. comfort one another

1 Th. 5 : 11. w. comfort yourselves
2 Th. 1 : 11. w. we pray always for
2 Ti. 1 : 6. w. I put thee in remembr.
Tit. 1 : 13. w. rebuke them sharply
Phm. 8. w. for love's sake I beseech
He. 2 : 17. w. it behooved him to be
3 : 1. w., brethren, partakers of
7. w., as Holy Ghost saith, To day
10. w. I was grieved wi. generation
7 : 25. w. he is able to save them
8 : 3. w. of necessity that this man
10 : 5. w. when he cometh into wor.
11 : 16. w. God is not ashamed to
12 : 1. w. seeing we are compassed
12. w. lift up hands which hang
28. w. we receiving a kingdom
13 : 12. w. Jesus suffered wi-t gate
Ja. 1 : 19. w. let ev. man be swift to
21. w. lay apart all filthiness⌊hear
4 : 6. w. saith, God resisteth proud
1 Pe. 1 : 13. w. gird up loins of mind
2 : 1. w., laying aside all malice
6. w. it is contained in Scripture
4 : 19. w. let them that suffer acc-g
2 Pe. 1 : 10. w., breth., give diligence
12. w. I will not be negligent to
3 : 14. w., seeing ye look for such
1 Jn. 3 : 12. w. slew he him ? ⌈deeds
3 Jn. 10. w. I will remember his
Re. 17 : 7. w. didst thou marvel ?

WHEREIN.

⌈life
Ge. 1 : 30. everything w. there is
6 : 17. to destroy all flesh w. is life
7 : 15. two of all w. is breath of life
17 : 8. give thee land w. thou art a stranger, 28 : 4. Ex. 6 : 4.
21 : 23. to land w. thou sojourned
37 : 1. land w. his father a stranger
Ex. 1 : 14. w. they made them serve
12 : 7. of houses w. they shall eat it
18 : 11. thing w. they dealt proudly
22 : 27. his raiment ; w. shall sleep ?
33 : 16. w. be known I have found
Le. 4 : 23. if sin w. he sinned, come
5 : 18. conc. ignorance w. he erred
6 : 28. vessel w. sodden be broken
11 : 32. vessel w. work is done unc.
36. pit w. is plenty of water be cl.
13 : 46. days w. plague sh. be in hou.
52. burn any thing w. plague is,
54. wash the thi. w. plague is⌊57,
18 : 3. Aft. doings of Eg. w. ye dwelt
Nu. 12 : 11. w. we have done foolish.
19 : 2. heifer w. is no blemish ⌊(2)
31 : 10. burnt all cities w. they dw-t
33 : 55. vex you in land w. ye dwell
35 : 33. not pollute land w. ye are
34. Defile not the land w. I dwell
De. 8 : 9. w. thou sh. not lack any thi.
12 : 2 places w. nations served gods
7. w. thy God hath blessed thee
17 : 1. not sacrifice sheep w. is blem.
Jos. 8 : 24. wildern-s w. they chased
10 : 27. into cave w. they been hid
22 : 19. w. Lord's tabern. dwelleth
33. destroy land w. Reuben dwelt
24 : 17. preserved in all way w. we
Ju. 16 : 5. see w. his great str., 6 : 15.
18 : 6. before Lord is way w. ye go
1 S. 6 : 15. coffer w. jewels of gold
14 : 38. see w. sin hath been this d.
2 S. 7 : 7. places w. I walked wi. Ier.
1 K. 2 : 26. hast been afflicted in all w. my father was ⌈2 Ch. 6 : 11.
8 : 21. ark w. is covenant of Lord,
36. way w. they sho. walk, 2 Ch. 6, 15.
50. forgive peo. w. have transgres.
13 : 31. bury me w. man of G. is bur.
2 K. 12 : 2. days w. Jehoiada instruc.
14 : 6. book of law w. L. commanded
17 : 29. made gods in cities w. they
2 Ch. 8 : 1. 20 years w. Solomon built
33 : 19. w. he set up graven images
Ezr. 5 : 7. sent letter, w. was written
Ne. 6 : 6. w. written, It is reported
9 : 12. light in way w. should go, 19.
13 : 15. in day w. they sold victuals
Es. 5 : 11. w. k-g had promoted him
8 : 11. w. k. granted Jews in ev. city
9 : 22. w. Jews rested from enemies
Jb. 3 : 3. Let day perish w. I was bo.
6 : 16. brooks w. the snow is hid
24. to understand w. I have erred
38 : 26. rain on wildern. w. no man
Ps. 74 : 2. Sion w. thou hast dwelt
90 : 15. days w. thou hast afflicted
104 : 20. night w. beasts creep forth
25. sea w. are things innumerable
142 : 3. In the way w. I walked
143 : 8. to know way w. I sho. walk
Ec. 2 : 19. labour w. I have shewed myself wise (2), 22. ⌈boureth ?
8 : 9. what profit in that w. he la-
8 : 9. w. one man ruleth to his hurt
Is. 2 : 22. w. is he to be accounted
14 : 3. give thee rest fr. bondage w.
33 : 21. w. sh. go no galley with oars
47 : 12. sorceries w. hast laboured
65 : 12. did choose w. I delighted
Je. 7 : 14. my name w. ye trust⌊not
16 : 19. lies, things w. is no profit
20 : 14. Cursed be day w. I was b.
31 : 9. straight way w. sh. not stum.
36 : 14. Take roll w. thou hast read
41 : 9. pit w. Ishmael had cast dead
42 : 3. that Lord may shew way w.
51 : 43. wildern. w. no man dwel-h
Eze. 20 : 34. countries w. scat-d, 41.
43. doings w. ye have been defiled
23 : 19. youth w. she played harlot
26 : 10. as men enter city w. breach
32 : 6. water with thy blood land w.
37 : 23. dwellingplaces w. sinned
25. in land w. your fathers dwelt
42 : 14. lay their garments w. they minister ; they are holy, 44 : 19.
Ho. 2 : 13. days of Baalim, w. she burned incense ⌈than 120,000
Jon. 4 : 11. Nineveh, w. are more
Mi. 6 : 3. w. have I wearied thee ?
Zph. 3 : 11. w. hast transg-d ag. me
Zch. 9 : 11. out of the pit w. no wat.
Mal. 1 : 2. ye say, w. hast loved us ?
6. w. have we despised thy name?
7. say, w. have we polluted thee ?
2 : 17. w. have we wearied him ?
3 : 7. ye said, w. shall we return ?
8. ye say, w. have we robbed thee ?
Mat. 11 : 20. upbraid cities, w. mighty
25 : 13. hour w. Son of man cometh
Mk. 2 : 4. bed w. sick of palsy lay⌈ed
Lu. 1 : 4. w. thou hast been instruct-
25. days w. he looked on me to take
11 : 22. taketh armour w. trusted
23 : 53. sepulchre w. never man before was laid, Jn. 19 : 41. ⌈born
Ac. 2 : 8. ev. man in our tongue, w.
7 : 4. him into land w. ye dwell
10 : 12. w. were all manner of beasts
Ro. 2 : 1. w. thou judgest another
7 : 6. being dead w. we were held
1 Co. 7 : 20. Abide in calling w., 24.
2 Co. 11 : 12. w. they glory, found as
12 : 13. what is it w. ye inferior⌊we
Ep. 1 : 6. w. he hath made us accep.
8. w. he hath abounded tow. us in
2 : 2. w. ye walked acc. to this world
5 : 18. drunk with wine, w. is excess
Ph. 4 : 10. w. ye were careful, but
Col. 2 : † 3. w. are hid treasures of
12. w. ye are risen with him ⌊wisd.
2 Ti. 2 : 9. w. I suffer trouble, as
He. 6 : 17. w. God confirmed it by
9 : 2. the first, w. was candlestick
4. w. was golden pot and Aaron's
1 Pe. 1 : 6. w. ye greatly rejoice⌊rod
3 : 20. w. few, eight souls were sav.
4 : 4. w. they think it strange ye
2 Pe. 3 : 12. w. heavens being on fire
13. earth w. dwelleth righteousn.
Re. 2 : 13. w. Antipas was martyr
18 : 19. city, w. all were made rich
See PLEASURE, STAND, TRUSTEDST, TRUSTEST, VESSEL.

WHEREINSOEVER.

2 Co. 11 : 21. w. any is bold, I am

WHEREINTO.

Le. 11 : 33. ev. vessel w. any falleth
Nu. 14 : 24. Caleb will I bring unto land w. he went ⌈ciples
Jn. 6 : 22. boat, save that w. his dis-

WHEREOF.

Ge. 3 : 11. Hast eaten of tree w. I
Le. 6 : 30. no sin offer'ng w. blood
13 : 24. in skin w. is hot burning
27 : 9. if a beast w. men bring off-g
Nu. 5 : 3. defile not camps in midst w. I dwell ⌈to Moses
21 : 16. the well w. Lord spake un-
De. 13 : 2. the wonder w. he spake
28 : 68. way w. I spake unto thee
Jos. 20 : 2. cities of refuge w. I spa.
22 : 9. land, w. they were possessed
1 S. 10 : 16. matter of kingdom w.
2 S. 12 : 30. crown, weight w. talent
2 K. 13 : 14. sickness w. Elisha died
2 Ch. 6 : 20. upon place w. hast said
24 : 14. money w. were made vessels
33 : 4. house, w. L. said, In Jerus.
Ps. 46 : 4. streams w. sh. make glad
126 : 3. great things w. we are glad
Ec. 1 : 10. Is any thing w. it may be said, this is new? ⌈twins
Can. 4 : 2. flock, w. every one bear
Je. 32 : 43. land, w. ye say, desolate
Eze. 39 : 8. the day w. I have spoken
Ho. 2 : 12. trees, w. she hath said
Ac. 2 : 32. w. we all are witn., 3 : 15.
17 : 19. what this doct. w. speakest
21 : 24. things w. they were inform.
24 : 13. things w. they accuse me
Ro. 4 : 2. if by works he hath w. to
6 : 21. things w. ye are now asham.
1 Co. 7 : 1. things w. ye wrote unto
2 Co. 9 : 5. bounty w. ye had notice
Ep. 3 : 7. w. I was made a minister acc. to, Col. 1 : 25. ⌈might trust
Ph. 3 : 4. if thinketh he hath w. he
Col. 1 : 5. hope, w. ye heard before
1 Ti. 1 : 7. nei. what they say nor w.
6 : 4. strifes of words, w. railings
He 2 : 5. world to come w. we speak
10 : 15. w. Holy Ghost is witness
12 : 8. chastisement w. all partak-s
13 : 10. altar w. they have no right
1 Jn. 4 : 3. antichrist w. ye heard

WHEREON.

⌈give
Ge. 28 : 13. land w. thou liest will I
Ex. 3 : 5. the place w. thou standest is holy, Jos. 5 : 15.
8 : 21. full of flies, and ground w.
Le. 6 : 27. that w. it was sprinkled
15 : 4. bed w. he lieth, is unclean, 24.
6. w. he sat that had the issue
17. garment w. is seed of copulation
23. If it be any thing w. she sitteth
26. Ev. bed w. she lieth be unclean
De. 11 : 24. Every place w. your feet tread shall be yours, Jos. 14 : 9.
1 S. 6 : 18 stone w. they set ark of L.
2 Ch. 4 : 19. tables w. shewbread was
32 : 10. saith Samuel, w. do ye trust
Es. 7 : 8. Haman upon bed w. Esther
Jb. 24 : 23. Tho. in safety w. he rest.
Can. 4 : 4. w. hang 1,000 bucklers
Is. 36 : 6. Egypt ; w. if a man lean
Eze. 37 : 20. sticks w. thou writest
Mk. 11 : 2. find colt tied, w. never man sat, Lu. 19 : 30. ⌈built
Lu. 4 : 29. brow of hill w. city was
5 : 25. he took up that w. he lay
Jn. 4 : 38. reap w. ye bestowed no la-

WHERESOEVER.

⌊bour
Le. 13 : 12. leprosy w. priest looketh
2 K. 8 : 1. go sojourn w. thou canst
12 : 5. repair w. breach be found
1 Ch. 17 : 6. w. I have walked wi. Isr.
Je. 40 : 5. go w. seemeth convenient
Da. 2 : 38. w. children of men dwell
Mat. 24 : 28. w. the carcass is, there eagles, Lu. 17 : 37.

Mat. 26 : 13. w. this gospel shall be preached, Mk. 14 : 9. [eth him
Mk. 9 : 18. w. he taketh him he tear-
14 : 14. w. he go in, say ye to good-

WHERETO. [man

Jb. 30 : 2. w. might strength of their hands profit me [I sent it
Is. 55 : 11. shall prosper in thing w.
Ro. 6 : † 17. doct. w. ye were deliv-d
Ph. 3 : 16. w. we already attained

WHEREUNTO.

Nu. 36 : 3. of tribe w. received, 4.
De. 4 : 26. land w. ye go over Jordan
2 Ch. 8 : 11. places holy w. ark come
Es. 10 : 2. greatness of Mordecai w. king advanced him [sort
Ps. 71 : 3. w. I may continually re-
Je. 22 : 27. w. they desire to return
Eze. 5 : 9. w. I will not do the like
20 : 29. What is the place w. ye go?
Mat. 11 : 16 w. shall I liken this genera-n, Lu. 7 : 31. [Lu. 13 : 18, 20.
Mk. 4 : 30. w. sh. we liken kingdom,
Ac. 5 : 24. doubted w. this wou. grow
13 : 2. Saul for work w. I ha. called
27 : 8. Fair Havens ; nigh w. Lasea
Ga. 4 : 9. beggarly elements, w. ye
Col. 1 : 29. w. I also labour, striving
2 Th. 2 : 14. w. he called you by gosp.
1 Ti. 2 : 7. w. I am ordained a preacher, 2 Ti. 1 : 11. [attained
4 : 6. good doctrine w. thou hast
6 : 12. w. thou art called, and hast
1 Pe. 2 : 8. disobedient ; w. appoint.
3 : 21. figure w. baptism doth save
2 Pe. 1 : 19. w. ye do well that ye

WHEREUPON. [take

Le. 11 : 35. ev. thing w. carcass fal-h
Ju. 16 : 26. pillars w. house standeth
1 K. 7 : 48. table w. shewbread was
12 : 28. w. the king took counsel
2 Ch. 12 : 6. w. princes, k. humbled
Jb. 38 : 6. w. foundations fastened?
Je. 7 : † 10. this house w. my name is
Eze. 9 : 3. up from cherub, w. he was
40 : 41. eight tables, w. slew sacrif.
42. tables w. they laid instrum-ts
Am. 4 : 7. w. it rained not, withered
Mat. 14 : 7. w. he promised with oath
Ac. 24 : 18. w. certain Jews found me
26 : 12. w. as I went to Damascus
19. w., Agrippa, I was not disob-t
He. 9 : 18. w. nei. the first testament

WHEREWITH. [fath.

Ge. 27 : 41. bec. of blessing w. his
Ex. 3 : 9. w. Egyptians oppress them
4 : 17. this rod w. thou sh. do signs
16 : 32. bread w. I fed you in wild-s
17 : 5. rod w. thou smotest the riv.
29 : 33. sh. eat things w. atonement
Nu. 3 : 31. vessels w. they minister, 4 : 9, 12, 14. [redeemed
48. money w. odd number is to be
16 : 39. censers w. they that were
25 : 18. wiles w. they beguiled you
30 : 4 bond w. she had bound (2), 5, 6, 7, 8, 9, 11. [die, 18, 23.
35 : 17. if smite with stone, w. he
De. 9 : 19. w. L. was wroth ag. you
15 : 14. that w. L. hath blessed thee
22 : 12. vesture w. coverest thyself
28 : 53. w. enemies shall distress thee, 55, 57. Je. 19 : 9.
67. for the fear w. thou shalt fear
33 : 1. w. Moses blessed chil. of Isr.
Jos. 8 : 26. w. he stretched out spear
Ju. 6 : 15. O Lord, w. shall I save Isr.?
9 : 4. w. Abim-h hired vain persons
9. w. by me they honour God
38. w. saidst, Who is Abimelech
16 : 6. Tell me w. thou mightest be bound, 10, 13. [to his place
1 S. 6 : 2. tell us w. we shall send ark
8 : 8 works w. they have forsaken
29 : 4 w. should he reconcile hims.
2 S. 13 : 15. hatred w. he hated her
21 : 3. w. shall I make atonement

1 K. 8 : 59. w. I made supplication
15 : 22. took away timber w. Baasha had builded, 1 Ch. 16 : 6.
26. sin, w. he made Isr. to sin, 34.
30. w. Jerob. provoked L., 21 : 22.
22 : 22. And the Lord said unto him, w.? 2 Ch. 18 : 20. [Amaz-h
2 K. 13 : 12 might, w. Joash fought
21 : 16. sin, w. he made Judah sin
23 : 26. fierceness w. his anger was
25 : 14. vessels w. they ministered, took they, Je. 52 : 18. [en sea
1 Ch. 18 : 8. w. Sol-n made the braz-
2 Ch. 2 : 17. numbering w. Da. num-
35 : 21. ag. hou. w. I have war [bered
Ne. 9 : 34. w. didst testify ag. them
Jb. 15 : 3. reason with speeches w. he can do no good? [89 : 51. (2)
Ps. 79 : 12. w. reproached thee, O L.,
93 : 1. strength w. he girded hims.
119 : 42. shall I have w. to ans. him
129 : 7. w. mower filleth not his ha.
Can. 3 : 11. w. his moth. crowned him
Is. 28 : 12. w. ye cause weary to rest
37 : 6. w. servants blasphemed me
Je. 18 : 10. good w. I would benefit
21 : 4. weapons w. ye fight ag. king
33 : 16. is name w. she sh. be called
La. 1 : 12. sorrow w. L. afflicted me
Eze. 13 : 12. daubing w. ye daubed
20. ag. pillows, w. ye hunt souls
16 : 19. oil and honey w. I fed thee
29 : 20. Egypt for labour w. he serv.
32 : 16. lamentation w. they lament
36 : 18. idols w. they polluted land
40 : 42. w. they slew burnt offering
Da. 2 : 1. dreams w. was troubled
Mi. 6 : 6. w. shall I come before Lord
Zch. 14 : 12. plague w. L. will smite
Mal. 2 : 5. fear w. he feared me [18.
Mat. 5 : 13. if lost savour, w. shall it be salted, Mk. 9 : 50. Lu. 14 : 34.
Lu. 17 : 8. make ready w. I may sup
Jn. 13 : 5. towel w. he was girded
17 : 26. love w. thou hast loved me
Ro. 14 : 19. w. one may edify another
2 Co. 1 : 4. w. we are comforted of G.
7 : 7. consolation w. he was comf-d
10 : 2. w. I think to be bold ag. some
Ga. 5 : 1. w. Christ hath made us
Ep. 2 : 4. great love w. he loved us
4 : 1. the vocation w. ye are called
6 : 16. w. ye be able to quench fiery
1 Th. 3 : 9. w. we joy for your sakes
He. 10 : 29. blood w. he was sanctif.

WHEREWITH soever.

Mk. 3 : 28. w. s. they sh. blaspheme

WHEREWITHAL.

Ps. 119 : 9. w. sh. a young man cleanse
Mat. 6 : 31. w. shall we be clothed?

WHET. [children

De. 6 : † 7. shalt w. them unto thy
32 : 41. If I w. my glittering sword
Ps. 7 : 12. If turn not will w. sword
64 : 3. who w. their tongue like a sw.
Ec. 10 : 10. If iron blunt and he w.

WHETHER. [not edge

Ge. 18 : 21. w. according to cry of it
24 : 21. w. his journey prosperous
27 : 21. w. thou be my very son Esau
31 : 39. w. stolen by day or by night
37 : 14. Go, see w. it be well wi. breth.
32. w. it be thy son's coat [you
42 : 16. be proved w. any truth in
43 : 6. to tell w. ye had a brother?
Ex. 4 : 18. and see w. they be alive
12 : 19. cut off, w. stranger or born
16 : 4. w. they will walk in my law
19 : 13. w. beast or man, sh. not live
21 : 31 w. he have gored a son or d.
22 : 4. theft, w. it be ox or sheep, 9.
8. w. he put hand unto neighb-'s
34 : 19. ev. firstling, w. ox [goods
Le. 3 : 1. if offer, w. male or female
5 : 1. w. he hath seen or known it
2. w. carcass of unclean beast, or
7 : 26. eat no blood, w. of fowl or

Le. 11 : 32. w. it be any vessel or sack
13 : 47. leprosy, w. woollen garm-t
48. w. it be in warp or woof, w., 52.
55. w. it be bare within or without
15 : 3. w. his flesh run with issue
16 : 29. w. one of own country, 17 :
18 : 9. w. she be born at home [15.
22 : 28. w. cow or ewe, not kill both
27 : 12. value it w. good or bad, 14.
26. w. ox or sheep ; it is the Lord's
30. w. seed of land or fruit, Lord's
33. not search w. it be good or bad
Nu. 9 : 21. w. by day or night, cloud
22. Or w. it were two days, or mo.
11 : 23. shalt see w. my word come
13 : 18. w. they be strong or weak
19. what the land is, w. good or bad ; w. in tents or strongh-s, 20.
20. w. there be wood therein (2)
15 : 30. w. he be born in land or
De. 4 : 32. w. hath been such thing
8 : 2. w. wouldest keep his com-ts
13 : 3. w. ye love the Lord with all
18 : 3. priest's due, w. ox or sheep
22 : 6. w. they young ones or eggs
24 : 14. needy, w. of thy brethren
Jos. 24 : 15. w. gods fathers served
Ju. 2 : 22. w. will keep way of Lord
3 : 4. w. would hearken unto com-ts
9 : 2. w. better for you that all sons
18 : 5. w. our way sh. be prosperous
Ru. 3 : 10. followedst not young men, w. poor or rich [may live?
2 S. 12 : 22. Who can tell w. child
1 K. 20 : 18. w. be come for peace (2)
33. w. any thing come from him
2 K. 1 : 2. w. I shall recover of this
2 Ch. 14 : 11. to help, w. with money
15 : 13. to death, w. small or gr., w.
Ezr. 2 : 59. not shew w. they were of Israel, Ne. 7 : 61. [of Cyrus
5 : 17. search w. a decree was made
7 : 26. w. unto death or banishm-t
Es. 3 : 4. w. Mord.'s matters stand
4 : 14. w. to kingd. for such a time
Jb. 34 : 29. w. done ag. nation or m.
33. w. thou refuse, or w. choose
37 : 13. w. for correction or mercy
Pr. 20 : 11. his work, w. pure or w.
29 : 9. foolish man, w. he rage or lau.
Ec. 2 : 19. who knoweth w. he shall be a wise man or fool? [or much
5 : 12. sleep sweet, w. he eat little
11 : 6. w. shall prosper this or th., or w. both shall be good [or w.
12 : 14. work into judgm., w. good
Can. 6 : 11. to see w. vine flourished
7 : 12. to see w. tender grape appear
Je. 30 : 6. see w. a man doth travail
42 : 6. w. good or evil, we will obey
Eze. 2 : 5. w. they will hear or w. will forbear, 7.-3 : 11. [fowl or b.
44 : 31. nor eat of thing torn, w.
Mat. 9 : 5. w. is easier, to say, Thy sins, Mk. 2 : 9. Lu. 5 : 23. [will
21 : 31. w. of them twain did the
23 : 17. w. is greater, gold or temple
19. w. is greater, the gift or altar
26 : 63. tell us w. thou be Christ
27 : 21. w. of twain will ye I release
49. let us see w. Elias will come to save him, Mk. 15 : 36. [Lu. 6 : 7.
Mk. 3 : 2. w. he would heal on sab.,
15 : 44. w. he had been any while d.
Lu. 3 : 15. mused w. he were Christ
14 : 28. counteth w. he have suffic-t
31. consulteth w. able wi. 10,000
22 : 27. w. is greater, he that sitteth
23 : 6. asked w. man were Galilean
Jn. 7 : 17. doctrine w. of God or w. I
9 : 25. w. he a sinner I know not
Ac. 1 : 24. shew w. of these 2 chosen
4 : 19 w. it be right in sight of Lord
5 : 8. Tell w. ye sold land for so
9 : 2. if found any, w. men or wom.
10 : 18. w. Simon were lodged there
17 : 11. Scriptures, w. things were

Ac.19 : 2. not heard w. be Holy Gh.
25 :20. I asked w.he wou.go to Jer.
Ro. 6 : 16. w. of sin unto death or of
12 : 6. Having gifts, w. prophecy
14 : 8. w. we live or die, we are (3)
1 Co. 1 : 16. I know not w. I bapti-d
3 : 22. w. Paul, or Apollos, or Ceph.
7 : 16. w. thou save thy husband ?
8 : 5. w. in heaven or in earth ⌊(2)
10 : 31. w. thf. ye eat or drink, do
12 : 13. into one body, w. we be Jews
or Gentiles, w. bond or fr.⌈bers
26. w. one memb. suffer all mem-
13 : 8. w. prophecies, w. tongues w.
14 : 7. w. pipe or harp, exc. they gi.
15 : 11. w. it were I or they, so we
2 Co. 1 : 6. w. we be afflicted, w. comf.
2 : 9. proof, w. ye be obedient in all
5 : 9. w. present or absent, we may
10. he hath done, w. good or bad
13. w. beside ourselves, or w. sober
8 : 23. w. any do inquire of Titus
12 : 2. w. in the body, I cannot
tell ; or w. out of the body, 3.
13 : 5. examine, w. ye be in the fai.
Ep. 6 : 8. receive of L., w. bond or fr.
Ph. 1 : 18. w. in pretence or truth
20. w. it be by life or by death
27. w. I come and see you, or else
Col. 1 : 16. w. thrones or dominions
20. w. things in earth or heaven
1 Th. 5 : 10. w. we wake or sleep, we
2 Th. 2 : 15. been taught, w. by word
1 Pe. 2 : 13. w. to king as supreme
1 Jn. 4 : 1. try spirits w. they are of G.

WHICH. ⌈mament

Ge. 1 : 7. waters w. were above fir-
29. every tree in w. is fruit (2)
3 : 17. of the tree w. I commanded
6 : 2. wives of all w. they chose
14 : 2. king of Bela, w. is Zoar
3. vale of Siddim, w. is salt sea
17. valley of Shaveh, w. is k.'s dale
18 : 13. shall I bear child w. am old
27. I, w. am but dust and ashes
19 : 29. overthrew cities in w. Lot
45 : 6. in w. be nei. earing nor harv.
Ex. 15 : 13. peo. w. thou redeemed, 16.
Le. 11 : 13. These are they w. ye shall
have in abomination, De. 14 : 12.
Nu. 3 : 3. w., 26. De. 4 : 19 -32 : 38.
Jos. 13 : 10, 12. Ju. 1 : 26. 1 K.
21 ; 25. 2 K. 17 : 15, 34. Jb. 3:
25.-15 : 14.-16 : 8 -22 : 15. -24:
16.-27 : 13.-36 : 24. Ps. 9 : 13, 16.
-17 : 7, 13, 14 -60 : 10. (2).-61 : 7.
-65 : 9.-66 : 20.-78 : 5.-83 : 10.-
91 : 9.-104 : 10, 16.-119 : 47, 48,
85, 165.-139 : 16.-141 : 5, 9 Pr.
11 : 22.-30 : 18, 21, 24, 29, 30.
Ec. 2 : 18.-4 : 2. (2).-5 : 13.-6 : 1,
12.-8 : 12, 13, 1 , 15. Is. 1 : 29.-
28 : 4. (2). Eze. 9 : 6. Mat. 2 : 9.
Lu. 8 : 16. Jn. 17 : 4. Ac. 7 : 37.-
10 : 37. Ro. 1 : 3. 27, 28.-2 : 2, 3,
14, 19, 20, 21.-3 : 22, 26.-4 : 11,
12, 17.-5 : 5.-7 : 5, 10, 19.-8 : 1, 18,
26.-9 : 23, 25. (2) 30. (2) 31.-10 :
5. (2) 6. - 11 : 2, 14, 22.-12 : 14.-
15 : 26.-16 : 1, 10, 11, 14, 15, 17,
25.-1 Co. 1 : 4, 24.-2 : 7, 8, 13. (2)
-3 : 11 -4 : 19. 2 Co. 8 : 22. 2 Ti.
1 : 6. He. 4 : 3.-7 : 28. (2) - 8 : 1.
1 Pe. 3 : 4. Re. 5 : 8.-7 : 9, 13, 17.
-10 : 8. (2)-21 : 24.-22 : 8.
Nu. 19 : 2. heifer upon w. nev yoke
De. 2 : 11. w. were accounted giants
3 : 13. w. was called land of giants
Ju. 20 : 18. w. sh. go up first to bat-
2 K. 9 : 5. Unto w. of all of us? ⌊tle
1 Ch. 23 : 4. Of w. 24,000 were to set
Ezr. 4 : 12. Jews w. came up fr. thee
Jb. 3 : 21. w. long for death ; com-h
22. w. are glad when find grave
5 : 9. w. doeth great things and
11. w. mourn may be exalted to
6 : 16. w. are blackish by ice⌊safety

Jb. 9 : 5. w. overturneth the mts. (2)
6. w. shaketh the earth out of uer
7. w. sealeth up the stars(2)⌊place
8. w. alone spreadeth out heav-s
9. w. maketh Arcturus, Orion
10. w. doeth things past finding
15 : 9. what . . . thou, w. is not in us
16. w. drinketh iniquity like wa.
18. w. wise men have told fr. fa-s
22 : 16. w. were cut down out of ti.
17. w. said unto God, Depart from
24 : 11. w. make oil within walls⌊us
28 : 7. w. vulture's eye not seen (2)
25 : 6. Son of man w. is a worm
34 : 8. Job, w. walketh with wicked
36 : 28. w. clouds do distil upon men
38 : 23. w. I have reserved ag. troub.
39 : 14. w. leaveth her eggs in earth
Ps. 9 : 15. in net w. they hid is own
19 : 5. w. is as bridegroom coming
32 : 8. teach in way w. thou sh. go
41 : 9. w. did eat of my bread ⌈ers
58 : 5. w. will not hearken to charm-
78 : 3. w. we have heard and known
104 : 8. place w. thou hast founded
106 : 21. w. had done great things
114 : 8. w. turned rock into water
119 : 49. upon w. caused me to hope
146 : 6. w. keepeth truth for ev (2
7. w. giveth food to hungry (2)
Pr. 2 : 17. w. forsaketh guide of her
6 : 7. w. having no guide provideth
Ec. 4 : 3. they, w. hath not yet been
7 : 28. w. soul seeketh, I find not
Is. 3 : 12. w. lead thee, cause to err
5 : 23. w. justify wicked for reward
50 : 1. w. of my creditors is it
Mal. 1 : 14. deceiver w. hath in flock
Mat. 6 : 27. w. of you can add to his
stature, Lu. 12 : 25. ⌈sheep's
7 : 15. false prophets w. come in
24. wise man w. built upon rock
26. foolish man w. built upon sand
11 : 14. this is Elias w. was to come
13 : 52. w. bringeth out of his treas
16 : 28. some here w. shall not taste
of death, Mk. 9 : 1. ⌈so born (3)
19 : 12. are some eunuchs w. were
18. He saith unto him w.? Jesus
20 : 1. w. went out to hire labour-s
21 : 33. householder w. planted vin.
41. husbandman w. shall render
22 : 2. king w. made marriage for
36. w. is the gr. com-t, Mk. 12 : 28.
23 : 27. sepulchres w. appear beau.
25 : 1. virgins w. took their lamps
27 : 55. many women w. followed J.
Mk. 3 : 17. w. is, The sons of thund.
4 : 16. are they w. are sown on, 18, 20
12 : 18. w. say, is no resurrection
42. threw in two mites w. make a
Lu. 1 : 20. words w. shall be fulfilled
2 : 10. good tidings w. be to all peo.
5 : 21. this w. speaketh blasphem-s
6 : 16. Judas w. also was the traitor
33. if to them w. do good to you
7 : 37. woman in city w. was sinner
42. Tell me, w. will love him most
8 : 3. many w. ministered unto him
13. w. for a while believe, fall (2)
26. country of Gadarenes, w. is
43. w. had spent all her living
9 : 30. two men, w. were Mos., Elias
46. w. should be greatest, 22 : 24.
10 : 36. w. of these three was neighb.
42. chosen good part, w. shall not
11 : 5. w. of you shall have a friend
12 : 1. leaven of Phari., w. is hypoc.
14 : 5. w. of you sh. have an ox or
28. w. of you intending to build
15 : 7. w. need no repentance ⌈ing
17 : 7. w. of you having serv. plough-
21 : 6. in w. not be left one stone
22 : 23. w. of them should do this
23 : 29. in w. shall say, Blessed are
55. women w. came with him from
24 : 19. Jesus, w. was a prophet

Jn. 6 : 39. of all w. he hath given(2)
8 : 46. w. of you convinc-h me of sin
53. thou greater than Abr. w. is
10 : 32. for w. do ye stone me⌊dead
18 : 1. garden into the w. he ent-d
21 : 20. Lord, w. is he th. betrayeth
25. many things w. Jesus did, the
w. if written ⌈them (2)
Ac. 1 : 16. Judas w. was guide to
3 : 23. soul w. not hear th. prophet
7 : 52. w. of prophets not persecuted
8 : 26. Jerus. unto Gaza, w. is des.
9 : 39. shew-g coats w. Dorcas made
10 : 44. Holy Gh. fell on all w. heard
47. w. have received Holy Ghost
11 : 6. Upon the w. I had fastened
20. men of Cyprus w. spake ⌊eyes
28. w. came to pass in days of Cl.
30. w. they did, and sent it by Sa.
12 : 10. iron gate w. opened of own
16 : 12. Philippi, w. is chief city of
16. damsel w. brought her masters
17. w. shew unto us way of salva.
23 : 21. forty men w. have bound
26 : 4. my life, w. was at first among
16. witness of things w. thou hast
seen, things in w. I will appear
Ro. 1 : 2. (w. he had promised afore)
32. they w. commit such things
2 : 15. w. shew work of the law
16 : 12. Salute Persis w. laboured
1 Co. 1 : 11. w. are of house of Chloe
6 : 20. body and spirit w. are God's
7 : 13. woman w. hath husband th.
15 : 2. By w. ye are saved ⌈eth
2 Co. 9 : 11. bountifulness w. caus-
11 : 28. w. cometh on me daily⌈w.
Ga. 2 : 10. remember the poor, same
3 : 17. law, w. was 430 years after
4 : 24. one from mount Sinai w.
gendereth to bondage, w. is Ag.
25. Agar ans-eth to Jerus. w. now
26. Jerus. w. is above is free, w. is
5 : 19. works of the flesh, w. are
Ep. 1 : 20. w. he wrought in Christ
23. w. is his body, fulness of him
3 : 13. tribulations, w. is y-r glory
6 : 2. w. is first com-t with promise
17. sword of Spirit, w. is word of G.
Ph. 1 : 28. w. is to them evident
token of perdition, 2 Th. 1 : 5.
30. Having same conflict w. ye saw
4 : 3. Help those women w. laboured
Col. 1 : 24. his body's sake, w. is ch.
27. w. is Christ in you, the hope
2 : 17. w. are a shadow of things to
22. w. are all to perish with using
3 : 5. covetousness, w. is idolatry
7. in the w. ye also walked someti.
14. charity, w. is bond of perfectn.
4 : 11. workers w. have been a comf.
2 Th. 1 : 5. kingd. of G. for w. ye suf-
1 Ti. 1 : 4. w. minister questions⌊fer
6. Fr. w. some have turned unto
3 : 15. w. is church of living God
6 : 9. w. drown men in destruction
2 Ti. 1 : 5. w. dwelt in thy grandmo.
3 : 11. Persecutions w. came unto
He. 1 : 5. unto w. of angels, 13. ⌈en
2 : 3. salva-n w. began to be spok-
5 : 12. teach you w. be first princi.
7 : 2. King of Salem w. is K. of pea.
13. of w. no man gave attendance
19. hope by w. we draw nigh God
8 : 6. w. was established upon bet-r
9 : 5. of w. we cannot now speak
9. w. was a figure for the time then
10 : 8. w. are offered by the law
10. By the w. will we are sanctified
11. sacrifices, w. can never take
32. days, in w. ye endured gr. fight
35. w. hath great recompense of
11 8. place w. he should aft. rec.
12 : 5. exhortation w. speaketh
14. holiness, without w. no man
Ja. 1 : 1. twelve tribes w. are scatt-d
2 : 7. that name by w. ye are called

1 Pe. 2 : 10. w. in time past not a peo.
11. lusts w. war ag. the soul ⌊(2)
3 : 19. by w. he preached to spirits
20. w. sometime were disobedient
2 Pe. 3 : 10. in the w. heavens pass
16. in w. are some things hard to
1 Jn. 1 : 2. life w. was with the Fath.
3 Jn. 6. w. have borne witness of
Re. 1 : 4. w. is, w. was, w. is to (4)
2 : 8. w. was dead and is alive ⌈tan
24. w. ha. not known depths of Sa-
7 : 4. number of them w. were saved
14. These are they w. came out of
9 : 4. men w. have not seal of God
11 : 17. w. art, wast, and art to come
12 : 13. woman w. bro-t forth man c.
17 : 9. seven mts. on w. wom. sitteth
12. k-s w. have received no kingd.
19 : 2. w. did corrupt earth with her
20 : 4. w. hath not worshipped beast
21 : 8. lake w. burneth ; w. is the
22 : 9. of them w. keep the sayings
11. he w. is filthy, let him be filthy
20. He w. testifieth, saith, I come
See CALLED, THING, THINGS.

That WHICH.

Ex. 18 : 8. of t. w. Lord did unto me
Le. 11 : 36. t. w. toucheth carcass unc.
Jb. 27 : 11. t. w. is with Almighty
will I not conceal ⌈hast wrought
Ps. 68 : 28 strengthen t. w. thou
Pr. 12 : 27. roasteth not t. w. he took
Ec. 6 : 10. t. w. hath been is named
7 : 24. t. w. is deep who find it out?
12 : 10. t. w. was written was upright
Is. 2 : 8. worship t. w. fingers made
Lu. 8 : 14. t. w. fell among thorns are
Ro. 1 : 26. unto t. w. is ag. nature, 27.
4 : 16. not to t. only w. is of law,
but to t. w. is of faith of Abra.
18. acc. to t. w. was spoken ⌈(2)
7 : 13. Was t. w. is good made death
11 : 7. not obtained t. w. he seeketh
12 : 9. Abhor t. w. is evil (2) ⌈ten
1 Co. 4 : 6. of men above t. w. is writ-
2 Co. 12 : 6. t. w. he seeth me to be
Ep. 1 : 21. this world, t. w. is to come
4 : 29. t. w. is good to the edifying
1 Pe. 3 : 4. t. w. is not corruptible
Re. 2 : 25. t. w. ye have, hold fast
See **THAT which.**
See **THEY which.**

WHICH was the son of.

Lu. 3 : 23. w. -, 24, (5) 25, (5) 26, (5)
27, (5) 28, (5) 29, (5) 30, (5) 31,
(5) 32, (5) 33, (5) 34, (5) 35, (5) 36,
(5) 37, (5)
38. w. - of Adam w. - of God (4)

WHILE.

Ge. 8 : 22. w. the earth remaineth
19 : 16. w. he lingered men laid hold
25 : 6. sent them aw. w. he yet lived
29 : 9. w. he yet spake Rachel came
45 : 1. w. Joseph made hims. known
Ex. 33 : 22. w. my glory passeth by,
I will cover thee w. I pass by
34 : 29. his face shone w. he talked
Le. 4 : 27. w. he doeth ag. comm-ts
26 : 43 w. desolate with-t sabbaths
Nu. 11 : 33. w. flesh yet betw. teeth
15 : 32. w. in wildern. found a man
23 : 15. Stand here w. I meet Lord
25 : 11. w. he was zealous for ⌈hot
De. 19 : 6. pursue slayer w. heart is
Jos. 14 : 10. w. Isr. wandered in wil.
Ju. 3 : 26. Ehud escaped w. they tarr.
11 : 26. w. Israel dwelt in Heshbon
14 : 17. she wept bef. him w. feast
16 : 27. beheld w. Sams. made sport
1 S. 2 : 13. w. the flesh was in seeth-g
7 : 2. w. ark abode in K. time long
14 : 19. w. Saul talked unto priest
20 : 14. w. yet I live shew me kindn.
2 S. 3 : 6. w. war betw. Saul and Da
35. David to eat w. it was yet day
13 : 30. w. in the way tidings came
15 : 8. a vow w. I abode in Geshur

2 S. 17 : 2. come upon him w. weary
19 : 32. king w. he lay at Mahan-m
24 : 13. wilt thou flee bef. enemies,
w. they pursue, 1 Ch. 21 : 12. ⌈k.
1 K. 1 : 14. w. thou yet talkest with
22. w. Bath-sheba yet talked with
42. w. he spake Jonathan came ⌊k.
3 : 20. took my son w. handm. slept
12 : 6. old men which stood bef. us
Sol. w. he yet lived, 2 Ch. 10 : 6.
2 K. 6 : 33. w. he yet talked wi. them
1 Ch. 12 : 1. w. David kept close bec.
2 Ch. 14 : 7. w. the land is yet bef. us
15 : 2. L. with you w. ye be wi. him
26 : 19. w. he was wroth wi. priests
34 : 3. w. yet young began to seek
Ne. 7 : 3. w. they stand by, shut d.
Es. 2 : 21. w. Mord. sat in k.'s gate
6 : 14. w. yet talking with Haman
Jb. 1 : 16. w. he was yet speaking
another said, The fire, 17, 18.
20 : 23. God shall rain wrath upon
him w. eating ⌈deliver
Ps. 7 : 2. tear my soul w. is none to
31 : 13. w. they took counsel ag. me
39 : 1. keep my mouth w. wicked
3. w. I was musing ⌊is before me
42 : 3. w. they say, where thy G., 10.
49 : 18. w. he lived blessed his soul
63 : 4. bless thee w. I live, 146 : 2.
69 : 3. eyes fail w. I wait for my G.
78 : 30. w. meat yet in their mouths
88 : 15. w. I suffer thy terrors I am
104 : 33. w. I have my being, 146 : 2.
Pr. 8 : 26. w. as yet not made earth
19 : 18. Chasten son w. is hope
31 : 15. She riseth w. it is yet night
Ec. 9 : 3. madness in heart w. they
12 : 1. w. evil days come not ⌊live
2. w. the sun be not darkened
Can. 1 : 12. w. King sitteth at table
Is. 28 : 4. w. yet in his hand eateth
55 : 6. Seek L. w. he may be found,
call upon him w. he is near
65 : 24. w. they are speaking I will
Je. 13 : 16. w. ye look for light
15 : 9. her sun gone down w. yet d.
38 : 1. w. Jeremiah was yet shut
up, 39 : 15. ⌈back
40 : 5. Now w. he was not yet gone
La. 1 : 19. w. they sought their meat
Eze. 9 : 8. w. they were slaying them
21 : 29. w. they see vanity unto
thee, w. they divine a lie ⌈court
44 : 17. w. they minister in gates of
Da. 4 : 31. w. word was in k.'s mou.
5 : 2. Belshazzar w. he tasted wine
9 : 20. w. I was praying, confessing,
Ho. 7 : 6. w. they lie in wait ⌊21.
Na. 1 : 10. w. they be folden as
thorns, w. they are drunken as
Mat. 1 : 20. w. he thought on these
5 : 25. agree w. in the way wi. him
9 : 18. w. he spake these things
12 : 46. w. he talked to the people
13 : 25. w. men slept enemy sowed
29. lest, w. ye gather up the tares
14 : 22. w. he sent the multitudes
away, Mk. 6 : 45. ⌈Lu. 9 : 34.
17 : 5. w. he yet spake, cloud,
22. w. they abode in Galilee, Jes.
22 : 41. w. Pharisees were gathered
25 : 5. w. bridegroom tarried, they
10. w. they went to buy, bridegr-m
26 : 36. sit here w. I go and pray
yonder, Mk. 14 : 32. ⌈Mk. 14 : 43.
47. w. he yet spake, Judas came,
28 : 13. stole him away w. we slept
Mk. 2 : 19. fast w. bridegroom is
with them? Lu. 5 : 34. ⌈Lu. 8 : 49.
5 : 35. w. he yet spake, came fr. ruler,
12 : 35. w. he taught in temple
Lu. 1 : 8. w. he executed priest's offi.
2 : 6. w. these days were accompl.
9 : 43. w. they wondered at all wh.
14 : 32 w. other is yet great way off
22 : 47. w. he yet spake, a multitude

Lu. 22 : 60. w. he spake, cock crew
24 : 15. w. they communed J. drew
32. w. he talked with us by way,
w. he opened Scriptures ⌈Joy
41. w. they yet believed not for
44. I spake w. I was yet with you
51. w. he blessed them, was parted
Jn. 5 : 7. w. I am coming, ano. stepp.
9 : 4. do work of him w. it is day
12 : 35. walk w. ye have the light, 36.
17 : 12 w. I was with them in wor.
Ac. 1 : 9. w. they beheld he was tak.
10. w. they looked toward heaven
5 : 4. w. remained, was it not thine
9 : 39. Dorcas made w. with them
10 : 10. w. they made ready he fell
17. w. Peter doubted what vision
19. w. Peter thought on vision
44. w. Peter yet spake these words
17 : 16. w. Paul waited at Athens
19 : 1. w. Apollos was at Corinth
22 : 17. w. I prayed in temple I was
24 : 20. any evil doing, w. I stood
25 : 8. w. he answered for himself
27 : 33. w. day was coming on, Paul
Ro. 5 : 8. w. were yet sinners, Christ
7 : 3. if w. husb. liveth she be marr.
1 Co. 3 : 4. w. one saith, I am of Paul
8 : 13. I will eat no flesh w. ⌈seen
2 Co. 4 : 18. w. we look not at things
9 : 13. w. by the experiment of this
Ga 2 : 17. if w. we seek to be justified
1 Ti. 5 : 6. is dead w. she liveth ⌈eted
6 : 10. money, which, w. some cov-
He. 3 : 13. w. it is called, To day
15. w. it is said, To day if ye will
9 : 8. w. 1st tabernacle was stand-g
17. is of no strength w. testator
1 Pe. 3 : 2. w. they beheld y-r chaste
20. waited, w. ark was preparing
2 Pe. 2 : 13. deceivings w. they feast
19. w. they promise liberty, are
See **Yet ALIVE.** ⌊serv-s

A WHILE. ⌈his wife

Ju. 15 : 1. a w. aft. Samson visited
1 S. 9 : 27. to Saul, stand still a w.
2 S. 7 : 19. hast spoken for a great w.
1 K. 17 : 7. aft. a w. brook dried ⌈w.
Mat. 13 : 21. not root, but dureth for a
26 : 73. aft. a w. came they th. stood
Mk. 6 : 31. into desert place, rest a w.
Lu. 8 : 13. for a w. believe, fall aw.
18 : 4. wou. not for a w. but afterw.
1 Co. 16 : 7. I trust to tarry a w.
1 Pe. 5 : 10. aft. we have suffered a w.

All the WHILE. ⌈up

Le. 14 : 46. into house - w. it is shut
1 S. 22 : 4. - w. David was in hold
25 : 7. - w. they were in Carmel, 16.
27 : 11. so will be his manner - w.
Jb. 27 : 3. - w. my breath is in me

Any WHILE. ⌈w. dead

Mk. 15 : 44. whether he had been a

Good WHILE. ⌈g. w.

Ge. 46 : 29. Jos. wept on his neck a
Ac. 15 : 7. g. w. ago God made choice
18 : 18. Paul tarried there a g. w.
See **GREAT while.**

Little WHILE. ⌈w.

2 Ch. 12 : † 7. I will grant them a l.
Jb. 24 : 24. they are exalted for l. w.
Ps. 37 : 10. yet a l. w. wicked not be
Is. 10 : 25. yet a very l. w., indigna-
29 : 17. Is it not yet a very l. w. ⌊tion
63 : 18. have possessed it but l. w.
Je. 51 : 33. yet a l. w., her harvest
Ho. 1 : 4. yet a l. w. I will avenge
8 : † 10. they shall sorrow in a l. w.
Hag. 2 : 6. Yet once, it is a l. w.
Lu. 22 : 58. after a l. w. another saw
Jn. 7 : 33. Yet a l. w. with you, 13 : 33.
12 : 35. Yet a l. w. is light with you
14 : 19. Yet a l. w. world seeth me no
16 : 16. A l. w. and ye shall not see
me, l. w. and ye sh. see me, 17, 19.
18. What is this he saith, A l. w.?
He. 2 : † 7. a l. w. inferior to angels

He. 10 : 37. yet a l. w. he will come
2 Pe. 2 : † 18. those for l. w. escaped

Long WHILE. [day
Ac. 20 : 11. talked l. w. till break of
See **MEAN while.**

WHILES = WHILE,
WHILST.

Jn. 6 : 31. put to death w. it is morn.
Ne. 6 : 3. why work cease w. I leave
Jb. 8 : 12. w. it is in his greenness
32 : 11. w. ye searched what to say
Ps. 141 : 10. wicked fall w. I escape
Je. 17 : 2. w. chil. remember altars
2 Co. 5 : 6. w. we are at home in body
7 : 15. w. he rememb-h obedience
He. 10 : 33. w. ye were made gazing-
stock; w. ye became compan-s

WHIP, S.

1 K. 12 : 11. my father chastised you
with w-s, 14. 2 Ch. 10 : 11, 14,
Pr. 26 : 3. A w. for a horse, a rod for
a fool's back [of wheels
Na. 3 : 2. The noise of a w., the noise

WHIRLETH.

Ec. 1 : 6. wind w. continually, and

WHIRLWIND, S.

2 K. 2 : 1. take up Elijah by a w., 11.
Jb. 37 : 9. Out of south cometh w.
38 : 1. answered Job out of w., 40 : 6.
Ps. 58 : 9. he shall take them away
as in a w., Pr. 10 : 25. Ho. 13 : 3.
Pr. 1 : 27. your destruction as a w.
Is. 5 : 28. and their wheels like a w.
17 : 13. like a rolling thing bef. w.
21 : 1. As w-s in the south pass
40 : 24. w. sh. take them as stubble
41 : 16. the w. shall scatter them
66 : 15. Lord will come with chariots like a w., Je. 4 : 13.
Je. 23 : 19. a w. of the Lord is gone
forth, even a grievous w. ; it
shall fall upon wicked, 30 : 23. (2)
25 : 32. a great w. shall be raised
Eze. 1 : 4. a w. came out of north
Da. 11 : 40. king ag. him like a w.
Ho. 8 : 7. sown wind, they sh. reap w.
Am. 1 : 14. with tempest in day of w.
Na. 1 : 3. Lord hath his way in w.
Ha. 3 : 14. came as w. to scatter me
Zch. 7 : 14. I scattered them with w.
9 : 14. Lord shall go forth with w-s

WHISPER, ED. [w-d

2 S. 12 : 19. David saw his servants
Ps. 41 : 7. All that hate me w. toge.
Is. 29 : 4. speech sh. w. out of dust

WHISPERER, S.

Pr. 16 : 28. a w. separateth friends
18 : † 8. words of w. are as wounds
26 : † 20. where no w. strife ceaseth
Ro. 1 : 29. full of murder, deceit, w-s

WHISPERINGS. [ings

2 Co. 12 : 20. lest there be w., swell-

WHIT.

De. 13 : 16. all the spoil, every w.
1 S. 3 : 18. Samuel told Eli every w.
Es. 6 : † 10. suffer not a w. to fall
Ps. 29 : † 9. ev. w. uttereth his glory
Jn. 7 : 23. made a man ev. w. whole
13 : 10. wash his feet is clean ev. w.
2 Co. 11 : 5. I was not a w. behind [w.

WHITE.

Ge. 30 : 35. every goat that had some
37. Jacob pilled w. streaks in th.,
and made the w. appear in rods
40 : 16. three w. baskets on my head
49 : 12. his teeth be w. with milk
Ex. 16 : 31. like coriander seed, w.
Le. 13 : 3. when hair in the plague is
turned w., 10. 20. 25. [19, 24.
4. If bright spot be w. in skin (2),
10. If rising be w. in skin, 19, (2) 43.
13. it is all turned w. ; he clean, 17.
16. If the flesh be changed unto w.
21. if be no w. hairs therein, 26.
38. If in their flesh w. bright spots
39. If spots in skin be darkish w.
42. if in bald head w. reddish sore

Ju. 5 : 10. ye that ride on w. asses
2 Ch. 5 : 12. Levites in w. linen
Es. 1 : 6. w., green, and blue hang-
ings, beds upon pavement of w.
8 : 15. Mordecai went in w. apparel
Jb. 6 : 6. any taste in w. of an egg?
Ec. 9 : 8. thy garments be always w.
Can. 5 : 10. My beloved is w., ruddy
Is. 19 : † 9. that weave w. works sh.
be confounded [wool
Eze. 27 : 18. Damascus traded in w.
Da. 11 : 35. some fall to make th. w.
12 : 10. Many be purified, made w.
Jo. 1 : 7. the branches are made w.
Zch. 1 : 8. red horses, speckled, w.
6 : 3. in third chariot w. horses
6. black horses; the w. go after
Mat. 5 : 36. not make one hair w. or
Mk. 16 : 5. a man in a long w. garm.
Jn. 4 : 35. fields w. already to harvest
20 : 12. seeth two angels in w. sit-g
Ac. 1 : 10. two stood by in w. apparel
Re. 1 : 14. his hairs were w. like wool
2 : 17. I will give him a w. stone
3 : 4. they shall walk with me in w.
6 : 2. and behold a w. horse, 19 : 11.
7 : 14. made robes w. in the blood
14 : 14. I looked, behold a w. cloud
15 : 6. seven angels in pure w. linen
19 : 8. be arrayed in linen, w., 14.
20 : 11. I saw a great w. throne
See RAIMENT, ROBES, SNOW.

WHITE, ED.

Mat. 23 : 27. ye are like w-d sepulch-s
Mk. 9 : 3. as no fuller can w. them
Ac. 23 : 3. God sh. smite thee, thou

WHITER. [w-d wall

Ps. 51 : 7. I shall be w. than snow
La. 4 : 7. Her Nazarites w. than milk

WHITHER.

Ge. 20 : 13. every place w. we come
Ex. 21 : 13. a place w. he shall flee
Le. 18 : 3. land of Canaan, w. I bring
you, 20 : 22. Nu. 15 : 18. [sent us
Nu. 13 : 27. we came unto la. w. thou
35 : 25. of refuge, w. he was fled, 26.
De. 1 : 28. ye said, w. sh. we go up?
3 : 21. all kingdoms w. thou passest
4 : 5. land w. ye go to possess it,
14.-6 : 1.-7 : 1.-11 : 8, 10, 11, 29.
-23 : 20.-28 : 21.-32 : 18, 47.
27. among heathen, w. Lord shall
23 : 12. a place without camp w. go
28 : 37. a byword among all nations
w. Lord shall lead thee, 30 : 1.
30 : 3. will gather thee from nations
w. Lord scattered thee, Je. 23 :
3, 8.-29 : 14.-32 : 37. Eze. 37 : 21.
1 S. 27 : 10. w. made a road to day?
2 S. 2 : 1. David said w. shall I go up
1 K. 2 : 36. go not thence any w.
42. day thou walkest any w. d-e
8 : 47. land w. they were carried
captives, 2 Ch. 6 : 37. [not sent
18 : 10. no nation w. my lord hath
12. Spirit carry thee w. I know not
21 : 18. vineyard of Naboth w. gone
2 K. 5 : 25. Thy servant went no w.
2 Ch. 10 : 2. Egypt, w. Jeroboam fled
Ps. 122 : 4. w. the tribes go up [(2)
139 : 7. W. shall I go fr. thy Spirit?
Can. 6 : 1. w. is thy beloved gone (2)
Is. 20 : 6. w. we flee fr. k. of Assyria
Je. 19 : 14. Tophet, w. L. sent Jere-h
22 : 12. die in place w. they led him
24 : 9. a taunt in all places w. I sh.
drive them, 29 : 18. Eze. 4 : 13.
29 : 7. w. I caused you to be carried
30 : 11. make a full end of nations
w. I scattered thee, 46 : 28.
40 : 4. w. it seemeth good to go, go
44 : 8. Eg., w. ye be gone to dwell
49 : 36. no nation, w. outcasts of El.
Eze. 6 : 9. remember me w. carried
10 : 11. w. head looked they foll-d
12 : 16. among heathen w. they co.
29 : 13. Eg-ns fr. people w. scattered

Eze. 47 : 9. sh. live, w. river cometh
Jo. 3 : 7. out of place w. ye sold them
Zch. 5 : 10. w. do these bear ephah?
Lu. 10 : 1. sent two and two w. he
Jn. 8 : 8. canst not tell w. it goeth
12 : 35. in darkness knoweth not
w. he goeth, 1 Jn. 2 : 11. [sort
18 : 20. temple w. Jews always re-
21 : 18. young, walkedst w. thou
wouldest; old, w. wouldest not
He. 6 : 20. w. forerunner is entered
11 : 8. Abr. went out not know-g w.
See DRIVEN, GO, GOEST, WENT.

WHITHERSOEVER.

Jos. 1 : 7. mayest prosper w. goest
9. Lord is with thee w. thou goest
16. w. thou sendest we will go
Ju. 2 : 15. w. they went, L. ag. them
1 S. 14 : 47. w. Saul turned, vexed th.
18 : 5. David went w. Saul sent him
23 : 13. David and men w. could go
2 S. 7 : 9. I was with thee w. thou
wentest, 1 Ch. 17 : 8.
8 : 6. Lord preserved David w. he
went, 14. 1 Ch. 18 : 6, 13. [est
1 K. 2 : 3. mayest prosper w., turn-
8 : 44. w. thou shalt send them
2 K. 18 : 7. Hez. prospered w. he w-t
Es. 4 : 3. w. king's com-t came, 8 : 17.
Pr. 17 : 8 w. it turneth, prospereth
21 : 1. he turneth it w. he will
Eze. 1 : 20. w. the spirit was to go
21 : 16. Go thee w. thy face is set
47 : 9. w. rivers sh. come shall live
Mat. 8 : 19. I will follow w. thou
goest, Lu. 9 : 57. [they laid sick
Mk. 6 : 56. w. he entered villages
1 Co. 16 : 6. on my journey w. I go
Ja. 3 : 4. turned w. governor listeth
Re. 14 : 4. follow Lamb w. he goeth

WHO. [naked?

Ge. 3 : 11. w. told thee thou wast
14 : 12. w., 24 : 15, 27.-30 : 2.-35 :
3.-36 : 1, 20, 35.-42 : 30.-48 : 14.
-49 : 25. (2). Ex. 4 : 28.-5 : 20.-
12 : 27, 40.-21 : 8. Le. 5 : 8.-12 :
7. Nu. 6 : 21.-7 : 2.-27 : 21.-31 :
27. De. 33 : 9. Jos. 12 : 2. 13 : 12.
-17 : 16.-21 : 10. Ju. 2 : 7.-6 :
35.-7 : 1.-8 : 34.-11 : 39.-17 : 4.
1 S. 10 : 19.-30 : 23. 2 S. 10 : 18.
-22 : 4.-23 : 1. 1 K. 14 : 14.-
19 : 19.-21 : 11. 2 K. 4 : 5.-7 : 17.
1 Ch. 8 : 13. (2)-9 : 18. 2 Ch. 32 :
31.-34 : 26. Ezr. 3 : 12. Es. 2 :
22. Jb. 27 : 2. (2).-34 : 7. Ps. 37 :
7. (2).-88 : 12.-105 : 17.-124 : 8.-
137 : 7. Can. 8 : 2. Is. 14 : 6.-40 : 14.-
65 : 16. Je. 26 : 20.-36 : 32. Ho. 3 : 1.
Am. 3 : 10. Mat. 10 : 2, 4.-25 :
14.-26 : 3.-27 : 57. Mk. 1 : 19.-
5 : 3.-13 : 34.-15 : 7, 41. Lu. 18 :
30.-23 : 19. Jn. 18 : 18. Ac. 4 :
36.-5 : 36.-7 : 46.-8 : 15.-10 : 41.
-11 : 23.-13 : 7.-21 : 32.-24 : 1.
Ro. 4 : 17.-8 : 1.-16 : 6, 7, (2) 22.
1 Co. 1 : 8.-4 : 17. (2). 2 Co. 3 : 10.
Ga. 1 : 15.-2 : 4. Ph. 2 : 20. He.
7 : 16, 26, 27, 28.-8 : 1.-9 : 14.-
10 : 29.-12 : 2. 1 Pe. 1 : 20.-3 : 5.-
5 : 10. 2 Pe. 2 : 15. Jude 18. Re.
1 : 2.-2 : 13.-4 : 9.-12 : 5. [Abr.
Ge. 21 : 7. w. would have said unto
26. I wot not w. hath done this
27 : 18. Isaac said, w. art thou, 32.
33. Isaac trembled and said, w.?
33 : 5. Esau said, w. are those with
43 : 22. cannot tell w. put our mon-
48 : 8. Israel said, W. are these? [ey
49 : 9. w. sh. rouse him, Nu. 24 : 9.
Ex. 2 : 14. w. made thee judge over
3 : 11. w. am I that I go unto Pha.
4 : 11. the Lord said, w. hath made
man's mouth, w. mak-h dumb?
5 : 2. w. is Lord I sh. obey his voice
6 : 12. w. am of uncircumcised lips
10 : 8. w. are they that shall go?

Ex. 15 : 11. w. is like unto thee, O
Lord ? w. like thee glorious in
holiness, Ps. 35 : 10.-71 : 19.-
113 : 5. Mi. 7 : 18.
32 : 26. w. is on the Lord's side?
Nu. 11 : 4. w. shall give us flesh, 18.
12 : 7. Moses, w. is faithful in all
16 : 5. Lord will shew w. are his, w.
23 : 10. w. can count dust of Jacob
24 : 23. w. live when G. doeth this ?
25 : 6. w. were weeping bef. taber.
De. 1 : 33. w. went in way before you
4 : 7. w. hath God so nigh unto th.
5 : 3. w. are all of us alive this day
26. w. hath heard and lived ?[ness
8 : 15. w. led thee thro. gr. wilder-
16. w. fed thee in wilderness with
9 : 2. w. stand before chil. of Anak?
21 : 1. If not known w. hath slain
30 : 12. w. go up for us to heaven
13. w. shall go over the sea for us
33 : 9. w. said unto his father and
29. w. is like unto thee, O peo. (2)
Jos. 9 : 8. w. are ye? from whence
15 : 19. w. ans-d, Give me a blessing
Ju. 1 : 1. w. go for us ag. Canaanites
3 : 19. king, w. said, Keep silence
6 : 29. said, w. hath done this thi. ?
9 : 28. Gaal said, w. is Abimelech
and w. is Shechem, 38. [vow
11 : 39. w. did with her acc. to his
15 : 6. Philis. said, w. hath done
18 : 2. w. when came to hou. of Mi.
3. they said, w. bro-t thee hither?
21 : 5. w. is there among all tribes?
Ru. 3 : 9. Boaz said, w. art thou ?
16. said, w. art thou, my dangh ?
1 S. 2 : 25. if man sin against Lord,
w. entreat for him ? [Gods ?
4 : 8. w. deliver us out of hand of
6 : 20. w. able to stand bef. this G.
10 : 12. one said, w. is their father?
11 : 12. w. is he said, Shall S. reign
14 : 17. number and see w. is gone
17 : 26. w. this uncircumcised Phil.
18 : 18. David said, w. am I that,
2 S. 7 : 18. 1 Ch. 17 : 16.[tell me?
20 : 10. David unto Jona. w. shall
22 : 14. w. is so faithful as David
23 : 22. Go, know w. hath seen him
25 : 10. w. is Da. ? w. son of Jesse ?
26 : 9. w. stretch hand ag. anointed
14. w. art thou criest unto king?
15. Abner, w. is like to thee in Isr.
30 : 24. w. hearken unto you in this
2 S. 1 : 24. w. clothed you in scarl.(2)
11 : 21. w. smote Abimelech son of
12 : 22. w. tell wheth. G. be gracious
16 : 10. w. sh. say, Wh f. hast done so?
22 : 32. w. is God save the L. ? w.
is a rock save our G.? Ps. 18 : 31.
1 K. 1 : 27 not shewed w. sh. sit on
3 : 9. w. able to judge this people ?
8 : 24. w. kept with David my fath.
14 : 8. David, w. kept my com-ts ;
w. followed me wi. all his heart
16. of Jeroboam, w. did sin, w.
20 : 14. w. shall order the battle ?
22 : 20. w. shall persuade Ahab
that he may go up, 2 Ch. 18 : 19.
2 K. 9 : 32. Jehu said, w. on my side?
10 : 9. I slew him ; but w. slew all
13. Jehu said, w. are ye? [these ?
18 : 35. w. are they among all the
gods, 2 Ch. 32 : 14. Is. 36 : 20.
1 Ch. 29 : 5. w. is willing to consecr.
14. w. am I and what is my people
2 Ch. 1 : 10. w. can judge this people
2 : 6. w. able to build him a house
26 : 5. w. had underst-g in visions
35 : 21. God, w. is with me [of God
36 : 23. w. is there among you of all
his people? Ezr. 1 : 3. [build, 9.
Ezr. 5 : 3. w. ha. commanded you to
Ne. 6 : 11. w. go into temple to save
7 : 7. w. came with Zerub-l [his life
13 : 26. Sol., w. was beloved of God

Es. 4 : 11. whosoever into the inner
court, w. is not called. [to kingd.
14. w. knoweth whe. thou art come
6 : 4. king said, w. is in the court ?
7 : 5. king said, w. is he that durst
Jb. 4 : 2. w. withhold from speaking
7. w. ever perished, being innoc-t
5 : 10. w. giveth rain upon earth
9 : 12. he taketh, w. can hinder
him ? w. will say, What doest
19. w. shall set me a time to plead
24. if not, where, and w. is he ?
11 : 10. if he cut off, w. can hinder
12 : 4. w. calleth upon G. [wrought
9. w. knoweth not that hand of L.
13 : 19. w. is he will plead with me ?
14 : 4. w. can bring clean thing out
17 : 3. w. will strike hands with me?
15. as for my hope, w. sh. see it?
21 : 31. w. declare his way to his
face? w. shall repay him ? [him
23 : 13. he is in one mind, w. turn
24 : 25. w. will make me a liar ?
26 : 14. his power w. can understand
27 : 2. G., w. hath vexed my soul (2)
30 : 4. w. cut up mallows by bushes
34 : 13. w. hath given him charge
over the earth ? or w. disposed
29. When he giveth quietness w.
make trouble? when hideth, w.
35 : 10. w. giveth songs in night ?
11. w. teacheth more than beasts
36 : 22. w. teacheth like him ?
23. w. hath enjoined his way ? w.
38 : 2. w. is this darkeneth counsel
5. w. hast laid the measures th-f?
or w. hath stretched the line
6. w. laid the corner stone thereof
8. w. shut up the sea with doors
25. w. hath divided a watercourse
28. w. hath begotten drops of dew?
29. hoary frost, w. gendered it ?
36. w. hath put wisdom in inward
parts? or w. given understadng
37. w. can number the clouds, or
w. can stay the bottles of heav.
41. w. provideth for raven his food
39 : 5. w. sent out wild ass free (2)
41 : 10. w. is able to stand bef. me ?
11. w. prevented th. I repay him?
13. w. can discover face of his
garment ? or w. come to him ?
14. w. open the doors of his face?
42 : 3. w. is he that hideth counsel
Ps. 4 : 6. w. will shew us any good
6 : 5. in grave, w. shall give thanks
8 : 1. w. set thy glory above heav-s
12 : 4. w. have said, w. is lord over
14 : 4. w. eat up my people as [us ?
15 : 1. w. shall abide in thy tabernacle? w. shall dwell in thy hill
19 : 12. w. can underst. his errors?
24 : 3. w. sh. ascend into hill of L.?
w. shall stand in his holy pla. ?
4. w. hath not lifted up soul unto
8. w. is this King of glory ? 10.
39 : 6. knoweth not w. sh. gather
59 : 7. w., say they, doth hear ?
60 : 9. w. bring me into strong city ?
w. lead me into Edom? Ps. 108 : 10.
64 : 3. w. whet their tongue like sw.
5. they say, w. shall see them ?
71 : 19. O God, w. hast done great
72 : 18. w. doeth wondrous things
73 : 12. ungodly, w. prosp. in world
76 : 7. w. may stand in thy sight
77 : 13. w. is so great a God as our
84 : 6. w. passing thro. val. of Baca
89 : 6. w. be compared unto L.? (2)
8. w. is a strong L. like unto thee
94 : 16. w. will rise for me ag. (2)
103 : 3. w. forgiveth all thine iniquities ; w. healeth diseases
4. w. redeemeth thy life, w.
5. w. satisfieth thy mouth wi. good
104 : 2. w. coverest thyself with
light; w. stretchest out heavens

Ps. 104 : 3. w. layeth beams of chambers in ; w. maketh clouds (3)
4. w. maketh his angels spirits
5. w. laid foundations of the earth
106 : 2. w. can utter mighty acts of
L.? w. shew forth all his praise
108 : 11. O God, w. hast cast us off
113 : 6. w. humbleth hims. to beho.
124 : 1. Lord w. was on our side(2)
130 : 3. O Lord, w. shall stand?
135 : 8. w. smote firstborn of Eg-t
9. w. sent tokens, wonders upon P.
10. w. smote great nations, and
136 : 23. w. remembered us in our
25. w. giveth food to all flesh[low
144 : 10. w. delivereth David from
147 : 8. w. covereth heaven wi. (3)
17. w. can stand before his cold ?
Pr. 2 : 13. w. leave paths of uprightn.
14. w. rejoice to do evil [bear?
18 : 14. a wounded spirit, w. can
20 : 6. a faithful man w. can find?
9. w. can say, I am pure from sin ?
23 : 29. w. hath woe? w. sorrow (6)
24 : 22. w. knoweth ruin of both ?
27 : 4. w. is able to stand bef. envy ?
30 : 4. w. hath ascended into heav. ?
w. hath bound the waters ? (4)
9. Lest I say, w. is the Lord ?
31 : 10. w. find a virtuous woman ?
Ec. 2 : 19. w. knoweth whe. he be wise
25. w. can eat, or w. hasten more
3 : 21. w. knoweth the spirit of man
22. w. shall bring him to see what
be after him ? 6 : 12.-8 : 7.-10 : 14.
4 : 3. w. hath not seen evil work
13. w. will no more be admonished
6 : 12. w. knoweth what is good for
7 : 13. w. can make that straight
24. That which is deep, w. find it
8 : 1. w. is as the wise man ? w.
4. w. may say unto k., What doest
10. I saw wicked, w. had come and
12 : 7. spirit unto God w. gave it
Can. 3 : 6. w. is this that cometh
out of wilderness, 8 : 5. [ing
6 : 10. w. she looketh forth as morn-
Is. 1 : 12. w. hath required this at
6 : 8. L. saying, w. will go for us ?
14 : 27. L. hath purposed, w. disannul it ? hand, w. sh. turn it?
23 : 8. w. hath taken coun. ag. Tyre
27 : 4. w. would set briers ag. me
29 : 15. say, w. seeth us? w. [(2)
33 : 14. w. dwell with devouring fire
40 : 12. w. hath measured waters
13. w. hath directed Spirit of L.
41 : 2. w. raised up righteous man
4. w. hath wrought and done it
26. w. hath declared fr. beginning
42 : 19. w. is blind but my servant?
w. blind as he that is perfect
23. w. among you will give ear to
24. w. gave Jacob for a spoil [(2)
43 : 9. w. can shew us former thi-s
13. I will work and w. shall let it?
44 : 7. w. as I shall declare it [en
10. w. hath formed a god or molt-
45 : 21. w. told it from that time?(2)
49 : 21. w. hath begotten me these,
and w. hath brought up these?
50 : 8. w. is mine adversary ? let
9. w. is he that sh. condemn me ?
10. w. among you that feareth L.
51 : 12. w. art thou afraid of a man
19. w. shall be sorry for thee?
53 : 1. w. hath believed our report ?
Jn. 12 : 38. Ro. 10 : 16. [8 : 33.
8. w. declare his generation? Ac.
60 : 8. w. are these, fly as a cloud
63 : 1. w. is this cometh from Edom
65 : 16. w. blesseth himself shall
66 : 8. w. hath heard such a thi. (2)
Je. 1 : 16. w. have forsaken me and
2 : 24. in her occasion w. can turn
9 : 12. w. is the wise man that (2)
10 : 7. w. would not fear thee, O K.

Je. 15 : 5. w. have pity upon thee, Jerus.? w. bemoan thee? (3)
17 : 9. heart deceitful, w. know it?
18 : 13. Ask, w. heard such things
21 : 13. wh. say, w. come ag. us (2)
23 : 18. w. hath stood in counsel of Lord, w. marked his word
30 : 21. w. is this engaged his heart
46 : 7. w. is this cometh as a flood
49 : 4. saying, w. sh. come unto me?
19. w. is chosen man I may appoint? w. is like me? w. will appoint me the time? w. is shepherd that will stand before me? 50 : 44. [heal thee?
La. 2 : 13. O dau. of Zion, w. can
3 : 37. w. is he th. saith and it com-
Eze. 10 : 7. w. took it and went [eth
Da. 3 : 15. w. is God that sh. deliver
6 : 27. w. hath delivered Daniel
Ho. 14 : 9. w. is wise sh. understand
Jo. 2 : 11. day of L., w. can abide it?
Am. 3 : 8. lion roared, w. will not fear? Lord hast spoken, w. can
Ob. 3. saith, w. shall bring me down
Jon. 3 : 9. w. can tell if God will turn
Mi. 3 : 2. w. hate the good and love evil; w. pluck off their skin
3. w. eat the flesh of my people
5 : 8. w. if he go thro. treadeth do.
6 : 9. hear the rod and w. appointed
Na. 1 : 6. w. can abide in his anger (2)
3 : 7. Nineveh waste, w. bemoan
Ha. 2 : 5. w. enlargeth desire as hell
Zph. 3 : 18. w. are of thee, to whom
Hag. 2 : 3. w. is left that saw house
Zch. 4 : 7. w. art thou, O great mt.?
Mal. 1 : 10. w. is there wou. shut doors
3 : 2. w. may abide day of his coming? w. shall stand when he
Mat. 3 : 7. w. hath warned, Lu. 3 : 7.
10 : 11. inquire, w. in it is worthy
12 : 48. w. is my mother? w. are my brethren? Mk. 3 : 33. [43.
13 : 9. w. hath ears to hear, let him,
46. w., when he had found pearl
18 : 1. w. is greatest in kingdom of
19 : 25. w. then can be saved? Mk. 10 : 26. Lu 18 : 26. [w. is this?
21 : 10. all city was moved, saying,
23. w. gave thee this authority? Mk. 11 : 28. Lu. 20 : 2. [12 : 42.
24 : 45. w. is a faithful servant, Lu.
26 : 68. w. is he that smote thee? Lu. 22 : 64. [4 : 34.
Mk. 1 : 24. I know w. thou art, Lu.
2 : 7. w. can forgive sins but God only? Lu. 5 : 21. [Lu. 8 : 45, (2)
5 : 30. w. touched my clothes, 31.
9 : 34. disputed w. sho. be greatest
16 : 3. w. sh. roll us away the stone
Lu. 5 : 21. w. is this speaketh blasp.
7 : 39. w. and what manner of wom.
49. w. is this that forgiveth sins
9 : 9. w. is this of whom I hear such
31. w. appeared in glory and spa
10 : 22. no man knoweth w. Son is but Fa.; and w. Fa. is, but S.
29. And w. is my neighbour?
12 : 14. w. made me judge ov. you?
16 : 11. w. commit to y-r trust true
12. w. sh. give you y-r own [riches
19 : 3. sought to see Jesus w. he was
23 : 51. w. waited for kingd. of God
Jn. 1 : 19. sent to ask him, w. art thou? 22.-8 : 25. [thee
4 : 10. if knewest w. it is saith to
5 : 13. healed wist not w. it was
6 : 60. a hard saying, w. can hear it
64. Jesus knew w. believed not, w. should betray him, 13 : 11.
7 : 20. w. goeth about to kill thee?
9 : 2. Master, w. did sin, this man
19. your son, w. was born blind?
21. w. opened eyes we know not
36. w. is he, L., that I might believe
12 : 34. w. is this Son of man?

Jn. 13 : 24. that he ask w. it sho. be
25. He saith, Lord, w. is it? [thou?
21 : 12. none durst ask him, w. art
Ac. 3 : 3. w. seeing Pet., asked alms
4 : 25. w. by mouth of David said
7 : 27. w. made thee ruler ov. us? 35.
38. w. received the lively oracles
53. w. have received law by angels
9 : 5. Saul said, w. art thou, Lord? 22 : 8.-26 : 15. [by, 10 : 32.
11 : 14. w. tell thee words, where-
13 : 31. w. are his witnesses unto
43. w. persuaded them [people
17 : 10. w. went into synagogue of
19 : 15. Paul I know, but w. are ye?
21 : 4. w. said to Paul thro. Spirit
33. chief captain demanded w. he
37. w. said, Canst speak Greek?
23 : 18. w. hath something to say
33. w. presented Paul before Felix
28 : 18. w. would have let me go
Ro. 1 : 25. w. changed truth into lie
32. w. not only do the same, but
2 : 6. w. will render to every man
4 : 16. w. is the father of us all
18. w. ag-t hope believed in hope
25. w. was deliv-d for our offences
7 : 24. w. sh. deliver me fr. this dea.
8 : 31. If God for us, w. can be ag. us
33. w. lay any thing to God's elect
34. w. is he that condemneth? (3)
35. w. sh. separate us fr. love of C.
9 : 4. w. are Israelites; to whom
5. w. is over all, G. blessed for ev.
19. w. hath resisted his will? [G.?
20. w. art thou that repliest ag.
10 : 6. w. shall ascend into heaven?
7. Or, w. shall descend into deep?
11 : 4. 7,000 w. have not bowed to
34. w. hath known mind of L., w. been counsellor? 1 Co. 2 : 16.
35. Or w. hath first given to him
14 : 4. w. thou that judgest, Ja. 4 :
16 : 4. w. for my life laid down [12.
1 Co. 3 : 5. w. is Paul, and w. is Ap.
4 : 7. w. maketh thee to differ
9 : 7. w. goeth a warfare at his own charges? w. feedeth flock (3)
10 : 13. w. will not suffer you to be
14 : 8. w. prepare himself to battle?
2 Co. 1 : 4. w. comforteth us in all
10. w. delivered us fr. so great dea.
2 : 2. w. is he that maketh me glad
16. w. is sufficient for these things?
10 : 1. w. in presence base am. you
11 : 29. w. is weak, w. is offended
Ga. 3 : 1. Gal-ns, w. hath bewitched
4 : 23. he w. was of the bondwoman
5 : 7. Ye did run well, w. did hinder
Ep. 4 : 19. w. past feeling, have given
Ph. 2 : 6. w. being in the form of God
2 Th. 1 : 9. w. shall be punished with
2 : 4. w. opposeth and exalteth him.
1 Ti. 1 : 13. w. was bef. a blasphemer
6 : 15. w. is the blessed only Potent.
16. w. only hath immortality
2 Ti. 2 : 2. w. shall be able to teach
18. w. concerning truth ha. erred
Tit. 1 : 11. w. subvert whole houses
He. 2 : 15. w. through fear of death
5 : 2. w. can have compassion on ig-
7. w. in days of his flesh [norant
8 : 5. w. serve unto example [doms
11 : 33. w. thro faith subdued king-
13 : 7. w. have spoken unto you
Ja. 3 : 13. w. is a wise man am. you?
4 : 12. w. is able to save and dest. (2)
1 Pe. 1 : 21. w. by him believe in G.
2 : 22. w. did no sin, nei. was guile
23. w. when he was reviled [sins
24. w. in his own self bare our
3 : 13. w. is he will harm you?
4 : 5. w. shall give account to him
2 Pe. 2 : 1. w. shall bring in heresies
1 Jn. 2 : 22. w. is a liar but he that
5 : 5. w. is he th. overcometh world
Re. 1 : 2. w. bare record of word of

Re. 5 : 2. w. is worthy to open book
6 : 17. w. shall be able to stand?
13 : 4. w. is like unto the beast? w.
15 : 4. w. shall not fear thee, O L.
7. God, w. liveth for ever and ev.

WHOLE. [Entire.]

Ge. 2 : 6. mist watered w. ground
47 : 28. w. age of Jacob 147 years
Ex. 19 : 18. w. m-t quaked greatly
29 : 18. burn w. ram upon altar
Le. 8 : 9. w. rump shall he take off
4 : 12. w. bullock sh. he carry forth
7 : 14. sh. offer one out of w. oblat-n
8 : 21. M. burnt w. ram upon altar
25 : 29. may redeem within w. year
Nu. 10 : 2. of w. piece make trumpets
11 : 20. Ye shall eat a w. month, 21.
14 : 29. fall acc. to your w. numb.
De. 33 : 10. w. burnt sacrifice upon
Jos. 10 : 13. sun hasted not w. day
Ju. 19 : 2. concubine there 4 w. mos.
20 : † 40. w. consumption of city
2 S. 14 : 7. w. family ag. handmaid
1 K. 6 : 22. w. altar overlaid wi. gold
11 : 34. I will not take w. kingdom
2 Ch. 15 : 15. sought him wi. w. desire
26 : 12. w. number of chief fathers
33 : 8. do acc. to w. law by Moses
Es. 3 : 6. destroy Jews thro-t w. k-m
Ps. 51 : 19. pleased wi w. burnt off-g
105 : 16. he brake w. staff of bread
Pr. 1 : 12. Let us swallow them w.
16 : 33. w. disposing is of the Lord
Ec. 12 : 13. conclusion of w. matter; Fear G.: this is w. duty of man
Is. 1 : 5. w. head sick, w. heart faint
3 : 1. from Jerus. w. stay of bread (2)
9 : † 5. w. battle, wi. confused noise
† 12. devour Israel with w. mouth
10 : 12. performed w. work upon Zi.
14 : 29. Rejoice not, w. Palestina
31. thou w. Palestina art dissolved
21 : 8. I am in my ward w. nights
Je. 4 : 29. w. city shall flee for noise
7 : 15. have cast out w. seed of Eph.
Eze. 5 : 10. w. remnant will I scatter
15 : 5. w. it was meet for no work
43 : 11. may keep the w. form th-f
12. w. limit th-f sh. be most holy
Da. 2 : 48. ruler over w. province
6 : 1. princes be over w. kingdom
3. thought to set him ov. w. realm
10 : 3. nei. I anoint till 3 w. weeks
11 : 17. strength of his w. kingdom
Am 1 : 6. w. captivity to Edom, 9.
Mal. 3 : 9. robbed me, this w. nation
Mat. 8 : 32. w. herd ran violently
34. w. city came to meet Jesus [21.
13 : 33. till w. was leavened, Lu. 13 :
27 : 27. unto him w. band, Mk. 15 : 16.
Mk. 6 : 55. they ran thro. w. region
12 : 33. more than w. burnt off-gs
15 : 1. consultation with w. counc.
Lu. 8 : 39. published thro-t w. city
11 : 36. the w. shall be full of light
Jn. 11 : 50. that w. nation perish not
Ac. 11 : 26. a w. year they assembled
13 : 44. almost w. city to hear word
15 : 22. pleased apostles with w. ch.
19 : 29. w. city filled with confus-n
28 : 30. two w. years in hired house
Ro. 8 : 22. w. creation groaneth in p-n
16 : 23. of the w. church, saluteth
1 Co. 5 : 6. leaveneth w. lump, Ga. 5 : 9.
12 : 17. if w. were hearing, where
14 : 23. If w. church come together
Ga. 5 : 3. a debtor to do the w. law
Ep. 3 : 15. of wh. w. family in heaven
6 : 11. Put on w. armour of G., 13.
Ja. 2 : 10. whoso. shall keep w. law

See ASSEMBLY.

WHOLE Body.

Eze. 10 : 12. their w. b. full of eyes
Mat. 5 : 29. w. b. be cast into hell, 30.
6 : 22. thy w. b. shall be full of light, Lu. 11 : 34, 36. [ness
23. thy w. b. shall be full of dark-

1 Co. 12 : 17. If w.b. were an eye
Ep. 4 : 16. From wh. w.b. fitly joined
1 Th. 5 : 23. I pray your w. spirit and b. be preserved blameless
Ja. 3 : 2. perfect man able to bridle
3. we turn about their w.b. [w.b.
6. so tongue, it defileth our w.b.

WHOLE congregation.

Ex. 16 : 2. w.c. murmured ag. Mos.
10. as Aaron spake unto w.c. of
Le. 4 : 13. If w.c. sin thro. ignorance
Nu. 3 : 7. shall keep charge of w.c.
14 : 2. w.c. said, Would God we
20 : 1. came w.c. into desert of Zin
22. w.c. of Isr. came unto m-t Hor
Jos. 18 : 1. the w.c. of Israel assembled at Shiloh, 22 : 12. [is this
22 : 16. saith w.c., What trespass
18. will be wroth with w.c. of Isr.
Ju. 21 : 13. w.c. sent some to speak
2 Ch. 6 : 3. k. blessed w.c. of Israel
Ezr. 2 : 64. w.c. was 42,360, Ne. 7:66.
Pr. 26 : 26. wickedn-s be shewed bef.

WHOLE earth. [w.c.

Ge. 8 : 9. waters were on face of w.e.
9 : 19 of them was w.e. overspread
11 : 1. w.e. was of one language
4. lest we be scattered upon w.e.
Ex. 10 : 15. locusts cov-d face of w.e.
2 Ch. 16 : 9. the eyes of the Lord run throughout w.e., Zch. 4 : 10.
Ps. 48 : 2. joy of w.e. is mount Zion
72 : 19. let w.e. be filled wi. his glo.
97 : 5. hills melted at Lord of w.e.
Is. 6 : 3. w.e. is full of his glory
14 : 7. The w.e. is at rest, quiet [e.
26. This the purpose upon the w.
28 : 22. a consumption upon w.e.
54 : 5. God of w.e. sh. he be called
Je. 15 : 10. a man of strife to w.e.!
50 : 23. How is hammer of w.e. brok.
51 : 41. is praise of w.e. surprised!
La. 2 : 15. call, The joy of the w.e.
Eze. 32 : 4 fill beasts of w.e. wi. thee
35 : 14. When the w.e. rejoiceth
Da. 2 : 35. the stone filled the w.e.
7 : 23. 4th kingdom sh. devour w.e.
8 : 5. he goat came on face of w.e.
Mi. 4 : 13. substance unto L. of w.e.
Zch. 4 : 14. two th. stand by L. of w.e.
5 : 3. This is curse goeth over w.e.
Lu. 21 : 35. that dwell on face of w.e.
See **Whole HEART.**

Under WHOLE heaven.

De. 2 : 25. fear upon nations u.w.h.
4 : 19. divided unto nations u.w.h.
Da. 7 : 27. greatness of kingd. u.w.
9 : 12. u.w.h. not been done as [h.
See **Under HEAVEN.**

WHOLE house, s.

Le. 10 : 6. let w.h. of Israel bewail
2 S. 3 : 19. seemed good to w.h. of B.
1 K. 6 : 22. w.h. he overlaid wi. gold
2 K. 9 : 8. w.h. of Ahab shall perish
Je. 35 : 3. I took w.h. of Rechabites
Jn. 4 : 53. himself believed and w.
Tit. 1 : 11. who subvert w.h-s [h.
See **HOUSE of Israel.**

WHOLE land. [gold

Ge. 2 : 11. w.l. of Havilah, where is
13. compasseth w.l. of Ethiopia
13 : 9. Is not the w.l. before thee?
De. 29 : 23. w.l. is brimstone, salt
Jos. 11 : 23. So Joshua took the w.l.
Is. 13 : 5. the Lord to destroy w.l.
Je. 1 : 18. brazen walls against w.l.
4 : 20. Destruction; w.l. is spoiled
27. The w.l. shall be desolate
8 : 16. w.l. trembled at neighing of
12 : 11. w.l. desolate bec. no man
25 : 11. This w.l. sh. be desolation
45 : 4. I will pluck up this w.l.
51 : 47. her w.l. sh. be confounded
Zph. 1 : 18. w.l. shall be devoured
Mk. 15 : 33. darkness over w.l. until
See MULTITUDE, STONES.
See **Whole WORLD.**

WHOLE. [Sound.]

Jos. 5 : 8. abode in camp till were w.
2 S. 1 : 9. bec. my life is yet w. in me
Jb. 5 : 18. his hands make w.. [w.
Je. 19 : 11. vessel th. cannot be made
Mat. 9 : 12. They that be w. need not physician, Mk. 2 : 17. Lu. 5 : 31.
21. If touch his garment, I shall be w., Mk. 5 : 28.
22. thy faith hath made thee w. And the woman was made w. from that hour, Mk. 5 : 34.-10 : 52. Lu. 8 : 48.-17 : 19.
12 : 13. hand was restored w., like the other, Mk. 3 : 5. Lu. 6 : 10.
14 : 36. as many as touched were made perfectly w., Mk. 6 : 56.
15 : 28. her daughter was made w.
31. they saw the maimed to be w.
Mk. 5 : 34. go in peace and be w.
Lu. 7 : 10. found the servant w. th.
8 : 50. Fear not, she sh. be made w.
Jn. 5 : 4. made w. of whatso. disease
6. Jesus saith, Wilt be made w.?
9. was made w. and took up bed
11. He th. made me w. said, Take
14. thou art made w., sin no more
15. Jesus, who had made him w.
7 : 23. bec. I made a man w. on sab.
Ac. 4 : 9. by what means is made w.
10. by him, this man stand here w.
9 : 34. Jesus Christ maketh thee w.

WHOLESOME. [life

Pr. 15 : 4. A w. tongue is a tree of
1 Ti. 6 : 3. If any consent not to w.

WHOLLY. [words

Le. 6 : 22. it shall be w. burnt, 23.
19 : 9. thou sh. not w. reap corners
Nu. 3 : 9. they are w. given unto him
4 : 6. over it a cloth w. of blue
8 : 16. Levites are w. given unto me
Ju. 17 : 3. I had w. dedicated silver
1 S. 7 : 9. offered a sucking lamb w.
1 Ch. 28 : 21. people w. at thy com-t
Jb. 21 : 23. One dieth, w. at ease
Is. 22 : 1. w. gone up to housetops?
Je. 2 : 21. planted thee w. right seed
6 : 6. she is w. oppression in midst
13 : 19. Judah be w. carried away
42 : 15. If ye w. set faces to enter E.
46 : 28. not leave thee w. unpunish-
50 : 13. Babylon be w. desolate [ed
Eze. 11 : 15. all the house of Isr. w.
Am. 8 : 8. rise up w. as a flood, 9 : 5.
Ac. 17 : 16. city w. given to idolatry
1 Th. 5 : 23. God of peace sanctify w.
1 Ti. 4 : 15. give thyself w. to them
See FOLLOWED.

WHOM. [formed

Ge 2 : 8. put the man w. he had
3 : 12. The woman w. thou gavest
4 : 25. instead of Abel, w. Cain slew
6 : 7. will destroy man w. I created
10 : 14. Casluhim (out of w. came Philistim) and, 1 Ch. 1 : 12.
15 : 14. nation w. they shall serve
21 : 3. called son w. Sarah bare Is.
22 : 2. Take son Isaac w. th. lovest
24 : 3. dau-s of Canaan, among w. I
14. damsel to w. I shall say, Let
44. be woman w. L. hath appoint.
47. Nahor's son, w. Milcah [ed
25 : 12. Ishmael, w. Hagar bare
30 : 26. wives for w. I served thee
43 : 27. the old man of w. ye spake
29. younger brother of w. ye spa.
44 : 10. he with w. cup is found, 16.
45 : 4. I am Joseph w. ye sold into
46 : 18. sons of Zilpah w. Laban
48 : 9. sons w. God hath given me
49 : 8. art he w. brethren sh. praise
Ex. 4 : 13. send by him w. thou wilt
6 : 5. w. Egyptians keep in bond-e
18 : 9. Israel w. he had delivered
22 : 9. w. judges condemn, he pay
23 : 27. destroy peo. to w. thou come
28 : 3. w. I have filled with wisdom [
Ex. 32 : 13. serv-ts, to w. thou swarest
33 : 12. w. thou wilt send with me
19. be gracious to w. I will, shew mercy on w., Ro. 9 : 15, 18 [ling
35 : 21. ev. one w. spirit made wil-
23. ev. man with w. found blue
24. ev. man, with w. shittim wood
36 : 1. in w. the Lord put wisdom
Le 6 : 5. him to w. it appertaineth
13 : 45. leper in w. the plague is
14 : 32. law of him in w. is plague
15 : 18. woman with w. man sh. lie
17 : 7. devils aft. w. gone a whoring
22 : 5. man of w. he may take uncl.
25 : 27. overplus to w. he sold it
Nu. 3 : 3. sons of Aa. w. he consecra.
4 : 45. w. Moses numb-d, 46.-26:64.
5 : 7. unto him ag. w. he trespassed
11 : 16. w. thou knowest to be elders
21. people am. w. I am are 600,000
12 : 12. of w. flesh is half consumed
16 : 5. w. he hath chosen to come
22 : 6. I not he w. thou blessest (2)
23 : 8. sh. I curse w. G. hath not (2)
36 : 6. marry to w. they think best
De. 7 : 19. people of w. thou afraid
9 : 2. Anakim w. thou knowest (2)
19 : 4. w. he hated not in time past
17. both betw. w. controversy is
32 : 20. children in w. is no faith
37. Where rock in w. they trusted
33 : 8. w. thou didst prove at (2)
Jos. 10 : 25. thus shall Lord do unto enemies ag. w. ye fight [ed
13 : 8. with w. Reubenites receiv-
24 : 15. choose you w. ye will serve
Ju 7 : 4. of w. I say, This shall go
8 : 15. with w. ye did upbraid me
14 : 20. w. he had used as his friend
Ru. 4 : 1. kinsman of w. Boaz spoke
1 S. 2 : 33. man, w. I shall not cut off
6 : 20. to w. sh. he go up from us?
9 : 17. man w. I spake to thee of
20. on w. is all the desire of Israel?
10 : 24. See ye him w. L. hath chos.
12 : 3. w. have I defrauded? w.
13. behold k. w. ye have chos. (2)
16 : 3. anoint unto me w. I name
17 : 28. with w. left those few sheep
24 : 14. After w. is king of Israel come? after w. dost pursue?
25 : 25. I saw not young men w.
28 : 8. bring him up w. I sh. name
11. woman said, w. sh. I bring up
29 : 5. Is not this David of w. they
30 : 13. To w. belongest thou? [sang
2 S. 14 : 7. kill him for bro. w. he sl.
15 : 33. Unto w. David said, If thou
16 : 18. w. people choose, his will I
19. again, w. should I serve? [be
17 : 3. man w. thou seekest is as if
20 : 3. concubines w. he had left to
23 : 8. of mighty men w. Dav. had
1 K. 9 : 21. w. Isr. not able to destroy
17 : 20. the widow with w. I sojourn
18 : 31. unto w. word of Lord came
20 : 14. Ahab said, By w.? by young
21 : 25. w. Jezebel his wife stirred
22 : 8. man by w. we may inquire
2 K. 6 : 19. bring you to man w. ye
8 : 5. son w. Elisha restored [seek
10 : 24. If any w. I brought unto your hands escape [17 : 11, 33.
16 : 3. heathen w. Lord cast out,
17 : 15. heathen, conc. w. Lord had
34. of Jacob, w. he named Israel
35. with w. Lord made a covenant
18 : 20. Now on w. dost thou trust?
19 : 10. Let not thy God in w. thou trustest deceive thee, Is. 37 : 10.
22. w. hast thou blasphemed? ag. w. exalted voice, Is. 37 : 23.
1 Ch. 2 : 21. w. he married wh. sixty
9 : 22. w. Samuel seer did ordain
2 Ch. 1 : 11. over w. I made thee king
Ezr. 2 : 65. ser-ts, maids of w., 7,337
4 : 10. nations w. great Asnapper

Ne. 8 : 10. portions for w. nothing
Es. 4 : 11. to w. k. hold out sceptre
6 : 6. what unto man w. king delighteth to honour? (2)7,9,(2)11.
Jb. 3 : 23. w. God hath hedged in
9 : 15. w. tho. I were righteous, yet
15 : 19. Unto w. alone earth was g.
19 : 27. w. I shall see for myself
25 : 3. upon w. doth not light arise?
26 : 4. To w. hast thou uttered w-s
30 : 2. me in w. old age was perished
Ps. 16 : 3. saints in w. is my delight
18 : 2. my God in w. I will trust
27 : 1. The Lord is my light and my
salvation ; w. shall I fear ? (2)
32 : 2. Blessed is man unto w. Lord
imputeth not iniq-y, Ro. 4 :6, 8.
41 : 9. own friend, in w. I trusted
73 : 25. w. have I in heaven but
89 : 21. with w. my hand he estab-d
94 : 1. O God, to w. vengeance (2)
95 : 11. Unto w. I sware in my wra.
106 : 34. nations concern-g w. Lord
144 : 2. shield, and he in w. I trust
146 : 3. nor in man, in w. no help
Pr. 3 : 12. w. L. loveth, he correcteth, as fath. son in w. delight-h
27. withhold not good from them
to w. it is due ⌈rising
30 : 31. and king, against w. is no
Ec. 4 : 8 nei. saith, For w. do I lab.
8 : 14. now, unto w. it happen-h (2)
Can 3 : 1. him w. my soul lov-h, 2, 3.
Is. 6 : 8. Lord, saying, w. sh. I send?
8 : 12. to w. peo. say, A confederacy
18. I and chil. w. Lord hath given
10 : 3. to w. will ye flee for help?
19 : 25. w. the L. of hosts shall bless
22 : 16. What hast thou here and w.
28 : 9. w. sh. he teach knowledge?
12. To w. he said, This is the rest
31 : 6. from w. Israel have revolted
40 : 14. with w. took he counsel
18. To w., then, will ye liken God?
25.-46 : 5. ⌈lighteth (2)
42 : 1. mine elect, in w. my soul de-
24. L., he ag-t w. we have sinned
44 : 1 hear, Israel, w. I ha. chosen
47 : 15. with w. thou hast laboured
49 : 3. Isr. in w. I will be glorified
7. to him w. man despiseth, to
him w. nation abhorreth ⌈(2)
50 : 1. which is it to w. I sold you
51 : 19. by w. shall I comfort thee?
53 : 1. and to w. is the arm of the
Lord revealed? Jn. 12 : 38.
57 : 4. Ag. w. do ye sport yours.?
ag. w. make ye wide mouth?
11. of w. hast been afraid, that lied
Je. 1 : 2. To w. word of Lord came
6 : 10. To w. shall I give warning
8 : 2. sun, moon, w. they loved (5)
9 : 12. who is he to w. Lord spoken
16. w. nei. they nor fa-s ha. known
11 : 12. cry unto gods unto w. offer
14 : 16. people to w. they prophesy
18 : 8. If nation ag. w. I pronounced
20 : 6. friends to w. prophesied lies
25 : 15. nations to w. I send thee, 17.
26 : 5. prophets w. I sent unto you
27 : 5. earth unto w. it seemed meet
29 : 20. Hear w. I have sent to Bab.
30 : 17. is Zion, w. no man seeketh
33 : 5. w. I have slain in my fury
39 : 17. not unto hand of w. afraid
42 : 9. saith L., unto w. ye sent me
11. Be not afraid of k. of w. ye are
50 : 20. pardon them w. I reserve
La. 1 : 10. heathen w. didst comm-d
14. from w. I am not able to rise
4 : 20. of w. we said, Under shadow
Eze. 9 : 6. not near any upon w. is
11 : 1. among w. I saw Jaazaniah
16 : 37. lovers with w. taken pleas.
20 : 9. heathen among w. ye were
23 : 22. lovers from w. alienated, 28.
28. into hand of them w. hatest (2)

Eze. 23 : 40. unto w. a messenger was
sent; for w. didst wash thyself
31 : 2. Pha:, w. like in greatn.? 18.
32 : 19. w. dost thou pass in beauty?
Da. 1 : 4. Children in w. no blemish
7. unto w. the prince gave names
3 : 12. Jews w. thou hast set over
4 : 8. in w. spirit of holy gods, 5 : 11.
5 : 19. w. he would he slew ; and
w. he would he set up (4) ⌈liver
6 : 16. God w. thou servest will de-
11 : 21. to w. not give honour of
Am. 7 : 2. by w. sh. Jacob arise? 5.
Na. 3 : 19. upon w. thy wickedness
Zch. 3 : 18. to w. reproach a burden
Mal. 1 : 4. The people ag-t w. Lord
2 : 14. wife ag. w. dealt treacher-ly
Mat. 3 : 17. my Son, in w. I am well
pleased, 17 : 5. Mk. 1 : 11. 2 Pe.
11 : 10. this is he of w. writ. ⌊1 : 17.
12 : 18. my servant w. I have chos-
en ; my beloved in w. my soul
27. by w. do your children cast
them out, Lu. 11 : 19.
16 : 13. w. do men say I am, Mk.
8 : 27. Lu. 9 : 18.
15. but w. say ye that I am, Mk.
8 : 29. Lu. 9 : 20. ⌈custom
17 : 25. of w. do kings of earth take
18 : 7. woe to that man by w. the
offence cometh. Lu. 17 : 1.
19 : 11. save they to w. it is given
20 : 23. for w. it is prepared, Mk. 10:
23 : 35. w. ye slew betw. temple ⌊40.
24 : 45. w. his lord hath made ruler
26 : 24. unto man by w. Son of man
is betrayed, Mk. 14:21. Lu 22:22.
27 : 9. him w. they of Isr. did value
17. w. will ye I release 15. ⌈would
Mk. 3 : 13. calleth unto him w. he
14 : 71. know not man of w. ye speak
15 : 12. What do unto him w. ye
40. among w. was Mary Magdal-e
Lu. 6 : 34. if lend to them of w. hope
47. will shew you to w. he is like
7 : 4. worthy, for w. he sho. do this
43. I suppose he to w. he ga. most
47. to w. little forgiven, loveth lit.
8 : 2. Mary, out of w. went 7 devils
35. found man, out of w. devils,
9 : 9. who is this of w. I hear ⌊38.
10 : 22. he to w. Son will reveal
12 : 5. forewarn you w. ye sh. fear
43. w. his lord shall find so doing
13 : 4. upon w. tower in Siloam fell
16. w. Satan hath bound 18 yrs.
23 : 25. released him w. th. desired
Jn. 1 : 15. This he of w. I spake, 30.
26. one among you w. ye know not
33. Upon w. thou shalt see Spirit
45. him of w. Moses did write, Jes.
47. an Israelite, in w. is no guile!
3 : 26. he to w. thou hearest witness
34. he w. God hath sent speaketh
5 : 21. so Son quickeneth w. he will
38. w. he hath sent ye believe not
45. accuseth, Moses, in w. ye trust
6 : 29. believe on him w. God sent
68. Lord, to w. shall we go? Thou
7 : 25. this he, w. they seek to kill?
28. sent me is true, w. ye know not
8 : 53. prophets dead ; w. makest
54. of w. ye say, he is your God
10 : 35. If gods, unto w. word of L.
36. Say ye of him w. Father sent
11 : 3. L., he w. thou lovest is sick
13 : 18. I know w. I have chosen
22. disciples, doubting of w. he
23. one w. he loved ⌊spake, 24.
26. He it is to w. I shall give a sop
14 : 26. Comforter w. Fa. will send
15 : 26. Comforter w. I will send
17 : 3. know Jes. Ch. w. thou sent
11. keep those w. thou hast given
18 : 4. Jesus said, w. seek ye? 7.
19 : 26. Jes. saw disciple w. he loved
37. look on him w. they pierced

Jn. 20 : 2. disciple w. Jes. loved, 21 : 20.
15. why weepest thou? w. seekest
Ac. 1 : 3. To w. he shewed himself
3 : 15. ye killed the Prince of life w.
God hath raised from dead, 13.-
4 : 10. (2).-5 30.-10 : 39.
16. made this man strong w. ye see
21. w. heaven must receive until
4 : 22. man on w. this miracle of
27. ag. Jesus w. thou hast anoint.
5 : 36. Theudas ; to w. about 400
6 : 3. seven men, w. ye may appoint
6. w. they set before the apostles
7 : 7. nation to w. sh. be in bondage
39. To w. fathers would not obey
52. Just One ; of w. ye betrayers
8 : 10. To w. they all gave heed
34. of w. speaketh prophet this?
9 : 37. Dorcas, w., when they had
10 : 21. Peter said, I am he w. ye
13 : 25. John said, w. think ye I am
14 : 23. to Lord on w. they believed
21 : 16 Mnason, wi. w. we sho. lodge
23 : 29. w. I perceived to be accus.
24 : 8. examining of w. mayest take
25 : 15. man in bonds about w., 24.
16. To w. I ans-d, It is not man-r
18. Ag. w. brought none accusat.
26. Of w. I have no certain thing
26 : 17. Gentiles, unto w. now I se.
27 : 23. God, whose I am, and w. I
Ro. 1 : 5. By w. we received grace
6. Am. w. are ye the called of Ch.
3 : 25. w. G. set forth a propitiation
4 : 17. before him, w. he believed
5 : 2. By w. we have access by faith
11. thro. Christ, by w. atonement
6 : 16. servants ye are to w. ye (2)
8 : 29. w. he did foreknow he also
30. w. he did predestinate, w. he
called, w. be justified
9 : 4. to w. pertaineth the adoption
5. of w. as concern-g the flesh Ch.
18. and w. he will he hardeneth (2)
10 : 14. on him in w. not beheved (2)
11 : 36. to w. be glory forever. Amen.
Ga. 1 : 5. He. 13 : 21. 1 Ti. 6 : 16.
2 Ti. 4 : 18. 1 Pe. 4 : 11.
13 : 7. tribute to w. tribute is due (4)
14 : 15. Destroy not him for w. Ch.
15 : 21. To w. he was not spoken of
16 : 4. unto w. I not only gi. thanks
1 Co. 1 : 9. G. faithful, by w. ye were
3 : 5. ministers, by w. ye believed
7 : 39. to be married to w. she will
8 : 6. one God, of w. are all things ;
one Lord Jes., by w. all things
11. sh. weak brother perish, for w.
15 : 6. 500 breth., of w. greater part
15. w. he raised not, if dead rise
2 Co. 1 : 10. in w. we trust he will ⌊not
2 : 3. sorrow fr. them of w. I ought
10. To w. ye forgive, I forgive (2)
4 : 4. In w. god of this world hath
8 : 22. w. we have proved diligent
10 : 18. he w. Lord commendeth
12 : 17. a gain by any w. I sent
Ga. 2 : 5. To w. gave place, no, not
3 : 19. till seed come to w. promise
4 : 19. chil. of w. I travail in birth
6 : 14. by w. the world is crucified
Ep. 1 : 7. In w. we have redemption
thro. blood, Col. 1 : 14. ⌈herit.
11. In w. we have obtained an in-
13. In w. ye trusted ; in w. ye
were sealed with Spirit ⌈sation
2 : 3. Among w. we had our conver-
21. In w. all building, fitly framed
22. In w. ye are builded for a hab.
3 : 12. In w. we have boldness by
15. Of w. whole family is named
4 : 16. From w. whole body fitly
6 : 22. w. I sent for same purpose
Ph. 2 : 15. amo. w. ye shine as lights
3 : 8. for w. I have suffered loss of
Col. 1 : 27. To w. make known riches
28. w. we preach, warning ev. man

Col.2 : 3, In w. are hid all treasures
11. In w. ye are circumcised with
4 : 10. (touching w. ye received)
2 Th. 2 : 8. Wicked, w. L. consume
1 Ti. 1 : 15. sinners, of w. I am chief
20. Of w. is Hymeneus and Alex.;
w. I have delivered unto Satan
6 :16. w. no man hath seen nor[ed
2 Ti. 1 : 12. I know w. I have believ-
15. turned fr. me; of w. Phygel-s
2 : 17. of w. is Hymeneus, Philetus
3 : 14. knowing of w. thou learned
4 : 15. Of w. be thou ware also
Phm. 10. w. I have begotten in bonds
He. 1 : 2. Son, w. he hath appointed
heir, by w. he made worlds
2 : 10. for w. are all things, by w.
3 : 17. with w. was he grieved 40 y.
18. to w. sware he they sho. not
4 :13. of him with w. we have to do
5 : 11. Of w. we have many things
7 :2. To w. Abr. gave tenth of all, 4.
8. of w. it is witnessed he liveth
13. he of w. these things are spok.
11 : 18. Of w. it was said, In Isaac
38. Of w. world was not worthy
12: 6. w. L. loveth he chasteneth (2)
13 : 23. Tim., with w. I will see you
Js. 1 : 17. with w. no variableness
1 Pe. 1 :8. w. having not seen ye love
12. Unto w. it was revealed, that
2 : 4. To w., as unto a living stone
5 : 8. seeking w. he may devour
9. w. resist, steadfast in the faith
2 Pe. 2 : 2. by w. truth be evil spok.
17. to w. darkn. reserved, Jude 13.
19. for of w. a man is overcome
1 Jn. 4 : 20. loveth not broth. w. he
hath seen, how can he love G. w.
3 Jn. 6. w. if thou bring forward on
Re. 7 : 2. to w. given to hurt earth
17 : 2. with w. kings . . . fornication
20 : 8. number of w. as sand of sea

Before WHOM.

Ge. 24 : 40. L. b.w. I walk will send
48 : 15. God b.w. fathers did walk
1 K. 17 : 1. As Lord liveth b.w. I
stand, 18 : 15. 2 K. 3 : 14.-5:16.
Es. 6 : 13. Mord-i b.w. hast begun
Da. 7 : 8. b.w. three of first horns
20. other which came, b.w. 3 fell
Ac. 26 : 26. king b.w. I speak freely

WHOMSOEVER. [gods

Ge. 31 : 32. With w. thou findest thy
44 : 9. With w. of thy servants [sue
Le. 15 : 11. w. he touch. that hath is-
Ju. 7 : 4. of w. I say, This sh. not go
11 : 24. w. Lord shall drive out bef.
Da. 4 : 17. kingdom, Most High giveth to w. he will, 25, 32.-5 : 21
Mat. 11 : 27. he to w. Son will reveal
21 : 44. on w. it fall, it will grind to
powder, Lu. 20 :18. [Mk. 14 :44.
26 : 48. w. I shall kiss, same is he,
Mk. 15 : 6. released one, w. desired
Lu. 4 : 6. devil said, to w. I will, I gi.
12 : 48. unto w. much is given, of
Jn. 13 : 20. that receiveth w. I send
Ac. 8 : 19. that on w. I lay hands
1 Co. 16 : 3. w. ye approve by letters

WHORE, S.

Le. 19 : 29. not cause her to be a w.
21 : 7. not take a wife that is a w.
9. if dau-r of priest profane herself
by playing the w. [house
De. 22 :21. to play the w. in father's
23 : 17. sh. be no w. of dau-s of Isr.
18. shalt not bring the hire of w.
Ju. 19 : 2. his concubine played w.
Pr. 23 : 27. a w. is a deep ditch, and
Is. 57 : 3. seed of adulterer and w.
Je. 3 : 3. thou hast a w.'s forehead
Eze. 16 :28. Thou hast played the w.
33. They give gifts to all w-s [w-s
Ho. 4 : 14. them[8]. are separated with
Re. 17 : 1. Judgment of the great w.
15. waters where the w. sitteth
Re. 17 : 16. these shall hate the w.
19 : 2. he hath judged the great w.

WHOREDOM.

Ge. 38 : 24. Tamar, with child by w.
Le. 19 : 29. lest the land fall to w.
Je. 3 :9. through lightness of her w.
13 : 27. have seen lewdn. of thy w.
Eze. 16 : 33. come unto thee for w.
23 : 8. they poured w. upon her
17. Babylonians defiled her wi. w.
27. make to cease thy w., bro-t
43 :7. Isr. not defile my name by w.
9. let them put their w. far fr. me
Ho. 4 : 11. w., wine take away heart
5 : 3. O Ephr. thou committest w.
6 : 10. there is the w. of Ephraim
See Commit WHOREDOM, S.

Committed WHOREDOM, S.

Eze. 23 : 3. two women; they c.w-s
in Egypt; they c.w-s in youth
7. Aholah c.w. with chosen men
Ho. 1 : 2. the land hath c. great w.
4 : 18. they have c.w. continually

WHOREDOMS. [w.

Nu. 14 : 33. your children shall bear
2 K. 9 : 22. w. of thy moth. Jezebel
2 Ch. 21 : 13. like w. of hou. of Ahab
Je. 3 : 2. polluted land with thy w.
Eze. 16 : 20. thy w. a small matter?
22. in w. not rememb-d thy youth
25. Thou hast multiplied thy w.
26. hast increased thy w., 23 :14.
34. contrary fr. women in thy w.
36. and thy nakedness discovered
through thy w., 23 : 29 (2) [Eg.
23 :8. Nei. left her w. brought from
11. in w. more than her sister in
18. So she discovered her w. [w.
19. Yet she multiplied her w.
35. bear thou thy lewdness and w.
Ho 1 : 2. Go take a wife of w., and
children of w. [her w.
2 : 2. not my wife, let her put away
4. not mercy, they be chil. of w.
4 :12. spirit of w. caused them to err
5 : 4. spirit of w. in midst of them
Na. 3 : 4. bec. of multitude of w. of
harlot, that selleth nations thro.

WHOREMONGER. [w.

Ep. 5 : 5. no w. hath inheritance in

WHOREMONGERS.

1 Ti. 1 : 10. law made for w., liars
He. 13 : 4. but w. God will judge
Re. 21 : 8. w. shall have their part in
22 : 15. without are w., murderers

Go a WHORING.

Ex. 34 : 15. lest they - w. after gods
16. their dau-s, thy sons - w. aft.
Le. 20 : 5. cut off all th. - w. after him
6. turneth after wizards to - w.
Nu. 15 :39. aft. which ye use to - w.
De. 31 : 16. peo. will - w. after gods
2 Ch. 21 : 13. hast made Judah - w.
Ps. 73 : 27. destroyed all that - w.
Eze. 6 : 9. eyes which - w. after idols

Gone a WHORING.

Le. 17 : 7. devils, after whom - w.
Eze. 23 : 30. hast - w. after heathen
Ho. 4 : 12. people - w. fr. their God
9 : 1. thou hast - w. from thy God

Went a WHORING.

Ju. 2 : 17. Israel - w. after other
gods, 8 : 33. 1 Ch. 5 : 25. [ephod
8 : 27. all Israel went - w. aft. the
Ps. 106 :39. - w. with own inventions

WHORISH. [bro-t

Pr. 6 : 26. by a w. woman a man is
Eze. 6 :9. broken with their w. heart
16 : 30. of an imperious w. woman

WHOSE. [earth, 12.

Ge. 1 : 11. w. seed is in itself upon
7 : 22. in w. nostrils breath of life
11 : 4. tower w. top may reach h-n
17 : 14. w. flesh is not circumcised
24 : 23. w. daughter art thou? 47.
32 : 17. w. art thou? w. are these?
Ge. 38 : 25. By man w. these are, am
I with child; discern w. are th.
49 : 22. w. branches run over wall
Le. 13 : 40. man w. hair is fallen off
15 : 32. law of him w. seed goeth
16 : 27. goat, w. blood was brought
24 : 10. son of woman, w. father E.
Nu. 24 : 3. man w. eyes are open, 15.
De. 28 : 49. nation w. tongue thou
shalt not understand, Eze. 3 : 6.
Ru. 2 : 5. Boaz said, w. damsel is this
12. under w. wing thou art come
1 S. 12 : 3. w. ox or w. ass have I
taken? of w. hand any bribe
2 S. 3 : 7. Saul a concubine w. name
1 K. 3 : 26. woman, w. the liv. child
2 K. 12 : 15. into w. hand the money
18 : 22. w. high places, w. altars
1 Ch. 9 : 35. Jehiel, w. wife's name
was Maachah, 8 : 29. [Jerusalem
Ezr 7 : 15. God, w. habitation is in
Jb. 3 : 23. Why to man w. way is hid
5 : 5. w. harvest hungry eateth up
8 : 14. w. hope shall be cut off, and
w. trust shall be as spider's web
26 : 4. and w. spirit came fr. thee?
38 : 29. Out of w. womb came ice?
39 : 6. w. house have I made wild.
Ps. 15 : 14. In w. eyes a vile person
17 : 14. w. belly fillest with treasure
26 : 10. In w. hands is mischief
32 : 1. w. transgression is forgiven,
w. sin is covered, Ro. 4 : 7.
2. in w. spirit there is no guile
105 :18. w. feet they hurt wi. fetters
144 : 15. w. God is the Lord [7.
146 : 5. w. hope is in the L., Je. 17 :
Pr. 2 : 15. w. ways are crooked [ceit
26 : 26. w. hatred is covered by de-
Is. 1 : 30. as an oak w. leaf fadeth
2 : 22. cease from man w. breath
14 : 2. take captives w. captives th.
26 : 3. w. mind is stayed on thee
Je. 22 :25. them w. face thou fearest
33 : 5. for w. wickedness I hid my
44 : 28. w. words stand, mine or
Eze. 17 : 16. w. oath he despised, w.
20 :9. in w. sight made mys known
Da. 4 : 8. Dan., w. name Belteshaz-r
5 : 23. the God in w. hand thy
breath, w. are all thy ways
7 : 20. w. look more stout than [8.
Jon. 1 :7. know for w. cause this evil,
Mat. 22 : 20. w. is this image and su-
perscrip-n, Mk. 12 :16. Lu. 20 :24.
28. w. wife shall she be of the
seven, Mk. 12 :23. Lu. 20 : 33. [be
Lu. 12 : 20. then w. sh. those things
Jn 1 : 6 man from God w. na. John
27. w. shoe's latchet I am not
worthy to unloose, Ac. 13 : 25.
11 : 2. w. brother Lazarus was sick
19 : 24. cast lots for it, w. it shall be
Ac. 27 :23. God, w. I am, wh. I serve
Ro. 2 : 29. w. praise is not of men
3 : 8. some, w. damnation is just
9 :5. w. are the fathers, and of wh.
2 Co. 8 : 18. w. praise is in the gospel
He. 3 : 6. Christ, w. house we are, if
7 : 6. he w. descent is not counted
11 : 10. city w. builder and maker
12 : 26. w. voice then shook earth
1 Pe. 2 : 24. by w. stripes are healed
3 : 3. w. adorning, let it not be that
6. w. daugh-s ye are, long as ye do
See Whose HEART, HEARTS.
See HAND, LAND, MOUTH, NAME, NAMES, SON.

WHOSESOEVER.

Jn. 20 : 23. w. sins ye remit: w. "

WHOSO.

Ge. 9 : 6. w. sheddeth man's blood
Le. 11 : 27. w. toucheth carcass be
22 : 4. w. toucheth any thing unc.
Nu. 35 : 30. w. killeth person [rantly
De. 19 : 4. w. killeth neighb-r igno-

Ps.50 : 23. w. offereth praise glorif-h
101 : 5. w. slandereth his neighb-r
107 : 43. w. is wise shall understand
Pr. 6 : 32. w. committeth adultery
8 : 35. w. findeth me findeth life
9. 4. w. is simple, let him turn in,
12 : 1. w. loveth instruction [16.
13 : 13. w. despiseth word be destro.
16 : 20. w. trusteth in L., happy is
17 : 5. w. mocketh poor reproach-h
13. w. rewardeth evil for g. [Maker
18 : 22. w. findeth a wife findeth g.
20 : 20. w. curseth father or mother, lamp be put out, Mk. 7 : 10.
21 : 13. w. stoppeth ears at cry of
23. w. keepeth mouth keep-h soul
25 : 14. w. boasteth of a false gift
26 : 27. w. diggeth a pit shall fall
27 : 18. w. keepeth fig tree shall eat
28 : 7. w. keepeth law is a wise son
10. w. causeth righteous astray
13. w. confesseth and forsaketh
18. w. walketh uprightly be saved
24. w. robbeth his father or moth.
26. w. walketh wisely sh. be deliv-d
29 : 3. w. loveth wisdom rejoiceth
24. w. is partner with a thief [fath.
25. w. putteth trust in L. be saved
Ec. 7 : 26. w. pleaseth God sh. escape
8 : 5. w. keepeth com-t fear no evil
10 : 8. w. breaketh hedge, serpent
9. w. removeth stones sh. be hurt
Da. 3 : 6. w. falleth not down, 11.
Zch. 14 : 17. w. not come to worship
Mat. 18 : 5. w. receive one little child
6. w. shall offend one of little ones
19 : 9. w. marrieth her put away
23 : 20. w. shall swear by the altar
21. w. shall swear by the temple
24 : 15. w. readeth let him underst.
Jn. 6 : 54. w. eateth my flesh and
Ja. 1 : 25. w. looketh into perfect l.
1 Jn. 2 : 5 w. keepeth his word, in
3 : 17. w. hath this world's good

WHOSOEVER.

Ge. 4 : 15. w. slayeth Cain, vengea.
Ex. 12 : 15. w. eateth leavened br., 19.
22 : 19. w. lieth with beast be put
30 : 33. w. compoundeth any like it, w. putteth it upon strang., 38.
31 : 14. w. doeth work therein, 15.
32 : 24. w. hath any gold left them
33. w. hath sinned him will I blot
35 : 5. w. is of a willing heart [out
Le. 7 : 25. w. eateth fat of beast, of
11 : 25. w. beareth aught of carcass, be unclean, 15 : 27. [dead
31. w. doth touch them when
17 : 14. w. eateth it shall be cut off
18 : 29. w. sh. commit these abomi.
19 : 20. w. lieth carnally with wom.
20 : 2. w. giveth seed unto Molech
21 : 17. w. he be hath any blemish
22 : 3. w. goeth unto holy things
5. w. toucheth any creeping thing
21. w. offereth a sacrifice of peace
24 : 15. w. curseth God sh. bear sin
Nu. 15 : 14. w. will offer offering of
17 : 13. w. cometh near unto taber.
19 : 13. w. toucheth dead body of
16. w. toucheth one that is slain,
31 : 19. w. hath killed person [31 : 19.
De. 18 : 19. w. will not hearken
Jos. 1 : 18. w. doth rebel ag. com-t
2 : 19. w. go out of thy house, his blood ; w. with thee in house
20 : 9. w. killeth person unawares
Ju. 7 : 3. w. fearful, let him return
2 S. 5 : 8. w. getteth up to gutter, smiteth Jebusites, 1 Ch. 11 : 6.
14 : 10. w. saith aught unto thee
17 : 9. w. heareth will say, slaught.
1 K. 13 : 33. w. would, he consecrated
2 K. 10 : 19. w. be wanting not live
21 : 12. w. heareth of it his ears shall tingle, Je. 19 : 3. [any thing
1 Ch. 26 : 28. and w. had dedicated
2 Ch. 13 : 9. w. cometh to consecrate
15 : 13. w. not seek L. be put to d.
23 : 7. w. else cometh into house
Ezr. 1 : 4. w. remaineth in any place
6 : 11. w. alter this word be hanged
7 : 26. w. will not do law of thy God
10 : 8. w. will not come wi-in 3 days
Es. 4 : 11. w. come unto k. not called
Pr. 20 : 1. w. is deceived, not wise
27 : 16. w. hideth her, hideth wind
Is. 54 : 15. w. shall gather ag. thee
59 : 8. w. goeth th-u not know pea.
Eze. 33 : 4. w. hear-h sound of trum.
Da. 5 : 7. w. shall read this writing
6 : 7. w. shall ask petition of any god
Jo. 2 : 32. w. shall call on name of L.
Mat. 5 : 19. w. sh. break one of these com-ts ; w. shall do and teach
21. w. shall kill shall be in danger
22. w. is angry with brother with-t cause, w. sh. say, Thou fool (3)
28. w. looketh on a woman to lust
32. w. shall put away his wife ; w. shall marry her that is divorced, 19 : 9. Mk. 10 : 11. Lu. 16:
39. w. sh. smite thee on right [18.
41. w. sh. compel thee to go a mile
7 : 24. w. heareth these sayings of
10 : 14. w. shall not receive you, Mk. 6 : 11. Lu. 9 : 5. [Lu. 12 : 8.
32. w. shall confess me bef. men,
33. w. shall deny me before men
42. w. give unto one of little ones
11 : 6. blessed, w. shall not be offended in me, Lu. 7 : 23.
12 : 32. w. speaketh a word against the Son, Lu. 12 : 10. [3 : 35.
50. w. do will of my Father, Mk.
13 : 12. w. hath to him be given, but w. hath not, Lu. 8 : 18.
15 : 5. w. sh. say to father or moth.
16 : 25. w. will save his life shall lose it ; w. will lose his life, Mk. 8 : 35. Lu. 9 : 24.-17 : 33. [child
18 : 4. w. shall humble himself as a
20 : 26. w. will be great among you, be minister, Mk. 10 : 43.
27. w. will be chief among you, let him be servant, Mk. 10 : 44.
21 : 44. w. shall fall on this stone, shall be broken, Lu. 20 : 18.
23 : 12. w. shall exalt himself shall be abased, Lu. 14 : 11. [(2)
16. w. shall swear by the temple
18. w. shall swear by the altar, w. sweareth by the gift upon it
Mk. 8 : 34. w. will come after me
38. w. be ashamed of me, Lu 9 : 26.
9 : 37. w. shall receive one of such chil., w. shall receive, Lu. 9 : 48.
41. w. give you cup of water in
42. w. shall offend one of these
10 : 15. w. shall not receive kingd. of God as little child, Lu. 18 : 17.
11 : 23. w. shall say unto this mt.
Lu. 6 : 47. w. cometh to me and
14 : 27. w. doth not bear his cross
33. w. he be that forsaketh not all
Jn. 4 : 13. w. drinketh of this water
5 : 4. w. first stepped in was made
8 : 34. w. committeth sin is servant
16 : 2. w. killeth you will think he
19 : 12. w. maketh himself a king
Ac. 2 : 21. w. shall call on name of Lord shall be saved, Ro. 10 : 13.
13 : 26. w. feareth God, to you is
Ro. 2 : 1. inexcusable, O man, w.
9 : 33. w. believeth on him shall not be ashamed, 10 : 11.
1 Co. 11 : 27. w. shall eat this bread
Ga. 5 : 4. w. of you are justified by
10. sh. bear his judgment w. he be
Ja. 2 : 10. w. shall keep whole law
1 Jn. 2 : 23. w. denieth the Son
3 : 4. w. committeth sin transgr-h
6. w. abideth in him, sinneth not ; w. sinneth, not seen him
1 Jn. 3 : 9. w. is born of God, doth not commit sin, 5 : 18. [not of God
10. w. doeth not righteousness is
15. w. hateth brother is murderer
4 : 15. w. shall confess Jesus is Son
2 Jn. 9. w. transgresseth hath not
Re. 14 : 11. w. receiveth mark of na.
20 : 15. w. was not found written
22 : 15. w. loveth and maketh a lie
17. w. will, let him take of water
See BELIEVETH, TOUCHETH.

WHY. [and w.

Ge. 4 : 6. Cain, w. art thou wroth ?
12 : 18. w. not tell me she thy wife
19. w. saidst thou, She is my sis.
25 : 22. If it be so, w. am I thus ?
27 : 45. w. sho. I be deprived of both
42 : 1. w. look one upon another ?
47 : 15. w. sho. we die in thy pres. ?
Ex. 1 : 18. w. have ye done this thi.
2 : 20. w. is it ye have left the man ?
3 : 3. will see w. bush is not burnt
5 : 22. w. is it thou hast sent me ?
14 : 5. w. have we done this, let Isr.
17 : 2. M. said, w. chide ye wi me ?
18 : 14. w. sittest thou thys. alone
32 : 11. w. doth thy wrath wax hot
Nu. 11 : 20. w. came we out of Egypt
20 : 4. w. bro-t cong. into wildern.
27 : 4. w. name of our fath. be done
De. 5 : 25. Now w. sho. we die? [away
Jos. 5 : 4. w. Joshua did circumcise
7 : 25. Joshua said, w. troubled us ?
17 : 14. w. given me but one lot to
Ju. 2 : 2. w. have ye done this ?
5 : 16. w. abodest thou am. sheepf-ds
17. and w. did Dan remain in ships
28. w. chariot so long in com-g (2)
6 : 13. w. then is all this befallen us?
8 : 1. w. hast thou served us thus
9 : 28. w. sho. we serve Abimelech?
11 : 7. w. unto me when in distress
26. w. did ye not recover them
13 : 18. angel said, w. askest my na.
15 : 10. w. are ye come up ag. us ?
21 : 3. w. is this, one tribe lacking
Ru. 1 : 11. Naomi said, w. go with me
21. w. then call ye me Naomi
2 : 10. w. have I found grace in
1 S. 1 : 8. Hannah, w. weepest thou ? w. eatest not ? w. thy heart
2 : 23. Eli said, w. do ye such things
6 : 3. w. his hand not removed from
17 : 8. w. are ye come to set battle
28. David, w. camest thou down
19 : 17. Michal, w. hast deceived me ? Let me go, w. should I kill
20 : 2. w. sho. my father hide this
8. w. bring me to thy father ?
21 : 1. w. alone, no man with thee ?
22 : 13. w. have ye conspired ag. me ?
27 : 5 w. thy servant dwell wi thee ?
28 : 12. Saul, w. hast deceived me ?
15. Saul, w. hast thou disquieted
2 S. 3 : 24. w. hast sent Abner away
7 : 7. w. build ye not me a house of cedar, 1 Ch. 17 : 6. [own house
11 : 10. w. didst not go down unto
21. w. went ye nigh the wall ?
13 : 4. w. art thou lean fr. day to d. ?
26. k. said, w. Amnon go wi. thee
16 : 9. w. this dead dog curse king
17. w. wentest not with thy friend
18 : 11. w. didst not smite Absalom
19 : 10. w. speak not of bringing k.
11. w. are ye last to bring k. back
36. w. should king recompense me
41. w. have men of Judah stolen
43. w. then did ye despise us ?
20 : 19. w. swallow up inherit. of L.
24 : 3. w. doth king delight in this
1 K. 1 : 6. not saying, w. hast done
13. w. doth Adonijah reign ? [so ?
2 : 22. w. ask Abishag for Adonijah?
43. w. hast not kept oath of Lord
9 : 8. w. hath Lord done thus unto this land, 2 Ch. 7 : 21.

1 K. 14 : 6. w. feignest to be another
21 : 5. w. is thy spirit so sad that
2 K. 1 : 5. w. are ye now turned back?
7 : 3. w. sit we here until we die?
8 : 12. Hazael said, w. weepeth my
12 : 7. w. repair ye not breaches of
14 : 10. w. shouldest thou meddle
to thy hurt, 2 Ch. 25 : 19.
1 Ch. 21 : 3. w. doth my lord require
this; w. be a cause of trespass
2 Ch. 24 : 6. w. not required of Lev-s
20. w. transgress com-ts of Lord
25 : 15. w. hast sought gods of peo.
16. forbear, w. sho. thou be smitt.
32 : 4 w. sho. kings of Assyria come
Ezr. 4 : 22. w. sho. damage grow to
7 : 23. w. be wrath ag. realm of king
Ne. 2 : 2. w. is thy countenance sad
3. w. not my countenance sad
6 : 3. w. should the work cease
13 : 11. w. is house of G. forsaken?
21. w. lodge ye about the wall?
Es. 3 : 3. w. transgresseth k.'s com-t
4 : 5. to know what it was and w.
Jb. 3 : 11. w. died I not fr. womb?(2)
12. w. did knees prevent me? (2)
23. w. is light to a man whose way
7 : 20. w. hast set me as a mark ag.
21. w. dost not pardon my trans
9 : 29. If wicked, w. labour I in va.
15 : 12. w. thine heart carry thee
19 : 22. w. do ye persecute me as
28. w. persecute we him ⌊God
21 : 4. w. not my spirit troubled?
24 : 1. w. do they not see his days?
27 : 12. w. are ye altogether vain?
31 : 1. w. sho. I think upon a maid
33 : 13. w. dost thou strive ag. him?
Ps. 2 : 1. w. do the heathen rage
10 : 1. w. standest afar off, O Lord?
w. hidest in times of trouble?
22 : 1. My God, w. hast forsaken
me, w. so far from helping me?
42 : 5. w. art thou cast down, O my
soul? w. disquieted, 11.-43 : 5.
9. w. hast thou forgotten me? w.
go I mourning, because of, 43 : 2.
43 : 2. w. dost thou cast me off?
44 : 23. Awake, w. sleepest thou, L.
52 : 1. w. boastest thou in mischief
68 : 16. w. leap ye, ye high hills?
74 : 1. O God, w. hast cast us off,
w. thine anger smote ag. sheep
80 : 12 w. hast broken down hedges
88 : 14. Lord, w. castest off my
soul? w. hidest thy face fr. me?
Pr. 5 : 20. w., my son, be ravished
22 : 27. w. take thy bed from under
Ec. 2 : 15. w. was I then more wise?
7 : 16. w. shouldest destroy thys.?
17. w. die before thy time? ⌈aside
Can. 1 : 7. w. be as one that turneth
Is. 1 : 5. w. ye be stricken any more
40 : 27. w. sayest, Jac., my way is
63 : 17. O L., w. made us to err ⌊hid
Je. 2 : 14. Israel, w. is he spoiled?
33. w. trimmest thy way to seek
36. w. gaddest about so much ⌊love
8 : 5. w. is this people slidden back
14. w. do we sit still? assemble
19. w. have they provoked me
22. w. not health of people recov.
14 : 8. w. be as a stranger in land?
9. w. thou be as a man astonished
15 : 18. w. is my pain perpetual
26 : 9. w. hast prophesied in name
27 : 13. w. will ye die, thou and peo.
29 : 27. w. hast not reproved Jer-h
30 : 15. w. criest for thine affliction
36 : 29. w. hast thou written th-in
46 : 15. w. valiant men swept away
49 : 1. w. doth their k. inherit Gad
Eze. 18 : 19. Yet say ye, w.? ⌈33 : 11.
31. for w. will ye die, O Israel?
Da. 1 : 10. w. see your faces worse
2 : 15. w. decree so hasty from king
Jon. 1 : 10 w. hast thou done this?

Mi. 4 : 9. Now w. dost cry aloud?
Ha. 1 : 3. w. dost shew me iniquity
Hag. 1 : 9. w.? saith Lord of hosts
Mat. 6 : 28. w. take ye thought for
7 : 3. w. beholdest the mote in
thy brother's eye, Lu. 6 : 41.
8 : 26. w. are ye fearful, Mk. 4 : 40.
9 : 11. w. eateth master wi. public-s
14. w. do we and Pharisees fast
oft, Mk. 2 : 18. Lu. 5 : 33. ⌈bles
13 : 10. w. speakest thou in para-
15 : 2. w. do thy disciples transgress tradition, Mk. 7 : 5. ⌈ment
3. w. do ye transgress command-
16 : 8. w. reason ye among yourselves, Mk. 8 : 17. ⌈Mk. 9 : 11.
17 : 10. w. say scribes, Elias must,
19. said, w. could not we cast
him out? Mk. 9 : 28. ⌈writing
19 : 7. w. Moses command to give
17. w. callest thou me good? Mk.
10 : 18. Lu. 18 : 19.
20 : 6. w. stand ye all the day idle?
21 : 25. will say, w. did ye not believe him? Mk. 11 : 31. Lu. 20 : 5.
22 : 18. w. tempt ye me, ye hypocrites, Mk. 12 : 15. Lu. 20 : 23.
26 : 10. w. trouble ye the woman?
she hath wrought a, Mk. 14 : 6.
27 : 23. w., what evil hath he done?
Mk. 15 : 14. Lu. 23 : 22.
46. My God, w. hast thou forsak-
en me? Mk. 15 : 34. ⌈blasphem.?
Mk. 2 : 7. w. doth this man speak
8. w. reason these in your hearts?
24. w. do they on sabbath day
that not lawful, Lu. 6 : 2.
5 : 35. w. troublest thou the Master
39 w. make ye this ado and weep
8 : 12. w. this generation seek sign?
17. w. reason ye, bec. ye have no
11 : 3. if any say, w. do ye this?
14 : 4 w. this waste of ointment
Lu. 2 : 48. Son, w. thus dealt wi. us?
5 : 30. w. do ye eat with publicans
6 : 46. w. call ye me, Lord, Lord
12 : 26. w. take ye thought for rest
57. w. judge ye not what is right?
13 : 7. w. cumbereth it the ground?
19 : 31. if ask w. ye loose him? 33.
22 : 46. w. sleep ye? rise and pray
24 : 5. w. seek ye living am. dead?
38. he said, w. are ye troubled?
w. do thoughts arise in hearts?
Jn. 1 : 25. w. baptizest thou then
4 : 27. w. talkest thou with her?
7 : 19. w. go ye about to kill me?
45. w. have ye not brought him?
8 : 43. w. not understand my speech
46. if I say truth, w. not believe
9 : 30. w. herein is marvellous thi.
10 : 20. He is mad; w. hear ye him?
12 : 5 w. was not this ointm-t sold
13 : 37. w. cannot I follow now?
18 : 21. w. askest thou me? ask th.
23. but if well, w. smitest thou me
20 : 13. they say, Woman, w. weep-t
Ac. 1 : 11. w. stand gazing ⌊thou? 15.
3 : 12. w. marvel ye at this? or w.
4 : 25. w. did the heathen rage
5 : 3. w. hath Satan filled heart
4. w. hast thou conceived this
7 : 26. w. do ye wrong one to ano.?
9 : 4. Saul, Saul, w. persecutest
thou me? 22 : 7.-26 : 14.
14 : 15. Sirs, w. do ye these things?
15 : 10. w. tempt ye G. to put yoke
22 : 16. w. tarriest thou? arise ⌈ble
26 : 8. w. be thought thing incredi-
Ro. 3 : 7. w. am I judged as a sinner?
8 : 24. seeth, w. doth he yet hope
9 : 19. w. doth he find fault? ⌈thus?
20. Shall thing say, w. made me
14 : 10. w. dost judge thy brother?
or w. set at nought thy brother?
1 Co. 4 : 7. w. dost thou glory, as if
6 : 7. w. do ye not take wrong? (2)

1 Co. 10 : 29. w. is my liberty judged
30. w. am I evil spoken of for th.
15 : 29. w. are they baptized for d.
30. w. stand we in jeopardy ev. h.
Ga. 2 : 14. w. compellest Gentiles to
5 : 11. w. do I suffer persecution
Col. 2 : 20. w. are ye subject to ordi-

WICKED. ⌊nances

Ge. 18 : 23. Wilt thou destroy the
righteous with w.? ⌈as w.
25. far fr. thee that righteous be
38 : 7. Er was w., Lord slew him
Ex. 9 : 27. I and my people are w.
23 : 1. put not thine hand with w.
7. I will not justify the w. ⌈cut off
Le. 20 : 17. a w. thing; they sh. be
De. 15 : 9. not a tho-t in thy w. heart
17 : 5. have committed that w. thi.
23 : 9. keep thee from ev. w. thing
25 : 1. judges shall condemn the w.
1 S. 2 : 9. w. shall be silent in darku.
24 : 13. Wickedn. proceedeth fr. w.
1 K. 8 : 32. condemning the w., to
bring his way, 2 Ch. 6 : 23.
2 K. 17 : 11. Israel wrought w. things
2 Ch. 7 : 14. If people turn fr. w. ways
24 : 7. of Athaliah that w. woman
Ne. 9 : 35. nei. turned k-s fr. w. works
Es. 7 : 6. adversary is this w. Haman
9 : 25. Haman's w. device return
Jb. 3 : 17. There w. cease fr. troubling
9 : 22. He destroy-h perfect and w.
29. If w. why labour I in vain?
10 : 7. Thou knowest I am not w.
15. If I be w., woe unto me ⌈old?
21 : 7. Whf. do the w. live, become
30. w. reserved to day of destruct.
27 : 7. Let mine enemy be as the w.
34 : 18. fit to say to king, Thou w.!
38 : 13. w. might be shaken out of
15. fr. w. their light is withholden
40 : 12. tread down w. in their pla
Ps. 7 : 11 God is angry with the w.
9 : 5. hast destroyed the w. for ev
16. w. is snared in work of his ha
9 : 17. w. shall be turned into hell
10 : 2. The w. doth persecute pool
3. w. boasteth of heart's desire
4. The w. will not seek after God
13. Whf doth w. contemn God?
11 : 2. For, lo, w. bend their bow
5. w. and violence his soul hateth
6. Upon the w. he sh. rain snares
12 : 8. The w. walk on every side
17 : 9. keep me fr. the w. th. oppress
13. L. deliver my soul from the w.
26 : 5. and I will not sit with the w.
27 : 2. When the w. came upon me
28 : 3. Draw me not away wi. the w.
31 : 17. let the w. be ashamed and
34 : 21. Evil shall slay the w.
37 : 7. bringeth w. devices to pass
10. yet a little, the w. sh. not be
12. The w. plotteth ag-t the just
14. The w. have drawn out sword
16. Is better than riches of many
20. But the w. shall perish ⌊w.
21. The w. borroweth, pay-h not
32. The w. watcheth the righte-s
34. when w. are cut off, thou sh.
35. I have seen the w. in gr. power
40. L. shall deliver them from the
39 : 1. I keep mouth while w. ⌊w.
58 : 3. w. are estranged from womb
59 : 5. be not merciful to any w.
68 : 2. let the w. perish at presence
75 : 8. the w. shall wring them out
92 : 7. When the w. spring as grass
94 : 3. how long shall w. triumph?
13. until pit be digged for the w.
101 : 3. I will set no w. thing bef.
4. I will not know a w. person
8. I will early destroy all the w.
104 : 35. and let the w. be no more
106 : 18. the flame burned up w.
112 : 10. w. shall see it, be grieved
119 : 95. The w. have waited for me

Ps. 119 : 110. w. laid a snare for me
119. Thou puttest away all the w.
155. Salvation is far from the w.
139 : 19. Surely thou wilt slay the
24. see if any w. way in me ⌊w.
140 : 8. further not his w. device
141 : 4. to practise w. works wi. men
10. Let w. fall into their own nets
145 : 20. all the w. will he destroy
147 : 6. he casteth the w. down to
Pr. 2 : 22. the w. shall be cut off fr.
5 : 22. His iniquities sh. take the w.
6 : 18. that deviseth w. imagina-
10 : 25. so is the w. no more ⌊tions
30. w. shall not inhabit the earth
11 : 5. w. sh. fall by his wickedness
8. righteous, w. cometh in stead
10. when w. perish is shouting
18. w. worketh a deceitful work
21. the w. sh. not be unpunished
31. much more the w. and sinner
12 : 2. man of w. devices condemn
7. The w. are overthrown, 21 : 12.
12. The w. desir-h net of evil men
13. The w. is snared by his lips
21. w. shall be filled wi. mischief
13 : 17. A w. messenger falleth into
14 : 17. man of w. devices is hated
19. w. bow at gates of righteous
32. w. is driven away in his wick-
15 : 29. Lord is far fr. the w.⌊edness
16 : 4. even the w. for day of evil
17 : 4. w. doer giveth heed to false
15. He that justifieth w. is abom.
18 : 3. w. cometh, then contempt
20 : 26. A wise king scattereth w.
21 : 18. w. be ransom for righteous
27. when bringeth it with w. mind
24 : 16. w. shall fall into mischief
19. nei. be thou envious at the w.
25 : 5. Take away the w. from king
26. A righteous man falling down
before the w. is as ⌈covered
26 : 23. w. heart is like a potsherd
28 : 1. w. flee, no man pursueth
4. that forsake the law praise w.
12. when w. rise a man is hidden
15. ranging bear ; so is w. ruler
28. When w. rise men hide thems.
29 : 2. w. beareth rule, peo. mourn
7. w. regardeth not to know it
12. hearken to lies, servants w.
16. When w. are multiplied ⌈w.
Ec. 3 : 17. God judge righteous and
7 : 17. Be not overmuch w., neith.
8 : 10. So I saw the w. buried, who
13. it shall not be well with the w.
Is. 5 : 23. justify the w. for reward
11 : 4. wi. breath of his lips slay w.
13 : 11. I will punish w. for iniquity
32 : 7. w. devices to destroy poor
53 : 9. he made his grave wi. the w.
55 : 7. Let the w. forsake his way
57 : 20. the w. are like troubled sea
Je. 2 : 33. thou hast taught w. ones
6 : 29. the w. are not plucked away
17 : 9. The heart is desperately w.
25 : 31. he will give the w. to sword
Eze. 3 : 18. nor speakest to warn w.
fr. wicked way, 19 (2).-33 : 8, 9.
8 : 9. behold the w. abominations
11 : 2. these give w. counsel in city
13 : 22. ye have strengthened w.
that he should not return from
his w. way ⌈shall live
18 : 21. if w. will turn from sins he
23. Have I pleasure w. sho. die
20 : 44. not acc. to your w. ways
21 : 3. cut off righteous and w., 4.
25. profane, w. prince of Israel
33 : 11. I have no pleasure in death
of w. ; but that w. turn, live
15. If the w. restore the pledge
19. if w. turn from wickedness
Da. 12 : 10. the w. shall do wickedly
Mi. 6 : 11. them pure with w. balan-
Na. 1 : 3. L. will not acquit w. ⌊ces?

Na. 1 : 11. There is one w. counsellor
15. w. shall no more pass through
Ha. 1 : 4. w. doth compass righteous
13. when the w. devoureth man
Zph. 1 : 3. and consume stumblingblocks with the w. ⌈and w.
Mal. 3 : 18. discern betw-n righteous
4 : 3. ye shall tread down the w.
Mat. 12 : 45. he taketh 7 spirits more
w. Even so shall it be unto this
w. generation, Lu. 11 ; 26.
13 : 49. angels shall sever w. fr just
16 : 4. w. generation seeketh sign
18 : 32. w. serv-t, 25 : 26. Lu. 19 : 22.
Ac. 2 : 23. Him ye by w. hands slain
18 : 14. if it a matter of w. lewdn-s
1 Co. 5 : 13. put aw. that w. person
Ep. 6 : † 12. we wrestle ag. w. spirits
Col. 1 : 21. were enemies by w. works
2 Th. 2 : 8. shall that W. be revealed
See **Wicked MAN.**
See **MEN with wicked.**

Of the WICKED.

Jb. 8 : 22. place - w. come to nought
9 : 24. earth is given into hand - w.
10 : 3. shine upon the counsel - w.
11 : 20. But the eyes - w. shall fail
16 : 11 turned me into hands - w.
18 : 5. light - w. shall be put out
21. Surely such are dwell-gs - w.
20 : 5. the triumphing - w. short
22. every hand - w. upon him
21 : 16. counsel - w. is far, 22 : 18.
17 How oft is candle - w. put
out, Pr. 13 : 9.-24 : 20. ⌈- w.?
28. where are the dwellingplaces
24 : 6. they gather vintage - w.
29 : 17. I brake the jaws - w. and
36 : 6. He preserveth not life - w.
17. hast fulfilled judgment - w.
Ps. 1 : † 1. Blessed is man walketh
not in counsel of the w. ⌈an end
7 : 9. let wickedness - w. come to
10 : 15. Break thou the arm - w.
22 : 16. assembly - w. inclosed me
36 : 1. transgression - w. saith in
11. let not hand - w. remove me
37 : 17. arms - w. shall be broken
28. the seed - w. shall be cut off
38. the end - w. shall be cut off
55 : 3. because of oppression - w.
58 : 10. wash his feet in blood - w.
64 : 2. Hide me from counsel - w.
71 : 4. Deliver me out of hand - w.
73 : 3. when I saw prosperity - w.
74 : 19. deliver not soul of . . . unto
multitude - w. ⌈cut off
75 : 10. All the horns - w. will I
82 : 2. How long accept persons - w.
4. rid the poor out of hand - w.
91 : 8. sh. thou see the reward - w.
92 : 11. shall hear my desire - w.
97 : 10. his saints out of hand - w.
109 : 2. mouth - w. is opened ag.
112 : 10. desire - w. shall perish
119 : 53. Horror hold of me bec. - w.
61. hands - w. have robbed me
125 : 3. rod - w. not rest upon just
129 : 4. Lord hath cut cords - w.
140 : 4. Keep me, O Lord, from the
hands - w. ⌈- w.
8. Grant not, O Lord, the desires
146 : 9. way - w. he turneth upside
Pr. 2 : 14. delight in frowardn. - w.
3 : 25. afraid nei. of desolation - w.
33. Curse of Lord is in house - w.
4 : 14. Enter not into the path - w.
19. The way - w. is as darkness
10 : 3. casteth away substance - w.
6. violence covereth mouth - w.,
7. the name - w. shall rot ⌊11.
16. the fruit - w. tendeth to sin
20. the heart - w. is little worth
24. The fear - w. it shall come
27. years - w. shall be shortened
28. expectation - w. shall perish
32. mouth - w. speak-h frowardn.

Ps. 11 : 11. city overthrown by mou. -
23. expectation - w. is wrath ⌊w.
12 : 5. counsels - w. are deceit
6. words - w. are to lie in wait
10. tender mercies - w. are cruel
26. the way - w. seduceth them
13 : 25. the belly - w. shall want
14 : 11. house - w. shall be overthr-n
15 : 6. in revenues - w. is trouble
15 : 8. sacrifice - w. is an abomination to the L., 21 : 27. ⌈to Lord
9. The way - w. is an abominat-n
26. thoughts - w. are abominat-n
28. mouth - w. poureth out evil
18 : 5. It is not good to accept the
person - w. ⌈iniquity
19 : 28. the mouth - w. devoureth
21 : 4. the ploughing - w. is sin
7. robbery - w. shall destroy th.
10. The soul - w. desireth evil
12. wisely considereth house - w.
Is. 14 : 5. L. hath broken staff - w.
Je. 5 : 28. they overpass deeds - w.
12 : 1. Whf. doth way - w. prosper
15 : 21. deliver thee out of ha. - w.
23 : 19. a whirlwind of Lord upon
head - w., 30 : 23. ⌈hands - w.
Eze. 13 : 22. ye have strengthened
18 : 20. wickedn. - w. be upon him
21 : 29. bring thee upon necks - w.
30 : 12. sell the land into hand - w.
33 : 11. no pleasure in death - w. (2)
12. as for the wickedness - w.
Da. 12 : 10. none - w. sh. understand
Mi. 6 : 10. Are treasures of wickedness in house - w.? ⌈thou. - w.
Ha. 3 : 13. woundedst head out of
Ep. 6 : 16. quench fiery darts - w.
2 Pe. 2 : 7. vexed wi. conversat-n - w.
3 : 17. lest ye be led away wi. error
See **Wicked ONE.** ⌊- w.

To or Unto the WICKED.

Jb. 31 : 3. Is not destruction **t. w.**?
Ps. 32 : 10. Many sorrows be **t. w.**
50 : 16. **u. w.** God saith, What hast
75 : 4. **t. w.** lift not up the horn ⌈ous
Pr. 24 : 24. saith **u. w.**, Thou righte-
29 : 27. upright is an abomina. **t. w.**
Ec. 9 : 2. one event to righteous, **t. w.**
Is. 3 : 11. Woe **u. w.** ! it shall be ill
26 : 10. Let favour be shewed **t. w.**
48 : 22. There is no peace, saith the
Lord, **u. w.**, 57 : 21.
Eze. 3 : 18. When I say **u. w.**, Thou
shalt die (4), 33 : 8 (4) 14.
7 : 21. I will give it **t. w.** for a spoil

WICKEDLY.

Ge. 19 : 7. Lot said, do not so w.
De. 9 : 18. of your sins in doing w.
Ju. 19 : 23. Nay, breth., do not so w.
1 S. 12 : 25. if still do w. be consumed
2 S. 22 : 22. I have not w. departed
from my God, Ps. 18 : 21.
24 : 17. Lo, I have sinned, done w.
2 K. 21 : 11. Manasseh hath done w.
2 Ch. 6 : 37. We have sinned, dealt
w., Ne. 9 : 33. Ps. 106 : 6. Da. 9 :
20 : 35. Ahaziah did very w. ⌊5, 15.
22 : 3. his mother counsellor to do
Jb. 13 : 7. Will ye speak w. for G. ⌊w.
34 : 12. surely God will not do w.
Ps. 73 : 8. speak w. conc. oppression
74 : 3. enemy done w. in sanctuary
139 : 20. For they speak ag. thee w.
Da. 11 : 32. as do w. ag-t covenant
12 : 10. the wicked shall do w. ⌈ble
Mal. 4 : 1. all that do w. be as stub-

WICKEDNESS, ES.

Ge. 6 : 5. God saw w. of man was gr.
39 : 9. how can I do this great w.
Le. 18 : 17. it is w., 20 : 14. ⌈of w.
19 : 29. lest the land become full
20 : 14. that there be no w. am you
De. 9 : 4. for w. of these nations, 5.
13 : 11. Isr. sh. do no more such w.
17 : 2 if any that hath wrought w.
28 : 20. because of w. of thy doings

Jos. 7 : †15. hath wrought **w.** in Isr.
Ju. 9 : 56. Thus G. rendered **w.** of A.
20 : 3. said, Tell us, how was this **w.**?
12. What **w.** is this among you?
1 S. 12 : 17. may see your **w.** is great
20. ye have done all this **w.** yet
24 : 13. **w.** proceedeth from wicked
25 : 39. **w.** of Nabal upon own head
2 S. 3 : 39. reward doer acc-g to **w.**
7 : 10 neither shall children of **w.** afflict them more, Ps. 89 : 22.
1 K. 1 : 52. if **w.** be found in him he
2 : 44. **w.** thine heart is privy to
8 : 47. saying, we have committed **w.**
21 : 25. Ahab sold hims. to work **w.**
2 K. 21 : 6. Manasseh wro-t much **w.**
1 Ch. 17 : 9. nei. chil. of **w.** waste them
Jb. 4 : 8. that sow **w.** reap the same
11 : 11. vain men; he seeth **w.** also
14. let not **w.** dwell in thy taberu.
20 : 12. Tho. **w.** sweet in his mouth
24 : 20. **w.** shall be broken as a tree
27 : 4. My lips shall not speak **w.**
34 : 10. far be it from God that he should do **w.** [ure in **w.**
Ps. 5 : 4. not a God that hath pleas-
9. their inward part is very **w.**
7 : 9. let **w.** of wicked come to end
10 : 15. seek out his **w.** till [ours
28 : 4. Give acc-g to **w.** of endeav-
45 : 7. Thou hatest **w.**: thf. thy G.
52 : 7. strengthened himself in **w.**
55 : 11. **w.** is in the midst thereof
15. **w.** is in their dwellings and
58 : 2. Yea, in heart ye work **w.**
84 : 10. than to dwell in tents of **w.**
107 : 34. land into barrenness for **w.** of them, Je. 12 : 4. [righte-s
125 : †3. rod of **w.** not rest upon
Pr. 4 : 17. they eat the bread of **w.**
8 : 7. **w.** is abomination to my lips
10 : 2. Treasures of **w.** profit noth.
†3. casteth away wicked for **w.**
11 : 5. wicked shall fall by his **w.**
12 : 3. man not be established by **w.**
13 : 6. **w.** overthroweth the sinner
14 : 32. wicked driven aw. in his **w.**
16 : 12. It is abomination to kings to commit **w.** [**w.**
†27. more when he bringeth it in
26 : 26. his **w.** shall be shewed bef.
30 : 20. she saith, I have done no **w.**
Ec. 3 : 16. place of judgm., **w.** there
7 : 15. wicked prolongeth life in **w.**
25. I applied to know **w.** of folly
8 : 8. neither shall **w.** deliver those
Is. 9 : 18. For **w.** burneth as the fire
58 : 4. ye smite with the fist of **w.**
6. the fast, to loose bands of **w.**
Je. 2 : 19. own **w.** shall correct thee
4 : 14. Jerus., wash thine heart fr.
6 : 7. so she casteth out her **w.** [**w.**
7 : 12. see what I did for **w.** of peo.
8 : 6. no man repented of his **w.**
14 : 20. We acknowledge, L., our **w.**
23 : 14. none doth return fr. his **w.**
33 : 5. for whose **w.** I hid my face
44 : 9. Have ye forgotten the **w.** of your fathers, **w.** of kings, **w.** of their wives, your own **w.**, and **w.** of y-r wives? † **w.**-s (ö)
Eze. 3 : 19. if he turn not from **w.**
5 : 6. changed my judgments into
7 : 11. Violence into a rod of **w.** [**w.**
18 : 20. **w.** of wicked shall be upon
27. when wicked turneth from **w.**
31 : 11. driven him out for his **w.**
33 : 12. as for **w.** of wicked he shall not fall in day he turn-h fr. **w.**
19. But if wicked turn from his **w.**
Ho. 7 : 1. was discovered **w.** of Sama.
9 : 15. for **w.** of doings I will drive
10 : 13. Ye have ploughed **w.** and
15. So shall Beth-el do bec. of **w.**
Mi. 6 : 10. Are treasures of **w.** in ho.
Zch. 5 : 8. he said, This is **w.** And
Mal. 1 : 4. call them The border of **w.**
Mal. 3 : 15. that work **w.** are set up
Mk. 7 : 22. out of the heart, **w.**, † **w.**-s
Lu. 11 : 39. inward part is full of **w.**
Ac. 25 : 5. accuse, if any **w.** in him
Ro. 1 : 29. Being filled with all **w.**
1 Co. 5 : 8. neither the leaven of **w.**
Ep. 6 : 12. ag-t spiritual **w.** in high
1 Jn. 5 : 19. whole world lieth in **w.**

Their WICKEDNESS.

De. 9 : 27. look not to **t. w.** nor sin
Ps. 94 : 23. God shall cut them off in **t.** own **w.** [ed for **t. w.**
Pr. 21 : 12. God overthroweth wick-
Je. 1 : 16. judgments touching **t. w.**
14 : 16 I will pour **t. w.** upon them
23 : 11. in my hou. I have found **t. w.**
44 : 3. are a desolation, Bec. of **t. w.**
5. inclined not to turn from **t. w.**
La. 1 : 22. Let **t. w.** come before thee
Ho. 7 : 2. that I remember all **t. w.**
3. They make king glad with **t. w.**
9 : 15. all **t. w.** is in Gilgal, there I
Jo. 3 : 13. get you down, **t. w.** great
Jon. 1 : 2. cry ag. Nineveh, for **t. w.**
Mat. 22 : 18. Jesus perceived **t. w.**

Thy WICKEDNESS.

1 K. 2 : 44. the L. shall return **t. w.**
Jb. 22 : 5. Is not **t. w.** great
35 : 8. **t. w.** may hurt a man as thou
Is. 47 : 10. hast trusted in **t. w.** [**w.**
Je. 3 : 2. hast polluted land with **t.**
4 : 18. this is **t. w.** bec. it is bitter
22 : 22. be confounded for all **t. w.**
Eze. 16 : 23. came to pass aft. all **t. w.**
57. Before **t. w.** was discovered
Na. 3 : 19. upon whom hath not **t. w.**
Ac. 8 : 22. Repent theref. of this **t. w.**

WIDE.

[11.
De. 15 : 8. shalt open thine hand **w.**,
1 Ch. 4 : 40. the land was **w.**, quiet
Jb. 29 : 23. opened their mouth **w.**
30 : 14. upon me as a **w.** breaking
Ps. 35 : 21. opened mouth **w.** ag. me
81 : 10. open thy mouth **w.**, I will
104 : 25. So is this great and **w.** sea
Pr. 13 : 3. he that openeth **w.** his lips
21 : 9. than with a brawling woman in a **w.** house, 25 : 24. [mouth?
Is. 57 : 4. ag-t whom make ye a **w.**
Je. 22 : 14. I will build a **w.** house
Na. 3 : 13. the gates be set **w.** open
Mat. 7 : 13. **w.** is the gate that lead- [eth

WIDENESS.

Eze. 41 : 10. between chambers **w.**

WIDOW.

[house
Ge. 38 : 11. Remain a **w.** in father's
14. she put her **w.**'s garments off
Le. 21 : 14. **w.** or a harlot not take
22 : 13. if priest's daughter be a **w.**
Nu. 30 : 9. vow of a **w.** shall stand
De. 24 : 17. nor take a **w.**'s raiment to
2 S. 14 : 5. I am a **w.** woman [pledge
1 K. 7 : 14. Hiram was a **w.**'s son
11 : 26. Jereb.'s mother a **w.** wom.
17 : 9. have commanded **w.** woman there to sustain thee [sticks
10. he came, **w.** woman gathering
20. evil upon **w.** with whom I soj.
Jb. 24 : 21. doeth not good to the **w.**
29 : 13. I caused **w.**'s heart to sing
31 : 16. or caused eyes of **w.** to fail
†18. guided **w.** from my mother's
Pr. 15 : 25. he will establish border of
Is. 47 : 8. I shall not sit as a **w.** [**w.**
La. 1 : 1. how is she become as a **w.**
Eze. 44 : 22. Nei. take for wives a **w.**, but maidens, or **w.** that had
Mk. 12 : 42. certain poor **w.** threw in 2 mites, Lu. 21 : 2. [Lu. 21 : 3.
43. poor **w.** cast more in than all
Lu. 2 : 37. Anna was a **w.** about 84
7 : 12. only son of his moth., a **w.**
18 : 3. **w.** in that city came unto
5. because this **w.** troubleth me
1 Ti. 5 : 4. if any **w.** have children
5. is a **w.** indeed trusteth in God
9. Let not a **w.** be taken under 60
Re. 18 : 7. I sit a queen, and am no **w.**

WIDOW, S, with fatherless.

Ex. 22 : 22. shall not afflict **w.** or **f.**
24. your wives shall be **w.**-s, your children **f.** [**w.**
De. 10 : 18. Judgment of the **f.** and
14 : 29. stranger, **f.** and **w.** shall come and eat, 26 : 12. [**w.**, 14.
16 : 11. rejoice in feast, thou, **f.** and
24 : 19. sheaf in field shall be for the **f.** and **w.**, 20, 21.-26 : 13.
27 : 19. Cursed he that perverteth judgm-t of stranger, **f.**, and **w.**
Jb. 22 : 9. hast sent **w.**-s away empty, arms of **f.** been broken
24 : 3. They drive away ass of **f.**, take **w.**'s ox [**w.**-s is God
Ps. 68 : 5. A father of **f.**, a Judge of
94 : 6. slay the **w.** and murder **f.**
109 : 9. Let his children be **f.**, and his wife a **w.** [and **w.**
146 : 9. The Lord relieveth the **f.**
Is. 1 : 17. judge the **f.** plead for **w.**
23. they judge not **f.**, neither doth cause of **w.** come [**f.** and **w.**-s
9 : 17. neither have mercy on their
10 : 2. **w.**-s be their prey, they rob **f.**
Je. 7 : 6. If ye oppress not the **f.** and **w.**, 22 : 3. Zch. 7 : 10.
49 : 11. Leave thy **f.** children; let thy **w.**-s trust in me [as **w.**-s
La. 5 : 3. We are **f.**, our mothers are
Eze. 22 : 7. have they vexed **f.** and **w.**
Mal. 3 : 5. against those that oppress the **w.** and **f.** [tion
Ja. 1 : 27. To visit **f.** and **w.** in afflic-

WIDOWS.

Jb. 27 : 15. and his **w.** shall not weep
Ps. 78 : 64. **w.** made no lamentation
Je. 15 : 8. Their **w.** are increased
18 : 21. let their wives be **w.**; men
Eze. 19 : †7. And he knew their **w.**
22 : 25. have made her many **w.**
Mat. 23 : 14. Woe unto you, ye devour **w.**s' houses, Mk. 12 : 40. Lu. 20 : 47. [of Elias
Lu. 4 : 25. many **w.** in Israel in days
Ac. 6 : 1. murmuring bec. **w.** neglect- [ed
9 : 39. the **w.** stood by weeping
41. when he called saints and **w.**
1 Co. 7 : 8. I said to **w.**, It is good if
1 Ti. 5 : 3. Honour **w.** that are **w.**
11. But the younger **w.** refuse
16. If any have **w.**, let th. relieve, that church relieve **w.** indeed

WIDOWHOOD.

[of **w.**
Ge. 38 : 19. Tamar put on garments
2 S. 20 : 3. concubines, living in **w.**
Is. 47 : 9. in one day loss of chil., **w.**
54 : 4. not remember reproach of [thy **w.**

WIFE.

Ge. 7 : 13. entered Noah, Noah's **w.**
11 : 29. Abram's **w.** was Sarai, 31.-12 : 17.-16 : 1, 3.-20 : 18. [**w.**
20 : 3. woman thou hast is a man's
21 : 21. Hagar took **w.** for Ishm. [37.
24 : 3. not **w.** unto my son of Ca-n,
4. go unto my kindred, take a **w.** unto my son Isaac, 7, 38, 40.
15. Milcah, **w.** of Nahor, 11 : 29.
36. Sarah, master's **w.**, bare son
51. Rebekah be thy master's son's
25 : 1. Abraham took a **w.** [**w.**
27 : 46. if Jacob take a **w.** of dau-s of Heth, what good, 28 : 1, 2, 6.
36 : 10. Adah, **w.** of Esau, Bashemath, **w.** of Esau, 12, 17. [18.
14. sons of Aholiba-h, Esau's **w.**,
38 : 6 Judah took a **w.** for Er, his
8. Go in unto brother's **w.**, marry
9. Onan went in unto brother's **w.**
12. dau-r of Shuah, Judah's **w.**
39 : 7. **w.** cast her eyes upon Joseph
8. he refused, said unto master's **w.**
46 : 19. sons of Rachel, Jacob's **w.**
Ex. 18 : 2. Jethro took Moses' **w.**

Ex. 20 : 17. thou shalt not covet thy neighbour's w., De. 5 : 21. [(2)
21 : 4. If his master hath given a w.
10. If he take anoth. w., her duty
Le. 18 : 8. nakedness of thy father's w. not uncover, 20 : 11. De. 27 : 20.
11. father's w.'s dau. not uncover
15. not uncover daughter in law, son's w. [w., 20 : 21.
16. shalt not uncover brother's
18. Neither take a w. to her sister
20. not lie with neighb.'s w. [(2)
20 : 10. adultery with ano. man's w.
14. if man take w. and her moth.
20. If a man lie with his uncle's w.
21 : 7. not take a w. that is whore
13. priest sh. take w. in virginity
Nu. 5 : 12. If man's w. go aside, 29.
26 : 59. Amram's w. was Jochebed
36 : 8. shall be w. unto one of tribe
De. 13 : 6. if w. of thy bosom entice
20 : 7. what man hath betrothed w.
22 : 13. man take w. and hate her
30. man not take his father's w.
24 : 1. taken w., found uncleanness
2. she may be another man's w.
5. taken a new w. he not go to war
25 : 5. w. of dead not marry stranger
7. if he like not take bro.'s w. (2)
9. sh. brother's w. come unto him
11. w. of the one draweth near
28 : 30. betroth a w., ano lie with
54. eye be evil tow. w. of bosom
Ju. 4 : 4. Deborah, w. of Lapidoth
17. Sisera fled to tent of Jael, w.
21. Jael, Heber's w., took a nail
5 : 24. Blessed above women, Jael,
11 : 2. Gilead's w. bare sons [w.
14 : 3. goest to take a w. of Philist.?
19 : † 1. Levite took a w. a concu.
21 : 18. Cursed giveth w. to Benj.
Ru. 4 : 5. buy it of Ruth, w. of dead
10. Ruth, w. of Mahlon have I purchased to be my w.
1 S. 4 : 19. Phinehas' w. with child
14 : 50. name of Saul's w. Ahinoam
2 S. 3 : 5. Ithream, by Eglah, David's w., 1 Ch. 3 : 3. [Solomon's w.
1 K. 9 : 16. present unto his dau-r,
14 : 2. be not known the w. of Jero.
4. Jeroboam's w. went to Ahijah
5. w. of Jerob. to ask for son, sick
6. come in thou w. of Jeroboam
17. Jeroboam's w. came to Tirzah
2 K. 5 : 2. she waited on Naaman's w.
22 : 14. unto Huldah, prophetess, w. of Shallum, 2 Ch. 34 : 22.
1 Ch. 2 : 24. Hezron's w. bare Ashur
26. Jerahmeel had ano. w., Atarah
29. w. of Abishur was Abihail
7 : 16. Maachah, w. of Machir, bare
9 : 35. Jehiel, whose w.'s name was Maachah, 8 : 29. [ash
2 Ch. 22 : 11. w. of Jehoiada hid Jo-
Ezr. 2 : 61. a w. of dau-s of Barzillai
Ne. 2 : † 6. king (w. sitting by him)
Pr. 6 : † 26. w. hunt for precious life
18 : 22. whoso findeth a w., findeth
19 : 13. contentions of w. continual
14. prudent w. is from the Lord
Ec. 9 : 9. Live joyfully with w. [w.
Is. 54 : 1. more than chil. of married
Je. 3 : 20. Surely as a w. departeth
6 : 11. husband with the w. taken
16 : 2. not take a w. in this place
Eze. 16 : 32. But as a w. that committeth adultery [whoredoms
Ho. 1 : 2 take unto thee a w. of
12 : 12. Israel served for a w. and
Mal. 2 : 14. is she w. of thy covenant
Mat. 1 : 6. had been w. of Urias
14 : 3. John in prison for Herodias' sake, Philip's w., Mk. 6 : 17. Lu. 3 : 19.
19 : 29. that hath forsaken w. or children for my name's sake, Mk. 10 : 29. Lu. 18 : 29.
Mat. 22 : 25. first married a w., deceased, Mk. 12 : 20. Lu. 20 : 29.
28. Thf. whose w. shall she be of the 7? Mk. 12 : 23. Lu. 20 : 33.
Mk. 1 : 30. Simon's w.'s mother lay sick, Lu. 4 : 38. [brother's w.
6 : 18. it is not lawful to have thy
Lu. 8 : 3. Joanna, the w. of Chusa
14 : 20. I have married a w., can-
17 : 32. Rememb. Lot's w. [not come
20 : 28. If man's bro. die, having w.
Jn 19 : 25. stood by cross, Mary, w.
1 Co. 5 : 1. that one have father's w.
7 : 3. Let the husband render unto the w, also w. to the husband
4. w. not power ov. her own body
10. Let not w. depart fr. husband
12. If any hath w. believeth not
14. unbelieving husband is sanctified by w., unbelieving w. by
16. knowest, O w., whe. thou save
27. Art loosed fr. a w. seek not w.
34. difference betw. w. and virgin
39. w. bound long as husb. liveth
9 : 5. to lead about a sister, a w.
Ep. 5 : 23. husband is head of the w.
33. let every one love his w. as himself, w. see th. she reverence
1 Ti. 3 : 2. bishop be husband of one w., 12. Tit 1 : 6. [of one man
5 : 9. a widow, having been the w.
1 Pe. 3 : 7. honour unto w. as weaker
Re. 21 : 9. I will shew thee Lamb's w.

His WIFE.

Ge. 2 : 24. a man shall cleave unto h.w., Mat. 19 : 5. Mk. 10 : 7.
25. they were both naked, man and h.w. [selves
3 : 8 Adam and h.w. hid them-
20. Adam called h.w.'s name Eve
21. Unto Adam and h.w. coats of
4 : 1. Adam knew Eve h.w., 25.
17. Cain knew h.w.; she conceiv-
7 : 7. Noah went in, and h.w. [ed
8 : 18. Noah went forth, h.w. and
12 : 5. Abram took Sarai h.w. and
11. Abr. said unto h.w. thou fair
12. Eg-ns shall say, This is h.w.
20. sent Abr. away, h.w., 13 : 1.
16 : 3. Hagar to Abr. to be h.w. [w.
19 : 16. laid hold upon hand of h.
26. h.w. looked back, bec. pillar
20 : 2. Abr. said of h.w., She sister
7. restore the man h.w., 14. [w.
17. God healed Abimelech and h.
23 : 19. Abr. buried Sarah h.w. in cave, 25 : 10.-49 : 31. [h.w.
24 : 67. Isaac took Rebekah, became
25 : 21. Isaac entreated L. for h.w.
26 : 7. men asked him of h.w. [w.
8. Isaac sporting with Rebekah h.
11. toucheth h.w. be put to death
28 : 9. took Mahalath to be h.w.
36 : 39. Hadar, h. w.'s name was Mehetabel, 1 Ch. 1 : 50.
39 : 9. nei. kept from me but thee, because thou art h.w. [w.
19. his master heard words of h.
Ex. 4 : 20. Moses took h.w. to Eg-t
18 : 5. Jethro with h.w. unto Mo.
21 : 3. if married h.w. go with him
22 : 16. shall endow her to be h.w.
Le. 18 : 14. shalt not approach h.w.
Nu. 5 : 14. jealous of h.w. (2). 30.
15 man shall bring h.w. unto p.
30 : 16. statutes betw. man, h.w.
De. 22 : 19. be h.w. all his days, 29.
24 : 3. die wh. took her to be h.w.
4. not take her again to be h.w.
5. taken new w. he sh. cheer h.w.
Ju. 13 : 2. Manoah; h.w. barren
11. Manoah went after h.w. to
19. Manoah and h.w., 20, 21. [die
22. Manoah said unto h. w., we
23. h.w. said, If L. were pleased
15 : 6. h.w. given to companion
21 : 21. catch you every man h.w.
Ju. 21 : 22. reserved not to each h.w.
Ru. 1 : 1. man in Moab, h.w., two
2. name of h.w. was Naomi [sons
4 : 13. Boaz took Ruth, she was h.w.
1 S. 1 : 4. to Peninnah h.w. and
19. Elkanah knew Hannah h.w.
2 : 20. Eli blessed Elkanah, h.w.
25 : 3. Nabal, name of h.w. Abigail
37. when h.w. had told him these
42. Abigail became h.w. [things
30 : 22. save to every man h.w. [w.
2 S. 11 : 27 Bath-sheba became h.
12 : 9 hast taken h.w. to be thy w.
24. comforted Bath-sheba h.w.
1 K. 14 : 2. Jerob. said to h.w., Arise
21 : 5. Jezebel h.w. came to him, 7.
25. whom Jezebel h.w. stirred up
2 K. 8 : 18. dau-r of Ahab was h.w.
1 Ch. 2 : 18. Caleb begat chil. of h.w.
4 : 18. h.w. Jehudijah bare Jered
19. sons of h.w. Hodiah, sister of
7 : 23. Ephraim went in to h.w.
8 : 9. Sha-m begat of Hodesh h.w.
Jb. 2 : 9. said h.w., curse God and
Ps. 109 : 9. let h.w. be a widow [die
Je. 3 : 1. If a man put away h.w. [w.
Mat. 1 : 24. Joseph took unto him h.
5 : 32. whosoever sh. put away h. w., saving for, 31.-19 : 9. Mk. 10 : 11. Lu. 16 : 18. [fever
8 : 14. saw h.w.'s mother sick of
18 : 25. to be sold, h.w., chil., all
19 : 3. Is it lawful for a man to put away h.w., Mk. 10 : 2. [h.w.
10. If the case of a man be so with
22 : 24. If man die, brother sh. marry h.w., Mk. 12 : 19. Lu. 20 : 28.
25. left h.w. unto bro., Mk. 12 : 19.
27 : 19. Pilate, h.w. sent unto him
Lu. 1 : 5. h.w. was of dau-s of Aaron
24. h.w. Elizabeth conceived
2 : 5. taxed with Mary h. espoused
14 : 26. If man hate not h.w. [w.
Ac. 5 : 1. Ananias with Sapphira h.w.
2. kept part, h.w. privy to it
7. h.w. not knowing what was
18 : 2. Aquila with h.w. Priscilla
24 : 24. Felix with h.w. Drusilla
1 Co. 7 : 2. every man have h. own w.
11. let not hush-d put away h.w.
33. car-h how he may please h.w.
Ep. 5 : 28. loveth h.w. love-h hims.
31. man shall be joined unto h.w.
33. let ev. one love h.w. as hims.
Re. 19 : 7. h.w. hath made herself
See MICHAL, NABAL. [ready

My WIFE.

Ge. 20 : 11. slay me for m.w.'s sake
12. she is my sister, became m.w.
26 : 7. he feared to say, She is m.w.
29 : 21. Jacob said, Give me m.w.
44 : 27. Ye know m.w. bare 2 sons
Ex. 21 : 5. if serv-t say, I love m.w.
Ju. 15 : 1. said, I will go in to m.w.
2 S. 3 : 14. Deliver me m.w. Michal
11 : 11. shall I go into mine house to lie with m.w.? [hou. of Da.
2 Ch. 8 : 11. m.w. shall not dwell in
Jb. 19 : 17. breath strange to m.w.
31 : 10. let m.w. grind unto anoth-
Eze. 24 : 18. at even m.w. died [er
Ho. 2 : 2. she is not m.w., nor I
Lu. 1 : 18. m.w. well stricken in yrs.
See His NEIGHBOUR, SAMSON, URIAH, ZERESH.

Thy WIFE. [t.w.

Ge. 3 : 17. hearkened unto voice of
6 : 18. come into ark, thou and t.w.
8 : 16. go forth of ark, thou, t.w.
12 : 18. why not tell me she was t.
19. behold t.w., take her [w.
17 : 15. t.w., sh. not call her Sarai
19 Sarah t.w. sh. bear son, 18 : 10.
18 : 9. Where is Sarah t.w. [dau-s
19 : 15. Arise, take t.w. and two
26 : 9. Of a surety she is t. w. [w.
10. one might have lain with t.

Ex. 18 : 6. unto thee, t. w., two sons
De.21 : 11. wouldest have her to t. w.
13. go in to her, she shall be t. w.
2 S. 12 : 9. taken his w. to be t. w., 10.
Ps 128 : 3. t. w. be as a fruitful vine
Am. 7 : 17. t. w. sh. be a harlot [w.
Mat. 1 : 20. fear not to take Mary t.
Lu. 1 : 13. t. w. Elizabeth sh. bear son
1 Co. 7 : 16. whether shalt save t. w.

To WIFE. [t. w.

Ge. 12 : 19. I might have taken her
25 : 20. when he took Rebekah t. w.
26 : 34. wh. Esau took t. w. Judith
29 : 28. Laban ga. him Rachel t. w.
30 : 4. Rachel gave him Bilhah t. w.
9. Leah gave Zilpah to Jacob t. w.
34 : 4. Get me this damsel t. w., 12.
8. I pray you, give her him t. w.
38 : 14. not given unto Shelah t. w.
41 : 45. gave Joseph t. w. Asenath
Ex. 2 : 1. took t. w. a dau-r of Levi
6 : 20. Amram took Jochebed t. w.
23. Aaron took Elisheba t. w.
25 took of dau-s of Putiel t. w.
Le. 21 : 14. virgin of own people t. w.
De. 22 : 16. I gave my daughter t. w.
25 : 5. husb.'s broth. take her t. w.
Jos. 15 : 16. to him will I give Achsah
my dau. t. w., 17. Ju. 1 : 12, 13.
Ju. 14 : 2. now get her for me t. w.
21 : 1. not give dau. unto Benj. t. w.
1 S. 18 : 17. Merab will I give t. w.
19. Merab was given Adriel t. w.
27. Saul gave David Michal t. w.
25 : 39. wi. Abigail to take her t. w.,
1 K. 2 : 17. give me Abishag t. w. [40.
21. Abishag be giv. to Adon. t. w.
4 : 11. had dau-r of Solomon t. w.
15. Ahimaaz took Basmath t. w.
7 : 8. Pha-h's dau. Sol. taken t. w.
11 : 19. to Hadad t. w. sister of own
16 : 31. Ahab took t. w. Jeze-l [w.
2 K. 14 : 9. thistle said to cedar, Give
thy daughter to my son t. w.,
2 Ch. 25 : 18. [to Jarha t. w.
1 Ch. 2 : 35. Sheshan gave his dau-r
7 : 15. Machir took t. w. dau. of S.
2 Ch. 11 : 18. Rehoboam took Mahalath t. w. [Ahab t. w.
21 : 6. Jehoram had daughter of
Ne. 7 : 63. which took one of daughters of Barzillai t. w. [20 : 33.
Mk. 12 : 23. the 7 had her t. w., Lu.
Lu. 20 : 30. second took her t. w. and

WIFE with youth. [died

Pr. 5 : 18. rejoice with w. of thy y.
Is. 54 : 6. grieved, a w. of y. refused
Mal. 2 : 14. Lord witness between
thee and w. of y. [w. of his y.
15. let none deal treacherously ag.

WILD.

Ge. 16 : 12. Ishm-l will be a w. man

WILD ass, es. [grass?

Jb. 6 : 5. w. a. bray when he hath
24 : 5. as w. a-s go they to work
39 : 5. Who hath sent out w. a.?
free? who loosed bands of w. a.?
Ps. 104 : 11. w. a-s quench thirst
Is. 32 : 14. forts sh. be a joy of w. a-s
Je. 2 : 24. A w. a. used to wilderness
14 : 6. w. a-s snuffed up wind like
Da. 5 : 21. his dwelling with w. a-s
Ho. 8 : 9. they are gone, a w. a. alone

WILD beast, s. [you

Le. 26 : 22. I will send w. b-s among
1 S. 17 : 46. carcasses of P-s to w. b-s
2 K. 14 : 9. a w. b. in Lebanon trode
down thistle, 2 Ch. 25 : 18.
Jb. 39 : 15. forget-h w. b. may break
Ps. 50 : 11. w. b-s of field are mine
80 : 13. the w. b. doth devour it
Is. 13 : 21. w. b-s of desert lie there
22. w. b-s of islands shall cry in
34 : 14. w. b-s of desert shall meet
with w. b-s of island, Je. 50 : 39.
Ho. 13 : 8. the w. b. shall tear them
Mk. 1 : 13. Jes. in wildern. with w. b-s
Ac. 10 : 12. Wherein were w. b-s and
creeping things and fowls, 11 : 6.
See BULL, GRAPES, GOURDS,
HONEY, OX, ROE, VINE.
See **Wild GOAT, S.**
See **OLIVE tree.**

WILDERNESS.

Ge. 14 : 6. El-paran, which is by w.
Ex. 14 : 3. w. hath shut them in
16 : 3. ye brought us into w. to kill
10. looked toward w., glory of L.
Nu. 14 : 2. would we had died in w.!
29. carcasses sh. fall in w., 32. [ed
35. in this w. they sh. be consum-
20 : 4. why bro-t cong-n into this w.
21 : 18. from w. they went to Mat-h
24 : 1. Balaam set face tow. the w.
De. 1 : 19 we went through all that
gr-t and terrible w., 8 : 15. [w.
2 : 7. he knoweth thy walking thro.
11 : 24. from w. unto the sea shall
your coast be, Jos. 1 : 4. [ing w.
32 : 10. found him in a waste howl-
Jos. 8 : 20. peo. that fled to w. turned
16 : 1. lot of Joseph fr. Jordan to w.
18 : 12. goings out at w. of Beth-av.
Ju. 11 : 16. Israel walked thro. w., 18.
22. possessed coasts fr. w. unto J.
20 : 45. fled tow. w. unto Rim-n, 47.
1 S. 13 : 18. valley of Zeboim tow. w.
26 : 2. Saul went down to w. of Z (2)
1 K 19 : 15. Go to w. of Damascus
2 K. 3 : 8. The way thro. w. of Edom
1 Ch. 12 : 8. unto David to the w. [el
2 Ch. 20 : 16 find them bef. w. of Jeru-
Jb. 1 : 19. wind from w. smote house
24 : 5. w. yieldeth for them and
38 : 26. to rain on w. wh-in no man
39 : 6. Whose house I made the w.
Ps. 29 : 8. voice of the Lord shaketh
w.; Lord shaketh w. of Kadesh
68 : 7. thou didst march through w.
74 : 14. be meat to peo. inhab-g w.
106 : 9. he led them thro. depths
as thro. w., 136 : 16. Am. 2 : 10.
107 : 33. He turneth rivers into w.
35. turneth w. into stand-g water
Can. 3 : 6. Who is this that cometh
out of the w.? 8 : 5. [a w.
Is. 14 : 17. Is this the man made world
16 : 1. lamb to ruler from Sela to w.
27 : 10. city shall be left like a w.
32 : 15. Until w. be a fruitful field
33 : 9. Sharon is like a w.; and
35 : 1. The w. shall be glad for th.
41 : 18. I will make w. pool of wat.
42 : 11. Let w. and cities lift voice
50 : 2. I make the rivers a w. [den
51 : 3. he will make her w. like E-
64 : 10. Thy holy cities are a w.;
Zion is a w., Jerusalem [w.
Je. 2 : 6. Where is L. that led us thro.
24. A wild ass used to the w. that
31. Have I been a w. unto Israel?
4 : 26. the fruitful place was a w.?
9 : 12. the land is burned like a w.
12 : 10. my pleasant portion a w.
12. The spoilers are come thro. w.
22 : 6. I will make thee a w., Ho. 2 : 3.
50 : 12. the nations shall be a w.
51 : 43. Her cities are a w. [w.
Eze. 6 : 14 land more desolate than
23 : 42. brought Sabeans fr. the w.
Ho. 13 : 15. wind of L. sh. come fr. w.
Jo. 2 : 3 behind them a desolate w.
3 : 19. Edom shall be a desolate w.
Am. 2 : 10. I led you 40 yrs. thro. w.
Zph. 2 : 13. make Nineveh like a w.
Jn. 11 : 54. Jes. unto country near w.

In the WILDERNESS.

Ge. 16 : 7. Hagar by fountain - w.
21 : 20. lad dwelt - w. became archer
36 : 24. Anah, that found mules - w.
37 : 22. Cast him into this pit - w.
Ex 5 : 1. hold a feast unto me - w.
7 : 16 that people may serve me - w.
8 : 28 that ye sacrifice to Lord - w.
Ex. 14 : 11. hast thou taken us to die
- w., 12. Nu. 16 : 13.-21 : 5.
15 : 22. went three days - w. [w.
16 : 2. peo. murmured ag-t Moses -
19 : 2. pitched - w., Nu 21 : 11, 13
Le. 16 : 22. shall let go the goat - w.
Nu. 10 : 31. we are to encamp - w.
14 : 16. saying, theref. he hath slain
them - w., De. 9 : 28. [and - w.
22. have seen my miracles in Eg-t
33. until carcasses be wasted - w.
15 : 32. while - w. found man gath-g
26 : 65. They shall surely die - w.
27 : 3. Our father died - w.; no sons
32 : 15. he will again leave them - w.
33 : 8. 3 days' journey - w. of E-m
De. 1 : 1. words Moses spake - w.
31. - w. seen how L. bare thee [6 : 78.
4 : 43. Bezer - w., Jos. 20 : 8. 1 Ch.
8 : 16. Who fed thee - w. with manna, Ex. 16 : 32. [edst Lord - w.
9 : 7. forget not how thou provok-
11 : 5. And wh. he did unto you - w.
29 : 5. I have led you 40 years - w.,
8 : 2. Jos. 5 : 6.-14 : 10. Ne. 9 : 21.
Jos. 5 : 4. All the males died - w.
5. people born - w. not circumci.
8 : 24 end of slaying inhabit-s - w.
12 : 8. a possession - w. and south
15 : 61. - w. Beth-arabah, Middin
24 : 7. ye dwelt - w. a long season
1 S. 4 : 8. smote with plagues - w.
17 : 28. with whom left sheep - w.
23 : 14. David abode - w. in strong
holds, in a mountain - w. of
Ziph 15.-26 : 2. (2) 3. (2)
24. David and his men were - w.
of Maon, 25. [Maon
25. Saul pursued David - w. of
24 : 1. David is - w. of En-gedi
25 : 4. David heard - w. Nabal did
21. in vain kept all fellow hath - w.
2 S. 16 : 2. that such as be faint - w.
17 : 29. peo. hungry and thirsty - w.
1 K. 2 : 34. Joab was buried in own
house - w. [2 Ch. 8 : 4.
9 : 18. Solomon built Tadmor - w.,
1 Ch. 21 : 29 tabernacle Moses made
- w., 2 Ch. 1 : 3. [tower - w.
2 Ch. 20 : 24. Judah came tow. watch-
24 : 9. collection laid upon Isr. - w.
Ne. 9 : 19. forsookest them not - w.
Ps. 55 : 7. then would I remain - w.
63.* Ps. of David when - w. of Ju.
72 : 9. that dwell - w. bow bef. him
78 : 15. He clave rocks - w., gave
17. provoking Most High - w., 40.
19. Can God furnish a table - w.?
52. guided them - w. like a flock
95 : 8. Harden not your heart as
in day of temptation - w., He.
106 : 14. lusted exceedingly - w. [3 : 8.
26. hand to overthrow them - w.
Pr. 21 : 19. better to dwell - w. than
Is. 23 : 13. for them that dwell - w.
32 : 16 judgment shall dwell - w.
35 : 6. - w. shall waters break out
40 : 3. The voice of him that crieth
- w., Prepare, Mat. 3 : 3. Mk.
1 : 3. Lu. 3 : 4. Jn. 1 : 23.
41 : 19. I will plant - w. the cedar
43 : 20. honour me because I give
water - w. [- w.
63 : 13. That led them as a horse
Je. 2 : 2. when wentest aft. me - w.
3 : 2. sat for them as Arabian - w.
4 : 11. A dry wind of h. places - w.
9 : 2. Oh that I had - w. lodging pl.
26. will punish all that dwell - w.
17 : 6. inhabit parched places - w.
31 : 2. people left found grace - w.
48 : 6. Flee, be like the heath - w.
La. 4 : 3. people cruel like ostriches -
19. they laid wait for us - w. [w.
Eze. 19 : 13. now she is planted - w.
20 : 13. Israel rebelled ag. me - w.,
I wou. pour fury upon th. - w., 21

Eze. 20 : 15. hand unto them - w., 23.
17. nei. did make end of them - w.
18. I said unto their children - w.
36. as I pleaded with fathers - w.
34 : 25. they shall dwell safely - w.
Ho. 9 : 10. found Isr. like grapes - w.
13 : 5. I did know thee - w. in dry
Am. 5 : 25. Have ye offered - w.
40 years? Ac. 7 : 42. [w. of Ju.
Mat. 3 : 1. John came preaching -
15 : 33. Whence should we have so
much bread - w., Mk. 8 : 4.
Mk. 1 : 4. John did baptize - w.
13. he - w. 40 days tempted of S.
Lu. 3 : 2. word came unto John - w.
15 : 4. leave the ninety and nine - w.
Jn. 3 : 14. Moses lifted serpent - w.
6 : 49. fathers did eat manna - w.
Ac. 7 : 30. appeared to him angel - w.
36. aft. had shewed wonders - w.
38. he that was in the church - w.
44. had tabernacle of witness - w.
13 : 18. suffered their manners - w.
1 Co. 10 : 5. were overthrown - w.
2 Co. 11 : 26. perils in city, perils - w.
He 3 : 17. whose carcasses fell - w.

Into the WILDERNESS.

Ex. 3 : 18. now let us go three days' Journey - w., 8 : 27. [ses
4 : 27. Aaron, Go - w. to meet Mo-
15 : 22. they went out - w. of Shur
18 : 5. Jethro came unto Moses - w.
Le. 16 : 10. let him go for scapeg-t - w.
21. send him by fit man - w. [w.
Nu. 21 : 23. Sihon went ag-t Israel -
33 : 8. passed thro. midst of sea - w.
Ju. 1 : 16. chil. of Kenite - w. of Ju.
1 S. 26 : 3. David saw Saul came - w.
1 K. 19 : 4. Elijah a day's jour. - w.
2 Ch. 20 : 20. they went - w. of Tekoa
Jb. 30 : 3. fleeing - w. in former tim.
Eze. 20 : 10. and I bro-t them - w.
35. I will bring you - w. of people
29 : 5. I will leave thee thrown - w.
Ho. 2 : 14. will allure, bring her - w.
Mat. 4 : 1. Then was Jesus led of the Spirit - w., Mk. 1 : 12. Lu. 4 : 1.
11 : 7. What went ye out - w. to see? A reed shaken, Lu. 7 : 24.
Lu. 5 : 16. he withdrew himself - w.
8 : 29. he was driven of devil - w.
Ac. 21 : 38. wh. leddest - w. 4,000 m.
Re. 12 : 6. the woman fled - w., 14.
17 : 3. he carried me in spirit - w.

Of the WILDERNESS.

Ex. 13 : 20. encamped in edge - w.
16 : 14. upon face - w. lay a small
Nu. 33 : 6. Etham is in edge - w.
De. 2 : 26. And I sent messengers out - w. of Kedemoth [- w., 16.
Ju. 8 : 7. tear your flesh wi. thorns
1 S. 25 : 14. sent messengers out - w.
2 S. 15 : 28. I will tarry in plain - w.
17 : 16. Lodge not in plains - w.
1 Ch. 5 : 9. unto entering in - w.
Ps. 65 : 12. drop upon pastures - w.
102 : 6. I am like a pelican - w.
Je. 9 : 10. for habitations - w. a lamentation because [wind - w.
13 : 24. stubble passeth away by
23 : 10. pleasant places - w. dried
La. 5 : 9. peril because of sword - w.
Jo. 1 : 19. devoured pastures - w., 20.
2 : 22. the pastures - w. do spring
Am. 6 : 14. afflict you unto river - w.
Mal. 1 : 3. laid waste for dragons - w.

WILDERNESS of Paran.

Ge. 21 : 21. ishmael dwelt in w. -
Nu. 10 : 12. the cloud rested in w. -
12 : 16. fr. Hazeroth, pitched in w. -
13 : 3. Mos. sent fr. w. - heads of Isr.
26. they went and came unto w. -
1 S. 25 : 1. David arose, went to w. -

WILDERNESS of Sin.

Ex. 16 : 1. took journey from Elim unto w. -, Nu. 33 : 11. [33 : 12.
17 : 1. journeyed from w. -, Nu.

WILDERNESS of Sinai.

Ex. 19 : 1. same day came into w. -
Le. 7 : 38. to offer oblations in w. -
Nu. 1 : 1. Lord spake unto Moses in w. -, 3 : 14.-9 : 1. [w. -, 26 : 64.
19. so Moses numbered them in
3 : 4. Nadab and Abihu died in w. -
9 : 5. Israel kept passover in w. -
10 : 12. took journeys out of w. -
33 : 15. fr. Rephidim, pitched in w. -

WILDERNESS with wander, ed.

Ge. 21 : 14. Hagar w-d in w. of Beer.
Nu. 14 : 33. your children shall w. in w. 40 years, 32 : 13. [in w.
Jos. 14 : 10. while chil. of Israel w-d
Jb. 12 : 24. he causeth them to w. in w., Ps. 107 : 40. [tary way
Ps. 107 : 4. They w-d in w. in soli-
Is. 16 : 8. lords of heathen w-d thro.

Way of the WILDERNESS.

[w. [sea
Ex. 13 : 18. led peo thro. - w. of Red
De. 2 : 8. we passed by - w. of Moab
Jos. 8 : 15. Josh. and Isr. fled by - w.
Ju. 20 : 42. turned backs before Israel unto - w. [- w. of Gibeon
2 S. 2 : 24. Ammah before Giah by
15 : 23. people passed over tow. - w.

WILDERNESS with way.

Nu. 14 : 25. get you into w-s by w. of Red sea, 21 : 4. De. 1 : 40.-2 : 1.
De. 1 : 19. terrible w-s ye saw by w.
8 : 2. rememb. w. L. led thee in w-s
1 K. 19 : 15. thy w. to w-s of Damas.
2 K. 3 : 8. Which w. shall we go? The w. through w-s of Edom
Is. 43 : 19. I will make a w. in w-s
Ps. 107 : 4. in w-s in a solitary w.
See Wilderness of ZIN.

WILES.

Nu. 25 : 18. they vex you with their [w.
Ep. 6 : 11. able to stand ag-t w. of [devil

WILFULLY.

He. 10 : 26. if sin w. after received [truth

WILILY.

Jos. 9 : 4. Gibeonites did work w.

WILL, WILLS.

De. 33 : 16. good w. of him in bush
Ne. 9 : † 24. do with them acc. to w.
Es. 9 : † 5. acc-g to their w. unto
Ps. 27 : 12. Deliver me not unto w. of mine enemies [his enemies
41 : 2. not deliver him unto w. of
Ec. 5 : † 8. marvel not at the w. [hate
Eze. 16 : 27. thee unto w. of them th.
Mal. 2 : 13. receiveth it with good w.
Mat. 7 : 21. but he that doeth the w. of my Father, 12 : 50. [ther
18 : 14. it is not the w. of your Fa-
21 : 31. Whe. of them did w. of fa.?
Lu. 2 : 14. on earth peace, good w.
12 : 47. nei. did acc. to his lord's w.
23 : 25. delivered Jesus to their w.
Jn. 1 : 13. born, not of the w. of flesh
4 : 34. meat is to do the w. of him
5 : 30. I seek the w. of the Father
6 : 38. I came fr. heaven to do w. of
39. this is the Fath.'s w., 40. [him
Ac. 21 : 14. The w. of Lord be done
Ep. 2 : † 3. fulfilling w-s of the flesh
5 : 17. understanding w. of Lord
6 : 7. With good w. doing service
Ph. 1 : 15. some preach Ch. of good w.
He 10 : 10. By wh. w. we are sanctif.
1 Pe. 4 : 3. wrought the w. of Gent.
2 Pe. 1 : 21. prophecy not by w. of [man

WILL of God.

Ezr. 7 : 18. do after the w. o. your G.
Mk. 3 : 35. whosoever shall do w. - is my brother [but o. G.
Jn. 1 : 13. born, not of the w. of man,
Ac. 13 : 36. served generat-n by w. -
Ro. 1 : 10. prosperous journey by w. -
8 : 27. maketh interces-n acc. to w. -
12 : 2. prove that acceptable w. -
15 : 32. unto you with joy, by w. -
1 Co. 1 : 1. Paul, an apostle of Jesus Christ, by w. -, 2 Co. 1 : 1. Ep. 1 : 1. Col. 1 : 1. 2 Ti. 1 : 1.
2 Co. 8 : 5. gave themselves unto us by the w. - [ing to w. -
Ga. 1 : 4. us from evil world accord-
Ep. 6 : 6. doing the w. - fr. the heart
Col. 4 : 12. stand complete in all w. -
1 Th. 4 : 3. this is the w. -, 5 : 18.
He. 10 : 36. after ye have done w. -
1 Pe. 2 : 15. w. - th. ye put to silence
3 : 17. it is better if the w. - be so
4 : 2. not to lusts of men, but w. -
19. them that suffer acc-g to w. -
1 Jn. 2 : 17. he that doeth the w. - [abideth

His WILL.

Da. 4 : 35. he doeth acc-g to h. w.
8 : 4. he did acc-g to h. w., became
11 : 3. king sh. do acc. to h. w., 36.
Lu. 12 : 47. servant, which knew his lord's w. nei. did acc. to h. w.
Jn. 7 : 17. If any man will do h. w.
9 : 31. if any man doeth h. w., him
Ac. 22 : 14. th. shouldest know h. w.
Ro 2 : 18. thou a Jew, knowest h. w.
9 : 19. For who hath resisted h. w.
1 Co. 16 : 12. h. w. was not to come
Ep. 1 : 5. to good pleasure of h. w.
9. made known mystery of h. w.
Col. 1 : 9. filled with knowl. of h. w.
2 Ti. 2 : 26. taken captive at h. w.
He. 13 : 21. Make perfect to do h. w.
1 Jn. 5 : 14. if we ask acc-g to h. w.
Re. 17 : 17. put in their hearts to ful- [fil h. w.

My WILL.

Lu. 22 : 42. not m. w., but thine be
Ac. 13 : 22. Da., who sh. fulfil m. w.
1 Co. 9 : 17. if I do this thing ag. m. [w.

Own WILL.

Le. 1 : 3. he shall offer it of his o. w.
19 : 5. ye shall offer it as your o. w., 22 : 19, 29. [his o. w.
Da. 11 : 16. he shall do according to
Jn. 5 : 30. bec. I seek not mine o. w.
6 : 38. from heaven, not to do o. w.
1 Co. 7 : 37. hath power over o. w.
Ep. 1 : 11. after counsel of his o. w.
He. 2 : 4. gifts, acc-g to his o. w.
Ja. 1 : 18. Of his o. w. begat he us
See SELFWILL.

Thy WILL.

[God
Ps. 40 : 8. I delight to do t. w., O my
143 : 10. Teach me to do t. w., my
Mat. 6 : 10. t. w. be done in earth as in heaven, Lu. 11 : 2. [be done
26 : 42. if cup may not pass, t. w.
He. 10 : 7. Lo, I come to do t. w., 9.

WILL. [Verb.]

De. 21 : 14. let her go whither she w.
Jb. 13 : 13. let come on me what w.
Pr. 21 : 1. he turneth the king's heart whithersoever he w.
Da. 4 : 17. God giveth it to whomsoever he w., 25, 32.-5 : 21.
Mat. 8 : 3. I w.; be thou clean, Mk. 1 : 41. Lu. 5 : 13. [I w.
20 : 15. Is it not lawful to do what
32. Wh. w. ye I shall do unto you?
26 : 39. not as I w., but as thou wilt, Mk. 14 : 36.
27 : 17. Whom w. ye that I release,
21. Mk. 15 : 9. Jn. 18 : 39. [John
Mk. 6 : 25. I w. thou give me head of
14 : 7. whenso. ye w. ye may good
15 : 12. What w. ye I sh. do to him?
Lu. 4 : 6. to whomso. I w., I give it
12 : 49. what w. I, if it be kindled?
Jn. 5 : 21. Son quickeneth wh. he w.
9 : 27. w. ye also be his disciples?
15 : 7. ask what ye w., it sh. be done
17 : 24. I w. they be with me where
21 : 22. If I w. that he tarry, 23. [w.
Ac. 18 : 21. I return unto you, if God
Ro. 7 : 18. to w. is present with me
9 : 18. hath he mercy on whom he w., whom he w., he hardeneth
1 Co. 4 : 19. to you shortly, if L. w.

1 Co. 4 : 21. What w. ye? sh. I come
7 : 36. do what he w., sinneth not
39. to be married to whom she w.
12 : 11. ev. man severally as he w.
2 Co. 8 : 11. as was a readiness to w.
Ph. 2 : 13. God in you, both to w.
1 Ti. 2 : 8. I w. men pray ev. where
5 : 14. I w. younger women marry
Tit. 3 : 8. these I w. th thou affirm
Ja. 4 : 15. If Lord w. we shall do this
Re. 11 : 6. to smite often as they w.
22 : 17. whosoever w. let him take

WILL be. [water

Ge. 16 : 12. Ishmael w.b. a wild
man; his hand w.b. ag. every
17 : 8 I w.b. their God, Ex. 29 :
45. Je. 24 : 7.-32 : 38. 2 Co. 6 : 16.
26 : 3. I w.b. with thee and will
bless thee, 31 : 3. Ex. 3 : 12. Ju.
6 : 16. 1 K. 11 : 38. [keep me
28 : 20. if God w.b. with me and
34 : 15. if ye w.b. as we, circumcis.
41 : 40. in throne w. I b. greater
43 . 9. I w.b. surety for him [than
44 : 9. we w.b. my lord's bondmen
47 : 19. we w.b. servants unto Pha.
Ex. 4 : 12. go, I w.b. wi. thy mouth
6 : 7. I w.b. to you a God; and ye
shall know, Le. 26 : 12. [enemies
23 : 22. I w.b. an enemy unto thine
Nu. 14 : 11. w. it b. ere they believe
Jos. 7 : 12. nei. w. I b. wi. you more
14 : 12. if Lord w.b. with me, then
22 : 18. it w.b., seeing ye rebel ag.
Lord, be w.b. wroth [oth. side
1 S. 14 : 40. I and Jonathan w.b. on
2 S. 2 : 26. w.b. bitterness in end
7 : 14. I w.b. his father, he shall b.
14 : 17. thf. thy G. w.b. with thee
1 K. 12 : 7. w.b. thy servants forev.
Ne. 4 : 12. fr. all places w.b. upon
Jb. 39 : 9. w. unicorn b. willing to
Ps. 48 : 14. he w.b. our guide even
Je. 7 : 23. Obey my voice, I w.b.
your God, 30 : 22. [be quiet
47 : 6. how long w. it b. ere thou
Eze. 11 : 16. w. I b. to them sanct-y
20 . 32. say, We w.b. as heathen
Ho. 5 : 12 w. I b. unto Ephr. moth
14. I w.b. unto Ephr-m as a lion
8 : 5. how long w. it b. ere they
13 : 7. I w.b. unto them as a lion
10. I w.b. their king; where is
14. O death, I w.b. thy plagues;
O grave, I w.b. thy [rael
14 : 5. I w.b. as the dew unto Is-
Jo 3 : 16 L. w.b. hope of his people
Zch. 2 : 5. I w.b. unto her a wall of
fire, w.b. the glory in midst of
Mat. 6 : 21. there w. your heart b.
20 : 26. whoso. w.b. great among
you, let, 27. Mk. 10 : 43, 44.
Lu. 21 : 7 what sign w. there b.
Jn. 9 : 27. w. ye b. his disciples?
Ac. 18 : 15. I w.b. no judge of such
27 : 10. voyage w.b. with hurt
2 Co. 6 : 18. I w.b. a Fath. unto you
10 : 11. such w. we b. also in deed
1 Ti. 6 : 9. they that w.b. rich fall
He. 1 : 5. I w.b. to him a Father
8 : 10. I w.b. to them a God, they
Ja. 4 : 4. Whosoever w.b. friend of
Re. 21 : 7. I w.b. his God [world

WILL not be. [ing

Ge. 24 : 5. Peradv. woman w. - will-
8. if woman w. - willing to follow
Nu. 14 : 43. thf Lord w. - with you
Ru. 3 : 18. man w. - in rest until he
Zch. 8 : 11. I w. - unto this people as
See **Will DO, We will DO, DO with not, DO with this.**

WILL have.

1 S 8 : 19. we w.h. king over us
Eze. 5 : 11. nei. w. I h. any pity, 7 :
4.-8 : 18.-9 : 10. [rifice, 12 : 7.
Mat 9 : 13 I w.h. mercy, not sac-
27 : 43. let him deliver if he w.h.

1 Ti. 2 : 4. Who w.h. all men saved

WILL not. [manded

2 S. 13 : † 28. w. ye n., since I com-
Ps. 80 : 18. So w.n. we go from thee
Eze. 20 : 3. I w.n. be inquired of by
Am. 6 : † 10. w.n. make mention
7 : 8. I w.n. again pass them, 8 : 2.
Mat. 15 : 32. I w.n. send them away
21 : 29. He said, I w.n., but afterw.
23 : 4. w.n. move them with one
26 : 35. Though I die, w. I n. deny
Mk. 14 : 29. tho. all offended, w.n. I
Lu. 19 : 14. We w.n. have this man
Jn. 5 : 40. ye w.n. come to me that
1 Co. 16 : 7. For I w.n. see you now
3 Jn. 13. I w.n. with ink and pen
See **SELFWILLED.** [write

WILLETH.

Ro. 9 : 16. it is not of him that w.

WILLING. [me

Ge. 24 : 5. woman not be w. to follow
8. if woman not w. to follow [(2)
Ex. 35 : 5. whoso. is of w. heart, 29
21. ev. one whom his spirit made
22. came as many as were w. [w.
29 chil. of Isr. brought a w. off-g
1 Ch. 28 : 9. serve God with w. mind
21. with thee every w., skilful man
29 : 5. who is w. to consecrate his
Jb. 39 : 9. Will unicorn be w. to
Ps. 110 : 3. Thy people shall be w.
Can. 6 : † 12. on chariots of w. peo.
Is. 1 : 19. If w. ye shall eat good of
Mat. 1 : 19. not w. to make example
26 : 41. spirit is w., flesh is weak
Mk. 15 : 15. Pilate w. to content peo.
Lu. 10 : 29. he, w. to justify himself
22 : 42. if thou be w. remove cup
23 : 20. Pilate w. to release Jesus
Jn. 5 : 35. ye were w. for a season
Ac. 24 : 27. w. to shew Jews pleasure
25 : 9. Festus w. to do the Jews a
27 : 43. centurion w. to save Paul
Ro. 9 : 22. What if God w. to shew
2 Co. 5 : 8. w. to be absent from body
8 : 3. were w. beyond their power
† 10. also to be w. a year ago [ed
12. if first a w. mind, it is accept-
1 Th. 2 : 8. we w. to have imparted
1 Ti. 6 : 18. w. to communicate [heirs
He. 6 : 17. God, w. to shew unto the
13 : 18. w. to live honestly in all
2 Pe. 3 : 9. not w. any should perish

WILLINGLY.

Ex. 25 : 2. offering of every man that
giveth w. [selves, 9.
Ju. 5 : 2. the people w. offered them-
8 : 25. We will w. give the earrings
1 Ch. 29 : 6. the princes of Israel,
with rulers, offered w., 9. (2)
2 Ch. 35 : 8. [so w.
14. that we should be able to offer
17. in uprightness have I offered
w.; thy people here to offer w.
2 Ch. 17 : 16. Amasiah w. offered h-f
Ezr. 1 : 6. besides all that was w. off.
3 : 5. every one that w. offered
Ne. 11 : 2. men that w. offered thems.
Pr. 31 : 13. worketh w. with hands
La. 3 : 33. he doth not afflict w. nor
Ho. 5 : 11. Ephraim w. walked after
Jn. 6 . 21. w. received him into ship
Ro. 8 : 20. subject to vanity not w.
1 Co. 9 : 17. if I do this thing w., I
Phm. 14. not as of necessity, but w.
1 Pe. 5 : 2. Feed the flock of God w.
2 Pe. 3 : 5. this they w. ignorant of

WILLOW tree. [w.t.

Eze. 17 : 5. by waters, and set it as a

WILLOWS.

Le. 23 : 40. ye shall take w. of brook
Jb. 40 : 22. w. of brook compass him
Ps. 137 : 2 We hanged harps upon w.
Is. 15 : 7 shall carry to brook of w.
44 : 4. they shall spring up as w.

WILL-WORSHIP. [w.

Col. 2 : 23. have a shew of wisdom in

WILT. [away

Ex. 18 : 18. Thou w. surely wear
Ju. 1 : 14. Caleb said unto her, What
w. thou? Es. 5 : 3.
1 S. 1 : 11. if thou w. look on thine
handmaid (2) [en?
14. How long w. thou be drunk-
Ps. 85 : 5. w. be angry for ever? (2)
6. w. thou not revive us again
108 : 11. lead me, w. not thou, O
G., w. not thou go with, 60 : 10.
Pr. 5 : 20. why w. thou be ravished?
Je. 3 : 4. w. thou not cry unto me?
13 : 27. w. thou not be made clean?
Eze. 20 : 4. w. thou judge them, Son
of man? (2).-22 : 2. (2)
24 : 19. w. thou not tell us what
28 : 9. w. thou say before him that
Mat. 8 : 2. Lord, if thou w., canst
make me clean, Mk. 1 : 40. Lu. 5 : 12.
13 : 28. w. thou we go and gather
15 : 28. O woman, be it as thou w.
17 : 4. if thou w. let us make three
19 : 17. if thou w. enter into life
21. If thou w. be perfect, go sell
20 : 21. What w. thou? She saith,
26 : 17. Where w. thou we prepare
passover? Mk. 14 : 12. Lu. 22 : 9.
39. not as I, but as thou w., Mk.
14 : 36. [thou w.
Mk. 6 : 22. Ask of me whatsoever
10 : 51. What w. thou I should do
unto thee? Lu. 18 : 41. [fire
Lu. 9 : 54. w. thou that we comm-d
Jn. 5 : 6. w. thou be made whole?
14 : 22. how w. manifest thyself
Ac. 1 : 6. w. thou restore kingdom?
7 : 28. w. kill me as thou didst Eg-n
9 : 6. what w. thou have me do?
13 : 10. w. not cease to pervert right
25 : 9. w. go to Jerus. to be judged
Ro. 13 : 3. w. not be afraid of power?
Ja. 2 : 20. w. thou know, O vain man

WIMPLES. [and w.

Is. 3 : 22. L. will take away mantles

WIN, NETH.

2 Ch. 32 : 1. he thought to w. them
Pr. 11 : 30. he that w-h souls is wise
Ph. 3 : 8. but dung, that I may w.

WIND. [Christ

Ge. 3 : † 8. in garden in w. of day
8 : 1. God made a w. to pass over
Ex. 10 : 19. west w. took aw. locusts
15 : 10. didst blow with thy w. [sea
Nu. 11 : 31. w. brought quails from
2 S. 22 : 11. he was seen upon wings
of the w., Ps. 18 : 10.-104 : 3.
1 K. 18 : 45. heaven was black wi. w.
19 : 11. a great w. rent the mountains, but the L. was not in w.
2 K. 3 : 17. ye sh. not see w. nor rain
Jb. 1 : 19. came a w. fr. wilderness
6 : 26. speeches which are as w.
7 : 7. O remember that my life is w.
8 : 2. how long words of thy mouth
be like a strong w.? [end?
16 : † 3. Shall words of w. have an
21 : 18. they are as stubble bef. w.
30 : 15. terrors pursue my soul as
22. Thou liftest me to the w. [w.
37 : 21. the w. passeth and cleanseth them, Ps. 103 : 16. [away
Ps. 1 : 4. like chaff which w. driveth
18 : 42. beat them as dust before w.
35 : 5. Let them be as chaff before
w., 83 : 13. [that passeth aw.
78 : 39. they were but flesh; a w.
135 : 7. he bringeth w. out of his
treasuries, Je. 10 : 13.-51 : 16.
147 : 18. he causeth his w. to blow
Pr. 11 : 29. He shall inherit w. [rain
25 : 14. like clouds and w. without
23. north w. driveth away rain
27 : 16. Whoso. hideth her, bid-h w.
30 : 4. who gathered w. in his fists?
Ec. 1 : 6. w. goeth toward the south,
and w. returneth again

Ec. 5 : 16. he that laboured for w.
11 : 4. He th. observeth w. not sow
Is. 7 : 2. as trees are moved with w.
11 : 15. with his w. shake his hand
17 : 13. nations be chased before w.
26 : 18. we have brought forth w.
27 : 8. he stayeth rough w. in day
32 : 2. a man shall be as a hiding place from the w. [57 : 13.
41 : 16. w. shall carry them away,
29. their molten images are w.
64 : 6. our iniquities, like w., have
Je. 2 : 24. ass that snuffeth up w.
4 : 11. a dry w. of the high places
12. a full w. from those places
5 : 13. prophets shall become w.
13 : 24. scatter them by w. of wild.
14 : 6. snuffed up w. like dragons
22 : 22. w. shall eat up thy pastures
51 : 1. ag-t Babylon destroying w.
Eze. 5 : 2. part thou sh. scatter in w.
12 : 14. I will scatter tow every w.
37 : 9. Prophesy unto the w., son of man, say to the w., Come
Da. 2 : 35. the w. carried them away
Ho. 4 : 19. w. hath bound her up
8 : 7. sown w. shall reap whirlwind
12 : 1. Ephraim feedeth on w., he
13 : 15. w. of the Lord shall come
Am. 4 : 13. lo, he that createth w.
Jon. 1 : 4. Lord sent out a great w.
Mi. 2 : † 11. If a man walk with w.
Zch. 5 : 9. the w. was in their wings
Mat. 11 : 7. A reed shaken with the w. ? Lu. 7 : 24. [48. Ac. 27 : 4.
14 : 24. w. was contrary, Mk. 6 :
30. saw w. boisterous, was afraid
32. w. ceased, Mk. 4 : 39.-6 : 51.
Jn. 3 : 8. w. bloweth where it listeth
6 : 18. sea arose by reason of w.
Ac. 2 : 2. a sound as of a mighty w.
27 : 7. w. not suffering us, we [w.
14. arose against it a tempestuous
15. could not bear up into the w.
40. hoised up mainsail to the w.
Ep. 4 : 14. with every w. of doctrine
Ja. 1 : 6. like wave driven with w.
Re. 6 : 13 as tree shaken of mighty w.
7 : 1. w. should not blow on earth

East WIND. [23, 27.

Ge. 41 : 6. ears blasted with e.w.,
Ex. 10 : 13. Lord brought e.w. all day, e.w. brought locusts, 14 : 21.
Jb. 15 : 2. wise fill his belly wi. e.w.
27 : 21. The e.w. carrieth him aw.
38 : 24. light which scattereth e.w.
Ps. 48 : 7. breakest ships with e.w.
78 : 26. He caused e.w. to blow
Is. 27 : 8. he stayeth his rough wind in day of his e.w. [w.
Je. 18 : 17. I will scatter as with e.
Eze. 17 : 10. wither wh e.w. toucheth
19 : 12. e.w. dried up her fruit
27 : 26. the e.w. hath broken thee
42 : † 16. He measured e.w. with
Ho. 12 : 1. Ephraim followeth e.w.
13 : 15 Tho. fruitful e.w. sh. come
Jon. 4 : 8. G. prepared vehement e.
Ha. 1 : 9. faces sh. sup as e.w. [w.

North WIND. [south

Can. 4 : 16. Awake, O n.w., come

See **SOUTH wind.**
See STORM, STORMY.

WINDS. [the w.

Jb. 28 : 25. To make the weight for
Je. 49 : 32. I will scatter into all w. them in utmost, Eze. 5 : 10, 12.
36. upon Elam will I bring the four w., and scatter them toward w.
Eze. 17 : 21. be scattered tow. all w.
Zch. 6 : † 5. These are 4 w. of heavens
Mat. 7 : 25. the w. blew, beat upon that house, 27. [Lu. 8 : 24.
8 : 26 he arose and rebuked the w.,
27. What man is this that w. obey him ? Mk. 4 : 41. Lu. 8 : 25. [w.
Ja. 3 : 4. ships, tho. driven of fierce

Jude 12. are clouds carried about of
See FOUR. [w.

WINDING. [stairs

1 K. 6 : 8. and they went up with w.
Eze. 41 : 7. a w. about still upward

WINDOW. [ark

Ge. 6 : 16. A w. shalt thou make to
8 : 6. Noah opened w. of the ark
26 : 8. k. of Gerar looked out at w.
Jos. 2 : 15. Rahab let spies thro. w.
21 bound scarlet line in w., 18.
Ju. 5 : 28. mother looked out at w.
1 S. 19 : 12. let David down thro. a w.
2 S. 6 : 16. Michal looked through a w., saw Da. dancing, 1 Ch. 15 : 29.
2 K. 9 : 30. Jezebel looked out at a w.
32. Jehu lifted face to w., said
13 : 17. he said, Open w. eastward
Pr. 7 : 6. at w. of my house I looked
Ac. 20 : 9. sat in a w. a young man
2 Co. 11 : 33. thro. a w. was I let down

WINDOWS.

Ge. 7 : 11. w. of heaven were opened
8 : 2. w. of heaven were stopped
1 K. 6 : 4. w. of narrow lights, Eze.
7 : 4. were w. in three rows [40 : 16.
5. doors were square, with the w.
2 K. 7 : 2. if L. make w. in heav., 19.
Ec. 12 : 3. those that look out of w. be darkened [at the w.
Can. 2 : 9. My beloved looketh forth
Is. 24 : 18. w. from on high are open
54 : 12. I will make thy w. of agates
60 : 8. that flee as doves to their w.
Je. 9 : 21. death is come into our w.
22 : 14. Woe unto him cutt-h out w.
Eze. 40 : 22. w. were after measure
25. w. in it, arches (2), 29, 33, 36.
40 : 16. w. were round about in w-d
41 : 16. door posts, narrow w., galleries ceiled, and w. covered, (3). 26. [Jerusalem
Da. 6 : 10. his w. being open toward
Jo. 2 : 9. enter in at w. like a thief
Zph. 2 : 14. their voice sh. sing in w.
Mal. 3 : 10. if I will not open w. of

WINDY. [storm

Ps. 55 : 8. I would hasten from w.

WINE. [drunken

Ge. 9 : 21. Noah drank of w. was
24. Noah awoke from his w. [w.
14 : 18. Melchizedek brought bread,
27 : 25. brought Jacob w., he drank
49 : 11. he washed his garments in
12. His eyes were red with w. [w.
Ex. 29 : 40. fourth part of hin of w. for offering, Le. 23 : 13. Nu. 15 : 5.
Nu. 6 : 3. shall separate hims. fr. w.
† 4. eat nothing made of vine of w.
15 : 7. offer third part of a hin of w.
10. offering, half hin of w., 28 : 14.
28 : 7. cause strong w. to be poured
De. 14 : 26. bestow money for w. or
29 : 6. neither have ye drunk w. or
32 : 33. Their w. poison of dragons
38. which drank w. of drink off-g
Ju. 9 : 13. w. wh. cheereth God, man
19 : 19. bread, w., for me and handm.
1 S. 1 : 14. Eli said, Put away thy w.
15. have drunk nei. w. nor strong
25 : 37. when w. was out of Nabal
2 S. 6 : 19. to every one a cake and a flagon of w., 1 Ch. 16 : 3.
13 : 28. when Amnon's heart is merry with w. [w., gave king
Ne. 2 : 1. w. was before him, I took
5 : 15. former governors taken w.
18. once in ten days store of w.
13 : 15. lading asses with w., grapes
Es. 1 : 7. gave royal w. in abund-e
10. heart of king merry with w.
5 : 6 Esther at banquet of w., 7 : 2.
7 : 7. k. arising from banquet of w.
8. k. returned into banquet of w.
Jb. 1 : 13 and drinking w. in eldest brother's house, 18. [no vent
32 : 19. my belly is as w. that hath

Ps. 75 : 8. is a cup, the w. is red [w.
78 : 65. that shouteth by reason of
104 : 15. w. maketh glad the heart
Pr. 9 : 2. she hath mingled her w.
20 : 1. w. is a mocker, strong drink
23 : 30. Who hath woe? They that tarry long at the w., they that go to seek mixed w. [red
31. Look not upon w. when it is
31 : 6. Give w. unto those of heavy
Ec. 2 : 3. sought to give mys. unto w.
10 : 19. w. maketh merry, but [10.
Can. 1 : 2. thy love better than w., 4:
4. remember thy love more th. w.
2 : † 4. He bro-t me to house of w.
5 : 1. I have drunk my w. wi. milk
7 : 9. roof of thy mouth like best w.
Is. 1 : 22. thy w. mixed with water
5 : 11. continue till w. inflame th.
12. pipe and w. are in their feasts
16 : 10. sh. tread out no w. in presses
22 : 13. eat-g flesh and drinking w.
24 : 11. is a crying for w. in streets
27 : 2. sing ye, A vineyard of red w.
28 : 1 that are overcome with w.
7. they have also erred thro w., are swallowed up of w. [51 : 21.
29 : 9. are drunken, but not wi. w.,
55 : 1. come, buy w. and milk with-
56 : 12. Come ye, I will fetch w. [out
Je. 23 : 9 I am like a man whom w.
35 : 5. bef. Rechabites pots full of w.
40 : 12. Jews gath-d w. very much
48 : 33. w. to fail from winepresses
51 : 7. nations ha. drunken her w.
Eze. 27 : 18. merchant in w. of Hel-
Da. 1 : 5. king gave of the w. [bou
8. Daniel not defile himself wi. w.
5 : 1. Belshazzar drank w. before
2. while he tasted the w. [thous-d
4. They drank w., praised gods
23. concubines have drunk w. in
10 : 3. nei. flesh nor w. in mouth
Ho. 2 : 9. take away my w. in season
3 : 1. who love flagons of w. [heart
4 : 11. whoredom, w., take away
9 : 4. not offer w. offerings to Lord
14 : 7. scent shall be as w. of Leb-n
Jo. 1 : 5. howl, all ye drinkers of w.
Mi. 2 : 11. I will prophesy unto thee of w. and strong drink [by w.
Ha. 2 : 5. because he transgresseth
Zch. 9 : 15. sh. make noise as thro. w.
10 : 7. heart sh. rejoice as thro. w.
Mat. 9 : 17. bottles break and w. runneth out, Mk. 2 : 22. [old w.
Lu. 5 : 39. No man having drunk
7 : 33. John came, nei. drinking w.
Jn. 2 : 3. when wanted w., mother of Jesus saith, They have no w.
9. tasted water that was made w.
10. at the beginning set good w., thou hast kept good w. until
4 : 46. Galilee, wh-e water was made
Ep. 5 : 18. be not drunk with w. [w.
1 Ti. 3 : 3. Not given to much w., 8.
Tit. 1 : 7.-2 : 3. [sake
5 : 23. use a little w. for stomach's
1 Pe. 4 : 3. we walked in excess of w.
Re. 16 : 19. give her w. of his wrath
17 : 2. drunk with w. of fornication
18 : 3. nations drunk w. of wrath

WINE with bottle, s.

Jos. 9 : 4. they took old sacks, w. b-s
13. b-s of w. wh. we filled were n.
1 S. 1 : 24. Han. took flour, b. of w.
10 : 3. another carrying a b. of w.
16 : 20. Jesse took bread, b. of w.
25 : 18. Abigail took two b-s of w.
2 S. 16 : 1. Ziba with loaves, b. of w.
Je. 13 : 12. Every b. be filled with w.
Ho. 7 : 5. king sick with b-s of w.
Mat. 9 : 17. Nei. do men put new w. into old b-s : else the b-s break and w. runneth out, and b-s perish ; they put new w. into new b-s, Mk. 2 : 22. Lu. 5 : 37, 38.

WINE cellars.
1 Ch. 27 : 27. over the w.c. was Zab-
See **CORN and wine.** ⌊di
See **DRINK wine.**
New WINE. ⌈w.
Ne. 10 : 39. sh. bring offering of n.
13 : 5. chamber wh. they laid n.w.
12. tithe of n.w. unto treasuries
Pr. 3 : 10. presses sh. burst wi. n.w.
Is. 24 : 7. n.w. mourneth ⌈n.w.
49 : † 26. drunken with blood as wi.
65 : 8. As n.w. is found in cluster
Ho. 4 : 11. n.w. take away heart
9 : 2. the n.w. shall fail in her
Jo. 1 : 5. howl, bec. n.w. is cut off
10. the n.w. is dried up, the oil
3 : 18. mountains shall drop down
n.w., Am. 9 : † 13. ⌈n.w.
Hag. 1 : 11. I called for drought upon
Zch. 9 : 17. make young men cheer-
ful, n.w. the maids⌈Lu. 5:37.(3)
Mk. 2 : 22. n.w. doth burst bottles,
Lu. 5 :39. No man also having drunk
old w. desireth n. ⌈w.
Ac. 2 : 13. These men are full of n.
See **OIL with wine.**
See **SWEET wine.**
See **WINE with bottles.**
WINES.
Is. 25 : 6. feast of w. on the lees, of
w. on the lees well refined
WINEBIBBER, S.
Pr. 23 : 20. Be not with w-s, eaters
Mat. 11 : 19. Behold a man a w.,
WINECUP.⌊Lu 7:34.
Je. 25 : 15. Take the w. of this fury
WINEFAT. ⌈w.
Is. 63 : 2. like him that treadeth in
Ho. 9 : † 2. the w. shall not feed th.
Mk. 12 : 1. he digged a place for w.
WINEPRESS, ES. ⌈30.
Nu. 18 : 27. as the fulness of the w.,
De. 15 :14. furnish him out of thy w.
16 : † 13. gathered in thy floor, w.
Ju. 6 : 11. threshed wheat by the w.
7 : 25. Zeeb they slew at w. of Zeeb
2 K. 6 : 27. sh. I help thee? out of w.?
Ne. 13 :15. some treading w-s on sab.
Jb. 24 : 11. tread w-s, suffer thirst
Is. 5 : 2. vineyard, he made a w. th-n
63 : 3. I have trodden the w. alone
Je. 48 : 33. wine to fail from the w-s
La. 1 : 15. trodden virgin as in a w.
Ho. 9 : 2. The w. sh. not feed them
Zch. 14 : 10. inhabited unto king's
Mat. 21 : 33. digged a w. in it ⌊w-s
Re. 14 : 19. it into great w. of wrath
20. w. was trodden, blood came
out of w. unto the horse bridles
19 :15. treadeth w. of wrath of God
WING. ⌈ark
Ge. 7 : † 14. bird of every w. into
1 K. 6 : 24. five cubits was one w. of
cherub, five cubits the other
w., 2 Ch. 3 : 11, 12.
27. w. of one touched one wall
w. of other touched other wall
Ps. 78 : †27. rain fowl of w. as sand
148 : † 10. birds of w. praise Lord
Pr. 1 :†17. every thing that hath w.
Is. 10 : 14. was none that moved w.
24 : † 16. From the w. of the earth
Eze. 17 :23. sh. dwell fowl of every w.
39 : †4. thee unto birds of every w.
† 17. Speak unto the fowl of ev. w.
WINGS. ⌈eagles' w.
Ex. 19 : 4. seen how I bare you on
25 : 20. cherubim stretch forth w.,
covering mercy seat with w.,
37 ; 9. 1 K. 8 : 7. 1 Ch. 28 : 18.
Le. 1 : 17. he shall cleave it with w.
De. 22 : † 12 fringes upon four w.
32 : 11. As an eagle spreadeth her
w., taketh young on her w.
Ru. 2 : 12. under whose w. to trust
2 S. 22 : 11. seen upon w. of wind
1 K. 6 : 27. stretched forth w. of
cherubim; w. touched one ano.
8 : 6. priests brought ark under w.
of cherubim, 2 Ch. 5 : 7, 8. ⌈w.
7. cherubim spread forth their 2
2 Ch. 3 : 13. w. of cherubim spread, 20.
Jb. 39 : 13. Gavest thou w. unto
peacocks? or w. unto ostrich
26. Doth hawk stretch w. south?
Ps. 17 : 8. hide me under thy w.
18 : 10. fly upon w. of wind, 104:3.
36 : 7. men put trust under shadow
of thy w., 57 : 1.-61 : 4.-91 : 4.
55 : 6 O that I had w. like a dove
63 : 7. in shadow of thy w. will I
68 : 13. shall ye be as w. of a dove
139 : 9. If I take the w. of morning
Pr. 23 : 5. riches make thems. w.
Ec. 10 : 20. that which hath w. tell
Is. 6 : 2. seraphim each had six w.
8 : 8. his w. shall fill thy land ⌈w.
18 : 1. Woe to land shadowing with
40 : 31. mount up with w. as eagles
Je. 48 : 9. Give w. unto Moab, it
40. shall spread his w. over Moab
49 : 22. shall spread his w. over Bozrah
Eze. 1 : 6. every one had four faces,
four w., 8.-10 : 21. ⌈10 · 8, 21.
8. hands of man under their w.,
11. Their w. were stretched upward; two w. of every one were
joined, 9. ⌈had two
23. their w. straight, every one
24. I heard noise of their w., they
let down w., 25.-3 : 13.-10 : 5.
5 : † 3. shalt bind them in thy w.
10 : 12. body, w. were full of eyes
16. cherubim lifted w., 19.-11 : 22.
17 : 3. A great eagle with great w.
7. another great eagle with gr. w.
Da. 7 :4. first, like a lion, had eagle's
w., I beh-d till w. were plucked
6. another, four w. of a fowl ⌈w.
Ho. 4 : 19. wind bound her up in her
Zch. 5 : 9. two women, wind was in
their w.; had w. like w. of stork
Mal. 4:2. arise with healing in his w.
Mat. 23 :37. as a hen gathereth chick-
ens under her w., Lu. 13 : 34.
Re. 4 : 8. four beasts had each six w.
9 : 9. sound of w. as of many horses
12 : 14. to woman two w. of eagle
WINGS of the earth.
Jb. 37 : † 3. his lightning unto w.-
38 : † 13. might take hold of w.-
Is. 11 : † 12. gather dispersed from
WINGED. ⌊w.-
Ge. 1 : 21. God created every w. fowl
De. 4 : 17. likeness of any w. fowl
Eze. 17 : 3. great eagle came, long w.
WINK, ED, ETH.
Jb. 15 : 12. what do thy eyes w. at?
Ps. 35 : 19. nei. let them w. with eye
Pr. 6 : 13. wicked man w-h with eyes
10 : 10. He that w-h causeth sorrow
Ac. 17 : 30. times of ignorance God
WINNETH. See WIN. ⌊w-d at
WINNOWED, EST, ETH.
Ru. 3 : 2. Boaz w-h barley to night
Ps. 139 : † 3. Thou w-t my path and
Is. 30 : 24. been w-d with the shovel
WINTER. [Noun.] ⌈w.
Pr. 20 : † 4. not plough by reason of
Can. 2 : 11. for lo, the w. is past
Mat. 24 : 20. pray your flight be not
in w., nei. on sab., Mk. 13 : 18.
Jn. 10 : 22. feast of dedication in w.
2 Ti. 4 : 21. Do diligence to come bef.
See SUMMER. [Noun.] ⌊w.
WINTER house.
Je. 36 : 22. the king sat in the w.h.
Am. 3 : 15. I will smite w.h. with
WINTER, ED.
Is. 18 : 6. beasts shall w. upon them
Ac. 27 : 12. haven not commodious
to w. in, to Phenice to w.
28 : 11. ship which had w-d in isle
1 Co. 16 : 6. may be I will w. wi. you
Tit. 3 : 12. I determined there to w.
WIPE, ED, ETH, ING.
2 K. 21 : 13. I will w. Jerusalem as
a man w-h a dish, w-g it and
Ne. 13 : 14. w. not out my good deeds
Pr. 6 : 33. his reproach not be w-d a-
30 : 20. w-h her mouth, saith⌊way
Is. 25 : 8. Lord will w. away tears
from all faces, Re. 7 : 17.-21 : 4.
Lu. 7 : 38. woman did w. them with
hairs of her head ⌈w-d them
44. washed my feet with tears and
10 : 11. very dust we do w. ⌈12 : 3.
Jn. 11 : 2. Mary w-d his feet with
13 : 5. he began to w. them with
WIRES. ⌊towel
Ex. 39 : 3. they did beat the gold into thin plates, cut it into w.
WISDOM. ⌈w., 36:2.
Ex. 31 : 6. in hearts of all I have put
35 : 26. women whose heart stirred
them up in w. spun ⌈to work
35. Them hath he filled with w.
2 S. 14 : 20. wise, acc-g to w. of angel
20 : 22. woman unto peo. in her w.
1 K. 3 : 28. saw w. of God was in him
4 : 29. God gave Solomon w., 5 : 12.
30. Solomon's w. excelled w. of
east country and w. of Egypt,
10 : 23. 2 Ch. 9 : 22.
34. came to hear w. of Solomon
from all kings which had heard
of his w., 10 : 24. 2 Ch. 9 : 23.
10 : 4. when queen had seen Solomon's w., 2 Ch. 9 : 3.
11 : 41. acts of Sol., his w., are they
2 Ch. 1 : 10. Give me now w. that
11. Bec. hast asked w. and knowl.
12. w. and knowledge is granted
Ezr. 7 : 25. Ezra, aft. the w. of thy G.
Jb. 4 :21. they die, even without w.
6 : 13. is w. driven quite from me?
11 : 6. shew thee the secrets of w.
12 : 2. w. shall die with you
12. With the ancient is w., 13, 16.
13 : 5. hold peace, it sho. be y-r w.
15 : 8. dost restrain w. to thyself?
26 : 3. counselled him hath no w.?
28 : 18. price of w. is above rubies
30 : †22. and thou dissolvest my w.
32 . 7. I said, years should teach w.
13. Lest ye say, We have found w.
33 : 33. hearken, I shall teach w.
34:35. Job's words were without w.
36 : 5. God mighty in strength, w.
38 : 37. Who number clouds in w.?
39 : 17. God hath deprived her of w.
Ps. 37 : 30. The mouth of righteous
speaketh w. ⌈my heart sh.
49 :3. My mouth shall speak of w.;
51 : 6. shalt make me to know w.
90 : 12. may apply hearts unto w.
104 : 24. thy works! in w. hast ma.
105 : 22. and teach his senators w.
107 : † 27. all their w. is swallowed
136 : 5. that by w. made heavens
Pr. 1 : 3. To receive instruct-n of w.
7. fools despise w., instruction
20. w. crieth without, she, 8 : 1.
2 : 6. For the Lord giveth w. ⌈ous
7. layeth up sound w. for righte-
10. When w. entereth thine heart
3 : 19. Lord by w. founded earth
21. son keep sound w., discretion
4 : 11. I taught thee in way of w.
8 : 5. O ye simple, understand w.
11. For w. is better than rubies
12. I w. dwell with prudence and
9 : 1. w. hath builded her house
10 : 21. but fools die for want of w.
31. mouth of just bring-h forth w.
11 : 2. with the lowly is w. ⌈hour
12. He void of w. despiseth neigh-
12 :8. man be commended acc-g to
13 : 10. with well advised is w.⌊w.
14 : 6. A scorner seeketh w. ⌈way
8. w. of prudent is to understand

Pr 15 : 21. joy to him destitute of w.
33. fear of L. is instruction of w.
16 : 16. better to get w. than gold
17 : 16. price in ha. of fool to get w.
18 : 1. man intermeddleth with w.
4. wellsp-g of w. as flowing brook
19 : 8. getteth w. loveth own soul
21 : 30. There is no w. ag. the Lord
23 : 4. cease from thine own w.
9. fool will despise w. of thy words
24 : 7. w. is too high for a fool
14. So shall w. be unto thy soul
29 : 3. Whoso loveth w. rejoiceth fa-
15. rod and reproof give w. ⌊ther
30 : 3. I nei. learned w., nor have I
31 : 26. She openeth mouth with w.
Ec. 1 : 13. to search out by w. all
16. I have gotten more w. than
all, had great experience of w.
17. I gave my heart to know w.
18. For in much w. is much grief
2 : 3. acquainting mine heart wi. w.
9. and my w. remained with me
12. I turned myself to behold w.
13. I saw w. excelleth folly as far
21. a man whose labour is in w.
26. G. giveth to man th. is good, w.
7 : † 10. dost not inquire out of w.
11. w. is good wi. an inheritance
12. w. is a defence; w. giveth life
19. w. strength-h more than ten
23. All this have I proved by w.
25. I applied heart to seek out w.
8 : 1. w. maketh his face to shine
16. applied my heart to know w.
9 : 10. no work nor w. in the grave
13. This w. have I seen under sun
15. by his w. delivered the city
16. w. is better than strength:
the poor man's w. is despised
18. w. better than weapons of war
10 : 1. that is in reputation for w.
3. his w. faileth, saith he is a fool
10. but w. is profitable to direct
Is. 10 : 13. I have done it by my w.
33 : 6. w. be stability of thy times
Je. 8 : 9. they rejected word of Lord;
what w. is in them? ⌈his w.
9 : 23. Let not the wise man glory in
10 : 12. estab-d world by w., 51 : 15.
49 : 7. saith Lord, Is w. no more in
Teman? is their w. vanished?
Eze. 28 : 12. sealest sum, full of w.
Da. 1 : 4. Children skilful in all w.
17. four chil., G. gave skill in w.
2 : 14. Daniel answered with w.
20. God, for w. and might are his
21. he giveth w. unto the wise
23. O God, who hast given me w.
30. not revealed for any w. I have
Mi. 6 : 9. man of w. sh. see thy name
Mat. 11 : 19. but w. is justified of
her children, Lu. 7 : 35.
12 : 42. queen of the south came to
hear w. of Solo-n, Lu. 11 : 31.
13 : 54 Whence hath this man w.
Mk. 6 : 2. what w. is this given him
Lu. 1 : 17. disobedient to w. of just
2 : 40. child grew, filled with w.
52. Jes. increased in w., stature
11 : 49. Theref. said the w. of God
21 : 15. I will give you mouth, w.
Ac. 6 : 3. look out 7 men full of w.
10. were not able to resist the w.
7 : 10. ga. Joseph w. in sight of Ph.
22. learned in all w. of Egyptians
Ro. 11 : 33. O the depth of w. of God
1 Co. 1 : 17. preach not wi. w. of words
19. I will destroy w. of the wise
20. made foolish the w. of world
21. after that in the w. of God
the world by w. knew not God
22. and Greeks seek after w.
24. Christ power and w. of God
30. who of God is made unto us w.
2 : 1. not with excellency of w.
4. my speech not with man's w.
1 Co. 2 : 5. faith not stand in w. of men
6. we speak w. among them that
are perfect, yet not w. of world
7. But we speak the w. of God ⌈eth
13. not in words man's w. teach-
3 : 19. w. of this world is foolishn-s
12 : 8. to one by Spirit word of w.
2 Co. 1 : 12. not with fleshly w., but
Ep. 1 : 8. abounded tow. us in all w.
3 : 10. be known manifold w. of G.
Col. 1 : 28. warning ev. man in all w.
2 : 3. In whom all treasures of w.
23. wh. things have a shew of w.
3 : 16. word dwell in you in all w.
4 : 5. Walk in w. tow. them without
Ja. 1 : 5. If any lack w. ask of G ⌈w.
3 : 13. shew works with meekness of
15. This w. descendeth not from
17. w. fr. above is first pure ⌊above
2 Pe. 3 : 15. acc. to the w. given him
Re. 5 : 12. Worthy is the Lamb to
receive w., glory ⌈our God
7 : 12. Blessing and glory and w. to
13 : 18. Here is w. Let him that
17 : 9. Here is the mind wh. hath w.

Spirit of WISDOM.

Ex. 28 : 3. whom I filled with – w.
De. 34 : 9. Joshua was full of – w.
Is. 11 : 2. shall rest upon him – w.
Ep. 1 : 17. That God may give – w.

Thy WISDOM.

1 K. 2 : 6. Do therefore acc. to t. w.
10 : 6. It was a true report that I
heard of t. w., 2 Ch. 9 : 5. ⌈fame
7. t. w. and prosperity exceedeth
8. happy thy servants wh. stand
bef. thee, hear t. w., 2 Ch. 9 : 7.
2 Ch. 9 : 6. half of t. w. was not told
Jb. 39 : 26. Doth hawk fly by t. w.?
Is. 47 : 10. t. w. hath perverted thee
Eze. 28 : 4. With t. w. got-n riches, 5.
7. draw swords ag. beauty of t. w.
17. corrupted t. w. by brightness

WISDOM with understanding.

Ex. 31 : 3. Bezaleel, filled with spirit of God in w. and u., 35 : 31.
36 : 1. in whom Lord put w. and u.
De. 4 : 6. your w. and u. in sight of
1 K. 4 : 29. God gave Sol. w. and u.
7 : 14. Hiram filled with w. and u.
1 Ch. 22 : 12. L. give thee w. and u.
Jb. 12 : 13. With him w., he hath u.
28 : 12. But where sh. w. be found?
and where is place of u., 20.
28. fear of the Lord, that is w.;
to depart fr. evil is u., Ps. 111 :
10. Pr. 9 : 10. ⌈words of u.
Pr. 1 : 2. To know w.; to perceive
2 : 2. incline thine ear unto w., and
apply thine heart to u.
3 : 13. Happy is the man that findeth w., the man that getteth u.
4 : 7. w. is the principal thing;
therefore get w., and get u.
5 : 1. My son, attend unto my w.,
and bow thine ear to my u.
7 : 4. Say unto w. thou art my sister; call u. thy kinswoman
8 : 1. Doth not w. cry? and u. put
14. Counsel is mine, and sound
w.; I am u. ⌈w. is found
10 : 13. In lips of him that hath u.
23. but a man of u. hath w. ⌈u.
14 : 33. w. in heart of him th. hath
17 : 24. w. is bef. him that hath u.
21 : 30. is no w. nor u. ag-t Lord
23 : 23. Buy truth; also w. and u.
24 : 3. Thro. w. is a house builded,
and by u. it is established ⌈u.
Is. 11 : 2. upon him spirit of w. and
29 : 14. w. of their wise shall perish, u. of their prudent be hid
Eze. 28 : 4. With w. and u. riches
Da. 1 : 20. in matters of w. and u.
ten times better than ⌈him, 14.
5 : 11. u. and w. like w. of gods in
Col. 1 : 9. be filled in all u. and spir-

WISE. ⌊itual w.

Ge. 3 : 6. and a tree to make one w.
41 : 39. none so discreet, w. as thou
Ex. 23 : 8. take no gift, gift bindeth
the w., De. 16 : 19. ⌈people
De. 4 : 6. this great nation is a w.
32 : 29. O that they were w. and
Ju. 5 : 29. Her w. ladies answ-d her
2 S. 14 : 20. my lord w. acc. to wisd.
1 K. 3 : 12. have given thee w. heart
5 : 7. Lord which hath given David
a w. son, 2 Ch. 2 : 12. ⌈sellor
1 Ch. 26 : 14 for Zechariah a w. coun-
Jb. 5 : 13. taketh w. in own crafti-s
9 : 4. He is w. in heart and mighty
11 : 12. vain man would be w. ⌊self
22 : 2. w. may be profitable to him-
32 : 9. Great men are not always w.
37 : 24. he respecteth not any w.
Ps. 2 : 10. Be w., O kings ⌊of heart
19 : 7. testimony making w. simple
36 : 3. he hath left off to be w., and
94 : 8. ye fools, when will ye be w.?
107 : 43. Whoso is w. and will obs.
Pr. 1 : 5. A w. man will hear; a
man of understanding shall attain unto w. counsels ⌈w.
6. To understand the words of the
3 : 7. Be not w. in thine own eyes
35 The w. shall inherit glory
6 : 6. Go to the ant and be w.
8 : 33. Hear instruction, and be w.
9 : 12. If thou be w. thou shalt be
w. for thyself ⌈father, 15 : 20.
10 : 1. A w. son maketh a glad
5. gathereth in summer is w. son
8. w. in heart will receive com-ts
19. he th. refraineth his lips is w.
11 : 29. fool shall be servant to w.
30. he that winneth souls is w.
12 : 15. hearkeneth unto counsel
18. tongue of w. is health ⌊is w.
13 : 1. A w. son heareth his fath.'s
14. law of the w. is a fountain
20. He that walketh with w. men
shall be w. ⌈them
14 : 3. lips of the w. shall preserve
24. crown of w. is their riches
35. king's favour is tow. w. serv-t
15 : 2. tongue of w. useth knowl-e
7. lips of w. disperse knowledge
12 nei. will scorner go unto w.
24. way of life is above to the w.
31. hear-h reproof abideth am. w.
16 : 21. w. in heart be called prud-
23. heart of w. teacheth mou. ⌊ent
17 : 2. A w. servant shall have rule
over a son ⌈is counted w.
28. a fool when he holdeth peace
18 : 15. ear of w. seeketh knowl-e
19 : 20. mayest be w. in latter end
20 : 1. deceived thereby, is not w.
26. A w. king scattereth wicked
21 : 11. scorner punished, simple is
made w.; when the w. is
20. is oil in the dwelling of the w.
22 : 17. hear words of the w. ⌈w.
23 : 15. my son, if thine heart be
19. Hear thou, my son, and be w.
24. begetteth w. child sh. have joy
24 : 6. by w. counsel sh. make war
23. These things belong to the w.
25 : 12. so is a w. reprover upon
26 : 5. Answer fool lest he be w. in
12. Seest a man w. in own conceit
27 : 11. son, be w., make my heart
28 : 7. keepeth the law is a w. son
11. rich man is w. in own conceit
30 : 24. be four things exceed-g w.
Ec. 2 : 15. why was I then more w.
16. no remembrance of w. more
19. wh-in I have shewed mys. w.
4 : 13. Better is a w. child than a
6 : 8. what hath w. more than fool?
7 : 4. heart of w. in hou. of mourn-
5. better to hear rebuke of w. ⌊ing

Ec. 7 : 19. Wisdom strengthen-h w.
23. I said, I will be w., but it was
9 : 1. the w. are in the hand of God
11. I saw nei. yet bread to the w.
12 : 9. Because Preacher was w.
11. words of w. are as goads [eyes
Is. 5 : 21. Woe unto them w. in own
19 : 11. how say ye, I am son of w.
31 : 2. Yet he is w., will bring evil
Je. 4 : 22. my people w. to do evil
8 : 8 How do ye say, We are w.
18 : 18. not perish counsel from w.
Da. 2 : 21. G. giveth wisdom unto w.
12 : 3. they that be w. shall shine
10. but the w. shall understand
Ho. 14 : 9. Who is w. sh. understand
Zc. 9 : 2. Tyrus and Zidon tho. w.
Mat. 10 : 16. be ye thf. w. as serpents
11 : 25. thou hast hid these things
fr. w. and prudent, Lu. 10 : 21.
24 : 45. Who is a faithful w. servant
25 : 2. five of them were w. and
4. the w. took oil in their vessels
8. foolish said unto w., Give us
9. But the w. answered, Not so
Lu. 12 : 42. Who, then, is w. steward
Ro. 1 : 14. I am debtor to the w. and
22 Professing themselves to be w.
11 : 25. lest ye be w. in own conceits
12 : 16. Be not w. in own conceits
16 : 19. I would have you w. unto
27. To God only w., 1 Ti. 1 : 17.
Jude 25. [the w.
1 Co. 1 : 19. I will destroy wisdom of
20. Where is the w.? [w.
27. foolish things to confound the
3 : 10. as a w. masterbuilder, I
18. If any man seemeth w., become a fool that he may be w.
19. taketh w. in own craftiness
20. Lord knoweth thoughts of w.
4 : 10. We are fools for Christ's sake, but ye are w. in Christ
2 Co. 10 : 12. They comparing themselves are not w. [ye are w.
11 : 19. ye suffer fools gladly, seeing
Ep. 5 : 15. walk not as fools: but w.
2 Ti 3 : 15. are able to make thee w.
Tit. 2 : † 4. teach young wom. be w.
See Wise MAN, Wise MEN.

Over WISE. [w.
Ec. 7 : 16. neither make thyself o.
See Wise WOMAN.

W SE. [Adverb.]

WISE hearted. [w.h.
Ex. 28 : 3. speak unto all that are
31 : 6. in all w.h. I have put wisd.
35 : 10 w.h. sh. make all that Lord
25. all the women w.h. did spin
36 : 1. Then wrought ev. w.h. man
2. Moses called every w.h. man
8. every w.h. man made ten curt.
See LIKEWISE, OTHERWISE.

WISE. [Noun]

In any WISE.
Ex. 22 : 23. if thou afflict them - w.
Le. 19 : 17 shalt - w. rebuke neighb.
27 : 19. if he will - w. redeem field
De. 17 : 15. shalt - w. set him king
21 : 23. shalt - w. bury him th. day
22 : 7. shalt - w. let the dam go
Jos. 6 : 18. - w. keep from accursed
23 : 12. if ye - w. go back an. clea
1 S. 6 : 3. - w. return tres. as. off-g
1 K. 11 : 22 howbeit, let me go - w.
Ps. 37 : 8. fret not - w. to do evil
Mk. 14 : 31. I will not deny thee - w.

In no WISE.
Le. 7 : 24. fat of beasts torn, - w. eat
1 K. 3 : 26. give child, - w. slay it, 27.
Mat 5 : 18. one tittle shall - w. pass
10 : 42. he shall - w. lose his reward
Lu. 13 : 11. could - w. lift up hers-f
18 : 17. sh. - w. enter therein [cast
Jn. 6 : 37. cometh to me I will - w.
Ac. 13 : 41. work ye sh. - w. believe
Ro. 3 : 9. are we better th. they? - w.
Re. 21 : 27. - w. enter that defileth
See LIKE wise.

On this WISE.
Nu. 6 : 23. - w. ye shall bless Israel
Mat 1 : 18. birth of Jesus was - w.
Jn. 21 : 1. - w. shewed he himself
Ac. 7 : 6. God spake - w., That his
13 : 34. he said, - w. I will give sure
Ro. 10 : 6. righteousn. speaketh - w.
He. 4 : 4. spake of seventh day - w.

WISELY.
Ex. 1 : 10. Come on, let us deal w.
Jos 1 : †7. mayest do w. whitherso.
1 S. 18 : 14. David behaved himself w. in all his ways, 5. [very w.
15. Saul saw he behaved himself
30. David behaved himself more
1 K. 2 : † 3. mayest do w. [w. than
2 Ch. 11 : 23. Rehoboam dealt w.
Ps. 58 : 5. charming never so w.
64 : 9. shall w. consider of his doing
101 : 2. I will behave myself w. [w.
Pr. 16 : 20. He that handleth matter
21 : 12. righteous w. considereth
28 : 26. whoso walketh w. shall be
Ec. 7 : 10. thou dost not inquire w.
Lu. 16 : 8. commended because he had

WISER. [done w.
1 K. 4 : 31. Solomon was w. than all
Jb. 35 : 11. maketh us w. than fowls
Ps. 119 : 98. w. than mine enemies
Pr. 9 : 9. wise man will be yet w.
26 : 16. sluggard is w. in conceit
Eze. 28 : 3. thou art w. than Daniel
Lu. 16 : 8. are in their generations w.
1 Co. 1 : 25. foolishness of G. w. than

WISH. [Noun.] [stead
Jb. 33 : 6. I am acc. to thy w. in G.'s

WISH, ED.
Ps. 40 : 14. put to shame that w. evil
73 : 7. ha. more than heart could w.
Jon. 4 : 8. Jonah fainted, w-d to die
Ac. 27 : 29. cast anchor, w-d for day
Ro. 9 : 3. I could w. myself accursed
2 Co. 13 : 9 we w. your perfection
3 Jn 2. I w. above all thou prosper

WISHING.
Jb. 31 : 30. Nei. to sin, by w. a curse

WIST. [what
Ex. 16 : 15. manna : for they w. not
34 : 29. Moses w. not his face shone
Le. 5 : 17. tho. he w. not, yet guilty
18. wherein he erred, w. it not
Jos 2 : 4. I w. not whence they were
8 : 14. he w. not were liers in amb.
Ju. 16 : 20. w. not L. was departed
Mk. 9 : 6. he w. not what to say
14 : 40. nei. w. they what to ans-r
Lu. 2 : 49. w. ye not I must be about
Jn. 5 : 13. healed w. not who it was
Ac. 12 : 9. w. not that it was true
23 : 5. said Paul, I w. not, brethren, that he was the high priest

WIT. [Verb.] [perous
Ge. 24 : 21. to w. whe. journey pros-
Ex. 2 : 4. sister, to w. what be done
2 Co. 5 : 19. To w. God was in Christ
8 : 1. we do you to w. of the grace

WITCH.
Ex. 22 : 18. not suffer a w. to live
De. 18 : 10. not be found among you a

WITCHCRAFT, S. [w.
1 S. 15 : 23. rebellion is as sin of w.
2 K. 9 22 Jezebel, her w-s so many
2 Ch. 33 : 6. Manasseh used w. and
Mi. 5 : 12. I will cut off w-s out of
Na. 3 : 4. mistress of w-s that selleth families thro. her w-s [atry, w.
Ga. 5 : 20. works of flesh are, Idol-

WITH.
See With CHILD, With GOD, HEART with all, With HER, With HIM, With ISRAEL. See LAY with, LIE with, LIETH with, LYING with.

WITH me. [w.m.
Ge. 3 : 12. woman thou gavest to be
Ge. 14 : 24. of men wh. went w.m.
21 : 6. that hear will laugh w.m.
23. swear thou not deal falsely w.
29 : 19. Laban said, Abide w.m. [m.
27. for service w.m. 7 oth. years
30 : 20. will husband dwell w.m.
33. shall be counted stolen w.m.
31 : 42. Except God of Abr. w.m.
33 : 10. thou wast pleased w.m.
13. herds with young are w.m.
15. Let me leave some folk w.m.
35 : 3. God who was w.m. in way
39 : 8. wotteth not what is w.m.
15. left his garment w.m., 18.
42 : 33. leave one of brethren w.m.
43 : 6. Whf. dealt ye so ill w.m.
16. these men shall dine w.m.
47 : 29. deal kindly and truly w.m.
Ex. 33 : 12. whom wilt send w.m.
Le. 25 : 23. ye are sojourners w.m.
Nu. 23 : 13. Balak said, Come w.m.
De. 1 : 37. Lord was angry w.m. for your sakes, 3 : 26.-4 : 21. [m.
Jos. 14 : 8. brethren that went up w.
Ju. 1 : 3. Come w.m. into my lot
6 : 17. shew sign thou talkest w.m.
18 : 4. Thus dealeth Micah w.m.
1 S. 15 : 25. pardon, turn w.m., 30.
16 : 5. come w.m. to the sacrifice
21 : 8. nei. sword nor weap-s w.m.
26 : 6. Who will go down w.m. to
29 : 3. Is not this Dav. w.m. [Saul
6. thy coming in w.m. is good
2 S. 3 : 12. Make thy league w.m.
15 : 33. if thou passest on w.m.
19 : 33. king said, Come w.m. (2)
38 Chimham shall go over w.m.
1 K. 11 : 22. what hast lacked w.m.
13 : 7. Come home w.m., 15.
22 : 4. Wilt thou go w.m. to battle to Ramoth gilead? 2 Ch. 18 : 3.
2 K. 3 : 7. wilt go w.m. ag-t Moab
10 : 16. Come w.m., see my zeal
18 : 31. Make an agreement w.m. by a present, Is. 36 : 16. [m.
1 Ch. 4 : 10. that thine hand be w.
2 Ch. 2 : 3. as with David deal w.m.
Ezr. 7 : 28. chief men to go up w.m.
8 : 1. genealogy of them w.m.
Ne. 2 : 9. king sent horsemen w.m.
12. I arose and few men w.m. (2)
12 : 40. I and half of rulers w.m.
Jb. 10 : 2. shew whf. contend. w.m.
13 : 19. Who is he will plead w.m.
17 : 2. Are not mockers w.m.?
3. who will strike hands w.m.?
31 : 13. when they contended w.m.
18. bro-t up w.m. as with a fath.
Ps. 34 : 3. O magnify L. w.m. [m.
35 : 1. Plead wi. them th. strive w.
142 : 7. sh. deal bountifully w.m.
Pr. 7 : 14. I have peace off-gs w.m.
Ec. 2 : 9. wisdom remained w.m.
Can. 1 : 6. mother's chil. angry w.m.
Is. 12 : 1. though thou angry w.m.
Je. 2 : 29. Whf. will ye plead w.m.?
3 : 20. ye dealt treacherously w.m.
18 : 19. to them that contend w.m.
20 : 17. womb to be always gr. w.m.
40 : 4. to come w.m. into Bab. (2)
Da. 8 : 18 as he was speaking w.m.
10 : 7. men w.m. saw not the vision
Zch. 1 : 14. angel communed w.m.
Mat. 15 : 32. bec. they continue w.m. three days, Mk. 8 : 2. [pay
18 : 29 Have patience w.m., I will
26 : 23. He that dippeth hand w.m. in dish, Mk 14 : 20. [w.m.
Mk. 14 : 18. One of you which eateth
Lu. 12 : 13. divide inheritance w.m.
Ac. 25 : 5. go down w.m., accuse
26 : 13. them wh journeyed w.m.
2 Co. 9 : 4. if they of Mac. come w.m.
11 : 1. Wou. ye could bear w.m. (2)
Ga. 1 : 2. all brethren w.m., Ph. 4 : 21.
2 : 1. I took Titus w.m. also, 3. [21.
Tit. 3 : 15. All w.m. salute thee

Re. 1 : 12. see voice that spake w. m.
22 : 12. I come quickly, my reward [is w. m.
See With ME.
See DEALT, SWORD, TALKED, TALKING, WHOM,
With THEE, With THEM, With US, With YOU.

WITHAL.

Ex. 25 : 29. make dishes and covers thereof to cover w., 37 : 16.
30 : 4. places for staves to bear it w., 37 : 27. [40 : 30.
18. a laver of brass to wash w.,
36 : 3. of sanctuary, to make it w.
Le. 5 : 3. if a man shall be defiled w.
6 : 30. to reconcile w. in holy place
11 : 21. which have legs to leap w.
19 : 24. fruit be holy to praise L. w.
Nu. 4 : 7. bowls, covers to cover w.
1 S. 16 : 12. ruddy and w. of beautif.
1 K. 19 : 1. w. he had slain prophets
2 K. 23 : 26. Manasseh provoked L. w.
1 Ch. 29 : 4. overlay walls of houses w.
2 Ch. 24 : 14. vessels to offer w. and
26 : 15. engines to shoot stones w.
Es. 6 : 9. array man w. whom king
Jb. 2 : 8. potsherd to scrape hims. w.
Ps. 141 : 10. wicked fall, I w. escape
Pr. 22 : 18. w. be fitted in thy lips
Is. 30 : 14. take water w. out of pit
23. that thou shalt sow ground w.
Lu. 6 : 38. same measure ye mete w.
Ac. 25 : 27. not w. to signify crimes
1 Co. 12 : 7. Spirit to every man to [profit w.
Col. 4 : 3. w. praying for us
1 Ti. 5 : 13. w. they learn to be idle
Phm. 22. But w. prepare me lodging

WITHDRAW.

1 S. 14 : 19. Saul said, w. thine hand
Jb. 9 : 13. If God will not w. anger
13 : 21. w. thine hand far from me
33 : 17. w. man from his purpose
Pr. 25 : 17. w. foot from neighbour's [hou.
Ec. 7 : 18. fr. this w. not hand
Is. 60 : 20. nei. shall moon w. itself
Jo. 2 : 10. stars sh. w. shining, 3 : 15.
2 Th. 3 : 6. w. from every brother
1 Ti. 6 : 5. fr. men of corrupt minds w.

WITHDRAWEST, ETH.

Jb. 36 : 7. w-h not eyes fr. righteous
Ps. 74 : 11. Why w-t thy right hand?

WITHDRAWING.

Ne. 9 : †29. they gave a w. shoulder

WITHDRAWN.

De. 13 : 13. w. inhabitants of city
Can. 5 : 6. my beloved had w. hims.
La. 2 : 8. not w. hand fr. destroying
Eze. 18 : 8. w. his hand fr. iniquity
Ho. 5 : 6. the Lord hath w. fr. them
Lu. 22 : 41. w. from them a stone's [cast

WITHDREW.

Ne. 9 : 29. they w. shoulder
Eze. 20 : 22. Nevertheless I w. mine [hand
Mat. 12 : 15. when Jes. knew it he w.
Mk. 3 : 7. Jesus w. hims., Lu. 5 : 16.
Ga. 2 : 12. when they were come, Pet. [w.

WITHER.

Ps. 1 : 3. his leaf also shall not w.
37 : 2. they shall w. as green herb
Is. 19 : 6. reeds and flags shall w.
7. every thing by brooks shall w.
40 : 24. they sh. w. and whirlwind
Je. 12 : 4. How long shall herbs w.?
Eze. 17 : 9. shall he not cut off fruit that it w., it shall w. in all
10. shall it not utterly w. when east wind? it sh. w. in furrows
Am. 1 : 2. the top of Carmel shall w.

WITHERED.

Ge. 41 : 23. behold, seven ears w.
Ps. 102 : 4. My heart is smitten, w.
11. and I am w. like grass
Is. 15 : 6. hay is w., the grass faileth
27 : 11. When boughs thereof are [w.
33 : † 9. Lebanon is w. away
La. 4 : 8. Nazarites, their skin is w.
Eze. 19 : 12. her strong rods were w.
Jo. 1 : 12. all trees of field are w.; bec. joy is w. from sons of men
17. barns broken down, corn w.
Am. 4 : 7. wh-upon it rained not w.
Jon. 4 : 7. it smote gourd that it w.
Mat. 12 : 10. a man which had his hand w., Mk. 3 : 1, 3. Lu. 6 : 6, 8.
13 : 6. because having no root, they w. away, Mk. 4 : 6.
21 : 19. presently the fig tree w., 20. Mk. 11 : 21. [moisture
Lu. 8 : 6. it w. aw. because it lacked
Jn. 5 : 3. blind, halt, w., waiting for
15 : 6. he is cast forth and is w.

WITHERETH. [herb

Jb. 8 : 12. flag w. before any other
Ps. 90 : 6. evening, it is cut down, w.
129 : 6. like grass that w. before
Is. 40 : 7. The grass w., the flower fadeth, 8. 1 Pe. 1 : 24. [w. grass
Ja. 1 : 11. the sun no sooner risen,
Jude 12. trees whose fruit w., dead

WITHHELD, EST. [me

Ge. 20 : 6. I w. thee fr. sinning ag.
22 : 12. hast not w. son fr. me, 16.
30 : 2. w. from thee fruit of womb?
Ezr. 9 : † 13. w. beneath our iniq-s
Ne. 9 : 20. w-t not thy manna from
Jb. 31 : 16. If I have w. the poor
Ec. 2 : 10. I w. not my heart fr. joy

WITHHOLD. [chre

Ge. 23 : 6. none shall w. his sepul-
2 S. 13 : 13. he will not w. me fr. thee
Jb. 4 : 2. who can w. fr. speaking?
30 : † 10. w. not spittle fr. my face
Ps. 40 : 11. w. not mercies from me
84 : 11. no good thing w. fr. them
Pr. 3 : 27. w. not good from them
23 : 13. w. not correction fr. child
30 : † 7. Two things w. not from me
Ec. 11 : 6. evening w. not thy hand
Jo. 2 : 25. w. foot fr. being unshod

WITHHOLDEN.

1 S. 25 : 26. Lord hath w. thee from
Jb. 22 : 7. hast w. bread fr. hungry
38 : 15. fr. wicked their light is w.
42 : 2. no thought can be w. fr. thee
Ps. 21 : 2. not w. request of his lips
Je. 3 : 3. The showers have been w.
5 : 25. sins have w. good things
Eze. 18 : 16. hath not w. pledge [G.
Jo. 1 : 13. drink offering is w. from
Am. 4 : 7. I have w. the rain fr. you

WITHHOLDETH.

Jb. 12 : 15. Behold he w. the waters
Pr. 11 : 24. w. more than is meet
26. that w. corn, people sh. curse
2 Th. 2 : 6. now ye know what w.

WITHIN. [tent

Ge. 9 : 21. he was uncovered w. his
18 : 12. Sarah laughed w. herself
25 : 22. children struggled w. her
39 : 11. none of the men of house w.
40 : 13. w. three days shall Pha-h lift thine head, 19. [holy place
Le. 10 : 18. blood of it not brought w.
14 : 41. cause house be scraped w.
25 : 29. w. a year may redeem it (2)
30. if it be not redeemed w. a year
26 : 25. when gathered w. cities
Nu. 4 : 10. w. cov-g of badgers' skins
De. 17 : 2. if w. thy gates a man hath wrought wickedness [gates
8. matters of controversy w. thy
23 : 10. man not clean not come w.
Jos. 19 : 1. w. inheritance of Jud., 9.
21 : 41. w. possession of Isr. 48 cities
Ju. 7 : 16. pitchers. lamps w. pitch.
11 : 18. came not w. border of Moab
26. recover them w. that time?
14 : 12. if declare riddle w. 7 days
15 : 1. it came to pass w. a while
1 S. 13 : 11. not w. the days appointed
14 : 14. slaughter w. half an acre
25 : 36. Nabal's heart merry w. him
37. told him, his heart died w. him
2 S. 7 : 2. ark dwelleth w. curtains
1 K. 6 : 15. built walls w. with cedar
16. he even built them for it w.
18. cedar of house w. was carved
19. oracle he prepared in house w.
21. Solomon overlaid house w. with gold, 2 Ch. 3 : 4. [ubim
23. w. the oracle he made 2 cher-
27. he set cherubim w. inner ho.
7 : 8. had another court w. porch
31. mouth of it w. chapiter, cubit
2 K. 4 : 27. her soul is vexed w. her
6 : 30. he had sackcl-h w. his flesh
7 : 11. told it to king's house w.
11 : 8. th. cometh w. ranges be slain
Ezr. 4 : 15. moved sedition w. same
Ne. 4 : 22. Let every one lodge w. Je.
6 : 10. Let us meet w. the temple
Jb. 20 : 13. keep it still w. his mouth
24 : 11. make oil w. their walls
41 : † 13. Who come w. his bridle?
Ps. 36 : 1. transgression of wicked saith w. my heart, no fear of G.
40 : 8. thy law is w. my heart
10. not hid thy righteousness w.
45 : 13. King's dau-r glorious w.
101 : 2. walk w. my house with
7. He that worketh deceit shall not dwell w. my house
122 : 7. Peace be w. thy walls; prosperity w. thy palaces [it
Ec. 9 : 14. a little city, few men w.
Can. 4 : 1. doves' eyes w. thy locks
3. like pomegranate w. locks, 6 : 7.
Is. 7 : 8. w. 65 years Ephr. broken
16 : 14. w. 3 years glory of Moab
21 : 16. w. year glory of Kedar fail
60 : 18. nor destruction w. borders
Je. 28 : 3. w. two years bring vessels
11. break yoke of Neb-r w. 2 yrs.
Eze. 1 : 27. appearance of fire w. it
3 : 24. shut thyself w. thy house
12 : 24. no more vain visions w. Isr.
40 : 7. porch of gate w. was one reed,
16. to their posts w. the gate [8.
43. And w. were hooks, a ha. broad
41 : 9. place of side chambers w.
44 : 17. while they minister w. [days
Da. 6 : 12. ask of man or God w. 30
11 : 20. w. few days he be destroyed
Mi. 3 : 3. pieces as flesh w. caldron
5 : 6. he treadeth w. our borders
Zph. 3 : 3. princes w. are roar-g lions
Mat. 3 : 9. think not to say w. yourselves, We have, Lu. 3 : 8.
9 : 21. said w. herself, If I but touch
23 : 25. w. they are full of extortion
26. cleanse first what is w. cup
27. are w. full of dead men's bones
28. w. ye are full of hypocrisy
Mk. 2 : 8. perceived they reasoned w.
7 : 21. fr. w. proceed evil thoughts
23. these evil things come from w.
Lu. 11 : 7. fr. w. sh. say, Trouble me
12 : 17. he thought w. himself [not
17 : 21. The kingd. of God is w. you
Jn. 20 : 26. after 8 days, disciples w.
Ac. 5 : 23. prison, found no man w.
Ro. 8 : 23. even we groan w. oursel-s
1 Co. 5 : 12. do not ye judge them w.
Re. 4 : 8. they were full of eyes w.
5 : 1. a book written w. and on back
See Three DAYS,
CITY, GATES, HIM, HIMSELF.

WITHIN me. [w. m.

Ps. 55 : 4. My heart is sore pained
109 : 22. my heart wounded w. m.
143 : 4. my heart w. m. is desolate
Jon. 2 : 7. When my soul fainted w. [m.
See Within ME.
See THEE, THEMSELVES, US, VAIL, YOU.

WITHIN and without.

Ge. 6 : 14. shalt pitch the ark w. -
Ex. 25 : 11. shalt overlay ark with pure gold w. -, 37 : 2. 1 K. 6 : 30.
1 K. 6 : 29. figures of open flowers w. -
7 : 9. stones sawed with saws w. -

Eze. 2 : 10. the book was writ-n w.-
41 : 17.all the wall w.- by measure
See WITHOUT with within.

WITHOUT. [23.

Ge. 1 : 2. earth was w. form, Je. 4 :
9 : 22. Ham told his two breth. w.
24 : 11. made camels kneel w. city
31. Come in, whf. standest w. ?
41 : 44.w.thee sh. no man lift hand
Le. 10 : 12. eat meat off-g w. leaven
Nu. 35 : 22. if he thrust him w. enmity, w. laying of wait [27.
26. slayer come w. border of city,
De. 8 : 9. eat bread w. scarceness
25 :5.wife of dead sh. not marry w.
32 : 4. a God of truth w. iniquity
Ju.2 :23.w.driving them out hastily
Ru. 4 : 14. not left thee w. kinsman
2 S.23 : 4.he as a morning w. clouds
1 K. 6 :6. w. in wall he made rests
8 : 8. ends of the staves were not
seen w., 2 Ch. 5 : 9. [and Isr.
22 : 1. 3 years w. war betw. Syria
2 K. 10 : 24. appointed 80 men w.
11 : 15. Have her forth w. ranges
16 : 18. covert in king's entry w.
18 : 25. Am I come w. the Lord
against this place, Is. 36 : 10.
23 :4.Josiah burned the vessels w.
6. Josiah brought grove w. Jeru.
25 : 16. brass of these vessels was
w. weight, Je. 52 : 20. [w. cost
1 Ch. 21 : 24. not offer burnt offer-gs
2 Ch. 15 : 3. long season Israel w.
true God, w. a priest, w. law
21 : 20.Jehoram departed w.being
24 : 8. set chest w. at gate of house
32 : 5. Hez-h built another wall w.
33 : 14. built wall w. city of David
Ezr. 7 : 22. oil, salt w. prescribing
Ne.13 :20.sellers were lodged w.Jer.
Jb. 4 : 20. perish w. any regarding
21. they die, even w. wisdom [it
7 : 6. My days are spent w. hope
8 : 11. Can the rush grow w. mire?
Can the flag grow w. water ?
10 : 22. of shadow of death w.order
12 : 25. grope in darkness w. light
24 : 7. naked to lodge w. clothing,
26 : 2. helped him is w. power [10.
30 : 28.went mourning w. sun[ing
31 :19.If I have seen poor w. cover-
33 : 9. I am clean w. transgression
34 :6.wound incurable w.transg-n
20. mighty be taken aw. w. hand
Ps. 17 : † 1. prayer w. lips of deceit
31 : 11. that did see me w. fled
59 : 4. prepare thems. w. my fault
Pr. 1 : 20. Wisdom crieth w. ; she
5 : 23. He shall die w. instruction
6 : 15. suddenly broken w. remedy
7 : 12. Now is she w.,now in streets
11 : 22. a fair woman w. discretion
15 : 22.w.counsel purposes disapp.
16 :8.than great revenues w. right
22 : 13. is a lion w. I shall be slain
24 : 27. Prepare thy work w.,make
25 :14.boasteth is like wind w.rain
29 :1.destroyed and that w.remedy
Ec. 10 : 11.serpent bite w. enchant-t
Can. 8 : 1. find thee w. I would kiss
Is. 5 : 14. Therefore hell opened her
mouth w. measure [prisoners
10 : 4. w. me they shall bow under
33 : 7. valiant ones sh. cry w. [end
45 : 17. not be ashamed, world w.
55 : 1. buy wine and milk w. price
Je. 2 : 32. forgotten me days w. nu.
5 : 21. Hear, O peo., w. underst-g
9 : 21.to cut off chil. from w.[price
15 : 13. treasures to the spoil w.
33.: 10. w. man, w. inhabitant,
w. beast, (5). 12.-32 : 43.[men ?
44:19. pour out drink off-gs w. our
49 : 31.nation th. dwelleth w. care
La. 1 : 6. princes are gone w. stren.
3 : 49.eye trickleth w. intermission

Eze. 17 : 9. w. great power to pluck
33 : 15. If wicked w. committing
40 : 19. forefront of inner court w.
40. at the side w. were two tables
44. w. inner gate were chambers
41 : 9. wall for the side chamber w.
17. unto inner house and w. (2)
25. planks upon face of porch w.
42 :7.wall w., length was 50 cubits
43 : 21.sh.burn bullock w.sanct-y
46 : 2. prince enter by th. gate w.
47 : 2. he led me about the way w.
Da. 2 :34.stone was cut out w. ha-s,
8 :25. shall be broken w. hand[45.
11 : 18. w. reproach he shall cause
Ho. 3 : 4. Israel w. a king, w. a
prince, w. a sacrifice, w. an
image, w. an ephod, and w. a
teraphim [w.
7 : 1. the troop of robbers spoileth
11. Ephr. like silly dove w. heart
Mat. 10 : 29. not fall w. your Fath.
12 : 46. his brethren stood w., 47.
Mk. 3:31, 32. Lu. 8:20.[Mk.4:34.
13 : 34. w. a parable spake he not,
57. prophet not w. honour save
in own country, Mk. 6 : 4.
15 : 16. Are ye yet w. understanding ? Mk. 7 : 18.
26 : 69. Now Peter sat w. in palace
Mk. 1 : 45. was w. in desert places
3 :32.mother and brethren w. seek
4 : 11. unto them w. these are done
7:15.nothing fr.w.a man can defile
18. whatso. from w. entereth (2)
11 : 4. found colt tied by door w.
14 : 58. will build anoth. w. hands
Lu. 1 : 10. multitude praying w.
6 : 49. w. a foundation built a hou.
22 : 35.I sent you w. purse, lacked
Jn. 1 :3.w. him not any thing made
8 : 7. He that is w. sin among you
18 : 16. Peter stood at the door w.
19 : 23. now the coat was w. seam
20 : 11.Mary stood w. at sepulchre
Ac.5 :23.found keepers standing w.
26. capt. bro-t them w. violence
9 : 9. he was three days w. sight
10 : 29. Thf. came I w. gainsaying
14 : 17. left not himself w. witness
25 : 17. w. any delay I sat on judg.
Ro. 1 :20.so that they are w. excuse
31. w. understanding, w. natural affection, 2 Ti. 3 : 3.[effect?
3 : 3. unbelief make faith of G. w.
28. is justified by faith w. deeds
4 6.imputeth righteousn. w.works
5 : 6. when we were yet w. strength
10 : 14. how hear w. a preacher ?
11 :29.gifts of G. are w. repentance
12 : 9. Let love be w. dissimulation
1 Co. 5 : 12. what have I to judge
13. them w. G. judgeth [them w.
6 : 18. Every sin is w. the body
7 : 32.I wou.have you w. carefuln.
35. attend upon L. w. distraction
9 :18. I may make gospel w. char.
11 : 11. nel. is the man w.wom. (2)
14 : 7. things w. life giving sound
10. voices, none w. significance
2 Co. 10 : 13. not boast w. meas.,15.
11 : 28. Beside things that are w.
Ep. 1 :4.that we be w. blame before
2 : 12. that time ye were w. Christ
and w. God in the world [end
3 : 21. Unto him be glory world w.
Ph. 2 : 14. Do all w. murmurings
15. ye be sons of God w. rebuke
Col. 2 : 11. circumcision w. hands
4 : 5.Walk in wisdom tow.them w.
1 Th. 4 : 12. walk honestly toward
them w. [wrath
1 Ti. 2 : 8. lifting up holy hands w.
3 : 7. a good report of them w.
16.w.controversy gr.the mystery
5 :21.w. preferring one bef. anoth.
Phm. 14. w. thy mind I do nothing

He. 4 : 15. tempted as we, yet w. sin
7 : 3. Melchisedec, w. father, w.
mother, w. descent [blessed
7. w. all contradiction the less is
20.not w.an oath made priest, 21.
9 : 7.not w. blood which he offered
18. nei. first testament w. blood
22. w. shedding of bl-d no remis-
28.appear w.sin unto salva.[sion
10 : 23.Let us hold fast w. waver-g
28. died w. mercy under two or 3
11 : 6. w. faith impossible to please
12 : 8. But if ye be w. chastisement
14. holiness w. wh. no man sh.see
13 :5.conversation be w. covetous-
12. Jesus suffered w. gate [ness
Ja. 2 : 13. have judgment w. mercy
18. shew me thy faith w. works
26. as body w. the spirit is dead,
so faith w. works is dead, 20.
3 : 17. w. partiality, w. hypocrisy
1 Pe. 1 : 17. w. respect of persons
3 : 1. may w. the word be won by
4 : 9. Use hospitality w. grudging
2 Pe. 2 : 17.These are wells w.water
Jude 12. feast, feeding themselves
w. fear : clouds they are w.
water,trees w.fruit, twice dead
Re. 11 : 2. court which is w, temple
14 : 5. are w. fault bef. the throne
10. the wrath of God w. mixture
22 : 15. For w. are dogs, sorcerers

WITHOUT with within.

Le. 13 : 55. it is fret inward whether
bare w-n or w-t [sh. destroy
De. 32 : 25. sword w-t, terror w-n
Eze. 7:15. sword is w-t, famine w-n
Lu. 11 : 40. did not he that made
that w-t make that w-n also
2 Co. 7 : 5. w-t fightings, w-n fears
See BLEMISH, CAMP, CAUSE,
CEASING, CHILDREN, CITY,
FAIL, FEAR, INHABITANT,
KNOWLEDGE, LAW, ME, MON-
EY, NUMBER, SPOT, STAND,
THEE, THEM, US, VAIL,
WALLS.

WITHS. [green w.

Ju. 16 :7.If they bind me with seven
8. lords brought her 7 green w.
9. he brake w. as thread of tow

WITHSTAND.

Nu. 22 : 32. I went out to w. thee
2 Ch. 13 : 7. Rehoboam could not w.
8.ye think to w. kingdom of Lord
20 : 6. that none is able to w. thee
Es. 9 : 2. no man could w. the Jews
Ec. 4 : 12. if one prevail, two sh. w.
Da. 11 :15.arms of south sh.not w.,
nei. be strength to w.[w. God ?
Ac. 11 : 17. what was I that I could
Ep. 6 : 13. able to w. in the evil day

WITHSTOOD.

2 Ch. 26 : 18. they w. Uzziah king
Da. 10 : 13. prince of Persia w. me
Ac. 13 :8. Elymas sorcerer w. them
Ga. 2 : 11. I w. Peter to the face
2 Ti. 3 : 8. as Jambres w. Moses
4 : 15. hath greatly w. our words

WITNESS. [Noun.]

Ge. 21 : 30. be a w. that I digged
31 : 44. let covenant be a w. between me and thee
48. This heap is a w. between me
and thee, 52. [thee
50. see, God is w. betwixt me and
52. This heap be w., pillar be w.
Ex. 22 : 13. if torn, bring it for w.
23 : 1. not to be an unrighteous w.
Le. 5 : 1. if hear swearing and is w.
Nu. 5 : 13. if be no w. against her
35 : 30. one w. shall not testify ag.
any person, De. 17 : 6.-19 : 15.
De. 19 : 18. if the w. be a false w.
31 : 19. this song may be w. for me
21. sons sh. testify ag. them as w.
26. this book be for a w. ag. thee

Jos. 22 : 27. altar, that it be a w.
between us, 28, 34. [to us (2)
24 : 27. this stone shall be a w. un-
Ju. 11 : 10. Lord be w. between us,
Je. 42 : 5. [you this day
1 S. 12 : 5. The Lord is w. against
20 : †42. L. be w. of that we sworn
Jb. 16 : 8. wrinkles, is a w. ag. me (2)
19. behold my w. is in heaven
29 : 11. when eye saw me, gave w.
Ps. 89 : 37. as a faithful w. in heaven
Pr. 14 : 5 A faithful w. will not lie,
but a false w. will utter lies
25. A true w. delivereth souls,
but a deceitful w. [Judgment
19 : 28. An ungodly w. scorneth
24 : 28. Be not w. ag. thy neighb-r
Is. 19 : 20. it sh. be for a w. unto L.
55 : 4. I have given him for a w.
Je. 29 : 23. I am a w., saith Lord
Mi. 1 : 2. let the Lord be w. ag. you
Ha. 2 : † 11. beam sh. w. ag. it [wife
Mal. 2 : 14. L. be w. betw. thee and
3 : 5. I will be swift w. ag. sorcerers
Mat. 24 : 14. be preached for a w.
Mk. 14 : 55. sought for w. ag. Jesus
56. their w. agreed not togeth., 59.
Lu. 22 : 71. What need we furth. w.?
Jn. 1 : 7. The same came for a w. to
bear w. of the Light [w.
3 : 11. We speak, ye receive not our
26. he to whom thou hearest w.
5 : 31. If I bear w. of myself, my
w. is not true [true
32. the w. he witnesseth of me is
36. I greater w. than that of John
Ac. 1 : 22. one be ordained to be w.
4 : 33. gave w. of the resurrection
10 : 43. To him give all prophets w.
14 : 17. left not himself without w.
22 : 15. thou sh. be his w. unto all
26 : 16. make thee a minister, a w.
Ro. 1 : 9. God is my w., 1 Th. 2 : 5.
Tit. 1 : 13. This w. is true, rebuke
He. 10 : 15. Holy Ghost is w. to us
11 : 4. by which Abel obtained w.
Ja. 5 : 3. rust of them be w. ag. you
1 Pe. 5 : 1. Peter a w. of suff-gs of C.
1 Jn. 5 : 9. If we receive the w. of
men, w. of God is greater, for
this is the w. of God [himself
10. He that believeth hath w. in
Re. 1 : 5. Christ, who is faithful w.
3 : 14. saith the Amen, the true w.
20 : 4. beheaded for the w. of Jesus

Bare, Bear, or Beareth WITNESS.

Ex. 20 : 16. not b-r false w. against
thy neighbour, De. 5 : 20. Mat.
19 : 18. Ro. 13 : 9.
1 K. 21 : 10. set two sons of Belial to
b-r w. against Naboth [my face
Jb. 16 : 8. my leanness b-h w. to
Pr. 25 : 18. A man that b-h false w.
is a maul [18 : 20.
Mk. 10 : 19. Do not b-r false w., Lu.
14 : 56. many b-e false w. against
him, their w. agreed not, 57.
Lu. 4 : 22. all b-e him w., wondered
11 : 48. ye b-r w. that ye allow deeds
Jn. 1 : 7. The same came for a w. to
b-r w. of the Light, 8. [he
15. John b-e w. of him, This was
3 : 28. Ye b-r me w. that I said, I
5 : 31. If I b-r w. of myself, my w.
is not true [of me
32. There is another that b-h w.
33. John, he b-e w. unto truth
36. works I do b-r w. of me, 10 : 25.
8 : 18. I b-r w. of myself, and Father that sent me b-h w. of me
15 : 27. ye sh. b-r w. bec. with me
18 : 23. If I have spoken evil b-r w.
37. into world th. I should b-r w.
Ac. 15 : 8. God b-e them w., giving
22 : 5. high priest doth b-r me w.
23 : 11. must thou b-r w. at Rome
Ro. 8 : 16. Spirit b-h w. with our sp.
1 Jn. 1 : 2. we have seen and b-r w.
5 : 6. it is the Spirit that b-h w.
8. are three that b-r w. in earth

Bearing or Borne WITNESS. [of me

Jn. 5 : 37. the Father hath b-e w.
Ro. 2 : 15. their conscience b-g w.
9 : 1. conscience b-g me w. in Holy
He. 2 : 4. G. b-g them w. with signs
3 Jn. 6. have b-e w. of thy charity
See **FALSE witness, es, TABERNACLE of witness.**

WITNESSES. [of w.

Nu. 35 : 30. be put to death by mou.
De. 17 : 6. At the mouth of two or
three w. be put to death [him
7. hands of w. shall be first upon
19 : 15. at the mouth of two or three
w. shall matter be established,
Mat. 18 : 16. 2 Co. 13 : 1.
Jos. 24 : 22. Ye are w. ag. yourselves,
they said, We are w. [10.
Ru. 4 : 9. Ye are w. that I bought,
11. peo. and elders said, We are w.
Jb. 10 : 17. Thou renewest w. ag. me
Is. 8 : 2. I took unto me faithful w.
43 : 9. let nations bring their w.
10. Ye are my w., 12.–44 : 8. [not
44 : 9. are their own w., they see
Je. 32 : 10. I sealed it, took w., 12.
25. Buy the field and take w., 44.
Mat. 23 : 31. Wheref. ye be w. unto
26 : 65. what further need have we
of w.? Mk. 14 : 63. [things
Lu. 24 : 48. And ye are w. of these
Ac. 1 : 8. shall be w. to me in Jerus.
2 : 32. raised, wh-f we are w., 3 : 15.
5 : 32. we are his w. of these, 10 : 39.
7 : 58. w. laid clothes at Saul's feet
10 : 41. unto w. chosen bef. of God
13 : 31. who are his w. unto people
1 Th. 2 : 10. Ye are w., how holily
1 Ti. 5 : 19. receive not an accusation
but before two or three w. [w.
6 : 12. a good profession bef. many
2 Ti. 2 : 2. heard of me am. many w.
He. 10 : 28. died without mercy under two or three w. [of w.
12 : 1. compassed with so gr. cloud
Re. 11 : 3. will give power unto my 2
See EYEWITNESSES. [w.

WITNESS. [Verb.]

De. 4 : 26. I call heaven to w. ag. you
1 S. 12 : 3. here I am; w. against me
Is. 3 : 9. countenance doth w. ag-t
La. 2 : 13. What take to w. for thee?
Mat. 26 : 62. what is it that these w.
against thee? Mk. 14 : 60.
27 : 13. saith unto him, Hearest thou
not how many things they w.
against thee, Mk. 15 : 4.

WITNESSED. [both

1 K. 21 : 13. men of Belial w. ag. Na-
Ro. 3 : 21. w. by law and prophets
1 Ti. 6 : 13. before Pilate w. a good
He. 7 : 8. it is w. that he liveth

WITNESSETH, ING.

Jn. 5 : 32. that he w-h of me is true
Ac. 20 : 23. Holy Gh. w-h in ev. city
26 : 22. w-g both to small and gr-t
Ro. 2 : † 15. conscience w-g wi. them

WIT'S. [w. end

Ps. 107 : 27. stagger and are at their

WITTINGLY. [w.

Ge. 48 : 14. Israel guided his hands

WITTY.

Pr. 8 : 12. I find out w. inventions

WIVES. [two w.

Ge. 4 : 19. Lamech took unto him
23. ye w. of Lamech, hearken (2)
6 : 2. took w. of all wh. they chose
18. into the ark thy sons, sons' w.
7 : 13. Noah's wife and 3 w. of sons
8 : 16. Go forth thy sons, sons' w.
11 : 29. Abram and Nahor took w.
28 : 9. Esau took unto the w. he had
Ge. 30 : 26. Give me my w., let me go
31 : 17. Jac. set his w. upon camels
50. if th. take w. beside my dau-s
32 : 22. Jacob rose, took his two w.
34 : 21. let us take their dau-s for w.
36 : 2. Esau took w. of Canaan, 6.
37 : 2. Bilhah, Zilpah, father's w.
46 : 26. all, besides Jac.'s sons' w.
Nu. 14 : 3. our w. should be a prey
32 : 26. our w. sh. be in cities of Gil.
36 : † 6. be w. to whom think best
De. 17 : 17. Nei. sh. he multiply w.
21 : 15. If man have two w., one be-
Ju. 8 : 30. Gideon had many w. [liev.
21 : 7. How shall we do for w., seeing we will not give our daughters to w., 16. [saved alive
14. gave them w. which they had
18. not give them w. of our dau-s
23. took w. of them that danced
Ru. 1 : 4. two sons took w. of Moab
1 S. 1 : 2. Elkanah had two w.; one
25 : 43. they were both David's w.
27 : 3. at Gath David with his 2 w.
30 : 5. David's w. were taken capt.
18. Da. rescued his two w. [two w.
2 S. 2 : 2. Unto Hebron, David and
5 : 13. David took more concubines
and w., 1 Ch. 14 : 3. [thy bosom
12 : 8. I gave thy master's w. into
1 K. 11 : 3. Sol-n had 700 w., prin-
cesses; w. turned away heart,
20 : 7. sent for my w. and chil. [4.
2 K. 4 : 1. a woman of w. of prophets
24 : 15. Neb-r carried away king's
w., 2 Ch. 21 : 17. [lah and N.
1 Ch. 4 : 5. Ashur had two w., He-
7 : 4. sons of Uzzi had many w.
8 : 8. Hushim, Baara were his w.
2 Ch. 11 : 21. Rehob. loved Maachah
above all his w. (he took 18 w.)
23. Rehoboam desired many w.
13 : 21. Abijah married 14 w. [w.
24 : 3. Jehoiada took for him two
29 : 9. our w. in captivity for this
Ezr. 10 : 3. a covenant to put away w.
44. some had w. by wh. had chil.
Ne. 12 : 43. the w. and chil. rejoiced
13 : 23. Jews married w. of Ashdod
Es. 1 : 20. the w. shall give to husbands honour [your sons
Je. 29 : 6. Take ye w., take w. for
23. adultery with neighbours' w.
35 : 8. to drink no wine, we, our w.
Da. 5 : 2. his w. might drink th-n, 3.
Mi. 2 : †9. w. of my peo. have ye cast
Lu. 17 : 27. They drank, married w.
Ac. 21 : 5. they brought us on our
way with w. [had none
1 Co. 7 : 29. that have w. be as tho.
Ep. 5 : 22. w. submit yourselves to
your husb-s, Col. 3 : 18. 1 Pe. 3 : 1.
24. so let w. be to their husbands
1 Ti. 4 : 7. refuse old w'. fables [w.
1 Pe. 3 : 1. Be won by conversation of

Strange WIVES.

1 K. 11 : 8. likewise for all his s. w.
Ezr. 10 : 2. we have trespassed and
taken s. w., 10, 14, 44.
11. separate yourselves fr. people
of the land and s. w. [s. w.
17. an end with all that had taken
18. sons of priests had taken s. w.
Ne. 13 : 27. to transgress in marrying

Their WIVES. [s. w.

Ge. 34 : 29. their wealth and t. w.
took they captive, 1 S. 30 : 3.
46 : 5. carried t. w. in wagons
Nu. 16 : 27. stood in the door t. w.
Ju. 3 : 6. took daughters to be t. w.
2 Ch. 20 : 13. all Judah with t. w.
31 : 18. genealogy of t. w. and sons
Ezr. 10 : 19. that they put away t. w.
Ne. 5 : 1. a great cry of peo. and t. w.
10 : 28. t. w. entered into an oath
Is. 13 : 16. be spoiled, t. w. ravished
Je. 8 : 10. give t. w. unto others, 6 : 12.

Je. 14 : 16. have none to bury t.w.
18 : 21. let t.w. be bereaved of chil.
44 : 9. ye forgotten wickedn. of t.w.
15. knew t.w. had burned incense
Eze. 44 : 22. Nei. take for t.w. a wid.
Da. 6 : 24. cast into den of lions t.w.
Zch. 12 : 12. mourn, ev family and
t.w. apart (2). 13, (2) 14, (2)
Ep. 5 : 28. to love t.w. as own bodies
1 Ti. 3 : 11. so must t.w. be grave,

Thy WIVES. [sober

2 S. 12 : 11. take t.w. before thine
eyes, he shall lie with t.w. in
19 : 5. saved this day lives of t.w.
1 K. 20 : 3. thy gold is mine ; t.w.
5. sh. deliver me, t.w., and chil.
2 Ch. 21 : 14. Lord will smite t.w.
Je. 38 : 23. So they shall bring t.w.
Da. 5 : 23. t.w. have drunk wine

Your WIVES.

Ge. 45 : 19. take wagons for y.w.
Ex. 19 : 15. said, come not at y.w.
22 : 24. y.w. sh. be widows [y.w.
32 : 2. Break off earrings in ears of
De. 3 : 19. y.w. and little ones shall
remain in cities, Jos. 1 : 14. [w.
29 : 11. Ye stand before L. with y.
Ne. 4 : 14. fight for y.w. and houses
Je. 44 : 9. forgotten wickedn. of y.w.
25. Ye and y.w. have spoken
Mat. 19 : 8. Moses suffered you to
put away y.w. [Col. 3 : 19.
Ep. 5 : 25. Husbands, love y.w.,

WIZARD.

Le. 20 : 27. a w. shall be put to death
De. 18 : 11. shall not be am. you a w.

WIZARDS.

Le. 19 : 31. seek after w. to be defiled
20 : 6. soul that turneth after w.
1 S. 28 : 3. Saul had put w. out of
the land, 9. [2 Ch. 33 : 6.
2 K. 21 : 6. Manasseh dealt with w.,
23 : 24. w. and idols Josiah put aw.
Is. 8 : 19. Seek unto w. that peep
19 : 3. they sh. seek to idols and w.

WOE, WOES.

1 S. 4 : 7. w. unto us, 8. Je. 4 : 13.-
6 : 4. La. 5 : 16. [sorrow?
Pr. 23 : 29. Who hath w.? who hath
Is. 3 : 9. w. unto their soul! [him
11. w. unto the wicked, be ill with
10 : † 5. w. to the Assyrian, rod of
17 : 12. w. to multitude of people
18 : 1. w. to land shadowing with
28 : 1. w. to the crown of pride
29 : 1. w. to Ariel, wh. David dwelt!
30 : 1. w. to the rebellious children
Je. 23 : 1. w. unto the pastors that
48 : 1. w. unto Nebo! it is spoiled
Eze 2 : 10. written, mourning and w.
13 : 3. w. unto foolish prophets
18. w. to women that sew pillows
24 : 6. w. to bloody city, 9. Na. 3 : 1.
30 : 2. Howl! w. worth the day, ye
34 : 2. w. be to shepherds that feed
Zph. 2 : 5. w. unto inhab-ts of sea
3 : 1. w. to her that is filthy [coast
Zch. 11 : 17. w. to idol shepherd th.
Mat. 18 : 7. w. unto world because
of offences! w. to man by whom
the offence cometh! Lu. 17 : 1.
26 : 24. w. unto man by whom Son
is betrayed, Mk. 14 : 21. Lu. 22 : 22.
Re. 8 : 13. angel saying, w., w., w.
to inhabiters of earth, 12 : 12.
9 : 12. One w. is past; behold there
come two w-s more [cometh
11 : 14. second w. is past; third w.

WOE
to him or unto him.

Ec. 4 : 10. w. - alone when he fall-h
Is. 45 : 9. w. - striveth wi. his Maker
10. w. - saith unto father, What
begettest thou [righteousness
Je. 22 : 13. w. - that buildeth by un-
Ha. 2 : 6. w. - increaseth that not
9. w. - that coveteth an evil [his
Ha. 2 : 12. w. - buildeth town wi. bl.
15. w. - giveth his neighb. drink
19. w. - saith to the wood, Awake

WOE is me. [Meshech

Ps. 120 : 5. w. - that I sojourn in
Is. 6 : 5. w. - ! I am undone, I am of
Je. 4 : 31. w. - ! my soul is wearied
10 : 19. w. - ! for my hurt, my
15 : 10. w. - ! my mother, that thou
45 : 3. w. - ! Lord hath added grief
Mi. 7 : 1. w. - ! I am as when they

WOE unto me.

Jb. 10 : 15. If I be wicked, w. -
Is. 24 : 16. I said, My leanness, w. -
1 Co. 9 : 16. w. - if I preach not gospel

WOE
to thee or unto thee.

Nu. 21 : 29. w. - Moab! Je. 48 : 46.
Ec. 10 : 16. w. -, O land, when k-g a
Is. 33 : 1. w. - that spoilest [child
Je. 13 : 27. w. -, O Jerusalem!
Eze. 16 : 23. w., w. - ! saith Lord G.
Mat. 11 : 21. w. -, Chorazin! w. -,
Bethsaida! for if, Lu. 10 : 13.

WOE
to them or unto them.

Is. 5 : 8. w. - that join house to hou.
11. w. - that rise early in morn-g
18. w. - draw iniquity with cords
20. w. - that call evil good, and
21. w. - wise in their own eyes
22. w. - are mighty to drink wine
10 : 1. w. - that decree unrighteous
29 : 15. w. - seek deep to hide coun.
31 : 1. w. - that go down to Egypt
Je. 50 : 27. w. - ! their day is come
Ho. 7 : 13. w. - ! they fled from me
9 : 12. w. - when I depart fr. them!
Am. 6 : 1. w. - that are at ease in Zi.
Mi. 2 : 1. w. - that devise iniquity
Mat. 24 : 19. w. - that are with child,
Mk. 13 : 17. Lu. 21 : 23. [Cain
Jude 11. w. - ! have gone in way of

WOE unto you. [Lord

Am. 5 : 18. w. - that desire day of
Mat. 23 : 13. w. - scribes and Pharisees, hypocrites! 14, 15, 23, 25,
27, 29. Lu. 11 : 44. [say, Whoso.
16. w. -, ye blind guides, which
Lu. 6 : 24. w. - that are rich [laugh
25. w. - that are full, w. - that
26. w. - when all men speak well
11 : 42. but w. - Pharisees, 43.
46. w. - also, ye lawyers! 47, 52.

WOEFUL. [w. day

Je. 17 : 16. nei. have I desired the

WOLF.

Ge. 49 : 27. Benj. shall raven as a w.
Is. 11 : 6. w. shall dwell with lamb
65 : 25. w. and lamb sh. feed toget.
Je. 5 : 6. w. of the evenings sh. spoil
Jn. 10 : 12. hireling seeth the w.
coming, the w. catcheth sheep

WOLVES.

Eze. 22 : 27. Her princes are like w.
Ha. 1 : 8. horses more fierce than w.
Zph. 3 : 3. her judges are evening w.
Mat. 7 : 15. inwardly are ravening w.
10 : 16. you as sheep in midst of w.
Lu. 10 : 3. I send you as lambs am. w.
Ac. 20 : 29. sh. grievous w. enter in

WOMAN. [am. you

Ge. 2 : 22. rib from man made he w.
23. she sh. be called w. bec. taken
3 : 1. serpent said unto w., 4. [eat
2. w. said unto serpent, We may
6. w. saw tree was good, she took
12. The w. whom thou gavest to
13. Lord said unto w. And w.
15. put enmity betw. thee and w.
16. w., I will multiply thy sorrow
12 : 11. I know thou art fair w., 14.
15. w. was taken into Pha-'s hou.
20 : 3. thou a dead man for w. taken
24 : 5. w. will not be willing to follow me, 8, 39. [appointed
44. let same be the w. Lord hath
Ge. 38 : 20. rec. pledge fr. w.'s hands
46 : 10. Shaul, the son of Canaanitish w., Ex. 6 : 15. [a son
Ex. 2 : 2. the w. conceived and bare
9. w. took the child and nursed it
3 : 22. every w. shall borrow of her
neighbour, 11 : 2. [with child
21 : 22. if men strive and hurt a w.
Le. 12 : 2. If w. have conceived seed
15 : 19. if a w. have an issue, 25. [19.
18 : 17. not uncover nakedn. of w.,
23. nei. any w. stand before beast
19 : 20. whoso. lieth carnally wi. w.
20 : 13. If lie with mank-d as wi. w.
16. if w. approach any beast and
lie down thereto, shalt kill w.
21 : 7. nei. shall take a w. put away
14. divorced w. or harlot not take
24 : 10. son of Israelitish w., 11. (2)
Nu. 5 : 18. priest shall set the w. bef.
L., and uncover w.'s head, 30.
19. priest say unto w., If no man
21. priest shall charge w. with an
oath of cursing, and say unto w.
22. the w. shall say, Amen, amen
24. cause w. drink bitter wat., 26.
25. take offering out of w.'s hand
27. w. shall be a curse am. people
28. if w. not defiled shall be free
31. this w. shall bear her iniquity
12 : 1. ag. Moses because of Ethiop.
ian w. whom he had married (2)
25 : 6. brought Midianitish w. in
sight of Moses [belly
8. Phinehas thrust w. through
14. slain with Midian-h w. was Z.
15. name of Midianitish w. Cozbi
30 : 3. If a w. vow a vow unto Lord
De. 15 : 12. if a Hebrew w. be sold
21 : 11. am. captives a beautiful w.
22 : 14. I took this w., not a maid
28 : 56. The tender and delicate w.
Jos. 2 : 4. w. took the two men, hid
6 : 22. into harlot's hou., bring out
Ju. 4 : 9. sell Sisera into ha. of w. [w.
9 : 53. w. cast a piece of millstone
upon Abim-h's head, 2 S. 11 : 21.
54. men say not of me, w. slew him
11 : † 1. Jephthah, son of w. a harlot
13 : 3. angel appeared unto w., 9.
6. w. came and told her husband
10. w. ran and shewed her hush-d
11. thou the man spakest unto w.
13. Of all I said unto w., beware
24. the w. bare a son, 2 K. 4 : 17.
14 : 1. Samson saw a w. in Timnath
2. I have seen a w. of dau-s of Ph.
3. Is there never a w. am. my peo.
7. S. went and talked with the w.
10. his father went down unto w.
16 : † 1. Samson saw a w. a harlot
4. Samson loved a w. in Sorek
19 : † 1. Levite, who took to him a w.
26. Then came the w. in dawning
20 : 4. husb-d of w. slain answered
Ru. 1 : 5. the w. was left of her sons
3 : 8. behold, a w. lay at his feet
14. Let it not be known a w. came
4 : 11. Lord make the w. like Rachel
1 S. 1 : 15. I am w. of sorrowf. spirit
18. w. went her way, no more sad
23. w. abode, gave her son suck
26. I am the w. that stood by thee
2 : 20. Lord give thee seed of this w.
20 : 30. thou son of rebellious w.
25 : 3. she a w. of good underst-g
28 : 7. Seek a w. that hath familiar
spirit; is a w. at En-dor
8. Saul came to the w. by night
9. w. said, thou knowest what S.
11. said w., whom sh. I bring up
12. when the w. saw Samuel, w.
spake to Saul, 13. [troubled
21. the w. came unto Saul, sore
23. servants with w. compelled
24. w. had fat calf in house [w.
2 S. 3 : 8. thou chargest me conc. this

2 S. 11 : 2. David saw a **w.** washing
herself; and **w.** was beautiful
3. David inquired after the **w.**
5. the **w.** conceived, and told Da.
21. Who smote Abim.? did not **w.**
13 : 17. Put now this **w.** out fr. me
14 : 2. be as a **w.** mourned for dead
4. the **w.** of Tekoah spake unto
the king, 9, 12, 13, 18, 19.
8. king said unto the **w.**, 18. ⌈ance
27. Tamar a **w.** of fair counten-
17 : 19. **w.** spread covering over⌈(2)
20. Absalom's servants came to **w.**
20 : 17. **w.** said, Art thou Joab?
21. the **w.** said, his head shall be
thrown to thee ⌈wisdom
22. **w.** went unto people in her
1 K. 3 : 17. one **w.** said, I and this
w. dwell in one house ⌈ered
18. third day this **w.** was deliv-
19. this **w.**'s child died in night
22. other **w.** said, Nay; living is
26 then spake **w.** whose the child
7 : † 14. Hiram son of a widow **w.**
14 : 5. shall feign herself another **w.**
17 : 17. the son of the **w.** fell sick
24. **w.** said to Elijah, I know thou
2 K. 4 : 1. cried a **w.** of wives of proph-
8. at Shunem, was a great **w.**⌊ets
6 : 26. cried a **w.**, Help, O king
28. This **w.** said, Give thy son th.
30. when king heard words of **w.**
8 : 1. Then spake Elisha unto **w.**
2 **w.** did after saying of man of G.
3. **w.** returned out of la. of Philis.
5. **w.** whose son he restored to life,
Gehazi said, O king, this the **w.**
6. when k. asked the **w.** she told
9 : 34. Go, see now this cursed **w.**
2 Ch. 2 : 14. son of **w.** of dau-s of Dan
24 : 7. Athaliah that wicked **w.**
Jb. 31 : 9. If been deceived by a **w.**
Ps. 48 : 6. pain as of a **w.** in travail,
Is. 13 : 8.-21 : 3.-26 : 17. Je. 4 :
31.-6 : 24.-13 : 21.-22 : 23.-30 :
6.-31 : 8. - 48 : 41. - 49 : 22, 24.-
50 : 43. Mi. 4 : 9, 10. ⌈w.
58 : 8. like the untimely birth of a
113 : 9. mak-h barren **w.** keep hou.
Pr. 6 : 24. To keep thee from evil **w.**
32. commit-h adultery with a **w.**
7 : 10. met him a **w.** subtile of heart
9 : 13. A foolish **w.** is clamorous
11 . 16. gracious **w.** retaineth hon.
22. So is a fair **w.** with-t discretion
21 : 9. with a brawling **w.**, 25 : 24.
19. than with a contentious **w.**
27 : 15. rainy day, contentious **w.**
30 : 20. Such is way of adulter-s **w.**
23. an odious **w.** when married
31 : 30. a **w.** feareth Lord be praised
Ec. 7 : 26. more bitter than death, **w.**
28. **w.** among all have I not found
Is. 45 : 10. to **w.**, What bro-t forth?
49 : 15. Can a **w.** forget her child?
54 : 6. called thee as a **w.** forsaken
Je. 6 : 2. dau-r of Zion to comely **w.**
31 : 8. with them **w.** with child and
La. 1 : 17. Jerus as menstruous **w.**
Eze. 16 : 30. work of an whorish **w.**
18 : 6. nei. come near menstru-s **w.**
23 : 44. unto her, as in unto a **w.**
36 : 17. as unclean-s of removed **w.**
Ho. 3 : 1. Go, love a **w.** beloved of
Zch. 5 : 7. a **w.** that sitteth in ephah
Mat. 5 : 28. whoso. looketh on **w.** to
9 : 20. a **w.** wh. was diseased twelve
years, Mk. 5 : 25. Lu. 8 : 43.
22. the **w.** was whole fr. that hour
13 : 33. like leaven which a **w.** took
and hid, Lu. 13 : 21. ⌈mercy
15 : 22. a **w.** of Canaan cried, Have
28. O **w.**, great is thy faith
22 : 27. And last of all the **w.** died
also, Mk. 12 : 22. Lu. 20 : 32.
26 : 7. came a **w.** having an alabaster box, Mk. 14 : 3.

Mat. 26 : 10. Why trouble ye the **w.**?
13. that this **w.** hath done, be told
Mk. 5 : 33. the **w.** trembling, fell
before him, told all, Lu. 8 : 47.
7 : 25. **w.** whose dau-r had an uncl.
26. The **w.** was a Syrophenician
10 : 12. if a **w.** put away her husb.
Lu. 4 : 26. Elias unto a **w.** a widow
7 : 37. a **w.** in city wh. was a sinner
39. who and what manner of **w.**
44. Simon, Seest thou this **w.** (2)
45. **w.** not ceased to kiss my feet
46. this **w.** hath anointed my feet
50. said to **w.**, Thy faith hath sav.
10 : 38. **w.** named Martha received
11 : 27. a **w.** said unto him, Blessed
13 : 11. a **w.** which had a spirit of
12. **w.** thou art loosed fr. infirmity
16. ought not this **w.**, a dau. of A.
15 : 8. what **w.** hav-g 10 pieces silv.
22 : 57. Peter saying, **w.**, I know
him not ⌈thee?
Jn. 2 : 4. **w.** what have I to do with
4 : 9. askest of me, **w.** of Samaria?
11. **w.** saith, Sir, 15, 19, 21, 25. ⌊7.
17. **w.** ans-d, I have no husband
27. marvelled that he talked with
28. **w.** left her water pot ⌊w.
39. many believed for say-g of **w.**
42. many said unto **w.**, we believe
8 : 3. a **w.** taken in adultery, 4.
9. Jesus left alone, **w.** standing
10. When Jesus saw none but **w.**,
he said, **w.**, Where thy accusers?
16 : 21. A **w.** in travail hath sorrow
19 : 26. saith, **w.**, behold thy son!
20 : 13. **w.**, why weepest thou? 15.
Ac. 9 : 36. **w.** full of good works⌈eas
16 : 1. Timotheus, son of **w.** a Jew-
14. a **w.** named Lydia, seller of ⌈ris
17 : 34. believed, **w.** named Dama-
Ro. 1 : 27. leaving natural use of **w.**
7 : 2. **w.** that hath husb. is bound
1 Co. 7 : 2. let ev. **w.** have own husb.
13. the **w.** which hath a husband
34. unmarried **w.** careth for Lord
9 : † 5. not power to lead ab. a **w.**?
11 : 5. **w.** that prayeth uncovered
6. if **w.** not covered, be shorn; if
shame for **w.** to be shorn ⌈head
10. **w.** ought to have power on
13. comely that a **w.** pray uncov-d
15. if a **w.** have long hair, a glory
Ga. 4 : 4. sent his son made of a **w.**
1 Ti. 2 : 11. Let the **w.** learn in si-
12. I suffer not **w.** to teach ⌊lence
14. **w.** deceived was in transgr-n
Re. 2 : 20. sufferest that **w.** Jezebel
12 : 1. a **w.** clothed with the sun
4. the dragon stood before the **w.**
6. the **w.** fled into the wilderness
13. the dragon persecuted the **w.**
14. to **w.** two wings of great eagle
15. cast water as a flood aft. the **w.**
16. And the earth helped the **w.**
17. dragon was wroth with the **w.**
17 : 3. I saw a **w.** sit upon a beast
4. the **w.** was arrayed in purple
6. **w.** drunken with blo. of saints
7. I will tell the mystery of the **w.**
9. 7 mts. on which the **w.** sitteth
18. **w.** thou sawest is that gr. city
See BONDWOMAN.

Born of a WOMAN.

Jb. 14 : 1. Man - **w.** is of few days
15 : 14. What is man, - **w.**, that he
25 : 4. how can he be clean th. is - **w**

Hebrew man or WOMAN.

De. 15 : 12. If a H. **m.o.w.** be sold

WOMAN with man.

Ex. 21 : 28. If an ox gore a **m.** or **w.**
29. ox have killed a **m.** or **w.** ⌈m.
Nu. 31 : 17. kill ev. **w.** hath known
Ju. 21 : 11. destroy ev. **w.** lain by **m.**
Pr. 6 : 26. by whorish **w. m.** is bro-t
† 36. **w.** of a **m.** will hunt ⌈m.
Je. 31 : 22. A **w.** shall compass a

1 Co. 11 : 9 Neither was **m.** created
for the **w.**; but the **w.** for **m.**
11. neither is the **m.** without the
w., neither the **w.** without **m.**
See MAN with woman.

Strange WOMAN.

Ju. 11 : 2. thou art the son of a **s.w.**
Pr. 2 : 16. To deliver thee from **s.w.**
5 : 3. lips of a **s.w.** drop as honey co
20. why be ravished with **s.w.**
6 . 24. To keep thee from the flattery
of a **s.w.**, 7 : 5. ⌈**s.w.**, 27 : 13.
20 : 16. take a pledge of him for a
23 : 27. a **s.w.** is a narrow pit
See TRAVAIL [Noun], TRAVAIL-
ETH, TRAVAILING.
See VIRTUOUS, WIDOW.

Wise WOMAN. ⌈**w.** (2)

2 S. 14 : 2. Joab fetched thence a **w.**
20 : 16. cried a **w.w.** out of the city
Pr. 14 : 1. Every **w.w.** buildeth her

Young WOMAN. ⌊hou.

Ru. 4 : 12 seed Lord shall give thee
of this **y.w.** ⌈same **y.w.**
Am. 2 : † 7. man and father in unto

WOMANKIND. ⌈**w.**

Le. 18 : 22. not lie with mank-d as wi.

WOMB, S. ⌈**w-s**

Ge. 20 : 18. Lord had closed all the
25 : 23. Two nations are in thy **w.**
24. were twins in her **w.**, 38 : 27.
29 : 31. Leah, Lord opened her **w.**
30 : 22. Rachel, God opened her **w.**
49 : 25. blessings of breasts and **w.**
Ex. 13 : 2. openeth the **w.** is mine
Nu. 8 : 16. of such as open every **w.**
Ju. 13 : 5. be a Nazarite fr. the **w.**, 7.
Ru 1 : 11. any more sons in my **w.**?
1 S. 1 : 5. Lord had shut up her **w.**, 6.
Jb. 3 : 11. Why died I not fr. the **w.**?
10 : 18. Whf. bro-t me forth of **w.**?
19. I sho. have been carried fr. **w.**
24 : 20. The **w.** shall forget him
31 : 15. Did not he that made me in
w. make him? did not one
fashion us in the **w.**? ⌈of **w.**
38 : 8. brake, as if it had issued out
29. Out of whose **w** came the ice?
Ps. 22 : 9. he that took me out of **w.**
10. I was cast upon thee fr. the **w.**
58 : 3. wicked are estranged fr. **w.**
71 : 6. By thee holden up fr. the **w.**
110 : 3. from the **w.** of the morning
Pr. 30 : 16. The grave; and barren **w.**
31 : 2. What, my son? and what,
the son of my **w.**? ⌈grow in **w.**
Ec. 11 : 5. knowest not how bones
Is. 44 : 2. Lord formed thee from the
w., 24.-49 : 5. ⌈from the **w.**
46 : 3. O Israel, which are carried
48 : 8. a transgressor from the **w.**
49 : 1. Lord hath called me from **w.**
15. not have compassion on the
son of her **w.**? ⌈and shut **w.**?
66 : 9. shall I cause to bring forth,
Je. 1 : 5. bef. thou camest out of **w.**
20 . 17. Bec. he slew me not fr. **w.**,
or her **w.** to be always great
18. came I forth of the **w.**? ⌈**w.**
Eze. 20 : 26. thro fire that openeth
Ho. 9 : 11. glory fly fr. birth and **w.**
14. give them a miscarrying **w.**
12 : 3. took his broth. by heel in **w.**
Lu. 1 : 31. thou shalt conceive in **w.**
41. the babe leaped in her **w.**, 44.
2 : 21. bef. he was conceived in **w.**
23 male that openeth **w.** be holy
11 : 27. Blessed is **w.** that bare thee
23 : 29. Blessed **w-s** that never bare
Ro. 4 : 19. nei. deadness of Sarah's

Fruit of WOMB. ⌊**w.**

Ge. 30 : 2. withheld from thee **f.o.w.**
De. 7 : 13. he will bless **f.o.** thy **w.**
Ps. 127 : 3. Lo, **f.o.w.** is his reward
Is. 13 : 18. have no pity on **f.o.w.**
Lu. 1 : 42. blessed is the **f.o.** thy **w.**
See MOTHER.

WOMEN. [w.
Ge. 14 : 16. Abr. brought again the
18 : 11. with Sarah aft. man-r of w.
24 : 11. time w. go to draw water
31 : 35. wisdom of w. is upon me
33 : 5. Esau saw w. and children
Ex. 1 : 19. Heb. w. not as Eg-n w.
15 : 20. w. went out after Miriam
35 : 25. all w. wisehearted did spin
26. all w. whose heart stirred th.
38 : 8. lookingglasses of the w.
Le. 26 . 26. ten w. shall bake bread
Nu. 31 : 9. took all w. of Midian cap.
15. Have ye saved all the w. alive?
18. all w. and children keep alive
35. 32,000 of w. not known man
De. 20 : 14. w. and little ones take
Jos. 8 : 35. read bef. cong-n with w.
Ju. 5 : 24. Blessed above w. sh. Jael
21 : 10. Smite with sword w. and c.
14. saved alive of w. of Jabesh-gil.
16. seeing w. are destroyed out of
Ru. 1 : 4. took wives of w. of Moab
4 : 14. w. said unto Naomi, Blessed
17. the w. gave the child a name
1 S. 2 : 22. how they lay with the w.
4 : 20. w. th. stood by said, Fear not
15 : 33. As sword made w. childless
18 : 6. w. came out of cities singing
7. w. answered as they played
21 : 4. if young men kept from w.
5. w. been kept fr. us three days
30 : 2. Amalekites had taken w.
2 S. 1 : 26. love passing love of w.
15 : 16. k. left ten w. to keep house
20 : 3. king took ten w., concubines
1 K. 3 : 16. two w., harlots, unto king
2 K. 8 : 12. wilt rip up their w. with
child, 15 : 16. Ho. 13 : 16. Am. 1 : 13.
23 : 7. w. wove hangings for grove
2 Ch. 28 : 8. Israel carried captive w.
Ne. 13 : 26. outlandish w. cause to
Es. 1 : 9. Vashti made feast for w.
17. deed come abroad unto all w.
2 : 3. all fair virgins to house of w.,
unto Hege, keeper of w. [of w.
8. Esther brought to Hegai, keeper
9. unto best place of house of w.
11. Mordecai walked bef. w.'s hou.
12. aft. 12 months, acc to manner
of w., things for purifying w.
13. go with her out of house of w.
14. returned into sec. house of w.
15. what keeper of w. appointed
17. loved Esther above all the w.
3 : 13. to slay all chil. and w., 8 : 11.
Jb. 42 : 15. no w. fair as dau-s of Job
Ps. 45 : 9. King's daughters among
thy honourable w. [to w.
Pr. 31 : 3. Give not thy strength un-
Can. 1 : 8. O thou fairest among w.
5 : 9.-6 : 1. [over them
Is. 3 : 12. as for my people, w. rule
4 : 1. seven w. shall take hold of
19 : 16. Egypt shall be like unto w.
27 : 11. w. come, set them on fire
32 : 9. Rise up ye w. at ease [w.
10. years be troubled, ye careless
11. tremble, ye w. at ease [cakes
Je. 7 : 18. w. knead dough to make
9 : 17. call for the mourning w.;
send for the cunning w. [w.
20. hear word of the Lord, O ye
38 : 22. all w. left shall be brought
to king, and those w. shall say
41 : 16. Johanan took the w., 43 : 6.
44 : 15. all the w. that stood by
24. Jeremiah said to w., Hear
50 : 37. they shall become as w.
51 : 30. men of Bab-n became as w.
La 2 : 20. Shall w. eat chil. span long?
4 : 10. pitiful w. have sodden chil.
5 : 11. They ravished w. in Zion
Eze. 8 : 14 w. weeping for Tammuz
9 : 6. slay utterly maids, chil., w.
13 : 18. Woe to w. that sew pillows
16 : 34. contrary from other w. in
Eze. 16 : 38. w. that break wedlock
41. judgment in sight of many w.
23 : 2. two w. dau-s of one mother
10. she became famous among w.
44. went they in unto the lewd w.
45. manner of w. that shed blood
48. w. not to do aft. your lewdn-s
Da. 11 : 17. shall give him dau. of w.
37. Nei. sh. regard the desire of w.
Mi. 2 : 9. w. of my peo ye cast out
Na. 3 : 13. thy people are w. [wings
Zch. 5 : 9. two w., wind in their
8 : 4. old w. shall dwell in streets
14 : 2. houses rifled, w. be ravished
Mat. 11 : 11. Among them born of w.,
not greater than John, Lu. 7 : 28.
14 : 21. about 5,000 men, beside
w., children, 15 : 38. [Lu 17 : 35.
24 : 41. Two w. shall be grinding,
27 : 55. many w. were there beholding, Mk. 15 : 40. Lu. 23 : 27, 49.
28 : 5. angel said unto w., Fear not
Mk. 15 : 41. Many other w. fr. Jerus.
Lu. 1 : 28. blessed thou among w., 42.
8 : 2. certain w. which been healed
23 : 55. w. from Galilee followed
24 : 10. Mary and other w. told
22. certain w. made us astonished
24. found it even so as w. said
Ac. 1 : 14. continued in prayer wi. w.
13 : 50. Jews stirred up devout w.
16 : 13. speak unto w. wh. resorted
17 : 4. believed, of chief w. not a few
12. of honourable w. not a few
Ro. 1 : 26. w. did change natural use
1 Co. 14 : 34. Let w. keep silence in
35. a shame for w. to speak in ch.
Ph. 4 : 3. help those w. wh. laboured
1 Ti. 2 : 9. that w. adorn in modest
10. becometh w. profess-g godlin.
5 : 2. entreat older w. as mothers
14. I will that young w. marry
2 Ti. 3 : 6. which lead captive silly w.
Tit. 2 : 3. The aged w. that they be
as becometh holiness, † holy w.
4. teach younger w. to be sober
He. 11 : 35. w. received dead raised
1 Pe. 3 : 5. manner holy w. adorned
Re. 9 : 8. they had hair as hair of w.
14 : 4. These are they not defiled
See BONDWOMEN. [wi. w.
See **Men, women, and CHILDREN.**
Hebrew WOMEN.
Ex. 1 : 16. office of midwife to H. w.
19. H. w. are not as Egyptian w.
2 : 7. Shall I call a nurse of H. w.?
See **MEN with women.**
WOMEN servants. [Abr.
Ge. 20 : 14. Abimelech gave w.s. to
32 : 5. I have men servants, w.s.
22. Jacob took his two w.s. over
WOMEN singers.
Ec. 2 : 8. I gat me men s. and w.s.
See **SINGING women.**
Strange WOMEN. [w.
1 K. 11 : 1. Solomon loved many s.
Pr. 22 : 14. mouth of s.w. deep pit
23 : 33. Thine eyes sh. behold s.w.
WON. [tles
1 Ch. 26 : 27. of the spoils w. in bat-
Pr. 18 : 19. broth. is harder to be w.
1 Pe. 3 : 1. be w. by conversation of
WONDER. [Noun.]
De. 13 : 1. if prophet give sign or w.
2. And the sign or w. come to pass
28 : 46. upon thee for a sign and w.
2 Ch. 32 : 31. sent to inquire of w.
Ps. 71 : 7. I am as a w. unto many
Is. 20 : 3. walked barefoot for a w.
29 : 14. a marvellous work and a w.
Zch. 3 : † 8. for they are men of w.
Ac. 3 : 10. they were filled with w.
Re. 12 : 1. appeared a gr. w. in heav-
WONDERS. [en, 3.
Ex. 3 : 20. I will smite Egypt with all
my w., 7 : 3.-11 : 9.
Ex. 4 : 21. see thou do those w., 11 : 10.
15 : 11. fearful in praises, doing w.
Jos. 3 : 5. to morrow Lord will do w.
1 Ch. 16 : 12. Remember his w. and
judgm-s, Ps. 105 : 5. [Ps. 78 : 11.
Ne. 9 : 17. nei. mindful of thy w.,
Jb. 9 : 10. doeth great things; yea,
w. without number [of old
Ps. 77 : 11. I will remember thy w.
14. Thou art the God th. doest w.
78 : 43. How he wrought w. in Zoan
88 : 10. Wilt thou shew w. to dead?
12. Sh. thy w. be known in dark?
89 : 5. heavens shall praise thy w.
96 : 3. Declare his w. among people
106 : 7. fathers underst. not thy w.
107 : 24. These see his w. in deep
135 : 9. Who sent w. in midst Eg-t
136 : 4. who alone doeth great w.
Je. 32 : 21. Israel out of Eg-t with w.
Da. 4 : 3. How mighty are his w.!
12 : 6. How long it be to end of w.?
Jo. 2 : 30. And I will shew w. in the
heavens, Ac. 2 : 19. [people
Ac. 6 : 8. Stephen did great w. amo.
15 : 12. w. God wro-t am. Gentiles
Re. 13 : 13. doeth great w. in sight
See **SIGNS and wonders.**
WONDER. [Verb.] [er
Is. 13 : † 8. they sh. w. one at anoth-
29 : 9. Stay yourselves and w.; cry
Je. 4 : 9. priests and prophets sh. w.
Ha. 1 : 5. regard and w. marvellously
Ac. 13 : 41. ye despisers w., perish
Re. 17 : 8. they on the earth sh. w.
WONDERED.
Is. 59 : 16. he w. was no intercessor
63 : 5. I w. there was none to uph.
Zch. 3 : 8. for they are men w. at
Mat. 15 : 31. multitude w. when
saw the dumb speak, Lu. 11 : 14.
Mk. 6 : 51. were sore amazed and w.
Lu. 2 : 18. all they that heard it, w.
4 : 22. all w. at the gracious words
8 : 25. they being afraid w.; for he
9 : 43. while they w., Jesus said
24 : 41. believed not for joy, and w.
Ac. 7 : 31. When Moses saw it he w.
8 : 13. Simon w., behold-g miracles
Re. 13 : 3. all the world w. aft. beast
17 : 6. saw her, I w. with admirat-n
WONDERFUL. [w.
De. 28 : 59. L. will make thy plagues,
Ju. 13 : † 18. Why askest my name,
seeing it is w. [was w.
2 S. 1 : 26. brother, thy love to me
2 Ch. 2 : 9. house I am to build, w.
Jb. 42 : 3. uttered things too w. for
Ps. 119 : 129. Thy testimonies w. [me
131 : † 1. nei. in things too w. for me
139 : 6. Such knowl. too w. for me
Pr. 30 : 18. three things too w. for me
Is. 9 : 6. his name shall be called W.
25 : 1. O Lord, hast done w. things
28 : 29. fr. Lord who is w. in counsel
Je. 5 : 30. A w. thing and horrible
Da. 8 : † 13. another saint said unto
the w. numberer [w. things
Mat. 21 : 15. when scribes saw the
See **Wonderful WORKS.**
WONDERFULLY.
1 S. 6 : 6. when he had wrought w.
Ps. 139 : 14. I am fearfully, w. made
La. 1 : 9. Jerusalem came down w.
Da. 8 : 24. he shall destroy w. and
WONDERING. [peace
Ge. 24 : 21. man w. at her, held his
Lu. 24 : 12. Peter w. at that which
Ac 3 : 11. the people ran, greatly w.
WONDROUS things. [10.
Ps. 72 : 18. God, who doeth w.t., 86 :
119 : 18. behold w.t. out of thy law
145 : † 5. I will speak of thy w.t. to
See **Wondrous WORKS.**
WONDROUSLY. [oah
Ju. 13 : 19. the angel did w.; Man-
Jo. 2 : 26. L. hath dealt w. with you

WONT. [with horns
Ex. 21 : 29. if ox were w. to push
Nu. 22 : 30. was I w. to do so unto
1 S. 30 : 31. Dav. and men w. to haunt
2 S. 20 : 18. w. to speak in old time
Da. 3 : 19. seven times more than w.
Mat. 27 : 15. governor w. to release
Mk. 10 : 1. as he was w. he taught
Lu. 22 : 39. went as he was w. to m-t
Ac. 16 : 13. where prayer was w. to

WOOD. [be made
Ge. 6 : 14. Make an ark of gopher w.
22 : 3. Abr. clave w. for burnt off-g
6. Abr. took w., laid it upon Isaac
7. said, Behold the fire and w. [w.
9. Abr. laid w. in order, son upon
Ex. 35 : 33. works in carving of w.
Le. 1 : 7. lay w. in order upon fire
8. lay head and feet upon w., 12.
17. priest sh. burn it upon w., 3 : 5.
4 : 12. [every morning
6 : 12. priest shall burn w. upon it
11 : 32 unclean ; whe. vessel of w.
15 : 12. ev. vessel of w. sh. be rinsed
Nu. 13 : 20. whe. be w. therein or not
31 : 20. purify all things made of w.
35 : 18. if smite with weapon of w.
De. 10 : 1. into m-t, make ark of w.
19 : 5. when a man goeth into the
w. to hew w. [country
Jos. 17 : 15. get thee up to the w.
18. mountain is a w., cut it down
Ju. 6 : 26. offer the w. of the grove
1 S. 6 : 14. they clave w. of the cart [26.
14 : 25. came to a w.; was honey,
23 : 15. David in wilderness in a w.
16. Jonathan went to Da. into w.
18. David abode in the w. [w.
19. Doth not David hide in the
2 S. 6 : 5. instrum-ts made of fir w.
18 : 6. battle was in w. of Ephr.
8. w. devoured more than sword
17. cast Absalom into pit in w.
24 : 22. instruments of oxen for w.
1 K. 6 : 15. cov-d walls inside with w.
18 : 23. lay bullock on w., no fire
33. he put the w. in order, laid
bullock on w., and said, pour
water on the w. [and w.
38. fire of Lord consumed sacrifice
2 K. 2 : 24. two she bears out of the w.
6 : 4. came to Jordan they cut w.
1 Ch. 16 : 33. sh. trees of the w. sing
21 : 23. threshing instrum-s for w.
29 : 2. prepared w. for things of w.
2 Ch. 2 : 16. cut w. out of Lebanon
Ne. 8 : 4. Ezra stood upon pulpit of w.
Jb. 41 : 27. He esteemeth brass as
rotten w. [waste it
Ps. 80 : 13. boar out of the w. doth
83 : 14. As the fire burneth a w.
96 : 12. shall all trees of w. rejoice
132 : 6. we found it in fields of w.
141 : 7. as when one cleaveth w.
Pr. 26 : 20. Wh. no w. is, fire . . . out
21. As w. to fire, so content-s man
Ec. 2 : 6. made pools to water the w.
10 : 9. cleaveth w. be endangered
Can. 3 : 3. As apple tree am. trees of
3 : 9. Sol-n made chariot of w. [w.
Is. 7 : 2. as trees of w. are moved
10 : 15. staff lift itself as if no w.
30 : 33. pile th-f is fire and much w.
45 : 20. that set up w. of image
60 : 17. for iron silver, for w. brass
Je. 5 : 14. my words fire, this peo. w.
7 : 18. chil gather w., fa-s kindle fire
28 : 13. Thou hast broken yokes of
La. 5 : 4. our w. is sold unto us [w.
13. children fell under the w.
Eze. 15 : 3. sh. w. be taken to do work?
24 : 10. Heap on w., consume flesh
39 : 10. take no w. out of the field
41 : 16. the galleries ceiled with w.
22. altar of w. 3 cubits high (2)
Mi. 7 : 14. flock which dwell solitarily in the w.
Ha. 2 : 19. Woe unto him saith to w.
Hag. 1 : 8. bring w., build house
Zch. 12 : 6. like hearth of fire am. w.
1 Co. 3 : 12. upon this foundation, w.
2 Ti. 2 : 20. in great house vessels of
gold, of w. [leth
Ja. 3 : † 5. great a w. little fire kind-
Re. 18 : 12. all thyine w., all manner of vessels of precious w.

Cedar WOOD.
Le. 14 : 4. two birds, c. w., scarlet,
hyssop, 6, 49, 51, 52.–19 : 6.
1 Ch. 22 : 4. bro-t much c. w. to Da.

Hewer, s of WOOD.
De. 29 : 11. fr. h. o. w. unto drawer
Jos. 9 : 21. let them be h-s o. w.
and drawers of water, 23.
27. Joshua made them h-s o. w.
Je. 46 : 22. ag-t Egypt as h-s o. w.

See **Wood OFFERING.**

See **SHITTIM wood.**

WOOD with stone. [s.
Ex. 7 : 19. blood in vessels of w. and
De. 4 : 28. serve gods, the work of
men's hands, w. and s., 28 :
36, 64.–29 : 17. 2 K. 19 : 18. Is.
37 : 19. Eze. 20 : 32. [and s., 23.
Da. 5 : 4. praised gods of gold, w.
Re. 9 : 20. not worship idols of s. and

WOODS. [w.
Eze. 34 : 25. they sh. safely sleep in w.

WOOF.
See **WARP or woof.**

WOOL. [floor
Ju. 6 : 37. I will put fleece of w. in
2 K. 3 : 4. rendered 100,000 rams wi.
Ps. 147 : 16. giveth snow like w. [w.
Pr. 31 : 13. She seeketh w. and flax
Is. 1 : 18. sins like crimson be as w.
51 : 8. worm shall eat them like w.
Eze. 27 : 18. was thy merchant in w.
34 : 3. ye clothe you with the w.
44 : 17. no w. shall come upon th.
Da. 7 : 9. the hair of his head like
the pure w., Re. 1 : 14. [w.
Ho. 2 : 5. my lovers that give me my
9. I will recover my w., my flax
He. 9 : 19. water and scarlet w. and

WOOLLEN.
See
LINEN. [Adj.] LINEN. [Noun.]

WORD. [Mat. 2 : 8.
Ge. 37 : 14. Go and bring me w.,
44 : 2. did acc. to w. Joseph spoken
18. O my lord, let thy servant
speak a w., 2 S. 14 : 12. [31.
Ex. 8 : 13. Lord did acc. to w. of M.,
12 : 35. Isr. did acc. to w. of Moses
32 : 28. Levi did acc. to w., Le. 10 : 7.
Nu. 13 : 26. they brought back w.
22 : 8. I will bring you w., De. 1 : 22.
20. w. I shall say unto thee, do
35. w. I sh. speak, thou sh. speak
De. 1 : 25. brought us w. again, 22.
4 : 2. Ye shall not add unto the w.
9 : 5. w. Lord sware unto fathers
15 : † 9. Beware there be not a w.
18 : 20. presume to speak a w. in
21. How shall we know the w.?
21 : 5. by their w. ev. controversy
Jos. 1 : 13. Remember the w. Moses
6 : 10. nei. any w. out of your mou.
8 : 35. not a w. wh. Josh. read not
14 : 7. espy ; I bro-t him w. again
22 : 32. princes bro-t them w. again
1 S. 3 : † 17. G. do so to thee if thou
hide any w. [Israel
4 : 1. And w. of Samuel came to all
17 : † 30. he spake after the same w.
2 S. 3 : 11. not ans-r Abner a w. again
7 : 7. spake I a w. with any of
tribes, 1 Ch. 17 : 6. [thy serv-t
25. w. thou hast spoken conc-g
13 : † 35. acc. to w. of thy servant
14 : 17. w. of my lord be comfort-e
15 : 28. until w. from you to certify
19 : 10. why not a w. of bringing k.
2 S. 24 : 4. the king's w. prevailed
against Joab, 1 Ch. 21 : 4.
1 K. 2 : 30. brought king w. again.
20 : 9. 2 K. 22 : 9, 20. 2 Ch. 34 :
42. w. I have heard is good [16, 28.
8 : 56. not failed one w. of all his
10 : † 6. It was a true w. I heard
of thy acts, 2 Ch. 9 : † 5 | 21 : 4.
18 : 21. people answered not a w.,
2 K. 18 : 36. Is. 36 : 21. [good
† 24. people answered, The w. is
20 : † 12. when Ben-hadad heard w.
2 K. 6 : 18. smote acc. to w. of Elisha
18 : 28. Hear w. of the great king
1 Ch. 16 : 15. w. he commanded to
thous-d generations, Ps. 105 : 8.
21 : 12. advise what w. I shall bring
Ne. 1 : 8. Remember w. thou com.
Es. 1 : 21. king did acc-g to w. of M.
Jb. 2 : 13. none spake a w. unto Job
4 : † 2. If a w. wilt thou be grieved?
Ps. 17 : 4. by w. of thy lips kept me
68 : 11. The Lord gave the w. [serv.
119 : 49. Remember w. unto thy
123. Mine eyes fail for the w. of
139 : 4. not a w. in my tongue, but
Pr. 12 : 25. good w. maketh it glad
13 : 13. Whoso despiseth the w.
14 : 15. simple believeth every w.
15 : 23. w. in due season how good
18 : † 13. He that returneth a w.
25 : 11. A w. fitly spoken is like
Ec. 5 : † 2. not hasty to utter w.
8 : 4. Where w. of a king is power
Is. 2 : 1. w. Isaiah saw conc. Judah
5 : 24. despised w. of Holy One
8 : 10. speak w., it shall not stand
9 : 8. Lord sent a w. unto Jacob
29 : 21. man an offender for a w.
30 : 21. shall hear a w. behind thee
41 : 28. no counsellor answer a w.
44 : 26. confirmeth w. of his serv-t
50 : 4. how to speak a w. in season
Je. 5 : 13. wind, the w. is not in th.
10 : 1. Hear ye w. Lord speaketh
18 : 18. not perish w. from prophet
23 : 36. ev. man's w. be his burden
26 : 2. speak, diminish not a w.
28 : 9. when w. of prophet sh. come
34 : 5. I have pronounced the w.
37 : 17. Is there any w. from the L.
44 : 16. As for the w. spok. unto us
46 : 13. The w. Lord spake to Jere.
50 : 1. The w. L. spake ag-t Bab-n
51 : 59. w. Jer-h commanded Ser-h
Eze. 9 : † 11. man returned the w.
12 : 25. w. I shall speak shall come
28. w. I have spoken shall be done
13 : 6. that they would confirm w.
33 : 30. hear what is w. fr. the Lord
Da. 3 : † 22. bec. king's w. urgent
28. who have changed king's w.
4 : 17. demand is by w. of holy ones
9 : † 23. At thy supplicat-n w. came
Jon. 3 : 6. w. unto king of Nineveh
Hag. 2 : 5. Acc. to w. I covenanted
Mat. 2 : 13. be there until I bring w.
8 : 8. speak the w. only, my servant shall be healed, Lu. 7 : 7.
12 : 32. whosoever speaketh a w.
against Son of man, Lu. 12 : 10.
36. every idle w. men gi. account
13 : 19. When any one heareth the
w. of the kingdom, 20, 22, 23.
Mk. 4 : 16, 18, 19, 20. Lu. 8 : 15.
21. when persecution ariseth, because of the w., Mk. 4 : 17.
15 : 23. Jes. answered her not a w.
18 : 16. that every w. may be established, 2 Co 13 : 1. [him a w.
22 : 46. no man was able to answer
26 : 75. Pet. rememb-d w. of Jesus
27 : 14. Jesus answered to nev. a w.
28 : 8. run to bring his disciples w.
Mk. 2 : 2. preached the w. unto th.
4 : 14. The sower soweth the w.
15. by way side where w. is sown

Mk 2 : 33. with parables spake he w.
14 : 72. Peter called to mind the w.
16 : 20. confirming the w. wi. signs
Lu. 1 : 2. were ministers of the w.
4 : 36. all saying, What a w. is this
8 : 12. taketh w. out of their hearts
13. hear, receive the w. with joy
24 : 19. Jes., a prophet mighty in w.
Jn. 1 : 1. In the beginning was the W., and the W. was with God, and the W. was God [dwelt
14. the W. was made flesh, and
2 : 22. they believed w. Jesus said
4 : 50. man believed the w. Jesus
12 : 48. w. I have spoken sh. judge
14 : 24. the w. ye hear is not mine
15 : 3. ye are clean through the w.
20. Remember the w. that I said
25. that the w. might be fulfilled
17 : 20. believe on me thro. their w.
Ac. 6 : 4. will give ourselves to the ministry of the w. [15 : 35.
8 : 4. ev. where preaching the w.,
10 : 36. w. wh. God sent unto Isr.
37. that w. I say ye know wh. was
11 : 19. preach-g w. to none but Jews
13 : 15. if any w. of exhortation
26. to you is w. of this salvation
14 : 3. gave testimony unto the w.
25. when had preached w. in Per.
15 : †27. Silas, who sh. tell you by w.
16 : 6. forbidden to preach w. in A.
17 : 11. received w. with readiness
20 : 32. you to the w. of his grace
28 : 25. aft. Paul had spoken one w.
Ro. 10 : 8. w. of faith wh. we preach
15 : 18. make Gentiles obed-t by w.
1 Co. 4 : 20. kingd. of G. is not in w.
12 : 8. w. of wisdom, to another w. of knowledge [yea and nay
2 Co. 1 : 18. our w. toward you, not
5 : 19. unto us w. of reconciliation
10 : 11. such as we are in w. by let.
Ga. 5 : 14. law is fulfilled in one w.
6 : 6. Let him that is taught in w.
Ep. 5 : 26. washing of water by w.
Ph. 1 : 14. are bold to speak the w.
2 : 16. Holding forth the w. of life
Col. 1 : 5. heard in w. of truth of gosp.
3 : 16. Let w. of Ch. dwell in you
17. whatsoev. ye do in w. or deed
1 Th. 1 : 5. our gospel not in w. only
6. received w. in much affliction
2 : 13. received it not as w. of men
2 Th. 2 : 2. be troubled neither by spirit nor by w. [or epistle
15. been taught, whether by w.
17. G. stablish you in ev. good w.
3 : 14. if any man obey not our w.
1 Ti. 4 : 12. be thou an example in w.
5 : 17. labour in the w. and doctrine
2 Ti. 2 : 17. their w. eat as canker
4 : 2. Preach the w.; be instant in
Tit. 1 : 9. Holding fast the faithf. w.
He. 1 : 3. upholding by w. of his
2 : 2. if w. by angels was steadfast
4 : 2. w. preached did not profit
5 : 13. useth milk is unskilful in w.
6 : †1. leaving w. of begin-g of Ch.
7 : 28. w. of the oath, which was
12 : 19. intreated w. not be spoken
13 : 22. suffer the w. of exhortat-n
Ja. 1 : 21. receive the engrafted w.
22. be ye doers of the w., and not
23. if any be a hearer of the w.
3 : 2. If any man offend not in w.
1 Pe. 2 : 2. desire sincere milk of w.
8. them which stumble at the w.
3 : 1. if any obey not the w., may without the w. be won [proph.
2 Pe. 1 : 19. We a more sure w. of
3 : 7. heavens by same w. are kept
1 Jn. 1 : 1. handled of the w. of life
3 : 18. let us not love in w. [one
5 : 7. Father, W., and Holy Ghost
Re. 3 : 10. kept w. of my patience [ny
12 : 11 overcame by w. of testimo-

WORD of God.

1 S. 9 : 27. stand still that I may shew thee the w. - [at w. -
2 S. 16 : † 23. as if a man inquired
1 K. 12 : 22. w. - came unto Shem-h
1 Ch. 17 : 3. w. - came to Nathan
Pr. 30 : 5. Every w. - is pure; he is
Is. 40 : 8. w. - shall stand for ever
Mk. 7 : 13. Making w. - of none eff.
Lu. 3 : 2. w. - came unto John in
4 : 4. not by bread alone, but w. -
5 : 1. people pressed to hear w. -
8 : 11. parable, The seed is the w. -
21. my breth. these th. hear w. -
11 : 28. blessed they that hear w. -
Jn. 10 : 35. If gods, unto whom w. -
Ac. 4 : 31. spake w. - with boldness
6 : 2. not reason that we leave w. -
7. w. - increased in Jerusalem
8 : 14. Samaria had received w. -
11 : 1. Gentiles had received w. -
13 : 5. preached w. - in synagogues
7. Sergius desired to hear w. -
44. came whole city to hear w. -
46. w. - sho. first have been spok.
17 : 13. w. - was preached at Berea
18 : 11. Paul teaching w. - among
19 : 20. mightily grew w. -, 12 : 24.
Ro. 9 : 6. Not as tho. w. - taken none
10 : 17. hearing by the w. - [effect
1 Co. 14 : 36. came w. - out fr. you?
2 Co. 2 : 17. as many wh. corrupt w. -
4 : 2. not handling w. - deceitfully
Ep. 6 : 17. sword of Spirit, wh. is w. -
Col. 1 : 25. is given me to fulfil w. -
1 Th. 2 : 13. when ye received w. -
1 Ti. 4 : 5. it is sanctified by w. - and
2 Ti. 2 : 9. but the w. - is not bound
Tit. 2 : 5. th. w. - be not blasphemed
He. 4 : 12. w. - is quick, powerful
6 : 5. who have tasted the good w. -
11 : 3. worlds were framed by w. -
13 : 7. have spoken unto you w. -
1 Pe. 1 : 23. Being born again by w. -
2 Pe. 3 : 5. by w. - the heavens were
1 Jn. 2 : 14. the w. - abideth in you
Re. 1 : 2. Who bare record of w. -
9. I was in isle Patmos for w. -
6 : 9. souls of them slain for w. -
19 : 13. his name is called The W. -
20 : 4. were beheaded for the w. -
See **HEARD** with word, s.

His WORD.

Nu. 27 : 21. at h. w. shall they go out, at h. w. they shall come in
30 : 2. If vow, shall not break h. w.
1 S. 1 : 23. only the Lord estab. h. w.
2 S. 17 : † 6. shall we do after h. w.?
2 S. 23 : 2. h. w. was in my tongue
1 K. 2 : 4. That Lord continue h. w.
8 : 20. Lord hath performed h. w., 2 Ch. 6 : 10. [of h. w.
2 K. 1 : 16. no God in Isr. to inquire
2 Ch. 10 : 15. that L perform h. w.
Ps. 56 : 4. In God I will praise h. w.,
103 : 20. hearkening unto h. w. [10.
105 : 19. Until the time h. w. came
28. they rebelled not ag-st h. w.
106 : 24. they believed not h. w.
107 : 20. He sent h. w., healed th.
130 : 5. I wait for L., in h. w. hope
147 : 15. h. w. runneth very swiftly
18. he sendeth out h. w., melteth
19. He sheweth h. w. unto Jacob
148 : 8. stormy wind fulfilling h. w.
Is. 66 : 5. ye th. tremble at h. w. (2)
Je. 20 : 9. h. w. in mine heart as fire
23 : 18. who hath marked h. w.
La. 2 : 17. he hath fulfilled h. w. [w.
Jo. 2 : 11. strong that executeth h.
Mat. 8 : 16. cast out spirits wi. h. w.
Lu. 4 : 32. for h. w. was with power
Jn. 4 : 41. believed bec. of h. own w.
5 : 38. ye have not h. w. abiding in
Ac. 2 : 41. that gladly received h. w.
Tit. 1 : 3. in due times manifested h.
1 Jn. 1 : 10. liar, h. w. not in us [w.
1 Jn. 2 : 5. whoso. keepeth h. w., in [him

WORD, S that came to Jeremiah.

Je. 7 : 1. w. - by the Lord, 11 : 1.-18 : 1.-21 : 1.-27 : 1.-30 : 1.-32 : 1.-34 : 1, 8.-35 : 1.-36 : 1.-40 : 1.
14 : † 1. w. - s of the dearths [dah
25 : 1. w. - concerning peo. of Ju-
27 : 1. in reign of Jehoiakim this w. - from the Lord, 26 : 1.-36 : 1.
44 : 1. w. - concerning Jews in E

WORD of the Lord came.

Ge. 15 : 1. w. - c. unto Abram, 4.
1 S. 15 : 10. Then c. w. - unto Sam-l
2 S. 7 : 4. w. - c. unto Nathan, 1 Ch.
24 : 11. w. - c. unto Gad [17 : 3.
1 K. 6 : 11. And w. - c. to Solomon
13 : 20. w. - c. unto the prophet
16 : 1. Then w. - c. to Jehu, 7.
17 : 2. w. - c. unto Elijah, 8.-18 : 1.-19 : 9.-21 : 17, 28. [be thy na.
18 : 31. unto Jacob w. - c., Isr. sh.
2 K. 20 : 4. w. - c. to Isaiah, Is. 38. 4.
1 Ch. 22 : 8. But the w. - c. to Dav.
2 Ch. 11 : 2. w. - c. to Shemaiah, the man of God, 12 : 7. 1 K. 12 : 22.
Je. 1 : 4. w. - c. unto me saying, 11, 13.-2 : 1.-13 : 3, 8.-16 : 1.-18 : 5.-24 : 4.-32 : 6. Eze. 6 : 1.-7 : 1.-11 : 14.-12 : 1, 8, 17, 21, 26.-13 : 1.-14 : 2, 12.-15 : 1.-16 : 1.-17 : 1, 11.-18 : 1.-20 : 2, 45.-21 : 8, 18.-22 : 1, 17, 23.-23 : 1.-24 : 1, 15, 20.-25 : 1.-26 : 1.-27 : 1.-28 : 1, 11, 20.-29 : 1, 17.-30 : 1, 20.-31 : 1.-32 : 1, 17.-33 : 1, 23.-34 : 1.-35 : 1.-36 : 16.-37 : 15.-38 : 1. Zch. 4 : 8.-6 : 9.-7 : 4.-8 : 1, 18.
2. To whom w. - c. in days of Jo.
14 : 1. w. - c. to Jeremiah, 28 : 12.-29 : 30.-32 : 26.-33 : 1, 19, 23.-34 : 12.-35 : 12.-36 : 27.-37 : 6.-39 : 15.-42 : 7.-43 : 8.-46 : 1.-47 : 1.-49 : 34. Da. 9 : 2. [16.
Eze. 1 : 3. w. - c. unto Ezekiel, 3 :
Ho. 1 : 1. w. - c. unto Hosea in days
Jo. 1 : 1. w. - c. to Joel, son of Peth.
Jon. 1 : 1. w. - c. unto Jonah, 3 : 1.
Mi. 1 : 1. w. - c. to Micah in days of
Zph. 1 : 1. w. - c. unto Zephaniah
Hag. 1 : 1. c. w. - by Haggai the prophet, 3.-2 : 1, 10, 20.
Zch. 1 : 1. In second year of Darius c. w. - unto Zachariah, 7.-7 : 1, 8.
See **Word of the LORD.**
See **MOUTH** with word, s.

My WORD.

Nu. 11 : 23. whe. m. w. sh. come to pass
20 : 24. bec. ye rebelled ag. m. w.
1 K. 6 : 12. will perform m. w. with
17 : 1. nor rain, but acc. to m. w.
Is. 55 : 11. so shall m. w. be that goeth
66 : 2. him that tremb-h at m. w.
Je. 1 : 12. I will hasten m. w.
23 : 28. he that hath m. w. let him speak m. w. [saith Lord
29. Is not m. w. like as a fire,
29 : 10. perform m. good w. tow.
Eze. 48 : † 11. priests wh. kept m. w.
Jn. 5 : 24. He that heareth m. w.
8 : 31. If continue in m. w. are ye
37. kill me bec. m. w. no place in
43. bec. ye can-t hear m. w. [you
Re. 3 : 8. hast kept m. w. not denied

This WORD. [tell thee

Ex 14 : 12. is not t. the w. we did
Jos. 14 : 10. L. spake t. w. unto Mos.
1 S. 9 : † 21. wh. speakest acc. to t.
2 S. 19 : 14. sent t. w. unto king [w.
1 K. 2 : 23 spoken t. w. ag. his life
Ezr. 6 : 11. whosoever sh. alter t. w.
10 : 5. swear they sh. do acc. to t.
Is. 8 : 20 if speak not acc. to t. w. [w.
24 : 3. the Lord hath spoken t. w.
30 : 12. Bec. ye despise t. w., trust

Je. 5 : 14. Bec. ye speak t.w., 23:38.
7 : 2. Stand in gate, proclaim t.w.
13 : 12. shalt speak unto them t.w.
14 : 17. shalt say t.w. unto them
22 : 1. L. said, go speak t.w. [5 : 1.
28 : 7. hear now t.w., Am. 3 : 1.-4 : 1.
Da. 10 : 11. had spoken t.w. unto me
Ac. 22 : 22. gave audience unto t.w.
He. 12 : 27. t.w. Yet once more

This is the WORD.

2 K. 19 : 21. - w. Lord hath spoken
conc. him, Is. 16 : 13.-37 : 22.
Je. 34 : 8. - w. unto Jeremiah fr. L.
38 : 21. - w. Lord hath shewed me
Zch. 4 : 6. - w. of L. unto Zerubb-l
Ro. 9 : 9. - w. of promise, Sarah sh.
1 Pe. 1 : 25. - w. which is preached

Thy WORD.

Ge. 30 : 34. I would it be acc. to t.w.
41 : 40. acc. unto t.w. peo. be ruled
Ex. 8 : 10. said, Be it acc-g to t.w.
Nu. 14 : 20. I pardoned acc. to t.w.
De. 33 : 9. they have observed t.w.
1 S. 9 : † 10. t.w. good, let us go
2 S. 7 : 21. For t.w.'s sake hast done
1 K. 8 : 26. let t. w., I pray thee, be
verified, 2 Ch. 6 : 17. [at t. w.
18 : 36. I have done all these things
22 : 13. let t. w. be like the w. of
one of them, 2 Ch. 18 : 12. [w.
Ps. 119 : 9. by taking heed acc. to t.
11. t.w. have hid in mine heart
16. I will not forget t.w. [101.
17. that I may live, and keep t.w.,
25. quicken acc. to t.w., 107, 154.
28. strengthen me acc unto t.w.
38. Stablish t.w. unto thy serv-t
41. unto me salvation acc to t.w.
42. answ. him ; for I trust in t.w.
50. affliction, t.w. quickened me
58. merciful unto me, acc. to t.w.
65. dealt with servant acc. to t.w.
67. astray, but now have kept t.w.
74. I have hoped in t. w., 147.
76 Let thy kindness be acc-g to t.
81. I hope in t.w., 114. [w.
82. Mine eyes fail for t.w. [tled
89. For ever, O Lord, t. w. is set-
101. that I might keep t. w.
105. t. w. is a lamp unto my feet
116. Uphold me acc-g unto t.w.
133. Order my steps in t.w., let
140. t.w. is very pure ; therefore
148. th. I might meditate in t.w.
158. grieved, they kept not t.w.
160. t.w. is true from beginning
161. heart standeth in awe of t.w.
162. I rejoice in t.w. as one [t.w.
169. give understanding acc-g to
170. deliver me according to t.w.
172. My tongue shall speak of t.w.
138 : 2. hast magnified t.w. above
Je. 15 : 16. t.w. was unto me the joy
Eze. 20 : 46. drop t.w. toward south
21 : 2. drop t.w. toward holy places
Am. 7 : 16. drop not t.w. ag. Isaac
Ha. 3 : 9. thy bow naked, even t.w.
Lu. 1 : 38. be it unto me acc. to t.w.
2 : 29. depart in peace, acc. to t.w.
5 : 5. at t.w. I will let down net
Jn. 17 : 6. thine, they have kept t.w.
14. I have given them t.w.
17. Sanctify them ; t.w. is truth
Ac. 4 : 29. with boldness speak t.w.

See **Word of TRUTH.**

WORDS. [one w.

Ge. 11 : † 1. whole earth of one lip,
44 : 24. we told him w. of my lord
49 : 21. Naphtali giveth goodly w.
Ex. 4 : † 10. I am not a man of w.
19 : 8. Moses returned w. of people
9. Moses told w. of peo. unto Lord
23 : 8. gift perverteth w. of righteous, De. 16 : 19. [De. 10 : 2.
34 : 1. w. that were in first tables,
† 28. He wrote upon tables ten w.
Nu. 22 : 7. spake unto him w. of B.
De. 2 : 26. unto Sihon with w. of p.
4 : 12. ye heard the w. but saw no
5 : 28. I have heard w. of this peo. (2)
10 : † 4. wrote on tables the ten w.
13 : 3. not hearken unto w. of that
28 : 14. not go aside fr. w. [dreamer
29 : 19. he heareth w. of this curse
31 : 30. Moses spake w. of th. song
Ju. 5 : † 29. returned her w. to hers.
11 : 28. king hearkened not unto w.
16 : 16. pressed him daily with w.
1 S. 2 : † 23. I hear evil w. of you [w.
17 : 23. Goliath spake acc-g to same
18 : 23. S.'s serv-ts spake those w.
24 : 9. Saul, Whf. hearest men's w.
25 : 9. to Nabal, acc. to all those w.
24. she said, hear the w. of thine
handmaid, 2 S. 20 : 17. [servant
26 : 19. Now let king hear w. of his
28 : 20. Saul afraid bec. of w. of S.
2 S. 3 : 8. Abner wroth for w. of Ish.
19 : 43. w. of men of Judah fiercer
22 : 1. David spake w. of this song
23 : 1. these be last w. of David
1 K. 10 : † 3. Sol. told her all her w.
7. believed not the w. until I came
12 : 7. If wilt speak good w. to this
people, 2 Ch. 10 : 7. [told to fa.
13 : 11. w. spoken unto king they
22 : 13. w. of the prophets declare
good unto king, 2 Ch. 18 : 12.
2 K. 6 : 12. Elisha telleth the w. thou
speakest in thy bedchamber
18 : 37. told Hezekiah the w. of
Rabshakeh, Is. 36 : 22. [Is. 37 : 17.
19 : 16. L., hear w. of Sennach-b,
22 : 13. inquire of Lord concerning
w. of this book (2), 2 Ch. 34 : 21.
23 : 24. might perform w. of law, 3.
1 Ch. 23 : 27. by last w. of David
Levites were numbered [of Sam-l
29 : † 29. acts of Dav. written in w.
2 Ch. 9 : † 29. acts of Solomon written in w. of Nathan [Shemaiah
12 : † 15. acts of Rehoboam in w. of
20 : † 34. acts of Jehoshaphat written in w. of Jehu [of David
29 : 30. to sing praise with the w.
32 : 8. peo. rested upon w. of Hez.
33 : 18. w. of the seers are written
35 : 22. hearkened not unto w. of
Ezr. 7 : 11. Ezra, scribe of w. of com.
Ne. 1 : 1. The w. of Nehemiah [me
2 : 18. I told them king's w. unto
8 : 12. bec. they understood w., 13.
Es. 4 : 9. Hatach told Esther w. of M.
12. They told Mord-i Esther's w.
9 : 30. sent letters with w. of peace
Jb. 4 : † 2. who can refrain from w.
6 : 10. not concealed w. of the Holy
25. How forcible are right w. [One
26. Do ye imagine to reprove w.
11 : 2. Sho. not mult. of w. be ans-d
12 : 11. Doth not ear try w.? 34 : 3.
15 : 13. lettest such w. out of mou.
16 : 4. I could heap up w. ag. you
18 : 2. How long will it be ere ye
make end of w.? [with w.?
19 : 2. How long will ye break me
23 : 5. I would know w. he would
31 : 40. The w. of Job are ended
32 : † 11. whilst ye searched out w.
† 18. For I am full of w. ; spirit
35 : † 4. I will return to thee w.
16. multiplieth w. without knowl.
36 : † 2. shew there are yet w. for G.
38 : 2. who darkeneth counsel by w.
Ps. 7. * David sang conc. w. of Cush
18. * David spake w. of this song
22 : 1. why so far fr. w. of my roar-g
52 : 4. lovest devour-g w., O tongue
59 : 12. for w. of lips let th. be taken
64 : 3. shoot their arrows, bitter w.
65 : † 3. w. of iniquities prevail ag.
105 : † 27. shewed w. of his signs
109 : 3. compassed me wi w. of hat
137 : † 3. required of us w. of song
Ps. 145 : † 5. speak of thy wondr-s w.
Pr. 1 : 2. to perceive w. of underst-g
6. To understand w. of the wise
2 : 16. flattereth with her w., 7 : 5.
10 : 19. In multitude of w. sin
12 : 6. w. of wicked to lie in wait
15 : 1. grievous w. stir up anger
26. w. of the pure are pleasant w.
16 : 24. Pleasant w. as honeycomb
18 : 8. The w. of a talebearer are
as wounds, 26 : 22. [with w.
19 : 7. the poor, he pursueth them
27. to err from w. of knowledge
22 : 12. overthroweth w. of transgr-r
17. hear the w. of the wise [edge
23 : 12. thine ears to w. of knowl-
29 : 19. servant not corrected by w.
30 : 1. The w. of Agur, son of Jakeh
31 : 1. The w. of king Lemuel, the
Ec. 1 : 1. The w. of the Preacher
5 : 3. fool's voice known by multitude of w., 10 : 14. [vanities
7. in many w. there are divers
12 : 10. The Preacher sought acceptable w., even the w. of tru.
11. w. of the wise are as goads
Is. 29 : 11. as the w. of a book sealed
18. shall deaf hear w. of the book
36 : 13. Hear ye w. of great king
Je. 1 : 1. The w. of Jeremiah, son of
12 : 6. though they speak fair w.
19 : 2. proclaim there w. I shall tell
23 : 9. because of w. of his holiness
16. Hearken not unto w. of the
prophets, 27 : 14, 16. [servants
26 : 5. To hearken to w. of my
35 : 14. w. of Jonadab performed
36 : 10. read Baruch w. of Jere., 27.
28. write in it all the former w.
32. added unto them many like w.
38 : 4. in speaking such w. unto th.
44 : 28. know whose w. shall stand
51 : 64. Thus far the w. of Jere-h
Eze. 3 : 6. w. canst not understand
Da. 5 : 10. by reason of w. of king
7 : † 1. Daniel told sum of the w.
11. great w. which the horn spake
25. speak great w. ag. Most High
10 : 11. understand the w. I speak
15. had spoken such w. unto me
12 : 4. O Daniel, shut up the w.
9. Go, Daniel, for the w. are closed
Ho. 10 : 4. spoken w. swearing falsely
14 : 2. Take with you w., turn to L.
Am. 1 : 1. The w. of Amos, who was
Hag. 1 : 12. peo. obeyed w. of Hag.
Zch. 1 : 13. ans-d with comfortable w.
7 : 7. Should ye not hear w. the Lord
12. lest they should hear the w.
Mat. 26 : 44. prayed third time, saying same w., Mk. 14 : 39. [saias
Lu. 3 : 4. written in book of w. of E-
23 : 9. questioned wi. him in many w.
Jn. 6 : 63. w. I speak, they are life
68. thou hast w. of eternal life
14 : 10. w. I speak, not of myself
17 : 8. unto them w. thou gavest
Ac. 2 : 40. with many w. did testify
6 : 11. blasphemous w. ag. Moses.
13. blasphemous w. ag. holy place
7 : 22. Moses was mighty in w. and
10 : 22. Cornelius to hear w. of thee
11 : 14. Peter, who shall tell thee w.
15 : 15. to this agree w. of prophets
24. certain troubled you with w.
32. exhorted brethren with many
18 : 15. if it be a question of w. [w.
20 : 35. to remember w. of L. Jesus
38. Sorrowing for the w. he spake
24 : 4. hear of thy clemency few w.
Ro. 16 : 18. by good w. deceive simple
1 Co. 1 : 17. not with wisdom of w.
2 : 4. not wi. enticing w. of man's, 13
14 : 19. I had rather speak five w.
Ep. 3 : 3. as I wrote afore in few w.
Col. 2 : 4. beguile with enticing w.
1 Th. 2 : 5. nei. used we flatter-g w.

1 Ti. 4 : 6. nourished in **w.** of faith
6 : 3. wholesome **w.**, oven **w.** of Jes.
4. doting about strifes of **w.** [w.
2 Ti. 1 : 13. Hold fast form of sound
2 : 14. not about **w.** to no profit
4 : 15. hath greatly withst-d our **w.**
He. 12 : 19. sound of trumpet, voice
13 : 22. have written in few **w.** [of w.
2 Pe. 2 : 3. with feigned **w.** make merchandise of you [ity, Jude 16.
18. speak great swelling **w.** of van-
3 : 2. be mindful of **w.** by prophets
3 Jn. 10. prating with malicious **w.**
Jude 17. remember ye **w.** of apostles
Re. 1 : 3. Blessed that hear **w.** of
22 : 18. every man that heareth **w.**
19. if any take from **w.** of the book

All the WORDS.

Ge. 45 : 27. told Jacob - **w.** of Jos-h
Ex 4 : 30. Aaron spake - **w.** L. had
De. 9 : 10. on tables, acc. to - **w.** L.
32 : 44. Moses spake - **w.** of song [spa.
46. Set hearts unto - **w.** I testify
1 S. 3 : † 18. Samuel told Eli - **w.**
2 K. 19 : 4. it may be the L. will hear - **w.** of Rabshakeh, and reprove the **w.**, Is. 37 : 4. [of book
22 : 16. bring upon this place - **w.**
Es. 9 : 26. Thf. for - **w.** of this letter
Ec. 7 : 21. take no heed unto - **w.**
Je. 26 : 2. speak - **w.** th. I command
20. according to - **w.** of Jeremiah
30 : 2. Write - **w.** I have spok., 36 : 2.
36 . 20. they told - **w.** in ears of k.
32. Baruch wrote - **w.** of b-k burn-
Ac. 5 : 20. speak - **w.** of this life [ed

All these WORDS.

Ex. 19 : 7. Moses laid bef. faces - **w.**
20 : 1. God spake - **w.**, De. 5 : 22.
24 : 8. covenant made cone-g - **w.**
Nu. 16 : 31. an end of speaking - **w.** De. 32 : 45. 1 S. 24 : 16. [com-d
De. 12 : 28. Observe and hear - **w.** I
Ju. 9 : 3. mother's breth. spake - **w.**
2 S. 7 : 17. According to - **w.** did Nathan speak, 1 Ch. 17 : 15.
Je. 7 : 27. Thf. speak - **w.** unto them
11 : 6. Proclaim - **w.** in cities of J.
16 : 10. when shalt shew people - **w.**
25 : 30. Prophesy against them - **w.**
26 : 15. Lord sent me to speak - **w.**
27 : 12. I spake to Zed-h acc. to - **w.**
34 : 6. Jer-h spake - **w.** unto Zed-h
36 : 16. We will tell king of - **w.**
18. He pronounced - **w.** unto me
38 : 27. Jer-h told them acc. to - **w.**
43 : 1. Je. made end of speak-g - **w.**
51 : 60. Jer-h wrote - **w.** ag. Bab.
61. When thou shalt read - **w.**

All WORDS of this law.

De. 17 : 19. may learn to keep **a. w.** -
27 : 3. sh. write upon stones **a. w.** -, 8.
26. Cursed, confirmeth not **a. w.** -
28 : 58. If wilt not observe **a. w.** - [12.
29 : 29. that we may do **a. w.** -, 31 :
31 : 24. end of writing **w.** - in book
32 : 46. command chil. to do **a. w.** -
Jos. 8 : 34. Joshua read **a. w. o.** the **l.**

WORDS of covenant. [-

Ex. 34 : 28. He wrote upon tables **w.**
De. 29 : 1. These are the **w.** - which
9. Keep therefore the **w.** - that ye
2 K. 23 : 2. Josiah read all the **w.** -, 2 Ch. 34 : 30. [Ch. 34 : 31
3. their heart, to perform **w.** -, 2
Je. 11 : 2. Hear ye **w.** -, do them, 6.
3. Cursed that obeyeth not **w.** -
8. I will bring upon them all **w.** -
34 : 18. wh. have not performed **w.** -

WORDS of God. [w. -, 16.

Nu. 24 : 4. He hath said, wh. heard
1 Ch. 25 : 5. king's seer in the **w.** -
Ezr. 9 : 4. that trembled at the **w.** -
Ps. 107 : 11. they rebelled ag. **w.** -
Je. 23 : 36. perverted **w. o.** living G.
Jn. 3 : 34. God sent, speaketh **w.** -
Re. 17 : 17. until **w.** - be fulfilled

God's WORDS. [G.'s w.

Jn. 8 : 47. He that is of God, heareth
See **HEARD** with **word, s.**

His WORDS. [for h. w.

Ge. 37 : 8. they hated him yet more
De. 4 : 36. heardest **h. w.** out of fire
1 S. 3 : 19. he let none of **h. w.** fall
1 K. 1 : † 7. **h. w.** were with Joab
2 Ch. 34 : 27. heardest **h. w.** ag. this
36 : 16. they despised **h. w.** [place
Jb. 22 : 22. lay up **h. w.** in thine h-t
32 : 12. was none that answ-d **h. w.**
14. hath not directed **h. w.** ag. me
34 : 35. **h. w.** were without wisdom
37. he multiplieth **h. w.** ag. God
Ps. 55 : 21. **h. w.** softer than oil, yet
106 : 12. Then believed they **h. w.**
Pr. 17 : 27. He that hath knowledge spareth **h. w.** [h. w.?
29 : 20. Seest thou a man hasty in
30 : 6. Add thou not unto **h. w.**
Is. 31 : 2. L will not call back **h. w.**
Je. 18 : 18. let us not give heed to **h.**
Da. 9 : 12. hath confirmed **h. w.** [w.
10 : 6. **h. w.** like voice of multitude
9. heard **h. w.**, was in deep sleep
Am. 7 : 10. land not able to bear **h.**
Mk. 10 : 24. astonished at **h. w.** [w.
12 : 13. send Pharisee to catch him in **h. w.**, Lu. 20 : 20. [of h. w.
Lu. 20 : 26. they could not take hold
24 : 8. And they remembered **h. w.**

WORDS of the Lord.

Ex. 4 : 28. Moses told Aaron all **w.** -
24 : 3. Moses told the people all the **w.** -, Nu. 11 : 24. [rose
4. Moses wrote all the **w.** - and
Jos. 3 : 9. Come, hear the **w.** - y-r G.
24 : 27. this stone hath heard **w.** -
1 S. 8 : 10. Samuel told **w.** - unto peo- [ple
Ps. 12 : 6. **w.** - are pure words
Je. 36 : 4. Baruch wrote all **w.** -
43 : 1. Jeremiah made end of speaking **w.** -, even all these words
Am. 8 : 11. a famine of hearing **w.** -
Ac. 20 : 35. ought to remember **w.** -
See **Words of the LORD.**

Lying WORDS.

Is. 32 : 7. to destroy poor with **l. w.**
Je. 7 : 4. Trust ye not in **l. w.**, say-g
8. Behold ye trust in **l. w.** that
29 : 23. spoken **l. w.** in my name
Da. 2 : 9. ye have prepared **l. w.**

My WORDS. [2.

Nu. 12 : 6. Hear now **m. w.**, Jb. 34:
De. 4 : 10. will make them hear **m. w.**
11 : 18. lay up **m. w.** in your heart
18 : 19. not hearken unto **m. w.**
1 K. 8 : 59. let **m. w.** be nigh unto G.
Jb. 6 : 3. **m. w.** are swallowed up
9 : 14. choose out **m. w.** to reason
19 : 23. Oh! that **m. w.** were writ.
29 : 22. After **m. w.** they spake not
33 : 1. Wherefore, Job, hearken to all **m. w.**, 34 : 16. [my heart
3. **m. w.** sh. be of uprightness of
34 : 2. Hear **m. w.**, O ye wise men
16. hearken to the voice of **m. w.**
36 : 4. truly **m. w.** sh. not be false
Ps. 5 : 1. Give ear to **m. w.**, O Lord
50 : 17. castest **m. w.** behind thee
56 : 5. Every day they wrest **m. w.**
141 : 6. hear **m. w.**, they are sweet
Pr. 1 : 23. I will make known **m. w.**
2 : 1. My son, if wilt receive **m. w.**
4 : 4. Let thine heart retain **m. w.**
20. My son, attend to **m. w.**
7 : 1. My son, keep **m. w.**, lay up
Je. 6 : 19. not hearkened unto **m. w.**
11 : 10. refused to hear **m. w.**, 13 : 10.
18 : 2. I will cause thee to hear **m. w.**
19 : 15. they might not hear **m. w.**
23 : 22. if caused peo. to hear **m. w.**
30. ag-t prophets that steal **m. w.**
25 : 8. bec. ye have not heard **m. w.**
13. will bring upon land all **m. w.**
29 : 19. hearkened not to **m. w.**
Je. 35 : 13. ye not hearken to **m. w.**?
39 : 16. I will bring **m. w.** upon city
44 : 29. **m. w.** shall surely stand
Eze. 2 : 7. thou shalt speak **m. w.** unto them, 3 : 4. [in heart
3 : 10. Son of man, all **m. w.** receive
12 : 28. none of **m. w.** be prolonged
Mi. 2 : 7. **m. w.** do good to him
Zch. 1 : 6. **m. w.**, did they not take
Mat. 24 : 35. **m. w.** shall not pass away, Mk. 13 : 31. Lu. 21 : 33.
Mk. 8 : 38. whoso. shall be ashamed of me and **m. w.**, Lu. 9 : 26.
Lu. 1 : 20 bec. believest not **m. w**
Jn. 5 : 47. how shall ye believe **m.**
12 : 47. If any man hear **m. w.** [w.
48. He that receiveth not **m. w.**
14 : 23. If love me will keep **m. w.**
15 : 7. If **m. w.** abide in you
Ac. 2 : 14. Ye men, hearken to **m. w.**

Soft or **Softer WORDS.**

Jb. 41 : 3. will he speak **s. w.** unto
Ps. 55 : 21. his **w. s-r** than oil [thee?
See SPAKE, SPEAK, ING, SPOKEN.

Their WORDS.

Ge. 34 : 18. **t. w.** pleased Hamor
2 Ch. 9 : 6. I believed not **t. w.** until
Ps. 19 : 4. their line, **t. w.** to the end of the world, Ro. 10 : 18. [of t. w.
Eze. 2 : 6. son of man, nei. be afraid
Lu. 24 : 11. **t. w.** seemed as idle tales

These WORDS.

Ge. 27 : 42. **t. w.** of Esau were told
39 : 17. spake unto him acc. to **t. w.**
43 : 7. we told him acc-g to **t. w.**
44 : 6. steward spake **t.** same **w.**
7. Wherefore saith my lord **t. w.**?
Ex. 19 : 6. **t.** the **w.** thou shalt speak
34 : 27. write **t. w.**; after tenor of **t. w.** a covenant [manded
35 : 1. **t.** are the **w.** Lord hath com.
De. 1 : 1. **t.** be the **w.** Moses spake
5 : 22. **t. w.** L. spake unto assembly
6 : 6. **t. w.** shall be in thine heart
31 : 1. Moses spake **t. w.** unto Isr.
28. elders, that I may speak **t. w.**
Jos. 24 : 26. Josh. wrote **t. w.** in book
Ju. 2 : 4. when angel spake **t. w.**
1 S. 18 : † 24. Acc. to **t. w.** spake Da.
26. servants told David **t. w.**, it
21 : 12. David laid up **t. w.** [pleased
24 : 7. Da. stayed servants with **t. w.**
2 K. 1 : 7. what man told you **t. w.**
18 : 27. Hath my master sent me to speak **t. w.**? Is. 36 : 12. [t. w.
23 : 16. man of God who proclaimed
Ne. 6 : 6. thou be king acc. to **t. w.**
7. be reported to king acc. to **t. w.**
Jb. 42 : 7. L. had spoken **t. w.** unto
Je. 3 : 12. proclaim **t. w.** tow. north
22 : 5. if ye will not hear **t. w.** [w.
26 : 7. heard Jeremiah speaking **t.**
29 : 1. **t.** are **w.** of letter Jeremiah
30 : 4. **t.** are **w.** L spake conc. Isr.
38 : 24. Let no man know of **t. w.**
45 : 1. had written **t. w.** in a book
Da. 6 : 14. k. heard **t. w.**, was disple.
Zch. 8 : 9. be strong that hear **t. w.**
Lu. 24 : 44. **t.** are **w.** I spake unto
Ju. 7 : 9. had said **t. w.** he abode [you
8 : 20. **t. w.** spake Jesus in treasury
30. As he spake **t. w.** many believ-
9 : 22. **t. w.** spake his parents [ed
40. heard **t. w.** said, Are we blind
10 : 21. **t.** not **w.** of him hath devil
17 : 1. **t. w.** spake Jes., lifted eyes
18 : 1. spoken **t. w.** went over Ced.
Ac. 2 : 22. men of Israel, hear **t. w.**
5 : 5 Ananias hearing **t. w.** fell do.
10 : 44. Peter spake **t. w.**, Holy Gh.
13 : 42. besought **t. w.** be preached
16 : 38. serjeants told **t. w.** unto
28 : 29. said **t. w.**, Jews departed
1 Th. 4 : 18. comfort one ano. wi. **t. w.**
Re. 21 : 5. **t. w.** are true and faithf.

Thine or **Thy WORDS.**

De 33 : 3. every one receive of **t. w.**

Jos. 1 : 18. not hearken unto t.w.
Ju. 11 : 10. if we do not acc. to t.w.
13 : 12. Now let t.w. come to pass
1 S. 15 : 24. I have transgressed t.w.
28 : 21. I have hearkened unto t.w.
2 S. 7 : 28. art God, t.w. be true
1 K. 1 : 14. I will come in, confirm t.
8 : 12. I have done acc. to t.w.⌊w.
Ne. 9 : 8. thou hast performed t.w.
Jb. 4 : 4. t.w. have upholden him
33 : 5. set t.w. in order before me
Ps. 119 : 57. I said I would keep t.w.
103. How sweet t.w. unto my taste
130. entrance of t.w. giveth light
139. mine enemies forgotten t.w.
145 : † 5. speak of t. wondrous w.
Pr. 23 : 8. shalt thou lose t. sweet w.
9. he will despise wisdom of t.w.
Ec. 5 : 2. not rash, let t.w. be few
Is. 58 : 13. nor speaking t-e own w.
Je. 15 : 16. t.w. were found, I did
28 : 6. the Lord perform t.w. ⌈32.
Eze. 33 : 31. hear t.w., but not do,
Da. 10 : 12. Daniel, t.w. were heard,
and I am come for t.w.
Mat. 12 : 37. by t.w. shalt be Justified, and by t.w. condemned
See **Words of TRUTH.**

WORDS
with utter, ed, eth, ing.

Ju. 11 : 11. Jephthah u-d his w. before the Lord in Mizpeh
Ne. 6 : 19. they u-d my w. to him
Jb. 8 : 10. Shall not they u.w. out of
26 : 4. To whom hast thou u-d w.?
Pr. 1 : 21. in the city she u-h her w.
Is. 59 : 13. u-g from the heart w. of falsehood ⌈be understood
1 Co. 14 : 9. except ye u. w. easy to

Vain WORDS.

Ex. 5 : 9. let them not regard v.w.
2 K. 18 : 20. Thou sayest (but they are but v.w.), Is. 36 : 5.
Jb. 16 : 3. Shall v. w. have an end?
Ep. 5 : 6. Let no man deceive wi. v.w.

Your WORDS. ⌈proved

Ge. 42 : 16. in prison, that y.w. be
20. bring bro., so y.w. be verified
44 : 10. let it be acc-g unto y.w.
De. 1 : 34. L. heard voice of y.w., 5 : 28.
Jos. 2 : 21. she said, Acc. unto y.w.
Jb. 32 : 11. I waited for y.w., I gave
Is. 41 : 26. is none that heareth y.w.
Je. 42 : 4. I will pray acc. unto y.w.
Eze. 35 : 13. multiplied y.w. ag. me
Mal. 2 : 17. wearied the L. with y.w.
3 : 13. y.w. have been stout ag. me
Mat. 10 : 14. whoso-r not hear y.w.

WORK. [Noun.] ⌈w.

Ge. 5 : 29. shall comfort us cone-g
Ex. 5 : 9. more w. be laid upon men
12 : 16. no manner of w. shall be done in them, Le. 16 : 29.-23 : 3, 28, 31. Nu. 29 : 7. ⌈must do
18 : 20. shew them the w. th. they
24 : 10. G., under his feet paved w.
28 : 8. girdle acc-g to w. th-f, 39 : 5.
11. With w. of engraver in stone
31 : 15. Six days may w. be done; whoso. doeth w. in sabb. be put to death, 14.-35 : 2. Le. 23 : 3, 20.
35 : 21. brought offering to the w. of tabernacle, 24, 29.-36 : 3.
35. wisdom to w. all manner of w. (3), 36 : 1. ⌈w.
36 : 2. heart stirred him unto the
4. wrought all w. of sanct-y (2) 8.
5. more than enough for the w., 7.
6. nor woman make any more w.
37 : 29. acc-g to w. of apothecary
38 : 24. gold for w. in holy place (2)
39 : 32, w. of tabernacle finished
42. children of Israel made all w.
43. Moses did look upon all the w.
40 : 33 So Moses finished the w.
Le. 11 : 32. vessel wh-in w. is done
13 : † 48. in skin or any w. of sk., 51.
Le. 23 : 7. a holy convocation, ye sh. do no servile w., 8, 21, 25, 35, 36. Nu. 28 : 18, 25, 26.-29 : 1, 12, 35.
Nu. 4 : 3. 30 years old until 50 to do w. in taberu-e, 23, 30, 35, 39, 43.
8 : 4 w. of candlestick of gold (2)
31 : 20. purify all w. of goats' hair
De. 4 : 28. shall serve gods, the w. of men's hands, 27 : 15. 2 K. 19 : 18. 2 Ch. 32 : 19. Ps. 115 : 4.-135 : 15. Is. 37 : 19.
5 : 14. sabbath, in it shalt not do any w., 13 -16 : 8. Je. 17 : 22, 24.
14 : 29. that Lord may bless thee in all w., 24 : 19.-28 : 12.-30 : 9.
15 : 19. do no w. with the firstling
27 : 15.. w. of hands of craftsman
31 : 29. provoke him thro. w. of your hands, 1 K. 16 : 7. Je. 32 : 30.
33 : 11. Lord, accept w. of his hands
Ju. 16 : † 11. ropes wh-h w. not done
1 K. 5 : 16. 3,300 over people that wrought in the w. (2), 9 : 23.
7 : 8. another court of the like w.
17. nets of checker w., wreaths of chain w. for chapiters
19. chapiters of lily w. in porch
22. so was w. of pillars finished
28. w. of bases was on this man-
29. additions made of thin w.⌊ner
31. mouth round after w. of base
33. w. of wheels like w. of chariot
40. Hiram made an end of all the w. for house, 51. 2 Ch. 4 : 11 ⌈w.
11 : † 28. Sol. seeing young man did
2 K. 12 : 11. money into hands that did the w., 22 : 5 (2), 9. ⌈Ne. 10 : 33.
1 Ch. 6 : 49. w. of place most holy,
9 : 13. able men for w. of house of
19. over the w. of the service ⌊L.
33. employed in that w. day and
16 : 57. as every day's w. required
22 : 15. cunning men for every manner of w. ⌈Ezr. 3 : 8.
23 : 4. to set forward w. of house,
24. did the w. for the service of house of Lord, 28.-28 : 13, 20.
2 Ch. 24 : 12. Ne. 11 : 12. ⌈field
27 : 26. them that did the w. of the
29 : 1. the w. is great, Ne. 4 : 19.
5. gold, silver for all manner of w.
6. rulers of king's w. offered ⌈w.
2 Ch. 3 : 10. two cherubim of image
4 : 5. sea, brim like the w. of a cup
5 : 1. all w. for house of L. finished
8 : 16. all w. of Sol-n was prepared
24 : 13. w. was perfected by them
29 : 34. Levites helped till w. ended
31 : 21. in every w. that he began
34 : 12. men did the w. faithfully
13. overseers of all that wro-t w.
Ezr. 2 : 69. gave unto treasure of the w., Ne. 7 : 71. ⌈of God
4 : 24. Then ceased the w. of house
5 : 8. w. goeth fast on, prospereth
6 : 7. Let w. of house of God alone
22. strengthen their hands in w.
10 : 13. nei. is this a w. of one day
Ne. 2 : 16. neither had I told it to rest that did the w. ⌈to the w.
3 : 5. but nobles put not their necks
4 : 11. slay them, cause w. to cease
16. half wrought in the w., other
17. every one with one of his hands
21. So we laboured in w. ⌊in w.
5 : 16. I continued in the w., my servants were gathered unto w.
6 : 3. I am doing a great w. : why should w. cease whilst I leave
9. hands sh. be weakened from w.
16. perceived w. was wro-t of God
7 : 70. chief of fathers gave unto w.
13 : 10. singers that did w. were fled
Jb. 1 : 10. blessed w. of his hands
10 : 3. despise the w. of thine hands
14 : 15. desire to w. of thine hands
24 : 5. as asses go they to their w.
Jb. 34 : 11. w. of a man sh. he render
19. they are all w. of his hands
36 : 9. he sheweth them their w.
Ps. 8 : 3. When I consider the w. of
9 : 16. wicked is snared in w. of his
28 : 4. give them after w. of hands
44 : 1. we heard what w. thou didst
90 : 17. establish w. of our hands
95 : 9. When your fath-s saw my w.
101 : 3. I hate the w. of them that
102 : 25. heavens w. of thy hands
143 : 5. I muse on w. of thy hands
Pr. 11 : 18. worketh a deceitful w.
Ec. 2 : 17. the w. wrought under sun is grievous ⌈maketh, 8 : 17.
3 : 11. no man can find out w. God
17. is a time there for every w.
4 : 4. I considered every right w.
5 : 6. wh f. God destroy w. of thine
8 : 9. applied my heart unto ev. w.
14. just, unto whom it happeneth acc-g to w. of wicked; wicked to whom acc-g to w. of righteous
9 : 10. is no w. in grave whither
12 : 14. bring every w. into judgm.
Can. 7 : 1. w. of cunning workman
Is. 2 : 8. worship the w. of their own hands, Je. 1 : 16. ⌈hands
17 : 8. shall not look to w. of his
19 : 14. caused Eg. to err in every w.
19 : 15. Nei. shall be any w. for Eg.
25. Assyria the w. of my hands
29 : 16. sh. w. say of him that made
23. seeth his chil. w. of mine ha.
32 : 17. w. of righteousn-s be peace
45 : 11. concern-g w. of my hands
49 : 4. surely is my w. with my G.
60 : 21. sh. inherit w. of my hands
61 : 8. I will direct their w. in tru.
64 : 8. we all are w. of thy hand
65 : 7. former w. into their bosom
22. elect sh. enjoy w. of their ha-s
Je. 10 : 3. cutteth tree, w. of workm.
9. silver into plates, w. of workman; all the w. of cunn-g men
15. They are vanity and the w. of errors, 51 : 18. ⌈wheels
18 : 3. he wrought a w. on the
32 : 19. Great in council, mighty in
50 : 29. recompense acc. to w. ⌊w.
La. 3 : 64. acc. to w. of their hands
4 : 2. w. of the hands of the potter
Eze. 1 : 16. w. was as it were a wheel
15 : 3. Sh. wood be taken to do any
4. Is it meet for any w.? ⌊w.?
5. whole, it was meet for no w., how much less for any w. when
16 : 30. the w. of an whorish woman
Ho. 13 : 2. all of it w. of craftsmen
14 : 3. nei. say to w. of our hands
Mi. 5 : 13. shalt no more worship the w. of thine hands ⌈days
Ha. 1 : 5. for I will work a w. in your
Hag. 1 : 14. did w. in house of Lord
2 : 14. so is every w. of their hands
Mk. 6 : 5. could there do no mighty
Jn. 7 : 21. I have done one w. ⌊w.
17 : 4. I have finished w. thou gav.
Ac. 5 : 38. if this w. be of men, it
13 : 2. w. whereunto I called them
41. for I work a w. in your days, a w. which ye shall not believe
14 : 26. the w. which they fulfilled
15 : 38. went not with them to w.
27 : 16. much w. to come by boat
Ro. 2 : 15. shew the w. of the law
9 : 28. he will finish the w.; a short w. will L. make upon earth
11 : 6. otherwise w. is no more w.
1 Co. 3 : 13. Every man's w. be made manifest; fire sh. try ev. man's
14. If any man's w. abide ⌊w.
15. If any man's w. be burned
9 : 1. are not ye my w. in Lord?
Ep. 4 : 12. some for w. of ministry
Ph. 2 : 30. for w. of Ch. nigh death
1 Th. 5 : 13. love for their w.'s sake

2 Th.1:11.God may fulfil **w.** of faith
2 Ti.4:5. do the **w.** of an evangelist
Ja. 1: 4.let patience have perfect **w.**
25. doer of the **w.** shall be blessed
1 Pe.1:17.judgeth acc. to man's **w.**
See AWORK.

Beaten WORK. [**b.w.**
Ex. 25: 18. two cherubim of gold of
31. pure gold; of **b.w.** shall candlest. be, 36.-37:17,22. Nu. 8:4.

Broidered WORK.
Eze. 16: 10. I clothed thee with **b.**
13. raiment of silk and **b.w.** [**w.**
27: 7. Fine linen wi. **b.w.** thy sail
16. in thy fairs wi. **b.w.** and agate
24. thy merchants in **b.w.**, and

Carved WORK, S. [**w.**
1 K. 6: 35. with gold fitted upon **c.**
Ps. 74: 6. they break **c.w.** wi. axes
Pr. 7:16.decked my bed with **c.w-s**

Cunning WORK, S.
Ex. 26: 1. with cherubim of **c.w.**
make them, 36: 8, 35.[6.-39: 3.
31. fine twined linen of **c.w.**, 28:
28: 15. breastplate of **c.w.**, 39: 8.
31: 4. wisdom to devise **c.w-s** in
gold and,35:35.**c.w.**[ner of **c.w.**
35: 33. wisdom to make any man-
See EVIL work, s.

WORK, S of God.
Ex. 32: 16. the tables were the **w.** -
Jb. 37: 14.consider wondrous **w-s** -
Ps. 64: 9. all men shall declare **w.** -
66: 5. Come and see the **w-s** -
78: 7. might not forget the **w-s** -
Ec. 7: 13. Consider the **w.** -: for
8: 17. Then I beheld all the **w.** -
11: 5. thou knowest not the **w-s** -
Jn. 6: 28.that we might work **w-s** -
29. This is **w.** - that ye believe on
Jn. 9: 3. th. **w-s** - be made manif-t
Ac. 2: 11. we hear them speak **w-s**-
Ro. 14:20.For meat destroy not **w.**-
See GOOD work.
See GREAT work.
See HANDIWORK.

His WORK.
Ge. 2: 2: on seventh day God ended
h.w.: he rested on the seventh
day from all **h.w.**, 3
Ex.36:4.came every man from **h.w.**
De. 32: 4. the Rock, **h.w.** is perfect
Ju. 19: 16. an old man from **h.w.**
1 S. 8: 16. your young men to **h.w.**
1 K. 7: 14. Hiram wrought all **h.w.**
1 Ch.4:23.dwelt with king for **h.w.**
2 Ch 8:9.of Israel no servants for **h.**
16: 5. Baasha let **h.w.** cease [**w.**
Ne 4:15.returned ev.one unto **h.w.**
Jb. 7: 2.looketh for reward of **h.w.**
33: †17. withdraw man from **h.w.**
36: 24.Remember thou magnify **h.**
37: 7. all men may know **h.w.**[**w.**
Ps. 62:12. thou renderest to every
man acc. to **h.w.**, Pr. 24: 29.
104:23.Man goeth forth unto **h.w.**
111: 3. **h.w.** is honourable and
Pr. 16: 11. weights of bag are **h.w.**
18: 9. He that is slothful in **h.w.**
20: 11. whether **h.w.** be pure or
21: 8. as for the pure **h.w.** is right
Is. 1: † 31. be as tow: **h.w.** as spark
5: 19. Let him hasten **h.w.** that
10:12.the Lord performed **h.**whole
w. upon mount Zion and Jerus.
28:21. may do **h.w.**,**h.**strange **w.**
40: 10. **h.w.** before him, 62: 11.
54: 16.forth an instrum-t for **h.w.**
Je. 22: 13. giveth him not for **h.w.**
Hab. 2: 18. maker of **h.w.** trusteth
Mk.13:34.who gave to ev.man **h.w.**
Jn. 4: 34. my meat to finish **h.w.**
Ga. 6: 4. let every man prove **h.w.**
Re.22:12.to give every man as **h.w.**
See **Work of the LORD.**
See **MARVELLOUS work, s.**
See NEEDLEWORK,NETWORK,S.

Thy WORK.
Ex. 20: 9. Six days sh. labour and
do all **t.w.**, 23: 12. De. 5: 13.
Ru.2:12.The Lord recompense **t.w.**
Ps. 77: 12. I will meditate of **t.w.**
90: 16. Let **t.w.** appear unto thy
92: 4. L. made me glad thro. **t.w.**
Pr. 24: 27. Prepare **t.w.** without
Is. 45: 9. Shall the clay say, or **t.**
w., He hath no hands?
Je. 31: 16. **t.w.** shall be rewarded
Ha. 3: 2. Lord, revive **t.w.** in midst
See WOVEN, WREATHEN.

Your WORK.[minish.
Ex. 5: 11. not aught of **y.w.** be di-
2 Ch. 15: 7. **y.w.** shall be rewarded
Is. 41: 24.ye nothing, **y.w.** nought
1 Th. 1: 3. Rememb-g **y.w.** of faith
He. 6: 10.G. not unrighteous to for-

WORKS. [get **y.w.**
Ex. 5:13.Fulfil your **w.**, daily tasks
35: 32. to devise curious **w.** in gold
Nu.16:28.L. sent me to do these **w.**
De.2:7.G. blessed thee in **w.**, 16:15.
Ju. 2: 10. generation which knew
not Lord nor the **w.** [they have
1 S. 8: 8. According to all the **w.**
1 K. 7: 14. cunning to work all **w.**
13: 11. told him all **w.** man of God
2 K. 22: 17. provoke me with all **w.**
of their hands, 2 Ch. 34: 25.
1 Ch.28:19.underst-d **w.** of pattern
Ne. 9: 35. nei. turned fr. wicked **w.**
Ps.8:6.dominion over **w.** of thy ha.
14: 1. have done abominable **w.**
17: 4. Concerning the **w.** of men
92: 4. triumph in **w.** of thy hands
111: 7. **w.** of his hands are verity
138: 8. forsake not **w.** of thi. hands
141: 4. practise wicked **w.** wi. men
Pr. 31: 31.let her own **w.** praise her
Ec. 1: 14. I have seen all the **w.** that
2: 11.I looked on all **w.** my hands
Is. 26: 12. wrought all our **w.** in us
Je. 7: 13. ye have done all these **w.**
25: 6. provoke me not with **w.** of
your hands, 7.-44: 8 [hands
14. recompense accord-g to **w.** of
Eze. 6: 6. that your **w.** be abolished
Da. 4: 37. all whose **w.** are truth
Mi. 6: 16.kept, **w.** of house of Ahab
Mat.11: 2.heard in prison **w.** of Ch.
Jn. 5: 20. he will shew greater **w.**
36. **w.** which father hath given
me, the same **w.** bear witness
7: 3. thy disciples may see the **w.**
7. because I testify the **w.** are evil
8: 39. if chil., ye would do **w.** of A.
9: 4. I must work the **w.** of him
10: 25. **w.** that I do in Fa.'s name
32. for wh. of these **w.** stone me?
37. If I do not the **w.** of my Fath.
38. But if I do, believe the **w.**
14: 10. Fath. in me, he doeth the **w.**
11. else believe me for **w.**'s sake
12. **w.** that I do shall he do; and
greater **w.** than these [did
15: 24. If I had not done **w.** none
Ac. 7: 41. rejoiced in **w.** of own ha-s
26: 20. do **w.** meet for repentance
Ro. 3: 27. By what law? of **w.**? Nay
4: 2. if Abr. were justified by **w.**
6. G. imputeth righteousness wi-t
9: 11. not of **w.** but him that [**w.**
32. not by faith, but **w.** of the law
11: 6. if by grace, it is no more of
w., but if of **w.** no more of grace
13: 12.let us cast off **w.** of darkness
Ga. 2: 16. a man is not justified by
w. of the law, but by faith (3)
3: 2. Rec-d ye Spirit by **w.** of law?
5. doeth he it by **w.** of the law, or
10.as many as are of the **w.** of the
law, are under curse [fest
5: 19. the **w.** of the flesh are mani-
Ep. 2: 9. Not of **w.** lest any boast
5: 11. with unfruitful **w.** of darkn.

Col.1:21.and enemies by wicked **w.**
2 Ti. 1: 9. saved us, not acc-g to **w.**
Tit. 1: 16. but in **w.** they deny God
3: 5. Not by **w.** of righteousness
He. 1: 10. heavens **w.** of thi. hands
2: 7. didst set him ov. **w.** of thy ha.
3: 9. your fathers saw my **w.** 40 y.
4: 3.although the **w.** were finished
6: 1. of repentance from dead **w.**
9: 14.purge conscience fr. dead **w.**
Ja. 2: 14.if he have not **w.** can faith
save him? [20, 26.
17. faith, if it hath not **w.** is dead,
18. a man may say I have **w.**;
shew me thy faith without thy
w., I will shew my faith by **w.**
21. Was not Abr. justified by **w.**
22. by **w.** was faith made perfect
24. Ye see by **w.** a man is justified
25. was not Rahab justified by **w.**
2 Pe. 3: 10. earth and **w.** be burned
1 Jn. 3: 8. destroy **w.** of the devil
Re. 2: 5. repent and do the first **w.**
23.will give unto ev. one acc. to **w.**
26. that keepeth my **w.** unto end
9: 20. repented not of **w.** of hands
18: 6. unto her double, acc. to **w.**
See **EVIL works, WORK of God, GOOD works, GREAT works.**

His WORKS. [good
1 S. 19: 4. **h.w.** to thee-ward very
2 Ch. 32: 30.Hez. prospered in **h.w.**
Ps. 33: 4. all **h.w.** done in truth
78: 11. forgat **h.w.**, wonders, 106:
103: 22. Bless the L., all **h.w.** [13.
104: 31. Lord shall rejoice in **h.w.**
107: 22. declare **h.w.** with rejoic-g
111: 6. shewed peo. power of **h.w.**
145:9.tender mercies over all **h.w.**
17. The Lord is holy in all **h.w.**
Pr. 8: 22. L. possessed me bef. **h.w.**
24: 12. shall not he render to every
man acc. to **h.w.**? Mat. 16: 27.
Ec. 3: 22. man rejoice in **h.** own **w.**
Da. 9: 14.God righteous in all **h.w.**
Ac. 15: 18.Known unto G. all **h.w.**
2 Ti. 4: 14. Lord reward Alexander
according to **h.w.** [**h.w.**
He. 4: 4. did rest 7th day from all
10. he hath ceased fr. **h.** own **w.**?
Ja. 2: 22. Seest thou how faith wro-t
with **h.w.**? [tion **h.w.**
3: 15. shew out of a good conversa-
See **Works of the LORD.**
See **MARVELLOUS work, s.**

Mighty WORKS. [done
Mat. 11: 20.most of his **m.w.** were
21.if **m.w.** done in you, had been
done in, 23. Lu.10: 13. [**w.**?
13: 54. Whence this man these **m.**
58. not many **m.w.** there, Mk.6: 5.
14: 2. John Baptist risen fr. dead,
thf. **m.w.** do shew, Mk. 6: 14.
Mk. 6: 2. that **m.w.** are wrought
Lu. 19: 37. praise God for all **m.w.**

Their WORKS.
Ex. 5: 4. Wh. let people from **t.w.**
23: 24.Thou shalt not do after **t.w.**
Ne. 6: 14. upon Tobiah, acc. to **t.w.**
Jb. 34: 25.Theref. he knoweth **t.w.**
Ps. 33: 15. he considereth all **t.w**
106: 35.heathen, and learned **t.w.**
39. were they defiled wi. **t.** own **w.**
Ec. 9: 1. **t.w.** are in hand of God
Is. 29: 15. **t.w.** are in the dark [ing
41: 29.are vanity, **t.w.** are noth-
59: 6. nei. shall cover themselves
with **t.w.**; **t.w.** are **w.** of iniq.
66: 18. I know **t.w.** and thoughts
Am. 8: 7. I will never forget **t.w.**
Jon. 3: 10. G. saw **t.w.** they turned
Mat 23: 3. but do not ye after **t.w.**
5. all **t.w.** they do to be seen of
2 Co 11: 15. whose end be acc. to **t.**
Re. 14: 13. **t.w.** do follow them[**w.**
20: 12. judged acc-g to **t.w.**, 13.

Thy WORKS.
De. 3 : 24. for what God is there in heaven can do acc-g to t.w.?
15 : 10. God sh. bless thee in t.w.
2 Ch. 20 : 37. Lord hath broken t.w.
Ps. 66 : 3. terrible art thou in t.w.
73 : 28. that I may declare all t.w.
86 : 8 nei. any w. like unto t.w.
92 : 5. O Lord, how great are t.w.
104 : 13. satisfied with fruit of t.w.
24. O Lord, how manifold are t.w.
143 : 5. I meditate on all t.w.
145 : 10. All t.w. shall praise thee
Pr. 16 : 3. Commit t.w. unto Lord
Ec. 9 : 7. God now accepteth t.w.
Is. 57 : 12. I will declare t.w. [t.w.
Je. 48 : 7. bec. thou hast trusted in
Eze. 27 : † 16. the multitude of t.w.
Ja. 2 : 18. shew thy faith with-t t.w.
Re. 2 : 2. I know t.w., 9, 13, 19.-3 : 1, 8, 15. [before God
3 : 2. have not found t.w. perfect
Wonderful WORKS. [w.
Ps. 40 : 5. Many, O Lord, are thy w.
78 : 4. shewing w.w. he hath done
107 : 8. would praise the Lord for his w.w. to the child-n of men, 15, 21, 31. [remembered
111 : 4. made his w.w. to be re-
Mat. 7 : 22. in thy name done w.w.
Ac. 2 : 11. Cretes, Arabians speak in our tongues w. w. of God
Wondrous WORKS.
1 Ch. 16 : 9. Sing psalms, talk ye of all his w.w., Ps. 105 : 2. [God
Jb. 37 : 14. Job, consider w.w. of
16. Dost thou know w.w. of him
Ps. 26 : 7. I may tell of all thy w.w.
71 : 17. have I declared thy w.w.
75 : 1. name near, thy w.w. declare
78 : 32. believed not for his w.w.
106 : 22. done w.w. in land of Ham
119 : 27. so shall I talk of thy w.w.,
145 : 5. speak of thy w.w. [w.w.
Je. 21 : 2. if Lord will deal acc. to his
WORK. [Verb.]
Ex. 5 : 18. Go therefore now and w.
31 : 4. wisdom to w. in gold, silver, and brass, 35 : 32. 2 Ch. 2 : 7, 14.
5. to w. in all manner of workmanship, 35 : 35.-36 : 1.
34 : 21. Six days shalt thou w., but
39 : 3. gold into wires to w. it in blue
Jos. 9 : 4. They did w. wilily and
1 S. 14 : 6. may be L. will w. for us
1 K. 7 : 14. to w. all works of brass
21 : 20 hast sold thys. to w. evil, 25.
Ne. 4 : 6. the peo. had a mind to w.
Jb. 23 : 9. On left where he doth w.
Ps. 58 : 2 in heart ye w. wickedn-s
119 : 126. time for thee, Lord, to w.
Is. 19 : 9. w. in flax be confounded
43 : 13. I will w., who shall let it?
Eze. 33 : 26. ye w. abomination and
Da. 11 : 23. he shall w. deceitfully
Mi. 2 : 1. that w. evil upon their beds
Ha. 1 : 5. I will w. a work in y-r days, Ac. 13 : 41. [saith the Lord
Hag. 2 : 4. w., for I am with you,
Mal. 3 : 15. they that w. wickedness
Mat. 21 : 28. Son, go w. to day in my
Lu. 13 : 14. six days in which men ought to w. [I w.
Jn. 5 : 17. My Father worketh, and
6 : † 27. w. not for the meat that
28. we might w. the works of God
30. they said, what dost thou w.?
9 : 4. I must w. while it is day, night cometh, no man can w.
Ro. 7 : 5. sin did w. in our members
8 : 28. all things w. togeth. for good
Ep. 4 : 19. to w. all uncleanness with
Ph. 2 : 12. w. out your own salvat-n
1 Th. 4 : 11. w. with y-r own hands
2 Th. 2 : 7. mystery of iniquity doth
3 : 10. if any would not w. [w.
12. that with quietness they w.

WORK iniquity. [i.
Ps. 141 : 4. works with men that w.
Is. 31 : 2. ag-t help of them that w. i.
32 : 6. his heart will w.i. [w.i.
Ho. 6 : 8. Gilead a city of them that
Mat. 7 : 23. depart from me ye that
WORKER, S. [w.i.
1 K. 7 : 14. man of Tyre a w. in brass
2 K. 23 : 24. w-s with familiar spirits
1 Ch. 22 : 15. w-s of stone and timb
1 Co. 12 : 29. are all w-s of miracles?
2 Co. 6 : 1. We then as w-s with him
11 : 13. false apostles deceitful w-s
Ph. 3 : 2. Beware of dogs, of evil w-s
Fellow WORKERS.
Col. 4 : 11. These only are my f.w.
WORKERS of iniquity.
Jb. 31 : 3. strange punishm-t to w.-
34 : 8. goeth in company with w.-
22. where w.- may hide thems.
Ps. 5 : 5. thou hatest all the w.-
6 : 8. Depart from me, all ye w.-; for the L., Lu. 13 : 27. [edge, 53 : 4.
14 : 4. Have all the w.- no knowl-
28 : 3. Draw me not away with w.-
36 : 12. There are the w.- fallen
37 : 1. nei. be thou envious ag. w.-
59 : 2. Deliver me from the w.-
64 : 2. Hide me fr. insurrect-n of w.-
92 : 7. when all the w.- do flourish
9. w.- shall be scattered [thems.?
94 : 4. How long shall w.- boast
16. who stand for me ag. the w.-?
125 : 5. L. lead them forth with w.-
141 : 9. Keep me fr. the gins of w.-
Pr. 10 : 29. destruction shall be to the w.-, 21 : 15.
WORKETH. [man
Jb. 33 : 29. all these w. God with
Ps 15 : 2. He that w. righteousness
101 : 7. that w. deceit not dwell in
Pr 11 : 18. wicked w. deceitful work
26 : 28. a flattering mouth w. ruin
31 : 13. w. willingly with her hands
Ec. 3 : 9. What profit hath he th. w.
Is. 44 : 12. smith w. in the coals, he w. it with strength of his arms
64 : 5. meetest him w. righteousn-s
Je. 8 : † 8. false pen of scribes w. for
Da. 6 : 27. he w. signs in heaven
Jn. 5 : 17. My Father w. hitherto
Ac. 10 : 35. he that w. righteousn-s
Ro. 2 : 10. peace to ev. man w. good
4 : 4. to him that w. is the reward
5. to him that w. not, but believ-
15. Because the law w. wrath [eth
5 : 3. that tribulation w. patience
13 : 10. Love w. no ill to neighbour
1 Co. 12 : 6. same God wh. w. all in all
11. all these w. that one Spirit
16 : 10. he w. the work of the Lord
2 Co. 4 : 12. So then death w. in us
17. w. for us a far more exceeding
7 : 10. godly sorrow w. repentance, sorrow of the world w. death
Ga. 3 : 5. He that w. miracles am-g
5 : 6. but faith, which w. by love
Ep. 1 : 11. w. all things after counsel
2 : 2. spirit that now w. in the children of disobedience [us
3 : 20. acc-g to the power that w. in
Ph. 2 : 13. it is God that w. in you
Col. 1 : 29. which w. in me mightily
1 Th. 2 : 13. effectually w. in you
Ja. 1 : 3. that the trying of y-r faith w. patience [eousness of God
20. wrath of man w. not right-
Re. 21 : 27. nei. whatso. w. abomina-
WORKFELLOW. [tion
Ro. 16 : 21. Timothy my w. saluteth
WORKING. [ly
Ps. 52 : 2. like a razor, w. deceitful-
74 : 12. w. salvation in the earth
Is. 28 : 29. L., who is excellent in w.
Eze. 46 : 1. gate be shut six w. days
Mk. 16 : 20. the Lord w. with them
Ro. 1 : 27. men w. that is unseemly

Ro. 7 : 13. sin w. death in me by th.
1 Co. 4 : 12. w. with our own hands
9 : 6. not we power to forbear w.?
12 : 10. To another, w. of miracles
Ep. 1 : 19. acc-g to w. of his power
3 : 7. me by effectual w. of his power
4 : 16. to effectual w. in every part
28. w. with hands thing wh. is good
Ph. 3 : 21. acc-g to w. whereby he is
Col. 1 : 29. acc. to his w. in me migh.
2 Th. 2 : 9. whose coming is after the w. of Satan [bodies
3 : 11. w. not at all, but are busy-
He. 13 : 21. w. in you, well pleasing
Re. 16 : 14. spirits of devils w. mir-
WORKMAN. [acles
Is 40 : 19. w. melteth graven image
Je. 10 : 3. work of the w. with axe
9. work of the w. and the founder
Ho. 8 : 6. w. made it, it is not God
Mat. 10 : 10. w. worthy of his meat
2 Ti. 2 : 15. w. needeth not be asha.
Cunning WORKMAN.
Ex. 26 : † 1. cherubim, work of c.w.
35 : 35. wisdom to work all manner of work of the c.w., 38 : 23.
Can. 7 : 1. like jewels, work of c.w.
Is. 40 : 20. he seeketh a c.w. to pre-
WORKMANSHIP. [pare
Ex. 31 : 3. wisdom in all manner of w., 5-35 : 31. 1 Ch. 28 : 21.
2 K. 16 : 10. acc. to all the w. th-of
Je. 7 : † 18. cakes to w. of heaven
Eze. 28 : 13. w. of tabrets and pipes
Ep. 2 : 10. we are his w. created in
WORKMEN. [Christ
Ju. 5 : 26. her hand to w.'s hammer
2 K. 12 : 14. they gave to w., and repaired house, 15. 2 Ch. 34 : 10, 17.
1 Ch. 22 : 15. w. with thee in abund.
25 : 1. number of w. acc. to service
2 Ch. 24 : 13. w. wro-t, work perfect-
Eze. 3 : † 7. gave money unto w. [ed
9. Jeshua to set forward the w.
Is. 44 : 11. the w. they are of men
Ac. 19 : 25. with w. of like occupation
WORLD.
1 S. 2 : 8. hath set the w. upon them
2 S. 22 : 16. foundations of w. were discovered, Ps. 18 : 15. [stable
1 Ch. 16 : 30. the w. also shall be
Jb. 18 : 18. shall be chased out of w.
Ps. 9 : 8. he shall judge w. in righteousness, 96 : 13.-98 : 9. [of w.
17 : 14. deliver my soul from men
19 : 4. gone out, their words to end of the w., Ro 10 : 18. [ber
22 : 27. All ends of w. shall remem-
24 : 1. earth is the Lord's; the w.
50 : 12. w. is mine and the fulness
77 : 18. lightnings lightened w., 97:
89 : 11 w. thou hast founded [4.
90 : 2. hadst formed earth and w.
93 : 1. w. also is stablished, 96 : 10.
98 : 7. Let sea roar, w. and they
Pr. 8 : 26. had not made dust of w.
Ec. 3 : 11. hath set w. in their heart
Is. 13 : 11. I will punish w. for evil
14 : 17. Is this he made w. as wild-s
23 : 17. fornication wi. kingdoms of
24 : 4. w. languisheth, fadeth [w.
34 : 1. let earth hear the w. and all
45 : 17. ye shall not be confounded, w. without end [end of w.
62 : 11. Lord hath proclaimed unto
64 : 4. since beginning of w., Mat. 24 : 21. Ac. 15 : 18. Ep. 3 : 9.
Je. 10 : 12. established w. by wisdom, 51 : 15. [drink
25 : 26. all kingdoms of w. shall
Na. 1 : 5. earth is burned, yea the w.
Mat. 4 : 8. devil sheweth him all kingdoms of the w., Lu. 4 : 5.
5 : 14. Ye are the light of the w.
13 : 38. The field is the w. [w.
39. the harvest is the end of the
18 : 7. Woe unto w. bec. of offences

WORLD to come.

See **FACE of the world, FOUNDATION of world.**

In or Into the WORLD.

Inhabitants of the WORLD.

This WORLD.

Whole WORLD. [w.?

WORLDS. [of w. w.

WORLDLY. [lusts

WORM. [uary

WORMS. [gourd

Mi. 7 : 17. out of their holes like w.
Ac. 12 : 23. Herod was eaten of w.

WORMWOOD. [w.

De. 29 : 18. lest a root that beareth
Pr. 5 : 4. her end is bitter as w. [15.
Je. 9 : 15. will feed peo. with w., 23:
La. 3 : 15. made me drunken wi. w.
19. rememb-g my misery, the w.
Am. 5 : 7. Ye who turn judgm. to w.
Re. 8 : 11. the name of the star W.,
third part of waters became w.

WORSE. [them

Ge. 19 : 9. deal w. with thee than
2 S. 19 : 7. w. than all th. befell thee
1 K. 16 : 25. Omri did w. than all
2 K. 14 : 12. Judah was put to the
w. before Israel, 2 Ch. 25 : 22.
1 Ch. 19 : 16. Syrians put to w., 19.
2 Ch. 6 : 24. if Israel be put to the
33 : 9. made Jerusalem do w. [w.
Is. 41 : † 24. ye are w. than nothing,
your work w. than of a viper
Je. 7 : 26. did w. than fath-s, 16 : 12.
Da. 1 : 10. why should he see your
faces w. liking [Mk. 2 : 21.
Mat. 9 : 16. the rent is made w.,
12 : 45. last state of this man is w.
than first, Lu. 11 : 26. [first
27 : 64. last error shall be w. than
Mk. 5 : 26. nothing bettered, grew w.
Jn. 2 : 10. g. wine, then that wh. is w.
5 : 14. sin no more, lest a w. thing
1 Co. 8 : 8. nei. if we eat not are we w.
11 : 17. ye come not for better, but
1 Ti. 5 : 8. he w. than an infidel [w.
2 Ti. 3 : 13. seducers wax w. and w.
2 Pe. 2 : 20. latter end is w. wi. them

WORSHIP. [Noun.]

Lu. 14 : 10. shalt have w. in pres-
See WILL-WORSHIP. [ence

WORSHIP. [Verb.]

Ge. 22 : 5. I and lad will go and w.
Ex. 24 : 1. Come up, w. ye afar off
34 : 14. thou shalt w. no other god
De. 4 : 19. lest be driven to w. them
8 : 19. if thou w. other gods, 11 :
16.-30 : 17. 1 K. 9 : 6. 2 Ch. 7 : 19.
26 : 10. w. before the Lord thy God
Jos. 5 : 14. Joshua fell on face did w.
1 S. 1 : 3. this man went yearly to w.
15 : 25. turn, that I may w. L., 30.
1 K. 12 : 30. people went to w. before
2 K. 5 : 18. house of Rimmon to w.
17 : 36. Lord shall ye fear, him w.
18 : 22. Ye shall w. before this altar
in Jerus., 2 Ch. 32 : 12. Is. 36 : 7.
1 Ch. 16 : 29. w. L. in beauty of holiness, Ps. 29 : 2.-96 : 9. [138 : 2.
Ps. 5 : 7. I will w. toward thy temple,
22 : 27. all the nations shall w. before thee, 86 : 9. Re 15 : 4.
29. All that be fat shall eat and w.
45 : 11. he is thy Lord, w. thou him
81 : 9. neither w. any strange god
66 : 4. All the earth shall w. thee
95 : 6. O come let us w., bow down
97 : 7. w. him, all ye gods [132 : 7.
99 : 5. w. at footstool, he is holy,
9. Exalt Lord, w. at his holy hill
Is. 2 : 8. w. the work of own hands
20. cast idols, made to w., to bats
27 : 13. w. L. in mount at Jerus-m
46 : 6. god ; they fall down, yea w.
49 : 7. princes shall w. bec. of Lord
66 : 23. shall all flesh come to w.
Je. 7 : 2. at these gates to w., 26 : 2.
13 : 10. they that w. other gods, be
25 : 6. go not after other gods to w.
44 : 19. did we make cakes to w.
Eze. 46 : 2. he shall w. at threshold
3. the people shall w. at the door
9. entereth by north gate to w.
Da. 3 : 5. w. the golden image, 10, 15.
12. cert. Jews serve not nor w. im.
14. do not ye w. the golden image
15. if ye w. not, ye shall be cast
18. O king, we will not w. image
Da. 3 : 28. not w. any god exc. own G.
Mi. 5 : 13. no more w. work of thine
Zph. 1 : 5. that w. the host of heaven
2 : 11. men shall w. him, every one
Zch. 14 : 16. to w. the King, 17. [him
Mat. 2 : 2. seen star, and come to w.
8. that I may come w. him also
4 : 9. if thou wilt w. me, Lu. 4 : 7.
10. Thou shalt w. the Lord thy
G., him only, Lu. 4 : 8. [Mk. 7 : 7.
15 : 9. but in vain they do w. me,
Jn. 4 : 20. ye say in Jerus. is place
where men ought to w. [w. Fa.
21. nei. in this mt. nor at Jerus.
22. Ye w., ye know not what ; we
know what we w.
23. shall w. the Father in spirit ;
Father seeketh such to w. him
24. they that w. him, must w. in
12 : 20. certain Greeks came to w.
Ac. 7 : 42. God gave them up to w.
the host, 43. [lem to w.
8 : 27. eunuch had come to Jerusa-
17 : 23. Whom ye ignorantly w.
18 : 13. to w. God contrary to law
24 : 11. Paul up to Jerus. to w. God
14. way they call heresy, so w. [
the God of my fathers [w. God
1 Co. 14 : 25. falling down, he will
Ph. 3 : 3. which w. God in the spirit
He. 1 : 6. let angels of God w. him
Re. 3 : 9. make them w. bef. thy feet
4 : 10. w. him that liveth forever
9 : 20. should not w. devils, idols
11 : 1. measure temple, and them
13 : 8. beast ; all upon earth shall
that w. therein [w. him, 12.
15. as many as would not w. be
14 : 7. w. him that made heaven
9. If any man w. the beast and
11. have no rest who w. the beast
19 : 10. I fell at his feet to w., 22 : 8.
22 : 9. Then saith the angel, w. God

WORSHIPPED. [26, 48.

Ge. 24 : 52. Abr.'s servant w. Lord
Ex. 4 : 31. the people w., 12 : 27.
32 : 8. they made a molten calf, and
w. it, Ps. 106 : 19. [door
33 : 10. w. every man in his tent
34 : 8. Mo. bowed tow. earth and w.
De. 17 : 3. hath served other gods
and w. them, 29 : 26. 1 K. 9 : 9.
2 K. 21 : 21. 2 Ch. 7 : 22. Je. 1 :
16.-8 : 2.-16 : 11.-22 : 9. [w.
Ju. 7 : 15. Gideon heard dream, he
1 S. 1 : 19. they w., returned to Ra.
28. the child w. the Lord there
15 : 31. and Saul w. the Lord [32.
2 S. 12 : 20 Then David arose, w., 15 :
1 K. 11 : 33. forsaken me, w. Asht-h
16 : 31. served Baal, w. him, 22 : 53.
2 K. 17 : 16. they w. all the host of
heaven, 21 : 3. 2 Ch. 33 : 3. [k.
1 Ch. 29 : 20. all cong-n w. Lord and
2 Ch. 7 : 3. Israel w. and praised the
Lord, 29 : 28, 29, 30.
Ne. 8 : 6. all the people w. the Lord
9 : 3. confessed and w. their God
Jb. 1 : 20. Job fell upon ground, w.
Eze. 8 : 16. they w. the sun tow. east
Da. 2 : 46. Then Nebneh-r w. Daniel
3 : 7. all people w. golden image
Mat. 2 : 11. saw young child they w.
8 : 2. came a leper and w. him [him
9 : 18. came a certain ruler, w. him
14 : 33. they in the ship w. him
15 : 25. woman of Canaan w. him
18 : 26. servant fell down, w. him
28 : 9. held him by the feet, w. him
17. disciples w. him, Lu. 24 : 52.
Mk. 5 : 6. saw Jesus afar, he ran, w.
15 : 19. spit upon him and w. him
Jn. 4 : 20. Our fathers w. in this mt.
9 : 38. man which was blind w. him
Ac. 10 : 25. Cornelius met Peter, w. h.
16 : 14. Lydia of Thyatira wh. w. G.
17 : 25. Nei. is w. with men's hands
Ac. 18 : 7. Justus, one that w. God
Ro. 1 : 25. w. creature more than C.
2 Th 2 : 4. Who exalteth hims. above
all that is w. [staff
He. 11 : 21. Jacob w. leaning upon
Re. 5 : 14. the four and twenty elders w., 11 : 16.-19 : 4. [w. God
7 : 11. angels fell before the throne,
13 : 4. they w. dragon, w. beast
16 : 2. a grievous sore upon them
which w. his image [his image
19 : 20. he deceived them that w.
20 : 4. souls that had not w. beast

WORSHIPPER.

Jn. 9 : 31. if any man be a w. of God
Ac. 19 : 35. Ephesus is a w. of Diana

WORSHIPPERS.

2 K. 10 : 19. Jehu might destroy w.
21. and all the w. of Baal came
22. Bring vestments for w. of Ba.
23. Jehu said unto w. of Baal that
there be but w. of Baal only
Jn. 4 : 23. when true w. sh. worship
He. 10 : 2. bec. th. the w. once purged

WORSHIPPETH.

Ne. 9 : 6. the host of heaven w. thee
Is. 44 : 15. maketh a god, w. it, 17.
Da. 3 6. And whoso falleth not down
and w., 11. [world w.
Ac. 19 : 27. whom all Asia and the

WORSHIPPING.

2 K. 19 : 37. w. in house of Nisroch,
his sons smote him, Is. 37 : 38.
2 Ch. 20 : 18. all Judah w. the Lord
Mat. 20 : 20. moth. with sons w. him
Col. 2 : 18. no man beguile you in w.

WORST. [of angels

Eze. 7 : 24. I will bring w. of heath.

WORTH. [w.

Ge. 23 : 9. for as much money as it is
15. land is w. 400 shekels of silver
Le. 27 : 23. reckon w. of thy estimat.
De. 15 : 18. w. a double hired servant
2 S. 18 : 3. thou art w. 10,000 of us
1 K. 21 : 2. give the w. of thy vine-
yard in money [nothing w.
Jb. 24 : 25. who will make thy speech
Pr. 10 : 20. heart of wicked little w.
Eze. 30 : 2. say, Howl ye, Woe w.

WORTHIES. [day !

Na. 2 : 5. He shall recount his w.

WORTHILY.

Ru. 4 : 11. do thou w. in Ephratah

WORTHY.

Ge. 32 : 10. not w. of least of mercies
De. 25 : 2. if wicked, w. to be beaten
1 S. 1 : 5. unto Hannah a w. portion
26 : 16. As Lord liveth, ye w. to die
2 S. 12 : † 5 done this, is w. to die
22 : 4. Lord, who is w. to be praised,
Ps. 18 : 3. [w. man
1 K. 1 : 52. If he will shew himself a
Je. 26 : 11. This man is w. to die
16. This man is not w. to die
Mat. 3 : 11. shoes I am not w. to bear
8 : 8. Lord, I am not w., Lu. 7 : 6.
10 : 10. workman is w. of his meat
11. inquire who in it is w., and
13. And if the house be w., let
peace ; but if it be not w.
37. loveth mother more than me,
he is not w. of me (2) [of me
38. taketh not his cross, is not w.
22 : 8. wh. were bidden were not w.
Mk. 1 : 7. shoes I am not w. to unloose, Lu. 3 : 16. Jn. 1 : 27. Ac.
Lu. 3 : 8. fruits w. of repent-e [13 : 25.
7 : 4. he was w. for whom he should
7. nei. thought I mys. w. to come
10 : 7. labourer is w. of his hire
12 : 48. commit things w. of stripes
15 : 19. no more w. to be thy son, 21.
20 : 35. be accounted w. to obtain
21 : 36. be accounted w. to escape
Ac. 24 : 2. very w. deeds are done
Ro. 8 : 18. are not w. to be compared
Ep. 4 : 1. walk w. of the vocation

Col. 1 : 10. That ye might walk w.
of the Lord, 1 Th. 2 : 12.
1 Ti. 1 : 15. a saying w. of all acceptation, 4 : 9. [ward
5 : 18. the labourer is w. of his re-
He. 10 : 29. sorer punishment shall
he be thought w. who hath
11 : 38. Of whom the world not w.
Ja. 2 : 7. Do not they blaspheme that
w. name [of God
3 Jn. † 6. bring on their journey w.
Re. 3 : 4. walk in white, they are w.
4 : 11. Thou art w. to receive glory
5 : 2. Who is w. to open the book, 9.
4. no man found w. to open book
12. w. is the Lamb that was slain
16 : 6. blood to drink, for they are

Count or Counted [w.
WORTHY. [suffer

Ac. 5 : 41. that they were c-d w. to
2 Th. 1 : 5. ye may be c-d w. of k-m
11. God would c. you w. of call-g
1 Ti. 5 : 17. elders be c-d w. of double
6 : 1. c. masters w. of all honour
He. 3 : 3. this man c-d w. of more glo.

See **Worthy of DEATH.**
See THANKWORTHY.

WOT, WOTTETH. [this

Ge 21 : 26. I w. not who hath done
39 : 8. master w-h not what is with
44 : 15. w. ye not that I can divine
Ex. 32 : 1. Moses, we w. not what
has become of him, 23. Ac. 7 : 40.
Nu. 22 : 6. I w. he wh. thou blessest
Jos. 2 : 5. whith. men went I w. not
Ac. 3 : 17. I w. thro. ignorance ye
Ro. 11 : 2. w. ye not what Scripture
Ph. 1 : 22. what I sh. choose I w. not

WOULD. [word

Ge. 30 : 34. I w. it be acc-g to thy
Nu. 22 : 29. I w. a sword in mine ha
1 K. 13 : 33. whoso. w. he consecrat.
Ne. 9 : 24. do with them as they w.
Es. 9 : 5. Jews did what they w. to
Jb. 6 : 3. it w. be heavier than sand
Ps. 81 : 11. Israel w. none of me
Pr. 1 : 25. ye w. none of my reproof
30. They w. none of my counsel
Da. 5 : 19. whom he w. he slew;
whom he w. he kept alive;
whom he w. he set up; and
whom he w. he put down
Mat. 7 : 12. whatsoever ye w. men
sho. do to you, do ye, Lu. 6 : 31.
27 : 15. was wont to release a prisoner whom they w. [he w.
Mk. 3 : 13. he calleth unto him whom
10 : 35. we w. thou should. do for us
36. What w. ye that I do for you?
Jn. 6 : 6. he knew what he w. do
11. of fishes as much as they w.
Ac. 18 : 14. reason w. I should bear
Ro. 7 : 15. what I w., that do I not
19. the good that I w. I do not
21. when I w. do good, evil is pres.
1 Co. 7 : 7. I w. all men were as I
14 : 5. I w. ye all spake wi. tongues
2 Co. 5 : 4. not th. we w. be uncloth-
12 : 20. not find you such as I w. [ed
Ga. 2 : 10. they w. we rememb. poor
5 : 12. I w. they were cut off which
17. so ye cannot do things ye w.
Col. 2 : 1. I w. ye knew conflict [noth.
Phm. 14. without thy mind w. I do
3 Jn. 10. forbiddeth them that w.
Re. 3 : 15. I w. thou wert cold or hot

See **Would GOD.**

WOULD have.

Ps. 35 : 25. Ah! so w. we h. it; let
Mk. 7 : 24. he w. h. no man know it
Lu. 1 : 62. how he w. h. him called
Ac. 16 : 3. Him w. Paul h. with him
28 : 18. Who w. h. let me go, bec.
Ro 16 : 19. I w. h. you wise unto
1 Co. 7 : 32. But I w. h. you without
carefulness [man is Ch.
11 : 3. I w. h. you know head of ev.

WOULD not.

1 S. 20 : 9. if I knew, w. n. I tell
31 : 4. armourb-r w. n., 1 Ch. 10 : 4.
2 S. 12 : 17. he w. n., neither did eat
13 : 16. Amnon w. n. hearken unto
25. David w. n. go, but blessed
14 : 29. Joab w. n. come to Abs-m
1 K. 22 : 49. But Jehoshaphat w. n.
2 K. 24 : 4. which Lord w. n. pardon
2 Ch. 35 : 22. Josiah w. n. turn face
Ne. 9 : 30. yet w. they n. give ear [ed
Jb. 9 : 16. w. I n. believe he hearken-
Is. 30 : 15. be saved; and ye w. n.
54 : 9. sworn I w. n. be wroth with
Mat. 2 : 18. Rach w. n. be comforted
18 : 30. Have patience. And he w. n.
22 : 3. that were hidden w. n. come
23 : 30. we w. n. have been partak-s
37. Jerusalem how often w. I and
ye w. n., Lu. 13 : 34. [brok.
24 : 43. w. n. have suffered hou. to be
27 : 34. had tasted, he w. n. drink
Mk. 6 : 26. oath's sake w. n. reject
9 : 30. he w. n. any man sho. know
Lu. 15 : 28. was angry, w. n. go in
18 : 4. he w. n. for a while, but aft.
13. publican w. n. lift up his eyes
19 : 27. w. n. I should reign over
Jn. 7 : 1. he w. n. walk in Jewry
Ac. 7 : 39. wh. our fathers w. n. obey
9 : 38. that he w. n. delay to come
20 : 16. he w. n. spend time in Asia
21 : 14. when he w. n. be persuaded
Ro. 1 : 13. Now I w. n. have you
ignorant, brethren, 11 : 25. 1 Co.
10 : 1. 12 : 1. 1 Th. 4 : 13. [do
7 : 19. the evil which I w. n., that I
20. If I do that I w. n., it is, 16.
1 Co. 10 : 20. I w. n. ye should have
fellowship with devils [rant
2 Co. 1 : 8. we w. n. have you igno-
12 : 20. I be found such as ye w. n.
1 Th. 2 : 9. we w. n. be chargeable
2 Th. 3 : 10. if any w. n. work, nei.
He. 4 : 8. w. he n. afterw. ha. spoken

See **Would not HEAR.**

WOULDEST. [thou?

Jos. 15 : 18. Caleb said, What w.
1 K. 1 : 16. king said, What w. thou?
2 K. 4 : 13. w. thou be spoken for to
Jn. 21 : 18. walkedst whither thou w.

WOULDEST not.

2 Ch. 20 : 10. w. n. let Israel invade
Jn. 21 : 18 carry thee whi. thou w. n.
He. 10 : 5. Sacrifice thou w. n., 8.

See **Wouldest not HEAR.**

WOUND. [Noun.]

Ex. 21 : 25. give w. for w., stripe
1 K. 22 : 35. blood ran out of the w.
Jb. 34 : 6. my w. is incurable wi-t
Ps. 64 : † 7. suddenly their w. shall
Pr. 6 : 33. A w., dishonour sh. he get
20 : 30. blueness of w. cleans-h evil
Is. 30 : 26. healeth stroke of their w.
Je. 10 : 19. Woe. my w. is grievous
15 : 18. why is my w. incurable?
30 : 12. thy w. is grievous, Na. 3 : 19.
14. I wounded thee with w. of an
Ho. 5 : 13. Judah saw his w.; yet
could Jareb not cure your w.
Ob. 7. eat thy bread laid a w. under
Mi. 1 : 9. her w. is incurable [thee
Re. 13 : 3. his deadly w. healed, 12.
14. beast, which had w. by sword

WOUNDS.

2 K. 8 : 29. Joram went to be healed
of the w., 9 : 15. 2 Ch. 22 : 6.
Jb. 9 : 17. multiplieth my w. with-
Ps. 38 : 5. My w. stink [out cause
147 : 3. healeth broken in heart,
bindeth up their w. [w., 26 : 22.
Pr. 18 : 8. words of talebearer are as
23 : 29. who hath w. with-t cause?
27 : 6. Faithful are but w. of friend
Is. 1 : 6. no soundn-s, but w. bruises
Je. 6 : 7. before me is grief and w.
30 : 17. I will heal thee of thy w.
Zch. 13 : 6. What these w. in hands?
Lu. 10 : 34. Samaritan bound his w.

WOUND. [Verb.] [linen

Jn. 19 : 40. took body of Jes., w. it in
Ac. 5 : 6. young men w. Ananias up

WOUND. [Verb.]

De. 32 : 39. I kill, I w., and I heal
Ps. 68 : 21. God shall w. his enemies
110 : 6. w. the heads over countries
Am. 9 : † 1. w. them in the head all
1 Co. 8 : 12. ye w. their weak con-

WOUNDED. [science

De. 23 : 1. He that is w. in stones
Ju. 9 : 40. many overthrown and w.
20 : † 31. smite of the peo. w., † 39.
1 S. 17 : 52. w. of Philist-s fell down
31 : † 1. men of Israel fell down w.
in mount Gilboa, 1 Ch. 10 : † 1.
3. Saul was sore w. of the archers, 1 Ch. 10 : 3. [Ps. 18 : 38.
2 S. 22 : 39. mine enemies I have w.,
1 K. 20 : 37. in smiting he w. him
22 : 34. carry me out of the host,
for I am w., 2 Ch. 18 : 33.
2 K. 8 : 28. the Syrians w. Joram
† 29. wounds wherewith Syrians
w. him (2). 2 Ch. 22 : † 6. [w.
2 Ch. 35 : 23. Have me aw., I am sore
Jb. 24 : 12. soul of the w. crieth out
Ps. 64 : 7. suddenly shall they be w.
69 : 26. to grief of those thou hast w.
109 : 22. I am poor, my heart is w.
Pr. 7 : 26. hath cast down many w.
18 : 14. w. spirit who can bear?
Can. 5 : 7. watchm. found me, w. me
Is. 51 : 9. thou not it that w. dragon?
53 : 5. he was w. for our transgr-ns
Je. 30 : 14. I w. thee with wound of
37 : 10. there remained but w. men
51 : 52. thro. all her land w. groan
La. 2 : 12. swooned as w. in streets
Eze. 26 : 15. isles shake when w. cry
28 : 23. w. shall be judged in her
30 : 24. groanings of deadly w. man
Jo. 2 : 8. fall upon sword, not be w.
Zch. 13 : 6. w. in house of my friends
Mk. 12 : 4. he sent another servant,
they w. him, Lu. 20 : 12. [him
Lu. 10 : 30. fell amo. thieves wh. w.
Ac. 19 : 16. they fled out naked, w.
Re. 13 : 3. I saw one of his heads w.

WOUNDEDST, ETH.

Jb. 5 : 18. he w-h, his hands make
Eze. 28 : † 9. thou no God in hand of
him that w-h thee [wicked
Ha. 3 : 13. w-t head out of house of

WOUNDING. [w.

Ge 4 : 23. I have slain a man to my
1 K. 20 : † 37. man smote, w. him

WOVE, WOVEN.

Ex. 39 : 22. ephod of w-n work, 28 : 32.
27. coats of linen, w-n work for A.
2 K. 23 : 7. women w. hangings for
Jn. 19 : 23. coat without seam w-n

WRANGLING. [w.

Ja. 3 : † 17. wisdom fr. above is wi-t

WRAP. [himself in

Is. 28 : 20. narrower than he can w.
Mi. 7 : 3. judge asketh for a reward;
so they w. it up

WRAPPED.

Ge. 38 : 14. Tamar w. herself, sat in
1 S. 21 : 9. sword of Goliath w. in cl.
1 K. 19 : 13. Elijah w. face in mantle
2 K. 2 : 8. Elijah took mantle, w. it
Jb 8 : 17. His roots are w. about heap
40 : 17. sinews of his stones are w.
Eze. 21 : 15. sword w. for slaughter
Jon. 2 : 5. weeds w. about my head
Mat. 27 : 59. Joseph w. body in linen, Mk. 15 : 46. Lu. 23 : 53.
Lu. 2 : 7. Mary w. him in swaddling
12. find babe w. in swad-g clothes
Jn. 20 : 7. napkin w. together in

WRATH. [cruel

Ge. 49 : 7. Cursed be their w., it was
Le. 10 : 6. lest w. come upon all peo.

Nu. 1 : 53. that be no w. upon the congregation, 18 : 5. [the Lord
16 : 46. there is w. gone out from
De. 29 : 28.L. rooted them out in w.
32 : 27. Were it not I feared w. of
Jos. 9 : 20. let them live, lest w. be
22 : 20. w. fell on all the congreg-n
2S. 11 : 20. if so be king's w. arise
1 Ch. 27 : 24.he finished not, bec. w.
2 Ch. 19 : 2.is w. upon thee fr. Lord
10.so w.come upon you and your
24 : 18. w. came upon Judah for
28 : 13. there is fierce w. ag. Israel
32 : 25. therefore was w. upon him
Ezr. 7 : 23.why be w. ag. the realm?
Ne. 13 : 18. ye bri. more w.upon Isr.
Es. 1 : 18.thus sh. arise too much w.
2 : 1.when w. of king was appeased
3 : 5.M.bowed not,Haman,full of w.
7 : 10. Then was king's w. pacified.
Jb. 5 : 2. For w. killeth foolish man
19 : 29. w. bring-h the punishment
21 : 20.sh. drink of w. of Almighty
36 : 13. But hypocrites heap up w.
18. is w., beware lest he take thee
Ps.37 : 8.Cease fr. anger, forsake w.
55 : 3. wicked ; in w. they hate me
59 : 13. Consume them in w. that
76 : 10. w. of man sh. praise thee, remainder of w. thou restrain
138 : 7. thine hand ag. w. of enem-s
Pr. 11 : 23.expecta-n of wicked is w.
12 : 16.A fool's w. presently known
14 : 29.He that is slow to w. is of gr.
15 : 1.A soft answer turneth aw. w.
16 : 14. w. of king as messeng-s of d.
19 : 12. king's w. as roaring of lion
19. A man of great w. shall suffer
21 : 14. a reward pacifieth strong w.
24.scorner,who deal-h in proud w.
27 : 3.fool's w. is heavier than both
4. w. is cruel, anger is outrageous
29 : 8. wise men turn away w.
30 : 33.forcing of w. bringeth strife
Ec. 5 : 17. much w. with his sickn-s
Is. 13 : 9. day of Lord cometh wi. w.
14 : 6. He who smote people in w.
54 : 8. In a little w. I hid my face
Je. 21 : 5. I will fight ag-t you in w.
32 : 37. whi. driven them in gr. w.
Eze. 7 : 12. w. is upon all multitude
Na. 1 : 2. he reserveth w. for enemies
Ha. 3 : 2.L.,in w. remember mercy
Zch. 7 : 12. came a great w. fr. Lord
Mat. 3 : 7. who warned you to flee from w. to come? Lu. 3 : 7.
Lu. 4 : 28. filled with w.. Ac. 19 : 28.
21 : 23. sh. be w. upon this people
Ro. 2 : 5. treasurest up w. against the day of w. [eousness, w.
8. unto them that obey unright-
4 : 15. Because the law worketh w.
5 : 9. we shall be saved from w.
9 : 22. endured the vessels of w.
12 : 19.but rather give pla. unto w.
13 : 4.minister of God to execute w.
5. ye be subject, not only for w.
Ga. 5 : 20. works of the flesh are w.
Ep. 2 : 3. we by nature chil. of w.
4 : 26.let not sun go down upon w.
31. Let all w., anger be put away
Col. 3 : 8. put off all these, w., mal.
1 Th. 1 : 10. us from the w. to come
2 : 16. w. upon them to uttermost
5 : 9. G. hath not appointed us to w.
1 Ti. 2 : 8. holy hands, without w.
He. 11 : 27. Moses not fearing w. of
Ja. 1 : 19. let ev. man be slow to w.
20. w. worketh not righteousn-s
Re. 6 : 16. hide us from w. of Lamb
12 : 12. devil is come down unto you, having great w. [3.
14 : 8.nations drink wine of w., 18:

Day of WRATH. [w.
Jb. 20 : 28.goods flow aw. in d. o. his
21 : 30. the wicked shall be brought forth to the d. w.
Ps. 110 : 5. Lord strike thro. kings in the d. o. his w.
Pr. 11 : 4. Riches profit not in d. w.
Zph. 1 : 15. That day is a w. and
18.Nei. gold deliver them in d.o. Lord's w. [d. w.
Ro. 2 : 5. treasurest up wrath against
Re. 6 : 17. the great d. o. his w. is

WRATH of God. [come
2 Ch. 28 : 11. fierce w. is upon you
Ezr. 10 : 14. until w. be turned
Ps. 78 : 31. The w. came upon th.
Jn. 3 : 36. the w. abideth on him
Ro. 1 : 18. w. is revealed fr. heav.
Ep.5 : 6.bec.of th. things cometh w.
Col. 3 : 6. For wh. cometh the w.
Re.14 : 10. shall drink of wine of w.
19. cast it into winepress of w.
15 : 1. in them is filled up the w.
7. seven golden vials full of w.
16 : 1.pour vials of w. upon earth
19 : 15. he treadeth winepress of

His WRATH. [w.
De. 29 : 23. Lord overthrew in h. w.
1 S. 28 : 18. h. fierce w. upon Am-k
2 K. 23 : 26. Lord turned not from fierceness of h. great w. [30 : 8.
2 Ch. 29 : 10. that h. fierce w. turn,
Ezr. 8 : 22. h. w. is ag. all them that forsake him [quet in h. w.
Es. 7 : 7. king arising from the ban-
Jb. 16 : 9. He teareth me in h. w.
20 : 23. cast fury of h. w. upon him
Ps. 2 : 5. speak unto them in h. w.
21 : 9. L. swallow them up in h. w.
58 : 9. sh. take them away in h. w.
78 : 38.did not stir up all h. w. [w.
49. cast upon them fiercen. of h.
106 : 23. had not Moses stood to turn away h. w. [cans-h shame
Pr. 14 : 35. h. w. is against him that
24 : 18.lest L. turn aw. h. w. fr. him
Is. 16 : 6. pride of Moab and h. w.
Je. 7 : 29.forsaken generat-n of h. w.
10 : 10.at h. w. earth shall tremble
48 : 30.I know h. w. saith the Lord
La. 2 : 2. L. thrown down in h. w. strongholds of Judah [h. w.
3 : 1.I have seen affliction by rod of
Am. 1 : 11.bec. he kept h. w. forev.
Ro. 9 : 22. What if God, willing to shew h. w., endured [of h. w.
Re. 16 : 19. cup of wine of fierceness
See KINDLED.
See Wrath of the LORD.

My WRATH.
Ex. 22 : 24. m. w. shall wax hot [hot
32 : 10.let me alone, that m. w. wax
Nu. 25 : 11. Phinehas turned m. w.
2 Ch. 12 : 7. m. w. shall not be poured upon Jerus. [on this place
34 : 25. m. w. shall be poured up-
Ps. 95 : 11. Unto whom I sware in m. w., He. 3 : 11. [m. w.
Is. 10 : 6. send him against people of
60 : 10. for in m. w. I smote thee
Eze. 7 : 14. m. w. is upon all multit.
13 : 15. accomplish m. w. upon wall
21 : 31. I will blow against thee in fire of m. w., 22 : 21. [of m. w.
22 : 31. I consumed them with fire
38 : 19. in fire of m. w. ha. spoken
Ho. 5 : 10.pour out m. w. like water
13 : 11. k., I took him aw. in m. w.
He. 4 : 3. As I have sworn in m. w.

Provoke, ed, edst to or unto WRATH.
De. 9 : 7. Remember how thou p-t the Lord t. w. [t. w.
8. Also in Horeb ye p-d the Lord
22. at Massah ye p-d Lord t. w.
Ezr. 5 : 12. fathers had p-d G. u. w.
Je. 44 : 8. ye p. me u. w. wi. works
Zch. 8 : 14.when fath-s p-d me t. w.
Ep. 6 : 4. p. not your children t. w.

Thy WRATH. [ed
Ex. 15 : 7. sentest t. w. wh. consum-
32 : 11. why t. w. wax hot ag. peo.?
12. Turn from t. fierce w. ag. peo.
Jb. 14 : 13. keep me secret until t. w.
40 : 11. Cast abroad the rage of t. w.
Ps. 38 : 1. rebuke me not in t. w.
79 : 6. Pour out t. w. on heathen
85 : 3. Thou hast taken aw. all t. w.
88 : 7. t. w. lieth hard upon me
16. t. fierce w. goeth over me
89 : 46. shall t. w. burn like fire ?
90 : 7. by t. w. are we troubled
9. all our days are passed in t. w.
11. acc-g to thy fear so is t. w.
102 : 10. thine indignation and t. w.
Je. 18 : 20.I stood to turn away t. w.
Ha. 3 : 8. was t. w. against the sea
Re. 11 : 18. t. w. is come, time of

WRATHS. [dead
2 Co. 12 : 20. I fear lest be w., strifes

WRATHFUL.
Ps. 69 : 24.let thy w. anger take hold
Pr. 15 : 18. A w. man stirreth up

WREATH, S. [strife
1 K. 7 : 17. w-s of chain work [mels
2 Ch. 4 : 12. two w-s to cover pom-
13. 400 pomegranates on the two w-s ; two rows on each w.

WREATHED. [them
Pr. 8 : † 8.nothing w. or perverse in
La. 1 : 14. my transgressions are w.

WREATHEN.
Ex. 28 : 14. two chains ; of w. work, and fasten the w. chains to the ouches, 22, 24, 25.-39 : 15, 17, 18.
2 K. 25 : 17. w. work upon chapiter of brass ; sec. pillar wi. w. work

WREST. [w. judgm.
Ex. 23 : 2. nei. decline after many to
6. not w. judgment of thy poor
De. 16 : 19.Thou shalt not w. judgm.
Ps. 56 : 5.Ev. day they w. my words
2 Pe. 3 : 16.they th. are unstable w.

WRESTED, ING. [ment
Eze. 9 : † 9. city full of w-g of judg-
Ha. 1 : † 4. w-d judgment proceed-

WRESTLE, ED. [eth
Ge. 30 : 8.have I w-d with my sister
32 : 24. Jac. alone w-d, man wi. him
25. thigh out of joint as he w-d
2 S. 22 : † 27. with froward thou wilt w., Ps. 18 : † 26. [and blood
Ep. 6 : 12. we w. not against flesh

WRESTLING, S.
Ge. 30 : 8. great w-s with my sister ; she called his name, My W.

WRETCHED.
Ro. 7 : 24. O w. man that I am, who
Re. 3 : 17. knowest not thou art w.

WRETCHEDNESS.
Nu. 11 : 15.and let me not see my w.

WRIED.
Ps. 38 : † 6. I am w. ; I am bowed

WRING, ED.
Le. 1 : 15. priest sh. w. off head, 5 : 8.
Ju. 6 : 38. w-d the dew out of fleece
Ps. 75 : 8. all wicked shall w. them

WRINGER. [out
Is. 16 : † 4. for the w. is at an end

WRINGING. [blood
Pr. 30 : 33. w. of the nose bringeth

WRINKLE, S.
Jb. 16 : 8.thou hast filled me with w-s
Ep. 5 : 27. church not having spot

WRINKLING. [or w.
Na. 3 : † 19. is no w. of thy bruise

WRITE.
Ex. 34 : 1. I will w. upon these tables the words, De. 10 : 2.
27. Lord said to Moses, w. words
Nu. 17 : 2. w. ev. man's name upon
3. w. Aaron's name upon rod [rod
De. 6 : 9. w. them upon posts, 11 : 20.
24 : 1. then let him w. her bill of divorcement, 3. Mk. 10 : 4. [8.
27 : 3. w. upon stones words of law,
31 : 19. w. ye this song for you [w.
2 Ch. 26 : 22. acts of Uzziah did Is-h

Ezr. 5 : 10. might w. names of men
Ne. 9 : 38. a sure covenant and w. it
Es. 8 : 8. w. ye for Jews as it liketh
Pr. 3 : 3. w. them upon the table of
thine heart, 7 : 3. [man's pen
Is. 8 : 1. w. in the great roll with a
10 : 1. that w. grievousness which
19. trees few, that a child may w.
30 : 8. w. it before them in a table
Je. 22 : 30. w. ye this man childless
30 : 2. w. words I have spoken, 36 : 2.
31 : 33. w. my law in their hearts
36 : 17. How didst w. these words
28. ano. roll, w. in it former words
Eze. 24 : 2. w. the name of the day
37 : 16. stick, w. upon it, For Judah; take another stick, w.,
For Joseph [sight
43. 11. w. the form of house in their
Ha. 2 : 2. w. vision, make it plain
Lu. 1 : 3. good to me to w. unto thee
16 : 6. take thy bill and w. fifty
7. said, Take thy bill, w. fourscore
Jn. 1 : 45. of whom Moses did w.
19 : 21. w. not, King of the Jews
Ac. 15 : 20. w. that they abstain fr.
25 : 26. Of whom no certain thing
to w.; might have somew. to w.
1 Co. 4 : 14. I w. not to shame you
14 : 37. things I w. are command-s
2 Co. 1 : 13. we w. none other things
2 : 9. to this end also did I w. that
9 : 1. superfluous for me to w. you
13 : 2. I w. to them which sinned
10. I w. these things, being abs-t
Ga. 1 : 20. the things I w. I lie not
Ph. 3 : 1. To w. same things is safe
1 Th. 4 : 9. ye need not that I w. un-
2 Th. 3 : 17. so I w. [to you, 5 : 1.
1 Ti. 3 : 14. These things w. I unto
thee, 1 Jn. 2 : 1. [hearts
He. 8 : 10. will w. my laws in their
10 : 16. in their minds will I w. th.
2 Pe. 3 : 1. I now w. second epistle
1 Jn. 1 : 4. these things w. we you
2 : 7. I w. no new commandment
8. Again, a new command-t I w.
12. I w. unto you, little chil. 1, 13.
13. I w. unto you, fathers, I w.
2 Jn. 12. many things to w. you; I
will not w. with paper, 3 Jn. 13.
Jude 3. when I gave diligence to w.
of salvation, needful to w.
Re. 1 : 19. w. things thou hast seen
2 : 1. Unto angel of the church of
Ephesus w. | 8. in Smyrna w.
12. Pergamos w. | 18. Thyatira w.
3 : 1. in Sardis w. | 7. Philadelphia w.
12. I will w. upon him name of
my God, I will w. my new name
14. unto church of Laodiceans, w.
10 : 4. I was about to w.; I heard
a voice, w. not [that die in L.
14 : 13. w., Blessed are the dead
19 : 9. w., Blessed are they which
21 : 5. w., for these words are true
See Book.

WRITER, S.

[w.
Ju. 5 : 14. that handle the pen of the
2 S. 8 : †16. was w. of chronicles
Ps. 45 : 1. is the pen of a ready w.
Is. 10 : †1. Woe to the w-s that write
grievousness [his side, 3.
Eze. 9 : 2. with a w.'s inkhorn by

WRITEST, ETH.

[me
Jb. 13 : 26. w-t bitter things against
Ps. 87 : 6. count when he w-h up
Eze. 37 : 20. sticks whereon thou w-t

WRITING.

[God
Ex. 32 : 16. the w. was the w. of
39 : 30. crown, wrote upon it a w.
De. 10 : 4. on tables, acc-g to first w.
31 : 24. made an end of w. the law
1 Ch. 28 : 19. made me underst. in w.
2 Ch. 2 : 11. Huram answered in w.
21 : 12. w. to Jehoram from Elijah
35 : 4. prepare acc-g to w. of Da. (2)
2 Ch. 36 : 22. Cyrus put the proclamation in w., Ezr. 1 : 1. [tongue
Ezr. 4 : 7. w. of letter in the Syrian
6 : †18. acc-g to w. in book of Mos.
Es. 1 : 22. he sent letters unto every
province, according to the w.
thereof, 3 : 12.–8 : 9. (2) [ed, 8 : 13.
3 : 14. copy of the w. was publish-
4 : 8. to Hatach a copy of the w.
8 : 8. the w. in the king's name [w.
9 : 27. keep those two days acc-g to
Is. 38 : 9. The w. of Hezekiah when
Eze. 13 : 9. not in w. of house of Isr.
Da. 5 : 7. Whosoever sh. read this w.
8. wise men could not read w., 15.
16. if read w. thou sh. be clothed
17. I will read the w. unto king
25. this is the w. was written, 24.
6 : 8. Now, O king, sign the w.
9. Darius signed the w. and decree
10. when Dan. knew w. was signed
Mat. 5 : 31. let him give her a w. of
divorcement, 19 : 7.
Jn. 19 : 19. w. was, Jesus the King
See Handwriting.

WRITING table.

Lu. 1 : 63. Zacharias asked for a w. t.

WRITINGS.

Jn. 5 : 47. if ye believe not his w.

WRITTEN.

Ex. 31 : 18. two tables w. with finger of God, De. 9 : 10. [sides (2)
32 : 15. tables were w. on both their
Nu. 11 : 26. they of them th. were w.
Jos. 1 : 8. do acc-g to all is w. therein
2 K. 22 : 13. not do that w. conc. us
1 Ch. 4 : 41. these w. by name smote
2 Ch. 13 : 22. acts of Abijah w. in
33 : 19. w. among sayings of seers
35 : 25. are w. in the lamentations
Ezr. 4 : 7. letter was w. in Syrian
5 : 7. sent letter wh-in was w. thus
6 : 2. therein was a record thus w.
8 : 34. weight was w. at that time
Ne. 6 : 6. open letter, wherein was w.
7 : 5. I found w. therein, These
8 : 14. w. in the law, Israel should
dwell in booths [into cong. of G.
13 : 1. w. th-in, Ammonite not come
Es. 1 : 19. w. among laws of Medes
3 : 9. let it be w., they be destroyed
12. w. acc. to all Haman com-ded
6 : 2. found w. that Mordecai told
8 : 5. w. to reverse letters by Ha-n
8. writing wh. is w. in king's nam.
9 : 23. as Mordecai had w. unto
Jb. 19 : 23. Oh th. my words were w.
Ps. 69 : 28. not be w. with righte-s
102 : 18. be w. for generation to
149 : 9. To execute judgment w.
Pr. 22 : 20. Have I not w. excellent
Ec. 12 : 10. what was w. was upright
Is. 4 : 3. holy, every one that is w.
Je. 17 : 1. sin is w. with pen of iron
13. they shall be w. in the earth
36 : 6. go read in roll thou hast w.
29. Why hast w. th-in, The king
of Bab-n shall come [and woe
Eze. 2 : 10. was w. th-in lamentations
13 : 9. nei. be w. in writing of Israel
Da. 5 : 25. the writ-g that was w., 24.
Mat. 27 : 37. set up his accusation
w., Mk. 15 : 26. Lu. 23 : 38. [en
Lu. 10 : 20. your names w. in heav-
18 : 31. all things w. conc. Son sh.
20 : 17. What is this that is w.?
21 : 22. that all things w. be fulfil-d
22 : 37. that is w. must be accompl-d
24 : 44. w. in law of Mos. conc. me
Jn. 10 : 34. Is it not w., I said, Ye
12 : 16. rememb-d these things w.
15 : 25. word w., They hated me
20 : 30. many signs did Jes. not w.
31. are w. that ye might believe
21 : 25. if they should be w., world
not contain the books w. [him
Ac. 13 : 29. fulfilled all th. was w. of
Ac. 21 : 25. As touching Gentiles, w.
Ro. 2 : 15. work of law w. in hearts
4 : 23. not w. for his sake alone
15 : 4. whatsoever things were w.
aforetime were w. for our learn.
1 Co. 4 : 6. of men above that is w.
9 : 10. For our sakes this is w.
10 : 11. are w. for our admonition
15 : 54. brought to pass that is w.
2 Co. 3 : 2. Ye are our epistle, w. in
3. w. not with ink, but the Spirit
7. if ministration of death w. in
He. 12 : 23. church of firstborn w.
2 Pe. 3 : 15. as Paul hath w. unto
Re. 1 : 3. keep those things w. th-in
2 : 17. in the stone a new name w.
13 : 8. names not w. in book of life
14 : 1. Fa.'s name w. in foreheads
17 : 5. upon forehead w. Mystery
19 : 12. a name w. no man knew
16. had name w. on his thigh,
King of Kings [twelve tribes
21 : 12. gates, names w. thereon of

As it is WRITTEN.

Ezr. 3 : 4. keep feast of taberna. – w.
Ne. 8 : 15. trees to make booths, – w.
Mat. 26 : 24. The Son of man goeth,
– w. of him, Mk. 14 : 21. [ger
Mk. 1 : 2. – w., I will send messen-
7 : 6. – w., This peo. honoureth me
9 : 13. whatso. they listed, – w. of
Lu. 3 : 4. – w. in book of Esaias [him
Jn. 6 : 31. – w., He gave them bread
12 : 14. – w., thy King cometh sit-g
Ac. 7 : 42. – w., O ye house of Israel
13 : 33. – w., Thou art my Son
15 : 15. – w., After this I will return
Ro. 1 : 17. – w., The just shall live
2 : 24. God is blasphemed, – w. [by
3 : 4. – w., That thou be justified
10. – w., There is none righteous
4 : 17. – w., I made thee father of
8 : 36. – w., For thy sake are killed
9 : 13. – w., Jacob have I loved
33. – w., Behold I lay in Sion [feet
10 : 15. – w., How beautiful are the
11 : 8. acc. – w., God given slumber
26. – w., There sh. come out of S.
15 : 3. – w., The reproaches fell on
9. – w., For this cause I will conf.
21. – w., they sh. see and underst.
1 Co. 1 : 31. acc. – w., He that glori-
2 : 9. – w., Eye hath not seen [eth
10 : 7. – w., The peo. sat down to eat
2 Co. 4 : 13. acc-g – w., I believed
8 : 15. – w., He that gathered much
9 : 9. (– w., He hath dispersed)
See BOOK.
See BOOK of the law.
See BOOK of life.
See Written in the BOOK.
See BOOK of Moses.

I have or Have I WRITTEN.

[h. w.
Ex. 24 : 12. will give thee comm-ts I
Ho. 8 : 12. I h. w. to him gr. things
Jn. 19 : 22. What I h. w. I h. w.
Ro. 15 : 15. I h. w. more boldly [pany
1 Co. 5 : 11. I h. w., not to keep com-
9 : 15. nei. h. I w. these things th.
Ga. 6 : 11. how large a letter I h. w.
Phm. 19. I, Paul, h. w. wi. own ha.
1 Pe. 5 : 12. I h. w. briefly, He. 13 : 22.
1 Jn. 2 : 14. I h. w. unto you fathers;
I h. w. unto you young men
21. I h. not w. unto you, because
26. These things h. I w. you, 5 :

It is WRITTEN.

[13.
Ps. 40 : 7. Lo, in the volume – w. of
me, He. 10 : 7. [ompense
Is. 65 : 6. – w. before me, I will rec-
Mat. 2 : 5. – w., And thou Bethle-m
4 : 4. – w., Man shall not live by
bread alone, Lu. 4 : 4. [Lu. 4 : 10.
6. – w., He sh. give angels charge,
7. – w., Thou sh. not tempt Lord
10. – w., worship the L., Lu. 4 : 8.

Mat. 11 : 10. is he, of whom - w. I send my messenger, Lu. 7 : 27.
21 : 13. - w., My house shall be called, Mk. 11 : 17. Lu. 19 : 46.
26 : 31. - w., I will smite shepherd, Mk. 14 : 27. [sunder, Lu. 24:46.
Mk. 9 : 12. - w., of the Son, he must
Jn. 6 : 45. - w., they shall be taught
8 : 17. - w. that testimony of 2 men
Ac. 23 : 5. - w., not speak evil of rul.
Ro. 12 : 19. - w., Vengeance is mine
14 : 11. - w., every knee shall bow
1 Co. 1 : 19. - w., I will destroy wisd.
3 : 19. - w., He taketh the wise in their craftiness [lips will I spe.
14 : 21. - w., With men of other
15 . 45. so - w., The first man Adam
Ga. 3 : 10. - w., Cursed is ev. one, 13.
4 : 22. - w. that Abr. had two sons
27. - w., Rejoice thou barren, for
1 Pe. 1 : 16. Because - w., Be ye holy

It was WRITTEN.

1 K. 21 : 11. elders, nobles did as - w.
2 Ch. 30 . 5. not of long time, - w.
18. eat passover otherw. than - w.
Es. 3 : 12. in name of Ahasuerus, - w.
8 : 9. - w. acc. to all Mordecai com.
Eze. 2 : 10. roll, - w. within, without
Lu. 4 : 17. found place where - w.
Jn. 2 : 17. disciples rememb-d - w.
19 : 20. - w. in Hebrew, Greek, Latin

See **Written in the LAW.**
See **LAW of the Lord.**
See PROPHET, PROPHETS.

WRONG. [on thee

Ge. 16 : 5. Sarai said, My w. be up-
Ex. 2 : 13. said to him th. did the w.
De. 19 : 16. testify ag. him wh. is w.
Ju. 11 : 27. doest me w. to war ag.
1 Ch. 12 : 17. is no w. in mine hands
16 : 21. he suffered no man to do them w., Ps. 105 : 14. [only
Es. 1 : 16. Vashti not done w. to king
Jb. 19 . 7. I cry out of w., am not
Ps. 35 : † 11. Witnesses of w. did rise
Je. 22 : 3. do no w. to the stranger
13. buildeth his chambers by w.
La. 3 : 59. O L., thou hast seen my w.
Ha. 1 : 4. thf. w. judgm. proceedeth
Mat. 20 : 13. Friend, I do thee no w.
Ac. 7 : 24. and seeing one suffer w.
26. why do ye w. one to another?
27. he that did his neighbour w.
18 : 14. If it were a matter of w. [w.
25 : 10. Paul said, Have I done no
1 Co. 6 : 7. Why do ye not take w.?
8. Nay, ye do w. and defraud
2 Co. 7 : 12. did it not for his cause that had done the w., nor for his that suffered w. [this w.
12 : 13. not burdensome, forgive me
Col. 3 : 25. But he that doeth w. shall receive for the w.

WRONGED, ETH.

Pr. 8 : 36. th. sinneth w-h own soul
2 Co. 7 : 2. we have w-d no man
Phm. 18. If he hath w-d thee, or

WRONGFULLY.

Jb. 21 : 27. devices ye w. imagine
Ps. 35 : 19. Let not enemies w. rejoice
38 : 19. that hate me w. are multipl.
69 : 4. destroy me, mine enemies w.
119 : 86. they persecute me w.
Eze. 22 : 29. oppressed stranger w.
1 Pe. 2 : 19. if endure grief, suffering

WROTE. [w.

Ex. 24 : 4. Moses w. all words of L.
34 : 28. Lord w. upon tables ten commandments, De. 4 : 13.-5 : 22.-10 : 4. [it, HOLINESS.
39 : 30. crown of gold and w. upon
Nu. 33 : 2. Moses w. their goings out
De. 31 : 9. And Moses w. this law
De. 31 : 22. Moses w. this song, taught it chil. of Israel [law
Jos. 8 : 32. Josh. w. upon stones the
2 S. 11 : 14. Da. w. letter to Joab, 15.
1 K. 21 : 8. Jezebel w. letters, 9. [5.
2 K. 10 : 1. Jehu w. letters to Sam-a,
17 : 37. law he w. for you, observe
1 Ch. 24 : 6. Shemaiah w. them
2 Ch. 30 : 1. Hez. w. letters to Ephr.
32 : 17. Sennach-b w. to rail on G.
Ezr. 4 : 6. w. accusation ag. Judah
7. in days of Artax-s w. Bishlam
8. Rehum and Shimshai w., 9.
Es. 8 : 5. Haman w. to destroy Jews
10. Mordecai w. letters, 9 : 20, 29.
Je. 36 : 4. Baruch w. from mouth of Jeremiah, 18, 27, 32. [wall
Da. 5 : 5. a man's hand w. upon the
6 : 25. Darius w. unto all people
7 : 1. Daniel w. the dream and told
Mk. 10 : 5. Moses w. you this precept
12 : 19. Moses w. unto us, Lu. 20 : 28.
Lu. 1 : 63. Zacharias w., His name is
Jn. 5 : 46 for Moses w. of me [John
8 : 6. Jesus w. on the ground, 8.
19 : 19. Pilate w. a title and put it
21 : 24. disciple wh. w. these things
Ac. 15 : 23. apostles w. letters by
18 : 27. the brethren w. exhorting
23 : 25. Lysias w. after this man-r
Ro. 16 : 22. I, Tertius, who w. epistle
1 Co. 5 : 9. I w. in an epistle
7 : 1. conc. things wh-f ye w. [row
2 Co. 2 : 3 I w. lest I sho. have sor-
4. I w. unto you with many tears
7 : 12. tho. I w. I did it not for his
Ep. 3 : 3. as I w. afore in few words
Phm. 21. I w., knowing thou wilt
2 Jn. 5. not as tho. I w. new com-t
3 Jn. 9. I w. unto church : but Diot-
See BOOK. [rephes

WROTH.

Ge. 4 : 5. And Cain was very w.
6. Lord said, Why art thou w.?
31 : 36. Jacob was w. with Laban
34 : 7. sons of Jacob were very w.
40 : 2. Pha-h w. with officers, 41 : 10.
Nu. 16 : 15. And Moses was very w., 31 : 14. Ex. 16 : 20. [gregat-n?
22. wilt thou be w. with all con-
De. 1 : 34. the Lord heard and was w., 9 : 19. Ps. 78 : 21, 59. [sakes
3 : 26. Lord w. with me for your
Jos. 22 : 18. w. with whole congr-n
1 S. 18 : 8. Saul was very w. [ev. lis
20 : 7. if he be very w., be sure that
29 : 4. princes of Philis. w. with him
2 S. 3 : 8. Then was Abner very w.
13 : 21. Dav. heard, he was very w.
22 : 8. heaven shook because he was w., Ps. 18 : 7. [away
2 K. 5 : 11. Naaman was w., went
13 : 19. man of God was w. wi. him
2 Ch. 16 : 10. Asa was w. with the seer
28 : 9. the Lord was w. with Judah
26 : 19. Uzziah, while w. wi. priests (2)
Ne. 4 : 7. Sanballat, Tobiah, very w.
Es. 1 : 12. Vashti refused; k. very w.
2 : 21. Bigthan, Teresh were w.
Ps. 78 : 62. was w. with inheritance
89 : 38. been w. wi. thine anointed
Is. 28 : 21. be w. as in valley of Gib-
47 : 6. I was w. with my people [eon
54 : 9. I would not be w. with thee
57 : 16. neither will I be always w.
17. For his covetousness was I w., I hid me, and was w. [sinned
64 : 5. thou art w.; for we have
9. Be not w. very sore, O Lord
Je. 37 : 15. princes were w. wi. Jere-h
La. 5 : 22. thou art very w. ag-t us
Mat. 2 : 16. Herod was exceeding w.
18 : 34. lord was w. delivered him
22 : 7. when king heard, he was w.
Re. 12 : 17. dragon was w. with the

WROUGHT. [woman

Ge. 34 : 7. Shechem had w. folly in
Ex. 10 : 2. things I have w. in Eg-t
36 : 1. Then w. Bezaleel, Aholiab
4. wise men w. work of sanct-y, 8.
39 : 6. they w. onyx stones in ouches
Le. 20 : 12. they have w. confusion
Nu. 23 : 23. What hath God w.?
De. 17 : 2. man th. hath w. wickedn.
22 : 21. she hath w. folly in Israel, Jos. 7 : 15. Ju. 20 : 10. [w. (2)
31 : 18. for evils which they sh. have
Ru. 2 : 19. man's name with whom I w. to day is Boaz [among them
1 S. 6 : 6. Lord hath w. wonderfully
11 : 13. L. hath w. salvation, 19 : 5.
14 : 45. Jonathan hath w. with G.
† 48. Saul w. mightily and smote
2 S. 18 : 13. Otherwise I should have w. falsehood [day, 12
23 : 10. Lord w. a great victory that
1 K. 5 : 16. over people th. w., 9 : 23.
16 : 20. Zimri, and the treason he w.
25. Omri w. evil in eyes of the L.
2 K. 3 : 2. Jehoram w. evil in sight of the Lord, 2 Ch. 21 : 6. [of L.
12 : 11. builders that w. upon hou.
17 : 11. Israel w. wicked things
21 : 6. Manasseh w. much wicked-ness, 2 Ch. 33 : 6. [fine linen
1 Ch. 4 : 21. house of them that w.
2 Ch. 3 : 14. he w. cherubim th-on
24 : 12. hired such as w. iron, brass
13. So the workmen w., 34 : 10, 13.
31 : 20. Hez-h w. that wh. was good
32 : † 24. Lord w. miracle for Hez.
Ne. 4 : 16. half of my servants w.
17. every one with one of hands w.
9 : 18. they w. great provocat-s, 26.
Jb. 12 : 9. hand of L. hath w. this
36 : 23. who can say, Thou hast w. iniquity? [trust in thee
Ps. 31 : 19. hast w. for them that
68 : 28. strengthen that thou hast
78 : 43. How he w. signs in Eg. [w.
Ec. 2 : 11. all works my hands had w.
Is. 26 : 12. hast w. our works in us
18. we have not w. deliverance
41 : 4. Who hath w. and done it? I
Je. 11 : 15. she w. lewdn. with many
18 : 3. he w. a work on the wheels
Eze. 20 : 9. But I w. for my name's sake, 14, 22, 44. [w. for me
29 : 20. given him Egypt, bec. they
Da. 4 : 2. wonders G. hath w. tow. me
Jon. 1 : 11. sea w., was tempest-s, 13.
Zph. 2 : 3. wh. have w. his judgm-t
Mat. 20 : 12. last have w. but one h.
26 : 10. she hath w. a good work upon me, Mk. 14 : 6. [w. 21 : 19.
Ac. 15 : 12. what wonders God had
18 : 3. Paul abode wi. them and w.
19 : 11. God w. special miracles by
Ro. 7 : 8. w. in me concupiscence
15 : 18. Christ hath not w. by me
2 Co. 5 : 5. he that hath w. us is G.
7 : 11. what carefulness it w. in you
Ga. 2 : 8. that w. effectually in Peter
Ep. 1 : 20. Which he w. in Christ
2 Th. 3 : 8. we w. with labour, night
He. 11 : 33. who w. righteousness
Ja. 2 : 22. faith w. with his works?
1 Pe. 4 : 3. w. the will of the Gentiles
2 Jn. 8. we lose not those things wh. we have w. [w. miracles
Re. 19 : 20. the false prophet that

WROUGHT. [Passive.]

Ex. 26 : 36. an hanging of linen w. with needlework, 27 : 16.
Nu. 31 : 51. Moses took of them all w. jewels [is w., 17 : 4.
De. 13 : 14. that such abomination
21 : 3. a heifer wh. hath not been w.
1 K. 7 : 26. with flowers brim was w.
1 Ch. 22 : 2. masons to hew w. stones
Ne. 6 : 16. this work was w. of our G.
Ps. 45 : 13. her clothing of w. gold
139 : 15. when I was curiously w.
Ec. 2 : 17. the work w. is grievous
Mat. 14 : † 2. risen, mighty works are w. by him, Mk. 6 : 2. [of God
Jn. 3 : 21. manifest that they are w.
19 : † 23. coat w. from top thro-out

Ac. 5 : 12. wonders w. among people
2 Co. 1 : †6. w. in enduring sufferings
12 : 12. signs of an apostle were w.

WROUGHTEST. [thou?
Ru. 2 : 19. said to Ruth, Where w.

WRUNG. [5 : 9.
Le. 1 : 15. the blood shall be w. out,
Ps. 73 : 10. waters are w. out to th.
Is. 51 : 17. hast drunken dregs of cup
of trembling and w. them out

Y.

YARN.
1 K. 10 : 28. Solomon had out of
Egypt linen y. (2), 2 Ch. 1 : 16. (2)

YE. [ing good
Ge. 3 : 5. y. shall be as gods, know-
24 : 49. if y. deal truly with master
29 : 4. My brethren, whence be y.?
31 : 6. y. know I have served your
34 : 15. If y. will be as we be [father
40 : 7. Wh. look y. so sadly to day
42 : 9. y. are spies ; to see nakedn-s
19. If y. be true men let one of
Ex. 19 : 5. if y. obey my voice y. sh.
Le. 11 : 44. y. shall be holy, for I am,
(2). 19 : 2.-20 : 7. 1 Pe. 1 : 16. [er
19 : 2. y. sh. fear ev. man his moth-
20 : 26. y. shall be holy, y. be mine
25 : 13. that y. sho. not be bondm.
23. if y. will not be reformed by
Nu. 12 : 8. wheref. were y. not afraid
1 S. 4 : 9. quit like men, O y. Philistines, that y. be not servants
14 : 40. Be y. on one side, I will
23 : 21. Blessed be y. of the L., y.
2 K. 3 : 17. y. sh. not see wind, nei.
rain, yet may drink, y. and (4)
11 : 5. This is the thing y. shall do
2 Ch. 30 : 6. y. child-n of Israel turn
8. Now be y. not stiffnecked as
your fathers were, 7. Zch. 1 : 4.
Ezr. 6 : 6. Now be y. far from thence
Ne. 2 : 20. y. have no portion in Je-
4 : 14. Be not y. afraid of them [rus.
Jb. 12 : 2. No doubt y. are the people
13 : 4. y. are forgers of lies, y. are
9. mocketh, do y. so mock him?
16 : 4. I also could speak as y. do
19 : 2. how long will y. vex my soul?
21. Have pity, O y. my friends
29. Be y. afraid of the sword
32 : 6. I am young, y. are very old
Ps. 32 : 11. Be glad in the Lord, y.
righteous, 33 : 1. [sons of men
58 : 1. do y. judge uprightly, O y.
62 : 3. as a bowing wall shall y. be
82 : 6. I have said y. are gods ; and
94 : 8. y. fools, wh. will y. be wise?
97 : 10. y. that love the L. hate evil
105 : 6. O y. seed of Abr., y. child-n
115 : 11. y. that fear the L., 135 : 20.
148 : 4. Praise him y. heavens, y.
Is. 28 : 22. Now thf. be y. not mockers
33 : 11. y. shall conceive chaff, y. sh.
41 : 23. we may know y. are gods
24. Behold, y. are of nothing, and
44 : 8. y. are even my witnesses
23. Sing, O y. heavens ; shout, y. (3)
50 : 11. y. sh. lie down in sorrow (4)
51 : 7. nei. be y. afraid of revil-gs (3)
52 : 11. go y. ou. of the midst of her,
be y. clean that bear vessels (5)
55 : 1. Ho, come y. to the waters
57 : 4. are y. not chil. of transg-n (3)
14. shall say, Cast y. up, cast y.
65 : 11. y. are they th. forsake Lord
13. eat, but y. shall be hungry (3)
Je. 2 : 12. O y. heavens, be y. desol.
Je. 25 : 29. y. shall not be unpunished
29 : 13. y. shall find me when y.
30 : 22. y. sh. be my people [search
36 : 19. let no man know where y. be
44 : 25. y. and wives have spoken
46 : 9. y. horses ; rage y. chariots
48 : 14. How say y., We are mighty
28. O y. that dwell in Moab
49 : 3. cry, y. daughters of Rabbah
50 : 11. O y. destroyers of heritage (4)
51 : 46. lest y. fear for the rumour
Eze. 13 : 11. y., O great hailstones
20. y. hunt souls to make them fly
34 : 31. y. my flock, are men [y. see
Da. 2 : 8. y. would gain time because
Ho. 1 : 9. y. are not my people, 10.
10. y. are the sons of living God
5 : 1. give y. ear, O house of king
Jo. 2 : 22. Be not afraid y. beasts
Am 4 : 3. this liketh you, O y. chil.
Mi. 2 : 10. Arise y. and depart for
Zph. 2 : 12. y. Ethiop-s, y. be slain
Zch. 8 : 13. as y. were a curse y. sh.
11 : 2. howl, O y. oaks of Bashan
Mat. 5 : 13. y. are the salt of earth
14. y. are the light of the world
48. Be y. thf. perfect as your Fath.
6 : 8. your Fa. knoweth bef. y. ask
9. After this manner pray y., Our
26. Are y. not better than they?
7 : 11. If y. being evil, know how to
give good gifts, Lu. 11 : 13.
12. whatso. y. would men do to
you, do y. even so, Lu. 6 : 31 (2)
9 : 4. Wheref. think y. evil in heart
10 : 16. be y. thf. wise as serpents
20. is not y. that speak, but Spirit
31. y. are of more value th. many
14 : 16. Jesus said, Give y. them to
15 : 3. Why do y. transgress com-t
7. y. hypocrites, well did Esaias
16. Are y. yet without underst-g?
16 : 15. But whom say y. that I am?
18 : 12. How think y.? 21 : 28.-26 : 66.
19 : 28. y. which have followed me,
y. shall sit upon twelve thrones
20 : 4. Go y. into the vineyard, 7.
21 : 13. y. have made it a den of
16. have y. never read, Out of mou.
22. Whatsoever y. ask in prayer, y.
24. one thing which, if y. tell me
25. Why did y. not then believe?
32. y., when y. had seen it repented not that y. might believe (4)
23 : 8. be not y. called Rabbi [(8)
13. y. shut up kingdom of heaven
14. y. devour widows' houses (2)
15. y. compass sea and land to (2)
16. Woe unto you, y. blind g., 24.
17. y. fools and blind : for whe., 19.
23. y. pay tithe of mint, anise (2)
25. y. make clean outside of cup
27. y. are like whited sepulchres
28. y. outwardly appear righteous
29. y. build tombs of prophets [(2)
32. Fill y. up measure of your
33. y. serpents, y. generation of
vipers, how can y. escape
34. some y. sh. kill and crucify (2)
35. blood of Abel whom y. slew
37. often would I and y. wou. not
24 : 33. So y., when y. see all, know
42. y. know not what hour L., 44.
44. be y. also ready, Lu. 12 : 40 (2)
25 : 6. bridegroom ; go y. out to
27 : 24. I am innocent : see y. to it
28 : 5. Fear not y. ; I know y. seek
Mk. 6 : 37. y., 7 : 11, 18.-8 : 29.-11 :
17, 26. - 12 : 27. - 13 : 11, 23, 29.
Lu. 9 : 13, 20, 55. - 10 : 23, 24. -
47, 49, 54.-9 : 19, 30.-10 : 26, 36
- 11 : 49. - 13 : 10, 13, 14, 15, 33,
34.-14 : 3, 17, 19, (2) 20. (2)-15 :
3, 4, 5, 14, 16, (2) 27.-16 : 20, (2)
22, 27. - 18 : 31. - 19 : 6, 35. Ac.
1 : 5. - 2 : 15, 33, 36. - 3 : 13, 14,
25.-4 : 7, 10.-5 : 30.-7 : 4, 26.-8 :
24.-10 : 28, 37.-11 : 16.- 15 : 7.-
19 : 15. - 20 : 18, 25. -22 : 3.-23 :
15.- 27 : 31. Ro. 1 : 6. - 8 : 9.-9 :
26.-11 : 30.-16 : 17. 1 Co. 1 : 30.
-3 : 17, 23.-4 : 10, (3)-5 : 2, 12. -
6 : 7, 8.-9 : 1, 2.-10 : 15.-12 : 27.
-14 : 9, 12.-16 : 1, 6. 2 Co. 1 : 14.
-6 : 13, 16, 18.- 9 : 4.-11 : 7.-12 :
11.-13 : 9. Ga. 3 : 28.-4 : 13.-5 :
13. Ep. 1 : 13.-2 : 11, 22.-4 : 20.
-5 : Ph. 2 : 18. - 4 : 15. (2)
Col. 3 : 4, 7, 8, 13.-4 : 1, 16. 1
Th. 1 : 6.-2 : 10, 14. (2) - 4 : 9.
2 Th. 1 : 12. He. 10 : 25, 29, 33
(2). Ja. 2 : 3, 6, 9, 24.-3 : 14.-
4 : 5, 14. -5 : 3, 5, 6, 9, 11, 12. 1
Pe. 2 : 24, 25.-4 : 13.-(2)-5 : 10, 12.
1 Jn. 1 : 3.- 2 : 20, (2) 21, 24, (3)
27, (2) 29. (2)-3 : 5, 11, 15.-4 : 3,
3. 2 Jn. 6. (2) Jude 17, 20.
Mk. 8 : 17. Why reason y. because y.
have no bread? (4)
18. Having eyes, see y. not? and
ears, hear y. not? (3)
21. How is it y. do not understand
14 : 64. Wh. think y.? (2) Jn. 11 : 56.
Lu. 6 : 20. Blessed be y. poor
32. if y. love them wh. love you (2)
33. if y. do good to them wh. do (2)
34. if y. lend to th. of whom y. (3)
36. Be y. merciful as your Father
12 : 29. seek not y. what y. sh. eat (3)
33. Sell that y. have and give alms
54. When y. see cloud rise (2), 55 (2)
56. y. hypocrites, y. can disc. sky
21 : 31. So y. wh. y. see these (3) [(3)
22 : 10. when y. are entered into the
Jn. 3 : 7. y. must be born again [city
9 : 27. would y. hear it again? will
y. be his disciples (3) [do them
13 : 17. If y. know, happy y. if y.
15 : 8. so shall y. be my disciples (2)
Ac. 3 : 25. y. are child-n of prophets
5 : 9. How is it that y. have agreed [y.
7 : 51. y. stiffnecked, do as fathers so
52. Just One ; of wh. y. murderers
13 : 15. if y. have word of exhort-n
14 : 15. that y. turn from vanities
17 : 22. perceive y. are too supersti.
19 : 36. y. ought to be quiet and
Ro. 1 : 11. to the end y. be established
7 : 4. that y. be married to another
11 : 25. not that y. be ignorant of
mystery, lest y. be wise in own
12 : 2. th. y. may prove what is good
1 Co. 1 : 7. that y. come behind in
3 : 2. meat y. were not able to bear
3. For y. are yet carnal (2) [(2)
4 : 8. Now y. are full, now y. are
rich, y. have reigned as kings
10. We are fools, but y. are wise
in Christ ; we are weak, y. are
strong (3) [Ep. 5 : 1.
16. be y. followers of me, 11 : 1.
5 : 4. when y. are gathered, 11 : 20.
10. must y. needs go out of world
6 : 11. y. are washed ; y. are sancti-
20. y. are bought with price [fied (3)
7 : 23. y. are bought with a price ;
be not y. the servants of men
10 : 7. Nei. be y. idolaters as some
13. that y. may be able to bear it
20. not that y. have fellowship wi.

2Co. 6 : 17. come out, be y. separate
7 :9. not that y. were made sorry(4)
11. y. sorrowed after a godly(2), 9.
8 : 9. y. know grace of our Lord (2)
13 : 5. Examine whether y. be in
the faith. Know y. not your
own selves, that Christ is in
you except y. be reprobates
7. I pray to God y. do no evil (2)
Ga. 3 :29. if y. be Christ's then are y.
4 : 12. I am as y. are ; y. have not
15. y. wou. have plucked out your
6 : 1. y. which are spiritual restore
Ep. 2 : 13. y. who sometime were far
4 : 17. that y. walk not as other
22. That y. put off the old man
32. be y. kind one to another, as
5 : 7. Be not y. partakers with them
17. be y. not unwise, but underst-g
6 : 11. that y. may be able to stand
21. that y. may know my affairs
Ph. 1 : 10. y. be without offence (2)
12. I would y. should understand
2 : 2. Fulfil y. my joy : that y. be
15. That y. may be blameless (2)
Col. 1 : 10. That y. walk worthy of L.
2 : 1. would y. knew what conflict
3 : 1. If y. be risen with Christ [ful
15. to wh. are called, be y. thank-
4 : 6. know how y. ought to answer
1 Th. 1 : 7. y. were ensamples to all in
2 : 8. bec. y. were dear unto us [Mac.
19. our crown ? Are not even y. in
20. For y. are our glory and joy
3 : 8. we live, if y. stand fast in Lord
5 : 4. y. brethren are not in darkn.
2 Th. 1 : 5. That y. be counted worthy
2 : 2. That y. be not soon shaken in
3 : 13. y. brethren be not weary in
He. 5 : 11. seeing y. are dull of hear-
6 : 12. That y. be not slothful [ing
12 : 8. if y. be without chastisem-t
Ja. 1 : 22. Be y. doers of the word
2 : 7. name by which y. are called
8. If y. fulfil royal law y. do well
12. So speak y., and so do as they
16. one of you say, be y. warmed
4 : 2. y. have not bec. y. ask not(5)
3. y. ask and receive not bec. y.(3)
4. y. adulterers, know y. not (2)
8. Cleanse your hands, y. sinners
13. Go to now y. that say, To day
15. y. ought to say, If the Lord
5 : 1. Go to now, y. rich men [will
8. Be y. also patient ; stablish
1 Pe. 2 : 3. If so be y. have tasted
5. y. as lively stones, are built
9. y. are a chosen generation (2)
20. when y. do well and suffer, y.
3 : 1. y. wives be in subjection to
6. Sarah, whose daughters y. are
as long as y. do well [to wife as
7. y. husbands giving honour un-
13. who harm you if y. be follow-s
14. if y. suffer for . . . happy are y.
17. better y. suffer for well doing
4 : 4. think it strange y. run not
7. be y. sober, watch unto prayer
2 Pe. 1 : 4. that y. might be partakers
8. that y. neither be barren nor
10. If y. do these y. sh. never fall
15. y. may be able aft. my decease
3 : 2. that y. be mindful of words
11. what persons ought y. to be in
17. y. beloved, seeing y. know
things, beware lest y. fall, 14.(2)
1 Jn. 2 : 14. unto you, young men,
because y. are strong (3), 13. (3)
4 : 4. y. are of God, little children
Jude 5. though y. once knew this
Re. 18 : 20. Rejoice over her, y. apos-

All YE or YE all. [tles

De. 29 : 10. y. stand a. before the L.
Jos. 8 : 4. go not far, be y. a. ready
Ju. 20 : 7. y. are a. child-n of Israel
Jb. 13 : 4. y. a. physicians of no val-
16 : 2. miserable comforters y. a. [ue
Jb. 27 : 12. a. y. yoursel-s have seen it
Ps. 22 : 23. a. y. seed of Jacob glorify him ; fear him a. y. of Israel
31 : 24. courage, a. y. th. hope in L.
32 : 11. shout for joy a. y. upright
49 : 1. Hear this a. y. people (2) Mi.
66 : 16. hear a. y. th. fear God [1 : 2.
100 : 1. Make joyful noise a. y. lands
103 : 21. Bless y. the Lord a. y. his
hosts; y. ministers of his 134 : 1.
117 : 1. Praise Lord a. y. nations (2)
148 : 2. Praise y. him a. his angels
3. Praise him a. y. stars of light [(2)
Is. 48 : 14. a. y. assemble and [fire
50 : 11. Behold a. y. that kindle a
56 : 9. a. y. beasts of field, come (2)
66 : 10. be glad a. y. that love her ;
rejoice a. y. that mourn for her
Je. 2 : 29. y. a. have transg-d ag. me
29 : 20. Hear a. y. of the captivity
48 : 17. a. y. about him bemoan
him ; a. y. that know his name
say, How is staff [at her, 29.
50 : 14. a. y. that bend bow shoot
La. 1 : 12. Is it nothing a. y. th pass
Eze. 22 : 19. y. are a. become dross
Jo. 3 : 11. come a. y. heathen, gath.
Mat. 11 : 28. Come unto me a. y. th.
23 : 8. and a. y. are brethren [labour
26 : 27. saying, Drink y. a. of it
31. a. y. shall be offended, because of me, Mk. 14 : 27. [ish, 5.
Lu. 13 : 3. Nay y. sh. a. likewise per-
27. depart a. y. workers of iniq-y
Jn. 7 : 21. done one work, y. a. marv.
13 : 10. y. are clean, but not a., 11.
Ac. 2 : 14. a. y. that dwell at Jerus.
20 : 25. y. a. sh. see my face no mo.
22 : 3. zealous tow. God, as y. a. are
Ro. 15 : 11. Praise the Lord a. y.
Gentiles ; laud him a. y. people
1 Co. 1 : 10. th. y. a. speak same thing
14 : 5. would y. a. spake wi. tongues
18. I with tongues more than y. a.
31. y. may a. prophesy one by one
Ga. 3 : 26. y. are a. children of God
28. y. are a. one in Christ Jesus
Ph. 1 : 7. y. a. partakers of my grace
1 Th. 5 : 5. y. are a. children of light
1 Pe. 3 : 8. be y. a. of one mind [ants
Re. 19 : 5. Praise God a. y. his serv-

See **BLESSED are ye, DECLARE ye, Ye DIE, Ye MEN, PRAISE Lord, SEE ye, Ye have SEEN.**

See FAITH, HEAR, HEARKEN, PRAISE, SEEK, YOURSELVES.

YEA. [not eat

Gen. 3 : 1. y., hath God said ye shall
17 : 16. y., I will bless her, she sh. be
20 : 6. y., thou didst this in integ-
De. 33 : 3. y., he loved the peo. [rity
Ju. 5 : 29. y., 1 S. 15 : 20. - 21 : 5. -
24 : 11. 2 S. 19 : 30. - 22 : 39. 2
K. 2 : 5. - 16 : 3. 2 Ch. 26 : 20.
Ne. 5 : 16. - 6 : 10. - 9 : 18, 21.
Jb. 1 : 15, 17. - 6 : 27, 29. - 9 : 10.
- 11 : 15, 18, 19. - 12 : 3. - 15 : 4. -
18 : 5. - 19 : 18. - 20 : 8. - 21 : 7. -
22 : 25. - 28 : 27. - 30 : 2, 8. - 31 :
8. - 32 : 12. - 36 : 7. - 41 : 24. Ps.
7 : 4, 5. - 8 : 7. - 18 : 10, 14, 48. -
19 : 10. - 27 : 6. - 29 : 10. - 35 : 10,
15, 21, 27. - 37 : 36. - 43 : 4. - 44 :
22. - 57 : 1. - 58 : 2. - 59 : 16. - 68
- 26 : 8, 9, 11. - 29 : 5. - 32 : 13
- 40 : 24. (3) - 41 : 10, 23, 26.(2) -
43 : 7, 13. - 44 : 8, 12, 15, 16, 19.
- 45 : 21. - 46 : 6, 7, 11. - 47 : 3. -
48 : 8, 15. - 49 : 15. - 55 : 1. - 56 :
9, 11. - 59 : 15. - 60 : 12. - 66 : 3.
Je. 2 : 37. - 8 : 7. - 12 : 2, (2), 6.
- 14 : 5, 18. - 23 : 26. - 27 : 21. -
31 : 3, 19. - 32 : 41. - 46 : 16. - 51 :
44. La. 1 : 8. Eze. 6 : 14. - 16 :
6, 8, 9, 28, 52. - 17 : 10. - 22 :
2, 21, 29. - 23 : 36. - 26 : 18. -
28 : 26. - 32 : 10, 28. - 34 : 6. - 36 :
12. - 37 : 27. - 39 : 13. Da. 8 : 11.
- 9 : 11, 21. - 10 : 19. - 11 : 22, 24,
26. Ho. 4 : 3. - 8 : 10. - 9 : 12, 16.
- 12 : 4, 11. Jo. 1 : 16, 18. - 2 : 3,
19. - 3 : 4. Am. 8 : 6. Ob. 13,
16. Jon. 3 : 8. Mi. 3 : 7. Na. 1 :
5. Ha. 2 : 5. Zch. 7 : 12. - 8 : 22.
- 10 : 7. - 14 : 5, 21. Mal. 2 : 2. -
3 : 15. (3) - 4 : 1. [for their sakes
1 Ch. 16 : 21. y., be reproved kings
Ne. 5 : 15. y., their servants bare rule
Jb. 2 : 4. y., all that a man hath
5 : 19. y., in seven sh. no evil touch
6 : 10. y., I would harden in sorrow
15 : 15. y., the heav-s are not clean
33 : 14. God speaketh once, y., twice
40 : 5. Once have I spoken, y., twice
Ps. 16 : 6. y., I have a goodly heritage
23 : 4. y., tho. I walk through valley
40 : 8. y., thy law is within my heart
41 : 9. y., mine own familiar friend
90 : 17. y., work of our hands establ.
102 : 13. y., the set time is come
26. y., all shall wax old like [gold
119 : 127. above gold, y., above fine
Ec. 6 : 6. y., tho. he live 1,000 years
Can. 5 : 1. y., drink abundantly O
16. y., he is altogether lovely
Is. 5 : 10. y., ten acres shall yield
Mat. 5 : 37. let your communication
be, y., y. ; Nay, nay [13 : 51.
9 : 28. Believe ye? They said y., L.,
11 : 9. A prophet? y., Lu. 7 : 26.
21 : 16. y., have ye nev. read, Out of
26 : 60. y., tho. false witnes-s came
Lu. 2 : 35. y., a sword sh. pierce thy
11 : 28. y., rather, blessed are they
12 : 5. y., I say unto you, Fear him
57. y., why judge not wh. is right?
14 : 26. If hate not his wife, y., his
24 : 22. y., certain women of [life
Jn. 11 : 27. y., L. I believe thou art
16 : 2. y., the time cometh that
whosoever killeth [be scattered
32. hour cometh, y., is now th. ye
21 : 15. He saith unto him y., Lord
16. y., L. thou knowest I love thee
Ac. 3 : 16. y., faith by him hath given
24. y., and all prophets fr. Samuel
5 : 8. Sapphira said y., for so much
7 : 43. y., ye took up tabernacle of
20 : 34. y., ye know th. these hands
22 : 27. thou a Roman? He said y.,
Ro. 3 : 4. y., let God be true but
31. God forbid : y., we estab-h the
14 : 4. y., be sh. be holden up [law
15 : 20. y., so I strived to preach
1 Co. 2 : 10. y., Spirit searcheth deep
4 : 3. y., I judge not mine own self
16 : 6. abide, y., winter with you
15 : 15. y., and we false witnes-s of
2 Co. 1 : 17. that with me be y., y.,
and nay, nay ?

2Ti. 3 : 12. y., and all that live godly
Phm. 20. y., brother, let me have joy
He. 11 : 36. y., of bonds, imprison-t
Ja. 2 : 18. y., may say, Th. hast faith
5 : 12. let your y., be y.; your nay
1 Pe. 5 : 5. y., all be subject, one to
2 Pe. 1 : 13. y., I think it meet, as
3 Jn. 12. y., and we also bear record
Re. 14 : 13. y., saith Spirit, that they
YEAR. ⌊rest
Ge. 17 : 21. Sarah shall bear next y.
26 : 12. received same y. hundred-fold
47 : 17. with bread for cattle that y.
18. when y. was ended they came
Ex. 12 : 2. it shall be first month of y.
23 : 14. Three times a feast in the y.
17. Three times in y. thy males sh.
appear, 34 : 23, 24. De. 16 : 16.
30 : 10. make atonement once a y.
with blood (2), Le. 16 : 34.
34 : 22. feast of ingathering at the
y.'s end, 23 : 16. ⌈in a y.
Le. 23 : 41. keep it a feast seven days
25 : 5. it is a y. of rest unto land
29. redeem it within a whole y. (2)
50. reckon from y. he was sold unto
Nu. 9 : 22. whe. a y. that cloud tarried
14 : 34. forty days, each day for a y.
28 : 14. burnt offering throughout
months of a y., 1 Ch. 27 : 1. ⌈of y.
De. 11 : 12. fr. beginning of y. unto end
14 : 28. all tithe of increase same y.
15 : 9. the y. of release is at hand
26 : 12. third y., wh. is y. of tithing
31 : 10. solemnity of y. of release
Jos. 5 : 12. eat fruit of Canaan th. y.
Ju. 10 : 8. that y. Ammonites vexed
11 : 40. to lament four days in a y.
17 : 10. give thee ten shekels by y.
19 : †2. concubine there y. four mos.
2 S. 11 : 1. after the y. was expired,
1 Ch. 20 : 1. 2 Ch. 36 : 10.
14 : 26. at every y.'s end he polled it
1 K. 4 : 7. each his month in a y.
9 : 25 three times a y. did Solomon
offer, 2 Ch. 8 : 13. ⌈full y.
17 : † 15. she and house did eat a
20 : 22. at return of y. the king, 26.
2 K. 13 : 20. invaded at coming of y.
19 : 29. Ye shall eat this y. such as
grow of them-s, Is. 37 : 30 ⌈Syria
2 Ch. 24 : 23. at end of the y. host of
27 : 5. Ammon gave him same y. ⌈y.
Es. 9 : 27. would keep two days every
Jb. 3 : 6. be not joined unto days of
Ps. 65 : 11. thou crownest the y. ⌊y.
Is. 6 : 1. In y. that king Uzziah died
14 : 28. In y. that king Ahaz died
20 : 1. In the y. that Tartan came
21 : 16. Within a y. glory of Kedar
34 : 8. y. of recompenses for Zion
37 : 30. Ye sh. eat this y. such as g.
61 : 2. to proclaim the acceptable
y. of the Lord, Lu. 4 : 19. ⌈come
63 : 4. the y. of my redeemed is
Je. 11 : 23. the y. of their visitation,
23 : 12. - 48 : 44. ⌈drought
17 : 8. shall not be careful in y. of
28 : 1. it came to pass the same y.
16. this y. thou shalt die, because
17. So Hananiah died the same y.
51 : 46. in another y. shall come
rumour (2) ⌈for a y.
Eze. 4 : 6. I appointed thee each day
40 : 1. captivity, in beginning of y.
46 : 17. sh. be his to the y. of liber-
Mic. 6 : 6. with calves of a y. old? ⌊ty
Lu. 2 : 41. his parents to Jerus. every
13 : 8 Lord, let it alone this y. ⌊y.
Ju. 11 : 49. Caiaphas high priest that
same y. said, 51. - 18 : 13. ⌈bled
Ac. 11 : 26. a whole y. they assem-
18 : 11. Paul a y. six mos. teaching
2 Cor. 8 : 10. to be forward a y. ago
9 : 2. Achaia was ready a y. ago
He. 9 : 7. high priest once every y., 25
10 : 3. a remembrance of sins ev. y.
Ja. 4 : 13. will continue a y. and buy
Re. 9 : 15. four angels prepared for an
hour, a day, a month, and a y.

YEAR after YEAR.

2 S. 21 : 1. was a famine three years

YEAR by YEAR. ⌊y. -

De. 14 : 22. tithe the increase of thy seed
15 : 20. eat it before Lord y. - ⌊y. -
1 S. 1 : 7. as he did so y. - she provok-
1 K. 5 : 11. gave Sol. to Hiram y. - ⌊ed
10 : 25. they brought every man a
rate y. -, 2 Ch. 9 : 24. ⌈done y. -
2 K. 17 : 4. no pres. to king as he had
Ne. 10 : 34. to bring wood offering y. -
35. bring firstfruits of all trees y. -
He. 10 : 1. sacrifices wh. they offered

YEAR to YEAR. ⌊y. -

Ex. 13 : 10. keep ordinance from y. -
Ju. 11 : †40. went from y. - to lament
daughter of Jephthah ⌈y. -
21 : †19. feast of Lord in Shiloh from
1 S. 1 : † 3. went from y. - to worship
2 : 19. a coat to him from y. - ⌈cuit
7 : 16. Samuel went from y. - in cir-
2 Ch. 24 : 5. to repair house of your
God from y. - ⌈ye y. -
Is. 29 : 1. Woe to Ariel the city! add
Zch. 14 : 16. go up from y. - to wor-

Full YEAR. ⌊ship L.

Ge. 24 : †55. damsel abide with us f. y.
Le. 25 : 29. within f. y. may redeem
30. if not redeemed within f. y. ⌊it
1 S. 27 : 7. David in country of Philistines a f. y. and four months
1 K. 17 : † 15. she and house did eat a

YEAR of jubilee. ⌊f. y.

Le. 25 : 13. y. o. j. 28, 33, 40, 50,
52, 54. - 27 : 17, 18 (2), 23, 24.
See It came to PASS.

One YEAR. ⌈o. y.

Ex. 23 : 29. nor drive them out in
De. 24 : 5. he shall be free at home
1 S. 13 : 1. Saul reigned o. y. ⌊o. y.
1 K. 10 : 14. gold that came to Sol-n
in o. y.; 666 talents, 2 Ch. 9 : 13.
2 K. 8 : 26. Ahaziah reigned o. y. in
Jerusalem, 2 Ch. 22 : 2. ⌈y.
Je. 51 : 46. a rumour shall come o.

First YEAR. ⌈f. y.

Ex. 12 : 5. without blemish male of
29 : 38. shalt offer two lambs of f.
y., Le. 23 : 19. Nu. 28 : 3, 9.
Le. 9 : 3. calf and lamb, both of f. y.
12 : 6. a lamb of the f. y., Nu. 6 :
12. - 7 : 15, 21, 27, 33, 39, 45, 51,
57, 63, 69, 75, 81. Eze. 46 : 13.
14 : 10. one ewe lamb of the f. y.,
Nu. 6 : 14. ⌈6 : 14.
23 : 12. offer he lamb of f. y., Nu.
18. offer seven lambs of f. y.
Nu. 7 : 17. five lambs of f. y., 23, 29, 35,
41, 47, 53, 59, 65, 71, 77, 83.
87. the lambs of the f. y. twelve
88. the lambs of the f. y. sixty
15 : 27. she goat of f. y. for sin off-g
28 : 11. seven lambs of f. y. without spot, 19, 27. - 29 : 2, 8, 36.
Le. 23 : 18. ⌈20, 23, 26, 29, 32.
29 : 13. fourteen lambs of f. y., 17,
2 Ch. 29 : 3. Hezekiah in f. y. of his
reign opened house of L., Ezr.
1 : 1. - 5 : 13. - 6 : 3. Da. 1 : 21.
36 : 22. in f. y. Cyrus king of Persia
Je. 25 : 1. was f. y. of Nebuchadrez-r
52 : 31. Evil-merodach in f. y. of
Da. 7 : 1. In f. y. of Belshazzar ⌊reign
9 : 2. In f. y. of Darius' reign, 1. -

Second YEAR. ⌊11 : 1.

Ge. 47 : 18. came unto Joseph s. y.
Ex. 40 : 17. first month in the s. y.
Nu. 1 : 1. s. y. after they were come
9 : 1. L. unto Moses first mo. of s. y.
10 : 11. in s. y. cloud was taken up
1 K. 15 : 25. to reign in s. y. of Asa
2 K. 1 : 17. reigned in s. y. of Jehoram
14 : 1. In s. y. of Joash, Amaziah
15 : 32. s. y. of Pekah began Joth.
2K. 19 : 29. eat in s. y. th. wh. springeth of same, Is. 37 : 30. ⌈s. y. ?
2 Ch. 27 : 5. did Ammon pay Jotham
Ezr. 3 : 8. in the s. y. of their coming unto Jerusalem ⌈Darius
4 : 24. it ceased unto s. y. of reign of
Da. 2 : 1. in s. y. of reign of Neb.
Neb. dreamed dreams ⌈Zch. 1 : 7.
Hag. 1 : 1. In s. y. of Darius, 15. - 2 : 10.

Third YEAR. ⌈ing

De. 26 : 12. t. y., wh. is year of tith-
1 K. 15 : 28. In t. y. of Asa, did
Baasha slay him, 33. ⌈t. y.
18 : 1. word of the Lord to Elijah in
22 : 2. in t. y. Jehosh. came to king
2 K. 18 : 1. in t. y. of Hoshea, Hez-h
19 : 29. in t. y. sow ye, reap, eat
the fruit, Is. 37 : 30. ⌈reign
2 Ch. 17 : 7. in t. y. of Jehosaphat's
27 : 5. Ammon pay him sec. y. and
Es. 1 : 3. In t. y. of reign Ahas-s ⌊t.
Da. 1 : 1. In t. y. of the reign of
Jehoiakim ⌈a vision
8 : 1. In t. y. of reign of Belshazzar
10 : 1. In t. y. of Cyrus a thing re-

Fourth YEAR. ⌊vealed

Le. 19 : 24. in f. y. fruit be holy
1 K. 6 : 1. f. y. of Sol-'s reign he began to build, 37. 2 Ch. 3 : 2.
22 : 41. began to reign in f. y. of
2 K. 18 : 9. in f. y. of Hezekiah ⌊Ahab
Je. 25 : 1. word to Jere-h in f. y. of
Jehoiakim, 36 : 1. - 45 : 1. - 46 : 2.
28 : 1. in the f. y. of Zedekiah,
Hananiah spake ⌈f. y. of reign
51 : 59. Zedekiah into Babylon in
Zch. 7 : 1. f. y. of Darius word unto

Fifth YEAR. ⌊Zech.

Le. 19 : 25. f. y. ye sh. eat the fruit
1 K. 14 : 25. f. y. of Rehob. Shishak
came ag. Jerus-m, 2 Ch. 12 : 2.
2 K. 8 : 16. in the f. y. of Joram ⌈fast
Je. 36 : 9. in the f. y. of Jehoiakim a
Eze. 1 : 2. f. y. of Jehoiachin's cap-

Sixth YEAR. ⌊tivity

Le. 25 : 21. blessing upon you in s. y.
2 K. 18 : 10. s. y. of Hez-h Samaria
was taken ⌈reign of Darius
Ezr. 6 : 15. house finished in s. y. of
Eze. 8 : 1. s. y. hand of L. fell upon

Seventh YEAR. ⌊me

Ex. 23 : 11. s. y. thou shalt let it rest
Le. 25 : 4. in s. y. a sabbath of rest
20. What shall we eat in the s. y.?
De. 15 : 9. s. y. of release is at hand
12. in s. y. shalt let him go free
2 K. 11 : 4. s. y. Jehoiada fetched
rulers with capt-s, 2 Ch. 23 : 1.
12 : 1. In s. y. of Jehu, Jeho. began to
18 : 9. s. y. of Hoshea, Shalmanes-r
Ezr. 7 : 7. in s. y. of Artaxerxes, 8.
Ne. 10 : 31. would leave s. y., and
exaction of ev. debt ⌈y. of reign
Es. 2 : 16. Esther unto Ahas-s in s.
Je. 52 : 28. people carried captive:
in the s. y. 3,023 ⌈inquire
Eze. 20 : 1. in s. y. elders came to

Eighth YEAR. ⌈and

Le. 25 : 22. ye shall sow the e. y.,
2 K. 24 : 12. took Jehoiachin in e. y.
of his reign ⌈while young
2 Ch. 34 : 3. Josiah in e. y. of reign,

Ninth YEAR. ⌈y.

Le. 25 : 22. eat of old fruit until n.
2 K. 17 : 6. In n. y. of Hoshea, 18 : 10.
25 : 1. in n. y. Zed-h's reign Neb-r
came, Je. 39 : 1. - 52 : 4. Eze.

Tenth YEAR. ⌊24 : 1.

Je. 32 : 1. word to Jeremiah in t. y.
of Zedekiah ⌈me
Eze. 29 : 1. In t. y. word of L. unto

Eleventh YEAR.

1 K. 6 : 38. in e. y. house finished
2 K. 9 : 29. e. y. of Joram, began A.
25 : 2. Jerus. was besieged unto e.
y. of Zedekiah, Je. 52 : 5. ⌈eh
Je 1 : 3. unto end of e. y. of Zedeki-

Je. 39 : 2. in e. y. city was broken up
Eze. 26 : 1. in e. y. word of the Lord unto me, 30 : 20. - 31 : 1.

Twelfth YEAR. [Ahaz
2 K. 8 : 25. In t. y. of Joram did
17 : 1. t. y. of Ahaz began Hoshea
2 Ch. 34 : 3. in t. y. Josiah began to purge Judah [Pur
Es. 3 : 7. in t. y. of Ahasuerus cast
Eze. 32 : 1. in t. y. word of L. came
17. in t. y. 15th day word of Lord
33 : 21. in the t. y. of our captivity

Thirteenth YEAR.
Ge. 14 : 4. in the t. y. they rebelled
Je. 1 : 2. To whom word of Lord in t. y. of Josiah's reign [and 20th
25 : 3. from t. y. of Josiah unto 3

Fourteenth YEAR.
Ge. 14 : 5. in f. y. came Chedorlao-r
2 K. 18 : 13. in f. y. of Hezekiah did Sennacherib, Is. 36 : 1. [ten
Eze. 40 : 1. f. y. after city was smit-

Fifteenth YEAR.
2 K. 14 : 23. In f. y. of Amaziah
2 Ch. 15 : 10. gathered at Jerusalem in f. y. of reign of Asa [rius
Lu. 3 : 1. in f. y. of reign of Tibe-

Seventeenth YEAR.
1 K. 22 : 51. to reign s. y. of Jehosh-t
2 K. 16 : 1. In the s. y. of Pekah, Aha- [ziah

Eighteenth YEAR.
1 K. 15 : 1. in e. y. of Jeroboam reigned Abijam, 2 Ch. 13 : 1.
2 K. 3 : 1. to reign in e. y. of Jehosh-t
2 Ch. 35 : 19. In e. y. of reign of Josiah, 34 : 8. 2 K. 22 : 3. - 23 : 23.
Je. 32 : 1. in e. y. of Nebu-r, 52 : 29.

Nineteenth YEAR.
2 K. 25 : 8. n. y. of Neb-r Nebuzaradan burnt house of L., Je. 52 : 12.

Twentieth YEAR. [Asa
1 K. 15 : 9. in t. y. of Jerob. reigned
2 K. 15 : 30. slew in t. y. of Jotham
Ne. 1 : 1. in t. y. as I was in Shushan
2 : 1. in t. y. of Artaxerxes wine
5 : 14. I governor fr. t. y. of Artax-s

Three and twentieth or **Twenty third YEAR.**
2 K. 12 : 6. in - y. of Jehoash, priests
13 : 1. In - y. of Joash, Jehoahaz
Je. 25 : 3. 13th y. of Josiah unto - y.
52 : 30. In - y. of Neb-r, captive, 745.

Five and twentieth YEAR. [of Lord
Eze. 40 : 1. In - y. of captivity hand

Twenty sixth YEAR.
1 K. 16 : 8. In - y. of Asa, Elah

Seven and twentieth or **Twenty seventh YEAR.**
1 K. 16 : 10. smote Elah - y. of Asa
15. In - y. of Asa did Zimri reign
2 K. 15 : 1. In - y. of Jerob., Azariah
Eze. 29 : 17. in - y. word of L. unto [me

Thirtieth YEAR.
Eze. 1 : 1. in t. y. as I was by Che- [bar

Thirty and first YEAR. [Omri
1 K. 16 : 23. In - y. of Asa began

Two and thirtieth YEAR. [taxerxes
Ne. 5 : 14. governor unto - y. of Ar-
13 : 6. in - y. of Artax-s came I unto [king

Five and thirtieth YEAR.
2 Ch. 15 : 19. was no more war unto - y. of the reign of Asa

Six and thirtieth YEAR.
2 Ch. 16 : 1. In - y. of reign of Asa

Seven and thirtieth or **Thirty seventh YEAR.**
2 K. 13 : 10. In - y. of Joash, Jehoash
25 : 27. in the - y. of the captivity of Jehoiachin, Je. 52 : 31.

Thirty eighth YEAR.
1 K. 16 : 29. In - y. of Asa began [Ahab
2 K. 15 : 8. In - y. of Azariah

Nine and thirtieth or **Thirty ninth YEAR.**
2 K. 15 : 13. began to reign in - y. of
17. In - y. of Azariah [Uzziah
2 Ch. 16 : 12. Asa in - y. of reign dis- [eased

Fortieth YEAR.
Nu. 33 : 38. Aaron died in f. y. after
De. 1 : 3. f. y. Moses spake unto Isr.
1 Ch. 26 : 31. f. y. of reign of David

One and fortieth YEAR.
2 Ch. 16 : 13. Asa died in - y. of his [reign

Fiftieth YEAR.
Le. 25 : 10. ye shall hallow the f. y.
11. A jubilee shall that f. y. be
2 K. 15 : 23. In the f. y. of Azariah

Two and fiftieth YEAR.
2 K. 15 : 27. In the - y. of Azariah

Four hundred eightieth YEAR. [build
1 K. 6 : 1. in - y. Solomon began to

Six hundredth YEAR.
Ge. 7 : 11. In - y. of Noah's life, all

Six hundredth and first YEAR. [off earth
Ge. 8 : 13. in - y. waters were dried

YEARS. [days, y.
Ge. 1 : 14. let them be for seasons,
23 : 1. 127 were y. of life of Sarah
25 : 7. these are y. of Abr-'s life (2)
8. Abr. died an old man, full of y.
17. are y. of life of Ishmael, 137 y.
41 : 35. gather food of those good y.
50. two sons before y. of famine
47 : †8. How many are y. of thy life
9. The y. of my pilgrimage 130 y.; few and evil the y. of my life, not attained unto y. of fathers
Le. 25 : 8. number seven sabbaths of y.; sabbaths of y. shall be forty nine y. (4)
16. Acc. to multitude of y. increase, price, acc-g to fewness of y. (3)
27. let him count the y. of the sale
52. if but few y. unto jubilee, acc. unto his y. sh. he give price, 51.
54. if not redeemed in these y.
27 : 18. money acc. to y. th. remain
De. 32 : 7. consider the y. of many generations [in y.
Jos. 13 : 1. Joshua was old, stricken
1 S. 29 : 3. David with me these y.
1 K. 1 : 1. David old, stricken in y.
17 : 1. not be dew nor rain these y.
2 Ch. 14 : 6. Asa no war in those y.
18 : 2. after certain y. went to Ahab
Jb. 10 : 5. are thy y. as man's days
16 : 22 When a few y. are come I go
32 : 7. multitude of y. should teach
36 : 11. spend their y. in pleasures
Ps. 31 : 10. grief, my y. with sighing
61 : 6. Thou wilt prolong his y. as many generations [times
77 : 5. I considered the y. of ancient
10. I will remember y. of right h-d
78 : 33. consume their y. in trouble
90 : 4. a thousand y. in thy sight are but, 2 Pe. 3 : 8. [told
9. we spend our y. as a tale that is
10. our y. are threesc. y. and ten
15. according to the y. wherein we have seen evil [erations
102 : 24. thy y. throughout all gen-
27. same, thy y. shall have no end
Pr. 3 : †2. y. of life shall they add to
5 : 9. Lest give thy y. unto the cruel
9 : 11. y. of thy life sh. be increased
10 : 27. y. of wicked sh. be shortened
Ec. 12 : 1. while evil days come not nor the y. draw nigh when [ling
Is. 21 : †16. according to y. of an hire-
38 : 10. deprived of residue of my y.
15. I shall go softly all my y.
Eze. 4 : 5. upon thee y. of their iniq-y
22 : 4. thou art come even unto thy [y.
38 : 8. in latter y. into the land
Da. 11 : 6. in end of y. sh. join thems.
Da. 11 : 8. continue mo. y. th. the king
13. king of north after certain y.
Jo. 2 : 2. to y. of many generations
25. will restore y. locust hath eat.
Ha. 3 : 2. Lord, revive thy work in the midst of the y. [mer y.
Mal. 3 : 4. offering pleasant as in for-
Lu. 1 : 7. both well stricken in y., 18.
Ga. 4 : 10. Ye observe months and y.
He. 1 : 12. same, thy y. shall not fail
11 : 24. Moses when come to y. re- [fused

Many YEARS.
Le. 25 : 51. If be m. y. behind [ago
Ezr. 5 : 11. house builded these m. y.
Ne. 9 : 30. m. y. didst forbear them
Pr. 4 : 10. y. of thy life shall be m.
Ec. 6 : 3. If a man beget 100 children and live m. y. [joice
11 : 8. if a man live m. y. and re-
Is. 32 : 10. m. y. sh. ye be troubled
Eze. 38 : 17. which prophesied m. y.
Zch. 7 : 3. weep, as I these so m. y.
Lu. 12 : 19. goods laid up for m. y.
15 : 29. Lo, these m. y. I serve thee
Ac. 24 : 10. thou of m. y. a judge
17. aft. m. y. I came to bring alms
Ro. 15 : 23. a desire these m. y. to [come
See NUMBER [Noun], OLD.
See It came to PASS.

Two YEARS. [flood
Gen. 11 : 10. begat Arph-d t. y. after
41 : 1 end of t. full y. Pha. dream
45 : 6. these t. y. hath famine been
1 S. 13 : 1. Saul had reigned t. y.
2 S. 2 : 10. Ish-bosheth reigned t. y.
13 : 23. after t. full y. Absalom had sheepshearers [Jerusalem
14 : 28. Absalom dwelt t. full y. in
1 K. 15 : 25. Nadab over Israel t. y.
16 : 8. Elah to reign over Israel t. y.
22 : 51. Ahaziah t. y. over Israel
2 K. 15 : 23. Pekahiah reigned t. y.
21 : 19. Amon reigned t. y. in Jerusalem, 2 Ch. 33 : 21. [out
2 Ch. 21 : 19. after t. y. bowels fell
Je. 28 : 3. Within t. full y. will I bring again vessels, 11. [earthq.
Am. 1 : 1. wh. Amos saw t. y. before
Mat. 2 : 16. slew children from t. y.
Ac. 19 : 10. t. y. they in Asia heard
24 : 27. after t. y. Festus came [word
28 : 30. Paul dwelt t. y. in hired [house

Three YEARS.
Ge. 15 : 9. Take me an heifer of t. y. old, a she goat t. y. old, and a ram t. y. old [cumcised
Le 19 : 23. fruit: t. y. it be as uncir-
25 : 21. shall bring forth fruit t. y.
De. 14 : 28. At end of t. y. bring tithe
Ju. 9 : 22. Abim-h had reigned t. y.
2 S. 13 : 38. Absalom to Geshur t. y.
21 : 1. famine in days of David t. y.
1 K. 2 : 39. end of t. y. two serv. ran
10 : 22. once in t. y. came navy of Tharshish, 2 Ch. 9 : 21.
15 : 2. t. y. reigned Abijam in Jerusalem, 2 Ch. 13 : 2.
22 : 1. continued t. y. without war
2 K. 17 : 5. besieged Samaria t. y.
18 : 10. at end of t. y. they took it
24 : 1. Jehoiakim his servant t. y.
1 Ch. 21 : 12. Choose t. y. famine or
2 Ch. 11 : 17. Rehoboam strong t. y.; t. y. they walked in way of David and Solomon [rusalem
13 : 2. Abijah reigned t. y. in Je-
31 : 16. males from t. y. old upward
Is. 15 : 5. shall flee unto Zoar, a heifer of t. y., Je. 48 : 34. [hireling
16 : 14. Within t. y., as y. of an
20 : 3. Isaiah walked barefoot t. y.
Da. 1 : 5. so nourishing them t. y.
Am. 4 : 4. bring your tithes aft. t. y.
Lu. 4 : 25. heaven shut up t. y. six
13 : 7. these t. y. seeking fruit [mos.
Ac. 20 : 31. t. y. I ceased not to warn
Ga. 1 : 18. aft. t. y. I went to Jerus-

Ja. 5 : 17. it rained not t. y. six
Five YEARS. ⌊months
Ge. 45 : 6. yet are f. y. of famine, 11.
Le. 27 : 5. if from f. y. old unto 20 y.
6. if from a month old unto f. y.
2 S. 4 : 4. Jonathan had son f. y. old
Six YEARS. ⌈cattle
Gen. 31 : 41. I served s. y. for thy
Ex. 21 : 2. s. y. he shall serve, and in seventh, De. 15 : 12. Je. 34 : 14.
Le. 25 : 3. s. y. shalt sow thy land; s. y. prune vineyard, Ex. 23 : 10.
De. 15 : 18. worth double hired servant, in serving s. y. ⌈s. y.
Ju. 12 : 7. Jephthah judged Israel
1 K. 16 : 23. s. y. reigned Omri in Tir.
2 K. 11 : 3. Joash was hid in house of the Lord s. y., 2 Ch. 22 : 12.
Seven YEARS. ⌈Rachel
Ge. 29 : 18. I will serve s. y. for
20. Jacob served s. y. for Rachel
27. service with me s. other y., 30.
41 : 26. seven good kine are s. y.; seven good ears are s. y.: dream
27. seven thin kine are s. y.; seven empty ears s. y. of famine
29. come s. y. of great plenty, 34,
30. sh. arise s. y. of famine, 36. ⌊47.
48. he gathered all the food of s. y.
53. s. y. of plenteous-s were end-
54. the s. y. of dearth began ⌊ed
Le. 25 : 8. number seven times s. y.
Nu. 13 : 22. Hebron built s. y. before Zoan ⌈lease, 31 : 10.
De. 15 : 1. at end of every s. y. a re-
Ju. 6 : 1. delivered Israel into hand of Midian s. y. ⌈old
25. Take second bullock of s. y.
12 : 9. Ibzan of B. judged Israel s. y.
2 S. 2 : 11. David was king in Hebron s. y. and six months, 5 : 5. 1 K. 2 : 11. 1 Ch. 3 : 4. - 29 : 27.
24 : 13. Shall s. y. of famine come
1 K. 6 : 38. Sol. s. y. in building tem-
2 K. 8 : 1. famine sh. come s. y. ⌊ple
2. she in land of Philistines s. y.
3. at s. y.' end woman returned
11 : 21. s. y. old was Jehoash when he began to reign, 2 Ch. 24 : 1.
Je. 34 : 14. At end of s. y. let go every man ⌈fire s. y.
Eze. 39 : 9. shall burn weapons with
Lu. 2 : 36. with husband s. y. fr. vir-
Eight YEARS. ⌊ginity
Ju. 3 : 8. Israel served Chushan-r. e.
12 : 14. Abdon Judged Isr. e. y. ⌊y.
2 K. 8 : 17. Jehoram reigned e. y. in Jerus., 2 Ch. 21 : 5, 20. ⌈34 : 1.
22 : 1. Josiah e. y. when he, 2 Ch.
2 Ch. 36 : 9. Jehoiachin e. y. old wh.
Ac. 9 : 33. Eneas kept his bed e. y.
Nine YEARS.
2 K. 17 : 1. Hoshea over Israel n. y.
Ten YEARS. ⌈Canaan
Ge. 16 : 3. Abr. had dwelt t. y. in
Ju. 12 : 11. Elon judged Israel t. y.
Ru. 1 : 4. Moab, they dwelt ab-t t. y.
2 K. 15 : 17. Menahem reigned t. y.
2 Ch. 14 : 1. In his days land quiet
Eleven YEARS. ⌊t. y.
2 K. 23 : 36. Jehoiakim reigned e. y. in Jerusalem, 2 Ch. 36 : 5.
24 : 18. Zedekiah reigned e. y. in Jerusalem, 2 Ch. 36 : 11. Je.
Twelve YEARS. ⌊52 : 1.
Ge. 14 : 4. t. y. served Chedorlaomer
1 K. 16 : 23. Omri over Israel t. y.
2 K. 3 : 1. Jehoram reigned t. y.
21 : 1. Manasseh t. y. old began to reign, 2 Ch. 33 : 1. ⌈governor
Ne. 5 : 14. t. y. I not eaten bread of
Mat. 9 : 20. with issue of blood t. y., Mk. 5 : 25. Lu. 8 : 43. ⌈8 : 42.
Mk. 5 : 42. she of age of t. y., Lu.
Lu. 2 : 42. when Jesus was t. y. old
Thirteen YEARS.
Ge. 17 : 25. Ishmael was t. y. old

1 K. 7 : 1. Sol. building his house t.
Fourteen YEARS. ⌊y.
Ge. 31 : 41. served f. y. for thy dau-s
2 Co. 12 : 2. I knew a man f. y. ago
Ga. 2 : 1. f. y. after I went to Jerus.
Fifteen or Sixteen YEARS. ⌈s. y.
2 K. 13 : 10. Jehoash in Sama. reigned
14 : 21. took Azariah s. y. old, made king, 15 : 2. ⌈27 : 1, 8.
15 : 33. Jotham reigned s. y., 2 Ch.
16 : 2. Ahaz reigned s. y. in Jerusalem, 2 Ch. 28 : 1. ⌈Is. 38 : 5.
20 : 6. will add unto thy days f. y.,
2 Ch. 25 : 25. Amaziah lived after death of Joash f. y., 2 K. 14 : 17.
26 : 3. Uzziah s. y. old began to, 1.
Seventeen or Eighteen YEARS. ⌊flock
Ge. 37 : 2. Joseph s. y. old feeding
47 : 28. Jacob lived in Egypt s. y.
Ju. 3 : 14. Israel served Eglon e. y.
10 : 8. oppressed chil. of Isr. e. y.
1 K. 14 : 21. Rehoboam s. y. in Jerusalem, 2 Ch. 12 : 13. ⌈s. y.
2 K. 13 : 1. Jehoahaz in Sama. reigned
24 : 8. Jehoiachin e. y. old when he
Lu. 13 : 11. woman had infirm-y e. y.
16. Satan hath bound these e. y.
Twenty YEARS. ⌈41.
Ge. 31 : 38. t. y. have I been wi. thee,
Ex. 38 : 26. from t. y. and upward, 30 : 14. Nu. 1 : 3, 18, 20, 22, 24, 26, 28, 30, 32, 34, 36, 38, 40, 42, 45. - 14 : 29. - 26 : 2, 4. - 32 : 11. 1 Ch. 23 : 24, 27. 2 Ch. 25 : 5. - 31 : 17. Ezr. 3 : 8. ⌈y. unto 60
Le. 27 : 3. estimation of male from t.
5. from 5 y. old unto t. y., estima.
Ju. 4 : 3. Jabin oppressed Isr. t. y.
15 : 20. Samson judged Isr. t. y., 16 :
1 S. 7 : 2. ark in Kirjath-m t. y. ⌊31.
1 K. 9 : 10. end of t. y. when Sol-n had built two houses, 2 Ch. 8 : 1.
2 K. 15 : 27. Pekah over Israel t. y.
16 : 2. t. y. old Ahaz began to reign, 2 Ch. 28 : 1. ⌈t. y. and under
1 Ch. 27 : 23. took not number from
Twenty and one YEARS.
2 K. 24 : 18. Zedekiah, - y. old began to reign, 2 Ch. 36 : 11. Je. 52 : 1.
Twenty two, three, or four YEARS. ⌈rael
Ju. 10 : 2. t. t-e y. Tola judged Is-
3. Jair judged Israel t. t-o y. ⌈y.
1 K. 14 : 20. Jeroboam reigned t. t-o
15 : 33. Baasha over Isr. t. f. y. ⌈y.
16 : 29. Ahab reigned over Isr. t. t-o
2 K. 8 : 26. t. t-o y. Ahaziah began
21 : 19. Amon t. t-o y. old began to reign, 2 Ch. 33 : 21. ⌈to reign
23 : 31. Jehoahaz t. t-e y. old began
Twenty five, eight, or nine YEARS. ⌈Terah
Ge. 11 : 24. Nahor lived t. n. y. begat
Nu. 8 : 24. Levites fr. t. f. y. upw-d
1 K. 22 : 42. Jehoshaphat reigned t. f. y., 2 Ch. 20 : 31. ⌈t. e. y.
2 K. 10 : 36. Jehu reigned over Isr.
14 : 2. Amaziah t. f. y. old began; reigned t. n. y., 2 Ch. 25 : 1.
15 : 33. Jotham t. f. y. old began to reign, 2 Ch. 27 : 1, 8.
18 : 2. Hezekiah t. f. y. old began to reign; reigned t. n. y., 2 Ch. 29 : 1. ⌈reign, 2 Ch. 36 : 5.
23 : 36. Jehoiakim t. f. y. began to
Thirty YEARS. ⌈Eber
Ge. 11 : 14. Salah lived t. y. begat
18. Peleg lived t. y. begat Reu
22. Serug lived t. y. begat Nahor
41 : 46. Joseph t. y. old stood bef.
Nu. 4 : 3. From t. y. and upward even until fifty, 23, 30, 35, 39, 43, 47. 1 Ch. 23 : 3. ⌈to reign
2 S. 5 : 4. David t. y. when he began
Lu. 3 : 23 Jesus, about t. y. of age

Thirty one, two, or three YEARS. ⌈Serug
Ge. 11 : 20. Reu lived t. t-o y. begat
2 S. 5 : 5. David reigned t. t-e y., 1 K. 2 : 11. 1 Ch. 3 : 4. - 29 : 27.
2 K. 8 : 17. Jehoram t. t-o y. old began to, 2 Ch. 21 : 5, 20. ⌈34 : 1.
22 : 1. Josiah reigned t. o. y., 2 Ch.
Thirty four, five, or eight YEARS. ⌈begat
Ge. 11 : 12. Arphaxad lived t. f-e y.
16. Eber lived t. f-r y. begat Pel.
De. 2 : 14. until over Zered t. e. y.
1 K. 22 : 42. Jehoshaphat t. f-e y. old began to reign, 2 Ch. 20 : 31
Jn. 5 : 5. had an infirmity t. e. y.
Forty YEARS. ⌈bekah
Ge. 25 : 20. Isaac f. y. old took Re-
26 : 34. Esau f. y. old took Judith
Ex. 16 : 35. Isr. did eat manna f. y.
Nu. 14 : 33. you children shall wander in wilderness f. y., 32 : 13.
34. shall bear your iniquities f. y.
De. 2 : 7. f. y. Lord been with thee
8 : 2. way God led thee f. y., 29 : 5.
4. neither did thy foot swell f. y.
Jos. 5 : 6. Israel walked f. y. in wild.
14 : 7. f. y. old when Moses sent me
Ju. 3 : 11. had rest f. y., 5 : 31. - 8 : 28.
13 : 1. Isr. into hand of Phil-s f. y.
1 S. 4 : 18. Eli had Judged Israel f. y.
2 S. 2 : 10. Ish-bosheth f. y. old wh.
5 : 4. David reigned f. y., 1 K. 2 : 11. 1 Ch. 29 : 27. ⌈the king
15 : 7. after f. y. Absalom said unto
1 K. 11 : 42. Sol. reigned f. y., 2 Ch.
2 K. 12 : 1. Jeho-h reigned f. y. ⌊9 : 30.
2 Ch. 24 : 1. Joash reigned f. y. in J.
Ne. 9 : 21. f. y. didst sustain them
Ps. 95 : 10. f. y. was I grieved with
Eze. 29 : 11. not be inhabited f. y.
12. her cities shall be desolate f. y
13. end of f. y. will gather Egyp-s
Am. 2 : 10. I led you f. y. thro. wild.
5 : 25. offered sacrifices in wilderness f. y., Ac. 7 : 42. ⌈miracle
Ac. 4 : 22. man above f. y. on whom
7 : 23. when Moses full f. y. old, to visit his brethren ⌈an angel
30. f. y. were expired appeared
36. wonders in the wilderness f. y.
13 : 18. f. y. suffered he their man-
21. God gave them Saul f. y. ⌊ners
He. 3 : 9. fathers saw my works f. y.
17. with wh. was he grieved f. y.
Forty one, two, or five YEARS. ⌈f. f. y.
Jos. 14 : 10. Lord hath kept me these
1 K. 14 : 21. Rehoboam f. o. y. old began to reign, 2 Ch. 12 : 13.
15 : 10. f. o. y. reigned Asa in Jerus.
2 K. 14 : 23. Jerob-m reigned f. o. y.
2 Ch. 22 : 2. f. t. y. old Ahaziah wh.
Forty six or nine YEARS. ⌈f. n. y.
Le. 25 : 8. 7 sabbaths of y. shall be
Jn. 2 : 20. f. s. y. temple in building
Fifty YEARS.
Nu. 4 : 3. from 30 years until f. y. old, 23, 30, 35, 39, 43, 47. ⌈ing
8 : 25. fr. age of f. y. sh. cease wait-
Jn. 8 : 57. Thou art not yet f. y. old
Fifty two or five YEARS.
2 K. 15 : 2. Azariah reigned f. t. y. in Jerus., 2 Ch. 26 : 3. ⌈Ch. 33 : 1.
21 : 1. Manasseh reigned f. f. y., 2
Sixty YEARS. ⌈to s. y.
Le. 27 : 3. estimation of male fr. 20
7. if from s. y. old and above
Threescore YEARS. ⌈ah
Ge. 25 : 26. Isaac t. y. old wh. Rebek-
1 Ch. 2 : 21. Hezron married t. y. old
1 Ti. 5 : 9. not widow taken und. t. y.
Threescore and two or five YEARS. ⌈broken
Is. 7 : 8. within t. f. y. Ephraim be

Da. 5 : 31. Darius about t. t. y. old

Sixty and five YEARS.

Ge. 5 : 15. Mahaleel lived - y. begat
21. Enoch lived - y. begat Methus.

Threescore and ten YEARS. [fulfil - y.

2 Ch. 36 : 21. she kept sabbath to
Ps. 90 : 10. days of our y. are t-e y. -
Zch. 1 : 12. ag. Judah indignat-n - y.

Seventy YEARS. [Mahal.

Ge. 5 : 12. Cainan lived s. y. begat
11 : 26. Terah lived s. y. begat Abr.
Ps. 90 : † 10. our days they are s. y.
Is. 23 : 15. Tyre sh. be forgotten s. y.
17. end of s. y. Lord visit Tyre [y.
Je. 25 : 11. sh. serve king of Bab-n s.
12. when s. y. are accomplished
I will punish, 29 . 10. [rusalem
Da. 9 : 2. s. y. in desolations of Je-
Zch. 7 : 5. those s. y. did ye fast

Seventy five YEARS.

Ge. 12 : 4. Abr. - y. old wh. out of Ha-

Fourscore YEARS. [ran

Ex. 7 : 7. Moses f. y. old spake unto
Ju. 3 : 30. land had rest f. y. [Pha.
2 S. 19 : 32. Barzillai very aged, f. y.
35. I am this day f. y. old [old
Ps. 90 : 10. and if they be f. y.. yet

Fourscore and three or four YEARS. [Pha.

Ex. 7 : 7. Aaron f. t. y. old, sp. unto
Lu. 2 : 37. Anna, a widow of f. f. y.

Fourscore and five or six YEARS. [bare

Ge. 16 : 16. Abram f. s. y. wh. Hagar
Jos. 14 : 10. I am this day f. f. y. old

Ninety YEARS. [nan

Ge. 5 : 9. Enos lived n. y. begat Cai-
17 : 17. shall Sarah n. y. old bear?

Ninety eight YEARS.

1 S. 4 : 15. Eli n. e. y. old, eyes dim

Ninety YEARS and nine.

Ge. 17 : 1. Abram n. y. old a. n.,
Lord appeared to Abr. [cumcised
24. Ab-m n. y. a. n. when cir-
See HUNDRED, with numerals.

Two hundred and thirty YEARS.

Ge. 11 : 20. Reu lived - y. begat Serug
See OLD, THOUSAND.

YEARLY. [be

Le. 25 : 53. as a y. hired servant he
Ju. 11 : 40. daughters of Isr. y. to la-
21 : 19. feast of L. in Shiloh y. [ment
1 S. 1 : 3. Elkanah up y. to worship
21. up to offer y. sacrifice, 2 : 19.
20 : 6. y. sacrifice for all the family
Ne. 10 : 32. to charge ourselves y. with
Es. 9 : 21. should keep 14th day of
month Adar and fifteenth y.

YEARN, ED. [brother

Ge. 43 : 30. bowels did y. upon his
1 K. 3 : 26. bowels y-d upon her son

YELL, ED, ETH. [him

Je. 2 : 15. young lions roared, y-d on
12 : † 8. mine heritage y-h ag-t me
51 : 38. they sh. y. as lions' whelps

YELLOW.

Le. 13 : 30. if be in it a y. thin hair
32. if there be in it no y. hair
36. priests sh. not seek for y. hair
Ezr. 8 : † 27. two vessels of y. brass
Ps. 68 : 13. her feathers with y. gold

YES. [come

Mat. 17 : 25. saith y. and wh. he was
Mk. 7 : 28. y., L. yet the dogs under
Ro 3 : 29. y., of the Gentiles also [all
10 : 18. y., their sound went into

YESTERDAY. [before

Ge. 31 : † 2. not tow. him as y. and
Ex. 5 : 14. wheref. not fulfilled task y.
1 S. 20 : 27. Wheref. not son of Jesse
to meat y. nor to day? [y.
2 S. 15 : 20. whereas thou camest but
2 K. 9 : 26. seen y. blood of Naboth
Jb. 8 : 9. we but of y. and know noth.
Ps. 90 : 4. a thousand years but as y.
Is. 30 : † 33. Tophet is ordained fr. y.
Mi. 2 : † 8. y. my people as an enemy
Jn. 4 : 52. y. the fever left him
Ac. 7 : 28. kill me as the Egyptian y.
He. 13 : 8. Jesus same y., to day and

YESTERDAY [forever **with third Day.**

Ex. 4 : † 10. I am not eloquent, neither since y. nor t. d. [t. d., 6.
De. 19 : † 4. he hated not from y. the
Jos. 3 : † 4. ye not passed this way
since y. and t. d. [y. or t. d.
1 S. 4 : † 7. hath not been such thing
19 : † 7. David in Saul's presence
as y. t. d. [and t. d.
2 S. 3 : † 17. Ye sought for David y.
2 K. 13 : † 5. Israel dwelt in tents as
y. and t. d. [dest Israel
1 Ch. 11 : † 2. y. and t. d. thou led-

YESTERNIGHT.

Ge. 19 : 34. I lay y. with my father
31 : 29. God of your fath. spake unto
32. God rebuked thee y. [me y.
Jb. 30 : † 3. fleeing into wilderness y.

YET. [to rain

Ge. 7 . 4. For y. seven days cause it
15 : 16. iniq-y Amorites not y. full
18 : 22. Abram stood y. before Lord
32. I will speak y. but this once
27 : 30. Jacob was y. scarce gone
40 : 13. y. within 3 days sh. Pha. lift
23. y. did not butler rememb. Jos.
Ex. 5 : 11. y. not work be diminished
9 : 17. y. exaltest thyself ag. people
34. Pharaoh sinned y. more and
10 : 7. knowest not y. Eg. is destroy.
Le. 25 : 22. eat y. of old fruits until
26 : 18. if ye will not y. hearken
44. y. for all that, when in land of
Nu. 22 : 20. y. the word I sh. say, do
De. 1 : 32. y. in th. ye did not believe
9 : 29. y. they are thy people and
29 : 4. y. Lord not given you eyes
Jos. 14 : 11. As y. I am strong as I
Ju. 7 : 4. people are y. too many [was
10 : 13. y. ye have forsaken me
15 : 7. y. will I be avenged of you
1 S. 15 : 30. y. honour me bef. elders
18 : 29. Saul y. more afraid of Dav.
2 S. 23 : 5. y. wi. me everlast-g covt.
1 K. 14 . 8. y. hast not been as David
19 : 18. y. I have left me 7,000 in
22 : 8. There is y. one by whom we
may inquire [ces, 2 K. 14 : 4.
43. people offered y. in high pla-
2 K. 3 : 17. y. valley be filled wi. water
8 : 19. y. L. wou. not destroy Judah
13 : 23. nei. from his presence as y.
14 . 3. y. not like David his father
19 : 30. remnant shall y. take root
2 Ch. 6 : 16. y. so thy chil. take heed
20 : 33. as y. peo. had not prepared
27 : 2. the people did y. corruptly
30 : 18. not cleansed, y. did they eat
Ezr. 3 : 6. foundat. of temple not y.
9 : 9. y. our God hath not forsaken
us, Ne. 9 : 19. [to Jews
Ne. 2 : 16. neither had I as y. told
5 : 18. y. required not I bread of gov.
13 : 18. y. ye bring more wrath
Es. 5 : 13. y. all this availeth noth-g
Jb. 1 : 16. While he y. speak-g, 17, 18.
6 : 10. Then sho. I y. have comfort
9 : 31. y. thou plunge me in ditch
20 : 7. y. he shall perish forever
29 . 5. When Almighty y. with me
35 : 15. y. he knoweth it not in gr-t
extremity [hill of Zion
Ps. 2 : 6 y. have I set my King upon
37 : 25. y. have I not seen righteous
forsaken [5. - 71 : 14.
42 : 5. I shall y. praise him, 11 - 43 :
44 : 17. y. have we not forgotten
78 : † 1. y. God is good to Isr. [thee
119 : 51. y. have I not declined
from thy law. 157. [109, 141.
83. y. do I not forget thy statutes,
Pr. 27 : 22. y. will not his foolishness
30 : 12. y. not washed fr. filthiness
Ec. 4 : 3. he which hath not y. been
8. y. is no end to all his labor
Is. 10 : 22. y. a remnant shall return
14 : 1. the Lord will y. choose Israel
17 : 6. y. gleaning grapes sha. be left
28 : 4. while y. in his hand he eat-
12. y. they would not hear [eth it
31 : 2. y. he is wise, will bring evil
49 : 5. y. shall I be glorious in eyes
15. they may forget, y. will I not
53 : 7. y. he opened not his mouth
Je. 2 : 9. I will y. plead with you
3 : 1. y. return to me, saith Lord
5 : 28. judge not cause, y. prosper
15 : 1. y. my mind not tow. people
23 : 21. I have not sent, y. they ran
25 : 7. y. ye have not heark-d unto
36 : 24. y. they were not afraid, nor
Eze. 8 : 18. cry, y. will I not hear th.
11 : 16. y. will I be as a sanctuary
28 : 2. I am a god, y. thou art a man
9. Wilt thou y. say I am God?
36 : 37. I will y. for this be inquired
Da. 4 : 23. y. leave stump of roots
5 : 17. y. I will read writing unto
9 : 13. y. made not our prayer [king
11 : 35. it is y. for a time appointed
45. y. he sh. come to his end [not
Ho. 7 : 9. gray hairs, y. he knoweth
13 : 4. y. I am the L. thy God from
Am. 4 : 6. y. have ye not returned
unto me, 8, 9, 10, 11. Hag. 2 : 17.
6 : 10. Is there y. any with thee
Jon. 2 : 4. y. I will look tow. temple
3 : 4. y. forty days Nineveh shall be
4 : 2. when I was y. in my country
Mi. 6 : 10. y. treasures of wickedness
Na. 3 : 10. y. was she carried away
Ha. 3 : 18. y. I will rejoice in Lord
Mal. 2 : 14. y. is she thy companion
Mat. 6 : 25. nor y. for y-r body, what
26. y. your heavenly Fath. feedeth
29. y. I say, Solomon was not arrayed like, Lu. 12 : 27. [people
12 : 46. while he y. talked to the
13 : 21. y. hath not root in himself
15 : 16. ye y. without underst-g, 17.
27. Truth, Lord, y. dogs eat
crumbs, Mk. 7 : 28. [y.?
19 : 20. these I kept, what lack I
24 : 6. the end is not y., Mk. 13 : 7.
32. branch y. tender, Mk. 13 : 28.
26 : 33. Tho. all, y. will I never be
offended, Mk. 14 : 29. [sake
Mk. 6 : 26. king sorry, y. for oath's
8 : 17. have ye heart y. hardened (2)
11 : 13. the time of figs was not y.
12 : 6. having y. therefore one son
15 : 5. but Jesus y. answ-d nothing
Lu. 3 : 20. Herod added y. this [him
9 : 42. as y. a coming, devil threw
11 : 8. y. bec. of his importunity he
14 : 22. serv. said, y. there is room
35. nei fit for land, nor y. dung-
15 : 20. he y. a great way off [hill
29. y. thou never gavest me a kid
18 : 5. y. bec. this widow troubleth
22. y. lackest thou one thing [me
19 : 30. colt, wh-on y. nev. man sat
22 : 37. y. be accomplished in me
23 : 15. nor y. Herod; I sent you to
24 : 6. spake unto you y. in Galilee
Jn. 4 : 21. in this mt., nor y. at Jerus.
27. y. no man said, What seekest
35. Say not ye, There are y. 4 mos.
7 : 8. I go not up y. unto feast (2)
19. y. none of you keepeth the law
39. (Holy Ghost was not y. given;
bec. Jesus was not y. glorified)
8 : 14. y. my record is true; for I
16. y. if I judge, judgment is true
55. y. ye have not known him
57. Thou art not y. fifty years old
9 : 30. y. he hath opened mine eyes
12 : 37. y. they believed not on him

Jn. 14 :9. y.hast thou not known me
16 : 12. I ha. y. many things to say
32. y. I am not alone, bec. Father
19 : 41. wh-in was man never y.laid
20 : 1. cometh Mary when y. dark
5. saw linen clothes, y. went not
9. as y. they knew not the Script.
17. for I am not y. ascended to[ed
29. have not seen, y. have believ-
21 : 11. y. was not the net broken
23. y. Jes.said not, He sh.not die
Ac. 7 : 5. y.promised he would give
8 : 16. as y. Holy Ghost upon none
9 : 1. Saul y. breathing out slaugh.
13 : 28. y.desired he should be slain
18 : 18. Paul tarried y.a good while
19 : 37. nor y. blasphemers of god-s
24 : 11. y. but 12 days since I went
25 : 8.Nei. ag-t law, nor y. ag.Cesar
28 : 4. y.vengeance suffereth not to
17. y.was I delivered prisoner[live
Ro. 3 : 7. why y. judged as a sinner?
4 : 11. faith,being y.uncircumci.,12.
19. nei.y.deadn-s of Sarah's womb
5 : 6. when we y. without strength
7. y. for a good man, dare to die
8 : 24. seeth, why doth he y. hope
9 : 11. for the children not y. born
19. why doth he y. find fault? [cy
11 : 30. y. now have obtained mer-
16 : 19. y. I would have you wise
1 Co. 2 : 6. y. not wisdom of world
15. y.he hims. is judged of no man
3 : 2. neither y. now are ye able
3. For ye are y. carnal [fire
15. he shall be saved, y. so as by
4 : 4. y. am I not hereby justified
15. y. have ye not many fathers
5 : 10. y. not with fornicators[not I
7 : 10. unto married I command, y.
25. y. I give my judgment, as one
8 : 2. knoweth noth-g y.as he ought
9 : 2. If not apostle unto others, y.
19. I free, y. made myself servant
12 : 20. many members,y. one body
31. y. shew I a more excellent way
14 : 19. y. I rather speak five words
21. y. for all that will not hear me
15: 10. y.not I,but the grace of God
17. faith vain; ye are y. in y-r sins
2 Co. 1 : 10. trust he will y. deliver
23. to spare you I came not as y.
4 : 8.We troubled,y. not distressed
16. y. inward man is renewed day
5 : 16. y.now know we him no more
6 : 8. as deceivers and y. true
9. as unknown and y. well known
10.as sorrowful,y.alway rejoicing,
8 : 9. tho. rich, y. became poor [(3)
9 : 3. y. have I sent brethren, lest
11 : 6. be rude in speech, y. not in
16. y. as a fool receive me [knowl.
12 : 5. y. of myself I will not glory
13 : 4.though crucified,y. he liveth
Ga. 1 : 10. if I y. pleased men [me
2 : 20. I live, y. not I, but Christ in
3 : 4. suffered in vain, if y. in vain
15. man's coven-t, y. if confirmed
5 : 11. if I y. preach circumcision,
why do I y. suffer [flesh
Ep. 5 : 29. no man ever y. hated own
Ph. 1 : 9. that love abound y. more
22. y. what I sh. choose I wot not
2 : 25. y. I supposed it necessary
Col. 1 : 21. enemies, y. now reconcil-
2 : 5. y. am I with you in spirit [ed
1 Th. 2 : 6. glory, nei. of you nor y.
2 Th.2 : 5. y, wi. you I told [of others
3 : 15. y. count him not as enemy
2 Ti. 2 : 5. y.he is not crowned except
Phm. 9. y. for love's sake I beseech
He. 2 : 8. not y.all things put under
4 : 15. tempted as we, y. without
7 : 10. y. in loins of his father [sin
15. it is y. far more evident
9 : 8. the way not y. manifest (2)
25.Nor y.that he offer hims. often
He. 11 : 4. he being dead y. speaketh
7. warned of things not seen as y.
12: 4. Ye not y. resisted unto blood
26. y. once more I shake not only
27. this word, y. once more, signi-
Ja.2: 10. y. offend in one point [fieth
11. y.,if thou kill,art a transgres-r
3 : 4. ships so great, y. are turned
4: 2. y. ye have not bec. ye ask not
1 Pe. 1 : 8. see him not, y. believing
4 : 16. y. if any suffer as Christian
1 Jn. 3 : 2. not y.appear what we sh.
Jude 9. y. Mich-l durst not bring[be
Re. 6 : 11. rest y. for a little season
8 : 13.voices which are y. to sound!
9 : 20. not killed, y. repented not
17 : 8. beast that was, is not,and y.
12. received no kingdom as y. [is
See **Yet ALIVE, Yet COME.**
See AGAIN, THOUGH, WHILE,
Little WHILE.

YIELD. [strength
Ge. 4 : 12. earth not hencef-h y. her
49 : 20. he shall y. royal dainties
Le. 26 : 20. nei. shall trees y. fruits
2 Ch.30 : 8.y. yourselves unto the L.
Ps. 107 : 37. plant vineyards which
may y. fruits of increase [to y.
Pr.7:21.With fair speech caused him
Is. 5 : 10. ten acres shall y. one bath
seed of a homer sh. y. an ephah
Ho. 8 : 7. the bud shall y. no meal :
if it y., stranger shall swallow it
Jo. 2 : 22. fig tree, vine y. strength
Ho.3 :17.Although fields y. no meat
Ac.23 : 21. do not thou y.unto them
Ro. 6 : 13. Nei. y. ye your members
unto sin, y. yoursel-s unto God
16. to whom ye y. yours. servants
19. y. your members servants to
righteousness [and fresh
Ja. 3 : 12. no fountain y. salt water
See **Yield, ed, eth FRUIT.**
See INCREASE, OBEDIENCE.

YIELDED.
Ge. 49 : 33. Jacob y. up the ghost
Nu. 17 : 8. rod of Aaron y. almonds
Da. 3 : 28. y. their bodies that they
Mat. 27 : 50. Jesus y. up the ghost
Ac. 5 : 10. Sapphira y. up the ghost
Ro. 6: 19. ly. members to unclean-

YIELDETH, ING. [ness
Ge. 1 : 11. bring forth herb y-g seed,
tree y-g fruit, 12. [y-g seed
29. I have given you every tree
Ne. 9 : 37. it y-h increase unto kings
Jb. 24 : 5. the wilderness y-h food
Ec.10 : 4. y-g pacifieth great offences
2 Th. 1 : † 8. In flaming fire y-g ven-

YOKE. [geance
Ge. 27 : 40. shalt break his y. off thy
neck, Is. 10 : 27. Je. 30 : 8.
Le. 26 : 13. I have broken the bands
of your y. and, Eze. 34 : 27.
Nu.19 : 2.bring heifer upon wh. never came y., De. 21 : 3. 1 S. 6 : 7.
De. 28 : 48. sh. put a y. of iron upon
thy neck, Je. 28 : 14. [them
1S.11 : 7. Saul took y. of oxen hewed
14 : 14. a half acre which a y. of
oxen might plough
1 K. 12 : 4. thy father made our y.
grievous, now make his heavy
y.lighter,10. 2 Ch. 10 :4.[10 : 9.
9. Make y. upon us lighter, 2 Ch.
11. My father did lade you with
heavy y., I will add to your y.,
14. 2 Ch. 10 : 11, 14. [of oxen
19 : 19. Elisha ploughing with 12 y.
21. he took a y. of oxen, slew them
Jb. 1 : 3. his substance 500 y.of oxen
42 : 12.he had a thousand y. of oxen
Is. 9 : 4.hast broken y. of his burden
10 : 27. his y. from thy neck,and y.
be destroyed bec. of anointing
14 : 25. Assyrian, his y. depart [y.
47 : 6. upon ancient heavily laid thy
Is. 58 :6.†undo the bundles of the y.
58 : 6. and that ye break every y.
9.If take from midst of thee the y.
Je. 2 : 20.of old I have broken thy y.
5 : 5. but these have broken thy y.
27: 8. not put neck under y. of Bab.
11. that bring neck under y., 12.
28 : 2. brok. y. of king of Bab.,4,11.
10.took y. off Jeremiah's neck,12.
31 : 18.bullock unaccustomed to y.
51 : 23. will I break his y. of oxen?
La. 1 : 14. y. of my transgression is
3 : 27. good that he bear y. in youth
Ho. 11 : 4. I as they that take off y.
Na. 1 : 13. will I break y. fr. off thee
Mat. 11 : 29. Take my y. upon you
30. my y. is easy, my burden light
Lu. 14 : 19. I bought five y. of oxen
Ac. 15 : 10. y. upon neck of disciples
Ga. 5 : 1. be not entangled with the
y. of bondage [are under y.
1 Ti. 6 : 1. Let as many servants as

YOKES. [28 : 13.
Je. 27 : 2. Make thee bonds and y.,
28 : 13. hast broken the y. of wood
make y. of iron [Egypt
Eze. 30 : 18. when I shall break y. of

YOKED.
2 Co. 6 : 14. Be not unequally y.

YOKEFELLOW. [with
Ph. 4 : 3. I entreat thee also true y.

YONDER.
Ge. 22 : 5. I and the lad will go y.
Nu. 16 : 37. Scatter thou the fire y.
23 : 15. Stand while I meet Lord y.
32 : 19.we will not inherit on y. side
2 K. 4 : 25. y. is that Shunammite
Mat. 17 : 20. Remove to y. place
26 : 36. Sit here while I go and

YOU. [pray y.
Jos. 3 : 4. be a space betw. y. and ark
Jb. 16 : 4. could shake my head at y.
Is.59: 2. separated betw. y. and God
Je. 49 :3. dau-s gird y. with sackc-th
Eze. 11 : 19. will put new spirit within y., 36 : 26, 27. [shame
36 : 7. heathen about y. shall bear
36. heathen about y. sh. know I
Am.2 :13.I am pressed und. y.[build
3 : 2. y. only have I known of all(2)
Zch. 11 : 7.I will feed flock of slaughter even y. [flee
Mat. 3 : 7. who hath warned y. to
11. I baptize y. with water (2)
4 : 19. I will make y. fishers of men
5 : 11. Blessed are ye when men
shall revile y. (3) [y. (4)
44. Bless them that curse y. ; hate
46. if ye love them which love y.
Lu. 10 : 16. He that heareth y. heareth me,despiseth y. despiseth me
13 : 28. y. thrust out of kingdom
Ro. 2 : 24. G. is blasphemed thro. y.
16 : 19. I would have y. wise unto
that which is good
2 Co. 1:7. Our hope of y. is steadfast
10 : 16. gospel in regions beyond y.
12 : 14. for I seek not yours but y.
Col. 1 : 21. y. that were alienated in
2 :13. y. dead in sins hath he quickened, having forgiven y., Ep.2 : 1.

After YOU. [a. y.
Ge. 9 : 9. covenant with y. and seed
Le. 25 : 46. as an inheritance for children a. y., 1 Ch. 28 : 8.
26 : 33. I will draw out a sword a. y.
De. 11 : 4. as they pursued a. y. [y.
29 : 22. generation that shall rise a.
1 S. 25 :19. go on before,I come a. y.
Je. 42 : 16. famine follow close a. y.
2 Co. 9 : 14. wh. long a. y., Ph. 1 : 8.
Ph. 2 : 26. For he longed a. y. be-

Against YOU. [cause
Ex. 10 : 16. said, I have sinned a. y.
Le. 26 : 17. I will set my face a. y.
ye be slain, Je. 44 : 11. [a. y.
Nu. 17 : 5. whereby they murmur

De. 1 : 44. Amorites came out **a. y.**
4 : 26. I call heaven and earth to
witness **a. y.** this day, 30 : 19.
8 : 19. I testify **a. y.** ye shall perish
9 : 19. wherewith Lord was wroth
a. y., 11 : 17. Jos. 23 : 16. ⌈**a. y.**
Jos. 24 : 11. men of Jericho fought
1 S. 12 : 5. Lord is witness **a. y.**,
12. king of Ammonites came **a. y.**
15. shall hand of Lord be **a. y.**
2 S. 17 : 21. Ahithophel counselled **a.**
2 Ch. 13 : 12. to cry alarm **a. y.** ⌊**y.**
Jb. 16 : 4. I could heap up words **a. y.**
Je. 18 : 11. I devise a device **a. y.** (2)
21 : 5. I will fight **a. y.** ⌈**a. y.**
26 : 13. L. repent of evil pronounced
37 : 10. the Chaldeans th. fight **a. y.**
19. king of Bab. sh. not come **a. y.**
38 : 5. king not do any thing **a. y.**
44 : 29. my words shall stand **a. y.**
49 : 30. Neb-r taken counsel **a. y.**
Eze. 13 : 8. I am **a. y.** saith Lord⌊(2)
36 : 2. Bec. enemy said **a. y.**, Aha
Am. 3 : 1. Hear word Lord hath
spoken **a. y.**, 5 : 1. Zph. 2 : 5.
6 : 14. I will raise up **a. y.** a nation
Mi. 1 : 2. let God be witness **a. y.**
2 : 4. take up a parable **a. y.** ⌈**y.**
Mat. 5 : 11. say all manner of evil **a.**
21 : 2. Go into village over **a. y.**, Mk.
11 : 2. Lu. 19 : 30. ⌈off **a. y.**
Lu. 10 : 11. dust of your city we wipe
Col. 2 : † 18. Let no man judge **a. y.**
Ja. 5 : 3. rust shall be a witness **a. y.**
1 Pe. 2 : 12. speak **a. y.** as evil doers

All YOU or YOU all. ⌈dan

Nu. 32 : 21. **a.** of **y.** armed over Jor-
De. 29 : 10. Ye stand **a.** of **y.** bef. L.
1 S. 6 : 4. one plague on **y. a.** ⌈tains
22 : 7. son of Jesse make **y. a.** cap-
8. **a.** of **y.** have conspired ag. me
2 K. 11 : 7. two parts of **a.** of **y.** that
Jb. 17 : 10. But as for **y. a.** come now
Ps. 62 : 3. ye shall be slain **a.** ⌈**y.**
82 : 6. **a.** of **y.** child. of Most High
Je. 7 : 25. sent unto **y. a.** prophets,
25 : 4. - 35 : 15. - 44 : 4. ⌈great
Lu. 9 : 48. he least among **y. a.** sh. be
Ac. 3 : 16. soundness in presence of
Jn. 13 : 18. I speak not of **y. a.** ⌊**y. a.**
Ac. 4 : 10. Be it known unto **y. a.** and
Ro. 1 : 8. I thank my God for **y. a.**
15 : 33. God of peace be with **y. a.**
16 : 24. The grace of our Lord Jesus
Ch. be with **y. a.**, 2 Co. 13 : 14.
Ph. 4 : 23. 2 Th. 3 : 18. Re. 22 : 21.
1 Co. 16 : 24. My love with **y. a.** in Ch.
2 Co. 2 : 3. having confidence in **y. a.**
that my joy is the joy of **y. a.**
5. that I may not overcharge **y. a.**
7 : 13. his spirit refreshed by **y. a.**
15. he rememb-h obedience of **y. a.**
Ep. 4 : 6. One Father of **a.** in **y. a.**
Ph. 1 : 4. every prayer of mine for **y.**
7. meet to think this of **y. a.** ⌊**a.**
8. how greatly I long after **y. a.**
25. I shall abide with **y. a.** for ⌈**a.**
2 : 17. if I be offered, I joy with **y.**
26. Epaphroditus longed aft. **y. a.**
1 Th. 1 : 2. We give thanks for **y. a.**
2 Th. 1 : 3. charity of **y. a.** abound-
3 : 16. The Lord be with **y. a.** ⌊eth
Ti. 3 : 15. Grace with **y. a.**, Amen,
He. 13 : 25. 1 Pe. 5 : 14. ⌈anoth.
1 Pe. 5 : 5. **a.** of **y.** be subject one to

Among or Amongst YOU.

Ge. 17 : 10. Every man child **a. y.**
shall be circumcised, 12. ⌈**y.**
23 : 9. money for burying place **a**-t
35 : 2. Put away the strange gods
a. y., Jos. 24 : 23. 1 S. 7 : 3.
Ex. 12 : 49. stranger that sojourneth **a. y.**, Le. 16 : 29. - 17 : 8,
10, 12, 13. - 18 : 26. - 25 : 45.
Nu. 9 : 14. Eze. 47 : 22.
35 : 5. Take from **a. y.** an offering
Ex. 35 : 10. wise hearted **a. y.** sh. come
Le. 19 : 34. stranger as one born **a. y.**
20 : 14. that be no wickedness **a. y.**
26 : 11. will set my tabernacle **a. y.**
12. I will walk **a. y.** be your God
22. I will send wild beasts **a. y.**
25. I will send pestilence **a. y.** ⌈**y.**
Nu. 11 : 20. despised the L. who is **a.**
12 : 6. If there be a prophet **a. y.**,
De. 13 : 1. ⌈De. 1 : 42.
14 : 42. Go not, Lord is not **a. y.**,
15 : 14. whoso. **a. y.** will offer an
32 : 30. possessions **a. y.** in Canaan
De. 4 : 3. God destroyed them **a. y.**
6 : 15. Lord is a jealous God **a. y.**
7 : 14. not be female barren **a. y.**
21. L. thy God is **a. y.**, Jos. 3 : 10.
13 : 11. no more such wickedn. **a. y.**
13. chil. of Belial gone out fr. **a. y.**
14. ask if such abomination **a. y.**
15 : 4. when shall be no poor **a. y.**
7. **a. y.** poor man of thy brethren
16 : 11. fatherless and widow **a. y.**
17 : 2. If **a. y.** man wrought wicked.
7. So put the evil away from **a. y.**,
19 : 19. - 21 : 21. - 22 : 21, 24. -
24 : 7. ⌈**a. y.**
19 : 20. henceforth commit no evil
21 : 9. put away the guilt from **a. y.**
23 : 10. If **a. y.** any man not clean
16. servant escaped sh. dwell **a. y.**
26 : 11. shalt rejoice and stranger **a.**
28 : 54. man that is tender **a. y.** ⌊**y.**
29 : 18. **a. y.** root th. beareth gall (2)
32 : 46. words which testify **a. y.**
Jos. 3 : 5. Lord will do wonders **a. y.**
4 : 6. this may be a sign **a. y.** ⌈13.
7 : 12. exc. ye destroy accursed **a. y.**,
18 : 7. Levites have no part **a. y.**
23 : 7. nations that remain **a. y.** ⌈**y.**?
Ju. 20 : 12. What wickedness this **a.**
2 S. 16 : 20. said Absalom, Give counsel **a. y.** ⌈Ezr. 1 : 3.
2 Ch. 36 : 23. Who is there **a. y.**,
Jb. 17 : 10. cannot find wise man **a. y.**
Is. 42 : 23. Who **a. y.** will give ear?
43 : 12. when no strange god **a. y.**
50 : 10. Who is **a. y.** feareth the L.?
Je. 8 : 17. I will send serpents **a. y.**
25 : 27. sword I will send **a. y.** ⌈**a. y.**
Eze. 11 : 9. will execute judgments
20 : 38. will purge fr. **a. y.** the rebels
47 : 22. strangers wh. beget children
Jo. 2 : 25. great army I sent **a. y.** ⌊**a. y.**
Hag. 2 : 3. Who **a. y.** that saw this
5. Spirit remaineth **a. y.** ⌊house?
Mal. 1 : 10. Who **a. y.** wou. shut doors
Mat. 12 : 11. What man **a. y.** that
shall have one sheep?
20 : 26. not be so **a. y.**; whosoever
shall be great **a. y.**, Mk. 10 : 43.
27. whosoever will be chief **a. y.**
let him, 23 : 11. Lu. 22 : 26.
Lu. 9 : 48. is least **a. y.** shall be great
22 : 27. I am **a. y.** as he th. serveth
Jn. 1 : 26. there standeth one **a. y.**
8 : 7. He that is without sin **a. y.**
Ac. 2 : 22. Jes. approved of God **a. y.**
6 : 3. Look ye out **a. y.** seven men
13 : 26. whosoever **a. y.** feareth God
20 : 29. grievous wolves enter **a. y.**
25 : 5. Let them which **a. y.** are able
27 : 22. shall be no loss of life **a. y.**
Ro. 1 : 13. might ha. some fruit **a. y.**
12 : 3. I say to every man **a. y.** ⌈**y.**
1 Co. 1 : 10. that be no divisions **a.**
11. are contentions **a. y.**, 11 : 18.
2 : 2. not to know anything **a. y.**
3 : 3. is **a. y.** envying, strife ⌊save
18. If any man **a. y.** seemeth wise
5 : 1. reported is fornication **a. y.**
2. that he might be taken fr. **a. y.**
6 : 5. Is it so, not a wise man **a. y.**
7. there is utterly a fault **a. y.**
11 : 19. must be heresies **a. y.** (2)
30. For this cause many sickly **a. y.**
15 : 12. say some **a. y.** is no resurr-n
2 Co. 1 : 19. Christ was preached **a. y.**
10 : 1. I in presence am base **a. y.**
11 : 6. we been made manifest **a. y.**
12 : 12. Truly signs of apostle **a. y.**
21. lest my God humble me **a. y.**
Ga. 3 : 1. set forth crucified **a. y.**
5. He that worketh miracles **a. y.**
Ep. 5 : 3. let it not be named **a. y.**
Col. 1 : † 27. Chr. **a. y.** hope of glory
4 : 16. when epistle is read **a. y.**
1 Th. 1 : 5. what men we were **a. y.**
2 : 7. we gentle **a. y.** as a nurse
10. how holily we behaved **a. y.**
5 : 12. to know them wh. labour **a. y.**
2 Th. 1 : 10. testimony **a. y.** believed
3 : 7. we behaved not disorderly **a.**
11. some walk **a. y.** disorderly ⌊**y.**
Ja. 1 : 26. If any **a. y.** seem religious
3 : 13. Who is a wise man **a. y.**?
4 : 1. From whence fightings **a. y.**?
5 : 13. Is any **a. y.** afflicted? ⌈elders
14. Is any sick **a. y.**? let him call
1 Pe. 5 : 1. The elders **a. y.** I exhort
2. Feed flock of God which is **a. y.**
2 Pe. 2 : 1. sh. be false teachers **a. y.**
Re. 2 : 13. Antipas, who was slain

Before YOU. ⌊**a. y.**

Ge. 34 : 10. land shall be **b. y.** dwell
45 : 5. God did send me **b. y.** to, 7.
Ex. 10 : 10. look to it; for evil is **b. y.**
Le. 18 : 24. nations defiled which I
cast out **b. y.**, 27, 28, 30. - 20 : 23.
26 : 7. your enemies sh. fall **b. y.**, 8.
Nu. 14 : 43. Canaanites there **b. y.**
32 : 29. land shall be subdued **b. y.**
33 : 52. drive out inhabit-s **b. y.**, 55.
De. 1 : 8. I have set the land **b. y.**
30. L. wh. goeth **b. y.** fight for you
33. God who went in way **b. y.**
4 : 8. law I set **b. y.** this day, 11 : 32.
11 : 23. will Lord drive out nations
b. y., Jos. 3 : 10. - 23 : 5, 9. - 24 :
12. Ju. 6 : 9. ⌈Jos. 23 : 9.
25. no man, be able to stand **b. y.**
26. I set **b. y.** blessing and curse
30 : 19. I have set **b. y.** life and d
Jos. 3 : 11. ark **b. y.** into Jordan
4 : 23. Lord dried up Jordan **b. y.**
9 : 24. destroy inhabitants **b. y.**, 24 : 8.
23 : 13. Lord will no more drive nations **b. y.**, Ju. 2 : 3. ⌈wh. drave
24 : 12. And I sent the hornet **b. y.**,
1 S. 9 : 12. he is **b. y.** make haste
12 : 2. behold, the king walketh **b. y.**
2 Ch. 7 : 19. if ye forsake my statutes
I set **b. y.**, Je. 26 : 4. - 44 : 10.
19 : 11. Levites shall be officers **b.**
Is. 52 : 12. the Lord will go **b. y.** ⌊**y.**
55 : 12. hills shall break forth **b. y.**
Je. 21 : 8. I set **b. y.** the way of life
Mat. 5 : 12. persecuted prophets **b. y.**
21 : 31. go into kingd. of God **b. y.**
26 : 32. am risen, I will go **b. y.** into
Galilee, 28 : 7. Mk. 14 : 28. - 16 : 7.
Lu. 10 : 8. eat such things as are set
b. y., 1 Co. 10 : 27. ⌈**y.**
23 : 14. I having examined him **b.**
Ac. 4 : 10. this man here **b. y.** whole
25 : 26. I have brought him **b. y.**

By YOU. ⌈**y.**, 31.

Eze. 20 : 3. I not be inquired of **b.**
Ro. 15 : 24. brought on my way **b. y.**
1 Co. 6 : 2. if world be judged **b. y.**
2 Co. 1 : 16. pass **b. y.** into Maced-a
7 : 13. his spirit was refreshed **b. y.**
10 : 15. we shall be enlarged **b. y.**

Concerning YOU.

Nu. 9 : 8. Lord will command **c. y.**
Jos. 23 : 14. which the L. spake **c. y.**
Je. 42 : 19. Lord hath said **c. y.**
2 Co. 8 : 23. Titus my partner **c. y.**
1 Th. 5 : 18. this is will of God **c. y.**

See **DELIVER You.**

For YOU.

Ge. 9 : 3. **f. y.**, 47 : 23. Ex. 7 : 9. -
10 : 5. - 16 : 4, 23. Le. 22 : 20,
25. - 23 : 11. Nu. 34 : 7. - 35 :

11. Jos. 18 : 6, 8. 1 S. 17 : 8. -
30 : 26. 2 K. 17 : 37. Je. 34 : 17.
Eze. 39 : 17, 19. Jo. 2 : 23.
Ge. 44 : 17. as f. y., 50 : 20. Nu. 14 : 32.
De. 1 : 40. Jos. 23 : 9. Jb. 17 : 10.
Le. 8 : 34. atonement f. y., 16 : 30. -
23 : 28. Nu. 28 : 22, 30. - 29 : 5.
25 : 6. sabbath of land be meat f. y.
Nu. 15 : 15. One ordinance f. y., 16.
De. 1 : 18. cause too hard f. y. bring
30. all that he did f. y., 4 : 34. ⌊me
31 : 19. Now write this song f. y.
32 : † 38. let them be a hiding f. y.
47. it is not a vain thing f. y. ⌈y.
Jos. 2 : 10. Lord dried up Red Sea. f.
23 : 3. God is he that fought f. y., 10.
Ju. 9 : 2. Whe. is better f. y., either
17. For my father fought f. y.
1 S. 12 : 24. how great things done f. y.
2 S. 7 : 23. to do f. y. great things
21 : 3. Dav. said, What sh. I do f. y.
4. What ye sh. say will I do f. y.
1 K. 12 : 28. too much f. y. to go to Je.
Ps. 127 : 2. vain f. y. to rise early
Is. 7 : 13. Is it small thing f. y. to
weary men ⌈idols
Eze. 20 : 39. As f. y. O Israel, serve
34 : 17. as f. y. my flock, I judge
36 : 9. I am f. y. and I will turn
Da. 2 : 9. is but one decree f. y. ⌈y.
Am. 5 : 18. day of L.! to what end f.
Mi. 3 : 1. Is it not f. y. to know
judgment ⌈houses?
Hag. 1 : 4. f. y. to dwell in ceiled
Mal. 2 : 1. priests, this com-t is f. y.
Mat. 11 : 22. be more tolerable for
Tyre than f. y., Lu. 10 : 14. ⌈y.
25 : 34. inherit kingdom prepared f.
Mk. 10 : 36. What would ye I do f. y.
Lu. 22 : 19. This my body given f. y.
20. my blood wh. is shed f. y. ⌈3
Jn. 14 : 2. I go to prepare place f. y.,
16 : 7. expedient f. y., 2 Co. 8 : 10.
26. I will pray the Father f. y.
Ac. 1 : 7. not f. y. to know the times
28 : 20. For this cause I called f. y.
Ro. 1 : 8. I thank my God f. y. all
1 Co. 1 : 13. was Paul crucified f. y.?
11 : 24. this is my body broken f. y.
2 Co. 7 : 12. that our care f. y. appear
8 : 16. care into heart of Titus f. y.
9 : 14. by their prayer f. y., Ph.
1 : 4. Col. 1 : 3, 9. - 4 : 12. 2 Th.
12 : 15. I gladly be spent f. y. ⌊1 : 11.
Ep. 1 : 16. Wherefore I cease not to
give thanks f. y., 1 Th. 1 : 2. -
3 : 9. 2 Th. 1 : 3. - 2 : 13. ⌈f. y.
3 : 13. faint not at my tribulations
Ph. 1 : 24. abide in flesh needful f. y.
3 : 1. not grievous, but f. y. safe
Col. 1 : 5. hope which is laid up f. y.
24. I rejoice in my sufferings f. y.
25. dispensation given to me f. y.
2 : 1. what great conflict I have f.
4 : 13. he hath a great zeal f. y. ⌊y.
He. 13 : 17. that is unprofitable f. y.
1 Pe. 1 : 4. inheritance in heaven f.
20. manifest in last time f. y. ⌊y.
5 : 7. care upon him, he careth f. y.
See **FIGHT for**, PRAY.

From YOU. ⌈y.

Ge. 26 : 27. ye have sent me away f.
Le. 20 : 25. separated f. y. as unclean
Jos. 9 : 22 We are very far f. y. ⌈y.
1 S. 6 : 3. his hand is not removed f.
2 S. 15 : 28. I will tarry until word
f. y. ⌈away f. y.
2 Ch. 30 : 8. his wrath may turn
9. Lord will not turn his face f. y.
Is. 1 : 15. I will hide mine eyes f. y.
59 : 2. your sins hid his face f. y.
Je. 5 : 25. withholden good thi. f. y.
34 : 21. Bab.'s army gone up f. y.
42 : 4. I will keep nothing back f. y.
Eze. 18 : 31. Cast f. y. transgressions
Jo. 2 : 20. I will remove f. y. army
Am. 4 : 7. withholden the rain f. y.
Mat. 21 : 43. kingd. of God taken f. y.
Jn. 16 : 22. joy no man taketh f. y.
Ac. 1 : 11. taken up f. y. into heaven
13 : 46. seeing ye put it f. y. we turn
1 Co. 14 : 36. came word of God f. y.
2 Co. 3 : 1. need we commendat. f. y.
Ep. 4 : 31. evil speaking be put f. y.
Ph. 4 : 18. things wh. were sent f. y.
1 Th. 1 : 8. f. y. sounded out word
2 : 17. we being taken f. y. a short
3 : 6. when Timotheus came f. y.
Ja. 4 : 7. Resist devil, he will flee f.
See **GET you.** ⌊y.

In YOU.

Ge. 42 : 16. wheth. be any truth i. y.
Ju. 9 : 19. let him also rejoice i. y.
Eze. 20 : 41. I will be sanctified i. y.
before heathen, 36 : 23. ⌈live, 14.
37 : 6. I will put breath i. y. ye sh.
Mal. 1 : 10. I have no pleasure i. y.
Mat. 10 : 20. the Spirit speaketh i. y.
11 : 21. if mighty works done i. y.
Jn. 5 : 38. have not his word i. y.
42. ye have not love of God i. y.
6 : 53. Except ye eat flesh of Son of
man no life i. y. ⌈place i. y.
8 : 37. kill me, because my word no
14 : 17. ye know him; he shall be i.
20. ye in me and I i. y., 15 : 4. ⌊y.
15 : 7. if my words abide i. y.
Ro. 8 : 9. if the Spirit dwell i. y.
10. if Christ be i. y. body is dead
11. if Spirit of him dwell i. y. (2)
12 : 18. as lieth i. y. live peaceably
1 Co. 1 : 6. testimony confirmed i. y.
3 : 16. Spirit of God dwelleth i. y.
6 : 19. Holy Ghost which is i. y.
14 : 25. will report that God is i. y.
2 Co. 2 : 3. having confidence i. y.,
7 : 16. - 8 : 22. Ga. 5 : 10. ⌈i. y.
4 : 12. death worketh in us but life
7 : 7. wherew. he was comforted i. y.
8 : 6. would finish i. y. same grace
9 : 14. exceeding grace of God i. y.
13 : 3. is not weak, but mighty i. y.
5. Know ye not how Christ is i. y.
Ga. 4 : 19. until Christ be formed i. y.
Ep. 4 : 6. one God above all, i. y. all
Ph. 2 : 5. Let this mind be i. y.
13. it is God which worketh i. y.
Col. 1 : 6. fruit, as it doth also i. y.
27. Christ i. y. the hope of glory
3 : 16. Let word of Christ dwell i. y.
1 Th. 2 : 13. effectually worketh i. y.
2 Th. 1 : 4. we glory i. y. in churches
12. Christ may be glorified i. y.
Phm. 6. acknowledging every good
thing i. y. ⌈pleasing
He. 13 : 21. i. y. that which is well
1 Pe. 3 : 15. a reason of hope i. y.
2 Pe. 1 : 8. if these things be i. y.
1 Jn. 2 : 8. is true in him and i. y.
14. the word of God abideth i. y.
24. Let that abide i. y. ye have
27. anointing abideth i. y. ⌊heard
4 : 4. greater is he that is i. y. than

Of YOU. ⌈(2)

Ge. 9 : 2. fear o. y. upon every beast,
27 : 45. why I be deprived o. y. both
34 : 15. ev. male o. y. be circumc-d
42 : 16. send one o. y. fetch brother
Ex. 12 : 16. that only be done o. y.
22. none o. y. go out of hou. until
Le. 18 : 6. none o. y. approach kin
26 : 36. upon them left alive o. y. I
Nu. 9 : 10. If any o. y. be unclean
De. 1 : 22. came near every one o. y.
2 : 4. and they shall be afraid o. y.
4 : 4. ye are alive every one o. y. ⌈y.
Jos. 2 : 9. inhabitants to faint bec. o.
11. our hearts did melt bec. o. y.
9 : 24. afraid of our lives bec. o. y.
23 : 3. done unto nations bec. o. y.
10. One man o. y. sh. chase a thou.
Ju. 8 : 2. What I in comparison o.
15 : 7. will I be avenged o. y. ⌊y.?
Ru. 1 : 9. each o. y. in hou. of husb.
1 S. 22 : 8. none o. y. is sorry for me
1 K. 22 : 28. Hearken every one o. y.
2 K. 11 : 5. third part o. y. be keep-
2 Ch. 15 : 2. will be found o. y. ⌊ers
30 : 6. will return to remnant o. y.
Ezr. 7 : 21. Whatso. Ezra required o. y.
Ne. 1 : 9. though were o. y. cast out
Je. 29 : 14. I will be found o. y.
Eze. 6 : 7. slain fall in midst o. y.
9. that escape o. y. sh. remember
Am. 4 : 11. I have overth. some o. y.
Mi. 1 : 11. receive o. y. his standing
Zch. 7 : 10. let none o. y. imagine
evil against his brother, 8 : 17.
Mat. 6 : 27. Which o. y. can add to
his stature? Lu. 12 : 25.
7 : 9. What man o. y. if son ask ⌈7 : 6.
15 : 7. Esaias prophesy o. y., Mk.
26 : 21. one o. y. shall betray me,
Mk. 14 : 18. Jn. 13 : 21.
Mk. 10 : 44. whoso. o. y. will be chief-
11 : 29. will ask o. y. question ⌊est
Lu. 6 : 26. Woe wh. all speak well o.
11 : 5. Wh. o. y. sh. have friend ⌊y.
13 : 15. doth not each o. y. lead ox
14 : 5. Which o. y. sh. have an ass
28. which o. y. intending to build
33. whoso. o. y. forsaketh not all
15 : 4. What man o. y. having hundred sheep, if he ⌈ploughing
17 : 7. which o. y. having servant
21 : 16. some o. y. be put to death
Jn. 6 : 64. some o. y. believe not
70. twelve, and one o. y. is a devil
7 : 19. none o. y. keepeth the law
8 : 26. many things to judge o. y.
46. Wh. o. y. convinceth me of sin?
Ac. 2 : 22. God did in midst o. y. ⌈y.
38. Repent be baptized ev. one o.
3 : 26. every one o. y. fr. iniquities
4 : 11. set at nought o. y. builders
27 : 34. not hair fr. head of any o. y.
Ro. 1 : 12. mutual faith o. y. and me
15 : 14. I am persuaded o. y. breth.
16 : 2. business she hath need o. y.
1 Co. 1 : 11. been declared unto me o.
14. I baptized none o. y. but ⌊y.
4 : 6. that no one o. y. be puffed up
6 : 1. Dare any o. y. go to law bef.
11. such were some o. y. but ye are
12 : 21. to feet, I have no need o. y.
14 : 26. ev. one o. y. hath a psalm
16 : 2. let every one o. y. lay by him
2 Co. 1 : 7. our hope o. y. is steadfast
16. o. y. to be brought on my way
2 : 9. I might know the proof o. y.
7 : 4. great is my glorying o. y.
14. if I have boasted to him o. y.
9 : 2. for wh. I boast o. y. to them
3. lest our boasting o. y. be vain
11 : 20. ye suffer if a man take o. y.
12 : 11. I to have been commended
17. Did I make a gain o. y.? ⌊o. y.
18. Did Titus make a gain o. y.?
Ga. 3 : 2. This would I learn o. y.
27. as many o. y. as been baptized
4 : 11. I am afraid o. y. lest I have
20. I stand in doubt o. y. ⌈by law
5 : 4. Whosoever o. y. are justified
Ep. 1 : 16. making mention o. y. in
my prayers, 1 Th. 1 : 2. ⌈wife
5 : 33. let every one o. y. so love his
Ph. 1 : 3. upon ev. remembrance o. y.
Col. 4 : 9. Onesimus who is one o. y.
12. Epaphras who is one o. y. ⌈y.
1 Th. 2 : 6. sought we glory neither o.
8. affectionately desirous o. y. we
9. would not be chargeable unto
any o. y., 2 Th. 3 ; 8. ⌈how
4 : 4. every one o. y. should know
Tit. 2 : 8. no evil thi. to say o. y. ⌈heart
He. 3 : 12. lest in any o. y. an evil
13. lest any o. y. be hardened ⌈lt
4 : 1. lest any o. y. come short of
6 : 11. ev. one o. y. shew, diligence
Ja. 1 : 5. If any o. y. lack wisdom
5 : 4. hire, which is o. y. kept back

Ja. 5 : 19. if any o. y. err from truth
1 Pe. 3 : 16. they speak evil o. y., 4 : 4.
2 Pe. 2 : 3. make merchandise o. y.
Re. 2 : 23. unto every one o. y. acc.
See **All YOU.** [to works

On or **Upon YOU.** [judge

Ex. 5 : 21. The Lord look u. y.,
12 : 13. plague shall not be u. y.
32 : 29. may bestow u. y. a blessing
Le. 10 : 7. anointing oil of L. is u. y.
19 : 28. nor print any marks u. y.
26 : 21. 7 times more plagues u. y.
25. I will bring a sword u. y. shall
avenge, Eze. 6 : 3. [u. y., 7.
Nu. 16 : 3. they said, Ye take too much
De. 7 : 7. L. did not set his love u. y.
29 : 5. clothes not waxen old u. y.
Jos. 23 : 15. as all good things u. y.
2 S. 1 : 21. neither let be rain u. y.,
2 Ch. 10 : 11. fa. put heavy yoke u. y.
19 : 7. let the fear of Lord be u. y.
28 : 11. fierce wrath of Lord is u. y.
Ne. 4 : 12. From all places be u. y.
13 : 21. do so, I will lay hands u. y.
Jb. 13 : 11. Sh. not his dread fall u. y.
Ps. 129 : 8. blessing of Lord be u. y.
Pr. 1 : 27 when anguish cometh u. y.
Is. 29 : 10. poured u. y. spirit of sleep
30 : 18. he may have mercy u. y.
Je. 3 : 12. not cause anger to fall u.
5 : 15. bring a nation u. y. [y.
15 : 14. a fire wh. shall burn u. y.
23 : 2. visit u. y. evil of doings [y.
17. they say, No evil shall come u.
40. an everlasting reproach u. y.
40 : 3. thf. this thing is come u. y.
42 : 12. he may have mercy u. y.
Eze. 5 : 16. will increase famine u. y.
22 : 21. will blow u. y. in wrath
22. I have poured my fury u. y.
23 : 49. recompense lewdness u. y.
36 : 10. I will multiply men u. y., 11.
12. will cause men to walk u. y.
25. will sprinkle clean water u. y.
29. I will lay no famine u. y.
37 : 6. will lay sinews u. y. (2) [y.
Ho. 10 : 12. till he rain righteousn. u.
Am. 4 : 2. lo, the days sh. come u. y.
Jon. 1 : 12. my sake, this tempest u. y.
Zph. 2 : 2. bef. day of L.'s anger u. y.
Mal. 2 : 2. I will send a curse u. y.
Mat. 11 : 29. Take my yoke u. y.
23 : 35. u. y. may come the blood
Lu. 11 : 20. the kingdom of God u. y.
21 : 12. they sh. lay their hands o. y.
34. that day come u. y. unawares
24 : 49. promise of my Father u. y.
Jn. 12 : 35. lest darkness come u. y.
Ac. 1 : 8. after HolyGh. is come u. y.
1 Co. 7 : 35. not that I cast snare u. y.
Ga. 4 : 11. lest u. y. labour in vain
Ja. 5 : 1. miseries that sh. come o. y.
1 Pe. 4 : 14. Spirit of God rest-h u. y.
Re. 2 : 24. I put u. y. none other

Over YOU. [burden

Le. 26 : 16. will appoint o. y. terror
17. that hate you shall reign o. y.
De. 1 : 13. make them rulers o. y. [y.
15. wise men, made them heads o.
28 : 63. L. rejoiced o. y. to do good,
he will rejoice o. y. to destroy
Ju. 8 : 23. I will not rule o. y., nei.
shall my son rule o. y.: the
Lord shall rule o. y. [or one?
9 : 2. is it better that 70 reign o. y.
15. If ye anoint me king o. y.
1 S. 8 : 11. manner of the king o. y.
12 : 1. I have made a king o. y.
13. Lord hath set a king o. y. [y.
2 S. 3 : 17. Ye sought Dav. to be k. o.
2 Ch. 19 : 11. Amariah priest is o. y.
Je. 6 : 17. Also I set watchmen o. y.
Eze. 20 : 33. with fury will rule o. y.
Hag. 1 : 10. heaven o. y. is stayed fr.
Lu. 12 : 14. who made me judge o. y.
Ro. 6 : 14. sin not dominion o. y.
1 Co. 9 : 12. partakers of power o. y.

2 Co. 11 : 2. I am jealous o. y. with
1 Th. 3 : 7. we were comforted o. y.
5 : 12. know them o. y. in the Lord
He. 13 : 7. Remember them which
have the rule o. y. [o. y.
17. Obey them that have the rule
24. Salute them have the rule o.

I Pray YOU. [y.

Ge. 18 : 4. I p. y., 19 : 2, 7, 8. - 24 :
8. - 37 : 6. - 40 : 8. - 50 : 4. Nu.
16 : 8, 26. - 22 : 19. Jos. 2 : 12.
Ju. 8 : 5. - 9 : 2. - 19 : 9, 23. Ru.
2 : 7. 1 S. 14 : 29. - 23 : 22. 2 S.
20 : 16. 1 K. 20 : 7. 2 K. 5 : 7.
Ne. 5 : 10, 11. - Jb. 6 : 29. - 32 :
21. Is. 5 : 3. La. 1 : 18. Eze.
33 : 30. Mi. 3 : 1, 9. Hag. 2 : 15.
Mal. 1 : 9. Ac. 27 : 34.
See **TEACH you, TELL you.**

To or **Unto YOU.**

Ge. 1 : 29. t. y. it shall be for meat
19 : 8. let me bring them out u. y.
22 : 5. t. y., 41 : 55. Ex. 12 : 2, 16.
- 14 : 13. 1 S. 6 : 21. - 14 : 9. -
18 : 23. 2 K. 17 : 13. Ne. 6 : 3.
Je. 29 : 27. Mat. 7 : 15. - 10 : 13.
Lu. 10 : 6. - 16 : 26. Ro. 1 : 15.
1 Co. 11 : 2. He. 18 : 19.
34 : 9. take our daughters u. y., 16.
42 : 14. u. y. 22. - 45 : 12 Ex. 7 : 4,
9. - 11 : 9. - 20 : 23. - 24 : 14. - 26 :
33. Le. 9 : 4, 6. - 19 : 23. - 20 : 24.
- 23 : 10, 15. Nu. 18 : 4. - 28 : 31.
De. 1 : 45. - 30 : 18. 1 S. 11 : 10.
(2) 2 Ch. 28 : 10. Ne. 13 : 27.
Jb. 42 : 8. Is. 21 : 10. - 29 : 11.
Je. 10 : 1. - 25 : 5. - 26 : 14. - 27 :
9, 14. - 29 : 12. - 35 : 14. - 42 : 10,
12, 21. Eze. 14 : 22. - 36 : 9. -
47 : 22. Zch. 6 : 15. Mal. 1 : 6. -
2 : 4. Mat. 10 : 23. - 21 : 31, 32. -
23 : 34. - 25 : 12. Mk. 6 : 11. - 9 :
41. - 16 : 7. Lu. 6 : 26, 27. - 7 :
32. (2) - 10 : 19. - 13 : 25. - 16 : 9.
- 24 : 6, 44. Jn. 6 : 63. - 8 : 25. -
10 : 26. - 18 : 34. - 14 : 25, 26. -
15 : 3, 11, 15, 20. - 16 : 1, 6, 33.
Ac. 2 : 29. - 3 : 14, 20. 1 Pe. 1 : 12.
Ex. 3 : 13. God of fath-s sent me u. y.,
14. I AM hath sent me u. y. [15.
16. seen that which is done t. y. in
6 : 7. I will be t. y. a God [Egypt
12 : 13. blood shall be t. y. a token
14. this day be u. y. for memorial
26. when your child-n sh. say u. y.
20 : 23. nei. make u. y. gods of gold
30 : 32. it is holy, and shall be holy,
u. y., 36. - 31 : 14. Le. 25 : 12.
Le. 11 : 4. unclean u. y., 5, 6, 7, 8,
27, 28, 29, 31, 35. [12, 20, 23.
10. be an abomination u. y., 11,
16 : 29. a statute forever u. y., 34.
31. It sh. be a sabbath of rest u. y.
23 : 21. holy convocat-n u. y., 27, 36.
25 : 10. it shall be a jubilee u. y.,
26 : 9. I will have respect u. y. [11.
16. I also will do this u. y. [y., 28.
24. Then will I walk contrary u.
Nu. 10 : 8. be t. y. for an ordinance
10. they be t. y. for a memorial
11 : 20. it shall be loathsome u. y.
15 : 39. it shall be u. y. for a fringe
18 : 6. Levites t. y. as a gift for Lord
33 : 56. I sh. do u. y. as I thought
Jos. 23 : 12. if ye go in unto them
and they t. y. [u. y.
13. they shall be snares and traps
24 : 15. if seem evil u. y. to serve
1 S. 4 : 9. not servants as they t. y.
2 Ch. 19 : 10. what cause shall come
Jb. 6 : 28. evident u. y. if I lie [t. y.
12 : 3. I am not inferiour t. y., 13 :
32 : 12. Yea, I attended u. y. [2.
Pr. 1 : 23. will pour my spirit u. y. (2)
8 : 4. u. y. O men I call [breach
Is. 30 : 13. iniquity be t. y. as a
18. that he may be gracious u. y.

Je. 7 : 23. that it be well u. y. [t. y.
29 : 27. Jer. maketh hims. prophet
44 : 23. thf. evil is happened u. y.
Eze. 34 : 18. seemeth it small thing u.
Da. 3 : 4. t. y. it is commanded [y.
Jon. 1 : 12. so shall sea be calm u. y.
Mi. 3 : 6. thf. night shall be u. y. (2)
Mal. 4 : 2. u. y. that fear my name
Mat. 6 : 33. all things shall be added
u. y., Lu. 12 : 31. [Lu. 6 : 31.
7 : 12. that men should do t. y. as,
9 : 29. Acc. to your faith be it u. y.
12 : 28. then the kingdom of God is
come u. y., Lu. 10 : 9, 11.
13 : 11. given u. y. to know mysteries of, Mk. 4 : 11. Lu. 8 : 10. [y.
20 : 32. What will ye I shall do u.
26 : 15. I will deliver him u. y. [21.
27 : 17. Whom will ye I release u. y.?
Mk. 4 : 24. ye mete be measured t. y.;
u. y. that hear more be given
Lu. 2 : 11. u. y. is born a Saviour
12. this shall be a sign u. y. [y.
6 : 33. if to them which do good t.
10 : 9. kingdom of God nigh u. y.
20. that the spirits are subject u.
11 : 41. all things are clean u. y. [y.
22 : 29. I appoint u. y. a kingdom
Jn. 13 : 15. do as I have done t. y.
14 : 18. not leave; I will come t. y.,
27. my peace I give u. y. [28.
15 : 7. ask, it shall be done u. y.
21. all these will they do u. y.
16 : 7. I will send Comforter u. y.
14. receive of mine, shew it u. y.
Ac. 2 : 39. promise is u. y. [7 : 37.
3 : 22. raise up u. y. of your breth.
26. u. y. first God sent his son Jes.
4 : 19 hearken u. y. more than God
10 : 29. came I u. y. with-t gainsay-
13 : 26. u. y. word of salvation [ing
17 : 23. wh. ye worship, declare I u. y.
1 Co. 9 : 2. if not to others I am t. y.
14 : 36. came word of God u. y. only
2 Co. 3 : 1. need we commendation t. y.
5 : 12. commend not ourselves u. y.
6 : 11. O ye, our mouth is open u. y.
18. I will be a Father u. y.
7 : 12. our care might appear u. y.
8 : 17. of own accord he went u. y.
9 : 5. breth., that they go bef. u. y.
10 : 13. measure to reach even u. y.
14. as tho. we reached not u. y.;
we are come as far as t. y. in
Ph. 1 : 28. is token t. y. of salvation
29. u. y. given not only to believe
1 Th. 1 : 5. gospel not u. y. in word
9. what entering in we had u. y.
2 : 1. our entrance u. y. not in vain
3 : 11. Now God direct our way u. y.
2 Th. 1 : 7. t. y. troubled, rest with us
1 Pe. 2 : 7. u. y. wh. believe precious
Re. 2 : 24. u. y. I say, and the rest
See **DO, DONE, GIVE, GIVEN, SAID, SENT, SPAKE, SPEAK, SPOKEN. PEACE be, I SAY unto you, TOLD you, WOE unto you.**

Toward YOU. [y.

Je. 29 : 10. perform my good word t.
11. I know thoughts I think t. y.
Ho. 5 : 1. give ear, judgment is t. y.
2 Co. 1 : 18. our word t. y. was not yea
7 : 4. my boldness of speech t. y.
15. affection more abundant t. y.
9 : 8. make all grace abound t. y.
10 : 1. being absent am bold t. y.
13 : 4. sh. live by power of God t. y.
1 Th. 3 : 12. abound in love as we t.
See **YOU-WARD.** [y.

With YOU.

Ge. 9 : 9. establish covenant w. y.,
11. Le. 26 : 9. Ju. 2 : 1. [y., 12.
10. with every creature that is w.
23 : 4. I stranger, sojourner w. y.:
give me a buryingplace w. y.
24 : 16. we will dwell w. y. one peo.
42 : 38. my son not go down w. y.

Ge. 43 : 3. except your brother be
w. y., 5. -44 : 23. ⌈be w. y.
48 : 21. Behold I die; but God shall
Ex. 10 : 24. let little ones go w. y.
13 : 19. sh. carry up my bones w. y.
20 : 22. th. I talked w. y. fr. heaven
24 : 8. covenant which Lord made
w. y., De. 4 : 23. - 9 : 9. 2 K. 17:
14. Aaron and Hur are w. y. ⌊38.
Le. 19 : 34. stranger th. dwelleth w. y.
25 : 45. buy of their families w. y.
Nu. 1 : 4 w. y. a man of every tribe
5. names of men that stand w. y.
15 : 14. if a stranger sojourn w. y.,
17 : 4. where I will meet w. y. ⌊15, 16.
22 : 13. refuseth me leave to go w. y.
32 : 29. if Gad will pass w. y. over
De. 9 : 8. Lord was angry w. y. ⌊Jor.
10. words L. spake w. y. in mount
12 : 12. he hath no inherit-e w. y.
20 : 4. God is he that goeth w. y.
29 : 14. Nei. w. y. only, this coven-t
31 : 27. while I am yet alive w. y.
Jos. 4 : 3. 12 stones carry over w. y.
7 : 12. nei. will I be w. y. any more
9 : 7. how sh. we make league w. y.
11. Take victuals w. y. for jour-
24 : 8. Amorites fought w. y. ⌊ney
Ru. 1 : 8. the Lord deal kindly w. y.
2 : 4. Boaz said the Lord be w. y.
1 S. 11 : 2. will I make a covenant w.
12 : 7. that I may reason w. y. ⌊y.
22 : 3. Let my father mother bo w. y.
23. come again I will go w. y.
2 S. 15 : 27. return and two sons w. y.
16 : 10. What ha. I to do w. y.? 19 : 22.
18 : 2. I will surely go forth w. y.
2 K. 10 : 2. your master's sons w. y.
23. look that there be w. y. none
of servants of Lord ⌈36 : 12.
18 : 27. drink own piss w. y., Is.
1 Ch. 22 : 18. Is not the Lord w. y.?
2 Ch. 13 : 8. are w. y. golden calves
15 : 2. L. is w. y. while ye with him
19 : 6. Lord who is w. y. in judgm-t
20 : 17. fear not, L. will be w. y. (2)
28 : 10 are there not w. y. even w.
Ezr. 4 : 2. Let us build w. y. ⌊y. sins
Jb. 12 : 2. wisdom sh. die w. y. ⌈folly
42 : 8. lest I deal w. y. after your
Is. 55 : 3. everlasting covenant w. y.
Je. 2 : 9. I will yet plead w. y., Eze.
20 : 35, 36. ⌈y.
5 : 18. will not make a full end w.
18 : 6. cannot I do w. y. as potter?
42 : 11. I am w. y., Hag. 1 : 13. -2 : 4.
Eze. 20 : 44. wh. I have wrought w. y.
47 : 22. sh. have inheritance w. y.
Jo. 2 : 26. G. dealt wondrously w. y.
Am. 5 : 14 God of hosts sh. be w. y.
Hag. 2 : 5. word I covenanted w. y.
Zch. 8 : 23. We will go w. y., for we
have heard God is w. y.
Mat. 17 : 17. O perverse, how long sh.
I be w. y., Mk. 9 : 19. Lu 9 : 41.
26 : 11. ye have the poor always w.
y., Mk. 14 : 7. Jn. 12 : 8. ⌈kingd.
29. when I drink it new w. y. in
55. I sat daily w. y. teaching,
Mk. 14 : 49. Lu. 22 : 53. ⌈of world
28 : 20. I am w. y. alway unto end
Lu. 22 : 15. to eat passover w. y. bef.
24 : 44. I spake while I was w. y.
Jn. 7 : 33. Yet a little while am I w.
y., 13 : 33. ⌈w. y.
12 : 35. Yet a little while is the light
14 : 9. Have I been so long w. y.?
16. Comforter, that he abide w. y.
17. Spirit of truth; ye know him;
for he dwelleth w. y. ⌈w. y.
25. have I spoken, being present
27. Peace I leave w. y., my peace
30. Hereaf. will not talk much w. y.
16 : 4. these I said bec. I was w. y.
Ac. 14 : 15. We of like passions w. y.
18 : 14. reason would I bear w. y.
20 : 18. manner I have been w. y.

Ac. 26 : 8. Why thought incredible w.
28 : 20. to see and speak w. y. ⌊y.
Ro. 1 : 12. I may be comforted w. y.
15 : 32. th. I may w. y. be refreshed
1 Co. 2 : 3. I was w. y. in weakness
4 : 8. that we might reign w. y. ⌈y.
9 : 23. that I be partaker thereof w.
16 : 6. may be I will winter w. y.
7. I trust to tarry a while w. y.
10. see he be w. y. without fear
2 Co. 1 : 21. establisheth us w. y. is G.
4 : 14. sh. raise and present us w. y.
7 : 3. ye in our hearts to die w. y.
11 : 9. when w. y. I was chargeable
to no man, Ga. 4 : 18. ⌈Ph. 4 : 9.
13 : 11. God of peace shall be w. y.
Ga. 2 : 5. that gospel continue w. y.
4 : 20. I desire to be present w. y.,
Col. 2 : 5. yet am I w. y. in spirit ⌊18.
1 Th. 3 : 4. w. y. we told, 2 Th. 2 : 5.
2 Th. 3 : 1. word be glorified w. y.
10. wh. w. y. this we commanded
He. 12 : 7. God dealeth w. y. as sons
1 Pe. 5 : 13. the church elected w. y.
2 Pe. 2 : 13. while they feast w. y.
See **GRACE of Lord Jesus,**
GRACE, WELL, **YOU all.**
Within YOU. ⌈36 : 26.
Eze. 11 : 19. put new spirit w. y.,
36 : 27. I will put my Spirit w. y.
Lu. 17 : 21. kingdom of God is w. y.
YOUNG. ⌈their y.
Ge. 31 : 38. she goats have not cast
33 : 13. herds with y. are with me
Ex. 23 : 26. sh. nothing cast their y.
Le. 9 : 2. take y. calf for sin offering
22 : 28. not kill it and her y. in one
De. 22 : 6. not take the dam with the
7. let the dam go, take the y. ⌊y.
28 : 50. nor shew favour to the y.
32 : 11. As eagle fluttereth ov. her y.
1 S. 9 : 11. y. maidens going to draw
2 S. 9 : 12. Mephibosheth had y. son
1 Ch. 22 : 5. Sol. my son is y., 29 : 1.
2 Ch. 13 : 7. when Rehoboam was y.
34 : 3. while yet y. began to seek G.
Es. 8 : 10. riders on y. dromedaries
Ps. 29 : 6. Sirion like a y. unicorn
78 : 71. follow-g the ewes great with
84 : 3. where she may lay her y. ⌊y.
147 : 9. he giveth food to y. ravens
Pr. 30 : 17. y. eagles shall eat it
Can. 2 : 9. My beloved is like a y.
hart, 17. - 8 : 14. ⌈7 : 3.
4 : 5. thy breasts like two y. roes,
Is. 7 : 21. man shall nourish y. cow
40 : 11. gently lead those with y.
Je. 17 : †11. as partridge gathereth y.
31 : 12. flow together for y. of flock
Eze. 17 : 4. cropped his y. twigs, 22.
31 : 6. beasts bring forth their y.
Mk. 7 : 25. y. dau-r had unclean spirit
Jn. 21 : 18. when y. girdedst thyself
Tit. 2 : 4. teach y. women to be sober
YOUNG ass, asses. ⌈a-s
Is. 30 : 6. carry their riches upon y.
24. the y. a-s that ear the ground
Jn. 12 : 14. when he found y. a., sat
YOUNG bullock, s. ⌊th-on
Ex. 29 : 1. Take one y. b. and two
rams, Le. 23 : 18. ⌈for sin off-g
Le. 4 : 3. priest sin, bring one y. b.
14. offer y. b. for the sin, Nu. 15 : 24.
16 : 3. Aaron with y. b. for sin off-g
Nu. 7 : 15. One y. b., one ram, one
lamb for, 21, 27, 33, 39, 45, 51,
57, 63, 69, 75, 81.
8 : 8. let them take y. b., another
y. b. thou take for sin off-g ⌈27.
28 : 11. ye shall offer two y. b-s, 19,
29 : 2. burnt offering; one y. b., one
13. ye sh. offer 13 y. b-s ⌊ram, 8.
17. on second day offer 12 y. b-s
Ju. 6 : 25. Take thy father's y. b. ⌈b.
2 Ch. 13 : 9. consecrate hims. with y.
Ezr. 6 : 9. y. b-s for burnt offering
Eze. 43 : 19. to priests y. b. for off-g

Eze. 43 : 23. offer y. b. with-t blemish
25. also prepare a y. b. and ram
45 : 18. take a y. b., cleanse sanct-y
46 : 6. in day of new moon a y. b.
See **Young CHILD.**
See **Young CHILDREN,**
Young LION, S, Young
MAN, Young MEN, OLD.
YOUNG one. ⌈y. o.
De. 28 : 57. eye be evil toward her
Zch. 11 : 16. nei. seek the y. o. nor
YOUNG ones. ⌊heal
De. 22 : 6. whether be y. o. or eggs
Jb. 38 : 41. his y. o. cry unto God
39 : 3. they bring forth their y. o.
4. Their y. o. are in good liking
16. she is hardened ag. her y. o.
30. eagle's y. o. suck up blood
Is. 11 : 7. y. o. sh. lie down together
La. 4 : 3. sea monsters give suck to
YOUNG pigeon, s. ⌊y. o.
Ge. 15 : 9. Take turtledove and y. p.
Le. 1 : 14. his offering of y. p-s, 14 : 30.
5 : 7. two turtledoves or two y. p-s,
14 : 22. - 15 : 14. Nu. 6 : 10. ⌈p-s
11. if he not able to bring two y.
12 : 6. she sh. bring a lamb and y. p.
8. if not bring lamb, bring two y.
p-s or, 15 : 29. ⌈y. p-s
Lu. 2 : 24. pair of turtledoves or two
See **Young VIRGIN, S.**
See **Young WOMAN.**
YOUNGER. ⌈done
Ge. 9 : 24. knew what his y. son had
19 : 31. firstborn said unto the y., 34.
35. the y. arose, and lay with him
38. y. also bear a son Ben-ammi
25 : 23. the elder shall serve the y.
27 : 15. put upon Jacob her y. son
42. she called Jacob her y. son
29 : 16. name of the y. was Rachel
18. serve 7 years for thy y. dau-r
26. not to give the y. bef. firstborn
43 : 29. Is this your y. brother of
whom ye spake ⌈head the y.
48 : 14. right hand upon Ephraim's
19. his y. brother shall be greater
Ju. 1 : 13. Caleb's y. bro. took it, 3 :
15 : 2. is not her y. sister fairer ⌊9.
1 S. 14 : 49. Saul's dau-s, y. Michal
1 Ch. 24 : 31. lots over ag. y. breth-n
Jb. 30 : 1. y. than I have me in deri-
Eze. 16 : 46. y. sister is Sodom ⌊sion
61. receive thy sisters, elder and y.
Lu. 15 : 12. y. said, Father give me
13. y. gathered all, took journey
22 : 26. great-t, let him be as the y.
Ro. 9 : 12. The elder sh. serve the y.
1 Ti. 5 : 1. entreat y. men as brethren
2. the y. as sisters, with purity
11. the y. widow's refuse, for when
14. I will that y. women marry
1 Pe. 5 : 5. ye y. submit unto elder
YOUNGEST. ⌈32.
Ge. 42 : 13. the y. is with our father,
15. ye shall not go except your
y. brother come, 44 : 23, 26, (2)
20. bring your y. bro. unto me, 34.
43 : 33. sat the y. acc. to his youth
44 : 2. put cup in sack's mouth of y.
12. began at eldest, left off at y.
26. if y. brother with us will we go
Jos. 6 : 26. in his y. son shall set up
gates of it, 1 K. 16 : 34. ⌈left
Ju. 9 : 5. yet Jotham the y. son was
1 S. 16 : 11. There remain-h yet the y.
17 : 14. David y., eldest followed S.
2 Ch. 21 : 17. never a son left save y.
22 : 1. made Ahaziah his y. son king
Ezr. 8 : † 12. Johanan y. son of Hak-
YOUR. ⌊katan
See BRETHREN, BROTHER, CAT-
TLE, CHILDREN, CITIES, EARS,
ENEMIES, EYES, FAITH, FATH-
ER, FATHERS, FLESH, GOD,
HEART, S, INIQUITIES, LAND,
MIND, MOUTH.

YOUR own. [seed
Ge. 47 : 24. four parts be y. o. for
Le. 18 : 26. nei. any of y. o. nation
19 : 5. ye shall offer it at y. o. will,
22 : 19, 29. [o. sight, 36 : 31.
Eze. 20 : 43. loathe yourselves in y.
Jo. 3 : 4. return your recompense
upon y. o. head, 7. [dition
Mk. 7 : 9. that ye may keep y. o. tra-
Lu. 16 : 12. who give you th. is y. o.?
Ac. 17 : 28. as certain of y. o. poets
18 : 6. blood be upon y. o. heads
Ro. 11 : 25. lest ye be wise in y. o.
conceits, 12 : 16. [o.?
1 Co. 6 : 19. know ye, ye are not y.
7 : 35. I speak for y. o. profit [els
2 Co. 6 : 12. straitened in y. o. bow-
Ga. 4 : 15. ye would have plucked out
y. o. eyes and given to me
Ep. 5 : 22. Wives submit unto y. o.
husbands, Col. 3 : 18. 1 Pe. 3 : 1.
Ph. 2 : 12. work out y. o. salvation
1 Th. 2 : 14. suffered in y. o. countrym.
4 : 11. study to do y. o. business and
to work with y. o. hands [ness
2 Pe. 3 : 17. ye fall fr. y. o. steadfast-
See SAKES, SEED.

YOUR own selves. [nigh
Lu. 21 : 30. know of y. - summer is
Ac. 20 : 30. of y. - shall men arise
2 Co. 13 : 5. prove y. - know ye not
y. - how Jesus is in you [y. -
Ja. 1 : 22. not hearers only, deceiving
See SIN, SINS, STRENGTH, WAY,
WIVES, WORDS, WORK, S.

YOURS. [y.
Ge. 45 : 20. good of land of Egypt is
De. 11 : 24. place soles of your feet
tread shall be y. [for y.
Jos. 2 : 14. answered her, Our life
2 Ch. 20 : 15. battle is not y. but G.'s
Je. 5 : 19. shall serve in land not y.
Lu. 6 : 20. y. is the kingdom of God
Jn. 15 : 20. if kept my say-g will keep
1 Co. 3 : 21. all things are y., 22. [y.
8 : 9. lest liberty of y. a stumblingbl.
16 : 18. they refreshed my spirit and
2 Co. 12 : 14. I seek not y. but you[y.

YOURSELVES. [tree
Ge. 18 : 4. wash and rest y. under
45 : 5. be not angry with y. that ye
49 : 1. Gather y. together, 2. Je. 6 :
1. Eze. 39 : 17. Jo. 3 : 11. Zph.
2 : 1. Re. 19 : 17. [to y. acc.
Ex. 30 : 17. perfume ye sh. not make
32 : 29. Consecrate y. to day to Lord
Le. 11. 43. ye shall not make y.
abominable, nei. make y. uncl-n
44. nei. sh. ye defile y., 18 : 24, 30.
19 : 4. nor make to y. molten gods
Nu. 16 : 3. wheref. then lift ye up y.?
21. Separate y. from congregation
31 : 3. Arm some of y. unto the war
18. women, children keep alive for
19. purify both y. and captives[y.
De. 4 : 16. lest ye corrupt y., 25.
11 : 23. sh. possess nations mightier
14 : 1. sh. not cut y. for dead[than y.
31 : 14. present y. in tabernacle [y.
29. I know ye will utterly corrupt
Jos. 2 : 16. hide y. there three days
6 : 18. keep y. from accursed thing,
lest ye make y. accursed
8 : 2. only the spoil take unto y.
23 : 7. nei. serve them nor bow y.
unto them, 2 K. 17 : 35. [them
16. ye have served and bowed y. to
24 : 22. ye are witnesses ag. y. [y.
Ju. 15 : 12. th. ye will not fall upon me
1 S. 4 : 9. quit y. like men, O ye Phil.
10 : 19. present y. before the Lord
14 : 34. Disperse y. among peo. [y.
1 K. 18 : 25. Choose one bullock for
20 : 12. Set y. in array. And they set
thems., 2 Ch. 20 : 17. Je. 50 : 14.
2 Ch. 29 : 31. ye have consecrated y.
32 : 11. to give y. to die by famine
2 Ch. 35 : 4. prepare y. by houses of
Ezr. 10 : 11. separate y. from people
Ne. 13 : 25. nor their daught-s for y.
Jb. 19 : 3. ye make y. strange to me
5. if ye will magnify y. against me
27 : 12. Behold, all ye y. have seen
42 : 8. offer for y. a burnt offering
Is. 8 : 9. Associate y., gird y., Jo. 1 :
29 : 9. Stay y. and wonder [13.
46 : 8. Remember and shew y. men
49 : 9. to them in darkness shew y.
50 : 1. for iniquities have ye sold y.
11. compass y. about with sparks
52 : 3. Ye have sold y. for nought
57 : 4. Against whom do ye sport y.
5. Inflaming y. with idols under
61 : 6. in their glory sh. ye boast y.
Je. 4 : 4. Circumcise y. to the Lord
25 : 34. wallow y. in the ashes [y.
26 : 15. bring innocent blood upon
37 : 9. saith the Lord, Deceive not y.
44 : 8. that ye might cut y. off and
Eze. 14 : 6. Repent, turn y. fr. idols,
18 : 30, 32. [Egypt, 18.
20 : 7. defile not y. with idols of
31. ye pollute y. with your idols
43. ye shall loathe y., 36 : 31. [y.
44 : 8. set keepers in sanctuary for
Ho. 10 : 12. Sow to y. in righteous-s
Am. 5 : 26. star of yo. God ye made to
Zch. 7 : 6. eat for y., drink for y. [y.
Mat. 3 : 9. think not to say within y.,
We have Abra., Lu. 3 : 8. [upon
6 : 19. Lay not up for y. treasures
20. lay up for y. treasures in heav-
16 : 8. Why reason ye among y. [on
23 : 13. ye nei. go in y., Lu. 11 : 52.
15. more the child of hell than y.
31. Whf. ye be witnesses unto y.
25 : 9. go ye rather, and buy for y.
Mk. 6 : 31. Come ye y. apart into a
9 : † 16. What question ye among y.
33. What was it ye disputed among
50. Have salt in y. and peace [y.
Lu. 11 : 46. ye y. touch not burdens
12 : 33. provide y. bags which wax
36. ye y. like men that wait [not
57. Why of y. judge ye not right
13 : 28. in kingdom ye y. thrust out
16 : 9. Make to y. friends of mam-
15. Ye are they wh. justify y.[mon
17 : 14. Go shew y. unto the priest
22 : 17. Take this, divide it amo. y.
23 : 28. weep for y. and your child-n
Jn. 3 : 28. Ye y. bear me witness
6 : 43. said, Murmur not among y.
16 : 19. Do ye inquire among y. of
Ac. 2 : 22. God did as ye y. know
40. Save y. from this generation
13 : 46. ye judge y. unworthy of life
15 : 29. if ye keep y. ye do well
20 : 10. Trouble not y., life is in him
34. ye y. know these hands minist.
Ro. 6 : 11. reckon ye y. to be dead
12 : 19. beloved avenge not y. [son
1 Co. 5 : 13. put from y. wicked per-
6 : 7. rather suffer y. to be defraud-
7 : 5. ye may give y. to fasting [ed
11 : 13. Judge in y. is it comely that
16 : 16. that ye submit y. unto such
2 Co. 7 : 11. what clearing of y.! In
all ye have approved y. clear
11 : 19. For ye suffer fools gladly,
seeing ye y. are wise
13 : 5. Examine y. whether ye be in
the faith; prove y. [of y.
Ep. 2 : 8. through faith, that not
5 : 19. Speaking to y. in psalms and
21. submitting y. one to another
1 Th. 2 : 1. y. breth. know our entrance
3 : 3. y. know that we are appointed
4 : 9. ye y. are taught of G. to love
5 : 2. y. know day of L. so cometh
11. Wherefore comfort y. together
13. And be at peace among y. [y.
15. follow that wh. is good among
2 Th. 3 : 6. command ye withdraw y.
2 Th. 3 : 7. y. know how ye ought to
He. 10 : 34. knowing in y. ye have
in heaven a better [the body
13 : 3. Remember as being y. in
Ja. 2 : 4. Are ye not partial in y.?
1 Pe. 1 : 14. not fashioning y. acc. to
2 : 13. Submit y. to every ordinance
4 : 1. arm y. with the same mind
8. have fervent charity among y.
1 Jn. 5 : 21. children keep y. fr. idols
2 Jn. 8. Look to y. that we lose not
Jude 20. building y. on most holy
21. Keep y. in love of God [faith
See ASSEMBLE.

Humble YOURSELVES.
Je. 13 : 18. Say unto king, queen h.
Ja. 4 : 10. h. y. in sight of Lord [y.
1 Pe. 5 : 6. h. y. under hand of God
See SANCTIFY, SUBMIT, YIELD,
OWN Selves, TAKE heed.

YOUTH. [y.
Ge. 8 : 21. imagination evil from his
43 : 33. youngest according to his
46 : 34. about cattle from our y. [y.
Le. 22 : 13. if returned unto father's
house as in her y. [y., 16.
Nu. 30 : 3. in father's house in her
Ju. 8. 20. the y. drew not his sword,
because yet a y. [of war from y.
1 S. 17 : 33. thou but a y., he a man
42. for he was but a y. and ruddy
55. Abner, whose son is this y.?
2 S. 19 : 7. th. befell thee from thy y.
1 K. 18 : 12. I fear the Lord from my y.
Jb. 13 : 26. possess iniquities of my
20 : 11. bones full of sin of his y. [y.
29 : 4. As I was in days of my y. [y.
30 : 12. Upon my right hand rise the
31 : 18. from y. brought up with me
33 : 25. sh. return to days of his y.
36 : 14. hypocrites die in y. [y.
Ps. 25 : 7. Remember not sins of my
71 : 5. O Lord, my trust from my y.
17. O God, hast taught me from y.
88 : 15. I am ready to die fr. my y. up
89 : 45. days of his y. hast shortened
103 : 5. thy y. renewed like eagle's
110 : 3. thou hast the dew of thy y.
127 : 4. as arrows, so chil. of thy y.
129 : 1. afflicted me from y., 2. [y.
144 : 12. sons as plants grown up in
Pr. 2 : 17. forsaketh guide of her y.
5 : 18. rejoice with wife of thy y.
Ec. 11 : 9. Rejoice, young man in thy
10. childhood and y. are vanity[y.
12 : 1 Remember thy Creator in
days of thy y. [from thy y.
Is. 47 : 12. wherein hast laboured
15. thy merchants from thy y.
54 : 4. shalt forget shame of thy y.
6. Lord called thee as a wife of y.
Je. 2 : 2. I remember kindness of thy
3 : 4. My Father, guide of my y. [y.
24. labour of our fathers fr. our y.
25. have sinned ag. Lord fr. our y.
22 : 21. This thy manner fr. thy y.
31 : 19. I did bear reproach of my y.
32 : 30. only done evil from their y.
48 : 11. Moab been at ease fr. his y.
La. 3 : 27. that he bear yoke in his y.
Eze. 4 : 14. not polluted: from y. up
I have not eaten of [thy y., 43.
16 : 22. not remembered days of
60. my covenant in days of thy y.
23 : 3. committed whoredoms in y.
8. in her y. they lay with her [21.
19. remembrance days of her y.,
21. lewdness of thy y., . . . by
Egyptians for the paps of thy y.
Ho. 2 : 15. sh. sing as in days of her y.
Jo. 1 : 8. lament for husband of her y.
Zch. 13 : 5. to keep cattle from my y.
Mal. 2 : 14. L. witness between thee
and wife of thy y. [of his y.
15. deal treacherously against wife
Mat. 19 : 20. All these have I kept fr.
my y. up, Mk. 10 : 20. Lu. 18 : 21.

Ac. 26 : 4. manner of life from my y.
1 Ti. 4 :12. Let no man despise thy y.

YOUTHS. [void of

Pr. 7 : 7. among the y. a young man
Is. 40 : 30. Even the y. shall faint

YOUTHFUL.

2 Ti. 2 : 22. Flee also y. lusts : but

YOU-WARD. [y.

2 Co. 1 : 12. and more abundantly to
13 : 3. Christ in me, to y. not weak
Ep. 3 : 2. grace of God given me to y.

Z.

ZAANA'IM. [of Z.

Ju. 4 : 11. pitched tent under plain

ZA'ANAN. [forth

Mi. 1 : 11. inhabitant of Z. came not

ZAANAN'NIM. [ami

Jos. 19 : 33. coast was to Z. and Ad-

ZA'AVAN or ZA'VAN.

Ge. 36 : 27. chil. of Ezer are these ;
Bilhan and Z., 1 Ch. 1 : 42.

ZA'BAD. [begat

1 Ch. 2 : 36. Nathan begat Z., 37. Z.
7 : 21. Z. Elead men of Gath slew
11 : 41. valiant men, Z. son of Ahlai
2 Ch. 24 : 26. these conspired, Z.
and Jehozabad, 2 K. 12 † : 21.
Ezr. 10 : 27. sons of Zattu, Z., Aziza
33. sons of Hashum ; Z., Jeremai
43. Of sons of Nebo ; Z. and Zebina

ZAB'BAI.

Ezr. 10 : 28. of sons of Bebai, Z. and
Ne. 3 : 20. Baruch, son of Z., repaired

ZAB'BUD. See UTHAI.

ZAB'DI. [of Z.

Jos. 7 : 1. Achan, son of Carmi, son
17. Zarhites and Z. was taken, 18.
1 Ch. 2 : †6. sons of Zerah ; Z., Dara
8 : 19. Jakim, Z., sons of Shimhi [Z.
27 : 27. over increase of vineyards
Ne. 11 : 17. son of Micha, son of Z.

ZAB'DIEL. [son of Z.

1 Ch. 27 : 2. Over first course was
Ne. 11 : 14. their overseer was Z.

ZA'BUD.

1 K. 4 : 5. Z. was principal officer

ZAB'ULON. See ZEBULUN.

ZAC'CAI. [14.

Ezr. 2 : 9. children of Z. 760, Ne. 7 :
Ne. 3 : †20 Baruch, son of Z. repaired

ZACCHE'US. [Z.

Lu. 19 : 2. there was a man named
5. Z., make haste and come down
8. Z. said, L., the half of my goods

ZAC'CHUR.

1 Ch. 4 : 26. Hamuel, Z. his son

ZAC'CUR. [son of Z.

Nu. 13 : 4. of Reuben, Shammua,
1 Ch. 24 : 27. sons of Merari ; Z., Ibri
25 : 2. Of the sons of Asaph ; Z., Jo-
10. they cast lots, third to Z. [seph
Ezr. 8 : †14. sons of Bigvai, Uthai, Z.
Ne. 3 : 2. next to them builded Z.
10 : 12. those that sealed were, Z.
12 : 35. Michaiah, son of Z., son of
13 : 13. next to them Hanan, son of

ZACHARI'AH, ZECHARI'AH. [Z.

2 K. 14 : 29. Jeroboam slept ; Za. his
son reigned, 15 : 8. [in Chron.
15 : 11. rest of acts of Za written
18 : 2. Abi dau-r of Za., 2 Ch. 29 : 1.

ZACHARI'AS. [Ze.

Mat. 23 : 35. blood of Z. whom ye slew
Lu. 1 : 5. priest, Z., of course of Abia
12. Z. saw angel he was troubled
13. Fear not Z., thy prayer heard
18. Z. said, Whereby shall I know
21. people waited for Z. and [this ?
40. Mary entered into house of Z.
59. called him Z., after name of fa.
67. Z. was filled with Holy Ghost
3 : 2. word of G. unto John, son of Z.
11 : 51. blood of Abel unto blo. of Z.

ZA'CHER or ZECHARI'AH

1 Ch. 8 : 31. father of Gibeon ; his
firstborn Abdon, Z-r, † Z-h, 9 :

ZA'DOK. [37. Z-h.

2 S. 8 : 17. Z. and Abimelech priests
15 : 24. Z. and Levites bearing ark
25. k. said unto Z., Carry back ark
27. k. said unto Z., Art not thou a
35. hast not wi. thee Z. ? (2) [seer ?
36. with them Ahimaaz, Z.'s son
18 : 19. said Ahimaaz, son of Z., 22.
27. like the running of son of Z.
1 K. 1 : 8. Z. not with Adonijah, 26.
32. David said, Call Z. the priest
34. let Z. anoint Solomon king, 38.
39. Z. the priest anointed Sol-n, 45.
44. k. hath sent with him Z. priest
4 : 2. princes : Azariah, son of Z.
2 K. 15 : 33. Jotham ; his mother
Jerusha, dau. of Z., 2 Ch. 27 : 1.
1 Ch. 6 : 8. Ahitub begat Z. ; Z. begat, 12, 53.-9 : 11.-18 : 16.
12 : 28. Z. a young man mighty of
16 : 39. Z., priest before tabernacle
18 : 16. Z. and Abimelech priests
24 : 3. Dav. distributed both Z. and
6. wrote them bef. k. and Z. priest
31. These cast lots in presence of
27 : 17. ruler of Aaronites, Z. [Z.
29 : 22. anointed Z. to be priest
2 Ch. 31 : 10. priest of house of Z.
Ezr. 7 : 2. son of Shallum, son of Z.
Ne. 3 : 4. repaired Z., son of Baana
10 : 21. those that sealed were, Z.
11 : 11. son of Z., son of Meraioth
13 : 13. I made treasurers Z. scribe
Eze. 40 : 46. sons of Z. which come
near to Lord, 43 : 19.-44 : 15. [Z.
48 : 11. priests sanctified, of sons of
See ABIATHAR, PRIEST.

ZA'HAM. See SHAMARIAH.

ZA'IR.

2 K. 8 : 21. Joram went over to Z.

ZA'LAPH. [son of Z.

Ne. 3 : 30. repaired Hanun, sixth

ZAL'MON. [Person.]

2 S. 23 : 28. one of the thirty ; Z. the
Ahohite, 1 Ch. 11 : †29.

ZAL'MON or SAL'MON.

Ju. 9 : 48. Abimelech gat up to m-t Z.
Ps. 68 : 14. was white as snow in S.

ZALMO'NAH. [in Z.

Nu. 33 : 41. departed, and pitched
42. departed from Z., pitched in

ZALMUN'NA. See ZEBAH.

ZAMZUM'MIM. [th. Z.

De. 2 : 20. giants, Ammonites call

ZANO'AH. [Person.]

1 Ch. 4 : 18. Jekuthiel, father of Z.

ZANO'AH. [Place.]

Jos. 15 : 34. cities of children of Judah, Z., 56. [habitants of Z.
Ne. 3 : 13. valley gate repaired in-
11 : 30. some of chil. of Judah at Z.

ZAPH'NATH-PAANE'AH

Ge. 41 : 45. Pharaoh called Joseph's

ZA'PHON. [name Z.

Jos. 13 : 27. coast in the valley, Z.

ZA'RA, ZA'RAH.

Ge. 38 : 30. had the scarlet thread,
his name was called Z-h
46 : 12. sons of Judah, Pharez, Z-h
Mat. 1 : 3. Judas begat Phares and Z-a
See ZERAH = ZARAH.

ZA'REAH = ZO'RAH.

Ne. 11 : 29. some of Judah dwelt at

ZA'REATHITES. [Z.

1 Ch. 2 : 53. of them came the Z.

ZA'RED or ZE'RED.

Nu. 21 : 12. pitched in valley of Za.
De. 2 : 13. get you over brook Ze. (2)
14. until over brook Ze. 38 years

ZAR'EPHATH = SAREP'TA.

1 K. 17 : 9. get thee to Z., dwell there
10. So he arose, went to Z. [to Z.
Ob. 20. host of Isr. shall possess un-

ZAR'ETAN = ZARTA'NAH

Jos. 3 : 16. from city Adam, beside Z.

ZA'RETH-SHA'HAR.

Jos. 13 : 19. Z., in m-t of the valley

ZAR'HITES. [20.

Nu. 26 : 13. Of Zerah, family of Z.,
Jos. 7 : 17. Josh. took family of Z. (2)
1 Ch. 27 : 11. 8th captain, Sibbecai
13. 10th capt-n, Maharai of Z. [of Z.

ZAR'TANAH = ZAR'THAN

1 K. 4 : 12. to Baana, Beth-shean by Z.

ZAR'THAN = ZARE'TAN.

1 K. 7 : 46. clay ground between
Succoth and Z. (See 2 Ch. 4 : 17.)

ZAT'THU = ZAT'TU.

Ne. 10 : 14. chief of people, Z., Bani

ZAT'TU = ZAT'THU.

Ezr. 2 : 8. chil. of Z. 945, Ne. 7 : 13.
10 : 27. taken strange wives ; sons

ZA'VAN. See ZAAVAN. [of Z.

ZA'ZA. See PELETH.

ZEAL. [z.

Nu. 25 : †11. he was zealous with my
2 S. 21 : 2. Saul sought to slay them
in his z. [Lord
2 K 10 : 16. Come, see my z. for the
19 : 31. the z. of the Lord of Hosts
shall do this, Is. 37 : 32.
Ps. 69 : 9. z. of thine house hath
eaten me up, Jn. 2 : 17. [me
119 : 139. My z. hath consumed
Is. 9 : 7. z. of Lord will perform this
59 : 17. and he was clad with z. as a
63 : 15. where is thy z. [cloak
Eze. 5 : 13. I have spoken it in my z.
Ro. 10 : 2. have a z. of God, but not
2 Co. 7 : 11. what z., what revenge
9 : 2. your z. hath provoked many
Ph. 3 : 6. Conc. z., persecuting ch-h
Col. 4 : 13. he hath a great z. for you

ZEALOUS. [sake

Nu. 25 : 11. while he was z. for my
13. he was z. for his God and
Ac. 21 : 20. they are all z. of the law
22 : 3. I was z. toward God as ye are
1 Co. 14 : 12. as ye are z. of spiritual
Ga. 1 : 14. exceedingly z. of tradit-ns
Tit. 2 : 14. people, z. of good works
Re. 3 : 19. I rebuke and chasten :

ZEALOUSLY. [be z.

Ga. 4 : 17. They z. affect you, but not
18. it is good to be z. affected [well

ZEBADI'AH. [ah

1 Ch. 8 : 15. Z., Arad, sons of Beri-
17. Z. and Hezeki sons of Elpaal
12 : 7. Joelah, Z., sons of Jeroham
26 : 2. sons of Meshelemiah, Z. 3d
27 : 7. 4th capt., Asahel, Z. his son
2 Ch. 17 : 8. to teach, sent Levites Z.
19 : 11. Z. ruler of house of Judah
Ezr. 8 : 8. chief of fathers, Z. [ani, Z.
10 : 20. taken strange wives ; Han-

ZE'BAH and ZALMUN'NA.

Ju. 8 : 5. I am pursuing Z. a. Z. [15.
6. Are hands of Z. a. Z. in thine,
7. when L. hath delivered Z. a. Z.
10. Z. a. Z. in Karkor and hosts
12. Z. a. Z. fled, he took the two
kings, Z. a. Z. [braid me
15. Z. a. Z. with whom ye did up-
18. said Gideon unto Z. a. Z.
21. Z. a. Z. said, Rise, fall upon
us. Gideon slew Z. a. Z. [Z. a. Z.
Ps. 83 : 11. Make all their princes as

ZEBA'IM. See POCHERETH.

ZEB'EDEE.

Mat. 4 : 21. saw James son of Z., and
John his brother, in a ship with
Z., mending nets, Mk. 1 : 19.
10 : 2. apostles, James son of Z.,
and John, Mk. 3 : 17. [children
20 : 20. came to him mother of Z.'s
26 : 37. J. took Peter, two sons of Z.
27 : 56. Mary and moth. of Z.'s chil.
Mk. 1 : 20. left father Z. in ship
10 : 35. sons of Z. unto him [Simon
Lu. 5 : 10. sons of Z. partners with

Jn. 21 : 2. together Peter and sons of
ZEBI'NA. See ZABAD. [Z.
ZEBO'IM, or ZEBOI'IM. [Z.
Ge. 10 : 19. as goest unto Admah and
14 : 2. war with Shinab king of Ad-
mah, Shemeber king of Z., 8.
De. 29 : 23. Admah, Z., L. overthrew
1 S. 13 : 18. looketh to the valley of Z.
Ne. 11 : 34. children of Benjamin
dwelt at Hadid, Z., Neballat
Ho. 11 : 8. how shall I make thee as
Admah ? how set thee as Z. ?
ZEBA'DAH. See RUMAH.
ZE'BUL. [cer?
Ju. 9 : 28. Abim-h, is not Z. his offi-
30. when Z. heard words of Gaal
36. Gaal said to Z., There (2)
38. said Z., Where is thy mouth
41. Z. thrust out Gaal and breth.
ZEB'ULONITE.
Ju. 12 : 11. Elon, a Z., judged Israel
12. Elon, a Z., died, was buried
ZEB'ULUN or ZAB'ULON.
Ge. 30 : 20. Leah called his name Z.
35 : 23. sons of Leah ; Reuben, Z.
46 : 14. sons of Z., Nu. 1 : 30.-26 : 26.
49 : 13. Z. shall dwell at the haven
Ex. 1 : 3. children of Israel into
Egypt, Issachar, Z., 1 Ch. 2 : 1.
Nu. 1 : 9. Of Z., Eliab the renowned
26 : 26. Of sons of Z. after families
De. 27 : 13. these upon mount Ebal
to curse ; Z., Gad, and [(2)
33 : 18. Rejoice Z. in thy going out
Jos. 19 : 27. Border reacheth to Z. 34.
Ju. 1 : 30. Nei. did Z. drive out inhab-s
4 : 10. Barak called Z. to Kedesh
5 : 14. out of Z. that handle the pen
18. Z. a people jeoparded lives [Z.
6 : 35. Gid-n sent messengers unto
12 : 12. Elon buried in country of Z.
1 Ch. 12 : 33. Of Z., expert in war
40. that were nigh Z. bro-t bread
27 : 19. ruler of Z., Ishmaiah son of
2 Ch. 30 : 10. posts passed unto Z.
11. divers of Z. humbled thems.
18. many of Z. had not cleansed
Ps. 68 : 27. princes of Z. and Napht.
Is. 9 : 1. lightly afflicted land of Z.
Eze. 48 : 26. of Issachar, Z. a portion
27. border of Z., Gad a portion
33. one gate of Simeon, one of Z.
Mat. 4 : 13. borders of Za., Nephth-m
15. land of Za. and Nephthalim
Children of ZEB'ULUN.
Nu. 1 : 30. Of - Z. able to go to war
2 : 7. Eliab shall be captain of - Z.
(2), 1 : 9 (2).-7 : 24.-10 : 16.
34 : 25. prince of - Z., Elizaphan
Jos. 19 : 10. third lot came for - Z.
16. This is the inheritance of - Z.
Ju. 4 : 6. Go, take 10,000 of - Z.
The tribe of
ZEB'ULUN or ZAB'ULON.
Nu. 1 : 31. numbered of - Z. 57,400
2 : 7. - Z. : Eliab sh. be capt., 10 : 16.
13 : 10. of - Z., Gaddiel to spy land
34 : 25. divide land, prince of - Z.
Jos. 21 : 7. children of Merari had
out of - Z. cities, 34. 1 Ch. 6 :
Re. 7 : 8. - Za. sealed 12,000 [63, 77.
ZEB'ULUNITES.
Nu. 26 : 27. These the families of Z.
ZECHARI'AH. [Z.
1 Ch. 5 : 7. Reubenites ; chief, Jeiel,
8 : † 31. chief men : Ahio, Z., 9 : 37.
9 : 21. Z. porter of tabernacle, 26 : 2.
15 : 18. with singers brethren of
second degree, Z. and [5.
20. Z., Aziel, with psalteries, 16 :
24. Z. Eliezer did blow wi. trumpets
24 : 25. Of the sons of Isshiah ; Z.
26 : 11. Hosah had sons ; Z. fourth
14. Z. a wise counsellor [Z.
27 : 21. ruler in Gilead, Iddo son of
2 Ch. 17 : 7. sent to Z. to teach [it
20 : 14. upon Jahaziel son of Z. Spir-

2 Ch. 21 : 2. Jehiel, Z., sons of Jehosh.
24 : 20. Spirit of God came upon Z.
26 : 5. Uzziah sought God in the
days of Z. [fied thems.
29 : 13. Z. and Mattaniah sancti-
34 : 12. overseers, Z., Meshullam
35 : 8. Hilkiah, Z., rulers of ho. of G.
Ezr. 5 : 1. Z. son of Iddo prophesied
unto Jews in Judah, 6 : 14. [11.
8 : 3. went up with me fr. Bab., Z.,
16. sent I for Z., chief men [Abdi
10 : 26. taken strange wives ; Z.,
Ne. 8 : 4. beside Ezra stood Z. and
11 : 4. Z. son of Amariah [honi
5. Joiarib son of Z., son of Shil-
12. Amzi, son of Z., son of Pashur
12 : 16. were priests. Of Iddo, Z.
35. priests, sons with trumpets, Z.,
Is. 8 : 2. witnesses, Uriah and Z. [41.
Zch. 1 : 1. came word of Lord unto
Z. son of Berechiah, 7.-7 : 1, 8.
See ZACHARIAH, ZACHARIAS,
ZACHER.
ZE'DAD. [to Z.
Nu. 34 : 8. goings forth of border,
Eze. 47 : 15. of Hethlon, as men go
ZEDEKI'AH. [to Z.
1 K. 22 : 11. Z. made him horns of
iron, 2 Ch. 18 : 10. [Ch. 18 : 23.
24. Z. smote Micaiah on check, 2
2 K. 24 : 17. k. changed his name to Z.
18. Z. 21 years old when he began
to reign, 2 Ch. 36 : 11. Je. 52 : 1.
20. Z. rebelled against king of
Babylon, Je. 52 : 3.
25 : 2. city was besieged unto
eleventh year of Z., Je. 52 : 5.
7. slew sons of Z., and put out eyes
of Z., Je. 39 : 6, 7.-52 : 10, 11.
1 Ch. 3 : 15. sons of Josiah, third Z.
16. Jehoiak. ; Jeconiah, his son Z.
2 Ch. 36 : 10. made Z. his brother k.
11. Z. was one and twenty
Je. 1 : 3. end of eleventh year of Z.
21 : 1. when Z. sent unto him Pa-
3. Thus shall ye say to Z. [shur
7. I will deliver Z. unto Neb-r [dah
24 : 8. So will I give Z. king of Ju-
27 : 3. hand of messengers unto Z.
12. I spake to Z. acc. to words [34.
28 : 1. beginning of reign of Z., 49 :
29 : 3. whom Z. sent unto Babylon
21 of Ahab and Z., wh. prophesy lie
22. thee like Z., wh. king roasted
32 : 1. word to Jer. in tenth year of
3. Z. had shut Jeremiah up [Z.
4. Z. shall not escape out of hand
5. he shall lead Z. to Babylon and
34 : 2. Go, speak to Z. and tell him
4. Yet hear word of the Lord, O Z.
6. Jer-h spake these words unto Z.
8. Z. had made a cov-t with people
21. Z., princes into hand of enem.
36 : 12. sat there Z. and all princes
37 : 1. Z. reigned instead of Coniah
3. Z. sent Jehucal to Jeremiah
17. Z. sent and took Jeremiah out
18. Jer-h said unto Z., What have
I offended against thee [Jer-h
21. Z. commanded they commit
38 : 5. Z. said, He is in your hand
14. Z. sent and took Jer. unto him
15. Jer. said unto Z., If I declare
16. So Z. sware secretly unto Jer.
17. said Jer. unto Z., Thus saith
19. Z. said, I am afraid of Jews
24. said Z., Let no man know
39 : 1. In ninth year of Z. came Neb.
2. in 11th year of Z. city broken up
4. Z. saw them, fled out of city
5. army overtook Z. in plains of
Jericho, 52 : 8. [Neb-r
44 : 30. as I gave Z. into the hand of
51 : 59. when Seraiah went with Z.
ZE'EB.
Ju. 7 : 25. Z. they slew at winepress
See OREB. [of Z.

ZE'LAH.
Jos. 18 : 28. cities of Benj., Z., Eleph
2 S. 21 : 14. Saul, Jonathan buried
ZE'LEK. [they in Z.
2 S. 23 : 37. one of the thirty ; Z.
the Ammonite, 1 Ch. 11 : 39.
ZELO'PHEHAD.
Nu. 26 : 33. Z. had no sons, but
dau-s (2), Jos. 17 : 3. 1 Ch. 7 : 15.
27 : 1. Then came daughters of Z.
7. The daughters of Z. speak right
36 : 2. give inherit. of Z. unto dau-s
6. L. command conc. daughters of
10. So did the daughters of Z. [Z.
11. daughters of Z. were married
1 Ch. 7 : 15. name second was Z. (2)
ZELO'TES. See SIMON.
ZEL'ZAH. [Z.
1 S. 10 : 2. by Rachel's sepulchre at
ZEMARA'IM. [Beth-el
Jos. 18 : 22. cities of Benjamin, Z.,
2 Ch. 13 : 4. Abijah stood upon m-t
ZEM'ARITE. [Z.
Ge. 10 : 18. And Canaan begat the
Arvadite, Z., and, 1 Ch. 1 : 16.
ZEMI'RA. [Joash
1 Ch. 7 : 8. The sons of Becher, Z.,
ZE'NAN. [ashah
Jos. 15 : 37. cities of Judah, Z., Had-
ZE'NAS.
Tit. 3 : 13. Bring Z. the lawyer and
ZEPHANI'AH.
2 K. 25 : 18. captain of guard took
Z., second priest, Je. 52 : 24.
1 Ch. 6 : 36. Of sons of Kohathites,
the son of Z., 6 : † 24. [ah Z.
Je. 21 : 1. Zedekiah sent unto Jeremi-
29 : 25. letters in thy name unto Z.
29. Z. read letter in ears of Jer-h
37 : 3. Z., son of Maaseiah priest
Zph. 1 : 1. The word of Lord unto Z.
Zch. 6 : 10. house of Josiah son of Z.
14. crown shall be to Hen son of Z.
ZE'PHATH. [ited Z.
Ju. 1 : 17. Canaanites that inhab-
ZEPH'ATHAH. [of Z.
2 Ch. 14 : 10. Asa set battle in valley
ZE'PHI or ZE'PHO.
Ge. 36 : 11. † sons of Eliphaz, Omar,
Z., 15. 1 Ch. 1 : 36. † [duke Z-o
15. these were dukes ; duke Omar,
ZE'PHON or ZIPH'ION.
Ge 46 : 16. † the sons of Gad ; Z., Ar-i
Nu. 26 : 15. † of Z., family of Zeph-s
ZEPH'ONITES. See ZEPHON.
ZER. [ah
Jos. 19 : 35. fenced cities, Z., Adam-
ZE'RAH.
Ge. 36 : 13. the sons of Reuel, Z.,
Mizzah, 17. 1 Ch. 1 : 37.
17. duke Z., duke Shammah
33. Jobab son of Z., 1 Ch. 1 : 44.
1 Ch. 6 : 21. Of Gershom ; Iddo, Z.
41. Of sons of Kohathites ; Z. son
2 Ch. 14 : 9. came against them Z.
See ZOHAR = ZERAH.
ZE'RAH = ZA'RAH.
Nu. 26 : 20. of Z. family of Zarhites
Jos. 7 : 1. son of Zabdi son of Z. [18
24. Joshua took Achan son of Z.,
22 : 20. Did not Achan son of Z.
1 Ch. 2 : 4. Tamar bare Pharez, Z.
6. sons of Z., Zimri, Ethan, and
9 : 6. sons of Z. ; Jeuel and breth-n
Ne. 11 : 24. of chil. of Z at k.'s hand
ZERAHI'AH.
1 Ch. 6 : 6. Uzzi begat Z., and Z. be-
gat Meraioth, 51. Ezr. 7 : 4.
Ezr. 8 : 4. Elihoenai the son of Z.
ZE'RED. See ZARED.
ZER'EDA. [of Z.
1 K. 11 : 26. Jerob., an Ephrathite
ZERED'ATHAH.
2 Ch. 4 : 17. clay ground between
Succoth and Z. (See 1 K. 7 : 46.)
ZER'ERATH = ZAR'THAN
Ju. 7 : 22. fled to Beth-shittah in Z.

ZE'RESH. [wife
Es. 5 : 10. Haman called for Z. his
14. Z. his wife said, Let a gallows
6 : 13. Haman told Z. his wife every
ZE'RETH. [thing (2)
1 Ch. 4 : 7. sons of Helah, Z., Jezoar
ZE'RI or IZ'RI.
1 Ch. 25 : 3. sons of Jeduthun; Z., † I
11. they cast lots, the fourth to I.
ZE'ROR. [Z.
1 S. 9 : 1. Kish, son of Abiel, son of
ZERU'AH. [name Z.
1 K. 11 : 26. Jeroboam mother's
ZERUB'BABEL.
1 Ch. 3 : 19. sons of Pedaiah, Z.,
Shimei; sons of Z. [7 : 7.-12 : 1.
Ezr. 2 : 2. Which came with Z., Ne.
3 : 2. Then stood up Jeshua, Z.,
and builded, 8.-5 : 2. [build
4 : 2. adversaries to Z. said, Let us
3. Z. said, Ye nothing to do wi. us
Ne. 12 : 47. Israel in days of Z. gave
Hag. 1 : 1. word of the Lord unto Z.
12. Z. obeyed voice of the Lord
14. Lord stirred up the spirit of Z.
2 : 2. Speak now to Z., Who is left
4. Yet now be strong, O Z., saith L.
21. Speak to Z., I will shake earth
23. that day will I take thee, O Z.
Zch. 4 : 6. This is word of L. unto Z.
7. bef. Z. thou shalt become plain
9. hands of Z. have laid foundat-s
10. shall see plummet in hand of
See ZOROBABEL. [Z.
ZERUI'AH.
1 S. 26 : 6. Abishai son of Z., 2 S. 16:
9.-18 : 2.-19 : 21.-21 : 17.-23 :
18. 1 Ch. 18 : 12.
2 S. 2 : 13. Joab son of Z., 3 : 16.-14:
1.-23 : 37. 1 K. 1 : 7.-2 : 5, 22. 1
Ch. 11 : 6, 39.-18 : 15.-26 : 28.-
27 : 24. [1 Ch. 2 : 16.
18. were three sons of Z., Joab and,
3 : 39. sons of Z. be too hard for me
16 : 10. What have I to do with you,
ye sons of Z.? 19 : 22. [to Z.
17 : 25. daughter of Nahash sister
1 Ch. 2 : 16. David, sisters, Z. and Abi-
ZE'THAM. [gail
1 Ch. 23 : 8. sons of Laadan; Z. and
26 : 22. Z. and Joel over the treasures
ZE'THAN. See TARSHISH.
ZE'THAR. See ABAGTHA.
ZI'A. See MICHAEL.
ZI'BA. [(2)
2 S. 9 : 2. David said, Art thou Z.?
3. Z. said, Jonath. hath a son lame
4. Z. said, he is in house of Machir
9. king called to Z., Saul's servant, 2.-19 : 17. [servants
10. Z. had fifteen sons, twenty
11. Z. said, So shall thy servant do
12. all in house of Z. serv-ts to M.
16 : 1. Z. met David with asses
2. Z. said, The asses be for k.'s (2)
3. Z. said, He abideth at Jerus-m
4. king to Z., thine are all that (2)
19 : 29. I said, Thou and Z. divide
ZIB'EON. [vite, 14.
Ge. 36 : 2. Anah dau. of Z. the Hi-
20. sons of Seir: Z., 1 Ch. 1 : 38.
24. children of Z.; Aiah, Anah;
Anah fed asses of Z., 1 Ch. 1 : 40.
29. duke Lotan, duke Z., duke A-
ZIB'IA. [nah
1 Ch. 8 : 9. Shaharaim begat Z., Jeuz
ZIB'IAH.
2 K. 12 : 1. Jehoash, his mother's
name was Z., 2 Ch. 24 : 1.
ZICH'RI. [Z.
Ex. 6 : 21. sons of Izhar; Nepheg,
1 Ch 8 : 19. Jakim, Z., sons of Shim-
23. Abdon, Z., sons of Shashak [hi
27. Eliah and Z. sons of Jeroham
9 : 15. Micah, son of Z. [son
26 : 25. Z. his son, Shelomith his
27 : 16. ruler of Reubenites son of Z.

2 Ch. 17 : 16. next was Amasiah son
23 : 1. took Elishaphat son of Z. [of Z.
28 : 7. Z. slew Maaseiah, king's son
Ne. 11 : 9. Joel, son of Z., overseer
12 : 17. were priests. Of Abijah, Z.
ZID'DIM. See RAKKATH.
ZIDKI'JAH. [ah, Z.
Ne. 10 : 1. that sealed were Nehemi-
ZI'DON. [Person.] See SIDON.
ZI'DON. [unto Z.
Ge. 49 : 13. Zebulun, his border be
Jos. 11 : 8. chased them unto great Z.
19 : 28. border goeth unto great Z.
Ju. 1 : 31. Nei. drive out inhabitants
10 : 6. Israel served gods of Z. [of Z.
18 : 28. no deliverer, bec. far from
2 S. 24 : 6. they came about to Z. [Z.
1 K. 17 : 9. Zarephath, belong-h to Z.
Ezr. 3 : 7. gave drink unto them of Z.
Is. 23 : 2. merchants of Z. replenished
4. Be thou ashamed, O Z. [Z.
12. O thou oppressed daughter of
Eze. 27 : 8. inhabit-ts of Z. mariners
28 : 21. set thy face ag. Z., prophesy
22. Behold I am against thee, O Z.
See SIDON [Place], TYRE.
See **TYRUS and Zidon.**
ZIDO'NIANS.
Ju. 10 : 12. the Z. did oppress you
18 : 7. careless, after manner of Z.
1 K. 11 : 1. Sol-n loved women of Z.
5. Sol. went after the goddess of Z.
33. Ashtoreth the goddess of Z.
16 : 31. Jezebel dau. of king of Z. [Z.
2 K. 23 : 13. Ashtoreth, abomina. of
1 Ch. 22 : 4. Z. bro-t cedar wood to Da.
Eze. 32 : 30. Z. gone down with slain
See SIDONIANS.
ZI'DON-RAB'BAH. [Z.
Jos. 11 : † 8. Isr. smote them unto
ZIF.
1 K. 6 : 1. month Z., which is second
37. foundation laid in month Z.
ZI'HA.
Ezr. 2 : 43. The Nethinim: the children of Z., Ne. 7 : 46. [inim
Ne. 11 : 21. Z., Gispa, over the Neth-
ZIK'LAG.
Jos. 15 : 31. cities of Judah, Z. [Z.
19 : 5. Simeon had in inheritance
1 S. 27 : 6. Achish gave David Z. (2)
30 : 1. Amalekites had smitten Z. (3)
14. an invasion, and we burned Z.
26. when David came to Z., he, 1.
2 S. 1 : 1. David abode two days in Z.
4 : 10. one told me Saul is dead, I
slew him in Z. [Ne. 11 : 28.
1 Ch. 4 : 30. they dwelt at Z. and at,
12 : 1. that came to David to Z., 20.
ZIL'LAH. [Adah, Z.
Ge. 4 : 19. Lamech took two wives,
22. Z. bare Tubal-cain, instructor
23. Lamech said unto Adah, Z.
ZIL'PAH.
Ge. 29 : 24. Laban gave unto Leah Z.
30 : 9. Leah gave Z. to Jacob to wife
10. Z., Leah's maid, bare a son, 12.
35 : 26. sons of Z. Gad and, 46 : 18.
37 : 2. lad was with the sons of Z.
ZIL'THAI.
1 Ch. 8 : 20. Z., Eliel, sons of [sands
12 : 20. Elihu, Z., captains of thou-
ZIM'MAH.
1 Ch. 6 : 20. Of Gershom; Libni, Z.
42. Kohathites; Z. son of Shimei
2 Ch. 29 : 12. Gershonites; Joah son
ZIM'RAN. [of Z.
Ge. 25 : 2. Keturah bare him Z.,
Medan, Ishbak, 1 Ch. 1 : 32.
ZIM'RI. [Person.]
Nu. 25 : 14. Israelite slain was Z., son
of Salu, a prince [of Z.
Jos. 7 : † 1. Achan son of Carmi, son
1 K. 16 : 9. Z. conspired against Elah,
10. Z. went in and killed Elah [16.
12. did Z. destroy house of Baasha
15. Z. reign seven days in Tirzah

1 K. 16 : 18. when Z. saw city taken
20. rest of acts of Z. are they not
2 K. 9 : 31. Had Z. peace who slew
1 Ch. 2 : 6. sons of Zerah; Z., Ethan
8 : 36. Jehoadah begat Z., Z. begat,
ZIM'RI. [Place.] [9 : 42.
Je. 25 : 25. made to drink; k-s of Z.
ZIN. [Jos. 15 : 3.
Nu. 34 : 4. your border on to Z.,
Desert or **Wilderness of ZIN.**
Nu. 13 : 21. searched land from w.
o. Z. unto Rehob [month
20 : 1. Israel into d. o. Z. in first
27 : 14. ye rebelled in the d. o. Z.,
at the water of Meribah, in w.
o. Z., De. 32 : 51. [wh. is Kadesh
33 : 36. they pitched in w. o. Z.,
34 : 3. south quarter be from w. o.
Z. along coast of Edom, Jos. 15 :
ZI'NA. See ZIZAH. [1.
ZI'ON.
2 S. 5 : 7. David took the stronghold
of Z., 1 Ch. 11 : 5. [2 Ch. 5 : 2.
1 K. 8 : 1. city of David, which is Z.,
Ps. 2 : 6. I set my King upon hill of
48 : 12. Walk about Z., go round [Z.
51 : 18. Do good in thy pleasure
69 : 35. God will save Z. [unto Z.
87 : 2. Lord loveth gates of Z. more
5. of Z. be said, This and that man
97 : 8. Z. heard and was glad [on Z.
102 : 13. Thou sh. have mercy up-
16. When the L shall build up Z.
126 : 1. When the Lord turned the
captivity of Z. [that hate Z.
129 : 5. let them be turned back
132 : 13. For the L. hath chosen Z.
133 : 3. dew upon mountains of Z.
137 : 1. wept, when we rememb-d Z.
3. Sing us one of the songs of Z.
146 : 10. shall reign, even thy God,
147 : 12. Praise thy God, O Z. [O Z.
149 : 2. let chil. of Z. be joyful in K.
Is. 1 : 27. Z. shall be redeemed with
12 : 6. shout, thou inhabitant of Z.
14 : 32. the Lord hath founded Z.
33 : 5. L. hath filled Z. wi. judgment
20. Look upon Z., city of our [of Z.
34 : 8. recompenses for controversy
40 : 9. Z. that bringest good tidings
41 : 27. first shall say to Z., Behold
49 : 14. Z. said, The L. hath forsaken
51 : 3. For the L. shall comfort Z.
11. the redeemed shall come with
singing unto Z., 35 : 10. [peo.
16. and say unto Z., Thou art my
52 : 1. awake, put on strength, O Z.
7. saith unto Z., Thy God reign-h!
8. When Lord shall bring again Z.
59 : 20. Redeemer shall come to Z.
60 : 14. The Z. of the Holy One of
62 : 1. For Z.'s sake will I not hold
64 : 10. Z. is a wilderness [brought
66 : 8. as soon as Z. travailed, she
Je. 3 : 14. and I will bring you to Z.
4 : 6. Set up the standard tow. Z.
14 : 19. hath thy soul loathed Z.?
26 : 18. Z. shall be ploughed like a
field, Mi. 3 : 12. [seeketh after
30 : 17. This is Z., whom no man
31 : 6. Arise ye, let us go up to Z.
12. they shall sing in height of Z.
50 : 5. They shall ask the way to Z.
51 : 35. sh. the inhabitant of Z. say
La. 1 : 4. The ways of Z. do mourn
17. Z. spreadeth forth her hands
4 : 2. sons of Z. comparable to gold
5 : 18. mountain of Z. is desolate
Jo. 2 : 23. Be glad, ye children of Z.
Am. 1 : 2. The Lord will roar from Z.
Mi. 3 : 10. They build Z. with blood
4 : 2. for the law sh. go forth of Z.
11. let our eye look upon Z. [slack
Zph. 3 : 16. to Z., Let not hands be
Zch. 1 : 14. I am jealous for Z., 8 : 2.
17. the Lord shall yet comfort Z.

Zch. 2 : 7. Deliver thyself, O Z. ⌈Z.
8 : 3. saith L., I am returned unto
9 : 13. When I have raised thy sons,
O Z., against thy sons, O Greece
See **DAUGHTER of Zion.**
See **DAUGHTERS of ZION.**

In ZI'ON, or SI'ON.

Ps. 9 : 11. Sing praises to Lord, who
dwelleth **i.** Z., 76 : 2. Jo. 3 : 21.
65 : 1. Praise waiteth for thee, O
God, **i.** S. ⌈before God
84 : 7. every one **i.** Z. appeareth
99 : 2. The Lord is great **i.** Z. ⌈Z.
102 : 21. To declare name of Lord **i.**
Is. 4 : 3. he that is left **i.** Z. shall be
called holy ⌈i. Z.
10 : 24. O my people that dwellest
28 : 16. I lay **i.** Z. for a foundation,
a tried stone, 1 Pe. 2 : 6.
30 : 19. the people shall dwell **i.** Z.
31 : 9. saith Lord, whose fire is **i.** Z.
33 : 14. The sinners **i.** Z. are afraid
46 : 13. I will place salvation **i.** Z.
61 : 3. appoint unto them th. mourn
Je. 8 : 19. Is not the Lord **i.** Z.? ⌊i. Z.
50 : 28. to declare **i.** Z. vengeance
51 : 10. declare **i.** Z. work of Lord
24. evil that they have done **i.** Z.
La. 2 : 6. sabbaths be forgotten **i.** Z.
4 : 11. Lord hath kindled a fire **i.** Z.
5 : 11. They ravished women **i.** Z.
Jo. 2 : 1. Blow ye trumpet **i.** Z., 15.
3 : 17. I am your God dwelling **i.** Z.
Am. 6 : 1. Woe to them at ease **i.** Z.
Ro. 9 : 33. I lay **i.** S. a stumblingstone

Mount
ZI'ON, or SI'ON.

2 K. 19 : 31. they that escape out of
m. Z., Is. 37 : 32. ⌈m. Z.
Ps. 48 : 2. joy of the whole earth is
11. Let **m.** Z. rejoice ⌈dwelt
74 : 2. **m.** Z. wherein thou hast
78 : 68. chose **m.** Z., which he loved
125 : 1. **m.** Z., wh. cannot be removed
Is. 4 : 5. upon every dwellingplace
of **m.** Z. a cloud ⌈m. Z., 18 : 7.
8 : 18. Lord of hosts wh. dwelleth in
10 : 12. his work whole upon **m.** Z.
24 : 23. when Lord sh. reign in **m.** Z.
29 : 8. so nations th. fight ag. **m.** Z.
31 : 4. so Lord shall fight for **m.** Z.
Jo. 2 : 32. in **m.** Z. shall be deliverance, Ob. 17. ⌈m. Z.
Ob. 21. saviours shall come up on
Mi. 4 : 7. Lord shall reign in **m.** Z.
He. 12 : 22. ye are come unto **m.** S.
Re. 14 : 1. a Lamb stood on the **m.** S.

Out of
ZI'ON, or SI'ON.

Ps. 14 : 7. Oh that salvation were
come - Z., 53 : 6. ⌈110 : 2.
20 : 2. Lord strengthen thee - Z.,
50 : 2. - Z. the perfection of beauty
128 : 5. L. sh. bless thee - Z., 134 : 3.
135 : 21. Blessed be the Lord - Z.
Is. 2 : 3. - Z. shall go forth the law
Je. 9 : 19. voice of wailing is heard
Jo. 3 : 16. Lord shall roar - Z. ⌊- Z.
Ro. 11 : 26. shall come - S. Deliverer

ZI'OR. ⌈bron, Z.
Jos. 15 : 54. in the mountains, He-

ZIPH. [Person.] ⌈of Z.
1 Ch. 2 : 42. Mesha, wh. was father
4 : 16. sons of Jehaleleel, Z., Ziphah

ZIPH. [Place.] ⌈55.
Jos. 15 : 24. cities of Judah, Z., Telem,
1 S. 23 : 14. Dav. in wildern. of Z., 15.
24. arose, went to Z. before Saul
26 : 2. Saul went to seek David in
wilderness of Z, (2) ⌈fence Z.
2 Ch. 11 : 8 Rehoboam built for de-

ZI'PHAH. See ZIPH. [Person.]

ZIPH'IM.

Ps. 54. * Z. said, Doth not Dav. hide

ZIPH'ION. See ZIPHON.

ZIPH'ITES. ⌈26 : 1.
1 S. 23 : 19. Then came Z. to Saul,

ZIPH'RON.

Nu. 34 : 9. border shall go on to Z.

Balak son of ZIP'POR.

Nu. 22 : 2. B. - Z. saw all Israel done
4. B. - Z. was king of Moabites
10. B. - Z. hath sent unto me ⌈der
16. saith B. - Z., Let nothing hin-
23 : 18. B., hearken unto me, - Z.
Jos. 24 : 9. B. - Z. warred ag. Israel
Ju. 11 : 25. Art thou better than

ZIPPO'RAH. ⌊B. - Z.
Ex. 2 : 21. Jethro gave Moses Z. his
4 : 25. Z. took a sharp stone, cut
18 : 2. Jethro took Z., Moses' wife

ZITH'RI. See MISHAEL.

ZIZ. ⌈of Z.
2 Ch. 20 : 16. they come up by cliff

ZI'ZA.

1 Ch. 4 : 37. Adiel, Z., were princes
2 Ch. 11 : 20. Maachah bare Rehob., Z.

ZI'ZAH or ZI'NA.

1 Ch. 23 : 10. sons of Shimei were
Jahath, Z-a, † Z-h, Jeush
11. Jahath was chief, Z-h the 2d

ZO'AN. ⌈before Z.
Nu. 13 : 22. Hebron built seven yrs.
Ps. 78 : 12. Marvellous things in Z.
43. How he wrought wonders in Z.
Is. 19 : 11. princes of Z. are fools, 13.
30 : 4. For his princes were at Z.
Eze. 30 : 14. I will set fire in Z. and

ZO'AR. ⌈Z.
Ge. 13 : 10. Eg. as thou comest unto
14 : 2. king of Bela, which is Z., 8.
19 : 22. name of the city called Z.
23. sun risen when Lot entered Z.
30. Lot went up out of Z. (2)
De. 34 : 3. valley of Jericho unto Z.
Is. 15 : 5. his fugitives sh. flee unto Z.
Je. 48 : 34. uttered their voice fr. Z.

ZO'BA or ZO'BAH. ⌈Z-h
1 S. 14 : 47. Saul fought ag. kings of
2 S. 8 : 3. David smote Hadadezer
king of Z-h, 1 K. 11 : 24. 1 Ch.
18 : 3, 9.
5. Syrians to succour Hadadezer
king of Z-h, 1 Ch. 18 : 5. ⌈Z-h
12. of spoil of Hadadezer, king of
10 : 6. children of Ammon hired
Syrians of Z-a, 1 Ch. 19 : 6. Z-h
8. Syrians of Z-a by thems. in field
2 S. 23 : 36. Igal son of Nathan of Z-h
1 K. 11 : 23. Rezon fled from king of
See ARAM-ZOBAH. ⌊Z-h
See HAMATH-ZOBAH.

ZOBE'BAH.

1 Ch. 4 : 8. Coz begat Anub and Z.

ZO'HAR, or ZE'RAH.

Ge. 46 : 10. † sons of Simeon, Jachin
and Z-r. Ex. 6 : 15. 1 Ch. 4 : 24.
Z-h, † Z-r ⌈hites, † Z-r
Nu. 26 : 13. Of Z-h family of Zar-

Son of ZO'HAR. ⌈- Z.
Ge. 23 : 8. entreat for me to Ephron
25 : 9. buried Abr. in field of Eph.

ZO'HELETH. ⌊- Z.
1 K. 1 : 9. slew cattle by stone of Z.

ZO'HETH. ⌈zoheth
1 Ch. 4 : 20. sons of Ishi, Z., Ben

ZO'PHAH.

1 Ch. 7 : 35. sons of brother Helem,
Z., Imna, Shelesh, and Amal
36. sons of Z.; Suah, Harnepher,
Shual, Beri, and Imrah

ZO'PHAI. See ZUPH.

ZO'PHAR.

Jb. 2 : 11. Z the Naamathite, 42 : 9.
11 : 1. Z. Naamathite answ-d, 20 : 1.

ZO'PHIM. ⌈of Z.
Nu. 23 : 14. brought Balak into field
See RAMATHAIM-ZOPHIM.

ZO'RAH. ⌈was Z.
Jos. 19 : 41. coast of inheritance
Ju. 13 : 2. certain man of Z., Manoah
25. camp of Dan between Z. and
16 : 31. buried Samson betw. Z. and
18 : 2. Dan sent from Z. to spy land
8. came unto their brethren to Z.
11. went out of Z. and Eshtaol 600
2 Ch. 11 : 10. Rehoboam built Z. and
See ZAREAH, ZOREAH.

ZO'RATHITES.

1 Ch. 4 : 2. These the families of Z.

ZO'REAH = ZO'RAH.

Jos. 15 : 33. cities of Judah, Z. and

ZO'RITES.

1 Ch. 2 : 54. The sons of Salma; Z.

ZOROB'ABEL.

Ezr. 3 : † 2. Z. builded altar of God
Mat. 1 : 12. begat Z. | 13. Z begat
Lu. 3 : 27. Rhesa, wh. was son of Z.
See ZERUBBABEL.

ZU'AR. See NETHANEEL.

ZUPH or ZO'PHAI.

1 S. 1 : 1. son of Tohu son of Z-h
1 Ch. 6 : 26. † sons of Elkanah; Z-i,

ZUPH. [Place.] ⌊35.
1 S. 9 : 5. when were come to land

ZUR. ⌊of Z.
Nu. 25 : 15. slain Cozbi daugh. of Z.
31 : 8. slew kings Evi, Rekem, Z.,
Hur, Reba., Jos. 13 : 21.
1 Ch. 9 : 36. Jehiel; his firstborn son,
Abdon, then Z., 8 : 30.

ZU'RIEL.

Nu. 3 : 35. chief of the house was Z.

ZURISHAD'DAI.

See SHELUMIEL.

ZU'ZIM = ZU'ZIMS. ⌈Ham
Ge. 14 : 5. the kings smote the Z. in

Lightning Source UK Ltd.
Milton Keynes UK
UKHW02n0047190818
327437UK00003B/117/P

9 780483 609310